MACKENZIE & SELBY'S HUNTER CHASERS & POINT-TO-POINTERS 2001

FORTY-SECOND EDITION

CHASE

Every effort is made to ensure that the information contained in this book is as accurate as possible. Nevertheless, some errors are certain to occur and a few of the opinions expressed about the horses will prove to be incorrect (it would be foolish for anyone to expect otherwise).

A book of this nature that made no conclusions would be valueless, one that was invariably correct miraculous.

The conclusions are those of the writers only (mostly of Iain Mackenzie and Martin Harris), and our team of correspondents play no part in the preparation of the horse commentaries beyond supplying their excellent race comments.

ISBN 1-872437-14-1

© 2000 Chase Publications

Published by Chase Publications
Stour House
68 Grove Road
Wimborne, Dorset BH21 1BW
Tel: (01202) 888200   Fax: (01202) 886090

Printed by
Graphikon, Gillingham, Dorset

Typesetting and Design by
Gazelle Design, Bournemouth

Cover Picture
by David Trundley

MACKENZIE & SELBY'S HUNTER CHASERS & POINT-TO-POINTERS 2001

Editors

IAIN MACKENZIE
TERRY SELBY
MARTIN HARRIS

CHASE

Contents

Acknowledgements

Together the writers of this book personally attended nearly 40 per cent of the 201 meetings held in 2000, but we rely on our nationwide team of correspondents to report the others.
The meetings they reported or areas covered were as follows:

Bob Bracher: South & West	**John Milburn**: Yorkshire
Scott Brinded: East Anglia, South East	**Jonathan Neesom**: South Midlands & South East
David Coulton: North West	**Darren Owen**: North West
Catriona Edwards: South & West Wales	**Steve Payne**: ubiquitous
David Gadian: Devon & Corwall	**John Rowden**: South East
Peter Mansell: West Midlands	**Granville Taylor**: Somerset, Devon & Cornwall
Lee & Myles McNulty: Northern	

We are very grateful to them all, and also to **Edward Dingle** (North Shropshire), **Allan Edwards** (South Pembs), **Brian Goodwill** (Tanatside), **Stewart Machin** (Tweseldown Racing Club), **Craig Reece** (South Notts), **John Storey** (Vine & Craven) and **Fern Thomas** (Four Burrow), and to all those who covered meetings exclusively for *Racing Post* or *Talking Point*.

Especial thanks to **Hugh Condry** for compiling the Review and his always excellent articles for Racing Post, to **Carolyn Tanner** (particularly for the many lifts to an always ungracious Mackenzie); and away from the racecourse to **Lucy**, **Kirstie** and **David** at Portman Square, all the Point-to-Point Secretaries; and not least **Jeanette Dawson** of the PPORA.

Our thanks to **Bob Bracher** for stepping into the breach late in the day to complete the course details, to **Brian Armstrong** for compiling the Quiz - and with **John Beasley** helping to sift the photographs, to **David Trundley** for allowing his painting to grace the dust jacket; to **Mel** for enthusiastically tackling numerous jobs in the hope of extracting enormous sums from her father to fund her gap year, and most of all to **Marian** who covers all the unsocial shifts and moods.
We are grateful to **James de Wesselow** of Raceform, Compton, Newbury RG20 6NL (01635 578101) and **Mike Barrett** of Formcard, Carrigtwohill Co Cork (00 353 21 613251) for permission to use their copyright material where necessary in the horse essays.

Photographers *Please support our photographers, all will be happy to supply copies of their work reproduced herein, and many have large portfolios of other racing pictures:*
Brian Armstrong, Pantiles, Penselwood, Wincanton, Somerset BA9 8NF (01747-841059)
Harry Armstrong, 127 Highfield Road, Nuneaton, Warwicks CV11 4PT (01203-344358)
Baths Photographic, 11 Allhalland Street, Bideford, Devon EX39 2JD (01237-479331)
John Beasley, 30 Thistlebarrow Rd, Bournemouth, Dorset BH7 7AL (01202-309489)
Steven Cargill, 11a Victoria Road, Aldershot, Hants GU11 1TQ (01252-343745)
Tim Holt, 21 Tarratt Rd, Yeovil, Somerset BA20 2LJ (01935-478982)
Nick Jay, Wynford Cottage, Chedington, Beaminster, Dorset DT8 3JA (01935 891005)
Mark Johnston, 9 Blackwater Road, Culmstock, Cullcompton, Devon EX15 3HF (01884 840670)
Alan Mitchell, 102 Redford Loan, Colinton, Edinburgh EH13 0AT (01314-416711)
John & Kathleen Munllen, Aintree, 67 Chartist Way, Blackwood, Gwent NP2 1WH (01495-227864)
Roy Parker, The Old Byre, Hutton Buscel, Scarborough, Yorks YO13 9LR (01273-862094)
Alun Sedgmore, 4 Pen-Yr-Allt, Watford Park, Caerphilly, Mid Glamorgan CF83 1NP (02920-866802)
Bill Selwyn, 164 Park Rd, Stapleton, Bristol BS16 1DW (01179-651596)
Peter & Marilyn Sweet, Lochinver, 21 Lymbridge Drive, Blackrod, Bolton BL6 5TH (01204-695793)
Colin Turner, PO Box 8, Ormskirk L39 3AA (01704-894220)
Clare Warwick, 11a Victoria Road, Aldershot, Hants GU11 1TQ (01252-343745)

— TRUNDLEY —

David Trundley has continued his Point-to-Point series with three new limited edition prints of Charing, Tweseldown and Holnicote.

The prints are limited to 250 full colour copies each numbered and signed by the artist, size 8" x 11¹/₂".

"Springtime, Charing"   *by David Trundley*

"Running Free, Tweseldown"   *by David Trundley*

A taste of Point to Pointing

Preview of 2001

Somehow the sport has survived the last five years of Labour government, and in 2001 we face another general election. As these words are written the best guess is that the Labour Party will form the next government with a reduced majority, and we fear it will need a miracle for hunting to survive for another Parliament without change. And any changes will have major ramifications for Point-to-Pointing.

That said, there has been too much change already. The Mildmay-White Report of 1986 which stated that 'Point-to-Pointing exists to make money for Hunting' sounded the death-knell of real amateurism, and the sport has become more and more mercenary ever since. Of course some meetings have always made money, but that was not their raison d'etre, and the halcyon days of '50s and '60s when the racing was what mattered, are a distant memory. If the sport does have to re-invent itself in the next few years then we must turn the clock back, at least a little.

Looking forward, 209 meetings are planned for the 2001 season. We have lost the West Shropshire Draghounds, the Thames Valley Club and the Cambridge University United Hunts Club from last season, but three others have immediately filled their places.

The Aldenham Harriers are returning at Cottenham (Feb 11), their first meeting since 7th March 1964. That was held on the famous and much missed course at Friars Wash (shared by the almost forgotten Hertfordshire Hunt, now assimilated into the Vale of Aylesbury), which closed for good the same year.

The North West Hunts Club (Tabley, May 20) have not been away so long, having raced at Wolverhampton as recently as 1st February 1998, and there will be a new meeting for the Countryside Alliance on Tudor Harries' land at Bonvilston (Jun 3). This is an overdue extra meeting in South Wales, and will end the local season, so a huge party is planned with everyone invited. The proceeds will benefit the Countryside Alliance and other racing charities, so make the effort and go along.

There are no fewer than five new courses in the 2001 programme. With Southwell no longer available, the Grove & Rufford (Feb 11) and Blankney (Mar 4) have moved to Nottingham racecourse - with the M1 close at hand. Neither meeting will be using the racecourse facilities, but will be based on the far side of the course around the stable lads' hostel, which will provide cover for declarations, etc. The course itself will be left-handed and is laid out inside the flat track, with eight brand-new metal-framed jumps which the Hunts are producing to their own design.

The Grove & Rufford have moved from one licensed racecourse to another, but the Eglinton are slightly different moving from the doggie-dirtied former flat track at Lanark into their own country at Ayr (Apr 28). The eight portable fences they share with the Lanark & Renfrew will be set out left-handed on the hurdles track. They too will not be using the racecourse buildings, but setting up their marquees inside the course.

The Pendle Forest & Craven are moving Hesslaker Farm, half a mile from A59 approaching Skipton from Preston. The course will be left-handed and on a slight grade - up one side and down the other, and times should be quite fast. The seven or eight fences will be portable, and races will comprise approximately two and three-quarter circuits.

The other two new courses are in South Wales, the Tredegar Farmers (May 26) and Ystrad Taf Fechan (May 5) have eventually cried enough at Bassaleg and are moving to Rhydygwern, five miles west of Newport on A468. This will be a new name to most people, but in fact it is the same course used until 1979 by the Gelligaer Farmers, when we knew it as Lower Machen. It will be left-handed with eight portable fences, and used to be described as 'undulating and sharp with long run-in'. We shall see.

The remaining new course is at Uplands Farm, Ystradowen, a mile north of Cowbridge on A4222. The Glamorgan are moving here (Easter Saturday, Apr 14) after more than 30 years at St Hilary, just a few miles away. The new course is a long left-handed undulating out-and-back rectangle with seven portable fences. Importantly it is all-grass (!), and is described as galloping with sweeping bends. Viewing will be superb with vantage points looking down to the course below.

The Jockey Club have come up with the usual crop of changes to the Regulations. Most are not of general interest, but as previously notified the penalty value above which winners in the past two seasons will be excluded from Point-to-Pointing has been raised to £10,500. After the ludicrous decision to end the NH year in April, it has been decided that for all Point-to-Point purposes, the last NH season will be deemed to have ended on 4th June 2000 (and for your information the previous season's date was 3rd June 1999).

Up to three Maiden races with differing conditions will now be permitted on any card, an increase from the two previously allowed.

There has never been a penalty for removing a tongue strap after it has been declared, but in an bizarre change, an owner may now run in a tongue strap not previously declared, but will pay a £75 fine - there's bound to be plenty of takers for that!

Horses will no longer be allowed to run in two races on the same day - excepting when one is a walkover – without getting the permission of the stewards. With the same general aim in mind, exhausted horses must always be pulled up (even if they are still leading, presumably), and failure to do so will be an offence.

The Sponsorship Committee is currently the most effective of any in the sport, and in 2001 they have again produced a full house of sponsors, who will pump more than £150,000 of vital revenue into the sport.

We welcome one completely new major sponsor. Intervet, the UK's leading animal health company, will support 24 Intermediate races around the country leading to a £5000 added Final at Cheltenham on Wednesday 2nd May. This is the first time the company has sponsored Point-to-Point racing though they have been active for many years under Rules, and Intervet certainly trips off the tongue a whole lot easier than Hoescht - the name by which they used to be known. Runners in the Final who have travelled over 75 miles to Cheltenham will be eligible for a travelling allowance of £100, £150 if their trip was over 200 miles, and £200 for 300 miles or more.

Land Rover enter their 16th year of continuous Point-to-Point sponsorship with no less than 30 individual sponsored races. As last year the winner of any Mens Open before 9th May will qualify for their £6000 Hunter Chase Final at the Towcester evening meeting on Monday May 14, and should the winner have finished first or second in any of Land Rover's own qualifiers they will receive a £6000 bonus. Runners travelling 75 miles or more to the Final will qualify for a £100 travel allowance.

Greig Middleton also retain their Ladies Open series, but having been acquired by Caple Cure Sharp (who had previously acquired Albert E Sharp - another financial house well-known to Point-to-Pointing), they will now be calling themselves Gerrard. So it is the Gerrard Ladies Championship Final Hunter Chase that will culminate their 24 race series at Stratford on 18th May. Similarly to the men's equivalent, should the winner of the Final have qualified in one of Gerrard's own qualifiers they will receive not only the £5000 prize money, but also a £5000 bonus. All runners in the Final will receive a £100 travel allowance.

After 14 years Dodson & Horrell have become synonomous with the PPORA Club races. Their support of these races has grown from 20 races in 1987 to 31 races in 2000, and they cover the country from John O'Groats to Lands End - well almost, Friars Haugh to Bratton Down.

Also aimed at PPORA members is the Marsh UK/Thoroughbred Breeders Association Mares series, successfully launched last season. All runners in

the 14 qualifiers will be eligible for the £4000-added Final at Stratford on 1st June). To qualify mares must be eligible to run in a Point-to-Point (not as silly as it sounds), and must not have won more than two Marsh/TBA races.

At the time we closed to press it was still not clear whether the Racing Channel would be broadcasting live coverage of Point-to-Pointing in 2001. Their coverage of the sport has been of high quality, but through no fault of its presenters, the company's image has been tarnished by its extreme reluctance to pay its way. Guests invited to appear can expect nothing more than a plastic cup of coffee for their efforts, and more than one local commentator persuaded to cut his fee to help the Hunt, has found his commentary broadcast to the nation without reward.

Sponsorship Chairman Nick Price had to rely upon the television for his Point-to-Pointing when ill-heath kept him away from the races for a long period. Now recovered, and besotted, he was delegated to handle the financial negotiations with the Racing Channel. He and Sponsorship Secretary, Jeanette Dawson, know better than anyone how attractive television coverage is to potential sponsors. Both have thrown their full weight behind the television station, with Mrs Dawson, a paid officer of the sport, acting directly on their behalf as intermediary with Point-to-Point Secretaries. It all seems frightfully cosy, and George Irvine, who runs the Racing Channel, must have had few qualms when Nick appeared at the office door with his hand out. It still remains to be seen whether the sport will benefit from his efforts.

Other agencies, however, have less to gain than the sponsors, and more to lose. To them increasing television coverage is a threat. Video coverage of the sport has already been drastically reduced, with the sport's small video companies going out of business. The West Midlands-based Review Video is a particularly grievous loss, and the excellent ACE Videos team from East Anglia have also been forced to give up. Despite their best endeavours their offerings could not compare with the standards set by the Racing Channel, whose generous donation of a broadcast quality tape to each winning owner inadvertently made things worse, and the little trade they survived on dried up. They have gone for good, and cannot be easily replaced when the Racing Channel have gone.

With free information becoming more generally available the widely appreciated Talking Point service is also under threat. Talking Point was designed to give practical assistance to the grass roots of the sport, whilst being an efficient information medium for the public, and a great number of Secretaries have come to rely on the free service it offers them. It operates

Fine Art of Feeding

SUPPORTING THE GRASS ROOTS OF RACING

In the year 2001, we celebrate our fourteenth year of support for all
Point-to-Point Owners and Riders Association races throughout Britain.

We will sponsor thirty-one races again this year with prize money, vouchers
and mementoes to owners and riders, plus a rug for the winning horse.

DODSON & HORRELL
LIMITED
Feed Specialists

FOR THE FRIENDLIEST HELP AND SERVICE CONTACT
JOHN SHARP ON 07802 236 277 OR 01832 731774

OR THE DODSON & HORRELL HELPLINE ON:
01933 624221

quietly behind the scenes, and has taken all the changes of the last six years in its stride, but now that entries are allowed to close so much later, and with the proliferation of Sunday racing, it has become extremely difficult and expensive to operate.

Chase Publications has funded the service completely since the end of its first year, but it can only do so if allowed to make money in other areas. The decision of the PPSA to exclude them from bidding for the National Planner (an astounding breach of faith), despite the succession of unsatisfactory past editions, may prove to be the straw that broke the camel's back. A decision on Talking Point's future will be taken at the end of the coming season, and if it closes, the official website (which made a halting start last year, despite vast sums of money being ploughed into it by Thus PLC) may follow.

There are other more serious concerns regarding the integrity of the sport once there is outside betting, and the standard of its officials. With all the recent changes in personnel, there is nobody in authority yet able to take a detached objective view. Short-termism reigns, and the sport badly misses former Controller Simon Claisse's experience and wise counsel.

These qualities were possessed in measure by our close friend, Eric Dymott. A correspondent of this publication for more than 30 years, he died a few weeks after the end of the season on the day following his 65th birthday. More than anybody, he was responsible for the formation of Mackenzie & Selby, knowing both of us well long before we had met each other. A gentle and caring man he took a boyish delight in the exploits of his Point-to-Pointing heroes, particularly ex-Champion, Richard Miller, and he loved to delve into his old formbooks to produce riding histories for anyone who cared to ask. He was the obvious choice to run the Point-to-Point Archive, and we looked forward to him playing an important role for Chase Publications in his retirement. We miss him deeply, and our journeys to the races, which were such an integral part of our enjoyment of the sport, will never be the same again.

For us an era has closed with Eric's passing, but another is set to begin with Martin Harris joining us to assist Iain in writing the horse summaries. We hope this will be the start of a long association with us. Like Iain, he is one of our foremost professional racing commentators, and when not writing is to be found on the racetrack, be it Point-to-Point, Arab, National Hunt or flat.

Michael Williams

An unfillable void was left in the world of Point-to-Pointing in October by the death of Michael Williams, the sport's distinguished, authoritative and enthusiastic chronicler for over half a century. He was 85.

So familiar round the courses, a large figure in somewhat crumpled brown tweed (mature sheepskin for early season cover), with silvery locks flowing free or curling up from beneath a cap, he had a huge circle of friends among owners, riders, officials and bookmakers, all avid readers of the comprehensive Point-to-Point coverage he provided every week in *The Sporting Life*. The passion for Hunt racing, which had developed when he was a schoolboy at Christ's Hospital in Sussex, shone from every paragraph.

His early freelance writing covered mainly non-sporting subjects, but his 'bread-and-butter' job was as a clerk at the Bank of England and it was after his appointment as Editor of the Bank's house magazine, *The Old Lady*, that his talent for sporting journalism emerged. This was about the time when Point-to-Pointing was restarting following its six-year wartime hiatus and his first reports on the sport were confined to *The Horseman's Year* — to which he contributed a seasonal review for more than 20 years — and the monthly magazine *Light Horse*, which he later quit *The Old Lady* to edit.

Then in 1950 he became chief Point-to-Point correspondent of *The Sporting Life* and his career blossomed. He recruited a countrywide band of local enthusiasts to supply news of every meeting, from which he painstakingly, lovingly crafted his column. In those days, too, he had to labour long into the night typing detailed results.

His reporting was not confined to Point-to-Points. A one-time chairman of the British Equestrian Writers' Association, he wrote on a variety of other equestrian activities, such as show jumping and horse trials. He penned a book on the former, *Show Jumping in Britain*, but will be best remembered for his two definitive volumes on the history and development of Hunt racing, *The Continuing Story of Point-to-Point Racing*, published in 1970, and its sequel, *Point-to-Pointing in Our Time*, in 1998.

Distinguished horsemen contributed forewords to both. In the first book the late Major Guy Cunard deplored the poor standards of Point-to-Point reporting which had existed 'before Michael Williams came on the scene to put one in the picture as one had never been put before'; in the second the late Capt, Tim Forster wrote: 'Michael has for so long been Mister Point-to-Pointing ... I have always felt that, when he gives up, the sport may well cease!'

That final volume was produced after his association with *The Sporting Life* ended in 1996. Though at first shocked to find himself suddenly demoted, he seemed to accept that all good things must come to an end. In a letter telling me the sad news he wrote, 'I think I would like to have the following epitaph inscribed on my tombstone: "He was given the bum's rush at the height of his prime" — even if it may not be strictly true.'

One of the founders of the national Point-to-Point dinner and its chairman for many years — his Latin grace was an institution — he was genuinely astonished to receive the committee's award for services to the sport at the 1993 dinner, after his fellow committee members had employed devious means to convince him that it was going to someone else. In 1996, to mark his enforced retirement, he received another award from the Point-to-Point Owners and Riders Association.

Throughout his long career Michael benefited beyond measure from the love and support of his wife Mary, who, among other things, chauffeured him to meetings all over the country, since driving was a skill he never bothered to acquire. They married in 1942 and had two daughters, Clare and Nicky, and seven grandchildren, to all of whom Michael was a much-loved 'Gampy'.

Mary, a devout Catholic, enjoyed a perfect partnership with her husband, despite his professed agnosticism. In recent years, however, his attitude towards her beliefs gradually changed and it gave her enormous comfort when, near the end, he requested baptism into the Catholic faith. Awaking after a brief sleep following the ceremony, he asked 'Is it time to go now?' Three days later it was.

Hugh Condry

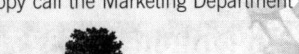

Review of 2000

by Hugh Condry

A SEASON which began with a victory on its opening afternoon for the horse destined to become the leading Point-to-Pointer of 2000, Balisteros, ended with the death on its last day of the country's top hunter chaser, Castle Mane, whose final moments came not in the hurly-burly of a race but after he had been found lying injured in his field at the Northamptonshire base of his trainer, Caroline Bailey. Veterinary surgeons battled unsuccessfully for five hours to save the life of Charles Dixey's illustrious chestnut even as, down in Devon, crowds were arriving at Umberleigh for the Torrington Farmers grand finale meeting. A post mortem revealed that his neck had been broken just in front of the withers.

Between Balisteros's first win and Castle Mane's end came another packed season, featuring 1537 races (one short of last year's highest figure) at 201 meetings, drawing 13,978 runners, the third largest total ever. Including Hunter Chases, new records were set for the number of races, 1676, horses competing, 4027, and runner total, 15,400.

Spring 2000 was very wet, with the downpours doing their worst in April and wreaking considerable disruption on the programme for Easter Saturday and the following weekend, which, it being a late Easter, included the May Day Bank Holiday. But most of the rained-off meetings, together with the few to suffer earlier, managed to fit in new dates; only eight abandonments occurred throughout the whole season. 'Season,' incidentally, still means January to June for Point-to-Pointing, despite the major boundary change in National Hunt racing. In its wisdom the British Horseracing Board decided that the NH season needed to 'go out with a bang' and therefore decreed a close on Whitbread Day at Sandown on April 29. So those Hunter Chases run from May 1 to the usual final meeting at Stratford in June now officially form part of the 2000/01 jumping season and will appear in next season's form-books — a peculiarity which this annual is ignoring!

Syndicate ownership, now given formal if slightly reluctant recognition, continued to spread – understandably encouraged by livery stable proprietors – and also spreading, though slowly, was the use of video evidence to assist stewards enquiries. Viewing of action replays had received sanction the previous year, but remains of limited value at Point-to-Points since, with all due respect to the various commercial video operators, their offerings cannot compare with the multi-camera power available on racecourses proper.

The Racing Channel continued to show interest and provided television coverage for its subscribers from a selected venue nearly every Sunday, though as yet with little obvious advantage to the host meetings. The company's cameras also operated again at the Heythrop's mid-week fixture.

Land Rover and Greig Middleton sponsorship of Mens and Ladies Open series with Hunter Chase Finals continued, as did the too-often unsung support from Dodson & Horrell for PPORA Club events. The news that *Horse & Hound* was pulling out of the Final Hunter Chase Championship at Stratford after 41 years was a major shock, but fortunately a new sponsor, Intrum Justitia, stepped in swiftly with offers of steadily-increasing prize money. *Horse & Hound* also ended its joint support (with the Thoroughbred Breeders Association) of the races for mares staged in each Area, for which winners receive stallion nominations, but the blank spot was thankfully filled when the TBA was joined by Marsh UK, which, as Bowring Countryside Insurance, had previously sponsored an Intermediate series.

New names topped both riders championship tables. Devonshire-based Les Jefford took the *Daily Telegraph* Cup, finishing streets clear of holder Julian Pritchard, after Tim Mitchell suffered cruel misfortune yet again, while Pip Jones, winner of the *Racing Post* Cup for the preceding two years, was deposed by Polly Gundry from Gloucestershire, runner-up in 1999. Another Polly — the renowned three-times champion Curling — announced her retirement just before the season started. She signed off with a career score of 220 in Point-to-Points alone and with Hunter Chase triumphs including the 1995 Cheltenham Foxhunters aboard Fantus.

PLATE 1   1137 Tiverton Staghounds Intermediate: Ardbei (L. Jefford), 1st, by a canvas from Fossy Bear (Miss S. Young), 2nd, after the second fence   PHOTO: Tim Holt

After the end of the season the chairmen of the Point-to-Point Secretaries Association and the Point-to-Point Owners and Riders Association both reached the end of their stints in office, Andrew Merriam being replaced at the PPSA by Libby Gilman while Richard Russell took over the PPORA reins from John Sharp.

Before the season started there had also been a change of command at the Jockey Club, necessitated by the departure of long-time Point-to-Point Controller Simon Claisse — a man who always put the sport first and who, thanks to his talent for leadership allied to tactful persuasion, had been responsible for numerous developments and improvements. He moved on to be Clerk of the Course at Britain's home of jumping, Cheltenham, and was succeeded in the hot seat by Charlie Lane, a former commander of the King's Troop.

Lane came to his new job from the Royal Agricultural College, where he was head of Equine Business Management. Though his active equestrian career had been principally in eventing (he won the British Open trials championship in 1975 and was *chef d'equipe* when Britain's three-day team beat the world), he had ridden a couple of Point-to-Point winners and done some stewarding. In early January he was quoted as saying he anticipated 'no dramatic problems' in the season ahead. But problems there must presumably have been — for him anyway — since in August it was announced that he had resigned after only eight months in office.

An immediate replacement for the post — officially manager of the Jockey Club's Racecourse and Point-to-Point Department — was found in the Windsor Clerk of the Course Fraser Garrity, who had previously spent some time as deputy to Simon Claisse at the Jockey Club.

The performancFe of Balisteros in winning the *Horse & Hound* Leading Horse title was little short of phenomenal. Though his score of 10 Ladies Open victories has been bettered, he also landed three Hunter Chases (including the Greig Middleton Ladies Final) and his overall 13 wins is the largest seasonal total of any previous Leading Horse since the award was first instituted by Grand Marnier back in 1971 — indeed *perhaps* by any horse, though early records are sketchy.

The tough 11-year-old faced the starter on no fewer than 17 occasions, more than any other runner in 2000 and equalled among previous Leading Horses only by Pensham, who won 11 of her 17 starts, all between the flags, in 1972.

Owner Mrs Billie Thomson deserves every credit for the training skills which kept Balisteros on the boil for five months, from the season's first day in January, when he travelled from Kelso to win at Tweseldown, to June at Stratford, where he just failed behind the highly-regarded Lord Harry (*qv* North Western) in the John Corbet Cup. Balisteros's score up to mid-April was only six (including two Hunter Chases), but then he hit a purple patch which brought six Ladies Opens in 22 days — two Saturday/Sunday doubles and two wins over the Easter weekend.

Effective at widely varying distances and on all types of going, he was placed in the four races he didn't manage to win and succeeded under four different pilots, Jill Wormall (six times), Pauline Robson (five) and Carrie Ford and Wilson Renwick (once each). Mrs Thomson, who gave up her racing saddle after breaking a leg in a non-racing accident, had won three times on him herself in 1998, after buying him two years earlier out of Richard Barber's Dorset stable — and allegedly being warned by the maestro: 'He'll never win you an Open!'

The remarkable Balisteros was the first to bring the Leading Horse prize to the **Northern** Area, where things began on a sombre note at the West Percy on January 23 when racegoers were stunned to learn of the death two days earlier of Dennis Waggott, aged only 52. Waggott was one of the most successful owners in the Area during the past decade and always remained loyal to the Geordie accent when naming his horses, none of whom cost more than 4500 guineas. Recent representatives Howayman and Sayin Nowt won 30 races between them.

A few weeks later the region in general and Galashiels-based handler Bill Hughes in particular suffered a devastating blow when the brilliant hunter chaser Jigtime collapsed and died after finishing third at Haydock in February. Some compensation for Hughes came from River Of Gold and Midsummer Glen, a couple of Irish Pointers sold on the same day at Doncaster the previous August for 4500 and 4600 guineas respectively, but the stable suffered again when Midsummer Glen died following an accident at home after having proved a model of consistency, landing a Maiden Hunter Chase at Kelso (under Marcus Armytage) and finishing second five times and third twice in his other seven outings. River Of Gold went hurdling after winning his Maiden impressively on his only run in February.

Hughes also saddled the diminutive Mystical Music, a seven-year-old daughter of dual *Horse & Hound* Cup winner Mystic Muse, who produced an impressive turn of foot from the last to collar Inglebrook Lad in a Dalston 2m4f Maiden.

Clive Storey secured the Area's Get Smart Men's Championship for the third successive year with a career-best 21 winners, including a memorable four-timer — his first — at the Jedforest in February, aboard three from his own Yetholm yard, Rainbow Times, Highland Monarch and Queen Biddy, and on one — Maximise — that Olympic silver medal event rider Ian Stark trained for his horse trials patron Lady Vestey. A six-year-old by Mandalus, Maximise did not reappear. He had been bought — for 1000 guineas as a four-year-old — for horse trials, in which sphere he had already won at pre-novice level, but in October, still carrying the Vestey colours, and now trained by Henrietta Knight, he finished third in a Novice Hurdle at Stratford. Seven-year-old Rainbow Times later triumphed in the Braes of Derwent Open on Easter Monday and won the Weatherby's Young Horse prize for the Area.

Storey nearly landed another quartet at the Lauderdale in May; there he followed success on two of his own training, Sunnycliff and Big Bark, by winning a Maiden for Nick and Kirsty Hargreave with Ardnut, but in the Open he and Dennett Lough went down by a length to Riverside Run, who benefited from a change of tactics and an inspired ride from Jimmy Walton. Ten days after the Lauderdale, Sunnycliff impressed when landing a 2m4f Perth Novice Hunter Chase under Luke Morgan, beating Storey and Blyth Brook by eight lengths.

PLATE 2   1029 Bedale Greig Middleton Ladies Open: That was win number seven for Billie Thomson and Balisteros, and they won again at Tranwell next day   PHOTO: Roy Parker

Other contributors to the northern champion's score from his own string included Blyth Brook, Dean Deifir and Happy Blake. Six-year-old Dun Rose, with Maiden and Restricted victories to her credit, completed a hat-trick for Storey in the Buccleuch Confined thanks to a slice of luck; she ran second to Love Actinium, only for this mare to be disqualified when her rider, Craig Niblo, omitted to weigh in.

Another Storey representative, Weejumpawud, took the Hurworth Land Rover in the capable hands of Barry Lusted, while it was also in Yorkshire that the rider-trainer notched up his 100th win (including Rules) when Queen Biddy won the Cleveland Restricted. Sadly Queen Biddy died in the summer, as did another in the yard, Ensign Ewart. One of Storey's top mounts of 1999, Faster Ron, was sidelined through injury, but his trainer, Rhona Elliot, enjoyed a relatively successful campaign, with Benefit-In-Kind, Dere Street, Mountain Thyne and the one-eyed Boris Brook all reaching the winner's enclosure.

Pauline Robson was the Area top lady for the eighth time in the last nine seasons, taking the R W Bruce Craigie Trophy by a street from Val Jackson, who had interrupted her sequence in 1998. Miss Robson's 21 successes eclipsed her previous best of 15 in 1994 and left her third nationally to Polly Gundry and Pip Jones. She might have had even more but for a couple of weeks on the sidelines after a crashing fall with Master Kit in the Borders National at Kelso.

She set the Balisteros run going at Tweseldown on the opening day and became the first northern lady rider to achieve a century between the flags when John Hogg's La Riviera scored at the Hurworth in March. La Riviera won three of his four starts, conceding only to Balisteros at Alnwick in February after having beaten Billie Thomson's wonder horse over the same course three weeks earlier.

The livery yard Miss Robson runs at Capheaton with just retired NH jockey David Parker enjoyed a remarkable strike-rate, with 18 winners from 40 runners. Apart from La Riviera, other three-time scorers were Riparius, Little Brockwell and Tea Box, while Allrite Pet won all her four starts between the flags for Dennis Waggott's widow. Syndicate-owned Tea Box, patiently restored to fitness, returned after a 21-month absence to win at Dalston and in Hunter Chases at Newcastle and Hexham; another returning from a year off, Denim Blue, was the only one of the yard's eight inmates who failed to score.

Mrs Jackson, who finished 41 points below Pauline Robson in the Area ladies table, extended her winning sequence in the Morpeth Members to five on Good and scored a brace of victories each with Nova Nita and Storm Alive, but the north's senior lady, Doreen Calder, had to settle for a solitary success in April at Balcormo Mains on her own Flaming Sunrise, an ex-novice hurdler who had been given a winning start in a February Alnwick Maiden by Luke Morgan.

Jimmy Walton rode his first winner over jumps at Ayr more than 30 years ago but is still a force to be reckoned with and finished runner-up again to Clive Storey when adding another seven wins to his career tally. The majority of Walton's victories have been gained under Rules and he now needs only five more for his double century overall. He won four times on his father's Excise Man and he also cruised home in the Eglinton Open on Snapper, who subsequently made 14,000 guineas at Doncaster.

After sending out 25 winners in the previous two campaigns, Simon Shirley-Beavan's Bonchester Bridge establishment suffered from 'the virus', though one to escape was Senso, who scored twice for Caroline Cox and deserved more. Another, The Alleycat, won first time out in the Jedforest Members under the promising Paul Robson, 16, and later scored for the same pilot at long odds in the South Durham Intermediate.

Ian and Ann Hamilton's horses emerged from under the previous season's virus cloud at Claywalls and the benefit of recently-installed all-weather gallops was duly reaped. Steel Rigg, Superior Weapon and Claywalls all scored once but the pick of the bunch was their home-bred six-year-old Divet Hill, who spreadeagled his rivals impressively at Lockerbie and Mosshouses. All four were partnered by Matthew Clayton, 25, who works in the Hamilton yard and deservedly won the Area Novice Riders Championship in his first season.

Marsh UK Ltd /
The Thoroughbred Breeders' Association
Mares Only Club Series (PPORA) -2001

are pleased to sponsor the third running of the Mares Only Club Series, with
qualifiers at the following meetings:

February

Sunday 4th	The Jedforest	Friars Haugh
Sunday 11th	The Badsworth	Wetherby
Sunday 11th	The Mid-Devon	Black Forest Lodge
Saturday 17th	The Granta Harriers	Higham
Sunday 18th	South East Hunts Club	Charing

March

Saturday 17th	Llangibby	Howick
Sunday 18th	Ross Harriers	Gamons
Saturday 24th	V.W.H.	Siddington
Sunday 25th	Fitzwilliam	Cottenham

April

Saturday 1st	Sir W. W. Wyan	Eaton Hall
Monday 16th	South Notts Hunt	Thorpe Lodge
Tuesday 17th	Croome & West Warwick	Upton-on-Severn
Sunday 29th	The Quorn	Garthorpe

May

Sunday 6th	Tedworth	Barbury Castle

Final to be held on Friday 1st June (evening) at Stratford Racecourse

For mares owned and ridden by members of the Point-to-Point Owners' and
Riders Association.

**A horse which has run in any of the above 14 races is qualified to enter the
March UK Ltd/TBA Mares Point-to-Point Championship Hunter Chase Final**

> The Marsh UK Ltd / TBA Mares Point-to-Point
> Championship Hunter Chase Final
> **£4,000 added to stakes**
> Stratford-On-Avon Racecourse on Friday (Evening), 1st June, 2001

**For further information or details on the TBA, please contact:-
Carrie Cherry, Stanstead House, The Avenue, Newmarket, Suffolk, CB8 9AA.
(01638 661321) email info@tbassoc.demon.co.uk
www.tbassoc.demon.co.uk**

Take a look at some

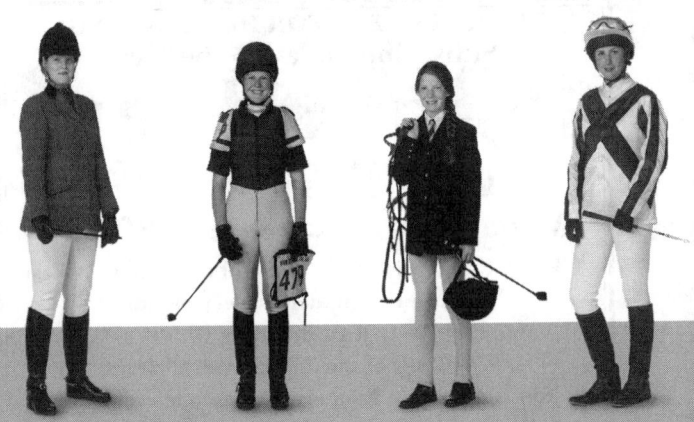

# of our customers

and you'll soon see why we tailor our insurance policies

Riders come in all shapes and sizes. And now, so does our insurance. Our knowledgeable, caring equine team will listen to you and design a policy to fit you and your horse. You can be confident you will receive:

- The benefits you need at competitive prices
- Straightforward cover with no hidden extras
- Fast, fair claims settlement

TAILORED INSURANCE FOR YOU & YOUR HORSE

The season's bargain buy was ex-selling hurdler Parade Racer, picked up for just 1100 guineas by Tim Butt at Doncaster the previous May. The nine-year-old won his first three starts to secure the Area's Confined Race Championship and could make his mark in Open company in 2001.

Another nine-year-old, former novice chaser Manhattan Rainbow, gave David Da Silva, 18, a memorable winning debut ride in a West Percy Maiden in January and then, after winning two Hunter Chases under Wilson Renwick at Kelso, scored again there for Da Silva in May. Renwick, 19, had ridden his first winner the previous year and, after adding another four between the flags in 2000, is now making a name for himself as a conditional.

Graham Murray's Bow Tie struck up a great bond with Corbridge land agent Ranald Morgan, winning Opens at Dalston, Lockerbie and Balcormo Mains, but the gelding has yet to prove himself over regulation fences and finished only third to Yorkshire horse Victoria's Boy and Weejumpawud in the Heart of All England Hunter Chase at Hexham. Morgan himself, who won the *Daily Telegraph* Novice Rider title in 1997, had his best season, with 11 successes, four of them on maidens, including Tim Reed's six-year-old Harleidalus, who has the scope to develop into a decent staying chaser and enhanced his reputation with a fine exhibition of jumping when he won at Lockerbie in April.

Other noteworthy youngsters included the five-year-old Wills Perk and the year older Another Handyman, who, after being just denied at Corbridge and Dalston, was again brought with a great rattle by the perhaps under-rated Peter Johnson to get off the mark deservedly in very testing conditions at Tranwell. He was subsequently knocked down for 10,500 guineas at Doncaster's May Sales to Harvey Smith.

Wills Perk made an impressive debut at the Berwickshire (the only Area meeting covered by the Racing Channel) and then went down narrowly to Lord Levi in the Eglinton Restricted, only to be promoted after rider Tom Oates's 'taking my ground' objection was upheld. However, this decision was subsequently reversed after Lord Levi's owner, Lisa Ogilvie, appealed to Portman Square. Lord Levi was beaten in three subsequent Hunter Chases but Wills Perk, trained by Kate Anderson, was put away and should be one to follow next season.

The Lanark & Renfrew was the Area's only abandonment from an 18-strong list; this was a result of a local riding club making rather too enthusiastic use of part of the old flat track at Lanark the week before. Fortunately all was literally smoothed over by the time of the Eglinton meeting there a month later.

One meeting was also lost from the scheduled 20 in the **East Anglian** Area, for a rather more conventional reason: waterlogging. The sufferer on May Day was the Enfield Chace and the following Saturday Area sport ended at High Easter on a high note with a tremendous Open race in which Dawn Alert just held off the 1999 leading horse Copper Thistle (*qv* Midlands), who had won all his previous eight starts in 2000 and was to triumph in the Land Rover Final nine days later.

Dawn Alert's stablemate Heathburn had won the same afternoon and this double set an appropriate seal on the remarkable achievement of the five-horse string owned by Anthony and Sue Howland-Jackson. Trained at Glemsford by Ruth Hayter (who also sent out Dry Highline to win three races for Clare Villar), the team contained only one who failed to get his head in front — the pricey ex-French recruit Gatchou Mains — but the other four won 15 Point-to-Points and a Hunter Chase between them.

Following the sad demise of St Gregory, winner of the 1998 leading horse title for the Howland-Jacksons, it would have required the foresight of Nostradamus (the soothsayer, not Ian McKie's old friend!) to have predicted that the stream of winners from this source would continue virtually unabated. But seven-year-old Heathburn, an Irish maiden bought at Doncaster the previous May for 7000 guineas, won two of his five starts and the year older Village Copper, a Cottenham Maiden winner in 1999, four from seven, while the two seniors did even better. Dawn Alert, after a belated start, won four out of four between the flags before failing in the Greig Middleton final, and Hatcham Boy topped up four Hunt racing wins from eight attempts by running second to Copper Thistle in the Land Rover Final and then landing a fine win over 4m2f at Uttoxeter.

Lisa Rowe, the new racing manager at Newmarket and married in September to Charlie Hancock, won once each on Dawn Alert, Hatcham Boy and Village Copper, but mostly the string was piloted by Christian Ward-Thomas. He registered a personal high of 12, though he missed the final High Easter double, where William Wales was on Dawn Alert and Heathburn was another for Nigel Bloom.

Bloom enjoyed his best season since he secured the national championship in 1994. His recent years have been blighted by injury, at least in part, but in 2000 the old wine flowed as freely as ever before, beginning on the Area's opening day at Cottenham aboard the useful South Wold-qualified Mr Freebie (*qv* Midlands) and continuing on a fairly regular basis until the end of March, when doubles on consecutive days at the Waveney and Fitzwilliam and another a fortnight later at the East Essex catapulted him to the head of the local table.

The best was yet to come. On Easter Monday, in a humble two-runner race at Marks Tey, Bloom passed his trainer father Mike's riding career score of 145 on the home stable's Mr Magget (a Welsh-qualified eight-year-old, bought for 4400 guineas at Ascot in February and sold again there in June for 100 guineas more after completing a Maiden/Restricted/Intermediate hat-trick) and the following Saturday at Fakenham brought up his 150 with a sensational four-timer.

Beginning with a determined, clever ride on Hugh Hodge's immensely-promising seven-year-old Sense Of Adventure (two wins from two starts), he then cajoled the former Henry Cecil-trained General Assembly into taking a sub-standard Open before winning both halves of the split-on-the-day Maiden, first nursing home the syndicate-owned Cradle Mountain and then scoring with Tod's Brother for Andrew Merriam, who, as mentioned earlier, has now handed over the PPSA reins but remains local supremo. Seven-year-old Cradle Mountain had been second on his only other run but the year younger Tod's Brother had been treated very tenderly in two previous starts.

Runner-up to Bloom locally, for the second consecutive year, was Andrew Sansome, who partnered most of Joe Turner's horses. They were busy from the opening day at Tweseldown to the close five months later at Umberleigh in Devon, proof indeed that Ampton enthusiasm remains undimmed since their championship glory days of the '70s. For all Sansome's efforts, however, it was the distaff side which took the plaudits, Zoe Turner's eight wins giving her a comfortable Area ladies title and a joint-sixth in the national table.

Five of her eight came aboard the stable's new recruit, Spring Gale, a winner over hurdles and fences during three seasons with Oliver Sherwood but whose recent form apparently indicated a loss of interest. As so often, Hunt racing rekindled enthusiasm and, after Emma Coveney had partnered him an initial third at Horseheath, he then oozed class as his owner's granddaughter rode him to win five out of six Ladies Opens, the odd one out being the fifth, in which he dropped his pilot two from home at Cottenham when looking held by Dawn Alert. His victories, all gained in facile style, were then supplemented by a Hunter Chase success at the family's beloved Fakenham and a fine second to the all-conquering Balisteros in the Greig Middleton Final.

Miss Turner's other three wins came once on the quirky Prince Of Saints, beyond the region's boundaries at Kingston Blount, and twice at Horseheath with gallant old servant Emsee-H, who later cast a cloud over the stable when breaking a pastern at High Easter on the Area's last day. It was Emsee-H who had helped Miss Turner back into winning form when she resumed the racing saddle in 1998 after breaking her neck at Charing two years before.

Sansome, whose final total was 11, had won earlier on the 15-year-old and gained other successes in the Turner colours on Squaddie (sold before the season's end to Patrick Millington), Persian Boy (twice), Prince Of Saints, the consistent Mister Audi and two youngsters who both took a fair while to lose their maiden certificates, Generous Deal (who made only 2200 guineas when sold at Doncaster in August) and five-year-old Always Trying.

Joe Turner's daughter, Mrs Gurney Sheppard, enjoyed her best season yet with her seven-year-old Fair Exchange, who won three of his five starts under Paul Taiano and took the Area's Young Horse prize.

The Area's other big family stable, that of Christopher Sporborg in Hertfordshire, seemed to have emerged shining brightly from its total virus eclipse of 1999 when landing a double on the season's opening day at Tweseldown with Rob Mine and Secret Streams, but if that gave Simon Sporborg hopes of another tilt at the national title they soon evaporated. Neither of his first-day winners could manage a repeat and, though the five-year-old Will Hill opened his account at the second attempt, he was not seen thereafter. Le Cabro D'Or, who had shown promise on his solitary 1999 outing, proved to have major steering problems.

Happiest Sporborg memories were provided by Rupert's Choice. He seemed revitalised by the application of blinkers and just won an exciting Coronation Cup when taken down to Larkhill in February. Subsequently the benefits of the headgear seemed to dwindle, though a late-season Hunter Chase win at Folkestone, under Alex Harvey, provided some compensation.

Simon Andrews had a relatively quiet time and it was a pity that one he rode and trained, seven-year-old Monty's Tag, appeared only twice. He made a winning debut on good ground at Horseheath in early February and seemed untroubled by the heavy at Marks Tey when easily landing a Restricted three weeks later. But that was all.

Monty's Tag, plus the afore-mentioned Sense Of Adventure and Will Hill, would be included on any list of those with a future, but the best of the lot might turn out to be another of Don Cantillon's charges, the scopey Zafan, who could follow in the hoofprints of his owner's Alpine Gale, a money-spinner under Rules since her East Anglian successes of 1999. Five-year-old Zafan, obtained unraced from Dermot Weld, looked far from the finished article but, after a quiet outing at the West Norfolk, he was rather surprisingly risked on the very firm ground when eased home in a Fernie Maiden at Dingley. Rider Harry Fowler reported him 'as green as grass' then, so there should be more to come.

From the future to the past: Robin Gill, who has had weight problems, announced his retirement and that of his mount, Aeolian, after they had won the Essex Hunt race together; third in the same event, Peanuts Pet, who had latterly raced for David Barnard and given great fun to his daughter, Hannah, also bowed out, after his 109th start, to be Newmarket trainer William Jarvis's hack. Also taking a deserved pension is Cache Fleur, who won the famous Warwick Vase at that same Essex meeting, just holding off Coral Grissell riding West Country challenger Baby Whale and giving Gi d'Angibau her 50th win in the process. Mrs d'Angibau, who needs another 30 to match the record of her mother, Fizz Chown, had earlier collected four Ladies' Opens — including at three of the four Highams — with Margaret Brightwell's Cracking Idea.

After three appearances in the fixture list (once early, twice late), the East Anglian Bloodhounds dropped out and as yet seem to have lost any desire to press claims for a return. But the Granta Harriers, granted a competitive date on a track (Higham) almost guaranteed to provide decent ground, staged an excellent first fixture and are set to return there in mid-February 2001. A major success was the move of the Easton Harriers to the Area's most scenic and rural-based track at High Easter in March. Devotees were rewarded with fresh ground, well-prepared facilities and an eight-race, 91-runner card, a runner total exceeded in the Area only by the 115 which turned out for the opening Cambridgeshire Harriers Hunt Club at Cottenham.

The early East Anglian meetings regularly attract raiders from afar and, true to form, five of the eight races at that first Cottenham went to horses based outside the Area, most notable of the winners being Secret Bay, who galloped away with the 21-runner Land Rover qualifier after the Sussex-based favourite Real Value (later second in the Cheltenham Foxhunters) had gone at the second ditch. Secret Bay moves this review conveniently into the **Midlands** Area, since he — bought for 10,500 guineas the previous summer after winning a Hunter Chase for a Yorkshire stable — was yet another of the top performers in Caroline Bailey's Northamptonshire establishment. After his Cottenham pipe-opener, Secret Bay moved into Hunter Chases, completing a hat-trick at Ludlow, Leicester and Newbury before being unable to cope with the Philip Hobbs-trained Bells Life at Aintree.

Only eight of the 26 horses Mrs Bailey sent out from Holdenby North Lodge failed to win; between them the other 18 collected 31 Point-to-Points and 11 Hunter Chases, with the star award again going to the ill-fated Castle Mane. Dreams of a Gold Cup tilt — entertained since his Cheltenham Foxhunters triumph the year before — were dashed after two early season disappointments, but a muscle enzyme problem was diagnosed and treated, leading to a triumphant return to the winner's enclosure at the Cheltenham evening meeting in early May.

Julian Pritchard rode him there, usual pilot Ben Pollock being absent at Punchestown, but Pollock was back for the horse's fourth and last run at Stratford a month later when he conquered Grimley Gale (*qv* West Midlands) in the Final Hunter Chase Championship, which, perhaps a little unfortunately for its new sponsor, Intrum Justitia, will ever be known as the *Horse & Hound* Cup. A week later, as previously related, Castle Mane was dead.

His final victory had taken Pollock's Hunter Chase score to seven, one ahead of Richard Burton, so he retained the Chase Publications Trophy for the third year. In addition to the one on Castle Mane, he won three on Secret Bay, once in February with Mr Branigan (who pulled up lame on his only other start) and twice aboard Gunner Welburn (Rowan Cope won another on him), with whom he fell at the last at Punchestown when a beaten third behind Ireland's champion Sheltering, Castle Mane's victim in the previous year's equivalent contest.

Pollock's wins for the stable between the flags numbered 11, the same as patron Richard Hunnisett, who enjoyed another wonderful season riding his Copper Thistle. Hunnisett had received the previous year's Leading Horse award after 10 wins on Copper Thistle and this time the 12-year-old was unbeaten in his first eight starts (all Opens) before just going under to Dawn Alert in that previously-described High Easter race. Consolation was not long coming; nine days later at Towcester Hunnisett and Copper Thistle scored their greatest triumph yet when making almost every yard in the Land Rover Final.

Hunnisett also won with his other horses. Inch Cross was successful for him at Market Rasen in January, while Shanavogh, a nine-year-old ex-chaser bought for 22,000 guineas at Doncaster the previous May, won Opens at Garthorpe and Clifton-on-Dunsmore and could be another sequence-provider in 2001.

Shanavogh's Garthorpe win in mid-March came the day after his trainer had taken seven horses to the Oakley meeting and won with five. One of them, Imperial Dawn, a successful ex-Irish Pointer who cost 13,500 guineas at Doncaster the previous August, was ridden exclusively in Ladies' Opens by Lisa Rowe, winning four from seven starts and finishing second twice.

Most of the Bailey stable horses qualified with the Pytchley, but there were exceptions. Castle Mane was hunted by his owner with the Meynell; three five-year-olds owned by former top amateur Chris Collins — the Maiden winners Hessac and Luckashan and the mare Dona Ferentis, who was restricted to a solitary run — all had Cottesmore certificates; Jim Cunningham's home-bred Oakley winner Right Company represented the Bicester; while Tom De Savoie was trained for a third year for East Anglian Area secretary William Barber and qualified with the West Norfolk before being ridden to win two Point-to-Points and a Hunter Chase by William Wales.

Mrs Bailey joined the action early and had led in winners at Tweseldown, Cottenham and Higham on the first three weekends before taking four runners to the first Area meeting, the Lincolnshire United Hunts Club fixture, and winning with three — Inch Cross, Red Rebel and Irisheyearesmilin. She had no runners in any of the five Maiden divisions, which all went to Yorkshire horses.

It was left to her sister-in-law trainer, Tik Saunders, to keep the local flag flying at the next two Area meetings, with Midnight Service, Hobnob and Starlight Fool (none of whom exactly set the pulses racing subsequently), but otherwise six of the 10 races at the Midlands Club fixture went beyond the region's boundaries, while at the Brocklesby a fortnight later two of the three Maidens were won by Yorkshire, the Wheatland-qualified Solba beat Shanavogh in the Open and Donnegale was another for Yorkshire in the Ladies' Open, in which Imperial Dawn had a decidedly off day.

Runner-up to Donnegale was the hurdle and chasing winner Cittadino, who had been given to Cliff Dawson when apparently soured of racing. With zest restored he followed with four Ladies' Open wins, ridden by Dawson's daughter-in-law Jill, at Market Rasen and at the first three of the four Garthorpe meetings, before being an 5-2 on loser at the fourth — the Melton — when handicapped by a lost shoe. Jill Dawson was beaten 22-21 on points as the Area's top lady rider by Louise Allen, but Cittadino won the local leading owner award for Cliff Dawson.

Matthew Mackley and Stuart Morris were inseparable for the men's prize; each scored 40 points, and each rode nine winners, eight within the Area. Mackley had his high point on Easter Monday with a treble at Thorpe Lodge; Morris rode a treble at the Atherstone and for him high points came every time he rode Bill Warner's charge Union Man. Philip Newton's seven-year-old by Teamster shed his maiden certificate on his debut run at Newton Bromswold and continued unbeaten through three more outings at Garthorpe to end as the Area's top Young Horse. He finished in great style in the Melton's Novice Championship from a field which included six winners last time out. Roll on 2001 for this one.

Warner, who sent out 10 winners in all (the others all for his principal patron, Mrs Judy Wilson), also introduced an impressive six-year-old, Shoemaker, who won both his starts under Morris impressively.

Other Area multiple winners include Ardeal, Gillone and Don't Tell The Wife, who all scored three times — the last-named speedily after a delayed return — while David Ingle, who ended the season planning to take out a licence, did well with Mr Freebie and Springfield Rex. The former collected wins under Nibby Bloom at the first Cottenham and in a Towcester Hunter Chase before running second in the Middleton's Grimthorpe Cup and then being short-headed by Overflowing River after a real thriller in the four-miler at the Cheltenham evening meeting; Springfield Rex, partnered by Fiona Needham, went to Yorkshire for a Ladies' race win on Easter Monday and then broke his Hunter Chase duck at Aintree in May.

Runner-up to Springfield Rex at Aintree was Baron Allfours, just about best — that may be damning with faint praise — of the 16-strong string operated by the irrepressible Patrick Millington; Baron Allfours was later responsible for a 21-day medical stand-down for champion jockey Tony McCoy when he fell at Southwell in July. The Millington horses ran in excess of 100 times during the season and gave their owner three wins. Without them things at the Fernie meeting — the poorest supported of any in an otherwise above-average Area for runners — would have been dire indeed. Millington provided nine of the day's 37 runners and won two races with horses he rode himself, Fortune Hunter in the Maiden (chased home by two stable-companions) and in the newly-instituted four-mile Dingley Gold Cup — the Area's double prize money prestige Open — on Polly Live Wire, who was, in fact, a maiden until then. She was taken home from Doncaster Sales when bids failed to pass 8000 guineas; 5000 guineas secured Fortune Hunter on the same day.

The Area's busiest meeting had come the week before the Fernie, when the Atherstone's 10-race race card (three divisions on the day) produced an enormous turnout of 125. Only one of the scheduled 17 meetings went west when the Woodland Pytchley was rained off on Easter Saturday. It was first postponed, but then abandoned when no medical cover could be arranged on the revised date. Sundays predominate in this part of the country, meetings on the sabbath outnumbering Saturdays by four to one.

By contrast **Wessex** remains more traditional, with just six Sunday fixtures as against 15 Saturdays. Inevitably this means clashes, but a wide catchment area prevents major problems, though on the last Saturday in March the Wilton's meeting on the good course at Badbury Rings drew only 37 runners compared with the 93 contesting the Mendip Farmers races about 35 miles away at Ston Easton. Next year the Mendip race on a Sunday.

The Area introduced an excellent new course at Chipley Park, used by the Tiverton in place of Stallenge Thorne, though sadly on a Sunday instead of its usual Wednesday, but the balance was maintained when the 14th Regiment Royal Artillery entered the calendar with a Wednesday evening gathering to ring down the Area curtain at Britain's most-used course, Larkhill. A very good try it was too, with a lot of silverware on offer and a 'celebrity' flat race won narrowly by Ron Hodges from Rose Vickery and Richard Linley, but unfortunately, on good to firm ground, only 38 runners turned out all told — against an average of 71 for the preceding six Larkhill meetings. On top of that the weather on the night took a decided turn for the worse. However, bloodied but unbowed, the Regiment will be having another go in 2001.

Larkhill had hosted the Area's first meeting in January, when the Army's Land Rover qualifier produced a 20-runner sizzler in which the Caroline Bailey-trained favourite, Gunner Welburn, crashed at the last with the race as good as won and Chism, left in front, was caught yards from the line by 25-1 shot Highway Lad, first winner of the season for eventual national champion Les Jefford.

Chism is a difficult individual (retirement would seem the only certain way to avoid further exasperation) and his partner, Robert Walford, was fined ú100 for failing to ride him out. Walford, son of Hunt racing trainer Tim Walford, was having his first Point-to-Point ride in the south since leaving his father in Yorkshire to join Robert Alner as stable amateur and ride Pointers for Alner's daughter, Louise.

She continued consistent, following the 17 successes gained in her debut training season in 1998 and the 18 (plus three Hunter Chases) in '99, with another 17 victories. The majority were ridden by Walford, though Richard Young, another Alner amateur, partnered Peasedown Tofana and the desirable five-year-old Priestthorn, while Michael Miller rode his aunt's Miss O'Grady — just about the stable star — to win Opens on successive Saturdays. In the Cheltenham Foxhunters Miss O'Grady was an early casualty, ridden by Walford as Miller was required for Skip'N'Time, trained by his father. Skip'N'Time finished the Foxhunters course but a long way behind and was generally a major disappointment after such a promising 1999.

In addition to Priestthorn, another five-year-old in the Alner yard on the 'reappearance eagerly awaited' list — and for both that will be in novice chasing — is Abbots Court, who won the last two of his three runs. Harry Wellstead owns them both.

The stable's most prolific winner was six-year-old Stoney River, who at Aintree in May was given his first try in a Hunter Chase — after completing a Maiden/Restricted/Intermediate hat-trick — and seemed set for second to Springfield Rex (*qv* Midlands) until ejecting Walford at the final fence.

Wessex is awash with livery stables and biggest of them all is that of Richard Barber at Seaborough in Dorset. He regained top spot in the national trainers table — from which he had been toppled the previous year by Caroline Bailey — sending out 35 Pointing winners to her 31. But 11 Hunter Chase victories to Barber's three gave Mrs Bailey overall honours.

Best of the Barber string was Lakefield Rambler, followed — not far behind — by 10-year-old Finnigan Free, who returned from a two-year absence and carried the colours of owner-breeder Sarah Rich through an unbeaten five-race sequence, starting in a Bishops Court Maiden in early March and ending in a Chepstow Hunter Chase in mid-May. One who might have risen to the top, seven-year-old Cash Man, had to be put down after pulling up distressed when leading a Great Trethew Restricted in his first run since being bought for 50,000 guineas after winning a Tranwell Maiden in 1998.

The front-running Lakefield Rambler had won his final three Point-to-Points of 1999 and continued where he left off in two early Ladies' Opens in Cornwall. Then he was thrown in at the Hunter Chase deep end at Cheltenham. Ridden as usual by Polly Gundry and starting at 33-1, he led the Foxhunters field until three from home and was still very much in contention before Cavalero's decisive run. Lakefield Rambler's worthy fourth soon earned compensation in the Aintree novice event on Grand National Day and he won the United Hunts Cup at Cheltenham before ending with a trailing third behind Lord Harry and Balisteros in the John Corbet Cup at Stratford.

Her home is in Gloucestershire, so strictly speaking Polly Gundry is a West Midlands rider and she will be mentioned further in the review of that Area, but clamouring for mention among numerous other horses she rode for Barber's multi-talented string are such as Mizyan, who won four times in Mixed or Ladies Open company and was placed in his other five starts, John Keighley's 10,000 guineas Doncaster purchase Rushing Again, a five-year-old winner of a Larkhill Maiden in April and a rosy prospect, being closely related to his owner's renowned Rushing Wild, and Roger (Earthmover) Penny's six-year-old We Move Earth, who pulled up lame in his first Hunter Chase at Cheltenham in May after three wins between the flags.

Barber's number one jockey, Tim Mitchell, rode his 100th winner for the stable on One Of The Natives in a United Services Maiden at Larkhill, but not long afterwards things turned sour for him yet again. Sidelined for six weeks by injury in 1999 and desperately unlucky the previous year — when the late cancellation of the Torrington Farmers had robbed him of his title chance — he broke a collar-bone at the beginning of March when leading the men's championship race on a score of 13. Though his first come-back ride — on another Barber inmate, Stillmore Business — was a winner at the Axe Vale in early April, the problems with his damaged shoulder returned after only one more mount and grounded him for the rest of the season.

His brother Nick, who had been out of action nearly all the previous year after dislocating a hip, enjoyed a sparkling spring, his tally of 19 (first time in double figures) giving him the Area men's title. Notable winners for Nick included Gamay, from the stable he runs with owner John Boulter and successful four times (one of them the Area's prestige Mixed Open at the Mendip), and his father's Noddadante, while he scored on several from the Kay Rees/Polly Curling yard and won six races on four of John Dufosee's string, including the final winner of the season, Inforapop in the second Torrington Maiden — though Sea Spirit's supporters insist that he didn't!.

Dufosee's best representative, seven-year-old Chasing The Bride, was kept to Hunter Chases after an initial Barbury Castle third, winning at Wincanton and Ascot under Michael Miller and finishing second three times.

Tim Mitchell's absence meant extra opportunities for several others, among them Anthony Honeyball, who won four times with Finnegan Free and finished on a personal best of 14 despite the early frustration of a 28-day medical stand-down resulting from a January fall, and, of course, Polly Gundry. She took the Area ladies' title by a country mile from joint runners-up Shirley Vickery, who suffered an injury-restricted season, and debutante rider Charlotte Tizzard, 16-year-old cousin of jockey Joe.

When he had started at 16 in 1996 Joe Tizzard carried off the *Daily Telegraph* Men's Novice award and in 2000 his cousin rode seven winners and shared the female equivalent with David Pipe's head-girl Olivia Green. Charlotte was also the first recipient of the PPORA's Princess Royal Trophy for the leading female novice under 21 (the Wilkinson Sword, formerly open to both sexes — Joe Tizzard had shared it with Stuart Morris in 1996 — is now confined to males), and all her wins came on nine-year-old Millyhenry, who took the Area's leading horse prize for her grandfather Les Tizzard, his owner-breeder. Trained by Les's daughter-in-law, Joe's mother Pauline, Millyhenry also won once under Tabitha Cave at Cothelstone, an hour or so after Charlotte had been stood down after taking a heavy fall with Lord Of The Rings.

Of Millyhenry's stablemates, Castle Lynch won four of her nine starts under a variety of riders (including a Wincanton Hunter Chase for Shirley Vickery), but Knight Of Passion, who landed the odds at the first Larkhill easily enough, was not seen after finishing a reasonable eighth in the Cheltenham Foxhunters.

Two places in front of him at Cheltenham was the former useful hurdler Gillan Cove, trained for Mike Lockyer by Susie Old and persistently whispered for the big race after he had secured late qualification by winning two Opens in February, in the first of them, at the South Dorset, trouncing Butler John (*qv* Devon and Cornwall) and Miss O'Grady. After Cheltenham Gillan Cove decamped to Ireland and ran fourth in the Irish Grand National at Fairyhouse. His stable-companion, six-year-old Here Comes Henry, was unbeaten in five starts, beginning as a maiden and finishing in the Cotley's Mixed Open on May Day, and took the Area's Young Horse award.

Best of two **Yorkshire** Area challengers for the Foxhunters was the gallant third, Grant Tuer's Trade Dispute, who was making his first trip south since blundering away his chance when favourite for the previous year's Land Rover Final. His other two outings in 2000 brought comfortable successes at Catterick in February and Newcastle in April and he could be one for the highest honours next season.

Another from the region to be confined to hunter chasing was Last Option. He made a belated winning seasonal debut at Towcester and, after being one of five to crash at the first fence in the Martell Fox Hunters, was placed in his other three runs in top company, second to Mighty Moss at Ayr, third (after Gunner Welburn's last fence fall) in Punchestown's championship won by Sheltering and then third again behind Castle Mane and Grimley Gale at Stratford, where on the same day Jo Foster brought off a 33-1 shock win for Yorkshire in the Ladies Hunter Chase aboard the Sinnington-qualified Vital Issue. Earlier Miss Foster had been three times successful and twice second in Ladies Opens with her own Monkey Ago, the Area's leading Open horse.

Last Option's rider, Fiona Needham, took the local ladies title, winning five races between the flags, including the Staintondale Ladies Open with subsequent Aintree winner Springfield Rex (*qv* Midlands). She also won Hunter Chases with Joint Account and Orswellthatenswell, the latter owned, like Last Option, by her father, Robin Tate.

Massive entries were once again a Yorkshire feature, with Maiden races divided at every meeting — sometimes split again at scale — and runners plentiful right to the end thanks to almost universal good going, though there were a couple of waterlogged exceptions in late April, the York and Ainsty (for the third year) and the Pendle Forest. New to the schedule was the West of Yore, who, formerly combined with the Bedale, staged a very successful first meeting at Hornby Castle in February, occupying the spot once filled by the South Durham, who this year, after having had to postpone in both preceding seasons, chose to end the Area programme.

The West of Yore's excellent day was packed with post-last-fence excitement. In two races the leader was caught on the flat, while in one of the Maidens Tricky Trevor's lead was unassailable until Holly Delahooke's leather broke and she came off 20 yards from the line. It took four more attempts before Tricky Trevor gave his rider consolation in a Bedale Maiden.

Prior to the Area start in February, Yorkshire owners had returned empty-handed from their raid on the first Cottenham meeting while a similar excursion the following week to Alnwick was rewarded only when Minden Rose — laid low from then on — justified favouritism in the Restricted. The picture changed next weekend when all five of the Lincolnshire Club meeting's Maiden divisions fell to Yorkshire horses, to the delight of supporters from the largest county who swamped Market Rasen.

Outstanding among the winners was Margaret Cooper's Key Debate, who was backed from 12-1 to joint-favouritism at 5-2 and, ridden by Guy Brewer, never looked in the remotest danger. This exciting eight-year-old possesses a relentless gallop and, after a second place at the Brocklesby, his front-running style brought him four consecutive victories, including Hunter Chases in May at Huntingdon and Hexham. He received the highest praise from Tim Walford, who finished as Yorkshire's top trainer and described Key Debate as the best he has ever handled.

Brewer, who works in the Walford yard and is in his third season race-riding, notched a personal best of nine Pointing wins. He also landed three other Hunter Chases besides his two on Key Debate, others for Walford being Donnegale and dual Pointing winner Victoria's Boy, who gave him the first leg of a Hexham double when he triumphed in the Heart of All England. Victoria's Boy failed to make his reserve in August at Doncaster, though the bidding reached 24,000 guineas. Brewer also steered Walford's Gildoran five-year-old Ambersam to an effortless win in one of the Middleton's 2m 4f Maidens. This youngster did not appear again but a lot is thought of him. The trainer's son Robert travelled up from his Dorset base with Robert Alner to ride another of the yard's hunter chasers, Hiltonstown Lass, to win at Sedgefield in May.

Others noteworthy among those five winning Lincolnshire maidens were Alan Moore's five-year-old Ella Falls, who won twice more before being snapped up for 26,000 guineas at Doncaster and winning first time out in a hurdle for his new stable (Heather Dalton's), and seven-year-old Jackson's Hole, who won cheekily under David Easterby and went on to score in three of his next four starts and finish as Area joint-novice champion with Polar King. This latter seven-year-old was trained by Easterby himself to win three races.

Only failure by Jackson's Hole came in the Holderness Confined, for which he started at 5-2 on but, with his rider perhaps a shade over-confident, succumbed to the flying finish of Lynne Ward and Insideout, who got up just before the line. Sadly Insideout had no chance to add further scalps; his neck was broken when he fell at the following week's Hurworth meeting.

Easterby gained another training success through the six-year-old lightly-raced novice hurdler Meadowbank. He legged up owner Milo Watson to win impressively on him in a Sinnington Maiden. Meadowbank soon galloped himself out of Restricted grade, scoring again under Watson at the Derwent a fortnight later, but he did not reappear.

The Area riding championship was retained by Easterby — though Clive Mulhall fought him all the way to the wire — which was just reward for dedication, since he had to slim down from a pre-season 14 1/2 stone and, despite continual weight-watching, frequently put up extra poundage. Stephen Swiers (who notched his 100th Pointing win when Mr Dick coasted home in the Holderness Open) deputised for him on Polar King to win the 12st Confined at the Zetland meeting on May Day. By that time Easterby's other mounts were beginning to dry up and Mulhall, who won a Maiden there on six-year-old debutant The Hussey's King (favourite on this his only run), then mounted a determined challenge with four rides at the concluding South Durham. But two seconds and a third were all he could manage, so he finished three points adrift.

One of Mulhall's earlier winners — in a Derwent Maiden — was the ex-Howard Johnson hurdler Noble Hymn, a first success for Marty Featherstone's livery yard at Scarcroft, for which the seven-year-old won the Middleton Restricted next time out. Celebrations were renewed in the summer when Marty and Mulhall tied the knot, followed by a wedding party so packed with Hunt racing friends that it was more akin to the Area dinner.

PLATE 3　　　504 Holderness Mens Open: Stephen Swiers' 100th Point-to-Point winner, Mr Dick
PHOTO: Roy Parker

Easterby's will to win was occasionally judged over-enthusiastic. When the Old Raby began the Area season at Witton Castle he was fined £50 for excessive use of the whip after six-year-old Scruton, on whom he put up 6lb overweight, got home by a neck from Andrew Dalton and Top Toy. A similar offence cost him £25 after Polar King, running a bit below par, failed to catch Chris Gibbon and Prime Style in the Bilsdale Confined.

Jackson's Hole was his biggest winner numerically, but the best was six-year-old Prominent, owned in partnership by his trainer, Mick Brown, and Nick Duxbury, an accountant. The winner of a Maiden and a Restricted from four runs as a five-year-old, Prominent scored first at the Old Raby under Kevin Prendergast and, after a third in a Musselburgh Hunter Chase, was taken over by Easterby to win his next three starts in Open company, culminating in scintillating style in the Grimthorpe Cup four-miler at the Middleton meeting, the highlight of Yorkshire's season, where the large crowd, bathed in hot sunshine, enjoyed a nine-race card on perfect going.

The one contentious note came in the first three-mile maiden. Six of the 10 starters, their riders blinded by the sun, passed the wrong side of a marker before the second fence and then, after Tiger King had beaten Joe Smoke in a hotly-disputed finish, a possible objection by the rider of the second foundered because it was (a) not made in writing within the time allowed and (b) not accompanied by the prescribed deposit.

Prominent's Grimthorpe victory (with Easterby carrying 4lb overweight) was gained easing down from Mr Freebie (*qv* Midlands) and the previous year's winner Overflowing River. These two had come to Whitwell-on-the-Hill after Hunter Chase victories and went on to enhance the form when Overflowing River repeated his previous year's success in the four-miler at the Cheltenham Hunter Chase evening, with Mr Freebie just a short-head away.

Rumours had been rife in mid-season that Prominent, the Area's top Young Horse, was about to be sold for big money into Heather Dalton's stable, but nothing came of it and he next appeared in Doncaster's sale ring in May, first to be knocked down for 36,000 guineas and then to be returned after failing to pass the vet. He is now in training with Mick Easterby and Duxbury still holds a share.

One buy which did hold up at that same sale was the 20,000-guinea bid of trainer Mark Bradstock for Monica Dickinson's five-year-old Never Wonder. He had taken four runs to win his Maiden, finally making it at the Bramham Moor, where one of the finds of the season, Quarterstaff, completed his hat-trick under Chris Wilson in the Intermediate, having started the season a maiden. The six-year-old was then sent hunter chasing, finishing a good third in a 20-runner maiden event at the Cheltenham evening meeting before running sixth in the Heart of All England.

Once again the Badsworth took the palm for runners: 95 of them at Wetherby in mid-February. One of the three Maiden winners was the afore-mentioned Polar King; another was Roger Marley's six-year-old Romantic Native (Clive Mulhall). Third at Market Rasen a fortnight earlier, he was put away after the Badsworth until Doncaster Sales in August, where he went to the 15,000-guinea bid of trainer Richard Fahey. A 5000-guinea offer at the same sale secured What A Fiddler, a seven-year-old who won all his three starts for brothers Richard and James Tate, sons of trainer Tom. Other siblings to share triumph were Richard and Ruth Clark, who rode both Open winners at the Cleveland, Richard on Private Jet and his sister aboard Japodene.

Frost threatened the Sinnington but the Duncombe Park course passed an early inspection and racing took place in glorious sunshine before a huge crowd, many of whom joined in the infectious gamble on Nigel Tutty's Murton Heights (25-1 to 6-1), who took the Open in some style when drawing clear of Concerto Collonges, who made the winner's enclosure himself after a Carlisle Hunter Chase on Easter Monday.

A rare sight on the Yorkshire circuit is a challenger from the **Welsh Border Counties** Area, but that splendid galloper Pharare, trained and ridden by Caroline Spearing, made the trip from the North Ledbury country to land the long odds laid on him in the Derwent Ladies' Open on the first Saturday in March. Pharare clearly travels well; his other Ladies' Open wins came at Thorpe Park, Kingston Blount (twice) and Weston Park (where he may have been treated kindly to be awarded a dead-heat after a tremendous battle with Hearts Are Wild); in fact, his one failure in six runs came the only time he stayed at home, when, with the South Herefordshire race at his mercy, he and Miss Spearing parted at the final

Garnons fence. His stable-companion Bankhead, returning from a not unsuccessful stint under Rules and racing with a Croome certificate, also travelled for two Ladies Open wins at Mollington — hard-pressed in January, very easily in March.

The North Ledbury was a newcomer to the Welsh Border schedule — the Hunt's races having been switched from Upton-on-Severn to Bitterley — and this brought other high-class horses within the boundaries in addition to Pharare, among them Distinctive, who will be mentioned later in the West Midlands review in connection with the Lady Dudley Cup.

Iron Pyrites was probably the most improved horse seen out in this part of the world and she collected the Area's Young Horse award. She began with victory in a division of the Brecon Maiden and, after transferring to the stable of her rider, Steve Lloyd, ended competently with wins at Bitterley and Bredwardine. The turn of foot possessed by this young mare should keep her to the fore in 2001.

The Radnor & West Hereford veteran Rusty Bridge, the horse on which Richard Johnson, Tony McCoy's only rival for the NH jockey title, gained early experience in the Point-to-Point field — and won his first Hunter Chase — carried off the first of the season's 'classics', the four-mile Lord Ashton of Hyde's Cup at the Heythrop fixture. The 13-year-old failed to get his head in front in his other four outings, all in Hunter Chases, but the marathon trip and the soft conditions at Dunthrop were set up for him as Richard Burton successfully adopted 'catch me if you can' tactics.

Sue Johnson also produced the winner's stablemate Raise And Gain, an unsuccessful novice hurdler, to score twice, though an 'improved form' inquiry followed his first victory in a Maisemore Maiden. The accepted explanation was that the Maisemore ground was good with soft patches, whereas it had been good to firm when he had been tailed off on his fencing debut at Chaddesley Corbett a fortnight before. Raise And Gain's only other run came a month later when he was sent up to win the Albrighton Restricted — on firm going.

In recent years Nick Shutts has probably not had the success his support for Point-to-Pointing deserves, but he may have unearthed a potential star in Mr Pistachio. The Penny Grainger-trained five-year-old's career did not begin well when he had to be withdrawn from a Ross Harriers Maiden at Garnons after unseating and injuring Alan Phillips on the way to the start. By the time Phillips returned to the saddle later in the season Mr Pistachio had won twice under Gary Hanmer in an Eaton Hall Maiden and in the Ludlow Members. In his only other outing he was still in contention when falling with Tim Stephenson at Sandon.

Another five-year-old in the same ownership, Cashew Crisis, overcame earlier jumping problems and finished second twice at Bitterley before being sold for 15,000 guineas at Doncaster to Richard Barber. Carrying the same colours stablemate Aegean Fanfare won two Ladies Opens, which would surely have been three had she not fallen foul of the last at Barbury Castle when well clear of her solitary rival.

Shutts's quartet with Karen Marks did not shine. Unrequited Love and Pancho's Tango failed to impress, New Yorker looks as though he will need time to fulfil potential, while Nouvalari's speed did not match that of his famous namesake and 500 guineas was accepted for him — presumably with gratitude — at Doncaster in August.

Scarlett Knipe rode very successfully in the 1960s — was that post-war Point-to-Pointing's golden age? — and she and husband Robin enjoyed continued success with horses from their Cobhall Court Stud, notably the Ardross mare Ardstown. She travelled to Cottenham in January, finishing second under Shirley Vickery to Imperial Dawn (*qv* Midlands) and was thereafter confined to Hunter Chases, showing plenty of gameness when ridden to victory by Frank Windsor-Clive at Chepstow and Leicester. She was placed in her other three outings. Six-year-old stablemate La Kabyle shaped like a non-stayer in her early appearances until Adrian Wintle (the Area's top rider) took over and managed to settle her at Garnons, where she confounded her critics by staying on strongly to win. But she had been bought in France with breeding in mind and racing is unlikely to figure on her future agenda.

Another with a North Ledbury certificate, Autumn Blunder, likewise offered little encouragement in his early runs from rider Tim Stephenson's stable at Castlemorton, but he improved as conditions firmed up and won at Woodford (giving Stephenson his 100th Point-to-Point winner) and Chaddesley Corbett.

Most of Andrew Dalton's string qualified in the North Western Area but Red Oassis was an exception. This son of Rymer had shown little in his first two seasons between the flags but now won an Upper Sapey Maiden and a Bitterley Restricted on his only starts. He qualified with the Ludlow, as did the debutant five-year-old Benson, ridden and trained by Dalton for Downton Hall pro trainer Henry Daly and third on his only start.

Dalton's presence in the saddle also seemed to revitalise the Mark Doyle-trained Good For A Loan to win the Area's prestige race, which was once again the *Confined* Championship at the Golden Valley. Qualification demanded completion in any Area Confined race and Good For A Loan just scraped in by virtue of a distant sixth at Cursneh Hill. Injury prevented his rider there, Robert Cooper, taking the mount in the championship, but under Dalton Good For A Loan ran on gamely to take the £350 prize at 25-1. Just four days later he (and Dalton) supplemented that with another success at the Teme Valley, whose meeting was restaged on a May Wednesday after being the Area's only casualty when waterlogged off on Easter Saturday. On the new date the going was firm and so slippery after showers that abandonment of the concluding Maiden divisions was forced.

Celtic Abbey may have dropped down the ratings since his *Horse & Hound* Cup win of 1997, but Christine Hardinge sent him from her Ballingham stable to win a Chepstow Hunter Chase impressively from Ardstown. That, though, was his only run, whereas another hunter chaser, Shafi, who joined Steve Flook after winning twice for David Pipe in 1999, contested seven after a pipe-opener at Barbury Castle and was never worse than fourth. His highlight came at the Cheltenham evening meeting when, despite running wide into the straight, he sprinted home in a 22-runner event over the extended two miles to give a first Rules win to his handler and a first win of any sort to his rider Mark Trott, a former conditional. Trott's first Point-to-Point win a fortnight later made fewer demands — it was a Teme Valley walk-over.

Clive Hitchings qualified a couple with the Kyre Bloodhounds which were prepared for him by Andy Morgan. Fontaine Again did not prove the most tractable sort at first but ran really well to win his Maiden when allowed to gallop on at the Golden Valley, while Thatsforeel did enough to win a Tanatside Intermediate, but that was his only outing and he has yet to suggest that he might ever give his owner adequate return for the 35,000 guineas he paid for him in 1998.

Three more with Kyre certificates were among those Annie Downes prepares in the Westhide yard she shares with her partner Mark Jackson, who held, but has now relinquished, a licence. One of them, Nevada Gold, finished third over 4m 2f at Uttoxeter under Richard Burton, after earlier carrying the North Hereford's amateur whip Ray Rogers, 46, to victory in a novice riders Mixed Open at Upton, while Flat winner Happy Minstral never failed to complete, beginnnig with a Garnons Confined win for Burton and ending with success in a Maisemore Mixed Open partnered by Adrian Wintle.

One in the yard with North Ledbury qualification, George Dillingham, is owned by Sue Gent, wife of avid supporter Peter, formerly of Interlink Express, and gave them both cause for celebration when sent up to Eaton Hall to be ridden by Carrie Ford to reverse his earlier Eyton-on-Severn placings — just — with Hersilia.

Others in the Jackson/Downes stable qualify with **West Midlands** Area packs, most notably — with the Clifton-on-Teme — star performer Grimley Gale. After unseating Shirley Vickery in the Cheltenham Foxhunters on her seasonal debut, she won three successive Hunter Chases at Ludlow and another at Exeter before finishing second to a rejuvenated Castle Mane when attempting to repeat her 1999 triumph in the Intrum Justitia *Horse & Hound* Cup. She will be 12 in 2001 but there is no reason to suppose she will slip from hunter chasing's top flight if her owners, Robin and Maureen Phillips, give her another year. Their colours were also carried by another Strong Gale mare, seven-year-old Miss Gale, who lost her maiden certificate on her only appearance of the season at Cursneh Hill on the last day of April.

This is a relatively small Area, with only 10 meetings, and three of the last four in the list, the Cotswold Vale, the Croome and the Berkeley, all had to find new slots in May after suffering waterlogging in April.

West Midlands rider Julian Pritchard tried hard to retain the national championship for a fourth year, but seemed to be fighting an uphill battle from the start and, though finishing runner-up, never managed to get his head in front at any stage. He won 28 races and was placed in no fewer than 47, too, which gives some indication of the frustration endured. He lost his top score record, too, when John Thomas McNamara rode an astonishing 52 winners in Ireland, but at least his British record remained intact when Jefford ended on 42, one short of Pritchard's 1999 figure.

His close association with the stables of Nickie Sheppard, Angelica (Jelly) Nolan and Jim Callow probably resulted in missing some 'spare' rides and the Sheppard yard at Eastnor, for one, dipped in fortune numerically, having to rest content with 11 winners, plus a Hereford Hunter Chase with Now We Know. Cruise A Hoop's loss and the absence of Stag Fight — between them they contributed seven to the Pritchard/Sheppard tally in 1999 — left the stable with limited resources for Open races, while its biggest winner, Peter Corbett's Upton Adventure, was ridden not by Pritchard but by Scott Joynes. Corbett's home-bred made significant progress, despite a tendency to make mistakes at the business end of her races; she won four of seven starts and received the Weatherbys Young Horse Award for the Area.

Next largest contributor for Mrs Sheppard was Graham Smith's Dawn Invader, who at last began to build on his Maiden success of 1997 and won three times. But when he scored in the Heythrop Intermediate Jamie Jukes was in the saddle, Pritchard being aboard Sue Nock's second-placed Burgundy Bob — more frustration — and when Pritchard got back on Dawn Invader at the Cheltenham Hunter Chase evening he appeared to be holding a double handful just behind Lakefield Rambler until his mount broke down three from home. Capstown Bay, Cowanstown Prince and Black Oak were other Sheppard winners for Pritchard, but Ard Na Carrig, who, after an inauspicious start, came good to win a Harkaway Maiden, was Adrian Wintle's ride.

Jim Callow and Pritchard enjoyed a fine season with Forest Fountain and his young half-brother Philtre. The former began successfully at Larkhill and ended with a Hunter Chase win at Stratford in May, in between times picking up some useful places in Open company and running third over four miles at Cheltenham, while Philtre won a Maiden and a Restricted before losing no kudos when going down to Key Debate (*qv* Yorkshire) on his Hunter Chase debut at Huntingdon.

Soft ground early on resulted in a quiet start for Jelly Nolan's Gloucestershire stable but the inmates came into their own when conditions grew more favourable. This yard, where Jayne Webber held sway until her departure for South Africa in 1998 and which receives major support from Patricia Duncan and her daughters, Caroline Mackness and Vanessa Ramm, is making an increasing impact, which could be even greater next year with the return of a trio who had to remain on the sidelines in 2000, Mountenry Star, Jimmy Greenspoon and Arctic Grey. 'Returnees' this year were Full Score and Haughton Lad, both winning again after a year off.

Full Score was one for Pritchard; others in the string who gave him single victories were Happen To Make It, Goawayoutofthat and Mick Mackie, but he rode the number one in the yard, Mrs Ramm's Fresh Prince, to win three times in Open company.

Miss Nolan herself had landed her first riding successes in 1999, winning three times with Look In The Mirror. This year, riding 20-1 shot Haughton Lad at Garnons in March, she benefited from the already-described Pharare upset (*qv* Welsh Borders), but then her luck ran out the following week. Look In The Mirror, with only three fences between him and victory in the Grafton Ladies race, fired her into the Mollington turf and she sustained a broken pelvis. Lucinda Sweeting proved an able deputy; she and Look In The Mirror won twice in May, in a Hereford Hunter Chase and when sent down west for the Dulverton East to beat Mizyan (*qv* Wessex). Finally Look In The Mirror was only caught on the flat in Stratford's Ladies Hunter Chase by Vital Issue (*qv* Yorkshire).

The West Midlands may no longer be able to boast the men's champion, but the *Racing Post* Cup for the top lady went to Gloucestershire rider Polly Gundry, though nearly all her 30 successes were notched either in the already-reviewed Wessex or the still-to-come Devon and Cornwall Areas. Seventeen of those wins, plus two Hunter Chases on Lakefield Rambler, came on horses trained by Richard Barber and she actually won only two races in her home Area — at the Beaufort on Just Bert for West Country trainer Mike Biddick and at the Berkeley for Susie Goess-Saurau on Libido (now with Henry Daly) — while even her own horse Hearts Are Wild, prepared for her near Wotton-under-Edge by 1961 men's champion John Daniell to win three times, raced with a Cattistock certificate.

PLATE 4   *Richard Barber, for once not directly involved, congratulates Ladies Champion Polly Gundry after another win on her own Hearts Are Wild, father Robin looks on*
PHOTO: Mark Johnston

Exceptionally talented and delightfully modest with it, the one-time event rider has been much-boosted by her link with the Barber yard but looked a championship long-shot in the first half of the season. Title-holder Pip Jones set a blazing early pace — indeed, bookies had closed their ledgers on *Racing Post* Cup betting by the end of February — but then the leader sailed into the doldrums. Miss Gundry, who rode her first winner at the Talybont as a 16-year-old in 1992 and had been runner-up for the title last year, drew level with a double on Easter Saturday, went ahead with two more on the Monday and gradually drew clear.

Alison Dare has brought the ladies title to the West Midlands six times and few can match her skills in the saddle, even after 20 years of riding winners, most of them for the acknowledged master of his art, Dick Baimbridge. This time her season was interrupted by a broken collar-bone incurred when falling with only her second ride (Play Poker at Black Forest Lodge) and she did not start winning until the Heythrop, but there her uncanny judgement of pace was never better demonstrated than in the Lyon Trophy, when Rip Van Winkle, a distance behind at halfway, scythed through tiring rivals, which included Mr Dow Jones, Grey Smoke and Hearts Are Wild, to lead before the second last.

Rip Van Winkle returned to his best form, winning four of his five starts (Claire Dyson substituting for the first of them), but he is approaching retirement and, though owner Dr

Paul Brown looked to have a ready-made replacement in Connors after his debut second at Whitwick, the seven-year-old broke down badly under Pritchard at Chaddesley Corbett in March. Another four-time winner for the Baimbridge/Dare partnership — after being comprehensively beaten by the useful Vestey horse Grey Smoke at Barbury Castle — was Split Second, while the evergreen Nether Gobions won three under Julian Pritchard, though sadly owner Pearce Clutterbuck died three weeks before the last of them. Well Ted looks a rising Baimbridge star; he won his last two outings in Confined class after early disappointments and could figure prominently in next year's Opens.

Tom Scudamore, son of former NH champion Peter and now establishing himself under Rules, enjoyed a great second season's Pointing, particularly with his mother's Cotswold-qualified Glevum. A disappointing hurdler and chaser, the eight-year-old found Hunt race opposition less formidable and ran up a sequence of six wins and was in contention for the Leading Horse award until Easter. At two West Country meetings she gave her 17-year-old rider the third leg of trebles set up on David Pipe horses.

Another Cotswold qualifier, former useful staying hurdler Newton Point, provided further NH connection; he won twice and was second in his other three starts to give a first taste of success to rider Belinda Keighley, wife of ex-jockey Martin, and trainer Dolly Maude, wife of still-going-jockey Chris.

Caroline Chadney has a good record with what might be termed 'problem' horses and Fintona Boy was another fine advertisement for her Mathon stable. Disappointing last year and making no special mark in his first two runs of 2000, he suddenly started winning under Richard Burton at the end of March and landed four consecutive victories. Miss Chadney can also claim some credit for the triumph of Distinctive in the Area's 'big' race, the Worcestershire's Lady Dudley Cup at Chaddesley Corbett. She helped with the preparation after the horse's owner-trainer, Debbie Jackson, broke a shoulder coming off him at Brampton Bryan. Until then Distinctive had been an intended runner in the Worcestershire's Ladies race — he had won over the course at the Harkaway under Mrs Jackson — but, switched to the 'classic' and with Adrian Wintle up, he led from flag fall and had the prize in safe keeping a mile from home.

It has to be admitted that, apart from the disappointing odds-on Solba, Distinctive did not have a lot to beat; the field of four was the smallest since this once-great race was established in 1897 — when the winner received 'a cup, value £50, presented by Lady Dudley, plus one third of the [2 sov] entrance fees' — and its star status has long gone. Can it be recovered? Suggestions of a mid-week date produce shudders from organizers at the thought of reduced attendances, though at this year's rain-hit meeting, four days after an extra-busy mid-week Heythrop, the crowd seemed not up to much anyway. In 2001 the fixture follows Easter, just four days after the Croome. The committee has a lot of thinking to do.

The Worcestershire Members winner Do It Once sported colours carried to so many successes by the famed Pat Tollit, and before that for her father, long-time races secretary Harold Rushton. Eight-year-old Do It Once, a discard from J P McManus after winning in Ireland in 1999 (5000 guineas at Doncaster), won again at the Croome and looks a useful acquisition. He is trained at home, but the 1996 Supreme Novice Hurdle winner Indefence, who won for Mrs Tollit at Brampton Bryan, beating Rip Van Winkle, is with Pip Hooley. Indefence had leg problems after his Festival win and they may have recurred, since he was not seen again.

Smile Pleeze's performances vindicated the judgement of Upton-on-Severn trainer Mike Daniell, who paid 5000 guineas for him when he was sent to Malvern after the 1999 season from the John Dufosee stable in Dorset. The eight-year-old began with a win at the PPORA fixture in January and then scored twice in May at Eyton-on-Severn and Woodford.

Janet Hughes, who has not enjoyed the best of luck in recent years with Rocket Radar and Hatterill Ridge, has a promising youngster in Cider Man, judging by his good effort at Upton in May, while Emma Baker's yard at Naunton houses two bright prospects in the Andoversford Maiden winner Ballyblack and five-year-old Brockbuster, who was going well until falling at the 15th on his only run.

Advancing years have not yet caught up with Granville Grill or his trainer-rider Johnnie Deutsch. Aged, respectively, 15 and 47, they won twice together and it would be no surprise to see them lining up to attempt a fifth victory in the Beaufort Members race next year.

Like Deutsch, Rory Lawther is of maturer vintage, but he showed far younger rivals a thing or two when the Berks and Bucks Draghounds brought **South Midlands** Area activities to a close at Kingston Blount on the last Sunday in May. The 43-year-old farrier from near Great Missenden won on all his four rides to set the seal on a personal best season (16 wins) and snatch Area and course championships from Jimmy Tarry. Remarkably, all his four mounts were saddled by John White, a former pro trainer from Upper Basildon, who sent out a fifth to win for Julian Pritchard. White trained four of this quintet for the Hunt's Master, Nick Quesnel, the best of them being Open winner Castle Folly, who had won earlier in similar class at the first meeting on the course in February and at the Beaufort in March.

Earlier Lawther had special reason to remember the 107-runner Heythrop meeting, where he rode Take The Brush to win one of the 2m 4f Maidens. The six-year-old mare — another of Quesnel's — was the first winner trained by Lawther's wife Karen. Both Heythrop Opens have been mentioned earlier; missing from the men's four-miler, the Area's prestige race, was the previous year's winner, Camp Bank. Gerard and Sue Nock's Strong Gale 10-year-old had won five consecutive races last year, but, following an easy win at Mollington in January and a vain chase of Copper Thistle over the Heythrop course at the Farmers' Bloodhounds meeting in February, he did not appear again. The Nocks also introduced six-year-old Burgundy Bob to win impressively at Larkhill and Mollington before being beaten by Dawn Invader at the Heythrop.

Leading South Midlands lady rider was Lucinda Sweeting, who rode three horses from her own stable to win four races and also, as related in the preceding West Midlands review, substituted successfully for the injured Jelly Nolan on Look In The Mirror. Best from her own yard was the eight-year-old Mr Custard, who, after an initial sixth, was never out of the first three in his next eight runs, winning Ladies Opens at the VWH and the Harborough Club.

The PPORA got the Area off to a spanking start in January at Barbury Castle, with sunshine for once drawing a record crowd. As to be expected here, winners came from a variety of countries, the only one from within the region being the Old Berks-qualified Rectory Garden, on whom young Robert Biddlecombe repeated his opening day victory at Tweseldown a fortnight before. He and Rectory Garden returned to win again at Tweseldown and, after several placings, ended their season with an Easter Open race double, at Kimble on the Saturday and Lockinge on the Monday. The young man also won a novice riders race at the Mendip Farmers for Nick Mitchell on Starpath.

Two lengths behind Rectory Garden in the PPORA's Mixed Open came Cavalero, who was returning after Highworth owner-trainer Johnny Manners had given him a not unsuccessful season in handicap chases, collecting some useful place money before a shot at the Grand National was ended by a slipping saddle. The year before, following a last-fence fall when victory was certain at the PPORA meeting, Cavalero had numbered the United Hunts Cup and the Aintree Fox Hunters among seven consecutive wins. This time, after a second at Haydock and a win at Warwick, he and Alex Charles-Jones — a painter who displays artistry in the saddle — swooped to win the Cheltenham Foxhunters, catching six rivals on the climb from the final fence. The VWH-qualified 11-year-old missed the cut in the Grand National and unseated early in the Scottish equivalent, but returned to Cheltenham in late April to win again, inflicting another defeat on Foxhunters runner-up Real Value (qv South East).

The Area suffered no major weather disruption, though the second Bicester meeting at Kingston Blount in mid-April fell victim to waterlogging and heavy rain made the Ashorne course unraceable on May Day for the Warwickshire's fixture. It was staged successfully on the Wednesday of the following week — by which time the ground rode firm. True Point-to-Point tradition was to the fore when meeting secretary Ann Cockburn won the Members race with Hehas, a home-bred representing the fifth generation descending from a mare called Shemight — Shewill's daughter Shedid was the best of them — who Mrs Cockburn had been given nearly 50 years before. Hehas and Charlie Wadland followed up in a Larkhill Intermediate a fortnight later.

PLATE 5   32 P-t-P Owners & Riders Club Mixed Open (Div 1): Mizyan (Miss P. Gundry), 3rd, leads from Cavelero (A. Charles-Jones), 2nd, La Kabyla (F. Windsor Clive), 7th, and Flying Imp (J. Barnes), 4th   PHOTO: Tim Holt

The Bicester — to be strictly correct the Bicester with Whaddon Chase — has two slots in the fixture list, a legacy of the amalgamation of the two Hunts 14 years before, and the going for the first, at Mollington in early March, was so deep that only 55 of 196 entries turned out and the Land Rover qualifier, in which Kites Hardwicke beat three rivals, was arguably the worst Open seen on the course in its 28-year history. None of the three Maiden winners seems likely to gain much greater glory, but at least local hero Jimmy Tarry, whose early-season efforts had frequently gone awry, finally got off the mark with Grecian Star, while the Master's wife, Tocky McKie, led in the Members winner Perfect Minstrel. Successful rider Fred Hutsby scored again on Perfect Minstrel at the Warwickshire but he was to end the season with a broken arm when the too-often disappointing True Hustler fell at Umberleigh's ditch on the final day.

Grecian Star won again later for Tarry but the Preston Capes stable, which qualifies its home-bred horses with the Grafton or Pytchley, had a quieter-than-usual season, with not much young blood apparent. Just Like Madge and Fawsley Manor were always among the finishers and contributed a couple of wins apiece, but time-honoured veteran Lucky Christopher, confined to Ladies races partnered by Jimmy's niece Rosie Goodwin, failed to add to his career total of 25 victories. The Tarry-bred Lily The Lark was the Area's biggest Ladies race winner, scoring five times from 11 runs for owner-rider Heather Irving, who now holds a training licence. The mare qualified with the Farmers Bloodhounds and scored four times beyond the Area's boundaries, at Parham (twice), Guilsborough and Flagg Moor, her one 'home win' being gained very easily at Kimble from My Best Man.

The latter was one of the few failures in the Aston Rowant establishment of Lawney Hill, whose husband, former rider Alan, is Master of the Vale of Aylesbury. Of the stable's seven individual winners Mr Snowman earned top spot. Ridden by the trainer herself, he began by taking a Confined at the Oxford University meeting and then went hunter chasing. Kept to shorter distance events, he won at Leicester and Towcester and finished second on his other two outings, going down by a short-head at Ascot to the Berks and Bucks-qualified and pro-trained Castle Court.

A new neighbour of the Hills, David Barlow, one of three riding brothers — William and Charlie are the others — who have done well in the North-West, now keeps his horses with them and his move south brought a best-ever season, with 11 wins. He had the distinction of winning the Cambridge University Club race on his own Cherrynut and the Oxford University equivalent on another from the Hills stable, Winters Tale, while he won twice on his own Oboedire and travelled to score for other connections in Herefordshire, Shropshire and Kent.

Seven-year-old Royal Estate, qualified with the Heythrop and the only horse trained by Tim Holland-Martin, looks an improving sort. A perhaps fortunate winner of the VWH Confined (Well Ted unseated his rider at the last when three lengths clear) he ended by beating the only other finisher in an Intermediate at Woodford. Two-length runner-up to Royal Estate at the VWH was another bearing a Heythrop certificate, Mike and Ginny Elliott's Gildrom. This was the Gildoran six-year-old's only appearance within the Area but he was never worse than second in five races, winning three and collecting the Young Horse award for the South Midlands.

PLATE 6   953 Blackmore & Sparkford Vale Intermediate: Elliewelliewoo and Champion Rider Les Jefford, 1st, lead Agile King and joint National Ladies Champion Novice Rider Charlotte Tizzard, 4th
PHOTO: Brian Armstrong

Elliewelliewoo, who took the equivalent prize in **Devon and Cornwall**, was one of the winning rides of new national champion Les Jefford, the one, indeed, on whom he chalked up his career century when the flying mare came up country to complete a seasonal hat-trick at the Blackmore Vale. Jefford, assistant to Cullompton trainer Gerald Cottrell, was the first to take the *Daily Telegraph* Trophy to the Area since Philip Scholfield set what was then a record 37 wins in 1988. Jefford's final score of 42 pushed his career total to 121 and there have been many more under Rules, not least those which brought him the 1999 Bollinger Amateur Championship on the Flat. Invitations to ride abroad are one of the perks of this title and he made a Sunday trip to France to ride in a chase there 24 hours after completing a double at the Dulverton East (from Mounsey Hill Gate to Auteuil, the mind boggles) but dashed back for the South Tetcott on the Bank Holiday, only to be narrowly beaten aboard the odds-on Georgetown, his only mount.

Devon and Cornwall also provided the joint-novice champion lady rider in Olivia Green, who shared this top spot with Charlotte Tizzard (*qv* Wessex). Miss Green, who is David Pipe's head girl, rode her first winner on Mike Biddick's Travel By Land in the North Cornwall Members in early February and added another six successes before the end of the season, despite 21 days on the sidelines resulting from a heavy fall at the Blackmore Vale.

Jefford also looked likely to miss several weeks after being taken to hospital strapped to a stretcher following a crash in January at the Royal Artillery meeting, when his mount suffered a fatal heart attack approaching the ninth fence and fell, crushing him against it. His name was even removed from championship betting lists by bookies, but in the event he was absent for only one weekend and, though drawing blank on his immediate return, rode a four-timer the following week at the South Pool, a feat he was to repeat later in the season at the Dartmoor.

West Country achievement was also recognised at the PPORA Awards lunch at Stratford in June when the Weatherbys Breeder of the Season prize went to Basil Young, who stands the 23-year-old stallion Lir, always prominent in the sires of winners list, at his stud near Liskeard. The Youngs provide enthusiastic support for racing and have enjoyed notable recent successes with such home-breds by Lir as Saint Joseph, Full Alirt and The Kimbler, all ridden by daughter Susan Young.

Saint Joseph collected two Hunter Chase wins on his favoured soft ground at Taunton. Other Hunter Chase winners from the Area included Palace Parade, who followed three Pointing victories by scoring at Fontwell on Spring Bank Holiday for Lewdown-based trainers Yvonne Watson and Jo Channon; John Papworth's grey Flying Maria, successful at Newton Abbot and Ludlow; and Lead Story, a well-backed winner of the Intermediate Final at Newton Abbot under Tabitha Cave. Lead Story's trainer, Gordon Chambers at Buckfastleigh, also saddled Blazing Miracle, Sagaville and Witney O'Grady to win Point-to-Points.

Caroline Egalton and Graham Stuart have produced an exceptional strike rate from their stable near Ottery St Mary in recent years and 2000 was no exception. The duo provided eight of Jefford's total, including Elliewelliewoo's three. Brave Noddy was another three-timer for them, culminating in the Torrington's Open on the final day; but he failed to make his Doncaster reserve in August, being led out unsold after bids petered out at 12,000 guineas.

David Pipe has wasted no time infiltrating the top-flight of Point-to-Point trainers since he retired from race-riding with 22 winners (21 more than father Martin) and in his second season achieved an impressive 28 successes, notably Well Armed (six wins), Slew Man (seven wins, three seconds from 10 runs), Iranos (three wins) and Brian Kilpatrick's home-bred five-year-old Horus, who started a maiden and completed his hat-trick in the Cattistock Open. Kingsbridge was another three-time winner (once each for Tom Scudamore, Les Jefford and Polly Gundry), for whom 20,000 guineas was not enough at the May Doncaster Sale.

Pipe's first triumphs came at the Area's opening meeting, the Silverton, thanks to Alice Shorelark and Well Armed, but Slew Man (Tim Mitchell) was just outbattled when 5-2 on for the Open there by the consistent Bells Wood, ridden by Charlie White, one of the most improved jockeys in the West after so long in the shadow of his now-grounded brother Richard. Bells Wood was placed in five of his next six outings and then, at the end of May, defeated another 5-2 on chance, Butler John, at Mounsey Hill Gate before signing off at Bratton Down on a day of swirling fog (that's Exmoor in June!) by beating Starpath and Possible Pardon in very soft ground. On that same foggy day Stewart Pike's home-bred Ardross six-year-old No Loss gave notice of Hunter Chase potential when winning the Restricted under Jefford. A stable accident had kept No Loss at home after his seasonal debut second at an early Larkhill, but he won his Maiden very easily on his return at Bredwardine in mid-May.

PLATE 7   *The season ended as it had begun, flaming June at Laleston for the Llangeinor*
PHOTO: Kathleen Mullen

Tim Mitchell partnered Iranos and the ill-fated Ibex (who broke his pelvis at Cothelstone in April) for another Pipe double at the second Area meeting, the North Cornwall — where one from Mike Biddick's string, Just Bert, scored the first of three Ladies Open wins — but the two winners for the stable a week later at the Mid-Devon, Slew Man and Well Armed (beat Bells Wood), were both ridden by Tom Scudamore, who went on to complete a treble aboard Glevum (*qv* West Midlands). This was the 17-year-old rider's first threesome, but he did it again at Holnicote at the end of the month, with Glevum again and two more of Pipe's, the then maiden Kingsbridge and the Open on Rossell Island, who was later killed in a first-fence fall in the Aintree Fox Hunters.

Pipe's horses gave Jefford his initial four-timer the following week at the first Buckfastleigh meeting, the South Pool, where Marion Turner's so-consistent No More Nice Guy landed his first success of the campaign in the Restricted. He followed in an Intermediate later and was never out of the first four in 10 races, helping Mandy Hand, daughter of his owner, to a 10th Area ladies' title. Needless to say Jefford took the men's.

Rain featured frequently in the West but the first of many wet days failed to spoil a good nine-race card put on by the East Cornwall at Great Trethew, when another of Mrs Hand's mounts, Sandra Turner's Solomans Sister (by Lir), gained the first of her three wins in one of the Maidens. Solomans Sister, now 10, was not broken until seven but is beginning to pay tribute to her staying dam, Cornish Princess. In 1996 another of identical breeding, Prince Soloman, gave Solomans Sister's trainer George Turner (Mrs Hand's uncle) the last win of an honourable career in the saddle.

The East Cornwall's Lemalla meeting (the Hunt has had two fixtures since its merger with the Bolventor Harriers) was also hit by rain and fog. Richard Barber came down from Dorset to win both Opens with The Hobbit and Lakefield Rambler (they had also scored at Great Trethew) and the Confined provided one of the closest finishes seen in the Area when Richard Woollacott forced Westcountry Lad up on the line to deny Baldhu Chance and Alex Ede by inches. Woollacott, 22, enjoyed his best season, his nine winners putting him second to Jefford for the local title, while Ede took the novice award after three successes on Terry Long's Baldhu-prefixed horses and has now joined Robert Alner.

It was Barber two, Pipe four, at the East Devon on Oliver Carter's course at Ottery St Mary, but local interest in one of the Maidens centred on Wibbley Wobbley, who gained the first of four wins. The eight-year-old, allegedly named after the course he tended to steer in dressage before a planned eventing career was aborted, was the mount of Jo Cumings, who married the horse's owner, Rory Davies, in September. Wibbley Wobbley, subsequently sold privately to a South Eastern owner, was a leading winner for the stable of his rider's father, Keith Cumings, whose other successes included the late season hat-trick by Mine's A Gin, also partnered by his daughter.

Numerous dogs had barked before the Phardante six-year-old Black Dante made his debut at the second Buckfastleigh. A short-priced favourite, he fell before halfway, but six days later made amends at Kilworthy. He was even more impressive the following month in very heavy ground at Bratton Down, where, elevated straight into Mixed Open company — for the Area's prestige race — he beat Wibbley Wobbley by five lengths and earned the highest praise from rider Alex Charles-Jones. Now in training with Philip Hobbs, he had earlier failed to reach his reserve at Doncaster May Sales, where owner Edward Retter's other entry, the seven-year-old S B S By Jove, also remained unsold after a final bid of 17,000 guineas. Picked up for a tiny fraction of that sum the year before, after bucking his way to notoriety in the North, S B S By Jove won a Maiden and a Restricted impressively under Charles-Jones in February but was not seen again.

Followers in the West certainly get their money's worth. The Lamerton's 11 races and 113 runners at the end of March were followed a week later by the Spooners & West Dartmoor's 12 races contested by 108 horses at rain-soaked Cherrybrook, where Saint Joseph lowered Mizyan's colours in the Ladies' Open (with favourite Just Bert well beaten) and riders Richard Woollacott and Neil Harris were both fined £175 after a Portman Square inquiry into their contretemps in one of the Restricteds. The Confined went to Rosa's Revenge, trained by Lucy Johnson, who provides Point-to-Point coverage in the *Western Morning News*, and the mare followed up at fortnightly intervals at the two Flete Park meetings — a splendid prelude for her retirement to stud.

Jefford notched up his second four-timer at the first Flete Park, taking the four-mile Open for the Lord Mildmay of Flete Cup with a vintage ride on Jane Walter's home-bred Funny Farm in ground made soft by heavy overnight rain. Next weekend relentless rain on the day forced abandonment after only three races of the Four Burrow's Easter Monday meeting, though the new course at Trebudannon had a full workout a fortnight later when it hosted the South Cornwall, postponed from Great Trethew in early March. The new line was well received, applauded for its compact layout of all facilities at the top of a hillside from which there was a perfect view of the flat, left-handed track on the valley floor. The Area's only other weather victim was the Stevenstone, rained off at Vauterhill on May Day.

A clash between Butler John and Elliewelliewoo promised the race of the season at the Tetcott in mid-May but, like many a keenly-anticipated title fight, ended inconclusively, with the mare's bridle coming adrift in Jefford's hands just as she lay down her challenge at the 16th fence, leaving Nick Viney's 11-year-old to collect his fifth win of the season at leisure. He made it six (a career 26 between the flags) the following weekend at Bratton Down before his already-mentioned defeat by Bells Wood at Mounsey Hill Gate.

With its 26 meetings, the Devon and Cornwall is the largest of all the Areas and has many hundreds of horses qualified with a plethora of packs. By far the smallest is **Sandhurst**, which schedules just six fixtures. Certificates issued within the Area number below three figures and, apart from the second Hackwood Park on Easter Monday, there was never a shortage of runners, thanks to the customary considerable influx of horses from elsewhere — particularly at the two early meetings at Tweseldown — and also to the fact that two of the Hunts race in adjacent Wessex, the Hursley Hambledon at popular Badbury Rings in Dorset and the Staff College at the busiest of all venues, Larkhill on Salisbury Plain. So the Area can boast a healthy runner average of 9.7 for its 44 races.

Tweseldown and Philip Scouller go together like gin and tonic. The long-time Area chairman, who has done so much to promote and defend this venue — latterly with a powerful ally in Steven Astaire — first won there in 1970 on Buacaill Breaga and landed his 61st course win in the Tweseldown Club race on Sulphur Springs. Now 53, he had previously announced his coming retirement and for this last Tweseldown ride the executive had a suitable presentation ready. Sulphur Springs, new to the Scouller string, had finished sixth in the 1999 Grand Steeple Chase de Paris; another of his horses, Blanville, also possesses sound French form and, with his owner-rider showing the benefit of advice from jumping guru Yogi Breisner — you're never too old to learn — went through the season unbeaten, three times in Open company and finally in the John and Nigel Thorne Hunter Chase at Stratford in May. The planned return to Stratford to bid for an even more glorious finale in the *Horse & Hound* Cup had to be aborted, but he had a jolly good party anyway and then, instead of hanging up his boots on a career total of 119, succumbed to the lure of Blanville in 2001, and put his retirement on hold for another year - at least.

For his contemporary Tim Underwood, another Tweseldown stalwart who started winning — in 1966 at Hackwood Park — even before Scouller, the season provided no such happy memories. His first ride on new acquisition Arleneseoin ended in an awful crash at the first fence in the Hursley Hambledon Confined in February, the resulting injuries keeping him out of the saddle thereafter. Philip York benefited, donning the Underwood colours to win twice on fading star What A Hand and once with Peafield. York had his best-ever season, finishing on a total of nine, principally thanks to one from his father Ray's string, Rustic Revelry, successful in three Point-to-Points and a Folkestone Hunter Chase and the Area's Young Horse prizewinner.

Arleneseoin never fully atoned for the Badbury Rings disaster, though he was placed in five Opens under York before being sold at Ascot for 8000 guineas and winning at summer jumping. A Hursley Hambledon-qualified seven-year-old to do well was David Rees's Ball In The Net, on whom Mick (Curly) Holdforth opened his winning account at 38 at Charing and staged repeats at Badbury Rings and Larkhill.

PLATE 8   343 Tivyside Confined: David Brace's National Champion Young Horse Dawn's Cognac helped former champion Pip Jones to the 200 winner mark, this was number 185
PHOTO: Alun Sedgmore

Among other trainers in the Sandhurst Area, John Porter had a quieter-than-usual season with about a dozen Vine and Craven-qualified horses, of which the best, Chris Bennett's former Arthur Moore chaser Tarthooth, knocked at the door several times before finally winning the Tedworth Open and then going to Ascot to make 12,500 guineas. Bennett's other old favourite, Ardbrennan, sadly died at Kingston Blount. Kate Buckett enjoyed herself with about 10 in her stable at Upham (she legged up Simon Claisse to win at Badbury Rings on Dear Emily), while Bill Smith saddled Glenpine to win at both Hackwood Park meetings.

The 1998 and '99 Ladies Champion Pip Jones travelled from Wales to begin her hat-trick bid at the first Tweseldown. She managed only a second there but won in Cornwall and in Devon before really getting under way when racing started on her home ground in the **South and West Wales** Areas. So well did she do initially that bookies ceased offering any odds on the ladies title from the last weekend in February, after she had registered a four-timer at the Tivyside; the only question that seemed to remain was whether she might exceed her personal best of 30. But then the picture changed. The winners were still coming, but slower. She reached 19 and still led when Coolwawn Lady won the Ladies Open at the Llandeilo on April 8, but it was April 30 before her next successes — on Dawn's Cognac and Sister Kit at Cursneh Hill. By that time Polly Gundry had gone by and was drawing clear. Miss Jones's departure for Australia — at the end of the Welsh season but with eight racing days to go nationally — removed all doubt.

Deposed she may have been, but for sheer consistency she ranks among the highest, having ridden in excess of 20 winners in each of the last six years, finishing champion twice, second three times and third once. And with her final ride of 2000, when Hal's Prince walked over on a miserably wet day at Bassaleg, she reached 200 wins between the flags; among lady riders only Alison Dare and Polly Curling have notched a double century. Hal's Prince was from the stable of her brother, Tim, who, as described in the South East review later, had previously sent High Guardian on the long trip to win the Kent Grand National.

Chief provider of Miss Jones's winners was once again owner-trainer David Brace. She won 13 times in his colours, principally with Dawn's Cognac, who had looked promising since 1998 and finally brought his talent to fruition. The seven-year-old's five wins (three in Ladies Opens) from 11 outings earned the Weatherbys National Young Horse Championship. His stable-companion Gunner Boon was, after a warm-up run at Cottenham, never out of the first three in seven attempts, winning four, once under Jamie Jukes after Miss Jones had gone Down-Under.

Jukes also scored once on Brace's tough-as-teak mare, the four-time winner Coolwawn Lady, who appeared in the first race of the season — second to Sulphur Springs at Tweseldown — and was still going strong at Stratford in June. She ran in the Foxhunters at Cheltenham — albeit finishing last — three days before being beaten at odds-on by African Warrior at Erw Lon; then, after being brought down at the first fence in the Aintree Fox Hunters (going on to complete the course riderless), she went back to Erw Lon, this time after a two-day interval, and won. Four days later she was at Chepstow to try, unsuccessfully, for the Championship Hunter Chase for the Area's Point-to-Pointers sponsored by Brace's company, Dunraven Windows. At Stratford she was reported in foal but has since been summer jumping — and winning.

Another of Brace's winners, seven-year-old Evan's Colliers Boy, was ridden exclusively by Jukes. He went to Cottenham in January to win one of the 2m 4f Maidens easily and was similarly untroubled next time out in a Vale of Clettwr Restricted, but he was not seen again after being pulled up when favourite for the Monmouthshire Open, on a day when the Llanvapley corn was stopping horses to a walk.

Jukes was equal third man nationally — he has not been lower than fourth since his championship year in 1996 — and took both Area titles. Christian Williams chased him home in South Wales while Grant Lewis was runner-up in the West, where Bridget Lewis was top lady. For the second successive year the national top male novice prize came to Wales, with Jason Cook succeeding Christian Williams. Cook, 19, had ridden just one winner in each of the two preceding season but blossomed in 2000, scoring eight times, on seven different horses, including three maidens. Probably best of the seven was John Flint's little 10-year-old Anorak, who was never out of the first three in nine runs and had scored twice under Williams before completing a seasonal hat-trick when Cook rode him in a novice riders race at the Tredegar.

Another good winner for Williams, trained by his father Robert, was Kinnefad King. Beginning in an Intermediate run in atrocious weather at Pantyderi in February, he followed up in two Confineds the next month and, after a St Hilary last-fence hiccup, beat Mr Dow Jones on Easter Monday at Lydstep. Also going well for the father/son team was No Fiddling, who, after scoring first in the Monmouthshire Open — untroubled by the Llanvapley corn — carried off the Dunraven Windows Championship at Chepstow and lost nothing when third to Cavalero and Real Value at Cheltenham's pre-Easter meeting. He looked less enthusiastic later and, after making 8200 guineas at Malvern, pulled up in his first run for his new stable in the Ladies Hunter Chase at Stratford.

Runner-up to Pip Jones in South Wales was Fiona Wilson, principally thanks to John Milton's horses. On his Karaburan she won four times, three in Open company plus the Ystrad Taf Fechan Members, while she supplemented her South Pembrokeshire Ladies race success on his Bullens Bay in a Newton Abbot Hunter Chase. At Bassaleg in early May she was lucky to escape serious injury when Not For Profit crashed through the wing of the eighth and almost catapulted her into the branches of a tree.

John Barton's bargain buy Secret Beauty (400 guineas) loved Erw Lon, winning there three times with the owner's son-in-law Mark Lewis on board. She and the John Moore-trained Merrie Jar, also a three-time winner, shared the West Wales Young Horse prize. Mark Lewis also won at the first Erw Lon on his father Dewi's Mister Horatio, who then reverted to hunter chasing and made the frame several times without reaching the winner's enclosure.

The Brecon & Talybont produced its customary marathon at Llanfrynach in March. The number of races — 14 — set an all-time record, though the number of runners, 159, has been bettered several times. Those hardy souls who stayed to watch the concluding five *Confined* Maiden divisions in the hope of seeing something with a future were rewarded only in the very last by Iron Pyrites (*qv* Welsh Borders); none of the other four winners even finished the course in subsequent runs.

Though torrential rains forced four meetings to postpone, all were eventually held more or less successfully. Next season at least two new courses will have to be found, as neither St Hilary nor Bassaleg will be available. A change of course is also scheduled in the **North Western** Area, with the Pendle (which also features in the Yorkshire schedule) quitting Gisburn, its home since 1925, for a new line just off the A59 at Skipton, where Skipton Horse Trials have been staged for many years. Unfortunately the final Gisburn meeting succumbed to waterlogging, a fate it had been near to suffering in 1999.

In what is something of a stop-start Area (this time six of its 16 meetings were crammed into the 10 days from Easter Saturday to May Day), the only other weather interruption was to the Tanatside, which had to be put back a week because of waterlogging at Eyton-on-Severn.

Gary Hanmer took the riding prize for men ahead of Alastair Crow, clinching the award with a treble at the closing meeting, the Wheatland, after Crow had missed rides after being shaken up in a fall with Open favourite Jacob's Wife. Hanmer's achievement is of no little magnitude since his Northwich yard does not possess the firepower of the Hadnall stable. But his talents are widely recognised and the majority of his successes were gained for others, in particular Paul Jones, for whom he rode several, including six-year-old Master Jock, impressive on his solitary appearance at the Bramham Moor. He also partnered another Jones six-year-old, Night Irene, to win both her outings.

Hanmer had ended 1999 celebrating a best-ever season and now did it again, riding 23 winners, which put him equal third nationally with Jamie Jukes. He achieved trebles twice and on the second Sunday in April won at two meetings, taking the Ludlow Members race on Mr Pistachio (qv Welsh Borders) before speeding to the Cheshire Forest to win the Restricted on one from his stable, Mister Moss. Of those he trained, Bucks View shone brightest. Both times he ran he met useful Crow performers in Eaton Hall Opens, first running a close second to Weak Moment at the Wynnstay and then beating Bishops Hall at the Flint and Denbigh.

The Hanmer stable also housed five-year-old Denney's Well, winner of his only start at Sandon in April and led out unsold at Doncaster the following month after being bid up to 12,500 guineas. Denney's Well had been a last-stride winner from Fanion De Nourry, whose rider, Jason Merry, works in the Hanmer yard and was fined £50 for easing his mount before the line. Fanion De Nourry, owned and trained by Edmund Haddock, lost his maiden certificate next time out and, after following up in a Restricted, scored easily in a Towcester Hunter Chase, ridden each time by lorry driver Len Hicks.

Alastair Crow had the Area's outstanding horse in Lord Harry. Unbeaten in six outings, he romped home in four successive Opens before triumphing in the NW Area Championship Final Hunter Chase at Bangor, a race he so nearly won two years earlier. Then Lord Harry went to Stratford to score an authoritative victory in the John Corbet Cup over national leading horse Balisteros, with Lakefield Rambler trailing. Next year's target for Lord Harry will surely be the Cheltenham Foxhunters, a race in which this year's Crow representative was Whatafellow. He finished only ninth but won four earlier Opens with some ease and was untroubled in a Maiden Hunter Chase at Cartmel.

The stable suffered a scare in January when the trainer and guiding light, Alastair's mother Sheila, took some hefty blows when one of the string dropped dead as she rode at exercise. Typically, she refused to allow the injuries to keep her at home for long and winners continued to flow, the final score being 28 races, plus three Hunter Chases, won by 16 horses. Not listed but not least of Crow's victories came in the Sandy Temple Memorial flat race which opened the Cheshire Forest card. His mount Harweld also scored in his only two runs over obstacles. Maiden winners in the stable who should go on to better things include three six-year-olds retired for the season after a single winning run, Fast Lane and Sams Day at the North Shropshire on Easter Monday under Brendan Foster (when Crow was 'resting' after a heavy fall two days earlier), and Acton Bank, who set the afternoon's fastest time when giving Joe Downes his initial success at the South Shropshire on May Day.

Another rider to win for the yard — twice on Glacial Trial — was Whitchurch farmer Michael Worthington, the news of whose death in a car accident in late summer shocked followers in the Area. His eight wins last season included two on the smart five-year-old Ella Falls, who, as mentioned in the Yorkshire review, was subsequently sold for 26,000 guineas and won in the summer for Heather Dalton. She is now a pro trainer, so husband Andrew took over responsibility for the Point-to-Pointers in consequence and saddled 11 horses to win 19 races, plus a Leicester Hunter Chase with Mickthecutaway.

Most he rode himself, though Ben Shaw, who was spending a pre-university year in the yard, landed an end-of-season hat-trick on his mother's The Crazy Bishop, while Sam

Beddoes took the South Shropshire Ladies race with Sun Surfer. The majority qualified with the Wheatland (one from the Ludlow, Red Oassis, is mentioned in the Welsh Borders review) and heading them was Solba. His Lady Dudley failure has been referred to, but he won three Opens, all out of the Area and once partnered by Richard Burton. Stablemate Wejem scored in three lesser contests and, of the maidens, six-year-old Azzante had his moment of glory at Market Rasen before being knocked down for 15,000 guineas to Robert Stronge at the Doncaster August sale. One victory that perhaps brought a lump to the Dalton throat came on his father's Shoon Wind in the Albrighton Members. Now 17, Shoon Wind has been racing since 1987 and this was his 22nd victory.

Dalton fell twice with Jane Thornton's Lochnomore, but the seven-year-old, trained by John Downes, won three times with Richard Burton in the saddle — slamming Mickthecutaway at Bitterley — to gain the Area's Young Horse prize.

Carrie Ford took riding honours among the ladies. Her Cheshire Forest Ladies Open victory was her fourth in the last five years (she missed the 1999 race), this time on Celtic Who, the horse who had given husband Richard his retirement victory in the Maiden at the previous year's meeting. Her best day came at the Wynnstay, where she trained three winners, riding two herself, Another Gentleman (by a short-head in a Maiden) and Melnik (a Ladies Open cruise), and legging up owner Alison Price, who works in the yard, to take the Confined aboard Aly Daley. Unfortunately Melnik, who was returning from a year off after winning all his four Ladies Opens of 1998, managed only the one run.

Mrs Ford had opened her scoring before the Area season started after a 480-mile round trip to partner Balisteros in the College Valley Open, while later she made the most of her ride at the Flint and Denbigh on the North Ledbury horse George Dillingham, trained by Annie Downes.

Runner-up to Mrs Ford was Sue Sharratt, who rarely does anything wrong. The only time she sat on Ita's Fellow was the only time he won — at 25-1 — and she completed a hat-trick with the mare Hatton Farm Babe. Mouse Barlow also won four races, two apiece on her father-in-law's Three Potato Four and Ian Anderson's Killatty Player, who took the Area's prestige race, the Scally Muire Ladies Open at the Wheatland. The Crooked Oak, owned by Vale of Lune secretary Keith Thomas and ridden by his son Gareth, was invincible in three outings between the flags but failed to trouble the judge in Hunter Chase grade.

And finally . . . the **South East**, where a feature was the large number of successes gained by horses from other Areas. They won half the 12 Men's Opens and Restricted as well as the solitary Mixed Open and five of the 12 Ladies races. Early on the locals fared little better against raiders in Maidens, with five of the nine races at the first four meetings going to horses from beyond the region's boundaries. But in return south easterners made a number of successful forays into East Anglia and it was an exceptional season for local hunter chasers, with Real Value taking the star. This Di Grissell-trained nine-year-old maintained his 100 per cent record (when completing) in English Point-to-Points, adding to the six consecutive wins gained in lesser contests in 1999 by winning Opens at Horseheath and Charing, after he had fallen in the lead at Cottenham on his seasonal debut. The step up to hunter chasing class was comfortably accomplished when he beat an admittedly below par Castle Mane at Newbury, and next stop was the Cheltenham Foxhunters.

Here, given another superb ride by Ben Hitchcott, he looked to have the race won until denied in the final 100 yards by the sprouting wings of Cavalero and after that came anti-climax. An early faller in the novice race at Aintree, he was favourite, on nine pounds better terms, to to reverse Foxhunters form with Cavalero in a rematch at Cheltenham, only to fail by one-and-a-quarter lengths, and then, in his final run, he was long odds-on at Folkestone — where Julian Pritchard rode him for the first time — but, unhappy on the firmish ground, was pulled up.

David Robinson's Struggles Glory has not been beaten in Point-to-Points since coming from Ireland and, ridden as usual by his 58-year-old owner, he stretched his Charing score to five in Opens there in February and April, winning each by over a fence. In between times he doddled a Plumpton Hunter Chase at 6-1 on but disappointed at Kempton and was among the covey caught out by the first fence in the Aintree Fox Hunters. The potential that was there may soon be lost for ever.

Robinson provided the Area with a new course on his land in a fold of the South Downs at Rodmell, near Lewes, for the two Southdown and Eridge meetings. A very sharp track, it suits speedsters, though the uphill climb from the second last may catch out those with suspect stamina. The going was surprisingly fast each time and Rodmell is clearly far less likely to suffer the waterlogging which so frequently affected its predecessor, Heathfield.

Fittingly the landowner won at the first meeting, when That's Dedication got up close home in the Confined, but he could not stage a repeat at the second with a returning Martha's Boy. This was the nine-year-old's first run since a breakdown at Folkestone in 1998 had ended a spectacularly successful campaign, starting as a maiden and completing five consecutive victories in three Hunter Chases to earn an 11st 7lb rating. But Robinson's son Stuart rode him that season; the owner himself had finished on the floor in both runs by Martha's Boy the previous year and now crashed again. The nine-year-old did not reappear.

Other Hunter Chase wins by Area horses included three by two sons of Buckskin, Prince Buck (at Wincanton) and Little Buck (at Plumpton and Kempton), while Brambledown won twice at Folkestone under owner Belinda Sillars. The mare was coming back from a year off — again — and lost no caste in defeat (her first) when third to Little Buck at Kempton, as her rider surely set her too tough a task; even so, she finished in front of Struggles Glory.

Four of the six races at the United Hunts meeting also went to local horses — Galeaway, Tidal Reef, Noyan and Young Nimrod — while a fifth was won by Rustic Revelry, who, though qualified from Ray York's stable with the Staff College, does much of his racing in the Area. Irish-based owner Gavin Wragg had an interesting prospect with Di Grissell in Satchmo, who had previously done well for him in Ireland. After an initial win at Charing (under Wragg) the eight-year-old was ridden by Ben Hitchcott to win a relatively undistinguished race at Sandown's Royal Artillery meeting. On the strength of that he was made favourite ahead of Real Value for the novice event at Aintree on Grand National Day, only to bounce Julian Pritchard off two fences before the exit of his Hitchcott-partnered stablemate. Then Satchmo travelled to Ireland for Punchestown's Champion Hunter Chase and was still within three lengths of Sheltering until nearly dislodging Brian Hassett with a terrible last-fence blunder. He recovered to finish a distant second, in front of Fiona Needham and Last Option (qv Yorkshire).

The effective David Dunsdon, who had won five times between the flags on his debut season as a 16-year-old in 1999, added another six to his tally, plus four Hunter Chases on three horses, Shekels, Finnow Thyne and Lochnagrain, all owned by his mother, Sarah. She is Josh Gifford's sister-in-law and the trio were saddled by Josh's son Nick, who, in his first season as a trainer, also sent out Belvento to win three Point-to-Points.

To illustrate the worth of Dunsdon and Hitchcott it is only necessary to survey the form of three horses, Jamies First, Lord Ellangowan and Jojo. The first two possessed appalling completion records before Dunsdon put a leg across them — and they both immediately won Maidens. Similarly Jojo, even with the benefit of Mrs Grissell's training, had looked an arch-villain last year, but Hitchcott persuaded him to win two of his first four races — albeit reluctantly — and be placed in the others. Then the diminutive rider took a tumble from a maiden at Charing and was prevented from riding Jojo, who promptly reverted to ways of old.

Open winners from the Area, apart from Struggles Glory and Real Value, were Prince Buck, Galaroi and Prime Course, while the best of those from afar were Gillan Cove (*qv* Wessex) and Blanville (*qv* Sandhurst). Farthest traveller of all was Tim Jones's out-and-out stayer High Guardian, who came from Wales to Detling in March to land the West Street-Tickham's four-mile Mixed Open, dubbed the Kent Grand National and the Area's prestige race.

In fact High Guardian only gained the outright verdict in the stewards tent; Prime Course led over the last to be caught on the line, but, after the judge had ruled a dead-heat, the stewards upheld the 'taking my ground' objection of High Guardian's rider, Julian Pritchard, and demoted Prime Course to second. An appeal to the Jockey Club against this decision by Prime Course's owner, John Farrant, was dismissed. The Kent Grand National had been won on a disqualification once before, when Holborn Head was stood down in favour of Architrade in 1986.

Gi d'Angibau repeated her successful 1999 raids from East Anglia with Cracking Idea and Cache Fleur in Ladies Opens at Charing and Penshurst and Heather Irving brought Lily The Lark from the Midlands to win at both Parham fixtures, but the only local lady to manage a similar double — at Bexhill and the second Penshurst — was Julie Wickens, and oddly enough she did it with a Worcestershire-qualified horse. This was My Wee Man, who had won his single start for Angela Rucker in 1999 and now gave Miss Wickens her first successes after being bought for 2500 guineas at Malvern in February. In their only other start together, in the Ashford Valley Ladies Open on Easter Saturday, they were caught just before the line by Caroline Holliday, who was scoring her solitary victory with her Ann Blaker-trained Danger Flynn.

Last year Emma Coveney and Native Venture were virtually invincible in south eastern Ladies races. This time they were beaten favourites in each of three runs, third at Cottenham, soundly trounced by Lily The Lark at Parham and then pulling up at Detling on Kent Grand National Day in the Confined Ladies race which gave Lisa Stock and Kincora their only success. Native Venture was clearly not relishing the fast ground that day but the stewards still cautioned Mrs Coveney when she gave the firm surface as her reason for pulling up. The gelding will be 13 next season and it is difficult to visualise a return to days of supremacy.

Jenny Grant won the Surrey Union Ladies race for Maxine Rigg on 25-1 chance For William. She had done likewise for the same owner in 1999 with Wednesdays Auction — at 33-1. In both cases the starting price fairly represented the horse's chance, but also in both cases it was the first time Miss Grant had ridden them, so watch out for a possible three-timer next year! Head-girl in Jeff Peate's yard, she rode four winners to take the Area ladies title; the men's went to six-time winner Chris Gordon, who also rides extensively for popular Peate, so that was a fitting double to mark the trainer's retirement year.

Sometimes retirement talk is premature. Last year it seemed that Nethertara had run her last race and was destined for motherhood, but the 13-year-old with a hatful of Pointing victories on her card came back for a season under Rules, winning twice for Ben Hitchcott and ending her campaign with an honourable eighth in the four-mile National Hunt Chase at the Festival meeting.

Youngsters of promise include the afore-mentioned Noah and Belvento, while seven-year-old Kenny Davis followed a Horseheath Maiden win by taking a Penshurst Restricted and was in with a strong chance in the Surrey Union Open until unseating his rider at the penultimate. Kenny Davis is hunted with the Stevenstone by his owner, Maria Askew, before being sent for racing to the small Hildenborough stable of trainer-rider-policeman Paul Blagg. Bright Approach, who took the Area's Young Horse prize, travelled in the reverse direction. Last seen locally when winning a Restricted at Aldington in 1999, he was qualified again with the Old Surrey and Burstow before owner John Burbidge moved down to the West Country and put the seven-year-old with Ollie Cann, who saddled him to win two races under Polly Gundry and be placed in five others.

To conclude on a note of hope: in 15 runs over three seasons eight-year-old Tidal Reef had earned nothing but a form-book squiggle; this time he completed a hat-trick under Chris Gordon, supplementing Maiden and Restricted wins with victory in the SE Championship Hunter Chase at Folkestone. So if at first you don't succeed ...

PLATE 9   1676 Torrington Farmers Open Maiden (Div 2): The end of the last race of the season and R to L Tabitha Cave seems to drive Sea Spirit past Nick Michell and Inforapop, but apparently not; Mustang Molly (Andy Martin) and Budghill (Colin Heard) know their fate for certain

PHOTO: Brian Armstrong

Results
Point-to-Point Meetings
& Hunter Chases 2000

A chronological numbered list of all British hunter racing results in 2000 with comments-in-running.

Meetings are arranged alphabetically for each day with Hunter Chases first.

The figure to the left of the horse's name is the number of the race in which it last appeared, and the superscript figure its fate.

In Hunter Chase results the weights shown are those actually carried.

In Point-to-Point results any penalty, allowance or overweight is shown alongside the horse's name, this is followed by the Starting Price.

Figures to the left of the finishing position are our correspondent's estimate of how far the horse was beaten.

All Tote returns are to a £1 stake unless stated.

These results include changes made after Jockey Club enquiries of which there is a full list near the back of this volume.

UNDER JOCKEY CLUB RULES

Index to Point-to-Point Fixtures in 2000

**Eight meetings were lost
completely in 2000:**

Lanarkshire & Renfrewshire (Lanark, Feb 19th – course not fit), Bicester with Whaddon Chase (Kingston Blount, Apr 15th – waterlogged), Woodland Pytchley (Dingley, Apr 22nd – waterlogged), York & Ainsty (Easingwold, Apr 22nd – waterlogged), Pendle Forest & Craven (Gisburn, Apr 29th – waterlogged), Enfield Chace (Northaw, May 1st – waterlogged), Stevenstone (Vauterhill, May 1st – waterlogged) and West Street–Tickham (Aldington, May 1st – waterlogged).

**Five meetings were held with
new entries after the original fixture
was abandoned:**

South Cornwall (Trebudannon, May 6th, after abandoning at Great Trethew on Mar 4th – waterlogged), Old Surrey, Burstow & West Kent (Penshurst, May 14th, after abandoning on Apr 16th – waterlogged), Pentyrch (Bonvilston, May 27th, after abandoning on Apr 22nd – waterlogged), Teme Valley (Brampton Bryan, May 17th, after abandoning on Apr 22nd – waterlogged) and Llangeinor (Laleston, 3rd Jun, after abandoning on Apr 29th – waterlogged).

**Eight postponed meetings
went ahead within 15 days
with entries standing:**

Vale of Clettwr (Erw Lon, Feb 19th, after postponement on Feb 12th – waterlogged), Carmarthenshire (Erw Lon, Mar 19th, after postponement on 4th Mar – waterlogged), Tanatside (Eyton–on–Severn, Mar 12th, after postponement on 5th Mar – waterlogged), Cotswold Vale Farmers (Maisemore Park, May 1st, after postponement on Apr 22nd – waterlogged), Croome & West Warwickshire (Upton–on–Severn, May 6th, after postponement on Apr 25th – waterlogged), Berkeley (Woodford, May 14th, after postponement on Apr 29th – waterlogged), Lauderdale (Mosshouses, May 7th, after postponement on Apr 30th – waterlogged) and Warwickshire (Ashorne, May 10th, after postponement on May 1st– waterlogged).

Index to Hunter Chases 2000

139 Hunter Chases were run in 2000, 145 had been scheduled (including four late additions), and six races were lost:

Ayr (March 9th – waterlogged), Exeter (April 4th – waterlogged), Hexham (April 17th – waterlogged), Towcester (April 24th – waterlogged), Wetherby (April 25th – waterlogged) and Perth (April 27th – waterlogged).

Thames Valley Club

Tweseldown (RH 8F,17J) Sun, 9 Jan (GOOD)

1 Club Members, 12st   10 ran

1		**SULPHUR SPRINGS (IRE)** 6-1 P Scouller *8s-6s; lw; went 2nd 3; ld 7; 4l clr 2 out; comf*
2	5	**Coolvawn Lady (IRE)** (5a) 7-2 Miss P Jones *6s-7/2; a.p; 2l 3rd ½way; went 2nd 4 out; rdn & no imp 2 out*
3	1	**Cahors (IRE)** 2-1F N Mitchell *Ww; 7l 9th ½way; 7l 8th 14; gd hdwy 4 out; 5l 3rd & rdn 2 out; nt qckn; btr for rce*
4	4	**Mendip Prince (IRE)** 20-1 A Lillingston *Chsd ldrs; 4l 6th ½way; 8l 5th & rdn 2 out; stayed on one pce*
5	1	**Rustic Revelry** 20-1 P York *Swtng; hld up; hdwy 9; 4½l 7th ½way; mist & rmdrs 11; 4l 5th 14; eff 4 out; 7l 4th & rdn 2 out; no ex*
6	15	**Leap Frog** 5-1 A Charles-Jones *Swtng; prom; 2½l 4th ½way; wknd 3 out; eased when btn aft 2 out*
7	1½	**Balance** 14-1 G Maundrell *Hld up; hdwy & 3½l 5th ½way; lost plce 12; bhnd frm 14*
8	7	**Gillone** 7-2 J Docker *2 handlers; unruly padd; swtng; ld to 7; 2nd til rdn & wknd qckly 4 out; t.o*
P		**Cabille (FR)** 14-1 J Owen *(xnb) Nvr gng wl; rdn 9; 12l 10th ½way; wl bhnd 12; t.o 14 til pu 2 out*
P		**Feel The Power (IRE)** 14-1 J Maxse *Hld up; mist 7; 6l 8th ½way; 6½l 7th 14; wknd aft 4 out; t.o & pu last*

OFFICIAL DISTANCES: 4l, 1l, ½l TIME: 6min 22.4s

Fences 4 & 13 were omitted from all races because of the state of the ground; the usual fence numbers have been retained in comments-in-running

2 Restricted (Div 1), 12st   12 ran

1		**JO JOS BEST FRIEND** (5a) 9-2 T Vaughan *Hld up; hmpd 1; stdy hdwy 8; 2½l 3rd ½way; went 2nd aft 12-14; ld 3 out; clr last; rdly*
2	10	**Ally Pally** 12-1 P York *Jmpd lft; prom til lost plce 5; rallied & 5l 5th ½way; 8l 6th 14; rdn 4 out; 7l 4th when hit 2 out; went 2nd at last; no ch w wnr*
3	5	**Mister Audi (IRE)** 14-1 A Sansome *Hld up & pulled hrd; 6l 6th ½way; went 2nd 14; ld 4 out-nxt; rdn & ev ch 2 out; no ex*
4	7	**Right Company** 9-4 B Pollock *Ld til hdd aft 9; 5l 4th 14; rallied & ev ch 3 out; wknd aft 2 out*
5	5	**Ten Bob Note** (bl) 14-1 M Walters *Oht; bhnd til hdwy 5; ld aft 9 til hdd 4 out; wknd app 2 out*
6	runin	**Wild Buck (IRE)** 20-1 B Kendellen *Lost plce & rmdrs 7; 10l 9th ½way; lost tch 12; t.o 15*
P		**Cloak And Dagger** 14-1 A Charles-Jones *Went 2nd aft 1-3; lost plce 8; mist 10; 9l 8th ½way; wl bhnd 14; t.o & pu 4 out*
R		**Icenfriendly (IRE)** 5-4F Miss P Jones *2s-5/4; hld up; 7th when rn out thro wing & ur 7*
F		**Newman's Conquest** (5a,2ow) 33-1 M Shears *4th when fell 1*
P		**Newtown Rambler (IRE)** 33-1 M Baldock *1st ride over fncs; hld up; hdwy 5; 3l 4th ½way; 7l 5th 14; wknd aft 4 out; bhnd when pu 2 out*
P		**Novasun** 33-1 J Barnes *Prom; went 2nd 3-9; lost plce & mist 10; 8l 7th ½way; rdn 12; bhnd when pu 4 out*
P		**Steel Gem (IRE)** 10-1 A Wintle *A bhnd; 15l 10th ½way; t.o & pu 3 out*

OFFICIAL DISTANCES: 10l, 2l, 3l TIME: 6min 32.0s

3 Ladies Open   10 ran

1		**BALISTEROS (FR)** 5-2 Miss P Robson *4s-5/2; hld up & bhnd; 11l 7th ½way; stdy hdwy 11; outpcd 4 out; went 8l 3rd nxt; rdn & stayed on wl 2 out; ld final 50yds*
2	1½	**Tom Snout (IRE)** (4x) 7-1 Miss S Vickery *Hld up; 4l 3rd ½way; went 2nd aft 14; ld 3 out; 3l clr aft 2 out; hdd & no ex u.p final 50yds*
3	12	**Lily The Lark** (5a,4x) 6-1 Miss H Irving *Hld up; hdwy 8; went 2nd app 10 til hmpd bad bend aft 14; 4l 3rd 4 out; sn rdn & outpcd; 13l 4th 2 out; lft 3rd at last*
4	2	**Persian Butterfly** (5a) 20-1 Miss T Habgood *Swtng; hld up; 9l 5th ½way; hdwy 11; 7l 6th 4 out; sn outpcd; 14l 5th & btn 2 out*
5	4	**Bel Lane** (5a) 16-1 Miss C Spearing *25s-16s; 2nd/3rd to 10; 6l 4th ½way; rdn aft 12; outpcd 4 out; wknd & 15l 6th 2 out*

6	20	**Fern Leader (IRE)** 12-1 **Mrs J Hughes** *Prom til lost plce 6; 17l 9th ½way; wl bhnd 14; t.o*
F		**Dawn's Cognac (IRE)** 11-10F **Miss P Jones** *Jmpd lft; went 2nd 5; ld 8-3 out; 3l 3rd & rdn when fell last*
P		**Ngala (IRE)** (5a) 33-1 **Miss J Tett** *Drpd to rr 6; mist 7; t.o & pu 12*
P		**Sip Of Brandy (IRE)** 12-1 **Miss E Jones** *Ld to 1; lost plce 6; 10l 6th & rdn ½way; rallied 11; wknd app 14; t.o & pu 2 out*
P		**Vital Shot** (5a) 33-1 **Mrs R Baldwin** *(xnb) Ld 2-8; sn wknd; 15l 8th ½way; t.o 14 til pu 2 out*

OFFICIAL DISTANCES: 2l, 8l **TIME:** 6min 27.4s

4 Mens Open, 12st 15 ran

1		**ROB MINE (IRE)** 8-1 **S Sporborg** *Lw; jmpd lft; ld 2; clr 2 out; impressive*
2	5	**Wishing William (IRE)** (7x) 10-1 **S Waley-Cohen** *1st ride; lw; hld up & bhnd; 18l 8th ½way; hdwy & 17l 5th 15; went 15l 3rd aft 2 out & 10l 2nd at last; r.o flat; nt rch wnr*
3	15	**My Shout** (7x) evensF **B Pollock** *Chsd ldrs; 10l 3rd ½way; rdn 15; no imp 4 out; wknd 2 out; lft 3rd at last*
4	20	**Tarthooth (IRE)** (7x) 14-1 **P Cowley** *A bhnd; 24l 12th ½way; t.o 4 out*
5	1½fs	**The Hatcher (NZ)** 33-1 **R Cope** *Bhnd frm 7; 21l 10th ½way; rdn 12; t.o 14*
B		**Arfer Mole (IRE)** (7x) 25-1 **D Dennis** *A bhnd; 19l 9th ½way; 24l 8th when mist 15; bd 4 out*
P		**Broguestown Pride (IRE)** 33-1 **P Blagg** *Sn wl bhnd; t.o 9 til pu 12*
P		**Cebu Gale (IRE)** 33-1 **M Hewitt** *Prom to 7; 16l 7th ½way; wl bhnd when pu 4 out*
F		**Celtic Silver** (4x) 16-1 **B Hitchcott** *12th when fell 1*
P		**High Guardian** 14-1 **Julian Pritchard** *25s-14s; nd; lost tch 9; 23l 11th ½way; t.o & pu 15*
P		**Ickford Okey** (7ow) 8-1 **T Illsley** *Swtng; hld up; mist 2; hdwy 8; 13l 5th ½way; 18l 6th & wkng when mist 15; bhnd when pu 4 out*
F		**Noyan** 12-1 **P York** *Swtng; ld to 2; ev ch 3 out; sn rdn & wknd; tired 2nd when pckd bad 2 out; 14l 3rd when fell last*
F		**Reign Dance** (7x) 33-1 **S Walker** *Hld up; 15l 6th ½way; no hdwy 12; 21l 7th 15; wl bhnd when fell 4 out*
F		**Welsh Warrior** 33-1 **T Vaughan** *Mist 2; 11l 6th when fell 6*
F		**Whispering Pines (NZ)** (7x) 7-2 **N Mitchell** *Chsd ldrs; 11l 4th ½way; no imp 4 out; wknd & 17l 5th 2 out; wl bhnd when fell last; lame; broke leg; subsq pinned*

OFFICIAL DISTANCES: 15l, 5l **TIME:** 6min 22.5s

5 Club Members 7yo&up (Vet & Nov Rdrs), 12st 11 ran

1		**RECTORY GARDEN (IRE)** (5x) 7-4JF **R Biddlecombe** *1st ride; trckd ldrs; 2l 3rd ½way; went 2nd 4 out; ld 3 out; sn wl clr*
2	30	**Royal Arctic (IRE)** (5x) 7-1 **J Oldring** *12s-7s; 2nd/3rd til lft in ld 10; hdd 3 out; sn rdn & no ch w wnr*
3	1½	**Strong Chairman (IRE)** 7-4JF **S Waley-Cohen** *9/4-7/4; prom; 2nd/3rd to 11; drpd to rr 14; stayed on 2 out; lft rem 3rd at last*
4	8	**Equity Player** 16-1 **T Underwood** *Rmdrs 9; bhnd til hdwy & 3½l 5th ½way; lost plce 14; hrd rdn 4 out; sn wknd; t.o*
5	3	**Northern Kingdom (USA)** 16-1 **J Diment** *Hld up; mist 7; drpd to rr 9; 12l 8th ½way; mist 12; eff 4 out; wknd app 2 out; t.o*
6	nk	**Paco's Boy** 6-1 **W Kirkbride** *10s-6s; bhnd til hdwy 9; 3l 4th ½way; went 2nd 11-14; rdn & wknd 4 out; t.o*
7	3	**Cawarra Boy** 25-1 **M Walters** *Hld up; 4l 6th ½way; hdwy 12; went 2nd 14-4 out; wknd app 2 out; t.o*
U		**Arise** 8-1 **T Abbott** *Lost plce 6; 10l 7th 4 out; hdwy 14; wknd app 2 out; rem 3rd when ur last*
U		**Gamay** 7-1 **T Atkinson** *(xnb) 5th when ur 2*
P		**Lord Ellangowan (IRE)** 25-1 **D Slattery** *Ld & pulled hrd; clr 5; 25l up when mist 9; pu 10 (thought unsound)*
U		**Walkers Point** 33-1 **Miss S Hutchings** *4th when ur 3*

OFFICIAL DISTANCES: dist, 2l **TIME:** 6min 29.6s

The stewards enquired into the running and riding of Lord Ellangowan; the rider's explanation that he had pulled up when well clear because the horse seemed to have hurt its back after making a mistake at the previous fence was noted

6 Restricted (Div 2), 12st   15 ran

1		**NOUGHTOSIXTY (IRE)** 5-2F B Pollock *Lw; made all; clr 3 out; stayed on wl*
2	10	**Possible Pardon (NZ)** 8-1 A Charles-Jones *2 handlers; hld up; 5l 6th ½way; 7l 5th 14; sn outpcd; stayed on 3 out; went 131 4th nxt & 2nd nr fin*
3	hd	**Rhyme And Chime** 10-1 Miss S Vickery *Hld up; hdwy & 3½l 5th ½way; went 3rd 12 & 8l 2nd 3 out; no imp; dem nr fin*
4	5	**Strong Ambition (IRE)** (5a) 4-1 J Owen *(xnb) Prom til lost plce 8; 8l 7th ½way; rdn 12; rallied & 5l 4th 14; 12l 3rd 2 out; no ex*
5	20	**Lyrical Seal** (5a) (bl) 25-1 J Maxse *Hld up; hdwy & 3l 4th ½way; wknd & 10l 7th 14; t.o*
6	10	**Gt Hayes Pommard** 33-1 D Howells *Sn prom; went 2nd 9 til aft 11; 8l 6th & wkng when mist 14; t.o*
7	5	**Effie Wood** (5a) 7-1 B Kendellen *Nt jw; drpd to rr 3; 13l 9th ½way; lost tch 12; t.o 4 out*
B		**Dinedor Charlie** 20-1 D Jones *33s-20s; 2nd til bd by loose horse app 6*
U		**Father Henry (IRE)** 7-2 P York *5s-7/2; hld up; 5l 7th when blun & ur 10*
P		**Indian Miller** 33-1 M Green *Pulled v hrd; fighting rdr in rr; 14l 10th ½way; t.o & pu 3 out*
U		**Jamies First (IRE)** 25-1 D Slattery *Hld up; 7th when tried to rn out 7 & threw rdr into fnce*
P		**Lady Buckland** (5a) 4-1 Julian Pritchard *Hld up; hdwy 8; mist & lost plce 9; 111 8th ½way; lost tch 12; t.o & pu last*
P		**Persian Boy (IRE)** 33-1 A Sansome *Trckd ldrs; lft 2nd 6-9; 2½l 3rd ½way; went 2nd aft 11 til wknd qckly 3 out; pu 2 out*
U		**Sleep Walker** (5a) 25-1 Mrs J Parris *8th when ur 2*
F		**Street Trader (IRE)** 25-1 P Cowley *5th when fell 1*

OFFICIAL DISTANCES: 10l, nk   **TIME:** 6min 32.4s

7 Open Maiden (Non-Rules Rnrs), 12st - 15J   13 ran

1		**SECRET STREAMS (IRE)** 5-4F S Sporborg *Lw; went 2nd 5; ld 14; qcknd clr flat; impressive*
2	5	**Billy Blakeney** 9-2 R Cope *2 handlers; a.p; 1½l 3rd ½way; went 3l 2nd 15; hrd rdn aft 4 out; mist last; no ch w wnr flat*
3	15	**Sir Wynham** (bl) 33-1 O Ellwood *Lw; hld up; 6l 7th ½way; hdwy 15; went 6l 3rd nxt; wknd frm 2 out*
4	1	**First Tenor** 9-4 Miss P Jones *Hld up; 3½l 5th ½way; 8l 6th & rdn 4 out; went 9l 4th nxt; no imp*
5	15	**General Typhoon** 6-1 Miss E Tory *Hld up; hdwy 8; 3l 4th ½way; 7l 4th 4 out; wknd 3 out; t.o*
6	10	**Wonastow** 25-1 D Jones *Chsd ldrs; 5l 6th ½way; wknd & 9l 8th 15; t.o*
7	25	**Just Reuben (IRE)** (7a) 14-1 R Young *A bhnd; 13l 12th ½way; t.o; easy rn*
P		**Doranslone** (5a) 33-1 N Docker *Swtng; lost plce 8; 8l 9th ½way; wknd 11; sn t.o; pu 4 out*
P		**Executive Blue (IRE)** (5a) 33-1 G Barfoot-Saunt *Rdn in padd; sn wl bhnd; t.o 11; school til pu 4 out*
P		**Sixth Sense (IRE)** 16-1 P McAllister *Hld up; 7l 8th ½way; hdwy 11; wknd & 10l 7th 4 out; t.o & pu last*
P		**Straight Baron** 33-1 C Gordon *(xnb) Ld til hdd 14; wknd 4 out; mist 3 out; t.o & pu last*
P		**Valentine King** 20-1 B Hitchcott *Swtng; a bhnd; 111 10th ½way; rdn & no resp 11; t.o & pu last*
P		**Witches Promise** (5a) 20-1 R Lawther *(xnb) Hld up & bhnd; 12l 11th ½way; t.o & pu 15*

OFFICIAL DISTANCES: 5l, 10l   **TIME:** 6min 28.9s

Fences 9 & 18 were also omitted from this race due to low sun

Army

Larkhill (RH 13F,18J) Sat, 15 Jan (GOOD)

8 Army Saddle Club Members, 12st   6 ran

1		**DESERT WALTZ (IRE)** 11-10F O Ellwood *Lw; ww; went 2nd 6; ld aft 12; drew clr 2 out; comf*
2	8	**Ardbei (IRE)** 4-1 D Alers-Hankey *Opened 5s; hld up; 7l 4th ½way; eff 11; went 2nd app 13; sn rdn; one pce 2 out*
3	25	**Archies Oats** (vis) 14-1 J Trice-Rolph *Chsd ldrs; mist 2; lft 2nd 5-6; 5l 3rd ½way; 7l 3rd 15; sn wknd*

4	runin	**Camitrov (FR)** 6-1 **R** Sturgis *Ld; lft 10l clr 5; hdd aft 12; rdn & wknd 13; t.o*
U		**Ballyea Boy (IRE)** (bl) 8-1 **R** Webb-Bowen *2nd til mist & rfo 5*
P		**Prince Teeton** 5-1 **J** Snowden *Tchd 6s; mist 3; drpd to rr 4; t.o & pu 8*

OFFICIAL DISTANCES: 10l, dist TIME: 6min 16.0s TOTE: £1.20 DF: £1.40

9 Ladies Open   9 ran

1		**KNIGHT OF PASSION** 4-6F Miss **P** Jones *Tchd 4/7 & 8/11; lw; made all; mists 3, 4 & 6; rdn out*
2	4	**Percy Smollett** 10-1 Miss **S** Vickery *(xnb) 14s-10s; a.p; went 2nd 6-13; rdn 14; chsd wnr 15; hit 3 out; one pce u.p 2 out*
3	40	**Tomcappagh (IRE)** 10-1 Miss **J** Grant *16s-10s; bit bckwd; chsd ldrs; 8l 4th ½way; went 3rd 10-11; 13l 4th & wkng 14; t.o when lft 3rd at last*
4	5	**Mr Golightly** (2ow) 14-1 Mrs **J** Reed *(xnb) Lw; sn prom; mist & lost plce 5; 11l 6th ½way; lost tch 12; wl bhnd 15; t.o*
r		**Abit More Business (IRE)** (bl) 7-2 Miss **P** Gundry *9/2-7/2; 2 handlers; hld up; hdwy 6; 9l 5th ½way; went 3rd 11 & 2nd 13-15; 5l 3rd & btn when ref last*
P		**Cabbery Rose (IRE)** (5a) 40-1 Miss **W** Southcombe *A bhnd; 13l 7th ½way; 17l 6th 14; t.o & pu 2 out*
P		**Hensue** 33-1 Miss **C** Prouse *Bckwd; sn wl bhnd; t.o 6; pu 13*
U		**Man Of Steele (IRE)** (1ow) 6-1 Miss **D** Harding *7th when blun & ur 3*
P		**Silver Sleeve (IRE)** 50-1 Miss **L** Bridges *2nd to 6; 7l 3rd ½way; wknd 12; 18l 7th 14; t.o & pu 3 out*

OFFICIAL DISTANCES: 5l, dist TIME: 6min 07.5s TOTE: £1.70 DF: £1.80

10 Land Rover Mens Open, 12st   20 ran

1		**HIGHWAY LAD** 25-1 **L** Jefford *Lw; hld up; 7l 9th ½way; hdwy 13; 3l 4th 15; went 6l 3rd aft 2 out; lft 3l 2nd at last; r.o to ld nr fin*
2	¾	**Chism (IRE)** (7x) 20-1 **R** Walford *Hld up; hdwy 7; 1½l 3rd ½way; went 2nd app 2 out; lft in ld last; nt rdn flat; hdd nr fin; rdr fined*
3	10	**Camp Bank** (4x) 3-1 **Julian** Pritchard *Tchd 7/2; sn outpcd & bhnd; 11l 13th ½way; eff 13; 9l 6th 15; stayed on 3 out; went 3rd flat; nvr nr to chall*
4	1½	**Bet With Baker (IRE)** (7x) 14-1 **T** Mitchell *A.p; went 2nd 5; ld 12-15; wknd qckly 2 out; btr for rce*
5	5	**Ruperts Choice (IRE)** (7x) 8-1 **S** Sporborg *Sn outpcd & bhnd; 14l 15th ½way; 17½l 12th 15; stayed on frm 3 out; nvr nrr*
6	½	**The Hobbit (IRE)** 20-1 **A** Honeyball *Hld up; hdwy 6; 6l 8th ½way; 8l 5th & rdn 15; btn when jmpd slow 3 out*
7	2½	**Epsilo De La Ronce (FR)** (7x) 50-1 **A** Harvey *Swtng; nd; 8l 10th ½way; lost tch 13; 16l 9th 15*
8	12	**Solo Gent** (7x) 25-1 **S** Bush *Hld up; mist 1; 3½l 5th & hdwy ½way; wknd 13; 15l 8th 15; t.o*
9	4	**Hillhead (IRE)** (7x) 50-1 **J** Barnes *Nd; 10½l 12th ½way; 17l 11th 15; t.o*
F		**Castle Lynch (IRE)** (5a) 25-1 **M** Miller *5th when fell 2*
F		**Copper Coil** (7x) 50-1 **G** Maundrell *2nd to 5; lost plce 8; 13l 14th ½way; t.o 14; pu last*
F		**Formal Invitation (IRE)** 14-1 **S** Joynes *Hld up; 5½l 7th & hdwy ½way; rdn 13; wknd & 14l 7th 15; bhnd when fell 3 out; broke fnce*
F		**Gunner Welburn** (7x) 9-4F **B** Pollock *Tchd 5/2; sn prom; 5l 6th ½way; went 2nd 13; ld 15; 3l clr when fell last*
[4ᴾ] P		**Ickford Okey** 16-1 **R** Cope *(bf) Prom; 3l 4th ½way; wknd 13; 16½l 10th 15; t.o & pu 2 out*
F		**Iranos (IRE)** (7x) (bl) 7-1 **A** Farrant *Tchd 8s; 15th when fell 8*
P		**Killeshin** 50-1 **A** Charles-Jones *Swtng; hmpd 2 & 6; sn wl bhnd; 30l 16th ½way; t.o 11; pu 13*
[5ᴾ] F		**Lord Ellangowan (IRE)** 33-1 **D** Slattery *15th when fell 6*
P		**Sister Lark** (5a) 100-1 **D** Jones *Sn wl bhnd; t.o 11; pu 13*
P		**Who Is Equiname (IRE)** (7x) 16-1 **S** Morris *Hld up; 10l 11th ½way; lost tch 13; t.o & pu 3 out*
P		**Wixoe Wonder (IRE)** 100-1 **A** Sansome *Made most to 12; wknd qckly 14; wl bhnd when pu 3 out*

OFFICIAL DISTANCES: ½l, 6l TIME: 6min 13.0s TOTE: £13.80 DF: c/f
The stewards fined the rider of the runner-up £100 for failing to ride the horse out to the finish

11 Open Maiden 567&8yo (Div 1), 12st - 17J   16 ran

1		**ABERFOYLE PARK (IRE)** 7-4F **R** Walford *6s-7/4; hld up; 6l 5th & hdwy ½way; went 2l 2nd app 15; rdn to ld nr fin*

2	¾	**No Loss** 3-1 **Miss S Vickery** *(xnb) Hld up; 5½l 4th & hdwy ½way; ld aft 12; hrd rdn flat; hdd nr fin*
3	8	**One Of The Natives (IRE)** 4-1 **T Mitchell** *Hld up & bhnd; 12l 9th ½way; hdwy 13; went 3l 3rd 15; no ex 2 out*
4	20	**Lost Your Marbles (IRE)** (5a) 33-1 **J Mead** *(bnh) Nvr on terms; 13l 10th ½way 15l 7th 15; lft 25l 4th 2 out*
P		**Black Oak** 5-1 **Julian Pritchard** *(xnb) 10s-5s; lw; ld til hdd & wknd qckly aft 12; wl bhnd when pu 14*
P		**Bonny Rigg (IRE)** (5a) 8-1 **D Jones** *Opened 10s; blun 3; 2nd to 12; sn wknd; 25l 8th 15; t.o & pu 2 out*
P		**Catchatan (IRE)** (7a) 20-1 **M Rimell** *Prom; 5l 3rd ½way; went 2nd at 12 til wknd app 15; bhnd when pu 2 out; btr for rce*
P		**Goforitgirl** (5a) 20-1 **L Jefford** *Chsd ldrs; mist 5; 7l 6th ½way; wknd 12; wl bhnd when pu 14*
P		**Horus** (7a) 5-1 **B Pollock** *Drpd to rr 4; 14l 11th ½way; mist 10; gd hdwy 13; 7l 5th & wkng when mist 15; bhnd when pu 2 out; btr for rce*
F		**Imperative** 14-1 **A Charles-Jones** *Fell 1*
P		**Joli Hardy** (5a) 33-1 **A Honeyball** *Hld up; 10l 7th ½way; eff 13; wknd & 12l 6th 15; t.o & pu last*
P		**Mountain Tae (IRE)** 25-1 **R Green** *Bckwd; wl bhnd when pu 8*
P		**Native Dawn (IRE)** 4-1 **P York** *(xnb) Hld up & bhnd; mist 8; 11l 8th ½way; lost tch 12; pu 14*
P		**Regal Wolf** 20-1 **J Snowden** *A bhnd; 18l 12th ½way; t.o & pu 14*
U		**Thecabbageflinger** 14-1 **J Young** *Ur 1*
F		**Whatacharlie** (tt) 25-1 **P Keane** *(xnb)Fell 1*

OFFICIAL DISTANCES: hd, 3l TIME: 6min 16.3s TOTE: £1.90 DF: £12.40
Fence 16 was omitted - damaged

12 Open Maiden 567&8yo (Div 2), 12st - 17J   17 ran

1		**FERRYHILL (IRE)** 8-1 **N Mitchell** *Tchd 6s; a.p; went 2nd 9-13; 5l 4th 15; went 8l 2nd aft 2 out; lft in ld at last; rdn clr*
2	6	**It's Beyond Belief (IRE)** 7-4F **T Mitchell** *Opened 2s; 2nd til ld 8; hdd 10; ld 12-13; chsd ldr 15 til wknd qckly aft 2 out; lft 11 2nd at last; fin tired*
3	8	**Prah Sands** 7-1 **J Young** *Sn prom; 2l 3rd ½way; ld 10-12 & 13 til hdd app 15; 6l 4th & wkng 2 out; btn when lft 3rd at last*
4	6	**Ard Na Carrig (IRE)** 16-1 **A Wintle** *Made most to 8; 3l 4th ½way; 12l 5th & wkng 14; stayed on*
5	6	**Border Light** 50-1 **A Charles-Jones** *Hld up & bhnd; 14l 9th ½way; 19l 7th 14; nvr on terms*
U		**Copper Valley** (5a) 12-1 **L Jefford** *Bhnd when hmpd & ur 3*
P		**Fireman** 25-1 **D Jones** *2 handlers; chsd ldrs; 6l 5th ½way; wknd aft 12; wl bhnd when pu 15*
F		**Gallatin (IRE)** 12-1 **R Walford** *6th when fell 3; dead*
P		**Harlequin Boy** 5-2 **Miss S Vickery** *4s-5/2 (opened 10s in plce); sn wl bhnd; t.o 5; pu 2 out; v green*
U		**Highland Pearl** (5a) 33-1 **M Bryant** *Last pr when ur 1*
U		**Idlewild (IRE)** (7a) 8-1 **Julian Pritchard** *10s-8s; bhnd when tried to ref & ur app 2*
F		**Lockett's Lamp (IRE)** 20-1 **J Barnes** *10th when fell 6*
U		**Play The King (IRE)** 7-1 **P Cowley** *Hld up; 9l 7th ½way; gd hdwy aft 12; went 3rd 14; ld app nxt; 10l clr when blun & ur last*
P		**Romany Chat** 33-1 **A Martin** *Bckwd; 2 handlers; nd; 12l 8th ½way; 15l 6th 14; wl bhnd when pu 15*
P		**Snowboy (IRE)** (tt) 10-1 **D I Turner** *Hld up; hdwy 6; 6½l 6th ½way; wknd aft 12; wl bhnd when pu 14*
B		**The First One** 16-1 **A Honeyball** *Towards rr til bd 3*
P		**Wise Examiner (IRE)** 14-1 **Richard Darke** *A bhnd; 15l 10th ½way; t.o & pu 14*

OFFICIAL DISTANCES: 5l, 8l TIME: 6min 18.1s TOTE: £27.10 DF: c/f
Fence 16 was omitted - fallen horse

13 Restricted (Div 1), 12st   12 ran

1		**RIVER SWILLEY (IRE)** 2-1F **R Walford** *5/2-2s; sn prom; mist 3; went 2nd 8; ld 13-14 & 15-3 out; qcknd to ld & mist last; rdn & r.o wl flat*
2	¾	**The Earth Moved (IRE)** 3-1 **Miss P Gundry** *Hld up; 8½l 8th ½way; stdy hdwy & 5l 4th 15; went 5l 3rd aft 2 out; str chall flat; nt qckn*
3	3	**Little Crumplin** 6-1 **J Owen** *Hld up; 9½l 9th ½way; gd hdwy 13; went 2nd 15; ld 3 out; hdd & hit last; no ex flat*

4 12 **Goawayoutofthat (IRE)** 5-2 **Julian Pritchard** *Hld up; 8l 7th ½way; hdwy 12; ld 14-15; rdn & wknd aft 2 out*
5 5 **Forever Dreaming (IRE)** 10-1 **M Rimell** *2nd/3rd to 5; 6l 5th ½way; 9l 6th & rdn 15; sn wknd*
6 12 **Cucklington** (bl) 16-1 **J Snowden** *Ld; mist 5; hdd 13; 7l 5th & rdn 15; sn wknd*
7 6 **See Me Shine** (5a) 14-1 **D Jones** *Hld up & pulled hrd; went 4l 3rd ½way; lost plce 12; 18l 8th 15; t.o*
[6U] P **Father Henry (IRE)** 12-1 **P York** *2nd/3rd til mist 8; 4½l 4th ½way; wknd qckly 13; wl bhnd when pu 15*
[2P] P **Novasun** 33-1 **J Barnes** *A bhnd; 11l 11th ½way; t.o & pu 14*
P **Raining Stairs (IRE)** 12-1 **J Trice-Rolph** *Lost plce 5; 6½l 6th & hdwy ½way; wknd 13; 23l 9th 15; t.o & pu 3 out*
P **Royal Orchard** 5-1 **A Martin** *Bckwd; hld up; 10l 10th ½way; eff 13; 13l 7th 15; sn wknd; t.o & pu last*
F **True Fred** 33-1 **A Evans** *Fell 1*

OFFICIAL DISTANCES: 1l, 2½l **TIME:** 6min 17.1s **TOTE:** £7.50 **DF:** £4.60
Simply Susie (P Keane, rdr inj in previous rce) was withdrawn after declarations closed

14 Restricted (Div 2), 12st — 11 ran

1 **GILDROM** 4-5F **M Rimell** *(xnb) Tchd evens; a.p; ld to 6; disp ld 9 til ld 11; qcknd 5l clr 14; blun last; all out*
2 2 **Shobrooke Mill** 9-2 **A Charles-Jones** *(xnb) Hld up; mist 3; 7l 4th & hdwy ½way; went 5l 2nd aft 14; eff when mist 2 out; kpt on*
3 40 **River Gala (IRE)** (1ow) 8-1 **T Mitchell** *2nd/3rd til lft in ld 8; hdd 10; wknd & 12l 4th 15; went poor 3rd nr fin*
4 4 **Timber Wolf (IRE)** 14-1 **N Mitchell** *Hld up; 2l 3rd & hdwy ½way; wknd & 10l 3rd 15; fin tired*
5 20 **Satori** 8-1 **Julian Pritchard** *Hld up & bhnd; blun 1; 15l 8th ½way; blun 10; t.o 13*
P **Bally Boy** 33-1 **D Jones** *Hld up; blun 9; 14l 7th ½way; wl bhnd 11; t.o & pu 13*
F **Bright Lady** (5a,1ow) 50-1 **M Green** *Swtng; nd; 8l 5th ½way; lost tch 11; wl bhnd when fell 14*
P **Iberian (IRE)** (5a,2ow) 8-1 **C Gordon** *Hit 2; 12l 6th ½way; wl bhnd 11; t.o & pu 13*
[6U] F **Jamies First (IRE)** 33-1 **A Martin** *Pulled hrd; went 2nd 2; ld 6 til fell 8*
P **Lillooet (IRE)** (5a) (bl) 50-1 **Miss J Grant** *Drpd to rr 6; lost tch & 18l 9th ½way; t.o 13; pu last*
F **Upton Adventure** (5a) 6-1 **T Stephenson** *(xnb) 2 handlers; 4th when fell 5*

OFFICIAL DISTANCES: 2l, dist **TIME:** 6min 19.0s **TOTE:** £5.10 **DF:** £18.50

Cambridgeshire Harriers Hunt Club

Cottenham (RH 9F,19J) Sun, 16 Jan (GOOD)

15 Club Members, 12st — 14 ran

1 **SCARLETT O'HARA** (5a) 4-5F **S Sporborg** *11/10-4/5; lw; hld up; gng str; 5l 7th ½way; hit 12; hdwy 15; went 2nd app 3 out; ld & mist nxt; rdn clr flat*
2 7 **Ann's Ambition** 25-1 **Miss C Fryer** *Hld up; 6l 8th ½way; outpcd 13; stayed on wl 3 out; went 15l 5th nxt & 2nd flat; no ch w wnr*
3 1 **Fire On Ice (IRE)** 12-1 **N King** *(xnb) Ld 3-14 & 4 out-2 out; 2nd til wknd flat*
4 ½ **John Tufty** 25-1 **B Hitchcott** *Hld up; 4l 6th & hdwy ½way; went 3rd 14 & 2nd w ev ch 4 out; rdn 3 out; sn outpcd*
5 ¾ **Ballyquintet (IRE)** (5a,1ow) 25-1 **N Bloom** *Ld to 3; 2nd to 7; 3l 5th ½way; went 2nd aft 13; ld 14-16; 5l 4th & rdn 3 out; kpt on one pce*
6 15 **Andermatt** (7x) (tt) 25-1 **J Cornwall** *Nt jw; prom til lost plce 9; 6½l 9th ½way; bhnd frm 13*
7 2 **Royal Raven (IRE)** (3ow) 10-1 **R Gill** *Hld up; hdwy 8; 2½l 4th ½way; rdn & wknd app 4 out*
8 20 **Just Jack** 25-1 **Miss F Jonason** *1st ride; lost plce 6; 8l 10th ½way; lost tch 14; t.o*
[4P] 9 30 **Broguestown Pride (IRE)** 33-1 **P Blagg** *A bhnd; 13l 12th ½way; t.o 13*
P **Arctic Revel** (5a,1ow) (tt) 16-1 **M Gingell** *25s-16s; hld up; hdwy 5; went 2nd 7; mist 8; 4l 5th & rdn when mist 4 out; wknd qckly & pu nxt*
F **Barna Boy (IRE)** 7-2 **S Morris** *Swtng; 13th when fell 1*
P **Buckman** (4ow) 12-1 **S R Andrews** *Prom; 2l 3rd ½way; rdn 13; sn wknd; t.o & pu 3 out*

| P | | **Primrose Hill** (5a) 25-1 **M Barnard** *Sn wl bhnd; t.o & pu 13* |
| P | | **Red Friday** 25-1 **A Pickering** *Bckwd; mist 9; 12l 11th ½way; wl bhnd when pu 13* |

OFFICIAL DISTANCES: 8l, ½l **TIME:** 6min 26.0s **TOTE:** £1.90 **DF:** £29.60

16 Restricted   11 ran

1		**VILLAGE COPPER** 5-2JF **C Ward-Thomas** *2 handlers; lw; ld to 2 & 4-6; 2nd til ld brief 10; lft in ld 13; hdd & mist 16; rdn & blun 2 out; lft wl clr at last*
2	40	**Rising Sap** 20-1 **A Dalton** *2 handlers; swtng; swerved at starters flag; lost plce 6; 6l 5th ½way; mist 11; lost tch 14; plodded on; t.o when went 2nd flat*
3	2	**Star Changes** 5-1 **T Stephenson** *Hld up; 8l 7th ½way; mist 12; eff 14; 8l 4th 4 out; sn wknd; hmpd bad last*
4	1	**Moor Lady** (5a) 8-1 **S Swiers** *Hld up & bhnd; 9½l 9th ½way; hdwy 14; 9l 5th 4 out; sn wknd; t.o when lft 2nd at last; dem flat*
5	½	**Duncaha Hero** 25-1 **Miss R Barrow** *Prom; 5l 4th ½way; outpcd 14; 7l 3rd 4 out; sn wknd; broke down*
P		**Al Jawwal** 20-1 **S R Andrews** *Chsd ldrs; mist 9; 7l 6th ½way; mist & rmdrs 10; bhnd when pu 12*
F		**Buckaholic** (IRE) 9-2 **P Bull** *6s-9/2; ss; hdwy 5; went 3rd 7; lft 2nd 13; ld 4 out; lft 3l clr 2 out; fell last*
F		**Coogee Bill** (IRE) 5-2JF **A Wintle** *Hld up; 7th when fell 6*
P		**Gerej** (POL) 20-1 **R Barrett** *(xnb) A bhnd; rmdrs 4; 9l 8th ½way; lost tch u.p 13; pu 14*
F		**Minino** (IRE) 16-1 **A Coe** *Ld 2-4, 6-10 & 11 til fell 13*
U		**Mrs Wumpkins** (IRE) (5a) 20-1 **Mrs F Needham** *8th when mist & ur 3*

OFFICIAL DISTANCES: dist, 1½l **TIME:** 6min 21.0s **TOTE:** £2.90 **DF:** £105.00

17 Land Rover Mens Open, 12st – 18J   21 ran

1		**SECRET BAY** (7x) 11-4 **B Pollock** *Lw; ld to 5; 2nd/3rd til ld 9; qcknd clr 3 out; v impressive*
2	25	**Cherrynut** (7x) 4-1 **D Barlow** *Hld up; 9l 11th & stdy hdwy ½way; 9l 7th 14; 10l 6th 16; went 12l 3rd app 2 out & 2nd at last; no ch w wnr*
3	nk	**Makin' Doo** (IRE) (4x) 16-1 **C Mulhall** *2nd til ld 5; hdd & mist 8; 2½l 4th ½way; lft 3rd 13; 8l 4th 16; sn outpcd; stayed on flat*
[4²] 4	hd	**Wishing William** (IRE) (7x) 13-2 **S Waley-Cohen** *8s-13/2; lw; hld up & bhnd; 15l 15th ½way; 16l 9th 16; stayed on wl 3 out; went 4th at last; nrst fin*
5	6	**General Assembly** (IRE) 33-1 **N Bloom** *Hld up; stdy hdwy to 5l 7th ½way; lft 3l 2nd 13; blun 3 out; sn outpcd; 2nd til wknd at last; hung rt & releg 5th flat*
6	8	**Pangeran** (USA) (7x) 12-1 **N King** *Chsd ldrs; mist 3; 3½l 5th ½way; went 4l 3rd 14; mist 16; wknd app 2 out*
7	4	**High Learie** (7x) 33-1 **A Harvey** *Chsd ldrs; 4½l 6th ½way; 7l 5th & rdn 14; wknd app 3 out; t.o*
8	10	**Saint Bene't** (IRE) (bl) 33-1 **A Coe** *A bhnd; 15½l 16th ½way; t.o*
P		**French Buck** (IRE) 33-1 **M Rimell** *A bhnd; 19th ½way; t.o & pu 13*
F		**Galant Des Epeires** (FR) (tt) 33-1 **S Brisby** *Nvr; 9½l 12th ½way; rdn 13; wl bhnd when fell 2 out*
U		**Hatcham Boy** (IRE) 16-1 **C Ward-Thomas** *Prom; 4th & mist 7; lost plce; 5½l 8th ½way; 10l 8th 14; wl bhnd when mist & ur 2 out*
P		**Jazz Track** (IRE) (7x) (bl,tt) 33-1 **G Brewer** *Nvr gng wl; rmdrs 1; 10½l 14th & rdn ½way; lost tch 11; t.o & pu 14*
U		**Jolly Jack** (IRE) 33-1 **A Wintle** *Swtng; pckd 1; 15th when blun & ur 3*
P		**Maltby Son** (IRE) 20-1 **T Lane** *Swtng; chsd ldrs; lost plce & 6l 9th ½way; wknd 11; wl bhnd when pu 14*
P		**Mighty Merc** (7x) 33-1 **S R Andrews** *(xnb) Prom til mist 7; mist 10; wknd & 10l 13th ½way; t.o & pu 13*
P		**Nawrik** (IRE) 33-1 **R Barrett** *A bhnd; 17th ½way; t.o & pu 13*
P		**Offshore** (IRE) 33-1 **R Guest** *Sn wl bhnd; 20th ½way; t.o & pu 14*
P		**Premier First** (IRE) 33-1 **G Pewter** *A bhnd; 18th ½way; t.o & pu 14*
F		**Real Value** (IRE) 9-4F **B Hitchcott** *Lw; hdwy 6; went 2nd 10; ld & fell 13*
P		**Shake Five** (IRE) (7x) (bl) 10-1 **S Sporborg** *Hld up; 8l 10th ½way; hdwy & 8l 6th 14; wknd 4 out; t.o & pu last*
P		**Tom Pinch** (7x) 33-1 **J Cornwall** *Went 2nd 7; ld 8-9; 3rd ½way; jmpd lft 11; wknd 13; t.o & pu 3 out*

OFFICIAL DISTANCES: 20l, nk **TIME:** 6min 16.0s **TOTE:** £6.00 **DF:** £20.50
Fence 12 was omitted - fallen rider

18 Intermediate, 12st   11 ran

1		**MR FREEBIE (DEN)** 7-1 N Bloom *(xnb)* Hld up; 12l 7th ½way; gd hdwy 13; went ½l 2nd nxt; ld 4 out; drew clr 2 out; r.o wl
2	15	**Mr Grimsdale (IRE)** 4-1 M Rimell A.p; went 2nd 7; ld 11-4 out; rdn 3 out; wknd aft 2 out
3	20	**Lord Knox (IRE)** 25-1 A Coe Sn prom; 7l 4th ½way; lost plce 11; lft 8l 4th 15; wknd 4 out; went 3rd nr fin
4	3	**Optimism Reigns (IRE)** 10-1 R Clark Hld up; 8l 5th ½way; 5l 4th & hdwy when hmpd 11; mist 12; lft 5l 3rd & hmpd 15; rdn nxt; wknd u.p app 2 out
5	25	**Murberry (IRE)** (5a) 14-1 A Barlow Ld til hdd & mist 6; lost plce; 10l 6th ½way; lost tch 12; t.o
P		**Charter** (bl) 20-1 N King A bhnd; mists 5 & 9; 15l 8th ½way; t.o & pu 13
F		**Dry Highline (IRE)** 7-2 C Ward-Thomas Lw; pulled hrd; went 2nd 5; ld 6-11; 2½l 3rd when fell 15
F		**Give It A Whirl** (5x) 9-1 T Lane 5th when unsighted & fell 1
F		**Lochnomore** 7-4F A Dalton Prom; 3l 3rd ½way; fell 11
P		**Mitchells Best** 16-1 T Stephenson Hmpd 1; lost tch 8; 20l 9th ½way; t.o 12; pu 2 out
P		**Orphan Olly** 25-1 P York 2nd til carried v wide by loose horse bend aft 4 & drpd to rr; blun & lost tch 8; 25l 10th ½way; t.o & pu 11

OFFICIAL DISTANCES: 15l, 20l   **TIME:** 6min 25.0s   **TOTE:** £5.60   **DF:** £17.70

19 Greig Middleton Ladies Open   12 ran

1		**IMPERIAL DAWN (IRE)** 7-2 Miss L Rowe 2nd til ld 14; rdn & r.o wl flat
2	3	**Ardstown** (5a) 2-1F Miss S Vickery 3s-2s; swtng; a.p; 3rd ½way; jmpd slow 16 & 3 out; went 2nd app nxt; sn wknd fin
3	2	**Donnegale (IRE)** 13-2 Mrs C Ford 8s-13/2; prom; 5l 4th ½way; outpcd 13; went 8l 3rd app last; stayed on wl flat
4	30	**Faha Gig (IRE)** (5a) 12-1 Mrs F Needham 20s-12s; nd; 10l 7th ½way; 12l 5th when hmpd by loose horse 13; wl bhnd 15
5	10	**Half Each** (5a) 20-1 Miss L Watson Nd; 9l 6th ½way; lost tch 13; t.o
6	½	**Amber Spark (IRE)** 33-1 Miss Carla Thomas Nd; 8l 5th ½way; hmpd & rdr lost iron 10; wl bhnd 13; t.o
7	8	**Damier Blanc (FR)** 33-1 Miss Rachel Clark A bhnd; 15l 9th ½way; t.o 14
8	40	**Spuffington** 33-1 Miss C Hall 1st ride; 2 handlers; sn wl bhnd; 25l 10th ½way; t.o 11
U		**Bally Clover** 14-1 Mrs T Hill Prom til lost plce 5; hdwy & 4l 5th when hmpd bad & ur 10
P		**Gunner Boon** 3-1 Miss P Jones Ld til hdd 14; 2nd til wknd app 2 out; sn eased; 4th when pu last
F		**Japodene** (5a) 14-1 Miss A Deniel Trckd ldrs; 3l 4th when fell 10
P		**Laughing Fontaine (IRE)** 33-1 Miss R Clark Nd; 111 8th ½way; wl bhnd when pu 13

OFFICIAL DISTANCES: 3l, 2l   **TIME:** 6min 20.0s   **TOTE:** £2.20   **DF:** £4.00

20 Open Maiden 8yo&up, 12st - 17J   18 ran

1		**GLEVUM** (5a) 5-2F T Scudamore 4s-5/2; ld 2; lft 6l clr 14-3 out; rdn clr flat
2	7	**Jobsagoodun** (2ow) 10-1 M Yardley Ww; 8½l 11th ½way; stdy hdwy 13; went 7l 2nd aft 15; eff 3 out; sn rdn; no ex flat
3	3	**Peacemaker (IRE)** 7-1 J Cornwall Prom & hdwy 5; 3½l 5th ½way; lost plce 12; 15l 7th 4 out; 12l 4th & rallying 2 out; stayed on flat
4	½	**Hya Prim** 16-1 M Mackley Hld up & bhnd; 10l 13th ½way; hdwy 15; went 10l 4th nxt; & 6l 3rd aft 3 out; sn rdn & one pce
P		**Arctic Lodge (IRE)** 33-1 M Hewitt Chsd ldrs; 4l 6th ½way; went 3rd 12; lft 6l 2nd 14; mist 15; sn wknd; t.o & pu last
U		**Bachelor-Carrasco (IRE)** (2ow) 8-1 S R Andrews Went prom 5; 2nd 9 til mist & ur 14
P		**Chaps** 33-1 Mrs F Needham 2 handlers; a bhnd; 9l 12th ½way; lost tch 13; t.o & pu last
F		**Country Barle** 12-1 N Bloom Fell 1
P		**Cumberland Youth** 33-1 R Cope Prom; lost plce & rmdrs 7; 5l 8th ½way; wknd u.p 13; t.o & pu last
U		**Deep Song** 33-1 Miss Carla Thomas Ld to 2; 2nd til mist 9; 2l 3rd ½way; mist 12; 8th & wkng when mist & ur 13
F		**Fine Stalker (IRE)** 5-1 M Nicolls Hld up & bhnd; 11l 14th & rmdrs ½way; rdn 13; hdwy & 11l 5th when fell 4 out
P		**Frosty Deal (IRE)** 33-1 R Fowler Prom; 3rd & blun 4; lost plce 7; 4½l 7th ½way; rdn 13; 12l 7th & wkng 15; t.o & pu last

P		**Howsyourluck (IRE)** 8-1 T Vaughan *(xnb) Hld up; mists 6 & 9; 8l 10th ½way; lost tch 13; wl bhnd when pu 15*
P		**Out By Night (IRE)** 12-1 D Barlow *Hld up; mist 2; gd hdwy 8; 2½l 4th ½way; lft 8l 3rd 14; wknd qckly 3 out; wl bhnd when pu last*
P		**Shouldhavesaidno (IRE)** (5a) 33-1 J Owen *Sn wl bhnd; t.o & pu 12*
F		**Squaddie** 8-1 A Sansome *Swtng; 2nd when fell 1; fell agn nxt when loose*
U		**Tellaporky** 12-1 Miss E Owen *(xnb) 20s-12s; blun & ur 2*
P		**Thunderbird** (5a) 6-1 A Harvey *Nd; 7l 9th ½way; bhnd frm 12; t.o & pu last*

OFFICIAL DISTANCES: 10l, 3l   **TIME:** 6min 28.0s   **TOTE:** £3.00 **DF:** £29.50
Fences 10 & 11 were omitted to protect fallen riders

21 Open Maiden 56&7yo (Div 1), 2m4f, 12st - 15J   15 ran

1		**THE RED BOY (IRE)** 6-1 K Edmunds *Hld up & bhnd; 20l 10th ½way; 12l 5th & gd hdwy 16; went 2nd nxt; ld on bit aft 2 out; qcknd clr flat; impressive*
2	7	**Noah** (7a) 33-1 P York *Hld up & bhnd; 16l 9th ½way; hdwy 10; 8l 3rd 16; rdn to jn ldrs 3 out; ev ch last; one pce*
3	20	**Light The Sky** 7-1 J Turcan *Prom; 7l 4th ½way; lost pce 10; stayed on frm 2 out; went poor 3rd flat*
4	1	**Just The Business** 14-1 P Bull *(xnb) Lw; hld up; mist 3; 12l 7th ½way; lost tch 10; stayed on 3 out; nvr able to chall*
5	3	**Morris Piper** (tt) 7-4F Miss S Vickery *(xnb)Swtng; ld til hdd aft 2 out; sn wknd*
6	10	**You Can Quote Me (IRE)** 8-1 A Harvey *Chsd ldrs; 9l 5th ½way; 9l 4th when mist 4 out; sn wknd; t.o*
7	6	**Flowing Fortune** 10-1 Miss R Clark *Prom; 3rd ½way; went 3l 2nd app 10-3 out; wknd qckly app 2 out; t.o*
8	6	**Grain Hill** (5a) 20-1 B McKim *A bhnd; 11th ½way; t.o*
9	2	**Henavos** (5a) 7-1 S Swiers *Ss; a bhnd; 13th ½way; t.o*
F		**Campden Kitty** (5a) 10-1 G Carenza *Ss; 11th when fell 5*
P		**Chop-Chop (IRE)** 12-1 P Cowley *16s-12s; lw; pulled hrd; went 2nd 4 til blun 9; 3rd & wkng when mist 10; bhnd when pu 4 out*
P		**Howling Jack** 10-1 A Dalton *Sn wl bhnd; t.o 8; pu 4 out*
P		**Shine A Little (IRE)** 33-1 D Cook *Nd; 10l 6th ½way; lost tch 10; t.o & pu 2 out*
P		**Sidney Street** 16-1 R Barr *A bhnd; mist 4; 12th ½way; t.o & pu 2 out*
P		**Three Monroes (IRE)** 10-1 M Munrowd *Chsd ldrs; lost plce & 14l 8th ½way; jmpd slow 9; bhnd when pu 10*

OFFICIAL DISTANCES: 10l, 20l   **TIME:** 4min 56.0s   **TOTE:** £9.40 **DF:** £3.00 (1+any)

22 Open Maiden 56&7yo (Div 2), 2m4f, 12st - 15J   13 ran

1		**EVAN'S COLLIER BOY (IRE)** 5-2 J Jukes *(xnb) 2 handlers; swtng; made all; 10l clr when hit 5 & 8; stdd 9; went 7l clr 4 out; unchall*
2	15	**Le Cabro D'Or** 13-8F S Sporborg *2 handlers; a chsng wnr; mist 11; rdn app 2 out; 5l 2nd when hung bad lft bend aft 2 out; sn wknd*
3	25	**Fistral Flame** (5a) 5-1 A Charles-Jones *Trckd ldrs; 13l 4th ½way; no hdwy frm 10; went poor 3rd 2 out*
4	10	**Viking Art** (5a) 8-1 P York *Hld up; 15l 6th ½way; rn wide bend aft 8; 8l 3rd & hdwy nxt; rdn 11; wknd u.p app 2 out; t.o*
5	8	**Missmass** (5a) 20-1 M Nicolls *(xnb) Prom; 3rd when mist 4; 14l 5th ½way; rdn & wknd 10; t.o*
6	10	**Glencloy (IRE)** 10-1 A Coe *2 handlers; mist 1; lost plce 6; 24l 8th ½way; t.o 10*
P		**Boozi Birthday** (5a) 20-1 E Linehan *A wl bhnd; 27l 10th ½way; t.o & pu 16*
P		**Fountain Bank (IRE)** 10-1 M Gingell *Sn wl bhnd; t.o 8; pu 16*
P		**Heavenly Seven** (5a) 12-1 F Windsor Clive *Prom; mist 7; 12l 7th ½way; wknd & 10l 5th 10; t.o & pu 3 out*
U		**Hijacked** 16-1 T Stephenson *20l 9th when blun & ur 6*
P		**Inns Of Court** 20-1 B Hitchcott *A wl bhnd; 25l 9th ½way; t.o & pu 11*
P		**Magicman** (7a) 8-1 G Brewer *Hld up; 16l 7th ½way; wl bhnd when blun 9; t.o & pu 11*
P		**Regal Role** (5a) 20-1 M Mackley *A wl bhnd; 28l 11th ½way; t.o & pu 4 out*

OFFICIAL DISTANCES: 20l, dist   **TIME:** 4min 50.0s   **TOTE:** £2.30 **DF:** £3.90

North Norfolk Harriers
Higham (LH 8F,19J) Sat, 22 Jan (GOOD)

23 Open Maiden (Div 1), 12st   16 ran

1		**BALLINURE BOY (IRE)** 9-4F A Hickman *(xnb) Hld up trckng ldrs; 5th 12; went 2nd 16; clsd nxt; ld 2 out; sn qcknd clr*

2	8	**The Herbivore (IRE)** 9-2 B Hitchcott	*Jmpd slow 5; hld up; prog in 4th 11; went 2nd 14; outpcd nxt; kpt on to 2nd aft 2 out; no ch w wnr*
3	5	**On Target** 16-1 N Bloom	*Tk keen hld in 2nd; ld app 12; 5l clr 15; wknd nxt; hdd 2 out*
4	20	**Call The Tune** (5a) 10-1 D Brightling	*Bhnd; rem by 8; drvn & kpt on flat; nvr nr ldrs*
5	½	**Fair Ally** 10-1 B Kendellen (xnb)	*Pulled hrd; ld 4-11; lost plce rap*
6	20	**Johnny Cool** 6-1 M Hewitt	*Tk keen hld & prom; ld brief app 12; 3rd & wkng 16*
	P	**Arry's Away** 12-1 M Gorman	*Midfield; wknd 11; t.o & pu 16*
[20U]	B	**Bachelor-Carrasco (IRE)** 33-1 S R Andrews	*Chsd ldrs; 6th & rdn 13; bd 15*
	P	**Casino Nell** (5a) 20-1 A Harvey	*Trckng ldrs when pu 8; saddle slpd*
	P	**City Run (USA)** 20-1 M Grange	*Last pr; t.o 8; pu 12*
	P	**County Derry** 20-1 A Sansome	*Jmpd slow 4; novicey in last trio; rem by 8; pu 12*
	P	**River Surprise (IRE)** 12-1 R Barrett	*A bhnd; lost tch 8; t.o & pu 15*
	F	**Second Thoughts** (5a) 12-1 W Wales	*Novicey in midfield; 8th & outpcd 12; fell 14*
[21F]	P	**Sidney Street** 8-1 A Coe	*Ld to 4; lost plce qckly; t.o & pu 13*
	P	**Teluk (IRE)** 20-1 M Gingell	*Chsd ldrs to ½way; wknd & pu 13*
	F	**Tom's Lad** 16-1 S Morris	*Cl up; 4th 12; prsng ldrs when fell 15*

OFFICIAL DISTANCES: 8l, 4l TIME: 6min 20.0s TOTE: £2.30 DF: £18.00

24 Open Maiden (Div 2), 12st
13 ran

1		**HELENA JUSTINA** (5a) 7-1 P Taiano	*Hld up & bhnd; mod 7th 12; gd prog in 12l 3rd 16; stayed on str to ld aft 2 out; sn clr*
[22P] 2	10	**Fountain Bank (IRE)** 10-1 M Gingell	*Hld up; impd to 2nd 8; lft in ld 13; rdn 16; tried to get clr nxt; wknd & hdd aft 2 out; fin tired*
3	8	**Highfurlong (IRE)** 6-4F J Oldring	*Ld to 3; 3rd 11; lost plce qckly; mod 6th when drvn & nt keen nxt; nvr gng wl & nd aft*
4	5	**Dorans Joy (IRE)** 7-1 B Hitchcott	*Hld up in midfield; eff to 3rd 12; lft 2nd & lkd outpcd nxt; w ldr 16; wknd nxt; fin tired*
5	20	**The Secret Grey** 6-1 A Coe	*Midfield; 4th & outpcd 12; lft 3rd nxt; sn lost tch*
[20P]	F	**Arctic Lodge (IRE)** 16-1 M Hewitt	*Prom; 4th 11; outpcd nxt; rem last when fell 2 out*
	P	**Cicero's Law (IRE)** 5-1 P Chinery	*Oht; rr when wrestled to halt aft 7*
	P	**Citizen Band (IRE)** 14-1 C Lawson	*Bckwd; a wl outpcd; t.o 12; pu 3 out*
	P	**Duke Of Tulla (IRE)** 25-1 R Barrett (xnb)	*Prom early; rr 11; t.o & pu 14*
	P	**Outside The Rain (IRE)** (5a) 20-1 T Macfarlane	*Ld brief aft 3; 6th 8; lost tch 11; t.o & pu 14*
	P	**Primulas Daughter** (5a) 20-1 B Kendellen	*Novicey in last pr; sn t.o; pu 14*
	F	**Spectre** 10-1 N Bloom (xnb)	*X-eventer; tk keen hld; ld 4 til fell 13*
	P	**Tuath Deuchainne** 20-1 Miss R Pask	*Fat; wl bhnd in last pr til pu 5*

OFFICIAL DISTANCES: 10l, 8l TIME: 6min 29.0s TOTE: £3.20 DF: £74.00
The stewards interviewed the rider of Tuath Deuchainne; they accepted that she had pulled up because the horse was lame after knocking itself; Second Amendment (S Morris, rdr inj in prev rce) was withdrawn not under orders - Rule 4 deduction 25p in pound

25 Dodson & Horrell PPORA Club Members (Nov Rdrs), 12st
11 ran

1		**APPLEY DAPPLY** (5a) 12-1 Miss C Jiggins	*Jw; trckd ldrs on outer; stdy hdwy to 3rd 11 & 2nd 15; ld app 2 out; sn clr; rdly*
2	10	**Commasarris** 2-1F P Blagg	*Bckwd; tk keen hld; lft in ld 4; 3l clr 16; drvn & hdd app 2 out; sn btn*
[36] 3	6	**Fern Leader (IRE)** (7x) 8-1 Mrs J Hughes	*A 3rd/4th; prsd ldrs to 14; 18l 4th & no ch 16*
4	¾	**Neelisagin (IRE)** 4-1 J Turcan	*Ld to 2; hmpd sltly 4; prom; 2nd 12; wknd 15; 13l 3rd nxt*
5	15	**Golden Mac** (4ow) 16-1 J Barnard	*A bhnd; 8th 11; plodded round*
6	4	**Borrow Mine (IRE)** 3-1 A Braithwaite	*Rr of midfield; 7th 11; strugg frm nxt*
7	30	**Master Chuzzlewit (IRE)** (7x) 5-1 M Baldock (xnb)	*Midfield; 6th 11; outpcd & nd frm nxt*
8	3	**Ishma (IRE)** 16-1 D Page	*Sn prom; 2nd when jmpd slow 8; mist 10 & u.p; sn wknd; 5th & btn 12*
	F	**Limited Liability** 12-1 Miss C Grissell	*Ld 2 til fell 4*
[52]	P	**Royal Arctic (IRE)** (7x) 5-2 J Oldring	*Lw; bhnd & reluct; drvn & no resp 9; poor 9th 11; t.o & pu 2 out*
	P	**Target Time** (5a) 10-1 Mrs L Stock	*Poor last by 7; t.o & pu 12*

OFFICIAL DISTANCES: 12l, 4l TIME: 6min 21.0s TOTE: £8.40 DF: £24.00

26 Mens Open
8 ran

[43] 1		**MY SHOUT** 4-5F B Pollock	*Lw; ld/disp at brisk pce; went 11 clr 16; drvn along frm nxt; kpt on wl; all out*

	2	2	**Prince Buck (IRE)** 7-2 B Hitchcott *Lw; prom; jnd wnr 11 til aft 15; r.o game frm 2 out; nt qckn flat*
	3	½	**Bas De Laine (FR)** 2-1 A Hickman *Prsd ldrs; hit 5; 5th 11; outpcd nxt; 20l 3rd 16; stayed on wl 3 out to flatt brief bef last; no ex flat*
	4	25	**Jack The Td (IRE)** 12-1 J Cornwall *Sn prom; ld/disp 4-10; disp 3rd app 12; sn wknd; rem 4th 16*
[15⁹]	5	runin	**Broguestown Pride (IRE)** 33-1 P Blagg *Fat; imm outpcd; t.o 8*
	P		**Airtrak (IRE)** 25-1 A Harvey *Rr but in tch; 6th 11; rdn 12; sn strugg; pu 14*
	P		**Prince Of Saints (IRE)** 16-1 A Sansome *Prom; 4th 11; lost plce qckly aft nxt; eased & pu 14*
	P		**Reuter** 25-1 C Ward *Rr & nvr gng wl; u.p 7; lost tch 9; t.o 11; pu 14*

OFFICIAL DISTANCES: 1l, ½l   TIME: 6min 15.0s   TOTE: £2.00   DF: £5.50
The stewards interviewed the trainer of Broguestown Pride which was late into the parade ring; they were not satisfied with her explanation and fined her £50

27 Intermediate, 12st   10 ran

[4⁹]	1		**CEBU GALE (IRE)** 8-1 M Hewitt *Settled cl 3rd/4th; ld aft 15 & qcknd 7l clr nxt; drvn & kpt on one pce frm 2 out; a hldng rnr-up*
	2	3	**Just One Question (IRE)** 5-2 A Harvey *Settled trckng ldrs; impd to 3rd 11 & 2nd 12; ev ch 15; outpcd by wnr nxt; drvn & no imp aft*
	3	8	**Kincora (IRE)** 2-1F Mrs L Stock *(xnb) Ld 2-9; cl 3rd 12; wknd 14; 13l 3rd & btn 16*
[2⁹]	4	25	**Newtown Rambler (IRE)** 6-1 M Baldock *Prsd ldrs til 6th & strugg 11; wl bhnd aft nxt*
	5	nk	**The Millmaster (IRE)** (bl) 10-1 A Coe *Ld til mist 2; chsd ldr til ld 9; hdd aft 15; 15l 4th & wkng rap nxt*
	P		**Barron Bay (USA)** 20-1 M Gorman *Bhnd; lost tch 7; t.o 10; pu 13*
	P		**Court Amber (IRE)** 5-2 G Cooper *Prsd ldrs; 5th 11; wknd nxt; nt pushed; pu 16*
	P		**Generous Deal (IRE)** 6-1 A Sansome *Turdy; nt jw & nvr gng wl in rr; t.o & pu 8 (rdr reported saddle slpd)*
[6ᶠ]	P		**Street Trader (IRE)** 20-1 B Kendellen *Nt jw in last pr; t.o 7; pu 9*
	P		**Sultan Of Swing** 20-1 D Brightling *A bhnd; t.o 8; pu 12*

OFFICIAL DISTANCES: 3l, 10l   TIME: 6min 17.0s   TOTE: £51.00   DF: £30.50
The stewards interviewed the riders of a) Just One Question (marked by the whip) - owner cautioned for not warning that horse marked easily; and b) Generous Deal (pulled up early) - rider warned and explanation that saddle had slipped recorded

28 Ladies Open   9 ran

	1		**STRONG MEDICINE** 5-4F Mrs E Coveney *Jmpd rt; made virt all; bad mist 12; went 3l clr 16; drvn & hdd last; ld agn flat; won on jockeyship*
	2	3	**Uron V (FR)** 12-1 Miss T Hayter *Bhnd; outpcd 9; impd to 18l 3rd 12 & 7l down 16; clsd to chall 2 out; rdn & ld last; one-pcd & sn hdd*
	3	1¾	**Andrelot** (bl) 16-1 Miss C Grissell *Sn chsng wnr; rdn 16; clsd & ev ch 2 out; nt qckn last*
[19⁹]	4	10	**Laughing Fontaine (IRE)** 25-1 Miss L Allan *Lw; sev posns; drpd to rr 5; 6th 11; plodded on & nd frm nxt*
	P		**Emsee-H** 7-1 Miss Z Turner *Prom; 4th 8; wknd nxt; 4th 11; eased & pu 12*
	U		**Haunting Music (IRE)** 4-1 Miss E Neyens *Impd to 3rd 8; 10l down when hit 11; wknd rap 13; jmpd rt & rfo in mid-air nxt*
	U		**Mill O'The Rags (IRE)** 3-1 Mrs A Hays *Ur 1*
	P		**Red Channel (IRE)** 12-1 Miss P Bryan-Brown *Pulled hrd; hld up in rr; last 11; u.p to when jmpd rt & nrly ur 15; sn pu*
	U		**Velka (5a)** 8-1 Miss P Ellison *Midfield when rn v wide aft 3; ur 4*

OFFICIAL DISTANCES: 3l, 2l   TIME: 6min 21.0s   TOTE: £3.60   DF: £16.50

29 Confined, 12st   7 ran

[15³]	1		**FIRE ON ICE (IRE)** 5-2 N King *Lw; lft in ld 2-7; ld aft 11; hrd prsd when bad mist 2 out; rcvrd wl & in comm flat; rdly*
	2	8	**Ballydesmond (IRE)** 4-6F S Sporborg *Oht; rn in snatches & nvr lkd gng wl; kpt clsng on ldrs & lsng plce agn; went 3rd 14; 8l down 16; hrd rdn to chall 2 out; nt r.o frm last*
	3	15	**Going Around** (3x) 14-1 M Gingell *Settled 3rd/4th til 2nd 12; ev ch 16; wknd qckly 2 out*
	4	10	**Carson City** 10-1 J Purllant *Rr & reluct frm 4; 5l 5th 11; last & lsng tch nxt; 18l 4th 16; sn wl bhnd*
	5	30	**Hizal** 25-1 A Coe *Cl up til 6l last 11; mod 4th 14; t.o frm 3 out*
	U		**Candle Glow (5a)** 4-1 N Bloom *Ld til bad mist & ur 2*

| P | | **Dynamite Dan (IRE)** 25-1 **T Bulgin** *(xnb) Tk keen hld; 2nd/3rd til ld 7; hdd aft 11; ev ch when mist nxt; wknd rap; pu 16* |

OFFICIAL DISTANCES: 8l, dist **TIME:** 6min 28.0s **TOTE:** £3.60 **DF:** £3.30

The stewards enquired into possible interference by Going Around after the 10th fence; the rider admitted that his horse had hung to the rails but the interference was found to be accidental and the result was allowed to stand

Point-to-Point Owners & Riders Club

Barbury Castle (LH 8F,18J) Sun, 23 Jan (GOOD)

30 Club Members Maiden 6&7yo (Div 1), 12st   14 ran

	1		**WE MOVE EARTH** 4-5F **Miss P Gundry** *Lw; jmpd rt; sn prom; lft 2nd 5; ld aft 8; drew clr 3 out; mist last; comf*
	2	15	**True Hustler** 16-1 **F Hutsby** *Ld to 2; ll 3rd ½way; hit 11; went 2nd nxt; rdn 3 out; wknd 2 out*
	3	10	**Cherokee Run (IRE)** (tt) 16-1 **M Keel** *Hld up; 6l 7th ½way; 9l 7th 12; hdwy 15; went 10l 3rd nxt; no imp; mist last; fin tired*
	4	20	**Labula Bay** 33-1 **P York** *Bckwd; hld up; 4th when mist 7; 4l 5th ½way; 6l 4th 13; wknd 15; t.o*
	P		**Azzante (IRE)** 5-2 **A Dalton** *(xnb) 4s-5/2; hld up; hdwy 8; 3l 4th ½way; mists 10 & 11; 6l 5th nxt; wknd & 13l 6th 14; t.o & pu last*
	F		**Brookthorpe** (5a) 33-1 **G Barfoot-Saunt** *Went 2nd 3 til fell 5*
	P		**Dozmary Pool** 33-1 **R Burton** *Bckwd; ld 2 til hdd aft 8; 2nd til wknd & 7l 6th 12; 14l 7th 14; t.o & pu last*
	U		**Fontaine Again (IRE)** 10-1 **T Stephenson** *(xnb) 14s-10s; 12th when hmpd & ur 1*
[21⁸]	U		**Grain Hill** (5a) 25-1 **B McKim** *Chsd ldrs; 5l 6th ½way; went 5l 3rd 12; wkng when mist 15; t.o when mist & ur last*
	P		**Lord Chamberlain** 14-1 **E Williams** *25s-14s; hld up; mist 6; 9l 8th ½way; lost tch u.p 11; 20l 8th when pu 12*
	P		**Moon Island** (5a) 33-1 **L Lay** *Mist 1; sn wl bhnd; t.o 9 til pu 12*
	U		**Okeford (IRE)** 7-1 **R Walford** *20s-7s; mist 2; bhnd when blun & ur 7*
	P		**Riverlord** 20-1 **B Hodkin** *2 handlers; tde; prom til mist 2; wl bhnd 7; t.o 9 til pu 14*
	P		**Well I Never** 33-1 **P Millington** *A bhnd; mist 4; 10l 9th ½way; lost tch 11; pu 12*

OFFICIAL DISTANCES: 15l, 15l **TIME:** 6min 43.2s **TOTE:** £1.80

31 Club Members Maiden 6&7yo (Div 2), 12st   14 ran

	1		**CAUGHT AT DAWN** 6-1 **A Phillips** *14s-6s; sn prom; lft 2nd 7 til mist 12; ld 13; mist 3 out; clr when wandered aft 2 out; jmpd v slow last; reluct flat & all out*
	2	5	**River Bloom** (5a) 4-1 **A Martin** *Bckwd; prom; mist 1; 4l 5th ½way; 7l 4th 15; sn outpcd; went 10l 3rd nxt; stayed on 2 out; lft 2nd last; nt rch wnr*
	3	20	**Jack Flash** 10-1 **A Dalton** *Hld up; mist 8; 4½l 6th ½way; lost plce 12; 12l 6th 14; sn wl bhnd; went 3rd nr fin*
	4	1½	**Need More Practice** 20-1 **R Burton** *Hld up; hdwy 8; 3½l 4th ½way; 5l 3rd when blun 15; wknd 15*
	F		**Balmoral Spring (IRE)** 12-1 **P Millington** *13th when fell 1*
	F		**Dunethna (IRE)** 3-1JF **Julian Pritchard** *Hld up; 6l 7th ½way; stdy hdwy 11; 7l 6th when fell 13*
	P		**Free To Conker (IRE)** 16-1 **M Hawkins** *(xnb) Tde; blun 1; mists 3 & 8; 10l 10th ½way; lost tch 11; pu 12*
[12ᵁ]	P		**Highland Pearl** (5a) 16-1 **J Barnes** *Hdwy 4; lost plce 7; 9l 9th ½way; mist 11; t.o & pu 13*
	P		**Mainlier** 3-1JF **A Wintle** *7s-3s; hld up; 7l 8th ½way; lost tch 12; 20l 7th 14; pu 15*
	P		**Mr Kettlestone** 5-1 **S Joynes** *(xnb) 2 handlers; swtng; ld 2 til hdd aft 12; wknd & 7l 5th 14; pu 15*
	F		**Ossie Dale (IRE)** 25-1 **D Jones** *Ld to 2; mist 6; 2nd til fell 7*
	U		**Quick Response (IRE)** 20-1 **Miss M Norledge** *(citation) Last til mist & ur 1*
	P		**Thatl Do** (5a) 33-1 **P Sheldrake** *Hld up; 6l 7th ½way; 15l 11th ½way; t.o & pu 14*
[11ᶠ]	F		**Whatacharlie** (tt) 16-1 **B Kendellen** *(xnb)Hld up; stdy hdwy 7; 2½l 3rd ½way; ld aft 12-13; ev ch aft 3 out; wknd & mist nxt; 10l 2nd & exhaust when fell last; winded for sev mins*

OFFICIAL DISTANCES: 6l, 20l **TIME:** 6min 57.1s **TOTE:** £29.10

32 Mixed Open (Div 1), 12st   9 ran

[5¹]	1		**RECTORY GARDEN (IRE)** 2-1 **R Biddlecombe** *Went 2nd 3-5; 4l 5th ½way; went 2l 3rd 14; qcknd to ld app 2 out; rdly*

2	2	**Cavalero** 11-2 **A Charles-Jones** A.p; went 2nd 7-10; ld aft 12-13; ev ch app 2 out; kpt on wl
3	15	**Mizyan (IRE)** 8-1 **Miss P Gundry** 14s-8s; a.p; hit 5; 3l 4th ½way; qcknd to ld 13; mist 15; hdd app 2 out; sn wknd
4	20	**Flying Imp** 20-1 **J Barnes** 33s-20s; lost plce & mist 4; 6l 7th ½way; eff & 3l 5th 14; wknd 15
5	5	**Muntafi** 16-1 **A Wintle** Hld up; 7l 8th ½way; rmdrs 11; wl bhnd 15; t.o
6	4	**The Crazy Bishop (IRE)** 20-1 **B Shaw** Rdr did nt carry whip; ld til hdd 5; 2nd/3rd til wknd 13; t.o
7	12	**La Kabyle (FR)** (5a) 33-1 **F Windsor Clive** Pulled hrd; hdwy to ld 5; mist 8; hdd aft 12; 6l 4th & rdn 15; sn wknd; t.o
F		**Manamour** 33-1 **R Cooper** 7th when fell 2
P		**Miss O'Grady (IRE)** (5a) evensF **M Miller** 6/4-evens; hld up; 5l 6th ½way; 7th & in tch when pu 14; bbv

OFFICIAL DISTANCES: 2¼l, 10l **TIME:** 6min 33.3s **TOTE:** £3.20

The stewards enquired into the running and riding of Miss O'Grady; the rider's explanation that the horse had been pulled up because it had burst a blood vessel was accepted

33 Club Members (Nov Rdrs) (Div 1), 12st   16 ran

1		**TURNING TRIX** 5-1 **Miss R Curtis** Trckd ldrs; 3½l 5th ½way; ld 13; 5l clr 2 out; just hld on
2	nk	**Encima Del Rio (IRE)** 6-1 **B King** A.p; 2l 3rd ½way; went 2nd aft 12; outpcd aft 3 out; r.o u.p frm 2 out; just failed
3	15	**The Whole Hog (IRE)** (tt) 12-1 **Miss M Lowndes** Hld up; bhnd to 8; 6½l 10th ½way; hdwy to ld 12; hdd 13; 10l 3rd & btn when hit 2 out
4	8	**Some Tourist (IRE)** 4-1JF **N Benstead** Hld up; hdwy 8; 4l 6th ½way; lost plce 12; 11½l 8th 14; stayed on one pce frm 3 out
[6⁶] 5	3	**Gt Hayes Pommard** 20-1 **D Howells** 2 handlers; prom til hit 3; lost plce 6; 9l 12th ½way; rallied & 11l 7th 14; went 15l 4th 3 out; wkng when mist 2 out
6	6	**Saffron Moss** 4-1JF **H Evans** Blun & nrly ur 2; 12l 14th ½way; 22l 13th 14; nvr nrr
7	s hd	**Paul (IRE)** 16-1 **Miss L Collins** Prom; 2½l 4th ½way; 4l 6th when mist & rdr lost irons 13; sn wknd
8	4	**No Dozing (IRE)** 33-1 **J Byrne** Spurs; a bhnd; 11l 13th ½way; 20l 11th 14
9	3	**Kingofnobles (IRE)** 20-1 **R Rogers** 2 handlers; ld til hdd aft 2; 2nd til lft in ld 7; hdd 12; 6l 4th 14; sn wknd; t.o
10	10	**Aralier Man (IRE)** (bl) 25-1 **S Graham** Chsd ldrs; 5½l 8th ½way; lost plce 10; 21l 12th 14; t.o
11	6	**Panda Shandy** (5a) 9-2 **H Froud** 1st ride; sn wl bhnd; t.o 9
U		**Ardbrennan** 7-1 **Miss R Porter** Ld aft 2 til blun & ur 3
[14⁵] U		**Bright Lady** (5a) 33-1 **M Green** Chsd ldrs; 6l 9th ½way; wknd 12; 18l 10th 14; wl bhnd when mist & ur 15
[5⁷] F		**Cawarra Boy** 6-1 **M Walters** (xnb) 20s-6s; hld up & bhnd; hdwy 8; 5l 7th ½way; same plce when fell 13
U		**Dante's Gold (IRE)** 25-1 **R Bliss** Stdd start; hld up & bhnd; hit 6 & 7; 8l 11th ½way; short-lived eff 11; wknd & 16l 9th 14; hmpd & ur 15
P		**Stratus** 12-1 **J Gallagher** 20s-12s; lft in ld 3 til pckd 7; 2nd to 12; mist 13; wknd & 10l 15th nxt; t.o & pu 2 out

OFFICIAL DISTANCES: nk, 15l **TIME:** 6min 44.6s **TOTE:** £3.75

34 Mixed Open (Div 2), 12st   17 ran

[10⁶] 1		**FORMAL INVITATION (IRE)** 14-1 **S Joynes** Jw; hld up; 12½l 8th ½way; hdwy & lft 3rd 11; went 2nd 14; lft in ld 3 out; drew clr 2 out; rdn out
[5⁵] 2	10	**Gamay** 33-1 **N Mitchell** (xnb) hld up wl bhnd; 28l 12th ½way; 15l 10th 12; hdwy 14; lft 10l 4th 3 out; stayed on; went 2nd flat; nt rch wnr
3	2½	**Chasing The Bride** (5a) 5-1 **M Miller** A.p; 10l 5th ½way; 5l 4th 12; went 4l 3rd & rdn 15; lft 2nd nxt; wknd app last
4	10	**Simple Arithmetic** 25-1 **Miss P Gundry** Hld up & bhnd; 20l 10th ½way; 13l 8th 12; gd hdwy & lft 7l 3rd 3 out; wknd app last
5	1½	**Shariakanndi (FR)** 14-1 **T Mitchell** Hld up & wl bhnd; 30l 14th ½way; 14l 9th 12; stayed on frm 3 out; nvr nrr
6	½	**Pontabula** 12-1 **A Charles-Jones** Tubed; trckd ldrs; 11l 6th ½way; 9l 6th 12; no hdwy frm 14
7	15	**Down The Mine** 6-1 **Miss A Dare** Prom; 9l 4th ½way; lost plce & 12l 7th 12; 15l 9th 14; sn wl bhnd

	8	12	**Better Future (IRE)** 8-1 T Stephenson *12s-8s; 2nd to 4; lost plce 6; 25l 11th ½way; 18l 11th 12; to 14*
	F		**Comme Une Fleur (FR)** (5a) 33-1 T Vaughan *9th when fell 2*
	P		**Karaburan** 33-1 Miss F Wilson *A bhnd; 29l 13th ½way; 23l 12th 12; to & pu 14*
	F		**Leave It Be (IRE)** 16-1 J Barnes *25s-16s; mist 4; bhnd til fell 5*
	R		**Mickthecutaway (IRE)** 6-1 A Dalton *Went 2nd 4; ld 5-10; lft in ld 11 til rn out & ur 3 out*
	F		**Minella Silver (IRE)** 5-2F M Rimell *5s-5/2; lft in ld 1; hdd 5; 2nd til ld 10; qcknd 10l clr when fell 11*
	F		**Mr Motivator** 14-1 T Scudamore *Ld til fell 1*
	P		**Savuti (IRE)** 33-1 J Jukes *Chsd ldrs; 12l 7th ½way; rdn & wknd 10; wl bhnd when pu 12*
	P		**Shafi (IRE)** 9-2 D Mansell *Sn prom; 6l 3rd ½way; lft 2nd 11-14; eased & 6l 4th when pu 3 out*
	P		**Thinkers Effort (IRE)** 9-2 M Rodda *Hld up & bhnd; 19l 9th ½way; gd hdwy 11; went 8l 5th nxt; blun 14; wknd app 3 out; pu 2 out*

OFFICIAL DISTANCES: 8l, 3½l   TIME: 6min 42.6s   TOTE: no wnr

35 Club Members (Nov Rdrs) (Div 2), 12st   16 ran

	1		**MILLYHENRY** 11-10F Miss C Tizzard *6/4-11/10; 1st ride; a.p; jmpd slow 8; 5l 4th ½way; lft 2nd 10; lft clr 12; 20l ahd 15; unchall*
	2	10	**Military Man** 12-1 M Keel *Ld to 1; lost plce 4; 16l 6th ½way; hdwy & 111 4th 11; lft 12l 2nd nxt; hit 14; stayed on u.p frm 2 out; no imp*
[5ᴜ]	3	8	**Arise (IRE)** 10-1 T Abbott *Sn wl bhnd; 30l 10th ½way; 23l 5th 13; went poor 4th 3 out; stayed on; nt rch ldrs*
	4	1	**True Fortune** 3-1 M Barber *Sn wl bhnd; 34l 12th 4th 13; went 25l 3rd 15; stayed on; nvr nr to chall*
	5	30	**Kites Hardwicke** 25-1 P Sheppard *A wl bhnd; 32l 11th ½way; 30l 6th when mist 13; to*
	F		**Bricanmore (IRE)** 7-1 P Dartnall *Bhnd til hdwy 5; went 2nd 9; ld & fell 10*
	P		**Bushehr (IRE)** 33-1 J Cook *(xnb) Ld 2; hit 5 & 6; hdd 9; wknd qckly 10; to & pu 12*
	P		**Coolree (IRE)** 20-1 M Shears *Prom; 5l 5th ½way; lft 3rd 10; rdn & wknd qckly 12; to 14 til pu 2 out*
	P		**Flickering Flame** 33-1 B Hodkin *Mist 5; sn wl bhnd; 37l 13th ½way; to 11; pu 2 out*
	P		**Haveafewmanners (IRE)** (5a) (tt) 14-1 Miss M Lowndes *(kineton)+mid$(hk$,14):goto 1290*
[10ᴾ]	P		**Killeshin** 12-1 S Sellars *Sn to; pu 7*
[3ᴾ]	P		**Ngala (IRE)** (5a) 33-1 Miss J Tett *Chsd ldrs til wknd 8; 22l 8th ½way; to & pu 13*
	P		**Parditino** (5x) 16-1 Miss J Nicholas *25s-16s; sn wl bhnd; 25l 9th ½way; hdwy & 18l 3rd 13; wknd 15; to & pu last*
[9ᴾ]	U		**Silver Sleeve (IRE)** 25-1 Miss L Bridges *Hld up & bhnd; 21l 7th ½way; hdwy & 15l 5th when mist & ur 12*
[3ᴾ]	F		**Sip Of Brandy (IRE)** 14-1 G Skone *5l 4th & drvn along when fell 3*
[5ᴜ]	U		**Walkers Point** 33-1 Miss S Hutchings *19l 6th when mist & ur 7*

OFFICIAL DISTANCES: 8l, 7l   TIME: 6min 53.0s   TOTE: £1.70

36 Club Members Intermediate (Div 1), 12st   11 ran

	1		**SMILE PLEEZE (IRE)** 4-1 T Stephenson *(xnb) Hld up & bhnd; 14l 10th ½way; hdwy & 8l 4th 13; went 8l 2nd 3 out; str rn to ld aft 2 out; r.o wl; rdly*
	2	3	**Dannicus** 13-8F A Honeyball *2s-13/8; jw; ld; qcknd 13; 8l clr 15; hdd aft 2 out; rdn & ev ch last; no ex*
	3	30	**Royal Rupert** 14-1 N Benstead *Hld up & bhnd; 15l 11th ½way; hdwy & 7l 5th 12; lost plce & 9½l 6th 14; wknd 15; lft poor 3rd last*
	P		**Badger Beer** 4-1 A Charles-Jones *Prom; mists 2, 3 & 6; 5l 4th ½way; 10l 7th & wkng 14; to & pu 2 out*
	P		**Blayneys Privilege** 14-1 Miss T Habgood *2nd til wknd qckly 15; to & pu last*
	P		**Ilandra (IRE)** (5a) 33-1 M Nicolls *Nd; 11l 8th ½way; lost tch u.p 11; pu 12*
[14]	P		**Mendip Prince (IRE)** 4-1 A Lillington *Mist 2; lost plce 4; mist 5; 10l 7th ½way; lost tch 12; 20l 8th 14; pu 15*
	P		**Perfect Finisher** 25-1 M Hawkins *Hdwy 4; 6l 5th ½way; wknd qckly 11; pu 12*
[31ᴜ]	P		**Quick Response (IRE)** 33-1 Miss M Norledge *(citation) Hld up; hdwy 5; 3l 3rd ½way; went 8l 2nd 13 til wknd 3 out; poor 3rd when hung rt & pu last*
	P		**Ryder Cup (IRE)** 12-1 G Maundrell *Hld up; 12l 9th & rdn ½way; eff & 8l 6th 12; 9l 5th 14; sn wknd; to & pu 2 out*
	P		**West Lutton** 33-1 M Dobson *Sn prom; lost plce 7; 8l 6th ½way; wknd qckly 11; to & pu 15*

OFFICIAL DISTANCES: 3½l, dist   TIME: 6min 43.5s   TOTE: £3.00

37 Club Members Intermediate (Div 2), 12st   10 ran

[1⁵]	1		**RUSTIC REVELRY** 12-1 P York *16s-12s; hld up; hdwy & 2½l 4th ½way; ld 11; r.o wl*
	2	4	**Seymour's Double** 12-1 A Dalton *Hld up & bhnd; 6l 7th ½way; stdy hdwy 11; went 11 3rd 15 & 2nd aft nxt; rdn & ev ch 2 out; nt qckn*
	3	5	**Kristal Haze** (5a) 14-1 E Williams *33s-14s; sn prom; lft 2nd 6; hit 8; rdn & ev ch 15; one pce 3 out*
	4	3	**Babbling Brook (IRE)** evensF L Jefford *Hld up; hmpd 6; 3½l 5th ½way; hdwy 11; 3l 5th when mist 15; one pce 3 out*
	P		**Catchphrase** 33-1 J Docker *Hld up; 5l 6th ½way; hmpd 11; sn rdn & wknd; wl bhnd when pu 13*
	P		**Executive Office (IRE)** 13-2 A Wintle *Ld 1-2; mist 5; 2l 3rd ½way; 2l 4th 15; wknd & eased 3 out; pu nxt*
	F		**Longmore (IRE)** 9-4 T Mitchell *4s-9/4; ld to 1; ld 2-3; 2nd til fell 6*
	P		**Pointed Remark (IRE)** 20-1 D Jones *Prom til lost plce 7; 9l 8th & rdn ½way; sn wknd; t.o & pu 12*
	U		**Rising Dawn (IRE)** 25-1 P Millington *Mist 5; 7th when blun & ur 8*
	F		**Tiotao (IRE)** 33-1 J Gallagher *Hdwy to ld 3; hld & fell 11*

OFFICIAL DISTANCES: 5l, 6l **TIME:** 6min 54.7s **TOTE:** £6.70

38 Club Members Restricted 67&8yo, 12st   18 ran

[20¹]	1		**GLEVUM** (5a) 5-2F T Scudamore *Ld to 1; 2nd til lft in ld 5; hdd 2 out; rdn to ld last; r.o wl*
	2	1½	**Sir Frosty** 14-1 L Jefford *20s-14s; stdd start; hld up & wl bhnd; hmpd 5; 12l 11th ½way; gd hdwy & 4l 5th 12; went 4l 3rd 14; rdn & ev ch last; r.o*
	3	½	**My Clean Sweep (IRE)** 3-1 Miss P Gundry *6s-3s; hld up; blun 1; hdwy 7; 6½l 7th ½way; mist 11; 7l 8th nxt; eff & 9l 5th 3 out; str rn to ld nxt; hdd last; one pce*
	4	8	**Paddy For Paddy (IRE)** 8-1 A Dalton *Hld up & bhnd; stdy hdwy & 9l 9th ½way; went 3rd 12-14; 7l 4th nxt; one pce 3 out*
	5	15	**Rise To It (IRE)** 16-1 G Hanmer *Got loose & rn amok padd; swtng; hld up; hdwy 7; 3l 3rd ½way; went 2nd 11; disp ld 13-15; wknd qckly 2 out*
	P		**Best Bitter** 25-1 A Charles-Jones *Prom; went 2nd aft 8-11; 5l 6th nxt; sn wknd; bhnd when pu 14*
	P		**Coddington Girl** (5a) 13-2 T Stephenson *(xnb) Prom; lft 2nd 5-8; 4½l 4th ½way; wknd & 8l 9th 12; bhnd when pu 14*
	F		**Crocked Again (IRE)** 6-1 Julian Pritchard *(xnb) Ld 1; 10l clr when fell 5*
	P		**Dyffryn Prince (IRE)** (tt) 25-1 D Jones *Chsd ldrs; mists 4 & 8; 9½l 10th ½way; eff & 6l 7th 12; sn wknd; bhnd when pu 14*
	P		**Gaelic Royale (IRE)** (5a) 33-1 T Vaughan *Prom; mist 5; 5l 5th ½way; wknd qckly 11; pu 12*
	P		**G-And-T** (5a) 16-1 M Cowley *A bhnd; 13th ½way; t.o & pu 12*
	F		**Joao Passos** (5a) 33-1 T Mitchell *Wl bhnd til fell 6*
[11⁷]	P		**Mountain Tae (IRE)** 33-1 R Green *A bhnd; mist 3; 30l 12th ½way; t.o & pu 12*
	P		**Not For Profit (IRE)** 10-1 C Williams *20s-10s; chsd ldrs; 8l 8th ½way; rdn 11; 8½l 10th nxt; sn wknd; t.o & pu 3 out*
	P		**Pure Air** 25-1 G Maloney *A bhnd; 14th ½way; t.o & pu 12*
	U		**Simply Susie** (5a) 16-1 B Kendellen *Hld up; 11th when hmpd bad & ur 5*
	P		**Smart Orange (IRE)** 6-1 M Rimell *Jmpd rt; hld up; mist 6; hdwy & 6l 6th ½way; jb rt 11; 2½l 4th nxt; 7l 5th & rdn 14; sn wknd; wl bhnd when pu 3 out (swallowed tongue)*
	U		**Teelyna** (5a) 25-1 G Marsh *Nt jw; wl bhnd til tried to ref & ur 6*

OFFICIAL DISTANCES: 1½l, ½l **TIME:** 6min 48.2s **TOTE:** £4.20

The rider of Gaelic Royale was fined £60 for failing to pass the doctor following a fall in an earlier race

West Percy

Alnwick (LH 9F,18J) Sun, 23 Jan (GOOD)

39 Hunt (with Percy), 12st   8 ran

	1		**CARNAVEN** 6-1 A Robson *Hld up; 6th ½way; prog in 3rd 13; sltly outpcd 15; rallied to ld 2 out; sn rdn clr*
	2	8	**Kings Token** (3x) 6-4F J Walton *Ld; 10l clr 5; hdd brief app 3 out; hdd agn nxt; rdn & sn outpcd*
	3	4	**Fingerhill (IRE)** (4x) 16-1 M Thompson *Settled 4th; went 2nd 8; hit 13; rdn to ld brief app 3 out; wknd nxt*

	4	12	**Paperback Writer** (5a) 14-1 R Green *Lw; last pr; 8l last 9; blun 13; some hdwy 15; mod 4th when blun 2 out*
	5	5	**Carnmoney (IRE)** (3x) 2-1 Mrs K Hargreave *Settled ab 6th; outpcd frm 13*
	6	2fncs	**With Respect** 2-1 Miss D Crole *Prsd ldr til mist 8; drpd rap to rr app 13; to 3 out*
	P		**Black Ice (IRE)** 10-1 T Oates *(xnb) Chsd ldrs to 13; sn wknd; to app 15; pu 3 out*
	P		**Wylup** 25-1 H Humble *Last pr; brief eff when hit 11; outpcd 14; to 3 out; pu last*

OFFICIAL DISTANCES: 8l, 8l   **TIME:** 6min 39.0s

40 Restricted   14 ran

	1		**MINDEN ROSE** (5a) 6-4F C Mulhall *(xnb) Hit 1; cl up & gng wl; 5th ½way; ld 12; lkd in comm when mist 2 out; eased cl home*
	2	1½	**Shingle Beach** (5a) 6-1 Miss P Robson *Hld up in rr; 10th ½way; gd prog 15; r.o str frm 2 out; sltly flatt by prox; promising*
	3	1	**Border Glory** 8-1 M Bradburne *Fat; cl up; 6th ½way; eff in 2nd 15; sn rdn; kpt on stdly frm 2 out; a hld*
	4	4	**Blyth Brook** 10-1 C Storey *(xnb) Hld up; impd to 3rd ½way; one pce & no imp frm 15*
	5	15	**Mini Cruise** 10-1 L Morgan *Chsd ldrs; 8th ½way; eff 14; 5th nxt; sn wknd*
	P		**Abbey Lad** 7-2 C Wilson *Midfield; 9th 9; mid-div when pu 12*
	P		**All Or Nothing** (5a) (bl) 33-1 Miss L Kendall *Drpd to rr 6; to when mist 8; pu 3 out*
	P		**Boris Brook** 10-1 T Oates *Tubed; midfield; 7th ½way; jmpd slow 10; outpcd 13; pu 3 out*
	P		**Harleidalus (IRE)** 10-1 R Morgan *Prom & pulled hrd; jmpd slow 5; 2nd/3rd to 9; mist 11; 5th & wkng 12; tired when pu 3 out*
	P		**Just Hoping** 12-1 S Charlton *Jw; last early; hdstrng & 3rd by 2; made most 3-12; prom to 15; nt pushed; pu 3 out; promising debut*
	P		**Luvly Bubbly** (bl) 16-1 Miss C Hall *Bhnd & nvr gng wl; 12th ½way; to & pu 3 out*
	P		**Mr Bossman (IRE)** 7-1 T Glass *Lw; prom; 4th ½way; hit 13; wknd nxt; pu 3 out*
	P		**Riverside Run (IRE)** 7-1 A Robson *(bf) Ld to 3; 3rd when saddle slpd & pu 5*
	P		**Storm Alive (IRE)** 14-1 Mrs V Jackson *A bhnd; 11th ½way; lost tch 13; to & pu 3 out*

OFFICIAL DISTANCES: 1l, 1l   **TIME:** 6min 34.0s

41 Ladies Open   13 ran

	1		**LA RIVIERA (IRE)** 9-2 Miss P Robson *Midfield & hld up; 20l 6th 9; 3rd & prog 15; 2nd nxt; rdn to ld aft 2 out; stayed on wl*
	2	4	**Pebble Beach (IRE)** 20-1 Miss C Savell *Pulled hrd in clr ld; 15l ahd ½way; still 15l clr 13; pegged back 15; nt hdd til aft 2 out; btn when blun last*
[3¹]	3	1½	**Balisteros (FR)** 4-7F Mrs C Ford *Wl bhnd; 22l 7th ½way; 5th & prog 15; stayed on frm 2 out; too much to do*
	4	5	**Houselope Beck** 12-1 Miss C Hall *(xnb) Lw; chsd ldr 3-10; handy til one-pcd app 3 out*
	5	5	**Marius (IRE)** 5-1 Miss V Russell *Prsd ldrs on outer; 5th ½way; handy til nt qckn aft 15*
	6	1	**Steel Rigg (IRE)** 10-1 Miss A Price *Prom in chsng group; went 2nd 10-13; wknd aft 15*
	7	15	**Tabriz** (5a,3ow) 16-1 Miss A Thompson *Mid-div; 8th ½way; in tch to 15; sn wknd*
	8	20	**Cab On Target** 4-1 Miss W Gibson *Trundled rnd in rr; 10th ½way; to 13; schoolmastering*
	9	12	**Nosmo King (IRE)** 12-1 Miss L Kendall *Wl bhnd in last trio; 11th ½way; to 12*
	P		**Gaelic Warrior** 20-1 Miss R Clark *(xnb) Chsd ldr to 3; lost plce 8; 9th ½way; to & pu 3 out*
	P		**Lyford Cay (IRE)** (4ow) 12-1 Miss A Turnbull *(xnb) Jmpd w hd in air; a last; 20l bhnd 6; to 10; pu 3 out*
	P		**Mullingar (IRE)** 12-1 Mrs V Jackson *Chsd ldrs; 5th ½way; wknd 13; to & pu last*
	P		**Sharp Thyne (IRE)** 8-1 Miss J Hedley *Bit bckwd; wl bhnd; 12th ½way; to 10; pu 3 out*

OFFICIAL DISTANCES: 3l, 2l   **TIME:** 6min 27.0s

42 Mens Open   9 ran

	1		**DENNETT LOUGH (IRE)** 2-1 C Storey *Bhnd; 15l 7th 6; 25l 7th ½way; stayed on wl frm 13; 2½l 3rd 15; hrd rdn to ld last; all out; won on jockeyship*
	2	½	**Jymjam Johnny (IRE)** (7x) 2-1 J Tate *Rdn in snatches; ld 3-7; 5l 3rd ½way; ld 12-13 & 14-15; ld agn 2 out; gng best when stumbled last; wkly rdn flat (ungenuine & can't be tchd w whip)*
	3	12	**Greenhil Tare Away** 5-1 S Swiers *Lw; tk str hld; ld to 3; cl 2nd/3rd til ld 15; hdd & wknd 2 out*
	4	3	**Sunrise Sensation** (7x) 6-1 C Denny *Midfield & chsng clr ldrs; 14l 5th & clsng ½way; eff & flatt brief 15; sn outpcd; rn wl*
	5	20	**Majority Major (IRE)** (7x) 12-1 T Glass *Chsd clr ldng trio; 12l 4th ½way; lost tch 15*

6	15	**Lottery Ticket (IRE)** (7x) 20-1 **S J Robinson** *Lw; midfield til 24l 6th ½way; mists 9 & 10 & rdr waving wildly; sn t.o*
[17ᵖ]	P	**Jazz Track (IRE)** (7x) (bl,tt) 8-1 **M McGhee** *Reluct & climbed fncs; 20l last 6; t.o & pu 8*
	F	**Jigtime** (5a,7x) 1-3F **M Bradburne** *Made most 7 til hdd & fell 14*
	P	**Judicial Field** (bl) 5-1 **G Moscrop** *Wl bhnd in last pr; 37l last ½way; t.o & pu 12*

OFFICIAL DISTANCES: ½l, 12l   **TIME:** 6min 30.0s

43 Confined, 12st   13 ran

1		**PARADE RACER** 7-1 **A Richardson** *In tch; 6th ½way; went 3rd 13; ld 15-nxt; drvn along & ld agn last; r.o wl*
2	½	**Midsummer Glen (IRE)** 4-1 **Miss M Bremner** *Sn cl up & gng wl; 4th ½way; chall 15; ld nxt; rdn when outj & hdd last; kpt on*
3	15	**The Caffler (IRE)** 6-1 **Miss R Ramsay** *Keen in 2nd/3rd; ld 10-13; ev ch 15; wknd aft nxt*
4	1	**Fragrant Lord** 8-1 **Mrs V Jackson** *Ld to 2; lft in ld 5; 6l clr 9; hdd 10; ld agn 13-15; no ex nxt*
5	4	**Poynder Park (IRE)** 3-1 **L Morgan** *Bhnd early; 8th ½way; nvr plcd to chall*
6	6	**Ballyboden** 14-1 **F Arthur** *Prom; 3rd 9; hdwy 13; lost plce nxt; btn 15*
7	6	**Claywalls** 3-1 **M Clayton** *Cl up; 7th 9; wknd 15; fin distressed*
8	15	**Excise Man** (7x) (tt) 5-1 **J Walton** *Sn bhnd; last 9; t.o 15*
	P	**Charlieadams (IRE)** 4-1 **J Muir** *Saddle slpd bef rce; tk str hld; ld 2 til saddle slpd agn & pu 5*
	P	**Damas (FR)** 2-1JF **Miss P Robson** *A bhnd; 9th 9; rem frm 14; pu 3 out; lame*
	F	**Fiscal Gale (IRE)** 6-1 **P Strang Steel** *Mist & nrly ur 2; prom; 4th 10; crashing fall 12; dead*
	U	**Kilminfoyle** 3-1 **P Robson** *12th when rfo 1*
	P	**Primitive Way** 2-1JF **P Maitland-Carew** *Easy rn in last pr; outpcd 13; t.o & pu 3 out*

OFFICIAL DISTANCES: ½l, 15l   **TIME:** 6min 37.0s

The stewards interviewed the Clerk of the Course about a delay in the rider receiving attention following the fall of Fiscal Gale, there being no medical cover at the fence; they accepted his assurance that this had been quickly remedied

44 Open Maiden (Div 1) - 16J   11 ran

1		**QUARTERSTAFF** 3-1 **C Wilson** *(xnb) Bckwd; handy; 3rd ½way; qcknd ahd 10; clr 3 out; easy*
2	12	**Menaldi (IRE)** 7-1 **T Glass** *Impd to 2nd/3rd frm 7; 2l 2nd 15; sn outpcd by wnr; hrd prsd & und str press flat to keep 2nd*
3	s hd	**Hooky's Treat** (5a) 7-1 **Miss J Hedley** *Ld to 10; disp 2nd aft; outpcd by wnr frm 15 but kpt on wl in sust duel for 2nd*
4	25	**Smiths Wynd** 2-1F **T Oates** *Cl up; 5th ½way; 3l 3rd 15; wknd qckly nxt*
5	2	**Blackchesters** 7-1 **J Walton** *Hld up in rr; 10l 8th ½way; sn lost tch & wl bhnd; easy rce*
	U	**Donard Son (IRE)** 6-1 **D Jewett** *Ur bend bef 4*
	P	**Escalate** 20-1 **Miss L Kendall** *Prom brief; 7th & wkng when mist 9; jmpd slow aft & sn t.o; pu 3 out*
	P	**Gallant Major** 6-1 **A Robson** *Handy til pu 6; saddle slpd*
	P	**Lothian Commodore** 10-1 **Miss L Bradburne** *Chsd ldrs; 4l 6th ½way; wknd 14; tired when pu 3 out*
	P	**Night Riot (IRE)** 16-1 **Mrs V Jackson** *Lw; sn strugg in rr; wl bhnd 7; t.o 10; pu 3 out*
	P	**What A Coincidence** (5a) 20-1 **M Williams** *(xnb) Prsd ldrs; 4th ½way; wknd 13; pu on flat 3 out; broke both forelegs; dead*

OFFICIAL DISTANCES: 20l, s hd   **TIME:** 6min 40.0s

Fences 3 & 12 were omitted - fallen horse; Hey Chief was withdrawn not under orders - rider injured; the rider of Menaldi was warned by the stewards concerning his use of the whip

45 Open Maiden (Div 2)   13 ran

1		**MORE JOY** 12-1 **S Bowden** *Ld 1; ld 4 til aft 14; ld agn 3 out; clr nxt; kpt on stdly*
2	8	**Do Justice (IRE)** 4-1 **C Wilson** *Trckd ldrs; 7l 4th ½way; outpcd 14; rallied app last; r.o wl flat*
3	2½	**The Other Half** 4-1 **Miss P Robson** *Hld up; 6th ½way; eff to 3rd 14; lkd dangerous app 3 out; tiring when jmpd slow 2 out & last*
4	½	**Briar Rose (IRE)** (12a) 5-2F **J Ewart** *5s-5/2; mist 4; rr div; 8th ½way; prog 15; kpt on wl aft 2 out*
5	25	**Farebit** (5a) 6-1 **C Storey** *Wl bhnd in last trio; mist 12; schooled on*
6	6	**Rye Rum (IRE)** 10-1 **J Walton** *Sn hld up in rr; 10th ½way; nvr put in rce aft*

7	6	**Superior Weapon (IRE)** 4-1 M Clayton *7s-4s; keen early; ld aft 1-4; chsd ldr to 11 & brief aft 14; wknd rap nxt*
U		**Dram Hurler (IRE)** 3-1 R Morgan *3rd til went 2nd & blun & ur 8*
P		**Go Nomadic** 8-1 P Atkinson *Erratic in last; bad mist 6; mist 7; t.o when blun 14; pu 3 out*
F		**Highbury** 4-1 G Brewer *Lw; oht; trckd ldrs; 5th 9; handy 4th when fell 15*
P		**Nisbet** 7-1 Miss M Bremner *Nvr trbld ldrs; 7th ½way; t.o & pu 3 out*
F		**Smiddy Lad** 6-1 T Oates *14s-6s; fat; mist 5; prom; 6l 3rd 9; 2nd 11 til ld aft 14; hdd 3 out; 5l 2nd & tired when fell nxt*
P		**Tricky Trevor (IRE)** 6-1 Miss H Delahooke *Lw; hld up & bhnd; 9th ½way; t.o & pu 3 out*

OFFICIAL DISTANCES: 12l, 1l TIME: 6min 42.0s

46 Open Maiden (Div 3)   15 ran

1		**MANHATTAN RAINBOW (IRE)** 7-1 D Da Silva *10s-7s; settled handy; went 2nd 10; ld 12; drew clr bef 3 out; stayed on wl; unchall*
2	8	**High Expectations (IRE)** (7a) 2-1 R Tate *Oht; ur bef start & bolted; chsd ldrs; 6th 10; eff in 4th 15; went 7l 2nd app 3 out; trying to cl when mist nxt; no imp; mist & nrly ur last*
3	8	**Ben Buckley** 10-1 W Renwick *A 3rd/4th til disp 2l 2nd 15; sn wknd to 15l 3rd; plodded on*
4	12	**Mount Gay** 6-4F M Bradburne *4s-6/4; tk keen hld; hdwy 6; 3rd when mist 9; lost plce tame aft 12; nd aft*
5	20	**Test Of Loyalty** 8-1 A Robson *Bhnd til 7th & eff 10; wknd 14; rem 3 out*
P		**Broken English** (5a) 12-1 Miss T Jackson *Drpd out & wl bhnd in last trio; t.o 12; pu 3 out*
P		**Cool Kevin** 5-1 R Morgan *7s-5s; midfield; 8th 10; outpcd aft 12; pu 3 out*
P		**French Bell** (5a) 10-1 A Richardson *Last trio & wl bhnd; t.o last 10; pu 3 out*
P		**Harleyburn** 8-1 Mrs A Hamilton *Chsd ldrs; 5th 10; outpcd 14; pu 3 out*
P		**Lady Alice** (5a) 8-1 L Morgan *Mists in rr; drvn 8; t.o 13; pu 15*
P		**Normandy Duke (NZ)** 14-1 Mrs K Hargreave *Mists; rr aft jmpd slow 6; t.o 12; pu 15*
R		**Senso (IRE)** 8-1 Miss P Robson *(xnb) Lw; tk str hld in rr til rn out 2*
P		**Slave's Choice** 12-1 S Swiers *Ld; 6l clr 5; hdd 8; wknd rap nxt; t.o & pu 12*
P		**Solway Saffy** (12a) (tt) 10-1 T Davidson *Midfield; hit 7; bhnd frm 10; t.o & pu 15*
F		**Tropnevad** 7-1 B Lusted *2nd til ld & mist 8; 6l clr 10; hdd 12; wknd rap aft 15; disp rem & v tired 4th when fell 2 out*

OFFICIAL DISTANCES: 10l, 6l TIME: 6min 37.0s

Lincolnshire United Hunts Club
Market Rasen (LH 7F,18J) Sat, 29 Jan (GOOD to FIRM)

47 Club Members, 12st   5 ran

1		**EVE'S TREASURE** (5a) 6-4 S Campion *Ld 2-4; 2nd til ld 8; hdd aft 10; ld app 14; drew clr 2 out; comf*
2	12	**Springfield Rex** 4-5F Mrs F Needham *Hld up; 2½l 3rd ½way; ld 13; hdd app 14; rdn 2 out; sn wknd*
3	20	**Ryders Wells** 10-1 S Walker *Nvr gng wl; jmpd slow & rmdrs 7; 3½l 4th ½way; lost tch u.p 13; went rem 3rd 2 out*
4	20	**Fontaine Fables (IRE)** (7x) 8-1 N Wilson *Hld up; 4½l 5th ½way; mist & rmdrs 11; lost tch u.p 13; lft 30l 3rd 15; dem 2 out; t.o*
P		**Sovereigns Match** 12-1 Simon Robinson *Ld to 2; ld 4-8 & aft 10 til wknd 13; 20l 3rd when pu 15*

OFFICIAL DISTANCES: 20l, dist TIME: 6min 36.7s

48 Confined, 12st   11 ran

1		**INCH CROSS (IRE)** (4ow) 10-1 R Hunnisett *14s-10s; a.p; 4l 3rd ½way; went 2nd aft 13; ld app 14; mist 15; drew clr 2 out; stayed on wl*
2	8	**Linlathen** 4-1 N Bell *(xnb) Hld up & bhnd; 22l 5th ½way; hdwy 13; went 15l 3rd nxt; stayed on frm 3 out; went 2nd at last; nt rch wnr*
[18F] 3	nk	**Give It A Whirl** (3x) 8-1 T Lane *Jmpd rt; prom; went 8l 2nd 4; ld 12 til hdd app 14; wknd aft nxt; one pcd*
4	25	**Drummond Warrior (IRE)** 12-1 Miss A Burton *2nd to 4; 15l 4th ½way; lost tch 13; 22l 4th nxt; cont wl bhnd*
5	20	**Just Charlie** (3x,1ow) 3-1JF D Easterby *Hld up; lost plce 7; 26l 7th ½way; no hdwy 12; t.o 14; easy rn*

[15F] P   **Barna Boy (IRE)** 3-1JF **R Armson** *Jmpd lft; ld; 8l clr 4; hdd 12; wknd qckly aft 13; 29l 5th nxt; wl bhnd when pu 15*

       P   **Cede Nullis** (5a) 10-1 **S Brisby** *(xnb) Hld up; 22½l 6th ½way; no hdwy & 20l 6th when pu 13*

       P   **Demoniac (FR)** (1ow) (tt) 20-1 **G Smith** *(xnb) Lost plce 6; wl bhnd 8; 35l 10th ½way; t.o 11; pu 13*

       P   **Springhill Quay (IRE)** 12-1 **R Clark** *Mist 5; wl bhnd 8; 30l 8th ½way; t.o 14; pu 2 out*
       P   **Take Two** 25-1 **S Pinder** *(xnb) Ss; wl bhnd til pu 5*
       P   **Tiderunner (IRE)** 20-1 **S Walker** *Wl bhnd 8; 33l 9th ½way; t.o & pu 13*

OFFICIAL DISTANCES: 10l, nk, 10l   **TIME:** 6min 32.5s

49 Dodson & Horrell PPORA Club Members, 12st   5 ran

       1   **RED REBEL** 1-3F **B Pollock** *Made all; drew wl clr frm 3 out; unchal*
       2   20   **Miss Ondee (FR)** (5a,7x) 14-1 **D Mansell** *Chsd wnr; jmpd slow 2 & 6; no imp 15*
       3   runin   **Moneghetti** 25-1 **R Armson** *Hld up; drpd to rr 4; 14l 5th ½way; wl bhnd 13; lft 3rd nxt; t.o*
       F   **Running Free (IRE)** 33-1 **M Williams** *Hld up; 9l 3rd ½way; eff & disp 4l 2nd when fell 14*
       P   **Vitaman (IRE)** 9-2 **G Barfoot-Saunt** *Hld up; mist 7; 13l 4th ½way; lost tch 12; jmpd v slow 13 & pu; bbv*

OFFICIAL DISTANCES: dist, dist   **TIME:** 6min 44.3s
       Dulas Bay (P Millington, 12-1, weighed-out without 7lb penalty) was withdrawn at start not under orders; the owner/rider was fined £60

50 Restricted, 12st   8 ran

       1   **IRISHEYESARESMILIN (IRE)** 2-5F **B Pollock** *A.p; went 2nd 4; blun 13; ld app 14; drew wl clr frm 15; unchal; fin tired*
       2   20   **Macfin (IRE)** 20-1 **Miss L Allan** *Ld 2 til hdd aft 3; lost plce & 6½l 6th ½way; went 9l 4th 12; lft 12l 3rd 14; went 20l 2nd app 2 out; no imp*
       3   25   **Yornoangel** 25-1 **R Clark** *Ld to 2; mist 9; 2l 3rd ½way; lft 6l 2nd 14; wknd 3 out; t.o*
       P   **Deer Park Lass (IRE)** (5a) 33-1 **D Thomas** *A bhnd; 13l 8th ½way; 25l 8th when pu 13*
       P   **Dorgan** 20-1 **A Sansome** *Hld up & bhnd; jmpd slow 2; 9l 7th ½way; short-lived eff u.p 12; t.o & pu 14*
       F   **Miorbhail** 20-1 **Miss T Gray** *(xnb) Pulled hrd; ld aft 3 til hdd aft 13; 4l 2nd when fell 14*
       P   **Primitive Charles** 6-1 **G Brewer** *Hld up; 6l 5th ½way; lost plce & 10½l 7th 12; wl bhnd when pu 14*
       P   **Vintage Choice (IRE)** 8-1 **N Kent** *Bckwd; hld up; mist 6; hdwy & 5l 4th ½way; wknd 12; wl bhnd when pu 14*

OFFICIAL DISTANCES: dist, dist   **TIME:** 6min 43.2s

51 Open Maiden (Div 1), 12st   16 ran

       1   **JACKSON'S HOLE** (4ow) 6-1 **D Easterby** *Ww; hdwy & 5l 7th ½way; lft 4th 13; went 2nd aft 2 out; ld app last; clever*
       2   1   **Primitive Man** 20-1 **S Charlton** *A.p; mist 9; 3l 4th ½way; ld 15 til hdd app last; r.o*
       3   8   **Lingham Lady** (5a) 7-1 **S Swiers** *Hld up & bhnd; 15l 14th ½way; 15l 9th 13; hdwy 14; 5l 5th 3 out; stayed on one pce*
       4   7   **C L B Jemilla** (5a) 9-2 **Mrs F Needham** *Chsd ldrs; lost plce & 6l 9th ½way; rallied 12; went 2nd 15 til wknd qckly aft 2 out*
       5   5   **Village Gossip** (5a) 33-1 **M Worthington** *Hld up; hdwy 7; went 2nd ½way; ld 11-12 & aft 13 til hdd 15; wknd app 2 out*
       6   1½fs   **Alston Fanfare (IRE)** (1ow) 12-1 **J Cookson** *(xnb) A bhnd; 18l 15th ½way; t.o 13*
       F   **Camden Kid (IRE)** 16-1 **Miss L Allan** *(xnb) Pulled hrd; 2nd til ld 5; hdd 11; ld 12 til aft 13; 4th & wkng when fell 14*
[7P]   P   **Doranslone** (5a) 14-1 **N Docker** *Swtng; lost plce 7; 14l 12th ½way; t.o 13; pu last*
       P   **Fine Times** 20-1 **M Mackley** *Hld up & bhnd; 12l 11th ½way; 10l 8th 13; nt rch ldrs; 12l 6th 3 out; pu last*
       P   **Guilsborough Gorse** (7a) 16-1 **G Brewer** *Hld up & bhnd; hdwy & 5½l 8th ½way; 6th & wl in tch when pu 12; easy rn*
       F   **Intrepid Gal** (12a) 16-1 **J Docker** *Chsd ldrs; lost plce & 6½l 10th ½way; eff & 7l 6th when fell 12*
       P   **Jambo Bwana** 8-1 **P Millington** *A bhnd; 14½l 13th ½way; lost tch & 20l 10th 13; t.o & pu 14*
       P   **Pee-O-Tempa** (5a) 7-1 **R Cope** *Prom; 3½l 5th ½way; sn lost plce; bhnd when pu & dism 12; bbv*
       U   **Run For The Mill** 4-1F **M Morley** *(xnb) Mounted outside padd; 11th when rfo 2*

U		**Shropshire Gale (IRE)** 6-1 N Kent *12s-6s; hld up; stdy hdwy 7; 4l 6th ½way; 3l 4th when blun & ur 13*
U		**The Noble Rebel (IRE)** 8-1 A Pennock *16s-8s; ld to 5; 2nd til 2l 3rd ½way; 10l 8th & wkng when hmpd & ur 12*

OFFICIAL DISTANCES: 1l, 1½l **TIME:** 6min 47.7s

52 Open Maiden (Div 2, Part 1), 12st - 17J   9 ran

1		**TRACEYTOWN (IRE)** (5a) 9-2 Miss Rachel Clark *A.p; lft 2nd 8; lft in ld 12; hdd 14; ld aft 2 out; r.o wl*
2	8	**Grey Gossip (IRE)** (1ow) 4-1 G Smith *Ld 2-4 & 6-7; 4l 3rd ½way; 2l 3rd 2 out; went 2nd app last; no ex*
3	20	**Round The Bend** 9-1 S Brisby *Hld up; 5l 4th ½way; lft 2nd 12; ld 14; mist 3 out; hdd & wknd qckly aft 2 out; fin tired*
F		**Blue Chip (IRE)** (5a) 12-1 D Mansell *Hld up; 5½l 5th ½way; 4th when mist 12; 3l 4th when fell 2 out*
F		**Mandalay Man (IRE)** 7-2F P Millington *Hld up; mists 5 & 9; 8l 6th ½way; mist 13; 8l 5th when fell 14*
U		**Miss Pink** (5a) 12-1 M Barnard *Mists; hld up; 7l 6th when mist & ur 10*
U		**Po Cap Eel** (5a) 16-1 Miss H Kinsey *(xnb) Sn wl bhnd; 20l 7th ½way; ur 12*
[22P] U		**Regal Role** (5a) 33-1 M Mackley *(xnb) Ld to 2; ld 7 til stumbled & ur 12*
F		**Stanwick Hall** (1ow) 4-1 K Needham *Pulled hrd; ld 4 til mist 6; 2nd when fell 8*

OFFICIAL DISTANCES: 8l, dist **TIME:** 6min 54.4s
Fence 15 was omitted - fallen planet

53 Open Maiden (Div 2, Part 2), 12st   7 ran

1		**MANDRIL (IRE)** 4-1 N Tutty *(xnb) Ww; 3½l 4th ½way; lft 2nd 12; ld aft 13; drew clr 2 out; rdly*
2	20	**Fair Farm Lad** 20-1 P Welsh *2nd til lft in ld 5; hdd 7; mist 9; lft in ld 12; hdd aft nxt; wknd 2 out*
3	8	**Sparebit** (5a) 10-1 R Armson *Ld to 2; lost plce & 8l 5th ½way; lft 12l 3rd 14; no ch aft*
4	2fncs	**Ron On The Run (IRE)** (bl) 5-2 S Charlton *Hld up; blun 6; 2½l 3rd ½way; went 2l 2nd & fell 14; rmtd*
U		**In The Van** 10-1 M Morley *(xnb) 7th when rfo 2 (cf Run For The Mill)*
P		**Perdix** (12a) 10-1 K Prendergast *Nt jw & oft bad lft; sn wl bhnd; t.o & pu 8*
P		**The Butcher Boy** (4ow) 13-8F D Easterby *3s-13/8; ld aft 2 til hit 5; ld 7; mist 8; blun bad & hdd 12; 5l 4th when blun 13; nt rec; wl bhnd when pu 15*

OFFICIAL DISTANCES: 20l, 15l, fence **TIME:** 6min 55.6s
Redmire was withdrawn not under orders - rider injured in previous race

54 Open Maiden (Div 3), 12st   15 ran

1		**ELLA FALLS (IRE)** (12a) 25-1 M Worthington *Hld up & declined mad early pce; 45l 9th ½way; 13l 5th & hdwy 14; went 8l 4th 3 out; str rn to ld aft 2 out; sn clr*
2	8	**Erni (FR)** 9-2 W Burnell *Hld up; 35½l 4th ½way; went dist 3rd 12; hdwy 14; went 2nd nxt til 2 out; no ch w wnr*
3	10	**The Happy Monarch (IRE)** 10-1 Mrs F Needham *Hld up; mist 2; 37l 6th ½way; went dist 4th 13; hdwy 14; went 6l 3rd nxt; ev ch 2 out; sn wknd*
4	5	**Scraptastic** 12-1 N Bell *Chsd ldr 2; 20l clr of rest when mist 7; ld app 14; 5l clr 15-2 out; sn hdd & wknd qckly*
5	12	**New Hope** (5a) 16-1 Mrs M Bellamy *2nd to 2; 35l 3rd ½way; 15l 6th & no hdwy 14; 20l 6th & wkng 2 out*
6	15	**Icantsay (IRE)** 8-1 D Thomas *Chsd ldrs; mist 1; lost plce & 47l 10th ½way; 26l 8th 14; t.o*
P		**Del The Lorry Man** 14-1 D Mansell *A wl bhnd; 49l 12th ½way; 38l 11th 14; t.o & pu 2 out*
P		**Fooled You (USA)** 12-1 E Andrewes *Chsd clr ldrs; 25l 3rd 7; 36l 5th ½way; wknd qckly 12; t.o & pu 14*
F		**Fountain Street (IRE)** 10-1 R Burton *(xnb) Hld up & wl bhnd; mist 12; no hdwy when fell 13*
P		**Grannies Delight (IRE)** 33-1 L Hicks *A wl bhnd; 48l 11th ½way; mist 11; 30l 9th 14; t.o & pu 2 out*
P		**Huntsbydale** (5a) 5-1 S Walker *A wl bhnd; 49½l 13th ½way; 35l 10th 14; t.o & pu 2 out*
P		**Joridi Le Forige (IRE)** 3-1 B Orde-Powlett *A wl bhnd; 53l 14th ½way; 39l 12th 14; t.o & pu 2 out*
F		**Mighty Monarch (IRE)** 16-1 P Millington *(citation) Sn t.o; mist 2; jmpd v slow 6; 60l 15th ½way; fell 12*

P		**Pharstar (IRE)** (4ow) 11-4F **D Easterby** *Set suicidal pce & sn wl clr w one rival; wknd & hdd app 14; 10l 5th 3 out; wl bhnd when pu last*
P		**Tom's Surprise** 6-1 **N Kent** *Bckwd; chsd ldrs; 39l 7th ½way; 25l 7th & no hdwy 14; t.o & pu last*

OFFICIAL DISTANCES: 6l, 6l **TIME:** 6min 46.3s

55 Open Maiden (Div 4), 12st   11 ran

1		**KEY DEBATE** 5-2JF **G Brewer** *Made all; sn wl clr; 40l ahd when blun 12; kpt up relentless gallop; unchall*
2	40	**Madame La Claire** (5a) 5-2JF **D Thomas** *A chsng wnr; no imp frm ½way; a clr of rest*
3	5	**Romantic Native (IRE)** 6-1 **C Mulhall** *Hld up & wl bhnd; 55l 4th ½way; went dist 3rd app 2 out; stayed on*
4	30	**Scruton** 5-1 **K Prendergast** *Ur & rn loose bef start; a wl bhnd; 64l 8th ½way; t.o*
[21⁷] 5	2	**Flowing Fortune** 14-1 **Miss R Clark** *Chsd clr ldr; mist 5; 50l 3rd ½way; wknd app 2 out; t.o & virt pu flat*
[7ᴾ] F		**Executive Blue (IRE)** (5a) 20-1 **G Barfoot-Saunt** *Hld up & bhnd; rem 7th when fell 7*
F		**Fortune Hunter (IRE)** 20-1 **P Millington** *Sn wl bhnd; t.o 5; pu 14*
U		**Mr Hook** 20-1 **P Halder** *Sn wl bhnd; 60½l 6th ½way; blun & ur 13*
P		**Steel My Song** (5a) 10-1 **R Armson** *A wl bhnd; 66l 9th ½way; t.o & pu last*
P		**The Boree Log** 14-1 **M Hewitt** *Chsd ldrs; 3rd when blun 6; wknd & 61l 7th ½way; t.o & pu 12*
[21ᴾ] P		**Three Monroes (IRE)** 6-1 **M Munrowd** *A wl bhnd; 60l 5th ½way; jmpd v slow 15; t.o & pu 3 out*

OFFICIAL DISTANCES: dist, 8l, dist **TIME:** 6min 35.0s

Royal Artillery
Larkhill (RH 13F,18J) Sat, 29 Jan (GOOD)

56 Hunt   3 ran

1		**COACH (NZ)** (7x) 4-5F **B Kendellen** *(xnb) Tchd evens; keen in ld; 8l ahd 5; 15l clr when hit 7; virt solo aft; hit last*
2	30	**Bathwick Bobbie** 9-2 **Jeremy Young** *A chsng wnr; dist bhnd aft 12; tired frm 14*
[8ᵁ] 3	12	**Ballyea Boy (IRE)** (bl) 9-4 **R Webb-Bowen** *A last; jmpd poor; hit 3; strugg 6; wl t.o aft 12*

OFFICIAL DISTANCES: dist, 15l **TIME:** 6min 25.7s **TOTE:** £1.60

57 Open Maiden 56&7yo (Div 1), 12st   8 ran

1		**BRODANTE KING (IRE)** 20-1 **P Cowley** *Prom & gng wl; 2nd 7 til ld 13; forged clr frm 3 out; rdly*
[11³] 2	30	**One Of The Natives (IRE)** (1ow) 4-5F **T Mitchell** *Opened evens; ld to 13; lkd tired & hanging when mist 3 out; no ch aft*
r		**Chasing A Bid** (7a) 33-1 **J Snowden** *Bckwd; novicey in last pr; lost tch 10; lft rem 4th when blkd & ref 13*
U		**Country Captain** 11-2 **L Jefford** *Prsd ldrs til stumbled app 9; collapsed on to apron & died*
[30ᵁ] r		**Fontaine Again (IRE)** 12-1 **T Stephenson** *Rr trio; lost tch 10; just lft poor 3rd when ref & ur 13*
F		**Gilt Air** (5a) (tt) 40-1 **J Diment** *Tk keen hld; mist 3; 2nd brief 6; cl 3rd 12; wkng qckly in 3rd when fell 13; down for sev mins*
F		**Hobby De Beyssac (FR)** (12a) (bl) 3-1 **T Scudamore** *(xnb) 9/2-3s; prom; jnd ldrs & fell 5*
P		**Royal Dew (IRE)** (1ow) (vis) 16-1 **D Evatt** *Grad lost plce; 5th 9; t.o last aft 12; inherited v rem 3rd 13; sn pu*

OFFICIAL DISTANCE: dist **TIME:** 6min 13.2s **TOTE:** £7.50 **DF:** £10.36

58 Open Maiden 56&7yo (Div 2), 12st   7 ran

1		**MONTY'S THEME (IRE)** (1ow) 3-1CF **T Mitchell** *Settled last til aft 12; smooth prog nxt; disp ld 14 til forged clr frm 2 out; easy*
[12³] 2	12	**Prah Sands** 3-1CF **J Young** *2nd/3rd til aft 12; w wnr til wknd bef 2 out; plodded on*
[12ᵁ] 3	20	**Copper Valley** (5a) 14-1 **A Honeyball** *Prsd ldrs til 3rd & ev ch aft 12; wknd 14; mist last*
[12ᴾ] P		**Harlequin Boy** 3-1CF **M Miller** *7s-3s,tchd 5/2(!); ld til app 6; nt fluent aft; 5th 7; wknd app 13; poor last when bad mist 14; pu nxt*
[22ᴾ] U		**Heavenly Seven** (5a) 20-1 **F Windsor Clive** *Pulled hrd; rr but cl up; mist 5; blun & ur 6*
[22⁹] U		**Viking Art** (5a) 6-1 **Y York** *Ld app 6 til aft 12; disp ld to 15; wkng when blun & ur 3 out*

| | F | | Yanto (7a) 5-1 Julian Pritchard Tchd 6s; bit bckwd; novicey; hld up in tch; wknd uphill aft 12; last when fell hvly 13 |

OFFICIAL DISTANCES: 20l, dist TIME: 6min 20.0s TOTE: £3.90 DF: £7.40

59 Mixed Open (Div 1), 12st
12 ran

	1		**FOREST FOUNTAIN (IRE)** 2-1F **Julian Pritchard** 5/2-2s; ld 1; stdd to rr of midfield; smooth prog on outer frm 14; 2nd nxt; ld 3 out; sn in comm; jmpd delib last
[4F]	2	3½	**Noyan** 3-1 **P York** 5s-3s; 2nd/3rd til ld 13; jnd 15; drvn but chsd wnr vain frm nxt
[10B]	3	3½	**Solo Gent** 14-1 **S Bush** 20s-14s; chsd ldrs til wknd app 13; 5th & btn 15; plodded on stdly frm 2 out
	4	6	**Pyr Four** 33-1 **B Pauling** 1st ride; settled in tch; eff to jn ldrs 13; ev ch 15; bhnd nxt; drpd dead aft rce
	5	6	**Stillmore Business** 12-1 **Miss P Gundry** Bit bckwd; hld up; 4th & eff 9; wknd app 13; rem last 15
	6	½	**Alex Thuscombe** (bl) 33-1 **P Shaw** Ld aft 1; hdd 13; sn lost plce; 4th & btn 15
	P		**Funny Farm** 9-2 **Miss S Vickery** Hanging bad; trckd ldrs to 12; wknd qckly; pu 13
	F		**Gaelic Blue** (tt) 25-1 **A Wintle** Last pr; 11th when fell hvly 11
	P		**Lie Detector** 16-1 **J Gasper** 2nd 4; lost plce 9; wknd app 13; pu 14
[34F]	F		**Mr Motivator** 9-1 **T Scudamore** Rr of bunch; in tch til app 13; mod 6th 15; fell 2 out
	P		**Radio Days (IRE)** 16-1 **Miss C Tizzard** Prom brief; lost tch by 6; hit 8; t.o 12; pu 13
[9³]	P		**Tomcappagh (IRE)** 8-1 **C Gordon** Hdwy 5; chsd ldr 7; wknd app 13; t.o & pu last

OFFICIAL DISTANCES: 3l, 10l TIME: 6min 11.1s TOTE: £4.30 DF: £4.40

60 Open Maiden 56&7yo (Div 3), 12st
9 ran

[11⁴]	1		**LOST YOUR MARBLES (IRE)** (5a) 4-1 **J Mead** (b4) Oht; sn 2nd; ld aft 12; pushed along & kpt on game frm 2 out
[12⁵]	2	3½	**Border Light** 7-2 **A Charles-Jones** Opened 10s in a plce; bckwd; settled in tch; mist 6; eff 13; last of 3 w ch 3 out; nt qckn aft til stayed on flat; clsd til no ex final 100 yds
	3	5	**Ballyblack (IRE)** 6-1 **N Mitchell** Settled rr; still last 12; went 2nd nxt; ev ch 2 out; rdn & prsng wnr when blun last; nt rec
[17P]	4	10	**Offshore (IRE)** 3-1F **R Guest** 4s-3s; mists; ld 1; prom; 4th 13; last & wkng when mist 15
	5	25	**Perking** 16-1 **M Foley** Bckwd; sn ld; hdd aft 12; lost tch 15; t.o
[12U]	P		**Idlewild (IRE)** (7a) 7-1 **Julian Pritchard** Opened 8s; jmpd erratic in detach last til pu aft 4; saddle tree broke
[14F]	P		**Jamies First (IRE)** 14-1 **A Martin** Nt fluent; tk keen hld & cl up til wknd rap aft 12; t.o & pu 13
	F		**Larry** (7a) 14-1 **P York** Prom; mist 8; fell 11
[12B]	F		**The First One** 9-2 **A Honeyball** Hld up gng wl in rr; smooth prog in 3rd 12; wknd 15; tired when crashing fall 2 out; winded bad & down for 20 mins

OFFICIAL DISTANCES: 2½l, 3l TIME: 6min 22.6s TOTE: £3.10 DF: c/f
The stewards enquired into the running and riding of Idlewild; the rider's explanation that the saddle tree had broken, possibly following a heavy fall in an earlier race, was accepted

61 Mixed Open (Div 2), 12st
14 ran

	1		**FRESH PRINCE** 5-1 **Julian Pritchard** Ld to 5; ld agn 12; 8l clr nxt; prsd app last; found ex flat & r.o wl
	2	10	**Blue Laws (IRE)** 16-1 **Miss C Tuffin** Tchd 20s; lw; settled in chsng group; stayed on wl aft 2 out; went 2nd flat; nt rch wnr
	3	½	**Glaisnock Lad (IRE)** 25-1 **J Barnes** Midfield; nt trble ldrs frm 14; stayed on frm 2 out; tk 3rd cl home
	4	3	**Skip'n'time** 4-5F **M Miller** 6s-4/5; trckd ldrs; mist 5; 3rd 7; chsd wnr frm 13; drvn to cl & flatt brief last; slowed dramatic & releg 4th nr fin
[10⁴]	5	15	**Bet With Baker** 5-1 **T Mitchell** Tchd 6s; cl up to 12
	P		**Blessed Oliver** 25-1 **J Trice-Rolph** Midfield; wknd 12; pu 3 out
[8⁴]	P		**Camitrov (FR)** 50-1 **R Sturgis** (xnb) Prom; 4th 7; wknd 12; t.o last when pu last
[4F]	F		**Celtic Silver** 20-1 **B Hitchcott** Towards rr when fell 3
[35P]	P		**Coolree (IRE)** 66-1 **M Shears** Strugg frm 12; pu 14
	P		**Gale Toi (IRE)** 13-2 **O Ellwood** Lw; hld up; eff in 5th 7; wknd 13; pu 3 out
	P		**Garethson (IRE)** 66-1 **B King** Bckwd; ld 5-12; chsd ldng pr frm 3 out; no imp; pu 2 out
[32F]	P		**Manamour** 66-1 **A Charles-Jones** In tch to 12; pu 2 out
	P		**Mr Edgar** 50-1 **M Bluck** Sn bhnd; to 7; pu 14
	P		**Mystery Aristocrat (IRE)** 33-1 **R Tory** Lw; sis; a last pr; t.o 7; pu 14

OFFICIAL DISTANCES: 10l, 2l TIME: 6min 10.2s TOTE: £3.90 DF: c/f

62 Confined, 12st
11 ran

	1		**BAVARD DIEU (IRE)** 20-1 *Miss V Sturgis Towards rr to 10; hdwy 13; 3rd 15; chsd ldr nxt; lkd hld til stayed on aft last; ld cl home*
[10^P]	2	2½	**Copper Coil** 14-1 *G Maundrell Prom; ld 12; 2l clr & lkd wnr when rdn last; r.o; hdd nr fin*
[1³]	3	15	**Cahors (IRE)** 4-1 *N Mitchell Opened 10s in plce; bckwd; hld up; 5th 9; eff 13; 2nd & ev ch 15; wknd 2 out; btn 3rd when blun last*
	4	20	**Capo Castanum** 16-1 *R Sturgis Tubed; prom ld 8-12; wkng when mist 14*
	5	2½	**Cardinal Gayle (IRE)** 8-1 *Miss D Harding Last pr; no ch frm 12*
	6	2½	**Single Man (NZ)** (2ow) (bl) 25-1 *Miss T Blazey Ld 1; stdly lost plce; rr 9; wl bhnd 13*
	P		**Arleneseoin (IRE)** (7x) 20-1 *C Gordon Sis; rr when mist 6; prsng in 4th 9; lost tch 13; pu 2 out*
[8¹]	P		**Desert Waltz (IRE)** 5-2 *T Mitchell A towards rr; wknd 13; pu 15; lame*
[11^F]	F		**Imperative** 33-1 *A Charles-Jones (xnb) Jmpd erratic in midfield til fell 8*
[1¹]	U		**Sulphur Springs (IRE)** evensP *P Scouller Lw; ld 2-8; prom to 13; 4th & outpcd 15; same & no ch when mist & ur last*
	P		**Tom Furze** 20-1 *D Dennis Nvr btr than midfield; 6th 9; mist 11; wl bhnd when pu 14*

OFFICIAL DISTANCES: 2l, 25l **TIME:** 6min 12.9s **TOTE:** £5.00 **DF:** c/f

63 Intermediate, 12st
18 ran

[10^F]	1		**CASTLE LYNCH (IRE)** (5a) 7-1 *Miss S Vickery Trckd ldrs; eff 13; 4th 15; str chall aft 2 out; ld & lft clr last*
	2	10	**Ross Cottage** 2-1F *A Bateman Tchd 5/2; hld up; eff 13; 4th & prsng ldrs 15; nt qckn 2 out; lft 2nd & hmpd last*
	3	2	**Another Junior (IRE)** 33-1 *M Miller Prom; ld 12-15; wknd nxt*
	4	4	**Shrewd Thought (USA)** 20-1 *J Trice-Rolph Hld up; eff 13; nt trble ldrs frm 15*
	5	1	**Hehas** 20-1 *C Wadland In tch to 13; nd frm nxt*
[7³]	6	10	**Sir Wynham** 33-1 *O Ellwood Lw; unruly & threw rdr padd; prsd ldrs; mist 7; ld 15; hdd 2 out; sn wknd*
	7	2	**Glendine (IRE)** 33-1 *D Smith Bhnd frm 12*
	8	10	**Toms Choice (IRE)** 25-1 *Miss T Blazey Bhnd frm 6; t.o*
	U		**Bally Wirral (IRE)** 10-1 *G Maundrell Tchd 8s; u r*
	P		**Bertie Bavard** 40-1 *P Cowley Bckwd; missed break & sn t.o; pu 14*
	P		**Hardy Weather (IRE)** 33-1 *C Smyth Missed break; a t.o; pu 13*
	C		**Ibex** 3-1 *Julian Pritchard 4s-3s; sn ld til carried out by loose horse 4*
[10^F]	F		**Lord Ellangowan (IRE)** 40-1 *A Martin Rr of ldrs; no ch frm 11; fell 14 & broke fnce*
	P		**Mendip Son** 25-1 *Miss P Gundry Prom; 2nd 1; wknd 13; t.o & pu 2 out*
	F		**Old Harry's Wife** (5a) 33-1 *N Mitchell Nvr btr than midfield; rem 10th when fell 3 out*
	P		**Royal Estate** 10-1 *M Rimell Chsng ldrs when mist 5; bhnd frm 12; pu 3 out*
	U		**True Chimes** 12-1 *J Owen (xnb) Lft in ld 4-12; prom til ld agn 2 out; sn rdn & hdd; btn 2nd when blun & ur last*
	P		**Young General** (bl) 12-1 *T Mitchell Lft & sn rem in trailing trio; pu 3 out*

OFFICIAL DISTANCES: 2l, 10l **TIME:** 6min 24.7s **TOTE:** £5.70 **DF:** c/f

64 King's Troop RHA Members, 2m4f - 15J
8 ran

	1		**HIGHNOON (U)** (5a,3ow) 4-1 *J Attrill Chsd ldrs; cl 3rd 6; disp ld 10 til stayed on str flat*
	2	2	**Highgate (U)** (5a) 2-1F *Miss D Humphreys A.p; disp when lft in ld 6; jnd 10 til hdd & no ex flat*
	3	25	**Homfray (U)** (3ow) 4-1 *C Gilbert Ld to 2; jmpd slow 4; trckd ldng pr til wknd 2 out; sn btn*
	4	1½fs	**Brummel (U)** 7-1 *C Whittaker Last trio 4; t.o 10; plodded on*
	5	2fncs	**Brigstock (U)** 7-1 *J Grantham Last 3 til fell 8; rmtd fncs bhnd*
	U		**Bugler (U)** (15ow) 7-1 *J Faulkner Last trio 4 til blun & ur 7*
	U		**Henley (U)** 5-2 *L Grey Ld 3 til jnd & ur 6*
	U		**Herzagova (U)** (5a) 3-1 *G Chanter Pulling in 4/5th til blun & ur 8*

OFFICIAL DISTANCES: 2l, 20l **TIME:** 6min 18.0s **TOTE:** £27.30 **DF:** £87.90
This race was scheduled to be third on the card, but was put back nearly four hours to allow the horses to arrive at the course (delayed by a road traffic accident)

Silverton
Black Forest Lodge (RH 8F,19J) Sun, 30 Jan (GOOD)

65 Hunt, 12st
6 ran

	1		**ALICE SHORELARK** (5a) 1-2F *T Greed (xnb) Lw; set off in false start & then reluct to line up; disp 2nd til ld aft 7; jmpd delib 16 & releg 3rd; 2nd agn nxt; ld on inner app last; rdn out*

	2	1½	**Mr Jervis (IRE)** (7x) 5-1 **Miss V Tremlett** *1st ride; rcd wide & tkn stdly; 8l 3rd 11; clsd 13; jmpd ahd 16; hdd aft 2 out; rallied game; outrdn (no disg)*
	3	15	**Clontoura (IRE)** 5-1 **David Dennis** *Ld & clr early; hdd aft 7; hit 10; rdn 13; disp ld brief 16; drvn & wknd nxt*
	P		**Chief's Example (USA)** (tt) 7-2 **E Chanin** *1st ride; rcd wide; last pr; 10l 4th 11; lost tch 13; wl t.o when pu 3 out; lame*
	P		**Starmont** 33-1 **S Kidston** *Mounted on course; unruly start; prom brief; 12l 4th & wkng 7; last when jmpd slow 8; t.o & pu 13*
	U		**Trooper Pippin** 16-1 **A Ede** *Last til blun & ur 6*

OFFICIAL DISTANCES: 1l, 20l   **TIME:** 6min 16.0s

66 Confined
7 ran

	1		**WELL ARMED (IRE)** (bl) 4-11F **T Mitchell** *Lw; hld up; 10l 5th 11; went 2nd 13; ld 16; hdd 2 out; drvn up on inner bef last; jmpd & ld cl home; v wl rdn*
	2	½	**Western Fort (IRE)** 6-1 **Miss J Cumings** *Hld up; 9l 4th 11; jmpd slow 14; 6l 4th 16; clsd nxt; ld 2 out til drvn & hdd nr fin*
	3	½	**Summit** 33-1 **Miss J Congdon** *Set stdy pce; 6l clr 11; hdd 16; 3rd & nt drdn 2 out til pushed along & stayed on agn flat*
	4	½	**Gypsy Gerry** 7-2 **T Clarkson** *1st ride; lw; disp 3rd; 5l 3rd 16; sltly outpcd 3 out; rallied last; kpt on*
	5	30	**It's Not My Fault (IRE)** 20-1 **Adam Jones** *Chsd ldr til hit 12 & rdn; lft last 13; nt r.o & rem frm 16*
	P		**Dfoursdream** 33-1 **A Holdsworth** *V novicey; school in last pr & a detach; mist 11; pu 12*
	P		**Spartans Last** (12a) 66-1 **J Young** *Bit bckwd; jmpd v erratic in last pr; t.o 6; over fnce bhnd when pu 13*

OFFICIAL DISTANCES: ½l, ½l   **TIME:** 6min 24.0s

67 Greig Middleton Ladies Open
10 ran

	1		**ROYAL MOUNTBROWNE** 6-1 **Miss E Jones** *2nd/4th; hit 10; ld aft 12 & went clr; 3l ahd when hit 16; lkd vulnerable 2 out; forged clr game app last*
[10⁹]	2	2	**Hillhead (IRE)** 10-1 **Miss S Sharratt** *Lw; midfield & off pce; 30l 5th 11; prog in 10l 3rd 16; went 2nd nxt; w nnr 2 out; rdn & nt qckn app last*
	3	6	**Warren Boy** 4-1 **Miss P Jones** *Lw; set blistering pce; mist 4 & rmdr; hdd aft 12; rallied 16; 3rd & ev ch nxt; nt qckn app last*
	4	1	**Cool Character (IRE)** 8-1 **Miss T Newman** *Rr div; 32l 6th 11; 17l 5th 16; plugged on stdly but unable to chall*
	5	½	**Court Master (IRE)** 4-1 **Mrs L Borradaile** *Off pce in mid-div; 23l 4th 11; 15l 4th 16; eff nxt; no imp when flr 2 out*
	6	30	**Chickabiddy** (5a) 12-1 **Miss G Edwards** *Nt fluent in last; t.o 7; drvn to snatch 6th*
	7	½	**Quiet Confidence (IRE)** (5a) 6-1 **Miss D Stafford** *2nd/3rd til 11l 3rd 11; sn lost plce; t.o aft 16*
	P		**Madam Rose (IRE)** (5a) 33-1 **Miss J Congdon** *Oht; a bhnd; 32l 7th 11; t.o & pu 14*
	F		**Play Poker (IRE)** 4-5F **Miss A Dare** *20l 8th 3; fell hvly 6*
	U		**Thomas Crown (IRE)** 14-1 **Mrs J Wilkinson** *Rfo 1*

OFFICIAL DISTANCES: 4l, 1l   **TIME:** 6min 08.0s

68 Land Rover Mens Open, 12st
8 ran

	1		**BELLS WOOD** 8-1 **C White** *Ldng pr; ld 2-5, 13-15 & agn aft nxt; jmpd v awkward 2 out; hdd brief app last; rdn & agn game flat*
	2	½	**Slew Man (FR)** (4x) 4-9F **T Mitchell** *Opened evens; lw; hit 4; settled last pr til prog 10; went 4l 3rd 16; 5l 2nd & drvn nxt; rallied to ld brief aft 2 out; just outbattled flat*
	3	20	**A Few Dollars More (IRE)** 14-1 **R Woollacott** *Trckd ldrs; mist 9; 7l 4th 11; hit 14 & outpcd; kpt on agn 2 out to tk mod 3rd*
[10⁹]	4	2	**Sister Lark** (5a) 16-1 **D Jones** *Cl up early; 7th & drvn 11; no ch frm 15*
	5	1	**Rootsman (IRE)** 12-1 **T Stephenson** *Bckwd; settled towards rr; 7th 11; nd frm 16*
	6	15	**Oneforwillie** (7x) 8-1 **J Snowden** (xnb) *Ld 5-13; hit nxt; 8l 4th & wkng 16; nd frm nxt*
	7	1	**Robert's Toy (IRE)** (7x) (bl) 7-2 **N Harris** *Lw; settled 3rd; ld 15 til outj nxt; drvn & nt keen aft 3 out*
	P		**Union Station (IRE)** 50-1 **B Parsons** *Nt jw in last pr; t.o 12; pu 13*

OFFICIAL DISTANCES: ½l, 8l   **TIME:** 6min 14.0s

69 Restricted, 12st
16 ran

	1		**FAIR WIND (IRE)** 5-2F **N Mitchell** *Hld up; prog in 7th 13; 4l 4th 16; ld app 3 out; clr when jmpd delib last*

2	4	**No More Nice Guy (IRE)** 4-1 **Mrs M Hand** *Settled mid-div; 9th 13; 10l 6th 16; rap prog nxt to chall 2 out; rdn & no imp app last*
3	10	**Market Springer (IRE)** 8-1 **Miss B Williams** *(xnb) Lw; prom; ld 9-11; hit 14; 6l 5th 16; r.o one pce frm nxt*
[13²] 4	12	**See Me Shine** (5a) 6-1 **D Jones** *Cl up; 3rd 13; chall & ev ch 16; rdn & wknd nxt*
5	12	**Peyton Jones** 5-1 **M Miller** *2nd/3rd til ld 11-13; cl 2nd 16; rdn & wknd nxt*
6	½	**Tiger Lord** 10-1 **S Blackwell** *Chsd ldrs; 8th 13; lost tch 15*
P		**Belski** 13-2 **R Woollacott** *Stdd start; hld up in rr til rap prog to 2nd 11; ld 13 til hdd app 3 out; wknd nxt; pu last*
P		**Don Luigi** 6-1 **N Harris** *Rr div; 10th 13; t.o & pu 16*
[6²] P	P	**Lady Buckland** (5a) 5-1 **Miss P Jones** *Prom; ld 8-9; 5th & wkng 13; t.o & pu 3 out*
	P	**Nodforms Inferno** 14-1 **D Alers-Hankey** *Tde; tk str hld; ld til aft 7; lost plce qckly; t.o & pu 13*
P		**O So Bossy** 6-1 **Miss J Congdon** *A rr; 11th 13; t.o & pu 3 out*
P		**Pachakutec (IRE)** 25-1 **Miss P Gundry** *Nvr btr than midfield; strugg 11; t.o & pu 14*
F		**Poet's Song (IRE)** 7-2 **T Vaughan** *Chsd ldrs; 7th when fell 12*
P		**Rossaleen** (5a) 10-1 **P Shaw** *Eary in rr; t.o & pu 13*
P		**Sagaville (IRE)** 12-1 **Miss T Cave** *Chsd ldrs; 6th 13; wknd 15; pu 3 out*
P		**Sporting Chance** 6-1 **C Heard** *(xnb) Stdd start; nt jw in rr; 12th 13; t.o & pu 3 out*

OFFICIAL DISTANCES: 3l, 8l TIME: 6min 11.0s

70 Open Maiden (Div 1, Part 1), 12st   8 ran

1		**NOBLE STAR** 5-2 **S Bush** *Prsd ldr to 11 & frm 16; sust chall 2 out; lft in ld last; drvn & just hld on*
2	s hd	**Mike's Dream** 2-1 **T Vaughan** *Set stdy pce; 2l clr 3 out; lkd wnr whn jmpd slow last; rallied & just failed; unlucky*
[14²] 3	25	**Bally Boy** 8-1 **D Jones** *Bckwd; 3rd til 2nd 11-16; wknd tame 3 out*
4	15	**The Islander** 7-1 **G Barfoot-Saunt** *Bckwd; settled 4th; hit 13 & 14 & outpcd; rallied 16; v one-pcd frm nxt*
5	5	**Soleil D'Ete** (5a) 16-1 **N Mitchell** *Lw; a last trio; strugg 15; mist nxt; t.o 3 out*
P		**Joli Eau** 14-1 **S Partridge** *5th 5 but wl t.o aft 7; pu 9*
P		**Lufah Wood** 10-1 **J Young** *Towards rr; in tch to 12; nt pushed; t.o & pu 3 out*
[14⁵] P		**Satori** 7-4F **T Mitchell** *Jmpd slow 2; erratic prog in rr; rdn aft 10; 15l last 15; t.o & pu 3 out*

OFFICIAL DISTANCES: s hd, 14l TIME: 6min 28.0s

71 Open Maiden (Div 1, Part 2), 12st   9 ran

1		**VELLATOR (IRE)** 11-2 **D Alers-Hankey** *Bit bckwd; hld up; cl 5th when blun 11; chall 16; went 2nd nxt; sn ld & clr; kpt on wl*
2	10	**Gunner B Special** 4-1 **Miss P Jones** *Lw; prom; ld/disp 4-8; ld brief 3 out; outpcd frm nxt*
3	5	**Luney River** (5a) 5-1 **Miss L Gardner** *Tk keen hld; chsd ldrs; went 3rd 11; 7l 4th 16; plodded on & nd aft; jmpd slow last*
4	6	**Sea Jay Son** 6-1 **Mrs M Hand** *Made nrly all til hdd 3 out; wknd rap; fin tired*
P		**Autumn Blunder** 7-1 **T Stephenson** *Last when mists 3 & 4; lost tch 5; t.o 8; pu 3 out*
F		**Kopain** 5-2 **J L Llewellyn** *(xnb) Hld up & bhnd; mist 7; mod 6th when fell 9*
P		**Namron (IRE)** 6-4F **R Woollacott** *Nfurnished; 3s-6/4; prom; lost 3rd 11; sn wknd; pu 13*
P		**Qu'appelle** 8-1 **M Miller** *Prom; mist 6; 6th 11; wknd rap 13; pu nxt*
P		**Stories Bold** 2-1 **Miss P Baker** *Bhnd; lost tch 11; jmpd lft 12; cont to; pu 3 out*

OFFICIAL DISTANCES: 6l, 4l TIME: 6min 17.0s

72 Open Maiden (Div 2), 12st   15 ran

[20²] 1		**JOBSAGOODUN** 11-10F **M Yardley** *Lw; hld up chsng ldrs; 6th 11; eff 14; 8l 2nd 16; chall aft 3 out; ld aft 2 out; pushed clr*
[11²] 2	6	**Bonny Rigg (IRE)** (5a) 3-1 **D Jones** *Prom; ld 13; 8l clr 16; drvn & hdd aft 2 out; wknd*
3	½	**Frank Naylar** 25-1 **H Froud** *2 handlers; hit 6; chsd ldrs; 5th 11; 18l 4th 16; stayed on wl frm nxt; no ch w wnr; wl rdn*
4	8	**Oaklands Wolf** 12-1 **Miss P Jones** *Ld to 13; 15l 3rd & wkng 16; plugged on*
5	½	**Carbonado** 10-1 **Miss P Gundry** *Rr early; 2nd by 7; 4th 11; wknd 14; 20l 5th 16*
6	30	**The Naughty Vicar** 6-1 **G Richards** *Bckwd; ld in start; midfield; 8th 11; rem 6th aft 16*
7	7	**Purslet** (5a) 6-1 **Miss N Stallard** *(xnb) A rr; 12th 10; t.o aft 15*
8	5	**Killerton Clover** (5a) 33-1 **Miss C Llewellin** *(xnb) Rr div; hit 9; 11th 11; t.o aft 15*
P		**Fernhill Blaze (IRE)** 33-1 **T Vaughan** *Prom; 3rd when mist 11; sn wknd; pu 14*
P		**Flushing Spirit (IRE)** (5a) 10-1 **R Woollacott** *7th 11; pu & dism 13*
P		**Josameric** 33-1 **T Stephenson** *Lw; 13th 11; t.o & pu 13*
P		**Judith Jones** (5a) 33-1 **Miss D Stafford** *Mists in rr; 14th 11; t.o & pu 13*
P		**Kinglassie** (5a) 4-1 **T Mitchell** *2 handlers; prom early; 9th & wkng 11; t.o & pu 13*

P		**Salford Quay (IRE)** 12-1 **G Barfoot-Saunt** *(xnb) Sn bhnd; 10th 10; t.o & pu 14*
P		**Sparties Image** (5a) 12-1 **J Young** *Fat; novicey; sn hopelessly t.o; pu 15*

OFFICIAL DISTANCES: 4l, ½l **TIME:** 6min 17.0s

73 Open Maiden (Div 3), 12st
9 ran

1		**SEA URCHIN** 10-1 **D Alers-Hankey** *(xnb) Arrived 10am & hacked rnd lanes; v late to padd; came in mounted & trotted one circ; settled rr but in tch; eff 13; 2nd 16; chall nxt; ld & qcknd 2 out; sn in comm*
2	4	**The Frosty Fox (IRE)** evensF **M Miller** *Tchd 5/4; prom; 3rd 11; lft disp ld 14; 5l clr 16; hdd 2 out; rdn & nt qckn*
3	1¼fs	**Royal Chip** 5-1 **Jeremy Young** *Lw; prom; 2nd 11; wknd 14; 25l 4th 16*
4	20	**Aint No Lady (IRE)** (5a) 10-1 **Miss S Robinson** *Rr div; hit 4; 8l 8th 11; t.o 15; rdn into v rem 4th flat*
5	3	**Grandpa Maurice (IRE)** 7-1 **G Shenkin** *Drpd out 8 til prog 11; 2nd 13; lft disp ld nxt; 6l 3rd 16; wknd bad app 3 out; climbed 2 out; t.o*
F		**Cherry Pie** (5a) 4-1 **Mrs M Hand** *2nd til ld 5; hrd prsd when fell 14*
P		**Iron Buck** 10-1 **R Hodges** *Novicey in detach last; t.o 9; pu 12*
P		**Mia Fort** (5a) 14-1 **T Vaughan** *Mist 1; cl up; 5th 11; pckd bad 13; pu 14*
P		**Super Rooster** 2-1 **G Barfoot-Saunt** *Tk keen; hld to 5; mist 6; wknd rap 11; mist 12; sn t.o; pu 15*

OFFICIAL DISTANCES: 3l, 10l **TIME:** 6min 19.0s

South Midlands Area Hunt Club
Mollington (RH 8F,18J) Sun, 30 Jan (GOOD to SOFT, HOLDING)

74 Club Members Confined
14 ran

	1		**LIVE WIRE (IRE)** 20-1 **G Kerr** *Prom til lost plce 8; 10th ½way; rallied 11; ld aft 12 til mist 15; rdn to ld flat; stayed on wl*
[1⁶]	2	1½	**Leap Frog** 4-1 **A Charles-Jones** *(xnb) Tde; a.p; went 2nd 5; ld 8-10; lft in ld 15; hdd & no ex flat*
[8³]	3	7	**Archies Oats** (vis) 14-1 **J Trice-Rolph** *Bhnd to 8; 11th ½way; hdwy 11; went 6l 4th 14; outpcd 15; stayed on frm 2 out; went 3rd flat; nt rch ldrs*
	4	20	**Templeroan Prince** (tt) 33-1 **M Cowley** *Rmdrs 4; hdwy 6; 3rd ½way; ld 10-11; 8l 5th & wkng 14*
[4⁵]	5	hd	**The Hatcher (NZ)** 33-1 **R Cope** *Prom; 4th ½way; lost plce & rdn aft 10; 12l 7th & u.p 14; cont wl bhnd*
	6	5	**Just Like Madge** 5-2F **J Tarry** *Swtng; mounted outside padd; tde; ld to 2; lost plce 5; 9th ½way; rallied 13; went 5l 3rd 14 & 2nd aft 3 out; ev ch nxt; wknd qckly; virt pu flat*
[19ᵁ]	P		**Bally Clover** 3-1 **Mrs T Hill** *5s-3s; ld 2-3; 2nd/3rd til lost plce aft 10; 8l 7th when mist 13; bhnd when pu 15*
	P		**Dolly Bloom** (5a) 20-1 **Miss N McKim** *Ld 3-4; lost plce 7; 12th ½way; wl bhnd when pu 13*
	U		**Drunkard's Corner** (12a) 33-1 **J Diment** *Hld up & bhnd; 13th ½way; gd hdwy 10; 2l 3rd when mist & ur 11*
[31ᴾ]	F		**Free To Conker (IRE)** 33-1 **M Hawkins** *(xnb,bh) Swtng; tde; rcd wide; ld 4; mist 6; hdd 8; mist & lost plce 9; 7th ½way; wkng when fell 10*
[17ᴾ]	P		**Nawrik (IRE)** 20-1 **R Barrett** *Chsd ldrs; 8th ½way; wknd qckly u.p aft 10; wl bhnd when pu 11*
	U		**Over The Master (IRE)** 4-1 **D Barlow** *Swtng; hld up; stdy hdwy 8; 6th ½way; 2l 4th when blun & ur 12*
[31²]	P		**River Bloom** (5a) 10-1 **A Martin** *Hld up & bhnd; 14th ½way; short-lived eff 11; 14l 8th when mist 14; pu 15*
	P		**Tango's Delight** 33-1 **J Gallagher** *Swtng; hld up & rcd wide; hdwy 7; 5th ½way; went 2nd aft 10; ld 11 til hdd aft 12; wknd & 11l 6th 14; wl bhnd when pu 3 out*

OFFICIAL DISTANCES: 1½l, 6l **TIME:** 6min 57.9s

75 Intermediate, 12st
18 ran

1		**INCH FOUNTAIN (IRE)** (5x) 10-1 **A Crow** *Swtng; ww; gd hdwy 7; 3½l 5th ½way; went 2l 3rd 15; ld 2 out; stayed on wl*
2	12	**Tiger Tina** (5a) 6-1 **Miss C Stucley** *(xnb) Hld up & bhnd; 7½l 12th ½way; hdwy 10; went 1½l 3rd 13; jmpd slow 15; lost plce 3 out; 14l 5th 2 out; stayed on wl flat; went 2nd nr fin*
3	1½	**King Of Clare (IRE)** 10-1 **A Martin** *Lw; a.p; lft 2nd 6; ld 10; blun 12; hdd 3 out; no ex 2 out; went 2nd flat til dem nr fin*
4	1	**Tirley Missile** 7-1 **Julian Pritchard** *Mist & lost plce 4; bhnd til hdwy 4; 4l 6th ½way; went 2l 4th 13; lost plce 15; 6l 4th & rdn 3 out; no ex 2 out*

	5	4	**Nearly A Beau** 10-1 **D Mansell** Hld up; hdwy & mist 5; 2l 3rd ½way; went 2nd aft 12; disp ld 14 til ld 3 out; hdd nxt; 2nd til wknd bad flat
	6	2	**Montecot (FR)** 8-1 **D I Turner** Hld up; stdy hdwy & 4½l 7th ½way; rdn 15; 10l 6th 3 out; no ex
[33⁵]	7	30	**Gt Hayes Pommard** 33-1 **D Howells** 2 handlers; a bhnd; 17l 15th ½way; 18l 11th 13; t.o
	R		**Ball In The Net** 33-1 **M Holdforth** Pulled hrd; went 2nd 3; ld 4; rdr lost iron 5; rn out 6
	P		**Benbulbin (IRE)** 12-1 **M Bluck** Chsd ldrs; lost plce & 7l 11th ½way; wknd 12; pu 13
	U		**Cool Work** 20-1 **B Ridge** Swtng; hld up; 5½l 9th ½way; hmpd 11; lost tch & 15l 9th 13; wl bhnd when pckd & rfo 14
	P		**Grecian Star** 3-1 **J Tarry** 2 handlers; nvr gng wl; 9l 13th ½way; 17l 10th 13; wl bhnd when pu 3 out
	U		**Hill Sprite** (5a) 33-1 **R Barrett** (xnb) Prom; lost plce & 5l 8th ½way; 9l 8th & wkng when ur 13
	F		**Its Murphy Man** 20-1 **C Wadland** Sn prom; 2½l 4th ½way; 5l 6th & wkng when fell 11
	U		**Mr Freeman (IRE)** 33-1 **J Diment** 2nd to 3; lost plce 7; 6l 10th & rdn ½way; bhnd when hmpd & ur 11
	F		**Mr Hatchet (IRE)** 33-1 **C Weaver** (xnb) Swtng; 4th when fell 4; broke nr hind; dead
[6¹]	P		**Noughtosixty (IRE)** 11-10F **B Pollock** Ld til hdd & mist 5; mist 5; lft in ld 6; hdd 10; lost plce & 6l 7th 13; pu 14
	P		**Stonebroke (IRE)** 20-1 **R Cope** Rdn 7; sn wl bhnd; 15l 14th ½way; pu 10
[13ᶠ]	P		**True Fred** 20-1 **A Wintle** A wl bhnd; t.o & pu 11

OFFICIAL DISTANCES: 12l, 1l **TIME:** 6min 51.1s
Gun Runner (A Barlow 20-1) was withdrawn after declarations had closed

76 Club Members Confined Maiden (Div 1), 12st   13 ran

	1		**SEVERN MAGIC** (5a) 10-1 **A Wintle** Hld up & bhnd; 8l 11th ½way; 12l 9th 13; 15l 6th 3 out; str rn 2 out; switched rt & ld flat; r.o wl
[12ᴾ]	2	3	**Romany Chat** 10-1 **A Martin** Pulled hrd; ld aft 2-7; lft 2nd 12; ld 2 out til hdd & no ex flat
	3	1½	**Dark Challenger (IRE)** 5-4F **R Lawther** Ld til hdd aft 2; lost plce 5; hmpd 6; 4½l 8th ½way; hdwy & 3l 4th 13; rdn 15; ev ch last; nt qckn
[20ᵁ]	4	4	**Tellaporky** 10-1 **Miss E Owen** (xnb) Ss; wl bhnd til gd hdwy 13; 6l 5th nxt; eff app 2 out; ev ch last; wknd flat
	5	8	**Top Trump** (5a) 5-1 **R Cope** 2 handlers; 2nd/3rd to 9; lft 3rd 12; rdn 3 out; wknd 2 out
	6	1½	**Whistling Rufus (IRE)** 5-1 **M Rimell** Jw; went 2nd 3; ld 7-10; lft in ld 12; hdd 2 out; wknd qckly
	7	12	**Music Class (IRE)** 10-1 **J Gallagher** 33s-10s; hld up; hdwy aft 8; 3l 6th ½way; 6l 5th & rdn 13; wkng when mist 14
	F		**Evenkeel (IRE)** 14-1 **D Smith** Hld up; hdwy 8; 2l 3rd ½way; ld 10 til fell 12
[24³]	P		**Highfurlong (IRE)** 5-1 **Miss H Irving** Prom; lost plce & 4l 7th ½way; 9l 7th & rdn when mist 12; wl bhnd 15; t.o & pu 2 out
[30ᴾ]	U		**Moon Island** (5a) 33-1 **J Diment** 2 handlers; prom; 3l 4th when ur 4
	P		**Quick Succession (IRE)** 10-1 **J Trice-Rolph** 16s-10s; jmpd rt; hld up; hdwy 8; 2½l 4th ½way; lost plce 11; 9l 7th 13; bhnd when pu 15
	U		**Shady Exchange (IRE)** (7a) 10-1 **M Baldock** (xnb) 2 handlers; hld up; mist 4; 6l 9th ½way; 11l 9th when mist & ur 11
	P		**The Merry Nun (IRE)** (5a) 14-1 **J Owen** A bhnd; 7l 12th ½way; pu 13

OFFICIAL DISTANCES: 4l, 1½l **TIME:** 7min 05.3s

77 Mens Open (Div 1)   11 ran

[10³]	1		**CAMP BANK** evensF **Julian Pritchard** A.p; 9l 3rd ½way; went 8l 2nd 12; eff 15; ld 3 out; sn wl clr; easy
[4⁴]	2	25	**Tarthooth (IRE)** (bl) 16-1 **P Cowley** Swtng; prom; hmpd 5; lost plce & rmdrs 7; 13l 7th & rdn ½way; wl bhnd 13; 25l 4th when hit 3 out; stayed on; went 2nd nr fin
	3	nk	**Grunge (IRE)** 12-1 **C Barlow** 16s-12s; hld up; 10l 4th ½way; mist 13; went 15l 3rd nxt; no imp 3 out; went poor 2nd flat; dem nr fin
	4	15	**Buonarroti** 12-1 **D Dennis** Hld up; 15l 8th ½way; rdn 11; wl bhnd 13; t.o
	5	7	**Against The Agent** 7-1 **A Wintle** Ld; mists 1 & 4; 8l clr 9-15; hdd 3 out; sn wknd; 2nd til aft last; virt bp nr fin; btr for rce
	P		**Artic Pearl** (5a) 33-1 **R Langley** A bhnd; t.o 11; pu 13
	P		**Castle Folly (IRE)** 5-2 **R Lawther** Went 2nd 2-12; 16l 4th & wkng 14; wl bhnd when pu 3 out
	P		**Gaelic (IRE)** (5a) (tt) 33-1 **L Lay** Hld up; lost tch 8; t.o & pu 12
	P		**Major's Law (IRE)** 20-1 **J Owen** Swtng; hld up & bhnd; 10½l 5th & hdwy ½way; wknd app 12; t.o & pu 3 out

	P		**Members Cruise** 14-1 *E Walker Sn prom; lost plce & 11l 6th ½way; 12l 4th when blun 12; nt rec; wl bhnd when pu 14*
	P		**Winter Belle (USA)** 14-1 *R Shepherd-Cross A bhnd; rmdrs & swished tail 4; t.o 10; pu 15*

OFFICIAL DISTANCES: dist, ½l TIME: 6min 49.4s

78 Greig Middleton Ladies Open
14 ran

	1		**BANKHEAD (IRE)** 4-1 *Miss C Spearing A.p; jmpd delib; went 2nd aft 8; ld aft 12; 3l clr 2 out; all out*
[9²]	2	1	**Percy Smollett** 11-4F *Miss S Vickery Hld up; 3l 5th ½way; rmdrs; went 10l 3rd 14; eff 3 out; hit doll benb bef 2 out; went 2nd app last; r.o u.p flat*
	3	6	**Stretchit** 4-1 *Miss T McCurrich Jnd ldrs 5; went 2nd 7; ld 8 til hdd aft 10; chsd wnr 13 til app last; wknd flat*
	4	15	**Alska (FR)** (5a) (vis) 33-1 *Miss W Southcombe 2nd to 5; 5l 6th ½way; ld aft 10 til hdd aft 12; 7l 3rd when mist 13; 17l 5th & wkng 15*
	5	5	**Roly Prior** 7-2 *Miss S Samworth Hld up; 6l 8th ½way; 12l 7th & no hdwy 13; 19l 6th 15; cont wl bhnd*
	6	1½	**Pongo Waring (IRE)** 10-1 *Miss T Habgood Hld up; 8l 9th ½way; 13l 8th 13; 14l 4th & hdwy 15; wknd 3 out*
[4ᴮ]	P		**Arfer Mole (IRE)** 33-1 *Miss J Grant Ld 2-7; hit 8; 2½l 4th ½way; wknd 13; 22l 7th 15; t.o & pu 2 out*
	U		**Dawn Mission** 20-1 *Miss L Pearce Ld to 2; 4th when rfo 3*
	P		**Grange Prize** 33-1 *Miss K Henry Sn wl bhnd; t.o 8; pu 11*
[28ᵁ]	P		**Haunting Music (IRE)** 25-1 *Miss E Neyens (xnb) Hld up; 5½l 7th ½way; 10l 5th 13; sn wknd; 25l 8th when pu aft 15*
[3³]	P		**Lily The Lark** (5a) 8-1 *Miss H Irving Prom; ld 7-8; 2l 3rd ½way; rdn & lost plce aft 10; wl bhnd 12; t.o & pu 15*
[17ᴾ]	P		**Maltby Son** (tt) 14-1 *Miss L Allan Nd; 9l 10th ½way; wl bhnd when pu 13*
	P		**Miss Pilkington** (5a) 33-1 *Miss T Hirst A wl bhnd; t.o & pu 10*
	P		**Shadowgraff** (5a) 33-1 *Miss T Spearing Swtng; a bhnd; t.o & pu 10*

OFFICIAL DISTANCES: 1l, 5l TIME: 6min 52.7s

79 Mens Open (Div 2)
10 ran

[17⁹]	1		**WISHING WILLIAM (IRE)** 5-2 *S Waley-Cohen Lw; hld up; hdwy 5; 1l 3rd ½way; went 2nd aft 10; mist 15; ld app 2 out; sn clr; easy*
	2	20	**Cariboo Gold (USA)** (bl) 2-1F *J Diment Sn prom; 2l 4th ½way; ld aft 10 til hdd u.p app 2 out; sn btn; fin tired*
[32⁵]	3	7	**Muntafi** 6-1 *A Wintle Swtng; jmpd rt; hld up & bhnd; 10l 5th ½way; 10l 3rd & hdwy 11; no imp 14*
	4	20	**Golden Savannah** 33-1 *A Maculan Sn wl bhnd; t.o 6*
	P		**Characteristic** 3-1 *C Stockton 2nd til ld 6; hdd 7; ld 8-10; sn lost plce; 16l 6th 12; wl bhnd when pu 13*
	P		**Credo Is King (IRE)** 20-1 *R Barrett Nvr gng wl; wl bhnd when pu 11*
	U		**Look In The Mirror** 33-1 *M Carter Nd; mist 1; 15l 8th ½way; went 13l 4th 12; no imp aft; blun & ur last*
	P		**Northern Bluff** (6ow) 25-1 *J Deutsch Ld aft 2-6; ld 7-8; ld 10; sn hdd & lost plce; 15l 5th 12; wl bhnd when pu 13*
	P		**Tanborough** 33-1 *A Tutton A bhnd; t.o & pu 11*
	P		**Titus Andronicus** 14-1 *J Oldring Ld to 2; lost plce 7; 12l 6th ½way; lost tch 11; wl bhnd when pu 12*

OFFICIAL DISTANCES: 30l, 10l TIME: 6min 57.9s

80 Club Members Confined Restricted, 12st
10 ran

	1		**OBOEDIRE (IRE)** 4-1 *D Barlow A.p; went 2nd 5-10; 3l 4th 13; went 2nd app 2 out; drvn & stayed on to ld nr fin*
	2	nk	**Final Analysis (IRE)** 7-1 *J Owen Hld up; gd hdwy & 2l 3rd ½way; went 2nd 10; rdn to ld aft mist 3 out; hrd drvn flat; hdd nr fin*
[33²]	3	3	**Encima Del Rio (IRE)** 7-4F *B King Hld up & rcd wide; 5l 7th ½way; went 3rd 13; rdn & mist 14; hdd aft 3 out; stayed on one pce*
	4	20	**Tranquil Lord (IRE)** 33-1 *D Smith 2nd til ld aft 2; hdd 14; rdn & wknd 3 out*
	P		**Benova Boy** 12-1 *J Diment Jnd ldrs 5; lost plce 8; 6l 8th ½way; rdn 11; 14l 7th & wkng 13; t.o & pu last*
	P		**Derryair** 12-1 *F Hutsby Hld up; gd hdwy 7; 3l 5th & rmdrs ½way; 11l 5th & wkng qckly 13; wl bhnd when pu 2 out*
[13⁵]	F		**Forever Dreaming (IRE)** 4-1 *M Rimell Prom; 2½l 4th ½way; fell 11*
	P		**Northern Yarn (IRE)** 16-1 *C Weaver Jnd ldrs 5; 3rd & blun bad 7; 4l 6th ½way; 13l 6th & wkng 13; t.o & pu last*

[13P]   P   **Royal Orchard** 6-1 A Martin *A bhnd; 8l 9th ½way; lost plce 11; 15l 8th 13; mist 14; t.o & pu 3 out*
[6U]   r   **Sleep Walker** (5a) 20-1 B McKim *(xnb) Tde; ld til hdd aft 2; 2nd to 5; sn lost plce; 9l 10th & rdn ½way; wl bhnd when ref 11*

OFFICIAL DISTANCES: nk, 3l   TIME: 7min 00.1s

81 Club Members Confined Maiden (Div 2), 12st   8 ran

1   **CLAYMORE LAD** 4-1 A Maculan *2nd/3rd to 6; lft 3rd 8 & 2nd 12; ld flat; r.o wl*
2   2   **Uncle Reginald** 2-1 B McKim *Went 2nd 4; lft in ld 12; hdd & no ex flat*
P   **Count Henry** 16-1 C Wadland *(xnb) Bckwd; hld up; 7l 5th ½way; wknd qckly aft 10; wl bhnd when pu 11*
F   **Folding** 16-1 M Hawkins *Rcd wide; ld aft 2 til fell 12*
[20P]   S   **Shouldhavesaidno** (IRE) (5a) 16-1 J Owen *Ld til hdd to 2; lost plce 6; 8l 6th ½way; lost tch u.p 14; 20l 4th when slpd up flat aft 3 out*
F   **Star Marshall** (IRE) (bl) 7-1 S Joynes *(xnb) 10s-7s; 2 handlers; lw; hld up; hdwy 6; ld & fell 8*
P   **Take The Brush** (IRE) (5a) 5-4F R Lawther *Lw; hld up; 5l 4th ½way; lft 3rd 12; mist & rmdrs 14; rdn & wknd aft 3 out; jmpd v slow 2 out; exhaust when pu last*
F   **Yodeller Bill** (7ow) 25-1 P Sheppard *Rdr chewing; 5th when fell 5*

OFFICIAL DISTANCE: 2l   TIME: 7min 12.1s

Suffolk

Ampton (RH 7F,20J) Sun, 30 Jan (GOOD, GOOD to SOFT in places)

82 Hunt   5 ran

[16¹]   1   **VILLAGE COPPER** 11-10F C Ward-Thomas *2 handlers; made all; jnd 15; drew clr app 2 out; comf*
2   5   **Bramblehill Buck** (IRE) 12-1 D Kemp *16s-12s; last but wl in tch; prog 13; jnd wnr 15; rdn 3 out; one pce aft*
3   8   **Remilan** (IRE) 6-4 A Sansome *Swtng; cl up; jmpd slow 9 & 11; 4l 3rd & rdn 16; no ch aft*
[17P]   4 runin **Premier First** (IRE) 33-1 G Pewter *(xnb) Tk keen hld; prom til mist & rmdrs 14; sn strugg; rdn 16; t.o 3 out*
[28U]   P   **Mill O'The Rags** (IRE) 9-2 N King *Trckd ldrs til last & rdn 14; lost tch 16; pu nxt*

OFFICIAL DISTANCES: 6l, 8l   TIME: 6min 52.0s   TOTE: £1.70

83 Confined, 12st   10 ran

[18F]   1   **DRY HIGHLINE** (IRE) 5-1 C Ward-Thomas *Mists; made all; 20l clr 4; blun 6 & 11; 3l clr & rdn 2 out; kpt on game; all out*
2   2   **Tom De Savoie** (IRE) (5x) 4-5F W Wales *7/4-4/5; ww; prog to ch wnr frm 12; 10l 2nd & blun 3 out; sn rdn; 3l down nxt; one pce aft*
3   40   **Oflaherty's Babe** (IRE) (5x) 3-1 S Sporborg *5s-3s; ww; some prog 13; rdn nxt; 25l 3rd 16; no prog; t.o*
4   8   **Popeshall** 10-1 A Coe *Prom in main group; rdn & wknd frm 14; t.o frm 16*
5 runin   **Cheryl's Lad** (IRE) 14-1 M Mackley *Jmpd rt; ld main group to 12; wkng when jmpd slow 16; t.o when blun 3 out; jb rt last*
[15⁴]   P   **John Tufty** 12-1 B Hitchcott *Mid-div in main group; lsng plce & rmdrs 10; no ch frm 16; t.o last when pu last*
P   **Major Man** (IRE) 14-1 C Ward *Prom in main group; 17l 3rd 9; 5th when pu qckly 14; lame*
[17P]   P   **Mighty Merc** 33-1 S R Andrews *(xnb) Blun 2; prom in main group til wknd 11; t.o & pu 13*
P   **Mister Main Man** (IRE) 7-1 K Edmunds *Sn bhnd; last & pushed along 7; sn lost tch; t.o & pu 12*
P   **Nibble** 25-1 G Cooper *(xnb) Stdd start; last when blun & rdr lost iron 1; pu aft*

OFFICIAL DISTANCES: 2l, dist   TIME: 6min 44.0s   TOTE: £7.20

84 Ladies Open   8 ran

1   **THURLES PICKPOCKET** (IRE) 6-1 Mrs S Hodge *Disp ld to 1; stdd; went 2nd & mist 13; ld gng wl app 15; lft 5l clr 17; 1½l up & still gng wl when lft clr nxt; hit 2 out*
2 runin   **Peanuts Pet** 14-1 Miss H Barnard *Ld 2; sn hdd; prom to 13; 15l 4th 16; no ch aft; lft rem 2nd by defections*
[25F]   3 25   **Limited Liability** 20-1 Miss C Grissell *(xnb) Tk keen hld; jnd ldrs 3-7; sn lost plce; t.o frm 14; lft v rem 3rd by defections*

	P		**Cracking Idea (IRE)** evensF **Mrs G d'Angibau** *Ld app 3 til outj & hdd 11; sn drpd out; last frm 14; pu 16*
	P		**Dockmaster** 33-1 **Miss A Stennett** *Mists; sn detach in last; t.o & pu 13*
	P		**Docs Dilemma (IRE)** 7-1 **Mrs E Coveney** *Rr; in tch til 5th & outpcd 13; t.o last when pu last*
[19⁴]	U		**Faha Gig (IRE)** (5a) 12-1 **Mrs F Needham** *Mid-div; prog to 3l 3rd 14; outpcd by ldng pr nxt; rallied & lft 5l 2nd 17; 1½l 2nd when blun & ur nxt*
	U		**Gatchou Mans (FR)** 3-1 **Miss L Rowe** *Disp ld to 2; trckd ldrs til ld 11; hdd aft 14; mist & rmdr nxt; 11 2nd when blun & ur 17*

OFFICIAL DISTANCES: dist, 20l **TIME:** 6min 48.0s **TOTE:** £16.60

85 Land Rover Mens Open, 12st
10 ran

	1		**COPPER THISTLE (IRE)** (7x) 4-6F **R Hunnisett** *Chsd ldr 3; ld 11; 10l clr 13; stayed on wl frm 3 out*
[17ᵁ]	2	2½	**Hatcham Boy (IRE)** 4-1 **C Ward-Thomas** *Patiently rdn; stdy hdwy frm 9; chsd wnr 14; 6l 2nd 16; rdn 3 out; wkng last; no imp flat*
[17ᴾ]	3	runin	**Shake Five (IRE)** (7x) (bl) 10-1 **S Sporborg** *Chsd ldrs; 10l 3rd 11; outpcd by ldrs frm 15; jmpd rt last; t.o*
	4	12	**Lonesome Traveller (NZ)** 33-1 **K Sheppard** *A bhnd; last 8; 5th & no ch 16; tk poor 4th 2 out; t.o*
[15⁶]	5	3	**Andermatt** (7x) 33-1 **J Cornwall** *A rr; rmdrs 6; no ch frm 11; t.o*
	P		**Dual Or Bust (IRE)** (7x) 33-1 **P McAllister** *Mid-div; 13l 5th 11; blun nxt; wkng when pu 14*
	R		**Punnett's Town** (5a,12ow) 33-1 **P Hickman** *Detach last when rn out 2*
[17⁸]	P		**Saint Bene't (IRE)** (bl) 33-1 **B Hitchcott** *Mid-div; rmdr 6; rdn when jmpd slow 9; t.o frm 11; last when pu last*
	P		**Torus Spa (IRE)** (7x) 9-2 **A Sansome** *Ld to 11; wknd qckly 13; pu nxt*
[10ᴾ]	P		**Who Is Equiname (IRE)** (7x) 10-1 **R Armson** *In tch; 5th & rdn 12; sn wknd; pu 15*

OFFICIAL DISTANCES: 2½l, dist **TIME:** 6min 48.0s **TOTE:** £1.80

86 Restricted, 12st
14 ran

	1		**ARDEAL** (5a) 5-1 **A Bealby** *Ld 2; mist 3; made rest; 4l clr app 3 out; stayed on wl*
[7¹]	2	2½	**Secret Streams (IRE)** 4-9F **S Sporborg** *Opened 4/7; prom; mist 6; chsd wnr frm 8; 3l down 2 out; unable to qckn u.p*
	3	8	**Tumlin Oot (IRE)** 16-1 **M Lurcock** *Chsd ldrs; mist 4; 4l 3rd 16; one pce aft*
	4	8	**Javelin Cool (IRE)** 14-1 **N King** *Ww in mid-div; stdy prog 9; 5l 3rd 3 out; wknd nxt*
	5	runin	**Therewearethen (USA)** 25-1 **D Parravani** *In tch til rdn & outpcd 10; sn wl bhnd; t.o*
	P		**Bakmalad** 33-1 **D Kemp** *Bhnd frm 7; t.o 12; pu 16*
	P		**Baron Allfours** 14-1 **P Millington** *(citation) 20s–14s; hld up; 11th & mist 9; nvr nr ldrs; no ch when pu 16*
	P		**Free And Equal (IRE)** 25-1 **S R Andrews** *Bhnd & rdn 6; t.o 10 til pu 16*
[16ᴾ]	P		**Gerej (POL)** 25-1 **M Gingell** *Ld to 2; chsd wnr 4-8; lost plce 10; t.o & pu 3 out*
	P		**Holiday Time (IRE)** (5a) 25-1 **Mrs S Hodge** *Bhnd; stdy prog to mid-div 7; no prog frm 13; 7th & no ch when pu 16*
[14ᴾ]	P		**Iberian (IRE)** (5a) 16-1 **C Gordon** *(boh) Chsd ldrs; mist 3; 4l 3rd when blun bad 15; sn wknd; t.o & pu 3 out*
[14ᴾ]	P		**Lillooet (IRE)** (5a) (bl) 20-1 **P Hall** *Nt jw; bhnd; last & rmdrs 7; t.o frm 10; pu 15*
[2³]	P		**Mister Audi** 8-1 **A Sansome** *Ww in rr; prog 11; 6th & in tch when blun 14; no prog aft; pu 16*
	P		**Skinsey Finnegan (IRE)** 16-1 **A Coe** *Ww in tch til 8th & wkng 14; t.o when blun 17; pu nxt*

OFFICIAL DISTANCES: 2½l, 5l **TIME:** 6min 56.0s **TOTE:** £4.70

87 Open Maiden (Div 1), 12st
12 ran

[20³]	1		**PEACEMAKER (IRE)** evensF **J Cornwall** *Lft 2nd 1; clr w rival til lft 12l clr 5; sn stdd pce; hdd app 11; 5l 3rd & rdn app 3 out; kpt on to ld last 100yds; all out*
	2	1	**King's Mandate (IRE)** 8-1 **P McAllister** *Lw; trckd ldrs gng wl; disp ld 13 til jmpd to ld 3 out; rdn app nxt; jmpd rt last; hdd & no ex last 100yds*
	3	20	**Ballad (IRE)** (tt) 5-1 **T Bulgin** *Chsd ldrs 8; 4l 4th 16; wknd app 3 out; lft 3rd at last*
	C		**Bannagh Express (IRE)** 20-1 **M Lurcock** *Lft in ld 1; sn clr w rival til carried out by loose horse 5*
	P		**Campbellhill (IRE)** 20-1 **M Mackley** *Stdd start; school in rr til pu 13*
[23ᴾ]	P		**Casino Nell** (5a) 20-1 **A Harvey** *Chsd ldrs; lft 2nd 5; ld app 11-13; 6l 5th 15; sn lost tch; pu 17*
[24ᴾ]	P		**Cicero's Law (IRE)** 10-1 **D Cook** *2 handlers; in tch; jmpd slow 4 & 8; 12l last & rdn aft 15; t.o & pu 17*

	P		**Dreamisle** (5a) 25-1 A Coe *Chsd ldrs; 4th when mist 8; wknd 11; t.o & pu 13*
	P		**Oak House** 16-1 R Fowler *Bhnd & pushed along 6; t.o & pu 13*
	P		**Polly Live Wire** (5a) 14-1 P Millington *Jmpd poor; sn wl bhnd; t.o & pu 14*
[20F]	P		**Squaddie** 7-1 A Sansome *Stdd start; hld up; prog to 5l 5th 11; jnd ldr 15; outj & hdd 3 out; ev ch til wknd qckly 2 out; 12l 3rd when pu last*
	F		**Tierna's Respect** 7-2 E Williams *5s-7/2; ld & fell 1*

OFFICIAL DISTANCES: 1l, 20l **TIME:** 7min 07.0s **TOTE:** £2.50

The stewards interviewed the rider of Squaddie (rode back vigorously after pulling up at the last in 3rd); his explanation that the horse was very tired & had fallen last time was accepted, but they warned him of his duty to achieve the best placing

88 Open Maiden (Div 2), 12st
10 ran

	1		**CLOUDY CREEK** (IRE) 7-2 P Bull *(xnb) Confid rdn; 10l 4th & gng wl 11; went 2nd 15; rdn to ld 2 out; sn drew clr; easy*
[20P]	2	15	**Frosty Deal** (IRE) 8-1 R Fowler *Cl up; ld 12; mist 14; hdd 2 out; sn btn; blun last; dism aft fin; lame*
	P		**Airborne Blue** 10-1 S R Andrews *Bckwd; ld to 5; bhnd frm 7; t.o & pu 14*
[23P]	P		**City Run** (USA) 8-1 D Cook *A rr; 30l 6th & rdn 13; no prog; pu 15*
	U		**Classic Ms** (IRE) 10-1 M Grange *A rr; 8th when blun & ur 10*
[23P]	P		**County Derry** 8-1 A Sansome *Mists; prom; cl 3rd & rdn 15; wkng & jmpd slow nxt; t.o & pu 3 out*
	P		**Eltrym Flyer** (5a) 8-1 A Coe *A mid-div; nvr trbld ldrs; t.o & pu 15*
	P		**Full Bore** (IRE) 6-1 P Taiano *(xnb) Mists; blun 2; bhnd; last frm 8; t.o & pu 15*
	P		**Out Of Actons** (IRE) (7ow) 20-1 C Jarvis *(xnb) Stdd start; rushed up to ldrs 3; ld 5-12; sn wknd; blun 14; pu nxt*
	P		**The Arkle Bar** (IRE) 2-1F T Bulgin *Nt jw; sn bhnd; mist 2; rmdrs 5; jmpd slow & rdn 9; no resp; t.o 11; pu 14*

OFFICIAL DISTANCE: 15l **TIME:** 7min 06.0s **TOTE:** £3.70

Kelso (LH 8F,19J)
Thu, 3 Feb (GOOD to SOFT)

89 Alba Country Foods HC
12 ran

[46¹]	1		**MANHATTAN RAINBOW** (IRE) 11-00 10-1 W Renwick *Jw; cl up; ld 6 til hit 12; ld 15; drew clr frm 3 out; 8l ahd last; drvn along & just hld on; game*
	2	hd	**Over The Hill** (IRE) 12-00 8-1 M Armytage *Hld up & bhnd; hdwy 13; 9l 3rd 2 out; rdn & chsd wnr aft last; wandered but kpt on wl cl home*
[17³]	3	¾	**Makin' Doo** (IRE) 11-02 6-1 C Mulhall *Cl up; ld 4-6; hit 14; niggled 16; disp 9l 3rd & outpcd 2 out; kpt on agn aft last*
[39¹]	4	20	**Carnaven** (IRE) 11-02 8-1 A Robson *Trckd ldrs; eff & 2l 2nd 3 out; wknd & lost 2 plces aft last*
	5	9	**Titan Thai** (IRE) 11-11 (bl) 14-1 L McGrath *Chsd ldrs; mist 15; sn outpcd*
[42¹]	6	5	**Dennett Lough** (IRE) 11-07 6-4F C Storey *Mists in rr; rdn in 11th 11; nvr gng wl or nr ldrs*
	7	8	**Stormy Session** 12-00 (vis) 14-1 J Alexander *Chsd ldrs; 6th 14; outpcd when blun nxt; sn btn*
[40²]	8	8	**Shingle Beach** (IRE) 11-07 6-1 Miss P Robson *Rmdrs aft 1; midfield; nvr gng wl; rdn 9; 8th & strugg 12; t.o*
	9	16	**Kentucky Gold** (IRE) 11-07 33-1 D Sherlock *Ld to 4; outpcd 9; 9th 12; t.o*
	10	1¼	**Snooty Eskimo** (IRE) 11-04 25-1 C Wilson *Cl up; ld 12-15; 7l 3rd 3 out; wkng when blun nxt; t.o*
	11	nk	**Rusty Blade** 11-07 40-1 T Davidson *A bhnd; 10th & strugg 12; t.o*
[46F]	12	dist	**Tropnevad** 11-00 (bl) 50-1 Miss D Aitken *Mists; a last pr; t.o 13*

TIME: 6min 46.2s **TOTE:** £13.10; places £2.50,£2.80,£1.50 **Ex:** £126.90 **CSF:** £80.93 **Tri:** £70.40

Wetherby (LH 9F,18J)
Sat, 5 Feb (GOOD with GOOD to SOFT places)

90 Nags Head at Pickhill 'Happy Birthday Janet' HC
11 ran

	1		**MR BRANIGAN** (IRE) 12-04 6-4F B Pollock *Chsd ldrs; ld 6; jmpd rt 9; drew clr frm 3 out; jmpd rt last; qcknd flat; impressive*

	2	14	**Carley Lad (IRE)** 11-11 9-4 L McGrath *Sn cl up; 3rd frm 12 til 2nd 15; rdn nxt; kpt on; no ch w wnr*
	3	4	**Dry Hill Lad** 11-11 20-1 N Kent *Cl up; 2nd 12 til rdn 15; one pce aft*
[42²]	4	1	**Jymjam Johnny (IRE)** 11-11 7-1 J Tate *Pulled hrd; sn ld; hdd 6; mists 11 & 13; 6l 6th aft 15; nd aft*
	5	1	**Valiant Warrior** 12-04 9-1 C Bonner *Prsd ldrs; 4th when mist 14; rdn nxt; r.o one pce*
	6	3½	**Master Boston (IRE)** 11-09 (6) 20-1 B Woodhouse *Hld up; hdwy & prom 10; outpcd 13; rallied to 4th & rdn bef 15; wknd app nxt*
	P		**Edge Of Night** 11-10 33-1 N Wilson *In tch; blun 9; wknd nxt; pu 11*
[41⁷]	U		**Gaelic Warrior** 11-03 66-1 Miss Rachel Clark *Mist 3 (water); prom til blun & ur 6*
[42³]	U		**Greenhill Tare Away** 11-10 11-1 S Swiers *Hld up in tch; mist & ur 6*
	F		**Shanballymore (IRE)** 11-03 100-1 D Sherlock *Hld up; 7th when fell 4*
	P		**Toarlite (IRE)** 11-03 66-1 R Trotter *Mists; a bhnd; strugg 10; t.o & pu 2 out*

TIME: 6min 52.7s **TOTE:** £2.20; places £1.10,£1.70,£2.70 **Ex:** £6.60 **CSF:** £4.49 **Tri:** £99.80

Cambridgeshire
Horseheath (RH 10F,18J) Sat, 5 Feb (GOOD - softish patches)

91 Hunt   **7 ran**

	1		**FAIR EXCHANGE** 2-5F P Taiano *Lw; tk keen hld; hld up til ld app 7; hit 9; 12l clr 14; unchall*
[86⁴]	2	25	**Javelin Cool (IRE)** 9-2 N King *Bckwd; handy; chsd wnr frm 10; flatt brief 15; v tired frm nxt*
[86⁷]	3	8	**Free And Equal (IRE)** 7-1 S R Andrews *Jmpd slow 3 & rdn; bhnd & nt keen; lost tch 8; 23l 5th 11; drvn to tk 3rd aft blun 2 out*
	4	10	**Spring Wheat** (5a) (tt) 25-1 T Lane *Bit bckwd; hld up & nvr btr than midfield; 12l 4th 11; 25l 3rd 14; plodded on & dem aft 2 out*
[88⁷]	P		**Airborne Blue** 33-1 Miss Carla Thomas *Fat; mist 4; ld til app 7; last aft 9; sn t.o; pu 14*
[19⁷]	U		**Damier Blanc (FR)** (bl) 20-1 D Cook *Bit bckwd; trckd ldrs til ur 8*
[15⁸]	P		**Just Jack** 14-1 Miss F Jonason *Hit 6; chsd ldr to 10; 12l 3rd & wkng nxt; lft t.o last 14; pu last*

OFFICIAL DISTANCES: dist, 5l **TIME:** 6min 44.0s **TOTE:** £1.40 **DF:** £1.70

92 Confined, 12st   **12 ran**

	1		**RUPERTS CHOICE (IRE)** (bl) 11-10F S Sporborg *Made nrly all frm 3; forged clr 12; unchall; canter*
[10⁵]			
[82²]	2	20	**Bramblehill Buck (IRE)** (3x) 5-1 D Kemp *2nd/3rd til outpcd aft 12; 25l 3rd 15; plodded on to tk 2nd at last*
[18³]	3	3	**Lord Knox (IRE)** 33-1 A Coe *Oht; chsd ldrs; 4th 10; outpcd 12; 40l 5th 15; plugged on frm nxt*
	4	½	**More Fun (USA)** 12-1 N Bloom *Lw; hld up; 5th & prog 10; 10l 2nd 13; nt rch wnr aft; v tired last & lost 2 plces*
[19⁸]	5	1½fs	**Spuffington** 33-1 Miss C Hall *Plodded rnd in rr; lost tch 10; wl t.o 14; trotted in*
	6	2	**Cropredy Lad** (1ow) 14-1 T Humphrey *Lw; rr div; lost tch 10; wl t.o frm 14; trotted in*
[26⁷]	P		**Airtrak (IRE)** 25-1 A Harvey *Hld up; 6th when hit 10; strugg nxt; t.o & pu 14*
[29⁴]	P		**Carson City** 14-1 J Purllant *Lw; bhnd; rdn 7; nvr gng wl; lost tch 10; t.o 12; pu last*
[86⁷]	P		**Holiday Time (IRE)** (5a) 33-1 Mrs S Hodge *Lw; tk keen hld; ld to 3; ld app 7-8; wknd aft 12; 30l 4th 15; t.o & pu 2 out*
	P		**Salmon Mead (IRE)** (6ow) 33-1 R Gill *Bckwd; prom v brief; nrly ref 4 & t.o aft; pu 7*
	P		**Spaceage Gold** 33-1 S R Andrews *Bckwd; rr div & nvr gng wl; lost tch u.p 9; t.o & pu 11*
	P		**Still In Business** 4-1 A Ayers *Bit bckwd; hit 3; a bhnd; lost tch 10; hit 12; t.o & pu 14*

OFFICIAL DISTANCES: 20l, ½l **TIME:** 6min 40.0s **TOTE:** £2.60 **DF:** £9.30

93 Dodson & Horrell PPORA Club Members, 12st   **10 ran**

	1		**TEETON BUILDS** 6-4F A Sansome *Settled trckng ldrs; eff 9; ld 10-11 & aft jmpd slow 12; drew clr app 3 out; rdly*
	2	3	**Fresh Ice (IRE)** (5x) 2-1 R Barrett *Hld up in midfield; clsd in 3rd 10; 3l 3rd 14; chsd wnr frm nxt; kpt on but no imp*
	3	15	**Royal Banker (IRE)** 5-1 N Bloom *Ld 4 til hdd & mist 7; 5th 10; nt r.o frm nxt; rem 4th 15*
[25⁶]	4	10	**Borrow Mine (IRE)** 16-1 A Braithwaite *Sn towards rr; 8th & outpcd 10; t.o 14*
[86⁷]	5	6	**Bakmalad** 33-1 D Kemp *Bhnd; 9th & outpcd 10; t.o 14*
	P		**Aeolian** (7ow) 12-1 R Gill *Last to 6; prog in 6th 10; chsng ldrs 12; sn wknd; pu 15*

	P	**Broadway Swinger** 7-1 **S R Andrews** *Charged tapes; got loose & galloped off bef start; mist 4; chsng ldrs til 6th & lsng tch 10; nt pushed; pu 13*
[35⁵]	P	**Kites Hardwicke** (7ow) 20-1 **P Sheppard** *Ld to 4; rr 6; t.o aft 10; pu 14*
	U	**Minor Key (IRE)** (tt) 20-1 **A Harvey** *(xnb)Lw; prom; ld 9-10; prsng ldrs when mist & ur 13*
	P	**Penrose Lad (NZ)** 20-1 **W Tellwright** *Sn prom; ld/disp app 7 til 2l 2nd 14; wknd aft nxt & v tired; lost 3rd aft climbing 3 out & nxt; pu last*

OFFICIAL DISTANCES: 3l, 15l TIME: 6min 41.0s TOTE: £2.40 DF: £2.50

94 Mens Open   10 ran

[17ᶠ]	1		**REAL VALUE (IRE)** 2-5F **B Hitchcott** *Lw; nt fluent 6; settled rr til qcknd to 3rd 8; ld 13; qcknd clr app 3 out; impressive*
	2	12	**Freedom Fighter** 8-1 **A Martin** *Bckwd; pulled hrd; sn stdd in rr; 6th 10; chsd ldrs aft til wnt 2nd bef 3 out; nvr nr wnr*
	P		**Beau Joueur (FR)** (bl) 33-1 **A Coe** *Fat; sn rr div; 7th 10; lost tch nxt; pu 13*
[10ᵖ]	F		**Epsilo De La Ronce (FR)** 14-1 **A Harvey** *Settled midfield; 5th 10; cl up til wknd qckly app 3 out; disp poor 3rd when crashing fall nxt*
[26⁴]	P		**Jack The Td (IRE)** (bl) 7-1 **J Cornwall** *Hdwy to ld aft 4; 10l clr 8; hdd 13; last & wkng qckly when pu 15*
	P		**Looks Like Reign** 16-1 **B McKim** *Nfurnished; lw; jmpd sketchy; mist 6; t.o & jmpd slow 7; pu 8; bbv*
[83ᵖ]	P		**Mighty Merc** (tt) 33-1 **S R Andrews** *(xnb)Prom early; 9th & wkng 10; pu 11*
	r		**No Quitting (IRE)** 4-1 **N Bloom** *Lw; hld up & cl up; 3rd 10; same & ev ch 15; wknd rap; t.o when ref 3 out*
[26ᵖ]	P		**Prince Of Saints (IRE)** 10-1 **A Sansome** *Still bckwd; ld to 2; 4th 10; pushed along nxt; chsd wnr 15 but sn wl outpcd; v tired 3rd when pu last*
[26ᵖ]	P		**Reuter** 25-1 **C Ward** *Ld 2 til aft 4; prom to 7; wkng when jmpd slow 9; nt keen; t.o & pu 12*

OFFICIAL DISTANCE: dist TIME: 6min 36.0s TOTE: £1.40 DF: £8.50

95 Ladies Open   8 ran

[84¹]	1		**THURLES PICKPOCKET (IRE)** 9-4 **Mrs S Hodge** *Settled handy; jmpd rather delib at times; 3rd 11; ld 13-14; disp ld frm nxt; drvn along flat to ld nr fin*
	2	nk	**Cache Fleur (FR)** 11-8F **Mrs G d'Angibau** *Bckwd; ldng trio; ld 11-12 & 14-15; w wnr aft; tk slt ld flat; drvn along & r.o game til hdd nr fin*
	3	8	**Spring Gale (IRE)** 3-1 **Mrs E Coveney** *Lw; reluct & ld in start; ldng trio; ld 7-11 & 12-13; disp ld 3 out; rdn & one pce nxt*
[84ᵁ]	4	25	**Faha Gig (IRE)** (5a) 8-1 **Mrs F Needham** *Rr div; 10l 4th 9; clsd 12; 4l 4th aft 15; sn wknd*
	5	15	**Ballyedward (IRE)** (6ow) 20-1 **Miss H Pewter** *Detach last; u.p 10; no resp & sn t.o*
[25³]	P		**Fern Leader (IRE)** (bl) 25-1 **Mrs J Hughes** *Lw; ld & sn clr; hdd 7; wkng when blun 8; last 11; t.o til pu 13*
	P		**Lets Twist Again (IRE)** 25-1 **Miss A Stennett** *Fat; lost tch 6; t.o aft 10; pu 14*
	U		**Royal Surprise** 25-1 **Miss L Ingram** *Mist & ur 1*

OFFICIAL DISTANCES: ½l, 5l TIME: 6min 37.0s TOTE: £3.60 DF: £2.70

96 Intermediate, 12st   10 ran

[27²]	1		**JUST ONE QUESTION (IRE)** (tt) 5-1 **A Harvey** *Settled rr to 5; impd to 2nd 9-13; 5l 3rd nxt; chsd ldr bef 3 out; lkd hld til r.o aft 2 out; lft w ev ch last; ld flat; all out*
[16ᶠ]	2	nk	**Buckaholic (IRE)** 4-5F **P Bull** *Nt a fluent; sn 3rd/4th; jmpd slow 7; chall 13; ld app 3 out & sn 10l clr; lkd wnr til scrambled last; drvn & hdd 100yds out; r.o u.p*
[36ᵖ]	3	12	**Ryder Cup (IRE)** 12-1 **G Maundrell** *Chsd ldrs; 7th 10; 20l 5th & wl outpcd 14; plodded on*
[27⁵]	4	25	**The Millmaster (IRE)** (bl) 25-1 **C Ward** *Ld; 4l clr 10; hdd app 3 out & wknd rap*
[29²]	P		**Ballydesmond (IRE)** 11-4 **S Sporborg** *Chsd ldr to 8; 5th 10; lsng plce 10; strugg when jmpd v slow 13; t.o & pu 13 out*
	P		**Blithe Spirit** 14-1 **N Bloom** *Lw; pulled hrd & novicey; sev posns til 9th & wkng 10; t.o & pu 13*
[27ᵖ]	r		**Court Amber (IRE)** 12-1 **G Cooper** *Lw; hld up & bhnd; 6th & in tch 10; 8l 4th & outpcd 14; rem when ref 3 out*
[27ᵖ]	P		**Generous Deal (IRE)** 12-1 **A Sansome** *Hld up til impd to 2nd 8-9; 4th when jmpd slow 10 & lost plce; pu 12*
	P		**Mackoy (IRE)** 14-1 **P McAllister** *Tk keen hld; prom early; 8th & wkng 10; sn t.o; pu 13*
[86ᵖ]	P		**Skinsey Finnegan (IRE)** 20-1 **A Coe** *Mostly last; blun 8 & drvn; lost tch 10; t.o & pu 13*

OFFICIAL DISTANCES: hd, 5l TIME: 6min 41.0s TOTE: £8.10 DF: £2.60

97 Open Maiden (Div 1), 12st   11 ran

[20ᶠ]	1		**COUNTRY BARLE** (vis) 3-1 N Bloom *Prom; ld 10; 10l clr 14; a gng best; unchall*
[22⁶]	2	25	**Glencloy (IRE)** 10-1 A Coe *2 handlers; oht; lw; chsd ldrs; 10l 3rd 10; chsd wnr 13; nvr able to cl; v tired frm 3 out*
	P		**Always Trying** (7a) 10-1 A Sansome *Bckwd; ld 3; mist 8; hdd 10; 3rd & wkng when pu 14*
	U		**Cardinal Bud (IRE)** (xnb) 8s-3s; *lw; unruly; blun & ur 3*
	P		**Colemore Green** 10-1 M Gingell *Slouched rnd padd; strugg in rr; t.o 5; pu 12*
	P		**Josh's Choice (IRE)** (7a) 5-2F S Sporborg *Lw; blatant school in last trio; t.o 5; blun 9; pu 13*
	P		**Malvern Lad** 10-1 T Lane *Fat; ld to 3; nrly fell 6; jb aft; wknd rap 9; pu 11*
	U		**Mr Matchit (IRE)** 7-1 I Hudson *Rr of bunch; mist 7; 8th when rfo 8*
	P		**Nosy Parker (IRE)** 10-1 A Harvey *School in last trio; t.o 5; pu 14*
	P		**Semliki** 8-1 S R Andrews *Cl up early; 25l 4th aft 10; pu 11*
[20ᶠ]	U		**Thunderbird** (5a) 10-1 P McAllister *Blun & ur 3*

OFFICIAL DISTANCE: dist TIME: 6min 45.0s TOTE: £5.90 DF: £16.10

98 Open Maiden (Div 2), 12st   12 ran

	1		**MONTYS TAG (IRE)** 3-1 S R Andrews *5s-3s; lw; jw; nt fluent; made virt all; 5l clr aft 14; breather nxt; sn clr agn & r.o str*
	2	15	**Uncle Buck (IRE)** 25-1 P Taiano *Lw; hld up; 4th & prog 10; outpcd 12; rallied to 2nd 14; outpcd agn nxt; mod 2nd frm 3 out*
[21⁶]	3	20	**You Can Quote Me (IRE)** 8-1 A Harvey *Mid-div; 5th when hit 10; outpcd 12; unable to chall aft*
[16ᶠ]	4	6	**Minino (IRE)** 7-2 A Coe *Hit 3; impd to 3rd 10 & 2nd 12; bad mist 13; rec & cl 2nd 15; wknd bad bef nxt*
	P		**David Bruce (IRE)** (tt) 10-1 S March *Prom til mist 8; jmpd slow 9 & drvn; lost plce rap; t.o & pu 12*
[88ᵖ]	P		**Full Bore (IRE)** 10-1 N Bloom *(xnb) Lw; hld up & bhnd; mist 7; 9th 10; lost tch 12; t.o & pu 3 out*
	P		**Here's Humphrey** (bl) 33-1 M Gingell *2 handlers; oht; lw; u.p app 1; 3rd 5; numerous rmdrs; wknd 6; last 7; t.o & pu 8*
	P		**Little Veralyn** (12a) 12-1 P Bull *Novicey in final trio; last when hit 10; t.o & pu 15*
[24ᵖ]	U		**Outside The Rain (IRE)** (5a) 33-1 T Macfarlane *Jmpd slow 2; poor last when ur 3*
	P		**Ruddy Marvel Lass** (5a) 8-1 P McAllister *Tk keen hld; went 2nd 5-10; 3l 3rd 12; wknd nxt; t.o & pu 15*
	P		**Stormhill Farmer** 9-2 M Keel *Prom brief; 8th & lsng tch 10; t.o & pu 15*
	P		**Tickle The Tiller (IRE)** (5a) 2-1F R Lawther *Jb in last pr til 6th & prog 10; outpcd 12; rallied to disp 2nd 14; wknd nxt; nrly stpd 2 out & pu*

OFFICIAL DISTANCES: 15l, 10l TIME: 6min 45.0s TOTE: £7.20 DF: £51.80

North Cornwall
Wadebridge (LH 8F,18J) Sat, 5 Feb (GOOD with FIRM patches)

99 Hunt, 12st   5 ran

	1		**TRAVEL BY LAND** 4-1 Miss O Green *Disp ld/cl 2nd til outpcd aft 14; lkd hld when lft clr 3 out; rdr's 1st wnr*
	2	5fncs	**Whitelegs (U)** (5a,35ow) 66-1 T Biddick *Heavy hunter; 1st ride; imm t.o; hunted rnd; disp rem last; sev fncs adrift when lft disp 2nd 3 out; went 2nd nr fin*
	3	1	**Sam (U)** (35ow) 66-1 M Biddick *Massive heavy hunter; imm t.o; sev fncs bhnd when lft disp 2nd 3 out; dem nr fin*
	U		**County Bash** (5a) 4-9F Miss L Gardner *Ld/disp til drew clr app 15; lkd wnr when blun bad & ur 3 out*
	P		**Kimber Hill Lad** 5-1 C Heard *(xnb) Swtng; fractious in padd; chsd ldrs til lost tch 13; poor 3rd when pu nxt; school*

OFFICIAL DISTANCES: dist, ¾l TIME: 6min 39.0s

100 Land Rover Mens Open, 12st   4 ran

[10ᶠ]	1		**IRANOS (FR)** (7x) 1-2F T Mitchell *Opened 8/11; lw; hld up in 3rd; hdwy to ld 13; slt ld til mist & hdd aft last; rallied u.p to ld cl home*
	2	1	**Baldhu Chance** 4-1 A Ede *Ld til hdd 13; sn outpcd in 3rd; rnwd eff 3 out; ld aft last & lkd wnr til no ex cl home*
	3	10	**Stalbridge Gold** (5a) 7-2 J Ferguson *1st ride; trckd ldr; cl up & ev ch til wknd 15*
	P		**She Wood She** (5a) 66-1 Richard Darke *Swtng; lost tch 8; t.o & pu 10*

OFFICIAL DISTANCES: ¾l, 10l TIME: 6min 22.0s

101 Greig Middleton Ladies Open
7 ran

	1		**JUST BERT (IRE)** 3-1 Miss J Cumings _Handy; ld aft 14; drew clr 2 out; r.o wl_
[3F]	2	3	**Dawn's Cognac (IRE)** 5-2 Miss P Jones _Lw; hld up; hdwy 10; 3rd frm 12; lkd hld when hit 2 out; stayed on to tk 2nd run-in_
	3	5	**Hearts Are Wild** 2-1F Miss P Gundry _Bit bckwd; ld to 3 & frm 9; jmpd lft & hdd aft 14; chsd wnr & ev ch til no ex 2 out; wknd flat_
	4	40	**Legal Artist (IRE)** 33-1 Miss J Congdon _Bit bckwd; midfield; 4th frm 12; nt chall ldrs; eased clsng stages_
	5	5	**The Bold Abbot** 6-1 Miss S West _Opened 8s; bit bckwd; sn rr & nt a fluent; t.o frm 11_
	6	5	**Crownhill Cross** 150-1 Miss O Green _Bckwd; sn rr; a last pr; t.o frm 11_
	P		**Ballymaloe Boy (IRE)** 16-1 Miss B Williams _Lw; rcd free; ld 3-9; lost plce qckly 11; rmdrs & no imp; poor 5th when pu 15_

OFFICIAL DISTANCES: 3l, 3l **TIME:** 6min 09.0s

102 Restricted, 12st
5 ran

[2R]	1		**ICENFRIENDLY (IRE)** 8-15F Miss P Jones _Tchd 4/7 & 1/2; lw; hld up in 3rd; lkd beaten til went 2nd aft 3 out; r.o u.p to ld cl home; dism aft post (reported sound later)_
	2	1½	**Chocolate Buttons (5a)** 12-1 H Thomas _Bit bckwd; ld at crawl to 7 & frm 10; pushed clr 3 out; 4l clr last & lkd cert wnr til stpd rap & hdd cl home_
	3	10	**Devonshire Lad** 33-1 Miss K Cook _Lw; in tch 4/5th; hdwy to 3rd 15; went 2nd nxt; wknd app 2 out_
	4	8	**Chasing Daisy (5a)** 8-1 J Snowden _Lw; oht; cl up on inner; ld 7-10; lost tch qckly 14_
	5	5	**Spartans Winney (5a)** 7-2 J Young _A 4/5th; in tch til outpcd aft 14_

OFFICIAL DISTANCES: ¾l, 3l **TIME:** 6min 34.7s

103 Confined, 12st
3 ran

	1		**PALACE PARADE (USA)** 11-4 C Heard _Tchd 3s; lw; cl up til disp ld 10-11; ld 14; drew clr aft nxt; unchall_
[66⁵]	2	25	**It's Not My Fault (IRE)** 9-4 Adam Jones _Bit bckwd; cl up/disp ld til slt ld aft 12; hdd & rdn 14; jmpd slow 15; reluct & sn wl btn_
	F		**Where's Sam (IRE)** (5x) 4-5F S Craddock _5/4-4/5; ld/disp; slt ld when fell 12_

OFFICIAL DISTANCE: dist **TIME:** 6min 28.9s

104 Intermediate, 12st
5 ran

[63C]	1		**IBEX** evensF T Mitchell _Lw; trckd ldr; ld brief 8; ld agn 13; hung lft nxt; sn pushed clr; easy_
	2	30	**Jeepers (IRE)** 10-1 S Kidston _Bckwd; mostly 4/5th; went 3rd 14; no ch w ldrs; lft poor 2nd 2 out_
[69P]	3	8	**Don Luigi** (bl) 25-1 N Harris _Mostly last; reluct & drvn along frm 11; lft poor 3rd 2 out_
	P		**King's Response (IRE)** 5-4 Miss P Jones _(xnb) Tchd 6/4; lw; ld; jmpd rt; hdd brief 8; hdd 14; lost ground stdly; 20l 2nd when pu 2 out_
	F		**Lucky Thursday** (bl) 50-1 R Woollacott _3rd frm ½way; lost tch & rdn 13; btn 4th when fell nxt_

OFFICIAL DISTANCES: dist, 6l **TIME:** 6min 19.0s

105 Open Maiden (Div 1), 12st
12 ran

	1		**BALDHU JACK** 20-1 A Ede _Bhnd; went 4th aft 14; kpt on frm 3 out; lkd hld agn nxt; r.o game to ld last stride; fin lame; rdr's 1st wnr_
	2	hd	**Tanglefoot Tipple** 6-1 N Mitchell _Lw; midfield; hdwy to ld 13-15; chall & mist 3 out; r.o to ld 50yds out; hdd on line_
	3	3	**Blackoid (FR)** 3-1 T Mitchell _Made most to 12; ld agn 15; slt ld last; wknd & hdd last 50yds; fin tired_
	4	5	**Durnford Bay (IRE)** 10-1 Miss C Stucley _A.p; cl 2nd 11-14; wknd; 3rd 3 out; no ch clsng stages_
	U		**Amazing Hill (IRE)** 25-1 Mrs R Morris _Bit bckwd; a rr; poor 6th 13; kpt on frm 15; 3rd when ur 2 out_
	F		**Broad Ink** 33-1 S Kidston _Bckwd; prom; jmpd violent rt 5; cl 2nd 9; lsng plce when fell 12_
	U		**Button Up Bill** 33-1 H Thomas _(xnb) Prom til ur 5_
	P		**Cauld Signal (IRE)** (5a) 14-1 Miss B Williams _Oht; midfield; 7th 11; rr when pu 13; school_
	P		**Hanukkah (5a)** 14-1 I Hambley _(bf) Mounted on course; sn bhnd; strugg in rr til pu 12_
	P		**High Sturt (5a)** 25-1 J Snowden _Lw; rr; 9th ½way; bhnd when pu 12_
	P		**Resource (IRE)** 13-2 Richard Darke _Trong; hmpd 5; hdwy to 3rd 9; cl up til lost plce 13; btn 6th when pu 3 out_

| U | | **Wibbley Wobbley** 13-8F **Miss J Cumings** Lw; in tch; hdwy to disp 2nd 11; cl up when hmpd bad & ur 12 |

OFFICIAL DISTANCES: hd, 1l **TIME:** 6min 29.6s

106 Open Maiden (Div 2), 12st   10 ran

	1		**S B S BY JOVE** 10-1 **A Charles-Jones** Prom; jw; ld aft 14; went 6l clr 3 out; easy
	2	12	**Brother Nero (NZ)** 9-2 **C Heard** Tchd 6s; lw; hld up towards rr; hdwy 14; went 2nd 15; hrd rdn & no imp frm 3 out; do btr
	3	2	**Versicium (FR)** 11-10F **T Mitchell** (xnb) 6/4-11/10,tchd evens; lw; hld up; prog to 3rd 11; ld & jmpd rt 12 & 13; cl up & ev ch til wknd 15
[11P]	4	10	**Regal Wolf** 6-1 **J Snowden** Lw; prom; 3rd ½way; lost ground 12; rdn & no imp frm 14
	5	2	**Scally Lane** (5a) **T Dennis** (xnb) Mounted course; sn prom; cl 2nd ½way; lost plce 14; mist 15; eased
	U		**Counsel** (7a) 8-1 **Miss S Vickery** (xnb) Stdd start; last til blun & ur 3
	F		**Georgetown** 14-1 **Adam Jones** Bckwd; tk keen hld; slt ld when fell 8
	U		**King Tudor** 50-1 **S Kidston** Bit bckwd; prom til ur 8
	U		**Soeur Marie** (5a) 7-1 **Miss J Cumings** Blun bad & ur 2 (reported inj whilst loose)
	P		**West Ashridge** (12a) 25-1 **R Woollacott** Bckwd; rr; btn 6th when pu 14

OFFICIAL DISTANCES: dist, 1l **TIME:** 6min 30.7s

Jedforest
Friars Haugh (LH 9F,18J) Sun, 6 Feb (GOOD)

107 Hunt - 17J   7 ran

	1		**THE ALLEYCAT (IRE)** 11-10F **P Robson** A handy; 6l 5th when mist & nrly ur 4; 5l last 6; 4l 4th & gng wl 11; gd prog app 3 out to ld aft nxt & nrly rn off course; mist last; stayed on wl
[44³]	2	5	**Hooky's Treat** (5a) 9-1 **Miss M Neill** 1st ride; a.p; mostly 3rd til prog aft 7; 2l 2nd 8-9; disp ld app 15-3 out; sn outpcd; kpt on; no ch w wnr
[46R]	3	5	**Senso (IRE)** 20-1 **Mrs C Cox** Ld early; hdd app 3; trckd ldr aft; 4l 3rd 9; prog to disp ld 13; outpcd app 15; stayed on agn app nxt; r.o flat to 3rd cl home
	4	nk	**Benefit-In-Kind (IRE)** 7-2 **Miss J Hedley** Trckd ldr early; til ld app 3; 2l up 10; jnd 13; ll ld agn 15; hdd & outpcd aft nxt; one pce flat; dem on line
	5	8	**Flying Arrangement** (5a) 20-1 **Miss L Hislop** Chsd ldrs; 5l 4th 3; 4l 3rd 8; outpcd 14; prog to disp ld nxt; ld brief app 16; short-lived eff & sn outpcd
	U		**Cool Yule (IRE)** (7x) 4-1 **Miss A Warden** 1st ride; a rr but in tch; mist 3; 10l of pce 5; 7l last app 10; 8l off pce when mist & ur 13
	F		**Pilmur Gold** (12a) 20-1 **Miss A Turnbull** Nt a fluent; a rr; mist 2; 10l last app 3; 12l last 7; 15l down when fell 8

OFFICIAL DISTANCES: 3l, 5l **TIME:** 6min 37.0s
Fence 15 omitted - fallen rider

108 Intermediate, 12st   8 ran

[40P]	1		**RIVERSIDE RUN (IRE)** 5-1 **A Robson** Rr early; 10l last 2; stdy prog to 6l 3rd 12; 2l 3rd 15; ld aft 3 out; ll ahd nxt; stayed on; r.o wl flat
	2	¾	**Boyup Brook** 3-1JF **T Morrison** Hld up in rr; 11l 5th 6; 14l 4th 8; went 6l 3rd app 11; 6l 5th & prog when mist 15; ld nxt; sn hdd; stayed on chall agn app last; r.o; just outpcd flat; btr for rce
[43⁷]	3	5	**Claywalls** 5-1 **M Clayton** Trckd ldrs in 3rd mostly; 8l 3rd 8; sltly outpcd 13; prog & ev ch 15; sn outpcd agn; stayed on agn app last; fin wl; btr for rce
[43⁴]	4	2	**Fragrant Lord** 3-1JF **Mrs V Jackson** Nt a fluent; prom; trckd ldr; 2l 2nd 8; disp ld 11-15; ev ch 2 out; sn outpcd
	5	3	**Thinkaboutthat (IRE)** 12-1 **J Muir** 5l; clr 9; jnd 11 til hdd aft 15; sn wknd & one pce
[39P]	P		**Black Ice (IRE)** 14-1 **T Oates** A rr; 20l bhnd 9; pushed along 12; 25l last 15; t.o & pu last
	U		**Driminamore (IRE)** 7-2 **Miss R Ramsay** (xnb) Chsd ldrs; 10l 4th 3; 16l 7th & wkng 8; wl bhnd when ur 15
[39⁶]	P		**With Respect** 5-1 **Miss D Crole** In tch early; sn bhnd; 10l 4th 4; 20l last 8; sn t.o; climbed 12; fnce bhnd when pu 15

OFFICIAL DISTANCES: ½l, 4l **TIME:** 6min 36.0s

109 Ladies Open   10 ran

| | 1 | | **RIPARIUS (USA)** 7-4F **Miss P Robson** (xnb) 2s-7/4; lw; mid-div; 6l 6th 3; 12l 4th 9; went 5l 3rd & mist 12; 1l 3rd 15; ld app 2 out; hrd prsd last; r.o; all out |

	2	1	**Astrac Trio (USA)** 2-1 Mrs A Hamilton *Handy; 5-8l 3rd 2-10; prog to ld 12; jnd 15; hdd app 2 out; chall & ev ch last; outpcd; btr f rce*
	3	10	**Kingennie** (5a) 7-1 Miss M Bremner *In tch in rr early; 18l 6th 10; stdy hdwy frm 13; nrst fin; improve*
[19³]	4	2	**Donnegale (IRE)** 5-1 Mrs C Ford *(xnb) Ld/disp; mist 2; ½l up 8; hdd 12; disp ld 15; sn hdd; 8l 3rd & outpcd when mist 2 out; wknd*
[41ᴾ]	5	8	**Mullingar (IRE)** 14-1 Mrs V Jackson *Oht; chsd ldrs; 8l off pce 7; 7l 4th nxt; 15l 5th 9; outpcd 14; kpt on one pce frm nxt*
[41ᴾ]	6	2½	**Sharp Thyne (IRE)** 10-1 Miss J Hedley *Ld/disp; 2l up 3; ½l 2nd 8; outpcd 13; one pce*
	7	25	**Buckaroo** (5a) 16-1 Mrs A Tweedie *In tch in rr 4; lsng tch 9; t.o 14*
[40ᴾ]		F	**All Or Nothing** (5a) (bl) 80-1 Miss L Kendall *Sn rr; t.o 14; rmdrs & 30l 7th aft 15; fell 2 out*
		P	**Craigdale** (tt) 80-1 Mrs M Robinson *(orbs)Oht; tde; a last; sn 25l down; fnce bhnd 10; t.o & pu 16*
		U	**Oat Couture** 6-1 Miss S Johnstone *(xnb) 7s-6s; in tch in rr til blun & ur 4*

OFFICIAL DISTANCES: ½l, 8l TIME: 6min 29.0s

110 Mens Open
11 ran

	1		**RAINBOW TIMES (IRE)** (5a) 6-4F C Storey *Lw; a handy; 5l 4th 10; 2l 4th & prog 15; ld app 2 out; drvn app last; sn clr*
[42ᴾ]	2	8	**Judicial Field (IRE)** 5-1 A Robson *(xnb) Cl up; 4th 5; 3l 2nd 8; disp 4l 2nd 10; ev ch til outpcd aft 3 out; 5l down at last; kpt on; fin lame*
	3	½	**Fordstown (IRE)** 12-1 J Alexander *(bf) A.p; 10l 3rd 3; disp 4l 2nd 10; disp ld 15; sn hdd & outpcd; kpt on flat*
	4	2	**Kings Lane** 10-1 M Bradburne *In tch; 4l 3rd 8; 6l 5th & pushed along aft 12; disp ld 15; rmdrs & sn outpcd*
	5	10	**Master Hyde (USA)** 7-1 J Tate *A rr; 12l last 3; mist 6; wl bhnd 14; t.o 16*
	6	10	**Whispering Steel** 12-1 M Armytage *Mid-div; 8l down 8; nvr nrr; btr f rce*
[43⁶]		P	**Ballyboden** 20-1 F Arthur *Sn rr; 10l last 8; 20l down aft nxt; wl bhnd 14; pu nxt*
[43ᴾ]		F	**Charlieadams (IRE)** 4-1 J Muir *Ld; 3l up 3; 4l ahd 9; mist nxt; hdd 13; disp ld agn nxt; ev ch when slpd & fell 3 out*
[43ᵁ]		U	**Kilminfoyle** 14-1 P Robson *(xnb) 10l down when mist & ur 2*
[42⁵]		P	**Majority Major (IRE)** 14-1 T Glass *Chsd ldrs; mist 6; pu nxt*
		P	**No Pain No Gain** 9-1 J Murphy *Trckd ldr early; 2l 2nd 3; sn strugg; rr by 10; t.o 12; pu 15*

OFFICIAL DISTANCES: 8l, 2l TIME: 6min 35.0s

111 Restricted, 12st
14 ran

	1		**HIGHLAND MONARCH** 7-2 C Storey *4s-7/2; lw; made all; 3l up 5; 2l up 16; hrd prsd app 2 out; rdn & stayed on wl*
	2	½	**Mountain Thyne (IRE)** 2-1F Miss P Robson *3s-2s; lw; mid-div; 8th 8; prog to 3l 4th 12 & 2l 2nd 3 out; chall last; just outpcd flat*
	3	6	**Geordies Express** 9-2 A Richardson *Oht; hld up in rr; 10l last 7; smooth prog 10 to trck ldrs 15; 6l 4th 3 out; stayed on; btr f rce*
	4	1	**Victoria's Boy (IRE)** 10-1 G Brewer *(xnb) A.p; 4l 3rd 5; 2l 3rd 8; ev ch 15; outpcd aft nxt; 4l 3rd & no ex app 2 out*
[40³]	5	2	**Border Glory** 7-2 M Bradburne *(xnb) Swtng; mid-div; 5l 5th 8; outpcd 3 out; kpt on*
[40ᴾ]	6	6	**Boris Brook** 10-1 T Oates *Tubed; mid-div; nvr nrr*
[40⁵]	7	2½	**Mini Cruise** 14-1 L Morgan *Prom early; 3l 2nd 5; outpcd 14; kpt on aft; eased flat*
[40ᴾ]	8	5	**Storm Alive (IRE)** 12-1 Mrs V Jackson *Prom early; 2l 2nd 4; 5l 4th 5; grad lost plce frm 9; wl bhnd 15*
	9	4	**Madame Bella** (5a) 20-1 Miss J Hollands *Trckd ldr early; 1l 2nd 2; in tch til wknd 13; wl bhnd 3 out*
		P	**Derring Dan** 10-1 R Morgan *(xnb) In tch in rr; mist 9; eff to 4th 11; sn lost tch; wl bhnd when climbed 15; pu nxt*
		U	**Grey Rock (IRE)** (5a) 10-1 Miss K Miller *Mid-div; 6l 7th when blun & ur 11*
		P	**Miss Bubbles (IRE)** (5a) 16-1 S Hughes *A rr; saddle slpd & pu 11*
		P	**Miss Portcello** (5a) 6-1 W Renwick *Rr when hit 2; sn bhnd; t.o & pu 15*
		F	**No Problem Jac** (5a) (tt) 12-1 T Davidson *Mid-div; 8l 10th 9; fell 11*

OFFICIAL DISTANCES: ½l, 10l TIME: 6min 36.0s

112 Open Maiden Mares
13 ran

| | 1 | | **QUEEN BIDDY (IRE)** (5a) 7-2 C Storey *9s-7/2; lw; oht; a handy; 1l 3rd 8; ld 9; unchall aft; 6l ahd aft 15; hit nxt; wandered aft 2 out; eased* |
| [46ᴾ] | 2 | 6 | **Lady Alice** (5a) 10-1 L Morgan *Mid-div; 6l 6th 10; went 8l 3rd app 16; kpt on; nt trble wnr; prsd for 2nd flat* |

[45⁴]	3	½	**Briar Rose (IRE)** (12a) 2-1F J Ewart *9/4-2s; oht; trckd ldrs; 3l 3rd 3; mist 8; 3l 4th 14; 3rd when tried to ref 15 & releg 15l 4th; nd aft; kpt on agn app last*
	4	15	**Iveston (IRE)** (5a) 7-1 M McGhee *A rr; 12l 9th 3; 25l 5th 2 out; kpt on; lft 4th at last*
	F		**Cleikumin (IRE)** (5a) 9-1 T Oates *10s-9s; swtng; in tch; 6l 5th 6; prog to cl 2nd 11; ll down & ev ch 15; sn wknd; hit nxt; btn 4th when fell last*
	B		**D V's Delight** (5a) 25-1 T Davidson *Bd 1*
	C		**Homo Dorney (IRE)** (5a) 7-1 Miss L Bradburne *Oht; in tch; 7l 7th 10; 3rd aft 13 til carried out by loose horse aft 14; unlucky*
	F		**Magical Poitin (IRE)** (5a) 5-2 G Armitage *Jmpd big & awkward & nrly ur 1; crumpled on landing & fell*
	P		**Myles Of Moss (IRE)** (5a) 12-1 D Reid *Ld early; prom; ll 2nd 3; 3l 4th 11; outpcd 14; sn wknd; t.o & pu 3 out*
	P		**Satin Flash** (5a) 12-1 J Walton *A rr; 15l last 3; rmdr nxt; nd 8; sn wl bhnd; pu & dism 14*
	F		**Solway Donal (IRE)** (5a) 5-1 M Bradburne *Cl up; 5l 4th 7; 2l 4th nxt; fell 11*
	U		**Spot The Music (IRE)** (5a) 20-1 R Trotter *(bf) In tch when blun & ur 2*
	P		**Tofino Swell** (5a) 7-1 Miss J Hedley *Tde; ld; ll up 4; mist 7; hdd 9; sn wknd; t.o & pu 15*

OFFICIAL DISTANCES: 8l, 1l   **TIME:** 6min 54.0s

113 Open Maiden (Div 1), 12st   11 ran

	1		**RIVER OF GOLD (IRE)** 9-4F Miss M Bremner *In tch in mid-div; 6l 5th 4; 15l 3rd 9; gd prog to disp ll 2nd 15; ld 2 out; sn clr*
	2	8	**Happy Blake** 7-1 C Storey *Chsd ldrs; 15l 4th 10; 12l 4th & hdwy 13; disp ll 2nd 15; ld 3 out; hdd nxt; sn btn & eased*
	3	12	**Roscoe Burn** 5-1 R Morgan *Got flier; jw; ld; 3l up 5; 10l clr 10; hdd aft 15 & dem 3l 3rd; one pce*
[44²]	4	1¼	**Menaldi (IRE)** 4-1 T Glass *Chsd ldr; 10l down 10; outpcd aft 14; 10l 4th 16; kpt on one pce; wknd flat*
	5	20	**Kirkharle (IRE)** 6-1 M Clayton *Mid-div; 10l 7th 3; 25l 6th 13; 40l 5th aft 16; fin wl; nt pushed*
	6	fence	**Good Profit** 33-1 T Davidson *A rr; lsng tch 9; t.o 14; mist & nrly ur last; brilliant rcvry*
	P		**Christiemouse** (5a) 25-1 Miss L Hislop *Lw; ss; 20l down app 3; sn t.o; pu 10*
	P		**Kelly Canyon** 7-1 Miss P Robson *Lw; a rr; t.o & pu aft 14*
	F		**Mystical Music** (5a) 8-1 M Bradburne *Sn rr; 20l off pce 6; school til fell 10*
[45ᶠ]	U		**Smiddy Lad** 100-30 T Oates *Swtng; chsd ldrs; 3rd 7; 2l 2nd nxt; in tch when mist ur 15*
	U		**Strong Focus (IRE)** 33-1 N Crookston *Lw; oht; in tch til wknd 10; 20l 5th 13; pu 16*

OFFICIAL DISTANCES: 6l, 15l   **TIME:** 6min 43.0s

114 Open Maiden (Div 2), 12st   10 ran

	1		**MAXIMIZE (IRE)** 7-4F C Storey *Jw at times; chsd ldrs til ld 9; ll up 12; qcknd 6l ahd 15; sn wl clr; unchall*
	2	15	**Tom's Man** (tt) 11-2 T Oates *Hdstrng in mid-div; 5l 5th app 10; 8l 4th 14; 15l 4th & rdn 15; sn one pce; lft 2nd by defectors*
[44ᴾ]	3	2	**Gallant Major** 5-2 A Robson *In tch in rr; 7l 7th 10; 12l 3rd 15; 5th & wkng when lft 3rd 2 out; chall for 2nd & hmpd bad last*
	U		**Border Farmer (IRE)** 6-1 Mrs V Jackson *Prom; ld 8; hdd nxt; 4l 4th 11; wkng when ur 14*
[46ᴾ]	U		**Harleyburn** 7-1 Mrs A Hamilton *Prom til mist & ur 2*
	U		**Hey Chief (IRE)** (bl,tt) 5-1 P Strang Steel *Patiently rdn in rr; 10l last 2; 8l 8th 8; some prog 15; btn 3rd but staying on when ur 2 out*
	P		**Liffey Lane** 12-1 M Clayton *Oht; sis; last 1; ld 3; 2l up 5; hdd 8; 4l 3rd 9; wknd 14; pu 3 out*
[45ᴾ]	F		**Nisbet** 5-1 Miss M Bremner *A.p; 4l 3rd 5; went 2l 2nd 9; mist 10; outpcd 13; 5l 2nd 15; btn 2nd when fell last*
[46ᴾ]	P		**Solway Saffy** (12a) (tt) 10-1 S Olley *Lw; prom; 2l 2nd 5; 6l 6th 10; sn wknd; lsng tch when pu aft 14*
	P		**The Dust Buster** 20-1 H Trotter *(bf) Sn rr; 15l last & jmpd slow 8; t.o & pu 15*

OFFICIAL DISTANCES: 15l, 2l   **TIME:** 6min 48.0s

Midlands Area Club

Thorpe Lodge (LH 7F,19J) Sun, 6 Feb (GOOD with STICKY patches)

115 Club Members Confined, 12st - 17J   13 ran

| | 1 | | **MIDNIGHT SERVICE (IRE)** (bl) 12-1 R Barrett *2nd/3rd til ld 14; sust duel w 3rd aft til forced ahd app last; drvn out* |

2	3	**Burntwood Melody** (3x) 14-1 *R Armson Bhnd; 8th aft 12; wl outpcd til rap hdwy app last; fin fast; too much to do*
3	hd	**Dulas Bay** 25-1 *P Millington Hld up early; prog to 4th aft 12; ld 15; ll up 3 out; jnd nxt; r.o u.p til hdd app last; nt qckn*
[48¹] 4	¾	**Inch Cross** (IRE) (3x,1ow) 4-6F *R Hunnisett Lw; prom; went 2nd aft 12; slpd app 14 & rdr lost irons for 2 fncs; 16l 3rd 3 out; rallied & kpt on flat; unlucky*
[27¹] 5	8	**Cebu Gale** (IRE) 7-2 *M Hewitt Stdy hdwy to 2nd 9; 5th aft 12; outpcd nxt; tried to rally for plce 3 out; no imp*
6	15	**Cormeen Lord** (IRE) 7-1 *J Sharp Midfield; 7th aft 12; pushed along & sn no ch*
[47³] 7	10	**Ryders Wells** (bl) 20-1 *S Walker Rr div; 9th & strugg aft 12; t.o 16*
[47⁴] 8	20	**Fontaine Fables** (IRE) (bl) 100-1 *A Pickering Ld; 10l clr aft 12; hdd 14 & gave up rap*
9	7	**Needwood Neptune** 20-1 *P Bennett Mists 4 & 8; sn rr; t.o last aft 12*
[85⁵] P		**Andermatt** 16-1 *J Cornwall Lw; chsd ldrs til 6th & outpcd aft 12; t.o & pu last*
P		**Nishvamitra** (3ow) 50-1 *A Woodward Bckwd; a bhnd; t.o 9; pu aft 12*
F		**Plunder Bay** (USA) 12-1 *Miss F Hatfield 11th when crashing fall 2*
F		**Regal Bride** (5a) 50-1 *M Mackley V bckwd; jb & v green; imm lost tch; hmpd 2 & wl t.o aft; crashing fall 6*

OFFICIAL DISTANCES: 1½l, hd **TIME:** 6min 26.0s
Fences 9 & 16 omitted - fallen rider

116 Intermediate, 12st - 17J 14 ran

1		**CAPSTOWN BAY** 9-2 *Julian Pritchard Lw; a cl up & gng wl; 2nd aft 12; ld 13; hrd prsd frm 3 out; fnd ex app last; rdn & r.o wl*
2	2½	**Sharsman** (IRE) (5x) 7-4F *A Crow Pulled hrd in 2nd/4th; blun 5; 3rd aft 12; ev ch frm 3 out til drvn & nt qckn bef last*
[48³] 3	1	**Give It A Whirl** (5x) 11-2 *T Lane Lw; tk str hld in ldng trio; ld 9-13; w wnr 2 out; drvn & nt qckn last*
4	30	**Distant-Port** (IRE) 20-1 *T Stephenson Hld up wl off pce; 10th aft 12; kpt gng stdly; nvr put in rce*
5	2	**Smart Rhythm** (5a) 25-1 *R Armson Midfield early; 9th & rdn aft 12; t.o 14*
P		**Ardkilly Warrior** (IRE) 16-1 *N Bloom Hld up; stdy prog 9; 5th aft 12; ev ch 15; 35th when pu qckly nxt*
P		**Cheval De Marly** (IRE) 10-1 *R Burton Prom to 10; 7th aft 12; strugg 14; hanging bad when pu 3 out*
P		**Diamond Market** 66-1 *A Davenhill (xnb) Bckwd; mists & pulled hrd; rr til hdwy 3; lost plce agn & 8th 5; t.o last when pu 13*
R		**Honeysuckle Lil** (5a) 100-1 *T Gardham Bckwd; strugg & sn wl bhnd; crashed out thro wing & ur 7*
P		**Mackabee** (IRE) (bl) 20-1 *G Hanmer Chsd ldrs; 6th aft 12; chall & ev ch nxt; wknd 14; pu 2 out*
[25⁴] P		**Neelisagin** (IRE) 16-1 *J Turcan Chsd ldrs; 8th & outpcd aft 12; t.o & pu 2 out*
P		**Priory Piper** (5x) 7-1 *L Hicks Lw; nt jw; made most til hit 9; 4th aft 12; sn lost tch; t.o & pu 2 out*
P		**Sandi Devil** 100-1 *D Dickenson A rr; t.o last 13; pu 16*
P		**Tudor Fellow** (5ow) (tt) 25-1 *M Wells Sn poor last; t.o 7; pu 8*

OFFICIAL DISTANCES: 3l, ½l **TIME:** 6min 33.0s
Fences 8 & 15 omitted - damaged

117 Mens Open 8 ran

1		**WHATAFELLOW** (IRE) (bl) 3-1 *A Crow Bhnd early; hdwy & lft 2nd aft 6; ld nxt; sn 5l clr; rdn along & stayed on wl frm 2 out; a in comm*
[34ᴿ] 2	10	**Mickthecutaway** (IRE) 3-1 *R Burton Cl 2nd til lft in ld brief app 7; chsd wnr vain aft; eff frm 3 out; no imp; pckd bad nxt*
3	4	**Sharimage** (IRE) 6-1 *Julian Pritchard Lw; jmpd delib early; last 5; some hdwy 9; 15l 4th aft 12; outpcd nxt; kpt on stdly*
4	15	**Casual Water** (IRE) 25-1 *L Hicks A 3rd/4th; 10l 3rd aft 12; 15l 3rd & tired 3 out; wl btn*
[55ᴾ] P		**Fortune Hunter** (IRE) 66-1 *P Millington (citation) Jb & wl bhnd in last pr; 22l 5th 12; t.o & pu 15*
[49³] P		**Moneghetti** 100-1 *R Armson Towards rr; lost tch 8; sn t.o; pu 14*
[49¹] S		**Red Rebel** evensF *B Pollock Lw; ld til slpd up turn bef 7*
[17ᴾ] B		**Tom Pinch** (IRE) 12-1 *J Cornwall Tk keen hld in 3rd til bd turn bef 7*

OFFICIAL DISTANCES: 12l, 5l **TIME:** 6min 26.0s

118 Ladies Open 11 ran

1		**PHARARE** (IRE) 1-3F *Miss C Spearing Prom & keen; ld app 7; sn spreadeagled field; 20l clr aft 12; nrly fnce ahd frm 14; v impressive*

	2	fence	**Count Of Flanders (IRE)** 50-1 **Mrs J Hughes** *Handy; went 2nd 9; chsd wnr in hopeless pursuit frm 12*
	3	10	**Blue Lyzander** (5a,4ow) 50-1 **Mrs E Staines** *Midfield & nd; 40l 4th aft 12; sn chsng ldng pr vain*
	4	30	**Bare Fisted** 14-1 **Miss H Phizacklea** *Sn wl t.o; 75l last aft 12; plugged on & fin fresh*
	5	15	**Rainbow Walk (IRE)** 16-1 **Miss A Burton** *Ld til app 7; lost 2nd 9; 30l 3rd aft 12; lkd v tired aft & t.o*
	6	1½	**Circus Colours** 9-2 **Miss J Elson** *Nt jw & nvr gng wl in rr; 66l 7th aft 12*
	U		**Faraday** 50-1 **Miss S Phizacklea** *Sn wl t.o; 65l 8th aft 12; blun & ur 13*
	F		**Hotscent (IRE)** (5a) 16-1 **Miss C Wilberforce** *A bad outpcd; 57l 6th aft 12; fell 14*
[78ᴾ]	B		**Lily The Lark** (5a) 7-1 **Miss H Irving** *15l 6th 5; bd 6*
	P		**Nowhiski** 25-1 **Miss C Tarratt** *Pulled hrd; prom to 8; 27l 4th & wkng rap aft 12; sn t.o; pu 3 out*
	F		**What's Your Story** 5-1 **Miss E Marley** *Cl 2nd/4th til fell 6; broke leg; dead*

OFFICIAL DISTANCES: dist, 12l TIME: 6min 27.0s

119 Dodson & Horrell PPORA Club Members Restricted (Div 1), 12st - 17J   11 ran

[14ᶠ]	1		**UPTON ADVENTURE** (5a) 5-2 **S Joynes** *Trckd ldrs; 4th aft 11; qcknd to ld app 3 out; rdn & r.o wl flat*
[86ᴾ]	2	2½	**Baron Allfours** 16-1 **P Millington** *Hld up & bhnd; prog in 6th aft 12; jnd ldrs 14; 2nd 3 out; sust chall frm nxt; no imp u.p flat*
	3	15	**Coming Through (IRE)** (1ow) 2-1F **A Crow** *2 handlers; mounted course; svs & lost 25l; grad rec & 7l 8th aft 12; rdn & no imp frm 16*
	4		**Cantango (IRE)** 8-1 **J Turcan** *Prom; 2nd aft 12; ev ch 16; sn outpcd*
[16³]	5	hd	**Star Changes** 5-2 **T Stephenson** *Prsd ldrs; cl 7th aft 12; eff 14; ld brief 16; wknd nxt*
	6	3	**Holmby Copse** 10-1 **R Burton** *Chsd ldr; ld 9-12; wknd app 3 out*
	7	20	**Neva-Agree** 7-1 **R Armson** *Bhnd; hdwy to 5th gng wl aft 12; ld 14-16; wknd rap; t.o*
[16ᴾ]	P		**Al Jawwal** 20-1 **R Cope** *Jmpd slow in rr & sn niggled along; 10l 9th aft 12; sn lost tch; crawled 15 & pu*
	P		**Grove Victor (IRE)** 25-1 **P Andrew** *(xnb) Fat; mists; ld at slow pce to 9; sn lost plce; last aft 12; cont t.o; pu 3 out*
	U		**Out Of The Blue** (5a) 8-1 **A Wintle** *7th 5; rdr went out side door 8*
	P		**Wotanite** 33-1 **E Walker** *Prom; 3rd aft 12; wknd rap 14; t.o & pu 3 out*

OFFICIAL DISTANCES: 3l, 20l TIME: 6min 38.0s

Fences 6 & 13 omitted from this and the rest of the meeting for 'safety reasons'; original fence numbers used

120 Dodson & Horrell PPORA Club Members Restricted (Div 2), 12st - 17J   10 ran

	1		**HARWELD** 8-1 **B Foster** *Hld up; mist 7; 5th 11; went 2nd nxt; ld app 14 & qcknd clr; kpt on wl frm 2 out; cheeky*
	2	¾	**Percy Medlicott** 9-2 **Julian Pritchard** *Lw; ld til app 3; lost plce stdly; 8th 11; hdwy in 6th aft 12; 8l 3rd 16; rdn to chall aft 2 out; a hld*
	3	25	**Thereandback (IRE)** 5-1 **L Hicks** *Hit 1; rn in snatches & many posns; went 2nd 11; 3rd 12; chsd wnr bef 14; chall 3 out-nxt; hrd rdn & nt r.o*
[52ᵁ]	4	4	**Po Cap Eel** (5a) 40-1 **Miss H Kinsey** *School in last to 12; outpcd 14; kpt on stdly aft 3 out*
[86ᴾ]	5	10	**Gerej (POL)** 16-1 **R Barrett** *(xnb) Jw; chsd ldr to 11; 4th nxt; outpcd app 14*
	6	12	**Buck Run (IRE)** 7-2 **C Barlow** *Hld up in midfield; 7th aft 12; lost tch 14*
[6ᴮ]	7	5	**Dinedor Charlie** 7-1 **D Jones** *Bhnd; jmpd slow 8; 8th aft 12; wknd 14; t.o*
	P		**Grants Carouse** 40-1 **M Mackley** *Prom; 3rd 11; last aft nxt; sn t.o; pu 14*
[75ᴾ]	P		**True Fred** 7-1 **J Brereton** *Ld app 3 til app 13; wknd rap; t.o & pu 3 out*
[50ᴾ]	P		**Vintage Choice (IRE)** 3-1F **N Kent** *Bckwd; bhnd early; sn cl up; 5th aft 12; sn strugg; t.o & pu 3 out*

OFFICIAL DISTANCES: 1l, 20l TIME: 6min 41.0s

121 Open Maiden (Div 1), 12st   11 ran

	1		**ROLY POLY (IRE)** 10-1 **M Mackley** *2nd/3rd; 8l 3rd aft 12; went 2nd 14; ld & gng best aft 2 out; sn rdn clr*
[23³]	2	10	**On Target** 7-2CF **N Bloom** *8s-7/2; trckd ldrs; 17l 5th aft 12; went 12l 3rd app 2 out; plodded into 2nd aft last; no ch w wnr*
	3	4	**Druids Dream** (5a) 20-1 **J R Barlow** *Tk keen hld; hdwy to ld aft 5; sn 10l clr; hit 16; 2l ahd 3 out; hdd aft 2 out; fin tired*
	4	12	**My Friend Billy (IRE)** 4-1 **Miss S Phizacklea** *W ldrs to 5; 7th & strugg aft 12; plodded on; 27l 4th app 3 out*
	5	2	**Philelwyn (IRE)** (5a) 9-2 **A Wintle** *Ld/disp to 5; 6th & strugg aft 12; 30l 5th app 3 out*
	6	8	**Kings Choir** 10-1 **K Needham** *Fat; strugg in rr; rem 9th aft 12; cont t.o*

[11P]	P		**Black Oak** 7-2CF **Julian Pritchard** *(xnb)* Hld up & nt jw; hrd hld in 15l 4th aft hit 12; outpcd when mist & rdr lost iron 15; t.o & blun 2 out; pu last; disapp
	P		**Celias Twink** (5a) 14-1 **R Barrett** Bckwd; school in last pr; last 12; t.o & pu 16
	U		**Grey Warrior** 7-2CF **M Hewitt** Fat; blun & ur 2
	P		**Mainvalley Queen (IRE)** (5a) 14-1 **L Hicks** Mists; in tch; went 2nd 7 til app 14; sn wknd; t.o & pu last
[37U]	P		**Rising Dawn (IRE)** 20-1 **P Millington** Jmpd slow 7; nt fluent in last trio; poor 8th aft 12; t.o & pu 14

OFFICIAL DISTANCES: 10l, 3l **TIME:** 6min 44.0s

122 Open Maiden (Div 2), 12st   13 ran

	1		**CATCHWORD** 8-1 **R Armson** 2 handlers; hld up & bhnd; 8th 12; qcknd & lft in ld 14; clr 2 out; sprinted up run-in; impressive
[22U]	2	20	**Hijacked** 10-1 **T Stephenson** Prom; 3rd aft 12; outpcd 14; 15l 4th 16; plugged into rem 2nd aft 2 out
[24F]	3	8	**Spectre** 7-2 **N Bloom** Pulled hrd in midfield; 6th & gng wl til aft 12; 3rd 15; wl outpcd nxt
	4	6	**Spumante** 5-2F **C Barlow** Midfield; 4th & gng str aft 12; lft 2nd & mist 15; lkd dangerous nxt; wknd rap 3 out; 8l down when blun nxt; fin v tired
[60P]	5	runin	**Idlewild (IRE)** (7a) 8-1 **Julian Pritchard** Lw; jb & imm lost tch; t.o 3; hunted rnd
	P		**Copper Thorn** (5a,5ow) 16-1 **K Needham** Novicey & detach in last trio; t.o 3; pu 13
	F		**Digitalis** (5a) 25-1 **R Burton** Hld up in midfield; 7th aft 12; outpcd 14; rem when fell last
	P		**Emperor Roscoe** (7a) 16-1 **N Docker** School in rr; t.o 3; pu 15
	P		**Far Forest** (bl) 7-1 **A Evans** Hit 2; sn prsng ldr; u.p aft 12; ev ch when tried to ref 15; slowed bad & pu nxt
[12P]	U		**Fireman** (bl) 33-1 **D Jones** Hit 8; made nrly all til blun & ur 14
	P		**Marquis Of Bedford** 3-1 **E Walker** Nt a fluent; jmpd slow 3; chsd ldrs; 9th & wkng aft 12; t.o & pu 3 out
[52U]	P		**Regal Role** (5a) 33-1 **M Mackley** Mostly 2nd/3rd til 4th 10; mist 11; 5th 12; wkng when pu & dism 14
	P		**The Last Shout (IRE)** 6-1 **P Millington** Hld up & bhnd; 10th & lsng tch aft 12; t.o & pu 14

OFFICIAL DISTANCES: 25l, 8l **TIME:** 6min 42.0s

123 Open Maiden (Div 3), 12st   11 ran

	1		**HOBNOB (IRE)** 5-1 **R Barrett** *(xnb)* 2nd/3rd til ld aft 5; 3l clr when hit 16; just hdd nxt; 2l up 2 out; drvn & much more determined than rival flat
	2	2½	**Vulpin De Laugere (FR)** (bl) 5-1 **Julian Pritchard** *(xnb)* Lw; sn cl up; went 2nd aft 5; hmpd by loose horse app 10; jnd wnr 3 out; rallied & ev ch last; ducked lft bhnd wnr & v doggy flat
[30P]	3	15	**Well I Never** 10-1 **P Millington** Mists in rr; eff in 6th aft 12; went 10l 3rd 3 out; drvn & no imp aft
	4	12	**Ginger Pudding** 6-1 **N Bloom** Hld up & bhnd; 8th aft 12; plodded into 20l 3rd 16; sn dem
[87C]	5	5	**Bannagh Express (IRE)** 16-1 **M Lurcock** 2nd/3rd til aft 12; wknd qckly 14
	6	½	**Rushes Lane** 40-1 **M Skinner** Fat; ld til aft 5; 4th aft 12; lost tch bef 14; plodded on game
[24F]	F		**Arctic Lodge** (vis,tt) 4-1F **M Hewitt** 12s-4s; hld up & bhnd early; hdwy 9; 5th aft 12; went 3rd 14; slowed rap nxt; rem 4th when crashing fall 16
[54P]	U		**Del The Lorry Man** 16-1 **K Needham** Pulled hrd cl up; 5th 5; blun bad & ur 7
[54P]	P		**Fooled You (USA)** (tt) 7-1 **E Andrewes** Strugg in detach last; t.o 9; pu 14
	P		**Grey Dante** (5a) 9-2 **R Burton** 8s-9/2; hld up towards rr; 7th aft 12; 5th when bad mist 14; nt rec; t.o & pu 2 out
[55P]	U		**Three Monroes (IRE)** 5-1 **M Munrowd** Blun & ur 1

OFFICIAL DISTANCES: 3l, 15l **TIME:** 6min 46.0s

124 Open Maiden (Div 4), 12st   14 ran

	1		**WHITEGATES WILLIE** evensF **G Hanmer** 8s-evens; confid rdn in rr; 8l 8th aft 12; qcknd to 2nd 15; cut down clr ldr & jmpd ahd 2 out; sn in comm; comf
	2	7	**Tom's Prize** (7a) 7-2 **S Joynes** *(xnb)* Lw; ld 2; rcd free & jmpd bold; qcknd 14; 10l clr nxt; rdn & hdd 2 out; no ch w wnr
[31F]	3	25	**Balmoral Spring (IRE)** 20-1 **P Millington** Bhnd & rn green; last 5; 10th aft 12; eff 14; 20l 4th & u.p 3 out; no ch w ldrs
[54S]	4	3	**New Hope** (5a) 12-1 **Mrs M Bellamy** Hld up; impd to 2nd 7; hit 9; chsd ldr to 14; wknd qckly nxt; fin lame
[53²]	5	6	**Fair Farm Lad** 8-1 **P Welsh** Cl up til aft 12; wknd qckly 14
[54P]	6	10	**Tom's Surprise** 10-1 **N Kent** Bckwd; prom; lost plce 10; 5l 7th aft 12; 4th 14; sn wknd; t.o

[21³]	7	10	**Light The Sky** 4-1 J Turcan *2 handlers; trckd ldrs; went 3rd aft 12; lost tch w ldng pr 15; t.o*
	P		**Ali's Lark** 25-1 K Needham *Tk keen hld to start; bhnd; 7th 5; rem when pu 11*
	P		**Alphabites** (5a) 25-1 T Gardham *Nt jw & strugg in last trio; lost tch 8; t.o & pu 14*
[23⁶]	F		**Johnny Cool** (bl) 8-1 M Hewitt *Hld up; cl 6th aft 12; outpcd by ldng pr 15; 15l 3rd 3 out; 4th & v tired when fell hvly & winded last*
	F		**Kelly's Island** (5a) 25-1 M Mackley *Bckwd; prom; 4th aft 12; 5th & wkng when fell 14*
	P		**Second Story** (5a) 12-1 L Hicks *Bckwd; jmpd v sticky in final trio; sn strugg; t.o last aft 12; pu 16*
[24ᴾ]	P		**Tuath Deuchainne** 33-1 Miss R Pask *2nd/3rd to 10; 9th & lsng tch aft 12; sn t.o; pu 3 out*
[51⁵]	R		**Village Gossip** (5a) 8-1 M Worthington *Hdstrng; ld to 2; drpd back 9th 5; rn out 7*

OFFICIAL DISTANCES: 6l, dist   TIME: 6min 39.0s

Mid Surrey Farmers Draghounds
Charing (LH 8F,19J) Sun, 6 Feb (GOOD)

125 Hunt (with Coakham Bloodhounds)   7 ran

	1		**PRIME COURSE (IRE)** (7x) 7-2 C Gordon *Settled 4th; hdwy to cl 2nd frm 8; hrd rdn & jnd ldr 4 out; outj nxt 2; kpt on und str drvng to ld last; hld on wl flat*
	2	1½	**Thats Dedication (IRE)** (tt) 4-5F D Robinson *Ld/disp til ld 6; made rest til jnd 4 out; outj wnr nxt 2; hdd app last; kpt on one pce w rdr wkng on flat*
	3	1½fs	**Mosta (IRE)** (5a) 16-1 P Bull *A last pr; 10l 5th 11; 20l 3rd 15; t.o frm nxt*
	P		**A Bit Extra** 33-1 R Goring *Nrly ur & lost irons 2; pu; cont t.o til pu 7*
	P		**Daddy Long Leggs** (6ow) 33-1 R Hubbard *Cl 2nd/3rd til wknd 11; rr when pu 13*
	P		**Half Moon Spinney** 4-1 Miss C Holliday *Prsd ldrs til wknd 11; rr when pu 13*
	P		**Parson's Way** (1ow) 14-1 S Fisher *A towards rr; last frm 7; 13l 6th 11; 25l 4th 15; t.o & pu nxt*

OFFICIAL DISTANCES: 1l, dist   TIME: 6min 33.0s   TOTE: £4.60; places £1.10,£2.80 DF: £1.90

126 Restricted   13 ran

[75ᴿ]	1		**BALL IN THE NET** 33-1 M Holdforth *Rr to 3; smooth hdwy to cl 3rd frm 9 til prsd ldr 15; ld 4 out; drew clr app last; easy*
[36³]	2	10	**Royal Rupert** 5-1 N Benstead *Prsd ldr til ld 15; hdd nxt; hrd rdn & ev ch 2 out; wknd app last*
[25⁸]	3	1	**Ishma (IRE)** D Page *A in tch; 10l 6th 11; 15l 5th aft 15; stayed on to tk 3rd 3 out; kpt on one pce*
[24¹]	4	30	**Helena Justina** (5a) 13-8F P Taiano *A in tch; 9l 5th 11; impd to 10l 3rd aft 15; no further prog; mist 4 out; wknd qckly aft nxt*
	5	15	**For Josh (IRE)** 33-1 P Townsley *A wl in tch; 5l 4th 11; wknd aft 15; fin tired*
[25ᴾ]	6	20	**Target Time** (5a) 25-1 Mrs L Stock *A rr; 35l 10th 11; t.o frm 13*
[27ᴾ]	7	5	**Barron Bay (USA)** 25-1 M Gorman *W ldrs to 8; 19l 8th & lsng plce 11; t.o frm 13*
[2²]	F		**Ally Pally** 7-4 P York *Midfield til fell 6*
	P		**Ballybollen (IRE)** 25-1 D Brightling *A towards rr; 14l 7th 11; wl bhnd frm 15; t.o & pu 2 out*
	U		**Belvento (IRE)** 3-1 D Dunsdon *Prsd ldrs til blun & ur 9*
	P		**I Do The Jokes (IRE)** 10-1 K Giles *Made most til wknd rap aft 14; 6th & no ch when pu 4 out*
	P		**Perripage** 20-1 Miss A Sansom *A rr; lsng tch in last 11; t.o & pu 13*
	P		**Winward** (bl) 25-1 P M Hall *A rr; 27l 9th 11; t.o & pu 2 out*

OFFICIAL DISTANCES: 7l, ½l   TIME: 6min 32.0s   TOTE: £16.00; places £4.30,£1.30,£56.20 DF: £37.00

127 Confined, 12st   13 ran

	1		**SATCHMO (IRE)** (5x) 6-1 G Wragg *A cl up; trckd ldr 10 til ld 12; made rest gng wl; kpt on str frm 2 out w rdr doing little*
	2	¾	**Seod Rioga (IRE)** (5x) 4-5F C Gordon *Ld to 11; prsd wnr rest of way; hrd rdn frm 4 out; blun nxt; kpt on app last; a wl hld*
[25²]	3	30	**Commasarris** 7-1 P Blagg *Trckd ldng pr; 6l 3rd aft 15; wknd frm nxt*
[1ᴾ]	4	8	**Feel The Power (IRE)** 33-1 J Maxse *A chsng ldrs; 10l 5th 11; 12l 4th aft 15; lost tch frm nxt*
	5	10	**Nossi Be** 7-2 D Parker *A midfield; 22l 5th aft 15; nvr able to get nr ldrs*
	6	1	**Touring-Turtle (IRE)** 20-1 D Dennis *Midfield; 13l 6th 11; 35l 7th & lsng tch aft 15*
	7	nk	**Nattico (IRE)** 10-1 Miss S Gladders *A towards rr; 15l 8th 11; nvr nrr*
[29⁵]	8	20	**Hizal** 25-1 A Coe *Prsd ldr to 9; 5l 4th 11; 32l 6th & wkng aft 15; t.o*

9	2	**How Friendly** 33-1 **D Brightling** *A wl bhnd*
P		**Bang On Target** (bl) 33-1 **J Stephens** *Qckly lost tch; t.o 7 til pu 11*
U		**Joyful Hero** (5a) 33-1 **Miss P Ellison** *Midfield whn ur 3*
r		**Moon Rising** 25-1 **P Bull** *Jmpd slow 1; ref 2*
P		**What A Hand** 10-1 **T Underwood** *Jmpd sticky; sn lost tch; t.o frm 8 til pu 12*

OFFICIAL DISTANCES: ½l, 15l **TIME:** 6min 25.0s **TOTE:** £3.20; places £1.10, £1.70, £1.40 **DF:** £3.70

128 Ladies Open   11 ran

[84⁷]	1		**CRACKING IDEA** (IRE) 6-4JF **Mrs G d'Angibau** *Midfield; hdwy 7; prsd ldr 9 til ld 12; made rest; 10l clr aft 15; stayed on str*
[27³]	2	15	**Kincora** (IRE) 6-1 **Mrs L Stock** *Ld to 11; chsd wnr to 15; lft 2nd agn 4 out; kpt on one pce*
	3	fence	**Strongalong** (IRE) (5ow) 6-4JF **Miss K Roncoroni** *Sn wl bhnd; 43l 9th 10; nvr lkd likely to get nrr; lft 3rd by default*
	U		**Danger Flynn** (IRE) 6-1 **Miss C Holliday** *Cl 3rd til chsd wnr frm 15; 10l down when ur 16*
[28⁷]	P		**Emsee-H** (2ow) 14-1 **Miss Z Turner** *A midfield; 15l 6th 10; same plce but wkng when pu 15*
	R		**Professor Page** (IRE) 33-1 **Miss J Grant** *Chsd ldrs; 10l 4th 10; lost tch frm 13; dist 3rd when rn out 2 out*
[28⁷]	P		**Red Channel** (IRE) 33-1 **Miss P Bryan-Brown** *Midfield; 31l 8th 10; wknd 13; t.o & pu 15*
[28²]	P		**Uron V** (FR) 10-1 **Miss T Hayter** *Sn wl bhnd; 47l 10th 10; t.o & pu 15*
[28ᵁ]	P		**Velka** (5a) 33-1 **Miss P Ellison** *Prsd ldr to 7; 23l 7th & wkng 10; rr when pu 13*
	P		**Wednesdays Auction** (IRE) 33-1 **Mrs C Andrews** *Sn wl bhnd; 49l 11th 10; t.o & pu 15*
	S		**Young Nimrod** (tt) 14-1 **Miss C Grissell** *Midfield; 12l 5th 10; chsng ldng trio when slpd up bend bef 16*

OFFICIAL DISTANCES: 12l, 20l **TIME:** 6min 29.0s **TOTE:** £7.50; places £6.70, £1.30, £1.80 **DF:** £13.00

The stewards enquired into the running and riding of Strongalong which was soon tailed off; the rider was cautioned as to her future riding

129 Mens Open   4 ran

	1		**STRUGGLES GLORY** (IRE) 2-7F **D Robinson** *Made all; drew clr frm 14; in comm frm 16*
	2	1¼fs	**Monks Soham** (IRE) 16-1 **D Parker** *Trckd wnr most of way til lost tch aft 14; eased aft 2 out; hacked in*
	r		**Cill Churnain** (IRE) 14-1 **A Sansome** *Nvr gng wl; a last; t.o 7; scrubbed along frm 10; jmpd slow 13; ref 14*
	U		**Nadjati** (USA) 3-1 **P Hall** *Trckd ldr in 2nd/3rd til ur 10*

OFFICIAL DISTANCE: 25l **TIME:** 6min 31.0s **TOTE:** £1.50 **DF:** £3.60

130 S.E. Hunts Club Members Moderate, 12st   15 ran

	1		**JOJO** (IRE) (bl) 12-1 **B Hitchcott** *Trckd ldrs; 4l 4th 11; ld 3 out; sn clr; 8l up when v reluct & almost jnd app last; kpt on to ld agn flat*
	2	1½	**Primitive King** (7x) 3-1JF **P Hacking** *A.p; 3l 3rd 11; chsd wnr frm 2 out; lft w ev ch app last; no ex flat*
[37¹]	3	6	**Rustic Revelry** (4x) 9-2 **Y York** *A cl up; prsd ldr 9 til ld 15-4 out; wknd app 2 out*
[56¹]	4	1	**Coach** (NZ) 6-1 **B Kendellen** *A cl up; 5l 5th 11; ev ch 4 out; no ex frm nxt*
[26⁵]	5	1½fs	**Broguestown Pride** (IRE) 33-1 **P Blagg** *Prsd ldr to 5; sn lost plce; 25l 9th 11; t.o frm 14*
	P		**Balmy Breeze** (5a) 33-1 **N Holdforth** *Sn wl bhnd; pu bef ½way*
	r		**Commuter Country** (7x) 3-1JF **A Coe** *Chsd ldrs; 8l 6th & rdn along 11; lost tch 15; rem 5th when ref last*
[5⁴]	P		**Equity Player** 20-1 **T Underwood** *Midfield; 9l 7th 11; lost tch frm nxt; pu 15*
[25⁵]	U		**Golden Mac** 25-1 **J Barnard** *A rr; 36l last 11; t.o when ur last*
	U		**Hatch Gate** 33-1 **M Gorman** *Towards rr but in tch til ur 6*
	P		**Loftus Lad** (IRE) 25-1 **D Dennis** *A rr; 27l 10th 11; no ch when pu 15*
	P		**Mister Spectator** (IRE) 7-1 **P Hickman** *Ld to 14; wknd aft nxt; 5th & no ch when pu last*
[27⁷]	F		**Sultan Of Swing** 12-1 **J Stephens** *Sn rr; t.o when fell 6*
	P		**The Bishops Sister** (IRE) (5a) 12-1 **Miss S Gladders** *A rr; 31l 11th 11; wl bhnd when pu last*
	P		**The Glow** (IRE) (7x) 10-1 **D Brightling** *Midfield; 15l 8th 11; pu 15*

OFFICIAL DISTANCES: 2l, 5l **TIME:** 6min 34.0s **TOTE:** £4.70; places £1.30, £2.30, £2.30 **DF:** £30.30

131 Open Maiden (Div 1), 12st   16 ran

[21²]	1		**NOAH** (7a) 3-1F **P York** *In tch; 5th 11; hdwy to ld aft 15; made rest; kpt on wl app last*
	2	3	**Kenny Davis (IRE)** 4-1 **P Blagg** *Hld up in rr; 11th 11; stdy hdwy frm nxt; prsd wnr 3 out; hrd rdn & ev ch app last; wknd flat*
	3	15	**Zaisan (IRE)** 6-1 **D Dunsdon** *Midfield; 9th 11; prsd ldrs 15 til no ex frm 3 out*
[21⁴]	4	3	**Just The Business** 7-1 **P Bull** *A in tch; 8th 11; ev ch app 4 out; kpt on one pce*
[23⁸]	5	1	**Bachelor-Carrasco (IRE)** 4-1 **S R Andrews** *Towards rr; 10th 11; hdwy to press ldrs app 4 out; no ex frm nxt*
	6	10	**Jo Bloggs (IRE)** 8-1 **A Lillingston** *Cl up til ld 8-15; wknd qckly aft 16*
[23⁵]	7	25	**Call The Tune** (5a) 10-1 **D Brightling** *Mists; a wl bhnd; 14th 11; t.o*
	F		**Lady Of Verse** (5a) (bl) 25-1 **M Gorman** *A towards rr; 13th 11; fell hvly 14*
[11⁷]	F		**Native Dawn (IRE)** 5-1 **C Williams** *Towards rr; 12th 11; fell hvly nxt*
	P		**Paddy Clyde (IRE)** 6-1 **C Gordon** *Prsd ldr; blun 5; 3rd 11; wknd 13; pu 15*
[6⁹]	P		**Persian Boy (IRE)** 8-1 **A Sansome** *Cl up; 4th 11; wkng when pu 15*
	r		**Rushenova** 8-1 **R Guest** *A rr; last 11; wl bhnd when ref 13*
	P		**Satellite Express (IRE)** 8-1 **P Hickman** *Rr til pu 9*
	P		**Sleipnir** 10-1 **B Hitchcott** *Midfield; 7th 11; pu 14*
[24⁵]	F		**The Secret Grey** 6-1 **A Coe** *In tch; 6th 11; fell 13*
[31⁶]	P		**Whatacharlie** (tt) 10-1 **P Keane** *Ld to 7; prsd ldr til wknd 15; 7th & no ch when pu last*

OFFICIAL DISTANCES: 4l, 10l **TIME:** 6min 40.0s **TOTE:** £2.80; places £1.10,£2.50,£13.90 **DF:** £11.20

132 Open Maiden (Div 2), 12st   9 ran

[30⁴]	1		**LABULA BAY** 6-1 **P York** *Sn prom; prsd 2nd frm 8; disp ld frm 15; ld nxt; drew clr app last*
	2	12	**Mister Chips** 4-1 **P Bull** *Ld/disp virt a way; ev ch 2 out; wknd rap app last*
	3	2	**Chill Factor** (1ow) (tt) 4-1 **A Sansome** *Chsd ldrs; 16l 5th 10; no prog til stayed on frm 16; nrst fin*
	4	fence	**Rag Bolt (IRE)** 8-1 **S R Andrews** *W ldrs to 7; 10l 3rd 10; lost tch frm 12; no ch frm 15*
	5	30	**Tom's Influence** (5a) 33-1 **D Parker** *Sn lost tch; 36l 6th 10; t.o frm 13*
[23⁹]	P		**Arry's Away** 12-1 **A Hickman** *Sn lost tch; 38l 7th 10; wl bhnd when pu 13*
	R		**Carraig Brol (IRE)** 2-1F **B Hitchcott** *Trckd ldrs; cl 3rd when rn out 8*
	P		**Schisandra** (5a,1ow) 33-1 **P Blagg** *Jb; sn lost tch; 41l last 10; pu 13*
	U		**Scottish Spirit** (5a) 12-1 **P Hall** *Chsd ldrs; 13l 4th 10; 5th when ur 12*

OFFICIAL DISTANCES: 12l, ½l **TIME:** 6min 42.0s **TOTE:** £11.00; places £5.50,£2.30,£1.30 **DF:** £7.70

Old Raby Hunt Club
Witton Castle (RH 7F,19J) Sun, 6 Feb (GOOD to SOFT)

133 Club Members Confined Maiden, 12st   8 ran

[20⁹]	1		**CHAPS** 20-1 **Mrs F Needham** *(pricker ns) Rr to 8; mist 9; went cl 5th 13; 3l 3rd 3 out; rdn to ld app last; r.o u.p; bbv*
	2	2	**Hazel Reilly (IRE)** (5a) 10-1 **L Bates** *Rr to 5; last 5-9; cl up 6th 14; 6l 4th 3 out; fin wl; tk 2nd flat*
	3	1	**Heather Lad** 20-1 **D Raw** *2 handlers; oht; unruly; chsd ldr to 11; ld 12-3 out; jnd nxt; sn wknd*
	4	8	**Wayward Buttons** 4-5F **S Swiers** *Last to 5; hdwy aft 6; handy 4th 12; 11l 2nd 16; disp ld 3 out-nxt; wknd aft; nt hrd pushed; will improve*
	P		**Mefein Boy (IRE)** (bl) 9-4 **W Burnell** *Midfield to 8; 3l 3rd 12; cl up til lsng tch 14; wknd qckly aft 15; t.o & pu 2 out*
	P		**Mr Speck** 4-1 **G Tuer** *Sn clr; 10l ld to 6; 2l clr 7-10; rmdrs & wknd qckly 12; last & lsng tch when pu 14*
	r		**Palmed Off** (5a) 14-1 **C Wilson** *(xnb) Handy to 5; rmdrs aft 6; midfield by 8; lsng tch 13; t.o when ref 14*
	P		**Thirkleby Skeena** (5a) 5-1 **N Tutty** *Handy to 4; 12l 4th 6; went 2l 2nd 9; outpcd & wknd 14; t.o & pu last*

OFFICIAL DISTANCES: 2l, ½l **TIME:** 6min 47.0s

134 Intermediate, 12st   11 ran

	1		**PROMINENT** 4-1 **K Prendergast** *A handy; 2l 2nd 12 til ld 15; 6l ld 3 out; stayed on wl; bltr for rce*
[51²]	2	2	**Primitive Man** 6-1 **S Charlton** *Mid-div to 13; went 5l 5th 14; stayed on wl; went 4l 2nd 2 out; chsd ldr til mist last; no ex flat*
	3	8	**Harbour Blaze** 5-1 **Miss R Clark** *Swtng; rr when bad mist 4; bhnd til hdwy frm 12; went handy 5th 14; outpcd nxt; r.o one pce*

	4	15	**Dromore Dream (IRE)** 7-2 S Swiers *(xnb) Rr to 11; stayed on past btn horses; nrst fin*
	5	2	**Orswellthatenswell** (5x) 8-1 Mrs F Needham *Cl up; ld frm 3; 2l ld 14; pushed along 16; wknd app 3 out; r.o one pce*
	6	8	**Blackwoodscountry** (5x) 8-1 N Wilson *Ld to 2; 3l 3rd frm 4-9; handy 3rd aft 12; pushed along & rmdrs 13; wknd 15; poor 6th 2 out*
	7	2fncs	**Childsway** 50-1 S J Robinson *(xnb) Sn bhnd; a pushed along; t.o 14; 2 fncs adrift 3 out*
	F		**Bold Fountain (IRE)** 3-1F C Wilson *6s-3s; rr div to 8; hdwy frm 11; mist 13; went 4l 4th 15; outpcd 3 out; hld in 3rd when fell 2 out*
[18⁴]	P		**Optimism Reigns (IRE)** 8-1 R Clark *Prom early; handy 4th 8; pushed along aft 11; mist & lsng tch 13; pu 14*
	P		**Prime Style** (7ow) 33-1 C Gibbon *(xnb) Prom early; 11 2nd 3-7; pushed along 8; sn wknd; rr & lsng tch 10; t.o 13; pu last*
	P		**Stellar Force (IRE)** (5x) 5-1 N Tutty *(xnb) A rr; last 6-8; bhnd & lsng tch 12; hrd rdn 14; no resp; t.o & pu 16*

OFFICIAL DISTANCES: 2l, 5l   TIME: 6min 41.0s

135 Ladies Open   11 ran

	1		**MONKEY AGO** 4-1 Miss J Foster *Handy to 6; went 3l 3rd 8-14; 2l 2nd 15; ld 3 out; sn clr; 8l ld last; wknd cl home; just hld on*
[41⁵]	2	½	**Marius (IRE)** 6-1 Miss V Russell *Midfield to 7; 10l 6th 8; outpcd & rr 13; pushed along when blkd 16; stayed on wl; 12l 4th 2 out; flew up run-in; just failed*
	3	8	**Misti Hunter (IRE)** 16-1 Miss Rachel Clark *(xnb) Cl 2nd to 5; ld 6-7; handy 2nd to 14; 3rd & pushed along 16; outpcd 3 out; 8l 4th nxt; stayed on to tk 3rd flat*
	4	3	**Insideout** 2-1F Mrs L Ward *(xnb) Rr to 2; nt settle; pulled to ldrs 5; disp ld to 7; cl up til outpcd & wknd 15; 15l 5th 3 out; r.o same pce*
[41⁷]	5	6	**Tabriz** (5a) 33-1 Miss A Thompson *Tde; a mid-div; nvr pce to chall; 12l 6th 13; r.o one pce*
[19ᶠ]	6	5	**Japodene** (5a) 4-1 Miss A Deniel *Ld to 5; cl 2nd to 8; ld agn 9 til jnd 15; 6l 3rd 3 out til virt stpd app last; clambered over & hacked home*
[41⁶]	7	1	**Steel Rigg (IRE)** 5-1 Miss A Price *Nd; a rr; t.o 16*
[41⁸]	8	4	**Scrabo View (IRE)** 50-1 Miss S Ward *A bhnd; lsng tch 8; t.o 16; slt late hdwy*
	U		**Cab On Target** 16-1 Miss W Gibson *Cl up to 8; outpcd 9; 8l 5th 10; 10l 5th 12; pushed along 14; 12l 4th when ur 15*
	P		**Holiway Star** 33-1 Miss T Jackson *Tde; planted at start; set off over fnce bhnd; jb lft; hopelessly t.o when pu aft 10*
	U		**Tudor Lodge (IRE)** (5a) 9-2 Miss S Swindells *Midfield when ur 2*

OFFICIAL DISTANCES: ¾l, 7l   TIME: 6min 37.0s

136 Mens Open   6 ran

	1		**RED SPECTACLE (IRE)** 2-1 N Tutty *Trckd ldr to 3 out; hrd rdn to 11 2nd nxt; chall last; gd j to ld & r.o wl*
	2	3	**On The Fly** (tt) 4-6F K Prendergast *(xnb) Made most; 3l up 3 out; jnd app last; hrd rdn & fnd nil; btr for rce*
[48ᴾ]	3	20	**Take Two** 25-1 S Pinder *Last to 10; lsng tch 12; rmdrs 13; poor 4th 16; lft dist 3rd 3 out*
[42⁶]	4	15	**Lottery Ticket (IRE)** 20-1 S J Robinson *Sn pushed along; 12l 4th 9; hrd rdn & rmdrs 13; rem 5th 16; plodded home*
	P		**Calleva Star (IRE)** 3-1 R Abrahams *Prom early; 2l 2nd to 6; wknd & rr by 7; t.o & pu 13*
	U		**Gikongoro** 20-1 B Orde-Powlett *(xnb) Last to 4; hdwy 5; 2l 2nd 7-15; pushed along & wknd 16; 15l 3rd when ur 3 out*

OFFICIAL DISTANCES: 2l, 20l   TIME: 6min 50.0s

137 Restricted, 12st   20 ran

	1		**TRIPLE EAVES** 5-1 C Mulhall *A.p; handy 4th to 7; ld 10; 1l up 15 til jnd 2 out; forged clr app last; r.o wl*
	2	4	**Young Ardross** 7-1 Mrs F Needham *Midfield to 8; stdy hdwy to 5l 4th 14; went 2nd 3 out; disp ld nxt til outpcd app last; r.o same pce*
[53ᴾ]	3	12	**The Butcher Boy** (7ow) 6-1 D Easterby *Rn in snatches; hld up & settled in last early; hdwy frm 9; went handy 6th 14 til bad mist 15; 10l 5th & wkng 16; stayed on; fin wl; sure to improve*
	4	8	**Just Takethe Micky** 12-1 S Charlton *Ld to 14; cl 3rd 16; outpcd & wknd 3 out; dem app last*
	5	4	**Priceless Sam** (5a) 4-1F Mrs L Ward *A mid-div; bad mist 2; nvr plcd to chall*
[40ᴾ]	P		**Abbey Lad** 6-1 C Wilson *A midfield; mist 9; lsng tch 11; t.o & pu 13*
[48ᴾ]	P		**Cede Nullis** (5a) 12-1 S Brisby *(xnb) Midfield to 8; pushed along frm 9 til hdwy 4th 15; stayed on to 3rd 2 out; wknd rap aft; came to crawl & pu last*

P		**China Lal** (5a) 12-1 **Mrs K Diggle** *2nd to 10; cl 3rd 12; wknd 14; t.o & pu 2 out*
P		**Computer Pickings** (5a) 20-1 **F Crawford** *A rr; lost tch 6; pu 7*
P		**Crimson Bow** (5a) 12-1 **G Thomas** *A rr div; lsng tch & pu 10*
P		**Efaad (IRE)** 10-1 **W Burnell** *Midfield; pushed along 12; outpcd & wknd qckly 13; t.o & pu 3 out*
P		**Ellerton Tony** 5-1 **S Swiers** *Prom in 3rd to 7; 4l 3rd 8; wknd aft 12; t.o 15; pu 3 out*
P		**Graceland** (5a) 50-1 **N Tutty** *A rr; lsng tch 7; t.o & pu 10*
P		**Gunmetal** (7a) 10-1 **P Halder** *(xnb) Tkn rnd gently in rr; lsng tch when pu 13*
P		**Just A Single (IRE)** 33-1 **K Prendergast** *Hacked rnd in rr til pu aft 14; nvr put in rce*
P		**Kanona** 6-1 **N Wilson** *Mid-div to 8; went handy 5th 9; in tch til wknd 13; rr & lsng tch 14; t.o & pu 3 out*
P		**Lord George** 14-1 **P Atkinson** *Midfield to 8; handy 4th 9-13; wknd 14; t.o & pu 3 out*
P		**Mrs Drummond (IRE)** (5a) 16-1 **G Markham** *Prom early; 5l 5th 6; rr by 10; lsng tch & pu 13*
P		**The Grey Bay** (5a) 20-1 **Miss T Jackson** *A rr; lsng tch when pu 13*
P		**The Hazel Harrier (IRE)** 12-1 **Miss A Deniel** *(bh) Jmpd terribly; mists 4 & 5; last 6; t.o 8; pu 13*

OFFICIAL DISTANCES: 4l, 15l **TIME:** 6min 44.0s

138 Open Maiden (Non-Rules Rnrs) (Div 1), 12st   10 ran

[55⁹]	1		**SCRUTON** (6ow) 5-2 **D Easterby** *Prom early; 2l 2nd 9-15; ld aft 16; 2l up 3 out; jnd nxt-last; hrd rdn & just hld on*
	2	½	**Top Toy (IRE)** 2-1F **A Dalton** *Patient rdn; rr to 10; stdy hdwy frm 11; trckng ldng pr 14; disp ld 2 out til just outpcd flat; gd rn; sure to improve*
	3	6	**Mighty Rising** (7a) 20-1 **S Charlton** *Midfield to 11; went cl 3rd 14; ½l 2nd 16; wknd 3 out; gd rn*
	4	15	**Tiger King** 4-1 **C Mulhall** *Ld til mist 14; wknd 15; 12l 4th 2 out; r.o one pce*
P			**Dragon Stout** 5-1 **C Wilson** *Midfield to 9; wknd & lsng tch 14; t.o & pu 2 out*
P			**Flashing Gale (IRE)** 6-1 **D Coates** *Last to 6; hdwy frm 7; rushed up to cl 3rd 10; in tch til wknd 14; t.o & pu last*
P			**Miss Jones** (5a) 16-1 **P Frank** *Jmpd erratic; bad mist 4; 6l 5th 7-10; rr & lsng tch 12; bad mist 13; pu 14*
P			**Oaklands Millie (IRE)** (5a) 10-1 **P Kinsella** *Ld to 2; cl 3rd til mist 7; rr by 13; t.o & pu 3 out*
P			**Primelle** (5a) 50-1 **Mrs F Needham** *A last; lsng tch 11; pu 13; lks slow*
P			**Surprise View** (5a) 12-1 **R Clark** *(xnb) Cl up; 2l 2nd 7; handy 3rd 11; wknd 12; sn lost tch; pu 16*

OFFICIAL DISTANCES: nk, 5l **TIME:** 6min 59.0s
The rider of the winner was fined £50 by the stewards for incorrect use of the whip, and causing the horse to be marked

139 Open Maiden (Non-Rules Rnrs) (Div 2), 12st   9 ran

	1		**ATOSKI** 4-7F **A Dalton** *Jw; made all; qcknd clr app 2 out; r.o wl; impressive*
[45ᶠ]	2	10	**Highbury** 2-1 **S Walker** *Mid-div to 10; 5l 5th 12; outpcd 15; 6l 3rd 3 out; rdn to 2nd app last; r.o one pce; no ch w wnr*
[44ᵁ]	3	3	**Donard Son (IRE)** 7-1 **N Wilson** *Rr to 6; hdwy 10; went 4l 3rd 12; cl 2nd & lkd danger 3 out; mist nxt; wknd*
P			**Ben From Ketton** (7a) 20-1 **S J Robinson** *Prom to 3; rr 7; lost tch 12; pu 16*
P			**Cape Crusader** 20-1 **C Mulhall** *Rr to 5; hdwy aft 7; went 6l 3rd 9; handy 3rd 11; rmdrs 12; wknd 13; dist 5th 15; pu 16*
P			**Heavenly Blues** 25-1 **C Wilson** *Trckd ldr to 6; disp ld 7-8; cl 2nd to 14; wknd nxt; pu 16*
P			**Morcan House** 16-1 **S Gibbon** *Cl 3rd to 8; handy to 11; wknd qckly aft 12; last & lsng tch when pu 14*
R			**Mr Norm** 33-1 **J Clare** *Rr when bad mist 2; pulled to ldrs & rn out 4*
[53ᴾ]	P		**Perdix** (12a) 14-1 **K Prendergast** *Jmpd novicey; jb lft; bad mist 1; a bhnd; pu 16*

OFFICIAL DISTANCES: 8l, 3l **TIME:** 7min 08.0s

Tiverton

Chipley Park (RH 7F,18J) Sun, 6 Feb (GOOD to FIRM with SOFT patches)

140 Hunt   5 ran

[35ᴾ]	1		**PARDITINO** 6-1 **Miss J Nicholas** *Nov rdn; a.p; 2l 3rd ½way; went 2nd 3 out; ld last; r.o wl; rdr's 1st wnr*

	2	2	**Jolson** (tt) 20-1 *R Woollacott 2nd til ld 8; hdd 13; ld 15-last; r.o*
	3	½	**Foxy Dawn** 13-8 *D Alers-Hankey 2s-13/8; 2 handlers; hld up; 3l 4th ½way; mist & rmdrs 12; last & rdn 14; stayed on u.p frm 3 out; went 3rd last; nvr able to chall*
[8²]	4	½	**Ardbei (IRE)** 4-5F *Miss J Cumings Lw; ld to 8; 2nd til ld 13; hdd 15; ev ch 3 out; sn rdn; one pce*
	5	12	**Stormhill Warrior** 33-1 *R Emmett Hld up; 4l 5th ½way; eff 13; 4th when mist 15; wknd 3 out*

OFFICIAL DISTANCES: 2½l, ½l **TIME:** 6min 31.3s

141 Mixed Open, 12st   7 ran

[19ᴾ]	1		**GUNNER BOON** 5-4F *Miss P Jones Lw; jmpd lft; ld to 8; 2nd til ld 11; 5l clr when jb lft 2 out; all out*
	2	2	**Ask Frank** 11-2 *F Hutsby Hld up; 9l 4th ½way; qcknd & went 2nd aft 12; mist & stayed on game*
	3	runin	**Via Del Quatro (IRE)** (5a,7x) 20-1 *J Barnes Bit bckwd; a bhnd; t.o 11; went dist 3rd aft 2 out*
	4	5	**Amtrak Express** 11-2 *H Froud 2 handlers; nov rdn; lw; went 2nd aft 2-7; 4l 3rd ½way; wknd 15; blun 2 out; t.o*
	U		**Mr Magnetic (IRE)** (7x) 4-1 *D Harvey 8s-4s; bckwd; nov rdn; oht; 3rd when mist & ur 5*
[8ᴾ]	P		**Prince Teeton** (bl) 14-1 *Jeremy Young Lw; lost plce & rmdrs 3; nt r.o; t.o & pu 6*
	P		**Shehab (IRE)** (7x) 16-1 *N Mitchell Tchd 20s; bit bckwd; hld up & pulled hrd; hdwy 6; went 2nd nxt; ld 8-11; 7l 4th & wkng when mist 13; wl bhnd when pu 15*

OFFICIAL DISTANCES: 2½l, 25l **TIME:** 6min 12.1s

142 Intermediate, 12st   6 ran

[63ᵁ]	1		**BALLY WIRRAL (IRE)** 7-4F *G Maundrell Tchd 2s; 2nd til ld 4; hdd 5; 5l 4th ½way; went 3rd 12; ld 13; drew clr 2 out; comf*
	2	6	**Belarus (IRE)** (bl) 4-1 *C White Drpd to rr 4; hdwy 6; went 2nd 8-13; outpcd 15; 8l 3rd 2 out; stayed on u.p; went 2nd flat*
	3	1½	**Bolshie Baron** (tt) 9-4 *J Jukes Ld to 4; ld 5-13; ev ch 3 out; sn hrd rdn; wknd app last*
[68³]	P		**A Few Dollars More (IRE)** 8-1 *R Woollacott 2nd/3rd to 12; sn rdn & lost plce; wl bhnd 15; t.o & pu last*
	P		**Flockmaster (IRE)** 16-1 *T Vaughan Bit bckwd; swtng; hld up; mists 6 & 9; 8l 6th & rdn ½way; lost tch u.p 12; t.o & pu 14*
	U		**Willie B Brave (IRE)** 8-1 *David Dennis Tchd 20s in plce; hld up; jmpd lft 5; jmpd slow 7 & 8; 7l 5th ½way; mist & ur 11*

OFFICIAL DISTANCES: 5l, 2l **TIME:** 6min 12.5s

143 Dodson & Horrell PPORA Club Members, 12st   6 ran

	1		**CAMERA MAN** 10-1 *C Heard Lw; 2nd to 6; went 2nd agn 10; ld aft 12 til hdd last; rallied u.p to ld nr fin*
	2	nk	**Hylters Chance (IRE)** (4x) 4-1 *D Alers-Hankey 8s-4s; lw; rcd v keen; made most til hdd aft mist 12; rdn to ld last; veered lft flat & hdd nr fin*
	3	5	**Perhaps (USA)** (5a) 4-1 *H Williams Ww; 4l 4th ½way; outpcd 14; stayed on u.p frm 2 out; went 5l 3rd app last; nt rch ldrs*
[36²]	4	8	**Dannicus** 4-5F *T Mitchell Lw; pulled hrd; went 2nd 6; ld 8; sn hdd; 3rd 10; blun 13; ev ch 15; rdn & wknd 2 out*
	5	12	**Ive Called Time** 10-1 *G Chanter Hld up; mist 5; 8l 6th ½way; lost tch 14*
[49ᴾ]	6	10	**Vitaman (IRE)** 20-1 *G Barfoot-Saunt Hld up; 5l 5th ½way; no hdwy frm 13; wknd 3 out; virt pu flat*

OFFICIAL DISTANCES: ½l, 4l **TIME:** 6min 22.7s

144 Restricted, 12st   8 ran

	1		**BALLINA** 11-2 *J Jukes Jmpd lft; ld; mist & rmdrs 13; hit 15; drvn clr 3 out; stayed on wl*
	2	5	**Pallingham Lad (IRE)** (tt) 33-1 *S Kidston Bit bckwd; swtng; hld up & bhnd; 8th ½way; last to 15; hdwy 9l 5th nxt; stayed on wl u.p 2 out; went 8l 2nd at last; nt rch wnr*
	3	5	**Primero (IRE)** (tt) 16-1 *R Woollacott Lw; hld up; mists 6 & 8; hdwy & 4th ½way; went 3rd 15; chsd wnr 3 out til wknd & hit last*
[6²]	4	1½	**Possible Pardon (NZ)** 7-2 *A Charles-Jones 6s-7/2; lw; hld up; mist 7; 7th ½way; rdn along 11; 4l 5th 14; sn outpcd; 111 6th 3 out; stayed on*
	5	8	**Nearly All Right** 100-1 *N Harris Prom; 3rd ½way; lost plce 11; rallied & 2l 3rd 13; wknd u.p & 8l 4th 3 out*
	6	6	**Securon Lady** (5a) 50-1 *J Barnes Bit bckwd; mist 5; 2nd/3rd to 8; 5th ½way; 5l 6th 14; wknd 15*

| | P | **Blondie Boo (IRE)** (bl) 33-1 **I Widdicombe** *Prom; went 2nd 6 til wknd qckly 3 out; bhnd when pu last* |
| [13²] | F | **The Earth Moved (IRE)** 4-7F **Miss P Gundry** *Tchd 4/6 & 1/2; lw; hld up; 6th ½way; stdy hdwy & 2l 4th when fell 12* |

OFFICIAL DISTANCES: 5l, 8l **TIME:** 6min 28.2s

145 Open Maiden (Div 1), 12st   14 ran

	1		**CARDINALS FOLLY (IRE)** 10-1 **E Williams** *12s-10s; a.p; went 2nd 4; ld 7; rdn when lft wl clr aft 2 out; fin tired*
	2	runin	**Porters Lodge** 10-1 **David Dennis** *Bckwd; hld up; mist 3; 6l 5th ½way; went 5l 4th 13; wknd u.p 15; lft dist 2nd aft 2 out*
	F		**Aherne** (7a) 25-1 **N Tucker** *Jnd ldrs 3; 5th when fell 6*
	P		**Aller Coombe** (5a) 6-1 **T Greed** *8s-6s; swtng; a bhnd; 20l 11th ½way; t.o 12; pu 3 out*
	U		**Beths Gift** (5a) 20-1 **Miss B Williams** *5th when rfo bend app 2*
	P		**Bid For Tools (IRE)** 12-1 **G Barfoot-Saunt** *Bit bckwd; hld up & bhnd; 17l 10th ½way; t.o & pu 13*
[31²]	P		**Highland Pearl** (5a) 33-1 **J Barnes** *Hld up; 7l 6th ½way; wknd 13; t.o & pu 2 out*
[57F]	P		**Hobby De Beyssac (FR)** (12a) (bl) 4-5F **T Scudamore** *Tchd evens; hld up & wl bhnd til hdwy 8; 8l 7th ½way; qcknd & lft 2nd 13; rdn & ev ch 3 out; pu lame aft 2 out; broke pelvis; dead*
	P		**John Robin** 20-1 **M Sweetland** *2 handlers; swtng; unruly padd; mounted course; 2nd/3rd til 6l 5th 13; lft 3rd nxt; wknd 15; sn eased; wl bhnd when pu 2 out*
	P		**Keldan Star (IRE)** 12-1 **T Vaughan** *Bit bckwd; a bhnd; mist 1; 14l 9th & drvn along ½way; t.o & pu 13*
	P		**Problematic** 4-1 **J Jukes** *5s-4s; bckwd; fractious in padd; ld to 7; chsd wnr 10 til blun 13; pu nxt*
[65P]	P		**Starmont** (bl) 50-1 **S Kidston** *Pulled hrd; prom; 5l 4th ½way; wknd qckly u.p 11; t.o & pu 14*
	P		**Summerbridge** 14-1 **N Mitchell** *Hld up; 12l 8th ½way; lost tch 11; t.o & pu 14*
[38U]	P		**Teelyna** (5a) (bl) 20-1 **G Marsh** *Jmpd v slow & rmdrs 1; wl bhnd when blun & smashed guardrail; sn t.o; pu 13*

OFFICIAL DISTANCE: dist **TIME:** 6min 25.6s
Fence 12 omitted - damaged

146 Open Maiden (Div 2), 12st   16 ran

	1		**KERRY GOLD MINE** 8-1 **Miss P Jones** *Tchd 10s; a.p; went 2nd 8; ld 11-13 & 14 til hdd aft 15; ld aft 2 out; comf*
	2	3	**Happy Team** (5a) 3-1 **David Dennis** *Lw; hld up; stdy hdwy & 7l 5th ½way; went 2nd 13; rdn to ld 3 out; hdd aft 2 out; one pce*
	3	2	**Kingsbridge (IRE)** 5-2F **T Mitchell** *Tchd 3s; lw; hld up & bhnd; 10l 8th ½way; hdwy 11; mist 12; 6l 7th nxt; smooth prog to ld on bit aft 15; hdd 3 out; rdn & ev ch 2 out; no ex*
	4	8	**Tedstone Fox** 40-1 **D Mansell** *Swtng; nt jw; hld up; 9l 7th ½way; mists 10 & 11; hdwy when hit 12; blun 14; ev ch 3 out; wknd u.p aft 2 out & eased*
	5	12	**La Tormenta (IRE)** (5a) 10-1 **N Harris** *Wl bhnd frm 6; 20l 13th ½way; hdwy 13; 12l 7th 15; one pce*
[30F]	P		**Brookthorpe** (5a) 33-1 **G Barfoot-Saunt** *Sn wl bhnd; t.o 6; pu 13*
	P		**Danny Dolittle (IRE)** 33-1 **R Pipe** (xnb) *Nov rdn; a bhnd; mist 2; 17l 11th ½way; 20l 9th 15; t.o & pu 3 out*
	U		**Humara (IRE)** (5a) 33-1 **T Greed** *Lw; chsd ldrs; pckd 3; 10l 6th when blun & ur 7*
[71³]	U		**Luney River** (5a) 8-1 **Miss L Gardner** *Hld up & bhnd; 13l 9th ½way; short-lived eff 11; 9l 10th when ur 13*
	P		**Merrie Jar (IRE)** 7-1 **T Vaughan** *12s-7s; ld 2-11; wknd & 5l 6th 15; pu & dism 3 out*
	P		**Murphys Mandarin** 5-1 **Miss P Gundry** *Nt fluent; ld to 2; 6l 4th ½way; went 2nd aft 12; ld 13 til hdd & mist 14; w ldrs when pu aft 15; lame*
[69P]	P		**Pachakutec (IRE)** 33-1 **R Woollacott** *Hld up; mist 9; 8l 6th & rmdrs ½way; wknd 13; t.o & pu 3 out*
	P		**Persian Dawn** (5a) 33-1 **A Holdsworth** *Sn wl bhnd; t.o 5; pu 11*
	P		**Talkalot (IRE)** 6-1 **F Hutsby** *10s-6s; pulled hrd; went 2nd 4 til aft 8; 5l 3rd ½way; 5l 6th & wkng when blun 13; hit 14; wl bhnd when pu 15*
	P		**Tiger Bell** 33-1 **Miss S Major** *Bhnd frm 8; 18l 12th ½way; t.o & pu 14*
	P		**Timber Top** (5a) 10-1 **D Alers-Hankey** *Hld up; 15l 10th ½way; lost tch 13; 17l 8th 15; t.o & pu 3 out*

OFFICIAL DISTANCES: 3l, 2l **TIME:** 6min 28.5s

147 Open Maiden (Div 3), 12st

12 ran

1		MAYBRIDGE LADY (5a) 5-4F N Mitchell *Opened 3s; lw; ww; hdwy 6; went 8l 2nd aft 8-10; lft 2nd 15; ld app 3 out; drew clr 2 out; comf*
2	15	Mr Robstee 8-1 J Jukes *Bckwd; swtng; a.p; went 8l 2nd 10; clsng when lft in ld 15; sn hdd; rdn & ev ch 3 out; wknd 2 out*
3	runin	Rosalee Royale (5a) 5-1 T Greed *Hld up; 15l 7th ½way; 19l 6th & no ch 13; went dist 3rd flat*
4	4	Rushaway 14-1 R Woollacott *(xnb) Ss; hld up; hdwy 6; 12l 5th ½way; went 13l 4th 13; no imp aft; went poor 3rd aft 15; dem flat; t.o*
5	25	Gunerkillinghurst 16-1 A Charles-Jones *2nd til aft 8; 10l 4th ½way; wknd & 14l 5th 13; t.o*
F		Forest Moss (IRE) (5a) 33-1 D I Turner *Lost plce & rmdrs 5; 17l 8th & rdn ½way; wl bhnd when fell hvly 12*
P		My Happy Lord 14-1 Miss V Nicholas *Hld up & bhnd; 21l 10th ½way; 25l 8th 13; t.o & pu 14*
P		Parsons Secret (5a) 12-1 T Vaughan *Rmdrs 2; mists; lost plce 5; sn drvn along; t.o 9; pu 11*
P		Piccadilly Wood 10-1 G Barfoot-Saunt *Bit bckwd; sn wl bhnd; t.o 8; pu 10*
P		Spirito (7a) 14-1 Jeremy Young *Jmpd lft; hld up & bhnd; hdwy & 14l 6th ½way; wknd qckly 11; t.o & pu 13*
P		The Greenkeeper (IRE) 13-2 C Heard *Hld up & pulled hrd; 18l 9th ½way; 20l 7th 13; went poor 4th app 3 out; t.o; pu 2 out*
P		Willsan 7-2 J Barnes *Tchd 9/2; lw; jmpd bold; ld; sn 8l clr to 13; blun & hdd 15; wknd qckly; t.o & pu 2 out (declared tongue-strap came off in padd)*

OFFICIAL DISTANCES: 15l, 25l **TIME:** 6min 27.1s

Warwick (LH 10F,20J)
Tue, 8 Feb (GOOD, GOOD to SOFT in places)

148 Air Wedding HC

7 ran

[10^F]	1		GUNNER WELBURN 12-02 1-2F B Pollock *Lw; jmpd sound; chsd clr ldr app 4; clsd 7; jnd ldr 10; ld 11; 5l clr 17; galloped on str aft*
	2	8	Hurricane Blake 11-09 20-1 J Young *Hld up; 16l 4th 10; hdwy to 11 2nd 14; hit nxt; rdn along & no imp on wnr*
[59^F]	3	22	Mr Motivator 11-13 20-1 T Scudamore *Ld; 12l clr 4; jnd 10; hdd 11; cl 3rd 14; rdn & sn wknd*
[5³]	4	28	Strong Chairman (IRE) 11-09 11-4 S Waley-Cohen *Chsd clng ldr pr; 15l 3rd 10; clsd 11 til jmpd slow 12; plodded on; t.o 14; rdn out for 4th*
	5	½	Grecian Lark 11-13 10-1 J Tarry *Hit 2; a toiling in rr & sn rdn; 20l 5th 10; t.o 14; lifeless*
	P		Manalesco (IRE) 11-09 100-1 S Graham *Bckwd; w ldr to 2; drpd to rr 4; t.o 8; fnce bhnd when pu 12*
	F		Pru's Profiles (IRE) 11-09 50-1 A Middleton *Fell 1*

TIME: 7min 7.0s **TOTE:** £1.50; places £1.60,£4.10 **Ex:** £8.90 **CSF:** £11.86

Chepstow (LH 11F,18J)
Wed, 9 Feb (SOFT, HEAVY in places)

149 Earthstoppers HC

12 ran

[19²]	1		ARDSTOWN 11-06 10-1 F Windsor Clive *Hdwy 5; 5th 8; 3rd & gng wl 14; jw aft; ld 3 out; drvn & qcknd clr aft last; impressive*
	2	12	Mr Dow Jones (IRE) 12-01 5-1 D O'Meara *Bhnd; 6th & hdwy 8; chsd ldrs frm 13; rdn nxt; staying on & disp 2nd but hld when lft chsng wnr last; outpcd*
[34⁶]	3	dist	Pontabula 11-12 25-1 A Charles-Jones *Jmpd slow 2; bhnd; detach 7th 8; no ch frm 13; lft rem 3rd at last*
	4	1¼	Rusty Fellow 11-08 20-1 T Stephenson *Wl bhnd; 10th 8; hdwy 11; no ch 14; running on stdly frm 3 out; t.o*
	5	4	Desperate 11-11 11-1 R Barrett *In tch; 3rd & eff 8; rdn to chse ldrs 12; 2nd 14; mist & wknd nxt; t.o*
	P		Apple John 11-13 33-1 Miss P Gundry *Ld at fast pce to 3; 10th & wkng rap 8; t.o & pu 12*
	P		Duchess Of Tubber (IRE) 11-03 66-1 Miss S Young *A bhnd; 11th 8; cont t.o; pu last*
[10¹]	P		Highway Lad 11-12 8-1 Julian Pritchard *Hdwy 6; 4th 8; wknd & pckd 11 (water); pu 12*
	P		Opera Fan (IRE) 12-01 5-1 Miss P Jones *Prom; 2nd 8; lost plce & blun 13; wknd nxt; 5th & no ch when pu 3 out*
	P		Pancho's Tango (IRE) 11-12 50-1 A Phillips *Prom early; sn bhnd; stpd to nil aft 7; t.o & pu 8*

| [4¹] | F | | **Rob Mine (IRE)** 11-08 7-4F S Sporborg *Ld 3; blun 15 & rdn; hdd nxt; disp tired 2nd & hld when fell last* |
| [33⁶] | F | | **Saffron Moss** 11-08 25-1 M Nicolls *Mists; a bhnd; hit 4 & 5; sn rdn; 8th & strugg 8; t.o when fell 15* |

TIME: 6min 47.2s **TOTE:** £8.60; places £2.10,£2.50,£3.10 **Ex:** £45.90 **CSF:** £50.19 **Tri:** £190.30

Ludlow (LH 8F,19J)
Wed, 9 Feb (GOOD to FIRM, GOOD in places)

150 Weatherbys Hunter Chase Planner HC   10 ran

[17¹]	1		**SECRET BAY** 12-07 4-9F B Pollock *Lw; prom & gng wl; 2nd 10; ld app 12; 4l clr 16; stayed on wl*
[34⁸]	2	6	**Shafi (IRE)** 11-07 12-1 D Mansell *Bit bckwd; drpd out last; stdy hdwy 12; chsd wnr 3 out; rdn & no imp when hit last*
	3	17	**Highway Five (IRE)** 11-07 66-1 D Dennis *Bit bckwd; sn pushed along in rr; clsd in 5l 6th 12; 3rd, rdn & wl outpcd 15; releg poor 5th; plodded on agn flat*
	4	2½	**Silverdalesureshot** 12-02 13-2 R Burton *Unclipped & rough; bit bckwd; hmpd start; bhnd; hdwy 11 to 3l 4th 12; wknd nxt; easy rn*
[33³]	5	1	**The Whole Hog (IRE)** 11-11 33-1 A Evans *Mist 2 (water); prom; 2l 3rd 12; went 2nd aft 15; sn ev ch & rdn; dem & wknd 3 out*
	6	2½	**Hee's A Dancer** 12-00 8-1 C Williams *Bit bckwd; chsd ldrs; ld brief 6; ld agn 8 til app 12; wknd aft 15*
[61⁸]	7	dist	**Manamour** 11-11 66-1 T Scudamore *Ld; 6l clr 2; made nrly all to 8; wknd qckly 12; t.o 16*
[79⁸]	U		**Characteristic** 11-11 20-1 A Wintle *Veered lft & ur start*
	U		**Miss Pennyhill (IRE)** 11-06 33-1 T Doyle *Cl up; jnd ldr & blun 5; 4l 5th when stumbled aft 11; wknd when ur 12*
[76⁴]	P		**Tellaporky** 11-07 50-1 J Owen (xnb) *Mists; sn rr & gng poor; t.o & pu aft 11*

TIME: 6min 20.6s **TOTE:** £1.60; places £1.30,£1.50,£15.90 **Ex:** £9.00 **CSF:** £5.74

Huntingdon (RH 9F,19J)
Thu, 10 Feb (SOFT)

151 Mascot Grand National Nov HC   12 ran

	1		**MIGHTY MOSS (IRE)** 11-09 11-10F F Hutsby *Ld to 3; w ldrs til ld agn 12; cantering frm 2 out; clr last; impressive*
[26¹]	2	3½	**My Shout** 12-00 7-4 B Pollock *Lw; ld 4-8; ld 10-12; drvn & ev ch bef when lft clr 2nd 2 out; kpt on but no match for wnr*
[18¹]	3	3	**Mr Freebie (DEN)** 11-09 12-1 N Bloom (xnb) *Hld up & bhnd; hdwy to trck ldrs 13; outpcd 16; hmpd 2 out; rallied & kpt on game aft last*
[17⁶]	4	1¼	**Pangeran (USA)** 11-11 25-1 N King *Lw; sn prom; ld 8-10; rdn & ev ch bef 2 out; nt qckn*
	5	29	**Danegeld (IRE)** 11-11 33-1 C Ward-Thomas *Prom til outpcd 13; 6th when hit 15; sn wl bhnd*
[83⁸]	6	dist	**John Tufty** 11-07 66-1 Miss R Illman *Jmpd slow 3; rr when hmpd 8; mists 12 & 14 (water); t.o aft*
	F		**Alston Antics** 11-07 25-1 D Flavin *Trckd ldrs; hit 13; eff 3 out; disp 2nd & ev ch when fell nxt; dead*
	P		**Butchers Minstrel** 11-07 50-1 D Mansell *Chsd ldrs; outpcd in 7th when pu 16; bbv*
[16⁸]	F		**Coogee Bill (IRE)** 11-11 33-1 A Wintle *Fell hvly 2*
[29³]	P		**Going Around** 11-07 66-1 M Gingell *Rr of bunch; strugg 12; t.o & pu 15*
[87¹]	P		**Peacemaker (IRE)** 11-07 50-1 J Cornwall *Prom til lost plce & mist 10; t.o & pu 2 out*
	U		**Raphael Bodine (IRE)** 11-11 15-2 Miss S Vickery *Tk keen hld; hld up trckng ldrs; pckd 8; blun & ur 11*

TIME: 6min 39.5s **TOTE:** £2.70; places £2.20,£1.10,£1.20 **Ex:** £5.20 **CSF:** £3.03 **Tri:** £14.20

Wincanton (RH 9F,19J)
Thu, 10 Feb (GOOD to SOFT, SOFT in places)

152 Somerset HC   7 ran

| [26²] | 1 | | **PRINCE BUCK (IRE)** 12-03 100-30 B Hitchcott *Ld 5-12; ld brief 15; drvn & ld agn 3 out; lft clr nxt & r.o wl* |
| [34³] | 2 | 12 | **Chasing The Bride** 11-13 5-2F M Miller *Cl up til lost plce 13; 8l 5th 16; rallied app 3 out; sn ev ch; 3rd & btn when blun bad nxt; 2nd agn last* |

	3	dist	**Madam Sioux (IRE)** 11-04 12-1 **T Dennis** *Set slow pce to 5; ld agn 12-15; ld brief nxt; wknd qckly app 3 out; blun nxt*
[10²]		P	**Chism (IRE)** 12-02 (vis) 8-1 **R Walford** *Trckd ldrs; 4th & rdn 13; wknd app 16; no ch when hmpd bad 3 out; pu 4*
[59²]		P	**Noyan** 12-03 13-2 **P York** *Hit 3; hld up; hdwy 11; rdn nxt; lost tch & mist 15; t.o & pu 3 out*
		P	**Punters Overhead (IRE)** 12-07 100-30 **T Mitchell** *Pu aft 1; lame*
		F	**Thinking Twice (USA)** 11-09 14-1 **Jeremy Young** *Hld up; hdwy 13; 4l 4th & rdn when fell 3 out*

TIME: 7min 22.8s **TOTE:** £4.40; places £2.20,£2.80 **Ex:** £12.60 **CSF:** £11.30
Water jump omitted on both circuits due to low sun

Bangor (LH 9F,15J)
Fri, 11 Feb (GOOD to SOFT, SOFT in places)

153 Gilbert Cotton Mem HC   9 ran

	1		**BELLS LIFE (IRE)** 12-07 4-5F **P Flynn** *Declined suicidal early pce; rr til clsd 6; chall 11; ld app 2 out; sn wl clr; canter*
	2	28	**Late Encounter** 12-04 16-1 **A Wintle** *Ldng trio; ld 5-6 & aft 9-12; ld 3 out til app nxt; rdn & no ch w wnr aft*
[9⁴]	3	25	**Mr Golightly** 12-02 16-1 **Mrs J Reed** *Set fast pce to 4; drpd rap to rr 6; mist 8 (water); sn t.o; plugged into 3rd game at last*
	4	16	**Desert Calm (IRE)** 12-04 14-1 **D Alers-Hankey** *Prom; ld 6-9 & 12-3 out; wknd rap; fin tired; t.o*
		P	**Ivy Boy (IRE)** 12-00 11-4 **D Mansell** *In tch to 6; sn drvn along; t.o & pu 10*
		P	**My Nominee** 12-02 (bl) 25-1 **R Burton** *Ld 4-5; 4th nxt; strugg aft 9; t.o & pu 3 out*
		P	**Not My Line (IRE)** 12-00 40-1 **M Foley** *Blun & nrly ur 1; nt rec; poor last til pu 6*
		P	**Private Jet (IRE)** 11-07 (bl) 50-1 **R Clark** *(xnb) Prom; 3rd 6; drvn & outpcd when hit 9; sn poor 4th; clambered 3 out & pu*
[34ᴾ]		P	**Savuti (IRE)** 12-00 100-1 **M Nicolls** *Bit bckwd; towards rr; mist 4; hrd rdn 8; sn t.o; pu 10*

TIME: 5min 55.2s **TOTE:** £1.70; places £1.60,£1.60,£1.20 **Ex:** £9.20 **CSF:** £12.01 **Tri:** £34.10

Newbury (LH 11F,18J)
Fri, 11 Feb (GOOD to SOFT)

154 Charles Higgins Mem HC   10 ran

	1		**MARCHING MARQUIS (IRE)** 11-11 5-1 **T Gibney** *Made nrly all; hdd brief 15; hrd rdn last; hld on game*
[61⁴]	2	¾	**Skip'n'time** 11-11 6-4F **M Miller** *Hld up; hdwy 7; lost plce 11; rallied nxt; chsd ldrs 15; rdn to chall last; kpt on; nt qckn nr fin*
[9ᵖ]	3	26	**Abit More Business (IRE)** 11-05 (bl) 12-1 **Miss P Gundry** *In tch; chsd ldrs 8; went 2nd 12; chall 15; w wnr nxt; wknd 2 out; lft poor 3rd & hmpd last*
	4	11	**Hall's Mill (IRE)** 11-02 7-1 **A Charles-Jones** *Chsd ldrs; hit 2; wknd 13; 5th & no ch when hmpd bad 14*
[25ᴾ]	5	dist	**Royal Arctic (IRE)** 10-12 50-1 **R Barrett** *Bhnd when jmpd slow 9; sn wknd; t.o*
[34¹]		P	**Formal Invitation (IRE)** 11-11 4-1 **S Joynes** *A bhnd; drvn & strugg 13; t.o & pu 15*
[94²]		P	**Freedom Fighter** 11-03 16-1 **A Martin** *Bhnd; blun 12; no ch aft; t.o & pu 2 out*
		F	**Six Clerks (IRE)** 10-12 66-1 **J Young** *Hld up in rr; hdwy & hit 10; chsd ldrs 12; ld 15; sn hdd; 3rd & btn when fell last*
		U	**Time Enough (IRE)** 11-10 (1) 25-1 **P Townsley** *Chsd ldrs; eff 7; cl 3rd 13; 5th & wkng when blun & ur nxt*
[59ᴾ]		F	**Tomcappagh (IRE)** 11-03 20-1 **B Hitchcott** *In tch when fell 5*

TIME: 6min 19.4s **TOTE:** £5.90; places £1.80,£1.10,£3.20 **Ex:** £13.20 **CSF:** £11.76 **Tri:** £170.14

Catterick (LH 8F,21J)
Sat, 12 Feb (GOOD)

155 Moulton HC   8 ran

| | 1 | | **TRADE DISPUTE (IRE)** 12-00 4-6F **G Tuer** *2nd/3rd til lft in ld 15; stayed on str frm 3 out; clr last; canter* |
| | 2 | 6 | **Gymcrak Tiger (IRE)** 11-07 40-1 **R Clark** *Tk keen hld; prom; ld 14 til pckd bad nxt; kpt on but no ch wnr aft 2 out* |

	3	8	**Overflowing River (IRE)** 11-11 9-2 **T Glass** *Trckd ldrs; rdn 17; outpcd aft nxt; 5th 2 out; kpt on to 3rd flat*
	4	1	**Ensign Ewart (IRE)** 12-04 6-1 **C Storey** *In tch; rdn & lost plce 13; rallied nxt; hit 15; 5l 5th aft 18; outpcd app 3 out*
[89⁵]	5	10	**Titan Thai (IRE)** 12-04 (bl) 14-1 **N Wilson** *Hld up & bhnd; lost tch 15; plodded on*
	6	1½	**Dromhana (IRE)** 11-07 20-1 **Miss J Wormall** *Ld to 14; cl up til lost 2nd & rdn 3 out; btn nxt*
	7	dist	**Mr Primetime** 11-07 66-1 **Miss A Armitage** *Jb; blun & nrly ur 4; hit 5; mist 7; blun 8; in tch til blun 14; sn btn; t.o 18; blun last; virt pu*
	P		**The Crooked Oak** 11-07 25-1 **G Thomas** *Mists; jmpd slow 6; sn bhnd; lsng tch when pu & dism aft 11*

TIME: 7min 48.0s **TOTE:** £1.60; places £1.40, £8.20, £1.50 **Ex:** £49.70 **CSF:** £31.37 **Tri:** £50.90

Haydock (LH 9F, 18J)
Sat, 12 Feb (HEAVY)

156 Walrus HC   **12 ran**

	1		**IT'S HIMSELF** 12-00 (tt) 10-1 **A J Martin** *Stdd start; tk keen hld; blun 1; mists; wl bhnd; blun 12; hmpd bad nxt; jmpd lft 14; 16l 4th app 3 out; relentless prog aft; jb lft 2 out & veered rt; stayed on to ld sn aft last; drew clr; impressive*
[32²]	2	9	**Cavalero** 12-04 14-1 **A Charles-Jones** *Hld up; mist 2; 5th & hdwy 10; hmpd & lost plce 13; releg 4th 2 out; rallied game u.p to tk poor 2nd flat*
[42ᶠ]	3	4	**Jigtime** 12-02 7-1 **M Bradburne** *Prom; lft 2nd 13; blun 3 out & outpcd; rdn & rallied w ev ch last; sn outpcd; collapsed & died*
	4	½	**Castle Mane (IRE)** 12-07 30-100F **B Pollock** *Ld at fast pce; stumbled & pckd bad 4; hit 7; hdd aft 10; ld 12; pckd 14; 3l ahd & lkd ab to draw clr app 3 out; hdd & wknd flat; v injudicious tactics*
[59¹]	5	20	**Forest Fountain (IRE)** 11-11 25-1 **Julian Pritchard** *A bhnd; 10th aft 10; no ch frm 14*
[90²]	6	28	**Carley Lad (IRE)** 12-00 (tt) 16-1 **L McGrath** *Hld up; hit 7; 7th aft 10; mist 12; hmpd bad 13; blun nxt; nd aft; t.o*
	7	2½	**Fiscal Policy** 11-07 66-1 **R Trotter** *Chsd ldrs; rdn aft 5; mist 9; 8th aft nxt; wknd 11; impeded 13; t.o nxt*
[90³]	8	dist	**Dry Hill Lad** 11-11 33-1 **N Kent** *Cl up; 6th aft 10; hmpd 13; wkng when hit 14; mist nxt; sn t.o*
	9	3½	**The Big Fella (IRE)** 11-07 66-1 **D Sherlock** *Bhnd; 11th when blun bad 10 (water); sn t.o*
	F		**Henry Bruce** 11-11 (bl) 25-1 **D Mansell** *Midfield; hdwy 9; 4th aft 10; cl 4th when fell 13*
[9¹]	F		**Knight Of Passion** 12-04 16-1 **M Miller** *Chsd ldr; ld aft 10; hdd & hit 12; w ldr when fell 13*
	P		**Whitby** 11-13 66-1 **C Mulhall** *Last when mist 5; t.o when nrly ref 11 & pu*

TIME: 7min 4.2s **TOTE:** £9.50; places £2.10, £2.00, £2.30 **Ex:** £198.90 **CSF:** £120.42 **Tri:** £433.40

East Cornwall
Great Trethew (RH 7F, 19J) Sat, 12 Feb (SOFT/HEAVY becoming HOLDING)

157 Hunt, 12st   **8 ran**

	1		**FOSSY BEAR** (5a) 10-11F **Miss S Young** *Opened 1/2; oht; trckd ldr til ld on inner 3 out; kpt on; easy*
	2	28	**Ledburian** 5-1 **S Craddock** *7s-5s; prom; hmpd 4; in tch til rdn & wknd 15; last & no ch frm 3 out; walked in; fin 3rd; promoted to 2nd*
	2d		**Pillmere Lad** 33-1 **Miss A Barnett** *Bckwd; ld; jmpd lft; mist 11; hdd 3 out; tired & btn when mist last; walked in; fin 20l 2nd; disq - nt weigh-in*
	F		**Border Rose** (5a) 6-1 **Mrs W Doyne-Ditmas** *3rd when fell 4*
	P		**Bridge House Boy** 4-1 **A Oliver** *(xnb) Bckwd; in tch; hit 11; wknd 14; btn 4th when pu 3 out*
	P		**Linton** (5a) 25-1 **W Smith** *Bhnd frm 7; sn t.o; 2 fnces adrift when pu 16*
	r		**Moorland Rose** (12a) 66-1 **Miss D Mitchell** *Ref 1 (twice); cont without jmpng; ref 2*
	P		**Sonnenski** 25-1 **Miss J Weeks** *Bckwd; nov rdn; hmpd 1 & sn bhnd; t.o 6 til pu 13*

OFFICIAL DISTANCES: Originally 10l, 7l. **TIME:** 6min 44.0s
Pillmere Lad finished 2nd, but was disqualified as the rider failed to weigh-in - she was fined £50

158 Confined Maiden (Div 1), 12st   9 ran

	1		**FRANKLY FEAR** 2-1F **J Young** *Lw; hld up in tch; jmpd lft 11; cl 4th 13; stdy hdwy to ld aft 3 out; tkn wide for btr ground; in comm when hit last*
	2	2½	**Alpine Castle (IRE)** (5a) 9-4 **Miss S Young** *(b4) Bit bckwd; ld; jnd 8 til slt ld 3 out; sn hdd outpcd; kpt on one pce*
	3	20	**Saucy's Wolf** 8-1 **Jeremy Young** *Bit bckwd; chsd ldr til disp ld 8; rdn & hdd 16; no ex frm 3 out*
[73F]	U		**Cherry Pie** (5a) 5-1 **Mrs M Hand** *Blun & ur 1*
	U		**Frankie Moneybags** 9-1 **T Dennis** *(xnb) Tk keen hld; wl in tch; 3rd 11; slt ld when pckd 13; ur some way aft; will improve*
	P		**Horton** 50-1 **W Smith** *Bckwd; bhnd til pu 12*
	R		**Jo's Wedding** 33-1 **Miss S Gaisford** *Swtng; pulling; missed marker aft 2*
	R		**Patrio (IRE)** (5a) 50-1 **J Cole** *Missed marker aft 2; cont without rtrcng & steered erratic; hmpd 11; to nxt; pu 16*
	P		**Thornbird** (5a) 12-1 **C Heard** *Mist 4; in tch; mist 10; 5th when blun 12; pu nxt*

OFFICIAL DISTANCES: 2l, dist   TIME: 7min 07.0s
The connections of Horton were cautioned for being very late in paddock

159 Confined Maiden (Div 2), 12st   12 ran

	1		**SOLOMANS SISTER** (5a) 4-1 **Mrs M Hand** *Bit bckwd; prom til disp aft 11; ld 3 out; stayed on str*
	2	1½	**Lydford Castle** 4-5F **C Heard** *Bit bckwd; opened 4/6,tchd 10/11; handy; disp aft 11-3 out; rdn & kpt on; btr for tce*
	3	2fncs	**The Ugly Duckling** 20-1 **R Woollacott** *Settled 5th; 3rd frm ½way; lost tch 16*
	F		**Baldhu Jay Arr** 12-1 **A Ede** *Midfield; 8th when fell 12*
	P		**Call Me Dickins** (tt) 33-1 **Miss A Barnett** *Bckwd; prom til wknd qckly 9; to & pu 13*
	P		**Classic Mistress** (5a) 6-1 **Richard Darke** *Lost ground frm 8; rr when pu 12*
	P		**Golden Sunset** (5a) 50-1 **Miss D Mitchell** *Bhnd frm 8 til pu 13*
	F		**Inlight** 20-1 **W Smith** *Scruffy; last when fell 3*
[106U]	P		**King Tudor** 16-1 **S Kidston** *Bit bckwd; 4th 12; in tch til wknd 14; btn 4th when pu 3 out*
	F		**No Need For Alarm** (12a) 4-1 **J Young** *Hld up & pulling; blun bad 4; hdwy to ld 9; fell 11; do btr*
[72P]	P		**Sparties Image** (5a) 33-1 **A Michael** *Bckwd; slt ld frm 5-9; wknd; jmpd lft 13; 5th when pu 14; may improve*
	P		**Woodys Widget** (12a) 25-1 **Miss K Baily** *Ld & jmpd lft til bad mist 5; lost ground stdly frm 10; 6th when pu 12; school*

OFFICIAL DISTANCES: ½l, dist   TIME: 6min 54.0s

160 Mens Open, 12st   6 ran

[106]	1		**THE HOBBIT (IRE)** 9-4 **T Mitchell** *Lw; hdwy 12; slt ld 15; pushed clr app last; stayed on wl*
	2	2	**Bitran** (7x) 11-2 **T Greed** *Slt ld 10 til hdd 15; stayed on dour aft 3 out; ev ch til no ex app last*
	3	1½fs	**Cool Clown** 4-1 **B Trickey** *6s-4s; lw; ld/disp; mist 5; prom til mist 11; lost tch 14; kpt on one pce; bad mist last*
[1002]	R		**Baldhu Chance** 10-1 **A Ede** *Cl up/disp ld til slt ld 9; missed marker on bend bef nxt*
	P		**Rasta Man** 2-1F **K Heard** *(xnb) Bit bckwd; hld up; 4th 12; lost tch 14; btn 4th when pu 3 out*
[345]	P		**Shariakanndi (FR)** (bl) 4-1 **N Mitchell** *6s-4s; hit 3; on & off bit; cl 3rd 10; wknd & hit 13; reluct & lost plce qckly; bhnd when pu 16*

OFFICIAL DISTANCES: 2l, dist   TIME: 6min 45.0s

161 Ladies Open   8 ran

	1		**LAKEFIELD RAMBLER (IRE)** 6-4F **Miss P Gundry** *Lw; jw; ld frm 7; drew clr 15; shkn up app last; unchall*
[612]	2	15	**Blue Laws (IRE)** 5-2 **Miss C Tuffin** *Sn bhnd; mist 7; to 12; hdwy 14; went 20l 2nd 3 out; stayed on clsng stages; too much to do*
	3	15	**Saint Joseph** 3-1 **Miss S Young** *Sn rr; bhnd frm 11; tk rem 3rd 3 out*
	4	12	**Southern Flight** 11-2 **Miss J Cumings** *Lw; ld/disp to 7; prom til wknd 14; bhnd frm 16*
	P		**Elle Flavador** (5a) 33-1 **Miss S Vickery** *(xnb) Handy; 5th 10; wknd; 6th when pu 15*
	P		**Native Alliance (IRE)** 6-1 **Miss O Green** *Lw; prom; 2nd frm 12; wknd 15; eased; to & pu 2 out*
	P		**Roving Rebel** 50-1 **Miss T Cave** *Bit bckwd; to & pu 13*

P   **Schlepp (IRE)** (5a) 10-1 **Mrs M Hand** *Bit bckwd; prom to 12; lost ground 14; last when pu 15*

OFFICIAL DISTANCES: dist, 3l **TIME:** 6min 42.0s

162 Intermediate, 12st   11 ran

[37F]	1		**LONGMORE (IRE)** 3-1 **T Mitchell** *4s-3s; lw; midfield; 5th 12; 4th & rdn 3 out; disp 2nd & staying on when lft clr at last (won on fitness)*
[63P]	2	fence	**Young General** (bl) 16-1 **Miss P Gundry** *Lw; in tch; 5th & rdn 14; wl btn 3 out; lft rem 2nd & blun bad last; walked in*
	r		**Baby Whale (IRE)** (5a) 10-1 **Miss J Cumings** *Lw; ld til hdd 3 out; kpt on; disp 2nd but tired when impeded & ref last*
	P		**Edge Ahead (IRE)** 50-1 **Mrs E Coveney** *Lw; sn prom; cl 2nd 7; wknd 11; bhnd 14 til pu 3 out*
	P		**Jimmy The One (NZ)** 50-1 **C Heard** *Lw; rr; t.o & pu 11; school*
	P		**Lead Story (IRE)** 6-1 **Richard Darke** *Bit bckwd; in tch to 10; sn eased; pu 13; quiet rn*
[13¹]	r		**River Swilley (IRE)** evensF **R Walford** *Opened 2s in plce; lw; handy; went 2nd 15; ld 3 out; tired & wandering aft 2 out; slt ld but exhaust when ref last*
	r		**Robbie Bee** 16-1 **R Young** *Bit bckwd; 4th & hdwy 12; rdn 15; cl 4th 3 out; kpt on one pce; ref last; broke down*
[66P]	P		**Spartans Last** (12a) 100-1 **J Young** *2 handlers; bad mist & rdr lost irons 4; sn t.o; pu 11*
	P		**Track O' profit (IRE)** 50-1 **Miss S Young** *Bckwd; mist 4; prom to 10; bhnd when pu 15*
	P		**Valley's Choice** (5a) 20-1 **C White** *9th ½way; bhnd til pu 15*

OFFICIAL DISTANCE: dist **TIME:** 6min 56.0s

163 Restricted (Div 1), 12st - 17J   8 ran

	1		**SMACKWATER JACK (IRE)** 11-10F **R Walford** *Lw; sn prom; disp frm 13 til drew ahd aft 3 out; stayed on str*
	2	15	**Damiens Pride (IRE)** 14-1 **T Dennis** *Tchd 16s; cl 3rd 10; disp 14 til rdn 3 out; wl hld frm 2 out; v tired run-in*
[14³]	3	2	**River Gala (IRE)** 9-4 **T Mitchell** *Lw; made most to 13; wknd & no ch frm 15*
	P		**Cool Million** 20-1 **N Mitchell** *Sn rr; bhnd frm 7 til pu 14*
	P		**Lirkimalong** 25-1 **Miss S Young** *2 handlers; blun bad 4; in tch to 13; pu 15; quiet rn*
[6³]	P		**Rhyme And Chime** 3-1 **Miss S Vickery** *Tchd 7/2; tk keen hld; 4th & bad mist 12; rdn & lost tch 14; wl btn 4th when pu 3 out*
	P		**Shameless Lady** (5a) 25-1 **Richard Darke** *Bit bckwd; prom to 10; lost plce 12; 6th when pu 15*
[65U]	U		**Trooper Pippin** 50-1 **A Ede** *Last when blun & ur 4*

OFFICIAL DISTANCES: 8l, ½l **TIME:** 6min 57.0s
    Fences 11 & 18 omitted - fallen ridres

164 Restricted (Div 2), 12st   10 ran

	1		**BLAZING MIRACLE** (5a) 12-1 **Miss T Cave** *Jw; hld up; hdwy 14; 4th 16; eff & ld aft nxt; sn clr; stayed on wl*
	2	6	**Think Positive (IRE)** 12-1 **G Maundrell** *Lw; ld/disp early; cl 2nd & ev ch 15; no ex frm 2 out; gd eff*
	3	2	**Spruce** (5a) 20-1 **Mrs S Fell** *Nov rdn; prom; cl 3rd when mist 11; 5th 16; r.o stdly clsng stages; nt disg*
	4	1½	**Genereux** 13-2 **Miss P Gundry** *Handy til ld 13; hdd & rdn aft 3 out; sn no ex; btr for rce*
[38²]	5	2	**Sir Frosty** 9-2 **L Jefford** *Lw; hld up; gd hdwy 14; went 2nd & ev ch 3 out; wknd qckly 2 out*
	P		**Cash Man (IRE)** 11-8F **T Mitchell** *(xnb) Tchd 2s; lw; hld up & pulling; mist 4; hdwy to ld 9; hit 12; pu & dism qckly bef nxt; destroyed*
	P		**King Of Cairo** 50-1 **I Hambley** *(xnb) Bckwd; rr til pu 11*
	P		**Nearly Fair** (5a) 16-1 **T Greed** *(bf) Bckwd; 9th 10; bhnd frm 15 til pu 2 out*
	U		**Phartoomanny (IRE)** (5a) 16-1 **R Woollacott** *Cl 2nd/disp to 9; cl 4th when ur 14*
	F		**Rakaposhi Ryme (IRE)** (5a) 9-4 **Miss S Vickery** *4th when fell 11*

OFFICIAL DISTANCES: 1½l, ½l **TIME:** 6min 58.0s

165 Confined, 12st   9 ran

	1		**WESTCOUNTRY LAD** 6-1 **R Woollacott** *In tch; cl 4th 10; hdwy to ld 16; disp ld nxt & tkn wide for btr ground; staying on when lft clr 2 out*
[66⁴]	2	10	**Gypsy Gerry** (6x) 7-4F **T Clarkson** *Lw; nov rdn; rr; stdy prog to 3rd but lot to do 16; stayed on stdly; nt trble ldr; lft 2nd 2 out*
	F		**Baldhu Luckystrike** 20-1 **A Michael** *Ch ride; fell 1; rmtd; ref 2; cont; t.o til pu 6*
	P		**Cornish Hope** 33-1 **Miss S Young** *(xnb) Jmpd novicey; ld & rn green to 8; still in tch when pu 11; school*

[101⁶]	P	**Crownhill Cross** 100-1 **Miss O Green** *Bckwd; rr & strugg frm 11; scrambled over 13; pu 14*
	P	**Eserie De Cores (USA)** 12-1 **S Kidston** *Midfield; 6th 10; t.o & pu 14*
	F	**Hold Your Ranks** (7x) 9-4 **D McKenna** *Tchd 5/2; lw; 1st ride; rcd free; ld 8 til jnd 14; disp nxt & ev ch til fell 2 out*
	P	**Queen's Award (IRE)** 10-1 **S Craddock** *Bckwd; hit 8; 5th ½way; lost tch 15; btn 4th when pu 3 out*
	P	**Rice Point** 6-1 **C Heard** *(xnb) Bit bckwd; hdwy to 2nd 10; cl 3rd whn pu 15*

OFFICIAL DISTANCE: 8l TIME: 6min 59.0s
> *The rider of Gypsy Gerry was fined £50 for being unable to produce his Medical Record Book*

Badsworth
Wetherby (LH 8F,18J) Sun, 13 Feb (GOOD to SOFT)

166 Hunt   **4 ran**

	1		**KIND PRINCE** 6-4 **S Harris** *Cl 2nd to 5; ld frm nxt; 2l up 10-14; just ld 3 out; chall last; r.o str flat*
	2	4	**Asked To Leave** (5a) 4-6F **I Bennett** *Ld to 3; mist 5; 10l 3rd 6-9; cl 2nd to 14; pushed along to chall app last; one pce flat*
	3	2fncs	**Bex Boy (IRE)** 5-1 **Miss K Fletcher** *Prom; ld 4-5; rn v wide bend app 7; cl 3rd to 10; lsng tch 11; cl 2nd 12; poor 3rd 14; hunted home*
	4	3fncs	**Cold Harbour Icicle (U)** (5a,50ow) 33-1 **J Peace** *Sn bhnd; t.o 2; fnce adrift 5; hunted rnd*

OFFICIAL DISTANCES: 5l, dist TIME: 7min 39.0s

167 Open Maiden 56&7yo (Div 1), 12st   **14 ran**

[55³]	1		**ROMANTIC NATIVE (IRE)** 5-1 **C Mulhall** *Trckd ldrs early; went 4l 5th 12 til outpcd 15; 20l 4th 3 out; stayed on str; lft 6l 2nd 2 out; fin wl; ld flat; rdn out*
	2	2	**Square One (IRE)** (5a) 7-1 **J Docker** *Pulled to cl 3rd 3; prom to 10; 2l 2nd 11; disp ld 3 out; lft clr nxt; jnd flat; outrdn & hdd cl home*
	3	10	**Eddie Rombo** (7a) 10-1 **B Woodhouse** *Midfield to 9; hdwy to 4l 5th 12; outpcd 14; 22l 4th 3 out; lft 3rd 2 out; r.o one pce*
[51³]	4	8	**Lingham Lady** (5a) 3-1 **S Swiers** *Midfield to 10; 12l 7th 12; outpcd & wl bhnd 14; stayed on wl frm 3 out; fin v fast; sure to improve*
	5	2	**Hattie** (5a) 12-1 **C Denny** *Cl 2nd to 6; ld 7-10; outpcd 11; r.o one pce*
	F		**Desert Boot** (7a) 14-1 **B Wharfe** *Mid-div to 6; 8l 7th 8-10; rr by 11; lsng tch 13; t.o when fell 2 out*
	F		**Emperor Ross (IRE)** (7a) 5-1 **A Dalton** *Trckd ldrs early; 4l 5th 5-8; ld frm 10; gng wl in 3l ld & lkd wnr when fell 2 out*
	P		**Fryup Digital** (7a) 25-1 **P Halder** *Rr div to 10; lsng tch 13; t.o 14; pu last; school*
	P		**Gentleman Charles (IRE)** 12-1 **S Walker** *Pulled hrd early; 3l 3rd 5-8; wknd 9; rr 10; lsng tch when pu 3 out*
[73ᵖ]	F		**Iron Buck** 14-1 **G Brewer** *Bad mist 1; ld frm 4 til fell 6*
[51ᵖ]	P		**Jambo Bwana** 14-1 **P Millington** *A.p; 1l 2nd to 12; trckd ldng pr in 3rd to 14; wknd qckly 15; pu 2 out*
	F		**Meadowbank** 4-5F **M Watson** *Ld til fell 4*
	P		**Norman Way** (7a) 14-1 **P Cornforth** *Sn bhnd; jmpd slow 3; t.o 6; jmpd novicey til pu 13*
	P		**Young Saffy** 7-1 **A Pennock** *A rr; bhnd by 6; lsng tch 10; t.o 14; pu 2 out*

OFFICIAL DISTANCES: 1½l, 10l TIME: 7min 38.0s
> *Gun Runner was withdrawn not under orders - unseated and injured the rider in paddock*

168 Open Maiden 56&7yo (Div 2), 12st   **16 ran**

	1		**POLAR KING (IRE)** 2-1 **D Easterby** *Midfield to 5; went 6l 6th 9; clsd to 3l 3rd 11 til outpcd 13; 15l 3rd 14; stayed on wl frm 3 out; 1l 2nd at last; hrd rdn flat; hrd drvn to ld nr fin*
[40ᵖ]	2	1½	**Mr Bossman (IRE)** 5-1 **T Glass** *Prom to 9; went 1l 2nd 10-13; disp ld 14-3 out; ld nxt; 1l up last; hdd & outpcd cl home*
[55²]	3	20	**Madame La Claire** (5a) 6-4F **C Mulhall** *Handy 3rd to 9; ld 10-14; jnd 15 & disp til wknd 3 out; r.o one pce*

[124ᴾ]	4	runin	**Tuath Deuchainne** 33-1 **Miss R Pask** *Cl 2nd to 2; ld frm 3-9; wknd 10; t.o & rem by 14*
[139ᴾ]	U		**Ben From Ketton** (7a) 33-1 **S J Robinson** *Ur 1*
	F		**Colonels Hatch** 20-1 **Mrs K Diggle** *Last by 5; lsng tch 10; t.o when fell 12*
	F		**Elver Spring** 4-1 **A Dalton** *Fell 1*
	F		**Fiery Jack** 10-1 **N Tutty** *Fell 1*
	P		**Handsome Is** (IRE) (12a) 8-1 **G Brewer** *A rr div; pu 13*
[21⁹]	U		**Henavos** (5a) 16-1 **S Swiers** *A rr div; rem 5th & exhaust when climbed over 2 out & ur*
	P		**Imperial Line** (IRE) 20-1 **Miss T Jackson** *Trckd runaway ldr in 2l 2nd to 7; wknd 8; sn rr; t.o & pu 3 out*
	P		**Ingleby Jack** 12-1 **P Frank** *Chsd ldng pr in 4th to 8; 8l 4th 11 til mist 14; wknd qckly & pu 15*
[52ᶠ]	U		**Mandalay Man** (IRE) 12-1 **P Millington** *Mid-div til ur 9*
[137ᴾ]	U		**Mrs Drummond** (IRE) (5a) 20-1 **K Prendergast** *Mid-div when ur 5*
	U		**Never Wonder** (IRE) (7a) 6-1 **J Tate** *Midfield til ur 9*
	P		**The Other Eye** (IRE) 12-1 **S Walker** *Blkd bad 2; rr by 3; jmpd big; tkn gently in rr til tired & pu 15*

OFFICIAL DISTANCES: 1½l, dist   TIME: 7min 13.0s

169 Open Maiden 56&7yo (Div 3), 12st   17 ran

[51ᴾ]	1		**GUILSBOROUGH GORSE** (7a) 3-1 **G Brewer** *Midfield to 9; went 3l 3rd 11; cl 2nd 14; ld 2 out; sn clr; eased flat; impressive*
	2	5	**Gemolly** (IRE) (5a) 10-1 **C Mulhall** *Rr early; hdwy to 20l 5th 14; stayed on wl to 4th 3 out & 2nd at last; no ch w wnr*
[45ᴾ]	3	6	**Go Nomadic** 20-1 **P Atkinson** *Midfield to 14; 22l 6th 15; stayed on to 3rd at last; r.o str flat*
	4	8	**Redmire** (5a) 10-1 **A Pennock** *A rr div; r.o past btn horses*
[137ᴾ]	5	3	**The Hazel Harrier** (IRE) 6-1 **Miss A Deniel** *A towards rr; nd*
	6	1	**Playlord** 7-2 **J Docker** *Ld to 3 out; wknd rap app nxt; exhaust & coaxed home*
[31³]	7	10	**Jack Flash** 3-1 **A Dalton** *Nt jw; chsd ldr to 8; mist 9; 3l 3rd 11; mist 12; trckd ldr to 3 out; wkng when mist nxt*
	P		**Brave Man** 6-1 **N Wilson** *Prom to 9; disp ld frm 8 til pu app 10; lame*
	P		**Captain Oates** 10-1 **M Watson** *A rr; lsng tch & pu 11*
	U		**Curtainsatchopwell** (IRE) 5-2F **S Swiers** *(xnb) Ur 1*
	P		**Howsham** (5a) 10-1 **S Walker** *A rr; lost tch by 9; bhnd when pu 11*
	P		**Imps Way** (12a,1ow) 33-1 **L McGrath** *A bhnd; t.o & pu 11*
	F		**Joe Smoke** 12-1 **Mrs F Needham** *Fell 1*
[54ᶠ]	F		**Mighty Monarch** (IRE) 12-1 **P Millington** *Mid-div when fell 2*
	F		**Miss Gloria** (5a) 12-1 **S Charlton** *Midfield til fell 6*
	P		**New Yorker** (USA) (7a) 12-1 **A Phillips** *Trckd ldrs to 8; 5l 4th 9-14; wknd & pu nxt*
	U		**Port Valenska** (1ow) 14-1 **B Woodhouse** *Handy 3rd to 10; went 2l 2nd 11 til ur 13*

OFFICIAL DISTANCES: 6l, 6l   TIME: 7min 21.0s

170 Ladies Open   6 ran

[135¹]	1		**MONKEY AGO** 1-2F **Miss J Foster** *Made all; 3l up 14; 12l clr when lft virt solo 2 out; canter*
	2	runin	**Stride To Glory** (IRE) 20-1 **Mrs H Arnold** *Handy 3rd to 7; outpcd 8; rr 9; rem 4th 15; lft poor 2nd at last*
[90ᵁ]	P		**Gaelic Warrior** 20-1 **Miss Rachel Clark** *Cl 2nd to 9; 2l 2nd 10 til outpcd & lost tch 13; t.o & pu 14*
	U		**Staigue Fort** (IRE) 8-1 **Miss V Stubbs** *Sn bhnd; last 10; poor 5th when ur 14*
	r		**Take The Buckskin** 12-1 **Miss C Holliday** *Prom in 3rd til 2l 2nd 12; mist 14 & dem; wknd 3 out; lft 3rd when lft 2nd agn 2 out; exhaust & ref last*
[135ᵁ]	F		**Tudor Lodge** (IRE) (5a) 2-1 **Miss S Swindells** *Last til hdwy 10; went 15l 3rd 14; 12l 2nd & clsng when fell 2 out*

OFFICIAL DISTANCE: dist   TIME: 7min 16.0s

171 Mens Open   16 ran

	1		**CLASS OF NINETYTWO** (IRE) 12-1 **C Stockton** *Made all; stayed on dour when chall 2 out; clr at last*
[42⁴]	2	2	**Sunrise Sensation** 20-1 **C Denny** *Rr early; hdwy 7 to 3l 4th 11; 11l 2nd 14; trckd ldr til chall 2 out; wknd & one pce app last*

	3	3	**Jr-Kay (IRE)** 12-1 N Bannister *A.p; chsd ldr in 2l 2nd to 13; sltly outpcd 15; 3l 3rd 2 out; r.o one pce*
	4	5	**Concerto Collonges (FR)** 3-1 R Hartley *(xnb) Midfield to 6; 5l 5th 8; outpcd 13; 8l 5th & pushed along 14; stayed on to 4l 4th 2 out; wknd app last; btr for rce*
	5	20	**Allerbank** 10-1 T Greenway *Trckd ldng pr to 10; 2l 3rd 11; outpcd 13; 6l 4th 15; wknd 3 out*
	6	1½fs	**Orton House** 50-1 S Kelly *Last by 3; t.o 11; 2 fncs adrift 15*
[90F]	7	1½	**Shanballymore (IRE)** 50-1 R Owen *Imm outpcd; lost tch frm 5; t.o 13; hunted home 15*
	P		**Be Brave** (1ow) 20-1 R Lochman *In tch in mid-div til outpcd 11; t.o & pu 15*
	P		**Blue Wave (IRE)** 12-1 D Sherlock *Handy; 3l 3rd & mist 10; wknd & pu nxt*
[18]	U		**Gillone** 12-1 J Docker *Cl 2nd til ur 6*
[110P]	U		**Majority Major (IRE)** 20-1 T Glass *Midfield to 12; outpcd & wkng when ur 13*
	P		**Nishkina** 33-1 C Cundall *In tch in midfield to 6; 6l 7th 8; pushed along 11; outpcd & wknd 12; t.o & pu 13*
	P		**Repeat Offer** 20-1 N Tutty *(xnb) Midfield to 10; lsng tch & pushed along 12; t.o & pu 13*
	U		**Solba (USA)** 1-2F A Dalton *Ur 1*
[136³]	U		**Take Two** 50-1 S Pinder *In tch in mid-div til blun & nrly ur 6; stdly lost tch; t.o when ur 2 out*
	P		**The Shy Padre (IRE)** 50-1 J Townson *Chsd ldrs in 4/5th til wknd 12; bhnd when pu 14*

OFFICIAL DISTANCES: 2l, 4l **TIME:** 7min 11.0s

172 Marsh UK/TBA PPORA Club Members Mares, 12st   5 ran

[86¹]	1		**ARDEAL** (5a) 4-1 A Bealby *Made all; 10l clr 3-9; 11 up 3 out; qcknd clr app last; impressive*
	2	20	**Flip The Lid (IRE)** (5a) 14-1 N Tutty *Chsd ldr to 10; went handy 2nd 13; pushed along & outpcd nxt; stayed on; ev ch 3 out; sn outpcd agn; mist last*
	3	3	**Hiltonstown Lass (IRE)** (5a) 1-2F C Mulhall *Last early; hdwy frm 7 to 8l 4th 10; 11 2nd 14 til wknd & dem 3 out*
	P		**Catch The Pigeon** (5a) 4-1 S Swiers *Last 3-10; chsd up to 6l 4th 11; outpcd & wknd 14; t.o & pu 3 out*
	P		**Tiger Paws (IRE)** (5a) 20-1 A Gribbin *Prom in ldng trio to 8; 3l 3rd 9; last 11; lost tch 14; t.o & pu 2 out*

OFFICIAL DISTANCES: 20l, 2l **TIME:** 7min 14.0s

173 Restricted, 12st   17 ran

	1		**RUBON PRINCE (IRE)** 7-2 L McGrath *(bh) Midfield to 8; hdwy aft 10 to 2l 2nd 12; chsd ldr til ld 2 out; r.o wl u.p*
[138¹]	2	6	**Scruton** (5x) 3-1 D Easterby *Hld up in rr til hdwy aft 12; went 15l 4th 14; stayed on str to 2nd flat; too much to do*
	3	8	**Mr Mark (IRE)** (5x) 12-1 D Sherlock *Ld; 8l up 6-11; 2l up 13-3 out; wknd & hdd nxt; dem flat*
	4	20	**Teme Willow (IRE)** (5x) 8-1 M Hammond *Midfield to 7; went cl 2nd 11; 3l 3rd 12 til wknd 15*
	5	6	**Up And Over (IRE)** 14-1 Miss J Foster *Prom early; cl 2nd to 5; 10l 3rd 9; in tch til wknd 13; t.o 15*
	P		**Fair Farm Boy** (5x) 20-1 J Handley *Rr by 2; t.o 8; pu 15*
	P		**Flashlight** (5x) 16-1 P Halder *(bf) Prom to 7; wknd 9; rr & lsng tch when pu 12*
[54P]	P		**Joridi Le Forige (IRE)** (5x) 16-1 B Orde-Powlett *Sn bhnd; rr & lsng tch 7; t.o & pu 13*
	F		**Keep A Secret** (5x) 10-1 P Atkinson *(xnb) Last pr when fell 3*
	F		**Lynx Marine (IRE)** 20-1 N Kent *Mid-div til fell hvly 2; dead*
	P		**Maltese Cross (IRE)** (5x) 12-1 C Stockton *Midfield to 9; outpcd & wknd 11; t.o when pu 13*
[16⁹]	P		**Moor Lady** (5a,5x) 12-1 S Swiers *Midfield when bad mist 4; lost tch; pu 9*
	F		**Nouvalari (IRE)** (5x) 12-1 A Phillips *Fell 1*
	F		**Offley Lucielastic** (5a,5x) 10-1 A Dalton *Fell 1*
[50P]	P		**Primitive Charles** (5x) (bl) 6-1 G Brewer *Trckd ldrs; went 8l 2nd 7 til wknd 11; t.o & pu 15*
	B		**Red Spice** 14-1 R Owen *Rr by 7; t.o when bd 14*
[137²]	U		**Young Ardross** (5x) 2-1F Mrs F Needham *Mid-div to 10; went 15l 6th 12; stdy hdwy to 3l 2nd 3 out; ev ch when ur last*

OFFICIAL DISTANCES: 8l, 8l **TIME:** 7min 15.0s
Fences 10 & 18 omitted - fallen horse

Cambridge University Draghounds
Cottenham (RH 9F,19J) Sun, 13 Feb (GOOD)

174 Hunt
8 ran

[91⁴]	1		**SPRING WHEAT** (5a) (tt) 6-4F **T Lane** *Jmpd safe; sn 2nd; hit 9; ld app 13; clr nxt; drvn rt out*
	2	runin	**Aughnacloy Rose** 9-1 **R Page** *Bckwd; toiling in last by 5; t.o 10; plodded on to jn 3rd 2 out; went clr of him flat*
[88ᵁ]	3	6	**Classic Ms (IRE)** 12-1 **M Grange** *Sn labouring; 30l 5th 10; lft rem 2nd 16; jnd nxt til releg last flat*
[87ᴾ]	U		**Campbellhill (IRE)** 12-1 **M Mackley** *Nrly fell & ur 1*
	P		**Nuclear Beach** (7a) 2-1 **M Gingell** *5s-2s; v bckwd; v novicey & nd; disp 20l 3rd 10; nt pushed aft; pu 15*
[15ᴾ]	r		**Primrose Hill** (5a) 12-1 **M Barnard** *Sn chsng clr ldng pr; disp 20l 3rd 10; lft rem 2nd 15; ref nxt*
	P		**Speedy Snaps Pride** 7-1 **N Page** *Fat; sn toiling in rr; t.o 10; pu 2 out*
	r		**Wardy Hill** (5a) 14-1 **Miss L Marriott** *1st ride; ld by 10-15l til hit 10; hdd & nrly ur 13; poor 2nd & exhaust when wisely ref 15*

OFFICIAL DISTANCES: dist, 5l **TIME:** 6min 50.0s **TOTE:** £2.20 **DF:** £4.00

175 Intermediate, 12st
13 ran

[18ᶠ]	1		**LOCHNOMORE** 3-1 **R Burton** *Settled 3rd; lft in ld 10; outj challenger frm 14; 4l up 3 out; lft virt solo nxt*
	2	30	**Courier's Way (IRE)** (5x) 25-1 **P McAllister** *2nd/3rd; 7l 3rd 10; blun 12; in tch to 14; 20l 3rd & btn 3 out; lft 2nd nxt*
[15ᶠ]	3	2	**Ann's Ambition** 20-1 **Miss C Fryer** *Bhnd; 30l 6th 10; plugged on & lft rem 3rd 2 out; nt fluent 2nd last*
[83ᴾ]	4	30	**Nibble** 25-1 **G Cooper** *(xnb) Lw; midfield & sn nd; 27l 4th 10; fin fresh; nvr put in rce*
[116ᴾ]	5	4	**Neelisagin (IRE)** (tt) 33-1 **J Turcan** *Bhnd; 35l last 10; t.o 14*
	F		**Barnadown (IRE)** 33-1 **S R Andrews** *Lw; midfield til drpd dead on flat app 10*
[83ᴶ]	U		**Dry Highline (IRE)** (5x) 9-4 **C Ward-Thomas** *Lw; set fast pce & sn clr; 10l ahd when bad mist & ur 9*
[96ᴾ]	P		**Generous Deal** 33-1 **A Sansome** *Jb & nvr gng wl in rr; 28l 5th 10; t.o 14; pu 3 out*
	U		**Lunar Dancer** 33-1 **B Durrell** *Rr; rdr unsafe at 1 & 2; threw himself off 3*
	U		**Majestic Queen** (5a) 33-1 **P Piddington** *(xnb) Bckwd; oht; ss; jmpd v erratic in last; t.o 6; ur 9*
	P		**Sweet Talker (IRE)** 33-1 **N Bloom** *V bckwd; outpcd in rr; 31l 7th 10; t.o 14; pu 3 out*
	F		**Tell Tale (IRE)** 12-1 **T Bulgin** *5th when fell 7*
[83²]	F		**Tom De Savoie (IRE)** (5x) 11-10F **W Wales** *Lw; hld up early; lft 2nd aft 9; chsd wnr but nt fluent final circ; 4l down 3 out; no imp when fell nxt*

OFFICIAL DISTANCES: dist, 1½l **TIME:** 6min 22.0s **TOTE:** £3.90 **DF:** £1.70 (1st&any)
The stewards enquired into the fall on the flat of Barnadown; having interviewed the rider who explained that 'having been going well the horse suddenly collapsed' they found there were no grounds for any further action

176 Mens Open
8 ran

[17⁵]	1		**GENERAL ASSEMBLY (IRE)** 5-2 **N Bloom** *5s-5/2; settled trckng ldrs; 3rd & eff 13; ld gng best 3 out; drew clr aft nxt; rdly*
	2	15	**Bishops Hall** 5-2 **A Crow** *Nt fluent; ld 4-6; pckd 8; ld 14 til hdd & hit 3 out; wknd aft nxt*
[85³]	3	8	**Shake Five** (bl) 6-1 **S Sporborg** *Ld to 4; prom til ld aft 10-14; 4l 3rd 3 out; wknd qckly nxt*
[85ᴾ]	4	10	**Torus Spa (IRE)** 7-4F **A Sansome** *Hit 1; chsng group to 11; 4th 13; nt keen & sn btn; 17l 4th 3 out*
	5	runin	**Ardshuil** (1ow) 33-1 **S Pile** *(xnb) Fat; oht; 2 handlers; nt fluent; tk str hld; ld 6 til pckd 10; hdd & virt pulled himself up bef nxt; lost plce rap; t.o 14*
[83⁵]	U		**Cheryl's Lad (IRE)** (bl) 20-1 **J Henderson** *Jmpd slow 2; prom; 2nd 10; wkng when blun & ur 12*
[92ᴾ]	P		**Spaceage Gold** 33-1 **S R Andrews** *Last by 5; lost tch 7; t.o 10; pu 11*
[92ᴾ]	U		**Still In Business** 16-1 **A Ayers** *Rr div; 7th when rfo 3*

OFFICIAL DISTANCES: 10l, 5l **TIME:** 6min 29.0s **TOTE:** £3.10 **DF:** £3.20

177 Greig Middleton Ladies Open - 18J   10 ran

[95³]	1		**SPRING GALE (IRE)** 7-2 Miss Z Turner *Lw; ld in start; settled mid-div; 15l 5th 10; stdy prog 14; chall 3 out; ld app nxt; sn clr; easy*
[78³]	2	15	**Stretchit** 7-4 Miss T McCurrich *(xnb) Hld up trckng ldrs; 10l 4th 10; clsd to ld 13; jmpd slow 3 out; hdd & outpcd bef nxt*
	3	5	**Native Venture (IRE)** 13-8F Mrs E Coveney *V bckwd; ld 5-6; 2nd/3rd aft; w ldr 14-3 out; qckly blew up*
	4	7	**Tighter Budget (USA)** 14-1 Miss G Hutchinson *Jmpd slow 5; made most to 13; outpcd nxt; sn nd but plodded on*
	F		**Hersilia (IRE)** (5a) 10-1 Miss S Hopkins *Last pr & nvr in rce; 25l last 10; t.o 13; fell 2 out*
[95ᴾ]	P		**Lets Twist Again (IRE)** 33-1 Miss A Stennett *Still fat; prom; ld/disp 6-9; lost plce 13; hit nxt & sn rem; pu 3 out*
[94ᴾ]	F		**Mighty Merc** (tt) 33-1 Miss Carla Thomas *Sn last & outpcd; fell 7*
[82ᴾ]	S		**Mill O'The Rags (IRE)** 14-1 Mrs A Hays *Chsng ldrs when slpd up aft 7*
	P		**Paparazzo** 14-1 Mrs M Barlow *Sn bhnd; 22l 6th 10; t.o 13; pu 2 out*
[84²]	U		**Peanuts Pet** 12-1 Miss H Barnard *Jmpd slow 4; a bhnd; 23l 7th 10; t.o 13; hmpd & ur 2 out*

OFFICIAL DISTANCES: 15l, 5l TIME: 6min 19.0s TOTE: £4.60 DF: £11.70
Fence 16 omitted - fallen rider

178 Marsh UK/TBA PPORA Club Members Mares, 12st   11 ran

[15¹]	1		**SCARLETT O'HARA** (5a) evensF S Sporborg *Lw; nt a fluent; hld up in midfield; 7th 10; prog to 10l 4th & hld 8th app nxt; eff & nt rdn app nxt; drvn to chall flat; ld & sn clr*
	2	3	**Jacob's Wife** (5a,7ow) 7-4 A Crow *Ld to 3; mists 4 & 6; chsd ldrs; 6th 10; rallied 14 to ld nxt; went 4l clr 2 out; rdn & hdd aft last; fnd nil*
	3	4	**Moonstone (IRE)** (12a) 33-1 D Mansell *(xnb) Hld up & bhnd; 9th 10; gd prog nxt; went 3rd 15 & 2nd nxt; chall & ev ch 3 out; sn btn; rn wl*
[15⁵]	4	15	**Ballyquintet (IRE)** (5a) 25-1 N Bloom *Tk keen hld; ld 3-5; cl 5th 10; 2nd agn brief 14; wknd nxt; no ch 3 out*
[86ᴾ]	5	1	**Iberian (IRE)** (5a) 33-1 Miss J Grant *Handy; 5th 7; hdwy to ld 10-15; 8l 3rd & wkng when blun 3 out*
	6	2	**Insulate** (5a) 6-1 S March *Bckwd; prom; 4th 10; 6th & wkng 14*
	7	6	**Mai Point** (5a) 33-1 Miss C Grissell *(xnb) Prom; ld 7-10; cl up til 5th & wkng 14*
[32⁷]	8	12	**La Kabyle (FR)** (5a) 4-1 F Windsor Clive *V hvly rstrnd & lost 30l start; pulled hrd & nt jw; hdwy 7; 8th 10; eff 13; wknd nxt*
[77ᴾ]	P		**Artic Pearl (IRE)** (5a) 33-1 R Langley *A wl bhnd; 10th 10; t.o 13; pu 16*
	r		**I Don't Think So** (5a) (bl) 33-1 Miss H Pewter *Ld in start & reluct to set off; u.p aft 1; rap prog to ld 5-7; 3rd 10; wknd rap aft 13; t.o & ref 3 out*
	P		**Waisu** (5a) 33-1 M Grange *Dwelt; jmpd poor in rr; jmpd slow 7 & lost tch; t.o 8; rn v wide bef 10; pu 12*

OFFICIAL DISTANCES: 3l, 4l TIME: 6min 27.0s TOTE: £1.50 DF: £2.30

179 Restricted, 12st   16 ran

[38⁵]	1		**RISE TO IT (IRE)** 7-1 G Hanmer *Ld 3 til hmpd by loose horse 12; 2nd til ld agn 16; jmpd best & in comm aft 2 out; rdn out*
[21¹]	2	2	**The Red Boy (IRE)** 11-10F K Edmunds *Trckd ldrs; 6th 10 & 3rd 13; chsd wnr but outj frm 16; outpcd aft 2 out; rdn & rallied flat; stayed on*
[82⁴]	3	runin	**Premier First (IRE)** 33-1 W Pewter *Midfield early; rr 10; t.o 13; plodded on v slow*
[1·19ᴾ]	P		**Al Jawwal** (tt) 20-1 D Cook *Jmpd poor & nvr gng wl; mist 7; lost tch 10; t.o & pu 12*
	U		**Cill Chuillinn (IRE)** 10-1 Miss J Knight *Ur 3*
[50ᴾ]	P		**Dorgan** (5a) 20-1 A Sansome *Ld in start; prsd ldrs to 10; bhnd frm 13; t.o & pu 3 out*
[119ᴾ]	U		**Grove Victor (IRE)** 20-1 P Andrew *Bckwd; ur 2*
	P		**Mannagar (IRE)** 33-1 D Page (East Anglia) *Fat; svs; a wl bhnd; mist 7; t.o & pu 11*
	P		**Man Of Antrim (IRE)** 3-1 A Hickman *Chsd ldrs; 5th 9; wknd 12; 11th when pu 14*
	F		**Miss Mouse** (5a) 33-1 C Ward-Thomas *Sn 2nd; pckd 10; lft in ld 12-16; 8l 3rd & wkng 3 out; lft 3rd agn & no ch nxt; fell last*
[75⁵]	P		**Nearly A Beau** 9-4 D Mansell *Ld to 3; 4th 10; wknd 12; t.o & pu 15*
[87ᴾ]	P		**Oak House** 20-1 R Fowler *Sn pushed along; strugg 5; last when climbed 8; pu 9*
[16²]	F		**Rising Sap** 10-1 R Burton *Oht; chsd ldrs; 5th 13; 15l 5th & btn 3 out; fell nxt*
	U		**Stormy Words** 10-1 Miss E Garley *Oht; drpd out in last pr; gd prog frm 13; 14l 4th 3 out; 3rd & still trying to cl when mist & ur nxt*
	P		**Tommy O'Dwyer** 20-1 Mrs T Hill *Chsd ldrs; mist 4; wknd 13; t.o & pu 3 out*
	P		**Warner For Sport** 20-1 A Harvey *Oht; 2 handlers; mist 9; nvr btr frm midfield; t.o & pu 15*

OFFICIAL DISTANCES: 1½l, dist TIME: 6min 29.0s TOTE: £8.80 DF: £8.60

180 Open Maiden 56&7yo (Div 1), 2m4f, 12st - 15J   11 ran

1		**AGASSI'S ACE** 8-1 A Harvey *(xnb) Lw; hld up in midfield; 4th & prog 11; qcknd to ld app 2 out; lft clr flat*
2	8	**Manna Brave (IRE)** 8-1 C Ward-Thomas *Chsd ldrs; 5th & eff 3 out; drvn & stayed aft 2 out; went 2nd flat; no ch w wnr*
[87P] 3	2	**Cicero's Law (IRE)** 5-2 P Chinery *Hld up early; went 2nd aft 6; mist 7; ld 11-12; ev ch 3 out; rallied aft nxt; ch when rdr unbalanced & hung bad lft flat; nt rec*
[88P] 4	10	**County Derry** 6-1 A Sansome *Prom; ld aft 6; jmpd slow 9; hdd 11; ld 12 til rdn & hdd aft 3 out; blun bad nxt; nt rec*
5	30	**Lady Nevada (IRE)** (5a) 3-1 Miss S Hopkins *Bckwd; ld 3-6; sn lost plce; t.o 3 out*
P		**About Time (IRE)** 16-1 P Taiano *Bhnd; hmpd 5; mist 9; t.o aft; pu 2 out*
[124P] F		**Ali's Lark** (bl) 14-1 K Needham *Bckwd; ur gng down; 6th when fell 5*
P		**Golden Knight** 20-1 P Piddington *Fat; jb; sn t.o; pu 9*
[52U] P		**Miss Pink** (5a) 4-1 M Barnard *(xnb) Jmpd abysmal; a gng bad in rr; t.o 9; pu last*
F		**Sire De Brumetz (FR)** (7a) 14-1 G Pewter *Cl up til fell 3*
r		**T'nightsthenight** 5-2F C Barlow *Cl up; ld brief 6; ev ch til wknd rap 3 out; rem 5th when ref & collapsed last*

OFFICIAL DISTANCES: 3l, 1l TIME: 5min 03.0s TOTE: £28.40 DF: £17.70 (1st&any)

181 Open Maiden 56&7yo (Div 2), 2m4f, 12st - 13J   10 ran

1		**SMURF (IRE)** 8-1 N King *Hld up in tch; 7th 6; qcknd to ld app 10; 4l clr 12; gng best when lft wl clr 2 out; mist last*
2	20	**Senior Partner (IRE)** 14-1 S R Andrews *Tk keen hld in 3rd; lft 2nd 9; 12l 3rd & wkng 12; lft 2nd 2 out*
3	20	**Fruit Crop** (5a) 6-1 B Foster *Hld up & bhnd; 9th 6; lost tch 10; non-trier*
[53³] 4	20	**Sparebit** (5a) 8-1 S Morris *Cl up; 4th 6; wknd 9; 24l 4th 14; plodded on*
U		**Banteen** (5a) 16-1 C Ward-Thomas *Bckwd; 8th 6; no ch frm 10; rem 4th when blun & ur last*
U		**Daydreamer (USA)** 8-1 D Brightling *V fat; midfield; 6th 6; impd to 3rd 10 & 4l 2nd 12; 2l down but lkd hld when blun & ur 2 out*
[51P] P		**Fine Times** 14-1 M Mackley *Bckwd; prom; 5th 6; wknd nxt; t.o & pu 3 out*
[51P] P		**Intrepid Gal** (12a) 7-1 A Sansome *Jmpd v slow in last; rdn 6; t.o 7; pu 9*
[22²] R		**Le Cabro D'Or** 4-6F S Sporborg *Lw; 2 handlers; ld; rn v wide bef 6 & nrly lft track; veered rt & sn ld agn; rn out to boxes & ur app 11*
[23P] F		**Sidney Street** (bl,tt) 20-1 R Barr *Went 2nd 4-6; wknd 9; jmpd v slow 10; sn t.o & crawling fncs til fell 3 out; appalling rdng*

OFFICIAL DISTANCES: dist, dist TIME: 4min 59.0s TOTE: £7.00 DF: £14.60 (1st&any)
Fences 7 & 8 omitted - low sun; the stewards enquired in the running and riding of Fruit Crop who finished strongly under an apparently tender ride; the rider's explantion that the horse had been interfered with and sustained an injury was accepted

College Valley & N. Northumberland
Alnwick (LH 9F,18J) Sun, 13 Feb (GOOD with GOOD/SOFT patches)

182 Hunt, 12st   3 ran

[89¹²] 1		**TROPNEVAD** (2ow) (bl) 5-4JF B Lusted *6/4-5/4; trckd ldrs in 2nd/3rd; mist 5; just ld 7-8; disp cl 2nd 9; l1 2nd 14; ld & qcknd clr 3 out; lft clr nxt*
2	bad	**Valley Hopper** (7a) 5-4JF C Storey *Green; trckd ldr in 2nd/3rd til 3rd & outpcd bef 3 out; lft 12l 2nd nxt; tired & 20l down when fell last; rmtd & walked in; imm distm*
U		**Big Bark (IRE)** 5-2 H Norton *Ld; set sedate pce; just hdd brief 7-8; just ld 14 til hdd 3 out; 5l 2nd & btn when mist & ur nxt*

OFFICIAL DISTANCE: dist TIME: 6min 48.0s

183 Dodson & Horrell PPORA Club Members Confined, 12st   11 ran

1		**MINELLA GOLD (IRE)** 4-1 Miss M Bremner *A handy; 5l 6th 14; prog u.p to disp ld 3 out; lft clr at last*
2	15	**Tea Box (IRE)** 10-11F Miss P Robson *Lw; chsd ldrs; 3l 3rd 14; 6l 3rd app 2 out; nt pce to chall; btn when lft 2nd at last; btr for rce*
3	4	**Rum Rebel** (2ow) 2-1 J Walton *Oht; chsd ldrs; 2l 2nd 11; outpcd 15; 8l down aft; 15l 4th & btn 2 out; lft 3rd at last*
P		**Branch End** 8-1 F Arthur *Cl up; 6l 7th 5; 2l 2nd 12; disp ld app 15; wknd qckly aft nxt; pu last*

	P	**Buck Lady (IRE)** (5a) 6-1 **Mrs V Jackson** *Lw; a rr; 15l 7th 9; t.o 14; pu 3 out*
[41⁴]	F	**Houselope Beck** 8-1 **Miss C Hall** *A.p; 2l 3rd 9; disp ld 3 out til fell last; unlucky*
	P	**Lindon Run** 14-1 **R Morgan** *A rr; hmpd 2; pushed along 7 & sn lost tch; t.o 14; pu 3 out*
[43⁵]	P	**Poynder Park (IRE)** 6-1 **L Morgan** *Prom; 11 2nd 4; ld 8; 2l ahd 11; 1l up when reins snapped 13; jnd app 15; pu & dism nxt*
[43ᴾ]	F	**Primitive Way** 14-1 **P Maitland-Carew** *Lw; oht; prom til fell 2*
[108⁵]	P	**Thinkaboutthat (IRE)** 20-1 **J Muir** *Ld 2; 1l up 4; hdd 8; sn wknd; t.o & pu 3 out*
[108ᴾ]	P	**With Respect** 50-1 **Miss D Crole** *Jmpd slow; a rr; 20l last 3; t.o 5; fnce bhnd 7; pu aft 9*

OFFICIAL DISTANCES: 13l, 5l   **TIME:** 6min 29.0s

184 Restricted, 12st   11 ran

[44¹]	1		**QUARTERSTAFF** 6-4F **C Wilson** *Prom; 6l 3rd app 6; 3l 2nd 11; went 1l 2nd 13-14; ld app 3 out; jmpd awkward nxt; 2l up at last; r.o wl*
[40⁴]	2	3	**Blyth Brook** 3-1 **C Storey** *(xnb) A.p; 4l 4th app 7; 2l 2nd 8; 3l 3rd aft 12; ev ch 3 out; outpcd bef nxt; fin wl to tk 2nd flat*
	3	nk	**How Burn** 14-1 **Mrs V Jackson** *Rr til 8l 5th 9; 4th 11; ev ch 15; outpcd bef nxt; stayed on frm 2 out; fin wl*
[45¹]	4	1	**More Joy** 8-1 **S Bowden** *(bf) Trckd ldr; 4l 2nd 4; cl 3rd & mist 9; 2l 3rd app 3 out; ev ch til outpcd app last; releg flat; reported sore*
[40ᴾ]	5	25	**Harleidalus (IRE)** 20-1 **R Morgan** *Oht; a rr; sis; detach 2; 20l last 6; mist 10; wl bhnd 3 out; fin wl; improve*
	6	nk	**Madame Defarge** (5a) 7-1 **Mrs K Hargreave** *In tch towards rr; 12l 8th & outpcd when hit 10; 10l last aft 14; wl bhnd 3 out; fin wl*
[40ᴾ]	7	2	**Luvly Bubbly** 14-1 **Miss C Hall** *Mid-div; 6l 4th app 5; outpcd 15; wl bhnd nxt; hvly eased & releg 7th flat*
	8	dist	**Hopies Delight** 5-1 **J Ewart** *(bf) Hdstrng; set gd pce; 1l up 14; hdd app 3 out; kpt on; tired but ch when jmpd slow & ur last; rmtd; lame*
	P		**Dunnellie** (5a) 12-1 **A Robson** *Lw; oht; mid-div; 10l 7th & outpcd 15; wl bhnd & pu 3 out*
[39²]	P		**Kings Token** (2ow) 6-1 **J Walton** *Mid-div; 15l last & lost tch app 9; t.o & pu 12*
	P		**Solwaysands** 33-1 **S Hughes** *Mid-div; 8l 5th 9; lost tch 12; pu aft 14*

OFFICIAL DISTANCES: 4l, hd, 3l   **TIME:** 6min 31.0s

The stewards enquired into the riding of Hopies Delight; they fined the rider £150 for remounting after a fall at the last when the horse was lame

185 Ladies Open   7 ran

[41³]	1		**BALISTEROS (FR)** 4-1 **Mrs C Ford** *Chsd ldrs; 7l 5th 4; 3l 4th 14; ld & rmdr 3 out; ½l up nxt; hrd prssd til jmpd btr last; rdn clr*
[41¹]	2	2½	**La Riviera (IRE)** 7-4F **Miss P Robson** *Lw; in chsng bunch; 18l 6th 4; prog to 3l 3rd & pckd 10; mist 11; 2½l 3rd 14; ½l down 3 out; prsd ldr til slt mist last; hld flat*
[109²]	3	15	**Astrac Trio (USA)** 9-4 **Mrs A Hamilton** *Chsd ldrs; 16l 4th 4; cl up by 9; 4l 5th app 3 out; sn outpcd*
	4	2½	**Sudden Sally (IRE)** (5a) 7-1 **Mrs M Bremner** *Oht; tde; ld/disp early; hit 2; chsd ldr 3; jmpd slow 9; ld brief app 10 & aft 15; 4l 3rd & outpcd 2 out*
[41²]	5	½	**Pebble Beach (IRE)** (tt) 5-1 **Miss C Savell** *Ld/disp til ld 3; 5l up 6; narrow ld nxt til hdd aft 15; wknd*
	P		**Dear Do** 12-1 **Miss J Hedley** *Fat; chsd ldng pr; 10l 3rd 2; 15l 3rd 4; drpd back to 6l last 9; 15l last 14; t.o & pu 3 out*
[109⁵]	P		**Mullingar (IRE)** (bl) 25-1 **Mrs V Jackson** *Oht; resaddled start; rr; 15l last 3; 20l down nxt; hdwy 6; cl up 9; 5th & mist nxt; 10l down & outpcd 12; 12l 6th 14; wl bhnd 3 out; pu nxt*

OFFICIAL DISTANCES: 2l, 20l, 2l   **TIME:** 6min 26.0s

186 Mens Open   6 ran

[43⁸]	1		**EXCISE MAN** 4-1 **J Walton** *Mid-div; 8l 4th 5; jmpd slow nxt; releg last by 10; 8l 5th & rdn app 3 out; 4th nxt; disp 2l 2nd at last; ld flat; r.o wl; wl*
[107ᵁ]	2	½	**Cool Yule (IRE)** 3-1 **W Renwick** *Rn in snatches; 8l 5th & rdn 5; disp 6l 2nd nxt; 7l 4th 13; mist & outpcd nxt; 10l last app 3 out; hrd rdn & stayed on to disp 2l 2nd app last; r.o flat*
[110ᶠ]	3	½	**Charlieadams (IRE)** 9-4 **J Muir** *Ld; 6l ahd 9; 1l up 14-3 out; hdd aft last; just outpcd & dem app flat*
[49ᶠ]	4	15	**Running Free (IRE)** 3-1 **C Wilson** *Lw; oht; chsd ldrs; 8l 3rd 3; went 3l 2nd app 6; 10l 3rd 10; 11 2nd 14 til outpcd aft 3 out; wknd qckly; virt pu flat*

	P		**Galzig** 8-1 **L Morgan** Oht; 2nd mostly til 5l 3rd 12; outpcd aft 15; no ex nxt; sn wknd; pu 2 out
[108¹]	F		**Riverside Run (IRE)** 2-1F **A Robson** (xnb) Oht; hld up in rr; 10l last 3; 12l off pce 6; prog 10; shkn up 13; 6l 3rd app 15; 4th & ev ch when fell 2 out

OFFICIAL DISTANCES: ½l, ½l, 10l   **TIME:** 6min 39.0s

187 Open Maiden (Div 1), 12st   11 ran

[112ᶠ]	1		**SOLWAY DONAL (IRE)** (5a) 11-4 **T Davidson** 4s-11/4; mid-div til prog to 5l 2nd 13; 2½l app 3 out; ld agn 15; ld app 3 out; sn clr; mist last; wl rdn
	2	25	**Bold Navigator** 10-1 **Miss M Bremner** In tch; outpcd 12; 15l 3rd 15; kpt on; nd
	3	3	**Whiskey Galore** 8-1 **R Morgan** (xnb) Ld; 4l up 6; hdd 8; lft 5l clr aft 9; 2l up 15; hdd bef nxt; sn wknd; 15l 2nd 2 out; tired & jmpd slow last
	U		**Alizarine Blue** 14-1 **Miss L Kendall** Jmpd sticky; ld early; 4l up 6; hdd & mist 8; mid-div when mist & ur 11
	P		**Anotherhandyman** 10-1 **P Johnson** School in rr; 20l off pce 4; t.o & pu 11
[114ᵁ]	P		**Border Farmer (IRE)** 4-1 **Mrs V Jackson** Sis; prog 9 to 20l 3rd 13; outpcd aft nxt; rem 4th when hmpd by loose horse & pu 3 out
[46ᴾ]	U		**Cool Kevin** (bl) 10-1 **S Hughes** (bf) Prom; ld 8; 2l up when rn v wide to boxes aft 9; rr when hmpd bad & ur 11
	F		**Delwood** 14-1 **J Ewart** (xnb) Oht; prom early; 5l 3rd 4; mist & nrly up 8; outpcd 11; fell nxt
	U		**Eastlands Twilight** 2-1F **T Morrison** (bf) Fat; prom; mist & ur 2
	U		**Katjack (IRE)** 5-1 **L Morgan** (xnb) Lw; mid-div; blun & ur 9
	P		**River Rising** 3-1 **C Wilson** Prom brief; sn rr; t.o & pu 15

OFFICIAL DISTANCES: 25l, 3l   **TIME:** 6min 45.0s

188 Open Maiden (Div 2), 12st   13 ran

	1		**FLAMING SUNRISE** 10-1 **L Morgan** Ld/disp til lft in ld 11; 1l up 13; hdd 3 out; ld agn last; sn clr; eased cl home
	2	8	**Sunnycliff** (tt) 5-1 **C Storey** A.p; 1l 2nd 13; 1l up 3 out; hdd but ev ch when bad mist & nrly ur last
[45ᵁ]	3	3	**Dram Hurler (IRE)** 5-2F **R Morgan** Lw; rr; prog 13; 7l 4th 15; outpcd aft nxt
	4	2	**Wester Lad** 16-1 **A Richardson** Chsd ldrs; 8l 5th 9; 8l 4th aft 15; kpt on one pce; nd
[45³]	5	3	**The Other Half** 3-1 **Miss P Robson** Mid-div; outpcd 13; some prog til no ex 3 out; kpt on
[46³]	6	4	**Ben Buckley** 7-2 **W Renwick** Chsd ldrs; 3l 3rd 5; 2l 3rd 15; sn wknd
[39ᴾ]	7	1½fs	**Wylup** 20-1 **H Humble** 2 handlers; mid-div; 6l 4th 9; outpcd 12; t.o 14
	U		**Carrie's Gift** (bl) 20-1 **S Hughes** Fat; oht; rr til jmpd awkward & ur 3
	P		**Dere Street** 20-1 **Miss J Hedley** Lw; school in rr; t.o 6; hmpd bad by loose horse & pu app 7
[114ᵁ]	U		**Harleyburn** 12-1 **Mrs A Hamilton** Cl up when ur 6
	P		**House Of Oasis (IRE)** 14-1 **C Wilson** Oht; prom early; 2l 2nd 4; strugg 8; wl bhnd & pu 11
	F		**Lord Torridon (IRE)** 5-1 **Mrs V Jackson** Lw; ld/disp; ld & mist 7; 3l clr aft; jmpd slow 10; fell hvly 11
	P		**Mesling** (2ow) 10-1 **J Walton** Sn rr; jmpd slow 2; t.o; 30l down when hmpd bad by loose horse & pu app 7

OFFICIAL DISTANCES: 8l, 3l, 2l   **TIME:** 6min 42.0s

189 Open Maiden Mares, 12st   7 ran

	1		**NICKYS PERIL** (5a) 6-4JF **W Renwick** (xnb) 2s-6/4; lw; trckd ldr; 3l 2nd 6; ld aft 14; qcknd 4l clr app 15; 10l up app 3 out; 20l clr when mist nxt; unchall; eased flat
	2	25	**Setting Sail** (5a) 6-4JF **Miss P Robson** (xnb) 6s-6/4; chsd ldrs in 6l 5th til lost tch 12; stayed on stdly frm 15; 20l 2nd & no imp 2 out
[112ᴮ]	P		**D V's Delight** (5a) 12-1 **T Davidson** Ld; 10l up 4; 3l clr 6; blun & nrly up 9; pu aft
	P		**Fairy Bell** (5a) 25-1 **A Richardson** Fat; rr; mist 2; 20l 4th 4; last 10; outpcd 12; wl bhnd & tired when pu 3 out
	U		**Lewesdon Countess** (5a) 7-1 **Miss C Savell** Oht; sis; 10l off pce when mist & ur 10
[112ᶠ]	P		**Magical Poitin (IRE)** (5a) 9-4 **T Oates** Lw; rr early; 20l 4th 3; prog to 2l 3rd & mist 13; 4l 3rd 14; sn outpcd; wl bhnd & v tired when pu & dism 2 out
	P		**The Early Bird** (5a) 14-1 **D Reid** Cl up; ld aft 9-14; sn wknd; wl bhnd & tired when pu 3 out

OFFICIAL DISTANCE: dist   **TIME:** 6min 52.0s

Farmers Bloodhounds

Dunthrop (RH 8F,18J) Sun, 13 Feb (GOOD)

190 Hunt
5 ran

[79P]	1		**TITUS ANDRONICUS** 4-5F J Oldring Ld to 11; ld 12; went 4l clr 3 out; just hld on
[36P]	2	hd	**Perfect Finisher** 20-1 Miss A Melvin Swtng; 1st ride; hld up; 1½l 3rd ½way; outpcd 12; sn 7l adrift; eff 15; went 4l 2nd & nrly ur 3 out; 1½l 3rd nxt; r.o flat; just failed
[119⁶]	3	5	**Holmby Copse** 5-2 F Hutsby Swtng; lft 2nd 3; ld 11-12; mist 14; rdn & ev ch aft 2 out; no ex flat
	4	runin	**In Place (USA)** (1ow) 5-1 G Whisker 2 handlers; oht; jmpd lft; 2nd til mist 3; 2l 4th ½way; outpcd 12; 15l 4th 14; t.o
	P		**Connie Foley** 14-1 M Rodda Hld up; 7l 5th ½way; mist & lost tch 11; pu 12

OFFICIAL DISTANCES: nk, 4l **TIME:** 7min 04.8s

191 Confined, 12st
18 ran

	1		**TRUE STEEL** 20-1 J Trice-Rolph Mounted course; ww; bhnd til stdy hdwy 8; 7l 8th ½way; 4l 5th 12; outpcd 14; went 7l 3rd 3 out; rdn to ld flat; stayed on wl
[50¹]	2	2	**Irisheyesaresmilin (IRE)** 10-11F B Pollock Hld up; 5l 7th ½way; went 2l 4th 12 & 2nd nxt; ld 14-15 & 2 out til hdd & no ex flat
[74U]	3	3½	**Over The Master (IRE)** (3x) 8-1 D Barlow A.p; 2l 4th ½way; went 2nd aft 11-13; ld 15-2 out; no ex flat
[63U]	4	2	**True Chimes** 16-1 J Owen (xnb) Swtng; hld up; 8l 9th ½way; 6l 7th 12; outpcd 15; went 15l 4th 2 out; stayed on wl flat; nt rch ldrs
	5	1½	**Sideliner** 33-1 T Stephenson Bhnd til hdwy 7; 4l 6th ½way; 7l 8th 12; mist 14; sn outpcd; 11l 6th 3 out; stayed on one pce frm nxt
	6	20	**Mr Custard** 7-1 Miss L Sweeting Swtng profuse; ld to 3; 2nd til ld 11; hdd 14; sn wknd; 8l 4th 3 out; fin tired; btr for rce
[18⁵]	7	20	**Murberry (IRE)** (5a,2ow) 33-1 A Barlow A bhnd; 16l 12th ½way; 20l 10th 12; t.o 14
[93P]	8	12	**Kites Hardwicke** (7ow) 33-1 P Sheppard A bhnd; 20l 16th ½way; t.o 13
	P		**Beans River** 33-1 Miss C Dyson Tde; prom; jmpd slow 5; wknd qckly & 10l 10th ½way; t.o & pu 13
	P		**Foodbroker Star (IRE)** 12-1 Julian Pritchard A bhnd; 17l 13th ½way; 25l 12th 12; t.o & pu 3 out
[63⁷]	P		**Glendine (IRE)** 20-1 D Smith Drpd to rr 3; sn wl bhnd; 30l 18th ½way; t.o & pu 12
[63⁵]	F		**Hehas** 25-1 C Wadland A bhnd; 21l 17th ½way; t.o when fell 15
[75³]	P		**King Of Clare (IRE)** 6-1 A Martin Lw; prom til lost plce 7; hdwy & 3l 5th ½way; 5l 6th 12; wknd & 8l 7th 14; 17l 7th 3 out; wl bhnd when pu 2 out
	P		**La Mon Dere (IRE)** (vis) 33-1 Miss T Spearing Sn prom; 11 3rd ½way; wknd 13; 25l 8th 3 out; t.o & pu 2 out
	P		**Le Meille (IRE)** 10-1 E Walker 33s-10s; swtng; ld 3-11; wknd qckly & 8l 9th nxt; wl bhnd when pu 13
	P		**Lift The Latch (IRE)** 33-1 M Cowley (xnb) A bhnd; 15l 11th ½way; 23l 11th 12; mist 14; t.o & pu 2 out
	U		**Persian Sword** 20-1 Miss P Swindin Bhnd frm 7; 18l 14th ½way; 26l 13th 12; t.o when mist & ur 14
[74⁹]	P		**Templeroan Prince** (tt) 33-1 P Cowley Lost plce & rmdrs 6; 19l 15th ½way; wl bhnd 11; t.o & pu 3 out

OFFICIAL DISTANCES: 3l, 2l **TIME:** 6min 58.9s

192 Ladies Open
10 ran

	1		**RIP VAN WINKLE** 5-2F Miss C Dyson Lw; sn prom; went 2nd 8; ld 10; lft 5l clr 3 out; stayed on wl
	2	15	**Lake Mission** 14-1 Miss G Browne Lw; prom til lost plce 8; 14l 8th ½way; lost tch & 16l 7th 12; lft 25l 4th 14 & 3rd 3 out; stayed on; went 2nd nr fin
	3	hd	**Hill Island** 5-1 Miss L Sweeting Tubed; drpd to rr 3; sn wl bhnd; 37l 10th ½way; t.o 10; stayed on 3 out; went dist 4th app 2 out; fin wl
	4	1½	**Aqua Star (IRE)** (vis) 7-2 Miss T Spearing Tde; hld up; mist 3; hdwy 8; 3rd ½way; went 2nd 11-15; wkng when lft 2nd nxt; dem 2 plces final 50yd
	5	20	**Just Marmalade** 25-1 Miss J Williams (xnb) Swtng; lost tch 5; 25l 9th ½way; mist 11; t.o 12
	6	30	**Erbil (IRE)** 20-1 Miss S Kelly (xnb) Went 2nd 3; ld 4-10; 8½l 5th & wkng 12; t.o 15
[78U]	P		**Dawn Mission** 7-1 Miss E Jones 12s-7s; prom til lost plce & 4½l 6th ½way; 8l 4th when mist 12; pu 13

	U		**Hostetler** 33-1 **Miss K Norris** *Went 2nd aft 1-3; lost plce 6; 12l 7th ½way; wl bhnd 12; to 14; rem 7th when rfo 3 out*
[118ᴮ]	R		**Lily The Lark** (5a) 6-1 **Miss H Irving** *Hld up; mist 9; hdwy & 4l 5th ½way; went 4l 3rd aft 11 & 2nd 15; rn thro wing & ur 3 out*
	U		**Wot No Cash** 20-1 **Miss T Habgood** *Ld to 4; 2nd to 8; 2l 4th ½way; wknd & 10l 6th 12; 20l 4th when mist & ur 14*

OFFICIAL DISTANCES: 20l, nk TIME: 7min 02.5s

193 Restricted (Div 1), 12st   10 ran

	1		**MAGGIES BROTHER** 14-1 **D Barlow** *Hld up; hdwy & 3l 4th ½way; lost plce 12; 6l 7th 14; rallied to 2nd aft 3 out; lft in ld nxt; stayed on wl*
[63ᴾ]	2	4	**Royal Estate** 5-1 **S Joynes** *Hld up; jmpd slow 5; 4l 6th ½way; hdwy & 3l 4th 12; lft 3rd 14; went 2nd nxt; ld aft 3 out til jmpd slow nxt; one pce*
[78ᴾ]	3	3	**Shadowgraff** (5a) 12-1 **T Stephenson** *Swtng; prom til lost plce & 4½l 7th ½way; 5l 6th 12; 4½l 6th 14; rallied aft 2 out; stayed on*
[33⁹]	4	3½	**Kingofnobles (IRE)** 20-1 **R Rogers** *2 handlers; jw; 2nd til ld 5; hdd aft 3 out; no ex frm nxt*
	5	8	**Derrys Prerogative** 33-1 **M Rodda** *Hld up & pulled hrd; went 2nd 6-15; sn wknd*
[31¹]	6	2	**Caught At Dawn (IRE)** 2-1JF **Julian Pritchard** *Ld to 5; 2l 3rd ½way; lost plce & 4l 5th 14; rallied 3 out; hdng qckly app last*
[13ᴾ]	7	3	**Raining Stairs (IRE)** 8-1 **J Trice-Rolph** *Hld up; 7l 9th ½way; 7l 8th 14; no hdwy 3 out*
[80²]	U		**Final Analysis (IRE)** 2-1JF **J Owen** *Hld up; 3½l 5th ½way; 4l 5th 12; 2l 3rd & drvn along when blun & ur 14*
	P		**Military Dreamer** 20-1 **R Cope** *Hld up; 6l 8th ½way; wknd qckly 11; pu 12*
	U		**Wolfie Smith** 14-1 **Miss W Houldey** *Bhnd til ur 7*

OFFICIAL DISTANCES: 3l, 2l TIME: 7min 06.4s

194 Confined Maiden (Div 1), 12st   18 ran

	1		**DARK KNIGHT** 14-1 **J Owen** *(xnb) 20s-14s; hld up & bhnd; 12½l 14th ½way; 9l 10th 12; gd hdwy to 2l 4th 14; went 3rd 3 out; lft in ld nxt; drew clr flat*
[30²]	2	12	**True Hustler** 5-2JF **F Hutsby** *Hld up & bhnd; 12l 13th ½way; 6l 8th & hdwy 12; 2½l 5th 14; went 2nd 3 out; ev ch when hmpd nxt; wknd flat*
	3	6	**Chadwick Bank (IRE)** 16-1 **R Cope** *Lw; prom; 2½l 4th ½way; went 2nd aft 11-14; wknd 3 out; lft 8l 3rd nxt*
[76ᴾ]	4	8	**Highfurlong (IRE)** 9-1 **J Oldring** *Ld aft 1-3; 5l 7th ½way; 4l 6th 12; 8l 10th & wkng 14*
[75ᴾ]	5	nk	**Benbulbin (IRE)** (vis) 14-1 **M Bluck** *Prom; 2l 3rd ½way; ld 11-14; 8l 5th & wkng 3 out*
[20ᴾ]	6	½	**Cumberland Youth** 33-1 **J Diment** *Chsd ldrs; 7l 9th & rdn ½way; 4½l 7th 12; 5½l 8th 14; 10l 7th & wkng 3 out*
	P		**Cherry Orchid** 33-1 **J Jukes** *Ld 3-7; 4l 6th & rdn ½way; bhnd when pu aft 12*
	P		**Hesgreen** 16-1 **C Wadland** *Bhnd til pu 11*
[36ᴾ]	P		**Ilandra (IRE)** (5a) 33-1 **G Carenza** *Jnd ldrs 6; ld 8-11; wknd rap; pu 12*
	P		**Nelsun** 5-1 **B Pollock** *Hld up; 10l 11th ½way; 14l 13th 12; wl bhnd when pu 14*
	P		**Queens Token** (5a) 14-1 **T Illsley** *Hld up & wl bhnd til pu aft 11*
[36ᴾ]	B		**Quick Response (IRE)** 5-2JF **M Nicolls** *(citation) 7s-5/2; mist 2; bhnd til bd 3*
	F		**Red Spark** 33-1 **E Walker** *(xnb) 11th when fell 3*
	P		**Thor's Phantom** 20-1 **A Martin** *2 handlers; pulled hrd; ld til hdd aft 1; ld 7-8; 2nd/3rd til wknd & 5l 7th 14; bhnd when pu 3 out*
	P		**Trueway Two** (5a) 20-1 **A Wintle** *Hld up; 9l 10th ½way; 7l 9th 12; no hdwy 14; wl 6th 3 out; wkng when lft 20l 4th 2 out; pu last*
	P		**Upanoff** (5a) 33-1 **B Pauling** *Hld up; 11l 12th ½way; 10l 11th 12; no hdwy 14; bhnd when pu 3 out*
	F		**Vital Hesitation** (5a) 16-1 **R Millar** *Chsd ldrs; 3½l 5th ½way; mist 11; 3l 5th nxt; 7l 6th when fell 15*
	F		**Wrens Island (IRE)** 12-1 **S Joynes** *Hld up & bhnd; 6l 8th & gd hdwy ½way; went 2l 4th 12; ld 14 til fell 2 out; unlucky*

OFFICIAL DISTANCES: 15l, 6l TIME: 7min 03.1s
Fences 4 & 13 omitted - damaged

195 Mens Open   15 ran

[85¹]	1		**COPPER THISTLE (IRE)** 5-2 **R Hunnisett** *Made all; went 5l clr 15; stayed on wl; eased nr fin*
[36¹]	2	2½	**Smile Pleeze (IRE)** 20-1 **T Stephenson** *Hld up & bhnd; 16l 10th ½way; 11l 7th 12; 14l 5th 3 app last; went 2nd flat; nt rch wnr*
[79¹]	3	3	**Wishing William (IRE)** 4-1 **S Waley-Cohen** *Lw; hld up & bhnd; 14l 8th ½way; 9l 6th & hdwy 12; went 7l 4th 14 & 7l 2nd app 2 out; no imp & dem flat*

[77¹]	4	7	**Camp Bank** 11-10F Julian Pritchard *Hld up; mist 2; 11l 6th ½way; 5l 4th & hdwy 12; 7l 3rd & rdn 3 out; sn btn*
[59ᵖ]	5	8	**Lie Detector** 12-1 J Gasper *Prom; went 2nd 7 til wknd app 2 out*
	B		**Across The Water** (5a) 33-1 A Wintle *Bd 2*
	F		**Bitofabuzz (IRE)** 33-1 D Birkmyre *Went 2nd 2-7; 4l 3rd ½way; 9l 6th & wkng when fell 14*
	P		**Buachaill Dana (IRE)** 33-1 R Cope *Nd; 15l 9th & rdn ½way; 25l 9th 12; t.o & pu 13*
[77ᵖ]	P		**Gaelic (IRE)** (5a) (tt) 33-1 L Lay (xnb) *2 handlers; hld up & pulled hrd; 12l 7th ½way; mist 10; wkng when jmpd v slow 11; wl bhnd when pu 12*
	P		**Granville Grill** (2ow) 25-1 J Deutsch *Tde; chsd ldrs; 10l 5th ½way; wknd 11; 15l 8th nxt; t.o & pu 14*
	U		**Have To Think** 25-1 A Morley *Prom til mist & ur 4*
	F		**Parman (IRE)** 14-1 R Dalgety *Fell 2*
	P		**Saffron Flame (IRE)** 33-1 M Rodda *A bhnd; t.o & pu 10*
	P		**Secret Truth** (5a) 33-1 A Martin *Oht; swtng; hld up; mist 7; 5l 4th & hdwy ½way; mist 11 & 7l 5th nxt; 8l 5th 14; sn wknd; 17l 6th when mist 3 out; wl bhnd when pu nxt*
	P		**Skeough (IRE)** 33-1 M Cowley *Bckwd; swtng; sn wl bhnd; t.o & pu 10*

OFFICIAL DISTANCES: 2l, 3l TIME: 6min 57.2s

196 Restricted (Div 2), 12st 16 ran

	1		**DAWN INVADER (IRE)** 7-1 Julian Pritchard *2nd/3rd til ld 10; qcknd 7l clr 13; stayed on wl frm 2 out*
[2⁴]	2	12	**Right Company** 6-1 B Pollock *A.p; 4l 5th ½way; went 4l 3rd 12 & 5l 2nd 15; no ex 2 out*
[72¹]	3	3½	**Jobsagoodun** (2ow) 5-2F M Yardley *Ld aft 2-10; 2nd to 15; 8l 3rd 2 out; no ch when mist last*
[2⁵]	4	15	**Ten Bob Note** (bl) 14-1 M Walters *Tde; bhnd til gd hdwy 7; 2l 3rd ½way; 5l 4th 12; wknd 14*
[71ᵖ]	F		**Autumn Blunder** 33-1 T Stephenson *2 handlers; 11th when fell 4*
	P		**Chalcuchima** 33-1 J Diment *Hld up; lost plce & 13l 9th ½way; bhnd when pu aft 11*
	P		**Grand Canyon (IRE)** 10-1 A Wintle *A bhnd; 16l 11th ½way; 24l 9th 12; t.o & pu 14*
	P		**Lady Kilton** (5a) 10-1 P Cowley *A bhnd; 20l 12th ½way; 26l 10th 12; t.o & pu 14*
	P		**Mismetallic** (5a) 25-1 C Wadland *Bhnd til hdwy 8; 10l 8th ½way; wknd & 18l 8th 12; pu 13*
[33⁸]	F		**No Dozing (IRE)** 33-1 J Byrne *Spurs; sn wl bhnd; jmpd v slow 8; 30l 13th ½way; t.o 11; fell 13*
	U		**Please Call (IRE)** 7-1 E Linehan *Hld up & bhnd; hdwy & 8½l 7th ½way; 9l 6th 12; 20l 6th & wkng when mist & ur 14*
	P		**Rickshaw** 7-1 S Sellars (xnb) *2 handlers; nd; 14l 10th ½way; wl bhnd when pu 12*
[80ᵖ]	U		**Royal Orchard** 6-1 A Martin *Chsd ldrs; 8l 6th ½way; 14l 7th & wkng 12; 24l 7th 14; t.o when tried to ref 2 out; ploughed thro it & ur*
[120ᵖ]	P		**True Fred** (vis) 14-1 S Joynes *Chsd ldrs til lost plce 8; nt r.o; misp 9; bhnd when pu 11*
	P		**Winters Tale (IRE)** (5a) 6-1 D Barlow *Swtng; prom; went 2nd 4-8; 3l 4th ½way; 8l 5th 12; 18l 5th & wkng when mist 14; t.o & pu last*
[119ᵖ]	F		**Wotanite** 20-1 E Walker *Ld til hdd aft 2; 4th when fell 3*

OFFICIAL DISTANCES: 15l, 3l TIME: 6min 59.3s
Fence 11 omitted - damaged

197 Confined Maiden (Div 2), 12st 14 ran

[30³]	1		**CHEROKEE RUN (IRE)** (tt) 10-1 M Keel *Hld up; 8l 7th ½way; 7l 7th 12; 3l 4th & hdwy 14; went 3rd 3 out & 2nd app last; stayed on to ld nr fin*
[76²]	2	hd	**Romany Chat** 7-2 A Martin *A.p; went 2nd 6-11; 4l 3rd nxt; went 2nd 15; ld aft 2 out til hdd nr fin*
[81²]	3	15	**Uncle Reginald** 3-1F B McKim *Bhnd til gd hdwy 8; 2l 3rd ½way; went 2nd 11-15; 8l 4th & wkng 2 out*
	4	1	**Happen To Make It (IRE)** 4-1 Julian Pritchard *8s-4s; lw; ld 2 til hdd aft 2 out; sn wknd*
[81ᶠ]	5	runin	**Yodeller Bill** (7ow) 33-1 P Sheppard *2nd/3rd to 5; lost plce 7; 11l 9th 9th 12; 15l 9th 12; t.o nr fin*
	6	4	**Strong Account (IRE)** 8-1 R Sealey *Prom; 3l 4th ½way; 5l 4th 12; wknd & 9l 7th 14; t.o nr fin*
			Abbey Flyer 5-1 T Illsley (b4) *Ld to 2; 4th when fell 3*
[81ᵖ]	P		**Count Henry** 25-1 R Cope *Bhnd til pu aft 10*
	P		**Maquilleux** 12-1 J Trice-Rolph *Blun 2; 17l 11th ½way; wl bhnd til pu 11*
	P		**Minty's Folly (IRE)** 14-1 A Wintle *Went 2nd 3 til blun 6; sn lost plce; bhnd when pu aft 10*
[97ᵁ]	P		**Mr Matchit (IRE)** 16-1 I Hudson *Chsd ldrs til mist 5; 12l 10th ½way; t.o & pu 12*

	P	**Musical Hit** 14-1 C Wadland *Hld up; hdwy 7; 7l 6th ½way; 10l 8th 12; 13l 8th & wkng 14; t.o & pu 2 out*
[20P]	P	**Out By Night (IRE)** 5-1 D Barlow *Hld up, mist 2; hdwy 7; 6l 5th ½way; 6½l 6th 14; wknd 3 out; wl bhnd when pu last*
	F	**Wood Buzzard** 12-1 M Morley *Bhnd til 9l 8th ½way; hdwy to 6l 5th 12 til fell 14*

OFFICIAL DISTANCES: hd, 4l **TIME:** 7min 03.2s
Fences 4 & 13 omitted - fallen horse from previous race

Mid Devon

Black Forest Lodge (RH 8F,19J) Sun, 13 Feb
(GOOD with GOOD/SOFT and loose patches)

198 Hunt   3 ran

[140⁴]	1		**ARDBEI (IRE)** 4-9F D Alers-Hankey *Tchd 4/7; lw; chsd ldr; lost tch ½way; niggled along & little imp; 30l adrift 16; stayed on but lkd hld when lft in ld app last; lucky*
	2	runin	**Strong Stuff (IRE)** 11-4 M Shears *Tchd 3s; bit bckwd; rcd in 3rd; bhnd frm 16; lft rem 2nd app last*
	P		**Ever So Windy** 5-1 David Dennis *Bit bckwd; ld & sn clr; 30l ahd 16; 15l up & lkd wnr when pu app last; lame*

OFFICIAL DISTANCE: dist **TIME:** 6min 28.2s

199 Confined, 12st   8 ran

[68²]	1		**SLEW MAN (FR)** (10x) 4-9F T Scudamore *(xnb) Opened 1/2; lw; hld up; hdwy 12; cl 2nd 15 til qcknd rdly 3 out; sn clr; easy*
	2	8	**Exe Cracker** 4-1 L Jefford *Lw; hld up; hdwy 11; slt ld 15 til aft nxt; tired & btn 2 out*
[142P]	3	3	**A Few Dollars More (IRE)** 10-1 R Woollacott *Lw; sn prom; disp ld 11-14; outpcd in 3rd 16; kpt on one pce clsng stages*
	4	5	**Manor Rhyme** (vis) 14-1 E Gretton *Slt ld til jnd 11; wknd & hdd aft 14; lost ground stdly frm 16*
[71P]	5	runin	**Stories Bold** 20-1 Miss P Baker *In tch to 12; wknd; bhnd frm 16*
[65³]	6	¾	**Clontoura (IRE)** 20-1 David Dennis *Bckwd; prom til lost plce 9; rdn & strugg 12; bhnd frm 16*
[66P]	7	6	**Dfoursdream** 50-1 A Holdsworth *Towards rr; 7th when bad mist 14; t.o*
	P		**Chili Heights** 33-1 S Craddock *(xnb) Bckwd; rr frm 9; mdrs 11; bhnd & pu 13*

OFFICIAL DISTANCES: 10l, 2l **TIME:** 6min 25.0s

200 Mens Open   7 ran

[66¹]	1		**WELL ARMED (IRE)** (bl) 5-2 T Scudamore *Tchd 3s; lw; went 3rd 8; ld 16; drew clr aft 3 out; comf*
[68¹]	2	4	**Bells Wood** 4-1 C White *Lw; jw; made most; hdd 16; outpcd in 3rd nxt; stayed on agn to 2nd 2 out; no ch w wnr*
	3	15	**Mostyn** 16-1 P Pritchard *Handy; disp ld 9-10; in tch til outpcd aft 16; plugged on*
[61P]	P		**Coolree (IRE)** 66-1 M Shears *Lw; 4th ½way; lost tch 14; bhnd when pu last*
	P		**Good For A Laugh** (tt) 33-1 G Shenkin *Lw; last frm 8 til pu 13*
	P		**Khayal (USA)** 4-6F L Jefford *Bit bckwd; swtng; ld in start; hld up; hdwy 13; went 2nd 16; ev ch til wknd 3 out; 4th when pu last*
[74²]	P		**Tango's Delight** 66-1 J Gallagher *Rr til pu 16*

OFFICIAL DISTANCES: 6l, 10l **TIME:** 6min 22.5s

201 Ladies Open - 18J   7 ran

[67¹]	1		**PLAY POKER (IRE)** 10-11F Miss J Cumings *Tchd evens; lw; went 2nd 7; chsd ldr til eff aft 16; ld nxt; sn pushed clr; comf*
[67³]	2	2½	**Warren Boy** 7-4 Miss P Jones *Lw; ld; 15l clr ½way; hdd 2 out; battled on game*
	3	40	**Doyenne** (5a) 12-1 Miss F Wilson *Lw; lft 3rd 11; 15l 3rd 15; lost ground stdly*
	4	1½	**Lady Lir** (5a) 12-1 Miss S Young *(b4) Bit bckwd; towards rr; went 4th 12; nd*
[106ᵁ]	U		**Counsel** (7a) 12-1 Miss L Hawkins *Blun & ur 2*
	F		**Its Grand** 50-1 Mrs J Wilkinson *(xnb) 12l 3rd when fell 11*
	P		**Southern Ridge** 33-1 Miss E Vince *Nov rdn; bckwd; prom; hmpd 3; lost tch 12; bhnd when pu 14*

OFFICIAL DISTANCES: 2l, 16l **TIME:** 6min 17.0s
Last fence omitted - fallen rider

202 Intermediate, 12st
                                                                                   8 ran

[38¹]	1		**GLEVUM** (5a) 4-6F T Scudamore *Opened 4/5; lw; jw; ld 4-9 & agn aft 11; rdn aft 16; drew clr 2 out; r.o*
[66²]	2	8	**Western Fort (IRE)** 5-2 Miss J Cumings *4th 14; stdy hdwy 16; went 2nd nxt; kpt on one pce*
[142ᴾ]	3	3	**Flockmaster (IRE)** 16-1 T Vaughan *Bit bckwd; swtng; handy; chsd ldr frm 11; 3rd & one pce frm 3 out*
[146ᵁ]	4	20	**Luney River** (5a) 25-1 Miss L Gardner *Prog to 3rd 14; lost ground 16; bhnd frm 3 out*
[140³]	5	1	**Foxy Dawn** 6-1 D Alers-Hankey *8s-6s; lw; blun bad 9 & releg last; poor 5th frm 16*
	U		**Bak To Bill** (7a) 50-1 S Kidston *In tch in last when blun & ur 6*
[102³]	P		**Devonshire Lad** 25-1 Miss K Cook *Rr; 5th when pu 13*
[69ᴾ]	U		**O So Bossy** 20-1 Miss J Congdon *Bit bckwd; ld; mist & hdd 3; trckd ldr til ld agn 9; pckd bad & ur 11*

OFFICIAL DISTANCES: 6l, 12l TIME: 6min 27.5s

203 Restricted, 12st
                                                                                   9 ran

	1		**FIDDLERS KNAP** 7-2 J Hobbs *(xnb) Ld/disp frm 9; def advant 3 out; r.o wl when prsd frm 2 out*
[69ᴾ]	2	5	**Belski** 17-2 R Woollacott *Lw; 5th ½way; hdwy 16; rdn to chall 3 out; ev ch til nt qckn app last*
[69²]	3	20	**No More Nice Guy (IRE)** 2-1F Mrs M Hand *5/2-2s; bit bckwd; hld up; 6th ½way; lot to do 15; kpt on stdly; lft 3rd 3 out; nrst fin*
[99ᵁ]	4	15	**County Bash** (5a) 14-1 Miss L Gardner *prog to 3rd 15; no outpcd; no ch frm 3 out*
	P		**Breeze-Bloc** (5a) 33-1 M Shears *Bckwd; swtng; midfield til pu 7*
	P		**Chilli Jo** 33-1 Miss S Robinson *Prog to jn ldrs 8; mist 10; 4th when bad mist 14; lost plce qckly; t.o & pu 2 out*
	P		**Donside** (tt) 10-1 T Scudamore *(bh)Ld to 9; wknd & rmdrs 11; bhnd 15 til pu 3 out*
	P		**Karlin's Quest** 16-1 Miss A Barnett *(xnb) Chsd ldr to 8; sn wknd; lost tch 11; t.o & pu 13*
[73¹]	F		**Sea Urchin** 9-4 D Alers-Hankey *(xnb) Tchd 5/2; v late & rdn into padd; sn prom; ld/disp frm 9 til aft 16; cl 3rd but lkd hld when fell 3 out*

OFFICIAL DISTANCES: 6l, 12l TIME: 6min 22.0s

204 Open Maiden (Div 1), 12st
                                                                                   14 ran

	1		**JABIRU (IRE)** 7-1 D Alers-Hankey *Midfield; prog to 3rd 14; disp 16 til ld aft 2 out; pushed clr app last; rdly*
[21⁵]	2	4	**Morris Piper** 4-1 L Jefford *(xnb) Lw; patient rdn; gd hdwy 12; 4th 16; eff to disp 17; slt ld nxt; ev ch til rdn & no ex app last*
	3	20	**Castle Chief (IRE)** 4-1 G Gretton *(bf) Bckwd; ld 5-16; disp nxt; wknd 2 out; eased; fair eff*
[71²]	4	3	**Gunner B Special** 7-2F Miss P Jones *Tchd 5s; lw; ld early; hmpd bend aft 4; cl 2nd to 16; wknd u.p 3 out; btn 4th when hit last*
	5	8	**Dedalus (FR)** (7a) (bl) 7-1 T Scudamore *A bhnd*
	F		**Caundle's Hand** (5a) 33-1 Mrs R Partridge *(xnb) Bckwd; some hdwy 10; 6th when fell 15*
	P		**Jestastar** 10-1 S Bush *Midfield; slt hdwy 12; sn wknd; bhnd & pu 3 out*
	U		**Kentlands Lad** (7a) 33-1 G Richards *Bit bckwd; ur 1*
[70²]	P		**Mike's Dream** 4-1 T Vaughan *Prom; hmpd bend aft 4; lost plce & rmdrs 12; bhnd & pu 16*
	P		**Miss Muckley** (5a) 12-1 G Barfoot-Saunt *Bit bckwd; rr; pu lame bend aft 10*
	P		**Sausalito** (5a) 16-1 Mrs M Hand *Bit bckwd; sn trailing; wl bhnd & jmpd novicey; t.o & pu 14*
	P		**Tony's Time** 20-1 S Kidston *Prom; 4th when mist 12; lost ground frm 14; t.o & pu 2 out*
	P		**Witney O'Grady (IRE)** 12-1 Richard Darke *Swtng; towards rr; mist 12; bhnd & pu 14*
	P		**Young Lucky** 33-1 L Tibbatts *rr group; bhnd frm 11 til pu 2 out*

OFFICIAL DISTANCES: 5l, 12l TIME: 6min 25.0s

205 Open Maiden (Div 2, Part 1), 12st
                                                                                   9 ran

	1		**REITERATE** (5a) 3-1JF R Emmett *Tchd 7/2; jmpd bold; sn prom; ld frm 5; clr 16; easy*
[146ᴾ]	2	15	**Persian Dawn** (5a) 14-1 David Dennis *Bit bckwd; chsd ldr frm 10; no imp frm 3 out*
	3	20	**So Peaceful** (5a) 8-1 Miss S Robinson *Hdwy & mist 10; 3rd 12; 4th & mist 16; no ch w ldrs aft; 3rd agn run-in*
	4	3	**Maid O'Tully (IRE)** (5a) 14-1 R Hodges *Midfield; 30l 4th 14; went 3rd but fnce bhnd 3 out; lost 3rd run-in*
[37¹]	5	1½fs	**Tiotao (IRE)** 14-1 J Gallagher *Prom to 9; t.o frm 14*

		U		**Frisky-Breeze** (5a) 33-1 **D Phelan** *Rdn into padd; tde; towards rr til blun & ur 6*
[72ᵖ]		F		**Kinglassie** (5a) 4-1 **T Scudamore** *(xnb) Lw; hit 3; bhnd frm 5 til fell 13*
[72⁷]		P		**Oaklands Wolf** 4-1 **Miss P Jones** *Lw; swtng; ld to 5; cl up to 10; pu nxt; lame*
[12ᵖ]		P		**Wise Examiner (IRE)** 3-1JF **Richard Darke** *Lw; hdwy 11; sn btn; rr when pu 16*

OFFICIAL DISTANCES: 15l, dist **TIME:** 6min 29.7s

206 Open Maiden (Div 2, Part 2), 12st   8 ran

	1		**PHAR LORD (IRE)** 7-2 **G Barfoot-Saunt** *Rr; 3rd frm 14; went 2nd 16; kpt on to ld last*
[67ᵖ]	2	4	**Madam Rose (IRE)** (5a) 3-1 **L Jefford** *(xnb) 4s-3s; tried to make all; lkd wnr til wknd & hdd last; no ex*
[72⁷]	3	6	**Purslet** (5a) 9-4F **Miss N Stallard** *(xnb) Sn prom; chsd ldr frm 10-16; sn one pce*
	4	runin	**Weycroft Valley** (5a) 6-1 **L Tibbatts** *Bckwd; midfield; trailing frm 15*
[146ᵁ]		U	**Humara (IRE)** (5a) 6-1 **Miss G Edwards** *Lw; clsng in 3rd when blun & ur 14*
[73ᵖ]		P	**Mia Fort** (5a) 5-1 **T Vaughan** *2nd frm 2-10; lost plce; bad mist 13; poor 5th when pu 16*
[147ᵖ]		P	**Parsons Secret** (5a) 5-1 **N Tucker** *Bhnd & hanging bad; wl bhnd frm 15; pu 3 out*
		F	**Tabula Rasa** 5-1 **M Foley** *Fell 6*

OFFICIAL DISTANCES: 1½l, 4l **TIME:** 6min 37.3s

207 Open Maiden (Div 3), 12st   10 ran

	1		**HAYDENS FIELD** 5-1 **J Cook** *Ld; drew 30l clr 16; virt stpd & hdd bef nxt; r.o agn to ld last*
[72³]	2	3	**Frank Naylar** 11-8F **H Froud** *Lw; chsd ldr frm 11; hopeless task til ldr stpd; ld 3 out; hdd & mist last*
	3	12	**Lighter Lord** 7-1 **D Alers-Hankey** *Nfurnished; midfield; went rem 3rd 15; 4th frm nxt til 3rd agn run-in*
[76⁷]	4	6	**Music Class (IRE)** 10-1 **J Gallagher** *Last & detach early; impd 9; 6th 13; went rem 3rd 16 til dem flat*
[145ᶠ]		P	**Aherne** (7a) 14-1 **T Vaughan** *Midfield; 3rd when blun 13; lsng ground in 5th when mist 15; t.o & pu nxt*
		P	**Check The Deck (IRE)** 5-2 **D Phelan** *Bit bckwd; went 2nd 6; prom to 11; pu nxt*
[72ᵖ]		P	**Judith Jones** (5a) 14-1 **Miss D Stafford** *Rr when pu lame 11*
		P	**Loxley-Lad** 16-1 **G Richards** *Bit bckwd; in tch to 8; t.o & pu 13*
		P	**Summerhouse** (5a) 7-1 **T Dennis** *Swtng; towards rr when blun bad 6; bhnd til pu 3 out*
[70⁴]		P	**The Islander** 7-1 **G Barfoot-Saunt** *Sn rr; bhnd til pu 14*

OFFICIAL DISTANCES: 2l, 12l **TIME:** 6min 31.2s

South Dorset
Milborne St Andrew (LH 8F,19J) Sun, 13 Feb (GOOD)

208 Restricted, 12st   14 ran

	1		**SEE MORE SENSE** 9-4 **T Mitchell** *Lw; jmpd rt; hld up in rr; rn wide bend app 3; prog 9; ld nxt; rn wide agn bend app 11; 4l up 13; lkd in comm 2 out; mist & hdd brief last; stayed on str flat; dism aft fin*
[11¹]	2	¾	**Aberfoyle Park (IRE)** 4-5F **R Walford** *Rstrnd in rr til gd prog 9; 3l 4th nxt; chsd wnr frm 14; eff to ld aft last; sn hld & no ex*
	3	4	**Westwinds** 20-1 **P Shaw** *(xnb) Trckd ldrs in 3rd mostly; disp 3½l 4th 5; chsd ldng pr vain frm 15*
[33ᵁ]	4	10	**Dante's Gold** 33-1 **R Bliss** *Nov rdn; hld up in rr til hdwy 11; 20l 4th 3 out; nt trble ldrs*
[102⁴]	5	3	**Chasing Daisy** (5a) 33-1 **J Snowden** *Tde; mid-div 5; stayed on past btn horses to 25l 5th 3 out; nd*
[38³]	6	6	**My Clean Sweep (IRE)** 6-1 **Miss P Gundry** *Chsd ldrs 2; sn lost plce; prog to 5½l 5th 11; grad wknd; no ex frm 2 out*
[6⁵]	7	1½	**Lyrical Seal** (5a) (bl) 50-1 **J Maxse** *Trckd ldrs; 2½l 3rd 5; grad wknd; bhnd frm 3 out*
[12¹]	8	4	**Ferryhill (IRE)** 12-1 **N Mitchell** *Swtng; ld 1; disp 3½l 4th 5; grad wknd frm 13; bhnd frm 3 out*
	9	4	**Lord Of The Rings** 50-1 **Miss C Tizzard** *Mid-div til prog to 5l 6th 5; ld 9-nxt; wknd 14; bhnd frm 3 out*
[33ᵁ]	10	runin	**Bright Lady** (5a) 66-1 **Miss R Green** *1st ride; imm last; t.o 6; plodded home*
[63³]		P	**Another Junior** (5a) 20-1 **M Miller** *Nt jw; prom to 3; sn lost plce; rr when mists 6 & 7; jmpd slow 13; pu nxt*
[38ᵖ]		U	**Best Bitter** 33-1 **A Charles-Jones** *Rcd in mid-div til blun & ur 9*
		P	**Butts Castle** 66-1 **J Barnes** *4th 3; ld 5-8; sn wknd rap; bhnd when pu 12*
		P	**Hemero (IRE)** (tt) 50-1 **Jeremy Young** *2 handlers; ld 2-4; wknd 10; sn rr; pu 13*

OFFICIAL DISTANCES: ¾l, 3l **TIME:** 6min 26.3s **TOTE:** £2.50

209 Hunt   7 ran

[34²]	1		**GAMAY** 4-5F N Mitchell *(xnb)* Hld up in 5th; 20l 4th 10; 3rd & clsng when bad mist 15; gd rcvry; lft 2nd 3 out; swept past ldr apr nxt; sn clr; easy
	2	8	**Spring Marathon (USA)** 5-2 Miss E Tory *Trckd clr ldr 8; 20l 3rd 4; prog to disp ld 15; lft in ld 3 out; hdd & brushed aside nxt; stayed on one pce*
	3	8	**Noddadante (IRE)** 9-1 T Mitchell *Tkn stdly in rr; 45l 6th 10; lft rem 3rd 3 out; plugged on but nt trble ldrs*
	4	25	**General Giggs (IRE)** (bl) 25-1 Mrs E Smith *4th to 9; 35l 5th nxt; jmpd wildly 11; lost tch & rem 6th 10; when lft 4th 3 out*
	P		**Blakeington** (bl) 50-1 Miss K Reynolds *(kineton) 1st ride; sn rem 6th; called cab 3; last 7; t.o 12; pu & dismt 3 out*
[61ᴾ]	U		**Mystery Aristocrat (IRE)** 7-1 R Tory *Swtng; chsd clr ldr; 12l down 10; clsd to ½l 13; disp ld 15; ev ch when blun 3 out; ur 50 yds aft*
	P		**Pharsilk (IRE)** 12-1 J Barnes *2 handlers; re-saddled & mounted late; pulled hrd & sn clr; mist 2; 15l up 4; still 5l up 13; hdd & wkng when bad mist 15; pu nxt*

OFFICIAL DISTANCES: 10l, 8l **TIME:** 6min 27.7s **TOTE:** £2.00
The stewards interviewed the owner and trainer of Pharsilk who was saddled without a number cloth; they were warned to exercise more care in future

210 Mixed Open, 12st   12 ran

	1		**GILLAN COVE (IRE)** 8-1 R Young *A.p; disp 3½l 3rd 3; 2l 2nd 9; ld 13; made rest; 4l up 3 out; drew clr aft nxt; impressive*
	2	10	**Butler John (IRE)** 6-4F N Harris *Ld 2; 2l up 5 til hdd & mist 13; releg 3rd 15; stayed on game frm 3 out; went 2nd agn flat; nt trble wnr*
[32ᴾ]	3	3	**Miss O'Grady (IRE)** (5a) 9-4 M Miller *Hld up in rr to 4; prog to 5th 7; 4l 3rd 13; chsd wnr 15; ev ch app 2 out; nt r.o & hld when blun last; dem flat*
	4	15	**Red Parade (NZ)** 25-1 Miss A Goschen *Mid-div mostly; 10th & outpcd 10; stayed on to rem 4th 15; no further prog*
	5	5	**Charden** 16-1 R Webb-Bowen *(bf) A towards rr; 6th 10; 5th & strugg 15; nd*
[141³]	6	40	**Via Del Quatro (IRE)** 8a (vis) 50-1 J Young *Chsd ldr 2-11; wknd qckly to rr nxt; t.o 15*
	U		**Dangerous Guest (IRE)** 10-1 T Mitchell *Last 1; 9th 10; jmpd slow 12; still towards rr when blun & ur 13*
[61³]	F		**Glaisnock Lad (IRE)** 8-1 J Barnes *Disp 3½l 3rd 3; grad lost plce; 8th 10; rmdrs 12; wkng when fell 14*
	P		**Go Universal (IRE)** 33-1 N Mitchell *Towards rr 4; 7th 10; disp 10l 4th 13; wknd bhnd when pu 3 out*
[70ᴾ]	P		**Joli Eau** (bl) 100-1 S Partridge *Mist 2; last & rmdrs 4; jmpd slow nxt & pu 6*
	P		**Penny's Prince** 20-1 Jeremy Young *(xnb) A rr; last 10; jmpd slow 13; pu nxt*
[3²]	P		**Tom Snout (IRE)** (bl) 14-1 Miss S Vickery *Chsd ldrs; 4l 3rd 5; 10l 4th 13; wknd 15; bhnd when pu nxt*

OFFICIAL DISTANCES: 15l, 3l **TIME:** 6min 18.0s **TOTE:** £8.00
The stewards cautioned the rider of Joli Eau for galloping on past the fences after pulling up

211 Countryside Alliance Club Members (Nov Rdrs), 12st   14 ran

[34⁴]	1		**SIMPLE ARITHMETIC** 12-1 B Clarke *Mid-div; grad prog to 5th 11; chsd ldr frm nxt; 5l down 3 out; sn ld; clr aft nxt; pushed out flat; rdr's 1st wnr*
[63ᴾ]	2	5	**Mendip Son** (bl) 20-1 D Crosse *(xnb) Trckd ldrs; 4th 3; ld 9; 5l up nxt; rdn & hdd 2 out; no ex frm last*
[35³]	3	nk	**Arise (IRE)** 14-1 T Abbott *Chsd ldr; disp 12l 4th 5; outpcd & lost plce 12; stayed on agn frm 3 out; nrly snatched 2nd*
	4	5	**Starpath (NZ)** 6-1 T Atkinson *Impd to 5th 7 & 7l 3rd 10; lost tch w ldng pr 16; stayed on one pce*
[67⁴]	5	8	**Cool Character (IRE)** 16-1 Miss T Newman *15l 6th 5; nd aft; stayed on one pce frm 3 out*
[63⁸]	6	20	**Toms Choice (IRE)** 20-1 Miss T Blazey *Trckd ldrs; 4th & wkng 12; rr 15*
	P		**Beechdown** 14-1 R Bliss *Nt jw; last 2; t.o when rdr called cab 5; fnce bhnd when pu 15*
[35ᶠ]	U		**Bricanmore (IRE)** 6-1 P Dartnall *Hld up towards rr; blun & lost irons 9; ur flat aft nxt*
	U		**Bright Approach (IRE)** 14-1 Miss A Bush *(xnb) A toiling towards rr; t.o when blun & ur 15*
[67⁵]	F		**Court Master (IRE)** 7-1 D Borradaile *Ld aft 2; 2l up when mist 5; hdd 9; chsd ldr til wknd 15; btn when fell 2 out*
[35¹]	U		**Millyhenry** 4-5F Miss C Tizzard *Disp 12l 4th 5; still trckng ldrs when blun & ur 8*
	P		**Mystic Moment** (5a) 20-1 Miss S Lane *A last trio; t.o 10; fnce bhnd when pu 16*
	P		**Our Wizzer (IRE)** 20-1 C Whittaker *(xnb) Ld to 2; 8l 4th 10; wknd 12; bhnd when pu 15*

[68ᴾ] F   **Union Station (IRE)** (2ow) 33-1 **B Parsons** *Last 1; prog to mid-div 4; rr agn when mist 7; fell hvly 9*

OFFICIAL DISTANCES: 6l, hd **TIME:** 6min 28.7s **TOTE:** £10.00
The stewards interviewed the rider of Mendip Son and cautioned him concerning his use of the whip

PLATE 10   211 South Dorset Countryside Alliance Club Members (Nov Rdrs): L to R Court Master, fell, and Mendip Son land ahead of Cool Character, Our Wizzer (at fence), Toms Choice, Arise, Millyhenry and Starpath   PHOTO: Bill Selwyn

212 Confined Maiden (Div 1), 12st   13 ran

1†		**LITTLE NATIVE (IRE)** (7a,7ow) evensF **T Mitchell** *(xnb) Hld up in rr til prog to 4th 9; 6l 3rd 11; jmpd to 2nd 14; disp ld 3 out; drew clr nxt; lkd in comm when mist last; rdn & edged rt flat; lkd to just hld on*
1†	s hd	**CONQUER THE KILT** 8-1 **D I Turner** *(xnb) Trckd ldrs; 4th 5; lft chsng ldr 9; 11 2nd 11; disp ld brief 3 out; stayed on str & clsd flat; lkd to just fail*
3	10	**Saltis (IRE)** 7-1 **J Barnes** *Disp 2nd 2; chsd ldr 4 til ld aft 7; 2½l up 10 til hdd 3 out; no ex u.p frm nxt*
4	40	**Freemount Boy (IRE)** 14-1 **N Mitchell** *Disp 2nd brief 2; chsd ldrs frm 7; 10l 3rd 10; jmpd slow nxt; grad lost tch 15; t.o frm 3 out*
5	8	**Vercheny** (12a) 5-1 **Miss P Gundry** *Rr 2; some prog to 6th 10; chsd ldrs til wknd 15; t.o frm 3 out*
	F	**Ballot Box** 16-1 **M Miller** *Ld & blun 2; crashing fall nxt*
	U	**Basil** 10-1 **Jeremy Young** *Mid-div when blun & ur 1*
[6ᴾ]	F	**Indian Miller** 33-1 **M Green** *Trckd ldrs; 3rd 4; still cl 3rd when fell 8*
[7ᴾ]	P	**Just Reuben (IRE)** (7a) 7-1 **R Walford** *Disp 2nd brief 2; grad lost plce; rr & wkng 11; t.o 13; pu 14*
	U	**Millcroft Regatta (IRE)** 5-1 **R McKenzie Johnston** *Trckd ldrs; lft in ld 3; jmpd rt 5; hdd 7; lost plce 9; 4th & staying on one pce when blun & ur 3 out*
	P	**Mister Deep (IRE)** 8-1 **R Young** *A towards rr; rmdrs 12; t.o when pu 16*
[106⁴]	P	**Regal Wolf** 14-1 **J Snowden** *Last 4; prog to 6th nxt; rr agn 9; last when pu 13*
[11ᵁ]	U	**Thecabbageflinger** 14-1 **J Young** *Rr 2; blun & ur 3*

OFFICIAL DISTANCES: d ht, 15l **TIME:** 6min 34.4s **TOTE:** LN:£2.00; CTK:£4.00
The stewards enquired into possible interference between the joint-winners before and after the last; having interviewed both riders they decided the placings need not be altered; the rider of Little Native was fined £50 for excessive use of the whip

213 Confined Maiden (Div 2), 12st

15 ran

1		STONEY RIVER (IRE) 8-1 **R Walford** *Mid-div til impd to 3rd 9; lft 2nd 14; disp ld 3 out; ld & drew clr nxt; easy*
2	5	Franklins Best (IRE) 8-1 **R Young** *2 handlers; towards rr 9; impd to 4th 13; lft disp 3rd nxt; stayed on frm 2 out; nt trble wnr*
3	12	Remember Ridemore (IRE) 7-1 **T Mitchell** *Lw; chsd ldr; jmpd rt 6; ld 9; jnd nxt til lft in ld 14; hdd app 2 out; 3rd & wkng when mist last*
4	20	Grey Jerry 20-1 **B O'Doherty** *Towards rr 9; bhnd frm 14; t.o frm 16*
F		Beckhill Lady (IRE) (5a) **D I Turner** *Rr quartet 3; some prog to mid-div 9; disp 3rd 15; staying on when fell nxt*
[58P]	**P**	Captain Dusty (bl) 66-1 **M Sweetland** *Fat; last 2; t.o 5; pu 7*
	P	Harlequin Boy 8-1 **Jeremy Young** *Ld 2; hdd nxt; lft in ld 7; hdd nxt; wknd & lost plce 9; bhnd when pu 3 out*
	r	Montepulciano (IRE) 10-1 **N Mitchell** *2 handlers; ref 1*
[13P]	**P**	Novasun (bl) 20-1 **J Barnes** *A towards rr; mist 5; pu nxt*
	P	Prussian Steel (IRE) 6-1 **T Greed** *Mid-div 9; stayed on to 5th 12; wknd 15; bhnd when pu 3 out*
	P	Ruben James (IRE) 14-1 **J Young** *Rr 2; mist nxt; last 10; t.o 15; pu 2 out*
	F	Shareton 4-1JF **Miss S Vickery** *Trckd ldrs frm 5; chsd ldr 9; disp ld nxt til fell 14*
[63⁶]	**F**	Sir Wynham 7-1 **J Case** *Mid-div til prog to 4th 9; grad lost plce; wkng when fell 13*
	F	Snowshill Harvest (IRE) 20-1 **Miss P Gundry** *(xnb) Prom; chsd ldr 12; ld nxt til fell hvly 7*
[73²]	**U**	The Frosty Fox (IRE) 4-1JF **Miss A Goschen** *2 handlers; ch ride; prom when blun & ur 2*

OFFICIAL DISTANCES: 5l, 15l **TIME:** 6min 32.2s **TOTE:** £7.00

214 Confined, 12st - 18J

9 ran

[9U]	**1**	MAN OF STEELE (IRE) 9-4F **Miss D Harding** *Ld to 4 & agn 9-10; ld 13; made rest til hdd aft 2 out; rallied to ld last; drew clr flat*
	2	3½ Malihabad (IRE) (5x) 5-1 **Miss A Goschen** *Chsd ldr; 3½l 3rd 5; lost plce 12; r.o str & chsd ldr frm 3 out; ld brief aft nxt; blun last; no ex flat*
[59⁵]	**3**	12 Stillmore Business 6-1 **T Mitchell** *Trckd ldr; 8l 7th 5; mist 9; 20l 3rd 13; 3rd when blun 3 out; no ex u.p last*
	4	2½ Avril Showers (5a,8x) 14-1 **R Atkinson** *Disp 3rd 3; 5l 4th 5; lost tch 15; stayed on one pce frm 3 out; nd*
[36P]	**5**	6 Badger Beer 20-1 **N Mitchell** *Disp 3rd 3; ld aft nxt-8; ld agn 11-nxt; wknd 16; bhnd frm nxt*
	6	1½fs Arabitan (5a) 20-1 **M Green** *A towards rr; 10l 8th 5; t.o 14; plodded home*
[62³]	**U**	Cahors (IRE) 5-2 **S Best** *1st ride; hld up in last to 3; 7½l 6th 5; prog to 4th 12; chsng ldng pr when blun & ur 16*
[63⁴]	**P**	Shrewd Thought (USA) 8-1 **T Greed** *Ch ride; a last pr; t.o & pu 12; disapp*
[62⁶]	**P**	Single Man (NZ) (1ow) (vis) 25-1 **Miss T Blazey** *5½l 5th 5; blun 10 & broke fnce; pu nxt*

OFFICIAL DISTANCES: 2½l, 16l **TIME:** 6min 28.7s **TOTE:** £4.00
Fence 18 omitted - damaged

Tweseldown Racing Club

Tweseldown (RH 9F,19J) Sun, 13 Feb (GOOD)

215 Club Members, 12st

11 ran

[62U]	**1**	SULPHUR SPRINGS (IRE) (tt) 7-4 **P Scouller** *Rdr nrly f.o 1; ld aft 2-14; lost plce & 7l 5th 3 out; rallied aft nxt; went 2nd app last; qcknd to ld nr fin*
	2	1½ Tooth Pick (IRE) 8-1 **J Hawksfield** *Unruly padd; hld up & bhnd; 12l 8th ½way; hdwy 13; went 2nd aft 3 out; ld aft 2 out til rdn & hdd nr fin*
[82¹]	**3**	2 Village Copper evensF **M Gorman** *2 handlers; oht; lw; went 2nd 5; ld 14 til hdd u.p aft 2 out; no ex last*
[36P]	**4**	10 Mendip Prince (IRE) 12-1 **A Lillingston** *Hld up; 10l 6th ½way; eff 13; went 5l 3rd 3 out; rdn aft 2 out sn wknd*
[1⁷]	**5**	8 Balance 5-1 **G Maundrell** *Tchd 8s; prom; 2l 3rd ½way; lost plce 4 out; 9l 6th & rdn 2 out; sn wknd*
[62P]	**P**	Arleneseoin (IRE) (7x) 6-1 **P York** *Swtng; bhnd til hdwy 6; 3l 4th ½way; went 2nd app 14 til wknd aft 3 out; bhnd when pu last*
	U	Exemplar (IRE) 33-1 **Mrs D Rowell** *Ld til hdd aft 2; 4l 5th when rfo 9*
	F	Grand Applause (IRE) 33-1 **M Legge** *Nd; 12½l 9th ½way; hit 12; 8th & no ch when fell 14*

	F		**Sharp Seal** 33-1 A Blanch *A bhnd; mist 1; 17l 10th ½way; fell 14*
	P		**Susies Melody** (IRE) 33-1 D Dennis *Hld up; 7l 5th ½way; rdn & lost plce 13; 16l 7th 15; wl bhnd when pu 3 out*
[35ᵁ]	P		**Walkers Point** 33-1 Miss N McKim *Pulled hrd; lost plce 6; 11l 7th ½way; bhnd when pu aft 12*

OFFICIAL DISTANCES: 1½l, 2l   **TIME:** 6min 30.0s

216 Club Members (Nov Rdrs), 12st   10 ran

[33⁴]	1		**SOME TOURIST** (IRE) 5-1 N Benstead *Hld up; 6l 5th ½way; went 3rd 11; qcknd to ld 4 out; edged lft u.p flat; just hld on; game*
[62¹]	2	nk	**Bavard Dieu** (IRE) evensF Miss V Sturgis *Hdwy 4; sn prom; rcd wide; chsd ldr 10; ld 13-16; 3l adrift 2 out; rallied & 1l down last; r.o game flat*
	3	20	**Trifast Lad** 20-1 Mrs L Baker *Bhnd; nt jw; mist 5 (water); stdy hdwy & 9l 6th ½way; went 6l 4th 13; outpcd 4 out; went 15l 3rd 2 out; no imp*
[62⁴]	4	4	**Capo Castanum** 8-1 R Sturgis *Ld 4-13; 2nd til 4 out; sn wknd*
	5	runin	**Master Comedy** (bl) 33-1 V Simpson *Prom; went 2nd 6-9; 4l 3rd ½way; wknd 13; t.o*
[80³]	P		**Encima Del Rio** (IRE) 11-2 B King *A bhnd; 12l 8th ½way; 17l 6th 13; t.o & pu 3 out*
	U		**Garrison Friendly** (IRE) 6-1 N Wilson (Hants) *Bad mist & nrly ur 1; 10l 7th ½way; bhnd when rfo 11*
[63ᴾ]	U		**Hardy Weather** (IRE) 33-1 C Smyth *Ld to 4; 5l 4th ½way; 8l 5th & wkng when mist & ur 12*
[125ᴾ]	P		**Parson's Way** (6ow) 33-1 S Fisher *Lost plce 7; 15l 9th & rdn ½way; wl bhnd 11; t.o & pu 14*
	r		**Sabre King** (bl) 7-1 Miss N McKim *Ref to rce*

OFFICIAL DISTANCES: ¾l, 15l   **TIME:** 6min 33.5s

> An objection by the runner-up to the winner for 'taking my ground after last fence - did not change whip' was overruled; the stewards found that slight interference had occurred but it was accidental and had not affected the placings

217 Mens Open, 12st   4 ran

[32¹]	1		**RECTORY GARDEN** (IRE) 1-5F R Biddlecombe *Jw; a gng wl; 3rd ½way; releg last 11 til qcknd & 2nd 4 out; ld 2 out; comf*
[77⁰]	2	4	**Tarthooth** (IRE) (bl) 9-2 M Bradburne *Ld to 2; 2nd til ld 7; hdd & hmpd 13; rdn to ld app 4 out; hdd 2 out; kpt on u.p*
[79⁴]	3	12	**Golden Savannah** 12-1 A Maculan *Hld up; mist 5 (water); hdwy to ld 14; hdd app 4 out; wknd 2 out*
[10ᴾ]	P		**Wixoe Wonder** (IRE) 16-1 K Burke *Tk keen hold & jmpd lft; ld 2-7; w ldr til ld 13; hdd 14; wknd qckly 4 out; pu nxt*

OFFICIAL DISTANCES: 6l, 6l   **TIME:** 6min 32.0s

218 Greig Middleton Ladies Open   11 ran

[85²]	1		**HATCHAM BOY** (IRE) 7-4F Miss L Rowe *Hld up; lost plce aft jmpd left & slow 4; stdy hdwy & mist 10; 10l 6th ½way; went 5l 3rd aft 11; rdn to chall 2 out; ld & jmpd slow & went lft last; drvn out*
	2	1	**Sam Quale** (IRE) 10-1 Miss C Thomas *Hld up & bhnd; hdwy; 9l 5th ½way; 7l 4th 15; jnd ldrs 2 out; rdn & ev ch flat; one pce*
	3	1	**Silk Vestments** (5a) 10-1 Mrs D Rowell *Opened 14s; jmpd lft; a.p; went 5l 2nd app 10; ld aft 2 out; hdd & mist last; feebly rdn flat; no ex cl home*
[216¹]	4	4	**Sabre King** (bl) 33-1 Miss N McKim *2nd outing; pulled hrd; ld to 3; mist & nrly ur 3; 2nd til ld 8; 5l clr 10; pckd & rmdrs 13; hit 15; hdd u.p aft 2 out; one pce*
[78⁴]	5	8	**Alska** (FR) (5a) (vis) 14-1 Miss W Southcombe *Hld up; hdwy 9; went 7l 3rd ½way; lost plce 13; 10l 6th 15; no imp 4 out*
[128³]	6	½	**Strongalong** (IRE) (1ow) 3-1 Miss K Roncoroni *Wl bhnd 7; virt to 10; 20l 9th ½way; stayed on frm 3 out; nvr nrr*
[75²]	7	12	**Tiger Tina** (5a) 3-1 Miss C Stucley *Lw; hld up mist 6; 11l 7th ½way; gd hdwy 12; 3rd when mist 13; lost plce & 9l 5th 15; wknd 4 out*
[60ᴾ]	8	5	**Jamies First** (IRE) 33-1 Miss L Parrott *Rcd wide; 2nd til ld 3; hdd & lost plce & 8l 4th ½way; 12l 7th & wkng 15*
	U		**Dalusman** (IRE) 25-1 Miss N Sturgis *Last when rfo 1*
	P		**Gay Ruffian** 33-1 Miss C Hicks *A bhnd; t.o 10; pu 12*
	P		**Mo's Keliro** (5a) 33-1 Miss A Meakins *Chsd ldrs to 9; 11½l 8th ½way; wkng when mist 11; wl bhnd when pu 13*

OFFICIAL DISTANCES: 1l, 1l   **TIME:** 6min 30.0s

219 Club Members Moderate, 12st
7 ran

	1		**CHATERGOLD (IRE)** (bl) 5-1 R Lawther *2nd/3rd to 9; went 5l 3rd ½way; outpcd aft hit 11; lft 20l 2nd 15; stayed on frm 3 out; rdn to ld aft 2 out; mist last; r.o*
[14¹]	2	3½	**Gildrom** (5x) 9-4 M Rimell *Ld til hdd aft 1; 2nd/3rd til ld & hit 9; lft 20l clr 15; rdn 3 out; 8l up & tiring when hit 2 out; sn hdd & no ex u.p*
	P		**Bit Of A Do** 33-1 D Slattery *Hld up; mist 3; 8l 5th ½way; sn outpcd; wl bhnd 12; t.o & pu 4 out*
	P		**Blanchland** 25-1 R Arnold *Nt jw; a bhnd; lost tch 5; blun 7; rmdrs 9; 15l 6th ½way; t.o 13; mist 15; pu 4 out*
	P		**Glen Cherry** 10-1 P Scouller *Ld aft 1-9; 6l 4th ½way; sn outpcd; wl bhnd 13; lft 40l 3rd & jmpd v slow 15; pu 4 out*
[78²]	F		**Percy Smollett** 8-11F A Evans *Hld up; went 2nd & rdr drpd whip app 10; disp ld 11-13; 1l 2nd & drvn along when fell hvly 15*
[2ᴾ]	F		**Steel Gem (IRE)** 25-1 Miss M Bartlett *Sn wl bhnd; t.o 5; pu 16*

OFFICIAL DISTANCE: 3l **TIME:** 6min 39.0s

220 Open Maiden (Div 1), 12st
15 ran

[20ᶠ]	1		**FINE STALKER (IRE)** 7-2 A Price *Hld up; 8l 7th ½way; lft 15l 3rd 13; 12l 2nd when blun 15; stayed on to ld app 2 out; sn clr; hld on wl*
[74ᵁ]	2	4	**Drunkard's Corner** (12a) 6-1 Miss N McKim *Hld up & bhnd; 18l 12th ½way; hdwy 12; sn outpcd; 25l 7th nxt; stayed on wl frm 3 out; 10l 4th nxt; 5l 3rd when hit last; went 2nd nr fin; nt rch wnr*
[33⁷]	3	nk	**Paul** (5a) 8-1 Miss L Collins *Hld up; 14l 9th ½way; outpcd & 28l 9th 13; went 30l 4th 15; stayed on wl frm 3 out; 9l 3rd nxt; went 6l 2nd app last; dem nr fin*
[23⁵]	4	runin	**Fair Ally** 25-1 B Kendellen *Keen when mounted padd; hld up & bhnd; 15l 10th ½way; outpcd & 27l 8th 13; t.o 15*
	P		**Above Suspicion (IRE)** 20-1 G Maundrell *Oht start; w ldrs til wknd qckly 9; 12l 8th ½way; t.o & pu 13*
	U		**Buckleberry Time (IRE)** 3-1JF B Hitchcott *Hld up; hdwy 9; ld 10-11; mist 12; lft 10l clr nxt; mist 15; rdn aft 3 out; sn hdd & wknd; 10l 4th when blun & ur last*
	P		**Fast Flow** (5a) 33-1 Miss A Meakins *A bhnd; 30l 13th ½way; t.o & pu 13*
	P		**Graphic Designer (IRE)** 12-1 P Hall *33s-12s; hld up; stdy hdwy & 6l 5th ½way; hit 11; lft 10l 2nd 13-15; wknd qckly 3 out; 20l 5th when pu aft 2 out*
[62ᶠ]	F		**Imperative** 20-1 A Charles-Jones *Jnd ldrs 5; went 2nd 10; ld 11 til fell 13*
	F		**Island Gift** (5a) 8-1 A Wadlow *9th when fell 2*
	F		**Mandalady (IRE)** (5a) (tt) 33-1 M Legge *Went 2nd 3; ld 4-10; wknd qckly 12; lft 23l 4th nxt; t.o when fell 4 out*
	U		**Royal Season** 4-1 M Gorman *Ld to 4; 3l 4th ½way; 9l 3rd when blun & ur 13*
	P		**Summer Haven** (5a) 3-1JF M Bradburne *8s-3s; hld up; mist 6; 9th when blun bad 7; sn t.o; pu 12*
	P		**Tidal Reef (IRE)** 25-1 C Gordon *A bhnd; 16l 11th ½way; t.o & pu 13*
	P		**Tufree** 8-1 A Maculan *2nd/3rd to 8; 7l 6th ½way; wknd qckly 12; 29l 10th nxt; t.o & pu 15*

OFFICIAL DISTANCES: 7l, ½l **TIME:** 6min 39.8s

221 Open Maiden (Div 2), 12st - 17J
10 ran

[126ᵁ]	1		**BELVENTO (IRE)** 5-1 D Dunsdon *Hld up & rcd wide; hdwy when mist 7; 2½l 4th ½way; ld 13; 6l clr when pckd bad 3 out & rdr lost iron; drew rt away; impressive*
	2	25	**Top Designer (IRE)** 5-2F A Wadlow *Ss; bad hmpd & rdr lost irons 3; wl bhnd til 12th ½way; hdwy 12; went 6l 3rd 4 out; chsd wnr 3 out; no imp*
	3	1¾	**Climb The Hill (IRE)** 7-2 P Young *Tchd 6s; novicey; prom; 2l 3rd ½way; went 2nd aft 11-14; wknd 4 out*
[87ᶠ]	4	8	**Tierna's Respect** 7-1 E Williams *Prom; lft 2nd 8; ld 11-13; chsd wnr til rdn & wknd qckly 3 out*
[63ᶠ]	5	20	**Lord Ellangowan (IRE)** 12-1 A Irvine *Ld to 2; ld 4; mist 7; hdd & rmdrs 11; 8l 5th & rdn 15; sn wknd; to*
	P		**Ashburton Lord (IRE)** 5-1 D Dennis *Ss; hld up & pulled hrd; novicey; 11l 7th ½way; hdwy & mist 12; wknd 14; t.o & pu last*
[85ᴿ]	r		**Punnett's Town** (5a,6ow) 33-1 P Hickman *Hld up; 9th when ref & ur 3*
[30ᴾ]	P		**Riverlord** 33-1 B Hodkin *Tde; nt jw; chsd ldrs; 4l 5th ½way; lost plce & mist 12; 12l 7th nxt; t.o & pu last*
[57ᴾ]	P		**Royal Dew (IRE)** (vis) 8-1 D Evatt *Ld 2-4; lost plce & 7l 6th ½way; bhnd when pu 12*
	P		**Silk Oats** (5a) 7-1 M Wilesmith *Opened 12s; went 2nd 4 til blun & virt fell 8; nt rec; pu 10*

OFFICIAL DISTANCES: dist, 2l, 5l **TIME:** 6min 32.7s
Fences 9 & 18 omitted - low sun: Muffled Mist was withdrawn after declaration - got loose and galloped off

Hereford (RH 9F,16J)
Mon, 14 Feb (GOOD, GOOD to SOFT in places)

222 Gold Ring HC
15 ran

	1		**NOW WE KNOW (IRE)** 11-11 8-1 **Julian Pritchard** Trckd ldrs; 6th & gng wl 8; 12l 3rd 12; drvn & one-pcd 2 out til stayed on aft last; ld passing omitted final fnce; all out; v wl rdn
[79U]	2	3	**Look In The Mirror** 11-07 16-1 **Miss A Nolan** Lw; jmpd bold in ld; clr 7; hit 12; still 7l ahd last; rdr turned to jelly on long run-in; hdd 200yds out; r.o game; unlucky
	3	nk	**Ticket To The Moon** 11-06 7-1 **Miss S Vickery** Bit bckwd; hld up in midfield; 7th 8; hdwy aft 10; mod 4th 12; stayed on to chse wnr app 2 out; ev ch 200yds out; nt qckn; btr for rce
	4	1¼	**Rusty Bridge** 12-05 10-1 **R Burton** Prom; 4th 8; drpd to rr & hit 9; jmpd slow 10 (water) & rdn; poor 5th 2 out; r.o u.p to flatt 200yd out; hung lft; kpt on wl
[150U]	5	2½	**Miss Pennyhill (IRE)** 11-06 25-1 **D O'Meara** Impd to 5th 6; went 2nd 11 til hit 3 out; 4th & btn nxt; kpt on stdly
	6	dist	**Boxing Match** 12-03 33-1 **S Lloyd** Prsd ldrs; 3rd 8; rdn & wkng when mist 3 out; t.o
[34P]	7	2½	**Karaburan** 11-07 20-1 **Miss F Wilson** Tk str hld & sn prom; went 2nd 8 til hit 10; wknd aft mist 11 (water); mist 12; t.o
		U	**Archer (IRE)** 11-07 (bl) 8-1 **A Price** Chsd ldrs; 6th when mist & ur 6
[3S]		P	**Bel Lane** 10-13 25-1 **D Jones** A rr; 12th 8; t.o & pu 3 out
[61S]		P	**Bet With Baker (IRE)** 11-00 8-1 **Jeremy Young** Bhnd; 9th 8; brief eff & hit 9; sn btn; t.o & pu 3 out
		P	**Comedy Gayle** 12-00 5-1 **Miss S Gaisford** Rcd wide in last trio; lost tch 9; t.o & pu 3 out
		P	**Detroit Davy (IRE)** 11-07 10-1 **Miss P Jones** Nt jw in rr; mist 7; 10th 8; t.o & pu 13
[89²]		P	**Over The Hill (IRE)** 11-11 3-1F **T Scudamore** Lw; tk str hld brief; prom & mists 1 & 2; drpd to rr & mist 4; last 8; t.o & pu 12
		P	**Poucher (IRE)** 12-04 16-1 **A Evans** (xnb) Mists in rr; 13th & wl bhnd 9; pu 10
		P	**Wake Up Luv** 12-03 66-1 **Miss S Talbot** 2 handlers; mist 1 & rdr lost iron; midfield; 8th 8; wknd nxt; t.o & pu 3 out

TIME: 6min 57.8s TOTE: £9.50; places £3.20,£5.40,£3.20 Ex: £149.70 CSF: £118.64 Tri: £not won
Last fence omitted each circuit

Plumpton (LH 6F,18J)
Mon, 14 Feb (HEAVY, SOFT in places)

223 Flyaway HC
9 ran

	1		**LITTLE BUCK (IRE)** 11-07 8-1 **K Culligan** Tk keen hld; ld at slow pce frm 2; hdd 11; ld agn 13; pckd 15; blun nxt; sn qcknd clr; easy
	2	dist	**Master Of Troy** 12-01 evensF **Miss T McCurrich** Rcd wide in tch; prog to ld 11; hdd 13; clr w wnr frm nxt; mist 15 & rdn; sn wknd; fin tired
[32⁴]	3	½	**Flying Imp** 11-07 10-1 **J Barnes** Nt jw; chsd ldrs; rmdrs 12; sn outpcd; went poor 3rd 15; jmpd rt 2 out; stayed on u.p to chall for rem 2nd flat; kpt on
[77⁴]	4	26	**Buonarroti** 11-07 6-1 **D Dennis** Hmpd bad 1; jmpd slow 4; pckd 9; rr til prog 10; rmdrs 11; wknd u.p aft 13; t.o
[17⁷]		P	**High Learie** 12-01 (bl) 9-1 **A Harvey** Lft in ld 1; hdd nxt; mist 4; prom til wknd 13; t.o & pu 2 out
[89⁹]		F	**Kentucky Gold (IRE)** 11-07 20-1 **D Sherlock** Ld til fell 1
		P	**Luke The Duke (IRE)** 11-11 25-1 **T Gibney** Prom til lost plce 7; strugg frm 12; t.o & pu 15
		P	**Newtown Rosie (IRE)** 11-02 12-1 **A Hickman** Tk keen hld early; a rr; last when hit 7; lost tch 9; t.o & pu 13
[83³]		B	**Oflaherty's Babe (IRE)** 11-09 12-1 **R Fowler** Bd 1

TIME: 7min 49.3s TOTE: £7.00; places £2.30,£1.40,£1.60 Ex: £29.60 CSF: £16.19 Tri: £100.00

Folkestone (RH 7F,19J)
Tue, 15 Feb (SOFT)

224 R E Sassoon Mem HC
5 ran

	1		**BRAMBLEDOWN (IRE)** 11-02 3-1 **Mrs B Sillars** Jw; ld 6-15; ld 3 out; ½l advant last; shkn up & dashed clr w rdr waving & saluting flat; impressive

[79²]	2	5	**Cariboo Gold (USA)** 11-07 (bl) 11-8F **J Diment** *Hld up last til nt fluent 12; hdwy 15; rdn to press wnr 2 out; ev ch last; sn outpcd*
[59³]	3	21	**Solo Gent** 12-04 9-1 **S Bush** *Jmpd slow 6; in tch til outpcd 15; poor last nxt; passed btn horses to tk 3rd run-in*
	4	3½	**Charmer's Well (IRE)** 11-11 3-1 **T Gibney** *Dived at 4; ld to 6; blun 12; narrow ld 15-3 out; wknd app nxt*
[154ᵁ]	5	dist	**Time Enough (IRE)** 11-07 20-1 **A Hickman** *Hdwy to chse ldrs 7; nt fluent 9; 2nd 10-12; drvn 15; wknd nxt; t.o*

TIME: 7min 2.4s **TOTE:** £3.90; places £2.40,£1.10 **Ex:** £12.00 **CSF:** £6.76

Musselburgh (RH 8F,18J)
Wed, 16 Feb (GOOD to SOFT)

225 Anderson Strathern Land Ventures HC   11 ran

	1		**COOLE ABBEY (IRE)** 12-07 8-11F **M Bradburne** *Ld til aft 2; ld agn 6; jnd 12-15; rdn app 3 out; 5l clr nxt; t.o str; pushed out*
[89¹]	2	5	**Manhattan Rainbow (IRE)** 12-00 10-1 **W Renwick** *Hld up; hdwy 6; went 2nd 8; jnd wnr 12 til app 3 out; one pce frm nxt*
[134¹]	3	7	**Prominent** 11-07 7-1 **K Prendergast** *Midfield to 10; clsd smooth on clr ldng pr aft 14; disp ld nxt; drvn & wknd aft 3 out*
	4	14	**Snapper** 12-00 12-1 **Miss M Bremner** *Nt fluent; chsd ldrs; went 2nd 7-8; rdn & outpcd frm 12*
	5	23	**Pablowmore** 11-07 16-1 **R Green** *Mist 1; jmpd slow 2; last & wl bhnd to 6; some hdwy in 9th; rdn along & strugg frm 13*
[44⁴]	6	1¼	**Smiths Wynd** 11-07 33-1 **T Oates** *Midfield; 6th 10; mod 4th 13; strugg aft; t.o*
[89¹¹]	7	dist	**Rusty Blade** 11-07 100-1 **T Davidson** *A bhnd; 8th 10; t.o 13*
	P		**Cardenden (IRE)** 11-07 100-1 **J Ewart** *Pulled hrd; ld aft 2; sn 6l clr; hit 3; mist 5; hdd & mist nxt; lost plce qckly & blun 8; sn pu*
[43ᴾ]	P		**Damas (FR)** 12-00 (bl) 50-1 **Miss P Robson** *Chsd ldrs; 5th mist 6; rdn along & lost plce nxt; t.o & pu 3 out*
	P		**Dashmar** 11-07 66-1 **Miss R Barrow** *Midfield; wkng when blun & nrly ur 9; last aft; t.o & pu 12*
	P		**Joint Account** 12-07 7-2 **Mrs F Needham** *Nt jw; prom til blun 5; nvr gng wl aft; poor 9th when pu aft 10*

TIME: 6min 19.3s **TOTE:** £1.60; places £1.10,£1.40,£2.30 **Ex:** £7.60 **CSF:** £9.38 **Tri:** £62.50

Sandown (RH 11F,17J)
Thu, 17 Feb (GOOD to SOFT, GOOD in places)

226 Claremont HC   14 ran

	1		**COULTON** 11-10 4-1 **M Bradburne** *Sn prsd ldr; mist 3; hit 5; ld 9; 12l clr bef 3 out; rdn out; unchal*
[150²]	2	19	**Shafi (IRE)** 10-13 7-2F **D Mansell** *Tk str hld; hld up; blun 4; gd prog frm 10; chsd wnr app 3 out; rdn & nvr within 12l of him aft*
[148³]	3	3	**Mr Motivator** 11-03 14-1 **T Scudamore** *Sn rr; lost tch 8; rdn nxt; kpt on u.p frm 14; 22l 4th 2 out; tk 3rd at last; nvr able to chall*
	4	10	**Tea Cee Kay** 12-01 16-1 **A Sansome** *Ld; clr w wnr frm 7; hdd 9; rdn 14; lost 2nd app 3 out; fdd*
	5	1½	**Caddy Man (IRE)** 11-10 9-1 **P Cashman** *Prom in chsng group; went 3rd 9-13; rdn & btn app 3 out; poor 5th nxt*
[67¹]	6	5	**Royal Mountbrowne** 11-07 6-1 **Miss E Jones** *Blun 2; prom in chsng group; mist 13; 4th & btn aft nxt*
	7	10	**Hawaiian Sam (IRE)** 11-08 13-2 **A Michael** *Rcd wide; prom in chsng group; 6th 12; nvr nr ldrs; wknd aft 14*
[78⁶]	8	5	**Pongo Waring (IRE)** 11-03 20-1 **S Morris** *Rr; blun 6; sn lost tch; t.o 11*
	9	20	**Tickerty's Gift** 11-07 20-1 **T Gibney** *Nt jw; a last trio; blun 8; t.o aft*
[118⁵]	10	dist	**Rainbow Walk (IRE)** 10-13 50-1 **Miss A Burton** *Mist 2; prom to 4; sn wknd; t.o 14*
	11	3½	**Charlie Hawes (IRE)** 10-13 66-1 **Miss G Russell** *Imm detach & jmpd v erratic; blun 2; sn t.o; 2 fncs bhnd by 9*
	F		**Ham N'eggs** 11-08 25-1 **M Gingell** *Prom; 3rd when mist 6; 4th when fell nxt*
	P		**High Park Lady (IRE)** 10-08 20-1 **T Vaughan** *Chsd ldng pr 5 til mist 6; wknd 9; bhnd when pu 12*

P　　　　**Pontoon Bridge** 11-05 20-1 **R Burton** *Mists; outpcd in mid-div; lost tch 8; poor 8th when pu last*

TIME: 5min 31.6s **TOTE:** £4.90; places £3.10,£1.80,£3.00 **Ex:** £22.20 **CSF:** £15.30 **Tri^£48.10**

Fakenham (LH 6F,16J)
Fri, 18 Feb (GOOD)

227 Redsock Country Fairs (Walter Wales Mem) HC　　　　　　　　**8 ran**

| [90⁶] | 1 | | **MASTER BOSTON (IRE)** 11-10 (3) 20-1 **B Woodhouse** *Lft 2nd aft melee 5; hit 11; ld 13; hdd brief app 2 out; rdn clr aft 2 out; stayed on game* |

| | 2 | 1¾ | **Tommys Webb (IRE)** 11-11 14-1 **L Lay** *Lw; lft 3rd 5; chsd ldng pr; mist 3 out; 8l 3rd & no imp when blun nxt; went 2nd at last; r.o* |

| [151⁴] | 3 | 5 | **Pangeran (USA)** 11-07 100-30 **N King** *Hld up til lft in ld 5; mists 7 & 11; mist 13 & hdd; ld brief app 2 out; rdn & no resp; lost 2nd at last* |

| [17²] | 4 | dist | **Cherrynut** 12-05 7-2 **D Barlow** *Towards rr; last pr aft hmpd 5; hit 11; outpcd aft 13; mist 3 out; t.o* |

| | F | | **Floruceva (IRE)** 11-08 4-1 **R Tate** *Ld to start early; tk fierce hld; ld & 5l clr til barely rose & crashing fall 5* |

| [78⁷] | B | | **Maltby Son** 11-07 50-1 **T Lane** *2nd/3rd til bd 5* |

| [117⁵] | U | | **Red Rebel** 12-00 11-4F **B Pollock** *Hld up in tch til hmpd & ur 5* |

| | P | | **Stoney Valley** 11-07 16-1 **M Gingell** *Bckwd; tk keen hld early; lft 4th 5; brief eff 10; last & strugg aft nxt; t.o & pu 3 out* |

TIME: 5min 59.6s **TOTE:** £14.30; places £4.10,£2.40,£1.10 **Ex:** £84.10 **CSF:** £208.05 **Tri:** £164.10

Brocklesby
Brocklesby Park (LH 8F,18J) Sat, 19 Feb (GOOD to SOFT)

228 Hunt, 12st　　　　　　　　**2 ran**

| | 1 | | **SPLODGE** 4-6F **M Bennison** *Mist 7; disp til ld frm 9; went clr aft 15; unchall* |
| | 2 | 35 | **Rare Betty** (5a) evens **Miss C Blakey** *Mists 8 & 9; w wnr to 15; tired & rem 2 out* |

OFFICIAL DISTANCE: dist **TIME:** 6min 57.0s
The start of this meeting was delayed by one hour because of the late arrival of the paramedic ambulance; the first three races were then run at 15min intervals

229 Confined, 12st　　　　　　　　**11 ran**

| [116³] | 1 | | **GIVE IT A WHIRL** (3x) 8-1 **T Lane** *Tk keen hld & sn prom; ld 7-11; ld agn aft 15; drvn & kpt on wl frm 2 out; wl rdn* |

| [48²] | 2 | 5 | **Linlathen** 9-1 **N Bell** *Settled towards rr; hdwy 10; went 3rd 14 & 2nd app 3 out; sn ev ch; wknd aft nxt* |

| [115⁴] | 3 | 7 | **Inch Cross (IRE)** (3x) 6-4F **R Hunnisett** *Bhnd; 7th & pushed along 14; rchd 5th app 3 out; rdn & no imp aft* |

| [137¹] | 4 | 4 | **Triple Eaves** 4-1 **C Mulhall** *(xnb) Tk str hld; ld aft 3-7; mist 3 out; rdn 10; drpd back 6th 14; rallied to 3rd app 3 out; sn btn* |

| [115¹] | 5 | 25 | **Midnight Service (IRE)** (bl) 5-1 **R Barrett** *Chsd ldrs; rdn 10; 5th 14; nt r.o & sn lost tch* |

| | 6 | 2 | **Barneys Gold (IRE)** 7-1 **A Bealby** *Bckwd; mists & rdr v ungainly; prom brief but strugg in rr 7; t.o 14* |

| [137⁷] | 7 | 12 | **Cede Nullis** (5a) 16-1 **S Brisby** *(xnb) Settled midfield; eff 12; 3rd brief nxt; wknd 3 out; blun last; virt pu* |

| [93⁸] | P | | **Broadway Swinger** 20-1 **S R Andrews** *3rd/4th to 10; lost plce rap & nt keen aft; 8th when pu 14* |

| [90⁷] | U | | **Edge Of Night** 14-1 **A Pickering** *Midfield til blun & ur 10* |

| [115⁷] | P | | **Ryders Wells** (3ow) 20-1 **S Walker** *Ld til aft 3; prom til ld agn 11; hdd aft 14 & imm gave up; t.o & pu 2 out* |

| [116⁸] | P | | **Tudor Fellow (IRE)** 33-1 **M Mackley** *Lkd dreadful (hatrack); a last & strugg; mist 5; t.o when jmpd v bad 6; pu 8* |

OFFICIAL DISTANCES: 3l, 5l, 3l **TIME:** 6min 24.0s

230 Ladies Open　　　　　　　　**8 ran**

| [109⁴] | 1 | | **DONNEGALE (IRE)** (bl) 7-2 **Miss P Robson** *Chsd clr ldr frm 4; lkd hld frm 3 out til drvn to cl app last; str rn to ld nr fin; wl rdn* |

	2	½	**Cittadino** 6-1 **Mrs J Dawson** Jmpd bold in clr ld; 20l ahd aft 7; 8l up aft 15; r.o game & still lkd wnr at last; hdd nr fin
	3	25	**Sun Surfer (FR)** 4-1 **Mrs C Ford** Midfield; 4th 10; 25l 4th 13; unable to cl; lft 3rd 3 out
	4	10	**Doctor Dunklin (USA)** 14-1 **Miss E Graham** A detach in last trio; t.o 8
[48⁴]	5	1	**Drummond Warrior (IRE)** 10-1 **Miss A Burton** Chsd ldr to 4; 3rd 10; wknd & drvn along app 13; 35l 5th aft 15
	P		**Afternoon Delight (IRE)** (5a) 25-1 **Mrs F Needham** (xnb) Tk mad hld in last pr & und iron grip; t.o 8; pu 13
[19¹]	R		**Imperial Dawn (IRE)** 4-5F **Miss L Rowe** Midfield; 5th 10; sn scrubbed along & no resp; 23l 3rd 13; 20l 3rd & no imp when rn out 3 out
[118ᵖ]	P		**Nowhiski** 33-1 **Miss C Tarratt** Jb & sn towards rr; t.o 8; pu 10

OFFICIAL DISTANCES: hd, 15l, 1l   TIME: 6min 22.0s

231 Mens Open
5 ran

[171ᵁ]	1		**SOLBA (USA)** 2-5F **R Burton** Jmpd delib; prsd ldr & wl clr of rest; hrd rdn to chall 3 out; ld aft nxt; all out; unimpressive
	2	6	**Shanavogh** 2-1 **R Hunnisett** Lw; outj wnr; ld til jnd 3 out; ev ch til wknd aft nxt
	3	1½fs	**Charming Moss (IRE)** 12-1 **N Kent** Bckwd; pckd 2; 30l last aft 7; went 4th 12 & lft v rem 3rd 14; plodded on
	4	10	**Juke Box Billy (IRE)** 20-1 **W Burnell** Bckwd; jmpd slow 4; hld up in rr; went 25l 3rd 8; no prog when nrly ref 14; wl t.o aft
[115ᴮ]	P		**Fontaine Fables (IRE)** 20-1 **A Pickering** Rmdrs 3; 25l 3rd aft 7; reluct & nvr gng wl; releg last & pu 14

OFFICIAL DISTANCES: 3l, dist, 8l   TIME: 6min 29.0s

232 Restricted
7 ran

	1		**STARLIGHT FOOL** 4-1 **R Barrett** Chsd clr ldr; clsd aft 10; ld 11 & drew clr stdly; 15l ahd app 3 out; unchall; fin tired
[55¹]	2	runin	**Key Debate** 1-2F **G Brewer** Tde; set furious pce in long ld; mists; 20l clr 6; blun 8; wknd 10; jmpd rt & hdd 11; 6l 2nd 14; 22l 4th & exhaust app 3 out; unwisely cont & nrly fell last
[120ᵖ]	3	2fncs	**Vintage Choice (IRE)** 20-1 **N Kent** Jmpd slow 2; nvr gng wl in rr; 35l 5th 10; t.o 12; pu 3 out; cont
	P		**Miss Caitlin (IRE)** (5a) 33-1 **T Lane** Jmpd v erratic in last trio; t.o 5; pu 11
[119⁷]	P		**Neva-Agree** 14-1 **R Armson** Lw; detach 6th & nvr gng wl; mist 11; t.o 12; pu 14
[47⁷]	P		**Sovereigns Match** 33-1 **Simon Robinson** Hld up in midfield; blun 8; 15l 4th 10; eff 12 to disp 10l 3rd 12; 20l 3rd & tiring when pu app 3 out
[47²]	P		**Springfield Rex** 4-1 **Mrs F Needham** Slpd bad 1; pckd 2; chsd clr ldng pr; clsd in 12l 3rd 10; rdn & no imp; 15l 2nd app 3 out; v tired when pu nxt

OFFICIAL DISTANCES: dist, dist   TIME: 6min 38.0s

233 Open Maiden (Div 1), 12st
12 ran

	1		**HEIR OF GOLD (IRE)** 9-2 **S R Andrews** (xnb) Tk keen hld in 2nd/3rd; ld 12; 2l up app 3 out; rdn & hld on game flat
	2	1	**Step Lively** (5a) 4-1 **S Swiers** (xnb) Hld up towards rr; 6th 10; eff 14 to chse wnr app 3 out; rdn & a just hld frm nxt
	3	25	**Grangewick Flight** 14-1 **K Needham** (xnb) Bckwd; chsd ldrs; 5th 10; in tch til 5th & outpcd app 3 out; plodded on
[139²]	4	15	**Highbury** 7-2F **S Walker** Bhnd; 8th 10; lkd strugg when mists 13 & 14; 10l 6th app 3 out; wknd aft; disapp
[122ᵖ]	5	7	**Copper Thorn** (5a) 20-1 **L Hicks** Cl 3rd 4 til jnd wnr brief 13; 4th & wkng app 3 out; plodded on
	6	10	**Hydro (IRE)** 20-1 **R Burton** Lw; rr early; prog to 2nd app 8; lft in ld app 10-12; 8th & wkng rap app 3 out; t.o
	P		**Aunty Norma (IRE)** (5a) 20-1 **Miss A Armitage** A und iron grip; jb & imm hopelessly t.o; over fnce bhnd when nrly ref 6; pu 11
[51ᶠ]	B		**Camden Kid (IRE)** 8-1 **Miss L Allan** (xnb) 2 handlers; oht; unruly; ld til hmpd & bd flat app 10
[20⁴]	P		**Hya Prim** 6-1 **M Mackley** Midfield; 7th 10; in tch to 14; poor 7th when nrly fell 3 out; t.o & pu last
[169ᶠ]	P		**Joe Smoke** 20-1 **S Charlton** (xnb) Hld up in rr; poor 9th 10; t.o & pu 2 out
	P		**Magnus Maximus** 20-1 **T Lane** Prsd ldrs; 4th 10; went 2l 2nd on long rn aft 15; outpcd & lft nxt; pu 2 out
[123³]	F		**Well I Never** 20-1 **C Weaver** Ss; jmpd mod in 11th til fell 10

OFFICIAL DISTANCES: 1l, 20l, 10l   TIME: 6min 38.0s

234 Open Maiden (Div 2), 12st   13 ran

[137P]	1		**GUNMETAL** (7a) 10-1 S Charlton (xnb) Hld up in rr; 5th & prog 10; 8l 5th 13; mist nxt; 6l 2nd app 3 out; chall & mist nxt; sn ld; drvn out
[54q]	2	5	**Scraptastic** 5-1 N Bell Bckwd; 2nd til ld 9-11; sn ld agn; 6l clr app 3 out; rdn & hdd aft nxt; hld when mist last
	3	10	**Harps Hall (IRE)** (2ow) 16-1 M Chatterton Prom; 2nd 10; 6l 4th 13; wknd nxt; 20l 3rd app 3 out
[54P]	4	4	**Huntsbydale** (5a) 6-1 S Walker Lw; cl up; 3rd 10; ld brief 13 til bad mist nxt; nt rec
	5	runin	**Jock** 20-1 J R Barlow Bckwd; rr div; 8th 10; lost tch 12; t.o & nrly fell last
	P		**Dillon** 10-1 F Hutsby Cl up; 5th when mist 6; 4th 10; 5l 3rd 13; wknd nxt; t.o & pu 2 out
	P		**Father's Joy** (5a) 20-1 C Weaver (citation) Hld up in rr; 11th 10; t.o 14; pu 2 out
	P		**Good Job** (5a) 10-1 S Morris 2 handlers; hld up last; strugg 10; t.o 14; pu 2 out
[124F]	F		**Kelly's Island** (5a) 12-1 M Mackley 7th when fell 5
	P		**Kerrisdale** (5a) 10-1 D Thomas Midfield; 6th 10; lost tch 12; t.o & pu 2 out
	P		**Nasayer (IRE)** 7-2F A Pickering Mist 3; bhnd; 9th 10; 25l 7th 13; t.o & pu 3 out
	P		**Tailormade** 12-1 Mrs F Needham 2 handlers; oht; tk str hld; hit 4; ld to 9; wknd rap to 7th nxt; t.o & pu 14
[122P]	P		**The Last Shout (IRE)** 6-1 A Bealby Nt jw in midfield; rmdrs 7; rdn 10; sn lost tch; t.o & pu 3 out

OFFICIAL DISTANCES: 2l, 8l, 3l TIME: 6min 38.0s
Alston Fanfare was withdrawn not under orders - hurt in box

235 Open Maiden (Div 3), 12st   15 ran

[134²]	1		**PRIMITIVE MAN** 5-4F S Charlton 2nd/3rd til lft in ld 6; 6l clr 14; hrd prsd frm 3 out; fnd ex nxt; rdn & kpt on game
	2	5	**He's A Lad** (7a) 4-1 B Pollock Unruly padd; prom; 3rd 10; 4th app 3 out; blun nxt; rallied & ch last; nt qckn
	3	4	**Another Man (IRE)** (7a) 9-2 R Burton Bckwd; settled 3rd/4th; mist 10; 5l 3rd app 3 out; chall & ev ch nxt; sn btn; promising
[124⁶]	4	2	**Tom's Surprise** 20-1 N Kent Fat; lft 2nd 6; chsd wnr aft; ev ch til rdn & wknd 2 out
[52³]	5	25	**Round The Bend** 5-1 S Brisby Chsd ldrs; 6th 10; 5th & outpcd app 3 out
	6	1	**Gymcrak Gorjos** (5a) 7-1 D Thomas Midfield & in tch til 7th & outpcd app 3 out; sn btn
[116R]	7	nk	**Honeysuckle Lil** (5a) 25-1 T Gardham Rr div & nd; mod 8th app 3 out; plodded on
[124³]	P		**Balmoral Spring (IRE)** 25-1 S Walker Last trio & nvr gng wl; blun 6; lost tch 13; t.o & pu 3 out
[123U]	P		**Del The Lorry Man** 33-1 K Needham Jb lft 1 eliminating 2 rivals; tk str hld; hdwy in 5th 9; wknd & mist 13; t.o & pu 3 out
[117P]	F		**Fortune Hunter (IRE)** 25-1 C Weaver (citation) Bhnd to 12; prog in 6th app 3 out; chall & ev ch nxt; cl up when fell last
	U		**Gale Blazer** (5a) 10-1 R Wakeham (xnb) Hmpd & ur 1
	B		**Patrington Boy** 25-1 M Mackley Jb 1
	P		**The Bee's Castle (IRE)** 10-1 R Armson Jb in last trio; blun 9 & 14; t.o & pu 3 out
	P		**Two Of Diamonds** 20-1 W Burnell Bckwd; rr div; 7th 10; lost tch 13; t.o & pu 2 out
	r		**Woodlands Star** 8-1 T Lane Jmpd v bad; ld & sn 15l clr; nrly fell 2; ref & ur 6

OFFICIAL DISTANCES: 2l, 3l, 3l TIME: 6min 52.0s

Granta Harriers
Higham (LH 8F,19J) Sat, 19 Feb (GOOD, GOOD to SOFT in places)

236 Open Maiden 56&7yo (Div 1), 12st - 18J   9 ran

[180²]	1		**MANNA BRAVE (IRE)** evensF N Bloom Lw; mid-div; 17l 4th 8; lft 3rd 12; sn chsng wnr; 4l 2nd 14; ld app last; rdn out; comf
	2	6	**Our Man Flin (IRE)** (tt) 4-1 D Cook (xnb)Opened 8s; ld; 12l clr 4; jnd & lft clr 12; 3rd out; hdd app last; no ex
[21P]	3	1½fs	**Shine A Little (IRE)** 25-1 Miss F Jonason (xnb) Tk keen hld; chsd ldr til aft 3; grad lost plce; last frm 11; wl to frm 15
	F		**Action Stations** 12-1 A Hickman Hld up bhnd; last when fell 10
[123⁵]	P		**Bannagh Express (IRE)** 14-1 M Lurcock Chsd ldrs; lft 2nd 12; 6l 3rd 14; wknd rap app 16; t.o & pu 3 out
[87F]	F		**Casino Nell** (5a) (tt) 12-1 A Harvey Mid-div; mist 2; 6th when fell 5
[87P]	P		**Dreamisle** (5a) 20-1 N King Bhnd frm 4; went 25l 3rd 16; no prog aft; pu 2 out
[97²]	P		**Glencloy (IRE)** 4-1 C Ward 2 handlers; mid-div; 20l 5th 8; mist 10; sn rdn along; lost tch app 12; t.o & pu 3 out

F   **Morph** 20-1 **P York** *Jmpd slow 2; chsd clr ldr 4; clsd aft 11; ½l 2nd when fell nxt*

OFFICIAL DISTANCES: 5l, dist **TIME:** 6min 14.9s **TOTE:** £2.00 **DF:** £8.00
Fence 17 omitted - damaged

237 Open Maiden 56&7yo (Div 2), 12st - 18J   9 ran

[178⁷]	1		**MAI POINT** (5a) 11-4JF **Miss C Grissell** (xnb) *A.p; ld to 4; chsd ldr 16; chall app last; jmpd btr to ld aft last; r.o wl*
[98⁸]	2	3	**David Bruce** (IRE) 12-1 **R Fowler** *Chsd ldrs; ld 16; 3l clr nxt; hrd prsd when jmpd slow & hdd last; no ex flat*
[24²]	3	runin	**Fountain Bank** (IRE) 11-4JF **M Gingell** *Ww; prog 6; disp cl 2nd app 12; rdn & outpcd 14; no ch aft; went poor 3rd app last*
[180³]	4	5	**Cicero's Law** (IRE) 7-2 **P Chinery** 2 handlers; *prom; ld 4 til app 16; sn wknd; t.o*
[97⁸]	5	12	**Always Trying** (7a) 4-1 **A Sansome** *Hld up; prog 11; 10l 6th & rdn 15; sn wknd; t.o*
	P		**Marsden** 14-1 **S March** *Chsd ldrs til aft 11; wkng when mist nxt; t.o & pu 4 out*
[97⁸]	P		**Nosy Parker** (IRE) (tt) 10-1 **A Harvey** *Bhnd but in tch; jmpd slow 5; rdn & jmpd rt 10; sn lost tch; pu 12*
[23⁸]	F		**Second Thoughts** (5a) 20-1 **W Wales** *Mid-div; prog 11; 4l 5th when fell 13*
[180ᶠ]	P		**Sire De Brumetz** (FR) (7a) 33-1 **G Pewter** *Nt jw; jmpd slow 2; sn detach last; t.o frm 7 til pu 16*

OFFICIAL DISTANCES: 3l, dist **TIME:** 6min 24.7s **TOTE:** £3.60 **DF:** £33.00
Fence 17 omitted - damaged

238 Mens Open   9 ran

[84⁸]	1		**DOCKMASTER** 14-1 **M Abrey** *1st ride; chsd ldr 2-11; 10l 4th & outpcd 16; rallied nxt; ld app last; sn clr*
[94⁸]	2	10	**Prince Of Saints** (IRE) 5-1 **A Sansome** *Ww in mid-div; prog 11; 3l 3rd 13; ld aft 15; 3l clr nxt; hdd app last; wknd*
[177⁵]	3	15	**Mill O'The Rags** (IRE) 3-1 **N King** *Ww in rr; some prog 12; 12l 5th 16; went 3rd app 2 out; no prog aft*
	4	20	**Raincheck** 10-1 **B Hitchcott** *Chsd ldrs; slt ld frm 12 til hdd aft 15; 3rd & wkng when blun 3 out*
[92⁸]	P		**Airtrak** (IRE) 25-1 **R Garrard** *A last; hmpd 5; rdn 8; t.o 11 til pu 14*
[85⁸]	F		**Dual Or Bust** (IRE) 10-1 **P McAllister** *In tch in mid-div; disp 5l 3rd when fell 12*
	P		**Lusty Light** 5-2F **A Harvey** *Ld to 12; prom til ev ch 16; rdn & wknd qckly nxt; no ch when pu 2 out*
	F		**Tan Hill Sparky** (5a) 33-1 **C Ward** *Chsd ldrs til fell 5*
[130⁸]	P		**The Glow** (IRE) 3-1 **D Brightling** *Prom to 3; sn lost plce; lost tch 11; t.o & pu 16*

OFFICIAL DISTANCES: 6l, 6l **TIME:** 6min 15.5s **TOTE:** £12.50 **DF:** £73.00

239 Restricted, 12st - 17J   13 ran

[23¹]	1		**BALLINURE BOY** (IRE) 4-5F **A Hickman** (xnb) *In tch; went 2nd 9; lft in ld 11; made rest; 6l clr & rdn 2 out; stayed on; a in comm*
	2	4	**Ask The Doctor** (IRE) 5-2 **P Bull** (xnb) 2 handlers; *tk keen hld; trckd ldrs til lft 11 2nd 11; outpcd by wnr 4 out; 6l down & mist 2 out; kpt on flat; nt rch wnr*
[121²]	3	12	**On Target** 12-1 **N Bloom** (xnb) *Mid-div; prog 9; lft 13l 4th 11; chsd ldng pr frm 16; no imp*
[87²]	4	1	**King's Mandate** (IRE) 16-1 **A Harvey** *Chsd ldrs; 4th when mist 10; lft 10l 3rd 11; nvr rchd ldng pr; 4th & no ch frm 4 out*
[91²]	5	12	**Javelin Cool** (IRE) 16-1 **N King** *Mid-div; eff & 15l 5th 13; no further prog*
	6	8	**Harry Tartar** 20-1 **D Parker** *Bckwd; a mid-div; 18l 6th 12; no prog*
[86⁵]	7	10	**Therewearethen** (USA) 20-1 **D Parravani** *A bhnd; t.o frm 11*
[13⁸]	U		**Father Henry** (IRE) 20-1 **P York** *Ld; 15l clr 8; 1l up when hmpd by loose horse & ur 11*
	P		**Ger's Girl** (IRE) (5a) 33-1 **C Ward** *Chsd ldrs to 6; sn lost plce; bhnd frm 8; t.o & pu 14*
	F		**Henpecked** (IRE) 25-1 **T Bulgin** *Tk keen hld; chsd ldrs; ld brief app 4; 2nd when fell nxt*
[178⁸]	P		**I Don't Think So** (5a) (bl) 33-1 **Miss H Pewter** *Reluct to rce; set off 2 furlongs bhnd; t.o til pu 15*
	U		**River Ferdinand** (IRE) 6-1 **P Andrew** *Oht; ur 2*
[23⁸]	R		**Teluk** (IRE) 25-1 **M Gingell** *In tch til rn out 4*

OFFICIAL DISTANCES: 3l, 10l **TIME:** 6min 22.9s **TOTE:** £2.10 **DF:** £5.00
Fence omitted - fallen rider

240 Ladies Open   9 ran

| [128¹] | 1 | | **CRACKING IDEA** (IRE) (7x) 1-2F **Mrs G d'Angibau** *Disp ld 2; ld app 4; made rest; clr app 16; 12l up 2 out; eased nr fin* |

[128ᴾ]	2	8	**Uron V (FR)** 12-1 Miss T Hayter *Bhnd; 10l 5th & rmdrs 10; outpcd 12; stayed on frm 16; 15l 3rd 2 out; went 2nd flat; nt trble wnr*
	3	1½	**Dance On Sixpence** 14-1 Mrs S Hodge *(xnb) Disp ld to 4; prom; chsd wnr app 4 out; no imp aft; dem flat*
[128ᴾ]	4	20	**Emsee-H** (4x) 12-1 Miss Z Turner *In tch; 6l 3rd 11; chsd wnr nxt til app 16; sn wknd*
	P		**Airecco (IRE)** 10-1 Miss J Kandalaft *Bckwd; bhnd; hmpd 7; pu 8*
[118²]	F		**Count Of Flanders (IRE)** 8-1 Mrs J Hughes *Prom; prsng ldr when fll 8*
[91ᴾ]	P		**Just Jack** 33-1 Miss F Jonason *Prom to 6; grad lost plce; last when blun 14; t.o & pu 4 out*
[84³]	U		**Limited Liability** 20-1 Miss C Grissell *(xnb) Swtng; tk keen hld; chsd ldrs til blun & ur 7*
[95ᵁ]	P		**Royal Surprise** 20-1 Miss L Ingram *(xnb) A wl bhnd; t.o & pu 12*

OFFICIAL DISTANCES: 6l, 1½l TIME: 6min 18.0s TOTE: £1.30 DF: £6.50

241 Countryside Alliance Club Members

10 ran

[130ʳ]	1		**COMMUTER COUNTRY** 9-4 C Ward *(xnb) A gng wl; chsd ldr til ld 10; made rest; drew clr app 3 out; easy*
[96¹]	2	10	**Just One Question (IRE)** 11-10F A Harvey *2 handlers; ww in tch; prog to disp cl 2nd gng wl 12; mist nxt; 1½l 2nd 16; sn outpcd*
	3	15	**Cut A Niche** 3-1 B Kendellen *Mists; in tch; 3l 3rd when blun 16; sn rdn & btn; fin tired*
[151ʳ]	4	3	**Going Around** 25-1 M Gingell *In tch; 4l 4th 13; sn outpcd; no ch aft*
	P		**Absolute Limit** 10-1 N Bloom *Ld; 8l clr 3; hdd 10; sn drpd out; t.o & pu 14*
[29²]	P		**Dynamite Dan (IRE)** 33-1 N King *(xnb) Bhnd; 12l 5th app 12; sn lost tch; pu 15*
	P		**Greybury Star (IRE)** (bl) 25-1 P Bull *Prom til lost plce 10; last app 12; t.o & pu 14*
[94²]	P		**Reuter** (bl) 33-1 R Barr *Reluct to rce & set off fnce bhnd; passed rival 8; t.o til pu 11*
[174ʳ]	U		**Wardy Hill** (5a) 33-1 C Lawson *3rd when ur 3*
	P		**Wise Point (IRE)** 33-1 G Lush *(xnb) 2 handlers; nt jw; a rr; last 8; t.o & pu 10*

OFFICIAL DISTANCES: 10l, 20l TIME: 6min 19.1s TOTE: £3.50 DF: £3.50

242 Hunt

4 ran

[176ᵁ]	1		**CHERYL'S LAD (IRE)** (bl) 1-2F D Cook *Jb rt; made all but lost ground at fncs; 11 up when lft clr at last; rdn out*
	2	3	**Nanda Devi** 3-1 D Maxwell *Chsd wnr 4-11; last nxt til went 12l 3rd 15; kpt on frm 3 out; lft 5l 2nd at last; nt rch wnr*
[174ᵁ]	F		**Campbellhill (IRE)** 6-1 M Gingell *Tk keen hld; prsd wnr on inner; ev ch & rdn 2 out; 11 down when fell last*
[174³]	P		**Classic Ms (IRE)** 5-1 M Grange *In tch; 5l 3rd 12; last 15; sn lost tch; t.o & pu 4 out*

OFFICIAL DISTANCE: 2½l TIME: 6min 44.0s TOTE: £1.60 DF: £1.40

Oxford University Hunt Club

Kingston Blount (LH 8F,18J) Sat, 19 Feb (GOOD to SOFT)

243 Confined, 12st

10 ran

	1		**MR SNOWMAN** 9-4 Mrs T Hill *Trckd ldrs gng easy; cl up 10; hdwy to just ld 14; jnd nxt; lkd gng best when lft 8l clr 2 out; rdn out*
[127ᴾ]	2	10	**What A Hand** 14-1 T Underwood *Set off in rr; last but in tch aft 5; hdwy 9; outpcd 14; r.o agn frm nxt past tired rivals; lft 8l 2nd 2 out; no ch w wnr*
[75⁶]	3	6	**Montecot (FR)** 14-1 D I Turner *Cl 4/5th; jmpd slow 6; ld 7-14; outpcd by ldng pr 3 out; stayed on aft*
[1ᴾ]	4	¾	**Cabille (FR)** 8-1 J Owen *(xnb) Trckd ldrs; cl up in pack til ld 13; jnd nxt; nt qckn 15; kpt on one pce frm 2 out*
	5	6	**Castle Arrow (IRE)** 6-4F R Lawther *Ld in start; hld up in rr; clsd 10; hdwy to press ldr brief aft 13; gng easy on inner 3 out; squeezed bad bend bef 2 out; imm btn*
[74⁵]	6	8	**The Hatcher (NZ)** 25-1 R Cope *Prsd ldr in 2nd/3rd til wknd qckly 14; rdn & no resp 4 out*
[61ᴾ]	P		**Blessed Oliver** (3x) 8-1 J Trice-Rolph *Towards rr but in tch; outpcd 14; last 3 out; pu flat*
[75ᶠ]	P		**Its Murphy Man** 33-1 C Wadland *Ld at slow pce to 6; drpd to mid-div 9; wknd qckly; pu 13*
	F		**Lottie The Lotus** (5a) 6-1 J Tarry *2 handlers; swtng; rcd wide in mid-div; trckd ldrs frm 10; drpd to rr of pack 13; rdn & qcknd to press ldrs nxt; disp ld when fell 2 out*
	F		**Uncle Den** 33-1 I Hudson *Mist 4; disp 2nd/3rd on inner til outpcd 9; lsng tch 11 when fell 12*

OFFICIAL DISTANCES: 15l, 8l TIME: 6min 42.0s

244 Land Rover Mens Open, 12st
6 ran

[77^P]	1		**CASTLE FOLLY (IRE)** evensF R Lawther Ld; nt fluent; jmpd rt 4 & 5; 4l ahd 5; hdd 8; ld agn bef 11; 5l up 13; virt jnd 15; 11 up nxt til jnd app last; drvn out; unimpresive
[77^P]	2	nk	**Major's Law (IRE)** (7x) 12-1 J Owen Rr to 6; hdwy 8; trckd ldrs in 5l 3rd 11; prsd ldrs frm 14; rdn 3 out; sust eff to chall 2 out; upsides & ev ch last; no ex cl home
	3	1	**Fair Crossing** (1ow) Trckd ldr in 2nd til ld 8-10; 2nd til releg 6l 3rd 15; rdn 3 out; r.o str to press ldrs last; no ex cl home
[148⁵]	4	15	**Grecian Lark** (7x) 7-2 J Tarry Trckd ldrs disp 3rd til outpcd 10; 10l 4th 11; some hdwy 14; no imp aft
[74³]	5	10	**Archies Oats** 14-1 M Wall In tch disp 3rd til outpcd 10; lost tch 13; plodded on
[77^P]	P		**Winter Belle (USA)** (7x) 8-1 R Shepherd-Cross Sn rr & off pce; lost tch 7; t.o 9; pu last

OFFICIAL DISTANCES: nk, 2½l **TIME:** 6min 40.0s

245 Ladies Open
8 ran

[118¹]	1		**PHARARE (IRE)** 1-4F Miss C Spearing Cl 2nd til ld 4; 2l ahd til qcknd 14; went 5l clr nxt; nt fluent & shkn up 3 out; rallied & in comm 2 out; rmdr & drew clr app last; comf
[78⁵]	2	10	**Roly Prior** 6-1 Mrs T Hill Settled rr but in tch; smooth hdwy to 2l 2nd 11; chsd ldr aft til outpcd 15; clsd brief 3 out; no ex app nxt; nt pushed aft
[128^U]	3	4	**Danger Flynn (IRE)** 16-1 Miss C Holliday Trckd ldrs; in tch in 4/5th til 4l 3rd 11; 8l 3rd & outpcd 14; wknd 15
[62⁵]	4	6	**Cardinal Gayle (IRE)** 16-1 Miss D Harding Cl up; ld 3-4; cl 3rd til drpd to last aft 9; 15l last when jmpd slow 14; no ch aft
	U		**Belafonte** 33-1 Miss A Elsey Cl up disp 3rd; slt mist 7; blun & ur 8; rdr event unseated 40yds aft
	F		**Bend Sable (IRE)** 33-1 Miss S Duckett Ld; jmpd big 1; cl 2nd frm 4; 2l 2nd til fell 13
[192⁶]	U		**Erbil (IRE)** 33-1 Miss S Kelly Cl up til drpd to rr 8; just last when blun & ur 10
	U		**Lucky Christopher** 10-1 Miss R Goodwin Cl up in rr; 3l 4th when blun & ur 11

OFFICIAL DISTANCES: 12l, 6l **TIME:** 6min 37.0s

246 Club Members
6 ran

[196^P]	1		**WINTERS TALE (IRE)** (5a) evensF D Barlow Ld to 3; nt fluent; drpd to 4th 6; mists 9 & 10; ld agn 14; sn clr; hit 2 out; easy; unimpressive
	2	20	**Major Bugler (IRE)** 8-1 S Bush Off pce in 3rd til clsd 11; ld aft 13; hdd app nxt; nt qckn & sn 10l down; one pce
[196^U]	3	runin	**Royal Orchard** 3-1 C Marriott Rn & jmpd v poor; last & sn wl bhnd; t.o 9; plugged on frm 15; passed a tired rival flat
[78^P]	4	3	**Grange Prize** 33-1 Miss K Henry Sn strugg; 10l 5th 7; t.o 9; lft rem 3rd by 15; dem flat
[33^F]	P		**Cawarra Boy** 8-1 M Walters (xnb) Cl up til ld 5; 8l clr nxt; slowed aft 13; 15l 3rd & barely cantering nxt; pu 15
	P		**Fencing Master** 5-2 R Sweeting Pulled hrd; settled rr; 6l 3rd 10; mists 12 & 13; lost tch qckly; pu nxt

OFFICIAL DISTANCES: 20l, dist **TIME:** 6min 52.0s

247 Restricted (Div 1), 12st
13 ran

	1		**DARK RHYTHAM** 4-1 R Lawther A lkd to be gng wl; in tch; trckd ldrs til ld 10; clr 14; unchall
[6⁷]	2	runin	**Effie Wood** (5a) 6-1 P Cowley Ld to 2; cl up til ld agn brief 6; lost plce & towards rr 10; rap hdwy uphill aft 13 to 20l 3rd nxt; kpt on to dist 2nd aft 2 out
[80^P]	3	4	**Derryair** 5-2F J Owen In tch; chsd ldr frm 10; 6l 2nd & outpcd 14; v tired when blun 2 out & releg 3rd
	4	10	**Melody Princess** (5a) 6-1 F Brennan Rr to 5; slt hdwy 8; 15l 3rd 13; wknd bef nxt
[98^P]	5	6	**Stormhill Farmer** 12-1 M Keel Prsd ldr in cl 2nd/3rd til outpcd 13; 10l 3rd & wkng nxt
[75^U]	6	4	**Cool Work** 8-1 E Walker Cl 3rd 5; stdly wknd frm 11; bhnd 13; no ch aft
	P		**Another Comedy** 8-1 N Earnshaw Sn rr; rn & jmpd v bad; t.o 5; pu 10
	P		**Bright Prospect (IRE)** (5a) 16-1 R Langley A strugg towards rr; nt fluent; wl bhnd when pu 3 out
	P		**Imperial Honors (IRE)** 20-1 B Hodkin Hit 2; cl up til ld 6-10; wknd nxt; t.o 14; pu 2 out
	P		**Red Leo (USA)** 14-1 J Harty Pulled to ld 2-6; wknd rap & rr 8; pu 11
	U		**Scallywag** (5a) 12-1 M Munrowd Nt fluent; a rr; blun bad & ur 9
	P		**Sunczech (IRE)** (5a) 5-1 J Trice-Rolph Nvr gng wl in rr; lft last by 14; pu nxt
	F		**Zarza** (5a) (bl) 25-1 D Dennis Tore up to 1 & fell; clueless

OFFICIAL DISTANCES: dist, 5l **TIME:** 6min 41.0s

248 Restricted (Div 2), 12st   12 ran

[80P]	1		**NORTHERN YARN (IRE)** 14-1 P Cowley *Handy in mid-div; hdwy to disp ld brief 13; outpcd; stayed on frm 3 out; lkd hld til ldr blun 2 out; lft in ld sn aft; lucky*
	2	5½	**Native Isle (IRE)** 10-1 A Phillips *Trckd ldrs gng wl; on heels of ldrs 11; ld 12; jnd 13; ld agn nxt; 3l clr when blun bad 2 out & hdd; rn wide last bend; r.o agn last; unlucky; fin 3rd; promoted*
[119S]	3	5	**Star Changes** 5-1 T Stephenson *Hit 1; mid-div to 10; rr 13; dist 6th & no ch 15; r.o strr frm 2 out; no ch w ldrs; fin 4th; promoted*
[6A]	5	12	**Strong Ambition (IRE)** (5a) 5-2F J Owen *(xnb) A handy bhnd ldrs; hit 12 & drpd to rr; rap hdwy app to virt disp 2nd 14; wknd & qckly btn 3 out*
	6	8	**Lady Emerald** (5a) 5-1 J Tarry *Prom; prsd ldr in 2nd/3rd til rdn & wknd qckly 3 out; no ch frm nxt*
[80P]	2d		**Benova Boy** 7-1 J Diment *Prom in 3rd/4th; disp 3rd & prsd ldrs frm 13; ev ch 3 out; no ex aft nxt; fin 5l 2nd; disq - nt weigh-in*
	U		**Clinking** 6-1 M Dobson *In tch in 4/5th til wknd 8; drpd to last 10; lsng tch when blun & ur 13*
	P		**Cuban Skies (IRE)** 20-1 A Barnett *A last; jb; blun 8; t.o & pu 10*
	P		**Friends Of Bernard (IRE)** 3-1 D Barlow *Ld til aft 13; stdly wknd frm nxt; 15l 6th & no ch when pu 2 out*
	P		**Furious Avenger** 16-1 L Lay *In tch in mid-div to 8; outpcd 13; bhnd nxt; t.o & pu 3 out*
[196S]	P		**Rickshaw** 16-1 S Sellars *2 handlers; in tch in mid-div to 6; sn wknd; virt to 10; pu 11*
[192U]	P		**Wot No Cash** 25-1 R Lawther *In tch in mid-div to 12; outpcd frm nxt; bhnd when pu last*

OFFICIAL DISTANCES: Originally 5l, 1l **TIME:** 6min 51.0s
Benova Boy finished second but was disqualified when the rider failed to weigh-in; he was fined £50

249 Confined Maiden (Div 1), 12st   12 ran

[76³]	1		**DARK CHALLENGER (IRE)** (bl) evensF R Lawther *Mid-div; cl up on heels of ldrs 8; ld 12; sn clr; unchall; nrly fnce ahd when lft solo last*
	U		**Aladdin Sane Too** (6ow) 7-2 Miss S Wesley *Chsng ldrs in 5/6th; 10l 5th when ur 8*
[196P]	F		**Chalcuchima** 20-1 J Diment *Rr & off pce til hdwy to jn main group 9; lft 25l last 12; rem 3rd when fell 14*
	F		**Charles The Third** 33-1 J Owen *Rr; hdwy to jn main group 9; 20l 5th when fell 10*
	F		**Country Concorde** 33-1 L Lay *Midfield when fell 1*
	F		**Happy Blade** 20-1 B Durrell *Towards rr when fell 5; rmtd & cont 2 fncs bhnd til fell agn 9*
	P		**Have A Break** (7a) 8-1 R Cope *Bckwd; ld to 5; 2nd aft til lft in ld 8; hdd 12; sn outpcd & no ch; 30l 3rd out; exhaust & pu bef nxt*
	P		**Muddled Monk** 33-1 J Trice-Rolph *Swtng; in tch at rr of main group til aft 5; lost tch rap & pu bef nxt*
	U		**Nearly A Jester** 5-1 P Cowley *Cl up til ld 6; 2l ahd when ur 8*
	P		**Penaword** 12-1 J I Pritchard *Cl 2nd/3rd to 9; 4th & nt qckn 9; wknd qckly & pu 11*
	P		**Stable Girl** (5a,1ow) 16-1 A Tutton *Sn rr; t.o & pu 10*
	U		**The Fluter** 12-1 Miss A Naylor *Towards rr when rfo bend bef 2*

OFFICIAL DISTANCE: Finished alone **TIME:** 6min 55.0s

250 Confined Maiden (Div 2), 12st   14 ran

	1		**DYNOUN** 10-1 D Crosse *Trckd ldrs til prog 8; prsd ldr til disp ld app 14; ld 2 out; drvn clr; easy*
	2	8	**Rolcap** 9-1 J I Pritchard *Prsd ldr in 2nd til ld 11; hdd brief app 14; hdd & nt qckn 2 out; one pce*
[12U]	3	12	**Play The King (IRE)** evensF P Cowley *Mid-div when blun 3 & drpd to rr; mist 4; pushed along 10; hdwy aft 13 to ld brief app nxt; sn wknd; no ch frm 3 out*
[76P]	4	½	**Quick Succession (IRE)** 14-1 J Trice-Rolph *2 handlers; a towards rr; no ch in rem 5th when blun bad 3 out; kpt on; tk 4th aft 2 out*
[81S]	5	15	**Shouldhavesaidno (IRE)** (5a) 33-1 C Wadland *Cl up bhnd ldrs in 4/5th to 9; lost plce 12; bhnd & no ch frm 14*
[197S]	6	6	**Yodeller Bill** (6ow) 33-1 P Sheppard *Sn bhnd; lft last by 12; t.o frm 14*
[197U]	U		**Abbey Flyer** 6-1 J Owen *Ld to 10; cl 2nd/3rd til blun & ur 12*
	P		**Down To Joe's (IRE)** 6-1 T Underwood *Stdd at start; t.o 3; pu 9*
[30U]	U		**Grain Hill** (5a) B McKim *Cl up; gng wl in 4th when blun & ur 9*
	F		**Itani** 33-1 R Cope *Mid-div & nt pce to rch ldrs; disp 15l 5th when fell 14*
[76U]	P		**Moon Island** (5a) 33-1 J Diment *Hit 5; rr & jmpd v big 6 & 7; jnd pack brief 10-11; sn bhnd; t.o & pu 14*
	P		**Safe Cottage** 33-1 M Cowley *Mid-div til drpd to rr 9; sn lost tch; pu 12*

[81ᴾ] P **Take The Brush (IRE)** (5a) 5-1 **R Lawther** *In tch; trckd ldrs to 11; outpcd 14; kpt on til wknd qckly 3 out; 4th & no ch when pu nxt*
[194ᴾ] F **Upanoff** (5a) 33-1 **B Pauling** *Fell 1*

OFFICIAL DISTANCES: 8l, 10l TIME: 6min 55.0s

South Pool Harriers
Buckfastleigh (RH 7F,19J) Sat, 19 Feb (GOOD to SOFT, sticky patches)

251 Hunt   4 ran

[200¹] 1 **WELL ARMED (IRE)** (bl) 1-5F **L Jefford** *Tchd 2/7 in plce; lw; hld up; eff 15; ld on inner 3 out; sn qcknd clr; rdr lkng rnd app last; easy*
[103²] 2 6 **It's Not My Fault (IRE)** 16-1 **Adam Jones** *Hanging; lft in ld 6; hdd 3 out; sn btn*
[163ᴾ] 3 20 **Shameless Lady** (5a) 10-1 **Richard Darke** *Lw; in tch; 3rd whn mist 14; lost ground stdly; no ch frm 16*
[69ᴾ] U **Sagaville (IRE)** 6-1 **Miss T Cave** *Ld til blun & ur 6*

OFFICIAL DISTANCES: 6l, 12l TIME: 6min 51.1s

252 Mens Open   5 ran

[100¹] 1 **IRANOS (FR)** (bl) 5-4JF **L Jefford** *Opened 6/4, tchd 11/10; lw; trck ldr; slt mist 7; ld & mist 15; drew clr 3 out; comf*
2 10 **Bear Claw** 5-4JF **Jeremy Young** *Jmpd lft at times; ld til hdd 15; sn outpcd; no ch w wnr clsng stages*
3 10 **Romalito** 50-1 **Richard Darke** *Bit bckwd; 3rd mostly; lost plce 15; r.o one pce*
[68⁷] 4 6 **Robert's Toy (IRE)** (xnb) **N Harris** *Lw; hld up; some hdwy 13; went 3rd 15; poor 4th & wl btn frm 3 out*
[103ᶠ] P **Where's Sam (IRE)** 6-1 **S Craddock** *10s-6s; swtng; bit bckwd; last pr mostly; in tch til wknd 15; bhnd when pu last*

OFFICIAL DISTANCES: 20l, 16l TIME: 6min 22.0s

253 Confined Maiden (Div 1), 12st   10 ran

[106²] 1 **BROTHER NERO (NZ)** evensF **C Heard** *Opened 6/4; lw; swtng; hdwy 9; went 2nd 14; delayed chall til app last; r.o to ld nr post*
[145ᴾ] 2 hd **John Robin** 6-1 **M Sweetland** *2 handlers; swtng; tde; jw; tried to make all; ld til hdd last few strides*
[158³] 3 30 **Saucy's Wolf** (5a) 16-1 **Jeremy Young** *Tchd 7s; bit bckwd; chsd ldr to 14; 3rd & grad lost tch frm 16; jmpd lft clsng stages*
[105ᵁ] 4 runin **Amazing Hill (IRE)** 6-1 **Mrs R Morris** *Sn rr; r.o frm ½way*
F **Alice Sunrise** (5a) 16-1 **T Greed** (xnb) *Lw; tk keen hld; prom til fell 6*
[202ᵁ] F **Bak To Bill** (7a) 33-1 **Miss L Gardner** *Midfield; 5th when fell 13*
F **Frankies Flutter** 33-1 **Miss S Young** *Bckwd; midfield; 20l 4th 11; 5th when fell 12*
P **Miltown Castle** 14-1 **L Jefford** *Rr til pu 5 (lost shoe)*
F **Playing For Money** (5a) 14-1 **A Bateman** *2 handlers; bit bckwd; prom; cl 3rd when fell 7*
F **Travelling Jack** (7a) 12-1 **J Young** *Rr; some prog ½way; 4th & running on when fell 14*

OFFICIAL DISTANCES: 1l, dist TIME: 6min 35.5s

254 Confined Maiden (Div 2), 12st   13 ran

[106³] 1 **VERSICIUM (FR)** evensF **L Jefford** (xnb) *Lw; hld up towards rr; went 6th 14; stdy prog to ld app last; sn clr; easy*
[162ᴾ] 2 15 **Jimmy The One (NZ)** 6-1 **C Heard** *Handy; 2nd frm 12; lft in ld 3 out; hdd app last; fin tired; promising*
[145ᴾ] 3 4 **Aller Coombe** (5a) 7-1 **T Greed** *Lw; midfield; 6th & in tch 15; hmpd 3 out; r.o stdly; nrst fin; do btr*
[140⁵] 4 20 **Stormhill Warrior** 10-1 **R Emmett** *Midfield; 7th 9; towards rr when hmpd 14; no ch clsng stages*
[72⁸] 5 3 **Killerton Clover** (5a) 20-1 **Miss C Llewellin** (xnb) *Sn prom; cl 2nd when slt mist 7; lft in ld 10; hdd 16; 3rd 2 out; wknd*
[204ᴾ] 6 4 **Sausalito** (5a) 20-1 **Mrs M Hand** *Mist 2 & sn towards rr; 11th ½way; jmpd lft 13; nrst fin; school*
P **Butler Didit** (5a) 20-1 **N Harris** *Mist 2; jmpd novicey in rr; bhnd & pu 14; lks v green*
F **Harvest Home (IRE)** 16-1 **T Dennis** *Disp 9th ½way; slt hdwy to 5th when fell 14*
[158ᴿ] P **Jo's Wedding** 12-1 **Miss S Gaisford** *Swtng; pulled hrd; ld/disp; mist & rdr lost iron 7; pu nxt*

[159ᶠ]	P		**No Need For Alarm** (12a) 9-2 J Young *(xnb) Lw; pulling; ld aft 4; saddle slpd & pu aft nxt*
[146ᴾ]	P		**Pachakutec (IRE)** 20-1 R Woollacott *6th ½way; hdwy to disp 3rd 14; lost ground stdly frm 3 out; btn 6th when pu last*
	F		**Swift Venture (IRE)** 12-1 Richard Darke *Sn prom; 3rd ½way; prog to slt ld 16; jnd when fell nxt*
[163ᵁ]	P		**Trooper Pippin** 25-1 A Bateman *Towards rr; t.o 9; pu 12; school*

OFFICIAL DISTANCES: 25l, 6l **TIME:** 6min 35.1s

255 Restricted (Div 1), 12st
10 ran

[11ᴾ]	1		**HORUS (IRE)** (7a) 5-4F L Jefford *Lw; confid rdn; midfield; hdwy on bit 14; ww til chall app last; sprinted clr; impressive*
[159¹]	2	4	**Solomans Sister** (5a) 9-4 Mrs M Hand *Ld 2-4; trckd ldr til ld 15; kpt on wl; hdd app last; nt disg*
	3	20	**Dancing Ranger** 8-1 Richard Darke *In tch; cl 4th 13; ev ch til nt qckn 16; fair eff*
	4	6	**Drumbanes Pet** 20-1 R Woollacott *Bckwd; mid-div; 6th & rdn 15; no hdwy; dism aft post*
[203⁴]	F		**County Bash** (5a) 14-1 Miss L Gardner *Disp 4th 11; bad mist 14; one pce frm 16; wl btn 4th when fell last; winded*
	P		**Media Luna** (5a) 33-1 M Sweetland *Sn last; pckd bad 9; bhnd til pu 14*
	F		**Mollycarrsbrekfast** (7a) 33-1 D Ridge *V fresh to post; rcd free; ld 4 til mist 14; wkng in 4th when fell 15*
[69ᴾ]	U		**Rossaleen** (5a) 33-1 P Shaw *8th 11; lost tch 15; poor 6th when hmpd & ur last*
	P		**Ru Bidding** (5a) 33-1 T Greed *School in rr til pu 14*
	P		**Silver Man** 15-2 N Harris *Opened 10s; handy; cl 2nd frm 15; ev ch til wknd 2 out; pu last; btr for rce*

OFFICIAL DISTANCES: 4l, 10l **TIME:** 6min 32.3s

256 Restricted (Div 2), 12st
6 ran

[203³]	1		**NO MORE NICE GUY (IRE)** 2-1 Mrs M Hand *Blun bad 3; jw aft; cl up til ld 7; made rest; hung on last bend; pushed out flat*
[102²]	2	4	**Chocolate Buttons** (5a) 13-2 H Thomas *Tchd 9s; in tch; went 2nd 15; chall & ev ch app last; sn no ex*
	U		**Debbie's Darling** (5a) 10-1 Miss S Gaisford *Bit bckwd; hmpd & ur 3*
[157¹]	U		**Fossy Bear** (5a) evensF Miss S Young *Cl 2nd when ur 7*
	P		**Friendly Viking** 25-1 I Hambley *Bckwd; 2nd 9; disp 2nd 14-15; wknd; btn 3rd when jmpd slow 2 out; pu last*
	P		**Mr Kevernair** 16-1 C Heard *(xnb) Unruly gng to post; pulled v hrd; ld 2; 20l clr 4 til stdd & hdd 7; pu 10; bbv*

OFFICIAL DISTANCE: 4l **TIME:** 6min 42.5s

257 Ladies Open
7 ran

[67²]	1		**HILLHEAD (IRE)** 11-8F Miss A Goschen *Opened 6/4; lw; swtng profuse start; jw; made virt all; drew clr 16; easy*
[65²]	2	30	**Mr Jervis (IRE)** 13-2 Miss V Tremlett *Nov rdn; in tch; cl 3rd when pckd 11; prog to chse ldr 15; outpcd & no ch w wnr frm 3 out*
	3	4	**Dunlir** 25-1 Miss S Young *Rr; impd 10; went 4th 14; nt rch ldrs; wl btn 3rd frm 2 out; rdn out flat*
	4	10	**Desert Run (IRE)** 33-1 Miss J West *Bckwd; ld early; handy til lost pce 12; no ch frm 14*
	P		**It'snotsimple (IRE)** (5a) 3-1 Miss T Messer-Bennetts *Bit bckwd; sn prom; disp ld 12-14; 3rd & wkng nxt; sn lost tch; tired & pu last; btr for rce*
[204⁴]	U		**Luney River** (5a) 33-1 Miss L Gardner *Rr; last frm 8; staying on past btn horses to rem 4th aft 2 out; ur last*
[103¹]	U		**Palace Parade (USA)** 3-1 Mrs M Hand *4s-3s; lw; hld up; 6th 10; some hdwy to 4th when mist & ur 14*

OFFICIAL DISTANCES: dist, 4l **TIME:** 6min 25.0s

258 Confined
6 ran

	1		**BROWN ROBBER** 5-1 T Dennis *(xnb) Made all; drew clr stdly frm 3 out; comf*
[162ᴾ]	2	7	**Valley's Choice** (5a) 9-1 C White *Lw; a chsng ldr; outpcd by wnr 3 out; stayed on stdly*
	3	4	**Lirsleftover** 9-1 Miss S Young *2 handlers; oht; hld up; 3rd & gng wl 13; mist & lost ground 15; r.o agn to 3rd aft 2 out; nt*
[165²]	4	6	**Gypsy Gerry** 5-2 T Clarkson *5s-5/2; nov rdn; lw; rcd wide; settled 3rd/4th; just in tch in 10l 3rd 3 out; sn one pce; schoolmaster*
[104²]	5	15	**Jeepers (IRE)** 12-1 Richard Darke *Bit bckwd; rcd 3rd/4th mostly; lost plce 14; no ch frm 3 out*

P		**Uckerby Lad** 15-8F C Heard *Opened 2s; bit bckwd; hld up in tch; short-lived eff to 3rd 14; sn btn & nt prsd aft; pu last*	

OFFICIAL DISTANCES: 8l, 6l **TIME:** 6min 32.0s

United Services
Larkhill (RH 13F,18J) Sat, 19 Feb (GOOD)

259 United Services Members, 12st   **6 ran**

[62²]	1		**COPPER COIL** 5-4F D Alers-Hankey *Settled cl 4th frm 3 til 3rd 8; jnd ldr aft 13 til ld 3 out; 5l clr app last; rdn & r.o flat*
[62ᴾ]	2	2½	**Desert Waltz (IRE)** (5x) 6-4 O Ellwood *Tchd 7/4; a.p; cl 3rd 5; went nk 2nd 7; ld 10; jnd aft 13; hdd app 3 out; 5l 2nd app last; rdn & clsd flat; a hld*
[143⁵]	3	20	**Ive Called Time** (5x) (tt) 10-1 G Chanter *Cl last frm 3; slt mist 6; went 4th 9; disp 2l 3rd 14; 9½l 3rd & wkng 3 out*
[212¹ᵘ]	U		**Conquer The Kilt** (5x) 8-1 A Michael *14s-8s; cl up in last pr; blun bad 4 & rdr round horse's nk; rec wl; mists 7 & 8; rr when blun agn 12 & ur some way aft*
	U		**Heathburn (IRE)** 40-1 C Ward-Thomas *Cl 2nd mostly til ld 7; jnd 9; drpd to last when blun & ur 11*
[83ᴾ]	U		**Mister Main Man (IRE)** 16-1 S Sporborg *Ld to 6; 6½l 3rd 7; 4th nxt; prog to disp cl 2nd brief aft 12; disp 2l 3rd 14; disp 5l 3rd & outpcd when blun & ur 3 out*

OFFICIAL DISTANCES: 1½l, 15l **TIME:** 6min 19.2s **TOTE:** £2.50

260 Restricted (Div 1), 12st   **15 ran**

[106¹]	1		**S B S BY JOVE** 5-1 A Charles-Jones *14s-5s; v edgy & oht; lw; jw; trckd ldrs in 3rd/4th til ld brief aft 12; cl 2nd nxt til ld aft 3 out; sn in comm; impressive (seems transformed)*
	2	37	**Butterwick King (IRE)** 8-1 D Alers-Hankey *Trckd ldrs; cl 6th 4; gd hdwy 13; 3rd 14; ch til outpcd app 3 out; 14l 3rd aft 2 out; wknd; fin 3rd; promoted*
[38ᴾ]	3	25	**Smart Orange (IRE)** (tt) 8-1 M Rimell *10s-8s; nt jw; trckd ldrs in 4/5th; hit 4 & 7; ev ch til outpcd 15; 30l 4th & plodding aft 2 out; fin 4th; promoted*
	2d		**Mr Ben Gunn** 10-1 S Joynes *16s-10s; tde; v sa; in tch w main body by 6; gd prog to 3rd 13; ld 15; hdd & imm outpcd app nxt; still 8l 2nd aft 2 out; fin 25l 2nd; disq - nt weigh-in*
	P		**Good Thyne Girl** (5a) 33-1 O Ellwood *A towards rr; 11th app 5; wl bhnd when pu 3 out*
	P		**Leamlara Rose (IRE)** (5a) 16-1 Miss S Vickery *Mid-div & nd; 10th app 5; drpd to last of main body & wkng 13; t.o when pu nxt*
	P		**Lord Spider** 6-1 M Miller *Swtng; midfield; 8th app 5; in tch til wknd 13; bhnd when pu 3 out*
[60¹]	P		**Lost Your Marbles (IRE)** (5a) 16-1 J Mead *(bnh) Mounted aft rest had lft padd; sn prom; cl 3rd aft 5; 5th & wkng 13; bhnd when pu 16*
	P		**Mister River (IRE)** 33-1 Miss P Gundry *Midfield; 9th aft 5; drpd to rr of main body 11; t.o when pu 3 out*
	P		**Mystic Legacy** (5a) 33-1 M Foley *Dwelt & lost 15l start; a last; t.o; fncs bhnd when pu 14*
	U		**Off The Cuff (IRE)** 7-2 T Mitchell *Lw; cl 2nd app 4-12; 4th & wkng nxt; 12l 6th 15; blun & ur nxt*
[63ᶠ]	P		**Old Harry's Wife** (5a) 20-1 N Mitchell *Ld to 3; cl 6th app 5; grad lost plce; last of main body 12; t.o & pu 16*
	P		**Playmore (IRE)** 3-1F David Dennis *Prom til ld 4-12; ld brief agn nxt; wknd qckly; 10l 5th & btn 15; last when pu aft 2 out*
	P		**Solomons Mines (IRE)** 33-1 Miss C Goatley *(xnb) Sa; sn t.o in last pr; virt out of sight when pu 15*
	P		**Springvilla (IRE)** 25-1 R Young *(bf) Bckwd; sn towards rr; disp 12th app 5; lost tch 12; bhnd when pu 14*

OFFICIAL DISTANCES: Originally 20l, 8l **TIME:** 6min 15.8s **TOTE:** £4.80 **DF:** £5.10
     Mr Ben Gunn finished 2nd but was disqualified when the rider failed to weigh-in; he was fined £75

261 Restricted (Div 2), 12st   **9 ran**

[213¹]	1		**STONEY RIVER (IRE)** 5-4F R Walford *V confid rdn; hld up in last pr to 12; eff to 5th 13 & 6l 4th nxt; clsd stdly to 3l 3rd 3 out; hrd rdn to chall on outer aft nxt; ld app last; r.o*
[120²]	2	2½	**Percy Medlicott** 6-1 Julian Pritchard *Towards rr; 7th 3; 9l 7th 7; prog to cl 2nd aft 12; ld 15 til hdd & no ex app last*

	3	12	**Cades Bay** 7-1 **S Joynes** *Ld til jnd aft 14; hdd nxt; still cl 2nd aft 3 out; wknd & nt prsd aft; btr for rce*
[80^F]	4	20	**Forever Dreaming (IRE)** 12-1 **M Rimell** *Trckd ldrs; disp 5th aft 5; 8l 5th 7; prog to cl 3rd 13; sn wknd; 6l 5th aft nxt; 111 4th when jmpd v slow 3 out; plodded on*
[221^3]	P		**Ashburton Lord (IRE)** 33-1 **M Legge** *Sn prom in 2nd/3rd; disp 1½l 2nd 7; 3rd 9; wknd 12; bhnd when pu 15*
[7^5]	U		**General Typhoon** 14-1 **Miss E Tory** *Midfield; 6½l 6th 7; no imp when ur 13*
	P		**Muffled Mist** (5a) 33-1 **Miss V Sturgis** *2 handlers; unruly & broke padd rail; prom in 2nd/3rd; disp 1½l 2nd 7; 4th 9; wknd 12; poor 6th when pu 15*
[14^2]	P		**Shobrooke Mill** 9-4 **A Charles-Jones** *(xnb) Trckd ldrs; 3l 4th 7; 2nd 9; disp ld aft 14; wknd rap; pu 2 out*
[14^4]	P		**Timber Wolf (IRE)** 33-1 **N Mitchell** *Nt fluent; last pr til detach aft 5; jmpd slow 8; t.o aft 12; pu 15*

OFFICIAL DISTANCES: 2½l, 20l **TIME:** 6min 19.1s **TOTE:** £2.50

262 Mixed Open (Coronation Cup), 12st

10 ran

[92^1]	1		**RUPERTS CHOICE (IRE)** (bl) 4-1 **S Sporborg** *6s-4s; lw; trckd ldrs; cl 3rd aft 5; 1½l 2nd 7; trckd ldrs; mist 14; 6l 2nd nxt; rallied und str press 2 out; ld app last; rdn & r.o str flat; just hld on*
[217^1]	2	nk	**Rectory Garden (IRE)** 4-7F **R Biddlecombe** *Tchd 4/6; v confid rdn; hld up in last; 12l off pce 10; rap prog uphill aft 12; 4th 13; ww & 9l 3rd 15; still 7½l 3rd 2 out; finally unleashed app last; went 2nd flat & clsd qckly; just too much to do (should have won)*
[63^1]	3	12	**Castle Lynch (IRE)** (5a) 7-1 **Julian Pritchard** *Jw; prom til ld 3; 6l clr 14 & tried to steal rce; hdd app last; wknd qckly (rn wl)*
	4	2½	**Kilmington (IRE)** 33-1 **J Barnes** *Jw; mid-div; cl 5th 6; 2½l 4th 7; went 3rd 13; ev ch nxt; 10½l 4th & outpcd 15; kpt on*
[152^P]	5	12	**Chism (IRE)** 12-1 **R Walford** *Hld up in tch at rr; disp 8l 8th aft 5; some hdwy to 5th aft 12; 14l 5th 15; no imp on ldrs aft*
[59^P]	6	5	**Funny Farm** 14-1 **M Miller** *Last pr mostly; hdwy to 5th 14; 21l 6th & btn 15; kpt on one pce*
	7	25	**Beck And Call (IRE)** 16-1 **Miss S Vickery** *Cl 4th mostly til 6th 8; lost tch frm 12; 30l 7th & wkng 15; t.o 2 out*
[141^4]	P		**Amtrak Express** 33-1 **H Froud** *Prom; 3rd 2; cl 5th aft 6; 3rd agn 11 til wknd rap app 13; 40l 8th 15; t.o & pu 2 out*
[219^P]	P		**Blanchland** 100-1 **R Arnold** *Ld/disp to 3; cl 3rd til wknd 12; 7th & btn 13; t.o in last pr when pu 3 out*
[68^6]	P		**Oneforwillie** 100-1 **J Snowden** *Towards rr; cl 7th 5; last pr 9; last & wkng aft 12; t.o & pu 3 out*

OFFICIAL DISTANCES: s hd, 20l **TIME:** 6min 13.9s **TOTE:** £3.90

263 Intermediate, 12st

8 ran

[69^1]	1		**FAIR WIND (IRE)** 7-4F **M Miller** *Tchd 5/4 & 2s; jw; chsd ldrs in 4/5th til 2l 3rd 7; rmdrs 13 & cl 2nd nxt; jnd ldr 15; just ld 3 out; 2l up at last; r.o str u.p; a hldng rnr-up*
[162^f]	2	2½	**River Swilley (IRE)** 2-1 **R Walford** *Tchd 9/4; nt a fluent & rmdrs; last trio early; went 3l 4th 7; prog 10; disp ld aft 12 til ld 14; jnd & blun nxt & 2 out; sn hdd; 2l 2nd at last; r.o game und str press flat; a hld; eased nr fin*
[211^U]	3	30	**Bright Approach (IRE)** 16-1 **Miss P Gundry** *Ld; jnd aft 12; hdd aft nxt; 6½l 3rd 9 & wkng qckly 3 out*
	P		**Castle Shelley (IRE)** 12-1 **R Smith** *Cl 3rd mostly til 5th 7; lost tch 12; last 13; bhnd when pu 15*
	P		**Kinlogh Gale (IRE)** 33-1 **G Barfoot-Saunt** *A last & nvr on terms; 5l adrift of rest 4; detach 9; t.o & pu 13*
[74^2]	P		**Leap Frog** 7-2 **A Charles-Jones** *(xnb) tde; chsd ldrs; disp 4th 5; in tch to 12; wknd & releg last 14; pu nxt*
	P		**Merry Shot (IRE)** 16-1 **R Young** *Last of main body but wl in in tch; 4l 6th 7; disp 3rd 13; 5l 3rd & wkng 15; dem 4th when jmpd v slow 2 out & pu*
[96^3]	P		**Ryder Cup (IRE)** 20-1 **G Maundrell** *Chsd ldr; jmpd slow 7; still cl 2nd 12; wknd qckly; detach 5th & btn 14; pu 3 out*

OFFICIAL DISTANCES: 3l, 25l **TIME:** 6min 11.7s **TOTE:** £3.60 **DF:** £5.90

264 Open Maiden 56&7yo (Div 1), 12st

15 ran

[57^2]	1		**ONE OF THE NATIVES (IRE)** 5-2F **T Mitchell** *(xnb) Towards rr; 11th 5; hmpd bad 8; went 4th aft 12; trckd ldrs til eff 15; lft 3nd 3 out; went 2nd nxt; rdn to chall & ld flat; all out*
[72^5]	2	2	**Carbonado** 5-1 **P Pritchard** *7s-5s; trckd ldrs; 5th 4; 6th 7; prog to 3rd 9 & 1½l 2nd aft 12; ld aft nxt til hdd & no ex flat*

	3	20	**Border Laird (IRE)** 16-1 **A Charles-Jones** *Mid-div; 8th & mist 6; prog to disp ld 11; ld aft 12-14; 3rd & one pce 15; hvly eased & lost sev lengths flat*
	4	25	**Shamrock Lad** 10-1 **Miss P Gundry** *Towards rr; mist 3; went 15l 6th aft 12; 5th & no imp 15; lft t.o 4th 3 out*
[220ᶠ]	5	40	**Mandalady (IRE)** (5a) 50-1 **M Legge** *Sn last; t.o 8*
	P		**Abbots Court (IRE)** (7a) 20-1 **R Walford** *Prom brief; sn settled in last pr; school & stdly lost ground til pu 13*
[12⁴]	F		**Ard Na Carrig (IRE)** 6-1 **A Wintle** *Prom til 4; fell 8*
	U		**Chancellors Vision** 10-1 **Miss S Vickery** *Chsd ldrs; 4th 4; cl 2nd 9 til 3l 3rd aft 12; 2nd & ev ch 15; blun & ur nxt*
[57ʳ]	P		**Chasing A Bid** (7a) 25-1 **J Snowden** *Midfield & nd; 9th 7; lost tch frm 12; bhnd when pu 15*
[60⁵]	P		**Perking** 25-1 **M Foley** *Mid-div; 9th aft 5; stdly lost tch; rem 7th 14; pu 3 out*
	P		**Seriously Smart** (5a) 25-1 **Miss A Bush** *Ld to 3; prom to 7; in tch til wknd 11; bhnd when pu 14*
	P		**So Frank** 5-1 **David Dennis** *7s-5s; chsd ldrs; 7th 4; mist 6; nd aft; wl bhnd frm 12; pu 15*
	P		**Summer Pudding** (5a) 3-1 **Julian Pritchard** *Pulled v hrd; saddle slpd forward & jmpd 2 out of control; pulled round 3*
	P		**The Ugly Gunner** 25-1 **E Gretton** *Cl 3rd mostly to 7; in tch 11; sn wknd; bhnd when pu 15*
[131ᴾ]	P		**Whatacharlie** (tt) 12-1 **P Keane** *Cl 2nd til lft in ld 8; jnd 11; sn hdd; 5th & wkng aft 12; pu 15*

OFFICIAL DISTANCES: 2l, 25l **TIME:** 6min 18.2s **TOTE:** £3.20
> *The stewards interviewed the rider of Summer Pudding which was pulled up - his explanation that the saddle slipped was reported to Portman Square as the rider had experienced similar tack problems previously when riding at this weight*

265 Open Maiden 56&7yo (Div 2), 12st   7 ran

	1		**BURGUNDY BOB (IRE)** 4-1 **Julian Pritchard** *Jw; made all; 3l up to 12; virt jnd nxt; drew clr frm 14; 15l ahd 3 out; unchall; canter*
[212ᵁ]	2	15	**Basil** 7-1 **D Alers-Hankey** *Tchd 6s; cl 3rd/4th til 10l 5th aft 12; went 3rd 14; sn outpcd; tk 15l 2nd aft 2 out; nvr any ch w wnr; nt disg*
	3	15	**Fasgo (IRE)** (7a) 5-4F **Miss P Gundry** *Tchd 6/4; jmpd v novicey; 6l 4th when blun 6; went cl 3rd 11 & 2nd aft nxt; dem 3rd when blun agn 13 & releg last; 25½l last 3 out; kpt on wl*
	4	8	**Mayfair Monarch** (7a) 14-1 **H Froud** *2 handlers; jw mostly; trckd ldr in 3l 2nd to 12; 2nd agn 14; hopelessly outpcd frm mxt; 15l 2nd when pckd v bad 2 out; picked up wl by rdr but dem 4th & no ch aft*
	5	25	**Jackpat (IRE)** 9-1 **D Mansell** *Chsd ldrs; 6½l 5th aft 6; disp 3rd 8; 4th 12; 20l 4th & wkng 3 out; plodded on*
[31ᴾ]	F		**Mainlier** 7-2 **G Barfoot-Saunt** *Opened 4s; cl 4th til fell 4*
	U		**Newby End (IRE)** 10-1 **A Blanch** *Towards rr but wl in tch; 7½l 6th aft 6; cl last when ur 11*

OFFICIAL DISTANCES: 15l, 20l **TIME:** 6min 31.6s **TOTE:** £5.80

Vale of Clettwr
Erw Lon (LH 8F,18J) Sat, 19 Feb (SOFT)

266 Hunt   6 ran

	1		**SHEEPHAVEN** 4-1 **D Davies** *Trckd ldrs; ld 9 til hdd aft 10; 2nd & ev ch til lft wl clr last*
	2	15	**Young Mariner** 4-1 **J Edwards** *(xnb) 1st ride; drpd to rr 5; 6l 5th ½way; 5l 4th 13; sn outpcd; 20l 4th 2 out; stayed on; went 2nd flat*
	3	4	**Plucky Punter** (tt) 5-1 **A Barker** *1st ride; ld 2-6 & 7 til mist 9; ld aft 10 til hdd 14; wknd aft 3 out; lft 20l 2nd at last; dem flat*
	4	25	**Terrano Star (IRE)** 5-1 **P Sheldrake** *Tubed; 2 handlers; ld to 2; mist 5; 2nd til ld 6; hdd 7; 1½l 3rd ½way; 12l 5th & wkng 13; mist 15; t.o*
	U		**Caribbean Dream** (12a) 6-1 **G Skone** *6th when ur 1*
	U		**Time To Share (IRE)** 8-11F **G Lewis** *Hld up; 5l 4th ½way; went 2l 3rd 11; ld 14 til blun & ur last*

OFFICIAL DISTANCES: 20l, 10l **TIME:** 6min 47.0s

267 Confined Maiden (Div 1), 12st   10 ran

	1		**SOVIET SIP** (7a) 4-1 **D Jones** *A.p; jmpd v slow 1; 2½l 3rd ½way; went 2nd 13; mist 14; chsd ldr aft 3 out; stayed on to ld flat; all out*

	2	¾	**Travel Safely (IRE)** 4-1 **J Keen** *Hld up; 6l 5th ½way; hdwy 11; went 2l 3rd 14; qcknd to ld 3 out; 4l clr nxt; hdd & no ex flat*
	F		**Artique Fish (IRE)** 2-1F **J Jukes** *Prom; 3l 4th ½way; 8l 5th & lsng plce when fell 11*
	P		**Be Bop Bentley** (7a) 5-1 **P Hamer** *A bhnd; mists 3 & 8; 12l 8th ½way; lost tch 11; t.o & pu 14*
	U		**Cresswell Quay** 4-1 **G Lewis** *6th when ur 1*
	P		**Daisy's Choice** (12a) 6-1 **P Sheldrake** *Bckwd; sn wl bhnd; t.o when tried to rn out & jmpd v slow 5; pu 6*
[220ᴾ]	F		**Fast Flow (IRE)** (5a) 7-1 **Miss A Meakins** *Ld to 4; 2nd to 13; 4th & wkng when mist 15; 20l 3rd when fell last*
[72ᴾ]	F		**Fernhill Blaze** 3-1 **T Vaughan** *2nd til ld 4; hit 5; hdd 3 out; 6l 3rd & wkng when mist 2 out; poor 4th when fell last*
	P		**Itsfreddie** 12-1 **A Price** *Bckwd & unclipped; a bhnd; 10l 7th ½way; lost tch 12; t.o & pu 14*
	P		**Just Ruffled** 12-1 **J Price** *Hld up; 9l 6th ½way; lost tch 12; wl bhnd when pu 14*

OFFICIAL DISTANCE: ½l **TIME:** 6min 51.3s

268 Confined Maiden (Div 2), 12st   11 ran

[20ᴾ]	1		**HOWSYOURLUCK (IRE)** 6-4F **T Vaughan** *(xnb) 7/2-6/4; lw; ld to 2; ld 4; mists 14 & 2 out; stayed on wl*
	2	1½	**Saxon Queen** (5a) 7-2 **E Williams** *(xnb) Lw; hld up; 7l 5th ½way; went 2½l 3rd 14 & 2nd nxt; ev ch frm 2 out; edged rt u.p flat; r.o*
[72²]	3	7	**Bonny Rigg (IRE)** (5a) 2-1 **D Jones** *Trckd ldrs; 5l 4th ½way; went 2nd 12-15; one pce 3 out*
	4	12	**Clonshire Castle (IRE)** 2-1 **S Blackwell** *Hld up; 10l 7th ½way; hdwy 11; 3l 4th when mist 14; wknd 3 out*
	P		**Billy Whizz** 14-1 **P Sheldrake** *Prom to 8; 9l 6th ½way; lost tch 12; t.o & pu 2 out*
	F		**Fair Charmeur (IRE)** (5a) 20-1 **Miss A Meakins** *Hld up; 7l 6th when fell 7*
	P		**I Dont Believe It (IRE)** 10-1 **G Richards** *Bckwd; lost plce 5; 18l 9th ½way; wl bhnd when pu 12*
	r		**Jesusa** 14-1 **J Keen** *Last til ref 2*
[71ᶠ]	P		**Kopain** 8-1 **J L Llewellyn** *(xnb) Prom; 3l 3rd ½way; 4l 5th 14; wknd 15; bhnd when pu 2 out*
	P		**Spot On Millie** (12a) 12-1 **James Tudor** *1st ride; a bhnd; 15l 8th ½way; blun 14; t.o & pu 2 out*
	U		**Weaver Square (IRE)** 12-1 **M Parry** *1st ride; ld 2-4; 2nd to 12; 5l 6th & wkng when blun & ur 14*

OFFICIAL DISTANCES: s hd, 5l **TIME:** 6min 42.7s

269 Confined Maiden (Div 3), 12st   8 ran

	1		**MECCA PRINCE (IRE)** (7a) 4-1 **James Tudor** *Chsd ldrs; 4l 3rd ½way; 5l 4th 11; went 7l 3rd 13 & 2nd 3 out; ld nxt; stayed on wl flat; 16yo rdr's 1st win*
	2	3	**Secret Can't Say (IRE)** (5a) 11-10F **G Lewis** *A.p; went 2nd 7; ld 9; 4l clr when pckd 15; hdd 2 out; ev ch last; no ex*
	3	12	**Bright Beacon** 7-2 **E Williams** *Hld up; hdwy 8; 4½l 4th ½way; went 3l 2nd 10-3 out; 7l 3rd & wkng nxt*
	P		**Baytownghost (IRE)** 4-1 **J Price** *Bckwd; hld up & bhnd; hdwy 8; 7l 5th ½way; went 4l 3rd 11; 12l 4th & wkng when mist 13; pu 14*
	P		**Fridays Child** (5a) 3-1 **J Jukes** *Ld; 10l clr 5; hdd 9; wknd qckly & pu 10*
	P		**Itsarchie** 10-1 **A Price** *Bckwd & unclipped; sn wl bhnd; blun 6; 30l 8th ½way; t.o & pu 11*
	P		**Marnies Song** (5a) 10-1 **J L Llewellyn** *A bhnd; 15l 7th ½way; pu 11*
[145ᴾ]	P		**Teelyna** (5a) 10-1 **G Marsh** *Jmpd rt; 2nd til jmpd v slow & lost plce 7; 8l 6th ½way; 6l 5th 11; sn wknd; bhnd when pu 13*

OFFICIAL DISTANCES: 2l, 5l **TIME:** 6min 45.0s

270 Confined Maiden (Div 4), 12st   10 ran

	1		**SECRET BEAUTY (IRE)** (5a) 4-1 **M Lewis** *A.p; 4l 3rd ½way; ld 15; clr at last; stayed on wl*
	2	8	**Alisha Bavard (IRE)** (5a) 4-1 **P Sheldrake** *Hld up; 7l 5th ½way; hdwy 11; ld 13-15; 2l 2nd 2 out; wknd app last*
	3	8	**Alicat (IRE)** 3-1JF **Miss E Jones** *Ld to 5; 2nd to 12; ev ch 15; 5l 3rd nxt; wkng when jmpd v slow 2 out*
	4	4	**Omar's Odyssey** (7a) 8-1 **G Maloney** *Chsd ldrs; mist 7; 6l 4th ½way; blun 14; 15l 4th & wkng 3 out*
	P		**Bold Knight** 8-1 **G Skone** *Last til pu aft 2*

	r		**D'nial** (5a) 3-1JF **G Richards** *A bhnd; mist 1; 16l 7th ½way; t.o when ref 14 & ended up in ditch*
	U		**Jevington (IRE)** 6-1 **N Jones** *2nd til ld 5; mist 6; hdd & mist 13; 4l 5th when blun & ur 14*
[145ᴾ]	P		**Keldan Star (IRE)** 8-1 **T Vaughan** *6th when brought to standstill 6; 15l 6th ½way; bhnd when pu 11*
[30ᴾ]	P		**Lord Chamberlain** 4-1 **E Williams** *A bhnd; 20l 8th ½way; pu 10*
[146ᴾ]	F		**Tiger Bell** 12-1 **Miss S Major** *5th when fell 6*

OFFICIAL DISTANCES: 5l, 5l   **TIME:** 6min 48.4s

271 Mens Open, 12st   10 ran

	1		**MISTER HORATIO** 4-5F **M Lewis** *Ld 3; 3l clr 2 out; just hld on*
	2	½	**Skomar Oddy** 2-1 **J Jukes** *2 handlers; hld up; mist 1; 3l 4th & hdwy ½way; 2l 3rd 13; went 2nd 3 out; stayed on und tender handling flat; fin lame*
	3	20	**Whistling Buck (IRE)** (tt) 20-1 **C Williams** *(bf)Hdwy 6; 3½l 5th ½way; went 2nd 12-3 out; wknd & 8l 3rd nxt*
	4	12	**Twilight Tom** 14-1 **A Price** *Sn bhnd; 12l 10th ½way; 20l 7th 14; went 30l 4th 3 out; nvr nr ldrs*
[222ᵁ]	P		**Archer (IRE)** (7x) 9-1 **J L Llewellyn** *Hld up; hdwy & 2½l 3rd ½way; lost plce 13; 16l 5th nxt; t.o & pu 2 out*
	P		**Moon Tiger** 14-1 **D Jones** *In tch to 12; wl bhnd when pu 15*
[149ᶠ]	P		**Saffron Moss** (7x) (bl) 12-1 **E Williams** *Drvn along 5; lost plce 7; 7l 8th ½way; lost tch 11; wl bhnd when pu 13*
	r		**Swinging Sixties (IRE)** 33-1 **G Richards** *Prom; went 2nd 5-12; 8l 4th & wkng when mist 13; rem 5th when ref 2 out*
	P		**Viardot (IRE)** 12-1 **S Blackwell** *Prom til lost plce u.p & 4l 6th ½way; lost tch 12; 21l 8th 14; pu 15*
	P		**Willchris** (7x) 12-1 **T Vaughan** *Tde; ld to 3; lost plce 6; 8l 9th ½way; bhnd when pu 11*

OFFICIAL DISTANCES: ½l, 10l   **TIME:** 6min 28.6s

272 Ladies Open   11 ran

[149ᴾ]	1		**OPERA FAN (IRE)** evensF **Miss C Thomas** *Tde; ld to 6; 2l 4th ½way; 3l down 2 out; rallied last; qcknd to ld nr fin*
[1²]	2	1	**Coolvawn Lady (IRE)** (5a) 3-1 **Miss P Jones** *A.p; went 2nd 7; ld 9-14; ld 15; went 3l clr 2 out; hdd nr fin*
	3	20	**Bullens Bay (IRE)** 10-1 **Miss F Wilson** *Chsd ldrs; mist 3; 9l 6th ½way; outpcd & 12l 4th 14; went poor 3rd at last*
[150⁶]	4	6	**Hee's A Dancer** 5-1 **Miss E Jones** *Prom; ld 6-9; 2nd to 14; sn rdn & no ex; 15l 3rd 2 out; fin tired*
[101ᴾ]	P		**Ballymaloe Boy (IRE)** (3x) 25-1 **Miss B Williams** *(xnb) Chsd ldrs; 6l 5th ½way; wknd 12; wl bhnd when pu 14*
	U		**Bancyfelin Boy** 33-1 **Miss J Hughes** *(xnb) Bckwd; 1st ride; 10th when ur 1*
	P		**Captain Khedive** 16-1 **Miss S Talbot** *Prom; went 1½l 3rd ½way; wknd 12; 15l 6th 14; wl bhnd when pu 3 out*
	P		**Mr Mad** 16-1 **Miss G Evans** *1st ride; sn wl bhnd; to 5; pu 14*
	U		**Palladium Boy** 14-1 **Miss L Pearce** *3rd when mist & ur 3*
[33¹]	P		**Sand Star** (5a) 33-1 **Miss A Meakins** *A bhnd; 15l 8th ½way; t.o & pu 2 out*
	P		**Turning Trix** 7-2 **Miss R Curtis** *Nd; 12l 7th ½way; wl bhnd 12; t.o & pu 2 out*

OFFICIAL DISTANCES: ½l, 15l   **TIME:** 6min 23.0s

273 Restricted (Div 1), 12st   11 ran

[218ᴾ]	1		**TIGER TINA** (5a) 6-4F **A Evans** *Lw; hld up; hdwy & 3l 4th ½way; went 2nd 10; ld 14; drew wl clr frm 3 out; easy*
	2	20	**Mr Magget (IRE)** 4-1 **Miss C Thomas** *A.p; went 2nd 6-10; 6l 3rd 14; outpcd when mist 15; plodded on; went poor 2nd at last*
	3	1	**Presuming Ed (IRE)** 8-1 **A Price** *Bckwd; ld to 3; clr w wnr 13; hdd 14; mist 15; sn wknd; 2nd til dem at last*
[69ᴾ]	4	10	**Lady Buckland** (5a) 4-1 **Miss P Jones** *Ld to 3; 2l 3rd ½way; 4l 4th 11; lost plce & 10l 5th 13; no ch aft*
[38ᴾ]	5	runin	**Pure Air** 10-1 **G Maloney** *2nd to 6; 5l 5th ½way; wknd & 9l 7th 11; t.o 14*
	P		**Cefn Woodsman** 12-1 **D Jones** *Hld up; 6l 7th ½way; 8l 6th 11; wknd to 17l 6th 13; pu 14*
[38ᴾ]	P		**Gaelic Royale (IRE)** (5a) 12-1 **T Vaughan** *Hld up; 7½l 8th ½way; lost tch 11; pu 12*
	P		**Just Supreme** 4-1 **G Lewis** *Mist & lost plce 6; 17l 10th ½way; wl bhnd when pu 11*

F			**Lostyndyke (IRE)** 5-1 J Jukes *Hld up; 5½l 6th ½way; 4½l 5th 11; 8l 4th when fell 14*
P			**Sea Search** 33-1 J Keen *Bckwd; mist 1; sn wl bhnd; jmpd v slow 6; t.o & pu 8*
P			**The Rural Dean (IRE)** 20-1 J Price *A bhnd; 12l 9th ½way; t.o & pu 13*

OFFICIAL DISTANCES: 20l, 1l **TIME:** 6min 35.2s

274 Restricted (Div 2), 12st   7 ran

[22¹]	1		**EVAN'S COLLIER BOY (IRE)** 4-6F J Jukes *(xnb) 2 handlers; tde; ld 1; sn 10l clr; mist 13; drew rt away frm 15; unchall*
	2	25	**Milly Le Moss (IRE)** (5a) 12-1 T Faulkner *Sn wl bhnd; 30l 6th ½way; lft 20l 4th 14; went 20l 2nd aft 15; no ch w wnr*
[69⁶]	3	25	**Tiger Lord** (vis) 7-1 S Blackwell *(xnb) Sn drvn along & wl bhnd; 25l 5th ½way; lft dist 4th 3 out & 3rd at last*
	P		**Absent Citizen (IRE)** (5a) 5-2 E Williams *Hld up; mist 1; went 15l 3rd 3; eff 11; went 10l 2nd 12; wkng when mist 15; rem 3rd when pu last*
[38ᴾ]	P		**Dyffryn Prince (IRE)** 4-1 D Jones *Nvr gng wl; 22l 4th & rmdrs ½way; 15l 4th 11; wknd u.p 13; pu nxt*
	P		**Itscinders** (5a) 8-1 A Price *Sn wl bhnd; 37l 7th ½way; t.o & pu 11*
[38ᴾ]	P		**Not For Profit (IRE)** (bl) 8-1 C Williams *Jmpd lft; ld to 1; 2nd til wknd 13; 15l 3rd nxt; poor 4th when pu 3 out*

OFFICIAL DISTANCES: 25l, 20l **TIME:** 6min 34.1s

275 Confined, 12st   11 ran

[141¹]	1		**GUNNER BOON** (5x) 4-6F Miss P Jones *Lw; went 2nd 3 til mist 8; 12l 3rd ½way; went 2nd aft 12; mist 3 out; 7l down & lkd hld nxt; rallied & lft clr last*
[35ᶠ]	2	12	**Sip Of Brandy (IRE)** 10-1 G Lewis *Chsd ldrs; mist 3; 16l 4th ½way; eff & 5l 3rd 13; one pce 15; 12l 3rd 2 out; lft 2nd last*
	3	20	**Same Difference (IRE)** 14-1 Mrs B Lewis *Sn outpcd & wl bhnd; 30l 7th ½way; 28l 6th 11; lft 30l 4th 14 & poor 3rd at last*
[272ᵁ]	4	1½fs	**Bancyfelin Boy** 33-1 Miss J Hughes *(xnb) Bckwd; 2nd outing; sn wl bhnd; t.o 8*
	5	20	**Teigr Pren** 16-1 P Sheldrake *Sn wl bhnd; 36l 8th ½way; t.o 11*
	P		**Alfion (IRE)** 8-1 D Jones *Bhnd til pu & dism 3*
[34ᶠ]	P		**Comme Une Fleur (FR)** (5a) 20-1 T Vaughan *(bnf) 20l 7th when mist 6; wl bhnd when pu 8*
	F		**Flutterbud** (5a,3x) 5-2 E Williams *Lw; sn prom; went 10l 2nd 8; blun 11; ld 12; mist 14; went 7l clr & lkd wnr 2 out; jnd & fell last*
[141ᴾ]	P		**Shehab (IRE)** 12-1 C Williams *Ld; 10l clr 5-10; hdd & wknd 12; 12l 4th nxt; pu 14*
	P		**Swan's Wish (IRE)** 7-1 S Blackwell *Mist 1; sn bhnd; 29l 6th ½way; t.o 11; pu 13*
	P		**Tilt Tech Flyer** 12-1 Miss F Wilson *Nvr on terms; 22l 5th ½way; wl bhnd when pu 12*

OFFICIAL DISTANCES: 10l, 15l **TIME:** 6min 37.1s
The final fence was omitted by 4th & 5th horses - fallen horse

Sinnington

Duncombe Park (RH 9F,18J) Sun, 20 Feb (GOOD/SOFT)

276 Hunt - 16J   7 ran

[169⁵]	1		**THE HAZEL HARRIER (IRE)** 6-4 Miss A Deniel *Settled chsng group; 4th 10; mist 12; 12l 3rd passing omitted 2 out; ld on v long rn to last; rdn & qcknd clr flat*
[50³]	2	12	**Yornoangel** 6-1 R Clark *(xnb) Mist 4; detach last to 10; prog 12 to ld aft omitted 2 out; sn hdd; rdn & hld when mist last*
[55ᵁ]	3	15	**Mr Hook** 33-1 P Halder *Chsng group; 5th 10; lost tch in 27l 4th aft 3 out; plodded on*
[169ᵁ]	4	15	**Curtainsatchophowell (IRE)** evensF S Swiers *(xnb) Ld & sn 15l clr; 1½ fncs ahd by 11; wknd rap 3 out & hdd passing omitted 2 out; sn v tired & rem*
	U		**Louis Renee** 16-1 B Woodhouse *Midfield when blun & ur 6; fell agn last when loose*
	P		**Mac's Blade (USA)** 12-1 R Edwards *Fat; mist 2; in tch in chsng group to 11; wkng when blun 12 & pu*
[168ᵁ]	U		**Mrs Drummond (IRE)** (5a) 8-1 K Prendergast *Mist 6; chsd v long ldr til rdn 10; sn wknd; t.o when ur last*

OFFICIAL DISTANCES: 12l, 20l **TIME:** 6min 59.0s
Fences 8 & 17 omitted - frozen ground

277 Confined, 12st   14 ran

	1		**PHARLINDO (IRE)** 6-1 Mrs F Needham *(xnb,pricker os) Bckwd; tk str hld; rr brief; 3rd by 7; ld 9-11; lft in ld 15; 10l clr app last; drvn & kpt on wl*

[134³]	2	7	**Harbour Blaze (IRE)** 5-1 Miss R Clark *Bit bckwd; chsd ldrs; hmpd 6; 6th 10; hmpd agn 15 & lft 2nd; 10l down app last; rdn & one pce*
[48⁸]	3	10	**Springhill Quay (IRE)** 16-1 R Clark *A bhnd; 30l 9th 10; plugged past btn horses frm 2 out*
[134⁶]	4	1	**Blackwoodscountry** 10-1 N Wilson *Lft 2nd 6 til app 9; 4th nxt; outpcd aft mist 2 out; disp 20l 3rd when mist last*
[135⁹]	5	10	**Holiway Star (IRE)** 25-1 N Tutty *(xnb) Midfield; 7th 10; some prog 3 out; rdn & fnd nil aft nxt; disp 20l 3rd app last; nt r.o*
	6	2	**Postage Stamp** 12-1 B Orde-Powlett *Rr early; 7th & eff aft 8; 5th & mist 10; hmpd 15; lost tch 3 out; plodded on*
[54⁶]	7	25	**Icantsay (IRE)** 33-1 D Thomas *Rem & reluct in last pr; t.o last & drvn along 10*
[155⁷]	8	7	**Mr Primetime (IRE)** 12-1 N Bannister *Mist 4 & rmdr; prom; 3rd 10; mist 11; strugg aft; t.o 2 out; rn deplorably*
[48⁵]		P	**Just Charlie** (3x) 5-2F D Easterby *Lw; hit 2; wl bhnd & nvr gng wl; last aft 8; t.o & pu 13*
[135³]		U	**Misti Hunter (IRE)** 6-1 Miss Rachel Clark *(xnb) Lw; mist 3; bhnd; poor 8th aft 8 til ur 12*
		F	**Mr McCarney (IRE)** (tt) 25-1 W Burnell *Pulled hrd; 5th when fell 8*
		F	**Pennywise** (5a) 5-1 S Charlton *Ld to 9; ld agn & blun 11; still gng wl in ld when fell 15*
		U	**Vital Issue (IRE)** 5-1 P Johnson *Prsd ldr til ur 6*
		r	**Watacon** 8-1 K Prendergast *Bckwd; veered rt start & tk no part*

OFFICIAL DISTANCES: 6l, 10l   **TIME:** 6min 55.0s

278 Restricted   6 ran

[51¹]	1		**JACKSON'S HOLE** 2-5F D Easterby *Lw; confid rdn; last to 9; ld 11; gng easy aft; prsd & hit last; sn rdn clr*
[171⁹]	2	6	**The Shy Padre (IRE)** 14-1 J Townson *Clup in bunch; rdn & last brief aft 10; kpt on to chse wnr aft 2 out; ev ch last; drvn & outpcd*
[50⁹]	3	2½	**Deer Park Lass (IRE)** (5a) 20-1 D Thomas *Prom; ev ch 2 out; 7l 3rd app last; plugged on stdly but nd*
	4	15	**Hidden Island** 11-2 C Wilson *Oht; handy in cl bunch; went 2nd app 2 out; ev ch when stumbled app last; wknd flat*
[166²]	5	15	**Asked To Leave** (5a) 10-1 I Bennett *Set slow pce to 11; drvn & lost tch app 2 out*
[137⁹]	6	5	**Lord George** 5-1 P Atkinson *Chsd ldr to 10; mist 12 & lost tch; wl bhnd aft 2 out*

OFFICIAL DISTANCES: 6l, 4l   **TIME:** 6min 58.0s

279 Land Rover Mens Open, 12st   9 ran

	1		**MURTON HEIGHTS** 6-1 N Tutty *2 handlers; bckwd; settled rr; 4th & prog 10; trckd ldrs aft til 4th rdn to ld app last; stayed on str uphill*
[171⁴]	2	3	**Concerto Collonges (FR)** (4x) 6-4F R Hartley *(xnb) Jmpd slow 3; bhnd; 8th 10; rdn 14; still 6l 5th app last; drvn & stayed on wl; snatched 2nd cl home; nt rch wnr*
[134⁹]	3	1	**Bold Fountain (IRE)** 8-1 C Wilson *Hld up in midfield; 7th 10; prog in 2nd 3 out; jnd ldr gng wl app last; rdn & nt qckn flat*
[171³]	4	8	**Jr-Kay (IRE)** 5-2 N Bannister *2nd/3rd til ld aft 2 out; hdd last; sn btn*
[171⁹]	5	40	**Be Brave** (7x) 20-1 R Lochman *Mist 5; cl up til drpd back last 12; t.o 3 out*
[173⁹]	6	25	**Keep A Secret** 33-1 P Atkinson *(xnb) Mists in last; strugg aft blun 12; t.o aft 2 out; walked frm last*
[136⁹]		U	**Calleva Star (IRE)** 25-1 R Abrahams *Jmpd lft 11; ld til aft 2 out; ev ch app last; 4th & btn when ur*
		P	**Fryup Satellite** 14-1 P Halder *Bit bckwd; cl up; 4th 8; lost plce aft 10; pu 15*
		P	**Supercharmer** 7-2 K Prendergast *Hdwy to 3rd 8 & 2nd 10; wknd 15; t.o & pu last*

OFFICIAL DISTANCES: 3l, 1½l   **TIME:** 6min 57.0s

280 Ladies Open   8 ran

[135²]	1		**MARIUS (IRE)** 5-2 Miss V Russell *Lw; prsd ldrs; 3rd 10; mist 15; 5l 2nd & rdn aft 2 out; clsd to jn ldr last; forged clr; game*
[170¹]	2	5	**Monkey Ago** 5-4F Miss J Foster *Ld aft 1; 8l clr 3 out; hrd prsd on long rn app last; hdd flat; rdn & nt qckn*
[135⁵]	3	10	**Tabriz** (5a) 25-1 Miss A Thompson *V keen gng down; hld up trckng ldrs; 7l 16th 10; eff 13; chall & ev ch app last; outpcd flat*
[135⁹]	4	15	**Cab On Target** 5-1 Miss W Gibson *Cl up; 4th 10; outpcd 13; dist 4th aft 2 out*
		P	**Double Tempo (IRE)** 8-1 Miss R Clark *Mostly 2nd to 13; wknd qckly aft mist 3 out; t.o & pu 2 out*
		P	**Miss Accounts (IRE)** (5a) 8-1 Miss A Armitage *Ld 1 but 7th 2; lost tch 11; sn strugg agn; t.o & pu 3 out*
		P	**Sharp Embrace** 33-1 Miss S Rodman *Bckwd; nt jw in last; lost tch 5; t.o 8; pu 3 out*

| | | P | | The Minister (IRE) 5-1 Miss T Jackson *Hld up; mist 7; 5th & cl up 10; rdn nxt; wknd 3 out; t.o aft 2 out; pu last* |

OFFICIAL DISTANCES: 3l, 7l TIME: 6min 48.0s

281 Open Maiden (Div 1) 12 ran

[46²]	1		HIGH EXPECTATIONS (IRE) (7a) 5-4F J Tate *20l 4th 7; clsd to ld aft 8; sn hdd; prom & gng wl til ld agn last; rdn & qcknd clr*
[46⁹]	2	5	Broken English (5a) 25-1 Miss T Jackson *Hld up towards rr; mist 8; impd to 5th 10; jnd ldrs & ld brief on long rn app last; drvn & outpcd flat*
	3	7	Pearly's Song 14-1 K Needham *Towards rr early; bumped 8; lft 8th 11; eff 15; blun 2 out; 5th & ev ch aft til no ex app last; passed 2 rivals flat*
[169ᵁ]	4	12	Port Valenska (IRE) 5-2 B Woodhouse *(xnb) Midfield; 7th 10; outpcd 14; tried to cl aft 2 out; sn btn*
[53⁴]	5	4	Ron On The Run (IRE) (bl) 4-1 S Charlton *Bhnd & numerous mists; prog aft 8; 4th 10; went 2nd 15; 2l 5th aft 2 out; nt r.o; eased flat*
[53ᵁ]	6	5	In The Van 12-1 M Morley *(xnb) Lw; tk keen hld & clr w one rival til hvly rstrnd & hdd brief aft 8; hdd agn aft 2 out; wknd qckly bef last*
[51ᵁ]	7	20	The Noble Rebel (IRE) 12-1 A Pennock *Towards rr; mist 8; brief eff in 6th 10; wknd 13; mist 3 out; t.o aft blun nxt*
	P		Ard Drum (IRE) (tt) 14-1 N Wilson *A detach last; blun 15 & nxt; t.o 2 out; pu last*
	F		Charlie Dazzle (IRE) 7-1 Mrs F Needham *Fell 3*
	U		Im Struggling (7a) 14-1 K Lupton *11th when ur 2*
[138⁹]	U		Oaklands Millie (IRE) (5a) 25-1 P Kinsella *Chsng group; mist 6; 8th & wkng when blun & ur 11*
[277⁹]	P		Watacon 5-1 G Markham *2nd outing (still bckwd!); pulled v hrd; jmpd alarm 1; 2nd/3rd til mist 10; lsng plce when bad mist 12 & pu*

OFFICIAL DISTANCES: 5l, 5l TIME: 7min 05.0s

282 Open Maiden (Div 2) 15 ran

[167ᶠ]	1		MEADOWBANK 6-4F M Watson *Settled rr & gng wl; stdy prog 15; ld app last; r.o wl; rdly*
[45ᶜ]	2	3	Tricky Trevor (IRE) 20-1 Miss H Delahooke *Made most to 11; ld agn app 2 out; hdd app last; kpt on one pce*
[168ᵁ]	3	2	Never Wonder (IRE) (7a) 7-1 J Tate *V novicey in rr early; last & mist 4; prog 11; mist 15; 6l 3rd aft 2 out; tried to chall app last; no ex*
	4	12	Sassy Street (IRE) 50-1 A Richardson *Mist 2; rr but in tch til blun bad 12; 15l 7th aft 2 out; no ex*
[138³]	5	6	Mighty Rising (7a) 2-1 S Charlton *Hld up & bhnd; blun 8; wl in tch 10; 12l 6th & wkng aft 2 out*
[169⁴]	6	10	Redmire (5a) 20-1 A Pennock *Settled trckng ldrs; qcknd to ld 11; hdd app 2 out; sn wknd*
	P		Cricketing 33-1 P Johnson *Mist & rdr lost iron 1; unable to regain it & pu 3*
	P		Early Dawn (5a) 16-1 J Davies *Bckwd; unruly; 2 handlers; hdwy to 3rd when saddle slpd & mist 7 & pu*
[54²]	F		Erni (FR) 5-1 W Burnell *Hld up at rr of bunch; 10l 4th aft 2 out; no prog; btn 4th when fell last*
[55⁵]	P		Flowing Fortune 50-1 Miss R Clark *Midfield; mists 10 & 13; sn wknd; t.o aft 2 out; pu last*
	P		Lewis 20-1 Miss T Jackson *2nd/3rd & ev ch til wknd qckly app 2 out; t.o & pu last*
	P		Over In McGanns (IRE) 33-1 C Mulhall *Bhnd but cl up to 11; sn wknd; t.o 3 out; pu last*
[139⁹]	F		Perdix (12a) 33-1 G Brewer *Jmpd lft & mists; 8l last & strugg when fell 11*
[133⁹]	U		Thirkleby Skeena (5a) 16-1 N Tutty *3rd when mist 8; chsd ldrs til bad mist 14; blun & ur nxt*
	U		Timeforanother (5a) 12-1 Mrs F Needham *5th when blun & ur 8*

OFFICIAL DISTANCES: 3l, 1l TIME: 7min 03.0s

283 Open Maiden (Div 3) 10 ran

[133²]	1		HAZEL REILLY (IRE) (5a) evensF L Bates *Midfield; 13l 6th 10; impd to 2nd 14; ev ch when mist 2 out; chall & ½l down last; outpcd & lkd btn flat; rallied game final 100yds; ld nr fin*
[138⁹]	2	hd	Flashing Gale (IRE) 4-1 D Coates *Lw; mist 1; 2nd/3rd til lft in ld app 13; rdn 3l clr flat; tied up & caught nr fin*
[168ᶠ]	3	100y	Fiery Jack 6-1 N Tutty *2 handlers; midfield; mist 7; 12l 5th 10; lft 25l 3rd 15; sn wl t.o*
	r		Can I Come Too (IRE) 10-1 I Bennett *Ld; 4l clr 10; thrashed but pulled himself up aft bad mist 12*
[169⁹]	P		Captain Oates 8-1 M Watson *School in rr; clsd aft 8; eased out aft 10; pu 12*

	U		**Daring Magic** (5a) 5-1 C Denny *Settled 2nd/3rd til mist 7; 10l 3rd & wkng when mist & ur 15*
[169ᴾ]	P		**Imps Way** (12a) 10-1 C Mulhall *Jmpd sketchy & sn strugg in last; t.o & pu 13*
[169ᶠ]	U		**Miss Gloria** (5a) 7-1 S Charlton *(xnb) Disp last when blun bad & ur 6*
[139ᴿ]	F		**Mr Norm** 16-1 J Clare *Mists; chsd ldrs; 9l 4th 10; mist & wknd 11; t.o last when stumb bad & fell app 2*
	F		**Rain Street (IRE)** 8-1 D Thomas *Bhnd; 8th when mist 8; fell 11*

OFFICIAL DISTANCES: nk, dist **TIME:** 7min 06.0s

South East Hunts Club
Charing (LH 8F,19J) Sun, 20 Feb (GOOD, sticky in places)

284 Club Members Maiden 56&7yo, 2m4f, 12st
10 ran

	1		**TUBBER ROADS (IRE)** 4-1 A Sansome *(xnb) Prsd ldg; ld 10; jnd aft nxt; hdd aft 2 out & lkd btn; drvn & stayed on frm last to ld agn nr fin*
	2	hd	**Phar From Chance** (7a) 5-1 Miss P Gundry *Trckd ldrs; prog 9; jnd wnr aft 11; ld aft 2 out & lkd wnr; 2l up at last; wknd & hdd nr fin*
[131²]	3	20	**Kenny Davis (IRE)** 2-1F P Blagg *Hld up; prog to trck ldrs 7; outpcd by ldng trio 11; tk mod 3rd 2 out; nd*
[22³]	4	6	**Fistral Flame** (5a) 5-1 A Charles-Jones *Trckd ldrs; outpcd aft 11; last & no ch 4 out; tk mod 4th nr fin*
[98⁴]	5	¾	**Minino (IRE)** 7-1 N King *Ld to 10; stdly wknd aft nxt; lost 2 plces frm 2 out*
	U		**Finnigan's Lot (IRE)** 25-1 M Walters *Prom to 4; sn lost plce; mist 8; hmpd nxt; disp last when bumped & ur 11*
[130ᵁ]	P		**Hatch Gate** 33-1 M Gorman *(xnb) Jmpd sticky; a last & sn detach; t.o & pu 4 out*
[131ᶠ]	P		**Native Dawn (IRE)** (tt) 10-1 P York *Ldng trio to 7; lost plce; pu 10*
[131ᶠ]	P		**Satellite Express (IRE)** (bl) 20-1 P Hickman *A rr group; wknd 10; pu nxt*
[131ᴾ]	F		**Sleipnir** 14-1 B Hitchcott *A rr; 7th & lsng tch when fell 9*

OFFICIAL DISTANCES: hd, 5l **TIME:** 5min 15.0s **TOTE:** £3.30; places £1.60,£3.20,£1.80 **DF:** £2.60
The owner of Le Cabro D'Or was fined £155 for withdrawing the horse 25min after declarations had closed (not on course - box had broken down)

285 Club Members Restricted, 12st - 18J
12 ran

[190²]	1		**PERFECT FINISHER** (1ow) 16-1 M Hawkins *20s-16s; hld up; prog 8; ld 12-15; ld agn 16; 4l clr aft 2 out; kpt on; rdr weak*
[126³]	2	6	**Ishma (IRE)** 25-1 D Page *Rn in snatches; 7th & in tch 11; outpcd 15; drvn & r.o frm 3 out; stayed on best; lkd to fin 3rd*
[88¹]	3	nk	**Cloudy Creek (IRE)** 2-1JF P Bull *Prom; lft 2nd 5; blun & lost plce 10; eff to ld 15-nxt; prsd wnr aft; mist 3 out; no imp aft; tired last; lkd to fin 2nd*
[126ᶠ]	4	3	**Ally Pally** 2-1JF P York *Towards rr; mist 7; blun 13; rdn when mist 15; kpt on 3 out; nvr able to chall*
[93³]	5	s hd	**Royal Banker** 3-1 N Bloom *In tch; trckd ldng pr 11; outpcd 15; no prog aft; kpt on one pce frm 2 out*
[127⁷]	6	15	**Nattico (IRE)** 20-1 Miss S Gladders *In tch til outpcd frm 15; wknd stdly frm 3 out*
[92ᴾ]	7	15	**Holiday Time (IRE)** (5a) 33-1 Mrs S Hodge *Ld; nrly carried out by loose horse 8; hdd 11; chsd clr ldng pr 15 til pckd nxt; wknd*
[126ᶠ]	P		**Ballybollen (IRE)** 33-1 D Brightling *(xnb) Sn detach in last pr; clsd brief 13; wknd; last when pu 15*
[127ᵁ]	U		**Joyful Hero** (5a) 33-1 Miss P Ellison *Mist 1; rr when ur 4*
[126ᶠ]	U		**Perripage** (vis) 25-1 Miss A Sansom *Chsd ldr til ur 5*
[126²]	U		**Royal Rupert** 7-1 N Benstead *In tch in rr til blun & ur 6*
[126⁶]	U		**Target Time** (5a) 33-1 Mrs L Stock *Sn last pr & detach; clsd brief 13; sn wknd; t.o when mist & rfo 3 out*

OFFICIAL DISTANCES: 5l, hd **TIME:** 6min 44.0s **TOTE:** £23.10; places £8.80,£2.20,£1.40 **DF:** £16.20
Fence 14 omitted - fallen rider

286 Mens Open, 12st
8 ran

[94¹]	1		**REAL VALUE (IRE)** 1-2F A Hickman *Wl plcd; trckd ldr 9; ld aft 12; 15l clr 15; r.o str; most impressive*
	2	45	**Call Home (IRE)** (7x) 8-1 T Hills *Bckwd; 2 handlers; jmpd rt; ld at gd pce til aft 12; 3rd & outpcd frm 15; kpt on agn to tk poor 2nd at last*
[129ᵁ]	3	4	**Nadjati (USA)** (7x) 6-1 P Hall *Hld up; gd prog frm 10 to jn ldr 12; chsd wnr app nxt; 15l down aft 15; mist 3 out; wknd & lost 2nd at last*

[127ᴾ]	P		**Bang On Target** 33-1 J Stephens *(xnb) Sn wl bhnd; t.o when mist 6; pu 9*
[130ˢ]	P		**Broguestown Pride (IRE)** 33-1 P Blagg *Prom to 4; sn rdn & wknd; t.o 8; pu 12*
	P		**Galaroi (IRE)** *(7x) (tt)* 16-1 D Robinson *Chsd ldr to 9; wknd 12; 35l 4th aft 15; t.o & pu last*
	P		**Pair Of Jacks (IRE)** *(bl)* 33-1 P York *Rr & strugg to stay in tch; wknd 10; pu 12*
[93ⁱ]	P		**Teeton Builds** 7-1 A Sansome *Chsd ldrs; strugg 10; sn wknd; 65l last 15; pu nxt*

OFFICIAL DISTANCES: 25l, 3l TIME: 6min 32.2s TOTE: £1.60; places £1.10,£2.10,£1.70 DF: £6.10

287 Ladies Open
4 ran

	1		**WHIPPERS DELIGHT (IRE)** 9-4 Miss J Grant *Made all; pushed along & qcknd sltly to 6l clr 4 out; kpt on; unchall*
[128ˢ]	2	10	**Young Nimrod** 7-2 Miss C Grissell *Hld up gng wl; outpcd but still gng wl aft 15; eff to chse wnr aft 2 out; no imp & tired last*
[84ᵁ]	3	1½	**Gatchou Mans (FR)** 11-8F Miss L Rowe *Prsd wnr; mist 10; upsides 15; sn nt qckn; lost 2nd aft 2 out; v one-pced*
[129ᶜ]	4	25	**Cill Churnain (IRE)** 5-1 Mrs E Coveney *Chsd ldrs; jmpd rt 7; mist 10; pushed along & nt gng wl 15; wknd aft 15; t.o; disapp*

OFFICIAL DISTANCES: 12l, 2l TIME: 6min 37.0s TOTE: £2.20 DF: £7.60

288 Club Members Moderate, 12st
16 ran

[91ⁱ]	1		**FAIR EXCHANGE** 5-2JF P Taiano *Prom; ld 10; drew wl clr frm 13; 50l up aft 15; tired frm 4 out; unchall*
[115⁶]	2	25	**Cormeen Lord (IRE)** *(4x)* 10-1 J Sharp *Hld up wl in rr; stdy prog frm 12 to jn chsng group 15; chsd wnr 3 out; no ch*
[130²]	3	2	**Primitive King** *(8x)* 5-2JF P Hacking *Hld up wl in rr; stdy prog frm 12; jnd chsng group 15; kpt on; no ch w wnr*
[96ᴾ]	4	5	**Ballydesmond (IRE)** 16-1 S Sporborg *2 handlers; tde; ld to 2; lost plce 6; rr when mist 8; wl bhnd aft 15; r.o frm 3 out*
[93ᵁ]	5	8	**Minor Key (IRE)** *(tt)* 14-1 A Harvey *20s-14s; lw; in tch; prog & prom in chsng group frm 15; no ch w wnr; fdd aft 2 out*
[93⁴]	6	2	**Borrow Mine (IRE)** 16-1 A Braithwaite *Nov rdn; a rr group; nrly ur 6; mists 9 & 10; wl bhnd final circ*
[125²]	7	½	**Thats Dedication (IRE)** *(tt)* 8-1 D Robinson *Prom; chsd ldr 7-8; chsng group aft til wknd frm 16*
[130ᵁ]	8	dist	**Golden Mac** 33-1 J Barnard *A wl in rr; t.o 13*
	P		**Bit Of An Idiot** 33-1 D Slattery *Mid-div; lost tch 12; no ch when pu rap app 15*
[127³]	P		**Commasarris** *(4x)* 33-1 P Blagg *2 handlers; ld 2; forced fast pce; hdd 10; clr 2nd 13; still 2nd 4 out; wknd rap nxt; pu last*
[175ᴾ]	P		**Generous Deal (IRE)** 33-1 A Sansome *Prom in chsng group; disp 3rd when dived at 11; eased & pu 15 (cont on heels of plcd horses rnd outside of fnces)*
[125ᴾ]	P		**Half Moon Spinney** 33-1 Miss C Holliday *(xnb) Nvr on terms w ldrs; wl t.o when pu 16*
[127⁹]	P		**How Friendly** 33-1 D Brightling *A rr; wl bhnd 13; t.o & pu 16*
[127⁵]	P		**Nossi Be** *(4x)* 8-1 D Parker *Chsd ldrs; wknd 13; wl bhnd when pu 16*
	P		**Sovereign Spray (IRE)** *(4x)* 14-1 C Gordon *Bit bckwd; a wl in rr; t.o & pu 12*
[130ᶠ]	P		**Sultan Of Swing** 33-1 J Stephens *Svs; t.o & pu 9*

OFFICIAL DISTANCES: dist, 2l TIME: 6min 44.0s TOTE: £2.10; places £1.10,£7.40,£2.40 DF: £11.30
The stewards enquired into the running and riding of Sovereign Spray (pulled up at halfway); as the trainer could offer no explanation they considered no further action was necessary

289 Marsh UK/TBA PPORA Club Members Mares, 12st
10 ran

	1		**CADBURY CASTLE** *(5a)* 9-4F Miss J Grant *Tk keen hld; jb rt; ld 4; 5l clr aft 15; kpt on frm 2 out; unchall but tired*
[131ᵖ]	2	4	**Call The Tune** *(5a)* 20-1 T Peoples *Prom; chsd wnr 10-15 & agn 2 out; kpt on; nvr able to chall*
[95⁴]	3	1½	**Faha Gig (IRE)** *(5a)* 3-1 N King *Hld up in rr; rmdr 12; prog nxt; 9l 4th aft 15; kpt on frm 3 out; unable to chall*
[125³]	4	30	**Mosta (IRE)** *(5a)* 4-1 P Bull *7s-4s (why?); ld to 4; prom to 13; 24l 5th aft 15; sn t.o*
	5	1	**Billie's Mate (IRE)** *(5a) (vis)* 7-2 J Hawksfield *6s-7/2; swtng; hld up; lost tch 14; wl bhnd aft nxt; t.o*
[130ᴾ]	6	½	**The Bishops Sister (IRE)** *(5a)* 6-1 Miss S Gladders *In tch; drpd to rr 12; 32l 7th aft 15; cont t.o*
[178ˢ]	P		**Iberian (IRE)** *(5a)* 8-1 C Gordon *Prom; chsd wnr 8-10 & agn 15; 5l down aft til mist 2 out; wknd rap; pu last*

[131F]	P		**Lady Of Verse** (5a) 33-1 M Gorman *Rr; lost tch 8; t.o & pu 12*
[24P]	P		**Primulas Daughter** (5a) 16-1 M Bradburne *In tch in rr; wknd 13; 27l 6th aft 15; pu 16*
[132P]	U		**Schisandra** (5a,2ow) 33-1 P Blagg *Nt jw in rr til mist & ur 7*

OFFICIAL DISTANCES: 2l, 4l **TIME:** 6min 52.0s **TOTE:** £1.80; places £1.10,£8.00,£2.10 **DF:** £35.10
The rider of Billie's Mate was fined £50 for being unable to produce his Riders Qualification Certificate

290 Club Members Maiden (Div 1), 12st   12 ran

[132³]	1		**CHILL FACTOR** (tt) 5-1 A Charles-Jones *A lndg group; jmpd to ld 15; stayed on to draw clr frm 2 out*
[132R]	2	6	**Carraig Brol** (IRE) 5-2JF N Bloom *A.p; ld 13-15; prsd wnr til no ex u.p frm 2 out*
[131P]	3	20	**Persian Boy** (IRE) 8-1 A Sansome *(xnb) Tk keen hld; lndg group; eff to 5l 3rd aft 15; rdn when mist 3 out; wknd nxt*
[97U]	4	10	**Cardinal Bud** (IRE) 7-1 P Taiano *Mounted on course; tde; nt fluent; chsd ldrs frm 6; nvr able to get on terms; 15l 4th 4 out; fdd*
	P		**Anns Request** (5a) 33-1 P Hickman *Lost tch w lndg group 5; t.o & pu aft 10*
	P		**Calipo Bello** (IRE) 8-1 S Sporborg *Oht; tde; prom; chsd ldr 7-12; wknd rap aft 15; last when pu nxt*
[81F]	P		**Folding** 25-1 M Hawkins *(xnb) Hvly rstrnd & svs; pulled to prom when mist 4; wknd 7; t.o & pu 11*
[132²]	F		**Mister Chips** 5-2JF P Bull *Ld to 13; cl up when fell nxt*
	P		**Our Man Ned** (IRE) 10-1 P York *Mid-div; lost tch 8; no prog aft; wl bhnd when pu 14*
	P		**Sarenacare** (IRE) 25-1 A Hickman *Rr; blun 5; sn lost tch; t.o & pu aft 11*
	P		**Smooth Silk** (IRE) 25-1 D Page *Mist 2; sn bhnd; t.o & pu 11*
[132⁵]	P		**Tom's Influence** 3-1 D Parker *Blun 3; rr; lost tch 8; blun 12; pu nxt*

OFFICIAL DISTANCES: 6l, 12l **TIME:** 6min 48.0s **TOTE:** £5.60; places £3.30,£2.40,£9.00 **DF:** £17.10

291 Club Members Maiden (Div 2), 12st   8 ran

	1		**MARTHA LEADER** (IRE) 5-2 Stuart Robinson *Prom til mist & lost plce 5; jnd ldrs agn 15; chall nxt; outj & lkd btn 2 out; rallied to ld last; stayed on*
[87P]	2	1½	**Squaddie** 7-4F A Sansome *Hld up in tch; prog to ld 15; jnd nxt; pushed 2l ahd aft 2 out; wknd & hdd last*
[98P]	3	3½	**Little Veralyn** (12a) 7-1 P Bull *In tch; mist 10; trckd ldrs 13; unable to qckn 4 out; kpt on one pce frm nxt*
	4	runin	**Uk Eurolad** 8-1 T Hills *(xnb) 33s-8s; ld to 13; wknd nxt; 15l 5th aft 15; cont t.o*
	P		**Granite's Surprise** 7-1 C O'Brien *In tch til wknd 13; sn wl t.o; bu 2 out*
	P		**My Son Tom** 16-1 P Hickman *(xnb) In tch til wknd rap 10; pu nxt*
	U		**Sliabh Foy** (IRE) 7-1 F Marshall *1st ride; rdr unstdy; tk keen hld; chsd ldrs; ld 13-15; nt qckn 4 out; kpt on; 6l 4th & btn when ur last*
	U		**Squerrey** 10-1 T Peoples *Last when blun 7; detach when rfo 8*

OFFICIAL DISTANCES: 3l, 3l **TIME:** 7min 00.0s **TOTE:** £3.70; places £1.10,£1.50,£4.60 **DF:** £3.50

West Shropshire
Weston Park (LH 7F,18J) Sun, 20 Feb (GOOD to SOFT)

292 Hunt   6 ran

	1		**CARRIG BOY** (IRE) 4-6F D Barlow *Chsd ldrs; lft 15l 2nd 9; eff 12; rdn aft 2 out; stayed on to ld nr fin*
[35P]	2	nk	**Haveafewmanners** (IRE) (5a) 12-1 Miss M Lowndes *Lw; ld; 15l clr 5-12; 4l clr 2 out; mist & rdr lost irons last; hdd nr fin; unlucky*
	3	8	**Mytton's Choice** (IRE) 7-2 C Barlow *Hld up; 17l 3rd ½way; eff 12; 6l 3rd when mist 15; no imp 2 out*
[120⁶]	U		**Buck Run** (IRE) 12-1 A Ralphs *Hld up & bhnd; mist 8; 24l 5th ½way; 15l 5th & no hdwy when mist & ur 14*
	U		**Cookie Boy** 16-1 Miss A Davies *Went 2nd 2 til mist & ur 9*
	P		**Marwoods Mandate** (IRE) 14-1 C Stockton *Lw; hld up & bhnd; mist 5; 22l 4th ½way; mist 12; gd hdwy & 4l 3rd when blun bad 14; nt rec; pu 15*

OFFICIAL DISTANCE: ½l **TIME:** 7min 05.4s

293 Confined   14 ran

	1		**ROSMARINO** 5-4F A Dalton *5/2-5/4; hld up; stdy hdwy & 9l 7th ½way; jnd ldrs 11; went 3rd nxt & 2nd 15; ld 2 out; edged lft last; stayed on wl*

	2	7	**Commercial Artist** 8-1 S Jackson *Tubed; lw; sn prom; 5l 3rd ½way; went 2nd 11; rdn to ld 14; hdd 2 out; btn when jmpd v slow & rdr lost irons last*
	3	3	**Weak Moment (IRE)** 5-2 A Crow *Hld up & bhnd; 17l 11th ½way; rdn along 13; eff u.p & 12l 7th 14; 13l 6th 3 out; stayed on; nvr nr to chall*
[153ᴾ]	4	2	**My Nominee** (bl) 12-1 R Burton *Ld to 2; 7l 5th ½way; 10l 6th & outpcd 14; 11l 5th 3 out; stayed on one pce*
	5	30	**King Paddy (IRE)** (tt) 33-1 R Bevan *Hld up & bhnd; 12l 9th ½way; eff & 10l 7th 13; wknd 14; t.o*
	6	15	**Kidlaw** 14-1 Miss T Clark *Bckwd; prom; went 4l 2nd ½way-11; wknd qckly 13; 25l 9th nxt; t.o*
	P		**All In The Game (IRE)** 25-1 C Stockton *Hld up; lost plce 6; 15l 10th ½way; 4½l 4th & gd hdwy 13; wknd & 7l 5th nxt; 18l 7th 3 out; pu 2 out*
	P		**Applefort (IRE)** 10-1 M Worthington *2nd til ld 4; hdd 14; wknd & 7l 4th 3 out; poor 5th when pu aft nxt*
[33¹⁰]	P		**Aralier Man (IRE)** 14-1 L Stephens *A bhnd; rmdrs 2; 17½l 12th ½way; t.o & pu 3 out*
	P		**Bee Moy Do (IRE)** 20-1 J R Barlow *Bckwd; a bhnd; 18l 13th ½way; mist 10; pu 11*
	S		**Glamdring** (5a) 20-1 I Clyde *Bckwd & unclipped; ld 2-4; 2nd til 6l 4th when slpd up bend aft 9*
[77³]	U		**Grunge (IRE)** 8-1 C Barlow *Hld up; 10l 8th ½way; hdwy 13; went 5l 4th nxt; 3l 3rd when stumbled & ur bend aft 3 out*
[148ᴾ]	P		**Manalesco (IRE)** 33-1 P Cranmer *Jmpd v slow 3; sn wl bhnd; t.o 8; pu 3 out*
[171⁷]	F		**Shanballymore (IRE)** 33-1 R Owen *2 handlers; chsd ldrs; 8l 6th ½way; same plce when fell 12*

OFFICIAL DISTANCE: 6l   TIME: 7min 01.0s
The stewards enquired into possible interference to the runner-up by the winner; they decided that interference had occurred but it was accidental and had not affected the result; therefore the placings remained unaltered

294 Mens Open, 12st   14 ran

[117¹]	1		**WHATAFELLOW (IRE)** (7x) (bl) 2-1JF A Crow *Bhnd til 8l 4th & hdwy ½way; jnd ldrs 13; 1½l 3rd nxt; went 2nd & mist 15; ld aft 3 out; sn 5l clr; drvn out*
	2	7	**Kissair (IRE)** (7x) 20-1 S Morris *Bit bckwd; hld up & bhnd; 16l 7th ½way; hdwy 13; lft 8l 4th nxt; went 7l 3rd 2 out & 2nd app last; nt rch wnr*
	3	12	**Well Ted** 5-2 Julian Pritchard *Lw; a.p; went 2nd 5; ld app 7; mist 8; hdd aft 3 out; wknd 2 out*
	4	1	**Erlemo** 33-1 S Joynes *(bf) A.p; 4l 3rd ½way; went 2nd aft 13-15; 5l 3rd 3 out; wknd 2 out*
	P		**Alaskan Heir** (bl) 33-1 D Mansell *Bckwd; a bhnd; 20½l 11th ½way; t.o 13; pu last*
[150ᵁ]	P		**Characteristic** 14-1 T Stephenson *Mist 3; prom til pu 6; lame*
	P		**Chicodari** 33-1 E Walker *A bhnd; 18l 9th ½way; t.o & pu 14*
[104¹]	F		**Ibex** 2-1JF L Jefford *Hld up; 13l 6th ½way; hdwy & mist 11; 6l 4th & rdn when fell 14*
	P		**I Haven't A Buck (IRE)** 14-1 D Barlow *Prom til lost plce 4; pu & dism aft 6*
	P		**My Sister Lucy** (5a) 25-1 M Rodda *Bckwd; ld aft 2; clr 4; hdd app 7; lost plce & 12l 5th ½way; wl bhnd 12; t.o & pu 14*
	P		**Rockville Pike (IRE)** 20-1 G Barfoot-Saunt *(xnb) A bhnd; 20l 10th ½way; mist 12; t.o 13; pu last*
[32⁶]	U		**The Crazy Bishop (IRE)** (7x) 14-1 B Shaw *Hld up; 8th when mist & ur 9*
	P		**Watchit Lad** 12-1 R Burton *Bckwd; swtng; ld til hdd aft 2; 2nd/3rd to 6; 17l 8th & lsng plce ½way; wl bhnd 11; t.o & pu 14*
	P		**Winters Cottage (IRE)** 14-1 A Evans *(bof) Hld up; hdwy & 2nd 7; wknd qckly aft 13; 14l 6th when pu nxt*

OFFICIAL DISTANCE: 8l   TIME: 6min 55.6s
Cead Mile Failte was withdrawn not under orders

295 Ladies Open   5 ran

	1		**KERRY SOLDIER BLUE** 4-9F Miss P Jones *(bf) Went 2nd 6; ld aft 9-12; outpcd & 6l 2nd 14; rallied 2 out; jnd ldr & lft clr at last*
[116ᴾ]	2	12	**Mackabee (IRE)** (bl) 14-1 Miss J Priest *Hld up; 2l 4th ½way; went 3rd 11; outpcd 13; rallied & 8l 3rd nxt; no ex 2 out; lft 2nd at last*
	3	15	**Well Arranged (IRE)** 4-1 Mrs C Boyes *Ld to 4; 1l 3rd ½way; lost plce 11; 14l 4th 13; no imp aft; wknd 2 out*
[192ᴾ]	P		**Dawn Mission** (bl) 16-1 Miss E Jones *Pulled hrd; nt jw; went 2nd 2; ld 4; jb ft 5; mist 8; lost plce & 4l 9th ½way; bhnd when pu 11*
	R		**Killatty Player (IRE)** (5a) 5-1 Miss C Thomas *Jmpd lft; 2nd/3rd til ld 12; went 6l clr 14; jnd when rn out & ur last*

OFFICIAL DISTANCES: 15l, 10l   TIME: 7min 06.1s

296 Intermediate (Div 1), 12st
15 ran

[116⁴]	1		**DISTANT-PORT (IRE)** 14-1 T Stephenson *Ww; hdwy & 7l 5th ½way; went 5l 4th 13; 10l down 3 out; qcknd & 2l 2nd nxt; ld app last; rdly*
[35²]	2	4	**Military Man** 16-1 A Phillips *Ld 2-11; mist 3 out; 2nd til ld app 2 out; hdd app last; no ex*
[37²]	3	2	**Seymour's Double** 7-1 R Burton *Hld up & bhnd; 13l 9th ½way; eff & 12l 7th 14; 11l 5th 3 out; went 3l 3rd nxt; one pce*
	4	12	**Coolflugh Hero (IRE)** 6-1 A Crow *(xnb) Ld to 2; 2nd to 7; 3l 3rd ½way; 4l 3rd & rdn 14; 3½l 4th 2 out; sn wknd*
[36ᴾ]	B		**Blayneys Privilege** 20-1 Miss T Habgood *Hld up; 12th when bd 9*
[75ᴾ]	F		**Grecian Star** 4-1 J Tarry *Chsd ldrs; 5th when fell 9*
[102¹]	P		**Icenfriendly (IRE)** 5-1 Miss P Jones *Hld up; 9l 6th ½way; 12l 6th 13; no imp frm 14; wknd & 14l 6th 3 out; pu 2 out*
	P		**Mister Moss (IRE)** 2-1F G Hanmer *5s-2s; rcd keen & sn prom; went 2nd 7; ld 11; went 3l clr 14; hdd aft 3 out; wknd qckly & 5l 5th nxt; stpd to nil & pu aft 2 out*
[75ᵁ]	P		**Mr Freeman (IRE)** (vis) 33-1 J Diment *Chsd ldrs; 6l 4th ½way; 7l 5th 13; wkng when mist 15; 20l 7th 3 out; pu 2 out*
	P		**Nutty Solera** 33-1 E Williams *2 handlers; hld up; 7th when hmpd bad 9; nt rec; pu 10*
[120⁴]	P		**Po Cap Eel** (5a) 33-1 Miss H Kinsey *(xnb) A bhnd; 16l 10th ½way; t.o 14; pu 2 out*
[116⁷]	P		**Priory Piper** (5x) 14-1 L Hicks *Prom; mists 4 & 8; lost plce; 10l 7th ½way; 27l 10th & wkng 13; pu 14*
[173ᴮ]	B		**Red Spice** 14-1 R Owen *Bhnd til bd 9*
[116⁵]	P		**Smart Rhythm** (5a) 14-1 R Armson *Nd; 11l 8th ½way; 18l 8th 13; pu nxt*
[119¹]	B		**Upton Adventure** (5a) 3-1 S Joynes *Hld up; 8th when bd 9*

OFFICIAL DISTANCES: 2½l, 6l **TIME:** 7min 00.3s

297 Intermediate (Div 2), 12st
10 ran

[101²]	1		**DAWN'S COGNAC (IRE)** 7-4JF Miss P Jones *Jw; went 2nd 4; ld 11; clr last; comf*
	2	8	**Hatterill Ridge** 4-1 Julian Pritchard *A.p; 6l 3rd ½way; chsd wnr 15; wknd app last*
[74⁶]	3	5	**Just Like Madge** (5a,5x) 7-4JF J Tarry *2nd to 3; lost plce & 8½l 7th ½way; rallied & 9l 5th 14; went 10l 3rd 2 out; no imp*
	4	12	**Innishfea (IRE)** (5a) 6-1 Miss S Vickery *Hld up & pulled hrd; 9½l 8th ½way; went 8l 4th 14; wknd app 2 out*
	5	10	**Ballyhannon (IRE)** 33-1 Miss J Froggatt *Chsd ldrs; 7½l 5th ½way; 6l 4th when mist 13; 14l 7th & wkng qckly nxt*
	6	3	**Merely Mortal** 33-1 R Owen *Chsd ldrs; 6½l 4th ½way; mist 10; lost plce 11; wknd; 12l 6th 14*
	P		**Eau So Sloe** 50-1 K Burke *Drpd to rr 7; 12l 9th ½way; lost tch & 17l 9th 13; pu 14*
	P		**Hill's Electric (IRE)** 16-1 T Stephenson *Nt jw; hld up & bhnd; stdy hdwy & 8l 6th ½way; jnd ldrs 11; went 11 2nd 13 til wknd qckly 15; poor 5th when pu aft 2 out; btr for rce*
	U		**Pinouli** (5a) 33-1 R Burton *A bhnd; 15l 10th ½way; blun & ur 12*
[116⁷]	P		**Sandi Devil** (bl) 33-1 D Dickenson *Ld til hdd 11; lost plce u.p & 7l 5th 13; pu 14*

OFFICIAL DISTANCE: 8l **TIME:** 7min 08.7s

298 Confined Maiden 56&7yo
12 ran

	1		**FRANGIPANE** (5a) 12-1 W Hill *(boh) A.p; 4l 3rd ½way; 2l 3rd 14; ld 3 out; sn clr; mist last*
[168ᶠ]	2	20	**Elver Spring** 6-4F R Burton *5/2-6/4; ld til hdd 3 out; sn wknd*
	3	½	**Vertical Air** 3-1 S Jackson *(xnb) 10s-3s; lw; hld up; 8½l 6th ½way; hdwy 11; mist 12; went 2nd 14-3 out; sn wknd*
	U		**Dealer Boy (IRE)** 16-1 G Hanmer *Hld up; 12l 9th when stumbled & ur bend aft 9*
	P		**Dunston Slick** 16-1 J R Barlow *Chsd ldrs; 7½l 5th ½way; wknd & 14l 7th 14; lft poor 4th 3 out; pu 2 out*
[54ᶠ]	P		**Fountain Street (IRE)** 20-1 S Morris *(xnb) Hld up & bhnd; 13l 10th ½way; eff 13; 11l 6th nxt; nt rch ldrs; wkng when pu 3 out*
	U		**Gilded Way** 25-1 L Hicks *Jmpd v slow 1; bhnd til blun & ur 5*
	P		**Gun Runner** 12-1 C Barlow *Mounted on course; tde; hld up; 9l 7th ½way; lft 8l 4th 14; sn wknd; pu 3 out*
[180⁵]	P		**Lady Nevada (IRE)** (5a) 8-1 Miss S Hopkins *Still bckwd; prom; 7l 4th ½way; wknd 11; 18l 9th 13; t.o & pu 13*
	F		**Pharpen (IRE)** 2-1 J Jukes *Lw; went 2nd 4; pckd 6; ev ch 13; releg 2½l 4th when fell 14*
	P		**Roundabout** (5a) 25-1 A Evans *Hld up; lost plce & 14l 11th ½way; bhnd when pu 11*
[124ᴿ]	P		**Village Gossip** (5a) 10-1 M Worthington *Prom til lost plce 5; 10l 8th ½way; lost tch & 13l 8th 13; pu 13*

OFFICIAL DISTANCE: 25l **TIME:** 7min 14.9s

Fontwell (L&RH 7F,19J)
Mon, 21 Feb (SOFT)

299 Fontwell Foxhunters Trial HC   **7 ran**

[148¹]	1		**GUNNER WELBURN** 12-00 7-4F **R Cope** *2nd/3rd til ld on bit 16; shkn up app last & nt fluent; idled flat but a in comm*
[156ᶠ]	2	7	**Knight Of Passion** 12-07 5-2 **Miss P Jones** *Hit 8 & 13; made virt all to 16; 6l 2nd nxt; rdn & no imp aft*
[149¹]	3	2	**Ardstown** 11-09 8-1 **F Windsor Clive** *Mid-div; chsd ldng pr frm 14; drvn & mist nxt; stayed on same pce*
[156ᶠ]	4	3	**Henry Bruce** 12-00 (bl) 13-2 **D Mansell** *A rr; hit 4 & rmdr; drvn 12; lost tch 13; stayed on frm 2 out*
[152³]	5	12	**Prince Buck (IRE)** 12-07 8-1 **B Pollock** *Chsd ldr til ld brief 12; rdn & outpcd nxt; sn strugg*
[149²]	P		**Mr Dow Jones (IRE)** 12-04 11-1 **D O'Meara** *Mid-div; blun 9; mist 12; hrd rdn & wknd 13; sn wl bhnd; pu 3 out*
[149³]	P		**Pontabula** 11-11 50-1 **A Charles-Jones** *A last pr; wl bhnd whn hit 11; mist 12; pu 14*

TIME: 7min 8.9s TOTE: £2.90; places £1.30,£2.30 Ex: £7.70 CSF: £5.71

Folkestone (RH 7F,15J)
Tue, 22 Feb (GOOD to SOFT)

300 Tenterden Maiden HC   **9 ran**

	1		**FINNOW THYNE (IRE)** 12-00 7-4 **D Dunsdon** *Ld aft 1; 10l clr 6; sn stdd; rdn app 2 out; stayed on wl*
[127¹]	2	6	**Satchmo (IRE)** 12-02 11-10F **G Wragg** *(xnb) Lw; rcd wide & rdr landing awkward at fncs; hld up; smooth prog to 3rd 8; jnd wnr & rdr nrly f.o 3 out & lost iron; nt rdn frm app 2 out but stayed on pluckily*
	3	10	**Novatara (IRE)** 12-04 9-1 **T Gibney** *Mists & rn in snatches; hit 4; 2nd/3rd to 7; lost tch & mist 9; blun 11; kpt on & lft 3rd 12; no imp; bad mist 2 out*
[125¹]	4	20	**Prime Course (IRE)** 12-00 16-1 **C Gordon** *Lw; jmpd lft; hld up; rmdr 8; went 3rd but outpcd aft nxt; lft 3rd & blun 12; drvn out*
[128²]	5	1¾	**Kincora (IRE)** 12-00 10-1 **Mrs L Stock** *Lw; bhnd; lost tch 8; t.o 10*
	P		**Leggies Legacy** 12-00 33-1 **P Hall** *Bckwd; last when jmpd slow 5; lost tch 8; t.o & pu 10*
[130³]	F		**Rustic Revelry** 12-00 16-1 **P York** *A 2nd/3rd; disp 2nd when fell 12*
[150ᴾ]	P		**Tellaporky** 12-00 40-1 **J Owen** *Ld til mist 1; nt fluent; rdn & lost tch 9; t.o & pu 11*
	F		**Vendoon (IRE)** 12-00 (tt) 33-1 **M Foley** *Last when fell 3*

TIME: 5min 38.8s TOTE: £3.10; places; £1.70,£1.10,£2.40 Ex: £5.80 CSF: £4.16 Tri: £84.80

Sedgefield (LH 8F,14J)
Tue, 22 Feb (GOOD to SOFT)

301 Sanyo South Durham Maiden HC   **15 ran**

[185¹]	1		**BALISTEROS (FR)** 11-07 7-4F **W Renwick** *Bhnd; last 4; hdwy in 7th 8; ld aft 3 out; clr nxt; stayed on wl*
[151⁵]	2	16	**Danegeld (IRE)** 11-11 16-1 **C Ward-Thomas** *In tch; went 4th 8; rdn to chse wnr bef 2 out; kpt on; a wl hld*
[115⁵]	3	26	**Cebu Gale (IRE)** 11-07 16-1 **M Hewitt** *In tch; 6th 8; ev ch 11; 4th & btn when hit 3 out; hit last*
	4	7	**Celtic Who (IRE)** 11-11 10-1 **Mrs C Ford** *2; ld til hdd aft 3 out; drvn & sn wknd*
	5	18	**Just Ned** 11-09 (2) 40-1 **M Douglas** *Last pr; no ch frm 8; t.o*
[225⁵]	6	6	**Pablowmore** 11-07 7-1 **R Green** *Prom to 5; 8th & wkng 8; t.o*
	7	9	**What The Heck (IRE)** 11-07 14-1 **T Glass** *Mist 2; prom; 3rd 8; drvn nxt; wknd qckly aft 3 out; t.o*
[167ᶠ]	8	dist	**Desert Boot** 11-02 (2) 66-1 **P Kirby** *Mists; sn bhnd; t.o last 11*
	P		**Auntie Alice** 11-04 20-1 **C Mulhall** *Rr div; 10th & strugg 8; t.o & pu 2 out*
[89⁴]	P		**Carnaven** 11-09 10-1 **A Robson** *Wl bhnd & nvr gng wl; mist 7 & rmdrs; hit 8 & hmpd; t.o & pu 2 out*
[53¹]	U		**Mandril (IRE)** 12-00 14-1 **N Tutty** *Rr til blun & ur 4*
[184³]	P		**More Joy** 11-07 20-1 **S Bowden** *Last by 5; pu 7*
[89¹⁰]	P		**Snooty Eskimo (IRE)** 11-11 14-1 **C Wilson** *Chsd ldr to 7; sn wknd; t.o & pu 2 out*

[187¹]   F   **Solway Donal (IRE)** 11-02 6-1 **T Davidson** *In tch; hdwy to 4th when fell 8*
        P   **Willy Wee (IRE)** 11-07 10-1 **L Morgan** *Prom til drvn aft 7; wknd qckly; 11th when mist 8; t.o & pu nxt*

    TIME: 5min 34.4s **TOTE:** £2.70; places £1.60,£2.60,£3.90 **Ex:** £25.60 **CSF:** £25.40
       2 fences omitted

Huntingdon (RH 9F,19J)
Thu, 24 Feb (SOFT)

302 Peterborough Chase Restaurant HC   10 ran

[151¹]   1   **MIGHTY MOSS (IRE)** 12-00 1-3F **F Hutsby** *Hld up; went 3rd 6 & 2nd 8; hit 10; pckd 11; ld 15; cantering frm 2 out; v easy*
[224³]   2   5   **Solo Gent** 11-07 (vis) 14-1 **D I Turner** *Ld; clr early; hdd 15; hrd rdn aft 3 out; plodded on in vain pursuit*
[89³]   3   9   **Makin' Doo (IRE)** 11-09 16-1 **C Mulhall** *Bhnd; rdn & hdwy 12; outpcd by ldng pr aft nxt; mod prog aft 2 out*
       4   13   **Rocket Radar** 12-05 11-2 **Julian Pritchard** *Hld up; stdy prog 8; 3rd 11; mist 14 (water); outpcd by ldng pr nxt; tired 3 out; btr for rce*
[148⁴]   5   5   **Strong Chairman (IRE)** 11-07 20-1 **S Waley-Cohen** *Prom in chsng group to 11; rr & wl outpcd 13*
[150⁵]   6   20   **The Whole Hog (IRE)** 11-11 40-1 **T Scudamore** *Detach in last; mist 3; jmpd slow 5 (water); t.o 8*
[29ᵁ]   P   **Candle Glow** 11-02 66-1 **D Cook** *W ldr 2 til mist 3; chsd ldr to 9; sn bhnd; 8th when pu 11*
[156⁸]   P   **Dry Hill Lad** 12-00 33-1 **N Kent** *Mounted on course; handy in chsng group; 4th 11; rdn nxt; bad mist 14 (water) & rdr lost iron; nt rec; pu 16*
[154ᴾ]   F   **Freedom Fighter** 12-00 33-1 **A Martin** *Midfield & hld up; 5th & rdn 13; outpcd nxt; 4th when crashing fall 16*
[190⁴]   P   **In Place (USA)** 11-07 100-1 **T Lane** *Sn rr; mist 7; t.o 10; pu 12*

    TIME: 6min 30.3s **TOTE:** £1.40; places £1.30,£1.40,£2.30 **Ex:** £6.10 **CSF:** £5.45 **Tri:** £52.70

Kempton (RH 10F,19J)
Fri, 25 Feb (SOFT)

303 Corinthian HC   13 ran

[223¹]   1   **LITTLE BUCK (IRE)** 11-11 10-1 **K Culligan** *Settled 3rd/4th; went 2nd 11; ld 3 out; clr aft nxt; pushed out; wl idea*
[152²]   2   3   **Chasing The Bride** 11-11 20-1 **M Miller** *In tch; 7th 9; chsd ldng pr frm 13; rdn & outpcd frm 16; rallied 2 out; stayed on wl to 2nd aft last; no ch w wnr; gd eff*
[224¹]   3   2½   **Brambledown (IRE)** 11-09 100-30 **Mrs B Sillars** *Cl up; 5th 9; lost plce 12; in chsng group frm nxt; 12l 5th 16; eff app 3 out; r.o str frm last; gd eff (gvn no ch by rdr)*
[129¹]   4   3½   **Struggles Glory (IRE)** 11-12 (5) 7-4F **D Robinson** *Rdr v untidy 1; ld to 2; ld agn 4; pckd 8; hdd 3 out; btn 2nd & tired when hit last; wknd*
[154ᶠ]   5   29   **Tomcappagh (IRE)** 12-01 33-1 **T Doyle** *Last when jmpd slow 3; hld up wl in rr; 12th 9; stdy prog 12; jnd chsng group 16; sn wknd u.p*
[149ᶠ]   6   11   **Rob Mine (IRE)** 11-07 9-1 **S Sporborg** *Hld up in rr; 6th & prog 9; cl up 12; rdn & wknd 16*
[153³]   7   12   **Mr Golightly** 11-09 50-1 **Mrs J Reed** *Rdr nodding on landing side of fnces; prom to 8; 10th 9; no ch frm 13*
       8   6   **Stay Lucky (NZ)** 11-11 25-1 **D Alers-Hankey** *A rr; jmpd slow 3; 11th 9; mist 11; no ch 12; hit 13; t.o*
[26³]   P   **Bas De Laine (FR)** 11-07 12-1 **A Hickman** *Blun 2; trckd ldrs; 8th 9; wknd 13; blun 15; wl bhnd when pu 3 out*
[301³]   P   **Cebu Gale (IRE)** 11-07 66-1 **M Hewitt** *Prom; 3rd 9; chsd ldr 10-11; wkng when blun 15; wl bhnd when pu 3 out*
[61¹]   P   **Fresh Prince** 12-00 8-1 **Julian Pritchard** *Mid-div; 9th 9; in tch 12; wknd rap nxt; pu 14*
       P   **Lakeside Lad** 11-07 40-1 **F Windsor Clive** *A rr; last & rdn & strugg 9; hmpd slt 12; t.o & pu nxt*
[177⁴]   U   **Tighter Budget (USA)** 11-07 50-1 **Miss G Hutchinson** *Ld 2-4; mist 7; chsd ldr to 10; 7th & wkng when blun & ur 12*

    TIME: 6min 19.8s **TOTE:** £9.80; places £3.40,£3.30,£1.60 **Ex:** £124.30 **CSF:** £158.42 **Tri:** £335.30

Chiddingfold, Leconfield & Cowdray
Parham (RH 8F,18J) Sat, 26 Feb (GOOD to SOFT)

304 Hunt (with Kent & Surrey Bloodhounds)　　　　　　6 ran

[216¹]	1	**SOME TOURIST (IRE)** 2-7F Miss C Benstead *Jw; made all; stayed on stdly frm 3 out; comf*
[162⁷]	2 3	**Edge Ahead (IRE)** 4-1 Mrs E Coveney *Prsd wnr most of way; pushed along 4 out; kpt on frm 3 out; a hld*
[86⁷]	3 fence	**Lillooet (IRE)** (5a) (bl) 10-1 C Gordon *Spurs; cl 2nd/3rd til lost tch aft 11; 20l 3rd 4 out; plodded home*
	4 3½fs	**Just Oz (U)** 33-1 Miss L Free *Spurs; imm lost tch; fnce adrift by 7; hunted rnd*
	P	**Dreamin George (IRE)** 33-1 J Sole *Cl 4th til wknd 9; rem 5th when pu aft 14*
	F	**Mr Fitz (IRE)** 33-1 M Sheridan *Hld up; hdwy frm 7 to 6l 4th 11; 3rd & ev ch when fell 14*

OFFICIAL DISTANCES: 3l, dist **TIME:** 6min 58.0s **TOTE:** £1.60; places £1.40,£2.00 **DF:** £2.40

305 Confined, 12st　　　　　　9 ran

[288⁷]	1	**THATS DEDICATION (IRE)** (tt) 20-1 D Robinson *Spurs; cl 2nd/3rd til ld 14; made rest; a hldng rnr-up frm 3 out*
[127²]	2 5	**Seod Rioga (IRE)** (5x) 1-2F C Gordon *Settled in cl 3rd; disp ld frm 9 til pckd 12; prsng wnr when outj 14 & 15; hrd rdn aft; chall 2 out; sn btn*
[130³]	3 2	**Jojo (IRE)** (bl) 9-2 B Hitchcott *Cl up; 4l 4th 10; chsd ldrs frm 14; ev ch 3 out; kpt on one pce*
[215⁰]	4 4	**Exemplar (IRE)** 20-1 Mrs D Rowell *Prsd ldrs; 10l 6th & lsng plce 10; stayed on frm 15*
[216³]	5 25	**Trifast Lad** 20-1 Mrs L Baker *A last pr; 20l 8th 10; t.o frm 13*
[239⁰]	P	**Father Henry (IRE)** 33-1 P York *Jb; a towards rr; 22l 9th 10; lsng tch when blun bad & pu 12*
	P	**Just Try Me (IRE)** 33-1 P Hall *Mists; a towards rr; 18l 7th 10; wkng when pu 13*
[223⁷]	P	**Newtown Rosie (IRE)** (5a) 8-1 A Hickman *Ld/disp to 13; 12l 4th & wkng 4 out; pu app nxt*
[238⁷]	P	**The Glow (IRE)** (6x) 20-1 D Brightling *Hld up; hdwy to 6l 5th 10; lost tch aft 14; rr when pu 3 out*

OFFICIAL DISTANCES: 4l, 3l **TIME:** 7min 00.0s **TOTE:** £8.50; places £1.10,£1.80,£1.10 **DF:** £32.50

306 Restricted, 12st　　　　　　14 ran

[131¹]	1	**NOAH** (7a) 5-1 P York *Impd to trck ldrs 7; cl 3rd 11; ld 13; made rest gng wl; easily drew clr app last; impressive*
[144⁴]	2 5	**Possible Pardon (NZ)** 5-1 A Charles-Jones *Cl up; 4th 11; pushed along 13; prsd wnr 15; ev ch when blun nxt; no ex app last*
[285⁰]	3 20	**Royal Rupert** 12-1 N Benstead *Rr early; stdy hdwy 7 to cl 6th 11; 10l 4th 15; kpt on one pce*
[289⁶]	4 25	**The Bishops Sister (IRE)** (5a) 33-1 Miss S Gladders *Prom to 6; 11th 11; wl bhnd 14; stayed on frm nxt*
[247⁷]	P	**Another Comedy** 25-1 N Earnshaw *rr; rem 12th 11; t.o & pu 3 out*
	P	**Arrogant Lord** 8-1 B Hitchcott *Ld to 12; wknd qckly in 15l 5th 15; wl bhnd when pu nxt*
[285⁷]	P	**Ballybollen (IRE)** 33-1 D Brightling *Midfield; 8th 11; sn lost tch; no ch when pu 15*
[221¹]	F	**Belvento** 6-4F D Dunsdon *A cl 2nd/3rd; prsd wnr 14 til fell nxt*
[219⁷]	P	**Bit Of A Do** (tt) 33-1 D Slattery *Midfield; 7th 11; lsng tch when pu 15*
	P	**Blue Marlin** (5a) 10-1 J Owen *A last pr; wl bhnd when pu 11*
[289⁷]	P	**Iberian (IRE)** (5a) 12-1 Miss J Grant *Prsd ldrs; 5th 11; wknd aft 14; bhnd when pu 3 out*
[285²]	U	**Ishma (IRE)** 14-1 D Page *Midfield; 9th & pushed along 11; ur 13*
[285⁰]	P P	**Perripage** (vis) 20-1 Miss A Sansom *Mist & drpd to rr 6; jmpd slow 8; t.o last 11; pu 13*
	P	**Viking Lily (IRE)** (5a) 9-2 A Hickman *A rr; 10th 11; no ch when pu 15*

OFFICIAL DISTANCES: 4l, 20l **TIME:** 6min 55.0s **TOTE:** £5.10; places £2.00,£1.10,£3.30 **DF:** £93.20

307 Ladies Open - 17J　　　　　　7 ran

[192ᴿ]	1	**LILY THE LARK** (5a) 10-1 Miss H Irving *Trckd ldng pr frm 8; hdwy 15; jnd ldr on long rn to last; sn drew clr*
[177³]	2 15	**Native Venture (IRE)** 4-7F Mrs E Coveney *Chsd ldr frm 6; mist 9; rdn & ld aft 15; hdd aft nxt; sn outpcd & btn*

	3	2fncs	**For William** 33-1 *Mrs M Rigg Sn detach last; t.o 8; lft 3rd by default at last*
[245³]	F		**Danger Flynn (IRE)** (vis) 6-1 *Mrs C Holliday Swtng; ld; set gd pce to 15; hdd & wknd rap app nxt; 30l 3rd when fell last; winded & down for 10min*
[218⁸]	U		**Jamies First (IRE)** 33-1 *Miss L Parrott Ur 1*
[218³]	P		**Silk Vestments** (5a) 9-2 *Mrs D Rowell Chsd ldr in 2nd/3rd to 7; 15l 4th 11; t.o & pu last*
[128⁷]	U		**Wednesdays Auction (IRE)** 33-1 *Mrs C Andrews Prom to 5; mod 5th whr ur 9*

OFFICIAL DISTANCES: 12l, dist **TIME:** 6min 56.0s **TOTE:** £8.60 places £2.60,£1.50 **DF:** £5.30
Fence 17 omitted - fallen rider

308 Mens Open, 12st   7 ran

[210¹]	1		**GILLAN COVE (IRE)** (7x) 1-2F *R Young Ld frm 5; narrow ld til drew clr frm 3 out; stayed on str*
	2	40	**Take My Side (IRE)** (7x) (bl) 10-1 *B Hitchcott In tch; impd to cl 3rd 8; prsd wnr 14 til hrd rdn & wknd 3 out*
[286ᴾ]	3	fence	**Galaroi (IRE)** (7x) (tt) 12-1 *D Robinson Spurs; prsd ldr til wknd qckly 13; 25l 4th 15; lft poor 3rd app 2 out*
[216ᴾ]	P		**Fitness Fanatic** 33-1 *D Dunsdon Prsd ldrs to 8; fdd 11; lsng tch when pu 13*
[211¹]	P		**Parson's Way** (vis) 33-1 *C Gordon Ld to 4; pushed along & lost plce aft 7; rr when jmpd slow 12; pu app nxt*
[190¹]	P		**Simple Arithmetic** 5-1 *B Clarke Detach last til hdwy 7; 10l 3rd 14; wknd aft 4 out; 30l 3rd when pu & dism app 2 out*
	P		**Titus Andronicus** (4x) 12-1 *J Oldring Prom to 5; sn lost plce; last frm 8; t.o & pu 14*

OFFICIAL DISTANCES: dist, dist **TIME:** 6min 53.0s **TOTE:** £1.80 places £1.60,£3.30 **DF:** £6.90

309 Open Maiden, 12st - 17J   15 ran

[221ᴾ]	1		**ROYAL DEW (IRE)** 16-1 *D Evatt Cl 2nd/3rd til ld aft 13; jnd 3 out; ld agn flat; hld on wl cl home*
[220ᶠ]	2	½	**Imperative** 13-2 *A Charles-Jones A in tch; hdwy to jn wnr 3 out; stdd last; ev ch flat; no ex cl home*
[181ᵁ]	3	15	**Daydreamer (USA)** 3-1F *D Brightling Hld up; stdy hdwy 8; prsd ldng pr 15; wknd aft nxt*
[300ᴾ]	4	25	**Tellaporky** (bl) 4-1 *Miss E Owen Hld up; a towards rr; pushed along 12; slt hdwy frm 15; nvr nr ldrs*
[290ᴾ]	P		**Anns Request** (5a) (bl) 33-1 *P Hickman A rr; t.o & pu 12*
[63ᴾ]	r		**Bertie Bavard** 20-1 *B Hitchcott Rr early; in tch 10; impd to trck ldrs 15; 4th & wkng when ref 2 out*
[220ᴾ]	P		**Graphic Designer (IRE)** 12-1 *C Gordon Prsd ldrs til wknd qckly 13; pu 15*
[147⁵]	P		**Gunerkillinghurst** 20-1 *A Hickman A rr; wl bhnd when pu 11*
	B		**Little Farmer** 12-1 *P Hall Bd 2*
[221⁵]	F		**Lord Ellangowan (IRE)** 12-1 *D Slattery Prom when fell 2*
	P		**One More Man (IRE)** 25-1 *K Culligan A rr; lost tch 9; no ch when pu 15*
	R		**Percy Arms** 16-1 *N Benstead Rr when jmpd slow 3; rn out 4*
[220ᵁ]	P		**Royal Season** 7-1 *M Gorman Mists; ld 3-7; prsd ldr til wknd 12; lsng tch when pu 15*
[131ʳ]	S		**Rushenova** 20-1 *P York Prsd ldrs til slpd up on flat aft 7*
	P		**Rush 'n Tear** 5-1 *Miss J Grant Ld to 2 & frm 7-13; ev ch 15; wknd qckly & pu nxt*

OFFICIAL DISTANCES: nk, 8l **TIME:** 7min 00.0s **TOTE:** £64.60 places £-,£10.90,£2.40 **DF:** £40.30
Fence 10 omitted - fallen rider; the stewards enquired into the improvement in form of the winner; they accepted the owner/rider's explanations of problems with the bit and being hampered at Larkhill, and the horse having run better without a visor

East Cornwall
Lemalla (RH 6F,19J) Sat, 26 Feb (HEAVY)

310 Intermediate, 12st   11 ran

[202ᵁ]	1		**O SO BOSSY** 14-1 *Miss J Congdon Tchd 16s; jw; ld 2-4 & agn aft 14; drew 5l clr 3 out; stayed on wl; comf*
[162ᴾ]	2	5	**Track O' profit (IRE)** 50-1 *Miss S Young Handy; cl 4th frm 12; went 2nd 3 out; sn no ch w wnr; fair eff*
[256¹]	3	8	**No More Nice Guy (IRE)** 7-1 *Mrs M Hand Sn prom; chsd ldrs in 3rd mostly; cl 3rd 15; sn outpcd; kpt on same pce clsng stages*
[202⁵]	4	3	**Foxy Dawn** 10-1 *R Woollacott Tchd 12s; lw; 2 handlers; midfield; 5th ½way; 5th & pushed along 14; kpt on one pce frm 16*
	5	8	**Contradict** 14-1 *Miss S Gaisford Tchd 20s; prom early; settled mid-div; 7th 9; lost tch 13; no ch frm 15*

[258P]	6	4	**Uckerby Lad** (5x) 4-1 C Heard *Lw; sn towards rr; slt hdwy to 7 & just in tch when mist 13; rdn & no hdwy 15*
[143q]	7	10	**Dannicus** 5-2 T Mitchell *Tchd 3s; slt stringhalt nr hind; lw; keen early; ld 1 & agn 4-14; chsd wnr nxt til lost plce stdly aft 3 out; eased clsng stages; bbv*
	P		**Ashloch** (5a) 66-1 N Harris *Towards rr; lost tch 10; bhnd when pu 13; quiet intro*
[164¹]	U		**Blazing Miracle** (5a) 2-1F Miss T Cave *Opened 2s,tchd 6/4; lw; nt a fluent; hld up in midfield; 6th 13; no real hdwy; blun & ur 16*
	P		**Tubb Corner** 33-1 T Greed *(xnb) Bckwd; fractious & ur gng to post; sn rr; bhnd frm 8 til pu 13; school*
	P		**Walton Street** 50-1 W Smith *Swtng; last when bad mist 2; bhnd frm 4; t.o when blun bad 11; pu 13*

OFFICIAL DISTANCES: 5l, 3l **TIME:** 6min 55.0s

311 Confined Maiden (Div 1), 12st   10 ran

[159²]	1		**LYDFORD CASTLE** 4-5F C Heard *Tchd evens; hdd chsng group but let tearaway ldr go; lft in ld aft 12; forged clr u.p aft 2 out; pushed out*
[254F]	2	6	**Swift Venture** (IRE) 5-2 Richard Darke *Lw; settled mid-div & off pce; 5th ½way; impd to cl 3rd 14; outpcd 3 out; eff u.p 2 out; no ex app last*
[159³]	3	4	**The Ugly Duckling** 6-1 R Woollacott *Sn prom in chsng group; lft 2nd aft 12; cl 2nd & ev ch to 3 out; kpt on one pce*
[254F]	4	15	**Harvest Home** (IRE) 10-1 T Dennis *(xnb) Midfield & wl off pce; lft 4th aft 12; just in tch to 3 out; wknd & wl btn when blun last*
[106¹]	5	1½fs	**Georgetown** 7-1 T Greed *6th 5; sn lost ground; last ½way; 5th & bhnd frm 14*
[159³]	6	½	**Golden Sunset** (5a) 50-1 Miss D Mitchell *Bit bckwd; 5th 8; rr by 10; last frm 11; bhnd when mist 14; t.o*
[165P]	P		**Baldhu Luckystrike** 25-1 A Ede *Sn rr; last when pu aft 5*
[165P]	R		**Cornish Hope** 7-1 Miss S Young *Tde; hdwy to 4th 6; still prom in 4th when rn out bend aft 11*
	P		**Gibraltar Lady** (5a) 25-1 S Craddock *Tchd 33s; bckwd; rcd v keen & set up long ld; fnce clr 8; still 40l clr 10; wkng rap but still slt ld when pu exhaust aft 12*
	P		**Henryson** 14-1 Miss A Barnett *Bckwd; rr when blun bad 4; bhnd when pu 8; school*

OFFICIAL DISTANCES: 6l, 2l **TIME:** 7min 20.0s

312 Confined Maiden (Div 2), 12st   12 ran

	1		**THE BANDON CAR** (IRE) 5-1 T Cole *Settled towards rr; 7th 13; gd hdwy aft 16; chall & lft in ld 3 out; sn clr; stayed on str*
	2	runin	**Battle Lord Cisto** 11-2 D Doyne-Ditmas *Bckwd; sn rr; 8th ½way; hdwy 13; 5th & in tch 15; lft 2nd 3 out; sn one pce*
[105P]	3	3	**Hanukkah** (5a) 5-1 I Hambley *Midfield; 5th ½way; hdwy to 3rd 12; in tch til outpcd 16; kpt on one pce u.p*
[159P]	4	12	**Call Me Dickins** (bl,tt) 12-1 Miss A Barnett *Bckwd; ld/disp til def ld but rdn aft 14; hdd 16; sn wknd u.p; walked in*
[159F]	P		**Baldhu Jay Arr** 14-1 A Ede *Sn rr; bhnd til pu 10*
[105F]	P		**Broad Ark** 4-1 Richard Darke *5th when mist 8; 6th & in tch 13; lost ground aft nxt; bhnd when pu 3 out*
[256U]	F		**Debbie's Darling** (5a) 10-1 Miss S Gaisford *(xnb) Bit bckwd; hdwy to disp 5; ld/disp to 14; ld agn 16; slt ld when fell nxt; rdr concussed*
[158U]	B		**Frankie Moneybags** 11-8F T Dennis *(xnb) Lw; trckd ldrs; cl 3rd 9; in tch when bd 3 out*
[253F]	P		**Frankies Flutter** 14-1 Miss S Young *(xnb) Bckwd; pu app 4 (rdr thought horse unsound)*
[157P]	P		**Linton** (5a) 16-1 W Smith *Disp ld early; lost plce qckly 7; bhnd frm 9; t.o & pu last*
[73³]	P		**Royal Chip** 10-1 J Young *Keen & prom early; cl 4th ½way; in tch til wknd rap 14; bhnd when pu 16*
	F		**Spirit Of Life** (5a) 25-1 K Rixon *Midfield; slt mist 2; 7th ½way; rr when fell hvly 11; rdr inj*

OFFICIAL DISTANCES: dist, 2l **TIME:** 7min 10.0s

313 Land Rover Mens Open, 12st   4 ran

[160¹]	1		**THE HOBBIT** (IRE) 1-2F T Mitchell *Tchd 4/7 & 4/9; disp ld at stdy pce to 6; trckd ldr til 4l down & outpcd aft 16; sn rallied; ld aft 3 out; drvn clr last; eased cl home*
[160²]	2	6	**Bitran** (7x) 2-1 T Greed *Hld up in cl 3rd; ev ch 3 out; went 2nd 2 out; nt pce to chall*
[252³]	3	20	**Romalito** 12-11 N Harris *Disp ld til ld 6; slt ld til qcknd 16; hdd aft 3 out; hrd rdn & wknd nxt; fin tired*

[198²] **4**   7   **Strong Stuff (IRE)** (7x) 40-1 **M Shears** *A last; mist 8; cl up til mist & lost ground 14; no ch frm 16*

    OFFICIAL DISTANCES: 6l, 7l **TIME:** 7min 08.0s

314 Ladies Open - 16J   7 ran

[161¹] **1**   **LAKEFIELD RAMBLER (IRE)** 2-7F **Miss P Gundry** *Lw; made all; bad mist 2; 2l up when hit 12; pushed clr aft 13; stayed on wl u.p when chall 2 out; drew clr last*

[162ʳ] **2**   5   **Baby Whale (IRE)** (5a) 7-1 **Miss T Cave** *Hld up; stdy prog aft 12; went 2nd 3 out; ev ch til no ex u.p aft 2 out*

[149ᴾ] **3**   20   **Duchess Of Tubber (IRE)** (5a) 33-1 **Mrs M Hand** *Cl 5th ½way; rdn 12; lost tch 13; snatched 3rd on post*

        4   nk   **Secret Four** 6-1 **Miss K Langdell** (xnb) *Cl 4th ½way; went 2nd 11; outpcd aft 13; blun & releg 3rd 3 out; no ch clsng stages; lost 3rd nr line; btr for rce*

        P   **Agent** 66-1 **Miss C Stucley** (xnb) *Cl 3rd ½way; in tch til wknd aft 13; bhnd when pu 2 out*

[201⁴] **F**   **Lady Lir** (5a) 7-1 **Miss S Young** (b4) *Last but in tch when fell 4*

[161¹] **P**   **Roving Rebel** (bl) 6-1 **Miss C Prouse** *Trckd ldr ½way; lost plce rap 11; btn when pu nxt*

    OFFICIAL DISTANCES: 5l, 8l **TIME:** 6min 56.0s
    Fences 3, 9 & 15 omitted from this and all subsequent races because of the state of the ground

315 Restricted, 12st - 16J   19 ran

[255²] **1**   **SOLOMANS SISTER** (5a) 5-1 **Mrs M Hand** *Swtng; ld 1; trckd ldr frm nxt til app 3 out; lft 2nd 2 out; stayed on str to ld cl home*

[164³] **2**   s hd   **Spruce** (5a) 7-1 **Mrs S Fell** *Ld 2; 8l clr 11; disp ld 3 out; hdd; cl 2nd when lft in ld 2 out; lkd wnr til hdd nr line; gd eff*

[204¹] **3**   20   **Jabiru (IRE)** 5-2F **R Woollacott** *4s-5/2; lw; hld up towards rr; 11th ½way; stdy prog to 4th but lot to do 3 out; lft 3rd nxt; nrst fin*

[164ᴾ] **4**   15   **Nearly Fair** (5a) 14-1 **T Greed** (bf) *Bit bckwd; in tch early; 5th 8; lost ground & wl bhnd frm 3 out*

        5   3   **Born Natural (IRE)** (5a) 20-1 **Miss P Gundry** *Sn handy; 6th ½way; in tch til wknd frm 13; t.o*

[158¹] **6**   8   **Frankly Fear** 10-1 **J Young** *Lw; towards rr & nt a fluent; 13th 8; nd*

[164ᵁ] **7**   ½   **Phartoomanny (IRE)** (5a) 25-1 **Miss N Snowden** (xnb) *Hit 2; trckd ldrs; 5th ½way; lost plce qckly 11; t.o*

[203ᴾ] **P**   **Breeze-Bloc** (5a) 50-1 **M Shears** *Swtng; rr; pu app 2 (rdr reported horse felt unsound)*

[163²] **P**   **Damiens Pride (IRE)** 10-1 **T Dennis** (5a) *Midfield; 8th 12; nd; bhnd when pu 3 out*

        P   **Flaming Cold (IRE)** (5a,5ow) 5-1 **T Mitchell** *Midfield; 12th 8; slt hdwy to 7th 12; nt rch ldrs; pu 2 out; nt pushed*

        P   **Kimbross** 20-1 **K Heard** (xnb) *Lw; a rr; 15th 8; bhnd when pu 3 out*

[164ᴾ] **P**   **King Of Cairo** 33-1 **I Hambley** (xnb) *Rr; 14th 8; t.o & pu 12*

[163ᴾ] **P**   **Lirkimalong** 33-1 **Miss S Young** *Bckwd; 2 handlers; tde; sn rr; t.o 4 til pu 12; quiet rn*

        F   **Miner's Bill (IRE)** 16-1 **Miss T Cave** (xnb) *Hld up in midfield; 8th ½way; stdy hdwy to 3rd 13; went 2nd 3 out; slt ld & gng wl when fell 2 out; promising*

        P   **Moorland Abbot** 50-1 **Miss D Mitchell** *Bhnd til pu 12*

[144⁵] **P**   **Nearly All Right** 14-1 **N Harris** *Prom early; 7th ½way; sn wknd; bhnd when pu 3 out*

        P   **Newlyn** 25-1 **T Cole** *Last when bad mist 3; t.o & pu 7*

[165ᴾ] **P**   **Rice Point** 10-1 **C Heard** (xnb) *Lw; towards rr; 10th 8; prog to 6th 12; nt trble ldrs; 6th when pu 3 out*

[251ᵁ] **P**   **Sagaville (IRE)** 10-1 **Richard Darke** *Prom; chsd ldrs in 3rd to 13; wknd; bhnd when pu 3 out*

    OFFICIAL DISTANCES: hd, 8l **TIME:** 7min 02.0s

316 Confined, 12st - 16J   6 ran

[165¹] **1**   **WESTCOUNTRY LAD** (3x) 5-4F **R Woollacott** *Hld up in tch; hit 7; poised in 3rd frm ½way; 3l 3rd 3 out; eff bet horses aft 2 out; nk 2nd at last; stayed on wl u.p; won on nod*

[160ᴿ] **2**   s hd   **Baldhu Chance** 6-1 **A Ede** *Made most; 10l clr 10; still 5l up 4 out; hdd nxt; rallied to ld app 2 out; slt ld last; edged rt u.p flat; hdd on post*

[157ᶠ] **P**   **Border Rose** (5a) 33-1 **D Doyne-Ditmas** *Lost tch stdly aft 7; bhnd when pu 9*

[257³] **P**   **Dunlir** 10-1 **Miss S Young** *Prom to ½way; lost ground 10; pu 12*

[160ᴾ] **P**   **Rasta Man** (5x) 3-1 **K Heard** *Hld up in tch; 4th & niggled along 11; sn rdn & no imp; 14l 4th 4 out; btn when pu 2 out*

        P   **Rosa's Revenge** (5a,3x) 3-1 **C Heard** *Oht; chsd ldr; blun bad 12; prog 4 out; slt ld inner 3 out; hdd nxt; tired 3rd when pu last*

    OFFICIAL DISTANCE: hd **TIME:** 7min 11.0s

Essex Farmers & Union
Marks Tey (LH 10F,20J) Sat, 26 Feb (HEAVY)

317 Hunt   **7 ran**

[127⁸]	1		**HIZAL** 2-1F **D Hayes** Trckd ldr in 3rd; 8l 2nd 14; ld 3 out; a gng best aft; forged clr last; rdr's 1st wnr
[236ᴾ]	2	3	**Dreamisle** (5a) 8-1 **C Ward** A in tch in 5th; gng wl 13; 4th & hdwy 16; went 3l 2nd 3 out; one pce aft; a hld
[88ᴾ]	3	30	**The Arkle Bar (IRE)** 6-1 **A Braithwaite** Ld 2-9; 2nd nxt til drpd to 3rd 14; lost tch 16; plugged into dist 3rd app last
	4	5	**Skirmishing** 8-1 **T Moore** (xnb) Ld 1; prsd ldr nxt til ld 10; 8l up 14; wknd 16; hdd bef nxt; tired & lost tch rap; dem last
[180ᴾ]	5	5	**Golden Knight** 5-1 **P Piddington** Imm detach in last pr; nt jw & rdr constantly waving; t.o frm 2; plodded rnd
	P		**Exarch (USA)** 4-1 **Miss J Landymore** Fat; chsd ldrs in 4th; wknd rap 14; rem 5th nxt; t.o & pu 16
	U		**On The Beer (IRE)** 9-2 **M Bailey** 1st ride; imm detach in last pr; t.o 2; lft 5th 16; plugged on & just hldng t.o rival when blun & ur last

OFFICIAL DISTANCES: 3l, dist TIME: 7min 42.0s

318 Confined, 12st   **12 ran**

[175ᵁ]	1		**DRY HIGHLINE (IRE)** (3x) 3-1 **C Ward-Thomas** Ld; sn clr; 20l clr 9; mist 16; unchall; eased flat
[175⁴]	2	20	**Nibble** 20-1 **G Cooper** (xnb) Mid-div; outpcd 13; kpt on 15; 25l 5th 17; r.o frm 3 out; stayed on past tiring rivals to 2nd flat
[178¹]	3	¾	**Scarlett O'Hara** (5a) 5-4F **S Sporborg** Hld up in 7/8th; stdy hdwy frm 5; clsd 10; 3rd nxt; chsd runaway ldr 13; 30l 3rd & no imp nxt
[241¹]	4	2	**Commuter Country** (6x) 5-2 **C Ward** Drpd to rr 1; stdy hdwy frm 4; 25l 2nd 11; chsd runaway ldr til wknd app last; dem flat
[92⁵]	5	1½fs	**Spuffington** 33-1 **Miss C Hall** Chsd ldrs in 15l 4th til drpd to rr 10; wknd rap; t.o frm 13; plodded on
	P		**Alfredo Garcia (IRE)** 10-1 **R Gill** A rr; wknd 10; lost tch nxt; wl bhnd when pu 12
[116ᴾ]	P		**Ardkilly Warrior (IRE)** 16-1 **W Wales** Mostly 5/6th; chsd ldrs vain frm 14; 30l 5th & no ch 3 out; wknd rap nxt; t.o & pu last
[175²]	P		**Courier's Way (IRE)** (3x) 12-1 **S R Andrews** Mid-div; rr of main group 9; wknd stdly; rem 8th when pu 16
[92⁶]	P		**Cropredy Lad** 20-1 **T Humphrey** 2nd 1; chsd clr ldr; 10l 2nd 7; wknd rap frm 9; t.o 11; pu 15
[92⁴]	P		**More Fun (USA)** 14-1 **N Bloom** Handy 5/6th; nt qckn 11; stdly wknd; detach 7th 15; wl bhnd when pu 3 out
[223⁸]	F		**Oflaherty's Babe (IRE)** (3x) 8-1 **R Fowler** Nvr beyond mid-div; one pce frm 14; wknd 3 out; rem 5th when fell last
[174ᴾ]	P		**Speedy Snaps Pride** 33-1 **N Page** Imm detach in rr; t.o last when pu 12

OFFICIAL DISTANCES: 15l, ½l TIME: 7min 13.0s

319 Ladies Open   **10 ran**

[177¹]	1		**SPRING GALE (IRE)** evensF **Miss Z Turner** Ld in start; rcd wide; trckd ldrs gng wl in 4/5th; 3l 5th 14; 3rd frm nxt; stdy hdwy to press ldr 17; jmpd to ld 3 out; forged clr app last; impressive
[95²]	2	6	**Cache Fleur (FR)** 3-1 **Mrs G d'Angibau** Ld to 4; prom in 2nd/3rd til 4l 4th 12; sn prsng ldr; lft 4l clr 15; jnd 3 out; sn hdd; nt qckn app last
[95¹]	3	8	**Thurles Pickpocket (IRE)** 4-1 **Mrs S Hodge** Prom; cl 2nd to 4; prsd ldrs in 3rd/4th aft; 2l 3rd 14; disp 1l 2nd 3 out; one pce nxt
[240ᵁ]	4	25	**Limited Liability** 20-1 **Miss C Grissell** (xnb) A rr of main group; nt trble ldrs; outpcd 14; lft 10l 4th nxt; sn lost tch
[289³]	5	10	**Faha Gig (IRE)** (5a) 14-1 **Mrs F Needham** Mid-div & nt able to go pce; bhnd frm 13; plodded on
[175³]			**Ann's Ambition** 12-1 **Miss C Fryer** Settled last; hdwy & in tch frm 11-12; outpcd nxt & sn lost tch; t.o 15; pu 2 out
[177ᴾ]	U		**Lets Twist Again (IRE)** 16-1 **Miss A Stennett** Prsd ldr in 2nd/3rd to 13; 2l 4th when blun & ur 14
	P		**My Best Man** (bl) 10-1 **Mrs T Hill** In tch at rr of main group til wknd 13; sn wl bhnd; t.o & pu 14
[240ᴾ]	P		**Royal Surprise** 33-1 **Miss L Ingram** (xnb) Imm rr; strugg in 9th til releg last aft 10; sn detach; t.o 12; pu 2 out

[240²]   F   **Uron V (FR)** 14-1 Miss T Hayter *Prom til ld 5; 2l up & still gng wl when fell 15*

OFFICIAL DISTANCES: 5l, 5l   TIME: 7min 15.0s

320 Mens Open   8 ran

[195¹]   1   **COPPER THISTLE (IRE)** 1-3F R Hunnisett *Ld; 2-3l ahd til qcknd 12; in comm frm nxt; 8l clr 17; v easy*

        2   15   **Mister Trick (IRE)** (bl) 20-1 N King *Prsd ldr in 2nd til nt qckn 12; 8l 2nd 14; lost tch stdly & no ch aft; fin tired*

[176¹]   3   15   **General Assembly (IRE)** 7-2 N Bloom *Hld up; drpd to last 6; hdwy to 8l 4th 14; kpt on one pce; 15l 3rd & no imp 17*

[223ᴾ]   4   8   **High Learie** (bl) 33-1 A Harvey *Trckd ldrs in cl 4th mostly; ev ch til outpcd 13; sn btn*

[178⁶]   5   2   **Insulate** (5a) 33-1 S March *In tch in rr; drpd to last 10; lost tch qckly; plodded on*

        6   15   **Karar (IRE)** 25-1 R Fowler *Trckd ldrs in 5th; jmpd slow 12; rdn & wknd nxt; no ch 14; kpt on one pce; releg last flat; walked in; collapsed & died aft*

        P   **Cinnamon Club** (5a) 20-1 D Cook *Oht; rr & hit 3; 4l 3rd & hdwy 7; rdn when blun 13; wknd rap nxt; t.o & pu 16*

[82³]   P   **Remilan (IRE)** 10-1 A Sansome *Imm detach in rr & nvr gng wl; 10l 6th 10; lost further ground; 30l 7th 17; pu 2 out*

OFFICIAL DISTANCES: 15l, 20l   TIME: 7min 17.0s

321 Restricted, 12st   9 ran

[98¹]   1   **MONTYS TAG (IRE)** 4-7F S R Andrews *Disp ld til ld 5-10; 2l 2nd til ld agn 15; 2-3l ahd til forged clr 2 out; easy*

[239⁷]   2   12   **Therewearethen (USA)** 12-1 N King *Trckd ldrs in 3rd/4th; clsd 12; 8l 3rd 14; kpt on to 5l 2nd 17; chsd wnr game; 2l 2nd 3 out; wknd*

[97¹]   3   40   **Country Barle** (vis) 4-1 N Bloom *Disp ld to 4; trckd ldr nxt; releg 3l 3rd 11; outpcd 13; strugg nxt; 25l 4th 16; nursed rnd aft; v tired 3 out; lft rem 3rd 2 out*

        P   **Bally Seamus (IRE)** 7-2 R Cope *Nt jw in detach last; mist 7; t.o & pu 10*

[94ᴾ]   P   **Beau Joueur (FR)** (bl) 6-1 C Ward *In tch in 5th; wknd 11; detach 13; pu 14*

        P   **Coolest By Phar (IRE)** 14-1 C Ward-Thomas *2 handlers; oht; off pce in 6/7th to 9; wknd nxt; wl bhnd 10; virt t.o & pu 11*

        U   **Handy Boy** (7a) 12-1 A Harvey *V late in padd; sa; ur 10yd aft start; rmtd & imm ur agn*

[96ᴾ]   P   **Skinsey Finnegan (IRE)** 10-1 K Edmunds (xnb) *In tch; 6l 5th 9; wknd qckly; virt t.o 8; pu 10*

        P   **Trojan Love (IRE)** (5a) 10-1 K Edmunds (xnb) *In tch; 6l 5th 9; wknd qckly; virt t.o 8; pu 10*

OFFICIAL DISTANCES: 10l, dist   TIME: 7min 26.0s

The stewards enquired into the running & riding of Bally Seamus; they accepted the rider's explanation that the horse was 'unable to act on or jump out of the ground'

322 Confined Maiden (Div 1), 12st   12 ran

[181ᴿ]   1   **LE CABRO D'OR** 5-2 S Sporborg (xnb) *Nt settle in rr; pulled to 11 2nd 5; ld 9; jmpd violent rt 13 & 14; 15l clr 16; jmpd rt aft but unchall; v easy*

[98³]   2   20   **You Can Quote Me (IRE)** 16-1 A Harvey *Nt fluent; prom in 3rd/4th; outpcd 13; kpt on to disp rem 2nd 3 out; stayed on best flat*

[179ᶠ]   3   6   **Miss Mouse** (5a) 3-1 C Ward-Thomas *Jmpd rt; ld to 9; prom til outpcd 13; lost tch qckly; lft dist 2nd 16; prsd for 2nd 3 out til no ex & dem flat*

[290³]   4   30   **Persian Boy (IRE)** 10-1 A Sansome *Nt fluent; a strugg towards rr; outpcd frm 12; t.o 15; lft 4th by defections*

        P   **Arbitrage Man (IRE)** 16-1 R Cope *Strugg in mid-div to 10; wknd & drpd to rr nxt; lost tch qckly & pu 13*

[131⁵]   P   **Bachelor-Carrasco (IRE)** 6-1 S R Andrews *In tch in 5th to 11; wknd qckly nxt; t.o & pu 16*

        P   **Curracloe Rose (IRE)** (5a) 10-1 D Cook *Trckd ldrs; 4l 3rd 7; in tch til outpcd 13; wknd qckly nxt; t.o & v tired when pu 16*

        P   **Lancaster Boy (IRE)** 20-1 C Ward *Mid-div; mostly 6/7th til chsd ldrs 13; jnd rem 2nd 3 out; wknd bef nxt; 4th & no ch when pu last*

[98ᴾ]   P   **Ruddy Marvel Lass** (5a) 10-1 K Edmunds *Prom in main group; chsd clr ldr frm 11 outpcd 13; 15l 2nd but exhaust 15; pu nxt*

[98²]   P   **Uncle Buck (IRE)** 2-1F P Taiano *Cl up on heels of ldrs; 3l 3rd & gng easy when pu 11*

[241ᵁ]   P   **Wardy Hill** (5a) 25-1 C Lawson *Imm rr & detach last 4; t.o 6; pu 11*

[241ᴾ] P   **Wise Point (IRE)** 33-1 G Lush *In tch in rr to 9; wknd rap; t.o & pu 11*

OFFICIAL DISTANCES: dist, 3l **TIME:** 7min 35.0s

The stewards enquired into the running and riding of Uncle Buck; the rider's explanation that he thought the horse might be lame was accepted

323 Confined Maiden (Div 2), 12st   10 ran

[87³]   1   **BALLAD** (tt) 7-1 A Harvey *Prom; mostly 4/5th; chsd ldrs 13; 6l 3rd & lkd outpcd 15; rnwd eff nxt; disp ld 17 til ld 2 out; drvn clr; fin tired*

        2 25 **Glad All Over** (5a) 10-1 C Ward *Ld to 10; cl 2nd nxt til ld agn 14; 5l up nxt; jnd 17-2 out; hdd & wknd qckly bef last*

[181²] 3 15 **Senior Partner (IRE)** 7-4F S R Andrews *Prom; cl 2nd 8-10; ld nxt til nrly carried out by loose horse 14 & dem 5l 2nd; rallied til disp ld 17-2 out; wknd qckly btn; eased when ch gone*

[88ᴾ]   4 fence **Out Of Actons (IRE)** (5ow) 20-1 C Jarvis (xnb) *In tch in 4/5th; outpcd 14; 8l 4th 16; sn t.o*

        P   **French Tale (IRE)** 7-1 C Ward-Thomas *Chsd ldr; 2l 2nd 7; prom til tost tch qckly frm 11; bhnd when pu 14*

[179ᴾ] P   **Mannagar (IRE)** 14-1 D Page (East Anglia) *2 handlers; in tch to 5; sn wl bhnd; t.o & barely galloping 10; pu 12*

[174ʳ] r   **Primrose Hill** (5a) 20-1 Miss R Barrow *Imm last; t.o 1; ref 8*
        F   **Sugar Love** (5a) 14-1 R Fowler *Imm rr; detach by 7; rem 9th when fell 8*

[175ᴾ] P   **Sweet Talker (IRE)** 8-1 N Bloom *Rr; detach 7; pu 12*
        U   **Will Hill (IRE)** (7a) 4-1 K Edmunds *Prom & gng wl in 4/5th; prog to 2l 3rd when blun & ur 13*

OFFICIAL DISTANCES: 15l, 10l **TIME:** 7min 33.0s

Hursley Hambledon

Badbury Rings (LH 10F,19J) Sat, 26 Feb (GOOD)

324 Hunt, 12st   5 ran

[126¹] 1   **BALL IN THE NET** (7x) 4-7F M Holdforth *Tchd 8/13; jw; cl up in last pr til jnd ldrs 8; lft in ld 9; carried wide by loose horse aft nxt; 2l ahd 11; drew away frm nxt; 15l clr 14; unchall*

[216⁵] 2 40 **Master Comedy** (bl) 100-1 V Simpson (citation) *Bckwd; ld til jnd 7; 5l last when mist nxt; went 2l 2nd 11; sn outpcd; 15l 2nd & no ch 14*

        3 35 **Amaranthine** (5a,7x) 16-1 Mrs J Butler *Cl 2nd til jmpd to ld 7; jnd nxt; sn hdd; disp 2½l 2nd 9; pckd nxt; last & wkng qckly 11; sn wl bhnd; t.o & jmpng v slow frm 14*

[78ᴾ]   R   **Arfer Mole (IRE)** 5-2 D Dennis *Tchd 11/4; cl 3rd til rn out to lft thro wing 4*
[130ᴾ] C   **Loftus Lad (IRE)** 7-1 S Claisse *9s-7s; cl up in last pr early; hdwy to disp ld brief app 7; ld on inner agn aft 8 til carried out by loose horse 9*

OFFICIAL DISTANCES: dist, dist **TIME:** 6min 25.7s **TOTE:** £1.40

325 Confined, 12st - 18J   13 ran

[219¹] 1   **CHATERGOLD (IRE)** (bl) 4-1 R Lawther *A.p; trckd ldrs; 3l 4th aft 4; disp 7½l 3rd aft 10; 3l 3rd & clsng 14; ld nxt; prsd 3 out; kpt on str; in comm last; eased nr fin*

[214ᵁ] 2   6 **Cahors (IRE)** 6-4F N Mitchell *9/4-6/4; ww in rr; 11th 4; 13l 6th & clsng 14; went 6l 4th nxt & 3l 3rd 3 out; 1l 2nd & jnd nxt; sn btn; still btr for rce*

[214⁵] 3   2 **Badger Beer** 20-1 J Snowden *Tchd 25s; a.p; cl 2nd mostly til ld aft 13; hdd 15; prsd ldr; level & ev ch 3 out; 3½l 3rd & no ex nxt*

[200ᴾ] 4   6 **Coolree (IRE)** 50-1 Miss A Goschen *Jmpd rt; trckd ldrs; 2½l 2nd aft 3; disp 7½l 3rd aft 10; 10l 5th & outpcd 14; stayed on to 4½l 4th & ch 2 out; wknd*

[265ᵁ] 5 20 **Newby End (IRE)** 7-1 A Blanch *25s-7s; mid-div; 8th aft 3; 10th & just in tch 10; outpcd frm 12; mod 7th & one pce 3 out*

[35ᵁ]   6 2½ **Silver Sleeve (IRE)** 25-1 Miss L Bridges *A towards rr; 9th 9; 7th & outpcd 12; wl bhnd; kpt on frm 3 out*

[130⁴] 7   5 **Coach (NZ)** 7-1 B Kendellen *Lft in ld 1-12; still cl 3rd 15; wknd; 7½l 5th & btn 3 out*

[214⁶] P   **Arabitan** (5a) 33-1 M Green *A rr div; poor 11th ½way; t.o last aft 10; plodded on til pu last*

[215ᴾ] U   **Arleneseoin (IRE)** (7x) 33-1 T Underwood (kineton) *2 handlers; oht; swtng; tde; ld & ur 1*

[209ᴾ] P   **Blakeington** (bl) 100-1 Miss K Reynolds *Sa; a last; 12l bhnd rest 2; t.o; pu aft 10*
[127⁴] P   **Feel The Power (IRE)** 33-1 J Maxse *Trckd ldrs in cl 5th mostly til 5l 4th 14; 6th & wkng qckly nxt; rem 8 3 out; wl bhnd when pu aft nxt*

[211ᴾ] U   **Our Wizzer (IRE)** (1ow) 12-1 C Whittaker *Handy 7th aft 3 til blun 10; ur some way aft*

| | P | | **You Said It (IRE)** 7-1 D Crosse *Trckd ldrs; disp cl 5th aft 4; 4th 9; disp 7½l 3rd app 11; still 4th 12; 20l 7th & wkng qckly when pu 14; public gallop* |

OFFICIAL DISTANCES: 6l, 2l **TIME:** 6min 17.9s **TOTE:** £4.00
Fence 11 omitted - fallen rider

326 Ladies Open   13 ran

	1		**GREY SMOKE** 12-1 Miss B Lloyd *Last pr early; gd prog to disp 4th 7; jnd ldr 9; ld nxt; made rest; 2½l clr 2 out; drew wl clr w rnr-up; kpt on game & a in comm*
[32³]	2	1	**Mizyan (IRE)** 5-1 Miss M Coombe *A,p; trckd ldrs in 3rd/4th til 2nd 5; disp ld brief 9; trckd ldr til chall & blun bad 3 out; rallied wl & ev ch last; r.o; a hld*
	3	15	**Split Second** 9-4F Miss A Dare *(pricker ns) Bit bckwd; hld up towards rr; 9th ½way; stayed on frm 15; 20½l 7th 2 out; kpt on wl; nvr nr ldrs; btr for rce*
	4	1½	**Pride Of Kashmir** 16-1 Mrs C Ford *(bf) Tchd 20s; mid-div; 8th & hdwy ½way; went 4th aft 13; eff 15; 7½l 3rd 2 out; wknd*
[214¹]	5	1½	**Man Of Steele (IRE)** 4-1 Miss D Harding *10s-4s; prom; chsd ldr aft 3; 2l 2nd 10; 3rd nxt; outpcd frm 15; 11½l 4th & no ex 2 out*
	6	3	**Mine's A Gin (IRE)** 5-1 Miss J Cumings *Trckd ldrs in 4/5th; cl 4th 9; 5th & wkng 13; 18l 6th & btn 2 out*
[214²]	7	1½	**Malihabad (IRE)** 10-1 Miss A Goschen *Tchd 12s; sn rr; last trio 7; 6th & hdwy aft 13; nvr able to chall; 13l 5th & no imp 2 out*
[209⁴]	8	25	**General Giggs (IRE)** (bl) 40-1 Mrs E Smith *A rr; mostly last of main body; poor 12th 10th; t.o 13; kpt on past tired horses frm 15; nvr any ch*
	9	½	**Olive Basket** (5a) 50-1 Miss W Southcombe *Midfield; fair 7th 10; 9th & lsng tch 13; t.o 15*
	10	15	**Willie Makeit (IRE)** 12-1 Mrs M Barlow *Prom; disp ld 2; cl 3rd 5; stdly lost tch; 7th 10; to 8th & no ch 15; poor eff*
[208¹⁰]	11	½	**Bright Lady** (5a) 100-1 Miss R Green *A rr; last 3; t.o 9; rdn out to gain a plce flat*
[245ᶠ]	F		**Bend Sable (IRE)** 100-1 Miss S Duckett *Jmpd big & slow; ld/disp to 4l clr aft 3; jnd 9; sn hdd; 4th & wkng 11; btn when fell 14*
[209²]	P		**Spring Marathon (USA)** 16-1 Miss E Tory *Keen to start; a last trio; t.o & mist 12; pu last*

OFFICIAL DISTANCES: 1l, 15l **TIME:** 6min 13.0s **TOTE:** £4.00

327 Land Rover Mens Open, 12st   10 ran

[210³]	1		**MISS O'GRADY (IRE)** (5a,7x) 10-11F M Miller *Ww in mid-div; 6th 7; went 3rd aft nxt; disp cl 3rd 10; mist 14; clr 3rd 15; stalked ldrs til qcknd to ld 2 out; drew clr flat; comf*
	2	5	**Aintgottime (IRE)** 4-1 R Lawther *(xnb) Tchd 9/2; ld/disp til ld 3 out; hdd nxt; kpt on; ev ch til tired & hung lft aft last*
[210ᵖ]	3	4	**Go Universal (IRE)** 25-1 N Mitchell *Handy til 3rd 5; l3 3rd 10; cl 3rd/4th aft; 4th & ev ch 3 out; 5½l 3rd & outpcd 2 out; kpt on but no ch aft; rn wl*
	4	10	**Man Of The Match** 8-1 B Kendellen *Tchd 10s; cl 2nd/disp ld; ev ch 3 out; wknd qckly; nt disg*
[100³]	5	10	**Stalbridge Gold** (5a) 12-1 J Ferguson *Cl 3rd to 4 & agn brief 10; 5½l 5th aft 13; lost tch frm 15*
[33¹¹]	6	30	**Panda Shandy** (5a) 20-1 H Froud *Tchd 33s; last pr early; 8th 7; prog to disp 5th 11; 7l 6th aft 13; lost tch frm nxt; t.o 3 out*
	F		**Ebullient Equiname (IRE)** 3-1 S Morris *(orbs) 5s-3s; last 1; gd prog to cl 4th & fell 6*
[59ᶠ]	P		**Gaelic Blue** 33-1 C Weaver *Mid-div early; last trio by 7; last of main body 9; rdn & wknd 11; t.o 14; pu 3 out*
[5⁵]	P		**Northern Kingdom (USA)** 33-1 J Diment *Handy; cl 3rd aft 4; cl 5th 10; 7th & wkng 15; bhnd when pu 2 out*
[160ᵖ]	P		**Shariakanndi (FR)** 12-1 A Honeyball *Sn last; rmdrs aft 2; detach & scrubbed along aft; lkng to stop & vigorously rdn aft 10; t.o 14; pu 2 out*

OFFICIAL DISTANCES: 5l, 4l **TIME:** 6min 22.4s **TOTE:** £2.00

328 Confined Maiden (Div 1), 12st   10 ran

	1		**HIGHTECH TOUCH** 10-1 D Flavin *(xnb) Mid-div; prog to 7l 4th 5; 6th 10; mist nxt; went cl 3rd aft 13; jnd ldr 15 til ld 2 out; sn clr; v easy*
[208⁴]	2	20	**Dante's Gold (IRE)** 5-2JF R Bliss *4s-5/2,tchd 5/4; a,p; cl 3rd frm 3 til ld 10-13; ld agn & outj 14; disp ld 15; cl 2nd & ev ch nxt til wknd aft 2 out; sn no ch*
	3	3	**Spanish River** 100-1 G Weatherley *Trckd ldrs; 5l 4th aft 3; drpd back 6th 8; 10l last 12; prog to mod 4th aft 13; 18½l 4th 16; went 3rd app last; no ch w ldrs*
[249ᵖ]	4	½	**Have A Break** (7a) 25-1 R Lawther *Lw; last pr; lost tch frm 13; poor 6th 16; 5th 2 out; stayed on wl aft; easy rce*

	5	15	**Dancing Barefoot** (5a) 25-1 J Maxse *Bit bckwd; mostly last trio; mist 9; 8th 10; lost tch frm 12; last 14; plodded on*
[105²]	6	10	**Tanglefoot Tipple** 5-2JF N Mitchell *Tchd 3s; disp ld 1; settled trckng ldrs; 6l 4th 5; hdwy 8; disp ld 12; ld aft nxt til outj 14; 3½l 3rd & ev ch 16; wknd qckly; v tired 3rd 2 out; exhaust & nrly fell last*
	R		**Barton Nic** 9-2 P Keane *Tchd 5s; swtng; mounted & tde; hld up in last pr; cl last 8; 5th & hdwy 10; cl 3rd when crashed thro rt wing & fell 13*
[212ᴾ]	R		**Just Reuben** (IRE) (7a) 33-1 Miss C Tuffin *Virt bolted in ld til rn out to rt 3; carted rdr for more than a circ*
[264⁵]	P		**Mandalady** (IRE) (5a) 50-1 M Legge *Prom til ld aft 3; hdd 5; jnd ldr agn 7-9; 2l prom nxt; 5th & wkng 13; last when pu 2 out*
	P		**Under The Carpet** (IRE) 11-4 D Dennis *Tchd 3s; trckd ldrs til went 2nd aft 3; ld 5; jnd 7-9; 4th 10; lost tch frm 13; t.o & pu 3 out*

OFFICIAL DISTANCES: 20l, 3l   TIME: 6min 30.7s   TOTE: £9.00

329 Confined Maiden (Div 2), 12st   9 ran

	1		**HERE COMES HENRY** 5-1 A Honeyball *10s-5s; trckd ldrs in 4th; 7l 4th 10; hdwy 13; jmpd to 3rd nxt; lft 3l 2nd 15; ld aft 3 out; drew clr aft nxt; easy*
[30ᵁ]	2	12	**Okeford** (IRE) 3-1 R Walford *6s-3s; sn prom; 3rd aft 3; 4½l 3rd aft 10; disp ld brief nxt; cl 2nd til lft in ld 15; hd up & blun 3 out; sn hdd; btn when mist last*
[213ᵁ]	3	12	**The Frosty Fox** (IRE) 2-1F M Miller *Cl 2nd mostly to 9; 4l 2nd nxt; 2l 3rd 11; sn outpcd; wkng when lft 1 l l 3rd 15; disapp*
[207⁴]	4	8	**Music Class** (IRE) 14-1 J Gallagher *Mid-div; disp 12l 6th 10; poor 7th 14; 26l 4th & no imp 16*
	P		**Branski** 12-1 G Weatherley *A last & nt fluent; detach 3; 26l last 10; pu nxt; school*
[250ᴾ]	P		**Down To Joe's** (IRE) 16-1 D Crosse *Opened 20s; nvr btr than midfield; 9½l 5th 10; 16l 5th & wkng 13; t.o & jmpd v slow frm 15; clambered 2 out & pu*
	F		**Greg's Profiles** 9-1 F Brennan *14s-9s; ld; 4l clr 10; jnd brief nxt; jnd agn but still gng wl when fell 15*
[212ᶠ]	F		**Indian Miller** 25-1 M Green *A mid-div; disp 12l 6th 10; 25l 6th & wkng when fell 14*
	P		**Last Gamble** 25-1 P Keane *School in last pr; jmpd rt at times; detach 7; 18l 8th 10; pu nxt*

OFFICIAL DISTANCES: 12l, 12l   TIME: 6min 24.1s   TOTE: £6.00

330 Restricted (Div 1), 12st   15 ran

[144ᶠ]	1		**THE EARTH MOVED** (IRE) evensF A Honeyball *Lw; confid rdn; settled in last pr; 25l 10th 10; still rem in last pr 14; 5th & gng wl nxt; went 3rd 16; ld aft 3 out; 1l up & lkd wnr when lft clr last; quite impressive*
[215ᴾ]	2	10	**Susies Melody** (IRE) (tt) 16-1 D Dennis *Midfield; hdwy to disp 4th 7; 7th 10; gd hdwy nxt; disp cl 2nd 13; jnd ldr 15; ev ch 2 out; sn btn; lft mod 2nd at last; rn wl*
	3	15	**Givry** (IRE) (bl) 50-1 N Parker *Chsd clr ldr in 2nd/3rd to 7; lost plce & 15l 6th 10; gd prog to disp ld 11; cl 3rd nxt til wknd 15; btn 4th 2 out; lft 3rd at last*
	4	10	**Keszam** (IRE) 12-1 A Bateman *A last pr; rem 10th 10; stayed on one pce frm 16*
[220⁴]	5	4	**Fair Ally** 33-1 B Kendellen *(bh) 2 handlers; mid-div; disp 6th 7; went 12½l 4th 10; outpcd 14; 6th & btn 16*
[208ᴾ]	P		**Another Junior** (IRE) 13-2 M Miller *Tchd 7s; midfield; disp 6th 10; disp 8th 10; wknd 15; last when pu 2 out*
[211ᴾ]	F		**Beechdown** 50-1 R Bliss *Rr & fell 1*
[208ᵁ]	F		**Best Bitter** 16-1 J Snowden *Tchd 20s; trckd ldrs; 6th 3; 13½l 5th 10-13; wkng when jmpd v slow 14; 7th & btn 16; fell hvly nxt*
	P		**Fast Run** (IRE) 33-1 Miss M Taylor *A last pr; t.o & pu 9*
[212⁴]	F		**Freemount Boy** (IRE) (tt) 50-1 N Mitchell *Fell 1*
	U		**Friar Waddon** 9-2 Miss J Cumings *(xnb) Oht; trckng ldrs when ur 2*
[226ᴾ]	P		**High Park Lady** (IRE) (5a) 12-1 P Keane *Tchd 14s; ch ride; towards rr; 8th & prog 10; 5th 14; wknd 16; btn 5th 2 out; pu last*
[260ᴾ]	U		**Lost Your Marbles** (IRE) (5a) 12-1 D I Turner *2 handlers; tchd 14s; cl 3rd to 4; lost plce; went 2nd 9; disp ld 11; ld nxt til jnd 15; hdd 3 out; ll 2nd & hld when blun & ur last*
	P		**Luke Skywalker** 14-1 J Richardson *(xnb) Sn clr; 15l up 7; pckd 9; 8l clr 10; hdd bef nxt & wknd rap; t.o 14; pu 16*
	F		**Silver Hill** (5a) 25-1 Miss B Fear *Chsd clr ldr; 8l 2nd 10; 3rd & wkng 11; poor 9th 14; t.o when fell last*

OFFICIAL DISTANCES: 10l, 15l   TIME: 6min 28.0s   TOTE: £1.80

331 Restricted (Div 2), 12st   9 ran

1			**LUCKY TANNER** 33-1 Miss G Young *(xnb) Mid-div; 17l 5th 4; drpd back to disp 17l last 8; 53l 6th 14; stayed on as ldrs faltered; 37l 6th 16; 23l 4th nxt; fin wl; 3rd at last; r.o to ld flat*

[213²]	2	1¾	**Franklins Best (IRE)** 6-1 R Walford _2 handlers; midfield; 17½l 6th 4; 23l 5th 10; disp 25l 3rd 14; went 3l 2nd & pckd bad 3 out; cl 2nd last; no ex cl home_
[163³]	3	5	**River Gala (IRE)** (bl) 14-1 N Mitchell _Chsd ldr 2; 10l 2nd 10; 20l 2nd & outpcd 13; prsng wkng ldr when mist 16; ld 3 out; sn hdd & one pce; dem flat_
[38F]	F		**Crocked Again (IRE)** 11-2 V Keane _(xnb,bnh) 7s-11/2; 2 handlers; ld 1; rn v free & sn 12l clr; 20l ahd 14; wknd qckly aft nxt; 3l up 16; sn hdd & wknd rap; rr & tired when fell slow_
	P		**Dear Emily** (5a) 16-1 J Snowden _Grad lost ground in 3rd; 17l 3rd 5; 20l 3rd aft 10; 33l 5th & btn 14; t.o & pu 2 out_
[35F]	P		**Ngala (IRE)** (5a) 14-1 H Tett _A last trio; 40l last 10; 63l last 14; pu 3 out_
[69⁵]	P		**Peyton Jones** 9-2 M Miller _8s-9/2; last pr 4; stdy hdwy to 22l 4th 11; 17 4th & btn 16; pu 3 out_
	P		**Spanish Jest** 50-1 M Frith _2 handlers; last to 9; 28l 7th 10; t.o last when pu 12_
[30¹]	F		**We Move Earth** 10-11F A Honeyball _Chsd ldrs; 16l 4th 4; went 111 3rd 8; fell 9_

OFFICIAL DISTANCES: 1¾l, 5l TIME: 6min 27.0s TOTE: £14.00

North Herefordshire

Whitwick Manor (LH 8F,18J) Sat, 26 Feb (GOOD to SOFT)

332 Hunt, 12st

8 ran

	1		**BASIL STREET (IRE)** 5-1 D Mansell _Settled 3rd/4th; went 2nd app 14; catching ldr when lft virt solo 3 out_
[193⁴]	2	20	**Kingofnobles (IRE)** 4-1 R Rogers _Nd in 3rd/4th; 20l 4th app 14; 3rd frm nxt; lft poor 2nd 3 out_
	P		**Gunners Dawn** (5a) 20-1 K Ford _T.o 4; fnce bhnd when pu 10_
	P		**Little Star** (5a) 12-1 T Stephenson _V novicey in last trio; t.o 4; fnce bhnd when blun 9; pu 13_
	F		**Perfect Light** (7x) 2-5F R Burton _(xnb) oht; mist 1; ld & tk str hld; 25l clr 6; 10l up app 14; only 4l ahd & tiring when fell 3 out_
	P		**Pushover (FR)** 16-1 M Worthington _T.o 4; fnce bhnd 9; pu 11_
	U		**Reg's Rocket** 16-1 N Oliver _Chsng group; pckd 3; 30l 5th when mist & ur 8_
	F		**Took A Chance (IRE)** 16-1 S Graham _Nt fluent; chsd clr ldr; rmdrs 12; dem app 14; sn wknd; last when fell nxt_

OFFICIAL DISTANCE: 25l TIME: 6min 50.0s

333 Confined, 12st

15 ran

[193¹]	1		**MAGGIES BROTHER** 11-2 D Barlow _Hld up & bhnd; 8th 10; same app 14; gd hdwy 3 out; stayed on wl to ld last; drvn out_
	2	1½	**Merger Mania** 8-1 D Mansell _(xnb) Tk keen hld in midfield; 7th 10; went 3rd app 14; ld & mist 3 out & hdd; ev ch aft til hrd rdn to ld & mist last; sn hdd & nt qckn_
[178⁸]	3	3	**La Kabyle (FR)** (5a) 20-1 A Dalton _(xnb) Hit 2; set off in rr but pulled hrd & rap hdwy to jn ldrs 4; ld 5; hdd & lft in ld 3 out; hdd agn u.p last; wknd_
	4	4	**Fintona Boy (IRE)** (tt) 20-1 R Burton _Ld to 5; 2nd/3rd to 15; one pce & no imp frm 15_
[294P]	5	5	**Alaskan Heir** (vis) 20-1 M Rodda _Prom; mist 8; 5th 10; 2nd brief app 14; rdn & wknd aft nxt_
[18P]	6	30	**Mitchells Best** 16-1 T Stephenson _Prom early; drpd back 8th 10; same & btn app 14_
[192⁵]	7	6	**Just Marmalade** (5a) 20-1 Miss J Williams _Fat; a rr; last 10; t.o aft 13_
[116¹]	P		**Capstown Bay** (tt) evensF Julian Pritchard _Mists; towards rr; 9th 10; 20l 9th app 14; no prog; pu 3 out_
[295P]	P		**Dawn Mission** (tt) 25-1 P Pritchard _Lw; bhnd; 10th 10; no ch 13; t.o & pu 3 out_
[294⁴]	P		**Erlemo** 5-1 S Joynes _Chsd ldrs early; drpd to rr & drvn 11; t.o 14; pu 2 out_
[37P]	P		**Executive Office (IRE)** 10-1 A Wintle _Bit bckwd; prom; 3rd 10; 7th & wkng app 14; pu last_
	P		**Norman Warrior** (bl) 20-1 N Oliver _Last quartet; no ch 13; t.o & pu 3 out_
	P		**Rolled Gold** 8-1 A Phillips _Cl up; 4th when mist 10; same app 14; sn wknd; pu 2 out_
	P		**Stormhill Recruit** 11-2 S Blackwell _A bhnd; 14th 10; t.o & pu 15_
[143⁶]	P		**Vitaman (IRE)** 25-1 A Price _Hit 2; cl up; 6th 10; mist 14; no ch aft; pu 3 out_

OFFICIAL DISTANCES: 1l, 2½l TIME: 6min 48.0s

334 Mens Open, 12st

15 ran

[117²]	1		**MICKTHECUTAWAY (IRE)** 6-4 A Dalton _2s-6/4; 2nd/3rd til ld aft 5; 3l clr 3 out; r.o str frm 2 out_
[156⁵]	2	5	**Forest Fountain (IRE)** (7x) 5-4F Julian Pritchard _Lw; chsd ldrs; pckd 10; 5th nxt; went 2nd app 14; 3l down 3 out; drvn & a hld aft_

	3	12	**Three Saints (IRE)** 33-1 M Worthington *Midfield; 8th 11; 18l 5th app 14; stayed on to chse ldng pr frm 3 out; no imp; fair eff*
	4	12	**Saxon Fair** (7x) 14-1 G Hanmer *Bit bckwd; ld to 5; 4th 11; 5l 3rd app 14; wknd nxt*
[223F]	5	12	**Kentucky Gold (IRE)** (7x) 25-1 D Sherlock *Prom early; 9th & rdn 11; no resp; plodded on & rem 8th app 14*
[195B]	P		**Across The Water** (5a) 33-1 D Mansell *Lw; a wl bhnd; 10th 10; t.o & pu 14*
	P		**Bucksfern** 14-1 R Bevis *A bhnd; 12th & to 10; pu 14*
	r		**Credon** 14-1 A Evans *Ld brief 5; 2nd/3rd til 6l 4th app 14; plodded on; poor 5th & v tired 2 out; ref last*
	P		**Greville Again (IRE)** 16-1 A Wadlow *Chsd ldrs; 6th 11; 22l 7th & wkng app 14; t.o & pu last*
[293U]	r		**Grunge (IRE)** 7-1 C Barlow *Chsd ldrs; 7th 11; 20l 6th & btn when mist 14; t.o when blkd & ref last*
[195U]	r		**Have To Think** 33-1 A Morley *Ref to rce*
	U		**Ita's Fellow (IRE)** 16-1 M Prince *Sn last; to to 5; ur 14*
	F		**Knockthomas (IRE)** 6-1 J Cook *Handy; went 3rd 11; ev ch when fell nxt*
[79³]	P		**Muntafi** (7x) 5-1 A Wintle *Hld up & bhnd; 11th 11; rem 9th app 14; pu 2 out*
	P		**Scarlet Berry** (5a) 16-1 S Blackwell *Lw; a rr; t.o & pu 10*

OFFICIAL DISTANCES: 5l, 12l **TIME:** 6min 44.0s

335 Greig Middleton Ladies Open

8 ran

[222⁷]	1		**KARABURAN** 8-1 Miss F Wilson *Lw; pulled hrd; last early; hdwy in 3rd 9; ld nxt; outj rival in final mile; r.o wl to forge clr frm 2 out*
[78¹]	2	4	**Bankhead (IRE)** 1-3F Miss C Spearing *Hit 3; prom; drew clr w wnr frm 12; jmpd v sloppy when ev ch frm 14; rdn & btn 2 out*
[218U]	3	30	**Dalusman (IRE)** 12-1 Miss N Sturgis *Rcd wide; prom; 4th 10; lost tch 12; 30l 4th app 14; fin w flourish*
[150³]	4	6	**Highway Five (IRE)** 6-1 Miss L Brooke *1st ride; bckwd; bhnd; t.o 6; pushed along & stayed on stdly frm 3 out; passed 2 rivals frm nxt*
[195P]	5	6	**Saffron Flame** (5a) 20-1 Miss N Rudge *Ld 2-3; trckd ldrs; 4l 6th 10; lost tch 12; 32l 5th app 14*
[222P]	6	3	**Poucher (IRE)** 10-1 Miss C Thomas (xnb) *Lw; tk keen hld; ld 3-10; outpcd 13; 25l 3rd app 14*
	S		**Fed On Oats** 12-1 Mrs D Powell *Cl up; 5th 10; outpcd aft 12; slpd up aft 13*
[218U]	P		**Gay Ruffian** 20-1 Miss C Hicks *Jmpd sticky in last pr; t.o 6; pu aft 8*

OFFICIAL DISTANCES: 4l, dist **TIME:** 6min 48.0s

336 Restricted (Div 1), 12st

19 ran

	1		**WEJEM (IRE)** 4-1 A Dalton *Trckd ldrs; impd to 3rd 11; ld app 14; drvn & hld on wl frm last; all out*
	2	½	**Connors (IRE)** 6-4F Julian Pritchard *3s-6/4; lw; hld up in midfield; 9th 11; stdy prog nxt; 5l 3rd app 14; prsd wnr app 2 out; tried to chall & ev ch last; just hld*
[190³]	3	20	**Holmby Copse** 8-1 R Burton *Oht; 2 handlers; ld to 3; chsd ldr til mist 10; lost tch app 14; plugged on*
[222P]	4	15	**Bel Lane** (5a) (vis) 6-1 D Mansell *Prom; 2nd 11; wknd app 14*
[196P]	5	15	**Lady Kilton** (5a) 20-1 P Cowley *Hld up & wl bhnd; t.o app 14*
[274³]	6	4	**Tiger Lord** 20-1 A Wintle *Lkd awful; a rr; 12th 11; t.o when handed whip by rdr of Cowarne Adventure app 14(!)*
	P		**Brown Esquire** 10-1 D Barlow *Prom; 4th 11; sn wknd; pu 13*
	P		**Camogue Bridge (IRE)** 20-1 N Oliver *A wl bhnd; t.o & pu 11*
[197¹]	P		**Cherokee Run (IRE)** (tt) 4-1 M Keel *Hld up; impd to 5th 11; last of 4 w ch 14; sn wknd; pu 2 out*
	P		**Cowarne Adventure** 10-1 R Barrett *Bckwd; prom; 3rd 5; wknd 9; t.o & pu 14*
[116P]	P		**Diamond Market** 20-1 A Davenhill (xnb) *Sn t.o; pu 13*
[30P]	P		**Dozmary Pool** 20-1 A Evans (xnb) *Blun 2; midfield; 8th when mist 11; no ch aft; t.o & pu 15*
[220¹]	F		**Fine Stalker (IRE)** 8-1 O Defew *Bhnd; 11th 11; t.o when fell hvly 15*
	P		**Gold Talisman** (5a) 25-1 S Prior *Bckwd; chsd ldrs early; lsng plce when blun 10; t.o & pu 13*
	P		**In The Future (IRE)** (5a) 25-1 F Hutsby *Nvr nr ldrs; t.o & pu 12*
	U		**Rusty Buck** 8-1 S Blackwell *Wl bhnd; mist 6; 18th when tried to ref & ur 8*
[193³]	P		**Shadowgraff** (5a) 6-1 T Stephenson *Bckwd; midfield; 7th 11; sn wknd; t.o & pu 14*
[219P]	P		**Steel Gem** (5a) 4-1 J Cook *Prom; ld 5; 8l clr 11; hdd app 14; wknd 3 out; pu last*
	P		**Wild Edric** 7-1 G Hanmer *Mist 2; sn towards rr; 13th 11; pu 11*

OFFICIAL DISTANCES: nk, 25l **TIME:** 6min 47.0s

337 Confined Maiden (Div 1), 12st
17 ran

[121⁵]	1		**PHILELWYN (IRE)** (5a) 10-1 A Wintle *Cl 3rd/4th; chall l4 aft 2 out; in comm when lft clr last*
[146⁴]	2	7	Tedstone Fox 6-1 D Mansell *Chsd ldrs; 5th 12; chall & ev ch frm 14 til disp ½l 2nd 2 out; sn wknd u.p; lft 2nd at last*
	3	6	All Things Nice (5a) 12-1 T Stephenson *Lw; prom; 4th 12; ld app 14; slt advant til hdd 3 out; sn btn; lft 3rd at last*
	4	1½fs	Rusty Flame 14-1 S Lloyd *Mist 4; chsd ldrs early; t.o 12*
	5	nk	Tibs Eve (IRE) 4-1F Julian Pritchard *Ld to 11; 5th & wkng app 14; t.o 3 out*
	P		A Bit Of Fluff (5a) 20-1 M Trott *Bhnd; 6th 12; lost tch nxt; t.o & pu 2 out*
[145ᴾ]	r		Bid For Tools 14-1 Miss J Houldey *Reluct & sn last; t.o 7; ref 8*
	P		Cool Spell (5a) 20-1 M Munrowd *(citation) Sn wl bhnd; t.o & pu 8*
[122ᴾ]	r		Far Forest (vis) 14-1 A Evans *Sn bhnd; nrly fell 6; t.o & ref 8*
	U		Humphrey 20-1 N Oliver *2 handlers; blun & ur 3*
[167ᶠ]	P		Iron Buck 16-1 G Hanmer *Pckd 1; jmpd v sticky in last trio; t.o 6; pu 11*
	F		Lord Lard 12-1 M Rodda *Bckwd; fell 2*
	F		Missed Call (IRE) 10-1 R Burton *Bckwd; mostly 2nd til ld 11; hdd app 14; ld agn 3 out; hrd prsd nxt; hdd & 2nd best when fell last*
	F		Nineteenofive (IRE) 11-1 A Dalton *V unruly & ur start; wl bhnd; 11th when fell 10*
[221ᴾ]	P		Silk Oats (5a) 8-1 M Wilesmith *(xnb) Mist 5; chsd ldrs til 8th & wkng 12; t.o & pu 15*
[146ᴾ]	P		Talkalot (IRE) 6-1 F Hutsby *Pulled v hrd & sn prom; w ldrs when pu 11*
	P		Without The Agent (IRE) 5-1 A Price *Lw; hld up towards rr; bad mist 10; 6th 12; sn lost tch; t.o & pu 15*

OFFICIAL DISTANCES: 7l, 2l **TIME:** 6min 59.0s

338 Restricted (Div 2), 12st
14 ran

	1		**ROLL WITH IT (IRE)** 10-1 D Barlow *Confid rdn; hld up towards rr til prog 12; went 2nd 14; ld app 2 out; sn clr; r.o wl*
[196⁴]	2	5	Ten Bob Note (bl) 12-1 M Walters *Tde; prom; ld 10; pckd 14; drvn & hdd app 2 out; one pce & sn btn*
[81¹]	3	12	Claymore Lad 4-1 A Maculan *Trckd ldrs; 3rd 7; 5l 3rd app 14; nt qckn nxt*
	4	½	Sugi 9-1 I Wynne *Sn midfield; drpd to rr 10; nd frm 14; stayed on stdly aft 3 out; nrly caught 3rd*
[75ᵁ]	5	15	Hill Sprite (5a) 7-2F R Barrett *(xnb) Chsd ldrs; rdn 10; 5th 12; lost tch app 14*
[31⁴]	6	2	Need More Practice 11-1 R Burton *Bhnd; jmpd v slow 12; wl bhnd aft nxt*
	7	12	Briary Boy (IRE) 10-1 A Price *Chsd ldrs; 6th 12; wknd nxt*
	P		Baptist John (IRE) 10-1 A Phillips *Lw; ld 5-8; 2nd 12; wkng when mist 14; t.o & pu 2 out*
[196ᴾ]	P		Grand Canyon (IRE) 12-1 A Wintle *Cl; 2nd 13; ev ch app nxt; wkng when blun 3 out; pu last*
	P		J'accuse (IRE) 6-1 Miss F Wilson *Returning aft slpng both rr tendons off hocks; tk keen hld; 2nd/3rd til ld 8; hdd 10; 4th nxt; pu 12*
	P		Le Vienna (IRE) 25-1 S Currey *Sn t.o; pu 12*
[119ᵁ]	P		Out Of The Blue (5a) 8-1 D Mansell *Midfield; 6th & drvn app 14; sn lost tch; t.o & pu 2 out*
[191⁵]	P		Sideliner 8-1 T Stephenson *Lw; prom early; lost plce & blun 9; t.o & pu 2 out*
[193ᵁ]	U		Wolfie Smith 25-1 Miss W Houldey *Rfo 2*

OFFICIAL DISTANCES: 4l, 10l **TIME:** 6min 53.0s

339 Confined Maiden (Div 2), 12st
13 ran

	1		**PHILTRE** 4-6F Julian Pritchard *Lw; pulled hrd; made all; a comm frm 3 out; r.o wl*
	2	5	Loc A Lua (IRE) 8-1 A Wintle *Tk keen hld & jmpd rt; a cl up; went 2nd 11; chall & outj 15; no imp aft nxt*
[196ᶠ]	3	25	Autumn Blunder 12-1 T Stephenson *2nd/3rd; bad mist 4; ev ch app 14; sn wknd; poor 3rd when mist 2 out*
	P		Bay Fusilier 8-1 A Phillips *Bad hmpd 2 & rdr lost control; pu 3*
[146ᴾ]	P		Brookthorpe (5a,2ow) 20-1 A Price *Hld up; hdwy 8; 4th 11; v reluct to rce u.p aft nxt; sn t.o; pu 13*
	P		Captain Rose 20-1 P Cowley *Jmpd appalling in rr; t.o & pu 7*
	P		Crewman (IRE) 20-1 M Munrowd *Prom; 2nd 8; lsng plce when pu 11*
	P		Lord Rymax 14-1 S Joynes *Unruly; hld up & wl bhnd; t.o last 8; pu 13*
	F		Miss Pharly (5a) 10-1 D Mansell *Mist 3; green & sketchy in last pr; wl bhnd 8; 20l last app 14; no prog & fell hvly nxt*
	F		Ole Gunnar (IRE) 14-1 M Wilesmith *Fell 2*
	U		Pulpits Edge 20-1 R Hodges *(xnb) Ur 2*
[123²]	R		Vulpin De Laugere (FR) (bl) 8-1 Miss A Sykes *(xnb) 2nd/3rd til rn out 9*
[7⁶]	P		Wonastow (tt) 8-1 A Evans *Hld up in tch; 5th 11; 10l 4th aft 13; wknd rap; pu nxt*

OFFICIAL DISTANCES: 3½l, 30l **TIME:** 7min 00.0s

340 Restricted (Div 3), 12st   **14 ran**

	1		**VIKING FLAME** (5a) 7-1 S Bush *Trckd ldrs; 3rd 11; ld brief 13; ld agn 14 & ld/disp aft; hrd rdn to forge clr aft last*
	2	4	**Lordinthesky (IRE)** 4-1 R Cooper *Bckwd; hld up & bhnd; 6th & prog 11; clsd 14; chall 3 out; w wnr & drvn nxt; ev ch til outpcd aft last*
	3	15	**Who's Your Man (IRE)** 5-1 Julian Pritchard *Lw; ld to 3; 2nd/3rd & ev ch aft til wknd rap bef 15; drvn out to hld 3rd*
	4	1	**Lothian Magic (IRE)** (5a) 20-1 D Phelan *Chsd ldrs & sn drvn along; 5th & u.p 11; 10l 5th & outpcd app 15; plodded on*
	P		**Bill To Follow (IRE)** 20-1 S Blackwell *Pu 3*
	P		**Buckley House** 20-1 A Price *Unruly padd & start; ss; tk mad hld & ld aft 3; hdd 8; hung rt aft 9; reluct to cont; t.o & pu 12*
[38ᶠ]	B		**Clerical Cousin (IRE)** 20-1 Miss J Froggatt *Fat; ss; detach in last pr; mist 10; t.o to 13*
	B		**Coddington Girl** (5a) 2-1F T Stephenson *(xnb) Hld up; prog 9; 4th 11; gng wl when bd nxt*
[75⁷]	U		**Come On Boy** 20-1 D Mansell *Tkn stdly in rr; mod 9th 11; bd nxt*
			Gt Hayes Pommard 20-1 D Howells *Rdr v unstdy; 3rd/4th to 9; lost plce to 7th 11; lft 3rd 12; ld aft 13; hdd & nrly ur nxt; disp ld when pckd & ur 3 out*
	P		**Netherbrook Lad** 20-1 S Lloyd *A strugg in rr; t.o 13; pu 3 out*
	F		**Roscoes Dinky** (5a) 14-1 A Evans *Prom; ld 8 til fell 12*
	P		**Social Vision (IRE)** 20-1 M Cowley *Midfield; wknd 11; pu 13*
	F		**Star Chaser** 7-2 D Stephens (Wales) *Fell 2*

OFFICIAL DISTANCES: 2½l, 12l **TIME:** 7min 05.0s

341 Confined Maiden (Div 3), 12st   **18 ran**

[122²]	1		**HIJACKED** 4-1JF T Stephenson *(has sired a foal) Lw; settled 2nd/3rd; ld 13-nxt; gd j to ld agn 3 out; clr & on bit aft nxt; r.o str*
	2	8	**Gorsey Bank (IRE)** 8-1 R Cooper *Hvly rstrnd & set off last; wl bhnd to 7; gd prog 13 to 4l 3rd nxt; went 2nd & ev ch 15; rdn & no imp 2 out*
	3	8	**Brown Wren** (5a) 20-1 S Lloyd *Prsd ldrs; 4l 3rd app 14; rdn & nt qckn aft nxt*
	4	5	**Winning Town** 9-2 Miss S Talbot *(xnb) Prom; made most 8-13; ld agn nxt; hdd & outj 3 out; wknd qckly*
	U		**Ath Carne Castle** (7a) 20-1 S Joynes *A wl bhnd; blun bad & nrly ur 2 & agn 8; finally succeeded 12*
	P		**Di's Dream** (5a) 12-1 M Rodda *V excited & 2 handlers; 9th aft 5; nvr nr ldrs; t.o aft 13; pu 3 out*
	F		**Dungannon Lad** 20-1 A St George *Chsd ldrs; 7th & in tch when fell 11*
	U		**Lastofthe Littles** 8-1 A Phillips *Sn lost tch; mist 10; 7th & no ch app 14; t.o when mist & ur 3 out*
	R		**Layback** 14-1 K Burke *(xnb) Jb; sn t.o; rn out & ur 15*
	U		**Magni Momenti** (12a) 10-1 D Mansell *Jmpd v erratic; impd qckly to ld aft 5 til blun & 8*
[147ᵖ]	P		**Piccadilly Wood** 14-1 A Price *Mist 1; a wl bhnd; t.o 9; pu 13*
	P		**Poppycock (IRE)** (5a) 14-1 M Keel *Sn lost tch; t.o when mrly fell 10; pu 11*
[206³]	P		**Purslet** (5a) 8-1 Miss N Stallard *(xnb) Mist 1; 8th aft 5; eff to handy 6th 11; sn wknd; t.o & pu 14*
	P		**Sallioko** (5a) 12-1 D Barlow *(xnb) Sn lost tch; t.o & pu 14*
	P		**Sergeant Miller** 14-1 R Hodges *Jb & sn wl t.o; pu 12*
	P		**Spirit Prince** 8-1 A Wintle *2 handlers; ldng trio; 3rd 12; 6th & wkng aft nxt; t.o & pu 2 out*
[123ᵁ]	U		**Three Monroes (IRE)** 12-1 M Munrowd *Sn lost tch; stdy prog 8; 8th 11; 5th & chsng ldrs app 14; sn wknd; t.o when blun 2 out; stood w hd down & rdr event fell over it*
[58ᶠ]	P		**Yanto** (5a) 4-1JF Julian Pritchard *Lw; ld/disp to 5; mist 10; 4th 11; wknd rap nxt; t.o aft 12; pu 14*

OFFICIAL DISTANCES: 7l, 8l **TIME:** 6min 59.0s

Tivyside

Pantyderi (LH 8F,19J) Sat, 26 Feb (GOOD to SOFT becoming HEAVY)

342 Hunt, 12st   **1 ran**

| | 1 | **BREWERY LANE (IRE)** Miss P Jones *Walked over* |

OFFICIAL DISTANCE: Walked over

343 Confined, 12st   **8 ran**

| [297¹] | 1 | **DAWN'S COGNAC (IRE)** 4-6F Miss P Jones *2 handlers; lw; hld up; last to 5; 12l 5th ½way; hdwy & 5l 4th 14; went 3rd 4 out & 2nd nxt; ld app 2 out; sn clr; comf* |

[271^P]	2	6	**Moon Tiger** 12-1 D Jones *Prom; 9½l 4th ½way; went 2l 2nd 14; ld aft 4 out til hdd app 2 out; no ch w wnr*
	3	4	**Anorak (USA)** (3x) 7-1 C Williams *2nd to 14; lost plce & 8l 4th 3 out; stayed on*
[275³]	4	8	**Same Difference (IRE)** (bl) 20-1 Mrs B Lewis *Ld; 8l clr 6-11; hdd aft 4 out; 8l 3rd 2 out; wknd*
[275^F]	U		**Flutterbud** (5a,3x) 5-2 E Williams *Lw; hld up; went 9l 3rd ½way; 4th when blun bad 11; 8l 5th 14; wkng when blun & ur 4 out*
	P		**No Fiddling (IRE)** 16-1 T Vaughan *Lost tch 8; 20l 6th ½way; wl bhnd til pu 4 out*
[275^P]	P		**Swan's Wish (IRE)** (bl) 10-1 J Jukes *Rmdrs 3; wl bhnd 8; 30l 8th ½way; t.o & pu 11*
[275⁵]	U		**Teigr Pren** 25-1 P Sheldrake *(boh) Lost plce 6; 21l 7th ½way; t.o 14; exhaust when blun bad & ur 3 out*

OFFICIAL DISTANCES: 6l, 4l TIME: 6min 01.6s

344 Intermediate, 12st
10 ran

	1		**KINNEFAD KING (IRE)** (tt) 5-1 C Williams *Hld up; 5l 6th ½way; hdwy & 3l 4th 14; tried to rn out 4 out; ld nxt; drvn out*
[37³]	2	1	**Kristal Haze** (5a) 2-1JF E Williams *Ld til jmpd slow 2; 2nd/3rd til ld 4 out; hdd 3 out; ev ch last; r.o u.p*
[296^P]	3	15	**Icenfriendly (IRE)** 2-1JF Miss P Jones *Hld up; hdwy & 3l 4th ½way; 2½l 3rd 14; ev ch 4 out; 4l 3rd 2 out; sn wknd*
[266⁴]	4	30	**Terrano Star (IRE)** 33-1 P Sheldrake *A bhnd; 12l 9th ½way; 22l 7th 14; lft rem 4th 3 out; t.o*
	P		**Alias Parker Jones** 25-1 M Lewis *Bckwd; nd; 8l 7th ½way; lost tch 11; pu 13*
	P		**Duke Of Hades (IRE)** 4-1 J Jukes *Went 2nd 3; ld 6-16; wknd qckly; pu 3 out*
[202³]	P		**Flockmaster (IRE)** 8-1 T Vaughan *Ld 2-3; 4l 5th & u.p ½way; wknd & 9½l 6th 14; bhnd when pu 4 out*
	P		**Hollow Sound (IRE)** (5a) 12-1 G Lewis *Bckwd; swtng; prom til lost plce 9; 111 8th ½way; bhnd when pu 12*
[68⁴]	P		**Sister Lark** (5a) 8-1 D Jones *A bhnd; t.o & pu 14*
	P		**Storm Man (IRE)** 14-1 N Jones *Bckwd; ld 3-6; 2l 3rd ½way; wknd & 9l 5th 14; bhnd when pu 4 out*

OFFICIAL DISTANCES: 1l, 6l TIME: 6min 10.8s

345 Mens Open, 12st
7 ran

	1		**BIT OF A CITIZEN (IRE)** (5a,4x) 2-1 E Williams *Lw; hld up; hdwy 9; 3rd ½way; lost plce & 7l 5th 14; went 6l 2nd aft 4 out; qcknd to ld app 2 out; sn clr; easy*
[35⁴]	2	12	**True Fortune** 4-6F J Jukes *Hld up; 4th ½way; went 5l 3rd 11; rdn 14; 6l 4th 3 out; sn outpcd; went 8l 3rd nxt & 2nd app last; no ch w wnr*
[271^P]	3	1	**Viardot (IRE)** 7-1 D Jones *Prom; lft 2nd 8-14; 4l 3rd & und str press 3 out; sn outpcd*
	4	5	**Silverfort Lad (IRE)** (vis) 6-1 C Williams *2nd til ld 3; hdd 6; ld 7; lft 6l clr 4 out; hdd app 2 out; sn wknd*
	5	2½	**Frown** 10-1 P Hamer *Ld to 3; lost plce 9; 6th ½way; 8l 6th 14; 7l 5th & rdn 3 out; sn wknd*
[271^P]	F		**Saffron Moss** (7x) 6-1 N Jones *Hld up; 5th ½way; hdwy 12; went 3l 2nd 14; rdn & ev ch when fell 4 out*
[275^P]	F		**Shehab (IRE)** (7x) 10-1 T Vaughan *Hld up & pulled hrd; ld 6-7; 2nd when fell 8*

OFFICIAL DISTANCES: dist, ½l TIME: 6min 14.2s

346 Ladies Open
6 ran

[272²]	1		**COOLVAWN LADY (IRE)** (5a) 1-3F Miss P Jones *Made all; drew wl clr 14; unchall*
	2	25	**Young Manny** 6-1 Mrs B Lewis *Chsd ldrs; 6l 3rd ½way; went 5l 2nd 11; outpcd 14; no ch aft*
	U		**African Warrior** (5a) 7-2 Miss B Williams *4th when ur 4*
	P		**Battleship Bruce** 10-1 Miss A Meakins *Bckwd; hld up; 10l 4th ½way; lost tch 12; went poor 3rd aft 13; t.o & pu 3 out*
[272^U]	F		**Palladium Boy** 8-1 Miss L Pearce *2nd til wknd 11; rem 4th when crashing fall 14*
[270^P]	P		**Tiger Bell** 33-1 Miss S Major *A bhnd; mist 9; 30l 5th ½way; t.o & pu 13*

OFFICIAL DISTANCE: dist TIME: 6min 03.0s

347 Restricted, 12st
12 ran

[273⁵]	1		**PURE AIR** 10-1 G Maloney *Hld up; 8½l 6th ½way; hdwy 11; 4l 3rd 14; went 4l 2nd 4 out; mist 2 out; stayed on u.p to ld last strides*
[268¹]	2	s hd	**Howsyourluck (IRE)** 6-4 T Vaughan *Ld to 2; 2nd til lft in ld 6; mist 11; 4l clr 4 out; hrd rdn aft 2 out; hdd last strides*

	3	2fncs	**Ten Past Eleven (IRE)** (5a) (tt) 8-1 *Miss C Williams* Nd; 12l 7th ½way; wl bhnd 12; rem 4th when ref 3 out; cont
	P		**Adventurus** 6-1 *J Liley* Bckwd; bhnd til pu 7
[273ᴾ]	P		**Gaelic Royale (IRE)** (5a) 6-1 *H Evans* Chsd ldrs; 4l 3rd ½way; wknd & 8l 5th 14; pu 15
	P		**Itspantotime** (5a) 8-1 *J Jukes* Bckwd; chsd ldrs; 5l 4th ½way; wknd & 9l 6th 14; bhnd when pu 4 out
[267ᴾ]	P		**Just Ruffled** 14-1 *J Price* A bhnd; 22l 9th ½way; t.o & pu 13
[146ᴵ]	U		**Kerry Gold Mine** evensF *Miss P Jones* Ld 2 til ur 6
[274ᴾ]	U		**Not For Profit (IRE)** (bl,tt) 10-1 *C Williams* Hld up; hdwy & 8l 5th ½way; jnd ldrs 11; went 2nd 12 til rdn & wknd app 4 out; 20l 3rd & v tired when blun & ur 2 out
	P		**Rue De Fort** 5-1 *G Lewis* 2 handlers; lft 4l 2nd 6 til rdn 12; 6l 4th 14; sn wknd; bhnd when pu 16
[273ᴾ]	P		**Sea Search** 25-1 *J Keen* Still bckwd; lost plce 6; 16l 8th ½way; t.o & pu 13
[266²]	P		**Young Mariner** 16-1 *J Edwards* (xnb) A bhnd; 25l 10th ½way; t.o & pu 3 out

OFFICIAL DISTANCES: s hd, dist   TIME: 6min 18.0s

348 Confined Maiden (Div 1), 12st   11 ran

[267ᵁ]	1		**CRESSWELL QUAY** 3-1 *G Lewis* Hdwy to ld 6; drew wl clr 3 out; unchall
[267ᶠ]	2	25	**Artique Fish (IRE)** 5-1 *J Jukes* Prom; mist 2; 5l 3rd ½way; went 4l 2nd 11; wknd 3 out
	3	20	**Lough Neagh (IRE)** 5-2 *P Sheldrake* Nd; 6th when blun 7; 13l 7th ½way; eff & 12l 4th 14; wkng when mist 15; lft 30l 3rd aft 16; t.o
[267ᶠ]	4	30	**Fast Flow (IRE)** (5a) 3-1 *Miss A Meakins* Chsd ldrs; 10l 5th ½way; wknd 11; 30l 7th 14; t.o
	5	nk	**Blazing Connie** (5a) 2-1F *G Perkins* A bhnd; 16l 8th ½way; 32l 8th 14; t.o
[270³]	P		**Alicat (IRE)** 3-1 *Miss E Jones* Ld 2-6; 2nd to 9; 6l 4th ½way; wknd & 13l 5th 14; t.o & pu 3 out
[145ᵁ]	U		**Beths Gift** (5a) 10-1 *Miss B Williams* 6th when ur 3
	P		**Lillies Buttler** (5a) 10-1 *T Vaughan* Hld up; 12l 6th ½way; hdwy u.p & 9l 5th 11; wknd & 15l 6th 14; blun bad 15; wl bhnd when pu 16
[31ᶠ]	P		**Ossie Dale (IRE)** 3-1 *D Jones* Ld til hdd & mist 2; went 2nd 9-11; 10l 3rd 14; wkng when blun bad 16; sn pu
	P		**Run To The Glen** (12a) 6-1 *M Lewis* A bhnd; 18l 9th ½way; t.o & pu 13
	R		**Tarian (USA)** 10-1 *C Williams* Rn out 4

OFFICIAL DISTANCES: dist, dist   TIME: 6min 26.0s

349 Confined Maiden (Div 2), 12st   10 ran

	1		**THEBETSONMARY** (5a) 4-1 *D Jones* Hld up & 2nd 9; ld 4 out; drew clr 2 out; comf
[268²]	2	15	**Saxon Queen** (5a) 1-2F *E Williams* Jnd ldrs 6; hmpd & mist 8; 5l 4th ½way; went 3rd 11 & 2nd aft 16; no ex 2 out
	3	12	**Itswillie** 6-1 *J Jukes* Bckwd; prom; lft in ld 5; hdd 6; ld 8-16; wknd qckly & 15l 3rd nxt
	4	1	**Twopintsahalfone (IRE)** 3-1 *J Hayward* Hld up; 9l 6th ½way; lost tch 11; 20l 5th 14; 30l 4th 3 out; nvr on terms
	R		**Annie's Alfie** 10-1 *G Marsh* (xnb) Pulled hrd; ld; rn v wide bend app 3; rn out 5
[269ᴾ]	P		**Baytownghost (IRE)** 4-1 *J Price* (xnb) Hld up & bhnd; mist 7; 10l 7th ½way; lost tch 11; 25l 6th 14; t.o & pu 3 out
[268ᴾ]	P		**Billy Whizz** 6-1 *P Sheldrake* Chsd ldrs; 4l 3rd ½way; wknd qckly u.p & 10l 5th 11; pu 12
[268ᴾ]	P		**I Dont Believe It (IRE)** 6-1 *J Keen* Bhnd til pu 10
	P		**Look Who's Calling (IRE)** 5-1 *D Hughes* Lft 2nd 5; ld 6 til blun 8; 7l 5th ½way; wknd & 15l 4th 14; mist 15; t.o & pu 3 out
	C		**Move The Clouds** (5a) 4-1 *G Lewis* 2nd til carried out 5

OFFICIAL DISTANCES: dist, 12l   TIME: 6min 31.6s

350 Confined Maiden (Div 3), 12st   11 ran

[204⁴]	1		**GUNNER B SPECIAL** evensJF *Miss P Jones* Made all; 8l clr ½way; 15l up 14; unchall
	2	1½fs	**Lumback Lady** (5a) 2-1 *D Jones* Hld up; mist 7; 15½l 6th ½way; lost tch 11; t.o when mist 15; lft dist 2nd 3 out
[267²]	3	2fncs	**Travel Safely (IRE)** evensJF *J Keen* Hld up; 11l 4th ½way; went 3rd 12 & 20l 2nd aft 15; exhaust when pu 3 out; cont
	P		**Black Dan** 10-1 *P Sheldrake* A bhnd; t.o 10; pu 12
[270ᴾ]	P		**Bold Knight** 8-1 *G Skone* Hld up & bhnd; 15l 5th ½way; mist 11; t.o 14; pu 3 out
[105ᴾ]	F		**Cauld Signal (IRE)** (5a) 2-1 *Miss B Williams* Chsd ldrs til fell 4
[268⁴]	F		**Clonshire Castle (IRE)** 3-1 *C Williams* Prom; mist 3; 9l 3rd ½way; went 8l 2nd 11; sn no imp; 25l 3rd & exhaust when fell 4 out
	P		**Itsjayemm** 5-1 *J Jukes* Prom til lost plce 7; pu 9
[268ʳ]	U		**Jesusa** (5a) 8-1 *G Maloney* Nt jw; bhnd til tried to ref & ur 3

[206^P]   U   **Parsons Secret** (5a) 3-1 T Vaughan *2nd to 11; 15l 4th & wkng when mist & ur 13*
      P   **Sally Rod (IRE)** (5a) 5-1 D Hughes *(xnb) Bhnd til pu 3*

OFFICIAL DISTANCES: dist, dist   TIME: 6min 30.7s

West Somerset & Minehead Harriers
Holnicote (RH 7F,19J) Sat, 26 Feb (GOOD to SOFT, SOFT patches)

351 Hunt, 12st   **4 ran**

[144^2]   1   **PALLINGHAM LAD (IRE)** (tt) 6-4 S Kidston *Lw; swtng; 5l 3rd 2; slt mist nxt; lft in ld 6; made rest; 2½l up 13; grad drew clr frm 2 out; unchall*
      2   8   **Jukino** (5a) 6-1 A Michael *(5a) 6l down 5; lft 2nd 6; 2l down 9; releg last nxt; disp 2nd agn 12-14; stayed on frm 16; snatched 2nd flat*
      3   ¾   **Nothing To Fear** 14-1 W White *1st ride; chsd ldr; 2l adrift 5 til hmpd bad & carried wide by loose horse nxt; releg last & lost 15l; sn rallied; 2l 2nd 12; chsd wnr til wknd u.p 2 out*
[200^2]   U   **Bells Wood** (5x) 4-5F C White *Ld at modest pce; 2l up 5 til rfo nxt*

OFFICIAL DISTANCES: 8l, 1½l   TIME: 7min 09.0s   TOTE: £2.50

352 Confined Maiden (Div 1), 12st   **14 ran**

[207^P]   1   **LOXLEY-LAD** (tt) 33-1 G Richards *Towards rr; last 9; prog to 5l 5th 14; impd to 3rd app 3 out; jmpd to ld nxt; hld on game u.p flat*
[147^P]   2   ½   **Spirito** (7a) 14-1 Jeremy Young *Lft trckng ldng pr 4; mist 6; 5th 9; prog to ld aft 13; jmpd slow nxt; hdd 15; disp ld agn 3 out-nxt; rnwd eff frm last; just failed*
[146^P]   3   1½   **Timber Top (IRE)** 10-1 D Alers-Hankey *5th til lft in ld app 4-6; ld agn brief bef nxt; chsd ldng trio bef 8; ev ch app 2 out; no ex u.p frm last*
[206^U]   4   5   **Humara (IRE)** (5a) 6-1 Miss G Edwards *Last to 5; 7th 9; 5th & staying on 3 out; nrst fin; nd*
[73^5]   5   20   **Grandpa Maurice (IRE)** (bl) 4-1 T Scudamore *Hld up in last pr; last 6; 6th & in tch 9; prog to 3l 3rd 14; jmpd to ld 15; jnd bef 3 out; hdd nxt & wknd tame; sn bhnd*
[201^U]   F   **Counsel** (7a) 8-1 Miss S Vickery *Lft chsng ldr 4-6; 3½l 3rd nxt; disp ld 11; hanging rt when fell 13*
      B   **Fever Pitch** 16-1 J Barnes *Towards rr when bd 2; caused havoc aft nxt when running loose*
      P   **Here Comes The Sun** (5a) 14-1 G Barfoot-Saunt *Lw; rr 3; lft 5th 4; prog to 1½l 2nd 6; jmpd slow nxt; 2l 2nd 14; rmdrs & wknd app 3 out; pu nxt*
      P   **Jazetason** (bl) 50-1 M Woodward *Lft 4th 4; forged into ld 6; rn wide bend bef nxt & hdd; sn ld agn; jmpd v lft 8-10; jnd nxt til lft in ld 13; rn wide agn bend & sn rr; t.o when jmpd slow & pu aft 15*
[207^3]   C   **Lighter Lord** 5-2F L Jefford *(bf) Chsd clr ldr til carried out in melee app 4*
      F   **Pendragon** 12-1 S Kidston *(bf) Chsng ldrs when fell 2; caused havoc aft nxt when running loose*
      C   **Second Bite** (5a) 20-1 Miss S West *Disp 3rd til carried out in melee app 4*
      C   **Slubberdegullian** (7a) 20-1 A Bateman *Tde; ld & sn 8l clr til mist 3; carried out by loose horses bef nxt*
      C   **State Medlar** 14-1 G Maundrell *Disp 3rd when carried out in melee app 4*

OFFICIAL DISTANCES: 2l, 2l   TIME: 7min 23.0s   TOTE: £19.40

353 Confined Maiden (Div 2), 12st   **11 ran**

[146^3]   1   **KINGSBRIDGE (IRE)** evensF T Scudamore *Ld til rn wide aft 6; sn ld agn to 9; ld agn aft 13; made rest; drew clr frm 16; unchall*
[72^6]   2   30   **The Naughty Vicar** (bl) 14-1 G Richards *Ld in start; chsd ldrs to 3; 5½l 3rd 5; grad lost plce & rr of main group 11; rmdrs nxt; lft rem 3rd 15; stayed on one pce frm nxt; nd*
      3   20   **Diamond Duck** (5a) 12-1 Miss K Allan *(xnb) Reluct to leave padd; pulled hrd & sn chsng ldr; ld brief aft 6 & agn nxt 9-13; tired & wknd qckly app 3 out; clambered over last; dism aft fin*
      P   **Anolyze** (5a) 33-1 A Bateman *A last pr; 25l last 7; t.o nxt til pu 10; school*
[105^U]   P   **Button Up Bill** 20-1 H Thomas *(xnb) Towards rr when hmpd & ur 3*
[205^F]   P   **Kinglassie** (5a) 16-1 L Jefford *(xnb) A last pr; 18l 8th 7; t.o & pu 10*
      U   **Moody's Star** (12a) 8-1 Miss S Vickery *Disp 6th 5; smooth prog 9; 7l 4th 14 & lkd u.p; staying on rem 2nd when dumped rdr app 3 out (horse tk fnce)*
[147^P]   F   **My Happy Lord** (tt) 20-1 Miss V Nicholas *Mid-div til 4l 4th 7; trckd ldrs aft; 3l 3rd 14; staying on when fell nxt*
      U   **River Carron (IRE)** 20-1 G Maundrell *Lft 4th 3; 2½l 3rd 7; still chsng ldng pr when blun & ur 13*
[73^P]   P   **Super Rooster** 7-1 G Barfoot-Saunt *Disp 6th 5; 12l 7th 7; last & lsng tch when rmdrs 12; t.o when scrambled over 15 & pu*

F			Telimar (IRE) 3-1 J Barnes *12s-3s; 4th when fell 3*

OFFICIAL DISTANCES: dist, 20l **TIME:** 6min 59.8s **TOTE:** £2.20 **DF:** £4.80

354 Ladies Open   9 ran

[199¹]	1		SLEW MAN (FR) 5-2 Miss O Green *(xnb) Hld up in last; jmpd slow 1; 15l bhnd 7; rap prog to 11 2nd 14; ld nxt til jnd 3 out; fnd ex u.p & forged clr flat*
	2	4	Forbidden Waters (IRE) 7-1 Miss S Vickery *A.p; disp 3rd 3; 5½l 4th 7; chsd wnr frm 15; disp ld 3 out-nxt; no ex u.p flat*
[211ᵁ]	3	1	Millyhenry 5-4F Miss C Tizzard *3rd 3; grad lost plce; 9l 7th 7; prog to 4th 12; chsd ldng pr frm 15; clsng & ev ch when blun & rdr rec wl 2 out; no ex u.p flat*
[192⁴]	4	20	Aqua Star (IRE) 12-1 Miss T Spearing *Tde & walked slow to start; hld up in last pr til 6½l 5th 7; prog to 3l 3rd 14; wknd nxt; bhnd frm 3 out*
[101⁵]	5	8	The Bold Abbot 10-1 Miss S West *Ld; jmpd slow 5; 5l up 8-14; sn lost plce & bhnd frm 16; stayed on one pce frm nxt*
[214ᴾ]	6	10	Single Man (NZ) (8ow) (bl) 50-1 Miss T Blazey *A towards rr; 7l 6th 7; last & strugg 13; bhnd frm 16*
[67⁶]	P		Chickabiddy (5a) 16-1 Miss G Edwards *Rcd in mostly 3rd; 5l down 7-10; grad lost plce & 6th 13; t.o & pu 16*
[143²]	F		Hylters Chance (IRE) 7-1 Miss J Buck *1st ride; rcd in mid-div; 6th 5; 10l 8th 7; still in tch towards rr when fell 11*
	P		Link Copper 16-1 Miss S Jackson *Chsd ldr; rdr called cab 4; 3l down 7 til wknd 14; t.o & pu 3 out*

OFFICIAL DISTANCES: 6l, 1½l **TIME:** 6min 45.4s **TOTE:** £4.30 **DF:** £4.20

355 Mens Open, 12st   6 ran

	1		ROSSELL ISLAND (IRE) (7x) evensF T Scudamore *Chsd ldr to 2; 3l down 5; lft in ld 8; made rest; 3l up 13; hit 15; drew clr frm nxt; lft virt solo frm 2 out*
[160³]	2	15	Cool Clown 10-1 B Trickey *Ld to 2; sn outpcd & last 7; jmpd slow 9; eff & clsd to 7l down 13; stayed on one pce frm 16; lft rem 2nd 2 out*
[212ᶠ]	F		Ballot Box 50-1 Jeremy Young *Dashed into ld 2; sn 10l clr; mist 3; stdd & 3l up 5; still 7l up when jmpd lft & fell 8*
	P		Fenny Prince 33-1 M Sweetland *Last; mist 5; impd to 4th 7; lft 3rd 8; wknd 12; pu aft nxt*
[141ᵁ]	U		Mr Magnetic (IRE) (7x) 5-1 D Harvey *Nov rdn; jmpd slow 1; 4th 3; mist 4; 3l 3rd 5; lft 2nd 8; chsd wnr; 3l 2nd 13 til outpcd frm 16; hld when ur 2 out*
[201¹]	F		Play Poker 7-4 L Jefford *Disp 4th when fell 2*

OFFICIAL DISTANCE: 20l **TIME:** 7min 10.9s **TOTE:** £2.60 **DF:** £5.60

356 Intermediate (Nov Rdrs), 12st   7 ran

[142²]	1		BELARUS (IRE) (bl) 7-4F C White *Chsd clr ldr til clsd to 3l down 7; ld 11; made rest; 10l clr 14; unchall*
	2	15	Picard (IRE) 14-1 Miss L Hawkins *Rem 4th 3; jmpd slow 7; prog to 4th 8; 13l 3rd 14; stayed on & chsd wnr vain frm 16; no imp frm nxt*
[199³]	3	30	A Few Dollars More (IRE) 9-2 Miss O Green *Rem 4th 4; rmdrs nxt; impd to 3rd 8; chsd wnr vain 13-16; one pce nxt*
	4	2½fs	Cool Weather (IRE) 20-1 B Parsons *Rem 6th 4; t.o 7; scrambled over 10 & rmdrs aft; plodded home fncs adrift; accompanied up run-in by stable girl*
[211²]	P		Mendip Son (bl) 9-4 R Arnold *(xnb) Trckd clr ldr to 7; releg 5th 8; lsng tch when climbed 10; bhnd when bu 13; disapp*
[69ᴾ]	P		Nodforms Inferno 14-1 A Bateman *Tde; sn in clr ld; 30l up 3; sn came back to field & only 3l up 7; hdd 11 & sn wknd; rem 4th when pu 15*
	P		Palace King (IRE) 14-1 M Wheeler *(xnb) A last pr; t.o 7; 2 fncs adrift when pu 16*

OFFICIAL DISTANCES: 15l, dist **TIME:** 6min 59.6s **TOTE:** £3.10 **DF:** £11.90

357 Marsh UK/TBA PPORA Club Members Mares, 12st   5 ran

[202¹]	1		GLEVUM (5a) 1-2F T Scudamore *Chsd ldr til disp ld 3; ld nxt; 1½l up 6 til mist & hdd 12; mist 16; rnwd eff & got up on line; rdr's strength told*
[214⁴]	2	½	Avril Showers (5a,7x) 5-2 R Atkinson *Jw; hld up in last til prog on inner to disp 2nd 6; jmpd to ld 12; 2½l up 14; lkd wnr til hdd & no ex nr line; nt disg*
[161⁵]	3	40	Elle Flavador (5a) 16-1 Miss S Vickery *(xnb) Rcd in 3rd til chsd ldr frm 5-nxt; 5l 3rd 12; grad lost tch & jmpd slow frm 14; t.o 3 out*
[210⁶]	4	runin	Via Del Quatro (IRE) (5a,7x) (vis) 14-1 J Barnes *Ld til jnd 3; hdd nxt & releg 4th 6; last 9; rmdrs aft but little imp; t.o frm 15*

P   **The Dancing Parson** (5a) 20-1 **G Barfoot-Saunt** *4th early; last 6 til 4th aft 9; 8l 4th 12; wknd & bhnd frm 15; t.o & pu 2 out*

OFFICIAL DISTANCES: ½l, dist **TIME:** 6min 51.5s **TOTE:** £1.10 **DF:** £1.40

Berwickshire

Friars Haugh (LH 9F,18J) **Sun, 27 Feb** (GOOD to SOFT becoming SOFT)

358 Hunt   7 ran

	1		**ACROSS THE CARD** 6-1 **W Ramsay** *In tch mid-div; cl 3rd 8; prog to 11 2nd 13; 2l 2nd aft 14; just ld nxt; 6l up 3 out; stayed on; rdly*
[156⁷]	2	5	**Fiscal Policy** 11-10F **H Trotter** *(bf) Last; 15l off pce 5; 12l last 9; 8l down & stdy prog 11; 2½l 3rd 15; chsd wnr vain frm 3 out; v one pcd*
[43³]	3	20	**The Caffler (IRE)** 14-1 **Miss R Ramsay** *Oht; tde; sn ld; hdd 5-6; jmpd lft 9; hdd & wknd bef 15; 20l 3rd app 2 out*
[90ᴾ]	4	8	**Toarlite (IRE)** 14-1 **R Trotter** *(bf) Trckd ldrs in 3rd/4th; 8l 4th & rmdr 9; 5l 4th app nxt; slt hmpd 11; outpcd aft 14; 15l down & wkng aft nxt*
	U		**Blaweary** (5a) 4-1 **Miss J Wight** *Prom; 3l 4th app 3; 2l 3rd when slt mist 5 & ur sn aft*
[111ᴾ]	F		**Derring Dan** 20-1 **Miss H Gray** *Oht; in tch in rr when fell 3*
[188¹]	U		**Flaming Sunrise** 7-2 **Miss D Calder** *Jmpd rt; ld 1; sn hdd; ½l 2nd & slt mist 2; ld 5-6; hdd & rn wide aft 7; 3l 3rd 10; jmpd rt & blun & ur nxt*

OFFICIAL DISTANCES: 4l, 20l **TIME:** 6min 57.0s

359 Confined, 12st   15 ran

[43¹]	1		**PARADE RACER** (3x) 6-1 **A Richardson** *Oht; mid-div; mist 4; prog to trck ldrs frm 8; hdwy & gng wl 14; 1l 2nd app nxt; ld bef 16; sn 5l clr; easy*
[43²]	2	10	**Midsummer Glen (IRE)** 7-1 **Miss M Bremner** *Rr; prog 12; rdn & bhnd aft 14; 5th 3 out; stayed on str aft; 1k 2nd flat*
[110⁶]	3	½	**Whispering Steel** 12-11 **M Bradburne** *A.p; cl 3rd 9; 11 off pce nxt; 5l 4th 12; prog aft 14 & 5l 2nd 16; one pce nxt; dem nr fin*
[89⁷]	4	2	**Stormy Session** (7x) (5a) 8-1 **J Alexander** *(bf) Ld/disp; 2l up jmpd slow 4; hit 9; 11 up when mist 10; 3l up 13; pushed along aft 14; 11 up nxt; sn hdd & btn in 4th; kpt on same pce*
[185ᴾ]	5	nk	**Dear Do** (5x) 12-1 **Miss J Hedley** *In tch in mostly 5l/6th; 3l 6th 8; 6l 4th 15; 3rd 3 out; nt qckn aft*
[108²]	6	15	**Boyup Brook** 4-1 **T Morrison** *Mid-div; 7th aft 14; sn outpcd; virt ft pu flat*
	7	2	**The Green Fool** 20-1 **H Humble** *(xnb) A bhnd; no ch aft 14; virt pu flat*
[182²]	8	10	**Tropnevad** (bl) 20-1 **B Lusted** *A rr; jmpd slow 5; 20l last 8; jmpd lft & lost tch aft 9; wl bhnd 3 out; virt pu flat*
	P		**Allrite Bonny Lass** (5a) 10-1 **Miss P Robson** *Oht; rr; 10l off pce 7; strugg 15; wl bhnd when mist 2 out; pu last*
	P		**Commanche Scout (IRE)** 10-1 **T Oates** *Oht; cl up in ldng bunch til mists 11 & 12; sn wknd; pu aft 14*
[225ᴾ]	P		**Damas (FR)** 12-1 **W Renwick** *Keen early; cl up in bunch; jmpd slow & to rt 11; prog to 11 2nd & outpcd aft nxt; wl bhnd when jmpd slow 3 out & pu; lkd sore*
[108⁴]	P		**Fragrant Lord** 10-1 **Mrs V Jackson** *Rr of main bunch; sn 20l down; 20l 12th app 10; eff 12; sn wknd; hit 15; t.o & pu 3 out*
[111¹]	P		**Highland Monarch** evensF **C Storey** *(xnb,bof) Mists & rcd free early; ld/disp; mist 2; ld 5; mist 10; 3l 3rd 12; outpcd aft nxt; rdn & 8l 4th 15; wknd & mist nxt; 5th & wl bhnd when pu 2 out*
	U		**Senora D'Or** (5a) 20-1 **Miss L Bradburne** *In tch in mid-div when nrly fell & ur 3*
	U		**Tursal (IRE)** 33-1 **A Crookston** *Mists; rr; blun 4; blun & ur 5*

OFFICIAL DISTANCES: 10l, hd **TIME:** 6min 53.0s

360 Restricted   17 ran

	1		**LOVE ACTINIUM (IRE)** (5a) 10-1 **W Renwick** *In tch in mid-div; prog to trck ldrs 14; 2l 3rd aft; 11 2nd 15; ld bef 3 out; 5l up when hit 2 out; stayed on wl*
[111⁵]	2	5	**Border Glory** 6-1 **M Bradburne** *Mid-div; 8l 9th 8; went 5th 14; 2l 3rd & rdn 3 out; sn drvn & outpcd; unable to qckn*
[184ᴾ]	3	2	**Kings Token** 6-1 **J Walton** *Mid-div; prog 9 to 2l 3rd app 10; ld nxt; ½l ahd 13; 3l up 14; hdd bef 3 out; kpt on one pce*
[112¹]	4	6	**Queen Biddy (IRE)** (5a) 7-2 **C Storey** *In tch in mid-div; prog to chse ldrs in 6th 14; 4l 5th & drvn nxt; sn btn*
	5	¾	**Trivial (IRE)** (5a) 16-1 **R Morgan** *Oht; rr; 20l last 2; prog to 7th & in tch 14; outpcd bef nxt; jmpd lft aft; fin wl to tk 5th flat*

[111⁶] 6   3   **Boris Brook** 12-1 **T Oates** *Cl 3rd/4th mostly; 4th 5; cl 2nd 9; 5l 3rd 13-14; eff nxt; wknd 16; 6th when slpd & slid over line; decanted rdr aft*

[184⁶] 7   10   **Madame Defarge** (5a) 12-1 **Mrs A Hamilton** *Prom early; 6l 3rd & mist 9; mist 11; wkng aft 12; lsng tch 14; wl bhnd 3 out*

[109⁷] P   **Buckaroo** (5a) 12-1 **Mrs A Tweedie** *A rr; wl bhnd 12; t.o & pu last*

[183ᴾ] P   **Buck Lady (IRE)** (5a) 10-1 **Miss R Barrow** *A rr; sn 20l last; 15l last 7; wl bhnd 12; t.o & pu 3 out*

[395] P   **Carnmoney (IRE)** 16-1 **Mrs K Hargreave** *Prsd ldr til ld 6; 5l clr 8; hdd 11; ½l 2nd 13; wknd qckly aft nxt; 25l 8th 16; pu nxt*

     P   **Flower Of Dunblane** (5a) 16-1 **B Lusted** *A rr; t.o & pu aft 14*

     P   **Full Of Chat (IRE)** (5a) 12-1 **D Jewett** *Ld to 6; sn lost plce; t.o & pu 14*

[111³] F   **Geordies Express** 6-4F **A Richardson** *Hld up in rr; mist 2; mist & nrly ur nxt; last 5; prog 7; 8l 6th when fell 10*

[184³] B   **How Burn** 5-1 **Mrs V Jackson** *In tch in mid-div whn bd 10*

[187ᵁ] F   **Katjack** 10-1 **T Scott** *Rr early; some prog in 8th when fell 11*

     P   **Lord Levi (IRE)** 20-1 **A Robson** *A rr; lsng tch when slow j 14; t.o & pu 3 out*

[111⁷] P   **Mini Cruise** 8-1 **L Morgan** *Mists; prom; mist 2; cl 5th 5; 3l 3rd & pckd 6; hit 8; hmpd 11; wknd 14; wl bhnd when pu aft 3 out*

OFFICIAL DISTANCES: 7l, 1l   **TIME:** 7min 01.0s

361 Ladies Open   9 ran

     1   **NOVA NITA** (5a) 9-4 **Mrs V Jackson** *Handy in 3rd til 3l 2nd 8; 1l 2nd 12; ½l down 15; rdn nxt; chall last; sn ld; r.o flat; wl rdn*

     2   1   **Little Santa** (5a) 14-1 **Mrs K Hargreave** *Fat; in tch in mid-div; 12l 4th 7; prog to 3l 3rd 9 & ld 14; 2l up 3 out; hung rt aft; lkd gng btr 2 out-last; sn hdd & nt qckn flat; btr for rce*

[109³] 3   25   **Kingennie** (5a) 6-4F **Miss M Bremner** *Oht; mid-div; 5th 8; 10l 4th app 10; 11l 4th 13; cont hmpd by loose horse; 15l 4th & one pce 15*

[109⁶] 4   1½   **Sharp Thyne (IRE)** (bl) 12-1 **Miss J Hedley** *Nt a fluent & jmpd slow at times in rr; in tch til outpcd 7; 20-25l 5th frm 14-3 out; fin wl*

[109ᴾ] 5   3   **Craigdale** 33-1 **Mrs M Robinson** *Rcd keen; trckd ldr; 2l 3rd 3; ld 8; 3l up nxt; ll up 12; hdd 14; 3l 3rd 15; wknd qckly & sn wl bhnd*

     F   **Muskora (IRE)** (bl) 3-1 **Miss P Robson** *Prsd ldr til fell hvly 4*

[109ᵁ] F   **Oat Couture** 8-1 **Miss S Johnstone** *In tch in rr til fell 4*

     P   **Reve De Valse (USA)** (tt) 20-1 **Miss V Burn** *A rr; jmpd slow 1; sn t.o; fnce bhnd 11; 2 fnces adrift when pu 14*

[112ᴾ] P   **Tofino Swell** (5a) 33-1 **Miss L Hislop** *Mounted on course; ld at gd pce; v wide bend aft 7; hdd 8 & wknd qckly; 15l 6th 11; t.o & pu 14*

OFFICIAL DISTANCES: 1l, dist   **TIME:** 6min 59.0s

362 Mens Open   7 ran

[186¹] 1   **EXCISE MAN** (tt) 5-1 **J Walton** *Lw; trckd ldrs; disp 10l 2nd 2; went cl 2nd 5; 3l 4th 15; 1½l 2nd 3 out; lft in ld 2 out; r.o wl flat; all out; wl rdn*

[110¹] 2   2½   **Rainbow Times (IRE)** (5a) 5-4F **C Storey** *Cl up 5; jnd ldr 9; just ld app nxt; jnd 14; cl 4l clr app 3 out but v slow j & hdd; drvn & fnd little aft*

[185¹] 3   1½fs   **Mullingar (IRE)** 16-1 **L Morgan** *Chsd ldrs; cl up 5; 3rd 8; 5l 5th & pushed along 13; outpcd in 6l 5th 14; wl bhnd aft nxt; 25l last app 2 out; lft 3rd by defectors*

     P   **Bow Tie** 5-1 **R Morgan** *Tk keen hld; prom early; 5th 8; ½l 2nd 11; disp ld 12-14; ev ch til outpcd 3 out; sn wknd & lft 3rd but pu 2 out*

[186³] R   **Charlieadams (IRE)** 8-1 **J Muir** *Rcd free; ld; 10l up aft 2; 15l clr when iron snapped & rn out 5*

[110ᵁ] F   **Kilminfoyle** 25-1 **P Robson** *Rn in snatches; rr til disp 10l 2nd aft 2; lft in ld 5; 3l clr app 8; hdd 9; ½l 2nd & ev ch 15; outpcd aft nxt; 3ln 3rd when fell 2 out*

[183¹] U   **Minella Gold (IRE)** 5-2 **M Bradburne** *Hld up in rr; 20l last app 3; 4l last 8 til blun & ur 11*

OFFICIAL DISTANCES: 1½l, dist   **TIME:** 7min 08.0s

363 Confined Maiden (Div 1) - 14J   15 ran

     1   **WILLS PERK (IRE)** (12a) 8-1 **T Oates** *A handy; mist 6; 4l 4th 8; prog to trck ldr 12-15; 4l off pce nxt; jnd ldr 2 out; ll up & in comm when mist & lft clr last; rdn out*

[113ᴾ] 2   25   **Christiemouse** (5a) 12-1 **Miss L Hislop** *(xnb) Chsd ldrs; mist 3; rn wide bend aft 7; 4l 5th app 10 where blun; cl 3rd 14-15; ev ch til outpcd app 2 out; sn btn; mist & nrly ur last; rdr losr irons at least twice during race; improve*

[189²] 3   4   **Setting Sail** (5a) 9-2 **Mrs V Jackson** *Rr; hmpd 4; some prog 10 to 7th 14; 10l 4th app 15; sn wknd; kpt on*

4	½	**Running Mute** 5-1 Miss P Robson *In tch in rr early; jmpd slow 8; some prog 10; wl bhnd 15; kpt on*
	P	**Aces High** 14-1 T Morrison *A rr; jmpd slow 1; 20l last app 4; jmpd slow 8; 40l down & strugg when pu 10*
	F	**Border Country** 10-1 J Murphy *Mid-div; mist 3; fell 4*
[112F]	F	**Cleikumin** (5a) 9-2 W Renwick *Ur start; rr to 7; prog to cl 3rd/4th 13; 2l 4th when fell 15*
	P	**Davey John (IRE)** 10-1 D Jewett *Mists in rr; some prog 6-7; lsng tch when mists 13 & 14; pu aft nxt*
[187F]	P	**Delwood** 20-1 J Ewart *Mists; prom early; mist 4; bad mist 7 & stpd; strugg 10; t.o & pu 2 out*
[188P]	U	**Dere Street** 4-1JF C Storey *12s-4s; hdstrng; trckd ldrs in mostly 3rd til ld aft 14; ll up nxt; jnd 2 out; 2l 2nd & wkng when blun & ur last; btr for rce*
[112C]	P	**Homo Dorney (IRE)** (5a) 4-1JF Miss L Bradburne *Chsd ldrs; some prog in 5th 7; strugg 14; pu aft nxt*
	P	**Meadowleck** (5a) 14-1 T Scott *(bf) Tk keen hold; ld til hit 8; sn ld agn; hmpd by loose horse aft 9; blun 13 & hdd; jmpd slow 14; wknd rap; pu nxt*
[456]	F	**Rye Rum (IRE)** 5-1 J Walton *Trckd ldrs til ld brief 8; 2nd when fell 10*
	P	**Speckles (IRE)** (5a) 10-1 L Morgan *Rr when mist 1; mid-div in 6th 7; bhnd & wkng 13; pu aft 15*
[114P]	P	**The Dust Buster** 20-1 H Trotter *(bf) A rr; blun bad 5; rdn along 13; pu aft 15*

OFFICIAL DISTANCES: dist, 3l **TIME:** 7min 08.0s
> *In this and all subsequent races, fences 2, 9 & 16 were omitted because of the state of the ground; fence 11 also omitted - fallen rider*

364 Confined Maiden (Div 2) - 15J   13 ran

[107²]	1		**HOOKY'S TREAT** (5a) 3-1 M Bradburne *Trckd ldr; cl up til outpcd aft 12; hit 14; 15l down & lkd btn when lft 11 up app 15; pushed along app 2 out; sn clr; eased run-in; lucky (but deserved a win)*
[112²]	2	20	**Lady Alice** (5a) 5-1 L Morgan *Mid-div; eff to chse ldrs aft 13; 22l 3rd 15; lft 5l 2nd & ev ch aft 15; 12l bhnd & v tired when v slow j 2 out*
[114³]	3	15	**Gallant Major** 7-1 A Robson *In tch in rr; eff to chse ldrs when mist 12; 25l 4th 15; wkng when lft 3rd aft; v tired aft*
	P		**Bold Irene (IRE)** (5a) 20-1 R Nichol *Rr to 7; slow j nxt; 20l off pce 10; pu 12*
[107⁵]	P		**Flying Arrangement** (5a) 10-1 Miss L Hislop *Bhnd til pu aft 3*
	F		**Male Order (IRE)** 13-8F R Morgan *Bit bckwd; lw; hld up in rr; hmpd 6; 8l 5th & rdn 10; fell nxt*
	F		**On Merit** 12-1 T Oates *Pulled hrd; prom; 2l 3rd 3; fell 6*
	P		**Political Bill** 10-1 T Scott *Ld; hdd aft 7; 3rd til 7l 4th 10; wknd 14; t.o & pu 15*
	P		**Poppers** 16-1 T Davidson *Fat; in tch in rr; prog to chse ldrs 8; 3l 3rd 10; wkng 13; wl bhnd when pu 3 out*
[107³]	S		**Senso (IRE)** 8-1 Mrs C Cox *In tch; prog to ld 8; hmpd by loose horse aft 9; 6l up 13; sn wl clr; 15l clr & in comm when slpd up on flat aft 15; v unlucky*
	P		**Snitton South** 6-1 J Walton *Unruly padd; a rr; mist 1; nt jw & schooling; 25l off pce 8; fnce bhnd 14; pu nxt*
	P		**Vernham Wood** 8-1 Mrs V Jackson *Prom early; cl up til wknd 12; t.o & pu 15; btr for rce*
[188⁷]	P		**Wylup** 33-1 H Humble *Prom early; in tch in 4th 7; drpd back 9; lsng tch 12; t.o & pu 15*

OFFICIAL DISTANCES: 20l, 8l **TIME:** 7min 13.0s
> *The stewards interviewed the rider of Senso who slipped up in the lead half a mile from home; they accepted her explanation that the 'horse lost its footing and fell'*

365 Confined Maiden (Div 3) - 15J   13 ran

	1		**DUN ROSE** (5a) 5-4F C Storey *Keen; chsd ldrs; 8l 8th app 3; blun 6; 4l 3rd 8; prog to disp 2l 2nd 12; trckd ldr til ld gng wl app 2 out; sn clr*
[187²]	2	8	**Bold Navigator** (5a) 5-1 Miss M Bremner *Prom; 7l 3rd aft 8; 4/5th mostly aft til 3l 3rd app 2 out where ev ch; 8l 2nd & tired when hit last*
[114U]	3	4	**Hey Chief (IRE)** 10-1 P Strang Steel *Lw; hld up in rr; 20l last 5; prog to 10l 5th 10 & 10l 3rd 15; rdn to 5l 4th passing 3 out; sn wknd*
[187³]	4	2	**Whiskey Galore** 9-2 W Renwick *(xnb) In tch; 12l 6th 10; rdn & outpcd 14; kpt on one pce*
[112P]	5	10	**Myles Of Moss (IRE)** (5a) 20-1 D Reid *Hrd hld in detach last; jmpd slow 1; 15l down 10; lost tch 14; bhnd nxt; nvr plcd to chall*
	P		**Billieburn** 7-2 L Morgan *Unruly padd; mists in rr; jmpd slow 1; prog to 111 5th 10; lost tch 14; 25l down nxt; pu 2 out*
	F		**Four North (IRE)** 25-1 Miss J Hedley *7th when fell 3*

	P	**Gladys** (5a) 25-1 **A Richardson** A rr; 25l last 10; pu 13
[114ᴾ]	P	**Liffey Lane** 20-1 **M Clayton** 2 handlers; ld; 6l up 3; hdd 7; disp 2l 2nd 12; trckd ldr aft til 12l 4th & rmdrs 14; wknd; blun when pu 2 out
	U	**Master Crook** 20-1 **N Crookston** 20l 8th when blun bad & ur 4
[112ᵁ]	P	**Spot The Music (IRE)** (5a) 20-1 **R Trotter** (bf) Mid-div; 5th aft 7; 10l 5th app 10; blun 11; wknd 13; bhnd & pu 15
	F	**Stronacroibh** 8-1 **R Morgan** Pulled hrd; prom in 3rd til ld app 7; drew clr frm 12; 6l up 14; nrly jnd nxt; hrd rdn & hdd aft omitted 3 out; wkng qckly when fell nxt; winded
	P	**Tekroc (IRE)** 12-1 **D Jewett** (xnb) Trckd ldr til wknd qckly aft 8; pu 10

OFFICIAL DISTANCES: 8l, 4l **TIME:** 7min 14.0s

Blankney
Southwell (LH 7F,18J) Sun, 27 Feb (GOOD to SOFT)

366 Hunt, 12st   **4 ran**

	1	**DEFENCE COUNSEL (IRE)** 5-2 **M Leach** (xnb) 1st ride; hld up & rcd wide; mist 7; 4th ½way; went 2nd 13; ld aft 15; 3l clr 2 out; hld on wl flat
	2	nk **Affair Of Honour (IRE)** 12-1 **Miss C Elkington** Bckwd; 1st ride; went 2nd 3-8; releg last 12; chsd wnr 3 out; r.o wl flat
	3	20 **Sigma Wireless (IRE)** 4-5F **N Squires** Ld til jmpd v slow 6; 2nd 8 til ld 10; mist & hdd 12; wknd 3 out
	P	**Ming** (5a) 9-2 **T Lane** 2nd/3rd til ld 6; hdd 10; ld 12; mist 15; sn hdd & wknd qckly; pu 2 out

OFFICIAL DISTANCES: nk, dist **TIME:** 7min 09.8s

367 Confined, 12st   **10 ran**

[115²]	1	**BURNTWOOD MELODY** 7-2 **R Armson** A.p; went 2nd 9; ld app 10; 5l clr 13; 15l ahd 3 out; unchall
[151³]	2	20 **Mr Freebie (DEN)** 10-11F **N Bloom** Nvr gng or jmpng wl; 26l 8th ½way; 25l 7th 12; went 22l 4th 15; stayed on frm 3 out; went 2nd last; nvr nr wnr
[171ᵁ]	3	2 **Gillone** 5-1 **L Lay** 2 handlers; swtng; hld up; 10l 5th ½way; hdwy 11; 5l 3rd nxt; went 7l 2nd 14; wknd 3 out; dem last
	4	20 **Zam Bee** 11-1 **N Bell** Nvr wnt pce; 21l 7th ½way; 21l 5th 12; went 20l 4th 13 til wknd 15; t.o
[115⁹]	5	runin **Needwood Neptune** 33-1 **P Bennett** Spurs; tk no interest & sn wl bhnd; t.o 8
	P	**Birdietoo** (5a) 50-1 **M Skinner** A bhnd; mists 6 & 7; t.o 8; pu 11
[229ᴾ]	P	**Broadway Swinger** (bl) 20-1 **S R Andrews** Chsd ldr; blun & rmdrs 7; ld aft 8 til hdd app 10; sn rdn & nt r.o; 20l 4th 12; pu 13
[231³]	P	**Charming Moss (IRE)** 33-1 **N Kent** Nvr on terms; 20l 6th ½way; 23l 6th 12; mists 13 & 14; blun 15; t.o & pu 3 out
	P	**Native Cove (IRE)** 12-1 **L Hicks** Bckwd; prom; 3rd ½way; went 2nd 10 til wknd 14; 15l 3rd nxt; wl bhnd when pu 3 out
	P	**Rich Tradition (IRE)** 100-1 **M Hewitt** Ld til hdd aft 8; 4th & rdn ½way; sn lost plce; 28l 8th 12; pu 13

OFFICIAL DISTANCES: 15l, 2½l, dist **TIME:** 6min 29.3s

368 Ladies Open   **10 ran**

[230ᴿ]	1	**IMPERIAL DAWN (IRE)** evensF **Miss L Rowe** Ld to 2; 2nd til ld app 12; sn 5l clr; drew away frm 3 out; unchall
	2	20 **Corner Boy** (7x) 2-1 **Mrs J Dawson** Jmpd rt; a.p; mist 6; 2l 3rd ½way; mist 12; went 7l 2nd aft 14; no imp 3 out
[118⁴]	3	1½fs **Bare Fisted** 16-1 **Miss H Phizacklea** A bhnd; 22l 5th ½way; t.o 12; lft 4th nxt & rem 3rd when landed on stricken rival last; virt fio flat
	F	**Black Book (IRE)** (5a) 50-1 **Miss A Burton** Fell 2
[118⁶]	P	**Circus Colours** 16-1 **Miss J Elson** Chsd ldrs til jmpd v slow 2; nt r.o; pu 6
	P	**Dotty Dolittle** (5a) 33-1 **Mrs C Hirst** Bckwd; jmpd v slow 1; t.o & pu 3
[28⁴]	P	**Laughing Fontaine (IRE)** 25-1 **Miss L Allan** Nd; 15l 4th ½way; mist 10; sn wl bhnd; 30l 4th when pu 13
[191ᵁ]	U	**Persian Sword** 50-1 **Miss P Swindin** Spurs; chsd ldrs til wknd 8; 17l 5th when mist & rfo 9
[115ᶠ]	F	**Plunder Bay (USA)** 20-1 **Mrs J Parris** Ch ride; ld 2 til hdd & blun 12; wknd 14; 12l 3rd nxt; rem 3rd & exhaust when virt ref last; straddled fnce & fell; dead

	U		**Sir George Chuffy (IRE)** 20-1 Miss M Mullineaux *6th when rfo 4*

OFFICIAL DISTANCES: dist, dist **TIME:** 6min 27.9s
The rider Plunder Bay was fined £50 for being unable to produce her Riders Qualification Certificate and Mediacal Record Book

369 Mens Open, 12st   11 ran

	1		**LORD HARRY (IRE)** 7-2 A Crow *Lw; jnd ldrs 5; 2l 3rd ½way; went 2l 2nd 14; ld 3 out; sn qcknd clr*
[229¹]	2	4	**Give It A Whirl** 9-1 T Lane *Sn prom; 3l 4th ½way; went 2nd 11; ld 12-3 out; no ch w wnr*
[117³]	3	8	**Sharimage (IRE)** (7x) 6-1 Julian Pritchard *Hld up; 10l 7th ½way; eff & 8l 7th 12; went 4l 3rd 15; no imp 3 out*
[294ᵁ]	4	30	**The Crazy Bishop (IRE)** (7x) 10-1 B Shaw *Ld 2-3; 2nd to 11; 6l 5th 12; wknd & 10l 6th 14; t.o*
[171¹]	5	10	**Class Of Ninetytwo (IRE)** 5-2 R Burton *Chsd ldrs; 5l 6th ½way; 3½l 4th 12; 7l 5th 14; rdn & wknd aft 15; mist 2 out; t.o*
[171ᴾ]	P		**Blue Wave (IRE)** 25-1 D Sherlock *A bhnd; to 8; pu 12*
	P		**Canaillou II (FR)** 50-1 A Wadlow *Nd; lost tch u.p & 17l 8th ½way; wl bhnd when pu 12*
[92ᴾ]	P		**Carson City** 50-1 J Purllant *Sn wl bhnd & u.p; 25l 9th ½way; t.o & pu aft 11*
[117ᴾ]	P		**Casual Water (IRE)** (7x) 33-1 L Hicks *Chsd ldrs; 4l 5th ½way; 6½l 6th 12; wknd & 12l 7th 14; wl bhnd when pu 3 out*
[121ᴾ]	F		**Rising Dawn (IRE)** 66-1 A Sansome *Fell 2*
[231²]	P		**Shanavogh** (7x) 7-4F R Hunnisett *Ld to 2; ld 3-12; wknd & 7l 4th 15; wl bhnd when pu 2 out*

OFFICIAL DISTANCES: 5l, 8l, dist **TIME:** 6min 28.7s
The rider of Shanavogh was fined £50 for being unable to produce his Riders Qualification Certificate and Medical Record Book

370 Dodson & Horrell PPORA Club Members   7 ran

[75¹]	1		**INCH FOUNTAIN (IRE)** 1-2F A Crow *Ld to 1; 3l 4th ½way; went 4l 2nd 12; ld aft 15; sn clr; blun last; easy*
[156ᴾ]	2	12	**The Big Fella (IRE)** (vis) 7-1 C Barlow *Ld 1; qcknd 4l clr 12; hdd aft 15; no ch w wnr*
[288²]	3	4	**Cormeen Lord (IRE)** 4-1 J Sharp *(pricker ns) Went 2nd 2-12; mist 14; 4l 3rd & rdn 15; plodded on*
[171⁵]	4	25	**Allerbank** 5-1 T Greenway *Sn prom; hit 8; 4l 5th ½way; wknd 14; 11l 4th nxt; blun 3 out; t.o*
	P		**Colemans River (IRE)** 50-1 M Gregory *Nd; 11l 6th ½way; t.o & pu 12*
[194ᴾ]	P		**Ilandra (IRE)** (5a) 50-1 M Cowley *Nt jw; rdn 4; t.o & pu 9; useless*
[134ᴾ]	P		**Optimism Reigns (IRE)** (bl) 16-1 Miss R Clark *Chsd ldrs; mist 5; went 2l 3rd ½way; wknd qckly & 8l 5th 12; pu 14*

OFFICIAL DISTANCES: 12l, 6l, dist **TIME:** 6min 42.6s

371 Restricted   13 ran

[122¹]	1		**CATCHWORD** 5-2JF R Armson *Lw; sn prom; went 8l 2nd 9; ld app 12; sn 5l clr; 15l up 3 out; unchall*
[38⁴]	2	10	**Paddy For Paddy (IRE)** 5-2JF A Dalton *Hld up; 17l 4th ½way; hdwy & 7l 3rd 12; went 2nd nxt; rdn & nt qckn aft 15; stayed on*
[173ᴾ]	3	25	**Fair Farm Boy** 25-1 B Foster *Nvr nr ldrs; 20l 5th & rdn ½way; short-lived eff & 12l 5th 12; went poor 3rd aft 15*
[175ᵁ]	4	15	**Lunar Dancer** 66-1 B Logan *Hld up & bhnd; 27l 8th ½way; some hdwy & 13l 6th 12; wknd & 19l 4th 15; t.o*
	P		**Bustoni (IRE)** 7-1 W Tellwright *Ld to 5; ld 6; 8l clr 9; hdd app 12; wknd 14; 18l 3rd nxt; pu 3 out*
[179ᴾ]	P		**Dorgan** (bl) 33-1 A Sansome *2 handlers; rmdrs 4; hmpd bad 7; nt rec; t.o & pu 9*
[120ᴾ]	P		**Grants Carouse** 50-1 M Wells *Prom til lost plce 5; t.o & pu 9*
[179ᵁ]	U		**Grove Victor** 20-1 P Andrew *(xnb) 2nd til rfo 2*
[191ᴾ]	P		**Lift The Latch (IRE)** 66-1 M Cowley *V late in padd; lost plce 5; 28l 9th ½way; t.o & pu 12*
[173ᶠ]	F		**Offley Lucielastic** (5a) 10-1 R Burton *Hld up; hdwy 6; 12l 4th when fell 7*
[151ᴾ]	P		**Peacemaker (IRE)** 7-1 J Cornwall *Lost plce 8; 24l 7th ½way; 28l 7th 12; t.o & pu 15*
	P		**Secret Alliance (IRE)** 7-2 A Crow *(xnb) Lw; pulled hrd; went 2nd 3; ld & mist 5; hdd 6; 10l 3rd ½way; 8l 4th 12; sn wknd; wl bhnd when pu 15*
	P		**The Quakers Wake (IRE)** 40-1 C Barlow *A bhnd; 23l 6th ½way; 30l 8th 12; pu 13*

OFFICIAL DISTANCES: 12l, dist, dist **TIME:** 6min 42.7s

372 Confined Maiden (Div 1), 12st - 17J   14 ran

	1		**GANGSTER** 2-1F **R Cope** *Sn prom; went 2nd 9; ld 12; drew clr 15; 10l ahd 3 out; easy*
[169⁶]	2	7	**Playlord** 3-1 **N Docker** *2nd til ld 5; hdd 12; no ch w wnr frm 15*
[121⁶]	3	10	**Kings Choir** 10-1 **Mrs C Boyes** *Chsd ldrs; 18l 6th ½way; eff & 10l 4th 12; 16l 4th & no hdwy 15; went poor 3rd nr fin*
[121ᵁ]	4	¾	**Grey Warrior** 7-2 **M Hewitt** *Jmpd rt; hld up & bhnd; mist 2; hdwy & 16l 5th ½way; went 8l 3rd 11; wkng when blun 2 out*
[123⁶]	5	25	**Rushes Lane** 16-1 **M Skinner** *33s-16s; 2 handlers; chsd ldrs; lost plce & 20l 7th ½way; 18l 6th 12; 23l 6th 15; t.o*
[124⁵]	6	15	**Fair Farm Lad** 12-1 **P Welsh** *Sn drvn along & wl bhnd; 22l 9th ½way; 19l 7th 12; 27l 7th 15; t.o*
	F		**Caromisu** 20-1 **S Cochrane** *(xnb) Fell 1*
[168ᵁ]	P		**Mandalay Man (IRE)** 5-1 **A Sansome** *Hld up & bhnd; 21l 8th ½way; eff & 14l 5th 12; wknd & 19l 5th 15; pu 3 out*
[232ᴾ]	P		**Miss Caitlin (IRE)** (5a) 20-1 **C Weaver** *A bhnd; 10th ½way; t.o & pu 12*
	B		**Royal Charger (IRE)** 33-1 **L Hicks** *Bd 1*
	U		**Saundby Swordsman** (7a) 14-1 **M Chatterton** *Prom; 12l 4th ½way; 15l 6th & wkng when mist & ur 11*
	P		**Shula** (5a) 33-1 **T Lane** *(xnb) A bhnd; 11th ½way; t.o & pu aft 11*
[234ᴾ]	P		**The Last Shout (IRE)** 12-1 **R Barrett** *Ld to 5; 5l 3rd & rdn ½way; wknd rap 11; 30l 8th nxt; pu 13*
[168⁴]	P		**Tuath Deuchainne** 33-1 **Miss R Pask** *Drpd to rr 5; t.o 7; pu 9*

     OFFICIAL DISTANCES: 7l, 10l, 1l   **TIME:** 6min 50.1s
        Fence 8 omitted - fallen rider

373 Confined Maiden (Div 2), 12st   16 ran

	1		**STINGING BEE** 20-1 **N Bell** *Hld up; 8l 6th ½way; 8l 8th 12; hdwy 14; went 5l 3rd aft nxt; lft 4l 2nd 3 out; ld app 2 out; sn clr*
[235ᶠ]	2	25	**Fortune Hunter** 4-1 **C Weaver** *Hld up & bhnd; 13l 10th ½way; gd hdwy & 2½l 3rd 12; went 2nd 15; rdn to ld 3 out; hdd app 2 out; wknd rap*
[180ᶠ]	P		**Ali's Lark** 50-1 **K Needham** *A bhnd; 27l 12th ½way; t.o & pu 12*
	P		**Batcho Missile** 33-1 **E Walker** *Nd; 11l 9th ½way; lost tch 11; pu 12*
	R		**Carr Dyke Castle** 20-1 **B Foster** *2 handlers; bckwd; rn out & ur 1*
	P		**Cashel Green (IRE)** 10-1 **M Hewitt** *Hld up; 9l 7th ½way; 7l 9th 12; wknd 13; wl bhnd when pu 3 out*
	P		**Crested Lass** (5a) 16-1 **L Hicks** *A bhnd; jmpd v slow & rmdrs 5; 23l 11th ½way; t.o & pu 11*
	P		**Erik The Viking** 3-1 **R Armson** *Ld to 1; 6l 4th ½way; mist 10; 4l 5th 12; wknd 14; 15l 5th nxt; pu 3 out*
	F		**Game Drive (IRE)** 20-1 **S Walker** *(bf) Fell 1*
[233ᴾ]	F		**Hya Prim** 12-1 **M Mackley** *Prom; 3l 3rd ½way; went 2nd 11; ld 14 til hdd & fell 3 out*
	P		**Metro Fashion (IRE)** 12-1 **T Lane** *2nd/3rd to 5; 6½l 5th ½way; 4½l 6th 12; wknd qckly 14; pu 15*
[169ᶠ]	P		**Mighty Monarch (IRE)** 33-1 **A Sansome** *Pulled hrd; went 2nd 4; ld 7-14; 4th & wkng when pu 3 out*
	F		**Nautical Lad** (7a) 8-1 **R Barrett** *Fell 1*
	P		**Nelti** 33-1 **L Lay** *ld 1-7; 2nd to 11; 3l 4th when mist 12; wknd 13; pu 15*
	F		**Sands Point** 12-1 **N Kent** *Fell 1*
	P		**Syrpiro** 5-2F **R Cope** *5s-5/2; bckwd; hld up; 9½l 8th ½way; hdwy 11; 5l 7th nxt; sn wknd; pu 14*

     OFFICIAL DISTANCE: dist   **TIME:** 6min 54.9s

West of Yore
Hornby Castle (LH 8F,18J) Sun, 27 Feb (GOOD to SOFT)

374 Hunt, 12st   4 ran

[173ᴾ]	1		**JORIDI LE FORIGE (IRE)** 10-1 **B Orde-Powlett** *Chsd ldr to 9; qckly lost tch w ldng pr; 12l 3rd 13; lft rem 2nd & cause lkd hopeless 2 out; drvn along to catch errant ldr on post*
[279ᵁ]	2	½	**Calleva Star (IRE)** (7x) 4-7F **R Abrahams** *Ld; gng best when lft wl clr 2 out; napped to boxes app last & tried desperate to pu; did same passing padd aft last; hdd on line; v unlucky but needs stronger handling*
	F		**Highmoor Lady (U)** (5a) 50-1 **Miss E Blane** *(xnb) Last aft jmpd poor 3; lost tch 7; t.o 13; fell 15*

[167⁴] F **Lingham Lady** (5a) 6-4 S Swiers *Hld up; went 2nd 9; gng wl to 15; hit 3 out & rdn; hld by ldr when fell nxt*

OFFICIAL DISTANCE: ½l **TIME:** 6min 52.0s

375 Confined, 12st 11 ran

[278¹] 1 **JACKSON'S HOLE** 6-4F D Easterby *Lw; rr til impd qckly to ld 6; rdn & qcknd clr frm 2 out; impressive*

[135⁴] 2 6 **Insideout** 4-1 Mrs L Ward *Handy; went 3rd 13; ev ch til 5l 3rd & outpcd 3 out; kpt on to snatch 2nd on line*

3 hd **Blank Cheque** 8-1 D Coates *Hld up & bhnd til rap prog app 13; 2nd nxt; ll down 3 out; hrd rdn & reluct to pass boxes app last*

4 20 **Final Beat (IRE)** 10-1 C Cundall *Midfield & chsng ldrs; nvr able to chall; 6th & btn 15*

[173¹] 5 1 **Rubon Prince (IRE)** 6-1 L McGrath *Trckd ldrs to 13; 10l 5th & outpcd 15*

[134⁷] 6 3 **Stellar Force (IRE)** 12-1 N Tutty *Hld up in midfield; wkng when mist 14; 7th & btn nxt*

[137⁷] P **Abbey Lad** 33-1 C Wilson *Ld 4-6; 4th 8; rmdr nxt & sn wknd; to & pu 15*

[277⁵] P **Mr McCarney (IRE)** 20-1 W Burnell *Ld to 4; wkng when mist 9; pu 10*

[136²] P **On The Fly** (3x) (ttt) 7-1 R Edwards *Chsd wnr 6-14; 9l 4th & wkng nxt; rr when pu last*

[277¹] P **Pharlindo (IRE)** (3x) 9-4 Mrs F Needham *Blun & nrly ur 1; rdr lost irons; hanging violent rt & unridable on track; last early; 3rd by 8; lost plce 10; rr when pu 14*

[137⁷] P **The Grey Bay** (5a) 50-1 Miss T Jackson *Jmpd poor & sn last; to 9; pu 11*

OFFICIAL DISTANCES: 8l, hd **TIME:** 6min 40.0s

376 Mixed Open, 12st 10 ran

[225³] 1 **PROMINENT** (2ow) evensF D Easterby *Lw; hld up & bhnd; impd to 6th 10; tk 3rd 12 & 2nd 15; ld & lft clr 2 out; eased*

[90ᵁ] 2 runin **Greenhil Tare Away** 3-1 S Swiers *Settled 3rd/4th; outpcd aft 13; 24l 4th 15; went 2nd app last; no ch wnr*

3 6 **Cross Cannon** 20-1 T Glass *Ld to 2; chsd ldr til ld agn 11; hdd 12; 10l 3rd when jmpd slow 15; nt r.o; lft mod 2nd 2 out til app last*

[135⁸] 4 8 **Scrabo View (IRE)** 66-1 Miss S Ward *Ld 2; 6l clr 7; hdd 11; lost plce qckly; 30l 5th 15; kpt on game*

[136⁴] 5 20 **Lottery Ticket (IRE)** 33-1 S J Robinson *Spurs; a bhnd; last & rdn 10; reluct; to 13*

[41⁹] 6 20 **Nosmo King (IRE)** (bl) 14-1 Miss L Kendall *Bhnd; 7th & drvn 10; nvr gng wl; to when mist 15*

P **Primitive Streak** 14-1 R Abrahams *Mist 3; trckd ldrs; 5th when mist 10; strugg 12; pu 14*

[171⁷] P **Repeat Offer** 14-1 N Tutty *Jmpd slow & v reluct in rr; to & pu 7*

[171²] F **Sunrise Sensation** 2-1 C Denny *Hld up towards rr; prog 9; ld 14; hdd & fell 2 out; broke leg; dead*

[171ᵁ] R **Take Two** 66-1 S Pinder *Ineptly rdn; mod last when allowed to rn out 5*

OFFICIAL DISTANCES: dist, 5l **TIME:** 6min 41.0s

377 Restricted (Div 1) 11 ran

[134⁷] 1 **PRIME STYLE** 20-1 C Gibbon (xnb) *Bckwd; tk str hld & nt a fluent; made most to 13; chsd ldr 15; lkd hld til lft clr by ldr's antics app last*

2 15 **Mount Faber** (bl) 7-1 S Charlton *Hld up in midfield; 5th & prog aft 13; ld 15; lkd in comm til v reluct to pass boxes aft 2 out; sn hdd u.p & nt r.o*

[133¹] 3 1 **Chaps** 7-4F C Mulhall *Mists in rr; poor 8th aft 13; passed btn horses but nvr nr ldrs*

4 ¾ **Tyndrum Gold** 10-1 Miss A Daniel *Nt fluent early; sn detach last; still last 13; stayed on frm 3 out; unable to chall*

[137⁷] 5 3 **Ellerton Tony** 4-1 S Swiers *Settled towards rr; 6th aft 13; eff in 6l 4th 15; sn rdn & no resp*

[173⁷] 6 ½ **Flashlight** 2-1 P Halder *Hld up chsng ldrs; mist 12; 5th aft 13; 12l 5th 15; no prog aft*

[139⁷] 7 ½ **Heavenly Blues** 16-1 C Wilson *Mostly 2nd til 13; hdd 15; wknd qckly; nt stay*

[283ᵁ] P **Daring Magic** (5a) 5-1 C Denny *Chsd ldrs til 7th & strugg aft 13; to & pu 3 out; dead*

[276⁷] P **Mac's Blade (USA)** 50-1 R Edwards *Unclipped & rough; 3rd/4th to 7; lost plce 10; to & pu 15*

P **Palm Gold** (5a) 20-1 R Wakeham *Rr but in tch to 10; pu 12; easy rn*

[276²] U **Yornoangel** 7-1 R Clark (xnb) *Nt jw; prom; 2nd aft 13; w ldr when blun & ur 14*

OFFICIAL DISTANCES: 20l, ¾l **TIME:** 6min 55.0s

378 Restricted (Div 2) 11 ran

[276³] 1 **MR HOOK** 50-1 R Clark *Midfield; eff to 3rd & rdn 12; outpcd in 12l 4th 3 out; kpt on nxt; hrd rdn to ld nr fin; lucky*

[173^U]	2	hd	**Young Ardross** 2-1 Mrs F Needham *Lw; trckd ldrs; 5th 12; ld app 15; drew clr aft 3 out; faltered & hdd flat; kpt on brave; broke down*
[282^F]	3	1½	**Lewis** (bl) 10-1 Miss T Jackson *(xnb) Mist 2; ld to 8 & 10 til app 15; sn u.p; 10l 3rd 3 out; rallied nxt; tried to chall last; one pce*
[50^F]	4	10	**Miorbhail** 8-1 G Brewer *(xnb) Hld up & nvr btr than midfield; outpcd frm 14*
[281^P]	5	6	**Watacon** 16-1 G Markham *Mists & pulled hrd; blun 11; cl 2nd/3rd to 12; wknd to 20l 5th 3 out*
[229^7]	P		**Cede Nullis** (5a) 8-1 S Brisby *Lw; chsd ldr; ld 8-10; lost plce 12; rallied to 11 2nd app 15; ev ch 3 out; hrd rdn & nt r.o; pu last*
	P		**Chief Engineer** 25-1 L McGrath *A wl bhnd; to 9; pu 14*
[137^P]	F		**Efaad (IRE)** 14-1 W Burnell *(xnb) Mist 2; nvr btr than midfield; strugg when fell 14*
	P		**Eye Of The Storm (IRE)** 10-1 M Morley *Nt jw & a wl bhnd; to 11; pu 14*
[168^1]	F		**Polar King (IRE)** 2-5F D Easterby *Fell 3*
[283^P]	P		**Rain Street (IRE)** 25-1 D Thomas *Strugg in last trio; to 9; hopelessly to when pu 2 out*

OFFICIAL DISTANCES: hd, 1l **TIME:** 7min 02.0s

379 Open Maiden 56&7yo (Div 1), 12st   16 ran

[169^2]	1		**GEMOLLY (IRE)** (5a) evensF C Mulhall *Hld up & bhnd; 6th & hdwy 13; 5l 4th 3 out; ld nxt; drvn & stayed on wl*
[114^2]	2	2½	**Tom's Man** (tt) 6-1 P Johnson *Hld up in midfield; gd prog in 4th 13; 3rd & chall when lft 2nd & impeded 3 out; ev ch aft nxt; drvn & nt qckn*
	3	25	**Hey Sam (IRE)** 8-1 T Glass *Sn handy; 4th 10; went 2nd 15; lft in ld 3 out; hdd nxt; nt r.o & slowed rap aft*
	4	15	**Tough Decision** 16-1 S Brisby *(xnb) Midfield; drvn 11; 8th & outpcd 13*
[168^U]	5	4	**Ben From Ketton** (7a) 33-1 S J Robinson *Pulled hrd & mists; set slow pce to 7; 2nd 10; drpd back 10th 13; sn r.o*
[233^P]	P		**Aunty Norma (IRE)** (5a) 14-1 G Brewer *Mists & pulled hrd; 2nd/3rd to 11; 5th & wkng 13; pu 14*
	P		**Bonnie Buttons** (5a) 20-1 L McGrath *Bckwd; school in rr; to 6; pu 11*
	U		**Bred For Pleasure** (5a) 14-1 Miss T Jackson *Midfield; 9th when blun & ur 8*
[189^U]	F		**Lewesdon Countess** (5a) 6-1 R Wakeham *4th when fell 7*
[283^U]	P		**Miss Gloria** (5a) 33-1 S Charlton *(xnb) School; last early; to 10; pu 14*
[167^P]	r		**Norman Way** (7a) 20-1 P Cornforth *Mists & a bhnd; to when ducked to padd gate & put brakes on aft 10*
	P		**Pause For Thought** 4-1 Mrs F Needham *Chsd ldrs; 4th 11; 7th & strugg when mist 13; pu 15*
[282^F]	P		**Perdix** (12a) 33-1 K Prendergast *Nvr btr than midfield; lost tch 10; mod 9th 13; pu last*
[187^P]	F		**River Rising** 16-1 C Wilson *2nd/3rd til ld 13; ½l up when fell 3 out*
	P		**Wandering Wild** (12a) 16-1 Mrs L Ward *(xnb,martin) School in rr & v green; to 6; pu 11*
[133^4]	P		**Wayward Buttons** 5-2 S Swiers *Hld up; gd prog in 3rd 11; 4l 2nd 13; 8l 5th & wkng 15; pu last*

OFFICIAL DISTANCES: 2½l, 25l **TIME:** 7min 04.0s

380 Open Maiden 56&7yo (Div 2, Part 1), 12st   10 ran

[133^3]	1		**MEFEIN BOY (IRE)** 6-1 W Burnell *Settled midfield; mist & rdr lost reins 11; outpcd 13; 5th & lkd btn 15; lft 2nd by 2 out; presented w rce by misfortune of long ldr*
[169^3]	2	20	**Go Nomadic** 3-1 P Atkinson *Jmpd sluggish early & rmdrs; wl bhnd til hdwy 9; rdn 10; tried to cl u.p 15; btn nxt; nt pushed frm 2 out*
[139^P]	3	6	**Cape Crusader** 16-1 K Green *Lw; a wl bhnd; to 13; v lucky 3rd*
	P		**Benn Wood** (7a) 16-1 Miss S Brotherton *V novicey in last trio; to 7; pu 11; school*
[282^P]	P		**Early Dawn** (5a) 10-1 J Davies *Mounted on course & tde; tk str hld; w clr ldr til lft 20l ahd 7; 6l up aft bad mist 13; sn hdd; 3l 2nd when mist 15; tired rap; pu 3 out*
[133^3]	U		**Heather Lad** 7-1 D Raw *Chasing group; lft 3rd 7; in tch when mist & ur 14*
	P		**Personal Guarantee** (12a) 33-1 G Markham *Veered & svs; v novicey in last trio; to 7; pu 10*
	F		**Sparkling Gift (IRE)** (5a) 33-1 J Townson *Chsng group; lft 3rd 7; went 2nd aft 15; 5l 2nd when fell 3 out; promising debut*
[138^4]	F		**Tiger King** 4-1 C Mulhall *Set fast pce til jnd & fell 7*
[282^2]	U		**Tricky Trevor (IRE)** evensF Miss H Delahooke *Chsd clr ldng pr; lft 20l 2nd 7; clsd 13 to ld nxt; drew rt away aft; swishing tail violent flat; unassailable when leather broke & rfo flat*

OFFICIAL DISTANCES: 20l, 8l **TIME:** 7min 01s

381 Open Maiden 56&7yo (Div 2, Part 2), 12st   9 ran

	1		SON OF SAM 20-1 L McGrath *2nd/3rd; mist 5; ld 13; 10l clr 15; stayed on wl; unchall*
[137³]	2	25	The Butcher Boy (2ow) 4-6F D Easterby *Last pr & und iron grip; jmpd erratic; way off pce til eff aft 13; 20l 3rd 15; drvn brief & little resp; went poor 2nd app 2 out*
[276⁴]	P		Curtainsatchopwell (IRE) 5-1 S Swiers *Lw; ld & spreadeagled field; 12l up 10; clr til slowed rap & hdd 13; t.o & exhaust 15; pu 3 out*
[45²]	P		Do Justice (IRE) 4-1 S Charlton *Midfield; 11l 4th 7; went 2nd aft 13; 10l down nxt; dem app 3 out; wl btn when pu & dism last*
[44ᴾ]	r		Escalate 25-1 Miss L Kendall (xnb) *Sn wl outpcd; 30l 5th 7; t.o 11; ref 3 out*
[281ᵁ]	U		Im Struggling (7a) 25-1 K Lupton *Jmpd erratic 1 & 2; poor last when rfo 3*
[276ᵁ]	P		Mrs Drummond (IRE) (5a) (bl) 50-1 G Markham *Settled 2nd/3rd to 9; drvn 11; 4th & lsng tch when pu qckly & dism 13*
[282ᵁ]	U		Timeforanother (5a) 10-1 Mrs F Needham *Nt jw & sn rem; 45l last 7; t.o 10; blun & ur 14*
	R		Wheresbob 5-2 S Hughes *Bckwd; rn out 1*

OFFICIAL DISTANCE: 20l **TIME:** 6min 55.0s

Ludlow (LH 8F,17J)
Thu, 2 Mar (SOFT)

382 Ludlow Gold Cup HC   13 ran

	1		FLYING MARIA 11-06 7-1 L Jefford *Hld up; hdwy 7; ld gng wl 13; clr 3 out; hvly eased flat*
[226⁶]	2	dist	Royal Mountbrowne 11-11 11-2 Miss E Jones *Tk keen hld; prom; hit 12; ld brief bef nxt; chsd wnr vain frm 3 out*
[226⁴]	3	9	Tea Cee Kay 12-00 7-2F A Sansome *Prom til lost plce 7; rem 4th aft 13; plodded on*
[77⁵]	4	7	Against The Agent 12-00 11-2 Julian Pritchard *Lw; blun bad & almost ur 1; lost sev plces; rallied to ld 7; hdd bef 13; hung bad lft & lost 3rd flat*
[150⁷]	5	1¾	Manamour 11-11 25-1 T Scudamore *Sn outpcd; no ch aft 9; t.o 13*
[245ᵁ]	6	dist	Belafonte 11-07 33-1 A Middleton *Jb & sn lost tch; t.o 10*
[272ᴾ]	P		Captain Khedive 11-07 (bl) 16-1 Miss S Talbot *Prom til rdn & wknd aft 9; bad mist 12; rem 6th when pu 14*
[153⁴]	P		Desert Calm (IRE) 12-01 14-1 D Alers-Hankey *Sn outpcd; t.o 10; pu 14*
[297ᴾ]	P		Eau So Sloe 11-07 (bl) 100-1 K Burke *Sn labouring in rr; t.o & rdn 9; pu 13*
	P		Hacketts Cross (IRE) 11-11 16-1 R Burton *Chsd ldrs to 8; sn lost tch; t.o 10 til pu 14*
[153²]	P		Late Encounter 12-01 9-1 A Wintle *Nvr gng wl & sn lost tch; t.o 10; pu 14*
	P		Princess Lu (IRE) 11-07 66-1 N Tucker *Unbalanced all way; sn lost tch; t.o 10; pu 14*
[201²]	P		Warren Boy 12-04 9-1 Miss P Jones *Set fast pce; hdd 7; lost tch 9; poor 5th when pckd 11; pu nxt*

TIME: 5min 25.8s **TOTE:** £6.10; places £2.40,£2.30,£2.60 **Ex:** £52.80 **CSF:** £38.95 **Tri:** £80.20
The rider of Warren Boy was suspended for two days for careless riding; this suspension was later quashed by the Jockey Club Disciplinary Committee as the interference caused had been accidental in that the horse had suffered an injury

Taunton (RH 8F,15J)
Thu, 2 Mar (SOFT, HEAVY in home straight)

383 Mitford Slade HC   13 ran

[161³]	1		SAINT JOSEPH 11-04 10-1 Miss S Young *Bhnd; last 10; gd hdwy 12; chsd ldr passing omitted 14; chall 3 out; ld & hit nxt; rdn clr flat*
[262⁴]	2	1¾	Kilmington (IRE) 12-05 16-1 J Barnes *Jmpd slow 4 & 11; 3rd/4th til ld 13; hdd 2 out; ch when jmpd delib last & outpcd; rallied u.p cl home*
[299ᴾ]	3	21	Mr Dow Jones (IRE) 12-01 5-1 D O'Meara *Mist 2; bhnd; 10th 10; hdwy & hit 12; stayed on to chse ldrs 3 out; sn wknd; mist last*
[262³]	4	4	Castle Lynch (IRE) 10-13 5-1 Jeremy Young *Chsd ldrs; 4th 10; ev ch til rdn & wknd 3 out*
[177²]	5	29	Stretchit 11-04 9-2JF Miss T McCurrich *Chsd ldrs; 5th 10; drpd to rr nxt & strugg aft; t.o*
[142ᵁ]	6	dist	Willie B Brave (IRE) 11-04 25-1 David Dennis *Chsd ldrs; lost plce 7; rdn & hdwy in 6th 10; lft in ld 12; hdd nxt; sn wknd; t.o*
[154³]	P		Abit More Business (IRE) 11-11 (bl) 15-2 A Honeyball *Bhnd; 8th & hdwy 10; rdn 12; no resp; lost tch app 3 out; t.o & pu nxt*
[211ᵁ]	P		Bricanmore (IRE) 11-06 9-2JF N Harris *In tch; hit 9; 7th nxt; sn wknd; t.o & pu 3 out*

[272³]	P		Bullens Bay (IRE) 11-11 14-1 *Miss F Wilson Hit 3; hdwy 5; lost plce & 9th 10; last when blun 12; t.o & pu last*
[334⁵]	U		Kentucky Gold (IRE) 11-11 50-1 *D Sherlock Ld to 2; 2nd til ld agn app 11; mist & ur nxt*
[34⁶]	P		Leave It Be (IRE) 11-08 20-1 *A Charles-Jones Sn t.o; mist 6 & pu*
[209⁶]	P		Pharsilk (IRE) 11-11 50-1 *H Ephgrave Tk keen hld; ld 2 til app 11; sn wknd; t.o & pu 3 out*
[152⁶]	U		Thinking Twice (USA) 11-11 10-1 *A Bateman Landed awkward & ur 1*

TIME: 6min 40.9s **TOTE:** £11.90; places £3.20,£4.00,£2.60 **Ex:** £157.80 **CSF:** £138.80 **Tri:** £90.80
Last fence on far side omitted each circuit

Doncaster (LH 11F,15J)
Fri, 3 Mar (GOOD to SOFT)

384 Hambleton Hills HC　　　　　　　　　　　　　　　　　　　　　**18 ran**

[226¹]	1		COULTON 12-08 8-11F *M Bradburne Cl up; went 2nd 5; ld 7; made rest; 6l clr 2 out; rdn flat; all out*
	2	½	Island Echo (IRE) 11-07 25-1 *J Tate Prom til 12l 3rd & outpcd aft 11; rallied 2 out; 5l 2nd last; r.o str u.p*
[154⁶]	3	1	Six Clerks (IRE) 11-11 10-1 *A Wintle Bhnd; 8th & hdwy 10; lft 3rd 2 out; 8l 3rd last; kpt on wl u.p*
[94⁶]	4	23	Epsilo De La Ronce (FR) 12-01 50-1 *A Harvey Mid-div; 7th 10; outpcd 12*
	5	2½	King Torus (IRE) 12-08 10-1 *J Jukes Chsd ldrs to 8; no ch frm 12*
	6	13	Pro Bono (IRE) 12-03 16-1 *C Weaver Mist 6; chsd ldrs to 8; bhnd frm 10*
[185⁵]	7	2½	Pebble Beach (IRE) 11-07 25-1 *R Wakeham Chsd ldrs til 6th & wkng aft 10*
[217⁶]	8	4	Wixoe Wonder (IRE) 12-00 50-1 *A Sansome Ld to 7; 3rd 10; wknd rap*
[151ᵁ]	9	dist	Raphael Bodine (IRE) 11-11 9-1 *Miss S Vickery Mist 6; mid-div; hdwy to 4th & rdn 10; wknd qckly aft 12; t.o*
[278⁵]	P		Asked To Leave 11-12 (10) 50-1 *I Bennett Hmpd 1 & rdr lost irons; pu 2*
	F		James The First 11-10 (3) 25-1 *G Tuer Hit 4; a 2nd/3rd; 2nd when fell hvly 9*
[124⁶]	P		Johnny Cool 11-07 50-1 *M Hewitt Mist 1; sn bhnd; t.o & pu 12*
[225⁶]	F		Joint Account 12-04 7-1 *Mrs F Needham Mid-div; gd prog to 2nd 10; mist 12; 8l 2nd & no imp when crashing fall 2 out*
[226⁶]	U		Pontoon Bridge 11-07 (bl) 20-1 *Miss S Swindells Sn towards rr; bad mist 7; wl bhnd when blun & ur 2 out*
[153⁶]	P		Private Jet (IRE) 11-11 (bl) 33-1 *R Clark Mists; strugg in last pr; t.o & pu 12*
[297⁶]	P		Sandi Devil 11-07 (bl) 66-1 *D Dickenson Chsd ldrs til mist 8; wknd rap; t.o & pu 2 out*
[227⁶]	P		Stoney Valley 12-01 33-1 *M Gingell Mist 7; t.o & pu 10*
[155⁶]	U		The Crooked Oak 11-07 100-1 *G Thomas Rr when ur 1*

TIME: 5min 11.3s **TOTE:** £1.90; places £1.40,£4.70,£2.70 **Ex:** £22.80 **CSF:** £29.35 **tri:** £161.40

Newbury (LH 11F,18J)
Fri, 3 Mar (SOFT, HEAVY in places)

385 Peter Hamer Mem HC　　　　　　　　　　　　　　　　　　　　　**4 ran**

[286¹]	1		REAL VALUE (IRE) 11-04 2-1 *B Hitchcott Tk keen hld; hld up 3; hit 11; eff 14; ld nxt; sn clr; ballooned 2 out; unchal*
[156⁴]	2	13	Castle Mane (IRE) 12-05 1-2F *B Pollock Set v slow pce; hdd 5; prsd ldr til rdn to chall aft 14; w wnr when blun 15; sn outpcd & strugg (muscle enzyme problem diagnosed subsq)*
[223²]	3	29	Master Of Troy 11-12 12-1 *Miss T McCurrich 2nd til ld 5; hdd 15; wknd tame*
[226¹¹]	4	9	Charlie Hawes (IRE) 11-02 100-1 *Miss G Russell A last; strugg aft mist 11; no ch frm 13; t.o*

TIME: 6min 43.2s **TOTE:** £2.60; **Ex:** £5.00 **CSF:** £3.27

Warwick (LH 9F,20J)
Sat, 4 Mar (SOFT)

386 Town of Warwick Foxhunters HC　　　　　　　　　　　　　　　　**4 ran**

[156²]	1		CAVALERO 12-00 4-7F *A Charles-Jones Mist 1; 2nd til jnd ldr 12; ld 14; rdn clr flat*
[272¹]	2	1¼	Opera Fan (IRE) 11-10 3-1 *C Williams Tk keen hld; ld; mist 6; hdd app 11; w wnr 12-14; hit 3 out; rdn to chall nxt; unable to qckn flat*

[149⁴] 3 dist **Rusty Fellow** 11-12 16-1 D Barlow *Drpd back last & jmpd slow 8; rallied to ld app 11; hdd nxt; wkng when jmpd slow 14 & 15; t.o*

[148²] 4 5 **Hurricane Blake** 11-10 11-2 J Young *jmpd slow 1 & 2; last to 8; rallied 9; last agn when hit 11; lost tch & jmpd slow 12; t.o 14; jmpd slow 3 out*

TIME: 7min 14.5s TOTE: £1.50; Ex: £3.00 CSF: £2.60

Beaufort

Didmarton (LH 10F,18J) Sat, 4 Mar (GOOD, SOFT in home straight)

387 Hunt - 17J
6 ran

[195ᴾ] 1 **GRANVILLE GRILL** 12-1 J Deutsch *Tde; lft in ld 2; hdd 6; 12l 2nd ½way; ld app 3 out; 5l clr nxt; stayed on wl*

[215⁵] 2 5 **Balance** 8-1 G Maundrell *A 2nd/3rd; hit 1; 15l 3rd ½way; mist 13; no imp til stayed on wl frm 2 out; went 2nd app last; nt rch wnr*

3 15 **Warrior Bard (IRE)** 2-1 M Portman *A 2nd-2s; pulled hrd; sn prom; went 2nd aft 4; ld 6; 15l clr 11; wkng when mist 15; hdd app nxt; 2nd til dem app last*

[216⁴] 4 20 **Capo Castanum** 16-1 R Sturgis *Tubed; 2 handlers; hld up; wl bhnd 9; 22l 4th ½way; mist 13; t.o*

[216²] F **Bavard Dieu (IRE)** evensF Miss V Sturgis *(bf) Hld up; last til fell 4; dead*

[211⁶] P **Toms Choice (IRE)** (bl) 33-1 Miss T Blazey *Ld til pu app 2; collapsed & died*

OFFICIAL DISTANCES: 6l, 15l TIME: 6min 24.3s
Fence 14 omitted - fallen horse

388 Intermediate, 12st
12 ran

[219²] 1 **GILDROM** 7-1 M Rimell *(xnb) 2 handlers; sn prom; 2l 4th ½way; went 1½l 3rd 12; ld 14; 3l clr 2 out; rdn out*

[196¹] 2 4 **Dawn Invader (IRE)** 3-1 Julian Pritchard *Ld to 2; 2nd/3rd til ld 8; hdd 12; ld 13-14; rdn & hld when mist last*

[247¹] 3 25 **Dark Rhytham** 5-1 R Lawther *(xnb) Hld up & bhnd; hdwy & 5½l 7th ½way; 4½l 5th 12; 7l 4th 15; sn wknd; lft poor 3rd at last*

[215⁴] 4 15 **Mendip Prince (IRE)** 25-1 A Lillingston *Went 2nd 3-7; 3l 5th ½way; pckd 11; lost plce & 10l 6th nxt; 17l 6th 14; t.o*

5 ¾ **Questionaire** (5a) 20-1 D Stephens (Wales) *Chsd ldrs; 5l 6th ½way; 11l 7th 12; sn wknd; 18l 7th 14; t.o*

U **Appeal Again (IRE)** 50-1 J Cook *(xnb,bf) Swtng; hld up; hdwy 8; 5l 6th when blun & ur 9*

[144¹] P **Ballina** 10-1 J Jukes *Ld 2-8; 2nd/3rd to 12; wknd & 15l 5th 14; t.o & pu 13*

[249ᶠ] P **Country Concorde** 50-1 L Lay *(xnb) A bhnd; mists 3 & 9; 13l 11th ½way; 24l 10th 12; pu 13*

P **Holloa Away (IRE)** 50-1 R Millar *Mounted on course; prom til lost plce & mist 5; 10l 9th ½way; wl bhnd when pu 12*

U **Minstrel's Quay (IRE)** 25-1 A Charles-Jones *Hld up; 6l 8th ½way; wknd & 15l 8th 12; mist & ur 13*

[163¹] U **Smackwater Jack (IRE)** 7-4F R Walford *Hld up; mist 1; hdwy 7; 1½l 3rd ½way; went 2nd 11; ld 12 til mist 13; 4l 3rd 15; sn wknd; poor 3rd when mist & ur last*

[352ᶜ] P **State Medlar** 50-1 G Maundrell *Hld up; mist 3; lost plce 7; 11l 10th ½way; 18l 9th & wkng 12; t.o & pu 14*

OFFICIAL DISTANCES: 5l, 25l TIME: 6min 15.4s
The rider of Appeal Again was fined £50 for being unable to produce his Medical Record Book

389 Mens Open, 12st
8 ran

[244¹] 1 **CASTLE FOLLY (IRE)** (bl) 4-6F R Lawther *Ld to 3; 2nd til lft in ld 9; went 4l clr 3 out; jnd aft 2 out; r.o u.p flat*

[209ᵁ] 2 1 **Mystery Aristocrat (IRE)** 10-1 R Tory *Lost plce 3; 12l 5th ½way; 20l 4th 12; hdwy 15; went 6l 3rd nxt; chsd wnr app 2 out; ev ch last; r.o*

[195⁵] 3 15 **Lie Detector** (4x) 4-1 J Gasper *Sn prom; lft 2nd 9; 15l clr wnr 12; wknd app 2 out*

[246²] 4 2 **Major Bugler (IRE)** 20-1 S Bush *Chsd ldrs; 8l 3rd ½way; sn outpcd; eff 15; 7l 4th nxt; wknd 2 out*

5 20 **Cruise Free** 25-1 S Sellars *A bhnd; 14l 6th ½way; 22l 5th 12; t.o*

[327ᶠ] P **Gaelic Blue** (7x) (tt) 33-1 A Wintle *Chsd ldrs; 10l 4th ½way; wknd qckly 11; 25l 6th nxt; t.o & pu 14*

[200³] U **Mostyn** 6-1 P Pritchard *Ld 3 til blun & ur 9*

P **Queens Curate** (5a) 33-1 D Luff *Jmpd rt; a bhnd; hit 4; 25l 7th ½way; t.o 11; pu 14*

OFFICIAL DISTANCES: 1¼l, 12l TIME: 6min 24.8s

390 Ladies Open
5 ran

[101¹]	1		**JUST BERT (IRE)** (4x) 4-6F Miss P Gundry Lw; hld up; hdwy & 2l 3rd ½way; went 2nd aft 13; ld aft 14; 7l clr 2 out; easy
[335³]	2	3	**Dalusman (IRE)** 20-1 Miss N Sturgis Chsd ldr 3-9; 5l 4th ½way; went 2nd 11-13; chsd wnr vain 15; kpt on wl
[34⁷]	3	25	**Down The Mine** (4x) 5-4 Miss A Dare 2nd to 3; sn lost plce; 8l 4th 7; hdwy 9; ll 2nd ½way; ld 13 til hdd aft 14; wknd 3 out; mist last
[326ᴾ]	4	10	**Spring Marathon (USA)** (4x) 10-1 Miss E Tory Ld til hdd 13; wknd 15
[333ᴾ]	5	15	**Norman Warrior** (bl) 50-1 Miss V Sturgis Rn in snatches; jmpd slow; wl bhnd 7; eff & 9l 5th ½way; wknd 11; t.o 14

OFFICIAL DISTANCES: 3l, 25l **TIME:** 6min 20.4s

391 Confined Maiden 56&7yo, 12st
13 ran

[220²]	1		**DRUNKARD'S CORNER** (12a) 4-1 J Diment Lw; hld up; mist 1; 7l 9th ½way; 8½l 8th 12; gd hdwy & 4l 3rd 14; qcknd to ld 3 out; drew clr nxt; quite impressive
[264ᶠ]	2	10	**Ard Na Carrig (IRE)** 7-1 A Wintle Lw; ld to 10; 4l 3rd 12; outpcd & 7l 4th 15; stayed on wl frm 2 out; went 2nd at last; no ch w wnr
	3	1½	**Cowanstown Prince** 5-1 Julian Pritchard A.p; ld 10 til hdd & mist 13; 4l 3rd & rdn 2 out; no ex
[194⁴]	4	1	**Wrens Island (IRE)** 7-4F S Joynes 2nd til ld 13; hdd 3 out; 3l 2nd nxt; no ex
[122ᴾ]	5	25	**Marquis Of Bedford** 8-1 E Walker Chsd ldrs; 3l 5th ½way; 5l 4th 12; wknd & 111 6th 15; wl bhnd when mist 2 out
	6	hd	**The Chain Gang** 25-1 C Weaver Hld up; hdwy & 5l 7th ½way; 7l 6th 12; 6l 5th 14; wknd 15
	P		**Bramley** 33-1 A Martin A bhnd; 22l 13th ½way; pu 11
	P		**Captain George** 25-1 M Wall (xnb) 2 handlers; bckwd; hld up; jmpd slow 2; lost plce 8; 9½l 10th 12; sn wknd; wl bhnd when pu 14
	P		**Catechist (IRE)** (7a) 20-1 E Williams Hld up; lost tch 8; 20l 11th ½way; t.o & pu 13
[78ᴾ]	P		**Miss Pilkington** (5a) 16-1 T Stephenson Hld up; hdwy & 4l 6th ½way; 7½l 7th 12; wknd & 12l 7th 14; wl bhnd when pu 3 out
[250⁴]	P		**Quick Succession (IRE)** 10-1 J Trice-Rolph W ldrs til mist 8; 6l 8th ½way; 9l 9th 12; sn wknd; wl bhnd when pu 14
	P		**Ripping Yarn (IRE)** 20-1 J Snowden A bhnd; 21l 12th ½way; t.o & pu 12
[264ᴾ]	P		**Whatacharlie** 25-1 P Keane (xnb) Tubed; prom; 2l 4th ½way; 6l 5th 12; wknd qckly; 20l 8th 14; pu 15

OFFICIAL DISTANCES: 10l, 2l **TIME:** 6min 22.9s

392 Restricted, 12st
15 ran

	1		**THE RIGHT ATTITUDE (IRE)** 10-1 A Wintle Hld up & bhnd; 10l 11th ½way; hdwy & 7l 6th 15; 4l 5th & clsng 2 out; ld last; drvn out
[249¹]	2	nk	**Dark Challenger (IRE)** (bl) 5-2 R Lawther 4s-5/2; ld to 4; 3l 4th ½way; 5l 4th 14; went 2nd nxt; rdn to ld aft 2 out; hdd last; nt qckn
	3	2½	**Mr Smudge** 7-1 A Martin 2nd to 3; blun 9; 2l 3rd ½way; went 2nd aft 13 til 3l 4th 15; cl 3rd 2 out; one pce
	4	½	**Dellone** 33-1 G Carenza Hld up; 5½l 8th ½way; hdwy & mist 12; 7l 6th 14; went 2½l 3rd nxt; 3½l 4th 2 out; one pce
[173⁴]	5	7	**Teme Willow (IRE)** 10-1 M Hammond Chsd ldrs; went 2nd aft 8; ld 10 til hdd aft 2 out; wknd last
[340ᴮ]	6	12	**Coddington Girl** (5a) 2-1F T Stephenson (xnb) lw; hld up; 3½l 5th & hdwy ½way; went 4l 3rd 14; rdn & wknd app 3 out
[193⁷]	7	2	**Raining Stairs (IRE)** 10-1 J Trice-Rolph Chsd ldrs; 5l 7th ½way; went 2nd 12 til aft 13; 9l 7th & wkng 15
	8	hd	**Vale Of Oak** (5a) 33-1 M Portman (bf) 2 handlers; nd; 9l 10th ½way; wl bhnd frm 15
[336ᴾ]	F		**Camogue Bridge (IRE)** 50-1 N Oliver 4th when fell 3
	F		**Drom Island** (5a) 33-1 Miss N McKim Hld up & bhnd; gd hdwy to 4l 6th ½way; wkng qckly when mist 12; pu 13
[250¹]	U		**Dynoun** 5-2 D Crosse Hld up; hdwy to 3l 5th when mist & ur 9
	P		**Lochchoire** 50-1 J Cook Tde; sn wl bhnd; t.o 7; pu 12
[247⁴]	P		**Melody Princess** (5a) 12-1 J Jukes Nd; 8l 9th ½way; 11l 9th 14; wl bhnd when pu 2 out
[341ᴾ]	P		**Spirit Prince** 14-1 Julian Pritchard Jmpd rt; went 2nd 3; ld 4-10; 4l 4th 13; 8l 7th & wkng nxt; wl bhnd when pu 2 out
[194⁴]	U		**Vital Hesitation** (5a) 50-1 R Millar 6th when ur 3

OFFICIAL DISTANCES: nk, 3l **TIME:** 6min 27.6s
Wotanite was withdrawn not under orders - kicked at start

Derwent

Charm Park (LH 9F,19J) Sat, 4 Mar (GOOD to SOFT)

393 Hunt
5 ran

[51ᵁ]	1		**RUN FOR THE MILL** 5-2 M Morley *Hvly rstrnd in rr; pulled hrd & throwing hd ab; mists 2, 5 & 12; went 2l 3rd 13; trckd ldr til qcknd clr 3 out; sprinted home*
[171ᴾ]	2	4	**Nishkina** (3x) 4-7F C Cundall *Chsd ldr in 4l 2nd til ld at crawl 11; jnd 3 out; sn hdd & easily outpcd*
[283ᴾ]	3	15	**Imps Way** (12a) 12-1 C Mulhall *Rr to 8; went 11 2nd 12-16; easily outpcd 3 out; 15l 3rd at last*
	U		**Lingcool** (5a) 7-1 J Morley *Set pedestrian pce til hdd aft 10; in tch in last til outpcd 15; bhnd when ur 2 out*
[377ᴾ]	U		**Palm Gold** (5a) 6-1 R Wakeham *Handy in 3rd til ur 8*

OFFICIAL DISTANCES: 4l, dist TIME: 7min 47.0s

394 Confined, 12st
10 ran

[375ᴾ]	1		**MR MCCARNEY (IRE)** 20-1 W Burnell *A.p; trckd ldr in 11 2nd 5-9; 2l 2nd 14; outpcd 15; rallied & rnwd chall 3 out; ld nxt; stayed on wl; all out*
[277⁸]	2	1	**Mr Primetime (IRE)** 14-11 N Bannister *Cl 3rd til outpcd 12; 8l 4th 15; went 4l 3rd 2 out; stayed on wl; chall last; just outpcd*
[277⁴]	3	1½	**Blackwoodscountry** 9-1 N Wilson *Ld til jnd 3 out; hdd & mist nxt; wknd; fin lame*
[279³]	4	nk	**Bold Fountain (IRE)** 4-6F S Swiers *Hld up in rr to 8; went 4l 3rd 10 & 3l 3rd 16; wknd 3 out; stayed on one pce*
	5	10	**Fettle Up** (bl) 14-1 Miss S Brotherton *Trckd ldrs in 5th to 11; outpcd & rr by 12; 15l 5th & no imp 3 out*
[170²]	6	30	**Stride To Glory (IRE)** 20-1 Mrs H Arnold *Cl 2nd to 8; rr & lsng tch 10; t.o 12*
	P		**Caman** 25-1 Mrs N Palfreeman *Sn bhnd; lost tch by 5; last 6; t.o & pu 12*
[277²]	U		**Harbour Blaze (IRE)** 7-2 Miss R Clark *Rr when mist 3; pushed along to trck ldrs in 5th 10; 3l 2nd when blun & ur 14*
[277⁵]	r		**Holiway Star (IRE)** 20-1 N Tutty (xnb) *Lft at start; tk no part*
[276ᵁ]	U		**Louis Renee (IRE)** 50-1 B Woodhouse *Last when blun & ur 3*

OFFICIAL DISTANCES: 1l, 2l TIME: 6min 53.0s

395 Mens Open
5 ran

[376¹]	1		**PROMINENT** 4-6F D Easterby *Cl 2nd to 9; ld 10 til jnd 13-16; ld agn 3 out; sn qcknd clr; 15l up at last; easy*
	2	12	**Mr Dick** 6-4 S Swiers *Handy 3rd til ld 6-10; disp ld 13-16; pushed along & easily outpcd 2 out; btr for rce*
[231⁴]	3	20	**Juke Box Billy (IRE)** 33-1 W Burnell *Trckd ldng pr; 4l 3rd 8; 6l 3rd 11; rdn to 4l 3rd agn nxt; sn outpcd; wl bhnd 3 out*
[279⁵]	4	30	**Be Brave** 50-1 R Lochman *Sn bhnd; last & pushed along 10; poor 4th 12*
[277ᵁ]	U		**Vital Issue (IRE)** 10-1 P Johnson *Ld to 4; wknd 5; last & lsng tch when blun & ur 8*

OFFICIAL DISTANCES: 15l, dist TIME: 6min 53.0s

396 Restricted, 12st
14 ran

[282¹]	1		**MEADOWBANK** 5-2 M Watson *Handy in 3l 3rd til ld 10-11; cl 2nd til ld agn 15; 2l clr 2 out; stayed on str*
[283¹]	2	4	**Hazel Reilly (IRE)** (5a) 6-1 L Bates *Midfield to 7; lost posn & rr by 10; stdy hdwy frm 13; went 8l 4th 2 out; nt rch wnr*
[173²]	3	10	**Scruton** (5ow) 4-1 D Easterby *Ld to 3; cl 2nd to 10; disp ld 13-15; 2l 2nd 2 out; r.o one pce; dem flat*
[301ᵁ]	4	6	**Mandril (IRE)** 12-1 N Tutty *Midfield to 9; went 6l 5th 11; cruised to 11 2nd 15; flatt but outpcd & wknd 3 out*
[378⁰]	5	2	**Efaad (IRE)** 20-1 W Burnell (xnb) *A rr; stayed on frm 15; nrst fin*
[377ᵁ]	6	8	**Yornoangel** 20-1 R Clark *Mid-div early; went 2l 2nd 11; cl up to 16; 5l 4th & wkng 3 out*
[52¹]	7	2	**Traceytown (IRE)** (5a) 10-1 Miss Rachel Clark (xnb) *Mid-div til pulled to ld 6-9; prom til wknd 14; rr & pushed along 16*
[279⁶]	8	12	**Keep A Secret** 20-1 P Atkinson (xnb) *A rr; last & lsng tch 11; t.o 16*
[378ᴾ]	P		**Cede Nullis** (5a) (tt) 10-1 S Brisby *Cl 2nd to 8; 3l 4th 12; 3rd & pushed along 3 out; wknd qckly & pu bef nxt*
[137ᴾ]	F		**Kanona** 14-1 N Wilson (bf) *Ld til fell 2*
[377ᴾ]	P		**Mac's Blade (USA)** 33-1 R Edwards *V scruffy & unclipped; a rr; t.o by 4; pu 11*
	F		**Normins Hussar (IRE)** 7-1 G Brewer *Rr early; hdwy frm 6 to 4l 5th 9; ld 13; fell nxt*
[235¹]	B		**Primitive Man** 2-1F S Charlton *Prom when bd 2*

[173⁵] **B**   **Up And Over (IRE)** 33-1 **Miss J Foster** *Mid-div when hmpd & bd 2*

OFFICIAL DISTANCES: 3l, 15l **TIME:** 6min 50.0s

397 Ladies Open   6 ran

[245¹] **1**   **PHARARE (IRE)** 1-3F **Miss C Spearing** *Nt a fluent; made virt all; ½l up when blun 12; jnd 2 out; sn qcknd clr; 4l clr at last; r.o wl*

2   3   **Marius (IRE)** 5-2 **Miss V Russell** *Mid-div til went 11 2nd 8; outpcd 10; 10l 3rd 16; fin str; tk 2nd flat*

[280¹]

[135⁶] **3**   4   **Japodene** (5a) 16-1 **Miss R Clark** *A.p; went 3l 2nd 11; trckd ldr til chall & mist 2 out; wknd app last*

4   20   **Temple Garth** 11-1 **Miss F Hartley** *Bad blun & nrly ur 1; mist 6; bhnd & lsng tch 9; poor 4th 3 out*

[19⁵] **5**   30   **Half Each** (5a) 33-1 **Miss L Watson** *Handy in 3rd til mist 11; rr & lsng tch 13; poor 4th 15; t.o last 16; hacked home*

[276¹] **U**   **The Hazel Harrier (IRE)** 16-1 **Miss A Deniel** *Bhnd when bad mist 3; hdwy 12 to 4l 4th 13; in tch when blun & ur 15*

OFFICIAL DISTANCES: 2l, 3l **TIME:** 6min 49.0s

PLATE 11   398 Derwent Open Maiden 5&6yo: Jolly Minster leads L to R Mr Norm and partly obscured Step Lively, behind Aunty Norma and Personal Guarantee dispute, ahead of (half of) Sir Ruscott, Flowing Fortune (just visible between horses), Saxon Moss, Two Of Diamonds (sash) and Handsome Is (light cap), Curtainsatchopwell is way behind - the rest are in there somewhere!
PHOTO: Roy Parker

398 Open Maiden 5&6yo, 12st   16 ran

[233²] **1**   **STEP LIVELY** (5a) 2-1 **S Swiers** *Confid rdn; prom to 7; rstrnd til 8l 4th 10; chsd ldr in 8l 2nd 15; chall 2 out; sn ld; qcknd rt away last; easy*

2   8   **Jolly Minster** 10-1 **P Atkinson** *Made virt all; 6l and 12; tried to spreadeagle field 14; 8l up 3 out; jnd nxt; hdd & wknd app last; brave rn*

[379ᴾ] **3**   runin **Aunty Norma (IRE)** (5a) 25-1 **D Thomas** *Mid-div; 6l 5th 9 & 12l 4th 15; wknd & poor 4th 3 out; lft rem 3rd nxt*

[381ᴾ] **4**   40   **Curtainsatchopwell (IRE)** 9-1 **N Wilson** *(xnb) V hvly rstrnd in rr; wl bhnd 13; r.o to rem 4th 3 out; exhaust & clambered last*

P   **Alena H Banks** 16-1 **L McGrath** *(xnb) Sn bhnd; t.o 3; fnce adrift when pu 11*

P   **Ambersam** (7a) 9-2 **C Mulhall** *Gentle school in rr; nvr put in rce; pu 14*

[380ᴾ] **U**   **Benn Wood** (7a) 50-1 **Miss S Brotherton** *Jmpd big in rr til ur 8*

[282ᵖ]	P	**Flowing Fortune** 20-1 Miss R Clark *A midfield; lsng tch 15; t.o & pu 3 out*
[168ᵖ]	P	**Handsome Is (IRE)** (12a) 14-1 G Brewer *Midfield til blun bad 16; sn wknd; pu 3 out*
[283ᶠ]	U	**Mr Norm** 66-1 J Clare *A.p; trckd ldr; 11 2nd & gng wl when ur 12*
[282³]	C	**Never Wonder (IRE)** (7a) evensF J Tate *Mid-div; hdwy 13 to 15l 4th 15; went 12l 3rd 3 out; hdwy when forced out 2 out*
[379ᵖ]	F	**Perdix** (12a) 50-1 K Prendergast *Fell 2*
[380ᵖ]	P	**Personal Guarantee** (12a) 50-1 G Markham *Ld to 3; chsd ldr in 6l 3rd 10; lft 8l 2nd 12; wknd 15; pu last*
	P	**Saxon Moss** 20-1 M Hewitt *A towards rr; t.o & pu 16*
	P	**Sir Ruscott (IRE)** 14-1 Miss A Deniel *Rr by 9; lsng tch 11; t.o & pu 14*
[235ᵖ]	P	**Two Of Diamonds** 20-1 W Burnell *A rr div; t.o & pu 3 out*

OFFICIAL DISTANCES: 8l, dist **TIME:** 6min 57.0s

399 Open Maiden 7yo&up (Div 1) 16 ran

	1	**NOBLE HYMN** 7-1 C Mulhall *Patient rdn in rr 14; went 8l 6th 16; stayed on to 2l 2nd & mist 2 out; rallied to chall last; sn ld & r.o u.p*
	2 1½	**Santa Barbara (IRE)** (5a) 3-1F L Bates *Midfield to 8; hdwy to 2nd 10; ld 3 out; jnd at last; sn hdd & outpcd*
[281⁶]	3 20	**In The Van** 6-1 M Morley *(xnb) Rr to 8; hdwy 10 to 3l 3rd 12; gng wl 3 out; wknd qckly nxt*
[283³]	4 8	**Fiery Jack** 7-1 N Tutty *Handy 3rd to 10; 8l 4th 15; poor 4th 3 out*
[234ᵖ]	5 3	**Kerrisdale** (5a) (tt) 7-1 D Thomas *33s-7s; mid-div to 9; outpcd 13; poor 5th 3 out*
[283ᵖ]	P	**Captain Oates** 5-1 M Watson *Blkd & rdr lost reins 1; pu 2*
[282ᵖ]	U	**Cricketing** (tt) 20-1 P Johnson *Ld til ur 2*
[233⁴]	U	**Highbury** 7-2 G Brewer *Ur 1*
[137ᵖ]	P	**Just A Single (IRE)** (tt) 20-1 G Markham *Handy 4th to 9; in tch to 14; 10l 5th 15; wknd 3 out; t.o & pu flat*
[138ᵖ]	P	**Miss Jones** (5a) 20-1 P Frank *Chsd ldr in 20l 2nd to 6; wknd 9; t.o when pu 14*
	P	**Nells Delight** (5a) (bl) 16-1 R Clark *A rr; last 9; t.o & pu 15*
[281ᵁ]	P	**Oaklands Millie (IRE)** (5a) 14-1 P Kinsella *A rr div; t.o & pu 2 out*
[54ᵖ]	P	**Pharstar (IRE)** 5-1 D Easterby *(xnb) Lft in ld 2; 20l clr 4-7; 2l up 16; sn hdd & wknd; pu 2 out*
[52ᶠ]	F	**Stanwick Hall** 8-1 Mrs F Needham *(xnb) Fell 2*
	P	**The Way North** 10-1 R Wakeham *(xnb) A rr; t.o 15; pu 2 out*
[377⁴]	P	**Tyndrum Gold** 6-1 Miss A Deniel *A rr; lsng tch 12; t.o & pu 2 out*

OFFICIAL DISTANCES: 1l, dist **TIME:** 6min 50.0s

400 Open Maiden 7yo&up (Div 2) 14 ran

	1	**WHAT A FIDDLER (IRE)** 3-1 R Tate *Midfield to 8; went 8l 4th 14; hdwy 16 to disp ld 2 out; sn ld; clr last; r.o wl*
[278²]	2 5	**The Shy Padre (IRE)** 7-2 J Townson *Midfield to 8; went handy 6th 11; outpcd 14; 8l 3rd 15; stayed on to ld & mist 2 out; wknd & no imp*
[277⁷]	3 50	**Icantsay (IRE)** 14-1 D Thomas *Rr 9; pushed along & strugg to go pce 13; stayed on past btn horses; mist last; tk rem 3rd flat*
[378ᵖ]	4 6	**Eye Of The Storm (IRE)** 14-1 M Morley *Prom; cl 2nd 12; ld 15-3 out; wkng & outpcd nxt; exhaust & clambered last; dem flat*
[281ᶠ]	P	**Charlie Dazzle (IRE)** 14-1 N Wilson *A rr div; t.o & pu 13*
[283²]	P	**Flashing Gale (IRE)** 2-1F D Coates *Midfield early; went 8l 6th 9; stdy hdwy to cl 3rd 3 out; pu qckly nxt; lame*
	P	**Hopeful Earl (IRE)** 10-1 N Tutty *Handy in 4th 8; outpcd & wknd 11; t.o & pu last*
[233ᵖ]	P	**Joe Smoke** 10-1 S Charlton *A rr div; lost tch 13; t.o & pu last*
	P	**Lulagh-B** (5a) 14-1 R Wakeham *Midfield; 10l 7th 9; outpcd & wkng 11; t.o & pu 13*
[139ᵖ]	P	**Morcan House** 20-1 S Gibbon *Sn rr; t.o when pu 12*
	P	**Reskue Line** 14-1 S Swiers *Ld to 14; sn lost tch; pu 3 out*
	F	**The Big Lad (IRE)** 12-1 M Hewitt *Midfield early; went 5th 8; trckng ldrs when fell 10*
[380ᶠ]	P	**Tiger King** 7-2 C Mulhall *Slow into fncs & jb; hld up in last early; bhnd 7; pushed along & hdwy 11; bad mist 16; pu 16*
[378⁵]	F	**Watacon** 6-1 G Markham *A.p; 11 2nd when fell 13*

OFFICIAL DISTANCES: 4l, dist **TIME:** 6min 54.0s

East Devon
Bishops Court (LH 7F,19J) Sat, 4 Mar (SOFT, becoming sticky)

401 Hunt   5 ran

[161⁷]	1		**NATIVE ALLIANCE (IRE)** 5-4F Miss O Green *V fit; oht; ld til jnd 7; jmpd slow 12; disp til ld 15; sn rjnd; lft solo 2 out*
[199²]	U		**Exe Cracker** (tt) 5-2 L Jefford *(martin)Went 2nd 5; jnd ldr on inner 7; level & lkd gng btr when blun & ur 2 out*
[253²]	P		**John Robin** 7-2 M Sweetland *Oht; mounted on course & tde; tk keen hld; cl up to 10; 12l last & wkng 12; pu 14*
[260⁷]	F		**Lord Spider** 5-1 M Miller *Clr 3l 3rd when fell 16*
	F		**Playing Away** (12a) 25-1 Miss S Auld *Bckwd; tk keen hld; cl last til fell 10*

OFFICIAL DISTANCE: Finished alone TIME: 6min 46.2s

402 Mens Open, 12st   10 ran

[327¹]	1		**MISS O'GRADY (IRE)** (5a,7x) 2-1 M Miller *Trckd ldrs; 3rd 8 & 2nd 11; ld 3 out; clr but drvn when mist last; rdn out*
[209¹]	2	5	**Gamay** (7x) 12-1 N Mitchell *(xnb) Nt fluent early; detach last to 6; stdy hdwy 12 to 3rd 16; 6l 3rd nxt; went 2nd aft 2 out; rdn & nt rch wnr*
[293¹]	3	5	**Rosmarino** 8-1 A Dalton *Ld to 7; 2nd til mist 10; cl up til rdn & one pce aft 16*
[383¹⁰]	4	1½	**Thinking Twice (USA)** 16-1 A Bateman *Midfield; 6th 12; jmpd slow nxt; in tch to 16; sn btn*
[252¹]	5	10	**Iranos (FR)** (7x) (bl) 7-4F T Mitchell *Lw; 2nd til ld 7; outj & hdd 3 out; lost 2nd aft nxt; wknd & blun last; eased*
[223³]	6	½	**Flying Imp** 20-1 J Barnes *Cl up til jmpd slow 2; sn rallied; prsng ldrs when jmpd slow 10 & rdn; lost tch 14*
[252²]	P		**Bear Claw** 7-1 Jeremy Young *Cl 3rd/4th to 12; 5th & wkng 14; t.o aft 16; pu 2 out*
[222⁷]	P		**Bet With Baker (IRE)** (7x) 25-1 A Honeyball *Cl up in mid-div; mist 7; lsng plce when nrly ref 13 & pu*
[313⁴]	P		**Strong Stuff (IRE)** (7x) (tt) 66-1 M Shears *(bf)Sn last pr; 11th 9; hmpd 13; t.o nxt; pu 3 out*
[310⁶]	P		**Uckerby Lad** 40-1 C Heard *Midfield & handy til wknd 12; wl bhnd in 8th when pu 15*

OFFICIAL DISTANCES: 4l, 4l TIME: 6min 31.7s

403 Confined, 12st   10 ran

[210ᵁ]	1		**DANGEROUS GUEST (IRE)** 9-4 T Mitchell *Reluct to line up; jmpd slow in detach 9th to 3; prog in 6th 10; 11 2nd 15; 3l down & nt fluent 3 out; rdn to ld aft nxt; hit last; stayed on; wl rdn (lkd v reluct early stages)*
[214³]	2	2½	**Stillmore Business** 6-1 A Honeyball *Mist 6; hit 9; 2nd/3rd til ld 11; pushed along 3 out; hdd aft nxt; nt qckn*
[140¹]	3	25	**Parditino** (8x) 7-1 Miss J Nicholas *Chsd ldrs; 5th 10; wknd 12; 20l 4th 3 out; plugged on*
[315⁷]	4	10	**Kimbross** 16-1 L Jefford *(xnb) Hld up in midfield; went 4th 10; mist 13; outpcd 15; 15l 3rd 3 out*
	U		**Air Command (BAR)** 33-1 P Phillips *Bckwd; midfield; 7th & outpcd when blun & ur 11*
[199ᵁ]	P		**Manor Rhyme** (vis) 20-1 E Gretton *Cl up early; drpd back 9th 10; lost tch 14; t.o & pu 2 out*
[59⁷]	P		**Radio Days (IRE)** 10-1 Miss C Tizzard *Mist 2; sn rr; lost tch 7; 9th 10; pckd 11; t.o & pu aft 13*
	U		**Rocky Park** 12-1 R Emmett *Bckwd; ld to 11; 4th & wkng when mist & ur 14*
[161⁴]	P		**Southern Flight** 2-1F Miss J Cumings *2nd/3rd; jmpd slow & to rt 7; ev ch til 3l 3rd 15; wknd tame; pu 3 out*
	P		**Spare On** (5a) 16-1 A Michael *Bit bckwd; sn t.o; pu 10; school*

OFFICIAL DISTANCES: 2l, 20l TIME: 6min 41.0s

404 Intermediate, 12st   9 ran

[255¹]	1		**HORUS (IRE)** (7a) 4-6F L Jefford *Hld up trckng ldrs; 4th 8; 2nd/3rd frm 14 til ld 3 out; sn in comm; rdn out*
[63²]	2	6	**Ross Cottage** 5-2 A Bateman *Lw; ld aft 1 til jmpd slow 3; ld agn 4 til hdd 3 out; rdn & kpt on but no ex app last*
[263³]	3	6	**Bright Approach (IRE)** 10-1 T Mitchell *Ld/disp to 4; 4th 12; 10l 6th & outpcd 15; went 3rd 3 out; hit trble ldrs*
[198¹]	4	10	**Ardbei (IRE)** 16-1 N Harris *Chsd ldrs; 6th 8; u.p 11; handy but nvr lkd keen aft; 8l 5th 15; no imp frm nxt*

[162^p]	5	10	**Lead Story (IRE)** 10-1 **Richard Darke** Tk keen hld; handy but sev posns; disp 2nd 14 til 3rd & hit 16; wknd nxt; nt pushed
[253^F]	P		**Alice Sunrise** (5a) 66-1 **T Greed** (xnb) Last pr; lost tch & mist 6; jmpd v slow 7 & rem aft; pu 14
[330^U]	P		**Friar Waddon** 20-1 **Miss J Cumings** Sn 20l last; passed rival 9 & another 12 but nvr in tch; t.o 15; pu 2 out
[311^1]	P		**Lydford Castle** 12-1 **C Heard** Bhnd; bad mist 4; 8th & strugg 12; t.o to pu 14
[162^2]	P		**Young General** (bl) 16-1 **A Honeyball** Nt fluent; cl up til went 2nd 8-13; 4th & rdn 15; nt r.o; t.o & pu last

OFFICIAL DISTANCES: 5l, 4l   TIME: 6min 39.0s

405 Ladies Open
4 ran

[257^2]	1		**MR JERVIS (IRE)** 1-2F **Miss V Tremlett** Jmpd safe; made all; 2l up when hit 3; sn forged clr; easy
[208^9]	2	20	**Lord Of The Rings** 3-1 **Miss C Tizzard** Lw; a chsng wnr; tried to chall & mist 3 out; sn outpcd & fnd nil
[257^4]	3d		**Desert Run (IRE)** 8-1 **Miss J West** Last pr & sn labouring; 30l last 9; fnce bhnd 12; fin 2 fncs last; disq - tk wrong course
[201^F]	R		**Its Grand** 8-1 **Mrs J Wilkinson** (xnb) Nt fluent & sn lost tch in last pr; 25l 3rd 9; rn out & ur 12

OFFICIAL DISTANCES: Originally 15l, dist   TIME: 6min 45.9s

Desert Run finished third but was disqualified for missing a marker at the end of the first circuit; the rider explained she did not know she should have pulled up after taking the wrong course; in view of her inexperience she was fined £50

406 Restricted, 12st
15 ran

[331^F]	1		**WE MOVE EARTH** evensF **T Mitchell** Jmpd rt; tkn stdly in rr til prog 8; 3rd 12 & 2nd 14; ld nxt; drew clr 3 out; r.o str; impressive
[163^P]	2	8	**Rhyme And Chime** 20-1 **Miss S Vickery** Trckd ldrs; 5th 12; 10l 4th & rdn app 16; 5l 3rd & eff 3 out; sn chsng wnr vain
[157^2]	3	8	**Ledburian** 66-1 **S Craddock** Mist 6; hdwy to 3rd 7; ld 8-14; sn u.p; disp ld app 16; 4l 2nd when mist 3 out; plodded on
[251^3]	4	6	**Shameless Lady** (5a) 50-1 **Richard Darke** Chsd ldrs; 6th 12; one pce & nd frm 15
[253^1]	5	3	**Brother Nero (NZ)** 12-1 **C Heard** Rr early; impd to 8th 12; outpcd 15
[164^4]	6	10	**Genereux** (tt) 10-1 **A Honeyball** Nt jw; chsd ldrs; mists 2 & 7; 7th 12; drvn along & nt keen 15; btn when blun nxt
[330^4]	7	3½	**Keszam** (5a) 14-1 **Miss A Goschen** Bhnd; some prog 9; 9th 12; lost tch aft nxt
[315^P]	F		**Damiens Pride (IRE)** 20-1 **T Dennis** (xnb) Prom; 4th 12; fell nxt
[104^3]	P		**Don Luigi** 33-1 **N Harris** Ld to 8; 2nd 12; ld agn 14-15; 6l 3rd & wkng app 16; t.o & pu last
[352^1]	P		**Loxley-Lad** (tt) 16-1 **G Richards** A last; mists 1 & 2 & imm lost tch; wl bhnd til pu 14
	P		**Prudent Miner (IRE)** 33-1 **R Skinner** Mist 9; chsd ldrs to 10; 13th & strugg 12; t.o 14; pu 2 out
[255^P]	P		**Run With Joy (IRE)** 50-1 **J Berwick** A rr; lost tch 10; t.o 14th 12; pu 14
[261^P]	P		**Silver Man** 25-1 **Mrs M Hand** Sn bhnd; rdn 11; 11th nxt; t.o & pu 3 out
	P		**Timber Wolf (IRE)** 33-1 **M Miller** Mostly 2nd to 8; lost plce qckly to 10th 10; t.o & pu 2 out
	P		**Wonford Boy** 3-1 **N Mitchell** (b4) Chsd ldrs til 5th & mist 8; 12th & strugg 12; t.o & pu 3 out

OFFICIAL DISTANCES: 5l, 10l   TIME: 6min 39.5s

407 Open Maiden (Div 1), 12st
14 ran

[105^U]	1		**WIBBLEY WOBBLEY** 7-4F **Miss J Cumings** Prom in chsng group til lft 2nd 15; 4l down 15; pushed into ld aft 3 out; sn clr; easy
	2	15	**Peasedown Tofana** (5a) 4-1 **R Young** Prom in chsng group til lft 3rd 5; ld 7; rdn & hdd sn aft 3 out; one pce & btn nxt
[204^5]	3	25	**Dedalus (FR)** (7a) 6-1 **L Jefford** Lw; chsng group; 4th 9; 3rd 12; nt r.o frm nxt; 15l 3rd 15
[72^P]	4	7	**Salford Quay (IRE)** 14-1 **G Barfoot-Saunt** Lw; chsd ldrs; 3rd 9; 4th 12; sn strugg; 20l 4th 15
[213^4]	5	25	**Grey Jerry** 10-1 **B O'Doherty** Plodded rnd in rr; poor 9th 9; 30l last 15
[254^3]	P		**Aller Coombe** (5a) 4-1 **T Greed** Sn strugg; t.o 8; pu 11
	F		**Bold Joker** 50-1 **K Burke** Chsng group; handy 5th 9; fell 10
	P		**Eskimo Gold** (5a) 33-1 **M Shears** Mid-div; bad mist 6; 7th 9; in tch when pu 12
	F		**Jug Of Wine** (5a) 25-1 **R Arnold** Hld up; 6th 9; prsng ldrs when fell 11

	P		**Magic Caller (IRE)** 33-1 Miss S Robinson *Fat; clambered fnces & sn wl t.o; pu aft 6*
[213¹]	P		**Montepulciano (IRE)** 12-1 N Mitchell *(xnb) Jmpd v slow & to rt; a t.o; pu aft 13*
[147⁴]	P		**Rushaway** 5-1 Miss J Congdon *(xnb) Chsd rushaway ldr til lft in ld 5-7; wknd rap to poor 8th 9; t.o 12; pu 14*
[206ᶠ]	P		**Tabula Rasa** 33-1 A Honeyball *Jmpd erratic in rr; 10th & t.o 9; pu 14*
	P		**Tolepa (IRE)** (5a) 33-1 L Tibbatts *Set lunatic gallop in 20l ld til crashing fall 5*

OFFICIAL DISTANCES: 15l, 15l TIME: 6min 39.0s

408 Open Maiden (Div 2), 12st   5 ran

[213³]	1		**REMEMBER RIDEMORE (IRE)** 1-3F T Mitchell *Lw; prsd ldr til ld aft 10; 12l clr 14; unchall aft*
[12ᶠ]	2	15	**Lockett's Lamp (IRE)** 14-1 J Barnes *3rd & 10l frm ldng pr til 12l 3rd 14; no imp; mist 2 out*
	3	20	**Indian Muse** (12a) 7-1 M Shears *Jmpd poor in 4th; 15l down 9; went rem 3rd aft 15*
[355⁵]	P		**Ballot Box** 5-1 Jeremy Young *(xnb) Pulled hrd & nt jw; ld til aft 10; grad wknd; releg last aft 15; cont v slow & t.o; pu 2 out*
[255ᵖ]	U		**Media Luz** (5a) 25-1 M Sweetland *Mist 1; 12l last til blun & ur 3*

OFFICIAL DISTANCES: 15l, 15l TIME: 7min 02.2s

409 Open Maiden (Div 3), 12st   10 ran

	1		**FINNIGAN FREE** 11-4 M Frith *Lw; drpd out in last pr to 6; 4th & prog 9; 20l 4th 12; clsd to 2nd 16; ld app 3 out; sn clr; mist nxt; unchall*
	2	25	**Knock Star (IRE)** 7-1 S Partridge *Ld til hdd app 3 out; imm outpcd; plodded on*
[158ᵁ]	P		**Cherry Pie** (5a) 10-1 Mrs M Hand *Negatively rdn & sn last; t.o 5; pu 7*
[329ᶠ]	F		**Indian Miller** 20-1 M Green *Handy; went 2nd 9-16; sn wknd & 10l 3rd nxt; poor 3rd when fell 2 out*
[352ᶜ]	P		**Lighter Lord** 9-4F L Jefford *Lw; cl up til pu qckly 5 (rdr thought horse unsound)*
[212ᵁ]	r		**Millcroft Regatta (IRE)** 5-1 R McKenzie Johnston *Rdr unstdy; drpd to rr 12; 25l last 9; t.o 14; ref 2 out*
[213ᵖ]	U		**Prussian Steel (IRE)** 6-1 T Greed *Hld up; 4th 5; blkd by loose horse & ur within wings of 7*
[70⁵]	P		**Soleil D'Ete** (5a) 10-1 N Mitchell *Sn 2nd til releg 3rd 9; 15l adrift 12; pckd bad 14 & cont to; pu 3 out*
	U		**Turn Up The Heat** 20-1 O Jackson *Ur 1*
[204ᵖ]	P		**Young Lucky** 33-1 L Tibbatts *Nt jw in midfield; mist 9; 25l 5th & strugg 12; t.o when nrly ref 15 & pu*

OFFICIAL DISTANCE: 20l TIME: 6min 55.1s

410 Open Maiden (Div 4), 12st   9 ran

[255ᵁ]	1		**ROSSALEEN** (5a) 20-1 P Shaw *2nd/3rd; mist 8; ld 9-11; outpcd in 12l 3rd & lkd strugg 14; lft 3rd nxt & sn 2nd; clsd qckly aft 16 to ld aft nxt; drew clr*
[204ᶠ]	2	30	**Caundle's Hand** (5a) 16-1 R Arnold *(xnb) Trckd ldrs; 3l 4th 9; ld 11 & made most til lft 10l clr aft 15; nrly fell nxt; 6l clr 3 out but sn hdd & btn; blun 2 out; mist last*
[206⁴]	3	runin	**Weycroft Valley** (5a) 16-1 L Tibbatts *Ld to 7; 10l 3rd & strugg 14; lft 2nd brief nxt; v tired aft & t.o 3 out*
	U		**All-Inclusive (IRE)** (5a) 16-1 J Scott *Blun & ur 3*
	P		**Country Madam** (5a) 9-2 L Jefford *Bhnd; lost tch 8; pu & dism 10*
	U		**Final Chance** (5a) 6-1 Miss C Tizzard *Nt fluent; prom; ld 7-9; hit 13; ld agn til hit nxt & hdd; ev ch when blun & ur 15*
[315ᶠ]	U		**Miner's Hall (IRE)** 4-5F Miss T Cave *(xnb) Drpd out 15l bhnd rest; clsng 9; blun & ur 10*
	U		**Pennys Boy** 20-1 E Gretton *Jmpd slow 1; midfield when blun & ur 3*
[253³]	F		**Saucy's Wolf** (bl) 12-1 Jeremy Young *Chsd ldrs til fell hvly 6*

OFFICIAL DISTANCES: 20l, 25l TIME: 6min 58.6s

Thurlow

Horseheath (RH 10F,18J) Sat, 4 Mar (GOOD to SOFT, SOFT in places)

411 Open Maiden (Div 1), 12st   12 ran

	1		**CLARET AND BLUE** 4-1 B Pollock *(xnb) Bit bckwd; nt fluent early; handy in 4/5th til 8l 3rd; stdy hdwy to press ldr 3 out; led nxt; forged clr frm last; improve*
[131⁴]	2	5	**Just The Business** 7-1 P Bull *(xnb) Hld up in 6/7th; in tch til 12l 5th & outpcd 14; r.o aft nxt; prsd ldr 3 out; led nxt*
[123⁴]	3	3	**Ginger Pudding** 20-1 W Wales *Off pce in 5/6th til stdy hdwy frm 11; 10l 4th 14; jnd ldr 3 out; one pce & btn nxt; much improved eff*

[180P]	4	3	**About Time (IRE)** 20-1 T Lane *Mid-div; in tch in 6th 12; chsd ldrs 14; hdwy 3 out; disp 8l 4th & no imp when lft 4th at last; much btr rn*
[290⁴]	U		**Cardinal Bud (IRE)** 6-1 P Taiano *Trckd ldrs; 6l 3rd when blun & ur 10*
[194³]	F		**Chadwick Bank (IRE)** 7-2F R Cope *A rr of main group & nvr gng wl; mist 8; fell 11*
[180⁴]	P		**County Derry** 16-1 A Sansome *Rr of main group; lft last 11; t.o 14; pu 16*
[373²]	P		**Fortune Hunter (IRE)** 4-1 P Millington *Imm rr; nt jw til ur 7*
	P		**Life Of A Star (IRE)** 10-1 P Piddington *Nt fluent & school in last; sn t.o; pu 10*
[284⁵]	F		**Minino (IRE)** (bl) 8-1 N King *Hit 1; trckd ldr in 2-3l 2nd frm 2; prsd ldr 3 out & ev ch til wknd nxt; disp 8l 4th when fell hvly last*
	U		**Sayonara** 4-1 C Ward *Nt jw in rr; pckd bad 6; blun & ur 9*
[372P]	P		**The Last Shout (IRE)** (bl) 20-1 R Armson *Ld 1; mostly 2-3l up til jnd 3 out; hdd & stpd to nil; exhaust & releg last when pu last*

OFFICIAL DISTANCES: 5l, 3l **TIME:** 6min 56.0s **TOTE:** £3.50 **DF:** £58.50

412 Open Maiden (Div 2), 12st
12 ran

[284³]	1		**KENNY DAVIS (IRE)** 3-1 P Blagg *Ww in mid-div; hdwy 9; cl up 12; ld 14; jnd nxt til ld 2 out; sprinted clr & in comm last; easy*
[194P]	2	25	**Nelsun** 2-1F B Pollock *Disp 3rd til 5l 3rd aft 10; outpcd 14 & sn no ch w wnr; 20l 3rd aft 2 out; kpt on; went mod 2nd aft last; all out*
[372P]	3	½	**Mandalay Man** 14-1 R Armson *Last early; slt hdwy frm 14; jnd tiring rivals app 2 out; kpt on one pce to 3rd flat; nvr any ch*
	4	½	**Hagon Beck** 12-1 W Wales *Hld up towards rr; gd hdwy frm 12; 5l 3rd 14; disp ld nxt-3 out; sn brushed aside by wnr; 15l 2nd & exhaust when virt stpd last; lost 2 plces flat; promising*
[237²]	5	½	**David Bruce** 5-2 R Fowler *Trckd ldr; 8l 2nd 6; ld 10-14; prsd ldr to 3 out; imm outpcd & sn no ch*
[373P]	P		**Ali's Lark** 20-1 J Oldring *Ld & mist 1; drpd back qckly; last when pu 10*
[237⁵]	P		**Always Trying** (7a) 20-1 A Sansome *Prom til ld 3; 5l clr 5; hung rt & v reluct app 10; sn hdd; cl 2nd 12; wknd v qckly; t.o 15; pu 3 out*
[237⁴]	P		**Cicero's Law (IRE)** 8-1 P Chinery *Trckd ldrs; 4l 3rd when blun 9 & rdr shot up horse's nk; lost plce qckly; rr when pu 12*
[97P]	P		**Colemore Green** 20-1 M Gingell *Sn towards rr & nvr gng wl; barely galloping 11; pu 13*
[97P]	P		**Josh's Choice (IRE)** (7a) 6-1 S Sporborg *A towards rr; lsng tch when mist 13; virt t.o when pu last*
[373P]	P		**Mighty Monarch (IRE)** 14-1 P Millington *Pulling in rr; mist 6; hdwy 13; 3l 4th when blun 15; wknd v rap; pu 3 out*
[132⁴]	P		**Rag Bolt (IRE)** 16-1 S R Andrews *Sn outpcd in mid-div; bhnd 13; t.o when pu 3 out*

OFFICIAL DISTANCES: dist, ½l **TIME:** 6min 55.0s **TOTE:** £9.00 **DF:** £11.00

413 Intermediate, 12st
8 ran

[75P]	1		**NOUGHTOSIXTY (IRE)** 5-2 B Pollock *Ld 3; 4l up 15; almost jnd & jmpd awkward 3 out; jnd agn & lft wl clr 2 out; hvly eased flat*
[318²]	2	12	**Nibble** 6-1 G Cooper *Mist 3; a rr & nvr gng pce; disp last 11; t.o 14; stayed on frm nxt; lft 2nd 2 out by defections*
[288⁶]	3	15	**Borrow Mine (IRE)** (bl) 20-1 A Braithwaite *Jb & nvr gng wl; mostly 6th; t.o 14; lft dist 3rd 2 out by defections*
[93⁵]	F		**Bakmalad** 33-1 D Kemp *A last pr; last 7-10; disp last nxt til fell 13*
[288¹]	F		**Fair Exchange** 4-9F P Taiano *Ld to 2; 2l 2nd aft; hit 8; eff 15; rdn to chall & outj 3 out; rnwd eff & level when fell nxt*
[288P]	P		**Generous Deal (IRE)** 25-1 A Sansome *Pulling; chsd ldng pr; 2l 3rd 7; jmpd slow & lost tch 10; wknd qckly 13; wl bhnd when pu 3 out*
[127ʳ]	P		**Moon Rising** 20-1 P Bull *Ab 5-6l 4th til outpcd 11; blun nxt & imm pu*
	P		**Regency Cottage** 20-1 W Wales *Mostly 5th; rdn & chsd ldrs 10; went 15l 3rd 14; no further hdwy; v tired 3 out; pu nxt*

OFFICIAL DISTANCES: 15l, 20l **TIME:** 6min 51.0s **TOTE:** £3.30 **DF:** £14.70

414 Greig Middleton Ladies Open
10 ran

[240⁴]	1		**EMSEE-H** 14-1 Miss Z Turner *Cl 2nd til disp ld 6-8; disp ld agn frm 10; 2l up aft 15; forged clr frm 3 out; amazing*
[305P]	2	6	**Newtown Rosie (IRE)** (5a) 25-1 Mrs S Hickman *Chsd ldrs in 5/6th; hdwy 11; 6l 3rd & mist 15; 4l 2nd nxt; jmpd slow nxt; stayed on; a hld*
[28³]	3	2	**Andrelot** (bl) 10-1 Miss C Grissell *Rr & wl off pce; rem 5th when hit 14; r.o frm nxt; stayed on past btn rivals frm 3 out*
[319F]	4	8	**Uron V (FR)** 5-1 Miss T Hayter *Sa; a rr; mist 5; wl bhnd 11; kpt on stdly frm 14*
[319U]	5	5	**Lets Twist Again (IRE)** 20-1 Miss A Stennett *Cl up til disp ld 6; ld 9-10; cl up til wknd qckly 13; wl in rr 15; one pce 3 out*

[368^F]	6	3	**Black Book (IRE)** (5a) 33-1 *Miss A Burton A rr; last 5; plodded on frm 14*
[240³]	7	2	**Dance On Sixpence** 7-1 *Mrs S Hodge (xnb) Chsd ldrs in 3-4l 3rd to 15; still 10l 3rd when wknd v rap 3 out*
[95⁵]	8	15	**Ballyedward (IRE)** 14-1 *Miss H Pewter Mid-div to 3; thrashed but drpd to rr nxt; thrashed agn 7; stdly lost tch; t.o 14 & thrashed agn; plodded on*
[319²]	P		**Cache Fleur (FR)** 2-5F *Mrs G d'Angibau Ld to 5; drpd to 4th nxt; 8l 6th & nt gng wl 10; pu 12; lame*
[287⁴]	r		**Cill Churnain (IRE)** 16-1 *Mrs E Coveney V keen to start; charged & broke tapes; charged tapes agn; 50yds back & facing wrong way when flagged drpd; tk no part*

OFFICIAL DISTANCES: 2½l, 3l **TIME:** 6min 51.0s **TOTE:** £10.40 **DF:** £130.20

415 Mens Open, 12st
4 ran

[218¹]	1		**HATCHAM BOY (IRE)** 5-2 *C Ward-Thomas Cl 2nd til ld brief 11; prsd ldr aft til ld & qcknd clr bef 3 out; sn clr & in comm; nt fluent 2 out; easy*
[286^F]	2	12	**Teeton Builds** 6-1 *A Sansome Ld; hdd brief 11; ld agn 12 til hdd app 3 out; nt qckn & sn no ch; kpt on one pce; fin tired*
[262¹]	3	10	**Ruperts Choice (IRE)** (7x) (bl) 1-2F *S Sporborg Clup rr; 4l 4th 7; eff to disp ld 12-13; releg 3rd nxt; nt qckn 15; wknd v tame; btn when hit 2 out; walked in*
	P		**Veryvel (CZE)** 7-1 *D Kemp Cl 3rd; pckd 11 & nt qckn; 8l 4th nxt; lost tch qckly; 15l last when pu 14*

OFFICIAL DISTANCES: 15l, 10l **TIME:** 6min 47.0s **TOTE:** £3.60 **DF:** £12.30

416 Restricted, 12st
19 ran

[285⁵]	1		**ROYAL BANKER (IRE)** 2-1F *N Bloom Trckd ldr; 3-4l 2nd frm 7 til eff 15; ld 3 out; jnd nxt; hrd rdn & just hld on*
[304³]	2	s hd	**Lillooet (IRE)** (5a) (bl) 12-1 *C Gordon Mid-div; 7/8th til stdy hdwy 12; 8l 4th 15; jnd ldr 2 out; hrd rdn & r.o wl last; a just hld (lost nothing in defeat)*
[306^U]	3	12	**Ishma (IRE)** (bl) 6-1 *D Page 2 handlers; 5/6th; hit 6; stdy hdwy frm 11; 12l 4th 14; one pce & no ch frm 3 out*
[285⁷]	4	8	**Holiday Time (IRE)** (5a) 10-1 *Mrs S Hodge Chsd ldrs in 3rd/4th to 14; 3rd & nt qckn nxt; sn no ch; dem 2 out*
	5	25	**White Smoke (IRE)** 25-1 *R Ross Sn wl in rr; 15th 9; t.o 15; plodded on*
[321^F]	P		**Beau Joueur (FR)** (bl) 10-1 *A Coe Rr to 8; hdwy to mid-div & mist 10; sn drpd to rr agn; t.o 14; coasted on til pu 3 out*
[290^P]	P		**Calipo Bello (IRE)** 10-1 *S Sporborg Swtng; tde; a rr & nvr gng wl; t.o 14; coasted on til pu 3 out*
[321^P]	P		**Coolest By Phar (IRE)** (tt) 20-1 *D Cook Ld 2-5; prom when hmpd by loose horse aft 9; stdly wknd frm 11; pu 14*
	P		**Coptic Dancer** (5a) 10-1 *W Wales Imm rr; hit 4; last nxt; barely galloping when pu 7*
[98^P]	P		**Full Bore (IRE)** 10-1 *T Lane Rr & outpcd; wl bhnd frm 11; t.o 14; pu 16*
[291^P]	P		**Granite's Surprise** 14-1 *C O'Brien Sn towards rr of main group; 12th & strugg 10; barely galloping 12; pu 13*
	P		**Here Comes Trouble** 16-1 *A Braithwaite A rr; nt fluent; wl bhnd when pu 12*
[285^U]	P		**Joyful Hero** (5a) 8-1 *Miss P Ellison Sn rr & nt gng wl; wl bhnd frm 11; t.o 14; pu 3 out*
[96^P]	P		**Mackoy (IRE)** 12-1 *M Gingell Chsd ldrs in mostly 5/6th; wknd 15 & lost tch rap; t.o 5th when pu last*
[321^P]	P		**Skinsey Finnegan (IRE)** 8-1 *A Sansome Prom; ld 6; 3-4l up til hdd & wknd v rap 3 out; exhaust 6th when pu last*
[321²]	P		**Therewearethen (USA)** 4-1 *N King Final trio & nvr gng wl; wl bhnd til pu 12*
	U		**Top Of The Range (IRE)** 12-1 *R Fowler (xnb) Towards rr when blun & ur 2*
[179^P]	P		**Warner For Sport** 25-1 *A Harvey 2 handlers; a wl in rr; blun 8; pu 14*
[322^P]	P		**Wise Point (IRE)** 25-1 *G Lush Mid-div 9/10th to 10; stdly wknd; wl bhnd 13; pu 15*

OFFICIAL DISTANCES: hd, 10l **TIME:** 6min 56.0s **TOTE:** £2.30 **DF:** £30.80

417 Confined, 12st
7 ran

[175^F]	1		**TOM DE SAVOIE (IRE)** (3x) 1-2F *W Wales A cl up & gng wl; trckd ldrs in 3rd; smooth hdwy to ld 14; drew wl clr 3 out; v easy*
[177^U]	2	25	**Peanuts Pet** (5x) 8-1 *Miss H Barnard Ld; 4l up 9; jmpd slow 9 & 10 & hdd; prsd ldr til outpcd 14; chsd ldr vain til wknd aft 3 out*
	P		**Chris's Lad** 10-1 *M Gingell On heels of ldrs; 2l 4th 12; pu nxt (bleeding frm off-fore hoof)*
[91^U]	R		**Damier Blanc (FR)** (bl) 20-1 *Miss J Slack Disp 2l 2nd when rn out thro wing & ur 4*
[241^P]	P		**Dynamite Dan (IRE)** 20-1 *N King Pulling; trckd ldr in cl 2nd til ld 10-13; wknd rap into 3rd 15; 20l down when pu 3 out*
[259^U]	U		**Mister Main Man (IRE)** 7-1 *S Sporborg Disp 2l 2nd when rfo aft 4*

[238²] P   **Prince Of Saints (IRE)** (7x) 4-1 A Sansome *Nvr gng wl in last; in tch til rdn & hung lft & rt 10; to & pu 11*

OFFICIAL DISTANCE: dist TIME: 6min 58.0s TOTE: £1.40 DF: £5.40

Tynedale
Corbridge (RH 9F,18J) Sat, 4 Mar (GOOD with SOFT patches)

418 Hunt   **7 ran**

[108³] 1   **CLAYWALLS** 6-4F M Clayton *Lw; ld/disp to 3; made most aft; jnd 6-8; 2l up 15; stayed on wl*

        2   4   **Denim Blue** 4-1 Miss P Robson *Prom; 4l 6th app 6; prog 12 to disp 2l 3rd 14; 2½l 4th nxt; 2l 2nd & ev ch last; one pce flat; btr for rce*

[363³] 3   nk   **Setting Sail** (5a) 6-1 Mrs V Jackson *In tch; 6th 5; prog to 2l 3rd 10; ev ch 2 out; 2½l down when hit last; kpt on u.p flat; improve*

[360⁷] 4   5   **Madame Defarge** (5a) (tt) 7-2 Mrs K Hargreave *Oht; a rr; 8l last 4; 6l 6th 13; outpcd 15; kpt on; nd*

[361⁵] 5   2fncs **Reve De Valse (USA)** (tt) 20-1 Miss V Burn *Cl up; 5l 6th 7; mist 9 & outpcd; nt fluent 11; sn 10l last; 25l down & wkng 13; sn fnce bhnd*

[110⁵] F   **Ballyboden** 10-1 F Arthur *Ld/disp early; 2l 3rd 4; handy when fell 15*

        U   **Tenella's Last** 10-1 L Morgan *Oht; ld/disp; 2l 3rd 3; disp ld 6 & 8; trckd ldr til outpcd 3 out; btn 4th when ur 2 out*

OFFICIAL DISTANCES: 5l, nk, 6l TIME: 6min 45.0s

419 Confined, 12st   **13 ran**

[359¹] 1   **PARADE RACER** (6x) 11-10F A Richardson *Rr early; 6th & gng wl 10; hdwy 12; mist 14; 1l 2nd nxt; ld & mist last; pushed out flat*

[362ᴿ] 2   ½   **Charlieadams (IRE)** 4-1 J Muir *Ld; 6l clr 13; 1l up 15; hdd aft 2 out; ½l down & lkd hld when gvn ev ch agn last; nt qckn*

[359⁷] 3   20   **The Green Fool** 25-1 H Humble *(xnb) Trckd ldr; disp 2l 2nd 5; outpcd 14; 8l 5th 16; wknd aft; fin tired*

[359ᵁ] 4   5   **Senora D'Or** (5a) 33-1 Miss M Bremner *In tch; 3½l 4th 15; sn outpcd; kpt on; wknd app last; tired flat; btr for rce*

[183⁵] 5   5   **Branch End** 12-1 F Arthur *A rr; outpcd; 20l off pce 6; t.o 16; kpt on wl app 2 out*

[183⁵] 6   runin **With Respect** 66-1 Miss D Crole *Mid-div til rr 11; lost tch nxt; sn t.o*

[186⁵] P   **Galzig** 16-1 P Maitland-Carew *Trckd ldrs; 5l 4th 6; in tch til outpcd 14; wknd 16; t.o & pu 2 out*

        P   **Givemeyourhand (IRE)** 33-1 D Jewett *Oht; swtng; chsd ldrs; rmdrs 8; lost tch 12; t.o & pu last*

        P   **Hollow Palm (IRE)** 10-1 R Morgan *(xnb) Ld rnd start; unruly; sa; a rr; 25l off pce 6; mist 8; school & sn t.o; pu last*

[110⁴] F   **Kings Lane** 6-1 Miss P Robson *Prom til fell 2*

        P   **Mandika** 20-1 J Walton *Mid-div; mist 6; outpcd when mist 12; sn bhnd; t.o & pu last*

        F   **Strathmore Lodge** (5a) 12-1 L Morgan *Lw; in tch; pushed along 9; fell 12*

        P   **Weejumpawud** (5a,5x) 5-1 B Lusted *Hdstrng; mostly 2nd/3rd; 3l down 4; disp 2l 2nd nxt; 3l 3rd 15; ev ch 3 out; wknd qckly aft 2 out; tired & pu last*

OFFICIAL DISTANCES: 1l, dist, 6l TIME: 6min 29.0s
The owner of Charlieadams, whose passport was found to be not in order, was fined £100

420 Intermediate, 12st   **11 ran**

        1   **LITTLE BROCKWELL (IRE)** (5a) (tt) 2-1F Miss P Robson *2 handlers; oht; reared over bckwds padd; settled rr; 6l 9th 6; 10l off pce 13; prog to 8l 5th 15; stayed on str nxt; chall & ld flat*

[183⁵] 2   ½   **Poynder Park (IRE)** 3-1 L Morgan *Prom; mist 9; went 4l 3rd 14; ev ch app last; sltly hmpd; tk 2nd flat; all out*

[188ᵁ] 3   ½   **Harleyburn** (bl) 40-1 Mrs A Hamilton *In tch in main group; 5l off pce 6; prog to ld app 13; 2l up 2 out; hrd prsd last; hdd flat; kpt on; improve*

[359⁵] 4   6   **Fragrant Lord** 6-1 Mrs V Jackson *Ld/disp til 1l up 4; mist 9; 6l 4th & ch 15; outpcd aft nxt; kpt on wl*

[168²] 5   3   **Mr Bossman (IRE)** 9-4 T Glass *Oht; ld/disp til ld 10; 1l 2nd 13; outpcd 2 out; kpt on one pce*

[359⁵] P   **Commanche Scout (IRE)** 6-1 T Oates *(xnb) Prom; outpcd 14; lsng tch when pu 2 out; improve*

[108ᵁ] F   **Driminamore (IRE)** 7-1 Miss R Ramsay *Oht; prom; trckd ldr frm 9; 1l 2nd nxt; fell 12*

	U		**Joss Bay** 14-1 **T Davidson** *2 handlers; oht; in tch in rr til pckd, slpd & ur 4*
[183ᴾ]	P		**Lindon Run** 16-1 **R Morgan** *Ld/disp til outpcd 9; rmdrs nxt; lsng tch 15; pu 2 out*
	P		**Noneofyourbusiness (IRE)** (5a) 20-1 **Miss C Metcalfe** *Jmpd lft; sn bhnd; jmpd slow 5; 25l last 6; t.o & pu 9*
	F		**Tin Cup** 20-1 **C Storey** *In tch in main group; 5l off pce when fell 11*

OFFICIAL DISTANCES: ¾l, ½l, 6l   **TIME:** 6min 35.0s

421 Ladies Open, 3m5f - 21J   12 ran

[301¹]	1		**BALISTEROS (FR)** 4-5F **Miss P Robson** *Rr; prog to 12l 4th 13 & 3l 2nd 16; 1l down 3 out; ld bef nxt; stayed on wl*
[358¹]	2	4	**Across The Card** (tt) 8-1 **Miss R Ramsay** *Rr; 15l 5th 9; prog 11 to 3l 3rd 18; stayed on; nt pce to chall*
	3	8	**Pharmistice (IRE)** 10-1 **Miss N Stirling** *(xnb) 2 handlers; oht; rcd wide; trckd ldrs; 11 2nd 7; qcknd to ld 9; mist 11; hdd aft 3 out; kpt on one pce; btr for pce*
[183ᶠ]	4	3	**Houselope Beck** 4-1 **Miss C Hall** *In tch in rr; outpcd 16; some prog aft; 6l 4th 18; stayed on; nt prsd when ch gone*
[280ᴾ]	5	nk	**Miss Accounts (IRE)** (5a) 9-1 **Miss A Armitage** *Prom; 8l 4th app 8; 17l 4th aft nxt; outpcd 17; kpt on*
[280⁴]	6	4	**Cab On Target** 12-1 **Miss W Gibson** *Ld/disp til ld 4; 2l 3rd app 8; chsd ldrs; mist 15; 5l 4th 18; sn outpcd; kpt on*
[218⁶]	7	12	**Strongalong (IRE)** 10-1 **Miss K Roncoroni** *Rr; 20l 11th 10; some prog 12; outpcd 16; kpt on*
[360ᴾ]	P		**Buckaroo** (5a) 50-1 **Mrs A Tweedie** *Ld/disp; 11 2nd 4; ld 5; qcknd pce 8; 11 2nd nxt; ld brief agn 10; outpcd 12; wknd 16; t.o & pu 2 out; improve*
	P		**Dun Law** (8ow) 66-1 **Mrs K Weir** *Mid-div; lost tch 13; t.o & pu last*
[111⁹]	P		**Madame Bella** (5a) 50-1 **Miss J Hollands** *Rr; 7l last 3; jmpd lft 5 & 6; lost tch 16; t.o & pu 2 out*
	P		**Mirror Melody** (5a) (tt) 50-1 **Mrs M Robinson** *(xnb,bf)Rr; mist 12; sn outpcd; t.o & pu 2 out*
[135⁷]	U		**Steel Rigg (IRE)** 12-1 **Mrs V Jackson** *Rr but in tch; 15l down 7; wkng when blun & ur 14*

OFFICIAL DISTANCES: 5l, 9l, 3l   **TIME:** 7min 57.0s

422 Land Rover Mens Open, 3m5f, 12st - 21J   8 ran

[186²]	1		**COOL YULE (IRE)** (7x) (bl) 6-1 **W Renwick** *A.p; 5l 5th 7; hdwy 10; ld/disp 12-15; cl 2nd til chall 18; ld 2 out; sn clr; stayed on str*
[89⁶]	2	15	**Dennett Lough** 8-1 **B Lusted** *(boh) In tch in rr; 7l 7th 9; 8l 3rd when mist 18; outpcd bef nxt; stayed on wl 4 out*
[279²]	3	10	**Concerto Collonges (FR)** (4x) 7-2 **R Hartley** *(xnb) A rr; 10l last 9; climbed 18 & outpcd; 25l 6th 3 out; stayed on wl flat*
[362³]	4	hd	**Mullingar (IRE)** 50-1 **L Morgan** *Prom; disp 3l 3rd 9; 4th 13; 12l 5th & outpcd 16; mist nxt; disp 20l 4th 18; kpt on*
[155³]	5	nk	**Overflowing River (IRE)** (7x) 7-4F **T Glass** *Chsd ldrs; 7l 6th aft 7; 3l 3rd 10; 5th & pushed along 13; disp 20l 4th 18; kpt on*
[155⁵]	6	s hd	**Ensign Ewart (IRE)** (7x) (bl) 2-1 **C Storey** *Trckd ldrs; disp 3l 3rd & hit 10; jmpd slow 12; 5l 4th & rmdrs aft; gd prog to disp ld 14; ld aft 16; mist 18; hdd & rmdrs app 2 out; 3l 2nd last; v tired & wandering flat; lost sev plces*
[376⁵]	7	runin	**Lottery Ticket (IRE)** (7x) 100-1 **S J Robinson** *Trckd ldrs; pushed along 3; cl 2nd 5-10; 10l last & wkng 13; rmdrs aft; sn lost tch; climbed last*
	P		**Thank U Jim** 12-1 **R Morgan** *Tde; nt a fluent; ld; mists 4 & 5; 2l up 8; outpcd & hdd 13; sn lost plce; climbed 18; t.o & pu last*

OFFICIAL DISTANCES: 20l, 12l, hd   **TIME:** 7min 56.0s

The rider of Overflowing River was fined £50 for excessive use of the whip

423 Restricted (Div 1)   13 ran

[111²]	1		**MOUNTAIN THYNE (IRE)** 6-4F **Miss P Robson** *Hmpd start; rr; 10l last 7; prog 13; disp cl 2nd 16; ld & jmpd rt last; rdn out*
[111⁸]	2	3	**Storm Alive (IRE)** 20-1 **Mrs V Jackson** *Chsd ldrs; 10l 4th 5; 3l 4th & ev ch 3 out; outpcd app last; rvo u.p to tk 2nd flat*
[184²]	3	2½	**Blyth Brook** 7-2 **C Storey** *In tch; prog to trck ldrs 9; ld 12; 2l up 14; ½l up 3 out; hdd but still ev ch last; wknd flat*
[184⁷]	4	15	**Luvly Bubbly** 10-1 **Miss C Hall** *Rr of main bunch; outpcd 14; nd; fin wl u.p*
[188³]	5	1½	**Dram Hurler (IRE)** 7-1 **R Morgan** *Chsd ldrs; prog & gng wl 13; 5l 5th 15; outpcd bef nxt*
[113⁶]	6	20	**Good Profit** 50-1 **T Davidson** *In tch early; pushed along & lsng tch 10; rmdrs aft; 25l last 15; t.o*
[364ᴾ]	7	10	**Wylup** 33-1 **H Humble** *Prom early; 2l 2nd 4; trckd ldr aft til outpcd 9; wkng 13; t.o*

[375ᴾ]	P	**Abbey Lad** 10-1 *L Morgan* Ld/disp early; 8l 3rd 5; 6l 6th 15; short-lived eff nxt; wknd qckly & pu 2 out
	P	**Beach Patrol (IRE)** 25-1 *T Oates* Lw; rr; pushed along 9; lsng tch nxt; rmdrs 11 & no resp; pu 12
	U	**Castle Bay (IRE)** 20-1 *P Johnson* (xnb,bf) Unruly start; jinked rt & ur
	P	**Disrespect** (5a) 12-1 *Miss M Macmillan* Prom til outpcd 13; lsng tch nxt; pu last
[189¹]	P	**Nickys Peril** (5a) 5-2 *W Renwick* (xnb) Mists; mid-div; hit 7; prog 14; disp ½l 2nd 16; wknd v qckly; pu last
[364ᴾ]	P	**Political Bill** 20-1 *T Scott* Ld; 3l up 5; hdd aft 11; wknd; t.o & pu 2 out

OFFICIAL DISTANCES: 4l, 3l, dist **TIME:** 6min 41.0s

424 Restricted (Div 2) 12 ran

[281²]	1		**BROKEN ENGLISH** (5a) 7-2 *R Morgan* In tch; 3l 4th 7; prog 12 to disp ld 15; ev ch 2 out; sn outpcd; hld when mist & lft clr last; rdn out
[89⁸]	2	3	**Shingle Beach (IRE)** (bl) 5-2 *Miss P Robson* Chsd ldrs; 5l 3rd 4; rmdrs 10; outpcd 15 & sn bhnd; stayed on wl app 2 out; ev ch app last; nt rch ldr
[184ᴾ]	3	1	**Dunnellie** (5a) 6-1 *A Robson* Rr; 6l 6th app 8; 8l 4th 16; kpt on wl app last
	4	8	**Notoobig** 10-1 *T Glass* Chsd ldrs; prog to 4l 3rd 10; ld/disp frm 12; ev ch 3 out; outpcd aft nxt; wknd app last
[363ᶠ]	5	25	**Rye Rum (IRE)** 5-1 *J Walton* In tch; 6l 4th 4; outpcd 12; lost tch nxt; t.o 2 out
[184²]	6	6	**Solwaysands** (bl) 20-1 *S Hughes* Ld til hdd 12; 8l 7th & wkng 14; t.o
	7	2fncs	**Cruise Around** 12-1 *S Ramsay* Unruly & reluct to start; set off 1½ fncs bhnd; a t.o
[182ᵁ]	F		**Big Bark (IRE)** 16-1 *H Norton* Rr; last of group 10; lost tch 14; wl bhnd when fell 3 out
[358ᶠ]	F		**Derring Dan** 16-1 *Miss H Gray* Mid-div til fell 5
[360ᶠ]	U		**Geordies Express** 5-4F *A Richardson* 6/4-5/4; hld up; 10l 10th aft 5; prog 10; ld/disp app 13; ld aft 2 out w rdr lkng rnd; in comm when blun & ur last; unlucky
[113²]	F		**Happy Blake** 8-1 *L Morgan* Hdstrng; settled mid-div 5; jmpd rt & fell 9
[360ᴾ]	P		**Mini Cruise** 14-1 *L Morgan* Prom early; 2l disp 13; wl bhnd when pu last

OFFICIAL DISTANCES: 5l, 1l, 10l **TIME:** 6min 45.0s

425 Confined Maiden (Div 1) 13 ran

[187ᴾ]	1		**BORDER FARMER (IRE)** 12-1 *Mrs V Jackson* (xnb) Chsd ldrs; pckd 4; prog 15; 8l 4th & staying on nxt; ½l 2nd at last; ld flat & r.o u.p
	2	1	**The Peeler (IRE)** 9-1 *W Renwick* In tch 10; prog to 1½l 3rd 14; just ld 2 out-last; sn hdd & hung lft u.p
[114ᶠ]	3	2	**Nisbet** 6-1 *Miss M Bremner* A.p; 1l 2nd 6; ld/disp aft 12; ½l up when pckd 14; ev ch 2 out-last; no ex flat
[112³]	4	1	**Briar Rose (IRE)** (12a) 5-1 *J Ewart* (bf) A.p; 2½l 3rd 5; ev ch 14; 10l 5th & outpcd 3 out; kpt on wl
	5	½	**Divet Hill** 5-1 *M Clayton* Sis; school in rr; 25l last 4; 10l 7th 16; improve
[187ᵁ]	6	6	**Cool Kevin** 12-1 *S Hughes* (bf) Mid-div; outpcd 14; 8l 6th nxt; sn wknd
[188²]	7	15	**Sunnycliff** (tt) 6-4F *C Storey* (xnb)Cl up; ld/disp frm 12; cl 2nd 14; ev ch 3 out; wknd rap app nxt; wl bhnd when climbed last; walked in
	F		**Ballylesson (IRE)** (7a) 4-1 *Miss P Robson* Mid-div til fell 9
[44⁵]	C		**Blackchesters** 5-1 *J Walton* Handy; 1½l 3rd 7; carried out by loose horse 9
	F		**Harry Laws** 20-1 *T Scott* (xnb) Ld; 1l up 6; cruising in ld when fell 8
	P		**Shenoso** (12a) 25-1 *R Robinson* Tubed; mid-div; sn strugg; wl bhnd when pu 9
	P		**Souden Lyric** 10-1 *A Richardson* Nt jw; sis; a rr; hit 5; mist 12; 25l last 15; t.o & pu 2 out
	F		**The Dyke Louper** (5a) 7-1 *B Lusted* Chsd ldrs; 5l 4th 6; cl up & gng wl when skidded & fell 14

OFFICIAL DISTANCES: 2l, 4l, 2l **TIME:** 6min 49.0s

426 Confined Maiden (Div 2) 6 ran

	1		**BORDER BURN** 2-1 *J Ewart* 100/30-2s; green; jmpd big 1; ld/disp at sedate pce; 2l 2nd 4; disp ld 6; lft in ld 9; napped for boxes & hdd 11; trckd ldr til ld app 2 out; stayed on str u.p; all out
[187ᴾ]	2	½	**Anotherhandyman** 5-1 *P Johnson* Rr; 20l last 5; still 20l 4th 3 out; rap hdwy aft; 3l down at last; 2nd & clsng flat; just too much to do
	3	3	**I Say Dancer (IRE)** (5a) 25-1 *Miss C Metcalfe* In tch; 10l 3rd 13; prog to 5l 3rd 15; ev ch app last; nt qckn flat
	P		**Naughty Feelings** 6-1 *T Scott* Trckd ldng pr; disp 10l 3rd 5; wknd 10; sn wl bhnd; t.o last when climbed 14 & pu
	U		**Shay Gap (IRE)** 11-10F *C Storey* (xnb) Ld/disp at sedate pce; 1l up 4; jnd when swerved & tried to duck out 6; ur 9

P   **Swiftly Supreme (IRE)** (5a) 3-1 T Davidson *2 handlers; hdstrng; disp 10l 3rd 5; hit 8; ld 11-3 out; hdd & outpcd when mist 2 out; sn pu & dism; exhaust*

OFFICIAL DISTANCES: ½l, 3l   TIME: 7min 11.0s

Bicester with Whaddon Chase
Mollington (RH 8F,18J) Sun, 5 Mar (HEAVY, sticky)

427 Hunt   4 ran

	1		**PERFECT MINSTREL (IRE)** 6-1 F Hutsby *Hld up in tch; eff to ld aft 15; clr app last; rdn & stayed str*
[296⁸]	2	25	**Blayneys Privilege** 4-1 Miss T Habgood *2 handlers; cl up til outpcd frm 3 out; kpt on slow frm last to tk poor 2nd nr fin*
[193ᵁ]	3	¾	**Final Analysis** 2-5F J Owen *Cl up; rmdrs 11; ld 12-14; mist 15; drvn to chall agn bef 2 out; btn when mist last; walking flat & dem nr fin*
[191⁷]	4	20	**Murberry (IRE)** (5a) 14-1 A Barlow *Made most to 12; ld agn 14 til aft nxt; wknd 3 out*

OFFICIAL DISTANCES: 15l, 1l   TIME: 7min 06.0s

428 Confined, 12st   10 ran

[243⁶]	1		**THE HATCHER (NZ)** 25-1 R Lawther *(bf) Ld to 9; ld agn 12; kicked on bef nxt; 6l up 3 out; rdn & stayed on frm 2 out*
[294⁹]	2	6	**Chicodari** 16-1 E Walker *25s-16s; rdn into fncs & jmpd lft 1st circ; prom; chsd wnr aft 12; rdn & no imp 3 out; kpt on*
[74¹]	3	15	**Live Wire (IRE)** 9-4 G Kerr *Chsd ldr to 8; outpcd bef 13; lost tch 15; kpt on one pce frm 2 out to tk 3rd nr fin*
[248¹]	4	1	**Northern Yarn** 5-1 C Weaver *Hld up in tch; prog 12; outpcd bef nxt; eff & lft 3rd 3 out; no imp aft; wknd flat; lost 3rd nr fin*
[243ᴾ]	P		**Its Murphy Man** 33-1 C Wadland *Mist 6; a rr; wknd 12; pu 13*
[297³]	F		**Just Like Madge** (5a,3x) 11-10F J Tarry *Mostly trckd ldrs; outpcd 13; rdn & eff to disp 6l 2nd when fell 3 out*
	P		**Silly Boy** (7a,3ow) 33-1 A Tutton *2 handlers; drpd to last 4; mist 8; wknd & pu 11*
	F		**Smart Teacher (USA)** 33-1 G Carenza *(xnb) Hld up; prog 5; trckd ldr 8; ld 9-12; wknd qckly; 6th when fell 13*
	P		**Tarry Awhile** 33-1 Miss R Goodwin *2 handlers; in tch; pushed along 10; wknd aft 12; t.o & pu 15*
[191ᴾ]	P		**Templeroan Prince** 33-1 M Cowley *Rmdrs aft 2; sn rr; wkng when mist & pu 12*

OFFICIAL DISTANCES: 4l, 12l   TIME: 7min 07.0s

429 Dodson & Horrell PPORA Club Members, 12st   9 ran

[296ᶠ]	1		**GRECIAN STAR** (7x) 1-2F J Tarry *Lw; hld up early; clsd 8; pushed along 11; ld aft 12; clr 2 out; r.o str*
[247⁶]	2	15	**Cool Work** 20-1 E Walker *A cl up; rmdr 11; 3rd 13; eff to chse wnr app 2 out; no imp; kpt on*
[248²]	3	3	**Furious Avenger** 8-1 L Lay *Swtng; ld to 2; w ldr til ld agn 9 til aft 12; mist 14; chsd wnr til app 2 out; one pce*
[246³]	4	15	**Royal Orchard** 9-1 A Martin *Hld up wl in rr; clsd 10; outpcd bef 13; disp poor 5th 3 out; kpt on*
[80⁴]	5	15	**Tranquil Lord (IRE)** 9-1 D Smith *Rn in snatches; lost plce 6; jmpd lft nxt; clsd agn 10; bhnd frm 13; disp poor 5th 3 out; walked in*
[250ᶠ]	6	5	**Upanoff** (5a) 33-1 B Pauling *Prom; rmdr 11; lost tch w ldng trio 14; 4th & no ch 3 out; wknd; walked in*
[246⁴]	7	30	**Grange Prize** 33-1 Miss K Henry *Bckwd; bhnd frm 6; wl t.o 9; 2 fncs bhnd 2 out*
	P		**Goforitmrsmulligan (IRE)** (5a) 14-1 P Hall *2 handlers; rcd wide; jmpd lft; made most 2-9; wkng when blun 13; pu nxt*
[336⁵]	F		**Lady Kilton** (5a) 8-1 M Cowley *(bf) 14s-8s; hld up wl in rr; lost tch frm 6; wl adrift in 8th when fell 12*

OFFICIAL DISTANCES: 15l, 2½l   TIME: 7min 07.0s

430 Land Rover Mens Open   4 ran

[191⁸]	1		**KITES HARDWICKE** 20-1 P Sheppard *Ld to 2; drpd to last & lkd strugg aft 10; slt tap w whip & r.o frm 12; ld 13; stdly plodded clr frm 3 out*
	2	20	**Deep Refrain (IRE)** 9-4 G Kerr *Ld to 2; set slow pce til hdd 13; mists nxt 3; tired bef 2 out; walked in*
[115ᴾ]	3	5	**Andermatt** (7ow) (tt) 10-1 A Cockerill *In tch til qckly outpcd aft 12; 25l last 15; brief eff bef 2 out; sn wknd; walked in*

[302F] U   **Freedom Fighter** 4-9F **A Martin** Swtng; jmpd slow 3 & 5; eff to disp 2nd when stumbled bad & ur 12

OFFICIAL DISTANCES: 15l, 4l **TIME:** 7min 29.0s

431 Ladies Open   6 ran

[335²] 1   **BANKHEAD (IRE)** (bl) 8-11F **Miss C Spearing** Ld & set gd pce; jnd & outj by rival 5-8; forged clr frm 11; 20l up 14; stayed on str; unchall aft

[245U] 2   60   **Lucky Christopher** 8-1 **Miss R Goodwin** Sn outpcd & wl bhnd; 46l 5th 7; went rem 3rd 10; 60l 3rd 3 out; kpt on to tk 2nd flat

[245²] 3   7   **Roly Prior** 3-1 **Miss S Samworth** Jnd wnr 3 & outj him 5-7; rmdr & nt r.o aft 10; 20l down 13; wl btn 3 out; lost 2nd flat

          4   45   **Supreme Dream (IRE)** (5a) 6-1 **Mrs P Adams** (bf) Sn wl bhnd; 51l last 7; cont t.o; jmpd 2 out as wnr crossed line; won sprint for 4th

[192U] 5   ¾   **Hostetler** 33-1 **Miss K Norris** Chsd wnr to 2; sn wl bhnd; 45l 4th 7; cont t.o; jmpd 2 out as wnr crossed line

[94P]   P   **Looks Like Reign** 33-1 **Miss S Mason** W ldng pr 3-5; lsng tch when blun 6; wknd rap 8; t.o & lost 3rd 10; last when pu nxt

OFFICIAL DISTANCES: dist, 5l **TIME:** 7min 02.0s

432 Open Maiden (Div 1), 12st   7 ran

[250²] 1   **ROLCAP** 4-5F **J I Pritchard** Disp ld til ld 12; jmpd slow 14; clr 3 out; stayed on; unchall

[249F] 2   40   **Chalcuchima** 20-1 **J Diment** 33s-20s; mists in last; lost tch 12; 23l 4th 3 out; lft poor 2nd last; v reluct & nrly pu nr fin

          3   3   **Minster Star** (5a) 20-1 **C Wadland** Tk keen hld; cl up; jmpd slow 13 & lost plce; 11l 3rd 3 out; crawled 2 out; lft poor 2nd & nrly ref last; stpd flat; cont & nrly caught reluct rnr-up

[261P] 4   2fncs **Ashburton Lord (IRE)** 7-1 **M Legge** 10s-7s; in tch when fell 3; rmtd; cont t.o

[289P] P   **Primulas Daughter** (5a) 12-1 **P Cowley** Disp ld to 8; wknd rap nxt; last when pu 11

[74P]   P   **River Bloom** (5a) 3-1 **A Martin** Last pr; lost tch 12; gd prog nxt; disp 2nd & clsng when pu 15; lame

[76U]   P   **Shady Exchange (IRE)** (7a) 8-1 **M Baldock** Made most to 12; chsd wnr aft; btn 3 out; 25l 2nd when pu rap last

OFFICIAL DISTANCES: dist, 2½l **TIME:** 7min 19.0s

433 Open Maiden (Div 2), 12st   9 ran

          1   **PENNCALER (IRE)** 8-1 **M Emmanuel** Prom; ld 4 til jmpd slow & hdd 7; ld agn nxt; jnd 10; def advant 14; 4l clr 2 out; 7l up last; rdn & stpng nr fin

[372³] 2   2   **Kings Choir** 12-1 **Mrs C Boyes** 20s-12s; cl up; ld 7-8; rdr called cab nxt; shuffled back to 5th aft 14; mist 3 out; r.o nxt; tk 2nd flat; fin wl

[197²] 3   3   **Romany Chat** 13-8F **A Martin** Oht; hld up last; hit 3; blun 11; gd prog 14; chsd wnr 3 out; no imp nxt; one pce & lost 2nd flat

          P   **Ballyaction** 25-1 **J Owen** Tk keen hld; ld til blun 4; wknd 9; last when pu 11

[328P] F   **Mandalady (IRE)** (5a) 33-1 **A Blanch** Rdr insecure; in tch in mid-div; 6th when fell 12

          U   **Miss Hoity Toity** (5a) 10-1 **J Tarry** Drpd to last 5; lsng tch when tried to ref & ur tk-off side 7

[249U] P   **The Fluter** 33-1 **Miss A Naylor** (bf) In tch; pckd 8 & drpd to last; still in tch 11; wknd & pu aft 12

[194²] P   **True Hustler** 2-1 **F Hutsby** Mounted on course; tk keen hld; hld up in rr; prog 9; trckd ldng pr 12; pckd nxt; hit 3 out & btn; poor 4th when pu last

[197F] r   **Wood Buzzard** (1ow) 5-1 **M Morley** Cl up; hld wnr 10 til blun 14; chall agn & outj nxt; hit 3 out & wknd; poor 5th when ref & ur last; collapsed

OFFICIAL DISTANCES: 1½l, 2l **TIME:** 7min 23.0s

434 Open Maiden (Div 3), 12st   6 ran

          1   **UNCLE BILLY (IRE)** (bl) 4-1 **E Walker** Mists; prom; disp 10-12; 3rd & outpcd frm nxt; 20l bhnd 3 out; lkd wl btn aft; still 15l down last; rdn & stayed on to catch toiling rivals final 20yds

[197P] 2   3   **Musical Hit** 3-1 **C Wadland** Cl up; ld 7-8; duelled w rival aft 12 & wl clr of rest; narrowly hdd aft 2 out; drvn to ld agn flat; walking last 100yds; hdd nr fin

[250⁶] 3   ½   **Yodeller Bill** 5-2F **J Diment** Prom; ld/disp frm 8; duelled w rnr-up aft 12; narrow ld aft 2 out; drvn & hdd flat; walking nr fin

[250⁵] 4   30   **Shouldhavesaidno (IRE)** (5a) 10-1 **J Owen** Ld til aft 2; rstrnd in rr aft; mist 11; no prog nxt; nt jw & lost tch frm 13; t.o

          P   **Bangagin** (3ow) 25-1 **M Buchan** Ld aft 2-7; wknd 9; t.o & pu 13

P   **Country Buzzard** 7-1 L Lay *Lkd awful; jmpd slow 7 & drpd to last; mist nxt; sn bhnd; t.o & pu 12*

OFFICIAL DISTANCES: 2l, nk **TIME:** 7min 28.0s

Burton

Market Rasen (LH 7F,18J) Sun, 5 Mar (GOOD to FIRM, GOOD in places)

435 Hunt, 12st
8 ran

[232ᴾ]	1		**SOVEREIGNS MATCH** 4-1 M Mackley *(bf) Cl 2nd til ld 13; 2l up 3 out; qcknd rt away aft nxt; easy*
	2	15	**Office Hours** 5-2F C Mulhall *6s-5/2; hld up til hdwy aft 6; ld 7-12; chsd ldr & ch til mist 3 out; wknd*
	3	10	**Trial And Error** 14-1 K Green *Ld to 4; chsd ldng til outpcd 12; 15l 4th 14; stayed on to dist 3rd 2 out*
	4	3	**Quiet Mistress** (5a) 7-2 S Charlton *Midfield; mist 10 & pushed along; outpcd aft 12; 12l 3rd 14; dem 4th 2 out*
	5	10	**Vimchase** 33-1 Miss N Chappell *A chsng group; 5th & lsng tch 13; t.o 3 out*
	6	runin	**Slobadam** (2ow) 33-1 Simon Robinson *A rr; bhnd & lsng tch 8; t.o 13*
	P		**Crucial Runner** (U) (4ow) 25-1 M Ollard *Sn detach; to 6; hunted rnd til pu 14*
	P		**Law Designer (IRE)** 6-1 N Kent *Rr by 5; pushed along & rmdrs 7; lsng tch 10; t.o when pu 15*

OFFICIAL DISTANCES: 20l, 7l **TIME:** 6min 43.0s

436 Open Maiden (Div 1), 12st
14 ran

[167²]	1		**SQUARE ONE (IRE)** (5a) 3-1 J Docker *Ld to 3; cl 3rd & mist 6; 3rd to 11; outpcd 13; 12l 2nd 2 out; lft 5l 2nd at last; hrd rdn flat; ld on line*
[281⁵]	2	½	**Ron On The Run (IRE)** 8-1 S Charlton *Ld frm 4; 5l clr 9; jnd & outpcd 2 out; 6l 2nd when lft 5l clr last; hdd on line*
	3	4	**Fanion De Nourry (FR)** 25-1 L Hicks *Chsd ldr; 5l 2nd 13-15; wknd 3 out; 6l 4th when lft 3rd at last; r.o one pce*
[168ᴾ]	4	15	**The Other Eye (IRE)** 33-1 D Thomas *Midfield; outpcd 13; 35l 6th 15; stayed on wl; nrst fin*
	5	20	**Colonel Carats** 25-1 N Bell *A midfield; poor 6th 14; r.o one pce*
[234³]	6	2	**Harps Hall (IRE)** 8-1 M Chatterton *Last by 6; lsng tch 10; t.o 14; disapp*
[234ᴾ]	7	8	**Father's Joy** (5a) 33-1 A Sansome *Midfield to 7; 20l 5th 14; t.o last 3 out*
[233ᴮ]	P		**Camden Kid (IRE)** 25-1 S R Andrews *(xnb) Midfield to 10; wknd & lsng tch 13; t.o & pu 14*
	P		**Mademist Jaz** (5a) 14-1 S Swiers *Hld up in rr; jmpd slow 3; bhnd & lsng tch 10; t.o & pu 13; nt hrd pushed*
[282⁵]	F		**Mighty Rising** (7a) 12-1 G Brewer *Midfield to 9; handy 5th when mist 11 & rmdrs; fell 12*
[138ᴾ]	P		**Primelle** (5a) 20-1 Mrs F Needham *A rr; bhnd when mist 7; lsng tch 10; t.o & pu 14*
[181⁴]	P		**Sparebit** (5a) 16-1 S Morris *A strugg in rr; pushed along & rmdrs 11; lsng tch 13; t.o & pu 15*
	P		**Timothy George (IRE)** 33-1 P Millington *A rr div; t.o & pu 3 out*
[138²]	F		**Top Toy (IRE)** evensF A Dalton *Nt jw; jmpd slow 1; mist 5; handy 3rd 9-14; ld 2 out; 6l clr & in comm when fell last; unlucky*

OFFICIAL DISTANCES: ½l, 6l **TIME:** 6min 39.0s

437 Open Maiden (Div 2), 12st
14 ran

[30ᴾ]	1		**AZZANTE (IRE)** 5-2F A Dalton *Rr & mist 6; hdwy 8; lft in ld 12; 4l up & pushed along frm 2 out; stayed on wl*
[51⁴]	2	4	**C L B Jemilla** (5a) 11-2 Mrs F Needham *Midfield to 10; went 12l 5th 13; outpcd 14; 20l 5th by 3 out; gd hdwy to 8l 3rd at last; went 2nd flat & fin wl; nt rch wnr*
[237ᶠ]	3	2	**Second Thoughts** (5a) 14-1 W Wales *A handy; chsd ldr 2nd 12; clsd to 2l 2nd 2 out; wknd app last; dem flat*
[247⁵]	4	6	**Stormhill Farmer** 8-1 M Keel *Ld to 3; cl 2nd 4-11; 6l 3rd 3 out; wknd aft*
[138ᴾ]	5	3	**Dragon Stout** 11-2 P Atkinson *Hld up in rr early; stdy hdwy to 6th 13; pushed along 15; outpcd & wknd 2 out*
	F		**Anneka Louise** (5a) 25-1 N Kent *Ld frm 4 til fell 12*
	U		**Aughrim Quest (IRE)** (5a) 25-1 M Worthington *Midfield when ur 2*
[242ᶠ]	F		**Campbellhill (IRE)** 33-1 M Grange *A rr; t.o by 5; poor 6th when fell 14*
	P		**Educate Me (IRE)** 12-1 J Burley *Midfield to 7; 8l 6th 9; wknd 11; rr & lsng tch 12; t.o & pu 3 out*

[167ᴾ]	B		**Gentleman Charles (IRE)** 8-1 S Swiers *Handy 3rd & mist 7; in tch til wknd v qckly aft 13; bhnd whn bd 14*
	R		**Minster Echo** (12a) 33-1 S Charlton *Sn bhnd; t.o when rn out 5*
[369ᶠ]	P		**Rising Dawn (IRE)** 33-1 A Sansome *A rr; t.o & pu 14*
	F		**Silent Snipe** 25-1 C Mulhall *Sa; last when fell I*
[235ᴾ]	F		**The Bee's Castle (IRE)** 16-1 R Armson *A rr; last by 7; t.o & tired when clambered 11 & fell*

OFFICIAL DISTANCES: 3l, 3l **TIME:** 6min 39.0s

438 Open Maiden (Div 3), 12st — 12 ran

[235⁶]	1		**GYMCRAK GORJOS** (5a) 4-1 D Thomas *A handy; 8l 6th 11; sltly outpcd 14; 12l 4th 3 out; 6l down nxt; gd rn & slpd thro on inner to ld app last; r.o wl; brilliant rdn*
[234²]	2	½	**Scraptastic** 7-4F N Bell (xnb) *Ld 6; 2l up 15; slt ld 2 out; jnd app last; outrdn & hdd flat*
[282⁴]	3	½	**Sassy Street (IRE)** 8-1 A Richardson *Rr & mist 6; hdwy aft 12 to handy 5th 14; pushed up to disp ld 2 out; ev ch last; just outpcd flat*
[233ᴾ]	4	4	**Magnus Maximus** 7-1 T Lane *A handy; 2l 2nd 14; disp ld 15-3 out; 1l 3rd & ev ch app last; wknd flat*
[235ᴾ]	5	1	**Balmoral Spring (IRE)** 16-1 P Millington *Mid-div to 10; outpcd 13; 15l 5th 3 out; r.o one pce*
	6	12	**The Bombers Moon** (1ow) 12-1 S R Andrews *Tk str hld; ld to 6; cl up 2nd to 12; outpcd 14; wknd 15*
[121³]	F		**Druids Dream** (5a) 12-1 J R Barlow *Last by 5; bhnd & lsng tch 9; t.o when fell 12*
[298ᵁ]	F		**Gilded Way** 25-1 L Hicks *Handy 5th to 7; gng wl when mist 10; ld 11; fell 12*
	P		**Hibou** 9-2 P Atkinson *Last & lsng tch 7; t.o 14; pu last*
[235ᵀ]	U		**Honeysuckle Lil** (5a) 25-1 T Gardham (xnb) *Midfield to 10; stdy hdwy to cl 2nd 15; 1½l 4th & ev ch when ur 2 out*
[242²]	P		**Nanda Devi** (1ow) 25-1 D Maxwell *Handy 4th to 6; disp ld 7-8; wknd 14; lsng tch when pu 3 out*
	P		**Pipistrella** (5a) 12-1 S Morris *A rr; lsng tch when blun bad 12; imm dism; broke shoulder; dead*

OFFICIAL DISTANCES: ½l, ½l **TIME:** 6min 49.0s

439 Open Maiden (Div 4), 12st — 15 ran

	1		**HANDFAST POINT** 10-1 C Vale *Mid-div til hdwy 15; 12l 4th 2 out; stayed on to 5l 3rd at last; fin str; ld on line*
	2	½	**O'flaherty's (IRE)** 7-4F A Dalton *Hld up in 7th to 10; gd hdwy aft 12; went 11 2nd 14-2 out; slpd thro on inner to ld last; 3l clr flat; wknd & hdd on line*
	3	4	**Flying On** 6-1 M Hewitt *Tried to make all; 6l clr 7; 2l up 15; jnd last; sn hdd & wknd; dem*
[181ᴾ]	4	6	**Fine Times** 14-1 M Mackley *Midfield to 8; rr & pushed along 12; stayed on frm 3 out; nrst fin*
	5	15	**Petrea** (12a) 7-1 G Brewer *Rr & rmdrs 6; hdwy 9 to 6th 13; 12l 4th 2 out; wknd app last; rn wl; will improve*
[235⁴]	6	20	**Tom's Surprise** 6-1 A Sansome *Cl 2nd/3rd to 11; wknd 13; rr & lsng tch 15; t.o 3 out*
	7	6	**Tenor Bet (IRE)** 14-1 N Wilson *Rr to 7; hdwy aft 8; 7th 10; chsng ldrs 13; wknd 15; nt hrd pushed app last*
[230ᴾ]	F		**Afternoon Delight (IRE)** (5a) 14-1 S Charlton *Prom in 5th to 10; outpcd 14; 10l 4th 3 out; fell nxt; broke nk; dead*
[168ᵁ]	R		**Henavos** (5a) 25-1 S Swiers *A midfield; 8l 7th 14; pushed along & wkng when rn out 15*
[234⁴]	R		**Huntsbydale** (5a) 10-1 T Lane *Cl 3rd to 12; outpcd aft 13; 15l 5th & wkng when rn out 14*
[180ᴾ]	P		**Miss Pink** (5a) 25-1 M Barnard *Handy 6th when mist 9; rr & lsng tch 11; pu 12*
[234ᴾ]	R		**Nasayer (IRE)** 5-1 A Pickering *Cl 4th when rn out 7*
[235⁵]	P		**Round The Bend** 4-1 S Brisby *Sa; sn bhnd; rap hdwy frm 7 to 6l 4th 10; wknd 14; sn detach; t.o & pu last*
[399ᶠ]	P		**Stanwick Hall** 10-1 Mrs F Needham *A strugg; sn bhnd; last 7; t.o & pu 11*
[298ᴾ]	P		**Village Gossip** 20-1 M Worthington *Rr til hdwy 9; cl 6th 11; outpcd & wknd 14; t.o & pu 3 out*

OFFICIAL DISTANCES: ½l, 3l **TIME:** 6min 41.0s

440 Restricted, 12st — 14 ran

[179ᵁ]	1		**STORMY WORDS** (5a) 8-1 S Morris *Hld up early; went 10l 5th 11; hdwy to 4l 4th 14; jnd ldr 3 out; ld aft nxt; forged clr app last*
[119²]	2	8	**Baron Allfours** 10-1 P Millington *Last early; gd hdwy frm 10 to 8l 5th 11; str rn to ld 2 out; wknd app last*

[284¹]	3	3	**Tubber Roads (IRE)** 6-1 **A Sansome** Ld to 3; cl 2nd til ld agn 8-15; ev ch 2 out; wknd app last
[54²]	4	1	**Ella Falls (IRE)** (12a) 10-1 **M Worthington** Rr to 7; gd hdwy to 5l 4th 12; cruising bhnd ldng trio 3 out; ev ch nxt; fnd nil
[396ᴮ]	5	10	**Up And Over (IRE)** 66-1 **Miss J Foster** A mid-div; outpcd 14; 12l 5th 3 out; r.o one pce
[232ᴾ]	6	6	**Neva-Agree** 33-1 **R Armson** Cl 5th to 7; wknd 11; rr by 14; t.o 3 out
[173ᴾ]	7	6	**Moor Lady** (5a) 33-1 **S Swiers** A midfield; nvr able to chall
[371ᴾ]	P		**Grants Carouse** (3ow) (bl) 66-1 **M Wells** Nt jw; jmpd slow 4; mists 7 & 9; t.o 11; pu 12
[234¹]	P		**Gunmetal** (7a) 4-1 **C Mulhall** A rr & nt fluent; bhnd & lsng tch 13; t.o & pu 15
[123¹]	P		**Hobnob (IRE)** 16-1 **R Barrett** (xnb) Trckd ldrs in 3rd til wknd 15; t.o & pu last
[50²]	P		**Macfin (IRE)** 33-1 **Miss L Allan** Mid-div early; 15l 10th 9; last 14; lsng tch when pu 15
[396ᴮ]	P		**Primitive Man** 5-2F **S Charlton** Set str pce; ld 4-7; ll 2nd to 10; wknd v qckly 13; pu 15; disappt
[239ᵁ]	P		**River Ferdinand (IRE)** 12-1 **T Lane** Handy early; mists 4 & 6; rr & lsng tch 7; t.o & pu 12
[86³]	P		**Tumlin Oot (IRE)** 10-1 **M Lurcock** Mid-div to 6; 8l 5th 11; wknd 13; t.o & pu 15

OFFICIAL DISTANCES: 8l, 5l **TIME:** 6min 32.0s

441 Land Rover Mens Open, 12st   7 ran

[229⁵]	1		**MIDNIGHT SERVICE (IRE)** (bl) 7-2 **R Barrett** Handy in 3l 3rd 8; ld 9; made rest; 5l up 14; qcknd rt away 3 out; v easy
	2	20	**Rule Out The Rest** 4-1 **N Tutty** 5th & outpcd 9; pushed along nxt; went 12l 2nd 15; chsng ldr & clsng when blun bad 3 out; no ex aft
	3	4	**The Flying Phantom** 9-2 **T Denniff** Last to 3; hdwy 6 to cl 3rd 8; outpcd aft 13; 8l 2nd 15; wknd nxt
[229⁶]	F		**Barneys Gold (IRE)** 5-2F **A Bealby** Ld til fell 6
[242¹]	U		**Cheryl's Lad (IRE)** (bl) 6-1 **J Henderson** Prom to 5; lft in ld 6-9; chsd along aft 12; poor 4th & wkng when ur 14
	F		**Dahiyah (USA)** 20-1 **R Barrett** Last & lsng tch 6; t.o when fell 10; dead
	P		**Just Bruce** 12-1 **S R Andrews** Trckd ldr to 6; lft cl 2nd 7-11; outpcd & chsd along when mist 13; sn wknd; pu 15

OFFICIAL DISTANCES: dist, 5l **TIME:** 6min 38.0s

442 Ladies Open   9 ran

[230²]	1		**CITTADINO** 4-5F **Mrs J Dawson** Made all; 4l ahd when mist 4; 10l up 11; dist clr by 3 out; galloped on relentless
[230⁴]	2	30	**Doctor Dunklin (USA)** 33-1 **Miss E Graham** Chsd ldr in 10l 2nd to 9; outpcd & wknd 13; 4th 14; stayed on to poor 2nd 2 out
[240ᶠ]	3	1½	**Count Of Flanders (IRE)** 12-1 **Miss F Hatfield** Bhnd by 4; hdwy 6 to 15l 4th 9; went 2nd 13 til dem app last
[378ᴬ]	4	30	**Miorbhail** 20-1 **Miss T Gray** In chsng group 1st circ; 12l 4th 10; last by 13; t.o 14; poor 4th 2 out
	5	12	**Kendor Pass (IRE)** 33-1 **Mrs N Wilson** Prom in chsng group to 9; 13l 5th 10; lost tch 13; poor 5th 2 out
[240ᴾ]	P		**Airecco (IRE)** 25-1 **Miss J Kandalaft** Last & lsng tch 7; t.o 11; pu 13
[368²]	r		**Circus Colours** (bl) 33-1 **Miss J Elson** Spurs; reluct to rce; coaxed to 1 & ref (blinkers removed & bolted 2 circs w helpless rdr)
[368²]	U		**Laughing Fontaine (IRE)** 33-1 **Miss L Allan** Bhnd to 6; hdwy 9 to 20l 3rd & ur 14
[230³]	U		**Sun Surfer (FR)** 2-1 **Mrs C Ford** Ur 1

OFFICIAL DISTANCES: dist, 1½l **TIME:** 6min 34.0s

The stewards enquired into the unruly behaviour of Circus Colours at the start and after its blinkers had been removed later; having interviewed the rider and trainer they reported the matter to the Jockey Club

443 Confined, 12st   5 ran

[277ᶠ]	1		**PENNYWISE** (5a) 4-6F **S Charlton** Made all; mists 10, 11 & 14; 2l up 12; qcknd wl clr 14; unextended
[441ᶠ]	2	25	**Barneys Gold (IRE)** 5-2 **A Bealby** Last & mist 10; hdwy 14; mist 15; went dist 2nd 2 out; r.o but no ch w wnr
	3	5	**Deel Quay (IRE)** 20-1 **M Chatterton** Cl last to 4; hdwy to cl 3rd 8; 15l 3rd 13; went 15l 2nd 3 out; sn dem
	4	runin	**Osgathorpe** 10-1 **A Woodward** Chsd ldr in 2nd til wknd 14; t.o 3 out
[95ᴾ]	U		**Fern Leader (IRE)** 6-1 **M Hewitt** Ur 4

OFFICIAL DISTANCES: 20l, 6l **TIME:** 6min 48.0s

Ross Harriers

Garnons (LH 7F,18J) Sun, 5 Mar (SOFT)

444 Hunt, 12st
2 ran

1		**GLOBAL LEGEND** 1-5F **A Wintle** Made all; blun 13; drew wl clr aft 15; unchall
2	25	**Fionnuala** (U) (12a,12a) 3-1 **W Jordan** Chsd wnr; mist 9; within 3l til blun 15; sn wknd

OFFICIAL DISTANCE: dist TIME: 7min 35.0s

445 Confined, 12st
6 ran

	1		**HAPPY MINSTRAL** (USA) 20-1 **R Burton** Mist 5; 2nd til lost plce aft 8; 23l 4th ½way; 25l 5th 12; stayed on wl frm 15; went 7l 2nd 2 out; mist last; ld flat; rdn clr
[332¹]	2	5	**Basil Street** (IRE) 3-1 **D Mansell** Hld up; jmpd slow 7; went 20l 2nd aft 8-11; 18l 3rd 14; ld app 3 out; sn clr; hdd & no ex u.p flat
[333³]	3	25	**La Kabyle** (FR) (5a) 8-1 **F Windsor Clive** (xnb) Swtng; rcd free; ld; 20l clr when mist 8; hit 11; blun 12; wknd 15; hdd app 3 out; fin v tired
[294³]	4	4	**Well Ted** (IRE) 8-11F **G Barfoot-Saunt** Ww; 20½l 3rd ½way; went 20l 2nd 11; ev ch aft 15; 1½l 2nd when mist 3 out; wknd rap; climbed last; fin exhaust
[173F]	P		**Nouvalari** (IRE) 33-1 **M Rodda** J rt; 3rd til blun 3; lost tch 7; t.o v game
	P		**Paddy Maguire** (IRE) 20-1 **A Phillips** Nd; 26l 5th & rdn ½way; 22l 4th 12; sn wknd; t.o & pu 15

OFFICIAL DISTANCES: 4l, 15l TIME: 7min 02.0s

446 Mens Open, 12st
6 ran

[271⁴]	1		**TWILIGHT TOM** 5-1 **A Price** 10s-5s; jw; 2nd til ld 7; hdd 9; ld 13-15 & app 3 out til hdd nxt; ld last; edged lft u.p flat; r.o v game
[333P]	2	5	**Stormhill Recruit** 2-1 **S Blackwell** A.p; ld 6-7; 2½l 3rd ½way; ld 10-13; ld 15; sn hdd; rdn to ld 2 out; hdd last; no ex flat
[334P]	3	12	**Muntafi** (7x) 13-8F **A Wintle** Hld up; 7l 5th ½way; went 5l 3rd 11; rdn 15; no imp
	P		**Chaceley Lass** (5a) 20-1 **T Stephenson** A bhnd; jmpd slow 2; 11l 6th ½way; t.o & pu 12
[334¹]	P		**Have To Think** (bl) 14-1 **A Morley** Ld to 6; ld 9-10; wknd & 10l 4th 12; t.o & pu 15
	F		**Sun Of Chance** 20-1 **A Evans** Bckwd; chsd ldrs; mist 7; 4l 4th ½way; fell 10

OFFICIAL DISTANCES: 3½l, 8l TIME: 7min 05.0s

447 Marsh UK/TBA PPORA Club Members Mares, 12st
11 ran

[296B]	1		**UPTON ADVENTURE** (5a) 5-2F **S Joynes** Lw; hld up; 15l 6th ½way; 9½l 6th 12; hdwy to 2½l 4th 14; went 2nd aft nxt; ld 3 out; sn clr; hung bad rt & slowed markedly flat; drvn out
[295R]	2	7	**Killatty Player** (IRE) (5a,7x) 6-1 **Miss C Thomas** 2nd to 6; 13l 3rd ½way; ld aft 13 til hdd 3 out; lft 7l 2nd last; no imp flat
	3	5	**Black Serene** (IRE) (5a) 8-1 **R Burton** (bf) Tde; ld til hdd app 7; 2nd til ev ch 15; sn no ex; 8l 4th nxt; lft 3rd at last
[337P]	r		**A Bit Of Fluff** (5a) 33-1 **M Trott** Jmpd v slow 1; bhnd til ref 4
[178P]	P		**Artic Pearl** (IRE) (5a) 33-1 **R Langley** Lost plce 6; blun 8; 23l 10th ½way; hmpd & rdr lost irons 14; t.o & pu 15
[201³]	F		**Doyenne** (5a) 14-1 **Miss F Wilson** Bckwd; hld up; mist 8; 16l 8th ½way; 12l 8th 12; gd hdwy 14; 6l 4th when mist nxt; 2nd out; 5l 2nd when fell hvly last
[49²]	P		**Miss Ondee** (FR) (5a) 10-1 **D Mansell** Chsd ldrs; jmpd v slow 7; 13½l 4th ½way; 8l 4th 12; lost plce 14; 7l 5th & wkng when blun 15; pu 3 out
	F		**Sally's Twins** (5a) 4-1 **A Wintle** (xnb) Swtng; ww; 17l 9th ½way; 13l 9th 12; eff to 7l 8th when fell 14
[357P]	P		**The Dancing Parson** (5a) (bl) 20-1 **G Barfoot-Saunt** Chsd ldrs; 14l 5th ½way; 11l 7th & rdn when mist 12; sn wknd; 15l 9th 14; t.o & pu 3 out
[273¹]	P		**Tiger Tina** (5a) 7-2 **A Evans** (xnb) Hld up; 15½l 7th & rmdrs ½way; eff to 8½l 5th 12; 4½l 6th & rdn 14; wknd & pu 15
	P		**Turrill House** (5a,7x) 7-1 **A Phillips** Lw; mist 2; went 2nd 6; ld app 7; 12l clr ½way; mists 11 & 13; sn hdd; 2l 3rd when mist 14; 10l 6th & wkng qckly nxt; pu 3 out

OFFICIAL DISTANCES: 6l, 6l TIME: 7min 00.1s

448 Intermediate, 12st
8 ran

[296²]	1		**MILITARY MAN** 4-1 **A Phillips** Ld; rmdrs 6 & 12; hdd 14; blun nxt; 8l 3rd 3 out; lft in ld nxt & wl clr last; f
[75⁴]	2	15	**Tirley Missile** 9-2 **T Stephenson** Chsd ldrs; 6l 5th ½way; hit 11; 11l 5th 14; sn no ex; 20l 4th 3 out; lft poor 2nd at last

[340ᵖ]	3	20	**Netherbrook Lad** 25-1 **S Lloyd** *Bckwd; lost plce 6; 12l 6th ½way; wl bhnd 11; t.o 14; plodded on*
	P		**Alkarine** 8-1 **G Lewis** *Bckwd; jmpd poor & nt keen; a.p; jmpd slow 2; 14l 7th ½way; t.o 14; pu 3 out*
[222ᵖ]	U		**Detroit Davy (IRE)** 2-1F **Miss P Jones** *Lw; 2nd/3rd til ld 14; 7l clr 3 out; mist & ur 2 out; v unlucky*
[333ᵖ]	r		**Executive Office (IRE)** 5-1 **A Wintle** *Swtng; hld up; hdwy 7; 5l 4th ½way; 6l 3rd 14; went 7l 2nd app 3 out; wknd rap; 12l 2nd & exhaust when ref & ur last*
	r		**Penny Appeal** (5a) 25-1 **M Scales** *Pulled hrd; 7th & mist 1; went 2nd 3 til rn wide bend aft 6; nt r.o; ref to rce aft 7*
[340ᶠ]	P		**Roscoes Dinky** (5a) 12-1 **F Windsor Clive** *Nt jw; prom; hit 4; 4l 3rd ½way; 8l 4th & wkng when mist 14; bhnd when pu 15*

OFFICIAL DISTANCES: 20l, 20l   TIME: 7min 09.5s

449 Ladies Open   6 ran

	1		**AEGEAN FANFARE (IRE)** 4-1 **Miss E Jones** *Ld to 2; 2nd til ld 6; hdd nxt; mist 8; ld 15; 4l clr nxt; stayed on wl*
	2	8	**Distinctive (IRE)** 4-1 **Mrs D Jackson** *10s-4s; lw; ld 2-6 & 7-15; pckd 3 out; no ex*
[191ᵖ]	3	20	**Foodbroker Star (IRE)** 5-1 **Miss S Vickery** *Prom; 4l 3rd ½way; rdn 15; sn wknd*
	4	1	**Outrageous Affair** (5a) 25-1 **Miss R Reynolds** *A bhnd; 18l 6th ½way; went 15l 4th 11; no imp frm 14*
[335ᴬ]	5	25	**Highway Five (IRE)** (7x) 9-2 **Miss L Brooke** *A plodding; rmdrs 8; 17l 5th ½way; wl bhnd 11; 34l 6th 14*
	6	12	**Blue Rosette** (bl) 2-1F **Miss A Gibbons** *Nd; hit 1 & 2 & rdr ungainly; 12l 4th ½way; mist 10; wl bhnd 12; 32l 5th 14; t.o*

OFFICIAL DISTANCES: 10l, 15l   TIME: 6min 54.6s

450 Confined Maiden (Div 1), 12st   13 ran

[205ᴬ]	1		**MAID O'TULLY (IRE)** (5a) 14-1 **R Hodges** *Lw; hld up; 5½l 6th ½way; hdwy 11; went 2l 3rd 13 & 4l 2nd aft 3 out; stayed on u.p & hmpd flat; ld nr fin*
[125ᴬ]	2	s hd	**Idlewild (IRE)** (7a) 10-1 **S Joynes** *a.p; 2½l 3rd ½way; went 2nd 10; mists 14 & 15; ld 3 out; 4l clr nxt; hung rt & nt r.o flat; hdd nr fin; swerved lft & ur aft line*
[339ᵖ]	3	12	**Wonastow** 5-1 **F Windsor Clive** *(xnb) Chsd ldrs; 6l 7th ½way; went 5l 4th 14; no imp frm 3 out; went 3rd flat*
	4	1	**Muckle Jack** (7x) 7-1 **S Blackwell** *Lw; a.p; 3½l 4th ½way; ld 12-3 out; sn wknd*
[339ᵖ]	P		**Brookthorpe** (5a,7x) (tt) 20-1 **G Barfoot-Saunt** *Prom; went 2nd aft 8-10; mist & rmdrs 11; sn wknd; bhnd when pu & dism aft 13*
	F		**Cashew Crisis (IRE)** (7a) 7-1 **M Rodda** *10s-7s; jmpd sketchy; hld up; mist 3; 8l 9th ½way; hit 7 & then fell 12*
	F		**Cherry Alley** (5a) 5-2F **S Lloyd** *7th when fell 1*
[340ᴮ]	P		**Come On Boy** 12-1 **D Mansell** *A bhnd; bumped rival & rmdrs 3; 10l 11th & jmpd sketchy ½way; 20l 6th 14; sn t.o; pu last*
	P		**Jack Cruise** 5-1 **K Burke** *Bckwd; ld til hdd 7; lost plce & 7l 8th ½way; bhnd when pu 11*
	P		**Loup Rouge** (5a) 16-1 **W Jordan** *Bckwd; ss; jb; sn wl t.o; pu 6*
	P		**Marauder (IRE)** (7x) (bl) 12-1 **R Cooper** *Lw; 2nd til ld 7; hdd 12; wknd rap; pu 14; lks most ungenuine*
	P		**Spartan Gold** (5a) 10-1 **T Stephenson** *(orbs) Lost plce 6; 9l 10th & rdn along ½way; bhnd when pu 11*
	P		**Unrequited Love (IRE)** (7x) 12-1 **A Phillips** *Hld up; mists 7 & 9; 5l 5th ½way; wknd & 8l 5th 14; bhnd when pu 15*

OFFICIAL DISTANCES: s hd, 4l   TIME: 7min 09.3s

451 Confined Maiden (Div 2), 12st   8 ran

	1		**RASH-GALE (IRE)** (5a,7x) 5-1 **R Burton** *Lw; hld up; last to 7; 7l 6th ½way; 8l 5th 12; wl outpcd & 20l 3rd 14; mist 15; lft rem 2nd 2 out; lft in ld last; rdn clr flat*
[55ᶠ]	2	7	**Executive Blue (IRE)** (5a) 14-1 **G Barfoot-Saunt** *2nd to 7; 6l 4th ½way; mist 11; sn wknd; 9l 6th nxt; t.o 14; inherited 4l 2nd at last; no ex*
[341ᶠ]	3	8	**Dungannon Lad** (7x) 9-1 **A St George** *Swtng; prom; 4l 3rd ½way; wknd & 22l 4th 14; jmpd v slow 15; lft 5l 3rd at last; fin tired*
[339ᵖ]	P		**Bay Fusilier** 6-1 **M Rodda** *Hld up; hdwy to 2nd 7; ld 3 out; lft 30l clr nxt; still clr when ground to halt & pu app last*
	P		**Cedor Hicks** (5a) 8-1 **M Trott** *Bckwd; hld up; 6½l 5th ½way; eff & 6l 4th 12; wknd rap 13; sn t.o; pu 2 out*
[169ᵖ]	P		**New Yorker (USA)** (7a) (tt) 7-1 **T Stephenson** *Bit bckwd; prom til lost plce 8; 8l 7th ½way; 15l 7th & lsng tch 12; pu aft 13*

| [341P] | P | | **Sergeant Miller** 12-1 R Hodges *Bckwd; mists; drpd to rr 7 & sn u.p; 20l 8th ½way; wl bhnd when pu 10* |
| [337²] | P | | **Tedstone Fox** 2-1F D Mansell *Ld; qcknd 8l clr 14; hdd & wknd rap 3 out; exhaust 2nd when pu 2 out* |

OFFICIAL DISTANCES: 8l, 8l **TIME:** 7min 27.0s

> Mr Pistachio was withdrawn not under orders - unseated going down and rider injured; Rule 4 deduction 25p in the pound

Staff College & RMA Sandhurst Draghounds

Larkhill (RH 13F,18J) Sun, 5 Mar (GOOD)

452 Hunt (with Garth & S. Berks) · 3 ran

[243²]	1		**WHAT A HAND** 4-9F P York *Chsd ldr til mist 3 & releg last; chsd ldr agn frm 5; jmpd untidy 8; mostly 2l adrift til eff to ld 15; sn in comm; pushed out flat*
[219P]	2	2½	**Glen Cherry** 2-1 P Scouller *Ld & set stdy pce; jmpd slow 3; 2½l up 5; jmpd slow 7; hdd 15; stayed on; a hld frm 2 out*
	U		**Rupert (U)** (3ow) 10-1 D Line *Last to 2; jmpd to 2nd nxt; 3l last 5; strugg 11 & qckly t.o; ur 13*

OFFICIAL DISTANCE: 5l **TIME:** 6min 35.7s **TOTE:** £1.40

453 Confined, 12st · 9 ran

[263P]	1		**RYDER CUP (IRE)** (1ow) 20-1 G Maundrell *Chsd ldr frm 3 til disp ld 5; ld 7-11; releg 3rd 13; chsd ldr nxt; jmpd to ld 15; jmpd best 3 out & nxt; kpt on wl*
[325⁷]	2	2½	**Coach (NZ)** 7-1 P Keane *Cl up til ld 3; jnd 5-7; ld agn 12 til hdd 15; hit nxt; cl 2nd last; no ex u.p flat*
[191⁶]	3	4	**Mr Custard** 2-1JF Miss L Sweeting *Hld up in rr; impd to 3l 5th 6; stayed on to 6l 3rd 15; r.o one pce frm nxt*
[195F]	4	20	**Parman (IRE)** (5ow) 2-1JF R Dalgety *Jmpd awkward; last to 7; stayed on to rem 4th 15; nvr nr to chall; nvr put in rce*
[325U]	5	15	**Our Wizzer (IRE)** 14-1 C Whittaker *(xnb) Prom early; 6th & lsng plce when mist 9; bhnd frm 13; 30l last 3 out*
[127⁶]	6	5	**Touring-Turtle (IRE)** 25-1 D Dennis *Ld 2-3; 11 3rd 6; hit 11; still disp 3rd 12; chsd ldr nxt; bad mist 14; gd rec but sn wknd; 25l 5th 3 out*
[324C]	P		**Loftus Lad (IRE)** 16-1 S Claisse *A towards rr; mist 3; last 8; t.o 11 til pu 14*
	P		**Taura's Rascal** 6-1 R Brennan *Swtng; bit bckwd; 2l 4th 6; mist 7; disp 3rd 12; mist & releg 4th 13; tired when jmpd slow 15 & imm pu*
	P		**Villains Brief** 33-1 J Kwiatkowski *Ld to 2; sn lost plce & rr 4; t.o 12 til pu 14*

OFFICIAL DISTANCES: 1½l, 4l **TIME:** 6min 28.3s **TOTE:** £6.50

454 Mixed Open, 4m, 12st - 22J · 13 ran

[161²]	1		**BLUE LAWS (IRE)** 7-1 Miss C Tuffin *Hld up in last pr; 14l 11th 11; smooth prog 18; chsd ldr nxt til ld aft 2 out; stayed on str*
[313¹]	2	1	**The Hobbit (IRE)** 4-1 T Mitchell *6s-4s; swtng; hld up towards rr; 12l 10th 11; 4l 5th & prog 3 out; chall & lkd dangerous last; no ex u.p flat*
[262²]	3	5	**Rectory Garden (IRE)** 4-5F R Biddlecombe *Hld up in rr til gd prog to 5l 5th 9; disp 7½l 7th when jmpd slow 11; pckd bad 13; impd & cl 3rd 18; 3l 4th 3 out; outpcd flat*
[4P]	4	½	**High Guardian** 10-1 Julian Pritchard *A.p; ld to 3; 5½l 6th 11; trckd ldrs til 2nd 18; 2½l 3rd & ev ch 3 out; outpcd u.p frm last*
[211⁴]	5	10	**Starpath (NZ)** 20-1 N Mitchell *Mid-div; 6th 6; disp 4l 4th 9; ld app 17 til aft 2 out; 5th & btn when mist 3 out*
[302⁵]	6	1½	**Strong Chairman (IRE)** 15-1 S Waley-Cohen *Lw; 2l 3rd 4; chsng ldng pr 16 til wknd to 10l 6th 3 out; stayed on one pce frm*
[262P]	P		**Amtrak Express** 50-1 H Froud *2 handlers; disp ld 3-9 & agn 16-nxt; sn wknd; bhnd when pu 19*
[195F]	P		**Bitofabuzz (IRE)** (1ow) 33-1 D Birkmyre *A towards rr; 9th 4; 10l 9th when mist 11; mists 12 & 13; rdr drpd reins aft blun nxt & pu*
	P		**Frozen Drop** 14-1 J Barnes *Swtng; prom; ld/disp 3-15; mist 11; wknd qckly 17; t.o & pu 19*
[192³]	P		**Hill Island** 50-1 Miss L Sweeting *Tubed; last 4; sn strugg frm 6; 32l adrift 11; t.o 15 til pu 19*
[354F]	P		**Hylters Chance (IRE)** 12-1 L Jefford *Rr early; prog to 4th 6; disp 7½l 7th 11; grad wknd frm 18; bhnd when pu 3 out*

| [325⁶] | P | | **Silver Sleeve (IRE)** 66-1 Miss L Bridges *Mid-div til grad lost plce; rr 6; jmpd slow nxt; 22l 12th 11; t.o 17 til pu 3 out* |
| [217²] | F | | **Tarthooth (IRE)** (bl) 10-1 M Bradburne *Nt a fluent; 5th 6; 4l 5th 11; 4th & in tch 16; 7th & wkng when fell hvly 3 out* |

OFFICIAL DISTANCES: 2½l, 15l **TIME:** 8min 23.2s **TOTE:** £4.90

455 Open Maiden (Div 1), 12st
18 ran

[265³]	1		**FASGO (IRE)** (7a) 8-1 Miss P Gundry *5th 5; chsd ldrs 13; sust rn frm 15; chsd ldr nxt til ld aft 2 out; clr last*
[212⁷]	2	4	**Mister Deep (IRE)** 11-2 R Young *Lft 3rd 5; chsd ldr 11 til disp ld 15; drew 10l clr 15; hdd aft 2 out; no ex flat*
[212³]	3	25	**Saltis (IRE)** 6-1 J Barnes *Trckd ldrs; 6th 5; prog to disp ld 13-14; chsd ldr til one pce frm 15; sn lost tch; hung rt flat*
	4	4	**Mel (IRE)** 16-1 Miss M Eames *7th 5; impd to 4th 13; sn outpcd; stayed on frm 15; nd*
[352⁵]	5	25	**Pendragon** 25-1 N Mitchell *A towards rr; t.o 12; stayed on past btn horses but nvr nr ldrs*
[392ᵁ]	6	½	**Vital Hesitation** (5a) 14-1 R Millar *Chsd ldr til disp & mist 5; pckd 9; lft in ld 11 til hdd & mist 13; wknd frm 15; bhnd frm nxt*
[328ᴿ]	7	8	**Just Reuben (IRE)** (7a) 20-1 R Walford *Towards rr 5; nvr btr than mid-div; wknd aft 14; t.o 3 out*
[213ᶠ]	8	20	**Sir Wynham** 10-1 J Case *Last 5; jmpd slow 8 & nxt; t.o 11; plodded home*
[220⁷]		F	**Above Suspicion (IRE)** 20-1 M Walters *Tde; fractious start; prom; 4th 5; 5th & wkng when fell hvly 14; winded*
[60³]		P	**Ballyblack (IRE)** 7-2JF T Scudamore *(xnb) A rr; 12th 5; t.o 12; pu 14*
[264⁷]		P	**Chasing A Bid** (7a) 25-1 J Snowden *10th 5; rr 12; t.o & pu 15*
[197⁴]		R	**Happen To Make It (IRE)** 7-2JF Julian Pritchard *Made most til rn out to lft 11*
		U	**Jolification** 25-1 A Honeyball *A towards rr; strugg 7; jmpd lft 9 til blun & ur 12*
		F	**King Hab (IRE)** 16-1 D Alers-Hankey *Prom; 3rd when fell 5*
[349⁷]		P	**Look Who's Calling (IRE)** 14-1 J Jukes *Mid-div when pu 4; saddle slpd*
[213⁷]		P	**Novasun** 33-1 O Ellwood *9th 5; wknd 10; t.o 12 til pu 15*
		P	**Pearly Loch** (5a) 25-1 A Charles-Jones *(xnb) 2 handlers; mid-div when hmpd 5; hit 8 & pu; severed tendons; destroyed*
		P	**Rushing Again** (7a,6ow) 4-1 T Mitchell *Lw; last to 5; slt prog when pu 9*

OFFICIAL DISTANCES: 4l, dist **TIME:** 6min 24.8s **TOTE:** £4.50

456 Countryside Alliance Club Members (Service Rdrs), 12st
3 ran

[259¹]	1		**COPPER COIL** (7x) 5-4 D Alers-Hankey *Jw; trckd ldr til disp ld 2; outj rival 7; jnd agn 12-14; ll up 15; drew clr frm 2 out; easy*
[259²]	2	10	**Desert Waltz (IRE)** 4-5F O Ellwood *Ld til jnd 2; hit 8; disp ld agn 12-14; chsng wnr vain when jmpd slow 2 out; sn no ex*
		P	**Jack Sun** 1 J Snowden *Stdd start & tk keen hld; a last; wknd qckly & nt fluent 11; pckd 12; t.o & pu 13*

OFFICIAL DISTANCE: 8l **TIME:** 6min 32.4s **TOTE:** £2.20

457 Open Maiden (Div 2), 12st - 17J
15 ran

[264⁷]	1		**ABBOTS COURT (IRE)** (7a) 11-10F R Walford *4s-11/10; hld up in rr; 12th 4; jmpd lft 7; jmpd rap to trck ldr 13; disp ld on long rn frm nxt; ld 3 out & sn clr; easy*
[58²]	2	15	**Prah Sands** 6-1 J Young *Hld up; last 5; stayed on to ldrs 13; 6l 3rd 15; chsd wnr vain aft 2 out; nvr able to chall*
[220⁷]	3	10	**Summer Haven** (5a) 16-1 F Brennan *Chsd ldrs; rdn 9; ld 12; jmpd slow nxt; hdd 3 out; sn brushed aside; r.o one pce frm nxt*
[220³]	4	10	**Paul (IRE)** 7-1 Miss L Collins *(bf) Mid-div; chsd ldrs til wknd 14; 20l 5th nxt; bhnd frm 2 out*
[60ᶠ]	5	15	**Larry** (7a) 16-1 P York *Chsd ldrs; 3rd 3 til disp ld 5; ld aft nxt-11; 2l 3rd 13; sn wknd; 22l 6th 15; bhnd frm 2 out*
[254⁴]	6	2	**Stormhill Warrior** 11-1 R Emmett *Trckd ldrs; 4th 3; grad lost plce frm 12; disp 22l 6th 15; bhnd frm 3 out*
		F	**Clare's Spring (IRE)** 33-1 J Barnes *Mid-div 4; 6th when fell 12*
[352ᴮ]		U	**Fever Pitch** 20-1 A Honeyball *Mid-div 3; prog to 5th 6; still prom when jb lft & ur 11*
[309ᴾ]		P	**Gunerkillinghurst** 33-1 A Charles-Jones *Disp ld to 2 & agn 5-nxt; w ldr 10 til hmpd bad 11; nt rec; t.o & pu 15*
[284⁷]		P	**Hatch Gate** 33-1 M Gorman *(xnb) Towards rr 4; nvr nr to chall; disp 22l 6th 15; bhnd when pu last*
[260⁷]		F	**Mister River (IRE)** 20-1 Miss P Gundry *Ld aft 2; chsd ldr nxt til mist 9; wknd 14; 15l 4th nxt; btn when fell last*

[38ᴾ]	B		Mountain Tae (IRE) 25-1 R Green *Disp ld to 2; sn lost plce & last trio 4; mist 9; bhnd when bd 12*
[213ᶠ]	F		Snowshill Harvest (IRE) 11-2 T Mitchell *8s-1112; mid-div when fell 2*
[264ᴾ]	P		Summer Pudding (5a) 10-1 Jeremy Young *(xnb) Towards rr 4; mist 8; t.o & pu 13*
	F		Team Captain 16-1 L Jefford *(xnb) Fell 1*

OFFICIAL DISTANCES: 25l, 8l TIME: 6min 31.2s TOTE: £1.20

Fence 15 omitted - fallen rider; the stewards enquired into the improved form of the winner; they accepted the owners explanation that after a mistake on his debut (when 20-1!) the horse cut into both his front legs and was unable to gallop properly

458 Restricted, 12st   12 ran

[208³]	1		WESTWINDS 11-4 Miss M Coombe *(xnb) 4th 3; 4l 4th 7; chsd ldr frm 11; 4l down 15; eff to disp ld last; drew clr flat; wl idn*
[265¹]	2	4	Burgundy Bob (IRE) 3-1 Julian Pritchard *Jw; ld to 2 & agn 4; 3l up 7; still 4l ahd 2 out; rdn & jnd last; sn hdd & no ex*
	3	30	Church Ride (IRE) 50-1 R Woollacott *Hld up towards rr; last & jmpd slow 7; prog to 3rd 13; 7l 3rd 15; outpcd nxt; no ch when mist 2 out*
[196³]	4	3	Jobsagoodun 10-1 M Yardley *Mist 3; 5th 6; trckd ldrs 13 til wknd 15; rem 4th frm nxt*
[56²]	P		Bathwick Bobbie 50-1 Jeremy Young *Mid-div 3; impd to 3rd 12 til wknd 15; bhnd when pu last*
[330ᴾ]	F		Fast Run (IRE) 66-1 Miss M Taylor *A rr; 9th 7; to 12; pu 14*
	F		Mill Copse Dilemma (5a) 50-1 D I Turner *Last pr 4; fell nxt*
[58¹]	P		Monty's Theme (IRE) 6-4F Miss P Gundry *Ch ride; mid-div til jmpd slow 10 & pushed along; jmpd slow 11; impd to 4th 13; 8l 4th 15; sn wknd; pu 2 out*
[260²ᵈ]	F		Mr Ben Gunn 16-1 Miss L Sweeting *(xnb) Tde; hld up in last; still last pr when fell 9*
[2ᶠ]	P		Newman's Conquest (5a) 100-1 M Shears *Ld 2-4; disp 3l 2nd 7; mist 8; grad lost plce; wknd 14; t.o & pu 2 out*
[260ᵁ]	P		Off The Cuff (IRE) 12-1 A Honeyball *6th 7; towards rr of main group 14; bhnd when pu 3 out*
[164⁵]	P		Sir Frosty 12-1 L Jefford *2nd/3rd to 12; sn wknd; bhnd when pu 3 out*

OFFICIAL DISTANCES: 5l, dist TIME: 6min 24.0s TOTE: £3.60

Leicester (RH 10F)
Tue, 7 Mar (GOOD to SOFT, SOFT in places)

459 Gary Wiltshire Queens Royal Lancers Mdn HC   7 ran

[243¹]	1		MR SNOWMAN 12-00 7-1 Mrs T Hill *Jw; chsd ldrs on outer; stdy prog 9; gd j to jn ldr 12; ld nxt; forged clr 2 out; rdn & r.o str flat*
[151²]	2	19	My Shout 12-07 1-2F B Pollock *Lw; jw in 2nd/3rd; bumped along to ld 6; jnd 12; rdn & hdd nxt; outpcd 2 out*
[275¹]	3	2	Gunner Boon 12-07 7-2 Miss P Jones *Nt jw; ld 3; mist 5 & hdd; prom til blun 9; 4th & outpcd 12; plugged on agn aft nxt; unable to chall*
[300³]	4	dist	Rustic Revelry 12-00 25-1 P York *Tk keen hld; hld up in tch; 4th aft 5; wknd 10; wl bhnd aft 12; t.o*
[306ᶠ]	5	18	Blue Marlin 11-09 66-1 J Owen *(xnb) Tk keen hld; ld to 3; lft in ld 5; w ldr to 12; wknd rap 3 out; blun nxt; t.o*
	P		Barney Bear 12-00 66-1 S Prior *Nt jw; mist 5 & sn lost tch; to 7; pu 11*
[371ᴾ]	P		Bustoni (IRE) 12-00 33-1 W Tellwright *(xnb) Hit 9; bhnd; lost tch bef 6; to & pu 3 out*

TIME: 5min 23.9s TOTE: £7.20; places £1.80,£1.20 Ex: £26.00 CSF: £10.18

460 Mallard Pawnbrokers HC   8 ran

[299³]	1		ARDSTOWN 11-08 4-1 F Windsor Clive *Trckd ldrs; outpcd 10; rdn 13; 5th & u.p 3 out; lkd hld til str rn u.p flat; ld 50yds out; game*
[90⁵]	2	3	Valiant Warrior 11-12 12-1 C Bonner *Jw; 2nd til ld 13; disp ld frm nxt til went 3l clr & lkd wnr flat; rdn & fnd little; caught cl home*
[226²]	3	1½	Shafi (IRE) 11-05 7-1 D Mansell *Settled rr; stdy prog gng wl 11; chall 15; w ldr nxt 2; drvn & hdd bef last; nt qckn flat*
[149⁵]	4	18	Desperate 11-09 40-1 R Barrett *Settled 3rd/4th; ev ch til hrd rdn 12; plodded on & nd frm nxt*
	P		China Gem (IRE) 11-07 33-1 V Keane *Nt fluent; last to 9; went cl up 11; mist 13; disp ld 14-15; rdn & wknd nxt; mist 2 out; pu last*
[155⁶]	P		Dromhana (IRE) 11-05 (bl) 50-1 Miss J Wormall *Pulled hrd; cl up til rdn & wknd 10; t.o 3 out; pu last*

| [90¹] | P | | **Mr Branigan (IRE)** 12-06 4-7F **B Pollock** Lw; ld; hit 4; rdn & ears back aft 8; nt fluent aft; hdd 13; wkng when mist 14 & imm pu; lame |
| [227³] | U | | **Pangeran (USA)** 11-09 16-1 **N King** Pulled hrd; midfield; in tch til 5th & pushed along when nrly fell & ur 12 |

TIME: 6min 16.7s **TOTE:** £3.80; places £1.10,£2.50,£1.60 **Ex:** £46.70 **CSF:** £41.63 **Tri:** £74.40

461 Clinton Racing-Away Racing No Tax Sherwood Rangers Yeomanry HC   9 ran

[150¹]	1		**SECRET BAY** 12-07 2-5F **B Pollock** Lw; jmpd v wl; disp ld to 3; ld app 6; drew clr aft 3 out; v easy
	2	23	**Nordic Spree (IRE)** 11-09 (bl) 33-1 **V Keane** Prsd ldrs; rmdrs aft 6; went 2nd 9; mist 11; drvn & outpcd aft 3 out
[244³]	3	19	**Fair Crossing** 11-07 6-1 **M Emmanuel** Rcd wide & in tch; disp 4th when stumbled bad 9 & rdr lost irons; lft poor 3rd 12; unable to chall aft
[224⁵]	4	20	**Time Enough (IRE)** 11-10 (1) 16-1 **P Townsley** (xnb) Chsd ldrs til rdn & outpcd 10; wl bhnd 12; t.o
[226⁹]	5	20	**Tickerty's Gift** 11-11 20-1 **T Gibney** Nt jw; chsd ldrs til mist 6 (water) & rmdrs; sn rr; hmpd 8; t.o 10; blun 2 out; climbed last
[153¹]	6	¾	**Not My Line** 12-00 66-1 **A Sansome** Disp ld; jmpd slow 2; w ldr when pckd 8; wknd 10; t.o 3 out
[443ᵁ]	F		**Fern Leader (IRE)** 12-00 66-1 **Mrs F Needham** Drpd to rr aft 5; 7th when fell 8
	F		**Knock It Back (IRE)** 11-09 10-1 **G Hanmer** Pulled hrd; prom; outpcd by ldng pr 10; 15l 3rd when fell 12
	P		**Macamore Star** 11-07 100-1 **Miss S Sharratt** Sn lost tch & drvn along; t.o 9; pu 12

TIME: 5min 25.5s **TOTE:** £1.40; places £1.00,£9.30,£1.20 **Ex:** £22.80 **CSF:** £19.26 **Tri^£124.60

462 Tom Fruit-Leicester Mdn HC   7 ran

[334¹]	1		**MICKTHECUTAWAY (IRE)** 11-12 4-5F **A Dalton** Lw; made most; mist 9 (water); jmpd delib 15; gng best nxt; pushed along aft 2 out; prsd brief last; drew clr agn flat
[367¹]	2	3½	**Burntwood Melody** 12-00 9-4 **R Armson** Ld 3-5; 2nd/3rd til hit 11 & releg 4th & outpcd; blun 14 & landed sideways; rallied aft 3 out; eff u.p & 2l 2nd last; stayed on game u.p but a hld
[305¹]	3	26	**Thats Dedication (IRE)** 11-12 11-1 **D Robinson** Spurs; lw; tk keen hld; trckd ldrs til 5th & outpcd aft 8; rdn to jn wnr brief 10; 2nd & u.p 15; btn nxt
[373¹]	4	5	**Stinging Bee** 11-12 14-1 **N Bell** Mist 13; prsd ldrs gng wl to 14; releg 5th nxt; rdn & outpcd 3 out; plodded on
[191⁴]	5	1¾	**True Chimes** 11-12 16-1 **J Owen** (xnb) Tk keen hld & sev posns; ld brief 8; releg 5th 12; rallied 15 & 2nd brief nxt; hrd rdn & sn wknd; mist last
[329⁴]	6	10	**Music Class (IRE)** 11-12 (bl) 50-1 **J Gallagher** Mist 1; imm detach in 6th; t.o 10; kpt on stdly aft last
[216ᴾ]	P		**Encima Del Rio** 11-12 25-1 **B King** Sn t.o; pu 9

TIME: 6min 21.0s **TOTE:** £2.10; places £1.10,£3.80 **Ex:** £2.30 **CSF:** £2.71

463 JIG - Coventry Thrusters HC   11 ran

[244²]	1		**MAJOR'S LAW (IRE)** 11-05 4-1JF **J Owen** Settled midfield; rcd wide far side; went prom 7; disp ld gng wl app 3 out; hdd bef nxt & sn outpcd; drvn along & rallied game flat; ld nr fin
	2	nk	**Halham Tarn (IRE)** 11-13 9-2 **M Foley** Drpd out last to 4; stdy prog to 5th 9; ld app 2 out; 5l clr last; rdn & flagged final 100yds; just caught
	3	26	**Us Four (IRE)** 11-12 (bl) 6-1 **M Armytage** Settled towards rr; mist 8; eff aft nxt; prsd ldrs 3 out; sn no ex
[79ᴾ]	4	8	**Northern Bluff** 12-02 7-1 **J Jukes** Prom; ev ch when blun 9; rallied & w ldrs nxt; rdn & btn app 2 out
[248ᴾ]	5	15	**Wot No Cash** 11-07 50-1 **R Lawther** Rr til hdwy 5; 2nd 7; jnd ldr 3 out; rdn & sn wknd
[384⁹]	6	25	**Raphael Bodine (IRE)** 11-09 (tt) 13-2 **Miss S Vickery** Tk keen hld; ld 3 til rdn & hdd 3 out; sn wknd; t.o
[300ᶠ]	7	5	**Vendoon (IRE)** 11-09 20-1 **T Gibney** A bhnd; lost tch 8; t.o
	U		**Caracol** 11-12 4-1JF **Miss P Jones** Drpd back to disp last when blun & ur 4
[137¹]	P		**China Lal** 11-00 20-1 **Mrs K Diggle** Ld to 3; sn lost plce; strugg in rr when mist 8; t.o & pu 12
[197ᴾ]	P		**Minty's Folly (IRE)** 11-09 (bl) 40-1 **A Evans** Prom til jmpd slow 5 & wknd rap; sn t.o; pu 7
[230ᴾ]	P		**Nowhiski** 11-05 50-1 **M Mackley** Prom til mist 6; wknd aft nxt; t.o & pu 3 out

TIME: 4min 17.4s **TOTE:** £4.70; places £2.10,£2.40,£1.70 **Ex:** £16.00 **CSF:** £18.72 **Tri:** £28.80

Bangor (LH 9F,18J)
Wed, 8 Mar (SOFT)

464 Hugh Peel HC   **5 ran**

[150⁴]	1		**SILVERDALESURESHOT** 12-04 evensF **R Burton** Handy & hld up; chsd ldr frm 12; mist 15 & outpcd; rdn app 2 out; stayed on to ld & hung lft flat; rdn out
[271¹]	2	1¼	**Mister Horatio** 11-07 6-4 **M Lewis** Set mod pce; drew 8l clr aft 3 out; rdn & hit last; slowed bad & hdd flat; kpt on agn cl home
[293²]	3	dist	**Commercial Artist** 12-00 10-1 **S Jackson** Tubed; ld to 2; 2nd til rdn & jmpd slow 12; wkng when hit 14; jmpd slow nxt; to 2 out
[293ᴾ]	4	dist	**Applefort** (IRE) 11-07 33-1 **M Worthington** Hld up; rdn & outpcd 12; to 2 out
	P		**Corkers Flame** (IRE) 11-07 16-1 **I Wynne** Hld up; drpd back last & hit 9; sn lost tch; to & pu 2 out

TIME: 6min 58.2s TOTE: £1.80; places £1.10,£1.90 Ex: £3.70 CSF: £2.59

Catterick (LH 8F,19J)
Wed, 8 Mar (GOOD to FIRM)

465 Colin Russell Nov HC   **10 ran**

[230¹]	1		**DONNEGALE** (IRE) 11-07 (bl) 7-2 **G Brewer** Handy; nt fluent 11 & 14; 4th 16; lft 3rd nxt; stayed on wl u.p to ld final 50yds
	2	1½	**Major Tom** (IRE) 11-07 9-4F **J Tate** Trckd ldrs; ld app 12; made most til hdd aft 16; lft 4th nxt; rallied last; kpt on u.p
	3	1¾	**Jalcanto** 11-07 4-1 **D Mansell** Hld up in tch; mist 7; eff 12; ld/disp 15 til ld 3 out; lkd wnr til rdn & wknd flat; caught 50yds out; bbv
	4	3	**Rascally** 11-04 8-1 **C Mulhall** Bhnd; mod 7th 16; gd prog to trck ldrs 2 out; kpt on same pce aft; btr for rce
[113ᵁ]	5	½	**Smiddy Lad** 11-07 12-1 **W Renwick** Nt fluent & wl bhnd early; stdy prog 12; lft 2nd 3 out; drvn & one pce nxt
	6	dist	**Eastlands Hi-Light** 11-07 8-1 **T Morrison** Rr div; strugg frm 12; to aft 16
[301⁵]	7	1½	**Just Ned** 11-07 33-1 **M Douglas** Chsd ldrs to 11; sn bhnd; to 16
[377⁶]	8	3½	**Flashlight** 11-07 16-1 **D Jewett** Ld; jmpd slow 4 & hdd brief; hdd agn app 12; ld brief 14; wknd rap aft 16; to
[365²]	P		**Bold Navigator** 11-07 16-1 **Miss M Bremner** 2nd/3rd to 11; wkng when pckd 12; mist 14; to & pu 2 out
[303ᴾ]	F		**Cebu Gale** (IRE) 11-07 12-00 16-1 **Mrs F Needham** Mist 1; sn trckng ldrs; ld aft 16 til hdd & crashing fall 3 out; dead

TIME: 6min 44.6s TOTE: £4.10; places £1.60,£1.90,£1.50 Ex: £12.70 CSF: £12.01

Towcester (RH 10F,18J)
Thu, 9 Mar (SOFT, HEAVY in places)

466 Ides of March HC   **4 ran**

[367²]	1		**MR FREEBIE** (DEN) 11-07 9-2 **N Bloom** Sn trckng ldr; outj 12; ld bef 2 out; wandered flat; r.o game; all out
[219ᶠ]	2	2	**Percy Smollett** 11-09 4-1 **Miss S Vickery** Trckd ldng pr; rdn 14; went 2nd bef 3 out; tried to chall & went rt u.p flat; nt qckn
[299⁴]	F		**Henry Bruce** 11-09 (bl) 2-1JF **D Mansell** (xnb) Detach in last; cajoled along final circ w little resp; drvn 15; still last when hmpd bad & fell last (rdr threw whip away in disgust & then tk off helmet which followed suit!)
[227ᵁ]	r		**Red Rebel** 12-02 2-1JF **B Pollock** Jmpd slow 2; ld til hdd & releg 3rd when jb rt 2 out; sn v tired; ref last

TIME: 7min 09.5s TOTE: £5.00; Ex: £16.30 CSF: £17.02

Wincanton (RH 9F,21J)
Thu, 9 Mar (GOOD to SOFT, GOOD in places)

467 Dick Woodhouse HC   **7 ran**

[303²]	1		**CHASING THE BRIDE** 11-11 (tt) 8-11F **M Miller** A handy; jmpd delib 5; ld app 14; mist 18; 4l clr & rdn 2 out; stayed on wl
[152³]	2	2½	**Madam Sioux** (IRE) 11-02 4-1 **D Dennis** Hld up in rr; hdwy to chse wnr 14; rdn app 3 out; nt fluent last; unable to qckn

[218⁵]	3	dist	**Alska (FR)** 11-02 40-1 *Miss W Southcombe Ld til app 4; ld agn 6 til hdd bef 14; wknd nxt; t.o app 3 out; fin rem 4th; subsq promoted*
[326⁷]	3d		**Malihabad (IRE)** 11-07 20-1 *Miss A Goschen Hld up; hdwy 11; chsd clr ldng pr frm 15; 20l down 18; t.o aft blun 2 out; fin dist 3rd; subsq disq*
[258¹]	P		**Brown Robber** 11-07 14-1 *T Dennis Prom; hit 3; 2nd when mist 11; rdn & wknd frm 13; t.o & pu 18*
[222ᵖ]	P		**Comedy Gayle** 12-00 15-2 *Miss S Gaisford In tch til wknd 14; 4th & btn nxt; t.o & pu 3 out*
[275²]	P		**Sip Of Brandy (IRE)** 11-11 20-1 *D O'Meara W ldr; ld app 4; mist & hdd 6; hit nxt; rdn & drpd to rr 12; t.o 15; blun 17; pu nxt*

TIME: 7min 05.1s **TOTE:** £1.70; places £1.40,£1.40 **Ex:** £2.90 **CSF:** £3.21
Malihabad finished third, but was subsequently disqualified by the Jockey Club Disciplinary Committee for testing positive to phenylbutazone and oxyphenylbutazone from a medication being given to another horse in the yard; the owner was fined £600

Hereford (RH 9F,19J)
Fri, 10 Mar (GOOD)

468 Bonusprint HC   **10 ran**

	1		**LOCHNAGRAIN (IRE)** 11-07 4-1 *D Dunsdon Lw; hit 5; settled midfield; 5th & prog 10; ld aft 16; 8l clr nxt; pushed along & stayed on wl*
[222⁴]	2	2½	**Rusty Bridge** 11-11 4-1 *R Burton Ld to 3; 4th 7; sn bhnd; last 11; rallied 3 out; went 2nd aft 2 out; drvn & nt qckn flat*
[449⁵]	3	6	**Highway Five (IRE)** 11-07 14-1 *D Dennis Prom brief; 7th 7; hit 10; rdn nxt; rallied in 5th aft 13; 3rd & btn 3 out; slogged on*
[271ᵖ]	4	2½	**Archer (IRE)** 11-11 (bl) 12-1 *A Price Ld 3 til outj 6; ld agn 10-15; 8l 2nd 3 out; rdn & nt r.o*
[210⁴]	5	7	**Red Parade (NZ)** 11-07 20-1 *Miss A Goschen (xnb) Chsd ldrs; 6th 10; outpcd & nd aft 13; 10l 6th aft 15; rdn & btn when lft 3rd & blun 2 out; wknd*
[345¹]	6	11	**Bit Of A Citizen (IRE)** 11-06 11-2 *E Williams Hld up & bhnd; 8l 8th 10; lost tch 16; hmpd 2 out; eased flat*
[270²]	P		**Alisha Bavard** 11-09 12-1 *J Jukes Jmpd v poor in last; t.o 7; pu 11*
[345⁵]	F		**Frown** 11-11 (bl) 33-1 *D O'Meara Hit 2 & 4; prom til ld 6-10; wknd aft 13; poor last when fell 3 out*
	F		**Harry Henbit (IRE)** 11-07 50-1 *P Sheldrake Pulled hrd in midfield; 3rd & eff 10; ld 15 til aft nxt; poor 6th & tired when fell 2 out*
[222¹]	U		**Now We Know (IRE)** 12-04 3-1F *Julian Pritchard Hld up in tch & gng wl; 8l 6th when blun & ur 12*

TIME: 6min 44.1s **TOTE:** £3.50; places £1.40,£1.40,£2.70 **Ex:** £12.00 **CSF:** £17.96 **Tri:** £173.80
Phaedair (J Diment, tde, ur & bolted & completed 1½ circs loose - should nvr be allowed on course) was withdrawn not under orders

Sandown (RH 11F,22J)
Fri, 10 Mar (GOOD)

469 Duke of Gloucester Mem (Past & Present) HC   **6 ran**

	1		**SHIPS DECANTER (IRE)** 11-07 (bl,tt) 5-2F *J Nicholl Ww; mist 5 (water); prog to trck ldr 13; ld 3 out; sn clr; 10l ahd last; easy*
[301²]	2	13	**Danegeld (IRE)** 11-11 (bl) 8-1 *C Ward-Thomas Ld to 4; mist 5 (water); ld 7-9 & agn aft 11; hdd 3 out; no ch w wnr frm nxt*
[303⁸]	3	11	**Stay Lucky (NZ)** 11-11 12-1 *D Alers-Hankey Cl up; 3rd & ev ch when mist 18; wknd aft 3 out*
[226³]	4	7	**Mr Motivator** 11-11 3-1 *O Ellwood Mists; in tch; ld 9 til aft 11; rdn & strugg 16; rallied to chall & ev ch 3 out; sn wknd*
[244⁵]	P		**Archies Oats** 11-11 (vis) 12-1 *J Trice-Rolph Jmpd slow & sn detach; u.p 4; clsd 9; wknd 11; t.o 12; pu 14*
[226⁷]	P		**Hawaiian Sam (IRE)** 11-13 3-1 *A Michael Ld 4-7; lost plce 12; mists aft; strugg 15; t.o when blun 2 out; pu last*

TIME: 6min 33.6s **TOTE:** £2.80; places £2.00,£2.20 **Ex:** £10.80 **CSF:** £16.81

Sandown (RH 11F,17J)

Sat, 11 Mar (GOOD, GOOD to FIRM in places)

470 Open Dick McCreery HC
6 ran

[384¹]	1		**COULTON** 12-07 11-10F **O Ellwood** (xnb) Chsd ldr; mist 11 (water); mist 13; clsd to ld 3 out; 2l and last; rdn & stayed on
[152ᴾ]	2	1½	**Noyan** 11-07 16-1 **Miss L Horner** Swtng; tk keen hld; ld; drew 5l clr aft 14; hdd nxt; chsd wnr aft; kpt on but no imp flat
[469¹]	3	20	**Ships Decanter (IRE)** 11-07 (bl,tt) 11-4 **J Nicholl** Rcd keen early; chsd ldng pr to 7; rdn nxt; sn strugg; poor 4th when blun 13; stayed on to rem 3rd agn 2 out
[191¹]	4	7	**True Steel** 11-11 8-1 **J Trice-Rolph** Last pr; lost tch 7; plodded round
[156⁶]	5	11	**Carley Lad (IRE)** 12-03 (tt) 10-1 **F Wheeler** Sn wl bhnd; 6th 3; lost tch 7; t.o 6th when pckd bad 12
[382ᴾ]	6	3	**Desert Calm (IRE)** 12-03 16-1 **D Alers-Hankey** Chsd clr ldng pr 7; nvr on terms; niggled along 10; wknd & lost 3rd 2 out

TIME: 5min 14.8s **TOTE:** £1.90; places £2.20,£4.10 **Ex:** £15.50 **CSF:** £13.81

Avon Vale

Barbury Castle (LH 8F,18J) Sat, 11 Mar (GOOD to SOFT becoming DEAD)

471 Open Maiden 567&8yo (Div 1), 12st
15 ran

[328ᴿ]	1		**BARTON NIC** 5-1 **P Keane** (xnb) Tchd 6s; swtng profuse; oht; tde; hld up; hmpd & rdr lost irons 1; blun 6; 8l 9th ½way; hdwy & 4l 5th 12; went 2nd 3 out; rdn to ld last; r.o wl
[264²]	2	1½	**Carbonado** 5-2F **P Pritchard** Tchd 3s; hld up & bhnd; 10l 11th ½way; hdwy 10; 6l 6th 12; went 2nd 4 2 out; hdd last; r.o
[284⁴]	3	12	**Fistral Flame** (5a) 6-1 **A Charles-Jones** Tchd 8s; a.p; 2l 3rd ½way; ld 13 til hdd 2 out; sn wknd
[341⁴]	4	12	**Winning Town** 8-1 **Miss S Talbot** Chsd ldrs; 4½l 6th ½way; 3l 4th when mist 12; 6l 5th 14; sn outpcd
	5	5	**Impenny** (5a) 50-1 **M Wall** Hld up; hdwy & 4l 5th ½way; lost plce & 10l 7th 12; no imp 14
	P		**Barton Bog (IRE)** 16-1 **A Evans** (xnb,b4) Prom; ld 3-11; 2nd & ev ch til blun 14; wkng when blun 15; 18l 5th when mist 3 out; pu 2 out
[391ᴾ]	P		**Bramley** 50-1 **A Martin** A bhnd; 13l 12th ½way; rdn 10; t.o & pu 12
[264ᵁ]	P		**Chancellors Vision** 4-1 **Miss S Vickery** Hld up; 7½l 8th ½way; lost plce 10; 15l 9th 12; t.o when mist 14; pu & dism 15
	F		**Crafty Phantom (IRE)** (12a,1ow) 10-1 **Julian Pritchard** Hld up; 9th when fell 8
[284ᵁ]	P		**Finnigan's Lot (IRE)** (5a) 50-1 **M Walters** Ld til hdd & mist 2; went 2nd 6; ld 11 til hdd & mist 13; sn wknd; bhnd when pu 3 out
	P		**Hickey's Gin Mill (IRE)** (5a) 50-1 **G Barfoot-Saunt** A bhnd; mist 7; 14l 13th ½way; 22l 10th 12; pu 13
[329ᴾ]	P		**Last Gamble** 50-1 **G Maundrell** (xnb) Ld 2-3; mist 5; 6½l 7th ½way; sn wknd; t.o & pu 12
[194ᴮ]	P		**Quick Response (IRE)** 7-1 **S Joynes** (citation) Hld up & bhnd; 9½l 10th ½way; rdn 11; pu 12
[221ᴾ]	B		**Riverlord** 50-1 **F Brennan** Tde; hld up; 10th when bd 8
[264⁴]	P		**Shamrock Lad** 33-1 **D Dennis** Chsd ldrs; 2½l 4th ½way; wknd 11; 13l 8th nxt; wl bhnd when pu 14

OFFICIAL DISTANCES: 1l, 12l **TIME:** 6min 49.3s **TOTE:** £7.50

472 Open Maiden 567&8yo (Div 2), 12st
12 ran

	1		**KANDLES-KORNER** 6-4F **Julian Pritchard** 2s-6/4; ww; 8l 5th ½way; hdwy 12; went 6l 3rd 14 & 4l 2nd app 2 out; ld last; rdn flat
[197ᴾ]	2	3	**Maquilleux** 11-1 **E Walker** (xnb) Went 2nd aft 1; ld 4; 4l clr aft 3 out; hdd & no ex flat
	3	runin	**Dunston Trigger** 10-1 **A Charles-Jones** Lost plce & mist 5; 11l 6th ½way; hdwy 10; 4l 3rd 12; wknd & 8l 4th 14; lft 3rd last
	4	6	**Lily Lane** 6-1 **Miss S Vickery** Chsd ldrs; 4l 3rd ½way; 7l 5th 12; sn wknd; 13l 6th 14; t.o
	5	8	**Mandy** (5a) 10-1 **G Weatherley** Tchd 12s; hld up & bhnd; 17l 9th ½way; eff & 8½l 7th 12; wknd & 12l 5th 14; t.o
	P		**Lily Brown** (12a) 16-1 **P Keane** Hld up; hdwy 4; 4th when blun 9; lost plce & mist 10; bhnd when pu 12
	P		**Madam Doris** (5a) 20-1 **G Barfoot-Saunt** Hld up & bhnd; hmpd 8; 14l 8th ½way; hdwy 10; 8l 6th 12; wkng when mist 13; pu 14

	F		**Miss Molly** (5a) 16-1 *S Joynes Lw; hld up; 6th when fell 8*
[247^P]	P		**Red Leo** (USA) 12-1 *J Harty Nd; 13l 7th ½way; bhnd when mist 11; pu 12*
	U		**Strike Accord** (IRE) 10-1 *M Dobson Mist 1; 7th when blun & ur 4*
[391^P]	P		**Whatacharlie** 8-1 *B Kendellen (xnb) Tubed; prom; lft 2nd 9 til wknd rap app 2 out; poor 3rd when pu last*
	U		**Wolfie's Daughter** (5a) 12-1 *M Wall Swtng; oht; ld to 4; 2nd til blun & ur 9*

OFFICIAL DISTANCES: 2½l, 25l TIME: 7min 02.2s TOTE: £2.60

473 Hunt
6 ran

[142¹]	1		**BALLY WIRRAL** (IRE) evensF *G Maundrell Jw; hld up; ld 5-6; 2nd til ld 8; r.o wl*
[302²]	2	1½	**Solo Gent** 6-4 *S Bush Ld to 1; ld 3-5 & 6-8; rdn & ev ch 2 out; nt qckn*
[38^U]	3	1½fs	**Simply Susie** (5a) 5-1 *P Keane 14s-5s; hld up; last to 5; hdwy 8; 4l 3rd ½way; wknd 14; t.o*
[247^P]	4	5	**Imperial Honors** (IRE) 50-1 *S Coady Prom; 5l 4th ½way; mists 11 & 12; sn wknd; wl bhnd 14; t.o*
	P		**Ask In Time** (IRE) 40-1 *S Goodings Drpd to rr 5; 12l 6th & rdn ½way; wl bhnd when pu 12*
[330^F]	P		**Silver Hill** 22-1 *Miss B Fear Ld 1-3; 4th when mist 7; sn lost plce; 10l 5th ½way; blun 11; wl bhnd when pu 12*

OFFICIAL DISTANCES: 1½l, dist TIME: 6min 46.5s TOTE: £2.00

474 Land Rover Mens Open, 12st
10 ran

[210²]	1		**BUTLER JOHN** (IRE) (7x) 1-2F *N Harris Tchd 4/7; nt jw; 2nd til ld 14; blun 15; 5l clr 2 out; jmpd v slow last; drvn out*
[154^P]	2	2½	**Formal Invitation** (IRE) (7x) 5-1 *S Joynes Tchd 6s; hld up & bhnd; 24l 7th ½way; hdwy & 6l 3rd 12; went 3l 2nd app 3 out; rdn 2 out; no imp*
[244^P]	3	15	**Winter Belle** (USA) (7x) (bl) 20-1 *R Shepherd-Cross Ld; sn 10l clr to 4; went 8l clr 11; hdd 14; 5l 3rd 3 out; no imp*
[299^P]	4	5	**Pontabula** (7x) 14-1 *A Charles-Jones Tubed; hld up; 22l 5th ½way; 18l 6th 12; went 15l 4th aft 14; no imp*
[454^P]	P		**Bitofabuzz** (IRE) (7x) 25-1 *D Birkmyre Chsd ldrs; jmpd slow 4; 20l 4th ½way; hit 10; eff 12; wknd & 13l 4th 14; mist 3 out; t.o & pu 2 out*
[333^P]	P		**Capstown Bay** (tt) 15-2 *Julian Pritchard Hld up & bhnd; 27l 9th ½way; mists 10 & 11; 25l 7th nxt; t.o 15; pu last*
[325⁴]	P		**Coolree** (IRE) (tt) 100-1 *M Shears Prom; 6l 3rd ½way; wknd rap 11; 29l 8th nxt; t.o & pu 15*
	P		**Golden Gunner** (IRE) 40-1 *P Young Chsd ldrs to 8; 23l 6th ½way; sn wknd; t.o & pu 12*
	P		**Good For A Loan** 20-1 *A Evans Hld up & bhnd; 26l 8th ½way; hdwy to 12l 5th when pu & dismt 12*
[294^P]	P		**Rockville Pike** (IRE) 50-1 *G Barfoot-Saunt (xnb) A bhnd; mist 8; 32l 10th ½way; t.o & pu 12*

OFFICIAL DISTANCES: 2½l, 15l TIME: 6min 48.2s TOTE: £1.60

475 Ladies Open
7 ran

[326¹]	1		**GREY SMOKE** 6-4 *Miss B Lloyd Tchd 2s; ld 2; 5l clr 9-13; mist 15; r.o wl*
[326³]	2	8	**Split Second** evensF *Miss A Dare (pricker ns) Went 3l 2nd 6; eff 13; rdn 2 out; no ex*
[262⁷]	3	15	**Beck And Call** (IRE) 14-1 *Miss S Vickery Ld to 2; 2nd to 6; 7l 3rd & rmdrs ½way; drvn along 12; sn outpcd; no ch 14; blun 2 out*
[262⁵]	4	1	**Chism** (IRE) 8-1 *Miss C Tuffin Prom til lost plce 6; 111 5th ½way; 16l 5th & no ch 14; went poor 4th aft 3 out; no imp*
[331¹]	5	6	**Lucky Tanner** 16-1 *Miss G Young (xnb) 20s-16s; lw; chsd ldrs; 9l 4th ½way; mist 10; 15l 4th 14; rdn & no imp when mist 3 out*
	6	20	**Khalidi** (IRE) 40-1 *Miss M MacGregor (xnb) Bckwd; rdr insecure; nd; 15l 7th ½way; wl bhnd 12; t.o*
[3⁴]	P		**Persian Butterfly** (5a) 50-1 *Miss T Habgood Swtng; a bhnd; 13l 6th ½way; pu 12*

OFFICIAL DISTANCES: 8l, 15l TIME: 6min 40.7s TOTE: £2.30

476 Countryside Alliance Club Members (Nov Rdrs)
15 ran

	1		**NEWTON POINT** 20-1 *Mrs B Keighley 1st ride; a.p; 3l 5th ½way; went 2nd 10; ld 12; comf*
	2	2½	**Celtic Town** 16-1 *P Kay 1st ride; hld up; 9l 11th ½way; hdwy to 4½l 6th 12; 5l 7th 14; went 3l 4th aft 3 out; chsd wnr 2 out; r.o*
[211³]	3	5	**Arise** (IRE) 14-1 *Miss T Harrison 1st ride; sn wl bhnd; 16l 13th ½way; 16l 9th 14; stayed on wl frm 3 out; went 3rd flat; too much to do*

[453⁴]	4	3½	**Parman (IRE)** 7-2 R Dalgety *Tchd 4s; sn prom; went 2nd aft 8; mist 9; lost plce & 5l 7th 12; rallied & disp 11 2nd 14; ev ch 3 out; wknd nxt*
[369⁴]	5	3	**The Crazy Bishop (IRE)** 3-1F B Shaw *10s-3s; chsd ldrs; 4l 6th ½way; 4l 5th 12; rdn 3 out; no ex*
[347ᴾ]	6	4	**Adventurus** 33-1 J Liley *Bhnd til hdwy 8; 5l 7th ½way; 3l 4th 12; 2l 5th when mist 14; wknd 3 out*
[241³]	7	1	**Cut A Niche** 4-1 M Baldock *Ld 3-12; 2nd & ev ch to 3 out; sn wknd*
[338ᵁ]	8	1½fs	**Wolfie Smith** 33-1 Miss W Houldey *Sn bhnd; 11l 12th ½way; 15l 13th 12; t.o*
	P		**Country Lord** 66-1 J Harty *Bckwd; swtng; sn wl bhnd; t.o 6; pu 13*
[389⁵]	U		**Cruise Free** 25-1 S Sellars *Hld up; 6½l 9th ½way; eff & 6l 8th 14; no imp 3 out; 6th & staying on u.p when mist & ur last*
[35ᴾ]	U		**Flickering Flame** 33-1 A Stainer *Swtng; rdr nrly f.o 1; 7th when succeeded 2*
[243³]	U		**Montecot (FR)** 4-1 R Biddlecombe *Tchd 9/2; sn prom; 2l 4th ½way; 1½l 4th 14; went 2l 3rd aft 3 out; 5l down & btn when mist & ur last*
[327⁵]	P		**Stalbridge Gold** (5a) 12-1 J Ferguson *Ld to 3; 2nd/3rd til wknd 10; 11½l 10th 12; wl bhnd 14; t.o & pu 2 out*
	P		**Trevveethan (IRE)** 16-1 N Sutton *Swtng; nd; 5½l 8th ½way; 11l 9th 12; lost tch 14; t.o & pu 2 out*
[340¹]	U		**Viking Flame** (5a) 10-1 Miss K Clift *2nd/3rd til lost plce 5; 8l 10th ½way; 12l 11th 12; wl bhnd 14; ur 3 out*

OFFICIAL DISTANCES: 1½l, 6l   **TIME:** 6min 54.2s   **TOTE:** £6.60

477 Restricted, 12st – 17J   18 ran

[329¹]	1		**HERE COMES HENRY** 5-1 R Young *Tchd 6s; hld up; mist 6; 3½l 6th ½way; hdwy & 2l 4th 12; ld 13; 5l clr 2 out; rdn & hld on wl flat*
[462ᴾ]	2	2	**Encima Del Rio (IRE)** 25-1 B King *Wdrs; 8l 8th ½way; eff & 2½l 5th 12; went 1½l 2nd by-passing 14; ev ch 3 out; stayed on wl flat*
[306²]	3	4	**Possible Pardon (NZ)** 8-1 A Charles-Jones *Tchd 10s; prom; mist 7; 4l 7th ½way; 4l 6th & rdn by-passing 14; lft 4l 3rd nxt; sn outpcd; stayed on wl frm 2 out*
[208²]	P		**Aberfoyle Park (IRE)** 4-6F R Walford *Opened 4/5; lw; prom; 1l 3rd ½way; lft in ld 10; hdd 13; wknd u.p 15; t.o & pu 2 out*
	F		**Bit Of A Character** 100-1 Miss R Porter *Bhnd til fell 6*
	P		**Courage II (FR)** 100-1 J Casemore *Mist 4; sn wl bhnd; t.o 7; pu 9*
	P		**Darzal** 100-1 F Brennan *A bhnd; mist 5; 9l 11th ½way; t.o*
	U		**Doujas** (5a) 100-1 S Sellars *Bhnd til hmpd, virt fell & ur 6*
[247²]	P		**Effie Wood** (5a) 16-1 D Crosse *Prom; 2½l 5th ½way; 11 3rd when mist 12; hit 13; 3½l 5th & rdn by-passing 14; wkng when mist 15; poor 4th when pu last*
	P		**Miss Madelon** (5a) 33-1 P Cowley *Ld til hdd 4; sn wknd; t.o 7; pu 11*
[392³]	F		**Mr Smudge** 10-1 A Martin *Hld up; hdwy & 2l 4th ½way; ld & fell 10*
[331ᴾ]	r		**Ngala (IRE)** (5a) 100-1 H Tett *Jnd ldrs; lost plce & 7l 9th ½way; 7l 8th 12; sn wknd; t.o 15; ref last*
[339ᶠ]	B		**Ole Gunnar** 22-1 Julian Pritchard (xnb) *Bhnd til bd 6*
[206¹]	P		**Phar Lord (IRE)** 12-1 G Barfoot-Saunt *Hld up & bhnd; 8l 10th ½way; hdwy & 5l 7th 12; went 4l 4th 3 out; sn wknd; poor 5th when pu last*
[406²]	U		**Rhyme And Chime** 20-1 Miss S Vickery *Prom; mist 4; went 2nd 5 til mist 13; 4l 3rd & rdn when mist & ur 15*
[193²]	F		**Royal Estate** 11-1 M Rimell *Tchd 12s; fell 2*
[260ᴾ]	P		**Solomons Mines (IRE)** 66-1 Miss C Goatley (xnb) *A bhnd; 12l 12th ½way; t.o & pu 13*
[328³]	P		**Spanish River** 100-1 G Weatherley *2nd til ld 5; hdd 10; wknd qckly & 10l 9th 12; t.o & pu 15*

OFFICIAL DISTANCES: 2l, 3½l   **TIME:** 6min 45.4s   **TOTE:** £3.60
Fence 14 omitted - fallen rider

Brecon & Talybont
Llanfrynach (RH 8F,18J) Sat, 11 Mar (GOOD)

478 Hunt, 12st   5 ran

[295¹]	1		**KERRY SOLDIER BLUE** (7x) 1-5F Miss P Jones *Made all; pushed out & kpt on wl flat; bit cheeky*
	2	1	**Twotensforafive** 6-1 Miss C Thomas *Jmpd slow 8; settled 3rd; 6l down 11; eff 15; went 2nd 2 out; drvn & ev ch last; no imp*
	3	12	**Sibor Star** 10-1 J Cook *Prsd wnr til releg 3rd 2 out; one pce & sn btn*
	P		**Eveies Boy (IRE)** (7a) 12-1 K Burke *Stdd aft 2 & cont last pr; eased hvly 7; pu 8*

[448ʳ]   P   **Penny Appeal** (5a) 20-1 M Scales *Last pr; mist 3; blun & almost ur 5; 15l last 11; t.o 14 & nt keen to cont; pu 2 out*

OFFICIAL DISTANCES: 1l, 8l   **TIME:** 6min 41.0s

479 Confined, 12st

                                         12 ran

	1		**RED NECK** (tt) 7-4 T Vaughan *(xnb)Pulled hrd in 2nd/4th; chall 3 out; ld nxt; in comm when jmpd delib last; rdn out*
	2	5	**Sebastopol** 12-1 G Lewis *Reins broke start & borrowed bridle frm Hunt horse; ld; 10l clr 12; hdd 2 out; one pce but nt able to game*
[340²]	3	6	**Lordinthesky** (IRE) 7-1 R Cooper *Still burly; hld up towards rr; prog to 15l 5th 12; still 5th 3 out; kpt on but unable to chall*
[333²]	4	2	**Merger Mania** 6-4F D Mansell *(xnb) Oht; swtng; tk keen hld in last trio to 12; prog to 5th app 15; 4th nxt; rdn & nt qckn aft*
	5	6	**Reeshloch** 9-1 Miss E Jones *Mostly 2nd & ev ch til wknd aft 3 out*
[343⁴]	6	4	**Same Difference** (IRE) (bl) 12-1 Mrs B Lewis *Mid-div; 10th & strugg 12; t.o app 15; some late prog*
	7	25	**Chiaroscuro** 10-1 S Lloyd *Settled trckng ldrs; 8th & wkng 12; t.o app 15*
	8	1	**Doctor-J** (IRE) (tt) 20-1 S Blackwell *Tk keen hld & prom; 2nd 6; 13l 4th & wkng 12; t.o app 15*
[275ᶠ]	P		**Comme Une Fleur** (FR) (5a) 20-1 E Williams *A rr; pckd 5; t.o 11; pu 12*
	F		**Danny Gale** (IRE) 10-1 T Faulkner *Lw; a bhnd; t.o 11; mist 12; fell 14*
[392ʳ]	P		**Lochchoire** 12-1 J Cook *Chsd ldrs til 7th & wkng 12; t.o & pu 15*
	P		**The Last Mistress** (5a) 20-1 J Price *Oht; hld up & bhnd til hdwy to midfield 6; 6th 12; lost tch 15 & pu 2 out*

OFFICIAL DISTANCES: 4l, 5l   **TIME:** 6min 28.0s

480 Mens Open, 12st

                                         15 ran

[271¹]	1		**WHISTLING BUCK** (IRE) (tt) 7-1 J Jukes *Bhnd & sn pushed along; 9th 12; still 8th app 15; str rn 2 out & forced ahd nr fin*
[343³]	2	hd	**Anorak** (USA) 5-1 C Williams *Rn in snatches; 2nd/4th to 8; 6th 12; 4th app 15; rallied to 6l 2nd 3 out; rdn & stayed on to ld flat; just caught*
[343²]	3	2	**Moon Tiger** 3-1JF D Jones *Mist 8; 2nd/4th til ld 14; 6l clr 3 out; lkd wnr nxt; rdn when mist last; sn hdd & no ex*
	4	15	**Tremendisto** (xnb) D Mansell *Reluct to line up & ss; stdy hdwy to 8th 12; eff when pckd bad 15; 4th & btn 2 out*
[294ᵖ]	5	3	**Watchit Lad** (tt) 3-1JF R Cooper *Midfield; 7th 12; 6th & eff 15; one pce & nd frm nxt*
	6	15	**Harbour Island** (bl) 7-1 J L Llewellyn *Bhnd; 10th 12; hdwy 14; 3rd & mist 15; sn wknd*
[296¹]	P		**Distant-Port** (IRE) 4-1 T Stephenson *Reluct & set off fnce bhnd; a t.o; nrly ref 5 & pu 12*
	P		**Maes Gwyn Dreamer** 20-1 G Lewis *Handy; impd to ld 8-13; lost plce rap; pu nxt*
	P		**Mags Super Toi** (IRE) 10-1 A Price *Prom; 2nd 12; ld 13-nxt; wknd qckly 15; pu 2 out*
	P		**Persian View** (7x) 8-1 T Vaughan *Ld to 8; wkng when mist 11; t.o & pu 2 out*
[334ᵖ]	P		**Scarlet Berry** (5a) 10-1 S Blackwell *Lw; pu & dism 5*
[345²]	P		**Shehab** (IRE) (7x) 20-1 M Trott *Ss; nt jw in rr; t.o 11th when mist 12; pu 14*
	P		**Side Bar** 25-1 J Phillips *A bhnd; t.o last 12; pu 2 out*
	P		**Tigersun** 10-1 D Hughes *(xnb) A bhnd but still just in tch then pu 12; school*
[271ᵖ]	P		**Willchris** 9-1 E Williams *Prom & tk keen hld; 4th 12; 7th & wkng app 15; pu 2 out*

OFFICIAL DISTANCES: nk, 2l   **TIME:** 6min 30.0s

481 Ladies Open

                                         11 ran

[343¹]	1		**DAWN'S COGNAC** (IRE) evensF Miss P Jones *Hld up towards rr til hdwy in 4th aft 7; 5l 4th 12; wl outpcd aft 14 & 16l 3rd 3 out; drvn along frm nxt & stayed on game to ld cl home*
	2	nk	**Busman** (IRE) 4-1 Miss L Pearce *Bit bckwd; trckd ldrs; 3rd aft 7; ld 15 & sn clr w event 4th; rdn app last & lkd wnr; overwhelmed nr fin*
	3	10	**Indefence** (IRE) 4-1 Miss C Thomas *Midfield; 6th 12; in tch aft 14; sn outpcd & 15l 3rd 3 out; mist nxt; no imp aft*
[382²]	4	1	**Royal Mountbrowne** (3x) 5-1 Miss E Jones *Tk str hld in 2nd/3rd; ld 11-13; sn ld agn; hdd 15; wknd 2 out*
[335¹]	5	15	**Karaburan** (5x) 5-2 Miss F Wilson *Lw; hld up in midfield; 5th 12; drpd back 7th aft 14; nd aft*
[346²]	6	2	**Young Manny** 12-1 Mrs B Lewis *Ld aft 1-11; ld brief 13; wknd qckly 15; poor 5th nxt*
[345³]	7	1	**Viardot** (IRE) 12-1 Miss G Roberts *Bckwd; a rr & nvr gng wl; 15l last 12; plodded on*
	P		**Chieftain's Crown** (USA) 16-1 Miss A Meakins *Ld 1; sn midfield; 12l 7th 12; lost tch aft 14; t.o & pu last*
	U		**Everso Irish** 14-1 Miss L Ryder *1st ride; bckwd; rdr insecure; 5th 5; rfo 7*

	P	**Herbert Lodge (IRE)** 14-1 *Miss M Bartlett A last; t.o to pu 10*
[272ᴾ]	P	**Sand Star** (5a) 50-1 *Miss J Gill 2nd 5; drpd back 8th aft 7; mist 9; t.o 10; nrly ref 11; pu 12; lame*

OFFICIAL DISTANCES: hd, 3l   TIME: 6min 27.0s

482 Intermediate, 12st   12 ran

[338¹]	1		**ROLL WITH IT (IRE)** evensF *D Barlow Trckd ldrs gng wl; 4th 11; went 2nd app 15; ld nxt; sn clr; easy*
	2	10	**Illineylad (IRE)** 2-1 *D Jones Ld 1; 2nd/3rd til ld agn 9; hdd 3 out; imm outpcd by wnr but a clr of rest*
[334ᴾ]	3	25	**Across The Water** (5a) 10-1 *A Wintle Drpd out in rr; still 7th app 15; r.o to pass btn horses aft; nvr nr ldrs*
	4	2	**Roman Gale (IRE)** 7-1 *S Blackwell Impd to 4th 7 & 2nd 9-14; wknd qckly app nxt; lkd to fin 5th*
[343ᵁ]	5	8	**Teigr Pren** 10-1 *P Sheldrake Ld 4-9; 2nd 14; lost plce qckly & v tired aft; lkd to fin 4th*
[275⁴]	6	1	**Bancyfelin Boy** 16-1 *J Keen Bckwd; a towards rr; jmpd slow 8; releg last & lsng tch app 15*
[344⁴]	7	12	**Terrano Star (IRE)** 25-1 *A Price Tubed; fat; ld aft 1-4; 6th 9; 5th app 15; wknd qckly; t.o*
	P		**Carraig-An-Oir (IRE)** 16-1 *R Hughes (xnb) Keen early; 2nd brief 5; 5th 7; rr 10; pu 12*
	P		**Cracker Ticket (IRE)** (7a) 8-1 *J Jukes Novicey & imm detach in last pr; stumbled 6; t.o 8; pu 12*
[344ᴾ]	P		**Hollow Sound** (5a) 14-1 *G Lewis Sn bhnd; lost tch 8; pu 12*
[343³]	P		**Icenfriendly (IRE)** 4-1 *Miss P Jones Lw; hld up in midfield; went 4th 9; ev ch app 15; sn outpcd; in bunch chsng clr ldng pr when pu & dism last*
	P		**Newchurch Lad** 8-1 *J Price Nt jw & imm detach in last pr; t.o 8; pu 12*

OFFICIAL DISTANCES: 8l, 6l   TIME: 6min 33.0s

483 Restricted (Div 1), 12st   13 ran

[273ᴾ]	1		**THE RURAL DEAN (IRE)** 20-1 *J Price Rr of mid-div; jmpd slow 8; prog in 4th 12 & 2nd 14; releg 4th brief; chall 3 out & sn ld; jnd nxt til drvn ahd flat*
[274ᴾ]	2	2	**Absent Citizen (IRE)** (5a) 6-1 *E Williams Lw; hld up & bhnd til 6th & prog 12; went 3rd aft 14; chall & ev ch 3 out; w wnr nxt til rdn & outpcd aft last*
[120⁷]	3	3	**Dinedor Charlie** (bl) 9-1 *D Jones Trckd ldrs; 7th 12; qcknd ahd aft 14; pckd 3 out & sn hdd; drvn along & fnd nil frm nxt*
	4	5	**Bel-De-Moor** (5a) 3-1 *T Vaughan A chsng ldrs; 5th 12; 6th & outpcd app 15; no imp aft*
[336ᵁ]	5	2	**Rusty Buck** 5-1 *S Blackwell 2nd/4th til ld 11-12; sn u.p; wknd 15 & no ch when hung bad lft & tried to rn off course app 2 out; forced to cont*
[218ᴾ]	6	1	**Mo's Keliro** (5a) 11-1 *Miss A Meakins Midfield & nd; 7th aft 14; unable to chall aft*
[338⁵]	7	30	**Hill Sprite** (5a) 12-1 *T Stephenson (xnb) Towards rr; u.p 10; nd frm 13 & nt keen*
	8	20	**The Gadfly** 14-1 *J Hayward Bckwd; ld til aft 3 & 7-8; wknd rap 11; t.o 13*
[332³]	9	3	**Gunners Dawn** (5a) 12-1 *K Ford A last & strugg; t.o 8*
[350¹]	P		**Gunner B Special** 5-4F *Miss P Jones Tk keen hld; ld aft 3-7; 2nd 12; wknd rap app 15; pu 2 out*
[274ᴾ]	P		**Itscinders** (5a) 20-1 *J Jukes Sn last but 1; t.o 11; pu 12*
[347ᴾ]	P		**Rue De Fort** 10-1 *G Lewis Tde; prom; ld 8-9 & 12 til aft 14; lost plce rap; t.o & pu 3 out*
[347⁵]	F		**Sea Search** 12-1 *J Keen V fat & lkd horrible; towards rr when fell 5*

OFFICIAL DISTANCES: 2l, 4l   TIME: 6min 34.0s

484 Restricted (Div 2), 12st   14 ran

[349¹]	1		**THEBETSONMARY** (5a) evensF *D Jones Midfield & gng wl; impd to 4th 7 & 2nd 10; chall 15; ld app 2 out; drvn & all out to hld rnwd chall of 2nd flat; game*
[69³]	2	nk	**Market Springer (IRE)** 3-1 *Miss B Williams (xnb) Lw; chsd ldrs; went 4th 11; 5l 3rd app 15; jnd ldng pr app 2 out; sn outpcd; rdn & rallied flat; stayed on wl*
	3	25	**Saywhen** 10-1 *R Cooper Lw; ld 1; ld 6 til imp jmpd slow 15; hdd app 2 out; sn wknd u.p*
	P		**Arctic Ridge** 8-1 *D Hughes Midfield; 7th 7; wkng when mist 11 & pu*
[332ᴾ]	P		**Little Star** (5a) 16-1 *T Stephenson A wl bhnd; t.o app 15; pu 2 out*
[204ᴾ]	P		**Mike's Dream** 10-1 *T Vaughan 3rd/4th til 8l 4th app 15; wknd qckly; pu 2 out*
	P		**Saronica-R** (5a) 20-1 *J Price (xnb) 2 handlers; mists in rr; t.o & pu 10*
[270¹]	P		**Secret Beauty (IRE)** (5a) 3-1 *M Lewis Midfield; mist 10; 5th nxt; 15l 5th & outpcd app 15; pu 2 out*
[392¹]	R		**Spirit Prince** 25-1 *R Hodges Swtng & oht; 2 handlers; 2nd/3rd & tk str hld; hung bad lft to boxes aft 4 & ref to steer; rn out 5*
[266ᵁ]	P		**Time To Share (IRE)** 6-1 *G Lewis Rr div; lost tch 12; t.o when crawled 3 out & pu*
[196ᴾ]	P		**True Fred** (bl) 25-1 *A St George Chsd ldrs til 6th & strugg 12; nt keen; t.o & pu 15*
	F		**Under Milk Wood** 25-1 *T Faulkner (xnb) Pulled hrd; ld aft 1-6; 7th & fdng when fell 13*

[268U]	P		Weaver Square (IRE) 25-1 M Parry *A last; t.o 10; pu 12*
[340³]	P		Who's Your Man (IRE) 2-1 A Wintle *Midfield; lost tch 12; t.o & pu 2 out*

OFFICIAL DISTANCES: nk, dist TIME: 6min 28.0s

485 Restricted (Div 3), 12st
14 ran

	1		THE ARCHDEACON (IRE) 5-2 T Stephenson *(xnb) Hld up; gd prog in 4th 10; 3rd 12; swept into ld 3 out & sn clr; quite impressive*
[336⁶]	2	8	Tiger Lord 7-1 S Blackwell *(xnb) A 2nd/3rd; chsd wnr aft 3 out; sn outpcd & btn aft nxt*
[340U]	3	1	Gt Hayes Pommard 7-1 D Howells *Sev posns; lost plce 8; 12l 9th 12; kpt on agn frm 3 out; 4th app nxt; stayed on & catching 2nd aft last*
[338⁷]	4	15	Grand Canyon 6-1 A Wintle *Hld up; hdwy 10; 5th 12; wknd 15*
[297⁴]	5	½	Innishfea (IRE) (5a) 6-4F F Windsor Clive *Ld app 2 til hdd 3 out; 3rd & wkng bef nxt; needlessly whipped home flat*
	6	12	Chantingo Lad 10-1 A Price *Ld 1; sn lost plce; 8th 12; lost tch nxt; plodded on*
	P		Andsome Andy (IRE) 10-1 T Vaughan *Chsd ldrs to 10; strugg when pu 12*
[349⁷]	P		Baytownghost 16-1 J Price *(xnb) Jb in final trio; t.o 11; nrly fell 13; pu nxt*
[349⁷]	P		Billy Whizz 20-1 P Sheldrake *Sn labouring in rr; t.o 11; pu 12*
[347⁶]	F		Gaelic Royale (IRE) (5a) 14-1 H Evans *Towards rr til fell 7*
[338⁷]	P		Le Vienna (IRE) 33-1 S Currey *Sn lumbering in rr; t.o 12; pu 2 out*
[347U]	P		Not For Profit (IRE) (bl,tt) 10-1 J Jukes *Sn handy; 3rd 10; 2nd 12; drvn & wknd app 15; climbed nxt; nt keen; pu 2 out*
	P		Out On The Town (5a) 12-1 James Tudor *Chsd ldrs; 7th 12; wknd qckly; pu aft 14*
[348R]	P		Tarian (USA) 20-1 C Williams *Prom til 8l 6th & wkng 12; mist nxt; wl bhnd when pu aft 14*

OFFICIAL DISTANCES: 6l, 2l TIME: 6min 36.0s

486 Restricted (Div 4), 12st
15 ran

[274⁴]	1		DYFFRYN PRINCE (IRE) 12-1 P Sheldrake *Midfield to 8; drpd back 16l 7th 12; still 12l 5th 3 out; str rn frm nxt; rdn to catch reluct ldr aft last*
[336⁴]	2	2	Bel Lane (5a) (vis) 4-1 D Jones *Ld to 2; ld 7; went 5l clr 3 out; lkd wnr but rdn & v doggy frm nxt; hdd flat*
	3	6	Dunsford Dazzler (5a) 3-1 D Hughes *Hld up trckng ldrs; 5th 11; 4th & eff 3 out; one pce bef nxt*
	4	6	Mister Jay Day 9-1 A Price *(xnb) Trckd ldrs; 4th 12; outpcd aft 15; tried to rally bef 2 out; drvn & sn no ex*
	P		Classic Fairy (IRE) 12-1 K Burke *(xnb) Nt jw in last & sn rem; t.o last when pu 13*
[337⁷]	P		Cool Spell (5a) 8-1 M Munrowd *A rem; t.o & pu 10*
[348¹]	P		Cresswell Quay 2-1 G Lewis *Lw; 3rd/4th til 2nd 11; disp ld when mist 14; 5l 2nd & outpcd 2 out; went out like a light; pu last*
[347²]	P		Howsyourluck (IRE) 6-4F T Vaughan *2 handlers; ld 2-7; 3rd 11; wkng when mist 13; t.o & pu 2 out*
[347⁷]	P		Just Ruffled 20-1 J Price *Chsd ldrs early; lost tch 7; t.o last when pu 13*
[274²]	P		Milly Le Moss (5a) 6-1 T Faulkner *Sn strugg in rr; rem 8th 12; t.o & pu 3 out*
[448³]	P		Netherbrook Lad (tt) 10-1 S Lloyd *Prom early; 3rd 7; 8l 6th 12; sn wknd; t.o 15; pu last*
[337⁷]	P		Nineteenofive (IRE) 14-1 F Windsor Clive *Tde; a wl bhnd; 9th & t.o 12; pu aft 14*
[341⁷]	P		Piccadilly Wood 14-1 E Williams *Mists in rr; wl bhnd when pu 9*
	P		Some Grey (5a) 12-1 J Hayward *Tde; pulled hrd & cl up brief; lost tch 7; rem 10th 12; pu aft 14*
[347⁷]	U		Young Mariner 16-1 J Edwards *(xnb) 14th when ur 3*

OFFICIAL DISTANCES: 2l, 4l TIME: 6min 33.0s

487 Confined Maiden (Div 1, Part 1), 12st
8 ran

[337⁷]	1		WITHOUT THE AGENT (IRE) 3-1 A Price *Lw; mist 5; hld up & cl up til ld aft 7; hdd 12; ld agn 3 out but hrd prsd aft; drvn & all out*
[267⁷]	2	½	Itsfreddie 7-1 J Jukes *Swtng; oht; 2nd til ld 12; hdd 3 out; hrd rdn & ev ch last; kpt on wl*
	3	25	Lady Palamon (5a) 4-1 P Sheldrake *Prsd ldrs in 3rd mostly; 3l down aft 14 but 6l bhnd & wkng 3 out; sn rem*
	4	runin	Western Pearl (5a) 10-1 Miss M Thomas *Jmpd slow; made most at funereal pce to 7; 10l 4th & wkng aft 14; t.o 3 out*
[350F]	P		Cauld Signal (IRE) (5a) 4-1 Miss B Williams *7th when blun 2 & pu*
	F		Gi Gi Brace (5a) 6-4F A Hardacre *Last pr but in & out of tch; 10l down aft 14; wknd rap & 26l last 3 out; t.o when fell nxt*
[350U]	P		Jesusa (5a) 10-1 G Maloney *A bhnd; t.o 8 & unable to gallop; pu 10*

[451ᴾ]	P	**Sergeant Miller** 6-1 R Hodges *Still bckwd; pckd bad 3; mist 6; handy til outpcd 11; rdr kpt waving aft; t.o 12; pu 2 out*

OFFICIAL DISTANCES: 1l, dist **TIME:** 6min 58.0s

488 Confined Maiden (Div 1, Part 2), 12st   9 ran

	1	**ITS A HANDFULL** 3-1 J Price *Lw; trckd ldrs in 4/5th to 11; impd to ld aft 14; rdn & kpt on flat; all out*
[70³]	2 nk	**Bally Boy** 2-1 D Jones *Prom & 2nd much of way; 3l 4th app 2 out; sust chall u.p aft; just hld nr fin*
	3 2	**Craigson** 3-1 C Williams *(xnb) Hld up in tch; 5th 11; chall 15; 11 3rd app 2 out; nt qckn last*
[269ᴾ]	4 8	**Marnies Song** (5a) 4-1 J L Llewellyn *3rd/4th til 2nd 10; rdn frm 14; nt r.o frm 3 out*
[341³]	5 4	**Brown Wren** (5a) evensF S Lloyd *Mist 4; hld up in tch; slpd bef 10; 6th 11; lft in ld 13-14; ev ch 2 out; sn wknd*
[349ᴿ]	r	**Annie's Alfie** 4-1 G Marsh *Ld & sn 12l clr; rn wide bef 4; mist 5; jmpd lft 6; hung bad lft bef 12 & sn hdd; wknd qckly aft 14; t.o when ref & threw inept rdr over 2 out*
[267ᴾ]	P	**Be Bop Bentley** (7a) 3-1 P Hamer *Sn stdd to rr & novicey; last frm 7; lost tch 9; t.o aft mists 12 & 13; pu 15*
[269ᴾ]	P	**Teelyna** 4-1 T Vaughan *Svs; sn in tch; jmpd slow 7; 7th 11; wknd qckly 14; mist 15 & pu*
	U	**Timmy Tuff** (IRE) 6-4 J Yeates *8th when ur 6*

OFFICIAL DISTANCES: ¾l, 2l **TIME:** 6min 51.0s

489 Confined Maiden (Div 2, Part 1), 12st   9 ran

[450ᶠ]	1	**CHERRY ALLEY** (IRE) (5a) 5-4F S Lloyd *Settled trckng ldrs; blun 9; 4th 11; went 2nd 14 but 5l 3rd nxt & 4th 2 out; sn rallied; ld bef last & went clr; comf*
	2 5	**Cold Snap** (IRE) 3-1 A Wintle *Midfield & handy; 5l 5th 14; brief outpcd 15; rallied & ev ch when mist 2 out; rdn & outpcd last*
	3 ½	**Julies Joy** (IRE) (5a) 8-1 I Johnson *Ld; drvn & hdd app last; nt qckn*
[348⁵]	4 10	**Star Island** 6-1 A Price *Impd to 3rd 7; went 2nd 15; ev ch nxt til mist 2 out; sn btn*
	P	**Blazing Connie** (5a) 4-1 G Perkins *Prsd ldr til rn wide & hung lft bef 12; wknd qckly 15; pu 2 out (originally plcd 3rd by Judge!); v disapp*
[270ᴾ]	P	**Keldan Star** (IRE) 10-1 J Phillips *Lft last 2; strugg when mist 10; climbed 11 & pu*
	P	**No Escape** 12-1 P Sheldrake *Mist 2; towards rr; last 11; t.o 13; pu 15*
	F	**Royal George** (IRE) 6-1 M Scales *Last when fell 2*
	F	**Up Your Street** (12a) 6-1 C Williams *Fell 3*

OFFICIAL DISTANCES: 1½l, 1l **TIME:** 6min 53.0s

490 Confined Maiden (Div 2, Part 2), 12st   7 ran

	1	**SCOTTISH CLOVER** (5a) 6-1 S Blackwell *2nd/3rd til ld 6-8; ld agn 14; hrd prsd when ploughed thro last; r.o game u.p*
	2 hd	**Tudor Flight** (5a) 6-4 M Munrowd *(xnb) Hld up til prog to ld 8-14; cl 3rd 3 out; kpt on u.p frm nxt; ev ch last; just hld nr fin*
[268ᴾ]	3 3	**Kopain** 5-4F J L Llewellyn *(xnb) Midfield; hit 8; 4th 11; chall 15; 2l 2nd & ev ch 3 out; no ex aft nxt*
	4 1½fs	**Greenfield Maid** (IRE) (5a) 5-1 J Keen *Hit 2; nt jw in last; 20l adrift 11; t.o 14*
	U	**Charlotte's Rose** (5a) 5-2 T Faulkner *Galloped flat out frm padd; ld to 6; 2nd 8; 5th & wkng when ur 12*
[269ᴾ]	P	**Itsarchie** 4-1 J Jukes *Settled 3rd 5-14; wknd rap; pu nxt*
	F	**Just Arnold** 6-1 D Jones *Bckwd; hld up in tch; 5th 11; 6th & wkng when fell 13*

OFFICIAL DISTANCES: hd, 3l **TIME:** 7min 01.0s

491 Confined Maiden (Div 3), 12st   15 ran

	1	**IRON PYRITES** (5a) 5-1 S Lloyd *Hld up in rr but gng wl; 9th 12; 6th & eff 15; str rn in 5th 2 out; drvn & stayed on wl to ld nr fin*
	2 nk	**Bohola Pete** (IRE) 3-1 F Windsor Clive *3rd/4th til 2nd 10; ld brief 2 out; hrd rdn & ld agn flat; caught nr fin*
[447ʳ]	3 1	**A Bit Of Fluff** (5a) 10-1 M Trott *Towards rr early; impd to 7th 12; 5th & eff 15; clsd to chall 2 out; ld app last; hdd & nt qckn flat*
[350³]	4 15	**Travel Safely** (IRE) 4-1 J Keen *Bhnd; 11th aft 14; passed btn horses frm 2 out; unable to chall*
	5 1	**Tommyknocker** (5a) 12-1 C Williams *A 4/6th; 4th & ev ch 2 out; rdn & sn wknd*
[348ᵁ]	6 1	**Beths Gift** (5a) 16-1 D Stephens (Wales) *Bhnd; 10th 12; some prog in fair 7th 15; sn btn*

[337⁴]	7	10	**Rusty Flame** 8-1 A St George *Ld 4 til drvn & hdd 2 out; wknd rap*
[388ᵁ]	8	runin	**Appeal Again (IRE)** 5-1 J Cook *Swtng; oht; ss & strangled in last; a t.o; public school*
	P		**Bit Of A Flutter** (5a) 8-1 I Johnson *Mist 3; a rr; t.o 5; 12th 12; pu 2 out*
	P		**Double Steal** 5-2 E Williams *Bhnd early; prog to 6th 12; 3rd 14; chall & 2l 3rd 3 out; drvn & sn wknd; pu last*
	r		**Gowenbacktodudley** (5a) 12-1 A Hardacre *Ss; hrd hld & wl t.o & jmpd erratic til ref & ur 5*
	P		**Guard A Dream (IRE)** 3-1 S Blackwell *Chsd ldrs; mist 6; 5th 12; wknd qckly aft 14; t.o & pu 3 out*
[450ᴾ]	P		**Jack Cruise** 8-1 K Burke *Ld to 3; 7th 7; 8th 12; wknd aft 14; t.o & pu 2 out*
[339²]	F		**Loc A Lua (IRE)** 5-4F A Wintle *Lw; tk keen hld; 4/5th til fell 10*
	P		**Mystery Belle** (5a) 8-1 D Jones *Bckwd; ld 2-4; 2nd/3rd to 12; lost plce rap to 8th aft 14; t.o & pu 2 out*

OFFICIAL DISTANCES: hd, 3l   **TIME:** 6min 48.0s

Cumberland Farmers
Dalston (RH 8F,18J) Sat, 11 Mar (GOOD to SOFT becoming DEAD)

492 Hunt, 12st   7 ran

[424³]	1		**DUNNELLIE** (5a) 2-1F A Robson *Cl up; 3l 5th & mist 6; last 8; mist 10 & pushed along; rmdrs aft 13; prog 15 to 3l 2nd aft nxt; ld aft 2 out; all out; bbv*
[426¹]	2	1¼	**Border Burn** 10-1 J Ewart *(bf) Green; nt a fluent; 8l last 11; rr but in tch til gd prog frm 3 out; ev ch nxt; 4l 2nd at last; nt qckn flat*
	3	4	**Kaz Kalem (IRE)** 7-1 S Hughes *(xnb,bf) Cl up; jmpd to disp ld 10; ld aft 15; 10l clr aft nxt; hdd aft 2 out; 2l 3rd & no ex last; improve*
[376⁶]	4	20	**Nosmo King (IRE)** (bl) 3-1 Miss L Kendall *(bf) Ld rnd at start; in tch in rr of chsng group; pckd 2; 7l last 5; went 10l 2nd 15; sn outpcd*
	P		**Dari (IRE)** 7-1 D Jewett *Lw; prom; 3l 3rd 5; ½l 2nd 13; 3l 2nd 15; pu nxt*
[360ᴾ]	P		**Full Of Chat (IRE)** (5a) 6-1 T Davidson *Swtng; ld; ll up 4; ll mid 4; jnd 10 til outpcd aft 14; wl bhnd 3 out; t.o & pu nxt*
	P		**Greenfinch (CAN)** 6-1 Miss R Barrow *Trckd ldrs; ll 2nd & jmpd slow 4; outpcd 13; sn lost tch aft; wl bhnd when pu last*

OFFICIAL DISTANCES: 1½l, 4l, 15l   **TIME:** 6min 43.0s   **TOTE:** £2.00

493 Confined, 12st   13 ran

	1		**ALLRITE PET** (5a) 5-1 Miss P Robson *Mid-div; chsd ldrs in 4l 4th 3 out; ld app 2 out; 2l up at last; r.o wl*
[376²]	2	2½	**Greenhil Tare Away** 4-1 P Atkinson *Trckd ldr; 2l 2nd 9; ld 12; ll up 3 out; hdd & mist 2 out; no ex u.p last*
[359⁵]	3	2	**Dear Do** (5x) 7-1 Miss M Neill *Mid-div; 12l 4th 6; prog to 3l 3rd 3 out; ev ch nxt; outpcd; r.o agn flat*
[186ᶠ]	4	3	**Riverside Run (IRE)** 7-2 A Robson *Oht; mid-div til prog 12; 10l 5th app 2 out; kpt on; nt pce to chall*
[360¹]	5	4	**Love Actinium (IRE)** (5a) 6-1 C Niblo *Mid-div; 10l 4th & pckd 4; mist 5th 9; prog when mist 3 out; outpcd app nxt; kpt on*
[359⁶]	6	10	**Boyup Brook** 7-1 T Morrison *Mid-div; 8l 6th 16; hit 2 out; nvr nrr*
[362ᶠ]	7	2	**Kilminfoyle** 10-1 J Mactaggart *Rr & nvr plcd to chall; 15l 10th 11; 15l 7th 16; kpt on*
[183³]	8	25	**Rum Rebel** (3ow) 9-4F J Walton *4s-9/4; mid-div; 12l off pce 9; 10l off pce 12; nvr nrr; 20l off pce 16; kpt on one pce*
[423ᵁ]	P		**Castle Bay (IRE)** 100-1 D Jewett *(bf) Ld; 5l and 8; hdd 12; wknd qckly & jmpd rt 14; pu aft*
[365ᶠ]	P		**Four North (IRE)** 100-1 T Scott *Rr; jmpd big 2; 25l last 5; to 8; pu aft 13*
	P		**Mr Fudge** 40-1 P Lentelink *Prom; 3l 3rd 3-4; 15l 3rd 8; sn outpcd; t.o & pu last*
[107ᶠ]	P		**Pilmur Girl** (12a,2ow) 100-1 A Richardson *Rr; 25l 12th 7; t.o & mist 9; pu 13*
	P		**Rebel King** 25-1 R Morgan *Mid-div early; lost plce 8; wl bhnd 11; t.o & pu 15*

OFFICIAL DISTANCES: 2l, 3l, 2l   **TIME:** 6min 31.0s   **TOTE:** £3.00

494 Ladies Open   9 ran

[421¹]	1		**BALISTEROS (FR)** 5-4F Miss J Wormall *Handy; 4l 4th 7; 4l 4th 14; disp ld frm nxt; duelled w 2nd til stayed on str to ld flat*
[109¹]	2	1	**Riparius (USA)** 7-4 Miss P Robson *Mists; handy; hit 3 & 11; 5l 4th nxt; 4l 5th 13; prog to disp ld aft 15; duelled w wnr til hdd flat; just hld*
[421⁵]	3	15	**Miss Accounts (IRE)** (5a) 14-1 Miss A Armitage *Ld; 2l up 2; 2l clr 8; 11 ahd 11; hdd & easily brushed aside aft 3 out; 10l 3rd & btn nxt*

	4	nk	**Good (IRE)** 80-1 Mrs V Jackson (orbs) Oht; in tch; 4l 4th 11; 8l 6th 14; outpcd aft nxt & sn bhnd
[361F]	5	20	**Oat Couture** (2ow) 16-1 Miss S Johnstone A rr; 10l last aft 2; detach 8; t.o 15
[225F]	6	4	**Dashmar** 5-1 Miss R Barrow Trckd ldr; disp 2l 2nd 4; 1l 2nd 13; outpcd aft nxt; t.o 2 out
	P		**Ifafa Beach (IRE)** 80-1 Miss L Bradburne A rr; mist 1; 15l off pce & lsng tch 8; pu aft 12
[111F]	P		**No Problem Jac** (5a) (tt) 16-1 Miss L Hislop Mists; pulling; mist & nrly ur 2; hit 3; 4l 4th 5; mist 9; jmpd big 10; 10l 7th 11; sn outpcd; bhnd when pu 2 out
	U		**Rallegio** 6-1 Mrs A Hamilton Cl up; disp 2l 2nd 4; chsd ldrs; 3l 3rd when mist & ur 14

OFFICIAL DISTANCES: 1l, 15l, 1l **TIME:** 6min 30.0s **TOTE:** £2.00

495 Mens Open, 12st
7 ran

[362P]	1		**BOW TIE** 5-2 R Morgan Cl up; disp 2l 2nd 8; 2l 5th nxt; just ld 14; 5l up app 2 out; sn wl clr; in comm when hit last; eased flat
[279⁴]	2	20	**Jr-Kay (IRE)** (4ow) 3-1 N Bannister Oht; 5l 3rd 3; 4l 4th & mist 13; disp 4l 3rd 3 out; sn outpcd; kpt on; tk 2nd flat
[419F]	3	½	**Strathmore Lodge** (5a) 10-1 D Jewett In tch; 3l 5th 7; 2l 3rd 13; prog to ½l 2nd 14; wkng when mist 2 out; sn btn; tired & dem flat
	4	2	**Dean Deifir (IRE)** 4-1 C Storey (xnb) Oht; hdstrng; ld 1; trckd ldr til ld agn app 12-13; 3l 3rd 15; disp 4l 3rd 3 out; wknd rpdly 2 out; tired flat
[301F]	5	1½fs	**Willy Wee (IRE)** (1ow) 33-1 R Westwood Sis; pulled to ld aft 1; ½l up & mist 11; sn hdd & wknd; 10l 5th 14; t.o 3 out
[362¹]	U		**Excise Man** (7x) (tt) 2-1F J Walton Swtng; cl up til mist & ur 3
	P		**Warner's Sports** 10-1 J Innes 1st ride; rr & mist 1; 10l last 6; mist & nrly ur 9; rdr lost irons & pu app nxt

OFFICIAL DISTANCES: 20l, ¾l, 2l **TIME:** 6min 39.0s **TOTE:** £3.00

496 Dodson & Horrell PPORA Club Members, 12st
7 ran

[183²]	1		**TEA BOX (IRE)** 4-7F Miss P Robson (bnh) Pulling; made virt all; 2l up frm 3; nrly jnd 9; drew 3l clr app last; stayed on
	2	5	**Sounds Strong (IRE)** (4x) 7-2 N Bannister Cl up; 5l 4th 5; 2l 3rd 9; prog to disp 2l 2nd 3 out; sn outpcd & no ch w wnr
[171U]	3	1¼	**Majority Major (IRE)** 20-1 T Glass Trckd ldr in cl 2nd to 14; disp 2l 2nd 16; rmdrs in 3rd & no resp app 2 out; kpt on flat
	5	2fncs	**Heavenly Citizen (IRE)** 16-1 Miss E Edminson A rr; 10l last 4; 20l last 8; 2 fncs bhnd 14
[420F]	4d		**Lindon Run** 20-1 Miss R Barrow Prom 5l 5th 7; 10l 5th & pushed along 11; sn bhnd; 25l 5th 14; tk poor 4th 2 out; beaten 25l for 3rd; disq - nt weigh-in
[418F]	P		**Ballyboden** 10-1 F Arthur In tch; 4l 6th 3; outpcd aft 10; 15l 4th & wkng 13; poor 5th 2 out; wl bhnd when pu last
	P		**Mick Man (IRE)** 8-1 S J Robinson 20s-8s; handy; 4l 4th 8; stumbled on landing 10; pu & dism

OFFICIAL DISTANCES: 4l, 1½l, dist **TIME:** 6min 38.0s **TOTE:** £1.20
Lindon Run finished fourth but was disqualified when the rider failed to weigh-in; the rider was warned as to her future conduct but no fine was imposed

497 Restricted (Div 1), 12st
11 ran

[365¹]	1		**DUN ROSE** (5a) 5-4F C Storey Lw; in tch in mid-div; prog to 2l 4th 15; chall aft 3 out; level last; r.o wl to ld nr line
[360⁵]	2	hd	**Trivial (IRE)** (5a) 9-2 R Morgan In tch in rr early; 10l 4th 4; went 3rd 6; prog to disp ld frm 3 out; level & ev ch last; r.o wl; just outpcd
[364⁵]	3	3	**Senso (IRE)** 3-1 Mrs C Cox Rr early; 12l 5th & hdwy 4; 7l 7th 15; 3l 3rd & ev ch 2 out; no imp nxt
[424⁷]	4	25	**Cruise Around** (8ow) 20-1 S Ramsay Reluct start; 15l last 2; bad mist & nrly ur 6; 15l 10th 9; blun & nrly ur 12; sn wl bhnd
[363F]	P		**Border Country** 20-1 Miss M Bremner A rr; 20l last 6; mist 8; climbed 11; t.o & pu nxt
[364¹]	S		**Hooky's Treat** (5a) 6-1 Miss L Hislop Nt a fluent; ld; 8l up & jmpd slow 4; jnd 9; hdd 11; ld agn 13; jmpd slow 15; hdd aft nxt; btn 3rd when slpd up app 2 out
[188F]	F		**House Of Oasis (IRE)** 20-1 D Jewett Oht; mid-div; outpcd 15; 15l 5th when fell 2 out
[420U]	P		**Joss Bay** 12-1 T Davidson 2 handlers; mid-div; prog to disp ld 9; ld 11; hdd 13; grad wknd aft; t.o & pu 2 out
[423⁴]	P		**Luvly Bubbly** 14-1 Miss C Hall Trckd ldrs; 4l 2nd 3; outpcd nxt; bhnd 11; t.o & pu 2 out
[188P]	P		**Mesling** (4ow) 16-1 J Walton Mid-div; mist 3; in tch til bad mist 13; outpcd; t.o & pu 2 out
	P		**Pennyman** 16-1 T Glass Prom; 6l 3rd 3; ½l 2nd 8; outpcd 14; wknd qckly aft; t.o & pu 3 out

OFFICIAL DISTANCES: hd, 3l, hd **TIME:** 6min 43.0s **TOTE:** £2.00

498 Restricted (Div 2), 12st   8 ran

[423²]	1		**STORM ALIVE (IRE)** 6-4F Mrs V Jackson Prom; mist 2; 4l 6th 7; prog to ld 12; jnd 15 til ld agn 2 out; 11 up at last; r.o wl
[365³]	2	1	**Hey Chief (IRE)** 10-1 **P Strang Steel** Mostly 3rd/4th; 3l 5th 11; rmdrs nxt; 4l 4th 15; ev ch frm 2 out; disp 11 2nd at last; r.o; a hld
[358ᵁ]	3	½	**Flaming Sunrise** 5-2 Miss D Calder Prom; disp ld 7 & agn 10; 4l 5th 13; drpd back & gvn breather; prog to 6l 5th 15; 4l 4th at last; clsd flat; just hld
[424ᴾ]	4	nk	**Mini Cruise** 8-1 L Morgan Ld/disp til hdd 12; disp ld agn 14 til hdd aft 2 out; disp 11 2nd & ev ch last; dem 4th nr fin
[360³]	5	10	**Kings Token** (3ow) 11-4 J Walton Handy towards rr til 2l 3rd 8; eff 15; 5l 5th & no imp nxt
	F		**Colisnova** (5a) 14-1 C Niblo A rr; 10l last 5; bhnd when fell 11
	U		**Javaman** 14-1 Miss L Bradburne Mounted on course; ld to start; prom; cl 5th when mist & ur 9
	P		**Overton Girl** (5a) 33-1 T Davidson Cl up early; lost tch 9; 25l last 11; pu 12

OFFICIAL DISTANCES: 1½l, 1l, 1l **TIME:** 6min 43.0s **TOTE:** £2.00

499 Open Maiden 56&7yo (Div 1), 2m4f, 12st - 15J   12 ran

[426ᵁ]	1		**SHAY GAP (IRE)** 7-1 C Storey (xnb) Chsd ldrs; 6l 4th & mist 10; rmdrs aft; prog to ½l 2nd 2 out; sn ld; 2l up at last; r.o
[364ᶠ]	2	1	**On Merit** 5-1 T Oates Ld; 3l clr aft 12; jnd aft 2 out; sn hdd; stayed on; btr for rce
[425ᶜ]	3	1	**Blackchesters** 4-1 J Walton In tch in mid-div; 4l 4th 5; 5l 6th 10; eff & ev ch app 2 out; sn outpcd; kpt on wl flat
[189ᴾ]	4	1	**Magical Poitin** (5a) 6-1 A Richardson Rr; 15l off pce 8; gd prog frm 12; 6l 5th aft nxt; kpt on wl; nt trble ldrs
	5	25	**Prince Of Perils** 5-2 T Davidson A rr; 10l off pce 10; 20l down aft 13; kpt on; tk poor 5th flat
[379³]	6	hd	**Hey Sam (IRE)** 5-1 T Glass Prom; mists 2 & 3; 3l 3rd 7; rmdrs nxt; cl up 12; sn wknd
	7	runin	**Reflective Way** (5a) 10-1 R Robinson Rr & mist 1; 25l down 6; fnce bhnd 12
[187ᵁ]	P		**Alizarine Blue** 10-1 Miss L Kendall A p; disp ld 7; 3l 3rd 9; sn wknd; wl bhnd 13; pu nxt
[425ᶠ]	F		**Ballylesson (IRE)** (7a) 6-4F Miss P Robson Jmpd novicey; rr & mist 3; hit 4; 15l 8th 5; fell 8
[187ᵁ]	P		**Eastlands Twilight** 5-1 T Morrison (bf) In tch in rr; 10l 6th 10; sn wknd; t.o & pu last
[364ᴾ]	P		**Poppers** 20-1 T Scott Prom early; 3l 3rd 5; grad wknd; lost tch frm 8; pu 11
[381ᴿ]	P		**Wheresbob** 10-1 A Robson (xnb) Rr; bad mist 1; sn t.o; pu aft 4; saddle slpd

OFFICIAL DISTANCES: 1½l, 1l, 1l **TIME:** 5min 39.0s **TOTE:** £9.00

500 Open Maiden 56&7yo (Div 2), 2m4f, 12st - 15J   10 ran

[380²]	1		**GO NOMADIC** 11-4F P Atkinson Nt a fluent; made most at mod pce; 11 up 9; hdd brief 3 out; ½l up at last; r.o wl
[426²]	2	2	**Anotherhandyman** (xnb) P Johnson Settled in tch in rr; mist 4; gd prog aft 3 out; cl 2nd nxt; ev ch last; r.o; a hld
[425⁵]	3	1	**Divet Hill** 7-2 M Clayton Lw; mid-div; disp 6l 5th 5; 8l 6th app nxt; prog to 3l 3rd 13; ev ch when blun 2 out; 3l down at last
[182²]	4	1	**Valley Hopper** (7a) 7-1 B Lusted Rr; 8l last 2; prog aft; 4th & ev ch app last; stayed on; nt trble ldrs
[363⁴]	5	¾	**Running Mute** 3-1 Miss P Robson Chsd ldrs; disp 6l 5th 5; prog 13; ev ch app last; switched flat; stayed on; nt rch ldrs; improve
	6	1	**Stygian Star (IRE)** (5a,8ow) 14-1 M Smethurst A p; ½l down 8; ld brief 13; sn hdd; kpt on app last
	7	1	**Wishing Ash (IRE)** 14-1 T Davidson Rr; mist & nrly ur 1; sn gng wl; prog to 4l 6th 8; 4th 11; ev ch 2 out; no exa app last; kpt on flat
	8	15	**Strictly Hard** (5a) 12-1 L Morgan Trckd ldrs; 3l 2nd 2; 2l 3rd 10; wknd 12; bhnd app last; eased flat
	P		**Foxwood Polo** (12a,5ow) 8-1 A Robson Oht; rr; mist 4; 8l last 9; wknd 11; to 13; pu 2 out
	F		**Juinevera (IRE)** (12a) 7-1 T Oates (xnb) Mists; in tch in mid-div when fell 10

OFFICIAL DISTANCES: 2l, 1½l, 1l **TIME:** 5min 52.0s **TOTE:** £3.00

501 Open Maiden 56&7yo (Div 3), 2m4f, 12st - 15J   9 ran

[113ᶠ]	1		**MYSTICAL MUSIC** (5a) 8-1 Miss M Bremner In tch; 3½l 3rd & hit 5; hmpd 8; outpcd 10; 30l 4th & prog 13; 10l down & plenty to do last; sprinted flat; ld nr line
	2	1	**Inglebrig Lad** 6-1 T Davidson Tried to make all; 3l up 5; 20l ahd 12; rmdrs 2 out; 6l clr & lkd wnr last; napped flat; kpt on agn; hdd nr line

[46⁵]	3	nk	**Test Of Loyalty** 4-1 A Robson *In tch in rr til 12l 3rd 11; rmdrs aft nxt; 15l 3rd & mist 2 out; r.o wl u.p flat*
	4	2	**Border Reiver (IRE)** evensF T Oates *5/2-evens; chsd runaway ldr frm 8; 12l 2nd 11; ev ch 2 out; outpcd app last*
	P		**Carefree Love (IRE)** 12-1 T Glass *Chsd ldrs; sn wknd; bhnd & pu 11*
[188⁰]	F		**Carrie's Gift** (bl) 14-1 S Hughes *A rr; 15l 8th apr 4; fell 7*
[112⁴]	P		**Iveston (IRE)** (5a) 16-1 S Brisby *In tch in rr; jmpd slow 1; 15l 4th 10; sn bhnd; t.o & pu 13*
[379F]	P		**Lewesdon Countess** (5a) 12-1 Miss P Robson *Nt jw; 10l last & mist 2; lost tch 5; mist nxt & pu*
[363P]	U		**The Dust Buster** 14-1 R Trotter *(bf) Trckd ldr; 3l 2nd 5; bad mist & ur 8*

OFFICIAL DISTANCES: ¾l, 1l, 2l TIME: 5min 45.0s TOTE: £4.00

Holderness

Dalton Park (RH 8F,20J) Sat, 11 Mar (GOOD to FIRM)

502 Hunt

4 ran

	1		**UBU VAL (FR)** 4-7F Miss S Brotherton *Made all; 2l up 4 til qcknd clr 15; 20l up 3 out; eased app last; canter*
[438U]	2	6	**Honeysuckle Lil** (5a) 2-1 T Gardham *Jmpd slow 1; last to 7; pushed along frm 11; 8l 3rd nxt; went 20l 2nd 3 out; clsd on eased wnr last; flatt by prox*
	3	1½fs	**Mr Eglantine** 3-1 D Thomas *Chsd ldr in 2l 2nd to 14; outpcd & wknd 16; t.o 3rd 3 out*
[435P]	4	2fncs	**Crucial Runner (U)** 12-1 M Ollard *6l 3rd til mist 7; last & wkng 8; t.o last 12*

OFFICIAL DISTANCES: 5l, dist, dist TIME: 7min 20.0s

503 Restricted

11 ran

[378F]	1		**POLAR KING (IRE)** 4-7F D Easterby *Ld to 6; trckd ldng pr in 3l 3rd to 15; ld 3 out; jnd at last; qcknd to ld agn flat*
[396⁶]	2	3	**Yornoangel** 10-1 R Clark *(xnb,boh) Cl 5th to 5; hdwy to ld 8; jnd 14; hdd aft 15; 2l 2nd 2 out; chall app last; outpcd flat*
[278³]	3	8	**Deer Park Lass (IRE)** (5a) 25-1 D Thomas *Mid-div to 9; hdwy to ½l 2nd 12; disp ld 14-15; 4l 3rd 3 out; wknd & one pce nxt*
[374¹]	4	1	**Joridi Le Forige (IRE)** (bl) 33-1 B Orde-Powlett *A.p; clr w ldrs 11; 4l 4th 13; pushed along & wknd 16; 8l 4th 2 out; r.o flat*
[396⁷]	5	4	**Traceytown (IRE)** (5a) 12-1 Miss Rachel Clark *(xnb) Hld up in rr to 7; outpcd 14; hdwy frm 3 out; fin rtr; nrst fin*
[377²]	6	½	**Mount Faber** (bl) 7-1 S Charlton *A midfield; 5l 6th 12; outpcd & wknd 17; bhnd 2 out*
[380¹]	7	12	**Mefein Boy** 8-1 W Burnell *A rr; outpcd & bhnd 13*
[378P]	P		**Chief Engineer** 33-1 L McGrath *Swtng; reluct to line up; bhnd by 3; lsng tch 7; t.o 11; more than fnce adrift when pu 16*
[379¹]	r		**Gemolly (IRE)** (5a) 4-1 C Mulhall *Reluct; kicked owner in stomach & hospitalised him when smacked at start; ref 1*
[381U]	P		**Im Struggling** (7a) 33-1 K Lupton *Blun bad & rdr lost irons 1; t.o 3; pu 13*
[396P]	P		**Mac's Blade (USA)** 33-1 R Edwards *(bh) Trckd ldrs to 6; prom when mist 10; 2l 4th 12; wknd qckly aft nxt; t.o & pu last*

OFFICIAL DISTANCES: 2l, 6l, 1l TIME: 7min 19.0s

504 Mens Open

9 ran

[395²]	1		**MR DICK** 1-2F S Swiers *Rr til hdwy aft 7; 4th 10; 3l 3rd 12 til qcknd to ld 15; 6l up 17; drew rt away; v easy*
[374²]	2	25	**Calleva Star (IRE)** 8-1 R Abrahams *Cl 2nd til ld 4-7; cl 2nd til outpcd 16; 15l 4th 3 out; stayed on to dist 2nd 2 out*
[375⁴]	3	4	**Final Beat (IRE)** 6-1 C Cundall *Midfield; 20l 5th 17; stayed on on pce; nrst fin*
[384P]	4	6	**Private Jet (IRE)** 33-1 R Clark *Rr to 8; gd hdwy frm 12 to 5l 3rd 12; cl 3rd 15; ev ch til outpcd & wknd 3 out*
[395⁴]	P		**Be Brave** 33-1 R Lochman *Last by 2; lsng tch when jmpd slow 7; t.o & pu 12*
	P		**General Brandy** 16-1 G Tuer *A midfield to rr; 8l 6th 13; outpcd 15; 22l 6th when pu 2 out; easy rn*
[277⁶]	P		**Postage Stamp** 14-1 B Orde-Powlett *Mid-div; 10l 7th & mist 12; pushed along 13; wkng 16; t.o & pu 2 out*
[377¹]	F		**Prime Style** 20-1 C Gibbon *(xnb) Ld to 3 & agn 8-13; 2l 2nd 14; 4th & wkng when fell 17*
[279P]	P		**Supercharmer** 4-1 D Easterby *Pulled hrd; chsd ldrs; 10l 3rd 4; hdwy 8; went ½l 2nd 12; jnd ldr 13-15; 6l 2nd & wkng 3 out; pu last*

OFFICIAL DISTANCES: 20l, 4l, 2l TIME: 7min 01.0s

505 Ladies Open
7 ran

[280P]	1		**THE MINISTER (IRE)** 11-4 Miss T Jackson *Trckd ldr in 2l 2nd to 15; chall 3 out; 1l up nxt; r.o wl*
[280²]	2	2½	**Monkey Ago** 4-6F Miss J Foster *Cl up; ld frm 6 til jnd 3 out; sn hdd; 2l 2nd & one pce last; badly cut on off-hind*
[277U]	3	6	**Misti Hunter (IRE)** 14-1 Miss Rachel Clark *(xnb) Mid-div to 8; 5l 5th nxt; hdwy to 4l 3rd 15-3 out; sn outpcd*
[397⁴]	4	4	**Temple Garth** 7-1 Miss F Hartley *(xnb) Ld to 5; cl up til wknd 9; rr 11; outpcd 14; 15l 5th 17; stayed on to 4th 2 out*
[397U]	5	runin	**The Hazel Harrier (IRE)** 10-1 Miss A Deniel *(bh) A last; mist 10; lsng tch 14; to 3 out*
[280P]	P		**Double Tempo (IRE)** 6-1 Miss R Clark *Pulled hrd; 5l 4th 6; rn v wide bend bef 7; 4l 3rd when bad mist 12; wkng when bad mist 16; to & pu nxt*
	P		**Dublin Hill (IRE)** 20-1 Mrs F Needham *A rr; in tch til outpcd & wknd 14; to & pu 16*

OFFICIAL DISTANCES: 2l, 4l, 2l TIME: 7min 04.0s

506 Confined
10 ran

[375²]	1		**INSIDEOUT** 7-2 Mrs L Ward *(xnb) Chsd ldr; 2l 2nd 9; ld 10; 8l clr 11; jnd 16; sn hdd; 2l 2nd when flew last; fin fast to ld on line*
[375¹]	2	1	**Jackson's Hole** 2-5F D Easterby *Ld to 9; trckd ldr; 8l 2nd 12; stdy hdwy to cl 2nd 16; ld agn 3 out; 2l up & gng wl when nt fluent last; outrdn flat & hdd on line*
[170P]	3	1½fs	**Gaelic Warrior** 50-1 Miss Rachel Clark *Mid-div to 11; 18l 4th nxt; pushed along & went 20l 3rd & lsng tch 15; r.o one pce frm nxt*
	R		**Markham Lad** 100-1 K Prendergast *Last when rn out 5*
[378¹]	P		**Mr Hook** 100-1 R Clark *Bhnd by 5; last 12; poor 5th 15; rem when pu 3 out*
[379²]	C		**Norman Way** (7a) 33-1 P Cornforth *Rr & mist 5; bhnd & lsng tch when carried out by loose horse on bend bef 7*
[370P]	P		**Optimism Reigns (IRE)** 33-1 S Charlton *Nt jw; chsd ldng pr in 8l 3rd til mists 8 & 9; wknd 11; to & pu 16*
	P		**Pashby Wood** (5a) 50-1 M Morley *Burly; rr by 3; jmpd slow 4; bhnd & lsng tch when pu 13; school*
[375P]	F		**Pharlindo (IRE)** 9-2 Mrs F Needham *(xnb) Sa; hld up in rr early; pulled to 12l 4th 6; 15l 3rd 11; chsng ldng pr when fell 14*
[277³]	P		**Springhill Quay (IRE)** 12-1 Miss R Clark *Rr & mist 9; hdwy to 22l 4th 14; poor 4th when pu 3 out*

OFFICIAL DISTANCES: ½l, dist TIME: 7min 04.0s

507 Countryside Alliance Club Members Maiden (Div 1)
13 ran

[282F]	1		**ERNI (FR)** 7-4 W Burnell *Mid-div til 4l 4th 8; trckd ldrs til 3l 3rd 16; rdn to ld app 2 out til outpcd app last; 1l 2nd & hrd rdn flat; ld on line*
[380U]	2	½	**Tricky Trevor (IRE)** 4-6F Miss H Delahooke *Mid-div to 11; went 6l 5th 12; mist 13; rushed into ld app 14-3 out; cl 2nd til ld app last; 1l up til outrdn & hdd cl home*
[439R]	3	15	**Nasayer (IRE)** 10-1 A Pickering *Ld to 4; cl 3rd to 14; ld brief 3 out; outpcd & wknd app nxt*
	4	25	**Russian Prince (IRE)** (7a) 14-1 D Thomas *Mid-div when bad mist 9; 8l 6th 12; chsd ldrs til wknd 14; poor 4th 3 out*
[399P]	5	runin	**Captain Oates** 12-1 M Watson *Nvr put in rce; sn bhnd; to 14; stayed on frm hopeless posn*
[400P]	U		**Hopeful Earl** 8-1 N Tutty *Blun bad & ur 1*
[168P]	F		**Imperial Line** 8-1 Miss T Jackson *Prom; ld 5-7; cl 2nd 10-12; handy 3rd when fell 13*
[399P]	P		**Just A Single (IRE)** 6-1 G Markham *25s-6s; mid-div; went 8l 6th 8; hdwy to 1l 2nd 12; wknd 15; to & pu 2 out*
	P		**Maggie Simpson** (5a) 25-1 C Mulhall *A rr; last pr 10; to & pu 14*
	P		**Miss Gloria** (5a) 20-1 S Charlton *(xnb) Sn bhnd; to last 10; pu 15*
	P		**Not So Prim** (5a) 25-1 S Swiers *Prom; pulled to ld 7-13; wknd 14; to & pu 2 out*
[379P]	P		**Perdix** (12a) 33-1 Miss J Foster *Tkn rnd gently in rr; bhnd & lsng tch 7; to 13; pu 15*
[398P]	P		**Sir Ruscott (IRE)** 14-1 K Green *Jmpd abysmal; jmpd slow 3 & 4; to & pu to*

OFFICIAL DISTANCES: ½l, 20l, 20l TIME: 7min 10.0s

The stewards enquired into how Tough Decison had been included as a runner for this race and had been bet on; the Clerk of the Course reported that an error by the Declarations Clerk was missed by the Paddock Stewards and Starter; no action was taken

508 Countryside Alliance Club Members Maiden (Div 2)
11 ran

[398⁴]	1		**CURTAINSATCHOPWELL (IRE)** 12-1 K Green *Settled wl in ld; pulled 15l clr 7; dist ahd 11; still 15l up 3 out; galloped on str*

[381²]	2	8	**The Butcher Boy** 4-5F D Easterby *Nt a fluent; chsd along in bunch; 20l 5th 8; went dist 2nd 11; chsd wnr vain aft; slt hdwy when mist 3 out; kpt on*
[399⁴]	3	12	**Fiery Jack** 12-1 N Tutty *4s-4/4m; poor 14; 20l 4th 16l; stayed on one pce; tk 3rd flat*
[436²]	4	8	**Ron On The Run (IRE)** (bl) 3-1 S Charlton *Chsd ldrs; 30l 3rd 11; poor 3rd out; wknd last; dem flat*
[399ᴾ]	5	10	**Tyndrum Gold** 10-1 Miss A Deniel *(bh) A bhnd; t.o 3 out*
[380³]	6	5	**Cape Crusader** 20-1 C Mulhall *Rr to 9; hdwy to poor 6th 12; kpt on one pce; nvr nrr*
[281⁴]	7	12	**Port Valenska (IRE)** 6-1 B Woodhouse *A rr; rem 6th 14*
[378³]	8	2	**Lewis** (bl) 4-1 Miss T Jackson *Chsd runaway ldr to 10; dist 3rd 13; wknd 14; 5th & pushed along 16; sn strugg*
[398ᵁ]	P		**Benn Wood** (7a) 33-1 Miss S Brotherton *Sa; last 10; mist 12; t.o last when pu 15*
[400ᴾ]	F		**Charlie Dazzle (IRE)** 16-1 R Edwards *Sa; rr when fell 2*
[437ᶠ]	P		**Silent Snipe** 20-1 W Burnell *Last by 7; slt hdwy 11 to 7th 13; wknd; pu 15*

OFFICIAL DISTANCES: 6l, 6l, 6l **TIME:** 7min 10.0s

Oakley
Newton Bromswold (RH 9F,19J) Sat, 11 Mar (GOOD)

509 Hunt   **5 ran**

[20ᵁ]	1		**DEEP SONG** 9-1 Miss Carla Thomas *14s-9s; hurdled fncs; ld to 2; ld 4-7; chsd ldr aft; eff to chall 2 out; ev ch last; outrdn flat; fin 1/2l 2nd; awarded rce*
	2	runin	**Glenselier (IRE)** 10-11F I Hudson *Sn detach frm ldrs; jmpd slow 6; 17l 3rd 10; wl bhnd 14; cont t.o; fin 3rd; promoted*
	3	runin	**The H'penny Marvel (IRE)** 6-1 G Tawell *Imm detach in last; t.o frm 1/2way; rem 4th 4 out; fin 4th; promoted*
[434ᴾ]	5	4	**Bangapin** 33-1 M Buchan *Ld 2-3; pckd nxt; stdly wknd; dist last frm 16*
	1d		**Vulgan Prince** 5-2 R Barrett *4s-5/2; chsd ldr 4; ld 7; clr 9-3 out; jnd nxt; drvn to hld on; won by 1/2l; disq - nt draw weight*

OFFICIAL DISTANCES: 1/2l, dist **TIME:** 6min 50.5s **TOTE:** £4.00 **DF:** £10.60
Vulgan Prince finished 1st but was disqualified when the rider was unable to draw the correct weight (weighed-in 9lb light having lost weightcloth)

510 Confined, 12st   **20 ran**

[413¹]	1		**NOUGHTOSIXTY (IRE)** 11-4F B Pollock *Hit 1 hrd; made virt all; clr 4 out; stayed on str; impressive*
[243ᶠ]	2	8	**Lottie The Lotus** (5a) 7-2 J Tarry *Lkd rough; sn rr; 14th & wl bhnd 1/2way; rap prog frm 15; scythed thro rivals frm nxt; tk 2nd aft last; no ch w wnr*
[85ᴾ]	3	2	**Who Is Equiname (IRE)** (bl) 33-1 S Morris *Hld up in rr; mist 9; prog 13; chsd wnr 3 out; no imp when mist last; lost 2nd flat*
[320²]	4	12	**Mister Trick (IRE)** (bl) 6-1 N King *Rr; jmpd slow 7; rdn & no resp 13 & lost tch ldng group; r.o frm 4 out; nrst fin*
[415²]	5	2	**Teeton Builds** 7-1 A Sansome *Mist 3; ldng trio to 15; one pce & btn aft nxt*
[93²]	6	hd	**Fresh Ice (IRE)** (3x) 7-1 R Barrett *Wl plcd; lft 2nd 13 til aft nxt; lft 2nd agn 4 out; fdd*
[246¹]	7	hd	**Winters Tale (IRE)** (5a) 14-1 T Lane *Prom in chsng group; wl on terms 14; rdn when mist 3 out; stdly wknd*
[454ᴾ]	8	5	**Hill Island** (3x) 20-1 Miss L Sweeting *Mid-div; nvr on terms w ldng group; outpcd aft 13; no ch aft*
[296ᴾ]	9	20	**Priory Piper** (3x) 25-1 L Hicks *Ldng trio to 13; sn wknd; wl bhnd 3 out*
[296ᴾ]	10	1/2	**Mr Freeman (IRE)** (vis) 33-1 J Diment *Mid-div; lost tch frm 13; no ch aft*
[371⁴]	11	15	**Lunar Dancer** 33-1 B Durrell *Set off 15l bhnd rest; a t.o; fin full of running*
	12	15	**Real Progress (IRE)** 14-1 D Renney *A wl in rr; no ch frm 11*
	13	25	**Pims Gunner (IRE)** 25-1 Mrs C Lees *Sn wl in rr; lost tch frm 5*
	P		**Apple Nicking** 33-1 E Linehan *Bit bckwd; jb; sn wl in rr; t.o & pu 11*
[248ᴾ]	U		**Cuban Skies (IRE)** 33-1 A Barnett *Mid-div; 10th when blun & ur 6*
[246ᴾ]	U		**Fencing Master** 25-1 T Illsley *Lw; trckd ldng group; prog to 2nd when mist & ur 13*
	P		**Hope's Delight (IRE)** 33-1 R Smith *Swtng; nvr nr ldrs; wl in rr 11; t.o & pu 14*
[428ᴾ]	P		**Its Murphy Man** 33-1 A Tutton *Chsd ldrs; mist 7; wknd rap 9; t.o & pu 12*
[92³]	P		**Lord Knox (IRE)** 25-1 A Coe *Swtng; a towards rr; wl bhnd when pu 14*
	U		**Scarba** (3x) 16-1 C Wadland *Ww; stdy prog frm 13; went 5l 2nd when blun & ur 4 out*

OFFICIAL DISTANCES: 4l, 2l **TIME:** 6min 38.0s

511 Mens Open   **8 ran**

[320¹]	1		**COPPER THISTLE (IRE)** 1-4F R Hunnisett *Lw; ld to 8; ld agn 13; gd j & drew clr frm 4 out; in comm when hit 2 out & last; r.o wl*

[244⁴]	2	20	**Grecian Lark** 8-1 J Tarry *Prom; ld 7-13; outpcd in 3rd when mist 15; stayed on to 2nd agn bef last*
[417ᴾ]	3	12	**Prince Of Saints (IRE)** (bl) 20-1 A Sansome *Ldng group; jnd wnr 14; upsides when outj 4 out; hrd rdn & nt r.o aft; lost 2nd app last*
[367ᴾ]	4	6	**Broadway Swinger** (tt) 33-1 S R Andrews *Set off 10l bhnd main group; rr; jmpd slow 6 (ditch); eff in 5th when mist 13; sn outpcd; jmpd slow 15 (ditch); r.o agn frm 2 out*
[243ᴾ]	5	10	**Blessed Oliver** 33-1 R Lawther *Set off 10l bhnd main group; mist 1; nvr on terms; mist 12; no ch frm 15*
	6	3	**Jasilu** (5a) 20-1 D Flavin *Cl up & gng wl til outpcd aft 13; wknd 3 out*
	7	8	**Limosa** (5a) 33-1 R Barrett *Set off 10l bhnd main group; a bhnd; lost tch 9; rdn 13; t.o*
[302ᴾ]	P		**In Place (USA)** 33-1 T Lane *Lw; jmpd lft; w ldrs to 11; sn wknd; last when pu 4 out*

OFFICIAL DISTANCES: 20l, 10l **TIME:** 6min 38.0s **TOTE:** £1.70 **DF:** £2.40

512 Ladies Open - 17J
11 ran

[368¹]	1		**IMPERIAL DAWN (IRE)** evensF Miss L Rowe *Declined early pce; prog to press ldr 9; sust chall frm 13; rdn to ld last 300yds; coaxed home w hands & heels final 100yds*
[453³]	2	1½	**Mr Custard** 10-1 Miss L Sweeting *Prom; ld 8; prsd frm nxt by wnr; slt ld last; hdd final 300yds; kpt on game*
[307¹]	3	7	**Lily The Lark** (5a) 6-1 Miss H Irving *Settled rr; prog to trck ldrs 9; 4th 13; outpcd nxt; 3rd agn aft 15; nvr able to chall; kpt on*
[414⁴]	4	20	**Cill Churnain (IRE)** 33-1 Mrs E Coveney *Mists; ss; sn in tch; prog to trck ldng pr 13 til aft 15; sn btn*
	5	½	**Boarding School** 4-1 Miss A De Lisle Wells *Mist 5; in tch in rr; outpcd 13; 19l 6th 15; one pce aft*
	6	35	**Awbeg Rover (IRE)** 33-1 Mrs S Hodge *Ww in tch; outpcd 13; sn no ch; nt pushed*
[192²]	7	hd	**Lake Mission** 10-1 Miss G Browne *Prom til drpd last aft 9; lost tch 13; t.o aft*
[245ᵁ]	U		**Erbil (IRE)** 33-1 Miss E Owen *Bit bckwd; 2 handlers; ld to 2; drpd to rr & 9th 9; eff to 5th 13; same & wl btn til rfo 2 out*
[197ᴾ]	P		**Mr Matchit (IRE)** 33-1 Miss A Burton *Ld 2-8; wkng when blun 13; t.o & pu 15*
[368ᵁ]	U		**Persian Sword** (bl) 33-1 Miss P Swindin *Wl in tch to 11; 9th & wkng when rfo 13*
[218⁴]	U		**Sabre King** (bl) 16-1 Miss N McKim *Ur 1*

OFFICIAL DISTANCES: 1l, 5l **TIME:** 6min 32.0s **TOTE:** £2.30 **DF:** £19.00
Fences 10 & 19 omitted - fallen rider

513 Dodson & Horrell PPORA Club Members Restricted, 12st
15 ran

[196²]	1		**RIGHT COMPANY** 5-1 B Pollock *2 handlers; trckd ldrs & a in tch; prog to 2nd 15; ld aft 3 out; jnd nxt; clr last; hrd prsd flat; fnd ex nr fin*
[440ᴾ]	2	¾	**Tumlin Oot (IRE)** 33-1 M Lurcock *Rdr calling cabs; in tch in rr; outpcd by ldrs 16; rap prog 2 out; str rn to press wnr & lkd likely wnr final 100yds; nt qckn und flapping drvng nr fin*
[458ᵁ]	3	10	**Mr Ben Gunn** 14-1 Miss L Sweeting *Lw; ss; hld up in tch; prog frm 14; jnd wnr brief 2 out; wkng when mist last*
[196ᵁ]	4	½	**Please Call (IRE)** 14-1 E Linehan *In tch; jmpd slow 7; mist nxt; outpcd by ldrs aft 4 out; r.o agn bef last*
	5	6	**Proud Fountain (IRE)** 5-1 T Lane *7s-5s; a wl in tch; 4th & ch aft 3 out; wknd nxt*
[248²ᵈ]	6	8	**Benova Boy** 16-1 J Diment *2 handlers; swtng; made most to 4; stayed wl in tch; lsng plce when pckd 16; no ch frm nxt*
[341¹]	7	1	**Hijacked** 4-1F R Lawther *Nt a fluent; w ldrs; lost plce sltly 12; still ch 16; btn & nt pushed aft nxt*
[247³]	8	3	**Derryair** 20-1 C Weaver *2 handlers; jmpd slow 3; in tch; prog to press ldr 13-15; sn rdn & wknd*
[194¹]	P		**Dark Knight** 5-1 J Owen *(xnb) Hld up in tch in rr; strugg frm 12; 11th when mist 15; no ch aft; pu 2 out*
[371ᴾ]	R		**Dorgan** 33-1 A Sansome *Svs; in tch in rr til blun 6 & rdr lost irons; rn out nxt; cont w rdr unable to pu*
	P		**Goforitkate (IRE)** (5a) 14-1 T Illsley *25s-14s; bckwd; ld 4-9; in tch til wknd 15; pu 3 out*
[429ᴾ]	F		**Goforitmrsmulligan (IRE)** (5a,5ow) 25-1 P Hall *Fell 1*
[260ᴾ]	P		**Playmore (IRE)** 9-2 David Dennis *Prom; ld 9; hdd aft 3 out; cl up when rn v wide bend app 2 out & lost all ch; pu 2 out*
[432¹]	P		**Rolcap** 8-1 J I Pritchard *Nvr gng wl; rdn 8; strugg 11; t.o & pu 14*
[429⁵]	P		**Tranquil Lord (IRE)** 33-1 D Smith *Bhnd frm 3; t.o & pu 9*

OFFICIAL DISTANCES: ½l, 10l **TIME:** 6min 43.5s **TOTE:** £3.70 **DF:** £31.60
The stewards interviewed the rider of Dorcan who had dangerously cantered the horse through racegoers after pulling up; considering an earlier report that he had appeared to run down a member of the public they warned him as to his future behaviour

514 Open Maiden (Div 1)   15 ran

[121P]	1		**CELIAS TWINK** (5a) 7-1 *R Barrett 14s-7s; a cl up; ld 12; drew 5l clr aft 3 out; lft virt solo bef nxt; rdn out unnecessarily flat*
[250U]	2	250yd	**Abbey Flyer** 7-2JF *T Illsley Nt jw; chsd ldr to 11; chsd wnr 13-14; blun 15; wknd; lft rem 2nd bef 2 out*
[233³]	3	1	**Grangewick Flight** 6-1 *K Needham (xnb) Trckd ldrs til rn v wide bend bef 9 & drpd to rr; gd prog frm 13; chsd wnr 16; 5l 2nd when rn off course bend app 2 out; event rtrcd & nrly caught tired 2nd*
	P		**Belldoran** 8-1 *F Hutsby 16s-8s; swtng; in tch; 4th ½way; wknd & pu 12*
	P		**Five O'One** (IRE) 10-1 *S R Andrews Mists in rr; t.o & pu 12; school*
[373F]	P		**Game Drive** (IRE) 12-1 *M Mackley 25s-12s; jmpd v slow; t.o til pu 6*
	P		**Gwen's A Singer** (5a) 10-1 *J Owen Nt jw; wl in rr til pu 11*
[250F]	P		**Itani** 8-1 *S Morris A rr; no ch 13; t.o & pu 16*
	P		**Magical Manor** (5a) 8-1 *J Tarry Swtng; in tch; 5th ½way; wknd aft 13; wl bhnd when pu 3 out*
	P		**More Mettle** 25-1 *J Diment In tch; 7th ½way; wknd 11; t.o & pu 14*
	P		**Phar Away Cruise** (5a) 25-1 *M Cowley Bckwd; sn wl bhnd; 2 fncs when pu 10*
[249P]	P		**Stable Girl** (5a) 33-1 *A Tutton Bckwd; prom to 9; sn wknd; t.o & pu 13*
[373P]	P		**Syrpiro** 7-2JF *B Pollock In tch; 6th ½way; prog to chse wnr 14-4 out; 3rd & btn when pu aft 3 out; dism*
[433P]	r		**The Fluter** 33-1 *Miss A Naylor Rr & 9th ½way; sn wknd; t.o frm 15 til ref & ur 2 out*
[411P]	P		**The Last Shout** (IRE) (bl) 20-1 *P Millington Nt jw; ld to 12; sn wknd; t.o & pu 16*

OFFICIAL DISTANCES: dist, 1½l **TIME:** 6min 51.0s **TOTE:** £17.40 **DF:** £33.50

515 Open Maiden (Div 2)   14 ran

	1		**LUCKASHAN** (IRE) (7a) 13-8F *B Pollock Jmpd slow 1; mid-div; prog 9; chsd ldr 12; ld 14; in comm aft 3 out; rn green & rdn out flat; promising*
[434³]	2	4	**Yodeller Bill** 20-1 *P Sheppard Chsd ldr & clr of rest til dem 12; stayed prom; 3rd 14; one pce aft 3 out; kpt on to tk 2nd nr fin*
[234P]	3	hd	**Dillon** 20-1 *F Hutsby Rr til prog frm ½way; 6th & nt on terms ldng group 14; kpt on frm nxt; chall for 2nd last; nrst fin*
	4	hd	**Green Leader** (IRE) (5a) 9-2 *S R Andrews Prom in chsng group; 4th 14; eff to press wnr nxt; ev ch when blun 3 out; rdn app nxt; no imp; lost 2nd flat*
[234P]	5	20	**Good Job** (5a) 20-1 *S Morris Mist 1; mostly last pr; 9th & t.o 14; kpt on stdly aft; nt disg*
	P		**Bakewell** 20-1 *T Illsley Bckwd; a rr group; t.o & pu 13*
[249F]	U		**Charles The Third** 16-1 *J Owen Bit bckwd; rr group; mist 8; 8th & no ch 14; poor 6th when blun & ur 2 out*
[76F]	F		**Evenkeel** (IRE) 10-1 *D Smith Jmpd erratic & a last trio; no ch 14; poor 7th when fell 2 out*
[411U]	P		**Fortune Hunter** (IRE) 8-1 *P Millington Nt jw; hld up rr; prog frm 13; 5th & tried to cl on ldrs nxt; sn wknd; pu 2 out*
	P		**Johnny Mu** (IRE) 14-1 *K Needham Bit bckwd; nt fluent; ld & sn wl clr; rn wide bend bef 9 (cf previous rce); hdd & wknd 14; t.o & pu 2 out*
	P		**Poets Corner** (IRE) 10-1 *R Lawther Nt jw; prom til wknd 11; t.o last when pu 15*
[124P]	P		**Second Story** (5a) 33-1 *L Hicks Bit bckwd; mid-div; 7th & strugg 14; no ch when blun 3 out; pu sn aft*
[264P]	F		**So Frank** 5-1 *David Dennis Mid-div; in tch when fell 10*
	P		**Tod's Brother** 14-1 *N Bloom Bit bckwd; mid-div til wknd & eased aft 12; pu nxt; school*

OFFICIAL DISTANCES: 5l, hd **TIME:** 6min 57.0s **TOTE:** £3.20 **DF:** £12.80

516 Open Maiden (Div 3, Part 1)   10 ran

[391⁴]	1		**WRENS ISLAND** (IRE) 7-4F *Miss L Sweeting Cl up; ld 7; gng easy in ld til stretched away app 2 out; easy*
[249U]	2	25	**Aladdin Sane Too** 5-2 *Miss S Wesley In tch; eff to cl 3rd/4th but outj 14-3 out; rdr immobile as wnr qcknd clr app 2 out; r.o to 2nd app last*
	3	8	**Truly Optimistic** (5a) 16-1 *C Wadland Swtng; a cl up; disp 2nd/3rd frm 13 til def 2nd 4 out; no imp on wnr app 2 out; wknd & dem app last*
[236P]	4	10	**Glencloy** (IRE) 14-1 *A Coe Cl up; disp 2nd/3rd frm 11 til 4th & btn 3 out; no ch aft; wknd flat*
[194⁴]	5	30	**Highfurlong** (IRE) 8-1 *J Oldring Ld to 7; lost tch ldng group 13; t.o 15*
[412³]	P		**Mandalay Man** (IRE) 8-1 *P Millington Hmpd by rival 2 & 3; a bhnd; t.o when needlessly hit w whip 12; pu 2 out*
[194P]	P		**Queens Token** 20-1 *T Illsley Prom; blun 6; wknd rap 10; pu 14*
	P		**Sock Hop** (IRE) (2ow) 12-1 *P Smith Bckwd; svs; pulled hrd & sn prom; mist 7 & wknd; pu nxt*
	P		**Stonehill Prospect** (5a) 10-1 *R Lawther Jmpd appalling; a bhnd; t.o & pu 12*

[243ᶠ] P   **Uncle Den** 20-1 I Hudson *Svs; trundled rnd miles bhnd til pu 2 out*

OFFICIAL DISTANCES: 15l, 6l **TIME:** 6min 49.5s **TOTE:** £2.20 **DF:** £1.80

517 Open Maiden (Div 3, Part 2)   9 ran

	1		**UNION MAN** 2-1F S Morris *Hld up bhnd; prog 9; chsd ld 2 out; ld app last; r.o str; promising*
	2	4	**Hessac (FR)** (7a) 5-2 B Pollock *Whinnying padd; jmpd slow 1; sn wl bhnd; gd prog frm ½way; jnd ldrs 16; ld app 2 out til app last; outpcd by wnr flat; promising*
	3	25	**Its Worth A Bob** 3-1 F Hutsby *Chsd ldng trio; clsd & ld 10; hdd app 2 out & stumbled bend; wknd; fair eff*
	4	runin	**Yasgourra (IRE)** (5a) 33-1 P Morris *Prom til wknd frm 16*
[290ᴾ]	U		**Folding** (tt) 14-1 N Hawkins *Ld; blun 6; hdd 10; mist 13; 4th & wkng when blun & ur 15*
	P		**Peatsville (IRE)** 14-1 J Gasper *Chsd ldng group; no prog 14; sn wknd; bhnd when pu last*
[250ᴾ]	P		**Safe Cottage** 33-1 M Cowley *Sn wl bhnd; last & t.o 9; pu 13*
	P		**Spiderdore** 10-1 R Barrett *School; hld up wl in rr; t.o & pu 13*
	F		**Tarjumaan (USA)** 8-1 A Brown *Chsd ldng trio to 9; rdn & wknd nxt; t.o last when fell hvly 15*

OFFICIAL DISTANCES: 2½l, 15l **TIME:** 6min 59.5s **TOTE:** £7.60 **DF:** £2.30

Seavington
Littlewindsor (RH 7F,19J) Sat, 11 Mar (GOOD with GOOD to SOFT patch)

518 Open Maiden 56&7yo, 2m4f, 12st - 16J   10 ran

	1		**RIMPTON BOY** (7a) 5-1 Miss P Gundry *Hld up in mid-div; prog to 10l 3rd 10; lft 1; 2nd nxt; ld 14; sprinted clr app nxt; r.o str*
[71ᴾ]	2	12	**Qu'appelle** 25-1 Miss A Goschen *(orbnf) Trckd ldrs; 22l 3rd 5; lft in ld 11 til hdd 14; sn outpcd; stayed on one pce frm nxt*
[60ᶠ]	3	3	**The First One** 7-2 A Honeyball *5th 4; lft 2l 3rd 11; trckd ldrs til one pce frm 3 out; jmpd slow last*
[352²]	4	6	**Spirito** (7a) 4-1 Jeremy Young *Mid-div til lft 4l 4th 11; chsd ldrs til wknd & no ex frm 3 out*
[254ᴾ]	5	8	**No Need For Alarm** (12a,2ow) 3-1F J Young *7/2-3s; 9th when jmpd untidy 3; stdy hdwy 7; 5th & in tch 3 out; sn no ex*
[404ᴾ]	P		**Alice Sunrise** (5a) 20-1 T Greed *Chsd clr ldr 3; 24l 4th 5; rr when mist 9; lost tch 11; t.o 13; pu 2 out*
[330ᶠ]	P		**Freemount Boy (IRE)** 12-1 N Mitchell *(xnb) 8th 3; last 7; impd to 6l 5th 11; wknd 13; t.o nxt; pu 2 out*
[353ᴾ]	R		**Super Rooster** 15-2 A Bateman *Lw; tde; chsd clr ldr 4 til clsd 8; ld sn aft nxt; crashed thro wing 11*
[407ᶠ]	P		**Tolepa (IRE)** (5a) 14-1 L Tibbatts *(xnb) Rcd free & sn 10l clr; jmpd lft 3; mist & hdd 9; sn wknd; last when clambered over 11 & imm pu*
	U		**Vic's Girl** (5a) 25-1 R Emmett *Last 3; rr trio when blun & ur 4*

OFFICIAL DISTANCES: 12l, 3l **TIME:** 5min 28.0s

519 Hunt, 12st   6 ran

[331²]	1		**FRANKLINS BEST (IRE)** 2-1F N Mitchell *2 handlers; hld up in rr; 6l last 9; impd to disp 3rd 11; chsd clr ldr 14 til grad clsd 2 out; disp last; drew clr flat*
[211⁵]	2	2	**Cool Character (IRE)** 9-4 Miss T Newman *3rd til chsd ldr frm 4; 3½l 3rd 9; ld nxt; 5l up 13 til jnd last; no ex flat*
[303⁷]	3	15	**Mr Golightly** 3-1 Mrs J Reed *Ld 1; disp 1½l 2nd 5; ld agn 7-nxt; grad lost plce & rr 10; 23l 5th 14; stayed on one pce frm 3 out*
[330³]	4	3½	**Givry (IRE)** (bl) 6-1 N Parker *Last pr; 5l 5th 5; last but in tch 12; slt prog to 20l 3rd 14; wknd aft 3 out*
	5	6	**Speck** 20-1 J O'Rourke *3½l 4th 5; mist nxt; prog downhill aft 7; ld nxt-10; untidy 13 & sn lost plce; 22l 4th 14; grad wknd frm 3 out*
[331ᴾ]	P		**Spanish Jest** 50-1 L Tibbatts *Chsd ldr til ld 2-6; 1½l 2nd 9; wknd qckly 12; rmdrs nxt; bhnd when pu aft 14*

OFFICIAL DISTANCES: 2½l, 25l **TIME:** 6min 27.1s

520 Open Maiden, 12st   13 ran

[265²]	1		**BASIL** 3-1 N Mitchell *Hld up towards rr; impd to 4th 12; 2½l 3rd 14; jmpd to ld 3 out; jmpd slow last; sn hdd; rallied to ld nr line*
[409ᵁ]	2	s hd	**Prussian Steel (IRE)** 6-1 T Greed *A.p; 5th 3; 4½l 4th 5; chsd ldrs til stayed on str frm 3 out; ld flat; hdd nr line*

	3	6	**Gemini Mist** (5a) 14-1 Miss C Stretton *20s-14s; in rr; 10l 9th 5; stayed on to 6th 15 & 4th 2 out; nrst fin*
[455ᴾ]	4	5	**Novasun** 33-1 P York *Ld/disp to 3; 2½l 3rd 5; ld agn 7-10; disp agn 12-3 out; stayed on one pce nxt*
[329³]	5	6	**The Frosty Fox** (IRE) 6-1 M Miller *2 handlers; swtng; prom; 2l 2nd 5; chsd ldr 12 til no ex frm 3 out*
	6	4	**Restless Native** (IRE) (5a) 5-1 Miss P Gundry *Mid-div early; 8l 8th 5; chsd ldrs 12 til grad wknd frm 3 out; nt disg*
	7	10	**Strawberry Hill** (IRE) 7-4F A Honeyball *5/2-7/4; lw; mid-div til 6½l 6th 5; eff to 4th 15; wknd 3 out; sn bhnd*
[409ʳ]	8	5	**Millcroft Regatta** (IRE) 16-1 R McKenzie Johnston *A last trio; nvr able to chall*
[353²]	9	3	**The Naughty Vicar** 7-1 G Richards *Ld in start; chsng ldrs in 6th 3; 7l 7th 5; grad lost plce frm 14; bhnd frm 2 out*
[326¹¹]	10	25	**Bright Lady** (5a) 25-1 Miss R Green *4th 3; grad lost plce frm 8; last 12; t.o frm 15*
	P		**Church Field** (IRE) 25-1 D Luff *(xnb) Prom; disp ld 2 til ld nxt; 2l up 5 til hdd nxt; 1½l 3rd 8; ld agn 10-12; sn wknd; t.o & pu 3 out*
	P		**Penthouse Minstrel** 16-1 B O'Doherty *2 handlers; a towards rr; t.o & pu 3 out*
[212ᵁ]	P		**Thecabbageflinger** 12-1 J Young *Sa; last to 11; mist 14 & sn last agn; t.o & pu 3 out*

OFFICIAL DISTANCES: hd, 3l TIME: 6min 28.0s

521 Mens Open, 12st   8 ran

[209³]	1		**NODDADANTE** (IRE) 10-1 N Mitchell *Hld up in 6th; 8l 6; clsd to 4th 13; stayed on to disp 2nd 16; jmpd to ld nxt; r.o u.p flat*
[357²]	2	2	**Avril Showers** (5a,4x) 2-1 R Atkinson *Tchd 5/2; a.p; ld/disp 1-6; 2nd til disp ld agn 13-15; stayed on agn frm 3 out; no ex frm last*
[402⁶]	3	4	**Flying Imp** 5-1 J Barnes *7s-5s; chsd ldr; 11 down 6 til disp ld nxt; ld 10; 1½l up 16 til hdd nxt; no ex u.p frm nxt*
[162¹]	4	20	**Longmore** (IRE) 7-4F A Honeyball *Chsd ldrs in 4th 6; trckd ldng pr 8; 7l 4th & no ex frm 3 out; disapp*
[403ᵁ]	5	1	**Air Command** (BAR) 33-1 P Phillips *A rr; last 6; 15l 7th 14; nd*
[262ᴾ]	P		**Blanchland** (tt) 20-1 J O'Rourke *Prom; 2l 3rd 6; disp ld 7-10; grad wknd frm 14; bhnd when pu 16*
[210ᴾ]	P		**Penny's Prince** 8-1 Jeremy Young *Rcd in 5½l 5th 6; rmdr 10; 10l 6th & wkng 15; bhnd when pu 2 out*
[211ᶠ]	P		**Union Station** (IRE) 66-1 B Parsons *A rr; last 8; jmpd slow 10; sn t.o; clambered over 12 & imm pu*

OFFICIAL DISTANCES: 2l, 3l TIME: 6min 24.3s

522 Ladies Open   8 ran

[310⁷]	1		**DANNICUS** 9-2 Miss P Gundry *Jw; made all; 1½l up 6 til hdd 16; ld agn last; hld on u.p flat*
[263³]	2	hd	**Fair Wind** (IRE) 2-1 Miss R David *Last 3; hdwy to disp 1½l 2nd 6; wknd to 17l 7th 7; stayed on frm rem 4th til ld nxt; rap prog & ev ch last; just failed*
[257¹]	3	4	**Hillhead** (IRE) 5-4F Miss A Goschen *2s-5/4; trckd ldr; disp 1½l 2nd 6 & 3½l 3rd 12; chsd ldr frm 14 til outj rival 16; hdd last; no ex u.p flat*
[324ᴿ]	4	12	**Arfer Mole** (IRE) 25-1 Miss J Grant *4th 3; impd to 1½l 2nd 6; 4th nxt til 1½l 2nd 12; chsd ldng pr 15 til no ex frm 3 out*
[245⁴]	5	5	**Cardinal Gayle** (IRE) 13-1 Miss D Harding *Towards rr 6; 7l 6th nxt; rmdr 12; lost tch w ldrs 16; stayed on one pce frm nxt*
	6	12	**Don't Light Up** (vis) 12-1 Miss M Burrough *Chsd ldr; 2l 2nd 7 til grad wknd frm 15; bhnd 2 out*
[324³]	7	3fncs	**Amaranthine** (5a) 50-1 Miss C Cowe *(xnb) A towards rr; last 4; 20l bhnd 7; t.o 10; plodded home*
[67ᵁ]	P		**Thomas Crown** (IRE) 50-1 Mrs J Wilkinson *Towards rr; 6l 5th 7 til wknd 15; bhnd when pu 3 out*

OFFICIAL DISTANCES: nk, 2l TIME: 6min 19.7s

523 Dodson & Horrell PPORA Club Members (Nov Rdrs), 12st   7 ran

[354³]	1		**MILLYHENRY** 4-6F Miss C Tizzard *A.p; chsd ldr til ld 13; jnd nxt til stayed on str frm 2 out; a hldng 2nd*
[389²]	2	1½	**Mystery Aristocrat** (IRE) 7-4 R Tory *Hld up in rr til prog 11; chsd ldr 13; disp ld nxt-3 out; no ex nxt*
[256ᴾ]	3	runin	**Mr Kevernair** 33-1 M Woodward *(xnb) Tde; ld to 13; sn lost tch w ldng pr nxt; stayed on one pce frm 16*

[74ᴾ] 4   7   **Nawrik (IRE)** 20-1 M Flynn *Chsd ldrs in mostly 3rd/4th to 12; 5th & outpcd 14; t.o 16*
[351³] 5   3   **Nothing To Fear** 16-1 W White *A towards rr of main group; lost tch 14; t.o frm 16*
[211ᴾ] 6   2fncs   **Mystic Moment (IRE)** (5a) 16-1 Miss S Lane *A towards rr; sn lost tch; t.o 11*
[354ᴾ] U   **Single Man (NZ)** 25-1 Miss T Blazey *Trckd ldrs; 4th & lsng tch when rfo 14*

OFFICIAL DISTANCES: 1¾l, dist   TIME: 6min 25.8s

524 Restricted, 12st   7 ran

[208⁶] 1   **MY CLEAN SWEEP (IRE)** 4-5F Miss P Gundry *Disp 7l 4th 7; impd to 3rd 9; chsd ldr 14 til ld brief nxt; disp ld 3 out; still level when dived at nxt but lft virt solo; coasted home*
[144⁴] 2   10   **Securon Lady** (5a) 20-1 J Barnes *Hld up in rr; disp 7l 4th 7; outpcd & lost tch 14; lft rem 2nd by defections 2 out*
[315⁴] 3   15   **Nearly Fair** (5a) 14-1 T Greed *(bf) Chsd ldr frm 3; disp 1½l 2nd 6; grad lost plce frm 11; bhnd frm 14; lft dist 3rd by defections 2 out*
[273ᴾ] U   **Cefn Woodsman** 16-1 Miss K Lovelace *Swtng; last to 5; mist nxt; disp 7l 4th 7; 5th & in tch when blun & ur 11*
[416²] F   **Lillooet (IRE)** (5a) (bl) 5-2 C Gordon *3s-5/2; spurs; chsd ldr; 1½l 2nd 6; ld nxt til brief hdd app 15; sn ld agn; jnd & rdn 3 out; still level when fell 2 out*
[408¹] P   **Remember Ridemore (IRE)** 5-1 A Honeyball *Ld til hdd 7; prsng ldr when jmpd slow 14; chsd ldng pr til wknd 3 out; bhnd when pu last*
[406ᴾ] P   **Timber Wolf (IRE)** 25-1 N Mitchell *4th early; last 6; detach 14; t.o & pu 16*

OFFICIAL DISTANCES: 15l, 15l   TIME: 6min 27.5s

Sir W.W. Wynn's
Eaton Hall (RH 6F,16J) Sat, 11 Mar (HOLDING)

525 Hunt   8 ran

[334³] 1   **THREE SAINTS (IRE)** 2-1 M Worthington *Jw; cl 3rd/4th; ld 7; made most aft; qcknd 4l clr 3 out; stayed on str*
[369⁵] 2   8   **Class Of Ninetytwo (IRE)** (7x) 5-4F C Stockton *Cl 2nd til ld 6; sn hdd; rmdr nxt; trckd ldng pr til 2nd 12; mist nxt; fnd nil u.p frm 3 out*
[293⁶] 3   20   **Kidlaw** 8-1 Miss T Clark *Jw; ld to 5; cl up til wknd to 17l 4th 12; no ch aft; kpt on one pce to 3rd app last*
       4   8   **Ambrose** 20-1 I Wynne *Cl up; went 2nd 7; ld brief 11; 6½l 3rd & wkng nxt; no ch aft; tired & lost 3rd app last*
       5   30   **The Corinthian (U)** 33-1 Miss E Hancock *Disp 4th early; rr by 4; stdly lost tch frm 9; 27l 5th 11; plodded on*
       6   ½m   **Jasper (U)** (7a,14ow) 40-1 D Bardell *A last; 20l adrift 2; 2 fncs bhnd 9; completed in own time*
        U   **Batty's Island** 4-1 D Sherlock *(xnb) Trckd ldng trio in 4/5th til blun & ur 9*
        U   **River Mandate** (7x) 8-1 Miss F Barnett *In tch when ur 3*

OFFICIAL DISTANCES: 7l, 20l   TIME: 6min 56.0s   TOTE: £5.00
Course modified for this meeting and Flint & Denbigh season because of the waterlogged state of the ground

526 Open Maiden (Div 1)   10 ran

       1   **ANOTHER GENTLEMAN** (tt) 8-1 Mrs C Ford *Midfield; went 2nd 11; ld app 2 out; hit last & hdd; rallied und vigorous ride to ld agn on line*
       2   hd   **Charlie Keay (IRE)** 4-1 C Stockton *Trckd ldrs in 4/5th; hdwy to 3rd 3 out; stdy prog to chall last; sn ld; r.o wl; caught on line*
[337⁵] 3   20   **Tibs Eve (IRE)** 2-1F G Hanmer *Cl 2nd til ld 7; hdd & rmdrs app 2 out; sn btn*
[297⁵] 4   10   **Merely Mortal** 8-1 R Owen *Ld to 5; cl up; 6l 6th 11; wknd nxt; lsng tch when mist 13; bhnd aft*
[437ᴾ] 5   15   **Educate Me (IRE)** (tt) 5-1 J Burley *(xnb) Towards rr of main group; outpcd & lost tch frm 13*
[437ᵁ] P   **Aughrim Quest (IRE)** (5a) 8-1 M Worthington *Cl up; 2nd 8-11; 5l 3rd 13; sn btn; pu last*
[301⁸] P   **Desert Boot** (7a) 20-1 B Wharfe *Prom; ld brief aft 6; mist 7; imm eased & pu nxt*
[234⁵] P   **Jock** 25-1 J R Barlow *Swerved & ur start; rmtd; cont 2 fncs bhnd til pu 7*
[338⁶] U   **Need More Practice** 5-2 R Burton *Hld up in last; still last & lkd no ch 13; hdwy nxt; went 10l 3rd & blun last; ur some way aft*
        P   **Pendil's Dream** (5a) 14-1 D Sherlock *Made no show; mist 12; sn lost tch; pu 2 out*

OFFICIAL DISTANCES: s hd, 20l   TIME: 7min 00.0s   TOTE: £4.50

527 Open Maiden (Div 2)   8 ran

1		**MR PISTACHIO (IRE)** (7a) 2-1 **G Hanmer** Hld up in midfield; hdwy to 2nd 10; chsd ldr aft; qcknd to ld app 2 out; sn in comm; promising
2	5	**The Legend Of Zeb** 12-1 **Miss S Sharratt** Tk keen hld; jmpd bold; ld 2; 15l clr 9; 7l up 11; hdd app 2 out; kpt on game
3	10	**Goddess** (5a) 16-1 **S Prior** Cl 3rd/4th; 12l 4th 12; kpt on same pce
U		**Loch Ash** 5-1 **R Burton** Cl 3rd/4th til blun & ur 9
P		**Mr Peoples (IRE)** 4-1 **C Stockton** Ld 1; chsd ldr nxt til dem 3rd 10; ev ch 12; wknd nxt; drpd out rap; pu 2 out
P		**Robert The Rascal** 20-1 **A Gribbin** A last; 10-15l adrift frm 9; t.o 13; pu 2 out
P		**Snitton Salvo** (7a) 20-1 **A Wadlow** Rr of main group; rdn along 11; wkng when mist nxt; eased & pu 3 out
[122⁴] **F**		**Spumante** 6-4F **C Barlow** Hld up in midfield; went 3rd 3 out; nt rch ldng pr; 10l down when fell 2 out

OFFICIAL DISTANCES: 6l, 10l TIME: 7min 06.0s TOTE: £9.50

528 Open Maiden (Div 3)   7 ran

[384ᵁ] **1**		**THE CROOKED OAK** 7-4F **G Thomas** Jw; made all; 5l up 11; drew wl clr frm 12; 30l clr app 2 out; unchall
2	75	**Caherlow (IRE)** 20-1 **B Foster** 2nd to 6; lost plce; went 16l 3rd 12; wknd 3 out; lft rem 2nd nxt
P		**French Melody (IRE)** 9-1 **C Barlow** Midfield; 17l 4th 11; bhnd frm nxt; went 3rd app 2 out; sn tired & pu
r		**Knocknashane (IRE)** 5-2 **G Hanmer** Trckd ldrs til went 2nd 7; ev ch til wknd 12; 30l down & v tired when ref 2 out
[337ᶠ] **P**		**Lord Lard (IRE)** 10-1 **M Rodda** Tkn quiet at rr of main body; 25l 6th 11; eased & pu nxt
P		**River Moy** (5a) 12-1 **R Owen** School in rr; 27l 7th 11; pu nxt
P		**The Hollow (IRE)** (5a) 10-1 **M Worthington** In tch; went 3rd 8; 4th & wkng when mist 12; pu nxt

OFFICIAL DISTANCE: dist TIME: 7min 00.0s TOTE: £2.50

529 Confined, 12st   10 ran

1		**ALY DALEY (IRE)** 16-1 **Miss A Price** Jw; ld to 5; wl in tch aft; 4l 5th app 3 out; went 3rd app last; stayed on str to ld last 20 yds
2	2	**Garryspillane (IRE)** (2ow) 4-1 **G Hanmer** Hld up; 2l 4th 11; went 2nd app 2 out; ld app last w rdr lkng round; hdd & no ex last 20 yds
[292³] **3**	¾	**Mytton's Choice (IRE)** 10-1 **C Barlow** A ldng quartet; went cl 2nd 9; ld 3 out til hdd & no ex app last; kpt on flat
[370¹] **4**	12	**Inch Fountain (IRE)** 7-4F **A Crow** Hld up; rmdrs 5; hdwy to 4th app 2 out; no ex app last; eased flat
[334ʳ] **5**	10	**Grunge (IRE)** 8-1 **C Stockton** Prom frm 4; ld 6 til hdd app 3 out; 2l 3rd nxt; wknd app last
[402³] **6**	12	**Rosmarino** (3x) 2-1 **A Dalton** Hld up; 1½l 3rd 11; lost plce nxt; 10l 6th app 2 out; no imp aft
[293ᴾ] **P**		**All In The Game (IRE)** 14-1 **S Prior** Cl 2nd/3rd to 8; lost plce; 8l 3rd 11; sn lost tch; t.o 13; pu 2 out
[369ᴾ] **F**		**Canaillou II (FR)** 20-1 **A Wadlow** Midfield; 6l 6th when fell 7
P		**George Ashford (IRE)** 33-1 **I Hooper** A last pr; hmpd 7 & lost tch; pu nxt
[334ᵁ] **U**		**Ita's Fellow (IRE)** (vis) 25-1 **M Prince** Nt keen; blun 3; last pr til hmpd & ur 7

OFFICIAL DISTANCES: 1½l, ¾l TIME: 6min 55.0s TOTE: £42.00

530 Land Rover Mens Open, 12st   7 ran

[293³] **1**		**WEAK MOMENT (IRE)** 7-2 **A Crow** Rdn in last pr; 10l 5th 11; stdy hdwy frm 13; chall 2 out; ld app last; stayed on str
2	1	**Bucks View** 6-4F **G Hanmer** Hld up til went 2nd 8; ld 12; 8l clr 3 out; jnd nxt; sn hdd; 3l down app last; rallied und str press flat
[334ᴾ] **3**	15	**Greville Again (IRE)** 20-1 **A Wadlow** Jw; a.p; ld brief 11; chsd ldr 12 til dem app 2 out; kpt on one pce
[442ᵁ] **4**	35	**Sun Surfer (FR)** 2-1 **A Dalton** A last pr; jmpd v slow 7 & 12 (same fnce); lft wl bhnd frm nxt
P		**Emerald Knight (IRE)** (vis) 10-1 **C Stockton** Ld to 3; cl 2nd to 8; 6l 3rd 13; wknd qckly nxt; pu 2 out

[332ᶠ] P **Perfect Light** (4x) 6-1 R Burton *2nd til ld 4; hdd app 12; wknd & drpd out tame frm nxt; pu 2 out*

P **Russian Castle (IRE)** (7x) 20-1 A McKay *In tch when mist & rdr lost irons 3; pu nxt*

OFFICIAL DISTANCES: 2l, 12l **TIME:** 6min 48.0s **TOTE:** £2.50

The rider of Bucks View was fined £50 for excessive use of the whip

531 Ladies Open 3 ran

1 **MELNIK** 1-4F Mrs C Ford *Ld/disp til went clr 6; 15l up 7; fnce ahd 3 out; unchall*

[296⁴] 2 60 **Coolflugh Hero (IRE)** 4-1 Miss S Hopkins *Rdn along in 3rd; prsd rival but oft outj frm 7; rdn to tk 2nd flat*

[177ᵖ] 3 10 **Paparazzo** 10-1 Mrs M Barlow *Jw; prsd wnr to 5; 15l 2nd nxt; nursed round to conserve stamina; v tired & lost 2nd flat*

OFFICIAL DISTANCES: dist, 7l **TIME:** 6min 58.0s **TOTE:** £1.50

532 Restricted, 12st 7 ran

1 **NIGHT IRENE (IRE)** (5a) 4-6F G Hanmer *A gng wl; trckd ldrs in 3rd; went 2nd 12; ld & qckly went clr app 2 out; drew rt away app last; easy (seemed on verge of collapse aft - oxygen deficiency; kpt moving & rcvrd)*

2 25 **Hatton Farm Babe** (5a) 20-1 Miss S Sharratt *Rr til hdwy to 4th app 12; outpcd nxt; stayed on frm 2 out to 2nd at last*

[336ᶠ] 3 7 **Cherokee Run (IRE)** (tt) 14-1 M Keel *Last trio; went 20l 4th 11; one pce; 3rd 3 out; no ch w ldrs; tired & dem last*

[371ᶠ] 4 15 **Offley Lucielastic** (5a) 20-1 R Burton *(xnb) A last pr; wknd 12; bhnd & no ch aft*

[173³] 5 15 **Mr Mark (IRE)** 6-1 D Sherlock *Chsd ldr in 2nd til rem 12; wknd rap frm nxt; last 2 out; fin v tired*

P **Analystic (IRE)** 20-1 C Stockton *3rd & mist 2; lost plce; 16l 4th 8; last 11; pu 2*

[119³] P **Coming Through (IRE)** (bl) 7-2 A Crow *(bnh) Ld; jmpd slow 11; went 11 up 3 out; floundering in mud bef nxt; sn hdd & btn; pu last*

OFFICIAL DISTANCES: 25l, 5l **TIME:** 6min 50.0s **TOTE:** £2.10

533 Intermediate, 12st 5 ran

[336¹] 1 **WEJEM (IRE)** 6-4 A Dalton *Hld up; jnd ldrs 10; ld 12; drew clr frm 2 out*

2 10 **Elwill Glory (IRE)** 25-1 M Rodda *Disp ld to 11; chsd wnr aft; one pce frm 2 out*

3 35 **Bubble N Squeek** 14-1 C Barlow *A bhnd; no ch frm 13; lft poor 3rd 2 out*

[179¹] P **Rise To It (IRE)** 4-7F G Hanmer *Ld/disp to 11; wknd rap app 13; poor 3rd when pu 2 out*

P **Running Frau** (5a) 20-1 G Thomas *A last pr; no ch frm 12; pu 14*

OFFICIAL DISTANCES: 10l, 15l **TIME:** 7min 00.0s **TOTE:** £2.00

Western
Wadebridge (LH 8F,18J) Sat, 11 Mar (GOOD)

534 Confined, 12st 8 ran

[257ᵁ] 1 **PALACE PARADE (USA)** (3x) 5-4F C Heard *A.p; ld 14; drew clr app 2 out; rdn out*

[255³] 2 3 **Dancing Ranger** 5-2 Richard Darke *Made most to 5 & 9-14; 2l 2nd when hit 2 out; rallied & stayed on to regain 2nd flat*

[252ᵖ] 3 5 **Where's Sam (IRE)** (5x) 6-1 S Craddock *A.p; hdwy to chall ldr 15; 1l 2nd 3 out; wknd aft 2 out; dem flat*

4 1 **Darren The Brave** 14-1 D Stephens (Devon) *Trckd ldrs; 4l 4th 3 out; rdn & sn btn*

[315ᵖ] 5 30 **Moorland Abbot** 50-1 Miss D Mitchell *Lost tch aft 8; t.o 12; plodded on*

[311ᵖ] P **Baldhu Luckystrike** 50-1 A Ede *Jmpd v slow 2; a rr; tried to rn out 12; t.o & pu 14*

[165ᵖ] P **Eserie De Cores (USA)** 10-1 S Kidston *Ld/disp 6-8; cl up til lost tch aft 13; sn rdn & wknd; t.o when pu 2 out*

P **Forest Musk (IRE)** Pu 5; cont; jmpd 2 more fences; ld field past 11 til halted event aft jumping ropes & scattering crowds

OFFICIAL DISTANCES: 1l, 2l **TIME:** 6min 30.0s

The stewards interviewed the rider of Forest Musk who continued jumping some fences after appearing to pull up; they accepted the rider's explanation that the martingale had broken and he had been unable to maintain control

535 Ladies Open 3 ran

[354¹] 1 **SLEW MAN (FR)** 1-5F Miss O Green *Hld up; 10l down til smooth hdwy on inner to ld 12; drew clr app 3 out*

| [310¹] | 2 | 10 | O So Bossy (8ow) 5-2 Miss J Congdon *Ld & clr; mist 7; hdd 12; easily outpcd app 3 out* |
| | F | | My Jess (5a) 25-1 Miss C Prouse *15l last when fell 3* |

OFFICIAL DISTANCE: 8l TIME: 6min 15.0s

536 Restricted, 12st   9 ran

[407¹]	1		WIBBLEY WOBBLEY 3-1 Miss J Cumings *Prom in chsng group; clsd 13; ld 15; drew clr aft nxt; impressive*
[406⁵]	2	10	Brother Nero (NZ) 8-1 C Heard *Prom in chsng group; 2nd brief 14; 5l 3rd & outpcd 3 out; kpt on stdly*
[353¹]	3	12	Kingsbridge (IRE) 6-4F T Scudamore *Rn free in clr ld; mist 9; hdd 15; hit nxt; 5l 2nd 2 out; wknd qckly aft*
[315²]	4	1	Spruce (5a) 4-1 Mrs S Fell *Sa; rr til rap hdwy to 2nd app 8; mist 9; outpcd 12; some late hdwy*
[203²]	5	15	Belski 12-1 R Woollacott *2nd to 7; sn lost plce; 10l 5th when hmpd 14; sn t.o*
[316ꟳ]	F		Border Rose (5a) 50-1 D Doyne-Ditmas *Trckd ldrs; still in tch in 4th when fell 14*
[255ꟳ]	F		County Bash (5a) 16-1 S Kidston *A rr; 12l last when fell 10*
[330ᵁ]	P		Lost Your Marbles (IRE) (5a) 7-1 J Mead *Lost tch aft 8; last when pu 12*
[408ᵁ]	P		Media Luz (5a) 50-1 M Sweetland *Imm lost tch; t.o & pu 8*

OFFICIAL DISTANCES: 8l, 6l TIME: 6min 15.0s

537 Mens Open, 12st   6 ran

	1		TEXAN BABY (BEL) 6-1 K Sheppard *14s-6s; lw; jmpd rt; tk keen hold & made all; drew 4l clr 3 out; stayed on wl*
[355¹]	2	5	Rossell Island (IRE) (7x) 1-2F T Scudamore *Trckd ldr; pushed along aft 11; drvn & fnd little frm 3 out*
[404⁴]	3	3	Ardbei (IRE) 8-1 R Woollacott *Prom to 15; 8l 3rd & outpcd nxt*
[256²]	4	25	Chocolate Buttons (5a) 8-1 H Thomas *Trckd ldrs; cl up to 15; outpcd in 9l 4th nxt*
	P		Beam Me Up Scotty (IRE) 33-1 C Heard *Lw; trckd ldrs til wknd aft 11; t.o & pu 3 out*
[313³]	P		Romalito 7-1 S Kidston *Lost tch aft 8; last 9; wl bhnd when pu 12*

OFFICIAL DISTANCES: 5l, 3l TIME: 6min 19.0s

538 Open Maiden (Div 1, Part 1), 12st   8 ran

	1		ELLIEWELLIEWOO (5a) 1-2F L Jefford *Made most; drew clr aft 14; 10l clr 15; eased; impressive*
[159ꟼ]	2	15	King Tudor 8-1 Miss O Green *Trckd ldrs; hdwy to 2nd 12; 4l down 14; 10l down & hopelessly outpcd nxt*
[311³]	3	4	The Ugly Duckling 9-4 R Woollacott *Trckd ldrs in mostly 3rd; 8l down 14; drvn & plodded on*
[312ꟼ]	F		Baldhu Jay Arr 16-1 A Ede *A rr; blun 5; 15l 5th when fell 10*
	P		Morgan's Rose (5a) 14-1 M Sweetland *Sn lost tch; t.o & pu 12*
	F		Sea Spirit (5a) 14-1 T Jones (Devon) *1st ride; towards rr; hdwy & lft 4th 12; sn strugg; 25l 4th when fell hvly 15*
	P		Take The Risk (5a) 10-1 D Stephens (Devon) *Sa; sn wl bhnd; t.o 5; pu 12*
[159ꟼ]	F		Woodys Widget (12a) 7-1 Miss K Baily *W wnr to 7; 4th & wkng when fell 12*

OFFICIAL DISTANCES: 15l, 2l TIME: 6min 23.0s

539 Open Maiden (Div 1, Part 2), 12st   8 ran

	1		TE AKAU DAN (NZ) 3-1 N Oliver *Hld up gng wl in rr; hdwy to 3rd 14; ld on bit app 3 out; 2l up when mist last; rdn & just hld on*
	2	nk	Woodland King (IRE) 4-1 Mrs M Hand *Ld to 6; 2nd til ld agn aft 13; rdn 10l clr; hdd app 3 out; r.o wl cl home; just failed*
[312³]	3	25	Hanukkah (5a) 9-2 I Hambley *Mid-div; lost tch 12; plodding on when lft 3rd 2 out*
	U		Bailey Gray (5a) 14-1 T Dennis *Climbed 2; novicey; 10l 4th when mist & ur 10*
	P		Lucky Coombe 9-4F Miss J Cumings *Rr when jmpd slow 6; t.o aft; pu 12; nt keen*
[158ᴿ]	P		Patrio (IRE) (5a) 20-1 J Cole *Mist 5; in tch to 11; t.o 13; pu last*
[145ꟼ]	P		Starmont (bl) 12-1 S Kidston *Tde; prom; ld 6 til aft 13; wknd rap; pu 15*
[158ꟼ]	P		Thornbird (5a) 8-1 C Heard *Trckd ldrs in mostly 3rd/4th; nrly fell 10 & brilliant rcvry; btn 3rd when blun 3 out; exhausted when pu nxt*

OFFICIAL DISTANCES: hd, dist TIME: 6min 29.0s

540 Open Maiden (Div 2), 12st - 17J   13 ran

| [352ꟳ] | 1 | | COUNSEL (7a) 9-2JF L Jefford *Ld til aft 4; chsd clr ldr; jmpd lft 7; mist 10; jmpd lft 14; sn ld on inner; lft clr when blun bad 3 out; r.o; unchall* |

	2	20	**Opera Festival (IRE)** 5-1 D Stephens (Devon) *Trckd ldrs; pushed along & outpcd aft 13; lft 30l 3rd app 3 out; r.o to 2nd app last*
[205ᴾ]	3	8	**Wise Examiner (IRE)** 9-1 Richard Darke *Prom in 3rd/4th mostly til outpcd aft 13; lft 25l 2nd app 3 out; jbnd 3 out; 3rd & wkng app last*
[311⁵]	4	4	**Georgetown** 6-1 K Heard *A towards rr; 8th 6; 7th 11; no ch frm 14*
[253⁴]	5	4	**Amazing Hill (IRE)** 25-1 Mrs R Morris *Rr; 9th 6; 8th 10; plodded on*
[312ᴾ]	U		**Broad Ink** 20-1 S Kidston *Towards rr when blun & ur 4*
	S		**Frankie Muck** 9-2JF Miss C Stucley *Ld aft 4; sn 10l clr; hdd aft 14; 5l 2nd when slpd up app 3 out*
[312ᴾ]	P		**Frankies Flutter** 14-1 D Doyne-Ditmas *Mid-div; lost tch aft 11; blun 12; t.o to pu 14*
[311⁶]	P		**Golden Sunset** 25-1 Miss D Mitchell *Sn rr; t.o pu 12*
[146⁵]	U		**La Tormenta (IRE)** (5a) 6-1 Miss K Cook *Chsd ldrs; 15l 5th when blun & ur 8*
[253ᴾ]	F		**Miltown Castle** 7-1 K Sheppard *Cl 4th when fell 2*
[213ᴾ]	P		**Ruben James (IRE)** 14-1 C Heard *Towards rr when reluct u.p & pu 5*
[312ᴾ]	U		**Spirit Of Life** (5a) 33-1 Miss O Green *Mid-div & nd; 20l 6th & no ch when blun & ur 12*

OFFICIAL DISTANCES: 20l, 2l **TIME:** 6min 27.0s
Fence 15 omitted - fallen rider

541 Intermediate, 12st   8 ran

[315¹]	1		**SOLOMANS SISTER** (5a) 2-1 Mrs M Hand *A.p; ld 4-5; ld aft 6; mist 11; blun & hdd 12; ld aft 14; drew clr app 15; r.o u.p*
[258⁵]	2	10	**Jeepers (IRE)** 12-1 S Kidston *Mid-div; clsd on ldrs app 10; hdwy to 3rd 14 & 2nd 3 out; kpt on; no ch w wnr*
[37⁴]	3	8	**Babbling Brook (IRE)** evensF L Jefford *Ld 5-6 but jmpd sticky; cl up to 14; sn outpcd; 15l 4th 15; r.o cl home*
[99¹]	4	2	**Travel By Land** 25-1 Miss O Green *Sn rr; some hdwy 10; outpcd aft 14; r.o wl cl home*
	5	6	**Bedtime Pixie** 14-1 D Stephens (Devon) *Ld to 4; cl up to 13; sn rdn & lost tch; plodded on*
[315ᴾ]	6	1	**Rice Point** 12-1 C Heard *Tk keen hold; hld up early; hdwy to 3rd 6; ld 12; hdd aft 14; lost 2nd app 3 out; wknd bad*
[353ᵁ]	P		**Button Up Bill** 50-1 H Thomas *Sn lost tch; t.o & pu 15*
	F		**Dark Venetian** (5a) 50-1 R Woollacott *Towards rr when fell hvly 3*

OFFICIAL DISTANCES: 5l, 7l **TIME:** 6min 25.0s

Cottesmore
Garthorpe (RH 8F,18J) Sun, 12 Mar (GOOD)

542 Hunt   5 ran

[463ᴾ]	1		**NOWHISKI** 5-2 M Mackley *2nd til ld 4; qcknd 13; hdd last; rallied u.p & ld nr fin*
[373ᴾ]	2	nk	**Nautical Lad** (7a) 8-1 J Docker *Hld up; jmpd slow 5; 3rd ½way; went 2nd 12; mist 14; jnd wnr nxt; ld last; hdd & nt qckn nr fin*
[97ᴾ]	3	30	**Semliki** 12-1 Miss L Allan *Hld up; mists 4 & 6; last to 8; 4th ½way; went 7l 3rd 15; sn wknd*
[438ᴾ]	4	½	**Nanda Devi** 5-1 Miss H Campbell *1st ride; rcd wide; ld 2-4; 2nd to 12; 5l 3rd & wkng when mist 14; t.o*
	5	15	**Trade Hill Shalamar** (U) 5-4F A Bealby *Fat hunter; ld to 2; drpd to rr 8; outpcd 13; wknd & 11l 5th 15; t.o*

OFFICIAL DISTANCES: nk, 20l **TIME:** 6min 25.6s **TOTE:** £4.00; places £2.60,£2.20 **DF:** £12.00

543 Intermediate, 12st   14 ran

[367³]	1		**GILLONE** 5-1 J Docker *Mounted on course; tde; swtng; jnd ldrs 5; 4l 5th ½way; 4½l 4th 15; sn ldd; ld 2 out; blun last; rallied game to ld nr fin*
[191²]	2	nk	**Irisheyesaresmilin (IRE)** 4-5F B Pollock *Sn prom; 2l 3rd ½way; went 3l 2nd 14; rdn to ld aft 3 out; hdd 2 out; ld flat; hdd & no ex nr fin*
[288⁴]	3	10	**Ballydesmond (IRE)** (bl) 12-1 S Sporborg *Ld; 3l clr 14; hdd aft 3 out; ev ch 2 out; sn wknd*
[229⁴]	4	hd	**Triple Eaves** 10-1 C Mulhall *(xnb) Hld up; eff & 5l 6th ½way; lost plce 11; 9l 7th 15; stayed on frm 2 out; nt rch ldrs*
[263⁴]	5	5	**Castle Shelley** 8-1 R Smith *W ldrs; 3l 4th ½way; 6½l 6th 15; no ex 3 out*
[333⁴]	6	7	**Fintona Boy (IRE)** (tt) 20-1 A Wintle *Prom til lost plce 7; 7½l 9th ½way; rallied 11; went 2nd 13-14; 7l 4th & rdn 3 out; sn wknd*
[296ᴾ]	7	1½	**Smart Rhythm** (5a) 7-1 R Armson *(bf) 2nd to 13; 6l 5th & rdn 15; sn btn*
[37ᴾ]	8	20	**Catchphrase** 33-1 N Docker *Prom til lost plce & 7l 8th ½way; 13l 9th & wkng 15; t.o*

[96']	9	4	**Court Amber (IRE)** 20-1 G Cooper *Chsd ldrs; 6l 7th ½way; wknd & 11l 8th 15; t.o*
[191⁸]	10	2	**Glendine (IRE)** (bl) 33-1 D Smith *Mist 2; lost plce 5; 12th ½way; t.o 14*
[175⁵]	11	7	**Neelisagin (IRE)** (tt) 33-1 J Turcan *A bhnd; 11th ½way; t.o 15*
[330⁸]	P		**Luke Skywalker** 33-1 J Richardson *A bhnd; 13th ½way; t.o 13; pu 2 out*
[115⁸]	P		**Nishvamitra** 33-1 A Woodward *A bhnd; 14th ½way; t.o 14; pu 2 out*
[285¹]	P		**Perfect Finisher** 8-1 M Hawkins *12s-8s; swtng; hld up; 9l 10th ½way; lost tch 13; t.o & pu 2 out*

OFFICIAL DISTANCES: hd, 8l **TIME:** 6min 16.8s **TOTE:** £9.80; places £3.00,£1.10,£2.20 **DF:** £5.70

544 Ladies Open
9 ran

[442¹]	1		**CITTADINO** 4-5F Mrs J Dawson *Lw; ld 2; 5l clr 8-12; blun 14; r.o wl frm 2 out*
[319³]	2	3½	**Thurles Pickpocket (IRE)** 5-2 Mrs S Hodge *Chsd wnr 3; ev ch 3 out; one pce*
[440⁵]	3	4	**Macfin (IRE)** 33-1 Miss L Allan *Bhnd til hdwy 8; 10l 4th ½way; outpcd 12; went 12l 3rd 3 out; stayed on wl; nt rch ldrs*
[230⁵]	4	10	**Drummond Warrior (IRE)** 20-1 Miss A Burton *Chsd ldrs; 7l 3rd ½way; rdn 15; sn outpcd*
[431³]	5	6	**Roly Prior** 9-2 Miss S Samworth *Hld up; 12l 6th & shkn up ½way; 14l 5th 15; sn wknd*
[442⁸]	6	25	**Airecco (IRE)** 33-1 Miss J Kandalaft *Nd; lost plce & rmdrs 8; 16l 8th ½way; wl bhnd 12; t.o*
[118³]	7	10	**Blue Lyzander** (5a) 25-1 Mrs E Staines *(xnb) Ld to 2; lost plce 4; rallied 8; 11l 5th ½way; wknd 12; t.o 15*
[118ᵁ]	8	5	**Faraday** 50-1 Miss S Phizacklea *Lost tch 5; 18l 9th ½way; t.o 13*
[368³]	P		**Bare Fisted** 20-1 Miss H Phizacklea *Prom til lost plce 8; 15l 7th ½way; wl bhnd when pu 13*

OFFICIAL DISTANCES: 4l, 5l **TIME:** 6min 13.0s **TOTE:** £2.80; places £1.40,£1.10,£5.00 **DF:** £2.50

545 Land Rover Mens Open, 12st
9 ran

[369⁸]	1		**SHANAVOGH** (7x) 4-1 R Hunnisett *Lft 2nd 3; disp ld 13 til ld 15; 5l clr app 2 out; comf*
[303⁶]	2	5	**Rob Mine (IRE)** (4x) 5-4F S Sporborg *Ld til hdd 15; ld 7; no imp*
[369⁵]	3	12	**Casual Water (IRE)** (7x) 25-1 L Hicks *Prom; mist 6; 2l 3rd ½way; rdn 15; wknd 2 out*
[294²]	4	15	**Kissair (IRE)** (7x) 2-1 S Morris *Spread plate gng to post & delayed rce 15min; hld up; 5l 5th ½way; eff 13; 6l 4th & rdn 15; wknd u.p 2 out; eased when btn*
[367⁵]	5	runin	**Needwood Neptune** (vis) 20-1 P Bennett *Spurs; nvr gng wl & freq & needless rmdrs; t.o 7; forced on*
[430³]	P		**Andermatt** (7x,5ow) (tt) 50-1 A Cockerill *A bhnd; 13l 6th ½way; t.o 12; pu & dism flat*
	P		**Bucket Of Gold** 33-1 T Denniff *A bhnd; mist 8; 15l 7th & rdn ½way; t.o & pu 13*
[94⁸]	U		**Jack The Td (IRE)** 14-1 J Cornwall *2nd til mist & ur 3*
	P		**South Westerly (IRE)** 12-1 M Mackley *(bf) Hld up; hdwy 8; 3l 4th ½way; wknd qckly & 10l 5th 13; pu 14*

OFFICIAL DISTANCES: 1l, 4l **TIME:** 6min 15.3s **TOTE:** £3.80; places £1.10,£1.10,£10.00 **DF:** £2.70

546 Restricted
15 ran

[440⁶]	1		**NEVA-AGREE** 12-1 R Armson *Hld up; 12l 6th ½way; hdwy 11; 8l 6th & rdn 15; eff 3 out; lft 2nd bend bef 2 out; mist last; stayed on u.p to ld nr fin*
[435¹]	2	¾	**Sovereigns Match** 7-1 M Mackley *Hld up; 13l 7th ½way; hdwy 12; went 3rd nxt; mist 15; went 2nd app 3 out; lft in ld bend bef 2 out; hrd rdn flat; hdd nr fin*
[301⁸]	3	8	**Auntie Alice** (5a) 5-2 C Mulhall *Hld up & bhnd; 16l 10th ½way; 9l 8th 15; eff 3 out; went 4l 3rd nxt; no ex*
[371⁸]	4	3	**Peacemaker (IRE)** 12-1 J Cornwall *Chsd ldrs; 7l 3rd ½way; lost plce 11; 8½l 7l 15; rallied 3 out; one pce*
[366¹]	5	2½	**Defence Counsel (IRE)** 16-1 T Lane *(xnb) Mists; ld 2-3; 9l 4th ½way; 6l 4th & rdn 15; no ex 3 out*
[459⁸]	6	4	**Bustoni (IRE)** 7-1 W Tellwright *Tde; pulled hrd; jnd ldrs 5; ld 7; 5l clr 9-12; hdd aft 15; wknd qckly 2 out; mist last*
[322¹]	7	3	**Le Cabro D'Or** 2-1F S Sporborg *(xnb) Pulled hrd; ld 3-7; hit 14; 2nd til ld aft 15; cocked jaw & rn v wide bend app 2 out; nt rec*
[119⁴]	8	10	**Cantango (IRE)** 12-1 J Turcan *Ld to 1; lost plce 7; 14l 8th ½way; wl bhnd 13*
[416⁵]	9	15	**White Smoke (IRE)** 25-1 R Ross *W ldrs; 10l 5th ½way; 6½l 5th 15; sn wknd; t.o*
[440⁵]	P		**Grants Carouse** 33-1 M Wells *A bhnd; 22l 13th ½way; t.o & pu 12*
[371ᵁ]	P		**Grove Victor (IRE)** 16-1 S Morris *(xnb) Prom til lost plce 7; 15l 9th ½way; blun 11; bhnd when mist 12; pu 13*
	P		**High Green** 14-1 A Wintle *Hld up; bhnd when bu 7; lame*
[440⁸]	P		**River Ferdinand (IRE)** 12-1 J Docker *A bhnd; 20l 12th ½way; t.o & pu 11*
[174¹]	P		**Spring Wheat** (5a) (tt) 20-1 Miss C Tuke *Swtng; a bhnd; 17l 11th ½way; t.o & pu 3 out*

[196ᶠ]   P   Wotanite 25-1 E Walker *Rmdrs 4; jmpd slow & drpd to rr 6; 24l 14th ½way; t.o & pu 12*

OFFICIAL DISTANCES: ¾l, 6l TIME: 6min 25.4s TOTE: £20.00; places £5.00,£5.00,£1.20 DF: c/f

547 Confined Maiden (Div 1), 12st   10 ran

[439ᴿ]	1		**HUNTSBYDALE** (5a) 4-1 T Lane *Lw; a.p; 3l 4th ½way; ld 11; drew wl clr frm 3 out; easy*
[372⁴]	2	20	**Grey Warrior** 6-4F M Hewitt *Many mists; hld up & bhnd; hdwy & 6l 7th 5th 15; jnd ldrs 11; lost plce & 8l 5th 15; rallied u.p 3 out; went 12l 2nd aft 2 out; no imp*
[373ᶠ]	3	2½	**Erik The Viking** 7-2 R Armson *Hld up & bhnd; hdwy 8; 4l 5th ½way; 4l 3rd 15; went 2nd nxt; no ex u.p*
	4	8	**On The Bone** (5a) 7-1 L Hicks *10s-7s; hld up; hdwy 7; 2l 3rd ½way; blun 10; went 2nd 12 til rdn & wknd 3 out*
	5	4	**Paradise Row (IRE)** 7-1 M Chatterton *2nd/3rd til ld 9; hdd 11; 7l 4th 15; sn wknd*
[436⁵]	6	15	**Colonel Carats** 10-1 N Bell *Swtng; went 2nd 2-5; lost plce 8; 5l 6th ½way; wknd 11; t.o when mist 13*
	7	4	**Pretty Boy George** 10-1 A Bealby *Swtng; ld til hdd 9; wknd qckly 13; 20l 6th 15; t.o*
[367ᶠ]	P		**Birdietoo** (5a) 20-1 M Skinner *Tde; sev posns; lost plce 8; 10th ½way; lost tch 11; sn t.o; pu 3 out*
[235ᶠ]	r		**Del The Lorry Man** 20-1 K Needham *Jmpd lft; 5th & blun 3; lost plce 6; 7l 8th ½way; 7th when blun 11; sn wknd; t.o when ref 3 out*
[235ᴮ]	P		**Patrington Boy** 14-1 M Mackley *A bhnd; 9th ½way; pu 11*

OFFICIAL DISTANCES: 20l, 3l TIME: 6min 23.8s TOTE: £8.00; places £3.40,£1.10,£1.10 DF: £10.50

548 Confined Maiden (Div 2), 12st   10 ran

[93ᶠ]	1		**PENROSE LAD (NZ)** 10-1 W Tellwright *A.p; went 2nd 6; mist 9; ld 11; r.o wl*
[373ᶠ]	2	5	**Metro Fashion (IRE)** 3-1 T Lane *7s-3s; a.p; mist 3; 8l 3rd ½way; rdn when mist 15; went 2nd app 2 out; no ex u.p*
[438²]	3	1	**Scraptastic** 4-1 N Bell *2nd til ld 5; 6l clr 7; hdd 11; chsd wnr til rdn app 2 out; no ex*
[372³]	4	15	**Playlord** 7-4F N Docker *3s-7/4; hld up; 14l 7th ½way; bhnd til hdwy 12; sn outpcd; 23l 5th 3 out; stayed on*
[373ᶠ]	5	10	**Cashel Green (IRE)** 12-1 M Hewitt *Hld up; 9l 4th ½way; hdwy 12; rdn 14; wkng when hit 15*
[436ᶠ]	P		**Camden Kid (IRE)** 25-1 Miss L Allan *Swtng; a bhnd; 18l 8th ½way; mist 10; t.o & pu 12*
[233⁵]	P		**Copper Thorn** (5a) 20-1 L Hicks *Ld to 5; lost plce 8; 13l 6th ½way; wknd 12; t.o & pu 15*
	P		**Henry Henbit** (7a) 5-1 S Morris *Jmpd novicey; a bhnd; 20l 9th ½way; t.o & pu 13*
[124⁷]	P		**Light The Sky** 8-1 J Turcan *Hld up; 12l 5th ½way; lost tch u.p 13; t.o & pu 3 out*
	P		**Up The Road (IRE)** 20-1 R Armson *Rmdrs 3; bhnd til pu 8*

OFFICIAL DISTANCES: 4l, ½l TIME: 6min 29.7s TOTE: £10.50; places £4.50,£1.10,£1.20 DF: c/f to Belvoir

Dunston Harriers
Ampton (RH 7F,20J) Sun, 12 Mar (GOOD)

549 Confined, 12st   6 ran

[83⁴]	1		**POPESHALL** 7-2 C Ward *2nd/3rd; lost plce 13; rallied to 6l 2nd & u.p 15; kpt on wl to ld 2 out; stayed on game*
[318²]	2	5	**Oflaherty's Babe (IRE)** (3x) 4-5F A Sansome *Ld 5; 6l clr 15; 4l up app 3 out; rdn & hdd nxt; no ex; lame; has been retired*
[417ᴿ]	3	25	**Damier Blanc (FR)** (bl) 14-1 D Cook *Trckd ldrs; rdn in 10l 3rd aft 15; lost tch 3 out*
[319⁴]	4	3	**Limited Liability** 4-1 Miss C Grissell *(xnb) Handy; hit 8; 4th 15; strugg nxt; wl bhnd 3 out*
[241ᶠ]	P		**Absolute Limit** (3x) 3-1 N Bloom *Tk str hld & ld to 5; 4th 8; strugg 13; rem when pu 16*
	P		**Omidjoy (IRE)** (5a) 20-1 M Polley *Bckwd; a last; sn lost tch; t.o 11; pu 13*

OFFICIAL DISTANCES: 3l, 20l TIME: 6min 44.0s TOTE: £4.80

550 Open Maiden (Div 1) - 19J   11 ran

[291²]	1		**SQUADDIE** 3-1 A Sansome *Swtng; awkward & knocked over handler padd; tk keen hld; ld 3 & sn clr; 10l ahd 15; virt solo when tired 2 out; clambered last; unchall; enterprisingly rdn*
[259ᵁ]	2	25	**Heathburn (IRE)** 9-2 C Ward-Thomas *Prom; 6l 2nd 8; lost plce & 18l 4th 15; kpt on stdly frm 3 out to poor 2nd at last*
[372ᶠ]	3	2	**Miss Caitlin (IRE)** (5a) 25-1 P Millington *Hld up & bhnd to 8; hdwy 12; 18l 4th aft 15; kpt on to rem 2nd 2 out-last*

[75ᴾ]	4	12	**Stonebroke (IRE)** 12-1 J Diment *Sn prom in chsng group; 3rd 8; 10l 2nd 15; chsd wnr vain til wknd & blun 2 out; fin tired*
[330⁵]	5	2	**Fair Ally** 12-1 B Kendellen *(xnb) 2 handlers; oht; hld up towards rr; rdn & nt keen aft 14; 23l 5th aft 15; no ch aft*
[412ᴾ]	P		**Colemore Green** 20-1 M Gingell *Fat; sn strugg in rr; pu 10*
[322ᴾ]	F		**Curracloe Rose (IRE)** (5a) 20-1 D Cook *Chsd ldrs; 5th 8; fell 10*
[416ᴾ]	P		**Full Bore (IRE)** 16-1 W Wales *(xnb) Chsd ldrs; 6th 8; rdn & nt keen aft 14; 36l 7th aft nxt; pu 17*
	P		**Midnight Dynamite** 16-1 P Chinery *Lkd v unruly app 1; jmpd most erratic & sn t.o; pu 12*
[273²]	P		**Mr Magget (IRE)** 6-4F Miss C Fryer *(xnb) Ld to 3; prom; 2nd 12; 30l 6th & lsng tch rap aft 15; wl t.o when pu 3 out*
[321ᴾ]	F		**Trojan Love (IRE)** (5a) 25-1 K Edmunds *Mists in final trio; hmpd & fell 10*

OFFICIAL DISTANCES: 20l, 1½l TIME: 6min 46.0s TOTE: £2.60
Fence 17 omitted - fallen riders

551 Open Maiden (Div 2)   14 ran

[322⁴]	1		**PERSIAN BOY (IRE)** 5-2F A Sansome *2nd/3rd til ld 11; hdd brief 3 out; rdn clr agn aft nxt; all out*
	2	6	**Just Chica** 4-1 N Bloom *Bckwd; ld 4-8; chsd wnr frm 14 til ld brief 3 out; tried to rally app last; sn btn; fin tired*
[131ᶠ]	3	25	**The Secret Grey** 5-1 A Coe *Settled 4/5th til 3rd 15; wknd qckly 3 out*
[322ᴾ]	P		**Arbitrage Man (IRE)** 16-1 P McAllister *A rr div; 7th & strugg 14; t.o & pu 17*
	P		**Chariot Man (IRE)** 5-1 N King *Midfield til wknd 8; poor 9th 14; t.o & pu nxt*
[412ᴾ]	P		**Cicero's Law (IRE)** 5-1 P Chinery *Sn towards rr; 8th & strugg 14; t.o & pu 17*
[416ᴾ]	P		**Coolest By Phar (IRE)** (tt) 20-1 C Ward-Thomas *Ld to 4; ld 8 & made most to 11; cl 3rd 14; mist nxt & 6l 5th aft; sn wknd; pu 17 (had blood in mouth)*
[322ᴾ]	P		**Lancaster Boy (IRE)** 6-1 C Ward *(xnb) Trckd ldrs; 5th when mist 14; outpcd app 3 out; tired last when climbed nxt; pu last*
[323ᴾ]	F		**Mannagar (IRE)** 33-1 D Page (East Anglia) *Ss; last trio til fell 10*
[87ᴾ]	F		**Polly Live Wire** (5a) 10-1 P Millington *(citation) Bhnd; last 8; fell 10*
[323]	r		**Primrose Hill** (5a) (bl) 25-1 M Barnard *Ref to rce*
[237ᴾ]	P		**Sire De Brumetz (FR)** (7a) 25-1 G Pewter *A wl bhnd; t.o last 14; pu 16*
	P		**Take It Easy (IRE)** 25-1 D Parravani *(xnb) A gng bad in rr; t.o & pu 8*
[239ᴿ]	P		**Teluk (IRE)** 25-1 M Gingell *Ur gng down; 4th 8; drpd back 6th 14; sn lost tch; pu 16*

OFFICIAL DISTANCES: 4l, 20l TIME: 6min 51.0s TOTE: £2.20

552 Intermediate, 12st   5 ran

[215³]	1		**VILLAGE COPPER** 1-2F C Ward-Thomas *Lw; ld 5-7; 8-10 & frm 14; a gng wl; drew clr aft 3 out*
[327⁴]	2	10	**Man Of The Match** 4-1 F Hutsby *Ld to 5; 6-8 & 10-14; rmdrs nxt; chsd wnr vain frm 3 out*
[319ᴾ]	3	6	**Royal Surprise** 20-1 Miss L Ingram *Jmpd safe in 4/5th; went 3rd 16; sn outpcd by ldrs*
[416¹]	4	2	**Royal Banker (IRE)** 3-1 N Bloom *Sn niggled along & nvr lkd keen; hit 11; 5l 3rd 14; nt r.o u.p frm 16*
[318ᴾ]	P		**Ardkilly Warrior (IRE)** 14-1 W Wales *Mist 2; nt a fluent; a chsng group; rdn & lost tch v tame 3 out; pu last*

OFFICIAL DISTANCES: 8l, 5l TIME: 6min 43.0s TOTE: £1.50

553 Mixed Open, 12st - 19J   5 ran

[415¹]	1		**HATCHAM BOY (IRE)** (4x) 1-2F C Ward-Thomas *Lw; made nrly all & a gng wl; 5l clr 15; stdd & 2l up; 3 out; sn clr agn; easy*
[320ᴾ]	2	38	**Cinnamon Club** (5a) 12-1 D Cook *Cl up til rdn & mist 14; 10l 3rd nxt; trckd ldrs til 6l 3rd & jmpd slow 3 out; imm strugg; fin tired*
[320ᴾ]	2d		**Remilan (IRE)** (4x) 4-1 A Sansome *Swtng; w wnr 3-5; niggled 8; hung rt & pushed out rival 10; chsd wnr final circ but nvr keen & lost tch u.p aft 3 out; fin 8l 2nd; dsq*
[195ᴾ]	F		**Buachaill Dana (IRE)** (7x) 20-1 J Diment *Bit bckwd; 3rd app 8; cl up when fell 10*
[238¹]	R		**Dockmaster** (7x) 3-1 M Abrey *Trckd ldrs; last & in tch when forced to rn thro wing & ur 10*

OFFICIAL DISTANCES: Originally 6l, dist TIME: 6min 46.0s TOTE: £1.60
Fence 17 omitted - fallen riders; the stewards enquired into the running out of Dockmaster; having interviewed those concerned they fined the rider of Remilan £100 for reckless riding and disqualified the horse from second

554 Restricted, 12st   6 ran

[236¹]	1		**MANNA BRAVE (IRE)** 5-4F C Ward-Thomas *Lw; settled 2nd/3rd; 3rd 3 out; str rn to ld app last; sn clr*
[86⁸]	2	15	**Mister Audi (IRE)** 6-1 A Sansome *Ld & jmpd v slow 1; lft in ld 3; blun 8; hdd aft 14; ld agn 3 out; hrd rdn & hdd app last; sn wknd*
[440²]	3	5	**Baron Allfours** 4-1 P Millington *(citation) Hld up & handy til dashed into ld aft 14; hdd & mist 3 out; wknd nxt*
[126⁴]	4	20	**Helena Justina** (5a) 4-1 P Taiano *Towards rr; rdn & lost tch 13; 10l 4th 15; to 3 out*
[416ᵖ]	P		**Coptic Dancer** (5a) 33-1 A Braithwaite *(xnb) Bckwd; reared start & lost 20l; sn in tch & pulled hrd; last when pckd 9; lost tch qckly 12; t.o & pu 3 out*
[237¹]	P		**Mai Point** (5a) 8-1 Miss C Grissell *(xnb) Lft in ld 1 til pu 3 - passed 4 fncs bef rdr able to stop (rdr thought horse had gone wrong)*

OFFICIAL DISTANCES: 10l, 5l **TIME:** 6min 50.0s **TOTE:** £1.90

555 Countryside Alliance Club Members 6yo&up (Nov Rdrs)   6 ran

[319ᵖ]	1		**ANN'S AMBITION** 2-1 Miss C Fryer *Cl up til ld 11; 8l clr 14; hdd aft 3 out; rallied nxt; ld agn last; r.o game*
[319⁵]	2	4	**Faha Gig (IRE)** (5a) 7-4F A Braithwaite *Ld to 11; chsd ldr til ld aft 3 out; rdn & hdd last; sn outpcd*
[241⁴]	3	27	**Going Around** 5-1 Miss A Webb *Last & sn 10l adrift; virt t.o 10; clsd 14 & 22l last 16; went 4th nxt but nvr plcd to chall*
[179³]	5		**Premier First (IRE)** 16-1 W Pewter *(xnb) Prsd ldr to 13; 10l 4th nxt; lost tch 16; t.o 3 out*
[414⁶]	3d		**Black Book (IRE)** (5a) 6-1 Miss Carla Thomas *Lkd v scruffy; nt fluent; mist 2; in tch; 9l 3rd 14; 15l 3rd & outpcd nxt; plodded on; fin 16l 3rd; disq - lost weight-cloth 2 out*
[317¹]	U		**Hizal** 5-1 D Hayes *3rd/4th til mist & ur 10*

OFFICIAL DISTANCES: Originally 3l, 8l **TIME:** 6min 51.0s **TOTE:** £1.80
Fence 17 omitted - fallen rider; Black Book finished 3rd but was disqualified when the rider was unable to draw the correct weight - had lost weight cloth

South Devon

Black Forest Lodge (RH 8F,19J) Sun, 12 Mar (FIRM)

556 Hunt   4 ran

	1		**BIG SEAMUS (IRE)** (bl) 5-4F David Dennis *Hld up in last; impd to 2nd aft 15; ld app 2 out; sn clr; slowed into last; comf*
[409²]	2	5	**Knock Star (IRE)** 11-4 S Partridge *3s-11/4; settled 3rd; hdwy to in ldrs 9; ld app 11; rdn 3 out; hdd app nxt; no ex; fair eff*
[406⁷]	3	25	**Run With Joy (IRE)** 33-1 J Berwick *Bit bckwd; ld & 10l clr by 2; hdd 8; disp ld 9-10; wknd 14; btn 3rd when pckd 16; no ch aft*
[314ᵖ]	U		**Agent** 9-4 Miss C Stucley *(xnb) 5/2-9/4; chsd ldr til ld on inner 8; cl 3rd when blun & ur 9; rdr inj*

OFFICIAL DISTANCES: 7l, 30l **TIME:** 6min 08.0s

557 Confined, 12st   10 ran

[202²]	1		**WESTERN FORT (IRE)** evensF Miss J Cumings *Lw; handy; cl 4th ½way; jmpd to ld 13; hdd aft 15; cl 2nd when lft in clr ld 16; 15l clr 2 out; easy*
[258²]	2	8	**Valley's Choice** (5a,3x) 4-1 C White *Towards rr; some hdwy to 6th 11; lot to do 15; lft 2nd nxt; clsd stdly to 8l 2nd 3 out; no further prog*
[354ᵖ]	3	10	**Chickabiddy** (5a) 16-1 Miss G Edwards *Lw; rr; last but in tch 7; nt nr ldrs; poor 7th 14; went 3rd 3 out; r.o; nrst fin*
[315ᵖ]	4	4	**Breeze-Bloc** (5a) 66-1 M Shears *(bf) Swtng; midfield; mist 6; 7th 11; bhnd frm 14*
[403ᵖ]	5	6	**Manor Rhyme** (7ow) (vis) 25-1 T Gretton *Ld 2; jmpd lft & rmdr 12; hdd & wknd nxt; bhnd frm 14*
[310⁴]	B		**Foxy Dawn** 10-1 D Alers-Hankey *Lw; hdwy to disp 3rd 8; cl 3rd 15; ev ch when bd 16*
[9⁸]	P		**Hensue** 12-1 Miss C Prouse *Ld 1; sn lost plce; last frm 9; t.o & pu 14*
[259³]	U		**Ive Called Time** (3x) 7-1 G Chanter *Sn prom; cl 2nd when ur 7*
[354ᵖ]	F		**Link Copper** 10-1 Miss S Jackson *In tch; went 2nd 8; cl up til ld aft 15; slt ld when fell hvly nxt*
[355ᵁ]	U		**Mr Magnetic (IRE)** 12-1 D Harvey *Lw; hdwy 7; 5th 11; stdy prog aft 13; 4th & in tch when hmpd & ur 16*

OFFICIAL DISTANCES: 10l, 8l **TIME:** 6min 06.0s

558 Ladies Open   8 ran

[101³]	1		**HEARTS ARE WILD** 8-11F **Miss P Gundry** *Lw; swtng; prom; 2nd frm 7; slt ld 9 til jmpd lft 12; ld agn 15; drew clr 2 out; eased flat*
[357³]	2	6	**Elle Flavador** (5a) 50-1 **Miss S Vickery** *(xnb) Rcd keen; ld to 9 & agn aft 12; pckd & hdd 14; chsd wnr til wknd 2 out; nt disg*
[310³]	3	6	**No More Nice Guy (IRE)** 10-1 **Mrs M Hand** *Settled 4th; 10l 4th ½way; pushed along 13; went 12l 3rd 15; nt pce to chall*
[355F]	4	15	**Play Poker (IRE)** 6-4 **Miss J Cumings** *Tchd 7/4; hld up just in tch; went 4th but lot to do aft 14; 26l 4th 16; no ch frm 3 out; wl below form*
[406P]	5	5	**Don Luigi** (bl) 100-1 **Miss O Green** *Ch ride; in tch in 5th til releg last 10; rmdrs 12; sn bhnd*
	U		**Just Mai-Bee** 100-1 **Miss C Hurst** *(bf) Towards rr when u r 1*
[203P]	P		**Karlin's Quest** 100-1 **Miss A Barnett** *Chsd ldr to 6; stayed prom in 3rd til wknd qckly aft 14; sn bhnd; strugg when jmpd slow 2 out; pu last*
[314⁹]	P		**Secret Four** 16-1 **Miss K Langdell** *(xnb) Sn strugg & jmpd slow; t.o & pu 6*

OFFICIAL DISTANCES: 8l, 10l **TIME:** 5min 50.0s (course record)

559 Restricted (Div 1), 12st   10 ran

[203F]	1		**SEA URCHIN** 2-1F **D Alers-Hankey** *(xnb) Tde; patient rdn; prog to 10l 5th 12; hdwy to 3rd 2 out; str rn to ld cl home*
[208P]	2	hd	**Hemero (IRE)** (tt) 8-1 **A Honeyball** *Lw; sn prom; trckd ldr til slt ld frm 16; drvn into 3l ld aft 2 out; hdd last strides*
[206²]	3	6	**Madam Rose (IRE)** (5a) 6-1 **L Jefford** *(xnb) Tk keen hld; ld 2-16; cl 2nd til wknd & one pce aft 2 out*
[356P]	4	8	**Palace King (IRE)** 20-1 **M Wheeler** *(xnb) Jmpd lft 4 & lost early plce; 7th 12; nt trble ldrs; went 4th aft 2 out*
	5	8	**The Stuffed Puffin (IRE)** 10-1 **Miss S Rowe** *(nosenet) In tch towards outer; 6l 4th 12; cl 3rd 15; outpcd aft nxt; no ch frm 3 out*
[163P]	P		**Cool Million** 33-1 **Miss L Bridges** *(xnb) Sn last & climbing fncs; t.o 8; wl bhnd when pu 13*
[13⁶]	P		**Cucklington** (bl) 4-1 **A Charles-Jones** *Lw; ld 1; cl 3rd when hit 10 & rmdr; drvn along to stay in tch frm 13; cl 3rd 16; mist 3 out; pu & dism nxt*
	P		**Nick's Way** 20-1 **C White** *Towards rr & nt a fluent; 8th 12; hdwy to 5th & in tch 16; sn eased; pu 2 out*
[69F]	F		**Poet's Song (IRE)** 7-2 **G Barfoot-Saunt** *Tchd 4s; midfield; lost ground 11; bhnd when fell 14*
[407P]	P		**Rushaway** 16-1 **R Woollacott** *(xnb) Tchd 20s; handy; 5th 8; in tch in 6th 11; pu & dism 13*

OFFICIAL DISTANCES: hd, 7l **TIME:** 6min 02.0s

560 Restricted (Div 2), 12st   10 ran

[208⁵]	1		**CHASING DAISY** (5a) 11-2 **J Snowden** *Mounted on course; in tch; tk keen hld; cl 4th ½way; trckd ldr frm 11; chall on inner 3 out; ld aft nxt; pushed clr last; comf*
	2	5	**Ribington** 4-1 **T Scudamore** *Ld 1 & agn frm 7; niggled along 12; 2l ld frm 9; rdn nxt; hdd aft 2 out; no ex*
	3	10	**Divine Inspiration (IRE)** 100-30 **P Pritchard** *A handy; cl 5th 11; stdy hdwy to 3rd & gng wl 16; ev ch til rdn & wknd aft 3 out*
[356P]	4	2½	**Nodforms Inferno** 8-1 **A Bateman** *(xnb) Tde; tk keen hld & hld 2-7; settled btr & trckd ldr clsly to 11; in tch til grad wknd frm 16*
[315P]	5	20	**Nearly All Right** 10-1 **N Harris** *Oht; sn prom; cl 3rd 10; lost ground 12; drvn along 15; no ch frm 16*
	6	1	**Lynphord Girl** (5a) 16-1 **J Barnes** *Towards rr; 6th ½way; no ch frm 15*
[165P]	7	runin	**Crownhill Cross** 33-1 **Miss Johanna Sleep** *Nov rdn; swtng; sn strugg in rr; last frm 12; t.o*
	P		**Jolirose** (12a) 25-1 **Miss V Stephens** *Sn trailing; t.o 4 til pu 12; school*
[356²]	U		**Picard (IRE)** 2-1F **Miss L Hawkins** *In tch til ur 6*
[147P]	P		**Willsan** (tt) 5-1 **A Honeyball** *Tchd 6s; tubed; lw; midfield; 6th 9; bhnd frm 13 til pu 16*

OFFICIAL DISTANCES: 8l, nk **TIME:** 6min 01.0s

561 Mens Open, 12st   13 ran

	1		**TUSKAR FLOP** (7x) 6-1 **D Alers-Hankey** *Hld up in midfield; gd hdwy to 2nd aft 16; ld nxt; qcknd clr 2 out; rdly*

[251¹]	2	8	**Well Armed (IRE)** (7x) (bl) 4-7F **T Scudamore** Lw; hld up towards rr; stdy prog to 4th 12; cl 3rd & poised to chall 16; eff nxt; qckly outpcd 2 out
[351ᵁ]	3	4	**Bells Wood** 3-1 **C White** Swtng; pulling; ld 3-10; cl 2nd 15; outpcd & lost plce qckly nxt; 7th 3 out; r.o agn to tk 3rd last
[389ᵁ]	5	4	**Mostyn** 14-1 **P Pritchard** Ld to 3; stayed prom; disp ld 10; cl up til wknd 3 out
[271¹]	6	8	**Swinging Sixties (IRE)** 66-1 **G Richards** Handy in midfield; cl 6th 15-16; lost ground nxt; no ch aft
[356³]	7	3	**A Few Dollars More (IRE)** (bl) 25-1 **R Woollacott** In tch; hdwy to 4th 11; 7th 16; one pce
[453ᴾ]	8	6	**Villains Brief (IRE)** (bl) 100-1 **J Kwiatkowski** Prom in ldng group to 10; sn wknd; lost tch 13; mist 14; t.o
	4d		**Hanging Grove (IRE)** 14-1 **M Bryant** In tch; cl 6th 10; hdwy to 3rd 3 out; nt trble ldrs; releg 4th last; fin 14l 4th; disq - nt weigh-in
	P		**Gallant Effort (IRE)** (bl) 66-1 **C Sclater** Rr; wl bhnd frm 8; t.o & pu last
[263ᴾ]	P		**Leap Frog** 10-1 **A Charles-Jones** Tde; handy; ld 11 til aft 16; wknd rap; pu 2 out
[104ᴾ]	P		**Lucky Thursday** 50-1 **A Holdsworth** Sn bhnd; t.o when jmpd lft 12; wl bhnd when pu 2 out
[262ᴾ]	P		**Oneforwillie** (tt) 50-1 **J Snowden** 8th ½way; bhnd; pu 14
	P		**Safety (USA)** (bl) 12-1 **G Wright** Prom early; lost plce & 10th 10; bhnd & pu 15

OFFICIAL DISTANCES: 6l, 8l **TIME:** 5min 58.0s

Hanging Grove finished fourth but was disqualified when the rider failed to weigh-in; he was fined £40

562 Confined Maiden (Div 1), 12st   12 ran

[204ᴾ]	1		**WITNEY O'GRADY (IRE)** 4-1 **Richard Darke** (xnb) Tchd 7s; unruly start; sn prom; chsd ldr 14 til ld 16; rdn & forged 2l clr 3 out; jmpd lft aft; all out
	2	2½	**Copastrop** 16-1 **R Woollacott** Ld in start; drpd out early; last ½way; eye-catching prog to 4th 16; tk 2nd & ev ch 3 out; nt qckn run-in; do btr
[410ᶠ]	3	4	**Saucy's Wolf** 12-1 **Jeremy Young** Oht; handy; cl 3rd 7 til trckd ldr frm 9-14; 6l 3rd 16; one pce
[257ᵁ]	4	6	**Luney River** (5a) 7-1 **Miss L Gardner** Midfield; 6th ½way; nd; nrst fin
	5	8	**Typical Woman (IRE)** (5a) 12-1 **C White** Tchd 16s; ch ride; ld 5-16; drpd out tame
[353ᶠ]	6	6	**My Happy Lord** (tt) 3-1 **David Dennis** Chsd ldrs & nt fluent; in tch in 5th 12; poor 5th 16; no ch aft
[409ᴾ]	U		**Cherry Pie** (5a) 16-1 **Mrs M Hand** Ld til jmpd lft 4; cl 4th when blun & ur 6
[352⁵]	P		**Grandpa Maurice (IRE)** 7-2 **T Scudamore** Tubed; sn strugg in rr; t.o & pu 14
	P		**Hayne Condor** 20-1 **S Kidston** Bit bckwd; 7th ½way; sn lost plce; bhnd when pu 14
[352⁴]	P		**Humara (IRE)** (5a) 5-2F **Miss G Edwards** Tchd 3s; lw; swtng; sn rr; 9th ½way; t.o & pu 14
	P		**Mount Keen** 16-1 **D Stephens** (Devon) In tch; 4th ½way; lost plce 13; rr when hmpd 14; scrambled over nxt & pu
	F		**Reving-Alice** (12a) 12-1 **G Richards** Mist 3; 8th ½way; 7th when fell 14

OFFICIAL DISTANCES: 2l, 2l **TIME:** 6min 11.3s

563 Confined Maiden (Div 2), 12st   10 ran

[204²]	1		**MORRIS PIPER** 4-7F **L Jefford** Lw; swtng profuse; hld up in tch; 5th ½way; impd 15; jmpd into ld 16; drew clr 2 out; easy
	2	10	**Veiled Dancer (IRE)** (5a) 7-1 **A Holdsworth** Prom; bad mist 3; cl 4th 10; cl up til went 2nd aft 16; nt pce of wnr; eased run-in
	3	3	**Green Anker** 33-1 **Miss O Green** Ch ride; ld/disp frm 4-9; chsd ldr nxt til wknd stdly aft 15; 4th & no ch 3 out; tk 3rd frm tired rival app last
[145²]	4	4	**Porters Lodge** 5-1 **David Dennis** Bit bckwd; sn prom; ld/disp 4 til ld 10; blun 14; hdd 16; tiring in 3rd when scrambled over 2 out; btn 4th when blun last
[158ᴾ]	5	1½fs	**Horton** 16-1 **S Parkin** Tde; sa; a last; to frm 7
	P		**Emerald Ecstasy** (5a) 20-1 **I Hambley** Ld 1; wl in tch to 11; wknd; btn 7th when pu 14
	P		**Jolifast** 3-1 **D Alers-Hankey** (xnb) Settled towards rr; hdwy 10; 6th 12; 5th & nd when pu 3 out; quiet rn
	P		**Knap Hand** (7a) 25-1 **A Ede** Rr til pu 9
	P		**North Newcombe** 25-1 **N Harris** Jmpd novicey; midfield; 6th 10; nt trble ldrs; btn 6th when pu 3 out; school
[255ᴾ]	P		**Ru Bidding** (5a) 33-1 **T Greed** Rr frm 7; 8th 10; t.o & pu 15

OFFICIAL DISTANCES: 5l, 12l **TIME:** 6min 13.3s

Tanatside

Eyton-on-Severn (LH 13F,18J) Sun, 12 Mar (GOOD)

564 Intermediate, 12st
7 ran

	1		THATSFOREEL 5-1 T Stephenson *Rcd in cl 3rd/4th; ld 12; r.o und str press*
[179F]	2	hd	Rising Sap 7-1 R Burton *Prom; 4l 5th 10; prog to 2nd 3 out; r.o u.p*
	3	30	Robero 4-1 D Mansell *Hld up; 15l last 7; 8l last 12; nt pce to chall*
	4	2	Dainty Man (IRE) 5-1 A Dalton *Bckwd; chsd ldr to 12; lost tch 3 out*
[367F]	5	3	Native Cove (IRE) 8-1 G Hanmer *Prom; 3l 4th 10; outpcd 3 out*
	F		Glacial Trial (IRE) (5a) evensF A Crow *Hld up in tch; ev ch when fell 12*
[293⁵]	P		Glamdring (5a) 33-1 I Clyde *Ld to 11; wknd qckly; t.o & pu 3 out*

OFFICIAL DISTANCES: hd, 25l **TIME:** not taken

565 Mens Open, 12st
9 ran

[369¹]	1		LORD HARRY (IRE) (4x) 1-2F A Crow *Mid-div; prog to cl 2nd 8; ld app 3 out; drew clr; eased flat*
	2	4	Nothing Ventured 4-1 A Beedles *Settled mid-div; went cl 2nd app 3 out; outpcd by wnr*
[293⁴]	3	12	My Nominee (bl) 16-1 R Burton *Nt fluent; prom; 4l 3rd 9; outpcd app 3 out*
	4	2½	Jelali (IRE) 50-1 S Prior *Hld up in tch; outpcd ½way*
[57ʳ]	5	8	Fontaine Again (IRE) 50-1 T Stephenson *Bckwd; hld up in last; slt prog 8; nvr rchd ldrs*
[171⁴]	6	20	Orton House 66-1 S Kelly *A rr*
	P		Ask Antony (IRE) (7x) 3-1 D Sherlock *Jw; ld til app 3 out; sn wknd; pu last*
	P		Bermuda Buck (3ow) 33-1 A Davenhill *A last pr; lost tch 8; t.o 10; pu 4 out*
	P		Walls Court 66-1 J R Barlow *Rcd in cl 3rd/4th; lost tch 13; bad mist nxt & imm pu*

OFFICIAL DISTANCES: 6l, 10l **TIME:** 6min 19.0s

566 Ladies Open
10 ran

[177F]	1		HERSILIA (IRE) (5a) 10-1 Miss S Hopkins *Settled mid-div; outpcd 9; 25l 5th 12; stdy prog to ld app last; pushed out*
	2	1½	George Dillingham 5-1 Miss C Spearing *Made most; lft 15l clr ldr 13; hdd app last; no ex*
[178³]	3	20	Moonstone (IRE) (12a) 7-1 Mrs C Ford *Chsd ldr; outpcd 10; lft 2nd 13; r.o one pce frm 2 out*
[170ᵁ]	4	runin	Staigue Fort (IRE) 25-1 Miss V Stubbs *Sis; school rnd in rr*
	5	20	The Boiler White (IRE) 25-1 Miss J Froggatt *Sis; prog to cl 6th 5; outpcd 9; t.o nxt*
[442²]	U		Circus Colours 25-1 Miss J Elson *Sis; t.o last when mist & ur 5*
	P		Fundy (IRE) 2-5F Miss T Spearing *Prom; cl 2nd when pu & dism app 13 (rdr thought horse lame)*
[447²]	B		Killatty Player (IRE) (5a) 6-1 Miss C Thomas *Prom; outpcd 9; crashed into puller-up & bd app 13*
	U		Manvulane (IRE) (7x) 20-1 Miss K Crank *Sis; nvr on terms; rem 6th when ur 11*
[170F]	P		Tudor Lodge (IRE) (5a) 10-1 Miss S Swindells *Sis; a last pr; t.o 8; pu 3 out*

OFFICIAL DISTANCES: 1½l, 12l **TIME:** 6min 15.0s

567 Restricted, 12st
17 ran

[248³]	1		STAR CHANGES 5-1 E Williams *A front rank; ld 4 out; stayed on best und str drvng*
[296³]	2	nk	Seymour's Double 5-2F R Burton *Rcd cl 4/5th; prom to chall 14; upsides frm 4 out; no ex flat*
	3	10	Bobbing Along (IRE) 12-1 M Worthington *Hld up; smooth prog to heels of ldrs 14; no ex frm 3 out*
	4	2	Uncle Tom 25-1 R Cooper *Hld up in last trio 3; r.o thro btn horses*
	5	3	The Honest Poacher (IRE) 12-1 I Wynne *Chsd ldrs; cl 6th 13; lost tch nxt; r.o one pce*
[293F]	6	6	Shanballymore 14-1 R Owen *2 handlers; a rr; outpcd frm 5; stayed on frm 4 out*
[292ᵁ]	7	4	Cookie Boy 6-1 S Prior *Prom; ld brief 4 & 6; ld/disp to 11; lost tch 14*
[336⁴]	8	1	Wild Edric 6-1 G Hanmer *Mid-div; cl 5th 13; lost tch nxt*
[338⁵]	9	5	Out Of The Blue (5a) 16-1 D Mansell *Settled mid-div; nvr rchd front rank*
[172ʳ]	10	2	Tiger Paws (5a) 16-1 A Gribbin *Hld up; plodded on*
[292ᵁ]	P		Buck Run 16-1 C Barlow *Rr of ldng bunch; mist 8; t.o 12; pu 4 out*
	P		Carbery Ministrel (IRE) 20-1 K Burke *Jb; a rr; sn t.o; pu 11*
	P		Hectors Way 16-1 T Stephenson *Prom; ld/disp 7-13; wknd qckly; pu 2 out*
	P		Henwyn 7-1 A Dalton *Mid-div; cl 5th 9; lost tch 11; pu 2 out*
[247ᵁ]	P		Scallymay (5a) 14-1 M Munrowd *Mid-div; lost tch 11; pu 2 out*
[197⁶]	P		Strong Account (IRE) 20-1 R Sealey *Nd; pu 13*

| | | | P | **Tantara Lodge (IRE)** (vis) 20-1 C Stockton *Lost tch ½way; t.o 14; pu 2 out* |

OFFICIAL DISTANCES: nk, 10l **TIME:** 6min 19.0s
Ballyhannon (Miss J Froggatt) was withdrawn not under orders - vet's advice

568 Open Maiden (Div 1)   17 ran

	1			**BALLYHARRY (IRE)** 20-1 I Wynne *Mid-div; prog to cl 2nd 3 out; ld app last; rdly*
[336⁶]	2	6		**Dozmary Pool** 16-1 R Burton *Hld up; smooth prog 14; lft in ld nxt; hdd app last; no ex*
[436³]	3	30		**Fanion De Nourry (FR)** 11-2 J Merry *Hld up; nvr nrr*
	4	8		**Blacon Point** 12-1 T Stephenson *Hld up; r.o thro btn horses*
	5	8		**Silver Sumal** 7-1 A Dalton *(xnb) 2 handlers; hld up; nvr plcd to chall*
			P	**Eecel** 11-1 A Wadlow *A rr; bad mist 7; pu nxt*
			U	**Ice N' Slice (IRE)** (5a) 14-1 J Cornes *Ur 2*
[293⁵]			R	**King Paddy (IRE)** 7-1 R Bevan *Hld up; prog to cl 3rd 13; ld nxt; slt ld when rn out 15*
			F	**New Lizzard** (5a) 10-1 J Hobbs *Hld up; nvr rchd ldrs; mid-div & no ch when fell 15*
			P	**Onesevenfour (IRE)** 8-1 C Stockton *Ld til app 14; wknd qckly; pu 3 out; broke down*
[297ᵁ]			P	**Pinouli** (5a) 16-1 L Stephens *A rr; t.o 5; pu 11*
			P	**Prempted** 8-1 G Hanmer *Mid-div; cl 3rd 14; wknd qckly; pu 3 out*
[298ᴾ]			P	**Roundabout** (5a) 33-1 M Worthington *A rr; t.o ½way; pu 3 out*
			P	**Supermister** 20-1 P Morris *Chsd ldr; lost tch 10; pu 3 out*
			P	**Sutton Lighter** 14-1 D Mansell *(xnb) A rr; t.o 12; pu 3 out*
			P	**Teal Bay** (5a) 5-2F R Cooper *Mid-div; ur 6*
[76⁶]			P	**Whistling Rufus (IRE)** 72 M Rimell *(xnb) Mid-div; cl 4th 8; 2l 2nd 12; wknd qckly 4 out; pu nxt*

OFFICIAL DISTANCES: 7l, 25l **TIME:** 6min 22.0s
Ultimate Option (S Prior, 16-1) was withdrawn at the start not under orders

569 Open Maiden (Div 2)   18 ran

	1			**ALSTACK (IRE)** (bl) 10-1 B Foster *Made virt all; canter; rdr saluting at fin*
[296ᴾ]	2	8		**Po Cap Eel** (5a) 10-1 Miss H Kinsey *Mid-div; cl 5th 10; prog to cl 3rd 13; lft 2nd 4 out; nt pce of wnr*
	3	runin		**Lightening Steel** 16-1 P Morris *A rr; t.o 6; plodded on final mile passing btn horses; tk 3rd app last*
[339ᴿ]	4	5		**Vulpin De Laugere (FR)** (bl) 5-1 R Burton *Prom; disp 7; cl 4th 10; wknd nxt; r.o one pce*
			F	**Arthur Henry** 5-1 L Stephens *A front rank; cl 3rd when fell 13*
			U	**Bobby Violet** 14-1 J Merry *Last when ur 3*
[168ᶠ]			P	**Colonels Hatch** 16-1 D Sherlock *A rr; t.o 12; pu 15*
			P	**Crunch Time (IRE)** 6-1 C Stockton *Oht; a rr; lost tch 10; t.o & pu 15*
[298ᵁ]			P	**Dealer Boy (IRE)** 12-1 G Hanmer *A rr; lost tch 11; pu 3 out*
[336ᴾ]			P	**Diamond Market** 16-1 A Davenhill *Prom; cl 4th 7; lost tch 10; pu 13*
[337ʳ]			r	**Far Forest** (bl) 20-1 R Cooper *A rr; ref 6*
[297ᴾ]			P	**Hill's Electric (IRE)** 7-4F T Stephenson *Prom; disp to 13; gng wl til pu & imm dism 4 out*
			P	**Ishereal (IRE)** 10-1 S Prior *Mounted early; mid-div; lost tch 12; pu nxt*
			P	**Mezzo Princess** (5a) 12-1 J R Barlow *A rr; lost tch 11; t.o nxt; pu 2 out*
			P	**Offley Thomas** 7-1 M Worthington *A rr; t.o & pu 11*
[296⁸]			U	**Red Spice** 5-1 R Owen *Mid-div when ur 2*
			P	**Take A Right** 16-1 J Cornes *A last trio; t.o ½way; pu 4 out*
[371ᴾ]			r	**The Quakers Wake (IRE)** 12-1 C Barlow *Ww; went 6l 3rd 4 out; flatt brief; rem 3rd & tired when ref 2 out*

OFFICIAL DISTANCES: 8l, dist **TIME:** 6min 25.0s

570 Confined Maiden 56&7yo, 2m4f, 12st - 14J   15 ran

	1			**HIGHBRIDGE (IRE)** 12-1 A Evans *Made most; drew clr flat; rdly*
	2	6		**Oh So Droll** 5-1 R Burton *Mid-div; sust chall frm 3 out; outpcd flat*
[298ᴾ]	3	15		**Gun Runner** 6-1 C Barlow *Prom; cl brief 8; r.o one pce frm 13*
[298ᴾ]	4	runin		**Lady Nevada** (5a) 10-1 Miss S Hopkins *Mid-div; cl 6th 6; lost tch 9; stayed on past btn horses*
	5	15		**Mrs Sherman** (12a) 33-1 D Sherlock *Hld up; cl 5th 10; r.o one pce*
			P	**Arden Bay** (5a,4ow) 3-1 G Hanmer *(b4) T.o 7; pu 3 out*
			P	**Dancing Paws (IRE)** (7a) 20-1 S Prior *A last pr; lost tch 4; pu 4 out*
			P	**Daneswell** 33-1 M Munrowd *A last trio; lost tch 4; pu 4 out*
[298ᴾ]			P	**Fountain Street (IRE)** 12-1 L Stephens *Pulled hrd; prom; wknd qckly 3 out; pu nxt*
			P	**Hamish** 5-2F M Worthington *Prom til wknd frm 10; pu 2 out*
			U	**Inglerise** (12a) 25-1 Miss G O'Callaghan *Ur 1*
			F	**S And O P** 14-1 D Mansell *Rcd keen; ld brief 5-6; on terms when fell 7*

	P		**Step Quick (IRE)** 5-1 A Dalton *A front rank; lost tch 9; t.o 3 out; pu nxt*
	P		**Uncle Ada (IRE)** (7a) 20-1 T Stephenson *A rr; dist last; pu 4 out*
[439ᴾ]	P		**Village Gossip** (5a) 25-1 J Morley *Lost tch 4; t.o & pu 4 out*

OFFICIAL DISTANCES: 8l, 15l **TIME:** 5min 05.0s

West Street-Tickham
Detling (LH 9F,21J) Sun, 12 Mar (GOOD to FIRM)

571 Hunt
6 ran

[288ᴾ]	1		**HOW FRIENDLY** 25-1 A Hickman *Hld up; in tch in last pr til hdwy app 3 out; chall last; kpt on wl to ld cl home*
	2	½	**Rose King** (7x) evensF T Hills *Trckd ldr frm 6 til ld aft 4 out; jnd, blun & hdd 2 out; rallied to ld agn flat; hdd cl home*
[305ᴾ]	3	3	**The Glow (IRE)** (7x) 9-2 D Brightling *Hld up; cl 3rd frm 8 til prsd ldr 3 out; qcknd & ld nxt; 3l clr agn last; jmpd slow; sn hdd & btn*
[126²]	4	8	**Winward** (bl) 33-1 P M Hall *Set stdy pce; ld to 4 out; outpcd app nxt*
[289ᴾ]	5	12	**Lady Of Verse** (5a) 33-1 M Gorman *Prsd ldr to 6; 4th when blun 15; lsng tch when jmpd slow 17*
[289²]	F		**Call The Tune** (5a) 7-4 B Hitchcott *Prom til fell 6*

OFFICIAL DISTANCES: ½l, 4l **TIME:** 6min 33.0s **TOTE:** £11.30; places £2.10,£1.10 **DF:** £6.10

572 Confined Mens, 12st
15 ran

[305²]	1		**SEOD RIOGA (IRE)** (5x) 7-2 C Gordon *Cl 2nd/3rd til ld 7; made rest; 4-6l clr frm 14 til prsd aft 3 out; rdn & drew clr frm 2 out*
[461⁴]	2	12	**Time Enough (IRE)** (2ow) (bl) 33-1 P Townsley *A in tch; 4th 12; chsd wnr frm 14; chall 3 out; 3l down when mist 2 out; wknd app last*
	3	2	**Posh Spice** (5a) (tt) 14-1 P York *Wl in tch in 4/5th til outpcd aft 4 out; stayed on frm nxt to tk 3rd flat*
[239¹]	4	2	**Ballinure Boy (IRE)** 3-1JF A Hickman *Hld up towards rr; stdy hdwy to 5th 12; chsd ldng pr aft 4 out; 8l 3rd when blun 2 out; wknd app last*
[318ᴾ]	5	4	**Alfredo Garcia (IRE)** 20-1 S R Andrews *Ld to 6; cl 3rd 12; lost plce aft nxt; slt hdwy frm 3 out*
[215²]	6	1	**Tooth Pick** (3x) 5-1 J Hawksfield *Towards rr; 8th 12; hdwy frm 4 out; nrst fin*
[317ᵁ]	7	2fncs	**On The Beer (IRE)** (1ow) 33-1 M Bailey *A towards rr; 10th 12; t.o frm 15*
	P		**Celtic Spark** (3x) 7-1 D Dunsdon *A towards rr; 10th 12; no prog; pu aft 4 out*
[125ᴾ]	P		**Daddy Long Leggs** (8ow) 33-1 R Hubbard *Chsd ldrs in midfield; 9th & lsng plce 12; wl bhnd when pu 3 out*
[308³]	P		**Galaroi (IRE)** (tt) 14-1 D Robinson *Cl 2nd/3rd til chsd ldng pr 15; wknd qckly 4 out; pu nxt*
[241²]	P		**Just One Question (IRE)** (tt) 8-1 A Harvey *Midfield; 6th 12; fdd u.p frm 14; rr when pu 4 out*
	P		**Rainbow Legacy** 33-1 P Hickman *A wl bhnd; dist 13th 12; pu aft nxt*
[288ᴾ]	U		**Sultan Of Swing** 33-1 M Gorman *Last til ur 3*
[308²]	U		**Take My Side (IRE)** (bl) 3-1JF B Hitchcott *Trckd ldrs; mist 3; blun & ur 7*
	P		**Valibus (FR)** 33-1 P Scouller *A rr; dist 12th 12; pu aft nxt*

OFFICIAL DISTANCES: 12l, 2l **TIME:** 6min 03.0s **TOTE:** £6.80; places £3.30,£10.00,£9.00 **DF:** £105.00
The stewards cautioned the trainer of Sultan Of Swing under Regulation 115(iii) that she should ensure the horse is correctly saddled

573 Confined Ladies
9 ran

[300⁵]	1		**KINCORA (IRE)** 4-1 Mrs L Stock *Cl 3rd til chsd ldr frm 14; ld brief bend to 3 out; ld agn 2 out; drew clr app last*
[287¹]	2	6	**Whippers Delight (IRE)** 5-4JF Miss J Grant *Prsd ldr/disp til ld 12; hdd 2 out; wknd app last*
	3	25	**Man Of Mystery** 12-1 Miss A Sansom *Ld til almost ur 12; chsd ldng pr frm 14; lost tch 16*
	4	6	**Polar Ana** (5a) 10-1 Miss S Gladders *Hld up; 37l 8th 12; some hdwy frm 15 to 20l 4th aft 4 out; no further prog*
[416ᴾ]	5	5	**Joyful Hero** (5a) 33-1 Miss P Ellison *A chsng ldrs; 21l 6th 12; 18l 4th 4 out; wknd app nxt*
[305⁵]	6	15	**Trifast Lad** 16-1 Mrs L Baker *Prom when mist 3; sn lost plce; 36l 7th 12; t.o frm 15*
[286⁷]	7	6	**Pair Of Jacks (IRE)** (bl) 33-1 Miss J Wickens *Prsd ldrs til 15l 4th & wkng 12; no ch frm 15*
[289⁵]	8	8	**Billie's Mate (IRE)** (5a) (vis) 25-1 Mrs S Hickman *A last; 50l 9th 12; t.o frm 14*

[307²]   P   **Native Venture (IRE)** 5-4JF Mrs E Coveney *Midfield; 20l 5th & pushed along 12;
                    no prog; pu 14*

OFFICIAL DISTANCES: 7l, 15l TIME: 6min 02.0s TOTE: £7.60; places £2.20,£1.10,£1.80 DF: £12.40
*The stewards interviewed the rider of Native Venture who reported that she
had pulled up because the horse was not going on the ground; she was
cautioned as to her future riding*

574 Mixed Open, 4m, 12st - 28J   12 ran

[454⁴]   1   **HIGH GUARDIAN** 6-4JF Julian Pritchard *Jmpd sticky at times; cl 5/6th til impd 14;
                    2nd frm 18; blun 24; hrd rdn & clsd app 2 out; 11 down when mist & hmpd last; jnd ldr
                    on line; subsq awarded rce*
[300⁴]   2   d ht **Prime Course (IRE)** 8-1 C Gordon *Cl up til ld 8; clr 16; 3-6l up frm 18 til prsd &
                    jmpd lft 2 out & last; jnd on line; subsq plcd 2nd & appealed unsuccessfully*
[286²]   3   10   **Call Home (IRE)** 6-4JF T Hills *Hld up in rr; hdwy 15; cl 5th 20; trckd ldng pr 24; wknd
                    3 out*
[286ᴾ]   4   10   **Broguestown Pride (IRE)** 33-1 P Blagg *A towards rr; 8th & rdn along 20; stayed
                    on frm 4 out; nrst fin*
[288³]   5   5   **Primitive King** 5-1 D Dunsdon *Trckd ldrs in midfield; impd to cl 4th 20; wknd 4 out*
[304²]   6   15   **Edge Ahead (IRE)** 33-1 Mrs E Coveney *Prsd ldng pr to 21; lost tch frm 23*
[288ᴮ]   U   **Golden Mac** 33-1 J Barnard *Rr til ur 8*
[320⁵]   P   **Insulate** (5a) 20-1 S March *Midfield; 6th & wkng 20; pu 22*
[288⁵]   P   **Minor Key (IRE)** 33-1 A Harvey *Midfield til lost plce frm 15; rr when pu 19*
[92ᴾ]   P   **Salmon Mead (IRE)** 33-1 S R Andrews *A towards rr; 7th 20; pu 22*
[285ᵁ]   P   **Target Time** (vis) 33-1 Mrs L Stock *A last pr; lost tch 9; wl bhnd when pu 20*
[175³]   P   **Tell Tale (IRE)** 12-1 P Hickman *Ld to 7; prsd ldr til wknd qckly 16; rr when pu 20*

OFFICIAL DISTANCES: Originally: d ht, 4l TIME: 8min 25.0s TOTE: £3.40; places
£1.90,£1.60,£1.10 DF: £25.40
*Following an objection by the rider of High Guardian to Prime Course for
'taking my ground at the last' and a stewards enquiry, Prime Course was
demoted to second; this decision was later upheld on appeal to the Jockey
Club Disciplinary Committee*

575 Restricted, 12st   15 ran

[248ᴾ]   1   **FRIENDS OF BERNARD (IRE)** 9-2 D Barlow *Jmpd rt at times; ld/disp til went on 9;
                    made rest; mist 2 out; all out*
[323¹]   2   2   **Ballad (IRE)** (tt) 8-1 A Harvey *Midfield; hdwy 13; prsd ldrs 4 out; no further prog til
                    stayed on wl aft nxt; went 3rd app last; tk 2nd flat*
[306³]   3   3   **Royal Rupert** 6-1 N Benstead *Rr to 9; gd hdwy to trck ldrs 12; prsd wnr 15-3 out;
                    rallied & ev ch last; wknd flat*
[285⁴]   4   1   **Ally Pally** 7-1 P York *A wl in tch; 6th & rdn along 15; kpt on one pce frm 3 out*
         5   6   **Shamron (IRE)** (5a) 7-1 Miss S Gladders *Hld up towards rr; gd hdwy 16; trckd wnr
                    gng wl 3 out; mist nxt; wknd qckly app last*
[306ᴾ]   6   10   **Bit Of A Do** (tt) 33-1 D Slattery *Midfield; rdn along to press ldrs 12; ch 4 out; wknd*
[306ᴾ]   7   2   **Another Comedy** 25-1 N Earnshaw *Midfield til wknd 13; no ch frm 4 out*
[291¹]   8   2   **Martha Leader (IRE)** 33-1 F Stuart Robinson *Trckd ldrs til wknd qckly app 3 out*
[306ᴾ]   P   **Ballybollen (IRE)** 33-1 D Brightling *A rr; no ch when pu 2 out*
[286ᴾ]   P   **Bang On Target** (bl) 33-1 M Gorman *Prom to 6; sn lost plce; wl bhnd when pu 4 out*
[290¹]   P   **Chill Factor** (tt) 7-1 Julian Pritchard *A towards rr; no ch when pu 3 out*
         P   **Clean Sweep** 33-1 P Hickman *Prsd ldr/disp to 14; ev ch til wknd qckly 4 out; pu nxt*
[328¹]   P   **Hightech Touch** 5-2F D Dennis *Settled rr; some hdwy frm 13 but nvr nr ldrs; pu aft 4 out*
[413ᴾ]   P   **Moon Rising** 20-1 P Bull *In tch to 10; wl bhnd when pu 4 out*
[306ᴾ]   P   **Perripage** (vis) 33-1 Miss A Sansom *Prom to 6; sn lost plce; wl bhnd when pu 4 out*

OFFICIAL DISTANCES: 2l, 4l TIME: 6min 10.0s TOTE: £7.30; places £3.30,£2.90,£2.70 DF: £53.60

576 Open Maiden 56&7yo (Div 1), 12st   10 ran

[304ᶠ]   1   **MR FITZ (IRE)** 10-1 M Sheridan *Detach last til stdy hdwy 12; went 5l 2nd aft 4 out;
                    mist nxt; gd rn to press ldr app last; ld & drew clr flat*
[411²]   2   2   **Just The Business** (bl) 5-2 P Bull *Ld to 5; prsd ldng pr til ld agn 16; mist nxt; drew
                    clr aft 4 out; 6l up 2 out; jmpd slow last; wknd & hdd flat*
[290²]   3   10   **Carraig Brol (IRE)** 2-1JF B Hitchcott *Hld up; mod 6th 11; hdwy in 8l 4th when mist
                    15; chsd ldng pr app 3 out; kpt on one pce*
[131³]   4   10   **Zaisan (IRE)** 2-1JF D Dunsdon *Midfield; 7th & making no prog 11; slt hdwy frm 18*
[236ᶠ]   P   **Action Stations** 20-1 A Hickman *Hld up; hdwy into 10l 4th 11; no further prog; rr
                    when pu 3 out*
         P   **Dunston Ben** 20-1 D Page *Ur gng to stsrt; sn rr; t.o & pu 9*

	P	**Fables Green** 25-1 D Dennis *A towards rr; wl bhnd when pu 18*
	P	**Little River Place** 14-1 A Lillingston *Sn prom; ld 6-15; wknd qckly 4 out*
[290^P]	P	**Our Man Ned** (IRE) 20-1 P York *Chsd ldng trio to 10; 12l 5th when blun bad & pu 13*
[131^P]	P	**Paddy Clyde** (IRE) 16-1 C Gordon *Prsd ldr to 15; ev ch til wknd qckly 4 out; pu nxt*

OFFICIAL DISTANCES: 2l, 10l **TIME:** 6min 16.0s **TOTE:** £20.70; places £9.10,£1.10,£1.10 **DF:** £27.00

577 Open Maiden 56&7yo (Div 2), 12st
10 ran

[323³]	1	**SENIOR PARTNER** (IRE) 5-1 S R Andrews *A cl up; 2l 3rd 11; chsd ldr frm 14; 4l down when lft solo 2 out; almost ref last*
[309³]	U	**Daydreamer** (USA) 3-1JF D Brightling *Hld up; 10l 5th 11; lft 12l 3rd 4 out; slt hdwy when ur nxt*
[309^B]	P	**Little Farmer** 20-1 P Hall *Bolted 1½ circs bef start; prom til wknd qckly aft 9; rr when pu 11*
[236^F]	F	**Morph** 3-1JF P York *Trckd ldr til ld 9; made rest; blun 3 out; 4l up & lkd wnr when fell hvly 2 out; down for 15 mins*
	U	**Newick Park** (7a) 9-2 Julian Pritchard *Hld up; 13l 6th 11; making hdwy when swerved & ur 15*
[237^P]	U	**Nosy Parker** (IRE) 20-1 A Harvey *Chsd ldrs; 8l 4th 11; 10l 3rd when jmpd v slow & rfo 4 out*
	F	**Oxendale** 5-1 P Bull *Midfield til fell 6*
[291^U]	U	**Sliabh Foy** (IRE) 16-1 F Marshall *Ld to 8; prsd ldr to 12; 6l 3rd when blun & ur 15*
[290^P]	P	**Smooth Silk** (IRE) 25-1 D Page *Swerved bad rt & reluct to rce at start; jnd field by 3; sn lost tch agn; pu 9*
	P	**Toni's Tiger** 25-1 M Gorman *Sn wl bhnd; t.o 6 til pu 12*

OFFICIAL DISTANCE: Finished alone **TIME:** 6min 21.0s **TOTE:** £3.90; place £4.00 **DF:** £1.40 (1+any)

578 Open Maiden 8yo&up, 12st
11 ran

[322^P]	1	**BACHELOR-CARRASCO** (IRE) 4-1 S R Andrews *Midfield; 5th & pushed along 11; some hdwy 15 to 10l 3rd aft 4 out; stayed on wl app nxt to ld 2 out; qckly drew clr*
	2	13	**Ell Gee** (5a) 8-1 P Townsley *A.p in 3rd/4th; lost tch aft 4 out; kpt on one pce frm nxt; fin 3rd; subsq promoted*
	3	1	**Environmental Law** 8-1 P Cowley *Prom to 6; 6th & lsng plce 11; 25l 7th aft 4 out; gd hdwy frm nxt; fin wl for 4th; subsq promoted*
[290^F]	5	1	**Mister Chips** 6-4F P Bull *Ld to 3; prsd ldr til ld agn 4 out; hdd aft nxt; wknd qckly app last*
[304^P]	2d	**Dreamin George** (IRE) 33-1 C Sherry *Midfield; hdwy to 3rd 11; ld 13-17; prsd ldr til ld agn aft 3 out; sn hdd; wknd app last; fin 12l 2nd; subsq disq - rdr nt qualified*
[309^P]	P	**Anns Request** (5a) (bl) 20-1 P Hickman *A rr; lost tch 9; t.o & pu 13*
[300^P]	r	**Leggies Legacy** 8-1 P Hall *Rr when jmpd v slow 2; ref 3*
	P	**One More Bill** (vis) 20-1 M Gorman *In tch towards rr; 7th 11; rdn 16; bhnd when pu 3 out*
[309^R]	P	**Percy Arms** 14-1 P York *Jmpd sticky; sn rr; t.o 11; pu 13*
[291⁴]	P	**Uk Eurolad** 5-1 T Hills *Ld 4-12; 4th & wkng 15; rr when pu 2 out*
[416^P]	P	**Warner For Sport** 33-1 A Harvey *A towards rr; 8th & rdn along 11; wl bhnd when pu 4 out*

OFFICIAL DISTANCES: Originally 10l, ½l **TIME:** 6min 16.0s **TOTE:** £6.20; places £1.60,£4.70,£3.60 **DF:** £3.30 (1or2+any)

The rider of Dreamin George could not produce his Medical Record Book and was fined £50, he was subsequently found not to hold a Riders Qualification Certificate and was fined £125 by the Jockey Club Disciplinary Committee; the horse was disqualified

Plumpton (LH 6F,18J)
Mon, 13 Mar (GOOD, GOOD to FIRM in places)

579 Clapper HC
5 ran

[303⁴]	1	**STRUGGLES GLORY** (IRE) 11-13 (6) 1-6F D Robinson *Spurs; nt fluent & jmpd rt; disp ld til ld 11; went 4l clr app 14; stayed on str frm 2 out*
[414²]	2	13	**Newtown Rosie** (IRE) 11-02 14-1 A Hickman *Hld up; jmpd rt 9; went 2nd 14; outpcd & jmpd rt nxt; rdn 2 out; no ch w wnr*
	3	dist	**Pinoccio** 11-09 14-1 B Hitchcott *Mist 3; last pr; lost tch 9; poor 3rd frm 14*
[383^U]	4	30	**Kentucky Gold** (IRE) 11-07 20-1 D Sherlock *W wnr to 4; last & pushed along when blun bad 7; sn wl bhnd & nt keen; t.o 10*
[327⁶]	5	¾	**Panda Shandy** 11-02 16-1 H Froud *W ldr 4 til mist & hdd 11; drvn along aft; 3rd & wkng when blun 14; eased to loose rem 4th*

TIME: 6min 48.2s **TOTE:** £1.20; places £1.10,£1.70 **Ex:** £3.50 **CSF:** £3.41

The rdr of Panda Shandy was suspended for two days for failing to ride the horse out for fourth place

Stratford (LH 8F,16J)
Mon, 13 Mar (GOOD)

580 Racing Channel Flat 50 To Follow Nov HC   15 ran

[300¹]	1		**FINNOW THYNE (IRE)** 11-13 7-2 **D Dunsdon** *Lw; pckd 1; nt fluent 8; prom til went 2nd 3 out; chall & ev ch when lft clr last; idled & rdn out*
[430ᵁ]	2	1½	**Freedom Fighter** 11-13 33-1 **A Martin** *Cl up til drpd back 7th & rdn 10; 12l 6th 2 out; rallied & lft 3rd at last; str chall flat; nt quite rch wnr*
[297²]	3	5	**Hatterill Ridge** 12-03 20-1 **Julian Pritchard** *Midfield; 5th & prog 10; 3rd when mist 3 out; 2l 3rd when hit nxt; lft 2nd at last; veered lft & wknd flat*
[294ᴾ]	4	7	**I Haven't A Buck (IRE)** 11-13 (1) 40-1 **D Barlow** *Ld til app 11; rdn & outpcd 13; rallied to 8l 5th 3 out; one pce aft*
[172¹]	5	11	**Ardeal** 11-05 9-2 **F Windsor Clive** *Lw; pckd 1; cl 2nd mostly to 13; drvn nxt; 5l 4th & wkng 2 out*
	6	7	**Beyond The Stars** 12-03 20-1 **M Rimell** *Lw; hdwy to chse ldrs 8; 6th & rdn 10; sn wknd; no ch 3 out*
[344²]	7	15	**Sister Lark** 11-09 66-1 **D Jones** *Prom brief; drpd back 9th & hmpd 11; rem aft*
	U		**Bugsy Moran (IRE)** 12-03 33-1 **A Sansome** *Stumbled 1; rr when blun bad & ur 2*
[432²]	P		**Chalcuchima** 12-00 66-1 **L Lay** *Bhnd when hit 6; 9th when blun bad 7; t.o & hmpd 11; blun 12; pu 13*
[325¹]	U		**Chatergold (IRE)** 11-12 (bl) 10-1 **R Lawther** *Lw; 2nd/3rd til ld app 11; ll ahd when blun 2 out; ½l up & hrd prsd when blun & ur last*
[303ᴾ]	U		**Lakeside Lad** 11-12 20-1 **R Cooper** *Ur 2*
[175¹]	F		**Lochnomore** 11-10 3-1F **A Dalton** *Lw; fell 1*
[18²]	U		**Mr Grimsdale (IRE)** 12-00 9-1 **T Scudamore** *Ur 1*
[261ᴾ]	U		**Shobrooke Mill** 12-00 33-1 **A Charles-Jones** *(xnb) Bhnd; 8th 10; prog to 10l 5th but no imp when bad mist & ur 3 out*
[384³]	F		**Six Clerks (IRE)** 12-00 9-2 **A Wintle** *Fell 1*

TIME: 6min 14.1s **TOTE:** £4.20; places £2.30,£10.00,£4.30 **Ex:** £119.20 **CSF:** £111.28 **Tri:** £390.80
2 fences omitted

Taunton (RH 8F,17J)
Mon, 13 Mar (GOOD, GOOD to SOFT in places)

581 Somerset HC   9 ran

[325²]	1		**CAHORS (IRE)** 11-07 (bl) 9-2 **N Mitchell** *Bhnd; hdwy to 2nd aft 10; ld app 3 out; clr but u.p when veered bad lft to padd gate on run-in; kpt on*
[382⁴]	2	6	**Against The Agent** 12-00 10-1 **T Dennis** *Ld; dived wildly at 1 (shades of Ludlow!); sn clr; 10l ahd 12; mist 13; hdd app 3 out; outpcd nxt; hung bad lft flat*
[303ᴾ]	3	7	**Bas De Laine (FR)** 11-07 11-2 **M Gorman** *In tch; hit 8; drpd to rr u.p 9; 20l 3rd agn aft 14; stayed on agn flat*
[383²]	4	1½	**Kilmington (IRE)** 12-00 5-2F **J Barnes** *2nd when jmpd slow 4 & 5; 3rd when hit 11; 15l 3rd 13; stayed on one pce frm 3 out*
[354⁵]	5	2½	**The Bold Abbot** 11-07 20-1 **Miss S West** *Chsd ldrs; hit 10; lost plce nxt; poor 5th aft 14; stayed on agn frm 2 out*
[383ᴾ]	P		**Abit More Business (IRE)** 12-00 (bl) 12-1 **A Honeyball** *Midfield; jmpd slow 4; pckd bad 10; hit 11; 6th & no ch when blun 14 & landed v awkward; t.o & pu nxt*
	P		**Buzz O'The Crowd** 12-00 4-1 **R Woollacott** *Chsd ldrs; hit 10; rdn nxt; blun 12 & sn strugg; t.o when pu & dism aft 14*
	P		**Full Alirt** 11-02 10-1 **Miss S Young** *Sn t.o; rdr lost iron brief 8; pu last*
[382²]	P		**Late Encounter** 12-00 14-1 **A St George** *Chsd ldr to 4; drpd to rr aft 10; t.o & pu 12*

TIME: 6min 13.2s **TOTE:** £5.70; places £1.70,£1.90,£1.90 **Ex:** £32.50 **CSF:** £44.62 **Tri:** £133.30

Sedgefield (LH 8F,18J)
Tue, 14 Mar (GOOD to FIRM)

582 Mitsubishi Diamond Vision HC   6 ran

[422⁵]	1		**OVERFLOWING RIVER (IRE)** 12-03 (tt) 3-1 **T Glass** *Jmpd bold; made all; rdn & r.o str frm 2 out; drew clr flat*
[172³]	2	4	**Hiltonstown Lass (IRE)** 12-00 11-10F **C Mulhall** *Hld up & handy; 5l last 9; went 2nd 11; gng wl 3 out; w wnr when hit nxt shkn up & no ex appt last*
[362ᵁ]	3	5	**Minella Gold (IRE)** 11-09 9-2 **W Renwick** *Settled handy; 6th 10; disp 2nd & ev ch when mist 14; nt qckn app 2 out*

[362²]	4	4	**Rainbow Times (IRE)** 11-09 5-1 **C Storey** *Prsd ldrs to 15; rdn & outpcd when hit 3 out; no imp aft*
[360²]	5	19	**Border Glory** 11-07 50-1 **Miss M Bremner** *Prsd ldrs til pushed along & outpcd 14; hit nxt*
[359⁴]	6	2	**Stormy Session** 12-00 (bl) 16-1 **J Alexander** *Prsd wnr to 10; sn last; outpcd 13*

TIME: 6min 54.7s **TOTE:** £5.50; places £2.20,£1.10 **Ex:** £12.80 **CSF:** £6.72
Fence at top of hill omitted

Newton Abbot (LH 7F,16J)
Wed, 15 Mar (GOOD, GOOD to SOFT in places)

583 Totnes And Bridgetown Nov HC   13 ran

[382¹]	1		**FLYING MARIA** 11-13 4-5F **L Jefford** *Trckd ldrs; 5l 5th 13; rmdr & impd qckly; ld 3 out; 10l clr nxt; rdn bef last; kpt on wl*
[310²]	2	3½	**Track O' profit (IRE)** 11-10 25-1 **Miss S Young** *Prom; 2nd 8-10; 4th 13; 8l 4th nxt; stayed on agn flat; snatched 2nd*
[325³]	3	hd	**Badger Beer** 11-10 12-1 **J Snowden** *Prom; 2nd 10-13; outpcd & mist nxt (water); rallied & kpt on agn aft 2 out; 2nd at last til nr fin*
[316²]	4	6	**Baldhu Chance** 11-10 20-1 **A Ede** *Hld up; hdwy & hit 9; 10l 6th 13; stayed on app 2 out; 4th & btn when hit last*
[154⁶]	5	3½	**Hall's Mill (IRE)** 12-00 13-2 **A Charles-Jones** *Ld to 6; ld agn nxt; hit 9; rdn & hdd 12; fdd aft 3 out; blun last*
	6	8	**Minella Derby (IRE)** 12-00 (bl) 7-1 **T Gibney** *Blun 3; mist 5; hit 8; settled midfield; 5th 13; rdn & qcknd to ld 12; 3l clr nxt; hdd 3 out; sn btn; 5th when mist last*
[568ᴿ]	7	28	**King Paddy (IRE)** 12-00 25-1 **R Bevan** *Prom early; sn midfield; nt fluent 7 (water) & rdn; 7th 9; btn nxt*
[457²]	8	14	**Prah Sands** 11-10 16-1 **J Young** *Mist 3; a wl bhnd; t.o 10*
[331ᶠ]	P		**Crocked Again (IRE)** 11-12 16-1 **V Keane** *A wl bhnd; t.o & pu 10*
	P		**For Christie (IRE)** 11-10 25-1 **Miss A Goschen** *Hld up & bhnd; lost tch 10; t.o & pu 2 out*
[311ᴾ]	P		**Gibraltar Lady** 11-05 66-1 **S Craddock** *Pulled v hrd & rcd v wide; rushed up out of control to 2nd 3; ld 6-7; wkng rap when hit 9; t.o & pu 10*
[315³]	P		**Jabiru (IRE)** 12-00 12-1 **D Alers-Hankey** *Mid-div; hit 6; pckd 10; sn strugg; mist 11; t.o & pu 3 out*
	P		**Venn Ottery** 11-04 12-1 **F Windsor Clive** *A wl bhnd; t.o & pu 10*

TIME: 5min 43.8s **TOTE:** £1.60; places £1.70,£6.90,£3.50 **Ex:** £62.60 **CSF:** £32.83 **Tri:** £176.00

Cheltenham (LH 10F,22J)
Thu, 16 Mar (GOOD to FIRM, GOOD in places)

584 Christie's Foxhunter HC   24 ran

[386¹]	1		**CAVALERO** 12-00 16-1 **A Charles-Jones** *Settled rr; 15th & rdn 12; wl adrift frm 13 til stdy prog 19; still mod 7th aft 2 out; rap prog aft last to storm past 6 rivals & ld final 100yds*
[385¹]	2	¾	**Real Value (IRE)** 12-00 8-1 **B Hitchcott** *Cl up; 3rd 12; trckd ldr 17; ld 19; hrd prsd frm 2 out; nt fluent last; hdd final 100yds; r.o game*
[155¹]	3	1¼	**Trade Dispute (IRE)** 12-00 9-1 **G Tuer** *Settled rr; mist 4; last 6; 17th 12; prog 19; clsd on ldrs gng wl 2 out; 4th last; chall flat; nt qckn final 100yds*
[314¹]	4	2½	**Lakefield Rambler (IRE)** 12-00 33-1 **Miss P Gundry** *Made most til pckd & hdd 19; prom til 3rd & ev ch last; nt qckn*
[302¹]	5	1½	**Mighty Moss (IRE)** 12-00 3-1F **F Hutsby** *Settled rr; 12th 12; pushed along & r.o frm 17; eff 2 out; disp 4th when mist last; nt qckn*
[308¹]	6	¾	**Gillan Cove** 12-00 14-1 **R Young** *Settled rr; 16th 12; t.o 19; fin fast*
[156¹]	7	¾	**It's Himself** 12-00 8-1 **A J Martin** *Many mists; hld up wl bhnd; 13th 7; stdy prog frm 14; jnd ldrs 3 out; chall nxt; disp ld last; wknd flat*
[299²]	8	8	**Knight Of Passion** 12-00 33-1 **Miss P Jones** *In tch; mist 7; jnd ldrs 10; went 2nd 12 til blun 17; cl up til 6th & blun last; wknd; dism*
[294¹]	9	13	**Whatafellow (IRE)** 12-00 (bl) 66-1 **A Crow** *Settled midfield; mist 3; 10th 7; lost tch w ldrs 13; no prog 18*
[303¹]	10	23	**Little Buck (IRE)** 12-00 14-1 **K Culligan** *Mid-div; prog to 6th 12; drvn 14; wknd aft 18; t.o*
[154²]	11	1	**Skip'n'time** 12-00 20-1 **M Miller** *Missed break; a wl bhnd; last 12; t.o aft*
[383³]	12	3½	**Mr Dow Jones (IRE)** 12-00 100-1 **D O'Meara** *Mid-div when blun 6; rr aft; 18th 12; t.o*
	13	nk	**Dan's Your Man (IRE)** 12-00 10-1 **P Cashman** *Jb; chsd ldrs til 7th 12; blun 18 & wknd; t.o*

[225²]	14	8	**Manhattan Rainbow (IRE)** 12-00 100-1 **M Bradburne** *Mid-div; 11th 12; rdn & strugg aft; t.o; dism*
[346¹]	15	30	**Coolvawn Lady (IRE)** 11-09 100-1 **J Jukes** *Chsd ldrs; 5th 12; lft 4th 16; wknd 18; t.o & virt pu flat*
[303²]	F		**Brambledown (IRE)** 11-09 25-1 **Mrs B Sillars** *Sn wl bhnd; 19th 12; wl to when fell 18*
[210⁵]	P		**Charden** 12-00 (vis) 100-1 **R Webb-Bowen** *Prom; 6th 9; 14th & wkng rap 12; t.o & pu 14*
[334²]	B		**Forest Fountain (IRE)** 12-00 100-1 **Julian Pritchard** *Jmpd sketchy in rr til bd 5*
	U		**Grimley Gale (IRE)** 11-09 12-1 **Miss S Vickery** *Cl up; 4th 12; mist 13; disp 4th when blun & ur 16*
[303²]	P		**Makin' Doo (IRE)** 12-00 100-1 **C Mulhall** *Prom brief; 10th 9; 20th 12; t.o & pu 3 out*
[402¹]	U		**Miss O'Grady (IRE)** 11-09 33-1 **R Walford** *Midfield & in tch blun & ur 8*
[386²]	P		**Opera Fan (IRE)** 12-00 50-1 **C Williams** *2nd/3rd to 11; 8th & wkng nxt; mist 15; t.o & pu last; dism*
	F		**Sheltering (IRE)** 12-00 11-2 **P Fenton** *Missed break; nt jw in rr til fell 5*
[231¹]	P		**Solba (USA)** 12-00 66-1 **R Burton** *Trckd ldng group; 9th 12; wknd 18; t.o & pu last*

TIME: 6min 36.6s **TOTE:** £43.80; places £8.00,£2.70,£2.70 **Ex:** £267.20 **CSF:** £129.04 **Tri:** £1151.26

Fakenham (LH 6F,16J)
Fri, 17 Mar (GOOD, GOOD to FIRM in places)

585 William Bulwer-Long Mem Nov HC   **8 ran**

[375ᴾ]	1		**ON THE FLY** 11-02 12-1 **G Markham** *Chsd ldrs; prsd wnr frm 10; rdn & one pce frm 2 out; fin 15l 2nd; subsq promoted*
	2	3½	**Chester Ben** 11-02 (vis) 11-2 **T Lane** *Rr div; rdn 5 & agn when 7th 11; went 7l 4th nxt; 4th & outpcd when mist 2 out; carried hd high aft; fin 3rd; promoted*
[232¹]	3	10	**Starlight Fool** 11-02 9-2 **R Barrett** *Lw; chsd ldrs til 6l 3rd & rdn 2; 4th & wkng when bad mist 2 out; fin 4th; subsq promoted*
[243⁵]	4	2½	**Castle Arrow (IRE)** 11-04 (bl) 3-1 **R Lawther** *Lw; 2nd 5; drpd back 6th 10 & 10l 5th & btn 12 (rn v flat); subsq promoted to 4th*
[459⁵]	6	23	**Blue Marlin** 10-13 16-1 **J Owen** *(xnb) Pulled hrd; chsd ldr to 5; mist nxt (water); mist 9; drvn app 12; sn wknd; mist 2 out*
[318⁴]	1d		**Commuter Country** 11-02 7-4F **N King** *(xnb) Jw; hld up til hdwy 8; ld 10; 3l clr 12; r.o str; unchall; won by 15l; subsq disq*
	P		**Mustang Molly** 10-11 33-1 **A Martin** *Pulled hrd; hit 7; ld til app 10; wknd nxt; t.o & pu last*
	P		**Worthy Memories** 10-11 66-1 **D Cook** *Mist 2; prom brief; last & drvn 5; mist 7; lost tch nxt; t.o 10; pu 12*

TIME: 5min 35.1s **TOTE:** £3.10; places £1.20,£3.00,£1.70 **Ex:** £18.70 **CSF:** £20.56 **Tri:** £153.60

Market Rasen (RH 8F,17J)
Sat, 18 Mar (GOOD to FIRM, GOOD in home straight)

586 Beaumontcote HC   **6 ran**

[225¹]	1		**COOLE ABBEY (IRE)** 12-09 evensF **T Doyle** *Ld to 2; prsd ldr til ld aft 10; rdn 5l clr when mist 3 out; stayed on game flat*
[155²]	2	1¼	**Gymcrak Tiger (IRE)** 11-12 6-1 **R Clark** *Settled gng wl; hit 6; eff to chse wnr 14; pckd last; kpt on but a hld*
	3	22	**Howayman** 12-05 (bl) 7-2 **T Oates** *Settled 3rd; nt a fluent final circ; rdn aft 14; btn bef nxt*
[302ᴾ]	F		**Dry Hill Lad** 12-05 16-1 **M Mackley** *Ld to 2; dived at 8; jmpd rt 10; sn hdd; cl 4th but lkd wkng when turned somersault 14*
	P		**Moobakkr (USA)** 11-12 20-1 **T Lane** *Prom; 3rd 9; hit 10; drvn & strugg nxt; t.o & pu run-in; dism*
[443¹]	P		**Pennywise** 11-07 8-1 **S Charlton** *Numerous mists in last; lost tch aft 10; t.o & pu 14*

TIME: 6min 18.6s **TOTE:** £1.80; places £1.10,£2.90 **Ex:** £6.50 **CSF:** £6.38
     Water jump omitted

Cheshire
Alpraham (RH 8F,18J) Sat, 18 Mar (GOOD, sticky patches)

587 Hunt   **5 ran**

[529⁵]	1		**GRUNGE (IRE)** 4-5F **C Barlow** *Jmpd sticky early; chsd clr ldng pr til clsd to 2nd 11; ld app 12; stayed on one pce frm 3 out*

[579⁹]	2	12	**Kentucky Gold (IRE)** 6-4 D Sherlock *2nd til ld 10; hdd app 12; hit nxt; chsd wnr vain & unenthusiastic aft*
	3	75	**Foxy Blue** 25-1 Mrs K Diggle *Bit bckwd; ld to 10; lft last 12; 30l bhnd 14; t.o & crawled frm nxt; btn 38secs*
[336⁹]	P		**Gold Talisman** (5a) 7-1 D Barlow *Bckwd; a labouring in 4th; 25l adrift when jmpd slow 7; t.o & pu 12*
	P		**Native Rain (IRE)** (7a) 25-1 Miss E Lea *1st ride; lw; a last & nt jw; sn lost tch; t.o when mist 8 & pu*

OFFICIAL DISTANCES: 10l, dist TIME: 7min 35.0s

588 Open Maiden, 12st
15 ran

[568ᵁ]	1		**TEAL BAY** (5a,1ow) 4-1 D Barlow *3rd/5th bhnd clr ldng pr; 40l 5th 10; lft 15l 3rd 15; sn 2nd; ld aft 2 out & rdn clr (gd ride)*
	2	10	**Quixotry** 5-1 L Hicks *(xnb) Midfield & wl off pce; 45l 7th 10; went 3rd 13; clsd nxt & lft 2nd 15; sn ld & 8l clr; hdd & no ex aft 2 out; fin tired*
[449⁹]	3	15	**Outrageous Affair** (5a) 20-1 Miss R Reynolds *Rem in last; dist 10th 10; mist 12; lft 55l 7th 15; fin best but impossible task*
[528⁹]	4	30	**French Melody (IRE)** 12-1 J Burley *Poor 5th 3; stdly lost plce & 48l 8th 10; lft 46l 6th 15; cont t.o*
	U		**Banner Year (IRE)** (2ow) 33-1 P Stanway *1st ride; nrly ur 2; rdr drpd reins & nrly f.o 3; 5th when succeeded 4*
	P		**Berties Landing** (2ow) 16-1 M Plant *Nvr nr ldrs; 50l 9th 10; mist 11; cont t.o; pu 3 out*
[528²]	C		**Caherlow (IRE)** 14-1 B Foster *Jmpd sticky in 4/5th til carried out by loose horse 9*
[526²]	P		**Charlie Keay (IRE)** (1ow) 6-4F C Stockton *Nd in chsng group; 38l 4th 15; lft 58l 4th 15; no ex; pu 2 out*
[564⁹]	F		**Glamdring** (5a,1ow) 33-1 I Clyde *Lkd awful; set lunatic pce & jmpd sketchy; 5l ahd 10 w rest spreadeagled; still ahd but tiring when crashing fall 15*
[528ʳ]	P		**Knocknashane (IRE)** 14-1 J Merry *Midfield & nd; 44l 6th 10; lft 45l 5th 15; pu 3 out*
	P		**Otter River** 14-1 P Morris *Bckwd; jmpd poor & sn rem; rdr kpt waving; pu 10*
[526²]	F		**Pendil's Dream** (5a) 20-1 D Sherlock *Impd to chse clr ldng pr 8; 35l 3rd 10-13; 5th & wkng when fell nxt*
	P		**Royal Fling** (5a) 9-1 C Barlow *School & a rem; 11th 10; pu 11*
[514⁹]	P		**The Last Shout (IRE)** (bl) 33-1 P Millington *Nt jw but clr w another lunatic tearaway; lft in ld brief 15 but sn hdd & wknd rap; pu last*
	P		**Tosawi's Girl** (5a) 33-1 Miss T Clark *Oht; sn rem; wl t.o last 10; pu 13*

OFFICIAL DISTANCES: 7l, 25l TIME: 7min 33.0s

589 Restricted, 12st
10 ran

[532²]	1		**HATTON FARM BABE** (5a) 5-1 Miss S Sharratt *Bit bckwd; hld up trckng ldrs; went 3rd & mist 10; ld 11-12 & 13-15; ld agn 2 out; sn drvn clr*
[532⁹]	2	12	**Analystic (IRE)** (2ow) 14-1 C Stockton *Handy; went 3rd 7; ld 10-11 & 13-15; ld agn 3 out; hdd nxt; nt qckn*
[567¹⁰]	3	3	**Tiger Paws (IRE)** (5a) 33-1 A Gribbin *Prsd ldrs; 5th 10; same & ch 15; sn strugg; plodded on agn 2 out*
[336⁹]	4	3	**Brown Esquire** 2-1F D Barlow *2nd til ld 6-10; 3rd 12; one pce aft; 10l 4th 3 out*
[567⁷]	5	½	**Cookie Boy** 12-1 S Prior *Lw; handy; 6th 10; went 3rd 15; 8l frm ldng pr nxt; no ex*
[371¹⁹]	6	6	**Secret Alliance** 4-1 A Crow *Jmpd sticky in 25l last; nvr nr ldrs; mod 8th 15*
[555³ᵈ]	7	15	**Black Book** (5a) 25-1 P Millington *Unimpressive padd; detach in last trio; 15l 6th & no ch 15*
	8	25	**Scally Hill** (5a) 6-1 L Stephens *Ld to 6; 4th 10; wkng when pckd 12; impeded 14; plodded on; t.o*
[371³]	P		**Fair Farm Boy** 20-1 B Foster *Detach in last pr; 9th when hit 10; t.o 15; pu last*
[338⁴]	F		**Sugi** 7-1 I Wynne *Chsd ldrs; 7th 10; still just in tch when fell 13*

OFFICIAL DISTANCES: 12l, 3l TIME: 7min 23.0s

The stewards enquired into the running and riding of Secret Alliance which never showed in the race; the rider's explanation that the horse had jumped the fifth fence badly, found nothing when asked and was being tried in a new bit was recorded

590 Ladies Open
9 ran

| | 1 | | **THREE POTATO FOUR** 4-1 Mrs M Barlow *Chsd ldrs; 12l 4th 10; lft 3rd 12; 14l down 15; stayed on wl 2 out to ld last; rdn out* |
| [566⁹] | 2 | 3 | **Tudor Lodge (IRE)** (5a) 16-1 Miss S Swindells *Cl up; mist 9; 9l 3rd 10; lft 2nd 12; ld 3 out; sn drvn along; r.o v game til hdd last; nt qckn* |

	3	10	**The Parish Pump (IRE)** 1-3F Mrs C Ford *Lw; cl up til ld 6; 5l ahd 10; hdd 3 out; btn aft nxt; eased flat*
[531²]	4	runin	**Coolflugh Hero (IRE)** 9-1 Miss S Hopkins *Ld to 2; lft in ld 4 til hdd & hit 6; 2nd & rdn 10; nrly ur 12 & lost 2 plces; wknd to 35l 4th 15*
[449³]	5	5	**Foodbroker Star (IRE)** 12-1 Miss C Spearing *Midfield & nd; jmpd slow 7; 15l 5th 10; strugg 12; 45l 5th 15*
[368ᵁ]	6	25	**Sir George Chuffy (IRE)** 25-1 Miss M Mullineaux *A rem; 45l 7th 10; cont to*
[280ᶠ]	7	3	**Sharp Embrace** 33-1 Miss S Rodman *Wl bhnd; rdr nrly f.o 5; 30l 6th 10; t.o 12*
	8	2	**Merlyns Choice** 20-1 Miss J Richardson *A t.o*
	R		**Hello Me Man (IRE)** 20-1 Miss K Crank *Bckwd; reared & ur padd; tk str hld & out of control; ld 2 til rn out 4*

OFFICIAL DISTANCES: 2½l, 8l   TIME: 7min 16.0s

591 Mens Open, 12st   2 ran

| [530¹] | 1 | | **WEAK MOMENT (IRE)** 1-4F A Crow *Ld to 2 & frm 6; drew clr 13; 25l ahd 3 out* |
| [533³] | 2 | 30 | **Bubble N Squeek** 5-2 C Barlow *Ld 2-6; mist 10 & rdn; jmpd slow 13 & drpd 6l bhnd; drvn & nt keen aft* |

OFFICIAL DISTANCE: dist   TIME: 7min 35.0s

592 Confined, 12st   6 ran

[529ᵁ]	1		**ITA'S FELLOW (IRE)** 25-1 Miss S Sharratt *3rd til 2nd 7; ld aft 14; 10l clr 3 out; drvn along & stayed on wl*
[464³]	2	20	**Commercial Artist (7x)** 7-1 Mrs C Ford *Tubed; ld; mist 10; hdd 12; releg 3rd aft 13 & 5l down 15; rallied to chse wnr vain frm app 2 out*
	3	8	**Whistling Jake (IRE)** 2-1 A Crow (xnb) *Lw; tk keen hld but drpd out 20l last; went 4th 10 but still 15l bhnd 12; tk 3rd app 2 out but nvr able to cl*
[529³]	4	25	**Mytton's Choice (IRE)** 4-1 C Barlow *2 handlers; unruly & difficult to mount; jmpd slow 2; hld up & handy; 3l 3rd 10; rmdr aft nxt; ld 12 til aft 14; releg 3rd aft mist 3 out; sn btn & eased*
[482¹]	F		**Roll With It (IRE)** 5-4F D Barlow *5th when fell 4 (got on to road when loose)*
	P		**Royal Segos** 33-1 S Shaw *1st ride; chsd ldr to 7; wknd qckly 9; t.o & tired when pu 13*

OFFICIAL DISTANCES: 15l, 2l   TIME: 7min 22.0s

593 Open Maiden 56&7yo, 2m4f - 14J   10 ran

[372ᶠ]	1		**CAROMISU (tt)** 14-1 B Foster *Lft in ld 2; mist 5; jmpd lft 7; 12l clr 10; hrd prsd aft 2 out; drvn & hit last; kpt on; all out*
	2	3	**Grey Mystery (5a)** 4-1 C Barlow *Bckwd; chsd ldrs; went 2nd 8; drvn to cl app & jmpd lft 2 out; chall & ev ch app last; nt qckn*
[515³]	3	6	**Fortune Hunter (IRE)** 5-1 P Millington *Midfield; 6th 6; eff in 15l 3rd 10; 12l down 3 out; tried to chall aft nxt; no imp und unorthodox press*
[400ᶠ]	4	12	**The Big Lad (IRE)** 10-1 G Smith *Tk keen hld; settled 3rd/4th; outpcd in 27l 4th 10; plodded on*
	F		**Cracksman** 14-1 S Prior *Mid-div; 5th when bad mist 6; chsng ldrs when fell 8*
[181³]	F		**Fruit Crop (5a)** 7-4F A Crow *Lw; ld til fell 2*
[292ᶠ]	F		**Marwoods Mandate (IRE)** 5-2 C Stockton *Lw; lft 2nd 2-8; 3rd when fell 9*
	P		**Mister Pimpernel (IRE)** 12-1 L Stephens *Mist 1; nt jw in rr; 8th 6; 35l 5th 10; t.o & pu 3 out*
	U		**Peover Eye (7a)** 10-1 A Gribbin *Towards rr; 7th 6; lsng tch when ur 8*
	r		**Wily Miss (5a)** 33-1 K Burke *A detach last & novicey; t.o 9; ref 2 out*

OFFICIAL DISTANCES: 2½l, 6l   TIME: 5min 34.0s

Curre

Howick (LH 9F, 18J)   Sat, 18 Mar (GOOD to FIRM)

594 Hunt   4 ran

[480ᶠ]	1		**MAGS SUPER TOI (IRE)** 1-2F A Price *Pulling; trckd ldr til ld 5; 8l clr ½way; 2l ld when blun 3 out; rdn app last; stayed on*
[450ᵁ]	2	1½	**Muckle Jack** 5-2 S Blackwell *Opened 7/2; hld up in tch; chsd wnr frm 10; eff u.p & 2l down 3 out; one pce*
[481ᶠ]	3	runin	**Herbert Lodge (IRE)** 8-1 Miss M Bartlett *Ld to 5; chsd wnr to 10; 7l 3rd & wkng nxt; t.o*
[485ᶠ]	P		**Le Vienna (IRE)** (bl) 16-1 S Currey *Last frm 2; detach frm 6; mist 9; t.o 12; jmpd v slow 3 out; pu nxt*

OFFICIAL DISTANCES: 1l, dist   TIME: 6min 32.0s

595 Restricted (Div 1), 12st   11 ran

[485⁶]	1		**CHANTINGO LAD** (tt) 20-1 **A Price** *Ld to 5; chsd wnr to 9 & agn 3 out; 12l down & wl hld when lft clr 2 out*
[483ᶠ]	2	25	**Sea Search** 20-1 **J Keen** *A bhnd; last 12; some prog to 30l 6th 15; lft 3rd 2 out; went 2nd nr fin; nvr nr ldrs*
[340ᶠ]	3	½	**Star Chaser** 4-1 **D Stephens** (Wales) *In tch; chsd ldr 6; 10l 4th 13; sn outpcd; lft 20l 2nd 2 out; dem nr fin*
[338ᴾ]	4	10	**J'accuse (IRE)** 5-1 **Miss F Wilson** *A bhnd; lost tch 9; last frm 14; lft poor 4th 2 out; nd*
[485ᴾ]	P		**Andsome Andy (IRE)** 12-1 **T Vaughan** *Chsd ldrs; 12l 4th 6; lsng plce & blun 9; jmpd slow & rmdrs nxt; wl bhnd when pu 12*
[486²]	F		**Bel Lane** (5a) (vis) 2-1F **D Jones** *Chsd ldr til ld 5; clr frm ½way; drew rt away app 15; 12l up when fell 2 out; unlucky*
	P		**Cosy Ride (IRE)** 10-1 **J Phillips** *Mist 1; mid-div; pckd 7; 15l 5th when blun 15; no prog aft; pu 2 out*
[347ᴾ]	B		**Itspantotime** (5a) 8-1 **J Jukes** *Chsd ldng pr til went 2nd 9-3 out; lft 6l 2nd & btn when bd 2 out*
	R		**Ivors Boy** 10-1 **N Tucker** *Jmpd novicey; sn detach; rn out & ur 7*
[485ᴾ]	P		**Tarian (USA)** (bl) 25-1 **C Williams** *In tch til drpd to rr & rdn 10; no resp; t.o & pu 12*
[346ᴾ]	U		**Tiger Bell** 25-1 **A St George** *Blun & ur 3*

OFFICIAL DISTANCES: 25l, ½l **TIME:** 6min 34.0s

596 Restricted (Div 2), 12st   10 ran

[485²]	1		**TIGER LORD** 4-1 **S Blackwell** *Ld; clr 4; hdd 8; ld agn 11-14; 3rd & wl hld when lft 20l clr & hmpd bad 2 out; lucky*
[476⁶]	2	20	**Adventurus** 8-1 **J Liley** *Mid-div; outpcd 13; 15l 4th app 15; lft 2nd 2 out*
[485ᶠ]	3	8	**Gaelic Royale (IRE)** (5a) 16-1 **H Evans** *Pulling; chsd ldrs 4; ld 8-11; wknd 13; sn no ch; lft poor 3rd 2 out*
[483²]	F		**Absent Citizen (IRE)** (5a) 5-4F **E Williams** *Patient rdn; mist 7; 14l 7th 11; prog to 3rd 13; ld & lkd wnr when fell 2 out*
[483³]	F		**Dinedor Charlie** (bl) 5-1 **D Jones** *Chsd ldrs; ld 14; rdn 3 out; just hdd when fell 2 out*
	P		**Don't Forget (IRE)** (5a) 12-1 **T Vaughan** *A rr; mist 8; lost tch 9; pu nxt*
	P		**Final Option (IRE)** 10-1 **I Johnson** *A bhnd; last & detach 7; t.o 12 til pu last*
[559ᶠ]	P		**Poet's Song** 8-1 **C Williams** *Ww; mid-div; 10l 5th 9; disp 6l 3rd when blun bad 12; great rcvry; no ch aft; pu 3 out*
	P		**Seethrough** (5a) 12-1 **J Davies** *Bhnd frm 3; 5th & no ch when blun bad 13; pu aft*
[480ᴾ]	P		**Tigersun** 14-1 **D Hughes** *Chsd ldrs to 11; stdly wknd; 5th & no ch when pu 3 out*

OFFICIAL DISTANCES: 20l, 8l **TIME:** 6min 34.0s

597 Confined, 12st   13 ran

	1		**RAVE-ON-HADLEY (IRE)** (8x) 6-4F **E Williams** *Made all; rdn & r.o str app last; comf*
[343ᴾ]	2	3	**No Fiddling (IRE)** (7x) 12-1 **C Williams** *Chsd ldrs; 7l 4th & rdn along 12; went 2l 2nd 3 out; unable to qckn app last*
[479²]	3	5	**Sebastopol** 5-1 **G Lewis** *Prom; chsd wnr 6; disp ld brief 10; rdn app 15; 3rd & one pce frm nxt*
[383ᴾ]	4	½	**Bullens Bay (IRE)** 5-1 **Miss F Wilson** *Hld up in rr; prog to 12l 4th 12; 3rd & ev ch app 3 out; btn nxt*
[479ᴾ]	5	12	**The Last Mistress** (5a) 16-1 **J Price** *Tde; bhnd; prog to 10l 5th ½way; outpcd app 13; nd aft*
[387⁴]	6	½	**Capo Castanum** 10-1 **R Sturgis** *Tubed; a mid-div; 20l 6th 14; no prog*
[482ᴾ]	P		**Carraig-An-Oir (IRE)** 33-1 **R Hughes** *In tch to 7; bhnd & u.p 10; t.o & pu 3 out*
[479ᴾ]	P		**Comme Une Fleur (FR)** (5a) 33-1 **T Vaughan** *In tch to 7; sn bhnd; pu 11*
[334ʳ]	P		**Credon** 14-1 **D Jones** *Chsd ldr to 3; prom to 11; sn wknd; t.o & pu 3 out*
	P		**Don Du Cadran (FR)** 12-1 **C Gundry** *A wl bhnd; last & detach frm 4; wl t.o when pu 15*
	P		**Kilgobbin (IRE)** 6-1 **D Stephens** (Wales) *Mid-div to 7; bhnd frm ½way; pu 14*
[481⁷]	P		**Viardot (IRE)** (3x) 6-1 **S Blackwell** *Chsd wnr 3-6; prom to 12; sn outpcd; t.o & pu 3 out*
[333ᴾ]	P		**Vitaman (IRE)** 20-1 **A Price** *Chsd ldrs; 4l 3rd 9; wkng when blun 12; pu 13*

OFFICIAL DISTANCES: 3l, 4l **TIME:** 6min 22.0s

598 Land Rover Mens Open, 12st   8 ran

	1		**CREAM SUPREME (IRE)** (bl) evensF **E Williams** *Ww in tch; chsd ldr 13; mist 15; rdn to chall 3 out; outj nxt; sn ld; qcknd clr flat*
[272ᴾ]	2	5	**Ballymaloe Boy** (7x) 5-1 **J Jukes** *Chsd ldr; ld 8 til app 10; ld agn 11; hrd prsd 3 out; hdd app last; one pce*

[480ᴾ]	3	20	**Persian View (IRE)** (7x) 10-1 **T Vaughan** Wrs & reluct to rce; set off fnce bhnd; grad clsd; 25l 6th 8; 12l 4th & u.p app 15; no further prog
[480⁶]	4	2	**Harbour Island** (bl) 20-1 **P Sheldrake** Mist 2; chsd ldrs; 4l 3rd 11; mist 14; sn btn
[345ᴸ]	5	runin	**Saffron Moss** (7x) 6-1 **H Evans** Sn wl bhnd; last & t.o frm 7
[566ᴸ]	r		**Circus Colours** (7x) 6-1 **D Jones** Ref to rce; tk no part
[480ᴾ]	P		**Shehab (IRE)** (7x) 25-1 **M Parry** Pulling; chsd ldrs til ld 5-8; ld agn app 10-11; sn wknd; t.o when jmpd slow 3 out; pu nxt
[345⁴]	P		**Silverfort Lad (IRE)** (bl) 8-1 **C Williams** Opened 14s; ld to 5; rdn ½way; sn drpd out; last when pu 12

OFFICIAL DISTANCES: 5l, 25l   **TIME:** 6min 24.0s

599 Ladies Open

5 ran

[481⁵]	1		**KARABURAN** (5x) 7-4 **Miss F Wilson** Prsd ldr; disp ld brief 4; jmpd slow 7; 3l 2nd & mist 11; drvn up to jn ldr nxt; ld 14; clr 3 out; in comm when hit last; wl rdn
[382ᴾ]	2	6	**Warren Boy** (5x) 4-7F **Miss P Jones** Ld to 14; 2l 2nd app 15; rdn & btn app 2 out
[382ᴾ]	U		**Captain Khedive** 16-1 **Miss S Talbot** 3rd when blun & ur 3
	P		**Obelos (USA)** 20-1 **Miss A Meakins** Lft 10l 3rd 3; same plce til lost tch 12; t.o pu 15
	U		**Our Eddie** (tt) 14-1 **Miss H Bendall** 4th when blun & ur 3

OFFICIAL DISTANCE: 6l   **TIME:** 6min 23.0s

600 Intermediate, 12st

9 ran

[388ᴾ]	1		**BALLINA** 5-1 **J Jukes** Cl up; jnd ldr 4; ld 8; made rest; qcknd app 15; 3l clr 3 out; stayed on wl; wl rdn
[388⁵]	2	4	**Questionaire** (5a) 4-1 **D Stephens (Wales)** 2 handlers; cl up til 6l 4th & outpcd 14; stayed on agn frm 2 out; went 2nd flat; nt rch wnr
	3	1½	**Longstone Boy (IRE)** 6-1 **D Jones** Ww; 8l 7th ½way; prog to 3l 3rd app 13; u.p when blun 15; chsd wnr app last; no imp; dem flat
[2¹]	4	5	**Jo Jos Best Friend** (5a) 6-4F **T Vaughan** Trckd ldrs; went 2nd 11; 3l 2nd & rdn 3 out; wknd app last
[392¹]	5	5	**The Right Attitude (IRE)** 6-1 **J Cook** (xnb) Ww in rr; mist 8; prog to cl 3rd gng wl 11; outpcd 13; nd aft
[388ᴾ]	U		**Holloa Away (IRE)** 33-1 **R Millar** Tde; bhnd frm 3; 10l last ½way; sn lost tch; blun & ur 12
[344²]	P		**Kristal Haze** (5a) 4-1 **E Williams** Ld til aft 1; handy aft ld 10l 5th & outpcd 13; no ch aft; pu 2 out
	P		**Lawsons Lady** (5a) 33-1 **J Price** Tde; nt jw; detach last frm 4; jmpd v slow 7; pu 8
[344ᴾ]	P		**Storm Man (IRE)** 33-1 **H Evans** Rcd wide; ld aft 1; hdd 8; wknd 12; t.o & pu 15

OFFICIAL DISTANCES: 4l, 2l   **TIME:** 6min 23.0s

601 Confined Maiden (Div 1), 12st

12 ran

[478²]	1		**TWOTENSFORAFIVE** 4-5F **E Williams** Trckd ldrs; disp ld 11; ld 14; 3l clr & mist nxt; r.o wl; easy
[349³]	2	8	**Itswillie** 7-1 **J Jukes** Chsd ldrs; 4l 3rd 14; went 2nd u.p 3 out; no ch w wnr
	3	20	**Preseli Heather** (5a) 12-1 **M Lewis** Mid-div; 12l 5th & outpcd 15; no ch aft; went poor 3rd last
[122ᵁ]	4	½	**Fireman** (bl) 16-1 **A St George** 2 handlers; prom; ld 4; clr w wnr 13; hdd nxt; wknd; lft 3rd 2 out; dem last
[450ᴾ]	U		**Brookthorpe** (5a) 20-1 **G Skone** Lkd awful; rr til blun & ur 3
[340ᴾ]	P		**Buckley House** 8-1 **A Price** Tde; rcd wide; ld to 4; prsd ldrs; rn n vide ½way; wknd 12; t.o last when pu 15
	P		**Colour Of Life** (5a) 20-1 **Miss A Meakins** Nt jw; last frm 2; t.o when jmpd slow 7; pu 11
[267ᶠ]	F		**Fernhill Blaze (IRE)** 12-1 **C Williams** Prom; disp ld 10-11; 3rd & outpcd 13; wl hld when fell 2 out
[489ᴾ]	P		**Keldan Star (IRE)** 33-1 **J Phillips** Rr of main group; lost tch 8; t.o & pu 12
[482ᴾ]	P		**Newchurch Lad** 33-1 **J Price** In tch; 7th when mist 8; wkng when mist 11; bhnd when pu 13
	R		**Nomoremissnicegirl** (5a) 20-1 **G Lewis** Mid-div til rn out 5
	U		**Satco Supreme (IRE)** 12-1 **G Marsh** Mid-div til tried to ref & ur 6

OFFICIAL DISTANCES: 10l, 15l   **TIME:** 6min 31.0s

Foxwyn was withdrawn not under orders - bleeding from nose in paddock

602 Confined Maiden (Div 2), 12st - 17J

16 ran

	1		**LILLIEPLANT (IRE)** (5a) 4-1F **A Price** (xnb) 2 handlers; wrs; sn rec; pulling; ld 4; 10l clr 13; drew rt away; easy

[491⁵]	2	25	**Tommyknocker (IRE)** 8-1 **T Faulkner** *Prom in main group til lost plce 8; rallied to 10l 2nd 14; nvr nr wnr*
[489³]	3	1	**Julies Joy (IRE)** (5a) 5-1 **I Johnson** *Jmpd rt; ld to 4; chsd wnr to 13; 5th & no ch nxt; r.o agn app last*
	4	6	**Roger (IRE)** 5-1 **C Williams** *Chsd ldrs to 8; 7th & rdn 12; 20l 3rd when mist 3 out; dem last*
[348⁵]	5	8	**Alicat (IRE)** 8-1 **D Stephens** (Wales) *In tch; 3rd & gng wl 8; outpcd by ldng pr app last; no ch aft*
[332F]	6	2	**Took A Chance (IRE)** 20-1 **J Price** *Ww in rr; prog ½way; 6l 5th 11; outpcd frm nxt; no ch aft*
[487³]	7	10	**Lady Palamon (IRE)** (5a) 10-1 **P Sheldrake** *Swtng; chsd ldrs; 4th 8; wknd 12; t.o frm 15*
	F		**Bill's Integrity** (12a) 12-1 **E Williams** *(xnb) Tde; rr but in tch til fell 9*
[451³]	P		**Dungannon Lad** 16-1 **A St George** *Mist 3; a rr; last when pu 15*
	U		**Ginger Duchess** (5a) 20-1 **G Marsh** *Last when ur 3*
[350P]	P		**Itsjayemm** 20-1 **J Jukes** *A bhnd; pu 13*
[349C]	r		**Move The Clouds** (5a) 6-1 **G Lewis** *Ld rnd at start; mounted at last moment; ref to rce; tk no part*
[486P]	R		**Piccadilly Wood** 20-1 **R Hughes** *Ch ride; ur gng to start; last frm 4 til rn out thro wing & ur 9*
	U		**Sleepy Boy** 33-1 **M Parry** *(bf) 8th when mist & ur 6*
[488P]	P		**Teelyna** (5a) 33-1 **T Vaughan** *Bhnd; 11th when mist 7; t.o & pu 11*
[491⁴]	P		**Travel Safely (IRE)** 5-1 **J Keen** *Mid-div; 7th & in tch 11; sn strugg; t.o & pu last*

OFFICIAL DISTANCES: 25l, 1l **TIME:** 6min 32.0s
Fence 18 omitted - fallen horse and rider

Easton Harriers
High Easter (LH 9F,19J) Sat, 18 Mar (GOOD, GOOD to FIRM in places)

603 Hunt   **8 ran**

	1		**MOORE'S MELODIES (IRE)** 6-4F **M Gingell** *Trckd ldrs in cl 3rd; nt fluent; eff to ld 16; jnd nxt & disp til drvn to ld last; eased flat; comf*
	2	8	**The Marmalade Cat** 8-1 **P Browse** *Jw; ld to 4; cl 2nd nxt til drpd to 3rd 12; r.o agn to press ldr 16; ev ch & outj 2 out; btn app last; completely outrdn*
[241P]	3	5	**Reuter** (vis) 16-1 **R Barr** *Ld 4; rdr constant waving; 4l up 13; hdd & wknd v rap 16; t.o 2 out*
	fence		**Arkay** 25-1 **R Kerry** *Imm rr; disp 25l 4th til 4th 10; t.o 12; blun 14; plodded on*
[555³]	P		**Going Around** 3-1 **Miss A Webb** *Cl up til pu 5*
[551F]	U		**Mannagar (IRE)** 25-1 **D Page** (East Anglia) *Sn strugg & detach; disp 25l 4th when ur 10*
	U		**Sands Of Gold** (5a) 9-4 **T Pickett** *Kpt wide but in tch til blun & ur 4*
	P		**Seewardy (U)** (7a) 16-1 **C Ward** *(xnb) Rr 3; t.o last 5; school til pu 13*

OFFICIAL DISTANCES: 8l, 10l **TIME:** 6min 46.0s **TOTE:** £2.30 **DF:** £6.70

604 Open Maiden 56&7yo (Div 1), 12st   **10 ran**

[322²]	1		**YOU CAN QUOTE ME (IRE)** 3-1JF **A Harvey** *Hld up in 5/6th; trckd ldng group til hdwy to ld 16; jnd 3 out til r.o str to ld last*
[237³]	2	2	**Fountain Bank (IRE)** (vis) 4-1 **M Gingell** *Prom in 4/5th; hdwy to jn ldrs frm 14; prsd ldr 3 out aft nxt; ev ch til no ex app last*
[411³]	3	10	**Ginger Pudding** 3-1JF **W Wales** *Prom; 3l 2nd 5; releg 6th 9; sn impd to 3l 2nd 9; disp 2l 2nd 13; ev ch til no ex aft 3 out*
[550F]	4	¾	**Curracloe Rose** (5a) 25-1 **D Cook** *Ld; 1-2l up til hdd & wknd qckly 16; wl bhnd 2 out; rdr lost whip*
[551P]	5	fence	**Sire De Brumetz (FR)** (7a) 25-1 **G Pewter** *Sn rr; rap hdwy on outer 5 to 2nd nxt; ld brief 8; drpd qckly to rr; t.o 15; hacked home*
[411⁴]	U		**About Time (IRE)** 7-2 **N Bloom** *In tch til drpd to rr 6; strugg & grad lost tch aft; t.o 14; ur nxt*
[411U]	F		**Cardinal Bud (IRE)** 5-1 **P Taiano** *(xnb) Trckd ldrs cl up & gng wl; disp 2l 3rd 13; ½l 2nd when fell 15*
[317⁵]	U		**Golden Knight** 25-1 **P Piddington** *Nt jw; last 2; horse went one way & rdr the other & ur 4*
	P		**Maltby's Charlie** 12-1 **A Tutton** *Hld up in 6/7th; hdwy to cl 3rd 10; sn outpcd & wknd qckly; rr & strugg 12; pu 14*
[412P]	R		**Rag Bolt (IRE)** 7-1 **S R Andrews** *Hld up in rr & nvr gng pce; lft rem 5th by 15; 30l 5th when missed marker bef 3 out*

OFFICIAL DISTANCES: 1½l, 5l **TIME:** 6min 34.0s **TOTE:** £3.90 **DF:** £7.40

605 Open Maiden 56&7yo (Div 2), 12st   10 ran

[323ᵁ]	1		**WILL HILL (IRE)** (7a) 5-4F S Sporborg Trckd ldrs on outer in 3rd/4th; ld 12; jmpd rt aft; jnd brief 15; drew wl clr app 2 out; eased flat; impressive
[411ᶠ]	2	10	**Chadwick Bank (IRE)** 7-4 M Gingell Mostly 5/6th; trckd ldrs til hdwy aft 9; chsd ldr in 4l 2nd 13; eff to prsd ldr brief 15; sn outpcd; no ch 2 out
[516ⁿ]	3	20	**Glencloy (IRE)** 3-1 A Coe 2 handlers; mostly 5/6th; 6l 3rd 14; chsd ldng pr nxt; 8l 3rd when blun 16 & bridle broke & bit slpd thro mouth; no reins & lost tch qckly aft
	4	2	**Yashwell (IRE)** 8-1 P Taiano Hld up; mid-div; hdwy 8; 6l 3rd 10; chsng ldrs in 8l 4th when mist 14; nt pushed aft; improve
	5	10	**Cerisier (IRE)** (5a) 16-1 D Cook Towards rr when blun bad 4; sn off pce & nt jw; detach 9th 8; plodded on
	P		**Ardluck** 16-1 C Ward-Thomas Cl up 2nd & hit 4; prom in 2nd/3rd to 9; wkng when blun 13; school & stdly lost tch; t.o last when pu last
	P		**Bandit Boy** 14-1 N King Cl up; 4l 3rd 5; prom til wknd aft 13; rem 5th when pu 3 out
[22ᴾ]	P		**Inns Of Court** 20-1 P McAllister Ld; nt fluent & jmpd lft; hdd 12; wknd v rap; strugg in rr 14; pu 15
[550ᴾ]	P		**Midnight Dynamite** 20-1 P Chinery Almost imm last & sn detach; t.o 9; fnce last 11; pu 2 out
[181ᶠ]	F		**Sidney Street** (bl) 20-1 C Ward A rr; strugg in 9th when fell 10

OFFICIAL DISTANCES: 15l, dist **TIME:** not taken **TOTE:** £2.10 **DF:** £3.10

606 Open Maiden 8yo&up, 12st   11 ran

[416ᴾ]	1		**CALIPO BELLO (IRE)** 7-2 S Sporborg A.p; mostly 3rd/4th; narrow ld 15 til jnd 3 out; rdn app last; pushed out flat; one pce; just hld on
[323ᵠ]	2	hd	**Out Of Actons (IRE)** 16-1 C Jarvis (xnb) A rr; 8th 8; 10l 6th 11; hdwy to chse ldrs in 6l 3rd 16; sust rn frm 3 out; 2l 2nd last; r.o wl und motionless rdr; just failed
[323ᴾ]	3	4	**Sweet Talker (IRE)** 7-1 N Bloom Mid-div in 5/6th; hdwy 13; cl up 15; prsd ldr 3 out; ev ch nxt; rdr drpd whip bend bef nxt; no ex
[322³]	4	3	**Miss Mouse** (5a) evensF C Ward-Thomas Prom; trckd ldrs in 4/5th; 6l 5th & blun 14; lkd strugg aft; one pce & no ch 2 out
[551ᴾ]	5	7	**Chariot Man** 3-1 A Sansome Ld to 14; outpcd bef nxt; wknd 16 & releg last; nd aft
	P		**Bozo Bailey** 16-1 M Polley Prom; 3l 3rd 5; stdly lost plce; rr & strugg 10; virt t.o when jb rt 12; pu 14
[98ᵁ]	P		**Outside The Rain (IRE)** (5a) 25-1 T Macfarlane 2 handlers; imm rr; t.o last by 5; trundled rnd til pu 3 out
[551ᴾ]	P		**Take It Easy (IRE)** 14-1 D Parravani Imm rr; toiling & t.o 10; pu 15
[97ᵁ]	U		**Thunderbird** (5a) 20-1 P McAllister (bf) Cl up bhnd ldr; 4l 3rd 10; hdwy to ld 14; narrow advant when ur app 15
[322ᴾ]	P		**Wardy Hill** (5a) 20-1 C Lawson Prom 1; imm wrestled to rr; 10th by 4; t.o 9; pu 2 out
[416ᴾ]	R		**Wise Point (IRE)** 20-1 G Lush Chsd ldr; 10l 4th 8; sn drpd to rr; disp rem 6th when rn thro wing & ur 16

OFFICIAL DISTANCES: hd, 2l **TIME:** 6min 35.0s **TOTE:** £4.80 **DF:** £3.80 (1+any)

607 Mens Open   14 ran

[417¹]	1		**TOM DE SAVOIE (IRE)** 6-4F W Wales Hld up in mid-div bhnd runaway ldr; stdy hdwy to 5l 5th 14; 3rd nxt; kpt on to disp ld 2 out; ld app last; stayed on wl
[511ᵠ]	2	½	**Broadway Swinger** (tt) 20-1 S R Andrews Mid-div; ab 7/8th til hdwy 11; disp 4l 3rd 15; hdwy to disp ld 2 out; ev ch til no ex app last
[510ᵠ]	3	4	**Mister Trick (IRE)** (bl) 5-1 N King Swtng; prom in chsng group in mostly 2nd/3rd til ld 14; hdd app 2 out; 3l 3rd & no ex app last
[384ᵠ]	4	8	**Epsilo De La Ronce (FR)** 14-1 A Harvey Sn towards rr & nt go pce; detach 7; grad hdwy frm 13; r.o frm 16; 10l 4th & no ch 2 out; kpt on
[553ᴿ]	5	3	**Dockmaster** 7-1 M Abrey A rr & nd; last & outpcd 6; slt hdwy 10; in tch 14; r.o past btn horses frm 3 out; nrst fin
	6	4	**Kelly's Original** 10-1 C Ward-Thomas Prom; chsd ldrs in mostly 5/6th til hdwy 13; 4l 4th nxt; chsd ldrs til wknd rap aft 3 out; btr for rce
[94ᶠ]	7	3	**No Quitting (IRE)** 5-1 D Kemp Mid-div; in tch to 11; rr & outpcd frm 16
[553²ᵈ]	8	2	**Remilan (IRE)** (bl) 12-1 A Sansome A towards rr & nvr gng wl; rmdrs & no resp 10; 12th 14; plodded rnd
[384ᵠ]	9	25	**Stoney Valley** (vis) 20-1 M Gingell Ld 1; blun 2; 10l clr 5; wknd rap 14; sn wl in rr; nd aft
	P		**Captain Marmalade** 20-1 A rr; 10th 9; wl bhnd when blun 13; pu 14
[430²]	P		**Deep Refrain** 20-1 G Kerr Prom in chsng group; 12l 3rd 5; outpcd 10; wl in rr when pu 2 out
[417ᴾ]	P		**Dynamite Dan (IRE)** 33-1 A Braithwaite (xnb) A strugg off pce in mid-div; 7th when blun 9; rr when pu 2 out

	P		**Son Of Iris** 10-1 A Coe *Mid-div; 6/7th til drpd to rr & outpcd 8; strugg & last 10; pu 12*
[176U]	U		**Still In Business** 20-1 A Ayers *Prom in chsng group bhnd clr ldr; eff 9; 3l 2nd 14; blun & ur 16*

OFFICIAL DISTANCES: 1l, 2l **TIME:** 6min 25.0s **TOTE:** £3.20 **DF:** £32.00

608 Ladies Open - 18J   11 ran

[319¹]	1		**SPRING GALE (IRE)** 4-9F Miss Z Turner *A gng easy; hld up in 5/6th; prog to 3l 4th 10; trckd ldr til hdwy to ld brief aft 14; prsd ldr til ld agn 3 out; 10l clr nxt; eased flat; v easy*
[240¹]	2	8	**Cracking Idea (IRE)** 5-2 Mrs G d'Angibau *Lft 25l; jnd pack 4; mid-div til hdwy 13; ½sl 2nd 15; wknd qckly nxt; no ch frm 3 out*
[549⁴]	3	15	**Limited Liability** 33-1 Miss C Grissell *(xnb) Ld to 3; prom in chsng trio til outpcd 14; 4th & no ch aft; lft 15l 3rd 3 out*
[417²]	4	10	**Peanuts Pet** 20-1 Miss H Barnard *Sn rr & strugg to go pce; dist 5th 15; stayed on one pce*
[414⁸]	5	6	**Ballyedward (IRE)** 33-1 Miss H Pewter *In tch in mid-div til drpd to rr & last 11; plodded rnd*
[240ᴾ]	6	4	**Just Jack** 33-1 Miss F Jonason *Outpcd in mid-div; rr & strugg 14; plodded rnd; schoolmastering*
[287³]	U		**Gatchou Mans (FR)** 8-1 Miss L Rowe *Trckd ldr in 2nd/3rd; disp 5l 2nd when blun & ur 9*
	P		**Hay Dance** 33-1 Mrs E Coveney *Lose-coupled; prom in 3rd/4th; disp 5l 2nd 9; wknd rap bef nxt; rr & tired 11; pu 13*
[442ᵁ]	P		**Laughing Fontaine (IRE)** 33-1 Miss L Allan *Sn rr; last when broke fetlock & pu app 5; destroyed*
[414⁵]	U		**Lets Twist Again (IRE)** 33-1 Miss A Stennett *Prom in 4/5th to 10; lost plce stdly; rr 14; wl bhnd when ur 15*
[238³]	R		**Mill O'The Rags (IRE)** 20-1 Mrs A Hays *Ld 4; hdd brief aft 14; missed marker bef 3 out*

OFFICIAL DISTANCES: 10l, 12l **TIME:** 6min 25.0s **TOTE:** £1.30 **DF:** £2.10
Fence 14 omitted - fallen horse

609 Intermediate, 12st   14 ran

[413²]	1		**NIBBLE** 5-1 G Cooper *(xnb) Trckd ldrs in 5/6th; 4l 5th 10; chsd ldr 16; sust rn uphill app 2 out; ld last; r.o wl*
[327²]	2	1	**Aintgottime (IRE)** 1-2F R Lawther *Handy; trckd ldrs in 5/6th; hdwy 13; rdn to ld 16; 2l up 2 out; jnd last; no ex flat*
[572⁵]	3	3	**Alfredo Garcia (IRE)** 5-1 S R Andrews *Off pce in mid-div to 12; stdy hdwy frm 15; 3l 3rd 2 out; stayed on; r.o hld*
[428³]	4	6	**Live Wire (IRE)** 3-1 G Kerr *Hld up in tch in mid-div to 10; chsd ldrs 12; stayed on frm 3 out; nt pce to chall*
[413ᴾ]	5	3	**Generous Deal (IRE)** 33-1 A Sansome *Positively rdn; pulling; cl 2nd 5; harried ldr til wknd qckly 16; btn nxt*
[552³]	6	5	**Royal Surprise** 33-1 Miss L Ingram *(xnb) Mid-div & nt pce to trble ldrs; 15l 7th 15; one pce aft*
[510ᴾ]	7	2	**Lord Knox (IRE)** 16-1 A Coe *Prom; ld 6-16; wknd rap; wl in rr 2 out*
[413³]	8	15	**Borrow Mine (IRE)** (vis) 33-1 A Braithwaite *Cl up; ld 4-6; drpd to rr 12; plugged rnd*
	9	1½fs	**Hot Chocoholic** 25-1 Miss L Spence *Fat; sn strugg; t.o 12; 2 fncs bhnd 15; collapsed & died aft rce*
[93ᴾ]	P		**Aeolian** 16-1 R Gill *Imm rr & nvr gng wl; blun 3; sn t.o; pu 9*
[24ᴾ]	P		**Citizen Deal (IRE)** 33-1 C Lawson *Anchored start; virt t.o 2; pu 14*
[318ᴾ]	P		**Courier's Way (IRE)** (5x) 16-1 C Ward *Ld to 3; prom til wknd qckly 10; hit 12 & drpd back; wl bhnd when pu 14*
[574ᴾ]	P		**Minor Key (IRE)** 10-1 A Harvey *2 handlers; off pce in mid-div to 10; wl in rr 12; pu 2 out*
	P		**Youcat (IRE)** 20-1 N Bloom *Trckd ldrs; in tch in 4/5th to 10; nt qckn nxt; wkng when blun 13; pu nxt*

OFFICIAL DISTANCES: 2l, 3l **TIME:** 6min 28.0s **TOTE:** £6.30 **DF:** £3.10

610 Restricted   13 ran

[546ᴾ]	1		**SPRING WHEAT** (5a) 33-1 Miss C Tuke *Towards rr 6; 10l 8th 9; stdy hdwy frm 12; 8l 5th 3 out; sust rn aft; prsd ldrs app last; drvn out to ld cl home*
[554²]	2	½	**Mister Audi (IRE)** 6-4JF A Sansome *Trckd ldrs in 5/6th to 13; hdwy to press ldr 15; chall 2 out til jmpd to ld last; hdd & no ex cl home*
[413ᶠ]	3†	3	**Bakmalad** 33-1 D Kemp *Outpcd in mid-div; chsd ldrs vain 15; stayed on frm 3 out; 6l 4th app last; r.o flat; nrst fin*

[416P] 3† d ht **Mackoy (IRE)** 25-1 M Gingell *Prom in chsng trio til hdwy to ld aft 15; jnd 2 out til hdd last; no ex flat*

[509¹] 5 1 **Deep Song** 16-1 Miss Carla Thomas *Prom in chsng trio; ld 9-11; cl 3rd/4th aft 2 out; no ex app last*

[416P] 6 5 **Beau Joueur (FR)** (bl) 16-1 A Coe *Swtng; ld to 8 & 12-15; prom til aft 3 out; wknd qckly & sn no ch; last aft 2 out*

P **Ar Aghaidh Abhaile (IRE)** 12-1 G Cooper *Prom in chsng trio; prsd ldr 5-7; cl up til outpcd 16; wknd qckly & no ch nxt; bhnd when pu 2 out*

[179U] P **Cill Chuillinn (IRE)** 16-1 Miss J Knight *2 handlers; chsd ldng group til wknd v qckly 9; rr & barely galloping 11; pu 14*

[91³] P **Free And Equal (IRE)** 12-1 S R Andrews *Imm last; pushed along & nt keen frm 3; t.o & pu 11*

P **Hazy Sea (IRE)** 7-1 R Lawther *Rr of main group; strugg of pce 10; t.o 14; pu 16*

[411P] P **Life Of A Star (IRE)** 25-1 A Braithwaite *In tch towards rr til wknd 11; bhnd when pu 14*

[555⁵] P **Premier First (IRE)** 25-1 W Pewter *A towards rr; lost tch 12; t.o 15; pu 2 out*

[181¹] F **Smurf (IRE)** 6-4JF N King *Handy in 5/6th til wknd 12; lost tch qckly; 25l 5th & no ch when fell 15; disapp*

OFFICIAL DISTANCES: ¾l, 2l **TIME:** 6min 38.0s **TOTE:** £44.60 **DF:** £1.30 (1+any)
The rider of the winner was informally cautioned concerning her use of the whip

Harkaway Club
Chaddesley Corbett (LH 8F,18J) Sat, 18 Mar (GOOD to FIRM)

611 Club Members, 12st   **13 ran**

[449²] 1 **DISTINCTIVE (IRE)** 4-1 Mrs D Jackson *Swtng; ld til hdd 3 out; cl 3rd nxt; rallied to ld flat; r.o wl*

[17P] 2 1 **French Buck (IRE)** (7x) 20-1 M Rimell *Sn prom; 4l 3rd ½way; went 2nd aft 12-14; rdn to ld 2 out; hdd & nt qckn flat*

3 4 **Forest Feather (IRE)** 10-1 A Dalton *Hld up; 11l 8th ½way; hdwy 11; went 3rd nxt & 2nd 14; ld 3 out-nxt; one pce*

[333⁵] 4 10 **Alaskan Heir** (vis) 25-1 M Rodda *Chsd ldrs; 10l 6th ½way; mist 12; 8l 7th 14; 11l 5th 3 out; one pce*

[383⁵] 5 1 **Stretchit** 3-1F E Gretton *5s-3s; lw; chsd ldrs; 9l 5th ½way; 6½l 5th 14; 10l 4th 3 out; no imp*

6 10 **Egypt Mill Prince** 10-1 E Walker *2nd/3rd to 5; 7l 4th ½way; 7½l 6th 14; sn wknd*

7 1 **Bally Parson** 33-1 C Wadland *Bckwd; went 2nd aft 1-12; 6l 4th 14; sn wknd*

[474P] 8 5 **Capstown Bay** (7x) (tt) 7-1 Julian Pritchard *A bhnd; mist 3; 16l 9th & rdn ½way; 20l 9th 14; cont wl bhnd*

9 5 **Nick The Biscuit** (7x) 7-1 D Mansell *Swtng; bckwd; nd; 10½l 7th ½way; 12l 8th 14; wl bhnd frm nxt*

[447P] 10 1 **Artic Pearl (IRE)** (5a) 50-1 Miss E Hill *Prom til lost pce 5; 18l 10th ½way; wl bhnd 11; t.o 14*

[190P] F **Connie Foley** 33-1 Miss N Rudge *A bhnd; 22l 12th ½way; mist 11; t.o 12; fell last*

P **Cool Off** 33-1 R Cooper *Nt jw; sn wl bhnd; t.o & pu 8*

P **Gold'n Shroud (IRE)** 6-1 A Wintle *Hld up & wl bhnd; 19l 11th ½way; 25l 10th 14; t.o & pu 3 out*

OFFICIAL DISTANCES: 1¼l, 5l **TIME:** 5min 56.5s

612 Club Members Restricted, 12st   **15 ran**

[339¹] 1 **PHILTRE (IRE)** evensF Julian Pritchard *6/4-evens; lft 2nd 1; ld 4-5 & 6-8; ld 10; qcknd 15; 3l clr nxt; r.o wl*

[371²] 2 2½ **Paddy For Paddy (IRE)** 4-1 R Burton *Lw; prom til lost plce 6; 3l 6th ½way; 5½l 5th 14; sn outpcd; went 7l 3rd & rdn 3 out; stayed on wl; went 2nd at last; nt rch wnr*

3 1½ **Banteer Bet (IRE)** (5a) 14-1 R Cooper *Hld up; hdwy 8; 1l 3rd ½way; went 2nd aft 10; ev ch 15; chsd wnr til mist last; kpt on*

[261⁴] 4 6 **Forever Dreaming (IRE)** 25-1 M Rimell *Hld up; 5l 9th ½way; eff & 7l 6th 14; sn outpcd; 12l 5th 3 out; stayed on; went 4th nr fin*

[392⁶] 5 hd **Coddington Girl** (5a) 12-1 T Stephenson (xnb) *Hld up; hdwy 5; 2l 4th ½way; went 3rd 12 til 3½l 4th 14; 9l 4th 3 out; one pce*

[337¹] 6 15 **Philelwyn (IRE)** (5a) 6-1 A Wintle *Hld up; hdwy 7; 2½l 5th ½way; went 2½l 3rd 14; wknd & 15l 6th 3 out*

P **Crab 'n Lobster** (5a) 33-1 R Hodges *Swtng; hmpd 1; sn wl bhnd; 25l 11th ½way; mist 11; t.o 12; pu 15*

[510U] U **Cuban Skies (IRE)** (1ow) 33-1 A Barnett *2nd when blun & ur 1*

F **Fountain Glen (IRE)** 25-1 G Carenza (bnh) *Oht; fell 1*

[567P]	U	Henwyn 8-1 S Joynes *8th when mist & ur 2*
	P	Kemiller (IRE) 14-1 F Hutsby *Swtng; ld to 4; ld 5-6 & 8-10; rdn & wknd qckly 12; wl bhnd when pu 14*
	P	Lindalighter (5a) 20-1 M Munrowd *Swtng; hld up; 4l 7th ½way; wknd 12; 16l 8th 14; pu 15*
	F	Master Welder (vis) 12-1 A Dalton *Fell 1*
[332P]	P	Pushover (FR) 33-1 D Mansell *Hld up; 4½l 8th ½way; lost plce 12; 14l 7th 14; pu 15*
	P	Rolpen 12-1 J J Pritchard *Bckwd; hdwy 6; lost plce & 6l 10th ½way; mist 11; lost tch 12; 23l 9th 14; t.o & pu 3 out*

OFFICIAL DISTANCES: 4l, 2l **TIME:** 6min 00.4s

613 Greig Middleton Ladies Open   9 ran

[475²]	1		SPLIT SECOND 11-10JF Miss A Dare *(bf,pricker ns) Hld up; hdwy 6; 4l 3rd ½way; went 2nd 12; ld 2 out; r.o wl*
[385³]	2	2	Master Of Troy 11-10JF Miss T McCurrich *Ld 4-6; ld 7; mist 10; hdd 2 out; unable to qckn*
[512U]	3	8	Erbil (IRE) 50-1 Miss S Kelly *Swtng; 2nd til lost plce 4; hdwy to ld 6; hdd 7; 5l 3rd 13; no ex 3 out*
[218²]	4	15	Sam Quale (IRE) 6-1 Miss C Thomas *Hld up; 7l 6th ½way; hdwy & 3½l 5th 12; outpcd in 8l 4th 14; wknd 3 out*
[226¹⁰]	5	3	Rainbow Walk (IRE) 66-1 Miss A Burton *Ld to 4; lost plce 7; 6l 5th ½way; 10l 6th 12; wl bhnd 14*
[335⁵]	6	1	Saffron Flame (IRE) 33-1 Miss N Rudge *Swtng; pulled hrd & rcd wide; sn prom; lost plce 7; 9l 7th ½way; 12l 7th 12; wl bhnd 14*
	7	3	Reach For Glory 66-1 Miss P Swindin *Prom; 5l 4th ½way; went 2nd aft 10 til 3l 4th 12; 13l 5th 14; sn wknd*
[191P]	P		Beans River 50-1 Miss C Dyson *Nd; 12l 8th ½way; rdn 12; wl bhnd when pu 14*
[194⁶]	P		Cumberland Youth 66-1 Miss J Garley *Sn wl bhnd; t.o 6; pu 8*

OFFICIAL DISTANCES: 2½l, 10l **TIME:** 5min 56.9s

614 Mens Open   9 ran

[580F]	1		LOCHNOMORE 3-1 R Burton *Lw; made all; rdn 3 out; mist 2 out; all out*
[584B]	2	1	Forest Fountain (IRE) 5-2F Julian Pritchard *Lw; a.p; went 2nd 3-10; chsd wnr 12; mist 15; rdn 2 out; unable to qckn*
[195³]	3	4	Wishing William (IRE) 5-1 S Waley-Cohen *Hld up; hdwy 8; 4l 4th ½way; went 2nd 10-12; 5l 4th 14; outpcd in 7l 4th 15; stayed on one pce*
[465³]	4	2	Jalcanto 7-2 D Mansell *Swtng; hld up; went 3rd 5-10; 3½l 4th 12; 4l 3rd 14; rdn 3 out; one pce*
[195²]	5	5	Smile Pleeze (IRE) 33-1 T Stephenson *Hld up; jmpd slow 4; 5½l 6th ½way; 6l 7th 12; outpcd in 8l 7th 14; nvr nr to chall*
	6		Barton Black (NZ) 20-1 M Keel *Hld up; 6l 7th ½way; 5½l 6th 12; 6l 5th 14; sn outpcd; no ch when mist last*
[486P]	P		Classic Fairy (IRE) (5a) (tt) 50-1 P Hanly *(xnb)Hld up & pulled hrd; 4½l 5th ½way; 7l 6th & rdn when mist 14; sn wknd; bhnd when pu 3 out*
	P		Rexy Boy 33-1 C Wadland *2 handlers; nt jw; prom til lost plce 5; 10l 9th ½way; wl bhnd 12; t.o & pu 3 out*
[454⁶]	P		Strong Chairman (IRE) 25-1 M Waley-Cohen *Prom til lost tch 8; 6½l 8th ½way; lost tch 12; t.o & pu 3 out*

OFFICIAL DISTANCES: 1¼l, 4l **TIME:** 6min 00.2s

615 Club Members Moderate, 12st   17 ran

[371¹]	1		CATCHWORD 3-1 R Armson *5s-3s; 2 handlers; swtng; hld up; mist 9; 4l 7th ½way; went 2l 3rd aft 11; ld 12; qcknd 14; clr 3 out; r.o wl*
[447¹]	2	7	Upton Adventure (5a) 5-2F S Joynes *Hld up; 5l 8th ½way; hdwy 12; went 3l 2nd 14; rdn 3 out; no imp*
[333¹]	3	1½	Maggies Brother (5x) 9-2 T Stephenson *Rn in snatches; lost plce 6; 6l 9th ½way; rallied 12; 7l 6th 14; 8l 4th & rdn 3 out; stayed on one pce*
[448²]	4	4	Tirley Missile 12-1 Julian Pritchard *Hld up; 7l 10th ½way; mist 11; hdwy to 6½l 5th 14; went 7l 3rd 3 out; no ex u.p*
	5	15	Money Don't Matter (5a) 16-1 D Mansell *(xnb) Lw; hld up; 9l 11th ½way; eff & 10l 7th 14; wknd & 15l 5th 3 out*
[448r]	6	2	Executive Office (IRE) 25-1 M Keel *Swtng; hld up; lost plce & 9½l 12th ½way; wl bhnd 14*
[191F]	7	¾	Hehas 20-1 C Wadland *10l 13th ½way; drpd to rr 11; wl bhnd 14*
[333⁷]	8	10	Just Marmalade 33-1 Miss J Williams *(xnb) Swtng; prom; went 2nd 4; ld 6-8; 2l 4th ½way; wknd qckly 12; t.o*

	9	8	**Mr Drake (IRE)** 16-1 R Burton Ld 3-6; 2nd/3rd to 10; wknd 12; t.o; fin lame
	10	2	**Upton Orbit** 33-1 J I Pritchard Prom; 2½l 5th ½way; ld 10-12; 4l 3rd & rdn 14; sn wknd; t.o; fin lame
[446ᶠ]	P		**Chaceley Lass** (5a) 50-1 A Evans Jmpd v slow 6; bhnd til pu 7
[296ᶠ]	P		**Nutty Solera** 33-1 R Cooper Ld to 3; 2nd/3rd til ld 8; hdd 10; wknd qckly 12; t.o & pu 3 out
[567⁹]	P		**Out Of The Blue** (5a) 25-1 S Graham Sn prom; 11 3rd ½way; went 2nd 11-12; wknd qckly 14; wl bhnd when pu 3 out
	P		**Roman Romany** 33-1 E Walker Prom; 3l 6th ½way; 6l 4th 14; sn wknd; wl bhnd when pu last
	P		**Royal Leader (IRE)** 25-1 M Rodda Hld up & bhnd; 12l 15th ½way; eff & 13l 8th 14; wknd & 22l 6th 3 out; wl bhnd when pu last; broke shoulder; destroyed
[447ᶠ]	P		**Sally's Twins** (5a) 8-1 A Wintle (xnb) Swtng; unruly start; nvr gng wl; 1 11 14th ½way; t.o & pu 3 out
	P		**Starting Again** 8-1 A Dalton Hld up & bhnd; mist 1; 14l 16th ½way; no hdwy when pu & dism aft 14

OFFICIAL DISTANCES: 7l, 2l **TIME:** 5min 58.1s

616 Club Members Maiden (Div 1), 12st   11 ran

[391²]	1		**ARD NA CARRIG (IRE)** 5-1 A Wintle Lw; jw; made all; 10l clr 12; lft wl clr 15; 20l up 3 out; unchall
[484ᶠ]	2	20	**Little Star** (5a) 20-1 T Stephenson Hld up wl bhnd; 32l 6th ½way; went 25l 4th 13; lft 20l 3rd 15; chsd wnr 3 out; no imp
	3	15	**Cosa Fuair (IRE)** 20-1 R Burton (xnb) Chsd wnr to 13; lft 15l 2nd 15; sn wknd
[569ᵁ]	4	7	**Red Spice** 8-1 R Owen Chsd ldrs til lost plce 7; lft 25l 4th 10-13; lft dist 4th 15; t.o
[12ᶠ]	5	nk	**Snowboy (IRE)** 8-1 D Mansell Swtng; a wl bhnd; 33l 7th ½way; t.o 15
[298ᶠ]	6	12	**Pharpen (IRE)** 8-1 A Dalton A wl bhnd; t.o 7
[391ᶠ]	R		**Catechist (IRE)** (7a) 20-1 A Evans Hld up; 20l 5th & rn out thro wing 5
	P		**Commanche Rebel (IRE)** E Walker 8th when pu aft 3; broke off-hind; destroyed
[336²]	P		**Connors (IRE)** 2-5F Julian Pritchard Lw; hld up; went 20l 3rd 6; eff 12; went 10l 2nd aft 13; pu & dism 15; lame
[337ᶠ]	P		**Talkalot (IRE)** 10-1 F Hutsby (xnb) Hld up; went 25l 4th 7 til pu 10
[341ᵁ]	P		**Three Monroes (IRE)** 20-1 M Munrowd A wl bhnd; 34l 8th & rdn ½way; t.o & pu 11

OFFICIAL DISTANCES: 20l, 15l **TIME:** 6min 07.4s

617 Club Members Maiden (Div 2), 12st   10 ran

	1		**ACHILL SOUND** 9-1 G Hanmer (xnb) Hld up; 8l 6th ½way; jnd ldrs 11; qcknd to ld 12; 5l clr 3 out; rdn out
[391ᶠ]	2	5	**Captain George** 20-1 M Wall (xnb) 2 handlers; 2nd til ld 3; hdd 4; chsd wnr 12; no imp 3 out
[570ᶠ]	3	1½	**Step Quick (IRE)** 6-1 A Dalton Hld up & bhnd; 17l 8th ½way; 15l 7th 14; went 12l 3rd 3 out; stayed on wl; nt rch ldrs
	4	10	**Millstock** (5a) 12-1 Miss N Stallard Rfo trying to mount; chsd ldrs; 7l 5th ½way; outpcd in 13l 6th 14; nd aft
[332ᵁ]	5	2	**Reg's Rocket** 11-1 N Oliver Ld; jmpd slow 2; hdd 3; 5l 4th ½way; 6l 4th & rdn 14; wknd 15
[194⁵]	6	12	**Benbulbin (IRE)** (vis) 7-1 M Bluck Hld up; 14l 7th ½way; hdwy 11; 8l 5th 14; wknd 15
[341²]	U		**Gorsey Bank (IRE)** 4-5F R Cooper Hld up; 13l 7th when mist & ur 8
	P		**Judicial Queen** (5a) 14-1 L Lay Prom; mist 4; went 4l 3rd ½way; 5l 3rd 14; wknd 15; bhnd when blun 2 out; pu last
	P		**Persevere** (5a) 14-1 M Gregory Swtng; prom; ld 4 til hdd & wknd rap 12; 30l 9th 14; t.o & pu 3 out
	P		**Raise And Gain (IRE)** 12-1 R Burton Jmpd lft; a bhnd; 19l 9th ½way; 23l 8th 14; t.o & pu 3 out

OFFICIAL DISTANCES: 5l, 1½l **TIME:** 6min 10.5s
Daisy Fay was withdrawn after declarations closed

618 Club Members Maiden (Div 3), 12st   16 ran

	1		**MORE PEOPLE (IRE)** 9-4JF Julian Pritchard Lw; jmpd lft; ld to 5; 3l 4th ½way; lft 4th bend aft 11; ld 13; 7l clr 3 out; comf
[221²]	2	10	**Top Designer (IRE)** (tt) 9-4JF A Dalton Hld up & bhnd; 8l 11th ½way; gd hdwy to 3½l 4th 12; chsd wnr 15; no imp
[31ᶠ]	3	1½	**Dunethna (IRE)** 9-2 R Burton 7s-9/2; lw; sn prom; 2l 3rd 13; went 2nd 13; lost plce; 7l 5th 15; one pce 3 out

	4	4	**Moscow Squeaker (IRE)** 25-1 M Rodda *Hld up & bhnd; l0l 13th ½way; hdwy to 7l 8th l2; l2l 7th l5; nd aft*
[567ᴾ]	5	1	**Strong Account (IRE)** (tt) 16-1 R Sealey *Swtng; prom; went 2nd 5; ld 7-13; 5l 3rd l5; wknd qckly 3 out*
	P		**Ben Gilmore** 33-1 L Tibbatts *Bckwd; prom; 4l 5th ½way; wkng when mist l0; t.o & pu l5*
	P		**Chasing Dreams** 25-1 M Cowley *Oht; lost plce & rmdrs 4; 25l 14th ½way; t.o & pu l2*
	P		**Gwenllian** (12a) 33-1 L Whiston *Chsd ldrs til wknd qckly 6; t.o & pu 9*
	P		**Kyarra** (5a) 25-1 C Wadland *Tocky; 2 handlers; hld up; hdwy & 6l 8th ½way; l0l 9th & wkng l2; wl bhnd when pu l5*
[341ᵁ]	P		**Lastofthe Littles** 14-1 T Stephenson *Hld up; 7l 9th ½way; eff & 6l 7th l2; 8l 6th l5; wknd 3 out; bhnd when pu last*
	R		**Mr Stackhouse (IRE)** (bl) 25-1 M Keel *(xnb) Ld 5-7; 2nd til rn out bend aft 11*
	P		**Northern Prince** 33-1 M Thorne *Hld up; 5½l 7th ½way; hdwy l0; 5½l 6th l2; wknd l4; 20l 8th nxt; t.o & pu 2 out*
	P		**Penaction** (5a) 14-1 F Hutsby *Chsd ldrs; 5l 6th ½way; lost plce 11; 13l 10th nxt; wl bhnd when pu 2 out*
[194ᶠ]	P		**Red Spark** 20-1 E Walker *(xnb) Hld up; 7½l 10th ½way; hdwy & 4l 5th l2; 6l 4th l5; bhnd when pu 2 out*
[341ᴾ]	U		**Sallioko** (5a) 16-1 S Joynes *(xnb) Hld up & bhnd; 9l 12th ½way; blun & ur l2*
[451ᴾ]	F		**Tedstone Fox** 8-1 D Mansell *Fell 3*

OFFICIAL DISTANCES: 10l, 1½l **TIME:** 6min 08.0s

Hurworth
Hutton Rudby (LH 8F,20J) Sat, 18 Mar (GOOD)

619 Hunt, 12st   5 ran

[504ᴾ]	1		**GENERAL BRANDY** (10x) 4-6F G Tuer *Trckd ldr in 2l 2nd to 3 out; hdwy nxt; disp ld last; easily drew clr flat*
	2	2½	**King Fly** (5x) 6-1 Mrs S Horner-Harker *(xnb) Cl up til ld 5; 2l up 13-17; ld agn app last; jnd & hung lft flat; sn hdd & wknd*
[399ᴾ]	3	1½fs	**Oaklands Millie (IRE)** (5a) 50-1 P Kinsella *Trckd ldng trio in 6l 4th to 7; outpcd 8; 20l 4th l0; t.o l4*
[377⁵]	F		**Ellerton Tony** (5x) (tt) 7-4 S Swiers *Ld to 4; cl 2nd til 6l 3rd l2; pushed along l5; 5l 3rd 4; hld when fell 3 out*
	P		**My Sam** (12a) 14-1 Mrs L Ward *(xnb) V sa; jmpd delib; fnce adrift 3; jmpd slow 4; v rem when pu 7*

OFFICIAL DISTANCES: 1l, dist **TIME:** 6min 25.0s

620 Restricted - 19J   11 ran

[440⁴]	1		**ELLA FALLS (IRE)** (12a) 3-1JF M Worthington *(xnb,bh) Chsd ldr early; l5l 2nd l3; lft in ld nxt; 2l up 2 out; qcknd clr app last; r.o str; easy*
[360⁴]	2	6	**Queen Biddy (IRE)** (5a) 4-1 C Storey *Mid-div early; 25l 4th 9; stdy hdwy to 2l 2nd l6; ev ch til outpcd aft 2 out; r.o one pce*
[278⁴]	3	5	**Hidden Island (IRE)** 20-1 Miss P Robson *Midfield to l2; went l0l 6th & pushed along l4; tk 8l 4th 3 out; stayed on wl to tk 3rd flat*
[301⁷]	4	4	**What The Heck (IRE)** 9-2 T Glass *Midfield to l0; 8l 5th l4; hdwy l5 to 4l 3rd 3 out; wknd & dem flat*
[360ᴾ]	5	8	**Carnmoney (IRE)** 20-1 Mrs K Hargreave *Chsd ldng pr in l6l 3rd to l3; lft cl 2nd l4; 3l 3rd l7; mist 3 out; wknd*
[278⁶]	6	15	**Lord George** 20-1 P Atkinson *Nvr gng wl; l2l 6th til outpcd & wknd 3 out*
[398ᴾ]	P		**Alena H Banks** 66-1 L McGrath *(xnb) Sa; mist & jmpd slow 1; last; t.o 9; pu l5*
[508¹]	U		**Curtainsatchopwell (IRE)** 3-1JF K Green *(xnb) Sn clr; l0l up 6; l5l clr when blun bad & ur l4*
[396⁵]	U		**Efaad (IRE)** 33-1 S Pinder *(xnb) Chsng ldrs in 3rd when ur 3*
	P		**Jac Del Prince** 5-1 R Walker *Midfield in 6th to 4; outpcd aft 6; rr & lsng tch 7; sn t.o; pu 11*
[393ᵁ]	P		**Palm Gold** (5a) 33-1 R Wakeham *A rr; lsng tch 3; bhnd by 4; t.o 9 til pu l3*

OFFICIAL DISTANCES: 5l, 3l **TIME:** 6min 19.0s
Fences 10 & 17 omitted - fallen rider

621 Ladies Open   10 ran

[185²]	1		**LA RIVIERA (IRE)** 4-5F Miss P Robson *Midfield to 6; went 3l 3rd 7-12; went 2l 2nd l7; rdn to disp ld last; qcknd wl to ld flat*
[397³]	2	2½	**Japodene** (5a) 7-2 Miss A Deniel *Cl 4th til ld frm 7; 2l up 13-17; jnd last; hdd & outpcd flat*

[505⁴]	3	8	**Temple Garth** 25-1 *Miss F Hartley (xnb) Prom in 5l 3rd to 8; outpcd 10; 8l 6th 14; went 5th 3 out; stayed on wl to tk 3rd flat*
[185³]	4	3	**Astrac Trio (USA)** 7-1 *Mrs A Hamilton A.p; 4l 4th 11; went 3l 3rd 15; in tch til outpcd 3 out; 12l 3rd last; dem flat*
[504³]	5	15	**Private Jet (IRE)** 50-1 *Miss R Clark (xnb) Rr & pushed along 5; mists 7 & 10; last 11; stayed on frm 3 out; nrst fin*
[442⁵]	6	3	**Kendor Pass (IRE)** 50-1 *Mrs N Wilson Ld to 6; 1l 2nd 7-11; wknd 12; rr 3 out; r.o one pce*
[421⁷]	7	2	**Strongalong (IRE)** (5ow) 25-1 *Miss K Roncoroni A midfield to rr; bhnd by 17*
	U		**Kralingen** (5a) 6-1 *Miss C Metcalfe Prom early; 5l 5th 11; mist 14; hdwy 16 to 2l 3rd when ur 2 out*
[361²]	U		**Little Santa (IRE)** (5a) (tt) 9-2 *Mrs K Hargreave Last to 2; rr 7-10; bhnd when blun bad & ur 15*
[376⁴]	U		**Scrabo View (IRE)** 100-1 *Miss S Ward Rr div when ur 2*

OFFICIAL DISTANCES: 2l, 10l **TIME:** 6min 12.0s

622 Land Rover Mens Open, 12st   **9 ran**

[419ᴾ]	1		**WEEJUMPAWUD** (5a) 8-1 *B Lusted A.p; ld to 3; cl 2nd 4-8; led frm 9; 2l clr 2 out; stayed on wl*
[504²]	2	6	**Calleva Star (IRE)** (7x) 7-1 *R Abrahams Cl 2nd til ld 4-8; chsd ldr in 2l 2nd to 2 out; pushed along & outpcd app last*
[493⁴]	3	10	**Riverside Run (IRE)** 8-1 *A Robson Midfield early; pushed along in 10l 6th 13; went 5th 2 out; stayed on wl; tk 3rd flat; nrst fin*
	4	2	**Ways And Means** (5a) 14-1 *K Green Hld up in rr; last 14; went 15l 6th 2 out; stayed on one pce*
[277ᴾ]	5	1	**Just Charlie** (3ow) 3-1F *D Easterby Hld up in rr early; last 13; pushed along; went 7th 15; r.o one pce; nvr nrr*
[384ᶠ]	6	1	**James The First** 4-1 *G Tuer Last & mists 2 & 4; rr 7; rap hdwy aft 10 to 10l 3rd 3 out-nxt; wknd app last*
[422⁷]	7	½	**Lottery Ticket (IRE)** (7x) 66-1 *S J Robinson Trckd ldrs 1st circ; 3l 3rd 13; pushed along in 8l 4th 17-3 out; wknd app nxt*
[375³]	8	3	**Blank Cheque** 7-2 *D Coates Midfield; 6l 4th 6 & 5th 12; outpcd 15; lost ground qckly; t.o 3 out; rnwd rn; fin fast*
[394⁴]	P		**Bold Fountain (IRE)** 4-1 *C Wilson Prom early; 4l 3rd 4-10; chsd along 14; wknd 15; rr & lsng tch 16; t.o & pu 2 out*

OFFICIAL DISTANCES: 5l, 10l **TIME:** 6min 20.0s

623 Confined, 12st   **11 ran**

[506²]	1		**JACKSON'S HOLE** (3x) 4-6F *D Easterby Rr early; hdwy to 4l 3rd 7; went cl 2nd 13; trckd ldr til chall last; gd j & sn ld; drew clr; rdn out*
[394²]	2	1½	**Mr Primetime (IRE)** 20-1 *N Bannister A handy; 4l 4th 5; in tch 11; 4l 4th 13; outpcd 16; 8l 4th 2 out; hrd rdn; fin fast*
[134⁵]	3	4	**Orswellthatenswell** (3x) 4-1 *Mrs F Needham Chsd ldr in 3l 2nd til lft in ld 13; 2l up til jnd & nt fluent last; sn hdd & wknd*
[279ᴾ]	4	10	**Fryup Satellite** 25-1 *P Halder Rr by 2; mist 4; detach by 6; bhnd to 16; gd hdwy aft nxt; stayed on wl; tk 4th flat; nrst fin*
[186⁴]	5	2	**Running Free (IRE)** 10-1 *M Worthington Midfield til hdwy 11; cl 5th 13; pushed along nxt; 3l 3rd & lkd dangerous 15; ev ch 2 out; wknd qckly app last*
[393²]	6	4	**Nishkina** 100-1 *C Cundall Cl up til pushed along & outpcd 8; rr & lsng tch 10; bhnd 13*
[394⁵]	7	15	**Fettle Up** (bl) 66-1 *Miss S Brotherton Midfield; 8l 5th 10; hdwy to 4l 3rd 11; wknd 15; t.o 2 out*
[506¹]	F		**Insideout** (3x) 11-4 *Mrs L Ward (xnb) Midfield til hdwy 12; 6l 5th 13; trckng ldng trio in 5l 4th & gng wl when fell 17; broke nk; dead*
[496ᴾ]	P		**Mick Man (IRE)** 33-1 *S J Robinson Nt jw; midfield & mists 7 & 9; rr & lsng tch 10; t.o & pu 12*
[506ᴾ]	F		**Pashby Wood** (5a) 66-1 *M Morley Sa; detach by 2; t.o when fell 5*
[504ᶠ]	F		**Prime Style** (4ow) 12-1 *C Gibbon 2l ld to 10; qcknd 11; 8l clr when fell 13*

OFFICIAL DISTANCES: ½l, 3l **TIME:** 6min 19.0s
        Prince Moshar was withdrawn not under orders - unseated going to start & injured the rider

624 Open Maiden (Div 1)   **14 ran**

[113⁹]	1		**MENALDI (IRE)** 7-1 *Miss K Roncoroni Cl 2nd til ld 7-9 & 14-16; ld agn app last; stayed on wl u.p; a in comm*

[380^U]	2	2	**Heather Lad** 5-1 D Raw *2 handlers; oht; cl 3rd to 15; outpcd 16; 5l 5th 2 out; rdn to chall app last; wknd & one pce flat*
[424^F]	3	1	**Big Bark (IRE)** 14-1 C Storey *Patient rdn; rr to 12; hdwy 13 to 7l 6th 3 out; ev ch nxt; 2l 3rd app last; r.o one pce*
[113^3]	4	4	**Roscoe Burn** 2-1F R Morgan *Lw; trckd ldrs til hdwy 9 to cl 2nd 10; ld aft 17-2 out; wknd app last*
[282^P]	5	6	**Over In McGanns (IRE)** 14-1 C Mulhall *Midfield early; 8l 6th 12; hdwy 13 to cl 4th 15; 4l 4th 3 out; ev ch nxt; sn wknd*
	6	4	**Sinbad's Secret** 12-1 N Tutty *Hld up til hdwy 11 to 6l 5th 13; went cl 3rd & lkd dangerous 3 out; sn wknd*
	7	5	**Deerhunter** 12-1 D Dickenson *Sa; t.o by 7; late hdwy; fin fast; nrst fin*
[379^4]	8	6	**Tough Decision** 20-1 S Brisby (xnb) *Midfield to 11; 12l 8th 12; outpcd & wknd 15; bhnd by 3 out*
[363^P]	P		**Aces High** 16-1 T Morrison *Nt a fluent; rr by 3; lsng tch 6; t.o 9; pu 3 out*
[501^P]	F		**Carefree Love (IRE)** 20-1 T Glass *Midfield to 8; hdwy 9 to 3l 4th 12; in tch & gng wl in 3l 4th when fell 15*
	P		**Henah Hill** 10-1 Miss P Robson *A bhnd; lsng tch 10; t.o 15; pu 2 out*
[379^P]	F		**Pause For Thought** 7-2 Mrs F Needham *A.p; ld frm 2-6 & 10-13; wknd 15; lsng tch when fell 2 out*
[378^P]	P		**Rain Street (IRE)** 20-1 D Thomas *Rr when bad mist & nrly ur 6; miraculous rcvry; jmpd slow 7; t.o by 9; pu 3 out*
	P		**Westhall Jonstan (IRE)** 12-1 G Markham *A strugg; t.o 13; pu 16*

OFFICIAL DISTANCES: 1l, ½l **TIME:** 6min 32.0s

625 Open Maiden (Div 2)　　　　　　　　　　　　　　　　14 ran

[420^5]	1		**MR BOSSMAN (IRE)** 6-4F T Glass *Midfield early; cl 6th 9; went 4l 4th 13; ld frm 16; 2l up 2 out; stayed on wl*
[399^3]	2	5	**In The Van** 6-1 M Morley (xnb) *Pulled to ld 2-3; cl 2nd to 7; rdn to disp ld 3 out; outpcd nxt; r.o one pce*
[380^P]	3	10	**Early Dawn** (5a) 14-1 J Davies *Midfield til hdwy 7; cl 4th 10; 4l 5th 16; outpcd nxt; 5th app last; hmpd bad by loose horse; pushed out for 3rd*
[437^5]	4	nk	**Dragon Stout** (tt) 7-2 C Wilson *A cl up; 3l 3rd & gng wl 14; trckng ldng pr 3 out; outpcd nxt; hld in 4th when lft 3rd at last; hmpd bad by loose horse & virt brought to standstill; dem cl home*
[393^3]	5	20	**Imps Way** (12a) 25-1 C Mulhall *A rr; lsng tch 7; t.o 14; nd*
[507^P]	6	30	**Perdix** (12a) 66-1 Miss J Foster *A midfield; 12l 8th 10; pushed along & mist 12; chsng ldng group in 7th 16; wknd nxt; t.o 2 out*
	r		**Ardnut** 10-1 C Storey (xnb) *Midfield early; 8l 8th 12; pushed along 14; rr & lsng tch 16; to when ref last*
[379^5]	R		**Ben From Ketton** (7a) 50-1 S J Robinson *Pulled hrd early; cl 3rd 6-11; handy 3rd 15; outpcd & wknd 16; 15l 5th when rn out 2 out*
[507^P]	P		**Just A Single (IRE)** (tt) 20-1 G Markham *Ld frm 4-15; wknd 16 & drpd back last; t.o & pu 3 out*
[507^P]	P		**Miss Gloria** (5a) (bl) 100-1 K Green (xnb) *Midfield to 4; blun bad & rr by 5; jb rt nr horseboxes 6; nrly ur & imm pu*
[39^4]	P		**Paperback Writer** (5a) 14-1 M Henney *Jmpd v novicey; last by 2; jmpd slow 5 & 7; t.o & pu 14*
[281^3]	P		**Pearly's Song** 7-2 K Needham *Nvr gng wl; rr of ldrs 6; rr by 7; t.o 8; pu 14*
	R		**Vals Castle (IRE)** (5a) 12-1 Miss R Clark *Sa; rr til hdwy 12; 5l 5th 15; went cl 3rd 17; outpcd 2 out; 8l 3rd & hld when rn out last*
[167^P]	P		**Young Saffy** 33-1 A Pennock *Ld to 2; cl up to 8; t.o & pu 14*

OFFICIAL DISTANCES: 6l, 10l **TIME:** 6min 30.0s

626 Open Maiden (Div 3)　　　　　　　　　　　　　　　　14 ran

[437^2]	1		**C L B JEMILLA** (5a) 3-1 Mrs F Needham *Midfield; stdy hdwy to cl 5th 13; went 2l 2nd 2 out; rdn to disp ld last; gd j & lft wl clr; r.o*
	2	10	**Young Rab** (7a) 6-1 G Markham *Prom in 4th to 11; 2l 2nd 12l 2nd 15-17; pushed along 3 out; 3l 3rd & wkng nxt; 12l 3rd & hld when lft 2nd at last; rn wl; sure to improve*
[497^P]	3	12	**Pennyman (IRE)** 20-1 T Glass *Midfield to 11; hdwy 15; cl 4th 3 out; outpcd & wknd app nxt; dist 4th when lft 3rd at last*
[384^4]	4	6	**Asked To Leave** (5a) 33-1 I Bennett *Rr to 15; went poor 5th 3 out; lft 4th at last*
[426^3]	5	25	**I Say Dancer (IRE)** (5a) 25-1 Miss C Metcalfe *A rr; t.o 17; stayed on one pce; nd*
[503^P]	6	3	**Chief Engineer** 16-1 S Brisby *Ld to 3; handy 2nd 4-11; 3l 3rd 15; wknd qckly nxt; t.o 3 out*
[399^3]	7	12	**Miss Jones** (5a) 50-1 P Frank *Oht; pulled hrd to ld 4; 8l clr 10; hdd & wknd 15; sn bhnd; t.o*
	P		**Glenelly (IRE)** 20-1 R Morgan *Midfield to 9; lost plce & rr 11; t.o 16; pu last*

[424F]	F		**Happy Blake** 6-4F C Storey (xnb) Handy; 4l 5th 5; went cl 2nd 6; ld 14; 2l up 2 out; jnd & still gng wl when fell last
[438P]	P		**Hibou** 14-1 C Wilson Midfield to 9; hdwy 10; went 3l 3rd 13; outpcd & wknd 16; pu 3 out
	P		**Mighty Wizard** 5-2 N Tutty Cl 3rd til qckly pu 4; lame
	P		**Tom Kirby** 33-1 N Wilson Sn bhnd; t.o by 5; climbed over 7; rem when pu 14
[379P]	P		**Wandering Wild** 33-1 Miss T Jackson (xnb) Last to 2; sn bhnd; t.o by 12; rem when pu last; nt hrd pushed; school
	P		**Wild Briar** (12a) 33-1 D Raw A rr; rn v green; lsng tch 8; t.o & pu 14

OFFICIAL DISTANCES: 15l, 15l TIME: 6min 26.0s

627 Open Maiden (Div 4) - 17J
17 ran

[399P]	1		**PHARSTAR (IRE)** 5-1 D Easterby (drop noseband & twisted snaffle) Disp ld til ld 3; settled wl in front; 2l up 15; r.o wl when chall last
	2	3	**Leg Beforum (IRE)** 6-1 L Bates Hld up in rr to 8; stdy hdwy 10 to 6l 5th 15; went 3l 2nd 2 out; rdn to chall last; outpcd on long run-in
[439P]	3	8	**Tenor Bet (IRE)** 4-1 N Wilson Mid-div to 8; went 3l 2nd 12-15; cl 3rd 2 out; outpcd & wknd app last
[424⁴]	4	15	**Notoobig** 4-1 T Glass Midfield to 9; went 4l 3rd 12; cl up & ev ch til outpcd & wknd 2 out
[108P]	5	1	**Black Ice (IRE)** 25-1 C Storey (xnb) Midfield to 9; rap hdwy to 3l 2nd 13; outpcd & wknd 15
[167⁵]	6	4	**Hattie** (5a) 10-1 C Denny A mid-div; r.o one pce
[400⁴]	7	1	**Eye The Storm (IRE)** 33-1 M Morley Pulled hrd early; cl 3rd 6-10; wknd 12; bhnd 15
[282⁶]	8	1	**Redmire** (5a) 20-1 A Pennock Prom early; rr & bhnd 7
[439⁷]	9	½	**Stanwick Hall** 33-1 K Needham (xnb) Nt jw; t.o by 5
[375⁵]	10	6	**The Grey Bay** (5a) 33-1 Miss T Jackson A rr; bhnd by 7; t.o 13
	11	15	**Right Ron Run** 14-1 R Wakeham Cl up; disp ld 5-9; wknd 12; rem by 2 out
	U		**Buster Buttons** (bl) 25-1 N Tutty Midfield to 6; hdwy aft 12; cl 3rd 14; chall & disp ld when blun bad & ur 2 out
	P		**Countess Rosie** (5a) 25-1 Miss J Foster Sn bhnd; t.o by 5; pu 11
[503P]	U		**Im Struggling** (7a) 25-1 K Lupton Ld to 3; prom til ur 7
[398²]	F		**Jolly Minster** 4-5F P Atkinson Trckd ldrs to 7; 7l 6th 12; 5th when fell 13
[437R]	P		**Minster Echo** (12a) 33-1 S Brisby Hairy ride; bhnd & lsng tch 5; t.o 6; pu 16
[399P]	U		**Nells Delight** (bl) 33-1 Miss Rachel Clark Mid-div when ur 2

OFFICIAL DISTANCES: 4l, 8l TIME: 6min 19.0s
Fences 6, 13 & 20 omitted - low sun

New Forest
Larkhill (RH 13F,18J) Sat, 18 Mar (GOOD to FIRM)

628 Confined, 12st
6 ran

[453²]	1		**COACH (NZ)** evensF P Keane (xnb) Opened 6/4 in a plce; trckd ldrs; 3rd & hit 5; went 2nd 8; eff to jn ldr & drew clr w him frm 12; ld app 15; sn in comm; hit last; easy
	2	15	**Street Kid** 6-1 Miss L Rope In tch in last to 8; 16l last 13; stayed on wl aft; went 14l 3rd 15; 18l 3rd 2 out; went 2nd flat; no ch w wnr
	3	2½	**Flapjack Lad** 9-4 J Barnes Opened 6s in a plce; pulling & rn free; ld 2; 5l clr 7; jnd & hdd aft 12; wknd qckly; 10l 2nd & btn 2 out; dem flat
[452²]	4	1	**Glen Cherry** 10-1 P Scouller Prom; trckd ldr 2-7; handy 3rd til outpcd 12; 15½l 4th & lkd wkng 15; stayed on one pce
[453⁶]	5	40	**Touring-Turtle (IRE)** 10-1 D Dennis Tchd 12s; handy in last pr to 11; 10l 3rd & chsng clr ldrs aft nxt; 15l 3rd 14; drpd to last nxt & wknd qckly; t.o 2 out
[518U]	U		**Vic's Girl** (5a) 50-1 S Hayes Prom; cl 3rd when rfo 2

OFFICIAL DISTANCES: 15l, 4l TIME: 6min 05.7s TOTE: £1.70 DF: c/f

629 Open Maiden (Div 1), 12st
6 ran

[457U]	1		**FEVER PITCH** 5-1 A Honeyball Tchd 6s; trckd ldrs til cl 2nd aft 5; ld 7-12; ld agn 14; drew clr aft nxt; 10l ahd 2 out; unchall
	2	12	**Quit The Creek** (5a) 16-1 A Martin In tch in last pr to 10; 16l 4th aft 12; stayed on wl frm 14; went 3rd & gng wl at 3 out; tk 2nd flat; promising
[147²]	3	6	**Mr Robstee** 5-2F N Mitchell Hand in last til hdwy 7; went 2nd 10 til 6l 3rd aft 12; 5l 2nd & gng wl 15; 10l 3rd & wkng 2 out; dem flat
	P		**Meat Loaf (IRE)** 3-1 A Charles-Jones (xnb) Cl 2nd/3rd til jmpd slow 8; releg last aft 12; 18l last & wkng qckly 13; t.o & pu 15
[477B]	r		**Ole Gunnar (IRE)** 7-1 M Wilesmith (xnb) Ref to rce; event set off 2 fncs bhnd; ref & ur 1

[457F]   F   **Snowshill Harvest (IRE)** 3-1 *Miss P Gundry* Jmpd lft at times; ld to 6; reluct & 4l 2nd nxt; chsd ldr til ld agn aft 12-13; cl 2nd & mist 14; wknd qckly; last & btn when fell 2 out (changed hands aft rce)

OFFICIAL DISTANCES: 15l, 6l   TIME: 6min 12.3s   TOTE: £3.80   DF: c/f

630 Open Maiden (Div 2), 12st - 17J   11 ran

[204P]   1   **JESTASTAR** 5-1 *S Bush* 8s-5s; a.p; trckd ldr 4 til disp ld brief 10; sltly outpcd & drpd back 4th 15; rallied & chall nxt; cl 2nd 2 out til lft in ld last; r.o

[260P]   2   2½   **Springvilla (IRE)** 6-1 *R Young* (bf) 8s-6s; ld; jnd brief 4 & 10; hdd 13; cl 2nd/3rd til dem 4th 3 out; lft 3rd at last; fin wl; a just hld

[477P]   3   6   **Darzal** 12-1 *A Charles-Jones* Trckd ldrs; 4th & bad mist 5; 5th 8 til eff aft 12; disp ld brief 15; cl 3rd & ev ch 2 out; btn when lft 2nd brief last; rn wl

[433³]   4   8   **Romany Chat** 2-1F *A Martin* 5/2-2s; trckd ldrs in 4/5th; 5l 4th 7; cl 5th & ev ch by-passing 14; 5th & no imp 3 out; btn when lft 4th at last

[477P]   P   **Courage II (FR)** 50-1 *J Casemore* Cl 3rd to 6; stdly lost tch aft; rr of main group 10; t.o last aft 12; pu 15

          P   **Dicks Darlin'** (5a) 100-1 *S Sellars* Bckwd & unclipped; cl up to 3; sn last of main body; jmpd v lft 10; pu 12

[249U]   P   **Nearly A Jester** 11-2 *D Flavin* Dwelt; set off fnce bhnd; last; in tch 10; lft t.o last agn 15; pu 2 out

[471P]   F   **Shamrock Lad** 5-1 *Miss P Gundry* (bf) In tch towards rr of main body til fell 3

[472U]   P   **Strike Accord** 16-1 *P Young* Mid-div; 7th 7; 6th & outpcd 13; t.o 15; pu 2 out

[309⁴]   F   **Tellaporky** (bl) 10-1 *Miss E Owen* Failed to tk off & crashed 1

          U   **Youmeandhim (IRE)** 7-1 *P York* Mid-div; prog to 4th & hit 6; 2l 3rd nxt; ld/disp aft 12 til slt advant 2 out; lkd likely wnr when blun bad & ur last

OFFICIAL DISTANCES: 2l, 3l   TIME: 6min 13.6s   TOTE: £4.20   DF: £27.30
Fence 14 omitted - fallen rider

631 Mixed Open, 12st   6 ran

[210F]   1   **GLAISNOCK LAD (IRE)** 11-2 *J Barnes* Tchd 6s; cl 2nd til disp 5l 2nd aft 12; 5l 3rd 14; went 2l 2nd 3 out; stalked ldr til rdn & qcknd impressive to ld flat

[263P]   2   1½   **Merry Shot (IRE)** 8-1 *R Young* Wl in tch towards rr; 5l 5th aft 4; jmpd to 3l 3rd 7; eff to ld aft 14; untidy nxt 2; 2½l up at last; hdd & no ex u.p flat

[326⁵]   3   6   **Man Of Steele (IRE)** 2-1F *Miss D Harding* 3s-2s; cl 2nd mostly til ld 8; 5l clr aft 12; jnd 14; sn hdd; dem 6l 3rd 3 out; kpt on; no imp on ldrs aft

[456¹]   4   2½   **Copper Coil** 9-4 *D Alers-Hankey* Cl 3rd/4th til 5th aft 5; went 4th 13; 10½l 4th & jmpd slow 15; no imp aft; lacklustre

          P   **Flying Fellow (IRE)** 25-1 *A Charles-Jones* Tchd 33s; swtng; ld to 7; 4th & wkng 10; last when pu 13; public gallop

[580²]   P   **Freedom Fighter** 11-2 *A Martin* Tchd 6s; nrly a last; mist 7; in tch to 12; 15l last & wknd 14; bhnd when pu 3 out

OFFICIAL DISTANCES: 1½l, 5l   TIME: 6min 01.5s   TOTE: £2.30   DF: £31.00

632 Intermediate, 12st   6 ran

[324¹]   1   **BALL IN THE NET** 7-4 *M Holdforth* Tchd 2s; handy in 4th til 2nd aft 5; pulled to ld 8-12; jnd ldr 14 til ll up 2 out; just hdd but ev ch when lft wl clr last

[404³]   2   12   **Bright Approach (IRE)** 8-1 *Miss P Gundry* 10s-8s; ld to 7; cl 2nd til aft 12; drpd to 5th 14; stayed on wl frm nxt; went 4th 3 out; 9l 3rd 2 out; no imp when lft 2nd at last

[462⁵]   3   25   **True Chimes** 13-2 *J Owen* (xnb) Tchd 7s; cl 2nd to 5; 1½l 3rd & mist 8; cl 4th 11; went 5l 3rd 14; wkng when mist 3 out; 15l 4th & hrd drvn nxt; lft poor 3rd at last

[388U]   4   3   **Minstrel's Quay (IRE)** 16-1 *M Gorman* In tch in last pr; jmpd slow 6; 6l 4th 14; sn wknd; 27l 5th & btn aft 2 out

          P   **Dick's Cabin** 50-1 *Miss A Goschen* A rr; last 3; detach 6; t.o 12; pu 14

[306¹]   F   **Noah** (7a) evensF *P York* Cl 3rd/4th til 2nd 11; just ld 13; jnd nxt til hdd app 2 out; sust chall on inner aft; slt ld & fell last; prob unlucky

OFFICIAL DISTANCES: 20l, dist   TIME: 6min 04s   TOTE: £1.90   DF: £9.60

633 Restricted, 12st   5 ran

[330²]   1   **SUSIES MELODY (IRE)** (tt) 9-2 *D Dennis* Hld up in cl last til jmpd to 2nd 7; imm stdd to last agn; 4l adrift 10; hdwy to ld app 13; made rest; 3l up 2 out; drew clr app last; eased flat

[458P]   2   5   **Newman's Conquest** (5a) 33-1 *M Shears* Cl 3rd mostly; blun bad & nrly ur 6; disp ld 10-12; releg last brief nxt; 3½l 3rd 14; 2l 2nd aft nxt; chsd wnr in vain frm nxt

[70¹]   3   15   **Noble Star** 5-2 *S Bush* Cl 2nd mostly til disp ld 10 til aft 12; cl 2nd to 14; 3rd & wkng nxt; sn btn

| [559²] | P | **Hemero (IRE)** (tt) 7-4F **A Honeyball** Ld; jmpd slow 7; jnd 10; hdd aft 12; cl 3rd 13; 4l last & wkng nxt; detach & struggled over 3 out; t.o nxt; pu last |
| [536ᵖ] | U | **Lost Your Marbles (IRE)** (5a) 3-1 **J Mead** (bnh) Ur l |

OFFICIAL DISTANCES: 5l, 15l **TIME:** 6min 07.6s **TOTE:** £5.40 **DF:** c/f

634 Dodson & Horrell PPORA Club Members, 12st   7 ran

[403²]	1		**STILLMORE BUSINESS** 11-4JF **Miss P Gundry** Hairy & needs clipping (yet won best-turned-out!); pulling & carried tail high; trck ldrs in cl 3rd til ef 15; ld nxt; made rest; r.o str flat; comf
[387²]	2	5	**Balance** 9-2 **G Maundrell** Cl 2nd; jmpd to ld brief 4; mist nxt; jnd ldr aft 12; ld 14; jnd nxt; chsd wnr vain frm 3 out
[510ᵁ]	3	1	**Scarba** 3-1 **J Owen** Tchd 7/2; hld up; last pr til last 7-11; rap hdwy to disp 2l 2nd 13; ev ch til 4l 3rd & rdn along 3 out; 7l 3rd & one pce nxt
[454ᵖ]	4	15	**Frozen Drop** 11-4JF **J Barnes** Ld; hdd brief 4; jnd 8 & 13; sn hdd; cl 4th 15; wknd nxt; 19l 4th & btn 2 out
[457⁴]	5	40	**Paul (IRE)** 20-1 **Miss L Collins** A last trio; lost tch frm 12; t.o 14; duelled for rem last; rdn out & fin fast
[473ᵖ]	6	5	**Silver Hill** (5a) 50-1 **Miss B Fear** A last trio; cl up to 11; detach last aft nxt; t.o 14; duelled for rem last aft; poor 5th 3 out til one pce & dem flat
[459⁴]	F		**Rustic Revelry** (bl) 6-1 **P York** 2nd 1; disp ld & fell 2 (chsd field loose & jmpd sev fncs)

OFFICIAL DISTANCES: 5l, 1l **TIME:** 6min 06.4s **TOTE:** £3.10 **DF:** £4.80

Quantock Staghounds
Cothelstone (LH 7F,19J) Sat, 18 Mar (FIRM)

635 Hunt   4 ran

[407⁴]	1		**SALFORD QUAY (IRE)** 1-2F **G Barfoot-Saunt** 4/6-1/2; ld 1; sn settled; ww wl off pce; 40l adrift when lft in ld 13; jnd out; sn ld agn; drew clr frm 2 out
[403ᵖ]	2	10	**Spare On** (5a) 7-2 **A Michael** Oht; ww in 3rd; lft 4l 2nd 13; hdwy to disp 16; slpd bend bef 2 out; hld when pckd bad 2 out; no ex
	F		**Capiche (IRE)** 6-1 **Miss G Browne** Bit bckwd; nov rdn; bolted bef start; ld 2; stdy pce but sn wl clr; 40l ahd when fell hvly 13
	U		**Polka** (7a) 6-1 **D Ridge** 3rd when ur l

OFFICIAL DISTANCE: 12l **TIME:** 6min 46.7s **TOTE:** £1.60 **DF:** £9.80

636 Ladies Open   7 ran

[354²]	1		**FORBIDDEN WATERS (IRE)** 2-1 **Miss S Vickery** 3s-2s; hld up gng wl; hdwy to 4th 8; went 3rd 10; cl 2nd & pckd bad 14; eff on inner 3 out; lkd htd til drvn to disp last; pushed clr
[535¹]	2	1½	**Slew Man (FR)** 1-2F **Miss O Green** (xnb) Tchd 4/7; lw; hld up in rr; hdwy to 5th 10; stdy prog to 3rd 14; ld aft nxt; slt mist 3 out; ½l ld 2 out; jnd last; sn hdd & no ex
[101⁴]	3	20	**Legal Artist (IRE)** (8ow) 33-1 **Miss J Congdon** Ld; rdr waving 4; disp aft 8; slt ld 12-13; wknd nxt & sn no ch; 8l 3rd 3 out; dism aft post
[475⁶]	4	12	**Khalidi (IRE)** 25-1 **Miss M MacGregor** Bit bckwd; nov rdn; in tch; cl 4th 10; lost ground 14; 13l 4th 15; bhnd clsng stages
[405²]	F		**Lord Of The Rings** 12-1 **Miss C Tizzard** Lw; chsd ldr; disp ld 8-12; cl up when pckd bad 13; disp ld when fell 15
[326⁹]	P		**Olive Basket** (5a) 10-1 **Miss W Southcombe** In tch til pckd 6; lost ground stdly frm 10; 17l 6th 12; bhnd when pu 14
[454ᵖ]	P		**Silver Sleeve (IRE)** (bl) 25-1 **Miss L Bridges** In tch til lost ground 8; last frm 10; t.o 14 til pu last

OFFICIAL DISTANCES: 1½l, 15l **TIME:** 5min 56.8s **TOTE:** £2.40 **DF:** £1.20

637 Land Rover Mens Open, 12st   4 ran

[401ᵁ]	1		**EXE CRACKER** (tt) 6-4 **L Jefford** Lw; stdd start; hld up; last but in tch; went 3rd 15; ld on inner aft 3 out; 1l ld last; r.o resolute
[143¹]	2	1	**Camera Man** (7x) 4-5F **C Heard** Trckd ldr in cl 2nd frm 4; disp ld 3 out; cl 2nd & ev ch frm 2 out; nt pce of wnr run-in
[258⁴]	3	1½	**Gypsy Gerry** (bl) 10-1 **T Clarkson** Slt ld on inner at stdy pce til jnd 3 out; outpcd; cl 3rd on inner 2 out; nt qckn u.p clsng stages
	4	12	**Scud Missile (IRE)** 14-1 **S Goodings** Rcd keen & sn prom; cl 3rd mostly; wknd 15; 8l 4th nxt; no ch frm 2 out

OFFICIAL DISTANCES: 1l, ½l **TIME:** 6min 12.0s **TOTE:** £2.00 **DF:** £2.60

638 Confined
7 ran

[523¹]	1	**MILLYHENRY** 6-4F Miss T Cave *Opened 2s; ch ride; jw; ld 2-15 & agn frm 3 out; drew clr 2 out; comf*
[356¹]	2	7 **Belarus (IRE)** (bl) 3-1 C White *Hld up in rr; last to 12; stdy hdwy frm rr aft 13; went 3rd app 2 out; r.o to tk 2nd run-in*
[210°]	3	2 **Tom Snout (IRE)** 5-2 Miss S Vickery *Tchd 3s; lw; ld 1; trckd ldr til ld agn 15-3 out; sn one pce; 4l 2nd at last; eased run-in; dism aft post*
[403²]	4	15 **Parditino** 16-1 Miss J Nicholas *3rd/4th mostly; lost plce 13; outpcd; poor 5th frm 15; lft 4th at last*
[454°]	U	**Amtrak Express** 25-1 H Froud *Tchd 33s; lw; tk keen hld; cl 5th ½way; went 3rd 15; wknd 3 out; btn 4th when bad mist 2 out; ur last*
	P	**Fellow Sioux** 16-1 R Woollacott *(pricker ns) Hdwy to disp 3rd on inner 9; niggled along 12; lost ground qckly 15; pu nxt; bbv*
	P	**James Pigg** 10-1 G Richards *12s-10s; in tch; cl 3rd 8; sn lost plce; bhnd frm 13 til pu 16*

OFFICIAL DISTANCES: 10l, 1l **TIME:** 5min 59.7s **TOTE:** £4.10 **DF:** £5.60

639 Intermediate, 12st
8 ran

[536³]	1	**KINGSBRIDGE (IRE)** 6-4 L Jefford *Tchd 7/4; made all; dictated stdy pce; mist 7; qcknd clr 16; unchall*
[557¹]	2	7 **Western Fort (IRE)** (5x) 11-8F Miss J Cumings *Lw; 4th 10; gd hdwy 13; outpcd nxt; tk 2nd 3 out; no imp on wnr; hld on to 2nd u.p run-in*
[406⁷]	3	nk **Keszam** (5a) 14-1 A Bateman *Sn prom; went 2nd 10; outpcd 16; 3rd frm 3 out; r.o stdly*
[259°]	4	nk **Conquer The Kilt** 7-1 Maj S Robinson *(xnb) 6th ½way; hdwy to disp 3rd 13; kpt on one pce frm 2 out*
[351²]	5	3 **Jukino** (5a) 8-1 A Michael *Tchd 12s; towards rr; 7th ½way; went 5th 15; no hdwy u.p; dism aft post*
[453⁵]	6	15 **Our Wizzer (IRE)** (5x) 9-1 C Whittaker *(xnb) Towards rr; 5th ½way; just in tch til 15; sn wknd*
	7	6 **Granstown Lake (IRE)** 50-1 J Young *Dwelt; a last und iron grip; detach 7; nvr put in rce*
	U	**Mountain-Linnet** 50-1 Mrs J Reed *Oht; 5th & in tch when blun & ur 11*

OFFICIAL DISTANCES: 7l, nk **TIME:** 6min 11.8s **TOTE:** £2.90 **DF:** £1.70

640 Confined Maiden (Div 1), 12st
10 ran

[353³]	1	**DIAMOND DUCK** (5a) 8-1 Miss K Allan *(xnb) Swtng; ld to 7; stayed prom; ld agn aft 12; kpt on when chall aft 17; pushed clr run-in*
[255°]	2	4 **Mollycarrsbrekfast** (7a) 10-1 D Ridge *Opened 33s; handy; cl 4th ½way; gng easy 12; cl 3rd & mist 13; hit 16; eff on outer & tk 2nd app last; nt qckn flat; do btr*
	3	2 **Legal Petition** (5a) 9-2 L Jefford *Lw; tk keen hld & sn prom; cl 2nd frm 7; ev ch frm 3 out; slt mist last; no ex run-in; should improve*
	4	10 **Acetylene** (5a) 10-1 Miss T Cave *(xnb) 6th ½way; lft 4th 13; 21l 4th 17; kpt on one pce*
[410°]	5	2 **All-Inclusive (IRE)** (5a) 25-1 J Scott *Bckwd; a rr; r.o stdly frm 16; nrst fin*
	U	**Audley Lass (IRE)** (5a) 2-1F A Bateman *Lw; hld up in midfield; 5th 10; 4th & in tch when blun & ur 13*
	P	**Charlie Smith** (7a) 9-1 Miss S Vickery *Rr; 7th ½way; just in tch to 14; mist nxt; pu 16; school*
[352²]	F	**Irish Brush (IRE)** (5a) 11-2 G Barfoot-Saunt *Towards rr when fell 4*
[265⁴]	P	**Jazetason** (bl) 33-1 M Woodward *Swtng; sn rr; bhnd frm 7 til pu 16*
	F	**Mayfair Monarch** (7a) 5-1 H Froud *10s-5s; strong; swtng; rcd keen; sn prom; slt ld 9 til fell 12*

OFFICIAL DISTANCES: 5l, 3l **TIME:** 6min 17.0s **TOTE:** £6.40 **DF:** c/f

641 Confined Maiden (Div 2), 12st
6 ran

[213°]	1	**SHARETON** 11-10F Miss S Vickery *Pulling early; cl 2nd til ld 6; made rest; drew clr stdly frm 11; unchall*
[207°]	2	12 **The Islander** 13-2 G Barfoot-Saunt *Lft in ld 2 til hmpd by loose horses bend app 6; lost tch frm 11*
	3	30 **Suba Lin** (5a) 25-1 D Luff *Virt a 3rd; lost tch aft 10; 27l 3rd 11; plodded rnd*
[410°]	U	**Final Chance** (5a) 6-4 Miss T Cave *Opened 7/4; ch ride; distracted & ur 1*
	F	**Persian Raider** 25-1 M Sweetland *Bckwd; a last & jmpd hesitant; bhnd frm 9 til fell hvly 13*
[352°]	R	**Slubberdegullian** (7a) 10-1 A Bateman *Ld & jmpd violent rt 1; lkd uncontrollable & crashed thro wing 2*

OFFICIAL DISTANCES: 15l, 30l **TIME:** 6min 36.7s **TOTE:** £2.50 **DF:** £10.80
Leonard's Dream (25-1, J Scott) was withdrawn after declarations closed; the owners of Shareton, whose passport was found to be not in order, were fined £100

Carmarthenshire
Erw Lon (LH 8F,18J) Sun, 19 Mar (GOOD)

642 Hunt
6 ran

[272ᴾ]	1		**MR MAD** (vis) 1-2F P Hamer *Ld to 8; settled cl 3rd til r.o frm 2 out; ld app last*
[344ᴾ]	2	6	**Alias Parker Jones** 7-1 M Lewis *A.p; 4th mostly; hdwy to 2nd 12; ld 2 out til hdd app last; outpcd*
	3	4	**Crafty Gunner** 5-2 G Lewis *Swtng; 2nd til ld 10-3 out; ll 2nd & ev ch nxt; no ex app last*
	4	12	**Black Magic** (5a) 14-1 H Evans *Rr early; settled 3rd 7; ll 2nd 10; mist 13; wknd qckly nxt; sn rem*
	r		**Annie's Magic** (12a) 14-1 Miss A Meakins *(xnb) A bhnd; t.o 7; fnce bhnd when hmpd, ref & ur 2 out*
[483ᴾ]	r		**Rue De Fort** 5-1 Miss M Davies *Sn rr; t.o 7; ref & ur 2 out*

OFFICIAL DISTANCES: 3l, 1l **TIME:** 6min 31.0s

643 Confined, 12st
10 ran

[344¹]	1		**KINNEFAD KING** (IRE) (tt) 7-2 C Williams *Hld up in 5th; prog 12; 2nd 14; ld app last; kpt on wl*
[480²]	2	2	**Anorak** (USA) (3x) 3-1 Miss P Jones *Ld 1-4; cl 2nd aft til ld agn 15; hdd app last; swishing tail & no ex flat*
[480³]	3	4	**Moon Tiger** 2-1F T Vaughan *Towards rr til hdwy 13; went 3rd 15; nt rch ldrs*
[482⁶]	4	10	**Bancyfelin Boy** 33-1 J Keen *Rr; 7th frm 4 til stayed on past wkng horses frm 14*
[480¹]	5	6	**Whistling Buck** (IRE) (5x) 7-2 J Jukes *(bf) Last early; t.o 6 til prog 13; went 5th 3 out; no imp aft*
[275²]	6	11	**Tilt Tech Flyer** (5x) (tt) 12-1 Miss F Wilson *Midfield; settled 3rd 6 til outpcd frm 3 out*
[467²]	7	8	**Sip Of Brandy** 7-1 G Lewis *Trckd ldrs in 3rd til jmpd slow 11; sn t.o*
[480ᴾ]	8	15	**Side Bar** (vis,tt) 33-1 J Phillips *2nd til ld 5-14; fdd rap; t.o last nxt*
[266³]	F		**Plucky Punter** (tt) 33-1 A Barker *Mist 1; rr when fell 2*
[479⁶]	U		**Same Difference** (IRE) (bl) 25-1 Mrs B Lewis *2nd when ur 2*

OFFICIAL DISTANCES: 2l, 5l **TIME:** 6min 14.0s

644 Marsh UK/TBA PPORA Club Members Mares, 12st
7 ran

[346ᵁ]	1		**AFRICAN WARRIOR** (5a) 5-2 C Williams *Trckd ldr 3; 4l 2nd 12; ld app last; kpt on game*
[584¹⁵]	2	3	**Coolvawn Lady** (IRE) (5a) 1-2F Miss P Jones *Made virt all; 4l up 12; hdd app last; no ex*
[447ᶠ]	3	20	**Doyenne** (5a) 14-1 Miss F Wilson *Last; 4l adrift 2; some prog 12; poor 4th 15; r.o 2 out; no ch w ldrs*
[580⁷]	4	10	**Sister Lark** (5a) 16-1 T Vaughan *A 3rd/4th; 8l 3rd 12; wknd; 30l 3rd & no ch 15; dem 2 out*
[483⁶]	P		**Mo's Keliro** (5a) 14-1 Miss A Meakins *(bf) Midfield; mist 8; wknd 10; t.o last 14; jmpd slow 2 out; pu last*
[347³]	P		**Ten Past Eleven** (IRE) (5a) (tt) 20-1 Miss C Williams *Last trio til pu aft 10; broke fetlock; destroyed*
[31ᴾ]	P		**Thatl Do** (5a) 33-1 P Sheldrake *A bhnd; t.o & rdn 9; pu 14*

OFFICIAL DISTANCES: 4l, 20l **TIME:** 6min 07.0s

645 Mixed Open, 12st
5 ran

[459³]	1		**GUNNER BOON** evens Miss P Jones *Ld 2-4; cl 4th & rmdrs 6; ld agn 10; ½l up 3 out; unchall*
[584¹²]	2	4	**Mr Dow Jones** (IRE) 4-5F G Lewis *A.p; cl 2nd 5; ev ch 3 out; sn outpcd*
[272ᴾ]	3	6	**Turning Trix** 10-1 Miss R Curtis *In tch in rr; mist 7; 1½l 3rd 14; 6l 3rd & outpcd 2 out*
[481⁶]	4	12	**Young Manny** 20-1 M Lewis *Ld 1 & 3-8; cl 2nd til lost tch 12; sn no ch*
[266¹]	5	15	**Sheephaven** 20-1 D Davies *Cl 3rd to 8; 7l last 10; wknd 13; sn t.o*

OFFICIAL DISTANCES: 3l, 5l **TIME:** 6min 12.0s

646 Restricted (Div 1), 12st
6 ran

[484ᴾ]	1		**SECRET BEAUTY** (IRE) (5a) 7-1 M Lewis *Hld up in 3rd frm 5; rdn & prog 15; 3rd 2 out; ld app last; kpt on game; dism aft fin (hdd over-reached)*
[347ᵁ]	2	1	**Kerry Gold Mine** evensF Miss P Jones *Hld up in rr early; settled 2nd 6 til ld 15; hdd & no ex 2 out*
[486³]	3	4	**Dunsfold Dazzler** (5a,1ow) 7-4 D Hughes *2 handlers; ld to 13; 2l 2nd til outpcd 2 out*
[485ᴾ]	4	runin	**Baytomneghost** (IRE) (tt) 33-1 J Price *A last pr; t.o 7; mist 9*

| [595²] | P | | **Sea Search** 33-1 **J Keen** (xnb,bf) 3rd to 4th 7; 18l 4th 10; wknd; pu 12 |
| [267¹] | P | | **Soviet Sip** (7a) 7-2 **J Jukes** Nvr gng wl; last frm 4; rem whn mist 8; poor 4th when pu last |

OFFICIAL DISTANCES: 1½l, 3l **TIME:** 6min 23.0s

647 Restricted (Div 2), 12st
4 ran

	1		**RUSNETTO (IRE)** (vis) 4-5F **G Lewis** Ld at slow pce til qcknd 9; hdd 3 out; 2l 2nd & hdwy when lft clr app last
	2	20	**Kays-Lass** (5a) 2-1 **C Williams** (xnb) 2 handlers; cl 3rd til 2nd 13; ev ch 15; wknd; 20l 3rd nxt; lft 2nd app last
[485ᴾ]	R		**Out On The Town** (5a) 4-1 **James Tudor** Chsd ldr; 3-4l 2nd til lost plce 13; cl up til ld 3 out; 2l up when rn wrong side of hurdle bef last
[486ᵁ]	U		**Young Mariner** 6-1 **A Barker** Last 1; t.o 4; rdr knocked off by marker post bef last

OFFICIAL DISTANCE: 15l **TIME:** 6min 32.0s

648 Confined Maiden 56&7yo (Div 1)
10 ran

[146ᴾ]	1		**MERRIE JAR (IRE)** 4-6F **T Vaughan** Trckd ldr in 2l 2nd til ld 15; kpt on game
[269²]	2	4	**Secret Can't Say (IRE)** (5a) 3-1 **G Lewis** Ld til hdd 15; chsd wnr vain aft
[468ᴾ]	3	4	**Alisha Bavard** (5a) 4-1 **P Sheldrake** Settled 3rd frm 5; nvr able to chall
[267¹]	4	2fncs	**Daisy's Choice** (12a) 20-1 **J Hayward** Rr & mist 1; last nxt; jmpd slow 3; t.o 6; fnce bhnd frm 11
[488ᴾ]	P		**Be Bop Bentley** (7a) 20-1 **H Evans** 3rd early; sn rr; blun 7; rem til pu 14
[487ᴾ]	P		**Cauld Signal (IRE)** (5a) 20-1 **G Maloney** Midfield; 15l 4th 10; pu 12
[482ᴾ]	P		**Cracker Ticket (IRE)** (7a) 10-1 **J Jukes** Chsd ldrs in 5th til rem 4th & wkng when jmpd slow 13; pu 15
	R		**Gypsy Haze** (12a) 10-1 **C Williams** 12l 6th when rn out 8
	R		**Power Unit** (7a) 10-1 **J Price** Last pr; t.o 2; rn out 5
[268ᴾ]	P		**Spot On Millie** (12a) 10-1 **James Tudor** In tch in 4th to 8; wknd; 25l 6th 10; bhnd til pu 2 out

OFFICIAL DISTANCES: 5l, 3l **TIME:** 6min 18.0s

649 Confined Maiden 56&7yo (Div 2)
7 ran

	1		**BLUE CHEESE** (5a) 4-5F **Miss L Pearce** Made all; mist 6; 4l up 13; jmpd delib nxt; lft solo 15; jmpd slow & tail swishing 2 out
	F		**Dai-Namic-Storm (IRE)** (5a) 7-2 **P Sheldrake** 2nd til fell 6
[268ᶠ]	P		**Fair Charmeur** (5a) 16-1 **Miss A Meakins** 3rd til lft 2nd & mist 7; 4l 2nd & lkd reluct 13; blun & nrly ur 14; rn wide aft; mist 15; pu 3 out
[487ᴾ]	P		**Jesusa** (5a) 25-1 **J Keen** Jmpd hairy; to 3; pu 7
	U		**Mission Lord (IRE)** 8-1 **G Maloney** T.o 3; hmpd & ur aft 6
[348ᵁ]	R		**Run To The Glen** (12a) 6-1 **M Lewis** (b4) Rn out & ur 1
[595ᵁ]	F		**Tiger Bell** 20-1 **C Williams** 4th when fell 2

OFFICIAL DISTANCE: Finished alone **TIME:** 6min 32.0s

650 Confined Maiden 8yo&up
11 ran

[350²]	1		**LUMBACK LADY** (5a) 5-4F **Miss P Jones** Hld up in midfield; 4th & prog 12; 2nd nxt til qcknd clr 2 out; comf
[268³]	2	6	**Bonny Rigg (IRE)** (5a) 5-2 **T Vaughan** A.p; 2nd 14; 3rd & ev ch 2 out; nt rch ldr
[349²]	3	4	**Twopintsahalfone (IRE)** 6-1 **J Jukes** Settled 2nd til disp ld brief 10; ld agn 13; hdd 3 out; outpcd
[350ᴾ]	4	runin	**Black Dan** 20-1 **J Keen** Mid-div; 7th & wkng 9; sn rem; stayed on past tiring horses to 4th flat
	5	4	**Laudation (IRE)** 8-1 **M Lewis** Ld; mist 6; jnd 10; hdd & mist 13; ld agn 2 out; tired & eased to lose 4th flat
	6	runin	**Sing Cherry Ripe** (5a) 10-1 **J Hayward** A last; 6l adrift 2; jmpd slow 4; t.o 9
[486ᴾ]	P		**Just Ruffled** 20-1 **J Price** 5th early; wknd 8; 9th & no ch 10; pu 14
[348³]	P		**Lough Neagh (IRE)** 4-1 **C Williams** 3rd early; sn mid-div; rem 4th 13; pu 15
[480ᴾ]	P		**Maes Gwyn Dreamer** 7-1 **G Lewis** 4/5th til rmdrs & lost tch 13; pu 15
	P		**Parliament House (IRE)** 10-1 **J Phillips** (bf) A last trio; pu & dism 7
[484ᴾ]	P		**Weaver Square (IRE)** 20-1 **M Parry** (bf) Handy; 3rd 5; in tch in mid-div til wknd 12; pu 14

OFFICIAL DISTANCES: 7l, 4l **TIME:** 6min 16.0s

Dart Vale & Haldon Harriers

Buckfastleigh (RH 7F,19J) Sun, 19 Mar (GOOD, GOOD to FIRM in places)

651 Hunt
6 ran

[561²]	1		**WELL ARMED (IRE)** (bl) 1-4F **L Jefford** Lw; hld up in tch; nt a fluent; hmpd 14; hdwy to ld aft 3 out; sn clr; pushed out
[310⁵]	2	2½	**Contradict** 8-1 **Miss S Gaisford** A.p; disp 8; cl up when mist 14; went 2nd 2 out; r.o one pce
	3	15	**Good King Henry** 12-1 **I Widdicombe** In tch; cl 4th ½way; ld 14-3 out; wknd nr last
[251²]	P		**It's Not My Fault (IRE)** 12-1 **Adam Jones** Pu aft 4; lost action
[315ᴾ]	F		**Sagaville (IRE)** 12-1 **Richard Darke** Ld to 4; trckd ldr clsly til fell 13
	U		**Scarlet Rambler** 25-1 **R Bateman** Bckwd; 2 handlers; mist 1; ld 4-13; disp ld when ur nxt; rdr removed by air ambulance

OFFICIAL DISTANCES: 2l, 20l TIME: 6min 16.0s

652 Mixed Open (Div 1), 12st
8 ran

[263²]	1		**RIVER SWILLEY (IRE)** evensF **R Walford** Lw; hld up; went 2nd 13; ld 15; r.o wl u.p aft 2 out; drvn out
[403¹]	2	½	**Dangerous Guest (IRE)** 6-4 **Miss P Gundry** 3s-6/4; lw; swtng; hld up; prog to disp 4th 9; went 2nd 15; sust chall frm 2 out; ev ch last; no ex cl home; dism aft post
	3	25	**Bomba Charger** 8-1 **Richard Darke** Bit bckwd; midfield; 5th 13; lot to do 3 out; r.o to 3rd aft 2 out; stayed on but nt trble ldrs; btr for rce
[165²]	4	½	**Hold Your Ranks** 8-1 **D McKenna** Sn last; bhnd frm 11; t.o when mist 14; nrst fin
[537ᵁ]	5	30	**Romalito** 40-1 **Miss K Cook** In tch towards rr; 7th 11; fdd when pce qcknd frm 15; t.o
	6	12	**Bill Of Rights** 100-1 **D Luff** (xnb) Mounted on course; ld; jmpd lft; hdd 15; wknd qckly u.p
	P		**Alpine Music (IRE)** 50-1 **I Hambley** Went 3rd 5; prom til wknd 12; bhnd when pu 14
[534⁴]	P		**Darren The Brave** 33-1 **D Stephens (Devon)** Swtng; sn prom; chsd ldr to 13; cl 3rd 15-3 out; wknd; pu aft nxt; lame

OFFICIAL DISTANCES: nk, 16l TIME: 6min 05.0s

653 Mixed Open (Div 2), 12st
10 ran

[326²]	1		**MIZYAN (IRE)** 4-7F **Miss P Gundry** Lw; jw; handy; went 2nd 9; ld 13; prsd app last; qcknd game inside last 100yds
[454²]	2	1	**Hylters Chance** 7-1 **D Alers-Hankey** Lw; sn prom; pckd 4; went 3rd 9; trckd ldr frm 14 til slt mist 2 out; rallied on outer & ev ch last; nt qckn cl home
[316²]	3	3	**Rasta Man** 8-1 **R Woollacott** Hld up; went 3rd 15; tk 2nd 2 out; ev ch til wknd app last
	4	runin	**Lavalight** 12-1 **A Charles-Jones** 4th ½way; lost tch frm 14; t.o
[211ᴱ]	C		**Court Master (IRE)** 10-1 **D Borradaile** Midfield; pushed thro wing by loose horse 8
[405³ᵈ]	P		**Desert Run** 50-1 **Miss J West** Sn bhnd; t.o & pu 14
[557ᵁ]	R		**Mr Magnetic (IRE)** 10-1 **D Harvey** Lw; 8th when rn out 7
[252⁴]	P		**Robert's Toy (IRE)** (bl) 10-1 **N Harris** Chsd ldr til disp 6; lft in clr ld 7; clr 9; rdn 13; sn hdd & wknd; poor 5th when pu last
[403ᴾ]	P		**Southern Flight** 10-1 **G Maundrell** Settled 3rd; 20l 3rd when pu 9; bbv
[66³]	F		**Summit** 12-1 **Miss J Congdon** Chsd ldr til ld 4; cont at fast pce; jnd 6; fell hvly 7

OFFICIAL DISTANCES: ½l, 4l TIME: 5min 56.0s
Fence 14 omitted - injured rider

654 Intermediate, 12st
11 ran

[261¹]	1		**STONEY RIVER (IRE)** 11-10F **R Walford** Lw; trckd ldrs; went 2nd 14; duelled w 2nd & clr of rest frm 2 out; chall last; qcknd clr u.p flat
[448ᵁ]	2	2½	**Detroit Davy (IRE)** 7-2 **N Mitchell** 9s-7/2; prom; went 2nd 10; disp ld 12 til ld 14; slt ld til jnd last; hdd & no ex flat; gd eff
	3	20	**The Criosra** 25-1 **Miss T Newman** Midfield; 6th 11; r.o stdly to tk 3rd aft 2 out; nt trble ldrs
	4	2½	**Vansell** (5a) 7-1 **L Jefford** Lw; 2 handlers; chsd ldrs; 5th ½way; one pce & no imp frm 4 out
[404⁵]	5	3	**Lead Story** 5-1 **Richard Darke** Handy; cl 4th 10; cl up when blun bad 13; 10½l 3rd 16; no ch aft
[467²]	6	2½	**Brown Robber** (5x) 5-1 **T Dennis** (xnb) Ld to 3 & agn aft nxt; disp ld 12 til blun 14; wknd
[254ᴾ]	R		**Jo's Wedding** 50-1 **Miss S Gaisford** (xnb) Fractious padd; mounted on course; pulled hrd; ld aft 3; crashed thro wing 4
[558ᵁ]	P		**Just Mai-Bee** 50-1 **A Bateman** Sn towards rr; 8th & bhnd 10; t.o; pu & dism aft 12
	P		**Master Buckley** 12-1 **C White** Settled 7th; outpcd ½way; 7th & out of tch when pu 12
[310ᴾ]	P		**Walton Street** 33-1 **W Smith** Mists; sn trailing; wl bhnd frm 5 til pu 12

[404ᴾ] r **Young General** (bl) 14-1 **A Honeyball** *Lw; frightened by shattering plastic wing & ref 4*

OFFICIAL DISTANCES: 1l, 12l **TIME:** 5min 59.0s
Fences 11 (damaged) and 18 (injured rider) were omitted; the stewards enquired into the riding of Jo's Wedding which was out of control and had given trouble before; the owner's undertaking that a stronger jockey would be used in future was accepted

655 Open Maiden 56&7yo (Div 1), 12st   8 ran

[254²]	1	**JIMMY THE ONE (NZ)** 1-2F **C Heard** (xnb) *Opened evens; lw; chsd ldr til lft in ld 7; made rest; r.o str frm 2 out; pushed clr last; comf*
	2 5	**Wink And Whisper** (12a) 10-1 **R Young** *In tch; cl 4th ½way; gd hdwy to 2nd 16; prsd wnr til fdd app last; gd eff*
[254ᴾ]	3 4	**Butler Didit** (5a) 10-1 **N Harris** *Chsd ldrs; cl 4th 12; slt mist & rmdrs 14; lft 3rd 16; cl 3rd & ev ch til rdn & wknd aft 2 out*
[562ᴾ]	P	**Hayne Condor** 10-1 **S Kidston** *Tchd 16s; prom; 2l 2nd 9; cl up til bad mist 15; pu nxt; saddle slpd*
	P	**Mr Baloo** 17-2 **A Charles-Jones** *Towards rr til pu 8; school*
[535ᶠ]	P	**My Jess** (5a) 25-1 **M Shears** *Pu 3; steering problems*
[457ᴾ]	P	**Summer Pudding** (5a) 7-2 **Jeremy Young** *5s-7/2; ld & rcd v free; 20l clr 5; hanging bad but still clr when pu 7*
[407ᴾ]	U	**Tabula Rasa** 12-11 **M Foley** *Tchd 16s; towards rr; hdwy to cl 5th 9; went 2nd & gng wl 12; cl 3rd when blun & ur 16*

OFFICIAL DISTANCES: 6l, 10l **TIME:** 6min 24.0s
Wild Dream (Miss S Vickery 3-1) was withdrawn not under starter's orders - lame; Rule 4 deduction 20p in pound

656 Open Maiden 56&7yo (Div 2), 12st   12 ran

[339ᴾ]	1	**CREWMAN** 8-1 **M Munrowd** (xnb) *2 handlers; swtng; hdwy to jn ldrs 6; trckd ldr gng wl frm 12; lft in ld 15-16; prsd ldr til hrd rdn & lft in ld flat; prob lucky*
[540³]	2 2	**Wise Examiner (IRE)** 5-2 **Richard Darke** *Prom; cl 3rd mostly; slt mist 14; ld 16; 4l clr 2 out; 2l up last; veered sharp lft u.p flat; hdd & no ex cl home*
[540ᴾ]	3 40	**Frankies Flutter** 16-1 **D Doyne-Ditmas** *Prsd ldrs; jmpd rt 7 & caused fav to fall; cl 5th 11; lost tch 13; lft poor 3rd 16; no prog; pushed out for rem 3rd*
[539ᵁ]	4 4	**Bailey Gray** (5a) 16-1 **A Honeyball** *Mist 1; rr & jmpd lft; 7th 11; t.o 14; r.o stdly clsng stages; tk 4th app last; rdn out*
	P	**Birch Tor** 16-1 **J Cole** *Fractious padd; swtng; dwelt; sn last & jmpd hesnt; t.o 4 til pu 13*
	F	**Black Dante (IRE)** 5-4F **A Charles-Jones** *Tk keen hld; cl 5th when hmpd & fell 7*
[407ᴾ]	P	**Eskimo Gold** (5a) 10-1 **M Shears** *Chsd ldrs; blun 8; prom til wknd 13; lft 4th but no ch 16; poor 5th when pu last*
[145ᴾ]	U	**Highland Pearl** (5a) 25-1 **Adam Jones** *8th when mist & ur 3*
[204ᵁ]	P	**Kentlands Lad** (7a) 12-1 **G Richards** *A towards rr; 8th ½way; no prog; t.o & pu 14*
[536ᴾ]	P	**Media Luz** (5a) 33-1 **J Young** *Midfield; 6th 11; lost tch 12; t.o & pu 3 out*
[254ᴾ]	P	**Pachakutec (IRE)** 14-1 **R Woollacott** *Ld; jw; slt ld 13; still ld when mist 15; pu & qckly dism; broke leg; destroyed*
	P	**Solo Trip** (5a) 14-1 **J Barnes** *Sn trailing & jmpd slow; t.o frm 4 til pu 11*

OFFICIAL DISTANCES: 2l, 20l **TIME:** 6min 17.0s
Ashloch (N Harris 14-1) was withdrawn at start not under orders

657 Restricted (Div 1), 12st   7 ran

[311²]	1	**SWIFT VENTURE (IRE)** 8-1 **Richard Darke** *Trckd ldrs; prog on inner 12; went 2nd 14; str rn to chall aft 2 out; ld last; drvn out*
[539²]	2 2	**Woodland King** 4-1 **Mrs M Hand** *Jmpd bold; disp ld til ld 5; went 8l clr 3 out; hdd & one pce app last; kpt on; promising*
	3 30	**King's Courtier (IRE)** 11-2 **Jeremy Young** *Tk keen hld; wl in tch; disp 3rd 12; lost ground stdly frm 15; nt disg*
[331³]	4 3	**River Gala (IRE)** (bl) 9-2 **A Honeyball** *Trckd ldrs; 3rd ½way; outpcd 13; lost tch 15; btn 4th when blun 2 out*
[540ᵁ]	F	**Broad Ink** 33-1 **M Shears** *Sn prom; trckd ldr to 13; cl 3rd when fell 14; jmpd on by rival & inj*
[412¹]	B	**Kenny Davis (IRE)** evensF **P Blagg** *Hld up; prog 11; cl 4th & gng wl when bd 14*
	P	**Masked Martin** 25-1 **S Kidston** *Sn detach last; mist 9; t.o & pu 14*

OFFICIAL DISTANCES: 1½l, 25l **TIME:** 6min 06.0s

658 Restricted (Div 2), 12st
9 ran

[144³]	1		**PRIMERO (IRE)** (tt) 4-7F A Honeyball *Tchd 4/6; lw; jmpd lft; hld up in tch; hdwy but hmpd aft 12; ld aft 13; clr when bad mist 2 out; rec wl; comf*
[406⁴]	2	15	**Shameless Lady** (5a) 11-4 Richard Darke *Towards rr; hdwy 8; lft in ld brief aft 12; lost tch w ldr 3 out; clsd 2 out; no ex app last*
[541⁵]	3	1½fs	**Bedtime Pixie** 8-1 D Stephens (Devon) *Rr when mist 8; poor 4th & jmpd slow 14; rem 3rd when climbed fncs frm 3 out; drvn & reluct flat*
	4	4	**Aadann (IRE)** 50-1 L Tibbatts *Ld/disp; hit 9; wknd & lost plce 12; tired 4th frm 15; jmpd slow clsng stages; rdn out*
[540⁵]	U		**Amazing Hill (IRE)** 50-1 Mrs R Morris *7th when blun & ur 6*
	P		**Bird** (5a) 25-1 Mrs M Hand *Sn wl bhnd; t.o & pu 7; school*
[539ᵖ]	P		**Lucky Coombe** 20-1 W Smith *Mist 1; prom til lost plce 10; 5th when pu 12*
[562³]	U		**Saucy's Wolf** 25-1 Jeremy Young *5th when blun & ur 7*
	P		**The Grey Friar** 33-1 J Barnes *Disp 5 til jmpd to ld 10; 4l clr aft 11; pu imm aft 12; broke leg; destroyed*

OFFICIAL DISTANCES: 10l, dist   TIME: 6min 08.0s

Eglinton
Lanark (RH 8F,18J) Sun, 19 Mar (GOOD, GOOD to SOFT in places)

659 Hunt
4 ran

[359ᵁ]	1		**TURSAL (IRE)** 7-4JF A Campbell *Ld/disp; jmpd lft & hdd 9; ld aft 11; 2l up when mist 13; qcknd agn 15; 2l up 3 out; mist last; kpt on wl u.p*
[423⁶]	2	3	**Good Profit** (bl) 7-1 T Davidson *Trckd ldng pr; disp 3l 3rd 6; ld 10; hdd aft 11; cl 2nd til outpcd & 5l down app 3 out; 1½l 2nd & rdn 2 out; ev ch last; eased cl home*
[493ᵖ]	3	6	**Mr Fudge** 5-2 P Lentelink *7/2-5/2; ld/disp; ½l up 4; 1l 2nd nxt; cl up til 10l 3rd & outpcd 13; stdy prog to 6l 3rd app 3 out-last; kpt on*
	P		**Strong Debate (IRE)** 7-4JF N Crookston *Trckd ldng pr; disp 4l 3rd 6; outpcd aft 11; 8l off pce & mist nxt; 15l 4th & wkng 14; pu 15*

OFFICIAL DISTANCES: 2½l, 6l   TIME: 6min 59.0s

660 Confined, 12st
8 ran

[420²]	1		**POYNDER PARK (IRE)** 2-1 L Morgan *In tch in rr early; 5l 4th 5; prog 10; ld app 12; 2l up when mist 14; hdd 2 out; ld agn last; r.o u.p*
[359⁵]	2	¾	**Midsummer Glen (IRE)** 13-8F Miss M Bremner *Lw; in tch in rr; 11l 5th 8; prog to trck ldr 12; 1l down 15; ld & hit 2 out; hdd & blun last; no ex flat; eased cl home*
[110³]	3	20	**Fordstown (IRE)** 11-2 J Alexander *(bf) 6s-11/2; prom til jmpd slow 5; mist 6; 12l off pce 8; 6th & pushed along 11; 11l 4th 14; kpt on; tk poor 3rd app last*
[493³]	4	10	**Dear Do** (5x) 7-2 Miss M Neill *Trckd ldrs; 2l 2nd 4; 8l 3rd 7; prog 12; cl 3rd & hit 15; 1l down 3 out; wknd qckly app nxt; fin lame*
[495⁵]	5	1½fs	**Willy Wee (IRE)** 20-1 R Westwood *Oht; ld/disp; 2l up 2; 2nd nxt; ½l 2nd 6; wknd 12 & sn bhnd; 40l 6th 15; completed in own time*
[419⁵]	r		**Branch End** 16-1 F Arthur *A rr; 15l last 8; jmpd lft nxt; 12l 7th 10; lost tch aft; t.o when ref 13*
[492ᵖ]	P		**Dari (IRE)** (tt) 25-1 D Jewett *Lw; oht; chsd ldrs; 5l 5th 4; 12l off pce 8; 15l last 10; strugg & pu aft nxt*
[183ᵖ]	P		**Thinkaboutthat (IRE)** 12-1 J Muir *Trckd ldrs; 2½l 3rd 4; ld nxt; ½l up 6; ld/disp aft til hdd app 12; 25l 5th & wkng 15; t.o & pu 2 out*

OFFICIAL DISTANCES: ½l, 25l   TIME: 6min 36.0s

661 Ladies Open
12 ran

[494²]	1		**RIPARIUS (USA)** 1-2F Miss P Robson *A handy; hdwy to disp 11 2nd 11; 2l 2nd 15; disp ld 3 out til jmpd to ld last; r.o u.p flat*
[361¹]	2	1½	**Nova Nita** (5a) 2-1 Mrs V Jackson *Mid-div; squeezed & hit marker post bef 9; hdwy to disp ld 10; ld aft nxt; jmpd to ld 3 out til hdd last; no ex flat*
[494ᵁ]	3	15	**Rallegio** 12-1 Mrs A Hamilton *Mid-div; prog to trck ldrs 10; outpcd aft nxt; hdwy aft 15 & in tch 3 out; stayed on; nt trble ldrs*
[494⁵]	4	nk	**Oat Couture** 14-1 Miss S Johnstone *Rr; 15l last 4; 10l last 12; 15l 9th 15; stayed on aft nxt; fin wl*
[492⁴]	5	nk	**Nosmo King (IRE)** (bl) 14-1 Miss L Kendall *(bf) Rr; mist 3; 10l 9th app 9; prog to chse ldrs 11; outpcd aft 15; stayed on one pce*
[421ᵁ]	6	½	**Steel Rigg** 20-1 Miss C Hall *In tch; mist 6; prog to trck ldrs 11; outpcd aft 15; stayed on one pce*
[494⁶]	7	15	**Dashmar** 33-1 Miss R Barrow *Prom; 2l 2nd aft 4; outpcd 13; 10l 9th aft 14; lsng tch aft*

	8	3	**Pennine View** 25-1 **Miss M Bremner** (bf) Prom; 11 2nd 7; lft in ld 8; jnd nxt til 4l 5th 13; outpcd aft; wl bhnd 2 out
		P	**Bavington** 33-1 **Mrs E Reed** Prom early; 11 2nd 4; rr nxt; 15l last 6; mist 8 & 20l down aft; pu nxt
[421ᴾ]		P	**Madame Bella** (5a) 25-1 **Miss J Hollands** Prom; ld 4; 11 up 7; pu bef nxt; inj
[421ᴾ]		P	**Mirror Melody** (5a) (tt) 33-1 **Mrs M Robinson** (bf)Swtng; prom; 3l 3rd 5; ld/disp aft 8-13; hdd & outpcd 14; grad lost tch; t.o & pu last
[494ᴾ]		P	**No Problem Jac** (5a) (bl,tt) 20-1 **Miss L Hislop** In tch; prog to 3l 4th 14; 4l 3rd nxt; wknd qckly aft; t.o & pu 2 out

OFFICIAL DISTANCES: 2l, 10l, nk **TIME:** 6min 37.0s

662 Mens Open
5 ran

[225⁴]	1		**SNAPPER** 9-4 **J Walton** Trckd ldng pr; 3l 3rd 3; went 4l 2nd aft 15; prsd ldr 3 out; ld nxt; qcknd & 6l up at last; rdly
	2	8	**Castleroyal (IRE)** 11-8F **D Jewett** (bf) Oht; swtng; ld; 2l up 13; 4l clr 14-15; hrd prsd 3 out; hdd bef nxt; rdn & rmdrs but no imp
	3	15	**Cyborgo (FR)** 5-2 **J Mactaggart** (xnb) Trckd ldr; 11 2nd 5-6; 4l 2nd 14; 6l 3rd nxt; sn one pce; 10l 3rd 2 out; 20l down app last
		P	**Boss Morton (IRE)** 20-1 **J Alexander** (bf) A rr; sn outpcd; jmpd lft 3; 15l 5th 4; jmpd lft 6; 20l last 7; sn t.o; mist 10; jmpd lft nxt; pu aft 12
		P	**Kalajo** 11-1 **T Oates** (bf) Swtng; oht; in tch mostly 4th; rmdrs aft 12; 12l 4th & mist nxt; climbed 12; sn lost tch; 30l down when pu 3 out; lkd sore

OFFICIAL DISTANCES: 12l, 20l **TIME:** 6min 38.0s

663 Restricted, 12st
8 ran

[360ᴾ]	1		**LORD LEVI (IRE)** 20-1 **A Robson** Cl up; 2½l 4th app 9; ld aft 15; 11 up at last; drifted lft flat; all out; won by nk; dem to 2nd; subsq reinstated
[363¹]	2	nk	**Wills Perk (IRE)** (12a) 8-11F **T Oates** Hld up in rr; mist 3; jmpd into rival nxt; 6l 8th 4; 4l last 11; prog to 5l 4th 15 & 11 2nd at last; kpt on; nt clr rn flat; fin nk 2nd; awarded rce on day; decision subsq overturned
[499¹]	3	4	**Shay Gap (IRE)** 11-4 **C Storey** (xnb) Rr; bumped by rival 2; mist nxt; 4l 6th 8; 5l 4th 11; ld/disp frm 15; 11 down 3 out; outpcd; stayed on
[424ᶠ]		F	**Derring Dan** 25-1 **Miss H Gray** Cl 3rd mostly til ld aft 11; hdd & outpcd 15; 8l 4th app 3 out; wknd qckly; nrly fnce bhnd & exhaust when ploughed last & fell; winded
[360ᴾ]		P	**Flower Of Dunblane** (5a) 20-1 **R Morgan** Oht; trckd ldr; 2l 2nd 8; outpcd 12; wknd aft; wl bhnd when pu last
[498⁴]		P	**Mini Cruise** 7-1 **M Williams** Ld/disp til 2l up 8; 11 ahd 10; hdd aft nxt; outpcd & lsng tch 13; pu 3 out; rdr inj
		P	**Regar (IRE)** 14-1 **D Jewett** Oht; in tch in rr; 8l off pce 6; 12l last when jmpd slow 12; pu aft nxt
		P	**Rock On Bud (IRE)** 12-1 **Miss R Barrow** (xnb) Ld/disp; 2l 2nd 8; 11 down 10; hit 11 & outpcd nxt; 10l 7th 13; pu sn aft

OFFICIAL DISTANCES: ½l, 4l **TIME:** 6min 43.0s
Lord Levi finished 1st but following an objection by the second for 'taking my ground after the last' and a stewards enquiry the placings were reversed; this decision was later overturned by the Jockey Club Disciplinary Committee

664 Open Maiden 56&7yo, 2m5f, 12st - 14J
15 ran

[499ᴾ]	1		**EASTLANDS TWILIGHT** 5-1 **T Morrison** (bf) In tch; 6l 5th app 12; gd hdwy to chall 2 out; ld last; stayed on
[45⁵]	2	2	**Farebit** (5a) 3-1 **C Storey** (xnb) In tch in rr; prog 6; ld 9; 2l up 12; 11 up 3 out; jnd nxt; hrd rdn & hdd last; no ex flat
	3	25	**Guy Mornay** 14-1 **T Davidson** 2 handlers; rr; stdy prog aft 12; tk poor 3rd flat; nvr nrr
	4	6	**Chubby Morton** 25-1 **A Richardson** In tch in rr; hmpd 3; prog & lft 20l 4th 12; nd; 10l 3rd 3 out; kpt on; no ex; dem flat
		P	**Bonnie B** (5a) 10-1 **P Strang Steel** V unruly padd; school; 25l last aft 1; fnce bhnd 4; pu aft 6
[501ᶠ]		P	**Carrie's Gift** (bl) 14-1 **S Hughes** (pricker ns) Swtng; mid-div; wknd 11; bhnd aft 12; dist 5th when pu 2 out
		F	**Coastley Lane** (7a) 10-1 **Miss C Hall** In tch in rr when fell 3; rdr inj
		B	**Dunston Ace** 8-1 **J R Barlow** Unruly padd; oht; swtng; prom early; in tch in 5th 2; 2nd 8 til bd 11
[500ᶠ]		F	**Juinevera (IRE)** (12a) 4-1 **T Oates** Prom; 5l 3rd 3; 4l 3rd when fell 11
[499ᶠ]		B	**Poppers** 20-1 **R Nichol** Trckd ldr; 4l 2nd 2; wkng 10; bd nxt; rdr inj
[425ᶠ]		P	**Shenoso** (12a) 12-1 **R Robinson** Tubed; hdstrng in rr; strugg aft 5; t.o 7; pu 9

[363ᴾ]	B	**Speckles (IRE)** (5a) (bl) 12-1 L Morgan *Prom early; 4l 7th 8; rdn aft nxt; in tch when bd 11*
[501ᵁ]	F	**The Dust Buster** 20-1 H Trotter *Rr; prog when fell 11*
	P	**Tipsy Laird (IRE)** 6-4F R Morgan *7/4-6/4; ld; 4l up 2; hdd 9; 2l ahd agn 11; mist & hdd 12; 5l 2nd aft; pu qckly & dism app nxt*
[499ᴾ]	P	**Wheresbob** 5-1 D Jewett *A rr; sn t.o; 25l down when pu 8*

OFFICIAL DISTANCES: 2l, 25l, 6l **TIME:** 5min 56.0s
Fence 10 omitted - fallen rider

665 Open Maiden   11 ran

[498²]	1		**HEY CHIEF (IRE)** 2-1 P Strang Steel *Mid-div; 8l 5th 6; 6l off pce 11; prog aft 15 to 3rd 3 out; disp ld nxt; ld last; rmdrs flat & swished tail; kpt on*
[364³]	2	1	**Gallant Major** 6-1 A Robson *A.p; 2½l 3rd 4; 3l 2nd 11; prog to disp ld 2 out; hdd & mist last; no ex flat*
[365³]	3	1	**Myles Of Moss (IRE)** (5a) 20-1 D Reid *Rr early; sn mid-div; prog 8 to 3l 2nd at 10; ld 12; 8l ahd 15; hdd 2 out; outpcd app last; kpt on & clsng flat*
[492³]	4	3	**Kaz Kalem (IRE)** 7-4F S Hughes *(xnb,bf) 2s-7/4; swtng; rr; 20l off pce 8; prog aft 11; 4l 3rd 15-nxt; drvn & no resp; 6l down app last*
	5	1	**Tweed Brig** 10-1 R Morgan *(xnb,boh) 2 handlers; rr; some prog to mid-div til outpcd 12; bhnd 15; kpt on wl aft*
[364³]	6	25	**Bold Irene (IRE)** (5a) 25-1 L Morgan *Prom early; 4l 4th 9; outpcd 14; wknd nxt; t.o 2 out*
[363³]	7	30	**Meadowleck** (5a) 20-1 T Davidson *(bf) Swtng; ld; 2l up app 5; 10l up 8; hdd & wknd 11; sn bhnd; 25l down 15; t.o*
[497ᴾ]	P		**Border Country** 20-1 Miss M Bremner *Prom early; 2l 2nd 4; chsd ldr frm 6; 10l 2nd 8; wknd 11; sn t.o; 30l down 15; pu 16*
[497ᴾ]	P		**House Of Oasis (IRE)** 8-1 D Jewett *Chsd ldrs til outpcd 13; sn strugg; wl bhnd when pu 2 out*
[526ᴾ]	U		**Jock** 14-1 J R Barlow *Ur padd; mid-div; hmpd & ur 5*
	P		**Steel Brae (IRE)** (5a) 10-1 A Richardson *Rr & a fluent; 10l last 4; bad mist 7; blun 9; detach 10; veered lft & pulled herself up aft 11*

OFFICIAL DISTANCES: 1½l, nk, 2l **TIME:** 6min 57.0s

South Herefordshire
Garnons (LH 7F,18J) Sun, 19 Mar (GOOD to FIRM)

666 Hunt, 12st   4 ran

[450³]	1		**WONASTOW** 5-2 A Wintle *(xnb) A.p; went 2nd 9; ld 12-14; ld app 3 out; sn 5l clr; comf*
[484ᴾ]	2	5	**Who's Your Man (IRE)** 11-10F Miss E Jones *Lw; ld to 5; ld 7-12 & 14 til drvn & hdd app 3 out; r.o one pce*
[448ᴾ]	3	runin	**Roscoes Dinky** (5a) 2-1 F Windsor Clive *Lw; mist 2; ld 5-7; 2nd to 9; rdn 11; wknd qckly 15; t.o*
	r		**Sea Patrol** (6ow) (bl) 25-1 R Pike *Mist 4; jmpd v slow & lost tch 6; 20l 4th when ref 7*

OFFICIAL DISTANCES: 5l, dist **TIME:** not taken

667 Confined, 12st - 17J   9 ran

[445³]	1		**LA KABYLE (FR)** (5a) 4-1 A Wintle *(xnb) 2nd when hit 1; 5l 4th ½way; 4½l 5th by-passing 14; went 2nd app 2 out; ld rdng; rdn clr flat; settled much btr for this rdr*
	2	6	**Verulam (IRE)** 6-1 Julian Pritchard *(xnb) Lw; ld til hdd last; rdn & one pce flat*
	3	3½	**Kingsthorpe** 4-1 S Joynes *Swtng; hld up; 6l 5th ½way; hdwy 13; 2l 3rd 15; went 3l 2nd app 3 out; one pce*
	4	7	**Cwm Bye** 20-1 M Hammond *(bf) Prom; went 2nd 7 til mist 11; hit 12; went 2nd agn 14 til app 3 out; wknd 2 out*
[68⁵]	5	8	**Rootsman (IRE)** 10-1 T Stephenson *Hld up & sev posns; 8l 7th ½way; 7l 7th by-passing 14; short-lived eff 15; sn wknd*
[533²]	6	10	**Elwill Glory (IRE)** 9-2 M Rodda *Swtng; tde; went 2nd aft 1-7; 4l 3rd ½way; lft 2nd 11 til 4l 4th by-passing 14; rdn & wknd 15*
	7	25	**Rustic Gent** 33-1 C Weaver *Chsd ldrs; 7l 6th ½way; 6l 6th & rdn by-passing 14; sn wknd; t.o & wknd pu 15*
[445²]	F		**Basil Street (IRE)** 5-2F D Mansell *Hld up; 6th when fell 3*
	P		**Persona Pride** 25-1 R Hodges *2 handlers; a bhnd; mist 6; blun 7; 9l 8th & rmdrs ½way; lost tch 11; t.o & pu 15*

OFFICIAL DISTANCES: 6l, 4l **TIME:** 6min 19.6s
Fence 14 omitted - damaged

668 Ladies Open
5 ran

	1		**HAUGHTON LAD (IRE)** 20-1 Miss A Nolan *Hld up; 7l 4th ½way; went 3rd 11 & 2nd 14; ev ch 15; btn whn lft wl clr last*
[476⁸]	2	30	**Wolfie Smith** 33-1 Miss W Houldey *Jmpd slow 4; 10l 5th ½way; lost tch 12; wl bhnd 14; snatched poor 2nd nr fin*
	3	hd	**Rap Up Fast (USA)** 4-1 Miss A Dare *Lw; ld 2-12; 7l 3rd 15; sn wknd; lft poor 2nd last; dem nr fin*
[447ᵖ]	P		**Miss Ondee (FR)** (5a) 25-1 Miss E Jones *Hld up; jnd ldrs 5; lost plce & drvn along 8; went 6l 3rd ½way; mist & lost plce 11; bhnd whn pu 12*
[397¹]	U		**Pharare (IRE)** 1-4F Miss C Spearing *Ld to 2; w ldr & outj 7; 2nd til ld 12; went 4l clr 3 out; drawing away when mist & event ur last*

OFFICIAL DISTANCES: dist, 1l   TIME: 6min 15.9s

669 Restricted, 12st
12 ran

	1		**PLAYING THE FOOL** (5a) 12-1 S Gordon-Watson *Ww; 8l 7th ½way; 10l 6th 14; gd hdwy 15; went 2nd app 2 out; ld last; r.o wl*
[261²]	2	3½	**Percy Medlicott** evensF Julian Pritchard *2nd when blun 1; settled mid-div; 7l 6th ½way; 7l 5th 14; eff when mist 3 out; sn hrd rdn; r.o flat; went 2nd nr fin*
[445ᵖ]	3	hd	**Paddy Maguire (IRE)** (bl) 10-1 T Stephenson *A.p; ld 6; went 3l clr 14-3 out; hdd last; rdn & no ex flat*
[336³]	4	4	**Holmby Copse** 5-1 T Humphrey *A.p; went 2nd 7-9; 2l 3rd ½way; 6l 4th 12; went 3l 2nd 14-15; one pce 2 out*
[450¹]	5	6	**Maid O'Tully (IRE)** (5a) 6-1 R Hodges *Went 2nd aft 1-7; chsd ldr 9-14; 3l 2nd when mist 15; ev ch app 2 out; wknd last*
[337¹]	6	7	**Bid For Tools (IRE)** (bl) 25-1 G Barfoot-Saunt *Ld to 6; 2½l 4th ½way; 5l 3rd & rdn 12; 6l 4th 14; wknd app 3 out*
[451¹]	7	10	**Rash-Gale (IRE)** (5a) 12-1 R Burton *Nd; mist 8; 9l 8th ½way; 13l 8th 14; wl bhnd 3 out*
	F		**Another Wag** (5a) 6-1 S Lloyd *Hld up; mist 4; 6l 5th ½way; fell 10*
[392ᵖ]	U		**Camogue Bridge (IRE)** (bl) 25-1 N Oliver *10th when blun & ur 5*
[341ᵖ]	P		**Di's Dream** (5a) 25-1 M Rodda *Hld up; mist 7; 12l 11th ½way; lost tch 12; 18l 9th 14; t.o & pu 3 out*
[339ᵖ]	P		**Lord Rymax** 20-1 D Mansell *(xnb) Swtng; hld up; 10l 9th ½way; eff & 9l 6th 12; 11l 7th & rdn 14; sn wknd; wl bhnd when pu 2 out*
[428ᵖ]	P		**Silly Boy** (7a) 25-1 R Barrett *School in rr; jmpd slow 3; 11l 10th ½way; wl bhnd 12; t.o & pu last*

OFFICIAL DISTANCES: 4l, hd   TIME: 6min 29.0s

670 Mens Open, 12st
6 ran

[476²]	1		**CELTIC TOWN** 11-2 P Kay *Ld 4-6; 2l 4th ½way; went 2nd 12-14; outpcd in 7l 4th 3 out; rallied u.p 2 out; went 2nd app last; ld flat; r.o wl*
	2†	3	**Topical Tip (IRE)** 6-1 P Cowley *Went 2nd 4; ld 6-9 & aft 11-14; 3l 2nd 3 out; kpt on*
[446²]	2†	s hd	**Stormhill Recruit** 7-1 S Blackwell *Hld up; went ½l 2nd 9; ld 10 til hdd aft 11; ld 14; 3l clr 3 out; sn hrd rdn; hdd & no ex flat*
[445¹]	4	1½	**Happy Minstral (USA)** 7-4F R Burton *Ld til hdd aft 1; lft in ld 2; hdd 4; lost plce 6; hit 8; 2½l 5th ½way; rdn along 12; 9l 5th 3 out; stayed on one pce*
[345³]	5	½	**True Fortune** (7x) 9-4 M Barber *Hld up; went 3rd 7; lost plce & 3½l 6th ½way; rallied & 2nd brief 14; 5l 3rd 3 out; one pce*
[598²]	6	runin	**Circus Colours** (7x) 20-1 L Hicks *Ld aft 1 til jmpd v slow 2; ld 9-10; 2nd/3rd til rdn 14; nt r.o; 15l 6th 3 out; t.o*

OFFICIAL DISTANCES: 3l, d ht   TIME: 6min 31.2s

671 Dodson & Horrell PPORA Club Members, 12st
4 ran

[388²]	1		**DAWN INVADER (IRE)** 2-5F Julian Pritchard *Made all; 15l clr 5; stdd ½way; qcknd 14; blun 15; drew wl clr 3 out; unchall*
[480ᵖ]	2	25	**Distant-Port (IRE)** 4-1 T Stephenson *Chsd wnr to 8; 7l 3rd ½way; went 6l 2nd aft 15; no imp 3 out; eased when btn flat*
[484³]	3	3	**Saywhen** 6-1 S Blackwell *Hit 6; went 12l 2nd 8; w wnr when mists 12 & 13; 4l 2nd when hit 14 & 15; sn wknd*
[389⁴]	4	5	**Major Bugler (IRE)** 14-1 S Bush *Wl bhnd frm 7*

OFFICIAL DISTANCES: 25l, 3l   TIME: 6min 16.9s

672 Open Maiden 56&7yo (Div 1), 2m4f, 12st - 15J
14 ran

| [471⁴] | 1 | | **WINNING TOWN** 7-1 Miss S Talbot *Ld 4-9; ld 10 til hdd aft 3 out; rallied flat; ld nr fin* |

[124²]	2	½	**Tom's Prize** (7a) 6-4F **S Joynes** A.p; 4l 3rd ½way; went 2nd 10; ld aft 3 out til hdd & mist last; lft in ld flat; hdd nr fin
[450²]	3	6	**Idlewild (IRE)** (7a) 4-1 **Julian Pritchard** Hld up; hdwy & 7l 5th ½way; went 4l 3rd 11 & 2nd app 2 out; ld & hit last; hung lft & hdd flat; nt r.o
[568³]	4	2	**Fanion De Nourry (FR)** (7a) 7-1 **L Hicks** A.p; 5l 4th ½way; 6½l 5th 11; one pce 3 out
	5	3	**Call Me Bertie** 25-1 **S Lloyd** (xnb) Hld up & sn bhnd; 17l 9th ½way; 16l 7th 11; stayed on frm 3 out; nvr nr to chall
	6	25	**Irish Kinsman** 20-1 **M Gregory** Chsd ldrs; 11l 6th ½way; wknd & 18l 8th 11; blun 12; sn t.o
[451³]	7	5	**New Yorker (USA)** (7a) (bl,tt) 10-1 **M Rodda** A bhnd; 20l 10th 11; 26l 11th 11; t.o
[451³]	P		**Cedor Hicks** (5a) 25-1 **M Trott** Hmpd 2; wl bhnd 6; 30l 12th ½way; t.o & pu 11
	P		**Heathyard's Flight** 20-1 **A Price** Ld to 4; 2nd til ld 9; hdd 10; 6l 4th nxt; wknd 12; bhnd when pu 3 out
	P		**Jims Flossy** (5a) 20-1 **N Oliver** Blun 4; wl bhnd when pu 5
[341ᵁ]	U		**Magni Momenti** (12a) 7-1 **A Wintle** Swtng; a bhnd; 25l 11th ½way; 22l 10th 11; t.o when blun & ur 3 out
[472ᶠ]	P		**Miss Molly** (5a) 20-1 **R Burton** Hld up; 11½l 7th ½way; wknd & 21l 9th 11; t.o & pu 2 out
	P		**No Quibble** (5a) 20-1 **J Owen** Hld up; jmpd slow 2; 12l 8th ½way; 12l 6th & no hdwy 11; bhnd when pu 3 out; lame; removed by horse ambulance
	P		**Once Is Enough** (12a,0w) 20-1 **M Hammond** A bhnd; 31l 13th ½way; t.o & pu aft 10

OFFICIAL DISTANCES: ½l, 1l TIME: 5min 23.0s

673 Open Maiden 56&7yo (Div 2), 2m4f, 12st - 15J   16 ran

	1		**CEAD MILE FAILTE** (7a) 12-1 **F Windsor Clive** Hld up; 10l 8th ½way; hdwy 10; lft 4l 3rd nxt; lft in ld 12; qcknd 6l clr 3 out; just hld on
[341³]	2	½	**Yanto** (7a) 5-1 **Julian Pritchard** Lw; hld up; 8l 6th ½way; hdwy & 6l 5th 11; lft 3l 2nd nxt; sn outpcd; str chall flat; r.o; stayed on
[616ᴿ]	3	6	**Catechist (IRE)** (7a) 20-1 **A Evans** Hld up; 9l 7th ½way; 10l 8th 11; lft 7l 5th nxt; stayed on frm 3 out; went 10l 3rd last; nvr able to chall
	4	5	**Bonny (GER)** (5a) 11-2 **A Wintle** Sn outpcd & bhnd; 17l 10th ½way; hdwy & 11l 9th 11; lft 6l 4th nxt; went 10l 3rd app 3 out; one pce
[22⁵]	5	nk	**Missmass** (5a) 6-1 **T Stephenson** (xnb) Swtng; ld to 3; 5l 4th ½way; 7l 6th 11; lft 4l 3rd nxt; no ex 3 out
	6	runin	**Wee Kelpie** (5a) 20-1 **K Burke** (xnb) A wl bhnd; t.o 7
			Calys Halo (7a) 12-1 **T Lane** (xnb,martin) Pulled hrd; mist 1; jnd ldrs 4; ld 5-10; 2l 3rd when blun 11; wknd rap; wl bhnd when pu 3 out
[569ᴾ]	S		**Dealer Boy (IRE)** (bl) 12-1 **L Hicks** Prom; went 2nd 5-9; wkng when slpd up flat aft 10
[569ʳ]	r		**Far Forest** (vis) 14-1 **R Hodges** Lw; prom til jmpd v slow 4; v reluct to rce aft 6; t.o when ref 8
	P		**Foxley Lad** 6-1 **D Mansell** (xnb,bf) 2 handlers; bckwd; hld up & bhnd; 13l 9th ½way; eff & 9l 7th 11; lft 9l 6th & rdn nxt; sn wknd; t.o & pu last
	F		**Hottentot** (5a) 5-1 **S Bush** Swtng; ld 4-5; 2l 3rd when fell 7
[527ᵁ]	P		**Loch Ash** 16-1 **R Burton** 2 handlers; oht; swtng; a wl bhnd; t.o 8; pu 12
[450ᶠ]	F		**Marauder (IRE)** (bl) 20-1 **S Blackwell** Hld up; hdwy & 6l 5th ½way; went 2nd 9 til fell 12
	F		**One Mans Legacy** (5a) 12-1 **S Joynes** Hld up; 7½l 6th when fell 6
[478ᶠ]	U		**Penny Appeal** (5a) 25-1 **M Scales** Mists 1 & 5; bhnd til hmpd & ur 7
[273³]	F		**Presuming Ed (IRE)** 2-1F **A Price** 2nd til ld 3; hdd 4; 2l 3rd ½way; ld 10 til fell 12

OFFICIAL DISTANCES: nk, 5l TIME: 5min 22.6s

Southdown & Eridge
Rodmell (LH 7F,19J) Sun, 19 Mar (GOOD to FIRM)

674 Hunt   2 ran

	1		**EASTERS EVE** (5a) 9-4 **D Evatt** Pulled hrd; oft jb rt; crawled rnd und iron grip; rdr's 100th wnr
[305ᴾ]	U		**Just Try Me (IRE)** (tt) 4-11F **P Hall** Jmpd sticky 1; ur 2

OFFICIAL DISTANCE: Finished alone TIME: 8min 00.0s TOTE: £1.70

675 Dodson & Horrell PPORA Club Members Restricted, 12st   5 ran

[546⁹]	1		**WHITE SMOKE (IRE)** 6-1 **R Ross** 3rd til 2nd 7; ld 12; 8l clr nxt; 12l ahd 16; hrd prsd 2 out; jnd last; forged nr fin

[554³]	2	1	**Baron Allfours** 6-4F **P Millington** *(citation)* Settled last pr to 12; eff & nt fluent 14; pckd 15; went 12l 2nd nxt; clsd & 11 down 2 out; drew level last; outpcd cl home
[289⁴]	3	25	**Mosta (IRE)** (5a) 9-2 **P Bull** Hld up in tch; outpcd when wnr qcknd aft 13; 15l 3rd 2 out
[285⁶]	4	10	**Nattico (IRE)** 14-1 **Miss S Gladders** Jmpd rt; pckd 9; ld to 12; 4th & strugg 15; 25l last 2 out
[416³]	U		**Ishma (IRE)** (bl) 5-2 **D Page** Hit 3 & 4; chsd ldr to 7; last by 12; strugg when mist & ur 15

OFFICIAL DISTANCE: 1½l **TIME:** 6min 26.0s **TOTE:** £4.10; places £1.90,£1.20 **DF:** £6.60

676 Confined, 12st
8 ran

[462³]	1		**THATS DEDICATION (IRE)** (3x) (tt) 4-5F **D Robinson** Spurs; lw; hacking towards rr; lft 6th & impeded 10; went 6l 3rd aft 13; 12l 4th 15; rallied & 5l 4th 2 out; stayed on uphill; passed both v unwilling ldrs nr fin
[308ᴾ]	2	nk	**Parson's Way** (vis) 16-1 **C Gordon** Nrly a 2nd/3rd til ld 14; blun nxt; rdn 2l clr 2 out; lkd wnr til stpd to climb last; reluct & hdd nr fin
[572ᴾ]	3	1½	**Celtic Spark** (3x) (vis) 7-2 **D Dunsdon** Hit 6; ld; 10l clr 9; blun 12; made nrly all to 14; prsng ldr when hit 16 & nxt; hrd rdn & ev ch last; wknd nr fin
[572ᴾ]	4	6	**Daddy Long Leggs** (6ow) 33-1 **R Hubbard** Midfield & in tch to 13; 16l 5th & wkng 15; plugged on frm 2 out but rdr no help
	5	12	**Peafield (IRE)** 9-2 **D Dennis** Midfield; jmpd v slow 13; went 10l 3rd 15; eff & 4l 3rd 2 out; outpcd app last
[575⁶]	6	3	**Bit Of A Do** (tt) 33-1 **D Slattery** Bhnd; in tch to 13; 20l 6th & strugg 15; plodded on
	P		**African Jazz (GER)** 10-1 **B Hitchcott** Pulled hrd; went prom 3; ld brief 6; prom til 5th & wkng aft 13; 30l last 2 out; t.o & pu 2 out
[674ᵁ]	F		**Just Try Me (IRE)** (tt) 33-1 **P Hall** 2nd outing; settled in last trio til fell 10

OFFICIAL DISTANCES: nk, 11 **TIME:** 6min 21.0s **TOTE:** £1.90; places £1.10,£2.60,£1.60 **DF:** £14.20

677 Ladies Open
5 ran

[287²]	1		**YOUNG NIMROD** (tt) 5-4F **Miss C Grissell** Lw; ld aft 2; made nrly all aft; drew clr aft 2 out; easy
[128ᴾ]	2	25	**Velka** (5a) 6-1 **Miss P Ellison** Mist 3; ld brief 6; 4l 2nd & mist 10; 5l 2nd 2 out; fdd uphill app last
[128ᴿ]	3	½	**Professor Page (IRE)** 11-2 **Miss J Grant** Ld to 2; 5l 3rd 10; 7l 3rd 15; outpcd & mist nxt; 17l 3rd 2 out; plugged on & nrly snatched 2nd
[128ᴾ]	4	40	**Red Channel (IRE)** 8-1 **Miss P Bryan-Brown** Drpd out last mostly; 11l down 10; 22l last 15; mist nxt; sn t.o
[512⁴]	S		**Cill Churnain (IRE)** 5-2 **Mrs E Coveney** Unruly; hrd hld; 4l last 8; slpd up aft 9

OFFICIAL DISTANCES: 20l, ½l **TIME:** 6min 17.0s **TOTE:** £2.60; places £1.10,£2.50 **DF:** £5.90

678 Mens Open, 12st
4 ran

[511³]	1		**PRINCE OF SAINTS (IRE)** (7x) (bl) 5-2 **A Sansome** Prsd ldr frm 4; ld & hit 2 out; rdn clr app last
[415ᴾ]	2	20	**Veryvel (CZE)** 7-4F **D Kemp** Made most; jmpd slow 12; hit 15; hdd 2 out; no ex app last
	3	25	**Lake Of Loughrea (IRE)** 6-1 **N Wilson (Hants)** Sn last & out of tch; hit 11; 15l adrift 13; made no eff to cl
[572⁴]	R		**Galaroi (IRE)** (7x) (tt) 3-1 **D Robinson** Spurs; cl up til rn out & ur 4

OFFICIAL DISTANCES: 8l, 12l **TIME:** 6min 23.0s **TOTE:** £4.00 **DF:** £4.20

679 Open Maiden, 12st
10 ran

[220ᴾ]	1		**TIDAL REEF (IRE)** 10-1 **C Gordon** Jmpd rt at times; hld up 2nd/4th; 9l 4th 15; clsd to 2l 2nd 2 out; ld last; rdn clr
[578⁵]	2	4	**Mister Chips** 7-2 **P Bull** Settled midfield; lft 2nd 10 aft chapter of incidents; ld 13; drvn & hdd last; nt qckn
[436³]	3	20	**Father's Joy** (5a,3ow) 8-1 **A Sansome** *(citation)* Hld up & nt jw; hdwy 8; lft in ld 10; nrly fell 11; jnd 13; 8l 3rd 15; mist nxt; rallied & 4l 3rd nxt; wknd qckly uphill
[329ᴾ]	P		**Down To Joe's (IRE)** 7-2 **D Dennis** Nt jw; hld up & bhnd; 8th 8; mist 9; lft 3rd 10; disp ld brief 13; mist nxt; 3l 2nd 15; mist 16 & wknd to 10l last 2 out; pu last
[576ᴾ]	P		**Dunston Ben** 20-1 **Mrs L Stock** Climbed 2; last 3; t.o 5; pu 10
	P		**Happy Chappy** 16-1 **M Gorman** Bckwd; hld up; bad mist 7 & rdr lost irons; 9th 8; lost tch 14; t.o aft nxt; pu 2 out
	U		**Oisin Dubh (IRE)** 12-1 **G Gigantesco** Tk keen hld in 3rd; rcd v wide aft 6; lft in ld 9; bad mist & ur 10
[284ᶠ]	F		**Sleipnir** 14-1 **B Hitchcott** Hld up; 6th 8; lft cl up 9; fell 10
[577ᵁ]	U		**Sliabh Foy (IRE)** 12-1 **F Marshall** Sn chsng clr ldr til mist & ur 9

F   **Tonrin** 3-1F **P York** *Unruly; bckwd; tk str hld; 20l clr by 3; 10l ahd 8; fell 9*

OFFICIAL DISTANCES: 4l, 5l **TIME:** 6min 33.0s **TOTE:** £13.60; places £1.40,£1.30,£2.40 **DF:** £66.60

Exeter (RH 11F,19J)
Tue, 21 Mar (GOOD to FIRM)

680 Robert Webb Travel Open HC
8 ran

[470²]	1		**NOYAN** 11-05 7-2 **P York** *Made all; pushed 8l clr 14; rdr lkng rnd app 16; shkn up & stayed on wl flat*
	2	¾	**Lankridge** 11-05 9-2 **P Shaw** *Keen hld & prom; chsd wnr 12-14; hit nxt; went 2nd agn 16; eff app last; chall flat; kpt on wl; a hld*
[454⁴]	3	4	**Blue Laws (IRE)** 11-05 5-1 **Miss C Tuffin** *Bhnd; last 8; 5th & rdn 14; stayed on frm 3 out til nt qckn aft last*
[534⁵]	4	12	**Palace Parade (USA)** 11-05 14-1 **C Heard** *Hld up & bhnd; hit 13; 10l 6th aft 15; rdn nxt; hit 3 out & wknd*
[386⁴]	5	dist	**Hurricane Blake** 11-05 20-1 **J Young** *Jmpd slow 1; a pushed along; mist 4; jmpd slow 10; chsd wnr to 12; nt keen & lost tch u.p 15; t.o*
	F		**Act Of Parliament (IRE)** 11-09 (bl) 7-2 **D Flavin** *Hld up; hdwy 10; prsng ldrs when fell 12*
[390¹]	F		**Just Bert (IRE)** 11-11 11-4F **Miss J Cumings** *Chsd ldrs; blun 9 (water); sn rcvrd; rdn 13; rallied nxt; no ex aft 3 out; disp 3rd & btn when fell 2 out*
[316¹]	P		**Westcountry Lad** 11-05 16-1 **R Woollacott** *Chsd ldrs; drpd to rr 8; 7th when blun 11; hdwy 13; 4th nxt; wknd 16; blun nxt & pu*

TIME: 6min 26.4s **TOTE:** £3.20; places £1.40,£2.70,£1.50 **Ex:** £21.80 **CSF:** £19.86 **Tri:** £124.70

Fontwell (L&RH 7F,16J)
Tue, 21 Mar (GOOD to FIRM)

681 Charlton Hunt Challenge Cup HC
7 ran

[384⁵]	1		**KING TORUS (IRE)** 12-00 (bl) 6-4F **J Jukes** *Ld 2; made rest; hrd rdn app last; stayed on wl; comf*
	2	5	**Cougar Run (IRE)** 11-07 14-1 **K Culligan** *Hld up; hdwy gng wl in 3rd 8; chsd wnr 3 out; hanging & nt qckn frm nxt*
[474⁴]	3	1¾	**Pontabula** 11-11 4-1 **A Charles-Jones** *Hld up in midfield; mist 8; 4th & rdn 10; eff 12; disp 2nd 2 out; kpt on one pce*
[222⁵]	4	nk	**Miss Pennyhill (IRE)** 11-06 4-1 **D O'Meara** *Ld to 2; mist 6; 5th & rdn 10; outpcd 13; kpt on agn frm 3 out*
[475⁴]	5	7	**Chism (IRE)** 12-03 (bl) 5-1 **R Walford** *Chsd wnr 3 til urged along & dem 3 out; nt r.o & sn btn*
[151⁶]	6	1½	**John Tufty** 11-07 20-1 **Miss R Illman** *Hld up in rr; eff & in tch 12; mist & rdr lurched forward nxt; unable to chall aft*
[463⁷]	U		**Vendoon (IRE)** 11-11 (bl) 20-1 **T Gibney** *A last; in tch when blun & ur 11*

TIME: 4min 55.8s **TOTE:** £2.30; places £3.00,£3.90 **ex:** £17.90 **DF:** £19.50

Sedgefield (LH 8F,18J)
Tue, 21 Mar (GOOD to FIRM)

682 Sunderland Open HC
7 ran

[496³]	1		**MAJORITY MAJOR (IRE)** 11-10 20-1 **T Glass** *Made all; drvn & stayed on str flat*
[376³]	2	4	**Cross Cannon** 11-12 14-1 **W Renwick** *Hld up last to 10; stdy hdwy 13; chsd wnr & eff app 2 out; edged lft & nt qckn frm last*
	3	dist	**Brownrath King (IRE)** 12-03 16-1 **N Tutty** *In tch til outpcd 9; mod 4th 11; mist 13; hmpd bad nxt; nd aft; rdn 15; t.o nxt*
[460⁹]	4	dist	**Dromhana (IRE)** 11-10 13-2 **Miss J Wormall** *Mists; chsd wnr 5 til blun 13; wkng when jmpd slow nxt; t.o 3 out*
[529¹]	U		**Aly Daley (IRE)** 11-10 4-5F **Miss A Price** *Chsd wnr to 5; 3rd til 2nd agn 13; outpcd & dem aft 3 out; 3rd & btn when rfo nxt*
[377³]	F		**Chaps** 12-03 10-1 **Mrs F Needham** *Bhnd; 5th & strugg 10; 15l 5th when fell hvly 13*
[301ᶠ]	P		**Solway Donal (IRE)** 11-12 100-30 **C Storey** *Mists; bhnd; blun & nrly fell 10 & releg last; t.o & pu 2 out*

TIME: 6min 59.0s **TOTE:** £22.40; places £5.80,£3.40 **Ex:** £98.00 **CSF:** £211.50
Fence at the top of the hill was omitted

Chepstow (LH 11F,18J)
Wed, 22 Mar (GOOD)

683 Tintern Abbey HC
14 ran

	1		**CELTIC ABBEY** 12-04 13-2 A Wintle *Settled 3rd/4th; ld app 14; clr 3 out; stayed on wl; easy; impressive*
[460¹]	2	5	**Ardstown** 11-09 9-4F F Windsor Clive *Hld up & bhnd; 10th 7; 7th & prog 13; chsd wnr frm 3 out; drvn & no imp*
[369³]	3	5	**Sharimage** 12-07 4-1 Julian Pritchard *Chsd ldrs; outpcd 10; rallied in 5th 13; 3rd when hit 15; no imp aft*
[468²]	4	3½	**Rusty Bridge** 11-13 9-1 R Burton *Ld 1; nt pushed frm 4; lost plce in 9th 7; rr 13; stayed on agn frm 3 out; unable to chall*
[581ᴾ]	5	½	**Full Alirt** 11-04 20-1 Miss S Young *Nt fluent; 8th 7; rap hdwy to ld aft 13; sn hdd; wknd aft 3 out*
[468⁴]	6	9	**Archer (IRE)** 12-00 (bl) 25-1 A Price *Hit 2; sn prom; hit 8; chsd ldr 10-13; wknd & hit nxt; no ch when blun 2 out*
[479³]	7	1¾	**Lordinthesky (IRE)** 11-11 25-1 S Blackwell *6th 7; chsd ldrs til 8th & outpcd 13*
[153ᴾ]	8	5	**Ivy Boy (IRE)** 12-00 14-1 J Cook *Prom; went 2nd 8 til hit 9; rp 10; 6th 13; wknd 15; mist nxt*
[389³]	9	9	**Lie Detector** 11-09 33-1 J Gasper *7th 7; nt trble ldrs frm 13*
[468³]	10	dist	**Highway Five (IRE)** 11-09 25-1 D Dennis *A drvn along; sn bhnd; 11th 7; t.o 14; fnce bhnd*
	P		**Ardell Boy** 11-11 9-1 Miss P Gundry *Ld aft 1; hdd aft 13; wkng when hmpd bend bef nxt; nt rec; t.o & pu last*
[469⁴]	P		**Mr Motivator** 11-13 14-1 T Scudamore *Bhnd; 12th 7; t.o & pu 2 out*
[386³]	P		**Rusty Fellow** 11-11 16-1 D Barlow *A bhnd; mist 4; last 7; t.o & pu 11*
	P		**Rymin Thyne** 11-09 20-1 M Rodda *A bhnd; lost tch app 8; t.o 14; pu 2 out*

TIME: 6min 07.0s TOTE: £8.60; places £3.90,£1.10,£1.70 Ex: £35.40 CSF: £19.57 Tri: £53,702.80

Ludlow (LH 8F,19J)
Wed, 22 Mar (GOOD)

684 Magnus-Allcroft Mem Trophy HC
17 ran

	1		**GRIMLEY GALE (IRE)** 11-13 8-13F Miss S Vickery *Settled handy; 5th 10; went 2nd & blun 12; releg 3rd til pushed into 2nd app 16; hit 3 out; ld nxt; clr last; easy*
	2	3½	**Stanmore (IRE)** 11-07 6-1 R Barrett *Tk keen hld; sn prom; ld 8; rdn & hdd 2 out; one pce flat*
[272⁴]	3	5	**Hee's A Dancer** 11-11 16-1 C Williams *Ld to 6; 2nd/3rd aft; 3rd & rdn app 16; one pce*
[474²]	4	6	**Formal Invitation (IRE)** 12-00 5-1 M Rimell *Bhnd to 11; kpt on stdly frm 16; nvr able to chall*
[326¹⁰]	5	12	**Willie Makeit (IRE)** 12-01 33-1 M Miller *Prom; 4th 10; rdn 13; 4th & wkng app 16*
	6	5	**This Is My Life (IRE)** 11-05 11-1 P York *Pulled hrd; chsd ldrs; 6th 10; mist 12; sn outpcd; poor 6th & u.p 16; blun last*
	7	3½	**Smart Song** 12-00 40-1 M Hammond *Nrly ur 2; nt jw in midfield; 8th & outpcd 10; no ch aft*
[461⁶]	8	2½	**Not My Line** 11-07 66-1 M Foley *Sn 2nd; ld 6-8; 2nd 10; wkng when mist 13; no ch aft*
[222⁶]	9	5	**Boxing Match** 11-07 33-1 S Lloyd *Sn bhnd; strugg frm 10*
[336¹⁰]	10	16	**Cowarne Adventure** 11-07 50-1 T Stephenson *Rr & strugg 10; t.o*
	P		**Aganerot (IRE)** 11-07 100-1 P Cranmer *Qckly lost tch & nt jw; mist 6 & u.p; cont t.o til pu 10*
[569ᵁ]	R		**Bobby Violet** 11-07 100-1 S Graham *Qckly lost tch; t.o when veered violent lft & rn out & threw rdr nearing 5*
[479⁴]	U		**Merger Mania** 11-07 25-1 D Mansell *Bhnd; mist 7; strugg when blun & ur 9 (water)*
[384ᵁ]	P		**Pontoon Bridge** 11-07 66-1 Mrs K Diggle *Nt jw; prom to 4; mist 6; wl bhnd 10; t.o & pu 3 out*
[474ᴾ]	P		**Rockville Pike (IRE)** 11-11 66-1 F Hutsby *Midfield early; rr 10; t.o & pu 12*
[153ᴾ]	P		**Savuti (IRE)** 11-07 (bl) 66-1 H Ephgrave *Chsd ldrs to 8; wknd qckly; t.o & pu 10*
[567ᴾ]	P		**Tantara Lodge (IRE)** 11-09 (vis) 50-1 B Hitchcott *Chsd ldrs; 7th 10; wkng when nt jw aft; t.o & pu 3 out*

TIME: 4min 58.6s TOTE: £1.60; places £1.40,£1.70,£3.30 Ex: £7.00 CSF: £4.34 Tri: £35,305.25

Six riders (including the rider of the winner) were each fined £65 for disregarding the Starter's instructions

Wincanton (RH 9F,17J)
Thu, 23 Mar (GOOD to SOFT)

685 Stewart Tory Mem Nov HC   10 ran

[383⁴]	1		**CASTLE LYNCH (IRE)** 11-06 5-1 *Miss S Vickery Lw; settled 3rd; 2nd 8; ld 14; 10l clr nxt; pushed along & kpt on wl*
[580ᵁ]	2	5	**Chatergold (IRE)** 11-07 (bl) 9-2 *D Dennis Settled rr; 6th 8; rdn & hdwy 11; 6l 3rd 13; sn outpcd; rallied to disp 2nd last; kpt on but nt rch wnr*
[563¹]	3	¾	**Morris Piper** 12-00 (tt) 14-1 *L Jefford (xnb)Last when mist 3; 7th 8; eff in 4th 13; sn outpcd; rallied 2 out; disp 10l 2nd last; kpt on stdly (gd eff)*
[440³]	4	4	**Tubber Roads (IRE)** 12-00 12-1 *A Sansome (xnb) Hld up; 4th & prog 8; ld app 11; hdd 14; wknd & mist 2 out & lost 2 plces; mist last*
	5	5	**Rose Garden** 11-12 9-1 *D O'Meara Bckwd; swtng; chsd ldrs; 5th when mist 8; in tch to 13; r.o one pce*
[583³]	P		**Badger Beer** 11-07 (tt) 10-1 *J Snowden Lw; chsd ldr to 8; wkng when mist 12; t.o & pu last*
[467²]	F		**Madam Sioux (IRE)** 11-02 7-4F *T Dennis Lw; fell 1; broke leg; dead*
[467³ᵈ]	P		**Malihabad (IRE)** 11-07 25-1 *Miss A Goschen Bhnd; mists 7; last nxt; no ch when mist 13; t.o & pu 3 out*
	F		**The Captain's Wish** 11-07 (tt) 9-1 *A Michael Tubed; bit bckwd; rr when fell 4*
	P		**Timarisk** 11-07 50-1 *J Barnes Pulled hrd; ld & sn clr; 20l ahd 5; jmpd slow 9 (water); hdd bef 11; lost plce qckly; t.o & pu 14*

TIME: 5min 40.4s **TOTE:** £6.90; places £2.20,£1.60,£2.00 **Ex:** £29.90 **CSF:** £26.92 **Tri:** £nt won

Kelso (LH 8F,19J)
Fri, 24 Mar (GOOD to SOFT)

686 Percy Arms HC   10 ran

[494¹]	1		**BALISTEROS (FR)** 11-09 6-5F *Miss J Wormall Hld up; hdwy 12; ld app 3 out; urged along flat & kpt on game*
[660²]	2	hd	**Midsummer Glen (IRE)** 11-03 10-1 *Miss M Bremner Chsd ldrs; blun 11; went 2nd 15; prsd wnr frm last; wildly rdn & kpt on; ev ch til just hld nr fin*
[419¹]	3	1¾	**Parade Racer** 11-03 4-1 *A Richardson Hld up & bhnd; hdwy 14; chall & ev ch last; kpt on wl but outrdn final 100yds*
	4	15	**Nothingtotellme (IRE)** 11-03 8-1 *R Morgan Midfield; eff in 7th & rdn 16; drvn aft 2 out; 2l 5th last; wknd flat*
[495³]	5	12	**Strathmore Lodge** 10-12 12-1 *D Jewett 2nd/3rd til ld app 14; hdd app 3 out; w wnr 2 out-last; wknd qckly*
[465⁶]	6	13	**Eastlands Hi-Light** 11-03 20-1 *T Morrison Ld/disp til app 14; 4th when mist 3 out; sn wknd*
[225⁷]	7	dist	**Rusty Blade** 11-03 (bl) 100-1 *T Davidson Sn lost tch; rmdrs 10; t.o 12*
[495²]	P		**Jr-Kay (IRE)** 11-13 (10) 14-1 *N Bannister Mists & rdr v ungainly; prom til mist 9; rdr lost iron 11; lost tch nxt; pu 3 out*
[301ᴾ]	P		**More Joy** 11-06 (3) 33-1 *S Bowden Mists; ld/disp til hdd & blun 9; ld brief 10; wkng when mist 13; pu nxt*
[222ᴾ]	U		**Over The Hill (IRE)** 12-02 10-1 *M Bradburne Hld up; hdwy & trckd ldrs 12; mist 15; 3l 4th when mist & ur 3 out*

TIME: 6min 57.7s **TOTE:** £1.80; places £1.10,£3.10,£1.80 **Ex:** £16.20 **CSF:** £13.19 **Tri:** £45.50

Newbury (LH 11F,17J)
Fri, 24 Mar (GOOD to FIRM)

687 Newbury Golf Centre HC   14 ran

[461¹]	1		**SECRET BAY** 12-05 1-2F *B Pollock Jw; trckd ldrs; ld 12; hdd nxt; sn ld agn; drvn along frm 14; drew clr frm 2 out; pushed out*
[464²]	2	14	**Mister Horatio** 11-05 (tt) 15-2 *M Lewis (xnb)Cl up; ld app 8-12; ld agn nxt; sn hdd but clr of rest; rdn & outpcd frm 2 out*
[469³]	3	1¾	**Stay Lucky (NZ)** 11-12 25-1 *Julian Pritchard Bhnd; drvn along frm 7; poor 8th app 13; stayed on frm 3 out; unable to chall*
[226⁸]	4	20	**Pongo Waring (IRE)** 11-05 33-1 *S Morris Chsd ldrs to 11; 7th & strugg 13*
[384⁶]	5	2½	**Pro Bono (IRE)** 11-12 33-1 *M Foley Prom; ld 4 til app 8; hit 10; wknd nxt; blun 12; 5th & no ch 13*
[583⁵]	6	2	**Hall's Mill (IRE)** 11-09 25-1 *A Charles-Jones Ld to 4; 2nd/3rd to 12; wknd to poor 4th nxt*

[384²]	7	1¼	**Island Echo (IRE)** 11-05 6-1 J Tate *Chsd ldrs; stayed on to 15l 3rd 13; chsd ldng pr vain aft til wknd qckly 2 out*
[327³]	8	23	**Go Universal (IRE)** 11-05 25-1 N Mitchell *Midfield & nd; wknd 11; poor 6th 13*
[385⁴]	9	27	**Charlie Hawes (IRE)** 11-05 66-1 Miss G Russell *Sn t.o*
[511⁶]	P		**Jasilu** 11-00 (bl) 50-1 D Flavin *Prom; w ldr 4-6; rdn & wknd 9; t.o & pu 13*
[513⁷]	P		**Playmore (IRE)** 11-12 33-1 A Sansome *Midfield; in tch til jmpd lft 9; hung lft aft & sn wknd; t.o & pu 13*
[580ᶠ]	P		**Six Clerks (IRE)** 11-09 10-1 A Wintle *Sn lost tch; blun 3; nvr gng wl; t.o & pu 2 out*
[96⁶]	F		**The Millmaster (IRE)** 11-05 (bl) 20-1 A Coe *Fell 1*
[227²]	P		**Tommys Webb (IRE)** 11-13 25-1 L Lay *A bhnd; mist 4 & rmdrs; 9th 13; t.o & pu last*

TIME: 5min 42.0s TOTE: £1.70; places £1.30,£1.70,£3.20 Ex: £5.20 CSF: £4.77 Tri; ^£54.50

Bramham Moor
Wetherby (LH 8F,18J) Sat, 25 Mar (GOOD with SOFT & FIRM patches)

688 Hunt
2 ran

[400¹]	1		**WHAT A FIDDLER (IRE)** 2-5F R Tate *Disp til ld 3-7; trckd ldr til chall 3 out; level last; best spd flat*
[507¹]	2	nk	**Erni (FR)** 6-4 W Burnell *Disp ld to 2; cl 2nd when bad mist 6; ld 10-15; jnd 3 out; level & ev ch last; r.o flat; just outpcd*

OFFICIAL DISTANCE: nk TIME: 8min 10.0s

689 Restricted
15 ran

	1		**MASTER JOCK** 2-1 G Hanmer *Mid-div til hdwy 11; went 30l 2nd 14; clsd qckly on tiring ldr; disp ld 2 out; sn ld & clr; hvly eased flat; v impressive*
[620ᵁ]	2	6	**Curtainsatchopwell (IRE)** 7-1 K Green *(xnb) Ld; 20l up 6; 25l ahd 11; 15l clr when bad mist 3 out; jnd nxt; sn hdd & outpcd*
[503⁷]	3	6	**Mefein Boy (IRE)** 25-1 Mrs F Needham *Midfield; 6th 11; went 35l 3rd 14; clsd to 15l 3rd 3 out; r.o one pce*
[505⁵]	4	5	**The Hazel Harrier (IRE)** 10-1 Miss A Deniel *A midfield to rr; outpcd & lsng tch 11; stayed on frm 15; nrst fin*
[620ᵁ]	5	1	**Efaad (IRE)** 33-1 W Burnell *A midfield; 40l 4th 14; stayed on one pce; 17l 4th 3 out; dem flat*
[393¹]	6	8	**Run For The Mill** 33-1 M Morley *Tde; a midfield; r.o one pce*
[503⁶]	7	4	**Mount Faber** (bl) 16-1 S Charlton *Cl up in chsng group 11; outpcd 12; 6th 14; wknd app 3 out*
[620ᴾ]	8	8	**Jac Del Prince** 12-1 R Walker *Chsd ldr early; 10l 2nd 4; 20l 2nd 6 til wknd 12; bhnd 15; t.o 2 out*
[500¹]	9	8	**Go Nomadic** 8-1 P Atkinson *A rr; nd*
[423ᴾ]	P		**Abbey Lad** 33-1 C Wilson *Cl up in chsng group; 22l 3rd 6-10; wknd 11; t.o & pu 15*
	P		**Dunston Laddie** 50-1 J R Barlow *Tkn rnd gently in rr; bhnd by 11; lsng tch & pu 13*
[169¹]	F		**Guilsborough Gorse** (7a) 6-4F G Brewer *Hld up in rr early; stdy hdwy to 7th & fell 9*
[393ᵁ]	P		**Lingcool** (5a) 50-1 J Morley *Last to 3; hdwy to 6th 9; lost tch 10; t.o & pu 12*
	P		**Lord Nick** 14-1 C Mulhall *Midfield to 5; bad mist 6; rr & lsng tch 11; still in tch when rdr tried to pu app 2 out & horse rn into fnce*
	P		**Prince Moshar** 66-1 L McGrath *Mounted on course; rr & pushed along aft 8; lost tch 10; t.o & pu 12*

OFFICIAL DISTANCES: 5l, 5l TIME: 7min 07.0s

690 Ladies Open
6 ran

[505²]	1		**MONKEY AGO** 7-4 Miss J Foster *Trckd ldr in 3rd to 10; ld 12; 2l up 15; jnd 2 out; qcknd clr app last; r.o wl*
[170⁰]	2	6	**Take The Buckskin** 33-1 Miss A Burton *Chsd ldr in 2l 2nd til bad mist 11; cl 2nd agn 13-3 out; rdn to chall 2 out; wknd app last; one pce*
[397²]	3	4	**Marius (IRE)** (1ow) 4-6F Miss V Russell *Last to 2; 8l 5th 6-10; outpcd 15; pushed along 3 out; stayed on one pce u.p*
[494³]	4	4	**Miss Accounts** (5a) 8-1 Miss A Armitage *Rr; last 4-9; went 8l 3rd 13; jnd & prsd for 3rd 2 out; dem app last*
	P		**Major Look (NZ)** 10-1 Miss H Kinsey *Last 3-4; went 6l 4th 6-9; last & wkng rap 10; pu & imm dism; broke down*
[422ᴾ]	P		**Thank U Jim** 8-1 Miss T Jackson *Ld; 3l up 4-8; 2l clr 9 til wknd 12; last 13; wl adrift when pu 15*

OFFICIAL DISTANCES: 5l, 4l TIME: 7min 01.0s

691 Mens Open
8 ran

[584⁹]	1		**WHATAFELLOW (IRE)** (bl) 4-7F **A Crow** *Hld up in rr to 3; pulled to cl 3rd 4; ld app 7; made rest easy; rdly drew clr frm 15; 15l ahd last; eased flat*
[443²]	2	8	**Barneys Gold (IRE)** 20-1 **A Bealby** *Rn in snatches; ld to 3; 2l 2nd 4-9; outpcd 13; 10l 5th 15; stayed on to disp 2nd at last; went 2nd flat*
[395³]	3	4	**Juke Box Billy (IRE)** 12-1 **W Burnell** *Last by 5-9; hdwy 12 to 4l 2nd 14; chsd ldr to 2 out; dem flat*
	4	6	**Albert Blake** 14-1 **W Kinsey** *Planted himself in padd; reluct to go to start; ld/disp til ld 4-6; cl 3rd to 11; 6l 5th & outpcd 12; wknd app 3 out*
	5	½	**Vicosa (IRE)** 33-1 **S Prior** *Mid-div to 8; rr by 12; last 13*
[504³]	6	8	**Final Beat (IRE)** 10-1 **C Cundall** *Prom; 3rd 6; went 2l 2nd 11; chsd ldr to 13; sn outpcd; last & lsng tch 15*
	P		**Larkshill (IRE)** (tt) 25-1 **C Mulhall** *Midfield to 6; lsng tch 10; t.o to pu 12*
[279¹]	P		**Murton Heights** 7-2 **N Tutty** *Last to 3; went 8l 5th 9 & 5l 4th 11; 5l 3rd & clsng when pu 13; lame*

OFFICIAL DISTANCES: 10l, 5l **TIME:** 7min 10.0s

692 Intermediate, 12st
4 ran

[184¹]	1		**QUARTERSTAFF** 4-6F **C Wilson** *Prom til ld frm 5; 4l up 6 til qcknd clr 3 out; 15l ahd app last; hvly eased flat; v easy*
[394⁰]	2	8	**Harbour Blaze (IRE)** 2-1 **Miss R Clark** *Prom in mid-div to 7; went 3l 2nd 10; trckd ldr til pushed along 14; 2l 2nd 3 out; easily outpcd; r.o same pce*
[424¹]	3	2	**Broken English** (5a) 9-2 **Miss T Jackson** *Last early; 8l adrift by 4 til rap hdwy frm 10; disp 2nd nxt; outpcd 13; 6l 3rd 15; wknd stdly*
[394⁶]	U		**Stride To Glory (IRE)** 20-1 **Mrs H Arnold** *Ld; jmpd slow 3; hdd 5; 4l 2nd 6-10; wknd 11; 15l 4th when ur 2 out*

OFFICIAL DISTANCES: 15l, 2l **TIME:** 7min 11.0s

693 Open Maiden (Div 1, Part 1)
10 ran

[508ᴾ]	1		**SILENT SNIPE** 8-1 **W Burnell** *Midfield to 7; rap hdwy 13; went 3l 3rd 2 out; hrd rdn app last; stayed on wl u.p; ld to 1 home*
[624²]	2	2	**Heather Lad** 6-4F **D Raw** *Tried to make all; 2l up 11; 3l clr last; hrd rdn & wknd flat; just caught nr fin*
	3	6	**Allten (IRE)** 3-1 **G Tuer** *Last by 9; hdwy 11 to 12l 6th 14; stayed on to 3rd app last*
[233²]	4	6	**Well I Never** 8-1 **P Millington** *Nt jw; rr to 4; mist 5; last 6-11; hdwy 14 to disp 2nd 2 out; wknd app last; dem flat*
[508⁵]	5	3	**Tyndrum Gold** 14-1 **Miss A Deniel** *Prom in 2l 2nd 1-14; 4l 3rd 15; wknd app 3 out*
[526⁵]	6	8	**Educate Me (IRE)** 14-1 **J Burley** *Cl up; 3l 3rd til went 2l 2nd & ev ch 15; wknd qckly 3 out*
	7	20	**Party Elephant** (5a) 16-1 **Miss F Hartley** *Rr by 3; t.o 10; wl adrift 3 out*
[373ᴿ]	P		**Carr Dyke Castle** 20-1 **M Mackley** *Fat; prom in 3rd to 10; wknd qckly aft 11; pu 12*
[400ᴾ]	F		**Morcan House** 33-1 **J Davies** *Midfield to 8; 6l 5th 10; wkng when fell 14*
[627¹¹]	P		**Right Ron Run** 5-1 **R Wakeham** (bh) *Last by 3; pushed along & lsng tch 14; t.o & pu 2 out*

OFFICIAL DISTANCES: 2l, 5l **TIME:** 7min 28.0s

694 Open Maiden (Div 1, Part 2)
9 ran

[508³]	1		**FIERY JACK** 4-1 **N Tutty** *Chsd ldng pr in 30l 3rd 6-10; stdy hdwy to 5l 3rd 14; stayed on; ld app 2 out; r.o u.p*
[624²]	2	4	**Deerhunter** 5-1 **G Tuer** *Midfield to 9; hdwy to 4l 2nd 10-14; sltly outpcd 15; cruising bhnd ldng pr 2 out; fnd nil app last*
[507ᶠ]	3	5	**Imperial Line (IRE)** 3-1F **Miss T Jackson** *Ld; sn clr; 5l up 6; 25l ahd 10; wkng app 13; just ld 3 out; hdd & wknd nxt*
[459ᴾ]	U		**Barney Bear** 5-1 **S Prior** *Rr early; stdy hdwy frm 8 to 5l 3rd 11; ur 12*
[569ᴾ]	P		**Mezzo Princess** (5a) 7-1 **J R Barlow** *Pulled hrd early; chsd clr ldr in 15l 2nd 4-9; wknd 11; t.o & pu 14*
[508⁷]	P		**Port Valenska (IRE)** 4-1 **B Woodhouse** *Midfield to 8; pushed along & rmdrs 10; outpcd 12; 15l 4th 13; poor 5th when pu 2 out*
[398ᴾ]	P		**Saxon Moss** 10-1 **G Smith** *A rr; last by 5; bhnd & lsng tch 9; t.o 14; pu 3 out*
[624⁸]	P		**Tough Decision** 10-1 **S Brisby** (xnb) *Midfield to 6; 35l 4th 8; qckly drpd to rr 9; lsng tch when pu 11*
[593ᴾ]	P		**Wily Miss** (5a) 14-1 **D Sherlock** *Midfield to 5; 36l 5th 8; rr by 11; lost tch 12; t.o & pu 14*

OFFICIAL DISTANCES: 3l, 3l **TIME:** 7min 22.0s

695 Open Maiden (Div 2, Part 1)   10 ran

[168³]	1		**MADAME LA CLAIRE** (5a) 4-5F C Mulhall *Hld up in rr til hdwy 7; 3l 3rd 10; went cl 2nd 12-15; ld 3 out; sn wl clr; wknd & hung bad flat; broke down*
	2	12	**Ladylands** (5a) 12-1 D Raw *Ld to 7; 2nd 9 til lft in ld agn 11; 2l up 13 til hdd & outpcd 3 out*
[507ᵁ]	3	5	**Hopeful Earl (IRE)** 12-1 N Tutty *Nt a fluent; prom when bad mist 10; lft 4l 3rd 11-14; rdn to disp 2nd 2 out; wknd app last*
[620ᴾ]	P		**Alena H Banks** 6-1 L McGrath *(xnb) Last to 3; bhnd by 6; stdy hdwy to 20l 4th 15; 22l 4th when pu 2 out*
	P		**Bright Reform (IRE)** 20-1 S Prior *Rr to 6; hdwy 9 to 12l 6th 13; sn wknd & pu 14*
[167³]	U		**Eddie Rombo** (7a,1ow) 12-1 B Woodhouse *Prom to 6; handy 3rd when ur 14*
[506ᶜ]	F		**Norman Way** (7a) 33-1 P Cornforth *Mostly prom; 2l 2nd 3-8; handy in 8l 4th when fell 13*
[547ᴾ]	P		**Patrington Boy** 20-1 M Mackley *Rr by 10; pushed along & wknd 13; t.o & pu 14*
	F		**Sally Scally** (5a) 12-1 Miss T Jackson *Rr to 3; hdwy frm 6; ld 9; sn clr & tk str hld; 8l up when fell 11*
[625ᴿ]	U		**Vals Castle (IRE)** (5a) 4-1 Miss R Clark *Rr div when ur 6*

OFFICIAL DISTANCES: 15l, 10l   TIME: 7min 29.0s

696 Open Maiden (Div 2, Part 2)   10 ran

[398ᶜ]	1		**NEVER WONDER (IRE)** (7a) 4-7F J Tate *Mid-div til hdwy 9; 30l 3rd 11; went cl 2nd 15; ld 3 out; lft wl clr nxt; hmpd by loose horses last & rdr lost iron; pushed out flat*
[551ᶠ]	2	10	**Polly Live Wire** (5a) 16-1 P Millington *Nt jw; last to 3; mist 4; jmpd slow 5; bhnd & lsng tch 12; poor 5th 15; stayed on & lft dist 2nd 2 out*
	3	50	**Sylcanny** (5a) 16-1 J Davies *Jmpd v novicey in rr; bad mist 4; jmpd big 6; lsng tch 12; went poor 4th 15; lft rem 3rd 2 out*
	U		**Almikino (IRE)** 5-1 S Brisby *(xnb) Sn clr; 20l abd 7; came back to field 10; qcknd agn app 11 & 25l up 12; stpd rap app 14; clambered over & ur*
	F		**Buddy Girie** 16-1 C Denny *Nt jw; jmpd slow 1; mist 4; mid-div when fell 8*
[398ᴾ]	P		**Handsome Is (IRE)** (12a) 10-1 G Brewer *Chsd runaway ldr to 11; wknd 14; hanging bad rt; hld in 4th when pu 2 out*
[400³]	U		**Icantsay (IRE)** 14-1 D Thomas *Prom in chsng group to 8; wknd 13; mid-div when hmpd bad & ur 14*
[400ᴾ]	R		**Lulagh-B** (5a) 16-1 R Wakeham *Mid-div early; stdy hdwy to cl 3rd when rn out 15; will improve*
[623ᶠ]	P		**Pashby Wood** (5a) 33-1 M Morley *A rr; lsng tch 13; t.o & pu 15*
[593⁴]	U		**The Big Lad (IRE)** 4-1 G Smith *A.p in chsng group; ld 14 til disp 3 out; disp ld but u.p when ur 2 out*

OFFICIAL DISTANCES: 20l, dist   TIME: 7min 27.0s

Clifton-on-Teme

Upper Sapey (RH 8F,18J) Sat, 25 Mar (GOOD to SOFT becoming SOFT)

697 Hunt   4 ran

	1		**HAVEN LIGHT** (4x) 1-3F C Stockton *Ww; lft 3l 2nd 8; ld 12; 4l clr 3 out; jnd aft nxt; ld flat; clever*
[673ᴾ]	2	1	**Loch Ash** 8-1 M Jackson *2 handlers; ld to 3; mist 6; 2nd til lft in ld 8; hdd 12; jnd wnr aft 2 out; rdn & ev ch last; one pce*
[618ᶠ]	3	1½fs	**Tedstone Fox** 7-2 T Stephenson *2nd til ld 3; 10l clr when rn out 8; rtrcd & cont t.o; lft 3rd 12*
	P		**Fiddler's Lane** (bl) 20-1 Mrs D Powell *Chsd ldrs; 8l 3rd ½way; wknd 11; 15l 3rd when pu 12*

OFFICIAL DISTANCES: 1l, dist   TIME: 6min 42.5s

698 Restricted, 12st   7 ran

[532³]	1		**CHEROKEE RUN (IRE)** (tt) 3-1 M Keel *Trckd ldrs; went 3rd 7; ld 9-13; ld 14; r.o u.p flat*
[485⁵]	2	1	**Innishfea (IRE)** (5a) 5-2F Julian Pritchard *Ww; 3l 5th ½way; 4l 3rd 15; went 2nd & ev ch last; rdn & fnd nil flat*
[567⁸]	3	2½	**Wild Edric** 7-2 A Beedles *Ld to 4; 2nd til ld 7; hdd 9; chsd wnr 14; 4th & ev ch last; one pce*
[484ᴾ]	4	15	**True Fred** (vis) 33-1 R Burton *Ld 4; hdd 7; 2½l 4th ½way; drpd to rr 11; 10l 6th 15; no imp*
	5	2	**Kanjo Olda** (5a) 4-1 D Mansell *Hld up; 5l 6th ½way; rdn 12; 5l 4th 15; wkng when blun 3 out*
[567ᴾ]	U		**Carbery Ministrel (IRE)** 20-1 K Burke *(bf) Spurs; 3rd to 7; 5th when ur 8*

[612P] **P**   **Lindalighter** (5a) 14-1 M Munrowd *Hld up; hdwy & 2l 3rd ½way; went 2nd 11; ld 13-14; 7l 5th & wkng rap when mist nxt; wl bhnd when pu 3 out*

OFFICIAL DISTANCES: 1l, 3l   **TIME:** 6min 45.5s

699 Ladies Open   6 ran

[192¹]	**1**		**RIP VAN WINKLE** 1-3F **Miss A Dare** *A.p; went 6l 2nd 8; ld 13; drew clr frm 3 out; comf*
[668¹]	**2**	12	**Haughton Lad (IRE)** 14-1 **Miss A Nolan** *Ld 2; clr 7-11; hdd 13; blun 14; 4l 3rd nxt; sn outpcd; 12l bhnd 2 out; went 2nd flat; no ch w wnr*
[613⁴]	**3**	2½	**Sam Quale (IRE)** 4-1 **Miss C Thomas** *Hld up; stdy hdwy & 5l 3rd ½way; jnd ldrs 12; chsd wnr 14; rdn 3 out; wknd app last; dem flat*
[544⁷]	**4**	30	**Blue Lyzander** (5a,4ow) 33-1 **Mrs E Staines** (xnb) *Ld to 1; lost plce 6; 12l 5th ½way; wl bhnd 12; t.o*
[481ᵁ]	**U**		**Everso Irish** 20-1 **Miss L Ryder** *Rcd wide; lost tch 7; 20l 6th ½way; wl bhnd when rfo 12*
	P		**Winter Breeze** 25-1 **Miss J Priest** (xnb) *Ld 1-2; 2nd to 8; 6l 4th ½way; wknd 12; wl bhnd when pu 15*

OFFICIAL DISTANCES: 12l, 3l   **TIME:** 6min 28.5s

700 Land Rover Mens Open, 12st   3 ran

	1		**NETHER GOBIONS** (7x) 1-3F **Julian Pritchard** *Made all; hung lft bend aft 10; unchall*
[34⁸]	**2**	10	**Better Future (IRE)** (7x) 5-2 **T Stephenson** (bnf) *Chsd wnr; jmpd slow 9; hrd rdn & no resp 14; mist last*
[529P]	**3**	runin	**George Ashford (IRE)** 16-1 **I Hooper** *A bhnd; t.o 9*

OFFICIAL DISTANCES: 8l, dist   **TIME:** 6min 33.0s

701 Intermediate, 12st   7 ran

[142³]	**1**		**BOLSHIE BARON** (tt) 7-2 **M Harris** *2nd til ld 8; hdd 9; ld 12; stayed on wl frm 2 out*
[354⁴]	**2**	6	**Aqua Star (IRE)** 100-30 **Miss T Spearing** *Tde; hld up; rmdrs 6; 3½l 5th ½way; rmdrs 10; went 3rd 12; rdn 14; went 2nd aft nxt; mist 3 out; nt qckn*
	3	5	**Full Score (IRE)** 3-1F **Julian Pritchard** *Ld to 8; hd 9-12; 2nd til aft 15; 4l 3rd 2 out; wknd last*
[615P]	**4**	4	**Starting Again** 9-2 **R Burton** *Trckd ldrs; 3l 4th ½way; lost plce & 8l 5th 15; sn u.p; 10l 4th 2 out; one pce*
[543⁸]	**5**	4	**Catchphrase** 25-1 **J Docker** *Swtng; prom; 2l 3rd ½way; lost plce 12; 6l 4th 15; wknd 3 out*
[564³]	**P**		**Robero** (tt) 4-1 **D Mansell** (xnb,bf)*Hld up; 7l 6th ½way; wknd & 12l 6th 15; wl bhnd when pu 3 out*
	P		**Wrenbury Farmer** 20-1 **K Burke** *Swtng; 4th when mist 3; drpd to rr 5; lost tch 7; 25l 7th ½way; t.o 12; pu 14*

OFFICIAL DISTANCES: 6l, 6l   **TIME:** 6min 36.9s

702 Confined   6 ran

[543⁶]	**1**		**FINTONA BOY (IRE)** (tt) 8-1 **R Burton** *14s-8s; ld to 3; ld 5-11; 2nd til ld agn 15; lft 15l clr 3 out; rdn out*
[667F]	**2**	12	**Basil Street (IRE)** 5-2JF **D Mansell** *Hld up; 3l 4th ½way; jnd ldrs 11; 4l 3rd & rdn 15; sn outpcd; hmpd & lft poor 2nd 3 out; no imp*
[449⁶]	**3**	2	**Blue Rosette** (bl) 7-2 **T Stephenson** *Went 3rd 4 til mist 9; 4l 5th ½way; hit 11; 8l 5th & rdn 12; 7l 4th 15; lft poor 3rd 3 out*
[428²]	**4**	3	**Chicodari** 5-2JF **E Walker** *2nd/3rd to 4; 2½l 3rd ½way; rdn 11; 7l 4th nxt; wknd 14*
[294P]	**P**		**My Sister Lucy** (5a) 33-1 **I Hooper** *Ss; sn wl bhnd; t.o & pu 8*
[476⁵]	**r**		**The Crazy Bishop (IRE)** 3-1 **B Shaw** *10s-3s; ld 3-5; 2nd til ld 11; hdd 15; ev ch when ref & ur 3 out*

OFFICIAL DISTANCES: 1l, 1½l   **TIME:** 6min 40.3s

703 Open Maiden (Div 1), 12st   13 ran

[439²]	**1**		**O'FLAHERTY'S (IRE)** evensF **A Dalton** *6/4-evens; a.p; ld 9; drvn out*
[264P]	**2**	3	**The Ugly Gunner** 33-1 **E Gretton** *Prom til lost plce 8; 5½l 7th ½way; rallied 11; went 5l 3rd nxt & 2nd aft 15; ev ch 2 out; no ex flat*
[337³]	**3**	4	**All Things Nice** (5a) 12-1 **T Stephenson** *Ld to 2; 4l 5th ½way; went 2nd aft 10-15; rdn 3 out; one pce*
[618²]	**4**	12	**Top Designer (IRE)** (tt) 5-1 **R Burton** *Hld up; 7l 8th ½way; eff 12; went 12l 4th 14; no imp*
	P		**Ask Elliot** 25-1 **F Hutsby** *Ld 2-6 & 8-9; wknd qckly 12; bhnd when pu 14*

	P		**Bonnie Amy** (12a,7ow) 33-1 **L** Hicks *A bhnd; jmpd v slow I; I III 12th ½way; lost tch 12; t.o & pu 15*
	F		**Cider Man** (7a) 10-1 **Julian Pritchard** *Hld up & bhnd; 10l 11th ½way; 8l 9th when fell 11*
[548²]	P		**Metro Fashion** (IRE) 4-1 **T Lane** *Hld up & bhnd; 5l 6th ½way; wknd qckly 12; wl bhnd when pu 15*
[432³]	P		**Minster Star** (5a) 10-1 **C Wadland** *(xnb) Mist 2; lost plce 6; 9l 10th ½way; wl bhnd when pu 11*
[337ᶠ]	P		**Missed Call** (IRE) 6-1 **C Stockton** *Prom; 3l 4th ½way; wknd 13; 13l 5th nxt; bhnd when pu 15*
	P		**Sister Jim** (5a) 33-1 **M Keel** *Lkd awful; sn bhnd; blun 9; pu 10*
	P		**Sister Sue** (5a) 33-1 **S Graham** *(xnb) Went 2nd 3; ld 6-8; 2l 3rd ½way; sn lost plce u.p; bhnd when pu 11*
[568ᶠ]	R		**Sutton Lighter** 33-1 **D Mansell** *(xnb) 2 handlers; hld up & bhnd; 8l 9th ½way; rdn 13; 17l 5th 15; wl bhnd when rn out 3 out*

OFFICIAL DISTANCES: 2l, 5l   TIME: 6min 48.1s

704 Open Maiden (Div 2), 12st   11 ran

	1		**RED OASSIS** 7-2 **A Dalton** *Chsd ldrs; 6l 5th ½way; eff 11; went 2nd 13; ld aft 15; rdn clr aft 2 out*
[484ᴿ]	2	5	**Spirit Prince** 5-1 **Julian Pritchard** *Swtng; ld til hdd aft 15; rdn & ev ch 2 out; btn when mist last*
[618ᴾ]	3	30	**Penaction** (5a) 8-1 **E Walker** *Prom; mist 2; went 2nd 8-11; wknd & 15l 4th 15; lft rem 3rd at last*
[486ᶠ]	F		**Cool Spell** (5a) 20-1 **D Mansell** *Hld up; 7th when fell 8*
	P		**Cracking Crumpet** (5a) 20-1 **M Keel** *Chsd ldrs til lost plce 7; 7l 6th ½way; wkng when blun 12; pu 13*
	P		**Gildorflame** (5a) 20-1 **T Stephenson** *9th when pu & dism aft 2; lame*
[220ᶠ]	P		**Island Gift** (5a) 20-1 **R Burton** *Nd; 10l 7th ½way; lost tch 13; 25l 5th 15; t.o & pu 3 out*
[341ᴿ]	P		**Layback** 20-1 **K Burke** *(xnb) Wl bhnd frm 7; 25l 9th ½way; t.o & pu 15*
[617³]	F		**Step Quick** (IRE) 5-2F **T Lane** *Hld up & bhnd; 12l 8th ½way; hdwy when mist 11; went 3rd 13; wknd qckly aft 15; 30l 3rd & v tired when fell last; winded*
[490²]	P		**Tudor Flight** (5a) 3-1 **M Munrowd** *(xnb) Hld up; hdwy 8; 5l 4th ½way; mist 10; went 2nd nxt; wknd rap 13; pu 14*
	P		**Wind And Stars** (5a) 12-1 **F Hutsby** *2nd to 8; 4l 3rd ½way; rdn & wknd qckly 11; bhnd when pu 12*

OFFICIAL DISTANCES: 6l, 30l   TIME: 6min 44.9s

Crawley & Horsham
Parham (RH 8F,18J) Sat, 25 Mar (GOOD to FIRM)

705 Restricted, 12st   7 ran

[551¹]	1		**PERSIAN BOY** (IRE) 7-4 **A Sansome** *Hdwy to cl 3rd 10; ld 14 til jnd 3 out; ld agn app last; drew clr flat*
[575³]	2	6	**Royal Rupert** 4-1 **N Benstead** *Slpd & nrly ur app 4; ld to 13; cl 2nd til jnd wnr 3 out; wknd when hung lft app last; wknd flat*
[288ᴾ]	3	25	**Bit Of An Idiot** 25-1 **D Slattery** *Trckd ldr to 11; 12l 3rd & wkng 4 out; plodded on*
	P		**And Why Not** 33-1 **D Dennis** *Prom to 7; rr & lsng tch 13; t.o 4 out til pu last*
[575ᴾ]	P		**Moon Rising** 25-1 **P Bull** *In tch 4/5th til wknd 14; no ch when pu 3 out*
[576¹]	U		**Mr Fitz** (IRE) 6-4F **M Sheridan** *Sn detach in last; 15l adrift of rest of field 7; still wl bhnd when mist & ur 12*
	P		**Paddy Casey** (IRE) 16-1 **C Gordon** *Prsd ldrs in 3rd/4th til wknd 13; wl bhnd when pu 3 out*

OFFICIAL DISTANCES: 7l, dist   TIME: 6min 41.0s   TOTE: £2.80; places £2.50,£1.60   DF: £2.90

706 Confined, 12st   10 ran

[572⁶]	1		**TOOTH PICK** (IRE) (3x) 3-1 **J Hawksfield** *Hld up in last; stdy hdwy frm 12 to 13l 5th 4 out; gd rn nxt; ld last; qcknd clr flat*
[288ᴾ]	2	2	**Sovereign Spray** (IRE) (3x) 5-2F **C Gordon** *A.p; made most frm 10 til hdd app last; no ex flat*
[678ᴿ]	3	6	**Galaroi** (IRE) 3-1 **D Robinson** *A cl 2nd/3rd; 5l 3rd 4 out; kpt on one pce frm nxt*
[130ᴾ]	4	8	**Equity Player** 20-1 **D Dennis** *Midfield; gd hdwy 12; ld brief aft 14; prsd ldr til ld brief agn app 3 out; wknd qckly app nxt*

	5	20	**American Eyre** 33-1 Miss S Gladders Ld to 9; lost plce qckly aft 13; t.o 4 out; some late hdwy
[676⁶]	6	12	**Bit Of A Do** 33-1 D Slattery A towards rr; 16l 6th & wkng 4 out; t.o
[574ᵁ]	7	1	**Golden Mac** (bl) 33-1 J Barnard Midfield til gd hdwy to press ldrs 10-13; 20l 7th & wkng qckly 4 out
[325ᵁ]		U	**Newby End (IRE)** 6-1 A Blanch Cl up in midfield til ur 8
[571³]		P	**The Glow (IRE)** (6x) 10-1 D Brightling Hld up in midfield; hdwy to 9l 4th 4 out; sn wknd; pu aft nxt
		P	**Wayward Mischief** (5a) 25-1 B McKim A towards rr; last frm 10; lsng tch when pu 13

OFFICIAL DISTANCES: 3l, 7l **TIME:** 6min 45.0s **TOTE:** £2.20; places £1.10,£2.60,£2.40 **DF:** £2.50

707 Ladies Open - 17J   9 ran

[512³]	1		**LILY THE LARK** (5a,5x) 7-4F Miss H Irving In tch; pushed along & hdwy to 8l 3rd aft 10; no prog til stayed on to chse ldr 3 out; clsd frm nxt; r.o wl flat; ld cl home
[289¹]	2	½	**Cadbury Castle** (5a) 5-2 Miss J Grant Ld 6; tried to make rest; 5l clr aft 10; 8l ahd 3 out; 2l up & wkng last; hdd & no ex cl home
[307ᴾ]	3	12	**Silk Vestments** (5a) 16-1 Mrs D Rowell A chsng ldrs; 13l 4th aft 10; 19l 4th 4 out; gd hdwy 3 out; wknd app last
[574⁶]	4	4	**Edge Ahead (IRE)** (bl) 10-1 Mrs E Coveney Prom; 2nd frm 6; 5l down aft 10; chsd ldr rest of way til wknd app 3 out
[573⁴]	5	15	**Polar Ana (IRE)** (5a) 16-1 Miss S Gladders Hld up towards rr; 18l 6th aft 10; nvr nr ldrs
[414³]	6	8	**Andrelot** (bl) 12-1 Miss H Grissell Sn lost tch; 33l 7th aft 10; t.o aft
		F	**Bilbo Baggins (IRE)** (bl) 20-1 Miss R Williams Midfield til fell 3
[414¹]		P	**Emsee-H** (4x) 5-2 Miss Z Turner Chsd ldrs til 15l 5th & lsng plce aft 10; wl bhnd frm 4 out til pu last
[307ᵁ]		F	**Jamies First (IRE)** 33-1 Miss L Parrott Ld to 5; cl 3rd when fell nxt

OFFICIAL DISTANCES: ½l, 7l **TIME:** 6min 35.0s **TOTE:** £4.50; places £1.60,£1.10,£2.30 **DF:** £2.40
Fence 11 omitted - fallen rider

708 Mens Open, 12st   3 ran

[299⁵]	1		**PRINCE BUCK (IRE)** (7x) 2-5F B Hitchcott Ld 4; made rest; lft clr 12; sn in comm
[607⁸]	2	40	**Remilan (IRE)** (4x) (bl) 6-1 A Sansome Ld til slpd app 4; last frm 6; lost tch 8; lft 20l 2nd 12; nvr nr wnr
[676¹]		U	**Thats Dedication (IRE)** 7-2 D Robinson Prsd wnr frm 6; hit 11; 4l down aft mist & ur 12

OFFICIAL DISTANCE: dist **TIME:** 6min 47.0s **TOTE:** £1.40 **DF:** £3.90

709 Open Maiden (Div 1), 12st   8 ran

[309ᶠ]	1		**LORD ELLANGOWAN (IRE)** 20-1 D Dunsdon Hld up; detach in last pr til impd to cl 3rd 12; jnd ldrs 2 out; ld app last; just hld on
[457⁵]	2	s hd	**Larry** (7a) 5-1 P York Trckd ldrs; hdwy 10; ld 12; pushed along frm 4 out; hdd app last; rallied flat; just failed
		U	**At It Again (IRE)** (6ow) 25-1 R Chelton Last pr til mist & ur 8
[578²]		U	**Ell Gee** (5a) 4-1 P Townsley Cl up til ur 8
[284ᴾ]		P	**Native Dawn (IRE)** 8-1 C Gordon Ld/disp to 8; cl 5th but wkng 12; wl bhnd when pu 14
[679ᵁ]		U	**Oisin Dubh (IRE)** 25-1 Mrs L Stock Mists; prsd ldr/disp til ld 8; blun & ur 10
[679ᵁ]		P	**Sliabh Foy (IRE)** 14-1 F Marshall Trckd ldrs; cl 4th when mist & almost ur 11 (rdr lost reins); pu nxt
[23²]		r	**The Herbivore (IRE)** 4-5F B Hitchcott Jmpd sticky; hld up; hdwy 6; prsd ldrs 8; lft in ld 10; jmpd slow & hdd nxt; rmdrs 12; prsd ldr aft; hrd rdn 14; cl 3rd & btn when ref last

OFFICIAL DISTANCE: s hd **TIME:** 6min 42.0s **TOTE:** £18.00; places £9.00,£1.70 **DF:** £25.90

710 Open Maiden (Div 2), 12st   9 ran

[578²ᵈ]	1		**DREAMIN GEORGE (IRE)** 7-2 C Sherry A.p; prsd ldr frm 10 til ld 3 out; made rest; lft clr last; rdr saluted crowd last 50yds
[576⁴]	2	25	**Zaisan (IRE)** 3-1F D Dunsdon In tch; impd to press ldr & jmpd slow 12; lost plce aft nxt; pushed along 15; hdwy to 12l 3rd app 3 out; lft poor 2nd at last
[290³]	3	25	**Sarenacare (IRE)** 14-1 A Hickman A last pr; lost tch 14; lft 3rd by default
[571ᶠ]		U	**Call The Tune** (5a) 6-1 N Morris Mist 2; blun & ur 3
		P	**Colonel Pedlar** 33-1 P Hall Trckd ldrs til wknd 14; wl bhnd when pu 3 out

[433ᶠ]	P		**Mandalady (IRE)** (5a) 12-1 D Dennis *Hld up in last pr; hdwy to press ldrs 13; ev ch til wknd qckly 15; wl in rr when pu 2 out*
[457ᴮ]	R		**Mountain Tae (IRE)** 33-1 R Green *Rr when rn out 3*
[577ᶠ]	F		**Oxendale** 4-1 P Bull *Pulled hrd; a.p; ld 15 til hdd 3 out; hit nxt; 11 2nd & hld when fell last*
[7ᴾ]	P		**Straight Baron** 4-1 C Gordon *Ld to 14; wknd qckly aft nxt; 4th & no ch when pu last*

OFFICIAL DISTANCES: 25l, 25l **TIME:** 6min 48.0s **TOTE:** £2.20; places £1.40,£1.30,£2.70 **DF:** £3.40

711 Hunt, 12st   **5 ran**

[306ᶠ]	1		**BELVENTO (IRE)** 4-5F D Dunsdon *Hld up in detach last early; cl 4th at 7; smooth hdwy to trck ldr 13; ld app 15; made rest; v easy*
[309ᴾ]	2	3	**Rush 'n Tear** 6-1 M Gorman *A.p; ld 13 til hdd aft nxt; rdn along to chse wnr rest of way; kpt on game; a wl hld*
[305⁴]	3	12	**Exemplar (IRE)** 3-1 Mrs D Rowell *Ld to 3; prsd ldrs til lost plce aft 12; 8l 3rd 4 out; pushed along & no resp; no ch when climbed 2 out*
	4	2fncs	**Doctor Edward** 33-1 Miss S Stephens *Hdwy to ld 4 & 5; sn lost plce; lost tch aft 7; t.o frm 10*
[573ᴮ]	P		**Billie's Mate (IRE)** (5a) (bl) 10-1 J Hawksfield *Cl up til ld 6-12; 10l 4th & wkng 15; wl bhnd when pu last*

OFFICIAL DISTANCES: 4l, 20l **TIME:** 6min 38.0s **TOTE:** £1.70; places £1.80,£1.50 **DF:** £3.90

Duke of Buccleuch's
Friars Haugh (LH 9F,18J) Sat, 25 Mar (GOOD)

712 Hunt   **9 ran**

[360⁶]	1		**BORIS BROOK** 7-1 R Morgan *Tubed; chsd ldrs; 5l 5th 8; went 2l 2nd 11; mist 14; chall aft 15; ld aft nxt; 3l clr last; stayed on*
	2	3	**Mudahim** 5-1 Miss V Simpson *10s-5s; swtng; ld; 2l clr 9; 11 ahd 14; hdd aft nxt; 2l 2nd til outpcd app last; stayed on*
[420³]	3	runin	**Harleyburn** (bl) 2-1F Mrs A Hamilton *Hdstrng; trckd ldr; mist 1; 2l 2nd 3; 4l 3rd 8; mist nxt & 11; 5l mist 12; sn lost tch; 25l 4th 15; kpt on to tk poor 3rd at last*
[499⁴]	4	2	**Magical Poitin (IRE)** (5a) 16-1 G Armitage *Oht; a rr; 8l last aft 3; lost tch aft 12; 20l 3rd 15; mist & dem last*
	5	1½fs	**My Young Pet** 66-1 J Manclark *(xnb) Pulling; a rr; sn lost tch; 20l 7th 9; fnce bhnd 14; sn 2 fncs bhnd*
			Border Glory 4-1 Miss M Bremner *Swtng; chsd ldrs; 4th 7; 4l 4th nxt; disp 2l 2nd 9; pu qckly nxt; iron snapped*
[363²]	F		**Christiemouse** (5a) 10-1 Miss L Hislop *Oht; trckd ldrs; 3l 3rd 4; 2l 2nd 8; cl 5th when fell 10*
	U		**Connor (U)** (6ow) 25-1 J Galbraith *Prom early; 10l off pce & wkng 6; fnce bhnd 8; 2 fncs bhnd when overj 10; ur 20yds aft*
[493⁵]	F		**Love Actinium (IRE)** (5a) 3-1 C Niblo *Fell 1*

OFFICIAL DISTANCES: 4l, dist **TIME:** 6min 46.0s

713 Restricted   **14 ran**

[111ᴾ]	1		**MISS PORTCELLO** (5a) 6-1 Miss J Hollands *Mid-div early; prog 10 to 2l 2nd 11; chall aft 15; 2l up nxt; jnd 2 out; just ld last; r.o wl flat*
[497²]	2	nk	**Trivial (IRE)** (5a) 2-1F R Morgan *3s-2s; rr early; prog to 4l 5th 9; went 11 2nd 15; disp ld brief app nxt & agn frm 2 out; just outpcd*
[111ᵁ]	3	8	**Grey Rock (IRE)** (5a) 8-1 Miss M Bremner *Handy to 3l 4th 8; prog 15; 3l 3rd nxt; ev ch aft til outpcd app 2 out; stayed on; btr for rce*
	P		**Another Islay** 25-1 P Strang Steel *Cl up til lost tch 14; wl bhnd when pu nxt*
	P		**Armet Prince** 6-1 J Walton *In tch; hit 4 hrd & lost tch; rmdrs til bhnd & pu 8*
[425¹]	U		**Border Farmer (IRE)** 7-1 Mrs V Jackson *Oht; prom; 2l 2nd 8; disp ld brief 11; ev ch 2 out; 6l 3rd & lkd hld when ur last*
	P		**Dino's Mistral** 10-1 M Clayton *(xnb) Rr early; ld/disp 3 til hdd & outpcd aft 10; wl bhnd 15; pu nxt*
[498³]	P		**Flaming Sunrise** 5-2 Miss D Calder *Prom til ld 4; jnd 11; 8l 5th & outpcd 15; wknd qckly aft; wl bhnd & pu 2 out*
[418⁴]	P		**Madame Defarge** (5a) 12-1 Mrs K Hargreave *(xnb) Mid-div; hit 3; rr & outpcd by 10; wl bhnd 14; t.o nxt; pu 2 out*

[624¹]	P		**Menaldi (IRE)** 8-1 Miss K Roncoroni *Ld early; 8l 8th 9; stayed prom til outpcd 12; lsng tch aft nxt; pu 15*
	U		**Polly's Lady** (5a) 12-1 T Morrison *Ld/disp early; jmpd slow 2; grad wknd; 15l 9th when ur 10*
	U		**Seldom Seen (IRE)** 12-1 L Morgan *(bf) Rr; 20l 13th when ur 8*
	P		**The Parlour Maid** (5a) 12-1 T Scott *A rr; 20l last 10; pu aft 12*
[359⁸]	r		**Tropnevad** (bl) 10-1 B Lusted *In tch; hit 5; stdy prog to 10l 5th 15; outpcd & bhnd aft nxt; t.o when ref last; lkd sore*

OFFICIAL DISTANCES: ½l, 6l   **TIME:** 6min 47.0s

714 Dodson & Horrell PPORA Club Members, 12st   11 ran

[660³]	1		**FORDSTOWN (IRE)** (4x) 10-1 J Alexander *(bf) A.p; 4l 3rd 6; 3l 3rd 9; prog to ld 15; 4l up nxt; 2l ahd 2 out; stayed on wl*
[423¹]	2	3	**Mountain Thyne (IRE)** 4-5F C Storey *Settled in tch in rr; 15l off pce when jmpd slow 6; 6l 8th 10; prog to 6l 4th 13; hrd rdn aft 15; went 11 2nd aft nxt; prsd ldr app 2 out; a hld; fin lame*
	3	25	**Everready Go** (5a) 25-1 A Richardson *Handy; 3l 3rd 3; 4th 10; 10l 5th & outpcd 15; went poor 3rd flat; improve*
	4	4	**Blair Castle (IRE)** 6-1 L Morgan *(bf) Ld; jnd brief 8 & agn 12; hdd aft 14; 10l 3rd & wkng aft 3 out; one pce & dem flat*
[660ᴾ]	5	2½	**Thinkaboutthat (IRE)** 20-1 J Muir *Trckd ldr; 11 2nd 4; disp ld brief 8 & 12; 2l 2nd 14; 8l 3rd & wkng nxt*
[364ᴾ]	6	runin	**Snitton South** 16-1 J Walton *A rr; last pr & 20l off pce 2; sn t.o; fnce bhnd 12*
[360ᴾ]	P		**Buck Lady (IRE)** (5a) 25-1 Mrs V Jackson *Rr til 6l 7th 10; lost tch 14; pu aft*
	P		**Master Rocky** 10-1 R Morgan *Chsd ldrs; 10l 8th 4; outpcd 13; sn lost tch; pu 15; lkd sore*
[419¹]	P		**Senora D'Or** (5a) 8-1 Miss M Bremner *(bf) Cl up; 3l 3rd & mist 6; 7l 3rd 8; rdn 13; lsng tch when pu 15*
[358³]	U		**The Caffler (IRE)** 8-1 Miss R Ramsay *Swtng; oht; tde; cl up; 3l 5th when mist & ur 10*
[419¹]	P		**With Respect** 33-1 Miss D Crole *A rr; 20l off pce in last pr 3; sn t.o; fnce bhnd 15; pu nxt*

OFFICIAL DISTANCES: 5l, 25l   **TIME:** 6min 50.0s

715 Greig Middleton Ladies Open   5 ran

[421³]	1		**PHARMISTICE (IRE)** 3-1 Miss N Stirling *2 handlers; jw; cl 3rd til ld/disp frm 3; ld 8; 2l clr 14; prsd 3 out; sn drew clr; hit last; easy*
[621⁴]	2	10	**Astrac Trio (USA)** 7-4F Mrs A Hamilton *2s-7/4; ld to 2; trckd ldr frm 3; 4l 3rd 8; mist 10; 2nd 2 out; no ch w wnr*
[361⁴]	3	8	**Sharp Thyne (IRE)** (bl) 5-1 Miss M Bremner *Disp ld/cl 2nd; rmdrs 12; 11 2nd 3 out; sn dem & outpcd; kpt on*
	P		**Earlymorning Light (IRE)** 4-1 Miss R Ramsay *Handy; 8l 4th & jmpd slow 6; disp 6l last 8; 4l 3rd app 10; cl last & eff 15; 15l 4th & wkng aft nxt; bhnd & pu 2 out*
[621ᵁ]	P		**Little Santa (IRE)** (5a) (tt) 4-1 Mrs K Hargreave *Reluct start & lost 20l; 12l last aft 2; 5l last 13; eff to 4l 4th & mist 15; wknd qckly; pu 2 out; dism & lkd sore*

OFFICIAL DISTANCES: 15l, 15l   **TIME:** 6min 41.0s

716 Mens Open   9 ran

[495ᵁ]	1†		**EXCISE MAN** 9-4 J Walton *Lw; patient rdn in rr; prog to cl 3rd 10; hdwy to disp ld 2 out; r.o wl to ld flat; jnd on line*
[424ᵁ]	1†	d ht	**GEORDIES EXPRESS** 3-1 A Richardson *Lw; hld up in rr; prog to 3l 3rd 8; disp ld 10-13; chall & gng wl app 2 out; hdd brief flat; r.o to jn ldr on line*
[582⁴]	3	1	**Rainbow Times (IRE)** (5a) 7-4F C Storey *Lw; 5l 5th 3; trckd ldrs til prog to 2l 5th 15; rdn & jnd ldr app nxt; ev ch last; r.o; just outpcd*
[422⁴]	4	5	**Mullingar (IRE)** 12-1 L Morgan *Unruly padd; chsd ldrs; 4l 4th 3; hit 8; cl 3rd 14; rdn 16; ev ch til outpcd 2 out; kpt on game*
[493⁶]	5	8	**Boyup Brook** 7-1 T Morrison *Ld at sedate pce; jnd 4 & 5; 3l ahd 9; jnd nxt til outpcd app 2 out*
	6	4	**Chummy's Saga** 8-1 R Morgan *Swtng; hld up in rr; 6l last 7; prog to 5l 4th when mist & nrly ur 12; lost plce; rallied to 5l 6th 3 out; 5th & mist nxt; dem app last*
[622⁷]	7	runin	**Lottery Ticket (IRE)** 20-1 S J Robinson *Prom til disp ld 4 & 5; cl 2nd 7; 3l 4th & mist 10; 8th outpcd 15; sn wknd; wl bhnd 2 out*
[420ᶠ]	8	10	**Driminamore (IRE)** 10-1 W Ramsay *Prom early; 3l 3rd 9; 8l last 9; outpcd 14; 15l 8th & lsng tch 15; t.o 2 out; walked in*

[110⁵] U   **Master Hyde (USA)** (5ow) 16-1 **J Brown** *Rfo l*
     OFFICIAL DISTANCES: d ht, ½l **TIME:** 6min 49.0s

PLATE 12   716 Duke of Buccleuch's Mens Open: L to R Lottery Ticket, Mullingar, Driminamore, Excise Man, Geordies Express, Rainbow Times and Chummy's Saga turn back towards Floors Castle   PHOTO: Alan Mitchell

717 Confined, 12st   17 ran

[497¹]	1		**DUN ROSE** (5a) 4-5F **C Storey** *6/4-4/5; oht; prom; disp ll 2nd 8; ld 9; 3l clr 15; hdd app 2 out; kpt on; fin 2l 2nd; awarded rce*
[493⁸]	2	8	**Rum Rebel** 10-1 **J Walton** *Oht; rr; 10l 9th 8; prog to 5l 5th 15; 12l 4th & outpcd app 2 out; nt pushed aft; fin 3rd; promoted*
[419³]	3	3	**The Green Fool** 12-1 **H Humble** *(xnb) Chsd ldrs; prog 10; ev ch til 10l 3rd & outpcd aft 3 out; fin 4th; promoted*
[420F]	5	20	**Tin Cup** 12-1 **L Morgan** *Rr; prog to 4l 6th 8; disp ld brief 11; 11 2nd 14; outpcd aft nxt; wl bhnd aft 2 out; walked in*
[419F]	6	1½fs	**Kings Lane** 8-1 **Mrs K Weir** *Mid-div; 10l off pce 7; grad wknd frm 12; t.o 2 out*
[712F]	1d		**Love Actinium (IRE)** (5a) 7-1 **C Niblo** *Prom early; sn settled rr; prog to 3l 3rd 10 & 2l 3rd 15; ld app nxt; r.o wl; cheeky; wl rdn; won by 2l; disq - nt weigh-in*
[662P]	P		**Boss Morton (IRE)** (7x) 16-1 **J Alexander** *(bf) Ld/disp; hdd 9; outpcd 12; 20l 7th 15; t.o & nrly ur 2 out*
	U		**City Buzz (IRE)** 16-1 **S Clark** *Prom; hit 5; prog to disp ld aft 15; ev ch til slpd & ur bend bef 2 out*
[359P]	P		**Damas (FR)** (bl) 8-1 **Miss J Hollands** *Prom; outpcd aft 8; lsng tch aft 12; wl bhnd & pu 15*
[420⁴]	F		**Fragrant Lord** 6-1 **Mrs V Jackson** *Handy; 10l 9th 11 til 8l off pce 12; rdn & outpcd aft; fell 14*
[492P]	P		**Full Of Chat (IRE)** (5a) 12-1 **D Jewett** *2 handlers; ld; hit 4; outpcd 7; 15l 4th 9; pu aft 14*
[418⁵]	P		**Reve De Valse (USA)** (tt) 16-1 **Miss V Burn** *A rr; sn bhnd; fnce bhnd 7; t.o & pu 15*
[621⁷]	F		**Strongalong (IRE)** 10-1 **Miss K Roncoroni** *A.p; 2l 3rd 2; 4l 4th when fell 12*
[659¹]	P		**Tursal (IRE)** 16-1 **A Crookston** *A rr; 15l 15th aft 2; mist nxt; t.o 8; fnce bhnd 10; pu 3 out*
	P		**Unor (FR)** (tt) 10-1 **D Reid** *(bf)Rr; 20l off pce 10; t.o & pu aft 3 out*
[359³]	P		**Whispering Steel** 7-1 **R Morgan** *(boh) Prom; 11 2nd 2; outpcd aft 13; bhnd when pu aft 3 out*

[423⁷] P   **Wylup** 33-1 Mrs K Hargreave *(bf)* A rr; 10l last 1; t.o 8; 1½ fncs bhnd 10; pu 3 out

OFFICIAL DISTANCES: Originally 2l, 15l **TIME:** 6min 48.0s
Love Actinium finished first but was disqualified when the rider failed to weigh-in; he was fined £125

718 Confined Maiden (Div 1)   13 ran

	1		**GOLF LAND (IRE)** 8-1 S Huggan *Trckd ldrs; 3½l 3rd 6; smooth hdwy to 1½l 2nd 15; ld aft nxt; 1l up 2 out; lkd wnr when lft clr last; r.o flat
[499³]	2	8	**On Merit** 3-1 C Niblo *Lw; ld; 1l up 11; jnd 3 out & sn hdd; outpcd nxt; 5l 3rd & btn when lft 2nd & hmpd last*
[225³]	3	10	**Smiths Wynd** 7-2 T Scott *Trckd ldr; 2l 2nd 8; outpcd aft 3 out; btn & eased app nxt; lft 3rd last*
[665³]	4	1	**Myles Of Moss (IRE)** (5a) 3-1 D Reid *Settled rr; some prog aft 14 to 6l 6th nxt; 12l off pce app 3 out; kpt on*
[501³]	5	2	**Test Of Loyalty** 4-1 A Robson *Rr; bad mist 3; 15l off pce 14; short-lived eff in 8l 7th 15; sn outpcd*
[497³]	6	25	**Mesling** 6-1 J Walton *Rr; jmpd slow 1; 15l last 8; 20l 8th 15; t.o 2 out; tk poor 6th flat*
[107⁴]	7	8	**Benefit-In-Kind (IRE)** 5-2F C Storey *3s-5/2; chsd ldng trio; 3l 4th & ev ch 15; wknd qckly aft nxt; virt pu flat*
	F		**Carlinare** 4-1 L Morgan *(bf)* Rr; prog to 6l 8th when mist & nrly up 9; 4l 4th aft 3 out; sn 2nd & ev ch; 1½l down & lkd hld when fell last
	F		**Mr McQuaker** 5-1 M Clayton *A rr; 20l last 1; prog in mid-div & fell 10*
[664ᴮ]	P		**Poppers** 12-1 T Davidson *Prom early; 3l 3rd 3; 4l 4th 6; wknd 10; bhnd when pu aft 14*
[425ᶠ]	F		**Souden Lyric** 8-1 A Richardson *Mid-div; 7l 6th 3; in tch when fell 11*
[365ᶠ]	P		**Spot The Music (IRE)** (5a) 10-1 R Trotter *(bf)* Swtng; oht; chsd ldrs; 6l 5th 3; sn strugg; 20l last 11; wl bhnd 14; pu aft nxt
[365ᶠ]	F		**Stronacroibh** 4-1 R Morgan *Oht; mid-div til prog to trck ldrs 8; bad mist 10; in tch when fell nxt*

OFFICIAL DISTANCES: 15l, 20l **TIME:** 6min 54.0s

719 Confined Maiden (Div 2) - 16J   15 ran

[497³]	1		**SENSO (IRE)** evensF Mrs C Cox *Mid-div; 7l 8th 8; stdy prog to ld 14; rn sltly wide app nxt; jnd 15; rn wide & hdd app 2 out; sn ld agn; ½l up at last; r.o flat*
[364²]	2	½	**Lady Alice** (5a) 8-1 L Morgan *Ld/disp; ½l 2nd 8; chall 15; ld nxt; sn jnd til ld agn brief 2 out; ev ch last; no ex u.p flat*
[365⁴]	3	10	**Whiskey Galore** 8-1 R Morgan *(xnb)* Chsd ldrs; 5l 6th 9; prog to 2l 3rd 14; 3l 3rd 15; sn rdn & outpcd; kpt on
[418³]	4	1	**Setting Sail** 7-1 Mrs V Jackson *Rr early; prog to trck ldrs 5; 5l 4th 15; 12l 4th & outpcd nxt; kpt on*
[497⁴]	5	10	**Cruise Around** 10-1 S Ramsay *Sis; 25l last 2; hit 5; still 25l last 15; stayed on wl past btn horses frm 3 out; improve*
[365ᶠ]	6	15	**Liffey Lane** 10-1 M Clayton *Oht; trckd ldrs til outpcd app 15; wl bhnd aft nxt*
[501ᶠ]	F		**Border Reiver (IRE)** 4-1 D Jewett *Fell 1; inj rdr*
[498ᶠ]	F		**Colisnova** (5a) 10-1 C Niblo *Trckd ldr; 1l 2nd 3; 10l off pce & strugg when fell 10*
[189ᶠ]	P		**D V's Delight** (5a) 16-1 T Davidson *Sis; a rr; sn t.o; 30l last 10; pu nxt*
[425ᶠ]	P		**Harry Laws** 10-1 T Scott *(xnb)* Made most til stpd alarm aft 14; sn pu nxt
	B		**Lethem Ghost** (12a) 10-1 A Richardson *Bd 1*
	B		**Mornay Des Garnes (FR)** 20-1 P Strang Steel *(xnb)* 2 handlers; swtng; in tch in rr; 10l 9th 8; bd 11
[424⁵]	B		**Rye Rum (IRE)** 4-1 J Walton *Mid-div; prog to 2½l 5th 9; bd 11*
[425ᶠ]	P		**The Dyke Louper** (5a) 4-1 B Lusted *Nt a fluent; mid-div; wkng in 10l 6th 15; strugg & pu bef nxt*
[188⁵]	U		**The Other Half** (bl) 10-1 S Swiers *A handy; 3l 8th 8; 2l 3rd 9; blun & ur 11*

OFFICIAL DISTANCES: ½l, 20l **TIME:** 6min 55.0s
Fences 8 & 15 omitted - fallen rider

Lamerton
Kilworthy (LH 8F,18J) Sat, 25 Mar (GOOD becoming SOFT)

720 Hunt   7 ran

| [654⁶] | 1 | | **BROWN ROBBER** 13-2 T Dennis *(xnb)* 2nd 5; ld 9; slt ld 2 out; drvn clr last; all out |
| [541¹] | 2 | 2 | **Solomans Sister** (5a) 4-6F Mrs M Hand *Tchd 4/7; lw; cl 4th mostly; hdwy to 2nd 15; chsd wnr & ev ch 2 out; stayed one pce run-in* |

[406³]	3	4	**Ledburian** 10-1 C Heard *In tch; 2nd frm 10-15; rdn & wknd 16; hrd rdn 2 out; stayed on stdly*
[534²]	4	20	**Dancing Ranger** 10-1 Richard Darke *Handy on inner; cl 3rd ½way; lost tch 15; no ch frm 3 out*
[312¹]	5	20	**The Bandon Car (IRE)** 100-30 T Cole *7s-100/30; lw; towards rr; 5th & in tch 12; 4th & rdn 15; lost ground; btn when jmpd lft clsng stages*
[560⁷]	6	30	**Crownhill Cross** 100-1 Miss Johanna Sleep *Nov rdn; sn last & strugg; bhnd frm 8; t.o*
[583ᴾ]	7	25	**Gibraltar Lady** (5a) 50-1 S Craddock *(xnb) Mounted on course; pulled hrd; sn clr; jmpd lft 8; hdd 9; wknd rap; bhnd frm 13; t.o*

OFFICIAL DISTANCES: 1¾l, 3l TIME: 6min 25.5s

721 Confined Maiden (Div 1, Part 1), 12st   9 ran

[556²]	1		**KNOCK STAR (IRE)** 7-4F S Partridge *Opened 2s; lw; ld 4; made rest; drew 4l clr 15; kpt on str app last; comf; rdr's 1st wnr*
[538²]	2	6	**King Tudor** 4-1 R Woollacott *In tch; 5th when slt mist 9; went 3rd 14; r.o stdly u.p frm 3 out; tk 2nd cl home*
[657ᴾ]	3	nk	**Masked Martin** 12-1 S Kidston *Sn prom; trckd ldr; outpcd 15; tried to chall 2 out; sn shrugged off; hrd rdn & wknd flat; dem nr line*
[312ᴾ]	4	1½	**Linton** (5a) 20-1 W Smith *Prom; lft in ld 2; sn hdd; 5l 3rd 10; lost ground aft 14; 4th & btn nxt; no hdwy u.p*
[540ᴾ]	5	40	**Golden Sunset** (5a) 20-1 Miss D Mitchell *Just in tch to 9; bhnd frm 12*
[656ᴾ]	6	25	**Birch Tor** 33-1 J Cole *Sn towards rr; slt mist 11; wl bhnd frm 12*
[311ᴿ]	R		**Cornish Hope** 5-1 Miss S Young *Rap hdwy to ld aft 1; swerved violent; rn out & ur 2*
[540ᴾ]	P		**Miltown Castle** 7-1 K Sheppard *Tk keen hld; 4th & jmpd untidy 9 & 10; lost plce 12; 6th when pu 14*
[162ᴾ]	P		**Spartans Last** (12a) 14-1 K Heard *Rr & school early; hdwy 12; 6th when pu 15; quiet rn*

OFFICIAL DISTANCES: 5l, hd TIME: 6min 47.5s

722 Confined Maiden (Div 1, Part 2), 12st   8 ran

[656ꟳ]	1		**BLACK DANTE (IRE)** 5-4F A Charles-Jones *Opened 2s; jw; hld up in tch; 6l 5th 10; smooth hdwy to 3rd 12; disp ld 16; ld 2 out; r.o strd and hands & heels; v easy; impressive; lks useful*
	2	6	**Henrys Song** 6-1 Richard Darke *(xnb) Oht; ld in start; prom; trckd ldr 10 til slt ld 15; disp ld 16; hdd nxt; jmpd lft last; kpt on u.p; fair ef*
[658ᵁ]	3	5	**Amazing Hill (IRE)** 16-1 Mrs R Morris *Ld to 15; wknd stdly frm nxt*
[562ᴾ]	4	30	**Mount Keen** 12-1 D Stephens (Devon) *Swtng; midfield; 6th when mist 10; nt rch ldrs; poor 4th frm 14*
	5	25	**Druid Merill** (5a) 12-1 Miss T Cave *Tchd 14s; sn trailing; a bhnd; school*
	P		**Calvary Hill** 12-1 D Doyne-Ditmas *Handy; 3rd 10; slt mist 11; wknd & pu 14*
[312ᴮ]	U		**Frankie Moneybags** 9-4 T Dennis *(xnb) Lw; pulled hrd in midfield & nt fluent; 5½l 4th ½way; in tch in 5th when blun & ur 11*
[253ꟳ]	P		**Travelling Jack** (7a) 6-1 J Young *Last when blun & nrly ur 3; bhnd; jmpd violent rt 13; pu nxt*

OFFICIAL DISTANCES: 6l, 5l TIME: 6min 32.8s

723 Confined Maiden (Div 2, Part 1), 12st   8 ran

[538³]	1		**THE UGLY DUCKLING** 7-2 R Woollacott *Lw; handy; went 2nd 9; ld 3 out; hrd rdn & forged clr app last; kpt on*
	2	12	**Change** 17-2 T Dennis *(xnb) Tchd 9s; rcd keen & nt a fluent; ld to 3 out; no ex; do btr*
	3	5	**My Prides Way** (5a) 7-1 T Greed *(xnb) Settled 5th; in tch to 13; went 12l 3rd 15; blun nxt; no ch clsng stages*
[158²]	4	3	**Alpine Castle (IRE)** (5a) 4-6F Miss S Young *(b4) Wl plcd; cl 4th 9; lost ground 13; lft 3rd 14; sn btn; no ch frm 16; rem 4th but r.o cl home*
[654ᴾ]	5	6	**Walton Street** 33-1 W Smith *Prom early; sn lost plce; rr frm 8; t.o frm 14; mist last*
	U		**B For Business** (12a) 33-1 S Kidston *(xnb) Bckwd; rr; refb when ur 10*
[253ꟳ]	P		**Playing For Money** (5a) 16-1 R Emmett *Oht; slt mist 3; rr when jmpd rt 4; bhnd til pu 15*
	F		**Warning Board** 33-1 J Berwick *Swtng; prom on outer; cl 3rd ½way; in tch til faltered aft 13; fell nxt*

OFFICIAL DISTANCES: 13l, 2l TIME: 6min 39.0s

724 Confined Maiden (Div 2, Part 2), 12st   9 ran

[539³]	1		**HANUKKAH** (5a) 8-1 I Hambley *Midfield; gd hdwy to 3rd 12; cl up; 1l 2nd & rdn 16; disp ld when lft clr 2 out; wandered app last*

	2	12	**Melroy (IRE)** 16-1 D Doyne-Ditmas *Handy; cl 2nd 5; mist 10; disp ld 12-15; lost tch; slty hmpd & lft 2nd 2 out; nt disg*
[540²]	3	30	**Opera Festival (IRE)** 2-1F D Stephens (Devon) *Sn prom; cl 3rd when slt mist 9; lost ground frm 12; 4th & btn frm 14; no hdwy u.p frm 15*
[539ᴾ]	4	7	**Patrio (IRE)** (5a) 33-1 J Cole *Lkd fitter; prom early; lost plce 8; 7th 11; no ch; lft poor 4th 2 out*
[540⁴]	F		**Georgetown** 5-2 L Jefford *Hld up in tch; prog to 3rd 10; cl up til slt ld 15; jnd & ev ch when fell 2 out*
	P		**Hendra Chieftain** 16-1 N Harris *Nfurnished; school in midfield; lost ground 11; 7th when pu 13*
[105ᴾ]	P		**Resource (IRE)** 3-1 Richard Darke *Oht; sa & lost 30l; t.o & pu 3 out*
	P		**Safara** 25-1 Miss A Barnett *Mists in rr til pu 6*
[540ᵁ]	P		**Spirit Of Life** (5a) 20-1 M Woodward *Prom; ld frm 5; blun 10; hdd nxt; ldng ground when blun bad 12; 6th when pu nxt*

OFFICIAL DISTANCES: 15l, 30l **TIME:** 6min 46.0s

725 Ladies Open   11 ran

[314²]	1		**BABY WHALE (IRE)** (5a) 5-1 Mrs M Hand *7s-5s; lw; 5th ½way; hdwy to 3rd 13; sust chall frm 15; disp ld 2 out; slt mist last; sn ld; r.o str u.p*
[326⁶]	2	nk	**Mine's A Gin (IRE)** 9-4 Miss J Cumings *Opened 3s; handy; 5l 3rd 11; cl 3rd 15; chall 2 out; slt ld last; sn hdd; nt much room but battled on game; nt quite get up*
[222³]	3	4	**Ticket To The Moon** (5a) 11-8F Miss T Cave *Lw; made most to 10; 2nd til ld agn 14; jnd 2 out; ev ch last; no ex last 150yds*
[519³]	4	30	**Mr Golightly** 20-1 Mrs J Reed *Ld 1; prom; cl 5th 12; outpcd & lost tch aft 14; snatched 4th cl home*
[316²]	5	¾	**Dunlir** 50-1 Miss S Young *Mid-div; 7th ½way; nd*
[405¹]	6	4	**Mr Jervis (IRE)** 14-1 Miss V Tremlett *Cl up til ld 10; hdd 14; in tch til wknd u.p frm 15*
[562³]	7	2	**Luney River** (5a) 66-1 Miss L Gardner *A midfield; 7th when mist 12; no ch clsng stages*
[455³]	8	1	**Mel (IRE)** 50-1 Miss M Eames *Swtng; towards rr; 9th & bhnd 12; t.o*
[558⁹]	9	15	**Secret Four** 20-1 Miss K Langdell *Sn last & strugg; t.o frm 11*
[205³]	P		**Persian Dawn** (5a) 50-1 Miss C Prouse *A rr; t.o & pu 15*
[402⁴]	R		**Thinking Twice (USA)** 6-1 Miss M Coombe *Prom; disp ld when jmpd rt 5; cl up til crashed thro wing 8*

OFFICIAL DISTANCES: hd, 1½ **TIME:** 6min 30.0s

726 Confined, 12st   8 ran

[583⁴]	1		**BALDHU CHANCE** 4-1 A Ede *Ld 2-7; agn frm 9; slt ld til drew clr 2 out; stayed on*
[536⁴]	2	4	**Spruce** (5a) 3-1JF Mrs S Fell *Settled 3rd; impd 9; trckd ldr frm 12; cl up & ev ch til no ex w rdr virt motionless frm 2 out*
[558³]	3	8	**No More Nice Guy (IRE)** 7-2 Mrs M Hand *Lw; 5th when rmdrs 8; 4th ½way; hdwy to 3rd 12; ev ch 15; sn one pce u.p*
[383⁶]	4	5	**Willie B Brave (IRE)** 10-1 D Alers-Hankey *Lw; midfield; 5th 10; nt rch ldrs; btn 4th frm 3 out*
[534³]	5	1	**Where's Sam (IRE)** 14-1 S Craddock *Lw; in tch in 6th 10; lost ground frm 12; no ch aft*
[556ᵁ]	P		**Agent** 12-1 C White *(xnb) Ld 1; cl 2nd to 12; lost plce qckly nxt; btn 5th when pu 14*
[258³]	P		**Lirsleftover** 3-1JF Miss S Young *Sn rr; poor 7th when pu 8*
[534⁵]	P		**Moorland Abbot** 50-1 Miss D Mitchell *Sn last; t.o 4; fnce bhnd 12; pu 15*

OFFICIAL DISTANCES: 3½l, 8l **TIME:** 6min 39.0s

727 Mens Open   9 ran

[474¹]	1		**BUTLER JOHN (IRE)** 4-5F N Harris *Tchd 10/11; made all; 2l up & rdn 2 out; r.o str u.p when chall aft 2 out; drew clr flat*
[561¹]	2	7	**Tuskar Flop** 11-2 D Alers-Hankey *Lw; 12l 3rd 9; stdy hdwy frm 15; rcd wide for btr ground; chall & ev ch aft 2 out; 2l down last; no ex u.p run-in*
[537¹]	3	3	**Texan Baby (BEL)** 5-1 K Sheppard *Tchd 6s; lw; chsd ldr; ev ch til tiring & jmpd rt 2 out; wknd app last; fair eff*
	P		**Certain Angle** 66-1 E Chanin *Bit bckwd; nov rdn; hdwy 9; went 4th 12; some hdwy aft 15; nt trble ldrs; btn 4th when pu 2 out*
[534ᴾ]	P		**Forest Musk (IRE)** 66-1 I Hambley *Sn rr; bhnd when pu 11*
[149ᴾ]	P		**Highway Lad** 5-1 L Jefford *Tchd 6s; hld up in midfield; hdwy to 4th But sn rmdrs 11; btn 5th when pu 13; lethargic display*
[165ᴾ]	P		**Queen's Award (IRE)** 66-1 S Craddock *Prom til jmpd rt 3; sn u.p; bhnd frm 8; rmdrs 10; t.o & pu 13*

	P		Ryming Cuplet 33-1 B Trickey *Rr when bad mist 2; t.o 6; pu 13*
	P		Valnau (FR) 25-1 C White *Chsd ldrs; 4th when jmpd rt 4; 6th 10; sn lost plce 111 btn 6th when pu 13*

OFFICIAL DISTANCES: 6l, 2½l TIME: 6min 32.0s

728 Restricted (Div 1), 12st
16 ran

[410U]	1		MINER'S BILL (IRE) 3-1 L Jefford *(xnb) Tchd 4s; lw; patient rdn in rr; stdy hdwy on outer 13; went 3rd 2 out; chall nxt; ld aft last; strode clr*
[256U]	2	2½	Fossy Bear (5a) 9-2 Miss S Young *Rr early; gd hdwy to 7th 11 & 2nd 16; disp ld 2 out; sltly outpcd app last; stayed on wl run-in*
[562²]	3	3	Copastrop 20-1 R Woollacott *Tde; ld in start & lost 10l; drpd out last to ½way; stdy prog frm 13; 4th 3 out; chall & ev ch app last; one pce*
[541⁶]	4	1	Rice Point 12-1 C Heard *(xnb) 2 handlers; lw; prom on outer in cl bunched field; 9th but wl in tch ½way; gd hdwy to 2nd 14; ld/disp 3 out til slt ld last; wknd*
[524³]	5	8	Nearly Fair (5a) 14-1 T Greed *Tchd 16s; sn prom; ld brief 7; cl 6th 11; lost ground 14; hld in 5th frm 3 out*
[351¹]	6	2½	Pallingham Lad (IRE) 6-1 S Kidston *Sn prom; ld 10-13; lost plce nxt*
[147¹]	7	2	Maybridge Lady (5a) 2-1F D Alers-Hankey *Lw; sn towards rr; slt prog frm ½way; nrst fin; may need faster ground*
[315⁶]	8	5	Frankly Fear 20-1 J Young *Prom & rcd keen; cl 4th 9 til ld 13-15; sn wknd*
[73⁴]	P		Aint No Lady (IRE) (5a) 66-1 Miss S Robinson *Nt fluent; 10th when mist 10; hit 12 & rmdrs; bhnd frm 13 til pu 2 out*
[202ᴾ]	P		Devonshire Lad 66-1 Miss K Cook *Midfield; hdwy to 5th but rdn 11; bhnd when pu 15*
[315ᴾ]	U		King Of Cairo 66-1 I Hambley *(xnb) Mist 2; prom on outer til lost ground stdly frm 11; bhnd when blun & ur last*
[523³]	P		Mr Kevernair 20-1 M Woodward *Tk keen hld; ld 4-7 & 8 til slt mist 9; in tch til lost plce 14; pu 2 out*
	F		Mystic Warrior (USA) (7a) 20-1 Richard Darke *Tchd 25s; rr when fell 5*
[538ᶠ]	P		Sea Spirit (5a) 33-1 T Jones (Devon) *A rr; 11th ½way; bhnd & pu 2 out*
	P		Sister Swing (12a) 33-1 C Barlow *(xnb) Towards rr; bhnd frm 9; pu 15; quiet intro*
	P		Uncle James (IRE) 25-1 C White *Handy; 6th ½way; lost pce frm 12; bhnd & pu 2 out*

OFFICIAL DISTANCES: 2½l, 3l TIME: 6min 37.0s

729 Restricted (Div 2), 12st
17 ran

[538¹]	1		ELLIEWELLIEWOO (5a) 8-11F L Jefford *Opened 5/4 in plce; made virt all & gng wl; qcknd clr when chall aft 2 out; impressive*
[580U]	2	5	Shobrooke Mill 6-1 A Charles-Jones *(xnb) Rcd on outer for btr ground; 6th ½way; stdy hdwy to 2nd 14; str chall app 2 out; sn outpcd*
[536²]	3	15	Brother Nero (NZ) 8-1 C Heard *Lw; sn prom; cl 3rd 11; lost tch w ldrs frm 14; disp 3rd 2 out; one pce*
[406ᴾ]	4	2½	Wonford Boy 11-2 K Heard *(xnb) 2 handlers; chsd ldrs; 2nd 13; cl 3rd & ev ch 3 out; one pce*
	5	15	Barton Rose 10-1 D Alers-Hankey *Tchd 14s; midfield; nt rch ldrs; hld in 5th frm 3 out*
[315⁷]	6	8	Phartoomanny (IRE) (5a) 20-1 Miss N Snowden *Prom; 4th ½way; lost tch 14*
	7	10	Mosside 33-1 N Harris *Sn rr; t.o frm 14*
[559⁵]	8	15	The Stuffed Puffin (IRE) 16-1 Miss S Rowe *(nosenet) Rr frm ½way; t.o frm 14*
	P		Baron Knayber 25-1 S Edwards *Bhnd 9 til pu 15*
[157ᴾ]	P		Bridge House Boy 20-1 A Oliver *(xnb) Rr when mist 11; bhnd 14 til pu 2 out*
[458³]	P		Church Ride (IRE) 25-1 R Woollacott *Sn rr; bhnd frm 9; btn 7th when pu 2 out*
[315ᴾ]	P		Lirkimalong 66-1 Miss S Young *2 handlers; towards rr; bhnd when pu 15*
[633U]	P		Lost Your Marbles (IRE) (5a) 14-1 J Mead *2 handlers; sn prom; cl 3rd 9; lost plce qckly frm 12; pu 14*
[315ᴾ]	P		Newlyn 50-1 J King *Rr til pu 15*
	P		Pixie In Purple (IRE) 20-1 D Stephens (Devon) *In tch; cl 5th 9; lost plce 11; rr when pu 13*
[353U]	F		River Carron (IRE) 20-1 C Barlow *Fell 2*
[314ᴾ]	P		Roving Rebel 33-1 Miss C Prouse *Prom early; rn v wide first bend; bhnd frm 9 til pu 14*

OFFICIAL DISTANCES: 4l, 20l TIME: 6min 32.0s

730 Intermediate, 12st
11 ran

[536¹]	1		WIBBLEY WOBBLEY 4-5F Miss J Cumings *Tchd evens; lw; cl 3rd 8; jnd ldrs 10; disp ld 11-15; drew clr 3 out; r.o str; v easy*

[654⁵]	2	40	**Lead Story (IRE)** 5-1 Richard Darke *Sn prom on inner; cl 2nd 8; disp ld 10-15 & drew clr w wnr; wknd 3 out; 10l 2nd 2 out; fin v tired*
[541²]	3	2	**Jeepers (IRE)** 20-1 S Kidston *Prom; 6th 10; went 4th 12; poor 3rd frm 15; clsng cl home*
[541³]	P		**Babbling Brook (IRE)** (bl) 4-1 L Jefford *Prom til mist 8; 5th & sharp rmdrs aft 10; sn reluct & wknd; pu 13*
[315⁵]	P		**Born Natural (IRE)** (5a) (tt) 33-1 R Woollacott *(xnb)Stdd start; rr til hdwy 10; 7th 12; rr nr ldrs; btn 4th when pu 2 out*
[557⁸]	P		**Foxy Dawn** 14-1 D Alers-Hankey *2 handlers; hdwy to 4th 8; prom til lost plce 12; 5th & wkng when pu 14*
	P		**Master Pan** 50-1 I Widdicombe *WI bhnd til pu 14*
[157ᶠ]	P		**Moorland Rose** (12a) 100-1 Miss D Mitchell *Bit bckwd; sn bhnd; t.o & pu 11*
[214ᶠ]	P		**Shrewd Thought (USA)** 12-1 T Greed *Lw; ld to 3; lost plce 11; bhnd & pu 15*
[147ᶠ]	P		**The Greenkeeper (IRE)** 33-1 C Heard *Lw; pulled hrd; ld 3 til jnd 10; cl 3rd 12; lost plce stdly; bhnd when pu 3 out*
[310ᶠ]	P		**Tubb Corner** 50-1 T Jones (Devon) *(xnb) WI bhnd til pu 14*

OFFICIAL DISTANCES: dist, 5l TIME: 6min 38.0s

Mendip Farmers
Ston Easton (RH 7F,18J) Sat, 25 Mar (GOOD becoming SOFT)

731 Hunt, 12st
4 ran

[406¹]	1		**WE MOVE EARTH** 1-4F Miss P Gundry *Jw; hld up til 2l 2nd 4; ww til ld 12; sn clr; 10l up 14; unchall*
[581⁵]	2	20	**The Bold Abbot** 5-2 Miss S West *Ld; 2l up 7 til hdd aft 11; sn brushed aside; r.o one pce frm 3 out*
[357⁴]	3	15	**Via Del Quatro (IRE)** (5a) (vis) 10-1 J Barnes *Chsd ldrs to 3; sn strugg; 15l last 6; nrly fnce bhnd 15; tk little interest agn*
[356⁴]	U		**Cool Weather (IRE)** (17ow) 25-1 P Thorner *Last til rfo 4*

OFFICIAL DISTANCES: 20l, 20l TIME: 6min 30.4s TOTE: £1.20 DF: £1.30

732 Open Maiden 56&7yo (Div 1), 2m4f, 12st - 14J
14 ran

[284²]	1		**PHAR FROM CHANCE** (7a) 6-4F Miss P Gundry *A.p; chsd clr ldr 3 til ld 12; sn 10l clr; v easy*
	2	12	**Mrs Duf** (5a) 10-1 R Walford *Rcd in mid-div; 7th & lkd hld 3 out; sust rn frm nxt; fin fast; went 2nd nr line*
[472³]	3	½	**Dunston Trigger** 16-1 Miss S Vickery *Chsd ldrs in mostly 4th; 3rd & staying on frm 3 out; chsd wnr vain frm nxt; dem nr line*
[353ᶠ]	4	½	**Telimar (IRE)** 7-1 J Barnes *Hld up in rr; 8th 5; grad impd to 6th & mist 8; stayed on str frm 3 out; fin fast*
	5	3	**Sacrifice** (7a) 12-1 G Barfoot-Saunt *(xnb) Hld up in rr; 10th 5; prog to 6th when mist 11; stayed on frm 3 out; nrst fin; nt disg*
	6	10	**Fursan (USA)** (tt) 50-1 P Phillips *Ld aft 2; dived at nxt; sn 10l clr; rdr called cab 7; pegged back & mist 11; sn hdd; 3rd & wkng when jmpd slow last; lost sev plces flat*
[541ᶠ]	7	12	**Button Up Bill** 40-1 H Thomas *2 handlers; last 5; a bhnd; t.o frm 3 out*
[656ᵁ]	P		**Highland Pearl** (5a) 50-1 M Shears *Last when jmpd lft 2; prog to trck ldrs in 5th 9 til wknd 11; bhnd when pu 2 out*
	F		**L'orphelin** (7a) 10-1 M Miller *Jmpd novicey 2; 5th when fell nxt; broke fnce*
[407ᶠ]	r		**Montepulciano (IRE)** *(xnb) Ref to rce*
[407³]	U		**Peasedown Tofana** (5a) 3-1 R Young *(xnb) Cl up when blun & ur 3*
[520ᶠ]	P		**Penthouse Minstrel** 25-1 B O'Doherty *2 handlers; a towards rr; 9th 5 til pu 9*
[264ᶠ]	P		**Perking** (5a) G Maundrell *Ld 1; chsd ldng pr aft; wkng when mist 3 out; bhnd & pu last*
	P		**Star General** 33-1 A Honeyball *Tde; pulled hrd; ld brief 2; grad lost plce; t.o 11 til pu 3 out*

OFFICIAL DISTANCES: 12l, ½l TIME: 5min 18.2s TOTE: £2.50 DF: £54.00
Fence 10 omitted - damaged

733 Open Maiden 56&7yo (Div 2), 2m4f, 12st - 13J
14 ran

	1		**MUDSLIDE** 5-1 Miss P Gundry *(xnb) Rcd in 3rd/4th mostly til chsd ldrs 8; ld nxt; 1½l up 11; made rest; easy*
[146²]	2	5	**Happy Team** (5a) 4-1CF David Dennis *Jmpd lft 2; last nxt; gd prog to 6th 9; stayed on frm 3 out; lft 2nd at last*
[204ᶠ]	3	30	**Tony's Time** 6-1 Miss O Green *Trckd ldrs to 2; sn lost plce; 10th 5; stayed on frm rr to 4th 3 out; lft rem 3rd at last*

	4	8	**Rapid Liner** 20-1 J Gallagher *Pulling hrd; ld aft 2-7; grad lost plce; bhnd frm 12; lft rem 4th by defections last*
[455⁷]	5	15	**Just Reuben (IRE)** (7a) 10-1 R Walford *Chsd ldrs til disp ld brief 4; wkng when rmdrs 9; t.o frm 12; walked in*
[641ᵁ]	P		**Final Chance** (5a) 4-1CF N Mitchell *Chsd ldrs; 6th 6; disp ld brief 8; grad lost plce; wknd 12; bhnd when pu last*
	F		**Fullofancy** (5a) 9-2 M Miller *Mid-div 6; prog to 5th 9; lft chsng ldr 11; ll down 3 out; 2nd & hld when fell last*
[408³]	P		**Indian Muse** (12a,4ow) 12-1 M Shears *Mid-div early; sn lost plce & last 5; mist 8; t.o 11 til pu last*
[640ᶠ]	P		**Mayfair Monarch** (7a) 5-1 H Froud *(bf) 2 handlers; ld to 2; rdr called cab 4; ld agn brief 8; sn lost plce; bhnd when pu aft 12*
[518⁴]	P		**Spirito** (7a) 5-1 Jeremy Young *11th when jmpd slow 5; a bhnd til pu 11*
[655⁷]	P		**Summer Pudding** (5a) 10-1 J Barnes *Rr when jmpd lft 2l; 9th 5; bhnd aft til pu last*
[518ᴿ]	P		**Super Rooster** 4-1CF G Barfoot-Saunt *Trckd ldrs; 5th 6; grad wknd frm 11; bhnd when pu & dism 2 out; lame*
[457ᶠ]	U		**Team Captain** 10-1 A Honeyball *Late in padd; rcd in mid-div; 7th 6; prog to chse ldr aft 9; 1½l down & gng wl when blun & ur 11*
	P		**Wild Oscar (IRE)** 10-1 G Richards *(xnb) A towards rr; 13th when mist 4; jmpd slow 6; t.o & pu aft 9*

OFFICIAL DISTANCES: 4l, 20l **TIME:** 5min 12.4s **TOTE:** £6.00 **DF:** £8.50
Fences 3 & 10 omitted - damaged

734 Restricted, 12st - 16J
14 ran

[409¹]	1		**FINNIGAN FREE** 5-1 A Honeyball *Hld up in rr til mid-div 9; hdwy to 4th 11; chsd ldr 14 til ld 3 out; sn drew clr; pushed out flat*
[513⁸]	2	2½	**Derryair** 33-1 J Owen *A.p; chsd ldr til ld 7; 2l up nxt til hdd 3 out; stayed on one pce frm nxt*
[410¹]	3	15	**Rossaleen** (5a) (bl) 14-1 P Shaw *Rr 5 til some prog to mid-div 9 & 3rd 11; 5l 4th 14; stayed on one pce frm 2 out*
[455¹]	4	30	**Fasgo (IRE)** (7a) 6-4F Miss P Gundry *Chsd ldrs; 6th 5; 3l 3rd 14; 4th & no ex frm 2 out; fin tired*
[260⁷]	5	1	**Old Harry's Wife** (5a) 25-1 N Mitchell *Ld 3-7; 3l 2nd 11; sn wknd; bhnd frm 3 out*
[477²]	6	½	**Encima Del Rio (IRE)** 6-1 B King *Rr 5; last 9; t.o frm 14*
[391¹]	7	6	**Drunkard's Corner** (12a) 5-2 Miss N McKim *A rr; last 7; 5th but nd 3 out; t.o frm nxt*
[537⁴]	P		**Chocolate Buttons** (5a) 33-1 H Thomas *Rr 5; prog to mid-div 9; wknd qckly 12; bhnd when pu 15*
[519⁴]	P		**Givry (IRE)** (bl) 33-1 N Parker *Prom; 4th 4; grad lost plce; rr 9; t.o & pu 2 out*
	P		**Italian Man (IRE)** 10-1 A Morley *2 handlers; rr 5; 13th 9; t.o frm 14 til pu 3 out*
[477ᵁ]	P		**Rhyme And Chime** 12-1 Miss S Vickery *Trckd ldrs; 5th 6; 4l 4th 8; grad lost plce; bhnd when pu aft 12*
[560²]	P		**Ribington** 16-1 M Miller *Ld to 3; 3l 3rd 8; grad lost plce; bhnd when pu aft 12*
[254¹]	U		**Versicium (FR)** 5-2 Miss O Green *(xnb) Early; prog to mid-div when blun & ur 11*
[36⁷]	P		**West Lutton** 66-1 P Young *Mid-div 5 til wknd 12; t.o & pu 3 out*

OFFICIAL DISTANCES: 4l, 12l **TIME:** 6min 22.2s **TOTE:** £5.50 **DF:** c/f
Fences 6 & 13 omitted from this and all subsequent races - damaged

735 Mixed Open, 12st - 14J
9 ran

[402²]	1		**GAMAY** 3-1 N Mitchell *(xnb) Hld up in rr; stdy hdwy to 6th 10; smooth prog to disp 3rd 13; chsd clr ldr nxt til swept into ld aft 3 out; sn clr; in comm when veered lft run-in*
[402⁵]	2	12	**Iranos (FR)** (bl) 6-4 Miss O Green *4th til chsd ldr 4; ld aft nxt; 4l up 8; 10l ahd 14 til jmpd slow 3 out; hdd bef nxt; sn no ex*
[262⁶]	3	3	**Funny Farm** (bl) 8-1 Miss S Vickery *Rstrnd in rr; outpcd aft 12; stayed on wl frm 3 out; nrst fin*
[522³]	4	6	**Hillhead (IRE)** 6-1 Miss S Sharratt *8l 5th 6; outpcd aft 12; stayed on frm 3 out; nd*
[584¹¹]	5	3	**Skip'n'time** 4-5F M Miller *(xnb) Chsd ldr; 4l 3rd 4; disp 12l 3rd 14; rdn & stayed on frm 3 out; tired & dem flat; walked in*
[149ᵖ]	6	2	**Apple John** 9-1 Miss P Gundry *Ld; sn 5l clr to 5; chsd ldr til wknd 14; bhnd frm 3 out*
[628³]	7	5	**Flapjack Lad** 10-1 J Barnes *(xnb) 5l 4th 4; chsd ldr frm 11-14; grad wknd; bhnd frm 3 out*
[521⁵]	8	20	**Air Command (BAR)** 20-1 P Phillips *Prom early; last 6; sn outpcd; t.o frm 12*
	P		**Earl Boon** 6-1 A Honeyball *Trckd ldrs; 4th 3 til wknd 9; bhnd when pu 12*

OFFICIAL DISTANCES: 12l, 2l **TIME:** 6min 21.4s **TOTE:** £6.70 **DF:** £42.50
Fences 10 & 17 omitted - damaged

Chase Publications

Stour House
68 Grove Road
Wimborne
Dorset
BH21 1BW

nts

PLATE 13   735 Mendip Farmers Mixed Open: Apple John leads from Iranos, Skip'n'time, Flapjack Lad, with the grey, Earl Boon just about visible   PHOTO: Nick Jay

736 Countryside Alliance Club Members (Nov Rdrs), 12st - 16J   13 ran

[454⁵]	1		**STARPATH (NZ)** 4-5F **R Biddlecombe** *Chsd ldrs; 2l 2nd 4 til ld 14; made rest; drew clr flat*
	2	4	**Zingibar** (bl) 6-1 **Miss J Houldey** *Prog frm mid-div to 3l 3rd 4; trckd ldng pr til 2nd 14; kpt on one pce; no imp frm 2 out*
[476³]	3	7	**Arise (IRE)** 6-1 **Miss T Harrison** *Ld in start; last to 2; prog to 7l 5th 8; chsd wnr frm 15 til no ex frm 2 out*
[653ᴾ]	4	20	**Desert Run (IRE)** 20-1 **Miss J West** *Prom to 3; sn lost plce; rr 11; stayed on one pce frm 3 out; nd*
[634⁴]	5	½	**Frozen Drop** 10-1 **T Bishop** *1st ride; mid-div early; rr frm 5; a bhnd; stayed on one pce frm 3 out*
[522⁶]	6	10	**Don't Light Up** (vis) 10-1 **Miss M Burrough** *Chsd ldr; disp 7l 5th 8; rmdr 12; 4th & wkng 3 out; fin tired*
[561ᴾ]	7	2½fs	**Gallant Effort (IRE)** (bl) 25-1 **C Sclater** *Last & sn outpcd 5; t.o 8; fncs adrift 15; scattered crowds aft last*
	P		**Loch Na Keal** (5a) 25-1 **P Young** *Ld; 2l up 4 til hdd 14; wknd v qckly; bhnd when pu 3 out*
[356ᴾ]	P		**Mendip Son** (bl) 8-1 **D Crosse** *Rcd in 5th 4; disp 5½l 3rd 8; wkng when jmpd slow 14; pu nxt*
[401¹]	U		**Native Alliance (IRE)** 2-1 **Miss O Green** *Trckd ldrs; disp 7l 5th 8; chsng ldng trio but lkd hld when blun & ur 3 out*
[523⁴]	P		**Nawrik (IRE)** 16-1 **M Flynn** *Mid-div til outpcd & rr frm 11; jmpd slow 14; bhnd when pu nxt*
[579⁵]	P		**Panda Shandy** (5a) 8-1 **H Froud** *Last 2; prog to mid-div 5; sn rr agn; t.o frm 12 til pu 3 out*
[200ᴾ]	U		**Tango's Delight** 10-1 **J Gallagher** *Rr trio when blun & ur 5*

OFFICIAL DISTANCES: 3l, 8l   **TIME:** 6min 24.6s   **TOTE:** £8.20 **DF:** c/f

737 Intermediate, 12st - 16J   4 ran

[477¹]	1		**HERE COMES HENRY** 10-11F **R Young** *Hld up in last; 4½l down 7; chsd ldng pr 13; eff to disp 15; ld aft 3 out; sn in comm; drew clr last*

[404²]	2	8	**Ross Cottage** 11-10 **A Bateman** *3rd til ld aft 4-7; disp agn 11-15; ld 3 out til hdd & no ex frm nxt*
[632²]	3	10	**Bright Approach (IRE)** 8-1 **Miss P Gundry** *Ld to 4 & agn 7 til jnd 11-14; sn outpcd; no ex frm 3 out*
[453¹]	4	15	**Ryder Cup (IRE)** (5x) 5-1 **G Maundrell** *Chsd ldr til 3l 3rd 7; releg last 13; sn wknd & bhnd frm 3 out*

OFFICIAL DISTANCES: 6l, 12l **TIME:** 6min 29.2s **TOTE:** £2.90

738 Open Maiden 8yo&up (Div 1), 12st - 14J
14 ran

[520³]	1		**GEMINI MIST** (5a) 2-1F **Miss C Stretton** *Hld up in rr til prog to 6th 8; rap hdwy to ld 14; 3l up aft 3 out; hld on u.p flat*
[455⁵]	2	hd	**Pendragon** 5-1 **N Mitchell** *Hld up in rr til impd to 7l 6th 11; chsd ldng pr app 14; sust rn frm 3 out; just failed*
[207²]	3	6	**Frank Naylar** 3-1 **H Froud** *Prom; impd to 3rd 8; chsd ldr 11 til ld aft nxt-14; chsd wnr til no ex frm 2 out*
[457F]	4	20	**Mister River (IRE)** (bl) 5-1 **Miss P Gundry** *Mid-div to 7; lost plce & towards rr 9; nvr nr to chall; bhnd frm 3 out*
[520⁸]	5	2	**Millcroft Regatta** 6-1 **R McKenzie Johnston** *Chsd ldrs til eff to disp ld aft 5-nxt; ld agn 10; blun bad nxt; hdd 12; sn wknd; bhnd frm 3 out*
[410²]	P		**Caundle's Hand** (5a) 10-1 **R Arnold** (xnb) *A rr; t.o 12 til pu 15*
[540⁵]	P		**Frankie Muck** 6-1 **Miss C Stucley** (xnb) *Rstrnd in rr til gd prog to 5l 4th 11; bhnd 15 & sn bhnd; pu last*
[11P]	F		**Goforitgirl** (5a) 9-2 **A Honeyball** *Prog frm mid-div 3; 5th when fell 7*
[472F]	F		**Lily Lane** 6-1 **Miss S Vickery** (xnb) *2 handlers; trckd ldrs in 3rd 3; mid-div when fell 7*
[462⁶]	P		**Music Class (IRE)** 4-1 **J Gallagher** *Ld til jnd brief 5; hdd 9; wknd qckly; bhnd when pu 12*
[540P]	P		**Ruben James (IRE)** 7-1 **Jeremy Young** *Trckd ldrs; cl 3rd 4; wkng when jmpd slow 14; bhnd when pu 3 out*
[434⁴]	P		**Shouldhavesaidno (IRE)** (5a) 8-1 **J Owen** *Chsd ldrs to 3; grad lost plce; t.o 12 til pu 15*
	P		**The Grey Shadow** 5-1 **G Barfoot-Saunt** *Prog frm mid-div to 4th aft 5; 2½l 3rd 11; chsd ldng trio til wknd 3 out; bhnd when pu nxt*
[410³]	B		**Weycroft Valley** (5a) 8-1 **L Tibbatts** *Prom 4; lost plce & mid-div aft nxt; bd 7*

OFFICIAL DISTANCES: hd, 6l **TIME:** 6min 30.6s **TOTE:** £3.20 **DF:** £34.00
Fences 8 & 15 omitted - damaged; Ballot Box was withdrawn not under orders

739 Open Maiden 8yo&up (Div 2), 12st - 16J
7 ran

[455U]	1		**JOLIFICATION** 6-1 **A Honeyball** *Chsd ldr; 1l down aft 5; disp ld & jmpd slow 7; disp agn 9 til ld 11; 15l clr 14; unchall*
[407⁵]	2	20	**Grey Jerry** 6-1 **B O'Doherty** *Disp 2l 3rd 6; jmpd into 2nd 8; mist 11; rdn nxt; chsd wnr vain frm 15*
[520P]	P		**Church Field (IRE)** 6-1 **D Luff** (xnb) *7l 5th 6 til wknd 11; t.o aft nxt til pu 15*
[562P]	P		**Devil's Sting (IRE)** 5-2 **B McKim** *4th to 4; a last aft; bhnd when pu 15*
	P		**Humara (IRE)** (5a) 8-1 **Miss G Edwards** *Last & jmpd slow 2-4; 5th & in tch 8; bhnd frm 14 til pu 3 out*
[401¹]	P		**Lord Spider** 4-6F **M Miller** *Rcd in 3l 4th 6; chsd ldng pr 9; 8l 3rd 12; rdn & lost tch 14; rem 3rd when pu 2 out*
[630F]	P		**Tellaporky** 3-1 **J Owen** *Ld; 5l up 2nd til jnd app 7 & 9-11; chsd ldr til wknd qckly 15; 4th & tired when pu 2 out*

OFFICIAL DISTANCE: 25l **TIME:** 6min 40.8s **TOTE:** £25.00

Monmouthshire
Llanvapley (LH 8F,18J) Sat, 25 Mar (GOOD to SOFT, HOLDING in corn)

740 Hunt, 12st
4 ran

	1		**BORING (USA)** 2-1 **J Cook** (xnb,bf) *Ld til hdd 13; in tch til wknd thro corn aft 15; 25l 2nd 3 out; lft solo nxt; lucky*
	F		**Going Solo (U)** 16-1 **D Harrison** *Mists in last til fell hvly 5*
[491⁷]	F		**Rusty Flame** 7-1 **S Lloyd** *2nd til mist 4; 7l 3rd aft; 2l 2nd 10; ld 13; drew clr thro hvy ground aft 15; in comm when fell 2 out; unlucky*
[595³]	P		**Star Chaser** 4-6F **D Stephens (Wales)** (bh) *3rd early; settled 2nd frm 7; rmdrs 13; wknd & jmpd slow 14; pu 3 out*

OFFICIAL DISTANCE: Finished alone **TIME:** 7min 35.0s

741 Confined, 12st
13 ran

[643¹]	**1**		**KINNEFAD KING (IRE)** (3x) (tt) 6-4F C Williams *Hld up in 7th; hdwy 11; 3rd 12; hrd hld frm 3 out til ld last; pushed clr; v cheeky*
[596²]	**2**	2	**Tiger Lord** 6-1 A Price *(xnb) Ld to 5, 8-12 & 13; drvn 2 out; hdd last; nt qckn*
[600ᴾ]	**3**	3	**Kristal Haze** (5a) 6-1 J Cook *Hld up in 6th; went 2nd 13 & ld 15; hdd thro mire bef nxt; no ex frm 2 out*
[482²]	**4**	4	**Illineylad (IRE)** 5-1 A Wintle *4th & mist 6; midfield; nt rch ldrs frm 15*
[479⁷]	**5**	2	**Chiaroscuro** 16-1 S Lloyd *A bhnd; hit 3; 10th 9; last pr frm 14; clsd sltly frm 3 out*
[446²]	**6**	3	**Sun Of Chance** 12-1 D Stephens (Wales) *2nd til ld 5-8; 3rd 11; no ex thro corn frm 15*
[448ᴾ]	**F**		**Alkarine** 20-1 N Jones *Rr; lost tch frm 4; last & mist 6; t.o 7; u.p 10; fell 13*
	P		**Mister McGaskill** 20-1 James Tudor *5th early; wknd thro corn frm 8 & last pr aft; t.o 9; pu 12*
	P		**Persian Mystic (IRE)** 14-1 T Vaughan *Cl up; 3rd when hit 8; mists 12 & 13; sn wknd; t.o & pu 3 out*
[382ᴾ]	**F**		**Princess Lu** 20-1 N Tucker *3rd til 2nd 9; slt ld 12 til fell 13*
[482⁴]	**P**		**Roman Gale (IRE)** 20-1 S Blackwell *Hld up in rr; t.o 12; pu 3 out*
[483¹]	**U**		**The Rural Dean (IRE)** 5-1 J Price *Bhnd early; prog 7; cl 4th when blun & ur 14*
	U		**You Make Me Laugh (IRE)** 20-1 J Jukes *(xnb) Hld up in rr; last pr 5; 9th 8; 15l 6th & slt prog when mist & ur 15*

OFFICIAL DISTANCES: 2l, 2l, 3½l **TIME:** 7min 00.0s

742 Mens Open, 12st
9 ran

[597²]	**1**		**NO FIDDLING (IRE)** (7x) 7-2 C Williams *Hld up in last trio; r.o frm 9; 5l 3rd 11; hit 13; cl 2nd 14; jmpd slow nxt; kpt on thro plough to ld app 3 out; sn wl clr; unchall*
[598⁵]	**2**	runin	**Saffron Moss** (5x) 12-1 J Price *Rdn aft 2; 4th til 11 2nd frm 8; ld 14 but sn hdd thro plough aft nxt; btn 3rd 3 out til lft 2nd at last*
[468⁶]	**r**		**Bit Of A Citizen (IRE)** (5a) 7-2 James Tudor *Last & 10l adrift; bhnd til r.o 13; stayed on thro mire aft 15; 25l 2nd 2 out; ref last (nvr put in rce)*
[597ᴾ]	**P**		**Credon** 14-1 D Stephens (Wales) *A 5/6th; lost tch thro hvy ground aft 15; t.o 4th when pu last*
[479⁸]	**P**		**Doctor-J (IRE)** 33-1 A Price *A last pr; lost tch frm 11; t.o & pu 3 out*
[274¹]	**P**		**Evan's Collier Boy** 7-4F J Jukes *Ld til hdd & hit 9; mist 10; wkng rap when pu & dism aft 11*
[581ᴾ]	**U**		**Late Encounter** 12-1 A Wintle *Hit 3; rmdrs in 3rd 4; cont u.p in 5th 9; wknd 11; 15l 4th when ur 13*
[643ᵁ]	**P**		**Same Difference (IRE)** (bl) 25-1 M Lewis *A rr; 6th til rdn & wknd 11; t.o last aft 15; pu last*
[599²]	**P**		**Warren Boy** 10-1 G Lewis *2nd til ld 9-14; sn rdn; virt stpd to walk thro plough app 3 out & pu*

OFFICIAL DISTANCE: dist **TIME:** 6min 58.0s

743 Ladies Open
10 ran

[597ᴾ]	**1**		**VIARDOT (IRE)** 14-1 Miss G Roberts *Trckd ldrs in 3rd mostly til ld aft 15; kpt on game thro gluepot aft 15 & sn wl clr; unchall (only rnr to handle ground)*
[446¹]	**2**	fence	**Twilight Tom** (3x) 3-1 Miss B Williams *(drop) Midfield & off pce; stdy hdwy 12; went 3rd aft 15; sn btn; lft disp rem 2nd when blun & nrly ur 3 out; lft 2nd by defection*
[335⁶]	**3**	runin	**Poucher (IRE)** 14-1 Miss A Price *(xnb) Ld to 5; sn lost plce; 6l 5th when mist 14; wknd rap; fnce bhnd when lft 3rd; out-waddled rival when prsd run-in*
[600ᴾ]	**4**	1	**Storm Man** 25-1 Miss C Williams *Trckd ldr til ld 5-10; lost plce qckly to 6th 12; t.o aft 15; out-waddled for 3rd run-in*
[481¹]	**P**		**Dawn's Cognac (IRE)** 4-5F Miss P Jones *2 handlers; midfield early; settled 2nd frm 6 til ld 10; stpd to walk thro plough aft 15 & hdd; pu nxt*
[594³]	**P**		**Herbert Lodge (IRE)** 20-1 Miss M Bartlett *Sis; 35l 8th 9; t.o 11; fnce bhnd when pu 15*
	P		**Name Of Our Father (USA)** 4-1 Miss E Bryan *(orbs) 1st ride; sis; a bhnd; 45l last 9; fnce bhnd 11; pu 3 out*
[599ᵁ]	**P**		**Our Eddie** (tt) 33-1 Miss H Bendall *Sis; a last trio; 30l 7th & lsng tch 9; pu 15*
	P		**Polo Kit (IRE)** 25-1 Miss L Pearce *Trckd ldrs; prog 7; ½l 2nd 11; mists 13 & 14; ev ch til outpcd nxt; 20l 2nd 3 out; g exhaust when pu last*
	P		**Rapid Rascal** 25-1 Miss R Athay *1st ride; handy til hit 5 & 6; unable to handle mudbath at 8 & pu*

OFFICIAL DISTANCES: dist, dist **TIME:** 7min 00.0s

744 Restricted (Div 1), 12st
16 ran

[483⁴]	**1**		**BEL-DE-MOOR** (5a) 5-1 T Vaughan *(bf) Chsd ldrs; hit 3, 6 & 7; prog to 5th aft 10; r.o to 10l 2nd 13; ld & hit 3 out; hdd app nxt; btn when lft in ld last; drvn & all out; v lucky*

[392⁵]	2	3	**Teme Willow (IRE)** 10-1 M Hammond *3rd/4th til ld 12; 10l clr to 14; hdd 3 out; sn tired; no ex; lft 2l 2nd last; no imp*
[596ᴾ]	P		**Annastate** (5a) 5-1 J Jukes *Rr; 11th & some hdwy 11; to 15; pu nxt*
	P		**Final Option (IRE)** 20-1 I Johnson *A bhnd; last frm 6; to 14; pu 3 out*
[595⁴]	U		**General George** 14-1 S Blackwell *Last pr early; prog to 8th 9; fdd frm 11; pu 14*
			J'accuse (IRE) 8-1 Miss F Wilson *Last group to 9; 9th 11; r.o frm 15; 3rd 3 out; ld app nxt; qcknd clr; 10l up & in nd when hit last & ur*
[490ᶠ]	P		**Just Arnold** 12-1 A St George *A rr; to & pu 9*
	P		**Khandys Slave (IRE)** (5a) 12-1 J L Llewellyn *10l 2nd 2; lost plce 6; 7th & wkng 11; to & pu 14*
[612ᶠ]	P		**Master Welder** (vis) 12-1 A Wadlow *6th when tried to rn out marker aft 7; releg to last trio; 13th 11; to & pu 15*
	P		**Minibelle** (5a) 2-1F C Williams *Bhnd; blun 10; 12th 11; prog to 5th 14; lost tch thro plough aft 15 & pu*
[649ᵁ]	P		**Mission Lord (IRE)** 12-1 G Maloney *A rr; 14th 11; to & pu 14*
[484ᴾ]	P		**Saronica-R** (5a) 20-1 J Price *2 handlers; 2nd/4th til mist 9; 6th & u.p aft mist 11; sn wknd & pu 13*
[646ᴾ]	P		**Sea Search** 25-1 J Keen *Mid-div; clsr in 4th 8; impd to 3rd 14; stpd rap in mire aft nxt; pu 3 out*
	P		**Seventh Symphony (IRE)** 5-1 Miss P Jones *Tk str hld in 5th early; 2nd 5-11; lost plce qckly & pu 12*
	F		**The Croppy Boy** 8-1 A Price *Ld; 10l up 2; hdd & fell 12*
[487¹]	P		**Without The Agent (IRE)** 10-1 R Cooper *Midfield & nd; 10th 11; to & pu 15*

OFFICIAL DISTANCE: 1½l **TIME:** 7min 10.0s

An objection by the rider of the second to the winner for striking his horse in the face with the whip was over-ruled; the stewards considered the incident was accidental and had not affected the result

745 Restricted (Div 2), 12st
8 ran

[483⁵]	1		**RUSTY BUCK** 6-4F S Blackwell *Hld up in 4th early; 6l 3rd 9; lft 2nd 11; hdwy to ld thro plough 15; jnd 3 out; ld agn & hit nxt; rdn clr frm last*
[485⁴]	2	5	**Grand Canyon (IRE)** 3-1 A Price *Pulled hrd; prom; ld 4 til jnd & lft 3l clr 11; hdd thro mud aft 15; disp ld agn 3 out; sn hdd & outpcd; u.p when blun last*
[601ᴾ]	P		**Colour Of Life** (5a) 16-1 T Vaughan *(bf) Cl up til fdd 8; 20l last 12; jmpd slow 13; pu aft*
[649ᴾ]	U		**Jesusa** (5a) 14-1 G Maloney *Jb in rr; jmpd slow 6; to when blun 9 & ur aft*
[269¹]	P		**Mecca Prince** (7a) 9-4 James Tudor *(boh) Handy til lost tch 11; 15l 3rd & wkng 12; pu 3 out*
[485ᴾ]	U		**Not For Profit (IRE)** (bl,tt) 10-1 J Jukes *Ld to 4; cl 2nd til ld & pckd & ur 11*
[527ᶠ]	r		**Snitton Salvo** (7a) 8-1 A Wadlow *Ss; poor last when ref 1*
	r		**Stonemoss** (5a) 16-1 A Hardacre *Ref & ur 1*

OFFICIAL DISTANCE: 7l **TIME:** 7min 18.0s

746 Confined Maiden 56&7yo (Div 1), 12st
11 ran

[269³]	1		**BRIGHT BEACON** 5-2JF S Blackwell *Midfield; 7th & mist 5; still 7th 11; kpt on frm 14; 2nd nxt; ld 2 out; slt advant when lft clr last; r.o*
[648ᴿ]	2	8	**Gypsy Haze** (12a) 14-1 J Cook *Trckd ldrs; 6th 11; 3rd & ev ch 3 out; disp ld & outj nxt; rallied to chall last but skidded on landing & dem 3rd; rallied to tk 2nd cl home; prob v unlucky*
[350ᵁ]	3	3	**Parsons Secret** (5a) 12-1 T Vaughan *8l 2nd til ld 14; an u.p; hdd 2 out; lft 2nd brief last; no ex & fin tired*
[491ᴾ]	4	20	**Bit Of A Flutter** (5a) 14-1 I Johnson *A last quartet; no ch frm 14*
	P		**Adams Gold** 7-1 J Jukes *Tk str hld in 5th til settled 3rd 11; 2l 3rd 15; stpd to nil thro mud aft 15 & pu*
[488³]	U		**Craigson** 5-2JF C Williams *(xnb) Trckd ldrs; went 3rd 11; cl 4th when mist 15; wknd u.p nxt; poor 4th when mist & ur 2 out*
	P		**Double Indemnity (IRE)** (bl) 10-1 R Hodges *(xnb) Ld at mod pce; jmpd w hd in air & rdr lurching; jmpd slow 4; mist 5; blun 10; hdd 14; wknd rap & pu 3 out*
[602ᵁ]	P		**Ginger Duchess** (5a) 12-1 J Price *Jmpd novicey; school in last pr; to & pu 13*
	P		**Listenup Lord** (7a) 8-1 S Lloyd *School in last pr; to frm 4; pu 14*
[488⁴]	P		**Marnies Song** (5a) (bl) 7-1 J L Llewellyn *2 handlers; mist 6; 4l/5th til mist 13; strugg aft; pu 15*
[489ᴾ]	P		**No Escape** (7a) 12-1 G Perkins *2 handlers; 6th til lost tch aft mist 9; to 11; pu 13*

OFFICIAL DISTANCES: 6l, 2l **TIME:** 7min 41.0s

Arctium (ur & got loose going to start) was withdrawn not under orders

747 Confined Maiden 56&7yo (Div 2), 12st   10 ran

	1		**SECRETROCK (IRE)** 3-1 J Jukes *(xnb) Last trio early; prog to 2nd 8; ld 9; 6l up nxt; drew 25l clr aft 15; unchall*
[489F]	2	30	**Royal George (IRE)** 10-1 A Wadlow *4th early; sn rr; 18l 4th 12; stayed on aft mist 13; tk rem 2nd 3 out & plodded on; just kpt 2nd*
[348S]	3	nk	**Lillies Buttler** (5a) 6-1 T Vaughan *Mostly 5th; 20l bhnd when mist 11; no ex thro plough aft 15; 30l 3rd 3 out; plodded on*
[488r]	U		**Annie's Alfie** 10-1 G Marsh *0ht; j erratic; ld to 3 & app 5 til tried to rn out 6 & ur*
[491B]	P		**Appeal Again (IRE)** 5-1 J Cook *(xnb) Ld & hit 1; chsd clr ldng pr; clsd to 2l 2nd & hit 11; wknd aft; bad mist 13; last 15; t.o & pu 3 out*
[672P]	P		**Heathyard's Flight** 12-1 R Hodges *2 handlers; ld 3 til app 5; nrly tk wrong course thro fin but corrected qckly when crowd shouted; ld agn 7-9; 14l 3rd 11; fdd qckly nxt; pu 13*
	P		**Poacher's Paddy (IRE)** (12a) 8-1 J Price *A last pr; blun 9; t.o & pu 12*
	U		**Rowling Sea (IRE)** 4-1 C Williams *(xnb) Towards rr til blun & ur 6*
	P		**Silver Joy** (12a) 10-1 J Phillips *Mists; midfield early; last pr frm 5 til pu 9*
[489⁴]	P		**Star Island** 6-4F A Price *Mostly 5th; mist 10; 16l 3rd 12; went 25l 2nd 14; lost tch rap thro plough aft 15 & pu*

OFFICIAL DISTANCES: dist, ½l **TIME:** 7min 27.0s
The rider of Rowling Sea was fined £60 for failing to report to the doctor after a fall in the previous race

V W H
Siddington (LH 10F,18J) Sat, 25 Mar (GOOD)

748 Hunt   8 ran

	1		**LEWESDON MANOR** 5-2F M Portman *Hld up; 15l 3rd 10; stdy prog to disp ld 3 out; went clr nxt; easy*
[338³]	2	8	**Claymore Lad** 3-1 Miss Z Howse *1st ride; sa; 5th mostly til prog frm 12 to 4th 3 out; stayed on wl frm 2 out; nrst fin*
	3	30	**Deinka (IRE)** (5a) 16-1 A Cowie *1st ride; ur padd; hdstrng; disp ld 1-3; went 20l clr 9; wknd frm 14; jnd nxt; no ex*
	4	4	**Holy Sting (IRE)** 5-1 A Maculan *Disp 5th 1st circ; outpcd frm 12; come home in own time*
[476⁵]	5	2fncs	**Country Lord** (14ow) 16-1 C Walwin *Nt jw; hunted rnd in rr*
[477U]	r		**Doujas** (5a) 7-2 S Sellars *Sev mists til ref 6*
[600⁴]	F		**Holloa Away (IRE)** (bl) 16-1 R Millar *Disp ld to 3; 20l 2nd 9; stdy prog to disp ld 15; 8l 2nd & wkng when fell 2 out*
[392⁴]	P		**Melody Princess** (5a) 8-1 B Clarke *Bhnd; 20l 7th when pu aft 5*

OFFICIAL DISTANCES: 7l, 20l **TIME:** 6min 15.0s **TOTE:** £3.90

749 Confined, 12st   18 ran

[477F]	1		**ROYAL ESTATE** 10-1 A Evans *Cl up; hdwy to 3rd 14; disp ld & ev ch 2 out; 2nd & btn when lft clr last*
[388¹]	2	2	**Gildrom** 5-4F M Rimell *Sev mists; cl 5th 10; prog to 3rd 14; ev ch nxt; unable to sust eff*
[477F]	3	10	**Mr Smudge** 12-1 A Martin *Bhnd; mod prog frm 10; eff frm 3 out to 4th nxt; lft 3rd at last*
[543⁵]	4	12	**Castle Shelley (IRE)** 12-1 R Smith *Outpcd 1st circ; stdy prog frm ½way to 20l 5th 15; mod late prog*
[387¹]	5	2	**Granville Grill** (3x) 8-1 J Deutsch *Cl up; disp ld ½way; lost plce frm 13; one pce*
[475⁵]	6	½	**Lucky Tanner** 16-1 Miss G Young *Outpcd 1st circ; r.o thro btn horses frm 3 out; nrst fin*
[461³]	7	8	**Fair Crossing** (5x) 5-1 M Emmanuel *Prom in ldng group to ½way; 5th 12; wknd stdly*
	8	6	**Ashmead Rambler (IRE)** 16-1 Miss A Bush *Ld; set str pce til jnd 13; sn hdd & grad wknd*
[336P]	9	20	**In The Future (IRE)** (5a) 20-1 M Cowley *Detach frm ldng group 6; last 14*
[511⁵]	P		**Blessed Oliver** 10-1 R Lawther *Mid-div til pu 2 out*
[246P]	P		**Cawarra Boy** 20-1 M Walters *A strugg in mid-div til pu 2 out*
[476U]	P		**Cruise Free** 20-1 S Sellars *Last frm 9 til pu 2 out*
[508B]	P		**Hill Island** (3x) 14-1 Miss L Sweeting *Disp ld 1-3; wknd frm 12; rr when pu 2 out*
[191P]	P		**La Mon Dere (IRE)** (tt) 20-1 Miss E Marley *Bhnd frm 2; 20l last when pu aft 9*
[428⁴]	P		**Northern Yarn (IRE)** 20-1 P Cowley *A strugg; wl bhnd when pu 2 out*
	P		**Perseverance** 20-1 Miss K Clift *Mid-div to ½way; grad wknd; pu 2 out*
[392⁷]	P		**Raining Stairs** 20-1 J Trice-Rolph *Wl bhnd til pu 15*
[445⁴]	U		**Well Ted (IRE)** 7-2 S Joynes *Confid rdn; cl 3rd 13; hdwy to disp ld aft nxt; forged clr frm 2 out; 3l up & staying on wl when ur last; unlucky*

OFFICIAL DISTANCES: 1l, 2l **TIME:** 5min 58.0s **TOTE:** £8.80

750 Mens Open, 12st · 6 ran

	1		**BLANVILLE (FR)** 3-1 P Scouller *Sev mists; impd to disp ld ½way; r.o str when chall frm 3 out; drew clr app last*
[217³]	2	6	**Golden Savannah** 4-1 A Macūlan *Trckd ldrs; impd to jn ldrs 14; ev ch til hdd 2 out; wknd app last; saddle slpd*
[227⁴]	3	2	**Cherrynut** (7x) 4-7F D Barlow *Hld up; 2l 3rd & mist 11; mist 14; prog & ev ch 3 out; no ex*
[463⁴]	4	25	**Northern Bluff** 5-1 J Deutsch *Set mod pce to 10; lost plce; 5th 14*
[597⁶]	5	2	**Capo Castanum** 8-1 R Sturgis *3rd mostly 1st circ; lost plce frm ½way; no ex frm 3 out*
[430¹]	6	3	**Kites Hardwicke** (4x) 14-1 P Sheppard *Last; mod prog to disp 5th brief 14; sn btn*

OFFICIAL DISTANCES: 7l, 1l **TIME:** 6min 03.0s **TOTE:** £4.60

751 Ladies Open · 5 ran

[512²]	1		**MR CUSTARD** 5-4F Miss L Sweeting *Ld; 2l up til jnd app last; r.o str u.p flat*
[476¹]	2	nk	**Newton Point** 5-2 Mrs B Keighley *15l 4th 10; stdy hdwy to 3rd 14; str rn 2 out; chall last; r.o str flat; q hld*
[390²]	3	2	**Dalusman (IRE)** 3-1 Miss N Sturgis *Cl 2nd/3rd; eff 3 out; wknd app 2 out*
[512³]	4	30	**Boarding School** 4-1 Miss A De Lisle Wells *Cl up at ld pce qcknd 9; no ex frm 12*
[481⁷]	P		**Chieftain's Crown (USA)** 10-1 Miss A Meakins *2l 2nd; wknd frm 13; detach last when pu 2 out*

OFFICIAL DISTANCES: ¾l, 4l **TIME:** 6min 01.0s **TOTE:** £2.20

752 Marsh UK/TBA PPORA Club Members Mares, 12st · 5 ran

[357¹]	1		**GLEVUM** (5a) 2-7F T Scudamore *Ld; rmdrs 6; drew clr frm 14; in comm 2 out; easy*
[427⁴]	2	8	**Murberry (IRE)** (5a) 3-1 T Illsley *Ww; 10l 3rd til hdwy 12; disp 2nd 3 out-nxt; r.o wl when chall flat*
[611¹⁰]	3	nk	**Artic Pearl (IRE)** (5a) 10-1 R Langley *2nd til wknd 12; drpd back 3rd brief 3 out; rnwd eff app last; just outpcd flat*
[429⁶]	4	30	**Upanoff** (5a) 10-1 B Pauling *Last; mod prog 10-12; wknd frm 14*
[455⁶]	R		**Vital Hesitation** (5a) 10-1 R Millar *Mists 3 & 9; 10l 4th when rn out 10*

OFFICIAL DISTANCES: 7l, nk, 15l **TIME:** 6min 11.0s **TOTE:** £1.20

753 Confined Maiden (Div 1) · 12 ran

[568⁷]	1		**WHISTLING RUFUS (IRE)** 7-2 M Rimell *W ldrs; qcknd 20l clr frm 12; 1l 2nd but gng wl when lft clr 15*
[629³]	2	12	**Mr Robstee** 3-1F J Trice-Rolph *Ldng group to 10; 20l 5th 14; rnwd eff frm nxt; r.o wl to 2nd 2 out*
[457³]	3	8	**Summer Haven** (5a) 4-1 L Lay *Ld/disp til outpcd frm 14; 20l 3rd 2 out; r.o wl flat*
[630⁷]	4	½	**Dicks Darlin'** (5a) 20-1 S Sellars *Prom in ldng group to 10; outpcd frm nxt; duelled w 3rd frm 2 out; dem 4th nr line*
[250⁷]	5	½	**Take The Brush (IRE)** (5a) 5-1 R Lawther *Mid-div 1st circ; stayed on frm 14; nrst fin*
	P		**Bombadier Brown** 20-1 A Macūlan *Lost tch frm 10; last when pu 3 out*
	F		**Brockbuster** (7a) 4-1 T Scudamore *Hld up; last pr til qcknd to disp ld frm 12; 1l up & gng str when fell 15*
	F		**Floorex Carpetman** (7a) 8-1 R Smith *Mid-div 1st circ; 6/7th 7th 13 til fell last*
	P		**Foxwyn** 20-1 C Wilson *Chsd ldrs to ½way; wknd qckly frm 12; t.o & pu 3 out*
[370⁷]	F		**Ilandra (IRE)** 20-1 N Pearce *Lost tch frm ½way; btn when fell 15*
[410ᵁ]	P		**Pennys Boy** 16-1 T Gretton *Nvr beyond mid-div; pu 3 out*
[81ᶠ]	F		**Star Marshall (IRE)** 16-1 S Joynes *Rr; prog to jn ldrs 7; cl 4th when fell 8*

OFFICIAL DISTANCES: 8l, 3l **TIME:** 6min 18.0s **TOTE:** £4.00

754 Confined Maiden (Div 2) · 11 ran

	1		**BRIDGE MAN** 7-1 S Bush *Made virt all; drew wl clr frm 12; wknd frm 14; lft wl clr nxt*
[22⁷]	2	30	**Boozi Birthday** (5a) 20-1 C Weaver *Mid-div; eff frm 12; lft dist 2nd 15; no ch w wnr 2 out*
[455ᶠ]	P		**Above Suspicion (IRE)** 10-1 M Walters *Disp ld at str pce; drpd back to 2nd 13; 40l 3rd when pu 2 out*
[309ʳ]	r		**Bertie Bavard** 16-1 P Cowley *Mists in mid-div; detach last when ref 13*
			Cluan Goill (IRE) 16-1 R Smith *A rr; last when pu 10*
[328⁴]	F		**Have A Break** (7a) 2-1F R Lawther *Rem 5th 1st circ; prog to disp 2nd 14; 15l down but clsng when fell 15*
	P		**La Tosca** (5a) 10-1 M Wall *Mists; lsng tch frm 13; pu 15*
[514⁷]	P		**More Mettle** 20-1 M Cowley *Wl bhnd frm 13 til pu 15*
	P		**Oneforthefrog (IRE)** 12-1 B Clarke *Chsng ldrs when bad mist 8; pu nxt*

| | B | | **Super Saffron** (5a) 7-1 **B Kendellen** *Chsd ldng pr; 25l 3rd 12; clsng when bd 15* |
| [433ʳ] | U | | **Wood Buzzard** 6-1 **A Maculan** *Ur 1* |

OFFICIAL DISTANCE: dist **TIME:** 6min 21.0s **TOTE:** £5.60
Catchacan was withdrawn not under orders (damaged bridle at start); Rule 4 deduction 25p in pound

Waveney Harriers
Higham (LH 8F,19J) Sat, 25 Mar (FIRM)

755 Hunt, 12st
6 ran

[129²]	1		**MONKS SOHAM (IRE)** (7x) 1-2F **D Parker** *Jmpd sticky & nvr gng wl; chsd ldrs; 28l 3rd & rdn 11; went 2nd 15; caught tired ldr app last; kpt on*
[549ᴾ]	2	5	**Absolute Limit** (7x) 5-2 **N Bloom** *Ld & sn 25l clr; 10l ahd but tiring when pckd 13; hdd aft 2 out; rdn & no ex*
[123³]	3	35	**Arctic Lodge (IRE)** (bl) 10-1 **M Hewitt** *Sn chsng clr ldr; clsd brief 13; wknd nxt; 20l 3rd & rdn 16; hung rt 3 out*
	P		**Simmie** 10-1 **Miss L Barrett-Nobbs** (xnb) *Sn strugg; t.o 8; fnce bhnd 11; pu 16*
[606ᴾ]	P		**Take It Easy (IRE)** 10-1 **D Parravani** *Laboured bad in last pr; t.o 8; pu 13*
[551ᴾ]	P		**Teluk (IRE)** 10-1 **M Gingell** *Settled 4th but nvr gng wl; 25l bhnd & rdn 13; nt keen; t.o & pu 15*

OFFICIAL DISTANCES: 5l, dist **TIME:** 6min 08.0s **TOTE:** £1.50 **DF:** £1.80

756 Confined, 12st
10 ran

[460ᵁ]	1		**PANGERAN (USA)** (7x) 4-5F **N King** *Jmpd erratic 1 & 2; last trio to 6; hdwy 9; ld app 12; 8l clr by 14; 15l ahd 16; unchall*
[549¹]	2	15	**Popeshall** (3x) 3-1 **C Ward** *Chsng group; lft 2nd 9-11; lft 2nd app 12 but no ch w wnr aft 15*
[603ᴾ]	3	40	**Going Around** (3x) 33-1 **M Gingell** *Prom brief; rr 6; lft 4th 9; 5th & wkng 14; 35l 3rd 16; t.o*
[302ᴾ]	F		**Candle Glow** (5a) 7-1 **D Cook** *Set brisk gallop & clr w one pursuer til fell 9*
[607ᴾ]	P		**Dynamite Dan (IRE)** 33-1 **A Coe** *In tch to 8; 6th & strugg 11; t.o last 14; pu nxt*
	U		**Koathary (USA)** 20-1 **A Harvey** *Jmpd slow 4; settled midfield; 5th 11; eff to 3rd when mist & ur 14*
[572⁷]	P		**On The Beer (IRE)** 25-1 **M Bailey** *Rn last; mist 5; t.o & pu 9*
	U		**Royal Action** 12-1 **P Chinery** (xnb) *Tk keen hld in 2nd & clr of rest; lft in ld 9; nrly fell 10; hdd aft 11; 2nd & wkng when ur nxt*
[574ᴾ]	P		**Salmon Mead (IRE)** 33-1 **S R Andrews** *Bckwd; a strugg in rr; last 11; t.o 14; pu 2 out*
[607ᵁ]	U		**Still In Business** 6-1 **A Ayers** *Chsng group; 20l 3rd when rfo 9*

OFFICIAL DISTANCES: 20l, dist **TIME:** 5min 59.0s **TOTE:** £3.50 **DF:** £2.70

757 Mens Open
3 ran

[607⁵]	1		**DOCKMASTER** 7-2 **M Abrey** *W ldr 4 til ld brief 8; releg last 12 & sn 8l bhnd; rallied 16; hd app 2 out; sn clr*
[607⁹]	2	15	**Stoney Valley** 16-1 **M Gingell** *Ld til jnd 4; disp til hdd brief 8; hdd app 16 & sn outpcd; lft 2nd 2 out*
[585¹ᵈ]	P		**Commuter Country** 2-7F **C Ward** (xnb) *Hrd hld last til gd j to 2nd 12; blun 14; ld app 16 til faltered aft nxt; sn rdn & wknd; pu & dism last*

OFFICIAL DISTANCE: 15l **TIME:** 6min 06.0s **TOTE:** £3.50

758 Greig Middleton Ladies Open
7 ran

[608²]	1		**CRACKING IDEA (IRE)** 1-2F **Mrs G d'Angibau** *Lw; made virt all; drew clr 13; 10l ahd 16l 16 but hrd prsd when lft virt solo 2 out*
[608ᵁ]	2	40	**Gatchou Mans (FR)** 4-1 **Miss L Rowe** *Sn drpd out detach last; virt to 9; 40l 6th 16; r.o to 3rd nxt & lft 2nd 2 out; nvr put in rce*
	3	10	**Riverstown Lad** 10-1 **Miss L Allan** *Bit bckwd; off pce in midfield; strugg 12; 35l 4th 16; lft rem 3rd 2 out*
[414⁷]	4	8	**Dance On Sixpence** 5-1 **Mrs S Hodge** *Ld 4-5; prsd wnr & clr of rest til wknd 16; lost 2nd app 16; plodded on*
[573⁷]	5	6	**Pair Of Jacks (IRE)** (bl) 33-1 **Miss J Wickens** *Pulled hrd early; nvr btr than midfield; rdn 11; no ch nxt; 50l last 16*
[608⁶]	U		**Just Jack** 33-1 **Miss F Jonason** *Midfield & nd; 25l 4th 13; 5th when ur 3 out*
[608ᴿ]	F		**Mill O'The Rags (IRE)** 7-1 **Mrs A Hays** *Settled ab 15l bhnd clr ldng pr til clsd to 12l 2nd app 16; cont prog & prsng wnr & ev ch when fell 2 out*

OFFICIAL DISTANCES: dist, 8l **TIME:** 6min 04.0s **TOTE:** £1.30 **DF:** £2.80

759 Open Maiden (Div 1)   **6 ran**

[239³]	1		**ON TARGET** 4-6F N Bloom *(xnb) Lw; tkn stdly in 3rd/4th; went 2nd 13; ld aft 2 out; sn in comm*
[551³]	2	6	**The Secret Grey** 5-1 A Coe *Prsd ldr til ld 13; rdn & hdd aft 2 out; fin v wkly*
[606²]	3	6	**Out Of Actons (IRE)** 4-1 C Jarvis *Keen in 3rd/4th; cl up til outpcd 14; 15l 3rd 16; kpt on agn aft nxt but rdr no help & unable to chall*
[55ᴾ]	4	20	**Steel My Song** 10-1 S Morris *Last pr & cl up; rdn aft 11; 5th when blun 12 & lost tch; 40l last 16*
[384ᴾ]	5	5	**Johnny Cool** (bl) 12-1 M Hewitt *Jmpd rt; ld at slow pce to 13; 30l 4th & wkng rap 16; useless non-stayer*
[551ᴾ]	6	7	**Cicero's Law (IRE)** 10-1 P Chinery *Last pr; cl up to 11; lft for dead aft nxt; 35l 5th 16*

OFFICIAL DISTANCES: 4l, 4l   TIME: 6min 21.0s   TOTE: £1.50 DF: £3.50

760 Open Maiden (Div 2)   **7 ran**

[550ᴾ]	1		**MR MAGGET (IRE)** 7-4 N Bloom *(xnb) Settled handy but nt a fluent; mist 6; 2nd 8 til jmpd ahd 16; kpt on wl frm last*
[604²]	2	6	**Fountain Bank (IRE)** (vis) 5-4F M Gingell *Made virt all to 16; cl up til hrd drvn & nt qckn app last*
[239ᴾ]	3	3	**Ger's Girl (IRE)** (5a) 20-1 A Coe *(xnb) Prsd ldrs; 4l 3rd 11; eff & 2l 3rd 16; ev ch 2 out; sn wknd*
	4	10	**Henry Tartar** (7a) 20-1 D Parker *Mists in rr div; 15l 4th when mist 11; kpt trying to clse frm nxt but foiled by mists; 12l 4th 16; rallied app 2 out; sn btn*
[609ᴾ]	P		**Citizen Band (IRE)** 25-1 C Lawson *Bckwd; pulled to ld brief app 4; hit 5; lost plce qckly & 15l 5th 8; t.o 12; mist 16; pu & dism 2 out*
[551ᴾ]	P		**Lancaster Boy (IRE)** 10-1 C Ward *(xnb) A labouring in last; 30l down 11; t.o nxt; pu 2 out*
[317³]	P		**The Arkle Bar (IRE)** 6-1 N King *Prom & pulling brief but sn drpd to rr; 6th 8; 20l 6th 11; t.o & pu 14*

OFFICIAL DISTANCES: 2l, 3l   TIME: 6min 17.0s   TOTE: £3.10 DF: £2.10

761 Restricted, 12st   **6 ran**

[554ᴾ]	1		**MAI POINT** (5a) 5-4F Miss C Grissell *(xnb) Made all & jmpd bold; 4l clr 16; stayed on wl; rdly*
[610ᴾ]	2	5	**Ar Aghaidh Abhaile (IRE)** 7-2 G Cooper *Settled cl up; went 2nd app 12; pushed along & no imp frm 3 out*
[239⁶]	3	8	**Harry Tartar** 7-2 D Parker *Mists 2; bhnd but in tch; mist 6; u.p nxt; 6l 5th 11; outpcd 13; 10l 3rd & btn 16*
[610ᴾ]	4	25	**Free And Equal (IRE)** 12-1 S R Andrews *Spurs; sn rdn & nvr keen; last mostly til brief eff in 4th 14; nt r.o 27l 5th 16*
	5	4	**Rathkeal (IRE)** Bckwd; last trio til went 3rd 10-14; 20l 4th & strugg 16*
	P		**Nursery Story** 14-11 M Polley *Bckwd; jmpd slow 4; blun 8; prsd ldr til app 12; wknd 14; 28l last 16; t.o & pu 2 out*

OFFICIAL DISTANCES: 5l, 2l   TIME: 6min 10.0s   TOTE: £2.50 DF: £3.00

Wilton

Badbury Rings (LH 10F,19J) Sat, 25 Mar (GOOD to FIRM)

762 Hunt, 12st   **5 ran**

[474ᴾ]	1		**COOLREE (IRE)** (tt) 5-2 O Ellwood *Cl last early; disp 11 2nd 6; jmpd to ld 8-9; ld agn 14; lkd vulnerable 3 out; 4l clr & in comm nxt*
[636ᴾ]	2	12	**Silver Sleeve (IRE)** 14s-10s; ld to 6; cl 3rd til rdn & wknd 3 out; kpt on agn to 8l 2nd at last; no ch w wnr*
[518²]	3	6	**Qu'appelle** 7-1 Miss A Goschen *Went 2nd 5; ld brief 7 & agn 10; jnd 13; chsd ldr frm nxt; 1¼l 2nd & ev ch 3 out; fdd tame*
	U		**Drumagolands Golden Envoy (U)** (tt) 40-1 J Kwiatkowski *Nt a fluent; last & jmpd slow 4; cl 4th 8; mist 12; lft last agn 14; 8½l last 15; eff 3 out; clsng when pckd & rfo front 2 out; rn wl*
	P		**Magic Mole** (5a) 4-5F Mrs M Batters *Cl 2nd to 4; releg last 8; lost tch frm 10; 10l last 12; wknd qckly & pu 14*

OFFICIAL DISTANCES: 15l, 8l   TIME: 6min 30.9s   TOTE: £4.00
The stewards enquired into the running and riding of Magic Mole; they accepted the rider's explanation that the horse had been off the course for a long time, had had leg trouble and was struggling to go the pace

763 Confined Maiden, 12st   8 ran

[328²]	1		**DANTE'S GOLD (IRE)** 7-4F **R Bliss** (xnb) Sa; hld up last; hit 6 & rdr waving; mist 9; 15l 4th 10; clsd to 2l 4th 14; ww til eff aft 2 out; 2l 2nd at last; r.o; ld last 20 yds; all out
[630²]	2	nk	**Springvilla (IRE)** 2-1 **M Green** Tchd 5/2; nt fluent; cl 3rd frm 5 til jmpd to 2nd 10; ld 11-13; cl 2nd til jmpd to ld agn 2 out; 2l up but tiring last; hdd & no ex last 20 yds
[519³]	3	8	**Spanish Jest** 40-1 **J O'Rourke** (drop) 2 handlers; ld 2; 8l clr whn tried to follow loose horses off course & hdd aft 10; rallied to cl 2nd 11; ld agn 14 til pckd bad & hdd 3 out; nt rec
[328⁵]	U		**Dancing Barefoot** (5a) 40-1 **J Maxse** Cl 3rd til pckd bad & ur 7
[457³]	U		**Gunerkillinghurst** 40-1 **J Snowden** Ld 1; ld/disp & hanging bad til slpd & ur bend aft 3; jmpd rnd loose w field aft & jmpd all fncs
[407³]	U		**Jug Of Wine** (5a) 4-1 **S Hayes** Jmpd sketchy; cl up whn ur 4
[212³]	U		**Regal Wolf** 9-1 **Miss A Goschen** 14s-9s; 2 handlers; cl 2nd/3rd til ur 4
[477³]	U		**Spanish River** 20-1 **G Weatherley** Lft cl 2nd 4 til 2l 3rd 11; trckng ldrs & ev ch when virt fell & ur 15

OFFICIAL DISTANCES: nk, 7l TIME: 6min 38.8s TOTE: £3.00

764 Mens Open, 12st   4 ran

[653ᶜ]	1		**COURT MASTER (IRE)** 4-6F **O Ellwood** Mostly cl 2nd til ld aft 13; made rest; prsd 16; drew clr aft nxt; canter
	2	10	**Indian Knight** 5-2 **M Green** 5s-5/2; last pr; cl 3rd 7; eff to disp 2nd 15; cl 2nd & ev ch nxt; sn outpcd; btn app last
	3	15	**Caundle Steps** 6-1 **J Snowden** Ld; jnd 7; hdd aft 13; disp 2l 2nd 15; 5½l 3rd & wkng 3 out; sn btn
	U		**Catwalker (IRE)** 7-1 **S Cobden** Cl 3rd til 4l last 7; 7½l last & outpcd 11; 20l adrift when blun & rdr f.o front 15

OFFICIAL DISTANCES: 9l, dist TIME: 6min 33.0s TOTE: £1.70

765 Greig Middleton Ladies Open   4 ran

[636³]	1		**OLIVE BASKET** (5a) 11-8F **Miss W Southcombe** Jw mostly; made all; 2l up & & mist 2 out; sn strode clr; canter
[522³]	2	15	**Thomas Crown (IRE)** 11-4 **Mrs J Wilkinson** Tchd 3s; jmpd rt & rn wide; cl 2nd/3rd; disp 1½l 2nd & ev ch 3 out; sn brushed aside; v tired at last
[458³]	3	10	**Fast Run (IRE)** 9-4 **Miss M Taylor** Cl 2nd/3rd; disp 1½l 2nd & ev ch 3 out; 5½l 3rd & wkng qckly nxt; pushed out to keep 3rd flat
[520¹⁰]	4	2½	**Bright Lady** (5a) 11-1 **Miss R Green** Last frm 2; in tch til outpcd 10; 18l last aft 13; t.o 15; rdn & clsd qckly flat; schoolmastering & capable of btr

OFFICIAL DISTANCES: 18l, 9l TIME: 6min 24.9s TOTE: £2.90

766 Countryside Alliance Club Members (Nov Rdrs), 12st   5 ran

	1		**BIT O'SPEED (IRE)** (7x) 5-1 **J Richardson** (xnb) Bit bckwd; hld up gng wl in cl 2nd/3rd; ½l 2nd 10; ld 13; sn 10l clr; unchall aft; 12l ahd 2 out; fin tired
[523²]	2	8	**Mystery Aristocrat (IRE)** 4-7F **R Tory** Jmpd v poor & sn last; nrly ur 4; 5l last 10; went 10½l 3rd aft 13; chsd wnr frm nxt; no imp; lacklustre eff
[639⁶]	U		**Our Wizzer (IRE)** 12-1 **C Whittaker** (xnb) Cl 4th til disp 2nd 5; disp 3l 3rd 10; cl last when blun & ur 12
[561³]	P		**Safety (USA)** (bl) 5-1 **G Wright** Ld 2-12; wknd rap; detach last 13; fnce bhnd 15; pu 3 out; bbv
[561⁸]	U		**Villains Brief (IRE)** (bl) 50-1 **J Kwiatkowski** Ld 1; cl 2nd to 6; disp 3l 3rd 10; 10l 2nd & outpcd 13; 3rd & lsng tch when ur 14

OFFICIAL DISTANCE: 9l TIME: 6min 29.1s TOTE: £4.00

767 Restricted, 12st   6 ran

[331³]	1		**DEAR EMILY** (5a) 6-1 **S Claisse** Cl 2nd/3rd til ld 8; made rest; 10l clr 10; 5l up & tiring 3 out; kpt on game; fin exhaust
[330³]	2	40	**Best Bitter** 6-1 **J Snowden** Last but wl in tch til ldrs qcknd 8; went 10l 2nd & hit 10; chsd wnr aft; clsd to 5l 2nd & ch 3 out; wknd bad nxt; exhaust & barely galloping aft last
[208³]	3	12	**Lyrical Seal** (5a) (bl) 14-1 **J Maxse** Handy til 12l last aft 8; sn lost tch; t.o & jmpd slow 14; no ch but staying on slow when lft dist 3rd 2 out
[330³]	F		**Another Junior (IRE)** 5-1 **Mrs M Barlow** (xnb) Made most to 7; qckly outpcd; 11½l 4th 10; jmpd rt nxt; lft mod 3rd 13; 13l 3rd 3 out; staying on one pce when fell nxt
[330³]	F		**Beechdown** 25-1 **R Bliss** Tchd 33s; blun & rdr waving 1; 3rd & jmpd rt 2; cl 2nd nxt; pckd 5; dem 9l 4th 8; 5th 9; fell nxt

[519¹] F   **Franklins Best (IRE)** 10-11F **O Ellwood** *2 handlers; last pr to 6; went 8l 3rd 8; 13l 3rd & rmdrs aft 10; no imp when fell hvly 13*

OFFICIAL DISTANCES: dist, dist   TIME: 6min 33.6s   TOTE: £3.70

768 Confined, 12st   5 ran

[628¹] 1   **COACH (NZ)** (3x) 11-10F **P Keane** *(xnb) Last til pulled to ld aft 3; made rest; 2l clr 10; 15l ahd 15; 5l up & lkd vulnerable brief 2 out; kpt on game*

     2   15   **Celtic Token** 6-1 **D Birkmyre** *(xnb) Tde; cl 4th; blun bad 4; 9l 4th 10; chsd ldng pr frm 13; blun nxt (same fnce); 15l 3rd & mist 16; plodded into 2nd aft 2 out; nvr any ch*

[325ᴾ] 3   3   **Arabitan** (5a) 10-1 **M Green** *Chsd ldr; jmpd lft 6; 2l 2nd 10; outpcd frm 13; 10l 2nd 15; clsd to 5l 2nd & ch app 2 out; fdd rap; 3rd & btn app last; lkd dem 4th on line*

[519²] 4   hd   **Cool Character (IRE)** (3x) 7-4 **Miss T Newman** *5/2-7/4; sn last pr & nd; last aft 4; 13l last 10; mist 13; 20l 4th & staying on 15; 11l 4th 2 out; lkd to snatch 3rd on line*

[561ᴾ] P   **Oneforwillie** (7x) 20-1 **J Snowden** *Tde; ld 1; cl 2nd to 4; stdly lost plce; 8l 3rd 10; 20l last 14; hrd rdn & no resp nxt; t.o when cat-jmpd 3 out; pu nxt*

OFFICIAL DISTANCES: dist, 1l   TIME: 6min 25.0s   TOTE: £2.00

Fitzwilliam (Milton)

Cottenham (RH 9F,19J) Sun, 26 Mar (GOOD)

769 Hunt   6 ran

[179ᴾ] 1   **AL JAWWAL** 8-1 **Miss L Allan** *(xnb) Chsd ldr 4-7; releg last 13; mist 4 out; shkn up & qcknd to ld aft nxt; clr aft 2 out; r.o str*

[546ᴾ] 2   8   **Grove Victor (IRE)** 8-1 **M Grange** *(xnb) Ld 3-7; 2nd to 13; hit 14; went 2nd 4 out; chsd wnr 2 out; no imp*

     3   8   **Bukehorn** 5-4F **M Barnard** *(xnb) 3s-5/4; hrd hld in rr; 5l 4th ½way; hdwy to ld 13; jmpd 3l clr 15; mist 4 out; hit nxt; sn hdd; wknd 2 out*

[544⁶] F   **Airecco (IRE)** 9-4 **Miss J Kandalaft** *3s-9/4; 3rd when fell 1*

     P   **Cast The Line** 16-1 **Mrs E Thomas** *Rdr drpd whip 1 & all over the place w reins; lost tch 5; t.o & pu 8*

[88ᴾ] U   **City Run (USA)** 16-1 **Mrs T Holditch** *1st ride; ld to 3; 2nd/3rd til ld 7; hdd 13; 3l 3rd when ur 4 out*

OFFICIAL DISTANCES: 8l, 6l   TIME: 6min 27.0s   TOTE: £9.00   DF: £25.10

     Fences 10 & 19 omitted - fallen rider; the owner of City Run, whose passport was found to be not in order, was fined £100

770 Confined, 12st   14 ran

[552¹] 1   **VILLAGE COPPER** 6-4F **Miss L Rowe** *Hit 2; jnd ldrs 7; 3rd ½way; went 2nd 14; ld 15; qcknd clr 3 out; unchal*

[555¹] 2   15   **Ann's Ambition** 25-1 **Miss C Fryer** *Lw; sn bhnd; 12l 8th ½way; hdwy 12; 8l 6th 14; mist 15; stayed on one pce frm 3 out; went 2nd flat; no ch w wnr*

[303ᵁ] 3   5   **Tighter Budget (USA)** 14-1 **Miss G Hutchinson** *Ld to 4; 2nd to 14; chsd wnr 15 til wknd 2 out; lft 15l 2nd last; dem flat*

[440¹] 4   6   **Stormy Words** (5a) 7-2 **S Morris** *Hld up; hit 2; stdy hdwy to 8l 6th ½way; blun 12; 5l 4th & blun 14; went 7l 2nd 2 out; wkng when rn w vide bend bef last; jmpd v slow & went bad lft; dem 2 plces flat*

[756ᶠ] 5   10   **Candle Glow** (5a) 25-1 **D Cook** *2nd til ld 4; hdd 15; wknd qckly 3 out*

[177ᶠ] U   **Mighty Merc** (tt) 33-1 **Miss Carla Thomas** *4th when mist & ur 2*

     P   **Mr Five Wood (IRE)** 33-1 **J Purllant** *(xnb) A bhnd; 25l 11th ½way; t.o & pu 12*

[443⁴] P   **Osgathorpe** 33-1 **A Woodward** *(xnb) Prom til lost plce 9; 10l 7th ½way; wl bhnd 12; t.o & pu 3 out*

     P   **Pearly Haze** (5a) 16-1 **N King** *Hld up & rcd wide; hdwy & 7l 5th ½way; blun 10 & 11; 9l 7th 14; wknd 4 out; bhnd when pu 3 out*

[318³] U   **Scarlett O'Hara** (5a) 5-2 **S Sporborg** *Lw; hld up & bhnd; 15l 9th ½way; hdwy 13; rdn 15; went 7l 5th 4 out; 10l 4th when blun 2 out; sn wknd; 17l 5th when hmpd bad & ur last*

[176ᶠ] P   **Spaceage Gold** (vis) 33-1 **A Harvey** *Sn drvn along & nt keen; 18l 10th ½way; 13l 9th 13; wl bhnd when pu 4 out*

[122³] P   **Spectre** 33-1 **N Bloom** *Chsd ldrs; 5l 4th ½way; 7l 5th 14; wknd & 9l 7th 4 out; bhnd when pu 2 out*

[318ᴾ] P   **Speedy Snaps Pride** 33-1 **N Page** *Sn wl bhnd; t.o 4; pu 11*

[318⁵] P   **Spuffington** 33-1 **Miss C Hall** *Nd; lost tch 7; 28l 12th ½way; t.o & pu 11*

OFFICIAL DISTANCES: 10l, 5l   TIME: 6min 12.0s   TOTE: £2.30   DF: £23.20

771 Mens Open
7 ran

[130ᴾ]	1		**MISTER SPECTATOR (IRE)** 9-2 P Hickman *Pulled hrd; jmpd rt; made all; r.o u.p flat*
[320³]	2	2	**General Assembly (IRE)** 4-5F N Bloom *5/4-4/5; hld up; 2½l 3rd ½way; hit 4 out; outpcd & jmpd slow nxt; rallied & lft 3l 2nd last; stayed on u.p flat*
	3	15	**Pantara Prince** 16-1 A Sansome *Hld up; hdwy & lft 2nd 9-4 out; sn rdn & one pce; eased when btn flat*
[607ᴾ]	4	30	**Son Of Iris** 12-1 A Coe *2nd til blun 9; 3l 4th ½way; 8l 5th & rdn 14; sn wknd; t.o*
[327ᶠ]	F		**Ebullient Equiname (IRE)** 4-1 S Morris *Hld up; jmpd into back of rival 5; 4l 5th ½way; went 2nd 4 out; hrd rdn & ev ch when fell last*
	r		**King High** 33-1 J Cooper *Drpd to rr 3; lost tch 6; t.o when ref 8*
[603³]	P		**Reuter** (vis) 33-1 M Gingell *Chsd ldrs til lost plce 9; 5l 6th & rdn ½way; lost tch und str press 13; t.o & pu 15*

OFFICIAL DISTANCES: 1½l, 20l TIME: 6min 18.0s TOTE: £6.00 DF: £5.30

772 Ladies Open
4 ran

[28¹]	1		**STRONG MEDICINE** 2-1 Mrs E Coveney *Jw; made all; rn v wide bend aft 3 & bend aft 12; r.o wl*
[512¹]	2	4	**Imperial Dawn (IRE)** 2-5F Miss L Rowe *Jmpd slow; 4l 3rd ½way; pushed along 11; rmdrs 13; drvn & no resp 3 out; went 2nd last; no imp; v moody eff*
[442³]	3	6	**Count Of Flanders (IRE)** 25-1 Miss F Hatfield *Chsd wnr; rdn 2; dem last; wknd flat*
[608ᵁ]	P		**Lets Twist Again (IRE)** 25-1 Miss A Stennett *5l 4th ½way; in tch til wknd 12; t.o & pu 2 out*

OFFICIAL DISTANCES: 3l, 4l TIME: 6min 11.0s TOTE: £2.10 DF: £1.20

773 Restricted, 12st - 18J
7 ran

	1		**SENSE OF ADVENTURE** 7-2 N Bloom *8s-7/2; hld up; 2l 3rd ½way; went 2nd 15; ld 3 out; sn qcknd 3l clr; comf*
[86²]	2	6	**Secret Streams (IRE)** evensF S Sporborg *Ld 2-4; 2nd til lft in ld 9; hdd 11; hit 12; chsd wnr 3 out; rdn app last; no imp; dism aft fin*
[416ᴾ]	3	8	**Skinsey Finnegan (IRE)** 33-1 A Coe *Pulled hrd; 2nd/3rd til ld 11; rn wide bend app 14; pckd 4 out; hdd 3 out; sn outpcd*
[554ᴾ]	4	40	**Coptic Dancer** (5a) 33-1 A Braithwaite *Ld to 2; lost plce 6; 5l 4th ½way; wknd 14; t.o*
[550¹]	F		**Squaddie** 11-4 A Sansome *Swtng; 6th when fell 2; rmtd; waved rnd 9; cont wl to til pu 11*
	U		**Ulvick Star (IRE)** 9-1 R Fowler *Pulled hrd; went 2nd 3; ld & hit 4; hit 7; blun & ur 9*
[178ᴾ]	P		**Waisu** (5a) 33-1 M Grange *Jb; sn wl bhnd; pu 7*

OFFICIAL DISTANCES: 5l, 5l TIME: 6min 21.0s TOTE: £3.00 DF: £3.80
Fence 18 omitted - fallen rider

774 Open Maiden (Div 1)
8 ran

[606³]	1		**SWEET TALKER (IRE)** evensF N Bloom *2s-evens; swtng; ld to 5; 2nd/3rd til ld 9; rdn 4l clr 2 out; all out*
[412ᴾ]	2	1½	**Always Trying** (7a) 8-1 A Sansome *Swtng; hld up; blun 7; 4l 5th ½way; jnd ldrs 12; went 2nd 14; ev ch 3 out; sn drvn along & one pce; kpt on u.p flat; nt rch wnr*
[605ᴾ]	3	40	**Sidney Street** (vis) 25-1 M Gingell *2nd/3rd til ld 7; hdd 9; chsd wnr 12-14; wknd 4 out; t.o*
[242ᴾ]	F		**Classic Ms (IRE)** 33-1 M Grange *Hld up; 6l 7th ½way; fell 11*
	P		**Fair Storm (IRE)** 16-1 D Cook (xnb) *2 handlers; prom til ld 6 & jmpd v slow 5; hdd 7; 2nd when mist 11; wkng when mist 13; 14l 4th 15; t.o & pu 15*
[416ᴾ]	P		**Here Comes Trouble** 16-1 A Braithwaite *Jmpd lft; hld up; 5l 6th ½way; lost tch 12; tried to ref 13 & pu*
[412ᴾ]	P		**Josh's Choice** (7a) 13-2 S Sporborg *Jnd ldrs 5; 3l 4th ½way; blun bad 13; nt rec; 15l 5th 15; t.o & pu 2 out*
	P		**Stick Or Bust** (7a) 12-1 Miss R Barrow *Lost plce 5; mist & releg last 9; 17l 8th ½way; wl bhnd when pu 11*

OFFICIAL DISTANCES: 1l, dist TIME: 6min 34.0s TOTE: £1.60 DF: £9.40
Sayonara was withdrawn not under orders - bolted a circ of course w rdr;
Rule 4 deduction 20p in pound

775 Open Maiden (Div 2)
11 ran

[411ᶠ]	1		**MININO (IRE)** (bl) 10-1 A Coe *Sn prom; went 2nd 7; ld 10 til rn v wide & lost plce bend aft 12; went 3rd 15; outpcd 3 out; 6l 3rd nxt; stayed on u.p to ld flat; just hld on*
[585ᴾ]	2	hd	**Worthy Memories** (5a) 25-1 A Sansome *Ld 3-10; 2nd til lft in ld bend aft 12; mist 2 out; hdd u.p & swished tail flat; rallied nr fin*

[236²]	3	3	Our Man Flin (IRE) (tt) 2-1F D Cook (xnb,bf)A 2nd/3rd; rmdrs 7 & 10; carried wide bend aft 12; chsd ldr 14; blun 4 out & 2 out; hrd rdn app last; nt qckn
	4	runin	Rafter 25-1 C Carman A wl bhnd; 28l 7th ½way; t.o 11
[91ᵖ]	U		Airborne Blue 33-1 Miss Carla Thomas Ld to 3; 3rd when mist & ur 4
[547ᵖ]	F		Birditoo (5a) 33-1 M Skinner 2 handlers; chsd ldrs; 15l 5th ½way; wkng & t.o when fell 11
[606ᵖ]	P		Bozo Bailey 33-1 M Polley Bckwd; a bhnd; 25l 6th ½way; mist 10; pu 11
[437ᶠ]	F		Campbellhill (IRE) 25-1 M Gingell Hld up; 111 6th when fell 9
	F		Carlton Brae (12a) 25-1 A Harvey Bckwd; hld up & bhnd; 17l 8th when fell 9
[551²]	P		Just Chica 7-2 N Bloom Sn prom; 5l 4th ½way; lft 2nd aft 12-14; wknd 4 out; 15l 4th when pu 2 out
[284ᵖ]	P		Satellite Express (IRE) (bl) 8-1 P Hickman Hmpd 9; bhnd til pu 10

OFFICIAL DISTANCES: hd, 3l **TIME:** 6min 22.0s

Bally Seamus was withdrawn not under orders - unseated going down & galloped off; Rule 4 deduction 20p in pound; the rider of Our Man Flin was fined £50 and severely cautioned for incorrect use of the whip and causing the horse to be marked

Flint & Denbigh

Eaton Hall (RH 6F,16J) Sun, 26 Mar (HOLDING - variable)

776 Hunt
6 ran

[567⁶]	1		SHANBALLYMORE (IRE) 7-2 G Lowe Lw; ld to 3, 7-10 & frm 11; rdn & hdd 2 out; nt fluent & ld agn last; rdn o.up
[565⁶]	2	1¼	Orton House 2-1F S Kelly Lw; handy; ld app 5; hdd & nt fluent 6; prom til ld agn 2 out; mist & hdd last; kpt on o.up
	3	runin	Miss Blue (12a) 10-1 R Owen Bckwd; jmpd slow 1; in tch; hdwy 7; ld 10-11; wknd 4 out; t.o
	U		Golden Saxon 20-1 S Shone Bckwd; bhnd til blun & ur 7
	U		St Athans Lad 5-1 B Seddon Bckwd; swtng; blun & ur 1
	U		Strong Mission (IRE) 9-2 G Halliday Bckwd; pulled hrd; prom; ld 3; jmpd lft nxt; hdd app 5; ld 6-7; wknd 11; pckd nxt; bhnd when blun & ur 4 out

OFFICIAL DISTANCES: 1¼l, dist **TIME:** 6min 57.3s

777 Open Maiden (Div 1), 12st
9 ran

[569ᶠ]	1		ARTHUR HENRY evensF S Prior Lw; hld up in tch; hdwy & mist 12; chall 2 out; ld last; r.o
[527ᵖ]	2	3½	Robert The Rascal 10-1 A Gribbin Rr; mist 9; hdwy 12; ld 2 out; hdd last; no ex run-in
[570ᵖ]	3	¾	Fountain Street (IRE) 4-1 R Burton Unruly padd; a cl up; jmpd slow 7; ev ch 2 out; stayed on same pce u.p
[568ᵖ]	4	20	Pinouli (5a) 16-1 L Stephens Bckwd; prom til rdn & wknd app 2 out
[527ᵖ]	5	20	Mr Peoples (IRE) (tt) 3-1 C Stockton Bckwd; ld; rdn & hdd 2 out; sn wknd; fin tired
[526ᵖ]	6	3	Desert Boot (7a) 8-1 B Wharfe Nt jw; in tch; bhnd aft 9; rallied brief 11; bhnd when blun 4 out; t.o
[528ᵖ]	7	20	River Moy (5a) 16-1 R Owen In tch; mist 8; hdwy aft nxt; bhnd 11; sn t.o
[665ᵁ]	P		Jock 14-1 J R Barlow Bckwd; hld up; hdwy 11; mist when wkng 12; t.o & pu 4 out
[745⁴]	r		Snitton Salvo (7a) 7-1 A Wadlow Nt jw; t.o when ref 4

OFFICIAL DISTANCES: 3½l, ¾l **TIME:** 6min 51.9s

778 Open Maiden (Div 2), 12st
10 ran

[570ᵖ]	1		HAMISH 5-1 M Worthington Lw; in tch; hdwy 12; strall chall frm 2 out; r.o game to ld cl home
[569⁴]	2	nk	Vulpin De Laugere (FR) (bl) 5-1 R Burton Ld; hdd app 12; ld agn aft 3 out; hdd nxt; rallied to ld agn last; hdd cl home
[593ᶠ]	3	2	Marwoods Mandate (IRE) 5-2 C Stockton Hld up; hdwy 12; ld 2 out; hdd last; r.o same pce run-in
[526⁴]	4	15	Merely Mortal 12-1 R Owen Chsd ldrs; jmpd lft 5; tk clsr ord app 10; wknd 4 out
	5	5	Maudette (IRE) (12a) 12-1 B Wharfe Bckwd; midfield; hit 1; bhnd & no ch frm 4 out
[568⁴]	P		Blacon Point 6-1 T Stephenson Prom til wknd qckly 12; sn t.o; pu 2 out
[568ᵖ]	P		Eecel 16-1 A Wintle Bckwd; hld up; strugg & bhnd 11; t.o & pu 2 out
[587ᵖ]	P		Native Rain (IRE) (7a) 20-1 Miss E Lea Bhnd; lost tch 7; t.o & pu 9
[499⁷]	P		Reflective Way (5a) 20-1 R Robinson Bckwd; rr; hdwy app 7; bhnd 11; mist 4 out; t.o & pu 2 out
[380ᶠ]	P		Sparkling Gift (IRE) (5a) 11-10F Mrs C Ford Prom; ld app 12; nt fluent 4 out; hdd aft nxt; wknd qckly; bhnd when pu last

OFFICIAL DISTANCES: nk, 2l **TIME:** 6min 49.8s

779 Mens Open, 12st   5 ran

[530²]	1		**BUCKS VIEW (IRE)** 2-1 G Hanmer *Lw; hld up; chsd ldrs 10; went 2nd 3 out; ld nxt & bumped rival; nt fluent last; r.o; cheeky*
[176²]	2	1½	**Bishops Hall** 9-2 A Crow *Handy; rdn & unable to qckn 2 out; chsd wnr run-in; flatt by prox*
[530³]	3	10	**Greville Again (IRE)** 16-1 A Wadlow *Burly; ld; hdd aft 2; ld 5; clr 12; hdd & hmpd 2 out; wknd app last*
[464¹]	4	20	**Silverdalesureshot** (4x) 8-11F R Burton *In tch; drpd to rr 5; plenty to do 4 out; some hdwy app 2 out; sn no imp & wknd*
[530³]	5	fence	**Russian Castle (IRE)** 66-1 D Sherlock *Bckwd; pulled hrd; ld aft 2; mist 3; hdd 5; w ldr when rmdrs aft 12; sn wknd; t.o*

OFFICIAL DISTANCES: 1½l, 10l   TIME: 6min 39.9s

780 Greig Middleton Ladies Open   5 ran

[566²]	1		**GEORGE DILLINGHAM** 3-1 Mrs C Ford *In tch; mist 3; chsd ldr 9; ld 2 out; all out*
[566¹]	2	hd	**Hersilia (IRE)** (5a) 4-1 Miss S Hopkins *Lw; trckd ldrs; ev ch frm 2 out; r.o*
[590ᴿ]	3	15	**Hello Me Man (IRE)** 25-1 Mrs K Diggle *Swtng; pulled hrd; ld 3; hdd 2 out; wknd qckly*
[466²]	4	15	**Percy Smollett** 4-6F Miss S Vickery *Ld to 3; handy til rmdrs aft 11; lft wl bhnd frm 3 out*
[588ᴾ]	P		**Tosawi's Girl (IRE)** (5a) 66-1 Miss T Clark *Bckwd; nvr gng wl; lost tch aft 6; t.o & pu 12*

OFFICIAL DISTANCES: hd, 15l   TIME: 6min 35.5s

781 Confined, 12st   9 ran

[116²]	1		**SHARSMAN (IRE)** (3x) 7-2 A Crow *Prom; pckd 8; nt fluent 11; chsd ldr 3 out; ld nxt; rdn out*
[525¹]	2	6	**Three Saints (IRE)** 7-2 M Worthington *Chsd ldrs; impd to ld 4 out; 6l clr aft nxt; hdd 2 out; no ex clsal*
[529²]	3	4	**Garryspillane (IRE)** 7-4F G Hanmer *Hld up in rr; eff & some hdwy to chse ldrs app 2 out; sn one pce*
[565³]	4	20	**My Nominee** (bl) 11-1 R Burton *In tch; lost plce 10; lost tch 3 out*
[525ᵁ]	P		**Batty's Island** (3x) 12-1 L Stephens *Bckwd; cl up til wknd app 3 out; lsng tch when pu last*
[530ᴾ]	P		**Emerald Knight (IRE)** (5x) 12-1 C Stockton *Bckwd; ld; hdd 4 out; wknd nxt; lsng tch when pu last*
	P		**Gavaskar (IRE)** 33-1 R Owen *In tch; mist 6; bhnd & strugg 12; t.o & pu 4 out*
	P		**Logical Fun** 50-1 L Brennan *Bckwd; bhnd; t.o & pu 9*
	R		**Rolier (IRE)** 5-1 S Kelly *Bckwd; rr til rn out 9*

OFFICIAL DISTANCES: 6l, 4l   TIME: 6min 45.3s

782 Restricted, 12st   9 ran

[528¹]	1		**THE CROOKED OAK** 100-30 G Thomas *Midfield; impd 5; ld 9-11; ld agn app 3 out; kpt on game when prsd flat*
[532³]	2	½	**Coming Through (IRE)** 8-1 A Crow *Hld up; niggled along 7; hdwy app 9; ld 11; hdd app 3 out; sust chall; just hld*
[532⁵]	3	20	**Mr Mark (IRE)** 20-1 D Sherlock *Sn w ldr; ld & jmpd slow 7; hdd 9; wknd bef 3 out; jmpd lft nxt; no ch when blun last*
[526¹]	4	30	**Another Gentleman** 5-1 Mrs C Ford *Cl up; nt fluent 8; wknd app 4 out; t.o*
[589⁸]	5	12	**Scally Hill** (5a) 14-1 L Stephens *Bckwd; oht; ld to 7; rmdrs & lost plce app 10; bhnd aft; t.o*
	P		**Pear Tree Percy** 7-1 C Stockton *Midfield; drpd to rr aft 4; brief eff agn 8; sn lost plce; t.o & pu 10*
[567ᴾ]	P		**Scallymay** (5a) 16-1 M Munrowd *In tch; bhnd frm 10; t.o & pu 12*
	P		**Tale Bridge (IRE)** 20-1 S Prior *Prom; drpd to midfield aft 4; bhnd 10; t.o & pu 12*
[124¹]	P		**Whitegates Willie** 11-10F G Hanmer *Lw; hld up in rr; hdwy 4 out; staying on in 8l 3rd when pu 2 out*

OFFICIAL DISTANCES: ½l, 20l   TIME: 6min 45.7s

783 Intermediate, 12st   3 ran

[120¹]	1		**HARWELD** 4-5F A Crow *Lw; pulled hrd; trckd ldr; jmpd slow 7; ld 8; mist 11; clr aft 3 out; easy*
[533ᴾ]	2	20	**Rise To It (IRE)** evens G Hanmer *Oht; swtng; ss; rr til prog 12; went 2nd 4 out; sn wl adrift of wnr; rdn app last; no imp*
[590⁴]	3	¾	**Coolflugh Hero (IRE)** 7-1 Miss S Hopkins *Set slow pce til hdd 8; drpd to rr 4 out; sn nd*

OFFICIAL DISTANCES: 20l, ¾l   TIME: 6min 52.0s

Grafton

Mollington (RH 8F,18J) Sun, 26 Mar (GOOD to FIRM)

784 Hunt
5 ran

[428ᶠ]	1		**JUST LIKE MADGE** (5a) 1-5F J Tarry *Cl up; chsd ldr 13; chall & outj 3 out; shkn up to ld app last; sn in comm*
[74ᴾ]	2	4	**Dolly Bloom** (5a) 14-1 Miss N McKim *Ld; qcknd 11; rdr called cab 14 & 15; jnd & outj wnr 3 out; hdd & no ex app last*
[510ᴾ]	3	25	**Hope's Delight (IRE)** 14-1 R Smith *25s-14s; jmpd slow; wl in tch til outpcd by ldng pr app 3 out; no ch aft*
[428ᴾ]	r		**Tarry Awhile** 25-1 Miss R Goodwin *Cl up to 14; lsng tch when ref & ur nxt*
[515²]	R		**Yodeller Bill** (2ow) 10-1 P Sheppard *W ldr to 4; last frm nxt; 10l last & nt gng wl when rn out 11*

OFFICIAL DISTANCES: 4l, 15l TIME: 6min 26.0s

785 Intermediate, 12st
13 ran

[634ᶠ]	1		**RUSTIC REVELRY** 10-1 P York *A.p; chsd ldr aft 10; rdn to ld last; hld on wl*
[429¹]	2	1	**Grecian Star** evensF J Tarry *Chsng group but sev posns; 7th when mist 14; wl off pce til str rn frm 2 out; chsd wnr flat; no imp last 50yds; too much to do*
[513³]	3	2½	**Mr Ben Gunn** 16-1 Miss L Sweeting *Hld up; prog 5 to jn chsng group; 6th when mist 14; r.o frm 3 out; eff nxt; stayed on one pce flat*
[510ᵁ]	4	3	**Fencing Master** 7-1 T Illsley *Prsd ldr til ld 10; mist 15; hdd & blun last; wknd flat*
[80¹]	5	4	**Oboedire (IRE)** 4-1 D Barlow *Hld up; 8th & last of those w ch 13; no prog til stayed on frm 2 out; nvr able to chall*
[388³]	6	3	**Dark Rhytham** 8-1 Miss N McKim *Hld up in last pr; prog frm 9; jnd ldng group 15; wknd aft 2 out*
[632⁴]	7	1	**Minstrel's Quay (IRE)** 33-1 M Gorman *Jmpd slow 5; prom; cl 3rd when mist 3 out; wknd nxt*
[543¹⁰]	8	30	**Glendine (IRE)** (bl) 33-1 D Smith *Jmpd slow 7; a rr; wkng when hmpd 11; t.o frm 13*
[543¹¹]	9	¾	**Neelisagin (IRE)** 25-1 J Turcan *In tch to 10; sn wknd; t.o 13*
[510ᴾ]	P		**Apple Nicking** 33-1 E Linehan *10th & in tch when blun 8; mist 10 & rdn; lsng tch when hmpd nxt; t.o & pu 15*
	F		**Latzio** (5a) 33-1 B McKim *2 handlers; made most to 10; 9th & wkng rap when fell nxt*
	P		**Mr Dennehy (IRE)** (5x) 20-1 David Dennis *Tk keen hld; prom til aft 3 out; wknd rap 2 out; pu last*
	P		**Sam The Sloth** (5a) 33-1 C Wadland *A towards rr; mist 4; wknd 9; t.o & pu 11*

OFFICIAL DISTANCES: 1l, 3l TIME: 6min 17.0s

786 Open Maiden (Div 1), 12st
11 ran

	1		**SECOND AMENDMENT** (5a) 10-1 J Oldring *16s-10s; a cl up; lft 2nd 14; chall frm 2 out; switched lft last; r.o wl flat; ld post(?)*
[520⁴]	2	s hd	**Novasun** 12-1 P York *Ld 4; made rest; prsd frm 2 out; lkd likely wnr aft last; kpt on; hdd post(?)*
[434²]	3	10	**Musical Hit** 8-1 C Wadland *A wl in tch; disp 2nd when mist 15; chall & ev ch 2 out; wknd last*
	4	12	**Game Gunner** 33-1 D Flavin *Bckwd; mist 4; rr til prog frm 10; 5th & in tch app 2 out; sn wknd; should improve*
[433²]	5	30	**Kings Choir** 4-1 Mrs C Boyes *A rr; lost tch frm 12; t.o nxt*
[471ᶠ]	6	5	**Crafty Phantom (IRE)** (12a,3ow) 4-1 Julian Pritchard *School in rr; wl bhnd 12; prog when mist nxt; mist 15; wl btn when jmpd slow 3 out*
[517ᴾ]	7	1	**Safe Cottage** 33-1 M Cowley *Prom til wknd & mist 11; t.o frm 13*
[617²]	U		**Captain George** 6-1 M Wall *(xnb) 2 handlers; lw; prom; def 2nd frm 10; prsng ldr when blun & ur 14*
	P		**Crack 'n' Run** 20-1 E Linehan *Ld to 4; sn lost tch & rdr calling cabs; last when blun 12 & pu*
[471³]	P		**Fistral Flame** (5a) 2-1F A Charles-Jones *Hld up mid-div; disp 3rd & wl in tch when hmpd 14; cl 4th when pu 2 out; dism*
	P		**Rio Santo (IRE)** (7a) 25-1 J Turcan *Bckwd; jmpd lft & slow early; detach frm 6; t.o & pu 11*

OFFICIAL DISTANCES: hd, 2l TIME: 6min 24.9s

787 Ladies Open
9 ran

[475ᴾ]	1		**PERSIAN BUTTERFLY** (5a) 12-1 Miss T Habgood *Chsd ldng pr frm 5; outpcd 12; 20l 3rd nxt; lft 8l 2nd 3 out; sn clsd; chall 2 out; ld last; stayed on wl*

[308²]	2	4	**Titus Andronicus** (5x) 7-1 **Miss H Irving** Chsd ldr frm 4; pushed along 11; 8l down 13; 15l down & no ch when lft in 8l ld 3 out; prsd nxt; hdd & nt qckn last; disapp
[431²]	3	6	**Lucky Christopher** (5x) 6-1 **Miss R Goodwin** Chsd ldng trio frm 7; outpcd frm 12; 24l 4th when lft 3rd 3 out; tried to cl nxt; one pce
[544⁵]	4	20	**Roly Prior** 4-1 **Miss S Samworth** Mid-div; outpcd 11; 26l 5th 13; no prog aft
[431⁵]	5	6	**Hostetler** 33-1 **Miss K Norris** Chsd ldr to 4; 5th ½way; sn lost tch & wl bhnd frm 15; r.o agn flat
[613⁶]	6	10	**Cumberland Youth** 33-1 **Miss J Garley** Jmpd lft 3; towards rr; wl bhnd frm 12; cont to
[544⁸]	7	30	**Faraday** 33-1 **Miss S Phizacklea** Chsd ldrs; mist 6 & wknd; t.o 10
	8	2½	**Colonel Fairfax** 33-1 **Miss K Matthews** (xnb) Mist 8; a wl in rr; no ch when nrly ur 13; cont to
[222²]	F		**Look In The Mirror** (5x) 8-11F **Miss A Nolan** Ld & sn 6l clr; drew away frm 14; 15l up & in comm when fell 3 out

OFFICIAL DISTANCES: 3½l, 5l **TIME:** 6min 13.7s

788 Confined, 12st   7 ran

[510⁹]	1		**PRIORY PIPER** (3x) 10-1 **L Hicks** Made all; prsd frm 13; jw aft; 4l clr last; rdn out & hld on; wl rdn
[510²]	2	1½	**Lottie The Lotus** (5a) 4-11F **J Tarry** Hld up; 6th when mist 14; wl off pce til r.o app 2 out; chsd wnr flat; too much to do
[511⁷]	3	2	**Limosa** (5a) 20-1 **R Barrett** 33s-20s; lw; in tch; prsd wnr 12; rdn 3 out; ev ch nxt; one pce app last; fair ef
[469⁹]	4	10	**Archies Oats** 10-1 **J Trice-Rolph** Mostly chsd ldng pr til outpcd frm 3 out; nt qckn app nxt
[428⁶]	5	3	**Smart Teacher** (USA) 33-1 **G Carenza** (xnb) Hld up last; stdy prog frm 12; chsd ldng pr aft 3 out & in tch; wknd aft 2 out
[428¹]	6	12	**The Hatcher** (NZ) (3x) 7-2 **L Lay** (bf) Chsd wnr til aft 12; sn lost plce; 5th & strugg when mist 15; no ch aft 3 out
[510¹⁰]	7	½	**Mr Freeman** (IRE) (bl) 33-1 **P Cowley** Jmpd slow 3; sn rdn & little resp; jmpd slow 12 & drpd to last; wl bhnd 3 out

OFFICIAL DISTANCES: 1½l, 2l **TIME:** 6min 20.8s

789 Mens Open   6 ran

	1		**FAWSLEY MANOR** (5a) 4-5F **J Tarry** A cl up; chsd ldr 12; chall & mist 3 out; ld app nxt; forged clr last; comf
[607⁹]	2	4	**Deep Refrain** (IRE) (tt) 8-1 **G Kerr** Tk fierce hld early; ld til hdd app 2 out; kpt on but no imp on wnr
[25⁷]	3	12	**Master Chuzzlewit** (IRE) 7-2 **F Hutsby** Prom; 3rd & rdn & flashed tail 13; outpcd aft 3 out
	4	8	**Professor Longhair** 10-1 **P Bennett** Cl up til pushed along & lost tch w ldng trio frm 12; no imp aft; kpt on
	P		**King Curan** (USA) 12-1 **J Oldring** Bckwd; settled last; jmpd slow & bhnd frm 8; t.o & pu 13
	P		**Phaedair** 5-1 **A Michael** Bckwd; tde; prom to 8; wknd rap & pu 11

OFFICIAL DISTANCES: 4l, 10l **TIME:** 6min 25.0s

790 Open Maiden (Div 2), 12st   13 ran

[471⁵]	1		**IMPENNY** (5a) 14-1 **M Wall** Hld up towards rr; disp 6th ½way; prog & cl up 13; chall aft 3 out; ld last; r.o wl
	2	8	**Cash Account** 33-1 **M Hewitt** Chsd ldr 4; ld 10; clr when blun 12; prsd frm nxt; hdd last; hung lft & wknd flat
[617⁶]	3	2	**Benbulbin** (IRE) (1ow) (vis) 16-1 **M Bluck** Prom; trckd ldr 11; ev ch 3 out; one pce aft nxt
[516³]	4	6	**Truly Optimistic** (5a) 10-1 **C Wadland** 2 handlers; swtng; hld up; prog frm 8; jnd ldrs 13; ev ch aft 3 out; wknd app last
[298²]	5	1	**Elver Spring** 9-4 **J Trice-Rolph** Jmpd slow 5; mid-div; disp 6th ½way; clsd on ldrs 13; outpcd app 3 out; no prog aft
[471⁹]	6	1	**Barton Bog** (IRE) 2-1F **T Scudamore** (xnb,b4) Lw; lost plce & rr when jmpd slow 4; nvr gng wl aft; 10th ½way; poor 8th 13; kpt on to 15l 7th 3 out; no prog aft
[437⁹]	7	¾	**Stormhill Farmer** 16-1 **M Keel** Chsng group; disp 6th ½way; nt on terms w ldrs frm 13; kpt on to 5th 3 out; wknd last
[526³]	8	8	**Tibs Eve** (IRE) 6-1 **Julian Pritchard** Ld to 2; chsd ldr to 4; stdly lost plce; 9th ½way; sn no ch
[514⁹]	9	fence	**Stable Girl** (5a) 33-1 **A Tutton** Still bckwd; in tch til wknd 9; t.o & jmpd slow frm 13
	F		**Festival** (FR) 10-1 **P York** (xnb) Ld 2; sn clr; hdd 10; 3rd & wkng when fell nxt
[514⁹]	P		**Magical Manor** (5a) 14-1 **J Tarry** In tch til drpd to rr 8; lost tch & pu 11
[629⁹]	P		**Ole Gunnar** (IRE) 25-1 **M Wilesmith** (xnb) Ld in start; svs; jmpd reluct & t.o til pu 12

[588F] **P**   **The Last Shout (IRE)** (bl) 33-1 P Millington *Unenthusiastic padd; in tch; mist 5; 5th & pushed along ½way; wknd rap & pu 11*

OFFICIAL DISTANCES: 7l, 2l TIME: 6min 25.2s

791 Restricted, 12st

12 ran

[458²] **1**   **BURGUNDY BOB (IRE)** 4-5F Julian Pritchard *Jw; made all; 4/5l ahd til drew away app 2 out; v impressive*

[427¹] **2**   12   **Perfect Minstrel (IRE)** 4-1 F Hutsby *(xnb) Chsng group; eff to def 2nd aft 15; 4l down aft 3 out; no ch w wnr frm nxt; kpt on; rn wl*

[248⁶] **3**   15   **Lady Emerald** (5a) 7-1 J Tarry *Chsd ldrs in 3rd/4th; outpcd app 3 out; lft 3rd 2 out; nd*

[433¹] **4**   15   **Penncaler (IRE)** 12-1 M Emmanuel *Chsd wnr til aft 15; sn btn; fin v slow; dism aft fin*

[509¹ᵈ] **5**   5   **Vulgan Prince** 12-1 R Barrett *Chsd ldrs in 3rd/4th til lost plce frm 13; no ch app 3 out*

[477F] **6**   25   **Bit Of A Character** 33-1 P Young *Mid-div; rdn ½way; lost tch 12; cont t.o*

[392ᵁ] **B**   **Dynoun** 7-1 D Crosse *Chsd ldrs; in tch when mist 13; rdn & eff 3 out; 5th & btn when bd 2 out*

[513F] **P**   **Goforitmrsmulligan (IRE)** (5a) 33-1 P Hall *Swerved lft start; jb; detach last when blun 1; cont t.o until inept rdng til pu 13*

P   **Lucky Joe** 14-1 David Dennis *20s-14s; sn rr; wknd ½way; t.o & pu aft 12*

[513⁴] **F**   **Please Call (IRE)** 10-1 E Linehan *Rdr calling cabs most fncs; chsng group; eff to 12l 3rd aft 3 out; same & btn when fell 2 out*

[429⁴] **F**   **Royal Orchard** 25-1 A Martin *Rr til fell 2*

[434¹] **P**   **Uncle Billy (IRE)** (bl) 20-1 E Walker *Mist 5; rr; lost tch 10; cont t.o til pu 2 out*

OFFICIAL DISTANCES: 15l, 20l TIME: 6min 14.4s

792 Open Maiden (Div 3), 12st

15 ran

[121⁴] **1**   **MY FRIEND BILLY (IRE)** 9-2 Miss S Phizacklea *Duelled w rnr-up til def advant frm 15; 5l clr last; wknd flat; all out*

[577F] **2**   ½   **Morph** 9-4F P York *Duelled w wnr til 2nd frm 15; lkd btn 2 out; 5l down last; rallied wl flat; just failed*

[340P] **3**   45   **Social Vision (IRE)** 16-1 M Cowley *Mists in rr; 9th ½way; last & t.o 3 out; kpt on to tk poor 3rd nr fin*

4   1   **Stormhill Soldier** 10-1 J Owen *Mid-div; rdr called cab 10; 7th & out of tch ½way; t.o 13; kpt on to tk poor 3rd aft 2 out til dem nr fin*

5   4   **Teachers Pet** 16-1 Miss L Sweeting *Trckd ldrs; cl up when lft 3rd 12; lost tch ldng pr nxt; scrambled over 3 out & nrly stpd; still 3rd when rn wide bend app 2 out & lost plce; wknd*

[593³] **6**   12   **Fortune Hunter (IRE)** 8-1 P Millington *(bh) Rdr nrly f.o 1; nt jw in last trio; eff to 15l 6th aft 10; sn no prog; t.o frm 15*

[509⁵] **P**   **Bangagin** 33-1 M Buchan *(xnb,b4) Reluct to go to post; reluct to rce; miles bhnd til pu 12*

[669⁶] **U**   **Bid For Tools (IRE)** (bl) 10-1 G Barfoot-Saunt *Trckd ldrs; pushed along frm 10; 5th & still in tch when hmpd & ur 12*

P   **Cottage Light** 33-1 D Flavin *A rr; wknd 9; t.o & pu 11*

[249F] **U**   **Happy Blade** 16-1 B Durrell *A rr; 10th & wknd ½way; t.o when rdr toppled off 12*

[433ᵁ] **F**   **Miss Hoity Toity** (5a) 8-1 J Tarry *Pulled hrd; trckd ldrs; cl 3rd when fell 12*

[588P] **P**   **Otter River** 33-1 P Morris *Last pr & sn t.o; pu 8*

P   **Piltdown Lady** (5a) 16-1 T Macfarlane *Prom to 8; sn wknd; t.o & pu 11*

P   **Watts The Point** (5a) 6-1 David Dennis *12s-6s; lw; in tch; rmdrs aft 4; lost plce & jmpd slow 7; nt r.o; pu nxt*

P   **Whistling Song** (12a,2ow) 10-1 J Trice-Rolph *Fractious padd; school in rr; 8th ½way; sn t.o; pu 14*

OFFICIAL DISTANCES: ½l, dist TIME: 6min 25.5s

South Wold

Brocklesby Park (LH 8F,18J) Sun, 26 Mar (GOOD)

793 Confined Maiden 56&7yo, 12st - 17J

16 ran

[439⁴] **1**   **FINE TIMES** (tt) 8-1 M Mackley *Hld up & bhnd; gd prog in 6th app 3 out; sust rn aft; ld flat; drvn out*

[437ᴮ] **2**   1   **Gentleman Charles (IRE)** 16-1 S Walker *Ld 1; cl up; 4th app 14; went 2nd aft nxt; ld 2 out; drvn & hdd aft last; nt qckn*

[436⁶] **3**   5   **Harps Hall (IRE)** 10-1 M Chatterton *Rr of midfield; kpt on stdly aft 15; 3rd app nxt; drvn along & no imp aft 2 out*

[437³] **4**   6   **Second Thoughts** (5a) 4-1 W Wales *Oht; sn ld & mostly ab 6l clr w one pursuer; rdn & hdd 2 out; no ex*

[436⁴]	5	5	**The Other Eye (IRE)** 6-1 D Thomas *Hld up & bhnd; outpcd frm 13; mod late prog*
[399ᵁ]	6	½	**Highbury** 6-1 W Burnell *Chsd ldrs on inside til pushed along & outpcd in 8th app 14; strug aft*
[439⁵]	7	7	**Petrea** (12a) 7-2F G Brewer *Hld up & bhnd; smooth prog 10 & sn 2nd/3rd; ev ch til 4th & wkng app 3 out; fin tame*
[437⁸]	8	3	**Anneka Louise** (5a) 16-1 S Charlton *Bckwd; chsd ldrs; 7th app 13; 5th & in tch app 3 out; one pce*
[507⁴]	9	8	**Russian Prince (IRE)** (7a) 16-1 Miss F Hartley *Last pr most of way; bad mist 6; lost tch 11*
[439⁶]	10	8	**Tom's Surprise** 8-1 N Kent *Bckwd; a bhnd; strugg 12*
[51⁶]	11	6	**Alston Fanfare (IRE)** 40-1 J Cookson *Midfield early; drpd to rr 11; no ch aft*
[398³]	P		**Aunty Norma (IRE)** (5a) 14-1 S Swiers *Swtng; school in last; wl bhnd when pu 12*
[508ᴾ]	U		**Benn Wood** (7a) 40-1 Miss S Brotherton *(xnb) Tk str hld; chsd ldr to 14; sn wknd; wl bhnd when mist & ur last*
[507⁵]	S		**Captain Oates** 16-1 M Watson *Prom til lost plce 10; rallied in 6th aft 13; 3rd & ev ch when slpd up aft 15*
[547⁶]	F		**Colonel Carats** 25-1 N Bell *(xnb) Prom til fell 2*
	P		**Sail On By** (5a) 20-1 R Armson *Bckwd; prom in chsng group; 5th app 14; sn eased out; pu nxt*

OFFICIAL DISTANCES: 1l, 3l TIME: 6min 35.0s
Fence 10 omitted - fallen rider

794 Confined, 12st   9 ran

[229²]	1		**LINLATHEN** 6-4F G Brewer *(xnb) Hld up & bhnd til 5th & eff 10; trckd ldrs gng wl til tk 2nd aft 15; jnd ldr 2 out; rdn but lkd wnr when lft clr last*
[438¹]	2	4	**Gymcrak Gorjos** (5a) 12-1 D Thomas *Prom til lost plce sltly 8; cl 6th 10; rallied in 5l 5th app 3 out; jnd ldng pr nxt; nt qckn; lft 2nd at last; hung rt aft*
[622⁴]	3	6	**Ways And Means** (5a) 10-1 K Green *Hld up & bhnd; 8l last 10; gd prog app 3 out; 4th & staying on wl when lft 3rd & hmpd last; game eff*
[505³]	4	2	**Misti Hunter (IRE)** 7-1 R Douro *(xnb) Trckd ldrs; went 2nd brief 10; cl 4th aft 15; one pce nxt*
[231³]	5	runin	**Fontaine Fables (IRE)** (bl) 50-1 M Bennison *Jmpd delib in midfield; 7th 10; lost tch 15; t.o*
[435⁴]	6	½	**Quiet Mistress** (5a) 25-1 S Charlton *Handy; 4th & u.p aft 10; wknd 15; t.o*
	P		**Sheelin Lad (IRE)** 20-1 C Vale *Bckwd; pulled hrd & 2nd mostly; hit 9; 2nd 14; ev ch til drvn & wknd aft nxt; pu 3 out*
[545³]	P		**South Westerly (IRE)** 6-1 M Mackley *Bhnd; 8th 10; wknd 14; pu 3 out*
	F		**Syd Green (IRE)** 4-1 S Walker *(xnb) Ld at brisk pce til jnd & drvn 2 out; 2nd & btn when fell last*

OFFICIAL DISTANCES: 2l, 6l TIME: 6min 24.0s

795 Ladies Open   7 ran

[397⁵]	1		**HALF EACH** (5a) 12-1 Miss L Watson *Settled 4th & wl off pce; 20l 4th & clsng 10; 10l 5th 14; went 2nd app 3 out; stayed on to ld app last; r.o wl*
[623³]	2	2½	**Orswellthatenswell** 9-4 Mrs F Needham *Tk off in false start; ld at fast gallop; 3l clr app 3 out; drvn nxt; hdd app last; nt qckn*
[441ᴾ]	3	4	**Just Bruce** 25-1 Miss L White *1st ride; prsd ldr at fast pce til releg 3rd app 3 out; kpt on stdly til btn aft 2 out*
[544⁴]	4	4	**Drummond Warrior (IRE)** 12-1 Miss A Burton *3rd but sn wl adrift of ldrs; clsd in 12l 3rd 10; 7l 4th 14; one pce aft nxt*
[505¹]	5	3	**The Minister (IRE)** 8-11F Miss T Jackson *Nt jw; drpd out in 25l last; 35l 5th aft 7; mist 9; clsd to 12l 3rd 12; 1½l down & ev ch when blun & nrly ur 14; lost plce & hit nxt; wknd to 8l 4th app 3 out*
[442²]	6	½	**Doctor Dunklin (USA)** 12-1 Miss E Graham *Detach in last trio; 20l 6th 10; no ch frm 14*
[366²]	P		**Affair Of Honour (IRE)** 33-1 Miss C Elkington *Mist 3; detach in last trio; t.o 9; pu 14*

OFFICIAL DISTANCES: 2l, 3l TIME: 6min 24.0s

796 Land Rover Mens Open, 12st   6 ran

[584ᴾ]	1		**SOLBA (USA)** (7x) 5-4 A Dalton *Made nrly all; 3l clr & gng best app 3 out; r.o str aft*
[504¹]	2	8	**Mr Dick** (7x) 4-6F S Swiers *Settled 3rd mostly; chall 13; went 2nd aft 15; sn kicked along & no imp; a hld frm 3 out; lame*
	P		**Khatir (CAN)** N Kent *(xnb) Prsd ldrs til 3l 4th 14; qckly outpcd aft nxt; pu 3 out*
[376³]	P		**Primitive Streak** (7x) 25-1 R Abrahams *Lw; oft jw & ld brief 4 & 5; hit 8; prsd wnr til wknd qckly on long rn to 3 out; poor 3rd when pu last*
[229ᴾ]	P		**Ryders Wells** (bl) 33-1 S Walker *Cl up til rdn & reluct 10; sn poor last; t.o & pu 15*

[48ᴾ] P   **Tiderunner (IRE)** (bl) 33-1 S Charlton *Rr but cl up til rdn aft 10; lost tch qckly 14;*
                1½ fncs bhnd when pu 2 out

OFFICIAL DISTANCE: 10l **TIME:** 6min 30.0s

797 Restricted, 12st   14 ran

[232²] 1   **KEY DEBATE** 7-2 G Brewer *Ld in start; tk str hld; prom til ld 6; 15l clr 10; 30l ahd aft*
                  15; unchall & impressive (spreadeagled field)
[228¹] 2   20   **Splodge** 33-1 M Bennison (xnb) *Bhnd; stdy hdwy 13; went 3rd app 3 out; chsd wnr*
                  nxt; kpt on game but unable to chall
[396²] 3   12   **Hazel Reilly (IRE)** (5a) 7-1 L Bates *Wl bhnd; last aft 7; stayed on past btn horses frm*
                  15; snatched 3rd flat
[121¹] 4   ½   **Roly Poly** 11-1 M Mackley *Trckd ldrs; 15l 4th aft 7; went 3rd 12 & 20l 2nd*
                  13; nvr nr wnr; lost 2nd & mist 2 out; dem agn nr line
[233¹] 5   15   **Heir Of Gold (IRE)** 7-2 S R Andrews (xnb) *Ld to 2; 15l 4th aft 7; chsd wnr 12-13;*
                  sn outpcd; 40l 4th app 3 out
[626¹] 6   20   **C L B Jemilla** (5a) 10-1 Mrs F Needham *A midfield; outpcd frm 13*
[503³] 7   20   **Deer Park Lass (IRE)** (5a) 33-1 D Thomas *Bhnd; 12th aft 7; no ch 12; t.o aft 15*
[139¹] U   **Atoski** 2-1F A Dalton *Stdd chsng clr ldrs; 16l 5th aft 7; 25l 3rd when bad mist & ur 14*
        P   **Brackenhill** 33-1 R Wakeham *Midfield; 6th aft 7; mist 11; sn wknd; pu 3 out*
[367ᴾ] P   **Charming Moss (IRE)** 33-1 A Pickering *Pulled hrd; jmpd erratic & sn wrestled to*
                  rr; blun bad 5; strugg when bad mist 13; pu nxt
[439¹] P   **Handfast Point** 12-1 C Vale *Wl bhnd to 10; prog 12; 40l 5th aft 15; pu nxt*
        F   **Kind Of Chic** (5a) 33-1 P Kinsella *Ld 2 til app 6; wkng when mist 9; last & tlng off*
                  when fell 12
        P   **Mail Shot (IRE)** (7a) 33-1 N Kent *Tk str hld; ld brief app 6; chsd wnr til bad mist 10;*
                  wknd nxt; wl bhnd when pu 15
[435⁵] W   **Vimchase** 66-1 K Green *Withdrawn and orders; lame*

OFFICIAL DISTANCES: dist, hd **TIME:** 6min 21.0s

798 Open Maiden 8yo&up, 12st   15 ran

[507ᴾ] 1   **NOT SO PRIM** (5a) 9-2 S Swiers *2nd til ld 11; 6l clr app 3 out; stdly drew clr; unchall*
[54³]   2   20   **The Happy Monarch (IRE)** 11-2 Mrs F Needham (xnb) *Midfield; 5th 10; outpcd*
                  15; lft 18l 2nd & mist nxt; nvr nr wnr
[399⁵] 3   8   **Kerrisdale** (5a) (tt) 16-1 D Thomas *Trckd ldrs; 4th 10; rdn & desperate one-pcd frm*
                  15; 20l 4th app nxt; lft 3rd 3 out
[281⁷] 4   runin **The Noble Rebel (IRE)** (1ow) 20-1 A Pennock *Nt fluent; trckd ldrs; 6th 10; wknd*
                  15; t.o
[373ᶠ] U   **Hya Prim** 13-2 M Mackley *Midfield; 7th 10; plodding on when mist & ur 14*
        P   **Look Sharpe** 6-1 N Wilson *Tk keen hld; ld; mist 2; hdd 11; wknd 15; pu & dism nxt*
[502³] r   **Mr Eglantine** 20-1 Miss F Hartley *A strugg in rr; bad mist 6; t.o last 11; ref & threw*
                  rdr over 14
[507³] F   **Nasayer (IRE)** 6-1 A Pickering *Fell 2*
[625ᴾ] F   **Pearly's Song** 6-1 K Needham *Settled 3rd/4th; 3rd 10; chsd wnr 15; ab 8l down &*
                  hld when fell 3 out
        P   **Prince Baltasar** 25-1 C Mulhall *Strugg in rr; 10th 10; t.o to pu 3 out*
[372ᴮ] P   **Royal Charger (IRE)** 33-1 R Armson *Oht; last trio & nvr gng wl; 9th 10; pu nxt*
        P   **Rymerole** 20-1 M Bennison (xnb) *A last; t.o 6; pu 11*
[373ᶠ] U   **Sands Point** 12-1 N Kent *Ur 2*
[399ᴾ] P   **The Way North** 20-1 R Wakeham (xnb) *Prom brief; 11th & strugg 10; t.o to pu 15*
        P   **Wotstheproblem** 4-1F S Charlton (xnb) *Midfield; 8th & rdn 10; no resp; t.o to pu 12*

OFFICIAL DISTANCES: 20l, 6l **TIME:** 6min 29.0s

Sandown (RH 11F,15J)
Tue, 28 Mar (GOOD to FIRM, FIRM in places)

799 Ubique HC   8 ran

[300²] 1   **SATCHMO (IRE)** 11-04 11-10F B Hitchcott *Tk keen hld; trckd ldrs; prog 6; went 2nd*
                  8; ld 9; drew 20l clr aft 3 out; eased flat; impressive
        2   dist **Verity Valentine** 11-01 33-1 T Gibney *Jmpd lft; ld to 9; chsd wnr to 12; sn*
                  hopelessly outpcd; kpt on game to rem 2nd bef last
[684²] 3   7   **Stanmore (IRE)** 11-10 11-4 R Barrett *Trckd ldrs; jmpd slow 7; pushed along 8; 8l*
                  3rd 10; eff to chse wnr 13; rdn & btn aft nxt; lost 2nd app last; eased flat
[685ᶠ] 4   27   **The Captain's Wish** 11-06 (tt) 9-1 A Michael *Tubed; last & sn wl bhnd; t.o frm 6;*
                  drvn into v rem 4th nr fin

[585P]	5	hd	**Mustang Molly** 10-11 40-1 **A Martin** A rr; mist 5; t.o nxt
[581²]	P		**Against The Agent** 11-10 13-2 **T Dennis** Mist 4; chsd ldr to 8; lost tch 13; rem 4th when pu app 3 out; dism (lost concen temporarily)
[226⁵]	P		**Caddy Man (IRE)** 12-00 12-1 **P Cashman** Hit 2; nt fluent 4; midfield; lost tch aft 5; t.o & pu 10; bbv
[468F]	P		**Frown** 11-10 (bl) 33-1 **T Doyle** Chsd ldrs til wknd 7; t.o nxt; pu 2 out

TIME: 5min 09.5s **TOTE:** £2.00; places £1.30,£4.10,£1.10 **Ex:** £61.00 **CSF:** £33.72 **Tri:** £207.80

Ascot (RH 10F,20J)
Sat, 1 Apr (GOOD)

800 Royal Ascot Cricket Club Nov HC   **9 ran**

[467¹]	1		**CHASING THE BRIDE** 12-04 (tt) 2-1 **M Miller** Bhnd; hdwy 9; hit 12; jmpd delib 14 (water); 4th & chsng ldrs 3 out; went 2nd nxt; stayed on to tk ll ld last; in control when lft clr
[300³]	2	9	**Novatara** 11-11 12-1 **T Gibney** Blun 4 (water); jmpd poor in rr & wl bhnd; mod 6th 15; stayed on stout frm 3 out; kpt on & lft 2nd last; no ch w wnr
[631³]	3	1¾	**Man Of Steele (IRE)** 11-07 13-2 **Miss D Harding** Ld aft 2-8; ld agn 12; hdd 16; rdn & prsd ldrs til wknd aft 2 out
[799⁵]	4	9	**The Captain's Wish** 11-07 (tt) 33-1 **A Michael** Tubed; hdwy & cl up 8; chsd ldr 17 til rdn & wknd aft 2 out
[59⁶]	U		**Alex Thuscombe** 11-07 (bl) 14-1 **P Shaw** Chsd ldr; ld 8-12 & agn 15; hdd & ll down when blun & ur last
[631⁴]	U		**Copper Coil** 11-07 14-1 **J Barnes** Mist 1; chsd ldrs; 4th when hit 8; rdn 10; rr when mist & ur nxt
	U		**Lingering Laughter (IRE)** 11-07 33-1 **M Foley** 6th when mist & ur 3
[459²]	P		**My Shout** 12-00 15-8F **B Pollock** Ld til aft 2; mist 3; lost plce 6; jmpd lft 8; rdn & no resp 11; t.o & pu 3 out (v lacklustre)
[711²]	P		**Rush 'n Tear** 11-11 66-1 **A Charles-Jones** Chsd ldrs; hit 7; rallied 11; wknd & blun 13; t.o & pu 17

TIME: 6min 27.4s **TOTE:** £3.00; places £1.50,£2.00,£1.90 **Ex:** £54.80 **CSF:** £20.93 **Tri:** £364.50

Market Rasen (RH 8F,15J)
Sat, 1 Apr (GOOD to FIRM)

801 Marc & Mary Wheatley Countryside Counts Nov HC   **6 ran**

[611³]	1		**FOREST FEATHER (IRE)** 11-11 4-1 **D O'Meara** Handy; 3rd 9; ld 10; jmpd v slow 11; drew clr apr nxt; 20l ahd when blun 3 out; unchall
[546¹]	2	18	**Neva-Agree** 11-09 7-2 **R Armson** Chsd ldrs; 5th 10; lost tch nxt; poor 4th 3 out; kpt on to 2nd 2 out; no ch w wnr
[461⁵]	3	24	**Tickerty's Gift** 11-11 (bl) 8-1 **T Doyle** Nt fluent; ld til aft 3; hit 8; rmdrs app 10; lost tch nxt; t.o
	P		**Admiral Villeneuve** 11-07 (bl) 20-1 **R Arnold** Bhnd; mist 5; lost tch & rdn 7; t.o & pu 10
[585¹]	P		**On The Fly** 11-07 (tt) 2-1F **G Markham** Blun 1; oft jmpd slow but made most aft 3-10; 6l 3rd & u.p 12; lost tch rap; t.o & pu 3 out
[546²]	P		**Sovereigns Match** 11-07 5-1 **M Mackley** Cl 2nd to 11; 20l 2nd when went bad lft & tried to ref 3 out; t.o & pu nxt

TIME: 6min 28.5s **TOTE:** £5.60; places £2.40,£1.70 **Ex:** £19.90 **CSF:** £15.56

Water jump and last fence omitted each circuit

Towcester (RH 10F,16J)
Sat, 1 Apr (GOOD)

802 Empress of Austria HC   **9 ran**

	1		**LAST OPTION** 12-08 4-6F **Mrs F Needham** Sn ld; hdd aft 4; hit 10; 2nd/3rd til ld agn 13; went 8l clr app 2 out; idled & drvn flat; hld on game
[680F]	2	shhd	**Act Of Parliament (IRE)** 12-01 (bl) 9-2 **D Flavin** Hld up & bhnd to 8; hdwy to 4th & hit 10; outpcd 12; mod 5th 3 out; rallied app nxt; sn hrd rdn; went 2nd flat; stayed on wl; just failed
[460⁴]	3	4	**Desperate** 11-11 16-1 **R Barrett** Bhnd; mist 5; last & drvn 8; 4th & prog 13; 2nd 2 out; chall u.p & ev ch last; no ex flat
[731²]	4	1¾	**The Bold Abbot** 11-07 16-1 **Miss S West** Chsd ldrs; 5th 13; outpcd 3 out; rallied nxt; kpt on flat

[681⁶]	5	3	**John Tufty** 11-07 50-1 *Miss R Illman Midfield; outpcd 13; 7th 3 out; kpt on w rdr bumping aft til no ex last (game eff w v novicey partner)*
[460ᴾ]	P		**China Gem (IRE)** 11-09 16-1 *V Keane Hld up; hdwy 6; cl 3rd when mist 13; wknd app 2 out; 5th when pu last*
[749ᴾ]	P		**Northern Yarn (IRE)** 11-09 25-1 *J Owen A bhnd; mist 4; jmpd v slow 8; t.o 9; pu last*
	F		**Pimberley Place (IRE)** 11-11 7-1 *T Scudamore Jmpd lft; hdwy to ld app 5; jmpd slow 10; hdd 13; rdn & wknd app 2 out; tired 6th when fell last*
	P		**Strewth** 11-09 50-1 *C Weaver Ld brief aft 4; 2nd 7; blun 9; wknd 10; bhnd when hit 13; t.o & pu last*

TIME: 5min 58.9s **TOTE:** £1.60; places £1.30,£1.30,£1.70 **Ex:** £3.20 **CSF:** £3.83 **Tri:** £33.80

Cleveland

Stainton (RH 7F,20J) Sat, 1 Apr (GOOD to FIRM)

803 Hunt Maiden
7 ran

[627ᵁ]	1		**BUSTER BUTTONS** (bl) 7-4 *N Tutty Mid-div to 6; 8l 3rd when bad mist 7; last 10; gd hdwy 15 to ld 3 out; 6l up last; r.o str*
[694³]	2	8	**Imperial Line (IRE)** 6-4F *Miss T Jackson Ld 2; 2l up 13; hdd aft 15; 3l 2nd nxt; outpcd aft 3 out; 6l 3rd at last; rallied str flat; snatched 2nd on line*
	3	hd	**Catton Lady** (5a) 3-1 *G Brewer Trckd ldr in 2l 2nd til ld 14; sn qcknd clr; 3l up 16; jnd 3 out; sn hdd; outpcd & wknd 2 out*
[695ᴾ]	4	35	**Alena H Banks** 7-1 *L McGrath (xnb) Tk str hld; 6l 4th 9; pushed along & rmdrs 13; wknd & rem 5th 16; lft poor 4th 3 out*
[626⁶]	U		**Chief Engineer** 12-1 *S Brisby Ploughed thro 1 & ur*
	P		**Oaklands Jimmy** 33-1 *P Frank Jmpd novicey; last & jmpd slow 2; trailing by 10; lsng tch when bad mist 11; t.o & pu 16*
[627¹⁰]	U		**The Grey Bay** (5a) 20-1 *T Glass Pulled hrd early; handy to 10; hdwy 13 to ll 2nd 14; outpcd & wknd 16; 4th & hld when ur 3 out*

OFFICIAL DISTANCES: 8l, nk **TIME:** 6min 22.0s

804 Confined, 12st
6 ran

[692ᵁ]	1		**STRIDE TO GLORY (IRE)** (bl) 10-1 *Mrs H Arnold Jw; made all; 3l clr frm 8; jnd app 2 out; hrd rdn & sn ld agn; clr last; r.o wl*
[396⁸]	2	2	**Keep A Secret** 3-1 *P Atkinson (xnb) Hld up early; went 6l 3rd 11; hdwy to cl 3rd 17; outpcd by ldng pr 3 out; 6l 3rd last; hrd rdn flat; snatched 2nd cl home*
[692²]	3	1½	**Harbour Blaze (IRE)** 2-5F *Miss R Clark A.p; chsd ldr & 3l 2nd 8-16; eff to chall & mist 2 out; pushed along app last; wknd & dem flat*
[394ᴾ]	4	50	**Caman** (2ow) (bl) 8-1 *Mrs S Palfreeman Last by 3; a bhnd; lsng tch 8; t.o 13; rem 4th 16*
[506ᴾ]	P		**Mr Hook** (bl) 10-1 *R Clark Spurs; nt jw; mid-div to 5; mists 7 & 9; wknd 10; 15l 4th 11; hrd rdn 13; t.o & pu 15*
[696ᴾ]	P		**Pashby Wood** (5a,2ow) 33-1 *M Morley A rr; 10l 5th 6; last by 9; 20l 5th 11; t.o & pu 16*

OFFICIAL DISTANCES: 2l, 2l **TIME:** 6min 16.0s

805 Mens Open
5 ran

[621⁵]	1		**PRIVATE JET (IRE)** 5-1 *R Clark 20s-5s; last to 5; 20l 3rd 11; hdwy 13 to ½l 2nd 17; ld 3 out; rdn & qcknd nxt; 6l up at last; r.o str*
[622⁵]	2	5	**Just Charlie** 4-6F *D Easterby Chsd ldr; 8l 2nd 8; cl 2nd 14; pushed along & outpcd 16; 20l 4th 3 out; stayed on one pce; tk 2nd flat*
[682²]	3	5	**Cross Cannon** 6-4 *T Glass Last 5 til hdwy aft 12; cl 3rd 14; ld 17-3 out; wknd nxt; dem 3rd flat*
	4	3	**Iveagh Lad** 9-1 *N Tutty (bf) Made most; 15l up 11; stdd & 2l ahd 14; jnd & wknd 16; easily outpcd 3 out; 10l 3rd 2 out; broke down*
[623⁶]	5	12	**Nishkina** (bl) 33-1 *C Cundall Mid-div 1st circ; 9l 3rd 8; rr & pushed along 14; sn wknd; lost tch 17*

OFFICIAL DISTANCES: 4l, 5l **TIME:** 6min 20.0s

806 Ladies Open
6 ran

[621²]	1		**JAPODENE** (5a) 6-4F *Miss R Clark Mid-div to 7; hdwy 10 to cl 2nd 11; trckd ldr til ld 17; 2l ahd 3 out; 4l clr last; r.o str*
[795⁵]	2	7	**The Minister (IRE)** 2-1 *Miss T Jackson A.p; 3l 3rd 8-15; went 2l 2nd 3 out; pushed along & outpcd nxt*

[795¹]	3	5	**Half Each** (5a) 3-1 **Miss L Watson** *Outpcd; last 5 til hdwy 13; 12l 5th 16; pushed along 3 out; stayed on to tk 3rd flat*
[621ᵁ]	4	½	**Kralingen** (5a) 9-2 **Miss C Metcalfe** *Last to 4; 10l 5th 9; last agn by 14; pushed along 3 out; r.o one pce; nrst fin*
[619¹]	5	4	**General Brandy** 12-1 **Miss A Thompson** *Chsd ldr; 2l 2nd 8-15; handy in 4th 16; kpt on one pce; 5l 3rd 2 out; wknd app last*
[361ᶠ]	6	10	**Muskora (IRE)** (bl) 6-1 **Mrs V Jackson** *Ld by around 2l to 17; wknd qckly 3 out; last nxt*

OFFICIAL DISTANCES: 7l, 3l **TIME:** 6min 07.0s

807 Restricted
15 ran

[620²]	1		**QUEEN BIDDY (IRE)** (5a) 2-1F **C Storey** *Mid-div to 13; went handy 4th 14; ld app 3 out; 1l up nxt; 4l clr last; r.o u.p*
[689²]	2	4	**Lord Nick** 20-1 **N Tutty** *A.p; cl 5th 13; went 3l 3rd 15; 2l 3rd 2 out; hrd rdn app last; r.o one pce*
[173ᵖ]	3	10	**Primitive Charles** (bl) 14-1 **G Brewer** *Prom in 4th to 8; went 1l 2nd 11; ld 13-3 out; 1l 2nd & mist 2 out; hrd rdn & wknd app last*
[503⁵]	4	6	**Traceytown (IRE)** (5a) 20-1 **Miss Rachel Clark** (xnb) *Mid-div when bad mist 14; rmdrs 15; 25l 6th 3 out; stayed on wl; tk 5th app last; snatched 4th in drvng fin*
[689⁶]	5	½	**Run For The Mill** (5a) 20-1 **M Morley** *Midfield 1st circ; went 2l 3rd 13-16; outpcd & mist 3 out; 10l 4th nxt; wknd app last; dem on line*
[396²]	6	4	**Normins Hussar (IRE)** 12-1 **N Wilson** *A.p; rushed up to ld aft 10; 2l ahd 11 til hdd aft 13; trckd ldrs til wknd 3 out*
[503²]	7	3	**Yornoangel** 6-1 **R Clark** *Cl 3rd to 8; mid-div til mist 14; rmdrs & wknd 15*
[689ᵖ]	8	30	**Prince Moshar** 20-1 **L McGrath** *Sn rr; chsd along 10; lsng tch 11; t.o 14*
[396²]	P		**Cato (IRE)** 20-1 **D Easterby** *Sa; sn bhnd; t.o 11; pu 17*
	P		**Cede Nullis** (5a) (tt) 6-1 **S Brisby** *A midfield; 15l 9th 12; pushed along 14; lsng tch when pu 17*
[619ᶠ]	P		**Ellerton Tony** 8-1 **S Swiers** *Ld to 2; cl 2nd 3-10; wknd 11; rr & lsng tch 15; pu 17*
[688²]	P		**Erni (FR)** 3-1 **W Burnell** *A outpcd; rr when mist 9; lsng tch 13; pu 14*
[620⁶]	P		**Lord George** (bl) 20-1 **P Atkinson** *Ld frm 3; 8l clr 9; wknd aft 10; grad drpd back; rr when pu 17*
[503ᵖ]	P		**Mac's Blade (USA)** (bl,tt) 33-1 **R Edwards** *A rr; t.o 13; pu 17*
	P		**Spectacular View (IRE)** (7a) 20-1 **T Glass** *Mid-div to 6; hdwy 7 to 5l 4th 9; wknd 10; rr & lsng tch when pu 14*

OFFICIAL DISTANCES: 1l, 10l **TIME:** 6min 16.0s

808 Open Maiden (Div 1) - 18J
15 ran

[438³]	1		**SASSY STREET (IRE)** 6-1 **K Needham** *Rr early; hdwy 7 to handy 4th 10; went 1l 2nd 13-13 out; disp ld 2 out; outpcd app last; rallied & jnd ldr flat; plcd 1st; plcd 1st*
[798³]	2	d ht	**Kerrisdale** (5a) 7-1 **D Thomas** *Rr div to 8; smooth hdwy 10 to 3l 3rd 14; 1l 3rd & gng wl 3 out; chall nxt; 2l up & nt fluent last; jnd flat; plcd 2nd - lkd to share spoils*
[627³]	3	6	**Tenor Bet (IRE)** 7-4F **N Wilson** *Mid-div to 6; 3l 3rd 7-9; went cl 3rd 10; ld 13-3 out; hung lft in straight & wknd*
[627²]	4	1	**Leg Beforum (IRE)** 5-4F **L Bates** *Midfield in 5th to 11; 8l 5th 13; stayed on to 4th 2 out; r.o one pce*
	5	4	**The Killaloe Run** (5a) 20-1 **Miss J Foster** *A midfield; outpcd 17; 10l 4th 3 out; wknd to 13l 5th nxt*
[626⁵]	6	6	**I Say Dancer** (5a) 16-1 **Miss C Metcalfe** *Rr to 4; hdwy 10 to 12l 6th 13; nvr nrr; r.o one pce*
[626³]	7	1	**Pennyman (IRE)** 6-1 **T Glass** *A mid-div; nt pce to chall*
	8	1	**Canny's Fort** (5a) 33-1 **J Davies** *Prom early; 4l 3rd 3 & 10l 5th 11; wknd 13; rr & lsng tch 16*
[696ᵁ]	P		**Almikino (IRE)** 7-1 **S Brisby** *Chsd ldr in 2l 2nd til bad blun 13; ploughed thro nxt (ditch) & imm pu*
[625ʳ]	F		**Ardnut** 10-1 **C Storey** *Fell 1*
	P		**Baltic Lake (IRE)** 7-1 **M Smethurst** *A rr; pushed along & lsng tch 9; t.o & pu 14*
[399ᵁ]	P		**Cricketing** 10-1 **D Easterby** *Sn ld; 2l up til hdd aft 12; sn wknd & qckly drpd back; rr 15; t.o & pu 2 out*
[398ᵁ]	P		**Mr Norm** 20-1 **R Clark** *A strugg; bhnd & lsng tch when bad blun & nrly ur 7; imm pu*
[624ᶠ]	P		**Westhall Jonstan (IRE)** 1-1 **L McGrath** *Hmpd badly 1; sn bhnd; lsng tch when pu 9*
[625ᵖ]	F		**Young Saffy** 33-1 **A Pennock** *Fell 1*

OFFICIAL DISTANCES: ¾l, 6l **TIME:** 6min 25.0s
Fences 8 & 15 omitted - slippery ground

809 Open Maiden (Div 2) - 18J
13 ran

[626F]	1		**HAPPY BLAKE** 5-4F C Storey Mid-div 1st circ; hdwy 9 to 5l 4th 13; ld 3 out; hrd rdn app last; stayed on u.p
[398P]	2	2½	**Flowing Fortune** 33-1 Miss R Clark Rr to 7; hdwy 12 to 6l 5th 13; gng easy in 3l 3rd 3 out; went 2nd app nxt; rdn last; r.o one pce
[625²]	3	15	**In The Van** 9-2 M Morley Prom in 3rd til lost plce 7; 7th 9; hdwy 12 to disp ld 14-3 out; wknd app nxt; r.o one pce
	4	3	**Farm Talk** 33-1 S Charlton Last to 2; rr to 11; went 12l 7th 13; stayed on one pce; tk 4th app 2 out; nrst fin
[695F]	5	25	**Sally Scally** 2-1 Miss T Jackson Cl 4th til pulled to ld 6; 5l up 8; jnd 14; wknd 3 out; t.o nxt
[798⁴]	6	8	**The Noble Rebel (IRE)** 7-1 A Pennock A mid-div; 10l 6th 14; pushed along & outpcd 15; t.o 3 out
[627P]	P		**Countess Rosie** (5a) 33-1 N Wilson Rr by 4; jmpd slow 7; t.o 10; pu 2 out
[625F]	F		**Dragon Stout** 6-1 C Wilson A.p; 4l 3rd 13; handy 4th when fell 14
[625P]	P		**Just A Single (IRE)** (bl) 4-1 D Easterby Ld to 5; prom til grad wknd frm 10; t.o & pu 2 out
[620P]	P		**Palm Gold** (5a) 33-1 R Wakeham Midfield to 5; bad mist 11; rdr round horse's nk & imm pu
	U		**Rievers Way** (7a) 33-1 J Clare Unruly padd & diff to mount; cl up; 3l 4th when ur 3
[627⁹]	P		**Stanwick Hall** 33-1 K Needham Rr & bad mist 6; hung lft 7; wknd & lsng tch 8; t.o & pu 13
	P		**Woodford Again** (5a) 33-1 M Smethurst A rr; lsng tch 11; t.o & pu 3 out

OFFICIAL DISTANCES: 2½l, 12l **TIME:** 6min 26.0s

Holcombe Harriers
Whittington (LH 8F,18J) Sat, 1 Apr (GOOD, GOOD to FIRM in places)

810 Hunt
1 ran

[694P]	1		**MEZZO PRINCESS** (5a) J R Barlow Walked over

OFFICIAL DISTANCE: Walked over

811 Intermediate, 12st
6 ran

[713²]	1		**TRIVIAL (IRE)** (5a) 6-4F R Morgan (xnb) Jmpd slow 1; last pr til went 3l 3rd 6; trckd ldrs til ld 11; hdd 2 out; sn ld agn; drew clr flat; comf
[359P]	2	10	**Allrite Bonny Lass** (5a) 9-4 L Morgan Trckd ldrs in cl 4th; went 2l 2nd 13; prsd wnr til slt ld 2 out; sn hdd; 1l down last; outpcd flat
[543⁴]	3d		**Triple Eaves** 5-2 C Mulhall Ld; went wrong side of hdle app 3 & nrly did so agn app 6; hdd 11; chsd ldng pr to 2 out; one pce app last; fin 12l 3rd; disq
[363P]	P		**Davey John (IRE)** 33-1 R Nichol (xnb) 3rd to 4; disp last til jmpd slow 14; imm lost tch; wl bhnd when pu 3 out
	R		**Horton-Cum-Peel (IRE)** 20-1 Miss H Kinsey 3l 2nd when followed ldr wrong side of hdle app 3; cont 2nd til pu 9
[498U]	U		**Javaman** 10-1 G Thomas Last pr til hdwy 10; chsd ldrs frm 13; disp 3rd & hld when blun & ur 2 out (horse tripped over rdr & event fell)

OFFICIAL DISTANCES: 8l, 2l **TIME:** 6min 47.0s
Triple Eaves finished third but was disqualified for having missed a marker approaching the 3rd fence; the rider was fined £80; the rider of Horton-Cum-Peel was fined £65 for continuing to race after missing the same marker

812 Confined
4 ran

[776¹]	1		**SHANBALLYMORE (IRE)** 6-1 R Owen Cl 2nd/3rd; chsd ldr frm 13; str chall last; r.o str to ld cl home
[496²]	2	½	**Sounds Strong (IRE)** (7x) 4-7F N Bannister Jw; set slow pce; hdd 9; ld agn 11; 4l ahd 3 out; virt jnd last; r.o flat; outrdn & hdd cl home
[664B]	3	35	**Dunston Ace** 12-1 J R Barlow Sa & lost 15l; in tch 2; cl 4th til outpcd app 3 out; plodded into 15l 3rd & mist 2 out; no ch w ldrs
	4	12	**Tidaro Fairy (IRE)** 5-2 G Thomas Sa & lost 15l; in tch by 2; 2nd/3rd aft til wknd rap app 2 out; v tired 4th when blun & nrly ur last

OFFICIAL DISTANCES: ½l, 30l **TIME:** 6min 54.0s

813 Ladies Open   5 ran

[525U] 1   **RIVER MANDATE** 7-2 **Miss T Clark** *Ld 1; settled 4th by 3; hdwy to press ldrs app 13; ld app 2 out; outj & hdd; str chall flat; ld final strides*

[566⁴] 2   s hd   **Staigue Fort (IRE)** 5-2 **Miss V Stubbs** *Jmpd v wl; ld/disp frm 2 til hdd aft 3 out; jw ld to agn 2 out; just ld last; r.o str flat; hdd nr line*

        3   15   **See You Always (IRE)** 2-1JF **Miss A Price** *Disp ld frm 2 til releg 3rd app 13; chsd ldrs til wkng when mist & nrly ur 3 out; no ch aft*

[494ᴾ] P   **Ifafa Beach (IRE)** 33-1 **Miss R Barrow** *Imm last; jmpd rt 1; jmpd slow 6; 10l detach when jmpd slow 9; t.o & pu 11*

[661⁵] U   **Nosmo King (IRE)** (bl) 2-1JF **Miss L Kendall** *Handy 3rd til releg app 14; no imp on ldrs frm 3 out; 13l 4th & btn when mist & ur last*

   OFFICIAL DISTANCES: hd, 15l **TIME:** 6min 53.0s
        Balisteros (1-5F, injured head in box) was withdrawn from the paddock (reason had been that going was too firm until owner informed a £500 fine would result!); Rule 4 deduction 75p in pound on bets struck before withdrawal - new market formed

814 Mens Open, 12st   4 ran

[691⁵] 1   **VICOSA (IRE)** (7x) 5-2 **S Prior** *Ld 2-3; cl 2nd til ld agn 9-13; ld brief 3 out; 2l down & rmdrs app last; chall on inner flat; qcknd to ld 100yds out; stayed on u.p*

[591¹] 2   ¾   **Weak Moment (IRE)** (4x) 1-3F **A Crow** *Ld 1; trckd ldrs in last pr frm nxt; tk 2nd 3 out; sn ld; 2l up when mist last; level til no ex last 100yds*

[493ᴾ] 3   15   **Rebel King** (7x) (bl) 10-1 **G Thomas** *Last pr; rmdrs 11; lft bhnd by ldng pr frm 3 out; kpt on same pce*

[691ᴾ] 4   7   **Larkshill (IRE)** (7x) 12-1 **J R Barlow** *(tt declared - nt worn)Last early; ld 4; hit nxt; hdd 9; prsd ldr til ld agn 14-15; wknd app 2 out; no ch aft; bbv*

   OFFICIAL DISTANCES: ¾l, 15l **TIME:** 7min 00.0s
        The owner of Larkshill was fined £50 for failing to run the horse in a tongue strap as declared; this fine was later returned as no Regulation had been infringed

815 Marsh UK/TBA PPORA Club Members Mares, 12st   5 ran

[493¹] 1   **ALLRITE PET** (5a) 4-6F **L Morgan** *Trckd ldrs til lft in ld 9; sn hdd; ld agn 11; made rest; drew clr app 2 out; unchall; easy*

[665⁶] 2   30   **Bold Irene (IRE)** (5a) (bl) 14-1 **R Nichol** *Handy 3rd/4th til ld 10; sn hdd; chsd wnr aft til outpcd app 2 out; tired & no ch aft*

[426²] 3   2min   **Swiftly Supreme** (5a) 16-1 **T Davidson** *Last til hdwy 6; cl 2nd nxt; releg 3rd 10; chsd ldng pr til lost tch app slow 13; sn wl bhnd; t.o & tired when ur 2 out; event rmtd*

[620¹] U   **Ella Falls (IRE)** (12a) 11-10 **M Worthington** *Ld by 1-2l til mist & ur 9*

[661ᴾ] U   **No Problem Jac** (5a) (bl,tt) 14-1 **Miss L Hislop** *Pulling in last pr; 7l last when mist 10; ur 30yds aft*

   OFFICIAL DISTANCES: 30l, dist **TIME:** 6min 55.0s

816 Open Maiden   10 ran

[423⁵] 1   **DRAM HURLER (IRE)** 3-1 **R Morgan** *6s-3s; ld/disp up to 7; ld 9 til hdd app 2 out; sn ld agn; lft 4l clr last; r.o str*

[492ᴾ] 2   5   **Greenfinch (CAN)** 12-1 **Miss R Barrow** *Sn prom; 2nd 6 til ld 8; hdd nxt; cl up til 3rd & outpcd aft 2 out; lft 2nd last; kpt on same pce flat*

[507²] 3   15   **Tricky Trevor (IRE)** 7-4JF **Miss H Delahooke** *Last trio til hdwy to 3rd 13; 4th & outpcd 3 out; lft 14l 3rd last*

[624ᴾ] P   **Aces High** 20-1 **T Morrison** *Prom w rdr upright in irons when pu 1*

[526ᴾ] r   **Aughrim Quest (IRE)** (5a) 20-1 **M Worthington** *Tde; ref 1*

[500ᴾ] P   **Foxwood Polo** (12a) 33-1 **Miss L Kendall** *Handy to 6; last trio 9; lost tch 13; bhnd when pu 3 out*

[776U] U   **Golden Saxon** 33-1 **S Shone** *Prom; disp ld 3-5; cl up til lost plce 9; last & strugg when hit 11 & ur*

[588ᴾ] P   **Royal Fling** (5a) 7-1 **C Barlow** *A last trio; 5th & strugg when rmdrs app 3 out; sn lost tch; clambered over 2 out & pu*

[400²] U   **The Shy Padre (IRE)** 7-4JF **J Townson** *Prom frm 3; cl 4th 7 til slt mist & ur 10*

[500⁷] F   **Wishing Ash (IRE)** 20-1 **T Davidson** *Rr til hdwy 9; prom til ld 2nd 14; chsd wnr til ld app 2 out; sn hdd; 2l 2nd & hld when fell last*

   OFFICIAL DISTANCES: 5l, 15l **TIME:** 7min 01.0s

Llangibby
Howick (LH 9F,18J) Sat, 1 Apr (GOOD to FIRM, FIRM patches)

817 Hunt, 12st
4 ran

[683⁶]	1		**ARCHER (IRE)** (7x) 4-6F A Price Spurs; ld 1; cl 2nd/disp ld 3-12; trckd ldr til eff aft 3 out; sn swept into ld; 1½l up & lkd in comm when slowed & jnd app last; r.o str flat
[599ᵁ]	2	2	**Captain Khedive** 16-1 Miss S Talbot (xnb,bf) Cl last til 3rd aft 6; pulled to disp ld 11; ld & rn wide aft nxt; qcknd 14; 2½l ahd 2 out; sn hdd & outpcd; handed ch at last; one pce flat
[595¹]	3	1	**Chantingo Lad** (tt) 3-1 D Stephens (Wales) Settled cl 3rd mostly; last 5; pckd 6; mist 7; 3l last 10; 7½l 3rd & chsng ldrs 13; 10½l 3rd & hdwy 2 out; kpt on wl; too much to do
[597⁵]	4	¾	**The Last Mistress** (5a) 6-1 J Price Ld 2; jnd 3; ld 4-10; releg 9l last 13; und str press 15; rdn & clsd flat; nt rch ldrs

OFFICIAL DISTANCES: 2l, 1l TIME: 6min 44.6s

818 Restricted, 12st
15 ran

[602¹]	1		**LILLIEPLANT (IRE)** (5a) 7-4F A Price (xnb) 3s-7/4; tde; backed away start & reluct to jn others; hmpd start; rap hdwy to ld 2; made rest; 5l up 8; 8l ahd 13; drew 10l clr frm 2 out; unchall
[672¹]	2		**Winning Town** 6-1 Miss S Talbot Hld up in rr; 12th 3; 6th & hdwy 10; 20l 6th 13; 12l 3rd & staying on str 2 out; 10l 2nd at last; r.o; gvn impossible task
[647²]	3		**Kays-Lass** (5a) 16-1 C Williams (xnb) 2 handlers; oht; mid-div til 5th 5; went 3rd 11 & 4l 2nd 14; blun bad 3 out; nvr able to chall; dem flat
[745ᴾ]	4		**Mecca Prince (IRE)** (7a) 7-1 James Tudor Sn outpcd in mid-div; mod 6th 10; 14l 5th 13; 16l 6th & no imp 2 out
[596²]	5		**Adventurus** 25-1 J Liley Cl up in chsng group; 6th 3; 5th ½way; went 3rd brief 13; 8l 3rd 15; 14l 4th & wkng 2 out
[740ᴾ]	6		**Star Chaser** 10-1 D Stephens (Wales) 2 handlers; trckd ldrs in 4th til 12l 2nd 6; clsd to 4l 2nd 10; sn outpcd; 9l 4th & wkng 15; 18l 6th & btn 2 out
[744ᴾ]	7		**Final Option (IRE)** 33-1 J Johnson handlers; last 2; to aft 3; plodded on
	P		**Colonel Frazer (IRE)** (bl) 33-1 Miss F Wilson Prom; cl 3rd 3; 8th & wkng 6; wl bhnd when pu 12
[488¹]	P		**Its A Handfull** 12-1 J Price Recoiled frm elastic gate & hmpd sev rivals; a rr; last trio til to in last pr 10; pu 15
[647ᴿ]	P		**Out On The Town** (5a) 16-1 Miss M Bartlett Sn outpcd in midfield; 7th 2; wknd 10; to 8th aft 12; pu 3 out
[744ᴾ]	P		**Saronica-R** (5a) 25-1 Miss G Barfoot-Saunt Tchd 40s; 2 handlers; swtng; towards rr early; mist 4; 9th 10; sn wknd; to in last pr 13; pu 15
[477ᴾ]	P		**Solomons Mines (IRE)** 33-1 Miss C Goatley (xnb) Sn bhnd; last pr & mist 4; blun 8; 10th 10; to 13; pu 3 out
[484ᶠ]	U		**Under Milk Wood** 33-1 N Jones (xnb) Ld 1; chsd clr ldr nxt; 12l 2nd 6; 3rd & ur 7
[392⁸]	F		**Vale Of Oak** (5a) 33-1 M Portman (bf) 2 handlers; hmpd bad start & a last pr; detach 3; to when fell 7
[666²]	P		**Who's Your Man (IRE)** 14-1 A St George (xnb) Cl 2nd 1; 4/5th til 10l 3rd 9; fair 4th 12; 26l 7th & wkng qckly 13; to & pu 3 out

OFFICIAL DISTANCES: 10l, 2l TIME: 6min 27.7s

819 Confined, 12st
10 ran

[741ᵁ]	1		**YOU MAKE ME LAUGH (IRE)** 11-2 D Stephens (Wales) (xnb) Towards rr; 8th 3; 15½l 5th & jmpd slow 6; cl 4th ½way; cl 3rd 11; dem 3½l 4th 15; hrd rdn nxt; rap hdwy to ld aft 2 out; hld on u.p flat
[741²]	2	1	**Tiger Lord** 5-1 C Williams (xnb) Ld; jnd 3; chsd clr ldr til 3rd 7; drpd back 5½l 5th 10; eff 13; cl 2nd nxt; 2l 2nd & ev ch 2 out; kpt on u.p flat; just hld
[598⁴]	3	nk	**Harbour Island** (bl) 25-1 J L Llewellyn Hld up in rr; 17½l 7th 9; 5th & chsng clr ldrs 12; 14l 5th & lot to do 14; 10l 5th & staying on 3 out; went 4th app last & 3rd flat; fin wl; nt quite rch ldrs
[643⁶]	4	nk	**Tilt Tech Flyer** 25-1 Miss F Wilson Jw; a.p; ld aft 2; 2l up 2 out; sn hdd; 2½l 2nd at last; r.o; dem 2 plces in v cl fin
	5	5	**Southern Cross** (bl) 14-1 A Price Nt fluent; last to 4; 20l 6th & jmpd lft 6; rap prog on outer aft 9 & 2nd nxt; trckd ldr til 11 3rd & blun bad 3 out; rdn in 6l 4th & fnd nil app last
[741ᶠ]	P		**Alkarine** 40-1 N Jones Towards rr; disp 10½l 6th 4; drpd to last pr agn 6; last & nt keen 8; pu 9

[683^P] P **Ardell Boy** (3x) 8-11F G Barfoot-Saunt (xnb,bnf hoof) Bit bckwd; chsd ldrs; 7½l 4th when pu & dism 4; lame

[597^P] U **Comme Une Fleur (FR)** (5a) 50-1 G Haines (orbs) Mid-div; 6th when ur 3; bolted & careered into hedge alongside 7 & trapped; event extricated & removed v slow by horse ambulance; reportedly damaged pelvis

[743^P] F **Rapid Rascal** 66-1 Miss R Athay Chsd ldrs; 13l 4th 6; wknd rap frm 9; 10l adrift in last 10; t.o; fell 15; broke nr-hind hock; destroyed

[643⁸] P **Side Bar** (vis,tt) 50-1 J Phillips Chsd ldrs; 6l 3rd 4 til wknd qckly 13; t.o & pu 2 out

OFFICIAL DISTANCES: ½l, hd   TIME: 6min 31.5s

820 Marsh UK/TBA PPORA Club Members Mares, 12st   4 ran

[644¹] 1   **AFRICAN WARRIOR** (5a) 5-6F C Williams Tchd 11/10; pulled hrd & nt settle; in cl 2nd mostly til disp ld 6; stdd; 1½l 2nd ½way; dem 3rd & rdr shouting at colleague trying to come up inner app nxt; qcknd to ld 12; made rest & oft jmpd superb; 3l up at last; pushed out

[742²] 2   3   **Bit Of A Citizen (IRE)** (5a) 7-2 A Price Cl last mostly til 2l 3rd 9; eff aft 14; prsd ldr nxt til mist 3 out; 3l 2nd 2 out; r.o; no ch

[600²] 3   7   **Questionaire** (5a) 2-1 D Stephens (Wales) Tchd 9/4; nt fluent; jmpd slow 1; cl 3rd mostly til dem 4l last & jmpd slow 10; tried to sneak up inner app nxt; went cl 3rd agn aft 12; mist 13; wknd 15; 9l 3rd & btn 2 out

[752³] 4   20 **Artic Pearl (IRE)** (5a) 25-1 R Langley Ld; jnd 5; hdd 8; ld agn 9-11; wkng when blun & nrly ur 12; nt rec; 13; last & no ch nxt; t.o 3 out

OFFICIAL DISTANCES: 3l, 10l   TIME: 6min 27.8s

821 Mixed Open, 12st   8 ran

[599¹] 1   **KARABURAN** 13-8JF Miss F Wilson Trckd ldrs; 3l 3rd & stdd 5; 3½l 4th ½; went cl 3rd 11 & 2½l 2nd aft 12; sn outpcd by ldr; 8l 2nd 15; hdwy & 3l 2nd 2 out; sn ld; 2½l up at last; r.o; easy

[561⁶] 2   4   **Swinging Sixties (IRE)** 33-1 A St George Cl up in mid-div; gd hdwy to disp 2nd 9; ld app nxt; 2½l up agn 12; qcknd 8l ahd frm 14 til mist 3 out; 3l ahd 2 out; no ex when hdd app last; gd eff

[479^F] 3   25 **Danny Gale (IRE)** 50-1 C Williams Wl in tch in last pr; disp 7l 6th ½way; prog to 9¾l 4th aft 12; 14l 3rd 15; kpt on; nt trble ldrs

[742^P] 4   ¾   **Credon** (bl) 16-1 D Stephens (Wales) 33s-16s; prom til ld 3; jmpd untidy 6; hdd aft nxt; 1l 2nd ½way; 5½l 4th & outpcd 11; 19l 4th & btn 15

         P   **Fast Freeze** 50-1 G Haines (bf - fastened w black insulation tape) A rr; 15l last aft 5; 12l adrift of rest 7; t.o 10; pu 12

[743^P] P **Our Eddie** 50-1 J Price (xnb) Chsd ldrs in 3rd/4th to 7; 5½l 5th ½way; 15½l 5th & lsng tch 11; pu 13

         P   **River Room** 13-8JF A Price (bh - fastened w white insulation tape) Lkd jaded padd; cl up in mid-div; mist 7; disp 7l 6th ½way; 18l 6th & wkng aft 12; jmpd slow 14; pu 15; broke down nr hind

[597³] P **Sebastango** 5-1 N Jones Opened 12s in a plce; oht when mounted; dism & re-saddled; ld to 2; cl 2nd til jnd ldr 7; ld 9; jnd 11; sn hdd & wknd rap; 13l 5th aft 12; pu nxt

OFFICIAL DISTANCES: 4l, 30l   TIME: 6min 28.1s

822 Confined Maiden (Div 1), 12st - 17J   10 ran

[673^F] 1   **PRESUMING ED (IRE)** 6-4F A Price (pricker ns) Ld 1; ld 3; made rest; jnd 10-11; 2l up 15; drew clr nxt; 6l cl & in comm last; easy

[594³] 2   15 **Le Vienna (IRE)** 20-1 D Stephens (Wales) A.p; cl 2nd 2 & frm 3; jnd ldr 10-11; dem 3rd brief ½way; 2l 2nd & ev ch 15; 6l 2nd & btn 2 out; fin tired

[490³] 3   4   **Kopain** 6-1 J L Llewellyn (xnb) Last pr til 4th aft 5; went cl 3rd brief ½way; lft 7l 3rd 11 & disp 2l 3rd 13; 7½l 3rd & wkng when jmpd rt 3 out; btn when bad mist next 15

[491^P] 4   1¼fs **Guard A Dream (IRE)** 20-1 J Price Sn rr; last pr & mist 7; drvn along 9; 6th ½way; mist 12; 25l 5th & no ch nxt; plodded on; t.o when jmpd v slow & rdr waved last

         P   **A Suitable Girl** (5a) 33-1 G Haines A rr; lft last 5; 22l last 8; t.o 12; pu 13

[489^F] U   **Blazing Connie** (5a) 10-1 G Perkins (xnb,bf) 2 handlers; towards rr when ur 3

         U   **Egg Well Boy** 14-1 J Liley (xnb) Detach last 2; ur 3

         F   **Jayarejay** 12-1 C Gundry (xnb) Sa; charged up & sn prom; ld brief 2; 4th when bad mist 4 & releg last; fell hvly nxt

[650^P] P **Parliament House (IRE)** 20-1 J Phillips Mid-div; 5th aft 5; 15l 5th 9; 23½l 4th aft 12; wknd & pu 13

[747^U] P **Rowling Sea (IRE)** 6-1 C Williams 12s-6s; prom; 3rd 5; 2l 3rd ½way; cl 4th when pu 11

OFFICIAL DISTANCES: 15l, 4l   TIME: 6min 39.2s
Fence 14 omitted - fallen horse

Mackenzie & Selby

823 Confined Maiden (Div 2), 12st

9 ran

[602³]	1		**JULIES JOY (IRE)** (5a) 2-1F **I Johnson** *Tchd 9/4; jmpd violent rt most fncs; ld to 9; disp ld aft 12; 5l 3rd & lkd btn 14; rallied und str press nxt; level 3 out; lft 3l clr nxt; prsd & lkd v vulnerable when knocked rival over at last; r.o; just hld on*
[491⁶]	2	½	**Beths Gift** (5a) 100-30 **D Stephens (Wales)** *Tchd 7/2; cl up in rr; 6th 7; 7¼ 6th aft 12; stdy hdwy frm 16; lft disp 3l 2nd & hmpd 2 out; dem 3l sn aft; lft 3l 2nd agn at last; rdn & r.o str flat; just failed*
[747ᴾ]	3	20	**Star Island** 9-2 **A Price** *Lw; cl 2nd/3rd; pckd 7; jnd ldr 12; ld 13-14; cl 3rd when blun bad 3 out; nt rec; btn when lft disp 3l 2nd 2 out; dem 5th till lft mod 3rd agn last*
[602⁵]	P		**Alicat (IRE)** 10-1 **J L Llewellyn** *14s-10s; cl 4th early; pulling & hdwy 7; ld aft 9-11; 4th & wkng qckly 13; pu 15*
[595ᴾ]	F		**Cosy Ride (IRE)** 12-1 **J Phillips** *(bf) 20s-12s; in tch in rr til 2½l 4th aft 9; 7l 4th 14; no imp when mist 3 out; btn 4th when fell last*
[746ᴾ]	F		**Marnies Song** (5a) (bl) 13-2 **James Tudor** *Trckd ldrs; cl 3rd 3; 4th 7; 8l 7th 12; stayed on stdly frm nxt; lft 4l 4th 2 out; went 2nd & lkd prob wnr when virt blkd by hanging wnr & knocked over at last; unlucky*
[601ᴾ]	F		**Newchurch Lad** 20-1 **J Price** *Nt fluent; nrly ur 3 & releg last; hdwy 10; went 1½l 3rd aft 12; ld 15; jnd nxt til fell hvly 2 out*
[746ᴾ]	P		**No Escape** 33-1 **G Perkins** *Towards rr; cl last 10; wknd qckly 13; t.o when jmpd slow 13; pu nxt*
[595ᴾ]	P		**Tarian (USA)** 33-1 **M Parry** *Last early; shot up to ldrs out control on wide outside aft 3; pulled out to rt nxt bend*

OFFICIAL DISTANCES: nk, 25l **TIME:** 6min 51.6s

The stewards enquired into possible interference caused by the winner at the last fence; having interviewed the riders involved they decided any interference was accidental and allowed the result to stand

Old Surrey, Burstow & West Kent

Penshurst (LH 7F,18J) Sat, 1 Apr (GOOD becoming GOOD/SOFT)

824 Confined, 12st

12 ran

[522⁴]	1		**ARFER MOLE (IRE)** 6-1 **D Dennis** *A cl up; 2nd frm 10; clr w ldr frm 12 til ld app 2 out; hld on wl flat*
[305³]	2	1	**Jojo (IRE)** (bl) 5-1 **B Hitchcott** *Trckd ldr 3 til ld 5; made rest til hdd app 2 out; rallied flat but reluct to pass wnr*
[288ᴾ]	3	1	**Nossi Be** 8-1 **D Parker** *Ld to 2; sn midfield; hdwy 11 to 10l 4th 14; gd rn frm 3 out; prsd wnr app last; no ex flat*
[706¹]	4	8	**Tooth Pick (IRE)** (6x) 6-4F **J Hawksfield** *Hld up in last pr; hdwy 10 to 12l 6th 12; pushed along frm nxt; 4th & ch app 2 out; wknd app last*
	5	6	**Lovely Lynsey** (5a) 6-1 **Miss S Gladders** *Handy; hdwy to 6l 3rd 12; chsd ldng pr aft til wknd app 2 out*
[628⁵]	6	15	**Touring-Turtle** 33-1 **S Claisse** *Midfield to 11; lost tch frm nxt*
[571¹]	7	6	**How Friendly** 33-1 **D Brightling** *A towards rr; no ch frm 13*
[609ᴾ]	P		**Courier's Way (IRE)** 20-1 **S R Andrews** *Prom til fdd 11; wl bhnd when pu last*
[579³]	P		**Pinoccio** 33-1 **D O'Brien** *A rr; last & out of tch; 11; t.o & pu 2 out*
[571²]	P		**Rose King** 14-1 **T Hills** *Midfield; 13l 7th 12; lost tch frm 14; wl bhnd when pu last*
	P		**Storm Drum** 33-1 **Mrs E Coveney** *Ld 3 & 4; prsd ldr to 10; lost plce qckly aft 13; tne wr when pu 4 out*
[572ᵁ]	U		**Sultan Of Swing** (vis) 33-1 **J Stephens** *Mists; last pr til ur 9*

OFFICIAL DISTANCES: ½l, 1l **TIME:** 6min 47.0s **TOTE:** £12.20; places £6.20,£1.10,£1.50 **DF:** £22.20

825 Restricted, 12st

16 ran

[657ᴮ]	1		**KENNY DAVIS (IRE)** 3-1JF **P Blagg** *Last to 6; rap hdwy 8; ld/disp frm 10; both wl clr of rest frm 12 til stdd app 15; rdn clr agn app last; kpt on wl flat*
[706ᵁ]	2	3	**Newby End (IRE)** 16-1 **A Blanch** *Towards rr; hdwy 11 to 13l 4th 14; prsd wnr 3 out; ev ch app last; kpt on one pce*
[575⁵]	3	4	**Shamron (IRE)** (5a) 5-1 **Miss S Gladders** *Towards rr; gd hdwy frm 13 to trck ldng pr 3 out; jnd wnr gng wl 2 out; wknd app last*
[575⁴]	4	12	**Ally Pally** 11-2 **P York** *Midfield mostly; 20l 8th 14; stayed on frm 3 out; nvr nrr*
[710ᵁ]	5	10	**Call The Tune** (5a) 8-1 **P Bull** *Chsd ldrs; hdwy to 10l 3rd 12; ev ch 15; wknd aft nxt*
[574ᴾ]	6	4	**Target Time** (5a) (vis) 33-1 **Mrs L Stock** *Prom to 10; lsng tch in 25l 9th 14; slt hdwy frm 3 out*
[575ᴾ]	7	3	**Chill Factor** 8-1 **A Charles-Jones** *Prsd ldrs; 15l 5th 14; ch 4 out; wknd*
[675ᵁ]	8	3	**Ishma (IRE)** 33-1 **D Page** *A towards rr; wl bhnd when pu 11; t.o 14; slt hdwy frm 3 out*

[306ᴾ]	F		**Arrogant Lord** 5-1 B Hitchcott *In tch in midfield; mist 12; 6th & wkng when fell 15*
[578¹]	B		**Bachelor-Carrasco (IRE)** (2ow) 3-1JF S R Andrews *In tch; hdwy to cl 3rd 8; bd nxt*
[575ᴾ]	P		**Ballybollen (IRE)** 33-1 A Hickman *Ld 7-9; clr w wnr frm 12 til wknd rap 4 out; no ch when pu 2 out*
	P		**Lisaleen Wren (IRE)** 20-1 G Gigantesco *A rr; last frm 6; lsng tch when pu 8*
[575ᴮ]	P		**Martha Leader (IRE)** 14-1 Stuart Robinson *Ld 3-6; trckng ldrs when fell 9*
[291ᴾ]	P		**My Son Tom** 33-1 P Hickman *A rr; wl bhnd when pu 13*
[575ᴾ]	P		**Perripage** (vis) 33-1 Miss A Sansom *Prom to 5; sn lost plce; rr frm 11; t.o & pu last*
[571⁹]	P		**Winward** (bl) 3-1 P M Hall *Ld/disp to 7; lost plce rap aft 9; rr when pu 13*

OFFICIAL DISTANCES: 2l, 4l **TIME:** 6min 47.0s **TOTE:** £6.40; places £2.30,£5.50,£2.10 **DF:** £1.80 (1+any)

826 Mens Open, 12st
5 ran

[706³]	1		**GALAROI (IRE)** (7x) 5-1 D Robinson *Trckd ldng pr til went 2nd 12; jnd ldr 15; tk narrow advant aft 2 out; 1l up when btr j last; rdn out flat*
[574²]	2	3	**Prime Course (IRE)** 2-1 C Gordon *Prsd ldr til ld 10-15; w wnr til hrd rdn & hdd aft 2 out; ev ch last; kpt on one pce*
[676³]	3	fence	**Celtic Spark** 6-1 D Dunsdon *Hld up in last pr; rmdrs in 15l 5th 14; no resp; blun 3 out; kpt on to tk rem 3rd cl home*
	4	hd	**Boll Weevil** 14-1 P Bull *Ld to 9; prsd ldr to 11; 10l 3rd & lsng tch 14; no ch frm 3 out*
[572ᵁ]	U		**Take My Side (IRE)** (7x) (bl) evensF B Hitchcott *Nt jw; hld up in last pr; pushed along 12; 13l 4th when mist 14; 15l 3rd & no hdwy when blun & ur 3 out*

OFFICIAL DISTANCES: 2l, dist **TIME:** 6min 50.0s **TOTE:** £6.70; places £3.70,£1.30 **DF:** £7.50

827 Ladies Open
8 ran

[414ᴾ]	1		**CACHE FLEUR (FR)** 5-4F Mrs G d'Angibau *Prsd ldr most of way; pushed along 3 out; ld on inner aft 2 out; jnd last; just prevailed flat*
[573¹]	2	hd	**Kincora** 6-4 Mrs L Stock *Trckd ldrs in cl 4/5th; impd to ld 12; made rest w narrow advant til hdd 2 out; rallied to jn wnr last; just outbattled flat*
[707⁵]	3	15	**Polar Ana (IRE)** (5a) 12-1 Miss S Gladders *Hld up in rr; 11l 6th 14; gd hdwy to ld 3rd 3 out; wknd app nxt*
[676¹]	4	8	**Daddy Long Leggs** 10-1 Mrs J Parris *Last til hdwy 9; 9l 5th 14; 7l 4th & ch 3 out; wknd*
[307³]	5	20	**For William** 16-1 Mrs E Coveney *Cl up in midfield; hdwy when lft cl 3rd 12; wknd 15*
[758⁵]	6	6	**Pair Of Jacks (IRE)** (bl) 33-1 Miss J Wickens *Hld up; in tch towards rr; 12l 7th 14; wknd rap 4 out; t.o & pu 2 out*
[307¹]	U		**Danger Flynn (IRE)** 10-1 Miss C Holliday *Swtng; ld/disp til hit 12 & ur*
[677³]	P		**Professor Page (IRE)** 16-1 Miss J Grant *Cl 3rd/4th til lost plce qckly aft 14; rr when pu 4 out*

OFFICIAL DISTANCES: nk, 10l **TIME:** 6min 47.0s **TOTE:** £2.90; places £1.50,£1.70,£1.50 **DF:** £3.00

828 Open Maiden (Div 1), 12st
10 ran

[707ᶠ]	1		**JAMIES FIRST (IRE)** 7-2 D Dunsdon *A cl up; 4l 4th 11; trckd ldng pr frm 14; ev ch app 2 out; 2nd & btn when lft in ld last*
[709ᵁ]	2	6	**Oisin Dubh (IRE)** 10-1 C Gordon *Rcd keen; ld to 2 & 8-14; prsng ldr when blun 2 out; wknd qckly; lft 2nd at last*
[577ᵁ]	3	15	**Newick Park** (7a) 2-1F P Bull *Midfield; 7l 6th 11; mist 12; lsng tch in 14l 4th 3 out; lft 3rd at last*
[432⁴]			**Ashburton Lord** 12-1 A Blanch *Ld 3-7; 3l 3rd 11; wknd 14; blun 4 out; pu aft nxt*
[709ᵁ]	U		**Ell Gee** (5a) 4-1 P Townsley *Trckd ldrs; 5l 5th 11; 3rd & ev ch when ur 14*
[571⁵]	P		**Lady Of Verse** (5a) 33-1 Mrs L Stock *Cl up to 7; lsng tch in 19l 9th 11; t.o & pu 13*
[710ᴿ]	F		**Mountain Tae (IRE)** 16-1 P York *Cl 3rd/4th til prsd ldr 11; ld 15; drew clr aft 2 out; 8l up when almost ref & fell last*
[289ᵁ]	U		**Schisandra** (5a) 20-1 P Blagg *A last pr; 17l 8th 11; mist & ur nxt*
	P		**Three B's** (5a) 5-1 P Hickman *A rr; last when rmdrs aft 6; lsng tch when pu 8*
[328⁷]	P		**Under The Carpet (IRE)** 4-1 D Dennis *A towards rr; 15l 7th 11; wl bhnd when pu 13*

OFFICIAL DISTANCES: 4l, 8l **TIME:** 7min 00.0s **TOTE:** £7.60; places £1.50,£1.80,£1.20 **DF:** £2.90 (1+any)

829 Open Maiden (Div 2), 12st
10 ran

[290ᴾ]	1		**TOM'S INFLUENCE** (5a) 12-1 D Parker *Ld to 2 & agn frm 8; made rest; 3-6l up frm 10 til prsd frm 15; a just hldng 2nd frm 2 out; rdn out flat*
[705ᴾ]	2	1	**Moon Rising** 10-1 P Bull *Midfield; hdwy to 5l 3rd 11; 2nd frm 13; pushed along bef nxt; chall last; no ex flat*
[578³]	3	fence	**Environmental Law** 2-1F P York *A cl up; 2nd when mists 9 & 12; lost tch w ldng pr 15*

[709U]	P		**At It Again (IRE)** (1ow) 20-1 **R Chelton** *Prom to 6; sn lost plce; t.o & pu 11*
[131⁶]	P		**Jo Bloggs (IRE)** 4-1 **A Hickman** *Rcd keen; ld 3 til mist & hdd 8; 11 4th & wkng 11; wl bhnd when pu 3 out*
[710ᴾ]	P		**Mandalady (IRE)** (5a) 20-1 **D Dennis** *Hld up; 2ll 6th 11; rmdrs bef nxt; no prog; rem 4th when pu 2 out*
	U		**Not Yet Decent (IRE)** 20-1 **P Hall** *In tch towards rr; some hdwy when ur 10*
	P		**Phantom Slipper** (bl) 4-1 **T Warr** *Prsd ldrs; 13l 5th 11; same plce when blun bad 14; no ch when pu 3 out*
[577ᴾ]	P		**Smooth Silk (IRE)** 12-1 **Miss S Robertson** *In tch til 33l 7th & wkng 11; pu sn aft*
[577ᴾ]	P		**Toni's Tiger** 20-1 **T Hills** *A wl bhnd; t.o & pu 11*

OFFICIAL DISTANCES: ½l, dist **TIME:** 6min 57.0s **TOTE:** £10.70; places £1.10,£4.50,£1.30 **DF:** £5.00 (1+any)

The stewards cautioned the rider of the third for improper use of the whip

830 S.E. Hunts Club Members (Nov Rdrs), 12st   10 ran

[705³]	1		**BIT OF AN IDIOT** 33-1 **D Slattery** *A.p; 12l 3rd 11; impd to trck ldr 14; lft in ld 3 out; made rest; drew clr aft 2 out*
[304¹]	2	15	**Some Tourist (IRE)** 4-6F **N Benstead** *Sn rr; 25l 7th 11; gd hdwy 13 to 5l 3rd 15; prsd wnr aft nxt; 6l down 2 out; wknd app last*
[711³]	3	10	**Exemplar (IRE)** 14-1 **Mrs D Rowell** *Sn wl bhnd; 36l 9th 11; no prog til stayed on wl frm 3 out; nrst fin*
[675³]	4	3	**Mosta (IRE)** 8-1 **A Veale** *A chsng ldrs; 13l 4th 11; kpt on one pce frm 3 out*
[610⁵]	P		**Deep Song** 10-1 **Miss Carla Thomas** *Chsd ldr frm 4; 6l down 11; 14l 4th & wkng 13; t.o & pu 2 out*
[706⁷]	U		**Golden Mac** (bl) 33-1 **J Barnard** *Rr til ur 3*
[676²]	P		**Parson's Way** (1ow) (bl) 7-1 **S Fisher** *3-6l ld most of way til jmpd v slow & hdd 3 out; wknd rap; pu nxt*
	P		**Regal Aura (IRE)** 11-2 **D O'Brien** *Nrly ur 1; chsd ldrs in midfield; 19l 6th & rmdrs 11; no resp; pu 12*
[706ᴾ]	P		**The Glow (IRE)** 10-1 **D Brightling** *Hld up in midfield; 14l 5th 11; wknd 14; no ch when pu 2 out*
[307ᵁ]	P		**Wednesdays Auction (IRE)** 33-1 **Mrs C Andrews** *A wl bhnd; 35l 8th 11; t.o & pu 13*

OFFICIAL DISTANCES: 12l, 4l **TIME:** 6min 58.0s **TOTE:** £120.60; places £5.60,£1.10,£1.80 **DF:** £1.10 (1+any)

Pembrokeshire

Lydstep (LH 8F,19J) Sat, 1 Apr (GOOD with FIRM patches)

831 Hunt, 12st   7 ran

[670⁵]	1		**TRUE FORTUNE** (7x) 2-5F **M Barber** *Hld up in 3rd; 2nd 5; prom til ld 14; kpt on u.p frm 2 out*
[645⁴]	2	3	**Young Manny** 3-1 **M Lewis** *Ld 1-3; 2nd aft til lft in ld 5-13; cont w ev ch; drvn 2 out; nt rch wnr*
[483⁸]	3	runin	**The Gadfly** 14-1 **J Hayward** *3rd/4th; lost tch frm 10; btn frm 14*
[650⁶]	4	4	**Sing Cherry Ripe** (5a) 20-1 **Miss T Stevens** *Nt fluent; 5th & jmpd delib 4; lost tch frm 7; no ch aft; 50l 5th 14*
[482⁵]	5	30	**Teigr Pren** 10-1 **Miss G Evans** (bnh) *Midfield early; sn lost tch; rr frm 7; 30l last 11; cont out of tch*
	P		**Lauras Conquest** 10-1 **P Sheldrake** *10l last to 6; 4th & in tch 8; 5l 3rd & mist 11; wknd aft; 20l away 14; pu 2 out*
	U		**Theairyman (IRE)** 3-1 **J Jukes** (bf) *A.p; ld 4 til ur 5*

OFFICIAL DISTANCES: 2l, 25l **TIME:** 6min 22.0s

832 Restricted, 12st   13 ran

[486ᴾ]	1		**CRESSWELL QUAY** 4-1 **G Lewis** *Nvr worse than 4th; ld 12; 3l ld 14; drew clr frm 3 out; unchal*
[649¹]	2	15	**Blue Cheese** (5a) 8-1 **Miss L Pearce** *Ld 1-4; settled 2nd frm 6; wknd frm 12 & 5th 14; r.o frm 16 to 2nd agn 3 out but no ch w ldr*
[648¹]	3	15	**Merrie Jar (IRE)** 1-2F **T Vaughan** *Hld up in 3rd; nt fluent & sev mists; 12l 3rd 14; r.o 16; no ex uphill & eased run-in*
[744ᴾ]	4	12	**Sea Search** 25-1 **P Sheldrake** *Generally 6th; lost tch frm 10; no ch w ldrs aft*
	P		**Albert Woods** 16-1 **Miss E Jones** *Midfield; 5th frm 8; cont prom tp app 16; broke leg; dead*
[646³]	P		**Dunsfold Dazzler** (5a) 9-2 **D Hughes** *2 handlers; 7th to 11; fdd; cont out of tch; pu 15*

	P		**Glenville Breeze (IRE)** 12-1 J Cook A rr; lost tch 11; pu 15
	P		**Hil Lady** (5a) 8-1 M Barber A bhnd; last to 6; clsr in 8th 11; wknd frm 12; t.o & pu 16
	P		**Our Harry** 20-1 J Keen Ld 6-11; prom aft; 3l 2nd 14; tired frm 16; pu 2 out
[596²]	P		**Poet's Song (IRE)** 8-1 J Jukes A rr; last pr frm 9; lost tch 12; pu 14
[642¹]	P		**Rue De Fort** 25-1 A Hardacre Rr; last frm 9; bhnd til pu 13
[484⁴]	P		**Time To Share (IRE)** 8-1 Miss P Jones Nvr nrr; a last 4 or 5; lost tch frm 11; pu 14
[647ᵁ]	U		**Young Mariner** 33-1 A Barker (xnb,bh) A bhnd; nvr btr than 9th; out of tch when ur 12

OFFICIAL DISTANCES: 15l, 15l   TIME: 6min 14.0s

833 Mens Open, 12st   7 ran

[643⁷]	1		**SIP OF BRANDY (IRE)** 10-1 G Skone (xnb) Hld up in last; 15l away 12; r.o str frm 16; 3rd 2 out; displ 3d last; r.o wl; wl rdn
[643³]	2	3	**Moon Tiger** 6-4 T Vaughan Settled 3rd; went 4l 2nd 10; ld 15; just hdd last; outpcd
[642¹]	3	3	**Mr Mad** (vis) 6-1 P Hamer Hld up in 4th; 16l 3rd 16; r.o uphill & just ld last; outpcd u.p run-in
[742⁹]	4	20	**Warren Boy** (7x) 3-1 G Lewis 2nd early; ld 2-13; chsd ldr aft; 8l 2nd 16; tired uphill frm 3 out; sn btn
[645⁵]	5	10	**Sheephaven** 20-1 D Davies Last early; settled 12l 5th; rdn aft 11; mist 14; 5th & no ch aft
[742²]	6	6	**Saffron Moss** (7x) 10-1 H Evans A last pr; dem last 10; mist & rmdrs 12; wknd & sn wl bhnd
[598²]	P		**Ballymaloe Boy (IRE)** evensF J Jukes Ld 1; hld up in 2nd aft; lost plce 10; 20l 4th when pu 3 out

OFFICIAL DISTANCES: 2l, 2l   TIME: 6min 14.0s

834 Open Maiden 56&7yo (Div 1), 12st   14 ran

[648²]	1		**SECRET CAN'T SAY (IRE)** (5a) 4-6F Miss E Jones 3rd til 2l 2nd 6; 4th & wkng aft; 20l 4th 15; lft 2nd by defections; 15l 2nd when lft virt solo at last; lucky
[649ᴿ]	2	2fncs	**Run To The Glen** (12a) 10-1 M Lewis A last; t.o 6; 2 fncs bhnd frm 13; plodded on
[348⁵]	3	runin	**Ossie Dale (IRE)** 4-1 J Jukes Made all; qcknd clr 15; 20l up nxt; 15l clr when ur last; rmtd; unlucky
[207ᴾ]	P		**Aherne** (7a) 14-1 T Vaughan Mostly mid-div; 15l 6th 8; lost tch frm 14; 30l 4th when pu 3 out
[350ᴾ]	P		**Bold Knight** 14-1 G Skone 5th til fdd frm 8; 20l 5th 11; t.o 14; pu 2 out
[648⁴]	U		**Daisy's Choice** (12a) 8-1 J Hayward Last trio til ur 5
[746⁶]	P		**Ginger Duchess** (5a) 14-1 G Marsh A bhnd; last pr 5; lost tch frm 7; pu 14
[746²]	R		**Gypsy Haze** (12a) 3-1 J Cook Trckd ldrs in 4th til 2nd 11; cl up til rn off course bend aft 15
[745ᵁ]	P		**Jesusa** (5a) (tt) 25-1 G Maloney Midfield early; poor 8th 5; sn rr; pu 10
[270ᴾ]	F		**Lord Chamberlain** 6-1 D Davies 2nd 1-8; rmdrs in 3rd 11; lft 2nd aft 15; 20l 2nd & wkng 16; btn when fell hvly 2 out; event staggered to feet
[648ᴿ]	P		**Power Unit** (7a) 8-1 P Hamer School in last trio; t.o frm 5; pu 16
	P		**Pryvate Time** (5a) 10-1 J Keen Midfield early; rr frm 6; scrambled over 11; pu aft
	P		**Stormhill Daydream** (5a) 12-1 G Lewis Nvr btr than 7th; fdd 10; pu 13
	P		**Willows Jaybe** (5a) 10-1 A Hardacre Carried wide bend bef 2; virt brought to standstill & pu

OFFICIAL DISTANCES: dist, dist   TIME: 6min 37.0s

835 Open Maiden 56&7yo (Div 2), 12st   8 ran

[602ᴾ]	1		**TRAVEL SAFELY (IRE)** 2-1 J Keen Hld up in 5th; prog to 3rd 12; ld 16; drew clr nxt; unchall
[601ᴿ]	2	25	**Nomoremissnicegirl** (5a) 8-1 G Lewis Settled 3rd; ld brief 14; 2nd aft; 4l 2nd 16; no ex aft; tired 3 out; jmpd slow last
[348²]	P		**Artique Fish (IRE)** 4-5F J Jukes A last trio; rdn frm 7; no imp; lost tch rap & pu 9; bbv
	P		**Cefn Tiger** (7a) 12-1 D Hughes Oht & reared padd; rr early; grad impd frm 9; 2nd 9-10; cl up til 2nd agn 14; wknd 15; pu 3 out
[596ᴾ]	P		**Don't Forget (IRE)** (5a) 2-1 T Vaughan Ld early; 3rd & mist 5; lost tch & last 10; pu 14
[649ᴾ]	F		**Fair Charmeur** (5a) 10-1 Miss A Meakins A.p; settled 2nd; mist 4; 5th 14; hdwy in 4th when fell 16
[744ᴾ]	S		**Mission Lord (IRE)** 8-1 G Maloney 2 young handlers; cl 2nd early; wknd to last pr aft 8 til slpd up bend bef 12
[747ᴾ]	F		**Silver Joy** (12a) 8-1 N Tucker (bf) Ld 3; mist 11; hdd at nxt; 4th til fell 15

OFFICIAL DISTANCE: 25l   TIME: 6min 45.0s

836 Ladies Open   6 ran

[743P]	1		**DAWN'S COGNAC (IRE)** (3x) 2-1 **Miss P Jones** *2 handlers; hld up in 4th; sent into ld 14; qcknd clr 2 out; sn in comm*
[645²]	2	12	**Mr Dow Jones (IRE)** 6-4JF **Miss E Jones** (b4) *In tch in 5th; hdwy 13; 2l 2nd nxt; ev ch til outpcd frm 3 out*
[481²]	3	1½	**Busman (IRE)** 6-4JF **Miss L Pearce** *Last early; settled 3rd frm 6; ld 11; mist nxt; ld 3rd 14; ev ch til outpcd frm 3 out*
[645³]	4	15	**Turning Trix** 8-1 **Miss R Curtis** *A 3rd/4th; hdwy to 2nd 11; 4th aft; no ex frm 3 out*
	5	runin	**Celtic Friend (IRE)** (bl) 20-1 **Miss J Gill** *Prom; ld 4 til mist & rdr lost irons 11; releg last; t.o frm 14*
[346P]	F		**Battleship Bruce** 20-1 **Miss A Meakins** *Ld 1-3; cl 2nd aft to 9; 4th aft; 8l 4th when fell 16*

OFFICIAL DISTANCES: 12l, 1l   TIME: 6min 15.0s

837 Intermediate, 12st   13 ran

[741³]	1		**KRISTAL HAZE** (5a) 3-1 **J Cook** *4th to 9; 2l 2nd 10; disp ld 14; sn ld; drew 10l clr; hrd drvn flat; just hld on*
[600⁴]	2	1	**Jo Jos Best Friend** (5a) 2-1 **T Vaughan** *Hld up in 9th; hdwy 10; 25l 3rd 14; stayed on frm 3 out; 10l 2nd nxt; rdn & clsng flat; nt quite rch wnr*
[600³]	3	15	**Longstone Boy (IRE)** 6-4F **P Hamer** *Last trio to 11; 35l 6th 14; r.o frm 16; nt trble ldrs*
[486¹]	4	15	**Dyffryn Prince (IRE)** 4-1 **P Sheldrake** *2 handlers; midfield; 30l 5th frm 8; nvr nr ldrs aft*
[743⁴]	5	20	**Storm Man (IRE)** 20-1 **Miss C Williams** *4th early; grad fdd; last trio frm 9; t.o & no ch 13*
[347¹]	6	6	**Pure Air** 5-1 **G Maloney** *A 6/7th; lost tch frm 12; t.o*
[643⁴]	P		**Bancyfelin Boy** (5x) 8-1 **J Keen** *Midfield early; settled 3rd frm 6; 14l 3rd 10; rn wide to boxes bend & pu aft 11*
	U		**Final Rose** (5a) 14-1 **N Tucker** *2nd til ld 5; mist 10; 8l clr 13; jnd nxt; sn hdd & wknd; 6l 2nd when ur 3 out*
[344P]	U		**Flockmaster (IRE)** 14-1 **N Tucker** *A rr; mist 4; last pr when ur 12*
[643F]	U		**Plucky Punter** 20-1 **A Barker** (xnb) *4th til ur 7*
[646¹]	P		**Secret Beauty (IRE)** (5a) 14-1 **N Harvey** (bf) *8th to 6; fdd & 30l 4th 14; t.o & pu 3 out*
[644⁴]	P		**Sister Lark** (5a) 6-1 **Miss P Jones** *Ld to 4; 6l 2nd to 9; wknd & sn bhnd; pu 15*
[831U]	P		**Theairyman (IRE)** 14-1 **J Jukes** *2nd outing; a last pr; rmdrs 10; no resp; t.o 12; pu 14*

OFFICIAL DISTANCES: 1½l, 15l   TIME: 6min 37.0s

838 Open Maiden 8yo&up, 12st - 17J   8 ran

[650²]	1		**BONNY RIGG (IRE)** (5a) 4-6F **Miss P Jones** *Hld up in 2nd; ld frm 8; 4l ahd frm 12; rdn clr frm 16; unchall*
[484P]	2	10	**Mike's Dream** 5-1 **T Vaughan** *Prom; ld 4-7; cl 2nd aft til mist & nrly fell 11; rcvrd wl; 4l 2nd aft; rdn frm 15; no ex frm 2 out*
[650⁴]	3	20	**Black Dan** 14-1 **J Keen** *2 handlers; ld to 4; grad wknd; 14l 5th 11; no ch aft*
[646⁴]	P		**Baytownghost (IRE)** (tt) 12-1 **M Lewis** (xnb) *A 4/5th; mist 10; 12l 4th & jmpd slow 13; fdd aft; pu 15*
[490U]	F		**Charlotte's Rose** (5a) 12-1 **G Marsh** *2nd early; rn wide app 2; rmdrs aft; mist 5; last til fell 10*
[650P]	P		**Maes Gwyn Dreamer** 6-1 **G Lewis** *A rr; 18l last 10; pu 12*
	P		**Redoran** (5a) 8-1 **G Skone** (xnb) *Sis; last pr; prog 9 to 8l 3rd 11; fdd 14; pu 2 out*
[650³]	F		**Twopintsahalfone (IRE)** evensF **J Jukes** *4th til fell 9*

OFFICIAL DISTANCES: 8l, 25l   TIME: 6min 28.0s
Fences 5 & 13 omitted - damaged

Puckeridge

Horseheath (RH 10F,18J) Sat, 1 Apr (FIRM)

839 Hunt, 12st   4 ran

[609⁷]	1		**LORD KNOX (IRE)** 4-7F **A Coe** *Ld 4; a gng wl aft; pushed clr flat*
[609⁸]	2	3	**Borrow Mine (IRE)** (vis) 6-4 **A Braithwaite** *Nt a fluent; ld to 4; chsd wnr to 10 & frm 12; ev ch & flatt when outj last; rdn & nt qckn*
[577U]	3	25	**Nosy Parker** 8-1 **A Harvey** *Hit 8; went 2nd 10-12; u.p 14; ev ch til rap lost tch nxt*
[7P]	U		**Sixth Sense (IRE)** 4-1 **Miss S Turner** *3rd when slt mist & ur 3*

OFFICIAL DISTANCES: 2½l, 20l   TIME: 6min 37.0s   TOTE: £1.70   DF: £1.70

840 Intermediate, 12st   **5 ran**

[413F]   1   **FAIR EXCHANGE** 1-3F **P Taiano** *(xnb)* Lw; hld up & cl up til qcknd to ld & mist 10;
                    drew clr app 3 out; v easy
[609³]   2   15   **Alfredo Garcia (IRE)** 3-1 **N Bloom** Made most 4-10; sn outpcd in 3rd; 22l 3rd 15;
                    rem 2nd agn 2 out
[609⁵]   3   8   **Generous Deal (IRE)** 10-1 **A Sansome** Nt v fluent; prom/ld at times to 10; chsd wnr
                    clsly til outpcd 15; wknd & dem 3rd 2 out
[609⁶]   4   25   **Royal Surprise** 20-1 **Miss L Ingram** *(xnb)* Ld to 4; last & outpcd 10; 47l last 15;
                    plugged on
[609ᴾ]   P   **Aeolian** *(5ow)* 20-1 **R Gill** Settled cl up til pce qckng 10; 111 3rd & strugg 12; 42l 4th
                    15; t.o & pu last

    OFFICIAL DISTANCES: 15l, 10l TIME: 6min 28.0s TOTE: £1.40 DF: £1.40

841 Ladies Open   **5 ran**

[707ᴾ]   1   **EMSEE-H** 5-4 **Miss Z Turner** Ld 3 til aft 6; ld aft 10 til app 15; rallied to ld agn 2 out;
                    rdn & r.o game
         2   2   **Larry The Lamb** 5-1 **Miss T Hayter** Hld up last to 10; eff 13; 10l 3rd 15; kpt on
                    game to chse wnr aft 2 out; rdn & no imp
[607⁶]   3   12   **Kelly's Original** 11-10F **Mrs T Hill** Rn in snatches; ld aft 6-7; niggled 8; 4th 9; 2nd
                    agn 11; dashed to ld app 15 & sn 5l clr; rdn & hdd 2 out & wknd
[756ᴾ]   4   20   **Salmon Mead (IRE)** (bl) 33-1 **Miss N Barnes** 1st ride; prom; ld 7; rmdrs 9; hdd aft
                    10; wknd 12; 30l 4th 15
[608³]   5   2   **Peanuts Pet** 12-1 **Miss H Barnard** Ld to 3; 8l last aft 10; nvr gng wl aft; 32l last 15

    OFFICIAL DISTANCES: 2l, 8l TIME: 6min 20.0s TOTE: £2.10 DF: £3.90

842 Mens Open, 12st   **6 ran**

[553¹]   1   **HATCHAM BOY (IRE)** (7x) 1-3F **C Ward-Thomas** Lw; ld to 4, aft 6-7 & 9-11; lost
                    plce of 4th 14; 2nd but rdn & outpcd app 2 out; rallied & stayed on to ld flat; all out
[678¹]   2   ¾   **Prince Of Saints (IRE)** (7x) (bl) **A Sansome** Hld up in tch; went 3rd 14; qcknd to
                    ld app nxt; rdn clr 2 out; jmpd slow last; hung rt & nt r.o flat; sn hdd; kpt on agn nr fin
[607³]   3   15   **Mister Trick (IRE)** (bl) 5-1 **N King** Prom; ld/disp 11-14; cl 4th app 3 out; sn wknd
[756ᵁ]   4   12   **Koathary (USA)** 12-1 **T Lane** Hld up; impd to ld 8-9; ld/disp agn 11 til app 15; wknd
                    rap 3 out
[756ᵁ]   5   2   **Royal Action** (7x) 33-1 **P Chinery** *(xnb)* Nt a fluent; prom; mist 5; last frm 9; 25l
                    adrift 15; fin fast frm 2 out
[417ᴾ]   P   **Chris's Lad** (7x) 20-1 **M Gingell** Ld 4 til aft 6; releg 5th 11; sn lost tch; 8l adrift 14;
                    wl bhnd when pu 3 out

    OFFICIAL DISTANCES: ¾l, 10l TIME: 6min 22.0s TOTE: £1.40 DF: £3.20
              Damier Blanc was withdrawn not under orders - bolted before start

843 Restricted, 12st   **6 ran**

[610²]   1   **MISTER AUDI (IRE)** 4-5F **A Sansome** Settled cl up; went 2nd 10 & sn clr w rnr-up;
                    ld 3 out; rdn & mist nxt; sn hdd; lft in ld flat & drvn clr
[761²]   2   3   **Ar Aghaidh Abhaile (IRE)** 3-1 **G Cooper** 2nd/3rd til ld 10; hdd 3 out; ld agn aft
                    nxt; clr when veered lft towards boxes aft last; hdd & threw it away
[669⁴]   3   15   **Holmby Copse** 4-1 **T Humphrey** 2 handlers; oht; pulled hrd & prom to 10; 12l 3rd
                    & outpcd aft 13; 20l 3rd 15
[761⁴]   4   12   **Free And Equal (IRE)** 25-1 **N Bloom** Jmpd slow 2 & 3; sn detach last & nt keen;
                    30l adrift 15; went 4th flat
[610³⁼] 5   8   **Bakmalad** 25-1 **D Kemp** Set stdy pce to 10; outpcd 12; 25l 4th when mist 15; plodded
                    on & dem flat
[769F]   P   **Airecco (IRE)** 14-1 **T Lane** Bckwd; jmpd slow 6; cl up to 7; 5th & strugg 10; t.o & pu 3 out

    OFFICIAL DISTANCES: ½l, 10l TIME: 6min 27.0s TOTE: £1.60 DF: £1.30

844 Open Maiden (Div 1), 12st   **7 ran**

[514²]   1   **ABBEY FLYER** 3-1 **T Illsley** Made virt all; drvn 2 out; ½l up at last; r.o stdly
[604⁴]   2   1   **Curracloe Rose (IRE)** *(5a)* 5-1 **D Cook** Mid-div; 10l 4th 9; went 3rd 11; chall 13; ev
                    ch frm 15 til rdn & nt qckn final 100yds
[696²]   3   15   **Polly Live Wire** *(5a)* 4-1 **P Millington** *(citation)* Settled last; jmpd slow 7; mist 10;
                    outpcd nxt & 12l 4th 13; blun & almost out 15; miraculous rcvry; kpt on game; no ch aft
[610ᴾ]   4   ½   **Life Of A Star (IRE)** 12-1 **A Braithwaite** *(xnb)* Prsd ldr to 15; wknd qckly; lost 3rd
                    cl home

[604F] 5   25   **Cardinal Bud (IRE)** 2-1F P Taiano (xnb) Lw; rr & nt a fluent; clsd brief 9; outpcd 11 & poor last 13; schooled on

[551F] 6   6   **Coolest By Phar (IRE)** 14-1 C Ward-Thomas Tubed; prom; 3rd 9; nt r.o & 15l 5th 12; sn wl bhnd

      P   **Dilly May Dally** (5a) 14-1 A Coe Bckwd; jmpd slow; a rr; lost tch 10; pu 11

OFFICIAL DISTANCES: 1l, 15l   TIME: 6min 43.0s   TOTE: £4.70 DF: £4.60

845 Open Maiden (Div 2), 12st   6 ran

[322P] 1   **UNCLE BUCK (IRE)** 1-2F P Taiano Jmpd bold & made virt all til hdd app 15; vied for ld aft; jmpd to ld agn last; sn clr & r.o game

[617P] 2   7   **Judicial Queen** (5a) 6-1 A Sansome Pulled hrd; jmpd slow 5; cl up til went 2nd app 11; ld brief & outj 15; drvn & outpcd app 2 out; went 2nd agn flat

[605³] 3   1½   **Glencloy (IRE)** 7-2 A Coe Blun & nrly ur 3; mostly cl 2nd/3rd til ld app 15; hrd prsd & blun last; sn hdd & wknd

[759⁴] 4   20   **Steel My Song** (5a) 8-1 S Morris Lw; sn last & detach; 10l bhnd & drvn 9; unable to cl frm 13

[515P] P   **Bakewell** 10-1 T Illsley V fat; prom; 3rd when hit 11; wknd nxt; pu 14

      U   **Craftbook Marchesa (IRE)** (5a) 12-1 P Millington Last pr til blun & ur 4

OFFICIAL DISTANCES: 3l, ½l   TIME: 6min 36.0s   TOTE: £2.30 DF: £5.50
Midnight Dynamite was withdrawn not under orders - ur going to start and bolted

Spooners & West Dartmoor
Cherrybrook (LH 7F,18J) Sat, 1 Apr (GOOD to SOFT becoming HOLDING)

846 Hunt   6 ran

[680⁴] 1   **PALACE PARADE (USA)** 4-11F C Heard Lw; tkn wide; hld up in tch; ld 12; drew clr 2 out; easy

[71⁴] 2   25   **Sea Jay Son** 10-1 Mrs M Hand Ld til blun bad 11; lost tch 3 out; r.o agn clsng stages

[656²] 3   1   **Wise Examiner (IRE)** 3-1 N Harris (xnb) A.p; bustled along 13; cl 2nd 15; rdn & wknd aft nxt; lost 2nd cl home

[407²] 4   1½fs   **Magic Caller (IRE)** 33-1 Miss S Robinson Sn strugg; t.o frm ½way

      U   **Budghill** 10-1 T Dennis Nt fluent; 5th when blun & ur 7

[724⁴] r   **Patrio (IRE)** (5a) 33-1 J Cole 4th mostly; slt hdwy 9; mist 10; bhnd when ref last

OFFICIAL DISTANCES: 15l, 1l   TIME: 6min 18.0s

847 Restricted (Div 1, Part 1), 12st   10 ran

[458P] 1   **SIR FROSTY** (tt) 7-2 N Mitchell Lw; sn prom; 2nd frm 15; chall & ld inner 2 out; drvn out

[729⁴] 2   8   **Wonford Boy** 4-7F K Heard 6/4-4/7; hld up; prog to 4th 9; ld 15; hdd 2 out; btn when ploughed thro last & broke fnce; fin tired

[730²] 3   20   **Born Natural (IRE)** (5a) (tt) 16-1 R Woollacott Rr; hdwy to 15l 5th 9; nd; rem 3rd frm 15

[722P] P   **Calvary Hill** 33-1 D Doyne-Ditmas (xnb) In tch; 3rd 9; lost plce 12; bhnd when pu 15

      P   **Fleet Mill** (5a) 16-1 Miss T Cave (xnb) A rr; t.o & pu 3 out; quiet rn

[560P] P   **Jolirose** (12a) 50-1 Miss V Stephens Midfield; 6th ½way; lost ground & pu 15; school

[409⁴] P   **Lighter Lord** 20-1 D Alers-Hankey Midfield; 7th ½way; poor 5th when pu 3 out

[729P] P   **River Carron** 20-1 G Maundrell Rr til pu 11; school

      P   **Tamar Lily** (5a) 10-1 Miss A Barnett (xnb) 2 handlers; ld; mist 3; clr 5; ld clr 10; hdd 14; wknd; t.o & pu last

[728P] P   **Uncle James (IRE)** 33-1 C White Towards rr til pu 12

OFFICIAL DISTANCES: 8l, 20l   TIME: 6min 11.0s

848 Restricted (Div 1, Part 2), 12st - 15J   10 ran

[651F] 1   **SAGAVILLE (IRE)** 7-1 A Holdsworth Chsd ldr; ld aft; stayed on wl when chall aft 2 out; just hld on u.p

[406F] 2   nk   **Damiens Pride (IRE)** 5-1 T Dennis (xnb) Opened 7s; lw; handy; trckd ldr frm 10; ev ch 2 out; unable to qckn; rallied cl home; just failed

[403⁴] 3   3   **Kimbross** 7-4F L Jefford (xnb) Midfield til hdwy 10; 4th nxt; ev ch last; kpt on one pce clsng stages

[729P] 4   10   **Bridge House Boy** 10-1 A Oliver (xnb) Mist 2; cl 6th 10; slt mist & rmdrs 12; sn btn

[720⁵] 5   15   **The Bandon Car (IRE)** 3-1 T Cole In tch; cl 4th 11; staying on in 4th but no ch w ldrs when blun last; wknd

[726P] 6   40   **Moorland Abbot** 66-1 Miss D Mitchell Rr; bhnd frm 8

[652P] P   **Alpine Music (IRE)** 14-1 I Hambley Opened 25s; rr til pu 13

	U		**Gay Cavalier** 14-1 **J Cole** (xnb) *Nt fluent & sn last; rr when blun & ur 7*
[560⁴]	P		**Nodforms Inferno** 12-1 **A Bateman** *Tde; rcd keen early & sn clr; hdd 10; wknd rap; pu 12*
	P		**Smudges Season** (5a) 25-1 **R Emmett** *Rr til pu 6*

OFFICIAL DISTANCES: nk, 3l   TIME: 6min 15.0s
Fences 4, 11 & 18 omitted - damaged in previous race

849 Restricted (Div 2, Part 1), 12st   11 ran

[728²]	1		**FOSSY BEAR** (5a) 2-1 **Miss S Young** (b4) *Gd hdwy 10; went 2nd 12; ld 13-16; cl up til impd to ld on outer 2 out; stayed on wl*
[383⁷]	2	4	**Bricanmore** (IRE) 4-1 **N Harris** *Stdy prog 9; cl 3rd 13; rdr hit rival jock w whip app nxt; slt ld aft 16 til outj nxt; ev ch til no ex u.p app last*
[518¹]	3	15	**Rimpton Boy** (7a) evensF **Miss P Gundry** *5/2-evens; lw; handy; cl 5th 9; chsd ldr 14 til wknd 3 out; wl btn when jmpd rt last; fin exhaust*
[723¹]	4	6	**The Ugly Duckling** 10-1 **R Woollacott** *Lw; prom; ld 6-9; hit 11; cl up & ev ch when intentionally impeded rival aft 13 (& got whack from his whip in retaliation!); sn wknd; no ch frm 15*
[658²]	5	3	**Shameless Lady** (5a) 20-1 **Richard Darke** *Ld to 6; in tch til wknd 14; no ch frm nxt*
[728⁷]	F		**Aint No Lady** (IRE) (5a) 66-1 **Miss S Robinson** *Nt fluent in rr; bhnd when fell hvly 12*
[729²]	F		**Baron Knayber** 25-1 **S Edwards** *Sn prom; slt ld 9-12; just in tch but wkng when fell 14*
	P		**I'm Foxy** (5a) (bl) 66-1 **T Dennis** *Towards rr til pu 13*
	P		**Little Buster** 33-1 **D Alers-Hankey** (xnb) *Oht; 6th 6; sn strugg; t.o & pu 9*
	P		**Pick-N-Cruise** (5a) 66-1 **D Stephens** (Devon) *2 handlers; tde; snrr & hanging; bhnd when hmpd 12; pu nxt*
	P		**Whinholme Lass** (IRE) (5a) 20-1 **L Jefford** *Towards rr til pu 12*

OFFICIAL DISTANCES: 4l, 15l   TIME: 6min 15.0s
The Jockey Club Disciplinary Committee enquired into interference between fences 13 and 14; the riders of Bricanmore (for striking rival rider with whip) and The Ugly Duckling (for causing intentional interference) were each fined £175

850 Restricted (Div 2, Part 2), 12st   10 ran

[540¹]	1		**COUNSEL** (7a) 3-1 **Miss S Vickery** *Tchd 7/2; lw; made virt all; qcknd 8l clr app 2 out; wl in comm when hit last; comf*
[657²]	2	12	**Woodland King** (IRE) 4-1 **Mrs M Hand** *6s-4s; handy; stdy hdwy aft 14; went 2nd nxt; ev ch til outpcd aft 3 out*
[726²]	3	6	**Spruce** (5a) 2-1F **Mrs S Fell** *Nt a fluent; sn prom; trckd ldr & hit 10; cl 2nd til blun 15; no ex frm nxt*
[541⁴]	4	5	**Travel By Land** 33-1 **Miss O Green** *Midfield; 8th 9; no prog; plugged on to tk 4th cl home*
[536⁵]	5	1	**Belski** 14-1 **R Woollacott** *Hdwy 12; 10l 5th 13; lost ground 15; sn one pce u.p; lost 4th cl home*
	P		**Harveysinahurry** 33-1 **G Richards** (xnb) *In tch; 4th 9; wknd 11; bhnd & pu 14*
[728ᵁ]	P		**King Of Cairo** 66-1 **I Hambley** (xnb) *Midfield; 7th ½way; nt trble ldrs; poor 7th when pu 3 out*
[728⁷]	P		**Maybridge Lady** (5a) 4-1 **N Mitchell** *Impd to 3rd 9; in tch til lost plce aft 14; btn 6th when pu 3 out*
[657⁴]	P		**River Gala** (IRE) (bl) 12-1 **A Honeyball** *Midfield; rdn & lost ground frm 10; t.o & pu 15*
[724⁷]	P		**Safara** 33-1 **T Cole** *Sn rr & nt fluent; t.o & pu 11*

OFFICIAL DISTANCES: 12l, 6l   TIME: 6min 14.0s

851 Ladies Open   5 ran

[383¹]	1		**SAINT JOSEPH** 5-2 **Miss S Young** (b4) *Hld up; went 2nd 13; chsd ldr; eff & ld last; stayed on game*
[653³]	2	½	**Mizyan** (IRE) 2-1 **Miss P Gundry** *Lw; ld to 10 & agn aft 12; went 5l clr 15; lkd wnr til no ex when chall app last*
[680ᶠ]	3	20	**Just Bert** (IRE) 6-4F **Miss J Cumings** *Tchd 7/4; trckd ldr; ld 10-12; lost plce nxt; 3rd & one pce u.p frm 3 out*
[725⁹]	4	runin	**Secret Four** 66-1 **Miss K Langdell** (xnb) *Prom; cl 3rd but rdn 9; sn lost tch; t.o*
[636¹]	P		**Forbidden Waters** (IRE) 9-2 **Miss S Vickery** *Tchd 5s; lw; 4th mostly; in tch til rdn 14; pu & dism nxt (reportedly muscle problem)*

OFFICIAL DISTANCES: ½l, 20l   TIME: 6min 07.0s

852 Confined, 12st   12 ran

[316⁷]	1		**ROSA'S REVENGE** (5a,3x) 4-1 **L Jefford** *Tde; hld up; stdy hdwy frm 13; 4th 15; went 3rd 2 out; chall & ld last; stayed on wl; superb ride*

[535²]	2	3	**O So Bossy** 8-1 Miss J Congdon *(bf) Lw; chsd ldrs til ld aft 12; sn clr; lkd wnr til wknd aft 2 out; ev ch when blun last; no ex; gd eff*
[727ᴾ]	3	nk	**Certain Angle** (5x) 10-1 E Dennis *Nov rdn; rr til prog 9; hit 11; went 3rd aft 13; tk 10l 2nd aft 3 out; no ex frm nxt; fair eff for schoolmaster*
[726¹]	4	10	**Baldhu Chance** (3x) 5-1 A Ede *Jmpd rt; ld to 12; chsd ldr til wknd 3 out*
[653³]	5	2	**Rasta Man** (5x) 5-2F R Woollacott *(xnb,bf) Tchd 4s in plce; rr; rmdrs 12; some hdwy to 6th 3 out; nt trble ldrs*
	6	s hd	**Some-Toy** 16-1 C Heard *Bckwd; settled 3rd; chsd ldrs til lost tch stdly 14; no ch 3 out*
[652⁴]	7	1½	**Hold Your Ranks** (7x) 6-1 D McKenna *Sn towards rr; 11th ½way; nd*
[536ᶠ]	8	10	**Border Rose** (5a) 33-1 D Doyne-Ditmas *Midfield; 7th 12; no prog*
[720²]	9	2	**Solomans Sister** (5a) 6-1 Mrs M Hand *Nt fluent; 7th 9; hdwy to disp 3rd 13; sn wknd; wl bhnd when blun bad last*
[720¹]	P		**Brown Robber** (3x) 5-1 T Dennis *(xnb) Midfield; 6th when hit 11; pu aft nxt*
[536ᶠ]	P		**County Bash** (5a) 50-1 S Kidston *Sn rr & strugg; t.o & pu 14*
[402ᴾ]	P		**Strong Stuff (IRE)** 33-1 M Shears *Mist 1; rr & constant rmdrs; reluct & bhnd til pu 15*

OFFICIAL DISTANCES: 3l, nk TIME: 6min 12.0s

853 Intermediate (Nov Rdrs), 12st
10 ran

[720³]	1		**LEDBURIAN** 6-4F S Craddock *Lw; in tch & rcd outer; 8l 4th 13; hdwy nxt; slt ld 3 out; disp nxt; ½l ld last; kpt on u.p*
[537³]	2	1	**Ardbei (IRE)** 9-2 R Woollacott *Tchd 5s; sn prom; handy on inner; slt ld 10-14; clr up til drvn to disp ld on inner 2 out; ev ch last; no ex*
[730ᴾ]	3	2½	**Foxy Dawn** 5-1 Miss C Prouse *In tch in midfield; 6th 10; went 3rd 13; ev ch til 4th & rdn aft 3 out; plugged on to tk 3rd run-in*
[560ᵁ]	4	1	**Picard (IRE)** (bl) 11-2 Miss L Hawkins *Lw; 5th when mist 4 & rdr lost iron; in tch; 5th ½way; prog aft to ld 14; outj & hdd 3 out; reluct & lost plce nxt; tried to rally app last; one pce*
[720⁶]	5	runin	**Crownhill Cross** 50-1 Miss Johanna Sleep *Rdr lurching; mid-div; blun bad 9; poor 7th 13; no ch*
[406ᴾ]	6	nk	**Prudent Miner (IRE)** (5ow) 20-1 R Skinner *Ld til mist 2; stayed prom; 4th 10; lost tch 14*
[561⁷]	P		**A Few Dollars More (IRE)** 10-1 G Richards *Mist 2; early rmdrs; towards rr; 8th ½way; rdn 11; nd; to & pu 2 out*
[658³]	P		**Bedtime Pixie** (bl) 33-1 Miss L Jackson *Tk keen hld; ld/disp to 10; hit 12; wknd rap; t.o & pu 15*
[721⁵]	P		**Golden Sunset** (5a) 50-1 Miss D Mitchell *Last frm 5; t.o 12; pu 3 out*
[654ᴾ]	P		**Master Buckley** 4-1 C White *Lw; rr when jmpd rt 5; rdn 11; to & pu 2 out*

OFFICIAL DISTANCES: 1l, 2½l TIME: 6min 26.0s

854 Mens Open
4 ran

[727¹]	1		**BUTLER JOHN (IRE)** 2-9F N Harris *Made all; hit 4; 6l clr when blun 15; drvn out clsng stages; unimpressive*
[313²]	2	2½	**Bitran** 7-2 T Greed *Opened 4s; a chsd ldr; clsd up app 2 out; sn no ex u.p*
[726⁵]	3	runin	**Where's Sam (IRE)** 16-1 S Craddock *A 3rd; 15l 3rd ½way; no ch frm 13*
[727ᴾ]	P		**Forest Musk (IRE)** 50-1 I Hambley *Last & detach til rmdrs & slt prog aft 12; sn strugg; t.o & pu 3 out*

OFFICIAL DISTANCES: 2½l, 30l TIME: 6min 18.0s

855 Confined Maiden (Div 1, Part 1), 12st
9 ran

	1		**ASHDOWN BOY** 5-1 R Woollacott *7s-5s; confid rdn; rr til hdwy 13; went 4th 15; ww til eff bet horses 2 out; ld app last; v easy*
[721⁴]	2	12	**Linton** (5a) 7-2 W Smith *Ld to 7 & agn 13-3 out; sn hrd rdn; 3rd & one pce 2 out; lft 2nd at last*
[722³]	3	15	**Amazing Hill (IRE)** 6-4F Mrs R Morris *Rr; last 13; poor 6th 3 out; r.o stdly to tk 3rd run-in; far too much to do*
[730ᴾ]	4	8	**Tubb Corner** 20-1 T Greed *(xnb) Swtng; bit bckwd; in tch; 4th 13; sn rdn; mod 4th frm 3 out*
[730ᴾ]	5	4	**Moorland Rose** (12a) 25-1 Miss D Mitchell *Lkd poor; prom til mist 12; bhnd frm 14*
[159ᴾ]	6	25	**Sparties Image** (5a) 7-1 J Young *Sn prom on outer; blun 4; cl 2nd 8-12; lost plce & rdn 14; bhnd 3 out; t.o when clambered over last*
[159ᴾ]	F		**Classic Mistress** (5a) 6-1 Richard Darke *Tchd 8s; hld up in midfield; 4th 13; gd hdwy to 2nd 15; ld aft nxt til hdd; 5l 2nd when & hld when fell last*
[205ᵁ]	P		**Frisky-Breeze** (5a) 33-1 M Shears *Rdn padd; rcd wide & nt fluent; cl 3rd frm 8; lost plce qckly 14; mist 15; pu nxt*

[312^r] P   **Royal Chip** 3-1 Mrs M Hand *Pulled hrd; ld 6; hdd & mist 13; lost ground qckly; btn 7th when pu 3 out; lks physically amiss*

OFFICIAL DISTANCES: 12l, 15l **TIME:** 6min 40.0s
The stewards informally enquired into the running & riding of Amazing Hill - taking account of the novice rider they decided to take no further action

856 Confined Maiden (Div 1, Part 2), 12st   9 ran

[725^7] 1   **LUNEY RIVER** (5a) 5-1 Miss L Gardner *Handy til disp 12-13; cl 2nd when blun 3 out; rallied & ld nxt; pushed clr flat; rdr's 1st wnr*
[105^3] 2   5   **Blackoid (FR)** 2-5F L Jefford *Tchd 4/7; lw; nt a fluent; ld 2; jnd brief 12; clr & lkd wnr aft 3 out; rdn & hdd nxt; fnd nil*
[658^U] 3   runin **Saucy's Wolf** 6-1 Jeremy Young *In tch; 5th 11; 3rd & rdn 13; cl 3rd & ev ch 15; plodded on one pce*
[312^4] P   **Call Me Dickins** (bl,tt) 25-1 Miss A Barnett *Ld 1; sn lost plce; jnd ldrs 6; cl 3rd 11; wknd 13; no ch when mist 15; t.o & pu 2 out*
[656^3] P   **Frankies Flutter** 8-1 D Doyne-Ditmas *(xnb) sn prom; cl 4th 10; lost ground 12; 6th when pu 13*
[655^r] F   **Hayne Condor** 8-1 S Kidston *Towards rr when fell 9*
[729^p] P   **Newlyn** 20-1 J King *Midfield; 6th 11; nd; t.o & pu 3 out*
         P   **Swincombe (IRE)** (7a) 14-1 Miss T Cave *Last til hmpd 9; pu nxt*
         F   **Wesleys Choice** 14-1 T Cole *Bad mist & releg last 4; bhnd when fell 8*

OFFICIAL DISTANCES: 5l, 30l **TIME:** 6min 32.0s

857 Confined Maiden (Div 2), 12st   12 ran

[407^3] 1   **DEDALUS (FR)** (7a) (bl) 13-2 L Jefford *hdwy 6; disp ld 10; ld 13; rdn clr u.p app 2 out; drvn out*
         2   5   **Cornish Fort** (5a) 4-6F Miss J Cumings *Tchd 4/5; hdwy to disp 10-13; trckd ldr & ev ch til no ex u.p aft 3 out*
[723^3] 3 10   **My Prides Way** (5a) 5-1 T Greed *Rr of main group to ½way; cl 3rd 10; outpcd 14; no hdwy clsng stages*
[728^p] 4 25   **Sea Spirit** (5a) 33-1 T Jones (Devon) *Prom; slt ld 8-9; cl up til rmdrs 11; sn outpcd; no ch frm 3 out*
[723^U] R   **B For Business** (12a) 9-2 S Kidston *Pulled hrd; rn out 2*
         P   **Frosty Jo** (5a) 12-1 T Dennis *Tde; sn rr; t.o & pu 9*
[720^7] P   **Gibraltar Lady** (5a) 33-1 S Craddock *Tk v keen hld; ld & 15l clr by 6; mists; hdd aft 7; blun 9; wknd rap; t.o & pu 12*
[721^2] P   **King Tudor** 6-1 Miss O Green *Midfield; 6th 10; no prog; rr when pu 13*
[563^r] P   **Knap Hand** (7a) 25-1 A Ede *Rr; mist 4; pu nxt*
[655^r] P   **My Jess** (5a) 25-1 M Shears *In tch; 5th 10; rmdrs & lost ground frm 12; bhnd & pu 15*
[724^5] P   **Spirit Of Life** (5a) 33-1 M Woodward *A rr; t.o & pu 13*
[723^5] P   **Walton Street** 14-1 W Smith *Bhnd when mist 11; rr til pu 13*

OFFICIAL DISTANCES: 5l, 10l **TIME:** 6min 25.0s

United
Brampton Bryan (RH 8F,19J) Sat, 1 Apr (GOOD)

858 Hunt   5 ran

[698^3] 1   **WILD EDRIC** 1-2F G Hanmer *Went 2nd 2; ld 8-15; 1l 3rd nxt; lft in 3 out; all out*
[615^r] 2   ½   **Out Of The Blue** (5a) 7-2 S Graham *(bh) Ld to 7; 2nd to 11; 3l 4th 16; rdn & ev ch 2 out; r.o flat*
[612^r] 3 10   **Crab 'n Lobster (IRE)** (5a) 6-1 R Hodges *Ss; sn prom; ld 7-8; 2l 3rd ½way; went 2nd 11; ld 15-16; ev ch when jmpd lft 3 out; wknd nxt*
         4 4fncs   **Paddington Bear** (U) 25-1 Mrs S Stafford *Sn wl bhnd; t.o 4*
[118^F] R   **Hotscent (IRE)** (5a) 10-1 Miss C Wilberforce *2nd/3rd to 3; 5l 4th ½way; hit 12; went 2nd aft 15; ld nxt til rn out & ur 3 out*

OFFICIAL DISTANCES: nk, 12l **TIME:** 7min 27.8s

859 Mens Open, 12st   8 ran

[796^1] 1   **SOLBA (USA)** (7x) 4-9F A Dalton *Hld up; 1ll 4th ½way; hdwy 12; 3l 2nd nxt; ld 16; sn 5l clr; comf*
[480^5] 2   5   **Watchit Lad** 6-1 S Blackwell *Ld to 6; 2nd til ld 11; hdd 16; kpt on wl; no ch w wnr*
[671^2] 3   8   **Distant-Port (IRE)** 9-1 T Stephenson *Hld up; 13l 5th ½way; hdwy & 7l 4th 13; mist 15; went 6l 3rd aft nxt; no imp 3 out*

[480⁴] 4 1 **Tremendisto** (7x) 12-1 D Mansell *(xnb) Chsd ldrs; 10l 3rd ½way; mist 10; went 2nd aft 12-13; cl up til 7l 4th & rdn aft 16; mist 3 out; sn btn; blun last*

[482³] P **Across The Water** (5a) 25-1 A Wintle *Lw; a bhnd; jmpd slow 5; 19l 7th ½way; drvn along 11; 15l 6th 14; t.o & pu 3 out*

[670¹] r **Celtic Town** (4x) 9-1 P Kay *(xnb) Sn outpcd & wl bhnd; distracted by loose dog, ref & ur 7*

[382⁵] P **Manamour** 20-1 R Cooper *Nd; 15l 6th ½way; 14l 5th & no hdwy 14; wl bhnd when pu 16*

[530⁷] P **Perfect Light** (4x) 8-1 M Jackson *Pulled hrd; blun 3; 2nd til ld 6; mist 7; hdd 11; wknd qckly 13; 20l 7th nxt; pu 15*

OFFICIAL DISTANCES: 10l, 6l **TIME:** 6min 52.1s

860 Ladies Open
10 ran

[481³] 1 **INDEFENCE (IRE)** 3-1 Miss C Thomas *Ww; 15l 6th ½way; hdwy & lft 7l 3rd 13; qcknd to ld aft 16; sn clr; comf*

[699¹] 2 4 **Rip Van Winkle** (7x) 6-4F Miss A Dare *Hld up & bhnd; 22l 7th ½way; 15l 5th when mist 15; hdwy & 7l 3rd 3 out; stayed on; went 2nd nr fin; nt rch wnr*

[743⁷] 3 nk **Name Of Our Father (USA)** (7x) 14-1 Miss E Bryan *(orbs) A.p; went 1½l 2nd 8; mist 12; chsd wnr 3 out; kpt on; dem nr fin*

[787ᶠ] 4 25 **Look In The Mirror** (7x) 3-1 Miss L Sweeting *2nd to 8; 2½l 3rd ½way; lft in ld 13; hdd aft 16; sn wknd*

[683¹⁰] 5 15 **Highway Five (IRE)** 33-1 Miss L Brooke *Sn wl bhnd; t.o 8*

[613⁶] 6 5 **Saffron Flame (IRE)** 33-1 Miss N Rudge *Swtng; a bhnd; 23l 8th ½way; 25l 6th 15; t.o*

P **Cheeky Pot** (bl) 33-1 Miss J Priest *A wl bhnd; 30l 9th ½way; t.o 13; pu 2 out*

[611¹] U **Distinctive (IRE)** 7-1 Mrs D Jackson *Ld til rfo 13*

[667ᶠ] U **Elwell Glory (IRE)** 33-1 Miss M Peterson *Lw; tde; chsd ldrs; 12l 5th ½way; mist & ur 11*

[335⁵] R **Fed On Oats** 33-1 Mrs D Powell *Chsd ldrs; rdr lost irons 1; 8l 4th ½way; 9l 4th 15; wkng when mist 3 out; 20l 4th when rn out thro wing & ur last*

OFFICIAL DISTANCES: 4l, ½l **TIME:** 6min 52.1s

861 Dodson & Horrell PPORA Club Members, 12st - 17J
8 ran

[615²] 1 **UPTON ADVENTURE** (5a) 8-11F S Joynes *Lw; a.p; 3l 4th ½way; mist 12; went 2nd 14; ld app 3 out; rdn clr by-passing nxt; r.o wl*

[564⁴] 2 3½ **Dainty Man (IRE)** 7-1 A Dalton *Hld up & pulled hrd; 6l 7th ½way; eff & 2½l 5th 16; chsd wnr 2 out; nt qckn u.p*

[701²] 3 2½ **Aqua Star (IRE)** 6-1 Miss T Spearing *Lw; tde; hld up; 3½l 5th ½way; went 2l 3rd 15; rdn 3 out; one pce*

4 1 **Nevada Gold** 12-1 D Mansell *Ld til hdd app 3 out; one pce*

[667⁵] 5 7 **Rootsman (IRE)** 14-1 T Stephenson *Prom; went 2nd 8-14; ev ch 4 out; wknd 3 out*

[464ᶠ] 6 8 **Corkers Flame (IRE)** 20-1 I Wynne *Went 2nd 2-8; lost plce & 4l 6th ½way; 3l 6th 16; sn outpcd*

[670²ᵘ] 7 12 **Stormhill Recruit** 4-1 S Blackwell *Nt fluent; hld up; 2l 3rd ½way; lost plce 14; 4l 7th & rdn 16; sn wknd*

F **Foxy Lass** (5a) 25-1 J Burley *Hld up; 7l 8th ½way; in tch til fell 12*

OFFICIAL DISTANCES: 4l, 3l **TIME:** 7min 03.8s
Fences 10 & 18 omitted - damaged

862 Confined, 12st - 16J
16 ran

1 **THE RUM MARINER** 8-1 Miss C Thomas *Ld; mist 1; hdd 3; 2nd to 15; outpcd 9l 5th 16; stayed on wl to ld app last; sn clr*

[611ᵖ] 2 7 **Gold'n Shroud (IRE)** 5-2F A Wintle *Hld up; 10l 12th ½way; stdy hdwy & 7l 9th 13; qcknd to ld 15; sn 3l clr; hdd app last; no ex u.p*

[617¹] 3 1 **Achill Sound** 4-1 G Hanmer *(xnb) Swtng; hld up & bhnd; 12l 14th ½way; 9l 12th 13; 13l 9th 16; stayed on frm 3 out; nrst fin*

4 2 **Perambulate (NZ)** 12-1 D Barlow *Chsd ldrs; 6l 5th ½way; hit 12; 5l 7th nxt; outpcd in 10l 6th 16; rallied aft*

[741⁵] 5 1½ **Chiaroscuro** (bl) 5-1 S Lloyd *Chsd ldrs; 6½l 6th ½way; 3½l 5th 13; lost plce nxt; 18l 11th 16; stayed on wl*

[671³] 6 ½ **Saywhen** 8-1 R Cooper *Hld up & bhnd; mist 7; 11l 13th ½way; 8l 11th 13; 12l 8th 16; stayed on; nvr*

7 nk **Ollardale (IRE)** (3x) (bl) 7-1 R Burton *Chsd ldrs; jmpd slow 6; 7l 7th ½way; 4½l 6th 13; went 3rd 16; no ex*

[615ᵖ] 8 15 **Roman Romany** 16-1 E Walker *(xnb) Prom; 4l 3rd ½way; disp 2l 2nd 13; 10½l 7th & wkng 16; to*

[615ᵖ] 9 20 **Nutty Solera** 20-1 M Keel *9l 10th ½way; 11l 13th 13; 25l 12th 16; t.o*

[611⁴] U **Alaskan Heir** (vis) 20-1 M Rodda *7th when blun & ur 3*

[474²]	P		**Good For A Loan** 20-1 D Mansell *Hld up; 9½l 11th ½way; 7½l 10th 13; hdwy 15; went 3l 2nd nxt; mist 3 out; sn wknd u.p; bhnd when pu last*
[292²]	P		**Haveafewmanners (IRE)** (5a) (tt) 4-1 D Sherlock *Swtng; ld 3-15; 6l 4th 4 out; wknd qckly; wl bhnd when pu last*
	P		**Just For A Reason** 20-1 A Phillips *Nd; 11l 9th ½way; drpd to rr & blun 12; nt r.o; pu 13*
[461⁷]	P		**Macamore Star** 20-1 J Merry *Swtng; hld up; 7½l 8th ½way; hdwy 11; 3l 4th 13; wknd qckly 15; 16l 10th nxt; pu 3 out*
[684ᵁ]	U		**Merger Mania** 5-1 A Wadlow *(xnb) Hld up & bhnd; 13l 15th ½way; 12l 14th when stumbled & ur bend app 14*
	P		**Tangle Baron** 20-1 A Evans *Prom; 4½l 4th ½way; lost plce u.p & 6l 8th 13; bhnd when pu 16*

OFFICIAL DISTANCES: 6l, 1l **TIME:** 6min 58.0s
Fences 2, 10 & 18 omitted - damaged in previous race

863 Restricted (Div 1), 12st

10 ran

[570¹]	1		**HIGHBRIDGE (IRE)** 4-1 A Evans *Lw; pulled hrd; went 2nd 2-8; ld 10-13; ld 15; rdn 2 out; stayed on wl*
[683⁷]	2	4	**Lordinthesky (IRE)** 7-1 S Blackwell *Sn prom; went 2nd 8; ld 9-10 & 13-15; rdn & ev ch 2 out; no ex flat*
[564²]	3	15	**Rising Sap** 7-4F R Burton *2 handlers; ld to 9; 2l 3rd & rdn 16; wknd u.p 2 out*
[568¹]	P		**Arrysu** 8-1 Miss S Sharratt *Bhnd til pu 9*
	U		**Ballyharry (IRE)** 7-1 I Wynne *(xnb) Tde; hld up; 7l 5th ½way; mist 13; 6l 5th when mist & ur 14*
[667⁴]	P		**Cwm Bye** 10-1 M Hammond *Prom; 3l 4th ½way; mist 14; 4l 4th 16; wknd qckly; pu 3 out*
[472¹]	P		**Kandles-Korner** 5-2 Julian Pritchard *Lw; hld up; mist 1; 10l 6th ½way; lft 7l 5th 14; wknd u.p 16; wl bhnd when pu last*
[669⁵]	U		**Maid O'Tully (IRE)** (5a) 8-1 R Hodges *Prom; 3½l 5th when mist & ur 9*
[445¹]	P		**Nouvalari (IRE)** 20-1 M Rodda *In tch til blun bad 8; 15l 8th ½way; wl bhnd when pu 12*
[513⁷]	P		**Tranquil Lord** 20-1 D Smith *(bf) A bhnd; 12l 7th ½way; pu 3 out*

OFFICIAL DISTANCES: 5l, 20l **TIME:** 6min 56.6s

864 Restricted (Div 2), 12st

11 ran

[612²]	1		**PADDY FOR PADDY (IRE)** 6-4F R Burton *2s-6/4; lw; sn prom; 2l 3rd ½way; went 2l 2nd app 16; rdn to ld 2 out; edged lft flat; stayed on wl*
	2	1½	**Wise Prince** 7-1 L Stephens *(citation) Hld up; hdwy 7; went 2nd 10; ld aft 15; jb lft 3 out; hdd nxt; nt qckn flat*
[669²]	3	12	**Percy Medlicott** 3-1 Julian Pritchard *Chsd ldrs; rmrdrs 3; 4l 4th & rdn 16; went 3rd app nxt; no imp*
[683⁷]	4	12	**Rymin Thyne** 12-1 D Mansell *Mist 2; bhnd when mist 9; 11l 9th ½way; eff u.p & ld 5th 13; no imp when mist nxt*
[589⁵]	5	10	**Cookie Boy** 10-1 M Wilesmith *Ld til hdd aft 15; wknd app 3 out*
[489¹]	P		**Cherry Alley (IRE)** (5a) 10-1 S Lloyd *A bhnd; 12l 10th ½way; 19l 8th 13; pu 14*
[588⁷]	P		**Glamdring** (5a) 20-1 I Clyde *2nd til mist 9; 9l 7th & wkng ½way; bhnd when pu 12*
[792⁶]	P		**Otter River** 20-1 P Morris *Still bckwd; jmpd lft; sn wl bhnd; t.o & pu 11*
[612⁷]	P		**Pushover (FR)** 16-1 T Stephenson *Hld up; hdwy & 7l 5th ½way; wknd & 11l 6th 13; wl bhnd when pu 15*
[490¹]	P		**Scottish Clover** (5a) 10-1 M Hammond *Chsd ldrs; 8l 6th & rdn ½way; drpd to rr & mist 12; pu 13*
[567⁵]	P		**The Honest Poacher (IRE)** 20-1 I Wynne *Swtng; prom til lost plce 8; 10l 8th ½way; 17l 7th 13; t.o & pu 3 out*

OFFICIAL DISTANCES: 1½l, 15l **TIME:** 6min 57.6s

865 Confined Maiden (Div 1), 12st

14 ran

[588³]	1		**OUTRAGEOUS AFFAIR** (5a) 8-1 Miss R Reynolds *Ww; 9l 8th ½way; 7l 5th 13; 8l 6th 16; qcknd to ld 3 out; r.o wl; rdr's 1st wnr*
[618³]	2	5	**Dunethna (IRE)** 2-1¹JF R Burton *3s-2s; hld up; hmpd 6; 4l 5th ½way; 3l 4th 13; qcknd to ld aft 16; hdd 3 out; one pce*
	3	12	**Holding The Fort (IRE)** 6-1 D Barlow *A.p; went 2nd 6; ld 7-11; 2l 3rd 13; ev ch 3 out; no ex; mist last*
[486⁷]	4	hd	**Nineteenonfive (IRE)** 16-1 M Scales *Prom; 2l 3rd ½way; went 2nd 13-16; no ex 3 out*
[617⁵]	5	4	**Reg's Rocket** 7-1 N Oliver *Ld to 7; 8l 11th; hdd aft 16; sn wknd*
[672⁵]	6	8	**New Yorker (USA)** (7a) (vis,tt) 10-1 M Rodda *Swtng; hld up; 8l 7th ½way; 10l 6th 13; hdwy 15; 9l 7th nxt; wknd 3 out*

[450P]   P   **Come On Boy** 14-1 *D Mansell* Swtng; hld up & bhnd; 11l 10th ½way; mist 12; 15l
                    9th nxt; 10l 8th when mist 16; pu 3 out

[568U]   P   **Ice N' Slice (IRE)** (5a) 12-1 *J Cornes* (xnb) Hld up; hdwy & 3l 4th ½way; wkng when
                    blun 12; bhnd when pu 13

[616²]   F   **Little Star** (5a) 2-1JF *T Stephenson* Mist 1; 8th when fell 4; broke shoulder; destroyed

[339U]   U   **Pulpits Edge** 16-1 *R Carey* (xnb) Mist & rdr lost iron 2; 3rd when ur 4
         R   **Royal Silk** 14-1 *S Graham* (xnb) Wl bhnd wn rn out 4
         R   **Rusty King** 14-1 *R Hodges* Mist 4; 2nd til mist 6; 5l 6th ½way; lost plce & 12l 7th
                    13; rallied 15; 7l 5th when rn out 16

[488U]   P   **Timmy Tuff (IRE)** 8-1 *R Cooper* Tde; reluct to rce & svs; 15l 11th ½way; wl bhnd til
                    pu 13

[517⁴]   P   **Yasgourra (IRE)** (5a) 16-1 *P Morris* Nd; 10l 9th ½way; 14l 8th 13; wl bhnd when pu
                    2 out

OFFICIAL DISTANCES: 6l, 15l **TIME:** 7min 12.3s
Far Glen was withdrawn after declaration

866 Confined Maiden (Div 2), 12st - 17J   16 ran

[526U]   1   **NEED MORE PRACTICE** (tt) 5-1 *A Evans* Hld up & bhnd; 9½l 8th ½way; 7l 8th 13;
                    stdy hdwy 15; went 5l 4th aft nxt; chall 2 out; ld flat; r.o ww

         2   1   **Border Barley** 5-1 *D Barlow* Trckd ldrs; 7l 5th ½way; 2l 3rd when mist 14; ld aft 15;
                    hdd flat; r.o; collapsed & died aft fin

[703R]   3   7   **Sutton Lighter** 12-1 *D Mansell* (xnb) 2 handlers; tde; hld up; 8½l 7th ½way; 6l 7th
                    13; 5l 7th 15; went 2l 2nd aft nxt; hrd rdn 2 out; one pce

[778P]   5   13   **Blacon Point** 16-1 *T Stephenson* (xnb) Swtng; ld to 3; 5l 4th ½way; went 2l 3rd 15
                    & 2nd brief nxt; ch when blun 2 out; nt rec

[488⁵]   4d   **Brown Wren** (5a) 12-1 *S Lloyd* Chsd ldrs; 8l 6th ½way; 5l 6th 13; outpcd 15; 6l 6th
                    nxt; one pce; fin 13l 4th; disq - nt weigh-in

[570P]   F   **Daneswell** 20-1 *M Munrowd* Fell 1
         P   **Diamond Light** 14-1 *Miss E Bryan* Sn wl bhnd; 15l 11th ½way; t.o 13; pu 2 out

[588⁴]   P   **French Melody (IRE)** 14-1 *J Burley* (bf) Mist & rmdrs 4; jnd ldrs 7; went 2nd nxt; ld
                    10; mist 12; hdd 14; 3l 4th nxt; sn wknd; wl bhnd when pu 2 out

[483⁹]   P   **Gunners Dawn** (5a) 20-1 *K Ford* Nd; 10½l 9th ½way; 8l 9th 13; wknd & 12l 9th
                    15; wl bhnd when pu 2 out

         P   **Hil's Bluff (IRE)** (12a,1ow) 20-1 *A Wadlow* 2 handlers; bckwd; a bhnd; 11l 10th
                    ½way; t.o & pu 13

[618R]   P   **Mr Stackhouse (IRE)** (bl) 10-1 *G Barfoot-Saunt* (xnb) 2 handlers; went 2nd aft 3;
                    ld 4-10 & 14 til hdd aft 15; 4l 4th nxt; wknd rap; pu 3 out

[570²]   F   **Oh So Droll** 7-4F *R Burton* Fell 1
         B   **Polly Buckrum** (12a) 14-1 *R Hodges* Lw; bd 1

[569¹]   U   **Take A Right** 20-1 *J Cornes* (xnb) Prom; 3rd when rfo 9
         P   **Whatamonkey** 20-1 *P Morris* Sn wl bhnd; t.o 5; pu 13

[673²]   P   **Yanto** (7a) 11-4 *Julian Pritchard* Prom; hld 3-4; 2nd to 8; 3l 3rd ½way; 4l 6th 15; wknd
                    nxt; bhnd when pu 2 out

OFFICIAL DISTANCES: 1½l, 7l **TIME:** 7min 09.3s
*Fences 9 and 17 omitted - fallen rider; Brown Wren finished fourth but was
disqualified when the rider failed to weigh-in; he was fined £40*

Belvoir

Garthorpe (RH 8F,18J) Sun, 2 Apr (GOOD)

867 Hunt   12 ran

[436¹]   1   **SQUARE ONE (IRE)** (5a) 3-1F *J Docker* 2nd/3rd to 11; went 2nd 15; ld on inside aft
                    3 out; r.o

[543⁷]   2   2   **Smart Rhythm** (5a) 20-1 *R Armson* Ld til hdd aft 3 out; rdn & ev ch last; one pce

[797⁴]   3   12   **Roly Poly (IRE)** 4-1 *M Mackley* (bf) Chsd ldrs; 5l 4th ½way; went 3rd 11-13; 6l 3rd
                    & rdn 3 out; no ex

[441U]   4   10   **Cheryl's Lad (IRE)** 16-1 *J Henderson* Went 2nd 4-7; 4l 3rd ½way; chsd ldr 10-15;
                    wknd 3 out

[367⁴]   5   10   **Zam Bee** 7-2 *D Thomas* Hld up; 7l 5th ½way; outpcd 13; wl bhnd 15

[443³]   C   **Deel Quay (IRE)** 20-1 *M Chatterton* In tch til carried out 6

[372⁶]   P   **Fair Farm Lad** 33-1 *Miss R Pask* Rcd wide; a bhnd; 20l 8th ½way; t.o & pu 3 out

[547¹]   P   **Huntsbydale** (5a) 5-1 *S Walker* Prom til pu & dism 6; lame

         U   **Just Might** 20-1 *D Cook* (xnb) Nt jw; last when blun & ur 3

[798U]   P   **Sands Point** 16-1 *N Kent* Bckwd; nd; 13l 6th ½way; wl bhnd 13; t.o & pu 3 out

| [794⁷] | P | | **Sheelin Lad (IRE)** 8-1 **C Vale** *Bckwd; blun 6; in tch til pu 7* |
| | P | | **Spin Lightly (IRE)** 25-1 **E Andrewes** *Bckwd; in tch til 14l 7th & rdn ½way; nt keen; t.o & pu 14* |

OFFICIAL DISTANCES: 2l, 10l **TIME:** 6min 21.0s **TOTE:** £2.80; places £1.30,£3.50,£1.70 **DF:** c/f

> *The stewards warned the rider of Huntsbydale to take more care in future not to cause any horse to run out; the rider of Roly Poly was later fined £100 by the Jockey Club Disciplinary Committee for riding in more than three Hunt Members races*

868 Confined, 12st   10 ran

[543¹]	1		**GILLONE** 3-1 **J Docker** *Mounted outside padd; tde; swtng; went 2nd 4-13 & agn aft 15; rdn & qcknd to ld app last; r.o wl*
[510¹]	2	3½	**Noughtonsixty (IRE)** (3x) 10-11F **B Pollock** *Ld to 2; ld 3 til hdd app last; nt qckn*
[771⁷]	3	10	**Ebullient Equiname (IRE)** 6-1 **S Morris** *Nt jw early; hld up; 6l 7th ½way; hdwy 12; rdn when lft 5l 3rd bend aft 15; wknd 2 out*
[787⁷]	4	runin	**Faraday** 66-1 **Miss S Phizacklea** *A bhnd; 15l 9th ½way; t.o 15*
[770⁷]	5	1	**Spuffington** 66-1 **Miss C Hall** *Chsd ldrs; 4l 5th ½way; lost plce 11; wl bhnd 13; t.o*
[794³]	6	3	**Quiet Mistress** (5a) 50-1 **S Charlton** *Rmdrs 8; 5l 6th ½way; rdn 12; wknd 14; lft 4th bend aft nxt; t.o*
[373⁷]	P		**Batcho Missile** 66-1 **A Sansome** *A bhnd; 8l 8th ½way; mist 12; pu 13*
[229³]	U		**Inch Cross (IRE)** (3x) 6-1 **R Hunnisett** *Prom; 2l 3rd ½way; mist 10; went 2nd 13 til 11 3rd when clipped heels of wnr & ur bend aft 15*
	P		**Piccolina** (5a) 66-1 **T Lane** *Rcd wide; ld 2-3; 3l 4th ½way; lost plce 12; 12l 6th when pu 14*
[234⁷]	P		**Tailormade** 33-1 **Mrs F Needham** *Ss; a wl bhnd; t.o & pu 12*

OFFICIAL DISTANCES: 4l, 8l **TIME:** 6min 16.0s **TOTE:** £3.00; places £1.40,£1.20,£1.60 **DF:** £5.10

869 Ladies Open   11 ran

[544¹]	1		**CITTADINO** 4-7F **Mrs J Dawson** *Lw; made all; r.o str*
[512ᵁ]	2	6	**Sabre King** (bl) 16-1 **Miss N McKim** *Sn prom; 7l 4th ½way; went 2nd & rmdrs aft 12; sn clr w wnr; ev ch 15; hrd rdn app 2 out; one pce*
[795³]	3	25	**Drummond Warrior (IRE)** 33-1 **Miss A Burton** *2nd til drvn along aft 12; sn outpcd; 10l 4th 15; went poor 3rd flat*
[427²]	4	1½	**Blayneys Privilege** (orbs) 50-1 **Miss T Habgood** *Chsd ldrs; 6l 3rd ½way; outpcd 13; 13l 3rd 3 out; no ex; eem flat*
[544³]	5	4	**Macfin (IRE)** 10-1 **Miss L Allan** *Sn outpcd & bhnd; 16l 7th ½way; wl bhnd 13; stayed on frm 3 out; fin str as usual*
[176⁴]	6	12	**Torus Spa (IRE)** 10-1 **Mrs S Hodge** *Nd; mist 1; 14l 6th ½way; wl bhnd 13; t.o*
[795⁶]	7	2	**Doctor Dunklin (USA)** 50-1 **Miss E Graham** *Sn wl bhnd; t.o 4*
[431⁸]	8	1	**Supreme Dream (IRE)** (5a) 14-1 **Mrs P Adams** *Prom til lost plce 6; 19l 9th ½way; t.o 13*
	9	runin	**Driving Force** 50-1 **Miss S Hutchings** *Bckwd; mist 1; sn wl bhnd; t.o 8*
	P		**Kenilworth Lad** 25-1 **Miss R Pask** *A bhnd; 17l 8th ½way; t.o & pu 3 out*
[506⁷]	U		**Pharlindo (IRE)** 7-1 **Mrs F Needham** *(xnb,pricker os) Hld up; 9l 5th ½way; outpcd 13; disp 10l 4th 15; 17l 5th & wkng when mist & ur 3 out*

OFFICIAL DISTANCES: 8l, 25l **TIME:** 6min 11.0s **TOTE:** £1.40; places £1.60,£5.00,£4.00 **DF:** £10.20

870 Mens Open, 12st   7 ran

[511¹]	1		**COPPER THISTLE (IRE)** (7x) 2-7F **R Hunnisett** *Sn prom & rcd wide; went 2nd 6-13; rdn 15; ld aft 2 out; just hld on*
[510⁶]	2	nk	**Fresh Ice (IRE)** 10-1 **R Barrett** *A.p; 2l 4th ½way; hrd rdn aft 15; kpt on wl u.p frm 2 out; went 2nd last; just failed*
[796⁷]	3	4	**Primitive Streak** (7x) (tt) 40-1 **R Abrahams** *Jw; hld up & sev posns; 1l 3rd ½way; ld 10 til hdd aft 15; stayed on one pce 2 out*
[607²]	4	12	**Broadway Swinger** (tt) 10-1 **S R Andrews** *(bf)Hld up; 2½l 5th ½way; hdwy 12; went 2nd nxt; ld aft 15; hrd rdn when mist 2 out; sn hdd; wknd last; eased when btn flat*
[510⁵]	5	8	**Teeton Builds** 8-1 **A Sansome** *(orbs) Ld to 10; lost plce u.p & 6l 5th 13; no ch 15*
[789⁴]	6	12	**Professor Longhair** 50-1 **P Bennett** *A wl bhnd & nvr gng keenly*
[549³]	7	15	**Damier Blanc (FR)** (bl) 100-1 **D Cook** *2nd to 6; lost plce 8; 7l 6th & drvn along ½way; nt o.s; wl bhnd 13; t.o*

OFFICIAL DISTANCES: hd, 3l **TIME:** 6min 22.0s **TOTE:** £1.30; places £1.50,£4.20 **DF:** £6.10

871 Restricted   20 ran

[517¹]	1		**UNION MAN** 3-1 S Morris 2nd to 6; 2½l 4th ½way; ld 12-14; ld app 3 out; r.o str
[232ᴾ]	2	3½	**Springfield Rex** 12-1 Mrs F Needham Hld up; 6l 9th ½way; hdwy 12; went 3rd aft 15; chsd wnr 2 out; stayed on one pce
[546⁴]	3	8	**Peacemaker (IRE)** 20-1 J Cornwall Sn prom; went 2nd 6; ld 7-11; ld & mist 14; hdd app 3 out; wknd app last
[372¹]	4	15	**Gangster** 7-4F R Cope Prom; 4l 6th ½way; went 2nd aft 12 til ev ch 15; wknd qckly 3 out
[462⁴]	5	s hd	**Stinging Bee** 7-1 S Walker Hld up; 5l 8th ½way; hdwy 11; 8l 5th & rdn 15; sn wknd
[548⁵]	6	10	**Cashel Green (IRE)** (tt) 50-1 M Hewitt Trckd ldrs; 4½l 7th ½way; rdn 13; 11l 6th 15; sn wknd
	7	3	**Colonel Wilkie** 50-1 Mrs E Staines Chsd ldrs til lost plce 6; 9l 11th ½way; wl bhnd 14; t.o
[542⁴]	8	½	**Nanda Devi** 40-1 Miss H Campbell Svs; hld up & rcd wide; 15l 16th ½way; t.o 15; some late prog (gvn no ch by rdr)
[689³]	9	½	**Mefein Boy (IRE)** 12-1 W Burnell Hld up; 10l 12th ½way; rdn 13; wknd & 15l 8th 15; t.o
[797ᵂ]	10	10	**Vimchase** 66-1 M Mackley A bhnd; 11½l 14th ½way; rdn 12; t.o
[792¹]	11	½	**My Friend Billy (IRE)** 12-1 Miss S Phizacklea Prom; 2l 3rd ½way; rdn & lost plce 12; 9th & wkng 14; t.o
[791ᴾ]	12	½	**Goforitmrsmulligan (IRE)** (5a) 40-1 E Andrewes Prom; 3l 5th ½way; ld 11-12; sn lost plce 14l 7th 15; sn wknd; t.o
	13	1	**Fearless Bertie** 12-1 A Sansome Swtng; hld up & a wl bhnd; 20th ½way; t.o
[548¹]	14	4	**Penrose Lad (NZ)** 14-1 W Tellwright Hld up & bhnd; hmpd 3; 11l 13th ½way; 10th & no ch 14; t.o
[547⁷]	15	8	**Pretty Boy George** 66-1 J Docker Ld to 7; wknd qckly 12; t.o
[546⁸]	P		**Cantango (IRE)** 50-1 J Turcan Chsd ldrs; lost plce & 7l 10th ½way; mist 10; wkng when blun 11; t.o & pu 13
[769²]	U		**Grove Victor (IRE)** 40-1 M Grange (xnb) Mists 2 & 4; 18th ½way; wl bhnd til mist & ur 11
[546ᴾ]	U		**River Ferdinand (IRE)** 40-1 R Barrett A bhnd; mist & rmdrs 2; hit 8; 14l 15th & rdn ½way; mist & ur 11
	P		**Tipping Away (IRE)** 66-1 D Flavin A bhnd; 19th ½way; t.o & pu 12
[232³]	P		**Vintage Choice (IRE)** 33-1 N Kent A bhnd; mist 6; 16l 17th ½way; t.o 13; pu 3 out

OFFICIAL DISTANCES: 3l, 5l **TIME:** 6min 18.0s **TOTE:** £5.30; places £2.00, £3.60, £3.30 **DF:** £63.00

872 Open Maiden 56&7yo, 12st   17 ran

[542²]	1		**NAUTICAL LAD** (7a) 4-1 J Docker Hld up; 8l 7th ½way; same 15; went 2nd aft 3 out; lft in ld 2 out; rdn out
[412⁴]	2	¾	**Hagon Beck** 10-1 W Wales Hld up; 8½l 8th ½way; stdy hdwy 12; 6½l 6th 15; chall when hmpd 2 out; hrd rdn & ev ch last; r.o
[548ᴾ]	3	8	**Light The Sky** 12-1 J Turcan Ld to 2; 2nd/3rd til lft in ld 11; hdd 15; rdn & ev ch 3 out; wknd flat
[517ᴾ]	5	30	**Spiderdore** 25-1 R Cope (xnb) Hld up; hdwy 6; pckd 8; 5l 4th ½way; mist 14; rdn & wknd qckly 3 out; t.o
	4d		**Well Matched** (7a) 16-1 E Andrewes Hld up & bhnd; 16l 13th ½way; short-lived eff 11; wknd 13; t.o; fin 33¾l 4th; disq - nt weigh-in
	F		**Bin Fishin (IRE)** (7a) 7-1 N Bloom 14s-7s; trckd ldrs; 6l 5th ½way; blun 11; went 3rd & mist 12; 8l 5th & wkng when fell 2 out; destroyed
[693ᴾ]	P		**Carr Dyke Castle** 33-1 M Mackley A bhnd; 20l 15th ½way; t.o & pu 12
[793ᶠ]	U		**Colonel Carats** 33-1 T Lane Tk ld when blun & ur 2
[123ᴾ]	P		**Fooled You (USA)** (tt) 20-1 A Sansome Prom til lost plce 6; 9l 9th ½way; mist 12; bhnd when pu 13
	P		**Goldsteane** (5a) 16-1 S Morris A bhnd; 18l 14th ½way; pu 11
	P		**Incbrush** 10-1 M Foley 16s-10s; bckwd; sn wl bhnd; t.o 5; pu 8
[672⁶]	U		**Irish Kinsman** 20-1 M Grange Mist 3; 15l 12th ½way; blun til blun & ur 11
	P		**Lady Mana Mou (IRE)** (5a) 20-1 M Hewitt Hld up; mist 9; lost plce & 10l 10th ½way; bhnd when pu 12
[412²]	P		**Nelsun** 3-1F B Pollock 5s-3s; went 2nd 3; ld 4-5; 4l 3rd ½way; blun 11; wknd & 6l 5th 15; bhnd when pu 3 out
[548⁴]	F		**Playlord** 4-1 N Docker Sn prom; ld 5 til hmpd by loose horse 11; 2nd til ld 15; fell 2 out
[542³]	P		**Semliki** 33-1 S R Andrews Lft in ld 2-4; blun 9; 7l 6th ½way; rdn & wknd 12; bhnd when pu 14

[435⁶]   **P**   **Slobadam** 25-1 Simon Robinson *Nd; 12l 11th & rdn ½way; lost tch 12; blun 14; t.o & pu 2 out*

OFFICIAL DISTANCES: ½l, 6l **TIME:** 6min 27.0s **TOTE:** £4.20; places £1.10,£4.00,£11.00 **DF:** £21.10
Well Matched finished fourth but was disqualified when the rider failed to weigh-in; he was fined £40

Cattistock

Littlewindsor (RH 7F,19J) Sun, 2 Apr (GOOD, GOOD to SOFT in places)

873 Hunt, 12st   2 ran

[521²]   **1**   **AVRIL SHOWERS** (5a,7x) 1-7F R Atkinson *Ld at mod pce; 2l up 4; jnd brief aft 14; qcknd & lft clr 3 out; sn in comm; easy*

      2   20   **Jolie Roslin** (5a) 6-1 S Hayes *Chsd rival; 3l down 5; jmpd slow & to lft sev times; disp ld brief aft 14; outpcd nxt; rdn & clsng when blun bad 3 out; nt rec*

OFFICIAL DISTANCE: 20l **TIME:** 7min 10.3s

874 Open Maiden 56&7yo (Div 1), 2m4f, 12st - 15J   10 ran

[329²]   **1**   **OKEFORD (IRE)** 1-2F R Walford *4l 4th 7; chsd ldr 10; sust rn to ld app 3 out; sn clr; stayed on wl*

      2   3   **Exmoor Forest** (5a) 33-1 B O'Doherty *(bh) Hld up in 8th 4; disp 15l 6th 9; stayed on to chse wnr frm 3 out; nvr able to chall*

[732F]   **3**   10   **L'orphelin** (7a) 7-1 M Shears *Disp ld 2-3; jmpd slow 4; lft in ld brief 5; 4l 3rd 9; ld aft 11 til wknd & hdd 15; stayed on one pce frm nxt*

      4   12   **I'm Convinced** 3-1 Miss P Gundry *Disp ld 2-3 & agn 6 til 11 up 9-nxt; ld agn brief 15; wknd nxt; bhnd frm 2 out*

      P   **Bogey Man** 25-1 C Heard *Disp ld 2-3; ld agn 4; sn hdd; disp ld 6-8 til ld 10-11; chsd ldrs til wknd qckly 3 out; pu nxt*

      R   **Golden Jester** (5a) 20-1 R Woollacott *(xnb) Nt jw; v sa & a last; t.o til crashed into wing & ur 9*

      P   **Never On Time** 16-1 M Wells *Pulling hrd & ld 3; qckly lost plce & rr nxt; jmpd slow 11; t.o & pu 13*

[723P]   **P**   **Playing For Money** (5a) 14-1 R Emmett *2 handlers; swtng; a towards rr; disp 15l 6th 9; wknd 11; t.o when clambered over 3 out & imm pu*

      P   **Sparkling Secret** (7a) 16-1 A Honeyball *Mists in rr; 2nd 9; 12l 5th nxt; chsd ldrs til wknd 13; bhnd when pu 2 out*

[628U]   **R**   **Vic's Girl** (5a) 50-1 S Hayes *Nov rdn; pulled hrd; rcd into ld aft 4; rn out to lft nxt (out of control)*

OFFICIAL DISTANCES: 4l, 12l **TIME:** 5min 33.5s
Last fence omitted - damaged

875 Open Maiden 56&7yo (Div 2), 2m4f, 12st - 16J   8 ran

      1   **PRIESTTHORN (IRE)** (7a) 5-1 R Young *Ww; last 4; 23l 6th 6; 4th 11 & lft 3rd nxt; stayed on str to ld aft 3 out; sn clr; easy*

[518³]   **2**   6   **The First One** 6-4F A Honeyball *8l 3rd 4; chsd ldr 10 til ld aft nxt; hit 13; mist & hdd 3 out; stayed on one pce frm nxt*

[732F]   **3**   8   **Montepulciano (IRE)** 16-1 N Mitchell *(xnb) Chsd ldr to 3; 28l 5th aft nxt; last 8; stayed on one pce & lft 3rd by defections 2 out*

      r   **Caundle Encore** (5a) 25-1 J Snowden *2 handlers; whinnying in padd; wrs; ref to rce*

[733³]   **U**   **Final Chance** (5a) 9-2 Miss C Tizzard *Chsd ldr; 6l 2nd 4-10; 2½l 3rd when blun & ur 12*

      F   **Speculative** 8-1 M Miller *Swtng; 4th when crashing fall 3*

[733P]   **P**   **Summer Pudding** (5a) 5-1 L Jefford *Last to 2; 15l 4th 4; chsd ldr aft 11; jmpd into ld 3 out; rn v wide & pu bef nxt*

[518P]   **P**   **Tolepa (IRE)** (5a) 33-1 L Tibbatts *Ld & sn clr; 6l up 4; 12l clr 7; pckd 9; hdd aft 11; wknd rap; t.o & pu 3 out*

OFFICIAL DISTANCES: 6l, 8l **TIME:** 5min 31.7s

876 Restricted, 12st   11 ran

[477³]   **1**   **POSSIBLE PARDON (NZ)** (bl) 10-1 N Mitchell *2 handlers; trckd ldrs; disp 5l 2nd 6; ld 14; stayed on str frm 3 out; sn in comm*

      2   10   **Brave Noddy (IRE)** 5-4F L Jefford *Chsd ldrs; 6l 4th 6; impd to 11 2nd 14 til mist 3 out; sn no ex u.p*

[728⁶]	3	hd	**Pallingham Lad (IRE)** (tt) 20-1 S Kidston *Hld up towards rr; prog to 4½l 4th 14; stayed on frm 3 out; nrly snatched 2nd on line*
[734ᵁ]	4	10	**Versicium (FR)** 7-4 Miss P Gundry (xnb) *Hld up in rr; impd to 5l 4th 7; chsd ldrs til wknd & r.o one pce frm 3 out*
[520¹]	P		**Basil** 6-1 D Alers-Hankey *Trckd ldrs; 9l 5th 6; 2½l 3rd 14 til wknd 3 out; 5th when pu nxt*
[524ᵁ]	P		**Cefn Woodsman** 200-1 Miss K Lovelace *Mounted late; swtng; 5th 3; sn lost plce & last 5; t.o 14 til pu 3 out*
[739¹]	P		**Jolification** (bl) 33-1 A Honeyball *Ld 2; sn 5l clr; 11 up 9 til hdd 14; wknd nxt; bhnd when pu 3 out*
[763ᵁ]	P		**Jug Of Wine** (5a) 33-1 S Hayes *A rr; mist 2; rdr waving nxt; mist 9; t.o & pu 11*
[524³]	P		**Lillooet (IRE)** (5a) (bl) 11-1 C Gordon *20s-11s; spurs; ld 1; 5l 2nd 6; sn lost plce & rr 10; pu aft 13; lacklustre eff*
[406ᴾ]	P		**Loxley-Lad** (tt) 66-1 G Richards *Mid-div; 10l 6th 6; wknd; bhnd & pu 14*
[639ᵁ]	P		**Mountain-Linnet** (13ow) 200-1 A Corrie *Mist 6; rdr nrly toppled off nxt; sn rr frm 6; t.o nxt; fncs adrift when pu aft 13*

OFFICIAL DISTANCES: 12l, nk TIME: 6min 24.7s

877 Ladies Open   7 ran

[636²]	1		**SLEW MAN (FR)** 2-1 Miss O Green (xnb) *Hld up in rr til impd to 5l 4th 7; jmpd into 2nd 12; 3l down 14; ld 16; drew clr 2 out*
[725ᴿ]	2	8	**Thinking Twice (USA)** 8-1 Miss T Newman *Jw; ld & sn clr; 4l up 7 til hdd 16; chsd wnr vain frm nxt*
[390⁴]	3	6	**Spring Marathon (USA)** (1ow) 12-1 Miss E Tory *Chsd ldrs to 3; 3l 3rd 5; disp 2nd 10-12; 6l 3rd 14; stayed on one pce frm 3 out*
[634¹]	4	2	**Stillmore Business** 6-1 Miss P Gundry *Chsd ldr frm 3; 2l down 5 til grad lost plce 11; 13l 5th 14; stayed on agn frm 3 out; nd*
[597⁴]	5	1	**Bullens Bay (IRE)** 40-1 Miss F Wilson *Last til 7l 5th 7; 8l 4th 14 til grad wknd frm 16*
[403ᴾ]	6	4	**Radio Days (IRE)** 100-1 Miss C Tizzard *8l 4th 2; disp 10l 6th 7; stayed on to 4th 3 out til wknd app nxt*
[680³]	7	30	**Blue Laws (IRE)** 6-4F Miss C Tuffin *10l 5th 2; disp 10l 6th 7; last & outpcd 13; t.o 3 out; walked in; imm dism; v lame*

OFFICIAL DISTANCES: 8l, 6l TIME: 6min 28.1s

878 Mens Open, 12st   3 ran

[404¹]	1		**HORUS (IRE)** (7a) 1-4F L Jefford *Hld up in last; 5l down 3; jmpd untidy 5 & nxt; chsd ldr aft 14; jmpd to ld nxt; sn clr frm 3 out; canter*
[766²]	2	12	**Mystery Aristocrat (IRE)** 9-2 R Tory *Chsd ldr til disp brief 6; 1½l down 8; jmpd to ld 9 til jnd 12-14; hdd nxt; outpcd frm 3 out*
[764³]	r		**Caundle Steps** 14-1 J Snowden *Set mod pce; 2l up 3; jnd brief 6 til jmpd slow & hdd 9; disp ld agn 12-14; sn wknd & 10l adrift nxt; t.o 16 til ref 2 out*

OFFICIAL DISTANCE: 15l TIME: 6min 35.1s

879 Intermediate, 12st   4 ran

[728¹]	1		**MINER'S BILL (IRE)** 8-15F L Jefford (xnb,bnh) *Lw; hld up in last; 12l down 3 til impd to 3rd aft 14; jmpd into 2nd nxt; chall 2 out; ld last; pushed out flat*
[522⁵]	2	1	**Cardinal Gayle (IRE)** 11-1 Miss D Harding *Ld; 3l up 3-6; chsd ldr til disp ld 12; 3l up nxt til jnd 2 out; hdd last; outrdn & no ex flat*
[654ʳ]	3	runin	**Young General** (bl) 11-1 A Honeyball *Nt jw; jmpd slow 3; chsd ldr to 7; mist 9; prog on inner to chse ldr 14; wknd 3 out & reluct; t.o nxt*
[636ᶠ]	4	12	**Lord Of The Rings** 8-1 Miss C Tizzard *8l 3rd 3; prog on outer to ld 7; jnd 12; hdd 14; last nxt & qckly outpcd; t.o frm 3 out*

OFFICIAL DISTANCES: 1l, 25l TIME: 6min 33.7s

880 Open Maiden (Div 1), 12st   9 ran

[738²]	1		**PENDRAGON** 4-5F N Mitchell *Hld up in last trio to 6; 9l 5th 7; chsd ldrs in 5½l 3rd 14; stayed on to 2l 2nd 16; ld nxt; sn clr; easy*
[738³]	2	5	**Frankie Muck** 9-1 Miss C Stucley (xnb) *Last; cat-jmpd 3; 13l 8th 8; prog to 9l 5th 14; staying on & chsd wnr vain frm 3 out; hld when mist last*
	3	30	**Artistic Plan (IRE)** 6-1 A Honeyball (xnb) *A towards rr; 11l 6th 7; rr & outpcd 14; t.o 16; staying on one pce when lft rem 3rd by defections 2 out*
[733ᴾ]	4	4	**Indian Muse** (12a) 33-1 M Shears *2 handlers; chsd ldr 3; 2l down 5-9; wknd to 6th 12; sn lost tch; t.o 3 out*
[559³]	P		**Madam Rose (IRE)** (5a) 4-1 L Jefford (xnb) *Ld; 5l up 7 til hdd aft 14; wknd rap 16 & stpd to nil; pu nxt*

	P	**Pulham Downe** (7a) 12-1 **R Walford** 2 handlers; a towards rr; mist 5; 15l last 7; bhnd when pu aft 13; school
[738ᴾ]	P	**Ruben James (IRE)** (bl) **Jeremy Young** Prom; 3l 3rd 5 til chsd ldr 13; ld aft nxt; 3l up 16; hdd nxt; wknd rap & pu nxt
[641³]	P	**Suba Lin** (5a) 20-1 **D Luff** 4l 4th 5; chsd ldr frm 12-nxt; 7l 4th 14; wknd 3 out; bhnd when pu last
	U	**Windyway** (5a) 16-1 **L Tibbatts** (xnb) 5½l 5th 5; grad lost plce & rr 10; last 14; t.o 16; disp rem 3rd & staying on stdly when blun & ur 2 out; broke fnce

OFFICIAL DISTANCES: 8l, 22l **TIME:** 6min 35.9s

881 Open Maiden (Div 2), 12st
8 ran

[732ᵁ]	1		**PEASEDOWN TOFANA** (5a) evensF **R Young** (xnb) Ww in mostly 6th to 6; 5l 5th nxt; gd prog 8; ld nxt; made rest; in comm 2 out
[520²]	2	2	**Prussian Steel (IRE)** 7-4 **T Greed** Trckd ldrs; 2½l 3rd 7 til chsd ldr 12; 2l down 14 til no ex u.p frm 2 out
[520⁶]	3	15	**Restless Native (IRE)** (5a) 9-1 **Miss P Gundry** Hld up in 7th to 7; 6½l 6th nxt; prog to 4l 4th 12; stayed on to 3rd 3 out; no ex nxt
[203ᴾ]	P		**Chilli Jo** 33-1 **Miss S Robinson** Chsd ldr til disp ld brief 5; 1½l 2nd 7; disp agn 8-nxt; chsd ldr til wknd 12; t.o 15 til pu 3 out
[409ᶠ]	P		**Indian Miller** (tt) 40-1 **M Green** 4th aft 2; 4l 4th 7; disp ld 8-9; 2l 3rd 12 til wknd qckly 3 out; pu nxt
[640ᴾ]	P		**Jazetason** 40-1 **M Woodward** Mostly 5th to 7; sn lost plce & rr frm 13; t.o 15; scrambled over nxt & pu
[635²]	P		**Spare On** (5a) 16-1 **A Michael** A last; 20l adrift 8; lost tch 14; t.o nxt; pu aft 3 out
[520⁵]	U		**The Frosty Fox (IRE)** 10-1 **M Miller** Ld til jnd brief 5; hdd 9; mist 12; 5l 4th when jmpd slow 14; 5th & hld when blun & ur 3 out

OFFICIAL DISTANCES: 3l, 14l **TIME:** 6min 34.2s

Hampshire
Hackwood Park (LH 7F,18J) Sun, 2 Apr (GOOD)

882 Hunt, 12st
6 ran

	1		**TEETON HEAVENS** (5a) 7-2 **D Dennis** Lw; settled off pce; clsd to 2nd 7; ld 14; clr aft nxt; eased flat (rdr much superior to rest)
[522⁷]	2	15	**Amaranthine** (5a) 14-1 **Mrs J Butler** (xnb) Spurs; lw; chsd clr ldr to 5; 14l 3rd 12; nd aft; went rem 2nd 2 out
	3	2	**Mere Class** 4-1 **Miss D Powell** Midfield & nd; 15l 4th 12; plodded on; mist 3 out; rdr nrly f.o nxt
[678³]	4	15	**Lake Of Loughrea (IRE)** 2-1F **N Wilson (Hants)** Ld & sn clr; 25l ahd 4; wknd 9; hdd 14; lost 2nd 2 out
	U		**Artful Aviator** (7ow) 12-1 **H Rowsell** Bckwd; ab 25l 4th til rfo 4
[325ᶠ]	R		**Feel The Power (IRE)** 5-2 **J Maxse** Stdd start; ab 30l last til rn out & ur 5; broke down

OFFICIAL DISTANCES: 10l, 1½l **TIME:** 6min 36.0s **TOTE:** £4.48 **SF:** £13.32

883 Confined, 12st
10 ran

	1		**GLENPINE (IRE)** (5a) 6-1 **C Weaver** 2nd/3rd til ld aft 2 out; sn forged clr; rdn out
[405ᴿ]	2	6	**Its Grand** 8-1 **R Lawther** Rn in snatches & sev posns; 9th when jmpd slow 5; went 4th & rdn 14; cajoled along to be 2nd at last; no ch w wnr
[676⁵]	3	8	**Peafield (IRE)** 3-1 **P York** Hit 4; cl up; 2nd/3rd frm 8; 2l 3rd & rdn app 2 out; sn outpcd
[33ᵁ]	4	6	**Ardbrennan** 5-1 **D Crosse** Ld 2; hdd aft 2 out; wknd qckly
[476⁵]	5	2	**Parman** (5x) 12-1 **R Dalgety** Nvr btr than midfield; 17l 6th 14; no prog aft
[476⁷]	6	5	**Cut A Niche** 10-1 **F Hutsby** Ld to 2; chsd ldrs; 7l 5th 14; sn wknd
[707ᶠ]	P		**Bilbo Baggins (IRE)** (bl) 25-1 **A Hickman** Jmpd rt & mist 2; last to 10; hdwy nxt to midfield; wknd agn in 20l 7th 14; pu 3 out
[461²]	P		**Nordic Spree (IRE)** (bl) 4-1 **N Benstead** Lw; hld up; hdwy in 4th aft 9; nt r.o & last by 12; t.o & pu aft 3 out
[737⁹]	P		**Ryder Cup (IRE)** (3x) 10-1 **G Maundrell** Chsd ldrs; 5th aft 9; outpcd 13; pu nxt
[634³]	P		**Scarba** (3x) 2-1F **C Wadland** Nvr btr than midfield; 8th 12; wl bhnd when pu 15; lame

OFFICIAL DISTANCES: 5l, 2l **TIME:** 6min 24.0s **TOTE:** £5.54 **SF:** £22.94

884 Mens Open, 12st
7 ran

[318¹]	1	**DRY HIGHLINE (IRE)** 7-4 **C Ward-Thomas** Lw; made all at fast gallop; sn 12l clr; 15l ahd when blun 14; 4l up & rdn when mist last; stayed on wl

[454^{3}] 2 4 **Rectory Garden (IRE)** (7x) 1-2F **R Biddlecombe** *Lw; jw; idly rdn in midfield; 19l 4th 11; went 17l 4th & rdn 14; chsd wnr app 2 out & tried to cl; no ex last*

[325^{U}] 3 12 **Arleneseoin (IRE)** (7x) 33-1 **P York** *Drpd out in last; hdwy in 3rd 7 & 2nd 12; nvr rchd wnr; releg 3rd & one pce app 2 out*

[454^{F}] 4 3 **Tarthooth (IRE)** (7x) (bl) 8-1 **D Crosse** *A chsng ldrs; 18l 3rd 11; rdn & no imp aft; 20l 4th & btn 14*

[611^{7}] P **Bally Parson** 33-1 **C Wadland** *Hit 3; chsd ldr to 4 & 6-9; sn wknd; t.o & pu 14*

[474^{P}] P **Golden Gunner (IRE)** 33-1 **P Young** *Went 2nd 4 til mist 6; 25l 5th & wkng 9; pu 13*

[324^{2}] P **Master Comedy** (bl) 33-1 **V Simpson** *Sn last; hit 3; t.o 7; broke down bad & pu 14*

OFFICIAL DISTANCES: 2l, 7l **TIME:** 6min 17.0s **TOTE:** £2.59 **SF:** £3.47

885 Ladies Open — 7 ran

1 **DAWN ALERT (IRE)** 5-2 **Miss C Grissell** *Lw; settled trckng ldrs; clsd on clr ldng pr frm 11; went 2nd 14; ld aft 3 out; rdly drew clr*

[772^{1}] 2 15 **Strong Medicine** 1-2F **Mrs E Coveney** *Jmpd rt; sn ld; rdn & hdd aft 3 out; fnd nil & a hld aft*

[685^{P}] 3 nk **Malihabad (IRE)** 6-1 **Miss A Goschen** *Midfield; 4th when blun 10; outpcd aft 12; 12l 4th & btn aft blun nxt; went 3rd aft 3 out*

[636^{4}] 4 12 **Khalidi (IRE)** 33-1 **Miss M MacGregor** *Chsd ldr 6-14; wknd qckly nxt*

[475^{3}] P **Beck And Call (IRE)** 10-1 **Miss T Cave** *Ld 1; chsd ldrs til 5th & rdn 9; nt r.o; blun & broke fnce 12; t.o & pu 14*

P **Panicked (IRE)** 20-1 **Miss S Wallin** *Prom early; last by 9; t.o 13; pu aft 3 out*

[765^{2}] P **Thomas Crown (IRE)** (tt) 16-1 **Mrs J Wilkinson** *Bhnd; hit 2; lost tch & jmpd rt 8; mist 12; 5th & t.o when climbed 13; pu nxt*

OFFICIAL DISTANCES: 10l, nk **TIME:** 6min 20.0s **TOTE:** £2.35 **SF:** £3.70

886 Countryside Alliance Club Members, 12st — 16 ran

[634^{2}] 1 **BALANCE** 6-1 **G Maundrell** *Sn 2nd/3rd; 4l 3rd aft 3 out; sust chall aft; ld flat; rdn clr*

[474^{3}] 2 6 **Winter Belle (USA)** (7x) (bl) 8-1 **R Shepherd-Cross** *Sn prom; 2nd 7; ld 11; jb rt 3 out & sn hdd; kpt on & ld agn last; sn hdd & wl outpcd*

[749^{4}] 3 2 **Castle Shelley (IRE)** 14-1 **C Weaver** *Settled 3rd/4th; mist 7; 10l 4th 11; eff 15; ld aft 3 out til rdn & hdd last; fin wkly*

[615^{7}] 4 12 **Hehas** 8-1 **C Wadland** *Nvr btr than midfield; 7th 11; 24l 5th 14; plodded on*

[585^{4}] 5 15 **Castle Arrow (IRE)** 3-1 **R Lawther** *Awkward & ld in start; detach in final trio; mod prog in 9th 11; nvr nr ldrs*

[558^{2}] 6 6 **Elle Flavador** (5a) 5-1 **Miss T Cave** *(xnb) Prom; 5th 9; same but outpcd 11; 25l 6th 14*

[632^{3}] 7 8 **True Chimes** 6-1 **J Owen** *(xnb) Tk str hld; ld to 11; 2nd & rdn 14; mist nxt; wknd rap 3 out*

[476^{P}] 8 1 **Stalbridge Gold** (5a,2ow) 6-1 **J Ferguson** *Chsd ldrs; 6th & outpcd when jmpd slow 11; 27l 7th 14; plugged on*

[429^{7}] 9 8 **Grange Prize** 25-1 **Miss K Henry** *Outpcd in final trio; t.o 12*

[682^{4}] 10 hd **Dromhana (IRE)** (7x) 33-1 **G Galpin** *A bhnd; 9th 11; t.o 12*

[632^{P}] P **Dick's Cabin** 25-1 **Miss A Goschen** *Sn t.o; pu aft 13*

[326^{8}] P **General Giggs (IRE)** (7x) (bl) 20-1 **Mrs E Smith** *A bhnd; 10th aft 9; pu qckly & dism aft 13*

[628^{4}] P **Glen Cherry** (7x) 8-1 **P Scouller** *Prom til lost plce in 7th 7; no ch 12; t.o & pu 15*

P **Gneveguilla** 25-1 **F Hutsby** *Tubed; midfield; 8th & strugg when mist 11; t.o when clambered 13 & pu*

[581^{4}] r **Kilmington (IRE)** (7x) 2-1F **J Barnes** *Unruly & ref to line up; tk no part*

[634^{6}] P **Silver Hill** (5a) 14-1 **Miss B Fear** *Jmpd slow & mists; towards rr & nvr gng wl; t.o & pu 13*

OFFICIAL DISTANCES: 3l, 2l **TIME:** 6min 21.0s **TOTE:** £3.00 **SF:** £27.38

887 Restricted, 12st - 17J — 8 ran

[427^{3}] 1 **FINAL ANALYSIS (IRE)** 2-1F **J Owen** *Hit 1; ld 3; 3l clr 14; drvn rest of way; hld on wl flat; all out; wl rdn*

[477^{P}] 2 ½ **Effie Wood** (5a) 4-1 **D Crosse** *Trckd ldrs; hmpd bend aft 9; went 2nd 14 til bad mist 3 out & rdr drpd reins; cl 3rd passing nxt; sust chall aft; r.o wl cl home*

[630^{1}] 3 5 **Jestastar** 5-2 **S Bush** *A.p; ld to 2; 2nd/3rd til tried to demolish 10; 3l 3rd app omitted 2 out; one pce aft*

[477^{r}] 4 5 **Ngala (IRE)** (5a) 25-1 **H Tett** *Hld up & bhnd; hdwy 7; 2nd 12; 1l 2nd & ev ch passing omitted 2 out; sn wknd*

[575^{7}] 5 30 **Another Comedy** 12-1 **N Earnshaw** *Prom til drpd back last 7; rmdrs 9; 8l last 12; hit nxt & lost tch; plodded on*

[247ᴾ]	6	12	**Suncech (IRE)** (5a) 6-1 **B Kendellen** (xnb) *Rn in snatches; last 4; went 2nd 7; mist 8; releg 4th 12; rdn & nt r.o aft 14*
[513⁶]	P		**Benova Boy** 5-1 **J Diment** *Ld 2-3; cl up til 5l 6th 14; wknd nxt; wl bhnd when pu last (impeded by rival ducking out)*
[748ᴾ]	R		**Melody Princess** (5a) 14-1 **A Charles-Jones** *Bhnd but in tch; rmdrs 9; 6l 7th 14; 6l 5th app omitted 2 out; one pce & btn when rn out & ur last*

OFFICIAL DISTANCES: ½l, 3l **TIME:** 6min 30.0s **TOTE:** £3.87 **DF:** £3.08
Fence 17 omitted - damaged

888 Open Maiden (Div 1), 12st - 15J
5 ran

[471ᴾ]	1		**CHANCELLORS VISION** 4-5F **J Barnes** *Hit 1; hld up & cl up; 5l 4th 14; mist 3 out; sn 2nd; rdn & trying to chall when jmpd v slow last; rallied to catch flagging ldr nr fin; fin lame*
[618ᴾ]	2	½	**Kyarra** (5a) 7-1 **C Wadland** *Fat; ld 5 til aft 9; ld agn 11; 4l clr aft 3 out; lft 4l clr agn last; blew up; rdn & just caught*
[710³]	3	1	**Sarenacare (IRE)** (tt) 5-1 **A Hickman** *Nt jw; in tch; jmpd slow 13; 6l last nxt; 1 1l 4th & outpcd 3 out; rallied last; kpt plodding on*
[629ᴾ]	4	4	**Meat Loaf (IRE)** 2-1 **A Charles-Jones** *V green & veering around; set crawl til climbed 5; ld agn 9-11; mist 14; ev ch til 10l 3rd & outpcd aft 3 out*
[472⁵]	5	10	**Mandy** (5a) 5-1 **G Weatherley** *Bckwd; jb 2; novicey; in tch in crawl til 4l 3rd 14; sn fdd; 15l last aft 3 out*

OFFICIAL DISTANCES: ¾l, 1l **TIME:** 6min 55.0s **TOTE:** £1.69 **SF:** £34.04
Fences 3, 10 & 17 were omitted from this and the last race - damaged

889 Open Maiden (Div 2), 12st - 15J
13 ran

[550⁵]	1		**FAIR ALLY** 16-1 **R Lawther** (xnb) *2 handlers; hld up & bhnd early; hdwy 7; 2nd aft 9; ld 11; qckly drew 12l clr aft 3 out; kpt on stdly; unchall*
[516ᴾ]	2	10	**Uncle Den** 16-1 **I Hudson** *2 handlers; sn wl bhnd in last trio; to 12; stayed on wl aft 3 out; went 3rd last & snatched mod*
[618ᴾ]	3	hd	**Ben Gilmore** 25-1 **J Diment** *Bit bckwd; a 2nd/3rd; ev ch til wnr kicked clr 3 out; one pce aft; 10l 2nd at last; dem flat*
[515³]	4	5	**Dillon** 5-2 **F Hutsby** *Ld to 2; chsd ldrs; 8l 5th 14; one pce & nd frm nxt*
[679ᶠ]	5	7	**Tonrin** 2-1F **P York** *Set off last but pulled hrd & rushed into ld 4; hdd 11; 4l 3rd 14; 12l 3rd aft 3 out; wknd qckly passing omitted nxt*
[763ᵁ]	6	12	**Spanish River** 9-1 **G Weatherley** *Mist 1; handy; 6th aft 9; wknd 13; 6th & btn nxt*
[207ᴾ]	F		**Check The Deck (IRE)** 8-1 **B Kendellen** *Unruly & reluct to line up; sis; nt jw in rr til nt much room & fell 13*
[763ᵁ]	P		**Gunerkillinghurst** 25-1 **D Dennis** *Jmpd slow 4; a toiling in rr; to 12; pu 14*
[471ᴾ]	P		**Last Gamble** 20-1 **G Maundrell** *Bckwd; chsd ldrs; 5th aft 9; wknd 11; to & pu 15*
[604ᴾ]	P		**Maltby's Charlie** 16-1 **A Tutton** *Mid-div til pu 10; lame*
[606⁴]	F		**Miss Mouse** (5a) 4-1 **A Charles-Jones** *Ld aft 2-4; lost plce to 7th aft 9; rallied to 6l 4th 14; fell nxt*
[763ᵁ]	R		**Regal Wolf** 16-1 **Miss A Goschen** *Lkd sulky & rn in snatches; lost tch 10; to 12; rn out & ur 14; demolished wing*
[629ᶠ]	P		**Snowshill Harvest (IRE)** (5ow) 14-1 **J Rice** (xnb) *Prsd ldrs; 4th aft 9; wknd 12; pu 14; bbv (prob nt for first time)*

OFFICIAL DISTANCES: 7l, hd **TIME:** 6min 31.0s **TOTE:** £3.67 **SF:** £22.20
The stewards cautioned two riders concerning their use of the whip: a) Ben Gilmore's for excessive use, and b) Uncle Den's for failing to give the horse time to respond

Ledbury
Maisemore Park (LH 7F,18J) Sun, 2 Apr (GOOD with SOFT patches)

890 Hunt, 12st
4 ran

[683ᴾ]	1		**RUSTY FELLOW** 7-2 **D Mansell** *Chsd ldr to 3; rdn 10; went 2nd 13; ld app 3 out; sn drvn clr*
[667²]	2	20	**Verulam (IRE)** 11-8F **Julian Pritchard** *Ld & jw; hdd app 3 out; 10l 2nd when hit nxt; v tired when climbed last*
[669¹]	3	40	**Playing The Fool** (5a) 4-1 **S Gordon-Watson** *Jmpd slow 4 & 7; cl up til last 13; lft 3rd 15; fin v tired & to*
[667³]	U		**Kingsthorpe** 3-1 **A Phillips** *Cl up; hit 4, 9 & 14; sn rdn & btn; 10l 3rd when bad mist & ur 15*

OFFICIAL DISTANCES: 20l, dist **TIME:** 6min 39.0s

891 Open Maiden 8yo&up (Div 1), 12st

15 ran

[617P]	1		**RAISE AND GAIN (IRE)** 5-1 R Burton *10s-5s; trckd ldrs; impd to 5th & blun 9; went 4th & gng wl aft 15; chall aft 3 out; drvn to ld app last; stayed on wl flat (made a noise - reportedly may require wind operation)*
	2	½	**Far From Perfect (IRE)** (5a) 12-1 A Wintle *Bhnd; 9th & prog when bad mist 14; str rn aft 3 out; went 2nd flat; kpt on wl*
[617U]	3	1	**Gorsey Bank (IRE)** 7-2F R Cooper *Hld up; hdwy 10 to 2nd/3rd frm 12; ld 3 out til drvn & hdd app last; nt qckn flat*
[339³]	4	10	**Autumn Blunder** 16-1 T Stephenson *3rd/4th til blun 13 & releg 5th; lost tch app 3 out*
[790⁷]	5	8	**Stormhill Farmer** 10-1 M Wall *Ld/2nd til app 9; 2nd/3rd til ld 15-nxt; sn wknd*
	6	8	**Make Up Your Mind (IRE)** 14-1 David Dennis *Trckd ldrs; ld app 9-15; wknd qckly frm 3 out*
[601P]	P		**Buckley House** 20-1 A Price *Pulled hrd; ld/2nd til app 9; wknd aft nxt; t.o & pu 2 out*
	P		**Champagne Thunder** (tt) 8-1 G Barfoot-Saunt *A strugg; pu 12*
[612F]	P		**Fountain Glen (IRE)** 12-1 D Mansell *A rr; mist 8; t.o & pu 11*
[487²]	P		**Itsfreddie** 4-1 J Jukes *Mid-div; hit 5; eff when mist 11; 4th & rdn 14; wknd aft nxt; 5th when pu 3 out*
[491P]	P		**Mystery Belle** (5a) 14-1 A St George *Rr div; mist 6; strugg when blun 13; pu nxt*
[517P]	P		**Peatsville (IRE)** 25-1 J Gasper *Cl up til wknd 7; t.o & pu 12*
[630⁴]	P		**Romany Chat** 4-1 A Martin *Sev mists in mid-div to ½way; 7th & strugg 14; pu 3 out*
	P		**Ruby Rosa** (5a,2ow) (vis) 20-1 M Harris *Mist 5; nvr nr ldrs; rr when pu 13*
	P		**Weldson** 25-1 J Trice-Rolph *Cl up til wknd & mist 7; mist nxt; pu 9*

OFFICIAL DISTANCES: ½l, 1l   TIME: 6min 53.7s

The stewards enquired into the improved form of the winner; they accepted the owner's explanation that its last run had been on firm ground and the horse had jumped badly; the owner of Gorsey Bank, whose passport was not in order, was fined £100

892 Open Maiden 8yo&up (Div 2, Part 1), 12st

9 ran

[744F]	1		**THE CROPPY BOY** 13-8F A Wintle *Ur start & jmpd 1 loose; jw but to lft; made all; drew rt away frm 3 out; unchall*
	2	30	**Seamac** 11-1 M Keel *Towards rr; outpvd 12; 12l 3rd when mist 14; jmpd slow nxt; sn t.o; lft 2nd last*
[618⁵]	3	12	**Strong Account (IRE)** 9-2 R Sealey *Midfield; strugg aft mist 7; jmpd v slow 11; sn t.o*
	U		**Don'tcallmegeorge** 10-1 D Phelan *10l 4th frm 5 til ur 7*
	U		**Final Quay** (5a) (bl) 5-1 M Carter *Tk keen hold; went 2nd aft 2; rn wide bend app 6; releg 4l 3rd & ev ch when ur 13*
[753P]	F		**Pennys Boy** 14-1 E Gretton *Slow j 2; mist 4; dist 8th when fell 6*
[618P]	r		**Red Spark** 14-1 E Walker *Settled 3rd; mist 12; sn 2nd; hit 14; outpcd when hit 3 out; 15l 2nd when ref last*
	U		**Royal Sweep** (3ow) 11-1 A Martin *Slow j; a last; t.o when ur 8*
[703P]	P		**Sister Jim** (5a) 12-1 D Mansell *Clumsy; chsd ldrs; went 4th 8; mist 9 & imm strugg; mist 10 & pu*

OFFICIAL DISTANCES: 20l, 10l   TIME: 6min 59.0s

893 Open Maiden 8yo&up (Div 2, Part 2), 12st

8 ran

[703P]	1		**MISSED CALL (IRE)** 11-2 J Jukes *Settled cl 3rd; hit 11; ld & mist 13; hdd nxt; ld gng wl aft 3 out; 10l clr nxt; rmdrs app last; unimpressive*
[704²]	2	12	**Spirit Prince** 3-1 Julian Pritchard *Swtng; ld; & rcd wide; hdd brief 13; hdd & rn wide bend app 2 out; no ch w wnr*
[669P]	U		**Di's Dream** (5a) 14-1 S Graham *Jmpd slow 1; 20l last by 3; prog 5 to detach 6th 10; 30l 4th when ur 14*
	U		**Geisha** (5a) 9-4F T Scudamore *Mostly 2nd; cl 3rd when mist & ur 13*
[337U]	P		**Humphrey** 14-1 N Oliver *Towards rr; drvn 9; sn strugg; t.o & pu 13*
	P		**Mcloughlin (IRE)** 11-2 M Rodda *A strugg; lft detach 5th ½way & 25l 3rd 14; fnce bhnd when pu last*
[790P]	P		**Ole Gunnar (IRE)** 11-1 M Wilesmith *Mist 1; numerous slow js & nvr gng wl in rr; last by 8; 40l bhnd when pu 13*
	F		**Take Achance On Me** 100-30 M Harris *Mist 4; 15l 4th 8; 10l 5th 10; strugg when fell 13*

OFFICIAL DISTANCE: 10l   TIME: 6min 52.0s

894 Restricted (Div 1), 12st

9 ran

[13⁴]	1		**GOAWAYOUTOFTHAT (IRE)** 4-1 Julian Pritchard *Confid rdn in rr; smooth prog to 5th 12; qcknd to ld 3 out; 3l clr app nxt; prsd agn bet last 2; r.o wl u.p frm last*

[580⁶]	2	2½	**Beyond The Stars** 7-1 M Rimell *Ld 5-12; cl 2nd/3rd aft; outpcd aft 3 out; rnwd eff & ev ch nxt; r.o game*
[484²]	3	12	**Market Springer (IRE)** 4-1 Miss B Williams *Hit 1; went 2nd/3rd 6 til ld 13; hdd 3 out; sn wknd; hit last*
[669⁹]	4	10	**Another Wag** (5a) 25-1 S Lloyd *Rr & outpcd 1st circ; detach 8th ½way; prog to 4th by 2 out; nvr nr ldrs*
[57¹]	5	nk	**Brodante King (IRE)** evensF T Scudamore *Jmpd slow early; chsd ldrs; prog to ld 12-13; 3rd when blun 14; nt rec; 4th & no ch when mist 3 out; tired & dem flat*
[612ᴾ]	P		**Kemiller (IRE)** 20-1 David Dennis *Prsd ldrs til 5th 7 rdn 13; outpcd when mist nxt; pu 3 out*
[741ᴾ]	P		**Mister McGaskill** 25-1 James Tudor *Ld to 5; lost plce aft mist 10; t.o to 14*
[513ᴾ]	P		**Rolcap** (bl) 14-1 J I Pritchard *3rd to 5; rdn & jmpd slow 6; reluct & t.o when climbed 7; pu 8*
[336ᴾ]	P		**Shadowgraff** (5a) 20-1 J Jukes *Midfield; rdn 8; nvr gng wl aft; lost tch 12; t.o when crawled over 14 & pu*

OFFICIAL DISTANCES: 1½l, 8l **TIME:** 6min 47.0s

895 Mixed Open, 12st
23 ran

[478¹]	1		**KERRY SOLDIER BLUE** 9-2 Miss P Jones *Jw; made virt all & set str pce; ll and 15; lkd vulnerable app 2 out; r.o str flat & sn clr*
[614²]	2	2	**Forest Fountain (IRE)** 5-4F Julian Pritchard *Hld up; eff frm 10 to 3rd 13 & 2nd nxt; str chall frm 2 out; lkd btn but str rn to press wnr when pckd last; just outpcd flat*
[683⁹]	3	20	**Lie Detector** 20-1 J Gasper *Cl up; outpcd 13; poor 5th 3 out; no ch aft*
[631⁹]	4	6	**Freedom Fighter** 14-1 A Martin *Prom til outpcd & jmpd slow 14; no ch aft*
[670²ᶜ]	5	12	**Topical Tip (IRE)** 11-1 S Joynes *Imm outpcd; 9th ½way; a bhnd*
[614⁶]	6	3	**Barton Black (NZ)** 10-1 M Keel *Mid-div; outpcd 14; poor 7th 3 out*
[474⁹]	7	25	**Bitofabuzz (IRE)** 10-1 D Birkmyre *A rr; nt jw; blun 5; t.o aft bad mist 15*
[749⁹]	P		**Blessed Oliver** (vis) 33-1 J Trice-Rolph *Chsd ldrs; 5th 10; sn wknd; pu 13*
[611⁶]	P		**Egypt Mill Prince** 20-1 E Walker *Wl bhnd ½way; t.o & pu 15*
	P		**Flashman** 33-1 Miss E Crawford *Mist 1; wl in rr til pu 12*
[611²]	P		**French Buck (IRE)** 10-1 M Rimell *Prom in 6th when blun 8 & 9; wknd frm 11; pu 13*
	P		**Furry Fox (IRE)** 50-1 G Barfoot-Saunt *Ld brief 2; prsd wnr 7 til app 14; sn wknd; t.o & pu 2 out*
	P		**Keep Clear (IRE)** 33-1 David Dennis *A strugg; t.o & pu 12*
	F		**Lancashire Legend** Ss; rn wide bend aft 2; bhnd when fell 5
	P		**Latest Thyne (IRE)** 25-1 T Stephenson *A mid-div; 7th & u.p 10; 15l 4th 3 out; pu nxt*
[599⁹]	P		**Obelos (USA)** 50-1 A Price *Mist 1; a t.o; pu 3 out*
	P		**Olympian** (bl) 8-1 A Wintle *Hld up; eff to 5th 13 & 3rd nxt; 12l 3rd & wkng when bad mist 3 out; poor 5th & eased when pu last*
	P		**Persian Sword** (bl) 40-1 M Wall *4th when nrly u.r 4; sn bhnd; t.o & pu 13*
[512ᵁ]	P		**Princess Lu (IRE)** 33-1 N Tucker *Nd; t.o by 10; fell 3 out*
[741¹]	F		**Raphael Bodine (IRE)** 20-1 F Windsor Clive *Rn out 2*
[463⁶]	R		**Rockville Pike** 50-1 D Mansell *2nd 5-7; 3rd 9; wknd rap; t.o & pu 14*
[684ᴾ]	P		**Rustic Gent (IRE)** 50-1 K Burke *A bhnd; t.o 5; pu 12*
[667⁷]	P		**Slightly Special (IRE)** 33-1 J Cook *A trailing; t.o & pu 12*

OFFICIAL DISTANCES: 3l, 8l **TIME:** 6min 50.0s

896 Restricted (Div 2), 12st - 17J
14 ran

[612⁴]	1		**FOREVER DREAMING (IRE)** (bl) 9-1 M Rimell *Chsd clr ldng pr; clsd & hit 10; ld aft 3 out; sn clr; rdn & r.o wl*
[491¹]	2	3	**Iron Pyrites** (5a) 4-1 S Lloyd *Mid-div; hit 11; 5th 14; eff 3 out; sn outpcd in 7l 4th; rallied to go 3rd aft 2 out; stayed on wl but a hld*
[516¹]	3	12	**Wrens Island (IRE)** 5-2 Miss L Sweeting *Ld to 3 out; sn wknd; lost 2nd aft nxt*
	4	15	**My Nad Knows** 12-1 J Baimbridge *Prsd ldr & clr of rest to 9; dem aft 3 out; wknd qckly*
	U		**Arzliza** (5a) 33-1 A St George *Mist 2; last by 5; t.o when ur 7*
[338⁷]	R		**Briary Boy** 25-1 A Price *Last pr til nt much room & rn out 6*
	P		**Brother Prim** 10-1 T Stephenson *Sn bhnd; t.o 10; pu 13*
[382⁹]	P		**Eau So Sloe** (bl) 12-1 K Burke *Strugg in rr; t.o 10; pu 13*
[513⁹]	P		**Hijacked** 6-1 A Wintle *3rd/4th chsng clr ldrs; wknd 12; 6th & btn when pu 14*
[595⁸]	F		**Itspantotime** (5a) 8-1 J Jukes *Mid-div; 9th when fell 5*
[618¹]	F		**More People (IRE)** evensF Julian Pritchard *Hld up; stdy rn frm ½way to 4th 14; 5l 5th when fell 3 out*
[684⁹]	P		**Tantara Lodge (IRE)** 33-1 R Cooper *Midfield; 6th 9; brief eff nxt; wknd frm 13; pu 15*
[734⁹]	P		**West Lutton** 20-1 D Phelan *Chsd ldrs til 7th & strugg 9; t.o & pu 13*

[546ᴾ] P   **Wotanite** 16-1 E Walker *Imm strugg & sev mists; t.o 10; pu nxt*

OFFICIAL DISTANCES: 4l, 6l   TIME: 6min 53.0s
Fence 13 omitted - fallen rider

897 Intermediate, 12st
11 ran

[485¹]	1		**THE ARCHDEACON (IRE)** 5-2 T Stephenson *Hld up; 9th ½way; smooth hdwy frm 12 to ld 3 out; hdd brief; ld & pckd 2 out; forged clr app last*
[741ᵁ]	2	4	**The Rural Dean (IRE)** 9-1 J Price *Hld up in rr; blun 9; mists 10 & 12; prog to 5th & mist 14; rdn & outpcd 3 out; rallied & stayed on wl frm 2 out; fin str flat*
[615³]	3	5	**Maggies Brother** 9-4F D Barlow *Rstrnd in mid-div; cl 6th; mist 12; prog frm 14 to ld aft 3 out; sn hdd; wknd app last; fin 4th; promoted*
[615⁴]	5	nk	**Tirley Missile** 11-2 Julian Pritchard *Mostly last to 11; prog in 7th app 3 out; sn no ex*
[543ᴾ]	6	8	**Perfect Finisher** 8-1 M Hawkins *Tk keen hold & prom; 4th mostly til wknd aft 15*
[683ᴾ]	7	10	**Mr Motivator** 7-1 T Scudamore *Ld 2 til aft 9; 2nd 11; wknd rap 14*
[567¹]	3d		**Star Changes** 5-1 J Jukes *Ld 12; hdd 3 out; nt qckn u.p; 5l 2nd last; short-headed for 4l 2nd; disq - nt weigh-in*
[447³]	P		**Black Serene (IRE)** (5a) 6-1 A Wintle *Walked to start; ld to 2; 2nd/3rd to 9; mist 12; rdn 13; wkng when blun nxt & lost tch; pu 3 out*
[615⁶]	P		**Executive Office (IRE)** 20-1 M Keel *Midfield; impd to 3rd 13; 4th when hit 15; wknd qckly frm nxt; pu 2 out*
[785⁸]	P		**Glendine (IRE)** 33-1 D Smith *Drpd rr 8; rmdrs 11; t.o & pu 13*
[195ᴾ]	P		**Secret Truth** (5a) 12-1 A Martin *Pulled hrd; sn 2nd/3rd; ld aft 9-12; 10l 7th when pu 3 out*

OFFICIAL DISTANCES: 1½l, 3l   TIME: 7min 00.0s
Star Changes finished third but was disqualified when the rider failed to weigh-in ; he was fined £50

898 Open Maiden 56&7yo (Div 1, Part 1), 12st
9 ran

[672²]	1		**TOM'S PRIZE** (7a) evensF S Joynes *Tk keen hold; ld to 2; 10l bhnd ldr when lft 20l clr 9; made rest; unchall*
	2	40	**Arctium** (5a) 16-1 G Barfoot-Saunt *Sa & 20l last by 3; 50l last 8; qcknd past btn horses frm 14 to 20l 2nd 3 out; no ex*
[528ᴾ]	3	25	**Lord Lard (IRE)** 14-1 M Rodda *Bhnd; jmpd slow 4; mist 5; lft 30l 3rd 9; mist 13; t.o 3 out*
	P		**Brother Simon** 20-1 M Wall *Rr div; t.o by 11; pu 13*
[450ᶠ]	U		**Cashew Crisis (IRE)** (7a) 16-1 David Dennis *12l 4th when hit 4 & ur*
	P		**Forestry** 3-1 A Wintle *Bhnd; some hdwy 7 & lft 20l 2nd 9; chsd wnr vain til wknd aft 15; pu 2 out*
[490ᴾ]	P		**Itsarchie** 8-1 J Jukes *Hld up & nd; lft poor 4th 9; 33l 4th 11; mist 14; no prog; pu 3 out*
[672ᵁ]	R		**Magni Momenti** (12a) 20-1 M Keel *Tore to ld aft 2; 10l clr frm 6 til followed loose horse past 9; cont in first but missing fncs til rdr finally able to pu 14*
[249ᴾ]	F		**Penaword** 5-1 J I Pritchard *Chsd ldr to 4; 20l 3rd 6; fell 7*

OFFICIAL DISTANCES: 25l, 20l   TIME: 7min 12.0s

899 Open Maiden 56&7yo (Div 1, Part 2), 12st
9 ran

[471²]	1		**CARBONADO** 6-4F P Pritchard *Cl 3rd/4th & a gng wl; chall & ld brief 3 out; ld agn nxt; gd l last; pushed along & r.o str; cheeky & impressive*
[391³]	2	s hd	**Cowanstown Prince** 7-2 Julian Pritchard *Ld to 4; cl 2nd til ld 13; hdd 3 out; sn ld agn; jnd 2 out-last; outj but drvn & stayed on wl; a hld*
[478³]	3	25	**Sibor Star** 5-1 J Cook *Slt ld 4-13; 4l 4th 15; 10l 3rd & outpcd aft 3 out*
[72ᴾ]	4	2 fncs	**Josameric** 20-1 T Stephenson *Sev mists; wknd to last by 10; sn t.o; climbed last 2 fncs*
[471³]	P		**Bramley** 16-1 A Martin *Cl up to 4; drpd back 6th 12; lost tch & mist 13; climbed nxt; pu 15*
	P		**Lord North (IRE)** (7a) 7-2 T Scudamore *Mid-div; prog to 4th ½way; 3l 3rd 15; pushed along & sn wknd; pu last*
[602ᴿ]	U		**Piccadilly Wood** 25-1 G Barfoot-Saunt *Mid-div & cl up; 6l 5th & lkng outpcd when mist & ur 14*
[618ᵁ]	P		**Sallioko** (5a,1ow) 12-1 D Barlow *Jmpd slow 3 & 4; rr aft; 20l 7th when pu 13*
	P		**St Helier** (12a,4ow) 25-1 D Stephens (Wales) *Novicey; mists & school in last pr; lost tch 10; t.o & pu 13*

OFFICIAL DISTANCES: s hd, 25l   TIME: 7min 12.0s
Mia Fort was withdrawn not under orders - vet's certificate

900 Open Maiden 56&7yo (Div 2), 12st - 17J   **15 ran**

[629²]	1		**QUIT THE CREEK** (5a) 7-1 A Martin *3rd/4th til 2nd 7; ld 8; a gng wl aft; rdn & kpt finding ex when chall frm 2 out; nt fluent last*
	2	1½	**Mr Max (IRE)** 4-1 M Wall *Ld to 3; prsd wnr aft; blun 12; rdn & kpt on game aft 3 out; a hld*
[489²]	3	5	**Cold Snap (IRE)** 11-2 A Wintle *Bhnd til hdwy frm 11 to chse ldng pr vain frm nxt; jmpd slow final mile; 9l 3rd 15; kpt on*
[618⁴]	4	4	**Moscow Squeaker (IRE)** 20-1 M Rodda *Wl bhnd 1st circ; hdwy frm 12; hit 13; 20l 5th 14; 12l 4th nxt; kpt on stdly*
[601ᵁ]	P		**Brookthorpe** (5a) 20-1 G Barfoot-Saunt *Tk keen hold; 2nd til ld 5-7; wknd rap 10; t.o & pu 13*
[703ᶠ]	F		**Cider Man** (7a) 4-1 Julian Pritchard *Midfield; 6th 8; prsng ldrs whem fell 10*
[491ᴾ]	P		**Double Steal** 14-1 J Jukes *Nt fluent in midfield; imp to 4th 11; sn wknd; t.o & pu 15*
[744ᴾ]	P		**General George** 25-1 D Mansell *Hdstrng & rstrnd; mist 5; 8th & rdn 11; pu 13*
[595ᴿ]	P		**Ivors Boy** 25-1 T Macfarlane *Rr til pu 7*
	P		**Master Banker** 20-1 J I Pritchard *Mists; prsd ldrs; 6th aft mists 9 & 10; sn lost tch; last when pu 15*
[673ᵁ]	P		**Penny Appeal** (5a) 20-1 M Scales *Mists; prom til wknd frm 8; pu 11*
	P		**Sales Dodger (IRE)** 20-1 R Hodges *Bhnd & nt jw; last 8; t.o pu 11*
	P		**Sandy Floss (IRE)** 7-2F S Joynes *Prsd ldrs; impd to 3rd 9; 12l 3rd 13; wknd tame nxt; pu 3 out*
[450ᴾ]	P		**Spartan Gold** (5a) 20-1 T Stephenson *A wl in rr; t.o & pu 13*
[630ᴾ]	U		**Strike Accord (IRE)** 20-1 D Phelan *Jmpd slow; trckd ldrs til blun & ur 10*

OFFICIAL DISTANCES: 1l, 5l   TIME: 7min 11.0s

Fence 17 omitted - fallen rider; the owner of Spartan Gold, whose passport was found to be not in order, was fined £100

Meynell & South Staffordshire
Sandon (RH 7F,19J) Sun, 2 Apr (GOOD to SOFT)

901 Hunt   **5 ran**

[564⁵]	1		**NATIVE COVE (IRE)** 3-1 L Hicks *Lw; ld 3; made rest; clr 12; easy*
[592¹]	2	20	**Ita's Fellow (IRE)** 4-7F M Prince *Ld to 3; chsd ldrs; 2nd 13; chsd wnr vain aft*
[297⁵]	3	runin	**Ballyhannon (IRE)** 16-1 Miss J Froggatt *Nt fluent; sn prom; wknd 14; t.o*
[592⁴]	4	30	**Royal Segos** 25-1 S Shaw *Bckwd; bhnd 6; t.o 13*
[588²]	F		**Quixotry** 9-2 Miss S Hogbin *Bhnd; t.o 4th & tired when fell last; winded*

OFFICIAL DISTANCES: 25l, dist   TIME: 7min 17.7s   TOTE: £4.00

902 Confined, 12st   **11 ran**

[589¹]	1		**HATTON FARM BABE** (5a) 9-4F Miss S Sharratt *Hld up; hdwy 13; went 2nd 3 out; ld app last; stayed on wl*
[589⁴]	2	3	**Brown Esquire** 20-1 S Prior *Bckwd; swtng; prom; ld 8; blun 2 out; sn hdd; nt fluent last; no ex*
[682ᵁ]	3	25	**Aly Daley (IRE)** (3x) 6-1 Miss A Price *Prom; niggled along & outpcd 14; kpt on agn app 2 out; nt trble ldrs*
[779²]	4	5	**Bishops Hall** 5-2 A Crow *Rr; mist 11; hdwy 13; mist 15; sn rdn; wknd aft 3 out*
[530⁴]	5	8	**Sun Surfer (FR)** 10-1 A Dalton *Midfield; drpd to rr 5; nd aft*
[587¹]	6	6	**Grunge (IRE)** 12-1 C Barlow *Hld up; bhnd & strugg frm 16*
[779³]	7	5	**Greville Again (IRE)** 20-1 A Wadlow *Prom; mist 4; ld app 7; hdd 8; jmpd slow 9; bhnd frm 13*
[781⁴]	8	7	**Batty's Island** (3x) 20-1 L Stephens *Bckwd; midfield; hmpd sltly 4; blun 12; lost plce nxt; sn rdn & bhnd*
[464⁴]	P		**Applefort (IRE)** 20-1 M Worthington *Swtng; chsd ldrs; drpd to midfield 6; hdwy & prom 11; wknd 16; t.o & pu 2 out*
[593¹]	P		**Caromisu** 10-1 B Foster *Towards rr; hdwy 7; lost plce 12; lsng tch when pu nxt*
[461⁴]	P		**Knock It Back (IRE)** (7x) 5-2 G Hanmer *Bckwd; ld; hdd app 7; still prom when pu 10*

OFFICIAL DISTANCES: 4l, 20l   TIME: 7min 11.1s   TOTE: £3.00

903 Mens Open   **7 ran**

[565¹]	1		**LORD HARRY (IRE)** 1-3F A Crow *Prom; ld 7-10; ld agn 14; drew clr app 3 out; easy*
[525²]	2d		**Class Of Ninetytwo (IRE)** (bl) 5-1 M Worthington *Swtng; prom; ld 3; jmpd slow & hdd 7; ld 10-14; wknd bef 3 out; fin 50l 2nd; disq - nt draw correct weight*

[670⁶]	r	**Circus Colours** 33-1 **L Hicks** *Reluct to rce; ref I*
[781⁹]	r	**Logical Fun** 33-1 **T Greenway** *Bckwd; in tch; tk clsr ord 8; lost plce & t.o 13; ref 15*
	P	
[334⁴]	P	**Royal Pocket** (5a) 10-1 **M Briggs** *(bf) Bckwd; bhnd; detach 8; t.o & pu aft 10*
		Saxon Fair 10-1 **G Hanmer** *(bf) Bckwd; ld to 3; handy til lost plce aft 6; wknd 14; t.o 3rd when pu nxt*
[436⁹]	P	**Timothy George (IRE)** 16-1 **D Sherlock** *Sn handy; lost plce 8; jmpd slow 10; sn t.o; pu aft 13*

OFFICIAL DISTANCE: Originally 25l **TIME:** 7min 18.3s **TOTE:** £1.20
Class Of Ninetytwo finished second but was disqualified for failing to draw the correct weight (weighed-in four pounds light having forgotten to put on the weight cloth); he was warned as to his future conduct

904 Ladies Open 7 ran

[590¹]	1		**THREE POTATO FOUR** 5-4F **Mrs M Barlow** *(bf) Swtng; hld up; nt fluent 4; impd to midfield 10; eff 14; ld 2 out; drew clr run-in*
[783³]	2	10	**Coolflugh Hero (IRE)** 20-1 **Miss S Hopkins** *Ld 2-9; handy til ld agn 3 out; hdd nxt; sn btn*
[566ᴮ]	3	3	**Killatty Player (IRE)** (5a) 7-1 **Miss C Thomas** *Prom; jmpd slow 8; ld 11; mist & hdd 3 out; wknd app nxt*
[301⁴]	4	15	**Celtic Who** 4-1 **Mrs C Ford** *Rcd keen in rr; hdwy & prom 7; ld 9-11; chsng ldrs when mist 15; wknd*
[615ᴮ]	P		**Just Marmalade** 20-1 **Miss J Williams** *Bit bckwd; swtng; in rr; jmpd slow 2; strugg when mist 12; t.o nxt; pu 2 out*
[590²]	U		**Tudor Lodge (IRE)** (5a) 3-1 **Mrs K Diggle** *Ld to 2; lost plce 4; rallied 12; strugg when blun & ur 15*
	P		**Very Daring** 14-1 **Miss S Sharratt** *Prom; lost plce app 7; sn bhnd; t.o 13; pu 16*

OFFICIAL DISTANCES: 8l, 3l **TIME:** 7min 14.8s **TOTE:** £1.50

905 Dodson & Horrell PPORA Club Members 9 ran

[533¹]	1		**WEJEM (IRE)** 6-4 **A Dalton** *Ld to 2; prom but jmpd slow; ld 16; r.o game when prsd run-in*
[781¹]	2	¾	**Sharsman (IRE)** 11-8F **A Crow** *Swtng; prom; ld 2; hdd 16; ev ch run-in; r.o*
[589ᴾ]	3	6	**Fair Farm Boy** 33-1 **B Foster** *Nt jw in rr; hdwy to chse ldrs 14; one pce frm 2 out*
[370³]	4	5	**Cormeen Lord (IRE)** 10-1 **J Sharp** *Lw; in tch; outpcd 3 out; rallied nxt; no ex last*
[532⁴]	5	5	**Offley Lucielastic** (5a) 20-1 **S Prior** *Hld up in tch; tk clsr ord 12; wknd frm 3 out*
	6	5	**Freestyler (IRE)** (tt) 6-1 **G Hanmer** *Lw; in rr; hdwy 9; lost plce nxt; eff agn 3 out; ev ch when mist 2 out; sn wknd*
[369ᴾ]	P		**Blue Wave (IRE)** 12-1 **D Sherlock** *Bckwd; trckd ldrs; lost plce aft 13; t.o & pu last*
[437ᶠ]	P		**The Bee's Castle (IRE)** 40-1 **R Armson** *Pckd 1; a rr; strugg 12; lost tch 13; t.o & pu 14*
[566⁵]	U		**The Boiler White (IRE)** 25-1 **Miss J Froggatt** *Swtng; prom til blun & ur 4*

OFFICIAL DISTANCES: 1l, 4l **TIME:** 7min 31.5s **TOTE:** £1.60

906 Confined Maiden, 12st – 17J 17 ran

	1		**DENNEY'S WELL (IRE)** (7a,2ow) 6-1 **G Hanmer** *Hld up; outpcd 14; hdwy agn frm 3 out; r.o to ld cl home*
[672⁴]	2	s hd	**Fanion De Nourry (FR)** 9-1 **J Merry** *Prom; ld aft 2 out; eased & hdd cl home - rdr fined*
[786⁵]	3	15	**Kings Choir** 10-1 **Mrs C Boyes** *Bckwd; handy til wknd aft 3 out*
[588ᶜ]	U		**Caherlow (IRE)** 5-2F **B Foster** *6s-5/2; midfield; pckd 11; blun & ur 13*
[569ᴾ]	P		**Colonels Hatch** 20-1 **D Sherlock** *Bckwd; midfield; jmpd slow & bhnd 7; t.o 13; pu 14*
[548ᴾ]	P		**Copper Thorn** (5a) 20-1 **T Greenway** *Bckwd; midfield; bhnd frm 10; t.o & pu 13*
[616³]	P		**Cosa Fuair (IRE)** 10-1 **A Dalton** *Bckwd; cl up til wknd 15; t.o & pu last*
[569ᴾ]	P		**Crunch Time (IRE)** 10-1 **L Stephens** *Bckwd; handy; lost plce & rmdrs 6; bhnd when mist 15; t.o & pu last*
[693⁶]	P		**Educate Me** 6-1 **J Burley** *Lw; a rr; t.o 14; pu last*
[547³]	F		**Erik The Viking** 7-2 **R Armson** *Hld up; hdwy 6; lft in ld nxt; hdd aft 2 out; rdn when fell last; winded*
[777³]	C		**Fountain Street (IRE)** 6-1 **R Burton** *Midfield; mists 13 & 15; hdwy aft 3 out; ll down & chall when hmpd by loose horse & crashed thro wing last*
[569ᴾ]	C		**Ishereal (IRE)** 10-1 **S Prior** *Bckwd; sn ld; carried out by loose horse 7*
[570⁴]	F		**Lady Nevada (IRE)** (5a) 10-1 **Miss S Hopkins** *Prom til fell 4*
[593ᴾ]	P		**Mister Pimpernel (IRE)** 10-1 **J Downes** *A bhnd; t.o & pu last*
[547³]	C		**On The Bone** (5a) 4-1 **L Hicks** *Handy til carried out by loose horse 7*
	P		**Rural Gossip** 20-1 **M Worthington** *Ss; t.o 8; pu aft 10*

[590⁷]　U　　**Sharp Embrace** 20-1 **Miss S Rodman** *Blun & ur 2*

OFFICIAL DISTANCES: s hd, 20l　**TIME:** 7min 30.6s　**TOTE:** £12.00
*Fences 11 & 18 omitted - fallen rider; the rider of Fanion De Nourry was fined
£50 for failing to ride right out and losing the race; the stewards enquired into
an incident at the last fence and decided no further action was required*

Percy
Alnwick (LH 9F,18J)　Sun, 2 Apr (GOOD to FIRM)

907 Hunt, 12st　　　　　　　　　　　　　　　　　　　　　　**4 ran**

[421⁷]　1　　**BUCKAROO** (5a) 2-1 **Mrs A Tweedie** *2 handlers; swtng; trckd ldng pr; 5l last aft 3; prog to disp ld brief 9 & agn 11; hdd aft 13; ld nxt; 4l up app 15; qcknd & sn clr; mist 2 out; 10l clr when hit last; stayed on*

[499³]　2　10　**Blackchesters** 4-7F **J Walton** *Hld up in last pr; 4l off pce 9; disp 3l 3rd 13; outpcd aft nxt; kpt on u.p; 12l 3rd aft 15; tk 2nd 3 out; rdn & no imp*

[717ᶠ]　3　1　**Wylup** (2ow) 14-1 **H Humble** *2 handlers; trckd ldr; til 2l 3rd & pushed along aft 9; disp 3l 3rd 13; outpcd aft nxt; 10l 2nd aft 15; dem nxt; kpt on*

　　　P　　**Fish Quay** (7x) 20-1 **Miss S Lamb** *(bf) Ld til hdd aft 9; sn ld agn; jnd 11-13; hdd 14; 8l 4th & wkng aft; 25l last 3 out; t.o & pu 2 out*

OFFICIAL DISTANCES: 15l, 1l　**TIME:** 6min 21.0s
Racing was delayed by 50 mins - second doctor failed to arrive

908 Restricted　　　　　　　　　　　　　　　　　　　　　**7 ran**

[620³]　1　　**HIDDEN ISLAND** 8-1 **Miss H Delahooke** *Hld up in rr til prog app 8; cl 2nd 11; disp ld brief nxt; 2l 2nd & gng wl aft 13; ld app 2 out; qckng clr when stumbled last; stayed on wl; comf*

[689⁹]　2　3　**Go Nomadic** (tt) 9-1 **P Atkinson** *Chsd ldrs; 2½l 3rd 4; 8l 5th 9; prog app 15; ev ch 2 out; sn outpcd; tk 3l 2nd at last*

[301⁷]　3　¾　**Carnaven** 5-2 **A Robson** *Mist 1; 5l last 2; 4l 4th 9; prog to cl 3rd 11; 4l down & ev ch 2 out; 6l 4th at last; fin wl*

[423³]　4　1　**Blyth Brook** 4-5F **C Storey** *Evens-4/5; oht; in tch; 4l 5th 3; 1l 2nd 7; disp ld 12; sn ld; hdd aft 3 out; 4l 2nd & ev ch til outpcd app last; dem flat*

[719ᶠ]　5　8　**Border Reiver** (IRE) 6-1 **W Renwick** *Prom; 2l 3rd 5; 3l 3rd aft 9; prog to disp ld app 3 out; sn btn & eased; 10l 5th app last; virt pu flat*

[659ᵖ]　6　10　**Strong Debate** (IRE) 14-1 **N Crookston** *Unruly padd; pulling & sn prom; disp 2l 3rd 5; 6l 3rd; stdly lost tch; 20l last 15; kpt on*

[419ᵖ]　U　　**Givemeyourhand** (IRE) 20-1 **T Davidson** *Swtng; ld/disp; 1l up 4; jnd 7-9; hdd aft 12; sn wknd; 15l 6th 15; wl bhnd when mist & ur 2 out*

OFFICIAL DISTANCES: 5l, ½l, 2l　**TIME:** 6min 20.0s

909 Open Maiden 56&7yo (Div 1), 2m4f - 15J　　　　　　　**11 ran**

[695²]　1　　**LADYLANDS** (5a) 3-1 **D Raw** *Ld; 3l up 3; 1l ahd 11; jnd 3 out; duelled in ld til r.o wl to ld nr fin*

[379²]　2　nk　**Tom's Man** 5-4F **A Robson** *6/4-5/4; a handy; 3l 3rd 6; 1l 2nd 11; prog to disp ld & lkd to be gng best in sust duel frm 3 out; r.o flat; hdd & outpcd nr line*

[712⁴]　3　8　**Magical Poitin** (IRE) (5a) 11-2 **G Armitage** *Chsd ldrs; 4l 3rd 8; 3l 3rd 11; outpcd aft nxt; hit 3 out; 6l 3rd 2 out; kpt on*

[499ᵖ]　4　20　**Alizarine Blue** 33-1 **Miss L Kendall** *(bh) Prom; 2l 4th 9; outpcd aft nxt; 8l 4th 12; 12l 4th 2 out; kpt on*

[664ᶠ]　5　6　**The Dust Buster** 20-1 **H Trotter** *(bf) Rr; strugg 10; 25l off pce nxt; sn t.o; fin wl*

[426ᵖ]　6　8　**Naughty Feelings** 12-1 **T Scott** *Mid-div early; sn rr & strugg 6; 30l down 12; t.o when mist last*

　　　P　　**Blushing Heugh** 10-1 **Miss M Bremner** *In tch til pu aft 6*

　　　P　　**Camden Carr** (IRE) 10-1 **T Glass** *Fat; chsd ldrs; 5l 4th 6; 4l 5th 9; wkng nxt; 25l down aft 11; t.o & pu 3 out*

[664⁴]　P　　**Chubby Morton** 12-1 **R Morgan** *(xnb) A rr; lost action & pu aft 6*

　　　P　　**Solway Spice** (12a) 6-1 **Miss L Hislop** *Imm t.o; climbed 2; 25l bhnd aft 3; pu aft 7*

[500⁶]　F　　**Stygian Star** (IRE) (5a,2ow) 10-1 **M Smethurst** *Prom; 1l 2nd 6; cl up when fell 9*

OFFICIAL DISTANCES: nk, 10l, dist　**TIME:** 5min 26.0s

910 Open Maiden 56&7yo (Div 2), 2m4f - 15J　　　　　　　**11 ran**

[425⁷]　1　　**SUNNYCLIFF** 11-4 **C Storey** *(xnb) Lw; in tch in mid-div; prog to disp ld 10; 1l up 3 out; qcknd 8l clr aft 2 out; fiddled last; eased flat; comf*

[500⁴]	2	4	**Valley Hopper** (7a) 5-1 B Lusted *Rr; 12l 8th 7; prog aft 12; 15l down 3 out; fin wl; tk 2nd on line; nt trble wnr*
[718⁵]	3	nk	**Test Of Loyalty** 7-1 A Robson *Chsd ldrs; 8l 4th 3; 4l off pce 6; 15l 5th & outpcd 3 out; fin wl; nt trble wnr*
[624ᴾ]	4	½	**Henah Hill** 16-1 L Bates *A.p; 11 2nd 3 out; ev ch til 5l down & outpcd app nxt; nt pce to chall aft; wknd & dem nr line*
[400ᴾ]	5	6	**Tiger King** 10-1 C Mulhall *(xnb) Ld/disp; 2l up 4; jnd 6; sn hdd; 3l 3rd 10; ev ch til outpcd app 3 out; kpt on*
[627ᶠ]	6	6	**Jolly Minster** 2-1F P Atkinson *Trckd ldrs; disp ld brief 6; 3l 3rd aft; cl up til outpcd 3 out; kpt on*
[624ᶠ]	7	8	**Carefree Love** (IRE) 7-1 T Glass *Ld/disp early; 4l off pce 6; ev ch 12; sn wknd*
[712ᶠ]	8	10	**Christiemouse** (5a) 7-1 Miss L Hislop *Mid-div; 8l 7th 6; 15l off pce nxt; sn strugg; t.o 12*
[664ᴾ]	P		**Bonnie B** (5a) 33-1 P Strang Steel *A rr; 20l down 6; strugg aft; t.o 9; pu 3 out*
[500⁸]	P		**Strictly Hard** (5a) 14-1 L Morgan *Lw; a rr; lsng tch 9; t.o & pu 3 out*
[718³]	P		**Stronacroibh** 6-1 R Morgan *A rr; strugg 9; t.o & pu 11*

OFFICIAL DISTANCES: 5l, hd, nk **TIME:** 5min 24.0s

911 Mixed Open, 4m, 12st - 24J   7 ran

[621ᵁ]	1		**SCRABO VIEW** (IRE) 14-1 Miss S Ward *Trckd ldr; 2l 2nd app 3; sn chsng runaway; 25l 2nd 12; disp 25l 2nd 15; 15l 2nd 17; hdwy to ld 3 out; stayed on*
[424²]	2	2½	**Shingle Beach** (IRE) (bl) 11-8F J Mactaggart *Chsd ldrs; 20l 6th 6; disp 25l 2nd & pushed along 15; ld brief app 21; hdd & 11 down 3 out; nt pce to chall; 2l down & no imp 2 out*
[497⁵]	3	15	**Hooky's Treat** (5a) 7-1 Miss J Hedley *Chsd ldng pr; 3l 3rd 2; 27l 3rd 15; 12l 4th 21; kpt on; nt pce to chall*
[496ᴾ]	P		**Ballyboden** 12-1 F Arthur *Chsd ldrs; 15l 4th 3; disp 20l 4th 6; pu & dism aft 9*
[492¹]	F		**Dunnellie** (5a) 7-2 A Robson *Chsd ldrs; disp 20l 4th 6; 26l 4th 15; disp 15l 3rd when fell 18*
[623ᶠ]	P		**Prime Style** 4-1 D Raw *(xnb) Tde; ld; 25l ahd 12; stdly came back to pack; 10l up 19; 4l ahd & wkng 21; sn hdd; 3l 3rd & hit 3 out; tired & bhnd when bad mist 2 out; pu last*
[713ᶜ]	P		**Tropnevad** (bl) 16-1 B Lusted *Ld to start; a rr; 20l last 3; mist 4; 30l last 15; hit nxt & strugg aft; t.o & pu 21*

OFFICIAL DISTANCES: 2l, 25l **TIME:** 8min 51.0s

912 Confined, 12st   7 ran

[359ᴾ]	1		**HIGHLAND MONARCH** 4-5F C Storey *(xnb) Trckd ldng pr; 5l 3rd 10; prog to 3l 2nd 14; jmpd to ld 2 out; 2l up last; stayed on wl; comf*
[717³]	2	3	**The Green Fool** (1ow) 6-1 H Humble *(xnb) Ld/disp til ld 7; 1l up & pckd 9; 3l up 13; hdd 2 out; kpt on game flat; a hld*
[714ᵁ]	3	25	**The Caffler** (IRE) 3-1 Miss R Ramsay *Mid-div; disp 10l 5th 5; 10l 4th app 15; prog to 5l 3rd app 3 out; sn outpcd & nd*
	4	4	**Mischievous Andy** (IRE) 5-1 Mrs K Hargreave *(xnb) Mid-div; 5l 5th 11; sn 12l down & outpcd; 10l 5th when mist 15; wknd; mist last*
[717ᴾ]	5	1	**Unor** (FR) (1ow) (tt) 7-1 D Reid *(bf,boh)Swtng; ld/disp til 2l 2nd 7; wknd 13; 4th 15; sn lost tch; mist last; drvn out*
[717ᴾ]	6	15	**Reve De Valse** (USA) (bl) 10-1 Miss V Burn *A rr; 10l last 7; 6l last app 9; lost tch aft nxt; 25l last 15; t.o*
[496⁵]	U		**Heavenly Citizen** (IRE) (1ow) 8-1 Miss E Edminson *A rr; mist & ur 5*

OFFICIAL DISTANCES: 5l, dist, 1l **TIME:** 6min 14.0s

913 Confined Maiden (Div 1), 12st - 17J   9 ran

[624⁴]	1		**ROSCOE BURN** 7-2 R Morgan *Trckd ldr til ld brief 4; 2l 2nd & mist 9; ld 12; made rest; 3l up & mist 2 out; kpt on wl*
[719ᴾ]	2	2½	**Harry Laws** 4-1 T Scott *Ld til hdd 12; 6l 2nd 14; 3l 2nd 2 out; kpt on; mist last; no ex flat; btr for rce*
[665²]	3	½	**Gallant Major** 9-4F A Robson *Chsd ldrs; 10l 4th 4; 10l 3rd 9; prog to 6l 3rd & ev ch 2 out; kpt on wl flat; a hld*
[714⁶]	4	8	**Snitton South** 3-1 J Walton *7/2-3s; tubed; a rr; 22l last 6; some prog 13 to 4th aft nxt; 10l 4th 15; sn 12l down; kpt on wl*
[625ᴾ]	5	5	**Paperback Writer** (5a) (vis) 6-1 M Henney *Oht; a rr; 15l 6th 5; 15l 4th 11; kpt on frm 15*

[423^P]	P		**Beach Patrol (IRE)** 8-1 Miss J Hedley *Prom; 3l 3rd 3; 7l 4th 4; 15l 4th & wkng 10; t.o 15; pu nxt*
[493^P]	F		**Castle Bay (IRE)** (tt) 6-1 W Renwick *(bf)Stdd start; chsd ldng pr; 6l 3rd 4 til fell 7; dead*
	P		**Jupiter Lord** 10-1 C Storey *Jmpd v slow 1; rr; 15l 7th 6; lost tch & pu 11*
	P		**Springfield Prince (IRE)** 12-1 L Morgan *Rr; 20l 8th 6; 25l down 9; 25l last 11; t.o 15; pu 2 out*

OFFICIAL DISTANCES: 4l, 1½l, 10l **TIME:** 6min 20.0s

914 Confined Maiden (Div 2), 12st   10 ran

[425²]	1		**THE PEELER (IRE)** 11-10F W Renwick *Oht; handy; prog 15; cl 2nd 3 out; ld 2 out; rmdrs aft; rdn app last; stayed on wl; wl rdn*
[624³]	2	2	**Big Bark (IRE)** 7-1 H Norton *(xnb) Chsd ldrs; 5l 5th 3; eff 15; 2l 4th 3 out; ev ch when blun nxt; 2l down last; stayed on; went 2nd flat*
[139¹]	3	2½	**Donard Son (IRE)** (tt) 8-1 T Glass *(bf)Unruly padd; in tch til 6l 3rd 13; ld 3 out; hdd & ev ch nxt; no ex last; dem flat*
[663^P]	4	10	**Regar (IRE)** 14-1 L Morgan *Chsd ldrs; prog 15 & 11 3rd 3 out; ev ch til hit nxt; wknd qckly aft; virt pu flat & walked in*
[718⁶]	5	runin	**Mesling** 20-1 J Walton *Chsd ldrs; 2l 2nd 10; hit nxt; outpcd 13 & sn lost tch; 25l 6th app 3 out; kpt on*
[425⁴]	P		**Briar Rose (IRE)** (12a) 6-1 J Ewart *Unruly padd; a rr; 8l 9th 8; wknd to 25l last 11; t.o & pu 3 out; dism*
	P		**Jack Dory (IRE)** 25-1 D Da Silva *Trckd ldrs; 8l 3rd 3; outpcd 10; lost tch 13; pu aft 15*
[365⁵]	P		**Tekroc (IRE)** 20-1 R Nichol *(xnb) Fat; swtng; ld/disp early; 3l 2nd 3; sn wknd; 20l down when pu 8; bbv*
[664^P]	F		**Tipsy Laird (IRE)** 6-1 R Morgan *Tde; ld/disp til ld 3-10; 7l 5th & wkng when fell hvly 3 out; winded*
	P		**Willoughby Moss** (xnb) 4-1 C Storey *6s-4s; oht; cl up; 2½l 3rd 9; 2l 2nd 11; cl 3rd when pu & dism aft 15; lame*

OFFICIAL DISTANCES: 2l, 4l, dist **TIME:** 6min 23.0s

Kelso (LH 8F,19J)

Mon, 3 Apr (SOFT, GOOD to SOFT in places)

915 Dryburgh Abbey Hotel Buccleuch Mdn HC   8 ran

[686²]	1		**MIDSUMMER GLEN** 12-00 7-4F M Armytage *Blun 3; hdwy to chse ldr app 8; lft in ld 12; 2l clr & shkn up when blun last; pushed along & kpt on game flat*
[712^P]	2	2	**Border Glory** 11-07 25-1 P Maitland-Carew *3rd early; stdd 4; hdwy 12; disp 2nd & ev ch frm 3 out; tried to rally flat; no imp final 100yds*
[465⁵]	3	27	**Smiddy Lad** 11-09 6-1 W Renwick *Hld up; stdy hdwy 9; disp 2nd & ev ch 3 out-nxt; wknd qckly last*
[358²]	4	27	**Fiscal Policy** 11-07 8-1 R Trotter *Hit 7; chsd ldr til app 8; pckd 11; blun 13 & nrly ur; sn last & strugg; t.o*
[495¹]	U		**Bow Tie** 11-07 5-2 R Morgan *Blun & ur 2*
[419²]	U		**Charlieadams (IRE)** 11-11 (4) 7-1 J Muir *Ld & clr to 8; 3l ahd when mist & ur 12*
[663¹]	P		**Lord Levi (IRE)** 11-07 20-1 F Windsor Clive *Mists; cl up; went 2nd 14 til wknd aft 16; pu last*
[714^P]	P		**Senora D'Or** 11-02 66-1 Miss L Bradburne *In tch; wknd & hit 10; t.o & pu 13*

TIME: 7min 01.7s **TOTE:** £1.90; places £1.10,£5.90,£1.50 **Ex:** £38.60 **CSF:** £37.48 **Tri:** £not won

916 J. Rutherford (Earlston) HC   6 ran

[584¹⁴]	1		**MANHATTAN RAINBOW (IRE)** 11-09 3-1 W Renwick *Made most frm 3; mist 14; 5l lst clear; hrd drvn flat; stayed on game; all out*
[686¹]	2	5	**Balisteros (FR)** 11-07 11-8F Miss J Wormall *Chsd ldrs; hit 13; went 2nd & ev ch 3 out; kpt on game frm last; a hld*
[227^F]	3	23	**Floruceva (IRE)** 11-02 4-1 J Tate *Tk keen hld; nt fluent 1; jmpd slow 3; w ldr; ld 11-13 & 14-15; wknd app 2 out*
[582³]	4	1	**Minella Gold (IRE)** 12-00 10-1 S Swiers *Chsd ldrs; 4th when mist 16 & rdn; sn 6l adrift; btn when hmpd bad & nrly fell 2 out*
[465¹]	P		**Donnegale (IRE)** 11-07 (bl) 4-1 G Brewer *Bhnd; nt fluent 2 & 4; jmpd slow 11 & rdn; sn lost tch & nt keen; t.o & pu last*
[717⁶]	U		**Kings Lane** 11-07 50-1 M Clayton *Mists in rr; hdwy app 5; hit 8; lost tch 9; t.o 12; blun & ur 16*

TIME: 6min 58.6s **TOTE:** £4.50; places £1.70,£1.60 **Ex:** £10.80 **CSF:** £7.75

Newcastle (LH 11F)

Tue, 4 Apr (GOOD to SOFT, GOOD in places)

917 Northumberland Hussars HC

7 ran

[584³]	1		**TRADE DISPUTE (IRE)** 11-13 (4) 4-11F **G Tuer** *Hld up in tch; hdwy to 5l 3rd 12; 2nd nxt; ld on bit app 17; hit nxt; shkn up & went clr flat; v easy*
[586¹]	2	6	**Coole Abbey (IRE)** 11-11 7-2 **W Renwick** *Ld til app 17; ev ch 2 out; 2l down last; wknd flat*
[662¹]	3	1	**Snapper** 11-11 14-1 **Miss S Forster** *Chsd ldrs; went 2nd 7; hit 8; dem 13; outpcd 15; drvn & stayed on agn frm 2 out*
[496⁴ᵈ]	4	dist	**Lindon Run** 11-03 (tt) 150-1 **T Davidson** *Chsd ldr to 7; rdn 10; outpcd 11; lost tch 14; t.o*
[691³]	5	dist	**Juke Box Billy (IRE)** 11-03 (tt) 50-1 **W Burnell** *Bhnd; rdn & outpcd 10; wknd 13; t.o*
[662²]	P		**Castleroyal (IRE)** 11-05 14-1 **C Mulhall** *3rd mostly to 11; lost plce qckly & pu 12*
[716⁴]	P		**Mullingar (IRE)** 11-03 33-1 **W Morgan** *Jmpd slow 2; in tch til mdbrks 6; mist 7; drvn 9; wknd 10; t.o 11; pu 13*

TIME: 6min 23.1s **TOTE:** £1.50; places £1.50,£1.10 **Ex:** £2.30 **CSF:** £2.03

918 Town & Country Nov HC

12 ran

[496¹]	1		**TEA BOX (IRE)** 12-00 9-4 **S Swiers** *Jw; prsd ldr; ld app 7; drew 6l clr 3 out; rdn & hld on wl flat*
[686⁵]	2	1½	**Strathmore Lodge** 11-04 4-1 **W Renwick** *Mists; hld up; hdwy & prom 10; eff when hit 2 out; drvn & nt qckn final 100yds*
[661⁶]	3	1¾	**Steel Rigg (IRE)** 11-07 25-1 **M Clayton** *Mists; 9th when blun 6; went 2nd 9; one pce frm 3 out; dem app last*
[396⁴]	4	10	**Mandril (IRE)** 12-00 25-1 **N Tutty** *Tk keen hld in rr; hdwy & 5th when blun 11; eff 14; sn outpcd*
[622³]	5	12	**Riverside Run (IRE)** 11-09 10-1 **A Robson** *Prom; 3rd 6; lost plce nxt; strugg 8; nd aft*
[717⁵]	6	9	**Tin Cup (IRE)** 11-09 (2) 100-1 **W Morgan** *Hld up; hdwy & 4th 8; drvn aft 13; sn strugg*
[626⁴]	7	dist	**Asked To Leave (IRE)** 11-02 25-1 **I Bennett** *Prom; 4th 6; lost plce 7; rallied 9; wknd bef 13; t.o*
[794⁵]	P		**Fontaine Fables (IRE)** 11-07 (bl) 100-1 **M Bennison** *Chsd ldrs; blun bad 5; wknd 10; t.o aft 13; pu aft 2 out*
[586²]	U		**Gymcrak Tiger (IRE)** 11-07 evensF **R Clark** *Hmpd bad by rising faller & ur 1*
[465⁷]	F		**Just Ned** 11-09 (2) 50-1 **M Douglas** *Fell 1*
[663ᵖ]	F		**Rock On Bud (IRE)** 11-07 (tt) 40-1 **T Davidson** *Ld til app 7; rdn & wknd 10; t.o & pu 14*
[361ᵖ]	F		**Tofino Swell** 11-02 33-1 **J Ewart** *Fell 1*

TIME: 5min 32.2s **TOTE:** £3.70; places £1.30,£1.50,£3.00 **Ex:** £15.40 **CSF:** £11.61 **Tri:** £272.90

Ascot (RH 10F,15J)

Wed, 5 Apr (SOFT)

919 Hat and Picture Mahonia HC

11 ran

	1		**CASTLE COURT (IRE)** 11-09 12-1 **V Keane** *Ld to 5; ld 7-9 & agn nxt; 6l clr 13; blun 14 & rdn; hdd flat; drvn to rgn advant nr line (won on jockeyship)*
[459¹]	2	shhd	**Mr Snowman** 11-11 100-30 **Mrs T Hill** *Settled midfield; eff & pckd 9; clsd to 2nd 3 out; ev ch frm nxt til ld flat; outrdn & hdd final strides; unlucky*
[583¹]	3	4	**Flying Maria** 12-03 5-2F **L Jefford** *Hld up in midfield; hit 8; went 3rd 11; hrd rdn & nt qckn app last*
[583⁶]	4	9	**Minella Derby (IRE)** 11-09 16-1 **T Gibney** *Lw; settled towards rr; drvn to cl app 13; sn lost plce*
[481⁴]	5	3	**Royal Mountbrowne** 11-11 16-1 **Miss E Jones** *Lw; tk keen hld w ldr; ld 5-7; jmpd v slow 8; rjnd ldr 10; 2nd til app 3 out; 4th & wkng when mist last*
[463¹]	6	2	**Major's Law (IRE)** 11-13 7-1 **J Owen** *Swtng; bhnd; 10th 6; nd frm 12*
[736ᵖ]	7	24	**Panda Shandy** 11-02 66-1 **H Froud** *Bhnd; str rmdrs aft 1; 9th & rdn aft 6; rmdrs aft 9; t.o 12*
	P		**Caballus (USA)** 11-11 25-1 **F Hutsby** *Bckwd; w ldrs til mist 4; rap drpd back last 6; t.o 7; pu 8*
	P		**Destin D'Estruval (FR)** 12-03 7-2 **C Weaver** *Hld up in midfield; mist 8; eff 11; sn btn; t.o & pu last*
	P		**Funcheon Gale** 11-07 50-1 **R Barrett** *Prom; 3rd 6; ld brief 9; wknd qckly nxt; t.o & pu 2 out*
[463⁵]	P		**Wot No Cash** 11-09 50-1 **R Lawther** *Hld up & bhnd; strugg aft mist 9; t.o 12; pu 13*

TIME: 5min 11.6s **TOTE:** £13.80; places £2.40,£1.30,£1.30 **Ex:** £40.00 **CSF:** £46.89 **Tri:** £152.90

Ludlow (RH 9F,19J)
Wed, 5 Apr (GOOD)

920 Abberley Hall Old Boys Association HC   6 ran

[684¹]	1		**GRIMLEY GALE (IRE)** 11-13 2-7F R Burton *Ld to 2; 2nd til ld agn 8; mist 12; sn prsd; drew 6l clr 2 out; easy*
[460³]	2	12	**Shafi (IRE)** 11-07 5-1 D Mansell *Hld up; hdwy 12; mist nxt; went 2nd 15; sn rdn; outpcd 2 out*
[580ᵁ]	3	13	**Lakeside Lad** 11-09 33-1 R Cooper *Settled 3rd; mist 5; went from 11-14; wknd app nxt*
[667²]	4	18	**La Kabyle (FR)** 11-06 14-1 A Wintle *Pulled hrd in 4th; nt fluent 4; lost tch 11*
	P		**Gallant Lord (IRE)** 12-00 100-1 A Sansome *Bhnd; rdn & strugg app 7; lo to 12; pu 16*
[448¹]	P		**Military Man** 11-11 33-1 A Phillips *Ld 2-8; 2nd to 11; rdn when mist 12; jmpd poor aft; wknd 14; blun 3 out; to & pu last*

TIME: 6min 12.6s **TOTE:** £1.40; places £1.00,£2.20 **Ex:** £2.20 **CSF:** £1.83

Aintree (LH 7F,17J)
Thu, 6 Apr (GOOD)

921 Martell Fox Hunters HC   26 ran

[153¹]	1		**BELLS LIFE (IRE)** 12-00 11-2 D O'Meara *Trckd ldrs; 4th 15; clsd to ld passing omitted 2 out; stayed on wl; rdly*
[687¹]	2	9	**Secret Bay** 12-00 7-2F B Pollock *Jw; mid-div; outpcd frm ½way & sn plenty to do; hdwy aft 3 out; stayed on str frm last; nvr able to chall*
[470⁵]	3	¾	**Carley Lad (IRE)** 12-00 (tt) 33-1 L McGrath *Jmpd bold; cl up; ld 7; 12l clr 11; 8l ahd 15; hdd passing omitted 2 out; kpt on game at one pce*
	4	7	**Shuil's Star (IRE)** 12-00 100-1 J Jukes *Chsd ldrs; 7th 15; stayed on frm nxt; unable to chall*
[586³]	5	2	**Howayman** 12-00 (bl) 25-1 T Oates *Lft in ld 1 til aft 4; prom; mists 9 & 10 (Bechers); 5th & outpcd 15; nd aft*
[584¹⁰]	6	2	**Little Buck (IRE)** 12-00 16-1 K Culligan *Cl up; ld 6-7; mist 10 (Bechers); 2nd 15; wknd aft nxt*
[582²]	7	1	**Hiltonstown Lass (IRE)** 11-09 25-1 R Walford *Sn prom; went 12l 2nd 12 (Canal Turn); 3rd 15; wknd aft nxt; btn when blun last*
	8	1½	**Spot Thedifference (IRE)** 12-00 9-2 P Fenton *Blun 3 (Chair); eff 10 (Bechers); 8th 15; nd aft*
[691⁴]	9	10	**Albert Blake** 12-00 (tt) 50-1 R Burton *Sn bhnd; passed btn horses frm 3 out*
[764¹]	10	11	**Court Master (IRE)** 12-00 33-1 O Ellwood *Chsd ldrs; wkng when blun 14; strugg aft*
	11	2	**Donickmore (IRE)** 12-00 33-1 E Gallagher *Chsd ldrs; mist 10 (Bechers); 6th 15; sn wknd*
[590³]	12	3	**The Parish Pump (IRE)** 12-00 33-1 Mrs C Ford *Chsd ldrs to 10; sn strugg*
[677¹]	13	hd	**Young Nimrod** 12-00 (tt) 50-1 Miss C Grissell *Cl up; ld 4-6; wknd aft 10*
[592²]	14	9	**Commercial Artist** 12-00 100-1 W Renwick *Tubed; sn bhnd; to*
[735²]	15	23	**Flapjack Lad** 12-00 66-1 J Barnes *Chsd ldrs til wknd aft 12; mist 14; to*
[463²]	16	18	**Halham Tarn (IRE)** 12-00 (tt) 33-1 T Gibney *Ss; a bhnd; to*
[819⁴]	17	14	**Tilt Tech Flyer** 12-00 100-1 Miss F Wilson *Hmpd bad 1; sn to*
	18	dist	**Garrison Commander (IRE)** 12-00 100-1 P Townsley *Sn bhnd; to 5*
[644²]	B		**Coolvawn Lady (IRE)** 11-09 33-1 Miss P Jones *Bd 1*
[714¹]	r		**Fordstown (IRE)** 12-00 66-1 J Alexander *Jmpd slow in rr; blun 3; to when ref 7*
[61ᴾ]	F		**Gale Toi (IRE)** 12-00 20-1 P York *Bhnd til fell 10 (Bechers)*
[795³]	P		**Just Bruce** 12-00 100-1 N Kent *Nvr nr ldrs; to & pu aft 3 out*
[802¹]	F		**Last Option** 12-00 11-2 Mrs F Needham *Fell 1*
[537²]	F		**Rossell Island (IRE)** 12-00 (bl) 25-1 T Scudamore *Ld til fell 1; broke back; dead*
[579¹]	F		**Struggles Glory (IRE)** 12-00 16-1 D Robinson *Fell 1*
[460²]	F		**Valiant Warrior** 12-00 12-1 K Cooper *Fell 1*

TIME: 5min 40.1s **TOTE:** £5.20; places £2.20,£2.40,£15.00 **Ex:** £20.00 **CSF:** £21.33 **Tri:** £5036.30
The second last fence was omitted - fallen horse

Taunton (RH 8F,17J)
Thu, 6 Apr (GOOD to SOFT, SOFT in places)

922 Royal Devon Yeomanry HC   13 ran

[851¹]	1		**SAINT JOSEPH** 12-00 5-1 Miss S Young *Bhnd w ldrs gng frantic pce; 16l 6th & prog 10; chall 14; ld aft 2 out; drvn & r.o str; game*

[683²]	2	2	**Ardstown** 11-09 5-4F **F Windsor Clive** _Lw; hld up; 14l 5th & hdwy 10; lft 2nd 12; rdn & ev ch frm 3 out til nt fluent last; nt qckn u.p_
[735³]	3	11	**Funny Farm** 11-11 12-1 **M Miller** _Sn 2nd; ld 8; hdd & lft in ld 12; edged lft & rdn app 3 out; hd aft nxt; sn wknd_
[56³]	4	14	**Ballyea Boy** (IRE) 11-07 (bl) 50-1 **R Webb-Bowen** _Midfield & nd; 20l 7th 10; rdn 12; plodded on_
[314³]	5	1½	**Duchess Of Tubber** (IRE) 11-02 66-1 **Mrs M Hand** _Rdn & rem in last pr; t.o 8_
[725⁴]	6	nk	**Mr Golightly** 11-09 25-1 **Mrs J Reed** _Lw; nt fluent; ld to 2; 8l 3rd 10; wknd 13_
[255⁴]	U		**Drumbanes Pet** 11-07 66-1 **David Dennis** _Ur 1_
[799⁷]	P		**Frown** 11-11 (bl) 66-1 **T Doyle** _Set furious gallop 2-8; 2nd til jmpd v slow 11; sn lost plce; t.o & pu 3 out_
[729⁷]	P		**Mosside** 11-09 66-1 **N Harris** _Reluct in rr; u.p 4; t.o 7; pu 12_
	F		**Professor Strong** (IRE) 11-07 (bl) 33-1 **P Cranmer** _Chsd clr ldng pr to 7; wkng rap in rr when fell 9_
	P		**Space Cappa** 11-07 33-1 **Miss V Stephens** _12l 5th aft 3; hit 6; wknd to 35l 8th 10; t.o nxt; pu 3 out_
[725³]	F		**Ticket To The Moon** 12-00 3-1 **Julian Pritchard** _Tkn stdly as ldrs set furious pce; prog to 10l 4th 10; clsd to ld & fell 12_
[651¹]	U		**Well Armed** (IRE) 12-00 (bl) 5-1 **L Jefford** _Lw; 5th when mist & ur 3_

TIME: 6min 33.1s **TOTE:** £5.50; places £1.30,£2.20,£2.60 **Ex:** £12.30 **CSF:** £11.62 **Tri:** £64.40

Sedgefield (LH 8F,21J)
Fri, 7 Apr (GOOD, GOOD to FIRM in places)

923 Stanley Thompson Mem HC
9 ran

[384ᶠ]	1		**JOINT ACCOUNT** 11-12 15-8F **Mrs F Needham** _(martin) Tk keen hld in 3rd til ld 11; 10l clr when mists 13 & 14; 20l ahd 2 out; unchall_
[682³]	2	25	**Brownrath King** (IRE) 11-12 16-1 **N Tutty** _2nd til ld 7-9; disp ld to 11; bumped along & lost tch nxt; chsd wnr hopelessly frm 3 out_
[682¹]	3	14	**Majority Major** (IRE) 11-10 (bl) 5-2 **T Glass** _Ld to 7 & frm 9; hdd 11; outpcd 14; lost poor 2nd 3 out_
[807⁷]	4	29	**Yornoangel** 11-05 25-1 **P Aspell** _Chsd ldrs; 5th & drvn 10; outpcd nxt; t.o aft 2 out_
[682⁶]	P		**Chaps** 11-12 14-1 **N Wilson** _Sn strugg; mist 4; t.o 6; pu 12_
[686⁶]	P		**Eastlands Hi-Light** 11-05 9-1 **T Morrison** _Sn wl bhnd; 20l 5th 11; disp 35l 3rd 2 out; broke down & pu last_
[465⁸]	S		**Flashlight** 11-12 20-1 **S Swiers** _Mists; bhnd til slpd up aft 9_
[419⁹]	F		**Mandika** 11-09 50-1 **C Wilson** _Midfield & in tch til fell 9_
[805¹]	P		**Private Jet** (IRE) 11-05 15-2 **R Clark** _Sn wl bhnd; t.o when blun 6; pu 7_

TIME: 6min 57.9s **TOTE:** £2.10; places £1.10,£2.80,£1.80 **Ex:** £31.70 **CSF:** £24.56 **Tri:** £35.60

Aintree (LH 7F,19J)
Sat, 8 Apr (GOOD, GOOD to FIRM in places)

924 Martell Reserve Nov HC
10 ran

[584⁴]	1		**LAKEFIELD RAMBLER** (IRE) 12-00 6-1 **Miss P Gundry** _Jmpd bold most of way; made all; hrd prsd frm 3 out; r.o game; all out_
	2	1	**Father Andy** (IRE) 12-00 14-1 **G Elliott** _Hld up in tch; impd to 4th 11; went 2nd 14; ev ch when blun last; r.o u.p_
[580¹]	3	½	**Finnow Thyne** (IRE) 12-00 16-1 **D Dunsdon** _Prom; prsd wnr 9-14; rdn app 2 out; 3l 4th last; r.o_
[584⁷]	4	½	**It's Himself** 12-07 6-1 **A J Martin** _Hld up & wl bhnd; 20l last 8; brief eff 9; hdwy agn when mists 13 & 15; 7l 4th when hit nxt; chall on bit 2 out; rdn & ev ch last; fnd litle flat_
	5	dist	**Mister Softie** (IRE) 11-05 11-1 **B Hamilton** _Hld up; hit 8; eff 11; 3rd when blun 12; mist 13; outpcd 15; rallied to 6l 5th 3 out; wknd nxt; virt pu flat_
[685²]	6	30	**Chatergold** (IRE) 12-00 (bl) 50-1 **D Dennis** _Prom; jmpd slow 5; rdn & lost plce 11; blun nxt; t.o 16_
[469²]	F		**Danegeld** (IRE) 12-00 (bl) 50-1 **N Wilson** _Mist 1; hld up early; went prom 5; lft 2nd 6; fell 7_
[584²]	F		**Real Value** (IRE) 12-00 3-1 **B Hitchcott** _Tk keen hld; jmpd into 2nd 5; fell 6_
[799¹]	U		**Satchmo** (IRE) 12-00 11-4F **Julian Pritchard** _Jmpd wildly 1 & 2 & rdr waving; pulled hrd; 6th when hmpd & ur 4_
	F		**Very Very Noble** (IRE) 12-00 20-1 **M Armytage** _3rd when fell 4_

TIME: 6min 33.0s **TOTE:** £9.40; places £2.60,£1.90,£2.40 **Ex:** £72.00 **CSF:** £67.83 **Tri:** £294.50

Hereford (RH 9F,12J)
Sat, 8 Apr (GOOD)

925 Victor Chandler HC
17 ran

	1		**DAYTIME DAWN (IRE)** 12-00 9-2 **S Morris** *Settled 2nd/3rd; hit 8; went 2nd nxt; ld 2 out; 8l clr at last; easy*
[580U]	2	11	**Mr Grimsdale (IRE)** 11-11 3-1F **T Scudamore** *Settled 3rd/5th; ld 7; hdd 2 out; sn outpcd; hit last*
[685⁴]	3	4	**Tubber Roads (IRE)** 11-07 7-2 **M Foley** *Bhnd; outpcd 6; stayed on frm 3 out; went 3rd at last; far too much to do*
[745²]	4	5	**Grand Canyon (IRE)** 11-09 10-1 **R Cooper** *Bhnd; mist 4; outpcd 6; stayed on aft 3 out; mist last; went poor 4th cl home*
[585⁶]	5	1	**Blue Marlin** 11-04 25-1 **J Owen** *(xnb) Nt fluent; ld; mist 6 (water); hdd nxt; wknd app 3 out; 15l 3rd & tired 2 out*
[897⁷]	6	7	**Mr Motivator** 11-07 8-1 **F Windsor Clive** *Poor last aft 3; nvr on terms*
[223⁷]	7	8	**Luke The Duke (IRE)** 11-11 40-1 **T Gibney** *Midfield & nvr in tch; strugg frm 6*
[384⁷]	8	12	**Sandi Devil** 11-07 (bl,tt) 66-1 **D Dickenson** *Hmpd 2; a bhnd; lost tch 6*
[865⁶]	9	1¾	**New Yorker (USA)** 11-04 (vis) 40-1 **M Rodda** *Towards rr; lost tch 6*
[754²]	P		**Above Suspicion (IRE)** 11-07 50-1 **M Walters** *Hmpd 2; a bhnd; lost tch 6; t.o & pu 3 out*
[755³]	P		**Arctic Lodge (IRE)** 11-07 (bl) 33-1 **M Hewitt** *Mid-div; outpcd 7; t.o aft 3 out; pu last*
	P		**Cashew Chaos (IRE)** 11-11 (bl) 25-1 **A Phillips** *Mist 1; rdn & lost tch 6; t.o & pu 3 out*
[747⁷]	U		**Heathyard's Flight** 11-07 100-1 **S Graham** *Rr til blun & ur 6*
[785⁷]	P		**Mr Dennehy (IRE)** 11-11 9-1 **A Charles-Jones** *Prom; 2nd when 7; 12l 4th 9; wknd & pu 2 out; bbv*
[740⁷]	P		**Rusty Flame** 11-11 12-1 **A Evans** *Pckd 2; a bhnd; lost tch 6; t.o & pu 3 out*
[697³]	P		**Tedstone Fox** 11-07 40-1 **D Mansell** *Prom til wknd 6; t.o & pu 3 out*
[685²]	U		**Timarisk** 11-07 33-1 **A Bateman** *Cl up to 5; drpd out qckly; t.o when blun & ur 9*

TIME: 4min 04.6s **TOTE:** £4.60; places £2.60,£1.70,£1.90 **Ex:** £32.50 **CSF:** £16.91 **Tri:** £80.30

Axe Vale Harriers
Stafford Cross (RH 8F,18J) Sat, 8 Apr (GOOD)

926 Hunt, 12st
5 ran

[730⁷]	1		**SHREWD THOUGHT (USA)** 4-1 **T Greed** *5s-4s; nt a fluent; prsd ldr til 3rd & eff 2 out; kpt on to ld last; rdn out*
	2	6	**Shotley Again** 28-1 **P Phillips** *(xnb) Trckd ldng pr; 15l 3rd 11; clsd 15; ld 2 out-last; rdn & nt qckn; game eff*
[633⁷]	3	6	**Hemero (IRE)** (tt) 9-4 **A Honeyball** *Tchd 5/2; jw; ld; rdn aft 3 out; hdd nxt; sn dem 3rd; plodded on*
[738¹]	R		**Gemini Mist** (5a) (bl) 4-5F **Miss C Stretton** *Tchd evens; imm lost tch; 17l 4th 3; t.o 11; fnce bhnd 13; rn out & ur 2 out (gvn no ch by rdr)*
	r		**Silverino** 33-1 **Miss S Kennard** *V dozy padd & lkd awful (examined by vet); sn t.o; ref 4*

OFFICIAL DISTANCES: 4l, 5l **TIME:** 6min 09.1s **TOTE:** £5.80 **DF:** £8.00

The stewards enquired into the running and riding of Gemini Mist; having heard the views of the owner they cautioned the rider - having only her third ride - for riding an injudicious race and warned her as to her future riding; no fine was imposed

927 Confined, 12st - 17J
10 ran

[877⁴]	1		**STILLMORE BUSINESS** 7-1 **T Mitchell** *Tchd 8s; lw (still bit hairy); settled 3rd/4th; lft 2nd 9; clsd to ld 12; bad mist 3 out; rdn clr aft nxt; kpt on*
[639¹]	2	8	**Kingsbridge (IRE)** 11-8F **L Jefford** *2s-11/8; tk keen hld & sn ld; blun 3 (broke fnce); tkn on by another tearaway & hdd brief when lft in ld 9; hdd 12; rdn & ev ch 2 out; no ex*
[873¹]	3	½	**Avril Showers** (5a,8x) 10-1 **R Atkinson** *Last 3; hdwy 7; 4th passing 11; outpcd 14; ll 3rd app 2 out; rdn & stayed on game eff*
[658¹]	4	4	**Primero (IRE)** (tt) 12-1 **A Honeyball** *Lw; midfield; mist 4; 5th passing 11; 15l 3rd & rdn app 2 out; no imp; hung lft flat*
[654⁴]	5	12	**Vansell** (5a) 11-7 **T Greed** *2 handlers; 3rd/4th bhnd tearaway pr; clsd 11; outpcd 14; 14l 3rd & btn app 2 out*
[735⁸]	6	5	**Air Command (BAR)** 50-1 **P Phillips** *Hit 3; last by 7; 12l adrift 12; nvr nr ldrs aft*
[653²]	7	8	**Hylters Chance (IRE)** (7x) 5-2 **D Alers-Hankey** *Rr div & nvr gng wl; 7th passing 11; rdn & nd frm nxt; mist 3 out*

[653⁴] P   **Lavalight** 33-1 J Snowden *Tchd 50s; lw; cl up early; drpd back 8th & rdn passing 11; t.o & pu 2 out*

     F   **One Boy** 50-1 J Barnes *(orbs) Pulled hrd; sn 2nd; mist 7; ld & fell 9*

[877³] U   **Spring Marathon (USA)** (7x) 20-1 Miss E Tory *Ld 1; drpd to rr 7; prog to 6th passing 11; chsng ldrs when ur 13*

OFFICIAL DISTANCES: 6l, 4l   TIME: 5min 55.8s   TOTE: £8.60   DF: £21.00
Fence 11 omitted - damaged

928 Mixed Open, 12st - 16J   9 ran

[200ᴾ] 1   **KHAYAL (USA)** 11-4 L Jefford *4s-11/4; lw; hld up in midfield; impd to 4th 12; lft 2nd 13; ld app 2 out; rdn clr aft 2 out; rdly*

[727²] 2   15   **Tuskar Flop** (7x) 5-2 D Alers-Hankey *Made most til mist 7; sn lost plce; 5th & rdn 12; rallied to 4l 3rd app 2 out; sn chsng wnr; drvn & no imp*

    3   5   **Verde Luna** (7x) (vis) 7-1 S Blackwell *Midfield til impd qckly to ld aft 8; 10l clr passing 11; hdd app 2 out; sn btn but kpt on stdly*

[725²] 4   25   **Mine's A Gin (IRE)** 9-4F Miss J Cumings *Tchd 5/2; chsd ldrs til 6th & rdn 12; wknd to rem 4th 3 out; lkd reluct & clambered over nxt*

[521ᴾ] U   **Blanchland** 66-1 J O'Rourke *Tubed; prom; 2nd til ur 13*

[922ᵁ] P   **Drumbanes Pet** 66-1 R Woollacott *Hld up & bhnd; hit 10; 7th 12; sn wknd; t.o & pu 2 out*

     P   **Renardine Boy (IRE)** 33-1 B O'Doherty *Hld up in last pr; lost tch 12; t.o & pu aft 3 out*

[852ˣ] F   **Strong Stuff (IRE)** (7x) (bl) 50-1 M Shears *(bf) Tk str hld; ld & jmpd slow 4 & hdd; lft in ld 7 til aft 8; 3rd 12; fell 13*

[653ᶠ] F   **Summit** (xnb,bf) 20-1 S Kidston *fell 1*

OFFICIAL DISTANCES: 10l, 4l   TIME: 5min 56.0s   TOTE: £2.80   DF: £6.50
Fences 3 & 11 omitted - damaged in previous race

929 Countryside Alliance Club Members (Nov Rdrs), 12st   14 ran

[877¹] 1   **SLEW MAN (FR)** 4-5F Miss O Green *(xnb) Tchd evens; settled midfield; 4th & eff 12; ld 14; 12l clr app 2 out; rdn on; unchal*

[727³] 2   20   **Texan Baby (BEL)** 2-1 K Sheppard *Rcd free & rdr oft unbalanced; ld & jmpd slow 4 & hdd; mists 7 & 11; cl 2nd/3rd til bad mist 13; chsd wnr vain aft*

[736³] 3   5   **Arise (IRE)** 20-1 Miss T Harrison *Tchd 25s; rr div; 7th 3; hdwy to 5th 12; stayed on to rem 3rd 2 out*

[638⁴] 4   5   **Parditino (IRE)** 11-1 Miss J Nicholas *Chsng group; last of 6 w ch 12; 25l 3rd app 2 out; plodded on*

[853⁶] 5   12   **Prudent Miner (IRE)** (6ow) 33-1 R Skinner *Sn virt t.o; poor 7th 12; kpt on stdly frm 15; nvr nr ldrs*

[638ᵁ] U   **Amtrak Express** 25-1 H Froud *2 handlers; rfo 3*

[886¹⁰] U   **Dromhana (IRE)** (4ow) 50-1 G Galpin *Ld to 4; ur by marker bale aft 8*

[725ᶜ] F   **Mr Jervis (IRE)** 12-1 Miss V Tremlett *Prom; ld 8-14; 3rd & btn when fell hvly 3 out*

[729ᴾ] F   **Roving Rebel** (bl) 33-1 Miss C Prouse *Mouth doused with wet sponge in padd; rcd free in ld 4-8; 2nd 12; fell 13*

[556³] U   **Run With Joy (IRE)** 66-1 J Berwick *Imm lost tch; t.o 9; ur 2 out*

[727ᴾ] P   **Ryming Cuplet** 25-1 B Trickey *Midfield; strug 9; rem 9th 11; t.o & pu 2 out*

[762²] U   **Silver Sleeve (IRE)** 50-1 Miss L Bridges *Chsd ldrs; 5th 9; ur 11*

[848ᴾ] P   **Smudges Season** (5a) 33-1 R Emmett *Bckwd; novicey & a wl bhnd; t.o 11; pu 15*

[521ᴾ] P   **Union Station (IRE)** 50-1 B Parsons *Tchd 66s; jb & rdr v ungainly; sn t.o; pu 2 out*

OFFICIAL DISTANCES: 20l, 4l   TIME: 5min 58.8s   TOTE: £1.60   DF: £1.70

930 Intermediate, 12st   7 ran

[734¹] 1   **FINNIGAN FREE** 10-11F A Honeyball *Tchd evens; settled cl up in rr; went cl 4th 12; chall 3 out; ld aft nxt; sn clr; easy*

[657¹] 2   10   **Swift Venture (IRE)** 4-1 Richard Darke *Disp ld 4 til ld aft 8; hdd aft 2 out; no ch w wnr*

[639²] 3   15   **Western Fort (IRE)** (5x) 3-1 Miss J Cumings *4s-3s; trckd ldrs; went 3rd 12 & 2nd & ev ch brief app 2 out; wknd qckly*

    4   15   **Arble March** (5a) 40-1 N Harris *Disp ld til 3rd aft 8; prom; rdn 15; ev ch app 2 out; wknd rap*

[726⁴] 5   25   **Willie B Brave (IRE)** 14-1 R Woollacott *Jmpd slow & mists; ev ch til 6th & u.p 12; nt r.o & sn wl bhnd; t.o*

[730³] 6   8   **Jeepers (IRE)** 25-1 S Kidston *Trckd ldrs; cl 5th 12; sn rdn & nt r.o; t.o*

    7   15   **Morchard Milly** (5a) (bl) 50-1 T Jones (Devon) *Disp ld to 8; ld brief 11 but rap drpd back last & sev rmndrs 12; sn t.o; lame*

OFFICIAL DISTANCES: 15l, 15l   TIME: 6min 00.2s   TOTE: £1.50   DF: £4.00

931 Restricted (Div 1), 12st - 17J
10 ran

[633²]	1		**NEWMAN'S CONQUEST** (5a) 20-1 M Shears *Ld 3; blun bad 4; jmpd slow 6; jmpd slow & hdd 12; ld agn 3 out; hrd prsd & lft clr last; r.o wl but lkd lucky*
[264¹]	2	5	**One Of The Natives (IRE)** 6-4F **T Mitchell** *Hld up & bhnd; 7l last 12; trckng ldrs when rn wide app 2 out (rdr put shoulder out); kpt on desp getting no assistance aft; lft 2nd at last*
	3	1½	**I Like The Deal** (5a) 25-1 L Jefford *(xnb) Hld up towards rr; 5th 12; went cl 3rd 14; drvn & nt qckn aft 2 out; hmpd last*
[729⁵]	4	6	**Barton Rose** 8-1 D Alers-Hankey *16s-8s; tk keen hld; ld to 3; 2nd/3rd til bad mist 11; lft in ld 12; hdd 3 out; rdn & wkng nxt*
[315⁶]	5	2	**Flaming Cold** (5a) 10-1 M Miller *Hld up towards rr; hdwy 9; 3rd 11; cl 4th 14; chall when bad mist last; nt rec & hung lft flat*
[767⁶]	6	12	**Franklins Best (IRE)** 7-1 N Mitchell *2 handlers; towards rr but cl up; 6l 6th 12; 8l last & wkng aft 3 out*
[849²]	F		**Bricanmore (IRE)** (tt) 9-4 N Harris *2nd/3rd til fell 9*
[486⁴]	U		**Mister Jay Day** 12-1 S Blackwell *(xnb) Trckd ldrs; 4th 12; blun & event ur 13*
[538⁶]	P		**Morgan's Rose** (5a) 100-1 M Sweetland *Jb; sn t.o; pu 9*
[635¹]	U		**Salford Quay (IRE)** 20-1 G Barfoot-Saunt *In tch hmpd & ur 9*

OFFICIAL DISTANCES: 5l, 2l **TIME:** 6min 05.9s **TOTE:** £31.00 **DF:** -
Fence 17 omitted - fallen rider

932 Restricted (Div 2), 12st
11 ran

[685³]	1		**MORRIS PIPER** (tt) 11-10F L Jefford *(xnb)Settled towards rr; 7l 7th 12; prog in 3rd aft 3 out; chall str when lft in ld last; sn drvn clr*
[850²]	2	10	**Woodland King (IRE)** 6-1 Mrs M Hand *Tchd 7s; prom; 3rd 12; ev ch 15; outpcd aft nxt; kpt on to 2nd agn cl home; no ch w wnr*
[728⁴]	3	hd	**Rice Point** 10-1 C Heard *(xnb,boh) Hld up & bhnd early; hdwy 9; 5th 12; went 2nd & ev ch aft 3 out til app last; wknd flat*
[102⁵]	4	6	**Spartans Winney** (5a) 25-1 J Young *(bof) A cl up; 6th 12; prsd ldrs til one pce & nd aft 3 out*
[733¹]	5	15	**Mudslide** 4-1 A Honeyball *(xnb) Tchd 9/2; oht; bad mist 1; pulled hrd & sn prom; ld 7 til bad mist 3 out; 6l 4th & wkng qckly app nxt*
[729⁸]	6	12	**The Stuffed Puffin (IRE)** 33-1 Miss S Rowe *(xnb) Cl up; 4th 12; ev ch 15; wknd rapidly aft nxt*
[563⁵]	7	40	**Horton** 100-1 S Parkin *Tde; sn t.o*
	P		**Helismad** (7a) 66-1 Richard Darke *Fat; rr but in tch til pu 11*
[583⁷]	F		**Jabiru (IRE)** 5-1 D Alers-Hankey *7s-5s; sn 3rd; 2nd 8 til ld 3; slt advant but lkd v vulnerable when fell last*
	P		**Mayhem** (5a) 50-1 T Dennis *Trckd ldrs; mist 10; lost tch nxt; 25l adrift when pu 14*
[763³]	P		**Spanish Jest** 33-1 J O'Rourke *(drop) Ld to 6; sn lost plce; rr 11; wl bhnd when pu 13*

OFFICIAL DISTANCES: 10l, hd **TIME:** 6min 01.2s **TOTE:** £1.80 **DF:** £6.80

933 Open Maiden 56&7yo (Div 1), 12st
10 ran

[725⁶]	1		**PERSIAN DAWN** (5a) 14-1 R Woollacott *Hld up; went 3rd 8 & 2nd 11; ld 14 til hdd 2 out; lkd hld when lft clr at last; idly rdn & just hld on*
[733²]	2	½	**Happy Team** (5a) 4-5F L Jefford *6/4-4/5; cl up; 3rd 12; bad mist nxt; mist 14; rallied to 2l 4th app 2 out; sn outpcd; hrd drvn & came agn flat; just failed (& nrly won on jockeyship)*
[655³]	3	3	**Wink And Whisper** (12a) 4-1 Miss E Tory *Settled towards rr; prog to cl 5th 12; 1l 2nd app 2 out; one pce app last*
[722⁵]	F		**Druid Merill** (5a) 20-1 Miss T Cave *Bit bckwd; trckd ldrs; 4th 12; disp 2nd & ev ch when fell hvly 3 out*
[355⁶]	P		**Fenny Prince** 50-1 M Sweetland *Virt a last; t.o 12; pu 14*
[733⁶]	U		**Fullofancy** (5a) 7-2 M Miller *(drop) Lw; trckd ldrs in midfield; 6th 12; chall 3 out; ld nxt; lkd wnr when mist & ur last*
	P		**Golden Saddle (USA)** 50-1 A Honeyball *Pulled hrd & prom til mist 11; 8th & wkng rap nxt; mist 13; pu 14*
[105⁶]	P		**High Sturt** (5a) 50-1 J Snowden *Ld til mist 13; wknd qckly 15; t.o & pu 2 out*
[732⁶]	P		**Pentheon Minstrel** 25-1 B O'Doherty *(xnb) 2 handlers; oht; mists; cl up til u.p 9; lost tch 11; t.o & pu 13*
[100⁶]	P		**She Wood She** (5a) 33-1 Richard Darke *Mists; chsd ldr to 11; 4l 7th nxt; wknd rap; pu 3 out*

OFFICIAL DISTANCES: 1l, 3l **TIME:** 6min 17.0s **TOTE:** £12.60 **DF:** £9.00

934 Open Maiden 56&7yo (Div 2), 12st   **14 ran**

[732⁶]	1		FURSAN (USA) (tt) 10-1 P Phillips *(xnb removed at start)25s-10s; unruly; swtng; mists; tk str hld; impd to 6th 8; 3rd 11; 2nd nxt; ld 14; r.o str aft 2 out; rdr did wl*
[733ᵁ]	2	6	Team Captain 2-1F L Jefford *Tchd 9/4; 2 handlers; lw; settled 4/5th til 2nd/3rd frm 9; 3l 3rd 12; ev ch & drvn app 2 out; no imp app last*
[846³]	3	7	Wise Examiner (IRE) 4-1 Richard Darke *(xnb) Prom; 4l 4th 12; one pce frm 3 out; disp 2nd at last; wknd*
[723²]	4	30	Change 9-2 T Dennis *(xnb) Bit bckwd; 2nd til ld 10; hdd 14; 2nd & ev ch app 2 out; wknd rap*
	5	12	Sula Spirit (5a) 7-1 Miss O Green *Erratic in rr; t.o 8*
[411ᴾ]	P		County Derry 14-1 C Heard *Nvr btr than midfield; 23l 8th & strugg 12; t.o & pu 3 out*
[855ᴾ]	F		Frisky-Breeze (5a) 40-1 M Shears *(kineton) Cl up early; mist 5; drpng to rr when fell 11*
[724ᴾ]	P		Hendra Chieftain 16-1 A Honeyball *Chsd ldrs til 15l 7th & outpcd 12; bad mist 15; t.o & pu 13*
	P		Inforapop (7a) 14-1 J Snowden *(xnb) School in rr; sn lost tch; t.o 11; pu 13*
[721ᴾ]	R		Miltown Castle 16-1 K Sheppard *Jb & sn t.o; rn out 6*
	P		Soldier's Song (5a) 14-1 Miss T Cave *(xnb) Mist 2; midfield; 8l 6th 12; sn wknd; t.o & pu 2 out*
[641²]	P		The Islander 14-1 G Barfoot-Saunt *Mists & chsng ldrs; 7l 5th 12; rdn & nt r.o; t.o & pu 2 out*
[875ᴾ]	P		Tolepa (IRE) (5a) 33-1 L Tibbatts *Tk str hld; ld til hdd & wknd rap 10; pu 12*
	P		Willet Wizard 33-1 Miss V Stephens *(xnb) Fat; swtng; prom brief; rr & strugg 9; t.o & pu 12*

OFFICIAL DISTANCES: 6l, 2l **TIME:** 6min 04.1s **TOTE:** £4.00

East Essex

Marks Tey (LH 10F,20J) Sat, 8 Apr (GOOD, GOOD to FIRM in places)

935 Hunt   **7 ran**

[756ᵁ]	1		STILL IN BUSINESS 3-1F A Ayers *Ww in last trio; 16l 6th ½way; gd prog nxt; went 2nd app 15; ld 17; a hldng rnr-up aft*
[775²]	2	2½	Worthy Memories (5a) 5-1 A Sansome *Ld to 4; stdd to 12l 4th 6; prog to ld agn 12; hdd 17; one pce aft*
[840⁴]	3	runin	Royal Surprise 20-1 Miss L Ingram *(xnb) Wl bhnd in last trio; prog 9; 3l 3rd 12; outpcd 14; no ch frm 16; lft poor 3rd at last*
[758⁴]	4	6	Dance On Sixpence (bl) 7-1 S March *(xnb) Oht; chsd ldrs; ld 10-12; 4l 4th app 15; wknd 17; t.o; fin tired*
[771⁴]	5	30	Son Of Iris (bl) 4-1 A Coe W ldrs; 2nd & rmdrs 10; lost plce qckly nxt; last frm 13; t.o*
[608³]	P		Limited Liability (bl) 4-1 Miss C Grissell *(xnb) Bolted bef start; rcd keen; w ldrs; ld 4; blun 9; hdd 10; wknd 13; t.o & pu 3 out*
[842⁵]	F		Royal Action 4-1 P Chinery *6s-4s; hld up; wl bhnd in last trio; mist 8; 14l 5th ½way; prog to disp 2nd & ev ch 16; wknd 3 out; 10l 3rd & tired when fell last*

OFFICIAL DISTANCES: 2l, 20l **TIME:** 6min 45.0s **TOTE:** £2.30

936 Confined, 12st   **12 ran**

[841³]	1		KELLY'S ORIGINAL 12-1 N Bloom *Prom to 13; 8l 6th & outpcd app 15; rallied 17; ld 2 out; stayed on wl*
[770¹]	2	4	Village Copper (3x) 1-2F C Ward-Thomas *2 handlers; ww in tch; 4l 5th ½way; eff & hmpd bend bef 3 out; rallied u.p to chse wnr 2 out; no imp flat (struck into & lost shoe)*
	3	10	Hillwalk 20-1 A Harvey *Chsd ldrs; cl 4th & ev ch 17; one pce frm nxt; wrnt 3rd flat*
[842⁴]	4	1½	Koathary (USA) 10-1 T Lane *Ww in mid-div; 6l 6th ½way; went 3rd & gng wl 12; ld 3 out; hdd nxt; wknd*
[757²]	5	5	Stoney Valley 25-1 M Gingell *Ld til app 3 out; sn wknd; no ch frm nxt*
[771¹]	U		King High 33-1 J Cooper *(bf,boh) Prom; 3l 4th 14; ur nxt*
	P		Lazy Acres (IRE) 33-1 C Lawson *(xnb) Sa; sn t.o; pu 16*
[609¹]	U		Nibble 5-1 G Cooper *Blun & ur 3*
	P		Regal Bay 20-1 W Wales *(xnb) In tch til rdn & outpcd 11; t.o & pu 16; lame*
[770ᵁ]	P		Scarlett O'Hara (5a) 6-1 S Sporborg *In tch; 8l 7th ½way; 9th & lsng tch when pu 15; lame*
[770ᴾ]	P		Spaceage Gold (vis) 33-1 K Edmunds *Rr of main group; lost tch 10; t.o & pu 17*
	P		Take A Flyer (IRE) 25-1 A Coe *Unruly start & ld in; sa; t.o 5th when pu 16*

OFFICIAL DISTANCES: 2l, 5l **TIME:** 6min 40.0s **TOTE:** £9.00

937 Intermediate, 12st   11 ran

[609²]	1		**AINTGOTTIME (IRE)** 9-4JF R Lawther *In tch in mid-div; 4l 4th 16; chall 3 out; ld 2 out; clr last; comf*
[705¹]	2	7	**Persian Empire (IRE)** 3-1 A Sansome *5s-3s; ww in rr; prog to 2l 3rd ½way; ld 3 out; hdd nxt; no ex u.p*
[770²]	3	10	**Ann's Ambition** 12-1 Miss C Fryer *In tch; 3rd ½way; jnd ldrs 16; ld 17-3 out; one pce*
[574ᴾ]	4	3	**Tell Tale (IRE)** 12-1 A Harvey *Mid-div; 6l 7th 11; sn drvn along; 5l 5th 16; outpcd frm nxt; stayed on flat*
[770ᴾ]	5	hd	**Pearly Haze** (5a) 14-1 N King *Chsd ldrs to 10; lost plce & bhnd 13; stayed on agn frm 2 out*
[761¹]	6	6	**Mai Point** (5a) 10-1 Miss C Grissell *(xnb) Prom; chsd ldr 3; disp ld 12 til ld 14; hdd 16; grad wknd*
[388⁴]	7	15	**Mendip Prince (IRE)** 14-1 A Lillingston *In tch; mist 7; outpcd frm 14; sn no ch*
[840²]	U		**Alfredo Garcia (IRE)** (3ow) 12-1 S R Andrews *Ld to 2; cl 4th when blun & ur 10*
[239ᶜ]	U		**Henpecked (IRE)** 25-1 A Braithwaite *(xnb) Unruly padd; ur 1*
[839¹]	P		**Lord Knox (IRE)** 20-1 A Coe *Prom; ld 2-14; sn wknd; t.o & pu 3 out*
[554¹]	P		**Manna Brave (IRE)** 9-4JF C Ward-Thomas *In tch; 3; 4th ½way; outpcd app 15; wl bhnd when pu 3 out; lame*

OFFICIAL DISTANCES: 4l, 6l **TIME:** 6min 37.0s **TOTE:** £3.70
Ballydesmond was withdrawn after declaration because of the state of the going

938 Mens Open, 3m4f - 21J   7 ran

[842³]	1		**MISTER TRICK (IRE)** (bl) 7-1 N King *Ld to 2; chsd ldr aft & clr of rest; rmdrs 13; ld app 3 out; sn 6l clr; rdn out*
[842¹]	2	4	**Hatcham Boy (IRE)** 1-2F C Ward-Thomas *In tch; mostly 5th; outpcd by ldng pr ½way; 15l 4th & rdn 18; 12l 3rd 18; went 2nd app 2 out; kpt on; nt rch wnr*
[708²]	3	15	**Remilan (IRE)** (bl) 16-1 A Sansome *Bhnd; 15l 6th & rdn 10; no prog; 20l 4th & no ch 3 out; went poor 3rd 2 out*
[678²]	4	10	**Veryvel (CZE)** 8-1 D Kemp *Bhnd; went 10l 4th 7; mist 9; no ch w ldrs frm 12*
[320⁵]	5	5	**High Learie** (5a) 33-1 A Harvey *Tk keen; disp ld 1 til ld 5; hdd app 3 out; wknd qckly app nxt*
[415³]	P		**Ruperts Choice (IRE)** (bl) 4-1 S Sporborg *Ld chsng group; 12l 3rd when blun 12; sn rdn & strugg; t.o last when pu 3 out*
[238ᶠ]	P		**Tan Hill Sparky** (5a) 33-1 A Coe *A last; 25l off pce 8; sn t.o; pu 12*

OFFICIAL DISTANCES: 3l, 8l **TIME:** 7min 21.0s **TOTE:** £7.10

939 Ladies Open   7 ran

[608¹]	1		**SPRING GALE (IRE)** 1-4F Miss Z Turner *Ld in start; ww; went cl 4th 10; chsd ldr app 3 out; ld 2 out; rdn out*
[758²]	2	1½	**Gatchou Mans (FR)** 10-1 Miss C Grissell *Ld to 4; chsd ldrs aft; 2l 3rd app 3 out; went 2nd app last; unable to qckn flat*
[544³]	3	12	**Thurles Pickpocket (IRE)** 5-1 Mrs S Hodge *Jmpd rt; made most frm 4 til hdd & hit 2 out; sn btn & nt prsd aft*
[772³]	4	runin	**Lets Twist Again (IRE)** 33-1 Miss A Stennett *Prom; chsd ldr 5-9; 5l 6th & lsng plce ½way; t.o 15; went poor 4th flat*
[608ᴾ]	5	2	**Hay Dance** 33-1 Mrs E Coveney *Chsd ldrs; went 2nd 9; prsd ldr 11-16; wknd nxt; t.o*
[841⁶]	6	5	**Salmon Mead (IRE)** (bl) 33-1 Miss N Barnes *Detach last frm 6; t.o 12; went 6th 2 out*
[756³]	7	12	**Going Around** 33-1 Miss F Jonason *Mid-div; in tch to 10; sn bhnd; t.o last 2 out*

OFFICIAL DISTANCES: 1l, 4l **TIME:** 6min 38.0s **TOTE:** £1.10

940 Restricted   10 ran

[760¹]	1		**MR MAGGET (IRE)** 7-2 N Bloom *Prom on inner; cl 2nd frm 9 til hdd 16; rdn & stayed on frm 2 out*
[843²]	2	2	**Ar Aghaidh Abhaile (IRE)** 5-2F G Cooper *Trckd ldrs; 3l 5th ½way; went 3rd 12; ev ch 3 out; unable to qckn app last; went 2nd nr fin*
[773²]	3	¾	**Squaddie** 7-2 A Sansome *Hld up in rr; prog 10; 3l 4th 15; 2nd & ev ch 3 out; hrd rdn nxt; no ex last; dem nr fin*
[773³]	4	3	**Skinsey Finnegan (IRE)** 6-1 A Coe *Ld in; pulling; hld up; prog to 5l 7th 11; 10l 5th & outpcd 16; stayed on agn frm 2 out*
[610³⁼]	5	12	**Mackoy (IRE)** 14-1 M Gingell *Prom; slt ld frm 6 til hdd 16; wknd qckly 3 out*
[843³]	6	8	**Holmby Copse** 14-1 T Humphrey *2 handlers; tde; prom; ld brief 16; cl 3rd 15; wknd nxt*
[705ᴾ]	7	5	**And Why Not** 25-1 T Lane *Ld 1 til app 5; prsd ldrs aft til wknd 14*
[843⁵]	8	2	**Bakmalad** 33-1 D Kemp *Ld til jmpd slow 1; bhnd frm 6; no ch frm ½way*
[791ᴮ]	P		**Dynoun** 7-2 D Crosse *In tch in rr; mist 3; blun 14; sn strugg; 8th & no ch when pu 3 out*

[761⁵] P **Rathkeal (IRE)** 16-1 D Parravani *Prom to 13; sn drpd out; t.o 16; pu 3 out*

OFFICIAL DISTANCES: ½l, ½l **TIME:** 6min 47.0s **TOTE:** £2.10

941 Confined Maiden (Div 1) 10 ran

[775⁴] 1 **RAFTER** 20-1 C Carman *In tch; mist 3; went 2nd 8; disp ld 13-15; 6l 3rd & lkd btn 16; went 2nd 3 out; r.o wl to ld last 100yds*

2 1 **Cradle Mountain** 9/2-3s; *ld 1-5; 6l 3rd & mist 11; went 2nd 16; ld nxt; 3l clr & rdn 2 out; hdd last 100yds*

[604ᴿ] 3 30 **Rag Bolt (IRE)** 7-1 S R Andrews *Ww in rr; 10l 8th ½way; prog to 4th & mist 12; outpcd 15; no ch when jmpd lft 2 out; went poor 3rd nr fin*

[759³] 4 nk **Out Of Actons (IRE)** 11-4 C Jarvis *(xnb) Pulling; jnd ldrs 4; ld 5; jmpd 13; ld 15 til hdd 17; wknd; lost 3rd nr fin*

[760³] 5 runin **Ger's Girl (IRE)** (5a) 6-1 A Coe *Chsd ldrs; 7l 5th app 15; sn wknd; t.o*

[605ᴾ] P **Bandit Boy** 12-1 N King *Ld to 1; in tch in mid-div; 8l 5th ½way; sn lost tch; t.o last when pu 15*

[775ᶠ] P **Carlton Brae** (12a) 12-1 A Harvey *School in last pr; a wl bhnd; pu 13*

[412⁵] P **David Bruce (IRE)** 6-4F R Fowler *(xnb) Cl up to 10; strugg frm nxt; 6th & no ch frm 16; pu last*

[605ᴾ] P **Midnight Dynamite** 20-1 S March *Last pr frm 6; t.o ½way; pu 13*

[755ᴾ] P **Teluk (IRE)** 20-1 M Gingell *Prom to 7; 15l 8th & rdn 10; no resp; last & jmpd slow 11; pu aft*

OFFICIAL DISTANCES: 1l, 2l **TIME:** 6min 51.0s **TOTE:** £68.00

942 Confined Maiden (Div 2) 10 ran

[775³] 1 **OUR MAN FLIN (IRE)** 6-4F A Sansome *(xnb) Chsd ldng pr; 10l 3rd 7; went 2nd 13; ld 17; 2l up & rdn app last; kpt on; wl rdn*

[839ᵁ] 2 2 **Sixth Sense (IRE)** 7-1 T Lane *Mid-div; 5th ½way; lft 6l 3rd 14; chsd wnr app 2 out; unable to qckn u.p*

[760ᴾ] 3 25 **Lancaster Boy (IRE)** 8-1 S R Andrews *(xnb) Ld to 3 & agn 13; hdd 17; rdn & btn app 2 out*

[760ᴾ] 4 10 **Citizen Band (IRE)** 14-1 C Lawson *A mid-div; lsng tch 13; lft 4th nxt; nd*

[605⁴] 5 runin **Yashwell (IRE)** 4-1 P Taiano *Jmpd rt; a bhnd; 15l last ½way; lost tch 12; t.o*

[775ᴾ] P **Bozo Bailey** 14-1 M Polley *Mid-div to 12; sn outpcd; t.o last 16; pu 3 out*

[844²] U **Curracloe Rose** (5a) 2-1 D Cook *Chsd ldrs; 3l 3rd when blun & ur 14*

[844ᴾ] P **Dilly May Dally** (5a) 14-1 Miss R Barrow *Jb rt 1; last aft; t.o & pu 10*

P **Play Alone** (12a) 10-1 W Wales *Unruly padd; bhnd; prog to 12l 7th 11; lost tch 14; pu nxt*

P **Secret Music** 10-1 D Parravani *Prom; ld 3-13; 5th & wkng 15; pu nxt*

OFFICIAL DISTANCES: 1l, 4l **TIME:** 6min 48.0s **TOTE:** £3.10

Llandeilo Farmers

Erw Lon (LH 8F,18J) Sat, 8 Apr (FIRM)

943 Hunt 5 ran

[837ᴾ] 1 **SECRET BEAUTY (IRE)** (5a,3x) 1-2F M Lewis *(b4 on fetlocks) 12l 3rd 2; hdwy 9; 2nd nxt; mist 14; jmpd to ld 15; kpt on game*

[742ᴾ] 2 6 **Same Difference (IRE)** (3x) 3-1 Mrs B Lewis *10l 2nd 2; dem 3rd 9; 15l 3rd 13; rallied 2 out; r.o; nt rch wnr*

3 6 **Snow Cloud** (5a) 10-1 Miss I Tompsett *(xnb,boh) Ld; mists; 11 up 10; blun 6; 6l clr til outj & hdd 15; outpcd*

[834ᴾ] 4 2fncs **Jesusa** (5a) 25-1 G Maloney *A last; t.o 6; jmpd v slow 9; sn fnce bhnd; v rem frm 14*

[832⁴] P **Sea Search** 5-1 J Keen *(bf) A last pr; 15l 4th when pu 2 out*

OFFICIAL DISTANCES: 5l, 3l **TIME:** 6min 21.0s

944 Intermediate, 12st 10 ran

[702¹] 1 **FINTONA BOY (IRE)** (5x) (tt) 1-2F R Burton *A.p; 1½l 3rd 6; ld 9; hdd nxt; ld agn 12; 2l up & mist 2 out; sn rdn clr*

[837⁴] 2 6 **Dyffryn Prince (IRE)** 6-1 P Sheldrake *2 handlers; hld up in 5th; cl 3rd 9 til 2nd 12; 2l 3rd & ev ch til no ex 2 out*

[647¹] 3 10 **Rusnetto (IRE)** (vis) 4-1 G Lewis *Slt ld to 8; 5l 3rd & ev ch 15; mist nxt; sn fdd*

[837ᴾ] 4 15 **Sister Lark** (5a) 12-1 T Vaughan *Cl 2nd to 7; prom to 9; grad wknd; no ch 14*

[819ᴾ] P **Alkarine** 18-1 N Jones *A last pr; lost tch frm 3; t.o when jmpd slow 7; pu 12*

P **Appeal** (5a) 33-1 Miss A Meakins *(bf) A strugg in rr; t.o 5; pu 12*

[837P]   P   **Bancyfelin Boy** 16-1 **J Keen** *(xnb) Midfield; 6th & wkng 8; 12l 6th 10; stdly lost tch; pu 13*

[837U]   P   **Plucky Punter** (tt) 33-1 **G Skone** *(xnb)4th & mist 2; sn rr; lost tch frm 9; t.o & pu 14*

[837G]   P   **Pure Air** 6-1 **C Williams** *A towards rr; drvn 10; 4th & mist 11; pu & dism 15*

[831⁵]   F   **Teigr Pren** 16-1 **Miss G Evans** *(bh) 6th when fell 2*

OFFICIAL DISTANCES: 5l, 12l   TIME: 6min 03.0s

945 Mens Open, 12st   7 ran

[833²]   1   **MOON TIGER** 2-1F **T Vaughan** *Cl 3rd/4th; mist 10; just ld 13; outj & hdd nxt; jnd ldr 2 out; r.o game to ld last*

[643²]   2   4   **Anorak (USA)** 5-2 **C Williams** *Ld to 2; prom til ld agn 9-13; jmpd to ld agn brief 15; 6l 3rd 2 out; swished tail but r.o to 2nd flat; nt rch wnr*

        3   8   **Laurel Seeker (USA)** (7x) 3-1 **James Tudor** *(bh fetlocks) 4th early; cl 2nd frm 2; disp ld 2 out; wknd*

[922P]   4   6   **Frown** (bl) 12-1 **P Hamer** *A last pr; cl 5th & mist 8; nvr able to chall aft; one pce 3 out*

[684U]   5   runin   **Savuti (IRE)** (tt) 20-1 **J Keen** *Tde; in tch 5th til fdd 12; 12l last 14; t.o 3 out*

[343U]   P   **Flutterbud** (5a,7x) (bl) 4-1 **J Jukes** *Mists in 2nd til ld & mist 5; hdd aft 8; dem 3rd nxt; pu 11*

[819³]   P   **Harbour Island** (bl) 6-1 **J L Llewellyn** *Last & rmdrs 1; 4l adrift nxt; t.o 10; pu 14*

OFFICIAL DISTANCES: 3l, 7l   TIME: 5min 55.0s

946 Ladies Open   6 ran

[921⁸]   1   **COOLVAWN LADY (IRE)** (5a,5x) 1-3F **Miss P Jones** *2nd til jmpd to ld 6; hdd 10; cl 2nd til ld agn 13; r.o wl frm 2 out; sn clr; comf*

[821P]   2   8   **Sebastopol** 6-1 **Miss F Wilson** *Ld 1; mist 3; hdd aft 6; ld agn 10-12; 2nd & ev ch til outpcd 2 out*

[836⁴]   3   25   **Turning Trix** 10-1 **Miss R Curtis** *In tch in 3rd/4th til wknd 13; 14l 3rd & btn 3 out*

[836⁷]   P   **Battleship Bruce** 20-1 **Miss A Meakins** *Last to 7; impd to 5l 5th 10; pu bend aft 12*

[743²]   P   **Polo Kit (IRE)** 13-2 **Miss L Pearce** *Badly rubbed & raw tail; 3rd mostly; tiring when mist 13; 9l 3rd & lsng tch when mist 14; pu 3 out*

[831²]   P   **Young Manny** 10-1 **Mrs B Lewis** *A rr; lost tch frm 9; 18l last 10; pu 12; saddle slpd*

OFFICIAL DISTANCES: 9l, dist   TIME: 5min 58.0s

947 Restricted (Div 1), 12st   5 ran

[832³]   1   **MERRIE JAR (IRE)** 4-9F **T Vaughan** *Mist 1 & rdr lost irons; 3rd til 2nd 10; jnd ldr & mist 15; ld & mist nxt; qcknd clr frm 2 out; r.o str*

[837U]   2   12   **Final Rose** (5a) 4-1 **G Lewis** *Unruly; ld; 2l up & mist 14; jnd & mist nxt; sn hdd & no ex; btn 2 out*

[818⁴]   3   6   **Mecca Prince (IRE)** (7a) 5-2 **James Tudor** *Prom; cl 3rd to 8; 4th & ev ch 3 out; 10l 3rd & wkng nxt*

[832P]   4   runin   **Hil Lady** (5a) 6-1 **M Barber** *4th & mist 2; last 6; lost tch 10; mist 11; sn t.o*

[744²]   P   **Seventh Symphony (IRE)** 8-1 **J Cook** *Trckd ldr; mists 5 & 8; lost tch 12; 15l 4th 14; nd aft; pu 2 out*

OFFICIAL DISTANCES: 8l, 5l   TIME: 6min 02.0s

948 Restricted (Div 2), 12st   5 ran

[834¹]   1   **SECRET CAN'T SAY (IRE)** (5a) evensF **J Jukes** *Made all; dived at 4; narrow advant til jnd 13; sn ld agn; rdn clr frm 2 out; comf*

[818P]   2   10   **Out On The Town** (5a) 5-1 **James Tudor** *Trckd ldr til disp ld 13; 11 2nd 14; one pce 2 out*

[896R]   3   12   **Briary Boy (IRE)** (xnb) 5-1 **A Price** *5l 3rd & mist 9 & 10; blun agn 14; bhnd & no ch aft*

[612U]   P   **Henwyn** 2-1 **A Dalton** *A last; 7l last 6; u.p & jmpd slow 13; sn tired; t.o when scrambled over 2 out; pu last*

        R   **Jack Boots** 6-4 **J Phillips** *Last when rn out & ur 2*

OFFICIAL DISTANCES: 8l, 6l   TIME: 5min 58.0s

949 Open Maiden (Div 1)   10 ran

[596³]   1   **TIGERSUN** 5-1 **D Hughes** *(xnb) A.p; ld 13; mist 2 out; kpt on game; just hld on*

        2   ¾   **Eurogreen (IRE)** 2-1 **A Price** *Settled 3rd; went 2nd 9; ld 10-11; 2nd & ev ch aft; just failed*

[822²]   3   4   **Le Vienna (IRE)** 5-1 **S Currey** *Ld to 9; staring at fncs; 5th 13; kpt on past wkng horses to 10l 4th 2 out; stayed on; nt trble ldrs*

[838P]   4   3   **Redoran** (5a) 3-1 **G Skone** *(orbs) 4th mostly; lost tch frm 15; one pce clsng stages*

5	5	**Tiny** (12a) 3-1 J Jukes (xnb) 2nd early; 6th & rdn 11; hdwy to 3rd 13-last; btn & eased flat
6	15	**Chesnut Wood** 10-1 M Barber Dragged unwillingly rnd padd; a rr; jmpd delib 2; last frm 6; t.o 11; stayed on frm 2 out
7	1	**Motu Tapu** 4-1 Miss A Meakins A last trio; last 4; impd to 6th 10; fdd 13; dem 7th aft 2 out
[834U] 8	4	**Daisy's Choice** (12a) 4-1 P Sheldrake Rr; jmpd slow 6 & last pr aft; lost tch frm 13; 7th 2 out; sn releg last
[747P] P		**Poacher's Paddy** (IRE) (12a) 10-1 J Price 7th & mist 4; in tch til wknd 13; pu 15
[602²] P		**Tommyknocker** (IRE) 6-4F T Faulkner Nvr gng wl in midfield; 4th 8-11; 6th & rdn 13; fdd; rem 6th when pu last

OFFICIAL DISTANCES: ½l, 2l TIME: 6min 21.0s

950 Open Maiden (Div 2, Part 1)   10 ran

[834³] 1		**OSSIE DALE** (IRE) 4-6F J Jukes Made all; mist 8; 2l up til drvn & qcknd clr frm last; comf
[834] 2	6	**Bold Knight** 7-1 G Skone Unruly padd; jw; hld up in 6th; prog 14; r.o wl to 11 2nd 2 out; ev ch last; outpcd
[831⁴] 3	4	**Sing Cherry Ripe** (5a) 7-1 Miss T Stevens A.p; 3rd frm 2 til 4th 10; blun 15; went 3rd agn 2 out; nt trble ldrs
[835⁵] 4	25	**Mission Lord** (IRE) 10-1 G Maloney 2 young handlers; 4/5th til prog to 2nd 9; wknd 3 out; sn btn; walked in
[823³] 5	12	**Tarian** (USA) 14-1 M Parry 4th; hdwy to 2l 2nd 7; fdd 14; sn t.o
[835P] P		**Cefn Tiger** (7a) 3-1 D Hughes Tk str hld in 6th til last trio 10; pu & dism 12; subsq destroyed
P		**Hot'n Sprouty** (5a) 5-1 J Price Midfield; mists in 7th til went 5th 10; fdd 13; pu 14
[455P] P		**Look Who's Calling** (IRE) 6-1 A Dalton Nvr gng wl; a last pr; pu 13
P		**Queenofthemountain** (5a) 10-1 T Vaughan Midfield & mist 5; releg last pr; rdn & no resp 14; pu 15
[822P] P		**Rowling Sea** (IRE) 6-1 C Williams Prom; 3rd when to pu 5; inj; dead

OFFICIAL DISTANCES: 8l, 3l TIME: 6min 18.0s

951 Open Maiden (Div 2, Part 2)   9 ran

[602⁴] 1		**ROGER** (IRE) 3-1 A Price A.p; 3l 2nd 5; ld 10; 6l clr 13; lft virt solo nxt
[834P] 2	fence	**Pryvate Time** (5a) 10-1 J Keen Rr early; prog to 8l 3rd 6; lost tch frm 10; t.o 11; lft v rem 2nd 14
[746P] P		**Adams Gold** 5-2F J Jukes Ld early; jmpd delib 2; 3rd when pu 5
[484P] P		**Arctic Ridge** 6-1 D Hughes A last pr; lost tch 10; t.o & pu 13
[491⁵] P		**Gowenbacktodudley** (5a) 4-1 J Price Blun 3; 6th & mist 6; sn rem; wl t.o when pu 12
[822³] P		**Kopain** 3-1 J L Llewellyn (xnb) 4th til pu qckly & dism 9; subsq destroyed
[834F] r		**Lord Chamberlain** (bl) 5-1 P Sheldrake 2nd til ld 4-9; 6l 2nd 11; tiring when ref & ur 14; horse stuck on fnce
[834²] P		**Run To The Glen** (12a) 4-1 M Lewis (xnb) A bhnd; last frm 4; 10l adrift 6; wl t.o when pu 11
[834P] U		**Stormhill Daydream** (5a) 6-1 G Lewis 5th; lost tch frm 10; 30l 4th 14; hmpd & ur 14

OFFICIAL DISTANCE: dist TIME: 6min 10.0s

Blackmore & Sparkford Vale
Charlton Horethorne (RH 8F,18J) Sun, 9 Apr (GOOD to FIRM)

952 Hunt, 12st   9 ran

[638¹] 1		**MILLYHENRY** 7-4 Miss C Tizzard A.p; chsd ldr til ld 4-5 & frm 9; jnd 10-12; sn 3l up; jnd brief 3 out; stayed on str u.p frm nxt
[208¹] 2	1½	**See More Sense** evensF Miss P Gundry (xnb) Hld up in last; jmpd lft early; 8½l 8th 4; smooth hdwy to 2l 3rd 10; chsng ldr & clsng when mist 14; chall brief 3 out; no ex u.p frm nxt
[631¹] 3	10	**Glaisnock Lad** (IRE) (5x) 4-1 J Barnes A.p; chsd ldrs; 4½l 5th 4; disp ld 10-11; rmdr 12; outpcd 15; stayed on one pce frm 2 out
4	3	**Jackson Hill** 25-1 Jeremy Young 5th & pulling hrd 3; lost plce & 8th 6; stayed on to disp 6l 4th 12; 12l 3rd but wkng 2 out
[736⁵] 5	4	**Frozen Drop** 33-1 T Bishop Ld to 3 & agn 5-8; disp 2l 3rd 10; outpcd 13; stayed on one pce frm 3 out
[736⁴] 6	8	**Desert Run** (IRE) 66-1 B Parsons Prom; 4l 4th 4; chsd ldr nxt; sn lost plce & rr frm 10; nd aft; stayed on one pce frm 3 out
[929U] 7	5	**Amtrak Express** 66-1 H Froud (bf) 2 handlers; 7l 7th 4; eff to disp 6l 4th 12; sn wknd; bhnd frm 2 out

[762^U]   P   **Drumagolands Golden Envoy (U)** (tt) 66-1 **J Kwiatkowski** *A rr; 12l last 4; mist 13; t.o & pu 2 out*

[456^P]   P   **Jack Sun** 50-1 **J Snowden** *2½l 3rd 4; ld brief app 9; disp 2l 3rd nxt; wknd 13; rr when mist 3 out; pu nxt*

OFFICIAL DISTANCES: 2l, 15l   **TIME:** 6min 50.3s   **TOTE:** £2.30 **DF:** £1.20

953 Intermediate, 12st   13 ran

[729¹]   1   **ELLIEWELLIEWOO** (5a) 1-2F **L Jefford** *5l 5th 3; chsd ldng pr frm 9; 1½l 2nd 12; jmpd into ld 14; 10l up aft 3 out; qcknd clr nxt; impressive*

[876¹]   2   25   **Possible Pardon (NZ)** (bl) 2-1 **N Mitchell** *2 handlers; mid-div early; 5th & clsng 8; 4l 4th 10; mist nxt; outpcd 13; stayed on to 20l 3rd 3 out; chsd wnr vain frm nxt*

        3   ¾   **Gypsy Luck** (5a) 33-1 **Miss A Bush** *Hld up towards rr; 18l 6th 12; stayed on frm 3 out; nd*

        4   20   **Agile King** 25-1 **Miss C Tizzard** *Chsd ldr til ld 4; 2l up 8 til hdd 14; wkng when pckd 3 out; bhnd frm nxt; fin tired*

[633¹]   5   5   **Susies Melody (IRE)** (tt) 10-1 **D Dennis** *A towards mid-div; 15l 6th 10; rr frm 15*

[739^P]   P   **Church Field (IRE)** 50-1 **D Luff** *(xnb) Disp 3l 3rd 3; chsd ldng pr til wknd & rmdrs 10; sn 5th & lsng tch; bhnd when pu 13*

[765³]   P   **Fast Run (IRE)** 66-1 **Miss M Taylor** *A last pr; 12th & outpcd 10; pu 10*

[263^P]   P   **Kinlogh Gale (IRE)** 33-1 **G Barfoot-Saunt** *A towards rr; disp 10th 4; rmdrs 10; no resp & pu nxt*

        P   **Leejay Luki (IRE)** 33-1 **A Honeyball** *2 handlers; disp 3l 3rd 3; chsd ldrs to 6; sn wknd; bhnd when pu 13*

[736^P]   P   **Mendip Son** (bl) 20-1 **Miss P Gundry** *(xnb) Ld to 4; chsd ldr; 2l 2nd 8; disp 3½l 3rd 12; wknd 15; bhnd when pu 2 out*

[876^U]   U   **Mountain-Linnet** (7ow) 100-1 **A Corrie** *Towards rr when ur 2*

[641^F]   F   **Persian Raider** 33-1 **R Emmett** *Nt jw; a rr; mist 5; t.o 7 til pu 11*

[675¹]   P   **White Smoke (IRE)** 33-1 **R Ross** *Disp 10th 4; wkng 18l 7th 10; bhnd when pu 13*

OFFICIAL DISTANCES: dist, 1l   **TIME:** 6min 48.7s   **TOTE:** £2.50 **DF:** £1.60

954 Mixed Open, 12st   12 ran

[854¹]   1   **BUTLER JOHN (IRE)** 6-4F **A Charles-Jones** *Ld 1; jmpd 2-4; virt made rest; ½l up 10; 2l clr aft 3 out; stayed on game frm nxt*

[886⁶]   2   2   **Kilmington (IRE)** 20-1 **J Barnes** *3l 3rd 4; trckd ldr frm 8; ½l down 10; rmdr 12; 2l 2nd 3 out; no ex u.p frm nxt*

[454²]   3   5   **The Hobbit (IRE)** 8-1 **A Honeyball** *Hld up in rr; last 5; impd to 5l 5th 12; chsd ldrs frm 14 til no ex frm 2 out*

[468⁵]   4   7   **Red Parade (NZ)** 80-1 **Miss A Goschen** *(xnb) 2l 3rd 2; outpcd & towards rr 8; stayed on to 8l 4th 12; trckd ldrs til no ex frm 2 out*

[652¹]   5   30   **River Swilley (IRE)** 4-1 **R Walford** *Hld up towards rr; prog to 6th 8 & 2l 3rd 10; chsd ldr 13 til jmpd slow & lost plce 14; 3l 3rd 3 out; tired when jmpd lft last; walked in*

[681⁵]   6   20   **Chism (IRE)** 20-1 **R Young** *6l 5th 4; trckd ldrs til wknd 14; t.o 3 out*

        P   **Bannagh Mor (IRE)** 20-1 **Miss P Gundry** *Tde; disp 2-4; jmpd to disp brief agn 5; chsd ldr til grad wknd 12; bhnd when pu 3 out*

[522²]   U   **Fair Wind (IRE)** 9-4 **M Miller** *8l 5th 5; ab same when blun & ur 9*

[727^P]   P   **Highway Lad** 20-1 **L Jefford** *Mid-div 5; prog to 4th 8; chsd ldrs til wknd 14; bhnd when pu 2 out*

[652⁵]   P   **Romalito** 150-1 **Miss K Cook** *A rr; last 9; t.o 10 til pu 13*

        P   **Todd (USA)** 150-1 **L Tibbatts** *(xnb) Last 2; a towards rr; jmpd lft 11; t.o 14 til pu 3 out*

[731³]   U   **Via Del Quatro (IRE)** (5a) (vis) 66-1 **J Young** *5th when blun & ur 4*

OFFICIAL DISTANCES: 2l, 6l   **TIME:** 6min 45.5s   **TOTE:** £2.20 **DF:** c/f

Penny's Prince was withdrawn not under orders - lame

955 Open Maiden 56&7yo (Div 1), 12st   8 ran

[559^P]   1   **COOL MILLION** 20-1 **M Miller** *Chsd clr ldr 2; 20l 2nd 4; clsd to 3l 2nd 8; eff to disp ld aft 2 out; ld last; sn clr*

[71^P]   2   15   **Namron (IRE)** 5-1 **L Jefford** *Ld 2 & set mod pce; 20l up 5; stdd & 3l ahd 8; still 3l clr 3 out; hdd last; no ex*

[310^P]   P   **Ashloch** (5a) 11-1 **S Kidston** *Ld brief 1; sn rr; 28l 6th 4; last 8; jmpd v lft nxt & imm pu*

[455^P]   P   **Chasing A Bid** (7a) (tt) 12-1 **J Snowden** *22l 3rd 4; chsd ldng pr til 15l 4th 9; 5th & wkng when hit 14; imm pu; broke hind leg; destroyed*

[733⁵]   F   **Just Reuben (IRE)** (7a) 3-1 **R Walford** *Fell 1*

[655^P]   P   **Mr Baloo** 7-1 **A Charles-Jones** *Lw; rr 3; stdy prog to 20l 5th 9 & 8l 3rd 12; wknd & bhnd nxt; 3rd & tired when jmpd lft 2 out; pu sn aft*

[732⁵] P   **Sacrifice** (7a) 6-4F **G Barfoot-Saunt** Hld up; rr 3; 26l 5th nxt; prog to 13l 3rd 8; jmpd lft 9 & 12; 13l last nxt; prog to 3rd 14; sn wknd; bhnd when pu 2 out

[656ᴾ] P   **Solo Trip** (5a) 20-1 **J Barnes** 24l 4th 4; wknd 9; t.o & pu 11

OFFICIAL DISTANCE: 12l   **TIME:** 7min 11.2s   **TOTE:** £11.00 **DF:** c/f

956 Open Maiden 56&7yo (Div 2), 12st   9 ran

[213ᴾ] 1   **HARLEQUIN BOY** (bl) 9-1 **M Shears** Jmpd lft; ld 1; jnd 2-3; 1l up 10; 5l ahd when jmpd violent lft 3 out & hdd; sn ld agn; pushed out flat; wl rdn

[732⁴] 2   5   **Telimar (IRE)** evensF **J Barnes** Hld up til stdy hdwy to 3½l 4th 5; jmpd to 2nd nxt; 4th & trckng ldrs 12; chsd ldr 15 til ld brief 3 out; sn hdd; no ex frm 2 out

[471ᴾ] 3   7   **Finnigan's Lot (IRE)** 16-1 **M Walters** 4th 4; 5l 5th nxt; chsd ldr 11 down 13 til releg 3rd 15; no ex frm 2 out

    F   **Dido's Dream** (5a) 25-1 **A Charles-Jones** Last 3; 7th & in tch when fell 9

    P   **Early Morning** (7a) 25-1 **G Richards** Bit bckwd; last pr 3; last 8; jmpd novicey 10; t.o & pu 12

    P   **Flowing Again** (12a) 9-2 **Miss P Gundry** Lw; 3rd 4; chsd ldr nxt; mist 6; disp 11 2nd 10; 4th & wkng when pu 14

[563ᴾ] U   **Jolifast** 11-2 **D Alers-Hankey** (xnb) Trckng ldrs when blun & ur 3

[540ᵁ] P   **La Tormenta (IRE)** (5a) 10-1 **S Kidston** Disp ld 2-nxt; sn releg 6th 4; lsng tch when jmpd lft 12; t.o & pu 13

[730ᴾ] P   **The Greenkeeper (IRE)** 4-1 **C Heard** 2 handlers; disp 2-3; 2l 2nd 5; chsd ldr til wknd & rr 13; t.o & pu 15

OFFICIAL DISTANCES: 6l, 8l   **TIME:** 7min 07.2s   **TOTE:** £6.10 **DF:** £93.00

957 Confined Maiden 8yo&up, 12st   15 ran

[261ᵁ] 1   **GENERAL TYPHOON** 7-2 **Miss E Tory** Tde; chsd ldrs; 9l 5th 12; chsd ldr 14 til ld 3 out; sn 5l clr; easy

[725⁸] 2   10   **Mel (IRE)** 8-1 **Miss M Eames** Jmpd lft; chsd ldr 2; 4l down 6; 4½l 3rd 8; chsd ldr agn 10; stayed on one pce frm 2 out

[739²] 3   hd   **Grey Jerry** (bl) 8-1 **A Honeyball** Ld 1; 3l up 4; still 5l ahd 12; hdd 3 out & sn brushed aside; stayed on one pce nxt

[753⁷] 5   42   **Foxwyn** 33-1 **C Wilson** Towards rr when jmpd lft 3; 25l 13th 4; rmdrs 10; jmpd lft nxt; t.o 3 out

[731ᵁ] 6   2½fs   **Cool Weather (IRE)** 25-1 **B Parsons** Last 3; 27l 14th 4; t.o frm 7; fncs adrift 13; plodded on

[738³] 4d   **Frank Naylar** 5-2F **H Froud** 2 handlers; 19l 12th 4; stdy hdwy to disp 8l 3rd 4 & mist 10; chsd ldrs til wknd & mist 3 out; wandering up straight; fin 22l 4th; disq - nt weigh-in

[473ᴾ] P   **Ask In Time (IRE)** 33-1 **J Rice** 2 handlers; trckd ldrs in 4th 2; 6l 3rd 4; 2nd brief 7-8; 7l 4th 9; grad wknd nxt; bhnd when pu 13

[763ᵁ] P   **Dancing Barefoot** (5a) 20-1 **A Charles-Jones** 7th 2; 17l 11th 4; strugg when pu 13

    P   **Gradient** 25-1 **B O'Doherty** A mid-div; 15l 10th 4; bad mist 13 & rdr rec wl; pu 15

[881ᴾ] U   **Indian Miller** (5a) 25-1 **M Green** Cl 3rd 2; 7l 4th 4; towards rr of main group when blun & ur 9

[881ᴾ] P   **Jazetason** 25-1 **M Woodward** 2 handlers; mid-div 2; 7th & trckng ldrs 7; wknd 14; t.o & pu 2 out

    P   **Jentar Equilibra (IRE)** (5a) 12-1 **R Woollacott** Disp 13l 7th 4; impd to disp 8l 3rd & mist 10; joining ldng pr when mist 13 & imm lost ground; nt rec & pu 15; nt disg

    P   **Micro Missile** (5a) 10-1 **Miss P Gundry** Mid-div 2; 9l 6th 4; prog to 4th 6; chsd ldr 8; 3l down nxt; lost plce 10; sn wknd; rr when pu 3 out

    P   **Santim** 33-1 **G Weatherley** Nt jw; a rr; mist 2; last 4; mist nxt & sn t.o; pu 11

[738⁸] P   **Weycroft Valley** (5a) 25-1 **L Tibbatts** 6th 2; disp 13l 7th 4; wknd 11; rr 13 til pu 15

OFFICIAL DISTANCES: 8l, ½l   **TIME:** 6min 58.3s   **TOTE:** £9.30 **DF:** £23.00

Frank Naylar finished fourth but was disqualified when the rider failed to weigh-in; he was fined £40

958 Restricted, 12st - 15J   13 ran

[734ᴾ] 1   **GIVRY** (vis) 25-1 **N Parker** Ld 2; rn wide bend aft 4; releg last nxt; stayed on to 4l 3rd 10; ld agn 12; 4l up 15; stayed on wl frm nxt; rdr's 1st wnr

[458ᴾ] 2   5   **Bathwick Bobbie** 50-1 **Jeremy Young** Chsd ldr to 4; 4l 4th 8; ld 10-12; chsd wnr vain frm 3 out

[616⁵] 3   12   **Snowboy (IRE)** 40-1 **P Keane** Hld up in rr; 7th 5; stayed on to 5l 3rd 12; releg 4th 15; lft 3rd nxt; stayed on one pce aft

[767³] 4   15   **Lyrical Seal** (5a) (bl) 33-1 **A Charles-Jones** Chsd ldr; 2l down 4; 5l 4th 10; outpcd & rr 13; stayed on one pce frm 3 out

[477F]	P	**Aberfoyle Park (IRE)** 1-2F R Walford 5th 2; chsd ldr 6; 2½l 3rd 8 til grad lost plce & rr 13; bhnd when pu 2 out; bbv
[749⁸]	P	**Ashmead Rambler (IRE)** 33-1 Miss A Bush (xnb) Oht; disp 3l 3rd 4; rn wide bend aft 4; ld nxt; 1½l up 8; hdd nxt; sn wknd & last 13; t.o & pu 15
[847F]	B	**Calvary Hill** 50-1 D Doyne-Ditmas (xnb) Mid-div when bd 3; rdr inj
[876³]	U	**Cefn Woodsman** 66-1 Miss K Lovelace Mid-div when ur 3
[728²]	U	**Devonshire Lad** 50-1 Miss K Cook Chsng ldrs when ur 3
[563³]	F	**Green Anker** 25-1 Miss O Green Swtng; mid-div when fell 2; rdr inj
[657³]	P	**King's Courtier (IRE)** 3-1 J Snowden 4th 2; 3l 3rd 4; prom til wknd to rr 10; bhnd when pu 13
[734⁵]	U	**Old Harry's Wife** (5a) 20-1 N Mitchell Trckd ldng pr to 3; hdwy frm mid-div to 3rd 7; 1½l 2nd 8; stdd & 6l 5th 10; clsng on ldng pr when blun & ur 3 out
	F	**Pharniskey (IRE)** 9-1 J Barnes Mid-div when fell 3

OFFICIAL DISTANCES: 6l, 8l **TIME:** 6min 52.6s **TOTE:** £101.00 **DF:** -
Fences 10, 11 & 18 were omitted - fallen riders; the rider of Lyrical Seal was cautioned by the stewards for failing to obey the Starter's instructions

Cheshire Forest
Tabley (RH 7F,19J) Sun, 9 Apr (GOOD to FIRM)

959 Hunt   **6 ran**

[781P]	1		**EMERALD KNIGHT (IRE)** (3x) 2-5F C Stockton Hld up in last; hdwy 11; ld 13; made rest; hrd prsd last; r.o flat
[777⁶]	2	4	**Desert Boot** (7a) 10-1 B Wharfe Prom; ld 4; outj & hdd 13; 5l 2nd app 2 out; ev ch last; no ex flat
	3	12	**Freddie Fox** 7-1 Miss G Garton Cl up; w ldr 8-10; wknd 15; lost tch 2 out
[811R]	U		**Horton-Cum-Peel (IRE)** 4-1 W Kinsey Prom; ld 3-4; handy til blun & ur 6
[173²]	F		**Maltese Cross** 5-1 A Gribbin Trckd ldrs; 10l 3rd when fell 2 out
	U		**Riot Lady (IRE)** (5a) 7-1 Miss K Crank Ld to 3; cl 2nd when blun & ur 6

OFFICIAL DISTANCES: 4l, 15l **TIME:** 6min 18.0s **TOTE:** £2.00

960 Confined, 12st   **11 ran**

[902³]	1		**ALY DALEY (IRE)** (5x) 4-1 Miss A Price Prom; went 2nd 10; lft in ld app 2 out; all out
[622⁸]	2	1	**Blank Cheque** 7-1 D Coates Hld up; hdwy 13; outpcd nxt; rallied 2 out; r.o
[780³]	3	6	**Hello Me Man (IRE)** 12-1 Mrs K Diggle Handy; rdn 3 out; one pce
[776²]	4	20	**Orton House** 20-1 T Greenway Prom; lost plce aft 10; sn bhnd
[901³]	5	8	**Ita's Fellow (IRE)** (5x) 4-1 M Prince A bhnd; strugg 8; nd
[777⁷]	6	12	**River Moy** (5a) 33-1 B Foster A bhnd; lost tch 13; t.o
[529³]	U		**All In The Game (IRE)** 25-1 S Prior Hmpd & ur 1
[902³]	P		**Applefort (IRE)** 8-1 M Worthington Prom; wknd 15; no ch when blun 3 out; t.o & pu nxt
[564F]	r		**Glacial Trial (IRE)** (5a,3ow) 7-4F A Crow Rr til ref 7
[864⁶]	F		**Glamdring** (5a) 33-1 I Clyde Pulled hrd; fell 1
[781⁴]	U		**My Nominee** (bl) 6-1 L Stephens Ld & still gng wl when hmpd by loose horse & ur app 2 out

OFFICIAL DISTANCES: 1l, 6l **TIME:** 6min 04.6s **TOTE:** £9.00

961 Land Rover Mens Open, 12st   **8 ran**

[178²]	1		**JACOB'S WIFE** (5a,5ow) 1-2F A Crow Made all; clr 7; 20l clr 11; jmpd lft 2 out; rdn out flat
[796P]	2	3	**Khatir (CAN)** (bl) 25-1 N Kent Rn in snatches; impd to 2nd 11; rdn app 2 out; r.o u.p aft last
[543F]	3	30	**Nishvamitra** 14-1 A Woodward (bf) Chsd ldrs; strugg frm 12; nd & sn btn; dism; lame
[902⁸]	4	10	**Batty's Island** 6-1 L Stephens Hld up in tch; outpcd frm 12; sn wl bhnd
[525³]	5	3	**Kidlaw** (7x) 10-1 W Turner Bhnd; blun 9; sn t.o; dism; lame
	F		**Johnstons Buck (IRE)** 25-1 T Marlow Unruly padd; ss; rr til fell 12
[779⁵]	P		**Russian Castle** (7x) 20-1 A McKay Chsd ldr; nt fluent 4; still 2nd when pu 8
[776⁶]	P		**St Athans Lad** (7x) 33-1 B Seddon Swtng; reluct to rce & a t.o; 3 fncs bhnd when pu 5

OFFICIAL DISTANCES: 3l, 30l **TIME:** 6min 09.8s **TOTE:** £1.30
Haveafewmanners was withdrawn not under orders - injured when tongue-strap fitted

962 Ladies Open
5 ran

[904⁴]	1		**CELTIC WHO (IRE)** 7-4 Mrs C Ford *Prom; ld app 7; hdd app 14; ld agn 16; all out towards fin*
[525⁵]	2	½	**Ambrose** 6-1 Miss T Clark *(bf) Bit bckwd; swtng; in tch; impd to ld app 14; hdd 16; outpcd app 2 out; rallied & r.o str flat*
[589²]	3	6	**Analystic (IRE)** (7x) 6-4F Miss S Sharratt *Lw; handy; mist 8; ev ch 2 out; no ex app last*
[463⁸]	4	30	**China Lal** (5a) 4-1 Mrs K Diggle *Pulled hrd; ld; hdd app 7; wknd aft 3 out*
[813³]	P		**See You Always (IRE)** 8-1 Miss A Price *A last plce; t.o 7; pu 3 out*

OFFICIAL DISTANCES: ¾l, 5l TIME: 6min 04.3s TOTE: £2.30

963 Restricted, 12st
11 ran

[296⁶]	1		**MISTER MOSS (IRE)** 7-4F G Hanmer *Lw; ld at gd pce; sn clr; 25l ahd 2 out; easy*
[589⁶]	2	15	**Secret Alliance (IRE)** 10-1 A Crow *Chsd ldrs; nt fluent 3; went 2nd app 2 out; no imp*
[782⁶]	3	4	**Tale Bridge (IRE)** 14-1 Mrs C Ford *Chsd ldr to 3; in tch in 3rd til outpcd final circ*
	4	12	**Serenze (IRE)** 7-1 J Downes *Bckwd; midfield; outpcd 10; plodded on*
[782⁸]	5	15	**Pear Tree Percy** 12-1 D Sherlock *Chsd ldr frm 3 til app 2 out; wknd*
[858ᴿ]	6	7	**Hotscent (IRE)** (5a) 20-1 Miss C Wilberforce *A bhnd*
[863ᵁ]	7	2	**Ballyharry (IRE)** 8-1 I Wynne *Midfield; mist 9; bhnd 10; no ch when blun 2 out*
[777¹]	U		**Arthur Henry** 5-1 C Barlow *Hld up til blun & ur 11*
[778¹]	P		**Hamish** 5-1 M Worthington *Lw; svs; wl bhnd; nt fluent 2; t.o 11; pu 13*
	U		**Lady Dot** (5a) 3-1 B Foster *Ss; no ch when blun & ur 3 out*
	P		**Train Lover (NZ)** 7-1 G Smith *Bckwd; a bhnd; t.o & pu 10*

OFFICIAL DISTANCES: 15l, 4l TIME: 6min 02.4s TOTE: £6.00

964 Open Maiden - 18J
16 ran

[906ᶜ]	1		**ISHEREAL (IRE)** 16-1 J R Barlow *Cl up; ld 3-7; ld agn 13; rdn when lft clr last*
[816ᵁ]	2	12	**The Shy Padre (IRE)** 3-1JF J Townson *Bit bckwd; midfield; hdwy 13; lft 2nd app last; no imp*
[570ᵁ]	3	4	**Inglerise** (12a,4ow) 4-1 G Hanmer *Lw; hld up in rr; r.o str frm 2 out; one to note*
	4	12	**Nagara Sound** 12-1 J Downes *Swtng; hld up; bhny 13; ev ch 3 out; wknd nxt*
[776ᵁ]	5	15	**Strong Mission (IRE)** 12-1 G Halliday *Pulled v hrd; prom; ld 7-13; still ev ch 3 out; wknd app nxt*
[583⁷]	6	12	**King Paddy (IRE)** 8-1 R Bevan *Hld up; hdwy 13; chall when rn out app last; cont*
[694ᵁ]	F		**Barney Bear** 12-1 J Merry *In tch; tkng clsr ord when fell 13*
[906ᵁ]	U		**Caherlow (IRE)** 6-1 Miss C Goodall *Blun & ur 1*
[588ᵖ]	U		**Charlie Keay (IRE)** 4-1 C Stockton *Midfield til blun & ur 9*
[570ᵖ]	P		**Dancing Paws (IRE)** (7a) 16-1 C Hoggart *A bhnd; blun 15; t.o & pu 2 out*
	F		**Frenchman** (tt) 16-1 D Sherlock *Ld to 3; still cl up when fell 11*
[593⁷]	F		**Fruit Crop** (5a) 3-1JF L Stephens *A bhnd; no ch when fell 3 out*
	S		**Mandela Square** 6-1 M Worthington *Bckwd; rdn in padd; midfield til slpd up bend bef 14*
[777⁵]	F		**Mr Peoples (IRE)** 12-1 T Greenway *Chsd ldrs; mist 8; fell 11*
[593¹]	P		**Peover Eye** (7a) 20-1 C Barlow *A bhnd; t.o & pu 13*
[616⁴]	U		**Red Spice** 10-1 R Owen *Rr 6; blun & ur 15*

OFFICIAL DISTANCES: 12l, 4l TIME: 6min 12.4s TOTE: £32.00

Fence 18 was omitted - fallen horse; the stewards enquired into the running and riding of Inglerise - the rider's explanation that having to avoid two fallers brought him almost to a trot and he could not get back into the race was recorded

965 Open Maiden 56&7yo (Div 1), 12st
10 ran

	1		**CASSIA GREEN** 3-1 M Worthington *Lw; prom; ld aft 3 out; lft clr nxt*
[906ᵁ]	2	20	**Sharp Embrace** 8-1 J Burley *In tch; trckd ldrs 11; outpcd 14; nd aft*
[906ᵖ]	3	3	**Mister Pimpernel (IRE)** 5-1 J Downes *Prom; ld app 7; hdd 8; handy when blun 15; sn wknd*
[695ᵖ]	4	1½	**Bright Reform (IRE)** 4-1 C Barlow *Bckwd; bhnd; hdwy & prom 13; lft 2nd when mist 2 out; sn wknd*
	U		**B J Bubbles** 8-1 G Thomas *Bckwd; nt jw; sn bhnd; blun & ur 5*
[778⁵]	F		**Maudette (IRE)** (12a) 6-1 D Sherlock *Lw; prom; ld 8; mist 3 out; sn hdd; rdn when fell 2 out*
[778ᵖ]	P		**Native Rain (IRE)** (7a) 8-1 Miss E Lea *Bckwd; ss; bhnd; hdwy to ld app 4; hdd app 7; bhnd 9; t.o & pu 11*

	P	**Pocket Oscar** 8-1 J R Barlow *Midfield; bhnd frm 13; t.o to pu 4 out*
[777²]	P	**Robert The Rascal** 5-2F A Gribbin *Ss; a bhnd; jmpd slow 7; t.o to pu 10*
[568⁶]	F	**Roundabout** (5a) 12-1 L Whiston *Bckwd; ld; hdd app 4; still in tch when fell 10*

OFFICIAL DISTANCES: 20l, 3l   **TIME:** 6min 14.0s   **TOTE:** £5.00

966 Open Maiden 56&7yo (Div 2), 12st   10 ran

[777⁴]	1		**PINOULI** (5a) 5-1 J R Barlow *Prom; ld app 4; made rest; blun last; r.o*
	2	2	**Little Brown Bear** (IRE) 2-1JF Mrs C Ford *Bckwd; handy; rdn to chall flat; r.o u.p*
	3	20	**Native Cannon** (IRE) 2-1JF A Crow *Rr; hdwy & prom 7; no ex frm 2 out*
	4	10	**Doug Eng** (IRE) 10-1 R Bevan *Ld; hdd app 4; handy til wknd 4 out*
[704⁵]	5	5	**Step Quick** (IRE) 5-1 G Hanmer *A bhnd*
[570⁵]	6	25	**Mrs Sherman** (12a,2ow) 8-1 M Worthington *Bckwd; trckd ldrs; mist 13; wknd 2 out*
	U		**Blakes Corner** (5a) 10-1 J Merry *Mist 2; bhnd when jmpd lft 4; blun & ur 6*
[588⁶]	F		**Pendil's Dream** (5a) 5-1 D Sherlock *A bhnd; mist 13; fell 3 out*
[694⁸]	P		**Saxon Moss** 12-1 G Smith *Bckwd; a bhnd; t.o & pu 14*
[694⁸]	P		**Wily Miss** 14-1 C Barlow *Nt jw; midfield; rmdrs aft 5; bhnd 12; t.o & pu 14*

OFFICIAL DISTANCES: 1½l, 20l   **TIME:** 6min 11.3s

Cotswold

Andoversford (RH 9F,19J) Sun, 9 Apr (GOOD with SOFT patches)

967 Hunt   3 ran

[752¹]	1		**GLEVUM** (5a,5x) 4-7F T Scudamore *4l5-4l7; ld til outj & hdd 7; ld agn 13; made rest; rdn clr app last; comf*
[751²]	2	4	**Newton Point** (5x) 11-8 Mrs B Keighley *Sn pushed along; chsd ldr til jmpd slow 5; 4l 3rd 3 out; went 2nd app last; no imp flat*
	3	6	**Pretoria Dancer** (vis) 16-1 F O'Brien *Last til went 2nd 6; jmpd to ld 7; rmdr 10; hdd 13; rdn & btn when dem last*

OFFICIAL DISTANCES: 5l, 6l   **TIME:** 6min 26.0s

968 Confined, 12st   18 ran

[749⁰]	1		**WELL TED** (IRE) 5-4F Julian Pritchard *7l4-5l4; last to 4; 12l 14th 9; went 8l 5th 3 out; smooth prog to ld nxt; rdn out*
[749⁵]	2	2	**Granville Grill** (3x) 8-1 J Deutsch *Tde; jmpd lft; ld 4-2 out; one pce aft*
[749⁵]	3	nk	**Royal Estate** (3x) 5-1 A Evans *Bhnd; prog to 6l 6th 10; cl 3rd 3 out; one-pcd u.p nxt*
[561⁵]	4	8	**Mostyn** 8-1 P Pritchard *Chsd ldrs; 4th & mist 12; went 2nd nxt; rdn aft 3 out; wknd nxt*
[701¹]	5	12	**Bolshie Baron** (tt) 5-1 M Harris *Ww; prog 10; 4l 4th 13; rdn & btn app 2 out*
[883⁵]	6	4	**Parman** (IRE) (5x) 14-1 R Dalgety *Bhnd; 16th 11; r.o frm 3 out; nvr nrr*
[702³]	7	2	**Blue Rosette** (3x) (bl) 14-1 R Biddlecombe *Chsd ldrs to 14; no ch frm 3 out*
[671⁴]	8	8	**Major Bugler** (IRE) 20-1 S Bush *Mid-div; mist 2; 8l 5th 14; wknd 16*
[895⁸]	P		**Bitofabuzz** (IRE) 20-1 D Birkmyre *Mists; rr & blun 2; mist 5; wl bhnd frm 10; t.o & pu last*
[895⁸]	P		**Blessed Oliver** (3x) (vis) 20-1 J Trice-Rolph *A bhnd; t.o & pu 13*
[702⁸]	P		**Chicodari** 8-1 E Walker *Bhnd; last 8; t.o & pu 13*
[631⁸]	P		**Flying Fellow** (IRE) 14-1 J Gasper *Swtng; prom; 5th & mist 8; wknd 12; bhnd when pu 16*
[895⁸]	P		**Furry Fox** (IRE) 20-1 J Baimbridge *Bhnd frm 11; t.o & pu last*
[884⁸]	P		**Golden Gunner** (IRE) 20-1 P Young *Ld to 4; prom til wknd 11; t.o & pu last*
	P		**Prophet's Thumb** (IRE) 20-1 L Lay *Chsd ldrs to 10; grad wknd; bhnd 14; t.o & pu last*
[510¹²]	P		**Real Progress** (IRE) 20-1 D Renney *W ldrs to 5; stdly lost plce; no ch 14; t.o & pu last*
[895⁸]	P		**Rustic Gent** (IRE) 20-1 M Keel *A bhnd; jmpd slow 4; last 14; t.o & pu last*
	r		**Young In Heart** (5a) 20-1 A Martin *Ref 1*

OFFICIAL DISTANCES: 1l, ½l, 1l   **TIME:** 6min 17.0s

969 Ladies Open   10 ran

[751⁴]	1		**BOARDING SCHOOL** (tt) 8-1 Miss A De Lisle Wells *Ld to 2; chsd ldng pr aft; 10l 3rd 14; hdwy aft 3 out; ld app last; r.o wl*
[751¹]	2	3	**Mr Custard** evensF Miss L Sweeting *Ld 4 til mist & hdd 7; hit nxt; chsd ldr aft; mist 16; ld aft 3 out; hdd app last; unable to qckn u.p flat*
[765¹]	3	30	**Olive Basket** (5a) 12-1 Miss W Southcombe *Chsd ldng trio frm 8; 18l 4th 14; nvr on terms; went poor 3rd app last*
[699⁴]	4	3	**Blue Lyzander** (5a) 20-1 Mrs E Staines *(xnb) A mid-div; 18l 6th 12; nvr on terms; went poor 4th nr fin*

[78^P]	5	2	**Haunting Music (IRE)** 14-1 *Miss E Neyens (xnb) Jmpd bold; ld 2-4; ld agn 7; 3l up 3 out; hdd app nxt; wknd rap*
[668²]	6	30	**Wolfie Smith** 20-1 *Miss W Houldey 2 handlers; nt fluent; a wl bhnd; t.o frm 13*
[390⁵]	7	15	**Norman Warrior** (bl) 16-1 *Miss V Sturgis Jmpd lft; last & jmpd slow 6; t.o frm 8*
	P		**Charlie's Gift** (5a) 20-1 *Miss E Lockwood A rr; 30l 7th 11; t.o & pu 16*
[699²]	U		**Haughton Lad (IRE)** 3-1 *Miss C Stucley Mid-div; 15l 5th when tried to ref & ur 13*
	P		**Quite A Miss** (5a) 12-1 *Miss S Duckett Sa & lost 20l; a wl bhnd; t.o & pu 13*

OFFICIAL DISTANCES: 4l, dist, 3l TIME: 6min 16.0s

970 Land Rover Mens Open, 12st   8 ran

[700¹]	1		**NETHER GOBIONS** (7x) 4-5F *Julian Pritchard Made all; 3l clr 15; hrd prsd 2 out; stayed on wl & clr agn last*
[652³]	2	3	**Bomba Charger** 3-1 *Richard Darke Chsd wnr til mist 3; went 2nd 11; chall on inner 2 out; unable to qckn app last*
[766¹]	3	4	**Bit O'Speed (IRE)** (7x) 5-1 *J Richardson (xnb) Ww; 10l 5th 7; prog to 4l 3rd 16; ev ch app 2 out; one pce aft*
[818⁵]	4	6	**Adventurus** 20-1 *J Liley Mid-div; 5th frm 14; 12l down 3 out; went 4th nxt; nvr able to chall*
[750²]	5	12	**Golden Savannah** 8-1 *A Maculan A bhnd; lost tch 12*
[895^P]	P		**Egypt Mill Prince** 20-1 *E Walker Prom; chsd wnr 4-11; sn wknd; bhnd & pu 13*
[895³]	P		**Lie Detector** (4x) 10-1 *J Gasper Nvr gng wl; last til some prog to 12l 6th 8; last agn & rmdrs 10; pu 13*
[384⁸]	P		**Wixoe Wonder (IRE)** (7x) 20-1 *T Scudamore Chsd ldrs; 3l 3rd 11; 4th & rdn 16; sn btn; pu 2 out*

OFFICIAL DISTANCES: 2l, 3l, 2l TIME: 6min 20.0s

971 Intermediate, 12st   8 ran

[701³]	1		**FULL SCORE (IRE)** 7-4F *Julian Pritchard Tchd 2s; made all; mist 11; pushed clr app last; easy*
[698¹]	2	8	**Cherokee Run (IRE)** (tt) 7-2 *M Keel Mid-div; prog 11; went 3l 3rd 14; chsd wnr & ev ch app 2 out; outpcd app last*
[429³]	3	8	**Furious Avenger** 12-1 *L Lay 2 handlers; prsd wnr til app 2 out; sn wknd*
[744^P]	P		**Annastate** (5a) 5-1 *R Biddlecombe Mists; ww in rr; prog to 12l 6th 8; lsng tch when blun 13; pu aft*
[748²]	P		**Claymore Lad** 9-2 *A Maculan Chsd ldrs til lost plce 7; rallied to 12l 4th 14; nd aft; pu last*
[748^F]	U		**Holloa Away (IRE)** (bl) 20-1 *R Millar Tde; chsd ldrs; mist 3; rdn & wkng 12; 20l 5th when blun & ur 15*
[669^P]	P		**Silly Boy** (7a) 20-1 *A Martin 2 handlers; last til prog to 6l 5th 10; wkng when jmpd slow 12; last when pu nxt*
[476^U]	P		**Viking Flame** (5a) 6-1 *S Bush A bhnd; 15l last 9; t.o 14; pu 2 out*

OFFICIAL DISTANCES: 10l, 8l TIME: 6min 19.0s

972 Open Maiden, 12st   13 ran

[455^P]	1		**BALLYBLACK (IRE)** 9-4F *T Scudamore (xnb) 3s-9/4; chsd ldrs til prog to ld 13; made rest; rdn clr app last; comf*
[754^U]	2	10	**Wood Buzzard** 7-1 *E Walker Prom; chsd ldr 3-6 & agn 14; ev ch 2 out; sn outpcd*
[891^P]	3	12	**Champagne Thunder** (tt) 16-1 *M Keel (xnb)Prom; chsd ldr 6-13; ev ch 3 out; wknd app nxt*
[893²]	4	20	**Spirit Prince** 5-1 *P Pritchard 2 handlers; tde; ww; prog to trck ldrs 9; wknd 14; no ch 16; crawled over last; trotted in; t.o*
[898^P]	P		**Brother Simon** 20-1 *M Wall Rr of main group; hmpd 2; blun 10; sn lost tch; pu 14*
[434^U]	U		**Country Buzzard** (5a) 20-1 *L Lay Swtng; blun & ur 1*
[786^P]	P		**Crack 'n' Run** 20-1 *J Gasper (xnb,b4) Pulling; hld up in tch to 10; last frm 12; pu 14*
[739^P]	P		**Devil's Sting (IRE)** 16-1 *J Richardson Ld to 13; chsd ldrs til 4th & btn aft 3 out; pu nxt*
[892^U]	r		**Final Quay** (5a) (bl) 8-1 *M Carter A bhnd; 10th when ref & ur 13*
[672³]	P		**Idlewild (IRE)** (7a) (bl) 3-1 *Julian Pritchard (xnb) 2 handlers; hld up & wl bhnd; mist 5; jmpd slow 7; 10l 7th 12; blun nxt; smooth prog to jn wnr 2 out; imm downed tools & pulled himself up app last*
[738⁴]	P		**Mister River (IRE)** (bl) 12-1 *P Young Chsd ldrs; went 2nd 13; blun bad nxt; nt rec; pu 15*
	C		**Pulkerry (IRE)** 14-1 *A Martin Prom; 2nd when carried out by loose horse 3*
[792^P]	P		**Whistling Song** (12a) 14-1 *J Trice-Rolph In tch to 10; sn bhnd; pu 14*

OFFICIAL DISTANCES: 10l, 8l TIME: 6min 32.0s

Dumfriesshire

Lockerbie (RH 9F,19J) Sun, 9 Apr (GOOD to FIRM)

973 Intermediate, 12st
10 ran

[495⁴]	1		**DEAN DEIFIR (IRE)** 3-1 C Storey (xnb) Mid-div; 15l 5th 6; 6l 5th 9; 12l 5th aft nxt; prog to disp ld 14; 2l up nxt; 2l up 2 out; 1l up last; stayed on wl
[716⁵]	2	2	**Boyup Brook** 9-4 T Morrison Trckd ldrs; 10l 3rd 4; hit 11; prog to ld aft 14; mist & 2l down 15; ev ch 2 out; stayed on; nt pce to chall
[716⁸]	3	20	**Driminamore (IRE)** (7ow) 16-1 W Ramsay Chsd ldrs; 8l 4th 10; outpcd frm 14; disp 15l 3rd nxt; kpt on; nt trble ldrs
[912⁴]	4	2½	**Mischievous Andy (IRE)** 10-1 Mrs K Hargreave (xnb) Disp 4l 6th 2; nvr btr than mid-div; 14l 6th 10; nvr nrr; 20l 4th 2 out
[714⁵]	5	15	**Thinkaboutthat (IRE)** 12-1 J Muir Trckd ldr; 2l 2nd 5; disp ld brief 8 & ld nxt; 1l up 10; hdd & outpcd app 14; 10l 3rd nxt; grad lost tch; t.o 2 out
	P		**Behavingbadly (IRE)** (7a,1ow) 7-1 R Morgan Lw; stdd start & 10l last 1; mists 2 & 3; just pr 4; some prog 9 & 15l 7th aft nxt; outpcd & lsng tch 14; pu 16
[497ᴾ]	U		**Luvly Bubbly** 20-1 M Clayton Ld brief 2; sn mid-div; strugg 11; 25l last & mist 13; blun & ur nxt
[501¹]	P		**Mystical Music** (5a) 2-1F Miss M Bremner 5/2-2s; rr; 8l 9th aft 1; still wl off pce 13; prog to disp 15l 3rd 15; just ld 16; hit nxt & pu
	P		**Silver Ellie** (5a) 20-1 J Ewart A rr; last pr 4; 25l last 6; mist nxt; t.o & strugg when pu 12
	F		**Thistlekicker (IRE)** 16-1 L Morgan (xnb) Oht; sn ld; 1½l up 5; jnd 8 & hdd nxt; trckd ldr in 2l 2nd frm 11 til outpcd 13; sn bhnd; fell 3 out; winded

OFFICIAL DISTANCES: 2½l, 20l **TIME:** 7min 02.0s

974 Ladies Open
5 ran

[661²]	1		**NOVA NITA** (5a) 1-2F Mrs V Jackson Rr early; last 1; 4l 4th 2; disp 2l 2nd 5; disp 3l 3rd 10; prog to 1l 2nd 14; chall aft 15; just ld 2 out; qcknd 3l clr app last; stayed on; comf
[715³]	2	4	**Sharp Thyne (IRE)** (bl) 6-1 Miss M Bremner Ld at sedate pce; 2l up app 2; jnd aft 15; just hdd 2 out; ½l down aft; rdn & nt qckn; easily outpcd app last
[418²]	3	10	**Denim Blue** 7-2 Miss P Robson Trckd ldrs in cl 3rd mostly; 3l 3rd & ev ch 15; hit nxt & outpcd; nt pushed; 15l 3rd 2 out
[661⁷]	4	10	**Dashmar** 33-1 Miss R Barrow Cl 2nd mostly til 3l 3rd 14; 8l 4th & outpcd nxt; 12l 4th & no imp 16
[815ᵁ]	5	15	**No Problem Jac** (5a) (bl,tt) 25-1 Miss J Hedley Rr; 6l last when bad mist 3 & rdr lost iron; trckd ldr nxt; releg 6l last agn 9; lsng tch when hit 12; t.o when climbed last

OFFICIAL DISTANCES: 5l, 15l **TIME:** 7min 22.0s

975 Mens Open
7 ran

[915ᵁ]	1		**BOW TIE** 6-4F R Morgan Chsd ldrs; 15l 3rd 4; went 2nd aft 11 & lft in ld nxt; 4l ahd 16; stayed on wl; comf
[716³]	2	6	**Rainbow Times (IRE)** (5a) 9-4 C Storey Hld up in rr; 12l 5th 10; prog to 1½l 2nd 13; chsd ldr aft; 4l down & hrd rdn 16; nt pce to chall
[421⁴]	3	3½	**Houselope Beck** 20-1 M Clayton Mid-div; 10l 4th 10; prog to 2l 3rd 13; outpcd aft 15; 6l 3rd 3 out; kpt on wl
[915ᵁ]	P		**Charlieadams (IRE)** 7-2 J Muir Jmpd sticky at times; set str pce; 4l up & jmpd slow 7; hit nxt; lkng to ref when mist & rdr lost iron 9; shot 10l clr 11; 15l up when pu
[716⁶]	P		**Chummy's Saga** 25-1 J Innes Swtng; a rr & nvr put in rce; mist 3; 30l last 4-5; sn t.o; pu aft 15
[716ᵁ]	U		**Master Hyde (USA)** (7ow) 33-1 J Brown Rr 1; sn pulled thro field; 10l 3rd when rfo 2
[659³]	F		**Mr Fudge** 20-1 P Lentelink Trckd ldr; 3l 2nd 10; outpcd 12 & 15l 4th aft 13; 20l 4th 15; wl bhnd when fell 16; winded

OFFICIAL DISTANCES: 8l, 4l **TIME:** 6min 56.0s

976 Restricted
19 ran

[908⁴]	1		**BLYTH BROOK** 6-1 C Storey Mid-div; prog to ld 3 out; sn qcknd clr; stayed on
[713ᵁ]	2	6	**Border Farmer (IRE)** 5-1 Mrs V Jackson Swtng; unruly & dism start; rr; 25l off pce 6; prog 13 to 10l 10th 15; 1l 2nd & ev ch 2 out; sn outpcd
[663ᴾ]	3	4	**Mini Cruise** 10-1 L Morgan Chsd ldrs; 4l 4th 10; no imp 16; 3rd & stayed on wl frm 2 out
[913¹]	4	2	**Roscoe Burn** 6-1 R Morgan Trckd ldr til ld 4; 1l ahd 10; hdd & outpcd 3 out; kpt on
[717ᴾ]	5	8	**Tursal (IRE)** 16-1 A Crookston Prom; 1l 2nd 10; 5l 3rd 13; outpcd 16; no imp when lft 5th aft 2 out

[418U]	6	3	**Tenella's Last** (5a) 16-1 T Mounsey-Heysham *Cl up early; 10l 11th app 11; in tch in mid-div til outpcd 15; 25l down 2 out; kpt on wl aft*
[918P]	7	2	**Rock On Bud (IRE)** (tt) 14-1 T Davidson *(xnb)Rr early; prog & in tch in mid-div 12; 8l off pce aft 15; sn outpcd; 25l down 2 out*
[713³]	8	8	**Grey Rock (IRE)** (5a) 7-1 Miss K Miller *(bf) Mists; mid-div; 10l off pce 4; lost tch 13; wl bhnd 16; kpt on; 30l down 2 out*
[713P]	9	5	**Flaming Sunrise** 8-1 Miss D Calder *Rr; mist 3; 25l last 6; some prog aft 14 but nd; 30l down 2 out*
[713U]	10	5	**Polly's Lady** (5a) 16-1 T Morrison *A rr; 20l off pce 5; nd; nt gvn hrd time; t.o 2 out*
[713P]	11	3	**Dino's Mistral** 12-1 M Clayton *(xnb) Sis; a rr; jmpd lft 3 & 4; 25l off pce 6; nt hrd prsd; t.o 2 out*
[908⁵]	F		**Border Reiver (IRE)** 8-1 W Renwick *Mid-div; prog to 7l 9th aft 14; hdwy & ev ch when fell on flat app 16; broke leg; dead*
[714P]	P		**Buck Lady (IRE)** (5a) 10-1 Miss R Barrow *(orbs) Mid-div; 8l 10th 9; wknd qckly aft 13; t.o & pu 15*
[420P]	P		**Commanche Scout (IRE)** 10-1 T Oates *Swtng; oht; prom; 11 2nd 5; mist & nrly ur 9; gd rcvry; wknd 13; pu aft 15; bbv*
[663P]	R		**Flower Of Dunblane** (5a) 20-1 B Lusted *(xnb) Rdr cab-calling; in tch; outpcd 16; rdn nxt; 12l 5th when landed awkward & ducked out aft 2 out*
[718¹]	R		**Golf Land (IRE)** 7-2F S Huggan *(xnb) Prom; disp 3rd 5; 2l 2nd 11; ld 14; ld/disp til hdd 16; 14l 7th & wkng when rn out aft 2 out*
[665¹]	P		**Hey Chief (IRE)** 8-1 P Strang Steel *Chsd ldrs; cl 3rd 9; 5l 5th nxt; outpcd 16; rdn nxt; 18l 8th when hit 2 out & sltly hmpd; pu aft*
[46P]	P		**Normandy Duke (NZ)** 14-1 Mrs K Hargreave *Ld; blun & nrly ur 1; mist 2; hdd aft 3; cl up til strugg 13; t.o when mist 14; pu 15*
[719¹]	P		**Senso (IRE)** 4-1 Mrs C Cox *Mid-div; 10l off pce when rdr lost irons 10; virt pu nxt & regained iron; cont t.o; 2 fncs bhnd when pu aft 14*

OFFICIAL DISTANCES: 8l, 6l **TIME:** 7min 03.0s

977 Confined Maiden (Div 1), 12st   11 ran

[500³]	1		**DIVET HILL** 9-2 M Clayton *Jw; hdstrng; made all; 2l ahd 13; qcknd clr nxt; 8l up 16; 15l clr 2 out; unchal; mist last; pushed out; comf*
[808⁶]	2	20	**I Say Dancer (IRE)** (5a) 12-1 Miss C Metcalfe *Unruly padd; prom; 4l 4th 10; prog to chse ldr 13; 3l 2nd nxt; sn outpcd & no ch w wnr; 5l 2nd 15; 15l down 2 out*
[659²]	3	3	**Good Profit** 16-1 T Davidson *Prom early; 4l 5th 4; 10l 5th 10; outpcd 13; sn t.o; kpt on frm 2 out; rdn to tk poor 3rd flat*
[719²]	4	2	**Lady Alice** (5a) 7-4F L Morgan *Trckd ldr; 2l 2nd aft 10; 2l 3rd & mist 14; 10l down & outpcd nxt; 25l down 3 out; mist last; tired & dem flat*
[719³]	5	8	**Whiskey Galore** 7-1 W Renwick *(xnb) Trckd ldr; disp 1l 2nd 4; 3l 3rd 5; outpcd 13; 15l 5th 15; strugg aft*
[665P]	6	1½fs	**Border Country** 33-1 Miss M Bremner *2 handlers; mid-div; 15l off pce 5; 20l 8th & strugg 10; sn t.o*
[816P]	P		**Aces High** 33-1 T Morrison *Reluct; nrly ref & jmpd slow 1; rmdrs aft; jmpd big 2; sn bhnd; 25l 10th 10; t.o & pu last*
[364F]	P		**Male Order (IRE)** 4-1 R Morgan *Stdd start; hdstrng; 10l last 1; prog to 15l 6th aft 9 & 10l 7th aft nxt; hit 12; lost tch 14; pu 15*
	P		**Rambling Mick (IRE)** 6-1 C Storey *2 handlers; oht; mists; mid-div; 10l 6th app 11; hit nxt; outpcd 13; wl bhnd when pu 2 out*
[909P]	P		**Solway Spice** (12a) 12-1 Miss J Hedley *Sn rr; mist 4; bhnd & strugg 9; 30l last 10; t.o & pu 13*
[713P]	P		**The Parlour Maid** (5a) 16-1 T Scott *Mid-div; 12l 8th 6; outpcd aft 12; sn t.o; pu 2 out*

OFFICIAL DISTANCES: 25l, 6l **TIME:** 7min 15.0s

978 Confined Maiden (Div 2), 12st   8 ran

[184⁵]	1		**HARLEIDALUS (IRE)** 10-11F R Morgan *6/4-10/11; lw; nt a fluent; trckd ldr til ld & hit 5; 3l 3rd 6; lft in ld nxt; 2l ahd 16; sn clr; 10l up at last; r.o*
[719³]	2	12	**Setting Sail** (5a) 2-1 Mrs V Jackson *Hung lft in mid-div; 5l 5th aft 10; 15l 4th & outpcd 13; gd hdwy to 2l 2nd nxt; sn lost plce; lft 3l 2nd 3 out; ev ch when hung bad lft & saddle slpd 2 out; trotted in*
[665⁷]	3	¾	**Meadowleck** (5a) (tt) 16-1 R Nichol *(bf)Trckd ldrs; disp 3l 2nd 9; outpcd 12; 8l 3rd nxt; 15l 4th 15; nd; rdn flat*
[365P]	F		**Billieburn** 8-1 L Morgan *2 handlers; reared up start & rdr jmpd off; stdd in rr; jmpd big 1; 10l last & jmpd btr aft; prog to 1l 2nd 10; 3l down & ev ch when fell 3 out; rdr inj*
[719F]	P		**Colisnova** (5a) 16-1 C Niblo *A rr; pulling; 15l last 6; wknd 11; 25l 5th 15; pu nxt*
[365P]	P		**Gladys** (5a) 20-1 T Scott *Prom early; disp 3l 2nd 9; 4l 4th aft 10; sn outpcd; 15l 5th & strugg aft 12; t.o 14; pu 3 out*

[908⁶] **R** **Strong Debate (IRE)** 13-2 N Crookston *Ld til rn wide & hdd brief bef 2; 2l up nxt; rn out thro wing 4 (rdr stuck in wing)*

[664ᴾ] **R** **Wheresbob** 20-1 T Davidson *(bf) Hdstrng; prom; 2l 2nd 3; lft in ld brief nxt; cl up til hung lft & rn out 7*

OFFICIAL DISTANCES: 15l, 1½l **TIME:** 7min 20.0s

979 Hunt
4 ran

[424⁶] **1** **SOLWAYSANDS** (bl) 7-4 S Hughes *Sn ld til stdd 3; lft in ld agn 5 til hdd aft 10; sn ld agn; 20l clr & jmpd slow 14; unchall*

  2 1½l **Red Fox (U)** 12-1 Mrs J Lancaster *Fat; jw; hvly rstrnd w rdr standing in irons; 8l 3rd 4; 10l 2nd 6; ld aft 10 til rn wide & hdd app nxt; 10l down & wkng qckly 13; fnce bhnd 2 out*

[664ᴾ] **P** **Shenoso** (12a) (vis) 6-1 R Robinson *Tubed; oht; sn t.o; jmpd slow 3; 20l last nxt; 30l 3rd 10; fnce bhnd 12; 2 fncs bhnd when pu 16*

[665⁵] **R** **Tweed Brig** 4-7F R Morgan *(citation) Hdstrng & hanging; 8l 2nd 1; sn ld; 1l up 4; ducked lft & rn out nxt*

OFFICIAL DISTANCE: dist **TIME:** 7min 36.0s

East Sussex & Romney Marsh
Bexhill (RH 8F,18J) Sun, 9 Apr (GOOD)

980 Restricted, 12st
8 ran

[679¹] **1** **TIDAL REEF (IRE)** 14-1 C Gordon *Ld 1; stdd to cl 4th 3; trckd ldr aft; hdwy 12 to 3l 3rd 14; prsd ldng pr 2 out; kpt on str to ld last; r.o best flat*

[710¹] **2** 2 **Dreamin George (IRE)** 7-2 C Sherry *In tch w 4/5th mostly; 5l 5th when blun 10; hdwy 11; prsd ldr nxt; ld 15 til hdd 2 out; ev ch last; rdn & no resp*

[825⁸] **3** ½ **Ishma (IRE)** (bl) 20-1 D Page *Trckd ldrs in cl 3rd/4th; 3l 3rd 10; outpcd 12; r.o agn 15; 3l 3rd app 3 out; r.o downhill to ld nxt; hdd app last; stayed on same pce*

[705²] **4** 2 **Royal Rupert** 7-2 N Benstead *Lkd asleep in padd; hld up last but in tch; 10l 7th 9; hdwy 14; chsd ldrs to 5l 5th 15; lft 4th nxt; nt qckn 2 out*

[416⁴] **5** 5 **Holiday Time (IRE)** (5a) 20-1 Mrs S Hodge *Pulled to ld 2-5; 3l 2nd nxt; prsd ldng 7-11; outpcd 13; 6th & btn 15*

[825⁸] **P** **Bachelor-Carrasco (IRE)** 2-1F S R Andrews *Mostly 4/5th; mist 4; cl up to 13; wknd nxt; completely lost tch 15; t.o when pu 2 out*

  P **Three Of Clubs (IRE)** 25-1 P Bull *Rr & in tch 7; drpd to last 9; jmpd lft 11; wknd qckly; virt t.o when pu nxt*

[829¹] **P** **Tom's Influence** (5a) 12-1 D Parker *Cl 6th til hdwy 4; ld 6; 3l clr nxt; virt jnd 12; hdd 15; wknd v rap & lost plce; pu nxt*

OFFICIAL DISTANCES: 1l, ½l **TIME:** 6min 50.0s **TOTE:** £18.20; places £2.70,£1.10,£8.30 **DF:** £14.00

981 Mens Open, 12st
9 ran

[750¹] **1** **BLANVILLE (FR)** (4x) 2-1F P Scouller *Confid rdn & a gng wl; cl 2nd/3rd; l1 2nd 10; prsd ldr & clr of rest 15; ld 3 out; jnd agn nxt; kpt on to ld app last; forged clr flat*

[572¹] **2** 6 **Seod Rioga (IRE)** 3-1 C Gordon *Mostly 2nd/3rd; 3l 3rd 11; hdwy to ld nxt; jnd 15; clr w wnr aft; hdd bef nxt; chall & nt fluent 2 out; btn app last*

[574⁴] **3** runin **Broguestown Pride (IRE)** 33-1 P Blagg *Last by 2; sn t.o; plodded rnd in rr; lft 4th by 15; went rem 3rd 2 out*

[842²] **4** 25 **Prince Of Saints (IRE)** (7x) (bl) 8-1 A Sansome *Prom; 3l 2nd 6; disp 4l 4th 11; sn 3rd & chsd lndg pr to 14; outpcd & lost tch qckly; 20l 3rd 15; nt keen aft; dem 4th 2 out*

  5 2fncs **Sand Hutton (IRE)** 10-1 C Sherry *Mid-div; 6l 5th & mist 7; releg 10l 7th 9; hit 12; lost tch rap & last 13; lkd to pu app nxt but forced over; t.o & thrashed rest of way*

[574³] **U** **Call Home (IRE)** (7x) 6-1 T Hills *2 handlers; ld 2; 1-2l up til blun & ur 11*

[826¹] **U** **Galaroi (IRE)** (7x) (tt) D Robinson *Spurs; mostly 6th & strugg to go pce; 6l 6th 10; chsng ldrs when blun & lost irons 13; ur 100 yds aft*

[771¹] **U** **Mister Spectator (IRE)** 4-1 P Hickman *Mist til blun & ur 1*

[785¹] **R** **Rustic Revelry (IRE)** 16-1 P York *Cl 4/5th; 5l 5th 10; disp 4l 4th & lkng for non-existent room on inner when rn out 11*

OFFICIAL DISTANCES: 9l, 25l **TIME:** 6min 26.0s **TOTE:** £5.00; places £4.30,£1.10,£6.20 **DF:** £3.90
  Monks Soham was withdrawn not under orders - state of going; the rider of Sand Hutton was fined £125 for excessive and frequent use of the whip on a horse that was clearly tired

982 Ladies Open
8 ran

  1 **MY WEE MAN (IRE)** 7-1 Miss J Wickens *On heels of ldrs; 4l 4th 7; hdwy to 2l 2nd 11; prsd ldr til ld aft 3 out; in comm app last; wandered flat but r.o wl*

[869⁶]	2	3	**Torus Spa (IRE)** (4x) 16-1 **Mrs E Coveney** *Prsd ldr til ld 3; set fast pce til hdd aft 3 out; rdn nxt; no ex last*
[707²]	3	5	**Cadbury Castle** (5a) 3-1 **Miss J Grant** *Trckd ldrs on inner in cl 3rd mostly; 3l 3rd 11; 6l down 15; no ex aft 3 out; disp 3rd when mist last; just kpt 3rd*
[758¹]	4	nk	**Cracking Idea (IRE)** (7x) 4-7F **Mrs G d'Angibau** *Unable to ld & force pce; 5l 6th 10; chsd ldrs 13; 7l 4th 15; nt qckn 3 out; stayed on to disp 3rd last; no ex & dem flat*
[830⁶]	5	fence	**Wednesdays Auction (IRE)** (4x) 33-1 **Mrs C Andrews** *Prsd ldr to 3; drpd to last by nxt; t.o 6; plodded on*
[512⁶]	P		**Awbeg Rover (IRE)** 33-1 **Mrs S Hodge** *Mid-div; in tch when mist 7; sn strugg; 10l 6th & pushed along 10; stdly lost tch; wl in rr 13; t.o 5th when pu 2 out*
[827ᵁ]	U		**Danger Flynn (IRE)** 14-1 **Miss C Holliday** (xnb) *Trckd ldr in 3rd/4th; hdwy to 11 2nd 7; blun & ur 9*
[677²]	P		**Velka** (5a) 25-1 **Miss P Ellison** *Ld to 2; 4th 4; stdly lost plce; 12l 6th 11; wknd 14; t.o 6th when pu 3 out*

OFFICIAL DISTANCES: 3l, 1l TIME: 6min 28.0s

983 Confined, 12st   11 ran

[824²]	1		**JOJO (IRE)** (bl) 3-1 **B Hitchcott** *Ld/disp til ld 4; jnd 2 out; r.o agn & in comm last; kpt on & kidded*
[706²]	2	6	**Sovereign Spray (IRE)** (3x) 5-2F **C Gordon** *Hld up in 4/5th; hdwy 10; disp 2l 2nd 13 til prsd ldr 3 out; mist nxt; wknd app last*
[824⁵]	3	6	**Lovely Lynsey (IRE)** (5a) 7-1 **Miss S Gladders** *A chsng ldrs; mostly cl 3rd/4th; 4l 4th 12; 6l 3rd & one pce app 3 out; dem 4th & wkng when lft 3rd nxt; dism aft line*
[830²]	4	5	**Some Tourist (IRE)** (5a) 7-1 **N Benstead** *Ld/disp to 3; 2l 2nd nxt; disp 2nd 13 til wknd 15; releg 10l 5th & no ch nxt; one pce app 2 out*
[676⁷]	P		**African Jazz (GER)** 16-1 **P York** *Pulling; prom to 5; qckly drpd to rr 9; t.o when pu 13*
[707⁴]	P		**Edge Ahead (IRE)** (bl) 25-1 **Mrs E Coveney** *Trckd ldrs in 5/6th; 8l 6th 10; wknd bef nxt; lost tch qckly 12; 25l 6th when pu 14*
	U		**Endeavour (FR)** 7-2 **T Hills** *Handy in 5/6th; chsd ldrs 12; 6l 4th aft 15; staying on in 10l 3rd but no ch when blun & ur 2 out*
	P		**Lucas Court** 20-1 **S Garrott** *2 handlers; sn in rr; lft last 8; t.o 11; pu 14*
	P		**Sugar Mill** 33-1 **P Hall** *Sn rr & strugg to go pce; detach 10; t.o & pu 12*
	P		**Tallage (FR)** 6-1 **P Scouller** *Nvr gng wl; last 2; lsng tch when hit 6; wl bhnd when pu imm aft nxt*
	P		**The Portsoy Loon** 33-1 **P Hickman** *Towards rr & sn pushed along; rmdr 6; detach 10; t.o & pu 12*

OFFICIAL DISTANCES: 10l, 8l TIME: 6min 29.0s TOTE: £2.80; places £1.30,£3.50,£1.70 DF: £4.90

984 Open Maiden, 12st   13 ran

[710⁶]	1		**OXENDALE** 3-1 **P Bull** *2 handlers; hit 1; trckd ldrs in 4/5th mostly; prog 10; 4l 4th 12; chsd ldrs aft; 2l 3rd 3 out; chall 2 out; ld last; stayed on game flat*
[578²]	2	½	**Uk Eurolad** 25-1 **T Hills** *Ld 2; 6l up nxt; 2l up 9; jnd & hdd 3 out; nrly level 2 out; drvn & r.o last; just failed*
[709²]	3	2	**Larry** (7a) 7-4F **P York** *Hld up in tch in mid-div; 6l 6th 10; chsd ldrs 14; 3l 4th 3 out; rdn to chall 2 out; no ex last*
[828ᵁ]	4	25	**Schisandra** (5a) 33-1 **P Blagg** *Sn in rr; bhnd when nrly fell 6; t.o 13; blun 15; plodded on; lft 4th by defections*
[829⁶]	P		**At It Again (IRE)** 33-1 **R Chelton** *Prom in 2nd/3rd to 11; wknd qckly nxt; wl in rr when pu 15*
[679⁶]	P		**Dunston Ben** 33-1 **D Page** *Last; nvr gng or jmpng wl; t.o 4; blun bad 5; plodded on til pu 11*
[457⁶]	P		**Hatch Gate** 33-1 **M Gorman** (xnb) *Sn strugg in rr & nt jw; detach 9; blun 10 & 14; t.o & pu 3 out*
[829⁶]	P		**Jo Bloggs (IRE)** (tt) 9-2 **B Hitchcott** *1mm rr & nvr gng wl; jmpd violent lft & nrly thro wings frm 3; event pu 15*
[829ᵁ]	P		**Not Yet Decent (IRE)** 16-1 **P Hall** *Rr; lost tch 10; wl bhnd 11; pu 12*
[829⁶]	P		**Phantom Slipper** 20-1 **T Warr** *Mostly 7/8th; 8l 7th 10; outpcd 13; lost tch 15; wl in rr when pu 2 out*
[432⁶]	P		**Primulas Daughter** (5a) 33-1 **C Gordon** *A strugg; in tch in mid-div to 9; wknd qckly 12; t.o & pu 15*
	F		**Sunley Spring** 7-1 **A Sansome** *Prom in 2nd/3rd til 2l 2nd 9; prsd ldr 11 til ld 3 out; jnd & ev ch when fell hvly 2 out*
[709ʳ]	P		**The Herbivore (IRE)** (bl) 5-1 **Miss C Jiggins** *In tch in 4/5th; 5l 5th 10; wknd aft 13; wl in rr when pu 3 out*

OFFICIAL DISTANCES: ½l, 2l TIME: 6min 35.0s TOTE: £7.80; places £3.20,£20.80,£1.30 DF: £3.60

985 Hunt, 12st 6 ran

[707⁶]	1		**ANDRELOT** (bl) 6-4F **Miss H Grissell** Settled in 5th; hdwy to 6l 3rd 9; 2l 2nd nxt; trckd ldr til chall 15; sn ld & forged clr; in comm app last; rdr's 1st wnr
[573⁶]	2	10	**Trifast Lad** 5-1 **Mrs L Baker** Lft 2nd 3; tkn stdly bhnd tearaway ldr til lft in ld 6; jnd 15; sn hdd; wknd app last
[825⁷]	U		**Chill Factor** (tt) 5-2 **A Veale** Tore off virt out of control; lft in ld 3; 15l clr nxt; rdr baled out as horse tk off 6
[577ᵁ]	P		**Daydreamer (USA)** 4-1 **D Brightling** Last 2 til 12l 4th 10; clsd to 6l 3rd 13; qckly lost tch; 30l 3rd 3 out; pu 2 out
[677⁴]	P		**Red Channel (IRE)** 8-1 **Miss P Bryan-Brown** Trckd ldrs; lft 2l 2nd 6; 4l 3rd 10; releg 4th 13; lost tch rap & t.o nxt; pu 3 out
[709ᴾ]	U		**Sliabh Foy (IRE)** 12-1 **F Marshall** Ld 1; blun & ur 3

OFFICIAL DISTANCE: 10l TIME: 6min 38.0s TOTE: £3.20; places £2.40,£1.10 DF: £5.90

Ludlow
Bitterley (LH 8F,18J) Sun, 9 Apr (GOOD to FIRM)

986 Hunt 5 ran

[527¹]	1		**MR PISTACHIO (IRE)** (7a) 4-5F **G Hanmer** 6/4-4/5; lw; settled 3rd; hit 3; went 2nd 9-11; lft 2nd 13; ld 14; rdr lkng rnd frm 2 out; easy
[898ᵁ]	2	3	**Cashew Crisis (IRE)** (7a) 20-1 **M Rodda** Hld up; mist 5; 7l 5th ½way; last til eff & 7l 4th 15; chsd wnr 2 out; no imp
[744ᴾ]	3	2½	**Master Welder** (vis) 8-1 **A Wadlow** Hld up; 6l 4th ½way; went 2l 3rd 14; one pce 3 out
	P		**Ledwyche Gate** (7x) (bl) 6-4 **R Bevis** (bf) Ld; mist 5; hdd 6; sn drvn along; 2nd to 9; went 2nd agn u.p 11 til mist 13; lost plce & mist 14; nt r.o; t.o & pu 2 out
	F		**Winter Game (IRE)** 20-1 **R Inglesant** 2nd til ld 6; hdd 14; wknd 2 out; 10l 4th when fell last

OFFICIAL DISTANCE: 4l TIME: 6min 19.7s

987 Confined, 12st 12 ran

[702⁷]	1		**THE CRAZY BISHOP (IRE)** (15x) 8-1 **B Shaw** Trckd ldrs; 3½l 5th ½way; went 2nd aft 11; ld 13-2 out; lft in ld last; r.o; rdr's 1st wnr
	2	2½	**Chassagne (FR)** 9-4F **J Price** Hld up & bhnd; stdy hdwy & 7l 7th ½way; 6l 5th 13; went 2nd nxt; ld 2 out til blun last; nt rec
[702²]	3	15	**Basil Street (IRE)** 9-1 **Miss P Jones** A.p; 2l 3rd ½way; 4l 3rd 13; outpcd 15; no imp frm 3 out
[670⁴]	4	2½	**Happy Minstral (USA)** (3x) (bl) 8-1 **R Burton** Ld to 3; 3l 4th ½way; lost plce & 7l 6th 13; went 11l 4th 15; nd aft
[615ᴾ]	5	4	**Sally's Twins** (5a) 12-1 **A Wintle** (xnb) Hld up & bhnd; 10l 8th ½way; eff & 7½l 7th 13; 13l 6th 15; no ch aft
[333⁶]	6	runin	**Mitchells Best** 20-1 **J Jukes** Sn outpcd; 22l 10th ½way; t.o 12
	P		**Burkean Melody (IRE)** 33-1 **M Munrowd** Ss; hld up; stdy hdwy & 4½l 6th ½way; 5l 4th 13; wknd qckly 14; 20l 7th when pu nxt
[529ᶠ]	P		**Canaillou II (FR)** 33-1 **A Wadlow** (bnf) A bhnd; 20l 9th ½way; 15l 8th 13; t.o & pu 15
[862ᵁ]	R		**Merger Mania** 14-1 **M Trott** (xnb) Swtng; pulled hrd; jnd ldrs 4; went 2nd nxt; lft in ld 7 til jmpd violent rt & lost plce 11; rn off course app 12
[745¹]	P		**Rusty Buck** 14-1 **R Bevis** Prom; mist 3; lft 2nd 7; lft in ld 11-13; wknd u.p & 12l 5th 15; bhnd when pu 2 out
[861⁷]	P		**Stormhill Recruit** 16-1 **S Blackwell** Prom til lost plce 6; 10l 8th when pu 9
[862¹]	P		**The Rum Mariner** (3x) 3-1 **Miss C Thomas** 4s-3s; 2nd til ld 3; pu 7 (hurt by post lvng padd)

OFFICIAL DISTANCES: 3l, 12l TIME: 6min 02.9s

988 Land Rover Mens Open, 12st 9 ran

[614¹]	1		**LOCHNOMORE** 11-10JF **R Burton** Lw; jw; went 2nd 6; ld 7; qcknd 12; drew wl clr 3 out; v impressive
[462¹]	2	25	**Mickthecutaway (IRE)** 11-10JF **A Dalton** Ld aft 2 til hdd 7; 2l 3rd ½way; went 2nd 11; sn drvn along; chsd wnr til mist 15; 2nd agn aft 2 out; no ch w wnr
[859⁴]	3	10	**Tremendisto** (7x) 20-1 **D Mansell** (xnb) W ldrs; 5l 5th ½way; 9l 5th 13; sn outpcd; went 15l 4th 15; no imp aft; went poor 3rd flat
[859²]	4	4	**Watchit Lad** 7-1 **S Blackwell** Ld til hdd aft 2; 2nd/3rd to 5; lost plce & 7l 6th ½way; lost tch 12; 19l 7th nxt; 28l 6th 15; went rem 4th flat

[702P] 5 5   **My Sister Lucy** (5a) 50-1 **K Burke** *A bhnd; 12l 8th ½way; 20l 8th 13; t:o*

[697¹] 6 3   **Haven Light** 20-1 **J Jukes** *W ldrs; 3l 4th ½way; went 5l 3rd 12; lft 6l 2nd 15; wknd 2 out; still poor 3rd last; exhaust & virt bu flat*

[862P] P   **Good For A Loan** 25-1 **R Cooper** *Hld up; 8l 7th ½way; lost tch 12; 17l 6th nxt; t:o & pu 15*

[741⁴] F   **Illineylad (IRE)** 25-1 **A Wintle** *2nd/3rd to 12; 8l 4th nxt; wknd qckly & 16l 5th 15; wl bhnd when fell last*

  P   **Stillorgan Park (IRE)** (3ow) 33-1 **J Hughes** *Wl bhnd frm 7; 25l 9th ½way; pu 10*

OFFICIAL DISTANCES: 25l, 10l **TIME:** 6min 02.1s

989 Open Maiden 56&7yo (Div 1), 12st   13 ran

  1   **CONQUER (IRE)** (7a) 7-2 **M Rimell** (xnb) *Lw; a.p; went 2nd aft 8; ld 15; sn clr; impressive*

[436F] 2 25   **Top Toy (IRE)** evensF **A Dalton** *Lw; hld up; 7½l 7th ½way; went 8l 3rd aft 11; eff 15; went 2nd nxt; no ch w wnr*

[900³] 3 25   **Cold Snap (IRE)** 7-1 **A Wintle** *Lw; hld up; hdwy & 8l 6th ½way; went 12l 4th 12; wknd 14; lft rem 3rd 2 out*

[899⁴] 4 4   **Josameric** 14-1 **T Stephenson** (xnb) *2 handlers; a bhnd; 20l 13th ½way; 36l 7th 13; t:o; fin wl*

[570P] 5 runin   **Village Gossip** (5a) 16-1 **M Trott** *2nd to 4; lost plce & 10l 8th ½way; rdn 11; t:o 13*

  U   **Act On Impulse (IRE)** (7a) 16-1 **R Burton** *Hld up & bhnd; 15l 11th ½way; 27l 7th & some hdwy when mist & ur 12*

[822U] P   **Blazing Connie** (5a) 16-1 **G Perkins** (bf) *Ld; rmdrs 5; hdd 5; 4l 3rd ½way; wknd rap 11; t:o & pu 14*

  P   **Broadbrook Lass** (5a) 20-1 **S Blackwell** *Bckwd; a bhnd; 18l 12th ½way; t:o & pu 12*

  P   **Lady Ping** (5a) 14-1 **J Cook** *Hld up & sev posn; 11l 9th ½way; wkng when mist 11; pu 12*

[697²] P   **Loch Ash** 5-1 **G Lewis** 8s-5s; *2 handlers; went 2nd 4; ld 5; qcknd clr w wnr 12; hdd 15; wknd qckly; 20l 3rd when pu 2 out*

[673F] F   **Marauder (IRE)** (bl) 10-1 **R Cooper** *Chsd ldrs; 7l 5th ½way; wknd qckly 11; 25l 6th nxt; t:o when fell 14*

[672P] P   **Once Is Enough** (12a) 14-1 **M Hammond** *Bckwd; a bhnd; 14l 10th ½way; t:o & pu 12*

[616⁶] P   **Pharpen (IRE)** 6-1 **J Jukes** (xnb) *Swtng; sn prom; 6l 4th ½way; wknd u.p 12; 18l 5th nxt; t:o & pu 3 out*

OFFICIAL DISTANCES: 25l, dist **TIME:** 6min 07.1s

The riders of Act On Impulse and Marauder were each fined £60 for failing to report to the doctor after falling in this race

990 Open Maiden 56&7yo (Div 2), 12st   13 ran

  1   **JAMES ISAAC (IRE)** 8-1 **J Jukes** *Jmpd lft; made all; drew clr frm 15; unchall*

[265F] 2 20   **Mainlier** 7-1 **A Wintle** *Hld up; 14l 8th ½way; hdwy 11; 8l 4th 13; went 12l 2nd aft 3 out; wkng when mist last*

  3 15   **Benson (IRE)** (7a) 4-5F **A Dalton** *Jmpd novicey; hld up; mist 6; 12l 5th ½way; went 6l 3rd 12; wknd 3 out; btr for rce*

[616F] 4 15   **Three Monroes (IRE)** 20-1 **M Munrowd** *Hld up; 13½l 7th ½way; hdwy 11; 9l 5th 13; wknd 14; t:o*

[438F] P   **Druids Dream** (5a) 25-1 **M Trott** *2nd til wknd rap aft 10; pu 11*

  P   **Far Glen (IRE)** (7a) 20-1 **S Blackwell** (xnb) *A bhnd; 19l 11th ½way; t:o & pu 12*

[673F] P   **One Mans Legacy** (5a) 20-1 **S Joynes** *Chsd ldrs; 11l 4th ½way; went 2nd aft 10-11; wknd & 12l 7th 13; wl bhnd when pu 15*

[866B] P   **Polly Buckrum** (12a) 20-1 **R Hodges** *Hld up; 12½l 6th & stdy hdwy ½way; went 3l 2nd 11; wkng when mist & rdr unbalanced 3 out; 15l 3rd when pu nxt*

[900P] P   **Sandy Floss (IRE)** 8-1 **T Stephenson** *Chsd ldrs; 10l 3rd ½way; wknd & 9½l 6th 13; pu 14*

[568P] P   **Supermister** 20-1 **P Morris** (xnb,bf) *Swtng; a bhnd; 23l 13th ½way; t:o & pu 12*

[703⁴] P   **Top Designer (IRE)** (tt) 3-1 **R Burton** 5s-3s; *hld up; 17l 9th ½way; no hdwy & 16l 8th 13; wl bhnd when pu 15*

[570P] P   **Uncle Ada (IRE)** (7a) 20-1 **A Price** *Chsd ldrs til lost plce 7; 20l 12th ½way; t:o & pu 14*

[673⁶] P   **Wee Kelpie** (5a) 20-1 **K Burke** *A bhnd; 18l 10th ½way; t:o & pu 12*

OFFICIAL DISTANCES: 25l, 20l **TIME:** 6min 15.3s

City Express was withdrawn after declaration

991 Ladies Open - 17J   11 ran

[613¹]	1		**SPLIT SECOND** (7x) 2-5F **Miss A Dare** (pricker ns) Lw; ld to 2; ld 4-9 & frm 11; clr 2 out; drvn out
[902⁵]	2	4	**Sun Surfer (FR)** (bl) 10-1 **Miss P Jones** A.p; 3l 4th ½way; went 2nd aft 11 til mist 14; releg 3l 4th nxt; rdn & nt qckn 3 out; went 2nd flat; stayed on
[904³]	3	2	**Killatty Player (IRE)** (5a,7x) 8-1 **Mrs M Barlow** Prom; went 2nd 5-8; lost plce & 5l 7th ½way; 9l 6th 13; rallied & 2½l 3rd when hit 15; one pce 3 out
[817²]	4	1	**Captain Khedive** 16-1 **Miss S Talbot** (xnb) Hld up; 4½l 6th ½way; hdwy 12; went 2nd 14; ev ch 3 out; sn rdn; wknd flat
	5	15	**All Weather** 5-1 **Miss E Wilesmith** Ld 2-4 & 9-11; 6l 4th 13; wknd & 7l 5th 14
[860ᵖ]	6	12	**Cheeky Pot** (bl) 33-1 **Miss J Priest** Jmpd slow 4; bhnd til hdwy & 4l 5th ½way; 7½l 5th 13; wknd 14
[740¹]	P		**Boring (USA)** 20-1 **Miss E Crawford** (xnb) Pulled hrd; w ldrs; 2l 3rd ½way; wknd & 10l 7th 13; wl bhnd when pu 15
[648ᵖ]	P		**Cauld Signal (IRE)** (5a) 33-1 **Miss L Pearce** Prom til mist 6; 7l 8th ½way; wknd 12; 20l 8th nxt; t.o & pu 15
[860ᵁ]	U		**Elwill Glory (IRE)** 16-1 **Miss M Peterson** Tde; lost plce & rdr lost iron 8; bhnd when mist & rfo 10
[860ᴿ]	P		**Fed On Oats** 20-1 **Mrs D Powell** A bhnd; 22l 9th 13; t.o & pu 15
[611⁵]	U		**Stretchit** (7x) 8-1 **Miss I Rabone** 1st ride; hld up; blun & ur 3

OFFICIAL DISTANCES: 3l, 1l **TIME:** 6min 08.7s
Fence 18 omitted - fallen rider

992 Restricted (Div 1), 12st   11 ran

[704¹]	1		**RED OASSIS** 5-1 **A Dalton** 2nd/3rd til ld 11; jnd 3 out; rdn clr flat
[567²]	2	5	**Seymour's Double** 3-1JF **R Burton** Lw; a.p; 1½l 3rd ½way; went 4l 2nd 14; ev ch 3 out; rdn & wknd last
[669³]	3	25	**Paddy Maguire (IRE)** 7-1 **T Stephenson** Ld to 8; 2l 4th ½way; lost plce 12; 11½l 7th nxt; 20l 7th 15; lft poor 3rd at last
[858²]	4	15	**Out Of The Blue** (5a) 6-1 **S Graham** A bhnd; 12l 11th ½way; 20l 10th 13; t.o 15
[744²]	5	5	**Teme Willow (IRE)** 10-1 **M Hammond** Hld up; 4l 7th ½way; eff & 7l 4th 13; 13l 4th 15; sn wknd; t.o
[896²]	U		**Brother Prim** 20-1 **D Mansell** Hld up & bhnd; 8l 10th ½way; 14l 8th 13; stayed on frm 15; went 15l 3rd app 2 out; blun & ur last
[698²]	P		**Innishfea (IRE)** (5a) 12-1 **A Wintle** Pulled hrd; sn prom; ld 8-11; 7½l 5th & wkng 13; wl bhnd when pu 15
[698ᵖ]	P		**Lindalighter** (5a) 20-1 **M Munrow** Prom; went 2nd 4-8; 2½l 5th ½way; 11l 6th & wkng 13; wl bhnd when pu 3 out
[747¹]	P		**Secretrock (IRE)** 3-1JF **J Jukes** (xnb) Hld up; hdwy & 3l 6th ½way; went 2nd 12-14; 6l 3rd nxt; sn wknd; wl bhnd when pu last
[588¹]	P		**Teal Bay** 4-1 **D Barlow** Hld up; mist 6; 7l 9th ½way; mist 12; 16l 9th nxt; wl bhnd when pu & dism 14
[744ᵖ]	P		**Without The Agent (IRE)** 12-1 **A Price** Nt jw; hit 2; 6l 8th & rdn ½way; mist 10; lost tch u.p & pu 12

OFFICIAL DISTANCES: 3l, 20l **TIME:** 6min 11.9s

993 Restricted (Div 2), 12st   10 ran

[862⁶]	1		**SAYWHEN** 10-1 **R Cooper** Hld up; 7½l 7th & rmdrs ½way; hdwy to ld 11; drew clr 3 out; rdn out
[818²]	2	8	**Winning Town** 8-1 **Miss S Talbot** (xnb) Trckd ldrs; went 4l 3rd ½way; rdn 3 out; went 2nd nxt; no imp
[248²]	3	4	**Native Isle (IRE)** 7-1 **T Stephenson** Hld up; hdwy 8; went 2nd 9-11; chsd wnr 12 til wknd 2 out
[863ᵁ]	4	5	**Maid O'Tully (IRE)** (5a) 14-1 **R Hodges** Chsd ldrs; 7l 6th & rmdrs ½way; 5½l 5th 13; rdn 3 out; no imp
[894²]	5	nk	**Beyond The Stars** evensF **M Rimell** Ld 2-5 & 6-11; 5l 4th & rdn 13; no ex u.p 3 out
	P		**Apple Saft (IRE)** 20-1 **M Wilesmith** (xnb) Prom til mist 5; 9l 8th ½way; wl bhnd when pu 13
	P		**Dandelion Lad (IRE)** 20-1 **R Rogers** Drpd to rr 4; t.o 10; pu 12
[866¹]	r		**Need More Practice** (tt) 3-1 **R Burton** 5s-3s; ref to rce; tk no part
[338⁷]	P		**Sideliner** 10-1 **A Price** Ld to 2; 5l 4th ½way; lost plce 11; 9l 7th & rdn 13; sn wknd; wl bhnd when pu 2 out
[701ᵖ]	P		**Wrenbury Farmer** 20-1 **K Burke** Swtng; prom; ld 5-6; 5½l 5th ½way; 6l 6th & rdn 13; sn wknd; t.o & pu last

OFFICIAL DISTANCES: 10l, 5l **TIME:** 6min 10.4s

994 Open Maiden 8yo&up (Div 1), 12st
14 ran

[567⁴]	1		**UNCLE TOM** 3-1 R Cooper *Hld up & bhnd; 12l 9th ½way; eff & 10l 7th 12; went 8l 3rd aft 14; no imp til stayed on frm 2 out; went 3l 2nd last; ld nr fin*
[893⁶]	2	1	**Ole Gunnar (IRE)** 20-1 M Wilesmith *(xnb) Hld up & bhnd; 16l 11th ½way; hdwy 15; stayed on wl frm 3 out; went 4l 3rd last; nt rch wnr; lkd to fin 2nd*
	3	hd	**Strapped For Cash** (5a) 6-1 M Hammond *10s-6s; a.p; 3l 3rd ½way; went 2nd 14 & sn clr w wnr; ld 2 out; 3l clr last; wknd & hdd nr fin; lkd to fin 2nd*
[568⁵]	4	15	**Silver Sumal** 3-1 A Dalton *(xnb) 2 handlers; hld up; hdwy 7; 5l 4th ½way; went 2nd 11; ld aft 12 til hdd 2 out; wknd qckly last*
[487⁴]	5	runin	**Western Pearl (IRE)** 14-1 Miss M Thomas *A bhnd; 25l 12th ½way; t.o 12*
[703⁶]	P		**Ask Elliot** 10-1 F Hutsby *Ld to 1; lost plce 8; 15l 10th ½way; wl bhnd when pu 12*
[488²]	P		**Bally Boy** 5-2F D Mansell *Hld up; 8l 7th ½way; 7l 6th when blun & went rt 12; sn pu*
	P		**Connemara Freeway** 5-1 J Jukes *(bf) 7s-5s; big; bckwd; hld up; 7l 6th ½way; hdwy & 4½l 5th 12; wknd & pu 14*
[601⁴]	P		**Fireman** (bl) 12-1 N Oliver *2 handlers; chsd ldrs; 6l 5th ½way; wknd 11; 12l 8th nxt; t.o & pu 15*
[617⁴]	P		**Millstock** (5a) 7-1 Miss N Stallard *Swtng; sn prom; lft 2nd 5-11; 7l 4th 14; sn wknd; wl bhnd when pu last*
[864²]	P		**Otter River** 20-1 P Morris *2nd til ld 5; hdd aft 12; 6l 3rd 14; wknd qckly; pu 15*
[865ᵁ]	P		**Pulpits Edge** 20-1 A Price *(xnb) A bhnd; 26l 13th ½way; t.o 12; pu 15*
[865⁶]	U		**Timmy Tuff (IRE)** 12-1 K Burke *Ld 1 til hdd & blun & ur 5*
[704⁶]	P		**Tudor Flight** (5a) 7-1 G Lewis *(xnb) Chsd ldrs; lost plce u.p & 9l 8th ½way; wl bhnd when pu 12*

OFFICIAL DISTANCES: 2l, hd **TIME:** 6min 22.1s
Fence 13 omitted - fallen rider

995 Open Maiden 8yo&up (Div 2), 12st
17 ran

[616⁶]	1		**TALKALOT (IRE)** 7-1 A Wintle *(xnb) Hld up; stdy hdwy & 5l 6th ½way; went 2nd 11; ld 2 out; r.o wl*
[778²]	2	4	**Vulpin De Laugere (FR)** (bl) 7-2 R Burton *(xnb) Lw; ld til hdd 2 out; rdn & nt r.o flat*
[703³]	3	¾	**All Things Nice** (5a) 4-1 T Stephenson *Hld up; 6l 7th ½way; hdwy 12; went 2l 3rd nxt; rdn 3 out; one pce*
[594²]	4	10	**Muckle Jack** 3-1F S Blackwell *Lft 2nd 1-11; lost plce & 7l 5th 13; nd aft*
[602³]	5	5	**Dungannon Lad** 20-1 D Mansell *Swtng; prom; 4l 5th & rmdrs ½way; 4l 4th 13; rdn & wknd 3 out*
[858³]	P		**Crab 'n Lobster (IRE)** (5a) 12-1 R Hodges *A bhnd; 13l 11th ½way; 10l 9th 13; t.o & pu 15*
[704⁶]	P		**Cracking Crumpet** (5a) 12-1 J Jukes *Prom; 2½l 3rd ½way; rdn 11; wknd & 11l 8th 13; mist 15; t.o pu 3 out*
[490⁴]	P		**Greenfield Maid (IRE)** (5a) 20-1 J Keen *Swtng; a bhnd; t.o 10; pu 12*
	F		**Hardy Wolf** 20-1 F Windsor Clive *Bckwd; 2nd when fell 1*
[753⁶]	P		**Ilandra (IRE)** (5a) 20-1 N Pearce *Sn wl bhnd; pu & dism 5*
[865⁴]	P		**Nineteenonfive (IRE)** 7-1 M Scales *Prom; 3l 4th ½way; 9l 6th & rdn when mist 13; sn wknd; t.o & pu 2 out*
[892⁶]	P		**Pennys Boy** (10ow) 33-1 T Gretton *Lost plce 5; bhnd when jmpd v slow 7; pu 8*
	P		**Scholar Green** 25-1 A Phillips *Nd; 12l 10th ½way; wl bhnd when pu 12*
[703⁶]	P		**Sister Sue** (5a) 20-1 S Graham *(xnb) A bhnd; 16l 13th ½way; blun 11; t.o & pu 12*
[866ᵁ]	P		**Take A Right** 20-1 J Cornes *(xnb) Hld up; 11l 9th ½way; lost tch & pu 12*
[602⁶]	P		**Took A Chance (IRE)** 14-1 J Price *Hld up & bhnd; mist 5; hdwy & 9l 8th ½way; mist 12; 10l 7th nxt; sn wknd; t.o & pu 2 out*
[704⁶]	P		**Wind And Stars** (5a) 7-1 F Hutsby *Chsd ldrs til wknd 8; 15l 12th ½way; blun 11; t.o & pu 12*

OFFICIAL DISTANCES: 4l, 1l **TIME:** 6min 16.5s

Middleton
Whitwell-on-the-Hill (RH 9F,18J) Sun, 9 Apr (GOOD)

996 Hunt, 12st
10 ran

[114⁴]	1		**VICTORIA'S BOY (IRE)** 3-1 G Brewer *Ld to 2; ld agn 5; 3l clr 8; rn v wide bend app 10; rdn 4l clr 3 out; stayed on wl*
[621⁶]	2	4	**Kendor Pass (IRE)** 20-1 Mrs N Wilson *Ld 2-5; cl 2nd to 10; 8l 4th 13; 2nd agn nxt; outrdn & chsd wnr vain aft*
	3	8	**Corbleu (IRE)** 10-1 M Walford *1st ride; prom; lost posn 10; 9l 5th 13; went 3rd nxt; r.o one pce & no imp aft*

[794²]	4	4	**Gymcrak Gorjos** (5a) 4-6F **D Thomas** *Trckd ldrs; 7l 3rd 13; 5th & outpcd 15; hrd rdn 3 out; stayed on one pce*
[797²]	5	½	**Brackenhill** (14ow) 66-1 **F Houghton Brown** *1st ride; mid-div; hdwy to 2nd 11-13; 4th & outpcd nxt; plodded on*
	6	1½fs	**Ruff Account** 16-1 **Miss E Brader** *A rr; lost tch 11; hunted rnd; t.o 14*
[689²]	7	4	**Lingcool** (5a) 66-1 **J Morley** *A rr; mist 7; last & lsng tch 10; t.o 14; hrd rdn & stayed on frm 2 out; snatched 7th on line*
	8	3	**Mountain Lion** 66-1 **Miss T Hall** *Sn last to 7; hdwy 10 to 10l 6th 11; pushed along & outpcd 13; t.o 15; dem last cl home*
[807²]	U		**Cede Nullis** (5a) (bl,tt) 14-1 **S Brisby** *(xnb)Chsd ldrs; 6th when bumped & ur bend bef 9*
	U		**Risky Dee** 5-1 **M Morley** *Ur 2*

OFFICIAL DISTANCES: 4l, 6l **TIME:** 6min 34.0s

The rider of Risky Dee was cautioned by the stewards for using foul language following his fall in this race; he apologised and explained that having suffered a bang on the head he had no recollection of the incident

997 Confined   7 ran

[815ᵁ]	1		**ELLA FALLS (IRE)** (12a) 5-4F **C Wilson** *(xnb) Hld up last to 5; hdwy 9 to cl 2nd 11; ld on bit 14; qcknd clr 3 out; 10l dhd last; eased down flat; v easy*
[691⁶]	2	10	**Final Beat (IRE)** 6-1 **C Cundall** *Mid-div to 7; went 2nd 9-11; rdn to rgn 2nd 15-nxt; stayed on one pce; tk 2nd aft last*
[693¹]	3	½	**Silent Snipe** 3-1 **W Burnell** *6th when bad mist 4; last 6; hdwy 10 to 5l 3rd 13; rdn to 2nd 3 out; outpcd nxt; dem aft last*
[804⁴]	4	runin	**Caman** (bl) 33-1 **Mrs S Palfreeman** *Ld to 2; lft in ld 8; hdd & wknd qckly 14; t.o 2 out*
	F		**Chez Catalan** (bl) 33-1 **Miss J Foster** *Ld 2-3; tk keen hld & prom til wknd 5; last when fell hvly 10*
[506³]	U		**Gaelic Warrior** 50-1 **Miss Rachel Clark** *(xnb) Trckd ldrs; mist 3; hmpd & ur 8*
[869ᵁ]	F		**Pharlindo (IRE)** 3-1 **Mrs F Needham** *(xnb) Pulled to ld 3; fell 8*

OFFICIAL DISTANCES: 8l, nk **TIME:** 6min 37.0s

998 Dodson & Horrell PPORA Club Members   5 ran

[622²]	1		**CALLEVA STAR (IRE)** evensF **R Abrahams** *Ld til jmpd lft & rn wide aft 3; dem 2nd; rn wide aft 10; ld 12; rdly drew clr 3 out; r.o str*
	2	10	**Seven Four Seven** (5a) 7-4 **K Rosier** *Mid-div to 8; last 10; hdwy aft 12; 8l 4th aft 13; went 2nd 3 out; a hld aft*
[794⁴]	3	6	**Misti Hunter (IRE)** 4-1 **Miss Rachel Clark** *(xnb) Lft in ld 3-12; wknd to last 15; 10l 3rd 2 out; r.o same pce*
[689⁵]	4	3	**Efaad (IRE)** 8-1 **W Burnell** *Hld up in rr; hit 10 went 6l 3rd aft 13; 2nd brief 15; nt fluent nxt; sn btn; releg 2 out*
[623ᴾ]	P		**Mick Man (IRE)** 14-1 **S J Robinson** *Pckd 1; pulled slow 4 in last; 3rd 10; rdn aft 13; last & lsng tch nxt; t.o & pu 15*

OFFICIAL DISTANCES: 8l, 6l **TIME:** 6min 42.0s

999 Mixed Open (Grimthorpe Gold Cup), 4m1f, 12st - 24J   13 ran

[395¹]	1		**PROMINENT** (4ow) 5-2 **D Easterby** *Patient rdn & hld up in rr; 9th 12; hdwy to 3rd 20; ld nxt; qcknd 8l clr 3 out last; rdn flat til eased nr fin*
[466¹]	2	5	**Mr Freebie (DEN)** 9-2 **N Bloom** *Bhnd; 8th 12; impd to 5th & rdn 21; kpt on game to 3rd 2 out but nvr gng wl enough; snatched 2nd on line*
[582¹]	3	hd	**Overflowing River (IRE)** (tt) evensF **T Glass** *Ld 5-7; 2nd/3rd til 5th & rdn & outpcd 19; went 8l 2nd aft 3 out; drvn & nt qckn; dem nr fin*
[691²]	4	8	**Barneys Gold (IRE)** 12-1 **A Bealby** *Ld to 5, 8-9 & 11-14; 2nd when mist 19; sn lost plce & nd*
[422³]	5	4	**Concerto Collonges (FR)** 5-1 **R Hartley** *Midfield w 11; went 5th nxt; pushed along 20; ev ch nxt; 2nd brief 22; outpcd 3 out; plodded on*
[502¹]	6	6	**Ubu Val (FR)** (bl) 12-1 **Miss S Brotherton** *Sn prom; ld 9-11, 14-16 & 17-21; rdn & grad wknd*
[690⁴]	7	3	**Miss Accounts (IRE)** (5a) 14-1 **Miss A Armitage** *Trckd ldrs; 7th 12; pckd 16; sn lost tch; no ch 21*
[493²]	P		**Greenhill Tare Away** 16-1 **S Swiers** *Towards rr til pu 8*
[696ᵁ]	P		**Icantsay (IRE)** 100-1 **D Thomas** *Sn strugg; a last; t.o 11; pu 14*
[506ᴾ]	P		**Optimism Reigns (IRE)** 66-1 **Miss R Clark** *Hit 5; trckd ldrs; 4th 12; 5l 4th when blun 15; wkng when bad mist 19; jmpd v slow nxt & pu*
	P		**Simply A Star (IRE)** 33-1 **M Watson** *Rr by 8; 10th 12; nd aft; t.o & pu 3 out*
[797²]	P		**Splodge** 33-1 **M Bennison** *Nt jw; a rr; mists 5 & 8; 10th & lsng tch 12; t.o & pu 16*
[506ᴾ]	P		**Springhill Quay (IRE)** 50-1 **R Clark** *Prom early; 6th 12; 7th & wkng 15; pu 17*

OFFICIAL DISTANCES: 6l, hd **TIME:** 9min 05.0s

1000 Restricted, 12st

12 ran

[399¹]	1	**NOBLE HYMN** (tt) 3-1 C Mulhall *Tk keen hld; 3rd/4th frm 5 til 2nd 12; ld 3 out; hdd last; hrd rdn & rallied flat; ld on line*
[798¹]	2 hd	**Not So Prim** (5a) 6-1 S Swiers *Ld til app 14; sn releg 4th; rallied to 2nd 2 out; drvn to ld last; lkd wnr til wknd & hdd on line*
[696¹]	3 10	**Never Wonder (IRE)** (7a) 5-2F J Tate *2nd/3rd til ld app 14-15; rdn & releg 3rd 2 out; no ex*
[689ᶠ]	4 2	**Guilsborough Gorse** (7a) 4-1 G Brewer *Trckd ldrs; 5th 9; disp 3rd 12-15; rdn & wknd nxt; blun 2 out*
[137⁴]	5 8	**Just Takethe Micky** 16-1 S Charlton *Last to 3; hdwy 6 to mid-div 11; 6l 5th app 14; nd & stayed on same pce*
[399²]	6 runin	**Santa Barbara (IRE)** (5a) 10-1 Mrs S Palfreeman *Sn towards rr; 8th 9; lost tch 12; t.o 14*
[694¹]	P	**Fiery Jack** 10-1 N Tutty *Chsd ldr 2-9; lost plce qckly; pushed along & lsng tch 13; t.o & pu 3 out*
[797³]	P	**Hazel Reilly (IRE)** (5a) 9-2 L Bates *A rr div; pushed along aft 12; lsng tch 13; t.o & pu 2 out*
[807⁶]	P	**Normins Hussar (IRE)** 8-1 N Wilson *Mist 1; bhnd; last 9; nd aft; t.o & pu 2 out*
[689⁴]	F	**The Hazel Harrier (IRE)** 25-1 Miss A Deniel *Nt fluent in rr; no ch frm 13; 25l 6th 2 out; fell last*
	P	**Tied For Time (IRE)** 20-1 S Walker *Mid-div; 6th 9; sn wknd; t.o & pu 14*
[807⁴]	P	**Traceytown (IRE)** (5a) 20-1 Miss Rachel Clark *Midfield; 7th 9; pckd 10; rr & pushed along 12; t.o & pu 2 out*

OFFICIAL DISTANCES: hd, 8l TIME: 6min 32.0s

1001 Open Maiden 56&7yo (Div 1), 2m4f, 12st - 15J

10 ran

[398ᶠ]	1	**AMBERSAM** (7a) 2-1 G Brewer *5s-2s (opened 10s in plce); midfield til hdwy to 2nd 10; ld 12; drew wl clr aft 3 out; v easy*
[626²]	2 12	**Young Rab** (7a) 7-4F G Markham *(xnb) Cl up; lft in ld 7-12; rdn & outpcd when mist 2 out; fin tired*
[910⁶]	3 8	**Jolly Minster** 7-1 P Atkinson *Ld til bad mist 7; cl up to 11; sn wknd; poor 4th 3 out*
[436ᴿ]	4 1	**Mighty Rising** (7a) 9-1 S Charlton *Midfield to 7; pushed along 9; sn outpcd; strugg 11*
[625³]	P	**Early Dawn** (5a) 12-1 J Davies *Tk keen hld; prom to 10; wknd app nxt; t.o & pu 2 out*
[793⁶]	P	**Highbury** (7a) 7-1 S Walker *Prsd ldr to 7; 4l 5th 10; 3rd & wkng tame 12; t.o & pu last*
[808ᵖ]	F	**Mr Norm** 33-1 R Clark *Jmpd poor in last pr; lsng tch when fell 8*
[695ᶠ]	r	**Norman Way** (7a) 25-1 P Cornforth *A rr; pushed along & hanging lft aft 6; t.o when ref 7*
[627⁸]	P	**Redmire** (5a) 16-1 A Pennock *Handy in midfield; show 8; 5l 6th 10; sn wknd u.p; lost action app 3 out; pu bef nxt*
[379ᶠ]	P	**River Rising** 5-1 C Wilson *Chsd ldrs to 10; sn lost tch; t.o & pu 2 out*

OFFICIAL DISTANCES: 8l, 10l TIME: 5min 33.0s

1002 Open Maiden 56&7yo (Div 2), 2m4f, 12st - 15J

10 ran

[695ᵁ]	1	**EDDIE ROMBO** (7a,7ow) 2-1F B Woodhouse *(xnb) Mid-div to 7; 7l 4th aft 10; went 2nd nxt; ld 3 out; 8l clr aft 2 out; idled & just hld on flat*
[793ᵖ]	2 1	**Aunty Norma (IRE)** (5a) 4-1 D Thomas *Prsd ldr to 9; 11 2nd agn aft nxt; sn outpcd & 4th & u.p aft 12; rallied aft 2 out; stayed on to 2nd aft 2 out; fin str; just failed*
[625ᴿ]	3 8	**Ben From Ketton** (7a,4ow) 16-1 S J Robinson *Ld; rdn 11; hdd & blun 3 out; hung bad lft & rdr all over the plce aft; v tired when lost aft 2 out*
[626ᶠ]	4 3	**Wild Briar** (12a) 16-1 D Raw *Trckd ldrs; 2nd brief 9; 5l 3rd aft nxt; outpcd aft mists 11 & 12; fin tired*
[379ᵁ]	5 10	**Bred For Pleasure** (5a) 4-1 L McGrath *Blatant school; hld up in rr; to 3; nvr put in rce*
	6 4	**Total Relief** (7a) 7-1 Miss S Brotherton *V bckwd & jmpd v green; t.o by 3; hung bad lft aft 6; schooling*
	F	**Mac's View (IRE)** 8-1 T Glass *3rd when fell 7*
[22ᶠ]	P	**Magicman** (7a) 8-1 G Brewer *Prom in mid-div when reportedly lost action & pu 7*
[627ᶠ]	P	**Minster Echo** (12a) 12-1 S Charlton *Midfield; 13l 5th & outpcd aft 10; bad mist nxt & pu*
[695ᵁ]	U	**Vals Castle (IRE)** (5a) 9-4 Miss R Clark *8th when jmpd sideways & ur 2*

OFFICIAL DISTANCES: 1l, 8l TIME: 5min 48.0s

1003 Open Maiden (Div 1), 12st

10 ran

[910⁵]	1	**TIGER KING** 5-1 C Mulhall *Ld aft 10 til aft 13; ld agn 14; rdn 3l clr 2 out; idled bef last; hung lft flat; hld on u.p; all out*
[400ᶠ]	2 1	**Joe Smoke** 16-1 S Charlton *(xnb) Ld 3-7 & app 14; sn hdd; prsd wnr aft; outpcd 2 out; rallied u.p flat; nt much room & r.o one pce*

[627ᵁ]	3	8	**Nells Delight** (5a) 33-1 R Clark *Ld to 4 & frm 8-10; cl up in 3rd til outpcd & wknd 15; btn when mist nxt; plodded on*
[499⁶]	4	6	**Hey Sam** (IRE) 7-1 T Glass *Mist 8; w ldng trio at v slow pce til rdn app 14; sn strugg*
[696ᶠ]	R		**Buddy Girie** 12-1 C Denny *Dazzled & missed marker bef 2*
[808⁴]	R		**Leg Beforum** (IRE) 5-2 L Bates *Dazzled & missed marker bef 2*
[798ᴾ]	R		**Look Sharpe** 7-1 N Wilson *Mist 1; ld til dazzled & missed marker bef 2*
	F		**Sand Track** 20-1 M Haigh *Dazzled & missed marker bef 2; cont without rtrcng; 3rd when fell 5*
	R		**Star Design** (IRE) 12-1 K Green *Dazzled & missed marker bef 2*
[816³]	R		**Tricky Trevor** (IRE) evensF Miss H Delahooke *Mist 1; dazzled & missed marker bef 2; cont without rtrcng; pu 3*

OFFICIAL DISTANCES: 1l, 8l **TIME:** 6min 54.0s
An objection by the second to the winner was overruled (then thrown out for not being in writing); low sun caused many riders to take the wrong course - all pulled up except Tricky Trevor (cautioned) and Sand Track (fined £30 for not knowing course)

1004 Open Maiden (Div 2), 12st   11 ran

[798²]	1		**THE HAPPY MONARCH** (IRE) 3-1 Mrs F Needham *A.p; cl 2nd 4-15; 3l 3rd 3 out; outpcd 2 out; rallied to 5l 2nd app last; fin str; ld on line*
[696ᴿ]	2	hd	**Lulagh-B** (5a) 7-2 R Wakeham *Mid-div to 6; went 4l 3rd 8-13; cl 2nd 14; ld & stdly drew clr frm 3 out; 5l clr last; wknd flat; hdd on line*
[798ᶠ]	3	4	**Nasayer** (IRE) 6-1 A Pickering *Ld to 3; prom til mist 7; 12l 7th 9; rr by 12; stayed on frm 15 to 8l 3rd 2 out; fin wl; nrst fin*
[627⁴]	4	6	**Notoobig** 5-1 T Glass *A midfield; 6l 4th 3 out; r.o one pce*
[693⁵]	5	4	**Tyndrum Gold** (bl) 7-1 Miss A Deniel *Ld frm 3-15; wknd 3 out*
[693²]	6	4	**Heather Lad** 2-1F D Raw *Handy in 5th to 6; went 3l 3rd 7-14; cl 4th 15; pushed up to 11 2nd 3 out; wknd v qckly app nxt*
[694ᴾ]	7	4	**Port Valenska** (IRE) 3-1 B Woodhouse *Rr & mist 4; a rr; pushed along 15; nd*
[809⁵]	8	3	**Sally Scally** (5a) 10-1 Miss T Jackson *Hld up in rr to 5; slt hdwy to mid-div 9; rr agn 12; lost tch 15*
[693⁷]	9	runin	**Party Elephant** (5a) 20-1 Miss F Hartley *A rr div; last by 9; outpcd & lsng tch 11; t.o 14*
[816²]	F		**Aughrim Quest** (5a) 10-1 K Green *Fell 1*
	F		**Kings Cup** 20-1 M Haigh *Fell 1*

OFFICIAL DISTANCES: hd, 5l **TIME:** 6min 44.0s
Before this race the stewards inspected the first fence and the road crossing to make certain that the low sun was not in the eyes of the riders or horses; all riders were asked and no problems were raised

Pytchley
Guilsborough (LH 8F,19J) Sun, 9 Apr (GOOD)

1005 Hunt   10 ran

[543²]	1		**IRISHEYESARESMILIN** (IRE) 5-4F B Pollock *Lw; jw & a gng wl; sn 2nd; ld 3 out; hrd prsd frm nxt but kpt fndng ex; game*
[788²]	2	½	**Lottie The Lotus** (5a) 2-1 J Tarry *Hld up & bhnd; 7th 13; prog nxt to 3l 3rd app 3 out; sust chall frm 2 out; ev ch flat; r.o but a just hld*
[868³]	3	30	**Ebullient Equiname** (IRE) (bl) 7-1 S Morris *Bhnd; rdn 10; went 4th 12; 6l 4th & u.p app 3 out; nt r.o but went 3rd flat*
[788¹]	4	3	**Priory Piper** 12-1 L Hicks *Ld 2; rdn 15; untidy nxt; hdd 3 out; wknd qckly*
[553²]	5	25	**Buachaill Dana** (IRE) 25-1 R Cope *Ld to 2; pckd bad 5; 3rd when mist 11; wknd 14; poor last frm 3 out*
	r		**Be On The Sly** (5a) 33-1 Miss H Leak *(xnb) Fat; ss; ss til ref 1*
[789²]	P		**Deep Refrain** (IRE) (tt) 25-1 G Kerr *Prom; 4th & rdn 12; sn wknd; pu 14*
[440²]	P		**Hobnob** (IRE) (tt) 7-1 R Barrett *25s-7s; bhnd; drvn & lost tch 10; lkd reluct aft; pu 13*
[869⁸]	U		**Supreme Dream** (IRE) 20-1 Mrs P Adams *Chsng group til stumbled & rdr lost irons app 5; jmpd fnce without f.o & f.o aft 6*
[784ʳ]	P		**Tarry Awhile** 33-1 Miss R Goodwin *Towards rr; 6th & in tch 13; sn drvn & no resp; pu 15*

OFFICIAL DISTANCES: ¾l, 25l **TIME:** 6min 32.0s

1006 Confined, 12st   15 ran

[749²]	1		**GILDROM** 9-4F R Lawther *(xnb) Went 3rd aft 4; ld 12 & sn clr w one rival; drew 8l ahd aft 3 out; r.o str*

[784¹]	2	10	**Just Like Madge** (5a,3x) 4-1 J Tarry *Hld up in midfield; 4th & prog 11; outpcd 13 & 15l 3rd app 3 out; stayed on wl to chse wnr nxt; drvn along & kpt on but no imp*
[609⁴]	3	12	**Live Wire (IRE)** 12-1 G Kerr *Cl up til lost plce 8; 7th 11; rem frm 14 til stayed on agn aft 3 out; too much to do*
[510³]	4	4	**Who Is Equiname (IRE)** (bl) 5-1 S Morris *8s-5s; chsd ldrs; 6th when mist 11; drvn & no resp 13; 20l 4th 15; little zest*
[785⁶]	5	8	**Dark Rhytham** 25-1 Miss N McKim *(xnb) Tk keen hld in 2nd; ld 11-12; prsd wnr til 3l down app 3 out; wknd qckly*
[788³]	6	10	**Limosa** (5a) 16-1 R Barrett *Sn rdn & lost tch; 30l 9th 11; stayed on frm 2 out; no ch w ldrs*
[905⁴]	7	10	**Cormeen Lord (IRE)** 16-1 J Sharp *Midfield & off pce; mist 5; 20l 8th 11; plodded on; t.o*
[770³]	8	10	**Tighter Budget (USA)** 25-1 Miss G Hutchinson *Jmpd rt; ld to 11; wknd 13; 25l 5th 15; t.o*
[701⁵]	F		**Catchphrase** 33-1 J Docker *Sn lost tch in 13; bad mist 7; crashing fall 9; rdr broke wrist*
	P		**Don Royal** 33-1 P Millington *(citation) Bckwd; novicey & sn t.o; pu 9*
[509²]	P		**Glenselier (IRE)** 20-1 J Hudson *2 handlers; drpd to rr & mist 4; t.o 8; pu 14*
	P		**Gowlaun** 33-1 T Lane *Sn towards rr; strug when pu 12*
[897⁶]	P		**Perfect Finisher** 20-1 M Hawkins *Sn cl up; 5th 11; wknd 13; t.o & pu last*
[614ᴾ]	P		**Rexy Boy** 33-1 C Wadland *Jmpd mod & sn rr; t.o 9; pu 13*
[513¹]	S		**Right Company** 100-30 B Pollock *2 handlers; cl up til slpd up turn app 5*

OFFICIAL DISTANCES: 10l, 4l **TIME:** 6min 25.0s

1007 Ladies Open 12 ran

[707¹]	1		**LILY THE LARK** (5a) 7-1 Miss H Irving *Bhnd til hdwy 9; went 2nd 10-11 but 5th aft 12; 10l 5th app 3 out; rallied nxt; str rn to ld bef last; sn rdn clr*
[772²]	2	10	**Imperial Dawn (IRE)** 5-1 Miss L Rowe *Chsd ldrs; 6th 11; drvn along 13 w little resp; 8l 4th app 3 out; stayed on late but nd; went 2nd nr fin*
[687⁴]	3	nk	**Pongo Waring (IRE)** 25-1 Miss N McKim *Towards rr early; impd rap to 4th 11 & 2nd 13; ld 16; r.o wl til hdd & outpcd app last*
	4	4	**Dont Tell The Wife** 4-1 Miss G Hutchinson *Hld up & bhnd; rap prog in 5l 7th 11; disp 2nd 12 til 3l 3rd app 3 out; nt qckn aft*
[869¹]	5	½	**Cittadino** 10-11F Mrs J Dawson *Lw; set str gallop til hdd & mist 16; prsd ldr & ev ch to 2 out; wknd last*
[787⁵]	6	40	**Hostetler** 33-1 Miss K Norris *Drpd to rr 5; last 11; t.o 13*
[613⁷]	7	20	**Erbil (IRE)** 20-1 Miss S Mason *Sn lost tch; 10th 11; t.o 13*
[544ᶠ]	P		**Bare Fisted** 33-1 Miss H Phizacklea *2nd/3rd to 8; 8th & lsng tch 11; mist 12; t.o & pu 2 out*
[227⁸]	P		**Maltby Son** 14-1 Mrs T Hill *2nd/3rd to 11; 6th & wkng qckly nxt; t.o & pu 2 out*
[549ᴾ]	P		**Omidjoy (IRE)** (5a) (bl) 33-1 Miss A Stennett *Sn detach; t.o 7; pu 9*
[613⁵]	U		**Rainbow Walk (IRE)** 33-1 Miss A Burton *Sn prom; 5th 11; blun 12 & wknd; t.o when ur 3 out*
[295³]	P		**Well Arranged (IRE)** 33-1 Mrs C Boyes *Chsd ldrs to 9; 9th & strugg 12; t.o & pu last*

OFFICIAL DISTANCES: 5l, 3l **TIME:** 6min 25.0s

1008 Mens Open 8 ran

[870¹]	1		**COPPER THISTLE (IRE)** evensF R Hunnisett *Lw; jw; made all; 5l clr app 3 out; r.o str; v impressive*
[462²]	2	15	**Burntwood Melody** 5-2 R Armson *Prsd ldrs; disp 2nd frm 8 til 5l 2nd app 3 out; r.o game but a wl hld aft*
[607¹]	3	3	**Tom De Savoie (IRE)** 4-1 W Wales *Lw; mist 1; settled 2nd/4th; 2nd 13; mist nxt; 1 11 3rd & outpcd app 3 out; no imp aft*
[79ᴾ]	4	15	**Credo Is King (IRE)** 20-1 R Barrett *Chsd wnr to 8; 3rd 11; 12l 4th & outpcd 13; plodded on*
[511²]	5	8	**Grecian Lark** 11-1 J Tarry *Nvr gng wl & rdn all way; midfield; 6th 11; lost tch 13*
[589⁷]	P		**Black Book (IRE)** (5a) 33-1 P Millington *Nt lw; bhnd; 8l 7th 11; mist 12 & lost tch; mist 14; t.o & pu 16*
[770ᴾ]	P		**Mr Five Wood (IRE)** 33-1 J Purllant *Tk keen hld; prom; 5th 11; lost tch qckly 13; t.o & pu last; lame*
[545⁵]	P		**Needwood Neptune** 33-1 P Bennett *Sn rdn & reluct; t.o 5; pu 15*

OFFICIAL DISTANCES: 12l, 4l **TIME:** 6min 26.0s

1009 Dodson & Horrell PPORA Club Members Restricted, 12st 15 ran

[734²]	1		**DERRYAIR** 8-1 J Owen *Oht; made all; 8l clr 9; 7l ahd app 3 out; r.o wl frm nxt; a hldng rnr-up*

[869⁵] 2 4 **Macfin (IRE)** 8-1 Miss L Allan *Chsd ldrs; 5th 11; went 2nd 16; tried hrd to cl frm nxt but rdn & a hld*

[905³] 3 ½ **Fair Farm Boy** 16-1 M Mackley *Midfield; 7th 11; lost tch aft nxt & sn rem; 30l 5th app 3 out; r.o str aft til no ex flat; impossible task*

[869⁴] 4 15 **Blayneys Privilege** 33-1 Miss T Habgood *Sn chsng clr ldr; releg 3rd 16 & 13l down nxt; wknd*

[871¹⁴] 5 30 **Penrose Lad (NZ)** 20-1 W Tellwright *Sn prom; 3rd when pckd 11; wknd 15; fin tired*

[843ᴾ] P **Airecco (IRE)** 33-1 T Lane *Spurs; mist 3 in midfield; wkng when mist 10; t.o last nxt; pu 15 (connections forgot to declare intended blinkers)*

[675²] P **Baron Allfours** 16-1 P Millington *(citation) Hld up in rr; 9th & prog 11; chsd ldrs to 15; sn wknd; pu 2 out*

[411¹] P **Claret And Blue** 4-1 R Cope *6s-4s; midfield & hld up; 8th 11; lost tch 13 & sn wl bhnd; t.o & pu aft 16 (lkd shin-sore)*

[734⁷] P **Drunkard's Corner** (12a) 8-1 J Diment *Hld up & wl bhnd; rap prog in 4th 11; gng str when broke knee & pu 14; dead*

[515¹] F **Luckashan (IRE)** (7a) 5-4F B Pollock *Midfield when fell 3*

     P **Mr Greengrass** 20-1 S Sporborg *Novicey & detach in last pr; school til t.o & pu 13*

[761ᴾ] P **Nursery Story** 33-1 M Polley *Impd to midfield 5; 12th & wkng rap 11; pu 12; lame*

     P **Over The Barrow (IRE)** 33-1 L Hicks *Handy early; lost tch 9; 10th 11; t.o & pu 13; dism*

[612ᴾ] P **Rolpen** 16-1 J I Pritchard *Sn lost tch; 11th 11; t.o & pu 15*

[615¹⁰] P **Upton Orbit** 33-1 R Lawther *Chsd ldr to 5; 6th & wkng 11; t.o & pu 14*

OFFICIAL DISTANCES: 4l, ½l **TIME:** 6min 33.0s

1010 Confined Maiden (Div 1, Part 1)   10 ran

[790ᴾ] 1 **MAGICAL MANOR** (5a) 7-1 J Tarry *2nd til ld 6; hdd aft 8; sn ld agn; hdd 15; prsd ldr til jnd for 2nd & lft clr last; v lucky*

[906³] 2 5 **Kings Choir** 7-2 Mrs C Boyes *Sn drpd rr & rn in snatches; 6th 11; hit 12 & wl outpcd; virt to 15 r.o str frm 2 out; lft 2nd at last; hopeless task*

[753ᴾ] 3 7 **Floorex Carpetman** (7a) 5-1 R Smith *Hld up; prog 9; 4th & gng wl 11; prsd ldrs til wknd tame 16*

[703ᴾ] P **Bonnie Amy** (12a) 33-1 L Hicks *Hld up; hdwy & cl 5th 11; wknd 13; t.o & pu 3 out*

[515⁵] P **Good Job** (5a) 11-4F S Morris *Prom; ld brief aft 8; 3rd when mist 13; 2l 3rd app 3 out but tired rap; pu last*

[872ᴾ] U **Incbrush** 12-1 M Foley *Prsd ldrs til 7th 11; sn outpcd & nt pushed; 12l 4th app 3 out; str rn frm nxt; disp 2nd & gaining when hit fallen rival & ur aft last; lkd wnr*

[790⁹] r **Stable Girl** (5a) 20-1 A Tutton *Mists & sn bhnd; t.o crawling aft 11; ref & ur 13*

[514ᴾ] U **Syrpiro** 7-2 R Cope *Hit 1; reld; cl 2nd/3rd til ld 15; 2l clr 2 out; rdn & diminishing advant when blun, lost hind legs & ur last*

[905³] P **The Bee's Castle (IRE)** 33-1 R Armson *Bhnd; lft last & strugg 13; t.o & pu 2 out*

[55⁷] P **The Boree Log** 33-1 M Hewitt *(xnb) Tk str hld; ld to 6; wknd rap & last aft 8; t.o & pu 11*

OFFICIAL DISTANCES: 5l, 6l **TIME:** 6min 50.0s

1011 Confined Maiden (Div 1, Part 2)   10 ran

[11ᴾ] 1 **CATCHATAN (IRE)** (7a) 7-2 R Lawther *(xnb) Lw; 2nd/3rd & gng wl; ld 3 out; r.o str*

[439ᴾ] 2 20 **Round The Bend** 8-1 Miss L Allan *2 handlers; oht; swtng; pulled hrd; prom; ld 8-10 & 13-15; lft in ld nxt; hdd 3 out; no imp aft*

[844³] 3 2 **Polly Live Wire** (5a) 6-1 P Millington *Drpd out rem last; hdwy in 10l 8th 11; eff 15; 5l 3rd when blun 3 out & rdn; no imp aft*

[792ᴾ] P **Bangagin** 33-1 M Buchan *(xnb) Mounted on course & tde; str hld; ld to 8; 7th & wkng rap 11; wl to 13; pu last*

     P **Dona Ferentis (IRE)** (12a) 11-8F B Pollock *Cl up; jmpd slow 5; 6l 6th 11; outpcd 14; mist nxt; nt pushed; pu aft 16*

[514ᴾ] F **Game Drive (IRE)** 20-1 P Newton *Tk keen hld & prom; ld 10 til jnd & fell 13 (rdr resplendent in earrings)*

[898ᴾ] P **Penaword** 20-1 J I Pritchard *Prsd ldrs; mist 6; 5th 11; wknd tame 13; pu 15*

     U **Proper Charlie** 5-1 T Lane *Trckd ldrs; went 4th 11; 3rd & gng wl 14; ld 15 til blun & ur nxt; promising*

[516ᴾ] P **Sock Hop (IRE)** (2ow) 20-1 P Smith *Pulled hrd brief; mist 7; t.o aft 8; pu 11*

[517ᴾ] P **Tarjumaan (USA)** 25-1 A Brown *9th when mist 4; a rr; last & lsng tch 11; t.o & pu 15*

OFFICIAL DISTANCES: 15l, 1½l **TIME:** 6min 44.0s

1012 Confined Maiden (Div 2)   15 ran

     1 **SHOEMAKER (IRE)** 6-1 S Morris *Hld up gng wl; 5l 8th & smooth prog 11; ld 16; clr nxt; unchall; impressive*

[679³]	2	15	**Father's Joy** (5a) 12-1 *Miss A Burton Mists in rr; hdwy to midfield but off pce 11; no ch frm 15; kpt on to chse wnr hopeless frm nxt*
	3	4	**Fisherman Jack** (7a) 12-1 *M Mackley Tk keen hld in midfield; cl 7th 11; outpcd aft nxt; mod 5th app 3 out; kpt on stdly; fair debut*
[703⁹]	4	10	**Metro Fashion (IRE)** 3-1F *T Lane Prom; 3rd 11; ev ch whn mist 16; 4th & wkng nxt*
[550⁴]	5	12	**Stonebroke (IRE)** 10-1 *D Flavin Hld up; eff & cl 6th 11; prsd ldrs til wknd qckly app 3 out*
[321⁹]	P		**Bally Seamus (IRE)** 11-2 *R Cope Hld up in midfield; wknd 10; pu 12*
	P		**Broad Statement** 11-2 *J Owen Ld/disp til ld 10; hdd 16; 4l 2nd app nxt; wknd rap; pu 2 out*
[792⁹]	P		**Cottage Light** (bl) 25-1 *N Ridout Prom to 8; rr 11; t.o & pu 14*
[845ᵁ]	P		**Craftbook Marchesa (IRE)** (5a) 12-1 *P Millington Drpd out last; lost tch 11; t.o & pu 3 out*
[373⁹]	P		**Crested Lass** (5a) 33-1 *L Hicks Rmdrs aft 2; nvr gng wl; bhnd frm 8; pu aft 12*
	P		**Dennis** 12-1 *R Armson Midfield til wknd 10; pu 12*
[194⁹]	P		**Hesgreen** 20-1 *C Wadland Lw; tk keen hld & prom; 5th 11; wknd tame aft 12; pu 14*
[516⁵]	P		**Highfurlong (IRE)** (bl) 6-1 *J Oldring Made most to 10; nt r.o & lost plce rap; rr & blun 13; t.o last 16; pu 2 out*
[754⁹]	P		**More Mettle** 12-1 *J Diment Fat; hld up; impd to 4th 11; wknd aft nxt; wl bhnd when pu 15*
[548⁹]	P		**Up The Road (IRE)** 33-1 *P Newton Sn strugg in last; pu 8*

OFFICIAL DISTANCES: 12l, 3l **TIME:** 6min 40.0s

Heythrop
Dunthrop (RH 9F,18J) Tue, 11 Apr (GOOD becoming SOFTER)

1013 Hunt   6 ran

[749³]	1		**MR SMUDGE** 2-1 *A Martin Went 2nd 7-11; rdn 14; ld aft 3 out; mist last; drvn & stayed on wl*
[898¹]	2	2	**Tom's Prize** (7a) 5-2 *S Joynes (xnb) 7/2-5/2; lw; jw; settled in tch til went 3rd 10; 2nd 11; ld 12; pckd 3 out & hld; rdn & kpt on one pce aft nxt (lkd outstayed though poss unlucky as rdr drpd whip app last)*
[896³]	3	20	**Wrens Island (IRE)** 6-4F *Miss L Sweeting Tk keen hld & ld 1; hdd 12; 8l 3rd & wkng qckly 15*
[897⁹]	4	20	**Glendine (IRE)** 33-1 *D Smith Prsd ldr to 7; rdn & lost tch 11; t.o 13*
[749⁹]	5	15	**Raining Stairs** 20-1 *J Trice-Rolph Mist 4; jmpd slow 5; chsd ldrs; 7l 5th 10; lost tch 12; t.o 3 out*
[787⁸]	P		**Colonel Fairfax** 33-1 *Miss K Matthews A last; mist 2; lost tch 11; t.o 13; crawling when pu 3 out*

OFFICIAL DISTANCES: 2l, 15l **TIME:** 7min 00.0s

1014 Ladies Open, 3m5f - 21J   14 ran

[860²]	1		**RIP VAN WINKLE** 3-1 *Miss A Dare Lw; pushed along & outpcd towards rr; 20l 8th 11; rap prog aft 16; prom when jmpd delib 18; ld app 2 out; rdn & r.o wl flat; wl rdn*
[836²]	2	4	**Mr Dow Jones (IRE)** 4-1 *Miss B Lloyd Lw; chsd ldrs; hit 8; 7l 5th & eff 13; sn outpcd & 16l 5th 15; rallied to chse wnr aft 2 out; nt qckn u.p & a hld flat*
[475¹]	3	3	**Grey Smoke** 9-4F *Miss B Lloyd Rcd wide & gd hdwy 6; 3rd nxt; chall 13; ld 15; mist & rdr lost iron 17; hdd app 2 out; one pce but kpt on game*
[749⁶]	4	12	**Lucky Tanner** 33-1 *Miss G Young Midfield; hit 10; 25l 7th 13; rap prog aft 16; 4l 4th 18; drvn & sn wl outpcd*
[787²]	5	7	**Titus Andronicus** 33-1 *Miss H Irving Lw; hit 3; prsd ldrs; pckd 6; 6l 4th 13; u.p nxt; 15l 4th & btn 15; 10l 7th when mist 17*
[865¹]	6	20	**Outrageous Affair** (5a) 33-1 *Miss R Reynolds Jmpd slow 1; sn t.o; stayed on frm 2 out; hopeless task*
[904⁹]	7	3	**Just Marmalade** 33-1 *Miss J Williams (xnb) Cl up early; lost plce 9; 11th 13; t.o 16*
[785³]	8	5	**Mr Ben Gunn** 16-1 *Miss L Sweeting A wl bhnd; hit 6; 13th when blun 9; 10th 13; t.o 16*
[736¹]	9	7	**Starpath (NZ)** 10-1 *Miss T Cave Rcd keen; ld 4-6, 11-12 & 13-15; mist 16; 2nd when blun 17; nt rec & lost plce rap; t.o*
[751³]	P		**Dalusman (IRE)** 25-1 *Miss V Sturgis Midfield; wknd & nd; 9th & outpcd 13; t.o & pu 3 out*
[699ᵁ]	P		**Everso Irish** 25-1 *Miss C Thomas Chsd ldrs; 9l 6th 13; outpcd 15; t.o & pu 3 out*
[868⁴]	P		**Faraday** 33-1 *Miss S Phizacklea Ldrs til outpcd 9; t.o 13; mist 17; pu nxt*
[558¹]	P		**Hearts Are Wild** 7-1 *Miss P Gundry 10s-7s; tk keen hld; ld to 4, 6-11 & 12-13; 3rd when mist 15; lft 2l 2nd 18; dem & wknd rap aft 3 out; pu last*

[802⁴] U   **The Bold Abbot** 33-1 *Miss S West 3rd/4th to 9; 7th & wkng qckly when mist & ur 12*

OFFICIAL DISTANCES: 3l, 2½l   **TIME:** 8min 01.0s

1015 Mens Open (Lord Ashton of Hyde's Cup), 4m - 23J   16 ran

[683⁴]	1		**RUSTY BRIDGE** 4-1JF *R Burton Ld by ab 6l til hdd brief 19; nk advant nxt; r.o str frm 2 out; v game eff*
[890¹]	2	5	**Rusty Fellow** 14-1 *D Mansell Bhnd early; prog 9; 13l 4th 15; went 2nd 17; ld brief 19; mist 3 out; ev ch & drvn nxt; nt qckn app last*
[574¹]	3	4	**High Guardian** 5-1 *Julian Pritchard Lw; jmpd slow 1; trckd ldrs; went 3rd 10; 10l down 15; clsd & 2l 3rd & drvn 18; hrd rdn & outpcd in 6l 3rd 3 out*
[820²]	4	10	**Bit Of A Citizen (IRE)** (5a) (vis) 14-1 *E Williams Chsd ldrs; 19l 5th 15; plodded on & nvr within 20l of ldng trio aft*
[614⁵]	5	4	**Smile Pleeze (IRE)** 4-1JF *T Stephenson Lw; rr div; 10th & strugg 15; mod prog to poor 5th 2 out; nvr nr ldrs*
[529⁶]	6	2	**Rosmarino** 10-1 *A Dalton Lw; nt jw towards rr; brief eff 13; 13th & strugg 15; plodded on*
[886⁴]	7	12	**Hehas** 33-1 *C Wadland Bhnd; last 8; 15th 15; u.p & t.o aft nxt*
[788⁶]	8	20	**The Hatcher (NZ)** 16-1 *R Lawther Midfield & nd; poor 9th 15; t.o 18*
[473²]	9	1¼	**Solo Gent** 6-1 *S Bush 3rd when nrly ref 4; sn lost plce; poor 8th 13; 30l 6th 17; t.o 19*
[833¹]	10	3	**Sip Of Brandy (IRE)** 12-1 *G Skone Lost 20l start; a bhnd; 12th 15; t.o 18*
[788⁸]	P		**Archies Oats** 25-1 *J Trice-Rolph Spurs; chsd ldrs; 25l 7th 15; nvr on terms aft; t.o & pu last*
[859⁹]	P		**Celtic Town** 16-1 *P Kay (xnb) Bhnd; 11th 15; rdn & no resp 16; sn t.o; pu 2 out*
[557⁵]	P		**Manor Rhyme** (2ow) 33-1 *T Gretton Prom in chsng group; 12l 3rd 8 til mist 10; 6th & rdn 13; 24l 6th 15; t.o & pu 19*
[771³]	P		**Pantara Prince (IRE)** 33-1 *A Sansome Chsd wnr to 16; 8l 4th & wkng rap nxt; t.o & pu 19*
[895⁵]	P		**Topical Tip (IRE)** 16-1 *T Scudamore Chsd ldrs early; lost plce 9; last 16; t.o & pu 20*
[814²]	P		**Weak Moment (IRE)** 6-1 *A Crow Wl bhnd & nvr gng wl; 14th & rdn 15; t.o & pu 18*

OFFICIAL DISTANCES: 3½l, 2½l   **TIME:** 8min 41.0s

1016 Confined, 12st   12 ran

[800ᵁ]	1		**COPPER COIL** 9-4F *D Alers-Hankey In tch; hdwy to ld 8; 8l clr 12; prsd nxt; mist 15; hdd 3 out; ld agn aft nxt; rdn & forged clr flat; game*
[770⁴]	2	4	**Stormy Words** (5a) 3-1 *S Morris Hld up & bhnd; 6th & prog 10; 11l 4th 12; jnd ldng pr 13; ld 16 til aft 2 out; rdn & edged rt flat; nt qckn*
[750⁴]	3	40	**Northern Bluff** 3-1 *J Jukes Lw; hld up trckng ldrs; clsd & lft 2nd 10; 1l down 14; wknd rap aft 3 out & 20l 3rd nxt; virt pulled himself up flat*
[749ᴾ]	4	7	**La Mon Dere (IRE)** (bl,tt) 16-1 *Miss T Spearing Trckd ldrs; went 2nd 6 til blun 10; rdn aft; 9l 3rd 12; jb & reluct frm nxt; t.o 3 out; lft 4th & impeded last*
[784³]	P		**Hope's Delight (IRE)** 8-1 *R Smith Bit bckwd; midfield til drpd back 8th 10; mist & u.p nxt; wl t.o 13; pu 15*
[510ᴾ]	P		**Its Murphy Man** 33-1 *C Wadland Prom; 4th 10; sn hrd rdn; 20l 6th & strugg 12; pu 13*
[552²]	F		**Man Of The Match** (bl) 3-1 *F Hutsby 8s-3s; prom til 5th 9; 15l 5th & outpcd 12; t.o 3 out; 4th when fell last*
	P		**Robsand (IRE)** 16-1 *M Wilesmith School in rr; lost tch 6; eased out & pu 9*
	P		**Rupert's Princess (IRE)** (5a) 20-1 *S Sellars Jmpd v slow & reluct in last; t.o 4; pu 7*
[788⁵]	P		**Smart Teacher (USA)** 20-1 *G Carenza (xnb) Tde; unruly & ld rnd & ur start; ss & lost 20l; a wl bhnd; mist 8; last 10; sn rdn; t.o & pu 12*
	P		**Templerainey (IRE)** (tt) 16-1 *G Maundrell Strugg in rr; t.o 8; pu 9*
[428ᴾ]	P		**Templeroan Prince** 33-1 *M Cowley Ld til jb lft 3 & 4; ld agn to 8; 7th & wkng rap 10; t.o & pu 13*

OFFICIAL DISTANCES: 3l, dist   **TIME:** 6min 51.0s

1017 Intermediate, 12st   8 ran

[671¹]	1		**DAWN INVADER (IRE)** 2-1 *J Jukes Went 2nd 6; ld 8; outj & hdd brief 2 out; sn drvn 5l clr; blun last; kpt on*
[791¹]	2	15	**Burgundy Bob (IRE)** 4-9F *Julian Pritchard Sn 2nd; ld 5-8; prsd wnr hrd aft but nt a fluent; rdn to ld & outj 2 out; sn hdd; a fighting losing battle aft; tired when blun last; eased*
[840³]	3	12	**Generous Deal (IRE)** 25-1 *A Sansome Hit 4; sn towards rr; impd to 3rd 11 but 8l frm ldng pr nxt & 15l 3rd 13; mists & rdn aft; t.o 15; some late prog*
[785ᴾ]	P		**Apple Nicking** 33-1 *E Linehan Nt fluent 3 & 5; chsd ldrs til 4th & rdn 10; wknd qckly & jmpd slow nxt; pu 12*
[791⁶]	P		**Bit Of A Character** 33-1 *T Young Ld aft 1-5; sn bhnd; hit 8; reluct & t.o 11; pu 13*
[871⁷]	P		**Colonel Wilkie** 33-1 *Mrs E Staines Ld 1; lost tch aft 4 & lkd v reluct; fnce bhnd when pu 9*

| [886⁷] | P | | **True Chimes** 25-1 J Owen *(xnb)* Tk keen hld; sn 3rd; 4l 3rd 10; outpcd when mist 12; 28l 4th & wkng rap nxt; t.o pu 3 out |
| [609⁹] | P | | **Youcat (IRE)** 33-1 N Bloom Sn toiling in rr; lost tch & jmpd slow 7; t.o & pu 11 |

OFFICIAL DISTANCES: 10l, 15l **TIME:** 6min 56.0s

1018 Open Maiden 6yo&up (Div 1), 12st

9 ran

[790⁶]	1		**BARTON BOG (IRE)** 9-4JF A Evans Novicey jumper; settled 4th til went 2nd 12; ld brief 15; ev ch when lft in ld 2 out; sn rdn clr
[889⁴]	2	20	**Dillon** 9-4JF F Hutsby Nvr btr than midfield; 10l 8th 10; rdn 11; went 13l 3rd 14; strugg nxt; lft 2nd 2 out
[753⁵]	P		**Bombadier Brown** (bl) 33-1 A Charles-Jones Rn in snatches; chsd ldr to 6; jmpd slow 7; drvn 9; went 3rd brief nxt; reluct frm 11; t.o & pu 13
[899⁹]	P		**Bramley** 16-1 A Martin Jmpd sketchy in midfield; 7th 10; eff 12 & 3rd nxt; 16l 4th & strugg when jmpd slow 14; rem 4th when pu 2 out
[787⁶]	P		**Cumberland Youth** 20-1 Miss J Garley Last pr til impd qckly to 2nd 6; jnd ldr 7-8; 3rd when mist 12; 4th & wkng when blun 13; t.o & pu 3 out
[891⁹]	P		**Fountain Glen (IRE)** 10-1 Julian Pritchard Jmpd poor & sn last pr; 18l last 10; t.o & pu 14
[866⁹]	r		**Mr Stackhouse** 20-1 G Barfoot-Saunt *(xnb)* Ld; 5l clr 14; hdd u.p nxt; sn ld agn; mist 3 out; jmpd slow 2 out & hdd; nt r.o; btn 2nd when ref & stuck hd thro wing last
[866³]	P		**Sutton Lighter** 4-1 D Mansell *(xnb)* Tde; pulled hrd; 3rd til mists 8 & 9; 6th & wkng 10; rdn 11; t.o & pu 13
[790⁴]	P		**Truly Optimistic** (5a) 7-1 C Wadland Lw; nvr btr than midfield; 5th & in tch 10; wknd nxt; t.o & pu 13

OFFICIAL DISTANCE: 25l **TIME:** 7min 08.0s

1019 Open Maiden 56&7yo (Div 1), 2m4f, 12st - 14J

10 ran

[753⁵]	1		**TAKE THE BRUSH (IRE)** (5a) 7-4F R Lawther Declined suicidal early pce; disp 25l 4th 6; went 20l 2nd 9; clsd qckly to ld 11; 20l ahd by 2 out; v easy
[899ᵁ]	2	20	**Piccadilly Wood** 33-1 G Barfoot-Saunt Mist 2; nt jw in rr; 35l 6th 6; plodded into rem 2nd aft 2 out; nvr in rce
[433⁹]	P		**Ballyaction** 12-1 J Owen 16s-12s; mists; keen early; 20l 3rd 6; rem 3rd & tired 11; pu 3 out
	P		**City Express** (7a) 20-1 J Jukes Sis & a rem; t.o 6; pu 3 out
[74ᶠ]	P		**Free To Conker (IRE)** 20-1 M Hawkins *(xnb)* Tk v str hld & sn ld; hdd 7; wknd rap aft mist nxt; t.o & pu 11
[57ᶠ]	P		**Gilt Air** (5a) (tt) 8-1 C Weaver Sis; jmpd v slow 1; rem 9th 6; mist 9; nrly ref 10; pu 11
[250ᵁ]	F		**Grain Hill** (5a) 8-1 M Wall Sn chsng ldr & clr of rest; ld 7; 20l ahd 9; wknd nxt & hdd 11; 20l 2nd when nrly stpd 2 out; exhaust 3rd when fell hvly last
[898ᴿ]	P		**Magni Momenti** (12a,3ow) 3-1 Julian Pritchard *(martin)* Lost 30l in v ragged start; jmpd indifferent in rr; 40l 7th & mist 6; t.o & pu 11
[515⁹]	P		**Poets Corner (IRE)** 10-1 Miss N McKim *(xnb)* Ss; jmpd slow & a rem; t.o last 6; plodded on & last of 4 w ch of 3rd when fell last
[900ᵁ]	r		**Strike Accord (IRE)** 33-1 P Young 25l 4th & u.p 6; no ch when nrly ref 8; ref 9

OFFICIAL DISTANCE: 25l **TIME:** 5min 27.0s

1020 Open Maiden 6yo&up (Div 2), 12st

16 ran

[900²]	1		**MR MAX (IRE)** 7-4F M Wall *(xnb)* Broke cannon bone 2yrs ago; 2nd/4th til ld 14; hdd & lft in ld 3 out; 3l clr nxt; a in comm aft; comf
[891⁹]	2	5	**Romany Chat** 8-1 A Martin Lw; oht; tk keen hld; chsd ldrs; 6th 10; pckd bad 13; went 3rd nxt & 5l 3rd 15; tk 2nd 2 out; drvn & hld app last
[893⁹]	3	40	**Mcloughlin (IRE)** 20-1 M Rodda Wl bhnd; 13th & strugg 10; plodded on as others gave up
[738⁹]	4	½	**Music Class** 14-1 J Gallagher Bhnd; 12th 7 strugg 10; t.o 15; plodded on
[786²]	5	15	**Novasun** 4-1 P York Ld 4; mist 5; hdd app 6; ld agn 10 til app 12; w ldr nxt; wknd qckly 14; 20l 4th 15
[784ᴿ]	6	25	**Yodeller Bill** (5ow) 14-1 P Sheppard A bhnd; 11th 10; t.o 13; plodded on
[845⁹]	P		**Bakewell** 33-1 T Illsley Still bckwd; hdwy 5; ld app 6-10; ld app 12 til 4th & mist 13; wknd rap; t.o & pu 3 out
[868⁹]	P		**Batcho Missile** 33-1 A Sansome 2 handlers; chsd ldrs; 7th 10; wkng when blun 12; pu 13
[892ᵁ]	P		**Don'tcallmegeorge** 33-1 P Young Bckwd; jmpd abysmal in last; pu 15
[845²]	P		**Judicial Queen** 33-1 A Charles-Jones Hld up; hdwy in rr 8; disp ld 13 til blun 3 out; 6l 3rd & fdng qckly when jmpd v slow nxt; exhaust & sn pu
[606⁹]	U		**Outside The Rain (IRE)** (5a) 25-1 T Macfarlane Rr when ur 4

[471^P]	P		**Quick Response (IRE)** 5-1 S Joynes *8s-5s; midfield; 12l 10th 10; hdwy 12; 7l 5th when mist 14; pu nxt*
[792⁵]	r		**Teachers Pet** 14-11 Miss L Sweeting *Midfield when blun 7; 8th 14; lost tch 12; mist 14; wl bhnd when ref 3 out*
[433^P]	P		**True Hustler** 7-1 F Hutsby *Hld up; 8l 9th 10; wknd 13; t.o & pu 15*
[752⁴]	P		**Upanoff** (5a) 33-1 B Pauling *Blun 3; prsd ldrs; 5th 10; sn wknd; t.o & pu 15*
[891^P]	P		**Weldson** 33-1 J Trice-Rolph *2 handlers; oht; lw; pulled hrd; ld to 4; drpd to rr 8; t.o & pu 11*

OFFICIAL DISTANCES: 2½l, dist **TIME:** 7min 10.0s

1021 Open Maiden 56&7yo (Div 2), 2m4f, 12st - 13J   16 ran

[121^P]	1		**BLACK OAK** 6-1 Julian Pritchard *(xnb) Ld; 10l clr 8; hdd 11; lft in ld 3 out; hdd brief nxt; rdn clr bef last; kpt on*
[733⁴]	2	8	**Rapid Liner** 33-1 J Gallagher *Hld up & bhnd; 9th 6; hdwy in 6th passing 10; rchd 12l 3rd 2 out & snatched 2nd on line; no ch w wnr*
[693⁴]	3	hd	**Well I Never** 12-1 L Hicks *Midfield & off pce; 7th 6; hdwy 8 to 2nd 9; 4th & ev ch nxt; mist 3 out; ld brie*
[696^U]	4	½	**The Big Lad (IRE)** (1ow) 6-1 G Smith *10s-6s; lw; chsd ldrs; hit 4; 26l 5th 6; eff 9; plodded on & 13l 4th 2 out; just lost out in rce for 2nd flat*
	5	15	**Beat The Bank (IRE)** (7a) 20-1 D Crosse *A towards rr; 8th 6; lost tch 7; plodded on*
[747^P]	P		**Appeal Again** 14-1 A Wintle *(xnb) Jmpd poor & qckly lost tch; t.o aft mist 4; rdr lost irons; pu 7*
[605²]	P		**Chadwick Bank (IRE)** 2-1F R Cope *3s-2s; prom in chsng group; 4th when blun 3; 17l 3rd 6; 4th when bad mist 9; rdn & wknd rap; pu 2 out*
	P		**Crewski** (7a) 20-1 S Sellars *Fat; hmpd 1; jmpd poor & qckly lost tch; t.o 4; pu 7*
[754^P]	P		**Have A Break** (7a) 5-2 R Lawther *Str hld in 2nd to 9; ev ch 11; sn eased & lost tch; pu 2 out*
	P		**Hobgoblin** 20-1 J Owen *(xnb,martin) Tde; svs & strangled; v novicey & a t.o; pu 11*
[431^P]	F		**Looks Like Reign** 16-1 B McKim *(xnb) Reared & ur padd; mounted outside; 6th when fell 1*
[250^P]	P		**Moon Island** (5a) 16-1 S Morris *A bhnd; 11th & strugg 6; climbed 8; t.o & pu 11*
[732^P]	P		**Perking** 20-1 M Foley *Sn strugg; t.o & pu 8*
[792^P]	P		**Piltdown Lady** (5a) 33-1 T Macfarlane *A bhnd; 10th 6; t.o 9; pu 3 out*
[515^F]	F		**So Frank** 4-1 David Dennis *Chsd ldrs; 6th 6; eff & 6l 4th passing 10; wknd nxt; poor 6th when fell 2 out*
[194^F]	F		**Thor's Phantom** 33-1 A Martin *20l 4th 6; clsd 8; slt ld 11 til fell 3 out*

OFFICIAL DISTANCES: 3l, hd **TIME:** 5min 21.0s
Fence 10 omitted - fallen rider

Chepstow (LH 11F,18J)
Wed, 12 Apr (SOFT)

1022 Dunraven Windows S. & W. Wales P-t-P Championship HC   15 ran

[742¹]	1		**NO FIDDLING (IRE)** 11-10 4-1 C Williams *In tch; went 3rd aft 7 & 2nd 12; pushed along to ld 14; drew clr aft 3 out; kpt on wl; easy*
[895¹]	2	18	**Kerry Soldier Blue** 12-05 4-1 Julian Pritchard *Ld 2-4; chsd ldr to 11; sn lost plce; 26l 6th app 14; rallied 3 out; kpt on wl to 2nd flat; no match for wnr*
[687²]	3	2½	**Mister Horatio** 11-12 3-1F M Lewis *Chsd ldr 3; ld 5; hdd 14; 3l 2nd 3 out; sn wknd; jmpd slow nxt; dem flat*
[877⁵]	4	10	**Bullens Bay (IRE)** 11-10 40-1 Miss F Wilson *Tk keen hld; mist 4; 8th 7; impd to 5th 11; 12l 4th app 14; nd aft*
[832¹]	5	2	**Cresswell Quay** 11-07 12-1 G Lewis *Sn prom; 7th 7; went 2nd 11; 6l 3rd app 14; sn rdn; 3rd & btn 3 out; exhaust & lost 4th flat*
[744¹]	6	7	**Bel-De-Moor** 11-04 33-1 R Cooper *Hld up in rr; poor last 7; prog to 9th when blun 12; no ch aft*
[743¹]	7	16	**Viardot (IRE)** 11-10 16-1 J Cook *Prsd ldrs; 5th 7; blun 9; nd aft; t.o*
[831¹]	8	dist	**True Fortune** 11-12 15-2 P Sheldrake *10th 7; hdwy nxt; chsd ldrs 9; 7th 12; wknd aft 13; sn t.o*
[946¹]	P		**Coolvawn Lady (IRE)** 12-00 7-1 Miss P Jones *Prom to 5; 12th & strugg 7; t.o & pu 14*
[479¹]	P		**Red Neck** 11-07 10-1 T Vaughan *Blun 6; 11th nxt; hdwy 8; 6th 12; wknd 13; t.o & pu 15*
[833⁶]	P		**Saffron Moss** 12-00 40-1 A Charles-Jones *Hit 2; chsd ldrs; 7th 7; wknd 12; t.o & pu 15*
[943^P]	P		**Sea Search** 11-02 100-1 Miss A Meakins *A bhnd; 14th & strugg 7; t.o to 8; pu 12*

[819²]	P	**Tiger Lord** 11-09 33-1 S Blackwell *Chsd ldrs; 6th 7; wknd 11; t.o & pu 15*
[743²]	P	**Twilight Tom** 11-10 33-1 A Price *Ld to 2; drpd back 9th & strugg 7; t.o & pu 12*
[643⁵]	P	**Whistling Buck (IRE)** 11-10 20-1 F Windsor Clive *A bhnd; drvn 6; 13th 7; t.o & pu 12*

TIME: 6min 51.8s **TOTE:** £4.90; places £2.00,£2.00,£1.40 **Ex:** £33.10 **CSF:** £19.86 **Tri:** £52.50

Ludlow (RH 9F,19J)
Thu, 13 Apr (GOOD)

1023 Chase Meredith Mem HC   10 ran

[920¹]	1		**GRIMLEY GALE (IRE)** 11-13 4-11F R Burton *Lw; made most & a gng wl; drew clr frm 3 out; easy*
[901¹]	2	6	**Native Cove (IRE)** 11-09 20-1 L Hicks *Lw; sn 2nd/3rd; prsd wnr frm 11; mist 12; 11 2nd aft pckng 15; nt qckn 3 out*
[920³]	3	3	**Lakeside Lad** 11-11 (bl) 25-1 R Cooper *Mostly 2nd/3rd; 4l 3rd & rdn 14; hit 16; one pce nxt*
[920²]	4	12	**Shafi (IRE)** 11-09 5-1 D Mansell *Keen hld in rr; 5l 4th & prog 11; 9l 4th aft 15; no ex when jmpd slow nxt; mists final 3 fncs*
[863²]	5	dist	**Lordinthesky** 11-11 25-1 S Blackwell *Bhnd; blun 4; rmdrs aft 8; mod 7th 11; no ch aft; t.o 16*
[944⁴]	6	8	**Sister Lark** 11-04 33-1 T Vaughan *Sn towards rr; 8th & strugg 11; t.o 16*
[698ᵁ]	P		**Carbery Ministrel (IRE)** 11-09 50-1 K Burke *In tch brief; drpd back last aft 6; blun bad 8; sn wl t.o; 2 fncs bhnd when rdr event pu 2 out*
[895⁴]	P		**Freedom Fighter** 12-00 20-1 A Martin *Pulled hrd; ld brief aft 2; 5th when pckd bad 3; t.o 5; impeded 7; mist 9; 6th & rdn 11; sn wknd; mist 13; pu nxt*
[1020³]	P		**Mcloughlin (IRE)** 11-09 50-1 M Rodda *Bhnd; mist 10; eff & 5th nxt; sn wknd; t.o 16; pu 2 out*
[852²]	F		**O So Bossy** 11-10 (1) 20-1 Miss J Congdon *Hdwy to press wnr when fell 7*

TIME: 6min 22.7s **TOTE:** £1.60; places £2.00,£1.80,£2.10 **Ex:** £13.20 **CSF:** £11.03 **Tri:** not won
The stewards suspended the rider of Carbery Ministrel for 7 days for failing to pull up tired mount when out of contention

Ayr (LH 9F,21J)
Fri, 14 Apr (GOOD)

1024 Royal Scots Dragoon Guards ILPH HC   9 ran

[584⁵]	1		**MIGHTY MOSS (IRE)** 12-05 4-5F F Hutsby *Settled midfield; went prom app 13 & ld brief; ld agn 16; rdn clr flat*
[921ᶠ]	2	2½	**Last Option** 12-08 3-1 Mrs F Needham *Ld 3-4; ld 11-12; blun 15; rdn nxt; went 2nd & ev ch 3 out; hit 2 out; one pce flat*
[915¹]	3	19	**Midsummer Glen (IRE)** 11-12 33-1 Miss M Bremner *In tch til pckd 13; 6th nxt & outpcd; nd aft*
[422⁶]	4	1½	**Ensign Ewart (IRE)** 12-05 33-1 C Storey *Hld up; nt fluent 12 & rdn; hdwy & prsd ldrs aft 15; drvn & wknd app 3 out*
[224²]	5	1	**Cariboo Gold (USA)** 11-07 (bl) 5-1 J Diment *Prsd ldrs; ld 13-16; ev ch til 6l 3rd & wkng 3 out*
[915⁴]	6	30	**Fiscal Policy** 11-07 100-1 R Trotter *Ld 4-11; rdn & wknd 13; blun 15; t.o aft 17*
[422²]	F		**Dennett Lough (IRE)** 11-07 33-1 R Morgan *Ld to 3; chsd ldrs til wknd 15; 5th & no ch when fell 2 out*
[686ᵁ]	P		**Over The Hill (IRE)** 12-05 25-1 M Armytage *Hld up & bhnd; hdwy & prom 15; jmpd slow 17 & sn wknd; nt r.o; t.o & pu last*
[918⁶]	P		**Tin Cup** 11-07 200-1 K Burke *Mists in rr; lost tch 8; t.o 9; pu 16*

TIME: 6min 54.3s **TOTE:** £1.70; places £1.20,£1.50,£2.10 **Ex:** £3.10 **CSF:** £2.91 **Tri:** £24.80

Bangor (LH 9F,18J)
Sat, 15 Apr (GOOD to SOFT)

1025 Jane McAlpine Mem HC   10 ran

[299¹]	1		**GUNNER WELBURN** 12-07 8-13F B Pollock *Hld up gng wl; gd prog in 3rd aft 9; prsd ldr app 13; nk down when lft wl clr 15; v easy*
[779⁴]	2	23	**Silverdalesureshot** 12-04 10-1 R Burton *Rn in snatches; drpd back 6th aft 9; hdwy 14; lft disp poor 2nd nxt; chsd wnr vain aft*
[812²]	3	12	**Sounds Strong (IRE)** 11-07 25-1 N Bannister *Bhnd & rdr v ungainly; 7th when mist 9; no ch frm 13; plodded into rem 3rd aft 2 out*

[802³]	4	2½	**Desperate** 11-11 16-1 R Barrett *Bhnd; drvn frm 7; went 5th aft 9; outpcd 13; lft disp rem 2nd 15; sn wknd u.p*
[782¹]	5	7	**The Crooked Oak** 11-07 16-1 G Thomas *Bhnd; last when mist 10; t.o 13*
[334ᴾ]	P		**Bucksfern** 11-09 (bl) 50-1 R Bevis *Sn bhnd; t.o 8; pu 11*
[224⁴]	P		**Charmer's Well (IRE)** 12-04 33-1 T Doyle *Ld; mists 10 & 11 (water); hdd aft 12; wknd qckly u.p nxt; t.o & pu 3 out*
[862ᴾ]	P		**Haveafewmanners (IRE)** 11-02 50-1 M Worthington *Blun 1; tk keen hld & handy; 6th 9; sn strugg; t.o & pu 3 out*
[117ᴮ]	P		**Tom Pinch (IRE)** 11-11 25-1 J Cornwall *Pulled hrd; w ldr to 3; mist 7; 2nd til 4th & wkng 9; t.o & pu 13*
[691¹]	F		**Whatafellow (IRE)** 11-08 (1) (bl) 11-4 A Crow *A handy; went 2nd aft 9; ld 12; hrd prsd frm nxt; nk advant when fell 15*

TIME: 6min 41.7s **TOTE:** £1.60; places £1.40,£1.50,£3.90 **Ex:** £9.30 **CSF:** £7.82 **Tri:** £33.70

Stratford (LH 8F,16J)
Sat, 15 Apr (GOOD)

1026 Baulking Green HC
16 ran

	1		**SHEKELS (IRE)** 11-07 11-2 D Dunsdon *Hld up in mid-div; hdwy 8; went 2nd 11; trckd ldr til ld last; drvn out*
[919¹]	2	1½	**Castle Court (IRE)** 12-02 2-1F V Keane *Nt fluent; ld to 3; ld agn 8; mist 10; 2l ahd when mist 3 out; hdd last; kpt on u.p*
[463ᵁ]	3	s hd	**Caracol** 11-09 12-1 B Hitchcott *Tk keen hld early; mist 3; hld up; 6l 4th & prog 11; 4l 3rd 3 out; chall when mist nxt; stayed on flat*
[687⁵]	4	11	**Pro Bono (IRE)** 11-07 10-1 M Foley *Tk keen hld & cl up; 5th 11; drvn 13; 8l 4th 3 out; sn btn*
[382³]	5	10	**Tea Cee Kay** 11-07 8-1 J Diment *Midfield; 8th 11; brief eff app nxt; sn wknd*
[919ᴾ]	6	23	**Destin D'Estruval (FR)** 12-02 5-1 C Weaver *In tch; rdn 9; 5l 3rd 11; lost tch app 3 out*
[920ᴾ]	P		**Gallant Lord (IRE)** 11-07 100-1 R Arnold *Nvr nr ldrs; t.o 9; 9th 11; pu 2 out*
[802⁵]	P		**John Tufty** 11-07 33-1 Miss R Illman *Blun 4; a bhnd; t.o 9; 10th 11; rem 7th when fell 2 out*
[789⁴]	F		**King Curan (USA)** 11-07 66-1 F Windsor Clive *15th when fell 2 out*
[742ᵁ]	P		**Late Encounter** 11-11 (bl) 20-1 D O'Meara *Rmdrs 3; a bhnd & nvr gng wl; t.o & pu 10*
[821ᴾ]	P		**Our Eddie** 11-07 66-1 G Carenza *A bhnd; blun 7; t.o & pu 9*
[802⁷]	P		**Pimberley Place** 11-07 12-1 J Harty *Reluct to rce; a t.o & u.p; mists; pu 3 out*
[897ᴾ]	P		**Secret Truth** 11-02 33-1 A Martin *Mid-div; 7th & strugg 11; t.o & pu 2 out*
[801³]	P		**Tickerty's Gift** 11-11 (bl) 33-1 T Gibney *Nt fluent; ld 3-8; 6th & wkng u.p 11; t.o & pu 2 out*
[687ᴾ]	P		**Tommys Webb (IRE)** 11-07 14-1 S Morris *Hld up towards rr; some prog when pu & dism 9*
[753¹]	F		**Whistling Rufus (IRE)** 12-00 14-1 M Rimell *Blun 5; a wl bhnd & nvr gng keen; fell 10*

TIME: 5min 44.6s **TOTE:** £7.20; places £1.70,£1.60,£4.90 **Ex:** £27.10 **CSF:** £16.59 **Tri:** £91.60

Bedale
Hornby Castle (LH 7F,16J) Sat, 15 Apr (GOOD)

1027 Confined, 12st
7 ran

[811³ᵈ]	1		**TRIPLE EAVES** 9-4F C Mulhall *(xnb) 2nd til ld 12; pushed 3l clr 3 out; stayed on wl; comf*
[911ᴾ]	2	10	**Prime Style** 11-2 C Gibbon *(xnb) Tk keen hld; ld to 12; releg 5th nxt; rallied 2 out to 2nd & blun last; no ch w wnr*
[908ᴾ]	3	2	**Hidden Island** 7-2 Miss H Delahooke *Hld up; prog & 3rd 9; 3l 3rd 13; rdr did v little aft; btn 2 out; kpt on to 2nd app last*
[804³]	4	8	**Harbour Blaze (IRE)** 5-1 Miss R Clark *Settled 3rd/4th; went 1l 2nd & mist 13; drvn & one pce nxt; dem 2 plces & blun last*
[803¹]	5	3	**Buster Buttons** (bl) 7-2 N Tutty *Pulling; mists; hld up; 5l 5th at 11; 4l 3rd & rdn 3 out; no imp when blun nxt & nrly fell; nt rec*
[804ᴾ]	6	4	**Mr Hook** 33-1 R Clark *Trckd ldrs to 10; outpcd nxt; lft poor last 13*
[505ᴾ]	P		**Dublin Hill (IRE)** 16-1 Mrs F Needham *Swtng; in tch; 8l last 9; rdn nxt; sn strugg; rem when pu 13*

OFFICIAL DISTANCES: 10l, 2l **TIME:** 6min 39.0s

1028 Restricted, 12st
13 ran

[1000ᴾ]	1		**TIED FOR TIME (IRE)** 6-1 S Walker *Hld up in midfield; eff 9; 4th aft 11; ld app 3 out; drvn & hld on wl flat*

[808¹]	2	1	**Sassy Street (IRE)** 10-1 K Needham *Sn cl up; disp ld frm 6 til 2l down app 3 out; ev ch frm nxt but wkly rdn (prob should have won)*
[871⁹]	3	4	**Mefein Boy (IRE)** 8-1 Miss A Deniel *Settled towards rr; mist 6; 8th aft 11; prog nxt to cl 3rd 13; 6l 3rd nxt; rallied 2 out; kpt on one pce aft last*
[689⁷]	4	25	**Mount Faber** (bl) 10-1 S Charlton *Trckd ldrs; eff to disp ld 8-11; 4l 4th & hrd rdn aft 13; nt r.o & 8l 4th & btn nxt*
[923⁴]	5	6	**Yornoangel** 14-1 R Clark (xnb) *Bhnd; lft 15l last aft 11; mist 13; 18l 5th nxt*
[909¹]	6	4	**Ladylands** (5a) 7-2 D Raw *Sev posns; drpd back 7th aft 11; sn lost tch; rem last 3 out*
[440⁵]	7	1	**Up And Over (IRE)** (4ow) 14-1 D Easterby *Prom; disp ld 8-12; rdn & drpd out qckly; 30l 6th 3 out*
[689⁸]	P		**Jac Del Prince** 6-1 R Walker *Ld to 5; lost plce rap to 12th &; t.o & pu aft 11*
[1004ᶠ]	P		**Kings Cup** 33-1 M Haigh *Excitable & oht; tk keen hld & cl up; 5th 9; fell 10*
	P		**La Maja (IRE)** (5a) 33-1 G Tuer *Rr div; rdn & lost tch 10; t.o & pu 11*
[440⁷]	P		**Moor Lady** (5a) 20-1 S Swiers *Lw; chsd ldr til made most 5-9; 6th & wkng aft 11; wl bhnd when pu aft 13*
[807⁵]	U		**Run For The Mill** 33-1 M Morley (xnb) *Drpd out last; some prog & in tch when mist & ur 10*
[1004¹]	U		**The Happy Monarch (IRE)** 7-4F Mrs F Needham *Hld up; eff 9; 5th aft 11; chsng ldrs when mist & ur 12*

OFFICIAL DISTANCES: ½l, 1l   **TIME:** 6min 38.0s

1029 Greig Middleton Ladies Open   5 ran

[916²]	1		**BALISTEROS (FR)** 1-3F Miss P Robson *Hld up gng wl; tk 2nd 11; ld aft 13; pushed 6l clr 3 out; easy*
[806²]	2	12	**The Minister (IRE)** 4-1 Miss T Jackson *Hld up; blun 3; jmpd slow 6; clsd 11 & ev ch frm nxt til jmpd delib 3 out; chsd wnr vain aft*
[804¹]	3	runin	**Stride To Glory (IRE)** 5-1 Mrs H Arnold *Ld to 2; chsd ldr to 11; sn strugg in 4th; 28l down 3 out; sn lft 3rd*
[911¹]	U		**Scrabo View (IRE)** 12-1 Miss S Ward *Ld 2 til hdd aft 13; releg 3rd aft rdr lost control on bend bef 3 out; hit marker & ur turn bef nxt*
[621³]	P		**Temple Garth** 12-1 Miss F Hartley *Last pr & nvr gng wl; outpcd 8; hit 12; t.o & pu 13*

OFFICIAL DISTANCES: 15l, dist   **TIME:** 6min 38.0s

1030 Land Rover Mens Open, 12st   7 ran

[998¹]	1		**CALLEVA STAR (IRE)** 7-2 R Abrahams *Lw; jmpd lft; made virt all til rdn & hdd 3 out; lft in ld app last; kpt on*
[660¹]	2	1	**Poynder Park (IRE)** 5-2 L Morgan *Settled 3rd/4th til 2nd 12; slt ld 3 out til hrd rdn & hung lft app last; sn hdd & nt rec*
[918ᵁ]	3	5	**Gymcrak Tiger (IRE)** evensF R Clark (xnb) *Hld up towards rr; mist 10; chall 12; 3rd & ev ch when mist nxt; rdn & wknd 3 out*
[716⁷]	4	25	**Lottery Ticket** 33-1 S J Robinson *Prsd ldrs; u.p 10; lost plce rap 12; 20l 6th nxt*
[917ᴾ]	5	3	**Mullingar (IRE)** 25-1 R Morgan *Cl up; rdn 7; 8l last aft 11; strugg 12; sn rem*
	6	5	**That Old Feeling (IRE)** (tt) 7-1 D Easterby *Bckwd; oht; cl up; ev ch in 3l 4th 13; pushed along when bad mist 3 out; virt pu aft*
[805³]	7	15	**Cross Cannon** 20-1 T Glass *Last pr; 7l 6th aft 11; lost tch rap; rem frm 13; drpd dead aft fin*

OFFICIAL DISTANCES: 1l, 2l, dist   **TIME:** 6min 39.0s

The stewards enquired into the riding of Cross Cannon; the rider said he knew the horse well, had been placed on him over 3m3f and felt him fully capable of completing; his attention was drawn to the Regulations concerning improper riding

1031 Hunt   6 ran

[807³]	1		**PRIMITIVE CHARLES** (bl) 8-1 G Brewer *Drpd out last & wl off pce; 8l down & clsng 8; chall aft 12; prsd ldr & confid rdn frm 3 out til ld last; r.o wl*
[694²]	2	3	**Deerhunter** 4-1 G Tuer *Settled disp 2nd; clsd aft 11; slt ld 3 out til rdn & hdd last; nt qckn*
[804²]	3	2	**Keep A Secret** 7-4 P Atkinson *2nd/3rd til hit 12; outpcd in 7l 4th aft nxt; kpt on agn flat*
[384⁷]	4	6	**Pebble Beach (IRE)** (tt) 6-4F S Brisby *Lft in ld 3; sn 20l clr; prsd frm 8; rdn aft 12; hdd 3 out; wknd nxt*
	U		**Gromit (U)** 25-1 F Crawford (xnb) *Pulled hrd; ld til blun & ur 3*
	U		**Uncle Tom Cobley (U)** 33-1 Miss L Pounder (xnb) *Poor last til hit 3 & ur*

OFFICIAL DISTANCES: 2l, 3l, dist   **TIME:** 6min 47.0s

1032 Open Maiden (Div 1)   18 ran

[1004⁶]	1		**HEATHER LAD** 8-1 **D Raw** Hld up in rr div; 9th & gd prog aft 11; chall in 11 3rd 13; 2nd 2 out; ld last; rdn clr
[793²]	2	2	**Gentleman Charles (IRE)** 2-1 **S Walker** Cl up; 2nd/3rd 6 til ld 12; hrd rdn & hdd last; v one-pcd
[1001²]	3	8	**Young Rab** (7a) (tt) 7-4F **G Markham** Nt jw; trckd ldrs; mist 7; 5th nxt; 3rd aft 11; ev ch when mist 13; 4l 3rd 2 out; wknd bef last
[809²]	4	2	**Flowing Fortune** 6-1 **Miss R Clark** Hld up & bhnd; prog in 8th aft 11; eff nxt; chall 13; outpcd 3 out; 4th & btn nxt
[1003²]	5	12	**Joe Smoke** 14-1 **S Charlton** (xnb) Cl up; 6th aft 11; eff & ev ch 13; wknd tame bef nxt
[619³]	6	½	**Oaklands Millie (IRE)** (5a) 25-1 **P Kinsella** Chsd ldrs; 7th 8; 10th & wkng aft 11
[693²]	7	25	**Morcan House** 25-1 **J Davies** A bhnd; 11th & strugg aft 11
[809²]	8	15	**Countess Rosie** (5a) 16-1 **N Wilson** Mists in rr; lost tch 8; rem 12th aft 11; schooled on
[803²]	P		**Alena H Banks** 33-1 **L McGrath** (xnb) Drpd out last; mist 10; no ch frm nxt; t.o & pu 2 out
[695³]	P		**Hopeful Earl (IRE)** 12-1 **N Tutty** Cl up til 7th aft 11; rr when pu aft 13; v lame
[803²]	U		**Imperial Line (IRE)** 8-1 **Miss T Jackson** (xnb) Lw; mist 3 & ur wl aft
	P		**La Emni (IRE)** 33-1 **M Mawhinney** Chsd ldrs; 10th & outpcd 8; t.o & pu 13
[719⁶]	P		**Liffey Lane** 25-1 **M Clayton** Tk keen hld; ld 4-12; wknd rap; pu last
[374³]	P		**Lingham Lady** (5a) 8-1 **S Swiers** Drpd out in rr; 8th & prog 8; 5th aft 11; wknd nxt; pu 2 out
[804⁷]	P		**Pashby Wood** (5a) 33-1 **M Morley** Mostly 2nd til 4th & wkng aft 11; drpd out qckly; pu 13
[1003ᶠ]	P		**Sand Track** 33-1 **M Haigh** Lkd awful; excitable & unruly; tk keen hld; prsd ldrs to 6; 12th & wkng 8; pu 2 out
[798⁷]	P		**The Way North** 16-1 **R Wakeham** Nvr btr than midfield; strugg 8; 13th aft 11; t.o & pu 2 out
[1004⁵]	P		**Tyndrum Gold** (bl) 12-1 **Miss A Deniel** (xnb) Mist 5; a rr & sn drvn along; nvr gng wl; t.o last aft 11; pu 13

OFFICIAL DISTANCES: 2l, 10l, 3l   TIME: 6min 50.0s

1033 Open Maiden (Div 2)   15 ran

[1003ᴿ]	1		**TRICKY TREVOR (IRE)** 6-4F **Miss H Delahooke** Lw; made most; hdd 3 out; sn swishing tail; ld agn nxt; wavering aft but kpt on flat
[619⁷]	2	1	**My Sam** (12a) 9-1 **C Mulhall** (xnb) Hld up & bhnd; 15l 7th aft 11; stayed on aft 13 to 4th nxt; trying to chall when carried rt app last; nt ckn flat
[1002⁵]	3	4	**Bred For Pleasure** (5a) 2-1 **L McGrath** Stdd start; pulled hrd in rr til hdwy aft 11; 12l 5th 13; clsd rap to ld nxt; hdd aft 2 out; drvn & hung rt app last; no ex
[1001ᶠ]	4	12	**Mr Norm** 33-1 **R Clark** Prom; 3rd 8; cl 4th aft 11; chall & ½l 2nd 13; ev ch when jmpd slow nxt; sn wknd
[1003⁴]	5	8	**Hey Sam (IRE)** (bl) 7-1 **T Glass** Mist 3; drpd back 10th to 6; went cl 4th 8; chall & ev ch when mist 13; nt r.o; 5th & btn nxt
[508ᶠ]	6	1	**Charlie Dazzle (IRE)** 20-1 **Mrs F Needham** Hld up & wl bhnd; prog 10 to 12l 5th aft 11; eff short-lived & no ch 13
[696³]	7	1	**Sylcanny** (5a) 11-1 **J Davies** Cl up; 2nd 8; ev ch to 12; 12l 4th & wkng nxt
[809⁹]	8	6	**Palm Gold** (5a) 50-1 **R Wakeham** Still bckwd; towards rr; 15l 7th 8; plodded on
[626⁷]	9	15	**Wandering Wild** (12a) 25-1 **Mrs L Ward** Midfield; 8th 6; lost tch 8; mist 9; t.o
[1001ᶠ]	P		**Norman Way** (7a) 25-1 **P Cornforth** 6th 6; outpcd 8; u.p 10; no resp; t.o & pu aft 13
	P		**No Time To Wait** 20-1 **D Easterby** Pulled hrd; ld brief 3; drpd back 7th 6; 13l 6th 8; lost tch aft 11; t.o & pu 2 out
	P		**Profiler (IRE)** 20-1 **Miss T Jackson** Hld up & a wl bhnd; t.o & pu 11
[809⁷]	U		**Stanwick Hall** 12-1 **K Needham** (xnb) Trckd ldrs; 5l 5th 8; ur 10
[1002ᵁ]	P		**Vals Castle (IRE)** (5a) 7-1 **G Tuer** A rem in last trio; jmpd v slow 4; pu last
[400ᶠ]	R		**Watacon** 10-1 **G Markham** Ld in start; tk strt hld in 2nd/3rd til ld aft 6; rn straight on at bend aft 7

OFFICIAL DISTANCES: 2l, 2l, dist   TIME: 6min 53.0s

Cambridge University United Hunts Club
Cottenham (RH 9F,19J) Sat, 15 Apr (GOOD to SOFT becomimg SOFT)

1034 Club Members   4 ran

[750³]	1		**CHERRYNUT** 1-4F **D Barlow** Trckd ldng pr; 6l 3rd 8; went 2nd 15; ld app last; rdn clr flat
[749⁷]	2	10	**Hill Island** 2-1 **Miss L Sweeting** Ld to 6; ld agn 9; 2l up & rdn 3 out; hdd app last; blun last; outpcd flat
[758ᵁ]	3	dist	**Just Jack** 12-1 **Miss F Jonason** Prsd ldr; ld 6; mist nxt; hdd 9; last frm 15; wknd nxt

[842ᴾ] **F**   **Chris's Lad** 12-1 **M Gingell** *Hld up in last; rmdr 8; 5l off pce when fell 11*

OFFICIAL DISTANCES: 10l, 30l **TIME:** 6min 29.0s **TOTE:** £1.40 **DF:** £1.40

1035 Countryside Alliance Club Members (Nov Rdrs) - 17J   12 ran

[513²]	1		**TUMLIN OOT (IRE)** 6-4F **M Lurcock** *Mid-div; prog to 2nd 11; ld app 14; sn 5l clr; stayed on wl frm 2 out*
[555²]	2	6	**Faha Gig (IRE)** (5a) 9-2 **A Braithwaite** *Ww in mid-div; mist 4; prog 9; 4l 3rd 13; sn chsng wnr 14; 2½l down 2 out; btn last*
[785⁹]	3	40	**Neelisagin (IRE)** (tt) 10-1 **J Turcan** *Chsd ldrs; 4l 4th 13; sn outpcd; 5th & no ch 16; went poor 3rd nr fin*
[543⁹]	4	nk	**Court Amber** 14-1 **D Hayes** *Bhnd; stdy prog frm 11; went 35l 3rd 2 out; nvr nr ldrs; dem nr fin*
[906ᴾ]	5	10	**Cosa Fuair (IRE)** 14-1 **C Jarvis** (xnb) *Chsd ldrs; 12l 4th 14; sn lost tch; 30l 3rd app 2 out; t.o*
[770⁵]	6	½	**Candle Glow** (5a) 9-2 **D Cook** *Ld til app 14; 3rd & wkng nxt; no ch 3 out; t.o*
[610ᴾ]	7	40	**Premier First (IRE)** 20-1 **W Pewter** (xnb) *A bhnd; 10th & rmdrs 7; t.o frm 10*
[1012ᵁ]	U		**Father's Joy** (5a) 10-1 **Miss A Burton** *A bhnd; hit 1; last frm 5; some prog 14; blun nxt; 7th & no ch when ur 3 out*
	F		**Fawn Prince (IRE)** (5x) 12-1 **A Lochore** (xnb) *Stdd start; rcd keen; rushed up to mid-div 4; fell 9*
[871⁸]	P		**Nanda Devi** 14-1 **Miss H Campbell** *Prsd ldr; mist 4; disp ld 9-10; wknd 11; t.o & pu 2 out*
[756ᴾ]	P		**On The Beer (IRE)** 20-1 **M Bailey** *In tch; 10l 5th 11; mist 12; wkng when jmpd lft 13; t.o & pu 2 out*
[766ᴾ]	F		**Safety (USA)** (bl) 12-1 **G Wright** *Chsd ldrs; 3rd when fell 10*

OFFICIAL DISTANCES: 8l, dist **TIME:** 6min 29.0s **TOTE:** £2.80 **DF:** £9.30
Fences 2 & 11 omitted - damaged in previous race

1036 Mens Open   4 ran

[756¹]	1		**PANGERAN (USA)** 7-4 **N King** *Ww in 3rd; blun 8; lft 4l clr nxt; drew rt away 13; mist 15; jmpd slow 2 out; unchall*
[870⁴]	2	30	**Broadway Swinger** (tt) 10-1 **S R Andrews** *Mostly last; lft 4l 2nd 9; lost tch w wnr frm 13*
[884¹]	F		**Dry Highline (IRE)** 4-5F **C Ward-Thomas** *Ld; sn clr; mist 2; 8l clr when fell 9*
[981ᵁ]	U		**Mister Spectator (IRE)** 6-1 **P Hickman** *Chsd ldr til hmpd & ur 9; rmtd; t.o & pu 11*

OFFICIAL DISTANCE: dist **TIME:** 6min 33.0s **TOTE:** £3.30 **DF:** £4.20

1037 Ladies Open   6 ran

[885¹]	1		**DAWN ALERT (IRE)** 9-4 **Miss L Rowe** *Chsd ldng pr til went 2nd 9; ld app 14; sn hdd; ld agn 3 out; 2l up when lft wl clr nxt*
[939⁴]	2	35	**Lets Twist Again (IRE)** 33-1 **Miss A Stennett** *Chsd ldr to 9; 10l 4th & wkng 13; no ch 15; lft 33l 3rd 2 out; went 2nd app last*
[1006⁸]	3	7	**Tighter Budget (USA)** 25-1 **Miss G Hutchinson** *Ld; mist 4; hdd app 14; 15l 3rd & wkng 3 out; lft 30l 2nd nxt; sn dem*
[841⁵]	4	35	**Peanuts Pet** 33-1 **Miss H Barnard** *4th to 6; 10l 5th 9; sn wl bhnd; t.o 13*
[939¹]	U		**Spring Gale (IRE)** 2-5F **Miss Z Turner** *Ww; mist 2; prog to 3rd 11; ld 14-3 out; 2l 2nd when blun & ur 2 out*
[414⁴]	P		**Uron V (FR)** 10-1 **Miss T Hayter** *Sn bhnd & bustled along; detach frm 4; 30l last 11; t.o & pu 3 out*

OFFICIAL DISTANCES: dist, 6l **TIME:** 6min 24.0s **TOTE:** £2.30 **DF:** £38.40

1038 Restricted   9 ran

[941¹]	1		**RAFTER** 6-1 **C Carman** *Bhnd; gd prog 14; 10l 5th when blun 3 out; went 2nd nxt; wl hld when lft clr last; lucky*
[687ᶠ]	2	5	**The Millmaster (IRE)** 14-1 **T Lane** *Ld til jmpd lft 2; chsd ldrs; 8l 3rd 3 out; 4th & btn nxt; lft 3rd at last; went 2nd nr fin*
[775¹]	3	2	**Minino (IRE)** (bl) 6-1 **A Coe** *Prom; ld 2-5; mist 9; disp 10½l 3rd & btn 2 out; lft 2nd at last; dem nr fin*
[940³]	4	10	**Mackoy (IRE)** 6-1 **D Cook** *Prom; 6l 3rd 9; chsd ldr 13; rdn & no prog 2 out; 5th & wl btn app last; lft 4th at last*
[769¹]	P		**Al Jawwal** 12-1 **Miss L Allan** (xnb) *Mid-div; 10l 5th when mist 10; 6th & no ch when blun 13; t.o & pu*
[575²]	P		**Ballad (IRE)** 2-1F **A Harvey** *Hld up; last 7; prog & 12l 7th when blun bad 9; nt rec; wl bhnd when pu 16*

[773⁴]	P		**Coptic Dancer** (5a) (vis) 20-1 A Braithwaite *Jmpd rt; bhnd; some prog & 12l 6th app 13; sn lost tch; t.o & pu 16*
[774¹]	F		**Sweet Talker (IRE)** 12-1 N Bloom *7th when fell 4*
[773ᵁ]	U		**Ulvick Star (IRE)** 6-1 R Fowler *Trckd ldrs; ld 5; drew clr frm 3 out; 10l up when jmpd rt, blun & ur last; unlucky*

OFFICIAL DISTANCES: 4l, 2l **TIME:** 6min 39.0s **TOTE:** £8.30 **DF:** £39.20

1039 Open Maiden (Div 1), 12st
12 ran

[770ᴾ]	1		**SPECTRE** 7-2JF N Bloom *Jmpd rt; mid-div; 8l 6th 9; outpcd 10; 12l 4th & hdwy 3 out; went 3l 2nd & lft wl clr nxt*
[845³]	2	35	**Glencloy (IRE)** 4-1 A Coe *2 handlers; ww in rr; 12l 8th 9; nvr on terms; 30l 5th app 3 out; lft 2nd nxt*
[775ᵁ]	3	6	**Airborne Blue** 20-1 K Sheppard *Rr of main group; in tch to 10; last frm 12; lft poor 3rd 2 out; t.o*
[774²]	P		**Always Trying** (7a) 5-1 A Sansome *Ww; jmpd rt 3; prog to 5l 4th 12; wkng when blun 15; t.o & pu 3 out*
[236ᶠ]	F		**Bannagh Express (IRE)** 12-1 M Lurcock *Ld to 6; cl up; 4l 4th & wkng when fell 2 out*
[236ᶠ]	P		**Casino Nell** (5a) 16-1 A Harvey *Cl up; 3l 3rd 5; wknd 12; 15l 6th nxt; t.o & pu 3 out*
[774ᶠ]	P		**Classic Ms (IRE)** 16-1 M Grange *Jb; sn t.o; pu 10*
[942ᵁ]	F		**Curracloe Rose (IRE)** (5a) 7-2JF D Cook *Chsd ldrs; went 2nd 11; ld app 13; 3l clr when fell 2 out*
[197ᴾ]	B		**Out By Night** 5-1 D Barlow *Prom; chsd ldr 4; ld 6 til app 13; chsd ldr aft; 3½l 3rd when bd 2 out*
[1011³]	F		**Polly Live Wire** (5a,2ow) 5-1 P Millington *Hld up in rr; 10th when fell 11*
[774³]	P		**Sidney Street** (vis) 12-1 T Lane *Chsd ldr til mist 4; bhnd frm 11; t.o & pu 15*
[825ᴾ]	P		**Winward** (bl) 14-1 P M Hall *Chsd ldrs; 8l 5th 7; rdn & wknd 10; t.o & pu 15*

OFFICIAL DISTANCES: dist, 4l **TIME:** 6min 50.0s **TOTE:** £6.50 **DF:** £7.40

1040 Open Maiden (Div 2), 12st
12 ran

[550²]	1		**HEATHBURN (IRE)** 7-4F C Ward-Thomas *Ld til aft 1; ld 7-9; ld agn 16; sn in comm; lft wl clr nxt*
[606ᴿ]	2	runin	**Wise Point (IRE)** 12-1 G Lush *(xnb) Chsd ldrs to 4; grad lost plce; bhnd frm 9; lft poor 3rd 3 out; t.o when went 2nd app last*
[941ᴾ]	P		**Bandit Boy** (3ow) (bl) 12-1 P Hickman *Ld aft 1 til hdd 7; wkng when blun 10; pu nxt*
[775ᶠ]	F		**Campbellhill (IRE)** 10-1 M Mackley *Trckd ldrs gng wl; ld 11; jmpd lft 13; hdd 16; sn wknd; 10l down when crashing fall 3 out*
[769ᵁ]	P		**City Run (USA)** 10-1 Mrs T Holditch *Mid-div when jmpd slow 4; wl bhnd frm 8; t.o & pu 3 out*
[1012ᴾ]	P		**Craftbook Marchesa (IRE)** (5a,4ow) 5-1 P Millington *A last pr; t.o 11; pu 3 out*
[942ᴾ]	P		**Dilly May Dally** (5a) 16-1 Miss R Barrow *Bhnd frm 7; last 12; t.o & pu 13*
[88ᴾ]	P		**Eltrym Flyer** (5a) 5-1 N King *In tch; mist 9; 4th when jmpd lft 10 & 11; 10l off pce 13; wkng when pu 16*
[937ᵁ]	P		**Henpecked (IRE)** 8-1 A Coe *(xnb) Mounted on course; chsd ldrs to 9; wknd 11; pu 13*
[936ᴾ]	P		**Lazy Acres (IRE)** (4ow) 8-1 C Lawson *Tde; unruly start; sa; a t.o; lft poor 2nd 3 out; dem aft nxt; pu last*
[941⁴]	U		**Out Of Actons (IRE)** (3ow) 3-1 C Jarvis *(xnb) Rcd keen; chsd ldrs 4; ld 9-11; lft 13l 2nd when hmpd & ur 3 out*
[515ᴾ]	P		**Tod's Brother** 6-1 N Bloom *Jmpd novicey; mid-div; 15l 5th & pushed along 11; sn lost tch; pu 13*

OFFICIAL DISTANCE: dist **TIME:** 6min 53.0s **TOTE:** £2.20 **DF:** £23.60

Dartmoor
Flete Park (RH 8F,20J) Sat, 15 Apr (SOFT)

1041 Hunt
6 ran

[730²]	1		**LEAD STORY (IRE)** 8-1 Miss T Cave *Hld up; hdwy to ld 17; just hld on u.p*
[970²]	2	hd	**Bomba Charger** 2-5F A Holdsworth *A.p; outpcd aft 3 out; r.o cl home*
[852³]	3	6	**Hold Your Ranks** 12-1 D McKenna *Trckd ldrs; no ex frm 3 out*
[726³]	4	10	**No More Nice Guy (IRE)** 5-1 Mrs M Hand *Disp ld to 10; lost tch aft 14*
	5	6	**Night Time** 20-1 G Shenkin *Hdwy to ld 11; hdd 17; wknd*
	P		**Fine Example** 50-1 Miss S Gaisford *Rn wide & pu 3*

OFFICIAL DISTANCES: s hd, 5l **TIME:** 7min 06.0s

1042 Restricted (Div 1), 12st
11 ran

[164²]	1		**THINK POSITIVE (IRE)** 3-1 **G Maundrell** *Ld 14; drew clr aft 2 out*
[852⁸]	2	10	**Border Rose** (5a) 12-1 **Miss S Young** *Hld up; late hdwy to 2nd aft last*
[849⁴]	3	1	**The Ugly Duckling** 10-1 **R Woollacott** *A cl up; outpcd by wnr aft 14; r.o one pce*
[848³]	4	15	**Kimbross** 5-1 **G Richards** *Hld up; hdwy til app 2 out; no ex*
[404⁷]	5	1	**Friar Waddon** 5-1 **Miss J Cumings** *Hld up; hdwy to 2nd 2 out; wknd app last*
[853⁷]	P		**Bedtime Pixie** (bl) 33-1 **D Stephens (Devon)** *Prom to 15; wknd; pu 3 out*
[850⁵]	P		**Belski** 7-1 **Mrs M Hand** *Trckd ldrs; lost tch aft 3 out; pu last*
[852⁷]	P		**County Bash** (5a) 33-1 **S Kidston** *A rr; pu 17*
[721¹]	P		**Knock Star (IRE)** 2-1F **S Partridge** *5s-2s; ld to 13; wknd & pu last*
[728⁶]	P		**Mystic Warrior (USA)** (7a) 25-1 **Richard Darke** *Pu 11*
[559²]	P		**Nick's Way** 10-1 **C White** *Hld up towards rr; pu 17*

OFFICIAL DISTANCES: 7l, 1l TIME: 6min 57.0s

1043 Restricted (Div 2), 12st
11 ran

[876²]	1		**BRAVE NODDY (IRE)** (bl) 2-5F **L Jefford** *Trckd ldrs; hdwy to ld 2 out; r.o wl*
	2	8	**Belitlir** (5a) 8-1 **Miss S Young** *Hld up; hdwy to 2nd run-in*
[848⁴]	3	3	**Damiens Pride (IRE)** 7-1 **T Dennis** *Cl up; ld 15 til app 2 out; r.o one pce*
[850⁴]	4	20	**Travel By Land** 20-1 **Miss C Stucley** *A mid-div; nd*
[729⁴]	5	25	**Lost Your Marbles (IRE)** (5a) 20-1 **J Mead** *Trckd ldrs til lost tch aft 14*
	F		**Can't Be Scrabble** 50-1 **R Emmett** *Fell 10*
[853⁷]	P		**Golden Sunset** (5a) 100-1 **Miss D Mitchell** *T.o & pu 13*
[850⁷]	P		**King Of Cairo** 100-1 **I Hambley** *T.o & pu 12*
[728⁵]	P		**Nearly Fair** (5a) 25-1 **T Greed** *Towards rr; t.o & pu 12*
[876³]	P		**Pallingham Lad (IRE)** (bl) 6-1 **S Kidston** *Lost tch frm 11; pu 15*
[847⁷]	P		**Tamar Lily** (5a) 20-1 **Miss A Barnett** *Ld to 14; wknd; rr when pu last*

OFFICIAL DISTANCES: 10l, 3l TIME: 6min 54.0s

1044 Mens Open, 4m - 25J
8 ran

[922³]	1		**FUNNY FARM** 5-4F **L Jefford** *7/4-5/4; cl 3rd mostly til ld app 2 out; r.o wl*
[638²]	2	2	**Belarus (IRE)** (bl) 3-1 **C White** *Trckd ldr; ld brief 13; 2nd til outpcd aft 20; r.o cl home*
[637³]	3	5	**Gypsy Gerry** (bl) 14-1 **T Clarkson** *Made most; ld 2-12 & 14 til app 2 out; no ex*
[852³]	4	15	**Rasta Man** 3-1 **R Woollacott** *Hdwy to chall frm 19; 2nd 21; cl 3rd 3 out; wknd rap frm 2 out*
[853⁷]	P		**A Few Dollars More (IRE)** (bl) 50-1 **G Maundrell** *Cl 2nd to 9; 4/5th til wknd aft 19; rr when pu 21*
[930⁴]	P		**Arble March** (5a) 14-1 **N Harris** *Ld early; rdn along & in tch to 16; wknd & pu 19*
	P		**If You Say So** 50-1 **I Widdicombe** *Sn rr; t.o & pu 19*
[848¹]	P		**Sagaville (IRE)** 8-1 **A Holdsworth** *Sn last; rr when pu 19*

OFFICIAL DISTANCES: 2l, 4l TIME: 8min 29.0s

1045 Greig Middleton Ladies Open
9 ran

[922ᵁ]	1		**WELL ARMED (IRE)** 4-5F **Miss J Cumings** *Hld up; hdwy to 4th 8, 3rd 12 & 2nd 17; prog on inner to ld app last; wl rdn*
[877²]	2	3	**Thinking Twice (USA)** 9-4 **Miss T Newman** *Made all til hdd app last; r.o agn cl home*
[922³]	3	10	**Space Cappa** 25-1 **Miss V Stephens** *In tch in 3rd/4th mostly til outpcd aft 13; r.o to 3rd aft last*
	4	3	**Bendor Mark** 12-1 **Mrs M Hand** *Cl 2nd mostly til wknd rap aft 2 out*
[651²]	5		**Contradict** 10s-5s; *hld up; slt hdwy to 6th 12; no further prog aft 14; wknd & rr when pu 3 out*
[725⁵]	P		**Dunlir** 33-1 **Miss S Young** *In tch in mostly 4/5th til wknd aft 14; rr when pu 2 out*
[856¹]	P		**Luney River** (5a) 33-1 **Miss L Gardner** *A mid-div; 6th 11; 6th 15; no prog & pu 3 out*
[848⁶]	P		**Moorland Abbot** 25-1 **Miss D Mitchell** *Sn rr; t.o & pu 15*
[729⁶]	S		**Phartoomanny (IRE)** (5a) (tt) 33-1 **Miss N Snowden** *Sn lost tch; rr when slpd up bend aft 14*

OFFICIAL DISTANCES: 3l, 12l TIME: 6min 57.0s

1046 Marsh UK/TBA PPORA Club Members Mares, 12st
3 ran

[852¹]	1		**ROSA'S REVENGE** (5a) 2-5F **L Jefford** *Jw; ld 7; set stdy pce; pushed out cl home*
[734²]	2	3	**Rossaleen** (5a) (bl) 10-1 **P Shaw** *Cl up til outpcd aft 6; hdwy to 2nd 14; nt pce to chall wnr*
[257⁷]	P		**It'snotsimple (IRE)** (5a) 2-1 **Miss S Messer-Bennetts** *Ld brief 2-4; mostly 2nd aft to 12; sn strugg; lost tch aft 17; pu 2 out*

OFFICIAL DISTANCE: 3l TIME: 7min 09.0s

1047 Confined, 12st　　　　　　　　　　　　　　　　　　　　　　　　10 ran

[726ᴾ]	1		**LIRSLEFTOVER** 5-1 **Miss S Young** *8s-5s; trckd ldrs; went 15l 2nd 7; 8l down 3 out; str rn to ld app last; hvly eased flat*
[651³]	2	15	**Good King Henry** 20-1 **I Widdicombe** *Bhnd; outpcd 11; still poor 5th 2 out; r.o str to 2nd aft last*
[852³]	3	2	**Certain Angle** (5x) 9-2 **E Chanin** *Hld up; hdwy to disp 2nd brief 11; sn wknd to mod 4th; lft 2nd at last; wknd run-in; fin tired*
	P		**Ardscud** 20-1 **Miss C Woodward** *Sn t.o; pu 7*
[537ᴾ]	P		**Beam Me Up Scotty (IRE)** 33-1 **C Heard** *A rr; pu 11*
	P		**Cornish Ways** 50-1 **T Greed** *A rr; t.o 12; pu 17*
	P		**Garnwin (IRE)** 20-1 **Miss T Messer-Bennetts** *Ld to 3; cl 3rd/4th mostly til lost tch aft 11; jmpd slow 13; t.o 15; pu last*
[651ᴾ]	P		**It's Not My Fault (IRE)** 20-1 **G Richards** *20l 3rd when blun bad & nrly up 9; 5th when mist 10; sn lost tch; rr when pu 17*
[930²]	P		**Swift Venture (IRE)** 5-2 **Richard Darke** *Rn wide bend aft 2; trckd ldrs in mostly 4th; outpcd 15; 15l 3rd when pu last*
[876⁴]	P		**Versicium (FR)** (bl) 6-4F **L Jefford** *Pulled into ld 3; sn clr; 8l up aft 3 out; hdd u.p bet last 2; 5l 2nd but v tired when pu app last*

OFFICIAL DISTANCES: 20l, 2l　**TIME:** 7min 09.0s

1048 Confined Maiden (Div 1), 12st　　　　　　　　　　　　　　　　10 ran

[157²ᵈ]	1		**PILLMERE LAD** 3-1 **Miss A Barnett** *Made most; 15l ahd 12; r.o game when chall aft 2 out*
[855ᶠ]	2	6	**Classic Mistress** (5a) 5-2 **Richard Darke** *Hld up; hdwy to 4th 15 & 3rd 3 out; went 2nd at last; no ex run-in*
[855⁵]	3	10	**Moorland Rose** (12a) 25-1 **Miss D Mitchell** *Mid-div til r.o into 4th 2 out; went 3rd run-in; no ch w ldrs*
[855³]	4	5	**Amazing Hill (IRE)** 9-4F **Mrs R Morris** *Hld up; hdwy to 3rd 9 & 2nd 15; chall 2 out; wknd qckly*
[933ᴾ]	P		**Fenny Prince** 20-1 **M Sweetland** *Mid-div til lost tch frm 11; towards rr when pu 13*
[932ᴾ]	P		**Horton** 5-1 **S Parkin** *A rr; t.o & pu last*
[846⁴]	P		**Magic Caller (IRE)** 14-1 **Miss S Robinson** *Rr when blun 13; pu 14*
[846ᴾ]	P		**Patrio (IRE)** (5a) 20-1 **J Cole** *Prom; mostly 2nd to 14; wkng in 3rd 15; 5th 2 out; pu last*
[856ᴾ]	P		**Swincombe (IRE)** (7a) 8-1 **Miss T Cave** *In tch to 11; rr when pu 15*
[849ᴾ]	P		**Whinholme Lass (IRE)** (5a) 10-1 **G Richards** *In tch to 12; rr when pu 17*

OFFICIAL DISTANCES: 6l, 8l　**TIME:** 7min 12.0s

1049 Confined Maiden (Div 2), 12st　　　　　　　　　　　　　　　　9 ran

	1		**SPARKLING CASCADE (IRE)** (5a) 7-4F **L Jefford** *Trckd ldrs mostly in 3rd/4th; still 3rd 2 out; hdwy to chall last; hrd rdn flat; ld on line*
[857³]	2	s hd	**My Prides Way** (5a) 5-2 **T Greed** *Made most; ld frm 3 til hdd cl home; lost on nod; unlucky*
[856³]	3	3	**Saucy's Wolf** 8-1 **A Holdsworth** *Hld up; hdwy to 4th 11; 3rd 14 & 2nd 15; no ex app 2 out*
	4	20	**Country Gem** 12-1 **T Dennis** *Trckd ldrs; 2nd 12-14; lost tch frm 16; plugged on*
[856ᴾ]	P		**Call Me Dickins** (bl) 33-1 **R Woollacott** *In tch in 5th when mist & wknd aft 15; rr when pu last*
[848ᵁ]	P		**Gay Cavalier** 33-1 **J Cole** *Prom when rn wide bend aft 2; jmpd violent 9; rn a long way off course bend aft 10; cont 3 fncs down til pu last*
[855²]	P		**Linton** (5a) 3-1 **W Smith** *Ld til 3; 9th by 10; lost tch aft 11; rr when pu 2 out*
[730ᴾ]	P		**Master Pan** 16-1 **I Widdicombe** *Trckd ldrs; 5th 12; lost tch aft 14; 35l down when pu 11*
[538ᴾ]	U		**Take The Risk** (5a) 20-1 **Miss L Jackson** *Jmpd novicey; sn rr; ur 7*

OFFICIAL DISTANCES: hd, 1l　**TIME:** 7min 22.0s
　　　　　The rider of My Prides Way was cautioned concerning his use of the whip;
　　　　　the stewards considered he had not given the horse time to respond

Glamorgan
St Hilary (RH 8F,19J)　Sat, 15 Apr (HEAVY)

1050 Hunt, 12st　　　　　　　　　　　　　　　　　　　　　　　　　　3 ran

[820¹]	1		**AFRICAN WARRIOR** (5a,5x) 1-4F **C Williams** *Hld up in cl 2nd; jmpd to ld 7-12; hdd brief; ld 14; mist nxt; qcknd 6l clr 16; in comm when mist 2 out; comf*

[821⁴] 2   runin   **Credon** (bl) 5-1 **Miss A Meakins** *Just ld 2; cl 2nd til ld agn 7; outj & ll 2nd aft; mist 15; 6l 2nd & outpcd nxt*

[951ᴾ] P   **Arctic Ridge** 14-1 **D Hughes** *Cl 3rd til ld 5-6; 3l 3rd 7 til ld agn 13; 4l last nxt; tired & 15l off pce 16; pu 3 out*

OFFICIAL DISTANCE: dist   **TIME:** 7min 01.0s

1051 Confined, 12st   12 ran

[945ᴾ] 1   **FLUTTERBUD** (5a,3x) 8-1 **J Jukes** *Ld l; trckd ldr til ld 14; kpt on valiant und str press frm 3 out; fin tired*

[897²] 2   2   **The Rural Dean (IRE)** 5-1 **J Price** *Last pr to 5; cont rr til r.o to 5th 11; 4th & clsng when mist 15; went 3rd 3 out; lft 2nd at last*

[944ᶠ] 3   runin   **Teigr Pren** 12-1 **P Sheldrake** *(bnh) Trckd ldrs in 3rd to 8; wknd & 6th ll; sn btn*

[817³] P   **Chantingo Lad** (tt) 33-1 **D Stephens (Wales)** *A bhnd; jmpd slow 9; wknd ll; pu 3 out*

[819ᵁ] P   **Comme Une Fleur (FR)** (5a) 50-1 **G Marsh** *Mostly 5th; rdn & hdwy ll; went ll 3rd nxt; wknd thro corn & pu 14*

        P   **Hal's Prince** (7x) 8-1 **Miss P Jones** *Ld; ll up to 14; wknd thro corn & pu 14*

[741¹] U   **Kinnefad King (IRE)** (5x) (tt) 4-7F **C Williams** *Kicked handler in padd; a.p; 4th to 15; blun 16; drvn in 2nd 3 out; 2l down & lkd hld when ur last*

[594¹] P   **Mags Super Toi (IRE)** 14-1 **A Price** *(xnb) Last to 6; r.o frm ll; 5th & mist 14; fdd; pu 3 out*

[833³] P   **Mr Mad** (bl) 14-1 **P Hamer** *Prom early; rr & mist 6; pu nxt*

[741ᴾ] P   **Roman Gale (IRE)** 16-1 **G Thorne** *(bf) 1st ride; a bhnd; last frm 8; t.o & jmpd v slow 13; pu 14*

[819ᴾ] P   **Side Bar** (vis,tt) 50-1 **J Phillips** *6th to 9; fdd; last trio 11; sn lost tch; t.o til pu 2 out*

[819⁵] P   **Southern Cross** (bl) 14-1 **J Cook** *3rd til jmpd slow 9; 7th frm 11; midfield aft til pu 14*

OFFICIAL DISTANCES: 2l, dist   **TIME:** 6min 51.0s

1052 Greig Middleton Ladies Open - 15J   4 ran

[1022⁷] 1   **VIARDOT (IRE)** 2-1F **Miss G Roberts** *3rd til 2l 2nd frm 9; 12l down 10; kpt on thro corn & ld u.p 14; sn clr*

[837⁵] 2   15   **Storm Man (IRE)** 5-2 **Miss C Williams** *2nd to 5; ld on ½mile rn to 6; 12l up 12; tired & ll and nxt; mist u.p 2 out; rdr lost whip; crawled over last; walked in*

         3   2fncs   **Llan Cross Lady (IRE)** (5a) 14-1 **Miss T Stevens** *Pulled hrd; ld; 10l up 3; mist nxt; hdd & hanging in ll 2nd but rdr in control 6; rn wide bend bef 7; lost tch & 22l last 9; sn t.o; scrambled over last*

         P   **Minstrel Fire (IRE)** 7-1 **Miss L Pearce** *Last to 6; went 3rd frm 8; 12l 3rd nxt; pu 11*

OFFICIAL DISTANCES: 20l, dist   **TIME:** 6min 36.0s

Fences 6, 7, 14 & 15 were omitted from this and all subsequent races - state of ground

1053 Mens Open, 12st - 15J   6 ran

[1022ᴾ] 1   **SAFFRON MOSS** (7x) 6-4F **J Jukes** *Oht; 2nd til jmpd slow to ld 4-9; 3rd & blun nxt; 2nd 11; disp ld 12 til ld aft 13; sn drew clr*

[598ᴾ] 2   15   **Silverfort Lad (IRE)** 7-2 **C Williams** *Last early; r.o to 2nd 8; ld 10; jnd 12; hdd aft 13; sn tired & no ex*

[741⁶] 3   runin   **Sun Of Chance** 5-1 **D Stephens (Wales)** *Ld to 3; grad fdd; last pr 8; t.o last 11; plugged on; tk v rem 3rd cl home; nvr nr ldrs*

[817⁴] 4   1   **The Last Mistress** (5a) 8-1 **J Price** *Last pr early; mostly 3rd aft; lost tch thro corn; t.o frm 11; dem flat*

[944³] P   **Rusnetto (IRE)** (vis) 5-1 **G Lewis** *3rd early; settled cl 4th & rmdrs; went 2nd 10; wknd in hvy ground on long rn to 11; t.o & pu 13*

[945⁵] P   **Savuti (IRE)** (tt) 20-1 **J Keen** *Tde; 4th early; last pr frm 6 & last 8; t.o frm 10; pu 12*

OFFICIAL DISTANCES: 15l, dist   **TIME:** 6min 49.0s

1054 Restricted, 12st - 15J   11 ran

[832ᴾ] 1   **DUNSFOLD DAZZLER** (5a) 2-1F **D Hughes** *2 handlers; chsd ldrs; 5th mostly; 7th ll; 3rd & drvn 12; ld 14; kpt on*

[485³] 2   4   **Gt Hayes Pommard** 4-1 **D Howells** *3rd til ld 4-6; 3rd til ld agn brief 11; ev ch aft; kpt on game flat; a hld*

        P   **Cranagh Moss (IRE)** 4-1 **T Vaughan** *Midfield til pulled to 2nd 4; ld brief 7; 4th aft til wknd 12; pu 13*

[818ᴾ] P   **Its A Handfull** 10-1 **J Price** *8th til hdwy 8; 2nd 9; wknd thro corn aft 11; pu 13*

[483ᴾ] P   **Itscinders** (5a) 20-1 **D Stephens (Wales)** *Ld to 2; sn rr; last trio 5; lost tch frm 11; pu 13*

[896^F]	P		**Itspantotime** (5a) 12-1 J Jukes *Prom; 5l 3rd 5; drvn to ld 7; mist nxt & tired thro hvy ground aft 11; pu 12*
[823¹]	P		**Julies Joy (IRE)** (5a) 6-1 I Johnson *Swerved rt at start & nrly knocked over Steward; a last & jmpng rt; lost tch frm 11; pu 14*
[744^P]	P		**Khandys Slave (IRE)** (5a) 12-1 J L Llewellyn *Last trio to 8; 5th & hdwy 11; fdd on ½mile rn to nxt; pu 12*
[486^P]	P		**Milly Le Moss** (5a) 12-1 T Faulkner *Saddle slpd & pu 4*
[745^U]	P		**Not For Profit (IRE)** (tt) 25-1 C Williams *(b4)Midfield 2; settled 5th frm 4; 3rd & hdwy 9; jmpd to ld 12; hdd aft 13; pu nxt*
[818^P]	P		**Saronica-R** (5a) 16-1 J Cook *5th & mist 2; fdd 6; last pr frm 8; t.o frm 11; pu 14*

OFFICIAL DISTANCE: 4l　TIME: 7min 03.0s

The stewards enquired into an incident between Khandys Slave and Milly Le Moss at the fourth fence; having interviewed both riders they were cautioned as to their future conduct

1055 Confined Maiden 56&7yo, 12st - 15J　　　　　　11 ran

[834^R]	1		**GYPSY HAZE** (12a) 6-4F J Cook *(bnf) Hld up in 6th; settled 3rd frm 8; ld 13; sn clr*
[747³]	2	15	**Lillies Buttler** (5a) 5-1 T Vaughan *A.p; 2nd early; 3rd frm 4; lost plce 9; lft 3rd agn by defections 13; stayed on past tiring horse to 2nd 2 out; nt trble wnr*
[746^U]	3	4	**Craigson** 7-2 C Williams *(xnb) Ld 1 & 3-5; cl 2nd til ld agn 9; hdd frm 10; cont 2nd aft til 3rd 13; one pce aft*
[747^U]	P		**Annie's Alfie** 12-1 J Price *pulled to ld 6; prom aft til 5th & mist 11; wknd & pu 12*
[835^P]	P		**Artique Fish (IRE)** 7-2 J Jukes *4th til ld 7; hdd 9; ld agn 10-13; hdd & no ex; last when pu last*
[949⁶]	U		**Chesnut Wood** 10-1 M Barber *Midfield; ab 7th mostly; mist 10; hdwy in 5th when ur 13*
[949⁸]	P		**Daisy's Choice** (12a) 16-1 P Sheldrake *Mists; a last pr; last frm 7; t.o & pu 14*
[898^P]	P		**Itsarchie** 20-1 D Stephens (Wales) *Ld 2; 2nd 4; sn midfield; 6th til pu 14*
[943⁴]	U		**Jesusa** (5a) 20-1 G Maloney *A bhnd; lost tch frm 11; t.o when ur 13*
	P		**Kyre Moss** (7a) 8-1 N Jones *Lsng tch when jmpd slow 2; sn t.o; pu 7*
[823^P]	P		**No Escape** 16-1 G Perkins *2 handlers; nvr btr than 7th; wknd frm 12; pu 13*

OFFICIAL DISTANCES: 10l, 4l　TIME: 7min 12.0s

1056 Confined Maiden 8yo&up, 12st - 15J　　　　　　11 ran

	1		**BANNAGH BEG (IRE)** (5a) 14-1 C Williams *Mounted outside padd; ld 4-6; cl 2nd aft til ld agn 9; disp ld 11 & 12; ll up 13; kpt on game frm last; fin tired*
[838²]	2	4	**Mike's Dream** 5-4F T Vaughan *Ld 1-3; hld up in 2nd til ld agn 6-8; cl 2nd & mist 10; disp ld 11 & 12; ev ch frm 3 out; hdd & no ex last; pursued up run-in by fast finishing terrier*
[650^P]	3	20	**Lough Neagh (IRE)** 6-1 P Sheldrake *Generally 6th; 15l 5th 9; stayed on to 4th thro corn frm 11; lft 3rd by defections; nvr nr ldrs*
	P		**Albert The Lion (IRE)** 12-1 S Blackwell *(xnb) Midfield to 3; snr nr; last frm 6; roared into wl t.o 5th 11 til pu 4 out*
[823^F]	P		**Alicat (IRE)** 14-1 Miss E Jones *3rd/4th to 7; 20l 7th 9; wknd thro corn & t.o 11; pu 13*
[838³]	P		**Black Dan** 8-1 J Keen *A bhnd; strugg in last pr frm 5; t.o 11; pu 13*
[823¹]	U		**Cosy Ride (IRE)** 10-1 J Phillips *(bf) 7th til ur 8*
[891^P]	P		**Itsfreddie** 3-1 J Jukes *Mostly 3rd/4th; lost tch 13; pu last*
	P		**Millbank Honey** (5a) 6-1 G Lewis *2 handlers; chsd ldrs in 4th mostly; 5th when mist 6 & rdr up horse's nk; 13l 4th 9; virt stpd to walk in deep ground aft 11 & pu*
[823^F]	P		**Newchurch Lad** 6-1 J Price *A last trio; lost tch frm 10; sn t.o; last when pu 13*
[950⁵]	P		**Tarian (USA)** 25-1 M Parry *(b4) A bhnd; lost tch frm 11; pu 13*

OFFICIAL DISTANCES: 3l, 25l　TIME: 7min 03.0s

Portman

Badbury Rings (LH 10F,19J) Sat, 15 Apr (GOOD)

1057 Confined, 12st　　　　　　9 ran

[581^P]	1		**ABIT MORE BUSINESS (IRE)** (bl) 7-1 Miss P Gundry *Hld up towards rr til stdy hdwy to 7l 6th 9; 6l 3rd 13; sust rn frm 3 out; ld final stride; wl rdn*
[654¹]	2	hd	**Stoney River (IRE)** 4-5F R Young *Tchd evens; hld up towards rr; smooth prog to 3l 3rd 9; chsd ldr frm nxt til disp ld 15; lft in ld 3 out til hdd & no ex nr post (made a noise)*
[952⁵]	3	25	**Frozen Drop** 33-1 T Bishop *Disp ld to 3; grad lost plce & towards rr 9; 25l 8th 13; stayed on frm rr 16; passed tired rival for poor 3rd flat*

[632¹]	4	5	**Ball In The Net** 3-1 M Holdforth *Reared & ur padd; ld aft 3; 2l up 7 til jnd 15; pckd bad & hdd 3 out; 3rd & wkng nxt; jmpd v slow last; dem flat; reported to have gurgled*
[824¹]	5	4	**Arfer Mole (IRE)** (3x) 9-1 D Dennis *Ld brief 3; chsd ldr in 3l 2nd to 10; 10l 5th 13; grad lost tch; bhnd frm 16*
[768³]	6	2½	**Arabitan** (5a) 100-1 O Ellwood *Trckd ldrs frm 4; 5½l 5th 9; still in tch in 8l 4th 13; wknd & bhnd frm 16*
[929ᵁ]	7	20	**Silver Sleeve (IRE)** 66-1 Miss L Bridges *Disp ld to 3; grad lost plce & rr 9; rmdrs nxt; last 11; t.o 13; plodded home*
[768²]	F		**Celtic Token** 50-1 D Birkmyre *(xnb) Tde; chsd ldrs frm 4; 4l 4th 9; outpcd in rr trio 11; 23l 7th 13; 6th & hld when fell 3 out*
[927ᶠ]	F		**One Boy** 33-1 A Honeyball *(orbs) 2 handlers; sa & last to 10; 6th & in tch nxt; 13l down 13; fell 15*

OFFICIAL DISTANCES: hd, 20l **TIME:** 6min 20.0s **TOTE:** £6.00

1058 Hunt, 12st
3 ran

[737¹]	1		**HERE COMES HENRY** 1-5F R Young *Made virt all; 1½l up 6 til jnd 9 & hdd brief 11; jnd agn brief 13; in comm when lft clr 3 out; v easy*
[767²]	2	30	**Best Bitter** 5-1 M Miller *Chsd ldrs to 3; 3½l last nxt; jmpd slow 10; eff to ld brief nxt; 4l last 14; clsd nxt; lft 2nd 16; rdn when mist & slpd bad 3 out; nt rec*
[953ᶠ]	F		**Fast Run (IRE)** 12-1 Miss M Taylor *Last til 1½l 2nd 4; disp ld 9-10 & 13-14; chsng wnr when fell 16*

OFFICIAL DISTANCE: dist **TIME:** 6min 36.7s **TOTE:** £1.20

1059 Intermediate, 12st
4 ran

[737³]	1		**BRIGHT APPROACH (IRE)** 4-1 Miss P Gundry *Tchd 5s; disp ld til jmpd to ld 3; jmpd rt & hdd 5; chsd ldr 9 til ld agn 11; made rest; hld on wl u.p flat*
[879²]	2	1¼	**Cardinal Gayle (IRE)** evensF Miss D Harding *Disp ld to 3 & 6 til ld 8-11; disp ld brief agn 14; chsd ldr til jmpd slow & releg last 2 out; stayed on str frm last; a just hld*
[685³]	3	½	**Badger Beer** (tt) 7-1 J Snowden *Chsd ldng pr; 1½l 3rd 4; disp ld 6-7; 3½l 3rd 13; disp 1½l 2nd & ev ch 2 out; no ex u.p flat*
[927⁴]	4	6	**Primero (IRE)** (tt) 7-2 A Honeyball *Chsd ldrs 4; hld up in last; 3l down 9; still 4l adrift 10; disp 3rd brief 13; clsng & ev ch 2 out; no ex u.p frm last*

OFFICIAL DISTANCES: 1½l, nk **TIME:** 6min 34.5s **TOTE:** £4.00

1060 Mixed Open, 12st
5 ran

[851²]	1		**MIZYAN (IRE)** 4-11F Miss P Gundry *1/2-4/11; ld; 2l up 5 til blun bad 9 & releg last; gvn time to rec; ld agn aft 13; made rest; 3l up 3 out; in comm when mist nxt; easy*
[325ᶠ]	2	15	**You Said It (IRE)** 11-1 D Crosse *Trckd ldrs in 2½l 3rd 4; disp ld 10-13; chsd wnr frm nxt; 2l down 16; sn brushed aside*
	3	12	**Factor Ten (IRE)** 10-1 J Richardson *(xnb) 3l 4th 4; jmpd to disp ld 10-13; 6l 3rd 16; stayed on one pce frm nxt*
[877⁶]	4	4	**Radio Days** 33-1 Miss C Tizzard *5l last 4; eff to disp 2nd 9; lft disp ld nxt; last agn 11; 10l 4th 16; stayed on one pce frm nxt*
[684⁵]	P		**Willie Makeit (IRE)** 13-2 M Miller *Chsd ldr; 1l 2nd 4-9; disp ld 11-13; jmpd slow nxt & releg last; 12l bhnd & wkng 16; pu aft 2 out*

OFFICIAL DISTANCES: 20l, 10l **TIME:** 6min 24.3s **TOTE:** £1.30

1061 Restricted, 12st
10 ran

[931²]	1		**ONE OF THE NATIVES (IRE)** 11-8 A Honeyball *(xnb) Hld up in rr; 14l 6th 8; 4th when mist 15; 3rd & staying on 3 out; eff to chall last; sn clr; comf*
[958⁶]	2	2½	**Ashmead Rambler (IRE)** 66-1 Miss A Bush *(xnb) 8l 4th 4; lft 2nd nxt; jmpd to ld 10-11; disp ld agn 16 til ld 2 out; hdd last; no ex flat*
[458³]	3	8	**Monty's Theme (IRE)** 11-10F Miss P Gundry *Tchd 6/4; hld up til prog to 3rd 6; 7l down 8; chsd ldng pr til ld 3 out; hdd nxt; 3rd & btn app last*
[767ᶠ]	4	runin	**Another Junior (IRE)** 25-1 R Young *Cl up; 5l 2nd 4; grad lost plce; 12l 5th 8; jmpd rt 13; t.o 15; lft rem 4th 2 out*
[882²]	U		**Amaranthine** (5a) 66-1 Mrs J Butler *(xnb) Spurs; tchd 100s; chsd ldr to 2; sn outpcd; rr 7; 18l 7th 8; hopelessly to 12 til virt ref & threw rdr over last then jmpd it*
[958ᵁ]	U		**Cefn Woodsman** 200-1 Miss K Lovelace *Trckd ldrs; 8l 4th 8; 5th & still in tch when ur 13*
[879⁴]	P		**Lord Of The Rings** 33-1 Miss C Tizzard *Tchd 50s; a last; lkd unenthusiastic; nrly fnce adrift 7; blun bad 9; pu 13*
[886ᶠ]	F		**Silver Hill** (5a) 100-1 M Miller *Ld; 5l up 4; hdd 10; ld agn 12; jnd 16; sn hdd; wkng & mist nxt; v tired when fell hvly 2 out*

[882¹]	F		**Teeton Heavens** (5a) (tt) 14-1 **S Claisse** *Lw; towards rr when fell 2*
[932⁶]	U		**The Stuffed Puffin (IRE)** 100-1 **Miss S Rowe** *(xnb) 6l 3rd 4; 2nd & chsng ldr when blun & ur nxt*

OFFICIAL DISTANCES: 2l, 5l   **TIME:** 6min 27.6s   **TOTE:** £2.00

1062 Open Maiden, 12st   8 ran

[889⁶]	1		**SPANISH RIVER** 7-1 **G Weatherley** *Made virt all; 2½l up 4; lft 15l clr 14; tiring when jmpd slow 2 out; stayed on game; rdr's 1st wnr*
[874⁴]	2	32	**I'm Convinced** 2-1F **Miss P Gundry** *Disp 8l 3rd 7; chsd ldng pr when lft 15l 2nd 14; tired & jmpd slow 2 out; no ex flat & dem 4th nr post; plcd 3rd & subsq promoted*
[889ᴾ]	3	nk	**Gunerkillinghurst** 33-1 **J Snowden** *10l 4th 4; towards rr when rmdrs 10; mist nxt; t.o 15; stayed on frm 2 out; fin fast & snatched 3rd on line; plcd 4th; subsq promoted*
[765⁴]	2d		**Bright Lady** (5a) 20-1 **Miss R Green** *8l 3rd 4; grad lost plce & rr 11; lft rem 3rd 16; stayed on to v rem 2nd flat; fin 12l 2nd; disq - nt draw weight*
[882ᵁ]	F		**Artful Aviator** 33-1 **S Cobden** *A last pr; mist 7; last when fell 9*
[888⁴]	P		**Meat Loaf (IRE)** 3-1 **M Shears** *Tchd 4s; rr & mist 1; 4th 6; 4th & rdn 13; wknd qckly; t.o & pu 15*
[630ᴾ]	F		**Nearly A Jester** 5-1 **D Flavin** *10s-5s; last pr; jmpd slow & releg last 4; grad prog to disp 4th 10; lft 3rd 14; disp 12l 2nd when fell 16*
[932ᴾ]	U		**Spanish Jest** 6-1 **J O'Rourke** *(drop) 2 handlers; disp ld to 2; 3l 2nd 5; still 4l down when blun & ur 14*

OFFICIAL DISTANCES: Originally 15l, dist   **TIME:** 6min 45.3s   **TOTE:** £5.00
    Bright Lady finished second but was disqualified when the rider was unable to draw the correct weight - had lost weight cloth and other tack after the second last fence; she was warned to be more careful with her tack in future

Worcestershire

Chaddesley Corbett (LH 8F,20J)   Sat, 15 Apr (GOOD to SOFT, SOFT in places)

1063 Hunt, 3m2f, 12st   8 ran

	1		**DO IT ONCE (IRE)** (7x) (tt) 6-4F **Miss C Dyson** *(xnb)Hld up & bhnd; gd hdwy & 8l 5th ½way; jnd ldrs 12; went 2nd 15; ld 3 out; stayed on wl*
[991ᵁ]	2	5	**Stretchit** 5-1 **Miss I Rabone** *Rcd wide; a.p; mist 4; 6l 3rd ½way; went 2nd aft 11; ld aft 12 til hdd 3 out; btn when hit last*
	3	3	**Zodiac Prince** 100-30 **M Harris** *4s-100/30; hld up & bhnd; mist 5; last to 7; 9l 7th ½way; hdwy 13; went 1½l 3rd 15; rdn 17; ev ch 3 out; wknd app last*
[987⁶]	4	10	**Mitchells Best** 12-1 **M Keel** *Sn outpcd & bhnd; 16l 8th ½way; 17l 6th 15; stayed on frm 17; went 15l 4th 2 out; nvr able to chall*
[820⁴]	5	4	**Artic Pearl** (5a) 10-1 **R Langley** *Ld to 1; 2nd/3rd to 5; 8½l 6th ½way; 7l 5th & rdn 15; sn btn*
	6	12	**Bumble Rock** 20-1 **D Mansell** *Chsd ldrs; 7l 4th ½way; went 2nd aft 12 til 5l 4th 15; rdn 17; wkng when blun nxt*
[194ᴾ]	7	30	**Cherry Orchid** 33-1 **Miss R Fletcher** *Rcd wide; went 2nd 2; ld 5 til hdd aft 12; wknd qckly aft 13; 25l 7th 15; t.o*
[892³]	P		**Strong Account (IRE)** 25-1 **R Sealey** *Ld 1-5; 2nd til blun 11; wknd rap; t.o 13; pu 15*

OFFICIAL DISTANCES: 6l, 2l   **TIME:** 6min 58.6s

1064 Confined, 3m2f, 12st   7 ran

[614ᴾ]	1		**STRONG CHAIRMAN (IRE)** 20-1 **S Waley-Cohen** *Ld to 2; 2nd to 9; chsd ldr 13-15 & frm 17; ld app last; hld on wl u.p flat*
[612¹]	2	½	**Philtre (IRE)** 5-2 **Julian Pritchard** *Ld 2; blun 2 out; sn hdd; ev ch last; r.o u.p*
[862ᵁ]	3	30	**Alaskan Heir** (vis) 16-1 **G Hanmer** *Prom; went 2nd 9-13; lost plce & 8l 5th 16; sn wknd*
[897¹]	4	4	**The Archdeacon (IRE)** 5-2 **T Stephenson** *(xnb) Hld up; 9l 6th ½way; last to 14; eff & 4l 4th 16; wknd 4 out*
[580³]	P		**Hatterill Ridge** 11-2 **A Wintle** *Hld up; 8l 5th ½way; mist 11; releg last 14; 10l 6th 16; sn wknd; wl bhnd when pu 3 out*
	F		**Lofty Deed (USA)** 33-1 **G Barfoot-Saunt** *Fell 1*
[905¹]	F		**Wejem (IRE)** 2-1F **A Dalton** *Hld up; 7l 4th ½way; hdwy 14; went 2nd nxt-17; 1½l 3rd & hrd rdn when fell last*

OFFICIAL DISTANCES: ½l, 30l   **TIME:** 6min 49.4s

1065 Mens Open (Lady Dudley Cup), 3m2f   4 ran

[860ᵁ]	1		**DISTINCTIVE (IRE)** 5-2 **A Wintle** *Jw; made all; qcknd 15; 10l clr 3 out; r.o str*

[859¹] 2 20 **Solba (USA)** 4-6F A Dalton *2nd til jmpd slow 5; chsd wnr 9 til jmpd slow & rmdrs 12; went 2nd app 14; hrd rdn aft 15; no imp 17*

[598¹] 3 7 **Cream Supreme (IRE)** (bl) 6-1 E Williams *Prom; went 2nd 5-9; lft 2nd 12 til 4l 3rd 14; rdn 15; wknd 17*

[700²] P **Better Future (IRE)** 12-1 T Stephenson (bnf) *Jmpd delib & nvr gng wl; lost tch u.p 10; 15l 4th ½way; wl bhnd 12; t.o 14; pu 3 out*

OFFICIAL DISTANCES: 20l, 10l TIME: 6min 47.2s

1066 Ladies Open, 3m2f
7 ran

[991³] 1 **KILLATTY PLAYER (IRE)** (5a) 12-1 Mrs M Barlow *Chsd ldrs; went 3rd 8; 2nd 10; ld aft 17; stayed on wl*

[860³] 2 7 **Name Of Our Father (USA)** 9-4 Miss E Bryan *(orbs) 2nd/3rd til ld 9; hdd aft 17; rdn 3 out; btn when hit last*

[821¹] 3 2 **Karaburan** 6-4F Miss F Wilson *Lw; nt jw; lost plce & blun 4; releg last 6; 8l 7th & rdn ½way; hdwy 13; went 4l 3rd aft 15; rdn 17; no imp*

[860⁶] 4 runin **Saffron Flame (IRE)** 50-1 Miss N Rudge *Ld to 4; 2nd/3rd to 8; 5½l 5th ½way; 6l 4th 14; sn lost plce; wknd & 9l 6th 16; t.o*

[821³] P **Danny Gale (IRE)** (2ow) 40-1 Miss B Williams *Hld up; hdwy 9; 5l 4th ½way; 4l 3rd 13; 6l 4th & rdn 16; sn wknd; wl bhnd when pu 3 out*

[991ᵁ] U **Elwill Glory (IRE)** 33-1 Miss R Reynolds *Tde; hdwy to ld 4; mist 8; hdd 9; 4l 3rd ½way; mist & rdr lost iron 11; 6th when rdr leapt off 12*

P **Night Wind** 3-1 Miss C Thomas *Hld up; 6l 6th ½way; eff & 6l 4th 14; wknd 16; wl bhnd when pu 3 out*

OFFICIAL DISTANCES: 7l, 2½l TIME: 6min 57.2s

1067 Restricted, 3m2f, 12st
6 ran

[797ᵁ] 1 **ATOSKI** 4-7F A Dalton *A.p; 2l 3rd ½way; went 2nd aft 13; ld 14; drew clr 17; easy*

[791ᴾ] 2 12 **Uncle Billy (IRE)** 14-1 E Walker *Chsd ldrs; mist & rmdrs 4; went 2nd 7-9; 3l 4th ½way; drvn along 12; lost plce 16; went 12l 3rd 17; stayed on; went 2nd nr fin*

[894ᴾ] 3 1 **Shadowgraff** (5a) 16-1 Julian Pritchard *2nd/3rd til ld 11; hdd 14; no ch w wnr frm 17; dem nr fin*

[992³] 4 7 **Paddy Maguire (IRE)** (bl) 11-2 T Stephenson *Ld til hdd 11; lost plce & 6l 5th 14; rallied u.p & 6l 3rd 17; wknd 3 out; mist last*

[992ᵁ] P **Brother Prim** 5-1 D Mansell *Hld up; 4l 5th ½way; eff & 2l 3rd 14; sn drvn along; wknd 16; wl bhnd when pu 3 out*

P **The Final Optimist** (5a) 10-1 C Wadland *Oht; 2 handlers; jmpd novicey; lost tch 6; t.o & pu 8*

OFFICIAL DISTANCES: 10l, 1l TIME: 7min 02.2s

1068 Open Maiden, 3m2f, 12st
15 ran

[906²] 1 **FANION DE NOURRY (FR)** 7-1 L Hicks *Hld up; 10l 9th ½way; stdy hdwy & 5l 7th 15; went 2l 3rd nxt & 2nd aft 17; ld 3 out; r.o wl*

2 5 **Cherry Gold** 10-1 E Williams *(xnb) A.p; ld 3-5; 1l 3rd ½way; went 2nd 15; ld 17-nxt; ev ch 2 out; one pce*

3 nk **Mick Mackie (IRE)** 7-4F Julian Pritchard *3s-7/4; 2 handlers; hld up; 11l 10th ½way; 8l 9th 15; hdwy & 5l 6th nxt; went 3rd aft 4 out; no imp when mist 2 out*

[786³] 4 12 **Musical Hit** 14-1 C Wadland *Hld up; hdwy 7; 7l 8th ½way; same plce 15; 5½l 7th nxt; wknd 17*

[703²] 5 6 **The Ugly Gunner** 7-2 E Gretton *Prom; 4½l 6th ½way; 4l 5th 15; wknd 17*

[898²] 6 12 **Arctium** (5a) 25-1 G Barfoot-Saunt *Mounted v early outside padd; hld up & bhnd; 16l 11th ½way; mist 12; some hdwy 15; 9l 10th nxt; wknd 17; nt pushed*

[891⁴] P **Autumn Blunder** 14-1 T Stephenson *2 handlers; sn prom; went 2nd 6-10; 3l 5th ½way; 4½l 6th 15; wknd & 7l 9th nxt; wl bhnd when pu 3 out*

[514ᴾ] P **Belldoran** 11-1 F Hutsby *10th when pu & dism 5*

[204³] P **Castle Chief (IRE)** (8ow) 12-1 T Gretton *(bf) Ld 2-3; 5-14; 3l 4th 16; wknd 4 out; wl bhnd when pu 2 out*

[866ᶠ] P **Daneswell** 33-1 D Mansell *A bhnd; 25l 14th 8; t.o & pu 12*

[790⁵] P **Elver Spring** 7-1 A Dalton *Ld to 2; 2l 4th 8; went 2nd 10-13; 3l 4th 15; wknd & 6l 8th nxt; wl bhnd when pu 3 out*

[898³] P **Lord Lard (IRE)** 33-1 M Rodda *Hld up; mist 4; 6l 7th ½way; blun 12; 14l 11th & wkng 14; wl bhnd when pu 16*

[472²] P **Maquilleux** 14-1 E Walker *(xnb) Prom; 1½l 4th ½way; went 2nd 13; ld 14-17; 10l 4th & wkng when pu 3 out*

P **Pigeon Hill Buck (IRE)** 20-1 Miss M Bartlett *A bhnd; mists 3 & 4; 24l 12th ½way; mist 12; t.o & pu 13*

[893F] P   **Take Achance On Me** 14-1 M Harris *A bhnd; 16l 11th 8; t.o & pu 12*

     OFFICIAL DISTANCES: 6l, ½l   **TIME:** 6min 59.6s

         Ivors Boy was withdrawn not under orders - unseated and injured rider going to post

Grove & Rufford
Southwell (LH 7F,18J) Sun, 16 Apr (SOFT)

1069 Hunt   4 ran

[545P]   1   **BUCKET OF GOLD** 7-4 T Denniff *Made all; slt ld til 4l clr 12; 6l up 15; stdly drew clr; r.o str*

       2   15   **The Tide Race** (5a) 7-1 S Walker *Chsd ldr in 5l 2nd to 15; pushed along aft; outpcd 3 out; nt hrd prsd when btn*

[793³]   P   **Harps Hall (IRE)** 4-7F M Chatterton *Jmpd slow & nvr gng wl; 8l 3rd 10; pushed along 11; lsng tch when climbed over 13; t.o when clambered over 15 & pu*

[871P]   U   **Tipping Away (IRE)** (bl) 14-1 D Flavin *Last til blun & ur 7*

     OFFICIAL DISTANCE: 20l   **TIME:** 6min 53.0s

1070 Open Maiden 56&7yo, 2m4f, 12st - 16J   13 ran

[872F]   1   **PLAYLORD** 5-4F N Docker *Made vrt all; 4l ld up 3; drew clr frm 3 out; r.o str*

[548P]   2   10   **Camden Kid (IRE)** 40-1 K Green *Mid-div early; went cl 3rd 6 & 4l 2nd 10; pushed along & outpcd 13; r.o one pce frm 3 out*

[792⁶]   3   1½   **Fortune Hunter (IRE)** 8-1 P Millington *Rr to 6; hdwy 10; stayed on to 8l 3rd 3 out; r.o one pce*

[793¹⁰]   4   20   **Tom's Surprise** 20-1 S Walker *(bf) Midfield to 7; lft 15l 6th 11 & poor 4th by 3 out*

[793⁸]   5   8   **Anneka Louise** (5a) 16-1 N Kent *Mid-div to 8; went 6l 3rd 11; pushed along & wknd 13; t.o 3 out*

[793¹¹]   P   **Alston Fanfare (IRE)** 40-1 J Cookson *Rr by 7; pushed along & lsng tch 9; t.o by 13; pu 3 out*

[872P]   P   **Carr Dyke Castle** 20-1 M Mackley *Cl up early; 5l 4th 5; pushed along aft 8; wknd to 5th 10; bad mist & pu 11*

[906P]   U   **Copper Thorn** (5a) 40-1 Mrs C Boyes *Cl 2nd to 4; 8l 5th 7; mid-div when hmpd bad & ur 9*

[1006P]   P   **Don Royal** 25-1 A Sansome *A rr; lsng tch 3; t.o 8; rem & pu 11*

[593²]   P   **Grey Mystery** (5a) 9-4 C Barlow *A mid-div; 12l 6th when blun bad 12; imm pu & dism*

[872P]   F   **Lady Mana Mou (IRE)** (5a) 25-1 M Hewitt *Ld to 2; 4l 2nd 3 til fell 9*

[793P]   U   **Sail On By** (5a) 4-1 R Armson *Midfield til hdwy 7; cl 2nd 8; 4l 3rd when ur 13*

[808P]   r   **Young Saffy** (bl) 40-1 A Pennock *Sa; lsng tch aft 2; pushed along 9; t.o when ref 12*

     OFFICIAL DISTANCES: 10l, ½l   **TIME:** 5min 43.0s

1071 Dodson & Horrell PPORA Club Members Restricted, 12st   7 ran

[905⁶]   1   **FREESTYLER (IRE)** (tt) 13-8 G Hanmer *Last to 4; 10l 4th 6; hmpd bad 10; lft in ld 11 til mist 14; ll 2nd 15; ld app 3 out; 5l clr nxt; r.o u.p; all out; bbv*

[871P]   2   6   **Cantango (IRE)** 33-1 J Turcan *Last to 5; outpcd 8; hdwy 10 to ld 12 til outpcd 3 out; r.o one pce*

[902P]   3   30   **Caromisu** (tt) 20-1 S Cochrane *Ld to 5; 6l ld 6-10; disp 12 til wknd 13; lsng tch 15; poor 3rd 3 out*

[782⁴]   F   **Another Gentleman** 6-1 Mrs C Ford *Pulled hrd early; 6l 3rd 4; hdwy 8; 3l 3rd when fell 10*

       U   **Downtheground (IRE)** 4-1 A Crow *Mid-div when ur 2*

[1009P]   P   **Over The Barrow (IRE)** 33-1 L Hicks *Mid-div to 6; 12l 5th 7; outpcd 8; 20l 5th 9; v tired 11; rem & pu 12*

[871²]   U   **Springfield Rex** 6-4F Mrs F Needham *A.p; 4l 2nd 8; hdwy to disp ld 9-10; cl 2nd when blun bad & ur 11*

     OFFICIAL DISTANCES: 4l, dist   **TIME:** 6min 44.0s

1072 Confined, 12st   5 ran

[868¹]   1   **GILLONE** (3x) 1-4F N Docker *Ld to 3; 2l 2nd 4-9; chsd ldr in 4l 2nd to 14; disp ld 15-3 out; ld nxt; 2l clr by last; r.o u.p*

[690²]   2   5   **Take The Buckskin** (tt) 3-1 M Briggs *Ld; 4l up 6 til jnd 15; hdd 2 out; outpcd & wknd app last*

[867C]   3   20   **Deel Quay (IRE)** 10-1 M Chatterton *Prom; disp 2nd 8-10; qckly outpcd & last 11; poor 4th 15; stayed on to dist 3rd at last*

[871¹⁰] **4**   12   **Vimchase** 66-1 M Mackley *Last 4-10; went 6l 4th 11; outpcd 13; lft 25l 3rd 15; dem 4th flat*
[1008ᴾ] **F**   **Black Book (IRE)** (5a) 28-1 P Millington *Handy in 3rd til 4l 2nd 8; 5l 3rd & mist 11; pushed up to cl 3rd when fell 14*

   OFFICIAL DISTANCES: 4l, 12l   **TIME:** 6min 47.0s

1073 Mens Open   8 ran

[903¹] **1**   **LORD HARRY (IRE)** 4-7F A Crow *Ld 3; jnd 10-15; rdly drew clr app 3 out; galloped on str; dist ahd at last hvly eased flat; impressive*
[1008²] **2**   15   **Burntwood Melody** 9-4 R Armson *Ld to 2; cl 2nd 3 til disp ld 10; mist 11; hdd aft 15; sn pushed along & outpcd; r.o one pce*
[996³] **3**   25   **Corbleu (IRE)** 20-1 M Walford *Jw; last 5; hdwy 7 to 12l 3rd 9; outpcd 12; poor 3rd 14; r.o one pce*
[461ᶠ] **4**   20   **Fern Leader (IRE)** 33-1 T Rogers *A rr; bhnd by 10; t.o 13*
[781ᴿ] **5**   25   **Rolier (IRE)** 7-1 C Barlow *Rr by 4; 15l 4th 10; bad mist 11; sn wknd; rem 4th 15; dem app 2 out*
   P   **Court Thyne (IRE)** 50-1 P Millington *Rr to 3; hdwy 5 to 4l 3rd 7; outpcd & wknd 9; hrd rdn 10; t.o & pu 14*
[789³] **P**   **Master Chuzzlewit (IRE)** 20-1 R Lawther *A rr; last & lsng tch 11; t.o & pu 13*
[229ᴾ] **P**   **Tudor Fellow (IRE)** 66-1 A Sansome *11 2nd to 3; rmdrs aft 4; v reluct & last by 5; clambered over 6 & pu*

   OFFICIAL DISTANCES: 20l, dist   **TIME:** 6min 35.0s

1074 Ladies Open   3 ran

[904ᵁ] **1**   **TUDOR LODGE (IRE)** (5a) evensF Miss S Swindells *Hld up in rr; 5l last 10; hdwy 11; cl 3rd & mist 12; 5l 2nd 14; hrd rdn app last; stayed on well; fin str; ld on line*
[869ᴾ] **2**   1   **Kenilworth Lad** 6-4 Miss L Allan *Chsd ldr in 11 2nd til ld 6; 2l up 7-13; drew 5l clr 3 out til jnd & one pce flat*
[869⁷] **3**   40   **Doctor Dunklin (USA)** 7-2 Miss E Graham *Ld to 5; cl up til ld agn 10-12; wknd 13; poor 3rd 3 out*

   OFFICIAL DISTANCES: 1l, dist   **TIME:** 6min 48.0s

1075 Open Maiden (Div 1)   3 ran

[867ᴾ] **1**   **SANDS POINT** 2-1 N Kent *Ld to 4; cl 2nd 5-14; outpcd 15; 4l 2nd 3 out; hrd rdn app last; ld flat; hld on u.p*
[696ᴾ] **2**   2   **Handsome Is (IRE)** (12a) 6-4F G Brewer *Cl up til ld 6; 2l ld 7-14; drew clr aft 15; 6l up 2 out; rdn app last; jnd, put hd in air & nt r.o flat; hdd nr fin*
[816ᴾ] **r**   **Royal Fling** (5a) 7-4 C Barlow *Trckng ldrs when jmpd slow & rmdrs 2; last to 4; ld brief & mist 5; jmpd slow 6 & lost tch qckly; ref 7 & dumped rdr on fnce*

   OFFICIAL DISTANCE: 1½l   **TIME:** 7min 06.0s

1076 Open Maiden (Div 2)   4 ran

[867ᴾ] **1**   **FAIR FARM LAD** 5-2 Miss R Pask *Made all; slt ld to 15; drew clr 3 out; 3l up nxt; clr last; hung rt flat; hrd rdn & just hld on; all out*
   2   nk   **Canny Curate (IRE)** 1-2F G Hanmer *Cl 2nd to 5; outpcd app 3 out; 3l 2nd app last; hrd rdn & stayed on flat; just failed; fin lame*
[1012ᴾ] **P**   **Crested Lass** (5a) 6-1 L Hicks *Cl 3rd to 9; pushed along 11; mist 13 & sn wknd; t.o 15; v tired & pu 3 out*
   P   **Imperial Tokay (USA)** 10-1 A Brown *Sn bhnd; last & lsng tch 5; t.o 9; pu 12*

   OFFICIAL DISTANCE: nk   **TIME:** 7min 02.0s

Morpeth
Tranwell (LH 9F,18J) Sun, 16 Apr (SOFT)

1077 Hunt, 12st   2 ran

[494⁴] **1**   **GOOD (IRE)** 1-10F Mrs V Jackson *Tk keen hld; ld app 8; clr 14*
[719ᴮ] **2**   25   **Mornay Des Garnes (FR)** 3-1 G Scantlebury *(xnb) Bckwd; ld til app 8; no ch w wnr frm 14*

   OFFICIAL DISTANCE: 30l   **TIME:** 7min 07.0s

1078 Confined, 12st   12 ran

[498¹] **1**   **STORM ALIVE (IRE)** 6-1 Mrs V Jackson *10s-6s; cl up; 4th 10; ld 12; 4l clr 15; r.o wl; quite comf*

[713¹]	2	6	**Miss Portcello** (5a) 5-1 **Miss J Hollands** *Lw; nt jw; mist 2; bhnd; 7th 10; kpt on wl aft 14; passed tired horses frm nxt; no ch w wnr*
[916⁴]	3	2	**Minella Gold (IRE)** (3x) 2-1F **Miss M Bremner** *Prom; 3rd 10; nt qckn frm 15*
[717²]	4	5	**Rum Rebel** 3-1 **J Walton** *8s-3s; prom; lft in ld 10-12; one pce frm 15*
	5	12	**Todcrag** 3-1 **T Scott** *Bit bckwd; prom; lft 2nd 10; hit 11; chsd ldrs til wknd aft 14*
[912ᵁ]	6	2fncs	**Heavenly Citizen (IRE)** 40-1 **Miss E Edminson** *A strugg in rr; t.o 10*
[975ᴾ]	U		**Charlieadams (IRE)** 5-1 **J Muir** *Ld & str hld; 10l clr 3; blun & ur 10*
[717ᴾ]	P		**Full Of Chat (IRE)** (5a) 33-1 **D Jewett** *Prom early; 8th & wkng 10; t.o & pu 15*
[420¹]	P		**Little Brockwell (IRE)** (5a) 3-1 **Miss P Robson** *V reluct to line up & delayed start; ss & nt keen in final trio; poor 9th 10; t.o & pu 15*
[912²]	P		**The Green Fool** 20-1 **H Humble** *(xnb) Prsd ldrs til 7th & wkng 10; t.o & pu 2 out*
[911ᴾ]	P		**Tropnevad** 33-1 **B Lusted** *Chsd ldrs; 5th 10; wknd & mist 12; t.o & pu 2 out*
[495ᴾ]	P		**Warner's Sports** 40-1 **J Innes** *Strugg in rr; nrly fell 9; t.o & pu 10*

OFFICIAL DISTANCES: 5l, 1l **TIME:** 6min 48.0s

1079 Ladies Open   9 ran

[1029¹]	1		**BALISTEROS (FR)** 9-4 **Miss J Wormall** *Lw; trckd ldrs; 30l 3rd 5; ld 13; hrd prsd frm nxt til rdn & qcknd clr aft last; rdly*
[974¹]	2	4	**Nova Nita** (5a) 4-1 **Mrs V Jackson** *Tk keen hld in midfield; hld up til clsd 10; chsd wnr 14; ev ch til rdn & nt qckn last*
[661¹]	3	10	**Riparius (USA)** 6-4F **Miss P Robson** *Trckd ldrs & hld up; eff 14; 3l 3rd app nxt; rdn & sn wknd*
[661⁴]	4	6	**Oat Couture** 10-1 **Miss S Johnstone** *Hld up last to 8; stdy hdwy 10; stayed on to trck ldrs app 15; one pce nxt*
[661³]	5	6	**Rallegio** 16-1 **Miss L Hislop** *Hld up; eff 9; trckd ldrs 10 til 5l 4th app 15; sn wknd*
[806⁴]	6	runin	**Kralingen** (5a) 20-1 **Miss C Metcalfe** *Jmpd rt; ld & ab 10l clr to 10; hdd app 12; wknd rap 14; t.o*
[715ᴾ]	P		**Little Santa (IRE)** (5a) 12-1 **Mrs K Hargreave** *Bhnd; 7th 10; mist 13 & lost tch; t.o & pu 15*
[974⁵]	P		**No Problem Jac** (5a) (bl,tt) 25-1 **Miss J Hedley** *Rcd keen & sn 2nd; ld app 12-13; wkng rap when blun nxt; pu 15*
[912⁶]	U		**Reve De Valse (USA)** 20-1 **Miss V Burn** *Prom early; drpd back last 8; tlng off when rfo 10*

OFFICIAL DISTANCES: 4l, 10l **TIME:** 6min 51.0s

1080 Mens Open - 17J   5 ran

[716¹ᵉ]	1		**EXCISE MAN** (tt) 4-5F **J Walton** *Lw; hld up; 3rd frm 3; 6l down aft 14; went 2nd aft 15; lft in ld nxt; sn clr; eased flat*
[998ᴾ]	2	15	**Mick Man (IRE)** 20-1 **S J Robinson** *Set stdy pce; rdn app 14; hdd nxt; lft 2nd 3 out; rdr v unbalanced & kpt administering needless rmdrs*
[975ᴾ]	P		**Chummy's Saga** 14-1 **J Innes** *(xnb) Swtng; lost tch 3; jmpd slow 5; t.o & jmpd rt frm 10; furlongs bhnd when pu aft 14*
	R		**Slip Away** 4-1 **B Lusted** *3rd when ducked out & put hd thro wing 3*
[918³]	U		**Steel Rigg (IRE)** 2-1 **M Clayton** *2nd til ld 15; jmpd big & ur nxt*

OFFICIAL DISTANCE: 30l **TIME:** 7min 07.0s
Fence 12 omitted - damaged

1081 Restricted   12 ran

[811²]	1		**ALLRITE BONNY LASS** (5a) 7-2 **Miss P Robson** *Hld up & bhnd; impd to 6th 9 & 4th 12; trckd ldng pr til ld aft 2 out; drvn clr flat*
[423ᴾ]	2	6	**Nickys Peril** (5a) 3-1 **T Davidson** *(xnb) Prom lft in ld 5; drvn & hdd aft 2 out; nt qckn flat*
	3	1	**Tindles Bible** 5-2F **D Jewett** *3s-5/2; prom; lft 2nd 5; rdn & ev ch 2 out; outpcd flat*
[907¹]	4	runin	**Buckaroo** (5a) 7-1 **Mrs A Tweedie** *10s-7s; chsd ldrs; drpd back 8th 9; t.o aft 14*
	R		**A Monkey For Dick (IRE)** 33-1 **J Dixon** *Oht & veteran rdr had difficulty mounting; tk str hld; ld 2 til went wrong side of marker app 5; veered at fnce & rfo*
[660ᴾ]	P		**Dari (IRE)** 33-1 **C Mulhall** *Jb in rr; tlng off when tried to demolish 11 & pu*
[911ᴾ]	P		**Dunnellie** (5a) 5-1 **Karen Robson** *Bhnd; 8th 9; pu 10*
	U		**Hetty Bell** (5a) 25-1 **P Strang Steel** *V fat; sn strugg in rr; last by 5; t.o when ur 10*
[420ᴾ]	U		**Noneofyourbusiness (IRE)** (5a) 33-1 **Miss C Metcalfe** *Chsd ldrs; 4th 9; in tch when ur 13*
[976ᴾ]	F		**Senso (IRE)** 5-1 **Mrs C Cox** *(xnb) Mist 1; hld up & bhnd early; impd to 5th 9; went 3rd 12; prsng ldrs when fell 15*
[976⁶]	S		**Tenella's Last** (5a) 12-1 **T Mounsey-Heysham** *Prom; 3rd 9; slpd up turn bef 12*

[907³] P   **Wylup** 33-1 H Humble *Lw; prom early; 7th 9; lost tch 14; t.o & pu 3 out*

OFFICIAL DISTANCES: 2l, 1l   TIME: 7min 04.0s

1082 Dodson & Horrell PPORA Club Members Maiden, 12st - 16J   8 ran

[719ᵁ] 1   **THE OTHER HALF** (bl) 2-1F Miss P Robson *Ld to 2; ld agn 11; 4l clr brief aft 13; prsd nxt but in comm 2 out*

[914⁵] 2   5   **Mesling** 5-1 J Walton *Hld up in tch; mist 6; 9l 4th 10; slpd 11 & nt jw aft; chall aft 14; chsd wnr vain frm 3 out*

[364ᴾ] 3   20   **Vernham Wood** 6-1 Mrs V Jackson *Ld aft 2-12; ev ch app 3 out; sn wknd*

[913⁵] 4   runin   **Paperback Writer** (5a) 5-2 M Henney *Cl up early; 18l 5th & reluct 10; sn to*

[1004ᶠ] r   **Aughrim Quest (IRE)** (5a) 5-1 C Wilson *12s-5s; ld til ref & threw rdr over 1*

[977⁶] B   **Border Country** 10-1 Miss M Bremner *Bd by refuser 1*

[661ᴾ] P   **Mirror Melody** (5a) (tt) 3-1 R Robinson *Prom; 3l 4th aft 14; wkng when mist nxt; mist 2 out; t.o & pu last*

[913ᴾ] P   **Springfield Prince (IRE)** 7-1 L Morgan *Last pr; lost tch 10 & reluct u.p; t.o & pu 12*

OFFICIAL DISTANCES: 5l, dist   TIME: 7min 07.0s
Fences 9 & 18 were omitted from this and subsequent races - state of the ground (revised fence numbers used in comments-in-running)

1083 Open Maiden 56&7yo (Div 1), 2m4f, 12st - 13J   7 ran

[45⁷] 1   **SUPERIOR WEAPON (IRE)** 7-4 M Clayton *Pulled hrd early; ld 2; drew clr 2 out; easy*

[719ᴾ] 2   20   **The Dyke Louper** (5a) 11-2 B Lusted *Mist 3; a 2nd/3rd; prsd wnr 10 til ev ch nxt; sn wknd; tired when mists 2 out & last*

[808ᴾ] P   **Almikino (IRE)** 8-1 S Brisby *(xnb) Lw; 4th 4; handy when blun 6 & pu*

U   **Seabright Sunset** 12-1 T Davidson *Trckd ldrs; 8l 4th when pckd bad & ur 8*

[977ᴾ] P   **Solway Spice** (12a) 12-1 Miss J Hedley *15l last when mist 4; t.o & pu 8*

[909⁵] r   **The Dust Buster** 14-1 R Trotter *Lw; last pr; lost tch 4; virt to 7; clsd brief 9; strugg agn nxt; t.o when ref last*

[909²] P   **Tom's Man** (tt) 13-8F A Robson *2nd/3rd; rdn 9; 4l 3rd 10; stpd to nil & sn t.o; pu 2 out*

OFFICIAL DISTANCE: 20l   TIME: 5min 51.0s

1084 Open Maiden 56&7yo (Div 2), 2m4f, 12st - 13J   10 ran

[500²] 1   **ANOTHERHANDYMAN** 6-4F P Johnson *(xnb) 3s-6/4; sn t.o; jmpd v slow 2; still last but catching rest qckly 10; went cl 3rd nxt; ld bef last; r.o u.p; all out*

[910³] 2   2   **Test Of Loyalty** 3-1 A Robson *Jmpd rt 1; prom; ld 3 out; hrd rdn & hdd app last; drvn & one-pcd; fin tired*

[114ᴾ] 3   7   **Solway Saffy** (12a) 12-1 B Lusted *Ld to 6; w ldr til ld agn 10-11; sn wknd; fin v tired*

[909³] 4   ½   **Magical Poitin (IRE)** (5a) 6-1 G Armitage *Cl up; 6l 5th aft 7; mist 9; chsd 4th 10; wknd nxt; fin v tired*

P   **Farthing Wood** 5-1 Miss P Robson *Tkn stdly in rr; 8l 6th aft 7; pckd bad 10 & pu*

[718ᶠ] F   **Mr McQuaker** 5-1 M Clayton *Settled trckng ldrs; cl 6th when fell 7*

[909⁶] F   **Naughty Feelings** 10-1 T Scott *Mist 4; 9th & strug when fell 5*

[778ᴾ] P   **Reflective Way** (5a) (tt) 16-1 R Robinson *Cl up; made most 6-10; wknd rap nxt; t.o & pu last*

P   **Sinch** (12a) 8-1 J Stonehouse *Prom brief; t.o by 6; pu 8*

[808ᴾ] P   **Westhall Jonstan (IRE)** 10-1 L Morgan *Sn 3rd/4th; mist 9; ev ch til wknd & mist 3 out; v tired when mist nxt; pu last*

OFFICIAL DISTANCES: 1l, 2l   TIME: 6min 05.0s

North Ledbury

Bitterley (LH 8F,18J) Sun, 16 Apr (GOOD, GOOD to SOFT in places)

1085 Hunt, 12st   5 ran

[968⁷] 1   **BLUE ROSETTE** (5x) (bl) 6-4 A Phillips *2nd/3rd til ld 10; mist 12; drew clr 3 out; rdn out*

[990⁴] 2   12   **Three Monroes (IRE)** 8-1 T Stephenson *Ld til hdd 10; ev ch 15; sn wknd; mist last*

[751ᴾ] 3   1½fs   **Chieftain's Crown (USA)** 10-1 Miss E James *Hld up; 9l 4th ½way; rdn 11; sn wl bhnd; to when mist 13; lft rem 3rd 2 out*

[704ᶠ] P   **Cool Spell** (5a) 33-1 Miss K Huckfield *1st ride; sn wl bhnd; to 6; mist 8; pu 13*

P   **Spearhead Again (IRE)** 4-6F M Munrowd *(xnb,bf) 2s-4/6; w ldr to 3; 2nd 5-9; ev ch til 3rd & rdn 12; wknd qckly 14; to when clambered thro 3 out; pu nxt*

OFFICIAL DISTANCES: 12l, dist   TIME: 6min 28.0s

1086 Confined, 12st
13 ran

[991⁵]	1		**ALL WEATHER** 7-4F M Wilesmith 5/2-7/4; 2nd/4th to 11; lost plce & 7l 6th 14; 7l 5th & rdn 3 out; stayed on u.p & ld last; all out
[988⁵]	2	2	**My Sister Lucy** (5a) 33-1 K Burke Hld up; mist 4; 6l 8th ½way; stdy hdwy 12; 6l 5th 14; went 3rd nxt & 2nd 3 out; rdn aft 2 out; stayed on u.p flat
[920⁷]	3	1½	**Military Man** 5-1 A Phillips Ld; shkn up 10; 4l clr 3 out; sn rdn; hdd & mist last; no ex flat
[566³]	4	4	**Moonstone (IRE)** (12a) 8-1 D Mansell Hld up; 7½l 10th ½way; 8l 7th 14; hdwy 15; 6l 4th 3 out; hrd rdn aft 2 out; mist last; wknd flat
[861⁵]	5	3	**Rootsman (IRE)** 20-1 T Stephenson Trckd ldrs; 3½l 4th ½way; went 3rd 11 & 2nd 14 til rdn 3 out; edged rt & wknd aft 2 out
[987⁴]	6	4	**Happy Minstral (USA)** (3x) (bl) 3-1 R Burton Hld up; lost plce & 7l 9th ½way; mist 10; drvn along when mist 13; 11l 9th nxt; stayed on one pce frm 3 out
[700³]	7	1	**George Ashford (IRE)** (bl) 33-1 I Hooper Swtng; prom; went 3rd 6-9; lost plce & 5l 7th ½way; 12l 10th 14; rallied u.p 3 out; no imp
[968⁷]	8	1	**Chicodari** (bl) 12-1 E Walker Went 2nd aft 3-14; 10l 6th 3 out; nt r.o
[862⁷]	9	10	**Macamore Star** 50-1 J Merry Swtng; hld up; 4l 5th ½way; mist 11; lost plce & 9l 8th 14; wknd 3 out
[895⁷]	10	7	**Latest Thyne (IRE)** 10-1 A Wadlow Hld up; 4½l 6th ½way; hdwy 11; 5l 4th 14; rdn & wknd 15
[860⁵]	11	30	**Highway Five (IRE)** 20-1 Miss L Brooke Sn plodding & bhnd; 20l 12th & rdn along ½way; t.o 11
[905ᵁ]	12	3	**The Boiler White (IRE)** 20-1 Miss J Froggatt A bhnd; 17l 11th ½way; t.o 11
[987ᴿ]	P		**Merger Mania** (bl) 10-1 S Graham (xnb) Swtng; jmpd violent rt 3; bhnd til pu 7

OFFICIAL DISTANCES: 2½l, 1l **TIME:** 6min 24.0s

1087 Mixed Open, 12st
10 ran

[987¹]	1		**THE CRAZY BISHOP (IRE)** 7-2 B Shaw 8s-7/2; sn prom; went 2nd 6; rdn to ld 2 out; r.o wl
[988²]	2	6	**Mickthecutaway (IRE)** 2-1 A Dalton 2nd til ld 4; hrd rdn & hdd 2 out; no ex flat
[860⁴]	3	20	**Look In The Mirror** 16-1 M Carter Lost plce 5; 5l 6th ½way; 10l 6th 13; nd aft; lft poor 3rd 2 out
[895²]	4	15	**Forest Fountain (IRE)** 6-4F Julian Pritchard Hdwy 5; went 3rd nxt til 3l 5th & drvn along ½way; lost plce & 8l 5th 13; wknd aft 14; t.o
[449¹]	U		**Aegean Fanfare (IRE)** 12-1 Miss E Jones 6th when blun bad & ur 1
[859³]	P		**Distant-Port (IRE)** 33-1 T Stephenson Hld up; 2½l 4th ½way; went 3rd 11; lost plce & 7l 4th 13; btn when pu 15
[446⁷]	P		**Have To Think** (bl) 100-1 A Morley Prom; went 2nd 4-6; lost plce 8; 10l 8th & rdn ½way; t.o 12; pu 3 out
[895⁷]	P		**Slightly Special (IRE)** 100-1 A Wintle Went prom & blun 4; drpd to rr 5; mists 7 & 8; bhnd when wisely pu 9
[988³]	P		**Tremendisto** 33-1 D Mansell (xnb) Hld up; hdwy 7; 2l 3rd ½way; mist 13; ev ch 15; sn rdn; wkng when mist 3 out; 7l 3rd when pu nxt
[988⁴]	P		**Watchit Lad** 33-1 S Blackwell Ld to 4; sn lost plce; 8l 7th ½way; wl bhnd when pu 12

OFFICIAL DISTANCES: 6l, 15l **TIME:** 6min 15.0s

1088 Restricted (Div 1), 12st
7 ran

[896²]	1		**IRON PYRITES** (5a) 6-4F S Lloyd 2s-6/4; hld up; mist 5; 6l 6th ½way; hit 10 & 12; 3l 5th 14; went 3rd aft 15; rdn aft 3 out; ld app last; r.o wl
[893¹]	2	1½	**Missed Call (IRE)** 4-1 J Jukes Lw; a.p; went 2nd 4-10; ld 14; hrd rdn & hdd app last; kpt on und hvy press flat
[822¹]	3	2½	**Presuming Ed (IRE)** 6-1 A Price 2nd/3rd tit hit 13; 2l 4th nxt; jnd ldr 15; rdn & ev ch when hung lft 2 out; stayed on one pce
[862³]	4	2	**Achill Sound** 7-2 R Burton (xnb) Hld up; mist 1; last to 6; mist 9; 5l 5th ½way; outpcd 12; 15l 6th 15; stayed on frm 3 out; went 12l 4th nxt; nt rch ldrs
[746¹]	P		**Bright Beacon** 10-1 E Williams Hld up; mist 5; hdwy 7; 3l 4th ½way; went 2nd 13-15; sn rdn & wknd; bhnd when pu last
[892¹]	P		**The Croppy Boy** 8-1 A Wintle Swtng; ld; qcknd when mists 12 & 13; hdd 14; wknd qckly nxt; 12l 5th when pu 3 out
[969⁶]	P		**Wolfie Smith** 50-1 Miss W Houldey Drpd to rr 7; 8l 7th ½way; lost tch 12; t.o & pu 14

OFFICIAL DISTANCES: 1½l, 2½l **TIME:** 6min 26.0s
The stewards fined the rider of Missed Call £70 for excessive use of the whip

1089 Restricted (Div 2), 12st   10 ran

[993ʳ]	1		**NEED MORE PRACTICE** (tt) 7-2 **R Burton** 5s-7/2; hld up; 3l 6th ½way; hdwy 11; went 3rd nxt; ld 3 out; clr last; edged rt flat; r.o
[894⁴]	2	4	**Another Wag** (5a) 4-1 **S Lloyd** Hld up; l 11 9th ½way; went 7l 5th 14; outpcd & 12l 4th 3 out; hmpd aft 2 out; str rn flat; went 2nd nr fin; nt rch wnr
[666¹]	3	½	**Wonastow** 7-1 **F Windsor Clive** (xnb) Prom; 2l 4th ½way; went 2nd 14; ld aft 15 til hdd 3 out; rdn & ev ch 2 out; one pce
[744ᵁ]	4	15	**J'accuse (IRE)** 5-4F **S Graham** Prom; went 2nd 8; ld 12 til hdd aft 15; sn rdn & btn; 3rd & wkng when hung lft u.p aft 2 out
[734ᴾ]	5	15	**Italian Man (IRE)** 12-1 **A Morley** 16s-12s; 2nd to 8; 2½l 5th ½way; lost plce 12; 14l 7th 14; sn wl bhnd
[901³]	6	2	**Ballyhannon (IRE)** 20-1 **Miss J Froggatt** Prom; l 3rd ½way; lost plce 14; sn wl bhnd
[1023ᴾ]	P		**Carbery Ministrel (IRE)** 25-1 **K Burke** Spurs; nt jw; 6l 7th ½way; rdn 11; 12l 8th 13; wl bhnd when pu 15
	P		**Hugo Henry (IRE)** (tt) 20-1 **D Mansell** (xnb) Hld up & pulled hrd; 9l 8th ½way; in tch til eased & pu 13
[948²]	P		**Out On The Town** (5a) 10-1 **James Tudor** Ld til hdd 12; 4l 4th 14; wknd & 8l 4th nxt; wl bhnd when pu last
[669ʲ]	U		**Rash-Gale (IRE)** (5a) 20-1 **J Cook** Chsd ldrs; 3l 5th when mist & ur 7

OFFICIAL DISTANCES: 4l, ½l   TIME: 6min 30.0s

1090 Intermediate, 12st   6 ran

[987⁵]	1		**SALLY'S TWINS** (5a) 8-1 **A Wintle** Ww; mist 6; 5l 6th ½way; hdwy 13; went 3rd nxt & 2nd 3 out; ld 2 out; 4l clr last; rdn & hld on wl flat
[897³ᵈ]	2	1	**Star Changes** 6-4F **J Jukes** 2nd til ld 11; hdd 11; sn drvn along; stayed on u.p flat
[600⁵]	3	2	**The Right Attitude (IRE)** 8-1 **J Cook** (xnb) Hld up; 2l 3rd ½way; lost plce 15; 8l 6th 3 out; stayed on wl flat; nt rch ldrs
[993¹]	4	¾	**Saywhen** 3-1 **R Cooper** Ld 3; mist 4; hdd & mist 11; 2nd til ld 15; hrd rdn & hdd 2 out; hit last; one pce
[862⁹]	5	10	**Nutty Solera** 33-1 **M Keel** Hld up; 2½l 4th ½way; went 3rd 12-14; 6l 5th 3 out; no ex
[862⁴]	6	3	**Perambulate (NZ)** (5x) 5-2 **D Barlow** 4s-5/2; ld to 3; 3l 5th ½way; went 5l 4th 3 out; wkng when mist last

OFFICIAL DISTANCES: 1l, 2l   TIME: 6min 46.0s

1091 Open Maiden (Div 1), 12st   10 ran

[899³]	1		**SIBOR STAR** 10-1 **J Cook** Ld 2-5; ld 7; pckd 15; full of running w rdr lkng rnd aft 3 out; drew clr app last; comf
[995⁴]	2	12	**Muckle Jack** 7-1 **S Blackwell** Ld to 2; ld 5-6; rdn & ev ch 3 out; pckd 2 out; sn wknd
[349²]	3	3	**Saxon Queen** (5a) 5-2F **E Williams** (xnb) 7/2-5/2; a.p; ld 6-7; l 3rd ½way; ev ch when blun bad 14; rdn 3 out; wknd nxt
[989ᵁ]	P		**Act On Impulse** (7a) 8-1 **A Dalton** Hld up; lost plce 7; 10l 7th ½way; wknd 10; wl bhnd when pu 12
[565⁵]	r		**Fontaine Again (IRE)** 7-2 **T Stephenson** 5s-7/2; swerved violent lft start; ref to rce; tk no part
[898ʳ]	F		**Forestry** 16-1 **A Wintle** Bhnd til fell 7
[866ʳ]	P		**Gunners Dawn** (5a) 20-1 **R Burton** Chsd ldrs; 8l 5th ½way; wknd 11; 25l 4th nxt; t.o & pu 3 out
	P		**Larkin About** (7a) 3-1 **S Joynes** (xnb) Hld up; hdwy 8; 3l 4th ½way; gng wl when pu 11; lame
	P		**Princess Scully** (12a,8ow) 20-1 **P Morris** A bhnd; mist 4; t.o & pu 9
[865ᴿ]	P		**Rusty King** 14-1 **R Hodges** Hld up; mists 4 & 5; 9l 6th ½way; wknd 11; pu 12

OFFICIAL DISTANCES: 14l, 3l   TIME: 6min 28.0s

1092 Open Maiden (Div 2), 12st   11 ran

[906ᶜ]	1		**FOUNTAIN STREET (IRE)** 6-4F **R Burton** (xnb) Hld up; 5l 6th ½way; hdwy 11; went 2nd nxt; ld 13; jmpd rt frm 15; rdn 2 out; all out
[986²]	2	¾	**Cashew Crisis (IRE)** (7a) 7-4 **M Rodda** 5/2-7/4; hld up & bhnd; 6l 7th & stdy hdwy ½way; went 3rd 13 & 2nd aft 15; ev ch aft 2 out; r.o (nt rdn frm 2 out til aft last - rdr lft it far too late)
	3	20	**Kota Tinggi** (5a) 8-1 **R Inglesant** (bnf) Prom; hmpd 7; 3l 4th ½way; ld aft 11-12; 7l 4th 14; wknd 15; went poor 3rd 2 out
[816ᵁ]	4	10	**Golden Saxon** 16-1 **M Merry** Hld up; 8th ½way; hdwy 12; mist 13; 8l 5th nxt; wknd 15

[865ᴾ]	5	5	**Come On Boy** 16-1 D Mansell *Hld up; drpd to rr & 11th ½way; hdwy 12; 9l 6th 14; sn wknd*
[900ᴾ]	P		**General George** 20-1 S Blackwell *Hld up; 8th when mist 6; 10th ½way; short-lived eff 12; wl bhnd when pu 15*
[900ᴾ]	P		**Sales Dodger (IRE)** 20-1 R Hodges *Prom; jmpd rt 7; 2l 3rd ½way; went 2nd aft 11; ld 12-13; blun 14; ev ch 15; sn wknd; bhnd when pu 2 out*
[995ᴾ]	P		**Scholar Green** 20-1 A Phillips *Chsd ldrs; mist & rmdrs 9; 3½l 5th ½way; wknd qckly & 15l 7th 14; pu 15*
[602ᴾ]	P		**Teelyna** (5a) 20-1 J Cook *Ld to 4; 2nd til ld 10; hdd aft 11; wknd rap; pu 12*
[994ᵁ]	P		**Timmy Tuff (IRE)** 12-1 K Burke *Mounted outside padd; went 2nd 2; ld 4-10; wknd qckly 12; mist 13; wl bhnd when pu 15*
[450ᴾ]	P		**Unrequited Love (IRE)** 20-1 M Munrowd *A bhnd; 9th ½way; mist & rmdrs 10; t.o & pu 12*

OFFICIAL DISTANCES: ¾l, 16l   **TIME:** 6min 36.0s

1093 Open Maiden (Div 3), 12st   9 ran

[891³]	1		**GORSEY BANK (IRE)** 7-4 R Cooper *Hld up; last to 5; 7th ½way; gd hdwy 11; ld 12; clr 3 out; rdn out*
[995⁵]	2	12	**Dungannon Lad** 25-1 A St George *2 handlers; swtng; a.p; 3rd ½way; 3l 4th 12; 4l 3rd 14; went 2nd nxt; rdn 3 out; sn btn*
[491²]	3	¾	**Bohola Pete (IRE)** 5-4F F Windsor Clive *Nt jw; pulled hrd; chsd ldr; jmpd slow 7; mist 14; dem nxt; chsd wnr 3 out; sn rdn & no imp; dem flat*
	P		**Georgie Grace** 33-1 A Price *A bhnd; 15l 8th ½way; blun 11; t.o & pu 12*
[866ᴾ]	U		**Hil's Bluff (IRE)** (12a) 25-1 A Wadlow *Chsd ldrs; 4l 5th ½way; 6th & wkng when blun & ur 10*
[569³]	P		**Lightening Steel** 16-1 P Morris *W ldrs; 2l 4th ½way; wknd & 9l 6th 12; t.o & pu 2 out*
	P		**Model Agent** (12a) 25-1 R Hodges *Hld up & pulled hrd; 7th when mist 5; releg last nxt; blun 7; t.o & pu 8*
[925⁹]	P		**New Yorker (USA)** (7a) (vis,tt) 25-1 M Rodda *Hld up; 7l 6th ½way; 6l 5th 12; wknd & 12l 5th 14; pu & dism 15*
[925ᴾ]	P		**Rusty Flame** 7-2 Julian Pritchard *6s-7/2; ch ride; ld til hdd 12; wknd & 9l 4th 14; t.o & pu 2 out*

OFFICIAL DISTANCES: 10l, 1l   **TIME:** 6min 35.0s

West Somerset Vale

Cothelstone (LH 7F,19J)   Sun, 16 Apr (GOOD, GOOD to SOFT patches)

1094 Hunt   7 ran

[880ᴾ]	1		**SUBA LIN** (5a) 12-1 D Luff *Chsd ldr; 8l 2nd ½way; lost tch 3 out; jmpd rt nxt; 12l 2nd when lft in ld last; v lucky*
	P		**Bright Flash (IRE)** 3-1 D Kenny *(xnb) Bit bckwd; settled 3rd; 9l 3rd 9; lost tch 12; rem 3rd when pu 3 out*
	U		**Goldoak** (7a) 5-1 Miss S Robinson *(xnb) Ur 1*
	F		**Gradient** 2-1F B O'Doherty *(bf) Ld; jmpd slow 2; went 5l clr; drew rt away frm 3 out; in comm when dived at last & fell hvly; winded; unlucky*
[639⁷]	R		**Granstown Lake (IRE)** 4-1 J Young *Settled 4th; 12l 4th 9; went 20l 3rd 13; poor 3rd when rn out bend aft 15*
[957ᴾ]	U		**Jazetason** 33-1 Miss A Barnett *Bit bckwd; oht; nov rdr v nervous; dwelt; imm t.o & dawdled rnd; fnce bhnd when ur 7*
	P		**Kiltonga** (1ow) 33-1 P Anderson *Fat; veteran nov rdn; bhnd frm 6; wl bhnd when jmpd slow 10; t.o & pu 11*

OFFICIAL DISTANCE: Finished alone   **TIME:** 6min 33.0s   **TOTE:** £8.20   **DF:** -

1095 Restricted, 12st   15 ran

[876ᴾ]	1		**JOLIFICATION** (bl) 14-1 A Honeyball *Tchd 20s; lw; handy on inner; jw; went 2nd 11; ld 14; drew clr aft 3 out; v easy*
[641¹]	2	8	**Shareton** 4-1JF L Jefford *Lw; hld up; nt a fluent; hdwy 12; hit nxt; went 2nd aft 15; blun 17; one pce & no ch aft*
[583ᴾ]	3	10	**For Christie (IRE)** 33-1 Miss A Goschen *Sn prom; jmpd rt; cl 2nd 6; cl up til ld 13-14; outpcd nxt; 4th 3 out; lft 3rd app 2 out*
	4	2½	**Chance Encounter** 25-1 R Young *Towards rr; 9th ½way; prog to 5th 14; no ex frm 16*
[728ˣ]	5	5	**Mr Kevernair** 7-1 M Woodward *(xnb) Prom til lost plce ½way; 8th 13; no ch*
[848⁴]	6	3	**Bridge House Boy** 20-1 A Oliver *(xnb) Sn rr; bhnd frm 11; mist 15; no ch*
[881ᴾ]	7	runin	**Chilli Jo** (tt) 50-1 Miss S Robinson *Midfield; 7th ½way; bhnd frm 13*

[931⁴]	U		Barton Rose 13-2 D Alers-Hankey Lw; towards rr when blun & ur 1
[639⁴]	P		Conquer The Kilt 4-1JF M Miller (xnb) Tchd 5s; in tch; 4th 11; lost ground stdly frm 14; bhnd when pu 2 out
	P		Crosswell Star (IRE) 25-1 J Scott Bit bckwd; sn last; t.o when bad mist 9; trailing til pu 13
[763¹]	r		Dante's Gold (IRE) 6-1 R Bliss (xnb) Bit bckwd; 2 handlers; reluct to line up; ref to rce
[958ᴾ]	P		King's Courtier (IRE) (bl) 11-2 N Mitchell Sn prom; disp 2nd 7; lost plce qckly 10; t.o & pu 13
[848ᴾ]	P		Nodforms Inferno 25-1 A Bateman Tde; tk keen hld; ld 2-13; in tch til wknd 15; pu 3 out; subsq destroyed
[734ᴾ]	U		Ribington 9-2 T Scudamore Ld when blun & ur 1
[931ᵁ]	S		Salford Quay (IRE) 33-1 G Barfoot-Saunt Midfield; 6th 11; hdwy 15; drvn to disp 10l 2nd aft 17; slpd up bend bef 2 out

OFFICIAL DISTANCES: 10l, 8l **TIME:** 6min 20.0s **TOTE:** £9.70 **DF:** -

1096 Mixed Open, 12st
10 ran

[952¹]	1		MILLYHENRY 6-4F Miss C Tizzard Disp ld til ld 3; made rest; drew clr aft 3 out; stayed on str; comf
[928²]	2	12	Tuskar Flop (7x) 3-1 D Alers-Hankey Prom; trckd ldr frm 10; cl up on inner 13; ev ch til rdn 3 out; one pce & no ch w wnr clsng stages
[557ᶠ]	3	6	Link Copper 16-1 S Kidston Handy; cl 3rd 11; 5l 3rd 15; outpcd frm 16; duelled for 3rd frm 3 out til lft clr 3rd app last
[638ᴾ]	P		Fellow Sioux 33-1 R Woollacott On heels of ldng group; 5l 5th 12; cl up til lost plce 15; btn 5th when pu 3 out
[680⁵]	P		Hurricane Blake (7x) (bl) 16-1 C Heard Rr & nt keen; niggled along ½way; poor 6th when jmpd slow 14; t.o & pu 3 out
[294ᶠ]	F		Ibex 5-2 L Jefford Hld up; stdy hdwy 12; cl 6th & ev ch when fell 13; broke pelvis; destroyed
	P		Lauren's Lad (7a) 33-1 G Barfoot-Saunt Bit bckwd; sn trailing; bhnd frm 6 til pu 3 out
[558⁴]	P		Play Poker (IRE) 3-1 Miss P Gundry In tch; cl 4th 12; rdn 14; sn lost tch; stayed on to disp 3rd til pu last; dism; lkd sound aft
	P		Touch Of Winter 50-1 Miss S West Prom til jmpd slow 3; lost plce 6; bhnd & pu 11
[954ᵁ]	P		Via Del Quatro (IRE) (5a,7x) (vis) 50-1 J Barnes Ld/disp to 3; stayed cl up to 10; wkng & rmdrs 12; bhnd & pu 14

OFFICIAL DISTANCES: 15l, 5l **TIME:** 6min 17.0s **TOTE:** £2.80 **DF:** £5.70

1097 Intermediate (Nov Rdrs), 12st
9 ran

[847¹]	1		SIR FROSTY (tt) 11-10F A Bateman Opened 4/5,tchd 6/4; lw; prom; cl 3rd 13; ld 15; 2l up when jmpd rt last; fnd ex run-in; comf
[560¹]	2	3	Chasing Daisy (5a) 3-1 J Snowden Lw; oht; mounted on course; tde; handy; cl 4th 10; trckd ldr frm 13; ll 2nd 2 out; ev ch til no ex app last
[556¹]	3	7	Big Seamus (IRE) (bl) 10-1 S Kidston Hdwy 11; went 4th 3 out; nt rch ldrs; tk 3rd u.p run-in
[640¹]	4	1	Diamond Duck (5a) 10-1 Miss K Allan (xnb) Ld 2-6; cl 3rd ½way; cl up & ev ch til wknd aft 3 out; lost 3rd run-in
[749ᴾ]	5	5	Perseverance 66-1 Miss A Bush Tde; sn rr; bhnd frm 10
[853³]	6	5	Foxy Dawn 4-1 R Woollacott Tchd 5s; in tch; 5th ½way; sn rdn; in tch in 6th frm 14-16; wknd
[561ᴾ]	P		Lucky Thursday (bl) 50-1 Miss H Best Rcd free & jmpd lft; cl 2nd when blun bad 3; ld 6-13; cl 3rd when jmpd slow 16; wknd rap; bhnd & pu 2 out
	P		Master Kiwi (NZ) 33-1 G Richards Sn rr; nt keen & rmdrs 12; t.o & pu 15
[953ᵁ]	U		Mountain-Linnet 100-1 A Corrie Ur 1

OFFICIAL DISTANCES: 3l, 12l **TIME:** 6min 20.0s **TOTE:** £3.00 **DF:** £2.30

1098 Dodson & Horrell PPORA Club Members, 12st - 17J
9 ran

[929¹]	1		SLEW MAN (FR) (7x) 4-5F L Jefford (xnb) Tchd evens; lw; patient rdn off pce; stdy hdwy 10; 3rd & poised to chal 14; ld on inner 3 out; pushed clr aft 2 out; comf
[967¹]	2	4	Glevum (5a) 6-4 T Scudamore Tchd 7/4; made most til blun bad 9; gvn time to rec in 3rd; prog agn 12; ld agn 14 til hdd 3 out; ev ch til no ex u.p aft 2 out
[561³]	3	15	Bells Wood (4x) 9-1 C White Sn prom; ld 9-14; cl up til outpcd 3 out; no ch w ldrs but clr 3rd frm 2 out; hvly eased run-in
[820³]	4	4	Questionaire (5a) 16-1 D Stephens (Wales) Towards rr but just in tch 10; 5th 14; no ch w ldrs
[929⁴]	5	5	Parditino (4x) 40-1 Miss J Nicholas 5th ½way; lost plce 13; nd clsng stages

[749[P]]	P		Cawarra Boy 50-1 M Walters (xnb) Went 2nd 8; rmdrs 11; wkng in 5th when mist 13; bhnd when pu 16
[561[4d]]	P		Hanging Grove (IRE) 16-1 M Bryant In tch; slt mist 6; 9l 4th ½way; prom in 4th but rdn 14; lost ground; mist 17; t.o & pu 2 out
[953[P]]	P		Kinloch Gale (IRE) (bl) 100-1 G Barfoot-Saunt Rr; bhnd frm 12 til pu 2 out
[929[P]]	U		Union Station (IRE) 100-1 B Parsons Rr when ur 1

OFFICIAL DISTANCES: 4l, 15l TIME: 6min 12.0s TOTE: £1.90 DF: £1.20
Fences 8 and 15 were omitted - fallen rider

1099 Open Maiden 5678&9yo (Div 1, Part 1), 12st - 18J   10 ran

	1		NILOUFER (5a) 8-1 A Charles-Jones Hld up; last 7; prog to 3rd 12; lft 2nd 14; jmpd to ld 3 out; stayed on wl when prsd frm 2 out
[850[P]]	2	4	Harveysinahurry 6-1 G Richards Mist 3; in tch; 2nd frm 10; lft in ld 14; hdd 3 out; rnwd eff & drvn to chall 2 out; switched to outer flat; no ex cl home; do btr
[792[U]]	3	runin	Bid For Tools (IRE) (bl) 10-1 G Barfoot-Saunt (xnb) Ld 1; prom to ½way; lost ground & jmpd slow in rr 13; poor 5th 15; drvn to rem 3rd 3 out
[876[P]]	4	runin	Jug Of Wine (5a) 25-1 G Weatherley Pulled hrd; 2nd/3rd til lft in ld 7; bad mist 10 & nrly fell & hdd; wknd 13; tired when jmpd rt 15; lft 25l 3rd when climbed 3 out; plodded home; clambered over last
[880[2]]	F		Frankie Muck 5-4F Miss C Stucley (xnb) Tchd 2s; hld up; hdwy & cl 3rd when fell 11; broke back; destroyed; mbr rd
[733[P]]	F		Mayfair Monarch (7a) 4-1 H Froud (xnb) Prom til lft in ld 10; 5l clr when fell 14
[559[P]]	R		Rushaway 10-1 Miss J Congdon Oht; pulled hrd & ld 2; 5l clr when rn out 7
	U		Speech Bubble (IRE) (5a) 12-1 M Woodward Midfield; 6th 12; bhnd & jmpd slow 13; last when blun & ur nxt
[520[P]]	F		Thecabbageflinger 20-1 R Young Rstrnd in rr; jmpd slow 2 & 3; pulling & rap hdwy aft 5; jnd ldr & fell 6
[880[U]]	F		Windyway (5a) 10-1 L Tibbatts (xnb) Towards rr; 5th aft 12; lft 15l 4th & blun 14; 20l 3rd & tired when fell hvly 3 out

OFFICIAL DISTANCES: 3½l, dist TIME: 6min 33.0s TOTE: £9.40 DF: £1.70
Fence 18 omitted - fallen rider

1100 Open Maiden 5678&9yo (Div 1, Part 2), 12st   10 ran

[640[2]]	1		MOLLYCARRSBREKFAST (7a) 6-1 Miss S Robinson Oht; ld 2; made rest; hit 3 out; rec wl; r.o str when prsd frm 2 out; game eff
[728[3]]	2	1½	Copastrop 4-7F R Woollacott Opened evens; lw; hld up in rr; gd hdwy to 3rd 12; went 2nd 3 out; chall & ev ch 2 out; nt qckn run-in
[899[P]]	3	12	St Helier (12a,3ow) 50-1 D Stephens (Wales) Nvr put in rce; rr; last ½way; r.o stdly frm hopeless posn aft 3 out; nrst fin
[847[P]]	4	4	Lighter Lord 12-1 L Jefford Prom; chsd ldr frm 6; cl up to 15; wkng & slt mist 16; fdd
[847[P]]	5	1	Uncle James (IRE) 20-1 C White Midfield; 6th ½way; wl hld in 5th frm 3 out
[880[P]]	6	5	Ruben James (IRE) (bl) 16-1 Jeremy Young Midfield; 6th when slt mist 10; in tch to 15; wknd
[518[P]]	7	20	Alice Sunrise (5a) 3-1 T Greed Lw; some hdwy 11; 7th 12; sn strugg; bhnd frm 15
[880[4]]	P		Indian Muse (12a) 20-1 Miss A Goschen Lw; prom; slt mist 5; cl 3rd 8; just in tch in 7th when mist & rdn 14; bhnd when pu last
[857[4]]	F		Sea Spirit (5a) 25-1 T Jones (Devon) Prom in closely bunched field; cl 3rd 11; eff 3 out; cl 3rd when fell nxt
[352[3]]	P		Timber Top (IRE) 12-1 D Alers-Hankey Lw; towards rr & nt a fluent; prog to 5th 12; wknd nxt; last when mist 15; pu nxt

OFFICIAL DISTANCES: 1½l, 12l TIME: 6min 35.0s TOTE: £5.40 DF: £1.40

1101 Open Maiden 5678&9yo (Div 2, Part 1), 12st   10 ran

[847[P]]	1		FLEET MILL (5a) 7-1 Miss T Cave (xnb) Lw; sn prom on inner; disp ld 13-15; ld 17; kpt on wl frm 2 out; comf
[147[3]]	2	5	Rosalee Royale (5a) 7-2 T Greed (xnb) Midfield; 5th ½way; hdwy 15; went 3rd but lot to do 3 out; r.o stdly to 2nd aft last; no ch w wnr
[889[R]]	3	2½	Regal Wolf (bl) 14-1 Miss A Goschen Oht; lft in ld 3; jmpd slow & hdd 6; chsd ldrs; went 2nd 15; slt ld 16; sn hrd rdn & hdd; dem aft
[934[P]]	4	40	County Derry 12-1 C Heard Lw; handy; 4th 10; cl 3rd 14; wknd 16; wl btn frm 3 out
[1094[U]]	5	10	Jazetason 33-1 M Woodward Bit bckwd; 2nd outing; sn rr; t.o frm 14
[353[P]]	P		Anolyze (5a) 16-1 G Richards Sn bhnd; t.o & pu 11; nt pushed; v green at present
[875[P]]	U		Caundle Encore (5a) 14-1 J Snowden Rcd keen; 5th 6; blun bad & ur 10
[849[P]]	P		Little Buster 8-1 D Alers-Hankey (xnb) Lw; 6th when hit 5; nvr gng wl; t.o & pu 11

[955²] P   **Namron (IRE)** 2-1F N Mitchell *Lw; reluct to go down; prom; slt ld 9 til jnd 13; cl 2nd 15 but wknd rap into 5th nxt; pu 3 out*

[875ᴾ] F   **Summer Pudding** (5a) 4-1 J Barnes *Rcd keen; ld til fell 3*

OFFICIAL DISTANCES: 6l, 2l   TIME: 6min 27.0s   TOTE: £9.00 DF: £1.40

1102 Open Maiden 5678&9yo (Div 2, Part 2), 12st   10 ran

[583⁸] 1   **PRAH SANDS** 7-2 J Young *Opened 4s; lw; handy; cl 3rd frm 9; hdwy to ld 13; drew 10l clr 16; unchall*

[881³] 2 25 **Restless Native (IRE)** (5a) 11-4 Miss P Gundry *7/2-11/4; lw; in tch in mid-div; 6th 12; lft poor 4th 15; kpt on stdly to 2nd aft 3 out; jmpd rt nxt; no ch w wnr*

[953²] 3 1½fs **Church Field (IRE)** 33-1 D Luff *Rcd keen early; cl 2nd til rdn 11; wkng in 5th & u.p 14; lft rem 3rd aft 2 out*

[856²] P   **Blackoid (FR)** (bl) 5-4F L Jefford *In tch but mists; 3rd when pckd 6; lft 8l 2nd 15; blun bad 16; 3rd & wkng when hit 2 out; imm pu*

[875ᵁ] F   **Final Chance** (5a) 8-1 Miss C Tizzard *Ld to 13; disp cl 2nd when fell 15*

[739ᴾ] F   **Humara (IRE)** (5a) 33-1 Miss G Edwards *Towards rr; 7th when mist 9; rr when fell 13*

     P   **Jolitan** (5a) 16-1 R Woollacott *Rr & mist 1; bhnd til pu 14*

[472ᴾ] P   **Madam Doris** (5a) 40-1 G Barfoot-Saunt *Sn rr; 8th 12; bhnd & pu 2 out; school*

[874ᴾ] P   **Sparkling Secret** (7a) 25-1 A Honeyball *Midfield; 6th 10; hdwy to 4th 14; lft 15l 3rd 15; wkng & mist nxt; pu 2 out; nt pushed*

[874ᴿ] P   **Vic's Girl** (5a) 100-1 G Weatherley *(xnb,boh) Sn bhnd; t.o & pu 11*

OFFICIAL DISTANCES: dist, dist   TIME: 6min 29.0s   TOTE: £1.30 DF: £1.10

Cheltenham (LH 10F,22J)
Thu, 20 Apr (SOFT, HEAVY in places)

1103 Griffin Nuumed HC   10 ran

[584¹] 1   **CAVALERO** 12-04 11-4 A Charles-Jones *Hld up; went 3rd 8 & 2nd 12-14; 2nd agn 17; hit nxt & blun 19; ld 3 out; stayed on game to edge clr flat*

[924ᶠ] 2 1¼ **Real Value (IRE)** 11-09 7-4F B Hitchcott *Lw; tk keen hld; ld 3; hdd 3 out; drvn & kpt on game; ev ch til outpcd final 100yds*

[1022¹] 3 16 **No Fiddling (IRE)** 11-10 13-2 C Williams *3rd/4th til went 2nd 14; mist 16 & rdn; releg 3rd & mist 17; prsd ldng pr til one pce 2 out*

[922¹] 4 25 **Saint Joseph** 11-10 9-1 Miss S Young *Scruffy; rr div; 9th 12; brief eff frm nxt; lost tch 16; went rem 4th 3 out*

[687³] 5 10 **Stay Lucky (NZ)** 12-00 16-1 Julian Pritchard *Mist 2; midfield; rmdrs 10; 4th 12; outpcd 14 & 12l 4th 16; lost rem 4th 3 out; t.o*

[800¹] 6 23 **Chasing The Bride** 12-00 13-2 M Miller *Hld up towards rr; mist 7; 6th 12; eff when jmpd slow 14 (water) & 15; strugg aft; t.o*

[1025ᴾ] 7 17 **Charmer's Well (IRE)** 12-00 33-1 T Gibney *Ld to 3; hit 8 & 9; prsd ldr to 12; lost nxt; sn outpcd; rem 4th when bad mist 17; t.o*

[922⁴] P   **Ballyea Boy (IRE)** 11-07 (vis) 50-1 R Webb-Bowen *2nd/3rd early; 5th when jmpd slow 7; mist 9; 8th & strugg 12; blun 15; pu aft nxt*

     P   **Itsforu** 11-11 20-1 A Wintle *Hdwy 4; sn lost plce agn; 7th 12; outpcd 14; t.o & pu 19*

[446³] P   **Muntafi** 11-10 20-1 M Keel *Nrly a last; mist 10; bad mist 11 & lost tch; t.o 13; pu 16*

TIME: 7min 22.0s   TOTE: £3.20; places £1.70,£1.10,£1.60 Ex: £7.20 CSF: £7.54 Tri: £32.50

Ashford Valley
Charing (LH 8F,19J) Sat, 22 Apr (GOOD)

1104 Restricted, 12st   11 ran

[1026ᴾ] 1   **GALLANT LORD (IRE)** 16-1 B Hitchcott *Cl up in midfield; hdwy to 4l 3rd 12; prsd ldr aft 15; hrd rdn 3 out; kpt on to ld flat*

[985ᵁ] 2 2 **Chill Factor** 8-1 Mrs E Coveney *Ld to 4; prsd ldr til ld agn 14; pushed along & 4l up 4 out; lkd wnr til wknd & hdd flat*

[830³] 3 fence **Mosta** (5a) 14-1 C Gordon *Ld 5-13; 5l 3rd aft 15; wknd frm nxt*

[709¹] 4 nk **Lord Ellangowan (IRE)** 4-1 D Dunsdon *Trckd ldrs; 6l 5th 12; lost tch 14; 25l 4th aft nxt; kpt on one pce*

[1039¹] 5 40 **Winward** (bl) 33-1 P M Hall *Prom til 10l 6th & lsng plce 12; t.o frm 15*

[706⁶] 6 6 **Bit Of A Do** 25-1 D Slattery *Hld up towards rr; 13l 7th 12; t.o frm 15*

[825⁴] U   **Ally Pally** 11-4 P York *Trckd ldrs; 5l 4th & rdn along 12; same plce when blun & ur 14*

[675⁴]	P		**Nattico (IRE)** 33-1 **Miss S Gladders** *A rr; 20l 8th & lsng tch 12; wl bhnd when pu 14*
[984¹]	U		**Oxendale** 9-4F **P Bull** *Swtng; ld til mist & ur 1*
[825ᴾ]	U		**Perripage** (vis) 33-1 **Miss A Sansom** *Ur 3*
[984⁷]	r		**The Herbivore (IRE)** (bl) 20-1 **Miss C Jiggins** *A towards rr; mist 8; jmpd slow 9; last & lsng tch when ref 12*

OFFICIAL DISTANCES: 2l, 8l **TIME:** 6min 30.0s **TOTE:** £13.20; places £3.20,£1.20,£2.60 **DF:** £9.90

1105 Open Maiden 56&7yo, 2m4f, 12st - 15J   8 ran

[576²]	1		**JUST THE BUSINESS** 7-4 **A Hickman** *Trckd ldrs in midfield; rap hdwy 7; ld 9; 10l up 11; made rest; mist 3 out; hrd rdn frm 2 out*
[709ᴾ]	2	12	**Native Dawn (IRE)** 7-1 **C Gordon** *Cl 2nd til ld 4-8; lost tch w wnr aft 10; 15l down 3 out; kpt on one pce*
	3	nk	**Relocate (IRE)** 14-1 **P York** *Hld up in last pr; hmpd 9; hdwy to 16l 4th 11; chsng wnr when jmpd slow nxt; kpt on one pce frm 3 out*
[985ᵁ]	4	½	**Sliabh Foy (IRE)** 33-1 **F Marshall** *Ld to 3; nrly ur 5; 15l 3rd & lsng tch 11; r.o agn app last*
	U		**Maximus (IRE)** (7a) 4-5F **B Hitchcott** *Rcd keen; hld up towards rr til mist & ur 8*
[775²]	P		**Satellite Express (IRE)** 20-1 **P Hickman** *Cl 3rd til chsd ldr 6-8; 18l 5th & wkng 11; no ch when pu 3 out*
[984⁴]	F		**Schisandra** (5a) 33-1 **P Blagg** *In tch in midfield til fell 9*
[829ᴾ]	P		**Toni's Tiger** 33-1 **M Gorman** *A last pr; lost tch 9; 43l 6th 11; t.o & pu 3 out*

OFFICIAL DISTANCES: 6l, ½l **TIME:** 5min 18.0s **TOTE:** £2.50; places £1.10,£1.40,£2.60 **DF:** £6.90

1106 Land Rover Mens Open, 12st   3 ran

[921ᶠ]	1		**STRUGGLES GLORY (IRE)** (7x) 8-13F **D Robinson** *Trckd rivals; impd to disp ld when lft wl clr 14*
[936ᴾ]	2	1½fs	**Spaceage Gold** (vis) 12-1 **K Edmunds** *A last; lost tch 8; lft rem 2nd 14*
[708¹]	F		**Prince Buck** (7x) 6-4 **C Gordon** *Set gd pce; 2-4l up most of way til jnd & fell hvly 14*

OFFICIAL DISTANCE: dist **TIME:** 6min 27.0s **TOTE:** £1.70 **DF:** £5.90

1107 Ladies Open   6 ran

[982ᵁ]	1		**DANGER FLYNN (IRE)** 8-1 **Miss C Holliday** *Swtng; hld up last; hdwy to press ldr 13; lkd hld aft 2 out; rallied flat; ld cl home*
[982¹]	2	hd	**My Wee Man (IRE)** (4x) evensF **Miss J Wickens** *Ld 4; made rest in narrow ld; went 2l up app last; no ex flat; hung lft & hdd cl home*
[827³]	3	30	**Polar Ana (IRE)** (5a) 6-1 **Miss S Gladders** *Hld up; impd to press ldr 11-13; 10l 3rd & lsng tch 15; no ch frm 3 out*
[824ᴾ]	4	12	**Storm Drum** (bl) 33-1 **Mrs E Coveney** *Ld 1-3; prsd ldr til lost plce 11; wl bhnd frm 15*
[985¹]	U		**Andrelot** (bl) 8-1 **Miss H Grissell** *Hmpd & ur 1*
[982³]	F		**Cadbury Castle** (5a) 3-1 **Miss J Grant** *Ld til fell 1*

OFFICIAL DISTANCES: nk, dist **TIME:** 6min 38.0s **TOTE:** £9.00; places £3.50,£1.60 **DF:** £10.20

The stewards enquired into possible interference between the first two after the last fence; they found the rider of My Wee Man had caused accidental interference to the winner and cautioned her as to her future riding

1108 S.E. Hunts Club Members, 12st   9 ran

[981ᴿ]	1		**RUSTIC REVELRY** 3-1F **P York** *Cl up; disp ld 7-13; prsd ldr til hrd rdn to ld aft 2 out; r.o flat; all out*
[708ᵁ]	2	1½	**Thats Dedication (IRE)** (7x) 5-1 **D Robinson** *Ld 5; jnd 7 til ld agn 14-2 out; 3l down last; rallied flat; clsng nr fin*
[883³]	3	15	**Peafield (IRE)** 8-1 **M Gorman** *Wl in tch in midfield; impd 12; chsd ldng pr 15; lost tch frm 16*
[825⁵]	4	15	**Call The Tune** (5a) 25-1 **P Hall** *Rr til hdwy 8; cl up 11; 20l 4th & lsng tch 15; kpt on one pce*
[830¹]	5	6	**Bit Of An Idiot** 12-1 **D Slattery** *Prom to 8; cl 7th 11; 25l 5th & wkng 15; no ch frm 4 out*
[886ᴾ]	P		**Glen Cherry** 14-1 **P Scouller** *A last pr; wl bhnd when pu 2 out*
[983¹]	P		**Jojo (IRE)** (7x) (bl) 7-2 **P Hickman** *Ld to 4; lost plce 8; last & lsng tch when pu 13*
[574⁵]	P		**Primitive King** (4x) 5-1 **Mrs E Coveney** *A towards rr; lsng tch when pu aft 13*

| [983²] | P | | **Sovereign Spray (IRE)** (4x) 9-2 **C Gordon** *Prsd lndg pr; rdn along 12; lsng tch when pu 15* |

OFFICIAL DISTANCES: 1l, dist **TIME:** 6min 28.0s **TOTE:** £7.00; places £2.30,£2.10,£2.60 **DF:** £20.50

1109 Hunt, 12st
6 ran

[980³]	1		**ISHMA (IRE)** (bl) 9-2 **D Page** *Hld up; trckd lndg pr frm 7; ld 11; made rest; 5l clr aft 15; rdn & drew rt away frm 2 out*
[982²]	2	30	**Velka** (5a) 6-4F **Miss P Ellison** *Ld to 2; cl up til lft in ld 8; hdd aft 10; chsd wnr rest of way; almost ur 15; wknd qckly aft 2 out*
[706⁵]	3	6	**American Eyre** 7-2 **Miss S Gladders** *Chsd ldrs in 3rd/4th; impd to cl frm 12; lost tch frm 14*
[983ᴾ]	4	fence	**Lucas Court** (bl) 5-2 **S Garrott** *W ldrs; ld 3-4; sn lost plce; 20l 4th 12; t.o 15*
	P		**Fergie (U)** (5a) 14-1 **D Brightling** *Settled last; 2 1l 5th 12; stdy hdwy to 6l 3rd app 15; eased & pu nxt*
[829ᴾ]	R		**Smooth Silk (IRE)** 33-1 **Miss S Robertson** *Hdwy to ld 5 til rn out 8*

OFFICIAL DISTANCES: dist, 10l **TIME:** 6min 34.0s **TOTE:** £5.30; places £2.10,£2.20 **DF:** £6.40

Essex & Suffolk
Higham (LH 8F,19J) Sat, 22 Apr (GOOD, GOOD to SOFT in places)

1110 Hunt
4 ran

[238ᴾ]	1		**LUSTY LIGHT** (bl) 1-3F **A Coe** *Ld 2; clr 10; fnce ahd 14; v easy*
[1007ᴾ]	2	fence	**Omidjoy (IRE)** (5a) 10-1 **M Polley** *Ld 1; cl 3rd 2-10; 10l 2nd & lsng tch 12; t.o 14; plodded on*
	3	40	**Blazing Times** (5ow) 7-1 **J Buckle** *A last; 8l last 3; 25l down nxt; t.o 12; fnce bhnd 14; plodded on*
[941⁵]	P		**Ger's Girl (IRE)** (5a) 4-1 **D Hayes** *Cl up; 1l 2nd & mist 5; drpd to dist 3rd by 11; 30l down when pu & dism aft 12; broke down*

OFFICIAL DISTANCES: dist, dist **TIME:** 6min 25.0s **TOTE:** £1.60

1111 Restricted, 12st
8 ran

[1038ᵁ]	1		**ULVICK STAR (IRE)** 7-2 **R Fowler** *Pulled up to ld 2; 2-3l up til jnd brief 15; 2l ahd nxt; jnd last; qcknd & r.o wl flat*
[940³]	2	1	**Squaddie** 2-1F **A Sansome** *Hld up in rr; 8l 6th 4; stdy hdwy frm 11; 4l 3rd 13; 1l 2nd 15; prsd ldr aft; level & ev ch last; hdd & no ex cl home*
[940²]	3	½	**Ar Aghaidh Abhaile (IRE)** 7-2 **G Cooper** *Trckd ldrs; 3l 2nd 8; hit 11; 4l 3rd 15; chsd ldr nxt; rallied to 2l 3rd 2 out; r.o; ev ch last; no ex cl home*
[1038ᴾ]	4	10	**Al Jawwal** 12-1 **Miss L Allan** (xnb) *Rr & jmpd rt 10; 10l last 11; in tch in 7th & forced along 12; lost tch 15; stayed on one pce*
[761³]	5	2	**Harry Tartar** 12-1 **N King** *In tch til outpcd & drpd to last 5; drvn along 13; little resp & no ch 15; one pce*
[759¹]	6	1	**On Target** 4-1 **N Bloom** *Trckd ldrs; 6l 5th 4; outpcd 10; wknd & strugg 14; no ch aft*
[940⁷]	7	30	**And Why Not** 33-1 **D Cook** *Chsd ldr; 3l 2nd 4; drpd to 8l 5th 12; lost tch 14; t.o 3 out*
[940ᴾ]	P		**Rathkeal (IRE)** 12-1 **D Parravani** *Chsd ldrs in 3rd/4th til wknd & drpd to rr 13; sn lost tch; t.o & pu 3 out*

OFFICIAL DISTANCES: 1l, ½l **TIME:** 6min 23.0s **TOTE:** £7.30 **DF:** £9.50

1112 Mens Open, 12st
4 ran

[1037¹]	1		**DAWN ALERT (IRE)** (7x) 1-6F **C Ward-Thomas** *Made all; 1-2l up til virt jnd 12-14; drew clr frm nxt; in comm 3 out; v easy*
	2	35	**Abuljjood (IRE)** (7a) 10-1 **M Hewitt** *Trckd ldr; 2l 2nd 8; prsd wnr 12-14; wknd 16; 15l 2nd & tired when jb rt 3 out; nursed home*
[938ᴾ]	3	1½fs	**Tan Hill Sparky** (5a) 12-1 **A Coe** *A last; mist 3; 15l down 4; jmpd v slow 8; sn t.o*
[936ᴾ]	R		**Take A Flyer (IRE)** 10-1 **N King** *Chsd wnr; 6l 3rd 5; 8l down when rn thro wing & ur 12*

OFFICIAL DISTANCES: dist, dist **TIME:** 6min 21.0s **TOTE:** £1.20

1113 Ladies Open
7 ran

[982⁴]	1		**CRACKING IDEA (IRE)** 4-6F **Mrs G d'Angibau** *Trckd ldrs; 4l 3rd 7; 2nd & clsng nxt; 1l 2nd 10; prsd ldr til ld 14; 5l up & in comm when lft wl clr 3 out; hvly eased flat*
[841²]	2	10	**Larry The Lamb** 6-1 **Miss T Hayter** *Trckd ldrs in 4/5th; hdwy to 3l 2nd 7; 5l 4th 11; hit 15; stayed on to 15l 2nd 2 out; chsd wnr vain aft*
	3	20	**Island Vision (IRE)** 25-1 **Mrs J Hughes** *Trckd ldrs in 3rd/4th; 2l 3rd 11; ev ch til wknd rap 16; dem mod 3rd 2 out; fin tired; btr for rce*

[841¹]	4	1	**Emsee-H** 4-1 *Miss Z Turner* Outpcd & sn detach in rr; hdwy to 8l 6th 8; lft 10l 4th app 3 out; one pce
[758F]	5	15	**Mill O'The Rags (IRE)** 3-1 *Mrs A Hays* Ld brief 2; 2nd nxt til drpd to 5th 9; nvr gng wl aft; t.o frm 13
[939⁷]	U		**Going Around** 33-1 *Miss A Webb* Ld 3 til jnd & mist 12; dem 3l 2nd 15; 5l down when rfo bend bef 3 out
[939⁶]	P		**Salmon Mead (IRE)** (bl) 25-1 *Miss N Barnes* Nvr gng wl; 4th & hit 4; drpd to last 6; 15l down 8; t.o when scrambled over 14 & pu

OFFICIAL DISTANCES: 8l, 20l TIME: 6min 20.0s TOTE: £1.50 DF: £4.30

1114 Confined, 12st   8 ran

[1017³]	1		**GENEROUS DEAL (IRE)** (bl) 3-1 *A Sansome* Pulling; 6th 3; 5l 4th & hdwy 11; 3l 3rd 12; ld 16; sn clr; stayed on wl; comf
[937⁵]	2	8	**Pearly Haze** (5a) 8-1 *N King* Pulling; ld 3-11; 4l 3rd & wkng nxt; lsng tch when lft 3rd 3 out; plugged into 8l 2nd nxt; no ch w wnr
[936¹]	3	2	**Kelly's Original** (3x) 4-7F *A Coe* Hld up off pce; 10l 4th 12; hdwy & lft 8l 3rd 3 out; 2nd brief nxt; wknd last
[1017F]	4	35	**Youcat (IRE)** (bl) 20-1 *N Bloom* Ld to 2; cl 4th aft til outpcd 14; 4l 5th & u.p when blun & nrly fell 16; sn lost tch
[1035⁴]	U		**Court Amber (IRE)** (bl) 16-1 *G Cooper* Trckd ldrs gng wl; 3rd til hdwy to 3l 2nd 8; ld 12; blun & nrly ur 14 & dem 3l 2nd; jmpd rt & ur 3 out
[935⁴]	F		**Dance On Sixpence** 16-1 *Mrs S Hodge* Cl up til fell 5
[318P]	P		**More Fun (USA)** 12-1 *W Wales* Rr 3; hmpd bad 5; nvr gng wl aft; t.o & pu 12
[935⁵]	U		**Royal Action** 20-1 *P Chinery* (xnb) Last when ur 1

OFFICIAL DISTANCES: 5l, 3l TIME: 6min 25.0s TOTE: £3.50 DF: £50.00

1115 Open Maiden (Div 1), 12st   9 ran

	1		**SHINING LEADER (IRE)** 7-4F *R Fowler* Jmpd rt; ld 2; made rest; prsd brief 15; qcknd 4l clr 16; 8l up when hit last; rdr lost irons & saddle slpd; just hld on und frantic drvng
[604U]	2	½	**About Time (IRE)** 4-1 *N Bloom* Trckd ldrs in 3rd frm 3; 5l 3rd til outpcd 10; 15l 5th 12; stayed on frm 3 out to 10l 3rd when lft w ev ch flat; r.o one pce; tk 2nd cl home
	3	½	**Clifford Bay** 5-1 *A Sansome* Hld up in last til hdwy 8; 8l 3rd 11; 2l 2nd 13; prsd ldr brief 15; nt qckn nxt; 6l 2nd & no imp 3 out; lft w ev ch aft ldr blun last; no ex & dem cl home
[1035⁵]	4	10	**Cosa Fuair (IRE)** 5-1 *C Jarvis* (xnb) Nvr gng wl & scrubbed along in mid-div; 5th 11; plodded on frm 13
[1039P]	P		**Casino Nell** (5a) 20-1 *A Harvey* Prom; 4l 2nd 3; chsd ldr aft; 2l down 11; outpcd nxt; dem 3rd 13; 10l 3rd 15; drpd to rr & pu 3 out; broke down
[1040P]	P		**Eltrym Flyer** (5a) 4-1 *N King* Pulling; trckd ldrs in 4/5th; 12l 5th & mist 13; wknd nxt; v tired 15; last when pu 3 out
[941⁷]	P		**Midnight Dynamite** 20-1 *P Chinery* Sn rr; last 7; t.o & pu 12
[1009P]	U		**Nursery Story** 20-1 *M Polley* A last pr; 7th when blun & ur 7
[755P]	P		**Take It Easy (IRE)** 20-1 *D Parravani* A strugg in rr; rem 7th when pu 12

OFFICIAL DISTANCES: ½l, ½l TIME: 6min 36.0s TOTE: £1.70 DF: £3.70

1116 Open Maiden (Div 2), 12st   9 ran

[760²]	1		**FOUNTAIN BANK (IRE)** (vis) 7-4 *A Coe* Prom; trckd ldng pr in 3l 3rd; jnd ldrs 16; sprinted into ld 3 out; sn wl clr; easy
[935²]	2	30	**Worthy Memories** (5a) 6-4F *A Sansome* Ld 2-3; cl 2nd til disp ld 8-16; rap outpcd & dem 3rd bef nxt; plodded on poor 3rd at last
[1039F]	3	5	**Bannagh Express (IRE)** 10-1 *M Lurcock* Nt fluent; prom; ld 4; jnd 8 til hdd & rap outpcd 3 out; v tired 2 out; dem poor 3rd at last
[1040P]	P		**City Run (USA)** 20-1 *Mrs T Holditch* A towards rr; lost tch 12; t.o & pu 15
[844⁶]	P		**Coolest By Phar (IRE)** 20-1 *C Ward-Thomas* Tubed; chsd ldrs in 3rd/4th til lost tch rap 11; releg last nxt; t.o & pu 13
[550P]	P		**Full Bore (IRE)** 20-1 *D Cook* Mid-div & strugg to go pce; lft 8l 4th 15; wknd rap; t.o & pu 2 out
[321U]	P		**Handy Boy** (7a) 20-1 *A Harvey* Rr 2; jmpd slow 5; sn bhnd; t.o & pu 12
[942P]	F		**Play Alone (IRE)** (12a) 4-1 *W Wales* 10s-4s; handy in 4th to 5; trckd ldrs frm 12; 6l 4th when fell hvly 15
[23P]	P		**River Surprise (IRE)** 20-1 *R Garrard* A last trio & rdr waving; no hdwy frm 12; bhnd when pu 14

OFFICIAL DISTANCES: 25l, 8l TIME: 6min 27.0s TOTE: £2.50 DF: £1.50

Fife

Balcormo Mains (RH 8F,18J) Sat, 22 Apr (GOOD to SOFT, SOFT in places)

1117 Hunt
4 ran

[921¹]	1		**FORDSTOWN (IRE)** (3ow) 4-6F **J Alexander** (bf) Ld/disp til 2nd 5; lft in ld 7; ½l up 9; 3l ahd app 3 out; 6l clr last; stayed on
	2	7	**Bells Hill Lad** 8-1 **M Alexander** (bf) Fat; a last; lft 4l 2nd 7; cl 2nd 9; 6l down & no ch 2 out; kpt on
	F		**Classic Crest (IRE)** (vis) 7-1 **S Clark** (bf) 8s-7s; ld/disp til 2l up app 5; fell 7
[717P]	B		**Whispering Steel** 9-4 **Miss L Bradburne** (boh) Trckd ldrs; 6l 3rd 4; 3½l 3rd when bd 7

OFFICIAL DISTANCE: 12l TIME: 7min 21.0s

1118 Restricted, 12st
10 ran

[976⁹]	1		**FLAMING SUNRISE** 8-1 **Miss D Calder** A.p; 2l 2nd app 5; disp ld nxt til ld app 2 out; stayed on wl
[976³]	2	2	**Mini Cruise** 4-1 **R Morgan** Cl up; 2½l 3rd 7; disp ld aft nxt til hdd & rdn 2 out; stayed on; a hld
[976ᴿ]	3	3	**Flower Of Dunblane** (5a) 8-1 **B Lusted** Trckd ldrs; 3l 3rd app 5; disp ld nxt; ev ch til hdd & outpcd app last; kpt on
[976⁷]	4	3	**Rock On Bud (IRE)** (tt) 10-1 **T Davidson** (xnb)In tch; 4l 6th 5; prog 15 & ev ch nxt; outpcd & rdn 2 out; kpt on
[915²]	5	1	**Border Glory** 6-4F **P Maitland-Carew** Chsd ldrs; 4l off pce 9; 3l 6th 3 out; sn outpcd; kpt on
[914P]	F		**Carbery Spirit (IRE)** (5a) 7-2 **L Morgan** (bf) Oht; rr til fell 2
	P		**Jack Dory (IRE)** 10-1 **D Da Silva** Cl up; 4l off pce & pushed along aft 9; rdn 11; wknd qckly app 13; 20l last when pu nxt
[1079P]	P		**No Problem Jac** (5a) (bl,tt) 12-1 **C Storey** Rr early; cl up 9; ev ch til wknd 16; 10l 6th when pu last
[498²]	F		**Overton Girl** (5a) 20-1 **R Nichol** A rr; 10l last 9; hrd rdn nxt; fell 11
[976⁵]	U		**Tursal (IRE)** 8-1 **A Crookston** Prom til bad mist & nrly ur 5; 6l 8th 6; 10l 7th & outpcd 13; wl bhnd 2 out; blun last & ur some way aft

OFFICIAL DISTANCES: 2l, 4l TIME: 7min 15.0s

1119 Greig Middleton Ladies Open
4 ran

[1079¹]	1		**BALISTEROS (FR)** 2-5F **Miss J Wormall** Lw; trckd ldr; 1l 2nd 9; ld aft 12; 7l up 15; 12l clr 2 out; unchal
[715²]	2	15	**Astrac Trio (USA)** 3-1 **Mrs A Hamilton** Oht; trckd ldrs; 8l 3rd 5; hit 12 & outpcd; 15l 3rd 15; nd; lft poor 2nd 2 out
[1079⁵]	3	2fncs	**Rallegio** 9-1 **Miss L Hislop** Swtng; a last; in tch til pushed along 11; sn lost tch; t.o 2 out
	P		**Ordog Mor (IRE)** 6-1 **Miss N Stirling** Ld; 2l up 5; 3l up 10; hdd aft 12; outpcd 15; kpt on wl til lost action & pu app 2 out; drpd dead

OFFICIAL DISTANCES: 25l, dist TIME: 7min 00.0s

1120 Land Rover Mens Open, 12st
7 ran

[975¹]	1		**BOW TIE** (7x) 5-4F **R Morgan** 6/4-5/4; lw; in tch; 4l 4th 5; prog 12 & 1l 2nd nxt; ld 15; rdn out flat
[1024⁴]	2	3	**Ensign Ewart (IRE)** (7x) 7-2 **C Storey** In tch in rr; 7l 6th 7; prog to 3l 3rd 14; 1l 2nd & rdn 3 out; ev ch last; no ex flat
[917³]	3	3	**Snapper** (7x) 2-1 **J Walton** Oht; swtng; hld up in rr; 7l last 8; stdy prog aft 12; 5l 5th 15; 8l 3rd app 2 out; one pce
[918⁵]	4	15	**Riverside Run (IRE)** 5-1 **A Robson** 6s-5s; oht; chsd ldrs; 5l 5th 8; 10l last & rdn 13; kpt on one pce frm nxt
[714⁴]	P		**Blair Castle (IRE)** (7x) 16-1 **L Morgan** (bf) Oht; swtng; ld; 2½l up 3; jnd 10; hmpd by loose horse & hdd aft; 20l 4th & wkng 14; pu nxt
[717P]	U		**Boss Morton (IRE)** (7x) 16-1 **J Alexander** (bf) Trckd ldr; 3l 2nd 4; 1l down when mist & ur 9
[973²]	P		**Boyup Brook** 8-1 **T Scott** Trckd ldrs; 5l 3rd 8; prog to disp ld 10; hmpd bad by loose horse (til rdr whipped it); ld 12; hdd & outpcd 15; 3l 3rd & mist nxt; pu 2 out

OFFICIAL DISTANCES: 3l, 3l TIME: 7min 06.0s

1121 Intermediate   5 ran

[1030²]	1		**POYNDER PARK (IRE)** evensF **L Morgan** Chsd ldrs; 2l 3rd 9; ld 12; jnd nxt; gng wl 16; ½l up & hrd prsd when lft clr 2 out
[917⁴]	2	15	**Lindon Run** (tt) 14-1 **T Davidson** Trckd ldr; 1l 2nd 8; hit nxt & pushed along; 3l 4th aft; hit 14 & rdn aft; tk poor 3rd 3 out; no ch when lft 15l 2nd nxt
[912³]	3	1½fs	**The Caffler (IRE)** 7-1 **W Ramsay** Oht; tde; ld; 1l up 5; jmpd lft & hdd 12; 2l 3rd nxt; sn wknd; 20l 4th aft nxt; t.o
[807¹]	F		**Queen Biddy (IRE)** (5a) 2-1 **C Storey** Cl up; 3l 4th 8; prog & 1l 2nd aft 10; disp ld 13; prsd ldr & ev ch when fell 2 out
[1080ᴿ]	P		**Slip Away** 4-1 **B Lusted** (bf) Oht; settled nr; 5l last 8; 10l down & outpcd 14; hit 16 & pu; btr for rce

OFFICIAL DISTANCES: 8l, dist TIME: 7min 10.0s

1122 Open Maiden 56&7yo   5 ran

[46⁴]	1		**MOUNT GAY** 2-1F **L Morgan** 3s-2s; hrd hld trckng ldr; ld aft 4; 2-3l up til qcknd clr frm 2 out; comf
[907²]	2	5	**Blackchesters** 9-4 **J Walton** Ld til hdd aft 4; trckd ldr; 1l 2nd 15; ev ch til easily outpcd aft 2 out; kpt on one pce
[1084³]	3	runin	**Solway Saffy** (12a) 5-2 **C Storey** 2 handlers; rr; pulling in 6l last 6; 4l 3rd & rdn 15; 10l 3rd & wkng nxt
[718ᴾ]	F		**Poppers** 12-1 **T Davidson** Prom; 3l 3rd app 5; disp 4l 3rd when fell 7
[910ᴾ]	P		**Stronacroibh** 4-1 **R Morgan** Oht; hld up in rr; 6l last 3; prog to disp 4l 3rd 6; mist 9; 6l 4th 13; sn wknd; 20l 4th 3 out; t.o & pu nxt

OFFICIAL DISTANCES: 8l, dist TIME: 7min 23.0s

1123 Open Maiden 8yo&up   11 ran

[718ᶠ]	1		**CARLINARE** 5-2JF **R Morgan** Rr; 10l 9th & rmdrs aft 2; prog 11; 3l 3rd at 3 out; ld aft nxt; stayed on u.p
[712³]	2	1½	**Harleyburn** (bl) 5-2JF **Mrs A Hamilton** Prom; 6l 5th 8; ld/disp aft 12 til 3l clr app 2 out; sn hdd; 2nd & ev ch til nt qckn flat
[915³]	3	1½	**Smiddy Lad** 7-2 **T Scott** (xnb) Swtng; rr; 10l last 8; stdy prog frm 10; 1l down & ev ch last; no ex
[718⁴]	4	5	**Myles Of Moss (IRE)** (5a) 6-1 **D Reid** In tch; 8½l 7th 7; 6l 8th 14; ev ch til outpcd 3 out; kpt on wl app last
[712⁵]	5	nk	**My Young Pet** 12-1 **J Alexander** Swtng; ld/disp; 1l 2nd 5; ev ch 2 out; outpcd app last; wknd & releg 5th flat
	6	3	**Crashballoo (IRE)** 12-1 **Miss K Roncoroni** Ld/disp early; 7l 7th at 9; lost tch 3 out; one pce
[978³]	7	3	**Meadowleck** (5a) (tt) 12-1 **B Lusted** (bf)In tch; 4l 3rd 6; ev ch til outpcd app 3 out; sn wknd
[977³]	P		**Good Profit** 6-1 **T Davidson** 10s-6s; a rr; 10l last & pushed along 10; lost tch 13; 20l last & rmdr nxt; t.o & pu 2 out
[913ᴾ]	P		**Jupiter Lord** 12-1 **C Storey** Mid-div; 6l 6th 8; prog to 4l 4th app 13; ev ch til mist 2 out; pu last; improve
[978ᴿ]	U		**Strong Debate (IRE)** 10-1 **N Crookston** Ld/disp til outpcd 15; staying on when ur last
[1024ᴾ]	P		**Tin Cup** (bf) 7-1 **L Morgan** Swtng; handy; 6l 4th 5; 5l 6th 3 out; wknd qckly app nxt; 15l down when pu last

OFFICIAL DISTANCES: 2l, 2l TIME: 7min 21.0s

The rider of Good Profit was fined £50 for incorrect use of the whip causing the horse to be marked

North Staffordshire
Sandon (RH 6F,16J) Sat, 22 Apr (HEAVY)

1124 Hunt   5 ran

[902¹]	1		**HATTON FARM BABE** (5a) 1-5F **Miss S Sharratt** Jmpd to ld 1; made rest at stdy pce; 10l clr 6; 25l up 12; stayed on str
	2	15	**Barley's Boy** (U) (1ow) 9-2 **Mrs S Tideswell** A 2nd; lost tch w wnr 6; 25l bhnd 12; clsd stdly frm nxt; 15l down last; no imp flat
[565ᴾ]	3	40	**Bermuda Buck** 9-1 **A Davenhill** A 3rd; stdly wknd frm 10; 40l bhnd 12; plodded on; slowed to walk last 25yds; collapsed & died sn aft rce
[972ᴾ]	4	20	**Crack 'n' Run** 25-1 **M Pennell** Hvly rstrnd & sn detach; 68l last 4; 2 fncs bhnd 7; r.o frm nxt; went rem 4th 12; nvr nr ldrs; eased to walk last 25yds

5   20   **Wolfgang Amadeus** (U) 25-1 R Dobney *Rdr had insufficient lead so consumed 2 bananas; chsd ldrs; t.o 4th 6; releg to 100l last 12; cont slow*

OFFICIAL DISTANCES: 15l, dist   **TIME:** 8min 12.0s   **TOTE:** £1.10

1125 Open Maiden, 12st   7 ran

[906F] 1   **LADY NEVADA (IRE)** (5a) 6-1 S Prior *A handy & gng wl; hdwy 12; went 2nd nxt; rdn to chall last; ld flat; r.o game*

[964F] 2   2   **Fruit Crop** (5a) 3-1 B Foster *Cl up; ld 3; mist & nrly ur 10; sn rec; 5l up 12-3 out; jnd last; hdd & no ex flat*

[1010²] 3   2   **Kings Choir** 2-1F Mrs C Boyes *A.p; ld to 2; chsd ldng pr frm 3 out; no ex app last; r.o flat*

[965²] 4   20   **Sharp Embrace** 6-1 J Burley *Cl up; disp 2nd 6-11; feeling pce nxt; bhnd frm 3 out*

[1010F] 5   25   **Bonnie Amy** (12a,3ow) 16-1 L Hicks *Last pr; outpcd 13; lost tch nxt; wl bhnd 2 out*

[801P] P   **Admiral Villeneuve** 10-1 Miss G O'Callaghan *Trckd ldrs in last pr til tired 11; lost tch & pu nxt*

[965P] P   **Robert The Rascal** 4-1 A Gribbin *Rn in snatches; prsd ldrs 11; sn lost plce; lost tch 3 out; bhnd when pu nxt*

OFFICIAL DISTANCES: 2½l, 2l   **TIME:** 7min 49.0s   **TOTE:** £6.00

1126 Ladies Open - 15J   5 ran

[1087U] 1   **AEGEAN FANFARE (IRE)** 7-2 Miss C Thomas *Jmpd v wl; ld 4; lft 10l clr 6; made rest; unchall*

[1014⁷] 2   30   **Just Marmalade** 16-1 Miss J Williams *Disp ld to 2; 3rd til lft 10l 2nd 6; chsd wnr vain aft; 20l down app 13; kpt on same pce*

        3   4½   **Sarcoid (IRE)** 4-1 Miss G O'Callaghan *A last pr; no ch frm 14; r.o flat; snatched 3rd cl home*

[1086¹²] 4 ½   **The Boiler White (IRE)** (6ow) 16-1 Miss J Froggatt *A last pr; lft 3rd 6; no ch frm 14; 3rd at last; dem cl home*

[431¹] U   **Bankhead (IRE)** (bl) 1-2F Miss C Spearing *Ld/disp to 3; 1½l 2nd when tk off too sn, blun & ur 6*

OFFICIAL DISTANCES: dist, 4l   **TIME:** 7min 38.0s   **TOTE:** £5.00
Fence 12 omitted - fallen rider

1127 Mens Open   3 ran

[1064³] 1   **ALASKAN HEIR** (vis) 9-4 G Hanmer *Ld 3; jmpd slow 6 & 12; clr frm nxt; tired but kpt on u.p frm 2 out*

[903²ᵈ] 2   6   **Class Of Ninetytwo (IRE)** 1-2F A Crow *Ld to 2; nt jw aft; reluct & rdn along frm 10; 6l down 3 out; hrd rdn & nt r.o frm 2 out*

[903ʳ] r   **Circus Colours** 6-1 L Hicks *Last when ref 1*

OFFICIAL DISTANCE: 6l   **TIME:** 7min 49.0s   **TOTE:** £2.50
The stewards interviewed the rider of the winner following a report from the Starter that he had anticipated the start; they warned him as to his future conduct

1128 Confined   9 ran

[781³] 1   **GARRYSPILLANE (IRE)** 6-4F G Hanmer *Cl up frm 5; trckd ldrs frm 11; 10l 3rd & lkd btn app 2 out; rap hdwy to chall last; sn ld; idled flat; hrd rdn & hld on cl home*

[960U] 2   1¾   **My Nominee** (bl) 2-1 L Stephens *Jw; ld; 2-3l up frm 2; went 6l clr 3 out; jnd last; sn hdd; v tired but r.o game flat; no ex cl home*

[1015⁶] 3   15   **Rosmarino** 2-1 A Dalton *Ld 1; trckd ldr aft; 6l 2nd & no imp 2 out; wknd & dem app last*

[1025P] 4   3   **Bucksfern** (bl) 16-1 R Bevis *Cl 3rd til mist 10; wknd nxt; lost tch 12; no ch aft*

[1086⁷] 5   6   **George Ashford (IRE)** 16-1 I Hooper *A last pr; detach frm 5; 30l last 11; plodded on at own pce*

[529⁴] P   **Inch Fountain (IRE)** 3-1 A Crow *Trckd ldrs in 4l/5th; short-lived eff 12; 15l down 3 out; wl btn 4th when pu 2 out*

[960⁵] P   **Ita's Fellow (IRE)** 8-1 M Prince *Mid-div; lost tch w ldrs app 12; bhnd when mist nxt; poor 5th when pu last*

[1008P] P   **Needwood Neptune** 25-1 P Bennett *A last pr; mist 1; detach by 3; 35l last when jmpd v slow 8; t.o & pu 10*

[901⁴] P   **Royal Segos** 25-1 S Shaw *Prom to 2; in tch to 10; stdly wknd; t.o last 3 out; pu last*

OFFICIAL DISTANCES: 2l, 15l   **TIME:** 7min 47.0s   **TOTE:** £2.50
The stewards enquired into the pulling-up of Inch Fountain; they accepted the rider's explanation that the horse had a history of lameness, but warned him for striking the horse on the shoulder with the whip in the forehand position

1129 Restricted, 12st   **11 ran**

[782P]   1   **WHITEGATES WILLIE** 7-2 G Hanmer *Rr til hdwy 6; disp ld when lft in ld 10; sn hdd; ld agn 12; drew wl clr frm nxt; 30l ahd last; eased last 20yds*

[902²]   2   25   **Brown Esquire** 2-1JF S Prior *Ldng trio til ld 11; hdd nxt; 2nd & outpcd 13; no ch w wnr aft*

[861⁶]   3   5   **Corkers Flame (IRE)** 20-1 R Bevan *Mid-div; hdwy 10; 5l 3rd 12; wknd nxt; nd aft*

[589P]   4   20   **Sugi** 16-1 I Wynne *Trckd ldrs in 5/6th; 7l 5th 12; wknd nxt; nd aft*

[782³]   5   15   **Mr Mark (IRE)** 12-1 D Sherlock *A towards rr; lost tch 9; t.o 12*

[1089⁶]   P   **Ballyhannon (IRE)** 25-1 Miss J Froggatt *A last pr; detach frm 4; jmpd slow 6; t.o 8 til pu 10*

[864⁵]   P   **Cookie Boy** 20-1 M Wilesmith *A towards rr; lost tch 9; 30l 6th when pu 12*

[986¹]   F   **Mr Pistachio (IRE)** (7a) 2-1JF T Stephenson *Trckd ldrs; 6½l 4th 12; disp 3rd & ev ch when fell nxt*

[966¹]   P   **Pinouli** (5a) 7-1 L Stephens *Prom; ld 3-4; cl 2nd til lost plce 9; eased & pu aft 11*

[782⁵]   P   **Scally Hill** (5a) 20-1 J Downes *Last frm start; blun & nrly ur 5; t.o nxt til pu 9*

[963²]   F   **Secret Alliance (IRE)** 14-1 A Crow *Ld 1-2; ld 5 til jnd & fell 10*

     OFFICIAL DISTANCES: 30l, 5l   TIME: 7min 33.0s   TOTE: £4.00

South & West Wilts

Larkhill (RH 13F,18J) Sat, 22 Apr (GOOD to SOFT becoming DEAD)

1130 Hunt, 12st   **6 ran**

[1057⁶]   1   **ARABITAN** (5a) 2-1 O Ellwood *Tchd 11/4; made virt all; drew clr 13; 12l ahd when pckd 15; mist 3 out; unchall*

[766ᵁ]   2   12   **Villains Brief (IRE)** (bl) 16-1 J Kwiatkowski *Went 2nd 4; rdn 14; no imp*

[764²]   3   15   **Indian Knight** (2ow) evensF J Green *Hld up; went 4l 3rd 7; outpcd 13; wl bhnd 15*

[1062²ᵈ]   U   **Bright Lady** (5a) 15-2 Miss R Green *14s-15/2; swtng; mist 3; 2nd/3rd to 7; 7l 4th when ur 9*

[732P]   U   **Highland Pearl** (5a) 50-1 Miss S May *(xnb) last ride; ld & ur 2*

     P   **Ifs And Buts** (12a,3ow) 8-1 G Weatherley *Bckwd; jmpd novicey; hld up last; 10l 4th ½way; went 12l 3rd 14; sn rdn & wknd; pu 15*

     OFFICIAL DISTANCES: 15l, 20l   TIME: 6min 44.8s   TOTE: £3.00   DF: c/f

1131 Open Maiden, 12st   **17 ran**

[455P]   1   **RUSHING AGAIN** (7a) 3-1 Miss P Gundry *8s-3s; bit bckwd; hld up; 12l 11th ½way; hdwy to 5l 4th 13; mist 14; went 3rd nxt; ld last; rdn out*

[825²]   2   2½   **Newby End (IRE)** 6-4F D Dennis *5/2-6/4; trckd ldrs; 7l 6th ½way; went 2nd 13; ld aft 2 out til hdd last; nt qckn*

[957²]   3   ½   **Mel (IRE)** 7-1 Miss M Eames *Swtng; jnd ldrs 6; 4l 3rd ½way; 4½l 5th 15; outpcd 3 out; 5l 5th nxt; stayed on wl flat*

[958³]   4   5   **Snowboy** 22-1 P Keane *A.p; went 2nd 6; ld 9; 3l clr 12 til hdd aft 2 out; sn rdn & wknd*

[455⁸]   5   20   **Sir Wynham** 20-1 J Case *Hld up & bhnd; 14th ½way; hdwy to 9l 8th 13; jnd ldrs 15; 7l 4th 2 out; wknd qckly*

[874³]   6   12   **L'orphelin** (7a) 8-1 M Shears *(xnb) Hld up; mist 1; blun 8; 7½l 7th ½way; hdwy 13; 5l 6th 15; wknd qckly & 15l 6th 2 out*

[958⁸]   P   **Calvary Hill** 33-1 Mrs W Doyne-Ditmas *(xnb) 2 handlers; nd; 10l 9th ½way; blun 10; 26l 11th 13; t.o & pu 3 out*

[933P]   r   **High Sturt** (5a) 50-1 J Snowden *Hld up; hdwy 8; 5l 4th ½way; 7l 7th 13; wkng when ref 14*

[1099⁴]   P   **Jug Of Wine** (5a) 40-1 G Weatherley *A bhnd; mist 8; 13th ½way; t.o & pu 14*

[955³]   P   **Just Reuben (IRE)** (7a) 33-1 A Ede *(xnb) Ld to 2; 2nd til ld 5; hdd 9; 6l 5th ½way; wknd qckly 11; t.o & pu 13*

[829P]   P   **Mandalady (IRE)** (5a) 50-1 M Legge *Tubed; a bhnd; 16th ½way; t.o 11; pu 13*

[753²]   P   **Mr Robstee** 6-1 J Trice-Rolph *Chsd ldrs; lost plce & 9l 8th ½way; 17l 9th 13; wl bhnd when pu 15*

[955P]   P   **Solo Trip** (5a) 50-1 J Barnes *Prom til lost plce 7; 12th ½way; t.o & pu 13*

[763²]   P   **Springvilla (IRE)** (1ow) 6-1 M Green *Prom; went 2nd & blun 9; 4l 3rd ½way; 10l 7th & wkng when pu 15*

[753³]   P   **Summer Haven** (5a) 8-1 L Lay *Nd; mist 1; 111 10th ½way; 25l 10th 13; t.o & pu 15*

     P   **The Handsome Friar** (tt) 66-1 O Ellwood *Tubed; ld 2; mist 3; hdd 5; wknd 7; 15th ½way; t.o 11; pu 13*

     U   **Wild Dream** (12a) 9-2 Miss S Vickery *Hld up; mist 3; 12th when ur 5*

     OFFICIAL DISTANCES: 1½l, ½l   TIME: 6min 34.5s   TOTE: £5.10   DF: £5.20

1132 Ladies Open   4 ran

[685¹]	1		**CASTLE LYNCH (IRE)** (5a) 4-7F **Miss P Gundry** Tchd 4/5; went 2nd 3; ld 4; drew clr 3 out; comf
[927ᵁ]	2	30	**Spring Marathon (USA)** 5-1 **Miss E Tory** 8s-5s; a 2nd/3rd; chsd wnr 9; ev ch 15; 5l 3rd & rdn 3 out; sn wknd; lft poor 2nd at last
[851ᴾ]	P		**Forbidden Waters (IRE)** (bl) 3-1 **Miss C Tuffin** Tchd 7/2; jmpd lft; ld til hdd 4; 5l 4th ½way; hit 11; rallied 13; rdn & wknd aft 14; bhnd when pu 3 out
[885³]	F		**Malihabad (IRE)** (bl) 7-1 **Miss A Goschen** 11s-7s; hld up in last; went 2nd 6-9; rdn 14; went 3l aft nxt; wknd 2 out; 12l 2nd when fell last

OFFICIAL DISTANCE: dist **TIME:** 6min 29.1s **TOTE:** £1.20 **DF:** £3.40

1133 Mens Open, 12st   7 ran

[968⁴]	1		**MOSTYN** 25-1 **P Pritchard** Ld 2; mist 14; sn hdd; ld 15; drew clr 2 out; stayed on wl
[954²]	2	12	**Kilmington (IRE)** (7x) 9-4 **J Barnes** Went 2nd 3 til rdn aft 14; chsd wnr 15; no ex 2 out
[521⁴]	3	25	**Longmore (IRE)** 5-1 **A Honeyball** Tchd 6s; lw; hld up; hdwy 6; 4l 3rd ½way; ld aft 14 til hdd 15; 7l 3rd & wkng 3 out; jmpd v slow last; fin tired
	P		**Berude Not To (IRE)** 7-2 **M Miller** Opened 4s; ld to 2; lost plce 6; 6l 5th ½way; w ldrs til wknd aft 14; pu 15
[631²]	P		**Merry Shot (IRE)** 7-1 **G Weatherley** Tchd 8s; hld up; 5l 4th ½way; w ldrs til rdn app 15; 8l 4th & wkng 3 out; blun 2 out; sn pu
[521ᴾ]	P		**Penny's Prince** 25-1 **Jeremy Young** Sn last & drvn along; lost tch & 18l 7th ½way; pu 10
[954⁵]	r		**River Swilley (IRE)** 2-1F **R Walford** Opened 5/2; swtng; hld up; 8l 6th ½way; jmpd slow & rmdrs 11; in tch til ref 13

OFFICIAL DISTANCES: 12l, dist **TIME:** 6min 30.0s **TOTE:** £6.60 **DF:** £14.80

1134 Countryside Alliance Club Members (Nov Rdrs), 12st   11 ran

[967²]	1		**NEWTON POINT** 4-1 **Mrs B Keighley** 6s-4s; a.p; 6l 4th ½way; went 3l 2nd & rdn aft 14; ld 3 out; drew wl clr aft nxt
[308ᴾ]	2	20	**Simple Arithmetic** 6-1 **M Goess-Saurau** Tchd 7s; hdwy to ld & pckd 6; hdd 8; 2l 3rd ½way; ld 13-3 out; wknd qckly 2 out
[749ᴾ]	3	½	**Cruise Free** (7x) 100-1 **S Sellars** Hld up; 10l 7th ½way; hdwy to 7l 6th 13; rdn 15; wkng when lft 10l 3rd 2 out
[1016¹]	4	3	**Copper Coil** (7x) 6-4F **M Walters** Lost plce 5; 8l 5th ½way; hdwy 11; 6l 5th 15; rdn & wknd 3 out
[878²]	5	20	**Mystery Aristocrat (IRE)** 7-2 **R Tory** 9/2-7/2; a bhnd; 20l 8th ½way; t.o 13
[929ᵁ]	6	2½	**Dromhana (IRE)** 50-1 **G Galpin** Drpd to rr 4; 25l 9th ½way; t.o 13
[953⁵]	7	5	**Mendip Son** (bl) 33-1 **R Arnold** (xnb) Ld 2-6 & 8-9; 2nd til ld 12; hdd 13; mist 14; 5l 4th & rdn nxt; wknd qckly aft 3 out; t.o & virt pu flat
[628²]	8	15	**Street Kid** 14-1 **Miss J Stewart** (xnb) Jnd ldrs 4; lost plce 8; 9l 6th ½way; lost tch 12; t.o 14
[1057³]	F		**Frozen Drop** 16-1 **T Bishop** (bf) Sn prom; lft 2nd 4-6; 9l 12-13; 4l 3rd when mist 15; wkng when fell 2 out
[931¹]	F		**Newman's Conquest** (5a) 8-1 **M Shears** 12s-8s; tde; 4th when fell 4; fell agn when tried to swerve into padd chute whilst loose
[1061ᶠ]	U		**Silver Hill** (5a) 50-1 **Miss B Fear** Ld to 2; 2nd til ur 4

OFFICIAL DISTANCES: 25l, ½l **TIME:** 6min 28.8s **TOTE:** £6.20 **DF:** £7.00

1135 Restricted, 12st   11 ran

[457¹]	1		**ABBOTS COURT (IRE)** (7a) 4-6F **R Walford** Tchd 4/5; ww; 7½l 8th ½way; hdwy to 5l 7th 13; went ½l 3rd 15; ld 3 out; drew wl clr 2 out; easy
[524ᴾ]	2	10	**Remember Ridemore (IRE)** 14-1 **A Honeyball** 2nd til lft in ld 5; hdd aft 14; 3½l 4th nxt; lft 6l 3rd 3 out; no ex; went 2nd app last
[748ᴾ]	3	7	**Doujas** (5a) 66-1 **S Sellars** Hld up; 10l 10th ½way; eff 6l 8th 13; 5l 6th & rdn 15; sn btn; 15l 4th 2 out; went 3rd flat
[629¹]	4	10	**Fever Pitch** 8-1 **Jeremy Young** Tchd 10s; w ldrs; 3½l 4th ½way; 4½l 6th 13; ev ch 15; lft 3l 2nd nxt; wknd rap aft 2 out
[958ᵁ]	5	12	**Old Harry's Wife** (5a) 40-1 **T Atkinson** Chsd ldrs; 4½l 5th ½way; lost plce & 8l 10th 13; 10l 9th & rdn 15; sn wknd; t.o
[828ᴾ]	6	3	**Ashburton Lord (IRE)** 40-1 **D Dennis** Tchd 50s; hld up; 5l 6th ½way; hdwy 11; went 2nd aft 12; ev ch 14; 4l 5th nxt; wkng when hmpd 3 out; t.o
[956¹]	P		**Harlequin Boy** (bl) 14-1 **M Miller** Jmpd lft; ld til jb lft 5; mist 9; 2nd/3rd to 13; wknd & 5½l 7th 15; pu 3 out

[212¹ᵉ]	U	**Little Native (IRE)** (7a) 3-1 **Miss P Gundry** (xnb) Tchd 7/2; lw; hld up; mist 6; last to 8; 7l 7th ½way; 6l 8th when mist & ur 15
[1043⁵]	P	**Lost Your Marbles (IRE)** (5a) 33-1 **J Mead** 2 handlers; swtng; rn in snatches; lost plce & 8½l 9th ½way; rallied 12; 4l 5th nxt; wknd 14; t.o & pu 2 out
[560⁶]	U	**Lynphord Girl** (5a) 50-1 **J Barnes** Ldn ldrs 4; 4th when hmpd & ur 5
[958ᶠ]	F	**Pharniskey (IRE)** 8-1 **O Ellwood** Tchd 10s; swtng; sn prom; lft 2nd 9 til mist 12; ld aft 14 til hdd & fell 3 out

OFFICIAL DISTANCES: 12l, 8l TIME: 6min 41.8s TOTE: £1.60 DF: £10.30

Tiverton Staghounds
Bratton Down (LH 8F,19J) Sat, 22 Apr (HEAVY)

1136 Hunt   7 ran

[727ᴾ]	1		**VALNAU (FR)** 4-5F **C White** Lw; in tch in 3rd; blun bad 12; jnd ldrs 14; ld nxt; forged clr 3 out; stayed on dour; all out
[1097³]	2	30	**Master Kiwi (NZ)** 12-1 **G Richards** Settled 4th; mist 11; 20l 4th 14; r.o stdly frm 16; tk 10l 2nd 2 out; no ch when hit last; fin tired
[932ᴾ]	3	4	**Mayhem** 4-1 **M Sweetland** Tchd 7s; last early; rdn 11; poor 5th when jmpd rt 13; rem 5th 3 out; stayed on up final hill to pass 2 tired rivals run-in
[954ᴾ]	4	10	**Romalito** 9-4 **N Harris** Ld/disp; blun 4; wknd stdly frm 16; no ch frm 2 out
	5	1	**Another Bula (IRE)** 33-1 **Miss S Robinson** Oht; ld/disp to 15; cl 3rd nxt; wkng when hit 3 out; blun bad nxt; tired
	6	40	**Mutual Memories** 33-1 **R Burrow** 2 handlers; bit bckwd; bhnd frm ½way; climbed fncs & wl t.o clsng stages
[563ᴾ]	P		**Ru Bidding** (5a) 50-1 **R Emmett** 5th ½way; bhnd frm 12; t.o when mist 16; pu nxt

OFFICIAL DISTANCES: 25l, 5l TIME: 7min 21.0s TOTE: £2.10

1137 Intermediate, 12st   3 ran

[853²]	1		**ARDBEI (IRE)** 5-2 **L Jefford** Lft in ld 1; set stdy pce; jw til hit 2 out; jnd last; drvn & hld on game run-in
[849¹]	2	nk	**Fossy Bear** (5a) 2-5F **Miss S Young** (b4) Opened 4/9; cl last; hdwy to chall 2 out; level & ev ch last; rdn & nt qckn cl home
[929⁵]	U		**Prudent Miner (IRE)** 12-1 **R Skinner** Ld; 2l up when rfo 1

OFFICIAL DISTANCE: nk TIME: 7min 25.0s TOTE: £2.60

1138 Mixed Open, 12st   8 ran

[722¹]	1		**BLACK DANTE (IRE)** 100-30 **A Charles-Jones** Lw; in tch & gng easy in 4th; eff 3 out; ld nxt; easily drew clr app last; stayed on str; v impressive
[730¹]	2	6	**Wibbley Wobbley** 7-2 **Miss J Cumings** Lw; prom; cl 3rd 10; disp ld nxt til hdd app 2 out; kpt on wl; gd eff
[954⁴]	3	8	**Red Parade (NZ)** 20-1 **D Alers-Hankey** (xnb) Lw; rcd keen; prom til slt ld 5; jnd 11 til outpcd 2 out; 4th & u.p app last; stayed on to tk 3rd run-in
[878¹]	4	20	**Horus (IRE)** (7a) 6-4F **L Jefford** Tchd 13/8; lw; hld up in tch; slt mist 4; hdwy 14; cl 3rd & slt mist 3 out; chall & ev ch app nxt; sn wknd; btn & hvly eased to lose 3rd run-in
[930⁵]	5	5	**Willie B Brave (IRE)** 33-1 **R Woollacott** Tchd 50s; in tch in 7th ½way; 5th & pushed along 14; nt rch ldrs; btn 5th 3 out; walked in
[854²]	6	1	**Bitran** (7x) 9-1 **T Greed** Slt ld to 5; prom til wknd 10; btn 6th 16; tired nxt; t.o
[683⁵]	P		**Full Alirt** (5a) 10-1 **Miss S Young** (b4) A last; bhnd frm 10 til pu 2 out
	P		**Leonard's Dream** (5a) 100-1 **J Scott** Midfield; slt mist 6; went 2nd 8; disp ld 10 til mist nxt; wknd qckly; rr & pu 14

OFFICIAL DISTANCES: 5l, 10l TIME: 7min 14.0s TOTE: £4.30

1139 Confined   2 ran

| [735²] | 1 | | **IRANOS (FR)** (bl) 1-4F **L Jefford** Made virt all; mist 10; in comm when hit 2 out; pushed clr run-in |
| [355²] | 2 | 20 | **Cool Clown** 3-1 **B Trickey** Cl up; disp ld 10-12; trckd ldr til eff & ev ch last; sn wknd; eased to walk last 100yds |

OFFICIAL DISTANCE: 8l TIME: 7min 22.0s TOTE: £1.20

1140 Confined Restricted, 12st - 16J   10 ran

| [729²] | 1 | | **SHOBROOKE MILL** 2-1F **A Charles-Jones** (xnb) Tchd 3s; lw; handy; mist 11; prog to jn ldrs 13; ld 16; drew clr aft nxt; v easy |

[932F]	2	20	**Jabiru (IRE)** 3-1 D Alers-Hankey *Opened 5s in plce; towards rr; 7th 12; staying on in 3rd but lot to do aft 16; went 15l 2nd app last; no ch w wnr*
[934¹]	3	12	**Fursan (USA)** (tt) 8-1 P Phillips *2 handlers; swtng; rstrnd at start; pulled hrd & went 2nd 5; pckd 9; cl 2nd 16; chsd wnr vain til wknd app last; fin tired*
[1042⁴]	4	15	**Kimbross** (vis) 12-1 G Richards *Sn rr & lkd reluct; bhnd frm ½way; walked in*
[958U]	P		**Devonshire Lad** (bl) 66-1 N Harris *Midfield; 7th when jmpd rt 11; bhnd when pu 16*
[728⁸]	P		**Frankly Fear** 20-1 J Young *Towards rr til pu 12*
[931³]	U		**I Like The Deal** (5a) 9-2 L Jefford (xnb) *Midfield; 6th ½way; just in tch in 5th when blun & ur 16*
[560⁵]	P		**Nearly All Right** 50-1 C White *Lw; ld & went clr early; hdd aft 12; lost ground stdly; btn 5th when pu last*
[1043P]	U		**Pallingham Lad (IRE)** (tt) 11-2 S Kidston *Prom; slt mist 7; 6th & pushed along 12; no imp; btn 4th when blun bad & ur last*
[880¹]	F		**Pendragon** 4-1 N Mitchell *Hdwy 9; 12l 4th nxt; jnd ldrs 13; slt ld when fell 16*

OFFICIAL DISTANCES: 15l, 10l TIME: 7min 15.0s TOTE: £3.50
Fences 2, 10 and 17 omitted from this and the last race - state of ground, original fence numbers used

1141 Confined Maiden (Non-Rules Rnrs) 56&7yo, 12st - 16J   3 ran

[733³]	1		**TONY'S TIME** 9-4 N Harris *Cl 2nd til ld 11; mist 15; lft virt solo nxt; cruised home; unchall*
[563P]	2	40	**North Newcombe** 10-1 T Greed (xnb) *In tch in 3rd til wknd 11; nt pushed & jmpd novicey; lft rem 2nd 16*
[933²]	F		**Happy Team** (5a) 4-9F L Jefford *Set slow pce; blun 8; hdd 11; mist 12; w wnr when fell 16*

OFFICIAL DISTANCE: dist TIME: 7min 31.0s TOTE: £1.90

Vale of Aylesbury
Kimble (LH 7F,15J) Sat, 22 Apr (SOFT, v SOFT)

1142 Hunt   6 ran

[785⁵]	1		**OBOEDIRE (IRE)** evensF D Barlow *6/4-evens; lw; trckd ldrs in 2nd/3rd; 3l 3rd 8; lft 100yds clr 10; plodded on*
[74P]	2	9sec	**Bally Clover** 10-1 Miss L Walter *1st ride; rdr unstdy; qckly lost tch in 5th; lft 100yds 2nd 10; plodded on*
	3	9sec	**Toytown King (IRE)** 33-1 R Betts *t.o; fnce bhnd by 9*
[1006⁵]	U		**Dark Rhytham** 9-2 S Atkins (xnb) *2nd/3rd til hmpd & ur 10*
[1009¹]	U		**Derryair** 100-30 J Owen *Oht; ld til blun & ur 10*
[514P]	P		**Five O'One (IRE)** 16-1 R Cope *Jmpd sketchy in 3rd/4th; wkng rap when pu aft 9*

OFFICIAL DISTANCES: 20l, 20l TIME: 7min 22.0s

1143 Intermediate, 12st   4 ran

[785⁴]	1		**FENCING MASTER** 5-1 A Barlow *Ld 2-4 & frm 5; just hdd but jmpd to ld agn last; hld on game*
[1006⁵]	2	1	**Right Company** 9-4 B Pollock *Lw; settled cl 3rd/4th; chall to 2nd 2 out; slt ld & jmpd delib last; tried to rally cl home; a hld*
[785²]	3	12	**Grecian Star** 11-8F J Tarry *2 handlers; oht; cl 3rd/4th; rdn bef 12; went 2nd brief 3 out & ev ch nxt; slowed qckly aft*
[887¹]	P		**Final Analysis (IRE)** 5-2 J Owen *4s-5/2; lw; ld; nt fluent & rmdr 1; hdd 3; ld 4-5; rdn 8 & aft 10; mist 11; ev ch til slowed rap aft 3 out; pu nxt*

OFFICIAL DISTANCES: 1l, 8l TIME: 7min 03.0s

1144 Mens Open   7 ran

[884²]	1		**RECTORY GARDEN (IRE)** 7-4F R Biddlecombe *Lw; jw; trckd ldrs; 4l 4th 9; idly rdn & sn 8l adrift; 10l 3rd 12; clsd to 7l 3rd 2 out; stayed on game; lft in ld 50yds out (horse does it all for rdr)*
[1064¹]	2	2	**Strong Chairman (IRE)** 4-1 S Waley-Cohen *Ld to 2; chsd ldr til ld agn 12; hdd aft 3 out; 3l down nxt; rallied & ev ch when hit last & rdr nrly f.o front; nt qckn aft*
[389¹]	3	hd	**Castle Folly (IRE)** (bl) 5-2 R Lawther *4s-5/2; ld 2-12; ld aft 3 out; 3l clr nxt; lkd wnr til threw in towel & swerved aft last; hdd & nt r.o final 50yds (must have a running rail)*
[749⁷]	4	7	**Fair Crossing** 8-1 M Emmanuel *Rr trio & adrift til clsd in 6l 5th 8; lost tch aft 10; no ch frm nxt but stayed on apps aft 2 out*
[919P]	P		**Caballus (USA)** 25-1 N Ridout *Set off last; pulled v hrd & 2nd by 4; lost plce 7; 6th 8; slowed rap frm 10; t.o & pu aft 11*

| [1016ᴾ] | P | | **Hope's Delight (IRE)** 33-1 **R Smith** *Blun 2; mists in last pr & sn lost tch; t.o when hit 8; u.p 10; pu aft 11* |
| [800ᴾ] | P | | **My Shout** 4-1 **B Pollock** *Lw; oht; settled 3rd; rmdrs aft 7; 3l 3rd 8; hit 10 & nvr gng wl aft; no ch 12; pu 2 out* |

OFFICIAL DISTANCES: 2l, hd **TIME:** 7min 01.0s

1145 Ladies Open　　　　　　　　　　　　　　　　　　　　　　6 ran

[1007¹]	1		**LILY THE LARK** (5a) 8-13F **Miss H Irving** *Lw; sn 2nd; jnd ldr 5-8; made rest; went 10l clr 12; drew rt away; hvly eased flat*
[319ᴾ]	2	25	**My Best Man** (bl) 3-1 **Mrs T Hill** *Last pr; jmpd slow 9 & rmdr; 8l 5th & outpcd when hit 11; disp 15l 3rd & rdn nxt; plodded into rem 2nd aft last*
[787³]	3	1	**Lucky Christopher** 5-1 **Miss R Goodwin** *Trckd ldrs; bumped along 8; went 10l 2nd 12; nvr nr wnr aft*
[886⁵]	P		**Castle Arrow (IRE)** 8-1 **Miss S Duckett** *Ld in start; final trio; disp 4l 3rd 8 & 15l 3rd 12; rap lost tch; t.o & pu 2 out*
[1007⁷]	P		**Erbil (IRE)** 33-1 **Miss S Mason** *Ld to 5; disp ld to 8; hit 10 & rdr drpd reins; wknd rap 12; pu 3 out*
[969ᴾ]	P		**Quite A Miss** (5a) 20-1 **Miss L Parrott** *2nd til hit 2; mist 6 & releg last; lost tch & jmpd slow 7; t.o & pu aft 11*

OFFICIAL DISTANCES: 12l, 1l **TIME:** 7min 03.0s

1146 Restricted, 12st　　　　　　　　　　　　　　　　　　　　12 ran

[610ᴾ]	1		**HAZY SEA (IRE)** 33-1 **C Weaver** *Hld up & bhnd; 14l 8th app 11; gd prog 3 out to 4th nxt; str rn to ld aft last; rdn clr*
[1009⁴]	2	3	**Blayneys Privilege** 20-1 **Miss T Habgood** *Ld 2; went clr 11; still 5l ahd app 2 out; hdd app last; rallied flat; nt rch wnr*
[871⁴]	3	3	**Gangster** 4-1 **R Cope** *Trckd ldrs; 6th 8; eff 11 to 3rd nxt; ev ch app 2 out; rdn & nt qckn*
[1009ᶠ]	4	1	**Luckashan (IRE)** (7a) 7-2 **B Pollock** *Nt jw in mid-div; 7th 8; eff aft 12 til 2nd app 2 out; sn ld & went 3l clr; lkd wnr til tied up dramatic flat & stpd to nil*
[734⁶]	5	4	**Encima Del Rio (IRE)** 8-1 **B King** *Ld to 2; sn lost plce & midfield; chsd ldrs til one pce aft 2 out*
[791³]	6	2	**Lady Emerald** (5a) 8-1 **J Tarry** *2nd/4th; mist 11; 6l 2nd 12; drvn & wknd app 2 out*
[940ᴾ]	7	½	**Dynoun** 10-1 **D Crosse** *Numerous mists; mid-div; u.p 10; 6th app 11; chsd ldrs til wknd aft 3 out*
[392²]	8	6	**Dark Challenger (IRE)** 5-2F **R Lawther** *Sn 2nd; prsd ldr til releg 4th app 12; drvn & nt r.o; btn app 2 out*
[513ᴾ]	U		**Dark Knight** (xnb) 4-1 **J Owen** *7th aft 3; mist & ur 5 (became tangled in wire when loose & cut bad)*
[886⁹]	P		**Grange Prize** 33-1 **Miss K Henry** *Sn strugg; lost tch 6; t.o 8; pu 2 out*
[1009ᴾ]	P		**Rolpen** 11-1 **J Gasper** *Hdwy app 5; 5th 8; wknd to 15l 9th app 11; t.o & pu aft 3 out*
[791ᶠ]	P		**Royal Orchard** 20-1 **C Marriott** *Nvr went a yard & rdn all way; last pr; 15l last 4; t.o 8; pu aft 10*

OFFICIAL DISTANCES: 2l, 3l **TIME:** 7min 06.0s

1147 Open Maiden　　　　　　　　　　　　　　　　　　　　　11 ran

[517²]	1		**HESSAC (FR)** (7a) 5-4F **B Pollock** *Hld up in midfield; 16l 4th aft 10; clsd rap 3 out to ld nxt; imm qcknd clr; impressive*
	2	12	**Bright Vulcan** 6-1 **T Illsley** *Prsd ldrs; went 2nd 8; ev ch 3 out; 3rd & drvn nxt; chsd wnr vain frm 2 out; mist last*
[754⁸]	3	25	**Super Saffron** (5a) 6-1 **P Young** *Ld; 3l clr 10; drvn & hdd 2 out; wknd rap & climbed last*
[1012⁹]	P		**Cottage Light** 33-1 **N Ridout** *Mist 1; sn rr & reluct; t.o 7; pu 3 out*
[1012⁹]	P		**Dennis** 12-1 **J Tarry** *Midfield; outpcd when blun 9; 18l 6th 12; t.o & pu last*
[785ᶠ]	P		**Latzio** (5a) 6-1 **R Cope** *(xnb) Oht; 2 handlers; pulled hrd; prsd ldr to 7; 15l 3rd & wkng rap nxt; pu 10*
[900ᴾ]	P		**Master Banker** 10-1 **J I Pritchard** *Rdn padd; nt jw; rr div; bad mist 2; blun 9; 20l 5th aft 10; t.o & pu 2 out*
	P		**Misblaize** (5a) 14-1 **M Wall** *Bckwd; novicey in last trio; t.o 7; pu 8*
[1039ᴮ]	P		**Out By Night (IRE)** 7-1 **D Barlow** *Hld up trckng ldrs; outpcd by ldng pr 8; 15l 3rd aft 10; brief eff in 10l 3rd 12; sn strugg; v tired when pu 2 out*
[738ᴾ]	P		**Shouldhavesaidno (IRE)** (5a) 20-1 **C Weaver** *Last trio & nvr gng wl; t.o 7; pu 3 out*
[792⁴]	P		**Stormhill Soldier** 16-1 **J Owen** *Mist 2; midfield; bad mist 5; strugg to 10; pu 3 out*

OFFICIAL DISTANCES: 12l, 20l **TIME:** 7min 13.0s

Vale of Lune Harriers

Whittington (LH 8F,18J) Sat, 22 Apr (GOOD, GOOD to SOFT patches)

1148 Hunt
4 ran

[1025⁵]	1		**THE CROOKED OAK** 1-2F G Thomas _Ld til aft 2; prom til ld agn app 6; hdd aft 10; ld agn 2 out; drew clr aft last_
[778ᴾ]	2	7	**Sparkling Gift (IRE)** (5a) 4-1 Miss A Price _Handy; ld aft 10; hdd 2 out; nt fluent when no ex last_
[814³]	3	25	**Rebel King** 10-1 J R Barlow _Bit bckwd; chsd ldrs; chall 4 out; sn rdn; wknd app 2 out_
[962ᴾ]	4	fence	**See You Always (IRE)** (2ow) 12-1 M Bowker _Ld aft 2; hdd app 6; bhnd aft 10; sn lost tch; t.o_

OFFICIAL DISTANCES: 7l, 25l TIME: 7min 16.7s

1149 Confined, 12st
8 ran

[960²]	1		**BLANK CHEQUE** 5-1 D Coates _Hld up & bhnd; 20l down 3 out; str rn to ld aft 2 out; jmpd rt last; forced wide by loose horse entering straight; all out_
[781²]	2	1½	**Three Saints (IRE)** 7-2 M Worthington _Prom; ld 3 out; hrd prsd when mist nxt; sn hdd; rallied flat; stayed on_
[661⁸]	3	12	**Pennine View** 20-1 Mrs C Ford _Ld; rdn & hdd 3 out; wknd qckly_
[960¹]	4	3	**Aly Daley (IRE)** (6x) 5-1 Miss A Price _Prom; lost plce app 11; sn rdn & outpcd; nd aft_
[1025³]	U		**Sounds Strong (IRE)** (5x) 9-2 N Bannister _Handy; mist 6; blun & ur 9_
[961ᴾ]	P		**St Athans Lad** 50-1 B Seddon _Unruly start; ss; sn t.o; pu 11_
[812⁴]	P		**Tidaro Fairy (IRE)** 12-1 J Townson _In tch; outpcd 13; sn wl bhnd; t.o & pu 15_
[811¹]	U		**Trivial (IRE)** (5a) 7-4F P Robson _In tch; hdwy 10; jmpd lft 12; ev ch when blun & ur 2 out_

OFFICIAL DISTANCES: 1½l, 12l TIME: 7min 00.5s

1150 Greig Middleton Ladies Open
7 ran

[960³]	1		**HELLO ME MAN (IRE)** 7-1 Mrs K Diggle _Swtng; in tch; nt fluent 9; prog 11; mist 15; sn ld; 5l clr 2 out; 2l ahd when lft clr last_
[963³]	2	15	**Tale Bridge (IRE)** 5-1 Mrs C Ford _Ld to 6 & brief 7; cl up aft til wknd app 3 out; lft rem 2nd at last_
[974²]	3	4	**Sharp Thyne (IRE)** (bl) 4-1 Miss M Bremner _Handy; ld app 8; hdd app 3 out; wknd app nxt_
[813²]	4	25	**Staigue Fort (IRE)** 7-2 Miss V Stubbs _Prom; ld 6-7; handy; nrly tk wrong course aft 10; rmdrs & wknd 12; lost tch 15_
[962²]	U		**Ambrose** 7-1 Miss T Clark _(bf) Trckd ldrs til blun & ur 5_
[974³]	P		**Denim Blue** 6-1 Miss P Robson _Jmpd rt sev times; hld up in tch; eff 14; wknd aft 15; t.o & pu 2 out_
[1079⁴]	U		**Oat Couture** 5-2F Miss S Johnstone _Hld up in last; hdwy 14; ev ch 3 out; 5l down 2 out; 2l down & clsng when blun & ur last_

OFFICIAL DISTANCES: 15l, 4l TIME: 6min 56.3s

1151 Land Rover Mens Open, 12st
9 ran

[592⁴]	1		**MYTTON'S CHOICE (IRE)** 4-1 C Barlow _Hld up in tch; hdwy 9; chall 14; ld on bit 3 out; nt fluent last; all out; fin lame_
[493⁷]	2	¾	**Kilminfoyle** 11-1 P Robson _Sis; hld up; hdwy & mist 9; sltly outpcd aft 13; eff agn app 3 out; went 2nd last; r.o flat_
[961ᴾ]	3	12	**Russian Castle (IRE)** (7x) 33-1 K Burke _Tk keen hld; mists; prom; ld aft 15; hd nxt; wknd aft 2 out_
[814¹]	4	3	**Vicosa (IRE)** (7x) 6-4F C Hoggart _Hld up in tch; eff 11; rmdrs nxt; wknd aft 15_
[812¹]	5	15	**Shanballymore (IRE)** 4-1 R Owen _In tch w chsng group; hmpd 9; strugg & no ch frm 14_
[1073³]	F		**Corbleu (IRE)** 6-1 M Walford _Chsd clr ldrs; mist 6; fell 9_
	P		**Crofton Lake** 33-1 D Jewett _Chsd ldrs; drvn along 12; wknd aft 15; t.o & pu 2 out_
[1025ᴾ]	P		**Haveafewmanners (IRE)** (5a) (tt) 7-1 M Worthington _Ld; mist 4 out; sn hdd & wknd; wl bhnd when pu 2 out_
[814⁴]	P		**Larkshill (IRE)** (7x) 14-1 J R Barlow _A bhnd; t.o & pu 3 out_

OFFICIAL DISTANCES: ¾l, 12l TIME: 7min 07.0s

1152 Intermediate, 12st   9 ran

[815¹]	1		**ALLRITE PET** (5a) 11-10F *Miss P Robson Confd rdn & a gng wl; handy; eff to chall 14; sn clr w rnr-up; blun & hdd 3 out; ld agn nxt; 4l up when idled & jmpd slow last; rdn & rallied flat (aided by loose horse); comf*
[1090⁶]	2	6	**Perambulate (NZ)** (5x) 9-1 *Miss T Clark Cl 2nd mostly til ld/disp frm 14; sn clr w wnr; lft in ld brief 3 out; hdd & one pce nxt; btr for rce*
[998²]	3	6	**Seven Four Seven** (5a) 5-2 *K Rosier Jw; nt keen & sn last; grad hdwy frm 10; went 15l 3rd aft 15; hmpd & switched rt app nxt; stayed on wl; nt rch ldrs; lame aft*
[816¹]	4	10	**Dram Hurler (IRE)** 9-2 *Mrs C Ford Set modest pce til jnd aft 14; 4th & one pce nxt; no ch frm 3 out*
[533ᵖ]	5	20	**Running Frau** (5a) 20-1 *G Thomas Sn towards rr & nd; lost tch 10; sn t.o*
[712ᵖ]	P		**Boris Brook** 8-1 *T Oates Nt fluent; trckd ldrs in 4th; hmpd 9 & lost sev lengths; rallied to 4th agn 11; wknd 14; t.o & pu 2 out*
[567ᵖ]	P		**Buck Run (IRE)** 10-1 *C Barlow Sn bhnd; t.o & pu 2 out*
[1028ᵖ]	U		**La Maja (IRE)** (5a) 50-1 *Miss J Foster 2nd & blun bad 1; trckd ldr to 12; 3rd when hmpd by loose horse, blun bad & ur 13*
[1081⁵]	U		**Tenella's Last** (5a,80w) 25-1 *T Mounsey-Heysham Rdr novicey & swerving around; nt fluent; trckd ldrs on outer til blun & ur 9*

OFFICIAL DISTANCES: 6l, 6l   **TIME:** 7min 05.3s

1153 Open Maiden   14 ran

[363ᵁ]	1		**DERE STREET** 4-1 *T Oates Swtng; ld; nt fluent 14; hdd 15; ld agn nxt app nxt; hrd rdn & edged lft flat; kpt on game*
[964ᵁ]	2	3	**Red Spice** 16-1 *R Owen Prom; jmpd rt 13; ev ch app 3 out; nt qckn w wnr app last; stayed on agn u.p flat*
[778³]	3	15	**Marwoods Mandate (IRE)** 4-1 *M Worthington Hld up; mist 4; hdwy 10; went 3rd 4 out; ev ch app nxt; mist 2 out; wknd last*
[965⁴]	4	1	**Bright Reform (IRE)** 14-1 *C Hoggart Rr; mist 4; hdwy 10; nt qckn 15; stayed on agn app 2 out; sn no imp; eased when btn app last*
[500⁵]	5	10	**Running Mute** 9-2 *P Robson Hld up & bhnd; some hdwy 14; sn no imp & wl btn*
	6	6	**Lardante (IRE)** 6-1 *J Ewart Midfield; lost plce 10; mist when strugg 13; sn wl bhnd*
[811ᵁ]	7	30	**Javaman** 9-1 *G Thomas Tk keen hld; prom; chall 13; ld 15; hdd app nxt; wknd qckly*
[815²]	8	4	**Bold Irene (IRE)** (5a) (bl) 5-1 *J R Barlow Midfield; eff to chse ldrs 14; wknd aft nxt*
[965ᵁ]	P		**B J Bubbles** 14-1 *K Burke Midfield; mist 1; hdwy to go prom app 5; nt fluent 9; wknd 13; t.o & pu nxt*
[811ᵖ]	P		**Davey John (IRE)** 14-1 *D Jewett Midfield; lost plce 8; drvn along 10; t.o & pu 14*
[1092⁴]	P		**Golden Saxon** 12-1 *J Merry Prom; lost plce aft 7; t.o & pu 15; broke pelvis; dead*
[816²]	U		**Greenfinch (CAN)** 3-1F *Miss R Barrow Handy til blun & ur 6*
[188ᶠ]	F		**Lord Torridon (IRE)** 6-1 *Mrs C Ford Fell 2*
[1075ʳ]	P		**Royal Fling** (5a) 14-1 *C Barlow Chsd ldrs; drpd to midfield 7; rmdrs 10; sn bhnd; t.o & pu 14*

OFFICIAL DISTANCES: 3l, 15l   **TIME:** 7min 13.1s

Carlisle (RH 9F,19J)

Mon, 24 Apr (GOOD to SOFT, SOFT in places)

1154 Dennis Waggott Mem Mdn HC   11 ran

[999⁵]	1		**CONCERTO COLLONGES (FR)** 11-13 10-1 *R Hartley Prom til lost plce ½way; hdwy 4 out; stayed on wl to ld nr fin*
[1024⁶]	2	½	**Fiscal Policy** 11-13 10-1 *R Trotter Prom; lost plce 10; hdwy 12; ld 3 out; hdd cl home*
[1078ᵁ]	3	2½	**Charlieadams (IRE)** 12-01 (2) 16-1 *J Muir Ld to 3 out; kpt on run-in*
[584ᵖ]	4	15	**Makin' Doo** 12-01 2-1F *C Mulhall Mists; cl up; outpcd 14; nd aft*
[716¹⁼]	5	dist	**Geordies Express** 11-06 7-2 *T Davidson Hld up; hdwy to chse ldrs 11; hit 15; sn outpcd*
[1153ᵁ]	P		**Greenfinch (CAN)** 11-13 33-1 *D Jewett Chsd ldrs; drpd to rr aft 10; pu 13*
[911³]	F		**Hooky's Treat** 11-08 33-1 *Miss L Hislop Lost tch ½way; t.o when fell last*
[1028⁶]	P		**Ladylands** 11-01 33-1 *D Raw Mists in rr; t.o & pu 13*
[714ᵖ]	F		**Master Rocky** 11-06 7-1 *R Morgan Hld up; hdwy & prom 12; outpcd 3 out; 4th & btn when fell last*
[1078¹]	P		**Storm Alive (IRE)** 12-03 4-1 *Mrs V Jackson Hdwy to chse ldrs 3; wknd app 15; pu 2 out*
[964²]	U		**The Shy Padre (IRE)** 11-13 20-1 *J Townson In tch; hdwy to chse ldr when blun & ur 11*

TIME: 7min 03.6s   **TOTE:** £10.40; places £3.40,£3.60,£7.10 **Ex:** £210.90 **CSF:** £95.06

Fakenham (LH 6F)

Mon, 24 Apr (GOOD, GOOD to SOFT in places)

1155 Hood, Vores And Allwood Nov HC   9 ran

[925³]	1		**TUBBER ROADS (IRE)** 11-05 14-1 M Foley *(xnb) Ld til bef 10; ld agn 13; clr & rdn along aft 2 out; kpt on wl*
[919²]	2	7	**Mr Snowman** 11-11 5-4F *Mrs T Hill Lw; prom; rdn to 5l 2nd when blun & nrly ur 2 out; pushed along & chsd wnr vain aft*
[843¹]	3	2	**Mister Audi (IRE)** 11-05 9-1 *Mrs E Coveney Jmpd slow 1; prsd ldrs to 13; one pce & nd aft*
[827²]	4	14	**Kincora (IRE)** 11-05 10-1 *Mrs L Stock Midfield; outpcd 12; eased frm 2 out*
[937²]	5	7	**Persian Boy (IRE)** 11-12 12-1 *A Sansome Chsd ldrs til drvn & lost tch 11*
[757³]	6	10	**Commuter Country** 11-13 9-2 *N King (xnb) Trckd ldrs; qcknd ahd bef 10; hdd 13; fdd rap app 3 out*
[919³]	7	27	**Minella Derby (IRE)** 11-09 14-1 *T Gibney Nt jw; sn rr; strugg & drvn 10; t.o 3 out*
[1074³]	8	8	**Doctor Dunklin (USA)** 11-05 (bl) 33-1 *Miss E Graham Poor last & a rdn; t.o 13*
[919⁶]	P		**Major's Law (IRE)** 11-13 12-1 *J Owen Mists; hit 5 & rdn; nvr gng wl aft; lost tch 10; t.o & pu 13*

    TIME: 5min 37.5s **TOTE:** £28.80; places £2.90,£1.20,£1.50 **Ex:** £53.50 **CSF:** £30.11

1156 The Queen's Cup Eastern Counties HC   5 ran

[1008³]	1		**TOM DE SAVOIE (IRE)** 11-08 6-4F *W Wales Nt fluent; jmpd slow 3; mist 10; settled cl up & chall 3 out; ld nxt; 2l clr & rdn when hit last; all out; unimpressive*
[982²]	2	¾	**Torus Spa (IRE)** 11-05 4-1 *Mrs E Coveney Ld & tk keen hld; jnd 3 out; hdd nxt; 3l down app last; rallied & kpt on wl cl home*
[981⁴]	3	dist	**Prince Of Saints (IRE)** 11-12 (bl) 8-1 *A Sansome Swtng; sn hld up last; rdn 13; reluct & sn lost tch; t.o aft 3 out*
[1036¹]	U		**Pangeran (USA)** 11-07 7-4 *N King Lw; tk keen hld; hld up & cl up; 3rd when mist & ur 9 (galloped off course & hit iron gate)*
	P		**Roscolvin (IRE)** 11-03 25-1 *R Fowler Lw; pulled hrd; prom to 13; fdd bad; lost rem 3rd 2 out; v tired when pu last*

    TIME: 6min 41.3s **TOTE:** £2.00; places £1.10,£2.80 **Ex:** £13.00 **CSF:** £7.32

Hereford (RH 9F,11J)

Mon, 24 Apr (SOFT, HEAVY in places)

1157 Oswald and Rowland Symonds HC   7 ran

[1026³]	1		**CARACOL** 11-09 10-11F *S Blackwell Hld up in tch; went 2nd 7; ld 8; sn clr; v easy*
[945⁴]	2	22	**Frown** 11-11 (bl) 14-1 *P Pritchard Rr; lost tch 8; stayed on to rem 2nd 2 out*
[919⁵]	3	11	**Royal Mountbrowne** 11-11 15-8 *Miss E Jones Ld 2-3; mist nxt; ld 6-8; sn wknd; jmpd v slow & lost 2nd 2 out*
[818⁴]	4	1½	**Who's Your Man (IRE)** 11-09 14-1 *D Dunsdon Ld to 2; chsd ldrs til drvn & lost tch 8*
[859⁴]	P		**Manamour** 11-09 14-1 *R Cooper Blun bad 2; sn wl bhnd; pu aft 5*
[1026⁴]	U		**Our Eddie** 11-07 33-1 *L Hamilton Last til ur 1*
[925⁸]	P		**Sandi Devil** 11-07 (bl) 40-1 *Miss S Sharratt Ld 3-6; mist nxt; sn strugg; wl bhnd when pu 9*

    TIME: 5min 05.2s **TOTE:** £1.90; places £1.60,£3.00 **Ex:** £12.80 **CSF:** £12.72
    3 fences omitted

Braes of Derwent

Corbridge (RH 9F,18J) Mon, 24 Apr (SOFT becoming HOLDING)

1158 Hunt   2 ran

[1078⁴]	1		**LITTLE BROCKWELL (IRE)** (5a) (tt) 1-4F *Miss P Robson Made all; 8l up 9; 3l up 15; qcknd & sn in comm*
[1084⁴]	2	bad	**Sinch** (12a) 3-1 *J Stonehouse Nt a fluent; 8l down 4; clsd on rival aft 14; 3l down nxt; sn outpcd; mist & ur last; rmtd*

    OFFICIAL DISTANCE: dist **TIME:** 6min 57.0s

1159 Intermediate, 12st   7 ran

[1031³]	1		**KEEP A SECRET** 12-1 P Atkinson (xnb) Hld up in rr; 8l off pce 7; 6l 6th app 15; gd prog aft to ld app last; sn clr
[912¹]	2	4	**Highland Monarch** (5x) 6-4F C Storey (xnb) Trckd ldrs; 3l 3rd 7; disp 3l 3rd 3 out; outpcd aft; 5l 2nd & mist last; one pce & dem flat; fin 3rd; subsq promoted
[1078ᴾ]	3	8	**Tropnevad** (bl) 33-1 B Lusted Oht; prom; disp 3l 3rd 3 out; wknd app nxt; fin 4th; subsq promoted
[973⁴]	5	8	**Mischievous Andy (IRE)** 14-1 Mrs K Hargreave (xnb) Chsd ldrs; releg last by 11; prog to 4l 5th app 15; hit nxt & sn strugg
[1078³]	2d		**Minella Gold (IRE)** (5x) 7-2 Miss M Bremner A.p; 2l up 12; hdd aft 15; stayed on agn app last; kpt on wl to tk 2nd flat; fin 2nd; subsq disq - nt qualified
[908³]	F		**Carnaven** 10-1 A Robson Mid-div; rmdrs 11; prog to 2l 2nd 13; ld aft 15; hdd aft 2 out; btn 4th & tired when fell last
[107¹]	P		**The Alleycat (IRE)** (5x) 9-4 Miss P Robson In tch; 4l off pce 8; 7l 6th 10; hit 12 & strugg; pu sn aft

OFFICIAL DISTANCES: Originally 4l, 1½l **TIME:** 6min 58.0s
Minella Gold finished second but was subsequently disqualified by the Jockey Club Disciplinary Committee as it won three Hurdle races in Ireland; the owner was fined £150

1160 Mens Open   6 ran

[975²]	1		**RAINBOW TIMES (IRE)** (5a) (bl) 4-1 C Storey Prom gng wl; 1l 2nd 13; ld aft 15; 3l up 2 out; clr last; eased flat; comf
[1080¹]	2	8	**Excise Man** 2-1 J Walton Swtng; oht; a handy; disp 1l 2nd 10; 3l 3rd 14; prog & ev ch 2 out; nt pce to chall
[1080ᵁ]	3	10	**Steel Rigg (IRE)** 4-1 M Clayton Chsd ldrs; disp 1l 2nd 10; 5l 4th 14; hdwy to cl 2nd & blun 3 out; 3l down & outpcd aft
[1078⁶]	4	4	**Heavenly Citizen (IRE)** 12-1 T Scott Ld; 2l up 4; 1l up 13; hdd app 15; no ex nxt; sn wl bhnd
[422¹]	5	2½	**Cool Yule (IRE)** (bl) evensF T Oates Prom; cl 4th when blun 6; prog to disp 1l 2nd 10; pushed along & outpcd 12; rdn & 10l 4th 14; strugg aft
[974⁴]	6	15	**Dashmar** 16-1 P Johnson Oht; a rr; 8l last 7; hit 9; 15l last aft 14; nvr nrr

OFFICIAL DISTANCES: 10l, 10l **TIME:** 6min 54.0s

1161 Ladies Open   4 ran

[1119¹]	1		**BALISTEROS (FR)** 1-3F Miss P Robson A handy; disp 1l 2nd 9; hit 11; 2l 3rd & mist nxt; ld app 2 out; clr app last; stayed on
[715¹]	2	3½	**Pharmistice (IRE)** 4-1 Miss N Stirling (xnb) 2 handlers; oht; ld; jnd 12-13; hdd & hit 15; 5l 3rd & outpcd nxt; stayed on u.p to 2nd flat; nt trble wnr
[1078²]	3	1	**Miss Portcello** (5a) 7-1 Miss J Hollands Tchd 8s; trckd ldrs; disp 1l 2nd 9; disp ld 12; fl 5l 3rd aft nxt; ev ch til outpcd app last; one pce & dem flat
[1079ᵁ]	4	1½fs	**Reve De Valse (USA)** 33-1 Miss V Burn A rr; 6l last 5; lost tch 9; 20l last nxt; sn t.o; fnce bhnd 14

OFFICIAL DISTANCES: 3½l, 1l **TIME:** 6min 42.0s

1162 Restricted   12 ran

[1081ᶠ]	1		**SENSO (IRE)** 9-2 Mrs C Cox A.p; cl 2nd 6; ld/disp nxt til ld 14; sn clr; stayed on wl; unchall
[908²]	2	7	**Go Nomadic** (tt) 6-1 P Atkinson Hld up in rr; 15l last 5; stdy prog frm 9; 8l 5th 14; disp 4l 2nd 3 out; hit nxt; no imp aft
[498⁵]	3	15	**Kings Token** 5-1 J Walton Rr; 15l last 10; 25l off pce 14; stayed on wl frm nxt; r.o u.p flat; tk 3rd cl home
[1082¹]	4	2½	**The Other Half** (bl) 7-1 Miss P Robson Prom; ld/disp frm 10; 1l up 13; sn hdd; disp 4l 2nd 3 out; wknd; 20l 3rd at last; rdn & dem flat
[423ᴾ]	P		**Disrespect** (5a) 12-1 Miss M Macmillan A rr; wl bhnd 14; sn 20l last; t.o & pu 3 out
[977¹]	P		**Divet Hill** 11-10F M Clayton 5/2-11/10; swtng; prom; jmpd to ld 7; disp 2l 4th app 10; 4l 4th 13; wknd qckly 15; bhnd when pu 2 out
[976ᴿ]	P		**Golf Land (IRE)** (tt) 9-1 S Huggan In tch; disp 2l 4th app 10; hit 12 & sn strugg; wl bhnd when pu last
[713ᴾ]	P		**Madame Defarge** (5a) (tt) 14-1 Mrs K Hargreave Oht; a rr; 13l off pce 5; wl bhnd 14; t.o & pu last
[1081ᵁ]	U		**Noneofyourbusiness (IRE)** (5a) 25-1 Miss M Blakey (boh) A rr; 12l off pce 5; mist 9; tried to ref & ur 11
[807⁸]	U		**Prince Moshar** 16-1 G Markham Tde; in tch when blun & ur 8

[1152^U] P   **Tenella's Last** (5a) 14-1 T Mounsey-Heysham *Chsd ldrs; 6l 6th 9; outpcd frm 12; 10l 6th & wkng 15; t.o & pu 2 out*

[1081^P] P   **Wylup** 33-1 H Humble *Prom early; wkng 11; wl bhnd 14; t.o & pu last*

OFFICIAL DISTANCES: 10l, 10l   TIME: 6min 50.0s

1163 Open Maiden (Div 1)   10 ran

[718⁷]	1		**BENEFIT-IN-KIND (IRE)** 7-1 T Oates *(orbs) Rr; prog to chse ldrs 7; 1l 2nd 9; disp ld 12; ld 14; in comm frm 2 out; eased flat*
[1083²]	2	12	**The Dyke Louper** (5a) 3-1 B Lusted *Oht; a.p; 3l 3rd 9; prog to disp ld 12; 3l 2nd & outpcd 14; ld brief nxt; 1l 2nd aft 3 out; sn btn; fin tired*
[719^B]	3†	15	**Rye Rum (IRE)** 4-1 J Walton *Mid-div; 6l off pce 8; 21l 4th 14; blun nxt; poor 4th 2 out; tired & drvn out flat; lkd to snatch 3rd*
[808^P]	3†	s hd	**Baltic Lake (IRE)** 6-1 M Smethurst *Chsd ldrs; 5l 4th & rmdrs 10; 20l 3rd 14; poor 3rd 2 out; tired & drvn out flat; lkd dem on line*
[714³]	P		**Everready Go** (5a) 9-4F S Huggan *Mid-div; 3½l 4th 9; outpcd aft; strugg & pu 12*
[1081^U]	P		**Hetty Bell** (5a) 14-1 A Robson *(b4) Oht; a rr; 9l last 7; 15l 9th & lsng tch when blun 10; pu nxt*
	P		**Just Felix** 14-1 Miss N Stirling *(xnb,bf) Swtng; unruly; hldstrng; ld; 4l up 5; hdd 11 & wknd qckly; 20l down when pu aft 13*
[976^P]	P		**Normandy Duke (NZ)** 6-1 Mrs K Hargreave *Chsd ldr; disp 6l 2nd aft 5; bad mist 8; reluct aft; wl bhnd when pu 10*
[1003^R]	P		**Star Design (IRE)** 6-1 T Glass *Mists; sn rr; 15l last app 6; wl bhnd when blun 10; pu aft nxt*
[1084^P]	P		**Westhall Jonstan (IRE)** 8-1 G Markham *Prom early; strugg when mist 9; sn lost tch; pu 11*

OFFICIAL DISTANCES: 15l, 20l, d ht   TIME: 7min 01.0s

1164 Open Maiden (Div 2)   5 ran

[913²]	1		**HARRY LAWS** evensF T Scott *Lw; ld; 3l up 4; lft 10l clr 7; hdd app 13; trckd ldr; 2l 2nd & no imp til ldr blun last; hrd drvn to ld flat*
	2	hd	**Sharpaman** (7a) 5-2 Miss P Robson *Chsd ldrs; 12l 4th 5; lft 10l 2nd 7; sn clsd; ld 13; 2l up 3 out til blun last; nt rec; rdn & hdd flat*
[909^P]	F		**Camden Carr (IRE)** 6-1 T Glass *Chsd ldrs; 15l 5th 5; 3l 3rd 9; rmdrs nxt; outpcd when fell 12*
[978^P]	F		**Colisnova** (5a) (bl) 8-1 T Oates *Trckd ldr; 1l 2nd app 5; cl up when fell 7*
[1082³]	U		**Mesling** 2-1 J Walton *Trckd ldr; 8l 3rd 6; blun, sltly hmpd & ur nxt*

OFFICIAL DISTANCE: hd   TIME: 7min 16.0s

1165 Open Maiden 56&7yo (Div 1)   5 ran

[977^P]	1		**THE PARLOUR MAID** (5a) 10-1 T Scott *In tch in rr; 7l 4th 7; mist 10 & pushed along; lft 4l 2nd nxt; ld aft 3 out; stayed on*
[499³]	2	15	**Ballylesson (IRE)** (7a) 7-4 C Storey *Trckd ldr; 2l 2nd 5; lft in ld 11; 3l up 15; pckd & hdd nxt; ev ch til wandered & wknd alarm aft 2 out; exhaust & walked in (rdr pushing & shoving to force him over line); imm dism*
	3	10	**Play An Ace** 6-1 B Lusted *Rr; 10l 5th aft 5; 5l 3rd 9; 15l 3rd & wkng 3 out; kpt on one pce; pushed out flat*
[910^P]	4	50	**Bonnie B** (5a) 4-1 L Morgan *Chsd ldrs; 8l 3rd 4; rmdrs & prog to 3l last app 10; 10l last & outpcd app 14; sn t.o; walked in*
[977²]	U		**I Say Dancer (IRE)** (5a) 2-1 Miss M Blakey *Oht; swtng; ld; 2l up 6; blun & ur 11*

OFFICIAL DISTANCES: 20l, 15l   TIME: 7min 20.0s
        Pillaging Pict (6-4F) was withdrawn not under orders - rider not fully fit; Rule 4 deduction 40p in pound

1166 Open Maiden 56&7yo (Div 2)   6 ran

	1		**JUST A DIAMOND** (5a) 6-1 Miss M Bremner *Chsd ldrs; 18l 4th 5; prog & cl up 10; 1l 2nd 13; prsng ldr when lft in ld 2 out; lft solo app last; eased*
[626³]	R		**Glenelly (IRE)** 11-2 L Morgan *Dism start; a rr; 15l last & pushed along 6; drvn along 9; rn out & ur 11*
[363^P]	U		**Homo Dorney (IRE)** (5a) 7-2 P Robson *Swtng; trckd ldr; 1l 2nd 3; lft in ld 10; ½l up 3 out; blun & ur nxt*
[501²]	P		**Inglebrig Lad** 5-2 C Storey *(bf) Oht; pulling; mostly 3rd; 12l 3rd 5; went 2nd nxt; ½l 2nd 10; 3l 3rd 13; outpcd aft 15; t.o & tired when lft 2nd & pu 2 out*
[718²]	U		**On Merit** 4-5F T Oates *Ld; 10l clr 4; 6l up when blun & ur 10*
[807^P]	P		**Spectacular View (IRE)** (7a) 8-1 T Glass *Rr; wl bhnd 5; prog to 4l last aft 12; sn bhnd; t.o & tired when lft 2nd app 2 out; pu last*

OFFICIAL DISTANCE: Finished alone   TIME: 7min 20.0s

East Kent
Aldington (LH 9F,19J) Mon, 24 Apr (SOFT)

1167 S.E. Hunts Club Members Moderate, 12st
4 ran

[983⁴]	1		**SOME TOURIST (IRE)** 1-2F N Benstead *Ld til hdd app 10; ld agn aft 13; 8l clr 15; pushed along 16; hit nxt; lft wl clr 2 out*
[1109⁴]	2	12	**Lucas Court** 8-1 S Garrott *Detach 3rd til gd hdwy 9; ld 10-13; sn outpcd; lft poor 2nd 2 out*
[824ᴾ]	U		**Rose King** 2-1 T Hills *Hld up in detach last; stdy hdwy 11 to 5l 2nd 16; 8l down & no imp when blun & ur 2 out*
[983ᴾ]	P		**The Portsoy Loon** (bl) 8-1 P Hickman *Trckd wnr til lost plce aft 9; last & out of tch when pu 13*

OFFICIAL DISTANCE: 12l TIME: 7min 10.0s TOTE: £2.30 DF: £6.00

1168 Restricted, 12st
2 ran

[825ᴾ]	1		**LISALEEN WREN (IRE)** 5-2 G Gigantesco *Crawled in ld til lft solo 8*
[1104ᴾ]	U		**Nattico (IRE)** 1-4F Miss S Gladders *Trckd wnr til jinked lft & ur 8*

OFFICIAL DISTANCE: Finished alone TIME: 8min 59.0s TOTE: £2.60

1169 Confined, 12st
2 ran

[824³]	1		**NOSSI BE** 4-7F D Parker *Made all at stdy pce; drew clr app 2 out; easy*
[830ᴾ]	2	8	**The Glow (IRE)** (6x) (bl) 6-1 D Brightling *Trckd rival; pushed along 3 out; 5l down when rmdrs aft 2 out; no resp*

OFFICIAL DISTANCE: 8l TIME: 7min 24.0s TOTE: £1.10
Retail Runner was withdrawn not under orders - lame at start; Rule 4 deduction 35p in pound

1170 Ladies Open
4 ran

[1107ᵁ]	1		**ANDRELOT** (bl) 5-4F Miss H Grissell *Chsd ldr most of way to 15; 6l 3rd nxt; gd hdwy frm 2 out; ld last; drew clr flat*
[985²]	2	2	**Trifast Lad** 3-1 Mrs L Baker *Hdwy to ld 10; jnd 15; ld agn aft 3 out; hdd last; kpt on one pce flat*
[1107³]	3	2	**Polar Ana (IRE)** (5a) 11-8 Miss S Gladders *Detach last til smooth hdwy 12; prsd ldr & gng wl 15; hit 3 out & hdd; rdn & wknd app last*
[827⁵]	4	30	**For William** 12-1 Mrs M Rigg *Ld til hdd & mist 10; lost tch qckly frm 12; no ch frm 15*

OFFICIAL DISTANCES: 3l, 2l TIME: 7min 16.0s TOTE: £1.90 DF: £4.70

1171 Mens Open, 12st
3 ran

[755¹]	1		**MONKS SOHAM (IRE)** (7x) 7-4 D Parker *In tch in last; hrd rdn & hdwy 2 out; went 6l 2nd app last; r.o wl to ld cl home*
[981ᵁ]	2	s hd	**Call Home (IRE)** (7x) 1-2F T Hills *Tried to make all; 3-6l up til drew 8l clr aft 2 out; rdr lkd rnd app last; in comm & nt pushed flat; hdd on line - rdr fined*
[883ᴾ]	3	5	**Nordic Spree (IRE)** (bl) 6-1 N Benstead *Chsd ldr; pushed along 3 out; no imp; dem app last*

OFFICIAL DISTANCES: s hd, 3l TIME: 7min 17.0s TOTE: £1.90 DF: £1.10
The stewards fined the rider of Call Home £150 for failing to ride his horse out to the finish

1172 Open Maiden, 12st
6 ran

[1105⁴]	1		**SLIABH FOY (IRE)** 6-1 F Marshall *2nd til lft in ld aft 7; hvly rstrnd aft 10; detach last 11 til impd 14; 5l 3rd nxt; qcknd to chall app last; ld flat; r.o wl*
[985ᴾ]	2	1	**Daydreamer (USA)** 5-4F D Brightling *Hld up in last; gd hdwy to ld app 11-12; trckd ldr til ld agn 2 out; hdd & no ex flat*
[710ᴾ]	3	8	**Straight Baron** 3-1 P Bull *Cl 2nd/3rd til ld 13; hdd & blun 2 out; wknd app last*
[416ᴾ]	4	40	**Granite's Surprise** 5-1 C O'Brien *In tch; prsd ldng pr 10 til rmdrs 15; wknd frm nxt; t.o*
[1105ᴾ]	P		**Satellite Express (IRE)** 7-1 P Hickman *Ld; clr 6; reluct to rce & pu aft nxt*
[1109ᴿ]	U		**Smooth Silk (IRE)** 10-1 D Page *Midfield til blun & ur 8*

OFFICIAL DISTANCES: 1½l, 5l TIME: 7min 30.0s TOTE: £9.50; places £2.20,£1.50 DF: £7.80

Eggesford

Bishopsleigh (RH 7F,19J) Mon, 24 Apr (HEAVY)

1173 Hunt, 12st
6 ran

[1044⁴]	1		**RASTA MAN** (tt) 11-8 **I Widdicombe** 5/2-11/8; hld up; hdwy to 3rd 11 & 2nd 13; ld 14; sn clr; unchall
[557²]	2	20	**Valley's Choice** (5a) 5-4F **C White** Prom; lft disp ld 8; ld aft 12; hdd & outpcd 14; r.o one pce frm 3 out
[730ᴾ]	3	bad	**Babbling Brook** (IRE) 4-1 **S White** Trckd ldrs; rdn to 2nd aft 14; wknd 3 out; btn 3rd when ur last; rmtd
[1047ᴾ]	P		**Ardscud** 33-1 **Miss C Woodward** Prom; lft disp ld 8 til blun 12; sn wknd; lost tch frm 13; rr when pu 15
[856ᴾ]	F		**Frankies Flutter** 16-1 **Miss K Baily** Sn ld; jmpd lft 5; mist 6; 3l up when fell 8
	P		**Windsocks** (U) (7ow) 66-1 **R Skinner** In tch til blun 9; t.o when pu 14

OFFICIAL DISTANCES: dist, dist TIME: 8min 01.0s TOTE: £1.80

1174 Ladies Open
5 ran

[1045³]	1		**SPACE CAPPA** 6-4F **Miss V Stephens** Trckd ldrs; cl 2nd frm 9 til ld 13; rdn clr app 15; drew away frm 2 out
[1057⁷]	2	15	**Silver Sleeve** (IRE) (bl) 12-1 **Miss L Bridges** Made most to 12; outpcd by wnr frm 14
	3	½	**The Kimbler** 7-4 **Miss S Young** Hld up; lost tch aft 14; 30l down when blun 2 out; fin fast
[922⁶]	4	15	**Mr Golightly** 5-1 **Mrs J Reed** Disp ld to 5; drpd back 3rd 9 & 4th 10; jmpd slow 11; 20l 3rd & mist 15; plodded on
[851⁴]	U		**Secret Four** 10-1 **Miss K Langdell** Trckd ldrs; cl 4th when ur 12

OFFICIAL DISTANCES: 15l, ½l TIME: 8min 15.0s TOTE: £2.70

1175 Confined, 12st
3 ran

[1023ᶠ]	1		**O SO BOSSY** 4-7F **Miss J Congdon** Made all; kicked clr aft 14; r.o wl when prsd agn aft 3 out; sn in comm
[402ᴾ]	2	12	**Uckerby Lad** (3x) 2-1 **C Heard** Jmpd slow; hdwy to 2nd 8; outpcd aft 14; hdwy & prsd ldr 3 out; btn when jmpd slow agn nxt; no ex
[720⁴]	3	50	**Dancing Ranger** 3-1 **Richard Darke** 2nd to 7; 12-15l last nxt til wknd 14; t.o when stumbled over 2 out & last

OFFICIAL DISTANCES: 15l, 25l TIME: 8min 02.0s TOTE: £1.80

1176 Restricted, 12st
8 ran

[1046²]	1		**ROSSALEEN** (5a) 5-1 **P Shaw** 7s-5s; a cl up; ld 3 out; r.o str
[1043²]	2	2	**Belitlir** (5a) 9-4F **Miss S Young** Hld up; hdwy to 4th 6 & 3rd 14; ld brief 16; outpcd by wnr frm 3 out
[729³]	3	25	**Brother Nero** (NZ) 5-2 **C Heard** Hld up; hdwy to 4th 15 & 3rd 16; no further prog
[1042³]	4	25	**The Ugly Duckling** 5-1 **Richard Darke** Mid-div but outpcd aft 14; no ex frm 3 out
[1137ᴾ]	5	10	**Prudent Miner** (IRE) (7ow) 33-1 **R Skinner** Prom; ld 7-15; sn wknd & lost tch
[922ᴾ]	U		**Mosside** 25-1 **Miss K Cook** Sn rr; rdn along frm 14; t.o when ur 16
[1097ᵁ]	P		**Mountain-Linnet** 50-1 **Mrs J Reed** Ld 3-6; still prom but tired when pu 12
[164ᶠ]	P		**Rakaposhi Ryme** (IRE) (5a) (bl) 4-1 **I Widdicombe** Hld up; mists; rr when pu 16

OFFICIAL DISTANCES: 1l, 25l TIME: 8min 08.0s TOTE: £3.70

1177 Mens Open
3 ran

[735¹]	1		**GAMAY** 1-3F **N Mitchell** Pulled hrd til ld 5; drew 10l clr 15; mist 2 out; rdn out
[521³]	2	7	**Flying Imp** 3-1 **J Barnes** Jmpd slow; trckd ldrs; outpcd aft 14; 2nd & r.o wl frm 2 out; nt tch wnr
[1136¹]	3	10	**Valnau** (FR) 11-2 **C White** Ld to 4; chsd ldr til wknd & dem 3rd aft 2 out

OFFICIAL DISTANCES: 7l, 10l TIME: 8min 17.0s TOTE: £2.00

1178 Open Maiden (Div 1), 12st - 13J
4 ran

[857ᴾ]	1		**SPIRIT OF LIFE** (5a) 12-1 **M Woodward** 3rd mostly til lft last 11; outpcd & outj by rival frm 15 til r.o wl 2 out; ld cl home
[401ᴾ]	2	1	**John Robin** 6-4 **M Sweetland** Jw; made most; 10l clr 2 out; wknd app last; hdd & no ex cl home
[929ᴾ]	P		**Smudges Season** (5a) 7-1 **R Emmett** Jmpd sticky in last til lost tch aft 8; jmpd slow 9 & imm pu

[934³] F   **Wise Examiner (IRE)** 4-7F **Richard Darke** *Trckd ldr; cl 2nd when fell 11 (feet stuck in mud)*

OFFICIAL DISTANCE: 1l   TIME: 8min 20.0s   TOTE: £17.50
Fences 4, 6, 10, 12, 16 & 18 were omitted - state of ground

1179 Open Maiden (Div 2), 12st   4 ran

[722²]	1		**HENRYS SONG** evensF **Richard Darke** *Chsd ldrs in 3rd mostly til lft 2nd 15; ld app last; r.o when prsd cl home*
[312²]	2	nk	**Battle Lord Cisto** 5-4 **Miss S Young** *Chsd runaway ldr til lft in clr ld 15; hdd 2 out; r.o wl cl home*
[849ᴾ]	3	25	**I'm Foxy** (5a) (bl) 8-1 **M Sweetland** *Sn rr; mist 8; 20l down 14; no prog; plodded on*
[538ᶠ]	P		**Woodys Widget** (12a) 4-1 **Miss K Baily** *Jmpd violent lft; hrd hld til pulled to ld 3; sn wl clr; 15l up 12; still 2l ahd but tiring when pu 15*

OFFICIAL DISTANCES: s hd, 20l   TIME: 8min 25.0s   TOTE: £3.80

Essex Farmers & Union

Marks Tey (LH 10F,20J) **Mon, 24 Apr** (GOOD to SOFT, SOFT in places)

1180 Open Maiden   8 ran

[1039ᶠ]	1		**CURRACLOE ROSE (IRE)** (5a) 4-1 **D Cook** *Trckd ldrs; disp ld 10 til ld 17; clr app 2 out; hit last; rdn out*
	2	3	**Edgar Gink (IRE)** 2-1 **N Bloom** *Ww in mid-div; prog to ld 11; hdd 17; 3l 2nd & mist nxt; 5l down 2 out; kpt on flat*
[942²]	3	2½	**Sixth Sense (IRE)** 7-4F **Mrs S Hodge** *Chsd ldr to 2; sn lost plce; 7th & pushed along ½way; 5th 15; went 8l 3rd 3 out; kpt on; nt rch ldrs*
[1040ᴾ]	4	20	**Lazy Acres (IRE)** 12-1 **C Lawson** *Tde; sn bhnd; prog frm 11; went 10l 3rd app 3 out; sn outpcd*
[941ᴾ]	5	15	**Carlton Brae** (12a) 14-1 **A Harvey** *In tch; 7l 4th & rdn 16; wknd nxt; t.o*
[995²]	6	10	**Vulpin De Laugere (FR)** (bl) 4-1 **C Jarvis** *Mid-div; in tch; went 3rd 11; ev ch 15; wknd 17; t.o*
[1040ᴾ]	P		**Bandit Boy** (bl) 14-1 **A Coe** *Ld to 11; wknd 13; t.o & pu 16*
[844⁴]	P		**Life Of A Star (IRE)** 8-1 **A Braithwaite** *Chsd ldr to 10; wknd 14; t.o & pu 17*

OFFICIAL DISTANCES: 3l, 2l   TIME: not taken   TOTE: £6.00 DF: £42.00

1181 Restricted, 12st   8 ran

[1038¹]	1		**BALLAD (IRE)** (tt) 3-1 **A Harvey** *Trckd ldrs til disp ld app 16; lft 8l clr 2 out; rdn out*
[940⁶]	2	8	**Holmby Copse** 8-1 **T Humphrey** *2 handlers; swtng; tde; prom; ld 4-12; cl 3rd 15; outpcd app 3 out; lft 12l 3rd 2 out; went 2nd nr fin*
[1054²]	3	½	**Gt Hayes Pommard** 4-1 **D Howells** *Rcd wide; jmpd rt; ld to 4; prom til outpcd 16; lft 8l 2nd 2 out; dem nr fin*
[980⁵]	4	25	**Holiday Time (IRE)** (5a) 12-1 **Mrs S Hodge** *Dwelt; sn rec & mid-div frm 3; 6l 5th 16; sn lost tch*
[940⁸]	5	8	**Bakmalad** 16-1 **D Kemp** *Chsd ldr to 4l grad lost plce; last frm 12; lost tch 15; t.o*
[1040¹]	F		**Heathburn (IRE)** 5-4F **C Ward-Thomas** *Chsd ldrs; ld 12; jnd app 16; ev ch when fell 2 out*
	P		**Master Page** 16-1 **A Coe** *A last; sn detach; t.o & pu 11*
	P		**Monere** 5-1 **G Cooper** *Bckwd; a last pr; 20l 7th when pu 11*

OFFICIAL DISTANCES: 15l, 1l   TIME: 7min 03.0s   TOTE: £3.00 DF: £6.50

1182 Mens Open   3 ran

[1008¹]	1		**COPPER THISTLE (IRE)** 2-7F **R Hunnisett** *Made all; drew clr frm 3 out; easy*
[938²]	2	7	**Hatcham Boy (IRE)** 3-1 **C Ward-Thomas** *Chsd ldr til mist 11; went 2nd agn 16; rdn 3 out; no imp*
[938⁴]	3	30	**Veryvel (CZE)** 7-1 **D Kemp** *Trckd rivals til went 2nd 11-16; sn wknd*

OFFICIAL DISTANCES: 8l, dist   TIME: 6min 58.0s   TOTE: £1.50 DF: £1.10

1183 Ladies Open   5 ran

[1007¹]	1		**IMPERIAL DAWN (IRE)** 11-10F **Miss L Rowe** *Chsd ldrs; ld 14; 5l clr 2 out; sn rdn; hld on last 50yds*
[827¹]	2	1	**Cache Fleur (FR)** 6-4 **Mrs G d'Angibau** *Ld to 5; 4th & pushed along ½way; 8l 3rd 16; went 2nd & str rn app last; no imp last 50yds*

[939²] 3 10 **Gatchou Mans (FR)** 3-1 Miss C Grissell *Chsd ldrs; went 2nd 5; ev ch 17; wknd app 2 out*
[608⁵] 4 runin **Ballyedward (IRE)** 16-1 Miss H Pewter *W ldrs to 2; last frm 5; t.o 14*
[1037²] F **Lets Twist Again (IRE)** 14-1 Miss A Stennett *Ld 4-14; 4th & wkng when fell 17; dead*

OFFICIAL DISTANCES: 1l, 8l TIME: 6min 52.0s TOTE: £1.50 DF: £1.40

1184 Confined, 12st
7 ran

[936⁰] 1 **NIBBLE** 5-4F G Cooper *Confid rdn; hld up in last; stdy prog 11; ld app 2 out; sn clr; r.o wl*
2 3 **Who's Next** 4-1 D Cook *Ww; 6th & pushed along ½way; went 2nd 16; ld 3 out; sn hdd; one pce aft*
[935³] 3 hd **Limited Liability** 12-1 Miss C Grissell *A.p; cl 3rd & ev ch 15; one pce app 2 out*
[937³] 4 30 **Ann's Ambition** 3-1 Miss C Fryer *Mid-div; lost plce & last 8; prog agn nxt to ld 10; hdd app 3 out; sn wknd*
[936³] P **Hillwalk** 4-1 A Harvey *Mid-div; went 2nd 9-13; rmdrs nxt; wknd app 16; pu last*
[936⁰] r **King High** 25-1 J Cooper *Chsd ldrs; went 2nd 6-9; ev ch 15; wknd 17; no ch when ref last*
[868⁵] P **Spuffington** 25-1 Miss C Hall *Ld to 10; in tch til last & wkng app 15; t.o & pu 17*

OFFICIAL DISTANCES: 4l, hd TIME: 7min 03.0s TOTE: £2.00 DF: £2.40

1185 Intermediate, 12st
2 ran

[940¹] 1 **MR MAGGET (IRE)** 1-6F N Bloom *Disp ld 6; ld 15; drew clr frm 3 out; easy*
[935³] 2 10 **Royal Surprise** 5-2 A Coe *Ld; blun 11; hdd 15; rdn & btn 3 out*

OFFICIAL DISTANCE: 10l TIME: 7min 11.0s TOTE: £1.10

Four Burrow
Trebudannon (LH 8F,19J) Mon, 24 Apr (SOFT with HEAVY patches)

1186 Hunt - 16J
6 ran

[1044⁰] 1 **ARBLE MARCH** (5a) evensF N Harris *Ld to 3; stdd; regained 2nd 8; ld 15; drew clr; easy*
[1042⁰] 2 30 **Bedtime Pixie** (bl) 5-1 D Stephens (Devon) *Rr early; 10l 3rd 13; lost tch nxt; plodded on; blun 16; went rem 2nd bet last 2*
[855⁰] 3 10 **Royal Chip** 5-1 Miss L Jackson *Ld 2 & sn clr; blun 4; hdd 15; tired bad; releg 3rd when mist last*
U **Beaumont (U)** 6-4 B Simmonds *7/2-6/4; went 2nd & mist 7; lft 3rd 10; 8l 3rd when slpd on landing & ur 13*
U **North Coast Girl** (5a) 8-1 A Ede *12s-8s; went 3rd 8; 5l 3rd when mist & ur 10*
[850⁷] P **Safara** 20-1 K Heard *Sn bhnd; wl t.o when pu 8*

OFFICIAL DISTANCES: dist, dist TIME: 7min 26.0s TOTE: £3.00
Fences 5, 11 & 17 were omitted from all races because of the state of the ground; original fence numbers have been retained in the comments-in-running

1187 Intermediate (Nov Rdrs), 12st - 14J
3 ran

[1045⁰] 1 **LUNEY RIVER** (5a) 1-2F Miss L Gardner *Ld til hdd 14; trckd ldr til hdwy to ld 2 out; rdr lkng rnd app last; pushed out*
[1140²] 2 5 **Devonshire Lad** (bl) 7-4 A Ede *Tchd 2s; 2l 2nd til pushed into ld 14; hdd 2 out; one pce app last*
[1048³] P **Moorland Rose** (12a) 8-1 Miss D Mitchell *Cl 3rd til pu aft 2; tack problems*

OFFICIAL DISTANCE: dist TIME: 7min 37.0s TOTE: £1.20
Fences 5, 10, 11, 16 and 17 were omitted

1188 Mens Open, 12st - 13J
6 ran

[680⁰] 1 **WESTCOUNTRY LAD** 3-1 R Woollacott *9/2-3s; hld up in rr; clsd to 8l 3rd 12; 3l 2nd 14; ld 2 out; hdd app last; stayed on agn flat; ld on line*
[954¹] 2 nk **Butler John (IRE)** 2-5F N Harris *Ld til jnd & outj 2 out; drvn up to ld on inner app last; hdd on line*
[1041³] 3 35 **Hold Your Ranks** 10-1 D McKenna *Trckd ldrs; 10l 4th 12; grad lost tch; fin v slow*
[852⁰] 4 8 **Brown Robber** 8-1 T Dennis *Ab 3l 2nd mostly to 14; sn strugg*
[852⁰] P **Baldhu Chance** 4-1 A Ede *Lost tch 9; pu 11*
[854⁰] P **Forest Musk (IRE)** 20-1 I Hambley *A bhnd; 20l bhnd when pu 6*

OFFICIAL DISTANCES: ½l, dist TIME: 7min 12.0s TOTE: £4.00
Fences 4, 5, 10, 11, 16 and 17 were omitted; the rest of the meeting was abandoned because the waterlogged ground had become dangerous

North Cotswold

Paxford (LH 8F,18J) Mon, 24 Apr (SOFT)

1189 Hunt
8 ran

[1086⁸]	1		**CHICODARI** (bl) 9-4JF E Walker *Hld up; cl 3rd frm 12; eff to disp ld 2 out-last; qcknd clr final 25yds*
[969⁴]	2	2	**Blue Lyzander** (5a) 7-1 Mrs E Staines *Ww; eff to disp ld frm 9; just ld last; nt qckn & hdd nr fin*
[790³]	3	15	**Benbulbin (IRE)** (vis) 9-2 M Bluck *Disp ld til outpcd frm 15; sn btn*
	4	30	**Just Destiny (IRE)** 6-1 Miss E Lockwood *Mist 3 & drpd back to last; hunted rnd t.o*
[429²]	S		**Cool Work** 9-4JF N Sutton *Cl up til wkng frm 9; 5th & wkng when slpd up bend aft 13*
[995ᴾ]	P		**Pennys Boy** (3ow) 12-1 T Gretton *Last pr; 10l adrift of ldng group by 6; t.o to pu 13*
[1020ᴾ]	F		**Quick Response (IRE)** 5-1 Miss N Norledge *Hld up; ld brief 6-7; lost plce; 12l 4th & clsng when fell 14*
[1020ᴾ]	P		**Weldson** (tt) 12-1 J Trice-Rolph *Ld to 3; wkncd; wl bhnd when pu 13*

OFFICIAL DISTANCES: 1¾l, 12l **TIME:** 6min 40.0s

1190 Confined, 12st
7 ran

[968¹]	1		**WELL TED (IRE)** (3x) 6-4JF G Barfoot-Saunt *Sa & lost 20l; stdy prog to ld 13; drew clr frm 3 out; r.o str*
[1063¹]	2	6	**Do It Once (IRE)** (7x) 5-1 M Keel *Hld up; eff to disp ld frm 13; ch til outpcd frm 3 out*
[971¹]	3	8	**Full Score (IRE)** 6-4JF Julian Pritchard *Ld; stdd 6; disp ld til hdd app 13; chall agn 15; sn 3rd & btn*
[1064²]	4	20	**The Archdeacon (IRE)** 4-1 T Stephenson *Trckd ldrs in 3rd/4th til lost plce frm 13; nt qckn frm 15*
[1015¹]	5	3	**Archies Oats** 25-1 J Trice-Rolph *Prom til wknd qckly frm 12*
[1016⁷]	6	25	**Templeroan Prince** 33-1 M Cowley *Disp ld 3-6; wknd stdly frm 12*
[1016ᴾ]	P		**Its Murphy Man** 33-1 C Wadland *Mid-div; eff to disp ld brief 11-12; wknd qckly; last when pu 2 out*

OFFICIAL DISTANCES: 6l, 8l **TIME:** 6min 28.0s

1191 Ladies Open
8 ran

[991¹]	1		**SPLIT SECOND** (7x) 1-3F Miss A Dare *Confid rdn; 25l 6th 7; hdwy frm 10 to disp ld 13; drew clr 3 out; eased flat*
[1014ᴾ]	2	12	**Dalusman (IRE)** 6-1 Miss N Sturgis *Mid-div; stdy prog frm 10 to disp ld brief 14-15; outpcd frm 3 out*
[1007ᵁ]	3	10	**Rainbow Walk (IRE)** 20-1 Miss A Burton *Disp ld to 10; prom til ldrs qcknd 14; one pce*
[1063²]	4	8	**Stretchit (IRE)** 6-1 Miss I Rabone *Disp ld til jnd 13; sn hdd; v one-pcd*
[869³]	5	40	**Driving Force** 20-1 Miss S Hutchings *Chsd ldrs til wknd qckly frm 12*
[611³]	6	2	**Connie Foley** 25-1 Miss N Rudge *Outpcd; last by 3; t.o*
[969ᴾ]	P		**Charlie's Gift** (5a) 25-1 Miss E Lockwood *30l 6th when pu 2 out*
[1066ᴾ]	P		**Night Wind** 7-2 Miss C Dyson *Hld up in 6/7th; mod prog frm 9-11; 5th & wkng when pu 13*

OFFICIAL DISTANCES: 8l, 8l **TIME:** 6min 29.0s

1192 Mens Open, 12st
5 ran

[968²]	1		**GRANVILLE GRILL** (4x) 11-10F J Deutsch *Ld to 11; ld agn 13; r.o str when chall app last*
[1015ᴾ]	2	2	**Celtic Town** (4x) 6-4 Julian Pritchard *Cl 2nd til pushed into ld 11; hdd 13; mist 14; 2l 2nd & eff agn 2 out; no ex flat*
	3	hd	**Northsprite** 3-1 A Martin *10s-3s; prom til mist & lost plce 11; 12l 4th 13; stayed on agn frm 3 out; unable to qckn frm 2 out*
[612ᵁ]	R		**Cuban Skies (IRE)** 20-1 A Barnett *Hdstrng; hld up til disp ld 11-12; 2l 3rd & ev ch when rn out 3 out*
	P		**Lord Kilton** 25-1 M Cowley *Cl 2nd/3rd til outpcd 12; 30l last when pu 2 out*

OFFICIAL DISTANCES: 1½l, nk **TIME:** 6min 44.0s

1193 Restricted, 12st
5 ran

[971³]	1		**FURIOUS AVENGER** 9-2 L Lay *Ld to 11; cl 3rd til rnwd eff 3 out; just ld nxt; drew clr app last*
[1026ᶠ]	2	12	**Whistling Rufus (IRE)** 11-8F M Rimell *Trckd ldrs; rmdrs 11; eff to ld 13-16; wknd app 2 out; fin tired*
[925⁴]	3	3	**Grand Canyon (IRE)** 5-2 S Joynes *Trckd ldrs in 4th; 12l bhnd ldrs 12; stayed on frm 3 out*

[896⁴]	4	5	**My Nad Knows** 7-2 J Baimbridge *Cl 2nd; ev ch til bad mist 15; wknd 2 out*
[992ᴾ]	P		**Lindalighter** (5a) 20-1 M Munrowd *Cl up til rmdrs 11; lost tch; 25l last when pu 14*

OFFICIAL DISTANCES: 12l, 4l **TIME:** 6min 35.0s

1194 Open Maiden, 12st   10 ran

[899²]	1		**COWANSTOWN PRINCE** 4-6F Julian Pritchard *Confid rdn; prog frm 10 to disp ld 14 til ld 3 out; sn forged clr; easy*
[994²]	2	10	**Ole Gunnar (IRE)** 7-1 M Wilesmith *Sa; last 3; prog to 5th 12 & 3rd 3 out; r.o wl; went 2nd flat; nt trble wnr*
[1068⁵]	3	½	**The Ugly Gunner** 9-2 M Keel *14s-9/2; prom; ld 10; jnd 14; ev ch til brushed aside 3 out; dem flat*
[1018ᴾ]	4	25	**Bramley** 16-1 A Martin *Hld up in rr; rmdrs 11; stayed on past btn horses frm 15*
[1020⁴]	5	1	**Music Class (IRE)** 14-1 J Gallagher *A.p; cl 2nd frm 11-12; wknd stdly frm 14*
[792³]	6	nk	**Social Vision (IRE)** 20-1 M Cowley *Disp ld to 9; drpd back stdly frm 10*
[949³]	P		**Le Vienna (IRE)** 12-1 S Currey *Cl 3rd/4th til disp ld 7-9; sn lost plce; crawled over 15 & 3 out; pu nxt*
[673⁵]	F		**Missmass** (5a) 6-1 T Stephenson *10s-6s; rstrnd in 2nd/3rd til wknd qckly frm 12; 15l 5th when fell 14*
[1011ᴾ]	P		**Penaword** 20-1 J Gasper *Disp 2nd/3rd til wknd qckly frm 11; pu 14*
[1067ᴾ]	P		**The Final Optimist** (5a) 20-1 C Wadland *Mid-div & sev mists; rmdrs 11; t.o when bad mist & nrly ur 13; pu nxt*

OFFICIAL DISTANCES: 10l, ½l **TIME:** 6min 40.0s

North Shropshire
Eyton-on-Severn (LH 13F,18J) Mon, 24 Apr (DEAD)

1195 Hunt, 12st   4 ran

[782²]	1		**COMING THROUGH (IRE)** (bl) 8-15F L Stephens *Jw; ld; set stdy pce; jnd brief 9; 6l clr 14; drew rt away frm nxt*
[964⁶]	2	runin	**King Paddy (IRE)** 9-4 R Bevan *A 2nd; jnd wnr brief 9; ev ch til outpcd frm 14*
[964⁴]	3	5	**Nagara Sound** 6-1 J Downes *Nt jw; mostly 3rd; dived at 6 (ditch); lost tch w wnr frm 15; fin tired*
	P		**The Rising Buck (IRE)** 14-1 B Foster *Nt jw; last & bhnd; virt t.o 5; went 12l 3rd brief 12 til wknd frm 14; poor last when pu 2 out*

OFFICIAL DISTANCES: dist, 5l **TIME:** 6min 37.0s

1196 Open Maiden (Div 1), 12st   11 ran

	1		**FAST LANE (IRE)** 5-1 B Foster *Hld up early; hdwy 7; ld 12; drew wl clr frm 3 out; mist nxt; impressive*
[167ᶠ]	2	15	**Emperor Ross (IRE)** (7a) 8-11F R Burton *Opened 5/4; lvw; mid-div early; 6th 8; went 3rd 11 & 2nd 12; drvn & outpcd aft 15; fin tired*
[1092³]	3	2	**Kota Tinggi** (5a) 16-1 R Inglesant *A.p; 5th 5; outpcd frm 12; went 3rd 3 out; kpt on u.p; no ch w wnr*
[866⁵]	4	6	**Blacon Point** 20-1 A Beedles *Blun 2; 6th 9; went 3l 4th 12 but one-pcd frm 13*
	5	10	**See More Action** 20-1 M Rodda *Ld; jmpd rt at times; hdd 12; ev ch til wknd qckly frm 14*
[673ʳ]	P		**Far Forest** 12-1 D Mansell *2nd when rmdrs aft 3; still 2nd 9; drpd rt out & reluct aft; nrly ref 10; t.o & pu 14*
	P		**Governor's Bay** 16-1 J Merry *Prom early; drpd out frm 8; t.o & pu 10*
[1093ᴾ]	P		**Lightening Steel** 16-1 P Morris *Jb; a wl bhnd; t.o 10 til pu 15*
[1011ᵁ]	P		**Proper Charlie** 9-4 T Lane *Mid-div early; 6th 5; ev ch when cl 5th 12; went 4th brief 14; wknd qckly frm nxt; pu 2 out*
[906ᴾ]	U		**Rural Gossip** 16-1 M Worthington *Lw; rr when blun & ur 6 (ditch)*
[527ᶠ]	P		**Spumante** 8-1 C Barlow *Nd; 7th 9; brief eff 11; t.o 14 til pu 2 out*

OFFICIAL DISTANCES: 20l, 2l **TIME:** 6min 37.0s

1197 Open Maiden (Div 2), 12st   10 ran

	1		**SAMS DAY (IRE)** 2-1F B Foster *3s-2s; confid rdn; last til grad hdwy frm 11; went 4th 3 out & 2nd nxt; hrd hld to ld flat; v cheeky; promising*
[964ᶠ]	2	2	**Barney Bear** 5-1 M Worthington *A.p; jmpd to 2nd 9; blun 11 & went lft off course into plough; 4th 12; hdwy to ld app 2 out til hdd flat; flatt by prox*

[900⁹]	3	3	**Moscow Squeaker (IRE)** 7-2 M Rodda *Hld up; went 5th 10; chsd ldrs frm 14; kpt on stdly frm 3 out; unable to chall*
[964⁵]	4	1	**Strong Mission (IRE)** 10-1 G Halliday *Ld til hdd app 2 out; v one-pcd aft*
[906²]	5	15	**Crunch Time (IRE)** 10-1 L Stephens *Chsd ldrs til drpd back last 14; strugg wkn jmpd slow nxt*
[528²]	6	20	**The Hollow (IRE)** (5a) 20-1 A Wadlow *2nd/3rd early; wknd bad frm 15; mist nxt*
[1068²]	P		**Daneswell** 20-1 D Mansell *Chsd ldrs; went 3l 3rd 12; rdn & wknd 15; rr when pu 3 out*
[601²]	U		**Keldan Star (IRE)** 20-1 G Marsh *Bhnd; 9th when ur aft gd j 8*
	P		**Lady's Pet** 20-1 J R Barlow *A rr; 9th 7; t.o 11; pu 12*
[990²]	P		**Mainlier** 5-2 A Wintle *Hld up; 7th 10; went 3rd app 3 out & ev ch but sn wknd; btn 4th when nrly ur bet last 2 & pu*

OFFICIAL DISTANCES: 2l, 4l TIME: 6min 45.0s

1198 Mens Open, 12st
6 ran

	1		**MURPHYS WAY** (5a) 5-1 J Burley *4th early; went 2nd 8; ld 11; 6l clr 14; in comm when lft virt solo*
[921⁹]	2	50	**Albert Blake** (7x) (tt) 4-6F W Kinsey *Evens-4/6; sis; a rem; last to 6; went dist 2nd app 3 out; v lacklustre*
[896²]	3	2fncs	**Eau So Sloe** (vis) 7-1 R Carey *Spurs; ld to 6; lost tch 11; releg last 12; plodded on reluct & nrly ground to halt flat*
[1127²]	P		**Circus Colours** (7x) 8-1 L Hicks *Prom early but pushed along & nt keen; drpd back last 6; v reluct aft; t.o & pu 8*
[903²]	r		**Logical Fun** (bl) 6-1 T Greenway *Prom early; rdn 7; nt keen aft; lost tch 11; 12l 3rd 12; t.o 3rd when ref lost*
[1149²]	U		**St Athans Lad** 7-1 F Giuliani *Ld 7-11; 2nd til tired frm 14; 8l 2nd & btn when blun & ur 15*

OFFICIAL DISTANCES: dist, dist TIME: 6min 41.0s

1199 Ladies Open
7 ran

[992²]	1		**SEYMOUR'S DOUBLE** 2-1 Miss T Clark *5s-2s; swtng; last 5; went 5th 8 & 3rd 11; cl 2nd frm 15 til jnd ldr nxt; ld flat; wl rdn*
[991²]	2	½	**Sun Surfer (FR)** (bl) 3-1 Miss S Beddoes *Sn 2nd/3rd; ld 14 til jnd 3 out; w wnr til outbattled & hdd flat*
[1066¹]	3	6	**Killatty Player (IRE)** (5a) 6-4F Mrs M Barlow *Ld 6-7; 3rd 9; lost plce frm 11; 12l 5th nxt; r.o agn frm 15; unable to chall*
[684²]	4	6	**Pontoon Bridge** 10-1 Miss S Swindells *Drpd back last aft 8; r.o frm 15; nd*
[991⁶]	P		**Cheeky Pot** (bl) 8-1 Miss J Priest *Hdwy to ld aft 7; hdd 14; wknd qckly 15; t.o & pu 2 out*
[1086¹⁰]	P		**Latest Thyne (IRE)** (vis) 10-1 Miss E James *Prom in 5th & mist 9; went 2nd 12; ev ch nxt; wknd qckly frm 14; t.o & pu 2 out*
[813¹]	U		**River Mandate** 14-1 Miss F Barnett *Rr when jmpd lft & rfo 3*

OFFICIAL DISTANCES: nk, 4l TIME: 6min 33.0s

1200 Dodson & Horrell PPORA Club Members Restricted, 12st
14 ran

	1		**ROLFES DELIGHT** 10-1 L Stephens *Hld up early; grad prog frm 9; went 2nd 12; ld 14; went 6l clr 3 out; hvly eased flat*
[963ᵁ]	2	¾	**Lady Dot (IRE)** (5a) 10-1 J Downes *Last early; still 13th 8; gd hdwy frm 14; went 4th 3 out & 2nd aft nxt; too much to do & v flatt by prox*
[963²]	3	12	**Ballyharry (IRE)** 8-1 I Wynne *A.p; 4th 8; kpt on one pce frm 15*
[963ᵁ]	4	4	**Arthur Henry** 4-1 S Prior *Nvr btr than mid-div; 6th 8; went 5th 14; 3rd & outpcd by wnr 3 out; disp 2nd & hit nxt; sn wknd*
[1129²]	5	3	**Secret Alliance (IRE)** 10-1 J Handley *Jmpd to ld 5; hdd 14; grad wknd*
[1068³]	6	½	**Fanion De Nourry (FR)** 3-1 L Hicks *11th 8; hdwy 9 to 6th 14; btn when hit 2 out*
[995¹]	7	8	**Talkalot (IRE)** 20-1 A Wintle *12th 8; prog to jn ldrs 13; 2nd 3 out; wknd rap*
[1071ᵁ]	R		**Downtheground (IRE)** 2-1F B Foster *Burly; reared over padd; jmpd to 3rd 8; went 2nd & ev ch 11; 4l 4th when rn thro wing 15*
[963²]	P		**Hamish** 8-1 M Worthington *5th & pckd bad 9; t.o 15; pu nxt*
[1089⁴]	P		**J'accuse (IRE)** 12-1 S Graham *A rr; mist 5; last 8; rem 8th 14; bhnd when nrly ur 2 out & pu*
[698⁵]	P		**Kanjo Olda** (5a) 12-1 D Mansell *Ld to 5; 2nd til wknd 11; t.o & pu 3 out*
[986³]	P		**Master Welder** (vis) 10-1 A Wadlow *6th early; mist 7; drpd back last 11; pu nxt; struck into himself*

[863³] P **Rising Sap** 6-1 R Burrow *Swtng; prom; 3rd 8; wknd qckly frm 12; bhnd when pu last*
[992⁵] P **Teme Willow (IRE)** 20-1 M Hammond *Nd; 7th 8; t.o & pu 13*

OFFICIAL DISTANCES: ½l, 5l **TIME:** 6min 30.0s

1201 Open Maiden 56&7yo, 2m4f, 12st - 14J   11 ran

[906ᵖ] 1 **COLONELS HATCH** 20-1 D Sherlock *5th early; lft 3rd 8; went 2nd 9; lft in ld 10; hrd prsd when lft clr 3 out; lft solo at last*
[593ᶠ] F **Cracksman** 4-1 L Stephens *Hld up & wl bhnd; 8th when blun 7; gd hdwy to 3rd 9 & lft 2nd but v tired 3 out; 25l 2nd when fell last; down for 10min*
        U **Grey Lodge** (5a) 16-1 J R Barlow *Towards rr early; gd prog & ev ch frm 9; prsng wnr when jmpd low & ur 3 out*
[1070ᵖ] P **Grey Mystery** (5a) evensF C Barlow *5/2-evens; hld up; 10th 4; went 6th 5; blun v bad 7; nt rec; pu 8*
        P **Jacks Dream** (5a) 10-1 J Burley *Nd; bhnd when pu 8*
        U **Kinsale Florale (IRE)** (5a) 7-1 M Rodda *2nd when blun & ur 4*
[206ᶠ] U **Mia Fort** (5a) 10-1 D Mansell *Prom; 10l 2nd 5; ld aft 7; 1l clr when fell 8*
[965³] P **Mister Pimpernel (IRE)** 7-1 J Downes *Bhnd when pu 6*
[966⁶] U **Mrs Sherman** (12a) 14-1 M Worthington *Chsd ldrs; 4th & in tch but lkng outpcd when mist & ur 9*
[990ᵖ] P **Supermister** 20-1 P Morris *Burly; 3rd early w rdr caling cabs; lft 2nd 8; ld aft 9 til virt ref 10; hdd & wknd rap; t.o when blun 3 out & imm pu*
        P **Wizadora** (12a) (bl) 12-1 A Wadlow *Bolted in ld; 10l clr 5; hdd aft 7; lft in ld agn 8-9; wknd rap frm 10; t.o & pu 3 out*

OFFICIAL DISTANCE: Finished alone **TIME:** 5min 37.0s

Old Berkshire

Lockinge (LH 9F,18J) Mon, 24 Apr (GOOD, GOOD to SOFT in places)

1202 Hunt   8 ran

[968⁶] 1   **PARMAN (IRE)** 2-1 R Dalgety *Chsd ldrs; 3½l 3rd 5; trckd ldr frm 7; jmpd to ld 14; stayed on str frm 2 out; comf*
[476ᵁ] 2 6 **Montecot (FR)** 7-4F R Biddlecombe *Lad resplendent in plus-fours & bow tie; 5l 4th 5; chsd ldng pr frm 7; 2½l 3rd 10; rdn 3 out; stayed on one pce frm nxt*
[327ᵖ] 3 3 **Northern Kingdom** 6-1 J Diment *Sa; 10l 6th 10; stayed on to 4th 14; chsd wnr frm 3 out; no ex frm nxt*
[968ᶠ] 4 10 **Prophet's Thumb (IRE)** 11-2 Miss T Good *Chsd ldrs to 7; 6l 5th 4 & wkng 10; outpcd & last 14; stayed on one pce; nd*
[736ᵖ] 5 1½ **Loch Na Keal** (5a) 20-1 Miss G Browne *2 handlers; swtng; hld up towards rr; hdwy to 4l 4th 10; eff to disp brief app 14; chsd ldr til wknd 3 out*
        R   **Aces Wild** 16-1 A Charles-Jones *Last 2 & jmpd novicey; tlng off when rn out 5*
[968ᵖ] P   **Golden Gunner (IRE)** (bl) 16-1 P Young *Ld; 2l up 5; 1½l up 10; hdd aft 13; wknd qckly; t.o & pu aft 15*
[1026ᶠ] r   **King Curan (USA)** (9ow) 33-1 M Curtis *Chsd ldrs; lsng tch when cat-jmpd 6; sn t.o; 2 fncs adrift when ref 11*

OFFICIAL DISTANCES: 6l, 3l **TIME:** 6min 27.8s **TOTE:** £3.90 **DF:** £3.00

1203 Intermediate, 12st   9 ran

[248ᵁ] 1   **CLINKING** 10-1 P Young *(xnb) 6th 5; chsd ldng pr 9 til ld on inner aft 13; made rest; 3l up 3 out; drew clr frm last; easy; rdr's 1st wnr*
[748¹] 2 10 **Lewesdon Manor** 7-2 M Portman *Prom; ld 4; jnd 8; hdd 10; ld agn brief 13; chsd wnr vain frm nxt; no ex frm 2 out*
[802ᵖ] 3 8 **Northern Yarn (IRE)** (2ow) 6-1 T Illsley *Last til prog to 5th 10; 7l down 14; chsd ldng pr frm 3 out; no ex frm nxt*
[953³] 4 1 **Gypsy Luck** (5a) 3-1 Miss A Bush *Chsd ldrs; 3rd 6; rdr called cab nxt; grad lost plce; 9l 6th 14; stayed on one pce frm 3 out*
[1059²] 5 ½ **Cardinal Gayle (IRE)** 5-2F Miss D Harding *Chsd ldrs; 4th 5; lost plce & 7th 9; still 12l adrift 14; stayed on one pce frm 3 out*
[1006ᵖ] 6 5 **Perfect Finisher** 8-1 M Hawkins *Swtng; chsd ldng pr 5 til wkng ld 8; 3½l 3rd 14; grad wknd frm 3 out*
[752²] 7 1 **Murberry (IRE)** (5a,6ow) 8-1 A Barlow *Chsd ldr til disp ld 5; grad lost ground; 5l 4th 14; wknd 3 out*
[788⁷] 8 5 **Mr Freeman (IRE)** (vis) 20-1 J Diment *Rr 5; rmdrs 10 & nxt; 14l 8th 14; bhnd frm 2 out*

[1013⁴] P   **Glendine (IRE)** 20-1 D Smith *Ld; jmpd slow 1; hdd 4; sn lost plce; rr 6; 20l last 14; t.o & pu last*

OFFICIAL DISTANCES: 8l, 6l **TIME:** 6min 32.4s **TOTE:** £20.00 **DF:** £39.00

1204 Open Maiden 56&7yo, 12st   12 ran

[956³]   1   **FINNIGAN'S LOT (IRE)** 7-1 R Walford *33l 7th 5; chsng ldrs in 5th 10; 6l 3rd 14; chsd ldr nxt til ld 2 out; stayed on wl u.p flat*
[933ᵁ]   2   3   **Fullofancy** (5a) 7-4 F M Miller *Disp 25l 4th 5; chsd ldr 9 til disp ld 15; ld nxt til hdd 2 out; no ex u.p frm last*
[880ᵖ]   3   runin **Pulham Downe** (7a) 16-1 R Young *Disp 25l 4th 5; chsd ldrs frm 10; 10l 6th 14; sn wknd; lft rem 4th 3 out; 3rd nxt*
[889³]   P   **Ben Gilmore** 3-1 J Diment *30l 6th 5; chsd ldrs frm 10 til wknd qckly 13; last nxt; t.o & pu 15*
[1012ᵖ] P   **Broad Statement** 6-1 R Cope *Trckd clr ldr; 20l 2nd 5; 9l 5th & wkng 14; t.o & pu nxt*
[221³]   P   **Climb The Hill (IRE)** 3-1 P Young *40l 8th 5; trckld ldrs frm 10; 7½l 4th 14; sn wknd; bhnd when pu 3 out*
[1021ᵖ] P   **Crewski** (7a) 16-1 A Charles-Jones *A towards rr; mist 6; pu 9; school*
[1019ᵖ] P   **Free To Conker (IRE)** 16-1 M Hawkins *(xnb,bh) Ld & set fast pce; 20l up 5; sn wknd; hdd 9; mist nxt; bhnd when pu 11*
[872ᵖ]   P   **Goldsteane** (5a) 16-1 S Morris *A rr; last 5; t.o & pu 11*
[754ᵖ]   r   **Oneforthefrog (IRE)** 12-1 B Clarke *V sa; imm t.o; jmpd rt til ref 4*
[516ᵖ]   P   **Stonehill Prospect** (5a) 20-1 Miss N McKim *A towards rr; rmdrs 12; 15l 7th 14; t.o & pu nxt*
[1020ᵖ] F   **True Hustler** (bl) 6-1 F Hutsby *Chsd ldrs; 22l 3rd 5; ld 9; 3l up 14; jnd nxt; sn hdd & tired when fell hvly 2 out; winded*

OFFICIAL DISTANCES: 4l, dist **TIME:** 6min 32.1s **TOTE:** £13.70 **DF:** £20.00

1205 Mixed Open, 12st   11 ran

[1144¹] 1   **RECTORY GARDEN (IRE)** 4-5F R Biddlecombe *Trckd ldrs; disp 7l 5th 5; chsd ldng pr 7; 3½l 3rd 10; chsd ldr nxt til disp ld 13; sn ld; drew away frm 3 out; easy*
[1144³] 2   12   **Castle Folly (IRE)** (bl) 5-2 R Lawther *2nd til disp ld 2; ld 4; 1½l up 10; jnd 13; hdd nxt; chsd wnr vain aft; lost tch frm 3 out*
[919ᵖ]   3   15   **Funcheon Gale** 16-1 A Charles-Jones *Disp 11l 8th 5; stayed on to chse ldng pr 12; 12½l 3rd 14; stayed on one pce frm 3 out; no imp*
[970⁵]   4   10   **Golden Savannah** 12-1 A Maculan *Disp 7l 5th 5; outpcd & rr 10; 25l 7th 14; nd aft*
[954⁵]   5   8   **Chism (IRE)** 8-1 R Walford *Trckd ldrs; 1 11 8th 5; outpcd & rr 10; stayed on to 20l 5th 14; nvr threatened*
[784²]   P   **Dolly Bloom** (5a) 16-1 Miss N McKim *4th 4; disp 8l 4th 10; wknd 12; 23l 6th 14; pu nxt*
[389ᵖ]   P   **Gaelic Blue** (bl,tt) 20-1 P Young *Reluct to leave padd; 3rd & mist 2; 1½l 2nd 5; disp ld nxt-8; rmdrs 10; sn wknd; t.o & pu 15*
[61ᵖ]   P   **Garethson (IRE)** 14-1 B King *Mid-div; 9l 7th 5; grad lost plce & rr 12; t.o & pu 15*
[789ᵖ]   U   **Phaedair** 20-1 R Cope *Mounted on course; ld in start; ld/disp to 4; 5l 3rd nxt; 4th & wkng when rmdrs 9; blun & ur 11*
[1016ᵖ] P   **Rupert's Princess (IRE)** (5a) 25-1 S Sellars *A rr; rmdrs 4; t.o & pu 6*
[637⁴]   P   **Scud Missile (IRE)** 14-1 S Goodings *Rr to 10; stayed on to rem 4th 12; 12l down 14; 3rd but wkng 3 out; bhnd when pu last*

OFFICIAL DISTANCES: 15l, 12l **TIME:** 6min 24.3s **TOTE:** £2.00 **DF:** £4.00

1206 Restricted, 12st   10 ran

[881¹]   1   **PEASEDOWN TOFANA** (5a) 6-4F R Young *(xnb) Hld up in rr; 17l 6th 10; stdy hdwy to 10l 2nd 14; clsd rap to ld 3 out; sn clr; eased nr line*
[887ᵖ]   2   12   **Benova Boy** (bl) 20-1 J Diment *2 handlers; swtng; disp ld 2; ld nxt; 6l up 5; made rest; 10l up 14 til hdd 16; stayed on one pce nxt*
[786¹]   3   6   **Second Amendment** (5a) 5-1 S Morris *Hld up towards rr; 14l 7th 5 til gd hdwy to disp 3l 2nd 8; chsd ldrs til wknd 15; tired & no ex frm 2 out*
[887ᴿ]   4   12   **Melody Princess** (5a) 16-1 Miss N McKim *A rr trio; last 5; t.o 12; stayed on one pce frm 15; nvr nrr*
[1017ᵖ] P   **Bit Of A Character** (bl) 16-1 P Young *12l 6th 5; wknd & bhnd 12; t.o & pu 2 out*
[971ᵁ]   U   **Claymore Lad** 7-1 A Maculan *Ld/disp 1-3; grad lost plce; 6th & wkng when ur 11*
[889¹]   P   **Fair Ally** 3-1 R Lawther *(xnb,bf) Rr trio to 2; prog to 7½l 3rd 5; 10l 2nd 10; chsd ldr til wknd 15; bhnd when pu last*
[931⁵]   P   **Flaming Cold (IRE)** (5a) 7-2 M Miller *Chsd ldrs; 10l 5th 5; mist 8; 15l 4th 10; in tch til wknd 15; pu aft nxt*

	P		**Irish Buzz (IRE)** 10-1 A Charles-Jones *Late in padd; disp 7½l 3rd 5; grad lost plce; rr 9; t.o 12 til pu 15*
[887⁶]	F		**Sunczech (IRE)** (5a) 16-1 R Cope *(xnb,bf) Mid-div when fell 4*

OFFICIAL DISTANCES: 10l, 6l **TIME:** 6min 41.9s **TOTE:** £3.60 **DF:** £31.00

1207 Open Maiden 6yo&up   12 ran

[1018²]	1		**DILLON** 5-2F F Hutsby *Chsd ldrs; 12l 5th 5; prog to 3rd 10; chsd ldr; 1½l down 13 til ld 3 out; drew clr nxt*
[630³]	2	10	**Darzal** 3-1 M Miller *Mid-div; 7th 6 til stdy hdwy to 4th 10; 2½l 3rd 14; 2nd & chsd wnr vain frm 3 out*
[517ᵁ]	3	2	**Folding** (tt) 8-1 J Oldring *Ld; 1½l up 5; still 3l up 14; hdd 3 out; stayed on one pce frm nxt*
[889²]	4	15	**Uncle Den** 3-1 I Hudson *Chsd ldr 3; 5l 3rd 5; disp 2½l 3rd 14; stayed on one pce frm nxt*
[972ᴾ]	5	¾	**Devil's Sting (IRE)** 14-1 J Richardson *Trckd ldrs; 6th 6 til outpcd & rr frm 13; stayed on one pce frm 15; nd*
[889ᴾ]	6	3	**Snowshill Harvest (IRE)** 20-1 J Rice *Hld up towards rr of main group; 6th 10; 4l 5th 14; 4th when mist 3 out; sn wknd & rr nxt*
[748⁵]	7	3fncs	**Country Lord** 33-1 Mrs S Walwin *Spurs; prom 1; lsng tch qckly when mist 2; sn t.o; fncs adrift 15; plodded home*
	P		**Blue And Royal (IRE)** 6-1 R Lawther *Chsd ldrs; 7l 4th 5 til wknd 10; bhnd when pu 12*
[580ᴾ]	P		**Chalcuchima** 16-1 M Curtis *(5a; a rr; t.o 5; slt prog to rr of field 13; wknd nxt; bu 2 out*
[1020ᴾ]	P		**Don'tcallmegeorge** 10-1 P Young *Prom when mist 3; 1½l 2nd 5 til wknd 10; bhnd when pu 15*
[1020ᴾ]	U		**Judicial Queen** (5a) 8-1 A Charles-Jones *Disp 12l 5th 5; blun & ur nxt*
[193ᴾ]	P		**Military Dreamer** 7-1 R Cope *A rr; mist 10; bhnd when pu 12*

OFFICIAL DISTANCES: 10l, 2½l **TIME:** 6min 32.8s **TOTE:** £2.20 **DF:** £10.00

Southdown & Eridge

Rodmell (LH 7F,19J) Mon, 24 Apr (GOOD, GOOD to FIRM patches)

1208 Hunt   3 ran

[982⁵]	1		**WEDNESDAYS AUCTION (IRE)** 6-4 Mrs C Andrews *Trckd ldrs; 8l 3rd til lft 2nd 3; clsd to 2l 2nd 14; prsd ldr 16; eff to chall app last; ld flat; just hld on*
[826⁴]	2	½	**Boll Weevil** 4-9F P Hall *Ur gng to start; ld; 6l clr 7; 2l up 14; jnd app last; sn hdd; r.o agn cl home; just hld*
[674¹]	P		**Easters Eve** (5a,4x) 5-1 D Evatt *4l 2nd when pu bend bef 3; broke down*

OFFICIAL DISTANCE: nk **TIME:** 6min 54.0s

1209 Countryside Alliance Club Members (Nov Rdrs), 12st   6 ran

[830³]	1		**EXEMPLAR (IRE)** 2-1F Mrs D Rowell *Hld up off pce; disp 3rd til 2l 3rd 14; 4l 2nd nxt; r.o str to ld last; sn clr*
[1109²]	2	6	**Velka** (5a) 3-1 Miss P Ellison *Pulling; ld; eased 6l clr 12; almost jnd app 14; qcknd & sn clr agn; wknd aft 2 out; hdd last; imm btn*
[1073⁴]	3	3	**Fern Leader (IRE)** 8-1 Mrs J Hughes *Hld up; 8l 5th 8; clsd to 3l 4th 13; 2l 2nd 14; dem 3rd agn & outpcd nxt; 6l 3rd & one pce 3 out*
[827⁴]	4	5	**Daddy Long Leggs** (4ow) 7-2 R Hubbard *Hld up off pce; disp 3rd til dem 4th 14; 15l 4th & outpcd 2 out*
[985ᴾ]	5	2	**Red Channel (IRE)** 7-1 Miss P Bryan-Brown *Prsd ldr & hit 4; trckd ldr til wknd 14; drpd to 5th nxt & imm outpcd; poor 6th 16*
[705ᵁ]	6	fence	**Mr Fitz (IRE)** 5-2 M Sheridan *V sa; nvr gng wl; 15l 6th 3; rdr waved 4 & 10; t.o; plodded rnd*

OFFICIAL DISTANCES: 6l, 3l **TIME:** 6min 34.0s

1210 Mens Open   4 ran

[826²]	1		**PRIME COURSE (IRE)** 11-10 C Gordon *Ld; hit 4; hdd brief 5; jnd 10 til stdd & hdd bend aft 13; lft in ld agn nxt; qcknd clr app 2 out; sn in comm; v easy*
[981³]	2	20	**Broguestown Pride (IRE)** 6-1 P Hall *Last 3; 5l 4th 9; detach last til clsd as ldrs slowed aft 13; lft 3rd nxt; stayed on one pce; passed idling rival cl home*
[981ᵁ]	3	¾	**Galaroi (IRE)** (tt) 4-5F D Robinson *Spurs; pulling; prsd ldr; ld brief 5; jnd ldr 10-13; drpd to 3rd but lft 2nd agn 14; prsd ldr til outpcd app 2 out; wknd rap; nt rdn & dem cl home*
[705ᴾ]	R		**Paddy Casey (IRE)** 14-1 C Sherry *3rd & jmpd slow 6; 9l 3rd 13; clsd to ld aft 13; nt much room & rn out & slpd up nxt; lame*

OFFICIAL DISTANCES: 20l, ¾l **TIME:** 6min 42.0s

1211 Ladies Open
5 ran

[1113³]	1		**ISLAND VISION (IRE)** 7-2 **Mrs J Hughes** *Prom til ld 4; mostly ½-1l ahd til prsd app last; rdn clr flat; rdr's 1st wnr*
[969⁵]	2	2½	**Haunting Music (IRE)** 7-1 **Miss E Neyens** (xnb) *Pulling; rstrnd in rr went 3l 2nd 6; clsd to ½l 2nd 8; prsd ldr til no ex last*
[827⁶]	3	15	**Pair Of Jacks (IRE)** (bl) 14-1 **Miss J Wickens** *Sa; 4th til last 7; 10l 4th 15; wknd 3 out*
[707³]	U		**Silk Vestments** (5a) 3-1 **Mrs D Rowell** *Ld til blun & ur 3*
[573²]	P		**Whippers Delight (IRE)** 1-3F **Miss J Grant** *Rn in snatches; prsd ldr til drpd to 8l 3rd 4; rallied to ½l 2nd 7; drpd to 3rd agn 9; jnd ldng pr 13; cl up til lost action & pu 3 out; lame*

OFFICIAL DISTANCES: 4l, dist TIME: 6min 35.0s

1212 Confined, 12st - 17J
8 ran

[711ᴾ]	1		**BILLIE'S MATE (IRE)** (5a) (bl) 20-1 **Mrs S Hickman** *Hld up in 5th; lft 5l 4th 6; lft 4l 3rd 9 & 5l 2nd 15; lft wl clr nxt; unchall; lucky*
[826³]	2	10	**Celtic Spark** (3x) 5-1 **Miss J Grant** *2-3l 2nd til dem 3rd brief & lft 2nd agn 9; 6l 3rd & pckd 15; btn when lft 8l 2nd 16; one pce*
[676ᶠ]	U		**Just Try Me (IRE)** (tt) 33-1 **P Hall** *In tch towards rr; 6l 7th when ur 6 (did 3 circs of track loose)*
	F		**Martha's Boy (IRE)** (2ow) evensF **D Robinson** *Spurs; pulled v hrd; went 3rd & hit 3; rdr lost iron; unable to settle; 4l 3rd when fell 6*
[827ᴾ]	R		**Professor Page (IRE)** 8-1 **C Gordon** *Ld; wandered & tried to rn out app 10; 8l clr 14; rn thro rt wing & ur 14*
[983ᴾ]	P		**Sugar Mill** 10-1 **C Sherry** *Got loose padd & bloodied nose of woman who tried to catch it; mounted bosses; tde; last pr; lft 12l 4th by 9; lost tch qckly; t.o when rdr stpd 13; cont; pu imm aft 14; broke down*
[824⁴]	U		**Tooth Pick (IRE)** (6x) 5-2 **J Hawksfield** *Last pr; just last when ur 5*
[953ᴾ]	F		**White Smoke (IRE)** 7-2 **R Ross** *Trckd ldr in 4th; lft 4l 3rd 8; fell nxt*

OFFICIAL DISTANCE: 14l TIME: 6min 40.0s
Fences 12 & 18 omitted - fallen rider; the stewards formally warned the owner of Sugar Mill concerning the horse's unruly behaviour in the paddock (knocked over an Official) and at the start (unable to be re-girthed)

1213 Open Maiden, 12st
4 ran

	1		**GENERAL JACKIE (IRE)** 4-1 **P Hall** *Jw; cl 2nd til ld 3-7; cl 2nd 8; disp ld 9 til ld 15; prsd brief 2 out; r.o wl & clr last*
[828ᵁ]	2	5	**Ell Gee** (5a) 2-1 **P Townsley** *Trckd ldrs; 4l 3rd 6; clsd to 2l 3rd 12; 3l 2nd 16; rdn & nt qckn 2 out; sn btn*
[925ᴾ]	P		**Arctic Lodge (IRE)** (vis) 4-1 **Mrs J Hughes** *V novicey & drpd out in last; 6l last 3; t.o 9; fnce bhnd by 11; pu 13*
[829³]	F		**Environmental Law** (bl) 5-4F **C Gordon** *Ld to 2; cl 2nd til ld 8; jnd 9-14; releg 3rd 16; 4l 3rd & lsng tch when fell 3 out; ungenuine*

OFFICIAL DISTANCE: 8l TIME: 6min 47.0s

South Notts

Thorpe Lodge (LH 7F,19J) **Mon, 24 Apr** (GOOD to SOFT becoming SOFT)

1214 Hunt
6 ran

[961³]	1		**NISHVAMITRA** 7-2 **A Woodward** *A.p; ld to 5; w ldrs til chall 15; ld 3 out; r.o wl*
[1070⁴]	2	1½	**Tom's Surprise** 6-4 **N Kent** *A.p; ld 6-8; ld agn brief 10; 3rd 12; disp ld 15; ev ch when mist 2 out; a hld aft*
[546ᴾ]	3	25	**Grants Carouse** 10-1 **M Wells** *Mid-div; trckd ldrs 10; ld 11; jnd 15; hdd aft nxt; wknd rap & sn no ch*
	4	4fncs	**Riverdale Henry** (U) (52ow) 33-1 **W Walker** *Ss; 10l last 3; 2 fncs adrift 8; stdly lost tch; outwobbled other heavyweight flat*
	5	4	**Bruce** (U) (34ow) 33-1 **I Price** *Ss; sn detach in last pr; 2 fncs bhnd 8; stdly lost ground but ld other heavyweight til dem last flat*
[963ᴾ]	F		**Train Lover (NZ)** 4-1F **G Smith** *Trckd ldrs til ld 9-10; 4th & wkng when fell 14*

OFFICIAL DISTANCES: 1½l, dist TIME: 6min 59.0s

1215 Marsh UK/TBA PPORA Club Members Mares, 12st
6 ran

[532¹]	1		**NIGHT IRENE (IRE)** (5a) 4-7F **G Hanmer** *Confid rdn; hld up; 4th 12; rap prog to ld 16; r.o; v easy*

[794³]	2	6	**Ways And Means** (5a) 7-1 K Green A;p; jnd clr 9; jmpd to ld 14; hdd 16; r.o; a hld
[1005²]	3	5	**Lottie The Lotus** (5a) 5-2 J Tarry 2nd 2; 4l 4th 5; disp cl 2nd 13; ev ch 16; 3rd & one pce nxt
[867²]	4	20	**Smart Rhythm** (5a) 10-1 R Armson Ld & sn 10l clr; jnd 9; hdd 12; rdn & wknd 14; 13l 4th & btn 3 out
[868⁶]	P		**Quiet Mistress** (5a) 50-1 N Kent A towards rr; last pr 5; 10l adrift 13; t.o & pu 16
[773⁷]	P		**Waisu** (5a) 66-1 M Mackley In tch; 3rd 5; last & wkng 12; t.o & pu 14

OFFICIAL DISTANCES: 6l, 5l **TIME:** 6min 43.0s

1216 Mens Open, 12st
6 ran

[48⁹]	1		**BARNA BOY (IRE)** 5-1 M Hewitt Jmpd immaculate; pulled hrd; ld; 25l ahd 6; fnce clr 7; pegged back & 8l up when lft clr agn 2 out; r.o wl flat
[789¹]	2	15	**Fawsley Manor** (5a) 2-1 J Tarry Nt fluent; 4th 5; disp 3rd when jmpd rt 13 & 16; no imp when lft 2nd 2 out; one pce
[615¹]	3	5	**Catchword** 4-5F R Armson Chsd clr ldr; prog in 8l 2nd & lkd dangerous when blun & nrly fell 2 out; nt rec; dem & one pce nxt
[1072³]	4	fence	**Deel Quay (IRE)** 16-1 M Chatterton A rr; rem 5th 5; fnce bhnd 8; last 11; nd
[229ᵁ]	5	20	**Edge Of Night** 10-1 M Bennison In tch brief; 3rd 5; fnce 3rd 7; last 15; plodded on
	P		**Breckenbrough Lad** 33-1 I Bennett Sa; a last; t.o 7; pu 11

OFFICIAL DISTANCES: 20l, 5l **TIME:** 6min 44.0s

1217 Ladies Open
4 ran

[1074²]	1		**KENILWORTH LAD** 1-2F Miss L Allan Trckd ldrs; cl last 5; prog 11; ld 12; jnd brief nxt; made rest; blun 14; 15l clr 2 out; unchall; lft solo at last
[796⁹]	2	bad	**Tiderunner (IRE)** 6-1 Miss C Elkington Sa; last 1; gd prog & just ld 3-11; disp ld brief 13; chsd wnr vain aft; 20l 2nd when ur last; rmtd
	U		**Guest Alliance (IRE)** 2-1 Miss H Phizacklea Prom; 2nd & mist 4; ld & ur 12
[1012⁹]	P		**Up The Road (IRE)** 20-1 Miss S Tacy Handy til wknd 12; 20l last 13; pu 15

OFFICIAL DISTANCE: dist **TIME:** 7min 00.0s

1218 Restricted, 12st
7 ran

[867³]	1		**ROLY POLY (IRE)** 2-1 M Mackley Mid-div; 5th 5; gd prog to 2nd 12; disp ld 15; 10l clr nxt; drew rt away; impressive
[1010¹]	2	30	**Magical Manor** (5a) 7-1 J Tarry Trckd ldr to 5; drpd to last pr 12; rdn & stayed on to 3rd 15 & 2nd aft 2 out; no ch w wnr
[1005⁹]	3	5	**Hobnob (IRE)** 6-1 R Barrett Ld; jnd brief 7 & agn 15; sn hdd & wknd; dem 3rd aft 2 out
[1076¹]	4	nk	**Fair Farm Lad** 7-1 Miss R Pask In tch in 4/5th til wkng qckly to last 12; no ch aft; kpt on clsng stages
[1040ᶠ]	U		**Campbellhill (IRE)** 25-1 M Grange Sa; 5l last when ur 3
[1009²]	U		**Macfin (IRE)** 5-4F Miss L Allan Mid-div til last 6; niggled along 10; went 8l 3rd 12; ur 13
[1069ᵁ]	P		**Tipping Away (IRE)** 25-1 A Pickering Trckd ldrs; 3rd 5; disp ld brief 7; mist 9; 4th & wkng 12; pu 14

OFFICIAL DISTANCES: dist, 5l **TIME:** 6min 59.0s

1219 Open Maiden (Div 1), 12st
9 ran

[1012³]	1		**FISHERMAN JACK** (7a) 5-4F M Mackley Jw; midfield; hdwy to disp ld 3 out; ld nxt; r.o game
[1011²]	2	2	**Round The Bend** 6-1 Miss L Allan Chsd ldrs; prog to disp ld 6 & pr sn 10l clr of rest; mist & hdd 10; ld brief 14; 2nd app 16; kpt on; a hld
[792ᶠ]	3	10	**Miss Hoity Toity** (5a) 7-1 J Tarry Trckd ldr; mist 4; qcknd to ld 15 til rn wide & hdd aft nxt; one pce & dem 3rd 2 out
[1070⁵]	4	20	**Anneka Louise** (5a) 16-1 N Kent Mid-div; 3rd & chsng ldrs 3 out; 4th & wkng qckly nxt
[918⁷]	5	5	**Asked To Leave** (5a) 12-1 I Bennett Ld 1; jnd 6 & pr sn wl clr; ld 10 til blun & hdd brief 12; hdd 14; sn wknd
[1035ᵁ]	6	8	**Father's Joy** (5a) 8-1 P Millington Trckd ldrs; in tch til wknd 16; sn btn
[1039ᶠ]	P		**Classic Ms (IRE)** 33-1 M Grange Ss; detach last til pu 13
[872³]	P		**Light The Sky** 3-1 J Turcan Trckd ldrs til wknd 13; bhnd 15; pu nxt
[1010⁹]	U		**The Bee's Castle (IRE)** 20-1 R Armson Towards rr til ur 6

OFFICIAL DISTANCES: 2l, 10l **TIME:** 6min 57.0s

The rider of Classis Ms was fined £60 for failing to report to the Doctor following a fall in the previous race

1220 Open Maiden (Div 2), 12st   **8 ran**

	1		**BE UPSTANDING** (7a) 7-4F M Mackley *Jw; hld up in tch towards rr; prog to 3rd 12; jnd ldr 14 til ld 16; 8l clr & in comm nxt*
[871⁶]	2	25	**Cashel Green (IRE)** 3-1 M Hewitt *Unruly & reluct go to start; mid-div; prog to ld 12; jmpd rt & hdd nxt; disp ld 14; hdd 16; sn outpcd & no ch w wnr*
[1070ᴾ]	F		**Carr Dyke Castle** 10-1 N Kent *2nd when fell 2*
[861ᶠ]	F		**Foxy Lass** (5a) 7-2 G Hanmer *Hld up towards rr; jmpd slow 6; eff 10; went rem 3rd 13; exhaust when crashing fall 2 out*
[1011ᶠ]	P		**Game Drive (IRE)** 5-1 P Newton *Nd in midfield; mists 11 & 16; t.o last when pu 3 out*
[54ᴾ]	P		**Grannies Delight (IRE)** 20-1 I Bennett *Ld to 2; trckd ldrs; last 9; pu 12*
[1076ᴾ]	P		**Imperial Tokay (USA)** 20-1 A Brown *Prom til ld 3-7; wknd qckly; last pr & pushed along 12; pu 14*
[798ᴾ]	P		**Rymerole** 8-1 M Bennison *Jw; prom til ld 8-11; lost ground qckly frm nxt; last when pu 15*

OFFICIAL DISTANCE: dist   TIME: 7min 07.0s

South Pembrokeshire

Lydstep (LH 8F,19J) Mon, 24 Apr (GOOD)

1221 Hunt, 12st   **5 ran**

[837³]	1		**LONGSTONE BOY (IRE)** 7-4 P Hamer *Cl up in rr early; 10l 3rd 15; impd to 4l 2nd 3 out; jnd ldrs nxt; pushed out run-in*
[1022⁵]	2	2	**Cresswell Quay** (3x) 6-4F G Lewis *Prom; 7l clr 11; 4l app 16; jnd 18; u.p app last; no ex flat*
[1015¹⁰]	3	15	**Sip Of Brandy (IRE)** (7x) 6-1 Miss J Hughes *Prom early; wknd; rn wide app 13; 30l 4th 15; r.o one pce*
[484¹]	4	10	**Thebetsonmary** (5a,3x) 2-1 J Jukes *Cl up; disp ld til ld 13-14; wknd frm 16*
[650ᴾ]	U		**Just Ruffled** (bl) 33-1 Miss J Gill *Cl up when ur 3*

OFFICIAL DISTANCES: 1½l, 20l   TIME: 6min 21.0s

1222 Open Maiden 56&7yo (Div 1), 2m4f, 12st - 16J   **13 ran**

	1		**MARISOL (IRE)** (5a) 3-1 C Williams *Mid-div early; impd to 4l 3rd 8; 3l 2nd 10; disp ld 12; lft clr last*
[478ᴾ]	2	20	**Eveies Boy (IRE)** (7a) 3-1 E Williams *Ld frm 1-12; wknd 13; r.o one pce*
[834ᴾ]	3	20	**Power Unit** (7a) 8-1 P Hamer *3rd/4th to 7; 20l 7th 10; r.o frm 12*
[950⁴]	4	8	**Mission Lord (IRE)** 3-1 J Jukes *Mid-div early; 15l 4th 10; r.o one pce*
	5	2fncs	**Dreamington Rovers** (5a) 7-1 Miss A Meakins *T.o 5; hacked rnd*
[1055ᵁ]	6	4	**Jesusa** (5a) 25-1 J Keen *T.o 5; hacked rnd*
	F		**A Class Apart (NZ)** 6-1 N Oliver *A.p; 4l 2nd 3rd; 3l 2nd 11; disp ld 12-16; ½l up when fell last*
[595ᴾ]	P		**Andsome Andy** 2-1F T Vaughan *Mid-div to 10; wknd 11; pu 14*
[1055ᴾ]	P		**Annie's Alfie** 12-1 A Price *Mid-div; 15l 6th 10; wknd & pu 14*
	P		**Danas** 10-1 G Maloney *A rr; t.o 5; pu 11*
	P		**Dream Holiday** (12a) 6-1 P Sheldrake *In tch to 10; wknd & pu 13*
	F		**Lady Murrhill (IRE)** (12a) 8-1 J Hayward *Midfield when fell 4*
[835²]	P		**Nomoremissnicegirl** (5a) 3-1 G Lewis *Rr early; wknd 8; pu 12*

OFFICIAL DISTANCES: 20l, 20l   TIME: 5min 11.0s

1223 Open Maiden 56&7yo (Div 2), 2m4f, 12st - 16J   **13 ran**

[270⁴]	1		**OMAR'S ODYSSEY (IRE)** (7a) 4-1 C Williams *Mid-div early; impd to cl 4th 8; disp ld 10; clr frm 13; mist last; nd*
[489ᶠ]	2	20	**Up Your Street** (12a) 4-1 Miss P Jones *Rr early; 10l 6th 11; r.o frm 12*
[950²]	3	10	**Bold Knight** 5-2F G Skone *Hld up early; impd to 3l 3rd 12; lft 2nd 13; no ex*
[823²]	4	3	**Beths Gift** (5a) 3-1 D Stephens (Wales) *Mid-div early; 8l 5th 9; 10l 7th 12; r.o one pce*
[951²]	5	2	**Pryvate Time** (5a) 8-1 J Keen *Mid-div; r.o frm 13*
[989ᴾ]	6	1	**Blazing Connie** (5a) 7-1 G Perkins *Mid-div early; 8l 5th 12; wknd 13*
[949⁵]	7	2	**Tiny** (12a) 8-1 E Williams *Ld to 7; cl 3rd 8-12; wknd*
	8	15	**Rubian Princess** (12a) 8-1 S Lloyd *T.o 5; school in rr*
	9	1	**Get The Gist (IRE)** 12-1 P Hamer *T.o 5; school aft*
	P		**Cresswell Cherry (IRE)** (12a) 6-1 T Vaughan *A rr; pu 14*
[900ᴾ]	F		**Double Steal** 4-1 J Jukes *Prom; ld 7-12; cl 3rd when fell 13*
[834ᶠ]	F		**Ginger Duchess** (5a) 14-1 Miss C Williams *Mid-div when fell 3; broke leg; dead*
[949⁷]	U		**Motu Tapu** 4-1 Miss A Meakins *Rr early; impd to 6l 4th 13; 10l 2nd when blun & ur last*

OFFICIAL DISTANCES: 20l, 15l   TIME: 5min 19.0s

1224 Greig Middleton Ladies Open   8 ran

[1022⁴]	1		**BULLENS BAY (IRE)** 8-1 **Miss F Wilson** *Lft cl 3rd 8; 2l 2nd 14; 6l 2nd 16; clsd agn 2 out; ld app last; all out*
[1051ᴾ]	2	hd	**Mr Mad** (vis) 6-1 **Miss C Thomas** *Ld frm 9 til hdd app last; r.o agn u.p; just hld*
[943²]	3	40	**Same Difference (IRE)** 20-1 **Mrs B Lewis** *50l last 5; some late prog*
[836⁵]	4	10	**Celtic Friend (IRE)** 12-1 **Miss J Gill** *40l 7th 5; t.o 8*
	5	10	**Local Customer** 20-1 **Miss S Matthews** *30l 6th 5; t.o by 8*
[836³]	P		**Busman (IRE)** 2-1 **Miss L Pearce** *Lft cl 2nd 8; 3l 3rd 14; wknd frm 16; pu 2 out*
[836¹]	B		**Dawn's Cognac (IRE)** 1-2F **Miss P Jones** *Mid-div when bd 8*
[1052³]	F		**Llan Cross Lady** (5a) 20-1 **Miss T Stevens** *Ld; clr 1-7; still ½l up when fell 8*

OFFICIAL DISTANCES: hd, dist   TIME: 6min 19.0s

1225 Open Maiden, 12st   13 ran

[1068²]	1		**CHERRY GOLD** 4-6F **E Williams** *Made all; 10l clr 15; 20l clr 2 out; easy*
[838ᶠ]	2	20	**Twopintsahalfone (IRE)** (bl) 3-1 **A Price** *A.p; cl 2nd 8; 2l down 14; 10l 2nd 15; no ex*
[1055ᴾ]	3	50	**Artique Fish (IRE)** 3-1 **J Jukes** *Rr early; 6th 11; 30l 5th 14; r.o*
[950³]	4	2	**Sing Cherry Ripe** (5a) 7-1 **Miss T Stevens** *Last 5; wl bhnd 10; some gd late prog*
	5	10	**Carbury's Case** 12-1 **H Evans** *Rr early; r.o one pce*
[838¹]	F		**Baytownghost (IRE)** (bl) 5-1 **J Price** *Prom; ld 6-7; 8l 4th 10; wkng when fell 16*
[835ᶠ]	F		**Fair Charmeur (IRE)** (5a) 8-1 **Miss A Meakins** *Cl 4th 8; bad mist 11; pu 14*
[1221ᵁ]	P		**Just Ruffled** 12-1 **Miss J Gill** *2nd outing; a rr; pu 16*
[1056³]	F		**Lough Neagh (IRE)** 6-1 **P Sheldrake** *Prom when fell 6*
[838ᴾ]	P		**Maes Gwyn Dreamer** 6-1 **Miss L Pearce** *Mid-div til wknd 8; pu 10*
[1056ᴾ]	F		**Millbank Honey** (5a) 6-1 **M Barber** *Mid-div when fell 6*
[486ᴾ]	P		**Some Grey** (5a) 14-1 **J Cook** *A rr; pu 16*
[951ᵁ]	P		**Stormhill Daydream** (5a) 14-1 **G Lewis** *Mid-div til wknd 14; pu 16*

OFFICIAL DISTANCES: 15l, dist   TIME: 6min 29.0s

1226 Mens Open   7 ran

[1051ᵁ]	1		**KINNEFAD KING (IRE)** 2-1 **C Williams** *Rr early; impd to cl 3rd 14; disp ld 2 out; ld last; pushed out*
[1014²]	2	2	**Mr Dow Jones (IRE)** 6-4F **J Jukes** *Ld/disp 12-3 out; jnd nxt; 1l down last; no ex*
[945¹]	3	2	**Moon Tiger** 4-1 **T Vaughan** *Mid-div early; cl 4th 14; 1l 3rd 16; 2l 3rd app last; no ex*
[1022⁸]	4	15	**True Fortune** 8-1 **M Barber** *Mid-div early; wknd frm 16*
[1053¹]	5	4	**Saffron Moss** (bl) 14-1 **J Price** *Ld/disp to 8 & agn 12-14; wknd 16*
[1065³]	6	5	**Cream Supreme (IRE)** (bl) 3-1 **E Williams** *In tch in rr early; wknd frm 14*
[946ᴾ]	P		**Young Manny** (3x) 33-1 **M Lewis** *Disp ld to 11; wknd frm 13; pu 3 out*

OFFICIAL DISTANCES: 2l, 1l   TIME: 6min 22.0s

1227 Intermediate, 12st   9 ran

[837²]	1		**JO JOS BEST FRIEND** (5a) evensF **T Vaughan** *Mid-div early; cl 3rd 8; disp ld 14-16; ld nxt; clr app last; easy*
[1053ᴾ]	2	20	**Rusnetto (IRE)** 8-1 **G Lewis** *Ld/disp frm 6-16; r.o u.p; no ex*
[943¹]	3	10	**Secret Beauty (IRE)** (5a) 4-1 **M Lewis** *4/5th to 8; 6l 4th 14; r.o one pce*
[1022¹]	4	3	**Tiger Lord** 2-1 **C Williams** *Disp 3rd/4th early; 4l 3rd 14; 10l 3rd 16; no ex*
[944ᴾ]	P		**Bancyfelin Boy** 12-1 **J Keen** *A rr; to 8; pu 12*
[1054ᴾ]	P		**Dunsfold Dazzler** (5a) 4-1 **D Hughes** *A rr; lost tch 12; pu 14*
	P		**John's Right (IRE)** 6-1 **J Cook** *A rr; pu 14*
[948¹]	P		**Secret Can't Say (IRE)** (5a) 2-1 **J Jukes** *Prom to 11; wknd frm 14; pu 14*
[1051³]	P		**Teigr Pren** 6-1 **P Sheldrake** *Disp 2nd/3rd to 8; wknd 10; pu 14*

OFFICIAL DISTANCES: 15l, 10l   TIME: 6min 21.0s

1228 Restricted, 12st   13 ran

[832²]	1		**OUR HARRY** 10-1 **J Keen** *Ld/disp to 16; 2l clr 2 out; 8l clr last; easy*
[947²]	2	10	**Final Rose** (5a) 10-1 **G Lewis** *Ld/disp to 16; r.o one pce frm 3 out*
[486ᴾ]	3	5	**Howsyourluck (IRE)** 3-1 **T Vaughan** *Prom; 10l 3rd 6; nvr able to chall*
[947⁴]	4	30	**Hil Lady** (5a) 10-1 **M Barber** *Detach last early; prog frm ½way; nrst fin*
[832ᵁ]	5	10	**Young Mariner** (5a) 10-1 **G Maloney** *Mid-div early; 6th 12; wknd frm 14*
	P		**Bonny Boy** (7a) 8-1 **P Sheldrake** *A rr; to 8; pu 14*
[342¹]	P		**Brewery Lane** (5a) 10-1 **Miss P Jones** *Mid-div early; wknd frm 11; pu 16*
[948³]	P		**Briary Boy** (5a) 8-1 **A Price** *Mid-div; 4th 6; 5th 11; wknd 15; pu 3 out*
[864ᴾ]	P		**Cherry Alley (IRE)** (5a) 5-1 **S Lloyd** *Rr early; prog to 7th 14; 4th 16; wknd & pu 2 out*

[642³]	P		Crafty Gunner 10-1 Miss L Pearce *In tch in 8th 9; wknd 11; pu 15*
[948ᴿ]	P		Jack Boots 10-1 J Phillips *Rr early; wknd 10; pu 15*
[1089ᴾ]	P		Out On The Town (5a) 10-1 James Tudor *Mid-div early; disp 5th 8; wknd 10; pu 15*
[601¹]	P		Twotensforafive 4-6F E Williams *Mid-div early; 20l 5th 8; 4th 11; wknd 16; pu 2 out*

OFFICIAL DISTANCES: 15l, 10l **TIME:** 6min 27.0s

Staintondale

Charm Park (LH 9F,19J) Mon, 24 Apr (GOOD with SOFT patches)

1229 Hunt, 12st

6 ran

[808²]	1		KERRISDALE (5a) (tt) 4-5F S Charlton *Handy in mid-div to 12; went 2l 2nd 3 out; disp ld nxt; easily qcknd clr app last; eased cl home*
[918⁴]	2	15	Mandril (IRE) 6-4 N Tutty *Prom in 3rd til ld 7; 6l clr 9; 2l up 10-16; jnd by wnr 2 out; sn hdd & brushed aside*
[809⁶]	3	1½fs	The Noble Rebel (IRE) 7-1 A Pennock *Ld to 6; 6l 2nd 9; pushed along 11; 4l 3rd when bad mist 14; lost tch qckly; poor 3rd 3 out*
[1033⁸]	P		Palm Gold (5a) 25-1 R Wakeham *Rr to 8; pushed along & lsng tch 11; t.o & pu 13*
	P		Polly Maid (5a) 25-1 M Haigh *Cl 2nd til disp ld 3-5; grad wknd frm 9; t.o & pu 13*
[1070²]	P		Young Saffy 25-1 P Halder *Last to 2; lsng tch 6; t.o 12; rem 4th when pu 15*

OFFICIAL DISTANCES: 10l, dist **TIME:** 6min 51.0s

1230 Restricted

18 ran

[688¹]	1		WHAT A FIDDLER (IRE) 2-1F R Tate *Midfield to 10; went 8l 4th 11 & 6l 3rd 15; gd hdwy to 2l 2nd 3 out; chall app last; qcknd clr flat*
[996¹]	2	4	Victoria's Boy (IRE) 4-1 G Brewer *Prom til ld 5-10; cl 2nd til ld agn 3 out; jnd app last; hdd & one pce flat*
[1000⁵]	3	20	Just Takethe Micky 8-1 S Walker *Midfield to 14; stayed on to 15l 3rd 2 out; r.o one pce; nvr trbld ldng pr*
[1028²]	4	12	Sassy Street (IRE) 5-2 K Needham *Handy 2nd to 10; ld 11-16; outpcd & wknd 3 out*
[1000⁹]	5	2	Hazel Reilly (IRE) (5a) 7-1 L Bates *Last to 2; rr & pushed along 13; stayed on wl frm 15; fin str; nrst fin*
[808⁵]	6	3	The Killaloe Run (5a) 25-1 Miss J Foster *(bf) Prom to 6; wknd 8; rr & scrubbed along 10; r.o one pce*
[1000⁹]	7	2	Fiery Jack 20-1 N Tutty *Ld to 4; cl 2nd 5-9; wknd 10; poor 6th by 3 out*
[1028⁴]	8	4	Mount Faber (bl) 25-1 S Charlton *A midfield; nd*
[996⁵]	P		Brackenhill 7-1 R Wakeham *A midfield to rr; lsng tch 14; t.o & pu 3 out*
[797⁷]	P		Deer Park Lass (IRE) (5a) 14-1 D Thomas *Midfield to 8; went 5l 4th 10; pushed along & strugg 12; grad wknd; t.o & pu app last*
[923⁵]	P		Flashlight 25-1 P Halder *(bf) Cl 6th to 9; trckng ldrs 10; wknd 11; rr & lsng tch when pu 13*
[797ᶠ]	P		Kind Of Chic (5a) 20-1 P Kinsella *(xnb) Mid-div to 4; rr by 11; t.o & pu 13*
[1028³]	P		Mefein Boy (IRE) 10-1 Miss R Clark *A midfield; pushed along aft 11; lost tch 13; t.o & pu 3 out*
[1028ᴾ]	F		Moor Lady (5a) 33-1 S Swiers *A midfield to rr; bhnd when fell 13*
[1028ᵁ]	P		Run For The Mill 33-1 M Morley *A rr div; pushed along aft 13; t.o & pu 15*
[1028ᵁ]	U		The Happy Monarch (IRE) 5-1 Mrs F Needham *Mid-div when ur 5*
[1000⁷]	P		Traceytown (IRE) (5a) 25-1 Miss Rachel Clark *(xnb) A rr; lost tch 14; t.o & pu 3 out*
[1028⁵]	P		Yornoangel 33-1 R Clark *(xnb) Mid-div to 8; 8l 6th 10; wknd 11; lsng tch when pu 13*

OFFICIAL DISTANCES: 3l, 12l **TIME:** 6min 35.0s

1231 Mens Open

6 ran

[797¹]	1		KEY DEBATE 1-2F G Brewer *Jmpd fast; made all; 20l clr 13; galloped on str; unextended; v impressive*
[870³]	2	12	Primitive Streak 7-2 R Abrahams *A chsng ldr; 20l 2nd 14; went in hrd pursuit 3 out; r.o one pce; nvr able to chall*
[805⁵]	3	runin	Nishkina 33-1 C Cundall *A rr; lsng tch 5; rem last 13; stayed on to poor 3rd 2 out*
[1030⁶]	4	15	That Old Feeling (IRE) 8-1 R Edwards *A midfield; outpcd 12; 40l 3rd 14; dem to poor 4th 2 out; exhaust & clambered over last*
[504ᴾ]	B		Be Brave 33-1 N Tutty *In chsng group to 8; 7l 3rd 9; mists 11 & 12; wkng & pushed along in 5th when bd 13*
[805²]	F		Just Charlie 4-1 D Easterby *Cl 2nd to 3; outpcd 4; 25l 5th 11; pushed along 12; went 20l 3rd & fell 13*

OFFICIAL DISTANCES: 12l, dist **TIME:** 6min 35.0s

1232 Ladies Open   6 ran

[1071ᵁ]	1		**SPRINGFIELD REX** 4-5F Mrs F Needham *Hld up in mid-div to 8; went 3l 3rd 10; ld 13; stdly drew clr; 10l up 2 out; r.o str*
[998³]	2	8	**Misti Hunter (IRE)** 4-1 Miss Rachel Clark *(xnb) A 2nd; 2l 2nd 9-13; outpcd 14; 10l down 15; chsd wnr vain aft*
[797⁶]	3	6	**C L B Jemilla** (5a) 7-2 Miss S Brotherton *Prom in 4th til 3rd 11; outpcd 13; 12l 3rd 3 out; r.o same pce*
[1029³]	4	30	**Stride To Glory (IRE)** (bl) 10-1 Mrs H Arnold *Ld at str pce to 12; wknd 14; poor 4th by 2 out*
[1029ᴾ]	5	8	**Temple Garth** 5-1 Miss F Hartley *Rr & outpcd 3; 10l adrift by 6; t.o 13*
[1028⁷]	P		**Up And Over (IRE)** (bl) 14-1 Miss J Foster *Cl 2nd to 8; wknd 9; rr & outpcd by 12; poor 5th 13; t.o & pu 3 out*

OFFICIAL DISTANCES: 10l, 5l   TIME: 6min 38.0s

1233 Open Maiden 56&7yo   10 ran

[1032²]	1		**GENTLEMAN CHARLES (IRE)** 5-4F S Walker *Prom to 10; went 2l 3rd 13; disp ld 3 out-nxt; drew clr app last; r.o u.p; fin tired*
[1032³]	2	5	**Imperial Line (IRE)** 6-1 Miss T Jackson *(xnb) Pulled hrd early; ld frm 3; 1l up 16; jnd 3 out; disp ld nxt; wknd app last*
[1002²]	3	15	**Aunty Norma (IRE)** (5a) 7-1 D Thomas *Last early; hdwy to mid-div aft 6; 6l 5th 11; went cl 3rd 3 out; outpcd & wknd nxt*
[1001ᴾ]	4	12	**Redmire** (5a) 20-1 A Pennock *A rr; last & outpcd 13; poor 5th 2 out; stayed on to 4th flat*
[1033²]	5	8	**My Sam** (12a) 9-4 L McGrath *A rr; last but gng wl 15; pushed along 16; dist 4th 2 out; dem flat*
[809ᶠ]	P		**Dragon Stout** (tt) 7-1 C Wilson *Ld to 2; cl 2nd 3-14; wknd qckly & pu aft 15*
	P		**Enigma Bell** 20-1 N Tutty *Prom to 9; 4l 4th 14; mist 12 & wknd; lsng tch when pu 15*
[1001⁴]	P		**Mighty Rising** (7a) 8-1 S Charlton *A rr div; outpcd 15; lsng tch & bhnd when pu 2 out*
[625⁶]	P		**Perdix** (12a) 20-1 Miss J Foster *Prom to 3; rr by 5; lsng tch 8; t.o & pu 11*
[809ᵁ]	P		**Rievers Way** (7a) 16-1 R Clark *Midfield to 3; went ½l 2nd 4-6; bad mist 9; wknd qckly & pu nxt*

OFFICIAL DISTANCES: 4l, 10l   TIME: 6min 48.0s

1234 Open Maiden (Non-Placed) (Div 1)   10 ran

[1033⁹]	1		**WANDERING WILD** (12a) 10-1 Mrs L Ward *A.p; went 2l 2nd 12 til ld app last; rdly drew clr flat; r.o wl*
[1032²]	2	5	**Pashby Wood** (5a) 14-1 M Morley *Mid-div to 8; 15l 4th 10; hdwy 11 to cl 3rd 15; ld 3 out til hdd & one pce app last*
[1002⁶]	3	10	**Total Relief** (7a) 9-4 Miss S Brotherton *Bad mist 2; 10l 5th 6; gd hdwy 12 to cl 4th 13; ev ch 3 out; r.o one pce*
[1028ᶠ]	4	12	**Kings Cup** 20-1 M Haigh *Ld to 8; qcknd 10l clr 9-11; 2l ld 12-16; mist 3 out; wknd*
	5	15	**Highland Symphony** (5a) 7-4F Mrs F Needham *Blkd bad 1; rr to 9; 12l 5th & pushed along 11; lost tch 14; poor 5th by 3 out*
	P		**Addington Sharragh** (5a) 10-1 Miss J Binks *Chsd ldr in 2l 2nd to 7; outpcd 8; 10l 2nd 10; wknd 11; t.o & pu 15*
[803ᵁ]	P		**Chief Engineer** 6-1 L McGrath *A rr; last by 3; lsng tch 11 & t.o 16; rem 6th when ploughed thro 2 out & imm pu*
[1032ᴾ]	U		**La Emni (IRE)** 12-1 M Mawhinney *Midfield til ur 10*
[1002ᴾ]	P		**Minster Echo** (12a) 14-1 P Halder *Bad mist 1; last by 6; mist 8; rr & lsng tch 11; t.o & pu 3 out*
	P		**Procol's Boy** (7a) 4-1 S Walker *School in rr til pu 15*

OFFICIAL DISTANCES: 3l, 10l   TIME: 7min 01.0s

1235 Open Maiden (Non-Placed) (Div 2)   9 ran

[1033ᴾ]	1		**VALS CASTLE (IRE)** (5a) 3-1 G Tuer *A.p; 3l 3rd 8-10; lft in ld 12; 4l clr 3 out; stayed on wl; 10l clr last*
[809⁴]	2	15	**Farm Talk** evensF S Charlton *(bh) A.p; went 1l 2nd 11; cl 2nd & gng wl 16; easily outpcd 2 out; fnd nil*
[1032ᴾ]	3	15	**Sand Track** 14-1 M Haigh *Ld to 2; handy 5th 9; wknd 13; poor 4th 16; hrd rdn & tk 3rd flat*
[1034³]	4	4	**Mr Norm** 4-1 R Clark *Ld 4-8; cl 2nd 11-14; outpcd 16; 12l 3rd 2 out; scrambled over last; exhaust & dem 4th flat*
	P		**Arctic Corner** (5a) 10-1 A Pennock *A rr; mist 9; lsng tch & t.o 12; rem when pu 16*
[501ᴾ]	F		**Lewesdon Countess** (5a) 14-1 W Burnell *Hld up in rr to 5; went handy 5th 11; trckng ldrs in 5th when fell 13*

[793⁹]	F		**Russian Prince (IRE)** (7a) 8-1 **D Thomas** *Cl 2nd til ld 9; fell 13*
[1033ᵁ]	U		**Stanwick Hall** 6-1 **K Needham** *Handy 4th when ur 5*
	P		**Trigger Castle** (12a) 7-1 **S Walker** *A rr; bhnd & lsng tch 11; mist 12 & wknd; t.o & pu 16*

OFFICIAL DISTANCES: 12l, 15l **TIME:** 7min 05.0s

Taunton Vale

Kingston St Mary (RH 8F,19J) Mon, 24 Apr (GOOD to SOFT, SOFT patches)

1236 Hunt
3 ran

[927²]	1		**KINGSBRIDGE (IRE)** 4-11F **Miss P Gundry** (xnb) *Lw; hung lft; tk keen hld & sn ld; jmpd lft & hdd 13; disp ld agn when lft clr 16; pushed out clsng stages*
[638ᴾ]	2	2	**James Pigg** 6-1 **G Richards** *Trckd ldr; cl 3rd & niggled along 13; sn outpcd in 3rd; lft poor 2nd 16; rallied & tried to chall 2 out; ½l 2nd last; no ex flat*
[1059⁴]	F		**Primero (IRE)** (tt) 3-1 **A Honeyball** *Lw; hld up in tch; ld on inner 13; disp ld & gng wl when fell 16*

OFFICIAL DISTANCE: 2½l **TIME:** 6min 53.5s **TOTE:** £1.10

1237 Confined, 12st
8 ran

[954ᴾ]	1		**HIGHWAY LAD** (5x) (bl) 7-2 **L Jefford** *Tchd 4s in plce; lw; jw; sn wl plcd; cl 4th 11; ld nxt; drew clr stdly frm 16; comf*
[921¹⁵]	2	8	**Flapjack Lad** 8-1 **T Bishop** (xnb) *Handy; jw; cl 3rd 11; 3l 2nd 16; chsd wnr frm 3 out; kpt on game; fair eff*
[1098³]	3	2½	**Hanging Grove** 12-1 **M Bryant** *Lw; last when hit 4; rmdrs 11; 7th 13; 18l 5th 16; went 3rd past wkng horses 3 out; hrd rdn & kpt on one pce clsng stages*
[1098⁵]	4	4	**Parditino** (8x) 8-1 **Miss J Nicholas** *Chsd ldr to 12; lost plce; 7l 4th 15; r.o one pce frm 3 out*
[886⁶]	5	10	**Elle Flavador** (5a) 20-1 **Miss J Cumings** (xnb) *Lw; in tch in midfield; mist 7; hdwy to 3rd 13; pushed along in 3rd 16; went 2nd brief bef nxt; sn wknd & lost plce qckly 3 out*
[927¹]	P		**Stillmore Business** (3x) 10-11F **Miss P Gundry** *Rr & nvr gng wl; 5th & rmdr 10; mist 12; lost ground stdly frm 13; poor 6th when pu 15*
[1014ᵁ]	U		**The Bold Abbot** (3x) 7-1 **Miss S West** *Ld to 12; 4th & wkng 13; just in tch in 5th but wkng when blun & ur 14*
[1098ᵁ]	P		**Union Station (IRE)** (2ow) 50-1 **B Parsons** *Rr; rap hdwy 4; 4th 6; lost plce aft 8; last when mist 10; t.o & pu 13*

OFFICIAL DISTANCES: 8l, 1½l **TIME:** 6min 41.3s **TOTE:** £4.50

1238 Mens Open, 12st
4 ran

[930¹]	1		**FINNIGAN FREE** 5-4 **A Honeyball** *Tchd 2s in plce; lw; tk keen hld; jw; went 2nd 6; cl up til ld aft 16; pushed 3l clr 3 out; stayed on str*
[1098¹]	2	3	**Slew Man (FR)** (7x) 10-11F **L Jefford** (xnb) *Lw; hld up in tch; hdwy 15; went 2nd aft nxt; eff 2 out; ev ch til no ex last*
[927³]	3	20	**Avril Showers** (5a,4x) 8-1 **R Atkinson** *A frm sn 10l clr; hdd aft 16; wknd stdly*
[1096²]	P		**Tuskar Flop** (7x) 5-1 **D Alers-Hankey** *3rd frm 6; in tch in 4th 11; lost ground stdly frm 16; bhnd when pu 2 out*

OFFICIAL DISTANCES: 3l, 20l **TIME:** 6min 36.3s **TOTE:** £1.70

1239 Ladies Open
4 ran

[1060¹]	1		**MIZYAN (IRE)** 2-5F **Miss P Gundry** *Hld up; prog to ld 11; hit 14; drew clr nxt; 15l clr 3 out; canter*
[953⁴]	2	30	**Agile King** 10-1 **Miss C Tizzard** *Ld til jmpd slow 6; ld agn aft 8-11; in tch til wknd 14*
[969³]	3	runin	**Olive Basket** (5a) 7-1 **Miss W Southcombe** *A last; 25l last 12; plodded rnd*
[885ᴾ]	P		**Beck And Call (IRE)** (bl) 3-1 **Miss J Cumings** *Tchd 7/2; nt a fluent; ld aft 6 til aft 8; cl 3rd & rdn 13; lsng ground when blun 15; poor 3rd when pu aft nxt*

OFFICIAL DISTANCES: 25l, 30l **TIME:** 6min 42.0s **TOTE:** £1.20

1240 Restricted, 12st
7 ran

[926ᴿ]	1		**GEMINI MIST** (5a) (bl) 3-1 **Miss C Stretton** *Tchd 7/2; sn prom; cl 4th 10; trckd ldr frm 12; eff & ld 2 out; sn pushed clr*
[1095ᵁ]	2	6	**Barton Rose** 5-2 **D Alers-Hankey** *5s-5/2; lw; ld early; sn stdd & handy; cl 4th frm 13; nt fluent 14 & 15; 3rd & hdwy u.p 3 out; went 2nd app last; no ch w wnr*

[876F]	3	3	**Basil** 2-1F **L** Jefford *Tchd 5/2; lw; disp ld to 6; stayed cl up; 3rd when slt mist 12; 3l 3rd & ev ch 15-16; outpcd; hrd rdn & no prog 2 out; tk 3rd run-in*
[1095³]	4	2	**For Christie (IRE)** 5-1 **B O'Doherty** *(xnb) Tk keen hld; prog 7; ld 8 til hdd 2 out; sn btn; lost 3rd run-in*
[1042F]	5	12	**Belski** 14-1 **Miss J Buck** *Nov rdn; disp ld to 8; cl up til rn wide on bend aft 13; 6th 14; lost tch stdly frm nxt*
[931⁶]	U		**Franklins Best (IRE)** 5-1 **J Snowden** *Lw; midfield; in tch in 5th 14; no prog; 5th when mist & ur 16*
[873²]	P		**Jolie Roslin** (5a) 14-1 **A Honeyball** *Sn last; jmpd novicey; lost tch t.o & pu 3 out; school*

OFFICIAL DISTANCES: 5l, 2l TIME: 6min 54.0s TOTE: £7.70

1241 Open Maiden, 12st   11 ran

	1		**SHARED-INTEREST** (5a) 33-1 **B O'Doherty** *Tchd 50s; bhnd til gd hdwy 12; went 2nd aft 14; ld 15; drew clr 3 out & rdr kpt lkng rnd; pushed clr flat; comf*
[732³]	2	3	**Dunston Trigger** 2-1JF **L Jefford** *(xnb) Midfield when blun bad 4; prog 9; jnd ldrs 16; sn outpcd; went 2nd aft 3 out; drvn & 2l down when mist last; kpt on one pce*
[1100³]	3	runin	**Timber Top (IRE)** 2-1JF **D Alers-Hankey** *4s-2s; lw; jmpd v poor; handy; hmpd slt 8; cl 4th 11; mist & lost ground 16; mist 2 out; btn when blun last*
[957³]	4	runin	**Weycroft Valley** (5a) 25-1 **L Tibbatts** *5th ½way; in tch til lost plce 13; bhnd when jmpd slow 16; t.o aft*
	U		**All Sewn Up** 9-2 **A Honeyball** *20s-9/2; 2 handlers; prom; ld aft 6-13; 2nd when mist nxt; 2l 3rd when blun & ur 15; do btr*
[1101F]	U		**Anolyze** (5a) 50-1 **Miss K Allan** *Towards rr when ur 6*
[956F]	P		**Early Morning** (7a) 14-1 **G Richards** *Bckwd; rr; mist 5; 6th ½way; lost tch 11; bhnd & pu 13; school*
[1102F]	U		**Final Chance** (5a) 7-1 **Miss C Tizzard** *Prom; lft in ld aft 4 til jmpd v slow 6; chsd ldr til ld agn 13; jmpd slow nxt; hdd 15; 5l 2nd 3 out; wknd & v tired when blun bad & ur 2 out*
[958F]	U		**Green Anker** 7-1 **Miss C Stucley** *Slt mist 4; 5th when ur 6*
[518⁵]	R		**No Need For Alarm** (12a) 3-1 **Miss P Gundry** *(xnb) Lw; pulling; ld 3; jmpd lft 4; veered lft & rn off course app nxt*
	U		**Oh So Trendy** 20-1 **Miss J Cumings** *Ld to 3; 4th when blun & ur 8*

OFFICIAL DISTANCES: 2l, dist TIME: 6min 52.9s TOTE: £105.30

Vine & Craven
Hackwood Park (LH 7F,18J) Mon, 24 Apr (SOFT)

1242 Hunt, 12st   5 ran

[1015F]	1		**TOPICAL TIP (IRE)** 4-6F **P Cowley** *Jw; ld/disp; went 4l clr frm 16; 2l up at last; wknd flat; just hld on*
[937³]	2	¾	**Mendip Prince (IRE)** 9-4 **A Lillingston** *Cl up; disp ld 4; chsd ldrs til mist 10; 4l down 16; rallied to clse last; str chall flat; just failed; game*
[887⁴]	3	30	**Ngala (IRE)** (5a) 4-1 **H Tett** *Sa; clsd to disp ld 6; grad wknd frm 11*
	P		**Normanstown (U)** 7-1 **Miss J Buck** *Unruly start; sa; clsd to disp ld 6; pu aft 7*
	P		**Southern Nights** 3-1 **M Walters** *Settled mid-div; grad wknd; pu aft 11*

OFFICIAL DISTANCES: ¾l, dist TIME: 6min 48.0s TOTE: £1.70

1243 Intermediate (Nov Rdrs), 12st   7 ran

[886³]	1		**CASTLE SHELLEY (IRE)** 9-4 **R Smith** *Rr early; prog to disp ld 11; drew clr frm 15; r.o str; comf*
[1108⁵]	2	12	**Bit Of An Idiot** evensF **D Slattery** *Rr early; jnd ldr & mist 12; chsd wnr; ev ch 15; sn wknd; no ch 2 out*
[1134ᵁ]	3	3	**Silver Hill** (5a) 12-1 **Miss B Fear** *Sn outpcd in mid-div; wknd 11*
[1097⁵]	4	5	**Perseverance** 12-1 **Miss V Sturgis** *Rr mostly; stayed on one pce*
[971ᵁ]	5	10	**Holloa Away (IRE)** 12-1 **R Millar** *Ld/disp til lft in ld brief 10; sn wknd; walked in*
[1061ᵁ]	P		**Amaranthine** (5a) (bl) 10-1 **Miss C Cowe** *Cl up til mist 5; grad wknd frm 7; pu aft 15*
[828¹]	F		**Jamies First (IRE)** 4-1 **Miss L Parrott** *Ld/disp til fell 10*

OFFICIAL DISTANCES: 12l, 3l, 3l, 10l TIME: 6min 53.0s TOTE: £4.50

1244 Mixed Open, 12st   6 ran

[981¹]	1		**BLANVILLE (FR)** 1-3F **P Scouller** *Rr early; bad mist 5; gvn time to rec; chsd ldr frm 10; clsd 3 out; ld nxt; r.o wl; fin tired*

[884⁴]	2	1½	**Tarthooth (IRE)** (bl) 5-1 G Maundrell *Ld & jw; set str pce; 8l up 10; 6-7l clr 13; hdd 2 out; one pce; game*
[884³]	3	30	**Arleneseoin (IRE)** 5-1 P York *Tde; ld in start; pulled hrd early; settled aft 5; outpcd frm 10*
[1057⁵]	4	30	**Arfer Mole (IRE)** 6-1 D Dennis *Jmpd slow 2; trckd ldrs til aft 10; wknd aft; strugg home*
[764ᵁ]	P		**Catwalker (IRE)** 12-1 S Cobden *Jmpd slow 1; a strugg; pu aft 6*
[762¹]	P		**Coolree (IRE)** 12-1 Miss A Goschen *Disp ld early; wknd frm 7; pu aft 3 out*

OFFICIAL DISTANCES: 2l, dist, dist TIME: 6min 34.0s TOTE: £1.90

1245 Open Maiden, 12st   10 ran

[1101³]	1		**REGAL WOLF** (bl) 6-1 G Maundrell *Patient rdn; chsd ldrs frm 10; clsd to ld app 2 out; r.o wl*
[828ᶠ]	2	2	**Mountain Tae (IRE)** 3-1 P York *Ld; set stdy pce; jmpd slow 10 & 14; hdd app 2 out; kpt on one pce*
[630ᵁ]	3	12	**Youmeandhim (IRE)** 6-4F A Lillingston *Sa; hld up in rr; 15l bhnd 11; clsd qckly 15; one pce frm 3 out*
[309ᴾ]	4	30	**Graphic Designer (IRE)** 12-1 S Claisse *Rr early; kpt on one pce; nvr nrr*
	F		**Principal Profile** (5a) 12-1 M Wells *Rr when fell 3*
[984ᴾ]	F		**At It Again (IRE)** 12-1 R Chelton *Rr til fell 7*
[1131ᴾ]	P		**Mandalady** (5a) 12-1 D Dennis *Cl up early; wknd; pu 10*
[762³]	P		**Qu'appelle** 3-1 Miss A Goschen *Trckd ldrs til wknd aft 11; pu aft 13*
	F		**Spike Barnes** (7a) 12-1 M Walters *Fell 1*
[752ᴿ]	P		**Vital Hesitation** (5a) 6-1 R Millar *Mid-div til clsd 6; wknd frm 10; pu 12*

OFFICIAL DISTANCES: 3l, 15l, dist TIME: 6min 55.0s TOTE: £15.00

1246 Confined, 12st   6 ran

[452¹]	1		**WHAT A HAND** 2-1 P York *Cl up early; chsd ldr frm 8; disp ld frm 10; ld 3 out; stayed on str*
[883²]	2	10	**Ardbrennan** 4-1 Miss A Goschen *Jw; ld/disp til ld 8; jnd by wnr 12 til hdd & wknd 3 out; one pce*
[706⁴]	3	20	**Equity Player** 10-1 D Dennis *Rr when mist 9; strugg most of way; one pce*
[882⁴]	4	5	**Lake Of Loughrea (IRE)** 4-1 N Wilson (Hants) *A rr; one pce; strugg most of way*
[886¹]	P		**Balance** evensF G Maundrell *Hld up in 3rd early; bad mist 12; sn strugg; pu aft 2 out*
	P		**Heathview** 12-1 M Portman *Cl up early; wknd frm 10; pu aft 3 out*

OFFICIAL DISTANCES: 7l, 15l, 3l TIME: 6min 51.0s TOTE: £2.10
The rider of Lake Of Loughrea was fined £50 for excessive and unnecessary use of the whip on a tired horse

1247 Restricted, 12st   5 ran

[1131²]	1		**NEWBY END (IRE)** 7-4F D Dennis *Jw; chsd ldrs; lft in ld 14; r.o wl*
[132¹]	2	1	**Labula Bay** 3-1 P York *4th early; clsd to chse ldr aft 12; w wnr frm 14; 2l down last; kpt on w*
[1095ʳ]	3	40	**Dante's Gold (IRE)** 4-1 R Bliss *Lkd reluct to start; ld in; a rr; jmpd poor; bad mists 1 & 2 out; a trailing*
[338²]	F		**Ten Bob Note** (bl) 5-2 M Walters *Tk strt hld; ld; 2l up & gng wl when fell 14*
[524ᴾ]	P		**Timber Wolf (IRE)** 12-1 G Maundrell *Cl up early; mists 2 & 7; pu aft 13*

OFFICIAL DISTANCES: 1l, dist TIME: 6min 48.0s TOTE: £2.90

1248 Marsh UK/TBA PPORA Club Members Mares, 12st   4 ran

[883¹]	1		**GLENPINE (IRE)** (5a) 4-5F Miss A Goschen *Jw; made all at gd pce; comf*
[572³]	2	40	**Posh Spice (IRE)** (5a) 7-4 P York *3rd mostly til prog to 2nd aft 14; one pce; no ch w wnr*
[1061ᶠ]	3	30	**Teeton Heavens** (5a) 3-1 D Dennis *Chsd ldr 3-10; jmpd slow 12 & 13; strugg frm nxt; fin v tired*
[919⁷]	P		**Panda Shandy** (5a) 8-1 Miss B Fear *Sn bhnd; strugg aft 7; pu aft 13*

OFFICIAL DISTANCES: dist, dist TIME: 6min 49.0s TOTE: £1.70

Uttoxeter (LH 8F,16J)
Tue, 25 Apr (HEAVY, SOFT in places)

1249 Mount Argus HC   4 ran

[925²]	1		**MR GRIMSDALE (IRE)** 11-11 7-2 T Scudamore *Ld; hdd & hit 4 out; sn outpcd; stayed on u.p to ld last stride*
[1025²]	2	hd	**Silverdalesureshot** 12-04 8-11F R Burton *A.p; chsd ldr 10; hit 12; ld nxt; jmpd v slow last 2 fncs; wknd & hung lft flat; hdd last stride*

[1025⁴] 3   2½   **Desperate** 11-07 4-1 **R Barrett** *Blun bad 1; bhnd & drvn along; hit 11; hdwy 5 out; ev ch frm nxt; jmpd slow last 2; wknd flat*

    4   26   **Sailor Jim** 11-09 (2) 9-1 **W Tellwright** *Chsd ldr to 10; wknd 4 out*

    TIME: 6min 40.9s TOTE: £3.40 Ex: £8.60 CSF: £6.34

High Peak Harriers
Flagg Moor (LH 9F,18J) Tue, 25 Apr (SOFT)

1250 Hunt (Cross Country), 3m4f
5 ran

    1   **WELSH LEGION** 1-2F **N Fogg** *Made all; clr early; prsd final ½mile; rdn & kpt on*

[368ᴾ] 2   3   **Dotty Dolittle** (5a) 13-2 **J Burley** *Fat; a chsng wnr; no imp final ½ mile but rdr lost ab 2l bg gng inside final fnce*

    3   3   **Single Man (IRE)** 4-1 **Miss S Rodman** *4th early then 3rd; r.o str final ¼mile but set impossible task by rdr (unlucky)*

    4   600y   **Blue Moon (U)** (5a,24ow) 14-1 **Miss A Andrews** *Podgy hunter; spurs; sn t.o*

    5   200y   **Griff (U)** 20-1 **Mrs I Smith** *(xnb) Spurs; 1st ride; t.o final 12f; ref 2 out; cont*

    OFFICIAL DISTANCES: 4l, 4l TIME: 7min 13.0s TOTE: £1.50

1251 Open Maiden, 12st
5 ran

[964ᵁ] 1   **CHARLIE KEAY (IRE)** 4-7F **S Prior** *(rce rn at funereal pce) Ld to 3; climbed 5; hrd hld til ld brief app 3 out; ld agn nxt; rdn clr*

[872ᴾ] 2   6   **Slobadam** (tt) 20-1 **M Mackley** *Cl up in last pr; still puling hrd app 15; went 2nd & ev ch when outj 2 out; nt qckn*

[906ᴾ] 3   1½   **Educate Me (IRE)** (tt) 2-1 **J Burley** *Ld 3; hit 7; hdd aft 9; ld 12 til mist 14; disp ld app 3 out; ev ch nxt; rdn & sn btn*

[966ᴾ] 4   8   **Saxon Moss** 5-1 **G Smith** *Ld aft 9 til mist 12; disp ld 14 til hdd & wknd 2 out*

[964ᴾ] U   **Peover Eye** (7a) 20-1 **D Sherlock** *W ldr when ur 3*

    OFFICIAL DISTANCES: 8l, 2l TIME: 9min 01.0s TOTE: £1.30

1252 Confined
3 ran

[905⁵] 1   **OFFLEY LUCIELASTIC** (5a) 8-11F **S Prior** *Lw; ld til jmpd slow 3; ld 8 til jmpd slow 12; ld agn 14; drew clr aft nxt; rdn aft 2 out; kpt on flat*

[959³] 2   1½   **Freddie Fox** 7-2 **Miss G Garton** *Rcd wide; jw; ld 3-8; jmpd ahd 12; hdd 14; sn 10l adrift; rallied to go 2nd app 2 out; kpt clsng game aft til no ex final 50yds*

[959ᶠ] r   **Maltese Cross (IRE)** 9-4 **A Gribbin** *2nd/3rd; chsd wnr app 15; 15l down when jmpd slow nxt & wknd rap; sn lost 2nd; ref last*

    OFFICIAL DISTANCE: 1½l TIME: 8min 24.0s TOTE: £1.50

1253 Ladies Open
9 ran

[1145¹] 1   **LILY THE LARK** (5a) 5-4F **Miss H Irving** *Lw; chsd ldrs; hmpd 6; drpd rr & rdn 7; hdwy 8 to 10l 3rd 9; rdn to 2nd app 15; ld bef nxt & sn clr; kpt on str; unchal*

[1127²] 2   15   **Class Of Ninetytwo (IRE)** (vis) 12-1 **Miss S Sharratt** *Swtng; ld by ab 8l; jmpd slow 7; mist 10; 11 up app 15; hdd bef nxt & reluct w exhaust bef 2 out; plodded on in rem 2nd*

[987ᴾ] 3   2½   **Canaillou II (FR)** 33-1 **Miss T Clark** *Midfield; 20l 4th & outpcd 9; lft poor 3rd 3 out; trying to catch 2nd when blun last & rdr drpd reins*

[1209³] 4   12   **Fern Leader (IRE)** 40-1 **Mrs J Hughes** *Lost tch 6; 25l 7th aft hit 9; plodded on in rr; mist 2 out*

[1126⁴] 5   20   **The Boiler White (IRE)** (6ow) 20-1 **Miss J Froggatt** *A rr; 30l last 9; t.o 11*

[921¹⁴] r   **Commercial Artist** 6-1 **Miss P Robson** *Tubed; jmpd slow 6; chsd ldr to 11; wkng when hit 12; poor 4th when climbed nxt; cont v reluct til ref 15*

[963⁶] U   **Hotscent (IRE)** (5a) 40-1 **Miss C Wilberforce** *Midfield; hit 7; 22l 6th 9; outpcd when mist 12; ur nxt*

[921¹²] P   **The Parish Pump (IRE)** 6-4 **Mrs C Ford** *Settled 3rd/4th; 11l 4th & niggled along 9; went 2nd 11 til app 15; drvn & sn lost tch; 20l 3rd when pu 3 out*

    P   **Zvornik** 40-1 **Miss J Richardson** *Bckwd; midfield til 25l 8th & wkng 9; t.o & pu 12*

    OFFICIAL DISTANCES: 15l, 2½l TIME: 7min 54.0s TOTE: £2.30

1254 Land Rover Mens Open, 12st
5 ran

[1015ᴾ] 1   **WEAK MOMENT (IRE)** (4x) 2-1 **B Foster** *Lw; jmpd best; ld/disp til went 8l clr app 15; virt solo aft*

[1087²] 2   1¼fs   **Mickthecutaway (IRE)** (7x) 1-2F **A Dalton** *Alternated in ld w wnr; mist 7; blun 14 & lost ground rap w tail carried high; rem 2nd when crawled over 3 out & pu; restarted to pass exhaust rivals frm nxt*

[1014⁵]	3	8	**Titus Andronicus** (7x) 7-1 J Oldring *Lw; 3rd/4th; 15l 3rd & rdn 9; t.o 12; lft v rem 2nd 2 out til app last*
[1151ᴾ]	F		**Haveafewmanners (IRE)** (5a) 20-1 M Worthington *Pulled hrd early; ld aft 2 til mist 3; outpcd 6; 22l 4th 9; 3rd & t.o 12; mist 14; crawling frm 3 out; releg 4th when crashing fall nxt; bad winded*
[343ᴾ]	P		**Swan's Wish (IRE)** 40-1 M Hewitt *A last; lost tch & mist 5; sn wl t.o; pu 10*

OFFICIAL DISTANCES: dist, 6l **TIME:** 7min 43.0s **TOTE:** £1.90

1255 Dodson & Horrell PPORA Club Members   3 ran

[1129ᴾ]	1		**BALLYHANNON (IRE)** 7-1 Miss J Froggatt *Lw; cl up; 2nd frm 13; outpcd aft 15; climbed nxt; rallied 2 out; kpt on game to ld flat; all out*
	2	2½	**Prologue (IRE)** 4-1 D Sherlock *2 handlers; jmpd v slow 4; made nrly all; drew 5l clr aft 15; 3l ahd when climbed nxt; sn lkd v tired; put hd in air u.p but kpt on til hdd & wknd aft last*
[1071ᶠ]	3	nk	**Another Gentleman** 1-3F Mrs C Ford *Jmpd slow 5; ld brief aft 9-11; jmpd v slow nxt; 6l last 14; climbed 3 out; drvn to cl bef nxt; lkd reluct aft but chall agn bef last; fnd nil flat*

OFFICIAL DISTANCES: 3l, nk **TIME:** 8min 21.0s **TOTE:** £4.70

Modbury Harriers

Flete Park (RH 8F,20J) Sat, 29 Apr (SOFT with Heavy Patches - drying)

1256 Intermediate (Nov Rdrs), 12st   7 ran

[1045ᴾ]	1		**CONTRADICT** 8-1 Miss S Gaisford *Tchd 9s; cl up; went 2nd & niggled along aft 12; ld 14-2 out; rallied & ld agn last; kpt on wl; wl hld*
[1041¹]	2	2½	**Lead Story (IRE)** 5-4F R Emmett *Lw; 3rd/4th & gng wl; tk 2nd aft 14; ld 2 out & lkd wnr; hdd last & outrdn*
[1134ᶠ]	3	12	**Newman's Conquest** (5a) 11-1 M Shears *Nt jw; ld; 8; clr 6; prsd when mists 13 & 14 & hdd; rdn & wknd 3 out*
[848⁵]	4	d ht	**The Bandon Car (IRE)** 7-1 T Cole *14s-7s; lw; hld up 6th til hdwy 14; went 3l 3rd 3 out; drvn when blun nxt; nt r.o (lkd dd-ht 3rd)*
[1173ᴾ]	5	½	**Valley's Choice** (5a) 3-1 C White *Tchd 7/2; jmpd slow 2; cl up 2nd/3rd to 14; 4th & outpcd 3 out*
[1187ᴾ]	6	15	**Moorland Rose** (12a) 100-1 Miss D Mitchell *Last pr & rdr v ungainly; niggled along aft 4; lost tch 8 but kpt gng game*
[1173³]	7	runin	**Babbling Brook (IRE)** 10-1 A Bateman *Sis; u.p 3; a final trio; 6th & lsng tch when blun 17; t.o aft*

OFFICIAL DISTANCES: 3l, 12l **TIME:** 7min 09.0s

1257 Pegasus Club Members, 12st   6 ran

[1188³]	1		**HOLD YOUR RANKS** 9-4 G Welch *5s-9/4; settled 3rd; 17l down 4; 10l 3rd 10; clsd 12 & ld app 15; 7l clr 3 out; unchall*
[1041²]	2	8	**Bomba Charger** 4-6F Mrs R Welch *Spurs; tk keen hld & rdr sometimes waving; ld til app 15; mist nxt; prsd wnr til one pce & wl hld frm 3 out*
[1049³]	3	5	**Saucy's Wolf** 14-1 M Treneer *Prsd ldr to 14; 12l 3rd & btn 3 out; plodded on*
[1204ᴾ]	4	runin	**Goldsteane** (5a) 20-1 S Brodie *Tchd 25s; 1st ride; detach in final trio; 30l 4th 10; t.o aft 14; rdn into 4th nr fin*
[1047ᴾ]	5	1	**It's Not My Fault (IRE)** (3ow) 12-1 R Sheehan *Jmpd slow 2; last pr & wl bhnd; 35l 5th 10; t.o aft 14; tried to pu last & sn took 5th*
	P		**Blame The Groom (IRE)** 20-1 G Opperman *Tchd 25s; detach in final trio; 40l last 10; t.o & pu 13*

OFFICIAL DISTANCES: 10l, 6l **TIME:** 7min 15.8s

1258 Restricted, 12st   9 ran

[1176²]	1		**BELITLIR** (5a) 9-4F Miss S Young *3s-9/4; swtng; last pr; 10l last 10; outpcd aft 14 & 12l 6th 3 out; still 4th nxt but str rn to ld last; sn rdn clr; game*
[1043³]	2	3	**Damiens Pride (IRE)** 7-1 T Dennis *(xnb) Settled midfield; 5th 12; prog 16 to 6l 2nd 3 out; rdn to ld aft nxt; hdd last; fnd nil*
[857¹]	3	2	**Dedalus (FR)** (7a) (bl) 5-2 L Jefford *Lw; settled trckng ldrs; 4th 12; went 7l 3rd & rdn 3 out; fnd little aft & no imp*
[1042²]	U		**Border Rose** (5a) 16-1 Mrs W Doyne-Ditmas *Went 2nd app 3 out; lost plce qckly; last when ur 7*
[1043ᴾ]	P		**King Of Cairo** 66-1 I Hambley *Hdwy 6; hit 8; 6th when hit 12; lost tch & mist 15; t.o & pu 3 out*

[1048¹]	F	**Pillmere Lad** 8-1 Miss A Barnett *Lw; went 7l clr app 15; 6l ahd 3 out; hdd & wknd qckly aft nxt; 4th when fell hvly last; bad winded*
[1102¹]	P	**Prah Sands** 5-1 J Young *Tchd 6s; lw; prsd ldr to 17; 10l 4th & wkng rap nxt; pu 2 out*
[849⁵]	P	**Shameless Lady** (5a) 20-1 Richard Darke *Jmpd slow 2; sn bhnd; 7th 10; strugg when pu 14*
[1049¹]	P	**Sparkling Cascade (IRE)** (5a) 10-1 R Woollacott *Tchd 12s; mostly 3rd to 12; outpcd aft 15; 11l 5th & btn 3 out; t.o & pu last*

OFFICIAL DISTANCES: 2l, 3l **TIME:** 7min 10.7s

1259 Ladies Open, 4m   7 ran

[1014⁹]	1		**STARPATH (NZ)** 3-1 Miss P Gundry *Hld up til prog 14; 8l 3rd nxt; went 2nd 17; ld brief app 3 out; outpcd & lkd btn bef nxt; rallied to ld last; drvn out*
[1173¹]	2	10	**Rasta Man** (tt) 3-1 Mrs M Hand *Made most to 6; ld agn 12; 8l clr 17; hdd app 3 out; sn ld agn & pushed 5l up; hdd last; tried to rally but no ex*
[1044¹]	3	1¼	**Funny Farm** 4-5F Miss S Vickery *Lw; hung lft all way; made most 6-12; releg 9l 3rd 17; drvn & no imp aft 3 out*
[1174ᵁ]	4	1½fs	**Secret Four** 33-1 Miss K Langdell *Towards rr; 19l 5th 15; wl t.o by 22*
[952⁶]	5	2½	**Desert Run (IRE)** 66-1 Miss J West *Tchd 100s in plce; lw; chsd ldrs early; 16l 4th 15; wl t.o by 22; drvn out*
[853⁵]	P		**Crownhill Cross** 100-1 Miss Johanna Sleep *Tchd 150s in plce; jmpd slow in deatch last; t.o when pu & dism aft 7*
[1045ᴾ]	P		**Moorland Abbot** 150-1 Miss D Mitchell *Ld brief 2; last by 11; 23l bhnd 15; t.o when saddle slpd & pu 19*

OFFICIAL DISTANCES: 1l, 6l **TIME:** 8min 40.0s
The owner of Moorland Abbot, whose passport was found to be not in order, was fined £100

1260 Mens Open, 12st   3 ran

[1045¹]	1		**WELL ARMED (IRE)** (7x) (bl) 2-5F L Jefford *Lw; jw; gng wl in 2nd til ld 2 out; rdly*
[1044²]	2	4	**Belarus (IRE)** 9-4 C White *Made virt all to 2 out (rdn 13); hrd drvn & no ch w wnr*
[1042³]	3	8	**Mystic Warrior (USA)** (7a) 20-1 Richard Darke *Unruly & finally mounted outside padd; virt a last; rmdrs 4; jmpd slow 7; outpcd 16 but kpt on stdly*

OFFICIAL DISTANCES: 4l, 8l **TIME:** 7min 24.5s

1261 Confined, 12st - 18J   8 ran

[1046¹]	1		**ROSA'S REVENGE** (5a,6x) 8-11F L Jefford *2 handlers; settled towards rr; 5th 12; went 3rd 16; mist 17; rdn & outpcd 2 out; stayed on game to pass 3 rivals & ld nr fin*
[1044ᴾ]	2	hd	**If You Say So** 25-1 J Young *Tchd 33s; made most to 7; ld agn 12-14; prsd ldr til ld aft 2 out; hrd drvn & caught nr fin*
[1047ᴾ]	3	1	**Swift Venture (IRE)** 5-1 Richard Darke *7s-5s; cl 3rd/4th; disp 3l 3rd passing omitted 3 out; drvn & ev ch aft nxt; nt qckn*
[726ᴾ]	4	3	**Agent** 66-1 Miss A Barnett *(xnb) ss on purpose; pulled hrd & jnd ldrs 2; ld 7-12 & 14; rdn & hdd aft 2 out; sn wknd*
[1047¹]	5	8	**Lirsleftover** (3x) 3-1 Miss S Young *Scruffy; oht; last pr; in tch to 16; hit nxt; 13l 6th & btn passing omitted 3 out; no prog*
[1047²]	6	10	**Good King Henry** 8-1 I Widdicombe *14s-8s; prom; 3rd 12; releg 5th aft 14; one pce & nd frm 3 out*
[1047ᴾ]	P		**Cornish Ways** 100-1 T Greed *Lw; a bhnd; 8l last when mist 13; t.o 16; pu 2 out*
[928ᶠ]	U		**Strong Stuff (IRE)** (bl) 33-1 M Shears *Tchd 50s; ur 2*

OFFICIAL DISTANCES: hd, ½l **TIME:** 7min 14.3s
Fences 10 & 18 omitted - fallen rider

1262 Open Maiden (Div 1), 12st - 18J   10 ran

[1049²]	1		**MY PRIDES WAY** (5a) 3-1 T Greed *(xnb) Made all; 3l clr 3 out; kpt on stdly; wl in comm when nt fluent last*
[875³]	2	15	**Montepulciano (IRE)** 5-2F N Mitchell *(xnb) sn 4s-5/2; nt jw; 3rd mostly til 2nd 16; hrd rdn aft 3 out; nt keen & fnd nil; btn passing omitted 2 out*
[1049ᴾ]	3	8	**Master Pan** 25-1 I Widdicombe *Bckwd; towards rr; pckd 7; 5th 10; lost tch aft 14; 26l 4th 3 out*
[1101⁴]	4	12	**County Derry** 20-1 C Heard *Hld up; imp to 4th 10; rdn to go 2ng bef 12; dem 16; 23l 3rd when bad mist 3 out; hrd drvn but v reluct aft*
[723⁴]	P		**Alpine Castle (IRE)** (5a) 4-1 Miss S Young *Scruffy (lkd appalling); jmpd slow in last; sn rdn & nt qckn; t.o 7; pu 12*
[1049ᴾ]	F		**Gay Cavalier** 12-1 J Cole *2 handlers; pulled hrd; cl up when fell 3*

[654ᴾ]	B		Just Mai-Bee 14-1 B O'Doherty *Cl up when bd 3*
	P		Mr Bumble 10-1 Richard Darke *Bckwd; towards rr til pu 12 (blatant school)*
[856ᴾ]	P		Newlyn 33-1 J King *Prom; 6l 3rd 12; blun 14 & rmdrs; sn wknd; t.o when pu & dism aft 3 out*
[934⁵]	U		Sula Spirit (5a) 8-1 L Jefford *Hld up towards rr; 7th & in tch 10; wkng when ur 15*

OFFICIAL DISTANCES: 15l, 8l TIME: 7min 19.9s
Fences 11 & 19 omitted - fallen rider

1263 Open Maiden (Div 2), 12st
10 ran

[932²]	1		WOODLAND KING (IRE) 5-4F Mrs M Hand *Lw; mostly chsng clr ldr; ab 40l down when lft 10l clr 15; rdn & wknd aft 2 out; slt advant but v vulnerable when lft solo last*
[1048²]	U		Classic Mistress (5a) 7-4 Richard Darke *3s-7/4; 12l 2nd 4; lost plce 9; 5th & strugg 12; mist 14; ur 15*
[1049¹]	r		Country Gem 20-1 T Dennis *Chsng group; 4th 12; lft 10l 2nd 15; clsd u.p frm 2 out; ev ch when ref last & threw rdr over*
[1048ᴾ]	P		Horton 33-1 S Parkin *Mounted course; ss; hdwy to midfield & mist 4; strugg 8; t.o 10; pu 12*
[654ᴿ]	F		Jo's Wedding 9-1 L Jefford (xnb) *Pulled hrd in clr ld; 30l ahd 12; fell 15 (would have been diff to catch)*
[1048ᴾ]	P		Magic Caller (IRE) 33-1 Miss S Robinson *A labouring in rr; t.o 10; pu 13*
[928ᴾ]	P		Renardine Boy (IRE) 9-1 B O'Doherty *Midfield; 3rd 10; lft 18l 3rd 15; tiring when mist 17; 35l 3rd when pu aft 3 out*
[1099ᶠ]	P		Thecabbageflinger (bl) 33-1 J Young *Lw; pulled hrd in midfield; lost tch aft 10; t.o & pu 13*
[106ᴾ]	P		West Ashridge (12a) 25-1 R Woollacott *Tchd 33s; bhnd; hdwy to midfield 7; wknd aft 10; pu & dism 13*
[1048ᴾ]	U		Whinholme Lass (IRE) (5a) 33-1 G Richards (xnb) *Midfield & in tch in chsng group til mist & ur 12*

OFFICIAL DISTANCE: Finished alone TIME: 7min 25.7s

Quorn
Garthorpe (RH 8F,18J) Sat, 29 Apr (SOFT)

1264 Hunt, 12st
6 ran

[580⁵]	1		ARDEAL (5a) 1-2F A Bealby *Made all; 7l clr 14; jnd brief app 3 out; sn qcknd away w rdr lkng rnd; 8l ahd last; eased prematurely flat; just hld on*
[1072ᶠ]	2	¾	Black Book (IRE) (5a) 12-1 P Millington *Hld up; last to 7; 5th ½way; hdwy 11; went 2nd nxt; mist 13; eff u.p & jnd wnr app 3 out; sn brushed aside; kpt on stdly & nrly caught napping ldr nr fin*
[1073³]	3	runin	Court Thyne (IRE) (4ow) 14-1 J Hayward *Hld up; 4th ½way; went 2nd 10-11; wkng when lft 12l 3rd 13; t.o*
[871¹⁵]	4	12	Pretty Boy George 40-1 Miss A Townsend *Went 2nd 3-7; mist 10; sn lost plce; t.o 14*
[1072²]	P		Take The Buckskin (tt) 9-4 M Briggs *2nd/3rd to 10; 8l 3rd when pu 13*
[1011ᴾ]	P		Tarjumaan (USA) 40-1 A Brown *4th when mist 2; releg last 7; lost tch 8; 15l 6th & rdn w no resp ½way; pu 11*

OFFICIAL DISTANCES: 1l, dist TIME: 6min 47.0s TOTE: £1.70; places £1.30,£3.70 DF: £7.40

1265 Mens Open
9 ran

[1182¹]	1		COPPER THISTLE (IRE) 1-2F R Hunnisett *Lw; made all; qcknd 12; drew wl clr frm 3 out; impressive*
[1072¹]	2	35	Gillone 3-1 N Docker *Tde; hld up; hdwy 5; went 2nd nxt; in tch w wnr to 15; wkng when pckd 3 out*
[999⁴]	3	5	Barneys Gold (IRE) 12-1 A Bealby *Lost plce 5; 15l 8th ½way; wl bhnd 12; 30l 8th 15; stayed on frm 3 out; went 3rd nxt; nvr nr to chall*
[1216⁴]	4	2½	Deel Quay (IRE) 50-1 M Chatterton *Hld up; 6l 7th ½way; outpcd 12; sn wl bhnd; 25l 5th 15; t.o*
[870⁵]	5	20	Teeton Builds 20-1 A Sansome (orbs) *Hld up; mist 9; 5l 6th ½way; lost tch 12; 20l 5th nxt; rdn 15; sn t.o*
[921⁵]	6	nk	Just Bruce 33-1 N Kent (bf) *Swtng; went 2nd 3-6; 3rd ½way; outpcd 12; 18l 4th nxt; went poor 3rd 15; wknd 3 out*
[870²]	P		Fresh Ice (IRE) 8-1 R Barrett *Chsd ldrs; 3l 4th ½way; rdn 11; sn lost plce & wl bhnd; 26l 6th 15; pu 2 out*
[750⁶]	P		Kites Hardwicke 40-1 J Diment *Hld up; mist 6; eff & 4l 5th ½way; went 3rd 10; drvn along & outpcd 12; 15l down nxt; wknd qckly 15; t.o & pu 2 out*

[1128^P]   P   **Needwood Neptune** (vis) 50-1 M Hewitt *Mist 1; drpd to rr 4; sn drvn along & nt keen; t.o 8; pu 12*

OFFICIAL DISTANCES: 30l, 4l   **TIME:** 6min 39.0s   **TOTE:** £1.50; places £1.50,£1.10,£3.00   **DF:** £1.70

1266 Greig Middleton Ladies Open   8 ran

[1007⁵]	1		**CITTADINO** 4-6F **Mrs J Dawson** *Lw; 2nd til ld 8; hdd & blun 11; ld aft 2 out; sn clr*
[1087³]	2	6	**Look In The Mirror** 4-1 **Miss L Sweeting** *Ld to 8; 2nd til ld 11; went 7l clr nxt; hdd aft 2 out; no ex*
[772³]	3	20	**Count Of Flanders** (IRE) 16-1 **Mrs J Hughes** *Went 6l 3rd 7; rdn 15; wknd app 2 out*
[869³]	4	10	**Drummond Warrior** (IRE) 33-1 **Miss A Burton** *Nd; 24l 5th ½way; rdn 12; went 25l 4th 14; no imp*
[1007⁵]	5	25	**Hostetler** 66-1 **Miss K Norris** *A bhnd; t.o 8*
[1005ᵁ]	6	3	**Supreme Dream** (IRE) (5a) 20-1 **Mrs P Adams** *A bhnd; t.o 9; releg last aft 15*
[1113⁴]	P		**Emsee-H** (1ow) 12-1 **Miss Z Turner** *3rd to 7; sn outpcd; 20l 4th ½way; 28l 5th when pu aft 15*
[997ᶠ]	F		**Pharlindo** (IRE) 10-1 **Mrs F Needham** *(xnb,pricker os) Fell 2*

OFFICIAL DISTANCES: 6l, 12l   **TIME:** 6min 38.0s   **TOTE:** £1.40; places £1.10,£1.40,£2.80   **DF:** £2.10

1267 Intermediate, 12st   11 ran

[871¹]	1		**UNION MAN** 13-8F **S Morris** *A.p; mist 2; ld 3-4; ld 6; drew clr frm 3 out; impressive*
[861³]	2	20	**Aqua Star** (IRE) 16-1 **Miss T Spearing** *Tde; hld up; 5l 8th ½way; hdwy 11; 5l 5th & rmdrs 13; went 6l 4th & rdn 3 out; stayed on; went 2nd flat; no ch w wnr*
[1142ᵁ]	3	2	**Dark Rhytham** 20-1 **R Lawther** *(xnb) Lw; hld up; hdwy 7; 5l 7th ½way; went 2l 3rd aft 12 & 2nd 15; brushed aside aft 3 out; dem flat*
[1155⁵]	4	3	**Persian Boy** (IRE) 8-1 **A Sansome** *Prom; went 2nd 6-15; 2½l 3rd nxt; wknd qckly app 2 out*
[1126³]	5	20	**Sarcoid** (IRE) 10-1 **G Hanmer** *Drpd to rr 7; 9l 11th ½way; 12l 8th 13; 23l 6th 15; t.o*
[1006³]	6	2	**Live Wire** (IRE) 12-1 **G Kerr** *Chsd ldrs; 3l 4th ½way; lost plce & blun 11; 10l 7th 13; 22l 5th 15; t.o*
[1006ᶠ]	P		**Catchphrase** 33-1 **R Armson** *Ld to 2 & 4-6; 11 3rd ½way; wknd qckly & 9l 6th 13; t.o & pu 3 out*
[894¹]	P		**Goawayoutofthat** (IRE) 7-4 **Julian Pritchard** *Hld up; last to 7; hdwy & 4l 5th ½way; 6l 4th 15; wknd u.p & 8l 5th 3 out; pu nxt*
[1128ᴾ]	P		**Royal Segos** 66-1 **S Shaw** *Drpd to rr 8; 8l 10th ½way; t.o 15; pu 2 out*
[585¹]	P		**Starlight Fool** 8-1 **R Barrett** *(xnb) Ld 2 til hdd & mist 3; lost plce 7; 4½l 10th ½way; drpd to rr u.p 11; jmpd v slow 12; sn pu*
[1072⁴]	P		**Vimchase** 100-1 **M Mackley** *Nd; 7l 9th ½way; lost tch & 15l 9th 13; pu 14*

OFFICIAL DISTANCES: 25l, 2l   **TIME:** 6min 41.0s   **TOTE:** £2.00; places £1.10,£5.00,£10.00   **DF:** £18.00

1268 Restricted, 12st   8 ran

[1009³]	1		**FAIR FARM BOY** 6-1 **M Mackley** *A.p; 2½l 4th ½way; went 11 2nd 15; ld app 3 out; sn clr; comf*
	2	12	**Witkowski** (IRE) 2-1F **G Hanmer** *Hld up in last to 6; 5l 7th ½way; hdwy & 2nd 13; ld 14 til hdd & mist 3 out; sn btn*
[1075¹]	3	3	**Sands Point** 20-1 **N Kent** *Hld up; 4l 6th ½way; eff & 3l 5th 15; went 5l 3rd app 3 out; one pce*
[585²]	4	3	**Chester Ben** 8-1 **T Lane** *Prom; went 2nd 8-10; ld 13-14; 2l 3rd nxt; sn rdn & btn*
[1017⁴]	5	2	**Colonel Wilkie** 16-1 **Mrs E Staines** *Ld to 2; 3l 5th ½way; ld 10 til hdd u.p 13; 2½l 4th 15; sn wknd*
[1214³]	P		**Grants Carouse** (5ow) 66-1 **M Wells** *A bhnd; 12l 8th ½way; mist 10; pu 11*
[1070¹]	F		**Playlord** 3-1 **N Docker** *2nd til ld 5; hdd aft 7; 2l 3rd ½way; w ldrs til fell 13*
[867¹]	P		**Square One** (IRE) (5a) 5-2 **A Bealby** *Ld 2-5 & aft 7-10; lost plce & 4l 6th 15; sn wknd; t.o & pu last*

OFFICIAL DISTANCES: 12l, 3l   **TIME:** 6min 49.0s   **TOTE:** £6.50; places £1.50,£1.10,£18.00   **DF:** £16.00

1269 Open Maiden (Div 1), 12st   8 ran

[1220²]	1		**CASHEL GREEN** (IRE) 5-2 **M Hewitt** *A.p; went 2nd 6; ld 15; sn clr; comf*
[1004³]	2	12	**Nasayer** (IRE) evensF **A Pickering** *Swtng; hld up & pulled hrd; last til 10l 6th ½way; eff to 12l 4th 13; went 15l 3rd 15 & 2nd app last; no ch w wnr*
[547⁵]	3	7	**Paradise Row** (IRE) 7-2 **M Chatterton** *Ld til hdd 15; wknd 2 out*

[872^U]	4	30	**Colonel Carats** 8-1 **T Lane** *Prom; 7l 4th ½way; 4l 3rd when mist 12; sn rdn & strugg; wknd 15; t.o*
[412^P]	R		**Ali's Lark** (bl) 20-1 **K Needham** *2 handlers; crashed thro wing & dumped rdr 1*
[1070^P]	P		**Alston Fanfare** (IRE) (bl) 12-1 **J Cookson** *Went 2nd 4-6; 6l 3rd & shkn up ½way; wknd & 15l 5th 13; t.o & pu 2 out*
[1076^P]	P		**Crested Lass** (5a) 14-1 **L Hicks** *Hld up; 9l 5th ½way; wknd 12; 17l 6th nxt; wl bhnd when pu 15*
[785^P]	P		**Sam The Sloth** (5a) 14-1 **C Wadland** *Swtng; nd; 12l 7th ½way; wl bhnd when pu 11*

OFFICIAL DISTANCES: 12l, 8l **TIME:** 6min 49.0s **TOTE:** £3.50; places £2.00, £1.10, £1.10 **DF:** £2.00

1270 Open Maiden (Div 2), 12st   11 ran

[872^{4d}]	1		**WELL MATCHED** (7a) 10-1 **E Andrewes** *A.p; 4l 5th ½way; went 2nd aft 11; ld 12; drew clr app last; rdly*
[438⁵]	2	8	**Balmoral Spring** (IRE) 8-1 **T Lane** *Hld up; hdwy 8; 3l 4th ½way; went 2nd 13; ev ch 2 out; wknd last*
[1021⁴]	3	20	**The Big Lad** (IRE) 3-1F **G Smith** *Lw; hld up; mist 5; 6l 7th ½way; hdwy & 3l 4th 13; sn outpcd; went 8l 3rd aft 15; plodded on*
[1068⁴]	4	5	**Musical Hare** 5-1 **C Wadland** *Hld up; mist 3; hdwy 8; 5l 6th ½way; lost plce & 12½l 8th 13; 25l 5th 3 out; no imp*
[1070^U]	5	12	**Copper Thorn** (5a) 20-1 **Mrs C Boyes** (boh) *Ld to 5; ld 7-12; blun 14; wknd 15; 20l 4th nxt; t.o*
	P		**Brave Jeanie** (12a) 8-1 **M Mackley** *Bckwd; school in rr; 12l 10th ½way; 15l 9th 13; pu 14*
[1010^P]	P		**Good Job** (5a) 5-1 **S Morris** *2 handlers; hld up; 7l 8th ½way; mist 10; 12l 7th & rdn 13; wl bhnd when pu 15*
	P		**Mr Tucker** 33-1 **Mrs E Staines** (xnb) *2 handlers; 2nd til ld 5; hdd 7; 2nd til aft 11; 4l 5th when mist 13; sn wknd; t.o & pu 2 out*
[438⁶]	R		**The Bombers Moon** 14-1 **N Kent** *Hld up; 7th when nt much room & rn out 8*
[903^P]	P		**Timothy George** (IRE) 14-1 **P Millington** *A bhnd; 10l 9th ½way; 17l 10th 13; t.o & pu 2 out*
[1020⁶]	P		**Yodeller Bill** 6-1 **J Diment** *Prom; 2l 3rd ½way; rdn when mist 11; wknd & 8l 6th 13; t.o & pu 2 out*

OFFICIAL DISTANCES: 8l, 12l **TIME:** 6min 50.0s **TOTE:** £6.80 **DF:** £60.00 **Jackpot:** £11.00 (50p) **Placepot:** £50.00 (50p)

Radnor & West Herefordshire
Cursneh Hill (LH 8F,18J) Sun, 30 Apr (SOFT with HEAVY patches)

1271 Hunt, 12st   3 ran

[987^P]	1		**RUSTY BUCK** 4-7F **S Blackwell** *Cl 2nd til jnd ldr 6; ld 14; 12l up 3 out; eased last 50yds*
[1086^P]	2	4	**Merger Mania** 3-1 **M Trott** *Jmpd rt; hld up last til jmpd slow & lost tch 11; prog to 2nd 15; fin str frm nxt; too much to do*
[491^P]	3	35	**Jack Cruise** 4-1 **R Cooper** *Ld; mist 2; jnd 6; matched strides w wnr til hdd 14; last & pushed along nxt; wknd qckly*

OFFICIAL DISTANCES: 2½l, dist **TIME:** 6min 36.0s

1272 Confined, 12st   8 ran

[944¹]	1		**FINTONA BOY** (IRE) (3x) (tt) 2-1 **R Burton** *Ld; qcknd 14 & 12l clr apt nxt; slt mist 3 out & nxt; eased flat; impressive*
[1267²]	2	15	**Aqua Star** (IRE) 6-1 **Miss T Spearing** *Chsd ldrs; went 2nd 11; outpcd aft 14; wl hld frm 3 out*
[987³]	3	10	**Basil Street** (IRE) 10-1 **A Brown** *Hld up in tch; mists 1, 2 & 10; outpcd in 12l 3rd 15; no imp aft; jmpd slow 2 out*
[862²]	4	10	**Gold'n Shroud** (IRE) 7-4F **A Wintle** *2s-7/4; hld up; mist 7; 12l last 10; mist 12; prog to 4th 14; unable to sust eff*
[666²]	5	12	**Sea Patrol** (bl) 33-1 **D Hughes** *Mid-div; rmdrs 11 & 12; strugg aft; went 5th 15; no ex; collapsed & died aft rce*
[988⁷]	6	8	**Good For A Loan** 33-1 **R Cooper** *Chsd ldrs in mid-div til mist 13; outpcd 14; wknd frm nxt; t.o*
[987³]	7	20	**Stormhill Recruit** 12-1 **S Blackwell** *Chsd wnr to 11; lost plce u.p nxt; t.o 3 out*
[988⁶]	P		**Haven Light** 9-1 **Julian Pritchard** *Hld up disp last; rdn 5; short-lived eff 12-13; wknd qckly; 15l last when pu 15*

OFFICIAL DISTANCES: 10l, 8l **TIME:** 6min 23.0s

1273 Mens Open, 12st

5 ran

[1087¹] 1 **THE CRAZY BISHOP (IRE)** (7x) 2-7F **B Shaw** *2nd 2 til ld brief 5; ld agn 12; 3l clr 15; hrd prsd frm 3 out; stumbled last; pushed out flat*

[968ᴾ] 2 2 **Furry Fox (IRE)** 14-1 **G Barfoot-Saunt** *Cl 3rd; eff frm 11 to disp ld on inner nxt; outpcd in 6l 3rd & hrd drvn 3 out; stayed on wl flat; just sntched 2nd*

[1087ᴾ] 3 s hd **Watchit Lad** 5-1 **S Blackwell** *Made nrly all to 12; sn drvn; 3l 2nd 15; stayed on u.p frm 3 out; one pce flat; dem final stride*

4 20 **Hurricane Andrew (IRE)** 14-1 **N Oliver** *Last til 4th & outpcd aft 7; t.o 15*

[480ᴾ] P **Scarlet Berry** (5a) 6-1 **A Wintle** *4th til lost tch qckly aft 7; t.o & pu 12*

OFFICIAL DISTANCE: 1l, nk TIME: 6min 25.0s

1274 Intermediate, 12st

1 ran

[987²] 1 **CHASSAGNE (FR)** J Price *Walked over*

OFFICIAL DISTANCE: Walked over

1275 Ladies Open

5 ran

[1224ᴮ] 1 **DAWN'S COGNAC (IRE)** (7x) 1-3F **Miss P Jones** *2nd 5 til ld 8; 4l clr 15; prsd brief nxt; drew clr 2 out*

2 8 **Tee Tee Too (IRE)** 12-1 **Miss E James** *Jmpd poor & rmdrs 4; chsd wnr frm 9; tried to chall 3 out; btn app 2 out*

[1086¹¹] 3 30 **Highway Five (IRE)** (7x) 12-1 **Miss L Brooke** *Sn last; u.p 4; detach 7; t.o 10; went rem 3rd aft 15; nvr nr ldrs*

[1066²] 4 15 **Name Of Our Father (USA)** (7x) 4-1 **Miss E Bryan** *Ld to 8; 3rd when nrly ur 9; 4th when mist 11; lost tch & mist 14; sn t.o*

[1045ᴾ] P **Dunlir** 20-1 **Miss T Spearing** *Cl 2nd/3rd to 7; wknd frm 11; mist 13; t.o 15; pu last*

OFFICIAL DISTANCES: 7l, 20l, 12l TIME: 6min 21.0s

PLATE 14 1275 Radnor & West Herefordshire Ladies Open: L to R Dunlir, Tee Tee Too, Highway Five (obscured), Name Of Our Father and Dawn's Cognac PHOTO: Bill Selwyn

1276 Restricted, 12st

9 ran

1 **LEON GARCIA (IRE)** (5a) 8-1 **M Rodda** *Confid rdn; hld up; eff 12 to cl 3rd nxt; str rn to ld last; qcknd clr; clever*

[1092¹] 2 3 **Fountain Street (IRE)** 7-4F **R Burton** *Trckd ldrs; 3rd 5 til 2nd 9; ld app 3 out-last; drvn & nt qckn*

[993⁴]	3	6	**Maid O'Tully (IRE)** (5a) 12-1 R Hodges *Mid-div; stdy prog to 4th 15; 9l 4th 2 out; went 3rd u.p; no ch when mist last*
[1021¹]	4	15	**Black Oak** 3-1 Julian Pritchard *Jmpd rt; ld & clr; 7l ahd 11; hdd app 3 out; wknd rap aft nxt*
[863ᴾ]	F		**Cwm Bye** 12-1 M Hammond *Chsd ldr til lost plce rap 8; rr when fell 9*
[1089ᴾ]	P		**Hugo Henry (IRE)** 16-1 M Trott *Hdwy 5; 10l 2nd brief 8; lost plce bend aft 10; last when pu & dism 11*
[1200ᴾ]	U		**J'accuse (IRE)** 8-1 Miss F Wilson *Hld up & bhnd; 6th & in tch when stumbled bend & ur aft 10*
[864ᴾ]	P		**Scottish Clover** (5a) 6-1 S Blackwell *Chsd ldrs; mist 7; 3rd 11; mist 12; bad mist nxt; lost tch & jmpd bad rt 14; 20l last when pu 3 out*
[992ᴾ]	P		**Without The Agent (IRE)** 12-1 A Price *Last by 5; sn t.o; pu 11*

OFFICIAL DISTANCES: 2l, 6l TIME: 6min 26.0s

1277 Open Maiden (Div 1), 12st   7 ran

	1		**MISS GALE (IRE)** (5a) 3-1 R Burton *Ld to 13; cl 2nd til ld agn aft 2 out; in comm when hurdled last*
[1085²]	2	3	**Three Monroes (IRE)** 3-1 T Stephenson *2nd 4 til ld 13; nt fluent 2 out & sn hdd; drvn & nt qckn*
[1223²]	3	20	**Up Your Street** (12a) 7-4F Miss P Jones *Nvr gng wl; jmpd novicey in 4th; outpcd 14; 10l 3rd nxt; strugg aft*
[990ᴾ]	P		**Far Glen (IRE)** (7a) (ttt) 16-1 S Blackwell *Unable to rce; jmpd slow & nrly ref 2; rdr leant forward & removed tongue-strap; cont fence bhnd til pu 11*
[995ᴿ]	P		**Hardy Wolf** 12-1 A St George *2nd til 3rd 4; outpcd 14 & sn poor 4th; v tired & pu 2 out*
[1201ᵁ]	r		**Kinsale Florale (IRE)** (5a) 4-1 M Rodda *6s-4s; planted herself start; ref to rce*
[990ᴾ]	P		**Wee Kelpie** (5a) 20-1 R Hodges *Disp ld when bit broke & pu bef 2*

OFFICIAL DISTANCES: 3l, 20l TIME: 6min 38.0s

1278 Open Maiden (Div 2), 12st   6 ran

	1		**SISTER KIT (IRE)** (5a) 11-2 Miss P Jones *Cl 2nd til ld 9-11; hit 14; releg 3rd nxt; 2nd agn 2 out; chall & ev ch when lft wl clr last*
[972⁴]	2	20	**Spirit Prince** 2-1JF Julian Pritchard *5/2-2s; ld; set mod pce; stumbled bend aft 3; hdd 9; 3rd til went 2nd 15; dem 2 out & wknd rap*
[989ᴾ]	P		**Broadbrook Lass** (bl) 7-1 S Blackwell *20s-7s; stumbled aft 3; cl up; 3rd brief 11; mist 12; swishewd tail u.p aft nxt & reluct; mist 14; 30l last when pu 15*
[1085ᴾ]	U		**Cool Spell** (5a) 20-1 S Graham *Nt jw; ld 5th when tried to m out & ur 6*
[1093²]	P		**Dungannon Lad** 7-2 A St George *Hit 3; last 8; rdn & strugg 11; pu 13*
[1194³]	U		**The Ugly Gunner** 2-1JF E Gretton *3rd til 2nd 10; ld 11; stumbled bend aft 2 out; nk up when rfo last*

OFFICIAL DISTANCE: 25l TIME: 6min 33.0s

Tedworth

Barbury Castle (LH 8F,18J) Sun, 30 Apr (SOFT becoming DEAD)

1279 Hunt   8 ran

[1014⁴]	1		**LUCKY TANNER** 100-30 Miss G Young *In tch; mist & rmdr 6; cl 4th 10; outpcd & frm rdn 12; 3rd 14; lft 2nd nxt; stdly clsd; hrd rdn 2 out; kpt on to ld last few strides*
[1060²]	2	½	**You Said It (IRE)** 2-1F D Crosse *Tchd 3s; lw; slt ld to 5 & frm 7; pushed 5l clr 12; 15l up 3 out; stdly pegged back & 1½l ahd last; no ex flat; hdd nr post*
[883ᴾ]	3	40	**Ryder Cup (IRE)** 11-2 G Maundrell *Lw; sn prom on inner; cl 3rd 10; lost ground 12; 4th & strugg 14; t.o 3rd & no ch 15*
[476ᵁ]	4	2½fs	**Flickering Flame** 50-1 M Tillett *Bckwd; last frm 4; lost tch 7; fnce bhnd 10; plodded on frm rdn 12; poor 5th when scrambled over 13; t.o*
[687⁸]	P		**Go Universal (IRE)** 5-2 N Mitchell *Bit bckwd; hld up in tch; prog to 3rd 12; 5l 2nd & hit 13; disp 10l 2nd when pu 15; lame*
[1246ᴾ]	P		**Heathview** 40-1 M Portman *Slt ld 5 til hit 7 & hdd; cl 2nd to 11; lost plce qckly nxt; poor 5th when scrambled over 13; pu nxt*
	F		**Play It Down** (5a) 66-1 Mrs B Kwiatkowska *Dwelt; sn bhnd & rcd v wide; fell 4*
[1096ᴾ]	P		**Touch Of Winter** 14-1 A Charles-Jones *Bit bckwd; hld up in tch; 5th 10; sn outpcd; poor 6th when pu 13*

OFFICIAL DISTANCES: ½l, dist TIME: 6min 43.3s TOTE: £3.60; places £1.30,£1.00,£2.60

1280 Restricted, 12st - 17J
7 ran

[899¹]	1		**CARBONADO** evensF **Miss P Gundry** Opened 2s in plce; lw; jmpd bold; made all; lft clr 13; 8l clr 15; unchall; made a noise
[1140ᶠ]	2	25	**Pendragon** 11-4 **N Mitchell** Tchd 3s; rr early; hdwy 7; cl 5th 11; outpcd nxt; 14l 3rd 15; one pce & no ch frm 3 out; tk 2nd u.p flat
[1095ᴾ]	3	1½	**Conquer The Kilt** 12-1 **M Miller** (xnb) Tchd 14s; lw; cl 5th & mist 5; prog on inner to 2nd 8; wl in tch til outpcd 13; poor 2nd & jmpd rt last; dem cl home
[955¹]	4	40	**Cool Million** 14-1 **Miss L Bridges** Rcd wide; chsd ldr to 8; cl 4th 12; sn niggled along; 18l 4th 15; plodded home
[1206ᴾ]	F		**Irish Buzz (IRE)** 7-1 **A Charles-Jones** (xnb) Lw; edgy; disp cl 6th when fell 4
[1135ᶠ]	U		**Pharniskey (IRE)** 9-2 **O Ellwood** Nt fluent; 5th & mist 8; prog to cl 3rd 11; 1½l 2nd when blun & ur 13
[1088ᴾ]	P		**Wolfie Smith** 50-1 **Miss J Houldey** Jmpd lft; last but in tch frm 7; bhnd frm 12; btn 5th when pu 14

OFFICIAL DISTANCES: dist, 2l **TIME:** 6min 35.6s **TOTE:** £2.00; places £1.50,£1.10
Fence 10 omitted - fallen rider

1281 Greig Middleton Ladies Open
2 ran

[885⁴]	1		**KHALIDI (IRE)** 4-1 **Miss M MacGregor** Keen & set fast pce to 3; ld agn 5 til hdd & rmdrs aft 10; lost tch w rival frm 14; 20l down & tried to rally 3 out; hld when lft clr at last; all out; rdr's 1st wnr
[1126¹]	2	bad	**Aegean Fanfare (IRE)** 2-9F **Miss E Jones** Mists; ld 3-5; blun bad & nrly ur 6; gd rcvry; hit 10; ld nxt; forged clr 14; 20l ahd when hit 2 out; in comm when fell last; rmtd

OFFICIAL DISTANCE: dist **TIME:** 6min 50.9s **TOTE:** £2.10

1282 Mens Open, 12st
6 ran

[1244²]	1		**TARTHOOTH (IRE)** (7x) (bl) 10-11F **G Maundrell** Tchd evens; made all; jw; drew clr 13; unchall
[1144⁴]	2	15	**Fair Crossing** 9-2 **M Emmanuel** Went 2nd 6; chsd ldr; 10l 2nd 13; slt mist 3 out; no imp
[1177²]	3	40	**Flying Imp** 11-2 **J Barnes** Kpt jmpng rt; cl 3rd when mist 4; in tch til rmdr 11; fdd; poor 3rd frm 14; eased flat; walked in
[216ᵁ]	4	20	**Garrison Friendly (IRE)** 10-1 **N Wilson (Hants)** (xnb) Prom to 8; disp 3rd & jmpd rt 9; lsng tch when rmdr 11; wl btn 4th frm 14; t.o
	P		**Blown Wind (IRE)** 4-1 **C Williams** 6s-4s; swtng; hld up; prog to 3rd 11; wl in tch 12; 111 3rd when hit 13; eased & pu nxt
[1205ᴾ]	U		**Scud Missile (IRE)** 33-1 **S Goodings** 4th when blun & ur 5

OFFICIAL DISTANCES: 20l, dist **TIME:** 6min 31.3s **TOTE:** £1.70; places £2.50,£1.50

1283 Intermediate, 12st
4 ran

[953²]	1		**POSSIBLE PARDON (NZ)** (bl) 4-1 **N Mitchell** 2 handlers; lw; went 2nd 8; trckd ldr; hit 12; cl 2nd & stdd aft 3 out; ld 2 out; stayed on game
	2	12	**Jilly Wig (IRE)** (5a) 4-6F **Miss P Gundry** Bit bckwd; tchd 10/11; jw; keen hld & tkn wide; ld 3; 2l up til pushed along aft 3 out; hdd nxt & jmpd rt 2 out & last; btr for rce
[1042¹]	3	1½fs	**Think Positive (IRE)** 4-1 **G Maundrell** Ld to 3; trckd ldr to 8; lost tch stdly; fnce bhnd 13; t.o
[1095¹]	F		**Jolification** (bl) 6-1 **A Honeyball** Lw; cl up when fell 2

OFFICIAL DISTANCES: 15l, dist **TIME:** 6min 42.8s **TOTE:** £7.30

1284 Open Maiden, 12st - 17J
9 ran

[1135⁶]	1		**ASHBURTON LORD (IRE)** 5-2 **M Legge** Swtng; tk keen hld; slt ld to 10; cl up til ld agn on inner 15; veered rt when chall by-passing last; kpt on game; rdr's 1st wnr
[972²]	2	nk	**Wood Buzzard** 7-4F **E Walker** Hld up in tch; 3rd frm 9; rap prog to trck ldrs 14; went 2nd 3 out; chall & blun bad 2 out; rallied & nt much room last 100yds
[957ᴾ]	3	30	**Ask In Time (IRE)** 20s-9/2; 2 handlers; cl 2nd til ld 10-15; sn wknd; 12l 3rd frm when mist 3 out; no ch aft
[995ᴾ]	4	40	**Ilandra (IRE)** (5a) 20-1 **N Pearce** Rr & nt a fluent; poor 4th frm 12; t.o
[1207⁷]	5	2fncs	**Country Lord** 33-1 **Mrs S Walwin** Spurs; sn bhnd; t.o when scrambled over 5; 2 fncs adrift 14; plodded on
[956ᶠ]	P		**Dido's Dream** (5a) 33-1 **J Barnes** (xnb) Prom early; 5th & bad mist 10; poor 5th & wl btn frm 14; t.o & pu 2 out
[260ᴾ]	F		**Good Thyne Girl** (5a) 13-2 **Miss J Rees** Bhnd when fell 10; dead
	P		**Polly Gunner** (5a) 5-1 **M Gorman** Bit bckwd; midfield; 4th when rmdrs 9; poor 6th when climbed 12; imm pu

PLATE 15   1280 Tedworth Restricted: Carbonado leads L to R Cool Million, Pharniskey, Conquer The Kilt, Wolfie Smith and Pendragon turn out of the back straight   PHOTO: Brian Armstrong

[1102P] **P**   **Vic's Girl** (5a) 50-1 G Weatherley *Swtng; 4th when mist 2; nt jw; lost ground frm 5; 6th ½way; bhnd when mists 13 & 14; pu nxt*

OFFICIAL DISTANCES: hd, dist **TIME:** 6min 47.6s **TOTE:** £4.60; places £2.00,£1.20,£2.30
Last fence omitted - fallen horse

West Norfolk
Fakenham (LH 6F,18J) Sun, 30 Apr (GOOD to SOFT)

1285 Hunt
6 ran

[872²]	**1**		**HAGON BECK** 4-5F W Wales *Settled 4th & gng wl; 2l 3rd 12; jmpd to ld 15; drew clr aft 2 out; v easy*
[1038¹]	**2**	15	**Rafter** 6-4 C Carman *Nt a fluent; 3rd early; 2nd when mist 7; ld aft 9; outj & hdd 15; no ch w wnr aft 2 out*
[1184P]	**3**	25	**Spuffington** 33-1 Miss H Steele *Chsd clr ldr to 7; 1l 2nd 12; releg 3rd nxt; mist 14 (water); lost tch qckly 15; plodded on*
	4	runin	**Classical Style** 33-1 Miss E Boone *Rem last til 5th 7; plodded rnd; game*
	5	1½fs	**Rovac** 14-1 J Fryer *Nt fluent & sn lost tch; releg last 7; cont to*
[1038P]	**P**		**Coptic Dancer** (vis) 20-1 A Braithwaite *Jmpd rt; tk keen hld; ld; sn 20l clr; 12l up 7; hdd aft 9; poor 4th by 13; t.o & pu 15*

OFFICIAL DISTANCES: 15l, dist **TIME:** 6min 32.0s **TOTE:** £1.35; **DF:** £1.20

1286 Confined - 17J
9 ran

[773¹]	**1**		**SENSE OF ADVENTURE** 5-4F N Bloom *Prom & keen early but ballooning some fncs; drpd back last 7; 7l 7th 12; rallied 14 & disp 2nd aft 3 out; drvn along til ld flat; rather cheeky (v wl rdn)*
[1155³]	**2**	hd	**Mister Audi** (IRE) 4-1 A Sansome *Prom in 3rd mostly; drvn to 2nd 3 out; ld aft nxt; hd advant last; collared flat but r.o wl cl home*
[1008P]	**3**	15	**Mr Five Wood** (IRE) 33-1 J Purllant *Ld to 3; chsd ldr to 15; wknd nxt; kpt on to tk 3rd flat*
	4	½	**Sign** 12-1 D Barlow *Ld 3 & jw; rdn & hdd aft 2 out; sn btn; gd eff*
[1184²]	**5**	12	**Who's Next** 6-1 T Lane *Sn trckng ldrs; 5th & u.p 12; outpcd 14; nd aft*
[543³]	**6**	1	**Ballydesmond** (IRE) (bl) 12-1 K Edmunds *2 handlers; oht; tk keen hld & prom; blun 11; 4th 12; hit 13; wknd 14*
[1184⁴]	**7**	10	**Ann's Ambition** 20-1 Miss C Fryer *Mostly last; 8l down 12; lost tch nxt*
[1036²]	**P**		**Broadway Swinger** (tt) 6-1 S R Andrews *Settled towards rr; 6l 6th 12; nt fluent nxt; wknd 14; 6th & no ch when blun 3 out; pu last*
[29¹]	**U**		**Fire On Ice** (IRE) 5-1 N King *(xnb) Bckwd; hld up in rr til blun & ur 3*

OFFICIAL DISTANCES: hd, 15l **TIME:** 6min 24.0s **TOTE:** £2.50; **DF:** £5.35
Fence 9 omitted - fallen rider

1287 Restricted, 12st
13 ran

[1009P]	**1**		**BARON ALLFOURS** 14-1 P Millington *(citation) Tk keen hld in rr; cl 8th 12; hdwy 15; ld aft 2 out; drvn along in typically unorthodox fashion & r.o game fzg*
[1111²]	**2**	2½	**Squaddie** 5-2CF A Sansome *Swtng; hld up towards rr early; 6th & prog 12; ld 15; hdd u.p aft 2 out; nt qckn*
[793¹]	**3**	10	**Fine Times** 5-1 M Mackley *Hld up & bhnd; 10l 11th 12; gd hdwy 15; 3rd & flatt brief aft nxt; sn rdn & no further imp*
[179²]	**4**	nk	**The Red Boy** (IRE) 5-2CF K Edmunds *Swtng; keen hld in rr; blun 9; 10th & wl in tch 12; pulling hrd in 6th 12; outpcd aft 3 out; kpt on agn app last*
[1181²]	**5**	10	**Holmby Copse** 14-1 T Humphrey *Prom; 3rd 12; outpcd when mist 3 out*
[1039¹]	**6**	2	**Spectre** 5-2CF N Bloom *Cl up; 5th 12; outpcd 15*
[1035⁷]	**7**	8	**Premier First** (IRE) (bl) 33-1 W Pewter *(xnb) 2nd/3rd to 15; rdn & wknd nxt*
[1111³]	**P**		**Ar Aghaidh Abhaile** (IRE) 10-1 G Cooper *Towards rr; mist 10; sn pushed along; 8l 9th 12; wknd aft nxt; pu 2 out*
[797⁵]	**P**		**Heir Of Gold** (IRE) 5-1 S R Andrews *Mist 1; towards rr til pu & dism 7*
[1038¹]	**P**		**Sweet Talker** (IRE) 16-1 A Harvey *Trckd ldrs; mist 3; 4th 12; hit 13; wknd aft 14; pu 2 out*
[980P]	**P**		**Tom's Influence** (5a) 16-1 D Parker *Ld; pckd 9; hld 15; wknd rap; pu last*
[1180⁶]	**P**		**Vulpin De Laugere** (FR) (2ow) (bl) 33-1 C Jarvis *Lw; 2nd/3rd til lost plce rap 11; last & keen nxt; t.o & pu last*
	P		**Zafan** (IRE) (7a) 8-1 R Fowler *Prsd ldrs gng wl; 7th 12; eased aft 14; pu 2 out; v promising*

OFFICIAL DISTANCES: 2l, 8l **TIME:** 6min 29.0s **TOTE:** £21.00; **DF:** £44.50

1288 Mens Open, 12st   5 ran

[771²]	1		**GENERAL ASSEMBLY (IRE)** 4-6F N Bloom *Trckd ldrs; went cl 2nd 12 but outpcd & scrubbed along 14; lkd hld til ldr blun nxt; clsd aft 3 out to ld app last; all out & unimpressive*
[607⁴]	2	2	**Epsilo De La Ronce (FR)** (bl) 5-1 A Harvey *Swtng; settled cl up; mist 9; mist 11 & rdn rest of way; outpcd 14 & 15l 3rd nxt; stayed on to 2nd flat; nvr keen*
[1156³]	3	4	**Prince Of Saints (IRE)** (bl) 9-4 A Sansome *Cl 2nd/3rd til ld 11; drew 10l clr aft 14 & gng wl til nrly fell 15; miraculous rcvry by rdr; horse lost interest & rdn along aft; hdd app last; reluct & lost 2nd flat*
[1113ᵁ]	4	runin	**Going Around** 12-1 C Ward *Jmpd v slow 4; jmpd slow agn 10; made most to 11; wknd rap 13; sn t.o & v tired*
[1182³]	P		**Veryvel (CZE)** 10-1 D Kemp *Reluct in last; climbed 3 & lost tch; sn t.o & jmpd slow; pu 10*

OFFICIAL DISTANCES: 2½l, 3l   TIME: 6min 33.0s   TOTE: £1.80; DF: £4.40

1289 Ladies Open   4 ran

[1037ᵁ]	1		**SPRING GALE (IRE)** 1-4F Miss Z Turner *Lw; jmpd rather delib at times to 12 but much btr when pce qcknd; hld up; 7l last 6; clsd 12; ld 14; drew clr app 3 out; v easy*
[1181⁴]	2	15	**Holiday Time (IRE)** (5a) 7-1 Mrs S Hodge *Pulled hrd; ld to 14; chsd wnr vain frm 3 out*
[939⁵]	3	25	**Hay Dance** 7-1 Mrs E Coveney *Tk keen hld in cl 2nd to 12; 4l 3rd app 15; wknd rap & fin tired*
[1034³]	4	1½fs	**Just Jack** 8-1 Miss F Jonason *Trckd ldng pr til wknd qckly aft 11; t.o 14 & cont v slow*

OFFICIAL DISTANCES: 20l, 25l   TIME: 6min 29.0s   TOTE: £1.20; SF: £1.60

1290 Open Maiden 56&7yo (Div 1), 12st - 15J   10 ran

[941²]	1		**CRADLE MOUNTAIN** evensF N Bloom *Chsd ldr; ld 13; rdn aft 2 out; hrd prsd when lft clr last; fin lame*
[844⁵]	2	2	**Cardinal Bud (IRE)** 6-1 P Taiano *(xnb) Lw; drpd out in rr; jmpd slow 3; hdwy 9; ld 12-13; rdn aft 2 out; rallied to chall & hit last; nt qckn*
[1070³]	3	½	**Fortune Hunter (IRE)** 12-1 P Millington *(citation) Pulled hrd in midfield; 5th 12; 3rd & eff 15; drvn & one pce frm 2 out*
[1116ᴾ]	4	2½	**River Surprise (IRE)** 33-1 R Garrard *Prom; mists 3 & 10; 3rd 12; outpcd aft 3 out; trying to stay on when mist last; nt qckn; dism sn aft fin*
[1040³]	5	15	**Craftbook Marchesa (IRE)** (5a) 33-1 A Sansome *Hld up & bhnd; 6th 12; went 4th 15; drvn & sn bhtn*
[1115²]	6	25	**About Time (IRE)** 9-4 D Cook *(xnb) Trckd ldrs but rdn all way & nvr keen; 5th 12; lost tch nxt; cont reluct*
	P		**Holy Moses (IRE)** 25-1 T Macfarlane *Bit bckwd; jb & last mostly; clsd bet fncs & lost ground at them; lost tch & blun 12; t.o & pu 13*
[1070ᵁ]	P		**Sail On By** (5a) 7-1 R Armson *Nt fluent in midfield; mist 6; 7th & rdn at 10; sn lost tch; t.o & pu 3 out*
[1039ᴾ]	P		**Sidney Street** (vis) 33-1 R Barr *Tk wild hld; lft in ld 2 & sn 20l clr; mist 6; hdd 10 & stpd as if shot; t.o & pu 14 (rdr is totally out of control)*
[774ᴾ]	U		**Stick Or Bust** (7a) 16-1 R Fowler *Ld til blun 3; ur 75yds aft*

OFFICIAL DISTANCES: 2l, 2l   TIME: 6min 39.0s   TOTE: £1.80; DF: £4.00
Fences 2, 8 & 14 (water) were omitted from this and the last race - poached ground

1291 Open Maiden 56&7yo (Div 2), 12st   10 ran

[1040ᴾ]	1		**TOD'S BROTHER** 20-1 N Bloom *Bit bckwd; sn 2nd; ld 12; blun 15 & sn hdd; tkn gently til ld agn aft 2 out; sn clr (v wl handled - rdr's 150th wnr)*
[516ᴾ]	2	5	**Mandalay Man (IRE)** 14-1 R Armson *Hld up & bhnd; 9l 6th 12; drvn app 15; went 3rd nxt; outbattled mate for 2nd flat; no ch w wnr*
[1180³]	3	17	**Sixth Sense (IRE)** 5-4F T Lane *Nt fluent; bustled along in midfield & nvr gng wl; bad mist 9; 10l 7th 12; nd frm 14; fin 4th; promoted*
[839³]	5	8	**Nosy Parker (IRE)** 14-1 A Harvey *Prom; 4th 12; same & drvn 3 out; sn wknd*
[1039ᴾ]	3d		**Polly Live Wire** (5a) 7-1 P Millington *Hld up & wl bhnd; prog to 8l 5th when bad mist 12; clsd to ld aft 15; hdd und wild waving aft 2 out; nt qckn & lost 2nd flat; fin 7l 3rd; disq - nt weigh-in*
[1039ᴾ]	P		**Always Trying** (7a) 4-1 A Sansome *Trckd ldrs; 3rd 12; drvn in 3rd app 15; wknd to 6th aft mist nxt; pu last*
[1220ᶠ]	r		**Carr Dyke Castle** (bl) 33-1 M Mackley *Reluct & rdn in rr; t.o 12; ref 13*
[1070ᴾ]	P		**Don Royal** 33-1 Miss A Burton *Lkd awful; a wl bhnd; last when blun 6; sn t.o; pu 13*

[793⁴] P   **Second Thoughts** (5a) 7-4 W Wales _Tk keen hld & sn ld; hdd 12; wknd app 14; 5th & btn 3 out; pu last_

     P   **There Be Demons** (USA) (7a) 25-1 A Coe _Str hld; jb early; prom til nrly fell 2; 5th 6; wknd 10; pu 13; bbv_

OFFICIAL DISTANCES: 5l, 2l **TIME:** 6min 37.0s **TOTE:** £11.80; **DF:** £88.20
> _Polly Live Wire finished third but was disqualified when the rider failed to weigh in - he was fined £50_

1292 Open Maiden 8yo&up - 15J   9 ran

     1   **DENARII** (IRE) (5a) 7-2 Miss L Cowan _1st ride; sn ld/2nd; blun 9; 11 2nd 15; ld 2 out; kpt on stdly & clr app last_

[1040ᵁ] 2   10   **Out Of Actons** (IRE) 6-4F C Jarvis _Rr early; shot into ld aft 10; nt a fluent; hdd 2 out; desperately one-pcd_

[1219⁶] 3   8   **Father's Joy** (5a) 5-2 A Sansome _Lkd v poor; detach w mate; 15l 4th & hdwy 12; drvn to flatt aft 15; sn fnd nil; btn nxt_

[1116ᴾ] 4   12   **City Run** (USA) 20-1 Mrs T Holditch _Prsd ldrs but nt a fluent & rdr novicey; 4l 3rd 15; sn outpcd_

[1110³] P   **Blazing Times** (5ow) 10-1 J Buckle _2 handlers; prom; 3rd app 9; wknd alarm 11; t.o & crawled nxt; pu aft 13_

[1116ᴾ] P   **Coolest By Phar** (IRE) (bl) 12-1 C Ward-Thomas _Tubed; pulled hrd & ld/disp brief; lost plce 5; t.o & pu aft 12_

     r   **Cottesmore** 14-1 A Campbell _(xnb) 1st ride; mist 3; ref 4_

[437ᴾ] P   **Rising Dawn** (IRE) 20-1 P Millington _(citation) Sn detach w mate in last pr; blun 7; 20l last 12; drvn along & wl to frm 14; pu last; galloped on & passed outside winning posts w rdr gesticulating_

[1112³] F   **Tan Hill Sparky** (5a) 12-1 A Coe _Fat; ld/2nd til fell 10_

OFFICIAL DISTANCES: 8l, 5l **TIME:** 6min 43.0s **TOTE:** £4.40; **DF:** £3.40

Ludlow (RH 9F,19J)
Mon, 1 May (GOOD)

1293 Gladys Edwards Ten Decades HC   13 ran

     1   **OZZIE JONES** 12-00 7-4F Miss L Pearce _Cl up; ld 5-7; ld agn app 12; hdd 15; ld agn 2 out; drew clr run-in_

[684³] 2   6   **Hee's A Dancer** 12-01 9-1 Miss E Jones _Cl up; ld 2-5; ld 7 til app 12; ld agn 15; mist 3 out; hd nxt; no ex_

[1249²] 3   2½   **Silverdalesureshot** 12-04 5-2 T Scudamore _In tch; hdwy 12; sn chsng ldrs; stayed on one pce frm 16_

[302⁴] 4   ½   **Rocket Radar** 12-01 5-1 G Barfoot-Saunt _Hld up; hdwy aft 11; rdn to chse ldrs 14; kpt on one pce frm 16; no imp when mist 2 out_

[1128⁵] 5   10   **George Ashford** (IRE) 11-07 33-1 J R Barlow _Rr; stdy hdwy 14; nvr able to chall ldrs_

[684⁷] 6   dist   **Smart Song** 11-11 25-1 M Hammond _Prom til wknd qckly 15; t.o_

[859ᴾ] P   **Across The Water** 11-04 33-1 R Armson _Hld up; midfield 6; lost plce & rdn 8; sn bhnd; t.o & pu 15_

[467³] U   **Alska** (FR) 11-02 25-1 Miss W Southcombe _Ld to 2; stayed cl up; lost plce 7; rallied 13; 5th & 8l off pce when blun & ur 3 out_

[1089²] P   **Another Wag** 11-02 25-1 S Lloyd _Rr; t.o & pu 12_

[1093¹] P   **Gorsey Bank** (IRE) 11-09 12-1 R Cooper _Bucking, plunging & unrideable; pu bef 1_

[961²] P   **Khatir** (CAN) 11-07 (bl) 16-1 N Kent _Midfield; blun 5; drpd to rr 7; t.o & pu 15_

[1023⁵] P   **Lordinthesky** (IRE) 11-09 20-1 S Blackwell _Mists; hld up; hdwy 12; cl 6th when blun bad 14; nt rec; pu bef nxt_

[993ᴾ] P   **Wrenbury Farmer** 11-07 33-1 S Graham _Hld up; hdwy to go prom 5; lost plce 8; t.o & pu 14_

TIME: 6min 11.7s **TOTE:** £3.00; places £1.80,£2.40,£1.10 **Ex:** £16.50 **CSF:** £17.34

Banwen Miners
Pentreclwydau (LH 7F,18J) Mon, 1 May (GOOD to SOFT)

1294 Hunt   1 ran

[947¹] 1   **MERRIE JAR** (IRE) T Vaughan _Lw; walked over_

OFFICIAL DISTANCE: Walked over

1295 Confined, 12st
13 ran

[945P]	1		**HARBOUR ISLAND** (bl) 20-1 J L Llewellyn *2nd til ld app 12; jmpd rt 14; drew clr aft nxt; 6l ahd when mist 2 out; blun bad last & picked up off floor; drvn out; wl rdn*
[945²]	2	8	**Anorak** (USA) (3x) 3-1 C Williams *Chsd clr ldng pr; clsd app 12; cl 4th 15; rdn & outpcd kpt on agn aft 2 out & drvn into 2nd nr fin*
[819¹]	3	nk	**You Make Me Laugh** (IRE) (10x) 6-4F E Williams (xnb) *Midfield; 4th & prog 8; chall 12; 11 2nd when checked aft 15; sn drvn along & chsng wnr vain; lost 2nd nr fin*
[1224²]	4	10	**Mr Mad** (vis) 5-1 P Hamer *Rr early; prog in 6th 8; trckd ldrs 12 til jmpd awkward & outpcd 14; nd aft*
	5	10	**Desmond Gold** (IRE) 16-1 M Barber *Chsd ldrs; 5th 11; rdn & wknd aft 15*
[275P]	P		**Alfion** (IRE) 16-1 D Hughes *Chsd ldrs; rdn 9; 14l 7th & strugg 11; pu 12*
[1051P]	U		**Comme Une Fleur** (FR) (5a) 10-1 G Marsh *Mist 2; 8th when ur 6*
[1050²]	P		**Credon** 16-1 Miss A Meakins *Lw; a bhnd; 35l 9th 11; t.o & pu 15*
[1051P]	P		**Hal's Prince** (7x) 6-1 Miss P Jones *Mist 1; ld at gd pce til app 12; 4l 3rd aft 15; sn eased & pu nxt*
[743P]	P		**Herbert Lodge** (IRE) 20-1 Miss M Bartlett *Sn bhnd; last 8; t.o & pu 12*
[482P]	F		**Hollow Sound** (IRE) (5a) 50-1 A Hardacre *Sn bhnd; strugg 11; t.o when fell 13*
[741P]	P		**Persian Mystic** (IRE) 14-1 Miss S Wallin *Rr div; 25l 8th 11; t.o & pu 14*
	F		**Slip Haven** (5a) 50-1 A Price (xnb) *Sis; mists & wl bhnd in last pr; t.o & mist 7; fell 13*

OFFICIAL DISTANCES: 4l, ½l **TIME:** 6min 25.0s

1296 Mens Open, 12st
5 ran

[1226²]	1		**MR DOW JONES** (IRE) (7x) 5-4F J Jukes *Ld; mist 12; nt fluent 14 & 15 & hdd; ev ch til lft in ld last; drvn & all out*
[1226¹]	2	½	**Kinnefad King** (IRE) (tt) 6-4 C Williams *Hld up; 2nd/3rd frm 5; blun 10; tk slt ld aft 15 til blun last; rallied & r.o u.p; unlucky (cut leg badly)*
[1015⁴]	3	25	**Bit Of A Citizen** (IRE) (5a,7x) 8-1 E Williams *Hld up in last pr; 8l 4th 11; sn lost interest; 25l last aft 15*
[1226³]	4	12	**Moon Tiger** (7x) 4-1 T Vaughan *Mostly 2nd to 12; rdn nxt; 10l 3rd & outpcd aft 15; wknd*
[945³]	P		**Laurel Seeker** (USA) 8-1 James Tudor *Swtng profuse; prom brief; last by 7; 16l bhnd & strugg 11; t.o & pu 14*

OFFICIAL DISTANCES: 1l, 30l **TIME:** 6min 19.0s

1297 Ladies Open
11 ran

[991³]	1		**CAPTAIN KHEDIVE** 12-1 Miss S Talbot (xnb) *Hld up in midfield; 10l 6th & prog 11; went 4l 3rd aft 15; 2nd nxt; kpt on to ld last; pushed out*
[1226P]	2	2	**Young Manny** 20-1 Mrs B Lewis *Jw; ld 3 til app 12; ll 2nd aft 15; releg 3rd & lkd btn nxt; rallied & r.o str to 2nd agn aft last*
[645¹]	3	4	**Gunner Boon** (5x) 2-5F Miss P Jones *Ld to 3; cl 2nd til ld app 12; drvn & hdd when mist last; wknd*
[1221³]	4	½	**Sip Of Brandy** (IRE) (3x) 10-1 Miss J Hughes (xnb) *Prom til nrly ur 3; rallied 5; 5l 5th 11; went 3rd nxt & prsd ldrs til 8l 4th aft 15; kpt on agn flat*
[1052¹]	5	15	**Viardot** (IRE) (5x) 5-1 Miss G Roberts *Midfield; hit 10; 7th nxt; sn outpcd; 26l 7th aft 15*
[1022P]	6	6	**Whistling Buck** (tt) 6-1 Miss C Thomas *Sn prom; 4th 11; lost plce app nxt; strugg when jmpd v slow 14; nt r.o & 23l 6th aft 15*
[1053³]	7	20	**Sun Of Chance** 12-1 Miss A Meakins *Prom early; 9th & strugg 11; t.o last aft 15*
[1224⁴]	P		**Celtic Friend** (IRE) (bl) 20-1 Miss E Jones *Reluct & ss; mist 2; hdwy to press ldrs & rn v wide aft 4; rr & rdn 8; sn t.o; pu 12*
[1085³]	F		**Chieftain's Crown** (USA) 33-1 Miss E James (xnb) *Prom; 3rd 11; 5th when fell 13*
[1066P]	P		**Danny Gale** (IRE) 20-1 Miss F Wilson *Sn bhnd; 8th & outpcd 11; no ch aft; 38l 8th when pu 3 out*
[895P]	P		**Flashman** 25-1 Miss E Crawford *A rr; t.o & pu 9*

OFFICIAL DISTANCES: 1½l, 3l **TIME:** 6min 22.0s

1298 Restricted, 12st
15 ran

[1276U]	1		**J'ACCUSE** (IRE) 14-1 Miss F Wilson *Hld up in midfield; 7th 11; eff 13; went 11 2nd aft 15; chall 2 out; ld last; sn clr*
[1225¹]	2	3	**Cherry Gold** 6-4F E Williams (xnb) *Ld/disp til def advant 12; went 3l clr 3 out; stumbled nxt & drvn; hdd last; nt qckn*
[1088⁴]	3	15	**Bright Beacon** 10-1 A Price *Midfield; 6th 11; eff nxt but nvr rchd ldrs; lft 16l 3rd aft 15; plugged on*
[1055¹]	4	8	**Gypsy Haze** (12a) 3-1 J Cook *Prsd ldrs til 4th 11; virt rn off course on bend bef nxt & lost all ch; 30l 7th aft 15; kpt on*

[947³]	5	nk	**Mecca Prince (IRE)** (7a) 14-1 James Tudor _Midfield; 8th 11; outpcd nxt; 2l l 6th & btn aft 15_
[1228⁵]	6	1½fs	**Young Mariner** 33-1 G Maloney _(xnb) Rr & reluct; sn lost tch; t.o 7_
[1056¹]	P		**Bannagh Beg (IRE)** (5a) 14-1 Miss P Jones _Lkd awful; strugg in rr; t.o to pu 10_
	P		**Colebrook Willie** (bl) 14-1 P Hamer _V reluct & drvn along; t.o 5; pu 12_
[1054ᴾ]	P		**Cranagh Moss (IRE)** (vis) 8-1 J L Llewellyn _Chsd ldrs; 5th 11; wknd nxt; 20l 5th aft 15; t.o & pu 2 out_
[1228³]	P		**Howsyourluck (IRE)** (vis) 7-1 T Vaughan _Ld/disp to 7; 3rd 11; lost plce nxt; strugg when pu 14_
[1228ᴾ]	F		**Jack Boots** 12-1 J Phillips _(xnb) Midfield; 9th when fell 11_
[951¹]	P		**Roger (IRE)** 7-1 C Williams _2nd/3rd til ld 11-12; w ldr when bad mist 14; wknd & 17l 3rd aft mist nxt; tired when pu 3 out_
[1022ᴾ]	P		**Sea Search** 25-1 Miss A Meakins _Lkd awful; barely galloping in last; t.o 5; pu 9; disgraceful_
[835¹]	P		**Travel Safely (IRE)** 5-1 J Keen _Sn bhnd; t.o 10th aft 11; pu 12_
	F		**Wanstead (IRE)** 5-1 J Jukes _Prom til fell 4_

OFFICIAL DISTANCES: 3l, 30l TIME: 6min 26.0s

1299 Intermediate, 12st

10 ran

[837ᵁ]	1		**FLOCKMASTER (IRE)** 10-1 E Williams _Ld/2nd til ld aft 11; 2l ahd when lft 15l clr aft 15; hrd rdn 2 out; all out_
[1052²]	2	1	**Storm Man (IRE)** 20-1 Miss C Williams _Ld/disp 5-9; 3rd 11; drpd back 6th 13; lft 19l 4th aft 15; disp 2nd nxt; r.o wl gng last; clsng to wnr flat_
[1051ᴾ]	3	6	**Roman Gale (IRE)** 16-1 G Thorne _Hld up in tch; 6l 7th 11; 5th & outpcd 13; lft 16l 3rd aft 15; disp 2nd nxt; nt qckn aft_
[1227²]	4	15	**Rusnetto (IRE)** (vis) 5-1 P Hamer _Mist 4; nt jw in rr til prog in 4th 9; 5th 11; drvn & outpcd 13; lft 20l 5th aft 15_
[944²]	5	1	**Dyffryn Prince (IRE)** 5-1 P Sheldrake _2 handlers; ld to 3; prom; ld agn brief 11; outpcd 13; 15l 3rd when lft 2nd aft 15; 15l 3rd when lft 2nd aft 15; wknd qckly nxt_
[1227³]	6	8	**Secret Beauty (IRE)** (5a) 5-1 M Lewis _Nt jw & nvr gng wl in rr; 16l 7th 11; unable to cl_
[1022⁶]	U		**Bel-De-Moor** (5a) 3-1 T Vaughan _Prom; drew clr w wnr 13; 2l down when impeded by loose horse & ur turn aft 15 (lkd gng best)_
[1051ᴾ]	P		**Chantingo Lad** (tt) 20-1 A Price _Prom brief; last & strugg when bad mist 10; t.o & pu aft 11_
[1051ᴾ]	U		**Southern Cross** (bl) 4-1 J Cook _Jmpd erratic in last; t.o 6; blun bad & ur 7_
[1051²]	C		**The Rural Dean (IRE)** 2-1F J Price _Unimpressive padd; bad mist 2; nt jw in rr; hdwy 9 & 5l 6th 11; 4th & drvn 13; sn wl outpcd; carried out by loose horse aft 15_

OFFICIAL DISTANCES: 2l, 4l TIME: 6min 33.0s
Secret Can't Say was withdrawn after declaration

1300 Open Maiden (Div 1, Part 1), 12st

11 ran

[1091³]	1		**SAXON QUEEN** (5a) 4-5F E Williams _(xnb) Lw; ld aft 1 & spreadeagled field; 10l clr 12; 20l ahd aft 15; mist 2 out & drvn; unchall but nt impressive_
[831³]	2	15	**The Gadfly** 5-1 J Hayward _Hld up early; 3rd & prog 9; 10l 2nd 11; dem & lft poor 2nd agn 13; chsd wnr vain aft; mist last_
[1225⁴]	3	runin	**Sing Cherry Ripe** (5a) 7-1 J Keen _Chsd ldrs to 9; 17l 4th & outpcd 11; t.o 14_
[1222⁶]	4	81sec	**Jesusa** (5a) 10-1 G Maloney _T.o aft 4; 3 fncs adrift by 12; event fin 81secs aft wnr_
	P		**Fortunes Leap** 10-1 R Hughes _Ss & lost 20l; t.o 5; pu 11_
[822⁴]	F		**Guard A Dream (IRE)** 10-1 N Jones _Chsd ldrs; mist 4; 2nd 9; 12l 3rd 11; 12l 2nd when fell 13_
[1225ᴾ]	P		**Just Ruffled** 20-1 J Price _Chsd ldr til pu 8 (rdr thought horse sore)_
[1055ᴾ]	P		**No Escape** 20-1 G Perkins _Jb rt in final trio; rdn when climbed 7; cont to; pu 11_
[746³]	P		**Parsons Secret** (5a) 8-1 T Vaughan _Chsd ldrs early; 30l 6th when pu aft 11_
	P		**Queen's Equa** (5a) 10-1 Miss S Major _Handy early; 42l 7th when pu aft 11_
[823³]	P		**Star Island** (5a) 5-1 A Price _Ld 1; prom to 9; 23l 5th & fdng 11; pu 12_

OFFICIAL DISTANCES: 25l, dist TIME: 6min 35.0s

1301 Open Maiden (Div 1, Part 2), 12st

11 ran

	1		**ENERGY MAN** 8-1 J Keen _Declined mad early pce & rem 9th aft 4; 5th 12; went 10l 2nd aft 15; stayed on to ld 2 out; hrd prsd when lft wl clr last_
[1225ᴾ]	2	15	**Stormhill Daydream** (5a) 10-1 J Jukes _T.o in last pr; last 11; plugged on as others departed & lft 2nd 14 til aft nxt; fnd nil aft; lft 2nd at last_
[1225ᴾ]	3	bad	**Lough Neagh (IRE)** 7-1 P Sheldrake _Midfield; 4th 11; lft 3rd 12 & sn 15l 2nd; lft 10l clr 14; drvn & hdd 2 out; wildly rdn & ev ch when mist & ur last; rmtd_
[834ᴾ]	P		**Aherne** (7a) 14-1 J Phillips _Nt jw; imm lost tch; rem 7th 4; cont to; pu 14_

[602ᶠ]	P	**Bill's Integrity** (12a) 4-1 **E Williams** *School in last pr; a t.o; pu aft 11*
[1223³]	F	**Bold Knight** 6-4F **G Skone** *Prsd ldrs til fell 11*
[951ᴾ]	P	**Gowenbacktodudley** (5a) 20-1 **J Price** *Jmpd appalling & imm lost tch; t.o when jb rt 9; bad mist 11 & pu*
[1068ᴾ]	P	**Pigeon Hill Buck** (IRE) 20-1 **J Cook** *Chsd ldr to 11; wkng when lft 2nd brief 12; strugg aft; pu 15*
[943³]	r	**Snow Cloud** (5a) 6-1 **Miss I Tompsett** *(xnb) Pulled hrd & ld at furious gallop; sn clr; pckd 2; mist 3; hdd 10; t.o 12; crawling when ref 14*
[949ᴾ]	r	**Tommyknocker** (IRE) 10-1 **T Faulkner** *Handy; ld 11; drew clr aft nxt; lft 15l ahd 12; ref 14*
[4ᶠ]	F	**Welsh Warrior** 4-1 **C Williams** *Settled back of ldng group; 6th 8; eff 11; went 5l 2nd & fell 12*

OFFICIAL DISTANCES: 8l, dist   **TIME:** 6min 41.0s

1302 Open Maiden (Div 2), 12st   16 ran

[1056ᴾ]	1		**BLACK DAN** 12-1 **J Keen** *20l 3rd 7; clsd & lft 2nd 11; 3l 3rd nxt; ld & mist 15; sn releg 3rd; rallied to ld app last & mist; drvn out & fnd ex flat*
[1223⁹]	2	½	**Get The Gist** (IRE) 10-1 **P Hamer** *Drpd out wl bhnd; 6th & prog 11; 20l 5th nxt; rdn to cl in 2l 3rd aft 15; went 2nd out; drvn & just outpcd aft last*
[1056ᶠ]	3	10	**Albert The Lion** (IRE) 10-1 **C Williams** *(xnb) Chsng group bhnd clr ldng pr; 5th 7; lft in ld 11 til hdd & nt fluent 15; sn ld agn; hdd & bad mist 2 out; wknd & fin tired*
[1222ᶠ]	4	bad	**Lady Murrhill** (IRE) (12a) 8-1 **J Hayward** *Pckd 5; 8th 7; lft 12l 4th 11; wknd 13; 25l last aft 15; fnce bhnd when blun & ur last; rmtd*
	F		**Baran Itsu** 10-1 **P Sheldrake** *3rd when fell 6*
[891ᴾ]	P		**Buckley House** 12-1 **A Price** *(xnb) Hung rt aft 1; midfield; 7th & strugg when nrly fell 11; pu 12*
[350ᴾ]	P		**Clonshire Castle** (IRE) 10-1 **J Cook** *7th 7; impd & lft 3rd 11; 2l 2nd 12; mist 14; wknd rap aft nxt; t.o & pu last*
[1055³]	P		**Craigson** 6-1 **T Faulkner** *Towards rr; mist 9; 25l 6th 12; pu 13*
[835ᴾ]	P		**Don't Forget** (IRE) (5a) 6-1 **J Phillips** *Sn lost tch; 9th 11; t.o & pu 13*
	F		**Hill Top Flyer** (IRE) 16-1 **G Marsh** *Rr when fell 3*
[1055²]	P		**Lillies Buttler** (5a) 3-1 **I Johnson** *Qckly lost tch; t.o & pu aft 11*
[746ᴾ]	P		**Listenup Lord** (7a) 16-1 **G Maloney** *Broke hind leg aft 2; dead*
[1201ᶠ]	P		**Mia Fort** (5a) 16-1 **J Price** *Burly; 15l 5th 11; pu nxt*
	P		**Migsy Malone** (12a) 6-1 **J Jukes** *School & rem in last pr til pu aft 11*
[1056²]	U		**Mike's Dream** evensF **Miss P Jones** *Ld/2nd til blun & ur 10*
	F		**Pull On** 14-1 **E Williams** *(xnb,pricker ns) Tk keen hld; ld/disp; 20l clr of 3rd when bad mist 7; lft in ld 10; stumbled & fell 11*

OFFICIAL DISTANCES: ½l, 6l   **TIME:** 6min 39.0s

Cotley

Cotley Farm (LH 9F,18J) Mon, 1 May (GOOD, GOOD to SOFT in places)

1303 Hunt   4 ran

[654³]	1		**THE CRIOSRA** (IRE) 5-1 **Miss T Newman** *(bf) Hld up in last; 5l 5th; made up ground on climb to 10; disp 2l 2nd nxt; chsd ldr til ld aft 14; jnd brief 3 out; stayed on str nxt; a hldng rnr-up*
[1131³]	2	1	**Mel** (IRE) 9-4 **Miss M Eames** *Chsd ldrs; 1l 3rd 5 til ld 9; 4l up 11; hdd aft 14; disp brief 3 out; stayed on one pce til no ex last*
[1138⁶]	3	15	**Bitran** 8-13F **T Greed** *Ld/disp to 6; 4½l 3rd 9; jmpd slow nxt; outpcd & 10l 3rd 15; stayed on one pce frm nxt; disapp*
[1241⁴]	4	1¼fs	**Weycroft Valley** (5a) 33-1 **L Tibbatts** *Ld/disp til jmpd lft 7 & 8; sn lost plce & last 10; t.o 15*

OFFICIAL DISTANCES: 1½l, 8l   **TIME:** 6min 47.9s   **TOTE:** £3.00

1304 Confined (Nov Rdrs)   12 ran

[1096¹]	1		**MILLYHENRY** 1-2F **Miss C Tizzard** *Chsd ldr til lft in ld 3; made rest; 7l up 9; grad drew clr frm 12; 20l up 15; outclassed rivals*
[1139²]	2	30	**Cool Clown** 14-1 **B Trickey** *Chsd ldrs; 17l 6th 9; stayed on frm mid-div 14; lft rem 3rd nxt; stayed on to rem 2nd 2 out; nd*
[1097¹]	3	10	**Sir Frosty** 7-2 **A Bateman** *5s-7/2; mid-div; 6th 4; 18l 7th 9; stayed on to 20l 2nd 15; hit nxt; sn wknd & dem 2 out*
[1237²]	4	30	**Flapjack Lad** 12-1 **T Bishop** *(xnb) 10th 2; stdy hdwy to 6th 6; jmpd into 7l 2nd 9; chsd ldr til wknd 14; bhnd frm nxt*

[523U] 5 ½ **Single Man (NZ)** 66-1 B Parsons Chsd ldrs; jmpd into 2nd 6; 8l 3rd 9 til grad wknd 11; bhnd frm 15

[1047³] 6 1½ **Certain Angle** 25-1 E Chanin (bf) A towards rr; 9th 2; 19l 8th 9; nvr nr to chall; bhnd frm 15

P **Abbotsham** 33-1 C White Nvr bttr than mid-div; rr trio 5; mist 9; 22l 9th nxt; wknd 13; bhnd when pu 3 out

[929³] U **Arise (IRE)** 33-1 Miss T Harrison Mid-div when ur 1

[1236²] P **James Pigg** 14-1 G Richards Trckd ldrs til lft 2nd 3; 12l 4th 9; grad wknd frm 12; bhnd when jmpd slow 3 out; nt dang

[1176P] U **Mountain-Linnet** 66-1 A Corrie Ld; 5l up 2 til rfo nxt

[1134⁵] U **Mystery Aristocrat (IRE)** 6-1 R Tory 14s-6s; a chsng ldrs; 4th 4; 15l 5th 9; outpcd & 25l 3rd 15; blun nxt & event ur some way aft

[523⁶] U **Mystic Moment (IRE)** (5a) 100-1 Miss S Lane A last; 40l adrift aft 9; t.o when blun & ur 2 out

OFFICIAL DISTANCES: 20l, 10l TIME: 6min 31.0s TOTE: £2.00

1305 Mixed Open, 12st

8 ran

[1058¹] 1 **HERE COMES HENRY** 3-1 R Young Lw; hld up in rr; 10l 7th 3; prog to disp 4th 8; 3rd & gng wl 12; ld aft 14 & sn 5l clr nxt; stayed on str frm 2 out; impressive

[928¹] 2 6 **Khayal (USA)** (5x) 4-7F L Jefford Hld up in last pr; stdy hdwy to 6th on climb aft 9 & 4th 13; chsd clr ldr 15; rdn & no ex frm 2 out

[1138²] 3 12 **Wibbley Wobbley** 7-2 Miss J Cumings 6l 4th 3; chsd lng pr 9 til ld 12-14; sn hdd & outpcd frm nxt

[1044³] 4 10 **Gypsy Gerry** (bl) 25-1 T Clarkson Trckd ldrs; 4l 3rd 3 til ld 6; jnd brief 9; hdd 12; outpcd 15; stayed on one pce frm nxt; no ex nxt

[926¹] 5 1¼fs **Shrewd Thought (USA)** 16-1 T Greed Disp 6l 4th 3; chsd ldrs til grad lost plce frm 11; t.o frm 15

[1174⁴] 6 12 **Mr Golightly** 50-1 Mrs J Reed Chsd ldr to 5; sn lost plce & rr 9; t.o 13; plodded home

[921¹⁰] U **Court Master (IRE)** 20-1 D Borradaile 7l 6th 3; impd to 5l 3rd 6; chsd ldr nxt til disp brief 9; grad lost plce frm 12; 5th & lkng hld when blun & ur 14

[1060⁴] P **Radio Days (IRE)** (5x) 66-1 Miss C Tizzard Ld; 3l up 3; hdd 6; lost plce qckly; last when pu aft 9

OFFICIAL DISTANCES: 6l, 12l TIME: 6min 34.0s TOTE: £3.50

1306 Countryside Alliance Club Members 10yo&up, 12st

9 ran

[1177¹] 1 **GAMAY** (7x) 4-9F N Mitchell (xnb) Last to 4; 23l 6th 5; stdy hdwy to 5l 4th 10; disp ld 12; ld nxt; sn 10l clr 15; r.o; easy

[1134F] 2 4 **Frozen Drop** (7x) 25-1 T Bishop Chsd ldrs; disp 18l 4th 5; outpcd 10; stayed on frm rr 15; chsd wnr frm 2 out; nd

[1238³] 3 2 **Avril Showers** (5a,7x) 5-1 R Atkinson Chsd lng pr; 17l 3rd 5 til outpcd 10; stayed on frm rr 15; nvr nr to chall

[735⁴] 4 3 **Hillhead (IRE)** 6-1 J Barnes Trckd ldrs; disp 18l 4th 5; clsd 3l 3rd 10; disp ld nxt; chsd ldr frm 13 -3 out; no ex u.p nxt

[1060³] 5 30 **Factor Ten (IRE)** (7x) 16-1 J Richardson Ld/disp til 1½l up 5-12; grad wknd frm 14; bhnd frm 3 out

[767⁵] 6 1½fs **Dear Emily** (5a) 12-1 Miss L Brack 1st ride; prom early; rr frm 6; last 9; t.o nxt; plodded on; blun last; fin tired

[1058F] P **Fast Run (IRE)** 66-1 Miss M Taylor Nvr bttr than mid-div; 28l 7th 5; mist 7; pu & dism 9

[1098P] P **Kinlogh Gale (IRE)** (bl) 66-1 Miss J Cumings Disp ld to 4 & agn 8-12; sn wknd; bhnd when pu 3 out

[1130²] P **Villains Brief (IRE)** (bl) 50-1 J Kwiatkowski A towards rr; last 4-8; t.o 12 til pu 15

OFFICIAL DISTANCES: 6l, 3l TIME: 6min 39.2s TOTE: £1.30

1307 Open Maiden (Div 1), 12st

8 ran

[934²] 1 **TEAM CAPTAIN** 4-5F L Jefford (boh) Trckd ldrs; 3½l 3rd 2; ld 8; 1½l up nxt; hdd 10; lft in ld 12; jmpd rt & rdr called cab nxt; 15l up frm 2 out

2 10 **Sun Lark** 8-1 Miss S Vickery Tubed; disp 4½l 4th 2; 6l 3rd 5; outpcd & 15l 5th 11; stayed on to disp 7l 3rd 15; chsd wnr frm 2 out; no ex frm nxt

[1101U] 3 3 **Caundle Encore** (5a) 25-1 J Snowden Trckd ldrs til jmpd slow & last 2; 5th & in tch 10; 12l 4th nxt; 10l last 15; stayed on to 3rd nxt; nd

[1102P] 4 1½ **Sparkling Secret** (7a) 8-1 J Barnes 4½l 4th 2; sn lost plce & rr 5; 20l 7th 11; stayed on to disp 7l 3rd 15; no ex frm 2 out

[1241U] U **Green Anker** 14-1 Miss C Stucley Ld; 3l up 5-8; ld agn 10; 8l up nxt til blun & ur 12

[1099²] P **Harveysinahurry** 5-2 G Richards (xnb,boh) Last to 2; prog to 7l 4th 5; mist nxt; 2½l 3rd 9; lft 5l 2nd 12; wknd 15; jmpd slow 3 out; pu nxt

[1136ᴾ] **P**   **Ru Bidding** (5a) 40-1 **T Greed** *Ur padd; chsd ldr to 2; grad lost plce & towards rr 9; 22l last 10; t.o & pu aft nxt*

       P   **Tony's Croney** 10-1 **R Woollacott** *2 handlers; last pr 2; in tch to 10; 16l 6th nxt; bhnd when pu 12*

OFFICIAL DISTANCES: 7l, 5l **TIME:** 6min 59.9s **TOTE:** £2.00

1308 Open Maiden (Div 2), 12st   16 ran

[1048ᴾ] **1**   **SWINCOMBE (IRE)** (7a) 50-1 **Miss T Cave** *Rcd in mid-div; 6th & clsng 3 out; sust rn frm nxt; ld flat; sn clr; wl rdn*

[105⁴] **2** 3   **Durnford Bay (IRE)** (tt) 7-4F **L Jefford** *Ld 2-5 & agn nxt; disp agn 9 til ld 12; 2l up 15 til wandered u.p last; hdd flat; sn no ex*

[881ᵁ] **3** ½   **The Frosty Fox (IRE)** 25-1 **M Miller** *Disp ld 1; 4½l 3rd 5; chsd ldrs til 2l 2nd 14; chsd ldr til no ex flat*

[875²] **4** 4   **The First One** 7-2 **Miss P Gundry** *6s-7/2; hld up in rr til gd prog to 4l 4th 9; jmpd into 2nd 12; staying on one pce when jmpd rt 3 out; no ex frm nxt*

[874²] **5** 1½   **Exmoor Forest** (5a) 8-1 **B O'Doherty** *(bh) A chsng ldrs; 5l 4th 15; stayed on to 4l 3rd nxt; no ex u.p frm 2 out; mist last*

[1095⁴] **6** 5   **Chance Encounter** 16-1 **J Young** *Mid-div to 8; 11th 10; stayed on frm rr 15; nvr nr to chall*

[519⁵] **7** 1½   **Speck** 16-1 **J O'Rourke** *Towards rr 4; mid-div 9; in tch 15 til no ex frm 2 out*

       P   **Dealer Del** 33-1 **G Richards** *Disp ld 1; pulled hrd; mist 2; 6l 4th 5; 2l 3rd when mist 9; wknd 13; bhnd when pu 3 out*

[1062³] **P**   **Gunerkillinghurst** 66-1 **J Snowden** *Mid-div 7; grad wknd 9; sn rr & bhnd nxt; t.o & pu 12*

[1141ᶠ] **S**   **Happy Team** (5a) 4-1 **A Honeyball** *6s-4s; chsd ldrs; 5th 3; disp 6l 4th 5; still in tch when clipped heels & slpd up bend aft 9*

[1102ᴾ] **P**   **Jolitan** (7a) 66-1 **R Woollacott** *Rr til prog 9; cl 3rd 10; wknd 13; bhnd when pu 15*

[881²] **U**   **Prussian Steel (IRE)** 7-2 **T Greed** *Mid-div; chsd ldrs til stayed on to cl 4th 14; disp 2l 2nd & clsng when stumbled on landing & ur 15*

       P   **Slippen-On** 50-1 **M Sweeetland** *Ur padd; a last pr; t.o 10; pu nxt*

       P   **Sparkling Elver** (12a) 25-1 **N Mitchell** *Trckd ldrs til ld brief 5 & agn 7; jnd 9-12; grad wknd; bhnd when pu 15; pleasing debut*

       R   **Vague Idea** 33-1 **I Widdicombe** *15th when rn out & ur 2*

[1099ᶠ] **P**   **Windyway** (5a) 33-1 **L Tibbatts** *(xnb) Rr 3; last when bad mist & nrly fell 7; t.o 9 til pu 13*

OFFICIAL DISTANCES: 2½l, 4l **TIME:** 6min 47.1s **TOTE:** £30.00

1309 Restricted, 12st   10 ran

[1101¹] **1**   **FLEET MILL** (5a) 3-1 **Miss T Cave** *(xnb) Trckd ldrs; 6l 4th 5 & 7l 5th 11; smooth hdwy to ld 14; sn 3l up; pushed out flat*

[1240ᵁ] **2** 5   **Franklins Best (IRE)** 12-1 **N Mitchell** *Last 2; disp 8l 7th 9; gd prog 14; chsd wnr frm nxt; no ex u.p frm 2 out*

[144ᴾ] **3** 10   **Blondie Boo** (IRE) 12-1 **I Widdicombe** *Last 4; 14l adrift 9; stayed on str frm rr 14; 5l 3rd & ev ch 3 out; no ex u.p 2 out*

[1140ᴾ] **4** 12   **Frankly Fear** 14-1 **J Young** *(bh) Rr trio to 4; 7l 6th 9; chsd ldrs til outpcd 14; stayed on frm 3 out; nd*

[957¹] **5** 1   **General Typhoon** 2-1F **Miss E Tory** *Chsd ldrs in 5th 5; 8l 7th 9; outpcd & last 11; stayed on frm 15; nvr nr to chall*

[1045⁵] **6** 8   **Phartoomanny (IRE)** (5a) 33-1 **J Snowden** *(xnb) Tde; 6th 2; 10l 5th 5; chsd ldrs til grad wknd frm 15*

[1061ᵁ] **7** 12   **The Stuffed Puffin (IRE)** 20-1 **Miss S Rowe** *(xnb) Chsd ldr; 11 2nd 5; ld nxt; jnd 8-10; 3l up nxt; hdd 14; grad wknd*

[1061ᵁ] **P**   **Cefn Woodsman** 33-1 **Miss K Lovelace** *Prom; 2½l 3rd 5; disp ld brief 10; chsd ldrs til wknd 14; bhnd when pu 2 out*

[1135ᴾ] **P**   **Harlequin Boy** (bl) 3-1 **Miss P Gundry** *Ld; 2½l up 3; hdd 6; jnd ldr 8; jmpd slow & hdd 10; wknd qckly 13; bhnd when pu 15*

[1095²] **F**   **Shareton** 3-1 **Miss S Vickery** *Last 1; 10l 9th 9; gd prog to 4th nxt; still 4th & in tch when fell 15*

OFFICIAL DISTANCES: 4l, 6l **TIME:** 6min 39.9s **TOTE:** £3.00

Cotswold Vale Farmers

Maisemore Park (LH 6F,15J) Mon, 1 May (GOOD to SOFT, SOFT in places)

1310 Hunt   2 ran

| [897⁵] | 1 | | **TIRLEY MISSILE** 1-6F **Julian Pritchard** *Jmpd rt; made all; drew wl clr frm 14; lft solo last; unchall* |
| [1019²] | P | | **Piccadilly Wood** 7-2 **G Barfoot-Saunt** *Chsd wnr; mists 7 & 9; 4l 2nd ½way; mist 14; wknd 14; almost ref 3 out; t.o & pu last* |

OFFICIAL DISTANCE: Finished alone   TIME: 7min 23.0s

1311 Confined, 12st   7 ran

[466ᶠ]	1		**HENRY BRUCE** (7x) (bl) 1-2F **Julian Pritchard** *Made all; drew 8l clr aft 3 out; rdn out*
[1134¹]	2	4	**Newton Point** 2-1 **Mrs B Keighley** *Jmpd delib; prom; 6l 5th ½way; went 2nd 11-12; 7l 4th & rdn 15; rallied app last; went 2nd flat; nt rch wnr*
[597ᴾ]	3	1½	**Don Du Cadran (FR)** 20-1 **C Gundry** *5th when hit 1; sn prom; 4l 3rd ½way; chsd wnr 12; one pce 3 out; dem flat*
[967³]	4	8	**Pretoria Dancer** (vis) 20-1 **F O'Brien** *Mists 4 & 8; chsd wnr to 11; 5l 3rd 15; rdn & no imp 3 out; wknd app last*
	P		**Native Rambler (IRE)** 20-1 **Miss C Stafford** *(xnb) Swtng; hld up; mist 9; 14l 7th ½way; mist 12; t.o pu 13*
[895ᴾ]	P		**Rockville Pike (IRE)** 20-1 **G Barfoot-Saunt** *(xnb) Hld up last; mist 8; 11l 6th ½way; mist 11; lost tch 13; wl bhnd when pu 14*
[1086⁵]	P		**Rootsman (IRE)** (vis) 16-1 **T Stephenson** *Hld up; 5l 4th & rmdrs ½way; lost plce & 12l 5th 13; wl bhnd 15; t.o & pu last*

OFFICIAL DISTANCES: 4l, 1¼l   TIME: 6min 53.0s

1312 Marsh UK/TBA PPORA Club Members Mares, 12st   6 ran

[861¹]	1		**UPTON ADVENTURE** (5a) 1-2F **S Joynes** *Ww; stdy hdwy & 2½l 4th ½way; went 2l 3rd 13 & 2nd nxt; lft in ld 15; clr when jmpd slow & hit last; shkn up flat; r.o*
[1026ᴾ]	2	4	**Secret Truth** (5a) 20-1 **A Martin** *2 handlers; swtng; hld up & pulled hrd; jmpd slow 4; hdwy 8; 2l 3rd ½way; went 2nd aft 11-14; lft 2nd nxt; no imp 3 out*
[971ᴾ]	3	runin	**Viking Flame** (5a) 20-1 **S Bush** *2nd/3rd to 8; 5l 5th ½way; rdn 12; sn btn; lft 15l 3rd 15; r.o*
[823ᶠ]	P		**Marnies Song** (5a) 7-1 **Julian Pritchard** *14s-7s; hit 2; went 2nd 4 til lost plce 8; 7l 6th ½way; lost tch u.p 12; mist 13; t.o & pu 15*
[1020ᵁ]	U		**Outside The Rain (IRE)** (5a) 20-1 **T Macfarlane** *Prom; went 2nd 8 til aft 11; 2½l 4th when ur 13*
[1098⁴]	F		**Questionaire** (5a) 7-2 **D Stephens (Wales)** *Swtng; ld til fell 15*

OFFICIAL DISTANCES: 5l, dist   TIME: 7min 05.8s

1313 Mixed Open, 12st   6 ran

[1086⁶]	1		**HAPPY MINSTRAL (USA)** 4-1 **A Wintle** *Prom; 2l 3rd & pushed along ½way; went 2nd aft 13; lft in ld 3 out; drvn along & stayed on wl*
[1192²]	2	5	**Celtic Town** 13-8F **Julian Pritchard** *(drop,orbs) 2nd to 5; chsd ldr 8-13; 5l 3rd & drvn along 15; lft 3l 2nd nxt; one pce*
[833ᴾ]	P		**Ballymaloe Boy (IRE)** 9-4 **A Martin** *Hld up & pulled hrd; went 2nd 5 til mist 6; 4l 4th ½way; wknd & 10l 4th when mist 11; pu 12*
[969⁷]	P		**Norman Warrior** 20-1 **S Joynes** *(bf) Ld til hdd 7; sn rdn & nt r.o; 10l 6th ½way; wl bhnd when pu 12*
[1203⁶]	F		**Perfect Finisher** 7-1 **M Hawkins** *Swtng; jmpd bold & rcd wide; hld up; went 2nd 6; ld 7; 3l clr 12 til fell 3 out*
[1087ᴾ]	P		**Slightly Special (IRE)** (bl) 20-1 **A St George** *W ldrs; 6l 5th ½way; went 12l 4th & rdn aft 11; sn wknd; wl bhnd when pu 14*

OFFICIAL DISTANCE: 5l   TIME: 6min 58.6s

1314 Restricted   2 ran

| [1063³] | 1 | | **ZODIAC PRINCE** 6-4 **M Harris** *2nd til ld 8; mist 11; lft 6l clr 13; hdd aft 3 out; rdn to ld last; stayed on wl* |
| [1088²] | 2 | 2½ | **Missed Call (IRE)** 1-2F **Julian Pritchard** *2 handlers; lw; ld to 8; 3l 2nd when blun 13; ld aft 3 out til hdd last; no ex* |

OFFICIAL DISTANCE: 2½l   TIME: 7min 08.7s

1315 Open Maiden (Div 1), 12st   5 ran

[891²] 1   **FAR FROM PERFECT (IRE)** (5a) 1-2F A Wintle *Hld up; 5l 5th ½way; last til went 4l 3rd aft 13; went 2nd 15; ld app last; comf*

[1068ᴾ] 2   4   **Autumn Blunder** 12-1 **T Stephenson** *Lw; oht; hld up & pulled hrd; mist 5; went 2nd 8; ld aft 9 til hdd app last; no ex*

[972ᴾ] 3   15 **Mister River (IRE)** 14-1 P Young *Prom; mist 5; rmdrs 8; 2l 3rd ½way; went 2nd 12-15; sn rdn; wknd aft 3 out*

[1091ᶠ] 4   40 **Forestry** 7-1 Julian Pritchard *Ld til hdd aft 9; 2nd til mist 12; wknd & 15l 4th 15; t.o*

[994ᴾ] U   **Bally Boy** 7-2 **A St George** *Mist 6; 2nd to 8; hit 9; 4l 4th ½way; rdn 12; 12l 5th & wkng when tried to ref & ur 14*

OFFICIAL DISTANCES: 5l, 15l TIME: 7min 08.7s

1316 Open Maiden (Div 2), 12st   5 ran

[989³] 1   **COLD SNAP (IRE)** 2-5F A Wintle *2nd/3rd to 8; 3l 4th ½way; went 2nd agn 11; ld 14; mist 15; drvn out*

[1056ᴾ] 2   4   **Newchurch Lad** 3-1 D Stephens (Wales) *(bf) 2 handlers; a.p; went 2nd 6; mist 9; 2l 3rd ½way; went 2nd aft 3 out; one pce*

[1021ᴾ] 3   25 **Piltdown Lady** (5a) 20-1 T Macfarlane *Ld til hdd 14; 2nd til wknd qckly aft 3 out*

[615ᴾ] U   **Chaceley Lass** (5a) 10-1 T Stephenson *Hld up; hdwy 8; went 2nd aft 9-11; 7l 4th & wkng when blun bad & ur 14*

[900ᴾ] P   **Ivors Boy** 12-1 Miss R Barrow *(pricker os) Hld up; jmpd slow 4; 4l 5th ½way; in tch til wknd aft 9; pu 15*

OFFICIAL DISTANCES: 4l, dist TIME: 7min 12.9s

South Shropshire
Eyton-on-Severn (LH 12F,16J) Mon, 1 May (DEAD with SOFT patches)

1317 Hunt, 12st   4 ran

[565²] 1   **NOTHING VENTURED** 2-5F A Beedles *Set stdy pce; hdd app 11; ld agn bef 13; drew clr frm 3 out; 10l up last; v easy*

[948ᴾ] 2   9   **Henwyn** 8-1 A Dalton *Trckd ldrs in cl 3rd 4; eff to chall on inner app 3 out; sn outpcd; lft 2nd at last*

[862ᴾ] 3   25 **Tangle Baron** 20-1 J Tanner *Bit bckwd; trckd ldrs in cl 3rd/4th; wknd qckly & lost tch 13; lft poor 3rd last*

[1200⁴] U   **Arthur Henry** (5x) 4-1 J Cornes *Ur when mounted; trckd ldr in ½l 2nd; jmpd rt sev fncs; ld 11-12; ev ch nxt til outpcd app 2 out; 10l 2nd when blun v bad & ur last*

OFFICIAL DISTANCES: 8l, 20l TIME: 6min 26.0s TOTE: £1.50
Fences 1 & 14 omitted in all races - state of ground; and start moved forward by 150yds

1318 Open Maiden (Non-Rules Rnrs), 12st   9 ran

[865²] 1   **DUNETHNA (IRE)** 5-2 R Burton *Trckd ldrs in 3rd; 2nd frm 9; prsd ldr 12; disp when lft in ld 13; 1l up 2 out; in comm last; stayed on u.p flat*

[1196³] 2   3   **Kota Tinggi** (5a) 3-1 R Inglesant *Trckd ldrs in 3rd/4th; prsd wnr frm 13; 1l down 2 out; no ex app last; kpt on wl*

3   20 **Knockfiarne Magic (IRE)** 7-1 G Hanmer *Hld up; 16l 6th 8; went 3rd 12; lft 2nd nxt; rdn & wknd app 3 out; sn v tired; eased & nursed home aft; improve*

[965²] 4   15 **Pocket Oscar** 20-1 J R Barlow *A rr; mist 5; detach frm 6; 26l 7th 8; wl bhnd frm 12; lft poor 4th 14*

[1197ᴾ] P   **Daneswell** 16-1 M Munrowd *Jmpd delib in last pr; sn detach; pu & dism 5; sltly lame bhnd*

[964ᶠ] P   **Frenchman (IRE)** 7-1 D Sherlock *Set str pce; 10-15l clr 2-9; wknd & hdd app 11; pu nxt*

[1125²] F   **Fruit Crop** (5a) 6-4F B Foster *Trckd ldrs in 5th; hdwy app 11; sn ld; made rest til wknd, jnd & fell 13*

[777ʳ] F   **Snitton Salvo** (7a) 20-1 A Wadlow *Chsd clr ldr in 2nd til wknd 9; lost tch 10; rem 7th & wkng rap when fell 11*

[866ᴾ] P   **Whatamonkey** 14-1 P Morris *Jmpd delib in last pr; sn detach; t.o last 5 til pu 13*

OFFICIAL DISTANCES: 4l, 15l TIME: 6min 27.0s TOTE: £3.00

1319 Mens Open, 12st   6 ran

[1015⁵] 1   **SMILE PLEEZE (IRE)** 5-4F R Burton *Trckd ldrs in 4th frm 6; gd hdwy to ld app 13; made rest; drew clr frm 3 ou*

[1198¹] 2   12 **Murphys Way** (5a) 7-4 J Burley *4s-7/4; disp ld til ld app 6; hdd app 13; chsd wnr vain aft*

[1198²]	P		**Albert Blake** (7x) (tt) 8-1 **W Kinsey** *Disp ld to 5; reluct & drpd himself out frm nxt; 15l last 8; t.o 11; pu 13*
[961⁴]	P		**Batty's Island** 8-1 **L Stephens** *Trckd ldrs; cl 3rd 6 til wknd qckly 13; 30l last & v tired when lft 3rd 2 out; pu last*
[959¹]	P		**Emerald Knight (IRE)** (vis) 8-1 **S Prior** *Disp ld to 5; chsd ldr til wknd 13; sn lost tch; 25l 3rd when pu 2 out; collapsed & died*
[1073⁵]	P		**Rolier (IRE)** 8-1 **J Merry** *Sn last; drpd himself out & 10l detach by 5; pu & dism nxt; sound aft*

OFFICIAL DISTANCE: 12l **TIME:** 6min 17.0s **TOTE:** £4.00

1320 Ladies Open
4 ran

[1199²]	1		**SUN SURFER (FR)** (vis) 6-4 **Miss S Beddoes** *Trckd ldr til ld app 13; jnd 2 out; fnd ex app last & went 1½l up; stayed on u.p flat*
[1199¹]	2	¾	**Seymour's Double** evensF **Miss T Clark** *Trckd ldng pr in cl 3rd; eff app 13; prsd wnr aft; level 2 out; no ex app last; rallied flat; clsng nr fin*
[962³]	3	25	**Analystic (IRE)** 7-2 **Mrs C Ford** *Ld; qcknd app 12; hdd app nxt; wknd app 3 out; no ch aft & eased*
	P		**Fibreguide Tech** 16-1 **Miss H Kinsey** *Trckd ldrs in cl 4th; feeling pce frm 12; sn lost tch; 25l last when pu 3 out*

OFFICIAL DISTANCES: 1l, 25l **TIME:** 6min 15.0s **TOTE:** £2.00

1321 Confined, 12st
5 ran

[960⁶]	1		**GLACIAL TRIAL (IRE)** (5a) (vis) 3-1 **M Worthington** *Hld up in last; hdwy 13; ld & qcknd 6l clr app 3 out; stayed on str*
[864¹]	2	6	**Paddy For Paddy (IRE)** 1-2F **G Hanmer** *7/4-1/2; trckd ldrs in 3rd; eff 13; drvn in 2nd & outpcd app 3 out; no imp on wnr aft*
[1200³]	3	12	**Ballyharry (IRE)** 6-1 **I Wynne** *Ld to 2; trckd ldr til ld agn 8; hdd 13; sn fdd; btn when mist 2 out*
[1152²]	4	30	**Perambulate (NZ)** 5-1 **Miss T Clark** *Trckd ldrs in 4th til outpcd 13; sn wl bhnd*
[1089ᴾ]	P		**Carbery Ministrel (IRE)** (bl) 20-1 **R Carey** *Ld 2; jmpd slow 4 & 7; hdd bef nxt; cl up til wknd rap 11; t.o & nrly ur 12; pu nxt*

OFFICIAL DISTANCES: 5l, 10l **TIME:** 6min 18.0s **TOTE:** £5.00

1322 Restricted, 12st
7 ran

[1088⁴]	1		**ACHILL SOUND** 6-4 **G Hanmer** *Hld up; hdwy 9; 1 11 3rd nxt; trckd ldng pr aft; ld 13; drew 5l clr app 2 out where jmpd rt & imm u.p; jmpd rt last & fin slow; unimpressive aft lkng likely to win v easy*
[1129ᴾ]	2	6	**Cookie Boy** 8-1 **M Wilesmith** *Disp til ld 6; hdd 13; kpt on one pce frm 3 out*
[1129⁵]	3	25	**Mr Mark (IRE)** 12-1 **D Sherlock** *Disp ld to 5; cl up til wknd 10; bhnd & no ch frm 12; lft poor 3rd aft 3 out*
[1129⁴]	4	30	**Sugi** 14-1 **I Wynne** *Bumped 2; last nxt; sn detach; jmpd slow 7; t.o frm 11; lft 4th by defections*
[1200²]	S		**Lady Dot (IRE)** (5a) 10-11F **J Downes** *Disp ld to 5; trckd ldr til wknd 13; 5l 3rd & btn when slpd up flat sn aft*
[963⁵]	P		**Pear Tree Percy** 12-1 **S Prior** *Cl up til wknd 10; lost tch nxt; bhnd 12; pu nxt*
[782ᴾ]	P		**Scallymay** (5a) 16-1 **M Munrowd** *Last early; jb rt 2; hdwy to 8l 3rd 9; 4th & lsng tch 11; pu nxt*

OFFICIAL DISTANCES: 4l, 20l **TIME:** 6min 21.0s **TOTE:** £2.00

1323 Open Maiden, 12st
15 ran

	1		**ACTON BANK** 5-2 **J Downes** *Jw; mid-div early; 22l 5th 5; smooth hdwy frm nxt; jmpd to ld 9; 5l clr nxt; qcknd rt away frm 3 out; dived thro last; fin full of running; most impressive; rdr's 1st wnr*
[1196⁵]	2	30	**See More Action** 12-1 **L Stephens** *A ldng quartet; chsd wnr frm 10; 4l down & rmdrs app 3 out; btn when mist 2 out; gd eff*
[1091²]	3	10	**Muckle Jack** (bl) 2-1F **A Dalton** *Midfield; hdwy to 20l 5th 8; went 3rd 11; 10l down 13; outpcd app nxt; no ch aft; kpt on one pce*
[1125⁴]	4	2	**Sharp Embrace** 14-1 **J Burley** *Midfield; jnd ldng group 11; 15l 5th app 13; kpt on one pce frm 3 out*
[1197²]	5	3	**Barney Bear** 7-2 **G Hanmer** *Mid-div; hdwy 12; 13l 4th app nxt; disp 20l 3rd 3 out; fdd app last*
[1196¹]	F		**Governor's Bay** (bl,tt) 20-1 **J Merry** *Pulling & sn prom; 8l 4th when mist 5; 25l 8th & wkng rap when fell 7*
[1153³]	P		**Marwoods Mandate (IRE)** 4-1 **M Worthington** *A last trio; wl bhnd when pu 12*

[964ᶠ]	P	**Mr Peoples (IRE)** 12-1 D Sherlock *Sn prom; 5l 2nd 4; chsd ldr til to 8; hdd nxt; wkng 5th 11; pu nxt*
[995ᴾ]	F	**Nineteenfive (IRE)** 14-1 M Scales *A bhnd & nd; 20l 6th when fell 10*
[1201ᴾ]	P	**Supermister** 20-1 P Morris *25l 7th 7; nvr btr plcd; bhnd when pu 12*
[569ᴾ]	P	**The Quakers Wake (IRE)** 6-1 C Barlow *Last quartet by 4; bad hmpd 7; still in rr 10; mod hdwy aft; lft 40l 6th 12; tired & jmpd slow nxt; pu 3 out*
[990ᴾ]	U	**Uncle Ada (IRE)** (7a) 20-1 A Wadlow *Towards rr; lost tch 7; rem 11th when rfo 10*
[989ˢ]	P	**Village Gossip** (5a) 20-1 M Trott *Last pr to 5; some hdwy 8; sn lost plce; to 10; pu 12*
[966ᶠ]	P	**Wily Miss** (5a) (vis) 20-1 C Hoggart *Mid-div to 5; wl bhnd 10; to & pu 12*
[1201ᴾ]	P	**Wizadora** (12a) (bl) 10-1 T Greenway *Pulled hrd; ld; 5l clr 2-6; hdd app 8; wknd rap & pu 10*

OFFICIAL DISTANCES: dist, 2l **TIME:** 6min 12.0s **TOTE:** £3.00

Zetland

Witton Castle (RH 6F,16J) Mon, 1 May (GOOD to SOFT)

1324 Hunt   **4 ran**

[1027²]	1		**PRIME STYLE** evensF C Gibbon *Made all; 6l up 9; mist 10; qcknd clr aft 12; 8l clr 2 out; galloped on str*
[1027³]	2	8	**Hidden Island** 11-10 Miss H Delahooke *10l 3rd & bad mist 5; 12l 3rd 12; chsd ldrs 3 out; 6l 2nd nxt; r.o one pce*
[1001ᴾ]	3	20	**Early Dawn** (5a) 14-1 J Davies *Chsd ldr in 6l 2nd to 2; rmdrs 11; wknd 3 out; dist 3rd by nxt*
[1080²]	4	1½fs	**Mick Man (IRE)** 6-1 S J Robinson *A last; pushed along 6; lsng tch 7; to 11; rem by 3 out*

OFFICIAL DISTANCES: 10l, dist **TIME:** 6min 26.0s
Fences 4, 11 & 18 were omitted from all races - state of ground; revised numbers used in comments-in-running

1325 Confined, 12st   **6 ran**

[503¹]	1		**POLAR KING (IRE)** 1-2F S Swiers *Hld up bhnd ldrs; went 3l 3rd 12; ld 13; 3l ld 2 out; nt fluent last; r.o u.p*
[395³]	2	4	**Vital Issue (IRE)** 25-1 G Markham *Mid-div to 10; 3l 3rd 11; pushed along 13; lft 3l 2nd 2 out; r.o one pce*
[1231²]	3	6	**Primitive Streak** (tt) 2-1 R Abrahams *Cl 2nd til mist 5; went 11l 2nd 12; pushed along & outpcd 3 out; r.o one pce*
[1150²]	4	20	**Denim Blue** 12-1 Miss P Robson *A towards rr; pushed along 11; wknd 13; to 2 out*
[997⁴]	5	35	**Caman** (bl) 50-1 Mrs S Palfreeman *Last by 4; pushed along & lsng tch 8; to 11*
[1231⁴]	F		**That Old Feeling (IRE)** (6ow) (tt) 20-1 D Easterby *Ld to 3 out; 2l 2nd & hld when fell 2 out*

OFFICIAL DISTANCES: 4l, 4l **TIME:** 6min 22.0s

1326 Restricted   **14 ran**

[1000²]	1		**NOT SO PRIM** (5a) evensF S Swiers *Ld til hung bad app 11; ld agn aft 13; sn clr; 15l up 2 out; r.o wl; fin lame*
[809¹]	2	8	**Happy Blake** 10-1 C Storey *Handy 3rd til bad mist 8; ld 11-12; 6l 2nd & mist 3 out; r.o one pce; no ch w wnr*
[1033¹]	3	5	**Tricky Trevor (IRE)** 6-1 Miss H Delahooke *Trckd ldr in 2l 2nd to 11; outpcd 12; 25l 4th 2 out; tk 3rd app last*
[713ᴾ]	4	4	**Menaldi (IRE)** 16-1 Miss K Roncoroni *Prom in 3rd to 9; 6l 3rd 12 til bad mist 3 out; wknd qckly*
[1230ᵁ]	5	3	**The Happy Monarch (IRE)** 10-1 Mrs F Needham *A rr; last by 5; lsng tch 7; mist 11; pushed along 13; slt late hdwy*
[1032¹]	6	4	**Heather Lad** 12-1 D Raw *Mid-div to 11; hdwy 12 to 20l 3rd 2 out; wknd app last*
[396³]	7	8	**Scruton** 3-1 D Easterby *Mid-div to 11; went 6l 3rd 12; wknd 3 out*
[1230ᴾ]	P		**Kind Of Chic** (5a) 100-1 P Kinsella *(xnb) Prom early; mid-div when mist 6; rr & lsng tch 10; to & pu 12*
[807ᴾ]	P		**Mac's Blade (USA)** (tt) 100-1 R Edwards *Last by 3; hdwy 5 to prom 6th 6; wknd 10; to & pu 13*
[1230ᶠ]	P		**Moor Lady** (5a) 100-1 C Wilson *Mid-div to 8; hdwy 9 to cl 2nd 10; mist 11; disp ld 12; climbed 13 & pu*
[1162ᵁ]	P		**Noneofyourbusiness (IRE)** (5a) (bl) 100-1 Miss C Metcalfe *Midfield to 7; rr & lost tch qckly 9; pu 10*
[1162ᵁ]	P		**Prince Moshar** 100-1 L Morgan *A rr; lsng tch 12; reluct 13; to & pu 14*

| [1000ᶠ] | U | | **The Hazel Harrier (IRE)** (bl) 14-1 **Miss A Deniel** *Rr when ur 5* |
| [1235¹] | F | | **Vals Castle (IRE)** (5a) 16-1 **G Tuer** *A rr; lsng tch 7; last when squeezed & fell 11* |

OFFICIAL DISTANCES: 10l, 8l   **TIME:** 6min 25.0s

1327 Mens Open   7 ran

[923³]	1		**MAJORITY MAJOR (IRE)** (bl) 6-1 **T Glass** *Pulled to ld aft 4 til jnd 2 out; disp ld last & nt fluent; rallied flat; ld on line*
[976¹]	2	½	**Blyth Brook** 3-1 **C Storey** *Last to 3; went 4l 5th 8; hdwy 10 to cl 3rd 13; rmdrs 14; disp ld 2 out; gd j last; ld flat; wknd & hdd near line*
[136¹]	3	6	**Red Spectacle (IRE)** 6-1 **N Tutty** *Mid-div to 8; went handy 3rd 11; disp ld 2 out-last; wknd flat*
[1030¹]	4	4	**Calleva Star (IRE)** 4-5F **R Abrahams** *Ld to 4; handy 2nd to 12; pushed along & outpcd 13; 8l 4th 2 out; r.o one pce*
[1030⁴]	5	30	**Lottery Ticket (IRE)** 50-1 **S J Robinson** *Mid-div to 9; 5l 4th 10; pushed along & outpcd 11; lost tch 12; rem 5th 2 out*
[997²]	6	15	**Final Beat (IRE)** (bl) 20-1 **C Cundall** *Handy 3rd to 6; outpcd 8; rr & pushed along aft 10; lost tch 11; t.o 13*
	P		**Mr Bureaucrat (NZ)** 14-1 **I Bennett** *(bf) Handy in 3rd to 3; rn wide app 4; last & bad mist 5; qckly t.o & pu 6*

OFFICIAL DISTANCES: ¾l, 4l   **TIME:** 6min 22.0s

1328 Ladies Open   6 ran

[621¹]	1		**LA RIVIERA (IRE)** 4-9F **Miss P Robson** *Mid-div to 9; went cl 3rd 11; outpcd 3 out; 4l 2nd 2 out; rdn to chall last; qcknd clr flat*
[806¹]	2	3	**Japodene** (5a) 5-2 **Miss A Deniel** *Cl 2nd til qcknd to ld 3 out; 3l up nxt; jnd & one pce flat*
[795²]	3	10	**Orswellthatenswell** 5-1 **Mrs F Needham** *Ld til jnd 3 out; outpcd nxt; r.o one pce*
[996²]	4	6	**Kendor Pass (IRE)** 14-1 **Mrs N Wilson** *Cl 3rd to 12; outpcd 13; 8l 4th 3 out; r.o one pce*
[996ᵁ]	5	8	**Cede Nullis** (5a) (bl) 33-1 **Miss L Eddery** *Chsd ldrs to 10; mist 12 & pushed along nxt; lsng tch 14; dist 5th 2 out*
[1152ᵁ]	P		**La Maja (IRE)** (5a) 66-1 **Miss J Foster** *Last by 3; lsng tch 4; mist 6; bhnd & hrd rdn 9; rmdrs 10; t.o & pu 12*

OFFICIAL DISTANCES: 2½l, 10l   **TIME:** 6min 19.0s

1329 Open Maiden (Div 1), 12st   16 ran

	1		**THE HUSSEY'S KING (IRE)** 2-1F **C Mulhall** *Rr to 6; hdwy 8 to cl 3rd 12; chall & bad mist 3 out; 2l 2nd at last; hrd rdn & rallied flat; got up on line*
[1001³]	2	½	**Jolly Minster** 10-1 **P Atkinson** *Mid-div to 10; hdwy 11; ld 12; jnd 3 out; 2l up nxt; prsd agn flat; just outpcd in drvng fin*
[1031²]	3	10	**Deerhunter** 5-2 **G Tuer** *Midfield to 6; went 3l 3rd 11-13; outpcd by ldng pr 3 out; r.o one pce*
[1033⁵]	4	6	**Hey Sam (IRE)** (bl) 20-1 **T Glass** *Mid-div to 9; went prom 5th 11; outpcd 13; 15l 4th 3 out*
[1230⁶]	5	4	**The Killaloe Run** (5a) 12-1 **Miss J Foster** *Cl 2nd til disp ld 10; ld 11-12; wknd 13; sn btn*
[1032ᶠ]	6	8	**Tyndrum Gold** (bl) 33-1 **Miss A Deniel** *A rr; lost tch 11; t.o 13; stayed on stdly frm nxt; nvr nr to chall*
[1235ᵁ]	7	12	**Stanwick Hall** 33-1 **K Needham** *Mid-div to 8; rr 10; sn wknd; t.o 14*
[1083ᶠ]	P		**Almikino (IRE)** 25-1 **S Brisby** *Rr early; prog to cl 4th 11; outpcd & wknd 13; lost tch 3 out; t.o & pu last*
[1082ʳ]	P		**Aughrim Quest (IRE)** (5a) (bl) 25-1 **N Tutty** *Nt jw; a rr; climbed 2 & 3; sn lost tch; t.o & pu 10; v unenthusiastic*
[1003ᴿ]	F		**Leg Beforum (IRE)** 14-1 **L Bates** *Prom to 9; handy 4th 10; outpcd 13; hld in 5th when fell 2 out*
[1004²]	P		**Lulagh-B** (5a) 7-2 **R Wakeham** *A rr; last by 6; pushed along & lsng tch 9; pu 10*
	P		**Oaklands Billy** 66-1 **P Frank** *Ld to 9; wknd 10; t.o when pu 12*
[1234ᶠ]	P		**Procol's Boy** (7a) 20-1 **S Walker** *A rr; lost tch 11; pu 12*
[1004⁸]	U		**Sally Scally** (5a) 20-1 **Miss T Jackson** *(xnb) Ur 2*
	P		**Who's The Man** 16-1 **J Ewart** *Prom to 8; handy 5th 10; outpcd & wknd 13; rem pu last*
[1002⁴]	S		**Wild Briar** (12a) 33-1 **D Raw** *Prom to 5; rr by 8; t.o 11; slpd up bend bef 12*

OFFICIAL DISTANCES: ½l, 10l   **TIME:** 6min 27.0s

1330 Open Maiden (Div 2), 12st
14 ran

	1		**LITTLE VERA** (12a) 4-1 N Wilson *Rr to 4; hdwy 7; ld 11 til outpcd 3 out; rdn to chall last; stayed on wl u.p to ld but hung lft fnl flat*
[909F]	2	2	**Stygian Star (IRE)** (5a) 20-1 M Smethurst *Prom to 11; went cl 2nd 13; ld 3 out; 3l up nxt; jnd last; hung lft & hdd flat; no ex cl home*
[1033³]	3	8	**Bred For Pleasure** (5a) 9-4F M McGrath *Rr & mist 2; mid-div 9; hdwy 13 to 8l 3rd & mist 2 out; r.o one pce; eased cl home & nrly lost 3rd*
[910⁴]	4	nk	**Henah Hill** 5-2 Miss P Robson *Mid-div to 12; went 12l 5th 13; stayed on to 4th 3 out; r.o one pce; nrly snatched 3rd*
[1033P]	5	10	**No Time To Wait** 33-1 Miss J Foster *Prom; ld frm 3-10; wknd 11; outpcd & bhnd 13*
[1123⁶]	6	4	**Crashballoo (IRE)** 12-1 Miss K Roncoroni *Last by 5; mist 6; to 9*
[809P]		P	**Just A Single (IRE)** 33-1 A Morris *Ld to 2; cl 2nd til disp ld 7-9; rn v wide app 11; wknd & bhnd 13; pu last*
[1084⁴]		U	**Magical Poitin** (5a) 8-1 T Oates *Mid-div til ur 7*
		P	**Market Poseur (IRE)** 3-1 C Mulhall *Midfield to 5; outpcd 7; pushed along 10; went handy 6th 12; outpcd & wknd 3 out; pu nxt*
[803P]		P	**Oaklands Jimmy** 50-1 P Frank *Mid-div to 8; went cl 4th 13; wknd & outpcd 13; pu last*
[1165³]		P	**Play An Ace** 10-1 C Storey *Mist 1 & rmdrs; rr by 6; bhnd & mist 12; to & pu 2 out*
[693P]		P	**Right Ron Run** 14-1 R Wakeham *Cl 3rd to 12; wknd 13; to & pu 2 out*
[713ᵁ]		U	**Seldom Seen (IRE)** 20-1 L Morgan *Midfield til ur 11*
[973P]		P	**Silver Ellie** (5a) 20-1 J Ewart *A rr; to 13; pu 2 out*

OFFICIAL DISTANCES: 3l, 10l **TIME:** 6min 37.0s

1331 Open Maiden (Div 3), 12st - 15J
11 ran

[1234³]	1		**TOTAL RELIEF** (7a) 6-1 Miss S Brotherton *Mid-div to 4; lft 6l 2nd 7; ld 12; 2l clr 2 out; qcknd rt away app last; r.o str; hrd hld*
[1153⁶]	2	8	**Lardante (IRE)** 3-1 J Walker *16s-3s; midfield to 8; went 5l 4th 10; outpcd by ldng pr 3 out; stayed on to tk 2nd app last; r.o one pce; no ch w wnr*
[1235P]	3	½	**Trigger Castle** (12a) 25-1 V Walker *rr stdy hdwy frm 9; 6l 3rd 12; cl 2nd 13 til bad mist 3 out; sn outpcd by wnr; dem 3rd app last*
[1163³⁼]	4	8	**Baltic Lake (IRE)** 2-1F M Smethurst *Prom to 4; outpcd & rr by 9; to 13; stayed on frm 2 out; nrst fin*
[1163P]	5	runin	**Westhall Jonstan (IRE)** 25-1 L Morgan *Cl 2nd to 10; wknd 11; poor 5th by 2 out; clambered over last; coaxed home*
[1002³]	6	5	**Ben From Ketton** (7a) 12-1 S J Robinson *Midfield to 9; went prom 2nd 12; pushed along 13; sn wknd; rem 6th 3 out; clambered over last; fin legless*
		P	**Big Horn (IRE)** 7-1 C Mulhall *V sa; sn bhnd; to by 11; pu 3 out; nvr in rce*
[1033⁶]		F	**Charlie Dazzle (IRE)** 7-1 Mrs F Needham *Rr div when fell 5*
[808P]		R	**Cricketing** (6ow) (tt) 7-2 D Easterby *Tk str hld; rr til pulled to ld 5; 6l clr when rn thro wing 6*
[1163P]		P	**Hetty Bell** (5a) 20-1 A Richardson *A midfield to rr; to & pu last*
[1003ᴿ]		F	**Look Sharpe** 7-1 N Wilson *Ld til fell 5*

OFFICIAL DISTANCES: 20l, nk **TIME:** 6min 38.0s
Fence 11 omitted - fallen rider

Huntingdon (RH 9F)
Tue, 2 May (GOOD)

1332 Countrywide Surveyors HC
5 ran

[1015⁹]	1		**SOLO GENT** 11-11 (vis) 15-2 T Doyle *Ld aft 1; jmpd bold; hrd rdn app last; r.o game*
[802²]	2	¾	**Act Of Parliament (IRE)** 11-07 (bl) 7-4 D Flavin *Prsd wnr frm 4; chall gng wl & blun 3 out; rallied app last & ev ch; hung fire & nt go thro flat*
[1103⁵]	3	12	**Stay Lucky (NZ)** 12-00 6-1 Julian Pritchard *Sn last; niggled along 8 & nvr gng wl aft; rdn 10; mist 11; to aft 3 out; drvn & stayed on to snatch 3rd*
[1026¹]	4	hd	**Shekels (IRE)** 12-02 11-8F D Dunsdon *Ld 1; chsd ldr to 4; releg 4th 11; outpcd 13 & nvr gng wl aft; went 10l 3rd 3 out; unable to clse; eased & dem on line*
[1007³]	5	18	**Pongo Waring (IRE)** 11-07 S Morris *Trckd ldrs; 3rd 11; rdn & outpcd 14; wknd 3 out; eased flat*

TIME: 6min 04.4s **TOTE:** £5.20; places £2.10, £1.80 **Ex:** £9.60 **CSF:** £19.11

1333 Abbotts Estate Agents Nov HC
9 ran

[1231¹]	1		**KEY DEBATE** 11-07 6-5F G Brewer *Ld to start early; set str gallop; stdd aft 8; hit 11; went clr agn aft 12; dived at nxt; 20l ahd when appalling mist & virt fell 3 out; picked up brilliant & cont clr; unchall; v impressive*

[1064²] 2 24 **Philtre (IRE)** 12-00 7-4 **Julian Pritchard** *Lw; nt fluent 1 & 2; hld up & bhnd; 8l 8th & wide 11; rdn & outpcd when wnr qcknd aft nxt; 20l 3rd 16; went 2nd 3 out; drvn along & nvr able to cl*

[1111¹] 3 1¼ **Ulvick Star (IRE)** 11-09 7-1 **R Fowler** *Pulled hrd; hit 5; chsd wnr but nt jw; hit 12; 10l down nxt; bad mist 16; 3rd & one pce 3 out; pckd last (rdr did wl to get him rnd)*

4 23 **Galeaway (IRE)** 11-09 20-1 **D Dunsdon** *Novicey in rr div; 6th when mist 11; strugg 13 but kpt on stdly; nt disg*

[1108⁴] 5 2½ **Call The Tune** 11-04 33-1 **P Bull** *Bhnd & nt a fluent; clsd aft 8; 7l 7th 12; outpcd 13; t.o 3 out*

[1038²] 6 14 **The Millmaster (IRE)** 11-07 (bl) 25-1 **T Lane** *Chsd ldrs; 4th 11; 20l 5th & outpcd 13; t.o 3 out*

[1005⁵] F **Buachaill Dana (IRE)** 12-00 50-1 **J Diment** *Prom; 3rd 11; 16l 3rd & outpcd 13; dem 4th & fell hvly 16*

[1106²] P **Spaceage Gold** 11-07 (vis) 50-1 **K Edmunds** *Reluct in last; sn rdn & lost tch; t.o 8; pu 13; drpd dead*

[1104⁵] F **Winward** 11-07 (bl) 40-1 **P M Hall** *Pushed along in rr when fell 3*

TIME: 6min 02.7s **TOTE:** £1.90; places £1.10,£1.10,£1.60 **Ex:** £3.30 **CSF:** £2.98 **Tri:** £7.50

1334 Taylors Estate Agents Confined Series Final HC   10 ran

[369²] 1 **GIVE IT A WHIRL** 11-07 7-1 **T Lane** *Jw; trckd ldrs; ld 10-14 & 15-3 out; sn rdn; 3l 3rd & lkd btn 100yds out; rallied u.p & lft in ld post*

[1016²] 2 hd **Stormy Words** 11-02 14-1 **S Morris** *Drpd out last; mist 5 (water); hdwy 12 to 6l 6th nxt; 7l 6th 3 out; stayed on to ld 2 out; drvn 3l clr 100yds out; spooked at plastic rails & tried to pu final 30yds; just caught; v unlucky*

[968³] 3 s hd **Royal Estate** 11-11 11-1 **C Evans** *Nt jw in midfield; hdwy 8; 3rd 10; mist 11; went 2nd 12; ld 14-15; mist nxt; ld 3 out-nxt; hrd rdn & ev ch last; outpcd til ldr slowed & lft w ev ch nr fin*

[868ᴸ] 4 4 **Inch Cross (IRE)** 11-11 (4) 5-1 **R Hunnisett** *Hld up in rr; hdwy 11 to go prom 13; bumped along aft 3 out; one pce when hit nxt*

[1005⁴] 5 10 **Priory Piper** 11-07 20-1 **L Hicks** *Blun 3; chsd ldr to 9; cl 5th 13; prsd ldrs til wknd aft 3 out*

[1027¹] 6 4 **Triple Eaves** 11-09 15-2 **C Mulhall** *(xnb) Jmpd slow 6; towards rr; 8th when mist 12; drvn & sn lost tch*

[936³] 7 1¾ **Village Copper** 11-11 3-1F **C Ward-Thomas** *Nt fluent in rr; nvr gng wl; rdn 10; 8th 12; sn lost tch*

[924⁶] 8 23 **Chatergold (IRE)** 11-07 (bl) 9-2 **D Dennis** *Lw; rn in snatches; prom til lost plce & rdn 8; rallied to 3 out; t.o nxt; wknd rap*

[1114³] P **Kelly's Original** 11-07 9-1 **A Coe** *Lw; sis; a rr; rdn 8; last & lost tch 12; t.o & pu 16*

[1037³] P **Tighter Budget (USA)** 11-07 40-1 **Miss G Hutchinson** *Set str gallop; jmpd slow 6; 10l clr 8; hdd 10; wknd rap aft 12; t.o & pu aft mist 15*

TIME: 6min 06.3s **TOTE:** £10.70; places £2.40,£3.70,£2.80 **Ex:** £275.50 **CSF:** £86.47 **Tri:** £88.30

1335 Bairstow Eves Estate Agents Nov HC   18 ran

[687⁷] 1 **ISLAND ECHO (IRE)** 11-07 8-1 **J Tate** *Trckd ldrs; hmpd 8; went 6l 3rd aft nxt; no imp & nt rdn til aft 2 out; clsd to ld last; qcknd & pushed out*

[1108¹] 2 1½ **Rustic Revelry** 11-07 16-1 **P York** *Trckd ldrs; prog to ld aft 9; drvn 2 out; hdd last; nt qckn*

[969²] 3 9 **Mr Custard** 11-07 33-1 **Miss L Sweeting** *Swtng; 3rd/4th til ld 8; blun 9 & sn hdd; cl 2nd til blun 2 out & rdr v unbalanced; nt rec & btn last*

[465⁴] 4 5 **Rascally** 11-04 10-1 **C Mulhall** *Midfield; 6th aft 9; eff 11; rdn & one pce aft 3 out*

[783²] 5 dist **Rise To It (IRE)** 11-09 40-1 **G Hanmer** *A wl bhnd; rem 13th aft 9; went dist 5th 2 out*

[800⁴] 6 1½ **The Captain's Wish** 11-11 20-1 **T Gibney** *Tubed; chsd ldrs; 4th aft 9; eff 11; mist nxt; rdn & sn wknd; t.o*

[261³] 7 hd **Cades Bay** 11-11 12-1 **T Scudamore** *Taken down v gently; set str gallop; ld til hdd & blun 8; wknd rap to 7th aft nxt; t.o*

[1105¹] 8 3½ **Just The Business** 11-09 (bl) 33-1 **P Bull** *(xnb) 2 handlers; nt jw in midfield; 10th & strugg aft 9; t.o 3 out*

[987ᴾ] 9 6 **Burkean Melody (IRE)** 11-07 66-1 **M Munrowd** *Rmdrs & ss; a rem; hmpd by rival pulling up 8; t.o aft*

[1159ᴾ] 10 dist **The Alleycat (IRE)** 11-11 20-1 **W Renwick** *Lw; nt jw & nvr went a yard; 25l last when bad mist 5; 9th & drvn aft 9; sn t.o*

[1112²] P **Abuljjood (IRE)** 11-04 33-1 **M Hewitt** *A labouring; t.o 9; pu 10*

[924³] P **Finnow Thyne (IRE)** 12-02 10-11F **D Dunsdon** *Lw; jmpd slow 2 (water); sn rr &; nt gng wl; pushed along 6; pu 8*

[1030³]	P		**Gymcrak Tiger (IRE)** 11-07 9-1 R Clark *(xnb) Hld up & bhnd; 8th & strugg aft 9; poor 6th when pu 16*
[1036ᵁ]	P		**Mister Spectator (IRE)** 11-07 16-1 C Gordon *Tk keen hld; prsd ldr to 9; wknd rap; t.o & pu 13*
[925ᴾ]	U		**Mr Dennehy (IRE)** 11-07 33-1 David Dennis *Chsd ldrs; 9th when ur 8*
[1031¹]	P		**Primitive Charles** 11-07 (bl) 50-1 G Brewer *A bhnd; strugg in 11th when bumped bend aft 9; drvn aft; t.o & pu 2 out*
[1013²]	U		**Tom's Prize** 11-08 33-1 S Joynes *(xnb) Lw; hld up in midfield; 8th when blun & ur 8*
[919ᴾ]	F		**Wot No Cash** 11-07 50-1 R Cope *Chsd ldrs; 8th & wkng when fell 9*

TIME: 5min 01.0s **TOTE:** £12.90; places £3.40,£7.30,£4.40 **Ex:** £87.50 **CSF:** £109.58

Cheltenham (LH 10F)
Wed, 3 May (GOOD, GOOD to SOFT in places)

1336 Gilders Transport & Ski Tyres Maiden HC   20 ran

[687⁶]	1		**HALL'S MILL (IRE)** 11-11 20-1 A Charles-Jones *Swtng; prom; 5th 10; outpcd 13; 6th & lkd btn 3 out; rallied nxt; 4th last; str rn to ld final 50yds; sn clr*
[1022²]	2	3	**Kerry Soldier Blue** 12-00 7-2JF Miss P Jones *Prom; ld 5-9; chsd ldr aft; outpcd 3 out; rallied nxt; ld last; lkd wnr til hung rt & caught final 50yds*
[692¹]	3	2½	**Quarterstaff** 11-11 15-2 C Wilson *Cl up; ld 9; mist 12; drew clr 3 out; rdn & wknd & hdd last; no ex*
[988¹]	4	1¼	**Lochnomore** 11-11 7-2JF R Burton *Lw; a handy; 3rd 9; outpcd 3 out; rallied in 5l 3rd nxt; eff & ch when blun last & stpd in tracks; nt rec*
[897ᴾ]	5	1¼	**Executive Office (IRE)** 11-07 66-1 M Keel *Midfield; impd to ch ldrs 13; hit 3 out; one pce & nd frm nxt*
[861²]	6	8	**Dainty Man (IRE)** 11-07 40-1 A Dalton *Midfield; 3rd & rap prog 13; drvn & wknd aft 3 out*
[837¹]	7	2½	**Kristal Haze** 11-02 25-1 J Cook *Nt a fluent; mid-div; eff 13; no imp frm 3 out*
[1227¹]	8	6	**Jo Jos Best Friend** 11-02 16-1 M Foley *Jmpd v slow 1; imm lost tch; hrd rdn 5; no ch 10*
[802ᴾ]	9	¾	**Strewth** 11-09 33-1 C Weaver *Nt fluent early; a wl bhnd; lost tch 10*
[1133¹]	10	1¼	**Mostyn** 11-11 16-1 G Barfoot-Saunt *Nt fluent; ld til hdd & blun 5; lost plce & blun 8; no ch aft*
	11	1¾	**Shillelagh Oak** 11-09 25-1 M Harris *Lw; chsd ldrs til rdn 11; sn wknd*
[1207ᴾ]	P		**Chalcuchima** 11-07 100-1 J Oldring *Mist 1; chsd ldrs to 9; sn wknd; t.o & pu 2 out*
[1135⁴]	P		**Fever Pitch** 11-07 40-1 Jeremy Young *Chsd ldrs til outpcd & bad mist 10; nt rec; pu nxt*
[863¹]	P		**Highbridge (IRE)** 11-11 14-1 A Evans *Bhnd early & nt a fluent; prog to trck ldrs 11; rdn & wknd nxt; pu last (lost a shoe)*
[580⁴]	P		**I Haven't A Buck (IRE)** 11-09 33-1 D Barlow *Bhnd; brief eff 8; t.o & pu 2 out*
[897³]	P		**Maggies Brother** 12-00 33-1 Julian Pritchard *Sn wl bhnd; no ch 10; t.o & pu 2 out*
[1225ᶠ]	P		**Millbank Honey** 11-02 66-1 Miss L Pearce *Went prom aft 3; wknd aft 7; blun 8 & pu nxt*
[1315³]	P		**Mister River (IRE)** 11-07 (bl) 66-1 P Young *Rr & reluct; u.p 4; mist 8; t.o aft; pu 2 out*
[1189ᶠ]	F		**Quick Response (IRE)** 11-07 66-1 A Honeyball *(xnb) Chsd ldrs; blun 3; eff 12; 8th & just in tch when fell 14*
[731¹]	P		**We Move Earth** 11-09 7-1 Miss P Gundry *Last away; hdwy 6; 4th 9; ev ch when pu lame aft 12*

TIME: 5min 20.9s **TOTE:** £58.50; places £7.30,£1.70,£2.30 **Ex:** £45.50 **CSF:** £74.51

1337 Faucets Perrin & Rowe Classical Bathroom Fittings Champion HC   6 ran

[385²]	1		**CASTLE MANE (IRE)** 12-00 2-5F Julian Pritchard *Jw & made all; a gng str; r.o str aft 3 out & in a comm; impressive*
[735⁵]	2	7	**Skip'n'time** 11-11 6-1 M Miller *Drpd out in rr; outpcd 13; rallied 16; lft chsng wnr 19; shkn up 3 out; wl hld aft; hung rt flat*
[1144²]	3	dist	**Strong Chairman (IRE)** 11-07 14-1 S Waley-Cohen *Lw; 2nd/3rd til bumped 10 & lost plce; outpcd 13; rallied aft 16; wknd aft mist 19*
[1133²]	4	21	**Kilmington (IRE)** 11-07 20-1 J Barnes *Ld in start; hld up trckng ldrs til rdn & outpcd 13; t.o aft 16*
[1023ᴾ]	P		**Freedom Fighter** 11-07 66-1 A Martin *Pulled hrd in rr; mist 3; mist & outpcd 13; last when bad mist 15 & rdr lost iron & drpd reins; t.o & pu 15*
[921⁶]	F		**Little Buck (IRE)** 11-13 11-2 K Culligan *Lw; nt fluent & jmpd rt in 2nd/3rd; 2nd frm 10; prsng wnr when fell 19*

TIME: 6min 54.4s **TOTE:** £1.50; places £1.60,£2.50 **Ex:** £4.70 **CSF:** £4.03

1338 Winning Post at Cheltenham HC   23 ran

[999³]	1		OVERFLOWING RIVER (IRE) 12-00 8-1 T Glass Mist 4; handy; 10th 7; hdwy 16 & 6th nxt; rdn 19; went 2nd 23; ld 3 out til hrd rdn & hdd aft last; rallied game to ld post
[999³]	2	s hd	Mr Freebie (DEN) 11-09 9-1 N Bloom Wl bhnd; poor 18th 7; 17th 7; gd prog nxt to 5th 24; 8l 5th 3 out; stayed on to 2nd app nxt; chall & outj last; ld 100yds out; hdd on post
[1087⁴]	3	8	Forest Fountain (IRE) 11-11 16-1 A Wintle Midfield; 13th 7; 7th & prog 17; 4th 24; sn rdn; no imp app 2 out
[1133ᴾ]	4	9	Berude Not To (IRE) 11-07 (bl) 33-1 R Young Prom; 3rd 7; jmpd slow 12; ld 17 til hdd 3 out; rdn & wknd nxt
[1015²]	5	6	Rusty Fellow 11-09 14-1 D Barlow Hld up; 11th 7; 8th 17; pushed up to 2nd 19-21; 6th & wkng 24; plodded on
[1015¹]	6	2	Rusty Bridge 11-11 5-1 R Burton Ld to 3; 4th 7; sn lost plce; 15th & rdn 17; poor 7th 24; mod late prog
[938ᴾ]	7	9	Ruperts Choice (IRE) 11-07 (bl) 25-1 A Harvey 12th 7; same & rdn 17; strugg 20; nd aft
[1086¹]	8	5	All Weather 11-07 14-1 M Wilesmith Lw; handy; 6th 7; 10th 17; lost tch 22; poor 8th 24
[1154¹]	9	1¼	Concerto Collonges (FR) 11-10 (3) 12-1 R Hartley A wl bhnd; 21st 7; 20th 17; plodded on & nvr got gng
[1103³]	10	1	No Fiddling (IRE) 11-11 100-30F C Williams Mists & nvr gng wl; blun 4; 16th 7; blun 11 & rdn; 13th & no ch 17
[1275³]	11	7	Highway Five (IRE) 11-07 66-1 M Trott Rr & sn rdn; 22nd 7; mists 10 & 15; 21st 17; plodded rnd
[800²]	12	7	Novatara 11-11 25-1 T Gibney Jb in rr; 20th 7; blun 15; impd to 11th 17; bad mist 21; no ch aft; poor 9th 24
[1188¹]	13	dist	Westcountry Lad 11-07 33-1 R Woollacott Hit 4; bhnd; 17th 7; mist 14; 18th 17; t.o 24
[968⁵]	P		Bolshie Baron 11-09 33-1 M Harris Prom; 7th 7; 5th 7; 3rd & ev ch when bad mist 22; nt rec; poor 10th 24; pu 3 out
[1129²]	P		Brown Esquire 11-07 40-1 S Prior Prom; 5th 7; 9th 17; wkng when mist 20; pu 23
[1224¹]	r		Bullens Bay (IRE) 11-07 25-1 Miss F Wilson A rr; mist 6; 14th 7; mist 10; 16th 17; no ch aft; 12th when ref last
[1024⁵]	F		Cariboo Gold (USA) 11-07 (bl) 11-1 J Diment Lw; trckd ldrs; 8th 7; went 4th 17; cl 3rd 23 til 2nd & ev ch 3 out; sn wknd; poor 5th when tried to ref & turned somersault last
[1134⁶]	P		Dromhana (IRE) 11-07 (bl) 66-1 J Barnes Tk keen hld; ld 3 til mist 17; wkng rap when blun nxt; t.o & pu 3 out
[896¹]	P		Forever Dreaming (IRE) 12-00 (bl) 33-1 M Rimell Mists & nd; 13th 7; mist 14 & rdn; 14th 17; strugg when blun 20; pu nxt
[1015³]	P		High Guardian 12-00 25-1 Julian Pritchard Wl bhnd & nvr gng; 19th 7; 22nd 17; t.o & pu 23
[1199ᴾ]	P		Latest Thyne (IRE) 11-09 66-1 R Bevis Lw; 15th 7; midfield when hmpd 14; 19th 17; t.o & pu 22
[993ᴾ]	P		Sideliner 11-07 66-1 J Best Ss; a t.o; pu aft 17
[294ᴾ]	P		Winters Cottage (IRE) 11-11 (vis) 40-1 A Evans Tk keen hld & prom; 2nd/3rd 5-18; wknd qckly nxt; pu 22

TIME: 8min 39.6s TOTE: £11.40; places £3.50,£2.30,£5.60 Ex: £84.90 CSF: £66.79 Tri: nt won

1339 Lynx Express HC   8 ran

[470¹]	1		COULTON 12-04 11-10F R Burton (xnb) Ld at gd pce frm 3 & jmpd bold; sn clr w rnr-up; hit 14; drew 8l ahd 2 out; unchall
[1065¹]	2	10	Distinctive (IRE) 11-11 5-2 A Wintle Lw; tk keen hld; slt ld to 3; chsd wnr & clr of rest aft; mist 8; rdn & eff 3 out; sn wl outpcd
[1132¹]	3	19	Castle Lynch (IRE) 11-08 11-2 Miss P Gundry Mists & sn strugg; blun 6 & rdn; 28l 7th aft blun 7; t.o 10; kpt on frm 2 out to tk poor 3rd flat
[970³]	4	8	Bit O'Speed (IRE) 11-07 40-1 J Richardson Mid-div & a outpcd; 20l 5th 7; 30l 4th 13; lft poor 3rd 14 til dem flat
[1026³]	5	3	Tea Cee Kay 12-04 25-1 A Sansome Sn bhnd; 22l 6th & rdn 7; t.o 10
[1244⁶]	6	dist	Coolree (IRE) 11-11 50-1 O Ellwood Nt fluent in ab 15l 3rd to 8; 20l 4th 12; t.o 14
[603ᵁ]	7	dist	Sands Of Gold (IRE) 11-07 (vis) 50-1 A Coe Jb & imm rdn in last; 40l adrift 7 & nt keen; nrly ref 3 out; jmpd 2 out as wnr fin
[1022³]	F		Mister Horatio 11-07 7-1 M Lewis Lw; nt fluent 2; 15l 4th 7; chsd clr ldng pr vain frm nxt; mist 11; 25l 3rd when fell 14

TIME: 5min 18.6s TOTE: £2.00; places £1.30,£1.10,£1.40 Ex: £3.80 CSF: £3.83 Tri: £9.10

1340 Colin Nash Mem Utd Hunts HC
10 ran

[924¹]	1		**LAKEFIELD RAMBLER (IRE)** 11-12 4-9F **Miss P Gundry** *Lw; many mists; set gd gallop; hrd prsd & lft clr app 3 out; rdn nxt; blun last & sn hdd; fnd ex to go clr final 100yds*
[921⁴]	2	2	**Shuil's Star (IRE)** 12-00 9-1 **E Williams** *Drpd out last to 6; went 4th & mist 9; mist 10; lft mod 3rd 3 out; gd prog to 2nd nxt; jnd wnr u.p flat; outpcd cl home*
[1103ᴾ]	3	23	**Itsforu** 12-00 33-1 **A Wintle** *Mostly 2nd til aft 16; 7l 3rd 18; lft poor 2nd 3 out; clsd brief but dem & wknd nxt*
[1134³]	4	9	**Cruise Free** 12-00 66-1 **A Charles-Jones** *Prom; 3rd 11; nt jw & mists 16 & 17; sn lost tch & wl bhnd*
[1023ᴾ]	5	dist	**Mcloughlin (IRE)** 11-10 100-1 **M Rodda** *Chsd ldrs til hmpd 8; 7th 11; strugg nxt; t.o 18*
[1103ᴾ]	6	3	**Muntafi** 11-10 33-1 **M Keel** *Oht; releg last 6; rdn 8; 20l adrift & rdn 11; t.o 13*
[600¹]	U		**Ballina** 12-03 33-1 **J Jukes** *Tk keen hld & chsd ldrs; drpd back 9th & strugg 11; blun 14; t.o when blun & ur 18*
[1203¹]	F		**Clinking** 11-10 12-1 **P Young** *(xnb) Tk keen hld; hit 2; prom til fell 8*
[1017¹]	P		**Dawn Invader (IRE)** 12-03 6-1 **Julian Pritchard** *Mist 2; hld up; prog in 5th 11; went 2nd aft 16; prsd ldr & gng wl when broke down bad & pu 3 out*
[1237ᵁ]	U		**The Bold Abbot** 11-10 50-1 **Miss S West** *Cl up; 4th when blun & ur 12*

TIME: 6min 46.3s **TOTE:** £1.60; places £1.10,£2.30,£3.30 **Ex:** £5.60 **CSF:** £4.36 **Tri:** £147.30

1341 Filly Park Right HC
22 ran

[1023⁴]	1		**SHAFI (IRE)** 11-05 8-1 **M Trott** *Trckd ldrs gng wl; went prom 7; ld on bit aft 10; a cruising aft; 4l clr when rn wide bend bef 2 out; qcknd flat; impressive*
[1016³]	2	18	**Northern Bluff (IRE)** 11-12 25-1 **J Jukes** *Midfield; hdwy 8 to press ldrs 10; lft 2nd 3 out; one pce & no ch w wnr aft*
[1155¹]	3	¾	**Tubber Roads (IRE)** 11-09 9-1 **M Foley** *(xnb) Trckd ldrs; eff 11; rdn nxt; one pce & no imp in 4th app 2 out*
[1022ᴾ]	4	8	**Red Neck** 11-07 20-1 **R Cooper** *Hld up; prog to ch ldrs & mist 10; hung rt bef nxt; eff & hmpd 3 out; nd aft*
[921¹⁶]	5	2½	**Halham Tarn** 11-13 12-1 **T Gibney** *Lw; hld up in mid-div; stdy hdwy 10; lft 3rd 3 out; wknd app nxt*
[1293²]	6	1¾	**Hee's A Dancer** 11-09 10-1 **C Williams** *Prom; w ldrs 4-5; lost plce bend aft 10; one pce frm nxt*
[1026⁴]	7	14	**Pro Bono (IRE)** 12-05 20-1 **A Sansome** *Ld 4-8; prom til wknd aft 3 out; mod 5th app nxt*
[470⁶]	8	4	**Desert Calm (IRE)** 11-13 16-1 **T Scudamore** *Midfield; u.p 7; no ch frm 11*
[735⁶]	9	s hd	**Apple John** 11-09 25-1 **P Young** *Tk str hld; ld to 4; ld 8 til aft 10; sn lost plce; wkng when hmpd 3 out*
[991ᴾ]	10	2½	**Boring (USA)** 11-05 33-1 **J Cook** *(xnb) Tk keen hld; prom to 5; wknd 7; mist 10 & lost tch; t.o when mist last*
[463³]	11	½	**Us Four (IRE)** 11-05 (bl) 25-1 **R Cope** *A wl bhnd; rdn & strugg 8; t.o*
[1205ᵁ]	12	1½	**Phaedair** 11-05 50-1 **J Oldring** *Tde; chsd ldrs to 6; wkng when mist 8; t.o*
[1191³]	13	5	**Rainbow Walk** 11-05 40-1 **Miss A Burton** *Cl up to 8; sn wknd; t.o*
[928ᵁ]	14	½	**Blanchland** 11-05 66-1 **R Young** *A wl bhnd; t.o 11; fnce bhnd*
[925¹]	15	3	**Daytime Dawn (IRE)** 11-12 5-1 **S Morris** *(xnb) Cl up; mist 5; eff 10; rdn & sn btn; eased frm 2 out; t.o & fnce bhnd*
[1311ᴾ]	16	27	**Rockville Pike (IRE)** 11-09 (bl) 66-1 **G Barfoot-Saunt** *A bhnd; t.o*
[1057¹]	F		**Abit More Business (IRE)** 11-11 (bl) 10-1 **Miss P Gundry** *Midfield; hdwy 7; went 2nd & fell 3 out*
[754¹]	P		**Bridge Man** 11-09 33-1 **S Bush** *(xnb) Mist 4; sn rr; t.o & pu 2 out*
[1144ᴾ]	r		**Caballus (USA)** 11-09 33-1 **A Charles-Jones** *Ref to rce*
[919³]	U		**Flying Maria** 12-00 3-1F **L Jefford** *Hld up towards rr; stdy hdwy 10; 8th & chsng ldrs when hmpd & ur 3 out*
[1202ᴾ]	P		**Golden Gunner (IRE)** 11-07 (bl) 66-1 **C Weaver** *Ss; a t.o; pu 11*
[925¹]	U		**Timarisk** 11-05 66-1 **M Nicolls** *Tde; blun & ur 1*

TIME: 4min 05.4s **TOTE:** £7.00; places £2.00,£9.10,£3.00 **Ex:** £796.00 **CSF:** £181.25 **Tri:** £nt won

Kelso (LH 8F,19J)
Wed, 3 May (GOOD to SOFT)

1342 Charlie Brown Utd Border HC
9 ran

[916¹]	1		**MANHATTAN RAINBOW (IRE)** 11-12 5-2F **D Da Silva** *2nd/3rd til ld app 8; 10l clr 14; 7l ahd when mist 3 out; hdd nxt; lkd btn when rdr lost iron last; kpt on game to ld final 150yds*

[1024³]	2	2½	**Midsummer Glen (IRE)** 11-12 9-2 **Miss M Bremner** *Trckd ldrs; 4th 13; rdn nxt; 22l 5th 16; hit 3 out; 10l 3rd 2 out; no imp til stayed on wl final 100yds*
[915ᴾ]	3	½	**Lord Levi (IRE)** 11-10 14-1 **W Renwick** *Hld up & bhnd; 5th & prog 9; went 3rd 12 & 10l 2nd 14; clsd gng wl 3 out to ld nxt; drvn clr app last; lkd wnr til tied up u.p & hdd & no ex final 150yds*
[465²]	4	5	**Major Tom (IRE)** 11-06 3-1 **R Tate** *Ld 3 til app 8; 5th & outpcd 15; 15l 5th 2 out; kpt on agn frm last; unable to chall*
[1120³]	5	15	**Snapper** 12-05 5-1 **J Walton** *Last early; eff in 3rd 9; lost plce to 6th 12; mist nxt; blun 15; no ch aft*
[587²]	6	5	**Kentucky Gold (IRE)** 11-06 20-1 **M Worthington** *Ld to 3; 2nd til jmpd slow 6; 2nd agn 12-14; 20l 3rd & rdn 16; 14l 4th 2 out; fnd nil aft*
[1154²]	7	1¼	**Fiscal Policy** 11-06 20-1 **R Trotter** *Bhnd; 7th & rdn 10; outpcd u.p 12; strugg when hit 16*
[1120³]	8	7	**Ensign Ewart (IRE)** 12-05 13-2 **C Storey** *Nt jw in rr; 8th & rdn 12; some hdwy when hit 14; sn btn*
[1118⁵]	9	1	**Border Glory** 11-06 20-1 **P Maitland-Carew** *Bhnd; hit 11; last & rdn 12; no ch aft*

TIME: 6min 22.4s **TOTE:** £3.60; places £1.10, £2.00, £4.90 **Ex:** £16.50 **CSF:** £13.46 **Tri:** £78.10

Bangor (LH 9F,18J)
Fri, 5 May (GOOD to SOFT)

1343 James Griffith Mem Nov HC   **16 ran**

[1200¹]	1		**ROLFES DELIGHT** 11-07 3-1F **S Prior** *Hld up; hdwy 6; mist 9; ld 11 (water); drew clr 3 out; rdn out*
[1050¹]	2	13	**African Warrior** 11-02 100-30 **C Williams** *In tch; hdwy 7; blun 8; went 2nd 4 out; rdn & no imp on wnr app 2 out*
[1254ᶠ]	3	4	**Haveafewmanners (IRE)** 11-02 66-1 **M Worthington** *Ld til aft 3; ld agn 5; hdd 11 (water); one pce frm 4 out*
[987ᴾ]	4	2	**The Rum Mariner** 11-09 25-1 **Miss C Thomas** *Chsd ldrs; hit 10; sn lost plce; stayed on agn frm 3 out; nt rch ldrs*
[902⁷]	5	12	**Greville Again (IRE)** 11-07 100-1 **A Wadlow** *Midfield; jmpd slow 3; rdn in rr nxt; mist 10; nd aft*
[1129³]	6	s hd	**Corkers Flame (IRE)** 11-07 100-1 **I Wynne** *A bhnd*
[1125³]	7	14	**Robert The Rascal** 11-07 100-1 **J R Barlow** *Midfield; prog 7; cl 5th when hmpd sltly 14; btn when lft 3rd 3 out; sn wknd*
[999³]	8	13	**Miss Accounts (IRE)** 11-02 33-1 **Miss A Armitage** *T.o frm 3*
[1151⁵]	9	1½	**Shanballymore (IRE)** 11-07 16-1 **R Owen** *Bhnd; niggled along ½way; t.o*
[1125³]	P		**Admiral Villeneuve** 12-00 100-1 **D O'Meara** *Prom; ld aft 3; hdd 5; mists 6 & 11 (water); wknd 13; bhnd when pu nxt*
[916ᴾ]	F		**Donnegale (IRE)** 11-11 (vis) 7-1 **G Brewer** *Chsd ldrs; rdn app 13; hmpd nxt; 3rd & btn when fell 3 out*
[959ᵁ]	F		**Horton-Cum-Peel (IRE)** 11-11 40-1 **R Burton** *Hld up in midfield; strugg & bhnd when fell 4 out*
[1023³]	U		**Lakeside Lad** 11-08 (bl) 11-2 **R Cooper** *Sn prom; disp 3rd when blun & ur 14*
[1252²]	P		**Maltese Cross (IRE)** 11-07 100-1 **D Sherlock** *In tch; mist 7; sn rdn & lost plce; bhnd 9; t.o & pu 11 (water)*
[1154ᵁ]	P		**The Shy Padre (IRE)** 11-09 40-1 **C Mulhall** *Bhnd; sn t.o; pu 4 out*
[1129¹]	P		**Whitegates Willie** 11-09 100-30 **G Hanmer** *Hld up; hdwy 12; rdn & wknd app 14; no ch when hmpd 3 out; t.o & pu nxt*

TIME: 6min 21.6s **TOTE:** £4.50; places £1.00, £1.40, £19.00 **Ex:** £16.60 **CSF:** £11.98

Folkestone (RH 7F,19J)
Fri, 5 May (GOOD, GOOD to FIRM in places)

1344 Stuart Adamson Mem HC   **4 ran**

[584ᶠ]	1		**BRAMBLEDOWN (IRE)** 11-09 11-4 **Mrs B Sillars** *Lw; jw; v enthusiastic & ld aft 1; clr most of way; stdd & 8l ahd aft 12; sn clr agn; lft virt solo 16*
[1026ᴾ]	2	dist	**John Tufty** 11-07 50-1 **Miss R Illman** *Poor 3rd; 22l down aft 5; t.o 10; clsd 12; outpcd by wnr nxt & lft rem 2nd 16; lame & distressed aft*
[1103²]	P		**Real Value (IRE)** 12-07 1-3F **Julian Pritchard** *Ld 1; jmpd lft & nvr gng wl; chsd wnr but a lkd unhappy; outpcd 13; 25l 2nd when pu 16*
[824ᵁ]	R		**Sultan Of Swing** 11-07 (vis) 50-1 **M Gorman** *Hit 3; nt jw in last & nvr gng wl; t.o 10; rn out thro wing & ur 11*

TIME: 6min 39.9s **TOTE:** £2.80 **Ex:** £11.70 **CSF:** £29.26

Sedgefield (LH 8F,16J)

Fri, 5 May (GOOD to FIRM, FIRM in places)

1345 Guy Cunard HC
8 ran

[921⁷]	1		**HILTONSTOWN LASS (IRE)** 11-13 5-2 **R Walford** *Coolly rdn; ww; 5th 11; gd hdwy to chall aft 13; slt ld frm 2 out & rdr drpd whip; urged clr flat*
[917²]	2	2¼	**Coole Abbey (IRE)** 12-04 8-11F **W Renwick** *Settled gng wl; pckd bad 4; went 2nd 11; ld 12; hrd rdn & just hdd 2 out; nt qckn flat*
[916³]	3	13	**Floruceva (IRE)** 11-09 5-1 **J Tate** *Tk str hld in 2nd/4th; mist 2; 5l 3rd 3 out; sn wl outpcd*
[622¹]	4	3	**Weejumpawud** 11-09 12-1 **C Storey** *Pulled hrd; chsd ldr frm 4 til ld 11-12; 8l 4th 3 out; wknd qckly; t.o*
[1154³]	5	dist	**Charlieadams (IRE)** 12-00 (7) 14-1 **J Muir** *Tk str str hld; ld to 11; sn wknd; poor 5th 13; t.o*
[1163³⁼]	6	30	**Rye Rum (IRE)** 12-00 66-1 **J Walton** *Blun 2; last by 5; t.o 7*
[1078ᴾ]	U		**Full Of Chat (IRE)** 11-02 66-1 **F King** *Jmpd awkward 1; sn rdn; 15l last 3; hit 7; 7th when blun & ur 10*
[1230ᴾ]	P		**Yornoangel** 11-07 66-1 **R Clark** *Drpd to rr 8; rdn & lost tch 9; t.o 11; bad mist 13 & pu*

TIME: 5min 03.7s **TOTE:** £3.00; places £1.10,£1.10,£1.60 **Ex:** £5.80 **CSF:** £4.88 **Tri:** £8.10

Hereford (RH 9F,19J)

Sat, 6 May (GOOD, GOOD to FIRM in places)

1346 Russell Baldwin & Bright HC
10 ran

[1266²]	1		**LOOK IN THE MIRROR** 11-07 11-2 **Miss L Sweeting** *Made all; drew 10l clr 14; pushed out; unchall*
[1293¹]	2	7	**Ozzie Jones** 12-00 8-13F **Miss L Pearce** *Mostly 2nd frm 6; rdn 16; one pce & nvr able to chall*
[1134⁴]	3	4	**Copper Coil** 11-11 9-2 **T Scudamore** *Rdn all way; a 2nd/3rd; hit 9; 13l 3rd 14; stayed on same pce frm 3 out*
[1306⁵]	4	26	**Factor Ten (IRE)** 11-07 12-1 **J Richardson** *In tch; went 4th 9; rdn 12; sn wknd*
[1157²]	5	3	**Frown** 11-07 12-1 **M Nicolls** *Prsd ldrs; hit 5; 5th 8; outpcd & mists 11 & 12; no ch aft*
[1273³]	6	dist	**Watchit Lad** 11-09 20-1 **S Blackwell** *Chsd wnr to 3; bhnd frm 9; t.o 11*
[1271²]	P		**Merger Mania** 11-07 20-1 **M Trott** *Sn wl bhnd; t.o & pu aft 7; saddle slpd*
	P		**Merino Waltz (USA)** 11-07 33-1 **J Cook** *Hit 2; a wl bhnd; mist 6; t.o 12; pu aft 2 out*
[1174¹]	P		**Space Cappa** 11-07 9-1 **Miss V Stephens** *Sn wl bhnd; t.o 12; pu aft 2 out*
[1131ᴾ]	P		**Summer Haven** 11-06 33-1 **L Lay** *Jmpd poor in rr; sn t.o; pu 11*

TIME: 6min 30.7s **TOTE:** £6.90; places £1.40,£1.10,£1.50 **Ex:** £23.90 **CSF:** £10.21 **Tri:** £10.21

Bilsdale

Easingwold (LH 8F,18J) Sat, 6 May (GOOD to FIRM)

1347 Hunt
4 ran

[1234ᵁ]	1		**LA EMNI (IRE)** 5-1 **S Charlton** *Hld up & bhnd early; 15l 3rd til hdwy 8; 4l 3rd 10; ld 13; 11 up 15; jnd 2 out; sn hdd; 2l 2nd & hld when lft solo last*
[1331ᶠ]	R		**Charlie Dazzle (IRE)** 5-1 **A Morris** *Sa; pulled v hrd; hvly rstrnd; t.o 5; rn out 7*
[624ᶠ]	F		**Pause For Thought** 4-5F **Mrs F Needham** *Tk keen hld; ld; 2l up til qcknd 6l clr aft 8; hdd & outpcd 12; 3l 3rd 3 out; chall nxt; drew 2l clr & lkd wnr when fell last; dead*
[1329ᶠ]	F		**Stanwick Hall** 5-2 **K Needham** *(xnb) Chsd ldr in 2nd to 7; outpcd aft 8; 6l 2nd 10; hdwy 11 to ld 13; mist & hdd nxt; 6l 3rd & wkng when fell 2 out*

OFFICIAL DISTANCE: Finished alone **TIME:** 6min 11.0s

1348 Confined
10 ran

[1324¹]	1		**PRIME STYLE** 5-1 **C Gibbon** *(xnb) Ld; 2l up 8; just ld & mist 11; ld agn aft 12; 2l up til jnd app 2 out; pushed out & sn clr; r.o str*
[1325¹]	2	2½	**Polar King (IRE)** *(3x)* 2-5F **D Easterby** *Nvr gng wl; mid-div to 5; bad mist 9 & drpd to rr; hrd rdn 11 to 3l 3rd 2 out; went 2l 2nd 2 out; easily outpcd by wnr*
[807ᴾ]	3	6	**Lord George** 20-1 **P Atkinson** *Chsd ldr in 2l 2nd to 14; mist & wknd 15; 6l 3rd by 3 out; r.o one pce*

[1326F]	4	20	**Vals Castle (IRE)** (5a) 10-1 G Markham *Mid-div to 6; stdy hdwy to handy 5th 14; sn outpcd; 6l 3rd & wkng 3 out*
[1325S]	5	5	**Caman** (bl) 66-1 Mrs S Palfreeman *A towards rr; sn strugg; lsng tch 11; to 15*
[1326U]	6	12	**The Hazel Harrier (IRE)** 8-1 Miss A Deniel *(bh) Last by 3; lost tch frm 5; hrd rdn 10; to 15*
[997U]	P		**Gaelic Warrior** 66-1 Miss Rachel Clark *(xnb) Mid-div; 10l 5th 9; outpcd & wknd 13; poor 5th when carried wide bend bef 2 out & pu*
[1027U]	U		**Harbour Blaze** 10-1 Miss R Clark *Chsd ldng pr in 4l 3rd to 9; 6l 3rd when blun & ur 13*
[1326F]	F		**Mac's Blade (USA)** (bl,tt) 66-1 R Edwards *Fell 1*
[999P]	P		**Optimism Reigns (IRE)** (tt) 50-1 R Clark *Prom to 4; outpcd 8; 12l 6th 9; wknd qckly & pu 11; bridle broke & saddle slpd*

OFFICIAL DISTANCES: 2l, 7l TIME: 6min 01.0s

The rider of Polar King Was fined £125 for excessive use of the whip and causing the horse to be marked; this being his second similar offence

1349 Mens Open
9 ran

[1327³]	1		**RED SPECTACLE (IRE)** 6-4F N Tutty *Cl up; went 2l 2nd 10-14; chall 3 out; ld nxt; qcknd rt away app last; easy*
[1231³]	2	15	**Nishkina** (vis) 50-1 C Cundall *Mid-div til outpcd 10; poor 3rd 11; hdwy 15; 6l 3rd 3 out; outpcd & sn no ch w wnr but stayed on to 20l 2nd app last*
[1215F]	3	4	**Quiet Mistress** (5a) (bl) 66-1 S Charlton *Chsd ldr in 11 2nd til lft in ld 10; 2l up 11 til jnd 3 out; hdd nxt; wknd qckly app last*
[358⁴]	4	25	**Toarlite (IRE)** (vis) 20-1 H Trotter *A rr; rem 5th 12; plodded on one pce*
[1230⁵]	5	6	**Hazel Reilly (IRE)** (5a) 6-1 S Swiers *A rr; 15l 6th 8; outpcd 13; poor 4th 14; dist 4th 3 out; dem 5th flat*
[1235F]	6	20	**Arctic Corner** (5a) 66-1 A Pennock *Sa; rstrnd in rr; lost tch 4; t.o 11; rem 6th 3 out*
[1327⁴]	U		**Calleva Star (IRE)** 5-2 R Abrahams *Cl 2nd til ur 5*
[1027⁶]	U		**Mr Hook** 66-1 R Clark *Mid-div to 6; 6l 4th 8; chsd along aft 9; 10l 5th when saddle slpd & ur flat app 11*
[1325F]	F		**That Old Feeling (IRE)** (vis,tt) 5-2 D Easterby *Ld; 11 up when fell 10*

OFFICIAL DISTANCES: 12l, 4l TIME: 6min 04.0s

1350 Ladies Open
11 ran

[1232⁵]	1		**TEMPLE GARTH** 20-1 Miss F Hartley *A.p; ld to 3; 4l 5th 5; went 4th 14-3 out; cl 5th 2 out; hrd rdn app last; fin fast on outer; ld on line*
[1328²]	2	½	**Japodene** (5a) 4-1 Miss A Deniel *Patiently rdn; 8l 7th 8; hdwy 11 to 3l 3rd 14; ld 3 out; 1l up last; jnd flat & hdd cl home*
[1199⁴]	3	½	**Pontoon Bridge** (5a) A.p; 3l 4th 5-10; went cl 3rd 11 & 1l 2nd 14; cl 2nd & ev ch app last; outpcd run-in
[1328³]	4	2	**Orswellthatenswell** 5-1 Mrs F Needham *Sa; last to 3; hdwy aft 4; ld 6; 1l up til jnd 3 out; ev ch app last; wknd flat*
[1325²]	5	2	**Vital Issue (IRE)** 4-1 Miss J Foster *Prom; ld 4-6; cl 2nd/3rd to 15; 4l 5th 2 out; wknd app last; r.o one pce*
[1217²]	6	35	**Tiderunner (IRE)** (bl) 33-1 Miss C Elkington *A rr; last by 5; lsng tch 6; t.o 13; plodded on*
[1328⁵]	F		**Cede Nullis** (5a) (bl) 50-1 Miss L Eddery *Mid-div til hdwy 9; 2l 2nd 11; cl up til outpcd & wknd 14; 25l 6th when fell 3 out*
[505P]	P		**Double Tempo (IRE)** 20-1 Miss R Clark *Last by 4; hanging bad app 5; pu rap & dism 6 (rdr thought horse lame)*
[1328⁴]	S		**Kendor Pass (IRE)** 16-1 Mrs N Wilson *Rr to 5; slt hdwy 7 to 12l 7th 10; outpcd & lost tch 14; dist 6th when slpd up bend bef 2 out*
[1232⁴]	P		**Stride To Glory (IRE)** (bl) 33-1 Mrs H Arnold *A strugg to go pce; rr 4; slt hdwy 6 to 10l 6th 9; grad wknd; rr by 11; t.o & pu 3 out*
[690P]	P		**Thank U Jim** 7-1 Miss T Jackson *Prom; 2l 4th 9 til wknd 11; outpcd aft 12 & sn lost tch; t.o 7th when pu 2 out*

OFFICIAL DISTANCES: 1l, ½l TIME: 5min 54.0s

1351 Dodson & Horrell PPORA Club Members Restricted
9 ran

[801P]	1		**SOVEREIGNS MATCH** (tt) 5-1 M Mackley *(bf)Cl 2nd to 5; ld 6; 2l up til qcknd rt away frm 13; 10l ahd 14; dist clr app last; eased flat; canter*
[1230⁸]	2	10	**Mount Faber** (bl) 25-1 S Charlton *Ld to 5; cl 2nd 6; hanging on bend app 11 & rmdrs; in tch til easily outpcd by wnr aft 13; 15l 2nd 2 out; r.o one pce*
[1230⁷]	3	4	**Fiery Jack** 25-1 N Tutty *Cl up; 4l 3rd 7; outpcd aft 8; pushed along 14; 15l 3rd & hrd rdn 3 out; r.o one pce*

[1232³]	4	4	**C L B Jemilla** (5a) 5-2 **Mrs F Needham** *Rr to 6; slt hdwy 8 to 8l 4th 12; outpcd 13; 20l 4th 3 out; r.o same pce*
[1326ᴾ]	5	25	**Moor Lady** (5a) (tt) 12-1 **S Swiers** *Last to 2; midfield 6-10; went 12l 4th 12; outpcd & poor 5th 15*
[1201¹]	F		**Colonels Hatch** 20-1 **D Sherlock** *Cl up; 4l 3rd 9 til fell 11*
[1229¹]	F		**Kerrisdale** (5a) 7-4F **D Thomas** *Rr when fell 3; rdr broke collar-bone*
[1326ᴾ]	P		**Kind Of Chic** (5a) (tt) 25-1 **P Kinsella** *Midfield; outpcd & wknd 9; last & rmdrs 10; sn lost tch; t.o & pu 13*
[1230ᴾ]	F		**Traceytown (IRE)** (5a) 12-1 **Miss Rachel Clark** (xnb) *Mid-div to 5; rdn along aft 6; rmdrs 10; last & reluct 14; t.o 3 out; tired when fell 2 out*

OFFICIAL DISTANCES: 12l, 3½l TIME: 6min 04.0s

1352 Open Maiden (Div 1) 14 ran

[1329ᵁ]	1		**SALLY SCALLY** (5a) 8-1 **Miss T Jackson** *Handy in mid-div til 6l 4th 6; hdwy 11; ld 13; 2l up 15; scooted clr app 3 out; 25l clr 2 out; hvly eased flat; canter*
[1329³]	2	20	**Leg Beforum (IRE)** 5-2F **S Swiers** *Prom; 2l 2nd 6-15; outpcd & 20l 4th 3 out; stayed on; lft 3rd 2 out & tk 2nd flat*
[1251³]	3	8	**Educate Me (IRE)** (tt) 16-1 **J Burley** *Prom early; 3l 3rd 6-12; outpcd 14; 10l 3rd 3 out; lft 2nd 2 out til wknd bad & dem flat*
[1234⁵]	4	12	**Highland Symphony** (5a) 14-1 **Mrs F Needham** *A rr; 15l 10th 8; outpcd 13; poor 6th 3 out; stayed on; nrst fin*
[798ᴾ]	5	12	**Prince Baltasar** 5-1 **C Mulhall** *Sa; a rr; last by 13; to 14; rem 7th 3 out*
[1235ᶠ]	6	25	**Lewesdon Countess** (5a) 6-1 **W Burnell** *A rr; to 14; rem 8th 5 out*
[1164ᶠ]	P		**Camden Carr (IRE)** 6-1 **T Glass** *Mid-div early; 8l 5th 9 til outpcd & wknd 14; to by 3 out; clambered over & pu nxt*
[1235²]	P		**Farm Talk** 4-1 **S Charlton** *A rr div; bad mist 9; poor 5th 3 out; dist 5th & v tired when pu last*
[627ᵁ]	F		**Im Struggling** (7a) 14-1 **G Markham** *Cl up; 5l 5th & gng wl when fell 11*
[1330ᴾ]	F		**Just A Single (IRE)** (tt) 14-1 **A Morris** *Ld 5; 2l up til hdd & wknd 13; lsng tch & bhnd when fell 14*
[1235⁴]	P		**Mr Norm** 14-1 **R Clark** *A rr group; rmdrs 9; drvn along & lsng tch 10; t.o & pu 11*
[1234²]	F		**Pashby Wood** (5a) 3-1 **M Morley** *Cl 3rd til fell 5*
[1233¹]	F		**Redmire** (5a) 14-1 **A Pennock** *Ld to 4; cl up in ldng group til outpcd 12; 15l 4th 15; stayed on to 25l 2nd when fell 2 out*
[1330ᴾ]	F		**Right Ron Run** (vis) 7-1 **R Wakeham** *Rr when put foot in hole & fell bend bef 6*

OFFICIAL DISTANCES: 20l, 8l TIME: 6min 02.0s

1353 Open Maiden (Div 2) 9 ran

[1233ᴾ]	1		**DRAGON STOUT** (tt) 4-1 **C Wilson** *Rr to 5; hdwy 11 to 4l 3rd 14; rdn to disp ld 2 out; ld app last; sn clr; r.o*
[803³]	2	12	**Catton Lady** (5a) 2-1JF **C Mulhall** *Mid-div to 6; 10l 6th & pushed along 11; went 4th 14; 12l 4th 3 out; stayed on u.p to tk 2nd app last*
[1329³]	3	2	**Oaklands Billy** 14-1 **P Frank** *Ld; qcknd clr aft 5; 10l up 9; stdd & 2l ahd 10-15; 3l clr 3 out; hdd app last; wknd & dem flat; all out*
[1329⁶]	4	5	**Tyndrum Gold** (bl) 6-1 **Miss A Deniel** *Lkd v hrd ride; last early; hrd rdn & pushed along 11; 20l 6th 14; rmdrs 15; went 15l 5th 3 out; stayed on*
[1002ᶠ]	5	15	**Mac's View (IRE)** 2-1JF **T Glass** *10s-2s; rr to 4; hdwy 6 to cl 5th 11; went cl 2nd 13; mist 15; 6l 3rd 3 out; wknd rap; bounced home; all out*
	6	5	**Another Daughter** (5a) 6-1 **N Tutty** *Prom early; outpcd 9; wknd 11; rr & lsng tch 13; t.o 15*
[1229³]	7	20	**The Noble Rebel (IRE)** 14-1 **A Pennock** *Stdd early; pulled to cl 2nd 4 til outpcd 6; 10l 2nd 9; wknd; rr to 3 out; last 13; to 15*
[1234ᴾ]	U		**Addington Sharragh** (5a) 8-1 **Miss J Binks** *Prom 1st circ; 10l 3rd when ur 11*
[808⁸]	P		**Canny's Fort** (5a) 14-1 **J Davies** *Rr to 4; hdwy 6; 8l 2nd 10 til wknd 13; t.o & pu 3 out*

OFFICIAL DISTANCES: 8l, 2l TIME: 6min 06.0s

Croome & West Warwickshire

Upton-on-Severn (RH 10F,18J) Sat, 6 May (GOOD, GOOD to SOFT in places)

1354 Hunt, 12st - 17J 6 ran

[1272¹]	1		**FINTONA BOY (IRE)** (5x) (tt) 1-4F **R Burton** *Ld; jw; jnd brief 7; 2l clr 12; slt mist 15; drew rt away frm 3 out; wl clr last; hvly eased run-in; impressive*

[1067P]	2	12	**Brother Prim** 8-1 **A St George** 5l 4th 5; disp ld 7; sltly wide & hdd bend aft 9; prog to 2l 2nd 12-14; wknd app 3 out; v tired frm nxt; kpt on wl to hld 2nd
[1016⁴]	3	15	**La Mon Dere (IRE)** (3x) (bl,tt) 6-1 **Miss T Spearing** 3l 3rd 5; mists 7 & 8; rmdrs nxt; drpd back 4th & jmpd slow 11; wknd to 20l 4th 14; duelled for 3rd frm 2 out; just prevailed flat
[891⁵]	4	1½	**Stormhill Farmer** 16-1 **M Wall** 2-3l 2nd to 9; 10l 3rd 12; wknd grad frm 14; lost duel for 3rd flat
[893P]	P		**Humphrey** 14-1 **M Wilesmith** Tubed; 6l bhnd by 6; detach frm ldng group by 10; wl t.o when pu 3 out
	R		**T Rex (U)** 16-1 **M Keel** Rn out 1

OFFICIAL DISTANCES: dist, 15l, ½l TIME: 6min 41.0s
Fence 11 omitted - damaged

1355 Restricted, 12st   11 ran

[864²]	1		**WISE PRINCE (IRE)** 2-1 **L Stephens** Cl 4/5th til lost sev plces 10; prog to 3rd 14 & 2nd nxt; eff to dispd ld 3 out; cl 2nr nxt; r.o str flat
[612⁵]	2	2	**Coddington Girl** (5a) 10-1 **T Stephenson** Hld up; 6th 8; prog to 2l 2nd 12; ld 13-15; jnd nxt; 2l down 2 out; r.o wl; a hld
[1206ᵁ]	3	12	**Claymore Lad** 10-1 **A Maculan** Chsd ldr; 10l 2nd 4; drpd back to 3rd 15; unable to qckn frm 2 out
[863P]	4	6	**Tranquil Lord (IRE)** 33-1 **D Smith** Cl 5th to 6; lost plce & 12l last 8-14; stayed on agn frm 3 out; nrst fin
[832P]	5	½	**Poet's Song (IRE)** 20-1 **D Mansell** Cl 6th to ½way; mod prog to 15; unable to chall frm 2 out
[616¹]	P		**Ard Na Carrig (IRE)** 13-8F **A Wintle** 2s-13/8; jmpd lft; ld & sn clr; 12l ahd 5; 2l up 12; jnd 13; hdd & wknd v qckly nxt; last when pu 3 out
[896P]	P		**Hijacked** 10-1 **Julian Pritchard** Mostly 3rd til 3l 2nd 9-11; cl 3rd to 13; 5th & wkng 15; rr when pu 2 out
[1194³]	r		**My Nad Knows** 12-1 **J Baimbridge** Wrs; ref to rce
[260³]	P		**Smart Orange (IRE)** 12-1 **M Rimell** Sev posns; went 4th brief 10; lost tch frm 14; 7th & wknd when pu 3 out
[994¹]	P		**Uncle Tom** 10-1 **R Burton** Last pr by 4; impd brief 8; detach frm ldng group by 14; rr when pu 2 out
[1089³]	U		**Wonastow** 14-1 **A St George** Rr & a strugg; 8th & wkng when ur 11

OFFICIAL DISTANCES: 1l, 4l TIME: 6min 31.0s

1356 Intermediate, 12st   6 ran

[1312³]	1		**VIKING FLAME** (5a) 14-1 **S Bush** Trckd ldrs in 3rd til 2nd 6; prsd ldr frm 11; ½l 2nd 2 out-last; hrd drvn & r.o wl flat; ld on line
[1090²]	2	s hd	**Star Changes** 5-4F **Julian Pritchard** Disp 3rd to 8; 6l 3rd 13; 2l bhnd ldrs 15; chall on inner aft 3 out; just ld nxt; ½l up & slt mist last; r.o str u.p flat; hdd cl home
[1336P]	3	2	**Maggies Brother** (5x) 2-1 **D Barlow** Hld up; in tch in 5th; 6l last 8; prog on inner to disp 3rd 15; ev ch 2 out; wknd app last
[615⁵]	4	4	**Money Don't Matter** (5a) 8-1 **D Mansell** 10l last by 3; 6l bhnd 8; prog 11; 3l 4th 3 out; grad wknd
[971²]	5	2	**Cherokee Run (IRE)** (tt) 4-1 **M Keel** 7s-4s; ld; 2l clr 8; jnd 11-13; slt ld nxt til bad mist 3 out; nt rec; sn hdd & wknd
[1203P]	6	15	**Glendine (IRE)** 50-1 **D Smith** Cl 2nd to 5; 3rd to 11; wknd nxt; detach 15

OFFICIAL DISTANCES: s hd, 2l TIME: 6min 30.0s

1357 Mixed Open (Nov Rdrs), 12st   7 ran

[861⁴]	1		**NEVADA GOLD** 3-1 **R Rogers** Disp ld to 9; 2l clr nxt; mist 13; eff to ld agn 15-2 out; forged clr app last; stayed on str
[1086³]	2	5	**Military Man** 6-4F **M Keel** Disp ld to 3; 2l 2nd frm 9; disp ld 14; jmpd to ld 3 out; hdd & wknd nxt
[1205⁴]	3	20	**Golden Savannah** 4-1 **A Maculan** Rr; 15l bhnd 4; 30l bhnd 6; disp 4th 10; eff to 20l 3rd 15; stayed on wl; nrst fin
[743³]	4	8	**Poucher (IRE)** 10-1 **A Wadlow** Disp ld to 9; 5l 3rd nxt; wknd qckly frm 13; one pce frm 3 out
[701P]	5	20	**Robero** (tt) 12-1 **Miss R Reynolds** Mostly 5th 1st circ; 30l bhnd 14; nt pce to chall
[1205³]	6	30	**Funcheon Gale** (14ow) 4-1 **Mrs A Lee** Last by 4; fnce bhnd ½way
[1242P]	P		**Southern Nights** 7-1 **P Young** Last pr; disp 4th brief 10; wknd qckly & pu 15

OFFICIAL DISTANCES: 2l, 10l TIME: 6min 27.0s

1358 Confined, 12st
7 ran

[1190²]	1		**DO IT ONCE (IRE)** (7x) (tt) 2-1 M Keel *5th 1st circ; 4l bhnd 9; prog to chall 3 out; stayed on str to ld last 50yds*	
[1293⁴]	2	1	**Rocket Radar** (7x) 4-5-4/7; *trckd ldrs; smooth rn on inner to disp ld 7-9; 3l 2nd frm 12; gd j to ld 15; 3l clr nxt; rdr lkng rnd app 2 out; rmdrs app last; hdd & nt qckn last 50yds* Julian Pritchard	
[890ᵁ]	3	5	**Kingsthorpe** 10-1 A Phillips *Ww; eff to 3rd 10; 2l 2nd frm 15 til outpcd app last*	
[1275²]	4	3	**Tee Tee Too (IRE)** 10-1 Miss E James *Disp 3rd til wknd frm 14; went 3rd agn brief 2 out; nt qckn w ldrs frm 2 out*	
[1085ᴾ]	5	20	**Spearhead Again (IRE)** 16-1 M Munrowd *Jw; ld 2; jnd 7-9; 3l clr nxt til mist 14; wknd qckly frm nxt*	
[1126²]	6	4	**Just Marmalade** 20-1 Miss J Williams *Pulled hrd; ld to 4; drpd back to 6th 9; detach last by 13*	
[895ᴾ]	P		**Keep Clear (IRE)** 20-1 G Barfoot-Saunt *Rr; 4th 10; wknd frm 13; wl bhnd when pu 3 out*	

OFFICIAL DISTANCES: ½l, 5l, 2l TIME: 6min 32.0s

1359 Open Maiden 8yo&up, 12st
7 ran

[1270⁴]	1		**MUSICAL HIT** 5-2F C Wadland *3rd to 6 & 2nd 7-10; ld nxt; 3l up 14; drew clr frm 2 out; easy*	
[1068ᴾ]	2	20	**Take Achance On Me** 5-1 T Stephenson *Cl 2nd; 3l 3rd 12; eff to 2nd nxt; nt qckn app 2 out*	
[738ᶠ]	3	8	**Lily Lane** 3-1 R Burton *Swtng; jmpd slow 3; 5l 4th frm 9; mist & lost sev lengths 12; lft 3rd 3 out; nvr in posn to chall*	
[1315ᵁ]	r		**Bally Boy** 3-1 A St George *Ref to start*	
[1189³]	U		**Benbulbin (IRE)** (2ow) (vis) 3-1 M Bluck *Wrs & ur (put off by antics of rival)*	
	P		**Buckley Beau** 5-1 M Keel *Ld brief 1; handy 4th mostly to 12; wknd nxt; wl bhnd when pu 3 out*	
[995ᴾ]	r		**Wind And Stars** (5a,2ow) 10-1 A Barnett *Jw; ld 3-10; 5l 3rd 13; wknd qckly 15; ref 3 out*	

OFFICIAL DISTANCES: 25l, 10l TIME: 6min 47.0s

The stewards enquired into the start of this race where the tape spooked one runner who caused another not to start; having interviewed the riders concerned, the Starter and Flagman they were happy that the correct procedure had been followed

1360 Open Maiden 56&7yo (Div 1), 2m4f, 12st - 15J
10 ran

[955ᴾ]	1		**SACRIFICE** (7a) 6-1 G Barfoot-Saunt *Pulled hrd; 8th 5; clsd to 3rd 9; chall bet horses 2 out; str rn frm last to ld last 50yds*	
[900ᶠ]	2	2	**Cider Man** (7a) 2-1JF T Stephenson *Hld up; 7l last 5; hdwy 9 to disp 2nd 11; str rn frm 2 out to ld app last; just outpcd flat*	
[1021ᶠ]	3	8	**Thor's Phantom** 7-2 A Martin *Ld on inner aft 3; 5th nxt; prog to 3l 3rd 11-12; stayed on one pce frm 2 out*	
[1021²]	4	15	**Rapid Liner** 2-1JF J Gallagher *4th 1st circ; prog to disp ld frm 9; ½l clr 12; ev ch til hdd one pce aft 2 out*	
[1092ᴾ]	5	2	**Sales Dodger (IRE)** 8-1 R Hodges *Mostly 6th 1st circ; eff to go 4th 11; wknd frm 3 out*	
[673ᴾ]	C		**Foxley Lad** 10-1 D Mansell *8th 5; smooth prog til carried out 10*	
[1019ᶠ]	R		**Grain Hill** (5a) 10-1 M Wall *Pulled hrd; ld brief 2; cl 3rd 6; wkng when rn out 10*	
[1068ᴾ]	P		**Lord Lard (IRE)** 14-1 M Rodda *Mostly 3rd to 5; mist nxt; 10l last 9; rr when pu 3 out*	
[955ᴾ]	r		**Mr Baloo** 4-1 M Rimell *7th 5; pckd 11; wknd grad & 20l 6th when ref 2 out*	
[900ᴾ]	P		**Penny Appeal** (5a) 20-1 M Scales *Ld 1 & 5-9; wknd qckly; rr when pu 15*	

OFFICIAL DISTANCES: 1l, 10l TIME: 5min 21.0s

1361 Open Maiden 56&7yo (Div 2), 2m4f, 12st - 15J
9 ran

[1222²]	1		**EVEIES BOY (IRE)** (7a) 5-2F G Hanmer *Ld; jnd brief 4 & 6; 3l clr 12; drew clr app last; easy*	
[990ᴾ]	2	7	**One Mans Legacy** (5a) 4-1 R Burton *Mostly 3rd to 7; went 4l 2nd 8; disp ld 13; 2l 2nd nxt; nt pushed when ch gone*	
[899ᴾ]	3	20	**Sallioko** (5a) 8-1 D Barlow *Last by pr 4; detach by 9; disp 3rd frm 14; 10l 4th 3 out; r.o wl to 3rd flat*	
[391ᴾ]	4	2	**Miss Pilkington** (5a) 6-1 A St George *Disp 3rd/4th to 10; outpcd frm 12*	
[673ᴾ]	U		**Hottentot** (5a) 3-1 S Bush *Mid-div when ur 3*	
	P		**Rodney Trotter** 10-1 E Walker *5th to ½way; outpcd frm 10; dist 5th when pu aft 3 out*	
[835ᶠ]	P		**Silver Joy** (12a,3ow) 5-1 Julian Pritchard *Ld 4-6; 2nd nxt; wknd qckly frm 9; mist 10; lost plce rap & pu 12*	

[655U] U   **Tabula Rasa** 3-1 M Foley *Rr to 7; prog to 2nd 9 & 3rd 12; wkng when bad mist & ur 14*
[834P] P   **Willows Jaybe** (5a) 10-1 M Worthington *Last by 4; t.o 9; pu nxt*

OFFICIAL DISTANCES: 6l, 14l, 2l   **TIME:** 5min 26.0s

Cumberland
Aspatria (LH 8F,19J) Sat, 6 May (GOOD to FIRM)

1362 Hunt   7 ran

[1149U] 1   **TRIVIAL (IRE)** (5a) 4-9F R Morgan *In tch in last early; prog to 3l 3rd 11 & 2l 2nd 14; ld 3 out; sn clr; 5l up when jmpd lft last*

[1153B] 2 3 **Bold Irene (IRE)** (5a) (bl) 8-1 S Prior *16s-8s; jmpd sticky; ld; 5l up & mist 2; hdd aft nxt; l1 2nd 10; 3l 3rd & rmdrs 14; 4th & outpcd 16; stayed on to 2nd app 2 out; nt trble wnr*

    3 15 **Brandon Bridge** 8-1 T Davidson *Prom til ld aft 3; l1 up 10; hdd aft 3 out; kpt on; nt gvn hrd time; 8l 3rd when nrly ur last; improve*

    P   **Bear Faced** 50-1 A Robson *Swtng; prom & hit 1; sn rr; 9l 4th 5; 3rd & jmpd slow 8; 5l last & rdn 11; wknd 13; 20l last aft 15; t.o & pu 3 out*

[1118P] F   **No Problem Jac** (5a) (bl) 11-1 B Lusted *In tch in rr when fell 2*
[1083U] P   **Seabright Sunset** 14-1 D Jewett *Hdstrng; hld up in rr; 12l last 7; outpcd 12; strugg when climbed 14; pu aft*

    P   **Solway Coaster** (bl,tt) 5-1 C Storey *Lw; 2 handlers; oht; in tch; 8l 3rd 5; mostly 5th til prog & gng wl 11; 3l 3rd 15; outpcd nxt & sn wknd; wl btn 4th when pu & dism last*

OFFICIAL DISTANCES: 4l, 15l   **TIME:** 6min 27.0s

1363 Restricted   8 ran

[1230²] 1   **VICTORIA'S BOY (IRE)** 6-4JF G Brewer *Jw; trckd ldr til ld 5; made rest; 2l up 10; 8l ahd 16; qcknd app 3 out; 10l clr 2 out; stayed on wl; comf*

[1162⁴] 2 10 **The Other Half** (bl) 10-1 Miss P Robson *Chsd ldng pr; 8l 3rd 5; cl up 11; disp 5l 2nd 16; sn outpcd; 10l 2nd 2 out; kpt on*

[1162P] 3 5 **Tenella's Last** (5a) 14-1 R Morgan *Mid-div; 15l 4th 7; prog to 8l 3rd 10; cl up nxt til outpcd 14; 4th 16; 20l 3rd app last; kpt on wl*

[976²] 4 5 **Border Farmer (IRE)** (4a) F Mrs V Jackson *Sis; rr; 12l 6th 7; prog to 5l 5th & hit 11; disp 5l 2nd 16; one pce aft; wknd & releg 4th aft nxt*

[1162P] P   **Disrespect** (5a) 20-1 Miss M Macmillan *A rr; mist 2; 20l last 6; sn t.o; 40l 7th 14; pu 16*

[1164¹] P   **Harry Laws** 6-1 T Scott *Lw; ld; l1 up 4 til hit 5 & hdd; 2l 2nd 10; mist 13; 8l 3rd when mist nxt; pu aft*

[973U] P   **Luvly Bubbly** 12-1 Miss C Hall *A rr; 20l last 9; strugg in last pr 11; 40l last 14; climbed nxt & pu*

[1326P] P   **Noneofyourbusiness (IRE)** (5a) 33-1 Miss C Metcalfe *(xnb) Rr; 13l 7th 7; prog to 5l 6th 11; outpcd 13; wknd qckly & pu 15*

OFFICIAL DISTANCES: 20l, 10l   **TIME:** 6min 10.0s

1364 Ladies Open   6 ran

[1161¹] 1   **BALISTEROS (FR)** 4-9F Miss P Robson *Handy; 6l 4th 3; l1 3rd 7; knocked over marker app 9; went 1½l 2nd 15; hit 2 out; chall app last; outj & ½l down aft; stayed on u.p to ld flat*

[1154P] 2 1½ **Storm Alive (IRE)** 8-1 Mrs V Jackson *Chsd ldr; 6l 3rd aft 3; disp ld aft 4; ld 5; ½l up 12; 2l clr nxt; hrd prsd frm 16; jmpd btr & ½l up aft last; sn hdd & outpcd*

[1119³] 3 runin **Rallegio** 20-1 Miss L Hislop *Rr; 8l last 3; 4l 4th 8; handy til outpcd aft 15; 10l down nxt; 20l 3rd 3 out; t.o & jmpd slow last*

[806³] U   **Half Each** (5a) 7-1 Miss L Watson *Ld early; l1 2nd 3; drpd back 5; 7l last 7; 6l 5th 11; outpcd nxt; 8l last 13; lsng tch 14; bhnd when ur 16*

[975³] R   **Houselope Beck** 12-1 Miss C Hall *Prom; ld 3; disp ld aft nxt til hdd 5; l1 2nd 8; ½l 2nd 12; 2½l 3rd 15; ev ch til jinked lft & rn out nxt*

[1161³] P   **Miss Portcello** (5a) 6-1 Miss J Hollands *Chsd ldrs; 4l 3rd 5; sn rr; mist 10 & 10l last nxt; nvr seemed to be gng wl & lsng tch when pu aft 12*

OFFICIAL DISTANCES: 1½l, dist   **TIME:** 6min 01.0s

1365 Mens Open   11 ran

[1158¹] 1   **LITTLE BROCKWELL (IRE)** (5a) 7-1 L Morgan *Tchd 8s; lw; a handy; 3l 3rd 3; 4l 3rd 5; 3l 3rd 7; prog to ld aft 16; 4l up & mist 2 out; sn clr; bad mist last; gd rec; stayed on wl*

[1160²] 2 4 **Excise Man** (tt) 9-4F J Walton *Trckd ldr; 2l 2nd when hit 5; 2l 3rd 11; ev ch til outpcd aft 16; stayed on; nt pce to chall*

[1149¹]	3	½	**Blank Cheque** 8-1 **D Coates** *Rr; 8l off pce 11; prog to chse ldr nxt; outpcd 14; stayed on agn app 3 out; tk 3rd flat*
[686³]	4	8	**Parade Racer** 3-1 **T Davidson** *Swtng; oht; hld up; 8l 8th 6 & 7; prog to 4l 4th 8; 6l 4th 15; outpcd nxt; kpt on; dem 4th flat*
[1151⁴]	5	10	**Vicosa (IRE)** 10-1 **S Prior** *Rr; 9l 9th 5; 8l off pce 8; outpcd 12 & lsng tch nxt; 15l 5th 15*
[1163¹]	P		**Benefit-In-Kind (IRE)** 20-1 **T Oates** *(orbs) Chsd ldrs; 4½l 5th 5; 10l 5th & outpcd 15; sn bhnd; pu & dism app last*
[660ʳ]	P		**Branch End** 33-1 **T Scott** *Lw; 11 up 6; hdd aft 16 & sn one pce; pu 2 out*
[1151ᴾ]	P		**Crofton Lake** 33-1 **D Jewett** *Chsd ldrs; 4l 4th & mist 4; 4l 4th 11; outpcd 15; wl bhnd when pu 2 out*
[973¹]	U		**Dean Deifir (IRE)** 5-1 **C Storey** *(xnb) 8s-5s; oht; hld up in mid-div; prog to cl 5th 11; 2l 4th when mist 14 & ur 25 yds aft*
[1151²]	P		**Kilminfoyle** 16-1 **P Robson** *Tde; a rr; 10l last aft 8; 15l last & pushed along 11; mist nxt & lsng tch 13; wl bhnd when pu 2 out*
[1148³]	P		**Rebel King** 25-1 **G Thomas** *Oht; a rr; 10l last & mist 3; 10l 11th 13; lsng tch nxt; wl bhnd & pu 16*

OFFICIAL DISTANCES: 5l, 10l **TIME:** 6min 07.0s

1366 Intermediate, 12st
10 ran

[1120ᴾ]	1		**BOYUP BROOK** 7-1 **T Scott** *Hld up in tch in rr; prog to cl up 10; 6th & mist nxt; ww til chall & btr j last; lft in comm flat; wl rdn*
[1149³]	2	3	**Pennine View** (5x) 8-1 **D Jewett** *(bf) 16s-8s; trckd ldr til ld aft 4; 2l up nxt; 11 ahd 12; 11 up 16; hdd 2 out; eff & ev ch app last; no ex flat*
[1121²]	3	8	**Lindon Run** 14-1 **T Davidson** *Mid-div; cl up 10; 4l 4th 13 & 3l 3rd nxt; 4th & outpcd app 16; kpt on wl app last; tk 3rd flat*
[1121³]	4	½	**The Caffler (IRE)** 25-1 **Miss R Ramsay** *Tde; ld to 4; trckd ldr aft; disp 2l 2nd 5; outpcd 16; 10l 4th 2 out; kpt on to 3rd app last; dem flat*
[1121ᴾ]	5	10	**Slip Away** (bl) 8-1 **B Lusted** *Prom; 2l 3rd 4; trckd ldr aft; disp 2l 2nd 5; 5l 5th 11; 8l 6th & outpcd 15; kpt on one pce*
[976ᴾ]	P		**Commanche Scout (IRE)** 20-1 **T Oates** *Mid-div; outpcd 13 & lsng tch aft; t.o when pu & dism 2 out*
[717ᶠ]	P		**Fragrant Lord** 7-1 **Mrs V Jackson** *Swtng; prom early; drpd back by 5; rmdrs & nvr gng wl aft; 9l 9th 7; strugg 11; t.o & pu 2 out*
[1159²]	U		**Highland Monarch** (5x) 7-4F **C Storey** *(xnb) In tch in rr; prog to 4l 4th 8; 4l 4th & mist 11; 2l 2nd 14; hdwy to ld 2 out; hrd prsd when mist & ur last*
[1152⁵]	P		**Running Frau** (5a) 50-1 **G Thomas** *Oht; mid-div; 4l 4th 7; rdn & strugg 11; 12l off pce nxt; t.o & pu 2 out*
[1162¹]	P		**Senso (IRE)** 3-1 **Mrs C Cox** *Tchd 7/2; a rr; 10l last & mist 3; sn bhnd; 20l down aft 14; t.o 16; pu & dism last*

OFFICIAL DISTANCES: 4l, 8l **TIME:** 6min 07.0s

1367 Open Maiden (Div 1)
10 ran

[913³]	1		**GALLANT MAJOR** (tt) 5-1 **A Robson** *Chsd ldrs; 5l 5th 5; prog to 3l 2nd 11; hit nxt; chall aft 16; sn ld; 3l up & mist 2 out; 11 up & prsd last; hrd rdn flat; all out*
[1148²]	2	½	**Sparkling Gift (IRE)** (5a) 6-1 **Miss A Price** *2 handlers; prom; ld 9; 3l up 15; jnd aft nxt & hdd 2 out; 11 2nd & ev ch last; rdn & no ex flat*
[1153⁵]	3	½	**Running Mute** 7-1 **Miss P Robson** *In tch; 5l 3rd 15; outpcd nxt; kpt on app last; fin wl; nt rch ldrs*
[808⁷]	4	1½	**Pennyman (IRE)** 8-1 **M Clayton** *(bof) Ld/disp til outpcd aft 12; stayed on wl frm 3 out*
[1153ᴾ]	5	2fncs	**Davey John (IRE)** 33-1 **J R Barlow** *Ld/disp til drpd back & outpcd 12; wl bhnd 15; t.o 3 out*
[1163ᴾ]	6	15	**Everready Go** (5a) 7-1 **S Huggan** *(bnh) Prom; 4l 4th 5; 3½l 4th nxt; outpcd 13 & 10l last nxt; t.o 3 out*
[978ᴾ]	P		**Gladys** (5a) 33-1 **A Richardson** *A rr; 10l last aft 2; lost tch 8; t.o & pu 10*
[1166ᵁ]	P		**On Merit** 6-4F **T Oates** *Handy; 2l 3rd 4; outpcd 13; 10l 5th & mist nxt; nd aft; 25l 5th 16; t.o & pu 2 out*
[1153ᴾ]	P		**Royal Fling** (5a) 20-1 **C Barlow** *2 handlers; trckd ldrs early; wkng 5; sn lost tch; rr when pu 9*
[1330ᵁ]	P		**Seldom Seen (IRE)** 20-1 **L Morgan** *(bf) Rr; mists 4 & 5; 10l last & pushed along 11; pu & dism aft nxt; dead*

OFFICIAL DISTANCES: ¾l, 1½l **TIME:** 6min 16.0s

> The stewards a) enquired in to the running and riding of On Merit - accepted rider's explanation that horse was 'would not act on ground'; and b) fined the rider of Gallant Major £50 for excessive use of the whip and not giving horse time to respond

1368 Open Maiden (Div 2)   **9 ran**

[664²] 1   **FAREBIT** (5a) 9-4JF **C Storey** (xnb) A handy; 3l 3rd 5; cl 2nd 8; 5l 4th 12; prog to ld
                aft 15; 1l up at last; r.o flat

[1164ᵁ] 2   3 **Mesling** 7-1 **J Walton** In tch; 5l 6th 9; prog & cl up 11; 2l 3rd 15; trckd ldr aft; prsng
                ldr when rdr lost whip app last; nt qckn flat

[1166ᵁ] 3   25 **Homo Dorney (IRE)** (5a) 8-1 **P Robson** Ld; 3l up 4; hdd & outpcd aft 15; sn 3rd & btn

[1165ᶠ] P   **Bonnie B** (5a) 20-1 **L Morgan** A rr; detach 8; 20l last 12; t.o & pu 15

[664³] P   **Guy Mornay** 16-1 **J R Barlow** A rr; detach when hit 4 & pu

[1153⁷] U   **Javaman** 16-1 **G Thomas** Swtng; unruly gng to post; trckd ldr; 1l 2nd 5; prog 12; mist
                13; 8l 4th & outpcd 15; nd aft; saddle slpd & ur aft last; horse slid und rails & over line

[1158²] P   **Sinch** (12a) 5-1 **J Stonehouse** Trckd ldr early; jmpd big in 2l 2nd 3; hit 7 & sn bhnd;
                25l last 12; pu aft

[1083ᶠ] F   **Solway Spice** (12a) 20-1 **B Lusted** Prom; mist 3; 4l 4th app 8; prog to trck ldrs when fell 11

[816ᶠ] P   **Wishing Ash (IRE)** 9-4JF **D Jewett** A handy; 4l 4th 6; prog to trck ldrs when pu &
                dism aft 11; lkd sore

OFFICIAL DISTANCES: 3l, dist TIME: 6min 22.0s

Devon & Somerset Staghounds
Holnicote (RH 7F,19J) Sat, 6 May (FIRM)

1369 Hunt   **4 ran**

[928⁴] 1   **MINE'S A GIN (IRE)** 4-5F **Miss J Cumings** Tchd evens; made virt all; dived at 13;
                forged clr app 3 out; comf

[1096³] 2   8 **Link Copper** 7-4 **S Kidston** Tchd 2s; 2nd til jnd wnr 14-15; rdn & outpcd app 3 out;
                wl hld aft

[1102²] 3 2fncs **Humara (IRE)** (5a) 50-1 **Miss G Edwards** 3rd/4th; 6l last 9; strugg when mist 13; t.o
                15; mist nxt

[1100²] U   **Copastrop** 5-1 **R Woollacott** (martin) Tchd 6s; 3rd/4th & in tch til mist & ur 7

OFFICIAL DISTANCES: 10l, dist TIME: 6min 20.7s TOTE: £1.40 DF: £2.40

1370 Intermediate, 12st   **13 ran**

[1059³] 1   **BADGER BEER** (tt) 10-1 **N Mitchell** Trckd ldrs in 3rd/4th til 2nd 9; ld 3 out; drvn app
                last; kpt on

[927⁵] 2   2 **Vansell** (5a) 16-1 **T Greed** Swtng; 2 handlers; chsd ldrs; 5th 12; 10l 5th at 16; eff nxt;
                drvn into 2nd when dived at last; nt tch wnr

[930³] 3   4 **Western Fort (IRE)** 12-1 **Miss J Cumings** Midfield; 7th 12; eff 14; disp 5l 3rd aft 16;
                rdn & r.o one pce

[561ᶠ] 4   6 **Leap Frog** 10-1 **Miss P Gundry** (xnb) Swtng; late to padd & tde; tk str hld; ld; 7l clr
                7; rdn & hdd 3 out; grad wknd

[1097³] 5   6 **Foxy Dawn** 50-1 **D Alers-Hankey** Sn 2nd/3rd; releg 4th aft mist 12; wknd 15; no ch aft nxt

[1239²] 6   7 **Agile King** 25-1 **Miss C Tizzard** (xnb) Tde; chsd ldrs; went 3rd 12; disp 5l 3rd aft 16;
                sn wknd

[1136²] 7   10 **Master Kiwi (NZ)** 66-1 **G Richards** Lw; mounted course; nvr btr than midfield; 8th
                12; outpcd 14; plodded on

[1283ᶠ] P   **Jolification** (bl) 7-2 **A Honeyball** 7s-7/2; 2 handlers; jmpd v slow 2; rr & nvr gng wl;
                rem when jmpd v slow 6; brief prog 10 to 6th 12; lost tch nxt; pu 3 out

[1131ᶠ] P   **Jug Of Wine** (5a) 250-1 **G Weatherley** A last trio; mist 10; 9th 12; strugg nxt; t.o &
                pu 2 out

[721³] P   **Masked Martin** 80-1 **S Kidston** Mist 4; chsd ldrs til jmpd slow 5; nt jw aft & sn lost
                plce; last 12; blun 13; pu 14

[853ᶠ] P   **Master Buckley** 66-1 **C White** Midfield early; 10th & strugg 12; t.o & pu 2 out

[932¹] r   **Morris Piper** (tt) 4-5F **L Jefford** (xnb)Tchd evens; ref to rce; tk no part

[953²] P   **Persian Raider** 200-1 **M Sweetland** Jmpd v poor in last pr & imm lost tch; t.o; pu 13

OFFICIAL DISTANCES: 1½l, 3l TIME: 6min 28.9s TOTE: £7.80 DF: £16.00

1371 Confined, 12st1lb   **10 ran**

[1238²] 1   **SLEW MAN (FR)** 8-13F **Miss O Green** Opened 4/7; lw; confid rdn in rr; 9th 5; prog
                in 12l 3rd 12; clsd 14 & ld nxt; hdd brief but in comm & gng wl 3 out; kpt finding ex

[1237ᶠ] 2   2 **Stillmore Business** 3-1 **Miss P Gundry** 13/2-3s; nt fluent in 3rd/4th bhnd clr ldng
                pr; 5l 3rd aft 16; chsd wnr aft 3 out; no imp

[1098³] 3   1 **Bells Wood** 7-1 **C White** Ld 5-10 & 14 til hdd & hit nxt; 12l 4th & outpcd aft 16;
                rallied 2 out; kpt on wl flat

[1096^P]	4	10	**Play Poker (IRE)** (bl) 7-1 *Miss J Cumings Ld to 5; 2nd til ld agn 10-14; ld brief 16; wknd 3 out & nt pushed; qckly dism aft fin*
[1044^P]	5	25	**A Few Dollars More (IRE)** 50-1 *G Maundrell Settled 4th; jmpd slow 8; 15l 5th 12; wknd 14; to 16*
[953^P]	6	hd	**Leejay Luki** 66-1 *A Honeyball Chsd ldrs; 2l l 6th 12; wknd aft nxt; to 16*
[1304^P]	7	10	**James Pigg** 40-1 *G Richards A bhnd; 28l 8th 12; to 16*
[1096^P]	8	15	**Fellow Sioux** 25-1 *R Woollacott Midfield; 23l 7th & rdn w no resp 12; to 16*
	P		**Captain Jack** (bl) 16-1 *B O'Doherty Legs smothered in grease; towards rr; hit 7; 30l last 12; mist 14; to & pu 16*
[641^R]	R		**Slubberdegullian** (7a) 100-1 *S Craddock (xnb) Imm lost tch but pulling wildly & jmpd erratic; slowed bad aft 6 & hung to boxes & rn off course*

OFFICIAL DISTANCES: ¾l, 3l TIME: 6min 21.9s TOTE: £2.10 DF: £1.30

1372 Open Maiden 56&7yo (Div 1), 12st   8 ran

[1240^P]	1		**JOLIE ROSLIN** (5a) 20-1 *A Honeyball Trckd ldrs; ld app 14 til app nxt; 2l 4th aft 16; rallied 2 out; chall & lft clr last; rdn out*
[934^P]	2	4	**Inforapop** (7a) 7-1 *N Mitchell (xnb) 20s-7s; pulled hrd & jb; hld up in bunch; 6th 12; ld gng wl aft 16; v green & nrly unrideable at 2 out; blun last; sn hdd & imm eased*
[1178^F]	3	10	**Wise Examiner (IRE)** 11-2 *R Woollacott Ld to 5; lft in ld 7; clr brief 9; hdd 12; ld app 15 til hdd 3 out; sn wknd; lft 3rd & hmpd last*
[640^U]	4	8	**Audley Lass (IRE)** (5a) 3-1 *A Bateman Tchd 100/30; hld up; cl 5th 12; jmpd slow 14; wknd qckly aft 16*
[857^P]	5	6	**Frosty Jo** (5a) 50-1 *M Sweetland Tde; ld 5 til aft 6; mostly cl 2nd til ld agn 12 til app 14; wknd qckly aft 16*
[640^S]	F		**All-Inclusive (IRE)** (5a) 40-1 *J Scott Swtng; hld up in bunch; 5l 3rd 12; 4l 5th aft 16; 3rd & btn when fell last*
[1284^P]	R		**Vic's Girl** (5a) 150-1 *G Maundrell Prom but pulled v hrd; bolted to ld aft 6; rn out 7*
[933^J]	U		**Wink And Whisper** (12a) evensF *R Young 5/2-evens; settled in tch; 4th 12; jnd ldrs aft 16; 3rd & rdn when blun & ur 3 out*

OFFICIAL DISTANCES: 4l, 9l TIME: 6min 38.4 TOTE: £11.50 DF: £23.00

1373 Open Maiden 56&7yo (Div 2), 12st   7 ran

[732⁷]	1		**BUTTON UP BILL** 8-1 *H Thomas (xnb) 2 handlers; trckd ldrs; 3rd 12; ld 15 & 15l clr aft nxt; rdn unbalanced 3 out & lkd unstdy as horse rose at last; unchall*
[1101^P]	2	15	**Namron (IRE)** 5-4F *N Mitchell (xnb) 2s-5/4; tubed; ld til aft 2; chsd ldr til ld 12; hdd & hit 15; blun nxt; sn 15l bhnd & strugg*
[1241^P]	3	1½	**Early Morning** (7a) 12-1 *G Richards Chsd ldrs; 4th 12; 12l 3rd & strugg 14; 27l 3rd aft 16; no prog*
[874^P]	P		**Bogey Man** 6-1 *C Heard Tchd 8s; got loose padd; 2 handlers; sn last; 10l last when pu 13; broke knee; dead*
[1043^P]	P		**Can't Be Scrabble** 14-1 *R Emmett Oht; nt jw; towards rr; 8l 5th 12; 18l 4th & fdng 14; to & pu aft 16*
[1094^U]	P		**Goldoak** (7a) 3-1 *L Jefford (xnb) Jmpd slow 1; crawled over 2; to & pu 3*
[934^P]	P		**Tolepa (IRE)** (5a) 33-1 *L Tibbatts Bolted to ld aft 2 & sn 15l clr; wknd 11; hdd 12; jmpd lft nxt; 30l last 14; to whn crashed over 16 & pu*

OFFICIAL DISTANCES: 20l, 1l TIME: 6min 41.5s TOTE: £5.60 DF: £2.40

1374 Mixed Open, 12st   6 ran

[1239¹]	1		**MIZYAN (IRE)** 8-11F *Miss P Gundry Lw; cl up; ld 7; 8l clr 12; blun 13; mist nxt; 3l clr & rdn 3 out; stayed on wl & a hldng rival*
[1139¹]	2	7	**Iranos (FR)** (bl) 3-1 *L Jefford Tchd 7/2; lw; hld up; eff in 8l 2nd 12; tried to chall 16; 3l down & drvn app nxt; no imp*
[1132^F]	3	1½fs	**Malihabad (IRE)** (bl) 33-1 *J Barnes 2nd when jmpd slow 2; 4th & rdn 5; nt keen aft; 20l 4th when mist & drvn 12; to when lft 3rd 15*
[1096^P]	4	20	**Via Del Quatro (IRE)** (5a) 50-1 *J Young Tchd 100s; ld 3-7; 2nd 9; lost ground rap to 25l last 12; sn wl to; drvn wead*
[467^P]	P		**Comedy Gayle** 7-1 *Miss S Gaisford A detach last; hit 4; stumbled aft 6; 10l frm rest when pu 10*
[927^J]	R		**Hylters Chance (IRE)** (bl) 8-1 *D Alers-Hankey 25s-8s; ld to 3; disp ld brief 7; hit 8; outpcd in 12l 3rd 12; poor 3rd when rn out & hit wing 15*

OFFICIAL DISTANCES: 8l, dist TIME: 6min 16.7s TOTE: £1.50 DF: £1.10

1375 Restricted (Div 1), 12st - 17J   10 ran

[847²]	1		**WONFORD BOY** 11-10F *K Heard Tchd 5/4; drpd out last to 9; impd to 6th 13; cl 3rd aft 16; ld app last; rdn & r.o wl*

[1206⁴]	2	1¼	**Melody Princess** (5a) 10-1 D Alers-Hankey *20s-10s; handy; 3rd 7; 5th 13; cl 4th & u.p aft 16; outpcd by 2 out; rallied last & snatched 2nd*
[876ᴾ]	3	d ht	**Loxley-Lad** 33-1 G Richards *Hld up towards rr; impd to 4th 13 & lft 2nd nxt; ld aft 15 til app last; one pce & lost 2nd nr fin*
[1240⁵]	4	2	**Belski** 16-1 R Woollacott *Tchd 20s; handy; 4th 9; 2nd 13; lft in ld nxt; hdd aft 16; one pce 2 out*
[1095⁶]	5	10	**Bridge House Boy** 10-1 A Oliver *(xnb) 16s-10s; hld up & bhnd; 7th 13; prog nxt to cl 5th aft 16; wknd*
[926³]	6	6	**Hemero** (IRE) (tt) 3-1 A Honeyball *6s-3s; midfield; eff 11 to 7l 3rd 13; cl 6th aft 16; wknd tame*
[1095¹]	7	1½	**Crosswell Star** (IRE) 20-1 J Scott *Tchd 40s; swtng; tk keen hld & prom; mists 4 & 7; drpd back; 7th 9; 15l last when rn wide aft 13; no ch aft*
[1309ᴾ]	U		**Cefn Woodsman** 66-1 Miss K Lovelace *Tchd 100s; tdy nt qckn*
[1304ᵁ]	P		**Mountain-Linnet** 100-1 Mrs J Reed *Prom; lft in ld 5 til aft 6; 8th & wkng 13; mist 15; t.o & pu 3 out*
[853⁴]	U		**Picard** (IRE) (bl) 6-1 Miss L Hawkins *Tchd 7s; swtng; handy; ld aft 6 til hit 14 & ur*

OFFICIAL DISTANCES: 1l, ¾l   TIME: 6min 29.6s   TOTE: £2.70   DF: £22.40
Fence 12 omitted - fallen rider

1376 Restricted (Div 2), 12st

14 ran

[1042⁵]	1		**FRIAR WADDON** 6-1 Miss J Cumings *Opened 7s, tchd 8s; hld up towards rr til prog 9; 3l 5th 12; went 2nd aft 16; ld aft 2 out; sn clr; rdly*
[1140²]	2	5	**Jabiru** (IRE) 13-8F D Alers-Hankey *Tchd 2s; prom but nt a fluent; 4th 12; chall 15; ld 3 out til aft nxt; drvn & nt qckn*
[1140ᵁ]	3	12	**Pallingham Lad** (IRE) 14-1 M Miller *Chsd ldrs; 6th 12; cl 5th aft 16; sn wknd*
[1058²]	4	10	**Best Bitter** 4-1 A Charles-Jones *Lw; hld up in midfield; hdwy 10 to 3rd 12; went 2nd & hit 15; ld aft nxt; hdd 3 out; drvn & wknd qckly*
[847³]	5	12	**Born Natural** (IRE) (5a) 25-1 R Woollacott *Hld up; hdwy to 2nd 7; ld 8 til aft 16; hdd & wknd rap 3 out*
[1042⁵]	6	3	**Knock Star** (IRE) 6-1 S Partridge *14s-6s; rr div; 8th 12; no ch frm 15*
[1061⁴]	7	runin	**Another Junior** (IRE) 25-1 R Young *Unruly when mounted; prom brief; drpd back 11th 9; nvr gng wl aft; t.o 15*
[1136⁵]	P		**Another Bula** (IRE) 50-1 B O'Doherty *Ld to 5; wkng when mist 11; 9th nxt; t.o & pu 16*
[1095⁷]	P		**Chilli Jo** (tt) 100-1 E Chanin *Swtng; prom; 3rd 5; wknd 9; 12th 12; t.o & pu 15*
[1061²]	U		**Lord Of The Rings** 14-1 Miss C Tizzard *Last pr & sn detach; poor last when rfo front 14*
[1135ᵁ]	P		**Lynphord Girl** (5a) 50-1 J Barnes *Hdwy to ld 5-8; 2nd 12; nt r.o frm 14; rem when hung bad lft & pu 15*
[850ᴾ]	P		**Maybridge Lady** (5a) 7-1 N Mitchell *Towards rr; 10th 12; lost tch & pu 15; lame*
[1140²]	P		**Nearly All Right** 33-1 C White *A towards rr; lost tch aft 13; pu 3 out; v lame*
[1176⁵]	U		**Prudent Miner** (IRE) (7ow) 40-1 R Skinner *Lost tch & rdn 4; wl adrift when lost hind legs & ur bend aft 6*

OFFICIAL DISTANCES: 4l, 20l   TIME: 6min 21.7s   TOTE: £9.20   DF: £7.00

Essex

High Easter (LH 9F,19J) Sat, 6 May (GOOD to FIRM, GOOD in places)

1377 Hunt, 12st

4 ran

[840ᴾ]	1		**AEOLIAN** (4x,7ow) 11-10F R Gill *Imm detach; 2 11l last 5; went 3rd 10; no prog til stayed on frm 15; still 3rd at last; r.o to ld nr fin (horse & rdr both retired)*
[1113ᴾ]	2	1½	**Salmon Mead** (IRE) (4x) (bl) 3-1 Miss N Barnes *Trckd ldr til ld 6; 8l clr aft 13; in comm til jmpd slow 2 out; still ld nxt; hdd last 25yds*
[1037⁴]	3	6	**Peanuts Pet** (4x) 2-1 Miss H Barnard *Ld; jmpd slow 5; hdd nxt; outpcd by ldr 13; clsd agn 2 out; ev ch last; wknd flat*
[1181ᴾ]	P		**Master Page** 11-1 R Fowler *(xnb) Mist 2; cl 3rd to 6; sn wknd; mist 9; last nxt; t.o & pu 15*

OFFICIAL DISTANCES: 1½l, 5l   TIME: 6min 44.0s   TOTE: £2.10   DF: £1.80

1378 Confined

10 ran

[1184¹]	1		**NIBBLE** 7-2 G Cooper *Settled last quartet; plenty to do 14; gd prog nxt to jn ldrs 16; disp ld 2 out; sn ld; drvn & stayed on wl*
[940¹]	2	2½	**Fair Exchange** 4-5F P Taiano *Swtng; jmpd rt; settled mid-div; prog to ld 9; jmpd slow & hdd 15; eff to disp ld 2 out; hrd rdn & btn last; hung rt run-in*
[74¹]	3	1	**Tell Tale** (IRE) 8-1 A Harvey *A.p; prsd ldr 10; ld 15; jnd 2 out; sn hdd; kpt on one pce u.p*

[1286⁶]	4	20	**Ballydesmond (IRE)** (bl) 14-1 K Edmunds *Tde; ldng trio til easily outpcd frm 15; no ch aft 3 out; fin tired*
[1112ᴿ]	5	20	**Take A Flyer (IRE)** 33-1 C Ward *Reluct to line up; a last quartet; jmpd slow 9; lost tch aft 14; t.o*
[1266ᴾ]	P		**Emsee-H** 10-1 Miss Z Turner *Ld 2-4; cl up til pu aft 11; dead*
[1286ᵁ]	P		**Fire On Ice (IRE)** 5-1 A Coe *Ld 4-9; stdly wknd; wl bhnd frm 13; pu 3 out*
[936ᴾ]	P		**Regal Bay** 25-1 W Wales *Rr group; lost tch rap & jmpd slow frm 11; t.o & pu 14*
[1114ᵁ]	P		**Royal Action** 25-1 P Chinery *(xnb) A last quartet; wl bhnd aft 14; pu 2 out*
[1114ᵁ]	P		**Youcat (IRE)** (bl) 25-1 N Bloom *Trckd ldrs til lost tch 14; jmpd v slow 16; pu nxt*

OFFICIAL DISTANCES: 2l, ¾l **TIME:** 6min 30.0s **TOTE:** £3.50 **DF:** £2.00

1379 Restricted, 12st
9 ran

[1181ᶠ]	1		**HEATHBURN (IRE)** 9-4F N Bloom *Ww; in tch in rr; stdy prog 14; pushed along to chse ldr 3 out; sn clsd; ld sn aft 2 out; stayed on str*
[1038⁴]	2	10	**Mackoy (IRE)** 20-1 C Ward *Trckd ldrs; prog to 8l 2nd frm 15-3 out; sn btn; kpt on agn to 2nd aft last*
[1333⁶]	3	10	**The Millmaster (IRE)** (bl) 5-1 T Lane *2 handlers; ld; drew 8l clr app 15; tired & collared sn aft 2 out; btn when propped on landing last; wknd & lost 2nd flat; fin slow*
[791⁵]	4	5	**Vulgan Prince** 12-1 R Barrett *Chsd ldrs in 3rd/4th; pushed along ½way; outpcd aft 14; plodded on*
[1181⁵]	5	3	**Bakmalad** 25-1 Miss A Stennett *Last pr; detach frm 6; 15l bhnd rest 10; no ch aft; plodded on*
[1111ᴾ]	6	10	**Rathkeal (IRE)** 33-1 D Parravani *A rr; jmpd slow 2; rmdrs 11; bhnd frm 13; no prog aft*
[1181ᴾ]	P		**Monere (IRE)** 16-1 G Cooper *Chsd ldrs in 3rd/4th til wknd 9; wl bhnd when pu 2 out*
[940⁴]	P		**Skinsey Finnegan (IRE)** 7-2 A Coe *Hld up in last pr; no prog 12; sn lost tch; t.o & pu 3 out*
[845¹]	P		**Uncle Buck (IRE)** 5-2 P Taiano *Tk keen hld; trckd ldr to 15; sn wknd; no ch when pu 2 out*

OFFICIAL DISTANCES: 10l, 10l **TIME:** 6min 33.0s **TOTE:** £4.00 **DF:** £18.50

1380 Ladies Open
9 ran

[1183²]	1		**CACHE FLEUR (FR)** 7-4 Mrs G d'Angibau *Chsd ldrs; pushed along ½way; eff to chse ldr 3 out; ld nxt; 2l ahd last; just hld on; game*
[725¹]	2	½	**Baby Whale (IRE)** (5a) 6-4F Miss C Grissell *Trckd ldrs gng wl; cl up when nt fluent 15, 16 & 3 out; 4l 3rd nxt; r.o to chall last; just hld*
[1211¹]	3	2	**Island Vision (IRE)** 10-1 Mrs J Hughes *In tch in rr; 10l 6th 13; r.o frm nxt; 6l 4th 2 out; kpt on; nrst fin*
[1113⁵]	4	7	**Mill O'The Rags (IRE)** 9-1 Mrs A Hays *Ld to 2 out; wknd app last*
[1113²]	5	7	**Larry The Lamb (IRE)** 10-1 Miss T Hayter *Rdr calling cabs at many fncs; in tch in rr; outpcd & 20l 7th whn nrly f.o 14; r.o frm 3 out; nvr nrr*
[1286⁷]	6	½	**Ann's Ambition** 25-1 Miss C Fryer *Lw; chsd ldr to 3 out; sn lost tch & btn*
[1183⁴]	7	runin	**Ballyedward (IRE)** 33-1 Miss H Pewter *Rmdrs aft 1; in tch to 6; sn drpd out; t.o*
[937ᵁ]	P		**Alfredo Garcia (IRE)** 10-1 Miss N Barnes *8th when jmpd awkward 4; same & detach ½way; t.o & pu 14*
[677⁵]	P		**Cill Churnain (IRE)** 20-1 Miss R Barrow *Wl in tch; mist 15; imm gave up; pu last*

OFFICIAL DISTANCES: ¾l, 5l **TIME:** 6min 28.0s **TOTE:** £2.40 **DF:** £2.10

1381 Mens Open, 12st
8 ran

[1112¹]	1		**DAWN ALERT (IRE)** (7x) 5-2 W Wales *Trckd ldrs; eff to jn ldr 14; ld on inner nxt; rdn 2 out; 2l up last; just hld on u.p*
[1265²]	2	s hd	**Copper Thistle (IRE)** (7x) 2-5F R Hunnisett *Ld at gd pce but nvr more than 2l up; jnd by wnr 14; hdd on inner nxt; cl 2nd & rdn 2 out; 2l down last; rallied game flat; just failed*
[1006⁷]	3	25	**Cormeen Lord (IRE)** 33-1 P Taiano *Prom; prsd ldr 10 til aft 13; 10l 3rd & btn 15; stdly lost tch*
[1185¹]	4	20	**Mr Magget (IRE)** 7-1 N Bloom *10s-7s; trckd ldrs til stdly lost tch frm 9; disp 22l 4th aft 13; no prog; t.o*
[1006⁷]	5	2½	**Limosa** (5a) 33-1 R Barrett *Last & sn detach; 28l 7th 13; t.o aft*
[937ᴾ]	P		**Lord Knox (IRE)** 33-1 A Coe *Prsd ldr to 10; sn wknd; disp 22l 4th aft 13; t.o & pu 3 out*
[1035ᴾ]	P		**On The Beer (IRE)** 33-1 A Braithwaite *Rr; nt fluent 7 & 8; sn lost tch; t.o last when pu 14*
[1156ᴾ]	P		**Roscolvin (IRE)** 33-1 R Fowler *Hld up; lsng tch in 12l 6th 13; 24l 6th aft 13; t.o & pu 2 out*

OFFICIAL DISTANCES: hd, 10l **TIME:** 6min 22.0s **TOTE:** £3.30 **DF:** £2.50

1382 Open Maiden (Div 1), 12st   10 ran

[1039²]	1		**GLENCLOY (IRE)** 4-1 A Coe *2 handlers; trckd ldr; ld 7; made rest; mist 12; gng best 3 out; prsd last; rdn & stayed on*
[1292²]	2	2	**Out Of Actons (IRE)** (5ow) 5-1 C Jarvis *Ld to 7; chsd wnr aft; mist 9; 3l down & rdn 2 out; rallied & ch last; kpt on und vigorous bumping; a hld*
[1115³]	3	30	**Clifford Bay (IRE)** 5-4F A Sansome *2s-5/4; oht; trckd ldrs; mist 11; eff to disp 3l 2 out 3 out; imm wknd; fin slow*
[1039³]	F		**Airborne Blue** 20-1 K Sheppard *Mists; w ldrs; cl 4th when fell 15*
	R		**Bright Torino (IRE)** (12a) 8-1 N Bloom *Bit bckwd; school in rr til rn out 7; jmpd nxt*
	P		**Camden Loch (IRE)** (7a) 12-1 W Wales *Trckd ldng group to 4; sn drpd to rr; pu 12; school*
[759⁶]	P		**Cicero's Law (IRE)** 10-1 P Chinery *2 handlers; trckd ldrs til wknd rap & pu 11*
	P		**Craighardie** (7a) 12-1 A Harvey *Fat; jmpd slow; sn detach; pu 11; school*
[1292³]	P		**Father's Joy** (5a) 12-1 P Millington *Mists; wl in tch til wknd frm 16; t.o 4th when pu last (originally plcd 4th by Judge)*
[1180⁴]	P		**Lazy Acres (IRE)** 16-1 C Lawson *Tde; sn detach in rr; t.o & pu 14*

OFFICIAL DISTANCES: 1½l, 20l **TIME:** 6min 39.0s **TOTE:** £5.50 **DF:** £5.90

1383 Open Maiden (Div 2), 12st   10 ran

[1291ᵖ]	1		**ALWAYS TRYING** (7a) (bl) 7-1 A Sansome *Cl up; eff to chall 3 out; ld brief app nxt; sn drvn; 2l down last; kpt on slow to pass hanging rival nr fin*
	2	½	**Sweet William** 8-1 A Harvey *Prom; trckd ldr 10; ld 15-nxt; ld agn aft 3 out; hdd brief app nxt; drvn 2l clr app last; hung bad rt & wknd flat; hdd nr fin*
[1270²]	3	20	**Timothy George (IRE)** 14-1 P Millington *A in tch; prog to ld 16; hdd aft nxt; wknd; fin slow*
[1040ᵖ]	4	runin	**Henpecked (IRE)** 20-1 A Coe *(xnb) Ld to 2; ld 4-15; sn wknd; t.o*
[1180⁷]	P		**Life Of A Star (IRE)** 4-1 A Braithwaite *(xnb) Hld up in rr; 7th & just in tch when mist 13; no prog nxt; t.o & pu 2 out*
	P		**Midnight Royal** (12a) 12-1 G Pewter *(xnb) 2 handlers; sn prom; chsd ldr 7-10; sn wknd; t.o & pu 14*
[828³]	U		**Newick Park** (7a) 5-2F Miss C Grissell *3s-5/2; trckd ldr; 4th frm 4 til jinked & ur tk-off side of 6; horse tk fnce*
[1287ᵖ]	P		**Vulpin De Laugere (FR)** (5ow) (bl) 3-1 C Jarvis *Pushed up to ld 2 til rn wide bend aft 4; drpd to last 7; t.o & pu 14*
[1040²]	P		**Wise Point (IRE)** 25-1 G Lush *(xnb) In tch in rr to 12; wknd aft 14; pu nxt*
[942⁵]	P		**Yashwell (IRE)** 4-1 P Taiano *10s-4s; rr; jmpd rt to 3; prog & prom 10; sn lost plce; jmpd rt 11 & 12; lost tch 15; pu 3 out*

OFFICIAL DISTANCES: 1l, 15l **TIME:** 6min 45.5s

South Cornwall

Trebudannon (LH 7F,20J) Sat, 6 May (FIRM, GOOD to FIRM patches)

1384 Hunt, 12st   5 ran

[930⁶]	1		**JEEPERS (IRE)** 4-5F D McKenna *Tk str hld; made all; jw; pushed out when prsd frm 2 out; rdr's 1st wnr*
[1258ᵖ]	2	2½	**King Of Cairo** 8-1 I Hambley *Tchd 10s; hld up in tch; hdwy to 2nd 15; eff & rdn 3 out; ev ch nxt; nt qckn*
[1263ᵖ]	3	2½	**Horton** 12-1 S Parkin *In tch; cl 2nd 5-12; lost plce 14; 1l1 3rd 15; no ch w ldrs; tk 3rd app last*
[1186²]	4	2	**Bedtime Pixie** (bl) 11-2 D Stephens (Devon) *Swtng profuse; prom on inner; cl 3rd ½way; outpcd 15; wl hld in 3rd 17; reluct & lost 3rd app last*
[1186ᵁ]	P		**Beaumont (U)** 3-1 T Cole *Jb; jmpd v slow 2 & lost 10l; bad mist 4; mdrs; bhnd when pu 7*

OFFICIAL DISTANCES: 3l, 3l **TIME:** 6min 25.4s
An informal enquiry was held into the running and riding of Beaumont who pulled up early in the race; the rider's explanation that the horse was jumping badly, did not enjoy the firm ground and felt wrong was accepted

1385 Confined, 12st   5 ran

[1175³]	1		**DANCING RANGER** 7-2 Richard Darke *Tchd 4s; lw; ld to 3; stayed wl in tch; chsd ldr frm 16; eff & ld on inner aft 2 out; sn clr; comf*
[1045⁴]	2	5	**Bendor Mark** (3x) 4-6F Mrs M Hand *Ld 3; nt a fluent; went 5l clr aft 17; jnd 2 out; no ex whn hdd*
[1041⁵]	3	2½	**Night Time** 9-2 G Shenkin *Lw; rr & jmpd slow 1; last but in tch ½way; went 4th 15; kpt on u.p; nt rch ldrs*

	4	10	**Broughton's Port** 14-1 T Dennis Rcd keen & hld up; prog to 2nd 9; wknd & lost tch 15
[849F]	P		**Baron Knayber** 8-1 I Hambley Prog to cl 3rd 13; rmdr nxt; 2nd brief 15; blun & lost ground 16; hld in 3rd when jmpd slow 3 out; pu nxt

OFFICIAL DISTANCES: 2l, 4l **TIME:** 6min 17.3s

1386 Ladies Open   3 ran

[851³]	1		**JUST BERT (IRE)** 1-2F Miss T Cave Ld 1; cl 3rd & slt mist 3; jw aft; hld up til disp ld on inner 12; flew fnces 15-17 & sn 5l clr; in comm 3 out; eased cl home; comf
[852⁹]	2	8	**Solomans Sister** (5a) 9-4 Mrs M Hand Tchd 5/2; swtng; cl 2nd; stumbled slt bend aft 14; cl up til outpcd & rdn 16; no ch w wnr aft
[1187¹]	P		**Luney River** (5a) 6-1 Miss L Gardner Lw; ld 2; jnd 12-14; sn hdd; lost tch stdly frm 16; fdg & dism flat

OFFICIAL DISTANCE: 7l **TIME:** 6min 09.8s

1387 Mens Open, 12st   4 ran

[1188P]	1		**BALDHU CHANCE** 8-13F A Ede Jw; made most; in comm frm 3 out; easy
[1257⁵]	2	5	**It's Not My Fault (IRE)** (7x) 6-1 Adam Jones 10s-6s; went 2nd 12; eff & ld aft 14-16; cl up & ev ch til rdn 3 out; no ex frm nxt
[1136⁴]	3	20	**Romalito** 3-1 N Harris In tch; cl 3rd when hit 14; 5l 3rd when blun nxt; sn drpd away
[1188P]	P		**Forest Musk (IRE)** 6-1 I Hambley Pulled hrd & hung lft; mist 7; rap hdwy to 2nd 8; disp ld 9-10; cl 4th & gng str when pu 14

OFFICIAL DISTANCES: 4l, 15l **TIME:** 6min 04.0s
The stewards interviewed the rider of Forest Musk; they accepted his explanation that he was too tired to go on as the horse had hung and taken such a fierce hold; they considered the horse should no longer race and warned the owner about any recurrence

1388 Intermediate, 12st   4 ran

[1041⁴]	1		**NO MORE NICE GUY (IRE)** 5-1 Mrs M Hand Hld up in tch; hdwy 16; cl 3rd til chall on inner 2 out; switched app last; r.o to ld last stride; game
[1097²]	2	hd	**Chasing Daisy** (5a) 2-1 J Snowden Tde; rcd keen; ld/disp & gng wl; ld aft 2 out; lkd wnr til drifted lft run-in; faltered last 50yds; hdd on post; bit unlucky
[1186¹]	3	3	**Arble March** (5a) 13-2 N Harris Ld/disp; slt ld 16 til jnd & mist 2 out; sn wknd
[1261³]	U		**Swift Venture (IRE)** 10-11F Richard Darke Tchd 6/4; swtng; hld up; cl 3rd w wnr blun & ur 9

OFFICIAL DISTANCES: nk, 2l **TIME:** 6min 03.3s

1389 Restricted, 12st   7 ran

[1043⁴]	1		**TRAVEL BY LAND** 6-1 Miss T Cave Prom til lost plce 9; rap hdwy to ld on inner (vital) 14; r.o wl when prsd frm 2 out; wl rdn
[406P]	2	1½	**Silver Man** 9-2 Mrs M Hand Lw; hld up in tch; went 2nd 16; str chall 2 out; ev ch last; nt qckn run-in
[1042P]	3	2½	**County Bash** (5a) 8-1 Miss L Gardner Lw; prom; cl 4th 10; outpcd 15; went 3rd 3 out; r.o; nt rch ldrs
[1176³]	4	15	**The Ugly Duckling** 4-1 Richard Darke Swtng; slt ld til hdd 14; cl 3rd w hit 17; wknd
[1245¹]	5	12	**Regal Wolf** (bl) 5-4F J Snowden Sn prom; hld up in tch; cl 3rd 12; ev ch til outpcd 16; no ch frm 3 out
[1186U]	P		**North Coast Girl** (5a) 16-1 A Ede Rr; blun bad 2; in tch towards rr to 14; last when pu nxt
[729P]	P		**Pixie In Purple (IRE)** 14-1 D Stephens (Devon) Hld up; cl 5th 10; hdwy 12; went 3l 3rd aft 17; sn wknd; pu 2 out

OFFICIAL DISTANCES: 1½l, 2l **TIME:** 6min 16.1s

1390 Open Maiden (Div 1), 12st   7 ran

[849P]	1		**PICK-N-CRUISE** (5a) 12-1 D Stephens (Devon) (xnb) Went 3rd 8; ld 12; 1½l up & edged rt 2 out; pckd last; r.o wl
[1186³]	2	1	**Royal Chip** 7-4F T Cole Opened 3s; tubed; swtng; tk keen hld; chsd ldr to 11; stdd & in tch til went 2nd 17; chall u.p frm 3 out; ev ch til no ex flat
[1131³]	3	25	**High Sturt** (5a) 4-1 J Snowden Lw; cl 4th 10; hdwy to 2nd & gng wl 14; cl up til wknd qckly 17; no ch aft
[1049P]	P		**Call Me Dickins** (bl,tt) 8-1 Miss A Barnett Sn bhnd & strugg; jmpd slow; fnce bhnd 12; t.o & pu last
[563P]	R		**Emerald Ectasy** (5a) 10-1 I Hambley Rn out, clipped wing & ur 3

[874R] P   **Golden Jester** (5a) 12-1 **Miss J Congdon** *(xnb) Pulled hrd & rn green; clr ld frm 2; hit 6; hdd 12; wknd rap aft 14; jmpd slow 15; pu nxt*

[934P] P   **Hendra Chieftain** 6-1 **N Harris** *Towards rr; mist 4; in tch til jmpd slow 8; 5th 13; rdn & lost ground 16; t.o & pu last*

OFFICIAL DISTANCES: 1l, dist **TIME:** 6min 12.4s

B For Business (Miss L Gardner, 7-1) was withdrawn not under orders - bolted with rider before start; Rule 4 deduction 15p in the pound

1391 Open Maiden (Div 2), 12st   8 ran

[1048⁴] 1   **AMAZING HILL (IRE)** 7-4F **Mrs R Morris** *Tchd 2s; lw; hld up; hdwy 12; stdy prog to 3rd but bit to do 17; disp 10l 2nd 3 out; str rn to chall last; ld last 100yds; rdr's 1st wnr*

[956P] 2   1½   **La Tormenta (IRE)** (5a) 3-1 **N Harris** *Tried to make all; went 5l clr 17; drvn 10l clr nxt; still 2l up & rdn 2 out; jnd last; no ex last 100yds*

[657F] 3   15   **Broad Ink** 5-1 **D McKenna** *Went 2nd 7; mist 12; 2½l 2nd when blun 16; wknd; lft poor 3rd at last*

[538F] U   **Baldhu Jay Arr** 7-1 **A Ede** *In tch; cl 3rd & gng wl 12; outpcd 15; hdwy to disp 2nd 3 out; kpt on; 3l 3rd & hld when blun & ur last*

[932P] R   **Helismad** (7a) 10-1 **I Hambley** *Bit bckwd; rr; jmpd sticky 2; rn out nxt*

[857P] U   **Knap Hand** (7a) 10-1 **Miss L Gardner** *Prom; cl 3rd 8; in tch in 4th when blun & ur 14*

[934R] R   **Miltown Castle** 9-1 **Miss A Barnett** *2nd when rn off course bef 3*

[1186P] P   **Safara** 16-1 **T Cole** *Last frm 7; lost tch 12; t.o & pu 3 out*

OFFICIAL DISTANCES: 1l, 17l **TIME:** 6min 20.0s

Surrey Union

Peper Harow (LH 8F,18J) Sat, 6 May (GOOD, GOOD to SOFT in places)

1392 Hunt   4 ran

[1243²] 1   **BIT OF AN IDIOT** (3x) 7-2 **D Slattery** *Pulling & a gng wl; trckd ldrs in 3-4l 3rd; chall app 3 out; qcknd to ld app nxt; r.o wl; wl rdn*

[1104⁴] 2   6   **Lord Ellangowan (IRE)** (3x) 3-1 **D Dunsdon** *Ld to 8; drpd to 2nd nxt; 2l down 13; ld app 3 out; sn hdd & nt qckn; no ch when hit last*

[572²] 3   8   **Time Enough (IRE)** (3x) (bl) 4-7F **P Townsley** *Pulling; cl 2nd til ld 8; 5l clr 12; 2l up nxt; hdd app 3 out; qckly dem 3rd & v one-pcd*

[888³] 4   fence **Sarenacare (IRE)** (tt) 16-1 **A Hickman** *A 4th; in tch til hit 10; lost tch stdly aft; bhnd when jmpd slow 14; t.o*

OFFICIAL DISTANCES: 6l, 8l **TIME:** 7min 00.0s **TOTE:** £3.20 **DF:** £4.90

1393 Restricted, 12st - 15J   15 ran

[711¹] 1   **BELVENTO (IRE)** 9-4F **D Dunsdon** *Confid rdn & a gng wl; on heels of ldrs; 2l 3rd 7; jmpd to ld 13; sn in comm; r.o wl when prsd brief 2 out*

[1104ᵁ] 2   2   **Oxendale** 12-1 **P Bull** *Swtng; tk str hld; ld to 4; prsd ldr aft; cl 2nd & ev ch 2 out; no ex nxt*

[894⁵] 3   1   **Brodante King (IRE)** (bl) 3-1 **P Cowley** *6l 7th 4; hdwy 5 to ld 7-13; 1l 3rd nxt; prsd ldrs aft; no ex 2 out*

[1172¹] 4   3   **Sliabh Foy (IRE)** 16-1 **F Marshall** *A.p; 2nd/3rd til ld 4-6; cl up aft; 6l 4th 15; r.o; nt able to chall*

[1213¹] 5   10   **General Jackie (IRE)** 20-1 **A Hickman** *Chsd ldrs; mostly 5l/6th; 10l 5th & outpcd 13; chsd ldrs vain aft*

[1243³] 6   30   **Silver Hill** (5a) 16-1 **Miss B Fear** *Mid-div; 15l 7th app 11; lft 25l 6th 14; plodded on*

[1242³] 7   20   **Ngala (IRE)** (5a) 20-1 **H Tett** *Imm rr & nvr gng wl; plugged rnd; t.o 11*

[1243P] P   **Amaranthine** (5a) 33-1 **Mrs J Butler** *(xnb) Sn rr & strugg to go pce; nvr btr than 9/10th; virt t.o by 10; pushed along 12; no resp; wl bhnd when pu 15*

[575P] U   **Bang On Target** (bl) 33-1 **J Stephens** *Imm rr; last 5; ur 6*

[575P] P   **Clean Sweep** (1ow) 20-1 **P Hickman** *Hit 1; sn towards rr & strugg to go pce; wl bhnd when pu 13*

[575P] U   **Hightech Touch** 16-1 **D Dennis** *Mid-div; mostly 6/7th; outpcd frm 11; 15l 6th when blun & ur 14*

      P   **Lady Goodwin** (5a) 20-1 **P York** *Imm rr; sn last & jmpd novicey; t.o when pu 13*

[274⁴] F   **Newtown Rambler (IRE)** 16-1 **Mrs C Ford** *Mid-div; 10l 6th when fell 8*

[1104ᵁ] P   **Perripage** (vis) 25-1 **Miss A Sansom** *Cl 4/5th to 7; wknd & drpd to rr 10; wl bhnd 12; pu 13*

[1019¹]   U   **Take The Brush (IRE)** (5a) 4-1 **R Lawther** Imm rr & nvr gng wl; ur 5 (rdr lkd to bail out bef fnce)

OFFICIAL DISTANCES: 3l, ½l **TIME:** 6min 45.0s **TOTE:** £3.20; places £1.60,£2.30,£2.60 **DF:** £21.20
Fences 4, 10 & 16 omitted - rabbit holes

1394 Mens Open, 12st
12 ran

[1246³]	1		**EQUITY PLAYER** 14-1 **P Bull** Hld up in mid-div; hdwy to 8l 3rd 11 & 3l 3rd 13; jnd ldr 2 out; ld last; drvn & r.o flat
[1210¹]	2	1	**Prime Course (IRE)** (4x) 5-2F **C Gordon** Trckd ldng pr; 8l 3rd 7; went 2l 3rd 13; blun 14; chall aft 3 out; ev ch til no ex cl home
[1279²]	3	¾	**You Said It (IRE)** 4-1 **D Crosse** Cl 2nd til ld 6; sn 4l up; 2l ahd 13; jnd 2 out; w wnr when blun last; no ex & dem 3rd cl home
[1057ᶠ]	4	8	**Celtic Token** (1ow) 33-1 **D Birkmyre** Chsd ldrs in 4/5th mostly; hit 3 & 4 & rdr waving; hdwy aft 12; 12l 5th 13; 10l 4th & no imp 3 out; kpt on one pce
[1208²]	P		**Boll Weevil** 25-1 **Stuart Robinson** Ld to 5; chsd ldr & clr of rest til wknd v rap 13; 15l 5th & exhaust when ploughed thro 15; imm pu
[1244ᴾ]	P		**Catwalker (IRE)** 33-1 **S Cobden** Imm strugg in rr; mists; wl bhnd when pu 15
[883⁶]	P		**Cut A Niche** 16-1 **R Lawther** Mid-div & nd; 6/7th & chsd ldrs vain frm 12; wknd 15; 20l last when pu 2 out
[824⁷]	P		**How Friendly** 20-1 **A Hickman** Sn towards rr; t.o 12; pu 13
[825¹]	U		**Kenny Davis (IRE)** 3-1 **P Blagg** Hld up wl off pce; 25l 9th 10; gd prog to 15l 6th 13; rap hdwy to 5l 4th aft 3 out; 3l 4th & clsng when blun & ur 2 out; prob unlucky
[1167ᵁ]	P		**Rose King** 16-1 **T Hills** A rr & sn wl off pce; nvr btr than 9th; t.o & pu 15
	P		**Sprintfayre** 16-1 **P York** Sn outpcd in rr; t.o & pu 15
[1212ᵁ]	P		**Tooth Pick (IRE)** 7-2 **J Hawksfield** A last trio; nvr gng wl; t.o & pu 13

OFFICIAL DISTANCES: ½l, ½l **TIME:** 6min 45.0s **TOTE:** £28.50; places £5.50,£1.70,£2.00 **DF:** £1.10

1395 Greig Middleton Ladies Open
10 ran

[1170⁴]	1		**FOR WILLIAM** 25-1 **Miss J Grant** V positively rdn; cl 5/6th; eff aft 12; ld 14-3 out; releg 3rd app nxt; rallied & chall agn 2 out; level flat
[1171³]	2	½	**Nordic Spree (IRE)** 14-1 **Miss A Goschen** Prom; cl 2nd/3rd til drpd to 4l 4th aft 3 out; eff to 2l 4th at last; r.o str flat; just failed
[1209²]	3	½	**Velka** (5a) 12-1 **Miss P Ellison** Ld to 10; drpd to 6l 7th nxt; hdwy to ld agn brief 13; prsd ldrs til chall & level last; just outpcd flat
[326⁴]	4	1	**Pride Of Kashmir** 3-1F **Mrs C Ford** Hld up in tch; 4l 5th 10; hdwy 12; prsd ldrs 15; ld 3 out; jnd nxt; level & ev ch last; no ex flat
[1107¹]	5	8	**Danger Flynn (IRE)** (4x) 7-2 **Miss C Holliday** Swtng profuse; handy; 5l 5th 10; chsd ldrs frm 12; wknd to 6th & no ch 15; one pce
[1242²]	6	10	**Mendip Prince (IRE)** 9-1 **Miss J Tett** Rr & nrly ur 1; sn cl up; 2l 2nd 10; ld 11-12; hdd app nxt; outpcd 14; last & no ch app 3 out
[1170¹]	P		**Andrelot** (4x) (bl) 4-1 **Miss H Grissell** Imm last; nvr gng or jmpng wl; sn t.o; pu 16
[1145²]	P		**My Best Man** (bl) 7-2 **Mrs T Hill** Cl up in mid-div when jmpd slow 4; lost tch rap & nvr gng wl aft; 15l 8th when pu 7
[1108ᴾ]	P		**Primitive King** 6-1 **Mrs E Coveney** W ldrs; mostly cl 3rd/4th til chall 14; ½l 2nd 15; prsd ldrs til blun 3 out; wknd v qckly; 10l 5th when pu 2 out
[1211ᵁ]	R		**Silk Vestments** (5a) 16-1 **Mrs D Rowell** Tk wrg hld; cl up in mid-div; nt much room & rn out 4

OFFICIAL DISTANCES: ½l, ½l **TIME:** 6min 54.0s **TOTE:** £7.30; places £2.10,£7.50,£1.80 **DF:** £2.70
The rider of For William was fined £50 for misuse of the whip, hitting the horse in the wrong place and causing it to be badly marked

1396 Open Maiden (Div 1), 12st
10 ran

[1245⁴]	1		**GRAPHIC DESIGNER (IRE)** 8-1 **C Gordon** Chsd ldrs in 8-10l 3rd; eff 12; 4l 3rd 13; ld aft 15; 4l up & in comm when hit 3 out; sn wl clr; hit last; unimpressive
[984²]	2	15	**Uk Eurolad** 2-1F **T Hills** (xnb) Ld; 8l up 4; 2l ahd 12; hdd aft 15; qckly lost tch; no ch frm 3 out
	3	3	**Strawberry Blossom** (5a) 8-1 **P York** Pulling; trckd ldr; 8l 2nd & mist 4; blun 6; 2l 2nd 12; dem 3rd app 3 out; wknd & no ch aft; promising
[1245²]	4	fence	**Mountain Tae (IRE)** 5-2 **R Green** Hit 1; rcd in 5th & sn lost tch w ldrs; lft 4th aft 6; 25l 4th 12; plugged on; nd
	5	30	**Clifton Match** (5a,1ow) 16-1 **J Casemore** Ood-looking; sn lost tch; rem 5th 7; fnce adrift by 13; cont wl t.o
[1104⁶]	6	2	**Bit Of A Do** (tt) 5-1 **D Slattery** Sn wl bhnd in last quartet; rr 7; t.o
[309ᴾ]	7	15	**One More Man (IRE)** (7ow) 6-1 **W Goulding** Qckly outpcd in rr w rdr leaning back; detach in last quartet 5; sn hopelessly t.o

[679F]	8	fence	**Sleipnir** 16-1 C Sherry _Jmpd appalling; lft last 7; t.o 14; ploughed on slow bet bad mists til all but fell at last; rdr kpt in saddle_
[984P]	P		**Not Yet Decent (IRE)** 16-1 Miss J Grant _Pulling; hit 3; 10l 4th 5; saddle slpd 6 & imm pu_
	P		**The Flying Dragon** (5a) 8-1 Miss P Ellison _Lkd v green; jmpd novicey in rr til pu 7_

OFFICIAL DISTANCES: 15l, 4l **TIME:** 6min 53.0s **TOTE:** £6.70; places £2.50,£1.10,£1.80 **DF:** £12.20

1397 Open Maiden (Div 2), 12st 11 ran

[828²]	1		**OISIN DUBH (IRE)** 14-1 Mrs E Coveney _Hld up in mid-div; 6l 5th 11; 4½l 4th 13; gd hdwy to ld 3 out; imm sent 3l clr; sn in comm_
[1213²]	2	6	**Ell Gee** (5a) 5-1 P Townsley _Hld up in 7/8th; hdwy & chsd ldrs frm 11; 4l 3rd 13; lft 2l 2nd nxt; outpcd app 3 out; wknd nxt_
[889⁵]	3	8	**Tonrin** 9-1 M Gorman _Ld unmounted most of way to start; ld 1 & 3-6; cl 2nd til ld agn 10; prsd 13; lft 2l clr nxt; hdd 3 out; 3rd & wkng rap nxt; blun 2 out; exhaust & scrambled over last_
[984³]	4	½	**Larry** (7a) 3-1F P York _Trckd ldrs; 5l 4th 11; lost plce nxt; pushed along & no resp; 20l 5th 15; plugged into 4th aft 3 out; drvn along nxt; nrly snatched 3rd_
[1105²]	5	25	**Native Dawn (IRE)** 12-1 D Dunsdon _Ld 2; trckd ldr til ld agn 7-9; lost tch frm 12; lft 10l 4th 14; wknd qckly; v tired when blun 3 out; sn releg last_
[1207P]	P		**Blue And Royal (IRE)** 14-1 R Lawther _Chsd ldrs; 2l 3rd 9; 7l 6th & wkng qckly 11; bhnd & pu 14_
[828P]	P		**Lady Of Verse** (5a) 6-1 Mrs L Stock _Sa; nt jw; last by 4; sn hopelessly t.o; almost ref 9; clambered over & pu_
[829²]	F		**Moon Rising** 13-2 P Bull _Trckd ldng pr; 3l 4th 9; 2l 2nd 12; ½l down & gng wl when fell 14_
[1172U]	P		**Smooth Silk (IRE)** 25-1 D Page _Imm rr & nvr gng wl; wl bhnd when pu 10_
[984F]	R		**Sunley Spring** 7-2 A Hickman _Tk str hld aft 3; rushed up to ldrs & rn out 4_
[1245³]	R		**Youmeandhim (IRE)** 7-2 A Lillingston _In tch in mid-div when rn out 4_

OFFICIAL DISTANCES: 5l, 7l **TIME:** 6min 58.0s **TOTE:** £17.40; places £4.10,£1.30,£16.40 **DF:** £7.80

1398 Confined, 12st - 17J 14 ran

[1212¹]	1		**BILLIE'S MATE (IRE)** (5a,3x) (bl) 10-1 Miss J Grant _Chsd ldrs in 5/6th til 6l 4th 13; hdwy to 2l 2nd 15; prsd ldr frm 3 out; nipped thro on inner to snatch ld app nxt; r.o wl; wl bhnd_
[1209¹]	2	2	**Exemplar (IRE)** 10-1 Mrs D Rowell _Mid-div & wl off pce; stdy hdwy frm 12 to 10l 4th 3 out; r.o str to 2l 2nd at last; a hld_
[1243F]	3	3	**Jamies First (IRE)** 33-1 D Dunsdon _Prom; 5l 4th 12; 3l 3rd 13; hdwy to ld 15; lkd gng best til rdr tk bend bef 2 out too sharp & lost all momentum; rallied app last but all ch gone_
[1169²]	4	2	**The Glow (IRE)** (6x) (bl) 16-1 D Brightling _Mid-div; chsd ldrs frm 12; 6l 3rd 14; pursued ldng pr vain til wknd & no ch aft 3 out; dem 4th app nxt_
[1210²]	5	25	**Broguestown Pride (IRE)** 20-1 P Blagg _Chsd ldrs in 5/6th to 9; sn wknd & rr by 11; plodded on one pce_
[1134⁸]	6	2	**Street Kid** 25-1 Miss L Rope _Imm bhnd & nvr gng wl; t.o rem 12_
[1108P]	7	1	**Jojo** (3x) (bl) 5-1 C Sherry _Rdr waving; ld til app 13; wknd rap; no ch when lft rem 5th 15; no ch but drvn along aft; releg 7th at last_
[1212F]	8	3	**White Smoke** (3x) 12-1 R Ross _A rr; nvr gng wl; 8th 11; lft last by 15; t.o_
[1212²]	P		**Celtic Spark** (3x) 9-1 Mrs E Coveney _Cl up when jmpd slow 3; nvr gng wl aft & numerous mists; sn drpd to rr; t.o & pu 13_
[1108³]	F		**Peafield (IRE)** 6-1 P York _Hld up of pce til hdwy 5; 2nd & chsd ldr 7; ½l 2nd 10; ½l up when fell 13_
[824P]	P		**Pinoccio** (4ow) 20-1 D O'Brien _(xnb) Nvr able to go pce & sn rr; rem 7th when pu 14_
[1167¹]	R		**Some Tourist (IRE)** 3-1F N Benstead _Prom; trckd ldrs in 3rd/4th; 4l 3rd 12; ½l 2nd when lft in ld 13; by-passed dolled-off 14 on wrong side; jmpd nxt; eased & pu 3 out_
[1107⁴]	U		**Storm Drum** 33-1 M Gorman _Sn strugg in mid-div; t.o 10th when blun & ur 8_
[983P]	r		**Tallage (FR)** 10-1 P Scouller _Mid-div; outpcd frm 11; rem 6th & tired when ref 15_

OFFICIAL DISTANCES: 2l, 3l **TIME:** 6min 54.0s **TOTE:** £7.00; places £5.30,£1.80,£2.40 **DF:** £2.00
Fence 8 was omitted - fallen rider; Professor Page (C Gordon, 7-2, kicked at start) was withdrawn not under orders - Rule 4 deduction 10p in the pound; the rider of Some Tourist was fined £65 for continuing in the race after taking the wrong course

Ystrad Taf Fechan

Bassaleg (RH 8F,19J) Sat, 6 May (GOOD/FIRM)

1399 Hunt, 12st
6 ran

[1066³]	1		**KARABURAN** 2-7F Miss F Wilson *Prom; ld 10; 2-3l up aft; leant on 2nd twice u.p app last; kpt on*
[1298ᴾ]	2	2	**Travel Safely (IRE)** (vis) 6-1 J Keen *Greased hind legs; 4th til lft 3l 2nd by defections 9; sust chall when hmpd twice by wnr app last; nt go thro*
[1055ᶠ]	P		**Kyre Moss** (7a) 25-1 D Hughes *A last; 10l off pce when jmpd slow 4; hung lft & nt keen 10; fnce bhnd 11; pu nxt*
[1052ᴸ]	U		**Minstrel Fire (IRE)** 33-1 Miss Z Livermore *1st ride; ld to 5; lft in ld 8; hdd & ur 9*
[1299³]	F		**Roman Gale** 4-1 G Thorne *3rd when fell 2*
[1254ᶠ]	R		**Swan's Wish** 20-1 J Norman *1st ride; 3rd when mist & rdr lurched forward 3; ld 5 til rn out 8*

OFFICIAL DISTANCE: 2½l TIME: 6min 29.0s

1400 Restricted, 12st - 18J
12 ran

[1298³]	1		**WANSTEAD (IRE)** 3-1 J Jukes *2nd til ld app 3 out; r.o u.p frm nxt; tired app last; just hld on; all out*
[1298³]	2	s hd	**Roger (IRE)** 7-1 C Williams *Ld til app 3 out; mist nxt; rallied app last; r.o u.p flat; just failed*
[818⁶]	3	10	**Star Chaser** 10-1 D Stephens (Wales) *Rr to 5; 3rd frm 9; 8l 4th 12; outpcd aft 14; lft 3rd 2 out; nt trble ldrs*
[931ᵁ]	4	15	**Mister Jay Day** 6-1 A Price (xnb) *Chsd ldrs; 5th 10; outpcd aft 14; poor 6th when lft 4th 2 out*
[1054ᶠ]	5	20	**Julies Joy (IRE)** (5a) 16-1 I Johnson (xnb) *Sn last & jmpd rt; lost tch frm 6; 12l bhnd rest & rdn 10; jmpd slow 12; cont rem*
[1301ᴸ]	P		**Energy Man** 10-1 J Keen *Midfield when mist 2; 8th frm 5; cont last pr; t.o 13; pu last*
[894³]	U		**Market Springer (IRE)** 5-2F Miss B Williams (xnb) *Mostly 4th frm 6; hit 9; wknd aft 15; 15l 5h when ur 2 out*
[1054ᶠ]	R		**Not For Profit (IRE)** (tt) 10-1 Miss F Wilson *3rd when jmpd slow 6; jnd ldr & crashed thro wing & ur 8*
[1228ᴾ]	P		**Out On The Town** (5a) 12-1 James Tudor *4th 2; grad wknd; 6th & u.p 10; rr frm 11; lost tch aft 14; pu 3 out*
[1054ᶠ]	F		**Saronica-R** (5a) 33-1 J Price *2 handlers; bad mist 2; 9th when fell 3*
[1298³]	P		**Sea Search** 40-1 G Maloney *Bhnd; 8th 10; brief prog in 5th 11; lost tch 14; t.o when pu & dism last; lame*
[539ᴸ]	U		**Te Akau Dan (NZ)** 4-1 N Oliver *Rr; 7th 10; hdwy 15 to 15l 3rd 3 out; 12l 3rd when blun & ur nxt*

OFFICIAL DISTANCES: s hd, 8l, 20l TIME: 6min 11.0s
Fence 16 omitted - damaged

1401 Confined, 12st
8 ran

[1295²]	1		**ANORAK (USA)** (3x) 6-4JF C Williams *A.p; ld 4; mist 7; hdd 10; chsd ldr aft; 5l down bet last 2 & drvn along; swished tail but kpt on game; ld app last; wl rdn*
[833⁴]	2	4	**Warren Boy** (10x) 4-1 Miss P Jones *Cl 2nd til ld 11; 4l up 14; 5l clr & rdn 3 out; lkd wnr til flagged & hdd app last; no ex*
[644³]	3	runin	**Doyenne** (5a) 8-1 J Keen *Nt fluent; rmdr aft 2; mist & rmdr nxt; went 3rd frm 8; mist & rmdr 11; 8l 3rd 14; nt r.o & outpcd frm 16; sn btn*
[944ᴾ]	P		**Appeal** (5a) 33-1 J Jukes *2 handlers; sn strugg in rr; stuttered into 8; cont t.o in last trio; pu 15*
[1299ᴾ]	P		**Chantingo Lad** 33-1 A Price *Sn rr; lost tch frm 6; t.o nxt; pu 14*
[1295ᶠ]	U		**Herbert Lodge (IRE)** 50-1 Miss M Bartlett *A 4/5th; 15l 5th 9; ur 10*
[1295ᶠ]	P		**Slip Haven** (5a) 50-1 P Sheldrake (xnb) *Pulled hrd; nt much room & mist 2; lost tch frm 7; t.o aft hit 9; pu 13*
[1295³]	P		**You Make Me Laugh (IRE)** 6-4JF E Williams (xnb) *Ld to 4; slpd slt bend bef nxt & dem 5l 3rd; nt fluent & nvr gng wl aft; poor 4th 11; mist 13; pu nxt*

OFFICIAL DISTANCES: 3l, 30l TIME: 6min 06.0s

1402 Mixed Open, 12st - 18J
8 ran

[1022ᴾ]	1		**COOLVAWN LADY (IRE)** (5a) 2-5F Miss P Jones *Made all; 8l clr 5; unchall aft; 15l up 3 out; lft virt solo nxt; unchall*
[1297⁷]	2	runin	**Sun Of Chance** 20-1 Miss A Meakins *Disp 3rd 3; fdd & 6th frm 7; 18l 5th 11; 50l 5th 3 out; stayed on past wkng horses; went rem 2nd last; nvr any ch*

[1053⁴]	3	2	**The Last Mistress** (5a) 20-1 **J Price** *Chsd ldr to 9; lost plce 11; rem 4th 4 out; lft 2nd bet last 2 til dem last*
[1296ᶠ]	4	4	**Laurel Seeker** (USA) 8-1 **James Tudor** *Swtng; last early; disp 3rd 7; lft 3rd nxt; 12l 2nd frm 9; tired frm 15; 20l 3rd when mist nxt; wknd bad*
[1224⁵]	5	8	**Local Customer** 50-1 **Miss S Matthews** *A last trio; last frm 10; 22l away 11; t.o frm 14*
[1282ᴾ]	P		**Blown Wind** (IRE) 10-1 **C Williams** *Last pr; 4th & hdwy 9; 12l 3rd 11; went 2nd aft 15; tired 2nd but clr of rest when pu last*
[1297ᴾ]	U		**Danny Gale** (IRE) 33-1 **T Faulkner** *Last pr 3; poor last frm 6 til blun v bad & ur 10*
[1022ᵁ]	U		**Twilight Tom** 5-1 **Miss B Williams** (xnb) *12l 3rd when ur 8*

OFFICIAL DISTANCES: dist, 2l, 10l **TIME:** 6min 04.0s
Fence 16 omitted - fallen rider; the stewards enquired into why Blown Wind had pulled up; they accepted that the horse 'had run out of energy'; Rave-On-Hadley was withdrawn not under orders - state of the ground'; Rule 4 deduction 65p in pound

1403 Intermediate, 12st   7 ran

[988ᶠ]	1		**ILLINEYLAD** (IRE) 6-1 **E Williams** (boh) *Trckd ldrs; went 2nd 6; ld 11; 5l clr 14; drew rt away frm 3 out; rdn out*
[1299²]	2	runin	**Storm Man** (IRE) 10-1 **Miss C Williams** *Last trio; lost tch 5; 17l 5th 11; stayed on past wkng horses frm 15; went 2nd 2 out; no ch w wnr*
[832ᴾ]	3	4	**Rue De Fort** 50-1 **J Keen** *Tde; ld 3-5; 3rd nxt; went 2nd agn 13; no ex & tired frm 3 out; virt stpd to walk app last; t.o*
[818⁷]	4	6	**Final Option** (IRE) 33-1 **I Johnson** (bf) *A detach in final trio; 23l last 11; cont o*
[818¹]	P		**Lillieplant** (IRE) (5a) 4-7F **A Price** (xnb) *Tde; wrs but pulled hrd & sn cl 3rd; hit 3; ld 5; pckd 10; hdd 11; 9l 3rd 16; wknd qckly app nxt; pu last*
[1227ᴾ]	P		**Secret Can't Say** (IRE) (5a) 4-1 **J Jukes** *A bhnd; mist 2; rmdrs in last pr 3; no resp; lost tch 5; 20l 6th 11; mist nxt & pu*
[1227⁴]	P		**Tiger Lord** 7-1 **C Williams** (xnb) *Ld to 3; jmpd slow 6; lost tch 11; sn t.o; last 15; pu 3 out*

OFFICIAL DISTANCES: 30l, 8l, 10l **TIME:** 6min 09.0s

1404 Open Maiden (Div 1), 12st   12 ran

[1300ᶠ]	1		**GUARD A DREAM** (IRE) 6-1 **A Price** *Chsd ldr; hit 5 & 12; ld & mist 3 out; rdn clr nxt; comf*
[1302³]	2	12	**Albert The Lion** (IRE) 7-1 **C Williams** (xnb) *Ur start; midfield; impd to 3rd/4th 8 til 2nd app 16; jnd wnr 3 out; rdn & fnd nil*
[1223ᶠ]	3	20	**Double Steal** (bl) 12-1 **J Jukes** *Chsd ldrs; wenr 3rd 11; blun 14; eff 16; 2l 3rd when hit 3 out; nt r.o; jmpd slow last*
[994ᴾ]	4	12	**Tudor Flight** (5a) 8-1 **S Blackwell** (xnb) *Sn last pr; last frm 6; t.o 11; no ch aft*
[1300ᶠ]	5	15	**No Escape** (tt) 33-1 **M Parry** *Mists; a rr; t.o frm 11*
[1222ᶠ]	P		**A Class Apart** (NZ) 4-5F **N Oliver** *Tk keen hold; wandering in ld to 4; 4l up til frm wide app 9; 4l up agn 13; mist 15; hdd app nxt; wknd rap; 15l 4th when pu 2 out; collapsed & died aft*
	P		**All For Tack** (5a) 33-1 **Miss A Meakins** *A strugg in last pr; t.o 11; pu 14*
[1301ᶠ]	F		**Bold Knight** 5-1 **G Skone** (xnb) *2 handlers; dwelt; nvt btr than midfield; last of 6 w ch 11; 12l 5th when fell hvly 15*
[1093¹]	P		**Georgie Grace** 33-1 **James Tudor** *3rd to 7; lost plce qckly; 8th when jmpd slow 11; t.o aft; pu 15*
[1223⁵]	P		**Pryvate Time** (5a) 14-1 **J Keen** *Chsd ldrs in 4/5th; 8l 5th 11; lost tch 14; 12l 5th when pu 16*
[892ᴾ]	R		**Sister Jim** (5a) 25-1 **S Graham** *5th when r.o 11*
[1056ᵁ]	U		**Tarian** (USA) 50-1 **M Parry** (bf) *Sis; last pr to 6; hdwy to 6th when pckd & ur 10*

OFFICIAL DISTANCES: 15l, 15l, 10l **TIME:** 6min 22.0s
The owner of A Class Apart, whose passport was found to be not in order, was fined £100

1405 Open Maiden (Div 2, Part 1), 12st   9 ran

[1302ᶠ]	1		**BARAN ITSU** 4-1 **P Sheldrake** *Prom; ld 4; just hdd when lft 3l clr 2 out; jnd & lft wl clr last; lucky*
[1300ᴾ]	2	15	**Queen's Equa** (5a) 20-1 **Miss S Major** (bf) *Pulled hrd; settled 3rd/4th; ev ch til 5l 4th 3 out; sn wknd; lft 2nd by defections*
[1302ᶠ]	F		**Clonshire Castle** (IRE) 6-1 **J Keen** *Bhnd; 6th 11; r.o to cl 2nd 14; tk ½l ld & lkd prob wnr when fell 2 out*
[1302ᴾ]	P		**Craigson** 6-1 **D Stephens** (Wales) (xnb) *Ld & hit 1; 2nd to 8; cl 3rd til 2nd agn 11; 3rd & u.p 14; hit nxt; no ex; sn bhnd; t.o 6th when pu 2 out*
[1302ᶠ]	F		**Hill Top Flyer** (IRE) 20-1 **G Marsh** *Rn wide bend aft 1; sev mists in poor last til fell 8*

[602⁷]	P	**Lady Palamon (IRE)** (5a) 12-1 **J Jukes** *Chsd ldrs; 4th when hit 11; 5th aft; fdd to last pr 15; pu 3 out*
[1018⁶]	R	**Mr Stackhouse (IRE)** (bl) 4-1 **S Blackwell** *(xnb) Pulled hrd; 2nd when jmpd rt & rn off course aft 2; sn pu*
[1316²]	P	**Newchurch Lad** 5-1 **J Price** *Nt jw; a bhnd; 8l adrift 9; t.o 11; pu 2 out*
[1301⁵]	U	**Welsh Warrior** 2-1F **C Williams** *Ld 2-4; 4th when hit 4 5; settled 2nd frm 9-11; 6th when mist 13; r.o to 4l 3rd 3 out; lft 2nd 2 out; drvn along to make 3l & jnd wnr when blun & ur last; would have won*

OFFICIAL DISTANCE: 20l TIME: 6min 20.0s
The owner of Hill Top Flyer, whose passport was found to be not in order, was fined £100

PLATE 16   1404 Ystrad Taf Fechan Open Maiden (Div 1): Guard A Dream leads Georgie Grace ahead of L to R Pryvate Time, the blinkered Double Steal, Albert The Lion, Tudor Flight, Bold Knight, Tarian and Sister Jim   PHOTO: Alun Sedgemore

1406 Open Maiden (Div 2, Part 2), 12st   8 ran

[1300⁷]	1		**STAR ISLAND** 3-1 **E Williams** *Hld up trckng ldrs; went 3rd 11 & 2nd 14; jmpd lft & nt fluent 15 & 16; rdn to ld on long rn to last; kpt on*
[949²]	2	2	**Eurogreen (IRE)** evensF **A Price** *Ld to 2 & frm 5; rdn & hdd bet last 2; nt qckn*
[1301⁶]	3	3	**Aherne** (7a) 14-1 **J Cook** *Ld 2-5; 2nd to 14; disp 2nd & ev ch 3 out; drvn & fnd nil aft nxt*
[1301⁵]	4	6	**Tommyknocker (IRE)** 4-1 **T Faulkner** *Jmpd slow & nt fluent; towards rr; strugg 8; went 4th 13; 7l 4th 3 out; sn u.p & no resp; mist last*
[1223⁶]	5	runin	**Blazing Connie** (5a) 8-1 **G Perkins** *(boh) 2 handlers; mostly 3rd to 11; 5th 13; to 16*
[1312²]	6	1	**Marnies Song** (5a) (bl) 5-1 **James Tudor** *5l 3rd 2; mist nxt; 4th & mist 9; wknd 13; sn t.o*
[1223⁸]	7	runin	**Rubian Princess** (12a) 20-1 **S Lloyd** *A last trio; bad mist 10; mist 12; lost tch 13; sn t.o*
	P		**Watchyourback (NZ)** 5-1 **N Oliver** *Ur start & galloped up & down hedge; a last; 6l adrift 5; pu & dism 8*

OFFICIAL DISTANCES: 1½l, 3l, 7l **TIME:** 6min 28.0s

Albrighton
Weston Park (LH 7F,18J) Sun, 7 May (FIRM)

1407 Hunt   4 ran

	1	**SHOON WIND** 8-13F **A Dalton** *Jw; made all at stdy pce; drew clr 14; v easy*

[1086²] 2 20 **My Sister Lucy** (5a) 9-4 I Hooper *Hld up last; hit 8; went 3rd 13; rdn & one pce nxt; went poor 2nd aft 2 out; fin lame*

         3 15 **War Whoop** 6-1 J R Barlow *2nd to 4 & frm 7; outpcd 14; dem aft 2 out; qckly dism aft fin & lashing out w hind leg*

[865ᴾ]   P   **Yasgourra (IRE)** (5a) 33-1 P Morris *Pulled hrd & nt fluent; 2nd 4-7; releg last 13 & qckly lost tch; pu & dism nxt*

OFFICIAL DISTANCES: 15l, 10l **TIME:** 6min 50.0s

1408 Confined, 12st   8 ran

[902⁴]   1   **BISHOPS HALL** 7-4 A Crow *Chsd clr ldr; clsd to ld app 11; hdd 14; lkd hld 3 out; rdn & rallied game to ld aft 2 out; sn in comm*

[1128²] 2 6   **My Nominee** (bl) 4-5F R Burton *8l clr 2; hdd app 11; ld agn 14 & 5l ahd nxt; 8l up 3 out; drvn & hdd aft nxt; fnd nil*

[1127¹] 3 30 **Alaskan Heir** (5x) (vis,tt) 7-1 G Hanmer *18l 5th 7; nvr nr ldng pr; 30l 4th 3 out; rem 3rd aft*

[1255²] 4 2   **Prologue (IRE)** 16-1 S Prior *12l 3rd 2; went poor 3rd 8 but nvr within 12l of ldng pr; rem whn dem aft 3 out*

[1252²] 5 40 **Freddie Fox** 16-1 Miss G Garton *Sn rem last; t.o last aft 13; plodded on*

[1255¹] 6 25 **Ballyhannon (IRE)** 25-1 Miss J Froggatt *22l 6th 7; plodded rnd & t.o 12*

[960ᵁ]   7 8   **All In The Game (IRE)** 33-1 D Sherlock *Nt fluent & rdn along; 15l 3rd 7; strugg 10; t.o 12; blun last*

[1321ᴾ] P   **Carbery Ministrel (IRE)** (bl) 33-1 R Carey *Nt jw; jmpd v slow 3; imm lost tch in last pr; mist 9; t.o aft; pu aft 12*

OFFICIAL DISTANCES: 5l, dist **TIME:** 6min 31.0s

1409 Mens Open   7 ran

[1025ᶠ] 1   **WHATAFELLOW (IRE)** (bl) 2-7F A Crow *Hld up; went 3rd app 7; ld app 11; 12l clr & in comm 2 out; eased flat*

[1087ᴾ] 2 20 **Tremendisto** 16-1 S Joynes (xnb) *Lw; pulled hrd; hld up; went 2nd 12; ev ch nxt; drvn & outpcd 15; all out to hld 2nd*

[302⁶]   3 nk **The Whole Hog (IRE)** 16-1 M Worthington *Last early; went 5th 9; 15l 5th 11; tk 18l 3rd 15; stayed on aft 2 out & nrly caught rnr-up*

[1319ᴾ] 4 8   **Albert Blake** (tt) 50-1 W Kinsey *Ld til app 11; releg 4th 13; no ch frm nxt but plugged on stdly*

[1151³] 5 hd **Russian Castle (IRE)** 16-1 K Burke *Chsd ldr app 6-9; 4l 4th 11; 7l 3rd & outpcd 13; no ch frm nxt*

[1152ᴾ] P   **Buck Run (IRE)** 50-1 G Hanmer *Last pr & nvr gng wl; rmdrs aft 5 & nt keen; mist 8; lost tch 10; t.o & pu aft 13*

[1336ᴾ] P   **I Haven't A Buck (IRE)** 6-1 D Barlow *2nd early; jmpd slow 6 & releg 4th; 16l 6th 11; t.o & pu aft 13; lame*

OFFICIAL DISTANCES: 20l, nk **TIME:** 6min 37.0s

1410 Ladies Open   9 ran

[1014ᴾ] 1†   **HEARTS ARE WILD** 3-1 Miss P Gundry *Lw; jw; ld at str gallop to 5; prsd ldr; chall agn 15; ld nxt; drvn & hdd app last; lkd hld til rallied flat; ld post*

[668ᵁ]   1† hd **PHARARE (IRE)** 7-4F Miss C Spearing *Lw; jw; 2nd til ld 5; 6l clr 11; 3l up 14; rdn & hdd 3 out; ld agn app last & lkd wnr but outj; r.o game til pipped on post*

[1275¹] 3 8   **Dawn's Cognac (IRE)** 2-1 Miss P Jones *Chsd ldng pr frm 5 but nt a as fluent as them; 10l 3rd 11; eff 14; outpcd nxt & 4l down 3 out; drvn to rally & nt much room aft nxt; no ex last*

[1150ᵁ] 4 20 **Ambrose** 33-1 Miss T Clark *Midfield; poor 4th frm 7; 25l 4th 11; nvr on terms*

[1199³] 5 5   **Killatty Player (IRE)** (5a) 20-1 Mrs M Barlow *Midfield til drpd to rr app 7; 40l 7th 11; unable to clse*

[1297ᶠ] 6 8   **Chieftain's Crown (USA)** 20-1 Miss E James (xnb) *Bhnd; disp 33l 5th 11; nvr able to clse*

[1199ᴾ] 7 dist **Cheeky Pot** (bl) 33-1 Miss J Priest *A last; 30l adrift 5; t.o 11*

[1014ᴾ] P   **Everso Irish** 25-1 Miss C Thomas *Jmpd slow 2; nd; disp 33l 5th 11; t.o & pu 3 out*

[1150¹] P   **Hello Me Man (IRE)** 33-1 Mrs K Diggle (xnb) *A bhnd & hld up; 42l 8th 11; t.o & pu 2 out*

OFFICIAL DISTANCES: dd-ht, 3l **TIME:** 6min 26.0s

1411 Restricted, 12st   13 ran

[891¹]   1   **RAISE AND GAIN (IRE)** 2-1 R Burton *Trckd ldrs; 5th when hit 11; went 3rd 14; chsd wnr app 2 out; hrd rdn to ld app last; stayed on wl*

[1150²]	2	3	**Tale Bridge (IRE)** 10-1 Mrs C Ford *Ld to 3; 2nd/3rd til ld agn 9-10; 4th nxt; rallied & ld agn 14; 3l clr 2 out; drvn & hdd app last; nt qckn*
[900¹]	3	8	**Quit The Creek** (5a) 6-1 J Cook *Prom; 2nd 11; ld 13-14; 4l 3rd 15; one pce & btn aft 2 out*
[992⁴]	4	12	**Out Of The Blue** (5a) 20-1 S Graham *Bhnd but in tch; 9th 11; 8l 7th 14; sn wknd*
[1317ᵁ]	P		**Arthur Henry** 14-1 S Prior *Hld up last & sn t.o; mist 12; pu 14*
[1251¹]	P		**Charlie Keay (IRE)** 12-1 G Hanmer *Lw; trckd ldrs; 6th 11; hit 13; eff in cl 4th nxt; wknd rap; t.o & pu 2 out*
[1322²]	P		**Cookie Boy** 10-1 M Wilesmith *Prom; lft in ld 6-9; ld agn 10-13; 5l 5th & wkng 14; t.o & pu 2 out*
[1193ᴾ]	P		**Lindalighter** (5a) 33-1 M Munrowd *Midfield & nd; 7th 11; strugg aft nxt; t.o & pu 2 out*
[1014⁶]	P		**Outrageous Affair** (5a) 10-1 Miss R Reynolds *Sn bhnd; lost tch 7; poor 10th 11; t.o & pu last*
[1009⁵]	P		**Penrose Lad (NZ)** 16-1 W Tellwright *Prom; hmpd aft 6 & lost plce; rallied 9; 3rd 11; 6th & wkng 14; t.o & pu 2 out*
[1129ᴾ]	U		**Pinouli** (5a) 7-1 L Stephens *Tk keen hld; slt ld 3 til blun & ur 5*
[963⁴]	P		**Serenze (IRE)** 7-4F M Worthington *Chsd ldrs; 8th 11; fair 8th 14; sn wknd; pu 3 out*
[1200ᴾ]	P		**Teme Willow (IRE)** 20-1 M Hammond *A bhnd; lost tch 10; t.o when reluct & blun 12; pu imm*

OFFICIAL DISTANCES: 3l, 5l **TIME:** 6min 39.0s

1412 Open Maiden (Div 1), 12st
13 ran

[1194²]	1		**OLE GUNNAR (IRE)** 6-4F M Wilesmith *(xnb) Hld up & towards rr; impd to 7l 7th 11 & 3rd aft 12; chall 2 out; level when blun last & rdr unbalanced; kpt on final 100yds*
[1197⁴]	2	2	**Strong Mission (IRE)** 5-2 G Hanmer *Rcd free & ld/disp til ld 10; nk ahd 3 out; hrd rdn frm nxt; jnd last & lkd 2nd best when rival rdr blun; nt qckn aft*
[1196⁴]	3	runin	**Blacon Point** 5-1 T Stephenson *(xnb) Hld up in midfield; went cl 5th 11; wknd app 14; t.o*
[966ᶠ]	4	1	**Pendil's Dream** (5a) 25-1 D Sherlock *Lw; tk keen hld in 3rd/4th to 10; 6th nxt; went 2nd brief 12; rdn & wknd 15*
[1323ᴾ]	5	20	**The Quakers Wake (IRE)** 12-1 R Burton *Trckd ldrs; went cl 4th 11; 1l 2nd brief 14; wknd bad aft; t.o & walked in*
	P		**Castle Nutter** 14-1 G Thomas *Unfit & dull; ss; jb; sn t.o; pu 7*
[1124⁴]	P		**Crack 'n' Run** 33-1 M Pennell *A bhnd; 20l 9th 11; t.o 14; pu 2 out*
[1250²]	P		**Dotty Dolittle** (5a) 20-1 J Burley *Bhnd; blun 7; mist 8; 40l 10th 11; wl t.o when blun 13 & pu*
[778ᴾ]	P		**Eecel** 25-1 A Wintle *Ss; nt jw & imm lost tch; t.o & pu 2 out*
[964⁵]	P		**Mandela Square** 25-1 M Worthington *2 handlers; pulled hrd in 3rd/4th; mist 4; 3rd 11; wknd nxt; t.o when jmpd v bad 15 & pu*
	F		**Mornder Romany** 5-1 N Oliver *Chsd ldrs; 8l 8th 11; fell 12*
[865ᴿ]	P		**Royal Silk** 20-1 S Graham *Unimpressive padd; ss; jmpd v bad; sn wl t.o; pu 6 (unschooled)*
[570ᶠ]	P		**S And O P** 25-1 M Rodda *(xnb) Pulled v hrd; ld/disp to 11; wknd nxt; t.o when blun 15 & pu*

OFFICIAL DISTANCES: 1l, 20l **TIME:** 6min 45.0s

1413 Open Maiden (Div 2), 12st
12 ran

[1196ᴾ]	1		**SPUMANTE** 7-1 G Hanmer *Hld up & wl bhnd; 7th 10; 9l 3rd & clsng app 14; chall nxt; ld app 2 out; sn clr; easy*
[1277²]	2	8	**Three Monroes (IRE)** 7-2 T Stephenson *Lw; hld up; prog in 3rd 10; ld 12 til app 2 out; drvn & no ch w wnr aft*
[1323ᵣ]	3	1½fs	**Village Gossip** (5a) 20-1 M Trott *Pulled hrd in 2nd/3rd; prsd ldr 8-14; stpd to nil u.p aft nxt; sn t.o & exhaust*
[1201ᵁ]	4	5	**Grey Lodge** (5a) 4-1 J R Barlow *Midfield; 6th 10; outpcd 12; 26l 5th 14; t.o aft*
[684ᴾ]	P		**Aganerot (IRE)** (tt) 20-1 P Cranmer *Bolted clr; 20l ahd 5; stpd to nil 7 & hdd 8; nrly ref 9; cont to til pu 11*
	P		**Brydferth Ddu (IRE)** (12a) 33-1 Miss P Jones *Novicey; stdd in rr til prog 8; 5th 10; 4th & outpcd 13; pu & dism nxt*
[972ᵣ]	P		**Final Quay** (5a) (bl) 10-1 E Williams *Lw; chsd ldrs; mist 5; handy 4th 10; pu aft 12; lame*
[1318ᴾ]	P		**Fruit Crop** (5a) 5-2F M Worthington *Lw; mists & wl bhnd; poor 8th 10; nrly collided w hdle aft 12; cont to til pu 2 out*
[1277ᵣ]	P		**Kinsale Florale (IRE)** (5a) 16-1 M Rodda *Tde; reluct to start & rce; t.o til pu 5*
[1196ᵣ]	P		**Lightening Steel** 20-1 P Morris *Mists & jmpd lft; midfield early; t.o 10; jb lft 12 & pu*
[472ᴾ]	P		**Red Leo (USA)** 20-1 J Harty *(xnb) Chsd clr ldr til releg 4th app 7; t.o 11; pu 14; lame*

[959ᵁ] P   **Riot Lady (IRE)** (5a) 20-1 D Sherlock *Prom in chsng group; clsd & ld 8-12; 10l 3rd & wkng rap nxt; pu & dism 15*

OFFICIAL DISTANCES: 5l, dist **TIME:** 6min 49.0s
The Stewards cautioned the rider of Village Gossip concerning his use of the whip between the last two fences

Atherstone

Clifton-on-Dunsmore (LH 8F,19J) Sun, 7 May

(GOOD, GOOD to FIRM, GOOD to SOFT patches)

1414 Hunt									**9 ran**

[1007ᴾ]	1		**BARE FISTED** 7-1 Miss H Phizacklea *Ld 2-5 & 7-10; ld 12; r.o wl*
[1268ᶠ]	2	1	**Playlord** 2-1 N Docker *A.p; mist 7; 3rd ½way; 6l 4th 12; went 2nd nxt; rdn aft 3 out; ev ch last; unable to qckn*
[1267ᴾ]	3	8	**Catchphrase** (vis) 12-1 R Armson *Hld up; hdwy 7; 4th ½way; went 4l 3rd 3 out; one pce*
[1073²]	4	5	**Burntwood Melody** 11-10F Mrs N Hadfield-Tilly *1st ride; went 2nd 4; ld 5-7 & 10-12; lost plce & 7l 4th 15; nd aft*
[1125³]	5	20	**Kings Choir** 8-1 Mrs C Boyes *Swtng; ld to 2; lost plce 4; 7th ½way; 11l 6th 12; lost tch 14; sn wl bhnd*
[870⁶]	6	10	**Professor Longhair** 33-1 P Bennett *Prom til lost plce 7; 6th ½way; 12l 7th & drvn 12; mist 13; sn wl bhnd*
[1269ᴾ]	P		**Crested Lass** (5a) 25-1 L Hicks *Swtng; chsd ldrs; mist 4; 5th ½way; mist 10; 10l 5th 12; wknd & 20l 6th 14; mist 15; t.o & pu last*
[1014ᴾ]	P		**Faraday** 33-1 Miss S Phizacklea *A bhnd; 8th ½way; 20l 8th 12; t.o 14; mist 16; pu 3 out*
	P		**Tamally** 33-1 Mrs J Manicom *Bckwd; a bhnd; t.o & pu 11*

OFFICIAL DISTANCES: 1l, 6l **TIME:** 6min 13.8s

1415 Confined, 12st							**14 ran**

[1006⁴]	1		**WHO IS EQUINAME (IRE)** (bl) 12-1 S Morris *Swtng; hld up & bhnd; 11l 10th ½way; mist 11; hdwy & 7½l 7th nxt; went 2nd 14; ld 2 out; all out*
[897ᴾ]	2	½	**Black Serene (IRE)** (5a) 16-1 A Wintle *Walked to post; ld to 2; hdd til ld 5; hdd 8; ld 11; qcknd 5l clr 13; hdd 2 out; r.o flat*
[1006²]	3	8	**Just Like Madge** (5a,3x) 5-2JF J Tarry *5s-5/2; swtng; prom; mist 2; 4½l 6th ½way; lost plce & 8½l 9th 12; rallied 14; 7l 5th 16; went 3rd aft nxt; no imp*
[1267ᴾ]	4	12	**Starlight Fool** 20-1 R Barrett *Hld up; 8l 9th ½way; hdwy & 6l 5th 12; 5l 4th 16; wknd 3 out*
[1266⁴]	5	3	**Drummond Warrior (IRE)** 33-1 Miss A Burton *Chsd ldrs; 5l 7th ½way; lost plce & 9l 10th 12; rdn 14; 15l 6th 4 out; plodded on*
[801²]	6	7	**Neva-Agree (IRE)** 16-1 R Armson *Hld up; mist 2; 7l 8th ½way; 7l 6th 12; outpcd 14; 16l 7th & no ch 16*
[1334⁵]	7	10	**Priory Piper** (6x) 7-1 L Hicks *10s-7s; ld 2-5 & 8-11; 2nd/3rd til mist 14; sn wknd; 17l 8th 16; t.o*
[1146ᴾ]	8	3	**Rolpen** 33-1 J I Pritchard *A bhnd; 17l 12th ½way; 15l 11th 12; 25l 10th 16; t.o*
[1265³]	P		**Barneys Gold (IRE)** 8-1 A Bealby *Lost plce 4; outpcd & wl bhnd ½way; t.o 12; pu 14*
[1008⁴]	P		**Credo Is King (IRE)** 33-1 R Cope *Nvr gng wl; lost plce u.p 7; 20l 13th ½way; t.o & pu 12*
[1005⁴]	P		**Deep Refrain (IRE)** (7x) (tt) 20-1 G Kerr *Prom; 2½l 3rd ½way; 5l 4th 12; wknd qckly 13; wl bhnd when pu 15*
[466ʳ]	P		**Red Rebel** 5-2JF B Pollock *2 handlers; sn prom; 3l 4th ½way; 4l 3rd 12; went 5l 2nd nxt; 4l 3rd & rdn 16; wknd 3 out; bhnd when pu last*
[869²]	P		**Sabre King** (bl) 9-2 Miss N McKim *Sn chsng ldrs; 4l 5th ½way; lost plce & 8l 8th 12; 23l 9th 16; t.o & pu last*
[867ᴾ]	P		**Sheelin Lad (IRE)** 33-1 C Vale *2 handlers; swtng; a bhnd; 15l 11th ½way; 23l 12th 12; t.o & pu 13*

OFFICIAL DISTANCES: ½l, 6l **TIME:** 6min 01.5s

1416 Land Rover Mens Open, 12st					**11 ran**

[545¹]	1		**SHANAVOGH** (7x) 7-4F R Hunnisett *2nd til ld 14; lft 10l clr 16; unchal aft*
[1013¹]	2	20	**Mr Smudge** 14-1 A Martin *Chsd ldrs; 20l 3rd ½way; 22l 5th 12; lft 20l 2nd 16; no ch w wnr*
[1216²]	3	nk	**Fawsley Manor** (5a) 6-1 J Tarry *Chsd ldrs til lost plce 7; 24l 6th ½way; went 20l 3rd 13; lft disp poor 2nd 16; no imp*

[1023^{2}]	4	10	**Native Cove (IRE)** 4-1 **T Lane** *5s-4s; lw; hld up; hdwy & 22l 4th ½way; went 20l 3rd 12; rdn 15; lft 22l 4th 16; wknd 3 out*
[441^{1}]	5	10	**Midnight Service (IRE)** (bl) 12-1 **R Barrett** *A bhnd; 29l 9th ½way; 33l 9th & rdn 12; t.o 14*
[1311^{4}]	6	3	**Pretoria Dancer** (vis) 25-1 **F O'Brien** *A wl bhnd; 35l 10th ½way; t.o 12*
[1216^{1}]	F		**Barna Boy (IRE)** 5-2 **M Hewitt** *Swtng; ld aft 1; 8l clr 7; hdd 14; 1½l 2nd when fell 16*
[1189^{1}]	P		**Chicodari** (bl) 16-1 **E Walker** *Chsd ldrs; jmpd slow 6; rdn 8; 23l 5th ½way; nt r.o; 32l 8th 12; t.o 14; pu last*
[1114^{U}]	r		**Court Amber (IRE)** (bl) 20-1 **G Cooper** *Swtng; a bhnd; 28l 8th ½way; 29l 7th 12; t.o 14; jmpd v slow 15; ref last*
[1265^{P}]	P		**Needwood Neptune** (vis) 33-1 **P Bennett** *Ld til jmpd v slow 1; sn lost plce; t.o 5; pu 12*
[1313^{F}]	P		**Perfect Finisher** 14-1 **M Hawkins** *Swtng; nd; 25l 7th ½way; 22l 6th 12; t.o 14; pu last*

OFFICIAL DISTANCES: 15l, nk **TIME:** 5min 59.0s

1417 Ladies Open — 17 ran

[1007^{4}]	1		**DONT TELL THE WIFE** 2-1 **Miss G Hutchinson** *5/2-2s; ww; 10l 9th ½way; gd hdwy & 4l 4th 12; went 3rd nxt; ld 15; sn in comm; 10l clr when mist 2 out; easy*
[1253^{4}]	2	12	**Fern Leader (IRE)** (vis) 33-1 **Mrs J Hughes** *Went 2nd 3; ld & mist 4; hdd 5; 5l 6th ½way; 5l 5th 12; went 5l 3rd 16 & 2nd last; no ch w wnr*
[1332^{5}]	3	1½	**Pongo Waring (IRE)** 12-1 **Miss N McKim** *Hld up; mist 2; 10½l 10th ½way; eff & 10l 7th 12; 8l 6th 14; went 7l 4th 16; one pce*
[1341^{13}]	4	½	**Rainbow Walk (IRE)** 33-1 **Miss A Burton** *Ld 2-5 & 5-15; 2nd til no ex app last*
[1253^{1}]	5	10	**Lily The Lark** (5a) evensF **Miss H Irving** *Swtng; ld to 2; 3rd ½way; went 2nd 12-14; lost plce & 9l 5th 16; wknd 3 out*
[969^{U}]	6	10	**Haughton Lad (IRE)** 12-1 **Miss L Sweeting** *16s-12s; prom; went 2nd 9-12; 7l 5th 14; wknd & 10l 6th 16*
[1265^{6}]	7	8	**Just Bruce** 33-1 **Miss L White** *Prom; went 2nd 5-9; 4th ½way; lost plce & 14l 8th 12; 18l 7th 14; t.o*
[787^{1}]	8	4	**Persian Butterfly** (5a) 20-1 **Miss T Habgood** *Swtng; a bhnd; 13th ½way; 25l 10th 14; t.o*
[1189^{2}]	9	8	**Blue Lyzander** (5a,4ow) 33-1 **Mrs E Staines** *(xnb) Hld up; 7l 8th ½way; lost plce & 17l 9th 12; 20l 8th 14; t.o*
[1335^{P}]	U		**Abuljjood (IRE)** (7a) 33-1 **Miss L Allan** *Hdwy & rmdrs 8; 6l 7th ½way; 7l 6th when ur 12*
[1266^{3}]	U		**Count Of Flanders (IRE)** 16-1 **Miss F Hatfield** *Hld up; hdwy 7; 4l 5th ½way; mist & ur 10*
[1191^{5}]	P		**Driving Force** 33-1 **Miss S Hutchings** *A bhnd; 15th ½way; t.o 12; pu 15*
	P		**Far Senior** 25-1 **Miss H Dickins** *Prom til lost plce 7; 14th ½way; wl bhnd when pu 11*
[1217^{U}]	P		**Guest Alliance (IRE)** 25-1 **Miss S Phizacklea** *Nt jw; sn t.o; pu & dism 13*
[1211^{2}]	P		**Haunting Music (IRE)** 25-1 **Miss E Neyens** *(xnb) Hld up; mist 3; 12th ½way; 20l 10th & rdn along 12; 23l 9th 14; t.o & pu last*
[1311^{P}]	P		**Native Rambler (IRE)** 25-1 **Miss C Stafford** *(xnb) Swtng; a bhnd; 11th ½way; 25l 11th when mist & rdr lost irons 12; pu 13*
[1217^{P}]	P		**Up The Road (IRE)** 33-1 **Miss S Tacy** *Sn t.o; pu 13*

OFFICIAL DISTANCES: 6l, 1½l **TIME:** 6min 05.1s

1418 Restricted (Div 1), 12st — 11 ran

[1200^{6}]	1		**FANION DE NOURRY (FR)** 7-1 **L Hicks** *Bhnd til hdwy 7; 5l 7th ½way; 7l 7th 12; eff 15; 3½l 4th nxt; went 4l 2nd 3 out; stayed on to ld nr fin*
	2	hd	**Button Boy** 9-2 **S Morris** *2nd til ld 12; jmpd rt frm 3 out; 2l clr last; edged rt flat; hdd nr fin*
[1111^{4}]	3	5	**Al Jawwal** 33-1 **Miss L Allan** *(xnb) Chsd ldrs; 3½l 5th ½way; 6l 6th 12; 5l 6th 16; stayed on; went 3rd flat*
[1147^{1}]	4	1	**Hessac (FR)** (7a) 4-5F **B Pollock** *Prom; 2l 3rd ½way; went 2nd 13; mist 14; dem & rdn 3 out; one pce*
[1264^{2}]	5	3	**Black Book (IRE)** (5a) 16-1 **P Millington** *Hld up; 7l 9th ½way; hdwy 11; 5l 4th nxt; rdn 14; 4l 5th 16; no imp*
[996^{4}]	6	½	**Gymcrak Gorjos** (5a) 9-2 **G Brewer** *7s-9/2; sn prom; 3l 4th ½way; 5½l 5th & rmdrs 12; went 3rd 14; rdn 3 out; sn btn*
[1206^{2}]	7	10	**Benova Boy** 14-1 **J Diment** *Swtng; ld to 12; rdn 14; wknd & 12l 7th 16*
[894^{P}]	P		**Kemiller (IRE)** 33-1 **F Hutsby** *Swtng; w ldrs; 4l 6th ½way; lost plce & 7½l 8th 12; wknd 15; 16l 9th nxt; wl bhnd when pu 3 out*
[791^{F}]	P		**Please Call (IRE)** 10-1 **G Barfoot-Saunt** *A bhnd; 10l 10th ½way; 12l 10th 12; t.o & pu last*
[971^{P}]	P		**Silly Boy** (7a) 33-1 **R Barrett** *2 handlers; swtng; a bhnd; 13l 11th ½way; t.o & pu 14*

[1215^P] P   **Waisu** (5a) 33-1 **R Garrard** *Swtng; chsd ldrs; 6l 8th ½way; 8l 9th & rdn 12; wknd & 15l 8th 16; t.o & pu last*

OFFICIAL DISTANCES: s hd, 1½l   **TIME:** 6min 14.5s

1419 Restricted (Div 2), 12st   11 ran

[1012¹]	1		**SHOEMAKER (IRE)** evensF **S Morris** *Ww; last to ½way; gd hdwy & 3rd 12; 5l down 16; rdn to ld app last; r.o wl*
[1146³]	2	1½	**Gangster** 5-1 **R Cope** *A.p; went 2nd 9; rdn 3 out; ev ch last; unable to qckn*
[1146²]	3	5	**Blayneys Privilege** 8-1 **Miss T Habgood** *2nd til ld 4; hdd & no ex app last*
[1218^U]	4	6	**Macfin (IRE)** 7-1 **Miss L Allan** *Last trio to 7; 8th ½way; 7l 6th 13; outpcd & 14l 6th 16; stayed on wl frm 2 out; nt rch ldrs*
[1287³]	5	5	**Fine Times** (tt) 8-1 **M Mackley** *(bf)Hld up; 6l 7th ½way; hdwy & 4½l 5th 12; 9l 5th 16; no ex*
[1204¹]	6	8	**Finnigan's Lot (IRE)** 11-2 **M Walters** *Hld up; 5l 6th ½way; hdwy & 4l 4th 12; 7l 4th 16; rdn & wknd 3 out*
[844¹]	P		**Abbey Flyer** 12-1 **T Illsley** *Ld to 4; 2nd/3rd to 11; wkng when blun 12; 19l 9th nxt; t.o & pu 16*
[1264³]	P		**Court Thyne (IRE)** 33-1 **P Millington** *Prom; 3l 4th ½way; wknd qckly 12; 20l 10th nxt; mist 14; t.o & pu 15*
[1071^P]	P		**Over The Barrow** 33-1 **T Lane** *Swtng; a bhnd; 10l 11th ½way; 24l 11th 13; pu & dism 14; lame*
[894^P]	P		**Rolcap** 20-1 **J Gasper** *Swtng; chsd ldrs; 4l 5th ½way; lost plce 12; 12l 8th nxt; t.o & pu 3 out*
[1146^P]	F		**Royal Orchard** (bl) 33-1 **A Martin** *Hld up; 10th ½way; eff 12; 9l 7th nxt; no imp when fell 15*

OFFICIAL DISTANCES: 1½l, 4l   **TIME:** 6min 09.1s

1420 Open Maiden (Div 1, Part 1), 12st   12 ran

[1270³]	1		**THE BIG LAD (IRE)** 9-2 **G Smith** *A.p; went 2nd 5; ld 6-8; ld 11; drew clr app last; rdly*
[1021³]	2	8	**Well I Never** 3-1F **L Hicks** *Trckd ldrs; 4l 5th ½way; wnt 5l 3rd 13 & 2nd 15; jnd wnr & mist nxt; ev ch 2 out; sn wknd*
[1290³]	3	20	**Fortune Hunter (IRE)** 4-1 **P Millington** *Hld up; 4½l 6th ½way; mist 10; 5l 4th when mist 12; blun 15; 10l 4th nxt; sn wknd; went poor 3rd flat*
[1219⁴]	4	1½	**Anneka Louise** (5a) 16-1 **N Kent** *(bf) Sn prom; 3l 4th ½way; went 2nd 12-15; 4l 3rd & rdn nxt; sn wknd*
[1270⁵]	5	15	**Copper Thorn** (5a) 12-1 **Mrs C Boyes** *(boh) Swtng; 2nd til ld & mist 4; hdd 6; blun bad & lost plce 7; 10l 8th ½way; 10l 7th 12; lost tch 14; 24l 7th 16; t.o*
[1070²]	P		**Camden Kid (IRE)** (tt) 4-1 **K Green** *2 handlers; swtng; prom; mist 4; 3rd ½way; 6½l 5th 12; sn lost plce; 20l 5th 16; t.o & pu last*
	P		**Fancy A Buck** (12a) 8-1 **T Lane** *Bckwd; hld up; mist 5; hdwy 8; 5l 7th ½way; wknd qckly & 14l 9th 12; pu 13*
[1220^P]	P		**Game Drive (IRE)** 16-1 **P Newton** *Swtng; a bhnd; 20l 11th ½way; 18l 10th 12; t.o when mist 14; pu 16*
[1284⁴]	P		**Ilandra (IRE)** (5a) 33-1 **N Pearce** *Nt jw; a bhnd; 16l 10th ½way; 21l 11th 12; t.o 14; pu 16*
[1021^P]	P		**Moon Island** (5a) 16-1 **J Diment** *Nvr on terms; 15l 9th ½way; rdn 11; 13l 8th 12; lost tch 14; 23l 6th 16; t.o & pu last*
[798^P]	P		**Royal Charger (IRE)** 33-1 **R Armson** *Swtng; ld to 4; 2nd/3rd til ld 8; hdd 11; 4l 3rd when mist 12; wknd rap & 20l 9th nxt; t.o & pu 14*
[786⁷]	P		**Safe Cottage** 33-1 **M Cowley** *A bhnd; 25l 12th ½way; t.o 12; pu 15*

OFFICIAL DISTANCES: 8l, 20l   **TIME:** 6min 10.8s

1421 Open Maiden (Div 1, Part 2), 12st   12 ran

[845⁴]	1		**STEEL MY SONG** (5a) 8-1 **S Morris** *Swtng; hld up & bhnd; 17l 8th ½way; hdwy & 7l 6th 12; went 2l 3rd 15; ld 3 out; 4l clr last; just hld on*
[1291^{3d}]	2	1	**Polly Live Wire** (5a) 7-2F **P Millington** *2 handlers; hld up & bhnd; 15l 16th ½way; 9l 7th 12; hdwy & 5l 6th when mist 14; went 4l 2nd 2 out; r.o*
[1147³]	3	3	**Master Banker** (2ow) 14-1 **J I Pritchard** *A.p; 4l 3rd ½way; went 2nd 11; ld 12; qcknd 4l clr when rn wide bend bef 3 out; sn hdd; mist 2 out; one pce*
[1219^P]	4	12	**Light The Sky** 9-2 **J Turcan** *Prom; went 2nd 7-16; rdn 3 out; sn wknd*
[1018^P]	5	10	**Cumberland Youth** 25-1 **Miss J Garley** *A wl bhnd; 22l 10th ½way; 25l 8th 12; plodded on*
[797^P]	6	5	**Mail Shot (IRE)** (7a) 7-1 **N Kent** *(xnb) Swtng; ld to 3; 5l 4th ½way; mist 12; went 3rd 13-15; 3l 5th nxt; rdn 3 out; wknd qckly*

[1218U]	P	**Campbellhill (IRE)** 10-1 R Garrard *Swtng; jmpd atrocious; rmdrs 3; 20l 9th & hrd rdn ½way; t.o & pu 12*
[1220P]	P	**Grannies Delight (IRE)** 25-1 L Hicks *2nd to 7; 6l 5th ½way; rmdrs 12; 4l 5th 14; 2½l 4th & rdn when mist 16; sn wknd; t.o & pu last*
[1220P]	P	**Imperial Tokay (USA)** 25-1 A Brown *Nd; mists 4 & 6; 16l 7th ½way; mist 10; wl bhnd when pu 11*
[1021F]	P	**Looks Like Reign** 10-1 B McKim *Went down v early; ur & rn loose bef start; ld 3-12; wknd & 8l 7th 14; pu 15*
[1292P]	P	**Rising Dawn** 10-1 A Sansome *Bumped to 8th & pu 5; lame*
	R	**Super Trouper (IRE)** 8-1 M Wall *Lw; hld up; 10l 7th when rn out 6*

OFFICIAL DISTANCES: 1l, 3l TIME: 6min 18.3s

1422 Open Maiden (Div 2, Part 1), 12st   15 ran

[1068³]	1		**MICK MACKIE (IRE)** 4-5F Julian Pritchard *A.p; ld 2-4; 2nd til ld 16; sn drew clr; comf*
[799⁵]	2	15	**Mustang Molly** (5a) 11-1 A Martin *Ld til hdd & mist 2; 2l 3rd ½way; 3l 3rd 16; went 5l 2nd nxt; wkng when mist last*
	3	1	**Moss Harvey** (7a) 12-1 R Barrett *(bh) Lw; hld up & bhnd; 16l 10th ½way; 7l 6th nxt; 4l 4th 16; no ex frm 3 out; promising*
[1147P]	4	12	**Out By Night (IRE)** 12-1 D Barlow *2nd til ld 4; hit 14; hdd 16; sn wknd; fin tired*
[1012P]	5	7	**More Mettle** 33-1 J Diment *Hld up & bhnd; 20l 11th ½way; 14l 11th 12; hdwy 13; 6l 5th when blun 16; sn wknd*
[1251⁴]	6	½	**Saxon Moss** 33-1 G Smith *Chsd ldrs; 3l 4th ½way; mist 11; 6l 5th nxt; 7l 6th 16; sn wknd*
[749⁴]	7	20	**In The Future (IRE)** (5a) 33-1 M Wall *Hld up; 11l 8th ½way; 11l 9th 12; lost tch 13; t.o*
[1012P]	P		**Bally Seamus (IRE)** (bl) 10-1 R Cope *Mounted on course; chsd ldrs; 8l 7th & rdn ½way; nt r.o; wl bhnd when pu 12*
	P		**Court Alert** (7a) 16-1 S Morris *Hld up & bhnd; 23l 13th ½way; hdwy 12; 8l 7th nxt; 15l 8th & wkng when pu 16*
[1290⁵]	P		**Craftbook Marchesa (IRE)** (5a) 33-1 P Millington *Hld up & bhnd; 15l 9th ½way; 12l 10th 12; hdwy 14; 9l 7th & rdn 16; wkng when mist 3 out; pu 2 out*
[1291P]	P		**Don Royal** 33-1 R Armson *A bhnd; mist & rmdrs 6; 28l 14th ½way; mist 10; t.o & pu 11*
[438F]	P		**Gilded Way** 20-1 J Merry *Swtng; ss; nt jw; sn t.o; pu 8*
[1012P]	P		**Highfurlong (IRE)** 33-1 Miss H Irving *Hld up; hdwy 7; 5l 6th ½way; mist 10; 9l 7th & rdn 12; sn wknd; wl bhnd when pu 15; lame*
[1012⁴]	P		**Metro Fashion (IRE)** 4-1 T Lane *Hld up; hdwy 8; 4l 5th ½way; 4l 4th 12; wkng when mist 14; blun 15; 20l 9th when pu nxt*
	P		**Southern Target** 20-1 A Coe *Bckwd; a bhnd; 22l 12th ½way; 25l 12th 12; pu 13*

OFFICIAL DISTANCES: 20l, 1l TIME: 6min 11.3s

1423 Open Maiden (Div 2, Part 2), 12st   13 ran

[1219²]	1		**ROUND THE BEND** 7-2 Miss L Allan *Swtng; pulled hrd; hdwy to ld 5; r.o wl frm 2 out*
[436⁵]	2	5	**Sparebit** (5a) 5-1 S Morris *Hld up; 7l 8th ½way; hdwy 11; went cl 3rd nxt & 2nd 15; ev ch 2 out; wknd flat*
[1204P]	3	1½	**Ben Gilmore** 20-1 J Diment *A.p; 3l 3rd ½way; went 2nd 12-15; 4l 3rd nxt; one pce 3 out*
[1196²]	4	7	**Proper Charlie** 7-4F T Lane *Hld up; hdwy 7; 4l 4th ½way; lost plce & 8l 6th 13; blun 14; 11l 6th 16; stayed on one pce*
[1270R]	5	6	**The Bombers Moon** 33-1 N Kent *Swtng; hld up; 6½l 7th ½way; 7½l 8th 12; hdwy 13; 4½l 4th 16; wknd 3 out*
[1207⁵]	6	4	**Devil's Sting (IRE)** 20-1 J Richardson *Chsd ldrs; 5l 5th ½way; 6l 5th 12; 7l 5th 15; wknd nxt*
[1291²]	7	8	**Mandalay Man (IRE)** (bl) 10-1 P Millington *Hld up; 6l 6th ½way; 6½l 6th 12; 14l 7th 16; no imp*
[786⁴]	8	30	**Game Gunner** (7a) 7-1 N Ridout *Bckwd; jmpd slow & lost plce 3; 9l 11th ½way; 12l 12th 12; t.o 15*
[1125⁵]	9	8	**Bonnie Amy** (12a) 20-1 L Hicks *A bhnd; 12l 13th ½way; 13l 13th 12; t.o 15*
[514F]	P		**Phar Away Cruise** (5a) 33-1 M Cowley *(pricker os) Ld 2-5; 2nd til lost plce & 7l 7th 12; wkng when mist 13; sn t.o; pu 3 out*
	P		**Politina** (5a) 20-1 J Turcan *Bckwd; prom til lost plce 6; 8½l 10th ½way; 10l 9th 12; sn wknd; t.o & pu 16*
[1290⁴]	P		**River Surprise (IRE)** 10-1 R Garrard *Nvr gng wl; 10l 12th & rdn ½way; wl bhnd 14; t.o & pu 3 out*
[1264²]	U		**Tarjumaan (USA)** 33-1 A Brown *Ld to 2; mist 6; lost plce & mist 8; 7½l 9th ½way; bhnd when saddle slpd & ur bend aft 12*

OFFICIAL DISTANCES: 2l, 2l TIME: 6min 16.2s

Slobadam was withdrawn not under orders

Lauderdale
Mosshouses (LH 8F,19J) Sun, 7 May (GOOD to FIRM)

1424 Hunt
4 ran

[1118²]	1		**MINI CRUISE** 1-2F L Morgan *Ld 1; trckd ldr aft; 5l 2nd 6; 2l 2nd 12; ld aft 14; qcknd & 6l up when mist 2 out; 4l clr at last; hrd prsd flat; all out*
[916ᵁ]	2	hd	**Kings Lane** (5ow) 7-2 M Dun *Trckd ldng pr in mostly 3rd til 9l 4th 11; hit 13; prog to 3l 3rd 15; went 1l 2nd 16; 2l 2nd nxt; str rn flat; just failed*
[421ᴾ]	3	10	**Dun Law** (5ow) 25-1 Miss Gina Hutchinson *Mostly last; 8l last 4; 7l 3rd 11; hit nxt; prog to 1l 2nd 14; 5l last & outpcd 16; 10l 3rd 3 out; kpt on one pce*
[973⁵]	4	10	**Thinkaboutthat (IRE)** 8-1 J Muir *Oht; ld 2; 3l clr 10; hdd aft 14; 3l 3rd & outpcd 16; releg last nxt; sn strugg; 15l last 2 out*

OFFICIAL DISTANCES: hd, 20l TIME: 6min 18.0s
*Just Felix (14-1) was withdrawn not under orders - unseated rider at start;
Rule 4 deduction 5p in the pound*

1425 Intermediate, 12st
6 ran

[1162ᴾ]	1		**DIVET HILL** 7-4 M Clayton *Jw; made all at gd pce; 4l ahd 6; 8l up 3 out; sn in comm; easy; quite impressive*
[717²]	2	20	**Dun Rose** (5a,5x) 6-4F C Storey *Lw; oht; a chsng wnr; 2l 2nd & jmpd rt 5; 6l 2nd 15; mist nxt; 8l 2nd & outpcd 3 out; tired & mist nxt; no ch w wnr*
[973³]	3	15	**Driminamore (IRE)** 10-1 Miss R Ramsay *Rr til prog in 10l 3rd aft 5-8; disp 15l 3rd 13-15; outpcd & nd aft; kpt on*
[1159⁵]	4	1	**Mischievous Andy (IRE)** 14-1 Mrs K Hargreave *(xnb) Prom early; 2l 2nd 2; mostly 4th aft; mist 11 & pushed along; 12l last 13; strugg nxt; kpt on; nd*
[1118¹]	F		**Flaming Sunrise** 7-2 Miss D Calder *Lw; prom early; drpd to rr 4; 8l last 5; sn wl bhnd; 20l 5th 8; some prog frm 12 to disp 15l 3rd 13; outpcd 15; bhnd when fell nxt*
[915ᴾ]	F		**Senora D'Or** (5a) 33-1 Miss M Bremner *A rr; 5l last 3; 12l l5th 6; 20l 6th & outpcd 8; strugg 14; btn 4th when fell hvly last; rdr inj*

OFFICIAL DISTANCES: dist, 15l TIME: 6min 03.0s

1426 Ladies Open
7 ran

[1364¹]	1		**BALISTEROS (FR)** 2-1JF Miss J Wormall *(bnh) Hld up in rr; 7l 6th 7; 8l 6th nxt; 5l 6th 12; prog to trck ldrs 15; ld brief nxt; 1l up 2 out; fnd ex when prsd*
[1161²]	2	1	**Pharmistice (IRE)** 7-1JF Miss N Stirling *(xnb) 2 handlers; oht; ld; mist 9; 1l up til jnd 12; hdd 16; cl 2nd & ev ch last; chall flat; sn outpcd*
[1079³]	3	½	**Riparius (USA)** 4-1 Miss P Robson *Mid-div; 8l 4th 8; mist 9; 5l 4th 13; prog & ev ch 16; 5l 3rd & outpcd app 3 out; stayed on app last; r.o flat*
[1150³]	4	8	**Sharp Thyne (IRE)** (bl) 10-1 Mrs K Hargreave *Trckd ldr; 1l 2nd 4; disp ld 12; eff til outpcd aft 16; 12l 4th nxt*
[1119²]	5	10	**Astrac Trio (USA)** 12-1 Mrs A Hamilton *Oht; trckd ldrs; 3l 3rd 3; 4l 4th 5; knocked marker over app 9; outpcd 13; a chsng ldrs aft; 15l 6th nxt; nd*
[1160⁶]	6	1½fs	**Dashmar** 33-1 Miss J Hedley *A rr; 15l last 8; 10l last 10; pushed along 12; one pce; t.o 15*
[1079²]	P		**Nova Nita** (5a) 4-1 Mrs V Jackson *Rr early; 3rd 6; prog to trck ldrs 11; disp ld nxt; ev ch til knocked flag frm marker post app 14; nd aft; 5l 3rd nxt; 10l 5th & wkng when pu 16*

OFFICIAL DISTANCES: ½l, 2l TIME: 6min 01.0s

1427 Restricted, 12st
13 ran

[910¹]	1		**SUNNYCLIFF** 4-1 C Storey *(xnb) A handy; 111 5th 8; 5l 6th 9; prog to 2l 2nd 15; sn ld; qcknd 3l clr 2 out; eased flat; comf*
[1083¹]	2	5	**Superior Weapon (IRE)** 6-4F M Clayton *(bnh) Ld & tried to make all; 3l ahd 6; hdd 16; 3l 2nd 2 out; 8l 2nd & hld when mist last*
[1342ᴾ]	3	4	**Border Glory** 7-1 P Maitland-Carew *Chsd ldrs; 4l 3rd 4; 8l 3rd 16; outpcd & bad mist 2 out; kpt on wl app last*
[1077¹]	4	8	**Good (IRE)** (tt) 12-1 Mrs V Jackson *Oht; chsd ldrs; prog 8 & 3l 3rd 11; 4l 4th 14; outpcd aft nxt; kpt on app 2 out*
[976⁴]	5	2	**Roscoe Burn** 8-1 R Morgan *Oht; rr; hit 5; pushed along to 12l 7th 11; some prog 14 & 12l 5th app 16; eff & sn one pce*
[1152ᴾ]	6	8	**Boris Brook** 9-2 T Oates *Tubed; a rr; 25l last 3; wl bhnd 7; t.o 12; kpt on wl aft 16; nd*
[1118ᵁ]	7	3	**Tursal (IRE)** 25-1 A Crookston *Mid-div; outpcd 13; nd aft; kpt on wl flat; tk 7th nr line*
[1081⁴]	8	½	**Buckaroo** (5a) 16-1 Mrs A Tweedie *2 handlers; swtng; a rr; 15l 11th app 9; nvr nrr; stayed on past btn horses frm 16; tk 8th nr line*

[1162³]	9	½	**Kings Token** 5-1 J Walton *Chsd ldrs; 4l 4th app 5; 8l 4th 6; 8l 6th 12; outpcd & 15l 4th 14; sn one pce; 7th til eased & dem nr line*
[976ᴾ]	10	nk	**Hey Chief (IRE)** 12-1 P Strang Steel *Mid-div; 6th 8; rmdrs nxt & nd aft; strugg 14; t.o 3 out*
[979¹]	11	10	**Solwaysands** 33-1 S Hughes *Chsd ldrs; 10l 4th 8; strugg 13 & nd; t.o 16*
[976¹⁰]	P		**Polly's Lady** (5a) 25-1 T Scott *Oht; a rr; 30l down 7; fnce bhnd 12; pu 13*
[1159³]	P		**Tropnevad** (bl) 25-1 Mrs K Hargreave *Prom; hit 2; 3l 2nd 6; 4l 5th 13; wknd aft; t.o 16; pu nxt*

OFFICIAL DISTANCES: 6l, 5l   **TIME:** 6min 06.0s

1428 Mens Open, 12st   8 ran

[1120⁴]	1		**RIVERSIDE RUN (IRE)** 10-1 J Walton *12s-10s; prom; disp 11 2nd 3; 3l 3rd app 5 & 2l 2nd nxt; ld app 3 out; 1l up & prsd last; stayed on wl flat*
[1024ᶠ]	2	1	**Dennett Lough (IRE)** 3-1 C Storey *(bh) Trckd ldrs; 6l 4th 5; disp 4l 3rd 12; 3l 2nd 16; rdn 2 out; prog u.p to 1l 2nd & ev ch last; nt qckn*
[1078⁵]	3	½	**Todcrag** (7x) 2-1F T Scott *Oht; trckd ldr; disp 1l 2nd & pulling 3; 5l 3rd 6; 5l 5th 12; 8l 6th 15; prog & ev ch aft 3 out; 3l 3rd app last; r.o*
	4	1	**Wudimp** 5-1 L Morgan *Oht; chsd ldrs; 6l 4th 6; 4l 4th 14; ev ch til outpcd aft 3 out; eff app last; kpt on wl flat*
[1345⁵]	5	½	**Charlieadams (IRE)** (2ow) 8-1 J Muir *Oht; ld; 2l up 6; hdd app 3 out; kpt on one pce*
[1159²ᵈ]	6	6	**Minella Gold (IRE)** 6-1 W Renwick *Oht; hld up in rr; 7l 6th 7; 10l off pce nxt; prog to 6l 5th 14; smooth hdwy & ev ch 3 out; rdn & sn outpcd*
[1117¹]	7	runin	**Fordstown (IRE)** (7x) 6-1 J Alexander *(bf) A rr; jmpd slow 5; 10l last nxt; 15l off pce 8; rmdrs in last aft nxt; lost tch app 13; detach nxt; t.o 16*
[1080ᴾ]	P		**Chummy's Saga** (7x) 25-1 R Morgan *A rr; 10l last 4; 8l 6th 8; pushed along aft 10; jmpd slow & strugg 14; sn 20l down; t.o & pu 3 out*

OFFICIAL DISTANCES: 1l, ½l   **TIME:** 6min 05.0s

1429 Marsh UK/TBA PPORA Club Members Mares, 12st   5 ran

[918²]	1		**STRATHMORE LODGE** (5a) 6-1 D Jewett *Cl up; 2l 4th 6; 4l 4th 8; disp 3l 3rd 11-13; 1l 2nd 16; ld app 2 out; 4l clr last; stayed on wl*
[1079ᴾ]	2	6	**Little Santa (IRE)** (5a) 8-1 Mrs K Hargreave *10s-8s; oht; trckd ldr; pulling; 1l 2nd 3; 5l 2nd nxt; ld 6; 3l up 13; 1l ahd 16; hdd & hit 2 out; sn outpcd*
[1160¹]	3	2½	**Rainbow Times (IRE)** (5a) (bl) 4-6F C Storey *Trckd ldrs; 6l 3rd 5; disp 3l 3rd 11; mist & rmdr aft nxt; 5l 3rd 12; outpcd app 3 out; kpt on one pce*
[1082⁴]	4	20	**Paperback Writer** (5a) (vis) 50-1 A Robson *Ld 1; reluct & rmdr 3; 3l up nxt; hdd app 6; cl 2nd til mist 10 & rmdr; 4l 3rd 14; 6l 4th nxt; wknd aft 3 out; 20l 4th & btn 2 out*
[1081¹]	S		**Allrite Bonny Lass** (5a) 7-4 Miss P Robson *Unruly padd; nt a fluent & nvr gng wl in rr; rmdr 2; 6l last 3; 12l last 5; 15l down 16; slpd up app nxt; rdr inj*

OFFICIAL DISTANCES: 5l, 3l   **TIME:** 6min 12.0s

1430 Open Maiden (Div 1), 12st   9 ran

[914²]	1		**BIG BARK (IRE)** 5-4F C Storey *(xnb) A.p; 6l 4th 4; cl 4th 14; ld brief 16; ld aft nxt til hdd agn 2 out; rdn to chall last; stayed on to ld flat*
[1084²]	2	1	**Test Of Loyalty** 4-1 A Robson *A.p; 3l 3rd app 5; disp 2l 2nd 11; pushed along 15; ld 3 out; hdd brief til ld agn 2 out; jnd last; hdd & no ex flat*
[1123⁴]	3	2	**Myles Of Moss (IRE)** (5a) 8-1 W Renwick *Hld up in rr; prog to 4l 6th 7 til eff app 2 out; drvn & r.o one pce app last*
[1084ᴾ]	4	2	**Farthing Wood** 10-1 Mrs V Jackson *Rr; 6l 6th 6; prog to 1l 2nd 8; disp 2l 2nd 11-13; mist nxt; ev ch til outpcd 2 out; kpt on one pce*
[1166⁵]	5	8	**Spectacular View (IRE)** (7a) 33-1 M Clayton *Ld; 2l clr 13; hdd 16; ev ch til outpcd app nxt; sn no ex; kpt on*
[1123⁷]	6	8	**Meadowleck** (5a) (tt) 33-1 T Davidson *(bf) A rr; 7l 7th 9; stdly lsng ground frm 12; 12l last & strugg app 3 out*
[1165ᵁ]	7	2	**I Say Dancer (IRE)** (5a) 4-1 Miss C Metcalfe *10s-4s; swtng; chsd ldrs; mist & nrly ur 1; disp 6l 4th 4; still 6l 4th 16; wknd qckly app 2 out; kpt on*
[1163ᴾ]	P		**Normandy Duke (NZ)** 33-1 Mrs K Hargreave *Oht; prom early; 2l 2nd 3; ld brief 5; sn drpd back; wknd 9; lsng tch 11; pu 13*
	P		**Primitive Satin** (7a,4ow) 14-1 J Walton *A rr; 10l last 2; 20l last 7; fnce bhnd when pu 10*

OFFICIAL DISTANCES: 1l, 2l   **TIME:** 6min 18.0s

1431 Open Maiden (Div 2), 12st   **10 ran**

[808F]	1		**ARDNUT** 16-1 **C Storey** *(xnb)* Tde; mid-div; 5th 6; prog to jn ldr 14; ld nxt; hdd aft 16; sn ld agn til hdd app last; rallied to ld agn cl home; btr for rce
[1122²]	2	½	**Blackchesters** 5-1 **J Walton** Trckd ldr; 3l 2nd 4; 1l 2nd 12; prog to ld aft 16; hdd brief; 1l up & pckd last; no ex & hdd cl home
[1163²]	3	8	**The Dyke Louper** (5a) 4-1 **B Lusted** Hld up; 12l last app 8; pushed along in 5l last 15; 7l down nxt; some prog aft & ev ch 3 out; kpt on one pce
[1082³]	4	3	**Vernham Wood** 7-1 **Mrs V Jackson** 10s-7s; prom; 2l 3rd 5; ld 10; disp 14; hdd nxt; ev ch app 3 out; sn outpcd
[978F]	F		**Billieburn** 2-1F **L Morgan** Unruly start; collided w rival & fell 2 (horse's hd hit Sledmere's rdr's hd)
[1123²]	P		**Harleyburn** 4-1 **Mrs A Hamilton** Wrs; started nrly fnce bhnd; fnce bhnd 3; pu aft 5
[1163P]	P		**Just Felix** 25-1 **M Clayton** *(xnb,bf)* Oht; ld; 3l up 4; hdd 10; prom til 2l 3rd 16; lost tch app 3 out; wknd qckly & pu nxt
	P		**Sledmere (IRE)** (7a) 10-1 **G Moscrop** Rr when rdr hit on hd by faller 2; 7l last 11; hit 12 & inj rdr; lsng tch (& prob consciousness) when rn wide aft; 20l last when pu app 13 & rdr plummeted to ground
[1123³]	F		**Smiddy Lad** 5-1 **T Scott** *(xnb)* Mid-div; 4l 4th 6; 10l off pce 8; prog to trck ldrs nxt; cl 5th & ev ch when fell 16
[1163P]	P		**Star Design (IRE)** 20-1 **T Glass** Mid-div; 7l 7th 7; 4l 4th 10; in tch til wknd qckly 16; pu 3 out

OFFICIAL DISTANCES: ½l, 5l **TIME:** 6min 17.0s

Exeter (RH 11F,19J)
Tue, 9 May (FIRM, GOOD to FIRM in places)

1432 Portman Financial Planners HC   **12 ran**

[1023¹]	1		**GRIMLEY GALE (IRE)** 11-11 2-5F **R Burton** Trckd ldr til ld 16; sn clr; eased flat; impressive
[680¹]	2	18	**Noyan** 11-12 7-2 **P York** Swtng; pulled hrd; jw; ld til hdd 16; kpt on but sn no ch w wnr; fin tired
[1306⁴]	3	3	**Hillhead (IRE)** 11-05 25-1 **J Barnes** A 3rd/4th; nt fluent 13; chall nxt; sn outpcd; poor 3rd frm 16
[583²]	4	1½	**Track O' profit (IRE)** 11-05 25-1 **Miss S Young** Hdwy 6; trckd ldrs 8; 4th 11; lost plce nxt; rallied 14; 8l 4th 15; outpcd & no ch frm nxt
[637²]	5	18	**Camera Man** 11-05 25-1 **C Heard** Mid-div; rdn 12; hdwy 14; 9l 5th nxt; sn wknd
[1261²]	6	27	**If You Say So** 11-05 50-1 **J Young** Prom; 3rd 6; nt fluent 9 (water); wknd & blun 10; t.o
[854²]	7	1	**Where's Sam (IRE)** 11-05 50-1 **S Craddock** Hit 6; bhnd; detach 10th 11; brief eff 12; sn wknd; t.o
[1256¹]	P		**Contradict** 11-05 25-1 **Miss S Gardner** Sn towards rr; 9th 11; no ch aft; t.o & pu 16
[768⁴]	P		**Cool Character (IRE)** 11-05 66-1 **Miss T Newman** Sn bhnd; t.o 11; pu last
[1304⁴]	P		**Flapjack Lad** 11-05 40-1 **Miss A Goschen** Chsd ldrs; 5th 11; wknd 14; t.o & pu last
[1340⁶]	P		**Muntafi** 11-05 (bl) 50-1 **M Keel** Ss; bhnd; hdwy 8; 7th 11; wknd nxt; t.o & pu 2 out
[928³]	P		**Verde Luna** (vis) 16-1 **A Wintle** Bhnd; mod 11th 11; some hdwy 13; sn wknd; t.o & pu 2 out

TIME: 6min 07.4s **TOTE:** £1.40; places £1.10,£1.10,£4.70 **Ex:** £2.00 **CSF:** £1.87 **Tri:** £14.80

Chepstow (LH 11F,18J)
Wed, 10 May (FIRM)

1433 Jorrocks Nov HC   **14 ran**

[1238¹]	1		**FINNIGAN FREE** 11-07 3-1F **A Honeyball** Hld up & bhnd; 9th 11; some prog at 13; prsd ldr aft 14 til ld last; rdn & r.o wl flat
[1103⁶]	2	1	**Chasing The Bride** 12-04 7-2 **M Miller** Settled trckng ldrs; 5th 11; lft 2nd aft 14; slt advant til hdd last; drvn & kpt on
[954³]	3	2½	**The Hobbit (IRE)** 11-07 8-1 **N Mitchell** Jmpd slow 1; in tch til 7th 11; outpcd 12; rallied app 14; jnd ldng pr nxt; 1l 3rd 2 out; nt qckn last
[1338¹]	4	9	**Bullens Bay (IRE)** 11-07 20-1 **Miss F Wilson** Chsd ldrs; 6th 11; eff & hit 14; sn outpcd
[1335²]	5	2½	**Finnow Thyne (IRE)** 12-02 5-1 **D Dunsdon** Ld til aft 1; hit 3; 4th 11; prom til rdn & wknd aft 13
[1340²]	6	½	**Shuil's Star (IRE)** 11-11 4-1 **E Williams** Hld up & bhnd; 10th 11; some hdwy 14; nvr rchd ldrs

[801¹]	7	¾	**Forest Feather (IRE)** 11-12 12-1 **A Dalton** *Trckd ldrs; went 3rd 11; ld 12 til aft nxt; wknd aft 14*
[1257²]	8	2	**Bomba Charger** 11-09 20-1 **A Holdsworth** *Stumbled aft 7; 2nd/3rd til w ldr 10-12; lost plce & mist 13; nd aft*
[1293ᵁ]	9	dist	**Alska (FR)** 11-02 50-1 **Miss W Southcombe** *Mist 5; bhnd frm 8; t.o aft 13; fnce bhnd*
[1137²]	P		**Fossy Bear** 11-02 20-1 **Miss S Young** *A bhnd; lost tch 12; t.o & pu 3 out*
[1176¹]	P		**Mosside** 11-09 50-1 **N Harris** *Jmpd v slow 1; sn bhnd & reluct; t.o 6; pu 15*
[1175²]	P		**Uckerby Lad** 11-07 50-1 **C Heard** *Hld up & bhnd; lost tch 12; t.o & pu 14*
[799²]	P		**Verity Valentine (IRE)** 11-06 25-1 **T Gibney** *Ld aft 1-12; wknd rap aft 13; pu nxt*
[1355ᵁ]	P		**Wonastow** 11-09 50-1 **F Windsor Clive** *Hld up; eff & jmpd slow 8; sn rdn; 8th 11; wknd 12; t.o & pu 14*

TIME: 5min 54.8s TOTE: £5.00; places £2.60,£2.00,£1.90 Ex: £42.30 CSF: £12.49 Tri: £142.50

Fakenham (LH 6F,18J)
Wed, 10 May (FIRM)

1434 Basil Cook 80th Birthday Essandem HC   7 ran

[1289¹]	1		**SPRING GALE (IRE)** 11-05 4-5F **Miss Z Turner** *A gng wl; chsd ldr 2; ld 5; hit 9; nt rdn flat; easy*
[1341¹]	2	2½	**Pro Bono (IRE)** 11-11 8-1 **M Foley** *Ld 2-5; chsd wnr aft; hit 10; mist 14 (water) & nxt; no ch w wnr aft*
[1156²]	3	8	**Torus Spa (IRE)** 11-12 9-4 **A Sansome** *Hld up & bhnd; hld up in last pr; hdwy 11; 3rd 14; 10l down & btn aft 3 out*
[1005³]	4	14	**Ebullient Equiname (IRE)** 11-05 11-1 **S Morris** *Prsd ldrs; rdn 14; wknd nxt*
[1418³]	5	dist	**Al Jawwal** 11-01 33-1 **R Garrard** *Nt jw; prsd ldrs til hit 10; rdn & strugg nxt; mist 13; t.o 3 out*
[1214²]	6	4	**Tom's Surprise** 11-01 25-1 **N Kent** *Last pr; hit 7; lost tch 11; t.o 3 out*
[796²]	7	4	**Ryders Wells** 11-01 (bl) 50-1 **S Walker** *Ld to 2; rdn frm 4; 4th 12; nt r.o lost tch nxt; t.o 3 out*

TIME: 6min 13.3s TOTE: £1.60; places £1.60,£2.20 Ex: £9.10 CSF: £6.84 Tri: £17.40

Warwickshire
Ashorne (RH 8F,18J) Wed, 10 May (FIRM)

1435 Open Maiden (Div 1), 12st   13 ran

[1207ᵁ]	1		**JUDICIAL QUEEN** (5a) 13-2 **A Charles-Jones** *Hld up & bhnd; 9th aft 10; 5th & prog 13; 5l 3rd 3 out; stayed on to chall aft nxt; ld last; rdn clr*
[1204ᶠ]	2	4	**True Hustler** (bl) 9-2 **F Hutsby** *Tk keen hld; ld to 2; prom til ld agn 12; hdd 15 & sn 7l down; kpt on to ld agn app last; sn hdd & outpcd*
[1360ᴿ]	3	5	**Grain Hill** (5a) (bl) 20-1 **M Wall** *Mounted outside padd; pulled hrd in midfield; 6l 7th aft 10; went 3rd 14; ld 15 & sn 7l clr; wknd & hdd aft 2 out*
[1421³]	4	½	**Master Banker** 4-1 **J I Pritchard** *Rdn padd; chsd ldrs; mist 5; cl 6th when blun 11; outpcd & mist 13; nd frm 15*
[1012ᶠ]	5	2	**Hesgreen** 16-1 **M Rimell** *Tk keen hld; ld 4-12; rdn & wknd 15*
[1018ᶠ]	6	4	**Truly Optimistic** (5a) 10-1 **C Wadland** *Lw; prom; 4th aft 10; went 11 2nd 13; wknd 15*
[1359ᵁ]	7	12	**Benbulbin (IRE)** (vis) 7-1 **M Bluck** *Hld up in midfield; impd to 3rd aft 10; wknd 13*
[994ᶠ]	8	1	**Millstock** (5a) 16-1 **G Barfoot-Saunt** *Rr div; 10th aft 10; no ch frm 13*
[1219³]	P		**Miss Hoity Toity** (5a) 100-30F **J Tarry** *2 handlers; unruly & lashed out w both barrels at rival in padd; pulled v hrd; jnd ldr brief & rn wide bef 3; mostly 2nd til aft 10; sn lost plce; pu 15*
[1301ᵁ]	U		**Pigeon Hill Buck (IRE)** 20-1 **D Pugh** *Bhnd; last & strugg when ur 10*
[1316³]	P		**Piltdown Lady** (5a) 20-1 **T Macfarlane** *Sn toiling in rr; pu 7*
[972ᶜ]	F		**Pulkerry (IRE)** 20-1 **A Martin** *Blun 2; bhnd; 10l 8th aft 10; last when mist 12; t.o when fell 15*
	P		**Shortcut Shorty** 14-1 **W Brown** *Bit bckwd; kicked in padd by Uncle Jimmy's horse; jmpd poor in detach last; t.o & pu 9*

OFFICIAL DISTANCES: 3l, 5l TIME: 6min 23.0s

1436 Confined, 12st   7 ran

| [1335ᵁ] | 1 | | **MR DENNEHY (IRE)** 9-4 **David Dennis** *7/2-9/4; ld at gd pce; went 6l clr 14; r.o str aft; unchall* |
| [1203⁷] | 2† | 20 | **Murberry (IRE)** (5a) 4-1 **T Lane** *Lw; trckd ldrs; 5th when hit 10; rdn & outpcd in 14l 4th 13; stayed on frm 2 out & snatched 2nd nr fin* |

[1087ᴾ]	2†	1½	**Distant-Port (IRE)** 5-4F T Stephenson *Pulled hrd in rr; 5l last aft 10; went 6l 3rd 13 & 2nd nxt; rdn & no imp on wnr; wknd flat; disapp*
[1017ᴾ]	4	10	**Apple Nicking** 20-1 T Illsley *Lw; hld up; 4th aft 10; wknd 11; 20l 5th 13*
[1144ᴾ]	r		**Hope's Delight (IRE)** 20-1 R Smith *Nt a fluent; cl up; 3rd 10; drpd back last & hit 11; t.o 14; ref last*
[1190ᴾ]	P		**Its Murphy Man** 33-1 C Wadland *Tk keen hld; sn 2nd; dem 3rd 14 & wknd qckly; pu 3 out*
[1064ᶠ]	r		**Lofty Deed (USA)** 20-1 B McKim *Ref 1*

OFFICIAL DISTANCES: 15l, dd-ht TIME: 6min 14.0s

1437 Open Maiden (Div 2), 12st 8 ran

[1020²]	1		**ROMANY CHAT** 9-4F A Martin *Oht; 2 handlers; hld up & cl up; lft 2nd 9; ld brief app 13; jmpd to ld agn 3 out; hrd rdn flat; all out*
[1021ᶠ]	2	1	**So Frank** 7-1 M Harris *10s-7s; nt fluent 2; hld up last til impd to 12l 5th aft 10; stdy prog to cl 2nd gng wl 3 out; ev ch last; drvn & nt qckn final 100yds*
[1131⁴]	3	8	**Snowboy (IRE)** 3-1 P Keane *5s-3s; sn 2nd; lft in ld 9; jmpd slow & hdd 3 out; sn outpcd*
	4	4	**Shedoes** (5a) 6-1 C Wadland *Hld up trckng ldrs; mist 3; 10l 4th aft 10; drvn & no imp frm 15; ev ch of 3rd when blun last*
[1021ᴾ]	5	6	**Chadwick Bank (IRE)** 8-1 R Cope *Trckd ldrs; jmpd slow 7; 8l 3rd aft 10; strugg frm 15*
[1147²]	6	2	**Bright Vulcan** 11-4 T Illsley *Hld up in rr; 15l 6th aft 10; blun 13 & t.o nxt; r.o wl aft last*
[1421ᴾ]	F		**Looks Like Reign** 33-1 B McKim *Mounted outside padd & tde; pulled hrd & nt jw; ld til fell 9*
[1010ᴾ]	P		**The Boree Log** 33-1 M Hewitt *Pulled hrd & prom to 6; wknd 8; t.o & pu 12*

OFFICIAL DISTANCES: 1l, 3l TIME: 6min 21.0s

1438 Hunt 9 ran

[1015⁷]	1		**HEHAS** 3-1 C Wadland *Lft 2nd app 5 til ld 9-11; 6l 3rd 13 & 8l 3rd 15; rallied 2 out; ev ch last; drvn & stayed on game to ld cl home*
[1419ᴾ]	2	hd	**Rolcap** 3-1 J I Pritchard *Rn in snatches; drpd back 6th 8; rallied to ld 12; 2l clr 15; hrd rdn & jnd by 2 rivals last; ev ch til no ex nr fin*
[1207¹]	3	5	**Dillon** 5-4F F Hutsby *Settled midfield; went 2nd 12; rdn to jn ldng pr last; wknd uphill; fin sore*
[1192ᴿ]	4	30	**Cuban Skies (IRE)** 10-1 A Barnett *16s-10s; hit 3; trckd ldrs; 6th 11; eff & 7l 4th 13; wknd 15*
[1146³]	5	1	**Grange Prize** 25-1 Miss K Henry *Last pr; in tch to 11; plodded on aft; rem frm 14*
[1147²]	6	30	**Cottage Light** (bl) 33-1 N Ridout *Prom; 3rd aft 10; rdn & reluct frm nxt; t.o 15*
[176⁵]	S		**Ardshuil** 20-1 S Pile *(xnb) Bckwd; pulled hrd; ld & 12l clr til slpd up turn bef 5*
[891ᴾ]	P		**Peatsville (IRE)** 25-1 J Trice-Rolph *Lft in ld app 5; hdd 9; ld agn 11-12; sn wknd; jmpd slow 14; t.o & pu 2 out*
[1009ᴾ]	U		**Upton Orbit** 33-1 Miss J Hitchman *Rcd wide in last w rdr's hd wagging frm side to side; lost tch 12; t.o 15; ur last*

OFFICIAL DISTANCES: nk, 2½l TIME: 6min 20.0s

1439 Open Maiden (Div 3), 12st 7 ran

[455ᴿ]	1		**HAPPEN TO MAKE IT (IRE)** evensF Julian Pritchard *Made all; hit 13; 2l clr 15; drvn when blun bad 2 out; hrd rdn & kpt on flat*
[1021ᴾ]	2	1	**Have A Break** (7a) 6-4 R Lawther *Lw; a 2nd; hit 14; eff 3 out; chall & ev ch last; kpt on u.p; a just hld*
[1245ᴾ]	3	4	**Vital Hesitation** (5a) 6-1 A Charles-Jones *8s-6s; nt fluent in midfield; went 3rd 8; 5l down 15; drvn & eff app last; fnd nil flat*
[964ᴾ]	P		**Dancing Paws (IRE)** (7a) 20-1 C Hoggart *Last pr; hit 9 & lost tch; t.o & pu 12*
[1147ᴾ]	P		**Dennis** 10-1 J Tarry *Pulled hrd early; stdd to 5th 5; lost tch in 20l last aft 10; mist 12; t.o & pu 13*
[1207ᴾ]	P		**Military Dreamer** 25-1 R Cope *Settled 3rd/4th; 7l 4th aft 10; hit 11 & wknd; t.o 13; pu 15; broke down*
[1251ᵁ]	U		**Peover Eye** (7a) 25-1 D Sherlock *Mist 2; slpd & ur app 3*

OFFICIAL DISTANCES: ¾l, 3l TIME: 6min 18.0s

1440 Mixed Open, 12st 3 ran

| [303ᴾ] | 1 | | **FRESH PRINCE** (7x) 2-7F Julian Pritchard *Lw; made all; in comm frm 14; v easy* |
| [970ᴾ] | 2 | 12 | **Egypt Mill Prince** 13-2 E Walker *(xnb) A 2nd; rdn 14; no ch w wnr aft* |

[1265⁵] **P**   **Teeton Builds** (bl) 5-1 R Barrett *Lw; detach last & nvr happy; 18l bhnd & pushed along 10; t.o 13; 1½ fncs bhnd when pu last; dism; sore*

OFFICIAL DISTANCE: 12l **TIME:** 6min 18.0s

1441 SMAC Club Members (Nov Rdrs), 12st   7 ran

[1243¹] **1**   **CASTLE SHELLEY (IRE)** 15-8F R Smith *Hld up; last 5; hdwy 10 to 2nd aft 12; slt ld frm 15 til rdn & forged clr flat*
[1145⁷] **2** 2½ **Castle Arrow (IRE)** 9-4 M Wall *8s-9/4; lw; tde & ld rnd start; trckd ldrs til ld aft 12; hdd 15; prsd wnr til ev ch last; rdr unbalanced & nt qckn flat*
3 7 **Drumstick** (tt) 6-1 Miss S Kelly *Tk keen hld & prom; ld 7 til aft 12; tried to rally 2 out; sn one-pcd*
[1145⁷] **4** runin **Erbil (IRE)** 14-1 Miss M Mason *Sn prom; 2nd 10; 10l 4th & wkng 13; t.o*
[1205⁷] **F**   **Dolly Bloom** (5a) 5-1 Miss N McKim *(xnb) 8s-5s; tde; cl up; pckd 7; lost tch 12; t.o when fell 15*
[1243⁵] **F**   **Holloa Away (IRE)** (bl) 33-1 R Millar *5th when fell 5; t.o 8; fell 9*
[1035⁵] **P**   **Safety (USA)** (bl) 14-1 G Wright *Ld to 7; last & strugg 10 to 12; pu 15*

OFFICIAL DISTANCES: 2½l, 5l **TIME:** 6min 08.0s

1442 Restricted, 12st   5 ran

[791²] **1**   **PERFECT MINSTREL (IRE)** 4-9F F Hutsby *(xnb) Hld up; mist 5; went 2nd 8; ld 14; 4l clr nxt; a gng best aft; comf*
[1145⁷] **2** 4 **Quite A Miss** (5a) 7-1 A Martin *Settled 3rd; went 2nd 14; drvn along 2 out; a hld*
[38⁷] **3** 20 **G-And-T** (5a) 5-1 M Cowley *(xnb) Numerous mists & last mostly; 5l bhnd 13; went 6l 3rd 15 but rdn & sn lost tch*
[196²] **4** 4 **Mismetallic** (5a) 8-1 C Wadland *Pulled hrd; ld til hdd & hit 14; wknd rap & last nxt*
[896²] **P**   **Wotanite** 14-1 E Walker *Chsd ldr to 8; 20l last & labouring bad aft 10; pu 11; lame*

OFFICIAL DISTANCES: 3l, 15l **TIME:** 6min 22.0s

Stratford (LH 8F,18J)
Fri, 12 May (GOOD, GOOD to FIRM in places)

1443 John & Nigel Mem HC   11 ran

[1244¹] **1**   **BLANVILLE (FR)** 11-07 2-1F P Scouller *Nt fluent & tkn off feet in rr; hdwy 12; rchd 12l 6th at 15; still 6th when mist 3 out; str rn to chall 2 out; ld & hit last; qcknd clr*
[1339⁴] **2** 3½ **Bit O'Speed (IRE)** 11-07 33-1 J Richardson *(xnb) Tk keen hld & trckd ldrs; went 3rd 10 & 2nd 15; ld 2 out-last; nt qckn*
[1335³] **3** ½ **Mr Custard** 11-07 5-1 Miss L Sweeting *Swtng bad; prom; 5th & outpcd 14; rallied 3 out; stayed on stdly aft nxt*
[1312²] **4** ½ **Secret Truth** 11-02 25-1 A Martin *Swtng profuse; oht; pulled hrd; hit 1; ld to 7; chsd ldr til ld agn 15; hdd 2 out; drvn & nt qckn*
[1249⁴] **5** 8 **Sailor Jim** 11-07 20-1 W Tellwright *Chsd ldrs; 6th & outpcd 14; tried to rally aft nxt; wknd app 2 out*
6 dist **Silver Standard** 11-07 14-1 Miss L Pearce *(xnb) Midfield til wknd & mist 12; t.o*
[1339⁴] **7** 3½ **Mister Horatio** 11-07 (tt) 7-2 M Lewis *(xnb) Prom; ld 7-15; wknd rap bef 2 out; t.o*
[993⁵] **P**   **Beyond The Stars** 12-00 25-1 M Rimell *Prom brief; outpcd when mist 8; pu nxt*
[794¹] **F**   **Linlathen** 11-07 15-2 N Bell *Lw; drpd out in rr; prog in 5l 6th 11; nt fluent nxt; 6l 4th & no imp when fell 15*
[1066⁴] **P**   **Saffron Flame (IRE)** 11-07 (bl) 50-1 Miss N Rudge *Nt fluent & sn labouring in last; t.o 8; pu 3 out*
[1293⁶] **r**   **Smart Song** 12-03 50-1 M Hammond *Swtng; dwelt; bhnd; mist 4; rdn & strugg 11; mist 2 out; t.o & ref last*

TIME: 5min 53.5s **TOTE:** £3.00; places £1.60,£2.50,£1.40 **Ex:** £49.80 **CSF:** £66.90

Wincanton (RH 9F,17J)
Fri, 12 May (FIRM, GOOD to FIRM in places)

1444 R.K. Harrison Insurance Brokers HC   12 ran

[681¹] **1**   **KING TORUS (IRE)** 12-04 (bl) 7-4F J Jukes *Ld to 3; ld agn aft 4; made rest; drvn & kpt on flat*
[1370¹] **2** 2 **Badger Beer** 11-07 (tt) 8-1 N Mitchell *Jmpd slow 2; hld up; hdwy 7; chsd wnr frm 10; rdn & eff app 3 out; no imp flat*

[1140³]	3	2	**Fursan (USA)** 11-07 (tt) 20-1 P Phillips *Ss; pulled hrd; hld up; 7th & prog 8; went 5l 3rd 14; rdn app 3 out; one pce nxt*
[1045²]	4	17	**Thinking Twice (USA)** 11-07 12-1 Miss T Newman *Trckd ldrs; 5th 8; lsng plce when blun 13 & rdr nrly f.o; lft poor 4th nxt*
[1433⁹]	5	3	**Alska (FR)** 11-02 40-1 Miss W Southcombe *Mist 3; t.o 5; last 8; slt late prog*
[1335⁶]	6	1½	**The Captain's Wish** 11-11 16-1 T Gibney *Tubed; hld up & bhnd; 8th 11; some hdwy when blun 13; sn wknd*
[1202⁵]	7	1¼	**Loch Na Keal** 11-04 50-1 R Lawther *Chsd wnr; ld 3 til aft 4; 3rd 8; rdn 11; sn wknd*
[1336¹¹]	8	20	**Shillelagh Oak** 11-09 40-1 N Harris *Bhnd frm 6; 10th 8; rdn 9; sn t.o; fnce bhnd*
[1248¹]	9	18	**Glenpine (IRE)** 11-04 5-1 C Weaver *Sis; a bhnd; hit 4; 9th 8; rdn 11; sn t.o fnce bhnd*
[1341⁶]	P		**Hee's A Dancer** 11-11 7-2 C Williams *Prom; hit 7; 2nd 8; 4th & wkng when hit 13; pu nxt*
[1375⁴]	P		**Hemero (IRE)** 11-07 (vis,tt) 40-1 A Honeyball *Chsd ldrs; 6th 8; sn strugg; t.o & pu 13*
[1133⁹]	P		**Merry Shot (IRE)** 11-07 12-1 R Young *Hld up & bhnd; hit 3; 11th & strugg 8; t.o & pu 13*

TIME: 5min 09.6s **TOTE:** £2.90; places £1.70,£1.10,£3.80 **Ex:** £14.10 **CSF:** £15.05

Hexham (LH 10F,19J)
Sat, 13 May (GOOD to FIRM)

1445 Dennis Waggott Builders Heart of All England Mdn HC　　　　　19 ran

[1363¹]	1		**VICTORIA'S BOY (IRE)** 11-07 12-1 G Brewer *Settled 3rd/4th; went 2nd 10; rdn to ld app last; kpt on wl; eased final 100yds*
[1345⁴]	2	6	**Weejumpawud** 11-04 20-1 Miss S Forster *Chsd ldr til ld 4; hdd app last; kpt on one pce*
[1120¹]	3	5	**Bow Tie** 11-07 5-1 R Morgan *In tch; hdwy 8; 4th 14; 7l 3rd & rdn when overj 2 out; no imp aft*
[1342³]	4	5	**Lord Levi (IRE)** 11-11 5-1 W Renwick *Bhnd; hdwy aft 16; 8th 3 out; drvn & kpt on frm nxt; too much to do*
[1428²]	5	2	**Dennett Lough (IRE)** 12-00 14-1 C Storey *Hdwy & in tch 8; 5th & eff when stumbled & checked aft 3 out; swished tail & sn no imp*
[1336³]	6	3	**Quarterstaff** 11-11 7-4F C Wilson *Mists; hdwy to chse ldrs 8; 4th 10; cl 3rd when blun bad 3 out; sn btn*
[1428¹]	7	½	**Riverside Run (IRE)** 11-09 10-1 A Robson *Nt fluent; chsd ldrs; blun 7; sn rdn; 6th 3 out; outpcd bef nxt*
[1427³]	8	8	**Border Glory** 11-07 33-1 P Maitland-Carew *Hld up; brief eff 14; wknd aft nxt*
[1363³]	9	12	**Lindon Run** 11-07 (tt) 33-1 T Davidson *Chsd ldrs; lost plce 8; bhnd when jb rt 13*
[807⁶]	10	2½	**Erni (FR)** 11-07 33-1 W Burnell *Hld up & bhnd; blun 6; nvr on terms*
[1342⁴]	11	2	**Major Tom (IRE)** 11-07 7-1 R Tate *Chsd ldrs; 6th 14; rdn in 7th 3 out; sn lost tch*
[1427⁶]	12	7	**Boris Brook** 11-07 50-1 T Oates *A wl bhnd; t.o*
[1428⁵]	13	13	**Charlieadams (IRE)** 11-13 (6) 25-1 J Muir *Hdstrng; ld til jmpd slow 4; chsd ldr to 9; sn lost plce; mist 13; t.o*
[1345⁶]	14	dist	**Rye Rum** 12-00 50-1 J Walton *Imm lost tch; t.o 5*
[1152¹]	P		**Allrite Pet** 11-09 5-1 Miss P Robson *Hdwy & in tch 8; 9th & rdn 11; sn strugg; t.o & pu 16*
[918⁶]	P		**Just Ned** 11-09 (2) 66-1 M Douglas *Jmpd v poor; sn wl t.o; pu 7*
[1430⁶]	P		**Meadowleck** 11-02 (tt) 100-1 P Aspell *Mists in rr; t.o 5; pu 10*
[1121¹]	P		**Poynder Park (IRE)** 11-07 10-1 W Morgan *Sn wl bhnd; t.o & pu 13*
[1162⁷]	P		**Wylup** 11-10 (3) 66-1 H Humble *Sn wl bhnd; t.o 6; pu flat; lame*

TIME: 6min 17.1s **TOTE:** £20.90; places £3.10,£7.00,£2.40 **Ex:** £733.60 **CSF:** £231.86

1446 George F. White HC　　　　　　　　　　　　　　　　　　　7 ran

[1333¹]	1		**KEY DEBATE** 11-12 8-13F G Brewer *Tk keen hld; sev fine leaps; ld 5; lft 12l clr aft 8; hit 14 & 16; eased flat; unchall & v impressive*
[1149ᵁ]	2	7	**Sounds Strong (IRE)** 11-07 16-1 R Morgan *Sn wl bhnd; went 20l 3rd 9 & rem 2nd 16; nvr nr wnr*
[1078⁶]	3	dist	**The Green Fool** 11-10 (3) 40-1 H Humble *Sn wl bhnd; rem last 14; nvr on terms; plodded into 3rd*
[917⁵]	4	5	**Juke Box Billy (IRE)** 11-07 (tt) 33-1 W Burnell *Mists; a wl bhnd; rem 4th 14*
[1335⁷]	5	25	**Gymcrak Tiger (IRE)** 11-07 8-1 R Clark *Chsd ldrs; hdwy & lft 2nd aft 8; sn wl outpcd by wnr; wknd 16; eased flat; t.o*
[1345ᵁ]	R		**Full Of Chat (IRE)** 11-02 50-1 F King *Ld to 5; 2nd til hit 7 & dem; tk wrong course aft nxt; pu 11*

[921⁵] **R**   **Howayman** 12-04 (bl) 9-4 **Mrs V Jackson** *Chsd wnr 7 til tk wrong course & pu aft 8*

TIME: 6min 11.4s **TOTE:** £1.50; places £1.10,£3.80 **Ex:** £8.00 **CSF:** £10.77
The rider of Full Of Chat was suspended for three days for continuing in the race without retracing after being carried out

Warwick (LH 9F,17J)
Sat, 13 May (GOOD to FIRM)

1447 Warwick HC   **12 ran**

[925⁶]	1		**MR MOTIVATOR** 11-09 14-1 **F Windsor Clive** *Made all; drew 8l clr app 11; nt fluent 15; rdn app 2 out; kpt on wl; drvn out*
[1341¹]	2	9	**Shafi (IRE)** 11-12 5-4F **M Trott** *Hld up & bhnd; hdwy to chse ldrs app 11; went 8l 2nd 12; rdn & no imp on wnr*
[1335¹]	3	5	**Island Echo (IRE)** 11-12 7-2 **J Tate** *Hld up & bhnd; nt fluent 9; 4th & hdwy app 11; rdn app 2 out; kpt on; nt rch ldrs; too much to do*
[1157³]	4	dist	**Royal Mountbrowne** 12-00 25-1 **David Dennis** *Handy; chsd wnr aft 7; rdn 11; dem 12; 14l 3rd & wkng when mist 14; t.o*
[1341¹²]	5	11	**Phaedair** 11-07 66-1 **J Oldring** *Tde; prom til aft 3; sn midfield; strugg app 11; t.o 13; fnce bhnd*
[799³]	6	½	**Stanmore (IRE)** 12-00 7-2 **R Barrett** *Hld up; mist 5; bumped 8; 7th & strugg 11; t.o 13; fnce bhnd*
[970ᴾ]	7	1	**Wixoe Wonder (IRE)** 11-12 66-1 **G Carenza** *Chsd wnr til aft 7; wknd qckly app 11; t.o 13; fnce bhnd*
[1053ᴾ]	8	3	**Savuti (IRE)** 12-00 (tt) 66-1 **M Nicolls** *Pulled hrd; mist 2; prom early; 6th 9; rdn & wknd aft 10; t.o 13; fnce bhnd*
[1155⁸]	9	17	**Doctor Dunklin (USA)** 11-07 (bl) 66-1 **Jeremy Young** *Imm rdn; cl up to 9; sn strugg in rr; t.o 13; 1½ fnces bhnd*
[1157ᴾ]	10	dist	**Sandi Devil** 11-07 100-1 **Miss S Sharratt** *Handy; til rdn & lost plce 5; sn bhnd; t.o aft 10; over 2 fncs bhnd*
	P		**Conti D'Estruval (FR)** 12-02 14-1 **T Smith** *Sn bhnd; mist 6; t.o & pu aft 10*
[1341ᴾ]	**P**		**Golden Gunner (IRE)** 11-07 (bl) 100-1 **P Young** *Handy; jmpd slow & lost plce 8; pu 9*

TIME: 4min 49.2s **TOTE:** £19.70; places £4.70,£1.10,£1.80 **Ex:** £49.80 **CSF:** £29.26

Gelligaer Farmers
Bonvilston (RH 7F,18J) Sat, 13 May (FIRM with GOOD to FIRM patches)

1448 Hunt, 12st   **4 ran**

[1222¹]	1		**MARISOL (IRE)** (5a) 5-2 **E Williams** *Tchd 3s; cl 2nd 1; sn ld & made rest; jmpd to 5l ld 14; kpt on wl frm 3 out; drvn out flat*
[1400⁴]	2	2½	**Mister Jay Day** 8-1 **A Price** (xnb) *Ld 1; cl 2nd mostly til dem 3rd 10; 10l 3rd & lkd wl hld 3 out; rallied u.p & prsd 2nd 2 out; 2nd at last; clsd flat; too much to do*
[1336⁸]	3	8	**Jo Jos Best Friend** (5a) 4-7F **T Vaughan** *Cl 3rd/4th til 1l 2nd 10; outj 14 & 5l 2nd aft; rallied & mist 3 out; 2½l 2nd & ch 2 out; sn rdn & wknd tame*
[1054ᴾ]	4	15	**Itspantotime** (5a) 9-1 **J Jukes** *Cl up in last pr mostly; 3l last 9; grad lost tch; 9l last 13; 14l last & no imp 3 out*

OFFICIAL DISTANCES: 2½l, 8l **TIME:** 5min 58.8s

1449 Intermediate, 12st   **11 ran**

[1399ᶠ]	1		**ROMAN GALE (IRE)** 16-1 **A Price** (bf) *4l 2nd 1; settled 4/5th; 5½l 5th 5; went 3½l 4th 14 & 2nd 3 out; dem cl 3rd app last; fin wl u.p flat; ld on line*
[1299⁴]	2	hd	**Rusnetto (IRE)** (vis) 16-1 **P Hamer** *Mid-div; 6l 6th & hit 5; went 5l 4th & rmdr 13; 4½l 4th 15; gd rn on outer to ld last; r.o flat; hdd nr line*
[1403²]	3	nk	**Storm Man (IRE)** 14-1 **Miss C Williams** *Tchd 16s; jw; a.p; 2l 2nd 3; jnd ldr 7; ld 9; nvr more than 2l up til hdd last; r.o flat; dem nr line; rn wl; deserved to win*
[1271¹]	4	½	**Rusty Buck** 8-1 **S Blackwell** *Last pr early; 10l 8th 9; 12l 6th 14; rdn & stayed on frm nxt; tried hrd to cl but little imp til went 4th app last; fin fast; just too much to do*
[654²]	5	4	**Detective Davy (IRE)** 5-2 **Miss P Jones** *Tchd 3s; trckd ldrs; 5l 4th 5; went cl 3rd 7 & 2nd 10; mist 12; rmdrs & sn dem 3rd; 3½l 3rd & ev ch 15; wknd qckly*
[1221²]	6	10	**Cresswell Quay** 2-1F **J Cook** *Tchd 5/2; chsd ldrs in 5th mostly til 3l 4th 10; smooth prog to 1l 2nd & gng wl 13; disp & outj nxt; v one-pcd aft; 5th & btn app 2 out*
[944ᴾ]		**P**	**Alkarine** 50-1 **J Keen** *A rr & nt keen; last & rmdrs aft 4; detach 6; t.o & pu aft 8*
[1401ᴾ]		**P**	**Chantingo Lad** 33-1 **J Jukes** (xnb) *Jmpd to ld 2; jmpd lft & jnd 6; hdd rdn along in 5½l 4th & wkng 11; fdd rap; last 14; t.o & pu last*

[1227ᴾ] P   **Dunsfold Dazzler** (5a) 12-1 D Hughes *2 handlers; swtng; nt fluent in mid-div; 7th 3; 15l 8th 9; to 12; pu 13*

[1298¹] P   **J'accuse (IRE)** 6-1 Miss F Wilson *Last pr to 5; hdwy to disp 7½l 6th 9; still 12l 7th 14; eased & pu 2 out*

[1403ᴾ] P   **Tiger Lord** 14-1 E Williams *Got flying start & 4l up 1; hdd nxt; 4½l 3rd 5; stdly lost plce; 15l 10th 9; detach last when pu aft 12*

    OFFICIAL DISTANCES: s hd, hd   TIME: 5min 52.3s
       Sister Lark (T Vaughan, 25-1, rdr indisposed) was withdrawn not under orders

1450 Confined, 12st   11 ran

[1401¹] 1   **ANORAK (USA)** (6x) 6-4F C Williams *A.p; ld 2; made rest but freq jnd; 5l up 14; ½l ahd 3 out; kpt on wl & in comm app last*

[1295ᴾ] 2   5   **Persian Mystic (IRE)** 33-1 T Vaughan *(xnb) Chsd ldrs; 6½l 4th 8; went 3l 3rd 13; 9l 3rd nxt; eff to jn ldr 3 out; ev ch nxt; sn btn*

[1297²] 3   8   **Young Manny** 7-1 M Lewis *Midfield; 7th 2; 7l 5th aft 8; went 5l 4th 13; 11l 4th 16; stayed on one pce*

[1341¹⁰] 4   25   **Boring (USA)** 16-1 J Jukes *(xnb) Mid-div til prog to 5½l 3rd 7; cl 4th 11; 11½l 4th & one pce 14*

      S   **Bon Voyage (USA)** 5-1 E Williams *8s-5s; mounted outside padd; towards rr; 8th 2; 7th 6; prog when slpd up bend bef nxt*

[1295ᵁ] P   **Comme Une Fleur (FR)** (5a) 50-1 P Sheldrake *A last pr; lft 20l 7th 7; to & pu aft 12*

[1295⁵] F   **Desmond Gold (IRE)** 25-1 M Barber *Swtng; cl 2nd til jnd ldr aft 3; fell hvly 5*

[1401ᵁ] P   **Herbert Lodge (IRE)** (tt) 100-1 Miss L Horner *Sa; a last; 27l last 8; wl to when pu aft 12*

      P   **Itsdigitalis (IRE)** 20-1 D Stephens (Wales) *Bckwd; last trio; 13½l 6th 7; 9l 6th & gng wl 13; 30l 6th & wkng rap nxt; sn t.o; pu 2 out*

[1336⁷] B   **Kristal Haze** (5a) 7-2 J Cook *(bf) Oht; trckd ldrs; 2½l 3rd 4; bd bend aft 6*

[1295⁹] F   **Mr Mad** (vis) 7-1 P Hamer *Ld 1; cl 3rd til 11 2nd 6; jnd ldr brief aft 8 & agn 13; 5l 2nd when fell 15*

    OFFICIAL DISTANCES: 4l, 6l   TIME: 5min 48.5s

1451 Mixed Open, 12st   7 ran

[1226⁶] 1   **CREAM SUPREME (IRE)** 5-2 E Williams *4s-5/2; trckd ldrs in cl 4/5th; 3¾l 4th 10; qcknd to 4l 2nd 15; sn prsng ldr; ld 2 out; r.o und str press flat*

[1297³] 2   2½   **Gunner Boon** evensF Miss P Jones *Jmpd slow & to lft at times; set modest pce; 3l up 8; qcknd 4l and 15; hdd 2 out but clr of rest; no ex app last*

[1296⁹] 3   10   **Moon Tiger** 7-1 D Hughes *Prom in 3rd/4th til 1½l 2nd 10; 3l 2nd 13; outpcd 15; rallied to 3l 3rd 3 out; 9l 3rd & btn nxt*

[1402ᵁ] 4   4   **Twilight Tom** 7-1 A Price *Bhnd early; pulled to 4½l 4th 4 & 2nd 6; cl 3rd 10 til 4th & outpcd 15; 12¾l 4th & one pce 2 out*

[1295ᴾ] P   **Credon** 33-1 J Cook *Handy in 4/5th til rmdrs 5; sn drpd out; 15l 6th aft 7; 17l 5th 11; nvr nr ldrs aft; to 5th 3 out; dem last app nxt; pu last*

[1399ᵁ] P   **Minstrel Fire (IRE)** 16-1 Miss L Pearce *Rcd keen in 2nd til jmpd slow 5; 3½l 3rd 8; wknd rap nxt; pu 11*

[1053²] P   **Silverfort Lad (IRE)** 16-1 C Williams *Nt keen in last; detach 7; 17½l last & rdn along 11; to 5th & jmpd slow 2 out; pu last*

    OFFICIAL DISTANCES: 2l, 10l   TIME: 5min 51.0s

1452 Restricted (Div 1), 12st   10 ran

[1400³] 1   **STAR CHASER** 5-1 D Stephens (Wales) *Trckd ldrs; 3l 3rd 4; 10l 3rd 9; 5l 3rd & hdwy 12; went 3l 2nd 14; prsd ldr 15; jmpd to ld nxt; sn clr; easy*

[1298⁵] 2   10   **Mecca Prince (IRE)** (7a) 14-1 James Tudor *Towards rr; 7th 2; prog to 9½l 4th aft 5; 6½l 4th 12; dem 5th 14; 8l 4th & staying on aft 3 out; went 3rd aft 2 out & 2nd at last; nt trble wnr*

[947ᴾ] 3   2   **Seventh Symphony (IRE)** (tt) 25-1 Miss P Jones *(bf)2l 2nd til jnd ldr 7; ld 10; 3l clr 14; hdd 3 out; sn btn; 8l 2nd aft 2 out; dem last*

[1223¹] 4   10   **Omar's Odyssey (IRE)** (7a) 3-1 J Jukes *4s-3s; 2 handlers; last pr to 3; stdy prog to disp 13½l 6th aft 5; 8½l 5th & gng wl 12; went 6l 3rd aft 14; 6l 3rd & hrd rdn 3 out; qckly btn (was travelling lke wnr most of rce but fnd nothing off bridle)*

[1298ᶠ] P   **Jack Boots** 50-1 J Phillips *(xnb,bh fetlock) Nrly a last; detach 7; to & pu aft 11*

[1400ᴾ] P   **Out On The Town** (5a) 33-1 A St George *(small boh) Chsd ldrs; disp 4½l 4th 4; 13½l 5th 9; 9l 6th & mist 12; 10l 5th & no imp aft 3 out*

[1300¹] P   **Saxon Queen** (5a) 2-1F E Williams *Ld; jnd 7; hdd aft 9; cl 2nd & mist 13; 5½l 3rd & wkng nxt; drpd out rap; 6th & strugg aft 3 out; pu aft nxt*

[1400^P]	P		**Sea Search** 50-1 G Maloney *A rr; last brief 4; 22l 7th 10; releg last 12; t.o 15; pu 2 out*
[1406¹]	P		**Star Island** 9-1 A Price *Chsd ldrs; disp 4½l 4th 4; drpd to last pr 6; 21l 7th 12; t.o 15; pu 3 out*
[1399²]	P		**Travel Safely (IRE)** (vis) 5-1 J Keen *Mid-div; 7th 4; disp 13½l 6th aft 5; drpd to last trio 7; pu 9*

OFFICIAL DISTANCES: 8l, 2l TIME: 5min 54.9s

1453 Restricted (Div 2), 12st   10 ran

[596^F]	1		**ABSENT CITIZEN (IRE)** (5a) 5-4F E Williams *Jw; hld up towards rr til jmpd to 4th 7; 1½l 3rd 9; trckd ldr til jmpd superb to ld 14; 3l clr 3 out; 6l clr aft nxt; tiring flat; all out*
[1054^P]	2	2½	**Itscinders** (5a) 25-1 J Jukes *Hld up in last; 15l last 5; hdwy at 12; went 3rd 3 out; disp 6l 2nd aft nxt; clsd on ldr flat; too much to do*
[864⁴]	3	¾	**Rymin Thyne** 7-1 J Cook *(xnb,bf) A.p; trckd ldr til jmpd to ld 7; jnd 9; just ld aft 12 til outj & dem 3rd 14; 3l 2nd 3 out; jnd for 6l 2nd aft nxt; sn dem; kpt on; a hld*
[1302¹]	4	6	**Black Dan** 10-1 J Keen *Last trio early; disp 4l 5th 9; 8½l 5th aft 12; went 4th 3 out; 11l 4th and one pce 2 out*
[1403⁴]	5	5	**Final Option (IRE)** 25-1 I Johnson *(bf) Chsd ldrs; 6l 4th when lft 3rd 6; cl 4th 9; 8½l 5th aft 12; gd hdwy to 2nd 14; ev ch nxt; sn outpcd; 13½l 5th & no imp 2 out*
[1298^P]	6	½	**Cranagh Moss (IRE)** (bl) 10-1 S Blackwell *Swtng; nd; cl 5th when blun bad & nrly ur 3; 8l 5th aft 5; 11l 6th aft 12; nvr able to chall; last & no imp 3 out*
[1298^P]	P		**Bannagh Beg (IRE)** (5a) 20-1 Miss F Wilson *Last pr; prog to 6l 4th 7; drpd back 17l last aft 12; wl bhnd when pu 2 out*
[1228^P]	P		**Brewery Lane (IRE)** 10-1 Miss P Jones *Ld til outj & hdd 7; cl 2nd/disp to 13; 6th & wkng rap nxt; t.o & pu 2 out; reportedly lame aft*
[818³]	P		**Kays-Lass** (5a) 5-1 C Williams *(xnb) 2 handlers; trckd ldrs; 2½l 3rd 3; 5l 3rd when pu & dism 6*
[818^U]	U		**Under Milk Wood** 33-1 Miss L Pearce *(xnb) Handy when ur 2*

OFFICIAL DISTANCES: 3l, ½l TIME: 6min 00.5s

1454 Open Maiden (Div 1, Part 1), 12st   11 ran

[1405^U]	1		**WELSH WARRIOR** 6-4F T Vaughan *A.p; 9l 5th 5; went cl 3rd 8; disp 2½l 2nd 12; 2l 2nd & pckd 14; jnd ldr 3 out; ld nxt; clr last; drvn out flat til rdr stood in irons & waved crossing line (obviously feeling much btr - see footnote Race 1449)*
	2	7	**Riches To Rags (IRE)** 8-1 J Cook *Mid-div; gd prog to 6l 3rd 5; lft 2l 2nd nxt; jmpd to ld 7; jnd 3 out; sn hdd & one pce; fin lame*
[1223⁴]	3	25	**Beths Gift** (5a) 8-1 D Stephens (Wales) *Trckd ldrs; 8l 4th 5; lft 3½l 3rd nxt; 6l 3rd 14; nt able to chall; 12½l 3rd & rdn aft 2 out; wknd*
[1300²]	4	2½	**The Gadfly** 4-1 J Hayward *10s-4s; swtng; ld 1; jnd 2; sn hdd; lft 2nd app 4 & lft in ld 6; hld nxt; 3l mid 12; disp 8½l 4th 3 out; hrd rdn & wknd nxt*
[1223⁷]	5	10	**Tiny** (12a) 7-1 E Williams *(xnb) In tch in last pr to 8; 8¾l 5th aft 12 til wknd 3 out; last & no ch nxt*
[1056^U]	R		**Cosy Ride (IRE)** 33-1 J Phillips *(bf) Trckd ldrs; cl 4th 2; hdwy & lft in ld app 4; 2l up when rn out 6*
[1300⁴]	P		**Jesusa** (5a) 50-1 G Maloney *Swtng; sn last; t.o & jmpd slow 7; 1½fncs adrift when hit 12 hrd & pu imm aft*
	P		**Joesownbelle** (5a) 14-1 R Hughes *Reared & ur padd; rr til hdwy to 10l 6th 7; 8¾l 6th aft mist 12; drpd out rap & t.o last 15; pu 3 out*
[1336^P]	R		**Millbank Honey** (5a) 12-1 Miss L Pearce *(bf) Disp ld 2; just ld nxt til rn out bend bef 4; rtrcd & cont 2 fncs bhnd til pu 7*
[1404^U]	U		**Tarian (USA)** 33-1 M Parry *Last when blun & lft rdr hanging off side 1; event f.o some way aft*
	P		**Verdi Edition** 4-1 A Price *10s-4s; mid-div; 11l 6th 5; 10½l 7th aft 12; wknd rap; t.o in last pr when jmpd slow 15; pu 3 out*

OFFICIAL DISTANCES: 5l, 20l TIME: 6min 03.6s

1455 Open Maiden (Div 1, Part 2), 12st   10 ran

[1302^F]	1		**PULL ON** 6-1 E Williams *(xnb,pricker ns) Mid-div; disp 12l 5th 5; disp 6½l 4th 9; lft cl 3rd 12; 2½l 2nd 14; chall 3 out; rdn & ld app last; v tired & hung lft flat; drvn & all out*
[1222⁴]	2	8	**Mission Lord (IRE)** 16-1 C Williams *Trckd ldrs; 7l 4th 4; 8l 2nd nxt; cl 3rd 7; rdn 11; ld 13; prsd 3 out; exhaust & hdd aft nxt*
[1300^P]	P		**Fortunes Leap** 33-1 R Hughes *Jmpd to 3rd 2; ld nxt; 4l clr 9; hdd 11; blun bad 12; wknd rap; last when pu 14*
[1404^P]	R		**Georgie Grace** 16-1 S Blackwell *A rr; last & mist 5; 21l last when rn out 6*

[1277ᴾ]	P		**Hardy Wolf** 25-1 A St George Trckd ldrs; 4th 2; disp 12l 5th 5; 15l 6th 10; lft 12l 4th 12; nrly ref 13; pu & dism app nxt
[1399ᴾ]	R		**Kyre Moss** (7a,2ow) 10-1 **D Hughes** Swtng; rr; 17l 9th 5; rn out 8
[1222³]	U		**Power Unit** (7a) 3-1 P Hamer 2 handlers - aft tugging one rnd padd; lw; ld/disp to 2; prom til 2½l 2nd 7; ld brief 11; cl 2nd 13; 3½l 3rd when & ev ch when blun bad & ur 15
[648ᴾ]	F		**Spot On Millie** (12a) 20-1 James Tudor Tongue lolling padd; ld to 2; sn chsng ldrs; 8½l 3rd 6; 6½l 4th 9; fell 12; winded
	B		**Tejaque** (12a) 12-1 Miss F Wilson (bf) Last trio; 15l 8th 5; 27½l last 9; bd 12
[1277³]	P		**Up Your Street** (12a) 5-4F Miss P Jones Chsd ldrs brief; 5th 2; drpd back 25l 7th 10; t.o last when pu aft 13

OFFICIAL DISTANCE: 8l **TIME:** 6min 10.9s

1456 Open Maiden (Div 2, Part 1), 12st - 17J   12 ran

	1		**LUCKY JIM** 6-1 Miss K Lovelace Chsd ldrs; 18l 5th 4; went 20l 3rd 7; chsd clr ldng pr til 2l 2nd 3 out; ld by-passing nxt; 1½l up at last; comf; gvn gd ride
[1055ᴾ]	2	¾	**Itsarchie** 14-1 J Jukes 25s-14s; confid rdn; mid-div; disp 19l 8th 5; 28½l 7th 9; gd hdwy to 13l 4th 13; went 2½l 3rd 3 out; hrd rdn to chse wnr by-passing nxt; nt able to chall; sltly flatt by prox
[1223ᴾ]	3	20	**Cresswell Cherry (IRE)** (12a) 16-1 J Cook 2 handlers; rn in snatches; hdwy to 5th 3; lft 3rd 5; drpd back last 7; prog to 5th agn aft 12; 25l 5th 14; kpt on one pce; nvr nr to chall
[1302ᴾ]	4	8	**Buckley House** 25-1 A Price (drop) Backed away start & escorted back bet Hunt horses; ld; jnd 3 & pr sn 20l clr; ld 6 til jnd agn 14; tiring & only 2l up 3 out; 3l 2nd but exhaust by-passing 2 out; sn wl bhnd
[1301²]	5	30	**Stormhill Daydream** (5a) 8-1 J Keen A rr; disp last 6; disp 30l last 9; t.o 14
[601ᵁ]	6	2	**Satco Supreme (IRE)** 16-1 I Johnson 2 handlers; swtng; rr; hdwy 6; disp 22½l 4th 9; mist 12; 7th & wkng 13; 33½l 7th & btn nxt
[1225⁵]	U		**Carbury's Case** 25-1 H Evans Last pr when ur 2
[1302ᴾ]	P		**Don't Forget (IRE)** (5a) (tt) 20-1 T Vaughan (xnb)Chsd ldrs; 5½l 5th 2; sn outpcd by ldng pr & disp 24l 4th 7; 31l 6th & no ch 14; t.o pu last
[1301³]	S		**Lough Neagh (IRE)** 8-1 P Sheldrake Cl up; 5l 4th 2; rmdrs 4; sn wknd; disp 30l last 9; last 11; slpd up bend aft 13
[1406⁶]	U		**Marnies Song** (5a) (bl) 10-1 James Tudor (bf) 2 handlers; sn prom; 4l 3rd 2; 10l 3rd 4; blun & ur 5
[1100³]	F		**St Helier** (12a) 2-1F D Stephens (Wales) Tchd 5/2; swtng; last pr early; prog to 27l 6th when blun bad & lost sev plces 7; rallied to disp 22½l 4th 9; fell nxt
	P		**Teeton Tango** (5a) 5-1 Miss P Jones 7s-5s; 2l 2nd til jnd ldr 3; pr sn 20l clr of rest; cl 2nd/disp til wknd aft 15; sn btn; t.o pu last; broke down both forelegs

OFFICIAL DISTANCES: ½l, 10l **TIME:** 6min 02.3s
Fence 17 omitted - fallen rider

1457 Open Maiden (Div 2, Part 2), 12st   10 ran

[1302²]	1		**GET THE GIST (IRE)** 7-4F P Hamer Jw; ld 2; hdd bet fncs but jmpd to front each time til slpd bend aft 6; gvn time to rec & drpd back 13l 5th 15; str rn nxt to 2nd aft 2 out; swept into ld flat; wl rdn
[1300³]	2	2½	**Sing Cherry Ripe** (5a) 10-1 Miss T Stevens Tried to make all but jmpd poor & hdd ev fnce til qcknd 5l clr 14; 1l up & blun agn last; hdd & brushed aside by wnr flat
[1406⁵]	3	5	**Blazing Connie** (5a) 14-1 Miss P Jones (bf) Opened 16s; 2 handlers; mid-div; disp 6th 2; 5l 5th 7; 3½l 4th 13; 13l 4th 15; kpt on wl; nt pce to chall
[1228ᴾ]	4	1	**Bonny Boy (IRE)** (7a) 16-1 P Sheldrake Hld up in last to 12; 14l 6th 14; kpt on wl frm 3 out; nt rch ldrs; promising
[1301ᴾ]	5	15	**Bill's Integrity** (12a) 5-1 E Williams Tde; last pr early; 10l 9th 5; disp 8½l 7th 13; kpt on one pce; school
[1050ᴾ]	6	20	**Arctic Ridge** (tt) 7-1 D Hughes 16s-7s; cl 3rd til lft 2nd bend aft 6; ½l 2nd 13; dem 8l 3rd nxt; 11l 3rd & wkng 15; sn no ch; t.o; walked in
[1302ᴾ]	7	6	**Migsy Malone** (12a) J Jukes Trckd ldrs gng wl; 2l 4th 5; went 3rd 10 & 5l 2nd 14; chsd ldr & lkd danger til wknd qckly 2 out; virt pu flat
[602ᵁ]	8	½	**Sleepy Boy** 12-1 M Parry Last 1; prog to 7½l 6th 7; 6l 6th 13; last pr & wkng nxt; t.o 2 out
[1405ᶠ]	P		**Hill Top Flyer (IRE)** 40-1 G Maloney Prom; cl 4th 2; grad wknd; 7l 7th 7; last 12; detach & jmpd v slow 13 & 14; t.o & pu 15
	P		**Too Phar To Touch** (12a) 8-1 C Williams Whinnying padd; last trio early; prog to disp 4th & mist 10; blun bad nxt; pu 12

OFFICIAL DISTANCES: 1½l, 3l **TIME:** 6min 13.7s

Golden Valley
Bredwardine (RH 8F,18J) Sat, 13 May (GOOD to FIRM)

1458 Hunt   4 ran

[1088¹]	1		**IRON PYRITES** (5a) 4-7F S Lloyd *Hld up 3rd/4th; hit 7 & 8; mist 10; went 2nd 14; jnd ldr aft 3 out; ld nxt; easy*
[1275⁴]	2	4	**Name Of Our Father (USA)** (7x) 7-4 Miss E Bryan *Ld to 9; 2nd to 14; 3l 2nd app 2 out; chsd wnr vain frm 2 out*
[1276³]	3	6	**Maid O'Tully (IRE)** (5a) 10-1 R Hodges *Swtng; 2nd til ld 9; stumbled app 2 out & hdd; drvn & sn wknd*
[862⁸]	4	15	**Roman Romany** 33-1 E Walker *(xnb) 3rd 6 til releg last & rdn 14; 15l bhnd when mist 2 out*

OFFICIAL DISTANCES: 4l, 6l TIME: 6min 38.0s

1459 Restricted (Div 1), 12st   8 ran

[1318¹]	1		**DUNETHNA (IRE)** 7-2 R Burton *Settled 3rd/4th; 10l 4th 13; jnd ldrs 15; ld 2 out; kpt on wl; rdly*
[1314²]	2	3	**Missed Call (IRE)** 7-4F Julian Pritchard *Chsd clr ldr til clsd to ld 15; hdd 2 out; hrd rdn & nt qckn flat*
[1293ᴾ]	3	8	**Another Wag** (5a) 5-1 S Lloyd *(xnb) Nt a fluent; settled midfield; 11l 5th 13; jnd ldrs 15; 2l 3rd app 2 out; sn rdn & no ex; lame*
[1018¹]	U		**Barton Bog (IRE)** 5-2 A Evans *(xnb) Settled towards rr; prog in 3rd 7; 7l 3rd 13; jnd ldrs when mist & ur 15*
[1351ᶠ]	P		**Colonels Hatch** 25-1 D Sherlock *3rd/4th to 7; rr 9; 15l last & rdn 12; t.o & pu 14*
[1276ᴾ]	P		**Hugo Henry (IRE)** (tt) 25-1 A Wadlow *Ld; ab 8l clr 6-13; hdd 15 & lost plce rap; t.o & pu last*
	P		**Rascaletto** (5a) 14-1 D Mansell *(xnb) A last trio; 23l 6th & strugg 13; pu 14*
	P		**Westington** 16-1 M Keel *A last trio; 24l 7th & strugg 13; pu 15*

OFFICIAL DISTANCES: 3l, 8l TIME: 6min 39.0s

1460 Restricted (Div 2), 12st   10 ran

[699³]	1		**SAM QUALE (IRE)** 3-1 Miss C Thomas *Swtng; hld up in midfield; disp 8l 4th 13; 6l 5th app 2 out; stayed on wl to ld last; rdn clr*
[1276²]	2	1	**Fountain Street (IRE)** 2-1F R Burton *(xnb) Rr early; impd to 10l 2nd 9; releg 3rd 14; 5l 4th app 2 out; drvn & rallied to jn wnr last; nt qckn*
[1276⁴]	3	3	**Black Oak** 8-1 Julian Pritchard *(xnb) Ld & sn 10l clr; 5l ahd 13; hdd brief app 2 out; drvn & hdd agn last; no ex*
[1411ᴾ]	4	6	**Lindalighter** (5a) 50-1 M Rodda *Settled 4/5th; 3rd 12 til 2nd 14; 2l 3rd app 2 out; sn wknd*
[1354²]	5	2	**Brother Prim** 8-1 D Mansell *Bhnd; 7th 12; hdwy u.p 14; drvn to ld app 2 out; sn hdd & wknd*
[993²]	6	3	**Winning Town** 9-2 Miss S Talbot *(xnb) 3rd to 7; 6th & lsng plce 9; 8th & strugg 13*
[1417ᴾ]	7	15	**Native Rambler (IRE)** 25-1 Miss C Stafford *(xnb) Handy; went 2nd 6-9; 7th 13; wknd nxt*
[673¹]	P		**Cead Mile Failte** (7a) 3-1 F Windsor Clive *Lw; jmpd slow 1; bhnd til prog to disp 8l 4th 13; chall nxt; ev ch 3 out; sn lost plce; pu & dism nxt*
[1054ᴾ]	P		**Its A Handfull** 10-1 J Price *2nd til lost plce & jmpd slow 6; mist 9; last & u.p 10; pu 12 (cut leg badly)*
[1276ᴾ]	P		**Scottish Clover** (5a) 10-1 S Lloyd *Bit bckwd; towards rr; 9th & strugg 13; t.o & pu 2 out*

OFFICIAL DISTANCES: 1½l, 2l TIME: 6min 33.0s

1461 Mens Open, 12st   3 ran

[970¹]	1		**NETHER GOBIONS** (7x) 1-6F Julian Pritchard *Lw; jw; made all; gng best frm 3 out; comf*
[611⁸]	2	6	**Capstown Bay** 7-1 S Joynes *Lw; a chsng wnr; 5l down app 2 out; rdn & no imp*
[1157ᵁ]	3	2fncs	**Our Eddie** 12-1 K Burke *(xnb) A last; lost tch u.p 10; wl t.o aft 13; fin 53 secs bhnd wnr; lame*

OFFICIAL DISTANCES: 4l, dist TIME: 6min 30.0s

1462 Ladies Open   7 ran

[1014¹]	1		**RIP VAN WINKLE** (7x) 2-7F Miss A Dare *Lw; jw; ld to 4; cl up til ld agn 12 (slow pce); 3l clr app 2 out; rdn out*

[1358⁴] **2** 2 **Tee Tee Too (IRE)** 12-1 Miss E James *Tail-swisher; settled cl up til chsd wnr app 3 out; stayed on wl aft but no imp flat*

[1074¹] **3** 8 **Tudor Lodge (IRE)** (5a,7x) 10-1 Miss S Swindells *Lw; handy; ld 9-12; prsd wnr til app 3 out; 9l 3rd & btn app nxt*

[1417⁹] **4** 30 **Blue Lyzander** (5a) 25-1 Mrs E Staines *(xnb) Ld 4-6; prsd wnr to 12; wknd aft nxt; poor 4th when mist 3 out; eased flat*

[1313ᴾ] **5** 10 **Slightly Special (IRE)** (bl) 33-1 Miss T Hirst *Blun 1; nt fluent & rn in snatches; 6l last 13; wl bhnd when mist 3 out; t.o aft*

[1297¹] **U** **Captain Khedive** (7x) 6-1 Miss S Talbot *(xnb) Lw; rdr unbalanced 2 & f.o 50 yds later*

R **Peter Pointer** 33-1 Miss E Crawford *(xnb) Swtng bad; reluct to go down; ss; pulled hrd; hdwy when crashed thro wing & ur 2; broke hind leg; dead*

OFFICIAL DISTANCES: 1l, 5l **TIME:** 6min 45.0s

1463 Confined, 12st   11 ran

[1272⁶] **1** **GOOD FOR A LOAN** 25-1 A Dalton *Prom; slpd app 3; lft in ld app 10; 8l clr 13; prsd frm 2 out; edged rt app last; r.o game; all out*

[1272⁴] **2** ½ **Gold'n Shroud (IRE)** 5-1 A Wintle *Settled rr; 6th 11; 12l 4th & prog 13; went 3rd 15 & chsd wnr 2 out; drvn to chall & nt much room & switched lft last; kpt on wl*

[1090⁴] **3** s hd **Saywhen** 7-1 R Burton *Midfield; 5th 9; lft 2nd by 11; chsd wnr to 3 out; drvn & nt qckn aft nxt til rallied & r.o wl flat*

[1358³] **4** 8 **Kingsthorpe** 6-1 A Phillips *Midfield & nd; 18l 5th 13; unable to clse aft*

[1346ᴾ] **5** 5 **Merger Mania** 14-1 A Wadlow *(xnb) Pulled hrd & jmpd rt; rushed to ld 3; hdd 9; sn lost plce; 21l 7th 13; no ch aft*

[1276ᶠ] **6** 6 **Cwm Bye** 20-1 Miss E James *Midfield & nd; 20l 6th & outpcd 13; plugged on*

[1338⁸] **P** **All Weather** (3x) 7-1 M Wilesmith *Jmpd reluct & sn t.o; pu 6*

[1274¹] **S** **Chassagne (FR)** 11-10F J Price *Hld up in last pr til slpd up turn bef 10*

[862⁵] **P** **Chiaroscuro** (bl) 14-1 S Lloyd *Lft last 6; drvn & reluct aft; t.o 13; pu 3 out*

[1311ᴾ] **S** **Rootsman (IRE)** 14-1 T Stephenson *Prom til ld 9; slpd up turn bef nxt*

[890²] **P** **Verulam (IRE)** 5-1 Julian Pritchard *(xnb) Ld to 3; 2nd/3rd aft; 11l 3rd 13; 4th 15; sn wknd; t.o & pu last*

OFFICIAL DISTANCES: ½l, nk **TIME:** 6min 29.0s

1464 Open Maiden (Div 1), 12st   7 ran

[11²] **1** **NO LOSS** 2-7F L Jefford *(xnb) Settled midfield; went 3rd 9 & 2nd 11; ld 14; 25l clr app 2 out; v easy*

[925ᴾ] **2** 30 **Tedstone Fox** 5-1 Miss R Reynolds *Tk str hld; ld 3; 10l clr 6; 15l ahd 9; hdd 14; no ch w wnr aft but a clr of rest*

[1271³] **3** 15 **Jack Cruise** 8-1 M Scales *3rd early; went mod 2nd 9-11; 15l 3rd 13; v tired frm 3 out & crawled home*

[1360⁵] **4** 2 **Sales Dodger (IRE)** 12-1 R Hodges *A strugg towards rr; lost tch 10; 22l 4th 13; t.o 15*

[1197ᵁ] **5** fence **Keldan Star (IRE)** 14-1 G Marsh *Virt a last & blun rnd w rdr out of sync; 20l adrift 6; 30l bhnd 13; jmpd v slow nxt & sn wl t.o; trotted in*

[972³] **U** **Champagne Thunder** (tt) 8-1 M Keel *(xnb) Ur 1*

[1404ᴿ] **P** **Sister Jim** (5a) 14-1 Julian Pritchard *Nt fluent; ld to 3; chsd ldr to 9; last & strugg 11; pu 12*

OFFICIAL DISTANCES: 20l, 10l **TIME:** 6min 38.0s

1465 Open Maiden (Div 2), 12st   9 ran

[1091ⁱ] **1** **FONTAINE AGAIN (IRE)** 5-1 T Stephenson *Pulled hrd & made virt all; 2l ahd app 2 out; drew clr app last; comf*

[866⁴ᵈ] **2** 5 **Brown Wren** (5a) S Lloyd *2nd/4th; 2½l 4th 13; went 2nd nxt; chsd wnr aft; drvn & v one-pcd aft 2 out*

[1153²] **3** 10 **Red Spice** 5-2JF R Owen *Tk keen hld; jnd wnr 6-8; 2l 3rd 13; rdn nxt; disp 4l 4th app 2 out; sn wknd*

[995ᴾ] **4** 1 **Crab 'n Lobster (IRE)** (5a) 12-1 R Hodges *Prom; disp ld brief 8; 11 2nd 13; dem nxt; 3½l 3rd & rdn app 2 out; sn wknd; disp mod 3rd when rdr waved wildly at last*

[337ᶠ] **5** 15 **Silk Oats** (5a) 7-1 M Wilesmith *(xnb) Midfield & nd; 15l 5th 13; some prog to 8l 6th app 2 out; sn wknd*

[1302ᴾ] **6** 20 **Mia Fort** (5a) 14-1 D Mansell *Nt jw in last; 12l adrift 6; 38l bhnd 13; t.o aft 15*

7 3 **Hot Toddy (IRE)** (7a) 5-2JF Julian Pritchard *Bit bckwd; school in rr; lost tch 6; 32l 8th 13; t.o aft 15*

[1315⁴] **F** **Forestry** 8-1 A Wintle *Hld up towards rr; 16l 6th 13; prog nxt; disp 4l 4th app 2 out; sn wknd; mod 5th when fell last*

[1223ᵁ]　P　　　**Motu Tapu** 5-1 Miss A Meakins *Pulled hrd in midfield; mist 8; wknd 11; 30l 7th 13; pu & dism 15*

OFFICIAL DISTANCES: 5l, 1l　**TIME:** 6min 47.0s

1466 Open Maiden (Div 3), 12st　　　　　　　　　　　　　**6 ran**

[989ᴾ]　1　　　　**PHARPEN (IRE)** 4-1 A Dalton *Pulled hrd; 2nd & clr of rest til lft in ld app 6; 10l clr 12; 30l ahd aft 3 out; v easy*

[1359²]　2　25　　**Take Achance On Me** 7-2 M Harris *Nt fluent; 3rd/4th bhnd clr ldrs; 15l 3rd 9; disp 17l 3rd 13; went rem 2nd 3 out; v unimpressive*

　　　3　25　　**Moondyne** (5a) 6-1 J Price *Half asleep padd; hld up & novicey in group chsng 2 clr ldrs; mist 12; 23l 5th 13; went rem 3rd & pckd 2 out*

[989ᴾ]　4　4　　**Loch Ash** 4-5F R Burton *(orbs) 2 handlers; pulled hrd; ld til rn wide app 6; chsd wnr vain til wknd bad 3 out*

[995ᴾ]　5　fence　**Sister Sue** (5a) 8-1 Miss R Reynolds *(xnb) Ss; tk keen hld; went 4th brief 9 but sn last agn; 38l last 13; sn wl t.o*

[667ᴾ]　P　　　**Persona Pride** 6-1 R Hodges *Detach in chsng group; rdn 11 to disp 17l 3rd 13; jmpd slow 15 & reluct aft; t.o & pu 2 out*

OFFICIAL DISTANCES: 17l, 15l　**TIME:** 6min 42.0s

Minehead Harriers & West Somerset
Holnicote (RH 7F,19J) Sat, 13 May (GOOD to FIRM)

1467 Restricted, 12st　　　　　　　　　　　　　　　　**11 ran**

[1057ᶠ]　1　　　　**ONE BOY** 16-1 A Honeyball *Tchd 25s in plce; 2 handlers; hld up towards rr; 7th 10; stdy hdwy frm 15; went 3rd 3 out; chall 2 out; ld app last; r.o*

[1376ᴾ]　2　1　　**Lynphord Girl** (5a) 33-1 J Barnes *Lw; prom; jmpd to ld 7; hdd 10; trckd ldr til ld agn 14; pushed 5l clr aft 16; one pce & hdd aft 2 out; kpt on u.p*

[1135⁵]　3　20　　**Old Harry's Wife** (5a) 7-1 N Mitchell *Ld 2-7 & agn 10-14; rdn & lost ground frm 16; lost tch w ldrs aft nxt*

[1373¹]　4　8　　**Button Up Bill** 10-1 H Thomas *Opened 12s; 2 handlers; last when mist 4; 7th 9; prog to 5l 3rd 15; wknd aft nxt; sn no ch*

[1375⁴]　F　　　**Belski** 9-2 R Woollacott *Opened 5s; sn prom; settled 3rd; 8l 3rd when fell 13*

[1375⁷]　U　　　**Crosswell Star (IRE)** 50-1 J Scott *Swtng; rr; ur 1*

[1309⁵]　P　　　**General Typhoon** 3-1 Miss E Tory *Lw; in tch early; 5th 7; sn lost plce; slt mist 12; t.o & pu 14*

[458ᴾ]　P　　　**Off The Cuff (IRE)** 9-4F Miss P Gundry *Tchd 5/2; lw; towards rr; went 5th 10; mist 15; no imp; btn 5th when pu 2 out; lame; subsq destroyd*

[1370ᴾ]　P　　　**Persian Raider** 50-1 M Sweetland *Sn rr; last when mist 8; bad mist 10; t.o & pu 14*

[1309⁶]　P　　　**Phartoomanny (IRE)** (5a) 50-1 Miss N Snowden *(xnb) Prom early; sn midfield; bhnd when pu & dism 16*

[1309⁷]　P　　　**The Stuffed Puffin (IRE)** 20-1 Miss S Rowe *(xnb) In tch; settled 4th; lft 3rd 13; outpcd 15; lost ground; btn 6th when pu 3 out*

OFFICIAL DISTANCES: nk, 8l　**TIME:** 6min 33.0s　**TOTE:** £11.60　**DF:** £18.00

1468 Open Maiden (Div 1), 12st　　　　　　　　　　　**12 ran**

[1308⁶]　1　　　　**CHANCE ENCOUNTER** 4-1F J Young *Sn prom; chsd ldr 5 til ld app 11; went 4l clr aft 16; kpt on when prsd 2 out; drvn out*

[1241ᵁ]　2　4　　**All Sewn Up** 5-1 A Honeyball *Lw; patient rdn; towards rr; 6th 13; hdwy to 3rd 16; went 2nd on inner 3 out; tried to chall & rdn 2 out; no ex run-in*

[1262²]　3　1½　**County Derry** 14-1 B O'Doherty *Swtng; blun bad 5; midfield when mist & rmdr 2; 6th 13; stdy prog to 4th 16; went 3rd nxt; stayed on one pce*

[1245²]　4　20　　**Qu'appelle** 5-1 Miss A Goschen *Midfield; 7th 9; hdwy 13; lft 3rd 14; went 2nd brief 16; sn wknd; no ch frm 3 out*

[658⁴]　P　　　**Aadann (IRE)** 20-1 L Tibbatts *Towards rr; 8th 9; t.o & pu 14*

[1099³]　P　　　**Bid For Tools (IRE)** (bl) 14-1 G Barfoot-Saunt *Ld 1; hdd til lost ground 7; 6th ½way; bhnd frm 13 til pu 3 out*

[1241ᵁ]　P　　　**Final Chance** (5a) 8-1 Miss C Tizzard *Rcd keen; ld 2 & sn 6l clr; hdd app 11; wknd qckly & 5th 13; poor 6th when scrambled over 15 & nxt; bhnd when pu 3 out*

[1307ᵁ]　F　　　**Green Anker** 5-1 G Maundrell *Handy on inner; cl 3rd 9; went 2nd 11; cl up when mist 15; wknd qckly; wl btn 5th & v tired when fell 3 out*

[1179³]　F　　　**I'm Foxy** (5a) (bl) 16-1 T Dennis *Prom when pckd 3; 4th ½way; went 3rd 13; 4l 3rd when fell 14*

[1138ᴾ]　P　　　**Leonard's Dream** (5a) 12-1 J Scott *Jmpd slow & rmdr 3; sn trailing & nt jw; pu 10*

[1131ᴾ]　P　　　**The Handsome Friar** 33-1 J Barnes *Prom early; 6th 6; sn lost plce; t.o & pu 12*

[1100⁵] P   **Uncle James (IRE)** (bl) 9-2 **C White** 6s-9/2; sn towards rr & nvr gng wl; 10th ½way;
                  bhnd & reluct when pu 15

OFFICIAL DISTANCES: 5l, 1½l TIME: 6min 45.0s TOTE: £5.20 DF: £9.10

1469 Open Maiden (Div 2), 12st   12 ran

[1373²] 1   **NAMRON (IRE)** 4-1 **N Mitchell** Tubed; ld to 7; ld agn 10; went clr 12; 6l clr 17; blun
                  last; pushed out
[1308ᴾ] 2   3½   **Dealer Del** 5-1 **G Richards** 7s-5s; hld up in midfield; 6th 9; prog to disp 2nd 14; rdn
                  aft 3 out; no imp on wnr; lft clr 2nd at last
[1263ᴾ] 3   25   **Thecabbageflinger** (bl) 25-1 **J Young** Rr; slt mist 2; 9th ½way; prog 16; 5th 3 out;
                  nt rch ldrs; lft 3rd af last
[1178ᴾ] 4 runin **Smudges Season** (5a) 25-1 **R Emmett** Towards rr; 8th ½way; bhnd frm 15; lft poor
                  4th 2 out
[1308ᴾ] 5   15   **Windyway** (5a) 12-1 **L Tibbatts** (xnb) Sn rr; bhnd frm 7; t.o
         P   **Annie Dipper** (12a,6ow) 20-1 **D Alers-Hankey** Bit bckwd; sn towards rr; bhnd frm
                  8; t.o & jmpd lft 13; pu aft; school
  [640ᴾ] P   **Charlie Smith** (7a) 14-1 **R Young** In tch in midfield; went 4th 9; in tch to 15; eased;
                  5th when pu aft 16; do btr
[1372⁵] P   **Frosty Jo** (5a) 10-1 **M Sweetland** Sn handy; 3rd frm 10 til lost plce 13; 7th 15; bhnd
                  & pu 3 out
[1369³] U   **Humara (IRE)** (5a) 12-1 **Miss G Edwards** Prom & rcd towards outer; slt mist 7; cl
                  2nd 9; disp 2nd & chsd ldr frm 15; saddle slpd & ur aft last
  [640ᶠ] P   **Irish Brush (IRE)** (5a) 4-1 **G Barfoot-Saunt** 6s-4s; ld 7 til bad mist 10 & lost sev
                  lengths; nt rec; brought rn wide aft 3 out; rn out nxt
[1101⁵] R   **Jazetason** 33-1 **M Woodward** Pulling; 5th 7; midfield til some hdwy aft 16; 4th when
                  rn wide aft 3 out; rn out nxt
[1136³] U   **Mayhem** (5a) 5-2F **T Dennis** Tchd 3s; prom; jmpd violent rt & rdr lost irons 4; blun &
                  ur nxt

OFFICIAL DISTANCES: 3l, 20l TIME: 6min 50.0s TOTE: £3.70 DF: £10.50

1470 Mixed Open, 12st   5 ran

[1304¹] 1   **MILLYHENRY** 2-7F **Miss C Tizzard** Opened 4/11; lw; trckd ldr & clr of rest; prog to ld
                  15; sn 4l clr; pushed out
[1374ᴿ] 2   8   **Hylters Chance (IRE)** (vis) 12-1 **D Alers-Hankey** Lw; rcd keen; ld aft 2; set str pce;
                  hit 8; 3l clr 9; hdd 15; rdn 3 out; kpt on
  [735ᴾ] 3   6   **Earl Boon** 5-1 **Miss P Gundry** Settled off pce in 4th; slt mist 12; hdwy 16; went 3rd
                  nxt; no ex
[1374⁴] 4   8   **Via Del Quatro (IRE)** (5a) 33-1 **J Barnes** Slt ld til 2; settled 3rd; in tch til wknd 16
[1132²] P   **Spring Marathon (USA)** 12-1 **Miss E Tory** A last; just in tch to 15; wknd; t.o & pu last

OFFICIAL DISTANCES: 8l, 6l TIME: 6min 29.0s TOTE: £1.30 DF: £4.50

1471 Countryside Alliance Club Members (Nov Rdrs), 12st   10 ran

[1260²] 1   **BELARUS (IRE)** (bl) 5-2JF **C White** Tchd 11/4; went cl 2nd 5 til ld 15; sent 6l clr 3
                  out; stayed on; comf
  [927ᴾ] 2   15   **Lavalight** 20-1 **J Ferguson** Sn prom; lft in ld aft 6; hdd 15; sn no ex
[1306²] 3   3½   **Frozen Drop** 8-1 **T Bishop** Prog to 3rd 11; cl up & ev ch til outpcd 16; wl hld in 3rd
                  when slt mist 2 out
  [846¹] 4   2   **Palace Parade (USA)** 5-2JF **S Craddock** Opened 3s; hld up; prog to 4th 11; lost tch
                  stdly frm 15
[1304³] 5   6   **Sir Frosty** (tt) 3-1 **A Bateman** Opened 7/2; ld til app 6; 5th & in tch 9; lost plce & slt
                  mist 12; no ch frm 15
[1304⁵] 6   8   **Single Man (NZ)** 25-1 **B Parsons** Prom; cl 3rd 9; lost plce stdly frm 12; bhnd frm 16
[1338ᴾ] U   **Dromhana (IRE)** 33-1 **G Galpin** Blun bad & ur 3
[1306ᴾ] P   **Fast Run (IRE)** 50-1 **Miss M Taylor** Rap hdwy to ld 6; rn v wide bend & releg to last;
                  t.o nxt til pu 13
  [557ᵁ] U   **Ive Called Time** 12-1 **B O'Doherty** Hmpd & ur 3
[1306²] U   **Villains Brief (IRE)** (bl) 50-1 **J Kwiatkowski** Hmpd & ur 3

OFFICIAL DISTANCES: 14l, 4l TIME: 6min 34.0s TOTE: £2.50 DF: £19.60

1472 Intermediate, 12st   5 ran

[1370⁵] 1   **FOXY DAWN** 6-4JF **D Alers-Hankey** Jw; ld to 4; jmpd to ld agn 14; jnd 2 out; agn
                  jmpd to ld 2 out; drvn out
[1371⁶] 2   2   **Leejay Luki** 6-4JF **A Honeyball** 2 handlers; ld; blun 12; hdd 14; outj by wnr aft but
                  rallied game to chall 2 out; drvn & level when outj agn & hdd last; kpt on

[1370⁷] 3 runin **Master Kiwi (NZ)** 20-1 *Miss T Hayes Lft 3rd 3; lost tch aft 10; t.o*

[1097⁸] U **Lucky Thursday** (bl) 10-1 *Miss H Best Dived lft & ur 3*

[1370⁵] P **Master Buckley** (bl) 6-1 *C White Went 2nd 7; cl up when virt fell 8; nt rec; bhnd when pu 13*

OFFICIAL DISTANCES: 2½l, 30l **TIME:** 6min 47.0s **TOTE:** £2.20 **DF:** £1.70

1473 Confined, 12st
6 ran

[1371²] 1 **STILLMORE BUSINESS** (3x) 5-4F *Miss P Gundry Lw; ld/disp til jmpd to ld 14; sent 3l clr 3 out; in comm when dived at last; drvn out*

[1371³] 2 4 **Bells Wood** (5x) 7-2 *C White Ld/disp 3-6; cl 3rd 12; rdn 14; 5l 3rd 3 out; went def 2nd 2 out; kpt on one pce*

[1236ᶠ] 3 3½ **Primero (IRE)** (tt) 3-1 *A Honeyball 5s-3s; lw; swtng; nt a fluent; hld up; slpd bend aft 9; prog to 4th 15; clsd u.p to 3rd 3 out; no ex frm nxt*

[1340ᵁ] 4 4 **The Bold Abbot** (3x) 11-1 *Miss S West Tchd 12s; cl up frm 7; slt ld/disp frm 9 til outj & hdd 14; chsd ldr til wknd 2 out*

[523⁵] 5 runin **Nothing To Fear** 50-1 *Miss J Buck Nov rdn; bhnd frm 10; v wide bend aft 13; t.o*

[1369²] P **Link Copper** 13-2 *G Barfoot-Saunt Blun 1; settled cl 3rd; wl in tch til wknd 13; bhnd frm 16 til pu last*

OFFICIAL DISTANCES: 4l, 5l **TIME:** 6min 35.0s **TOTE:** £1.80 **DF:** £4.20

South Durham
Mordon (LH 8F,19J) Sat, 13 May (FIRM)

1474 Hunt, 12st
6 ran

[1327¹] 1 **MAJORITY MAJOR (IRE)** (bl) 1-3F *T Glass Ld & sn 8l clr; tried to rn out & dem 3l 3rd 3; sev rmdrs; ld agn 7; jnd 2 out; hrd drvn to ld agn last; r.o*

[1326⁶] 2 4 **Heather Lad** 4-1 *D Raw Chsd ldr til ld 4-6; 4l 3rd 7; hdwy 3 out; jnd ldr nxt; outpcd & 11 2nd when mist last; no ex flat*

[1331⁴] 3 15 **Baltic Lake (IRE)** 20-1 *M Smethurst Prom; cl 2nd 4; pushed along 15; outpcd & wknd nxt; 8l 3rd 2 out; r.o one pce*

[1348⁵] 4 1 **Caman** (bl) 33-1 *Mrs S Palfreeman A towards rr; 8l 4th 10; pushed along 12; outpcd & lsng tch 13; stayed on frm 2 out & nrly caught wkng 3rd on line*

[1326ᴾ] r **Prince Moshar** 33-1 *L McGrath Last by 3; 20l adrift when ref 6*

U **Say Sadie** (5a) 12-1 *M Clayton Rr by 3; 15l 5th when ur 5*

OFFICIAL DISTANCES: 4l, 15l **TIME:** 6min 05.0s

1475 Restricted, 12st
8 ran

[1352¹] 1 **SALLY SCALLY** (5a) 7-4F *Miss T Jackson (xnb) Hld up in rr; 8l 5th 8; last 12; hdwy to 5l 6th 14; 2l 3rd 3 out; ld nxt; qcknd 5l clr app last; r.o wl*

[807²] 2 4 **Lord Nick** 2-1 *C Mulhall Last to 4; 9l 6th & hdwy 8; 2l 3rd 11; cl 2nd 14; ev ch 2 out; sn outpcd; r.o*

[1348³] 3 2 **Lord George** 6-1 *P Atkinson A.p; 6l 3rd 5 & 4l 4th 11; hdwy 13; ld 16; jnd 2 out; sn hdd & outpcd*

[1347¹] 4 3 **La Emni (IRE)** 33-1 *S Charlton Handy in midfield to 8; went 11 2nd 13; ev ch 3 out; outpcd nxt*

[1230ᴾ] 5 12 **Mefein Boy (IRE)** 14-1 *L McGrath Nt jw; jmpd big at times in last; clambered over 6; rmdrs 7; slt hdwy 14 to 20l 6th 2 out; r.o one pce; snatched 5th on line*

[1154ᴾ] 6 ½ **Ladylands** (5a) 10-1 *D Raw Ld to 15; outpcd & stdly wknd frm 3 out; dem last on line*

[1351ᴾ] F **Kind Of Chic** (5a) 66-1 *P Kinsella Trckd ldr in 2l 2nd til ½l 2nd 9; sn wknd; lsng tch when fell 11*

[1326ᵠ] U **Menaldi (IRE)** 9-1 *Miss K Roncoroni Midfield to 6; rr by 8; last & outpcd 13; lsng tch when bad mist & ur 16*

OFFICIAL DISTANCES: 4l, 2l **TIME:** 6min 02.0s

1476 Mens Open
7 ran

[1349¹] 1 **RED SPECTACLE (IRE)** 7-4F *N Tutty Hld up in rr; hdwy 8 to 3l 3rd 11; went 11 2nd 2 out; sn ld & qcknd clr; r.o wl*

[1325³] 2 5 **Primitive Streak** (tt) 5-1 *R Abrahams Cl 3rd til ld 8; 2l up 11; cl 2nd 12 til ld agn 3 out; hdd & outpcd app last*

[1327³] 3 60 **Lottery Ticket (IRE)** 33-1 *S J Robinson Ld to 7; trckd ldr in 2l 2nd to 11; pushed along & wknd 13; lft rem 3rd 2 out*

[1151ᴾ] 4 8 **Larkshill (IRE)** 33-1 *C Mulhall Rr; last 6-9; went 8l 5th 12; pushed along 13; sn outpcd & wknd; poor 5th 15; lft rem 4th 2 out*

[1365ᴾ]	P	**Branch End** 50-1 T Scott *Trckd ldr in 11 2nd til wknd 8; last 10; t.o & pu 13*
[794ᶠ]	F	**Syd Green (IRE)** 5-2 S Walker *Last to 3; pulled hrd to handy 4th 5; bad mist 10 & brilliant rcvry; eff to ld 12; jnd 3 out; sn hdd; 2l 3rd & u.p when fell 2 out*
[1350⁵]	F	**Vital Issue (IRE)** 3-1 D Easterby *Ld til fell 6; rdr dislocated thumb*

OFFICIAL DISTANCES: 6l, dist TIME: 5min 59.0s

1477 Ladies Open   4 ran

[1350¹]	1		**CEDE NULLIS** (5a) (bl) 16-1 Miss L Eddery *Last to 9; 8l 4th 10; slt hdwy 13 to 5l 3rd 14; chsng ldr in 3l 2nd 3 out; str rn frm 2 out to chall last; stormed clr flat*
[1350²]	2	4	**Japodene** (5a,2ow) 4-7F Miss R Clark *Trckd ldr in 2l 2nd til ld 10; 3l up 3 out; 4l ahd & rdr lkng rnd app last; hdd & outpcd flat*
[1350¹]	3	1	**Temple Garth** 6-4 Miss F Hartley *Sn clr; ld to 9; wknd 11; last 13; 8l 4th 2 out; lft 3rd app last; fin str; nrly snatched 2nd*
[717ᶠ]	P		**Strongalong (IRE)** 10-1 Miss H Delahooke *Chsd ldng pr in 3rd to 5; 4l 3rd 10; pushed to 4l 2nd 12; outpcd 16; 6l 3rd when pu & dism last*

OFFICIAL DISTANCES: 2½l, ½l TIME: 6min 01.0s

1478 Intermediate   7 ran

[1335¹⁰]	1		**THE ALLEYCAT (IRE)** 12-1 P Robson *A.p; 3l 3rd 5-11; 4l 4th 13; hdwy 16 to disp ld 3 out; ld nxt; sn clr; r.o str; wl rdn*
[1000¹]	2	12	**Noble Hymn** 4-7F C Mulhall *Cl up; went 3l 3rd 10 & cl 2nd 15; ld 16-3 out; ev ch nxt; outpcd & wknd app last*
[1350⁴]	3	6	**Orswellthatenswell** 8-1 Mrs F Needham *Ld to 6; cl 2nd to 15; outpcd & wknd 3 out; 15l 4th 2 out; r.o one pce*
[1348ᵁ]	4	2	**Harbour Blaze (IRE)** 12-1 Miss R Clark *A rr; bhnd by 8; poor 5th 12; plodded on one pce; nrst fin*
[1349⁵]	P		**Hazel Reilly (IRE)** (5a) 5-1 S Swiers *Handy 3rd to 6; drpd to last 7; pushed along & lsng tch 11; t.o & pu 14*
[1328ᴾ]	U		**La Maja (IRE)** (5a) 66-1 Miss T Jackson *Last til ur 4*
[1351¹]	P		**Sovereigns Match** 4-1 M Mackley *Prom; 2nd til ld 7; jnd 16; hdd & outpcd 2 out; 8l 3rd when pu & dism last; lame*

OFFICIAL DISTANCES: 15l, 10l TIME: 5min 59.0s

1479 Open Maiden (Div 1), 12st   11 ran

[1352²]	1		**LEG BEFORUM (IRE)** 7-4F S Swiers *Ld to 5 & frm 7; 3l up 14; jnd 16-2 out; qcknd 5l ahd app last; stormed clr flat*
[1330²]	2	15	**Stygian Star (IRE)** (5a) 3-1 M Smethurst *Rr to 10; hdwy 12 to 12l 6th 14; disp ld 16 til outpcd aft 2 out; 5l 2nd at last; wknd bad flat*
[1037³]	3	20	**Sylcanny** (5a) 10-1 J Davies *A rr; nmped 12; went 15l 4th 16 & dist 3rd 2 out; v one-pcd*
[1352³]	4	35	**Educate Me (IRE)** (tt) 10-1 J Burley *Prom; 5l 4th 11; outpcd 14; lft 10l 3rd 16; pushed along & sn wknd; poor 4th by 2 out*
[1330⁵]	5	4	**No Time To Wait** 25-1 Miss J Foster *Cl 2nd til ld 5-6; in tch til wknd 13; poor 5th 2 out*
[1329ᴾ]	F		**Aughrim Quest (IRE)** (5a) 25-1 T Glass *Midfield to 10; 6l 5th when fell 12*
[1352³]	P		**Highland Symphony** (5a) 25-1 Mrs F Needham *A rr; last by 10; t.o 14; v rem 6th 2 out; pu last*
[1352³]	P		**Just A Single (IRE)** (tt) 25-1 A Morris *Sa; t.o & fnce adrift by 2; pu 8; saddle slpd*
[1330ᴾ]	P		**Oaklands Jimmy** 25-1 P Frank *Midfield; in tch til outpcd 13; wknd qckly; t.o & pu 14*
[1235³]	P		**Sand Track** 25-1 M Haigh *Rr by 7; bad mist 9; pushed along 10; last by 12; t.o & pu 3 out*
[1164²]	P		**Sharpaman** (7a) 7-2 T Scott *Prom in 3rd to 9; 3l 3rd 11 til did splits 14; pu nxt*

OFFICIAL DISTANCES: 10l, 20l TIME: 6min 05.0s

1480 Open Maiden (Div 2), 12st   15 ran

[1430⁵]	1		**SPECTACULAR VIEW (IRE)** (7a) 9-1 M Clayton *Jw; handy 3rd to 9; 4l 4th 10; ld 15; 8l up 2 out; r.o str; v easy*
[1367³]	2	12	**Running Mute** 3-1F T Scott *Handy in midfield to 10; hdwy 12 to 3l 3rd 14; cl 2nd & ev ch 3 out; easily outpcd aft*
[1353²]	3	3	**Catton Lady** (5a) (tt) 9-2 C Mulhall *A handy; went 2l 2nd 10; ld 11-14; sn wknd; 12l 3rd 2 out; r.o one pce*
[1324³]	4	8	**Early Dawn** (5a) 6-1 J Davies *Cl 2nd to 9; handy to 14; 5l 4th 15; outpcd & 20l 4th 2 out*
[1343ᴾ]	5	12	**The Shy Padre (IRE)** 5-1 Miss J Foster *Cl up til ld 6-10; 3l 5th by 14; outpcd 15; dist 5th 3 out*
[1329ᴾ]	6	10	**Almikino (IRE)** 20-1 S Brisby *In tch in rr til pushed along 12; poor 6th 3 out*

[1352⁶]	7	2	**Lewesdon Countess** (5a) 33-1 N Kent *A rr; outpcd & lsng tch 13; t.o 16*
[1352⁶]	8	4	**Right Ron Run** (vis) 20-1 R Wakeham *Handy; 6l 6th 10; gng wl 13; 4l 6th nxt; wknd qckly 15; poor 7th 3 out*
[1251²]	9	1	**Slobadam** (tt) 14-1 M Mackley *Rr til hdwy 9; 6l 5th 11; wknd 14; t.o 3 out*
[1330⁴]	U		**Henah Hill** 7-1 S Swiers *Cl up when hmpd bad & ur 5*
[1331⁶]	P		**Hetty Bell** (5a) 50-1 A Richardson *Last by 3; rem by 10; pu 2 out*
[1233⁵]	P		**My Sam** (12a,4ow) 6-1 L McGrath *A rr; pushed along 14; lsng tch when pu app 16; broke leg; dead*
[1353³]	F		**Oaklands Billy** 8-1 P Frank *Ld til fell 5*
[1032⁶]	P		**Oaklands Millie (IRE)** (5a) 50-1 P Kinsella *A towards rr; lsng tch 14; t.o & pu 2 out*
[1000⁶]	P		**Santa Barbara (IRE)** (5a,4ow) 6-1 Mrs S Palfreeman *Sn bhnd; t.o by 5; rem last when pu 11*

OFFICIAL DISTANCES: 15l, 3l TIME: 6min 04.0s

Vale of Aylesbury
Kingston Blount (LH 8F,18J) Sat, 13 May (GOOD to FIRM)

1481 Confined, 12st
11 ran

[1282²]	1		**FAIR CROSSING** (5x) 9-2 M Emmanuel *Ld to 3; prom; jnd ldr 10; duelled in ld & clr of rest til def advant 3 out; clr nxt; 8l up last; rdn & hld on*
[1215³]	2	3	**Lottie The Lotus** (5a) 2-1F J Tarry *Swtng; lost plce 6; 7th ½way; eff app 14; 4th aft nxt; drvn 2 out; 2nd & clsng flat; too much to do*
[1034²]	3	5	**Hill Island** (3x) (bl) 8-1 Miss L Sweeting *Chsd ldrs; 6th ½way; eff to chse ldng pr aft 14; chsd wnr 12 out; no imp when mist last; sn dem*
[572⁶]	4	20	**Valibus (FR)** 33-1 P Scouller *Bit bckwd; ld 3 til bef 6; chsd ldng pr brief app 14; sn wknd*
[1394⁶]	5	½	**Cut A Niche** 14-1 T Lane *(boh) Swtng; mist 3; in tch; 4th ½way; lost plce 14; no prog aft*
[1340⁶]	6	10	**Clinking** 9-2 P Young *(xnb) Lkd rough; tk keen hld; ld app 6; 8l up & mist 9; jnd nxt; duelled in ld til hdd & wknd rap 3 out; mist last*
[1381⁵]	7	1	**Limosa** (5a) 12-1 R Barrett *Hld up; a wl in rr; rdn aft 11; no prog*
[1441²]	U		**Castle Arrow (IRE)** 9-2 R Lawther *Swtng; tde; reluct to line up & ld in start; last til stumbled & ur aft 5*
[968⁶]	P		**Flying Fellow (IRE)** 25-1 A Charles-Jones *Bit bckwd; swtng; a towards rr; lsng tch when jmpd slow 14; wl bhnd when pu 3 out*
[1436⁵]	P		**Hope's Delight (IRE)** (bl) 33-1 T Illsley *Mist 2; chsd ldrs; wkng when mist 11; pu nxt*
[1016⁶]	P		**Smart Teacher (USA)** 25-1 G Carenza *(xnb) Hld up; stdy prog 7; chsd ldng pr 12 til wknd app 14; wl bhnd when pu 3 out*

OFFICIAL DISTANCES: 3l, 6l TIME: 6min 14.5s

1482 Restricted
8 ran

[874¹]	1		**OKEFORD (IRE)** 9-4F R Walford *In tch; trckd ldr 10; ld aft 13; 4l clr when jmpd slow 3 out; 2l up & jmpd slow last; pushed out & a hldng rnr-up; broke down*
[887²]	2	2	**Effie Wood** (5a) 5-2 D Crosse *Swtng; trckd ldrs; rdr called cab 13; eff to chse wnr aft 14; hrd rdn 2 out; kpt on flat; a hld*
[1146⁶]	3	½	**Lady Emerald** (5a) 9-2 J Tarry *In tch; chsd ldng pr 15; rdn 2 out; 4l 3rd last; kpt on flat*
[1419⁶]	4	15	**Abbey Flyer** 8-1 T Illsley *Ld til aft 2; lft in ld 8; hdd aft 13; outpcd easy aft 15; one pce aft*
[1419⁵]	5	12	**Royal Orchard** (bl) 16-1 A Martin *Last pr; rdn 11; lost tch 14; no ch aft*
[1206³]	6	15	**Second Amendment** (5a) 9-2 S Morris *Trckd ldrs; rdn to chse wnr app 14; wknd sn aft; fin tired*
[1438⁵]	P		**Grange Prize** 33-1 Miss K Henry *Swtng; ld aft 2 til pu 8; tack broke*
[1355⁴]	U		**Tranquil Lord (IRE)** 20-1 D Smith *Last pr til ur 6*

OFFICIAL DISTANCES: 2l, ½l TIME: 6min 24.5s
Newtown Rambler was withdrawn not under orders - state of ground

1483 Ladies Open
9 ran

[1410¹ˢ]	1		**PHARARE (IRE)** 1-3F Miss C Spearing *Lw; ld 2 til aft 5; ld 8; qcknd clr frm 15; impressive*
[1007⁶]	2	20	**Maltby Son** 6-1 Mrs T Hill *14s-6s; ss; hld up; prog 10; chsd wnr 12; 6l down 3 out; no ch aft; rn wl*
[1145³]	3	10	**Lucky Christopher** 12-1 Miss R Goodwin *Chsd ldrs; 3rd ½way; 4th & outpcd aft 13; went 3rd agn aft 15; no ch ldng pr*

[1417⁸]	4	15	**Persian Butterfly** (5a) 10-1 **Miss T Habgood** *Swtng; jmpd slow 3; prom; ld 6-8; chsd wnr to 12; eff agn 14; sn wknd*
[1380⁵]	5	25	**Larry The Lamb** 9-1 **Miss T Hayter** *Last pr & detach frm 6; t.o aft 13*
[1174²]	6	6	**Silver Sleeve (IRE)** (bl) 25-1 **Miss L Bridges** *Ld to 2; 7th & wkng when jmpd slow 11; mist & rdr nrly f.o 13; miles bhnd aft; snatched 6th cl home*
[1417ᴾ]	7	1	**Driving Force** 33-1 **Miss S Hutchings** *Prom; ld brief aft 5; 4th ½way; sn wknd; t.o aft 13; dem last nr fin*
[1380ᴾ]	P		**Cill Churnain (IRE)** 25-1 **Mrs E Coveney** *Chsd ldrs; 6th when blun 7; rr aft; blun 13; t.o & pu 3 out*
[753⁴]	P		**Dicks Darlin'** (5a) 25-1 **Miss N McKim** *Swtng; last & nt jw; t.o 6; pu 12*

OFFICIAL DISTANCES: 25l, 8l **TIME:** 6min 04.0s

1484 Mens Open, 12st   9 ran

[1416³]	1		**FAWSLEY MANOR** (5a) 2-1F **J Tarry** *Swtng; cl up; jnd ldr 14; duelled in ld aft; ½l up 2 out; hrd rdn last; sn clr*
[1286⁴]	2	10	**Sign** 9-4 **D Barlow** *Ld to 2; lft in ld 11; jnd 14; duelled w wnr til 2 out; 2l 2nd & jmpd slow last; fin tired*
[1244³]	3	4	**Arleneseoin (IRE)** (7x) 6-1 **P York** *Tde; pulled hrd; ld 2 til blun bad 11 lvng rdr hanging off side; miraculous rcvry & spontaneous applause frm crowd; cl up til outpcd by ldng pr 14; kpt on agn flat*
[938³]	4	25	**Remilan (IRE)** (4x) (bl) 8-1 **A Sansome** *Prom; rdn 11; nt r.o & sn lost tch; t.o 14*
[1304ᵁ]	5	250y	**Mystery Aristocrat (IRE)** 16-1 **R Tory** *Sn last; t.o ½way*
[1246²]	P		**Ardbrennan** 10-1 **D Crosse** *(xnb,bf) Hld up; clsd on ldrs 9; 4th & rdn 12; no prog; 4th when pu 13; dead*
[884ᴾ]	P		**Bally Parson** 25-1 **C Wadland** *Wl in tch til wknd rap 12; t.o & pu 14*
[1341ʳ]	r		**Caballus (USA)** (7x) 25-1 **A Charles-Jones** *Ref to rce; tk no part til rest had jmpd 3 fncs; ref 1; galloped lap of course missing fncs*
[886²]	P		**Winter Belle (USA)** (7x) (bl) 10-1 **R Shepherd-Cross** *Rr; detach frm 6; jmpd slow 8; wl bhnd when pu 13*

OFFICIAL DISTANCES: 10l, 4l **TIME:** 6min 13.0s
The Stewards interviewed the rider of Caballus who having dwelt and then refused the first fence was cantered a circuit of the course missing the fences; he was severely cautioned and the owner reported he would not be running the horse again

1485 Intermediate, 12st   10 ran

[1143³]	1		**GRECIAN STAR** 5-2 **J Tarry** *A cl up; ld aft 13; made rest; 4l up 2 out; r.o str*
[1286²]	2	8	**Mister Audi (IRE)** 2-1F **A Sansome** *Ww; prog on rvr 11; chsd wnr aft 13; 4l down 2 out; tried to rally app last; sn no imp*
[1272²]	3	8	**Aqua Star (IRE)** 10-1 **Miss C Spearing** *Tde; hld up in tch in rr; rmdr 10; prog 13; 4th 3 out; same & btn when mist 2 out; kpt on*
[1143ᴾ]	4	¾	**Final Analysis (IRE)** (bl) 5-1 **J Owen** *Prom; ld 6 til aft 13; 3rd when blun 15; wknd 2 out; dem flat*
[1378³]	5	3	**Tell Tale (IRE)** 11-2 **A Harvey** *Swtng; cl up; chsd ldr 8-9; sltly outpcd aft 13; eff agn nxt; one pce & no prog frm 3 out*
[953⁵]	6	7	**Susies Melody (IRE)** (tt) 8-1 **D Dennis** *Prom; sltly outpcd aft 13; eff agn nxt; wknd aft 3 out*
[1203⁵]	7	25	**Cardinal Gayle (IRE)** 14-1 **Miss D Harding** *Mist 7; in tch; chsd ldr 9 til mist 11; wknd aft 13; t.o nxt*
[1356⁶]	8	5	**Glendine (IRE)** 33-1 **D Smith** *Ld til jmpd slow & hdd 6; wknd 12; t.o*
[1203³]	P		**Northern Yarn (IRE)** 14-1 **T Illsley** *Lkd poor; hld up rr; in tch til wknd 13; t.o & pu 15*
[1005ᴾ]	P		**Tarry Awhile** 33-1 **Miss R Goodwin** *Mist 7; a rr; last & wkng when pu 13*

OFFICIAL DISTANCES: 8l, 6l **TIME:** 6min 15.0s

1486 Open Maiden   13 ran

[1020ʳ]	1		**TEACHERS PET** 33-1 **Miss L Sweeting** *Chsd ldng pr 6; clsd 10; 8l 3rd & outpcd aft 13; r.o 3 out; ld nxt; sn clr; pushed out*
[1422⁴]	2	12	**Out By Night (IRE)** 5-1 **D Barlow** *Ld at fast pce; clr w rival aft 13; hdd nxt; ld agn brief 3 out; sn btn; fin tired*
[1423⁶]	3	3	**Devil's Sting (IRE)** 33-1 **J Richardson** *Chsd ldr; clr of rest aft 13; ld 14-3 out; wknd nxt; fin tired*
[1207²]	4	25	**Darzal** 4-1 **A Charles-Jones** *Trckd ldrs; 5l 4th & clr of rest when blun 11; sn lost tch w ldng trio; no prog frm 13*
[1435ᴾ]	5	runin	**Shortcut Shorty** 16-1 **W Brown** *Mid-div; lost tch frm 8; 25l 6th 11; t.o aft 13*

[1423³]	P	**Ben Gilmore** 7-2 R Lawther *Swtng; a wl in rr & nvr gng wl; 25l 8th 10; no ch aft; t.o & pu 14*
[1437⁶]	P	**Bright Vulcan** 3-1F T Illsley *5s-3s; nt fluent & nvr gng wl; sn rr; mist 6; last & no ch when pu 12*
[1439ᴾ]	F	**Dennis** 16-1 J Tarry *Mist 2; rmdr aft 3; a wl in rr; no ch ½way; last when fell 13; dead*
[1257⁴]	P	**Goldsteane** (5a) 16-1 S Morris *25s-16s; swtng; chsd ldrs; 5th 8; 12l down 11; wl bhnd aft 13; t.o & pu 2 out*
[1382ᴾ]	P	**Lazy Acres (IRE)** 33-1 C Lawson *Tde; ss; imm t.o; pu 11*
[1147ᴾ]	F	**Misblaize** (5a) 33-1 M Wall *Swtng; chsd ldrs; wknd 8; rem last when fell hvly 12*
[1131ᴾ]	P	**Mr Robstee** 4-1 J Trice-Rolph *A rr; jmpd slow 3; no prog ½way; t.o 13; pu 15; dism*
[1147ᴾ]	P	**Stormhill Soldier** 33-1 A Middleton *A rr; blun 2; no ch when mist 11; t.o & pu 15; dism*

OFFICIAL DISTANCES: 15l, 6l **TIME:** 6min 16.5s

1487 Hunt, 12st   6 ran

[1146⁵]	1		**ENCIMA DEL RIO (IRE)** 10-1 B King *Swtng; in tch til 17l 4th aft 7; clsd 13; chsd ldr 15 til dem aft nxt; rallied 2 out; ld sn aft last; just hld on; rdr's 1st wnr*
[1142ᵁ]	2	hd	**Derryair** 5-4F J Owen *7/4-5/4; ld; 15l clr 2; stdd & hdd 6; ld agn 10; mist nxt; prsd frm 14; hrd rdn 2 out; hdd sn aft last; kpt on unr str press; just hld*
[1142²]	3	4	**Bally Clover** 2-1 Mrs T Hill *3s-2s; chsd ldr to 5; 10l 3rd 7; clsd 13; 3l 4th nxt; sn outpcd & btn; kpt on agn flat*
[1142³]	4	250y	**Toytown King (IRE)** 33-1 R Betts *Sn bhnd; t.o ½way*
[1267³]	U		**Dark Rhythm** 4-1 S Atkins *(xnb) Ss; sn rec; ld 6-10; prsd ldr til 2l 3rd 15; 2nd agn aft 3 out; w ldr nxt; 3l 3rd & btn when blun & ur last*
[1393ᵁ]	P		**Take The Brush (IRE)** (5a) 8-1 R Lawther *Hld up; mist 3; 20l 5th when mist 11 & rmdrs; clsd 13; wknd nxt; t.o & pu last*

OFFICIAL DISTANCES: hd, 10l **TIME:** 6min 27.0s

Berkeley

Woodford (LH 10F,19J)   Sun, 14 May (FIRM)

1488 Restricted, 12st   5 ran

[1088ᴾ]	1		**THE CROPPY BOY** 10-1 A Wintle *2 handlers; swtng; jmpd lft; ld; hdd brief 16; drvn out*
[896ᶠ]	2	2	**More People (IRE)** 5-4JF Julian Pritchard *7/4-5/4; 2nd to 6; went 2l 2nd ½way; hit 14; ld 16; hdd nxt; hrd rdn & ev ch last; nt qckn*
[734⁹]	3	10	**Fasgo (IRE)** (7a) 5-4JF Miss P Gundry *Swtng; hld up; releg last 6; 7l 5th ½way; mists 12 & 13; went 5l 3rd & hit 15; hrd rdn 3 out; btn when mist nxt*
[1061²]	4	15	**Ashmead Rambler (IRE)** 7-1 Miss A Bush *(xnb) Swtng; hld up; went 5l 2nd 6 til 2½l 3rd ½way; 6l 4th 15; wknd nxt*
[1355⁵]	P		**Poet's Song (IRE)** 25-1 T Stephenson *Hld up; mist 8; 5l 4th ½way; wknd qckly aft 14; t.o & pu 16*

OFFICIAL DISTANCES: 2l, 12l **TIME:** 6min 26.0s

1489 Hunt   7 ran

	1		**SALMON POUTCHER** (5a) 9-4 Miss A Dare *3s-9/4; swtng; made all; hit 8; lft 7l clr 16; easy*
[1311³]	2	15	**Don Du Cadran (FR)** 8-1 C Gundry *Chsd wnr to 5; 6l 3rd ½way; lft 7l 2nd & rdn 16; no imp*
	3	1½fs	**Marquis (U)** 33-1 H Wallace *1st ride; lost tch 6; 23l 6th ½way; t.o 14; went rem 3rd flat*
[892ᵁ]	4	12	**Royal Sweep** 33-1 J Martin *A bhnd; 17l 5th ½way; t.o 15; lft rem 3rd at last; dem flat*
	5	25	**Master Joey** 25-1 R Shute *A wl bhnd; 24l 7th ½way; t.o when fell 15; rmtd*
[1280¹]	P		**Carbonado** 4-7F P Pritchard *A.p; went 2nd 5; mist 13; jnd wnr nxt; ev ch til pu 16; lame*
[1096ᴾ]	P		**Lauren's Lad** (7a) 33-1 G Barfoot-Saunt *Chsd ldng trio; lost tch 6; mist 10; 15l 4th ½way; wl bhnd 13; t.o 15; lft 3rd nxt; pu last*

OFFICIAL DISTANCES: 15l, dist **TIME:** 6min 28.0s

1490 Intermediate, 12st   3 ran

[1334³]	1		**ROYAL ESTATE** (5x) 2-1 A Evans *Swtng; hld up; 4l 3rd ½way; went 2nd aft 14-16; ld app 2 out; rdn 3l clr app last; all out*
[1064ᴾ]	2	½	**Hatterill Ridge** 10-1 A Wintle *Chsd ldr; mists 11 & 12; dem aft 14; hit 15; went 2nd nxt; ld & mist 3 out; hdd app nxt; rallied u.p flat; r.o*

[1283²] P   **Jilly Wig (IRE)** (5a) 4-7F **Julian Pritchard** *Ld til hdd app 3 out; sn btn & eased; pu 2 out*

    OFFICIAL DISTANCE: 1½l **TIME:** 6min 21.0s

> *The stewards enquired into the running and riding of the favourite Jilly Wig;*
> *they accepted the rider's explanation that the horse was changing its legs*
> *from three out and he had pulled up to avoid possible injury*

1491 Greig Middleton Ladies Open   3 ran

[1191¹] 1   **SPLIT SECOND** 1-3F **Miss A Dare** (bf) *2nd til ld 16; 7l clr 2 out; easy*

[1191⁴] 2   8   **Stretchit** 12-1 **Miss I Rabone** (xnb) *Ld; 5l clr when mist 7; hdd 16; no ch w wnr*

[969¹]   3   ½   **Boarding School** (tt) 11-4 **Miss A De Lisle Wells** *Hld up; mist 8; 7l 3rd ½way; outpcd 15; sn rdn & no imp*

    OFFICIAL DISTANCES: 6l, ½l **TIME:** 6min 43.0s

1492 Mens Open, 12st   8 ran

[1319¹] 1   **SMILE PLEEZE (IRE)** 7-2 **T Stephenson** *Hld up; rmdr 7; pushed along 9; hdwy to 2½l 4th ½way; 2½l 3rd 13; rdn 16; still cl 3rd last; str rn to ld nr fin*

[1337²] 2   hd   **Skip'n'time** (7x) 4-5F **M Miller** *Sn prom; went 2nd 8; rdn to ld aft 2 out; hdd nr fin*

[1311¹] 3   1   **Henry Bruce** (7x) 3-1 **Julian Pritchard** *Ld til hdd aft 2 out; rdn & nt qckn flat*

[895⁶]   4   15   **Barton Black (NZ)** (7x) 8-1 **M Keel** *20s-8s; hld up; hdwy 8; 3l 5th ½way; 4½l 4th 13; rdn 3 out; sn wknd*

[1273²] 5   10   **Furry Fox (IRE)** 50-1 **G Barfoot-Saunt** *Prom to 7; 5l 7th ½way; 8l 7th 13; rdn & wknd 16*

[895ᶠ]   6   2   **Princess Lu (IRE)** 50-1 **G Marsh** *Chsd ldrs; blun 5; 4l 6th ½way; 6l 6th 13; mist 14; rdn & wknd app 3 out*

[1016ᴾ] P   **Robsand (IRE)** 25-1 **M Wilesmith** *Hld up & bhnd; 8l last ½way; lost tch 14; pu 15*

[1402³] P   **The Last Mistress** (5a) 33-1 **J Price** *2nd to 8; 2l 3rd ½way; lost plce & 5l 5th 13; mist 15; sn wknd; wl bhnd when pu 3 out*

    OFFICIAL DISTANCES: hd, 1½l **TIME:** 6min 22.0s

PLATE 17   1492 Berkeley Mens Open: L to R Smile Pleeze, Furry Fox, Henry Bruce, Skip'n'time, mostly obscured The Last Mistress, Barton Black and Princess Lu race towards the castle with Robsand bringing up the rear   PHOTO: John Mullen

1493 Open Maiden 8yo&up, 12st 6 ran

[1315²]	1		**AUTUMN BLUNDER** 5-4F T Stephenson *2 handlers; swtng; pulled hrd; ld 1 til rn wide bend bef 11; ld 13; mist 14; hdd app 16; btn when lft clr 2 out*
[451²]	2	12	**Executive Blue (IRE)** (5a) 5-1 G Barfoot-Saunt *Hld up; 8l 5th ½way; eff & 4l 3rd 15; rdn 3 out; sn wknd; lft 10l 2nd nxt*
[1284³]	3	30	**Ask In Time (IRE)** 12-1 P Young *Ld to 1; mist 4; 2nd til lft in ld bend bef 11; hdd & mist 13; 5l 4th 15; wknd qckly; lft rem 3rd 2 out; t.o*
[1464ᵁ]	P		**Champagne Thunder** (tt) 3-1 M Keel *Chsd ldrs; mists 5 & 9; 5l 3rd ½way; 7l 4th 13; 5th & btn whn pu 15; lame*
[1284⁵]U			**Country Lord** 33-1 Mrs S Walwin *Spurs; nt jw; sn wl bhnd; t.o 6; mist & rmdrs 8; cont v reluct; ¼mile bhnd when tried to ref & ur 15*
[1336ᴾ]	P		**Mister River (IRE)** (bl) 5-1 Miss P Gundry *Hld up; mist 3; 6l 4th ½way; went 6l 3rd 12 & lng aft 14; ld app 16; 8l clr nxt; pu 2 out; lame*

OFFICIAL DISTANCES: 10l, 30l **TIME:** 6min 39.0s

1494 Confined Maiden 56&7yo, 12st 3 ran

	1		**LIBIDO** (7a) 6-4JF Miss P Gundry *Jmpd delib; 2nd til disp ld 7-10; mist 11; ld 15; 4l clr 3 out; r.o str*
[1068⁶]	2	6	**Arctium** (5a) 6-4JF G Barfoot-Saunt *Rdn frm boxes; hld up; blun 5; 2½l 3rd ½way; eff & 2nd 16; blun 3 out; drvn to cl aft nxt; no ex flat*
[1361⁴]	3	15	**Miss Pilkington** (5a) 2-1 T Stephenson *Swtng; ld; qcknd 5l clr 13; hdd 15; rdn 3 out; sn btn*

OFFICIAL DISTANCES: 7l, 20l **TIME:** 6min 46.0s

Border

Corbridge (RH 9F,18J) Sun, 14 May (FIRM)

1495 Intermediate, 12st 4 ran

[504ᴾ]	1		**SUPERCHARMER** 2-1 G Markham *Hld up in last; prog to 3l 3rd 7; went 2l 2nd 3 out; ld aft nxt; ½l up last; r.o wl; comf*
[1429²]	2	1½	**Little Santa (IRE)** (5a) 5-1 Mrs K Hargreave *Swtng; ld; jmpd lft 2; jnd 7; mist & hdd brief 8; drew clr frm 14; hdd aft 2 out; eff & ev ch last; nt qckn*
[1121ᶠ]	3	15	**Queen Biddy (IRE)** (5a) 4-6F C Storey *Evens-4/6; prom; 1½l 3rd 4; ld brief 8; cl 2nd to 3 out; wknd*
[1366ᴾ]	4	4	**Fragrant Lord** 10-1 Mrs V Jackson *Swtng; prom til hit 5; 6l last nxt; rdn 10; lost tch 13; 20l last app 2 out*

OFFICIAL DISTANCES: 2l, dist, 6l **TIME:** 6min 12.0s

1496 Restricted 3 ran

[1424¹]	1		**MINI CRUISE** 6-4 L Morgan *Made all; 2-3l up til rmdr & drew clr app last; rdn out*
[1326²]	2	10	**Happy Blake** 4-7F C Storey *Mists; trckd ldr; bad mist 9; 1½l 2nd & hit nxt; ev ch til hrd rdn aft 2 out; sn btn & eased*
[1162ᴾ]	U		**Madame Defarge** (5a) (tt) 8-1 Mrs K Hargreave *A last; rdn along 11; strugg when blun & ur 13*

OFFICIAL DISTANCE: 12l **TIME:** 6min 16.0s

1497 Ladies Open 3 ran

[1426²]	1		**PHARMISTICE (IRE)** 4-9F Miss N Stirling *(xnb) 2 handlers; oht; made all; qcknd 4l clr & when hit 2 out; r.o wl; easy*
[1427ᴾ]	2	20	**Tropnevad** (bl) 20-1 Miss J Hollands *Oht; a chsng wnr; cl 2nd & hit 14; wknd aft 2 out; nt prsd*
[1426⁴]	3	20	**Sharp Thyne (IRE)** (bl) 6-4 Mrs K Hargreave *Last; jmpd slow 4; 10l down nxt; hit 10; lost tch aft 12; 25l adrift 14; t.o*

OFFICIAL DISTANCES: 20l, dist **TIME:** 5min 57.0s

1498 Mens Open 6 ran

[1365ᵁ]	1		**DEAN DEIFIR (IRE)** 10-11F C Storey *(xnb) Oht; hdstrng; trckd ldrs til disp ld aft 10; ld aft 12; slpd on bend bef nxt; prsd aft 3 out; 2l clr last; r.o wl; easy*
[1349⁴]	2	1¼	**Toarlite (IRE)** (vis) 40-1 R Trotter *(bf) Prom; ld/disp frm 7-12; cl 2nd & ev ch 2 out; r.o; a hld*
[1342⁷]	3	1½	**Fiscal Policy** 3-1 H Trotter *(bf) Ld; 2l up 3 & 4; jmpd 7; hdd aft 12; 5l 4th & outpcd nxt; kpt on frm 3 out; went 3rd app 2 out; nt rch ldrs*

[1030⁵]	4	4	**Mullingar (IRE)** 11-1 L Morgan *Oht; mostly 3rd/4th; rmdrs 10; rdn & outpcd 13; 8l 3rd 3 out; dem 4th app last*
	R		**Chan The Man** 25-1 S Huggan *Swtng; a rr; last 5; in tch when ducked thro rt wing 7*
[1159¹]	F		**Keep A Secret** 7-2 S Charlton *(xnb) 5s-7/2; sis; jmpd sideways & fell 1*

OFFICIAL DISTANCES: 2l, 2½l, 5l TIME: 6min 08.0s

1499 Open Maiden (Div 1)   4 ran

[1352ᶠ]	1		**IM STRUGGLING** (7a) 6-1 G Markham *Swtng; last; 15l down & hit 7; jmpd rt 11; went 5l 2nd 14; lft in ld aft 3 out; sn clr; jb lft last*
[1368²]	2	12	**Mesling** 4-6F J Walton *Oht; nt fluent; chsd ldr; 12l 2nd & jmpd slow 5; dem 6l 3rd 14; lft disp ld aft 3 out; sn hdd & wknd; fin tired*
[1154ᵖ]	r		**Greenfinch (CAN)** 2-1 Miss R Barrow *Sis; ref 1*
[1430²]	U		**Test Of Loyalty** evens A Robson *Oht; tried to make all; 15l up & hit 7; jmpd slow 9; 3l clr 13; 1l up when blun & ur 3 out*

OFFICIAL DISTANCE: 12l TIME: 6min 17.0s

1500 Open Maiden (Div 2)   8 ran

[1431²]	1		**BLACKCHESTERS** 4-1 J Walton *W ldr; bumped 10; ld 3 out; r.o wl*
[1429⁴]	2	1	**Paperback Writer** (5a) 12-1 L Morgan *Ld; mist 1; jmpd rt & bumped rival 10; hdd 3 out; ev ch til nt qckn flat*
	3	10	**Rysanshyn** (5a) 12-1 P Johnson *Mid-div; prog 8; 4l 3rd 13; ev ch 15; sn outpcd; one pce*
[1331²]	4	2½	**Lardante (IRE)** 7-2 J Ewart *Rr til hdwy 5; 5l 4th 13; ev ch til 10l 4th & outpcd 3 out*
[1431ᵖ]	U		**Harleyburn** (bl) 2-1F Mrs A Hamilton *(bf) Pulled hrd; 5l 3rd 4; 1l up when blun & ur 6*
[1445²]	P		**Meadowleck** (5a) (tt) 20-1 T Scott *(bf)Prom early; 5l 5th 10; wknd qckly aft 14; pu 2 out*
[1330ᵖ]	P		**Play An Ace** 20-1 Miss M Blakey *Sn last; mist & rdr called cab 3; in tch to 11; t.o 14; pu nxt*
[1083ʳ]	U		**The Dust Buster** 20-1 R Trotter *(bf) Trckd ldrs; 4l 3rd 7; 12l 5th 15; sn rdn & wknd; btn 4th when blun bad & ur 2 out*

OFFICIAL DISTANCES: 1l, 10l, 2l TIME: 6min 16.0s

1501 Hunt, 12st   7 ran

[1427⁸]	1		**BUCKAROO** (5a) evensF Mrs A Tweedie *6/4-evens; swtng; made all; 10l up 4; sn wl clr; 20l ahd 13; unchall*
[1431ᵖ]	2	runin	**Sledmere (IRE)** (7a) 2-1 T Scott *5s-2s; chsd ldrs in mostly 3rd; 15l 3rd 4; lft 25l 2nd 13; to 3 out*
[1363ᵖ]	3	runin	**Noneofyourbusiness (IRE)** (5a) (bl,tt) 14-1 Miss C Metcalfe *Sn bhnd; jmpd lft 11; 50l 3rd 14; t.o*
[1160⁴]	4	3fncs	**Heavenly Citizen (IRE)** 5-1 Miss E Edminson *Chsd ldr; 10l 2nd 4; wknd 7; 25l 6th nxt; t.o 11; 2 fncs bhnd 3 out*
	5	5fncs	**Trudys Birthday (U)** (5a,18ow) 33-1 M MacGregor *1st ride for veteran; sn t.o last; fnce behind 8; ref 10; cont; 3 fncs bhnd when pu for breather aft 3 out; event cont*
[1427⁹]	U		**Kings Token** 5-1 J Scratcherd *Rr; prog to 15l 2nd 7; 20l 2nd when mist & ur 13*
	F		**Price Of Gold** (5a) 8-1 J Walton *Rr; jmpd big 1; 15l 5th when fell 10*

OFFICIAL DISTANCES: dist, dist TIME: 6min 10.0s

Fernie
Dingley (RH 8F,18J) Sun, 14 May (FIRM)

1502 Hunt   7 ran

[1417¹]	1		**DONT TELL THE WIFE** 2-11F Miss G Hutchinson *Confid rdn at rr of bunch; went 4th 9; ld 3 out & imm qcknd 15l clr; v easy*
[790ᵖ]	2	15	**The Last Shout (IRE)** (bl) 33-1 Miss A Burton *Hld up in tch; eff & jmpd slow 10; rdn & outpcd 14; mod 3rd 3 out; kpt on to chse wnr vain frm nxt*
[1268⁵]	3	8	**Colonel Wilkie** 16-1 J Dillon *Cl up; 5th 11; outpcd 13; poor 4th 3 out*
[1417ᵖ]	4	10	**Far Senior** 5-1 C Millington *Prom til drpd to rr & rmdrs 6 & 7; drvn to ld app 9-11; outpcd 14; poor 5th 3 out*
[1417ᵖ]	5	2	**Up The Road (IRE)** 33-1 Miss S Stacy *Lost tch 3 & plodded rnd in last*
[1419ᵖ]	P		**Court Thyne (IRE)** 20-1 P Millington *Lkd awful; prom; ld 11 til hdd & blun 3 out; drvn aft; dem nxt & wknd; pu last*
[1270ᵖ]	P		**Mr Tucker** 33-1 Mrs E Staines *2 handlers; jw; ld til app 9; 3rd 11; drvn & wknd 13; t.o & pu 2 out*

OFFICIAL DISTANCES: 20l, 10l TIME: 6min 28.0s TOTE: £1.30 DF: £28.50

1503 Confined, 12st
6 ran

[1266⁵]	1		**HOSTETLER** 16-1 **Miss K Norris** *Made most to 6; drpd back 5th 9; outpcd 13; 5l 3rd 15; rallied to 2nd 2 out; ld app last; kpt on wl*
[1434⁴]	2	3	**Ebullient Equiname (IRE)** evensF **S Morris** *Lw; rdn 2; cl up; rmdr 7; went 2nd 12 & ld 14; gng v easy aft tk shkn up & hdd app last; imm jacked it in*
[1414³]	3	20	**Catchphrase** (vis) 9-2 **R Armson** (xnb) *Pushed along 2; cl up; lft 2nd 10; ld 11-14; ev ch nxt; drvn & fnd nil aft 3 out; lost 2nd nxt*
[1414¹]	4	5	**Bare Fisted** (5x) 2-1 **Miss H Phizacklea** *Imm lost tch; clsd v brief to be 10l down 10; nt r.o & wl bhnd aft; fin lame*
	P		**Nuns Cone** 33-1 **T Lane** *Hit 1; ld 3-4, 6-9 & 10-11; lost plce & blun 12; sn t.o; pu 2 out*
[1350⁶]	U		**Tiderunner (IRE)** (bl) 14-1 **S Walker** *Trckd ldrs; ld 9; just hdd when blun & ur 10*

OFFICIAL DISTANCES: 3l, 12l **TIME:** 6min 26.0s **TOTE:** £7.80 **DF:** £5.00

1504 Confined Maiden 56&7yo
6 ran

[1420³]	1		**FORTUNE HUNTER (IRE)** 7-2 **P Millington** *Pulled hrd; hld up in tch; 3l 4th 15; still pulling hrd 15; dashed to ld app 2 out; sn 7l clr aft; urged wildly flat & just hld on*
[1270²]	2	1	**Balmoral Spring (IRE)** 4-5F **T Lane** *Made most frm 7 til hdd aft 3 out; mist & lost momentum nxt; nursed along til rallied app last; stayed on flat & clsng qckly nr fin*
[1422ᴾ]	3	¾	**Craftbook Marchesa (IRE)** (5a) 20-1 **Miss A Burton** (citation) *Settled last; 8l down 12; kpt on frm 2 out; clsng w rnr-up flat*
[1069ᴾ]	4	6	**Harps Hall (IRE)** 6-1 **M Chatterton** *Swtng profuse; jmpd delib at times; cl up; 4l 5th 12; outpcd 14*
[1423⁷]	5	10	**Mandalay Man (IRE)** 5-1 **R Armson** (citation) *Ld at crawl to 7; cl 2nd 12; wknd & mist 14; wl bhnd 3 out*
[1422⁵]	P		**More Mettle** 10-1 **J Diment** *Hld up & cl up; ld app 11-12; disp ld 15-16; 3rd & rdn app 2 out; 4l 2nd & u.p when broke leg app last; dead*

OFFICIAL DISTANCES: ½l, ½l **TIME:** 6min 57.0s **TOTE:** £3.50 **DF:** £1.90

1505 Mixed Open, 4m, 12st - 24J
3 ran

[1421²]	1		**POLLY LIVE WIRE** (5a) 7-2 **P Millington** (citation) *Settled last; mist 17; qcknd to ld app 3 out; sn clr; jnd last; lft clr; drvn & all out*
[1268¹]	2	¾	**Fair Farm Boy** 4-7F **M Mackley** *Trckd ldr; hit 6; ld brief 13; hit 14; ld agn 20-21; flat-footed when wnr qcknd app 2 out; rallied & w wnr outj last; nt rec in time; rapped knee*
[1286³]	3	25	**Mr Five Wood (IRE)** 3-1 **J Purllant** *Set slow pce & jmpd slow at times; blun 5; hdd brief 13 & agn 20; rdn & lost tch rap app 2 out*

OFFICIAL DISTANCES: 1l, 20l **TIME:** 8min 47.0s **TOTE:** £3.20 **DF:** £2.20

1506 Restricted
4 ran

[1418ᴾ]	1		**PLEASE CALL (IRE)** 7-4JF **T Illsley** *Ld to 2; last & nt fluent 6; outpcd 13; 8l last 14; no prog til kpt on app last; sust rn flat; just fail; fin lame*
[1418⁵]	2	hd	**Black Book (IRE)** (5a) 2-1 **P Millington** *Swtng; hld up & cl up; blun 10; went 2nd 11; drvn along 3 out & nt much room twice when trying for rn on inner; wildly rdn to ld flat w rein flapping; lkd to just hld on*
[1012⁵]	3	½	**Stonebroke (IRE)** 10-1 **J Diment** *Ld & hit 2; made nrly all; drvn app last; hdd flat; nt qckn*
[1287ᴾ]	P		**Sweet Talker (IRE)** N Bloom *Ld 8-9; drpd back last 11; pu & dism 12; lame*

OFFICIAL DISTANCES: s hd, ½l **TIME:** 6min 35.0s **TOTE:** £3.00 **DF:** £3.80

Be Upstanding was withdrawn by permission of the Stewards after declarations had closed because the course had dried out rapidly; no fine was imposed

1507 Open Maiden
11 ran

[1287ᴾ]	1		**ZAFAN (IRE)** (7a) 10-11F **R Fowler** *Jmpd delib 1 & 2; settled 2nd/3rd; ld gng wl 15 til hdd brief & 2l down aft 2 out; rallied & sn ld agn; nursed along & kpt on wl*
[1269²]	2	1	**Nasayer (IRE)** 5-2 **A Pickering** *Hld up in tch; 4l 4th & rdn when mist 12; eff 2 out & sn 2l clr; hdd app last; rdn in characteristic fashion & became v unbalanced; r.o flat; a hld*
[1420³]	3	30	**Royal Charger (IRE)** (bl) 16-1 **R Armson** *Swtng; hld up; impd to 3rd 11; ld aft 12; hdd & mist 3 out; fdd rap app nxt*
[942⁴]	4	½	**Secret Music** 10-1 **D Parravani** *Ld 5; mist 11; hdd aft 12; wknd qckly 3 out*
[412⁵]	5	½	**Mighty Monarch (IRE)** 20-1 **Miss A Burton** (citation) *Bhnd; hit 10; some prog in 12l 5th 13; sn strugg*
[1383³]	6	8	**Timothy George (IRE)** (tt) 9-1 **P Millington** *Impd to jn ldrs 9; 4th nxt; sn rdn; drpd back 5th 12 & drvn; nvr gng wl aft*

[1292⁴]	7	10	**City Run (USA)** 14-1 **Mrs T Holditch** Chsd ldrs to 10; sn wl outpcd; no ch 12; t.o 15
[1414ᴾ]	U		**Crested Lass** (5a) 33-1 **Mrs C Boyes** Pulled hrd & rdr barely in control; nvr btr than midfield; 15l 6th when blun bad & ur 15
[1116ᴾ]	P		**Full Bore (IRE)** 16-1 **D Cook** Ld 1; 2nd 8; lost plce rap nxt; mist 10; nt r.o & no ch frm 13; t.o pu last
[1420ᴾ]	P		**Moon Island** (5a) 20-1 **J Diment** Sn ld; hdd 5; last by 9; t.o 15; pu last
	R		**Zam Bam** (12a) 12-1 **M Lurcock** Bckwd; v dozy padd; lost tch 2; rn out 3

OFFICIAL DISTANCES: 4l, 20l **TIME:** 6min 30.0s **TOTE:** £2.30 **DF:** £5.20

Old Surrey, Burstow & West Kent
Penshurst (LH 7F,18J) Sun, 14 May (GOOD)

1508 Hunt 5 ran

[1398⁵]	1	**BROGUESTOWN PRIDE (IRE)** 2-1F **P Blagg** Prsd ldr/disp to 11; rdn along frm 12; 3l down 14; rmdrs 3 out; stayed on; narrow ld when lft solo 2 out
[1209⁴]	U	**Daddy Long Leggs** 11-4 **R Hubbard** Ld/disp til ld 12; lkd gng btr til hdd, mist & ur 2 out
[60⁴]	P	**Offshore (IRE)** 3-1 **P Cowley** Cl up in last pr til 8l 3rd 11; lsng tch when pu & dism bef nxt
[1210ᴿ]	r	**Paddy Casey (IRE)** 5-1 **Mrs E Coveney** A last pr; 9l 4th 11; 15l 3rd when jmpd slow 13; ref nxt
[1393ᴾ]	R	**Perripage** (bl) 12-1 **Miss A Sansom** Ld & jmpd slow 1; prsd ldng pr to 4; last & lsng tch when rn out 7

OFFICIAL DISTANCE: Finished alone **TIME:** 6min 54.0s **TOTE:** £2.00; places £2.90 **DF:** £1.10 (1+any)

1509 Confined, 12st 9 ran

[1398ᶠ]	1		**PEAFIELD (IRE)** 5-2JF **P York** Hld up in midfield; cl 6th 11; impd to press ldr 3 out; ld bef nxt; sn drew clr; easy
[1394ᴾ]	2	8	**Rose King** 12-1 **T Hills** Made most til hdd aft 3 out; 4l down 2 out; kpt on one pce
[1282⁴]	3	2	**Garrison Friendly (IRE)** (7x) 12-1 **N Wilson (Hants)** A cl up; ld brief aft 11; prsd ldng pr 13 til wknd app 2 out
[1181¹]	4	5	**Ballad (IRE)** 5-2JF **A Harvey** Cl up in midfield; 5th 11; prsd ldr 13-4 out; fdd frm nxt
[1108ᴾ]	5	5	**Sovereign Spray (IRE)** (3x) 7-2 **C Gordon** Rn in snatches; prsd ldr til jmpd slow & lost plce 4; rdn & hdwy 8; prsd ldr 10 til stumbled app 13; 6l 5th & hrd rdn 15; wknd aft nxt
[1398⁸]	6	25	**White Smoke (IRE)** 12-1 **R Ross** Towards rr; gd hdwy 9; prsd ldr 11 & 12; rmdrs & wknd aft nxt; wl bhnd frm 3 out
[1109³]	P		**American Eyre** 33-1 **Miss S Gladders** Ld 3 & 4; lost plce qckly 6; 20l 9th 11; t.o & pu 3 out
[1211³]	P		**Pair Of Jacks (IRE)** (bl) 33-1 **Miss J Wickens** A last pr; 12l 8th 11; t.o 13 til pu 3 out
[1344ᴿ]	P		**Sultan Of Swing** (vis) 33-1 **M Gorman** Rr to 3; rap hdwy to press ldr 5-9; 10l 7th & wkng 11; t.o & pu 13

OFFICIAL DISTANCES: 5l, 2l **TIME:** 6min 40.0s **TOTE:** £4.20; places £1.30,£4.70,£1.50 **DF:** £31.00
The rider of Garrison Friendly was cautioned for misuse of the whip and not giving the horse time to respond

1510 Mens Open, 12st 7 ran

[1247¹]	1		**NEWBY END (IRE)** 7-2 **D Dennis** Cl 3rd/4th frm 5 til prsd wnr 3 out; lkd hld when lft in ld nxt; kpt on wl u.p
[1394¹]	2	2	**Equity Player** 4-1 **P York** Cl 2nd/3rd frm 5 til 6l 4th & pushed along 13; rmdrs 3 out; lft 11 2nd 2 out; kpt on one pce
[1393ᵁ]	P		**Bang On Target** (bl) 33-1 **J Stephens** Rr til pu 5
[1392¹]	r		**Bit Of An Idiot** 8-1 **D Slattery** Hld up in last; gd hdwy 10; cl 2nd when hmpd 12; chsd ldr til wknd 15; 10l 4th when blkd & ref 2 out
[1416⁴]	r		**Court Amber (IRE)** 16-1 **A Coe** Cl up til ld 9; jb rt frm 12; 4l up & gng best when ref 2 out; cont; ref agn last desp thrashing w whip
[1398ᴾ]	P		**Jojo (IRE)** (bl) 7-2 **B Hitchcott** Ld 3 til jmpd slow & hdd 8; cl up til lost plce aft 10; t.o 12 til pu 14
[1394²]	P		**Prime Course (IRE)** (4x) 2-1F **C Gordon** Ld to 2; prsd ldr til pu & dism app 5

OFFICIAL DISTANCE: 2l **TIME:** 6min 43.0s **TOTE:** £3.00; places £1.60,£2.40 **DF:** £10.70
The rider of Court Amber was fined £75 for improper riding - repeated severe use of the whip when the horse had refused at the penultimate and last fences

1511 Ladies Open - 17J   9 ran

[1107²] 1 **MY WEE MAN (IRE)** 3-1F Miss J Wickens *Towards rr; gd hdwy 8 to 4l 2nd aft 11; lost plce 13; 12l 5th 3 out; rap hdwy app nxt; str rn flat; ld cl home*

[1398²] 2 nk **Exemplar (IRE)** 14-1 Mrs D Rowell *In tch; 9l 6th aft 11; hdwy 13; chsd ldr aft 3 out; ld & went clr app nxt; 6l up last; hdd cl home*

[799²] 3 10 **Caddy Man** 6-1 Mrs E Coveney *Ld 4; 3-6l up frm 11 til wknd & hdd app 2 out*

[1288³] 4 1 **Prince Of Saints (IRE)** (bl) 6-1 Miss Z Turner *Midfield most of way; 10l 7th aft 11; hdwy to 9l 4th 3 out; kpt on one pce frm nxt*

[1395ᴿ] 5 ½ **Silk Vestments** (5a) 7-1 Mrs S Hickman *Ld to 3; 7l 5th aft 11; impd to chse ldr 14; 3l down when hit 3 out hrd; wknd app nxt*

[1107ᶠ] 6 10 **Cadbury Castle** (5a) 9-2 Miss J Grant *Midfield when jmpd v slow 1 & 2; rap hdwy to press ldr 5-10; 6l 4th aft 11; lost plce 13; no ch frm 15*

[1170³] 7 12 **Polar Ana (IRE)** (5a) 20-1 Miss S Gladders *A detach; 20l 8th aft 11; nvr nrr*

[1395ᴾ] P **Andrelot** (bl) 20-1 Miss H Grissell *Detach last frm 4; 35l 9th aft 11; t.o & pu 13*

[1395ˢ] P **Danger Flynn (IRE)** 6-1 Miss C Holliday *Cl up in midfield; hdwy to 5l 3rd aft 11; chsd ldr 13 til wknd qckly 15; wl bhnd when pu last*

OFFICIAL DISTANCES: ½l, 5l **TIME:** 6min 36.0s **TOTE:** £3.50; places £1.60,£1.30,£4.30 **DF:** £10.20
Fence 17 omitted - damaged

1512 Restricted, 12st   4 ran

[1398³] 1 **JAMIES FIRST (IRE)** 7-4F D Dunsdon *A gng wl; disp ld 1 & 2; cl 2nd/3rd til jnd ldr 14; qcknd clr aft 2 out; easy*

[1284¹] 2 4 **Ashburton Lord** 3-1 M Legge *Stdd start; hdwy to ld 3; made rest til hdd 2 out; sn outpcd*

[1396¹] 3 6 **Graphic Designer (IRE)** 2-1 C Gordon *Disp ld 1 & 2; cl 3rd/4th til prsd wnr 11-14; hrd rdn 3 out; ch app nxt; sn btn*

[1379ᴾ] P **Monere** (bl) 7-1 G Cooper *Cl up til lost plce aft 10; jmpd slow 11; pu sn aft*

OFFICIAL DISTANCES: 5l, 6l **TIME:** 6min 45.0s **TOTE:** £2.50 **DF:** £6.50

1513 Open Maiden, 12st   13 ran

[1105ᵁ] 1 **MAXIMUS (IRE)** (7a) 2-1F B Hitchcott *Hld up last to 9; smooth hdwy to settle in cl 5th 11; same plce til gd rn to ld 2 out; 3l up last; eshl rn flat*

[1397ᴺ] 2 4 **Moon Rising** 6-1 P Bull *Cl up in midfield til gd hdwy 9; w ldr 11 til ld 3 out; hdd nxt; no ex app last*

[1290²] 3 8 **Cardinal Bud (IRE)** 12-1 P Taiano *Midfield til hdwy 9; cl 4th 11; prsd ldng pr 13 til wknd app 2 out*

[1397²] 4 12 **Ell Gee** (5a) 20-1 P Townsley *A wl in tch; 3rd 11; disp ld frm nxt til hdd & wknd aft 15*

[1396³] 5 6 **Strawberry Blossom** (5a) 6-1 P York *Hld up in rr; 10th 11; nvr nr ldrs*

[1105ᴸ] 6 8 **Schisandra** (5a) 33-1 P Blagg *A rr; 11th 11; t.o frm 14*

[1172ᴷ] P **Granite's Surprise** 33-1 C O'Brien *In tch til drpd to rr 10; last frm nxt; t.o 14 til pu 3 out*

[1397ˢ] P **Native Dawn (IRE)** 20-1 D Dunsdon *Tubed; ld 2 til lost plce qckly app 10; last when pu aft nxt*

[1396ᴾ] P **Not Yet Decent** 33-1 Miss J Grant *Cl up; prsd ldr 6; ld 10-12; wknd 14; rr when pu 2 out*

[1284ᴾ] P **Polly Gunner** (5a) 33-1 M Gorman *A towards rr; 9th 11; wl bhnd when pu 2 out*

[1105³] P **Relocate (IRE)** 14-1 D Dennis *Towards rr; 8th 11; hdwy frm nxt to cl 4th aft 14; wknd app 3 out; pu 2 out*

[1422ᴾ] P **Southern Target** 33-1 A Coe *Midfield; 7th 11; lost tch 14; no ch when pu 2 out*

[1397ᴿ] P **Sunley Spring** 6-1 A Hickman *Prsd ldr 2-5; cl 6th 11; lost tch 14; no ch when pu 2 out*

OFFICIAL DISTANCES: 4l, 5l **TIME:** 6min 37.0s **TOTE:** £2.50; places £3.30,£2.30,£2.50 **DF:** £10.20

Tetcott

Lifton (RH 7F,19J) Sun, 14 May (GOOD to FIRM)

1514 Confined, 12st   11 ran

[1388ᵁ] 1 **SWIFT VENTURE (IRE)** 5-1 Richard Darke *8s-5s; sn handy; cl 3rd frm 7; 1l 3rd 12; ld 16; qcknd rdly aft 3 out; clr nxt; kpt on u.p*

[1188⁴] 2 5 **Brown Robber** (3x) 7-1 T Dennis *(xnb) Lw; prom; hit 5; disp ld 6-16; outpcd & 3rd nxt; kpt on cl home*

[1259²] 3 2 **Rasta Man** (5x) (tt) 9-4F R Woollacott *Hld up; hdwy 9; 4th 15; chall & ev ch nxt; wkng & hld in 2nd when mist 2 out*

[1370³]	4	1½	**Western Fort (IRE)** (3x) 3-1 *Miss J Cumings 9/2-3s; lw; midfield; slt prog 13; 5th & rdn 3 out; nrst fin*
[1385³]	5	6	**Night Time** 25-1 *G Shenkin (xnb) Lw; towards rr; 8th 12; nd*
[1275ᴾ]	6	10	**Dunlir** 50-1 *Miss S Young Ld/disp to 14; wknd stdly*
[1261⁶]	7	3	**Good King Henry** 20-1 *I Widdicombe Midfield; slt prog to 5th 10; outpcd 14; sn wknd*
[1256⁶]	8	runin	**Moorland Rose** (12a) 100-1 *Miss D Mitchell Sn last; t.o frm 12*
[1385²]	P		**Bendor Mark** (3x) 8-1 *Mrs M Hand Prom; cl 3rd 5; 8th 10; lost tch 15; bhnd & pu 2 out*
[1261ᴾ]	P		**Cornish Ways** (bl) 100-1 *T Greed Prom frm 7; disp 3rd 10; lost plce 12; 6th & rdn 15; bhnd & pu 3 out*
[852⁶]	P		**Some-Toy** 14-1 *C Heard Towards rr; mist 7; 10th 12; blun 14; bhnd when pu 3 out*

OFFICIAL DISTANCES: 5l, 2l **TIME:** 5min 55.0s

1515 Mixed Open, 12st
6 ran

[1188²]	1		**BUTLER JOHN (IRE)** 7-4 *N Harris Made most at str pce; jw; r.o str when prsd frm 15; lft clr aft 16; impressive*
[1387¹]	2	runin	**Baldhu Chance** 33-1 *A Ede (bh) Sn cl up; disp 4-6; 3rd & outpcd 9; 4th & bhnd frm 13; lft 3rd 2 out; drvn out to tk 2nd clsng stages*
[1260¹]	3	3	**Well Armed (IRE)** (bl) 4-1 *Miss J Cumings 13/2-4s; lw; swtng; settled 4th; went 12l 3rd 13; nt rch ldrs; lft 30l 2nd app 2 out; eased & dem clsng stages*
[1261ᵁ]	4	8	**Strong Stuff (IRE)** 66-1 *N Mitchell 5th & sn strugg off pce; no ch frm ½way*
[953¹]	P		**Elliewelliewoo** (5a) 4-5F *L Jefford Lw; settled cl 3rd; went 2nd 7; trckd ldr clr of rest; 2l 2nd 13; 2½l 2nd when pckd bad & lost bridle 16; pu 2 out*
	U		**Rosewood Lady (IRE)** (12a) 150-1 *J Young Last & getting detach when blun & ur 7*

OFFICIAL DISTANCES: 20l, 2l **TIME:** 5min 44.0s

The stewards enquired into the riding of Elliewelliewoo; they accepted the rider's explanation that he had been forced to pull up because the horse had completely lost its bridle and he had no control

1516 Intermediate, 12st
11 ran

[1256³]	1		**NEWMAN'S CONQUEST** (5a) 16-1 *N Mitchell Lw; sn handy; ld 7; clr frm 12; hit 3 out; r.o str frm 2 out*
[559¹]	2	2	**Sea Urchin** 8-1 *D Alers-Hankey (xnb) Rdn to padd; tde; ld in start; tk keen hld; chsd ldr frm 8; eff & cl up aft 3 out; ev ch til no ex frm 2 out*
[1385¹]	3	1½	**Dancing Ranger** (5x) 16-1 *Richard Darke Lw; prom; cl 4th 8; went 9l 3rd 15; kpt on clsng stages*
[1309¹]	4	½	**Fleet Mill** (5a) 3-1 *Miss T Cave (xnb) Lw; ld in start & dwelt; midfield; went 5th 13; 4th but nt rch ldrs 3 out; nrst fin*
[1384¹]	5	7	**Jeepers (IRE)** 25-1 *D McKenna Lw; prom when blun bad 3; 8th ½way; 5th & kpt on same pce frm 3 out*
[1043¹]	6	2	**Brave Noddy (IRE)** (bl) 4-5F *L Jefford Tchd 5/6; lw; nt fluent; 5th 8; hdwy 11; mist 4l 2nd 13; mist nxt; sn rdn & reluct; wknd tame*
	7	25	**Sansnip** 66-1 *B O'Doherty (xnb) Prog to 4th 9; in tch til rdn 16; wknd; dism aft post*
[1371⁵]	P		**A Few Dollars More (IRE)** 33-1 *G Maundrell Lw; ld to 3 & agn aft 4; hit 7 & hdd; lost plce 12; 7th when pu 14*
[1472ᵁ]	P		**Lucky Thursday** 66-1 *Miss J Congdon Sn bhnd; jmpd slow 3; t.o & pu 7*
[1044ᴾ]	P		**Sagaville (IRE)** 33-1 *A Holdsworth Sn towards rr; 9th ½way; sn rdn & outpcd; rr when hit 3 out; pu nxt*
	R		**Soon Come (USA)** 66-1 *S Craddock Pulled hrd; mist 2; ld 3 til crashed thro wing 4*

OFFICIAL DISTANCES: 2l, 1l **TIME:** 5min 57.0s

1517 Restricted (Div 1), 12st
11 ran

[1176³]	1		**BROTHER NERO (NZ)** 5-4F *L Jefford Tchd 7/4; in tch; cl 5th 10; went 3rd 13; slt mist nxt; 4th & rdn 3 out; gd hdwy to slt ld 2 out; hrd rdn last; just hld on*
[1389²]	2	nk	**Silver Man** 9-1 *Mrs M Hand Tchd 10s; lw; sn handy & jw; chsd ldr til lft in ld 12; went 5l clr 15; hdd 2 out; rallied game cl home*
[404ᴾ]	3	½	**Lydford Castle** 3-1 *C Heard Tchd 7/2; lw; midfield & gng wl; prog to 4th 12; went 3rd 15; eff 2 out; r.o wl cl home; dism aft post*
[1391¹]	4	8	**Amazing Hill (IRE)** 16-1 *Mrs R Morris Rr; 9th ½way; poor 7th 16; nrst fin*
[931ᴾ]	5	1½	**Morgan's Rose** (5a) 66-1 *M Sweetland Swtng; last ½way; hdwy to 5th 13; nt rch ldrs*
[1384⁵]	6	2	**Bedtime Pixie** 33-1 *D Stephens (Devon) V agitated padd & declared blinkers removed); swtng; midfield; 6th ½way; no prog*
[933¹]	7	10	**Persian Dawn** (5a) 4-1 *David Dennis 9s-4s; lw; hdwy 9; lft 2nd 12; chsd ldr nxt; 4l 2nd 3 out; wknd rap; dism qckly aft post; lame*

[1187²]	R		**Devonshire Lad** (bl) 20-1 N Harris *Ld 2; cont hmpd by loose horse til rn out 12*
[1258⁸]	P		**Shameless Lady** (5a) 12-1 **Richard Darke** *16s-12s; swtng; 6th ½way; lost tch 14; bhnd & pu 3 out*
[1389⁴]	F		**The Ugly Duckling** 16-1 R Woollacott *Ld til fell 2*
[723ᶠ]	U		**Warning Board** 33-1 J Berwick *Tchd 50s; swtng; prom; cl 4th 10; slt mist 12; lost ground nxt; last when blun bad & ur 14*

OFFICIAL DISTANCES: hd, ½l **TIME:** 6min 04.0s
> The owner of Bedtime Pixie (who became very agitated in the paddock) was given permission by the Stewards to run the horse in this race without blinkers despite having been declared to run in them; the normal fine was waived

1518 Restricted (Div 2), 12st   12 ran

	1		**FOR PAUL (IRE)** 11-8F N Harris *Tchd 2s; lw; rcd keen; sn ld/disp; slt ld 3 out; disp 2 out til ld last; edged lft run-in; drvn out*
[1258²]	2	½	**Damiens Pride (IRE)** 10-1 T Dennis *(xnb) Swtng; lw; sn prom; cl 3rd frm ½way; 3½l 3rd 3 out; eff to disp on outer 2 out; jmpd lft last; no ex cl home; dism aft post*
[1140ᵁ]	3	¾	**I Like The Deal** (5a) 15-2 L Jefford *Tchd 10s; lw; hld up in midfield; jmpd slow 14; 5th 3 out; tk 3rd app last; fin wl*
[1263¹]	4	5	**Woodland King (IRE)** 8-1 **Mrs M Hand** *Ld 1; handy; cl 2nd on inner 12; disp ld 15-17; no ex app 2 out; eased when btn run-in*
[1389³]	5	2	**County Bash** (5a) 16-1 Miss L Gardner *Tchd 20s; lw; midfield; 6th ½way; prog 13; cl 4th 15; one pce frm 3 out*
[1240⁴]	6	25	**For Christie (IRE)** 10-1 B O'Doherty *(xnb) Lw; 6th when slt mist 8; 8th ½way; 6th & just in tch 15; wknd 3 out*
[1256⁴]	7	8	**The Bandon Car (IRE)** 8-1 T Cole *Blun bad 2; jmpd slow nxt; sn bhnd; t.o*
[855¹]	F		**Ashdown Boy** 12-1 R Woollacott *(xnb) Rr til fell 11*
[558¹]	P		**Karlin's Quest** 50-1 Miss A Barnett *Tde; prom; cl 5th 11; 6th & rdn 13; lsng ground in 7th when pu 16*
[1384²]	P		**King Of Cairo** 50-1 I Hambley *Swtng; towards rr til pu 11*
[1390¹]	U		**Pick-N-Cruise** (5a) 16-1 D Stephens (Devon) *(xnb) Lw; oht; pulled hrd; ld/disp til veered lft & ur 11*
[1263ᵁ]	P		**Whinholme Lass (IRE)** (5a) 50-1 G Richards *(xnb) Sn towards rr; bhnd when pu 14*

OFFICIAL DISTANCES: ½l, ½l **TIME:** 5min 54.0s

1519 Confined Maiden 56&7yo (Div 1), 12st   11 ran

[1308²]	1		**DURNFORD BAY (IRE)** (tt) 1-2F L Jefford *Tchd 4/6; lw; hld up in midfield; prog to 3rd 12; mist 14; cruising in 3rd til eff & ld 2 out; sn qcknd clr; easy*
[563⁴]	2	6	**Porters Lodge** 12-1 David Dennis *Lw; hdwy 7; cl up til ld 12; slt ld 16 til hdd 2 out; hrd rdn & no ex app last*
[1260³]	3	4	**Mystic Warrior (USA)** (7a) 5-1 Richard Darke *Midfield; prog to 4th 12; 8l 4th 16; nt trble ldrs; tk 3rd cl home; dism aft post*
[846ᵁ]	4	¾	**Budghill** 25-1 C Heard *Tchd 33s; lw; hdwy 7; 5th ½way; disp cl 2nd when collided w rival 11; ev ch til outpcd aft 3 out; lost 3rd cl home; do btr*
[541ᶠ]	P		**Dark Venetian** (5a) 33-1 M Sweetland *Swtng; ld early; cl 2nd when blun bad 7; lost plce; mist 10; 8th 12; bhnd & pu 15*
[1173ᶠ]	P		**Frankies Flutter** 16-1 D Doyne-Ditmas *Hdwy to 3rd 7; cl 2nd ½way; lost plce 12; bhnd frm 15; poor 5th when jmpd slow 16; pu nxt*
[1390ᴾ]	R		**Golden Jester** (5a) 50-1 Miss J Congdon *(xnb) Pulled hrd & prom; cl 2nd when rn out bend bef 6*
[933ᴾ]	P		**Golden Saddle (USA)** 50-1 B O'Doherty *(bf) Sn rr; 9th 8; 7th when blun 14; bhnd & pu nxt*
[1391ᴿ]	R		**Miltown Castle** 50-1 Miss L Jackson *Midfield til rn out 6; tore thro infield out of control & jnd in agn 12 til threw rdr nxt bend & trotted back to box*
	P		**Son Of Courage** 8-1 N Harris *Tchd 12s; swtng; tde; slt ld when rn wide bend app 6; hmpd 7; cl 4th 10; sn wknd; rr when pu 14*
[857ᴾ]	P		**Walton Street** 25-1 W Smith *Swtng; lft in ld app 6; mists 11 & 12; wknd qckly; bhnd frm 15 til pu 2 out*

OFFICIAL DISTANCES: 4l, 3l **TIME:** 6min 08.0s
> The stewards interviewed the rider of Miltown Castle; her explanation that she had been squeezed up and was unable to control the horse thereafter was accepted; the owner was advised that the horse needed much stronger handling

1520 Confined Maiden 56&7yo (Div 2), 12st   13 ran

| [1372³] | 1 | | **WISE EXAMINER (IRE)** 7-2 Richard Darke *(xnb) Tchd 4s; oht; fractious lvng padd; handy; 7l 3rd ½way; went 2nd 15; ld on inner nxt; jnd 2 out-last; r.o wl u.p* |

[563²]	2	2	**Veiled Dancer (IRE)** (5a) 3-1F A Holdsworth *Tchd 7/2; 5th ½way; prog to 2nd 12; slt ld 14-16; cl up til disp 2 out-last; no ex run-in; dism aft post*
	3	5	**Impetuosity (IRE)** (5a) *Sn handy & gng wl; cl 5th 14; lft 3rd aft 16; nt rch ldrs frm 2 out; dism aft post* David Dennis
[1179ᴾ]	4	runin	**Woodys Widget** (12a) 20-1 Miss K Baily *Lw; ld/disp; tended to j lft 12; jmpd slow & hdd 13; wkng & jmpd slow nxt; sn btn*
[1048ᴾ]	5	8	**Patrio (IRE)** (5a) 33-1 J Cole *Sn last & strugg; a bhnd*
[857ᴿ]	P		**B For Business** (12a) 16-1 Miss L Gardner *(xnb) Tchd 20s; tde; rr; slt mist 6; 11th ½way; bhnd when pu 15; lame; removed by horsebox w off fore in splint*
[1263ᵁ]	B		**Classic Mistress** (5a) 4-1 A Charles-Jones *In tch; cl 5th 12; wl in tch in 4th when bd 16*
	P		**Ever Eddy** 33-1 T Dennis *Swtng; midfield; 7th 13; 6th when bad hmpd 16; pu nxt*
	P		**Ivans Dream** 5-1 L Jefford *Towards rr; 10th ½way; nd; bhnd & pu 2 out*
[857ᴾ]	F		**My Jess** (5a) 33-1 M Woodward *(xnb) Ld/disp; chsd ldr frm 6; lost plce brief 13; cl 3rd when fell 16; horse walked away feelingly 30mins later*
[1389ᴾ]	P		**North Coast Girl** (5a) 33-1 A Ede *Towards rr; 9th ½way; no prog; bhnd when pu 3 out*
[1141²]	P		**North Newcombe** 16-1 N Harris *(xnb) Midfield; 7th 9; bhnd frm 13 til pu 2 out*
	P		**Packitin Parky** 14-1 Miss S Young *Bhnd & school til pu 11*

OFFICIAL DISTANCES: 2l, 4l TIME: 6min 01.0s

1521 Confined Maiden 8yo&up (Div 1), 12st

9 ran

[724ᶠ]	1		**GEORGETOWN** 6-4F L Jefford *Tchd 7/4; ld aft 2; jw; clr frm 10; 5l clr but nt fluent 2 out & last; eased flat*
[1263ᶠ]	2	2	**Country Gem** 12-1 David Dennis *3rd mostly; lft to disp 2nd aft 12; tk def 2nd u.p aft 3 out; r.o; no ch w wnr*
[846²]	3	15	**Sea Jay Son** 14-1 Mrs M Hand *Tchd 20s; tde; sn prom; disp 2nd frm 12; 3rd aft 3 out; fdd frm 2 out*
[1384³]	4	runin	**Horton** 50-1 S Parkin *Sn rr; wl bhnd frm 10; plodded rnd; lft rem 4th 3 out*
[857²]	P		**Cornish Fort** (5a) 5-2 Miss J Cumings *(xnb) Lw; pu & dism app 3*
	P		**Elegant Wolf** 50-1 R Emmett *Sn bhnd; virt ref & banked 7; imm pu*
[1263ᶠ]	P		**Jo's Wedding** 11-4 N Mitchell *(xnb) Tchd 3s; swtng; tde; ld; pckd bad 2; pulled hrd & sev mists; chsd ldr; 10l 2nd when pu 12*
[1370ᴾ]	P		**Masked Martin** 25-1 Miss K Cook *Swtng; rr frm 8; 20l 6th 10; poor 4th 12; rem 4th when pu 3 out*
[1099ᴿ]	P		**Rushaway** 33-1 Miss J Congdon *(xnb) 5th 8; 17l 5th 10; pu 12; lame; removed by horsebox*

OFFICIAL DISTANCES: 1l, 8l TIME: 5min 53.0s

The stewards enquired into the running of a) Cornish Fort - accepted rider's explanation that she thought horse had broken down; and b) Jo's Wedding - accepted the rider's explanation that the horse could not act on the ground

1522 Confined Maiden 8yo&up (Div 2), 12st

9 ran

[1390²]	1		**ROYAL CHIP** 7-2 T Cole *Tubed; swtng; made all; 2-3l up frm 15; drvn clr u.p frm 2 out*
[1385⁴]	2	4	**Broughton's Port** 4-1 T Dennis *Opened 9/2; in tch & keen early; 5l 3rd 9; went 2nd 13; chsd ldr & ev ch til no ex frm 2 out; dism aft post*
[1391³]	3	1½	**Broad Ink** 10-1 D McKenna *Keen & hld up early; 5th ½way; hdwy to 3rd 16; ev ch til rdn & no ex app 2 out*
[1390ᴿ]	4	25	**Emerald Ectasy** (5a) 25-1 I Hambley *(xnb) Tchd 33s; handy; 4th & gng wl 13; wknd 15; no ch frm 3 out*
[1043ᴾ]	P		**Golden Sunset** (5a) 33-1 Miss D Mitchell *Sn strugg in last; a bhnd til pu 2 out*
[1262ᴮ]	P		**Just Mai-Bee** 14-1 B O'Doherty *Sn prom; trckd ldr to 13; sn lost plce; 4th & rdn 16; btn 4th when pu last; dism*
[1049ᴾ]	P		**Linton** (5a) 10-1 W Smith *Sn rr; 8th ½way; bhnd & pu 3 out*
[1257³]	P		**Saucy's Wolf** 6-4F A Holdsworth *Tchd 3s; midfield; 6th frm 8; no prog; hit 13; bhnd nxt til pu 2 out*
[1308ᴾ]	P		**Slippen-On** 20-1 M Sweetland *Rr; pckd 6; blun bad nxt; bhnd & rmdrs 11; t.o & pu 15*

OFFICIAL DISTANCES: 5l, ½l TIME: 6min 07.0s

Wheatland

Wolverhampton (LH 7F,19J) Sun, 14 May (GOOD to FIRM)

1523 Countryside Alliance Club Members, 12st

10 ran

| [1200ᴾ] | 1 | | **RISING SAP** (bl) 4-1 W Hill *Cl up; mist 7; went 2nd at 13; chsng clr ldr when hit nxt; clsd aft 16; sn chall; ld & hung sltly lft flat; r.o* |

[1416⁶]	2	1	**Pretoria Dancer** 6-1 F O'Brien *Prom; ld 10; lft 12l clr 12; prsd frm 3 out; hdd flat; r.o u.p*
[1358⁶]	3	30	**Just Marmalade** 16-1 Miss J Williams *In tch early; strugg 12; plodded on aft*
[476⁷]	4	3½	**Trevveethan (IRE)** 8-1 N Sutton *Bckwd; in rr; lost tch final circ; nvr on terms*
[960⁵]	5	20	**Orton House** (tt) 7-1 G Hanmer *Handy; rmdrs aft 7; lost tch 13; nd aft*
[1414⁶]	6	50	**Professor Longhair** 20-1 P Bennett *Lw; mists; to frm 8*
[1412⁷]	P		**Dotty Dolittle** (5a) 20-1 J Burley *Lw; a jmpd slow; sn bhnd; to 13; pu nxt*
[1343⁵]	P		**Greville Again (IRE)** 8-1 A Wadlow *Prom; ld 3-10; 2nd when pu 12; lame*
[1312ᵁ]	P		**Outside The Rain (IRE)** (5a) 12-1 T Macfarlane *Lw; wl bhnd; to 8; pu aft 13*
[1321⁴]	P		**Perambulate (NZ)** 6-4F D Barlow *Ld to 3; lft 2nd 12; wknd aft 13; eased aft 16; pu nxt*

OFFICIAL DISTANCES: 1l, 30l **TIME:** 6min 32.3s

1524 Mens Open, 12st   7 ran

[614⁴]	1		**JALCANTO** (4x) 7-2 D Mansell *Cl up; nt much room & hmpd sltly aft 13; went 2nd aft 16; 1l down when mist & lft in ld nxt; sn clr; drvn out*
[1416⁴]	2	5	**Native Cove (IRE)** 8-1 L Hicks *Lw; cl up; 2nd 15; outpcd 4 out; lft 2nd nxt; kpt on u.p flat; no imp on wnr*
[963¹]	3	½	**Mister Moss (IRE)** 6-4 G Hanmer *Ld to 13; prom til outpcd 16; hrd drvn & kpt on u.p flat*
[1320³]	P		**Analystic (IRE)** 25-1 S Prior *Lw; bhnd; to 7; mist 10; pu aft 13*
[1319⁷]	P		**Batty's Island** 25-1 L Stephens *Mists; cl up; rdn along aft 13; sn wknd; to & pu 16*
[1416⁷]	P		**Chicodari** 20-1 E Walker *Lw; a bhnd; ref & ur 6*
[961¹]	F		**Jacob's Wife** (5a,4ow) evensF A Crow *Prom; ld 13; 1l up & gng wl when fell 3 out; winded*

OFFICIAL DISTANCES: 5l, ½l **TIME:** 6min 26.7s
The owner of Jacob's Wife, whose passport was not in order, was fined £100

1525 Ladies Open   12 ran

[1410⁵]	1		**KILLATTY PLAYER (IRE)** (5a,7x) 8-1 Mrs M Barlow *Prom; ld 8-10; ld agn 14; made rest; prsd frm 3 out; r.o wl flat*
[1380³]	2	6	**Island Vision (IRE)** 6-1 Mrs J Hughes *In tch; hdwy 13; ev ch 3 out; rdn & pckd nxt; one pce flat*
[1253²]	3	30	**Class Of Ninetytwo (IRE)** (vis) 6-1 Miss S Sharratt *Spurs; hld up; hdwy 8; ld aft 13; hdd nxt; wknd 16*
[591²]	4	6	**Bubble N Squeek** 25-1 Mrs K Diggle *Sis; bhnd; lost tch 8; eased clsng stages*
[611⁹]	5	hd	**Nick The Biscuit** 7-1 Miss R Reynolds *Handy; mist 6; wknd aft 13*
[1408⁶]	6	4	**Ballyhannon (IRE)** (3ow) 20-1 Miss J Froggatt *A bhnd; lost tch 8*
[1281²]	P		**Aegean Fanfare** (7x) 5-2 Mrs C Ford *Prom til mist & rmdrs 13; sn wknd; to & pu 16*
[1313⁷]	P		**Ballymaloe Boy (IRE)** (7x) 20-1 Miss L Pearce *Ld to 8; ld agn 10 til aft 13; sn wknd; to & pu 16*
[1410⁷]	P		**Cheeky Pot** (bl) 25-1 Miss J Priest *Prom early; rmdrs aft 6; sn lost plce; still in tch when pu aft 13; lost shoe*
[1150⁴]	U		**Staigue Fort (IRE)** 20-1 Miss V Stubbs *Cl up; drpd to rr aft 7; mist 11; lost tch aft 13; no ch when blun & ur last; damaged check ligament*
[1320¹]	F		**Sun Surfer (FR)** (vis) 7-4F Miss P Jones *In tch; drpd to rr aft 7; hdwy 14; ev ch when fell 3 out*
[1253⁵]	P		**The Boiler White (IRE)** 25-1 Miss S Phizacklea *A bhnd; to 8; pu 16*

OFFICIAL DISTANCES: 6l, dist **TIME:** 6min 30.8s
The owner of The Boiler White, whose passport was not in order, was fined £100

1526 Open Maiden (Div 1), 12st   14 ran

[966³]	1		**NATIVE CANNON (IRE)** 10-1 B Foster *In tch; hdwy 12; lft in ld app 14; made rest; drvn out flat*
	2	2	**Master Will** (7a) 6-4F G Hanmer *Hld up in rr; hdwy 11; lft 2nd app 14; shkn up to chall app last; nt qckn flat*
[1406²]	3	20	**Watchyourback (NZ)** 6-1 N Oliver *In tch; tk clsr ord aft 13; sn outpcd; nd aft*
[1318⁷]	4	10	**Whatamonkey** 20-1 P Morris *Ss; a bhnd; nvr on terms w ldrs*
[1318⁷]	P		**Daneswell** 20-1 D Mansell *A bhnd; to & pu 13; dism*
[1422ᵁ]	P		**Gilded Way** 20-1 L Hicks *Rr; strugg when blun 15; to & pu 16*
[1201⁷]	P		**Jacks Dream** (5a) 8-1 J Burley *Mists; handy til wknd 10; to & pu 14*
[1413⁷]	R		**Kinsale Florale** (5a) 2-1 M Rodda *Ld to 4; prom til ld agn aft 7; hdd aft 10; ld agn aft 11; rn out 14*
[1435⁷]	P		**Piltdown Lady** (5a) 10-1 T Macfarlane *A bhnd; to 9; pu aft 13*

[1196U]	F		**Rural Gossip** 20-1 M Worthington *Ss; trckd ldrs frm 4 til fell 11*
	P		**The Devils Kandi** 25-1 Miss S Sharratt *Mist 2; cl up early; t.o 9; pu aft 13*
	U		**Tobias (IRE)** (7a) 8-1 M Munrowd *Blun & ur 1*
[1413³]	P		**Village Gossip** (5a) 8-1 M Trott *A bhnd; t.o & pu 2 out*
[1323P]	U		**Wily Miss** (5a) (vis) 20-1 C Hoggart *Prom; ld 4; hdd aft 7; rmdrs 9; ld aft 10; hdd aft nxt; mist 12; blun & ur 13*

OFFICIAL DISTANCES: 2l, 20l   **TIME:** 6min 41.6s
The stewards enquired into the running and riding of Master Will; the rider's explanation that the horse was having its first ever run, had nearly stopped at the first fence and was very green was accepted

1527 Open Maiden (Div 2), 12st - 18J   15 ran

[964³]	1		**INGLERISE** (12a,5ow) 7-4F G Hanmer *Stdd start; hld up; hdwy 8; cl 2nd 14; ld on bit 2 out; drew clr flat; canter*
[865³]	2	6	**Holding The Fort (IRE)** 8-1 D Barlow *Prom; rdn & outpcd app 2 out; stayed on agn flat; tk 2nd cl home; no ch w wnr*
[1412³]	3	hd	**Strong Mission (IRE)** 6-1 J Merry *Mists; pulled hrd; ld to 2; lft in ld 7; clr when mist 11; blun 14; rdn & hdd 2 out; no ex flat; eased & dem cl home*
[1323⁵]	4	8	**Barney Bear** 12-1 M Worthington *Ld 2; blun & hdd 7; gd rcvry; upsides nxt; blun 11; wknd aft 13*
[1340⁵]	5	3	**Mcloughlin (IRE)** 10-1 M Rodda *Midfield; hdwy to chse ldrs 14; wknd 16*
[1207⁶]	6	30	**Snowshill Harvest (IRE)** 16-1 J Rice *Hld up in midfield; rdn along aft 13; wknd 15; eased; t.o*
[1412P]	P		**Crack 'n' Run** 25-1 M Pennell *Prom; lost plce aft 7; bhnd 10; t.o 14; pu 3 out*
[990P]	P		**Druids Dream** 12-1 Miss S Sharratt *Mist 7; t.o & pu nxt*
[1290P]	P		**Holy Moses (IRE)** 25-1 T Macfarlane *Mists 1 & 2; pu 3*
	U		**May Rose** (5a) 12-1 D Mansell *Ss; blun & ur 1*
[1361²]	P		**One Mans Legacy** (5a) 8-1 R Burton *Midfield early; bhnd 10; hmpd bad 12; pu nxt*
[994P]	P		**Otter River** 8-1 J R Barlow *Handy til lost plce 10; t.o & pu 14*
[1439U]	P		**Peover Eye** (7a) 25-1 D Sherlock *Mists; midfield; rmdrs aft 6; t.o & pu 14*
	P		**Remember Equiname** (12a) 20-1 J Burley *In rr; wl bhnd 10; t.o & pu 14*
[1323²]	F		**See More Action** 2-1 L Stephens *Midfield til fell 12*

OFFICIAL DISTANCES: 6l, hd   **TIME:** 6min 33.4s
Last fence omitted - damaged; the stewards enquired into the running of the third place horse which had lost second near the line; they accepted the rider's explanation that the horse was hanging

1528 Restricted, 12st   11 ran

[1413¹]	1		**SPUMANTE** 2-1F G Hanmer *Hld up; stdy hdwy app 14; went 2nd 3 out; ld on bit flat; cheeky*
[1524P]	2	1½	**Analystic (IRE)** (vis) 8-1 M Worthington *Lw; in tch; hmpd 1; sn handy; chsd clr ldr 8; clsd gdft 10; lft in ld app 12; mist 14 & 16; hrd prsd when blun last; hdd flat; sn no ch w wnr*
[1408⁴]	3	8	**Prologue (IRE)** 8-1 T Greenway *In tch; mist 5; rdn to chse ldrs app 3 out; one pce app last*
[1253U]	4	5	**Hotscent (IRE)** (5a) (bl) 20-1 Miss C Wilberforce *Lw; in tch; chsd ldrs 5; lft 2nd app 12; wknd 3 out*
[1411⁴]	5	10	**Out Of The Blue** (5a) 12-1 S Graham *Mist 1; towards rr 7; nvr on terms*
[964¹]	6	7	**Ishereal (IRE)** 5-1 S Prior *Ld to 2; stdly lost ground frm 11; wl bhnd 14*
[1338P]	P		**Brown Esquire** 3-1 D Barlow *Nt jw; trckd ldrs early; bhnd & blun 11; t.o & pu aft 13*
[669U]	P		**Camogue Bridge (IRE)** 33-1 M Rodda *A bhnd; t.o & pu 13*
[1322³]	P		**Mr Mark (IRE)** 16-1 D Sherlock *Handy; mists 1 & 2; sn lost plce; bhnd when pu 9*
[1411U]	P		**Pinouli** (5a) 3-1 L Stephens *A bhnd; mist 3; blun 4; no ch when pu 3 out*
[1322P]	P		**Scallymay** (5a) 10-1 D Mansell *Pulled hrd; jmpd rt; ld 2; clr 7; pu 12*

OFFICIAL DISTANCES: 1½l, 8l   **TIME:** 6min 37.3s

1529 Hunt, 12st   5 ran

[1128¹]	1		**GARRYSPILLANE (IRE)** (bl) 4-11F G Hanmer *Hld up in tch; chall on bit 2 out; ld aft last; drvn out*
[1253¹]	2	¾	**Canaillou II (FR)** 4-1 A Wadlow *Chsd ldrs; chall 16; ld app nxt; rdn app 2 out; hdd aft last; nt qckn*
[1198³]	3	25	**Eau So Sloe** (bl) 14-1 R Hodges *Ld; rdn & hdd app 3 out; wknd app nxt*
	4		**White Willow** (5a) 8-1 R Carey *Bckwd; trckd ldr; pckd 11; wknd aft 16*
[922³]	5	15	**Professor Strong (IRE)** 6-1 P Cranmer *(bf) A bhnd; mist 5; lost tch 8*

OFFICIAL DISTANCES: ¾l, 25l   **TIME:** 6min 46.9s

Towcester (RH 7F)
Mon, 15 May (GOOD to FIRM)

1530 Land Rover Freelander Nov HC   7 ran

[1155²]	1		**MR SNOWMAN** 11-12 evensF *Mrs T Hill* Lw; jmpd v wl mostly; cl up; ld 8-10; disp ld 11 til ld & nt fluent 2 out; sn rdn clr; r.o wl
[1156¹]	2	14	**Tom De Savoie (IRE)** 11-12 9-4 *R Cope* Lw; prom; drew clr w wnr frm 11; ev ch til rdn & wknd 2 out
[1024ᴾ]	3	15	**Over The Hill (IRE)** 12-05 6-1 *M Armytage* Hld up & bhnd; lost tch 10; 26l 4th 13; poor 3rd frm nxt; floundered near last
[1421⁵]	4	12	**Cumberland Youth** 11-05 100-1 *J Diment* Sn 2nd; ld 6-9; wl outpcd frm nxt; rem 5th 3 out
[1447⁵]	5	6	**Phaedair** 11-05 50-1 *J Oldring* Tde & ld rnd dism at start; tk keen hld; ld to 6; ld 10 til jmpd slow 11; sn wl outpcd by ldng pr; lost 25l 3rd 3 out
[1194⁵]	6	dist	**Music Class (IRE)** 11-05 100-1 *J Gallagher* Mists in rr; rdn 5; lost tch nxt; t.o aft 9
[1269¹]	U		**Cashel Green (IRE)** 11-05 10-1 *M Hewitt* Trckd ldrs; 3l 5th when mist & ur 8

TIME: 5min 38.4s **TOTE:** £1.90; places £1.10,£1.70 **Ex:** £3.30 **CSF:** £2.96

1531 Hartwell Land Rover Discovery HC   14 ran

[1341¹¹]	1		**US FOUR (IRE)** 11-05 (bl) 20-1 *S Morris* Hld up; 28l 6th 5; hdwy to 3rd app 2 out; drvn to ld flat; sn clr
[1341⁸]	2	6	**Desert Calm (IRE)** 11-09 10-1 *W Renwick* Settled 3rd/4th; clsd to ld app 2 out; drvn & hdd flat; nt qckn
[1341⁵]	3	2½	**Halham Tarn (IRE)** 11-09 11-2 *T Gibney* Impeded 2; 20l last 3; hdwy 3 out; went 2nd app nxt; chall & ev ch when mist last; nt r.o
[1343ᴾ]	4	4	**Admiral Villeneuve** 11-09 66-1 *A Wintle* Outpcd; 30l 7th 5; hdwy 3 out; 4th nxt; one pce & sn btn
[1335ᶠ]	5	8	**Wot No Cash** 11-07 66-1 *R Lawther* Prom; hmpd 2; mist 4; outpcd in 20l 3rd 5; rallied aft 3 out; 5th & btn app nxt
[1293ᴾ]	6	dist	**Wrenbury Farmer** 11-07 (2) 66-1 *S Graham* Swtng; blun 1; mist 6; a bhnd; t.o 7
[1323ᶠ]	7	26	**Supermitten** 11-05 66-1 *J R Barlow* A wl bhnd; poor 8th 6; t.o 3 out; btn lame
[1438⁵]	8	18	**Ardshuil** 11-07 (2) 33-1 *S Pile* (xnb) Tk str hld; ld aft 3 & spreadeagled field; 10l clr 6 til stpd to nil uphill & hdd app 2 out; exhaust & blun over; forced to cont
[1413ᴾ]	P		**Aganerot (IRE)** 11-05 66-1 *P Cranmer* Hmpd 1; wl bhnd; t.o aft 5; pu 2 out
[1441⁴]	F		**Erbil (IRE)** 11-07 33-1 *J Owen* Ld til aft 1; 2nd when fell 2
[921ᶠ]	P		**Gale Toi (IRE)** 11-05 11-10F *P York* Lw; midfield; 25l 4th 5; mod 3rd when pckd bad 9; strugg aft; t.o & pu last
[1341²]	U		**Northern Bluff** 11-12 4-1 *J Jukes* Chsd ldrs; 7th when mist & ur 4
[736ᵁ]	P		**Tango's Delight** 11-05 66-1 *J Gallagher* Imm strugg; t.o 9; pu 2 out
[1323²]	P		**Wizadora** 10-12 (bl) 50-1 *T Greenway* Tore into ld aft 1 & sn clr; mist 4; hdd & hit 5; 25l ahd of rest nxt; mist 9; 2nd til stpd to nil aft 3 out; t.o & pu 2 out

TIME: 4min 10.9s **TOTE:** £26.90; places £3.70,£2.20,£1.50 **Ex:** £198.90 **CSF:** £167.10 **Tri:** £nt won

The rider of Ardshuil was banned from riding for 7 days for improper riding (earlier his crash helmet had been found to contravene the Regulations)

1532 Land Rover Gentlemans Championship HC   9 ran

[1381²]	1		**COPPER THISTLE (IRE)** 11-13 (2) 5-4F *R Hunnisett* Lw; jmpd brilliant; ld to 7; ld agn aft 9; drew 5l clr 15; r.o str; impressive
[1182²]	2	11	**Hatcham Boy (IRE)** 12-01 5-1 *C Ward-Thomas* Lw; hld up; 5th 7; outpcd 12; 13l 4th 15; rallied to chse wnr app 2 out; nvr able to chall
[1416²]	3	12	**Mr Smudge** 11-02 11-2 *A Martin* Hdwy to 4th aft 6; hit 8; 5th & outpcd 12; rallied & blun 14 (water); mist nxt; stayed on wl frm 2 out; 5th & u.p last; snatched 3rd
[1349ᵁ]	4	nk	**Calleva Star (IRE)** 12-00 16-1 *R Abrahams* Prsd wnr to 7; 6l 3rd & outpcd 12; rdn to go 8l 2nd 3 out; dem & nt qckn app nxt
[1416⁵]	5	3	**Midnight Service (IRE)** 11-02 (bl) 15-2 *R Barrett* 3rd til ld 7; hdd agn 9; chsd wnr to 3 out; sn wknd; hit last
[1205⁵]	6	25	**Chism (IRE)** 11-11 25-1 *R Walford* Midfield; 5th when blun 11; no ch aft; t.o
[1265ᴾ]	7	7	**Kites Hardwicke** 12-04 (16) 50-1 *P Sheppard* Bhnd; lost tch & jmpd awkward 8; t.o 11
[1237¹]	8	¾	**Highway Lad** 11-09 (bl) 10-1 *L Jefford* Bhnd; outpcd & mist 12; sn t.o
[441²]	P		**Rule Out The Rest** 11-09 25-1 *N Tutty* Drpd to rr & rdn 7; t.o & jmpd slow 10; pu 11

TIME: 6min 29.2s **TOTE:** £2.20; places £1.50,£1.30,£1.20 **Ex:** £6.20 **CSF:** £6.92 **Tri:** £9.30
The stewards suspended the rider of Mr Smudge for six days for misuse of the whip

1533 Range Rover HC 8 ran

[1418¹]	1		**FANION DE NOURRY (FR)** 11-05 7-1 L Hicks *Hld up & wl bhnd; 45l last 5; hdwy aft 11; went 2nd 15; ld nxt & sn 6l clr; nt fluent 2 out & hung lft; nt fluent last; unchall*
[1249³]	2	16	**Desperate** 11-05 6-1 R Barrett *Wl bhnd; 35l 5th 5; u.p frm 9; hdwy 11; chall & ev ch 3 out; sn wl outpcd bywnr*
[1332²]	3	1	**Act Of Parliament (IRE)** 11-05 (bl) 6-4F D Flavin *Chsd clr ldr & clr of rest; clsd & 3l down when pckd 11; mist 13; 4th & rdn when mist 15; nt keen aft; 15l 4th aft 3 out; drvn & plugged on flat*
[1343ᵁ]	4	2	**Lakeside Lad** 11-09 (bl) 7-2 A Wintle *20l 4th 5; nd frm 11; strugg on*
[1339⁵]	5	6	**Tea Cee Kay** 11-12 9-1 A Sansome *Sn 12l clr & spreadeagled field; checked twice by loose horse aft 8; jmpd delib 11; hdd 3 out; fdd imm; fin tired*
[1357⁶]	P		**Funcheon Gale** 11-12 16-1 A Charles-Jones *13l 3rd 5; chsd clr ldng pr til wknd aft 11; t.o 15; pu 2 out*
[1268³]	P		**Sands Point** 11-05 50-1 N Kent *42l 6th 5; last 9; t.o 11; pu 15*
[1266⁶]	U		**Supreme Dream (IRE)** 11-00 50-1 Mrs P Adams *Pckd 1; 4th when pckd sltly & rfo 2*

TIME: 6min 30.7s **TOTE:** £5.10; places £1.20,£1.30,£1.70 **Ex:** £55.60 **CSF:** £39.74 **Tri:** £137.50

Hereford (RH 9F,19J)
Tue, 16 May (GOOD)

1534 Ivor Johnson Mem HC 3 ran

[1293³]	1		**SILVERDALESURESHOT** 12-04 1-3F R Burton *Cl last til 2nd 12; ld 16; rdn clr aft 3 out; v easy*
[1336⁵]	2	26	**Executive Office (IRE)** 11-07 5-2 M Keel *Set slow pce; ld til jmpd slow 5; jmpd slow 6; lost 2nd 12; jmpd slow 14; chsd wnr aft 16; no ch aft 3 out*
[1309⁴]	3	dist	**Frankly Fear** 11-07 11-1 J Young *Jmpd lft; ld 5 til hdd & hit 16; imm rdn & lost tch; t.o app 2 out*

TIME: 6min 50.6s **TOTE:** £1.10; **Ex:** £1.50 **CSF:** £1.61

Exeter (RH 11F,15J)
Wed, 17 May (GOOD to FIRM, FIRM in places)

1535 West Country Nov HC 8 ran

[1334⁸]	1		**CHATERGOLD (IRE)** 11-05 (bl) 9-2 D Dennis *Chsd ldr frm 4 til ld app 12; drvn & stayed on frm nxt; all out*
[1256²]	2	1¼	**Lead Story (IRE)** 11-05 9-2 Richard Darke *Jw; trckd ldrs; lost plce 8; hdwy 10; went 2nd 12; outpcd nxt; 5l down 2 out; stayed on flat; nt rch wnr*
[1134⁷]	3	9	**Mendip Son** 11-07 (bl) 16-1 Miss P Gundry *Ld 2; clr 8; rdn 9; 6l ahd 10; hdd app 12; sn outpcd*
[1299³]	4	nk	**Flockmaster (IRE)** 11-05 8-1 M Foley *Ld to 2; drpd to rr 8; 5th 12; stayed on u.p frm nxt; nd*
[1432⁷]	5	25	**Where's Sam** 11-05 25-1 S Craddock *Wl bhnd frm 6; t.o app 12*
[1448¹]	P		**Marisol (IRE)** 11-04 9-2 E Williams *In tch; chsd ldrs 7; hit 10; wknd qckly & pu 12*
[1454ᴿ]	P		**Millbank Honey** 11-00 25-1 C Williams *Bhnd; eff 8; sn wknd; t.o & pu 12*
[1370⁷]	P		**Morris Piper** 11-12 (tt) 7-4F L Jefford *Bhnd 5; drvn & hdwy to chse ldrs in 4th 12; sn wknd; t.o & pu last*

TIME: 4min 11.4s **TOTE:** £6.10; places £1.30,£1.90,£2.50 **Ex:** £26.80 **CSF:** £23.48 **Tri:** £31.60

Folkestone (RH 7F)
Wed, 17 May (GOOD, GOOD to FIRM in places)

1536 Guy Peate Mem Nov HC 10 ran

[1333⁴]	1		**GALEAWAY (IRE)** 11-09 6-1 B Hitchcott *Sn trckng ldng pr; went 2nd 16; chall 3 out; lft in ld nxt; drvn out*
[1378⁴]	2	2½	**Ballydesmond (IRE)** 11-07 (bl) 25-1 K Edmunds *Made most; jnd 3 out; sn drew 5l clr; 2l ahd when jmpd slow 2 out; sn hdd; nt qckn frm last*
[1156ᵁ]	3	2½	**Pangeran (USA)** 11-12 6-5F N King *Nt fluent & jmpd lft; prsd ldr 3-3 out; rdn & eff aft nxt; ch when nt fluent last; nt qckn*
[1155⁴]	4	16	**Kincora (IRE)** 11-07 6-1 Mrs L Stock *Cl up; mist 10; nt fluent 14; outpcd nxt; 16l 4th aft 16; mist 3 out; no ch aft*

[1510[P]]	P		**Bit Of An Idiot** 11-07 20-1 D Slattery *Sn pushed along & bhnd; 6th & some prog 12; rdn 14; wknd nxt; wl bhnd when pu 3 out*
[1135[P]]	U		**Lost Your Marbles (IRE)** 11-02 50-1 R Arnold *Chsd ldrs til blun & ur 9*
[578[P]]	P		**One More Bill** 11-07 (vis) 66-1 M Gorman *In tch in midfield; rdn 7; wknd 11; t.o & pu 13*
[1377[2]]	P		**Salmon Mead (IRE)** 11-09 (bl) 25-1 R Fowler *A rr; rdn 10; wknd 12; jmpd slow aft & sn t.o; pu 3 out*
[1108[2]]	P		**Thats Dedication (IRE)** 12-01 (8) (tt) 7-2 D Robinson *Prom; mist & lost plce 6; no imp on ldrs aft 14; poor 5th nxt; pu aft last; dism*
[1333[F]]	P		**Winward** 11-10 (1) (tt) 66-1 P Townsley *Rdn 4; wknd 5; hit 6 & u.p; t.o 7; pu 9*

TIME: 6min 39.9s **TOTE:** £6.90; places £2.20,£6.00,£1.10 **Ex:** £139.70 **CSF:** £110.43

1537 Grants Cherry Brandy SE Champ HC 12 ran

[980[1]]	1		**TIDAL REEF (IRE)** 11-07 5-1 C Gordon *Jmpd slow 2; rr; mist 7 & rmdrs; gd prog 10; 4th & rdn nxt; ld brief 3 out; drvn to ld agn nxt; stayed on wl*
[1510[1]]	2	3½	**Newby End (IRE)** 11-07 7-2F D Dennis *Sn prom; chsd ldr 8; ld sn aft 3 out; jmpd slow & hdd nxt; led little aft*
[1267[4]]	3	2½	**Persian Boy (IRE)** 12-00 11-2 A Sansome *Chsd ldrs; pushed along frm 9; outpcd 11; kpt on agn u.p frm 2; went 3rd at last*
[576[3]]	4	1¾	**Carraig Brol (IRE)** 11-09 7-1 B Hitchcott *Jb lft; chsd ldr; ld aft 6-3 out; ev ch 2 out; one pce*
[1206[9]]	5	19	**Fair Ally** 11-09 16-1 R Lawther *Trckd ldrs; 5th 10; mist 11; sn btn; no ch aft 3 out*
[1207[4]]	6	11	**Uncle Den** 11-07 33-1 D Flavin *Rr; prog to chse ldng pr 9; rdn whn hmpd 11 & nxt; sn wknd*
[1292[1]]	U		**Denarii (IRE)** 11-04 5-1 F Windsor Clive *Mists; lost plce 3; 10th & rdn but in tch when blun & ur 8*
[980[2]]	F		**Dreamin George (IRE)** 11-07 8-1 C Sherry *Cl up til wknd & mist 12; 8l 6th & strugg when turned somersault 3 out & crashed und rails*
[1513[9]]	P		**Ell Gee** 11-07 (3) 20-1 P Townsley *In tch til rdn & wknd & mist 9; last when mist 10; t.o & pu 11*
[1396[4]]	U		**Mountain Tae (IRE)** 11-07 33-1 R Green *Rdr v cumbersome; nrly ur 5; mist 6; 9th & in tch when ur 7*
[1396[2]]	P		**Uk Eurolad** 11-07 10-1 T Hills *Ld til blun 6; sn wknd; rn wide bend bef 9 & pu*
[1284[2]]	P		**Wood Buzzard** 12-00 6-1 A Charles-Jones *Mist 1; in tch til wknd aft 8; t.o when jmpd v slow 12; pu nxt*

TIME: 5min 24.1s **TOTE:** £5.20; places £1.70,£1.50,£1.60 **Ex:** £32.80 **CSF:** £23.60 **Tri:** £18.60

1538 Www.racing-network.co.uk Open HC 4 ran

[1432[2]]	1		**NOYAN** 12-06 1-2F Miss L Horner *Jw; ld 3; drew wl clr frm 14; unchal*
	2	dist	**Ruth's Boy (IRE)** 12-06 10-1 F Windsor Clive *Ld to 3; chsd wnr to 12; rdn when mist nxt; went poor 2nd agn 3 out; mist last; gng up & down on spot on run-in*
[286[3]]	3	3	**Nadjati (USA)** 12-04 5-2 P Hall *Mist 2; bhnd til clsd 4; outpcd 10; clsd agn 11; chsd wnr 12; no imp & 15l bhnd & btn 14; lost poor 2nd 3 out; fin r tired*
[1392[3]]	4	hd	**Time Enough (IRE)** 12-01 12-1 P Townsley *A bhnd; rdn 12; t.o frm 14; plugged on frm 2 out; clsng on 2nd & 3rd flat*

TIME: 6min 35.1s **TOTE:** £1.40; **Ex:** £5.60 **CSF:** £5.26

1539 Shepherd Neame United Hunts Open Champ HC 5 ran

[1338[7]]	1		**RUPERTS CHOICE (IRE)** 11-07 (bl) 8-1 A Harvey *Hld up last; pushed along 7; drvn aft 9; prog 14; chsd ldr aft 17; ld 3 out; 4l clr nxt; idled & drvn app last; stayed on agn flat*
[1338[P]]	2	2	**Bolshie Baron** 11-09 (tt) 7-2 M Harris *Cl up; chsd ldr 13 til hit 17; rdn 3 out; went 2nd nxt; clsd & ev ch aft last; sn outpcd*
[1106[F]]	3	7	**Prince Buck (IRE)** 11-12 evensF B Hitchcott *Tk keen hld; jmpd lft; w ldr til ld 7; hdd & rdn when jmpd lft & mist 3 out; 6l 3rd & wkng app nxt*
[1434[3]]	4	hd	**Torus Spa (IRE)** 11-07 9-2 Mrs E Coveney *Chsd ldrs; rmdrs aft 16; lost tch & jmpd slow 3 out; kpt on agn frm nxt*
[1484[4]]	5	1¼	**Remilan (IRE)** 12-00 (bl) 12-1 A Sansome *Ld to 7; stdly lost plce; last & rdn 15; sn strugg; kpt on agn frm 2 out*

TIME: 8min 00.4s **TOTE:** £10.90; places £3.00,£1.40 **Ex:** £40.10 **CSF:** £30.86

1540 Ross & Co Mdn HC 8 ran

| [1335[2]] | 1 | | **RUSTIC REVELRY** 11-10 2-5F P York *Chsd ldrs; hit 3; pushed along aft 6; ld 7; hrd prsd frm 12; rdn & kpt on wl flat* |

[1381ᴾ]	2	1½	**Lord Knox (IRE)** 11-10 16-1 A Coe *Pulled hrd; prom; chsd wnr 7; chall 3 out; sn rdn; rallied app last; a hld*
[958²]	3	27	**Bathwick Bobbie** 11-10 10-1 Jeremy Young *Prom; chsd ldng pr frm 8; hit 10; wknd & mist 11; 15l 3rd when mist 3 out*
[1395³]	4	14	**Velka** 11-05 9-2 Miss P Ellison *Hld up & bhnd; eff to chse ldng trio 9; lost tch 11; strug aft*
[1394ᴾ]	5	1¼	**How Friendly** 11-10 25-1 A Hickman *Rmdrs aft 1; a towards rr; rdn & lost tch 10; sn wl bhnd*
[1287⁷]	6	dist	**Premier First (IRE)** 11-10 (bl) 25-1 G Pewter *Mostly 3rd to 7; wknd 9; wl to frm 11*
[578⁶]	U		**Leggies Legacy** 11-10 20-1 P Hall *Rmdrs aft 1; last when tried to ref & lft rdr on tk-off side 2*
[1397³]	P		**Tonrin** 11-10 14-1 M Gorman *Ur bef start; ld at fast pce; blun bad 6; hdd & wknd 7; t.o & jb aft; pu last*

TIME: 5min 22.1s **TOTE:** £1.60; places £1.10, £2.50, £1.80 **Ex:** £27.70 **CSF:** £8.18

1541 Regency Marquees United Hunts Open HC   8 ran

[921¹³]	1		**YOUNG NIMROD** 11-05 (tt) 10-1 Miss C Grissell *Chsd ldr to 6; outpcd frm 8; 10l 3rd 11; eff to chse clr ldr aft 3 out; clsd nxt; ld last; drew clr flat*
[768¹]	2	8	**Coach (NZ)** 11-05 7-2 P Keane *Tk keen hld; 4th til trckd ldr 6; ld 9; mist 12; 8l clr & lkd wnr 3 out; 3l up nxt; hdd & wknd last*
[1395²]	3	8	**Nordic Spree (IRE)** 11-05 (bl,tt) 10-1 Miss A Goschen *Hld up in rr; rdn & no resp frm 8; some prog aft 3 out; nvr nr ldrs*
[1246⁴]	4	5	**Lake Of Loughrea (IRE)** 11-05 25-1 N Wilson (Hants) *A rr; wl bhnd 8; no ch aft; poor 7th 3 out; mod prog frm nxt*
[1288²]	5	5	**Epsilo De La Ronce (FR)** 11-05 (bl) 13-2 A Harvey *Hld up in rr; 7l 4th & rdn 8; sn outpcd; nd frm 11*
[885²]	6	s hd	**Strong Medicine** 11-05 9-4F Mrs E Coveney *Ld; clr w rival aft 8; hdd 9; cl 2nd to 11; wknd 3 out*
[802ᴾ]	7	½	**China Gem (IRE)** 11-07 5-2 B Hitchcott *Bhnd; rdn 8; brief eff to chse clr ldrs 10; sn no prog & btn*
[1510ᴾ]	P		**Bang On Target** 11-05 (bl) 100-1 M Gorman *Chsd ldrs; mist 5; sn wknd; to 9; pu 12*

TIME: 5min 20.9s **TOTE:** £13.10; places £2.30, £1.10, £3.40 **Ex:** £62.80 **CSF:** £43.24 **Tri:** £40.20

Huntingdon (RH 9F,19J)
Wed, 17 May (GOOD to FIRM)

1542 Norwich & Peterborough HC   8 ran

[1332¹]	1		**SOLO GENT** 12-07 6-5F T Doyle *Nt fluent 7; made most til hdd & rdn 10; hit 13; rdn along frm 15; ld app last; r.o game*
[1346⁴]	2	2½	**Factor Ten (IRE)** 11-07 16-1 J Richardson *In tch; 2nd/3rd frm 6 til ld 14; clr 3 out; rdn & 4l ahd app nxt; hdd & hit last; no ex*
[1443ᶠ]	3	½	**Linlathen** 11-07 5-1 N Bell *Hld up; hdwy to press ldrs 10; rdn app 3 out; 6l 3rd app nxt; kpt on same pce und feeble handling*
[1441¹]	4	8	**Castle Shelley** 11-07 8-1 R Smith *Chsd ldrs; hit 6; mist 9; rdn frm 3 out; 12l 4th & btn app nxt*
[1344²]	5	dist	**John Tufty** 11-07 25-1 Miss R Illman *A bhnd; outpcd 8; t.o 11*
[1149⁴]	U		**Aly Daley (IRE)** 11-07 11-1 Miss A Price *Hld up trckng ldrs; blun & ur 12*
[997ᶠ]	P		**Chez Catalan** 11-07 (bl) 66-1 R Wakeham *Bhnd frm 4; lost tch 8; t.o & pu 11*
[1334¹]	P		**Give It A Whirl** 12-00 9-2 T Lane *Prsd ldr; nt fluent 5 (water); ld 10 til broke down app 14 & pu imm aft (will nt rce agn)*

TIME: 6min 02.2s **TOTE:** £2.00; places £1.10, £2.70, £1.80 **Ex:** £28.30 **CSF:** £18.08 **Tri:** £51.80

Teme Valley
Brampton Bryan (RH 8F,17J) Wed, 17 May (FIRM)

1543 Hunt   3 ran

[1463⁶]	1		**CWM BYE** 2-1 M Hammond *Made all; kpt on game frm 3 out; hit nxt*
[1272⁷]	2	10	**Stormhill Recruit** 4-5F S Blackwell *Chsd wnr; drvn app 3 out; fnd nil & a hld*
[1338¹¹]	3	20	**Highway Five (IRE)** (7x) 4-1 Miss L Brooke *A last; 6l down & rdn 10; nt keen aft; 18l adrift 14*

OFFICIAL DISTANCES: 7l, 20l **TIME:** 7min 18.0s
Fences 5 & 13 omitted from all races - ground unraceable after leaking fertiliser vehicle had been parked near fence

1544 Confined, 12st   4 ran

[1463¹]	1		**GOOD FOR A LOAN** (3x) 2-1 **A Dalton** Hld up & cl up; ld 11-13 & frm nxt; sn clr; hung rt & slowed flat; rdn out
[1403¹]	2	8	**Illineylad (IRE)** 2-1 **A Wintle** Ld to 2 & aft 4 til slpd aft 8 & releg last; 2nd agn 11; ld brief 13; rdn & outpcd aft nxt; nt fluent frm 3 out
[1356⁵]	P		**Cherokee Run (IRE)** (tt) 8-1 **A Phillips** Lw; lft in ld aft 8-11; 15l last & strugg 13; pu nxt (incorrectly bitted)
[1343⁴]	S		**The Rum Mariner** 5-4F **Miss C Thomas** Ld 2 til slpd up turn aft 4

OFFICIAL DISTANCE: 10l   TIME: 6min 50.0s

1545 Mens Open, 12st   3 ran

[1273⁴]	1		**HURRICANE ANDREW (IRE)** 12-1 **N Oliver** Lw; nt jw; last til 2nd app 13; 3l down 14; clsd to ld & dived over 3 out; hdd nxt; level last; drvn into ld flat; all out (rdr saluted Judge)
[1357¹]	2	hd	**Nevada Gold** 4-9F **R Rogers** Jmpd best; ld til hdd 3 out; ld agn nxt; jnd last; ev ch til outrdn nr fin
[1346⁶]	3	runin	**Watchit Lad** 2-1 **S Blackwell** Lw; 2nd til stumbled & releg last app 12; 9l down & strugg 14; t.o & virt pu flat

OFFICIAL DISTANCES: hd, dist   TIME: 6min 54.0s

1546 Intermediate, 12st   1 ran

[1463⁵]	1	**MERGER MANIA M Trott** Walked over

OFFICIAL DISTANCE: Walked over

1547 Ladies Open   4 ran

[1544⁵]	1		**THE RUM MARINER** 5-4F **Miss C Thomas** 2nd outing; set slow pce app 5-13; 4l down when lft fnce ahd aft 14
[1357⁷]	2	30	**Military Man** 5-2 **Miss S Talbot** Ld til app 5; ld agn 13; 4l clr when missed marker aft 14; rtrcd & cont fnce bhnd (rdr had hd down & 'lkng where she was gng')
[1410⁷]	U		**Everso Irish** 14-1 **Miss F Wilson** Ur 1
[736²]	S		**Zingibar** 2-1 **Miss J Houldey** Last til went 2nd & slpd up turn aft 7

OFFICIAL DISTANCE: 30l   TIME: 7min 01.0s
> The stewards interviewed the rider of Military Man; she explained that she had missed a marker on the last bend as she had her head down and was not looking where she was going; she was fined £65

1548 Restricted, 12st   6 ran

[1355²]	1		**CODDINGTON GIRL** (5a) 4-7F **T Stephenson** (xnb) Lw; set v careful & slow pce til app 7; chsd clr ldr gng wl til clsd app 3 out; ld nxt; hld hld
[1459⁷]	2	6	**Hugo Henry (IRE)** 14-1 **M Trott** Mounted on course; settled 4th til pulled hrd to ld app 7; 8l clr aft 14; prsd & mist 3 out; hdd nxt; no ch w wnr
[863³]	3	25	**Nouvalari (IRE)** 6-1 **M Rodda** Mists; 2nd til app 7; 20l 3rd when jb rt 10; mist 11; 40l last aft 14; rdn to snatch 3rd
[1228⁷]	4	nk	**Crafty Gunner** 8-1 **J Keen** Bckwd; detach last; jmpd slow 5 & 6; lft 16l 3rd aft 11; 28l down aft 14; drvn & dem nr fin
[1355¹]	r		**My Nad Knows** 3-1 **J Baimbridge** Reluct to rce; ref 1
[698⁴]	U		**True Fred** (vis) 8-1 **R Burton** (pricker os) Hld up; 16l 4th 10; went 3rd & slpd & ur turn aft nxt

OFFICIAL DISTANCES: 5l, 30l   TIME: 7min 12.0s
> The last two races were abandoned as rain falling onto the firm ground had made the course dangerously slippery

Weston & Banwell Harriers
Cothelstone (LH 7F,19J) Wed, 17 May (FIRM)

1549 Hunt   3 ran

[1237⁵]	1		**ELLE FLAVADOR** (5a) 1-6F **Miss T Cave** (xnb) Set mod pce; made all; 3l up 5; grad drew clr frm 15; 10l up & in comm nxt; canter
	2	15	**Choc (U)** 6-1 **E Kenny-Herbert** 1st ride; last til disp 2nd 4; trckd ldr nxt; 6l down 9; chsd wnr vain til outpcd frm 16
	3	30	**Shrimbelle** (5a) 16-1 **J Young** Chsd ldr til releg last 5; 8l adrift 5; 8l adrift 9; grad lost tch frm 14; plodded home

OFFICIAL DISTANCES: 10l, 20l   TIME: 6min 32.3s   TOTE: £1.60   DF: £1.60

1550 Countryside Alliance Club Members (Nov Rdrs), 12st   8 ran

[952⁷]	1		**AMTRAK EXPRESS** 14-1 **H Froud** 5½l 4th 5; disp 2nd 8; lft in ld aft 10; 1½l up 12; drew 6l clr 14; stayed on str frm 2 out; rdr's 1st wnr
[1417²]	2	1½	**Fern Leader (IRE)** (vis) 7-4 **Mrs J Hughes** Hld up in last pr; impd to 6l 5th 5; lft chsng ldr 10; 8l down 15; stayed on frm 3 out; no ex frm nxt
[1471³]	3	8	**Frozen Drop** 6-4F **T Bishop** Trckd ldr; 4½l 3rd 5; 14l 4th 12; stayed on one pce frm 15; nvr able to chall
[1393⁶]	4	15	**Silver Hill** (5a) 33-1 **Miss B Fear** Lw; ld to 3; 5l down 6; 3½l 3rd 12; grad wknd frm 16
[1306ᴾ]	5	2	**Kinlogh Gale (IRE)** (bl,tt) 33-1 **Miss A Bush** A towards rr; 7th 8; 22l 6th 12; t.o 2 out
[1239ᴾ]	6	½	**Beck And Call (IRE)** 7-1 **D Ross** Virt a last; jmpd slow 3; 25l adrift 12; to 2 out
[1015ᴾ]	P		**Manor Rhyme** (7ow) (bl) 16-1 **T Gretton** (orbs) Chsd ldr til ld aft 8; 4l clr 5; still 3l up when pu aft 10; destroyed
[1471ᵁ]	P		**Villains Brief (IRE)** (bl) 20-1 **J Kwiatkowski** 4th to 4; grad lost plce; 20l 5th 12; wknd frm 15; bhnd when pu last

OFFICIAL DISTANCES: 2l, 6l   TIME: 6min 08.2s   TOTE: £16.00   DF: £20.00

1551 Restricted, 12st   10 ran

[331ᴾ]	1		**PEYTON JONES** 11-4JF **M Miller** Chsd ldr; 3½l 4th 5; 2l 3rd 12; chsd ldr 15 til ld app 2 out; stayed on u.p flat
[1097⁴]	2	4	**Diamond Duck** (5a) 11-4JF **Miss K Allan** (xnb) Mounted late; sa; rap hdwy to 2nd 5; disp ld 11-nxt; ld 13 til hdd app 2 out; no ex frm last
[1467ᴾ]	3	3	**The Stuffed Puffin (IRE)** 20-1 **Miss S Rowe** (xnb) Trckd ldrs; 4l 5th 5; stayed on frm 15; nvr able to chall
[1375ᵁ]	4	10	**Cefn Woodsman** 33-1 **Miss K Lovelace** Prom early; sn lost plce & last pr 5; stayed on frm 14; nrst fin
	5	1½	**Crestwood Lad (USA)** 4-1 **M Yardley** Swtng; ld; 3l up 7 til jnd 11; hdd 13; grad wknd frm 16
[1467ᵁ]	6	7	**Crosswell Star (IRE)** 14-1 **J Scott** 8th 5; a bhnd; nd
[1376ᴾ]	7	7	**Chilli Jo** (tt) 100-1 **Miss S Robinson** 9th 2; prog to 7l 4th 7; grad wknd frm 14; bhnd when mist 2 out
[1468¹]	8	20	**Chance Encounter** 4-1 **J Young** 3l 3rd 5; sn lost plce; mid-div 10; grad wknd frm 16; t.o frm 2 out
[1393⁷]	P		**Ngala (IRE)** (5a) 25-1 **H Tett** 9th 3; last 5; to 12 til pu 16
[1389⁵]	P		**Regal Wolf** (bl) 5-1 **G Maundrell** 8th 2; hdwy to 5th 7; grad lost plce; 8th & strugg when pu 14

OFFICIAL DISTANCES: 4l, 3l   TIME: 6min 06.7s   TOTE: £4.00   DF: £10.00

1552 Mens Open, 12st   5 ran

[1371⁴]	1		**PLAY POKER (IRE)** (bl) evensF **R Woollacott** Jw; hld up in last; 23l adrift 5; prog to disp 5½l 4th 12; hdwy when jmpd to ld 16; sn clr
[1306³]	2	8	**Avril Showers** (5a,4x) 5-4 **R Atkinson** Chsd ldrs; 16l 3rd 5; impd to trck ldr 11; ld nxt til hdd 16; sn brushed aside
[1371⁷]	3	12	**James Pigg** (7x) 12-1 **G Richards** Swtng; 8l 4th 5; disp 2nd 10; 3l 3rd 12; chsd ldng pr til outpcd frm 16
[1440²]	4	2	**Egypt Mill Prince** 9-1 **E Walker** (xnb) Disp ld to 3; 8l down 7; ld aft 10-12; grad wknd frm 3 out
[1470⁴]	5	10	**Via Del Quatro** (5a,7x) 16-1 **J Barnes** Ld/disp; 2l up 4; sn 10l clr nxt; hdd 10; releg qckly to 4th; rmdrs 12; last nxt; bhnd frm 16

OFFICIAL DISTANCES: 6l, 12l   TIME: 6min 06.2s   TOTE: £2.00   DF: £2.00

1553 Ladies Open   2 ran

| [1410¹ˢ] | 1 | | **HEARTS ARE WILD** 1-9F **Miss P Gundry** Jw; made all; 1½l up 5; outj rival; 4l up 12; grad drew clr frm 16; 10l up 3 out; in comm when eased flat |
| [1281¹] | 2 | 8 | **Khalidi (IRE)** 7-1 **Miss M MacGregor** Chsd rival; 1½l down 5; 3l adrift 14; strugg frm 3 out; no ex |

OFFICIAL DISTANCE: 6l   TIME: 6min 01.8s   TOTE: £1.20

1554 Confined, 12st   7 ran

[1473³]	1		**PRIMERO (IRE)** (tt) 3-1 **A Honeyball** Hld up in last; blun bad 7; remarkable rcvry but lost 10l; stdy hdwy to disp 5l 5th 12; stayed on to 5l 2nd 3 out; disp ld last; r.o wl flat
[1388²]	2	2	**Chasing Daisy** (5a) 3-1 **J Snowden** Tde; chsd ldr til ld 5; 2l up 8; 5l up 3 out; u.p & jnd last; no ex flat
[1246ᴾ]	3	6	**Balance** (3x) 6-4F **G Maundrell** 9/4-6/4; chsd ldrs; disp 2nd 6; 2l 3rd 12; chsd ldr frm 14 til one pce frm 2 out

[1473⁴]	4	2	**The Bold Abbot** (3x) 11-2 *Miss S West* 10s-11/2; in last pr til impd to 3rd 6; 3½l 3rd 8; chsd ldrs til no ex frm 2 out
[1130¹]	5	3	**Arabitan** (5a) 16-1 *O Ellwood* Swtng; trckd ldrs; 4th & in tch 11; 1½l 2nd 12; grad wknd frm 3 out
[1394⁴]	6	4	**Celtic Token** 22-1 *D Birkmyre (xnb)* Tde; ld to 4; 4l 4th 8; 3l 4th 12; grad wknd to last frm 15
[1371ᴾ]	P		**Captain Jack** (bl) 14-1 *B O'Doherty* 20s-14s; chsd ldr to 5; mist 6; jmpd slow 10; sn last; pu aft 12

OFFICIAL DISTANCES: 2½l, 6l   TIME: 6min 00.6s   TOTE: £3.00 DF: £5.00

1555 Open Maiden, 12st - 17J   8 ran

[1131⁵]	1		**SIR WYNHAM** 9-2 *J Case* Ld & set fast pce; 2½l up 5; still 1½l up 12; lft virt solo 14; easy; rdr's 1st wnr
[1284ᴾ]	2	2fncs	**Dido's Dream** (5a) 50-1 *J Barnes (xnb)* 25l 7th 5; lft chsd 4th 9; passed flagging rival when lft 2nd 14; t.o frm nxt
[1370³]	3	20	**Jug Of Wine** (5a) 16-1 *R Emmett* 20l 5th 5; lft rem 3rd by defections 9; t.o frm 15
[1372⁴]	S		**Audley Lass (IRE)** (5a) 3-1 *A Bateman* Trckd ldrs; 18l 3rd 5 til slpd up bend aft 8
	U		**Comic Turn** (7ow) 25-1 *T Gretton* In last trio; 23l 6th 5 til blun & ur nxt
[957ᶠ]	U		**Dancing Barefoot** (5a) 14-1 *M Miller* 19l 4th 5; still rem 4th when blun & ur 8
[880ᴾ]	U		**Madam Rose (IRE)** (5a) 6-4F *L Jefford (xnb)* Chsd ldr; 2½l 2nd 5; trckng ldr when blun & ur 14
[1062ᴾ]	P		**Meat Loaf (IRE)** 5-2 *N Mitchell* Last; 30l adrift 5; nvr able to cl; pu 12

OFFICIAL DISTANCES: dist, 15l   TIME: 6min 02.3s   TOTE: £4.00 DF: £10.00
Fences 12 & 19 omitted - damaged

Perth (RH 8F,15J)
Thu, 18 May (GOOD to SOFT, SOFT in places)

1556 Nimrods Country And Equestrian Nov HC   11 ran

[1427¹]	1		**SUNNYCLIFF** 11-07 4-1 *L Morgan* Rr early; 3rd & prog 9; chall 11; ld gng wl aft nxt; 8l clr when mist 2 out; jmpd rt last; stayed on wl; rdly
[1327²]	2	8	**Blyth Brook** 12-00 5-1 *C Storey* Bhnd; hdwy in 6th & mist 7; 10l 5th 10; lost tch & jmpd rt 12; kpt on frm 2 out; tk 2nd flat; nt rch nr
[918¹]	3	¾	**Tea Box (IRE)** 12-05 6-4F *Miss P Robson* 2nd til ld 3; rdn & hdd aft 12; btn aft nxt
[1429¹]	4	2½	**Strathmore Lodge** 11-02 7-2 *D Jewett* 2nd/3rd; 3rd & ev ch when hit 12; sn outpcd; plugging on one pce when blun last
[1445⁵]	5	dist	**Just Ned** 11-11 (4) 50-1 *M Douglas* Mid-div; drpd back last 8; t.o 11
[1117ᶠ]	P		**Classic Crest (IRE)** 11-07 (vis) 25-1 *R Morgan* Ld to 3; chsd ldr til lost plce rap 6; t.o by pu 10
[1330ᵁ]	P		**Magical Poitin (IRE)** 11-02 25-1 *J Richardson* Towards rr; mist 5; to 11; pu 2 out
[1430³]	P		**Myles Of Moss (IRE)** 11-06 25-1 *Mrs V Jackson* Hit 1; mist 4; a rr; t.o & pu 7
[1362ᶠ]	P		**No Problem Jac** 11-02 (bl,tt) 25-1 *Miss L Hislop* Tk keen hld; prsd ldrs til wknd & mist 9; wl bhnd when pu nxt
[301ᴾ]	P		**Snooty Eskimo (IRE)** 11-11 25-1 *C Wilson* Sn bhnd; t.o & pu 9
[1083ᴾ]	P		**Tom's Man** 11-09 (tt) 25-1 *A Robson* Prom til 4th & outpcd 10; strugg nxt; pu 12

TIME: 5min 19.2s   TOTE: £4.20; places £1.40,£1.60,£1.70   Ex: £19.90 CSF: £21.49 Tri: £50.90

Aintree (LH 7F,19J)
Fri, 19 May (GOOD to FIRM)

1557 Graphic Connection Nov HC   7 ran

[1232¹]	1		**SPRINGFIELD REX** 12-00 8-1 *Mrs F Needham* Chsd ldrs; clsd 14; ld app 16; a gng wl aft; pushed along app 2 out; kpt on str
[1287¹]	2	4	**Baron Allfours** 12-00 8-1 *A Sansome* Hld up & bhnd; hdwy & mist 13; rdn in 8l 3rd 3 out; hit nxt; no imp aft; 6l 4th when lft 2nd at last
[800³]	3	dist	**Man Of Steele** 11-07 4-1 *Miss D Harding* Chsd ldr; eff to disp ld 13; lost plce 15; sn bumped along; hit 3 out & lost tch; t.o
[1365³]	4	1	**Blank Cheque** 11-07 9-1 *D Coates* Bhnd; jmpd slow 6; last frm 7; wl bhnd 13; t.o app 16; r.o str flat
	5	22	**Winsome Wallace (IRE)** 12-00 4-1 *M Bradburne* Hld up; 5th when blun 10; rdn & lost tch nxt; nt jw aft; t.o when blun bad 16

[1409P]	P		I Haven't A Buck (IRE) 11-11 (vis) 33-1 A Evans Ld; rdn 14; hdd app 16; sn wknd; t.o & pu 3 out
[1057²]	U		Stoney River (IRE) 11-11 7-4F R Walford Settled 3rd; hit 5 & 11; eff 14; rdn along to chse wnr app 16; 3l 2nd & hld when mist & ur last

TIME: 6min 28.3s TOTE: £19.70; places £4.30,£3.90 Ex: £93.50 CSF: £56.63

Stratford (LH 8F,18J)
Fri, 19 May (GOOD to FIRM)

1558 David Smith Farrier Nov HC
11 ran

[1338³]	1		FOREST FOUNTAIN (IRE) 12-00 9-2 Julian Pritchard Lw; jw; trckd ldrs; went 2nd 12; ld 14; pushed clr app 2 out; wl in comm when veered bad lft flat
[1443³]	2	7	Mr Custard 11-07 15-2 Miss L Sweeting Prom; ld aft 5; hdd 14; one pce & no ch w wnr frm 2 out
[1337P]	3	¾	Freedom Fighter 11-07 12-1 A Martin Oht; pulled hrd; prom; rdn & outpcd by ldng pr 15; drvn & kpt on to 3rd nr fin
[1336²]	4	1½	Kerry Soldier Blue 12-00 5-2F Miss P Jones Ld til aft 5; prom til 5l 3rd & outpcd 15; kpt on one pce aft; lost 3rd nr fin
[1343²]	5	11	African Warrior 11-02 9-1 Miss L Horner Bhnd; hdwy 8; chall 13; 5th & btn when hit 3 out
[1490²]	6	16	Hatterill Ridge 11-11 11-1 A Wintle Bhnd; mist 10; brief eff 12; 6th & strugg 15
[1338³]	7	3½	Sideliner 11-07 100-1 T Stephenson Lw; a bhnd; outpcd when jmpd slow 12; no ch aft
[1249¹]	8	10	Mr Grimsdale (IRE) 12-02 11-2 T Scudamore Lw; prom til rdn 9; nt r.o frm 12; rem 7th 15
[1400¹]	9	16	Wanstead (IRE) 12-00 16-1 J Jukes Midfield early; drpd to rr 10; t.o 15
[871U]	10	2	River Ferdinand (IRE) 11-07 100-1 Miss R Illman A towards rr; strugg 11; t.o when blun 15
[1336²]	P		Dainty Man (IRE) 11-07 25-1 A Dalton Bhnd; some hdwy 9; wknd 12; t.o & pu 3 out

TIME: 5min 57.8s TOTE: £5.50; places £1.80,£1.90,£4.10 Ex: £38.10 CSF: £32.86 Tri: £84.30

Bangor (LH 9F,18J)
Sat, 20 May (GOOD)

1559 North Western Area P-t-P Championship Final HC
10 ran

[1073¹]	1		LORD HARRY (IRE) 11-08 (1) 10-11F A Crow Sn 2nd/3rd; 4th 13-15; eff nxt; ld & jmpd untidy 2 out; 6l clr last; stayed on wl; comf
[1408²]	2	7	My Nominee 11-11 (bl) 25-1 R Burton Ld; rdn & hdd app 12; no ex app last
[1529¹]	3	1¼	Garryspillane (IRE) 11-09 16-1 G Hanmer Hld up towards rr; eff to chse ldrs 16; 7l 4th app 2 out; stayed on one pce
[1319²]	4	6	Murphys Way 11-02 40-1 J Burley Settled in tch; hit 8; went 3rd 9; mist 11 (water); chsd ldr aft til wknd 3 out; 4th when mist last
[1148¹]	5	5	The Crooked Oak 11-07 33-1 G Thomas Hld up in tch; eff 15; 5th & btn nxt
[1343¹]	6	11	Rolfes Delight 11-11 9-4 C Williams Handy; disp 3rd & rdn 14; wknd qckly 3 out; disapp
[904¹]	7	dist	Three Potato Four 11-07 20-1 Mrs M Barlow Mist 2 (water); sn lost tch; t.o 7
[1343⁶]	P		Corkers Flame (IRE) 11-11 100-1 R Bevan Cl up; 4th 9; 6th & wkng when blun 12; t.o & pu 3 out
[1317¹]	P		Nothing Ventured 11-07 9-1 A Beedles Trckd ldrs til lost plce 9; t.o & pu 3 out
[1465³]	P		Red Spice 11-07 100-1 R Owen Bhnd; lost tch 7; sn pushed along; t.o when jb rt 10; pu 15

TIME: 6min 09.9s TOTE: £2.20; places £1.10,£1.70,£1.80 Ex: £19.10 CSF: £26.74

Dulverton West
Bratton Down (LH 8F,19J) Sat, 20 May (GOOD to FIRM)

1560 Confined
5 ran

[1515¹]	1		BUTLER JOHN (IRE) 1-5F N Harris Opened 1/3; lw; went 2nd 4; ld 6; blun 9; 3l clr & gng wl 3 out; r.o str; pushed out flat
[1514³]	2	15	Rasta Man 14-1 R Woollacott Ld to 6; chsd wnr rest of way; in vain pursuit frm 14; 3l down 3 out; no ch aft nxt

[1433^P]	3	50	**Mosside** 100-1 *Miss K Cook Nt keen in 4th; 12l down 6; 27l bhnd & u.p 11; t.o aft 15; lft 3rd 2 out*
[1472³]	4	4	**Master Kiwi (NZ)** 100-1 *Miss T Hayes (xnb) Tde; jmpd novicey & a poor last; 30l bhnd 10; t.o 15*
[1374²]	F		**Iranos (FR)** (bl) 9-2 *L Jefford Hit 2 hrd; chsd ldr to 4; 10l 3rd 6; same & no prog when fell 2 out*

OFFICIAL DISTANCES: 15l, dist TIME: 6min 10.0s

1561 Mixed Open, 12st   5 ran

[1470¹]	1		**MILLYHENRY** 8-11F *Miss C Tizzard Tchd 10/11; lw; ld 2-7; cl up til ld agn 16; drew 6l ahd 3 out & 12l clr nxt; kpt on wl; rdn out*
[1374¹]	2	20	**Mizyan (IRE)** 7-4 *Miss P Gundry Tchd 2s; lw; prom; ld til outj 16; rdn & outpcd nxt; hld when nt fluent 2 out & last*
[1386¹]	3	20	**Just Bert (IRE)** 5-1 *Miss T Cave Ld til hit 2; rdn 3; nt fluent 7; jmpd slow 8; 8l 3rd 10; rdn nxt; nvr nr ldrs aft; 20l 3rd 3 out*
[1417⁶]	U		**Haughton Lad (IRE)** 50-1 *Miss L Sweeting Lw; detach 4th; blun 5; 15l adrift 7; blun 9 & ur some way aft*
	P		**Newt** (5a) 200-1 *D Doyne-Ditmas Jmpd competent in last; sn outpcd; t.o 10; pu 12*

OFFICIAL DISTANCES: 15l, 15l TIME: 6min 03.8s

1562 Dodson & Horrell PPORA Club Members, 12st   11 ran

[1369¹]	1		**MINE'S A GIN (IRE)** (7x) 2-1F *Miss J Cumings Tchd 3s; sn ld & oft jw; jnd brief 2 out; drvn & kpt fndng ex flat*
[1059¹]	2	2½	**Bright Approach (IRE)** 12-1 *M Miller Hld up; hdwy 8; 4th 12; 8l 3rd 14; eff to chall 3 out; 2½l 3rd aft nxt; went 2nd last; rdn & no imp*
[1467¹]	3	12	**One Boy** 11-2 *A Honeyball 12s-11/2; drpd out last to 6; hdwy 8; last agn 12; outpcd 16; str rn frm 2 out to snatch 3rd*
[1432³]	5	hd	**Hillhead (IRE)** (7x) 7-1 *J Barnes Prsd wnr; nt fluent 14; 3l down 3 out; dem nxt & one pce; lkd to fin 4th - btn hd for 3rd*
[1433^P]	6	4½	**Uckerby Lad** 20-1 *C Heard Chsd ldrs; outpcd in 10l 5th 14; rallied to cl 5th 3 out; wknd aft nxt*
[883²]	7	4	**Its Grand** (bl) 33-1 *Mrs J Wilkinson (xnb) Rr til prog 6 & hdwy 12; sn lost plce agn; no ch frm 3 out*
[1433⁸]	8	4	**Bomba Charger** 16-1 *Richard Darke Prom; stumbled aft 5; hit 7; 4th 12; wknd aft nxt; mist 15; no ch 3 out*
[1471⁶]	9	3	**Single Man (NZ)** 50-1 *B Parsons 3rd 5; drpd back 8th 12; strugg aft; no ch 3 out*
[1473¹]	4d		**Stillmore Business** 5-2 *Miss P Gundry Lw; hld up; impd to 3rd 8; drpd back 7th 12; mist 16; rallied 3 out & w wnr nxt; 3rd & rdn when mist last; sn btn; officially 4th (lkd to fin hd & nk bhnd 3rd in 5th); disq - nt weigh-in*
[1388³]	P		**Arble March** (5a) 33-1 *N Harris Last by 8; lost tch & jmpd slow 10; t.o & pu 12*
[1370²]	P		**Vansell** (5a) 11-2 *L Jefford Towards rr but in tch til pu & dism 12; lame*

OFFICIAL DISTANCES: 2l, 5l TIME: 6min 10.6s
Stillmore Business was adjudged to have finished 4th, but was disqualified as the rider failed to weigh-in (had actually finished 5th); she was fined £40

1563 Restricted, 12st   11 ran

[1307¹]	1		**TEAM CAPTAIN** 13-8F *A Honeyball (xnb) Trckd ldng pr; 10l 3rd 14; clsd stdly gng wl aft 3 out; lft 2nd nxt; pushed into ld flat; rdly*
[1258^P]	2	3	**Prah Sands** 8-1 *J Young Lw; tk keen hld; chsd ldr aft 2 til lft in ld 2 out; rdn & hdd aft last; nt qckn*
[1376³]	3	15	**Pallingham Lad (IRE)** (tt) 7-1 *M Miller Tchd 10s; trckd ldrs; 5th 12; 15l 4th & outpcd 14; lft mod 3rd 2 out; unable to cl*
[1240²]	4	4	**Barton Rose** 6-1 *D Alers-Hankey 12s-6s; nt a fluent; chsd ldrs; 4th 12; 18l 3rd & outpcd 14; nvr on terms aft*
[1456¹]	5	8	**Lucky Man** 10-1 *Miss K Lovelace 20s-10s; midfield; 6th 12; wknd nxt & strugg in rr frm 14; plodded on*
[1206^P]	P		**Flaming Cold (IRE)** (5a) 6-1 *Miss P Gundry Ld & jmpd v slow 1 & 2; sn lost plce; towards rr when pu & dism 6*
[655¹]	F		**Jimmy The One (NZ)** 6-1 *C Heard (xnb) Chsd ldrs; mist 10; 7th 12; lft last & lsng tch when fell 14*
[1376⁶]	U		**Knock Star (IRE)** 16-1 *S Partridge Hdwy to ld aft 2; 1l ahd but lkng vulnerable when ur 2 out*
[1376^U]	P		**Prudent Miner** (3ow) 33-1 *R Skinner Last when hit 4 & lost tch; t.o 7; pu 13*
[1258^P]	P		**Sparkling Cascade (IRE)** (5a) 10-1 *R Woollacott A bhnd; 8th 12; wl bhnd aft; t.o & pu flat*

[1094¹] P   **Suba Lin** (5a) 25-1 D Luff *Sn strugg; 20l 10th 6; t.o 10; pu 12*

OFFICIAL DISTANCES: 2l, 12l **TIME:** 6min 16.6s

1564 Open Maiden (Div 1), 12st
12 ran

[1303²] 1   **MEL (IRE)** 7-4F Miss M Eames *Prom; ld 2-9; ld agn 16 til hdd & lft in ld nxt; 6l clr 2 out; plugged on game*

[1376ᴾ] 2   8   **Another Bula (IRE)** 20-1 Miss S Robinson *Chsd ldrs; 4th 12; in tch 16; lft 4th nxt; 12l 4th 2 out; kpt on; went 2nd aft last; no ch w wnr*

[1469ᵁ] 3   hd   **Mayhem** (5a) 8-1 M Sweetland *Ld to 4; lost plce to 6th 9; rallied to 4th 16; lft 3rd nxt; 9l down & no imp 2 out*

[1131ᴾ] 4   10   **Calvary Hill** 25-1 D Doyne-Ditmas *(xnb) Prom; ld 12-14; lft 2nd 3 out; 6l down nxt; wknd last*

[1519⁴] 5   20   **Budghill** 5-1 C Heard *Nt jw in rr; 18l 9th 10; nvr nr ldrs aft*

[1469ᴿ] 6   12   **Jazetason** 33-1 M Woodward *Mist 4; nt fluent in midfield; 6th 12; lost tch 14*

[1372ᶠ] F   **All-Inclusive (IRE)** (5a) 6-1 J Scott *A wl bhnd & nt jw; last & mist 6; 25l 10th 10; t.o 14 til fell 2 out; rmtd & went crashing thro crowd on run-in*

[1468³] U   **County Derry** 7-1 B O'Doherty *Towards rr when nrly fell & ur 2*

         P   **Holcombe Handsel** (5a) 12-1 A Honeyball *School in rr; 15l 8th 10; t.o 16; pu last*

[1469ᴾ] P   **Irish Brush (IRE)** (5a) 6-1 G Barfoot-Saunt *Bhnd early then tk str hld in midfield; mist 5; 13l 7th 10; wl bhnd when pu 14*

[1308ᶠ] F   **Speck** 6-1 J O'Rourke *Rcd keen; ld/disp frm 4; 11 up when fell 3 out*

[722ᴾ] F   **Travelling Jack** (4a) 10-1 J Young *Sn bhnd; terrible mist 8 & t.o aft; jmpd violent rt 13; hopelessly t.o when crawled nxt; fell 16*

OFFICIAL DISTANCES: 8l, 3l **TIME:** 6min 28.8s

1565 Open Maiden (Div 2), 12st
14 ran

         1   **COOL WAGER** 14-1 D Alers-Hankey *Prom; ld 6 & jw aft; 3l ahd 2 out; rdn along & kpt on wl aft; quite comf*

[957ᴾ] 2   10   **Jentar Equilibra (IRE)** (5a) 6-1 R Woollacott *Tchd 9s; midfield; 6th 10; eff in 4th 15 & 3l 3rd 3 out; chsd wnr frm nxt; rdn & no imp*

[1278ᵁ] 3   12   **The Ugly Gunner** 5-1 E Gretton *Settled 3rd/4th; lft 2nd 14; 11 down nxt; dem 4l 3rd 2 out; rdn & no resp last; edged lft flat*

[1100ᶠ] 4   5   **Sea Spirit** (5a) 10-1 Miss T Cave *Hld up towards rr; 7th 10; eff to 3rd 15; 4l 4th 3 out; wknd nxt*

[1373ᴾ] U   **Can't Be Scrabble** 33-1 R Emmett *Mist 5; jmpd sketchy in rr aft til mist & ur 8*

[1102³] P   **Church Field (IRE)** 50-1 D Luff *Ld 2-6; prom; 4th when mist 10; wknd 13; t.o last when jmpd v slow 15; lkd to pu 3 out; cont; pu flat*

[1521ᴾ] P   **Elegant Wolf** 50-1 J Young *Sn t.o; pu 12*

[738ᶠ] F   **Goforitgirl** (5a) 4-1 Miss P Gundry *10s-4s; ld til jmpd slow 2; prsd wnr aft; cl 2nd when slpd & fell 14*

[1468ᶠ] P   **Green Anker** 14-1 G Maundrell *Midfield; 5th 10; wkng when pu 14*

[724²] P   **Melroy (IRE)** 10-1 D Doyne-Ditmas *Sn bhnd; t.o & pu 10*

[1308ᵁ] S   **Prussian Steel (IRE)** 5-4F M Miller *5th 4; slpd up turn aft 5*

[539ᶠ] P   **Thornbird** (5a) 20-1 C Heard *Bhnd; poor 9th 10; pu 12*

[562⁵] F   **Typical Woman (IRE)** (5a) 14-1 C White *Bckwd; fell 2*

         P   **Wayward Spree** 20-1 A Honeyball *Novicey in rr; 8th 10; lft t.o 5th 15; pu 3 out*

OFFICIAL DISTANCES: 8l, 10l **TIME:** 6min 24.4s

1566 Hunt (with Exmoor)
5 ran

[1305³] 1   **WIBBLEY WOBBLEY** 1-3F Miss J Cumings *Ld to 2; chsd tearaway til lft 10l clr 9; jmpd slow 12 & hrd prsd aft; jmpd slow 3 out; drew rt away aft nxt; v easy*

[1467⁴] 2   30   **Button Up Bill** 16-1 H Thomas *3rd til lft 2nd 9; chall 13; jnd wnr brief 3 out; hopelessly outpcd frm nxt*

[1111⁷] 3   8   **And Why Not** 50-1 P Picton-Warlow *Poor 4th til lft 25l 3rd 9; plodded on & gvn little assist*

[1280²] 4   150yd   **Pendragon** (vis) 6-1 A Jackson *(xnb) Jmpd poor in rem last; 33l adrift 10; wl t.o 14*

         U   **Move A Minute (USA)** 9-2 G Shenkin *10s-9/2; ld aft 2 & bolted clr; furlong ahd when nrly fell & ur 9*

OFFICIAL DISTANCES: 30l, 6l **TIME:** 6min 40.7s

Tredegar Farmers
Bassaleg (RH 8F,19J) Sat, 20 May (FIRM becoming GOOD/FIRM)

1567 Hunt, 12st 1 ran

[1295^P]	1		HAL'S PRINCE (7x) Miss P Jones Walked over (rdr's 200th P-t-P wnr)

OFFICIAL DISTANCE: Walked over

1568 Restricted, 12st 11 ran

[1405¹] 1   BARAN ITSU 5-2 P Sheldrake 4s-5/2; ld 4; clr 2 out; r.o wl
[1454¹] 2 5 Welsh Warrior 2-1F T Vaughan A.p; mist 6; 2l 3rd ½way; went 5l 2nd & rdn aft 2 out; no imp
[1453²] 3 20 Itscinders (5a) 13-2 J Jukes Went 2nd 5; ev ch 3 out; rdn & wknd rap aft nxt
[1298P] 4 1 Colebrook Willie 40-1 J Cook Lw; hld up; 10l 8th ½way; mist 11; 12l 8th 13; lost tch 15; stayed on frm 2 out; nvr nr to chall
[1404¹] 5 6 Guard A Dream (IRE) 9-2 A Price 2nd til lost plce 4; 5l 7th ½way; 10l 7th 13; eff in 9l 4th 15; wknd 3 out
[1452P] 6 12 Sea Search 50-1 Miss L Pearce Chsd ldrs; 3l 4th ½way; 6l 4th 13; wknd to 10l 5th 15; t.o
[1453U] 7 ½ Under Milk Wood 50-1 G Maloney (xnb) Chsd ldrs; mist 1; 4l 6th ½way; 7½l 6th 13; wknd to 12l 6th 15; t.o
[1453P] P   Brewery Lane (IRE) 10-1 Julian Pritchard Ld to 4; lost plce 6; rallied & 3½l 5th ½way; 7l 5th 13; wknd to 15l 7th 15; t.o & pu 3 out
[1400R] P   Not For Profit (IRE) (tt) 10-1 E Williams Hld up; 14l 9th when pu 9; lame
[1400F] P   Saronica-R (5a) 40-1 J Price A bhnd; 20l 9th ½way; t.o 13; pu 15
[1452P] P   Travel Safely (IRE) 10-1 J Keen Hld up; 10th when mist 5; 12l 9th when pu aft 10; dead

OFFICIAL DISTANCES: 4l, 12l **TIME:** 6min 14.7s

1569 Confined, 12st 5 ran

[1449¹] 1   ROMAN GALE (IRE) 5-1 A Price (bf) Hld up; 5l 3rd ½way; jnd ldrs 11; went 2nd aft nxt; ld 14; drvn out
[1297⁶] 2 4 Whistling Buck (IRE) (5x) (tt) 12-1 J Jukes Hld up; 7l 4th ½way; hdwy to 4l 3rd 15; jnd wnr 16; rdn & ev ch when jmpd slow last; nt rec
[597¹] 3 30 Rave-On-Hadley (IRE) (11x) 4-9F E Williams Ld to 6 & 7-10; 4l 3rd & shkn up 14; went 3l 2nd nxt; 2l 3rd when mist 4 out; sn wknd
[1450F] P   Desmond Gold (IRE) 25-1 M Barber Mist 2; sn wl bhnd; t.o 7; pu 10
[1567¹] P   Hal's Prince (7x) 5-1 Julian Pritchard Mist 3; 2nd til ld 6; hdd & hit 7; ld 10; hit 13; hdd 14; wknd to 6l 4th nxt; bhnd when pu 3 out

OFFICIAL DISTANCES: 4l, dist **TIME:** 6min 13.3s

1570 Mixed Open, 12st 5 ran

[1402¹] 1   COOLVAWN LADY (IRE) (5a) 11-10F J Jukes 6/4-11/10; jw; ww; hdwy 6; went 2nd 9; ld 14; drew wl clr 16; easy
[1451¹] 2 25 Cream Supreme (IRE) 13-8 E Williams Hld up & bhnd; 20l 4th ½way; went 15l 3rd 14; no imp when mist 15; went poor 2nd aft 2 out
[1401²] 3 15 Warren Boy 7-2 Julian Pritchard Ld til hdd 14; 7l 2nd & wkng when mist 16; v tired & dem aft 2 out
[1447⁸] 4 15 Savuti (IRE) (tt) 100-1 Miss E Jones Tde; 2nd to 9; 5l 3rd ½way; wknd 13; t.o
[1402²] P   Sun Of Chance 66-1 Miss A Meakins Sn wl bhnd; t.o 5; blun 9; pu last

OFFICIAL DISTANCES: dist, 12l **TIME:** 6min 05.8s

1571 Dodson & Horrell PPORA Club Members (Nov Rdrs), 12st 7 ran

[1450¹] 1   ANORAK (USA) 4-9F J Cook Ww; went 2nd 7; ld 9-11; ld 12; qcknd 8l clr 16; comf
[1451¹] 2 10 Silverfort Lad (IRE) 10-1 T Faulkner 14s-10s; ld til hdd 7; 2nd/3rd til ld 11; hdd 12; outpcd 15; rdn 2 out; no imp
[1051P] 3 15 Side Bar 50-1 M Parry Mist 3; drpd to rr & rmdrs 6; 5th ½way; went 10l 4th 12 & 3rd 15; plodded on
[1402⁵] 4 20 Local Customer 50-1 Miss S Matthews Steered erratic course; sn prom; went 2nd 6; ld 7-9; 3rd ½way; wknd 12; 17l 5th 14; t.o
[1338P] P   High Guardian (7x) 9-4 A Hardacre Nvr gng wl; 7th ½way; wl bhnd 11; 25l 6th 13; t.o & pu 15
[1451P] P   Minstrel Fire (IRE) 33-1 D Hughes Rmdrs 3; 6th ½way; wl bhnd 11; 30l 7th 13; t.o & pu 14

[1399R] F   **Swan's Wish (IRE)** 25-1 **G Thorne** *2nd/3rd to 7; 4th ½way; 2l 3rd 13; wkng when mist 15; rem 4th & v tired when fell last*

OFFICIAL DISTANCES: 8l, 12l   **TIME:** 6min 25.7s

1572 Intermediate, 12st

3 ran

[1452¹]   1   **STAR CHASER** 2-5F **J Cook** *2nd til ld 3; hdd 5; ld 6; 8l clr ½way; went 12l up 11; unchall*

     2   12   **Itsstormingnorma** (5a) 11-4 **J Jukes** *Swtng; ld to 3 & 5-6; no imp frm 12; rdn 2 out; no ch w wnr*

[1449P]   3   4   **Chantingo Lad** 6-1 **A Price** (xnb) *Hld up; 15l 3rd ½way; eff & disp 15l 2nd 3 out; no ex*

OFFICIAL DISTANCES: 12l, 3l   **TIME:** 6min 33.8s

1573 Open Maiden (Div 1), 12st

6 ran

[1302U]   1   **MIKE'S DREAM** 5-4F **T Vaughan** *Made all; mist 14; drew clr 2 out; mist last; unchall*

[1404⁴]   2   6   **Tudor Flight** (5a) 8-1 **S Blackwell** (xnb) *Hld up; 6l 3rd ½way; went 2nd & mist 11; 4l 3rd 13; 7l 3rd when mist 16; went 8l 2nd aft 2 out; no imp*

[1404²]   3   15   **Albert The Lion (IRE)** 6-4 **C Williams** (xnb) *5n-6/4; sn prom; lft 2nd bend aft 4-11; chsd wnr 13 til wknd qckly aft 2 out*

[1404³]   4   10   **Double Steal** (bl,tt) 6-1 **E Williams** *10s-6s; hld up & bhnd; mist 8; 8l 4th ½way; mist 11; lost tch & mist 13; blun 14; wknd 16*

[1405²]   F   **Queen's Equa** (5a) (bl) 14-1 **Miss S Major** *5th when fell 4; broke leg; dead*

[1464P]   S   **Sister Jim** (5a) (bl) 33-1 **S Graham** *2nd til slpd up bend aft 4*

OFFICIAL DISTANCES: 6l, 10l   **TIME:** 6min 44.3s

           Fence 12 omitted - fallen horse; Georgie Grace (T Faulkner 33-1) was withdrawn not under orders

1574 Open Maiden (Div 2), 12st

10 ran

     1   **ITSTHEJONESBOY** 7-1 **J Jukes** *Made virt all; r.o game u.p frm 2 out*

[1406⁴]   2   ¾   **Tommyknocker (IRE)** 4-1 **C Williams** *A.p; 2l 3rd ½way; went 2nd 11; disp ld 14; mist 16; rdn & ev ch last; nt qckn*

[1405F]   3   3   **Clonshire Castle (IRE)** (tt) 6-4F **J Keen** (bh)*Ww; 5l 7th ½way; 8l 5th 14; 5l 6th 3 out; eff on bit 2 out; ev ch app last; fnd nil*

[1456⁶]   4   4   **Satco Supreme (IRE)** 25-1 **I Johnson** *Hld up; 6l 4th ½way; jnd ldrs; disp ld 14; lost plce & 4l 5th when mist 3 out; one pce*

[1457⁶]   P   **Arctic Ridge** (tt) 25-1 **D Hughes** *Sn prom; went 2nd 6; disp ld 8-10; 5l 4th when mist 14; eff & 2l 3rd when mist 3 out; wknd qckly nxt; pu last*

[1055U]   U   **Chesnut Wood** 10-1 **M Barber** *8th when ur 1*

[1457P]   S   **Hill Top Flyer (IRE)** 25-1 **G Maloney** *Ss; jmpd v slow 1; bhnd til slpd up bend aft 4*

[1300P]   P   **Parsons Secret** (5a) 6-1 **T Vaughan** *2nd til mist 5; mists 7 & 10; lost plce & 9l 5th ½way; lost tch u.p 11; pu 12*

[1454U]   P   **Tarian (USA)** 40-1 **M Parry** (bf) *Ss; wl bhnd til pu 8*

[1454⁵]   P   **Tiny** (12a) 6-1 **E Williams** (xnb) *Hld up; jmpd slow 6; blun bad 7; 12l 6th ½way; mist 13; hdwy & 7l 5th 15; 3½l 4th 3 out; wknd 2 out; pu flat*

OFFICIAL DISTANCES: ½l, 3l   **TIME:** 6min 51.0s

Haydon

Hexham (LH 8F,19J)   Sun, 21 May (GOOD to SOFT becoming SOFT)

1575 Hunt, 12st

1 ran

[1363P]   1   **LUVLY BUBBLY** (5x) **Miss C Hall** *Walked over*

OFFICIAL DISTANCE: Walked over

1576 Confined, 12st

7 ran

[1445P]   1   **ALLRITE PET** (5a) 6-4F **Miss P Robson** *Mid-div; 3l 5th app 10; eff to ld aft 16; 3l clr nxt; 1l up last; hld on wl*

[1364P]   2   ½   **Miss Portcello** (5a) 3-1 **Miss J Hollands** *Trckd ldrs; 5l 3rd 2; jmpd to ld 9; hdd 12; 4l 4th & sltly outpcd aft 16; rallied aft nxt to 1l 2nd at last; r.o flat; just hld*

[1429⁵]   3   12   **Allrite Bonny Lass** (5a) 7-1 **L Morgan** *Chsd ldrs; rmdrs aft 7; 3l 3rd 16; 6l 3rd & no ex 2 out*

[1498¹]   4   20   **Dean Deifir (IRE)** 3-1 **C Storey** (xnb) *In tch in rr til trckd ldrs 7; 2l 3rd 9; ld aft 11; jnd 16 & sn hdd; tired & jmpd slow last; virt bu flat*

[1476P]   r   **Branch End** (bl) 33-1 **T Scott** *Ld aft 1; 4l up 4; mist & hdd 9; mist nxt; 6l last & pushed along 11; lsng tch when ref 13*

[1325⁴] **P**   **Denim Blue** 20-1 M Clayton *Rr; 9l last 2; 5l 6th 11; outpcd 14; 15l 5th & strugg nxt; wl bhnd when pu 2 out*

[1366⁴] **P**   **The Caffler (IRE)** 33-1 Miss R Ramsay *Tde; ld to 1; trckd ldr; ½l 2nd 4; 4l 4th 9; mist nxt; rdn 12; 16l 6th & outpcd 15; wl bhnd when pu 3 out*

OFFICIAL DISTANCES: ¾l, 15l TIME: 7min 10.0s

1577 Restricted, 12st   13 ran

[1445¹⁰]	**1**		**ERNI (FR)** (vis) 8-1 W Burnell *12s-8s; rr; pulled to ld 9; jnd 16; 4l up 2 out; stayed on wl; mist last*
[1230ᴾ]	**2**	6	**Deer Park Lass (IRE)** (5a) 3-1 C Mulhall *Rr; 4l 7th 8; prog to disp ld 16; 4l 2nd & outpcd app 2 out*
[1081²]	**3**	15	**Nickys Peril** (5a) 5-4F T Davidson *(xnb) Prom; ½l 2nd 6; ld/disp 7-16; sn dem 3rd; 5l 3rd & no ex 2 out*
[1335ᴾ]	**4**	8	**Primitive Charles** (bl) 11-2 G Brewer *Hld up in rr; last 7; 3l 6th 8; outpcd aft 14; 12l 4th & wkng 16; 20l 5th 3 out; drvn out for poor 4th*
[1445⁸]	**5**	2	**Border Glory** 8-1 P Maitland-Carew *In tch; 8l off pce 8; 4l 5th 10; outpcd 14; 15l 5th & btn 16; went 4th 3 out til dem flat*
[1575¹]	**6**	15	**Luvly Bubbly** 33-1 Miss C Hall *2nd outing; prom; 2l off pce 7; outpcd 14 & sn bhnd; kpt on one pce*
[1479ᶠ]	**P**		**Aughrim Quest (IRE)** (5a,2ow) 66-1 T Glass *Prom early; 4l 4th 4; outpcd aft 12; sn lost tch; pu 3 out*
[1363ᴾ]	**P**		**Disrespect** (5a) 100-1 Miss M Macmillan *Chsd ldrs; 8l last app 9; lost tch; pu aft 14*
[1501ᵁ]	**P**		**Kings Token** 14-1 J Walton *Trckd ldrs; 1l 3rd 6; 2l 3rd nxt; wknd 11; bhnd when pu aft 14*
[1475⁴]	**P**		**La Emni (IRE)** 10-1 S Charlton *A rr; 8l last app 2; outpcd 14 & strugg aft; sn bhnd & pu 2 out*
[686ᴾ]	**P**		**More Joy** 12-1 S Bowden *(bf) Chsd ldrs; ld aft 2; ½l up 6; sn hdd & strugg; pu aft 11*
[1474²]	**P**		**Prince Moshar** 50-1 L Morgan *Mounted on course; tde & ld to start; a rr; lsng tch when blun 12; pu aft*
[1363³]	**P**		**Tenella's Last** (5a) 25-1 R Morgan *Prom early; mist & rmdr 5; pushed along 9; lsng tch 11; strugg & pu aft 14*

OFFICIAL DISTANCES: 8l, 12l TIME: 7min 16.0s

1578 Mens Open, 12st   8 ran

[1160³]	**1**		**STEEL RIGG (IRE)** (7x) 7-2 M Clayton *4s-7/2; 2½l 4th 3; 7l 7th app 10; prog to 2l 2nd 12; 1l 2nd & mist 16; sn ld; 6l clr last; stayed on wl u.p*
[1428⁴]	**2**	4	**Wudimp** 9-4F C Storey *In tch; disp 5th 4; 5l 4th aft 8; outpcd app 3 out; stayed on agn frm 2 out; rdn to 2nd at last; nt rch ldr*
[1498³]	**3**	3	**Fiscal Policy** 4-1 R Trotter *(bf) 9/2-4s; ld/disp til 2l 3rd 6; 3l 3rd & ev ch 3 out; outpcd*
[1151ᶠ]	**4**	3	**Corbleu (IRE)** 10-1 M Walford *Hld up in rr; last 8; prog to 8l 5th 16; short-lived eff 3 out; one pce*
[1476³]	**5**	3	**Lottery Ticket (IRE)** (7x) 100-1 S J Robinson *Trckd ldrs til disp ld aft 8; ld 10-16; 2l 2nd & wkng 3 out*
[1498ᴿ]	**P**		**Chan The Man** 25-1 A Richardson *In tch in rr; 8l 7th 8; pulling & some prog aft 9; 5l 6th & rmdr 10; lsng tch when mist 12; strugg & pu 14*
[1365²]	**P**		**Excise Man** (7x) (tt) 3-1 J Walton *Oht; chsd ldrs; disp 5th 4; pushed along & mist 12; 15l 6th & lsng tch aft 14; t.o 6th 3 out; pu 2 out*
[1428⁷]	**P**		**Fordstown (IRE)** (7x) 12-1 J Alexander *20s-12s; ld/disp til ld 6; jnd 8; hit 9; hdd 10; mist 11; outpcd aft 13; 20l 7th & lsng tch 14; t.o 3 out; pu nxt*

OFFICIAL DISTANCES: 3½l, 2½l TIME: 7min 18.0s

1579 Ladies Open   7 ran

[1426³]	**1**		**RIPARIUS (USA)** 5-2 Miss P Robson *4s-5/2; sn handy; prog to ½l 2nd 15; prsd ldr til ld app 2 out; sn clr; eased flat*
[1426ᴾ]	**2**	6	**Nova Nita** (5a) 8-1 Mrs V Jackson *Trckd ldr 6; ld 7; hdd aft 8; 6l 3rd & outpcd 15; 10l 3rd & staying on 3 out; went 2nd flat; nt trble wnr*
[1426¹]	**3**	5	**Balisteros (FR)** 1-2F Miss J Wormall *Rr; 4th & hdwy 7; ld 9; hrd prsd 16; hdd & mist 2 out; wknd & dem flat*
[1497¹]	**4**	12	**Pharmistice (IRE)** 8-1 Miss N Stirling *2 handlers; hld up; 8l last 2; prog to disp ld aft 8; 2½l 4th nxt; 10l 4th & outpcd 15; kpt on*
[1343⁸]	**5**	25	**Miss Accounts (IRE)** (5a) 33-1 Miss A Armitage *Unruly gng to post; ld early; 11 up 3; lost plce 6 & 7l last nxt; 12l last & lsng tch 10; t.o frm 3 out*
[1364ᴿ]	**P**		**Houselope Beck** 12-1 Miss C Hall *Collided w running rail gng to start; trckd ldrs; 3l 3rd 3; mostly 4/5th aft; 2½l 5th app 12; outpcd & lsng tch 13; pu 15*

[1497²] P   **Tropnevad** (bl) 33-1 Miss J Hollands *Cl up til ld aft 4; hdd & outpcd 8; 7l 6th nxt; 10l 6th & wkng 11; pu 13*

OFFICIAL DISTANCES: 8l, 6l TIME: 7min 07.0s

1580 Open Maiden 8yo&up   8 ran

[1329³] 1   **DEERHUNTER** 5-2 G Tuer *(bf) Handy; gng wl in 6l 5th 8; prog to ½l 2nd aft 14; ld app 3 out; sn qcknd 10l clr; eased flat*

[1500ᴾ] 2   25   **Meadowleck** (5a) (tt) 25-1 T Davidson *(bf) Trckd ldrs; disp 11 2nd 4; lft disp ld aft 10; ld 12; sn hdd; 8l 3rd 3 out; kpt on to 2nd at last*

[1480ᴾ] 3   25   **Hetty Bell** (5a) 50-1 A Richardson *In tch in rr; 6l 7th 8; outpcd 12 & sn bhnd; 25l 5th 3 out; one pce & lft to.3rd by defectors*

[1500²] 4   25   **Paperback Writer** (5a) (vis) 3-1 A Robson *Spurs; trckd ldr; 11 2nd 9; lft disp ld aft nxt; hit 12 & outpcd; 15l 6th & wkng qckly 15; to 3 out*

[1081ᴿ] U   **A Monkey For Dick** (IRE) 50-1 J Dixon *Oht; 3 handlers; unruly; mounted on course; jmpd big at times; pulled to ld aft 1; 2l up 6; blun & ur 15yds aft 10*

         P   **Desert Devil** 6-1 M Clayton *Pulling & prom; disp 11 2nd 4; wknd 9; pu 11*

[1500ᵁ] P   **Harleyburn** (bl) 7-4F Mrs A Hamilton *Prom; trckd ldr 6; 2l 3rd 9; lft disp ld aft nxt; ld app 13-16; wknd qckly; strugg in 2nd when pu last*

[1353⁷] P   **The Noble Rebel** (IRE) 50-1 A Pennock *A rr; 8l last 3; hit 11 & lost iron; pushed along & sn bhnd; 25l 4th 3 out; pu last*

OFFICIAL DISTANCES: 30l, 20l TIME: 7min 40.0s

1581 Open Maiden 56&7yo (Div 1), 2m4f, 12st - 14J   8 ran

[1556ᴾ] 1   **MAGICAL POITIN** (IRE) (5a) 8-1 A Richardson *(bnh) Oht; disp cl 3rd til prsd ldr 11; ld aft 12; 2l up last; r.o; comf*

         2   5   **Pillaging Pict** (7a) 2-1 J Walton *5/2-2s; chsd ldrs; 3l 4th & mist 3; prog to ld app 10-12; cl 2nd til mist 2 out; 2l down & hld last; improve*

[1499ᵁ] 3   30   **Test Of Loyalty** evensF A Robson *5/4-evens; went to 3m start; ld early; cl 2nd 3 til 3l 3rd 11; sn outpcd; 15l last 3 out*

[1480⁶] P   **Almikino** (IRE) 12-1 S Brisby *16s-12s; rr; 6l last 3; 4l 6th 6; mist nxt; outpcd 9; lsng tch when hit 11; 20l 4th 3 out; strugg & pu nxt*

[1331⁶] r   **Ben From Ketton** (7a,4ow) 10-1 S J Robinson *Ld aft 1 til hdd app 10; sn outpcd; wl bhnd when ref & ur last*

[1153ᴾ] P   **B J Bubbles** 12-1 J R Barlow *20s-12s; oht; disp cl 3rd early; strugg & lsng tch 7; 15l off pce when pu aft 9*

[1474ᵁ] P   **Say Sadie** (5a) 8-1 M Clayton *A rr; 8l last 2; jmpd slow nxt; some prog to 5l 6th & mist 7; sn strugg; pu aft 10*

[1501²] P   **Sledmere** (IRE) (7a) 4-1 T Scott *6s-4s; rr early; sn disp cl 3rd; outpcd & lsng tch 9; pu aft 11*

OFFICIAL DISTANCES: 6l, dist TIME: 5min 45.0s

1582 Open Maiden 56&7yo (Div 2), 2m4f, 12st - 14J   8 ran

[499⁵]   1   **PRINCE OF PERILS** 10-1 T Davidson *Hld up; 15l 7th aft 3; prog to cl 6th 8; drpd back 15l 4th aft 11; smooth hdwy to 8l 4th aft 3 out; chall last; sn ld; r.o*

[1367ᴾ] 2   3½   **On Merit** 5-2F T Oates *Ld; jmpd sticky at times; hdd 3 out; disp when lft in ld agn nxt; 2l up app last; one pce & hdd flat*

[1480⁷] 3   5   **Lewesdon Countess** (5a) 20-1 W Burnell *Chsd ldrs; 6l 4th 4; 10l 3rd 11; eff to 4l 3rd 3 out; ev ch til outpcd app last; one pce*

[913⁹]   4   30   **Snitton South** 6-1 J Walton *Tubed; prom; 3l 2nd 3; disp 3l 3rd 7; outpcd 9; 15l 7th & wkng aft nxt; to 2 out*

[1349⁶] F   **Arctic Corner** (5a) 7-2 A Pennock *4s-7/2; dism start; sis; a rr; 20l last 2; jmpd lft 6 & sn t.o; rmdr app 9; fell 10; winded*

[1431ᶠ] P   **Billieburn** 7-2 L Morgan *Bleeding frm chest & mounted late; unruly & ur start; ld in; pulling in 12l 5th app 4; 2l 2nd 9; ev ch til wknd qckly 11; 25l 5th when pu 3 out*

[1122³] P   **Solway Saffy** (12a) (tt) 3-1 C Storey *Trckd ldrs; disp 3l 3rd 7; outpcd 9 & sn bhnd; strugg when pu 3 out*

[1431ᴾ] F   **Star Design** (IRE) 8-1 M Clayton *Chsd ldrs; 9l 4th & jmpd slow 4; prog to trck ldr nxt; 3l 2nd 10; ld 3 out; jnd & fell nxt*

OFFICIAL DISTANCES: 3½l, 8l TIME: 5min 55.0s

Melton Hunt Club

Garthorpe (RH 8F,18J) Sun, 21 May (GOOD to SOFT)

1583 Club Members 12yo&up, 12st   10 ran

[1502¹]	1		**DONT TELL THE WIFE** 30-100F Miss G Hutchinson *Lw; v confid rdn; detach in last trio to 7; 111 5th & prog 10; went 2nd 14; ld app 3 out; sn 10l clr; r.o v str & virt solo aft; hvly eased flat; impressive*
[1503ᴾ]	2	35	**Nuns Cone** 66-1 T Lane *Ld 2-6; chsd ldr to 14; sn gave up & 25l 3rd 3 out; drvn & kpt on flat to snatch rem 2nd*
[1478ᴾ]	3	nk	**Sovereigns Match** (bl) 5-1 M Mackley *Tk keen hld & sn prom; pulled to ld 6; 7l clr 13; hdd app 3 out; imm outpcd; nt r.o frm 2 out; drvn out & dem flat*
[1285³]	4	30	**Spuffington** 50-1 A Campbell *Bhnd; 15l 8th 10; t.o 12*
[1503ᵁ]	5	6	**Tiderunner (IRE)** (bl) 40-1 A Sansome *Ld to 2; 9l 4th 10; lost tch aft nxt; 28l 4th 13; sn r.o*
[1523⁶]	6	1½	**Professor Longhair** 50-1 P Bennett *Nt keen & detach in last pr; rmdrs 3; jmpd poor; t.o 11*
[1482ᶠ]	7	½	**Grange Prize** 66-1 Mrs J Parris *Detach in last pr; 20l last 7; t.o 11; rdn & kpt on flat*
[968ᴾ]	8	15	**Real Progress (IRE)** 25-1 D Renney *Chsd ldrs early; 14l 7th & strugg 10; t.o 12*
[1349²]	R		**Nishkina** (vis) 20-1 C Cundall *Lw; prsd ldrs; 8l 3rd 10; jmpd slow nxt; 15l 4th & rdn when tk wrong course aft 12*
[1383ᴾ]	P		**Vulpin De Laugere (FR)** 66-1 N King *Mist 2; prsd ldrs til 12l 6th & rdn 10; nt r.o; t.o & pu 14*

OFFICIAL DISTANCES: dist, ½l **TIME:** 6min 23.0s **TOTE:** £1.20; places £1.10,£8.00,£1.10 **DF:** £nt won

1584 Club Members Conditional   16 ran

[1415³]	1		**JUST LIKE MADGE** (5a) 2-1F J Tarry *Trckd ldrs; 3rd 10; chall 3 out; ld nxt; rdn & kpt on game flat*
[1415ᶠ]	2	2	**Red Rebel** 4-1 B Pollock *Settled trckng ldrs; 7th 10; stdy hdwy 15 to 11 3rd 3 out; sust chall & ev ch frm nxt; rdn flat & nt go thro*
[1215⁴]	3	hd	**Smart Rhythm** (5a) 12-1 R Armson *Ld; rdn & hrd prsd 3 out; hdd nxt; drvn & kpt on wl flat*
[1415ᴾ]	4	6	**Barneys Gold (IRE)** 7-1 A Bealby *Prom; 5th 10; went 2nd aft 14; dem aft nxt & sn outpcd by ldng trio*
[1379²]	5	6	**Mackoy (IRE)** 25-1 M Gingell *Midfield; 8th 10; eff 13 to chse ldrs in 6th aft 15; 4th nxt; sn lost tch*
[1550²]	6	5	**Fern Leader** (bl) 20-1 Mrs J Hughes *Sn chsng ldrs; 6th 10; 5th & in tch aft 15; sn strugg*
[1416ᶠ]	7	8	**Needwood Neptune** 50-1 A Sansome *Nvr keen in rr & rdn most of way; 10th 10; lost tch 12*
[1421¹]	8	5	**Steel My Song** (5a) 20-1 S Morris *Tkn stdly in rr; 11th 10; eff in 8l 8th 15; drvn & btn nxt*
[1438ᵁ]	9	6	**Upton Orbit** 33-1 J Gasper *A wl bhnd; 13th 10; plodded rnd*
[1327⁵]	10	¾	**Final Beat (IRE)** 33-1 C Cundall *Sn bhnd; rdn aft 7; sev rmdrs & no resp aft; 12th 10; plodded on*
[1503³]	P		**Catchphrase** (vis) 20-1 L Hicks *Midfield; 9th 10; sn lost interest & strugg; t.o & pu 3 out*
[1207³]	P		**Folding** (tt) 33-1 J Oldring *Went 2nd 2 til wknd rap u.p 12; t.o & pu aft 15*
[1349³]	P		**Quiet Mistress** (5a) (bl) 33-1 T Lane *Prom in 3rd/4th; jmpd slow 10; went 3l 2nd 12; sn dem; rdn & wknd qckly 14; t.o & pu last*
[1415⁸]	P		**Rolpen** 25-1 R Lawther *Reluct & sn t.o in last pr; pu aft 15*
[1292ᶠ]	P		**Tan Hill Sparky** (5a) 50-1 A Coe *Fat; jmpd slow & poor; sn t.o; pu 13*
[798⁵]	P		**Wotstheproblem** 14-1 N Kent (xnb) *Lw; reluct; last trio & nvr gng wl; 14th & rdn 10; t.o & pu 12*

OFFICIAL DISTANCES: 1l, nk **TIME:** 6min 24.0s **TOTE:** £2.30; places £1.60,£1.30,£2.40, **DF:** £7.20

1585 Mens Open   8 ran

[1440¹]	1		**FRESH PRINCE** 2-5F Julian Pritchard *Lw; jw; made all; jmpd 3l clr 3 out; pushed out flat; rdly*
[1476ᶠ]	2	5	**Vital Issue (IRE)** 7-1 G Markham *Hld up; jmpd slow 5; went cl up 10; tk 3rd 12 & 2nd aft 15; chall & 11 down when outj 3 out; rdn & a hld aft*
[1436¹]	3	25	**Mr Dennehy (IRE)** 5-1 David Dennis *Prsd wnr to 8 & agn 11; dem 10l 3rd & wkng app 3 out*
[1232²]	4	½	**Misti Hunter (IRE)** 10-1 S Swiers *Ld rnd start; settled prom; 2nd 9-11; outpcd 13; 25l 4th app 3 out*

[1492ᴾ]	5	20	**Robsand (IRE)** 66-1 M Wilesmith *Sn 6th; clsd brief to press ldrs 10; wknd nxt; t.o aft 15*
[1378ᴾ]	6	4	**Royal Action** 25-1 P Chinery *Prom; 2nd when hit 8; ev ch 11; wkng when mist 13; jmpng went to pieces aft; t.o 3 out*
[1502ᴾ]	P		**Court Thyne (IRE)** 66-1 P Millington *A bhnd; rdn & lost tch 10; sn t.o; pu 12*
[1192ᴾ]	P		**Lord Kilton** 66-1 M Cowley (xnb) *Nt keen in last; clsd brief & wl in tch 10; sn gave up; t.o 13; pu aft 15*

OFFICIAL DISTANCES: 4l, 15l **TIME:** 6min 19.0s **TOTE:** £1.20; places £1.40,£1.50,£1.50 **DF:** £3.00

1586 Club Members Novices   11 ran

[1267¹]	1		**UNION MAN** 4-9F S Morris *Lw; made all; dived at 13; qcknd 15l clr on bridle 3 out; unchall aft; mist 2 out*
[1285¹]	2	12	**Hagon Beck** 16-1 W Wales *Settled 4/5th; outpcd 15; 2 11l 4th nxt; went 2nd aft 2 out; r.o wl but nvr nr wnr; fin lame*
[1504¹]	3	10	**Fortune Hunter (IRE)** 20-1 Miss A Burton *Hld up & detach in final trio; nt a fluent & mist 8; 10th 10; poor 6th 3 out; bst last but hopeless task*
[1530⁴]	4	8	**Cumberland Youth** 100-1 J Diment *Hit 7; prsd wnr & ev ch to 15; 20l 3rd & wl outpcd nxt; plodded on*
[1530ᵁ]	5	3	**Cashel Green (IRE)** (tt) 33-1 M Hewitt *Midfield; went 3rd 10; prsd ldrs til 5th, rdn & wkng aft 15; poor 5th nxt*
[1218¹]	6	nk	**Roly Poly (IRE)** 7-1 M Mackley *Jmpd slow 2; prsd ldrs & sn 3rd/4th; eff & 2nd 15; imm outpcd by wnr; wknd 2 out*
[1288¹]	7	6	**General Assembly (IRE)** 8-1 N Bloom *Lw; midfield; 6th 10; lost tch 12; t.o 3 out*
[1146⁴]	P		**Luckashan (IRE)** (7a) 6-1 B Pollock *Lw; hld up towards rr; 7th when mist 10; lsng plce when jmpd lft 11; 10th when pu 12*
[1505¹]	P		**Polly Live Wire** (5a) 14-1 P Millington (citation) *Unimpressive padd; hit 2; detach in last pr til 8th & eff 10; lost tch 12; t.o 15; pu 2 out*
[1438²]	P		**Rolcap** 25-1 R Lawther *Prom brief; drpd to rr & jmpd slow 8; 9th 10; nt keen aft & sn t.o; pu 13*
[1423ᵁ]	P		**Tarjumaan (USA)** 100-1 A Brown *Sn labouring in rr; t.o 8; pu 13*

OFFICIAL DISTANCES: 15l, 10l **TIME:** 6min 23.0s **TOTE:** £1.60; places £2.40,£1.70,£40.00 **DF:** £6.00

1587 Ladies Open   5 ran

[1483²]	1		**MALTBY SON** 9-2 Mrs T Hill *Cl up; 4l 3rd 3 out; ld nxt; rdn & duelled w rival aft; kpt on wl cl home; all out*
[1483ᴾ]	2	½	**Cill Churnain (IRE)** 33-1 Mrs E Coveney *Ld rnd start; lft in ld brief 3; nt fluent 5; kpt prsng til ld aft 11; rdn & hdd 3 out; drvn & kpt on wl; ev ch til no ex final 50yds (v ungenuine - gvn fine ride)*
[1266¹]	3	2¼	**Cittadino** 2-5F Mrs J Dawson *Lw; ld til blun bad & nrly ur 3; ld agn app 4 til nt fluent 11; mist 13 & a lkd in trble aft; blun 15; 8l 4th nxt; tried to rally in 3rd aft 2 out; no imp (lost shoe)*
[1477¹]	4	5	**Cede Nullis** (5a) 8-1 Miss L Eddery (xnb) *Jmpd slow 1; pulled hrd; last to 6; cl up aft; went 2nd 15; 2l down 3 out; rdn & fnd nil nxt*
[1525²]	U		**Island Vision (IRE)** 13-2 Mrs J Hughes *Drpd back last 6; 6l down 10; lsng tch when leather broke & ur 3 out*

OFFICIAL DISTANCES: ½l, 1l **TIME:** 6min 25.0s **TOTE:** £6.00; places £1.50,£5.20 **DF:** £49.00

1588 Intermediate, 12st   12 ran

[1415ᴾ]	1		**SABRE KING** (bl) 8-1 Miss N McKim *Prom & rcd keen; ld aft 7 til app 9; 3rd/4th til 2nd agn aft 15; sust chall frm 2 out; stayed on wl to ld cl home*
[1264¹]	2	½	**Ardeal** (5a) 5-2F A Bealby *Ld til aft 7; ld agn 11; nt fluent 13; kpt on game & lkd wnr frm 2 out til outrdn & caught cl home*
[1322¹]	3	2½	**Achill Sound** 7-1 G Hanmer (xnb) *Lw; oht; tk keen hld in rr; lft last aft 10; hdwy to 4th 13; went 4l 3rd aft 15; veered lft final turn; sust chall u.p aft; no imp*
[1485³]	4	2	**Aqua Star (IRE)** 10-1 Miss T Spearing *Tde & ld rnd start; hld up & bhnd; 8th 10; checked aft 12; 6th & eff 13; outpcd nxt & 18l 4th aft 15; rallied & kpt on frm 2 out*
[1355ᴾ]	5	20	**Smart Orange (IRE)** 25-1 M Rimell *Midfield; 5th 13; sn wknd; poor 5th aft 15*
[1415⁴]	6	nk	**Neva-Agree** (vis) 12-1 R Armson *Midfield & nd; 10l 7th 13; rem aft 15*
[1220¹]	U		**Be Upstanding** (7a) 11-2 M Mackley *Swtng; stdd start; novicey in rr; 11th when blun bad & ur 7*
[797¹]	P		**Charming Moss (IRE)** (bl) 25-1 N Kent *Jb & reluct; sn rr; t.o 7; pu 9*
[1331ᴿ]	F		**Cricketing** (tt) 50-1 G Markham *Pulled hrd in rr; impd qckly to ld app 9; hdd 11; 4th & wkng when fell 15*
	P		**Prestige Lord (IRE)** 8-1 Miss L Sweeting *Jb; w ldr to 7; 2nd app 9; eased aft 10; pu 11*
[1348¹]	P		**Prime Style** (5x) 5-1 C Gibbon *Chsd ldrs early; drpd back last 9; t.o 12; pu 3 out*

[997³]	P	**Silent Snipe** 9-1 S Swiers *Bhnd; 12l 8th 13; t.o & pu 3 out*

OFFICIAL DISTANCES: nk, 1l **TIME:** 6min 24.0s **TOTE:** £18.00; places £4.60,£2.30,£1.40 **DF:** £8.10

1589 Open Maiden 56&7yo (Div 1), 2m4f, 12st - 15J   13 ran

[1422³]	1		**MOSS HARVEY** (7a) 9-4F G Hanmer *Lw; pulled hrd; settled handy; 6th 10; 4th app 3 out; sn 3rd & clr of rest; qcknd app last; str rn to ld flat; sn clr*
[1423⁴]	2	2	**Proper Charlie** 4-1 T Lane *Settled trckng ldrs; 7th when mist 10; eff 12; qcknd ahd app nxt; 5l clr 2 out; rdn & jmpd slow last; hdd & nt qckn flat*
[1420ᴾ]	3	6	**Camden Kid (IRE)** (tt) 20-1 Miss L Allan *Oht; 2 handlers; pulled hrd; prom til ld 12; hdd app 3 out; 5l 2nd & rdn aft nxt; one-pcd & sn btn*
[1420⁴]	4	8	**Anneka Louise** (5a) 25-1 N Kent *Hld up towards rr; 8th 10; passed btn horses frm 3 out; nvr nr ldrs*
[1435³]	5	12	**Grain Hill** (5a) (bl) 12-1 M Wall *Mounted course; cl up; jmpd lft 8; 4th 10; 4l 3rd app 3 out; wknd qckly*
[1423²]	6	3½	**Sparebit** (5a) 5-2 S Morris *Made most to 11; drpd back tame aft nxt to 7th app 3 out; no ch aft; disapp*
	P		**Aldington Annie** (5a) 12-1 M Rimell *Mists & novicey in rr; 9th & out of tch 10; t.o & pu 3 out*
[1504³]	P		**Craftbook Marchesa (IRE)** (5a) 33-1 P Millington *Wl bhnd; rdr lkng rnd for mate aft 6 (which reqd binoculars); hmpd 8; cont t.o; pu 2 out*
	F		**Daisy Fay** (12a,4ow) 33-1 E Walker *Hanging lft all way; prom; ld 5 but rn wide bef nxt & hdd; 3rd 10; ld 11-12; 5th & wkng when fell hvly 3 out*
[1422ᴾ]	P		**Don Royal** 33-1 Miss G Harriss *1st ride; nt fluent 1; a last; blun 4 & sn wl t.o; ab ½mile bhnd when event pu last*
[1423ᴾ]	P		**Phar Away Cruise** (5a) 14-1 M Cowley *(pricker os) Wl bhnd; lost tch & jmpd slow 9; t.o & pu 2 out*
[1527ᴾ]	U		**Remember Equiname** (12a) 25-1 J Burley *Nt jw in rr; 11th & strugg when blun & ur 8*
[1010ᵁ]	P		**Syrpiro** 6-1 R Cope *Mostly 2nd to 10; 6th & wkng app 3 out; wl bhnd when pu nxt*

OFFICIAL DISTANCES: 2l, 5l **TIME:** 5min 27.0s **TOTE:** £4.60; places £1.20,£3.40,£2.20 **DF:** £4.00

1590 Open Maiden 56&7yo (Div 2), 2m4f, 12st - 15J   12 ran

[1531ᴾ]	1		**WIZADORA** (12a) 33-1 K Burke *Hld up; 7th 8; rdn to 3rd aft 12; ld app nxt & dashed 8l clr app 2 out; wknd flat; just hld on; wl rdn*
[1269⁴]	2	hd	**Colonel Carats** 25-1 T Lane *Tk keen hld; hld up towards rr; prog in 4th 8 & 2nd aft 12; outpcd when wnr qcknd clr; rallied app last; veered rt flat & unable to chall*
[1437²]	3	12	**So Frank** 5-4F M Harris *Trckd ldrs; eff 11; mist nxt; went 3rd app 3 out; rdn & btn app nxt*
[1421⁴]	4	8	**Grannies Delight (IRE)** 25-1 L Hicks *2nd til ld 8; hdd app 3 out; fdd rap; sn poor 4th*
[1480⁹]	5	2	**Slobadam** (tt) 8-1 M Mackley *Midfield; 5th 8; rdn & outpcd 12; plodded on*
[1421⁴]	6	10	**Light The Sky** 5-1 J Turcan *Ld til aft 3; ld 5-8; 2nd & rdn 11; fdd rap app 3 out*
[872ᵁ]	7	8	**Irish Kinsman** 8-1 M Gregory *A bhnd; 9th & rdn 10; lost tch 10; sn rem*
	8	nk	**Space Hopper (IRE)** (7a) 14-1 M Wall *Novicey; handy early; drpd back 8th 8; lost tch 12*
[1290²]	9	25	**Sidney Street** (vis,tt) 33-1 R Barr *Last pr; blun 7; nt jw aft & sn t.o*
[1437²]	F		**Looks Like Reign** 16-1 A Tutton *Pulled hrd; ld aft 3-5; chsd ldr to 8; lost tch 11; rem when fell hvly last*
[1504⁵]	U		**Mandalay Man (IRE)** 6-1 P Millington *(citation) Hmpd & ur 1*
[1507ᴿ]	R		**Zam Bam** (12a) 33-1 M Lurcock *Rn out 1*

OFFICIAL DISTANCES: s hd, 12l **TIME:** 5min 30.0s **TOTE:** £52.50; places £12.50,£1.50,£1.50
Placepot: £8.00 **Jackpot:** £49.00
Princess Scully (25-1) was withdrawn not under orders

Kelso (LH 8F,19J)
Wed, 24 May (GOOD to FIRM)

1591 Hinchliffe HC   9 ran

[1446²]	1		**SOUNDS STRONG (IRE)** 11-07 7-2 R Morgan *Trckd ldrs; 3rd frm 6; 4l 3rd when lft in ld aft 15; drew clr frm 3 out*
[1447³]	2	12	**Island Echo (IRE)** 11-11 3-1 J Tate *Last pr & wl bhnd; 40l 6th 13; 32l 4th 16; stayed on str to chse hrne aft 2 out; 15l 2nd at last; veered rt flat & unable to chall*
[1342²]	3	10	**Midsummer Glen (IRE)** 12-04 6-4F M Armytage *Bhnd; nt fluent 5; mist 8; 30l 4th 13; went poor 3rd 16; slt hdwy aft 3 out; no prog frm nxt*

[1556²]	4	24	**Snooty Eskimo (IRE)** 11-02 66-1 **T Davidson** *Ld to 10; cl 2nd til lft in ld & hmpd 15; sn hdd; wknd bad aft 3 out*
[1342⁸]	5	3½	**Ensign Ewart (IRE)** 12-07 8-1 **M Bradburne** *Early rmdrs; nt jw; sn wl bhnd; t.o 13*
[1498⁴]	6	dist	**Mullingar (IRE)** 11-07 33-1 **M Clayton** *Chsd ldrs to 7; lost tch frm 10; 35l 5th & rdn 13; t.o*
[1542ᴾ]	P		**Chez Catalan** 11-02 (bl) 9-1 **R Wakeham** *A rr; t.o 9; pu 14*
[908ᵁ]	P		**Givemeyourhand (IRE)** 11-02 66-1 **D Jewett** *Strugg 7; t.o 9; pu 14*
[1478¹]	U		**The Alleycat (IRE)** 11-02 9-1 **P Robson** *Cl up; slt ld 10 til terrible mist & ur 15*

TIME: 6min 10.1s TOTE: £4.30; places £1.10,£1.40,£1.10 Ex: £13.90 CSF: £13.36 Tri: £25.80

Uttoxeter (LH 8F)
Wed, 24 May (GOOD to FIRM)

1592 Spot On Open HC   14 ran

[1532²]	1		**HATCHAM BOY (IRE)** 11-11 100-30F **C Ward Thomas** *Chsd ldrs; hit 3; lost plce 5; 9th 8; poor 11th & cause lkd hopeless aft 16; gd prog app 21; went 2nd app last; stayed on u.p to ld final 100yds*
[1533¹]	2	1¾	**Fanion De Nourry (FR)** 11-10 7-2 **L Hicks** *Hld up & bhnd; last 8; 5th & prog aft 16; 8l 3rd & rdn when blun & pckd 20; clsd to ld app 2 out; sn 3l clr; rdn & wknd last; hdd 50yds out*
[1545²]	3	10	**Nevada Gold** 11-11 14-1 **R Burton** *Ld 2-5; ld 9-15 & agn aft 16-17; ld agn 20 til hdd app 2 out; drvn & sn btn*
[1338⁵]	4	1½	**Rusty Fellow** 11-11 14-1 **D Barlow** *Chsd ldrs; 6th 8; 10th & u.p aft 16; hmpd 17; stayed on frm 3 out; nvr able to chall*
[1542²]	5	17	**Factor Ten (IRE)** 11-07 14-1 **J Richardson** *Hld up gng wl; 8th 8; hdwy 10; ld 15 til mist nxt; ld agn 17-20; wknd 3 out; tired 4th when mist last*
[1293⁵]	6	3½	**George Ashford (IRE)** 11-07 25-1 **J R Barlow** *Midfield; 7th 8; 9th aft 16; sn lost tch*
[986ᴾ]	7	8	**Ledwyche Gate (IRE)** 11-09 (bl) 20-1 **R Bevis** *Ld 2-5; ld 5 til jmpd slow 9 & rmdr; jmpd slow 10 & 12; chsd ldr to 15; 8l 3rd 18; nt r.o; wl bhnd when mist last*
[1226⁵]	8	5	**Saffron Moss** 12-00 25-1 **J Jukes** *Bhnd; 10th 8; 12th 16; wl bhnd aft*
[1157⁹]	9	4	**Who's Your Man (IRE)** 11-09 66-1 **D Dunsdon** *Prsd ldrs; 5th 8; 6th 16; a strugg aft*
[1443⁶]	10	22	**Silver Standard** 11-07 (bl) 25-1 **Miss L Pearce** *Numerous mists; prom; 4th 16; mist nxt; wknd & mist 18; blun 19; t.o*
[1525⁶]	P		**Ballyhannon (IRE)** 11-07 50-1 **Miss J Froggatt** *A rr; 12th 8; t.o & pu 17*
[1321³]	F		**Ballyharry (IRE)** 11-07 25-1 **I Wynne** *Hld up; hdwy 7; 6th when blun 10; hit 14; 8th & wkng 16; fell 17*
[1506²]	U		**Black Book (IRE)** 11-02 33-1 **Miss A Burton** *13th when blun & ur 3*
[1332³]	P		**Stay Lucky (NZ)** 12-00 7-1 **Julian Pritchard** *Bhnd; jmpd slow 4; 11th & rdn 8; 7th & u.p 16; no resp; t.o & pu 21*

TIME: 8min 41.4s TOTE: £3.30; places £1.20,£1.90,£1.70 Ex: £11.40 CSF: £12.29

1593 Greig Middleton Ladies Open Championship Final HC   7 ran

[1579³]	1		**BALISTEROS (FR)** 11-11 6-1 **Miss J Wormall** *Hld up; 6th 6; blun 7; hdwy nxt; disp 3rd frm 13; hit 15; tk 2nd 3 out; ld nxt; stayed on str*
[1434¹]	2	1	**Spring Gale (IRE)** 11-11 13-8F **Miss Z Turner** *Trckd ldrs; went 2nd 12; ld nxt; rdn & hdd 2 out; kpt on flat*
[1399¹]	3	11	**Karaburan** 11-02 16-1 **Miss F Wilson** *2nd 2 til ld 11-13; cl 2nd to 16; rdn & hit nxt; wknd 3 out*
[1561³]	4	nk	**Just Bert (IRE)** 11-07 14-1 **Miss T Cave** *Handy til lost plce 9; mist 12; rallied 16; sn rdn & outpcd; stayed on agn flat*
[1583¹]	5	4	**Dont Tell The Wife** 11-11 4-1 **Miss G Hutchinson** *Hld up last to 9; hdwy & bumped along aft 12; disp 2nd when mist 16; 3rd & wkng when mist 3 out*
[1381¹]	6	dist	**Dawn Alert (IRE)** 11-11 11-4 **Miss L Rowe** *Chsd ldrs; drpd to rr 9; lost tch 14; t.o*
[1449³]	7	dist	**Storm Man (IRE)** 11-02 40-1 **Miss C Williams** *Ld to 11; wknd 14; t.o*

TIME: 6min 33.3s TOTE: £7.80; places £3.50,£1.20 Ex: £13.70 CSF: £15.40

14th Regiment Royal Artillery
Larkhill (RH 13F,18J) Wed, 24 May (GOOD to FIRM)

1594 Restricted, 12st   5 ran

| [1555¹] | 1 | | **SIR WYNHAM** 6-1 **J Case** *Mounted outside padd; tde; made all; sn wl clr; 30l ahd 13; fnce clr 3 out; unchall* |

[1435¹]	2	30	**Judicial Queen** (5a) 5-1 A Charles-Jones *Opened 6s; mist 3; went 25l 3rd 5; no imp frm 12; tk rem 2nd & mist last; no ch w wnr*
[1531⁵]	3	3	**Wot No Cash** 16-1 R Cope *Went 20l 2nd 3; chsd wnr vain to last; tired & hung lft flat*
[1020¹]	4	runin	**Mr Max (IRE)** evensF M Wall *(xnb) Opened 5/4; 2 handlers; mist 3; 2nd/3rd to 5; releg last 7; t.o 10*
[1280ᵁ]	U		**Pharniskey (IRE)** 3-1 O Ellwood *(xnb) Tchd 4s; hld up; blun 7; 30l 4th when mist & rfo 10*

OFFICIAL DISTANCES: dist, 5l TIME: 6min 15.9s TOTE: £3.40

1595 Confined, 12st　　　　　　　　　　　　　　　　　　5 ran

[1132ᴾ]	1		**FORBIDDEN WATERS (IRE)** (5x) 4-5F L Jefford *Tchd evens; ww; last to 8; 5l 4th ½way; went 3rd 11 & 2nd aft 14; ld 15; drew clr 2 out; stpng & rdn out flat*
[1108ᴾ]	2	8	**Glen Cherry** 20-1 P Scouller *Ld til hdd 15; no ex 2 out*
[1471²]	3	7	**Lavalight** (3x) 9-4 N Mitchell *Tchd 3s; tde; pulled hrd; went 2nd 4-6; chsd ldr 8 til rdn aft 14; 4l 3rd when mist nxt; wknd 3 out*
[1550ᴾ]	4	25	**Villains Brief** 33-1 J Kwiatkowski *Prom; went 2nd 6-8; 4l 3rd ½way; rdn & lost plce 11; 12l 5th 14; sn wl bhnd; t.o*
[1130³]	U		**Indian Knight** 7-1 M Green *Prom to 4; lost plce 6; 6l 5th ½way; 8l 4th 14; nd aft; 17l 4th when blun & ur last*

OFFICIAL DISTANCES: 10l, 6l TIME: 6min 21.6s TOTE: £1.80

Another Junior (R Young, 12-1, reluct to leave padd, planted himself bef rchng course, reared & event ur; rdr seemed inj but recovered immediately when horse withdrawn!) was withdrawn not under orders; Rule 4 deduction 5p in pound

1596 Open Maiden 56&7yo, 12st　　　　　　　　　　6 ran

[1241²]	1		**DUNSTON TRIGGER** (tt) 4-6F L Jefford *(xnb)2nd til ld 4; hdd 6; ld 8-12; ld agn 2 out; sn clr; comf*
[1390³]	2	8	**High Sturt** (5a) 7-1 N Mitchell *10s-7s; hld up; mist 4; last til hdwy 12; lft 3rd 14; rdn & no imp 3 out; went 2nd last; wknd & hung lft flat*
[1507⁶]	3	5	**Timothy George (IRE)** (bl,tt) 9-1 A Sansome *Sn prom; lost plce & mist 8; hdwy & 2nd nxt; ld 12; mist 14; hdd 2 out; sn rdn & wknd*
[1526ᴾ]	4	1¼fs	**Piltdown Lady** (5a) 25-1 T Macfarlane *Ld til hdd 4; 2nd/3rd til lost plce 9; 5th ½way; wknd 12; t.o 14; jmpd v slow 3 out*
[1483ᴾ]	F		**Dicks Darlin'** (5a) 4-1 A Charles-Jones *Tchd 5s; prom; jmpd slow 2; went 2nd 5; ld 6-8; 3rd ½way; ev ch til fell 14*
[1291⁵]	P		**Nosy Parker (IRE)** 14-1 A Harvey *Hld up; 4th ½way; in tch til wknd 12; pu 13*

OFFICIAL DISTANCES: 15l, 5l TIME: 6min 27.0s TOTE: £1.30

1597 Mixed Open, 12st　　　　　　　　　　　　　　　6 ran

[1339³]	1		**CASTLE LYNCH (IRE)** (5a) 4-7F Miss P Gundry *Ld; mist 2; hdd aft 6; 2nd til ld 11; qcknd 10l clr 3 out; mist last; easy*
[1463²]	2	15	**Gold'n Shroud (IRE)** 4-1 A Wintle *Tchd 5s; hld up; 8l 4th ½way; hdwy 13; went 2nd nxt; outpcd 3 out; eased when btn flat*
[1346³]	3	nk	**Copper Coil** 4-1 D Alers-Hankey *Mist 3; 2nd til ld aft 6; hdd 11; lost plce 14; 7l 4th & rdn nxt; went 3rd aft 2 out; no imp*
[1585⁵]	5	4	**Robsand (IRE)** 33-1 M Wilesmith *Chsd ldrs; 7l 3rd ½way; rdn 14; 11l 5th nxt; nd aft; lkd to fin 18½l 4th*
[1402ᴾ]	4d		**Blown Wind (IRE)** 20-1 C Williams *Hld up; last to 8; 9l 5th ½way; hdwy 11; went 3rd 14 wknd qckly aft 2 out; lkd to fin 19½l last; plcd 4th; disq - nt weigh-in*
[1532ᴾ]	P		**Chism (IRE)** 12-1 R Walford *Hld up; lost tch & 14l 6th ½way; t.o 12; pu 13*

OFFICIAL DISTANCES: 15l, 2l TIME: 6min 11.8s TOTE: £1.40

Blown Wind was officially placed 4th and disqualified when the rider failed to weigh-in (had looked to finish fifth); the rider was fined £40

1598 Open Maiden, 12st　　　　　　　　　　　　　　12 ran

[1486⁴]	1		**DARZAL** 5-1 A Charles-Jones *Tchd 6s; hld up; 5th ½way; went 3rd 12 & 4l 2nd 14; ld 2 out; sn clr*
[1555ᵁ]	2	20	**Madam Rose (IRE)** (5a) 7-1 L Jefford *(xnb) Lw; pulled hrd; ld aft 1; mist 9; up to 12l clr 12; wknd & hdd 2 out*
[1308³]	3	1	**The Frosty Fox (IRE)** 3-1F M Miller *9/2-3s; 2 handlers; blun 3; 2nd to 11; 8l 5th 13; wl bhnd 15; went poor 3rd app last*
[1437³]	4	12	**Snowboy (IRE)** 4-1 P Keane *Tchd 5s; nt jw; hld up; 7th ½way; hdwy 11; disp 6l 2nd 13; 14l 3rd & wkng 15*

[1527⁶]	5	5	**Snowshill Harvest (IRE)** 20-1 **J Rice** Hld up; mist 7; 6th ½way; went 2nd 11 til wknd qckly 14; wl bhnd when mist 3 out; t.o
[1555ᵁ]	6	hd	**Dancing Barefoot** (5a) 50-1 **J Barnes** Sn prom; 3rd ½way; wknd qckly 12; 20l 8th nxt; t.o
[1270ᴾ]	7	runin	**Yodeller Bill** (9ow) 50-1 **P Sheppard** Lost plce 4; mist 7; 11th ½way; t.o 12
[1486³]	8	30	**Devil's Sting (IRE)** 8-1 **J Richardson** A bhnd; 17l 7th 13; t.o 15; virt pu flat
[1435⁵]	P		**Hesgreen** 16-1 **C Wadland** Ld til hdd aft 1; 4th ½way; wknd qckly 12; t.o & pu 14
[1359³]	P		**Lily Lane** (xnb) Tchd 22s; a bhnd; 9th ½way; t.o & pu 14
[1465⁵]	P		**Silk Oats** (5a) 16-1 **M Wilesmith** Hld up; 8th ½way; 11l 6th 13; sn wknd; wl bhnd when pu 15
[1439³]	P		**Vital Hesitation** (5a) 7-1 **A Wintle** A bhnd; 10th ½way; t.o & pu 14

OFFICIAL DISTANCES: 20l, 1½l **TIME:** 6min 18.9s **TOTE:** £4.50
Millbank Honey was withdrawn not under orders

1599 Intermediate, 12st
4 ran

[1438¹]	1		**HEHAS** 13-8JF **C Wadland** Tchd 7/4; settled 3rd; outpcd 7; 7l 3rd ½way; rdn to ld 15; drew clr 2 out; stayed on wl
[1370⁶]	2	8	**Agile King** 11-4 **Miss C Tizzard** Opened 3s; 2nd til ld 10; hdd 15; rdn & ev ch 2 out; no ex
[1554⁶]	3	4	**Celtic Token** (1ow) 9-1 **D Birkmyre** Ld til hdd 10; 2nd til rdn aft 14; no ex 3 out
[1303¹]	4	15	**The Criosra (IRE)** (5x) 13-8JF **Miss T Newman** A last; 10l 4th ½way; wl bhnd frm 12

OFFICIAL DISTANCES: 8l, 3l **TIME:** 6min 27.2s **TOTE:** £2.30

Newton Abbot (LH 7F,16J)
Thu, 25 May (GOOD to FIRM)

1600 J C Milton Contractors First Ever HCap HC
15 ran

[1433⁴]	1		**BULLENS BAY (IRE)** 10-00 16-1 **Miss F Wilson** Rdn aft 4; blun 5; mod 6th 12; 12l 6th app 3 out; str rn to ld last; sn pushed clr
[1444³]	2	5	**King Torus (IRE)** 10-10 (bl) 5-1 **J Jukes** Rmdrs aft 4; bhnd til hdwy 7; ld 10; 5l clr app 2 out; hdd last; fnd nil u.p
[1296¹]	3	1¾	**Mr Dow Jones (IRE)** 10-04 14-1 **C Williams** Chsd ldrs; rdn aft 9; 4th & outpcd when hit 12; hrd drvn frm 3 out; kpt on agn flat
[1060ᴾ]	4	1¼	**Willie Makeit (IRE)** 10-04 50-1 **R Young** Ld til aft 1; prom; hit 10; chsd ldr frm 11; rdn & outpcd aft 3 out; kpt on agn flat
[1444ᴾ]	5	1½	**Hee's A Dancer** 10-06 16-1 **Miss E Jones** Ld aft 1 til hdd 3; 2nd til rdn & jmpd slow 10; outpcd 12; some rnwd prog aft 2 out
[1339¹]	6	9	**Coulton** 12-04 7-4F **R Burton** Ld 3-10; 3rd & rdn when blun 13; wknd aft 3 out
[1538¹]	7	10	**Noyan** 11-08 7-1 **Miss L Horner** Chsd ldrs; hit 5; outpcd in 6th when hit 9; nd aft
[1341³]	8	4	**Tubber Roads (IRE)** 10-00 6-1 **M Foley** Bhnd most of way; nd frm 9
[1444²]	9	16	**Badger Beer** 10-04 (tt) 14-1 **R Walford** Bhnd; hit 4; eff 7; sn strugg in rr
[1570³]	10	6	**Warren Boy** 10-04 20-1 **B Hitchcott** Bhnd; 8th & rdn 9; sn wknd; t.o
[1432ᴾ]	11	13	**Verde Luna** 10-07 (vis) 20-1 **T Doyle** Bhnd; mist 5; lost tch 9; t.o
[1531²]	12	dist	**Desert Calm (IRE)** 10-04 16-1 **T Scudamore** Rr & nvr gng wl; lost tch & rdn 8; t.o
[1157¹]	P		**Caracol** 10-08 11-1 **S Blackwell** Chsd ldrs to 9; lost plce qckly; t.o & pu 11
[1026ᴾ]	P		**Late Encounter** 10-00 50-1 **D Dennis** Sn bhnd & rdn; nvr gng keen; t.o & pu last
[1447¹]	P		**Mr Motivator** 10-03 8-1 **F Windsor Clive** In tch early; rdn aft 6; strugg 9; pu 11

TIME: 5min 17.8s **TOTE:** £44.80; places £10.50,£1.50,£5.70 **Ex:** £446.20 **CSF:** £100.36 **Tri:** £1114.46

Cartmel (LH 6F,18J)
Sat, 27 May (GOOD to SOFT)

1601 Worthington Mdn HC
13 ran

[1409¹]	1		**WHATAFELLOW (IRE)** 11-10 (3) 8-13F **A Crow** Lw; a gng wl; tk 2nd app 7; ld 13; clr frm 2 out; virt pu final 100yds
[1559⁷]	2	19	**Three Potato Four** 11-09 12-1 **D Barlow** Lw; chsd ldrs; went 6l 3rd 11; tk 2nd app 15; rdn & wl outpcd aft 2 out but wl clr of rest
[1343ᶠ]	3	26	**Horton-Cum-Peel (IRE)** 11-11 50-1 **R Burton** (xnb) Nt jw towards rr; bad mist 7; blun 12; 28l 8th nxt; 5th last; tk rem 3rd & staying on flat
[1525⁴]	4	7	**Bubble N Squeek** 11-08 (1) 33-1 **C Barlow** Swtng; kicked trnr padd; ld in & sis; sn rec to chse ldrs; 8l 5th 13; drvn & nt wl; lft poor 4th 3 out
[1445²]	5	7	**Weejumpawud** 11-04 20-1 **Miss S Forster** Ld til hdd & hit 13; 10l 3rd 15; sn wl outpcd; lost 2 plces flat; t.o

[1577⁵]	P		**Border Glory** 11-07 33-1 *P Maitland-Carew* Jmpd slow 1; chsd ldrs; mist 10; 12l 6th & outpcd when bad mist 13 & rdr lost irons; pu nxt
[959²]	U		**Desert Boot** 11-00 33-1 **B Wharfe** Svs; rem last & v erratic til blun bad & ur 6
[1537F]	P		**Dreamin George (IRE)** 12-00 20-1 *T Doyle* (martin) Jb in rr; 25l 7th 13; blun nxt & rdr lost irons; pu 15
[1071¹]	U		**Freestyle (IRE)** 11-09 (tt) 16-1 *G Hanmer* Hld up in midfield; eff in 7l 4th 13; rdn & no ex aft nxt; mod 4th when blun & ur 3 out
[1445P]	P		**Poynder Park (IRE)** 11-07 12-1 *L Morgan* Mists in rr & nvr gng wl; blun bad 6; 40l last 13; pu 15
[1498²]	P		**Toarlite (IRE)** 11-07 (vis) 25-1 *R Trotter* Bhnd; strugg aft mist 6; broke down & pu 10
[1334⁶]	U		**Triple Eaves** 11-09 16-1 *C Mulhall* (xnb) Cl up til blun & ur 6
[1462³]	F		**Tudor Lodge (IRE)** 11-02 20-1 *Miss S Swindells* Bhnd; last when fell 7

TIME: 6min 40.6s TOTE: £1.60; places £1.40,£2.10,£14.80 Ex: £13.40 CSF: £8.31

Hexham (LH 9F,17J)
Sat, 27 May (GOOD, GOOD to SOFT in places)

1602 Flying Ace HC   **7 ran**

[1556³]	1		**TEA BOX (IRE)** 12-07 evensF *Miss P Robson* Handy; ld app 9; a gng best frm 2 out; rdn & kpt on flat
[1531¹]	2	1½	**Us Four (IRE)** 12-00 (bl) 2-1 *S Morris* Hld up in tch; chsd wnr aft 9; nt fluent 2 out; kpt on u.p flat but carried hd awkward & nt go thro
[1445⁹]	3	23	**Lindon Run** 11-11 (tt) 12-1 *C Wilson* Chsd ldrs; 8l 3rd 12; no imp & rdn when hit 3 out; wknd nxt
[1446R]	4	dist	**Full Of Chat (IRE)** 11-02 33-1 *D Jewett* Ld; hdd & rmdrs app 9; 4l 3rd 11; wknd rap; t.o
	5	6	**Ruecastle** 11-07 10-1 *R Morgan* 2nd/3rd to 8; wknd 10; t.o
[1591⁵]	6	19	**Givemeyourhand (IRE)** 11-07 20-1 *P Aspell* Rmdrs 1; nvr gng wl; last & rdn 6; lost tch aft 7; t.o 10
[1580P]	F		**Desert Devil** 11-07 20-1 *L McGrath* A rr; rdn 7; t.o 12; fell last

TIME: 5min 22.9s TOTE: £2.00; places £1.60,£1.30 Ex: £2.90 CSF: £3.00 Tri: £2.80

Market Rasen (RH 8F,12J)
Sat, 27 May (GOOD to SOFT, SOFT in places)

1603 Geostar HC   **8 ran**

[1447⁶]	1		**STANMORE (IRE)** 11-07 2-1F *R Barrett* Ww; hit 2; hdwy aft nxt; ld 8; clr 2 out; r.o wl
[1585²]	2	2½	**Misti Hunter (IRE)** 11-07 16-1 *R Douro* Hld up; eff & pckd 3 out; stayed on wl frm 2 out; nt rch wnr
[1535¹]	3	15	**Chatergold (IRE)** 12-01 (bl) 100-30 *B Hitchcott* Cl up; rdn & one pce frm 9; no ch when hit last
[1542³]	4	1½	**Linlathen** 11-07 3-1 *N Bell* W ldr; blun bad & lost plce 5; rallied 8; mist 3 out; sn btn
[1507²]	5	1¼	**Nasayer (IRE)** 11-03 12-1 *A Pickering* Cl up til rdn & lost plce 7; some rnwd prog aft last
[1495¹]	6	4	**Superchamer** 11-03 10-1 *S Walker* Hit 1; hld up in rr; hdwy 6; u.p bef 3 out; fdd
[1409²]	7	¾	**Tremendisto** 11-07 16-1 *S Joynes* Prsd ldrs; blun 5; sn bhnd
[1443⁵]	8	¾	**Sailor Jim** 11-07 10-1 *W Tellwright* Ld to 8; wknd qckly frm 3 out

TIME: 5min 52.9s TOTE: £3.30; places £2.00,£3.60,£1.10 Ex: £38.90 CSF: £30.87
The water jump and the last fence in the back straight were omitted because of the state of the going

Dulverton East
Mounsey Hill Gate (RH 7F,20J) Sat, 27 May (SOFT, GOOD to SOFT in places)

1604 Hunt, 12st   **6 ran**

[1471¹]	1		**BELARUS (IRE)** (bl) 1-3F *M Miller* Trckd ldr til ld 12; clr frm 3 out; stayed on; comf
[1376⁵]	2	30	**Born Natural (IRE)** (5a) (tt) 10-1 *R Woollacott* Hld up in rr; hdwy to 3rd 14; r.o stdly to 8l 2nd 3 out; unable to chall wnr; pushed out to keep 2nd
[1518³]	3	1	**I Like The Deal** (5a) 4-1 *Miss O Green* (xnb) Jmpd slow 3; settled 3rd; 12l 3rd 11; went 2nd 13; chsd ldr til fdd 3 out; one pce
[1560³]	4	1½fs	**Mosside** 33-1 *M James* Nov rdn; nt fluent in rr; rmdr 6; t.o 11; poor 4th frm 3 out; jmpd awkward last

| [1560⁴] | 5 | 25 | **Master Kiwi (NZ)** 25-1 Miss T Hayes (xnb) Mounted on course; hit 6; sn strugg in rr; poor 4th 14-3 out; t.o |
| [1517ᴿ] | P | | **Devonshire Lad** 33-1 Miss K Cook Sn slt ld; dived at 6; jw 9 & 10; hdd 12; tired qckly nxt; poor 4th & lsng ground when pu 14 |

OFFICIAL DISTANCES: 30l, 1l TIME: 7min 09.0s

1605 Ladies Open
7 ran

[1346¹]	1		**LOOK IN THE MIRROR** 2-1JF Miss L Sweeting Ld frm 6; jw; forged clr 15; stayed on dour
[1561²]	2	15	**Mizyan (IRE)** 9-4 Miss O Green Ch ride; hld up in tch; 3½l 3rd 13; jmpd slow & lost ground 15; 12l 3rd when nt jw 17; kpt on stdly to 2nd app last; no ch w wnr
[1386²]	3	10	**Solomans Sister** (5a) 28-1 Mrs M Hand Ld l; stayed cl up; 4th & pushed along 13; went 2nd & running on 16; sn u.p & no imp; dem 3rd app last
[1346ᴾ]	4	15	**Space Cappa** 25-1 Miss V Stephens Nvr threatened ldrs; 12l 5th ½way; bhnd frm 14
[1261⁵]	P		**Lirsleftover** 14-1 Miss S Young Sn last & strugg; t.o & pu 12
[1461¹]	P		**Nether Gobions** 2-1JF Miss A Dare Jw; in tch; cl 2nd 7; cl up til rdn 14; lost ground stdly frm 15; btn 4th when pu 3 out
	P		**Paris Of Troy** 33-1 Miss S Wallin Towards rr; 6th ½way; poor 6th when pu 14

OFFICIAL DISTANCES: 15l, 10l TIME: 7min 08.0s

1606 Mens Open, 12st
9 ran

[1473²]	1		**BELLS WOOD** 14-1 C White Ld frm 2; slt mist 12; outj & hdd 14; chsd ldr jmpd btr til ld agn 3 out; sn drvn clr; in comm nxt; stayed on wl
[1560¹]	2	15	**Butler John (IRE)** (7x) 2-5F N Harris Chsd ldr frm 4; rmdr 13; ld 14 & sn 2l clr; pushed along 16 til hdd 3 out; tired & no ex frm 2 out; lkd jaded
[1523²]	3	12	**Pretoria Dancer** (bl) 25-1 F O'Brien Rr early; prog to 4th but rmdr 13; went mod 3rd 15; no ch w ldrs
[1378¹]	4	10	**Nibble** 6-1 G Cooper In tch in 4/5th to ½way; lost tch 13; poor 5th 15; t.o when blun last
[1562⁵]	5	8	**Hillhead (IRE)** (7x) 10-1 J Barnes Lw; trckd ldrs; 10l 3rd 9; rdn 13; sn lost tch
[1304²]	U		**Cool Clown** 14-1 B Trickey Lw when blun & ur 5
[1387²]	P		**It's Not My Fault (IRE)** (7x) 25-1 L Jefford Dwelt; sn rr; 25l 5th 9; bhnd when pu 14
[1489ᴾ]	P		**Lauren's Lad** (7a) 100-1 G Barfoot-Saunt Ld l; 5th when jmpd slow 8; lost ground stdly; last when pu 14
[1566ᵁ]	U		**Move A Minute (USA)** 6-1 Julian Pritchard (xnb) Dwelt; pulling & hld up in rr; last when blun bad & ur 6

OFFICIAL DISTANCES: 15l, 10l TIME: 7min 12.0s

1607 Intermediate, 12st
8 ran

[1516⁶]	1		**BRAVE NODDY (IRE)** (bl) 6-4F L Jefford Tchd 7/4; jmpd rt; ld aft 1; made rest; went 6l clr 16; pushed out
[1258¹]	2	10	**Belitlir** (5a) 11-4 Miss S Young Cl up in midfield; 7l 4th 13; went 2nd 16 but sn rdn & no imp
[1203⁴]	3	2	**Gypsy Luck** (5a) 10-1 Miss A Bush Ld l; last by 3; in tch in 5th 13; duelled for 2nd but no ch w wnr frm 16
[1240¹]	4	10	**Gemini Mist** (5a) (bl) 3-1 Miss C Stretton Tchd 100/30; in tch; 6l 3rd 13; went 2nd 14; 3l 2nd 15; sn wknd; bad mist last
[1599²]	P		**Agile King** 20-1 Miss C Tizzard (xnb) Lw; sn prom; 2nd to 7; lost plce but just in tch to 13; wknd nxt; bhnd when pu 3 out
[886ᴾ]	P		**Gneveguilla** 25-1 M Harris In tch towards rr to 11; pu nxt
[1472ᵁ]	U		**Leejay Luki** 14-1 A Honeyball Hdwy on outer 8; went 2nd 10; cl up til wknd 14; sn rdn; btn 5th when blun & ur 16
[1256⁵]	P		**Valley's Choice** (5a) 8-1 C White In tch; cl 4th 10; pu & dism 12

OFFICIAL DISTANCES: 10l, 2l TIME: 7min 09.0s

1608 Restricted, 12st - 19J
12 ran

[1375²]	1		**MELODY PRINCESS** (5a) 12-1 D Alers-Hankey Hld up in mid-div; hdwy to 4th 11; cl 3rd frm 13; str rn aft 3 out; drvn 3l clr & gd j last; comf
[1518⁵]	2	6	**County Bash** (5a) 20-1 Miss L Gardner Lw; prom til lost plce 8; hdwy agn to 6th 13; ld 14; slt ld til hdd by-passing 2 out; kpt on to 2nd agn cl home
[1488²]	3	nk	**More People (IRE)** 9-4 Julian Pritchard Tchd 5/2; lw; hdwy to 7th 9; gd prog & went 2nd 16; eff u.p & slt ld by-passing 2 out; sn hrd rdn; wknd & hdd app last; tired & dem nr post
[1179¹]	4	8	**Henrys Song** 17-2 Richard Darke (xnb) Sn prom; cl 3rd 11-13; outpcd nxt; 4th but nt trble ldrs frm 17

[1375³]	5	3	**Loxley-Lad** 20-1 A Honeyball *Midfield in tight bunch; hdwy to cl 4th 14; 8l 5th 17; nd clsng stages*
[1517⁴]	F		**Amazing Hill (IRE)** 33-1 Mrs R Morris *Towards rr til fell hvly 12*
[1517⁶]	P		**Bedtime Pixie** 40-1 Miss L Jackson *Last til tried to duck up padd chute aft 13 & pu*
[1519¹]	P		**Durnford Bay (IRE)** (tt) 4-6F L Jefford *5/4-4/6; lw; hld up in rr & pulling; 9th ½way; some hdwy to 5th 16; nt rch ldrs; btn when pu aft 3 out*
[1375ᵖ]	P		**Mountain-Linnet** 66-1 Mrs J Reed *Prom & keen hld early; in tch in 5th 11; wknd 13; bhnd 14; jmpd slow 16; t.o & pu last*
[1469¹]	P		**Namron (IRE)** (tt) 14-1 R Woollacott *Tubed; lw; rcd keen; ld 3; disp ld 8 til ld agn 11; hdd & wknd v rap aft 13; pu nxt*
[1176ᵖ]	P		**Rakaposhi Ryme (IRE)** (5a) 14-1 Miss T Cave *Ld to 3; disp frm 8; rmdr 13; lost plce 14; bhnd when pu 3 out*
[1444⁸]	P		**Shillelagh Oak** 25-1 M Harris *10th ½way; slt prog to 7th 13; lost tch 15; jmpd slow 17; pu nxt*

OFFICIAL DISTANCES: 8l, nk **TIME:** 7min 14.0s
Fence 19 was omitted - fallen rider

1609 Open Maiden (Div 1), 12st

9 ran

[1469²]	1		**DEALER DEL** 6-4F L Jefford (xnb) *Hld up in tch; cl 3rd 10; jmpd lft nxt & lost ground; sn handy agn & jmpd to 2nd 16; ld 3 out; rdn & wandered u.p app last; jw & sn clr*
[1583ᵖ]	2	6	**Vulpin De Laugere (FR)** (bl) 12-1 C Jarvis *Ld to 6; prom til ld agn 11; hdd 15; sn lost plce; 10l 3rd 3 out; rallied to 4l 2nd 2 out; tried to chall but hld when blun last*
[933ᵖ]	3	nk	**Penthouse Minstrel** 9-1 B O'Doherty (xnb) *2 handlers; hld up in midfield; prog to 4th & gng wl 13; jmpd 2nd 16; slt ld when hit nxt; outj 3 out; sn one pce u.p*
[1390ᵖ]	P		**Hendra Chieftain** 25-1 N Harris *Sn rr; bhnd when pu 13*
[1391ᵁ]	R		**Knap Hand** (7a) 16-1 Miss L Gardner *Lw; 5th when rmdr 5; in tch in 6th 10; rn out & ur 12*
[1598ᵖ]	P		**Lily Lane** 16-1 R Young (xnb) *Sn ldng trio; lft in ld 9; hdd 11; cl 3rd when hit 13; 2nd when mist 14; ld 15 til rdn & wknd nxt; 8l 3rd when pu 3 out*
[1520ᵖ]	U		**North Newcombe** 20-1 Miss K Cook (xnb) *8th when ur 3*
[1520ᵖ]	P		**Packitin Parky** 10-1 Miss S Young *Ld brief 7; 4th ½way; lost plce 14; btn 5th & nt pushed when pu 15*
[1564ᶠ]	P		**Speck** 7-4 J O'Rourke (bf) *2 handlers; sn prom; ld when hit 9 & lost 4 plces; kpt in tch; rmdr 13; wknd rap & pu nxt*

OFFICIAL DISTANCES: 6l, nk **TIME:** 7min 33.0s

1610 Open Maiden (Div 2), 12st

8 ran

[1262ᵖ]	1		**ALPINE CASTLE (IRE)** (5a) 4-1 Miss S Young *Tchd 5s; chsd ldr; outpcd frm 15; drvn & no prog 3 out; hld in 2nd when ref last; event cont by-passing last when procedure allowed; lucky wnr*
[1521ᵖ]	F		**Jo's Wedding** 4-1 J Young (xnb) *Ld; sn 5l clr; kpt up stdy gallop; drew 8l clr 3 out; lkd cert wnr when fell last; winded*
[1101ᵖ]	P		**Little Buster** 20-1 Miss S Robinson (xnb) *15l 4th 7; rr when mist 9; t.o 11 til pu aft 13*
[1564³]	F		**Mayhem** (5a) 9-4F M Sweetland *Settled 3rd; in tch; 7l 3rd 13; rdn 15; lost ground & 12l 3rd 3 out; wl btn & exhaust 3rd when lft in ld but fell hvly last; winded*
[1204ᶠ]	P		**Oneforthefrog (IRE)** 16-1 D Alers-Hankey *Settled 5th; rmdr 6; 4th but nt nr ldrs aft 8; bhnd in 5th when pu aft 13*
[847ᵖ]	F		**River Carron (IRE)** 9-2 G Maundrell *Fell 1*
	P		**Sir William** 4-1 R Woollacott (xnb) *Fat; bhnd & jmpd novicey early; prog to 5th & dived frm 9; went mod 4th 12; pu 14; winded*
[1469⁵]	P		**Windyway** (5a) 33-1 L Tibbatts (xnb) *Sn jmpd sticky in rr; t.o 8 til pu aft 13*

OFFICIAL DISTANCE: Finished alone **TIME:** 8min 08.0s

Pentyrch
Bonvilston (RH 7F,18J) Sat, 27 May (SOFT)

1611 Hunt

1 ran

[1450ᴮ]	1		**KRISTAL HAZE** (5a) J Cook *Walked over*

OFFICIAL DISTANCE: Walked over

1612 Confined, 12st

12 ran

[1341⁴]	1		**RED NECK** (3x) (tt) 11-4F T Vaughan (xnb) *Ww in mid-div; prog to 8l 4th 13; went 3rd 3 out; ld nxt; qckly went clr; rdn out*

[895ᴾ]	2	20	**Olympian** 9-2 A Wintle *7s-9/2; ww; 15l 8th 7; rdn app 13; no prog; 20l 4th 2 out; stayed on past btn horses; went 2nd nr fin; nvr nr wnr*
[1571²]	3	2½	**Silverfort Lad (IRE)** 14-1 C Williams *Ld to 2 out; imm outpcd by wnr; v tired flat & dem nr fin*
[1572¹]	4	12	**Star Chaser** 4-1 J Cook *A.p; went 2nd 6; ev ch 3 out; wknd qckly app nxt*
[1401ᴾ]	P		**Appeal** (5a) 33-1 J Jukes *Chsd ldrs; 6l 4th & rdn 11; 6th & wkng when pu 13*
[1450ᴾ]	P		**Comme Une Fleur (FR)** (5a) 33-1 G Maloney *Sn bhnd; t.o & pu 10*
[1569ᴾ]	P		**Desmond Gold (IRE)** 33-1 D Hughes *A rr; mist 4; t.o & pu 3 out*
[1297ᴾ]	P		**Flashman** 33-1 Miss E Crawford *A rr; t.o 14 til pu 3 out*
[1051¹]	P		**Flutterbud** (5a,6x) 3-1 E Williams *Trckd ldrs; 4th & rdn 3 out; wknd qckly; pu nxt*
[1450ꟳ]	P		**Mr Mad** (vis) 10-1 Miss C Thomas *Chsd ldrs; mist 10; 12l 5th & outpcd 14; last when pu out*
[1571ꟳ]	U		**Swan's Wish (IRE)** 25-1 G Thorne *Bhnd til blun & ur 5*
[1450³]	U		**Young Manny** 12-1 M Lewis *6th when blun & ur 5*

OFFICIAL DISTANCES: 20l, 2½l TIME: 6min 26.0s

1613 Intermediate, 12st
11 ran

[1449²]	1		**RUSNETTO (IRE)** (vis) 12-1 Miss C Thomas *Ww in mid-div; 15l 6th gng wl 12; rap hdwy aft 13; lft in ld nxt; sn clr; 10l up 2 out; rdn out; unchall*
[1299ᵁ]	2	7	**Bel-De-Moor** (5a) 5-1 T Vaughan *In tch; 4th when mist & rmdr 12; lft 3rd & hmpd bad 14; rallied & chsd wnr 2 out; kpt on; unable to rch wnr*
[1449ᴾ]	3	25	**Dunsfold Dazzler** (5a) 33-1 D Hughes *Bhnd; prog in mid-div 10; 7th & outpcd 12; no ch aft; went poor 3rd flat*
[1558⁹]	4	12	**Wanstead (IRE)** 6-1 J Jukes *Chsd ldr to 6; cl up til 4th & wkng aft 13; went poor 3rd aft 2 out; dem flat*
[1453¹]	P		**Absent Citizen (IRE)** (5a) 7-1 E Williams *Ww in mid-div; 16l 7th 7; prog nxt; went 6l 2nd 15; 3rd & wkng qckly when jmpd slow 2 out; pu last*
[1568¹]	P		**Baran Itsu** 2-1 P Sheldrake *Ld to 13; disp 2nd when hmpd & lost all ch nxt; t.o & pu 3 out*
[1572²]	P		**Itsstormingnorma** (5a) 25-1 S Blackwell *A bhnd; 15l 8th 11; sn lost tch; t.o & pu 14*
[1221¹]	U		**Longstone Boy (IRE)** 7-4F P Hamer *2 handlers; hld up; last when blun & ur 5*
[1299ᴾ]	P		**Secret Beauty (IRE)** (5a) 33-1 M Lewis *A bhnd; t.o & pu 12*
[1403ᴾ]	F		**Secret Can't Say (IRE)** (5a) 12-1 C Williams *Prom; went 2nd 6; ld 13; 11 up when fell nxt*
[1023⁶]	P		**Sister Lark** (5a) 33-1 A Price *Bhnd frm 4; t.o & pu 13*

OFFICIAL DISTANCES: 6l, 20l TIME: 6min 28.0s

1614 Mixed Open, 4m, 12st - 24J
7 ran

[1592⁸]	1		**SAFFRON MOSS** 10-1 J Jukes *Disp 2nd bhnd clr ldr; went 12l 2nd 18; clsd to 1l 2nd 20; ld last; stayed on u.p*
[1336¹⁰]	2	2	**Mostyn** 12-1 A Wintle *Ld & sn wl clr; blun 4; 25l clr 7; blun 11; 12l clr 18; hrd prsd frm 20; hdd last; no ex*
[1571ᴾ]	3	20	**High Guardian** 10-1 T Vaughan *Disp 2nd bhnd clr ldr til 14l 3rd & u.p 18; no ch w ldng pr frm 20*
[1411ᴾ]	4	1½fs	**Outrageous Affair** (5a) 33-1 Miss R Reynolds *A last; t.o frm 11*
[1296³]	P		**Bit Of A Citizen (IRE)** (5a) (vis) 9-2 E Williams *6s-9/2; nvr gng wl; a last pr; 30l 5th 12; 4th & no ch when pu last*
[1611¹]	P		**Kristal Haze** (5a) 10-1 J Cook *Hld up in mid-div; 17l 4th & gng wl 18; wknd nxt; pu 3 out*
[1338¹⁰]	P		**No Fiddling (IRE)** 4-7F C Williams *Mid-div; 30l 4th 8; pu nxt; rdr inj*

OFFICIAL DISTANCES: 2l, 20l TIME: 8min 45.0s

The stewards enquired into the running and riding of the favourite, No Fiddling; the rider's explanation that he had pulled up because his shoulder 'slipped out during the race' was accepted and he was taken to hospital

1615 Restricted (Div 1), 12st
12 ran

[1453⁶]	1		**CRANAGH MOSS (IRE)** (bl) 14-1 S Blackwell *Chsd ldrs; mist 7; ld 10 til blun & lost plce 12; rallied u.p 14; ev ch frm 3 out; ld nxt til hung lft & hdd flat; forced back in front nr fin; wl rdn*
[1457¹]	2	hd	**Get The Gist (IRE)** 7-2 P Hamer *Hld up; stdy prog 11; went 3l 3rd gng wl 3 out; chall nxt; ld flat; hdd & no ex nr fin*
[1454⁴]	3	10	**The Gadfly** 16-1 J Hayward *Ld to 2; cl up til outpcd 13; 10l 5th 15; lft 4th nxt; plodded into 3rd aft last*

[1298²]	4	½	**Cherry Gold** 7-4F E Williams *(xnb) In tch; 3rd 8 til went 2l 2nd 13; ld nxt; hdd 2 out; sn wknd; tired & dem flat*
[1454⁴]	5	6	**Omar's Odyssey (IRE)** (7a) 10-1 S Lloyd *Ww in mid-div; 6th & outpcd 14; no ch aft*
[1453³]	6	15	**Rymin Thyne** 10-1 J Cook *A bhnd; 15l 10th & rdn 11; nd*
[1454ᴿ]	7	20	**Cosy Ride (IRE)** 25-1 J Price *Pulling; hld up in rr; 10l 9th when blun 12; lost tch nxt; t.o*
[1181³]	F		**Gt Hayes Pommard** 10-1 D Howells *2 handlers; trckd ldrs on inner; mist 7; 4l 3rd when fell 13*
[1568³]	F		**Itscinders** (5a) 14-1 J Jukes *Ww; 8l 8th when fell 12*
[1456⁵]	P		**Lough Neagh (IRE)** 33-1 P Sheldrake *A bhnd; blun 2; last frm 4; t.o & pu 15*
[1573¹]	F		**Mike's Dream** 6-1 T Vaughan *Ld; mist 2; hdd 14; 3l 3rd & rdn when fell 3 out*
[1568⁶]	P		**Sea Search** 40-1 J Keen *Prom; 3rd 6; outpcd frm 12; t.o & pu last*

OFFICIAL DISTANCES: hd, 10l TIME: 6min 35.0s

1616 Restricted (Div 2), 12st
13 ran

	1		**PRIDEWOOD GOLDING** 4-1 Miss E James *Chsd ldrs; 4l 5th 10; 1l 3rd 3 out; ld nxt; a hldng rivals aft*
[1551⁴]	2	1½	**Cefn Woodsman** 20-1 Miss K Lovelace *Prom; disp 2nd frm 8 til ld 14; hdd 2 out; one pce*
[1448²]	3	nk	**Mister Jay Day** 4-1 A Price *(xnb) Trckd ldrs on inner; ld 13-nxt; ev ch aft til one pce u.p frm 2 out*
[1456ᵁ]	F		**Carbury's Case** 40-1 H Evans *Last when fell 5*
[1543¹]	U		**Cwm Bye** 8-1 M Hammond *Cl up til rdn 12; sn drpd out; no ch when ur 14*
[1568⁵]	P		**Guard A Dream (IRE)** 7-1 J Keen *Hld up; prog 10; 15l 5th & outpcd 14; no ch when pu last*
[1298ᴾ]	P		**Howsyourluck (IRE)** (vis,tt) 3-1F T Vaughan *Pulling; chsd ldrs til ld app 7; blun & hdd 12; 8l 4th & btn 3 out; v tired when pu last*
[1574¹]	P		**Itsthejonesboy** 5-1 J Jukes *Tubed; ld til app 7; cl up til wknd 13; no ch nxt; pu last*
[831ᴾ]	P		**Lauras Conquest** 20-1 P Sheldrake *Hld up in rr; lost tch 12; t.o & pu last*
[633³]	P		**Noble Star** 4-1 S Bush *In tch; 10l 9th 9; rdn & outpcd app 13; no ch when pu 3 out*
[1568ᴾ]	P		**Saronica-R** (5a) 40-1 J Price *A wl bhnd; lsng tch when pu 12*
[1574²]	P		**Tommyknocker (IRE)** 10-1 T Faulkner *A bhnd; no ch frm 14; pu last*
[1568⁷]	P		**Under Milk Wood** 40-1 G Maloney *In tch; 5l 6th 10; wknd app 13; no ch when pu 15*

OFFICIAL DISTANCES: 1½l, nk TIME: 6min 37.0s

1617 Open Maiden 56&7yo (Div 1), 12st
10 ran

[1455ᵁ]	1		**POWER UNIT** (7a) 2-1F P Hamer *Tk keen hld; disp ld to 4; lft in ld nxt; made rest; jnd app last; pushed out & r.o best flat*
[1574³]	2	1	**Clonshire Castle (IRE)** 3-1 J Keen *Ww; stdy prog to 2l 3rd 3 out; chall on bit app last; fnd nil flat*
[1457³]	3	25	**Blazing Connie** (5a) 6-1 Miss F Wilson *2 handlers; prom; 3rd when jmpd slow 9; rmdrs 11; 4th when mist 12; wknd 2 out*
[1302⁴]	4	20	**Lady Murrhill (IRE)** (12a) 16-1 J Hayward *Disp ld til ld 4; hung bad lft & hdd nxt; bhnd aft; 8l last 11; mist 12; lost tch 14; t.o*
[1457⁵]	P		**Bill's Integrity** (12a) (bl) 5-1 E Williams *Hld up in tch; 1l 3rd whn blun 12; gng wl til wkng rap when jmpd v slow 14; t.o & pu nxt*
[1405ᴾ]	P		**Craigson** 8-1 T Vaughan *Pulling; prsd ldrs til 3l 3rd & rdn 14; wknd app 3 out; pu 2 out*
[1574⁵]	P		**Hill Top Flyer (IRE)** 25-1 G Maloney *Mid-div when blun & lost irons 4; pu nxt*
	P		**Lady Clifford** (5a) 16-1 M Hammond *Last when jmpd slow 1 & 2; prog to 6l 3rd 13; sn strugg; t.o & pu 3 out*
[1457⁷]	P		**Migsy Malone** (12a) 5-2 J Jukes *Ww in tch; prog to 4l 5th 14; btn 3 out; 10l 4th nxt; pu run-in*
	F		**Phar Top (IRE)** (12a) 12-1 P Sheldrake *7th when fell 5*

OFFICIAL DISTANCES: 1½l, 25l TIME: 6min 45.0s

1618 Open Maiden 56&7yo (Div 2), 12st
7 ran

[1456²]	1		**ITSARCHIE** 5-4F J Jukes *Ld/disp to 6; prsd ldr aft; blun 12; rdn 2 out; ld last 100yds*
[1457⁴]	2	nk	**Bonny Boy (IRE)** (7a) 6-4 E Williams *Ld/disp til slt ld frm 6; rdn 2 out; hdd & no ex last 100yds*
[1456ᵁ]	3	10	**Marnies Song** (5a) (bl) 4-1 James Tudor *Chsd ldrs til outpcd 15; 13l last 3 out; r.o agn frm last*
[1406⁷]	4	10	**Rubian Princess** (12a) 14-1 S Lloyd *(xnb) Jmpd slow 2; hld up; cl 3rd frm 11 til outpcd by ldng pr app 3 out; dem flat*
[1454ᴾ]	P		**Jesusa** (5a) 20-1 J Keen *A last; 12l adrift 8; lsng tch when pu 12*

| [949^P] | P | **Poacher's Paddy** (IRE) (12a) 12-1 **J Price** *Rr but in tch; 6l 5th & rdn 14; 12l 4th & btn 3 out; pu nxt* |
| | P | **Polly Watt** (5a) 10-1 **Miss E Crawford** *2nd when jmpd slow 2; blun nxt; jmpd v slow 5 & imm pu* |

OFFICIAL DISTANCES: ½l, 10l TIME: 7min 03.0s

Berks & Bucks Draghounds
Kingston Blount (LH 8F,18J) Sun, 28 May (GOOD, GOOD to FIRM in places)

1619 Hunt
5 ran

[791^P]	1		**LUCKY JOE** (IRE) 4-5F **R Lawther** *Swtng; hld up; lft 2nd 5; ld 10 til hdd app 14; ld 3 out; comf*
[1346^P]	2	2½	**Summer Haven** (5a) 2-1 **L Lay** *5/2-2s; ld to 2; ld 3 til jmpd v slow & blun 5; 1½l 3rd ½way; went 2nd & rdn 14; 2l 3rd when blun 3 out; nt rec; rallied & went 2nd flat; rdr almost forgot to weigh-in*
[1279^4]	3	1½	**Flickering Flame** 12-1 **M Tillett** *16s-12s; went 2nd 3; ld 5-10 & app 14 til hdd 3 out; sn rdn & one pce*
[1206^P]	P		**Bit Of A Character** 6-1 **P Young** *Ld 2-3; mist 5; jmpd slow & rmdrs 6; 2l 4th ½way; rdn 11 & jmpd lft aft; 5l 4th 14; pu & dism nxt*
	P		**Daisy** (U) (5a,26ow) 33-1 **N Lampard** *Sn wl bhnd; t.o 6; pu 13*

OFFICIAL DISTANCES: 2½l, 1½l TIME: 6min 54.0s

1620 Confined, 12st
4 ran

[1481^U]	1		**CASTLE ARROW** (IRE) (bl) 5-1 **Julian Pritchard** *Lw; tde; ld in start; jw; made all; rdn out*
[1509^1]	2	5	**Peafield** (3x) 3-1 **P York** *Hld up; 4l 3rd ½way; jmpd slow 10; lft 5l 2nd nxt; jnd wnr aft 13 but constantly outj; drvn along 15; no imp*
[1487^3]	3	1½fs	**Bally Clover** 20-1 **Miss L Walter** *Hmpd start (by wng trnr); bhnd til hdwy 4; went 2nd aft 5-8; lost plce & 6l 4th ½way; lft 12l 3rd 11; sn wl bhnd; t.o*
[1485^1]	U		**Grecian Star** 1-2F **J Tarry** *2nd til aft 5; chsd wnr 8 til blun bad & ur 11*

OFFICIAL DISTANCES: 5l, dist TIME: 6min 35.8s

1621 Mens Open
6 ran

[1205^2]	1		**CASTLE FOLLY** (IRE) (bl) 7-4 **R Lawther** *Lw; 2nd til ld aft 10; mist & rmdrs 15; rdn 6l clr 2 out; r.o wl*
[1484^3]	2	15	**Arleneseoin** (IRE) 10-1 **P York** *Hld up & pulled hrd; 7l 3rd ½way; went 2nd 11; hit 13; releg 5l 3rd 3 out; btn when mist 2 out; went 2nd agn flat*
[1484^1]	3	1½	**Fawsley Manor** (5a) 6-4F **J Tarry** *Hld up; hit 2; 8l 4th ½way; went 3rd 11; mist 13; rdn 14; chsd wnr app 3 out; wkng when hit nxt; dem flat*
[1539^5]	4	20	**Remilan** (IRE) (bl) 20-1 **A Sansome** *Lw; nvr gng wl; 15l 5th & drvn along ½way; went 25l 4th 14; t.o*
[1481^1]	5	25	**Fair Crossing** 3-1 **M Emmanuel** *Sn outpcd & bhnd; releg 20l last 5-11; hdwy & 10l 4th nxt; wknd aft 13; t.o*
[1531^8]	P		**Ardshuil** 33-1 **S Pile** *(xnb,orbs) 2 handlers; pulled hrd; ld; 10l clr 5 til mist 9; hdd & wknd qckly aft 10; t.o & pu 14*

OFFICIAL DISTANCES: 12l, 2l TIME: 6min 18.6s

1622 Ladies Open
7 ran

[1511^4]	1		**PRINCE OF SAINTS** (IRE) (bl) 6-4F **Miss Z Turner** *Lw; a.p; 1½l 3rd ½way; ld aft 14; rdn 4l clr 2 out; all out*
[1483^3]	2	1	**Lucky Christopher** 5-1 **Miss R Goodwin** *Drpd to rr aft 5; 3½l 5th ½way; outpcd 13; rallied u.p 15; went 6l 4th nxt & 4l 2nd app last; nt rch idling wnr flat*
[1587^2]	3	5	**Cill Churnain** (IRE) 3-1 **Mrs C McCarthy** *Ch ride; lw; ld rnd start; pckd 4; 2nd til ld 11; blun 13; sn hdd; 2l 3rd 3 out; one pce*
[885^P]	4	7	**Thomas Crown** (IRE) 25-1 **Mrs J Wilkinson** *Rdn in snatches; 5l 6th ½way; hdwy to ld aft 13; hdd aft nxt; ev ch app 2 out; no ex*
[1395^P]	R		**My Best Man** 3-1 **Mrs T Hill** *Ld til hdd 11; sn drvn along; 3l 4th 15; 6l 5th & und str press when cocked jaw & rn out to rt 2 out*
[1558^10]	U		**River Ferdinand** (IRE) 33-1 **Miss J Grant** *Hld up; blun 9; 3l 4th ½way; mist 13; 3l 5th & rdn when tried to rn out & ur 14*
[1462^5]	U		**Slightly Special** (IRE) (bl) 33-1 **Miss T Hirst** *Last til rfo 3*

OFFICIAL DISTANCES: 1l, 3l TIME: 6min 30.9s

1623 Restricted, 12st   9 ran

[1146⁸]	1		**DARK CHALLENGER (IRE)** (bl) 7-4F R Lawther *5/2-7/4; lw; hld up; mist 3; 3½l 5th ½way; hdwy to 2l 3rd 14; mist nxt; rdn to ld app 3 out; r.o u.p*
[1437¹]	2	2½	**Romany Chat** 3-1 **A Martin** *2 handlers; pulled hrd; ld to 2; 2nd/3rd til ld 8; hdd 11; mist nxt; outpcd 14; 4l 4th & rdn when mist 15; went 2nd aft 2 out; no ex u.p*
[1588⁵]	3	6	**Smart Orange (IRE)** 5-1 **M Rimell** *Jmpd rt; sn prom; 2nd/3rd 5 til ld 11; hdd 14; rdn & ev ch 3 out; wknd app last*
[1418⁷]	4	7	**Benova Boy** (bl) 8-1 **J Diment** *2 handlers; swtng; ld 2-8; rdn 12; 2nd/3rd til ld 14; hdd und str press app 3 out; wknd nxt*
[1460⁷]	5	runin	**Native Rambler (IRE)** 25-1 **Miss C Stafford** *(xnb) Went 2nd til mist 4; lost plce 7; 10l 6th ½way; wl bhnd 13; t.o*
[1583⁷]	6	runin	**Grange Prize** 33-1 **Miss K Henry** *A bhnd; 18l 8th ½way; t.o 12*
[1453⁷]	P		**Kays-Lass** (5a) 10-1 **S Blackwell** *(xnb) 2 handlers; lw; blun 1; sn wl bhnd; mist 5; t.o & pu 6*
[1482³]	P		**Lady Emerald** (5a) 3-1 **J Tarry** *Hld up; mist 4; hdwy 8; 2½l 4th ½way; mist 12; outpcd 14; 6l 5th & rdn nxt; sn wknd; bhnd when pu 2 out*
[1482ᵁ]	P		**Tranquil Lord (IRE)** 20-1 **D Smith** *(bf) A bhnd; mist 7; 16l 7th ½way; pu 12*

OFFICIAL DISTANCES: 3l, 5l **TIME:** 6min 31.3s

1624 Open Maiden, 12st   14 ran

[1439²]	1		**HAVE A BREAK** (7a) 6-4F R Lawther *Lw; hld up; 6th when blun 5; hdwy 6; 3½l 4th ½way; went 3l 2nd aft 15; lft in ld 2 out; hung rt flat & unrideable nr fin; just hld on*
[1540²]	2	nk	**Tonrin** 20-1 **C Gordon** *Pulled hrd; ld 2; mist 8; hdd aft 13; 4l 3rd & rdn 3 out; lft w ev ch frm nxt; nt much room flat; kpt on*
[1323³]	3	20	**Muckle Jack** 6-1 **S Blackwell** *Hld up; 11l 11th ½way; 12l 8th & hrd rdn 13; 10l 5th 15; lft poor 3rd 2 out*
[1435⁴]	4	15	**Pulkerry (IRE)** 12-1 **A Martin** *16s-12s; hld up; 5l 6th ½way; w ldrs til blun bad 13; 30l 8th 15; lft 4th 2 out; t.o*
[1486ᴾ]	P		**Ben Gilmore** 14-1 **J Diment** *Lw; sn prom; went 2nd 8; rdn when mist 11; wknd qckly u.p & 10l 5th 14; wl bhnd when pu 3 out*
[1468ᴾ]	P		**Bid For Tools (IRE)** (vis) 25-1 **G Barfoot-Saunt** *Prom; rdn aft 5; 4½l 5th ½way; lost plce & mist 10; nt r.o; t.o & pu 14*
[1396⁵]	P		**Clifton Match** (5a) 25-1 **J Casemore** *A bhnd; 18l 12th ½way; t.o & pu 13*
[679ᴾ]	P		**Down To Joe's (IRE)** 20-1 **D Dennis** *Hld up; mist 4; 5½l 7th ½way; hdwy 10; mist 12; eff to disp ld 14; wknd qckly & 7l 4th 3 out; pu nxt*
[1455ᴾ]	P		**Hardy Wolf** 25-1 **F Windsor Clive** *Bhnd til eff 8; 8l 10th ½way; rdn & mist 11; sn lost tch; t.o 14; pu 3 out*
[1435ᴾ]	P		**Miss Hoity Toity** (5a) 7-1 **J Tarry** *2 handlers; v unruly padd; lw; pulled hrd; 2nd to 8; lost plce & 6l 8th ½way; bhnd when mist 11; pu 12*
[1537ᵁ]	S		**Mountain Tae (IRE)** 10-1 **R Green** *(bnh) Nt jw; sn wl bhnd; t.o 7 til slpd up flat bef 14*
[1486⁵]	P		**Shortcut Shorty** 33-1 **W Brown** *Jb; sn wl bhnd; t.o & pu 4*
[1435²]	F		**True Hustler** (bl) 6-1 **F Hutsby** *Ld til hdd aft 1; 2½l 3rd ½way; ld aft 13 til rdn & fell 2 out*
[1397ᴿ]	P		**Youmeandhim (IRE)** 5-1 **P York** *Hld up & bhnd; hdwy & 7l 9th ½way; 8l 7th & rdn 13; sn wknd; 23l 7th 15; t.o & pu 2 out*

OFFICIAL DISTANCES: ½l, 12l **TIME:** 6min 35.6s

The stewards enquired into possible interference between the 1st and 2nd after the last; having interviewed both riders they decided that the winner had drifted to the right but that the interference was accidental and had not affected the result

Fontwell (L&RH 7F,19J)

Mon, 29 May (GOOD, GOOD to FIRM in places)

1625 Alfred Day Open HC   7 ran

[1471⁴]	1		**PALACE PARADE (USA)** 11-07 8-1 **C Heard** *Hdwy to chse ldrs 6; blun 14; rdn to ld last; stayed on*
[1538³]	2	2½	**Nadjati (USA)** 12-00 5-1 **P Hall** *Sn trckng ldrs; ld 14-last; nt qckn*
[1554⁴]	3	18	**The Bold Abbot** 11-07 12-1 **Miss S West** *Ld 5-14; outpcd frm 4 out*
[1537¹]	4	1¾	**Tidal Reef (IRE)** 11-12 11-4 **C Gordon** *Hld up; hdwy to chse ldrs 4 out; rdn & wknd nxt*
[1511ᴾ]	5	15	**Andrelot** 11-07 (bl) 20-1 **Miss C Grissell** *Rr 3; bhnd & strugg frm ½way*
[1304ᴾ]	P		**Abbotsham** 11-07 25-1 **M Wilesmith** *Chsd ldrs to 10; sn wl bhnd; pu aft 4 out*

[1542¹] P   **Solo Gent** 12-07 (bl) 6-4F **T Doyle** *Jmpd mod; ld 4-5; reluct to rce aft; wknd 14; wl bhnd when pu aft 16*

TIME: 6min 52.4s **TOTE:** £10.80; places £2.70,£2.50 **Ex:** £63.70 **CSF:** £40.12

Hereford (RH 9F,19J)
Mon, 29 May (GOOD to SOFT)

1626 Clive Mdn HC   16 ran

[958⁴]   1   **LYRICAL SEAL** 11-04 (bl) 25-1 **P York** *Hld up; hdwy 5; lft 2nd 12; ld 5 out; rdn app last; hld on wl*
[1604¹] 2   1½   **Belarus (IRE)** 11-09 (bl) 9-2 **C White** *Hld up in rr; hdwy 13; hmpd 3 out; rdn & stayed on to 2nd run-in*
[1418²] 3   1¼   **Button Boy** 11-09 5-1 **S Morris** *Ld til aft 1; stayed in tch; sltly hmpd 12; went 2nd 4 out; rdn app last; one pce*
[1465²] 4   25   **Brown Wren** 11-04 14-1 **S Lloyd** *In tch til wknd 5 out; sn wl bhnd*
[1293ᴾ] P   **Across The Water** 11-04 40-1 **M Appleby** *In tch to 10; bhnd when pu 15*
[1592ᶠ] P   **Ballyharry (IRE)** 11-09 20-1 **I Wynne** *A bhnd; t.o to 14*
[1204ᴾ] P   **Broad Statement** 11-11 33-1 **J Owen** *Prom to 9; t.o & pu 15*
[1586⁴] r   **Cumberland Youth** 11-09 50-1 **J Oldring** *In tch to 10; t.o when ref last*
[1356³] F   **Maggies Brother** 11-11 8-1 **D Barlow** *Fell 3*
[1524²] F   **Native Cove (IRE)** 11-09 5-2F **L Hicks** *Mid-div; hdwy 10; cl 3rd when fell 3 out*
[1461³] P   **Our Eddie** 11-09 25-1 **B Wharfe** *A bhnd; t.o & pu 2 out*
[1569¹] P   **Roman Gale (IRE)** 11-09 13-2 **A Price** *A bhnd; t.o & pu 2 out*
[1613ᶠ] P   **Secret Can't Say (IRE)** 11-04 20-1 **Miss L Pearce** *Chsd ldrs; ld app 11; jmpd lft; hdd 5 out; sn wl bhnd pu 2 out*
[1547¹] U   **The Rum Mariner** 11-11 11-1 **Miss C Thomas** *Ld aft 1; hdd app 11; blun & ur nxt*
[1307ᴾ] U   **Tony's Croney** 11-09 25-1 **J R Barlow** *Blun & ur 2*
[1598⁷] B   **Yodeller Bill** 11-09 40-1 **J Diment** *Bd 3*

TIME: 6min 40.3s **TOTE:** £83.80; places £13.00,£2.10,£2.10 **Ex:** £617.60 **CSF:** £126.68

Uttoxeter (LH 8F,16J)
Mon, 29 May (GOOD, GOOD to SOFT in places)

1627 Parkers Executive Travel Nov HC   10 ran

[1536³] 1   **PANGERAN (USA)** 12-01 2-1F **N King** *Prom; ld 6-9; ld agn 10; prsd frm 3 out; pushed out & r.o run-in*
[1444³] 2   4   **Fursan (USA)** 11-07 (tt) 9-4 **P Phillips** *Ss; hld up & bhnd; hdwy 11; ev ch frm 3 out; rdn app last; no ex run-in*
[1534³] 3   dist   **Executive Office (IRE)** 11-09 7-1 **M Harris** *Mists; prom; ld 9-10; handy til wknd app 3 out*
[1590¹] 4   ½   **Wizadora** 10-13 20-1 **K Burke** *Hld up; hdwy 11; chsng ldrs when mist 13; wknd app nxt*
[1592ᴾ] 5   7   **Ballyhannon (IRE)** 11-07 50-1 **Miss J Froggatt** *Midfield; bhnd frm 6; nvr on terms aft*
[904ᴾ]   6   29   **Very Daring** 11-07 40-1 **Miss S Sharratt** *Midfield early; bhnd final circ; t.o*
[1592ᵁ] B   **Black Book (IRE)** 11-09 40-1 **A Sansome** *Bhnd; mist 1; bd 9*
[1340³] P   **Itsforu** 11-11 9-2 **A Wintle** *Ld to 9; wknd & pu 13*
[1464³] F   **Jack Cruise** 11-11 16-1 **T Scudamore** *Chsd ldrs; niggled along aft 8; fell 9*
[1480¹] B   **Spectacular View (IRE)** 11-04 9-1 **M Clayton** *In tch til bd 9*

TIME: 5min 23.3s **TOTE:** £3.30 **places** £1.40,£1.40,£2.10 **Ex:** £5.90 **CSF:** £6.66

Wetherby (LH 9F,15J)
Mon, 29 May (GOOD to SOFT)

1628 Guy Cunard HC   10 ran

[1478³] 1   **ORSWELLTHATENSWELL** 11-07 14-1 **Mrs F Needham** *Ld 2; blun 12 & rdr lurched forward; kpt on & stayed on wl flat*
[1556⁴] 2   1½   **Strathmore Lodge** 10-10 (1) 6-1 **D Jewett** *Jmpd slow 2; hld up; went 2nd & jmpd slow 9 (water); tk 2nd aft nxt; mist 12; hit 3 out; kpt on wl flat; a hld*
[1345¹] 3   6   **Hiltonstown Lass (IRE)** 11-11 13-8F **R Walford** *Hld up; mist 3; 5th & rdn aft 11; eff to flatt nxt; sn one pce & no imp*
[1559²] 4   1¾   **My Nominee** 11-09 (bl) 6-1 **R Burton** *Ld til hmpd bad 2; chsd ldrs til 10l 6th aft 11; tried to rally nxt; plugged on & nd aft*
[1476¹] 5   dist   **Red Spectacle (IRE)** 11-07 3-1 **N Tutty** *Chsd ldrs; 4th aft 11; wknd nxt; t.o*

[1446⁴]	6	12	**Juke Box Billy (IRE)** 11-05 (tt) 20-1 W Burnell *Last pr; rdn aft 8; lost tch 11; t.o when blun 2 out*
[1531⁴]	U		**Admiral Villeneuve** 11-00 20-1 P Robson *Mist 10; 2nd/3rd til 3rd & rdn aft 11; 6th & wkng rap when blun & ur 12*
[1331ᶠ]	P		**Look Sharpe** 11-02 25-1 C Mulhall *Jmpd rt; a bhnd; t.o & pu 12*
[1434²]	F		**Pro Bono (IRE)** 12-02 11-2 A Charles-Jones *2nd when fell 2*
[1537⁶]	P		**Uncle Den** 11-00 33-1 T Lane *Mists; towards rr; lost tch 7; t.o & pu 12*

TIME: 5min 27.6s TOTE: £24.60; places £2.80,£2.60,£1.40 **Ex:** £272.90 CSF: £91.08

Albrighton Woodland
Chaddesley Corbett (LH 8F,18J) Mon, 29 May (GOOD)

1629 Hunt, 12st
8 ran

[1523³]	1		**JUST MARMALADE** 8-1 Miss J Williams *Jw; prom; ld 5-7; chsd wnr frm 12; ev ch frm 3 out; nt pce to chall; fin 3½l 2nd; subsq promoted*
[1525⁵]	2	6	**Nick The Biscuit** (4x) 5-2 Julian Pritchard *Trckd ldrs; mist 9; hdwy 12; lost plce 14; stayed on one pce frm 3 out; no threat to ldrs; fin 3rd; subsq promoted*
[864³]	3	7	**Percy Medlicott** 8-1 P Needham *1st ride; in tch; disp 3l 4th 10; lost tch 12; stayed on to 4th nr fin; subsq promoted*
[1547²]	5	s hd	**Military Man** (4x) 10-11F M Keel *Ld to 4; ld agn 9-11; cl up til outpcd app 15; trying to rally when blun nxt; 4th & no ch aft; dem cl home*
[1090⁵]	6	20	**Nutty Solera** 14-1 E Williams *Cl up; disp 3l 4th 10; chsd ldng pr frm 12; ev ch 15; wknd app nxt*
[1335⁹]	1d		**Burkean Melody (IRE)** (tt) 33-1 M Munrowd *Last pr til hdwy 7; ld nxt; sn hdd; ld agn 12; made rest; r.o wl u.p frm 2 out; won by 3½l; disq - rdr nt qualified*
[995⁷]	P		**Cracking Crumpet** (5a) 33-1 M Rodda *Cl up 4/5th; wkng 6l last 11; lost tch nxt; bhnd when pu 3 out*
[790⁸]	P		**Tibs Eve (IRE)** (21ow) 33-1 M Rose *1st ride; imm last; mists; lost tch 4; 25l detach 6; t.o & pu 8*

OFFICIAL DISTANCES: 3l, 5l TIME: 6min 13.2s
> An objection by the Secretary of the Hunt to the rider of the winner was referred to the Jockey Club Disciplinary Committee; he was found not to be qualified and fined £100, the horse was disqualified and the placed horses promoted

1630 Confined, 12st
8 ran

[1585³]	1		**MR DENNEHY (IRE)** (3x) 9-2 J Jukes *Prom; prsd ldr in cl 2nd 5 til disp 12; ld app 3 out til just hdd app last; lft clr*
[1463⁵]	2	8	**Chassagne (FR)** 9-4 J Price *Last & sltly detach to 4; some hdwy whn bad mist 6; 111 7th 10; 4th 3 out; stayed on to 3rd aft 2 out; no ch when lft 2nd at last*
[1358⁵]	3	3	**Spearhead Again (IRE)** 25-1 M Munrowd *Made most til jnd 12; disp til outpcd & releg 3rd app 3 out; nd aft; dem 4th aft 2 out; lft 3rd at last*
[1272ᶠ]	4	25	**Haven Light** 10-1 Julian Pritchard *Cl 3rd/4th til wknd app 15; no ch frm 3 out*
[1529³]	5	2½fs	**Eau So Sloe** (bl) 33-1 R Carey *Spurs; disp ld 3; prom to 8; last by 10; lost tch nxt; t.o 12; clambered over 14*
[1408¹]	F		**Bishops Hall** (3x) evensF A Crow *Midfield; hdwy to 4th 12; rdn along in 3rd app 15; chall frm 3 out; just ld & fell last; unlucky*
[1463⁴]	P		**Kingsthorpe** 10-1 A Phillips *Rr early; w ldrs 8; 5l 4th 10; wknd 12; lost tch 14; bhnd & pu 3 out*
[1460⁴]	P		**Lindalighter** (5a) 33-1 M Rodda *Rr; mist & releg last 4; 7l 6th 10; short-lived eff app 12; lost tch 14; bhnd & pu 3 out*

OFFICIAL DISTANCES: 8l, 4l TIME: 5min 57.2s

1631 Mixed Open, 12st
9 ran

[1416ᶠ]	1		**BARNA BOY (IRE)** 5-1 M Hewitt *Jmpd bold; ld; up to 25l clr; pegged back uphill app 3 out; 10l up 2 out; kpt on game*
[1524¹]	2	15	**Jalcanto** 4-1 D Mansell *Handy in chsng group; hdwy 12; 2nd frm 14; chsd wnr & tried hrd to clse; 10l down 2 out; no imp aft; eased last 25yds*
[1583⁸]	3	25	**Real Progress (IRE)** (bl) 33-1 D Renney *Chsd clr ldr til wknd 13; 3rd & no ch ldng pr frm 15*
[1545¹]	4	25	**Hurricane Andrew (IRE)** 10-1 Miss V Price *1st ride; imm detach last; t.o 6; jmpd v slow 7; fnce bhnd 10; r.o frm hopeless posn to poor 4th 3 out*

[1492⁵] 5 10 **Furry Fox (IRE)** 20-1 G Barfoot-Saunt *A towards rr; lost tch 11; sn t.o; releg last 3 out; snatched 5th cl home*

[19⁶] 6 ½ **Amber Spark (IRE)** 33-1 M Rodda *A last trio; lost tch 11; t.o frm nxt; dem last cl home*

[1552⁴] S **Egypt Mill Prince** 25-1 E Walker *Prom; 3rd to 10; 5th & wkng when slpd up bend bef 12*

[1585¹] P **Fresh Prince** 1-2F **Julian Pritchard** *Rr & nt fluent til hdwy 10; lft 3rd app 12; sn wknd; pu 14*

[1014³] S **Grey Smoke** 4-1 Miss B Lloyd *Handy in chsng group; hdwy in 3rd when slpd up bend bef 12*

OFFICIAL DISTANCES: 20l, 25l TIME: 5min 53.3s

The stewards enquired into the running and riding of the favourite, Fresh Prince; they accepted the rider's explanation that the horse was never jumping or travelling well

1632 Intermediate, 12st   16 ran

[1321¹] 1 **GLACIAL TRIAL (IRE)** (5a,5x) (bl) 2-1F M Worthington *Trckd ldrs in mid-div to 8; 6½l 4th 10; chall frm 3 out til hit last; sn rec; ld & forged clr last 50yds*

[1588³] 2 2½ **Achill Sound** 4-1 G Hanmer *Hld up; 10l 7th 10; hdwy to 2nd 13; ld 15; slt advant nxt til hdd & no ex u.p last 50yds*

[1523¹] 3 1½ **Rising Sap** (bl) 8-1 A Wadlow *A.p; ld 12 til hdd app 15; cl 3rd & ev ch frm nxt; one pce*

[1548¹] 4 10 **Coddington Girl** (5a) 9-2 T Stephenson *Trckd ldrs; 8l 6th 10; cl 3rd 13 til wknd 3 out*

[1588⁷] 5 1 **Prestige Lord (IRE)** 8-1 Miss L Sweeting *Tde; prom; chsd ldrs frm 13; one pce frm 3 out*

[1601⁴] 6 10 **Bubble N Squeek** 20-1 C Barlow *Midfield; 11l 8th 10; hdwy app 12; 4th nxt; wknd stdly frm 14*

[1460¹] 7 4 **Sam Quale (IRE)** 6-1 M Rimell *A rr; lost tch 11; bhnd aft*

[1459⁷] 8 20 **Rascaletto** (5a) 12-1 M Keel *A rr; detach 9; wl bhnd frm 12*

[1436⁴] P **Apple Nicking** 33-1 E Linehan *Mist 2; prom to 4; bhnd 8; sn detach; t.o & pu 12*

[1459¹] P **Dunethna (IRE)** 6-1 A Evans *Rr when jmpd v slow 4 (ditch); 15l adrift 7; t.o & pu 11*

[1317²] P **Henwyn** 33-1 A Dalton *In tch; cl 3rd 8 til 2nd & hit 12; sn lost plce; bhnd 15 til pu 2 out*

[1356⁴] P **Money Don't Matter** (5a) 16-1 D Mansell *A rr; detach 9; wl bhnd 12 til pu 3 out*

[668³] P **Rap Up Fast (USA)** 7-1 Julian Pritchard *Ld to 3; prom to 8; lost plce qckly & 13l 9th 10; eased & pu 12*

[1357⁵] P **Robero** (tt) 20-1 M Munrowd *Rr when blun bad 3; 10l detach when jmpd slow 4 (ditch); pu nxt*

[1528⁷] P **Scallymay** (5a) 33-1 C Wadland *Prom & pulling; ld 4; hdd app 12; lost plce qckly; pu 11*

[1615⁷] P **Sea Search** 33-1 J Keen *Rr; blun 8; sn detach; t.o 11; pu nxt*

OFFICIAL DISTANCES: 3½l, 1½l TIME: 5min 58.5s

1633 Dodson & Horrell PPORA Club Members Restricted   5 ran

[1493¹] 1 **AUTUMN BLUNDER** 9-2 T Stephenson *Trckd ldrs; disp cl 2nd 8-13; chsd ldr aft; str chall frm 2 out; hit last; rallied flat; ld last 25yds*

[569¹] 2 hd **Alstack (IRE)** (bl) 4-6F A Crow *Trckd ldrs til ld 7; slt mist 13; jnd 2 out; gd j last; r.o flat; hdd & no ex last 25yds*

[1551⁵] 3 15 **Crestwood Lad (USA)** 3-1 M Yardley *Swtng; jw; ld to 6; cl up til wknd app 15; nd aft*

[1528⁵] 4 12 **Out Of The Blue** (5a) 11-1 S Graham *A last pr; in tch to 14; plugged on one pce frm nxt*

P **Prince Itsu** 25-1 J Jukes *Pulling in cl 2nd; lost plce 7; disp last frm nxt; in tch til wknd 14; pu nxt*

OFFICIAL DISTANCES: hd, 15l TIME: 6min 07.5s

1634 Open Maiden (Div 1), 12st - 16J   17 ran

[1056⁷] 1 **ITSFREDDIE** 12-1 J Jukes *Settled rr; 9th 10; hdwy frm 12; cl 4th 14; prsd ldr 2 out til ld flat; r.o u.p*

[1589⁷] 2 2½ **Craftbook Marchesa (IRE)** (5a,4ow) 12-1 P Millington *(xnb) Mid-div; hdwy app 12; cl 2nd nxt; ld 2 out; hdd & no ex flat*

[1537⁷] 3 10 **Wood Buzzard** 5-1 E Walker *A.p; 2nd 10-12; ev ch 3 out til no ex frm nxt; btn when blun last*

[1465⁴] 4 10 **Crab 'n Lobster** (5a) 8-1 R Hodges *Tde; wl in rr; 11th 10; hdwy frm 15; nt rch ldrs; went 4th flat*

[1527ᵁ] 5 1 **May Rose** (5a) 11-1 Julian Pritchard *(xnb) Ld til wknd & hdd 2 out; 4th when mist last; dem flat*

[1412⁵] 6 1½ **The Quakers Wake (IRE)** 14-1 C Barlow *Rr most of way; r.o one pce frm 3 out; best plce fin*

[901ᶠ] 7 3 **Quixotry** 3-1JF S Joynes *(xnb) Mist 1; midfield til hdwy 10; sn prom; went 3rd 12; cl up til wknd qckly app 3 out*

[1589ᴾ]	P	**Aldington Annie** (5a) 8-1 **M Rimell** *Jmpd slow 4; prom 6 til mist 12; bhnd 15; pu 2 out*
[1555ᵁ]	F	**Comic Turn** 14-1 **C Wadland** *(xnb) Rr div til fell 6; dead*
[1526ᶠ]	B	**Daneswell** 16-1 **M Worthington** *Rr til bd 6*
[1589ᶠ]	P	**Don Royal** 16-1 **Miss G Harriss** *Midfield early; wl in rr 8; detach 10 til pu 12*
[1465ᶠ]	P	**Forestry** 10-1 **G Barfoot-Saunt** *W ldrs to 10; wknd stdly frm nxt; bhnd when jmpd v slow 15; pu nxt*
[1197³]	P	**Moscow Squeaker (IRE)** 3-1JF **M Rodda** *A rr; lost tch 10; pu 12; lame*
	P	**Ron Miel (IRE)** 5-1 **A Phillips** *A rr div; lost tch 11; t.o 12 til pu 3 out*
[1573ˢ]	R	**Sister Jim** (5a) (bl) 20-1 **S Graham** *V late to saddle & start; jmpd sticky & rstrnd in detach last to 4; in tch nxt; hdwy on outer 7; rn thro wing & ur nxt*
[1464²]	S	**Tedstone Fox** 10-1 **Miss R Reynolds** *Handy to 10; slpd up flat bef 14*
[1277ᶠ]	P	**Wee Kelpie** (5a) 20-1 **A Wadlow** *(xnb) Cl 2nd to 10; wknd app 12; bhnd when pu last*

OFFICIAL DISTANCES: 3l, 10l   **TIME:** 6min 11.7s

Fence 14 was omitted - fallen horse; fence 16 was omitted - fallen rider

1635 Open Maiden (Div 2), 12st   8 ran

[1527⁴]	1		**BARNEY BEAR** 4-1 **M Worthington** *Trckd ldrs in 5th til hdwy 9; cl 3rd nxt; ld 13; made rest; went clr 2 out; r.o wl flat*
[1412³]	2	5	**Blacon Point** 4-1 **T Stephenson** *Pulled hrd; cl 2nd to 8; prom; prsd wnr 3 out; one pce frm nxt*
[1435⁸]	3	6	**Millstock** (5a) 10-1 **Miss N Stallard** *In tch towards rr; 7l 6th 12; lost tch 15; kpt on same pce frm 3 out; went 3rd at last*
[1527ᶠ]	4	5	**See More Action** 5-4F **A Wadlow** *Ld; jmpd low at times; hdd 13; ev ch til wknd 3 out; 3rd & btn when mist 2 out; dem at last*
[1596³]	5	25	**Timothy George (IRE)** (1ow) 20-1 **P Millington** *In tch; rdn along frm 11; wknd 14; wl bhnd frm 3 out*
[1092⁵]	P		**Come On Boy** 5-1 **D Mansell** *A last of main bunch; mists 2 & 4; 8l 7th 12; wknd 14; lost tch nxt; pu 3 out*
[1464⁴]	P		**Sales Dodger (IRE)** 10-1 **R Hodges** *Prom; went 2nd 9; ½l down 12; wknd rap frm nxt; sn lost tch; pu 15*
[1466⁵]	P		**Sister Sue** (5a) 20-1 **Miss R Reynolds** *A last; 10l adrift & jmpd slow 6; 28l last 10; t.o 12; clambered over 14; pu nxt*

OFFICIAL DISTANCES: 6l, 6l   **TIME:** 6min 09.0s

South Tetcott

Lifton (RH 7F,19J) Mon, 29 May (GOOD with SOFT patches)

1636 Confined, 12st   7 ran

[1046ᶠ]	1		**IT'SNOTSIMPLE (IRE)** (5a,3x) 7-2 **Miss T Messer-Bennetts** *7s-7/2; rr early; prog 9; ld 12; prsd str frm 3 out; slt ld 2 out; pushed clr run-in; wl rdn*
[1515⁹]	2	2	**Strong Stuff (IRE)** 25-1 **N Mitchell** *(bf) Lw; sn prom; disp ld 7-12; trckd ldr nxt; sust chall frm 3 out; ev ch til drvn & no ex frm 2 out*
[1514²]	3	6	**Brown Robber** (3x) **T Dennis** *(xnb) Tchd evens; prom; nt a fluent; cl 3rd ½way; rdn 14; 3½l 3rd 3 out; one pce*
[1514⁷]	4	5	**Good King Henry** 33-1 **I Widdicombe** *Handy; 6th & in tch 12; prog to 3rd brief aft 3 out; no ch frm nxt*
[1514ᶠ]	5	5	**Bendor Mark** (3x) 10-1 **Mrs M Hand** *Rcd just in tch; cl 4th 13; stdly outpcd frm 15; nd clsng stages*
[1174³]	P		**The Kimbler** 7-2 **Miss S Young** *Sn rr; last frm 4; bhnd frm 12; t.o & pu last*
[1389¹]	P		**Travel By Land** 6-1 **Miss T Cave** *Ld til disp 7; lost plce stdly frm 11; 6th when nt jw & rmdr 13; bhnd when pu 3 out*

OFFICIAL DISTANCES: 2l, 4l   **TIME:** 6min 07.0s

1637 Mens Open, 12st   6 ran

[1516¹]	1		**NEWMAN'S CONQUEST** (5a) 4-5F **N Mitchell** *Tchd evens; tde; jw; prom til ld aft 4; slt ld til forged clr frm 3 out; easy*
[1550¹]	2	8	**Amtrak Express** 8-1 **H Froud** *Lw; hld up; prog to 2nd 12; trckd ldr & ev ch til wknd stdly 3 out; one pce*
[1560²]	3	25	**Rasta Man** (tt) 6-4 **R Woollacott** *Cl up frm 6; lsng tch & rmdr 9; 2l 3rd 14; wkng 14; reluct & sn no ch*
[1552³]	4	15	**James Pigg** (7x) 16-1 **G Richards** *Rr; bhnd & last frm 8; fnce bhnd 11; wl adrift but drvn out to snatch 4th*

[1516⁵]   5   2   **Jeepers (IRE)** 12-1 D McKenna *In tch in 3rd 9; sn outpcd; 13l 4th 14; lost ground & hit 16; jmpd slow nxt; t.o; dem cl home*

          F   **Hopefull Drummer** 9-2 N Harris *14s-9/2; ld til bad mist 4; lost plce aft 7; 5th when fell 9*

OFFICIAL DISTANCES: 12l, dist   TIME: 6min 05.0s

1638 Ladies Open   10 ran

[1562²]   1   **BRIGHT APPROACH (IRE)** evensF Miss P Gundry *Opened 5s in plce; lw; hld up; 6th & hdwy 12; went 4th 3 out; 3rd nxt; str rn frm last to ld last 75yds*

[1444⁵]   2   1½   **Alska (FR)** (5a) 16-1 Miss W Southcombe *Lw; midfield; 17l 4th 8; prog to 3rd & gng wl 12; chsd ldr frm 14; sust chall frm 3 out; slt ld & lkd wnr last; hdd & no ex flat; gd eff*

[1444⁴]   3   3   **Thinking Twice (USA)** 100-30 Miss T Newman *Lw; disp 3rd til ld 6; hrd prsd frm 3 out; jnd 2 out; sn hdd; no ex flat*

[1515²]   4   5   **Baldhu Chance** 10-1 Miss L Gardner *(bh) Hdwy to 4th 9; slt mist 14; went 3rd nxt; 4l 3rd 3 out; one pce app 2 out*

[1470²]   5   5   **Hylters Chance (IRE)** (vis) 4-1 Miss J Cumings *Lw; declined early pce & settled 3rd; hdwy 8; went 2nd 12-14; sn rdn & outpcd; no ch frm 3 out*

[1138ᴾ]   6   1½   **Full Alirt** (5a) 10-1 Miss S Young *(b4) Dwelt; rr; 9th & bhnd 12; nd; went rem 6th 3 out; nrst fin*

[1472¹]   7   25   **Foxy Dawn** 16-1 Miss O Green *Outpcd in rr 9way; 8th ½way; just in tch in 8th 12; bhnd & no ch frm 15*

[1549¹]   8   3   **Elle Flavador** (5a) 20-1 Miss T Cave *Ld & set fast pce; jnd 3; hdd aft 6; chsd ldr til mist 11; sn rdn & lost ground; bhnd frm 15*

[1047ᴾ]   P   **Garnwin (IRE)** 14-1 Miss T Messer-Bennetts *Sn towards rr; 7th ½way; no prog; rr when pu 15*

[1522ᴾ]   P   **Golden Sunset** (5a) 100-1 Miss D Mitchell *Sn strugg in rr; bhnd frm 5; t.o & pu 12*

OFFICIAL DISTANCES: 1l, ½l   TIME: 6min 02.0s

1639 Restricted, 12st - 18J   13 ran

[1467²]   1   **LYNPHORD GIRL** (5a) 10-1 J Barnes *(xnb) Hld up; prog to 3rd 9; smooth hdwy to press ldr 3 out; disp nxt; slt ld last; r.o game u.p*

[1521¹]   2   1   **Georgetown** 8-11F L Jefford *Opened 4/5; prom til ld 5; slt ld til jnd 2 out; hrd rdn & ev ch last; nt qckn cl home*

[1518²]   3   3   **Damiens Pride (IRE)** 3-1 T Dennis *(xnb) Tchd 4s; lw; hld up in midfield; 7th 10; hdwy to 3rd 12; cl up & ev ch 3 out; wknd u.p 2 out*

[1518⁷]   4   3   **The Bandon Car (IRE)** 20-1 T Cole *Last early; 11th 8; hdwy 12; went 4th & rdn 15; kpt on stdly*

[1563ᵁ]   5   12   **Knock Star (IRE)** 10-1 I Widdicombe *Midfield; 9th ½way; prog to 6th 15; went 5th & just in tch when mist 3 out; no ex aft*

[1444ᴾ]   6   15   **Hemero (IRE)** (tt) 20-1 Miss P Gundry *Lw; sn prom; cl 5th 10; lost ground 14; pushed along & nt fluent 16; sn btn*

[1608ᶠ]   P   **Amazing Hill (IRE)** 25-1 Miss L Gardner *Sn rr; last ½way; poor 9th 15; bhnd & pu last*

[1608ᴾ]   U   **Bedtime Pixie** (bl) 66-1 Miss L Jackson *Last frm 5 til blun & ur 7; rdr inj*

[1551²]   P   **Diamond Duck** (5a) 16-1 Miss K Allan *(xnb) Prom; cl 4th 10; lsng ground when mist 13; bhnd when pu 16*

[1467³]   P   **Old Harry's Wife** (5a) 33-1 N Mitchell *9th 8; strugg & bhnd frm 12 til pu 2 out*

[1258ᶠ]   P   **Pillmere Lad** 14-1 Miss A Barnett *Cl to 5; chsd ldr to 10; sn lost plce; rr when pu 13*

[1522¹]   P   **Royal Chip** 16-1 Mrs M Hand *Tubed; midfield early; in tch in 6th ½way; outpcd 7; 8th & bhnd 15; t.o & pu last*

[1520¹]   P   **Wise Examiner (IRE)** 8-1 Richard Darke *(xnb) Lw; bolted & ur lvng padd; prom til lost plce 8; hdwy agn to 5th 14; just in tch in 6th ½way; no prog; pu 2 out*

OFFICIAL DISTANCES: ½l, 1l   TIME: 6min 07.0s
          Fence 14 omitted - injured rider

1640 Open Maiden (Div 1), 12st   10 ran

[1520²]   1   **VEILED DANCER (IRE)** (5a) evensF A Holdsworth *Tchd 5/4; patient rdn in rr; 7th & off pce 10; hdwy 13; went 2nd 15; pckd nxt; ld 2 out; r.o; comf*

[1565⁴]   2   4   **Sea Spirit** (5a) 6-1 Miss T Cave *Sn handy; cl 2nd frm 10; disp ld when lft 15l clr 14; grad wknd frm 16; hdd 2 out; no ex*

[1564⁵]   3   8   **Budghill** 9-2 Mrs M Hand *Lw; handy; 4th 9; lft 3rd nxt; outpcd 13; some prog to 12l 3rd 3 out; no imp aft*

[1062ᵁ]   4   25   **Spanish Jest** 7-1 L Tibbatts *2 handlers; oht; lft in ld 4; hdd 12; wknd rap nxt; poor 4th & rdn 16; sn no ch*

[1522³]	F		**Broad Ink** 7-1 D McKenna *Sn rr; last ½way; lft rem 5th 15; bhnd in 5th when fell 2 out; winded*
[1551⁷]	U		**Chilli Jo** (tt) 20-1 Miss S Robinson *Pulled hrd; sn prom; disp ld 6; cl 2nd 7-9; lsng plce when blun & ur 11*
[1469⁹]	P		**Frosty Jo** (5a) 14-1 T Dennis *Tde; midfield; mist 8; 6th 10; 5th & out of tch when pu 15*
[1610ᶠ]	F		**River Carron** (IRE) 12-1 G Maundrell *Prog to 3rd 10; slt ld 12; jnd & fell hvly 14; dead*
	F		**Tilleys Orchid** (5a) 66-1 A Cooksley *Fat; sn last & detach; wl bhnd til fell 7*
[1519⁹]	U		**Walton Street** 33-1 W Smith *Ld til blun & ur 4*

OFFICIAL DISTANCES: 4l, 6l TIME: 6min 16.0s
Golden Saddle (B O'Doherty - 50-1) was withdrawn at the start not under orders

1641 Open Maiden (Div 2), 12st   13 ran

[1519⁹]	1		**FRANKIES FLUTTER** 14-1 T Cole *Tchd 16s; hld up in midfield; 7th 8; rdr cab-hailing 11; went 3rd 12; 8l 3rd nxt; chall & mist 16; ld nxt; sn clr; jmpd lft 2 out & last; rdr ecstatic*
[1372²]	2	10	**Inforapop** (7a) 10-11F N Mitchell *Tchd evens; lw; settled last; sn wl off pce; 9th 10; some prog 13; went 5th & lot to do 15; 5th 3 out; r.o stdly to 2nd 2 out; kpt on; hanging app last*
[1520⁵]	3	8	**Patrio** (IRE) (5a) 33-1 J Cole *Ld 4-8; hit 11; disp ld & rmdr 12; ld 13-16; outpcd frm 3 out; tired & blun 2 out; just kpt 3rd*
[1178²]	4	½	**John Robin** 5-2 M Sweetland *Tde; prom til disp ld 9-12; 7l 3rd & niggled along 15; sn wknd; 20l blun & last 3 out; no ch*
[1522⁹]	5	10	**Just Mai-Bee** 33-1 B O'Doherty *5th ½way; lost tch w ldrs 13; plodded on u.p & 22l 4th 3 out; one pce*
	P		**Dawn Caller** (IRE) 10-1 Richard Darke *(xnb) Ld to 3; still prom in 4th 12; wkng & pckd nxt; pu 15*
[1520⁹]	U		**Ever Eddy** 4-1 T Dennis *10s-4s; mid-div when blun & ur 7*
[934ᶠ]	P		**Frisky-Breeze** (5a) 33-1 L Tibbatts *Tde; 8th 8; last frm 10; bhnd when pu 13*
[1519ᴿ]	P		**Golden Jester** (5a) 20-1 J Young *(xnb) Sn rr; slt prog to 7th 9; nd; rr when jmpd slow 13; pu nxt*
[1522⁹]	P		**Linton** (5a) 25-1 W Smith *Prom early; 4th ½way; wknd 12; 8th & bhnd when pu 14*
[1519ᴿ]	R		**Miltown Castle** 33-1 D Stephens (Devon) *(xnb) Rr; slt mist 6; bhnd when rn out 9*
[1520⁹]	P		**North Coast Girl** (5a) 33-1 A Ede *Midfield; 7th 10; no prog; bhnd when pu 16*
[1517ᵁ]	P		**Warning Board** 33-1 J Berwick *A rr; 10th 9; bhnd & pu 13*

OFFICIAL DISTANCES: 8l, ½l TIME: 6min 25.0s

1642 Hunt   3 ran

[1262¹]	1		**MY PRIDES WAY** (5a) 3-1 Miss D Penwill *Opened 7/2; made all; hrd prsd & drvn aft 12; lft clr 14; 6l up 3 out; in comm when mist nxt; unchall; rdr's 1st wnr*
[1522²]	2	runin	**Broughton's Port** 9-4 T Dennis *Tchd 100/30; hld up in tch; lft 2nd 14; sn rdn & wknd; v tired & wl btn when climbed last; walked in*
[1521²]	r		**Country Gem** 4-5F Miss K Baily *Trckd ldr; hdwy 12; cl up til mist 13; reluct to cont; ref & threw rdr over nxt*

OFFICIAL DISTANCE: dist TIME: 6min 28.0s

Cartmel (LH 6F,18J)
Wed, 31 May (GOOD to FIRM)

1643 Guinness HC   16 ran

[1477³]	1		**TEMPLE GARTH** 11-07 33-1 G Brewer *Chsd ldrs; went 3rd 13 & 2nd nxt; sust chall aft last; stayed on dour u.p to ld 100yds out; all out; wl edn*
[1559⁴]	2	1¾	**Murphys Way** 11-02 20-1 J Burley *Sn chsng ldrs; ld 7; mist 10; went clr aft 12; 7l ahd last; rdn & kpt on game til tired & hdd final 100yds*
[1445⁵]	3	2	**Dennett Lough** (IRE) 12-00 16-1 C Storey *8th & rdn 6; eff 8; bumped along to chse ldrs aft 12; 4th 15; 3rd at last; no imp til stayed on u.p final furlong*
[1542ᵁ]	4	nk	**Aly Daley** (IRE) 11-07 20-1 Miss A Price *Ld 3-7; prsd ldr to 14; 4th when rdn & outpcd last; kpt on agn final furlong*
[1534¹]	5	1¼	**Silverdalesureshot** 12-04 9-4JF R Burton *Bhnd; 9th when jmpd slow 7; nvr gng wl aft; 20l frm ldr 14; mod prog u.p nxt; sn btn; rallied & stayed on final furlong*
[1031⁴]	6	11	**Pebble Beach** (IRE) 11-07 (tt) 25-1 N Kent *Mist 1; chsd ldrs; 6th 14; rdn & strugg aft; eased aft last*
[1578¹]	7	1½	**Steel Rigg** (IRE) 11-07 10-1 P Aspell *5th when jmpd slow 7 & rdn; scrubbed along & strugg frm 13*

[1578[P]]	8	dist	**Excise Man** 12-04 (tt) 16-1 J Walton *Bit bckwd; bhnd; mist 7; prog in 6th 13; wknd nxt; mist 3 out; t.o*
[1253[r]]	r		**Commercial Artist** 12-01 20-1 T Scudamore *Tubed; sn drvn along & reluct; prom; 4th 7; lost plce qckly & jmpd v slow 8; t.o when ref 14*
[1602[4]]	U		**Full Of Chat (IRE)** 11-02 50-1 D Jewett *Swtng; ld to 3; blun bad & ur 4*
	P		**Little-Nipper** 11-07 50-1 Miss A Armitage *Cl up early; drpd to rr aft 6; sn t.o; pu 9*
[1578[5]]	U		**Lottery Ticket (IRE)** 11-07 50-1 S J Robinson *Mostly 3rd til mist 13; drvn along in most ungainly fashion aft; 10l 5th 15; 6th when rfo 2 out*
[1530[3]]	F		**Over The Hill (IRE)** 12-04 8-1 M Armytage *Nt fluent & bhnd early; 6th & prog when fell 12*
[1500[3]]	P		**Rysanshyn** 11-02 33-1 L McGrath *(xnb) A last trio; t.o & rdn aft 12; pu 2 out*
[1591[1]]	U		**Sounds Strong (IRE)** 11-11 9-4JF R Morgan *Lw; rr til stumbled aft 3 (water) & ur*
[1578[2]]	P		**Wudimp** 12-00 14-1 Miss P Robson *A bhnd; t.o last 12; pu 14*

TIME: 6min 37.9s **TOTE:** £61.10; places £11.20,£5.90,£3.50 CSF: £502.55

Newton Abbot (LH 7F,20J)
Thu, 1 Jun (GOOD, GOOD to SOFT in places)

1644 Newton Abbot Racecourse Final HC   9 ran

[1535[2]]	1		**LEAD STORY (IRE)** 11-00 11-4F Miss T Cave *Trckd ldrs; hit 6; went 2nd 15; ld nxt; clr aft 17; nt fluent last; easy*
[1432[4]]	2	25	**Track O' profit (IRE)** 11-00 5-1 Miss S Young *Chsd ldrs; chall 13; chsd wnr frm 3 out but no imp; hung lft u.p run-in*
[1388[1]]	3	1¼	**No More Nice Guy (IRE)** 11-00 14-1 Mrs M Hand *Bhnd; hdwy 15; chsd ldrs frm 17; staying on for 2nd but no ch w wnr when hmpd run-in; one pce*
[1175[1]]	4	5	**O So Bossy** 11-03 (3) 4-1 Miss J Congdon *Ld; hit 8 & 13; hdd 16 & lost plce; rallied app 3 out; wknd nxt*
[1516[3]]	5	nk	**Dancing Ranger** 11-07 10-1 L Jefford *A in tch; hit 13; wknd 3 out*
[1449[5]]	6	5	**Detroit Davy (IRE)** 11-04 6-1 E Williams *Chsd ldrs; chall 13; wknd aft 3 out*
[1636[3]]	P		**Brown Robber** 11-00 12-1 T Dennis *Bhnd; hdwy 6; hit 7 & mists aft til wknd & pu 14*
[1535[4]]	P		**Flockmaster (IRE)** 11-02 10-1 M Foley *Hdwy 6; wknd 14; t.o & pu last*
[1562[6]]	P		**Uckerby Lad** 11-00 10-1 C Heard *Bhnd; rdn 13; sn lost tch; t.o & pu 2 out*

TIME: 6min 51.4s **TOTE:** £3.00; places £1.50,£1.70,£3.50 **Ex:** £21.60 CSF: £16.21 Tri: £72.30

Stratford (LH 8F)
Fri, 2 Jun (GOOD)

1645 Marsh UK Ltd/TBA Mares Club Championship Final HC   8 ran

[1558[5]]	1		**AFRICAN WARRIOR** 11-03 8-1 Miss L Horner *Lw; tkn stdly in rr; still 15l 4th 13; stayed on wl frm nxt; ld 2 out; rdn & kpt on game*
[1248[2]]	2	4	**Posh Spice (IRE)** 11-07 16-1 B Hitchcott *Lw; towards rr; 12l 4th & rdn aft 10; drvn to cl frm 3 out; went 2nd & nt fluent last; nt qckn*
[1098[2]]	3	10	**Glevum** 11-07 7-2 T Scudamore *Rdn at sev stages; set fast pce to 5; ld agn 10; hit 12; blun 13 & hdd; ld aft 3 out-nxt; fin tired*
[1524[4]]	F	dist	**Jacob's Wife** 11-12 (bl) 100-30JF R Burton *Ld 5-10; sn rdn & no resp; toiling in last app 13; t.o*
[1588[2]]	P		**Ardeal** 11-05 100-30JF F Windsor Clive *Swtng; handy til mist 7; rdn & strugg nxt; poor 7th when pu 10*
[1618[3]]	P		**Marnies Song** 11-06 (bl) 66-1 P York *Hit 1; detach in last plce til pu aft 10*
[1443[4]]	P		**Secret Truth** 11-03 9-1 A Martin *Swtng; prom early; outpcd 8; strugg when pu 11*
[1628[2]]	P		**Strathmore Lodge** 11-03 9-1 P Aspell *Went 3rd 8; 2nd & rdn 11; hit 12; ld aft nxt; drvn along aft; tired when hdd aft 3 out; sn pu*

TIME: 6min 08.6s **TOTE:** £9.90; places £2.10,£2.30,£1.20 **Ex:** £293.70 CSF: £89.18

1646 Weatherbys (John Corbet Cup) Champion Nov HC   16 ran

[1559[1]]	1		**LORD HARRY (IRE)** 11-08 (1) 7-2 A Crow *Lw; settled towards rr; prog & mist 11; 5th 17; qcknd aft 3 out; ld app nxt; kpt on str; impressive*
[1593[1]]	2	1½	**Balisteros (FR)** 11-07 6-1 Miss J Wormall *Lw; settled midfield; hit 10 & rdn; mist 13; went 4th 16 & 2nd nxt; ld 3 out til app nxt; kpt on game; no ext*
[1340[1]]	3	30	**Lakefield Rambler (IRE)** 11-09 2-1F Miss P Gundry *Set str gallop; hit 10; rdn & hdd 3 out; sn btn; jmpd slow last*
[1433[6]]	4	7	**Shuil's Star (IRE)** 11-11 16-1 E Williams *Hdwy to chse ldrs 5; outpcd aft 14; mist 18; no ch aft*

[1492¹]	5	6	**Smile Pleeze (IRE)** 11-07 16-1 T Stephenson *Swtng; bhnd; hit 12; nvr nr ldrs*
[1540¹]	6	2½	**Rustic Revelry** 11-09 20-1 P York *Prom; pckd 4; 6th & u.p 16; wknd nxt*
[1558³]	7	¾	**Freedom Fighter** 11-07 33-1 A Martin *Swtng; prom early; rr 12; no ch aft*
[1537³]	8	dist	**Newby End (IRE)** 11-07 50-1 D Dennis *Chsd ldrs to 14; sn strugg; t.o*
[1557²]	U		**Baron Allfours** 12-00 40-1 A Sansome *(citation) Last pr til virt fell & ur 4*
[1539²]	P		**Bolshie Baron** 11-09 (tt) 40-1 M Harris *Swtng; sn bhnd; last 9; t.o & pu 14*
[1621¹]	P		**Castle Folly (IRE)** 11-09 (bl) 12-1 R Lawther *Lw; prsd ldr; mist 2; hit 10; releg 3rd 17; wkng when mist nxt; rr when pu 2 out*
[1410³]	U		**Dawn's Cognac (IRE)** 12-00 12-1 J Jukes *Nvr btr than midfield; blun 11; lost tch 14; 11th when mist & ur 3 out*
[1533⁴]	P		**Lakeside Lad** 12-00 33-1 T Doyle *Chsd ldrs to 13; wknd nxt; t.o & pu 2 out*
[1532³]	P		**Mr Smudge** 11-11 50-1 J Trice-Rolph *Sn lost gd plce; rr 7; t.o 13; pu 15*
[1333²]	P		**Philtre (IRE)** 12-00 14-1 Julian Pritchard *Lw; sn chsng clr ldng pr; hit 12; wknd aft 16; mist 18; rr when pu 2 out*
[1586ᴾ]	F		**Polly Live Wire** 11-09 50-1 A Charles-Jones *Last pr til fell 4*

TIME: 7min 08.7s **TOTE:** £4.40; places £2.00,£1.80,£2.00 **Ex:** £19.40 **CSF:** £22.10 **Tri:** £16.10

Stratford (LH 8F)
Sat, 3 Jun (GOOD)

1647 Intrum Justitia (Horse & Hound Cup) Champion HC   7 ran

[1337¹]	1		**CASTLE MANE (IRE)** 12-00 11-10F B Pollock *3rd/4th til went 2nd 10-12 & agn 13; ld 16; disp nxt; drvn & r.o str; impressive*
[1432¹]	2	4	**Grimley Gale (IRE)** 11-09 2-1 R Burton *Settled 3rd/4th; chsd wnr brief aft 16; rdn to 2nd agn 18; tried to cl & hit 2 out; sn no imp; rn wl*
[1024²]	3	2½	**Last Option** 12-00 11-2 Mrs F Needham *Ww; mist 12; hit 16; eff to chse wnr 17-nxt; ev ch 3 out; sn rdn & outpcd; btn when blun 2 out*
[1561¹]	4	dist	**Millyhenry** 12-00 12-1 Miss C Tizzard *Chsd ldr to 10 & frm 12 til mist nxt; rdn 15; lost tch 16; mist 17; t.o*
[1533ᴾ]	P		**Funcheon Gale** 12-00 100-1 A Charles-Jones *A last & sn bad outpcd; t.o 11; pu 14*
[1600ᴾ]	U		**Mr Motivator** 12-00 50-1 F Windsor Clive *Ld; hit 12; drvn nxt; blun 15 & rdn; hdd 16; wknd rap & blun 17; poor 5th when blun & ur 18; dead*
[1601¹]	P		**Whatafellow (IRE)** 12-00 (bl) 11-1 A Crow *Hld up 6th & detach frm main group; clsd brief aft 13; hit nxt & rdn; no resp; t.o & pu aft 17*

TIME: 7min 07.4s **TOTE:** £1.90; places £1.70,£1.70 **Ex:** £3.60 **CSF:** £3.57 **Tri:** £3.70

1648 Horse & Hound Ladies HC   18 ran

[1585²]	1		**VITAL ISSUE** 10-07 33-1 Miss J Foster *Trckd ldrs; 8th & mist 9; 10l 5th when mist 15; still 10l 5th 3 out; gd hdwy app nxt; ld sn aft last; pushed clr*
[1605¹]	2	2½	**Look In The Mirror** 10-10 4-1F Miss L Sweeting *Made most; hit 11; hdd & lft in ld 2 out; hdd agn sn aft last & no ex*
[1600³]	3	7	**Mr Dow Jones (IRE)** 10-10 12-1 Miss L Pearce *Chsng ldrs when jmpd slow 8; 4th 10; went 2nd 11; rdn to ld when blun & nrly ur 2 out; sn hdd & nt rec*
[1603²]	4	7	**Misti Hunter (IRE)** 10-11 20-1 Mrs C Ford *Trckd ldrs; 7th 10; outpcd 14; no ch frm nxt; kpt on agn frm 2 out*
[1579²]	5	4	**Nova Nita** 10-02 16-1 Miss J Wormall *Hld up in rr; prog 9; 9th 10; eff to disp 3rd 14; wknd 3 out*
[1600¹]	6	3	**Bullens Bay (IRE)** 10-10 14-1 Miss F Wilson *Mid-div; mist 4; 10th when mist 10; 7th & strugg 14; nd aft*
[1593⁴]	7	17	**Just Bert (IRE)** 10-10 16-1 Miss T Cave *A rr; impeded 12; brief eff nxt; sn btn*
[1541¹]	8	29	**Young Nimrod (tt)** 10-10 20-1 Miss C Grissell *Prom to 6; sn lost plce; 12th & rdn 10; no ch frm nxt; t.o*
[1542²]	9	8	**John Tufty** 10-07 66-1 Miss R Illman *Sn in rr; t.o 14*
[1626²]	10	1¼	**Native Cove (IRE)** 10-05 33-1 Miss S Sharratt *Rcd wide; mid-div; mist 7; 11th 10; lost tch nxt; t.o*
[1597¹]	U		**Castle Lynch (IRE)** 10-12 7-1 Miss P Robson *Cl up; nt much room on inner & lost plce bend bef 4; prog 8; 6th 10; 5th & gng wl when mist & ur 12*
[1587⁴]	U		**Cede Nullis** 10-02 (bl) 50-1 Miss L Eddery *Ss to 6; ur 2 out*
[1570²]	P		**Coolvawn Lady (IRE)** 10-04 8-1 Miss C Thomas *Prom; 5th 10; wknd rap aft nxt; t.o & pu 3 out (in foal)*
[1553¹]	F		**Hearts Are Wild** 10-09 13-2 Miss P Gundry *Rcd wide; prom; chsd ldr 4-11; prom to 3 out; 4th & btn when fell nxt*
[1446ᴿ]	P		**Howayman** 11-04 (bl) 11-1 Miss V Jackson *Trckd ldrs; went 3rd 10; wknd 13; mist nxt; 8th when jmpd delib 15; pu nxt*
[1587¹]	U		**Maltby Son** 10-08 (1) 20-1 Mrs T Hill *Sn bhnd & nvr gng wl; t.o 6; mist & ur 9*

[1305⁶] U   **Mr Golightly** 10-09 66-1 **Mrs J Reed** *Chsd ldr to 4; lost plce 7; t.o 11; ur 2 out*
[1614ᴾ] P   **No Fiddling (IRE)** 11-00 9-2 **Miss E Jones** *Nvr gng wl; sn drvn along; t.o & reluct frm 6; pu 9*

TIME: 6min 01.6s TOTE: £91.40; places £15.10,£1.90,£3.20 Ex: £1689.50 CSF: £161.10

Exmoor

Bratton Down (LH 8F,19J) Sat, 3 Jun (SOFT becoming HEAVY)

1649 Countryside Alliance Club Members Confined, 12st   4 ran

[1472ᴾ] 1   **MASTER BUCKLEY** 8-1 **R Woollacott** *In tch; 3rd & niggled along 11; prog 15; disp ld 16 til jmpd to ld 2 out; 3l clr last; hrd rdn & r.o flat*
[1177³] 2   3   **Valnau (FR)** (3x) 2-7F **C White** *Opened 1/3; lw; ld; jmpd rt; hdd 16 & sn reluct; chsd ldrs in 8l 3rd 2 out; kpt on u.p to tk 2nd run-in*
[1566²] 3   8   **Button Up Bill** 3-1 **H Thomas** (xnb) *Tchd 7/2; oht; hld up in tch; trckd ldr frm 10; disp ld 16; ev ch when bad mist 2 out; one pce & dem run-in*
[1604⁵] 4   2½   **Master Kiwi (NZ)** 20-1 **Miss T Hayes** (xnb) *Mounted on course; in tch in last; mist 9; outpcd aft 15; no ch; 23l 4th 2 out*

OFFICIAL DISTANCES: 4l, 8l TIME: 7min 09.0s TOTE: £5.20 DF: £1.40

1650 Restricted, 12st   10 ran

[1464¹] 1   **NO LOSS** 4-6F **L Jefford** (xnb) *Opened evens; lw; hld up towards rr; 8th 10; gd prog on inner aft nxt; went 3rd 12; pushed along 3 out; stayed on wl app last; went 2nd aft last; led inside last 150yds*
[1563²] 2   4   **Prah Sands** 8-1 **J Young** *Jw; chsd ldr frm 3; clsd up 3 out; ld on inner 2 out; drvn 3l clr u.p app last; sn hdd & outstayed*
[1565¹] 3   2½   **Cool Wager** 9-4 **D Alers-Hankey** *Tchd 5/2; lw; tried to make all; 2l up 16; hdd 2 out; sn no ex; 3l 2nd at last; one pce & dem flat*
[1258³] 4   20   **Dedalus (FR)** (7a) (bl) 16-1 **Miss O Green** *Sn in tch; 3rd ½way; cl 4th 13; slt mist 15; 8l 4th & wkng when rdn 3 out; no resp; fdd*
[1610¹] 5   8   **Alpine Castle (IRE)** (5a) 50-1 **Miss S Young** (b4) *Trckd ldrs; cl 4th ½way; lost tch stdly frm 13; 5th & no ch frm 3 out*
[1551⁸] 6   3   **Chance Encounter** 33-1 **J Barnes** *Midfield; 6th ½way; 15l 7th 13; no ch frm 3 out*
[1473⁷] 7   8   **Nothing To Fear** 50-1 **Miss J Buck** *Nov rdn; sn towards rr; 9th 12; no prog; t.o frm 16*
[260⁷]   P   **Butterwick King (IRE)** 10-1 **M Miller** *Midfield; 6th when mist 12; 111 5th 13; sn lost tch w ldrs; btn 5th when pu 3 out*
[1608⁵] P   **Loxley-Lad** 25-1 **A Honeyball** *Towards rr; 9th ½way; no prog; slt mist 14; bhnd when pu 2 out*
[1604⁴] P   **Mosside** 66-1 **N Harris** *Sn last & drvn along; reluct & bhnd frm 13; t.o & pu 2 out*

OFFICIAL DISTANCES: 4l, 10l TIME: 6min 41.0s TOTE: £1.50 DF: £4.20

1651 Intermediate, 12st   10 ran

[1607³] 1   **GYPSY LUCK** (5a) 7-1 **Miss A Bush** *Lw; hld up on heels of ldrs; cl 5th 10; 2½l 3rd 12; disappeared into fog 14; ab 4l clr when reappeared at last; eased & nrly caught 100yds out; rdn agn & just hld on*
[1607²] 2   ¾   **Belitlir** (5a) 3-1 **Miss S Young** *Hld up towards rr; 6th 10; gd hdwy to disp 3l 3rd aft 13; chsng ldr & u.p when reappeared frm fog at last; hrd rdn & nrly caught eased wnr*
[1599⁴] 3   15   **The Criosra (IRE)** (5x) 16-1 **Miss T Newman** *Sn w ldrs; cl 3rd ½way; disp 3rd & wl in tch when disappeared into fog 14; wl hld in 3rd when reappeared at last*
[1485⁷] 4   20   **Cardinal Gayle (IRE)** 14-1 **Miss D Harding** *Sn towards rr; 7th & bhnd 10; 10l 7th 12; nt trble ldrs*
[1551¹] 5   3   **Peyton Jones** 6-1 **M Miller** *Prom; 2l 2nd 10; slt ld when disappeared into fog 14; bhnd & no ch when reappeared at last; virt pu run-in*
[1550⁵] 6   1½   **Kinlogh Gale (IRE)** (bl) 50-1 **G Barfoot-Saunt** *Ld to 5; trckd ldrs; 5th & just in tch 13; fdd*
[1563ᴾ] 7   6   **Prudent Miner (IRE)** 50-1 **R Skinner** *Jmpd rt at times; ld 5; hdd 14; wknd; t.o*
[1604³] P   **I Like The Deal** (5a) 8-1 **L Jefford** (xnb) *Tchd 12s; lw; prom early; 7th 6; pu 8 (rdr reported horse was hanging & jmpng rt)*
[1608¹] U   **Melody Princess** (5a) 5-2F **D Alers-Hankey** *Lw; midfield when hmpd & ur 5*
[1562³] F   **One Boy** 5-1 **O Nelmes** *1st ride; rr early; some hdwy when fell 8*

OFFICIAL DISTANCES: ½l, 8l TIME: 6min 54.0s TOTE: £6.40 DF: £4.20
Fences 1-2, 7-10 & 14-18 were obscured by fog during this race

1652 Ladies Open
6 ran

[1562¹]	1		**MINE'S A GIN (IRE)** 8-11F **Miss J Cumings** *Lw; jw; cl 2nd; ld app 14; went clr aft 2 out; r.o str; comf*
[1562⁷]	2	10	**Its Grand** (bl) 66-1 **Mrs J Wilkinson** *Trckd ldng pr; cl 3rd 9; 8l 4th & outpcd 14; went 3rd 3 out; r.o to 2nd 2 out; no ch w wnr; eased last 100yds*
[1605⁴]	3	15	**Space Cappa** 10-1 **Miss V Stephens** *Slt ld til hdd 9; kpt on; 2½l 2nd 3 out; one pce app nxt*
[1236¹]	4	25	**Kingsbridge (IRE)** 5-1 **Miss O Green** *Hld up; prog 7; cl 4th 9; 3rd & in tch 14; nt fluent & dem 3 out; wl btn clsng stages (lkd unable to act in v soft ground)*
[1636¹]	P		**It'snotsimple (IRE)** (5a) 3-1 **Miss T Messer-Bennetts** *Last early; prog to cl 4th 10; lost plce aft 12; 12l 5th 14; wknd & pu 16*
[1637⁴]	P		**James Pigg** 33-1 **Miss S Young** *Settled 4th; lost plce stdly frm 7; bhnd frm 9 til pu 12*

OFFICIAL DISTANCES: 8l, 10l **TIME:** 6min 46.0s **TOTE:** £1.60 **DF:** £3.85

1653 Mens Open, 12st
6 ran

[1606¹]	1		**BELLS WOOD** (4x) 5-2 **C White** *Tchd 3s; ld til mist & hdd 12; cl up til ld agn aft 16; 3l up nxt; drew clr 2 out; stayed on game u.p up final hill*
[1259³]	2	20	**Starpath (NZ)** (7x) evensF **N Mitchell** *(bf) Tchd 5/4; lw; handy; went 2nd 7; trckd ldr til ld on inner aft 12; slt ld til hdd aft 16; grad fddd; wl hld frm 2 out; fin tired*
[1283¹]	3	5	**Possible Pardon (NZ)** (bl) 7-2 **J Barnes** *Tchd 4s; lw; chsd ldr 4-7; cl 3rd when mist 8; nt fluent aft; lost tch w ldng pr aft 14; 25l 3rd 2 out; r.o agn up final hill*
[1625ᴾ]	P		**Abbotsham** 50-1 **K Burke** *Settled 5th; sn strugg; last frm 9; hit 12; bhnd when pu 15*
[1606ᵁ]	P		**Cool Clown** 33-1 **B Trickey** *Chsd ldr early; feeling pce 7; 4th & off pce ½way; 4th & bhnd til pu 16*
[1595¹]	P		**Forbidden Waters (IRE)** (tt) 7-1 **L Jefford** *(xnb)Sn towards rr; nt fluent; last til went mod 5th 7; nt trble ldrs; pu 15*

OFFICIAL DISTANCES: 15l, 6l **TIME:** 6min 48.0s **TOTE:** £2.10 **DF:** £4.40

1654 Open Maiden (Div 1), 12st - 17J
10 ran

[1565²]	1		**JENTAR EQUILIBRA (IRE)** (5a) 3-1 **R Woollacott** *Tchd 4s; confid rdn in rr; 8th ½way; stdy prog to 5th 14; hdwy to 2nd on inner 2 out; str chall & blun last; stayed on wl u.p; drew clr last 150yds; improve further*
[1564²]	2	3	**Another Bula (IRE)** (5a) 3-1 **M SS Robinson** *In tch; cl 3rd 9; hdwy to ld aft 13; 2l up 2 out; slt ld last; sn hdd & no ex; gd eff*
[1596²]	3	2	**High Sturt** (5a) 10-1 **N Harris** *16s-10s; lw; hld up in rr; 7th ½way; hdwy to cl 4th 14; outpcd 16; 6l 4th 2 out; stayed on; nt trble ldrs*
[1307²]	4d		**Sun Lark** 5-2F **M Miller** *Tubed; tchd 3s; handy; 4th ½way; ld 11 til aft 13; cl up & ev ch til 2 out; wknd u.p app last; fin 4th; disq - nt weigh-in*
[1519ᴾ]	P		**Dark Venetian** (5a) 50-1 **M Sweetland** *Rr; 8th & last frm 9; t.o & pu 13*
[1555²]	P		**Dido's Dream** (5a) 50-1 **J Barnes** *(xnb) Midfield; 6th & lsng ground 9; 7th 12; bhnd & pu 14*
[1565ᶠ]	P		**Goforitgirl** (5a) 3-1 **L Jefford** *Lw; tk keen hld & hld up; prog to 4th 12; cl 4th & ev ch when mist 3 out; wkng when hit 2 out; imm pu*
	P		**Shannons Charm** (5a) 9-2 **N Mitchell** *(xnb) Tchd 6s; pulled hrd & ld aft 3; went 25l clr 8; wknd rap & hdd 11; stpd qckly & pu 12*
[1626ᵁ]	P		**Tony's Croney** (bl) 16-1 **K Burke** *Tchd 25s; blun bad 1; bhnd til pu 8; severed tendon; subsq destroyed*
[1565ᶠ]	P		**Typical Woman (IRE)** (bf) 9-1 **C White** *Tchd 12s; rcd keen & ld to 3; chsd ldr to 10; lost plce 13; poor 6th when pu 16*

OFFICIAL DISTANCES: 4l, 3l **TIME:** 7min 02.0s **TOTE:** £9.60 **DF:** £6.30

Fences 7 and 15 were omitted from this and the last race - state of the ground; Sun Lark finished fourth but was disqualified when the rider failed to weigh-in; he was fined £40

1655 Open Maiden (Div 2), 12st - 17J
4 ran

[1308ᴿ]	1		**VAGUE IDEA** 5-1 **K Burke** *Tchd 7s in plce; rn & jmpd green early; slt ld 5-7; rstrnd in cl 3rd til jmpd to ld bet horses 2 out; 1½l up last; sn clr; eased last 100yds*
[1609ᵁ]	2	6	**North Newcombe** 7-2 **N Harris** *(xnb) Ld & hit 1; set funereal pce til hdd 5; nt fluent 8 & 9; ld agn 13 til disp aft 17; hrd rdn & ev ch on inner til no ex last*
[1519²]	3	20	**Porters Lodge** 10-11F **R Woollacott** *Lw; hld up last; went cl 2nd 13; trckd ldr til eff to disp ld 3 out-nxt; sn dropd & btn; walked in*
[1564ᶠ]	P		**Irish Brush (IRE)** (5a) 11-4 **G Barfoot-Saunt** *(xnb) 4s-11/4; oht; tk keen hld; dashed into ld app 8; hdd 13; lost tch nxt; t.o & pu 16*

OFFICIAL DISTANCES: 5l, 25l **TIME:** 7min 21.7s **TOTE:** £9.80 **DF:** £11.90

Llangeinor
Laleston (LH 7F,19J) Sat, 3 Jun (GOOD)

1656 Hunt   4 ran

[1450²]	1		**PERSIAN MYSTIC (IRE)** 6-4 T Vaughan _(xnb) 3s-6/4; ld to 5; jmpd slow 6; ld 7 til jmpd slow 11; ld agn 13; made rest; drew 5l clr 3 out; jmpd slow nxt; sn in comm_
[1571¹]	2	10	**Anorak (USA)** (5x) 4-5F James Tudor _Lw; ld 5-7 & 11-13; rdn & no resp 3 out; 8l down nxt; fnd nil aft_
[1612ᴾ]	3	runin	**Desmond Gold (IRE)** 25-1 Miss S Major _Last pr; jmpd slow 12; lost tch rap 15; sn rem_
[949¹]	P		**Tigersun** (3x) 10-1 D Hughes _(xnb) Rcd keen early; hld up & cl up til hit 14 & wknd qckly; pu nxt_

OFFICIAL DISTANCES: 6l, dist **TIME:** 6min 58.0s

1657 Confined, 12st   8 ran

[1613¹]	1		**RUSNETTO (IRE)** (vis) 3-1 P Hamer _Last pr til 12l 6th 12; hdwy 15; 3l 3rd 2 out; stayed on u.p frm last; ld cl home_
[1593⁷]	2	½	**Storm Man (IRE)** 5-2F J Jukes _4s-5/2; ld 2-6; chsd ldr to 10 & agn 16; drvn into ld aft 2 out; hrd rdn & hdd cl home_
[1614ᴾ]	3	6	**Kristal Haze** (5a) 7-2 J Cook _Prom; ld 6; 5l clr 16; drvn & hdd aft 2 out; one pce_
[1569ᴾ]	4	25	**Hal's Prince** (7x) 14-1 A Price _Trckd ldrs; hit 5; 6l 5th 12; outpcd 15; 18l 4th 2 out_
[1612³]	5	8	**Silverfort Lad (IRE)** 16-1 T Faulkner _2nd/3rd to 12; sn outpcd; 25l 5th 2 out_
[1612ᵁ]	6	½	**Swan's Wish (IRE)** 20-1 G Thorne _A last trio; 14l 7th 12; strugg 15_
[1612ᴾ]	P		**Flashman** 33-1 Miss E Crawford _4th 6; mist 7 & rdr lost iron; releg last 10; t.o & pu 14_
[1401ᴾ]	P		**You Make Me Laugh (IRE)** (10x) 3-1 E Williams _(xnb) Hld up towards rr; impd to 5th 10; 3rd 12; hit nxt; wknd aft 14; wl bhnd when pu 3 out_

OFFICIAL DISTANCES: nk, 3l **TIME:** 6min 45.0s

1658 Mixed Open, 12st   9 ran

[1451²]	1		**GUNNER BOON** 7-4F J Jukes _Settled 3rd; ld app 9; 6l clr 12; hdd 15; ld agn 3 out; rdn & kpt on flat_
[1621²]	2	2	**Arleneseoin (IRE)** 7-2 P York _7s-7/2; ur start; trckd ldrs; went 2nd app 9; ld 15; hdd 3 out; 3l 2nd nxt; rdn & kpt on but a hld_
[1569³]	3	25	**Rave-On-Hadley (IRE)** 3-1 E Williams _A 2nd/4th; 10l 3rd 12; nvr gng wl enough aft; 15l 3rd & wl btn 2 out_
[1597⁴ᵈ]	4	3	**Blown Wind (IRE)** 12-1 V Keane _Towards rr; mist 9; 23l 5th 12; tried to cl 14-15; sn btn; 35l 4th 2 out_
[1612ᵁ]	5	3	**Young Manny** 12-1 M Lewis _Chsd ldrs; 5th 6; mist 8 & strugg; 37l 6th 12; rdn & kpt on stdly_
[1571⁴]	6	2½fs	**Local Customer** 50-1 Miss S Matthews _Imm rdn in last; jmpd slow 4 & cont t.o; climbing sev fncs aft; walked in_
[1570⁴]	P		**Savuti (IRE)** (tt) 40-1 P Hamer _A bhnd; 47l 7th 12; t.o & pu 14_
[1571³]	P		**Side Bar** 50-1 M Parry _A rr & nvr gng wl; 8th & rdn 6; t.o 11; pu 14_
[1600¹⁰]	P		**Warren Boy** 8-1 J Cook _Ld til app 9; 20l 4th & fdng rap 12; t.o & pu 3 out_

OFFICIAL DISTANCES: 2l, 10l **TIME:** 6min 39.0s

1659 Restricted   10 ran

[1535ᴾ]	1		**MARISOL (IRE)** (5a) 7-4F E Williams _Prom; ld 9; hrd rdn frm 2 out; kpt on wl flat; all out_
[1615ᴾ]	2	3	**Itscinders** (5a) 7-1 J Jukes _Chsd ldrs; 3rd 14; went 2nd nxt; 1l down & drvn 2 out; no imp aft & a just hld_
[1615³]	3	12	**Gt Hayes Pommard** 14-1 D Howells _Blun 3; last to 10; prog in 4th 13; flatt brief 16; sn wknd; 16l 3rd 2 out_
[1453⁴]	4	15	**Black Dan** 12-1 J Keen _Bhnd; 6th 10; mist 12; prog in 2nd 14; wknd qckly nxt; 40l 4th 2 out_
[1568⁴]	U		**Colebrook Willie** 12-1 James Tudor _Ur 1_
[1452ᴾ]	F		**Jack Boots** (vis) 20-1 J Phillips _A towards rr; mist 9; 5th nxt; wknd 13; sn last; 50l last 2 out; fell last_
[1633ᴾ]	P		**Prince Itsu** 33-1 A Price _Swtng; oht; pulled hrd; lft in ld aft 4; hdd 9; 5th & wkng 14; t.o & pu 2 out_
[1632ᴾ]	S		**Sea Search** 33-1 G Maloney _Lkd v poor w raw patch above tail; towards rr; 7th 10; 5th & in tch 14; fdng when slpd up bef 3 out_
[1452³]	S		**Seventh Symphony (IRE)** (tt) 7-1 J Cook _Clr ldr til slpd up aft 4_
[1568²]	C		**Welsh Warrior** 2-1 T Vaughan _Mists; blun 8; mostly 2nd til carried out by loose horse 13_

OFFICIAL DISTANCES: 3l, 10l, dist **TIME:** 6min 58.0s

1660 Open Maiden 56&7yo   11 ran

[1617³]	1		**BLAZING CONNIE** (5a) 9-1 **G Perkins** *Settled 4th; 3rd 11; 8l 3rd nxt; lft 2nd 14; rdn to ld aft 2 out; drvn & all out; unimpressive*
[1465⁶]	2	2	**Mia Fort** (5a) 10-1 **E Williams** *Ld; 6l clr 3 out; 2l up & hrd pdn nxt; sn hdd; plodded on*
[1455⁵]	3	20	**Up Your Street** (12a) 7-2 **J Cook** *Bhnd; 8th 6; clsd to 9l 4th 12; poor 3rd & plodded on frm 3 out*
[1404²]	P		**All For Tack** (5a) 33-1 **Miss A Meakins** *A bhnd; mist 5; 9th 6; 11th 9; t.o & pu 13*
[1617⁹]	P		**Craigson** 6-1 **T Vaughan** (xnb) *Mid-div; 6th 6; mist 8 & rmdrs; nvr gng wl; lost tch 11; t.o & pu 15*
[1617⁹]	P		**Hill Top Flyer (IRE)** 20-1 **M Parry** *Jmpd abysmal; sn wl t.o; pu 14 (appalling display by horse & rdr – cf Sidebar in Race 1658)*
[1618⁹]	P		**Jesusa** (5a) 40-1 **G Maloney** *Jmpd slow; sn hopeless t.o; 3 fncs bhnd & crawling when made to pu 15 (course blocked by vets attending seriously inj horse)*
[1617⁴]	F		**Lady Murrhill (IRE)** (12a) 25-1 **J Hayward** *Mid-div; impd to 2nd 10; bad mist 13; fell nxt*
[1645²]	P		**Marnies Song** (5a) (bl) 8-1 **James Tudor** *Midfield; mist 5; 7th nxt; strugg 11; t.o & pu 15*
[1455²]	P		**Mission Lord (IRE)** 9-4F **J Jukes** *Mists; 3rd mostly til rdn & wknd aft 11; t.o & pu 15*
[1454⁹]	P		**Verdi Edition** 5-2 **A Price** *6s-5/2; mists; 2nd til pu 9; broke leg; dead*

OFFICIAL DISTANCES: 2l, 12l **TIME:** 7min 15.0s

1661 Open Maiden 8yo&up (Div 1)   8 ran

[1615³]	1		**THE GADFLY** (bl) 5-4F **J Jukes** *Ld to 3; ld 6; drew clr w rnr-up frm 14; 20l ahd 2 out; unchall*
[1624²]	2	30	**Youmeandhim (IRE)** 5-1 **P York** *Numerous mists; last pr to 6; 4th & eff 12; chsd wnr frm 14; rdn & lost tch tame 16*
[1615⁷]	3	12	**Cosy Ride (IRE)** 20-1 **J Price** *V free to post; midfield; went 3rd & nrly fell 12; mist 14; sn strugg; 35l 3rd 2 out*
[1457²]	4	7	**Sing Cherry Ripe** (5a) 16-1 **Miss T Stevens** *Mostly 3rd to 6; pckd bad 11 & drpd back 6th 12; sn bad outpcd; t.o 16*
[1456⁴]	P		**Buckley House** 14-1 **A Price** *Ld 3-6; prsd ldr to 14; sn gave up; 40l 4th when bad mist 2 out & pu*
[1624⁷]	P		**Hardy Wolf** 16-1 **D Mansell** *Numerous mists in rr; 12l last 6; t.o 11; pu 15*
[1615⁹]	P		**Lough Neagh (IRE)** (bl) 7-1 **E Williams** *Reluct & sn rdn; 5th 6; 6th & strugg 12; pu 14*
[1401⁹]	P		**Slip Haven** (5a) 3-1 **T Stephenson** (xnb,martin) *20s-3s; nt jw; chsd ldrs; 4th 6; 3rd 11; 5th & strugg 12; t.o & pu 15*

OFFICIAL DISTANCES: dist, dist, 10l **TIME:** 6min 56.0s

1662 Open Maiden 8yo&up (Div 2)   9 ran

[1573²]	1		**ALBERT THE LION (IRE)** 3-1 **T Vaughan** (xnb) *Tkn stdly bhnd tearaway ldng pr; 28l 3rd 6; same 12; went 2nd 14; clsd to ld app 2 out; in comm when blun last*
[1634⁵]	2	12	**Tedstone Fox** 7-2 **Miss R Reynolds** (xnb) *Ld & wl clr; 30l ahd 8; 20l up 14; wknd 16; hdd app 2 out; sn no ch w wnr*
[1574³]	3	12	**Satco Supreme (IRE)** 12-1 **I Johnson** *Midfield but nvr nr ldrs; 32l 4th 6; 32l 5th 12; plodded on unenthusiastic & 28l 3rd 2 out*
[1616⁹]	4	12	**Lauras Conquest** 20-1 **J Keen** (xnb) *Chsng group & nd; 30l 4th 12; went 3rd 14 & flatt brief; wknd 16; 28l 3rd 2 out*
[1225⁹]	5	1½fs	**Some Grey** (5a) 20-1 **J Hayward** (xnb) *Jmpd slow in poor 2nd; dem 14; sn hopeless t.o; crawling frm 2 out*
[1616⁹]	P		**Carbury's Case** 4-1 **P Hamer** *Midfield & nd; 37l 6th 12; t.o 16; pu 2 out*
[1624⁹]	P		**Down To Joe's (IRE)** 10-1 **D Dennis** *Rr whn pu & dism 4*
[1634⁸]	P		**Sister Jim** (5a) (bl) 20-1 **S Graham** *Jmpd v poor in last; bad mist 8; t.o 12; crawled 15; pu nxt; appalling*
[1616⁹]	P		**Tommyknocker (IRE)** 5-2F **V Keane** *Last trio & nvr went a yard; t.o 11; pu 12*

OFFICIAL DISTANCES: 6l, 12l, 5l **TIME:** 7min 14.0s

Harborough Hunts Club
Dingley (RH 8F,18J) Sun, 4 Jun (DEAD)

1663 Club Members   4 ran

[1584²]	1		**RED REBEL** 5-2 **B Pollock** *Made virt all; 6l clr 13 til rdn aft 2 out; kpt on but fnd little flat*
[1503¹]	2	runin	**Hostetler** 10-1 **Miss K Norris** *Ld 2-3; 8l 3rd 7; nt keen aft; lunged over 11; 40l 3rd 13; promoted to 2nd*

| [1593⁵] | 2d | | **Dont Tell The Wife** 1-3F Miss G Hutchinson *Drpd out last til 3rd 9; went 2nd 12; rdn aft 15; no resp til clsd app last; nt qckn flat; fin 1¾l 2nd; disq - lost weight-cloth app 3 out* |
| [1485ᴾ] | r | | **Tarry Awhile** 25-1 Miss R Goodwin *Hdwy to ld 7-8; releg 3rd & outpcd 12; blun bad 14 & reluct to cont; forced along to try to catch 3rd; still last when ref last* |

OFFICIAL DISTANCES: Originally 2l, dist **TIME:** 6min 41.0s **TOTE:** £2.10 **DF:** £5.50
Dont Tell The Wife finished second but was disqualified when the rider was unable to draw the correct weight - had lost weight cloth before three out

1664 Restricted, 12st   15 ran

[1623⁵]	1		**NATIVE RAMBLER (IRE)** 20-1 S Joynes *2nd til ld 10; hdd brief 3 out; jmpd 4l clr nxt; hrd rdn & wknd flat; just hld on*
[1577²]	2	s hd	**Deer Park Lass (IRE)** (5a) 14-1 D Thomas *Mid-div; impd to 4th 10; went 11 3rd 15; prsd wnr & outj 2 out; drvn & clsd slow flat; just failed*
[1623³]	3	15	**Smart Orange (IRE)** 7-1 M Rimell *Cl up; 3rd 10; disp 2nd frm 12 til ld brief 3 out; outpcd app nxt; sn btn*
[1626²]	4	8	**Cumberland Youth** 20-1 Miss J Garley *Wl bhnd; 11th 10; some prog frm 13; nvr nr ldrs*
[1597⁵]	5	5	**Robsand (IRE)** 8-1 M Wilesmith *Chsd ldrs til 9th & rdn 10; no ch aft; plodded on*
[1627ᴮ]	6	30	**Spectacular View** (7a,2ow) 3-1JF L McGrath *Hld up; stdy prog 8; 5th 10; 4th & wknd 13; t.o*
[1633²]	F		**Alstack (IRE)** (bl) 3-1JF A Crow *Lw; ld til hdd & mist 10; lost plce 12; 6th & strugg when fell 14*
[1287ᴾ]	P		**Ar Aghaidh Abhaile (IRE)** (bl) 8-1 G Cooper *Pulled hrd early; 3rd 5; drpd to rr & nt keen 10; t.o & pu 12*
[1442²]	P		**Quite A Miss** (5a) 20-1 A Martin *Sn bhnd; t.o & pu 13*
[1632ᴾ]	P		**Scallymay** (5a) 33-1 J Merry *2 handlers; chsd ldrs to 5; labouring in rr when pu 10*
[1287²]	U		**Squaddie** 4-1 P Millington *(citation) Wl in rr til mist & u 9*
[1584ᴮ]	P		**Steel My Song** (5a) 14-1 S Morris *Bhnd; 10th 10; mod prog 12; nvr nr ldrs; por 4th 2 out; pu last*
[1486¹]	P		**Teachers Pet** 7-1 Miss L Sweeting *Chsd ldrs; 8th 10; eff to 10l 4th 15; no imp when blun bad nxt & great rcvry; pu 2 out*
[1548ᵁ]	P		**True Fred** (vis) 33-1 G Barfoot-Saunt *Cl up to 9; drpd back 8th nxt; plodded on reluct; t.o & pu last*
[1584⁹]	P		**Upton Orbit** 33-1 Miss J Hitchman *Sn t.o; pu 9*

OFFICIAL DISTANCES: s hd, 15l **TIME:** 6min 43.0s **TOTE:** £14.00; places £15.00,£2.20,£3.00

1665 Ladies Open   10 ran

[1558²]	1		**MR CUSTARD** 4-5F Miss L Sweeting *Hld up; 5th 10; 4th 15; went 2nd aft 3 out; stayed on to ld app last; lft clr & patted home*
[1441³]	2	6	**Drumstick** 20-1 Miss S Kelly *Chsd long ldr; clsd & lft in ld 10; hdd aft 3 out; sn btn; 4th when lft 2nd at last*
[1410⁶]	3	1	**Chieftain's Crown (USA)** 33-1 Miss E James *(xnb) Bhnd; 8th 10; eff in 7l 6th 15; sn rdn; nt r.o frm 2 out; lucky 3rd*
[1622³]	4	30	**Lucky Christopher** 12-1 Miss R Goodwin *A bhnd; poor last 10; 30l last 15; lucky 4th*
[1626ᵁ]	5	1½	**The Rum Mariner** 4-1 Miss C Thomas *Towards rr & nvr gng wl; 7th & strugg 10; 20l 7th 15*
[1623ᴾ]	F		**Lady Emerald** (5a) 16-1 Mrs C McCarthy *Trckd ldrs; 6th 10; 3rd & eff 11; 2nd 15; ld aft 3 out; rdn & hdd aft nxt; 2l 2nd when fell last*
[1583ᴾ]	P		**Nuns Cone** 33-1 Miss T Habgood *Prsd ldrs; 3rd 10; 4th 13; mist nxt & sn pu (inj)*
[1622¹]	P		**Prince Of Saints (IRE)** (bl) 6-1 Miss Z Turner *Prsd ldrs; 4th 10; 3rd 15; nt r.o & lost plce qckly nxt; pu last*
[1603⁶]	F		**Supercharmer** 5-1 Mrs F Needham *Hld up in last pr to 10; stdy prog in 6l 5th 15; rdn 2 out; 3l 3rd & hld when fell last*
	F		**Tellherpatit (IRE)** (5a) 33-1 Miss N Leggatt *Dashed wl clr; 25l ahd 3; wkng rap & jnd when fell hvly 10*

OFFICIAL DISTANCES: 6l, ½l **TIME:** 6min 39.0s **TOTE:** £1.40; places £1.10,£6.50,£4.40 **DF:** £40.00

1666 Mens Open   8 ran

[1584⁷]	1		**NEEDWOOD NEPTUNE** 10-1 A Sansome *Trckd ldrs; prom frm 9; ld aft 3 out; hrd rdn & fnd little flat; won on jockeyship*
[1578⁴]	2	nk	**Corbleu (IRE)** 6-4F M Walford *Opened 5/2; made most at crawl to 11; lost plce qckly; 7l 6th aft 13; rallied 3 out; 5l 2nd nxt; nt rdn app last; stayed on flat*
[1585⁶]	3	1½	**Royal Action** 16-1 P Chinery *Tk keen hld & prom; ld brief 8; ld aft 13 til aft 3 out; rallied & ev ch when hit last & rdr lurched forwards; nt rec*
[1583ᴿ]	4	2	**Nishkina** (vis) 5-1 C Cundall *Settled handy; 3rd brief 13; rdn & no resp 15; plugged on agn aft 3 out*

[1621^P] **5** 12 **Ardshuil** 25-1 S Pile *Strangled in 20l last & nvr put in rce*
[1583⁶] **6** 10 **Professor Longhair** 33-1 P Bennett *Cl up; mist 7; lost tch 13; plodded on*
[1293^F] **7** 12 **Khatir (CAN)** (bl) 5-2 N Kent *Towards rr but cl up; 5th aft 13; lost tch aft 15*
[1646^F] **P** **Polly Live Wire** (5a) 5-1 P Millington *(citation) Hld up in rr; hdwy on inner to ld 11-13; wknd aft 3 out; pu last*

OFFICIAL DISTANCES: nk, ¾l **TIME:** 6min 56.0s **TOTE:** £7.50; places £1.30,£4.50,£2.70 **DF:** £27.50

1667 Intermediate, 12st　　　　　　　　　　　　　　　　　7 ran

[1355¹] **1** **WISE PRINCE (IRE)** 11-10F L Stephens *(citation,sheepskin side pieces) Drpd out last to 7; 6l 6th 13; smooth prog 15; ld aft 3 out; sn 5l clr; rdn app last; kpt on*
[1616¹] **2** 10 **Pridewood Golding** 14-1 Miss E James *Hld up trckng ldrs; eff in 4th 13; last of 3 w ch app 2 out; nt qckn aft but went 2nd app last*
[1601^U] **3** 8 **Freestyler (IRE)** (tt) 5-2 G Hanmer *Lw; sn ld; rdn & hdd aft 3 out; wknd app last; fin tired*
[1623²] **4** 4 **Romany Chat** 6-1 A Martin *Opened 10s; 2 handlers; oht; prom & pulled hrd; bad mist 6 & lost plce; sn rallied; cl 3rd 13; wknd aft 15*
[1627^B] **5** 15 **Black Book (IRE)** (5a) 25-1 P Millington *(citation) Towards rr but cl up; 5l 5th 13; wknd aft 15*
[1414^P] **P** **Faraday** 33-1 Miss S Phizacklea *Prom brief; drpd back last 7; jmpd slow nxt & lost tch; t.o & pu 2 out*
[1537³] **P** **Persian Boy (IRE)** 9-2 A Sansome *Lw; oht; tk keen hld & prom; 2nd & ev ch 15; wknd qckly aft nxt; pu last*

OFFICIAL DISTANCES: 6l, 6l **TIME:** 6min 48.0s **TOTE:** £2.00; places £1.50,£6.00 **DF:** £8.60

1668 Open Maiden (Div 1)　　　　　　　　　　　　　　　12 ran

[1437⁵] **1** **CHADWICK BANK (IRE)** 33-1 R Cope *2nd/3rd til ld app 9; jw final mile til slow at last; kpt finding ex when prsd; all out*
[1526²] **2** ¾ **Master Will** (7a) 4-5F G Hanmer *Hld up in midfield til blun & lost plce 6; rr til prog 12 to 3rd nxt; tk 2nd on bit aft 3 out; hung aft nxt; drvn & rallied flat; clsng nr fin*
[1506³] **3** 20 **Stonebroke (IRE)** 8-1 J Diment *Cl up; hit 6; went 2nd 10; ev ch til rdn & wknd aft 3 out; dism aft fin*
[1609²] **4** 20 **Vulpin De Laugere (FR)** (bl) 20-1 C Jarvis *Prom til 7th & wkng 10; nt r.o; sn wl bhnd; t.o 3 out*
[1502²] **5** dist **The Last Shout (IRE)** (bl) 10-1 P Millington *Bhnd til 5th & prog 10; 6l 4th 13; sn lost tch; rem 4th 3 out; walked in*
[1598⁸] **P** **Devil's Sting** 33-1 R Lawther *Last & nvr went a yard; t.o & pu 9*
[1527⁵] **P** **Mcloughlin (IRE)** 12-1 M Rodda *Prsd ldrs; 3rd 10; 5th & wkng when mist 13; pu nxt*
[1091^P] **U** **Princess Scully** (12a) 20-1 P Morris *Bhnd; last when mist 10; outpcd 13; t.o when ur 2 out; crashed thro rails when loose & returned in horse ambulance*
P **Pure Grit (IRE)** 5-2 J Merry *Tde; 2nd til ld 6; hdd app 9; 8l 4th nxt; wkng when pu & dism 13*
[1447¹⁰] **P** **Sandi Devil** 33-1 Miss S Sharratt *Ld to 6; 6th 10; lost tch 13; t.o & pu 2 out*
[1635⁵] **P** **Timothy George (IRE)** (bl,tt) 33-1 A Sansome *Bhnd; 9th 10; rem when pu 13*
[1526^U] **r** **Tobias (IRE)** (7a) 8-1 Julian Pritchard *(xnb) Last when ref & threw rdr over 2; rdr climbed back over & rmtd; ref & f.o agn 3 (but on tk-off side)*

OFFICIAL DISTANCES: ¾l, dist **TIME:** 6min 55.0s **TOTE:** £19.50; places £6.00,£1.10,£1.10 **DF:** £10.30

1669 Open Maiden (Div 2)　　　　　　　　　　　　　　　7 ran

[1624^P] **1** **SHORTCUT SHORTY** 16-1 C Wadland *Ld til jmpd slow 10; ld agn 12; drew 6l clr 3 out; plugged on stdly*
[1582³] **2** 12 **Lewesdon Countess** (5a) 7-2 W Burnell *Hld up in tch; impd to 2nd/3rd frm 13; 6l 2nd 3 out; rdn & unable to cl*
[1634^P] **3** 1 **Don Royal** (bl) 25-1 Miss G Harriss *Cl up til lost plce 12; 15l 5th aft 3 out; staying on to chall for poor 2nd when mist last; kpt on flat*
[1624^P] **4** 15 **Miss Hoity Toity** (5a) 2-1F J Tarry *Oht; 2 handlers; tk str hld; jmpd slow 1 & 2; prom to 12; mist 15; disp 10l 3rd aft nxt; nd aft*
[1197⁶] **5** 3 **The Hollow (IRE)** (5a) 6-1 S Joynes *Last most of way; in tch to 13; strug on*
[1634^P] **6** 8 **Ron Miel (IRE)** 5-1 A Phillips *Hld up & handy; went 4l 2nd 3 out; hit 15; disp 10l 3rd & rdn aft 3 out; sn btn*
[1626^B] **P** **Yodeller Bill** 4-1 J Diment *Prom; ld 10-12; last & fdng 14; t.o & pu 2 out*

OFFICIAL DISTANCES: 12l, 1l **TIME:** 7min 09.0s **TOTE:** £6.60; places £5.60,£2.00
Lightening Steel (12-1, lame in padd) was withdrawn not under orders - Rule 4 deduction 5p in pound

Torrington Farmers
Umberleigh (LH 6F,18J) Sat, 10 Jun (GOOD to FIRM - with stretch of arable)

1670 Hunt, 12st
3 ran

[1606⁶] 1   **IT'S NOT MY FAULT (IRE)** 2-5F **Miss J Congdon** (sheepskin side pieces) Jw; settled last til 2l 2nd 6; sn stdd to last agn; went 2nd aft 10; stdd to hld 2nd aft 12; ld aft 15 & sn wl clr; unextended

[1654⁶] 2   runin   **Dark Venetian** (5a) 8-1 **M Sweetland** Warm; ld at crawl; pckd 12; slpd bend bef 13; hdd aft 15; wknd rap; 15l 2nd & exhaust when clambered over 2 out; t.o

[1515ᵁ] P   **Rosewood Lady (IRE)** (12a) 9-4 **K Burke** 6s-9/4; swtng; nt fluent; 2nd; mist 5; 2nd/3rd til last aft 10; sn outpcd; 10l last 3 out; t.o when pu nxt

OFFICIAL DISTANCE: dist **TIME:** 6min 58.3s **TOTE:** £1.10

1671 Restricted, 12st
16 ran

[1655¹] 1   **VAGUE IDEA** 16-1 **K Burke** Mid-div; 15l 9th 6; still 13½l 7th 11; 7½l 4th & hdwy nxt; went 3rd 14; ld brief 2 out; chall & ld agn last; r.o str; comf

[1608²] 2   2½   **County Bash** (5a) 12-1 **Miss L Gardner** Chsd clr ldrs; 12l 3rd 8; went 2nd aft 10; 4l 2nd 12; ld app 13; hdd brief aft 3 out; no ex when hdd agn last

[1095ᵁ] 3   5   **Ribington** 16-1 **Miss O Green** Chsd ldrs in 5th; 17l 5th 8; 4th 14; went 3rd aft 2 out; stayed on; nt rch ldrs

[1604²] 4   7   **Born Natural (IRE)** (5a) (tt) 16-1 **R Woollacott** Tchd 20s; sa; detach last to 6; stdy hdwy to 30l 11th 11 & 5th 14; lft 4th aft 2 out; nt rch ldrs

[1660¹] P   **Blazing Connie** (5a) 8-1 **G Perkins** (bf) 25s-8s; 2 handlers; last pr; 30l 14th 6; last 7; t.o 12; pu 3 out

[1659ᵁ] P   **Colebrook Willie** 33-1 **G Richards** Midfield; 11th 5; 24l 10th 11; wl bhnd when pu 13

[1639²] P   **Georgetown** 4-5F **L Jefford** 11-10-4/5; a.p; 9l 4th 5; went 7l 3rd 12 & jmpd to 2nd nxt; wknd rap uphill aft 3 out; btn 4th when went wrong & pu imm aft 2 out; damaged stifle; subsq destroyed

[1639⁶] P   **Hemero (IRE)** (tt) 25-1 **A Honeyball** Mid-div & nd; 7th 5; 19l 9th 12; 7th 14; lft poor 5th & pu aft 2 out

[1280ᶠ] P   **Irish Buzz (IRE)** 8-1 **A Charles-Jones** (xnb) Tchd 10s; chsd ldrs; 6th 5; 17½l 8th 11; sn wknd; pu 15

[1659²] P   **Itscinders** (5a) 10-1 **J Jukes** A last trio; 37l last 11; t.o & pu 2 out
     P   **Medias Maid** (5a) 100-1 **M Woodward** Mist 1; 2nd nxt til jnd ldr app 7; ld 8; 6l clr 11; hdd aft nxt; wkng qckly; bhnd when blun bad 15; pu 2 out

[1616³] P   **Mister Jay Day** 9-1 **A Price** (xnb) (2s-9s; lkd unenthusiastic padd; mid-div; 7th 6; drpd to 31l 12th 11; t.o & pu 2 out

[1650⁷] U   **Nothing To Fear** (bl) 50-1 **Miss J Buck** A rr; 12th 5; 32l 13th 12; t.o when blun & ur 3 out

[1614⁴] P   **Outrageous Affair** (5a) 20-1 **D Mansell** Swtng; handy; 5th 5; 13l 6th 11; 8th & wkng 14; t.o & pu 2 out

[1651⁷] P   **Prudent Miner (IRE)** (3ow) 50-1 **R Skinner** A towards rr; 10th 6; 33l 14th 11; lft poor 8th & pu 2 out

[1659⁵] P   **Seventh Symphony (IRE)** (tt) 20-1 **J Cook** (bf) Ld to 6; 6l 2nd & outpcd aft 10; drpd out rap; 10th aft 12; t.o & pu 2 out

OFFICIAL DISTANCES: 2½l, 5l **TIME:** 6min 23.0s **TOTE:** £15.80 **DF:** £2.80

1672 Mens Open, 12st
12 ran

[1607¹] 1   **BRAVE NODDY (IRE)** (bl) 11-4 **L Jefford** Tchd 3s; jw mostly; ld 2-6 & frm 7; prsd aft 10; ld 12; made rest; 4l up when blun 2 out; 2l clr at last; r.o game

[1606³] 2   2½   **Pretoria Dancer** (bl) 16-1 **F O'Brien** A.p; 3l 3rd 5; disp ½l 2nd aft 12; 2l 2nd & ev ch 2 out; r.o; a hld

[1570²] 3   15   **Cream Supreme (IRE)** (4x) 11-4 **E Williams** Mid-div & nvr gng wl; 9½l 8th 6; 20l 8th & rdn along aft 12; clsd to 14l 3rd 2 out; no ex

[1614¹] 4   1½   **Saffron Moss** (7x) 7-1 **J Jukes** Oht & trnr had to rn rnd padd; chsd ldrs; dem 8½l 6th 7; pckd 9; 10l 6th & wkng 11; 19l 4th & pushed along 2 out; no imp

[1630³] 5   10   **Spearhead Again (IRE)** 14-1 **M Munrowd** (xnb,bf) Trckd ldrs; 7l 4th 7; 4½l 5th aft 12; btn aft 3 out; releg last nxt

[1637²] U   **Amtrak Express** 12-1 **H Froud** Mid-div; went 8½l 5th 7 & 2½l 3rd aft 10; jmpd to ld 12; hdd & mist nxt; cl 2nd when put down app 14 & shot rdr over fnce; horse followed him over

[1666⁵] P   **Ardshuil** 50-1 **S Pile** (kineton) A last pr; 15l last 6; 25l 11th 11; t.o last when pu aft 3 out

[1448⁴] P   **Itspantotime** (5a) 50-1 **G Richards** A towards rr; 24l 11th 7; 30l 9th aft 12; t.o & pu 2 out

[1552¹]	P		**Play Poker (IRE)** (bl) 2-1F R Woollacott *9/2-2s; hld up in last pr to 6; 16l 8th & hdwy nxt; 111 7th 11; sn wknd; wl bhnd when pu 2 out*
[1657⁶]	P		**Swan's Wish (IRE)** (7x) 50-1 G Thorne *A rr; 9th 6; 211 9th 11; wl bhnd when blun bad 3 out; pu nxt*
[1600¹¹]	F		**Verde Luna** (7x) (vis) 8-1 A Wintle *(xnb) 12s-8s; prom til cl 2nd 5; ld brief nxt; jnd ldr brief aft 10; 6l 3rd when fell 13*
[1595⁴]	P		**Villains Brief (IRE)** 50-1 M Shears *Ld brief 1; jmpd slow 3; stdly lost plce; 111 7th 7; last 11; t.o & pu 2 out*

OFFICIAL DISTANCES: 4l, 15l TIME: 6min 19.5s TOTE: £4.20 DF: £4.20

1673 Ladies Open   8 ran

[1462²]	1		**TEE TEE TOO (IRE)** 7-2 Miss E James *Trckd ldrs in ab 15l 3rd til 2nd 8; clsd to 3l 2nd 12; jnd ldr app nxt; ld 14; 8l clr 15; flashing tail frm nxt; only 2½l up & lkd vulnerable 2 out; rallied & in comm last*
[1644³]	2	5	**No More Nice Guy (IRE)** 9-1 Mrs M Hand *Trckd ldrs; 19l 4th 6; 25l 4th aft 10; went 12l 3rd app 13 & 8l 2nd 3 out; clsd to 2½l 2nd & lkd prob wnr 2 out; sn rdn & wknd*
[1638⁵]	3	25	**Hylters Chance (IRE)** (vis) 6-1 Miss J Cumings *Chsd clr ldr til dem 3rd 8; 19l 3rd 12; lost plce; 15l 5th 3 out; stayed on one pce to poor 3rd nxt; no imp on ldrs*
[1547ᵁ]	P		**Everso Irish** 40-1 Miss L Ryder *A last & sn strugg; 6l adrift 4; 38l last aft 6; t.o & pu 13*
[1608ᴾ]	P		**Mountain-Linnet** 66-1 Mrs J Reed *(b4) A last pr; 33l 7th aft 6; t.o 13; pu 15*
[1622⁴]	P		**Thomas Crown** 20-1 Mrs J Wilkinson *Trckd ldrs; 21l 5th 5; went 12½l 4th 13; 17l 4th when blun & rdr lost iron 3 out; pu nxt*
[1658ᴾ]	P		**Warren Boy** 12-1 Miss F Wilson *Pulling; ld & sn 12l clr; jnd 13 but still 12l clr of 3rd; hdd 14; 8l 2nd & btn 3 out; stpd to nil nxt; poor 4th when pu last; lame*
[1515³]	P		**Well Armed (IRE)** (bl) 8-11F Miss O Green *Evens-8/11; a last trio; 22l 6th 6; 25l 6th & no imp 12; went poor 4th app 2 out; pu last; dismal*

OFFICIAL DISTANCES: 5l, dist TIME: 6min 17.2s TOTE: £6.10 DF: £13.30

1674 Intermediate, 12st   13 ran

[1554²]	1		**CHASING DAISY** (5a) 7-2 J Snowden *Lw; tde; a.p; cl 2nd/3rd til dem 4th aft 11; 2l 3rd agn 13 & 2nd nxt; ld aft 3 out; drew clr app last; comf*
[1535ᴾ]	2	4	**Morris Piper** 5-2F L Jefford *(xnb) 7/2-5/2; lw; hld up towards rr; 10th 5; 8th & hdwy aft 10; cl 4th 14; 2l 3rd & ev ch 3 out; 4l 2nd & hld last*
[1514⁴]	3	6	**Western Fort (IRE)** 10-1 Miss J Cumings *Tchd 12s; mid-div; 7th 5; 6th & hdwy 11; 10l adrift in 5th 14; clsd to 3½l 4th & ev ch 3 out; 12l 3rd & btn last*
[1607ᴾ]	4	2½	**Agile King** 25-1 Miss C Tizzard *(xnb) Trckd ldrs; disp 4½l 5th 6; 4l 5th 13; gd rn to disp ld brief 15; 11 2nd aft 3 out; wknd*
[1645ᴾ]	5	1½	**Secret Truth** (5a) 8-1 A Martin *2 handlers; swtng profuse; trckd ldrs in 3rd/5th to 10; hdwy to ld 13-14; 5th & one pce nxt*
[1562ᴾ]	P		**Arble March** (5a) 33-1 N Harris *Last pr til releg last 12; t.o & pu 2 out*
[1613ᴾ]	P		**Baran Itsu** 7-2 A Price *10s-7/2; prom; 2l 2nd 5; disp ld brief 10; 7th & wkng qckly 13; pu 15*
[1629ᴵᵈ]	P		**Burkean Melody (IRE)** (tt) 16-1 M Munrowd *Handy in midfield til cl 4th 7; 3l 4th 13; wknd qckly; pu 15*
[1613ᴾ]	P		**Itsstormingnorma** (5a) 33-1 J Jukes *Ld; jnd ldr app 12; hdd nxt; drpd out qckly; pu 15*
[1607ᵁ]	F		**Leejay Luki** 20-1 A Honeyball *Towards rr; 9th 7; no imp when crashing fall 13*
[1649⁴]	P		**Master Kiwi (NZ)** 5-1 G Richards *Tde; trckd ldrs; 3½l 5th 5; wknd 7; last aft 12; sn t.o; pu 2 out*
[1651ᶠ]	P		**One Boy** 12-1 O Nelmes *(orbs) 2 handlers; sa; detach last to 9; t.o in last pr til pu app 13; dism; destroyed*
[1664ᵁ]	P		**Squaddie** 9-1 P Millington *(citation) Last trio to 7; some hdwy to mid-div & hit 12; sn wknd; t.o & pu 2 out*

OFFICIAL DISTANCES: 5l, 5l TIME: 6min 21.0s TOTE: £4.90 DF: £9.10

1675 Open Maiden (Div 1), 12st - 16J   13 ran

[1598³]	1		**THE FROSTY FOX (IRE)** 4-1 M Miller *A.p; cl 3rd til 2nd 5; ld 11; hdd brief 15; disp nxt til drew wl clr frm 3 out; 12l up when clambered over 2 out; sn in comm agn*
[1598⁵]	2	15	**Snowshill Harvest (IRE)** 20-1 J Rice *Handy in mid-div; 6th & staying on 3 out; scrubbed along & lft 2nd app last; rdn all way to line; no ch w wnr*
[1641ᴾ]	3	10	**Dawn Caller (IRE)** 6-1 Richard Darke *(xnb) Mid-div; 9th 5; 7th 10; 7¾l 7th 13; went 15l 3rd aft 3 out; 2nd & tired 2 out; sn dem; fin exhaust*
[1668ᴾ]	4	4	**Timothy George (IRE)** (bl,tt) 12-1 P Millington *(bh)Mid-div; went 3rd 5; hdwy to 2nd 11; ld nxt; sn jnd; hdd 15; wknd aft 3 out*

[1661³] 5 15 **Cosy Ride (IRE)** 20-1 **J Price** *(bf) Trckd ldrs in 5th til 2nd 11; 6l 3rd nxt; sn drpd back 5th; went 16l 4th app 2 out; 2nd & staying on wl when lost action app last; virt pu flat & walked in; lame*

[1640ᴾ] P **Frosty Jo** (5a) 25-1 **T Dennis** *(bf) Ld to 2; wknd grad; detach 8th 12; sn t.o; 1½ fncs last when pu aft 2 out*

[1654ᴾ] P **Goforitgirl** (5a) 3-1 **L Jefford** *4s-3s; mid-div; 7th 5; 5th & hdwy 12; 4¾l 4th 13; 18l 5th & btn when pu 2 out*

[1555³] F **Jug Of Wine** (5a) 20-1 **R Emmett** *(boh) Trckd ldrs in cl 4th til 2¾l 3rd 13; wknd 3 out; t.o last when fell last; dead*

[1609ᴿ] F **Knap Hand** 25-1 **Miss L Gardner** *Prom; cl 2nd 5; crashing fall 8*

[1555ᴿ] r **Meat Loaf (IRE)** 16-1 **N Mitchell** *A rr; swerved bad aft 4 & releg last; sn detach & nt fluent; t.o last when ref 11*

[1662ᴾ] r **Sister Jim** (5a) (bl) 33-1 **S Graham** *Last 3; rap hdwy to ld 7; jmpd slow & hdd nxt; cl 3rd & blun 9; wknd rap; 10l bhnd ldng group when ref 11*

[1661ᴾ] P **Slip Haven** (5a) 20-1 **A Charles-Jones** *Chsd ldr til ld 3; hdd 7; ld agn aft 9-10; sn wknd; pu 13*

[1624ᶠ] U **True Hustler** (bl) 6-4F **F Hutsby** *Mid-div til blun & ur 4; rdr broke arm*

OFFICIAL DISTANCES: 15l, 10l **TIME:** 6min 35.2s **TOTE:** £3.20 **DF:** £2.80
Fences 10 & 16 omitted - fallen rider

1676 Open Maiden (Div 2), 12st

13 ran

[1641²] 1 **INFORAPOP** (7a) 6-4F **N Mitchell** *(xnb) 2s-6/4; trckd ldrs; jmpd to 1 111 4th 7; cl 4th & gng easy aft 12; went 11 2nd 13; ld aft 3 out; 1½l up at last; r.o; lkd to be hdd on line*

[1640²] 2 s hd **Sea Spirit** (5a) 6-1 **Miss T Cave** *Mid-div; 12l 7th 7; cl 4/5th 10 til 2nd aft 3 out; clsd to 1½l 2nd at last; r.o str flat; lkd to ld on line*

[1422²] 3 2 **Mustang Molly** (5a) 6-1 **A Martin** *(kineton) Pulling; ld 1; 7l 3rd 7; cl 2nd 10; 8½l 4th & outpcd 13; rallied to 3rd 2 out; 2l 3rd & ch last; rdn & nt qckn flat*

[1640³] 4 10 **Budghill** 12-1 **C Heard** *A.p; cl 3rd/4th til 2½l 2nd 6; 11 2nd 13; 3rd aft 3 out; 4th & btn nxt*

[1517⁵] 5 30 **Morgan's Rose** (5a) 14-1 **M Sweetland** *(bf) 2 handlers; a last pr; t.o 12; plodded on*

[1642ᶠ] r **Country Gem** 12-1 **R Woollacott** *Mid-div early; 7th 5; 8th & jmpd v slow 7; drpd to last when ref & threw rdr over 9*

[1634²] P **Craftbook Marchesa (IRE)** (5a,4ow) 9-1 **P Millington** *(citation) Trckd ldrs; 4th 4; 4½l 5th aft 10; 18½l 6th & wkng 13; blun bad & nrly stpd 15; pu 2 out*

[1641ᵁ] P **Ever Eddy** 12-1 **T Dennis** *Mid-div; 6th 4; drpd back to last trio 7; t.o & pu 14*

[1641ᴾ] U **Frisky-Breeze** (5a) 50-1 **L Tibbatts** *(kineton) Tde; chsd clr ldr 2 til 1 111 4th & lsng plce 7; 20l 8th 11; bhnd when ur 3 out*

[1564ᴾ] P **Holcombe Handsel** (5a) 20-1 **A Honeyball** *Mid-div til wknd 4; last pr 7; 25l last 11; t.o & pu 14*

[1617ᴾ] F **Lady Clifford** (5a) 20-1 **M Hammond** *Mid-div when fell 7*

[1598²] P **Madam Rose (IRE)** (5a) 9-2 **L Jefford** *(xnb,Belgian gag bit) Ld 2; sn 8l clr; 2½l up 6; jnd brief aft 12; hdd aft 3 out; wknd rap uphill; v tired when pu 2 out*

[1660³] P **Up Your Street** (12a) 14-1 **J Cook** *(bf) A towards rr; 9th 7; disp 2ll 9th 11; t.o & pu 3 out*

OFFICIAL DISTANCES: s hd, 1l **TIME:** 6min 29.0s **TOTE:** £4.10 **DF:** £5.60

Runners

An alphabetical list of all the horses
that raced in Hunter Chases and
Point-to-Points in 2000
together with a list of Handicap Ratings
for all horses with measurable form

How to Read the Form

The description of each horse commences with details of age (from January 1st 2001), colour and sex. All male animals have been assumed to be geldings in the absence of definite knowledge to the contrary. Complete details of pedigree are given for all except unregistered horses (when any part of the pedigree is omitted it is non-thoroughbred or not registered). The latter, indicated by the abbreviation (U) after their name, may run only in Members races and such details of age and breeding as have appeared on racecards are given for them. Horses performing *only* in 'Cross-Country' Hunt races are not included.

Pedigrees are given conventionally with the sire's name first, then the dam's, and the damsire in brackets. The letters and numbers following this signify the form of each animal in 2000; the numbers indicating finishing positions and the letters the non-completions. The following abbreviations are used:

b:	brought down	**R:**	ran out
c:	carried out	**s:**	slipped up
d:	disqualified (after finishing position)	**u**	unseated rider
f:	fell	**v:**	void
p:	pulled up	**w:**	withdrawn under orders
r:	refused, took no part		

Form figures in italics refer to races, other than Hunter Chases, under NH Rules from 1st February 2000 to the end of the Point-to-Point season. A synopsis of the horses previous racing history under all Rules, together with that of the dam and near relatives where notable, follows a brief physical description. When relative's names are given without qualification ie. flat winner, Hurdles winner, etc.) they have at some time appeared in *Hunter Chasers & Point-to-Pointers* (back editions of the Annual are available from Chase Publications - see advertisement at back of book).

Past form details are given thus

FLAT r4 w1 (12f) p1 (2nd) = ran four times on flat, won once (at 12 furlongs) and placed once (second).
NH '80/2 r6 w1 (2m Ch) p2 = ran six times under National Hunt rules from 1980 to 1982, won once (a two mile Chase) and placed twice.
P-t-P/HUNT CH '82 r12 w2 (Maiden and Restricted) p6 = ran 12 times in Point-to-Point or hunter chases in 1982, won a Maiden and a Restricted Open and placed six times.

All Sales prices are in guineas unless otherwise stated.

Many details will, of course, remain unchanged from year to year and pressure of space necessitates some abbreviation and omission. Generally the most comprehensive histories will be given in the horse's first season of Point-to-Pointing.

All races are run over three miles unless specifically stated otherwise. The following abbreviations have been used for races under NH Rules:

Amat:	Amateur Riders	**Nov:**	Novices	**HCap:**	Handicap
Mdn:	Maiden	**Ch:**	Chase	**Sell:**	Seller
Condit:	Conditions	**Opp:**	Opportunity	**Hdle:**	Hurdle

The owner's name and the qualifying Hunt(s) complete the description followed by the trainer's name or qualifying livery yard, where applicable, and finally the numbers and types of races in which the horse appeared. Owners and trainers are not officially recorded and we cannot guarantee the accuracy of this information. The following race type abbreviations or combinations are used:

C:	Club Members	**MO:**	Mixed Open	**Cf:**	Confined
Mod:	Moderate	**CG:**	Gentlemen Members	**N:**	Novices
CL:	Ladies Members	**NCM:**	Natural Country Members	**H:**	Hunter Chase
nr:	Novice Riders	**I:**	Intermediate	**O:**	Open
L:	Ladies Open	**P:**	P-t-P Owners & Riders Club	**m:**	Mares
R:	Restricted	**M:**	Members	**Vetr:**	Veteran Horses
Ma:	Maiden	**yr:**	Young Riders		

These abbreviations are prefixed by the race distance for races not run over three miles. The corresponding races with detailed comments-in-running can be found in the Results section.

HANDICAP MARKS, where merited, appear after the horse's names. These are expressed in stones and pounds, and are derived directly from Geoffrey Sale's original Handicap first published in 1959, but based on work going back several years previously. They are intended to represent the merit of the horse at the beginning of 2001, but should give a valuable guide to racing throughout the season. Some ratings include the symbols § which means ungenerous or unreliable – cannot be relied on to do its best or run up to its rating, and §§ – totally ungenuine – unrateable and to be avoided.

As the season progresses some horses will be seen to have improved, some to have deteriorated, and new horses will appear and the Handicap is updated accordingly. The new and revised ratings are issued in Weekly and Fortnightly Supplements which may be obtained from Chase Publications, *qv* advertisement at back of book).

MODIFYING THE RATINGS
The higher the handicap mark given, the better is the previous form. If all the handicap marks are listed for all the runners in a level weight race, the highest-rated will have the best chance on previous form, though due consideration must be given to any qualifying remarks given in the Annual regarding going preferences, riders, etc.

Where a horse has incurred a penalty his chance is theoretically diminished in comparison with the others by the amount of the penalty, whilst an allowance increases the animal's chance. In practice, the good horses are usually capable of giving more weight to their opponents in Point-to-Points than would be expected – class tells.

It is therefore suggested that Handicap Marks (ratings) should be reduced for Point-to-Point penalties, on the following scale:

penalty	deduction
1lb – 4lb	0
5lb – 9lb	1
10lb – 14lb	2

Deductions in Hunter Chases should be greater, since the task is more testing and the following scale should be applied:

penalty	deduction	penalty	deduction
1lb	1lb	**5lb**	3lb
2lb	2lb	**6lb**	4lb
3lb	2lb	**7lb**	4lb
4lb	3lb		

and for higher penalties 4lb should be deducted from the rating for each whole 7lb extra carried and to scale for any balance. Overweights should be treated in the same way.

All horses carrying more weight than the lowest-weighted are considered to be carrying a penalty of the difference and their ratings modified using the above table. An example of this is given below.

Having worked out the top-rated horses in this fashion, the comments on each horse in the Annual must be checked to discover any other factors that might affect the result. Despite the small profit which might accrue from blindly backing the top-rated, the discriminating punter using his own discretion to decide between the top few horses will be much more successful.

LUDLOW – Thursday 2nd March 2000

382 LUDLOW GOLD CUP HUNTER CHASE

	Original Handicap Rating	Actual Weight Carried	Weight Carried in excess of Bottom Weight	Adjustment Necessary (from table)	Revised Handicap Rating	Fate
FLYING MARIA	11-06	0	0	10-5	10-5	1
ROYAL MOUNTBROWNE	11-11	5	-3	10-4	10-1	2
TEA CEE KAY	12-00	8	-5	10-5	10-0	3
AGAINST THE AGENT	12-00	8	-5	10-6	10-1	4
MANAMOUR	11-11	5	-3	9-5	9-2	5
BELAFONTE	11-07	1	-1	NR	-	6
CAPTAIN KHEDIVE	11-07	1	-1	NR	-	P
DESERT CALM (IRE)	12-01	9	-6	10-6	10-0	P
EAU SO SLOE	11-07	1	-1	NR	-	P
HACKETTS CROSS (IRE)	11-11	5	-3	10-2	9-13	P
LATE ENCOUNTER	12-01	9	-6	10-2	9-10	P
PRINCESS LU (IRE)	11-07	1	-1	NR	-	P
WARREN BOY	12-04	12	-7	10-5	9-12	P

Flying Maria (top-rated at 10-5) won from Royal Mountbrowne (joint second top-rated at a modified 10-1), with Against The Agent (the other joint second top-rated) fourth (having lost third on the flat). The winner was returned at 7-1 (Tote £6.10), the Computer Straight Forecast paid £38.95, and the Tote Exacta ú52.80.

Over the years many different schemes have been put forward involving further rating changes to account for the wide variation in rider skill etc. These generally have not resulted in any significant increase in top-rated winners and in our list of winners predicted in 2000 (*qv* Performance of the Handicap) the ratings have been modified only as described above.

AADANN (IRE) ..8-4.. 9 b.g. Mazaad — Ceann-Na-Bann (Doulab USA) 4p. Rangy. IR 2,500y. FLAT r1 p0. P-t-P '98 r3 p0 (4th, and fell 2). NH '98 (for S.G. Knight) r1 p0 (pulled up). Crash-landed in his first two Pointing ventures, and beaten out of sight in both completions since. Clearly not easy to train, but a clumsy sort when he does reach the track in any case, and his prospects do not seem bright. *I.P. Adams — Taunton V. (Alison Handel).* 658 (R), 1468 (OMa).

ABBEY FLYER ..9-8.. 9 b.g. Minster Son — Miss Felham (Malinowski USA) fu21p4. Unfurnished. Dam won 2m Hdle. P-t-P '97/8 r2 p1 (2nd); and pulled up 1. Frequently let down by his fencing until making all in the slowest time of the day at Horseheath, but had managed just two outings in three seasons prior to 2000, and will need to improve to have any chance in Restricteds. *Mrs J. Woollatt — Bicester with Whaddon (Shirley Brazier).* 197 (CfMa), 250 (CfMa), 514 (OMa), 844 (OMa), 1419 (R), 1482 (R).

ABBEY LAD ..9-12.. 11 b.g. State Diplomacy (USA) — Another Pin (Pinza) ppppp. Strong compact half-brother to Byland Pin, Byland Princess, Politico Pot and Is Red There. Dam won Maiden and 3rd twice. P-t-P '97/8 r9 w1 (Maiden) p2 (2nds, inc Hunt Ch); failed to finish 4 (unseated 2, and slipped up 1). Lost no caste in defeat when second to Coole Abbey in a Newcastle 2m4f Hunter Chase in '98, but failed to reappear the following season, and judged on his efforts this year still remains under a cloud. Has looked an awkward ride on occasions and whilst he would skate up in a Restricted on his best form, he seems unlikely to return. *E. Fenwick — Zetland.* 40 (R), 137 (R), 375 (Cf), 423 (R), 689 (R).

PLATE 18   457 Staff College & RMA Draghounds Open Maiden (Div 2): Abbots Court (R. Walford), 1st, jumps the 2nd last   PHOTO: Brian Armstrong"

ABBOTS COURT (IRE) ..10-9.. 6 b.g. Hallowed Turf (USA) — Coronea Sea Queen (IRE) (Bassompierre) p11. Big strong. The first debutant Pointer to appear alphabetically in these pages, but few novices to follow will gain such rave reviews. All his three appearances were at Larkhill, schooled for two miles when 20-1 on his debut, he started a hot favourite for his next two outings (backed from fours to 11/10 in the Maiden!) and beat little, but in most emphatic fashion. Looks a star of the future, particularly as he has plenty more maturing to do, and must be followed when he reappears on Robert Alner's side of the wall. Three mile Chases under Rules should be easy meat for him. *H. Wellstead — Portman (Louise Alner).* 264 (OMa), 457 (OMa), 1135 (R).

ABBOTSHAM ..—.. 16 b.g. Ardross — Lucy Platter (FR) (Record Token) ppp. Lengthy half-brother to Charlieadams (IRE) (*qv*). Has string-halt on the near-hind. FLAT r8 p0 (visored in Sell once, ran at Ascot twice '91/2!). NH '89/90, '93/6 and '98/9 r31 w2 (2m1f Hdle and 3m3f HCap Ch) p8 (6 2nds, inc a match). P-t-P/HUNT CH '90/2, '94/5 and '97/9 r34 w4 (inc 2 Hunt Chses, 3m-3m2f100y, and Ladies) p8 (6 Hunt Chses, inc 3rd in '91 Horse and Hound Cup); failed to finish 8 (fell/unseated 5).

A grand old servant for Oliver Carter over the years, and could probably have achieved even more, but for his tendency to root the odd fence, but gave every indication that he had reached the end of the road in 2000. *O.J. Carter — E. Devon.* 1304 (Cfnr), 1625 (3m2f110yH), 1653 (O).

ABERFOYLE PARK (IRE) ..10-2.. 7 b.g. Riverhead (USA) — Go For Doe (Whistling Deer) 12pp. P-t-P '99 r1 p1 (3rd). Looked a useful prospect when landing a touch on his seasonal reappearance and both the placed horses scored twice apiece subsequently, but beaten at odds-on in his next three starts, and it transpired that he had burst blood vessels at both Barbury Castle and Charlton Horethorne. Better than he was able to show, but in a top yard, and will win plenty more races if connections can find a cure. *A.J. Sendell — Portman (Louise Alner).* 11 (OMa), 208 (R), 477 (R), 958 (R).

A BIT EXTRA ..—§.. 10 ch.g. Broadsword (USA) — Lamdant (Redundant) p. Half-brother to Tickle-Tut and Home Girl. P-t-P '98 (for Mr J. Van Praagh) r6 p0 (pulled up 3, fell 2, and ran out 1. Related to two of the worst Pointers ever, and emerged from a year off to extend this dismal non-completion record. *R.H. Goring — Coakham Bloodhounds.* 125 (M).

ABIT MORE BUSINESS (IRE) ..10-6.. 10 b.g. Henbit (USA) — Driven Snow (Deep Run) r3pp1f. Small unfurnished half-brother to jumping winners, Lackendara and Slush Puppy (IRE) (in Ireland), and to Hurdles winner, Chelworth Raider. Dam won 2m Hdle. P-t-P/HUNT CH '96/8 r9 w4 (inc 2m5f Hunt Ch, and Ladies) p2; and pulled up 3. Beaten just once when completing from seven starts '98/9, but not as classy as his record suggests and seems to suffer from intermittent lameness. Brought Stoney River's winning run to an end at Badbury Rings under a persistent drive from Polly Gundry, but may have been lucky, as the runner-up was making a noise. Acquired blinkers on his final outing of '99, and has sported them ever since, but their effect seems to be minimal now. Would probably have been a creditable second at Cheltenham on his final start, but for falling two out, and though he still possesses plenty of ability it would be unwise to trust him implicitly. *R.G. Williams — Taunton V. (Richard Barber).* 9 (L), 154 (3mH), 383 (3mH), 581 (3mH), 1057 (Cf), 1341 (2m110yH).

A BIT OF FLUFF ..9-0.. 9 b.m. Green Adventure (USA) — Cantabile (Bustino) pr3. Small light sister to Adventure Princess. Dam, half-sister to Denberdar (*qv* '95 Annual), won 3 2m Hdles (hat-trick, including a Sell) and a 2m Ch and 2 Ladies and placed total of 8 for Sue Brooke. P-t-P '97 r1 p0 (fell). NH FLAT '98 (for R.J. Price) r1 p0. NH '98 r3 p0. Out of a most resilient mare, but failed to reappear following her promising third at the Brecon & Talybont, and is obviously nigh on impossible to train. Lacks substance (like the fences at Llanfrynach), but just about good enough to find an opening if she were able to stand a normal campaign. *Lady Susan Brooke — Teme V.* 337 (CfMa), 447 (Cm), 491 (CfMa).

ABOUT TIME (IRE) ..9-2§.. 8 br.g. Good Thyne (USA) — Cathy's Girl (Sheer Grit) p4u26. Compact. Dam, half-sister to Let Me Think (*qv* '95 Annual). P-t-P '99 r1 p0 (pulled up). Showed improved form though ultimately failed to take advantage of the long leader's tack going awry at Higham, but looked decidedly unco-operative when tailed off last of six finishers at Fakenham subsequently. May be able to take advantage of one of the bad Maidens that proliferate in East Anglia, but don't bet on it. *T.P. Whales — W. Norfolk.* 180 (2m4fOMa), 411 (OMa), 604 (OMa), 1115 (OMa), 1290 (OMa).

ABOVE SUSPICION (IRE) ..—.. 9 b.g. Henbit (USA) — Cash Discount (Deep Run) pfpp. Unfurnished half-brother to Cash Man (IRE) (*qv*). 5000 4-y-o. NH FLAT '96/7 r3 p0. NH '96/8 (from C. & E. James') r6 p0 (last only Ch). An excitable sort and a hard puller, and shows plenty of toe for one and a half miles, but devoid of stamina, and was 50-1 when tried in a 2m Hunter Chase. Running him again would appear to be a waste of time. *Mrs J.N. Humphreys — Beaufort (Richard Smith).* 220 (OMa), 455 (OMa), 754 (CfMa), 925 (2mH).

ABSENT CITIZEN (IRE) ..10-0.. 8 b.m. Supreme Leader — Boreen Citizen (Boreen FR) p2f1p. Workmanlike lengthy half-sister to Bit Of A Citizen (IRE) (*qv*). IRISH P-t-P '98/9 r9 w1 (5yo plus mares Maiden) p1 (3rd); pulled up 2, unseated 2, and fell at last when clear. A fair novice who has scored in soft and on firm, and looked unlucky for the second time when falling in the lead at Howick, but reappeared after a two month absence to score at Bonvilston. Her jumping can be rather hit and miss, and possibly best at a bare three miles, but should be able to score again. *R.A. Mason — Glamorgan (Evan Williams).* 274 (R), 483 (R), 596 (R), 1453 (R), 1613 (I).

ABSOLUTE LIMIT ..9-7.. 9 gr.g. Absalom — Western Line (High Line) pp2. Good-bodied half-brother to Pere Bazille, and to flat winner, Merryhill Madam. FLAT r4 p0. NH '96/8 r11 w1 (2m3f Hdle) p1 (2nd); remote last and fell 2 in Chses; failed to finish in 4 Hdles. P-t-P '99 (for Mr J.M. Turner) r6 w1 (Confined) p2, and fell 1. Held on to win a poor contest at Higham, after being 20 lengths clear at halfway in '99, but has always been a tearaway, and had run himself into the ground after about two miles in each of his races in 2000. Will need to seek out an equally hard race to stand the chance of repeating the dose in future. Remains a wholly unsuitable mount for an inexperienced jockey. *J.M. Bowles — Waveney H. (John Ibbott).* 241 (C), 549 (Cf), 755 (W).

ABULJJOOD (IRE) ..9-5.. 6 b.g. Marju (IRE) — Midway Lady (USA) (Alleged USA) 2pu. Strong-topped half-brother to flat winners, Umniyatee and Alasad (in Ireland — also successful over Hurdles there), and to jumping winner, Fatehalkhair (IRE). Dam won 5 flat, 7-12f, including 1000 Guineas, Oaks and Prix Marcel Boussac, and was subsequently sold to the Maktoums for $3,300,000. FLAT (often blinkered; final for I. Williams; unplaced 2 previously for M. Waring, claimed for £10,000; won previously for P. Haslam, bought for £13,500; previously for B. Hanbury, who trained the dam) r13 w1 (12f) p4. Bred in the purple, but his flat victory makes matters difficult for him in Points, and there is no guarantee that he will stay three miles. Got tired in the closing stages and was nursed home for a meaningless 35 lengths second, and unable to complete the course since. Showed signs of temperament in previous yards. *Mrs J. Hughes — Cranwell Bloodhounds (Paul Blockley).* 1112 (O), 1335 (2m4f110yH), 1417 (L).

ACES HIGH ..—.. 7 b.g. Crowning Honors (CAN) — Secret Storm (Secret Ace) pppp. Owner-bred half-brother to Secret Bay (*qv*). Related to a supremely game performer, but has so far looked far from enthusiastic himself, and verging on a squiggle. *Miss A.L.B. Vaughan — Buccleuch.* 363 (CfMa), 624 (OMa), 816 (OMa), 977 (CfMa).

ACES WILD ..—.. 8 b.g. Lightning Dealer — Barle Express (Pony Express) R. Dam, half-sister to three Rachel Matheson Pointers, won O. Berks Members (when tubed) and placed 6, and grandam, Barle Fantasy, ran in three Ladies for her. Ran out after a mile when tailing off in his Members. *Mrs R.C. Matheson — O. Berks.* 1202 (M).

ACETYLENE ..9-3.. 9 b.m. Miner's Lamp — Cherry Morello (Bargello) 4. Unfurnished half-sister to American Black, Quick Quick Sloe, Mazzard (IRE) and Second Bite. Dam won a Maiden and placed 3 for Simon Cave. P-t-P '97/8 r5 p1 (3rd); pulled up 2, and fell 1. NH '98 (from R.H. Alner's) r1 p0. Made a fleeting return from a season off when a well beaten fourth at Cothelstone. Named after a foul gas that can burn brightly, and whilst she has the ability to win there seems to be a darker side to her, and it would be no surprise if she were to remain a maiden. *Dr S.G.F. Cave — Blackmore & Sparkford V. (Penny Cave).* 640 (CfMa).

ACHILL SOUND ..10-2.. 8 b.g. Broadsword (USA) — Casino Cassie (Netherkelly) 134132. Smallish compact. Grandam, Old Mary, won 3 Points and placed 5 (inc Hunt Ch). P-t-P '98/9 r8 p3 (2nd of 3 once; 2 3rds, of 4 once and last once); failed to finish 4 (unseated 1, and ran out 1). Much improved in his third season — previously a weak finisher — though probably ran his best races in defeat. Keen (wears a cross-noseband), and always held up, but can produce a turn of foot that should enable him to win more minor Points. Benefits from the presence of Gary Hanmer in the saddle. *K.T. Hamer & Mrs A.C. Swarbrick — United (Corinne Swarbrick).* 617 (CMa), 862 (Cf), 1088 (R), 1322 (R), 1588 (I), 1632 (I).

A CLASS APART (NZ) ..9-8.. 7 b.g. Truly Vain (AUS) — Lampetia (AUS) (Nonoalco USA) fp. Half-brother to five winners in the Antipodes. NZ FLAT r9 p1 (3rd). NH Oct '99 (for N. Mason) r2 p0 (inc Sell). Fell at the last while leading narrowly at Lydstep, but weakened rapidly, collapsed and died when odds-on at Bassaleg. *N.H. Oliver — N. Ledbury.* 1222 (2m4fOMa), 1404 (OMa).

ACROSS THE CARD ..10-5.. 13 b.g. Lir — Cornish Susie (Fair Season) 12. Neat brother to Ewhonosebest. FLAT r4 p0. NH '91/4 (sometimes blinkered/visored) r21 p8 (inc 2 Sells). P-t-P/HUNT CH '95/9 r39 w10 (inc 3m1f Hunt Ch, and 2 4m Mixed Opens) p13 (7 2nds; and inc 4 Hunt Chses 2m5f-3m2f); unseated 3, and pulled up 1. Totally reformed by Pointing (was very ungenuine under Rules), and has won at least once in each of his six seasons racing between the flags. A sound jumper who is best suited by a thorough test of stamina (stays four miles), and is the ideal ride for a novice. Unbeaten in four attempts at the Berwickshire Members, and that race will surely be his prime target in 2001. *Major General C.A. Ramsay — Berwicks.* 358 (M), 421 (3m5fL).

ACROSS THE WATER ..9-6.. 7 b.m. Slip Anchor — Stara (Star Appeal) bp3ppp. Leggy lengthy. FLAT r8 p0 (inc Sells). P-t-P '99 r3 w1 (Maiden) p0; pulled up 1. Rather lucky, but did well to win as a five-year-old in her first season (left clear two out by the falls of her two nearest rivals), but apart from a fair third at Llanfrynach proved disappointing in 2000. A heavy fall on her reappearance could not have helped her confidence, and running her in Hunter Chases was a fruitless exercise, but is a steady jumper and still young enough to atone. *P.J. Sanderson — Kyre (Corinne Swarbrick).* 195 (O), 334 (O), 482 (I), 859 (O), 1293 (3mH), 1626 (3m1f110yH).

ACTION STATIONS ..—.. 7 b.g. High Estate — Toast (IRE) (Be My Guest USA) fp. Workmanlike. FLAT r6 p0. P-t-P '99 r1 p0 (pulled up). An unimpressive mover, and on the evidence to date seems most unlikely to make his mark in the Pointing arena. *A. Greig — E. Sussex & Romney Marsh (Sara Hickman).* 236 (OMa), 576 (OMa).

ACT OF PARLIAMENT (IRE) ..10-5§.. 13 br.g. Parliament — That's Show Biz (The Parson) f223. Compact unfurnished brother to Parlebiz. Dam won 3 Hdles (2m-2m2f) and 2 Chses (2m-2m2f) in Ireland. NH FLAT '93 r1 p0. NH '93/7 r23 w7 (2 2m5f Hdles, and 5 Chses, 2m4f-3m1f) p8. NH '99 r2 w1 (beat Cedar Square and Spring Double a short head and 1¾l in Worcester HCap Ch). HUNT CH '99 r1 p0. A decent animal on good ground over the years, but moody at best, and becoming very hard to win with (could have done so if he had wished at Huntingdon). Capable of superb jumping, but all too liable to make errors. Usually blinkered nowadays, and cannot be relied upon for betting purposes. *J. Perriss — Vine & Craven (Kim Bailey).* 680 (3m1fH), 802 (2m6fH), 1332 (3mH), 1533 (3m1fH).

ACTON BANK ..10-12.. 7 b.g. Teenoso (USA) — Lavenham Blue (Streetfighter) 1. Dam is half-sister to Mohock (*qv* '90 Annual). Bred from an apparently useless mare who fell three out when clear in a Hurdle once, but who fell or unseated in her three Chases, but made a sensational debut on dead ground at Eyton, where he led from halfway, quickened three out, and finished full of running to score in the fastest time of the day. His jumping was remarkably fluent, and he provided Jo Downs with his first success. There seems no reason to suppose that the result was a fluke, and his next appearance is awaited with eager anticipation. Surely has a future under Rules. *E.H. Crow — N. Salop (Sheila Crow).* 1323 (OMa).

ACT ON IMPULSE (IRE) ..—.. 6 b.rg. Jurado (USA) — Windara (Double-U-Jay) up. Big good-looking half-brother to Wolf Winter and Farney Glen, to Irish Pointing winner, Different Tune, and to Irish NH flat winner, The Bourda. Dam won 2m Hdle in Ireland. Bought Tattersalls (Ireland), Jun for 4642. Only went two miles at Bitterley twice, but well-related, and probably the sort who needs more time. Should do better eventually. *Mrs H. Dalton & D.M. Hughes — Wheatland (Andrew Dalton).* 989 (OMa), 1091 (OMa).

ADAMS GOLD ..—.. 7 br.g. Vital Season — Loranorda (Mandamus) pp. Small half-brother to Wyeside. Dam is half-sister to Double Silk (*qv* '99 Annual). Bought Ascot, Feb '97 for 875. Started favourite at Erw Lon in early April, but pulled up lame in the first mile, and not seen again. *R.A. Mason — Glamorgan (Evan Williams).* 746 (CfMa), 951 (OMa).

ADDINGTON SHARRAGH ..—.. 10 ch.m. Gildoran — Hands Off (Nearly A Hand) pu. Strong compact half-sister to Handy Oats, and to Irish NH flat winner, Handy Julie. Dam, half-sister to Monastic Calm (*qv* '94 Annual), was 3rd in Maiden. NH '96 r2 p0 (last, and pulled up 1). P-t-P '97 and '99 r3 p0 (pulled up 3). Ruined her row of pulled-ups when the owner toppled off at Easingwold, and appears devoid of talent. *Miss J. Binks — York & Ainsty N.* 1234 (OMa), 1353 (OMa).

ADMIRAL VILLENEUVE ..10-0.. 13 b.g. Top Ville — Great Tom (Great Nephew) ppp4u5. Tall rangy windsucker. Half-brother to Sugar Mill, and to 4 flat winners (2 abroad). Dam won at 6f. NH '93 and '96 (for C.R. Egerton) r8 p3 (15*l* 2nd in Hdle, and about 20*l* 3rd twice in Chses); last twice after unseating once, and fell 1 in other Chses. P-t-P '97 (for Miss C. Dudley) r1 p0 (pulled up). NH Jun '00 (for B.P.J. Baugh) r1 p0 (5th in 2m Nov HCap Ch: *prom, rdn and wknd 3 out*). Had plenty of ability, but incredibly lightly raced in the past (presumably due to a physical infirmity), and though he deserves to find a race it looks as though his best efforts will be thwarted. Often makes the running, and a fine jumper until his suspect stamina gives way. *A.J. Deakin — North East Cheshire Drag.* 801 (3m1fH), 1125 (OMa), 1343 (3m110yH), 1531 (2m110yH), 1628 (2m4f110yH).

ADVENTURUS ..10-0.. 9 b.g. Green Adventure (USA) — Florella (Royal Fountain) p6254. Half-brother to Gillie's Fountain. Dam is an unraced sister to Royella. P-t-P '97 (for Mr A.N. Dalton & Mr D. Doolittle) r3 w1 (Maiden) p2 (2nds). NH '99 (for M.D. Hammond) r5 p1 (3rd). Looked destined for better things following his Maiden success, but performed dismally in five starts for Mickey Hammond (having been bought for 15,000gns), and plodded badly on his return to Pointing. Tried in blinkers under Rules, and still a troubled and possibly ungenuine soul. *J.D. Liley — Llangeinor.* 347 (R), 476 (Cnr), 596 (R), 818 (R), 970 (O).

AEGEAN FANFARE (IRE) ..10-4.. 12 br.g. Trojan Fen — Sweet Melody (Alcide) 1u12p. Small neat half-brother to Irish flat and jumping winner, Derrymore Boy (also won Chasing in England). IRISH FLAT (to 7) r28 w3 (10-17f) p4. IRISH NH '92/6 r36 w3 (2m-2m6f Hdles) p11; 5th only Ch. P-t-P '97/8 r6 p4 (3 2nds); fell/unseated 2. NH '98 (from Miss K. Marks') r1 p1 (3rd). Finally gained compensation for some excellent placed efforts in Ladies Opens when dominating proceedings at Garnons and Sandon, and would have made it three, but for tipping up when unassailable at Barbury Castle subsequently. Suited by plenty of cut in the ground, but remains prone to diabolical blunders. Should win again if he can continue to dodge the better Ladies horses. *N. Shutts - Ludlow (Penny Grainger).* 449 (L), 1087 (MO), 1126 (L), 1281 (L), 1525 (L).

AEOLIAN ..9-9.. 10 b.g. Ovac (ITY) — Snare (Poaching) ppp1. Lengthy sparely-made hobdayed half-brother to Battue, Word Game (dam of Willmoss), Salehurst, Sweeting and Shouldofdone, and to Hurdles winner, Unguarded. NH FLAT '95/6 r2 p0 (tailed off). NH '96/7 r9 p1 (23*l* 3rd in Ch); last, pulled up 3 (inc Sell), and unseated in other Chses; pulled up all 3 Hdles. P-t-P '98/9 r14 w4 (Maiden, Restricted and 2 Members) p4 (2nds); pulled up 1. Next to useless under Rules (was tried tubed), and found his niche in lowly Points, and produced with a wet sail to capture his Members for the third year running. Has been retired, as has pilot, Robin Gill. *Mrs J. Pearl, K. Biltoo & D.L. Gill — Essex (David Gill).* 93 (C), 609 (I), 840 (I), 1377 (M).

A FEW DOLLARS MORE (IRE) ..9-8.. 11 ch.g. Tremblant — Spanish Natalie (Imperial Fling USA) 3p337pp5p. Rangy good-bodied half-brother to Carna Lady (IRE), and to Irish NH flat winner, Rostrevor Shore (IRE). Dam won Irish NH flat. NH FLAT (visored 1) r2 p0. NH '95 r1 p0 (pulled up). P-t-P '97/9 r17 w2 (Maiden and Restricted) p5 (3 3rds; also disqualified from 2nd once);

pulled up 2, and fell/unseated 2. Bought for an expensive 7000gns having won a bad three-finisher Maiden on firm ground, and has won just once in three seasons for present connections. Often features prominently for two and a half miles, but back pedals rapidly, and his losing sequence has now been extended to 19. Has been tried in an off-side pricker and blinkers. *R.G. Westacott — Devon & Somerset (Keith Cumings).* 68 (O), 142 (I), 199 (Cf), 356 (Inr), 561 (O), 853 (Inr), 1044 (4mO), 1371 (Cf), 1516 (I).

AFFAIR OF HONOUR (IRE) ..7-13.. 13 ch.g. Ahonoora — Good Relations (Be My Guest USA) 2p. Small half-brother to flat winner, Tacoma Heights. Dam won 2 Irish flat, 7-12f. FLAT r13 w1 (7f) p4. NH '91/3 r10 w2 (2m4f Hdles) p2. P-t-P '94/6 and '98/9 r16 w1 (Ladies) p1 (3rd); failed to finish 10 (unseated 2). Had ability until he broke down in '96, but went to pot completely in '99, and carried a gallery having her first ride when second of three finishers in a joke race for his Members on his reappearance. Deserves honourable retirement. *Mrs M. Morris — Blankney.* 366 (M), 795 (L).

AFRICAN JAZZ (GER) ..—.. 9 b.g. Kafu — An-An (GER) (Andrang GER) pp. Sturdy. GERMAN FLAT '95/7 r29 w3 (6-8f; one on dirt — 'Sandbahn') p3. Took a strong hold in both Confineds, but gave the impression of being completely unable to stay three miles. *C.E. Van Praagh — O. Surrey & Burstow (Richard Parker).* 676 (Cf), 983 (Cf).

AFRICAN WARRIOR ..10-6.. 9 b.m. Exodal (USA) — Sandy Looks (Music Boy) u41u11251. Small neat. Dam won 3 Hdles, 2m1f-2m3f. P-t-P '97/9 r21 w5 (up to Confined) p7 (4 2nds — looked winner once); failed to finish 9 (fell/unseated 5). NH Mar '00 r2 p0 (4th in Grand Military Gold Cup: *wknd 4 out*), and unseated in R.A. Gold Cup: *no ch when hmpd & ur 2 out*). Maintained her progression into her fourth season when landing a hat-trick under Christian Williams, and gelled nicely with Lucy Horner on her final two starts, culminating in a first Hunter Chase success at Stratford. Diminutive, but with terrier-like qualities, and can produce reasonable acceleration. Might not improve her rating much in future, but looks sure to win again. Acts on any going. *R.H.P. Williams — D. Griffiths — D.L. Williams — Miss L. Horner — Glamorgan (Robert Williams; Dai Williams).* 346 (L), 644 (Cm), 820 (Cm), 1050 (M), 1343 (3m110yH), 1558 (3mH), 1645 (3mH).

AFTERNOON DELIGHT (IRE) ..9-1.. 8 ch.m. Un Desperado (FR) — Miysam (Supreme Sovereign) pf. Small neat. Dam won at 5f. P-t-P '99 r3 p0 (5th, pulled up 1, and brought down 1). Showed speed in all her races, but used to pull too hard to get the trip and was beating a retreat when she fell fatally at Market Rasen. *Mrs S.R. Hardy — Derwent.* 230 (L), 439 (OMa).

AGAINST THE AGENT ..10-5.. 11 ch.g. Buckley — Calametta (Oats) 542p. Big rangy brother to NH flat and jumping winner, Skillwise. P-t-P/HUNT CH '95 and '97/9 r9 w4 (inc 2m Hunt Ch, and Confined) p3 (2nds). Unbeaten in three visits to Whitwick Manor '97/9, and added a Hereford 2m Hunter Chase on the final start of '99, but has never managed more than four outings in a season (missed '96 entirely), and is no easy ride, as his fencing can be hair-raisingly erratic at times. Tends to jump right-handed and hang left-handed, but has struck up a decent relationship with Adrian Wintle. Usually needs a run to put him spot-on, but might have to lower his sights to get back on the victory trail. *J.P. Price — Radnor & W. Herefords (Clive Davies).* 77 (O), 382 (2m4fH), 581 (3mH), 799 (2m4f110yH).

AGANEROT (IRE) ..—.. 11 b.g. Torenaga — Silly Company (King's Company) ppp. Big strong. NH '96 and '99 r6 p0 (inc fell 1 in Hdle; brought down 1, and pulled up 2 in Chses). P-t-P/HUNT CH '98 (for Mr D. Walker) r4 p0 (7th, pulled up 2, and fell 1). Hopelessly outclassed in Hunter Chases and does not stay in Points, so it seemed quite natural that he would end up with his present trainer, where predictably abysmal. Sure to attract a cult following in future. *M.A. Hill — Wheatland (Frank Matthews).* 684 (2m4fH), 1413 (OMa), 1531 (2m110yH).

AGASSI'S ACE ..9-13.. 8 b.g. Vital Season — Welsh Flower (Welsh Saint) 1 0. Tall brother to Chasing winner, Celtic Season, and half-brother to Comedie Fleur, to Chasing winner, Snowdon Lily, and to flat and Hurdles winner, Flower Of Tintern. P-t-P '99 (for Mr A.J. Cottrell) r6 p0 (pulled up 3, and fell/unseated 3). NH May '00 (from N. Twiston-Davies') r1 p0; last in 2m4f110y Mdn Hdle: (*pulled hard, ld frm 2, hdd 6, wknd*). Served up plentiful double faults in his debut season, but well bred, and made no mistake on his return in a youngsters short Maiden at Cottenham. Failed to reappear, but the runner-up boosted the form, and if his absence is not the sign of trouble then he should be up to winning a Restricted in 2001. *Mrs K. Pilkington — Enfield Chace (-; N. Twiston-Davies).* 180 (2m4fOMa).

AGENT ..9-12.. 8 ch.g. Anshan — Maria Cappuccini (Siberian Express USA) pup4. Small light close-coupled. Dam won 2 5f races. 21,000. FLAT (won for L Eyre, bought for 16,000; previously for W. Haggas) r19 w1 (7f) p7. NH '98 (for S. Cole; bought for 1350) r5 p0 (inc Sells; broke blood vessel and withdrawn on intended debut). His only success from 29 attempts was gained on the Lingfield equitrack, but gave a decent display (when 66-1) in his only Pointing completion, when he finished four lengths third at Flete Park. Headstrong and does not find it easy to get the trip, but it might just be worth trying him in Ladies company. *I.S.G. Lang — R. Oliver — S. Devon (Janita Scott; Emma Oliver).* 314 (L), 556 (M), 726 (Cf), 1261 (Cf).

AGILE KING ..10-0.. 10 b.g. Rakaposhi King — My Aisling (John De Coombe) 4262p4. Small unfurnished half-brother to Bridge House and The Ugly Gunner, to Hurdles winner, Lady Remainder, and to flat winner, Petal's Jarred. Dam won 2 flat, 7-10f, including a Seller, but was disqualified from both for causing interference. P-t-P/HUNT CH '96/9 (for Mr J.W. Evans) r21 w2 (3m2f Maiden and Restricted) p9 (6 3rds, last twice); fell 3, and pulled up 1. Took 13 races to get off the mark, and looked a non-stayer, but then won two weak races taking over seven minutes in quick succession. Has been let down by his lack of stamina since, and his losing run now stands at 13. Has been tried in a cross-noseband and taken to post early in the current yard. *A. & Mrs L. Tizzard — Blackmore & Sparkford V. (Alan Tizzard).* 953 (I), 1239 (I), 1370 (I), 1599 (I), 1607 (I), 1674 (I).

AHERNE ..8-6.. 6 b.g. Nalchik (USA) — Zoomar (Legend Of France USA) fppp3. Workmanlike lengthy. FLAT r4 p) (inc 4th in 2 Sells, dwelt on debut); visored and refused to enter stalls on intended debut. NH '99 (for B. Palling) r2 p0 (ran out at 1st after trying to refuse — very unruly and rearing at start; and tailed off and pulled up 1). Has at least been more tractable in Points, and finished five lengths third at Bassaleg (the fifth has scored since), but further improvement will be required if he is to get off the mark. *S. Jones — Llangeinor.* 145 (OMa), 207 (OMa), 834 (OMa), 1301 (OMa), 1406 (OMa).

AINTGOTTIME (IRE) ..10-7.. 9 ch.g. Decent Fellow — Spoonbender (Mr Bigmore) 221. Tall. Dam, half-sister to Crozbridge (*qv* '90 Annual), won 2 Points and placed 5 (inc 2 Hdles). P-t-P/HUNT CH '97/9 r10 w3 (Maiden, Restricted and PPORA) p2; pulled up 3, and fell 1. Surprisingly mown down by Nibble, who was just running into top form, after a promising seasonal debut behind Miss O'Grady, but landed his fourth Pointing success when scoring in the fastest time of the day at Marks Tey. Has had all kinds of problems in the past which have restricted his activities, and four outings in a season is his record. Not a straightforward ride, but would not look out of place in a Novice Hunter Chase, although he was disappointing on his only start in that sphere so far. *Mrs F. Kehoe — Bicester with Whaddon.* 327 (O), 609 (I), 937 (I).

AINT NO LADY (IRE) ..8-0.. 8 b.m. Brush Aside (USA) — Nelly Gleason (Gleason USA) 4pf. Workmanlike half-sister to Bonus Number (IRE). P-t-P '99 (for Mrs L. Ward) r2 p0 (pulled up 2). Beaten out of sight in her only completion, and has shown scant respect for the obstacles to date. *Miss S.E. Robinson — Quantock.* 73 (OMa), 728 (R), 849 (R).

AIRBORNE BLUE ..8-7.. 10 gr.g. Kuwait Beach (USA) — Sobralia (Sunley Builds) ppu3f. Lengthy well-made. NH FLAT '97 r2 p0. NH '97 (for J. Jenkins) r3 p1 (2nd); pulled up 1 and fell 1. His two placings (three years apart) are comprised of a distant second of four in a Hurdle (hung violently left on the run-in), and a remote last of three in a Maiden. Seems to be little better than useless, and was very fat in early season in 2000. *J. Worth — Cambs.* 88 (OMa), 91 (M), 775 (OMa), 1039 (OMa), 1382 (OMa).

AIR COMMAND (BAR) ..9-6.. 11 br.g. Concorde Hero (USA) — Hubbardair (Town And Country) u586. Close-coupled attractive half-brother to a winner in Barbados. Dam won at 8f. FLAT (tried blinkers and eyeshield; one win from C. Nash's; previously won Sell for J. Bridger, sold for 5000; also ran for R. Hannon, S. Dow and R. Hodges) r40 w2 (5-8f; Sell and Amat) p3 (3rds). NH '94, '96 and '98 (bought for 900; from E. James'; previously from C. Nash's; debut for D. Burchell) r8 p2 (inc 3rd in Sell). Very unreliable on the flat, but did manage to win a 23-runner Amateur race (by a short head, at 50-1) when ridden by Paul Phillips. His placings over Hurdles were gained in '96, and showed little aptitude or enthusiasm for Points, in which he was a remote finisher at best. Probabably the first Pointer to have been bred in Barbados. *P. & E. Phillips — Axe V.H. (Paul Phillips).* 403 (Cf), 521 (O), 735 (MO), 927 (Cf).

AIRECCO (IRE) ..—§.. 10 ch.g. Air Display (USA) — Echo Repeating (Ballymore) pp6fpp. Strong half-brother to 2 Hurdles winners (one in Ireland, and one in Italy). IRISH P-t-P '97 r5 p1 (last of 3); pulled up, and fell 2. P-t-P '98/9 (for Miss W.E. Hollowell) r7 w1 (Maiden) p4 (3 2nds); and fell/unseated 2. Well supported when opening his account for the previous yard, but became rather disappointing for them, and never went a yard in 2000 — though never looked race-fit. Was to have run blinkered on his final appearance having looked decidedly unwilling on his previous start, but connections forgot to declare them. Has since been booted out. *T.F.G. Marks — Fitzwilliam.* 240 (L), 442 (L), 544 (L), 769 (M), 843 (R), 1009 (CR).

AIRTRAK (IRE) ..9-7.. 12 b.g. Strong Gale — Deep Khaletta (Deep Run) ppp. Lengthy unfurnished brother to Hurdles winner, Strong John, and half-brother to Irish Pointing winners, Dont Rough It (also a successful Hurdler there) and Eyre Street Lady, and to Irish NH flat winner, Thyne Will Tell. NH FLAT r4 p0. NH '94/6 (tried tongue-tied) r14 w1 (3m Ch) p4 (inc 3 Hdles, distant last of 2 once). P-t-P/HUNT CH '97/9 r19 w1 (Confined) p6 (3 3rds, last once, and inc last of 2 once); pulled up 4, and fell 1. Generally disappointing under Rules, and gained his only Pointing success in a three-runner Confined on firm ground at High Easter in '97. Had had a soft-palate operation by then, and his lamentable performances suggest he has gone in the wind again. *Mrs K. Pilkington — Enfield Chace.* 26 (O), 92 (Cf), 238 (O).

ALADDIN SANE TOO ..9-8.. 13 b.g. Shaunicken — Tee-Eff-Ess (Tudor Flame) u2. Rangy plain ex-eventer. P-t-P '99 r3 p3 (2 2nds). Only eight lengths behind Camp Bank on his debut, but the first venture into race-riding for Sophie Wesley, and her lack of experience has been all too apparent. An ancient maiden, but has next to no miles on the clock, and good enough to win if getting some guidance from above. Clearly under-rated on his best form. *Miss S. Wesley — Grafton.* 249 (CfMa), 516 (OMa).

ALASKAN HEIR ..9-12.. 10 b.g. Northern State (USA) — Royal Meeting (Dara Monarch) p54u313. Leggy workmanlike half-brother to 3 flat winners, including Tonka and Woodland Nymph (both also sucessful Hurdlers). Dam won 8f Sell and 2m1f Hdle. FLAT (for breeder, D. Murray-Smith, who won with the dam) r10 w1 (8f) p2 (3rds). NH '94/9 (for A. Streeter; previously for T. Forbes, bought for 1500) r39 w2 (2m-2m4f Hdles) p14 (inc 9 Chses, inc Sell). Completed a double over hurdles to January '95, but was ending a losing run of 38 when he plodded round to beat two reluctant opponents in heavy at Sandon (one of them had declined the first fence). Unimpressive and had to be driven along to beat the other survivor, and was extremely lucky to find an opportunity to end his sequence. Wears headgear and has been tongue-tied, and was tubed latterly under Rules. Needs an abundance of mud to slow the opposition down. *Miss W.M. Bayliss — Albrighton Woodland.* 294 (O), 333 (Cf), 611 (C), 862 (Cf), 1064 (3m2fCf), 1127 (O), 1408 (Cf).

ALBERT BLAKE ..10-1§.. 14 b.g. Roscoe Blake — Ablula (Abwah) 492p4. Strong owner-bred brother to Lula Blake, and half-brother to Scorpotina. Dam was 3rd in Maiden for Richard Kinsey. NH '94/6 and '98/9 (visored 1) r11 w1 (3m1f HCap Ch) p4 (2 2nds, beaten head once); failed to finish 4 (fell 1). P-t-P/HUNT CH '92, '94/5 and '98/9 r19 w4 (inc 3m2f Hunt Ch) p4 (short-headed once, and inc last of 3 in Hunt Ch); failed to finish 7 (refused 1, carried out 1, ran out 1, and fell 1). Has always had more talent than most, but incredibly temperamental, and likes nothing better than making a total nuisance of himself before the race. Particularly lacklustre on his return to Pointing in 2000, especially in both jaunts to Eyton, where he squandered a golden opportunity to record a fifth victory (odds-on-favourite). A strange character who has been on the go for nine years, and the North West Area will not be the same when he goes, though Starters will breathe a huge sigh of relief. Usually wears a tongue-strap. *Mrs T.R. Kinsey — Cheshire Forest.* 691 (O), 921 (2m6fH), 1198 (O), 1319 (O), 1409 (O).

ALBERT THE LION (IRE) ..8-12.. 9 gr.g. Celio Rufo — Esker Lady (Gala Performance USA) p3231. Plain angular. NH FLAT '96 r2 p0. NH '96/8 (for J. Neville; visored 2) r8 p0 (inc Sells); ran out 1. Does not seem to get the trip too well and prone to make the odd bad mistake (may also be Albert The Cowardly Lion), but made the most of a simple opportunity in an eight-plus Maiden at Laleston, in which he recorded a time 18 seconds slower than the other division. Well handled by Tim Vaughan on that occasion, but as always he marred the performance with his childish victory salute. Will need to improve to have a chance in Restricteds. *T. Faulkner — Tredegar F. (Deborah Faulkner).* 1056 (CfMa), 1302 (OMa), 1404 (OMa), 1573 (OMa), 1662 (OMa).

ALBERT WOODS ..9-3.. 8 b.g. Tigerwood — Venus Saga (Sagaro) p. Small owner-bred. Dam, half-sister to Rainbow Legacy (*qv*), pulled up 3 and fell 2 in Points ('devoid of stamina and a terrifying ride'). NH FLAT '97 r1 p0 (tailed off). NH '97 r1 p0. P-t-P '98/9 r9 w1 (Maiden) p2; pulled up 6. Failed to finish in his first six starts, but showed steady improvement, and proved more resolute than the runner-up when successful at Bonvilston on his final outing in '99. Had to be destroyed after breaking a leg at Lydstep on his reappearance. *D.R. Thomas — Llangeinor.* 832 (R).

ALDINGTON ANNIE ..—.. 7 gr.m. Baron Blakeney — Aldington Princess (Cavo Doro) pp. Small lengthy sister to Aldington Baron and Aldington Charlie, and half-sister to Aldington Spot. Had a foal as a three-year-old. Novicey and made plenty of mistakes before pulling up in May Maidens, but possibly capable of better eventually. *Mrs H. Gwin — Heythrop (Mark Rimell).* 1589 (2m4fOMa), 1634 (OMa).

ALENA H BANKS ..8-7.. 7 b.g. Milieu — Widow Trellerne (Cool Guy USA) ppp4p. Workmanlike good-topped. Dam is sister to Davy Blake (*qv* '99 Annual). Had an uninspiring first season, and was a remote last on his only completion. *A. Jackson — Cleveland (Lynne Ward).* 398 (OMa), 620 (R), 695 (OMa), 803 (MMa), 1032 (OMa).

ALEX THUSCOMBE ..10-1.. 13 ch.g. Takachiho — Portate (Articulate) 6u. Small compact brother to Ben Tirran and Wayward Edward, and half-brother to Eborneezer's Dream. NH FLAT r1 p0. NH '93/4 r7 p0. P-t-P/HUNT CH '95/9 r31 w4 (up to Confined) p12 (7 2nds, inc Hunt Ch); failed to finish 8 (on floor 5, and carried out 1). Successful twice apiece '96/7, and placed seven times in 12 starts since, and would have been no worse than second but for unseating Peter Shaw when duelling with Chasing The Bride at Ascot (had been runner-up in the race 12 months earlier). Deserves to find another opportunity, but becoming more and more lightly raced, and is no longer in the first flush of youth. A sound leaper who is suited by top of the ground. Wears blinkers, and has previously been visored, including when successful. *Mrs F. Shaw — Cattistock (Fiona & Peter Shaw).* 59 (MO), 800 (3m110yH).

ALFION (IRE) ..9-12.. 12 b.g. Saxon Farm — Knockeevan Girl (Tarqogan) pp. Tall strong-topped half-brother to smart Hurdles winner, Miracle Man. Dam is sister or half-sister to 6 Pointers, including Father Delaney (*qv* '88 Annual). NH FLAT r1 p0. NH '94/6 (blinkered 2) r13 p0 (inc pulled up 4, and fell 1 in Hdles; 6th, pulled up 2, unseated 1, and refused 1 in Chses). P-t-P '97/9 r14 w3

(Maiden, Restricted and Confined) p6 (5 2nds); pulled up 1. Took well to Pointing after a dreadful career under Rules, but hindered by his enormous bulk, and after managing just three outings apiece '98/9 failed to go further than two miles in just two forays (ten weeks apart) in 2000. Would need to be treated with caution were he to reappear. *D.R. Thomas — Llangeinor.* 275 (Cf), 1295 (Cf).

ALFREDO GARCIA (IRE) ..9-12.. 11 b.g. Lancastrian — The Tame Fairy (Bluerullah) p532up. Big rangy half-brother to Cluricaune (IRE). Dam won an Irish Point. IRISH P-t-P '94/5 r7 w1 (Maiden) p2; pulled up 2. P-t-P '96 and '98/9 r12 w1 (Restricted) p5 (3 3rds); pulled up 2, and fell 1. Often unsound and raced sparingly since crossing the Irish Sea, and his solitary success owed much to the skill of Simon Andrews, but a weak finisher who will need to find a bad race in order to score again. A steady jumper, and suited by a sound surface — Catch 22? *The Marriage Family — Essex (Simon Marriage).* 318 (Cf), 572 (CfO), 609 (I), 840 (I), 937 (I), 1380 (L).

ALIAS PARKER JONES ..9-0.. 10 gr.g. Alias Smith (USA) — Fidessa (Fine Blade USA) p2. Rangy half-brother to Bertraghboy Bay. P-t-P/HUNT CH '97/9 r24 w2 (Maiden and Restricted) p2 (3rd of 4 twice); failed to finish 17 (on floor 3). Incredibly adept at non-completion, and is greatly flattered by two successes in dire contests: finished alone once, and reduced to a trot by the finishing line in the other. Often amazingly fat, and the odds of lightning striking for a third time must be astronomical. Rather busy '97/9, but disappeared after his Members, and may have suffered a setback. *D.W. Parker — Carms (Linda Parker).* 344 (I), 642 (M).

ALICAT (IRE) ..8-7.. 10 b.g. Cataldi — Sweet Result (Owen Dudley) 3p5pp. Close-coupled half-brother to a winner in Spain. NH FLAT '95/6 r2 p0. NH '96/9 (for N. Babbage, bought for 3400; previously for J. Curtis) r15 p4 (3rds, inc distant last thrice in Chses); pulled up 8, inc 5 consecutively and in Sell Ch final. Bought Ascot, May for 1400. A sour individual under Rules (tried in headgear on four occasions), and ran badly in Points after finishing 16 lengths third of four on his first attempt. Does not seem to stay more than 2m4f. *E. Parry — Gelligaer F.* 270 (CfMa), 348 (CfMa), 602 (CfMa), 823 (CfMa), 1056 (CfMa).

ALICE SHORELARK ..9-12.. 10 ch.m. Newski (USA) — Alice Woodlark (Sir Lark) 1. Small lengthy lop-eared half-sister to Alice Sunrise. Dam, half-sister to 3 Pointers including Devonshire Lad (qv), won 4 Points and placed 11 for Mrs Greed. Grandam, Alice Rairthorn, won a Members and placed 6 (inc 2 Hdles). NH FLAT '95/6 r3 p0. NH '97 r3 p0 (tailed off in Hdles — pulled up 2). P-t-P '98/9 r14 w1 (Maiden) p7 (6 2nds, last once); last pair 4, fell 1. Beaten in her first eight Maidens and struggling in Restricted company since, but capitalised on a relatively simple opportunity in her Members on her first start for David Pipe. Reserves her best for Black Forest Lodge, but presumably met with trouble there as she failed to reappear. Appears to go well fresh, but typically chestnut mare-ish and may not always put it all in — blinkers could still be worth a go. *Mrs J.M. Greed — Silverton (David Pipe).* 65 (M).

ALICE SUNRISE ..8-5.. 7 ch.m. Vital Season — Alice Woodlark (Sir Lark) fpp7. Small neat owner-bred half-sister to Alice Shorelark (qv). NH FLAT '98/9 (from G. Knight's) r2 p0 (tailed off). Shows nothing yet and was a poor last when eventually achieving a completion, but better jumping would help. *Mrs J.M. Greed — Silverton (M. Hollis).* 253 (CfMa), 404 (I), 518 (2m4fOMa), 1100 (OMa).

ALISHA BAVARD (IRE) ..9-8.. 8 gr.m. Le Bavard (FR) — Our Katy (Dragonara Palace USA) 2p3. Sparely-made. Dam won 2 6f Sells. P-t-P '98 (for Mr J.L. Lewis) r2 p0 (pulled up 2). Not disgraced when beaten a maximum of eight lengths in two Erw Lon Maidens, but was way out of her depth in Hunter Chases (jumped very poorly at Hereford). Lacks scope, but probably good enough to win a Welsh Maiden. *M.A. Watts — Pembs.* 270 (CfMa), 468 (3m1f110yH), 648 (CfMa).

ALI'S LARK ..—.. 8 b.g. Crested Lark — Ali's Chandy (Chandulal) pfppR. Rangy unfurnished half-brother to Late Discovery. Dam was placed in 3 Points and 2nd in a Hunt Ch. P-t-P '99 r2 p0 (pulled up 2). A thoroughly nasty piece of work to date (not even safe on the way to post), and has yet to go more than two miles without doing something totally deranged. Stronger handling might help, but blinkers have twice sent him into total apoplexy. *Mr & Mrs J.L. Marks — Fitzwilliam.* 124 (OMa), 180 (2m4fOMa), 373 (CfMa), 412 (OMa), 1269 (OMa).

ALIZARINE BLUE ..8-13.. 8 b.g. Tina's Pet — Rhiannon (Welsh Pageant) up4. Rangy workmanlike brother to successful Hurdler, Alcian Blue, and half-brother to King of Shadows and Malachite Green, to flat winner, Prince Of The Lake, and to a winner in Italy. NH '98 (for M. Hammond) r1 p0. Showed slight signs of improvement when 28 lengths fourth in early April, but not seen since, and may be difficult to train. Could conceivably provide his dam with another winner if able to appear in 2001. *R. Kendall — Cumberland F.* 187 (OMa), 499 (2m4fOMa), 909 (2m4fOMa).

AL JAWWAL ..9-8.. 11 ch.g. Lead On Time (USA) — Littlefield (Bay Express) ppp1p435. Sturdy half-brother to flat and Hurdles winner, Hayaain, and to flat winners, Dahik, Ebraaz and Moalem (in Malaysia). Dam, useful, won 3 flat, 6-8f. P-t-P/HUNT CH '95/7 (for Mrs P. King) r8 w1 (Maiden) p1 (3rd); failed to finish 6 (fell 2). Too backward to race on the flat, and off the track for two years following just eight starts in three Pointing seasons, but managed a full campaign in 2000, and rewarded his new connections with a win. Inclined to be lackadaisical at the fences from time to time, and often looks unwilling, but can shift when he wants to, and has produced his best efforts for Louise Allan. Far from disgraced in a fair Restricted on his penultimate start, and may consent to win one eventually. Wears a cross-noseband, and has been tried in a tongue strap. *Miss K. Thory — Fitzwilliam.* 16 (R), 119 (CR), 179 (R), 769 (M), 1038 (R), 1111 (R), 1418 (R), 1434 (3m110yH).

ALKARINE ..9-0§.. 9 gr.g. Alias Smith (USA) — Colly Cone (Celtic Cone) pfppp. Lengthy good-bodied. FLAT (at 4) r1 p0. NH '95/6 r3 p0 (pulled up 3; soon tailed off 2 inc Sell, and looked difficult ride final). P-t-P '97/9 r22 w2 (Maiden and Restricted) p4 (3 2nds); failed to finish 11 (refused 1, and fell/unseated 2). Won a dreadful Maiden in '97, but performed dismally in Restricteds the following year, and was a 20-1 chance when outstaying Detroit Davy in a Garnons bog on his '99 return. Has never looked 100 per cent co-operative, and did not go a yard in 2000. Often carries plenty of condition, and has been tried in headgear. Might revive if his health allows (covered in warts in early season), but one to treat with caution. *M.W. Lasper — Ystrad Taf Fechan.* 448 (I), 741 (Cf), 819 (Cf), 944 (I), 1449 (I).

ALLERBANK ..9-11.. 10 b.g. Meadowbrook — Allerdale (Chebs Lad) 54. Good-sized robust brother to Hurdles winner, Allerbeck, and half-brother to Hurdles winners, Allerlad (also won NH flat) and One Stop. Dam won 7 2m Hdles. NH '97/8 r11 p1 (2nd of 10 in Mdn Ch); pulled up in Sell Ch. P-t-P '96 and '99 (for Mr N.P. & Mr J.P.L. Williams) r9 w3 (Maiden, Restricted and Confined) p1 (3rd); fell/unseated 3. Did well to win thrice for the previous yard in '99, but presumably laid low after two below par efforts in February. Has abundant stamina and suited by soft ground, but still seems inclined to bolt the odd fence. Can win more races if present connections can restore him to full fitness. *R. Greenway — Cheshire (Reg Crank).* 171 (O), 370 (C).

ALLER COOMBE ..9-0.. 7 b.m. Teamster — Ragsi (Amerian USA) p3p. Small weedy half-sister to Huffin And Puffin, and to Chasing winner, Ragamuff. Dam was placed in a Ladies and 3 Restricteds (rarely tried Maidens, or could probably have won). P-t-P '99 r2 p1 (3rd); and pulled up 1. Beaten a minimum of 19 lengths in her placings, and does possess some ability, but disappeared after a dismal effort at Bishops Court, and is clearly not easy to get right. Lacks the scope for much improvement, though better ground would help. *S.O. Sampson — Tiverton Stag (Sarah Kinnon).* 145 (OMa), 254 (CfMa), 407 (OMa).

ALL FOR TACK ..—.. 8 b.m. Tigerwood — Roushane (Rustingo) pp. Small sister to Tiger Lord (*qv*). Did not look much good when 33-1 in late season Maidens. *Mrs G.A. Davies & B. Hill — Carms (A. Davies).* 1404 (OMa), 1660 (OMa).

ALL-INCLUSIVE (IRE) ..9-1.. 8 ch.m. Buckskin (FR) — Minimum Choice (IRE) (Miner's Lamp) u5ff. Small light-framed lengthy. Dam is half-sister to Buckland Filleigh (*qv* '97 Annual). NH '98/9 (for H. Daly; debut for I. Williams) r3 p0 (5th, pulled up and fell — tailed off thrice). Would have finished over eight lengths third had she not fallen at the last at Holnicote, but seemed to have lost her confidence next time, and gave a poor display of jumping until eventually crashing two out when tailed off. James Scott remounted and ploughed through the crowd who were crossing the run-in, but escaped the severe reprimand such stupid behaviour should have warrented. A watching brief is advised when she reappears. *H.F.T. & Mrs E. Scott — Minehead H. (Liz Scott).* 410 (OMa), 640 (CfMa), 1372 (OMa), 1564 (OMa).

ALL IN THE GAME (IRE) ..8-0.. 13 b.g. Carlingford Castle — Royal Bonnet (Beau Chapeau) ppu7. Rangy good-topped half-brother to Think Positive (IRE) (*qv*). IRISH P-t-P '97/8 r7 w1 (6yo plus Maiden) p2; pulled up 1, and fell 1. IRISH NH FLAT '93/4 r3 p0. IRISH NH '95/8 (tried blinkered) r24 w3 (2m6f Chses) p3 (3rds); inc Hunt Ch. Won four Irish races in mud, but was best at 2m6f, and when he resumed as a veteran in the new yard he definitely looked to be gone at the game. *S. Carter — Cheshire Forest (Reg Crank).* 293 (Cf), 529 (Cf), 960 (Cf), 1408 (Cf).

ALL OR NOTHING ..9-0.. 13 ch.m. Scorpio (FR) — Kelton Lass (Lord Nelson FR) pf. Lengthy. Dam won 2m Nov Ch. P-t-P/HUNT CH '93/9 r41 w1 (Maiden) p6 (3 2nds, dead-heated once); failed to finish 15 (fell/unseated 8). Took 16 attempts to get off the mark, and has been beaten 27 times since. Likely to extend that record further if reappearing. Wears blinkers nowadays, and remains a consistently shaky jumper. *R.S. Kendall — Cumberland F.* 40 (R), 109 (L).

ALLRITE BONNY LASS ..10-1.. 7 b.m. Nomination — Sense Of Pride (Welsh Pageant) p21s3. Small unfurnished half-sister to 3 flat winners (one prolific in Italy), including Sense Of Priority (20 victories, principally on all-weather) and Ottavio Farnese. Dam won 2 12f races in Ireland. P-t-P '99 r5 w1 (2m4f Maiden) p0; pulled up 2, and unseated 1. Appeared to relish the cut in the ground when winning her Restricted at the first time of asking, and would appear to be suited by plenty of cut in the ground (all at sea when conditions were fast next time), but it is questionable whether she has the scope to improve enough for the Ladies Opens that would suit her stature. Sure to be placed to advantage come what may. *Mrs A. Waggott — Tynedale (Pauline Robson).* 359 (Cf), 811 (I), 1081 (R), 1429 (Cm), 1576 (Cf).

ALLRITE PET ..10-6.. 10 b.m. Alias Smith (USA) — Munster Glen (Furry Glen) 111p1. Tall rangy half-sister to Need A Ladder. Dam won 2m Hdle. P-t-P/HUNT CH '97/9 r13 w2 (Maiden and

Restricted) p5 (4 2nds); pulled up 2, and unseated 1. A big mare who has taken time to come to herself physically, but did so in no uncertain terms in 2000, and would have gone through the season unbeaten had she not found the terrain too lively at Hexham. A thorough stayer and sound jumper, but yet to beat anything out of the ordinary, and Pauline Robson deserves credit for placing her so well. Benefits from having top riders at her disposal, and should be capable of winning in Open company. *Mrs A. Waggott — Tynedale (Pauline Robson)*. 493 (Cf), 815 (Cm), 1152 (I), 1445 (3m1fH), 1576 (Cf).

ALL SEWN UP ..9-3.. 9 ch.g. Jazetas — Rose Of Bradford (Levanter) u2. Lengthy. Dam half-sister to three Pointers, walked over for Taunton Vale Members. NH FLAT '96 r2 p0; also withdrawn not under orders once. NH '96 (for R. Baker) r4 p1 (20*l* 3rd of 5). Resumed four years after pulling up in a Hurdle, and was backed from 20s to 9-2 in a Maiden, but unseated at the 15th when weakening. Finished four lengths second next time, and there may be a small race to be had with her eventually. *N. & Mrs S.D. Dalgren — Quantock (Kay Rees & Polly Curling)*. 1241 (OMa), 1468 (OMa).

ALLTEN (IRE) ..9-1.. 8 br.g. Buckskin (FR) — I'll Say She Is (Ashmore FR) 3. Half-brother to Hurdles winner, Tax Exempt (IRE). Gave an apparently encouraging display when eight lengths third on his belated debut, but appears to be yet another difficult to train animal by Buckskin. A potential winner if ever fit enough to do himself justice. *E. Tuer — Hurworth*. 693 (OMa).

ALL THINGS NICE ..9-6.. 10 ch.m. Sweet Monday — Penny's Affair (Chingnu) 333. Small compact sister to Monday Country, and half-sister to Kettles, Fairy Favours and Miss Pilkington. Dam won Ladies and placed 7 for Joanna Daniell. P-t-p '97/9 r13 p3 (3rds, 4 once); failed to finish 8 (fell/unseated 5). Has now been placed on six occasions, but a surprisingly (in view of Kettles) weak finisher and does not get too many opportunities. Her fencing has become far more proficient, but though she deserves to find a race will surely struggle to do so. *Mrs M.R. Daniell — Ledbury (Mike Daniell)*. 337 (CfMa), 703 (OMa), 995 (OMa).

ALL WEATHER ..10-3.. 15 b.g. Air Trooper — Modom (Compensation) 518p. Very big strong brother to Hurdles winner, Out Yonder, and half-brother to Balmy Breeze, to flat and Hurdles winner, Bwana Kali, and to Chasing winner, In The Zone. Dam won 3 flat, 10-11f. P-t-P/HUNT CH '93/9 r32 w10 (inc 3m1f110y Hunt Ch, and 6 Nov Rdrs Clubs) p10 (8 2nds, inc 3 Hunt Chses); pulled up 6. Had his finest hour when beating Last Option at Cheltenham in '98, but was gaining his first success since when landing a gamble at Bitterley. Responded gallantly to Mark Wilesmith's urgings after looking held at the foot of the hill, and refused to accept defeat. Has to go left-handed, and always turned out looking a picture. Makes few concessions to age, but has now completed eight Pointing campaigns, and will be very hard to replace when his doting connections decide to retire him. *M.S. Wilesmith — Ledbury (Emma Wilesmith)*. 991 (L), 1086 (Cf), 1338 (4m1fH), 1463 (Cf).

ALLY PALLY ..9-10.. 10 ch.g. Town And Country — Drivers Bureau (Proverb) 2f444u. Lengthy. P-t-P '97 and '99 r5 w1 (Club Maiden) p3 (last of 3 once); unseated 1. Went wrong in his first season, and emerged from a year off to land a three-finisher Maiden at Charing in '99, but has found life frustrating in Restricted company since. Jumped left-handed on his reappearance forfeiting as much ground as he was eventually beaten by, and kept to left-handed courses since, but frequently kicks the fences out of the way, and will need to treat them with much more respect if he is to score again. *R.H. York — Surrey U*. 2 (R), 126 (R), 285 (CR), 575 (R), 825 (K), 1104 (R).

ALMIKINO (IRE) ..8-4.. 8 b.g. Altountash — Lucky Penny Lass (Kampala) uppp6p. Sturdy. IRISH P-t-P '99 r5 p1 (2nd); pulled up 4. Bought Doncaster, May for 1800. Prone to shocking errors and may lack stamina, and nothing he has achieved so far suggest he is going to be able to win (pulls up with monotonous regularity). *S.A. Sinclair — Braes (Russell Ross)*. 696 (OMa), 808 (OMa), 1083 (2m4fOMa), 1329 (OMa), 1480 (OMa), 1581 (2m4fOMa).

ALPHABITES ..—.. 9 b.m. Primitive Rising (USA) — Jay-Bee Windows (Revlow) p. Small neat. Dam was very remote 3rd twice in Points (pulled up once for Tim Gardham subsequently). Jumped poorly and soon struggling in an early February Maiden. *Mrs V. Gardham — Holderness*. 124 (OMa).

ALPINE CASTLE (IRE) ..9-3.. 9 ch.m. Carlingford Castle — Kakala (Bargello) 24p15. Good-topped half-sister to Belmount Beauty (IRE) and Relocate (IRE). IRISH P-t-P '96 r2 p0 (pulled up 2). P-t-P '99 r8 p2; pulled up 4. Booked for a poor second until the clear leader capsized at the last at Mounsey Hill Gate, but promptly put the brakes on — not for the first time — as mayhem followed. However Sue Young cunningly waited for the fence to be dolled off, and with the need to have a second crack at it removed continued merrily to the luckiest win of the season. Likely to struggle more in Restricteds. Wears bandages all round, and usually looks as though she has been fetched straight in from the field. *R. Ford — E. Cornwall (Sue Young)*. 158 (CfMa), 723 (CfMa), 1262 (OMa), 1420 (OMa), 1650 (R).

ALPINE MUSIC (IRE) ..—.. 7 b.g. Tirol — Holy Devotion (Commanche Run) pp. Good-topped half-brother to flat winner, Honorable Estate. FLAT r10 p1 (10*l* 3rd in Sell). NH '97/8 (for S. Mullins; previously for M. Bradley) r5 p1 (2nd). Bought Malvern, Sept for 400. Not seen under Rules after being short-headed in a Novice Claimer (pulled hard), and looked to have problems when finally reappearing two years later. Would theoretically be interesting if dropped to a Maiden. Tried in headgear on four occasions in previous yards. *Mrs J. Goudge — S. Cornwall (A. Goudge)*. 652 (MO), 848 (R).

ALSKA (FR) ..10-3.. 8 b/br.m. Leading Counsel (USA) — Kolkwitzia (FR) (The Wonder FR) 453.2u952. Tall. FRENCH FLAT '95/8 r18 w2 (1200m) p13. FRENCH NH '96/8 r21 w3 (2m Hdles) p7 (inc 2 Chses). HUNT CH '99 r6 p1 (3rd); last pair 2, unseated 2, and pulled up 1. NH Mar '00 r1 p1 (20l 2nd to Noyan in R.A. Gold Cup, Sandown, 3m110y: *outpcd 12; kpt on one pce*). A decent mare in France (won F695,000, around £70,000, including a flat race as recently as August '98), and looks up to winning races over here now that she has acclimatised, but requires more dynamic handling than she has been used to. Stamina does not seem to be her strong suit, and appears best with some cut in the ground, but remains liable to make the odd jumping error. Has been tried in a visor. *P.L. Southcombe — Cattistock*. 78 (L), 218 (L), 467 (3m1f110yH), 1293 (3mH), 1433 (3mH), 1444 (2m5fH), 1638 (L).

ALSTACK (IRE) ..9-12.. 10 ch.g. Mister Lord (USA) — Laura Nore (Laurence O) 12f. Lengthy. P-t-P '98/9 r3 p0 (pulled up 3). Clearly extracting the proverbial in his first three starts, as he showed massive improvement when tried in blinkers, although he beat little of note in a slow time at Eyton. Failed to justify favouritism on his final start (the rider came back to report that the horse needs further) when outbattled by Autumn Blunder, and seems to need everything to go his own way. Was losing interest having been headed when making his exit on his latest appearance. *E.H. Crow — N. Salop (Sheila Crow)*. 569 (OMa), 1633 (CR), 1664 (R).

ALSTON ANTICS ..10-10.. 8 gr.g. Daring March — Illustrate (Bustino) f. Strong lengthy. Dam is half-sister to Supercollege (*qv* '95 Annual). IRISH P-t-P '98 r3 w1 (5yo Maiden) p0; pulled up 1, and fell 1. NH '98 r2 p1 (8½l last of three in Ch — hampered, and deserved 2nd); and pulled up 1. Fell two out when in the process of giving an excellent display at Huntingdon (race won by Mighty Moss), but tragically died. *J. Stanley — Vine & Craven (Kim Bailey)*. 151 (3mH).

ALSTON FANFARE (IRE) ..7-12.. 8 b.g. Brush Aside (USA) — Rambling Rector (IRE) (The Parson) 60pp. Workmanlike. IRISH P-t-P '98 r5 p1 (35l 2nd); pulled up 1, and unseated 1. Last in both Maiden completions, and if he has any ability he is keeping it very well hidden. Blinkered on final start, and surely has a problem. *J.M.B. Cookson — S. Wold (David Ingle)*. 51 (OMa), 793 (CfMa), 1070 (2m4fOMa), 1269 (OMa).

ALWAYS TRYING ..8-10.. 6 b.g. Always Fair (USA) — Bassita (Bustino) p5p2pp1. Lengthy half-brother to useful jumping winner, Blowing Wind (FR), to NH flat winner, Nahla, and 2 winners abroad. Dam is an unraced half-sister to Pebbles. 65,000 francs y, 6400 2-y-o. FLAT (for M. Johnson) r4 p1 (11l 2nd); inc Sell. NH '98/9 (for M. Hammond, bought for 6800) r3 p0. Does not like racing and is certainly inappropriately named, but forced to score (in the slowest time of the day) by Andrew Sansome when blinkered for the first time on firmish at High Easter (his main rival hung badly right on the run-in and threw the race away). Needs a great deal of driving, and will have to show a much better attitude to follow up. *J.M. Turner — Suffolk*. 97 (OMa), 237 (OMa), 412 (OMa), 774 (OMa), 1039 (OMa), 1291 (OMa), 1383 (OMa).

ALY DALEY (IRE) ..10-2.. 13 ch.g. Roselier (FR) — Roses In June (Timobriol) 1u314u4. Small flashy brother to Lady Steel (IRE). Dam is an unraced half-sister to Grand National winner, Rag Trade. IRISH P-t-P '93/4 r7 w1 (6yo plus Maiden) p4; fell 2. NH '94/9 (for H. Johnson, bought for 32,000; 2 runs for P. Mooney in '97; blinkered once in '96) r32 w5 (2m5f-3m Chses) p8 (short-headed once). Bought Doncaster, Aug for 3600. Formerly a very game front runner at best, but gave seven poor unplaced displays on his final outings under Rules. Staged something of a revival in the new yard, and Alison Price did well to win on him twice, although she did not make the best of an apparently simple task when 4-5 at Sedgefield (eventually fell off two out when third and beaten). Acts on any ground and has no stamina worries, and may continue to give some fun at 13. *Miss A. Price — W. Salop (Carrie Ford)*. 529 (Cf), 682 (3m3fH), 902 (Cf), 960 (Cf), 1149 (Cf), 1542 (3mH), 1643 (3m2fH).

AMARANTHINE ..9-0.. 14 b.m. Sunley Builds — Warm Up (Hot Brandy) 372upp. Tall plain half-sister to Warm Blade. Dam, half-sister to prolific jumping winners, won Maiden and 2nd 2. Grandam, Ronbridge, was last of 3 in a Point. NH '93 r3 p0 (pulled up 3). P-t-P/HUNT CH '97/9 r13 w1 (Maiden) p6 (5 2nds); pulled up 5. Placed in each of her Members races in the last two seasons, but beaten a minimum of 15 lengths in 2000, and is unlikely to add to her Peper Harow success. Gave her normal partner her first win for 17 years, but became increasingly cheesed off with her upright wild waving, and dropped her at the last at Badbury, and never did a tap on final two starts (for newcomer, Clare Cowe in one). Tried in blinkers, a cross-noseband and spurs! *Mrs J.M. Butler — Hampshire, & Hursley Hambledon (Kate Buckett)*. 324 (M), 522 (L), 882 (M), 1061 (R), 1243 (Inr), 1393 (R).

AMAZING HILL (IRE) ..9-6.. 11 b.g. Amazing Bust — Cox Hill (Rarity) u45u33414fp. Strong lengthy. IRISH P-t-P '96 r2 p0 (pulled up 2). IRISH NH FLAT r2 p0. P-t-P '97 and '99 r10 p3 (2 2nds); pulled up 5, and fell 2. Finally got off the mark at the 18th attempt in a three-finisher affair when he finally got it all right. Deserved his moment of glory as he had been the victim of some injudicious riding previously, but Rebecca Morris (riding her first winner) deserved credit for not panicking when the runner-up shot ten lengths clear three from home. Takes a while to run himself fit, but will need to improve to become competitive in anything other than the most modest Restricteds. *R. T. & Mrs W.S. Cook — N. Cornwall*. 105 (OMa), 253 (CfMa), 540 (OMa), 658 (R), 722 (CfMa), 855 (CfMa), 1048 (CfMa), 1391 (OMa), 1517 (R), 1608 (R), 1639 (R).

AMBERSAM ..10-1.. 6 b.g. Gildoran — Golden Valley (Hotfoot) p1. Half-brother to Half Each (*qv*). Given a blatant school on his debut, but reaped the benefit when 2-1 (early birds snapped up the tens) in a 2m4f Maiden at Whitwell. Others in his family have done the Walfords proud, and must be noted for further successes, particularly as his sire Gildoran is doing so well. Potentially under-rated by several pounds. *Mrs G.B. Walford — Middleton (Tim Walford)*. 398 (OMa), 1001 (2m4fOMa).

AMBER SPARK (IRE) ..9-4.. 12 ch.g. The Parson — La Dragoniere (Hot Spark) 66. Small compact brother to Lantern Spark (IRE). IRISH P-t-P '94 r1 p0 (pulled up). IRISH NH FLAT '94 r3 p1 (3rd). IRISH NH '94/5 r9 p0. NH '96/8 r17 w1 (2m5f Ch) p7 (beaten a head in Hdle; and 6 Chses). P-t-P/HUNT CH '99 r5 p0; pulled up 2, and unseated 1. Successful only once from 37 starts, and beaten an aggregate of 121 lengths in his two spins in 2000, 19 weeks apart. Has shown minimal zest for much of his career, and there is surely something wrong with him. *The Whitestick Partnership — Miss H. Poole — Cambs (Simon Andrews; Kevin Ball)*. 19 (L), 1631 (MO).

AMBROSE ..10-2.. 14 b.g. Ile De Bourbon (USA) — Famous Band (USA) (Banderilla USA) 42u4. Compact half-brother to Irish flat and English Chasing winner, Famous Lad, and to flat winner, Bold Elect. FLAT (tried blinkers) r13 w1 (12f) p7 (short-headed once). NH '91/3 r17 w2 (2m Hdles) p7 (inc 3 Chses, last of once). P-t-P/HUNT CH '94/6 and '98/9 r21 w5 (3 Members and 2 Confineds; inc hat-trick '96) p2 (2nds, inc Hunt Ch); pulled up 7, and fell 2. In fine form in '96, but missed the following season, and returned a pale shadow of his former self until perking up for Tessa Clark at Tabley. Used to pull hard and often sweats up, but becoming elderly, and unlikely to achieve much outside of his Members (which he has won three times) should he return. Usually bandaged in front. *W.A. & Mrs T. Ritson — Sir W.W. Wynn's*. 525 (M), 962 (L), 1150 (L), 1410 (L).

AMERICAN EYRE ..9-5.. 16 gr.g. Step Together (USA) — Jane Eyre (Master Buck) 53p. Tall rangy brother to Irish NH flat and Hurdles winner, Step On Eyre (IRE), and half-brother to 3 Irish winners, including Noble Eyre (NH flat — subsequently won English jumping). Dam won an Irish Point. IRISH NH FLAT r18 w1 p5. IRISH P-t-P '93 r2 p1 (3rd). IRISH NH '90/1 and '93/5 (blinkered 4) r29 w4 (3 Hdles, 2m4f-3m, and 2m4f Ch) p5. P-t-P/HUNT CH '96/9 r25 w4 (inc 2 Confineds) p7 (3 2nds; and inc last of 3 once); pulled up 7. Won five Irish races in soft/heavy to '93, but became disappointing until revived by the current yard when winning four races '97/8. A precision jumper, but has simply got too old to keep up nowadays. *Mrs G.M. Gladders - Ashford V*. 706 (Cf), 1109 (M), 1509 (Cf).

A MONKEY FOR DICK (IRE) ..—.. 12 br.g. Monksfield — Maggie's Turn (Garda's Revenge USA) Ru. Tall half-brother to Irish Chasing winner, Merchants Road, and to Irish Pointing winner, Onthelist. IRISH NH FLAT Dec '93/4 r4 p0. IRISH P-t-P '97 r4 p0; pulled up 1, and fell 1. IRISH P-t-P '98 r1 p0 (pulled up). A more than passable fourth of 18 in a Down Royal bumper on his racecourse debut in '93, but has been seen on just a handful of occasions since, and would appear to have major problems (has had a tie-back operation). Attracted some market support on his English Pointing debut, but presumably went wrong and the veteran owner-rider could not hold one side of him on his return after a year off. It would be interesting to see what a strong pilot would make of him. *J. Dixon — College V. & N. Northumberland*. 1081 (R), 1580 (OMa).

AMTRAK EXPRESS ..10-3.. 14 ch.g. Black Minstrel — Four In A Row (Cracksman) 4ppuu712u. Light-framed angular brother to NH flat & Chasing winner, Golden Drum (IRE), and to successful Irish Pointers, Mightyatom, Cush Maid and Mighty Royal, and half-brother to Irish Pointing and jumping winner, Irish Fountain. IR 7400 4-y-o. NH FLAT Oct '92 r2 w1 p0. NH '93/8 (unplaced 4 for Mrs J. Pitman; previously for N. Henderson) r27 w8 (3 Hdles, 2m-2m2f, and 5 Chses, 2m1f-3m1f, inc £20,381 Agfa Diamond Ch, 3 ran) p6 (inc earned £10,477 when 3rd in '96 Whitbread — lame); on floor 6. Beat Earth Summit in a Bumper on his debut and went on to amass £88,756 under Rules. Formerly smart, but has shown almost nothing since his bout of lameness, although he did manage to give 16-year-old Hugo Froud his first winner in a Novice Riders event at Cothelstone (14-1 against opposition he would have gobbled for breakfast when in his prime). Despite his years can still be a careless jumper. His partner seems extremely enthusiastic (sometimes excessively so), and looks booked for further successes. *Mr & Mrs P.E. Froud & Mr & Mrs M. Taylor — Blackmore & Sparkford V. (Peter Froud)*. 141 (MO), 262 (MO), 454 (4mmMO), 638 (Cf), 929 (Cnr), 952 (M), 1550 (Cnr), 1637 (O), 1672 (O).

ANALYSTIC (IRE) ..9-10.. 11 br.g. Kambalda — Burlington Miss (Burlington II) p233p2. Compact light-framed half-brother to Another Stubbs, Rugged Baron and Cool It A Bit, to jumping winners, Golden Raider and Ennereilly River (in Ireland), and to Irish Pointing winner, Caffery's Park. Dam won an Irish Point. P-t-P '96/7 and '99 (for Mrs K. Liscombe) r10 w1 (Maiden) p1 (2nd); fell/unseated 5, and pulled up 1. Sent the rider into orbit on five occasions prior to losing his maiden status, but knocking at the door in Restricteds (runner-up in three of the five he has contested '99/2000), and should be concentrating exclusively on them. A thorough stayer, but not helped by his jumping, which remains as sketchy as ever. Acquired a visor on his final start. *Mr K. Liscombe — R.P. Hankey — Cheshire Forest.* 532 (R), 589 (R), 962 (L), 1320 (L), 1524 (O), 1528 (R).

ANDERMATT ..9-12.. 14 b.g. Top Ville — Klarifi (Habitat) 65p3p. Well-made good-looking half-brother to flat winners, Ezy Koter (in Ireland) and Kashteh (IRE). Dam won at 7f in Ireland. FRENCH FLAT r5 p2. NH '90/7 (blinkered 1 in '91) r50 w6 (2 Hdles, 2m5f-2m7f, and 4 Chses, 2m5f-2m6f) p18. HUNT CH '98/9 r13 w1 (2m4f110y) p3 (2nd once); unseated 3, and pulled up 1. The veteran of 73 races and used to love Bangor (gained his last win there in a Hunter Chase), but he plodded badly in his last two campaigns, and presumably went wrong at Garthorpe. Runs tongue-tied. *J.R. Cornwall — A.J. Cockerill — Belvoir.* 15 (C), 85 (O), 115 (CCf), 430 (O), 545 (O).

ANDRELOT ..9-9.. 14 b.g. Caerleon (USA) — Seminar (Don ITY) 3361u1pp5. Small short-backed half-brother to 10 winners at home and abroad, including Soiree (smart on flat). Dam won 3 5f races, and subsequently won at 8f in USA. FLAT r10 p1 (2nd). NH '90/3 and '95/8 r64 w6 (2 2m Hdles, and 4 Chses, 2m4f-3m) p26 (inc 2nd and 3rd at Galway). P-t-P/HUNT CH '94/5 and '99 (for Miss R. Porter in '99) r18 w4 (3 Hunt Chses, 2m3f-2m4f110y, and Open) p4 (3 2nds; and 3rd in Hunt Ch); unseated 3. Hero and villain, and has combined high talent with a very dodgy temperament throughout a lengthy career. Purchased as a schoolmaster by his last two yards and has filled the role admirably providing Hannah Grissell with her first winners, but would not go a yard in any of his last three appearances. Wears blinkers for good reason, and it is a feather in Miss Grissell's cap that the last two jockeys to win on him were Richard Dunwoody and A P McCoy. In the right area to find another simple opportunity or two if he is in the right frame of mind. *Magellan Partnership — E. Sussex & Romney Marsh (Di Grissell).* 28 (L), 414 (L), 707 (L), 985 (M), 1107 (L), 1170 (L), 1395 (L), 1511 (L), 1625 (3m2f110yH).

ANDSOME ANDY (IRE) ..—.. 8 ch.g. Orchestra — Nofert (USA) (Graustark) ppp. Tall rangy half-brother to Noble Minister. Pulled up in Maidens, but evidently thought to possess some ability, as he was sent off favourite on final start, and connections do not usually entertain angels unawares. *P.S. Payne — Banwen Miners (John Moore).* 485 (R), 595 (R), 1222 (2m4fOMa).

AND WHY NOT ..9-1.. 13 ro.g. Baron Blakeney — Tamana Dancer (Gay Fandango USA) p773. Sparely-made weak-necked. Dam won 7f Sell and 2m1f Hdle. NH '94 and '96 r11 p0 (5th of 6, 6th, last 2, and fell/unseated 3 in Chses). P-t-P/HUNT CH '97/9 r13 w2 (Maiden and Members) p2 (2nds); failed to finish 7 (fell/unseated 4). Stumbled across two bad three-finisher races on sound surfaces in '97 (raced 9-7), but beaten upwards of 30 lengths when completing since, and can be safely ignored for betting purposes. *P. Picton-Warlow — Exmoor (Penny Picton-Warlow).* 705 (R), 940 (R), 1111 (R), 1566 (M).

ANNASTATE ..9-7.. 10 b.m. Northern State (USA) — Portway Anna (Hot Brandy) pp. Small lengthy half-sister to Cashaban. Dam, sister to 4 Pointers, inc Portway Grey (*qv* '93 Annual), unseated in a Point. P-t-P '98/9 r4 w2 (Maiden and Members) p0; unseated 1, and pulled up 1. Successful on the only two occasions that she has produced a clear round, but the form of her wins does not amount to much and her infrequent visits to the track are a worry — reported to have a wind problem, and has been tried in a tongue-strap. Tends to pepper her rounds with jumping errors, and probably one to watch rather than back if she reappears. *Miss E.J. Lloyd — Ross H.* 744 (R), 971 (I).

ANNEKA LOUISE ..8-9.. 7 ch.m. Jendali (USA) — Scotgavotte (FR) (Dunbeath USA) f85444. Leggy owner-bred sparely-made. NH FLAT Jun '98 r1 p0. NH '98 r4 p0 (inc Sell). Beaten 16 lengths or much more when completing, and is extremely moderate. Does not seem to have a trip, and three miles looks too far. *F.S. Jackson — S. Notts (R.J. Jackson).* 437 (OMa), 793 (CfMa), 1070 (2m4fOMa), 1219 (OMa), 1420 (OMa), 1589 (2m4fOMa).

ANNIE DIPPER ..—.. 6 ch.m. Weld — Honey Dipper (Golden Dipper) p. Sturdy owner-bred half-sister to Celtic Dipper, Blue Sunday (dam of Sweet Blue, *qv* '97 Annual), Dip The Lights and Our Adventure, and to jumping winner, Sonny Hill Lad. Taken very steadily on a May debut. *Miss H. Day — W. Somerset.* 1469 (OMa).

ANNIE'S ALFIE ..—.. 7 b.g. Afzal — Annie's Daughter (Majestic Maharaj) Rrupp. Small. Dam won 4 Points inc a Ladies and placed 5 for Shan Farr ('only a titch, but has often tried very hard'). Grandam, Aldington Honey, was last, pulled up 1, and fell 2 in Points. P-t-P '99 r2 p0 (pulled up 1, and fell 1). Probably has some ability, but impetuous and a hard ride to date, and pairing him with a jockey who could not ride one side of him beggars belief. The air in the changing room at Pantyderi was turning blue after the antics of Gwyn Marsh on his debut, and the local stewards should act before his fellow jocks do it for them. *T.R.R. Farr — Ystrad Taf Fechan (Shan Farr).* 349 (CfMa), 488 (CfMa), 747 (CfMa), 1055 (CfMa), 1222 (2m4fOMa).

ANNIE'S MAGIC ..—.. 6 b.m. Abutammam — Martina's Magic (Martinmas) r. Small sparely-made owner-bred. Dam is half-sister to Another Lucas (*qv* '95 Annual). NH FLAT Oct '99 (from M. Quinn's) r1 p0 (very remote last — virtually pulled up). Yet to show any ability to gallop. *Mrs S.A. Meakins — Carms.* 642 (M).

ANN'S AMBITION ..9-12.. 14 b.g. Ovac (ITY) — Faultless Girl (Crash Course) 23p123476. Tall good-bodied hobdayed half-brother to jumping winner, Course Doctor (IRE). IRISH P-t-P '94 r6 p1 (last of 3, after falling); fell 3, pulled up 1, and ran out 1. IRISH NH FLAT r1 p0 (pulled up). IRISH NH

'95/6 r4 p1 (3rd in Ch); last twice, and pulled up after breaking blood vessel. P-t-P/HUNT CH '97/9 r26 w1 (Restricted) p8 (6 3rds, inc 2 Hunt Chses); failed to finish 7 (unseated 5). It took Caroline Fryer 22 attempts, and several boxes of Persil, to get him into the winners enclosure, but did the job well enough at Ampton after several commendable placed efforts. Tends to run in snatches and look a non-stayer at times, but has done well to hold his form for a veteran. *R.P. & Miss C. Fryer — Dunston H. (Mike Bloom).* 15 (C), 175 (I), 319 (L), 555 (Cnr), 770 (Cf), 937 (I), 1184 (Cf), 1286 (Cf), 1380 (L).

ANNS REQUEST ..8-6.. 12 b.m. My Treasure Chest — My Quintessence (Malt) ppp. Sturdy lengthy. NH FLAT '94 and '95 r4 p0. NH '95/6 r4 p0. P-t-P '98 r5 p1 (2nd); unseated 2, and pulled up 2. Thirty lengths last of two on her only completion, and returned from a year away to perform without distinction. Not worth bothering with, like the other Drury donkeys. *Mrs G. Drury — O. Surrey & Burstow (Peter Broad).* 290 (CMa), 309 (OMa), 578 (OMa).

ANOLYZE ..—.. 7 b.m. Zambrano — Pardilyza (Pardigras) ppu. Neat. Dam, half-sister to Stephen Langton (*qv* '87 Annual), won 3 Points (inc a Ladies) and placed 3 (last 2 placings for Mr Legg). Very green and has shown nothing so far, but should get the trip well if she ever cottons on. *K.J. Legg — Taunton V. (Carroll Gray).* 353 (CfMa), 1101 (OMa), 1241 (OMa).

ANORAK (USA) ..10-8.. 11 b.g. Storm Bird (CAN) — Someway Somehow (USA) (What Luck USA) 322221112. Small compact brother to prolific flat winner, Cape Pigeon (USA), and half-brother to 4 winners in USA and one in France. Dam won 3 flat in USA. FLAT r37 w2 (8-9f on Wolverhampton all-weather) p13. NH '93/7 r25 w1 (2m2f Hdle, probably lucky) p8 (2nd in dire Sell final). P-t-P '98/9 r13 w2 (PPOA Nov Rdrs and Confined) p6 (4 2nds, of 3 once); pulled up 2, and unseated 1. Famed as a tail-twirling shirker until teenage prodigy Christian Williams took over in '99, and the combination have won 50 per cent of their races since. Faced a simple task when ridden by the much improved Jason Cook at Bassaleg, but typically let supporters down when held by the well-backed Persian Mystic on his final start. Occasionally visored flat and hurdling, and worn blinkers once in '99. Has made the frame in 17 of his 22 Points, and sure to use his rudder to propel himself first past the post again in the future. Usually needs his first run of the season. *J.L. Flint — Llangeinor.* 343 (Cf), 480 (O), 643 (Cf), 945 (O), 1295 (Cf), 1401 (Cf), 1450 (Cf), 1571 (Cnr), 1656 (M).

ANOTHER BULA (IRE) ..9-6.. 10 b.g. Cardinal Flower — Celtic Lace (Celtic Cone) 5p22. Plain angular goose-rumped brother to Dewdrop Lady (IRE) and Hil's Bluff (IRE). NH FLAT Jun '96 r1 p0. NH '97/8 (for S. Howe) r5 p0 (Hdles, last 2, pulled up 2, and fell 1). Awful under Rules and in his first two Points, but did much better when second twice at Bratton Down, and looks to be on the verge of a modest success. Another Bula he certainly ain't. *D.J. Richards & Miss N. Dickenson — Tiverton Stag (D. Richards).* 1136 (M), 1376 (R), 1564 (OMa), 1654 (OMa).

ANOTHER COMEDY ..9-0.. 11 b.g. El Conquistador — Miss Comedy (Comedy Star USA) pp75. Leggy lengthy half-brother to Three And A Half and Master Laughter, and to flat winner, Miss Laughter. NH '96/8 r15 p3 (btn 24*l* to 30*l* in Chses); inc 2 Hdles. P-t-P '96 and '99 r10 w1 (Maiden) p6 (5 3rds, of 4 twice and last twice); and pulled up 3. Provided Police Sergeant Nick Earnshaw with his first success in '99, but likely to be detained in custody indefinitely if he performs again as poorly as he did in 2000. Often fails to have a cut at his fences, and blinkers might give him some confidence (wore them occasionally under Rules). *NCE Partnership — Staff College (Nick Earnshaw).* 247 (R), 306 (R), 575 (R), 887 (R).

ANOTHER DAUGHTER ..8-7.. 10 b.m. Royal Vulcan — Dereks Daughter (Derek H) 6. Leggy close-coupled. Dam won 2 Points and placed 4 for Anne Askew, and subsequently won 2m4f Ch and placed 8. NH FLAT '96 r1 p0. NH '98 r4 p0 (Hdles; inc last pair twice, and pulled up 1; Sell final). P-t-P '97/9 r4 p0; last pair 2, pulled up 1, and fell 1. Has only beaten two rivals in five Pointing attempts spread over four seasons, and never given any signs of encouragement. *Mrs A. Askew — Farndale (Nick Smith).* 1353 (OMa).

ANOTHER GENTLEMAN ..9-6.. 8 gr.g. Buckley — Another Spring (Town Crier) 14f3. Tall rangy half-brother to Young Spring, and to a Hurdles winner. Dam won 8f Sell, and won 4 Hdles at around 2m. 11,500 4-y-o. NH FLAT '98 (from R. Stronge's) r3 p0. Looks the part, and scraped home under a vigorous ride from Carrie Ford in holding at Eaton Hall (wore a tongue-strap), but was bitterly disappointing when 1-3 in a race taking 8min 21s in soft at Flagg. Looked very slow, and there is not much hope for him in future if this is the best that he can do. *G.B. Barlow — Cheshire (Carrie Ford).* 526 (OMa), 782 (R), 1071 (CR), 1255 (C).

ANOTHERHANDYMAN ..9-7.. 7 ch.g. Jupiter Island — Handbelle (Nearly A Hand) p221. Sturdy compact. Dam is sister to Bow Handy Man. 4800 4-y-o. NH FLAT '99 r2 p0 (tailed off). NH '99 r1 p0 (tailed off). Followed two creditable seconds with a win over 2m4f in mud at Tranwell (was tailed off for a long way, but stayed on under pressure to win all out), and may be suited by further. Possibly not an easy ride, but may have possibilities in a Restricted. *J.L. Gledson — N. Tyne.* 187 (OMa), 426 (CfMa), 500 (2m4fOMa), 1084 (2m4fOMa).

ANOTHER ISLAY ..—.. 10 b.g. Tobin Lad (USA) — Coincidence Girl (Manacle) p. Tall half-brother to What A Coincidence. NH FLAT r1 p0. NH '95/6 r2 p0. P-t-P/HUNT CH '97/9 r10 w1 (Maiden) p0; failed to finish 6 (fell 1). Won a bad Maiden on firm in '97, but has pulled up in six of eight attempts in the last three years, and lack of stamina is his downfall. Possibly nursing a wind problem. *D. Scott — Border.* 713 (R).

ANOTHER JUNIOR (IRE) ..9-0§§.. 9 gr.g. Over The River (FR) — Mine Head (Pragmatic) 3ppf47. Light-framed hobdayed. Dam is half-sister to Ronlees (*qv* '97 Annual). P-t-P '98/9 r12 w1 (Maiden) p2 (2nds); pulled up 5. Had luck on his side when opening his account on firmish, but well beaten when completing in 2000, and should not be trusted. Planted himself in the paddock, and then dropped and apparently injured the rider when eventually persuaded to go down for his final intended start at Larkhill (the stricken Richard Young rose like Lazarus the instant the horse's withdrawal was announced!). Has been tried in blinkers, but totally gone at the game, and surely the last has been seen of him (thinking back his naming was in some ways prophetic, *qv* '98 Annual). *N.R. Freak — Portman (Ali Tory).* 63 (I), 208 (R), 330 (R), 767 (R), 1061 (R), 1376 (R).

ANOTHER MAN (IRE) ..9-0.. 6 gr.g. Cataldi — Steal On (General Ironside) 3. Compact well-made half-brother to Wejem (IRE) and Our Little Man (IRE), to jumping winner, One Man (IRE) (won 3 Hdles and 17 Chses and £459,304 for John Hales), and to NH flat and Chasing winner, Steel Blade (IRE). Looked backward, but made a promising debut when nine lengths third in mid-February, but like the runner-up failed to appear again. Had two subsequent winners well behind him, and might eventually prove to be useful. Certainly his pedigree would be difficult to better. *J.R. & Miss L. Hales — Wheatland (Andrew Dalton).* 235 (OMa).

ANOTHER WAG ..9-8.. 10 b.m. Scallywag — Andantino (Another River) f42p3. Workmanlike lengthy half-sister to Cruise Ann and Derring Ann. Dam, half-sister to Jasitomcat (*qv* '88 Season Annual), won 2 Points and placed 4 (inc 3rd of 4 in Hunt Ch) from 8 starts. P-t-P '98 r2 w1 (Maiden) p0; and fell. Took little time in getting off the mark, and returned from a year off (in which she produced a foal by Alderbrook) to record two decent placings in Restricteds. Clearly good enough to win particularly with better fencing, but ended the season lame, and it could be that she will have to rest on her laurels and return to being a mum. *Mrs A. Dawes & J. Williams — Radnor & W. Herefords (Steve Lloyd & Angharad Watkins).* 669 (R), 894 (R), 1089 (R), 1293 (3mH), 1459 (R).

APPEAL ..—.. 11 ch.m. Sunley Builds — Pastures Green (Monksfield) ppp. Owner-bred. P-t-P '96/7 r7 p0 (last, pulled up 4, and fell/unseated 2). Failed to beat a rival in her first two Pointing campaigns (though beaten less than four lengths when last of 4 once), and returned from a two year hiatus to pull up in races she had no chance of winning. Will need to concentrate on Maidens if she reappears in 2001. *C. Wall — V. of Clettwr (Norman Jones).* 944 (I), 1401 (Cf), 1612 (Cf).

APPEAL AGAIN (IRE) ..—.. 8 br.g. Mujtahid (USA) — Diva Encore (Star Appeal) u8pp. Good-topped half-brother to 5 flat winners (2 abroad), including sprinters, Encore M'Lady and Don't Worry (smart, including abroad), and Magical Dancer. Dam won 2 flat, 12-14f. IRISH FLAT (tried blinkered) r12 p0. NH '96 r3 p0 (inc 2 Sells). P-t-P '99 r4 p1 (3rd); pulled up 1. Can show good speed for up to two miles, but not bred to stay, and does not get a yard further. Error-prone, and tends to get himself worked up before the race. *late M.J. Probert — Gelligaer F. (D. Probert).* 388 (I), 491 (CfMa), 747 (CfMa), 1021 (2m4fOMa).

APPLEFORT (IRE) ..—.. 11 b.g. Over The River (FR) — Sweet Apple (Menelek) p4pp. Brother to Irish Pointing winner, Riverfort. Dam won 2m2f Hdle in Ireland (on a disqualification). IRISH P-t-P '94/5 r2 w1 (5yo Maiden) p0; fell 2 out (probable winner). IRISH NH FLAT Spr '95 r2 p1 (2nd). IRISH NH '95 and '97/9 (blinkered final) r23 w1 (2m5f Ch) p5. Sold Tattersalls (Ireland), Nov for 3750. A dual winner in Ireland (heavy ground once), but unsuccessful since '97. His English efforts to date have been rather woeful. *Mrs A.P. Glassford — Cheshire.* 293 (Cf), 464 (3m110yH), 902 (Cf), 960 (Cf).

APPLE JOHN ..9-7.. 12 b.g. Sula Bula — Hazelwain (Hard Fact) p69. Tall sparely-made. Dam, half-sister to Saxony (*qv* '91 Annual), won 3 Points and placed 3. Grandam, Donington Queen, won 2 Points and placed 3. NH '96 r2 p1 (distant 3rd of 4 in Ch) and fell 1. P-t-P/HUNT CH '94, '96 and '98/9 r11 w4 (inc 3m Hunt Ch) p0; failed to finish 7 (fell/unseated 3). Was capable of useful front-running performances, but running out of gas long before the finish in 2000, and would appear to be on the decline. Has won three of the four Points he has completed, and needs to concentrate on them if he is to buck the trend. Has managed a mere 16 outings in his life, and it would be no surprise if that was that. *A.J. Whiting — Berkeley (Kevin Whiting).* 149 (3mH), 735 (MO), 1341 (2m110yH).

APPLE NICKING ..8-10.. 14 b.g. Nickel King — Apple Crumble (Pony Express) ppp4p. Light-framed lengthy. Dam won 2 Points and placed 4 (inc 2nd in Hunt Ch) for Mary Upstone. P-t-P '93/7 and '99 r26 w2 (Maiden and Restricted) p8 (4 2nds, short-headed once); failed to finish 13 (fell/unseated 5). Hit top form at the end of the '96 season, but on a downward spiral since, and failed to beat a rival in 2000. Jumping has never seemed to come naturally to him, and is unlikely to achieve anything if he returns. Has been very slow to get fit in his three most recent campaigns. *Mrs M.E. Upstone — Bicester with Whaddon.* 510 (Cf), 785 (I), 1017 (I), 1436 (Cf), 1632 (I).

APPLE SAFT (IRE) ..—.. 10 b.g. Arapahos (FR) — Why Cry (Pry) p. Half-brother to Irish Pointing winner, Tearfull. IRISH P-t-P '97/8 r7 w1 (6yo plus Maiden) p0; pulled up 3, fell 2 and unseated 1. P-t-P '99 r2 p0 (pulled up 2). Came from another parish to win the last of his seven Irish Points, but has failed to get round otherwise, and appears nigh on impossible to train. *M.S. Wilesmith — Ledbury (Emma Wilesmith)*. 993 (R).

APPLEY DAPPLY ..10-3.. 12 b.m. Broadsword (USA) — Susan's Mistake (Fine Blade USA) 1. Lengthy workmanlike half-sister to Fierce Bad Rabbit and Kellys Mouse. Dam, half-sister to Garrison Savannah, won 3 Points and placed 7 (inc 4 Hunt Chses, 2m-2m6f). An eventer who like many from that sphere before her put her jumping to good use when winning a Novice Riders event at Higham in January, and gave Catherine Jiggins a first success, but was not seen again. Could probably have been a decent racehorse had she been aimed in that direction when younger. Like Fierce Bad Rabbit, her name will delight all fans of Beatrix Potter. *M.J. Roberts — Mid Surrey F.* 25 (Cnr).

AQUA STAR (IRE) ..10-0.. 8 b.g. Village Star (FR) — First Water (FR) (Margouillat FR) 44232234. Leggy half-brother to 2 French flat winners (one also successful over jumps). Dam won at 7f in France. FLAT r2 p0. P-t-P '98/9 (for Mr A.J.K. Dunn) r5 w2 (Maiden and Restricted) p2. A quirky character who has to be led to post very early, and gives the impression that he might be saving a bit for himself. Usually ridden from off the pace, but seems to have no problems getting the trip, so it could be worth bouncing him out in front. Had by far and away his busiest season to date, and his reliable jumping should enable him to win again. Has been tried in a visor. *J. Eaton — N. Ledbury (Teresa Spearing)*. 192 (L), 354 (L), 701 (I), 861 (C), 1267 (I), 1272 (Cf), 1485 (I), 1588 (I).

ARABITAN ..9-10.. 9 ch.m. Lord Of Arabia — Pantaya VII (unknown) 6p3615. Rangy. P-t-P '99 r5 w1 (Restricted) p1 (2nd); last 2, and brought down 1. Has done well for a half-bred, and led two has-beens home at long intervals in her Members, but has her limitations, and usually put in her place in competitive races. *Miss S. Brine — S. & W. Wilts.* 214 (Cf), 325 (Cf), 768 (Cf), 1057 (Cf), 1130 (M), 1554 (Cf).

AR AGHAIDH ABHAILE (IRE) ..9-12§.. 10 ch.g. Henbit (USA) — Gaoth Na Bride (Strong Gale) p2223pp. Workmanlike half-brother to Oisin Dubh (IRE) and Ar Aghaidh Leat. Dam is an unraced half-sister to Lean Ar Aghaidh. IRISH P-t-P '96 r1 p1 (2nd). NH '96/8 r5 p0; pulled up 3. P-t-P/HUNT CH '98/9 r10 w1 (Maiden) p1 (2nd); failed to finish 7 (fell/unseated 2, and ran out 1). Won an awful race on firm at Marks Tey in '99, but always looking for a way out, and shirked the issue every time push came to shove in 2000 — could have won on three occasions had he wanted to. Regained blinkers on his final start, but pigged it furiously and tailed himself off, and is surely rapidly running out of chances in the current yard. *Miss S. Wallace — E. Anglian Bloodhounds (Cheri Cunningham)*. 610 (R), 761 (R), 843 (R), 940 (R), 1111 (R), 1287 (R), 1664 (R).

ARALIER MAN (IRE) ..—§.. 10 ch.g. Roselier (FR) — Ara Go On (Sandalay) 0p. Small flashy. P-t-P '96/9 r14 w3 (up to Confined) p3 (3rds, last once); failed to finish 5 (fell/unseated 2). Won once apiece '97/9 when a Crow inmate, but modest and moody and never travelling with any fluency in 2000. Tried blinkered on his reappearance. A revival in fortunes seems a long shot. *D. Manning — Cheshire Forest (K. Crank)*. 33 (Cnr), 293 (Cf).

ARBITRAGE MAN (IRE) ..—.. 9 b.g. Mandalus — Snow Rose (Deep Run) pp. Compact. IRISH NH FLAT '97/8 r4 p0. Ruddy awful. *J.S. Ruddy — Enfield Chace (Sue Ruddy)*. 322 (CfMa), 551 (OMa).

ARBLE MARCH ..9-9.. 12 gr.m. Baron Blakeney — Eventime (Hot Brandy) 4p13pp. Small lengthy light-framed half-sister to My Best Man and Mr Snowman. Dam won 3 Points (inc 4m Ladies) and placed 3. Grandam, Hunting Eve, won 3 Chases (2-3m) and 4 Points and placed 11 in total. P-t-P/HUNT CH '94/9 r32 w3 (Maiden, Restricted and Members) p10 (4 2nds, beaten head once, last once; and inc two fences last of 3 once); failed to finish 11 (fell 2). Has a commendable record in her Members (two wins, a second and a third '97/2000), but mostly lacklustre otherwise. Stays well, but not good enough for Opens, and her local will remain her best chance of a fifth success. *D.G. Congdon — Four Burrow (Mandy Hand)*. 930 (I), 1044 (4mO), 1186 (M), 1388 (I), 1562 (C), 1674 (I).

ARCHER (IRE) ..10-5§.. 13 b.g. Roselier (FR) — Suir Valley (Orchardist) up461*0*. Sturdy workmanlike brother to Irish NH flat and brilliant jumping winner, Carvill's Hill. Dam won an Irish Point. IRISH NH FLAT '94 r4 p0. IRISH NH '94 r2 p1 (3rd). NH '95/6 (blinkered last 3) r7 w1 (3m Hdle) p0; 5th of 6, 6th, last twice, and unseated 2 out (possible winner) in Chses. P-t-P/HUNT CH '97/9 r22 w3 (inc 3m1f110y Hunt Ch) p12 (10 2nds, and inc 4 Hunt Chses); fell/unseated 2, and pulled up 2. NH May '00 r1 p0 (12th in 3m1f110y HCap Ch: *chsd ldrs, mists 8 and 12, wknd 14, t.o and virt pu flat*). Has managed an annual success in four Pointing campaigns (a Hereford Hunter Chase being his crowning glory), and is unbeaten in three cracks at his Members, but often shows no zest for the job, and occasionally has to be spurred into action. Sometimes blinkered '99/2000, and remains a clumsy jumper of regulation fences. Could have achieved a lot more in his career had he been willing to try harder. *R.W. Lewis — Llangibby*. 222 (3m1f110yH), 271 (O), 468 (3m1f110yH), 683 (3mH), 817 (M).

ARCHIES OATS ..9-12.. 12 ch.g. Oats — Archetype (Over The River FR) 335p46p5. Lengthy lop-eared half-brother to Big Jim. NH '97/9 r3 p0 (last in '99 R.A. Gold Cup). P-t-P/HUNT CH '95/9 r21 w2 (2m4f110y Hunt Ch, and dead-heat for Club Maiden) p6 (4 2nds; inc Hunt Ch); failed to finish 7 (unseated 1). NH 'Mar '00 r1 p0 (6th in R.A. Gold Cup: *t.o 12*). Extended his losing sequence to 22 and even failed to plod into the Military money at Sandown. Occasionally visored in the last two seasons and tried in spurs once. A dependable jumper who has only ever lost his partner once in 32 races, but not an easy ride, and will continue to struggle for another success. *J.C. Trice-Rolph — Heythrop.* 8 (C), 74 (CCf), 244 (O), 469 (3m110yH), 788 (Cf), 1015 (4mO), 1190 (Cf).

ARCTIC CORNER ..8-8.. 7 b.m. Arctic Corner — Chatty Corner (Le Bavard FR) p6f. Dam is half-sister to Bignor Girl (*qv*). Sold Doncaster, Nov for 800. Has tended to start slowly, and gave a very erratic display before she fell heavily and was winded on final start (surprisingly, was supported in the market). *J. McGuinness — Staintondale (Andrew Pennock).* 1235 (OMa), 1349 (O), 1582 (2m4fOMa).

ARCTIC LODGE (IRE) ..8-0.. 9 b.g. Arctic Lord — Mogen (Adonijah) pff3pp. Compact. NH FLAT '98 r3 p0. NH '98 (for G. Thorner) r2 p0 (inc Sell). Bought Ascot, Nov for 925. Useless, and doubtless rendered so by a wind infirmity (has been tongue-tied). Fades rapidly if showing early speed, and was 40 lengths last on his only completion. Wore headgear on last three appearances. *Mrs J. Hughes — Waveney H. (Paul Blockley).* 20 (OMa), 24 (OMa), 123 (OMa), 755 (M), 925 (2mH), 1213 (OMa).

ARCTIC REVEL ..9-8.. 9 b.m. Arctic Lord — Festive Season (Silly Season) p. Workmanlike sister to Polar Party, and half-sister to Country Festival (dam of Rustic Revelry, *qv* 2000 Annual), Phaedair and Gemini Mist, and to jumping winner, D'Naan (IRE). Dam won 5 Points and 2nd twice. P-t-P '99 r7 w1 (2m4f Maiden) p2; fell/unseated 3, and pulled up 1. Tried in a tongue-strap for the first time when successful on her final outing in '99, and was in the process of running a good race on her return, but presumably went awry as she failed to reappear. Speedy enough to win a Restricted if all is well, though her jumping still requires some attention. *Miss T.V. Jenkins — Easton H. (Matthew Gingell).* 15 (C).

ARCTIC RIDGE ..8-3.. 9 b.g. Arctic Lord — Bally Small (Sunyboy) ppp6p. Workmanlike lengthy half-brother to Plowshare Tortoise. P-t-P '98/9 r6 p1 (3rd); fell/unseated 3, and pulled up 2. Previously appeared just about good enough to win a Maiden, but seems to have developed a wind infirmity, and stopped very quickly after holding every chance on his last two starts — ran tongue-tied on both occasions. *G.W. & N. Jervis — Glamorgan (L. Burrows).* 484 (R), 951 (OMa), 1050 (M), 1457 (OMa), 1574 (OMa).

ARCTIUM ..8-11.. 7 b/br.m. Gildoran — Orange Spice (Orange Bay) 262. A modest second of three twice in Maidens, and the rider had to survive a couple of blunders in the latest. Possibly capable of going one better. Like Gillone, who shares her sire, she can look very fractious in the preliminaries, and has been mounted very early and outside the paddock, and also ridden from the boxes. *M. Ley — Cotswold V.F.* 898 (OMa), 1068 (3m2fOMa), 1494 (CfMa).

ARDBEI (IRE) ..9-13.. 12 ch.g. Le Bavard (FR) — Blackrath Girl (Bargello) 2414321. Rather angular brother to Local Manor, and half-brother to Majestic Player. IRISH P-t-P '95/7 r7 p5; pulled up 2. P-t-P '98/9 r7 w2 (Maiden and Restricted) p3 (2 2nds); pulled up 1. Spent much of '99 on the sidelines, but returned for a full campaign and doubled his Pointing tally, though was lucky once, and had the benefit of Les Jefford in the saddle on his final start. Has looked rather faint-hearted on occasions, but a most reliable jumper, and suited by plenty of give in the ground. Will find winning opportunities harder to come by in the future. *C. de P. Berry — Tiverton, & Mid Devon (Sarah Kittow).* 8 (C), 140 (M), 198 (M), 404 (I), 537 (O), 853 (Inr), 1137 (I).

ARDBRENNAN ..9-13.. 14 b.g. Deep Run — Callan River (Harwell) u42p. Short-legged good-bodied brother to Kilkenny Gorge (dam of Farm Talk, *qv* '99 Annual) and Barracks Run, to Irish NH flat winner, Prince Of Cliona, and to Irish Pointing winner, Tassagh Lady. IRISH P-t-P '93/5 r16 w3 p3; pulled up 7, and fell 1. IRISH HUNT CH '95 r1 p0. P-t-P/HUNT CH '96/9 r22 w5 (3 Opens and 2 Mixed Opens) p11 (5 2nds; and inc 5 Hunt Chses); and fell/unseated 4. An expert jumper who was adept at getting into the money, but went into decline following a bout of lameness at the end of '98, and met his end at Kingston Blount. *C.C. Bennett — Vine & Craven (John Porter).* 33 (Cnr), 883 (Cf), 1246 (Cf), 1484 (O).

ARD DRUM (IRE) ..—.. 9 b.g. Febrino — Miss Maraise (Grange Melody) p. Lengthy light-framed half-brother to Fardross and Drummard (IRE). IRISH P-t-P '98 r3 p0 (pulled up 3). IRISH NH '98 r1 p1 (3rd in Ch). NH Sep '99 (from W.S. Cunningham's) r3 p0 (Nov Hdle and 2 Nov Chses). P-t-P '99 r2 p0 (pulled up 1, and fell 1). Showed plenty of speed in both '99 Pointing ventures, but had acquired a tongue-strap for his reappearance and trailed the field throughout. Clearly still a troubled soul. *Mrs J.N. Askew — Farndale (Nicky Smith).* 281 (OMa).

ARDEAL ..10-4.. 9 ch.m. Ardross — Rare Deal (Pitpan) 11512p. Compact. Dam, half-sister to Slice ofthe Action (*qv* '96 Annual), 'continually looks gutless', was 2nd in 2 Maidens and 2m Hunt Ch.

P-t-P '98/9 r4 w1 (Members) p1 (last of 3); pulled up 1, and fell 1. A genuine stayer who loves to set the pace and can gallop on strongly, and unbeaten in four consecutive Points (was eight lengths clear at the final fence in the latest, but eased prematurely, and only just held on). Has not impressed in Hunter Chases so far, and conceivably dislikes the bigger fences, but may have had a physical excuse on her most recent attempt. Appreciates give in the ground, and has the ability to score in Open company. Ashley Bealby's last two rides on her should be compulsory viewing for budding jockeys (in the 'How Not To Do It' section). *Mrs S.M.V. Bealby — Quorn (Chris Bealby).* 86 (R), 172 (Cm), 580 (3mH), 1264 (M), 1588 (I), 1645 (3mH).

ARDELL BOY ..10-8.. 13 b.g. Cisto (FR) — Muses Doom (Fate) pp. Tall rangy. P-t-P/HUNT CH '94 and '96/9 r19 w4 (up to Confined) p3 (2 2nds, inc Hunt Ch); failed to finish 6 (fell/unseated 3). Never able to run much, but a dependable front-runner who has improved with age, and ran the race of his life when runner-up in a Stratford Hunter Chase in '99. Sadly appeared to break down when odds-on at Howick and connections, who have done well with him, may be forced to bring down the curtain on his racing activities. *J.E. Grey — Berkeley.* 683 (3mH), 819 (Cf).

ARDEN BAY ..—.. 8 b.m. Buckley — Corny Story (Oats) p. Small compact half-sister to jumping winners, Cornet and Star Of Oughterard, and to Hurdles winners, Chiropodist and Monica's Story (latter also won Irish NH flat). P-t-P '98 r1 p0 (pulled up). Soon tailed off in two Maidens 22 months apart (bandaged all round in the most recent), and though she resides in a decent yard appears impossible to train. *P.S. Burke — Wheatland (Paul Jones).* 570 (2m4fCfMa).

ARDKILLY WARRIOR (IRE) ..—.. 8 b.g. Commanche Run — Dream Of Gold (Golden Love) ppp. Smallish compact hobdayed. Dam won Mares Maiden and NH flat in Ireland. IRISH NH '98 r2 p0. IRISH P-t-P '98/99 r11 w2 (Confined, and Winners of One) p2 (3rds); pulled up 5, unseated 1, and refused 1. Bought Doncaster, Aug for 11,000. His Irish wins include one in heavy, but was stopping rapidly when he pulled up thrice in 2000, and there is clearly something ailing him badly at present. *Mrs G. Fryer — W. Norfolk (William Wales).* 116 (I), 318 (Cf), 552 (I).

ARDLUCK ..—.. 8 b.g. Ardross — Trust To Luck (Mandamus) p. Tall strong. Dam, half-sister to Wodehouse (*qv* '98 Annual), won 2 Chses, 2m-2m4f; and won 7 Points (6 at Marks Tey; inc 2 Opens, 3m4f-4m) and placed 11 for Wilf Tolhurst (finished in all 27 attempts for him). Pulled up in March on a belated debut. Has an ideal pedigree, and it might be interesting to see him again. Could hardly have been named anything else. *W.J. Tolhurst — Essex & Suffolk.* 605 (OMa).

ARD NA CARRIG (IRE) ..9-13.. 8 ch.g. Mister Lord (USA) — Coxtown Lass (IRE) (Selko) 4f21p. Tall lengthy. IRISH NH '98/9 r3 p0 (inc 14th of 15 and pulled up in Chses). Finished an encouraging second at Didmarton, and confirmed the promise when jumping well and making all for a 20 length success at Chaddesley, but was diving away to the left before pulling up when a disappointing favourite next time. Should be able to atone in a Restricted if he does not have a problem. *S. Gegg — Ledbury (Nicky Sheppard).* 12 (OMa), 264 (OMa), 391 (CfMa), 616 (CMa), 1355 (R).

ARDNUT ..9-8.. 9 b.g. Phardante (FR) — Lady Tut (Fine Blade USA) rf1. Small unfurnished. Dam won 3 flat, 7-12f (inc 2 Sells) and 3 Hdles, 2m-2m6f. NH FLAT '98 r2 p0. P-t-P '99 r7 p1 (2nd of 3); last, pulled up 3, and fell/unseated 2. NH Jun '99 (for Mr J.W. Tudor) r1 p0 (pulled up in Hdle). Tried in blinkers and looked a non-stayer in the previous yard, but battled on well for Clive Storey to open his account, and as the runner-up gave the form a boost subsequently he might be good enough to stand a chance in Restricteds. Wears a cross-noseband and taken to post early before his success. Might not care for cut in the ground. *Mrs K.A. Hargreave — W. Percy (Nick & Kirsty Hargreave).* 625 (OMa), 808 (OMa), 1431 (OMa).

ARDSCUD ..—.. 14 b.g. Le Bavard (FR) — Tudor Lady (Green Shoon) pp. Lengthy half-brother to Satshoon (IRE) and Strawberry Hill (IRE), to jumping winner Supreme Lady (IRE), and to Hurdles winner, Captain Tancred. IRISH P-t-P '91 and '93 r6 w2 (inc Winners of Two) p1 (2nd); pulled up 1. IRISH NH FLAT '93 r1 p1 (3rd). NH '93/4 and '97 r4 p0 (last in only Ch — tailed off after mistakes). P-t-P '98/9 (for Mr J.C. Peate & Mr S. Tindall) r6 w2 (inc Ladies) p0; pulled up 2, and fell 1. Formerly a fair performer, but has had more than his fair share of problems, and did no more than adequately fill the job of schoolmaster in 2000. *R. & Mrs S.J. Hays — Eggesford.* 1047 (Cf), 1173 (M).

ARDSHUIL ..9-3.. 12 b.g. Pennine Walk — Ordina (FR) (Northfields USA) 5s8p5p. Tall rangy half-brother to 2 winners abroad. IRISH NH FLAT '94 r2 w1 p0. IRISH NH '94/8 r22 w2 (2m Hdle and 2m Ch) p5; inc 2 visits to England. NH '98 (for R. Buckler, bought for 6000) r3 p0. Stormed off at a rate of knots in all but his final two starts (strangled and never put into the contest at any stage once), but stops alarmingly, and Simon Pile was banned for seven days after forcing his mount to continue when exhausted over the final two fences at Towcester. Does not even stay two miles now, at least for the current clueless pilot, and also looks much too fat. *Mrs P.M. Pile — Warwicks (Mrs D. Mitchell).* 176 (O), 1438 (M), 1531 (2m10yH), 1621 (O), 1666 (O), 1672 (O).

ARDSTOWN ..10-6.. 10 b.m. Ardross — Booterstown (Master Owen) 313122. Compact sparely-made half-sister to Celtic Town (*qv*). P-t-P/HUNT CH '98/9 r11 w4 (inc 3m Hunt Ch) p5 (4 2nds;

and inc 3 Hunt Chses); pulled up 1, and fell 1. A useful and resilient mare who has now made the frame in her last 15 races, which includes three Hunter Chase successes under Frank Windsor-Clive. Stays well and can produce a fine burst of acceleration, but requires plenty of cut in the ground, and avoids anything livelier than good. An improved jumper, and her willingness to battle should ensure that she moves her winning tally towards double figures in 2001. A credit to connections. *Mrs R.F. Knipe — S. Herefords (Robin Knipe).* 19 (L), 149 (3mH), 299 (3m2f110yH), 460 (2m7f110yH), 683 (3mH), 922 (3mH).

ARFER MOLE (IRE) ..10-0.. 13 b.g. Carlingford Castle — Sharpaway (Royal Highway) bpR4154. Lengthy rather unfurnished half-brother to Deep Dawn and Sound Of Islay, to NH flat and smart Hurdles winner, Mole Board, and to Irish NH flat and Hurdles winner, Beacon Lane. Dam won Irish NH flat. NH FLAT Feb '93 r1 p0. NH '95/9 (for J. Old) r20 w4 (2m1f Hdle, and 3 Chses, 2m1f-3m) p5 (beaten head 1); possibly unlucky when fell last in Ch once; pulled up in 2 of final 3 attempts. Put a string of disappointments behind him when landing a Penshurst Confined, but unconvincing in two attempts since, and there is probably something not quite right with him. All his successes have been gained on good or easy surfaces. Connections probably did well to extract another win at 12. *Mrs K. Buckett — Hursley Hambledon.* 4 (O), 78 (L), 324 (M), 522 (L), 824 (Cf), 1057 (Cf), 1244 (MO).

ARISE (IRE) ..9-13.. 12 b.g. Rising — What's The Point (Major Point) u33333u. Workmanlike. IRISH NH FLAT r2 p0. IRISH P-t-P '94 r3 w1 (4&5yo Maiden) p1 (2nd); and fell 1. NH '97 r1 p0 (33/4th of 5 in Ch). P-t-P/HUNT CH '95, '97 and '99 (for Mr J.J. & Mrs L.M. Boulter) r15 w2 (Confineds) p6 (3 2nds, last once, and inc Hunt Ch); fell 3, and pulled up 1. Produced a decent turn of foot to score a ready double on firm ground in his first English Pointing season, but disappointingly beaten in his last 17 starts. Employed as a schoolmaster in the new yard, and though both riders managed to fall off him once apiece both did well, and his Barbury Castle placings were particularly meritorious as he came from miles back on each occasion. Deserves to find another race in 2001. *T. Abbott — D.E. Harrison — Blackmore & Sparkford V. (Rose Vickery).* 5 (Cv&nr), 35 (Cnr), 211 (Cnr), 476 (Cnr), 736 (Cnr), 929 (Cnr), 1304 (Cfnr).

ARKAY ..7-0.. 11 ch.g. Good Times (ITY) — Evening Crystal (Evening All) 4. Small compact. P-t-P '95/9 r15 p4 (remote last of 2; 3rd of 4; and last of 3 twice); failed to finish 8 (fell/unseated 5). Contested his Members for the sixth consecutive year, and bumbled round to finish tailed off last for the fourth time. Four outings in a season is his record, and has no pretensions of being a racehorse. *R.C. Kerry — Easton H.* 603 (M).

ARLENESEOIN (IRE) ..10-5.. 9 b.g. Aristocracy — Lady Flair (Flair Path) ppu33322. Tall workmanlike. IRISH P-t-P '97 r2 w1 (4&5yo Maiden) p1 (2nd). IRISH NH FLAT Oct/Nov '97 r2 p0. IRISH NH '97/9 r11 w1 (2m Ch) p0. A difficult ride who gets on his toes and goes to post early, and injured Tim Underwood when dumping him at the first on their only outing together, but has given some good displays in defeat for Philip York since. Unlucky to come up against some useful performers on occasions, probably his best opportunity was when 14 lengths third at Kingston Blount, where his partner's recovery from an alarming error was nothing short of miraculous. Looks as if he will always be a handful and threw the rider in the preliminaries when beaten only two lengths by Gunner Boon in much the fastest time of the day at Laleston. Thoroughly deserves a success. *T.D.B. Underwood — Garth & S. Berks.* 62 (Cf), 215 (C), 325 (Cf), 884 (O), 1244 (MO), 1484 (O), 1621 (O), 1658 (MO).

ARMET PRINCE ..—§.. 10 b.g. Ovac (ITY) — Verona Queen (Majestic Streak) p. Half-brother to Abernethy Pearl, Prince Of Verona and Price War. Dam pulled up in 3 Points for Sheila Dun. Great-grandam, Bright Beach, won 10 Hunt Chses, inc '68 Cheltenham Foxhunters. Great-great-grandam, Badger's Beech, won Pointing. P-t-P '97/8 r3 w1 (Maiden) p0; ran out 1, and refused 1. Awarded a Corbridge Maiden after the winner had weighed in light, but a total menace in three other Pointing forays and presumably pulled himself up after losing interest with an early blunder in the latest. Likely to remain as unco-operative as ever if he returns. Wore a near-side pricker when successful. *Mrs G.R. Dun — Lauderdale.* 713 (R).

ARROGANT LORD ..9-9.. 9 b.g. Arctic Lord — Warham Fantasy (Barolo) pf. Tall lengthy brother to Dream Lord, and half-brother to Torre Trader, and to jumping winners, Pennymoor Prince and The Bakewell Boy. Dam, a highly temperamental hurdler, fell at 2nd in a Point. NH FLAT Mar '96 (for R.G. Frost) r1 p0 (tailed off). P-t-P '97/8 r4 w1 (Maiden) p1 (2nd); pulled up 1. Looked set for a bright future when winning for the peerless Caroline Egalton in Devon as a five-year-old, and changed hands for 8400gns, but has stopped quickly in all three starts for present connections (missed the entire '99 campaign), and clearly stricken. In a top yard and worth another look only if they persevere with him. *A. Cowing & B. Cockerell — E. Sussex & Romney Marsh (Di Grissell).* 306 (R), 825 (R).

ARRY'S AWAY ..—.. 8 b.g. Picea — Top Of The Barley (Oats) pp. Light-framed angular half-brother to Jersey Hurdles winner, Wollboll. NH FLAT '98 r2 p0. P-t-P '99 r3 p0 (5th, pulled up 1, and fell 1). Quickly turfed out of Pipe's and boasts nothing better than a modest last-but-one in five Maiden attempts since. Would be a most unlikely winner. *Lady Huntly — Surrey U. (Brian Tetley).* 23 (OMa), 132 (OMa).

ARRYSU ..—.. 10 b.g. Derring Rose — New Dawning (Deep Run) p. Compact half-brother to New Cruiser and to Hurdles winner, First light. NH FLAT '95/6 r2 p0. NH '96 and '98 r2 p0. P-t-P '97 (for Miss S. Sharratt) r2 w1 (Maiden) p1 (short head 2nd). NH Oct '99 r2 p1 (2nd in a 2m6f Mdn Hdle); and pulled up 1. Won a moderate youngsters Maiden at Southwell in '97, but has had his problems since, and failed to get to halfway on his return to Pointing at Brampton Bryan. Would be a certainty for a Restricted on his best form (worth 10-2), but might not get the chance again. *F.M. Barton — Albrighton.* 863 (R).

ARTFUL AVIATOR ..—.. 13 b.g. Precocious — Mumtaz Flyer (USA) (Al Hattab USA) uf. Rangy half-brother to several flat winners (some abroad), including Bold Frontier. Ironically for one sired by Precocious he was making his debut at the age of 12, and predictably never flying high. Did provide Hamish Rowsell (substantially enlarged since last we saw him) with a comeback ride, but it only lasted as far as the fourth fence. *C. Aikenhead — Hampshire.* 882 (M), 1062 (O).

ARTHUR HENRY ..9-8.. 9 b.g. Scallywag — Firwood (Touching Wood USA) f1u4up. Lengthy unfurnished pin-fired half-brother to Tyndrum Gold. P-t-P '98/9 r6 p0 (fell/unseated 2, and pulled up 2). Let down by his jumping on several occasions before finally getting his act together at Eaton Hall, but promptly went back to fence-bending, and will need to improve to take a hand in future. Often gets wound up in the paddock, and has had two handlers. *F.D. Cornes, J. Whittall, J. Wynne & D. Gore — S. Salop (Gordie Edwards).* 569 (OMa), 777 (OMa), 963 (R), 1200 (CR), 1317 (M), 1411 (R).

ARTIC PEARL (IRE) ..9-5.. 11 ch.m. Le Bavard (FR) — Arctic Mistress (Quayside) ppp0345. Lengthy unfurnished half-sister to Irish Pointing winner, Ozone Lass. IRISH P-t-P '94 and '96 r6 w1 (5&6yo Mares Maiden) p1 (3rd); pulled up 2, and fell. IRISH NH FLAT '96/7 r2 p0. IRISH NH '96/8 r22 w1 (2m6f Ch) p3 (3rds, inc 2 Hdles). Won a couple of Irish races on easy surfaces to '97, but does not seem to have much ability now, and would need a bad race to score again. Looked unfit in early season, but has at least proved to be a safe ride for novices. *R.G. Langley — Worcs.* 77 (O), 178 (Cm), 447 (Cm), 611 (C), 752 (Cm), 820 (Cm), 1063 (3m2fM).

ARTIQUE FISH (IRE) ..8-6.. 8 ch.g. Gone Fishin — Above Age (IRE) (Horage) f2pp3. Small. IRISH NH FLAT '97/8 r4 p0. IRISH NH '97/8 r2 p0. Beaten 25 lengths and 70 lengths when placed in Maidens, and was also a most disappointing favourite twice, including when 4-5 and pulled up at halfway. Will need to make substantial improvement if he is ever to win. *A. Simpson — S. Pembs (Beverley Thomas).* 267 (CfMa), 348 (CfMa), 835 (OMa), 1055 (CfMa), 1225 (OMa).

ARTISTIC PLAN (IRE) ..9-6.. 9 b.g. Creative Plan (USA) — North Rose VII (unknown) 3. Tall brother to Hotscent (IRE) (*qv*). NH '97/8 r6 p1 (distant last of 3 in Ch); 5th, pulled up 1, and fell 1 in other Chses. P-t-P '99 r5 p1 (last of 2); 4th, fell 2, and carried out 1. Beaten between 12 and 35 lengths in his Pointing completions, and likely to fall when his stamina evaporates. Has been tried tongue-tied. *M.T. Lockyer & S. Vass — Portman (Rose Hicks).* 880 (OMa).

ARZLIZA ..—.. 8 br.m. Arzanni — Liza Ridd (Tycoon II) u. Dam, sister to John Ridd (*qv* '87 Season Annual), won 2 Points (lucky once) and placed 6; great-grandam, Lorna Doone, won 3 Points and placed 19. Bought Malvern, Oct '98 for 1550. Departed after a mile at Maisemore. Has been at stud, and produced a filly by Trainbleu in '97. *M.B. Bent — N. Cotswold.* 896 (R).

ASHBURTON LORD (IRE) ..9-5.. 10 br.g. Lord Americo — Fiona's Wish (Wishing Star) pp4p612. Strong-topped brother to Prestige Lord (IRE) (*qv*). IRISH P-t-P '96/8 r7 p2 (inc last of 3); inc pulled up 1, slipped up 1, and brought down 1. Sold Ascot, Sep '98 for 1450. Goes a reasonable gallop, but moderate and usually a weak finisher, and there were elements of luck when he gained an overdue first success on dead ground at Barbury Castle (the runner-up made a bad blunder when challenging two out, and did not receive much room when rallying in the final hundred yards — was eventually beaten only a neck). Provided Matthew Legge with his first win. Will have more to do in Restricteds. *P.E. Legge — I. of W.* 221 (OMa), 261 (R), 432 (OMa), 828 (OMa), 1135 (R), 1284 (OMa), 1512 (R).

ASHDOWN BOY ..9-1.. 10 ch.g. Karlinsky (USA) — Charmezzo (Remezzo) 1f. Stocky owner-bred brother to Sir William, and half-brother to Westcountry Lad. Dam is half-sister to Romany Anne (*qv* '00 Annual). P-t-P '98/9 r7 p0 (last, fell/unseated 4, and pulled up 2). Hit the deck in his first three Points, and had performed abysmally until trotting up in a poor Maiden on his 2000 reappearance — looked fitter than before. Given a very confident ride by Richard Woollacott, but the opposition was weak and the time was poor, so his prospects in Restricteds do not appear too bright. Returned to his error-prone ways of old on his final outing, and could not be backed with any confidence in future. *L. Bond — Stevenstone (Pen Bond).* 855 (CfMa), 1518 (R).

ASHLOCH ..—.. 7 b.m. Lochnager — True Princess (Eastwood Prince) pp. Good-bodied half-sister to Princess Senang, True Match, Trolly and Trueloch. Dam, half-sister to Air Truth (*qv* '95 Annual), unseated in a Point for Mr Norman, and grandam, Burrow Truth, was placed in 2 Points (inc tailed off last of 3) for him. From a family of losers, and yet to give the impression that she can redress the balance. *D.J. Norman — Tiverton (Neil Harris).* 310 (I), 955 (OMa).

ASHMEAD RAMBLER (IRE) ..9-11.. 11 b.g. Henbit (USA) — Bramble Lane (Boreen FR) 8p24. Very tall rangy. NH FLAT '96 r1 p0. NH '96 r8 p1 (23*l* 2nd of 3 in Ch); fell 2 out when close last of 3 in Ch won by Strong Promise once. P-t-P/HUNT CH '98/9 r6 w1 (Maiden) p0; 5th, and pulled up 4. A free-running individual who tends to waste a lot of nervous energy in the preliminaries, and is proving hard to settle. Capable of the odd decent effort, and ran much his best race for some time when chasing home One Of The Natives at Badbury Rings. Won his Maiden in mud, but better suited by top of the ground conditions. Has broken a blood vessel at least once. *W. Bush — Beaufort (Nick Bush).* 749 (Cf), 958 (R), 1061 (R), 1488 (R).

ASK ANTONY (IRE) ..10-4.. 11 gr.g. Roselier (FR) — Lady Casita (Paddy's Stream) p. Tall. P-t-P/HUNT CH '95 and '97 (for Mr J.R. Burns) r7 w3 (Maiden, Intermediate and 4m Mixed Open) p4 (3 2nds. inc 2 Hunt Chses). NH '97/9 (for P.F. Nicholls; debut for T.D. Walford) r4 w1 (3m1f110y Mdn Ch) p3 (2 2nds). Rated 11-0 after impressively winning the '97 Grimthorpe Gold Cup, and looked set for a bright future under Rules. Joined Paul Nicholls for 15,000gns and won a 3m1f Hereford Chase, but failed to reappear after finishing runner-up in the '99 Mandarin. Returned to Pointing after more than a year off, and led a useful Open field for a long way until lack of fitness told in the last half mile. Did not reappear, and clearly not going to reach the heights, but can still win more Points if he can be nursed back to health. A thorough stayer, and suited by soft ground. *L. Brennan — Cheshire Forest (Reg Crank).* 565 (O).

ASKED TO LEAVE ..8-11.. 9 ch.m. Montelimar (USA) — The Parson Fox (The Parson) 25p475. Small compact. NH FLAT '97 r1 p0. NH '97 r1 p0 (last in Hdle). P-t-p '98/9 r7 p3 (2 3rds); and pulled up 1. Her placings were gained whilst eligible for short distance Maidens, but does not get the full trip in Points (even outstayed by a son of Kind Of Hush in her Members), and is hopelessly outclassed in the Hunter Chase arena. *Mrs M.R. Bennett — Badsworth (Ian Bennett).* 166 (M), 278 (R), 384 (2m3f110yH), 626 (OMa), 918 (2m4fH), 1219 (OMa).

ASK ELLIOT ..—.. 12 ch.g. Librate — Limerick Lace (Pall Mall) pp. Dam won at 10f in Ireland. A late starter, and pulled up after about two miles twice. *H.W. Wheeler — N. Cotswold.* 703 (OMa), 994 (OMa).

ASK FRANK ..10-4.. 15 b.g. Seymour Hicks (FR) — West Bank (Martinmas) 2. Good-bodied half-brother to flat and Hurdles winner, Gunner's Hill. Dam won 2m 3yo Hdle in Ireland. IRISH P-t-P '90 r1 w1 (4yo Maiden). NH '91/3 r14 w2 (3m Hdle and 3m2f Ch) p3. P-t-P '94/9 r20 w6 (5 Opens) p10 (8 2nds); unseated 1. A useful Open horse in his prime, but remarkably lightly raced over the years, and restricted to just a single outing in 2000. Used to possess an impressive turn of foot, and was suited by plenty of cut in the ground. Lost no caste in defeat against Gunner Boon (five years his junior) at Chipley Park, and owes his connections nothing after seven seasons of continual service. Would be deserving of another win if he reappeared, but retirement seems more likely. *Mrs K.M. Price — N. Cotswold (Harry Wheeler).* 141 (MO).

ASK IN TIME (IRE) ..8-8.. 9 br.g. Jeu De Paille (FR) — C B M Girl (Diamonds Are Trump USA) pp33. Rangy half-brother to Witney O'Grady (IRE). Dam won 4 flat (6-8f, inc a Sell) and 2m Sell Hdle. NH FLAT '99 r1 p0. NH '97/8 r4 p0 (inc 9th and last in Hdles, and pulled up and fell in Chses). P-t-P '99 r3 p0 (last 2, and pulled up 1). In two of the major yards under Rules, and was twice sent off favourite (also the subject of a gamble at Barbury Castle in 2000), but has always let his supporters down. Most imposing, but does not get the trip in Points, and beaten at least 30 lengths when completing. Looks to be on the verge of erupting in the paddock, and usually tows two handlers round with him. *S. Usher — Avon V. (Jane Clifford).* 473 (M), 957 (CfMa), 1284 (OMa), 1493 (OMa).

ASK THE DOCTOR (IRE) ..9-8.. 8 ch.g. Black Minstrel — Lovely Tartan (Push On) 2. Angular half-brother to Injectabuck (IRE) (subsequent Hurdles winner) and Tartan Buck (IRE). P-t-p '98 r2 w1 (Maiden) p0; and 4th. NH Mar '99 (for Miss A.M. Newton-Smith) r1 p0 (pulled up). Overcame a few fencing errors to land a two-finisher Maiden at Fakenham in '98, but has seen the racecourse on just two occasions since. A hard-puller, but easily good enough for Restricted success if connections ask the veterinary how to get him right. *Dr D.B.A. Silk, N. Fordham & Miss E. Warren — Kent & Surrey Bloodhounds (Heather Silk).* 239 (R).

ASTRAC TRIO (USA) ..10-2.. 11 ro.g. Timeless Moment (USA) — Fairway Flag (USA) (Fairway Phantom USA) 234225. Tall lengthy. Dam won at 6f in USA. FLAT r14 w1 (6f, on all-weather) p0. NH '93/5 (tried blinkered/visored) r20 w1 (2m Sell Hdle) p3; 7th, last, and unseated 2 in Chses. P-t-P/HUNT CH '96/9 r22 w8 (inc 2m4f110y Hunt Ch, and 6 Ladies, dead-heated once; hat-trick '98) p10 (6 2nds, dead-heated once); unseated 3. Developed into a useful Ladies horse in '98, but reportedly suffering from a virus in '99, and has not been able to show his best form since. Likes to be able to dominate proceedings, and may yet revive in 2001. Usually gets on his toes in the preliminaries. *Mrs A.C. Hamilton — Buccleuch (Jim Bowie).* 109 (L), 185 (L), 621 (L), 715 (L), 1119 (L), 1426 (L).

A SUITABLE GIRL ..8-4.. 10 b.m. Reprimand — No Jazz (Jaazeiro USA) p. Leggy lengthy light half-sister to Stormy Session, and to Hurdles winner, Marx Mistress. FLAT r12 p2 (beaten 7½-10*l*, inc Sell). NH '94/5 r11 p0 (Hdles, inc Sells). P-t-P '98 (for Mr S.N. & M. Shinton & Mr I. Mason) r2 p1 (3rd); and 5th. NH '99 (for J. Neville) r3 p0 (pulled up 3). Twenty-five lengths last of three in her only placing on her Pointing debut, and has been tried in headgear and with her tongue-tied down. Highly unlikely to break her duck at the 30th attempt when she next reappears. *Mrs E. Smith — Gelligaer F. (K. Smith).* 822 (CfMa).

ATH CARNE CASTLE ..—.. 6 b.g. Carlingford Castle — Brookside Rose (Beldale Flutter USA) u. Rangy light. Ejected Scott Joynes at the 12th at Whitwick, having made strenuous attempts to do so at the second again at the eighth. *L.A.R. Lynch — Ledbury.* 341 (CfMa).

AT IT AGAIN (IRE) ..—.. 12 ch.g. Regular Guy — Pollys Grind (Crash Course) uppf. Very tall rangy. NH '95/6 and '98 (for W. McKenzie-Coles) r5 p0 (pulled up 5, inc 3 Chses — never less than 50-1). Extremely lightly raced and has a deplorable record of non-completions, and it would be amazing if anybody ever bothered to run him again. *Mrs D.J. Chelton & W.G. McKenzie-Coles — Taunton V. (Richard Parker).* 709 (OMa), 829 (OMa), 984 (OMa), 1245 (OMa).

ATOSKI ..9-12.. 7 b.g. Petoski — Culm Valley (Port Corsair) 1u1. Compact half-brother to Valley's Choice (*qv*). P-t-P '99 r2 p1 (2nd). Showed plenty of ability in his debut season, and won well at Witton Castle and Chaddesley despite feeble opposition and slow times, but unlikely to have troubled Key Debate in-between. Will surely win more Points in the future unless connections decide that he is good enough to race under Rules. *Mrs H. Dalton & D.M. Hughes — Wheatland (Andrew Dalton).* 139 (OMa), 797 (R), 1067 (3m2fR).

AUDLEY LASS (IRE) ..8-12.. 8 b.m. Strong Gale — Audley Lady (Deep Run) u4s. Workmanlike. NH FLAT '97 r1 p0. NH '97/8 r2 p0 (tailed off). P-t-P '99 r1 p1 (2nd). Had three subsequent winners behind her when second on her Pointing debut, but has twice failed to master Cothelstone since, and a well beaten fourth of five at Holnicote. Has raced exclusively on fast ground to date. Probably worth another chance in Maiden company. *Mrs E.J. Taplin — Minehead H.* 640 (CfMa), 1372 (OMa), 1555 (OMa).

AUGHNACLOY ROSE ..—§.. 14 gr.g. Derring Rose — Tower Road (Polaroid) 2. Plain rangy ewe-necked half-brother to Nothingtotellme (IRE), and to Irish Pointing winner, Copper Tower. IRISH P-t-P '93/5 r12 p2 (3rds — tailed off last 1); pulled up 5. P-t-P '96/8 r26 w1 (Maiden) p5 (2nd of 3 twice; and 3 3rds, last once, and of 3 once); failed to finish 11 (unseated 2, and refused 1). Soundly thrashed in 19 races since he carried the veteran trainer to success in '96, but returned from a long holiday to wobble home the length of the run-in behind the winner in her Members. Occasionally blinkered in the past, and is ungenuine and not worth the effort. *D. Etheridge, Miss K. Williams & N. Page — Cambridge Univ. (Russell Page).* 174 (M).

AUGHRIM QUEST (IRE) ..—§§.. 8 br.m. Royal Fountain — Giving Out (No Argument) uprfrpfp. Compact half-sister to Irish Pointing winners, Lisaleen Miss (also won jumping there) and For Donal. IRISH P-t-P '98/9 r5 p1 (3rd); inc pulled up, and fell. Bought Doncaster, Oct for 1600. Third on her racecourse debut, but thoroughly ungenuine ever since, and failed to successfully negotiate the first fence on three occasions in 2000 (also eliminated at the second once). Should have been banned by the middle of the season — how do they get away with it? Blinkered once. *J.A. Moore — S. Durham.* 437 (OMa), 526 (OMa), 816 (OMa), 1004 (OMa), 1082 (CMa), 1329 (OMa), 1479 (OMa), 1577 (R).

AUNTIE ALICE ..9-10.. 11 b.m. Uncle Pokey — Fortalice (Saucy Kit) p3. Compact good-looking half-sister to Snapper (*qv*). NH FLAT '95/6 r4 p1 (3rd). NH '96/7 r10 p2 (3rds in Hdles, beaten 1*l* in only Sell); 4th 4 inc only Ch, when beaten 25*l*. P-t-P/HUNT CH '98 r6 w1 (Maiden) p3 (2 2nds, inc a Hunt Ch); fell 1, and brought down 1. Placed on six occasions before she eventually got her head in front, but subsequently ran well in a Wetherby Hunter Chase, though that effort now appears to flatter her. Had just two outings in 2000, but showed at Garthorpe that another success should be forthcoming if she is able to stand a full campaign next year. Might not be entirely genuine. *Mrs D.D. Osborne, Mrs Dufton & Mr Byas — Sinnington (Cas Lawson).* 301 (2m5fH), 546 (R).

AUNTY NORMA (IRE) ..9-4.. 7 b.m. Satco (FR) — Torus Court (Torus) pp3p23. Workmanlike. Gave an appalling display when trainer-ridden on her debut, and she wisely handed over the reins to strong men subsequently. Has been tiring in the closing stages except when finishing a length second over 2m4f, but may be able to break her duck if she can find extra stamina. *J. Veitch — Middleton (Annabele Armitage).* 233 (OMa), 379 (OMa), 398 (OMa), 793 (CfMa), 1002 (2m4fOMa), 1233 (OMa).

AUTUMN BLUNDER ..9-13.. 9 ch.g. Brotherly (USA) — Thetford Chase (Relkino) pf34p211. Neat half-brother to Highland Chase. NH FLAT '97 r3 p1 (3½l last of 3). NH '98 (from A. Carroll's) r3 p0; 5th, pulled up 1, and unseated 1 in Hdles. An impetuous sort who sometimes requires two handlers, and has been slow to show his form, but improving. Lucky when winning a Maiden at Woodford (the clear leader broke down two out), but gained a more meritorious success when getting up close home at Chaddesley to surprise the odds-on favourite. May be capable of scoring again, although he is possibly over-rated. *K.G. Hughes — N. Ledbury (Tim Stephenson).* 71 (OMa), 196 (R), 339 (CfMa), 891 (OMa), 1068 (3m2fOMa), 1315 (OMa), 1493 (OMa), 1633 (CR).

PLATE 19   1493 Berkeley Open Maiden 8yo&up: Autumn Blunder (T. Stephenson), 1st, takes the second last and will give Tim Stephenson his 100th winner   PHOTO: Brian Armstrong

AVRIL SHOWERS ..10-2.. 12 b.m. Vital Season — April's Crook (Crozier) 42213332. Small plain sister to Westwinds. Dam won 2 Points and placed 4 for June Atkinson. Grandam, April Flash, won 3 Points and placed 12 for her. Great-grandam, April Pennant, won 7 Points and a Nov Ch. P-t-P '94/9 r37 w12 (inc 2 Mixed Opens, one a match, and Open) p11 (6 2nds, beaten neck once, and last once); failed to finish 7 (fell/unseated 3, and ran out 1). Landed the 13th success of her career when taking the Cattistock Members for the fourth time, and did well to maintain her form for the fifth consecutive year. Has stumbled across some weak races in recent seasons and usually has to play second fiddle in competitive events, but has an outstanding completion record, and is as game as the day is long. A smashing mare who will hopefully throw the Atkinson family some equally likeable foals when her racing days are over. *R. & Mrs N. Atkinson — Cattistock.* 214 (Cf), 357 (Cm), 521 (O), 873 (M), 927 (Cf), 1238 (O), 1306 (C), 1552 (O).

AWBEG ROVER (IRE) ..—.. 13 b.g. Deep Run — Kilbrogan (Menelek) 6p. Small half-brother to Saffron Gale (IRE), and to Irish Pointing and Chasing winner, Emerald Gale (won £19,550 Ch in '99). Dam won 5 Points and Hunt Ch in Ireland. IRISH NH FLAT '92/3 r2 p0. IRISH NH '92/4 r24 w1 (2m5f Hdle) p2 (3rds). IRISH P-t-P '95/7 and '99 r22 w4 (Opens) p8; inc pulled up 2, and fell. Won five races to '97, but has suffered from wear and tear since. Retired by the present yard after a couple of abortive attempts. *Mrs S.A. Hodge — Puckeridge (Hugh Hodge).* 512 (L), 982 (L).

AZZANTE (IRE) ..9-10.. 7 b.g. Phardante (FR) — Lady Bluebird (Arapaho) p1. Workmanlike half-brother to Weston Moon (IRE), to Chasing winner, Athnowen (IRE), and to Irish Pointing winner, Irish Perri. P-t-P '99 r1 p1 (3rd of 4). Followers of the Dalton yard are not afraid of putting their money down, but they got their fingers well and truly burnt on his reappearance (backed from fours to 5/2). Made no mistake when odds-on at Market Rasen, and two of those who finished behind went on to win themselves later in the season. Probably has a fair bit more scope for improvement, but his infrequent trips to the races are cause for concern. *Mrs H. Dalton & Mrs L. Windsor — Wheatland (Andrew Dalton).* 30 (CMa), 437 (OMa).

BABBLING BROOK (IRE) ..9-9§.. 9 ch.g. Meneval (USA) — Sparkling Stream (Paddy's Stream) 43p37. Plain angular half-brother to Irish NH flat and jumping winner, Royal Albert (IRE). NH FLAT '97 r1 p0. NH '97 r1 p1 (3rd in 2m4f110y Hdle). P-t-P '99 r2 w2 (Maiden and Restricted). Won two minor races in May '99, but a beaten favourite twice on his return, and downed tools in no uncertain terms when blinkered for the first time at Kilworthy. Never went a yard on his final start, and a watching brief is advised when he reappears. *Optimistic Partnership — Eggesford (Kay Rees & Polly Curtis).* 37 (Cl), 541 (I), 730 (I), 1173 (M), 1256 (Inr).

BABY WHALE (IRE) ..10-6.. 11 b.m. Supreme Leader — Determined Sara (Yellow River) r212. IRISH P-t-P '96 r5 w1 (mares Maiden) p0; pulled up 3, and fell 1. P-t-P '98/9 r11 w3 (Restricted, Members and Confined, hat-trick) p4 (3 2nds; and last of 3); fell/unseated 3. Only once out of the frame when completing on the mainland, and put up a smart performance when winning at Kilworthy (Jo Cumings and Tabitha Cave, who had partnered her on her first two starts in 2000, were on the placed horses), but seems likely to remain a sketchy jumper. Speedy and evidently suited by the lighter weights in Ladies races, so can confidently be expected to win again. Can handle top of the ground, but appreciates plenty of give. *F.D.A. Snowden — Tiverton (G. Snowden).* 162 (I), 314 (L), 725 (L), 1380 (L).

BACHELOR-CARRASCO (IRE) ..9-9.. 10 b.g. Le Bavard (FR) — Harvull (Harwell) ub5p1bp. Rangy. Dam won Irish Maiden. P-t-P '97 (Andrews-trained for Mr O. Brolly) r1 p1 (last of 2). Ventured to deepest Kent to lose his maiden status and appeared to appreciate the livelier ground (previously failed to cope with heavy going at Marks Tey), but the form of the race does not amount to much and has since failed to justify favouritism in two Restricteds (not his fault once). Does not seem blessed with limitless stamina, but might just be capable of finding another opportunity through superior jockeyship if nothing else. *S.R. Andrews & Miss J. Cook — Cambs (Simon Andrews).* 20 (OMa), 23 (OMa), 131 (OMa), 322 (CfMa), 578 (OMa), 825 (R), 980 (R).

BADGER BEER ..10-1.. 9 b.g. Town And Country — Panda Pops (Cornuto) p533p3129. Compact half-brother to Nearly A Pop, Panda Shandy, Hops And Pops (subsequent useful jumping winner), Best Bitter and Inforapop. Dam won 2 Points and placed 5 for Susan Woodhouse. Grandam, Queen's Bounty, half-sister to Royal Heath, Armagnac Queen and April Gypsey (themselves the dams of several successful Pointers), won 2 Points and placed 7 (including 2 3rds for her). Great-grandam, April Queen, won Liverpool Foxhunters, 2 other Chases and 6 Points. P-t-P/HUNT CH '97/9 r16 w2 (Maiden and Restricted) p5 (3 2nds); fell 2. Won two minor contests stylishly in '98, but generally a weak finisher and had clocked up 16 consecutive defeats prior to his Holnicote win. Had luck on his side as the odds-on favourite refused to race, and the second-in never went a yard on the ground, but deserved to find another race. Seems to have problems with his wind, and ran tongue-tied on his last five starts. Suited by firm ground, and worth persevering with in sub-3m Hunter Chases. *Mrs R.H. Woodhouse — Portman (John Dufosee).* 36 (Cl), 214 (Cf), 325 (Cf), 583 (2m5f110yH), 685 (2m5fH), 1059 (I), 1370 (I), 1444 (2m5fH), 1600 (2m5f110yH).

BAILEY GRAY ..7-12.. 7 gr.m. Baron Blakeney — Celtic Express (Pony Express) u4. Sister to Baroness Express, and half-sister to Butts Castle. Dam, half-sister to Bramble Pink (qv '97 Annual), won 6 Points and placed 11 for John Symes. Grandam, Celtic Pink, was a useless Pointer (11th of 12, pulled up 6, and fell 1). Jumped left before finishing a remote last, but can possibly do better in her second season. *Mr & Mrs J.F. Symes — Cotley (John Symes).* 539 (OMa), 656 (OMa).

BAKEWELL ..—.. 9 gr.g. Satin Wood — Apple Tart (FR) (Carwhite) ppp. Strong good-looking. Showed early speed on his last two appearances, but was well cooked when he pulled up. Far too gross to have any realistic hope of staying three miles. *Mrs J. Woollatt — Bicester with Whaddon (Shirley Brazier).* 515 (OMa), 845 (OMa), 1020 (OMa).

BAKMALAD ..8-11.. 15 ch.g. Kambalda — Joyspir (Master Buck) p5f35855. Tall. P-t-P '92/9 r33 w1 (Maiden) p9 (4 2nds); failed to finish 11 (fell 3). Formerly able, but usually plods away showing little zest these days. Made an exception when a creditable joint third at High Easter, and is only of use as a schoolmaster. *M.A. Kemp — Suffolk.* 86 (R), 93 (C), 413 (I), 610 (R), 843 (R), 940 (R), 1181 (R), 1379 (R).

BAK TO BILL ..—.. 6 b.g. Nicholas Bill — Kirstins Pride (Silly Prices) uf46. Angular owner-bred half-brother to Hasten Bak. Dam is half-sister to 4 Pointers, including Sergent Kay (qv '97 Annual). NH Mar/May '00 r2 p0 (remote 4th in 2m6f Mdn Hdle: *stayed on, nt rch ldrs*; and 6th in 2m6f Nov Hdle: *hdwy app 7, wknd nxt*). Needs to have more respect for the fences, but may benefit from the hurdling experience if returned to Points. *D.V. Gardner — Silverton (Lucy Gardner; Richard Frost).* 202 (I), 253 (CfMa).

BALANCE ..10-3.. 13 b.g. Balinger — Dance Partner (Manicou) 75221p3. Compact well-made home-bred half-brother to New Part, Dancing Doris and Tango Tom. Dam won 3 Points (disqualified once) and 3rd of 4. P-t-P '93/9 r26 w6 (up to Confined) p9 (5 2nds); and failed to finish 11 (fell/unseated 6). Looked really promising in his youth, and still a decent performer on his day, but his somewhat erratic fencing has prevented him from scaling the heights. Tends to hit a flat spot in his races, and did well to record his seventh success in quite a competitive event at Hackwood. Another win at 13 is a distinct possibility, and his Members seems the obvious target after three seconds in the past three years. Most effective on good ground, but had never managed more than six outings in a season until 2000. *R.J. Smith — Beaufort.* 1 (C), 215 (C), 387 (M), 634 (C), 886 (C), 1246 (Cf), 1554 (Cf).

BALDHU CHANCE ..10-0.. 13 ch.g. Chaparly (FR) — Galla Currency (Galeopsis) 2R2414p124. Small neat half-brother to Daisy Duke. Dam, sister to St Barbe (dam of Sancreed, *qv* '98 Annual) won very bad Maiden and placed 8 (7 3rds for Terry Long). Grandam, Lonesome Lass (who ran as Penny III), won 2 Maidens over banks and placed 5 for him. NH '94/5 r3 p0. P-t-P/HUNT CH '93/4 and '96/9 r47 w6 (inc an Intermediate) p9 (8 3rds, last once); failed to finish 20 (on floor 10). A busy little chap through the years, and has done well in minor company. Ended a losing sequence of 13 when successful at Kilworthy, and went in again at a dried out Trebudannon. Likes to dominate, and has struck up a good relationship with Alex Ede, but his efforts in Ladies races have been particularly praiseworthy (suited by the lighter weights), and would be a deserving winner of one. Liable to hang and jump right-handed. Appreciates fast ground. *T. Long — Four Burrow (Stephen Long).* 100 (O), 160 (O), 316 (Cf), 583 (2m5f110yH), 726 (Cf), 852 (Cf), 1188 (O), 1387 (O), 1515 (MO), 1638 (L).

BALDHU JACK ..9-7.. 8 b.h. Baldhu Cavalier — Little Stella (I'm Alright Jack) 1. Good-topped home-bred brother to Baldhu Jay Arr, and half-brother to Tinstreamer Johnny. Dam won a Maiden and 2nd for Terry Long. Sire is an unbroken brother to Baldhu Belle, and half-brother to Sancreed (*qv* '97 Annual). P-t-P '98 r5 p0 (6th, pulled up 3, and fell 1). One of very few entries to have Pointed, and primarily an Eventing stallion. Hinted at ability in his debut season, and despite a year off duty provided former conditional jockey Alex Ede with his first winner when getting up in the last stride at Wadebridge. Lamed himself and did not reappear, but might win another little race if connections can drag him from his destiny again. *T. Long — Four Burrow (Stephen Long).* 105 (OMa).

BALDHU JAY ARR ..—.. 7 b.g. Baldhu Cavalier — Little Stella (I'm Alright Jack) fpfu. Small narrow home-bred brother to Baldhu Jack (*qv*). Wild jumping has caused problems so far, but would have finished a respectable third had he not departed at the final fence on his latest attempt, and may yet do better if the penny drops. *T. Long & M.J. Stocker — Four Burrow (Stephen Long).* 159 (CfMa), 312 (CfMa), 538 (OMa), 1391 (OMa).

BALDHU LUCKYSTRIKE ..—.. 7 ro.g. Almoojid — St Christabelle (Golden Passenger) fpp. Compact half-brother to Baldhu Prospector. Dam, half-sister to the dam of Baldhu Chance (*qv*), won her Members for Terry Long. Does not seem to have been fully schooled (like JR), and pulled up after less than a mile on his first two attempts (conspicuously disastrous on his debut, in which he had fallen at the first and refused the second). *T. Long — Four Burrow (Stephen Long).* 165 (Cf), 311 (CfMa), 534 (Cf).

BALISTEROS (FR) ..11-4.. 12 b.g. Bad Conduct (USA) — Oldbury (FR) (Fin Bon) 13111112111111312. Workmanlike. Dam won 2 races in France, including Grande Steeplechase de Lyon. NH FLAT r2 p0. NH '93/4 r7 p0 (fell/unseated 2 in Chses). P-t-P/HUNT CH '95/6 and '98 r22 w6 (inc 3 Ladies) p12 (8 2nds, inc Hunt Ch; and inc 3rd in Hunt Ch); fell/unseated 2. A complete disaster under Rules, but transformed by Pointing and enjoyed a truly remarkable campaign when the leading horse in 2000 (at the expense of previous hero, Copper Thistle). Began the season with a successful 800-mile round trip to Tweseldown, and had accrued a further 12 victories prior to his excellent second to Lord Harry in the John Corbet. Missed the entire '99 season allegedly because Billie Thomson was cracked, and she is justifiably proud to boast of her successes with 'Seve', who had been an abject failure when with Richard Barber. Ably handled by both Pauline Robson and Jill Wormall. An heroic battler and a very thorough stayer who acts on any going, and is a fine tribute to the skill of his connections. A tougher individual is impossible to imagine — he appeared twice in a weekend on no fewer than three occasions! *Mrs B.K. Thomson — Berwicks.* 3 (L), 41 (L), 185 (L), 301 (2m5fH), 421 (3m5fL), 494 (L), 686 (3m1fH), 916 (3m1fH), 1029 (L), 1079 (L), 1119 (L), 1161 (L), 1364 (L), 1426 (L), 1579 (L), 1593 (3m2fH), 1646 (3m4fH).

BALLAD (IRE) ..9-9.. 9 b.g. Salluceva — Song Of Love (Raise You Ten) 312p14. Compact attractive half-brother to Hurdles winner, Torboy (IRE). P-t-P/HUNT CH '97 and '99 r4 p2 (twice last of 2; and last of 3); pulled up 1, and unseated 1. Much improved when getting his act together in 2000 (had previously not finished in front of another rival), and the acquisition of a tongue-strap was clearly what made the difference. A thorough stayer, but the form of his Marks Tey double does not amount to much, and firmly put in his place on his first venture into Confineds. Might improve his rating a little. *Mrs N.H. Bulgin — Essex F. & U.* 87 (OMa), 323 (CfMa), 575 (R), 1038 (R), 1181 (R), 1509 (Cf).

BALLINA ..10-5.. 9 b.g. Ayyabaan — Nicolene (Nice Music) 1p1u. Unfurnished brother to Swahili Run, and half-brother to Nicolene's Hope, and to NH flat and Hurdles winner, Ballet-K. Dam won 2 flat (10-12f) and placed 11. NH FLAT '96/7 r4 p0. NH '97 r2 p0. P-t-P '99 r5 w1 (Maiden) p2; and fell/unseated 2. Intelligently handled by Jamie Jukes in 2000, and responded with two early season successes, but has never particularly impressed with his fencing, and the Cheltenham faux pas was rather predictable. Blessed with more speed than stamina, and probably has to get clear in the final mile to succeed, but should find more opportunities. Yet to prove that he can cope with ground much softer than good. *S. Gallagher — Curre (Pat Hayes)*. 144 (R), 388 (I), 600 (I), 1340 (3m1f110yH).

BALL IN THE NET ..10-5.. 8 b.g. Arctic Lord — Courtlands Girl (Crimson Beau) R1114. Dam won 3 Hdles at around 2m. IRISH P-t-P '99 r2 p0 (fell 2). IRISH NH FLAT '99 r1 p0. Ran out after the rider had lost an iron on his English debut, but soon went on to notch a hat-trick, and gave Mick 'Curly' Holdforth his first winners. The first two successes were gained in poor company, and may then have been lucky in the Intermediate, in which he was left clear at the last when apparently just held. Goes a fair gallop (rather headstrong) and stays on, and can find other opportunities. His Members should again present a particularly simple task. *D.A. Rees — Hursley Hambledon*. 75 (I), 126 (R), 324 (M), 632 (I), 1057 (Cf).

BALLINURE BOY (IRE) ..10-2.. 8 b.g. Meneval (USA) — Sweet Cahore (General Ironside) 114. Workmanlike. IRISH P-t-P '98/9 r8 p4 (beaten a head once); fell 3. Came very close to scoring in Ireland, and duly ran away with a Maiden at Higham before returning there to follow-up in a Restricted. Did not show the same speed when a little disappointing on final start, but possibly had excuses, and it could be worth following him if he returns to his favourite track in 2001. *Mrs N.E. Turtle — E. Sussex & Romney Marsh (Sara Hickman)*. 23 (OMa), 239 (R), 572 (CfO).

BALLOT BOX ..—.. 9 b.g. The Bay Briar — Pillbox (Spartan General) ffp. Small ewe-necked half-brother to Spartan Times, and to smart Chaser and winning Hurdler, General Wolfe (earned over £100,000 to date). Dam won 3m Chase. NH '99 r1 p0 (tailed off and pulled up halfway). Makes some alarming mistakes, and gets a huge vote of no confidence. *L. Snook — Blackmore & Sparkford V. (Pauline Tizzard)*. 212 (CfMa), 355 (O), 408 (OMa).

BALLYACTION ..—.. 7 ch.g. Fearless Action (USA) — Ballytina (Rugantino) pp. Workmanlike home-bred half-brother to True Chimes (*qv*). NH FLAT '99 (from J. Cullinan's) r1 p0. Takes a keen hold, but does not jump fluently, and failed to get round in Maidens in which only three and two went clear. *T. Cardew — Bicester with Whaddon (Herbie Owen)*. 433 (OMa), 1019 (2m4fOMa).

BALLYBLACK (IRE) ..9-6.. 7 b br.g. Brush Aside (USA) — Buck Away (Buckskin FR) 3p1. Workmanlike. Ran well until blundering at the last when pressing the winner on his debut, but was tailed off next time. Returned to form to land a Maiden at Andoversford decisively, and should continue to progress in his second season. *M.J. & J. Arnold — N. Cotswold (Emma Baker)*. 60 (OMa), 455 (OMa), 972 (OMa).

BALLYBODEN ..—.. 14 ch.g. Over The River (FR) — Dadooronron (Deep Run) 6pfpp. Rangy half-brother to Young Parson. IRISH P-t-P '92 r1 p0. IRISH NH FLAT '93/4 r4 p0. IRISH NH '94/7 r23 w2 (2m-2m4f Chses) p3. P-t-P/HUNT CH '98/9 r13 p3 (2nds); fell/unseated 3, carried out 1. Employed as a schoolmaster to the young Arthurs for the last three seasons and has done an accomplished job but pulled up and dismounted on his final start, and reported dead. *Mrs R. Arthur — Tynedale*. 43 (Cf), 110 (O), 418 (M), 496 (C), 911 (4mMO).

BALLYBOLLEN (IRE) ..—.. 9 b br.g. Air Display (USA) — Clair The Lune (Martinmas) ppppp. Half-brother to a flat winner. IRISH P-t-P '97 r4 w1 (4&5yo Maiden) p1 (3rd); pulled up 2. NH '99 (for M. Pipe, bought for 24,000) r4 p1 (very distant and exhausted 3rd); pulled up in another Hdle, and pulled up 1, and unseated 1 in Chses. Sold Ascot, Jun for 775. Won his Irish Maiden despite tail-swishing, and then sold for a king's ransom, but looked defective when useless for Pipe, and has now failed to finish in his last eight attempts. *Mrs B. Ansell — W. Street/Tickham*. 126 (R), 285 (CR), 306 (R), 575 (R), 825 (R).

BALLY BOY ..8-12§.. 9 b.g. Green Adventure (USA) — Gold Willow (Goldfella) p32pur. Compact half-brother to Hurdles winner, San Giorgio. P-t-P '97 r5 p1 (2nd of 3); last, and pulled up 3. Looked faulty as a five-year-old, and two years off the track would not appear to have remedied the problem. Would struggle to find a more feeble race than when second at Llanfrynach, but liable to stop quickly, and declined to jump off at all on his final outing. Has the looks, but his temperament is most suspect, and usually makes mistakes. *M.R. Watkins — S. Herefords (Christine Hardinge)*. 14 (R), 70 (OMa), 488 (CfMa), 994 (OMa), 1315 (OMa), 1359 (OMa).

BALLY CLOVER ..9-11.. 14 ch.g. Deep Run — Miss De Jager (Lord Gayle USA) up233. Rangy good-topped half-brother to Life Of Brian (IRE), and to Irish Pointing winner, Fandangold. IRISH P-t-P '91 r1 p0 (pulled up). NH FLAT '92 r2 p0. NH '92/8 (for Miss W. Williams, bought for 11,000, 4 wins; previously for N. Henderson) r27 w7 (3 Hdles, 2m1f-2m6f, and 4 3m2f Chses, very lucky once) p13. Flattered by his multiplicity of prizes over the years, but acts well in the mud, and has a fine completion record (despite having been prone to the odd bad mistake under Rules). Very much a plodder at 13, but gave Louise Walter (not in the first flush of youth herself) a decent introduction when getting round for two very remote placings. Played a more positive role when four lengths clear of his trainer once, but it is difficult to envisage him being able to score again. *Miss L. & Mrs S.D. Walter — V. of Aylesbury (Lawney Hill)*. 19 (L), 74 (CCf), 1142 (M), 1487 (M), 1620 (Cf).

BALLYDESMOND (IRE) ..10-1.. 10 br.g. Forties Field (FR) — Tony's Mount (Choral Society) 2p43642. Tall rangy. Dam won an Irish Maiden. IRISH P-t-P '96 r6 w1 (4&5yo Maiden) p2 (remounted 2nd once); pulled up 2. P-t-P '97/8 r6 w3 (Restricted and 2 Clubs) p3 (2 2nds). Won at the opening meeting of '98 in the fastest time of the day, and looked a useful prospect, but failed to reappear, and missed the following season completely. Never really looked happy on his return, and acquired blinkers on his last four starts, but still remains capable of decent front-running efforts when the mood takes. Prone to getting himself worked up before the race, and has been taken to post early. *Sir C. Keswick & C.H. Sporborg — P.A. Bennett — Puckeridge (Christopher Sporborg; -).* 29 (Cf), 96 (I), 288 (CMod), 543 (I), 1286 (Cf), 1378 (Cf), 1536 (3m2fH).

BALLYEA BOY (IRE) ..9-12.. 11 gr.g. Sandalay — Nesford (Walshford) u3u4p. Close-coupled half-brother to Tom Snout (qv). NH FLAT Aut '94 r3 p2 (2nds). NH '94/8 (for S. Mullins; wins previously for D. Nicholson) r19 w2 (3m-3m1f Chses) p7 (inc 5 Hdles). NH '00 (from S. Mullins') r1 p0 (unseated in Grand Military Gold Cup: bhnd, mist ½ to til blun & ur 15). Completed a double in his first two Chases, but has not scored since '96. A very shoddy jumper, and was severely hampered by the rider in 2000. Probably faint-hearted, and often wears headgear. *Miss S. Cotterill — R.A. (Sally Mullins; Seamus Mullins).* 8 (C), 56 (M), 922 (3mH), 1103 (3m2f110yH).

BALLYEDWARD (IRE) ..9-8.. 11 b.g. Roselier (FR) — Paico Ana (Paico) 58547. Workmanlike angular. Dam is an unraced half-sister to prolific Chasing winners, My Buck and Givus A Buck. IRISH P-t-P '95 r1 w1 (4&5yo Maiden). NH FLAT '95 r1 p0. NH '95/8 r14 w1 (3m3f Hdle) p1 (3rd in Ch). P-t-P '99 r10 w1 (Members) p3 (2 2nds); 4th, last 3, and pulled up 2. Won a very weak Hurdle in '96, but suffering from injury problems since, and made very heavy weather of winning his Members in '99 — finished lame. Looked very sour in 2000, not surprising considering how frequently he experienced stinging felt on flesh. Beat just one rival home and looks finished. *N.J. Pewter & J.C. Chambers — E. Essex (Norman Pewter).* 95 (L), 414 (L), 608 (L), 1183 (L), 1380 (L).

BALLYHANNON (IRE) ..9-7.. 12 b.g. Strong Gale — Chestnut Fire (Deep Run) 536p166p5. Compact well-made half-brother to NH flat and jumping winner, Abbot Of Furness, to jumping winner, Plastic Spaceage, to Hurdles winner, Flaming Hope (IRE), to Irish Pointing and Hurdles winner, Lisaleen River, and to NH flat winner, Lisaleen Lady. Dam won NH flat and 2m2f mares Mdn Hdle in Ireland. IRISH NH FLAT r4 p1 (2nd). IRISH NH '94 r1 p0. IRISH P-t-P '94 r2 w1 (5yo Maiden) p0; disqualified from 2nd — no Hunters Certificate! P-t-P/HUNT CH '96 and '98/9 r22 p5 (4 3rds, last once); failed to finish 12 (on floor 5). Beaten in all but one of his 31 starts this side of the Irish Sea, but managed to outbattle two exhausted shirkers in a race taking well over eight minutes at Flagg. Otherwise not better than last-but-one in his 17 most recent attempts, and wasting his time in Hunter Chases. *E.W. Froggatt — Meynell & S. Staffs (Jane Froggatt).* 297 (I), 901 (M), 1089 (R), 1129 (R), 1255 (C), 1408 (Cf), 1525 (L), 1592 (4m2fH), 1627 (2m5fH).

BALLYHARRY (IRE) ..9-12.. 11 b.g. Phardante (FR) — Oakville Lady (Menelek) 1u733fp. Well-made half-brother to 2 winners in Ireland. Dam half-sister to Arctic Love (qv '87 Season Annual), won 4&5yo Maiden in Ireland. NH '97/9 (for P. Winkworth; regularly blinkered/visored, and been tongue-tied) r9 p3 (inc last of 3 in Ch — tailed off final mile). Sprang a 20-1 shock in a Maiden at Eyton, but beaten at least 12 lengths in his two thirds, and is basically very slow. Reported to have had breathing problems in the past. Sometimes makes errors, and needs to concentrate on Restricteds — flying far too high in Hunter Chases. *P. Grindley — W. Salop.* 568 (OMa), 863 (R), 963 (R), 1200 (CR), 1321 (Cf), 1592 (4m2fH), 1626 (3m1f10yH).

BALLYLESSON (IRE) ..8-11.. 6 b.g. Erdelistan (FR) — Three Dieu (Three Dons) ff2. Half-brother to Hand Over, Top Pryal and Bear's Picnic. Bought Doncaster, May for 5000. Fell at halfway in his first two Maidens (favourite for the second of them), and then finished an exhausted 15 lengths second in holding ground at Corbridge. Had to be forced past the post at a walk, and was immediately dismounted. Possibly possesses some ability, but will have to be regarded with suspicion until he proves it. *Mrs S.H. Shirley-Beavan — Jedforest (Simon Shirley-Beavan).* 425 (CiMa), 499 (2m4fOMa), 1165 (OMa).

BALLYMALOE BOY (IRE) ..9-12.. 8 b.g. Cataldi — Tartan Sash (Crofter USA) pp2ppp. Tall brother to Garethson (IRE) (qv). NH FLAT Nov '98 r1 p0. NH '98/9 (for M. Pipe; blinkered final) r7 w1 (2m7f Ch) p1 (3rd). Has only beaten one horse in eight of his last nine attempts, but finished five lengths second to Cream Supreme in the exception. A free-running sort who could clearly win Points on that sort of form, but obviously possesses a major defect which usually stops him in his tracks. Ran to 10-3 at Howick, but that is no longer warranted. *G. Richards — Tregear F.* 101 (L), 272 (L), 598 (O), 833 (O), 1313 (MO), 1525 (L).

BALLY PARSON ..9-7.. 15 b.g. The Parson — Ballyadam Lass (Menelek) 7pp. Tall rangy brother to top-class NH flat and jumping winner, Large Action (IRE) (earned £276,330, inc Tote Gold Trophy, also won in Ireland; and 2nd and 3rd in Champion Hurdles), and half-brother to One More Knight. NH FLAT '92 r1 p0. NH '92/8 r54 w6 (2m2f-2m5f Chses, on disqualification once; inc hat-trick) p6; broke blood vessel final. P-t-P '99 (for Mr G. Hutsby) r2 p1 (3rd); and 4th. A well-known performer under Rules, but has never pretended to stay three miles, and ran out of gas after two miles maximum in 2000. Gained all his wins bar one in April (the other was in April). *R.D. Green — Warwicks.* 611 (C), 884 (O), 1484 (O).

BALLYQUINTET (IRE) ..9-10.. 10 ch.m. Orchestra — Ollie's Pet (Tiepolo II) 54. Lengthy half-sister to Light The Wick, and to Irish Pointing winner, Distillery Hill. NH FLAT '96 r2 p0 (tailed off in both). P-t-P '98/9 r14 w1 (Maiden) p0; failed to finish 8 (fell/unseated 5). Made a more than respectable reappearance when less than ten lengths fifth to Scarlett O'Hara at Cottenham, but failed to emerge from another beating from the Sporborg mare on the same course a month later. A speedy mare (sometimes pulls too hard for her own good), and has the ability to win again particularly if her once very suspect jumping holds. *A.H.B. Hodge — Puckeridge.* 15 (C), 178 (Cm).

BALLY SEAMUS (IRE) ..—.. 8 b.g. Castle Keep — Four Roads Pet VII (unknown) ppp. Compact. A poor performer to date, and looked none too genuine on his latest appearance, when he sported blinkers and was mounted on the course before pulling up for the third consecutive time. *Mr & Mrs D.H. Gibbon — Pytchley (Caroline Bailey).* 321 (R), 1012 (CfMa), 1422 (OMa).

PLATE 20   *473 Avon Vale Hunt Members: Bally Wirral (G. Maundrell), 1st, holds off Solo Gent (S. Bush), 2nd*   PHOTO: Bill Selwyn

BALLY WIRRAL (IRE) ..10-8.. 9 b.g. Carlingford Castle — Jillie James (The Parson) u11. Workmanlike. IRISH P-t-P '98 r3 w1 (5&6yo Maiden) p0; fell after a mile twice. P-t-P '99 r2 w1 (Restricted) p0; and 4th. Successful in half his racecourse appearances, and clearly talented, but equally difficult to train — off the track for two and a half months between his two '99 outings, and has yet to manage a full campaign. Returned a decent time in both his 2000 successes, and might have prospects in a Novice Hunter Chase. A sound jumper nowadays. *G.C. Maundrell — Avon V.* 63 (I), 142 (I), 473 (M).

BALMORAL SPRING (IRE) ..9-5.. 8 b.g. Royal Fountain — The Best I Can (Derring Rose) f3p522. Narrow angular half-brother to Hurdles winner, Purple Ace (IRE), and Irish Pointing and Hurdles winner, No Messin'. NH '98/9 (for K. Bailey) r5 p1 (3rd); 20th in only Hdle. Bought Doncaster, Aug for 700. His Maiden placings have been reasonable, and should probably have won the latest, but was surprised when the winner made a dash for it at the top of the hill at Dingley, and could not quite recover in time (ironically, his vanquisher was the former owner). Should gain compensation eventually. *P.J. Millington — C.R. Millington — Fernie.* 31 (CMa), 124 (OMa), 235 (OMa), 438 (OMa), 1270 (OMa), 1504 (CfMa).

BALMY BREEZE ..7-6§.. 14 b.m. Idiot's Delight — Modom (Compensation) p. Very small compact half-sister to All Weather (*qv*). NH FLAT r3 p1 (20l 3rd on all-weather). NH '92/3 and '98 r8 p0. P-t-P '94 and '99 r7 w1 (Maiden) p2 (3rds, last after refusing once); and pulled up 4. Won a Maiden in '94, but reportedly at stud since, and has done nothing in four outings for present connections to suggest that she is happy at having her motherly duties interrupted. Half the size of her half-brother, but not half as good. *D.A. Rees — Hursley Hambledon.* 130 (CMod).

BALTIC LAKE (IRE) ..9-6.. 9 ch.g. Henbit (USA) — Deepwater Woman (The Parson) p343. Half-brother to Hurdles winner, Miss Bertaine (IRE). IRISH P-t-P '97 r1 p0 (pulled up). NH '98 r1 p0 (42/ 6th in Nov Hdle). P-t-P '99 r3 p2 (2nds); and pulled up 1. Has given Matthew Smethurst a decent feel for race-riding, and is capable of staying on in lowly company, but has yet to look like scoring (never within 15 lengths of the winner in his placings), and may not have the necessary resolve to do so. Might be worth trying in blinkers. *Mrs J. Smethurst — S. Durham.* 808 (OMa), 1163 (OMa), 1331 (OMa), 1474 (M).

BANCYFELIN BOY ..9-2§.. 14 ch.g. Old Lucky — Eve Darlin (Arcticeelagh) u464ppp. Deep-girthed strong-quartered half-brother to Official Eve. P-t-P/HUNT CH '92/7 and '99 r21 w3 (Maiden, Members and Confined) p4 (3 3rds, of 4 once, and last once); pulled up 11. Successful once apiece '94/6, but ran just once the following year, and has performed with a complete lack of zest since missing the '98 season. Ran in a cross-noseband when novice ridden (not for long once) at Erw Lon, but wouldn't have pulled the skin off a rice pudding. Very porky in early season, and highly unlikely to stage a revival at 14. *Miss A.L. Williams — S. Pembs.* 272 (L), 275 (Cf), 482 (I), 643 (Cf), 837 (I), 944 (I), 1227 (I).

BANDIT BOY ..8-2.. 8 gr.g. Robellino (USA) — Patraana (Nishapour FR) pppp. Neat brother to a winner in Hungary, and half-brother to Promethean Singer and Trap Dancer (jumping winner since Pointing). FLAT r1 p0 (last). NH Mar '97 r1 p0 (pulled up). P-t-P '98 r4 p0 (last, and pulled up 3). Tailed off last in his only Pointing completion, and is completely devoid of stamina. Has never contested a short Maiden, and no longer has that option open to him. Blinkers have made no difference. *Mrs R.M. Parris — Thurlow (Neville King).* 605 (OMa), 941 (CfMa), 1040 (OMa), 1180 (OMa).

BANGAGIN ..—§.. 15 b.g. Balinger — Rapagain (Deep Run) p5pp. Small neat half-brother to Deep Song (qv). NH '90/3 (for late J. Webber) r4 p0 (last in both Hdles, and in one of 2 Chses). Returned from obscurity after a seven year absence to finish two fences last in his Members, and subsequently caused plenty of problems in the preliminaries. *M.J. Buchan — Oakley.* 434 (OMa), 509 (M), 792 (OMa), 1011 (CfMa).

BANG ON TARGET ..—§.. 13 ch.g. Cruise Missile — Airy Fairy (Space King) pppupp. Sturdy. Dam, Selling class, won 7 Hdles, 2m-2m4f. NH '93 and '94/5 r9 p2 (3rds). P-t-P/HUNT CH '94, '96 and '99 r17 w1 (Maiden) p1 (3rd); failed to finish 10 (refused 1, and fell/unseated 3). Won on his Pointing debut in '94, but most unwilling since, and stretched his dire losing sequence to 22 in 2000. Has enjoyed taking the mickey out of Jeremy Stephens, and regularly tailed off at an early stage when partnered by him. Wears blinkers. *Mrs M.B. Stephens — E. Kent.* 127 (Cf), 286 (O), 575 (R), 1393 (R), 1510 (O), 1541 (2m5fH).

BANKHEAD (IRE) ..10-10.. 12 gr.g. Roselier (FR) — Coolcanute (Hardicanute) 121u. Small sturdy brother to Hurdles winner, Not For Turning (IRE), and half-brother to Irish jumping winner, Aughnavilla. Dam won 2m1f Hdle in Ireland. IRISH P-t-P '94 r3 w1 (4&5yo Maiden) p0; pulled up 1. NH '94/5 r7 w2 (3m-3m2f Hdles) p3. P-t-P '96 (for Mr A.J. Brazier) r7 w6 (Ladies) p0; and unseated 1. NH '96/9 (for J.L. Spearing) r13 w4 (2 Nov Chses, 3m110y-3m1f; and 2 HCap Hdles, 3m-3m110y) p2 (2nds); pulled up 2. Returned to racing under Rules following an unbeaten run in Ladies races in '96, but lost his confidence over fences following a November double, and reverted to hurdling. Made an immediate impact on his re-introduction to Pointing, but suffered his first defeat at the hands of Karaburan, and ran blinkered on his last two appearances. A thorough stayer and a powerful galloper, but has always been deliberate over birch. Acts on any going, but particularly fond of soft ground. Well handled by Caroline Spearing, and seems certain to win again. *Mrs N.F. Williams — Croome & W. Warwicks (Caroline Spearing).* 78 (L), 335 (L), 431 (L), 1126 (L).

BANNAGH BEG (IRE) ..9-0.. 11 b.m. Amazing Bust — Castle Ita (Midland Gayle) 1pp. Small light half-sister to Bannagh Mor (IRE) (qv). P-t-P '99 (for Mr G.G. Lewis) r6 p0 (6th, pulled up 3, and fell/unseated 2). A latecomer to Pointing, and it was no coincidence that Christian Williams was in the saddle when she lost her maiden status in a bad race in desperate ground at St Hilary. Cut no ice in Restricteds subsequently, and lacks scope and may have to rest on her laurels. Has been awkward at the start on occasions. *R. Williams-Jones — Llangeinor.* 1056 (CfMa), 1298 (R), 1453 (R).

BANNAGH EXPRESS (IRE) ..8-11.. 8 br.g. Detroit Sam (FR) — Castle Ita (Midland Gayle) c5pf3. Workmanlike brother to Bannagh Mor (IRE) (qv). IRISH P-t-P '99 r5 p0 (4th of 5, last, and pulled up 3). Bought Doncaster, Aug for 1400. Usually prominent for 2m4f in poor company, but fades alarmingly, and was very tired when claiming 35 lengths last of three. Stoutly bred, so presumably there is something wrong with him. *Miss K. Thory & M.J. Lurcock — Fitzwilliam (Katie Thory).* 87 (OMa), 123 (OMa), 236 (OMa), 1039 (OMa), 1116 (OMa).

BANNAGH MOR (IRE) ..10-5.. 10 b.g. Detroit Sam (FR) — Castle Ita (Midland Gayle) p. Sturdy attractive brother to Bannagh Express (IRE), and half-brother to Ita's Fellow and Bannagh Beg (IRE). IRISH P-t-P '96/7 r4 w1 (5&6yo Maiden, by short head) p1 (head 2nd). IRISH NH FLAT '96 r2 p0. IRISH NH '97 r1 p0. P-t-P/HUNT CH '98/9 r9 w5 (inc 3 Opens, inc 4-timer) p0; unseated 1, and pulled up 1. Unbeaten when completing in Kent Opens in '98, but restricted to just three outings since pulling up in the John Corbet that year, and is clearly still troubled. A strong-galloping front-runner in his prime, but has it all to prove if he reappears. *J.H. Burbidge — O. Surrey & Burstow (Ollie Cann).* 954 (MO).

BANNER YEAR (IRE) ..—.. 10 b.g. Lancastrian — Stunted Reina (Reformed Character) u. Small compact mare half-brother to Chasing winner, Free To Roam (IRE), and to Irish Pointing winner, Super Buck. Dam won NH flat and 2m5f Hdle in Ireland (won another NH flat, but demoted to 2nd). IRISH P-t-P '96 r7 p0 (5th of 6, last 2, and pulled up 4). NH FLAT Dec '96 r1 p0. NH '97 and Jun '99 (for A. Lockwood, bought for 1200; previously for T. Carr) r8 p2 (3rds in Chses). Beaten eight lengths and 34 lengths in Hexham thirds over 2m5f in May '97, but tailed off and pulled up on all three subsequent attempts under Rules. Partnered by a jockey having his first ride at Alpraham, and he fell off at the fourth fence, having almost done so at the two preceding obstacles. Looks very faulty. *Mrs G. Culleton — Derwent.* 588 (OMa).

BANTEEN ..8-6.. 7 b.m. Teenoso (USA) — Breac Ban (Laurence O) u. Small compacy half-sister to Bantry Bay. Dam, half-sister to Mossiman (*qv* '98 Annual), won an Irish NH flat (promoted from 2nd); and won 4 Hdles (2m6f-3m) and 3 Chses (3m1f-3m2f, inc a walk-over) in England; and placed total of 9 (including when 3rd in a Members for Wilf Tolhurst — would have won in similar company but for refusing 2 out). P-t-P '99 r1 p0 (last). A typically tiny Teenoso who would have been a remote fourth but for unseating at Cottenham, but two outings in two years does not bode well. *W.J. Tolhurst — Essex & Suffolk.* 181 (2m4fOMa).

BANTEER BET (IRE) ..10-1.. 9 ch.m. Black Minstrel — Deirdre Elizabeth (Salluceva) 3. Sturdy half-sister to Lordinthesky (IRE) and Roll With It (IRE). P-t-P/HUNT CH '97/9 r10 w1 (Maiden) p2 (3 3rds, inc Hunt Ch); pulled up 3, fell/unseated 2. Had three subsequent winners in her wake when successful in a seven minute Maiden at Brampton Bryan in '99, and not entirely flattered by a Hunter Chase placing, but disappeared after a promising reappearance at Chaddesley in 2000. A good thing to win a Restricted when the emphasis is on stamina if her enforced absence is not a bad omen, and could improve further with more fluency at the fences. *C.H. Gittins — N. Salop (John Groucott).* 612 (CR).

BAPTIST JOHN (IRE) ..9-11.. 13 b.g. The Parson — Corrielek (Menelek) p. Big rangy brother to Butler John (IRE) (*qv*). P-t-P '96/9 r11 w1 (Maiden) p5 (3rds); pulled up 2, and fell/unseated 2. Only embarked on a racing career aged eight, but won a Whitwick Maiden in his second season. Has done well in the circumstances, but stands his racing badly, and only manages an average of just over two races per annum. Deserves to win a Restricted — has been placed in two of three attempts — but prone to mistakes, and becoming elderly. *P.R.M. Philips — Worcs.* 338 (R).

BARAN ITSU ..9-12.. 7 br.g. Itsu (USA) — Adelbaran (FR) (No Pass No Sale) f11pp. Good-bodied owner-bred. Dam won 8f Claimer in France (awarded race). NH FLAT Feb '98 r1 p0 (favourite). NH '99 (from K Burke's) r4 p0; pulled up final 2. A free-running individual who was in front for most of the way when completing a double on sound surfaces at Bassaleg, but looked lucky in the Maiden, as a live danger fell two out. Badly hampered after 2m2f and lost all chance when bidding for the hat-trick, but should be quick enough to find compensation before too much longer. *F.H. Williams — Gelligaer F.* 1302 (OMa), 1405 (OMa), 1568 (R), 1613 (I), 1674 (I).

BARE FISTED ..9-13.. 13 ch.g. Nearly A Hand — Ba Ba Belle (Petit Instant) 43pp14. Small half-brother to Funny Farm and Frys Lane. Dam, half-sister to Chita's Cone and 5 other Pointers, won 2 Hunt Chses and 2 Ladies and placed 13. Grandam, Conchita II, won 2 Hunt Chses and 6 Points and 2nd 3. NH '93 r7 p0 (pulled up only Ch; inc last twice, pulled up 1, and fell 1 in Hdles). P-t-P/HUNT CH '95/6 and '98/9 r26 w5 (inc Open) p3 (2 3rds); pulled up 6, and fell/unseated 2. Moody and inconsistent, but put some modest efforts behind him when winning his Members for the second year running. Likes to dominate if he can, but quite happy to lag round in the ruck these days, and ended the season on a low by finishing lame. Sure to remain unpredictable if he returns in 2001. The announcer at the Atherstone was most impressed by Hannah Phizacklea's two enormous cups — perhaps the horse should be renamed. *Miss H.L. Phizacklea — Atherstone.* 118 (L), 368 (L), 544 (L), 1007 (L), 1414 (M), 1503 (Cf).

BARLEY'S BOY (U) ..7-0.. 9 b.g. Milk Of The Barley — Cemberlitas (unknown) 2. Not in the same parish as the winner in his Members, but at least finished a long way ahead of three others, giving the owner a very enjoyable ride in the process. *Mrs S. Tideswell — N. Staffs.* 1124 (M).

BARNA BOY (IRE) ..10-12.. 13 b.g. Torus — Barna Beauty (Gala Performance USA) fp1f1. Big rangy brother to Irish Pointing winner, Barna Lad (IRE). Dam won NH flat and 4 Hdles (2m-2m4f) in Ireland. IRISH NH FLAT '93 '93 r5 w1 p2 (3rds, demoted from 2nd once). NH '93/9 (from N. Henderson's) r31 w4 (3 Hdles, 2m1f-2m4f,and 2m1f Ch; inc hat-trick '94/5) p8; blundered badly last and unlucky once. Formerly smart at best under Rules, but had not scored since landing the £26,615 County Hurdle at the Cheltenham Festival in '97. Never tried beyond 2m5f in that sphere, but got the trip well in both Pointing successes, and gave splendid displays of jumping and never headed in either. Not always so foot-perfect, and seems to be vulnerable if he is headed. The Chaddesley victory was a splendid display, but has almost certainly led to an inflated rating. *Mrs J. Wilson — Pytchley (Bill Warner).* 15 (C), 48 (Cf), 1216 (O), 1416 (O), 1631 (MO).

BARNADOWN (IRE) ..9-11.. 11 b.g. Gallic Heir — Tricias Pet (Mandalus) f. Strong-topped compact brother to Must Be Murphy (IRE). IRISH P-t-P '96/8 r18 w2 (6yo&up Maiden; and Winners of One — poor 2nd when left well clear 2 out) p6; pulled up 3, ran out 2, refused, and fell 2. P-t-P/HUNT CH '99 r7 p1 (3rd); pulled up 2, and ran out 1. Appeared to have trouble getting the trip in England, and dropped dead in mid-race at Cottenham on his seasonal reappearance. Miss J.E. Cook — Cambs (Simon Andrews). 175 (I).

BARNEY BEAR ..9-7.. 10 b.g. Scorpio (FR) — Nutt's Corner (Cantab) puf2541. Strong rangy half-brother to Blakes Corner. Dam won 3 Irish Points and placed 6; and was placed in 2 English Points for Mrs Garton (was a hot ride, and had breathing problems). P-t-P '97/9 r8 p2; pulled up 3. Lightly-raced and a weak finisher, but gained reward for some meritorious performances when winning a bad Maiden at Chaddesley on his final outing. Often clumsy at his fences, and not good enough for sub three-mile Hunter Chases, so unless he finds some more stamina he will find life tough in Restricteds. *Mrs A.B. Garton — Cheshire Forest (Tim Garton).* 459 (2m4f110yH), 694 (OMa), 964 (OMa), 1197 (OMa), 1323 (OMa), 1527 (OMa), 1635 (OMa).

BARNEYS GOLD (IRE) ..10-1.. 12 ch.g. Orchestra — Fair Corina (Menelek) 6f2243p4. Tall half-brother to Waverley Mill, to English Hurdles and Irish Chasing winner, Programmed To Win, and to an Irish NH flat winner. NH FLAT '95 r2 p0. P-t-P/HUNT CH '96/8 r16 w4 (up to Confined) p5 (4 3rds, of 4 twice inc Hunt Ch, and last of 3 once); ran out 3, and fell 1. Almost unmanageable in his first season, but sorted out in the hunting field, and won four races in competent fashion '97/8. Missed the following season, and would appear to have gone backwards judged by this year's efforts. A thorough stayer, but tends to run his race in snatches, and has lost the acceleration he once possessed. No longer in harmony with the rider, and might be worth a whirl in blinkers. *I.S. Naylor — Cottesmore (Chris Bealby).* 229 (Cf), 441 (O), 443 (Cf), 691 (O), 999 (4m1fmO), 1265 (O), 1415 (Cf), 1584 (CCond).

BARON ALLFOURS ..10-6.. 9 gr.g. Baron Blakeney — Georgian Quickstep (Dubassoff USA) p2232p12u. Small close-coupled. NH FLAT '96/7 r2 p0 (veered badly left and ran out at start on debut, and unruly and virtually bolted to start and unseated next time). NH '97 r1 p0 (pulled up in Hdle). P-t-P '99 r13 w1 (Maiden) p2; pulled up 4, and fell 2. A total nutter under Rules, and bought cheaply (850gns), but has done Patrick Millington proud in Points, and landed his Restricted at the 14th attempt with a typically unorthodox success at Fakenham. Showed much improved form when second under Andrew Sansome at Aintree subsequently, and deserves to have his assistance on a more regular basis. Wears a citation and is usually anchored out the back in order to preserve his stamina. Once again the Millington horsebox wins the prize for the most miles on the clock in any one season. Tried Sunday racing in July (the lure of £300 appearance money proving irresistible), and gave A.P. McCoy a nightmare fall which led to an automatic three week suspension. *A. Waters & P.J. Millington — Fernie (Patrick Millington).* 86 (R), 119 (CR), 440 (R), 554 (R), 675 (CR), 1009 (CR), 1287 (R), 1557 (3m1fH), 1646 (3m4fH).

BARON KNAYBER ..—.. 12 b.g. Karlinsky (USA) — Moon Girl (Impersonator) pfp. Dam was placed in 2 Maidens. P-t-P '94, '96 and '98 r6 w1 (Maiden) p0; pulled up 3, and fell 1. Only emerges every other season, and apart from his success on firmish at Cothelstone in '98 (rated 9-8) has achieved nothing tangible. Is he a tax exile in his barren years, and will he make it back for 2002? *S.G. Edwards — S. Cornwall.* 729 (R), 849 (R), 1385 (Cf).

BARRON BAY (USA) ..—.. 9 br.g. Track Barron (USA) — In Bay (ARG) (Halpern Bay USA) p7. Workmanlike half-brother to a winner in USA. Dam won 10 races in Argentina, including 7 Group races. NH FLAT '96 r1 p0. P-t-P/HUNT CH '98/9 r7 w1 (Maiden) p2 (3rds); pulled up 3. Won a poor Maiden in much the slowest time of the day at Peper Harow in '98 (rated 9-3), but not better than last in five attempts since (pulled up in four), and seems to have developed a major defect. *B. Tetley — Surrey U. (Pam Tetley).* 27 (I), 126 (R).

BARTON BLACK (NZ) ..9-13.. 9 br.g. Tristrams Heritage (NZ) — Catena Heights (NZ) (Marceau AUS) 664. Big rangy. NH FLAT Oct '97 r1 p0. NH '97/9 (from S. Brookshaw's) r9 w1 (2m5f Hdle) p0; pulled up in all 3 Chses. Made all when winning a bad Hurdle on firmish (only five ran), but his jumping of regulation fences was far from convincing. Gets round in more competent fashion in Points, but faced some stiff opposition in Opens, and was found wanting at the business end. Was tubed for his final appearance under Rules. *Mrs H.J. Clarke — Worcs (Barry Key).* 614 (O), 895 (MO), 1492 (O).

BARTON BOG (IRE) ..9-9.. 7 gr.g. Roselier (FR) — Al's Niece (Al Sirat USA) p61u. Tall angular half-brother to Irish Pointing winner, Pops Academy. Sold Doncaster, May '98 for 27,000. Obviously no bargain, and appeared to hate the firmish ground once, but was able to make the most of a simple task in a two-finisher Maiden at Dunthrop. Clearly stays well, but his jumping has been very novicey to date. Likely to improve his rating if becoming more fluent. *Mrs J. Mould — Heythrop (Cathy Twiston-Davies).* 471 (OMa), 790 (OMa), 1018 (OMa), 1459 (R).

BARTON NIC ..10-1.. 8 b.g. Nicholas Bill — Dutch Majesty (Homing) R1. Big strong. Dam won 2m2f Hdle. NH FLAT '98/9 r3 p1 (2nd). NH '99 (from A. Streeter's) r2 p0. A handful who sweats profusely and goes to post early, but won quite a competitive Maiden in softish at Barbury Castle (returned a time 13 seconds quicker than the other division), and should have clear claims in a Restricted. Not seen since mid-March. *Mrs H.B. Clarke — R.A. (Don Harrington).* 328 (CfMa), 471 (OMa).

PLATE 21   471 Avon Vale Open Maiden 567&8yo (Div 1): Barton Nic (P. Keane), 1st, jumps in front of Carbonado (P. Pritchard), 2nd, at the last
                                                                    PHOTO: Tim Holt

BARTON ROSE ..9-7§.. 10 b.g. Derring Rose — Barton Sauce (Saucy Kit) 54u24. Workmanlike good-bodied half-brother to Saucy's Wolf. Dam won 2 Points. P-t-P '97 and '99 r5 w1 (Maiden) p0; pulled up 1, and fell/unseated 2. Won his Maiden in extraordinary circumstances in '99 (refused to leave the starting area until the others had jumped the first fence), but despite being less unruly has managed to avoid Restricted success. Remains a tricky ride, but often the subject of a move in the market, and will possibly reward his supporters one day. *Mrs S.J. Evans — Devon & Somerset (Mike Trickey).* 729 (R), 931 (R), 1095 (R), 1240 (R), 1563 (R).

BAS DE LAINE (FR) ..10-1.. 15 b.g. Le Pontet (FR) — La Gaina (FR) (New Chapter) 3p3. Tall good-looking. NH '91/7 (often blinkered/visored; for M. Hammond, 3 wins; previously for O. Sherwood) r40 w8 (4 Hdles, 2m-2m4f, and 4 Chses, 2m5f-3m1f) p16; penultimate run in Ireland. NH '99 r1 p0. HUNT CH '99 r1 p0 (disqualified from win because had won too-valuable race). Fell victim to a Weatherbys clanger in '99, but has always been tainted by bad luck, and even anno domini now seems to have it in for him. Was a smart front-running performer under Rules — earned £61,447 — and could have been even better had he been dealt a kinder hand. Did well to finish third at Taunton, but would have eaten the winner and runner-up for breakfast in his prime, and deserves to be able to put his feet up. *Mrs P.A. Tetley — Surrey U.* 26 (O), 303 (3mH), 581 (3mH).

BASIL ..9-8.. 8 br.g. Lighter — Thrupence (Royal Highway) u21p3. Half-brother to Goodfellow's Folly, to jumping winner, Flow, and to Hurdles winner, Amber Realm. P-t-P '99 r2 p0 (pulled up 1, and fell 1). Got up near the line to win a ten-finisher Maiden in the slowest time of the day at Littlewindsor, but the third Gemini Mist turned the tables well and truly the next time they met. Seems a steady enough jumper, and with normal improvement should be capable of winning an average Restricted. *Mrs C.J. Dunn — Cotley (Philip Greenwood).* 212 (CfMa), 265 (OMa), 520 (OMa), 876 (R), 1240 (R).

BASIL STREET (IRE) ..10-0§.. 9 b.g. Glenstal (USA) — Pockatello (Commanche Run) 12f233. Workmanlike good-bodied. FLAT r6 p1 (2nd). NH '95/6 (broke blood vessel 1) r8 p3 (2nds). P-t-P/HUNT CH '97/9 r15 w3 (2m4f Maiden, Restricted and Members) p3 (2 3rds, inc Hunt Ch); pulled up 3, and fell/unseated 3. Successful on his reappearance in three out of four Pointing seasons, but otherwise beaten in all but one of his 17 races, and is by far and away at his best fresh. Capable of decent efforts, but ungenuine and should always be treated with suspicion and not one to take too short a price about. Sometimes blinkered to '97. *B. Jackson — N. Herefords (Peter Hicks).* 332 (M), 445 (Cf), 667 (Cf), 702 (Cf), 987 (Cf), 1272 (Cf).

BATCHO MISSILE ..—.. 12 ch.g. Cruise Missile — Peticienne (Mummy's Pet) ppp. Sparely-made brother to Grange Missile, and half-brother to Pets Pride and Colonel Wilkie. P-t-P '95/6 and '98 r10 p0 (fell/unseated 4, and pulled up 6). Returned from a year's sabbatical as bad as ever, and remains in no fit state to be on a racecourse. *I.S. Gilbert — Fernie.* 373 (CfMa), 868 (Cf), 1020 (OMa).

BATHWICK BOBBIE ..9-10.. 14 b.g. Netherkelly — Sunwise (Roi Soleil) 2p23. Tall well-made half-brother to NH flat and jumping winner, Wise King. NH '93/4 (blinkered 4) and '96/7 (visored 1) r25 p7 (inc 3 Chses); unseated 2. P-t-P/HUNT CH '96 and '98/9 r15 w1 (Maiden) p5 (3 3rds, last once); unseated 5, and pulled up 1. Finally got off the mark as an 11-year-old, but struggling in Restricteds since, and does not appear to be the doughtiest of stayers. A steady jumper, and his reliable fencing might tip the scales in his favour again, though age is against him. Suited by top-of-the-ground conditions. *Dr J.R.J. Naylor — R.A.* 56 (M), 458 (R), 958 (R), 1540 (2m5fH).

BATTLE LORD CISTO ..9-1.. 13 ch.g. Cisto (FR) — Battle Lady Ivor (Bigivor) 22. Tall strong. NH '96 r3 p0 (17th of 18, and pulled up in Hdle, and pulled up in Ch). P-t-P '97/8 r7 p1 (3rd); pulled up 1, and fell/unseated 3. Kept going gallantly when runner-up in three and four-finisher Maidens in hock deep ground (took over eight minutes once), but desperately one-paced, and the form amounts to little. Has always been lightly-raced (missed the '99 season), and unlikely to get any simpler opportunities. *Miss E.A. Cork — E. Cornwall.* 312 (CfMa), 1179 (OMa).

BATTLESHIP BRUCE ..9-12.. 9 b.g. Mazilier (USA) — Quick Profit (Formidable USA) pfp. Robust attractive half-brother to flat winner, Smokey Pete. Dam won at 7f. £21,000y. FLAT (wins for N. Callaghan; unplaced 2 for Miss G. Kelleway) r25 w4 (8-10f, 2 on equitrack) p4. NH '95/9 (for B. Llewellyn; previously for P. Bowen — lame; previously for T. Casey; previously for N. Callaghan; ran once apiece '95 and '98/9) r16 p5 (inc 2 Sells). Would have completed a five-timer on the flat had he not been eased and short-headed, but has not scored since he was three, and generally very lightly raced and looks blighted since. Failed to get round in three Ladies Opens, despite there only being six runners each time. Sometimes wore headgear in previous yards, and was very inconsistent and found little at best. Named after Bruce Hobbs who won the Grand National on Battleship in 1938. *Mrs A.P. Davies — Carms.* 346 (L), 836 (L), 946 (L).

BATTY'S ISLAND ..9-2.. 12 b.g. Town And Country — Just Something (Good Times ITY) up84pp. Compact half-brother to Just Andy. NH '93/3 r3 w2 (all-weather) p0. NH '93/8 r26 w3 (2m1f Hdles) p4 (inc distant last of 3 in Ch); 6th, pulled up 1, and unseated 1 in other Chses; pulled up in Sell Hdles final 2 starts. P-t-P '99 (for Mr M.J. Langford) r3 w1 (Confined) p2 (3rds). Revived under the care of Sheila Crow in '99 (had trained-off badly under Rules after winning four of his first six races), but declined 17 pounds in the ratings in 2000, and managed to beat just one rival home. Looked portly even on his third start, and might be breaking blood vessels again. *K. Wynne — Sir W.W. Wynn's.* 525 (M), 781 (Cf), 902 (Cf), 961 (O), 1319 (O), 1524 (O).

BAVARD DIEU (IRE) ..10-7.. 13 ch.g. Le Bavard (FR) — Graham Dieu (Three Dons) 12f. Sparely-made hobdayed brother to Hurricane Tommy, and to Irish NH flat winner, Noeleens Delight, and half-brother to Mac's Glen, and to Irish NH flat and jumping winner, Graham Course. Dam won 2m Chase. IRISH NH FLAT '92/3 r9 w1 (2m3f) p5 (3 2nds). IRISH NH '93/5 r21 w5 (2m3f Hdle, and 4 Chses, 2m1f-2m4f; inc £9675 prize) p8 (beaten a mead once). NH '95/7 and '99 (for N. Gaselee; blinkered 1 — tried in them in Ireland) r20 w3 (2m6f-3m Chses) p4 (3rds). Sold Ascot, June for 2600. Earned over £50,000 under Rules, and took his total haul of wins into double figures when getting Tor Sturgis off the mark in a Confined at Larkhill, but met a sad end when taking a fatal fall in his Members. Had been looking rejuvenated by a change of yard, which made his demise even more distressing. *Miss V.C. Sturgis — Beaufort (Gail Sturgis).* 62 (Cf), 216 (Cnr), 387 (M).

BAVINGTON ..—.. 10 b.g. Meadowbrook — Bargello's Lady (Bargello) p. Small half-brother to Sword Beach, Divet Hill and Lady Manello (dam of Claywalls, *qv*). Dam won 3m Hdle and 7 Chses (2m-3m3f) and placed 12. P-t-P/HUNT CH '96/9 (for breeder, Mr I. Hamilton) r14 w1 (Maiden) p3 (2 2nds); fell 1, and pulled up 4. Much improved in '98 (rated 9-11), but clearly under the weather since, and has been pulled up in four of five subsequent attempts. Ran as though something was badly amiss at Lanark (the scene of his solitary success), and failed to reappear. *J.K. Huddleston — Tynedale.* 661 (L).

BAY FUSILIER ..8-2§§.. 8 b.g. Mazilier (USA) — Kingsfold Flash (Warpath) pp. Lengthy half-brother to Flashing Steel, and to 5 other winners, including Miltonfield (Irish flat, NH flat and hurdles), Kingsfold Flame (flat), Wensleydalewilliam and On The Sauce (both Hurdles). 25,000 3yo. NH FLAT '97 r1 p0. NH '98 r4 p0 (tailed off final 3). P-t-P '99 r5 p0 (pulled up 3, refused 1, and fell 1). Has twice managed to let certain Maiden success slip from his fingers at Garnons (ground to a halt at the last when well clear in the latest), and is an ungenuine non-stayer in Points. Has been tried in blinkers, but beyond redemption, and his disappearance in early March could mean that connections have finally cut their losses. *Miss J.M. Green — Ludlow (Penny Grainger).* 339 (CfMa), 451 (CfMa).

BAYTOWNGHOST (IRE) ..8-7.. 11 gr.g. Salluceva — Little Duckling (Pals Passage) ppp4pf. Tall rangy. IRISH P-t-P '97 r1 p0 (pulled up). IRISH NH FLAT '97 r1 p0 (remote 24th of 25). P-t-P '99 r7 p1

(2nd); fell/unseated 5, and pulled up 1. Went crash-bang-wallop in his first three Points and continues to jump with wreckless abandon, and though he may have some latent ability he is more likely to keep the Welsh St John's boyos and girls busy if he reappears. Has been tried in blinkers and a tongue-strap. Even Scooby Doo wouldn't fancy checking this spectre out. *Mrs K.B. Thomas — S. Pembs (Owen Thomas).* 269 (CfMa), 349 (CfMa), 485 (R), 646 (R), 838 (OMa), 1225 (OMa).

BEACH PATROL (IRE) ..—.. 13 b.g. Thatching — Waveguide (Double Form) pp. Sturday compact half-brother to flat winners, Surf City, Waveband and One of The Old Ones. 33,000y. FLAT (for W. Jarvis at 2) r2 p0. NH '93/4 (visored final; for R. Allan; previously for Mrs S. Taylor; previously for W. Storey; previously for A. Batey, bought for 2000) r10 p1 (3rd) inc Sells. A veteran maiden who has no ability, and was certainly not improved by a six-year holiday. *Mrs N.K. Leggate — Jedforest.* 423 (R), 913 (CfMa).

BEAM ME UP SCOTTY (IRE) ..9-6.. 12 br.g. Orchestra — Bright Path (He Loves Me) pp. Small robust attractive. FLAT r22 w1 (12f, all-weather) p5 (inc Sell). NH '92/6 r29 w2 (2m2f Hdles, inc Sell) p8. P-t-p '98/9 r9 p2; last pair 3, pulled up 3, and fell 1. Won twice at Exeter in September '94, and has run some fair races in Points, but regularly fails to stay. Tried blinkered/visored in the past. Has dematerialised just three times in the last two seasons and been pulled up on each occasion. *Mrs K. Heard — N. Cornwall.* 537 (O), 1047 (Cf).

BEANS RIVER ..—.. 12 ch.g. Deep River — The Danstan (The Brianstan) pp. Half-brother to Two-Halfs, and to 2 flat winners. Dam won 5f Seller. P-t-p '99 r1 p0 (pulled up). A latecomer to racing, and has shown no aptitude for Pointing. *Mrs N.J. Bird — Worcs (Claire Dyson).* 191 (Cf), 613 (L).

BEAR CLAW ..10-4.. 12 b.g. Rymer — Carmarthen Honey (Eborneezer) 2p. Compact sparely-made brother to Hurdles winner, Cockpit Crew, and half-brother to top-class Hurdler, Cruising Altitude. Dam, quite useful, won 2 Ladies and placed 4. NH FLAT '94 r3 w2 p0. NH '94/5 r12 w4 (3 Hdles, 2m4f-2m5f, and 3m Ch) p4 (3rds); fell/unseated in 3 of 7 Chses. P-t-p '99 r5 w1 (Mixed Open) p3 (2nds); and refused 1. A former smart hurdler who completed a hat-trick in '95 by collecting the EBF Final at Cheltenham worth £22,665, but lost his way latterly under Rules. Runner-up in four of his seven Pointing ventures, but can be moody and may have suffered a setback when pulled up at Bishops Court in the first week of March. Suited by plenty of give in the ground, but will probably struggle to add to his solitary Open haul if he returns in 2001. Usually blinkered under Rules. *C.G. Roach — N. Cornwall.* 252 (O), 402 (O).

BEAR FACED ..8-0.. 8 b.g. Majestic Streak — Dizzy Dora (Rubor) p. Small owner-bred half-brother to Gladys (*qv*). P-t-p '99 r6 p1 (last of 3); pulled up 3, unseated 1, and ran out 1. Error-prone and generally awful to date, and always fails to take the eye in the paddock to boot. *Miss Z.A. Green — Cumberland.* 1362 (M).

BEAT THE BANK (IRE) ..8-13.. 6 br.g. Good Thyne (USA) — Must Clear (Al Sirat USA) 5. Tall rangy. Bought Doncaster, May for 13,000. Probably just testing the water when 25 lengths last on his debut. *C. Munro — Vine & Craven (John Porter).* 1021 (2m4fOMa).

BEAU JOUEUR (FR) ..—..§§.. 8 ch.g. Tagel (USA) — Bille En Tete (FR) (Green Dancer USA) ppp6. Sturdy. FRENCH FLAT r3 p0. FRENCH NH '96 r2 p0. P-t-p '99 (for Mrs J.H. Docker) r7 w1 (Maiden) p1 (nk and sh hd 3rd); and pulled up 5. Won a bad youngsters Maiden at Dingley, but overwhelmed by his Gallic temperament since, and seems to begrudge putting one foot in front of the other these days. Blinkered to no avail on his last five starts, during which time he has failed to beat a rival. The prizest of prize pigs, and should definitely remain in the poke. *D. Heath — Essex & Suffolk (Keith & Colin Coe).* 94 (O), 321 (R), 416 (R), 610 (R).

BEAUMONT (U) ..—.. 9 b.g. Shaab — Turtur Ni (unknown) up. Sparely-made. Dam, 2nd twice on flat, was subsequently 3rd in a Maiden for John Weldhen, but otherwise extremely mulish, and refused to race properly in all her other Points. Sent off second favourite for Members races at Trebudannon, but failed to complete, and jumped badly and only went a mile on the second occasion. If the owner decides to register his name he will need a change, as there is already a Beaumont currently performing under Rules. *J.F. Weldhen — Four Burrow, & S. Cornwall.* 1186 (M), 1384 (M).

BE BOP BENTLEY ..—.. 6 br.g. Arms And The Man — Playful Touch (Lepanto GER) ppp. Unfurnished. Dam, half-sister to Moonbribe (*qv* '90 Annual), pulled up 4, and fell 1 in Points. Very novicey at present and coming close to equalling his dam's record, but looks to have some physical scope, and may eventually do better if he can improve his jumping. *G. Phillips — Ystrad Taf Fechan (Debbie Hamer).* 267 (CfMa), 488 (CfMa), 648 (CfMa).

BE BRAVE ..9-6§.. 11 b.g. Never So Bold — Boo (Bustino) p54pb. Good-bodied. Dam is half-sister to Chickabiddy (*qv*). NH FLAT '94/5 (first 3 for C. Thornton) r4 p1 (2nd). NH '95/99 (blinkered/visored since '98; for T. Etherington, bought for 5400) r31 w3 (2m-2m1f Hdles, the last 2 Sells) p8 (inc 3rd once in 7 Chses; beaten head once, and neck once). Three Hurdling wins in soft included two Sellers in '99, but flattered, as he often finds nil and certainly does not live up to his name. Was outclassed behind some smart performers in Open company, and surprisingly did not wear headgear. Seems unlikely to do more than plod round in future. *R.S. Lochman & D. Parsons — York & Ainsty S.* 171 (O), 279 (O), 395 (O), 504 (O), 1231 (O).

BECK AND CALL (IRE) ..9-4.. 12 ch.g. Buckskin (FR) — Kilmurray Jet (Le Bavard FR) 73pp6. Lengthy half-brother to Lancastrian Jet (IRE) (subsequent Chasing winner). NH FLAT '94 r2 p1 (3rd). NH '94/5 and '97 r8 w1 (3m1f Hdle) p3 (3rds). P-t-P '99 r3 p2 (2nds); and last. A modest winning hurdler, but did well to split Gaysun and Play Poker at Lifton on his final '99 start, and looked a good thing to go one better. Has since looked most unenthusiastic, and never went a yard for his novice partner on his latest start. Acts on top of the ground, but can be clumsy, and has been tried in blinkers. Will need to perk up radically if he is to stage a revival at 12. *Mrs E. Target — Mrs M.A. Counsel — Blackmore & Sparkford V. (Rose Vickery; Miss H. Counsel).* 262 (MO), 475 (L), 885 (L), 1239 (L), 1550 (Cnr).

PLATE 22   356 West Somerset & Minehead Harriers Intermediate (Nov Rdrs): Belarus (C. White), 1st, resolutely ignores the crock of gold at the end of this Somerset rainbow

PHOTO: Brian Armstrong

BECKHILL LADY (IRE) ..—.. 10 b.m. Welsh Term — Early Blossom (The Canon) f. Unfurnished. IRISH P-t-P '98 r1 p0 (fell). P-t-P '99 r2 p0 (5th, and fell 1). Not without ability, but has fallen in each of her four races (remounted to finish last once), and David Turner will probably wear a parachute if they ever meet again. Capable of springing a surprise, but may have encountered trouble in the latest spill, and has never managed more than two outings in a season. *Mrs J.M. Bailey — R.A.* 213 (CfMa).

BEDTIME PIXIE ..9-4§.. 9 ch.g. Lir — Celerity Lady (Lighter) 53pp246pu. Half-brother to Budghill. P-t-P '97/9 r11 w1 (Maiden) p2; pulled up 3, and unseated 1. Rather fortunate to collect a Wadebridge Maiden in '99 as the likely winner fell when clear two out, but the success was not undeserved following several fair efforts. Has patently failed to put his best foot forward since, and his behaviour is becoming increasingly recalcitrant. Tends to get in a muck sweat in the preliminaries, and regularly blinkered in 2000. One to treat with extreme caution, and only consents to race (half-heartedly) when the ground rides fast. Not a horse on which to learn the art of race-riding. *D. Stephens — S. Cornwall, & Four Burrow.* 541 (I), 658 (R), 853 (Inr), 1042 (R), 1186 (M), 1384 (M), 1517 (R), 1608 (R), 1639 (R).

BEECHDOWN ..—.. 9 b.g. Arctic Lord — Save It Lass (Nicholas Bill) pff. Half-brother to Hurdles winner, Moonraker's Image. A clueless jumper, and his arm-waving partner Ryan must be totally blissed off with him. *R.K. Bliss — Avon V. (Michael Blake).* 211 (Cnr), 330 (R), 767 (R).

BEE MOY DO (IRE) ..9-0.. 13 b.g. Kambalda — Gentle Goose (Push On) p. Compact. IRISH NH FLAT r2 p1 (3rd). IRISH P-t-P '93/4 r5 w1 (6yo plus Maiden) p2; fell 2. NH '94-July '95 and '99 (for T. Caldwell in '99) r10 p2 (3rds); pulled up both Chses. P-t-P '96 (for Mr A.K. Leigh) r3 p1 (3rd); pulled up 1, and fell 1. Made all to record the only success of his career in Ireland but a headstrong sort who has run in a nosenet, and has shaped like a non-stayer since his arrival here.

Off the track for ages following his exploits in Wales, and has looked unfit in both his subsequent starts. Can be safely ignored if he reappears. *Mrs M. Thomas — Albrighton.* 293 (Cf).

BEHAVINGBADLY (IRE) ..—.. 6 b.g. Lord Americo — Audrey's Turn (Strong Gale) p. Half-borther to Irish Pointing winner, Ebony Reef. Bought Goffs, (Ireland), Jun for 13,392. Made early mistakes and never got into contention in an Intermediate, but would be worth another look when he drops to a Maiden. *R.A. Bartlett — Fife.* 973 (I).

BELAFONTE ..9-1-.. 14 br.g. Derrylin — Ulla Laing (Mummy's Pet) u6*880*. Small neat half-brother to flat winner, Domulla. Dam won 3 2-y-o races, 5-6f. 13,500y. FLAT (wins for late R. Holder at 3; placed 3 for D. Morley) r26 w3 (11-12f) p9. NH '91/6 and '98 (2 wins for Karen George, bought for 3600, inc 2 runs from J. White's; 2 wins previously for C. Brooks; 2 wins previously for late R. Holder, bought for 10,500) r31 w6 (3 Hdles, 2m-2m1f, and 3 Chses, 2m-2m7f), p4 (inc 2nd at San Siro in '93). NH Mar/May '00 r3 p0 (last in Sell Hdle: *sn bhnd*; 15th in Sell Hdle: *bhnd frm 6*; and 8th in Sell HCap Ch: *made most to 9, sn wknd*). Did more than his share of winning as a youngster, but hopeless in just five outings since May '96 (endured a 22 month absence before reappearing). Occasionally wore headgear in the past. Jumped badly in his Hunter Chase. *Miss K. George — Oxford.* 245 (L), 382 (2m4fH).

BELARUS (IRE) ..10-1§.. 9 b.g. Waajib — Kavali (Blakeney) 21222112. Workmanlike compact half-brother to Mr Busker (IRE), to Chasing winner, Careysville (IRE), and to Irish jumping winner Market Mover. NH '97/8 r8 p0 (pulled up only Ch). P-t-P '99 r6 w2 (Maiden and Restricted) p0; 6th, pulled up 2, and unseated 1. Did not like the hurly-burly of racing under Rules, but has taken to Pointing, and enjoyed a fruitful campaign in 2000. Likes to dominate, and can battle willingly when inclined, but the blinkers he wears are no fashion accessory, and is not an armchair ride. A thorough stayer (the Dartmoor four-miler held no terrors for him), and appears to handle all ground alike. Got going too late on his Hunter Chase debut (probably should have won in hindsight, though not aided by the favourite falling in front of him three out), but otherwise ridden more than adequately by Charlie White. Capable of winning again in minor company. *Mrs S. Ashburner — Dulverton E. (Tessa White).* 142 (I), 356 (Inr), 638 (Cf), 1044 (4mO), 1260 (O), 1471 (Cnr), 1604 (M), 1626 (3m1f110yH).

BEL-DE-MOOR ..10-1.. 9 br.m. Macmillion — Bel Creation (Creative Plan USA) 416u2. Lengthy unfurnished. Dam won 2m Hdle. NH FLAT '96 r3 p1 (21*l* 3rd). NH '96/8 r9 p0; inc Sells. P-t-P '99 r4 w1 (Maiden) p3 (2 3rds, of 4 once). Gained her latest success in fortuitous circumstances as J'Accuse was clear when unseating at the last, but luck was against her subsequently, and the rider was knocked out of the plate by a loose horse when looking likely to succeed at Pentreclwydau. Out of her depth in the Hunter Chase arena, but a willing partner for Tim Vaughan, and should win again in her turn. Seems to act on any going. *Mrs J. Howells — Llangeinor (William Howells).* 483 (R), 744 (R), 1022 (3mH), 1299 (I), 1615 (I).

BELITLIR ..10-0.. 9 b.m. Lir — Kimberley Ann (St Columbus) 22122. Small neat home-bred sister to The Kimbler (*qv*). P-t-P/HUNT CH '97/9 r25 w1 (Maiden) p7 (5 3rds, last once); pulled up 13. A game little mare who finally gained a Restricted success at the 13th attempt when landing a bit of a touch at Flete Park. Becoming most adept at course completion, ploughs through soft ground and is a reliable jumper, so will probably find another minor race. *B.R.J. Young, Miss S. Young & Mrs K. Rogers - E. Cornwall (Sue Young).* 1043 (R), 1176 (R), 1258 (R), 1607 (I), 1651 (I).

BEL LANE ..10-1§.. 12 b.m. Brotherly (USA) — Bow Lane (Idiot's Delight) 5p42f. Compact half-sister to Peppermill Lane. P-t-P/HUNT CH '95/9 r25 w2 (Maiden and Members) p8 (5 2nds, last after refusing once; and 2 3rds in Hunt Chses); failed to finish 9 (refused 1, and unseated 1). Galvanised by the application of a visor when successful for the first time, but connections presumably lost them in the tack room as they were not used again for another 17 starts. Should have won when similarly equipped at Llanfrynach, but dogged it furiously after the last, and was assured of victory (possibly not, knowing her) when tipping up for the first time in her career at Howick. Presumably injured in her tumble as she failed to reappear. Would theoretically be a good thing for a Restricted if she returned, though her supporters have long been inmates of the poor house, and she will doubtless let them down again. *M.R. Watkins — S. Herefords (Christine Hardinge).* 3 (L), 222 (3m1f110yH), 336 (R), 486 (R), 595 (R).

BELLDORAN ..—.. 10 ch.g. Gildoran — Bellecana (Take A Reef) pp. Robust half-brother to Chasing winner, Ceridwen. NH FLAT Jan/Feb '96 r2 p0. NH '96/8 (for T. Greathead; previously for C.H. Jones) r5 p0 (tailed off and pulled up only Ch). Stands his racing very badly, carries a lot of condition, and has displayed no ability. Appeared to suffer yet another setback when pulled up and dismounted in the first mile on his latest appearance. *P.A. Britten — Croome & W. Warwicks (Harry Wheeler).* 514 (OMa), 1068 (3m2fOMa).

BELLS HILL LAD ..9-7.. 14 ch.g. Buckskin (FR) — Laiton Peni (Laurence O) 2. Angular brother to My Last Buck, and NH flat and jumping winner, Shagreen (IRE). IRISH NH '92/3 r8 p1 (3rd) NH '93/8 (from J. Barclay's, bought for 8000) r19 w1 (2m7f Hdle) p4 (4 or 5 finished each inc 2 3rds in Chses). Beat Scotton Banks by a neck in soft when gaining the sole win of his long career, but that dates way back to December '93. Fat when revived for a jolly in his Members, and plugged home last of two behind the other Alexander runner. *M. Alexander — Fife.* 1117 (M).

BELLS LIFE (IRE) ..11-7.. 12 b.g. The Parson — Affability (Royal Buck) 11. Compact good-bodied half-brother to Irish Pointing winner, Yakity Yak. Dam, half-sister to Afterkelly (qv 2000 Annual), won 2m Hdle in Ireland. IRISH NH FLAT '93/4 r2 w1 p0. IRISH NH '93/5 r7 w2 (2 2m4f Hdles) p2 (2nds). NH '95/7 and '99 (bought for 25,000) r20 w7 (2m5f Hdle, and Chses, 2m4f-2m6f, inc hat-trick '96) p4; pulled up Grand National final start. A classy performer at up to 2m6f (unproven over further, although he has tried longer trips on several occasions), but never able to run much, and had not scored under Rules since capturing the '97 John Hughes Chase over the Aintree National course, a race in which he triumphed despite having been badly hampered by loose horses at the Elbow and nearly squeezed into the Chair. Having only his fifth outing since when he sauntered home against vastly inferior opponents at Bangor, but then returned to Aintree for a great triumph in the 26-runner Foxhunters, in which he was given an excellent ride by David O'Meara, and was always carrying too many guns for Secret Bay. The £15,015 prize took his career earnings to £77,422, and is a fine tribute to the training of Philip Hobbs, who had to endure some nerve-racking moments on the eve of the big race when his charge was found to be suffering from a poisoned foot. Needs good or easy surfaces, and is not risked on firm. Has never fallen, and might still be able to compete successfully at the top level at 12. *R. Gibbs — Taunton V. (Philip Hobbs).* 153 (2m4f110yH), 921 (2m6fH).

PLATE 23   921 Martell Foxhunters HC, Aintree: Bells Life (D. O'Meara), 1st, is clear at the last
PHOTO: Steven Cargill

BELLS WOOD ..10-6.. 12 br.g. Sousa — Virtuosity (Reliance II) 12u333211. Neat. NH '96/7 and '99 r9 p1 (3rd of 4); pulled up 3, fell/unseated 3. P-t-P/HUNT CH '96 and '99 (for Mrs P.A. Dunn) r9 w2 (Maiden and Restricted) p2 (2nds); pulled up 3, and fell/unseated 2. Of little account over regulation fences where his jumping was not up to scratch, but his new connections concentrated their efforts on Points, and predictably reaped the dividends with three Open victories, although he is rather flattered by his defeat of Butler John. Stays well, and is best suited by plenty of cut in the ground though can handle quicker conditions. Insulted by blinkers once in '99. May be able to win again in 2001 — at an early Black Forest Lodge fixture? *C.A.L. White — Minehead H. (Tessa White).* 68 (O), 200 (O), 351 (M), 561 (O), 1098 (C), 1371 (Cf), 1473 (Cf), 1606 (O), 1653 (O).

BELSKI ..9-5§.. 8 br.g. Arctic Lord — Bellekino (Relkino) p255p54f. Lengthy unfurnished half-brother to Telephone. Dam won 5 Sell Hdles at around 2m. P-t-P '98/9 r10 w1 (Maiden) p1 (head 2nd); fell 3, and pulled up 5. Made the perfect start to his Pointing career when landing a gamble in a long race in softish at Lemalla, but a major disappointment since, and is clearly temperamentally unsound. Has been last or failed to finish in 11 of his last 13 outings, but surely worth trying in headgear as he does possess a fair degree of ability. Goes best fresh, and can probably be ignored after a couple of outings in 2001. *S.W. Dusting — Taunton V. (Kay Rees & Polly Curling).* 69 (R), 203 (R), 536 (R), 850 (R), 1042 (R), 1240 (R), 1375 (R), 1467 (R).

PLATE 24   1653 Exmoor Mens Open: Bells Wood (C. White), 1st, just leads the bespattered Starpath (N. Mitchell), 2nd, at the fourth last   PHOTO: Tim Holt

PLATE 25   1375 Devon & Somerset Staghounds Restricted (Div 1): L to R Hemero (A. Honeyball), 6th, and Belski (R. Woollacott), 4th, have a private duel in midfield
                    PHOTO: Brian Armstrong

BELVENTO (IRE) ..10-6.. 9 b.g. Strong Gale — Salufair (Salluceva) u1f11. Half-brother to NH flat winner, Mister Sandrovitch (IRE). Dam is half-sister to Random Traveller (*qv* '93 Annual). NH FLAT Dec '96 r1 p0. NH '97/9 (from J. Gifford's) r8 p0 (inc last, pulled up and fell in Chses — moderate jumper). Did not show any aptitude for racing under Rules, but much more at home in Points, and generally jumped well apart from a couple of blips. A real galloper who was confidently handled when winning three modest races decisively, and should certainly have scope to score again as he rises in grade. Could be worth trying in a Maiden Hunter Chase. His young trainer Nick Gifford made a splendid start in his first season, and will surely take over the reins from father Josh with great success eventually. *Mrs J. Plackett — Crawley & Horsham (Nick Gifford).* 126 (R), 221 (OMa), 306 (R), 711 (M), 1393 (R).

BEN BUCKLEY ..9-6.. 9 b.g. Buckley — Koritsaki (Strong Gale) 36. Sturdy. Dam was unbeaten in 2 Points, and subsequently won 2 2m4f Hdles; also placed total of 4, inc 2 Chses. P-t-P '99 r3 p0 (pulled up 2, and fell 1). Out of a decent mare (the sire is a worry though), but struggling to get the trip to date, and his infrequent trips to the racecourse do not augur well. *J.C. Hogg — Buccleuch.* 46 (OMa), 188 (OMa).

BENBULBIN (IRE) ..8-10§.. 11 b.g. Supreme Leader — Loose Key (Distinctly USA) p5633u7p. Workmanlike half-brother to Balancer and Willow Brook (IRE). Dam won Irish NH flat. IRISH P-t-P '94 r2 p2 (2nds, last once). NH '95/8 r17 p5 (3rds); pulled up 5, unseated 4, and refused 1. P-t-P '95 and '99 (for Mr C.D. Tilly & Mr J.W. Mullins) r6 p2 (2nds); unseated 1, and refused 1. NH Jun '00 (from R.J. Smith's) r1 p0 (pulled up in Nov Ch: *mist 5, chsd ldrs to 9, mist 11, t.o & pu 3 out*). A real softie who seems determined to remain a maiden despite having run in 32 races. Visored latterly under Rules (also tried blinkered) in his last six Points, and must be kept at arms length as far as punting is concerned. *R.M. Bluck — N. Cotswold (Jon Trice-Rolph; R.J. Smith).* 75 (I), 194 (CfMa), 617 (CMa), 790 (OMa), 1189 (M), 1359 (OMa), 1435 (OMa).

BENDOR MARK ..9-12.. 12 b.g. Lighter — Montana (Mossborough) 42p5. Workmanlike half-brother to Alabama and Iowa, and to flat and Hurdles winner, Wisconsin, and to a winner in Sweden. NH '94/8 r19 w2 (2m5f-3m Chses) p5 (inc 3rd in Hdle). P-t-P/HUNT CH '99 r4 w1 (Confined) p2 (2nd of 3; and last of 3); and pulled up 1. Ultimately disappointing under Rules, and an expensive investment for current connections as he has managed to recoup about £200 of his 8000 gns purchase price. Only once better than last in 2000 when his rating dropped by seven pounds, and future prospects do not seem rosy. *R. & Mrs M. Hand — Lamerton (Mandy Hand).* 1045 (L), 1385 (Cf), 1514 (Cf), 1636 (Cf).

BEND SABLE (IRE) ..9-12.. 11 b.g. Mtoto — Chrism (Baptism) ff. Compact good-bodied half-brother to 3 flat winners (2 abroad), including Eagle Canyon. FLAT r6 p0. NH '93/8 r38 w4 (2m-2m6f Hdles) p13. P-t-P '99 r2 p0 (last pair twice). Gained all four victories including a hat-trick in '94, but never tried over three miles under Rules, and has failed to stay in Points. Presumably suffering wear and tear after a hectic career as a youngster, and disappeared after trying to bend Sally Duckett for the second week running in February. Beaten in his last 29 races, and likely to extend the sequence if he reappears. *G. Deacon & N.D. Quesnel — Berks & Bucks (Geoffrey Deacon).* 245 (L), 326 (L).

BENEFIT-IN-KIND (IRE) ..9-5.. 9 br.g. Executive Perk — Tanarpa (Dusky Boy) 471p. Big workmanlike half-brother to Manor Ranger. Dam won 3 Irish Chses, 2m4f-2m6f. 23,000 4-y-o. NH FLAT Dec '96 r1 p1 (2nd). NH 98/9 (for Miss H. Knight) r5 p2 (distant last of 2 and 2 fences last of 3 in Chses). Disappointingly slow in the previous yard and hardly ever able to run, but found a Maiden much more appropriate, and ploughed through the mud at Corbridge to win readily. Soon in trouble again, and was pulled up lame on final start. *P.W. Henman & A. Scott — Jedforest (Rhona Elliot).* 107 (M), 718 (CfMa), 1163 (OMa), 1365 (O).

BEN FROM KETTON ..—§.. 6 b.g. Cruise Missile — Saucy Girl (Saucy Kit) pu5R36r. Tall plain. Bought Malvern, May for 2000. Shows early speed, but unsurprisingly already sickened by the rider thrashing around ineptly in the saddle, and is desperately seeking an escape route now. Gives the impression that he might achieve something for a sympathetic and competent jockey. *S.J. Robinson — Zetland.* 139 (OMa), 168 (OMa), 379 (OMa), 625 (OMa), 1002 (2m4fOMa), 1331 (OMa), 1581 (2m4fOMa).

BEN GILMORE ..9-3.. 7 b.g. Derrylin — Sweet Ryme (Rymer) p3p3pp. Strong-topped. Dam is an unraced half-sister to Star Changes (*qv*), who is by Derrylin. Grandam, Sweet Linda, won Members and placed 7. P-t-P '99 r3 p0 (7th, pulled up 1, and brought down 1). Has been backward and novicey, but a fair third at Clifton-on-Dunsmore, and a potential winner if he can find some extra stamina in his third season. Top of the ground might be essential to him. *Mrs M. Kimber — Grafton (Simon Gilmore).* 618 (CMa), 889 (OMa), 1204 (OMa), 1423 (OMa), 1486 (OMa), 1624 (OMa).

BENN WOOD ..—.. 6 b.g. Green Adventure (USA) — Greenhill's Girl (Radetzky) pupupp. Small neat half-brother to Hurdles winner, Sail On Sid. Dam won at 5f, and won 2m Sell Hdle. NH May '00 r2 p0 (tailed off and pulled up in Nov Hdles). A difficult ride and as green as grass so far, and has a great deal of improving to do if he is to achieve anything. *Mrs D.R. Brotherton — Middleton (Serena Brotherton; Sue Smith).* 380 (OMa), 398 (OMa), 508 (CMa), 793 (CfMa).

BENOVA BOY ..9-4.. 9 ch.g. Ra Nova — Alithorne (Kinglet) p2d6p274. Big strong half-brother to Broad-Thorne. Dam, half-sister to Bear's Flight (*qv* '98 Annual), won Maiden and placed 5 (raced latterly for Brian Gurney). P-t-P '99 r5 w1 (Maiden) p0; last pair 2, unseated 1, and pulled up 1. Looked an interesting prospect when successful at Brocklesby Park in '99, but has not progressed, and seems held in check by his volcanic temperament — appears on the verge of erupting in the paddock, and usually arrives awash with sweat with two handlers in tow. Good enough to win a Restricted on his best behaviour, and it is probably worth retaining the blinkers on a regular basis in future. *Mr & Mrs L. Owen & B. Gurney — Grafton (Simon Gilmore).* 80 (CCfR), 248 (R), 513 (CR), 887 (R), 1206 (R), 1418 (R), 1623 (R).

BENSON (IRE) ..9-0.. 6 b br.g. Hawkstone (IRE) — Erin St Helen (IRE) (Seclude USA) 3. Big good-looking. Sold Doncaster, May for 6600. Odds-on for his debut, but gave a novicey display, and finished 35 lengths third. Likely to benefit substantially from the experience, and should recoup losses. *H. Daly — Ludlow (Andrew Dalton).* 990 (OMa).

BE ON THE SLY ..—.. 12 ch.m. Battle Hymn — Bonny Meld (Charlottown) r. Neat attractive half-sister to Swillbrook Lad. P-t-P '99 r1 p0 (refused). Twice foiled by the first at Guilsborough when in no fit state to be at the races. *P.J. Walton — Pytchley.* 1005 (M).

BERMUDA BUCK ..—.. 15 b.g. Quayside — Lougharue (Deep Run) p3. Half-brother to Our Survivor, to Irish NH flat and Hurdles and English jumping winner, Trimleigh, and to successful Irish Hurdler, Lay One On Ya (IRE). IRISH NH FLAT '92 r2 w1 p1 (2nd). IRISH NH '92/7 r37 w4 (2 Hdles, 2m4f-3m, and 2 3m Chses) p9. IRISH P-t-P '98 r5 p2 (2nds, beaten neck once, and last once); pulled up 2, and unseated 1. P-t-P '99 r3 p0 (fell/unseated 2, and pulled up 1). Enjoyed a long and rewarding career in Ireland, but had declined badly in the current year, and sadly collapsed and died after finishing a remote third in his Members. *A.J. Davenhill — N. Staffs (Jackie Moule).* 565 (O), 1124 (M).

BERTIE BAVARD ..—§§.. 9 ch.g. Le Bavard (FR) — Acushla Macree (Mansingh USA) prr7. Small half-brother to Hurdles winner, Too Clever By Half. Dam won 4 flat, 8-10f, inc 2 Sells, and 2m1f Hdle for G. Johnson-Houghton. NH FLAT '97 r2 p0; also withdrawn not under orders after bolting once. NH '98 r1 p0 (tongue-tied when pulled up in Hdle, after hanging badly all way). NH APr '00 r1 p0 (7th in Mdn Hdle: *prom to 4 out*). A horrible little thing who has absolutely no intention of trying, and a nightmare ride for his partners. *Mrs R.F. Johnson Houghton — O. Berks (R.F. Johnson Houghton).* 63 (I), 309 (OMa), 754 (CM).

BERTIES LANDING ..—.. 7 ch.g. Safawan — Miss Pisces (Salmon Leap USA) p. Close-coupled ewe-necked brother to Young Saffy (*qv*). NH FLAT '99 (for Mrs M. Reveley) r4 p0. Bought Doncaster, June for 550. Looked a hopeless case on his Pointing debut. *M. Plant — Cheshire.* 588 (OMa).

BERUDE NOT TO (IRE) ..10-7.. 12 b.g. Roselier (FR) — Decent Debbie (Decent Fellow) p4. Well-made half-brother to Harry Lauder (IRE). NH FLAT Spr '94 r2 w2. NH '94/8 (for O. Sherwood) r15 w7 (4 Hdles, 2m1f-2m5f, and 3 3m Chses) p3 (2nds, short-headed once, and headed in final strides of £41,824 Sun Alliance Nov Hlde); last, and pulled up final 2, only runs since '97. A cracking performer in his early career, and was unbeaten in his first six races, and only once missed the frame in his first 15. Earned a total of £76,515, but has obviously had major training difficulties since '97, and in the circumstances did quite well to finish 17 lengths fourth over 4m1f at Cheltenham. Usually blinkered nowadays. May have to dine out on golden memories in future. *J. & Miss B. Cullen, Miss M. Malgrin & P. Moore — Portman (Ali Tory).* 1133 (O), 1338 (4m1fH).

BEST BITTER ..9-7.. 7 b.g. Petoski — Panda Pops (Cornuto) puf224. Workmanlike compact owner-bred half-brother to Badger Beer (*qv*). NH FLAT '98 r2 p0 (tailed off last twice). P-t-P '99 r5 w1 (Maiden) p0; pulled up 2, and fell/unseated 2. All out to win a Maiden in a slow time at Holnicote in '99, and like his half-brother is a very weak finisher. Beaten at least 30 lengths in his 2000 placings, and even fails to last home when the ground rides firm. *Mrs R.H. Woodhouse — Portman (John Dufosee).* 38 (CR), 208 (R), 330 (R), 767 (R), 1058 (M), 1376 (R).

BETHS GIFT ..8-9.. 8 ch.m. Blaze O'Gold (USA) — Lyns Legend (Marengo) uu6243. Small compact quite attractive half-sister to Lynwood Lad, Lyns Magic and Lyningo. Dam won 2 2m Hdles (inc Sell). NH FLAT Spr '98 r2 p0. NH '99 (for breeder, Colin Price) r1 p0. Bought Malvern, Sep for 1500. Beaten half a length in her first placing (the probable winner was knocked over at the last), but has not appeared to stay well when beaten more than 30 lengths since. Might struggle home in front eventually, but it would have to be a bad contest. *E. Ford — Tredegar F. (Lyndon Williams).* 145 (OMa), 348 (CfMa), 491 (CfMa), 823 (CfMa), 1223 (2m4fOMa), 1454 (OMa).

BETTER FUTURE (IRE) ..10-3§.. 12 br.g. Good Thyne — Little Else (Abednego) 82p. Smallish compact. IRISH P-t-P '94/5 r10 w2 p3; pulled up 3. NH '97 r4 p0 (tailed off in Chses — pulled up final). P-t-P '96 and '98/9 r16 w9 (inc 6 Opens and 4m Open, hat-trick '98) p4 (3 3rds, last once); and pulled up 3. Formerly useful on his day and ideally suited by a stamina test in mud, but tends to jump deliberately, and can look totally disinterested in proceedings as he has on his last five appearances. Due another change of heart, but has always been a highly risky betting proposition, and one to treat with caution if he returns. *C.J. Hitchings — Kyre (Gerald Dartnall).* 34 (MO), 700 (O), 1065 (3m2fO).

BET WITH BAKER (IRE) ..10-0.. 11 br.g. Ovac (ITY) — Moate Gypsy (Fine Blade USA) 45pp. Lengthy workmanlike half-brother to Chasing winner, Tuckers Town (IRE). P-t-P '96/8 r15 w7 (inc 2 Opens, inc hat-trick '98) p5 (3 2nds, beaten neck once, and last once); pulled up 2, and unseated 1. The speedy winner of seven races and looked all geared up for another successful season following a promising reappearance at Larkhill after a year off, but performed dismally on his Hunter Chase debut, and presumably went wrong at Bishops Court. Has shown a propensity to jump or edge right, and clearly has big problems to overcome. *G.W. Baker — Mendip F. (Richard Barber).* 10 (O), 61 (MO), 222 (3m1f110yH), 402 (O).

BE UPSTANDING ..9-11.. 6 ch.g. Hubbly Bubbly (USA) — Two Travellers (Deep Run) 1u. Rangy home-bred half-brother to Minden Rose (qv). Sold Doncaster, Nov for 2000, but returned. Won a slowly-run two-finisher Maiden in soft at Thorpe, but lacked fluency before unseating after a mile next time. Did well to make a winning start, and may be able to justify his rating in Restricteds. *M. Holmes — Belvoir (Helen Harvey).* 1220 (OMa), 1588 (I).

BEX BOY (IRE) ..—.. 10 ch.g. Mon Tresor — Calcine (Roan Rocket) 3. Leggy half-brother to several winners, including Viking Rocket (jumping). FLAT (blinkered latterly; inc Sell) r10 p2 (3rds). NH '94/5 r3 p0. P-t-P '97 (for Mr C. Warde-Aldam) r3 p0 (fell/unseated 3). Useless. Previously an awful jumper, but at least finally managed a Pointing completion when two fences third of four in his Members. *Mrs D. Fletcher — Badsworth (Katie Fletcher).* 166 (M).

BEYOND THE STARS ..9-12.. 10 b.g. Jupiter Island — MCA Lucky Star (Lucky Wednesday) 625p. Compact good-bodied half-brother to Mr Bumble. Dam won at 5f, but proved a madam after. FLAT r1 p0 (last). NH '94/6 (blinkered 1) and '97 r11 p2; inc last 6, and pulled up 2. P-t-P/HUNT CH '97/9 r5 w1 (Members) p1 (2nd); pulled up 2, and fell 1. Possesses the ability to win a Restricted, but incredibly lightly raced (has had leg problems), and may well have suffered another setback at Stratford. Has only completed once in four Hunter Chases, and should concentrate on Points with if he is able to return in 2001. *M.G. Rimell — Heythrop.* 580 (3mH), 894 (R), 993 (R), 1443 (3mH).

B FOR BUSINESS ..—.. 6 ch.m. Nicholas Bill — Little Beaver (Privy Seal) uRp. Plain light half-sister to Sharp Seal. Dam, half-sister to Dan De Lyon (qv '99 Annual), was 3rd in a Point, but subsequently won 2m Chse, and was also placed in 2 Hdles and 5 Chses. Had a torrid first season, which ended when she injured herself and had to be removed by horse ambulance. *Mrs W.S. Cook — N. Cornwall.* 723 (CfMa), 857 (CfMa), 1520 (CfMa).

BID FOR TOOLS (IRE) ..9-0§§.. 9 b.g. Don't Forget Me — Running Feud (Prince Tenderfoot USA) pr6u3pp. Close-coupled half-brother to George Ashford (IRE), and to Irish flat winner, Baby Elegance. NH FLAT '96 r3 p0. NH '96/7 r2 p0 (pulled up in 2 Hdles; blinkered final). P-t-P '98/9 (for Mr A. Witcomb in '99) r7 p1 (2nd); refused 2, and pulled up 3. Utterly ungenuine for three different Pointing yards, and shirks the issue as soon as hard work looms. Blinkered or visored nowadays, and would be a most undeserving winner. *Mr & Mrs M. Ewing — Ledbury (Debby Ewing).* 145 (OMa), 337 (CfMa), 669 (R), 792 (OMa), 1099 (OMa), 1468 (OMa), 1624 (OMa).

BIG BARK (IRE) ..9-7.. 9 b.g. Cataldi — Winter Cherry (Brave Invader USA) uf321. IRISH P-t-P '99 r1 p0 (pulled up). Lacks acceleration, but has been consistent in Maidens, and kept on steadily to open his account on firmish at Mosshouses. Seems to do best when trainer-ridden. Should at least get placed in Restricteds. *T.R.P.S. Norton — College V. & N. Northumberland (Clive Storey).* 182 (M), 424 (R), 624 (OMa), 914 (CfMa), 1430 (OMa).

BIG HORN (IRE) ..—.. 7 b.g. Little Bighorn — Fast Girl (IRE) (Tumble Gold) p. Lost a great deal of ground at the start and was always lagging on a May debut. Might do better if willing to extend himself. *P. Sadler — Rockwood H. (Stephen Wiles).* 1331 (OMa).

BIG SEAMUS (IRE) ..9-10§.. 11 ch.g. Carlingford Castle — Galla's Pride (Quayside) 13. Big strong. IRISH P-t-P '95 r4 p0 (pulled up 4). P-t-P '96/9 r18 w2 (Maiden and Restricted) p6 (4 2nds, last once; and last of 3); pulled up 5, and fell/unseated 2. Made the most of a simple opportunity when successful in his Members (his first win since '96), but consistently finds nothing off the bridle, and has generally stood few outings. Wears blinkers. *Mrs J.M. Whitley — S. Devon (John Bragg).* 556 (M), 1097 (Inr).

BILBO BAGGINS (IRE) ..—§.. 13 ch.g. Beau Charmeur (FR) — Hiking (Royal Highway) fp. Tall half-brother to Lennel Bank. NH FLAT r1 p0. NH '92/3 (blinkered 1) r6 p0. P-t-P/HUNT CH '95/9 r30 w3 (inc Mixed Open) p3 (2 2nds, last once); fell/unseated 2, and pulled up 5. Completed a double on firm for current connections in '97, but lacking in enthusiasm since and beaten in his last 13 starts — generally tailed off. Only once better than last '99/2000, and not worth bothering with again. Occasionally blinkered. *Mrs P.A. Tetley & Lady E. Huntly — Surrey U. (Brian Tetley).* 707 (L), 883 (Cf).

BILLIEBURN ..—.. 7 ch.g. Henbit (USA) — Birniebrig (New Brig) pfp. Strong half-brother to Chasing winner, Taramoss. Dam, half-sister to Earls Brig and Bronzeknowe, won a Maiden and 2nd 3 (inc 2 Chses; all her starts over fences). Grandam, Naughty Tara, won Maiden and Hunt Ch and 2nd thrice (after unseating once) — fell in 8 of her 14 races. May have some ability, but a frightful menace in the preliminaries, and invariably goes loopy and has twice got rid of Luke Morgan at the start. Fell three out when three lengths second once and injured him, and collided with George Moscrop's horse next time, causing him to be hit on the head, he fell off later when probably barely conscious. No wonder Doreen Calder never partners him! *Miss D.M.M. Calder — Berwicks.* 365 (CfMa), 978 (CfMa), 1431 (OMa), 1582 (2m4fOMa).

BILLIE'S MATE (IRE) ..10-0.. 10 b.m. Roselier (FR) — Toevarro (Raga Navarro ITY) 58p11. Small half-sister to NH flat and jumping winner, Beatson (IRE), to Irish NH flat winner, Geray Lady, and to jumping winner, Misty Class (IRE). Dam won Irish NH flat, and is half-sister to Weddicar Lady (*qv* '97 Annual). IRISH NH FLAT '95/6 r3 p0. IRISH NH '96/8 r10 p0 (finished in all 3 Hunt Chses). IRISH P-t-P '97/8 r8 w2 (Mares Maiden, and Winners of Three) p2; pulled up 2. NH'98/9 (for J. Portman, bought for 8500) r10 p0. Takes absolutely no interest under Rules, and needs plenty of kidding in Points, but was left a lucky winner at Rodmell, and then seemed ideally suited by Peper Harow when scoring on her merits under an enterprising ride from Jenny Grant. Wears headgear, and has not consented to race properly on the two occasions Jamie Hawksfield partnered her. *Mrs P.J. Hawksfield — Crawley & Horsham (Ian Cobb).* 289 (Cm), 573 (CfL), 711 (M), 1212 (Cf), 1398 (Cf).

BILL OF RIGHTS ..8-7§.. 13 b.g. Nicholas Bill — Cold Line (Exdirectory) 6. Small neat half-brother to NH flat and Hurdles winner, Give Best. Dam won at 12f. NH FLAT '92 and '94 r3 p0. P-t-P/HUNT CH '96/4 r4 p0 (last 2, and pulled up 2). NH '96 and '98 r5 p0 (last 2, and pulled up 2). NH '96 and '98 r5 p1 (3rd); unruly and withdrawn not under orders once. Very lightly raced and quirky throughout his undistinguished career, and promptly went back into hiding after finishing a remote last at Buckfastleigh. Might have achieved something tangible had he been sensibly placed in the past, but having a mind of his own hasn't helped. *Mrs E.B. Scott — Weston & Banwell H.* 652 (MO).

BILL'S INTEGRITY ..8-4.. 6 b.m. Bold Fox — Emlyn Princess (Julio Mariner) fp5p. Small compact sister to Hurdles winner, Gallant Taffy. Dam won her first 4 Hdles (2m-2m2f), and won 2 Chses (2m), but became reluctant to start latterly. Beaten over 20 lengths when completing, and seems to have inherited her dam's temperament, but none of her ability. Has been taken to post early, and blinkered on her latest outing. *W.E. Prichard — Glamorgan (Evan Williams).* 602 (CfMa), 1301 (OMa), 1457 (OMa), 1617 (OMa).

BILL TO FOLLOW (IRE) ..—.. 8 br.g. Roi Guillaume (FR) — Follow Lightly (Light Thrust) p. Small lengthy half-brother to Ojonnyo (IRE), to an Irish flat and Hurdles winner, and to Irish Chasing winner, Follow Lion. IRISH P-t-P '99 r7 p0 (6th, last, pulled up 2, and fell/unseated 3). IRISH NH FLAT '99 r1 p0. IRISH NH '99 r1 p0 (pulled up in Hdle). Bought Doncaster, Aug for 1100. Dismal so far, and only jumped two fences before pulling up in February. Neatly named. *K.C. Lewis — Gelligaer F.* 340 (R).

BILLY BLAKENEY ..10-3.. 8 b.g. Baron Blakeney — Flaxen Tina (Beau Tudor) 2. Half-brother to Mister Kingston. Dam won 8 Chses (2m-3m1f) for Colin Gee. P-t-P '99 r2 p1 (3rd). Displayed ability in both his '99 starts and again when runner-up at Tweseldown (with three subsequent winners well behind him), but failed to reappear, and is clearly extremely fragile. Will hopefully return to face a full season in 2001. *Mrs S. Gee — Pytchley (Caroline Bailey).* 7 (OMa).

BILLY WHIZZ ..—.. 10 ch.g. Push On — Dougy Bunny (Bunny Boy) ppp. Compact owner-bred. P-t-P '98 r3 p0 (pulled up 3). Returned from a bout of lameness as consistently pathetic as he was before. Has shown speed for up to two miles, but then Billy wheezes. *Mrs D.M. Hoe — V. of Clettwr (Emlyn Rhodes).* 268 (CfMa), 349 (CfMa), 485 (R).

BIN FISHIN (IRE) ..—.. 6 b.g. Gone Fishin — Toranoda (Torenaga) f. Medium-sized. Dam is sister to Prince of Baroda (*qv* '93 Annual). Backed from 14s to sevens at Garthorpe, and ran a tidy race until weakening and falling two out, but sadly suffered fatal injuries. *Mrs I. Hodge — Puckeridge (Sam Hodge).* 872 (OMa).

BIRCH TOR ..7-0.. 8 b.g. Access Travel — Two Parts (Pardigras) p6. Strong. Dam won South Devon Members and placed 10 for Mrs Irish ('tends to run ungenuine ... goes best for the owner'). Very green and hopelessly tailed off twice, including when (remarkably) managing to be 25 lengths behind one partnered by Dawn Mitchell. Fractious in the paddock on his debut. *Mrs S.L. Irish — S. Devon.* 656 (OMa), 721 (CfMa).

BIRD ..—.. 10 gr.m. Habs Lad — Abdication (Nickel King) p. Dam is sister to In The Clink, and half-sister to Hand Out (*qv* '98 Annual). Grandam, Stolen Ember, refused 2 and fell 3 in Points. Tailed off and pulled up after a mile on a belated debut. *E. Wonnacott — Spooners & W. Dartmoor.* 658 (R).

BIRDIETOO ..—.. 9 ch.m. Nad Elshiba (USA) — Wylie Hill VII (unknown) ppf. Angular. NH FLAT '96 r1 p0. P-t-P '99 (for Mr N. Wakefield) r2 p0 (unseated 1, and pulled up 1). Used to bolt under a novice rider in the previous yard, and has yet to even look likely to complete. Remains a poor jumper, appears to have stamina limitations, and is still a waste of time. Taken to post early once. *Mrs L.J. Matthews — Cottesmore.* 367 (Cf), 547 (CfMa), 775 (OMa).

BISHOPS HALL ..10-7.. 15 br.g. Pimpernels Tune — Mariner's Dash (Master Buck) 2241f. Rangy half-brother to Marathon Man and Jolly Boat, to Irish Chasing winner, What Do You Know, and to Irish NH flat and Hurdles winner, Knockerra. IRISH NH FLAT Nov '90 r2 p0. IRISH NH '90/9 r67 w10 (2m4f-3m1f Chses; inc £27,900 Kerry National and £16,350 prize) p11 (inc £9625 when 2nd in Galway Plate); fell at 1st in '95 Grand National. NH '96/7 (for R. Alner) r7 w1 (3m2f Ch) p1 (2nd); unseated 1st and pulled up in Grand National. IRISH P-t-P '99 r1 p1 (2nd — caught 50yds out). A lovely old horse who has enjoyed a splendid career, and has crossed the Irish Sea many times, but was gaining a first success for four years when he scored at Weston Park. Unlucky not to follow up at Chaddesley, where he fell at the final fence when just in front. It seemed to take the new stable a while to clear out his tubes, but retains plenty of enthusiasm, and there seems no reason to suppose that he could not score again if returned at 15. *G. Samuel — N. Salop (Sheila Crow)*. 176 (O), 779 (O), 902 (Cf), 1408 (Cf), 1630 (Cf).

BITOFABUZZ (IRE) ..—.. 10 b.g. Electric — Dowdstown Miss (Wolver Hollow) fpp7p. Tall hobdayed half-brother to Legal Artist (IRE) (*qv*). IRISH NH FLAT '96/7 r3 p1 (3rd). IRISH NH '96/7 r7 w1 (3m Hdle) p1 (3rd). Bought Doncaster, May for 2800. Signed off in Ireland with a win, but obviously sorely troubled since, and was hopelessly tailed off last on his only completion three years later. A dreadful jumper, and Dominic Birkmyre has to contend with countless mistakes. *Miss K. Waddington — Vine & Craven (Alex Hales)*. 195 (O), 454 (4mMO), 474 (O), 895 (MO), 968 (Cf).

BIT OF A CHARACTER ..—§.. 14 b.g. Orchestra — Royal Character (Reformed Character) f6ppp. Tall half-brother to Little Native (IRE), to Hurdles winner, Establish (IRE) and to Irish Pointing winner, Erins Banker. IRISH NH FLAT '92/5 r9 p1 (3rd). IRISH NH '96 r1 p0. IRISH P-t-P '97/8 r10 w1 (7yo plus Maiden) p3; pulled up 4, and fell 1. P-t-P '99 r4 p1 (2nd); fell 2, and pulled up 1. Fluked the solitary success of his career — was 20 lengths third approaching the final fence where both leaders indulged in synchronised falling — and has proved most irresolute otherwise. Tried in blinkers on his penultimate start, but appeared to go lame subsequently. *J. Conifey — Berks & Bucks*. 477 (R), 791 (R), 1017 (I), 1206 (R), 1619 (M).

BIT OF A CITIZEN (IRE) ..10-2§.. 10 b.m. Henbit (USA) — Boreen Citizen (Boreen FR) 16r243p. Strong workmanlike half-sister to Absent Citizen (IRE). Dam won a Maiden in Ireland. IRISH P-t-P '95/6 r10 w1 (5yo mares Maiden) p2 (2nds); pulled up 3, and unseated 1. IRISH HUNT CH '96 r1 p0. P-t-P/HUNT CH '97/9 r18 w5 (inc 2 Opens, 3-4m) p4 (3 2nds); pulled up 3, unseated 2, and brought down 1. Managed a success for the fourth season running when making a winning reappearance at Pantyderi, but has become most unreliable, and turned in some lack-lustre efforts subsequently. Unimproved by the application of a visor twice (has won in blinkers), and can probably be disregarded after her first couple of starts in 2001. Stays well, and suited by easy ground. *R.A. Mason — Glamorgan (Evan Williams)*. 345 (O), 468 (3m1f110yH), 742 (O), 820 (Cm), 1015 (4mO), 1296 (O), 1614 (4mMO).

BIT OF A DO ..8-0.. 11 b.g. Idiot's Delight — Deep Dora (Deep Run) pp66666. Tall very rangy brother to Bit Of An Idiot (*qv*). P-t-P '97/9 r13 p2 (last pair 4, pulled up 6, and fell 1). Plods badly due to a wind infirmity (wears a tongue-strap), and invariably tailed off for new connections. *A. Simpson — Surrey U. (Sarah Dawson)*. 219 (CMod), 306 (R), 575 (R), 676 (Cf), 706 (Cf), 1104 (R), 1396 (OMa).

BIT OF A FLUTTER ..8-1.. 8 ch.m. Henbit (USA) — Walnut Way (Gambling Debt) p4. Lengthy. Dam, sister to 2 Pointers, won 2 Points and placed 4; and subsequently won 5 Chses (2m-2m5f) and 2nd 4 (all her starts) when sent to Martin Pipe (previously placed in 2 Hdles). NH '99 (for H. Daly) r3 p0 (tailed off). Bought Malvern, Oct for 500. Bred from a good mare, but does not seem to have any ability herself, and was 30 lengths last at Llanvalley. *G.A. Fynn — Tredegar F. (Ian Johnson)*. 491 (CfMa), 746 (CfMa).

BIT OF AN IDIOT ..9-9§.. 13 b.g. Idiot's Delight — Deep Dora (Deep Run) p31521rp. Very big strong brother to Bit Of A Do and Auntie Dora (dam of Larkin About, *qv*), and half-brother to Hard To Fathom and Derryair. P-t-P/HUNT CH '95/9 (for breeder, Mrs D.E.S. Surman) r15 w1 (Maiden) p2; pulled up 2, fell/unseated 3, and refused 1. A hulking giant of a horse who accompanied his brother to new premises, but unlike him managed to resurrect his flagging career with victories in two poor four-finisher events. Easily brushed aside by half decent animals, and is moody, but at least gets decent assistance from David Slattery who looks promising. *A. Simpson — Surrey U. (Sarah Dawson)*. 288 (CMod), 705 (R), 830 (Cnr), 1108 (C), 1243 (Inr), 1392 (M), 1510 (O), 1536 (3m2fH).

BIT O'SPEED (IRE) ..10-7.. 10 b.g. Henbit (USA) — Speedy Debbie (Pollerton) 1342. Strong-topped half-brother to Irish Chasing winners, Dudley Do Right and Amble Speedy (latter also won Hurdling there). IRISH NH '95/8 r16 w2 (2m2f Hdle, and 2m1f Ch) p4. NH '98 (for J.J.O'Neill) r1 p0 (pulled up in Ch). Gained a first success for three years when upsetting the 4-7 favourite in a two-finisher Novice Riders event at Badbury, but later gave a much more modest display when only outpaced from the last by the flying Blanville at Stratford. May only stay a bare three miles, but goes kindly for James Richardson, and it could be worth seeking out some shorter Hunter Chases for him. Has worn a tongue-strap in the past. *J. Richardson — Cotswold (Susan Richardson)*. 766 (Cnr), 970 (O), 1339 (2m5fH), 1443 (3mH).

BITRAN ..9-12.. 11 gr.g. Midyan (USA) — Bishah (USA) (Balzac USA) 22263. Smallish sturdy fired. Dam won at 11f. FLAT r3 p0. NH '93/4 and '97/8 r 18 w3 (2m2f-2m3f Hdles, inc Sell) p8. IRISH NH '96 r4 p2; pulled up lame only Ch. P-t-P '99 r6 w1 (Open) p1 (3rd); 4th thrice, and fell 1. Has a fair record in Points, but betrayed by a lack of acceleration, and has found success a hard commodity to come by since '94. Stays well and suited by soft ground, but disappointed when odds-on in his Members, and will get few easier opportunities in the future. *A. Palmer — Cotley (Philip Greenwood)*. 160 (O), 313 (O), 854 (O), 1138 (MO), 1303 (M).

B J BUBBLES ..—.. 7 b.g. Pocketed (USA) — Song Bird (True Song) upp. Half-brother to Harvest Singer and Blues Singer. Dam won 2 bad Points and placed 3 for Christine Forber; also failed to finish 18, inc both Chses. A poor jumper who is struggling to get his act together at present. The Pointing efforts of his siblings set a gloomy precedent. *Mrs C.T. Forber — Saddleworth*. 965 (OMa), 1153 (OMa), 1581 (2m4fOMa).

BLACK BOOK (IRE) ..9-7.. 8 br.m. Detroit Sam (FR) — French Note (Eton Rambler) f63d7pf252ub5. Small sparely-made half-sister to Nevada Gold (*qv*). IRISH P-t-P '98 r3 w1 (Hunt) p0; last once, and pulled up 1. NH '98/9 (for E.Elliott, bought for 3000) r6 p0 (pulled up 2, and fell 1 in Chses — very poor jumper). Bought Doncaster, Aug for 900. A tough sort who had a busy campaign, but generally performed very poorly, and normally scrawny and unimpressive in the paddock. A couple of her displays were better efforts, and nearly caught the prematurely eased Ardeal in a Members, whilst she was undoubtedly unlucky in a four-runner Restricted at Dingley, where she was twice checked when trying for a run on the inner, but led under a wild ride after the last and appeared to everyone on the line to just hold on (the Judge differed; as did the two 'experts' on the Racing Channel — who were miles away). Was lucky when landing her Irish Point (all out to beat Lillooet), and is not finding it at all easy to follow up. Reportedly covered by Classic Cliche. *P.J. Millington — Fernie, & Quorn.* 368 (L), 414 (L), 555 (Cnr), 589 (R), 1008 (O), 1072 (Cf), 1264 (M), 1418 (R), 1506 (R), 1592 (4m2fH), 1627 (2m5fH), 1667 (I).

BLACKCHESTERS ..9-7.. 8 bl.g. Genuine Gift (CAN) — Newgrove (Cantab) 5c32221. Tall unfurnished home-bred. P-t-P '99 r2 p0 (4th, and pulled up 1). Given the kid glove treatment in his first three races, and followed three decent placings (beaten five lengths or less on three occasions) with a win on firm ground at Corbridge. A reliable jumper, and should have the scope to cope when upgraded. *J.M. Sordy — Percy.* 44 (OMa), 425 (CfMa), 499 (2m4fOMa), 907 (M), 1122 (OMa), 1431 (OMa), 1500 (OMa).

BLACK DAN ..9-2.. 9 b.g. Bay Spirit — Sian Melody VII (unknown) p43p144. Lengthy good-bodied owner-bred half-brother to Sing Cherry Ripe. P-t-P '98/9 r13 p0 (last pair 6, pulled up 5, and fell/unseated 2). Showed marked improvement to get off the mark at Pentreclwydau (the second and third have both won subsequently), but well held in two Restricteds, and needs to prove that success was not a flash in the pan. *Mrs A. James — Pembs.* 350 (CfMa), 650 (CfMa), 838 (OMa), 1056 (CfMa), 1302 (OMa), 1453 (R), 1659 (R).

BLACK DANTE (IRE) ..10-8.. 7 b.g. Phardante (FR) — Orchardstown (Pollerton) f11. Lengthy hobdayed brother to Irish Pointing and Hurdles winner, Queenofclubs (IRE), and half-brother to Chasing winner, Chicago City (IRE). Dam won 3 Irish Points. Bought Ascot, Nov '98 for 1500. Fell after a mile when favourite on his debut, but then streaked to an impressive double. Did not beat that much, including in a Mixed Open in heavy at Bratton Down (Horus, who was bidding for a four-timer, seemed to be below par), but the manner of the victories could hardly have been more sensational, and has already proved himself to be a thorough stayer and a smart novice. Will be an exciting prospect if he continues to improve at the current rate. Led out unsold at 44,000gns at Doncaster in the summer, but has now joined the powerful team of Philip Hobbs. *E. Retter — Dartmoor.* 656 (OMa), 722 (CfMa), 1138 (MO).

PLATE 26   1138 Tiverton Staghounds Mixed Open: Black Dante (A. Charles-Jones), 1st, is an impressive winner from Wibbley Wobbley (Miss J. Cumings), 2nd   PHOTO: Mark Johnston

BLACK ICE (IRE) ..9-4.. 10 b.g. Cataldi — Turbulent Lass (Pitpan) pp5. Big. NH '96/8 r7 p1 (3rd); 7th of 8, and pulled up 1 in Chses. P-t-P '99 r1 p0 (unseated). A promising third in a Kelso 2m6f Amateur Riders Maiden Hurdle in December '96, but bitterly disappointing since, and beaten 27 lengths on his sole Pointing completion. Has yet to manage more than three outings in a year, and is clearly hard to keep right. *Mrs A.E.J. Barnett — W. Percy (Nick & Kirsty Hargreave)*. 39 (M), 108 (I), 627 (OMa).

BLACK MAGIC ..8-8.. 7 br.m. Cigar — Mossage (Ballymoss) 4. Plain sparely-made half-sister to 2 flat winners. NH FLAT '98 (for P. Howling; homebred) r2 p0 (well tailed off last 2). FLAT r1 p0. Bought Ascot, Jul for 850. Last in her Members, and has nobody under her spell so far. *N. Evans — Carms*. 642 (M).

BLACK OAK ..9-11.. 8 b.g. Zambrano — Indian Election (Sula Bula) pp1435. Tall rangy half-brother to So Peaceful and Goldoak. Dam is half-sister to Indian Knight (*qv*). NH FLAT r1 p0 (tailed off after pulling hard). NH FLAT '99 r2 p0 (pulled up 1, and fell 1). NH May '00 (from M. Sheppard's) r1 p0 (5th in 2m Nov Ch: *ld, mist 2, hit 7 & hdd, wkng when mist 9*). A confirmed bolter who made most to win a short Maiden at Dunthrop, but has yet to prove conclusively that he has the stamina required for the regular trip. Looks the part, but has shown a tendency to jump right-handed, and despite the advantages of being Sheppard-trained and Pritchard-ridden may not rise much above Restricted class. *D.J. Eaton — Ledbury (Nicky Sheppard; Matt Sheppard)*. 11 (OMa), 121 (OMa), 1021 (2m4fOMa), 1276 (R), 1460 (R).

BLACKOID (FR) ..9-4.. 7 br.g. Labus (FR) — Marchka (FR) (Go Marching USA) 32p. Compact half-brother to 4 French jumping winners. Dam won on flat (9-11f) and over Hurdles in France. NH FLAT Nov '98 r1 p0. NH '98/9 (for M. Pipe) r2 p0. Three lengths third on his Pointing debut, and was only caught 50 yards out (finished tired), but has been most disappointing and expensive to follow when 2-5 and 5-4 since. His jumping is poor and enthusiasm suspect (blinkered on final start), but if the stable persevere with him there is a chance he might score. *B.A. Kilpatrick — Silverton (David Pipe)*. 105 (OMa), 856 (CfMa), 1102 (OMa).

BLACK SERENE (IRE) ..10-4.. 10 b.m. Black Minstrel — Saucy Serene (Tarqogan) 3p2. Compact sister to Brian Og, and half-sister to Scarteen Lower (both Irish Pointing winners), and to Irish NH flat and Hurdles winner, Leaping Lord. Dam won an Irish Point. IRISH P-t-P '97/8 r10 w1 (5yo plus mares Maiden) p4; pulled up 2. P-t-P '99 r3 w1 (Restricted) p0; 6th, and ran out 1. A headstrong mare who has to be walked to the start early nowadays, but not lacking in ability, and made a revitalised Who Is Equiname pull out all the stops at Clifton-on-Dunsmore. Speedy enough to win again, but gets few opportunities, and has only once managed more than three outings in a year. A winner on firm and in softish, but not an out-and-out stayer. *Mrs R. Evans — Croome & W. Warwicks (Charlotte Evans)*. 447 (Cm), 897 (I), 1415 (Cf).

BLACKWOODSCOUNTRY ..9-12.. 11 b.g. Town And Country — Sweet Spice (Native Bazaar) 643. Light-framed brother to Country Tarrogen, and half-brother to Cinnamon Cruise. P-t-P/HUNT CH '95/9 r20 w3 (Maiden, Restricted and Confined) p9 (6 3rds); failed to finish 6 (fell/unseated 3). Won three races '96/7 (rated 10-2), but seemingly under the weather since, and ended the 2000 season lame. A willing battler, but may be hard to patch up, and unlikely to ever be as good as he once threatened to be. *Mrs W.A. Birkinshaw — York & Ainsty S. (Tim Sharpe)*. 134 (I), 277 (Cf), 394 (Cf).

BLACON POINT ..9-4.. 10 b.g. Rakaposhi King — Doris Blake (Roscoe Blake) 4p5432. Small brother to China Lal. Dam, sister to Old Brig (*qv* 2000 Annual), was 3rd in a Hunt Ch (in '95) and a Point (also disqualified from 2nd in a Point). NH '99 r1 p0 (pulled up). P-t-P/HUNT CH '97/9 (for breeder, Mr J.S. Swindells) r9 p1 (2nd); pulled up 6, and fell 1. Very headstrong and struggles to get the trip in Points, and not nearly good enough for sub-3m Hunter Chases. Placed in three Maidens, and might just get lucky one day, particularly if retaining the services of Tim Stephenson. Wears a cross-noseband, and has been tried tongue-tied. *J.F. Evans — W. Salop (Tracey Mactaggart)*. 568 (OMa), 778 (OMa), 866 (CfMa), 1196 (OMa), 1412 (OMa), 1635 (OMa).

BLAIR CASTLE (IRE) ..9-2.. 10 b.g. Waajib — Caimanite (Tap On Wood) 4p. Workmanlike. Dam is half-sister to Tsagairt Paroiste (*qv* '97 Annual). NH FLAT (win hers: I. Balding) r12 w2 (8f) p1 (2nd). NH '95 and '97/9 (for Lucinda Russell, bought for 13,500; all wins previously for G.B. Balding) r48 w9 (5 Hdles, 2-2m2f, and 4 Chses, 2m2f-2m4f, inc hat-trick '95, and four-timer '97) p14 (just caught after being 20l clear at the last at Cartmel once); one run at Galway; would have completed five-timer but for unseating at last. Did well on sound surfaces to '97, but has always been an enigmatic character, and sometimes a sketchy jumper (although perfectly capable of fencing well on his day). Gone in the wind, and was tubed latterly under Rules. Has now taken his losing sequence to 21, with no sign of an end. *P.J.S. Russell — North West Draghounds*. 714 (C), 1120 (O).

BLAKEINGTON ..8-0§.. 15 b.g. Baron Blakeney — Camina (Don Carlos) pp. Strong compact half-brother to Catman. Dam won 10f Claimer and 2m Nov Hdle. NH '91/4 r24 p2 (distant 2nd of 3 and 20l last of 3 in Chses); 5th of 6, last 2, pulled up 8, unseated 2, and ran out 1 in other Chses. P-t-P '96 and '99 (for Miss C. Chutter, Mr M.R.T. & Mrs J. Bugg) r10 w1 (Maiden) p0; last pair 8, and pulled up 1. Wears blinkers. A lucky winner in '96, and revived to act as a schoolmaster in the past two seasons - a job he has done with reluctance. Not worth bothering with again as the latest pilot can have learnt little about travelling at speed from him. *Mrs R.H. Reynolds — S. Dorset*. 209 (M), 325 (Cf).

BLAKES CORNER ..—.. 8 b.m. Roscoe Blake — Nutt's Corner (Cantab) u. Owner-bred half-sister to Barney Bear (*qv*). Steered an erratic path until unseating after a mile at Tabley. *Mrs A.B. Garton — Cheshire Forest (Tim Garton).* 966 (OMa).

BLAME THE GROOM (IRE) ..—.. 11 b.g. Shy Groom (USA) — Peak (High Top) p. Strong hobdayed half-brother to Irish Hurdles winner, Brae (IRE). P-t-P '97/8 r5 p1 (last of 3); pulled up 3. Hobdayed before he set foot on a racecourse, and has performed like a physical wreck since joining his present handler (has run just three times in three seasons — missed '99 entirely). *D. Cocks — Devon & Somerset (Linda Blackford).* 1257 (C).

BLANCHLAND ..—.. 12 gr.g. Bellypha — Premier Rose (Sharp Edge) pppu0. Lengthy half-brother to George Dillingham (*qv*). FLAT '92/6 (for K. Ivory; wins previously for breeder, P. Harris; hung badly right when blinkered once) r18 2w (9-10f, one on equitrack) p1 (head 2nd). NH '96 and '99 (from P. Richens, bought for 5000) r5 w1 (2mHdle) p1 (distant 3rd in Ch). Put his head in front on the line in a Hurdle in '96, but unable to breathe properly nowadays, and although he can show speed for about two miles, a tongue-strap and tubing have brought no relief. It would be surprising to see him in action again. A visit to the village he is named after (nearest Pointing course, Witton Castle) is highly recommended. *Mrs S. Watson & J. Cullen — Wilton (Linda Syckelmoore).* 219 (CMod), 262 (MO), 521 (O), 928 (MO), 1341 (2m110yH).

BLANK CHEQUE ..10-2§.. 11 b.g. Idiot's Delight — Quickapenny (Espresso) 382134. Small half-brother to Sneakapenny, Catchapenny and Shining Penny. Dam, from a great jumping family, won 7 Hdles (2-3m) and 2 3m1f Chses. NH '95 r4 p1 (3rd). P-t-P/HUNT CH '96/9 r23 w5 (inc 2 Confineds) p8 (6 2nds); failed to finish 5 (refused 1, ran out 1, and fell/unseated 2). Ended a run of 12 consecutive defeats when successful at Whittington, but has been a thoroughly dodgy character throughout his career, and David Coates has sometimes excelled on him. Has to be held up for as long as possible as he idles in front, but often drops right out of contention, and sometimes loses interest completely. Still possesses a tidy turn of foot, and capable of scoring again if he co-operates fully. *J.J. Coates — Pendle Forest & Craven (David Coates).* 375 (Cf), 622 (O), 960 (Cf), 1149 (Cf), 1365 (O), 1557 (3m1fH).

PLATE 27　　750 V W H Mens Open: Blanville (unretiring P. Scouller), 1st, jumps ahead of Golden Savannah (smiling A. Maculan), 2nd　　　　　　　　PHOTO: Bill Selwyn

BLANVILLE (FR) ..10-12.. 12 b.g. Pot D'Or (FR) — Nordica III (FR) (Orvilliers) 1111. Small stocky. FRENCH FLAT '93/8 r10 w6 (1m3f-2m4f) p2. FRENCH NH '93/8 r24 w4 (2m2f-2m6f Chses) p7. P-t-P '99 r3 w1 (Open) p0; and unseated 2. Very close to the top of the French jumping tree, and has quickly acclimatised to English conditions and become a useful Pointer. Usually ridden with supreme confidence by the owner, but not a fluent jumper, and those who had lumped on him at

Stratford were looking decidedly uneasy until he hit top gear on the approach to the home straight — even then they had their hearts in their mouths as the combination had a disagreement as to when to take off at the last. Has recorded the fastest time of the day in three of his Pointing victories, and further success looks a formality. Best suited by some cut in the ground (was taken off his feet when encountering a lively surface at Stratford), and would be of great interest in a Handicap under professional guidance. Reports of the owner hanging up his boots at the end of the season were premature, despite a most agreeable retirement party being held for him by his wife Gaye on Horse & Hound Cup day, but he is likely to confine his activity in 2001 to Hunter Chases on this horse. Well, that's what he's saying at the moment! *P.A.D. Scouller — Garth & S. Berks (Nigel Allen).* 750 (O), 981 (O), 1244 (MO), 1443 (3mH).

BLAWEARY ..10-1.. 9 b.m. Rakaposhi King — Mount St Mary's (Lochnager) u. Rangy home-bred sister to Blue Chequer, and half-sister to Monynut. Dam, half-sister to Price Of Peace (*qv* '90 Annual), won 2m Ch. P-t-P/HUNT CH '98/9 r12 w3 (Maiden, Restricted and Intermediate) p0; pulled up 2. Looked like developing into a decent stayer after decisive wins at Alnwick and Aspatria in '99, but presumably suffered a setback after dumping the rider in her Members on her return. A pity as she has probably reached her physical peak after being big and backward in her first two seasons. Young enough to atone if all is well in 2001. *A.J. Wight — Berwicks.* 358 (M).

BLAYNEYS PRIVILEGE ..10-2.. 14 b.g. Morston (FR) — Flying Sister (St Paddy) pb24423. Tall attractive. NH '93/5 r9 p1 (2nd); 7th of 8 and fell in Chses. P-t-P/HUNT CH '98 r3 w1 (Maiden) p1 (3rd); and pulled up 1. Spent three years in a field prior to a successful Pointing campaign in '98 and then promptly went inactive for another year, but enjoyed his busiest season to date in 2000, and ran several fair races in defeat. Very much in the veteran stage now, but still sprightly enough to bustle up horses half his age, and would not be begrudged another win. *C. Bailey, W. Adams & Miss T. Habgood — Bicester with Whaddon (Tracey Habgood).* 36 (CI), 296 (I), 427 (M), 869 (L), 1009 (CR), 1146 (R), 1419 (R).

BLAZING CONNIE ..8-10.. 8 b.m. Blaze O'Gold (USA) — Drumconrath (Hawaiian Return USA) 5pup65331p. Tall. P-t-P '98 r4 p1 (2nd); unseated 1, and pulled up 1. Looked destined for better things after a decent second at Bonvilston in '98, but endured a long absence and looked troubled at times on her return. All out to win a bad three-finisher Maiden at Laleston, but had stopped very quickly on a couple of occasions earlier, and presumably has an intermittent fault. Attracted plenty of market support on her Restricted debut, but backers soon knew their fate, and is clearly not going to live up to expectations. Usually has two paddock attendants. *G. Perkins — Gelligaer F. (W. Perkins).* 348 (CfMa), 489 (CfMa), 822 (CfMa), 989 (OMa), 1223 (2m4fOMa), 1406 (OMa), 1457 (OMa), 1617 (OMa), 1660 (OMa), 1671 (R).

BLAZING MIRACLE ..9-10.. 9 b.m. Shaab — Cottage Blaze (Sunyboy) 1u. Small neat. Dam, half-sister to Ross Cottage (*qv*), won a Maiden and 2nd 2 for Rosemary Henderson. Grandam, Flavias Cottage, was useless in 5 Points, but is half-sister to Tied Cottage (and several awful Pointers). NH '96/7 r15 p2 (2nd in Hdle; and last of 3 in Ch — runner-up remounted); fell 2 out when 15l clear but tired in Hdle once. P-t-P/HUNT CH '99 (for Mrs R.G. Henderson) r4 w1 (Maiden) p2. Won her Restricted at only the second attempt showing improved form into the bargain, but looked unlikely to be involved in the finish when unshipping Tabitha Cave at the fourth last on her subsequent start at Lemalla. Had looked a short-runner in the previous yard, but the Great Trethew race took nearly seven minutes, so stamina no longer seems a problem. Handles holding ground well. Relatively busy as a four and five-year-old, but averaging just three runs per annum recently. *D.W. & N. Heard — Silverton (Gordon Chambers).* 164 (R), 310 (I).

BLAZING TIMES ..8-0.. 9 b.g. Good Times (ITY) — Skycap Lady (Derek H) 3p. Strong-topped half-brother to Norman Way (*qv*). Dam, sister to Capalice (*qv* '93 Annual), was placed in 3 Points (unlucky not to have won). Grandam, Skyvan, won 5 Irish Points. P-t-p '98 (for breeder, Mr J. Cornforth) r3 p0 (5th, pulled up 1, and fell 1). Incredibly slow. Tailed off twice on his return when carrying overweight, but at least the rider did not become unbuckled. *J.K. Buckle — Essex & Suffolk (Lesley White).* 1110 (M), 1292 (OMa).

BLESSED OLIVER ..—.. 11 ch.g. Relkino — Oca (O'Grady) pp5ppp. Strong-topped workmanlike owner-bred half-brother to Codger, Grovelands and Bold King's Hussar, to jumping winners, Wings Ground and Rostra, and to 3 other winners (one in Trinidad). NH '95/6 r8 w1 (2m6f Hdle) p2 (3rds, inc beaten 30l in Ch); unseated only other Ch (when 3rd and rallying 2 out). P-t-P '97 and '99 r4 w1 (Confined) p1 (3rd); fell 1. Stood a far busier campaign than normal in 2000, but unfortunately went to pieces totally, and acquired a tube as well as a visor on his two most recent attempts. Physical disabilities have always prevented him from realising his full potential. *O.D. Plunkett — Heythrop (C. Plunkett).* 61 (MO), 243 (Cf), 511 (O), 749 (Cf), 895 (MO), 968 (Cf).

BLITHE SPIRIT ..—.. 9 b.g. Sand Sedge — Cribbs Jerella (Pardigras) p0. Unfurnished. NH Apr '00 r1 p0 (tailed off last in Nov Hdle: *in tch* to 4). Looked well on his debut (although novicey jumping had Nigel Bloom hailing to thee), but does not appear to have any pretentions to being a racehorse. *F.D. McInnes Skinner & Countess Cathcart — W. Norfolk (-; John McConnochie).* 96 (I).

BLONDIE BOO (IRE) ..9-5.. 10 b.g. Henbit (USA) — Hamers Flame (Green Shoon) p3. Tall strong half-brother to Notary-Nowell and Nobodys Flame (IRE), and to NH flat and Hurdles winner, Strong Flame (IRE). Dam won 3 flat (11-16f), 4 2m Hdles, and 4 Chses (2m-2m5f) in Ireland. IRISH NH FLAT '96 r1 p0 (last). P-t-P '98 (for Mr R.A. Mason) r4 w1 (Maiden) p0; pulled up 1, and fell 1. Looked temperamentally suspect in his previous yard and reappeared after a season off equipped with blinkers, but presumably went wrong (again?) at Chipley Park as he spent the next 12 weeks on the sidelines. Flattered only to deceive subsequently and remains one not to place any faith in. *M. Weir — Dartmoor.* 144 (R), 1309 (R).

BLOWN WIND (IRE) ..9-12.. 10 b.g. Strong Gale — Raise A Queen (Raise You Ten) pp4d4. Workmanlike lengthy half-brother to Bleanahouree, to 2 Irish NH flat and Hurdles winners (one also successful on flat there), and to jumping winner, Bruton Street. NH FLAT '96 r2 p0. NH '96 and '98/9 (from O. Sherwood's) r8 w1 (2m Hdle) p1 (2nd); 5th of 6, last, pulled up and unseated 2 in Chses. Made an impressive start to his Hurdling career when beating 17 rivals on firm in September '96, but promptly disappeared for 26 months, and has been a major disappointment since returning. Made plentiful mistakes over regulation fences, and although he is safe enough in Points he does not get the trip, presumably because of a physical defect. Would have finished second at Bassaleg had the jockey not pulled up at the last, and the stewards accepted his explanation that 'the horse had run out of energy'! It is rather ironic that something as rare as a Welsh stewards enquiry should have concerned a horse from as far afield as the Sandhurst Area. This is a mild case of Kentish Disease, which can be easily recognised, one has only to see the locals' misdemeanours being ignored, and the Rule Book being thrown at anyone from away. This disease is endemic in the South East Area where fortunately anyone who's anyone is above the law — so we don't have to worry. *B.T. Stewart-Brown — Vine & Craven (Caroline Goatley).* 1282 (O), 1402 (MO), 1597 (MO), 1658 (MO).

BLUE AND ROYAL (IRE) ..—.. 9 b.g. Bluebird (USA) — Cat Girl (USA) (Grey Dawn II) pp. Leggy half-brother to 3 flat winners, including Snickersnee (also a successful Hurdler). Dam won at up to 8f in USA. FLAT (placing for R. Hannon) r14 p1 (3rd of 4). NH '96/7 (for V. Soane; previously for Miss J. Doyle, bought for 12,000) r5 p0. Hardly ever runs, and does not even stay two miles. Blinkered on occasions in the past. *G. & R. Whisker — Farmers Bloodhounds.* 1207 (OMa), 1397 (OMa).

BLUE CHEESE ..10-0.. 7 gr.m. Mystiko (USA) — Legal Sound (Legal Eagle) 123. Compact attractive half-sister to 2 flat winners, including Legatee (also a successful Hurdler). Dam won 5 6f races, the first a Seller. FLAT r8 p0 (visored when last in Sell final). NH '97/8 r5 p1 (2nd). P-t-P '99 r2 p1 (2nd). NH May '00 r1 p1 (8½f 3rd in 2m6f110y Nov Hdle; *prom, rdn 2 out, no ex*). A frantic puller over Hurdles when among a bunch of stiffs ragged when coming home alone in a youngsters Maiden at Erw Lon, but finished exhausted herself, and was no match for Cresswell Quay subsequently. Failed to reappear following a spin over Hurdles, and is clearly not easy to train. *K.R. Pearce — Carms.* 649 (CfMa), 832 (R).

BLUE CHIP (IRE) ..8-7.. 8 b.m. Executive Perk — Bluejama (Windjammer USA) f. Unfurnished half-sister to Cabin Hill, and to Irish flat winner, Northern Frontier (IRE). Dam won 2 2m Hdles in Ireland. IR 3200 4-y-o. NH FLAT Nov '98 r1 p0. NH '99 (final for C. Morlock; previously for T. M Jones) r3 p0 (12th of 13 and pulled up 2 in Hdles). Bought Malvern, July for 1100. Useless under Rules, but seemed to be doing a bit better until she fell two out in a January Maiden. Presumably hurt herself, because she hasn't been seen since. *E.D. Bailey — Ludlow.* 52 (OMa).

BLUE LAWS (IRE) ..10-7.. 11 b.g. Bluebird (USA) — Claretta (USA) (Roberto USA) 22137. Small compact half-brother to 6 flat winners (3 abroad, and one in Ireland), including smart Sapience. Dam won at 7f. FLAT r10 p2. NH '93/6 and '98 r17 w1 (2m5f Hdle) p7; remote finisher in all 3 Chses. P-t-P '99 r8 w1 (Ladies) p4 (2 3rds, last once); fell/unseated 2. Ran up a long losing sequence under Rules, but has taken well to Pointing, and provided Caroline Tuffin with her second winner when successful at Larkhill. A secure jumper, and best suited by some cut in the ground. Not bred to get much beyond a mile, but appreciated every yard of the four mile journey. Future appearances depend on the extent of the lameness incurred on his latest start. *L.R & Mrs C.J. Tuffin — Blackmore & Sparkford V. (Caroline Tuffin).* 61 (MO), 161 (L), 454 (4mMO), 680 (3m1fH), 877 (L).

BLUE LYZANDER ..9-8.. 12 b.m. Petrizzo — Ol' Blue Eyes (Bluerullah) 3744294. Small neat. Dam won 2 Ladies and placed 11, and earlier won a Point in Ireland. FLAT r2 p0. NH '93/5 r12 p2 (inc 2nd in Sell); pulled up final 2 (last race declared void). P-t-P '98/9 r9 w1 (Maiden) p1 (2nd); pulled up 4, and fell 1. Flattered by her win in a three-finisher Maiden, and regularly tailed off in Ladies races since — lacks the substance to carry the bigger weights in Restricteds. Overwhelmed by a confirmed villain in her Members, and usually fails to get the trip. *Mrs R.E. Walker — N. Cotswold.* 118 (L), 544 (L), 699 (L), 969 (L), 1189 (M), 1417 (L), 1462 (L).

BLUE MARLIN ..9-8.. 10 gr.m. Nishapour (FR) — Miss Pisces (Salmon Leap USA) p565. Tall strong-topped half-sister to Young Saffy (*qv*). NH FLAT May '96 r2 p0. P-t-P '98 r6 w1 (2m4f Maiden) p2 (2nds); fell/unseated 2, and pulled up 1. An impetuous galloper who seems to have trouble lasting home whatever the trip, and remains an unaccomplished jumper. Missed the '99 season entirely and obviously not right since. Her astute trainer has done well in the Pointing arena and has designs on taking out a permit, so perhaps Selling Hurdles might be an option in future. *W.J. Kelly — Bicester with Whaddon (Herbie Owen).* 306 (R), 459 (2m4f110yH), 585 (2m5f110yH), 925 (2mH).

BLUE ROSETTE ..9-12.. 12 b.g. Lucky Wednesday — Cadenette (Brigadier Gerard) 6371. Lengthy angular fired half-brother to Big Buckley. Dam won 10f Sell. NH '92 and '97 r6 p3 (2m3f-2m6f Hdles, inc Sell). P-t-P '94 and '96/9 (for Mr K.R. Dance) r15 w5 (up to Confined) p4 (2nds, beaten head once); pulled up 2, and fell/unseated 4. Did not win a Maiden until he was nine, and has had five different trainers in six years, but has ultimately made the most of his opportunities, and took advantage of the gambled-on favourite's poor showing to romp home in his Members. No longer a force in more competitive races, and well held otherwise in 2000. Has always been lightly raced, and blinkered without exception on his last 12 appearances. *P. Hibbard — N. Ledbury (Anita Gibbons).* 449 (L), 702 (Cf), 968 (Cf), 1085 (M).

BLUE WAVE (IRE) ..—.. 9 b.g. Project Manager — Over The Seas (North Summit) ppp. Tall good-looking brother to Hurdles winner, Just An Excuse (IRE). Dam won 2 flat (10-11f; also won at 12f, but demoted to 3rd) and 3 Hdles (2m-2m11f) in Ireland. IRISH NH FLAT '96/7 r3 w1 p0. IRISH NH '96/7 r4 w1 (2m4f Hdle) p0. NH '98 r2 p0 (tailed off and pulled up in Chses). P-t-P '99 r3 p3 (2 2nds, last once; and 3rd of 4). Sold to Anne Duchess of Westminster for a reputedly enormous sum after winning twice in Ireland, but performed as though faulty in Chases, and though placed in all of his Points in '99 was still under-achieving. Fared even worse in 2000, and his physical problems appear insurmountable. *R.B. Francis — Sir W.W. Wynn's.* 171 (O), 369 (O), 905 (C).

BLUSHING HEUGH ..—.. 8 b.g. Genuine Gift (CAN) — Haley Heugh (Montreal Boy) p. Owner-bred. Dam is sister to 4 Pointers, including McNay (*qv* '98 Annual), and half-sister to another. In touch when pulled up after a mile at Alnwick. *C. Graham - College V. & N. Northumberland.* 909 (2m4fOMa).

BLYTH BROOK ..10-6.. 9 b.g. Meadowbrook — The Bean-Goose (King Sitric) 4234122. Compact owner-bred brother to Beanley Brook, and half-brother to Victor Charlie. NH '97/8 r3 p0. P-t-P '99 r5 w1 (2m4f Maiden) p3 (2 3rds); and fell 1. A consistent sort, but still not a convincing stayer, and took six attempts before he finally landed his Restricted — in a seven minute race! Showed improved form when second to winning Hunter Chaser Majority Major at Witton Castle, and a fair second to a potentially useful stable companion at Perth subsequently, so worth campaigning in sub-3m events on a regular basis. Appears to handle most types of ground (successful in holding and on firmish). *Mrs S. Sutton — College V. & N. Northumberland (Clive Storey).* 40 (R), 184 (R), 423 (R), 908 (R), 976 (R), 1327 (O), 1556 (2m4f110yH).

BOARDING SCHOOL ..10-4.. 14 b.g. Glenstal (USA) — Amenity (FR) (Luthier) 5413. Tall rangy half-brother to 3 flat winners (one in Ireland), and to flat and jumping winner, Clifton Beat (USA). Dam won at 10f, and comes from a high-class family in France. IRISH FLAT r3 w2 (2m Listed race; head and neck defeats). IRISH NH '90/1 r8 w2 (2m Hdles) p3 (inc 3rd in Triumph). FLAT r2 p1 (2nd). NH '91/8 r42 w7 (2m-2m4f Chses) p9. P-t-P '99 r4 w2 (Ladies) p2. A tip-top 2m4f specialist in his prime, and has had his enthusiasm rekindled by Pointing when acting as schoolmaster to Anna de Lisle Wells. Outstayed Mr Custard (who had finished around 27 lengths in front of him when they met at Newton Bromswold) at Andoversford, and still capable of decent efforts, but is beginning to find the pace of Ladies races all too speedy. Owes his connections nothing, but Harry Wheeler does well with his veteran charges — Ask Frank, Bolshie Baron, etc, and it would be no surprise to see him back in 2001. Often tongue-tied. *Mrs A. De Lisle Wells — N. Cotswold (Harry Wheeler).* 512 (L), 751 (L), 969 (L), 1491 (L).

BOBBING ALONG (IRE) ..9-13.. 10 ch.g. Over The River (FR) — Ballymore Status (Status Seeker) 3. Tall brother to Rivers End (IRE). P-t-P '97 and '99 r3 w1 (Maiden) p0; pulled up 1. Had reportedly broken down before winning the fastest of four Maidens at Brampton Bryan in '99, and his 2000 campaign lasted just one race. Plenty good enough to win a Restricted, but a case of nice engine shame about the wheels. *Mrs A.P. Glassford — Cheshire.* 567 (R).

BOBBY VIOLET ..—§§.. 9 b.g. Starch Reduced — Otterden (Crooner) uR. Close-coupled brother to Violet's Boy and Red Breaker. Dam won 3m1f Sell Hdle in a long and generally dismal career. NH FLAT Dec '97 r1 p0 (tailed off). NH '98/9 (for A. Juckes, who won with the dam) r3 p0 (pulled up in 3 Hdles; 66-1 once, and 100-1 thrice). An appalling brute (and mirror image of Red Breaker) who went less than a mile before jettisoning his riders in bizarre circumstances twice. Veered violently and ran off the course at Ludlow, and the stewards should have immediately told Matthews that he was never to run the animal again. *J.E. Wood — Wheatland (Frank Matthews).* 569 (OMa), 684 (2m4fH).

BOGEY MAN ..—.. 7 b.g. Teamster — Alice Passthorn (Rapid Pass) pp. Workmanlike lengthy. Dam, half-sister to I've Called Time (*qv*), pulled up in a Point (after reluctantly clambering over 3 fences). Grandam, Alice Rairthorn, won a Members and placed 6 (inc 2 Hdles, and one a Sell). Broke a knee at Holnicote, and had to be destroyed. *Mrs P. Shaw — Dulverton W. (Lucy Roberts).* 874 (2m4fOMa), 1373 (OMa).

BOHOLA PETE (IRE) ..9-3.. 10 ch.g. Orchestra — Deep Link (Deep Run) 23. Good-topped half-brother to Dublin Hill (IRE) (*qv*). IRISH NH FLAT Apr '96 r1 p0. IRISH NH '96 r9 p1 (3rd). Sold Goffs, Feb '97 for 1386. Just caught when beaten a neck by Iron Pyrites at Llanfrynach on his first appearance for four years, but was a disappointing favourite next time, and did not jump well and pulled too hard before finishing 13 lengths last of three. A certainty to score were he ever to recapture his best form — on his penultimate start in Ireland, he was third of 20 with Hersilia (*qv*) fourth and the subsequently quite useful English Hurdler Miss Bertaine fifth. *A.M. Lloyd — Golden V.* 491 (CfMa), 1093 (OMa).

BOLD FOUNTAIN (IRE) ..9-12.. 10 b.g. Royal Fountain — Glitter On (Even Money) f34p. Lengthy angular half-brother to Lurriga Glitter (IRE) and Conna Moss (IRE), and to Irish Pointing winners, Lovely Glitter (also won NH flat there) and Glittering Moon. NH FLAT Spr '95 r2 w1 p1 (3rd). NH '95/6 (for G.M. Moore) r2 p2 (2 Hdles). Has had a very stunted career punctuated by huge absences, and was returning from a four year vacation in 2000. Made favourite twice, including at odds-on once, but gave his best display when four lengths third in an Open. Has no finishing speed, and disappeared after pulling up on the rough ground at Hutton Rudby in mid-March. *Mrs C. Dennis — Zetland (Chris Dennis).* 134 (I), 279 (O), 394 (Cf), 622 (O).

BOLD IRENE (IRE) ..8-7§.. 10 gr.m. Peacock (FR) — Bold And True (Sir Herbert) p6282. Small light sister to Irish NH flat and jumping winner, Bold Flyer, and half-sister to Cosa Fuair (IRE). IRISH NH FLAT '96 r2 p0. IRISH P-t-P '97 r5 p2 (2nds); pulled up 1. P-t-p/HUNT CH '98/9 r7 p2 (2nds); last pair thrice, refused 1, and pulled up 1. Has now been matron of honour on no fewer than six occasions, but rarely looked like winning, and blinkers brought no improvement on her last three starts. Lacks resolve, and will need a bad race to open her account. *F. Jestin — Cumberland.* 364 (CfMa), 665 (OMa), 815 (Cm), 1153 (OMa), 1362 (M).

BOLD JOKER ..—.. 10 b.g. Jester — Bold Difference (Bold Owl) f. Small compact. Dam won 3 flat, 6-10f, inc 2 Sells. 3000 2-y-o. FLAT (early runs for J. Wharton; tried blinkered) r13 p0. NH '95/6 (for G. Oldroyd) r4 p0 (inc Sell). Useless flat and Hurdling, and 50-1 when falling at halfway in a Maiden four years later. *R. Witney & I.P. Wardle — Mendip F. (R. Witney).* 407 (OMa).

BOLD KNIGHT ..8-7.. 8 b.g. Bold Fox — Harwall Queen (Tobique) ppp23ff. Sturdy rangy. Dam, half-sister to Royal Oats (*qv* 2000 Annual), won a Restricted and a Members and placed 3 for Tudor Harries (to '97), and grandam, Knights Queen, won 11 Points (inc 2 dead-heats) and placed 10 (inc 3rd in Hunt Ch) for him. P-t-P '99 r2 p0 (pulled up 2). Pulled up in his first five starts (after less than a mile three times) before chasing home Ossie Dale on firm at Erw Lon, and would appear not to be able to handle too much cut in the ground. Sent off favourite twice subsequently, but let supporters down, and encountered jumping problems on his final two forays. A bit of a handful to date, but might find an opportunity in his third season. *E.T. Harries - S. Pembs (Dawn Harries).* 270 (CfMa), 350 (CfMa), 834 (OMa), 950 (OMa), 1223 (2m4fOMa), 1301 (OMa), 1404 (OMa).

BOLD NAVIGATOR ..9-6.. 11 b.g. Lighter — Drummond Lass (Peacock FR) 22p. Half-brother to Nisbet (*qv*). Ran quite well for a ten-year-old newcomer in Maidens, but not seen after pulling up in a Hunter Chase in early March (made mistakes). Could yet score in the lowest grade if problem-free. *A.M. Crow — Buccleuch.* 187 (OMa), 365 (CfMa), 465 (3m1f110yH).

BOLL WEEVIL ..9-7.. 15 b.g. Boreen (FR) — Lavenham Lady (Precipice Wood) 42p. Rangy light-bodied. Dam won 2m5f Hdle and 2 2m4f Chses (all Novs). NH '91/6 r22 w5 (2 Hdles, 2m-2m5f, and 3 Chses, 2m4f-2m6f) p4. P-t-P/HUNT CH '97/9 r8 w3 (3 Members) p2 (fence last of 2 once); pulled up 3. Formerly a decent if somewhat unreliable performer, and farmed three weak Members races at now defunct Heathfield '98/9, but could not quite muster the energy to get past another veteran at the replacement, Rodmell. Of no account in competitive races (something of a contradiction in terms in the South East), and appeared to suffer a reverse on his final start. *N. Bowman — Southdown & Eridge (Sally Bowman).* 826 (O), 1208 (M), 1394 (O).

BOLSHIE BARON ..10-3.. 12 b.g. Baron Blakeney — Contrary Lady (Conwyn) 315p22p. Small neat half-brother to Contradict. Dam, half-sister to Roman Sea (*qv* '92 Annual), won 4 Points consecutively (beaten a neck but awarded dead-heat once) and placed 7 (inc 2 Hunt Chses, one 4m). P-t-P '95/6 (for breeder, Mr M.H. Weston) r10 w2 (Maiden and Restricted) p3 (neck 2nd; and 2 3rds); pulled up 2, and fell 1. NH '96/9 (for M.H. Weston) r14 p3 (2nds). Lost his way under Rules after finishing second in a 3m2f Chase at Fontwell in March '97 (subsequently last or pulled up in six of seven starts), but appreciated the return to Pointing, and stuck on well at Upper Sapey to land the third success of his career. In the process of running a big race in the Cheltenham four-miler until a bad blunder put paid to his chances, but again revealed his appreciation for a test of stamina when runner-up at Folkestone subsequently. Suited by top-of-the-ground, and has shown his best form going right-handed. Wears a tongue-strap. *E.O. Steward — Croome & W. Warwicks (Harry Wheeler).* 142 (I), 701 (I), 968 (Cf), 1338 (4m1fH), 1539 (3m7fH), 1646 (3m4fH).

BOMBA CHARGER ..9-10.. 9 b.g. Prince Of Peace — Lady Guinevere (Tormento) 322288. Smallish sturdy half-brother to Badon Hill. Dam is half-sister to 6 Ogle/Welch Pointers. Grandam, Bright Reply, was placed in 3 very bad Points for late Michael Ogle. NH FLAT '97 r2 p0. NH '97/8 r7 p1 (3rd); fell only Ch. P-t-P '99 r8 w4 (up to Confined) p3 (3rd of 4 twice); and pulled up 1. Made an immediate impact in Points, but did not reappear until the third week in March (Michael Ogle and his wife having died tragically at Christmas), and did not seem to be firing on all cylinders for their daughter subsequently. Despite his tenacious displays the previous year was presumably thought to be saving a bit for himself, as he was ridden in spurs when beaten at odds-on once, and nearly tripped over his own feet on his last two starts. Worth 10-3 on his best '99 form and might yet return to that sort of figure if his dip in fortune is just a temporary one — running Lead Story to a head at Flete Park was no disgrace. *Mrs R. Welch & Mrs D.J. Treneer — Dartmoor (Rebecca Welch).* 652 (MO), 970 (O), 1041 (M), 1257 (C), 1433 (3mH), 1562 (C).

BOMBADIER BROWN ..—§.. 10 b.g. K-Battery — Peace Keeper (Wolver Hollow) pp. Compact. Dam was 2nd in a Restricted (and a Sell Hdle ('her career is generally a catalogue of villainies and disasters'). P-t-P '97 r3 p0 (pulled up 2, and unseated 1). Resurfaced after being awol for three years but with the same dismal results, and quickly sloped back into the ranks. Looked ungenuine when tried in blinkers on his final start. *Major P. Greenwood — V.W.H.* 753 (CfMa), 1018 (OMa).

BONNIE AMY ..8-4.. 6 b.m. Syrtos — Bonnie Ivy (Ivotino USA) pp59. Compact owner-bred. Finished tailed off last twice, but is a sensible jumper for a baby, and may be able to go faster at six. *Mrs J.M. Jones — Atherstone (Roger Harvey).* 703 (OMa), 1010 (CfMa), 1125 (OMa), 1423 (OMa).

BONNIE B ..6-7.. 8 b.m. Gunner B — Dancing Jenny (Goldhill) pp4p. Half-sister to Jenny Wood, and to jumping winner, Alice Smith. Dam is half-sister to 3 Pointers, including The Pride Of Pokey. Grandam, Vikrom, won 4 Hdles at around 2m, and 10 Chses, 2m-2m4f. Tailed off in Maidens, and walked up the run-in when 75 lengths last on her only completion. Very unruly in the paddock on her debut. *Miss J. Fisher — Lauderdale.* 664 (2m5fOMa), 910 (2m4fOMa), 1165 (OMa), 1368 (OMa).

BONNIE BUTTONS ..—.. 8 br.m. Lord Bud — Lady Buttons (New Brig) p. Small neat home-bred sister to Buster Buttons (qv). P-t-P '99 r1 p0 (pulled up). Too backward to break into a gallop on the two occasions she has made it to the racecourse, and time passes her by whilst she remains inactive. *S.G. Jones — Cleveland.* 379 (OMa).

BONNY (GER) ..9-4.. 8 b.m. Esclavo (FR) — Bonny Brae (Cure The Blues USA) 4. Compact half-sister to 5 winners (2 abroad), including Solid Steel (Hurdles), Highlander (Irish NH flat and Hurdles) and Avoid The Rush (Irish flat and Hurdles). IRISH FLAT r11 p1 (3rd). NH '98/9 (for D. Wintle, bought for 750, blinkered last 3) r11 p2 (Sells). A disappointing sort, but could probably win a Welsh Maiden if she consented to put her best foot forward (was 12 lengths fourth over 2m4f at Garnons in mid-March, but not seen again). *R.J. Peake — Gelligaer F.* 673 (2m4fOMa).

BONNY BOY (IRE) ..8-9.. 6 b.g. Bustino — Dingle Bay (Petingo) p42. Half-brother to Henfield, and to 2 flat winners (one in Ireland; the other, Assessor (IRE) won Prix Du Cadran and '95 Italian St Leger, and earned £424,061). Dam won 2 Irish flat, 8-10f. Bought Doncaster, May for 6000. Has an interesting pedigree, and showed promise on his last two starts. Only caught in the final 100 yards at Bonvilston, and should have little difficulty going one better very soon. *D. Rees — Tivyside.* 1228 (R), 1457 (OMa), 1618 (OMa).

BONNY RIGG (IRE) ..9-11§.. 9 b.b.g. Phardante (FR) — Open Your Eyes (Beau Charmeur FR) p2321. Lengthy half-sister to Rovac (qv). NH FLAT Mar '96 r2 p0. NH '97/9 (for L. Lungo, blinkered 2) r19 p3 (inc 2 2nds in Chses). Bought Doncaster, June for 9000. Beaten seven lengths and two and a half lengths in Novices Handicap Chases in June '99, from out of the handicap in both (and despite the rider being five pounds overweight), but proved incredibly disappointing in Points until she won a three-finisher Maiden at Lydstep. Can front-run at a good clip, but a very weak finisher and no battler, and there is no guarantee that she will produce the goods again. *N.B. Jones — Llangeinor (Paul Haskins).* 11 (OMa), 72 (OMa), 268 (CfMa), 650 (CfMa), 838 (OMa).

BON VOYAGE (USA) ..—.. 9 b.g. Riverman (USA) — Katsura (USA) (Northern Dancer) s. Close-coupled little brother to 2 flat winners (one in France), including River Captain, and half-brother to 7 flat winners (4 abroad), including Rambushka. Dam won 2 Irish flat, 7-12f. FRENCH FLAT '95 r5 p2 (3rds). FLAT '98 r1 p1 (2nd in Sell). NH '95/9 (for P. Hobbs, bought for 10,000; wins previously for G. Grissell, bought for 20,000) r25 w2 (2m1f-2m4f Hdles) p9 (inc 3rd in Sell). Doncaster, Aug for 500. Backed from eights to fives at Bonvilston, but punters waved goodbye to their money when he slipped up on a bend after a mile (was mounted outside the paddock). A blinkered Hurdler who last scored in May '96, and hung right on the run-in and did not look keen when 16 lengths third in his most recent placing (June '99). May retain ability, but needs sweetening. *Mrs C.A. Williams — Glamorgan (Evan Williams).* 1450 (Cf).

BOOZI BIRTHDAY ..8-6.. 7 b.m. Crested Lark — Pollygloss (Doctor Pangloss) p2. Dam, sister to Valentines Day (qv '93 Annual), pulled up 2 and fell/unseated 3 in Points, principally for Mark Styles ('it will be no sadness if Potty Polly is never seen again'). Grandam, Wicken Folly, was placed in 2 bad Points (also pulled up, and on deck 5). Not bred for glory, and was left a lucky 30 lengths last of two by departures at Siddington. *M.R.P. Styles — Grafton (Sharon Kelly).* 22 (2m4fOMa), 754 (CfMa).

BORDER BARLEY ..9-3.. 10 ch.g. Scallywag — Centaura (Centaurus) 2. Workmanlike brother to Taura's Rascal and Teal Bay, and half-brother to Sonnaura. Dam won 6 Points and placed 6 for Paul

Jones, and is half-sister to 4 Pointers, including Major Star. Grandam, Tucute, won 2 Points and placed 6. P-t-P '99 r2 p0 (disqualified from 4th, and fell 1). Given a gentle introduction when 20 lengths fourth on his Pointing debut (the four horses to finish behind him all scored subsequently), and would almost certainly have won at Brampton Bryan on his return, but faltered near the line and collapsed and died walking back. It was a great pity he should lose his life in such circumstances, especially on the track where his dam had some of her finest moments. *P.A. Jones — W. Salop.* 866 (CfMa).

BORDER BURN ..9-6.. 7 ch.g. Safawan — Burning Ryme (Rymer) 12. Dam is half-sister to 5 Pointers, including Burning Scally (*qv* 2000 Annual). Made a pleasing start in his two races in the space of eight days in March, and followed a narrow win in a very slow run three-finisher Maiden at Corbridge with a very respectable second in his Members. Should progress to better things. *N.M.L. Ewart — Cumberland F.* 426 (CfMa), 492 (M).

BORDER COUNTRY ..7-9.. 9 ch.g. Town And Country — Queen Beyan (Laurence O) fpp6b. Plain lengthy. Dam, half-sister to River Saint (*qv* '92 Annual), won 4 Points (inc 3 Ladies, 3-4m) and placed 7 (one in Ireland). NH '97 r1 p0 (pulled up). P-t-P '99 (for Mr J.W. Hughes) r2 p0 (last pair 2). Only once better than last in three Pointing completions, and does not inspire confidence. His dam won four races (lost one at Portman Square) as a reformed 12-year-old in 1990, but the chances of him emulating her feat seem remote. *J. Murphy — Lanarks & Renfrews.* 363 (CfMa), 497 (R), 665 (OMa), 977 (CfMa), 1082 (CfMa).

BORDER FARMER (IRE) ..9-11.. 8 b.g. Riverhead (USA) — Double Figures (FR) (Double Form) up1u243. Lengthy half-brother to Can You Just (IRE), and to Irish flat winner, Mugnano. NH FLAT '98/9 (for D. Eddy) r2 p0. NH '99 (first for D. Eddy) r4 p0. NH May '00 r1 p1 (8l 3rd in 2m4f110y Hexham Nov Hdle: *stayed on frm 2 out*). Fairly slow, but has no stamina worries, and won a division of the Corbridge Maiden in a 22 seconds faster time than Border Burn. Can give trouble in the preliminaries, and has been seen to swish his tail. None too reliable, but would win a Restricted at best. *D. Carr — Haydon (Tim Reed).* 114 (OMa), 187 (OMa), 425 (CfMa), 713 (R), 976 (R), 1363 (R).

BORDER GLORY ..9-9.. 10 ch.g. Derrylin — Boreen's Glory (Boreen FR) 3525p259385p. Strong half-brother to Saffron Glory. P-t-P/HUNT CH '96/9 r21 w1 (Maiden) p2; failed to finish 12 (unseated 4). Beaten on 25 occasions since losing his maiden status, and Hunter Chasing him is generally a waste of time (the exception being an honourable second at Kelso in 2000) but gave Peter Maitland-Carew plenty of experience, and is at least a fairly reliable jumper. Needs to return to Points to win again, though no certainty for Restricted success. Has been tried in a visor. Clearly a good doer, and takes a run or two to get fit. *Mrs W.M. Scott — Hon. G. Maitland-Carew — Buccleuch (-; Clive Storey).* 40 (R), 111 (R), 360 (R), 582 (3m3fH), 712 (M), 915 (3m1fH), 1118 (R), 1342 (3m1fH), 1427 (R), 1445 (3m1fH), 1577 (R), 1601 (3m2fH).

BORDER LAIRD (IRE) ..9-9.. 8 b.g. Be My Native (USA) — Sonlaru (Deep Run) 3. Smallish half-brother to Carriglawn and Fellow Countryman (subsequent Chasing winner). Twenty-two lengths third on an apparently encouraging debut (heavily eased, or could have been a lot closer), but approaches eight with just the one outing under his belt. *A.D. Wardall — O. Berks (Caroline Gordon).* 264 (OMa).

BORDER LIGHT ..9-2.. 8 ch.g. Lighter — Border Cherry (Deep Run) 52. Smallish unfurnished half-brother to Moondyne. NH FLAT '98 r2 p0. P-t-P '98/9 r8 p0; failed to finish 7 (fell/unseated 3). A complete disaster in his first two seasons, but indicated that there might be light at the end of the tunnel when runner-up in a poor youngsters Maiden at Larkhill. Failed to reappear, but worth getting fit (has looked too fat to date), as he has some ability. *H.J. Manners — V.W.H.* 12 (OMa), 60 (OMa).

BORDER REIVER (IRE) ..9-6.. 8 ch.g. Moscow Society (USA) — Go In Peace (The Parson) 4f5f. Tall rangy. Dam is sister to Saints Alive, and half-sister to Cumberland Basin (*qv* both '88 season Annual). NH FLAT Apr '98 r1 p0 (tailed off). NH '99 (for N. Twiston-Davies) r3 p0 (last, and pulled up 2 in Hdles). Was showing signs of ability in Points, but ended a tempestuous career when he broke a leg at Lockerbie (had earlier fallen at the first at Friars Haugh, and injured Dale Jewett, who was stood down for 21 days). *R.J. Kyle — Jedforest.* 501 (2m4fOMa), 719 (CfMa), 908 (R), 976 (R).

BORDER ROSE ..9-13.. 12 b.m. Meadowbrook — Cornish Spirit (Flandre II) fpf82u. Small neat. Dam won Tynedale Members on Cherry Seage's first ride (was basically an eventer). P-t-P '99 r2 w1 (Maiden) p0; and pulled up 1. Won the quickest of four divisions of a Wadebridge Maiden on just her second racecourse appearance, and shows the ability to land a Restricted if her jumping can be sorted out. Acts in soft. *Mrs C.A. Seage — E. Cornwall.* 157 (M), 316 (Cf), 536 (R), 852 (Cf), 1042 (R), 1258 (R).

BORING (USA) ..9-12§.. 12 ch.g. Foolish Pleasure (USA) — Arriya (Luthier) 1p04. Tall rangy half-brother to 5 winners in France (including over jumps), and to Hurdles winner, Frontager (USA). Dam won 3 11f races in France. FLAT r17 w1 (12f) p4. NH '92/6 r21 p5 (inc 3 Chses, beaten ½l after hanging left once); inc Sell Hdle. P-t-P/HUNT CH '99 r6 p1 (2nd); pulled up 4, and ran out 1. Landed his first success over obstacles when fortuitously left solo in his Members, but otherwise fails to settle in Points, and patently does not stay. His rating remains suspect, and the chances of a follow up are negligible. *Mrs S.Y. Farthing & Miss P. Caudell — Monmouths (Shirley Farthing).* 740 (M), 991 (L), 1341 (2m110yH), 1450 (Cf).

BORIS BROOK ..9-7.. 10 ch.g. Meadowbrook — Crella (Cagirama) p661p60. Rangy workmanlike half-brother to Royella. Dam won a Maiden and placed 4. NH FLAT '96 r3 p0 (25-1 plus each time). NH '96/8 r5 p0. P-t-P '99 r6 w1 (Maiden) p0; ran out 1, and pulled up 1. Has gained both his wins at Friars Haugh, but the opposition has been modest, and has struggled in competitive events. Spooky-looking, with his one eye and a tube, and gives the impression that he is quite a character. *Mrs V. Scott Watson — Buccleuch (Rhona Elliot).* 40 (R), 111 (R), 360 (R), 712 (M), 1152 (I), 1427 (R), 1445 (3m1fH).

BORN NATURAL (IRE) ..9-5.. 10 b.m. Dromod Hill — Rossmire (Smartset) 5p3524. Unfurnished. Dam is half-sister to Smith's Lad (*qv* '94 Annual). IRISH P-t-P '97/8 r4 w1 (5yo plus mares Maiden) p1 (3rd); pulled up 2. P-t-P '99 r2 p0 (pulled up 1, and fell 1). Slogged her way through desperate ground when successful in Ireland, but beaten upwards of 14 lengths in her English completions, and worryingly has acquired a tongue-strap. *Mrs C.M. Woollacott — Dulverton E. (D. Woollacott).* 315 (R), 730 (I), 847 (R), 1376 (R), 1604 (M), 1671 (R).

BORROW MINE (IRE) ..9-7.. 9 b.g. Borovoe — Jasmine Girl (Jasmine Star) 646382. Sturdy compact half-brother to Shalik (IRE). P-t-P '97/9 (for Mrs C.H. Sporborg & Mr J. Pembreke) r11 w2 (Maiden and PPORA Restricted) p1 (3rd); pulled up 2, and fell 2. Enjoyed his busiest season to date, but has become a disappointing individual (beaten in his last 13 starts), and though he generally looked after his novice partner Andrew Braithwaite (slight promise, but much to learn) he did so in an unwilling manner. Visored on his last two starts (unimproved by blinkers previously), and remains an unconvincing jumper. *J.K. Braithwaite — Puckeridge (Christopher Sporborg).* 25 (Cnr), 93 (C), 288 (CMod), 413 (I), 609 (I), 839 (M).

BOSS MORTON (IRE) ..—.. 10 b.g. Tremblant — Sandy Kelly (Ovac ITY) ppu0. Compact good-topped half-brother to Irish Pointing winner, Instant Queen. Dam is half-sister to Melton Park (*qv* '97 Annual). IRISH P-t-P '95 r1 p0. IRISH NH FLAT '95 r2 p0. IRISH NH '95/9 r30 w2 (2m Hdle and 2m1f Ch) p5. Bought Doncaster, Oct for 6000. NH May '00 (from J. Barclay's) r1 p0 (tailed off over 3m: *wknd qckly 2 out*). In good heart when gaining all his seven prizes in '98 (the wins were on firmish), but unseated on his final two appearances in Ireland, and his jumping in the new yard remains very sketchy. Faced some difficult tasks, but nevertheless is disappointing considering he cost a tidy sum. Might be worth trying in blinkers. *J. Alexander - Fife.* 662 (O), 717 (Cf), 1120 (O).

BOW TIE ..10-8.. 10 b.g. Meadowbrook — Teviot Lady (New Brig) p1u113. Tall half-brother to Moss Peeble and Kinlochaline. Dam was placed in 4 Ladies. P-t-P '97/9 r17 w4 (inc 2 Opens) p3 (2 3rds); failed to finish 8 (fell/unseated 4, and refused 1). A late-maturing horse who enjoyed another fruitful season with three more Open wins to his credit, and a respectable third in the Heart of All England at Hexham. Usually needs an outing to get fit, but splendidly resolute once in the groove, and worth persevering with in Hunter Chases despite his tendency to hit the odd fence. Stays extra well, and appears to handle most surfaces. *J.G.B. Murray — Liddesdale.* 362 (O), 495 (O), 915 (3m1fH), 975 (O), 1120 (O), 1445 (3m1fH).

BOXING MATCH ..9-9.. 14 b.g. Royal Boxer — Mutchkin (Espresso) 69. Robust half-brother to Mutch Lark, Fiddle Nikhctum and One-T-Corbet. Dam won 10f Seller. NH '90/7 and '99 r49 w5 (3 Hdles, 2m6f-3m, and 2 Chses, 2m5f-2m6f; inc 4 Sells) p6. P-t-P/HUNT CH '98/9 (for Mr A.G. & Mr S.J. Merrick in '99) r11 w2 (inc 3m Hunt Ch) p2 (2nds, inc beaten neck in Hunt Ch); fell/unseated 2, and pulled up 2. The shock winner of the Greig Middleton Final at Huntingdon in '98, but has always lacked consistency, and the ravages of old age would appear to be catching up with him nowadays. Stays an easy three miles, but has gained his best results at shorter trips. Highly unlikely to achieve much were he to resurface. *Miss E. Saunders — Monmouths (Reg Brown).* 222 (3m1fH1oW), 684 (2m4fH).

BOYUP BROOK ..10-4.. 12 ch.g. Meadowbrook — Terrona Lady (unknown) 26652p1. Lengthy owner-bred half-brother to Polly's Lady. P-t-P '95 and '97/9 r18 w2 (Maiden and Restricted) p5 (3 2nds); failed to finish 7 (fell/unseated 3). Much improved in his fourth season thanks in no small measure to more accurate fencing, but has now probably reached the zenith of his powers. No easy ride as he tends to go in fits and starts, and given a confident drive by Thomas Scott in his latest success, might be capable of finding another race once he has had an outing or two in 2001. All his wins have been achieved on good ground or faster. *J.J. Paterson — Jedforest.* 108 (I), 359 (Cf), 493 (Cf), 716 (O), 973 (I), 1120 (O), 1366 (I).

BOZO BAILEY ..—.. 11 gr.g. Hadeer — Perceive (USA) (Nureyev USA) ppp. Strong parrot-mouthed. IRISH FLAT r4 p0. NH '94 (for M.H. Tompkins; visored 1) r7 p4 (inc 2). P-t-P '96/7 r8 p2; last 1, and pulled up 5. Gave the impression that he was not very keen over hurdles, and his thoughts are being brought back into training after three years off through injury would probably be unprintable were they known. The grub at Gibbon Towers must be good as he has never looked fit Pointing. The owner remains as svelte as ever, and still hopes to resume her glorious, but recently severely curtailed, riding career. *Mrs L. Gibbon — Essex & Suffolk.* 606 (OMa), 775 (OMa), 942 (CfMa).

BRACKENHILL ..9-7.. 8 b.g. Henbit (USA) — Havenwood Lady (Fair Season) p5p. Very tall rangy half-brother to Mirror Image. P-t-P '98/9 (for Mrs A.M. Easterby) r5 w1 (2m4f Maiden) p0; ran out 1, and fell/unseated 3. Quickened stylishly to win a three-finisher 2m4f Maiden at Southwell on his first Pointing completion, but disappeared after a February tumble in '99, and has proved disappointing since. Looked after the owner when not disgraced in his Members, but possibly another Henbit who would rather look after number one, and should be treated with caution at present. *F. Houghton Brown — Middleton.* 797 (R), 996 (M), 1230 (R).

BRAMBLEDOWN (IRE) ..10-12.. 10 b.m. Sheer Grit — Kilbeg Jackie (Beau Chapeau) 13f1. Good-bodied. P-t-P/HUNT CH '96 and '98 r5 w5 (inc 3m2f Hunt Ch and 2 Ladies). A high class mare who suffered her first defeat when given a dubious ride at Kempton, but bounced back from a spill in the Cheltenham Foxhunters to record a bloodless victory at Folkestone. Taken off her feet at Prestbury Park, but otherwise a determined galloper with the ability to quicken. Capable of spectacular jumping, and seems to cope with all types of going. Only manages light campaigns, and has missed alternate years to date, so may be absent in 2001. Glorious fun for her devoted owner-rider. *Mrs B.L.M. Sillars — W. Street/Tickham.* 224 (3m2fH), 303 (3mH), 584 (3m2f110yH), 1344 (3m2fH).

BRAMBLEHILL BUCK (IRE) ..10-1.. 12 gr.g. Roselier (FR) — Buckybrill (Buckskin FR) 22. Tall. IRISH P-t-P '94/5 r2 w1 (6 plus Maiden) p0. NH FLAT '95 r1 p1 (3rd). NH '95/8 r18 w4 (2m6f-3m3f Chses) p5 (inc 3rd in Hdle). P-t-P/HUNT CH '99 r7 w1 (Confined) p1 (3rd); pulled up 2, and unseated 1. A thorough stayer and suited by lashings of mud, but has always been a difficult ride, and needs everything to go his own way. Had a curtailed season in 2000, and probably only of interest in a Marks Tey mudbath if he resurfaces. Often blinkered under Rules, but not since. *M.A. Kemp — Suffolk.* 82 (M), 92 (Cf).

BRAMLEY ..8-9.. 7 ch.g. Fearless Action (USA) — Great Granny Smith (Fine Blue) pppp4. Sturdy close-coupled. Dam, half-sister to 9 Pointers including Royal Orchard (*qv*), won 7 Points (inc an Open) and placed 11 for the Marriotts. Was beaten 35 lengths when finally achieving a completion at the fifth attempt, but given the welter of success enjoyed by his family it would be surprising if he did not manage to win a race eventually. *C.J.W. Marriott — Heythrop (Fran Marriott).* 391 (CfMa), 471 (OMa), 899 (OMa), 1018 (OMa), 1194 (OMa).

BRANCH END ..—§§.. 9 b.g. Alias Smith (USA) — Besciamella (Foggy Bell) p5rppr. Workmanlike brother to Shawwell, and to Chasing winner, Kings Ketchup, and half-brother to Hurdles winner, Stagshaw Belle. Dam won 2m Hdle. NH FLAT '97/8 r2 p1 (3rd). NH '98/9 (for A. Charlton) r9 w1 (2m5f Hdle) p0; finished in both Chses. Won an appalling three-runner Hurdle on firm (a contest run at a crawl), but has proved to be thoroughly ungenuine in Points, and as well as defeating the novice Freddie Arthur, he also proved more than a match for Thomas Scott. Blinkered on his latest appearance. It would be most surprising if connections bothered with him again. *Mrs R. Arthur — Tynedale.* 183 (CCf), 419 (Cf), 660 (Cf), 1365 (O), 1476 (O), 1576 (Cf).

BRANDON BRIDGE ..8-2.. 10 b.g. Primo Dominie — Victoria Mill (Free State) 3. Compact half-brother to a French flat winner. NH FLAT '95 and '97 (first 3 for I. Balding) r4 p1 (2nd). NH '97 and '99 (final from T. Cuthbert's, bought for 550; previously for D. Geraghty, bought for 1500) r8; inc Sells. Only stands his racing in brief spurts, but was not wholly disgraced when 18 lengths last in his Members (would have been about 10 lengths closer had he not almost unseated at the final fence). A bad animal previously, and has pulled hard, but might conceivably have a squeak in a Maiden. *G.E. Davidson — Cumberland.* 1362 (M).

BRANSKI ..—.. 10 b.g. Newski (USA) — Lady Cognac (NZ) (Smuggler) p. NH FLAT '95 (for P. Nicholls) r2 p0. Sold Doncaster, Nov '95 for 1450. Surprisingly returned to the fray after a five year absence, but was never out of last place and jumped moderately before pulling up at halfway. *Mrs S. Baxter — R.A.* 329 (CfMa).

BRAVE JEANIE ..—.. 6 b.m. Alhaatmi — Jean Jeanie (Roman Warrior) p. Looked burly and given a quiet time before pulling up after 2m4f at Garthorpe. At least the rider did not end up flat on his back, which seemed to be the fate of those who encountered the Jean Jeanie. *Mrs K. Hughes — Cambridge Univ (Robert Mackley).* 1270 (OMa).

BRAVE MAN ..—.. 7 b.g. Arzanni — High Affair (High Line) p. Tall rangy half-brother to High Green (*qv*). NH FLAT Feb '98 (for M.W. Easterby) r1 p0. NH '98/9 (for J. Curtis; previously for M.W. Easterby; tried tongue-tied) r9 p2 (3rds in Chses, distant of 4 and of 5). Bought Doncaster, Aug for 3000. Pulled up lame at Wetherby, and subsequently had to be destroyed, compounding the miserable luck of our Yorkshire correspondent, John Milburn, whose previous runner suffered a similar fate. *J. Milburn & Mrs K.A. Jackson — Middleton (Nicky Wilson).* 169 (OMa).

BRAVE NODDY (IRE) ..10-6§.. 9 ch.g. Noalto — Running Brave (Brave Invader USA) 21611. IRISH P-t-P '97/8 r10 p2 (2nds); pulled up 1, and fell/unseated 2. P-t-P '99 r1 w1 (2-finisher Maiden). Acquired blinkers after failing to justify favouritism on his reappearance and gave three praiseworthy performances in them, but did not appear to be enjoying himself at Lifton, and a doubt remains about his total enthusiasm, though the firm ground that day probably had some bearing. Sure to win again if remaining in the present yard as he gets excellent assistance from the champion jockey, and is trained to near perfection by Caroline Egalton, but rarely sent off at a working man's price. *Mrs C. Egalton (Noddy Partnership) — Mid Devon (Caroline Egalton).* 876 (R), 1043 (R), 1516 (I), 1607 (I), 1672 (O).

BRECKENBROUGH LAD ..9-4.. 14 b.g. Uncle Pokey — Fabulous Beauty (Royal Avenue) p. Angular tubed brother to flat winner, Uncle Wilko. Dam won 3 5f races. FLAT r17 w1 (10f) p5 (3rds). NH '91/2 and '93/5 (blinkered 1) r10 w1 (2m Sell Hdle on all-weather) p0. P-t-P/HUNT CH '96/8 r12 w2 (match for Members, and Open) p2 (2nd of 3, and last of 3); pulled up 3, and unseated 1. Returned to the scene of his greatest Pointing achievement (winning the South Notts Open at 25-1 in '97) for his reappearance after two years absence, but quickly tailed off, and promptly drew his pension. *Mrs M.R. Bennett — Badsworth (Ian Bennett).* 1216 (O).

BRED FOR PLEASURE ..9-7.. 8 b.m. Niniski (USA) — The Fink Sisters (Tap On Wood) u533. Leggy spare-made. Dam won 2 2m4f Hdles, inc 3-runner Sell. NH FLAT '97 (for S. Cunningham) r2 p0. Unseated on her Pointing debut and given a blatant school next time (the jockey should have been fined), but has done better since, and has the ability to win a modest contest. Pulls hard and does not look an easy ride, and hung right in the closing stages before finishing five lengths third on her penultimate appearance. *A. Jackson — Cleveland (Tina Jackson).* 379 (OMa), 1002 (2m4fOMa), 1033 (OMa), 1330 (OMa).

BREEZE-BLOC ..9-0.. 11 ch.m. Sunley Builds — Sunny Breeze (Roi Soleil) pp4. Small light-framed owner-bred half-sister to Miss Melbury and Frisky-Breeze. Grandam, Softly Softly, was 2nd in 2 Points (disqualified once), and won 3m1f Ch. P-t-P '95/9 r14 w1 (Members) p2 (2nds, last once); last, and failed to finish 10 (refused 3, and fell/unseated 2). Lightly raced, exceptionally moderate, and most fortunate to have stumbled across a winning opportunity. Pulled up in her first two starts in 2000 when the rider injured himself, and then thought the horse was lame, but well beaten in a modest Confined when completing, and future winning prospects look dim. *J.B. Shears — Mid Devon.* 203 (R), 315 (R), 557 (Cf).

BREWERY LANE (IRE) ..—.. 8 b.g. Orchestra — Knight's Maid (Giolla Mear) 1ppp. Dam won 2m2f Mares Nov Ch in Ireland. IRISH P-t-P '97 and '99 r7 (6yo plus Maiden) p0; pulled up 5, and fell 1. Bought Doncaster, Aug for 1200. Has failed to complete in nine of 11 attempts, but has won the two exceptions — the Members was a walk-over. Has otherwise appeared to be devoid of stamina. *A. Hardacre — Tredegar F. (Tim Jones).* 342 (M), 1228 (R), 1453 (R), 1568 (R).

BRIAR ROSE (IRE) ..9-3.. 6 gr.m. Roselier (FR) — Born Lucky (Deep Run) 434p. Small unfurnished. Sold Tattersalls (Ireland), June '98 for 6782. Looks a thorough stayer in the making, and her first three efforts were all creditable (beaten a maximum of 11 lengths). Generally running on steadily in the closing stages, but has not been seen since pulling up and dismounting at the beginning of April. Should soon win a Maiden if sound in 2001. *N.M.L. Ewart — Liddesdale, & Cumberland F.* 45 (OMa), 112 (OMam), 425 (CfMa), 914 (CfMa).

BRIARY BOY (IRE) ..—.. 9 ch.g. Mister Lord (USA) — Aprolon Princess (IRE) (Duky) 7R3p. Workmanlike. Dam is an unraced half-sister to Many A Slip (*qv* '94 Annual). IRISH P-t-P '97 r3 p0 (5th of 6, and pulled up 2). IRISH NH '97/8 r3 p0. P-t-P '99 (for Mr N.W. Padfield) r7 w1 (Maiden) p4 (3rd of 4 thrice); last, and pulled up 1. Won a dreadful race in the previous yard, but gave new connections no grounds for encouragement in 2000 when failing to beat a rival, and looks suspect. *Mrs M. Murphy - Curre (Lyndon Williams).* 338 (R), 896 (R), 948 (R), 1228 (R).

BRICANMORE (IRE) ..9-7.. 9 b.g. Black Minstrel — Repetitive (USA) (Tell USA) fup2f. Workmanlike. Dam completed hat-trick in 2-2m2f Sell Hdles for Martin Pipe. IRISH P-t-P '96/7 r4 w1 (5yo Maiden) p1 (3rd); fell 1. IRISH NH '97 r3 p0. NH '99 r1 p0 (pulled up). His best form would entitle him to win a Restricted, but disappointing, and his jumping gets him into all sorts of trouble. Lost the rider at about halfway on three occasions, including on both Paddy Dartnall's attempts. Remarkably, started joint-favourite for a Hunter Chase, but was pulled up when tailed off. Tongue-tied on his latest appearance. *V. Dartnall — Dulverton W.* 35 (Cnr), 211 (Cnr), 383 (3mH), 849 (R), 931 (R).

BRIDGE HOUSE BOY ..9-3.. 10 ch.g. Sunyboy — Danny D'Albi (Wrens Hill) pp465. Sturdy half-brother to Danny Rhy. Dam dead-heated for 2m Irish Hdle and placed 6 (inc 3rd in English Adjacent). Grandam, Annie Babu, won Irish Members. P-t-P '97/9 r11 w1 (Maiden) p2; fell/unseated 2, and pulled up 3. Lost his maiden status at the 11th attempt on firm ground at Holnicote, and should be suited by a test of stamina, but does not appear to be getting the trip, and a Restricted success seems unlikely. Wears a cross-noseband, and has been tried in a tongue-strap. *A. Oliver — E. Cornwall.* 157 (M), 729 (R), 848 (R), 1095 (R), 1375 (R).

BRIDGE MAN ..9-6.. 11 gr.g. Scallywag — Starbridge (Space King) 1p. Big rangy owner-bred. Dam, half-sister to Rhodbridge (*qv* '94 Annual), won Maiden and placed 2. Great-grandam, Ronbridge, was 3rd in Point. NH '98/9 r5 p1 (2nd of 4 in Ch); pulled up 3. P-t-P/HUNT CH '97 and '99 r4 p0 (pulled up 3, fell 1). Made all in a clear lead to win in a bad two-finisher Maiden at Siddington, but was tiring visibly in the last half mile, and undoubtedly aided by the fall of the market leader at the fourth last. Another headstrong Scallywag who usually runs himself into the ground, and is not good enough for sub-3m events. Has been incredibly lightly raced, and sure to struggle in Restricteds. *N. Bush — Beaufort.* 754 (CfMa), 1341 (2m110yH).

BRIGHT APPROACH (IRE) ..10-4.. 8 gr.g. Roselier (FR) — Dysart Lady (King's Ride) u3323121. Unfurnished half-brother to Irish NH flat winner, It Takes Time (IRE). Dam won 2 Points (one at Castletown Geoghegan, scene of Bright Approach's victory), a NH flat, 2 2m Hdles and 3 Chses (2m3f-3m) in Ireland. IRISH P-t-P '98 r11 w1 (4&5yo Maiden) p3; pulled up 4, and unseated 1. P-t-P/HUNT CH '99 r5 w1 (Restricted) p2 (3rds). Cost current connections 14,000gns which looked money down the drain after his first English season, but has acclimatised well now, and landed a few nice bets when produced with a strong late run by Polly Gundry to win at Lifton on his final start. Seems to possess more speed than stamina, and can win again, particularly if retaining the services of the champion. *J.H. Burbidge — O. Surrey & Burstow (Ollie Cann)*. 211 (Cnr), 263 (I), 404 (I), 632 (I), 737 (I), 1059 (I), 1562 (C), 1638 (L).

BRIGHT BEACON ..9-9.. 7 br.g. Lighter — Pennulli (Sir Nulli) 31p3. Compact brother to Don'tcallmegeorge, and half-brother to Eighty Eight, Folly Furlong and Get On Lottie. Dam is an unraced daughter of Pensham (won 44 Points and Hunt Ch and placed 26 for Pat Tollit). P-t-P '99 r1 p0 (pulled up). Benefited from a gentle introduction, and in particular the last fence blunder of the runner-up to win at Llanvapley, but disappointingly faded tamely on his debut in Restricted company. Showed an abundance of stamina when scoring and not disgraced in a fair race on his final start, so ought to be capable of further success. *Mrs P. Tollit — Glamorgan (Evan Williams)*. 269 (CfMa), 746 (CfMa), 1088 (R), 1298 (R).

BRIGHT FLASH (IRE) ..—.. 8 b.g. Executive Perk — Bright Note (Buckskin FR) p. Sturdy half-brother to Irish NH Flat and Hurdles winner, Mrs Battle. Dam, half-sister to Pepys, won 4 Irish Hdles, 2m-2m4f. IRISH P-t-P '99 r1 p1 (20/3rd). IRISH NH '98 r1 p0. IRISH NH FLAT '98/9 r3 p0. An apparently poor performer who pulled up three out when a remote third in a Members in which only one of the runners got round. *Mr & Mrs K. Smith — W. Somerset V. (Dennis Kenny)*. 1094 (M).

BRIGHT LADY ..9-0.. 14 ch.m. Sunyboy — Rare Game (Raise You Ten) fu00042du. Half-sister to Last Gamble (qv). P-t-P '94/5 and '98/9 r12 p1 (2nd); fell/unseated 2, and pulled up 4. A slow old mare, and tailed off last four times consecutively when ridden by a novice girl, but got slightly more involved on her penultimate outing. Clearly some brave souls thought her Members was there for the taking as she was the subject of a (misplaced) gamble. Tends to sweat up, and not error free, but probably a good friend to Rachael Green. *M.S. Green — S. & W. Wilts (Jane Green)*. 14 (R), 33 (Cnr), 208 (R), 326 (L), 520 (OMa), 765 (L), 1062 (OMa), 1130 (M).

BRIGHT PROSPECT (IRE) ..9-4.. 10 ch.m. Arapahos (FR) — Oldcourt Lass VII (unknown) p. IRISH P-t-P '96/8 r8 w1 (dead-heat for 5&6yold mares Maiden) p2; pulled up 2, and unseated 1. IRISH NH FLAT '97 r1 p0. IRISH NH '98 r3 p0 (unseated in Hunt Ch). P-t-P '99 (for Mr T.D.B. Underwood & Mr A. Parrish) r4 p1 (3rd); unseated 1, and pulled up 1. Gained the only success of a five-year career in soft in '97 (actually appeared to have been beaten a head, but Judge awarded a dead-heat), but has been lightly raced and shown little since. *R.G. Langley — Worcs.* 247 (R).

BRIGHT REFORM (IRE) ..84.. 8 ch.g. Lancastrian — Clogheen Lucy (Sheer Grit) p44. Lengthy well-made half-brother to Irish Pointing winner, Clogheen Lass. Dam is an unraced half-sister to Time Traveller (qv '92 Annual). P-t-P '98 r1 p0 (pulled up). Has shown a little ability each time he has raced, but needs to improve further to be considered winning material. Missed the '99 season, and has looked to be carrying too much condition to date, so might achieve his goal if he can be produced fighting fit. *H.A. Shone — Cheshire*. 695 (OMa), 965 (OMa), 1153 (OMa).

BRIGHT TORINO (IRE) ..—.. 6 b.m. Febrino — Bright Toro (Proverb) R. Half-sister to Glynn Brae (IRE). Bought Doncaster, Nov for 1100. Was hacking round at the back when she ducked out at the seventh in a Maiden, and later found to be shin-sore. *Mr & Mrs M. Plinton & M.J. Bloom — Dunston H. (Mike Bloom)*. 1382 (OMa).

BRIGHT VULCAN ..9-2.. 10 b.g. Royal Vulcan — Bright Swan (Will Hays USA) 26p. Plain lengthy brother to Hurdles winner, Henrys Port, and half-brother to Hurdles winner, Lumumba Days. Dam was placed in 6 flat, 2nd in a Sell Hdle; and 2nd in Ladies ('has long given the distinct impression of being ungenuine'). P-t-P '98/9 (for breeder, Mrs J. Bradbery) r6 p1 (last of 3); pulled up 4. Stepped up on previous efforts when runner-up at Kimble on his reappearance but did not appear to appreciate the fast ground on his last two starts, and remains a lightly-raced maiden. *J.G. O'Neill — Bicester with Whaddon*. 1147 (OMa), 1437 (OMa), 1486 (OMa).

BRIGSTOCK (U) ..—.. a b.m. unknown 5. Remounted to complete one of the slowest ever circuits of Larkhill, finishing about a mile behind the winner of the King's Troop jolly. *Capt G. Chanter — R.A.* 64 (2m4fC).

BROADBROOK LASS ..—.. 7 ch.m. Broadsword (USA) — Netherbrook Lass (Netherkelly) pp. Rangy owner-bred half-sister to Netherbrook Lad (qv). Remote when pulling up twice, and evidently already has an attitude problem, as she was blinkered on her second start (the subject of an uninspired plunge from 20s to sevens). *M.H. Ings — Teme V. (Billie Brown)*. 989 (OMa), 1278 (OMa).

BROAD INK (IRE) 11 b.g. Broadsword (USA) — No Ink (No Mercy) fpuf33f. Robust quite attractive owner-bred half-brother to Oxford Quill and Godfrey Firstaider. NH FLAT '96 r1 p1 (3rd). P-t-P '98 r3 p0 (4th, and pulled up 2). Appeared to go wrong in '98, and resurfaced in the West

Country after two years off, but managed to beat just one rival in two completions. In the wars generally (missed six weeks after being jumped on whilst on the floor at Buckfastleigh, and winded on his final appearance), and his jumping technique needs polishing before he returns. *Mrs H.D. Power — S. Cornwall.* 105 (OMa), 312 (CfMa), 540 (OMa), 657 (R), 1391 (OMa), 1522 (CfMa), 1640 (OMa).

BROAD STATEMENT ..8-8.. 8 br.g. Broadsword (USA) — Spartiquick (Spartan General) ppp. Close-coupled half-brother to Newlands-General and No Quibble, and to Chasing winners, Highland Poacher and Quick Quote. Dam, half-sister to Hunter Chase and Pointing winner, Optomism, won Maiden and 2m4f Chase and placed total of 3 for Chubb Castle, and grandam, Quick Answer, won Hunt Ch and 5 Opens for him. P-t-P '99 r5 p0 (last, pulled up 2, and fell/unseated 2). Possibly unlucky at Ashorne in his first season (a length in front but ridden when falling two out), but looks to have a hole in him somewhere, and has compounded quickly after running prominently for a long way otherwise. Not easy to train, and did not reappear until April. Hunter Chasing him was wildly optimistic, but from a good family, and might be worth another chance in Maiden company. *J.M. Castle — Bicester with Whaddon.* 1012 (CfMa), 1204 (OMa), 1626 (3m1f110yH).

BROADWAY SWINGER ..9-12.. 10 b.g. Sulaafah (USA) — River Culm (Royal Salmon) ppp4242p. Tall good-looking half-brother to Semliki. Dam, half-sister to Culm Sovereign (*qv* '92 Annual), won 4 Points and placed 9. Grandam, Copper Plate II, was a useless Pointer, but great-grandam, Fonteray, won 3 Points. P-t-P '96/8 r11 w3 (Maiden, Restricted and Intermediate) p3 (2 2nds; and last of 3); failed to finish 4 (unseated 2). Showed plenty of tenacity to win three times '97/8, but off the course the following year, and clearly troubled on his return. Looked most unenthusiastic when tried in blinkers once, and acquired a tongue-strap on his last five starts, but finished weakly in the main despite the best efforts of Simon Andrews. Should be watched until he shows signs of a return to form. *P.E.D. Cooke — Cottesmore (Charlotte Cooke).* 93 (Cf), 229 (Cf), 367 (Cf), 511 (O), 607 (O), 870 (O), 1036 (O), 1286 (Cf).

BROCKBUSTER ..9-6.. 6 b.g. Syrtos — Ruby's Vision (Balinger) f. Brother to Elliewelliewoo (*qv*). Fell four out when leading in a poor Maiden at Siddington. An interesting recruit, as his sister completed a hat-trick in her first three Points in 2000, and will be short odds to gain compensation when next he appears. *M.J. & Mrs J. Arnold — N. Cotswold (Emma Baker).* 753 (CfMa).

BRODANTE KING (IRE) ..10-3.. 7 b.g. Phardante (FR) — Pedigree Corner (Pollerton) 153. Small neat half-brother to Bredinthepurple (IRE), and to Irish Pointing winner, Bramble Wood. IRISH P-t-P '99 r3 p1 (20*l* last of 3); pulled up 1. Won a youngsters Maiden at Larkhill in January in which only two of the eight starters were still going in the final mile, but made too many mistakes when a disappointing favourite next time. His first attempt in blinkers resulted in a respectable four lengths third, and would pick up a Restricted on his best form. *A.J. Hales (Merrylegs Racing) — Vine & Craven (Alex Hales).* 57 (OMa), 894 (R), 1393 (R).

BROGUESTOWN PRIDE (IRE) ..9-4.. 13 b.g. Kemal (FR) — Una's Pride (Raise You Ten) p955p43251. Lengthy half-brother to More Action and Dante's Pride, to Hurdles winner, Cantamega, to Irish jumping winner, Daring Double, and to Irish Pointing winners, Mount Leinster Lad and Your A Star (also successful Hunter Chaser). Dam won Hunt Ch and Point in Ireland. IRISH NH FLAT r1 w1(2m4f). IRISH NH '94 r7 w1 (3m Hdle) p3. NH '94/5 r2 p0 (remote 5th of 6 and pulled up 1 in Chses). P-t-P/HUNT CH '97/9 r17 p3 (2 2nds; and last of 3); pulled up 6. A veteran plodder, but still prepared to try hard, and gained his first success for six years when left solo to land his Members on his final start. Has had terrible problems with his wind, and is a waste of time in competitive races. *P. Blagg — O. Surrey & Burstow (Maggie Howie).* 4 (O), 15 (C), 26 (O), 130 (CMod), 286 (O), 574 (4mMO), 981 (O), 1210 (O), 1398 (Cf), 1508 (M).

BROKEN ENGLISH ..9-13.. 8 ch.m. Say Primula — Elitist (Keren) p213. Plain lengthy half-sister to Beyond Mombasa and Kralingen. P-t-P '99 r2 p0 (pulled up 2). Much improved in her second season, but needed luck on her side when successful at Corbridge (the favourite was clear when departing at the last), and found herself pitched into Intermediate class rather quicker than was probably intended. None of those who finished behind her have yet to emulate her feat in Restricteds, and she herself was last in her only subsequent race. *Mrs G. Sunter — Cleveland.* 46 (OMa), 281 (OMa), 424 (R), 692 (I).

BROOKTHORPE ..—.. 8 ch.m. Rakaposhi King — Hejera (Cantab) fpppup. Small light-framed half-sister to Po Cap Eel (*qv*). 1000 4-y-o. NH FLAT '98 (from R. Mitchell's) r2 p0. A very unattractive herring-gutted pony, and her form matches her looks. Was very reluctant to race after two miles once, and was subsequently tried in a tongue-strap. *J.S. Warner — Cotswold V.F.* 30 (CMa), 146 (OMa), 339 (CfMa), 450 (CfMa), 601 (CfMa), 900 (O).

BROTHER NERO (NZ) ..9-13.. 9 b.g. Roman Empire — End Of The Road (NZ) (Double Nearco CAN) 2152331. Compact good-bodied brother to a winner in New Zealand. NH FLAT '97 r2 p1 (3rd). P-t-P '97 (for Mr D.H. Barons) r3 p0 (fell/unseated 3). NH '99 (for A.G. Hobbs) r3 p0 (Hdles). Cut no ice over hurdles (looked too backward), but his previous jumping deficiencies did not manifest themselves again, and enjoyed a profitable season. Took five attempts to win a Restricted (had after all only beaten two long-standing maidens at Buckfastleigh), and seems to prefer decent ground, as softer surfaces appear to sap his stamina. Might prove good enough to win another minor race or two. *Mrs Y. Watson, K. Champion & P. Rattenbury — Lamerton (Yvonne Watson & Jo Channon).* 106 (OMa), 253 (CfMa), 406 (R), 536 (R), 729 (R), 1176 (R), 1517 (R).

BROTHER PRIM ..9-7.. 12 gr.g. Brotherly (USA) — Tudor Primrose (Tudor Sam) pup25. Big rangy owner-bred. P-t-P/HUNT CH '95/6 and '98/9 r12 w1 (Maiden) p2; pulled up 3, and fell/unseated 4. Won a remarkably well contested Chaddesley Maiden in '99, but has always been prone to errors, and still gives the impression that he does not get the trip. Looks likely to struggle further in Restricteds. *A.G.L. Taylor — Croome & W. Warwicks.* 896 (R), 992 (R), 1167 (3m2fR), 1354 (M), 1460 (R).

BROTHER SIMON ..—.. 8 b.g. St Columbus — The Tooth Fairy (Black Sovereign) pp. Half-brother to Recoco and Joe's Birthday. Dam was 2nd in a Point for the Wards. Poorly-bred, and was pulled up twice in the space of eight days in early April. *Mrs A. Ward — Bicester with Whaddon (Jon Trice-Rolph).* 898 (OMa), 972 (OMa).

BROUGHTON'S PORT ..9-3.. 11 b.g. Reesh — Tawnais (Artaius USA) 422. Strong-topped half-brother to flat winner, Bakers Daughter. FLAT '93/6 r19 p2. NH '96 (for W. Musson) r3 p0 (inc Sell). Sold Ascot, Nov '96 for 750. Placed twice as a three-year-old, including a three-quarters of a length second at Sandown, but unrewarded for the next seven years. Ran reasonably when beaten four lengths in an eight-plus Maiden, but a remote last next time, and it could be that he struggles to stay three miles. *T. Bricknell-Webb — S. Tetcott.* 1385 (Cf), 1522 (CfMa), 1642 (M).

BROWN ESQUIRE ..10-0.. 10 b.g. Broadleaf — Ana Brown (Souvran) p422pp. Tall plain. Dam, half-sister to Chestnut Prince (*qv* '90 Annual), pulled up and unseated in Points for Gemma Dewhurst (was previously distant last of two in a Maiden). NH '98 r3 p0 (tailed off in Hdles — pulled up 2). P-t-P '98/9 r6 w1 (Maiden) p3 (2 2nds); ran out 1, and pulled up 1. Has accrued five placings since winning a gruelling Maiden taking 8min 20s in heavy at Sandon, but very one-paced, and showed an instant dislike for fast ground on his final appearance. Deserves to win a Restricted, and Flagg Moor could be the place for him. *Miss G. Dewhurst — Cheshire.* 336 (R), 589 (R), 902 (Cf), 1129 (R), 1338 (4m1fH), 1528 (R).

BROWNRATH KING (IRE) ..10-2.. 12 b.g. Henbit (USA) — Selham (Derring-Do) 32. Workmanlike lengthy brother to jumping winner, Hedgehopper (IRE), and half-brother to Derring Assassin, and to 3 flat winners. Dam won at 8f. IRISH NH FLAT '93/4 r7 p1 (3rd). IRISH NH '93/8 r37 w2 (2m3f Hdle, and 2m6f Ch) p4. NH '99 (for C. Grant) r5 p2 (3rds in Chses, inc Sell). Achieved a couple of remote placings over 3m3f at Sedgefield, and was a distance behind Majority Major once, but 14 lengths ahead of him next time! Busy in Ireland (tried in blinkers), but sparingly raced now. Has not scored since '97, but might be able to rectify the situation if dropped to Points. *P. Sawney — Cleveland (Jackie Sawney).* 682 (3m3fH), 923 (3m3fH).

BROWN ROBBER ..9-12.. 13 gr.g. Baron Blakeney — Brown Veil (Don't Look) 1p61p423p. Rangy brother to Brown Blake, and half-brother to Brown Bala and Brown Wren. Dam won 2m4f Hdle and 4 Chses, 3m1f-3m4f. NH '93/4 and '95/7 r15 p3 (2nds in 2m3f Chses); lame final. P-t-P/HUNT CH '98/9 r9 w2 (Maiden and Restricted) p3 (2 2nds); unseated 1. Doubled his previous victory total in 2000, and usually makes the bulk of the running when successful, but does not put up much of a struggle when hard work looms, and finds regulation fences too demanding. Seems to act on any going, but further success might be elusive. *Mrs S.J. Batchelor — Lamerton.* 258 (Cf), 467 (3m1f110yH), 654 (I), 720 (M), 852 (Cf), 1188 (O), 1514 (Cf), 1636 (Cf), 1644 (3m2f110yH).

BROWN WREN ..9-4.. 10 b.m. Kinglet — Brown Veil (Don't Look) 354d24. Small unfurnished half-sister to Brown Robber (*qv*). NH FLAT '96 r1 p0. NH '96/7 r8 p1 (3rd). P-t-P '99 r4 p0 (4th, and pulled up 3). Improved for the change of scenery, but modest in the extreme, and will struggle to find a race though her reliable jumping should continue to be an asset. Regularly got into a challenging position in 2000, but like her half-sister found little when push came to shove. *Mrs A.G. Lawe — Radnor & W. Herefords (A. Charlesworth).* 341 (CfMa), 488 (CfMa), 866 (CfMa), 1465 (OMa), 1626 (3m1f110yH).

BRUCE (U) ..—.. 9 b.g. unknown 5. Waddled round four fences behind when hefting nearly 15 stone in his Members, and just got the worst of a needle match with a rival who was carrying 18 pounds more. *I.W. Price — S. Notts.* 1214 (M).

BRUMMEL (U) ..—.. 9 bl.g. unknown 4. P-t-P '99 r1 p0 (pulled up). Managed to complete the course this year — after taking all that time to get there it would have been rude not to — but only beat a remounter, and darkness was descending as he finished. *Capt G. Chanter — R.A.* 64 (2m4fC).

BRYDFERTH DDU (IRE) ..—.. 6 b.m. Supreme Leader — Mantas Melody (IRE) (Orchestra) p. Tall. Dam is half-sister to Lislary Lad (*qv* '97 Annual). Sold Tattersalls (Ireland), June for 5357. Looks the part and was sent off second favourite for a May debut, but gave a novicey display before pulling up and dismounting. May do better eventually if she is unscathed. Her name translates as Black Beauty, which might be useful information for anybody searching for Anna Sewell's heart-wrenching saga in a Welsh library. *D. Brace — Llangeinor.* 1413 (OMa).

BUACHAILL DANA (IRE) ..9-7.. 11 gr.g. King Persian — June The Tenth (Lord Gayle USA) pf5f. Tall strong-topped half-brother to an Irish flat and Hurdles winner, and to a winner in Hong Kong. P-t-P/HUNT CH '98/9 r17 w3 (inc 2m6f Hunt Ch) p2; fell/unseated 6, and pulled up 4. Unraced until he was eight, and has done well to win three races including an awful 2m6f Hunter Chase at Towcester, but has crashed in three of his last five starts, and is becoming most unsafe. Achieved nothing tangible in 2000, and will need a total overhaul if he is to get back on track. At least Jenny Garley (who has fallen off him on the five occasions she has partnered him) has given up the unequal struggle! *Miss J. Garley — Pytchley*. 195 (O), 553 (MO), 1005 (M), 1333 (3mH).

BUBBLE N SQUEEK ..9-12§.. 12 ch.g. Celtic Cone — Booterstown (Master Owen) 32446. Sparsely-made brother to Celtic Town (*qv*). P-t-P '95/9 r21 w3 (Maiden, Restricted and Club) p12 (7 2nds, last once); pulled up 2, and fell 2. Regularly in the frame, but tainted by an evil personality, and is becoming more and more unenthusiastic — beat just five home in 2000 and only three in '99. A thorough stayer, but can get bolshie in the preliminaries, and sometimes declines to jump off on terms. Beat Whatafellow first time out in '98, but has avoided winning all 17 starts since, and likely to try to extend the sequence if he returns. Surprisingly never tried in blinkers on the racecourse. *C.J.B. Barlow, S. Jones & Mrs J.C. Pepworth — Cheshire (Peter Morris)*. 533 (I), 591 (O), 1525 (L), 1601 (3mH), 1632 (I).

BUCKAHOLIC (IRE) ..10-6.. 8 b.g. Buckskin (FR) — Dunacarney (Random Shot) f2. P-t-P '99 r3 w1 (Maiden) p1 (2nd); and fell 1. A useful tool at best, but finds little at the business end, and pulled defeat out of the jaws of victory at Horseheath. This lends credence to the theory that he was coming to the end of his tether when departing at the last at Cottenham previously. Yet another Buckskin who stands his racing badly, but should romp a Restricted at least if all is well in 2001. *Dr D.B.A. Silk, W. Meadows & B. Warren — Kent & Surrey Bloodhounds (Heather Silk)*. 16 (R), 96 (I).

PLATE 28   907 Percy Hunt Members: Buckaroo (Mrs A. Tweedie), 1st, are in command at the last
PHOTO: Alan Mitchell

BUCKAROO ..9-9.. 10 b.m. Escapism (USA) — Come On Clover (Oats) 7pp1481. Smallish compact half-sister to Lady Clifford. Dam is half-sister to Welsh Clover. P-t-P '96/9 (for Mr K. Anderson) r17 w1 (Maiden) p7 (3 2nds); fell/unseated 4, and pulled up 3. Took 17 races and five years to break her duck, and has no more than an honest plodder, but finally captured both her Members races, and did so in respectable times. An excitable mare who tends to get warm in the paddock, in which she has two handlers. *Mrs A. Tweedie — Dumfries, Border, & Percy*. 109 (L), 360 (R), 421 (3m5fL), 907 (M), 1081 (R), 1427 (R), 1501 (M).

BUCKET OF GOLD ..9-6§.. 11 b.g. Buckskin (FR) — Among The Gold (Giolla Mear) p1. Tall rangy angular half-brother to Hurdles winner, Saint Cecilia. Dam won Irish NH flat. NH '95/7 r10 w1 (2m5f Hdle) p2 (2nds); 5th, and pulled up 3 in Chses. P-t-P '98/9 r7 w1 (Members) p1 (last of 2); pulled up 2, and fell 1. Landed his Members for the second year running (would be going for a four-timer in 2001 but for a race-losing error two out in '98), but it is one of the worst contests in the calendar, and he has looked decidedly irresolute otherwise. Blinkered once in '99. *Mr & Mrs A.S. Denniff — Grove & Rufford (Fiona Denniff).* 545 (O), 1069 (M).

BUCK LADY (IRE) ..—.. 8 b.m. Brush Aside (USA) — Parson Money (The Parson) pppp. Lengthy. Dam is sister to Supreme Dealer (*qv* '99 Annual), and half-sister to 3 other Pointers. IRISH P-t-P '98 r2 w1 (5yo Mares Maiden) p0. NH '98/9 (for P. Webber) r2 p0 (tailed off and pulled up twice). Bought Doncaster, Aug for 2500. Scored in very soft in Ireland, but has done nothing but pull up since she left her homeland. Gave the impression of being very shin-sore in 2000. *Mrs T.M. Gibson — Tynedale.* 183 (CCf), 360 (R), 714 (C), 976 (R).

BUCKLEBERRY TIME (IRE) ..9-6.. 10 b.g. Buckskin (FR) — Spring Chimes (Slippered) u. Half-brother to Le Belle Avril (IRE), and to Hurdles winner, Ballymana Boy (IRE). Sent off joint favourite (admittedly with the ghastly Summer Haven!) in a 15-runner Maiden in February, and gave a prominent display until fading after three out and unseating at the last. Seems to have another agenda, and was not seen again. *M.J. Roberts — Worcs* (Theresa McCurrich). 1359 (OMa).

BUCKLEY BEAU ..—.. 9 b.g. Buckley — Somay (Tarkhun) p. Half-brother to Basincroft. Dam won 3 Hdles, 2m-2m4f. Pulled up after 2m4f when struggling on a belated debut in May. *P.T. & Mrs S. Cartridge & T. Cartridge — Worcs* (Theresa McCurrich). 1359 (OMa).

BUCKLEY HOUSE ..—§§.. 9 b.g. Buckley — Reperage (USA) (Key To Content USA) pppp4p. Good-topped lenthy brother to Heavenly Seven (*qv*). NH FLAT Spr '97 r2 p0. NH '97/8 (for A. Charlton) r4 p1 (2nd). Sold Doncaster, Aug '98 for 1000. A thoroughly nasty piece of work (in the mould of so many by Buckley), and is regularly unruly in the preliminaries. Pulls very hard and hangs badly to the right, and gives up as soon as he thinks he has done enough. Pulled up in five Points, and 28 lengths fourth in the other. Maddeningly, he is perfectly capable of winning a Maiden, as he showed when second in a Hurdle in which he threw his chance away by veering badly on the run-in and almost leaving the course. Cannot be trusted an inch. *W.M. Kathrens & A. Jenkins — Curre (Lyndon Williams).* 340 (R), 601 (CfMa), 891 (OMa), 1302 (OMa), 1456 (OMa), 1661 (OMa).

BUCKMAN ..—.. 11 b.g. Buckley — Mangro (Mandamus) p. Tall strong fired brother to Hurdles winner, Glandalane Lady, and half-brother to Grayrose Double (dam of Grayrose Fleur, *qv* '99 Annual) and Watermead, and to successful Hurdler, Miss Mangaroo. NH '95/6 and '98 r7 p0 (last, and pulled up 1 in Hdles; and last, pulled up 3, and unseated 1 in Chses). P-t-P '99 r7 w2 (Maiden and Intermediate) p0; fell 2, and pulled up. Woken up by Simon Andrews for a late season double in '99 (worth 9-11; walked over once), but disappeared after pulling up at the opening East Anglian fixture in 2000. Indolent and will doss around to his hearts content if allowed, and only twice better than last in 15 career starts. *Mr & Mrs M.S. Burman — Cambs* (Michael Burman). 15 (C).

BUCK RUN (IRE) ..9-6.. 11 b.g. Buckskin (FR) — Aughclogeen Run (Deep Run) Rangy brother to Irish Pointing winner, Hoolby Skint. IRISH NH '94/6 r4 p0. IRISH NH FLAT '96 r1 p0. IRISH P-t-P '94 and '97 r5 p2. P-t-P '98 (for Mr S. Bradburn) r3 w1 (Maiden) p0. Never runs much (typical Buckskin), but won a stamina test at Sandon in '98, since when he has not finished within 30 lengths of the winner in two completions. Hated the firm ground on his latest appearance. *P.H. Morris & partners — W. Salop* (Peter Morris). 120 (CR), 292 (M), 567 (R), 1152 (I), 1409 (O).

BUCKSFERN ..—.. 14 b.g. Buckskin (FR) — Deep Fern (Deep Run) pp4. Tall hobdayed half-brother to Irish Pointing and English jumping winner, Mossy Fern, and to Irish NH flat and jumping winner, Coq Hardi Affair (IRE). Dam won Irish NH flat. IRISH P-t-P '92/5 r15 w7 (inc dead-heat) p5 (2nds); pulled up 2, and fell last when 1l up but tiring. IRISH HUNT CH '94/5 r6 w1 (3m) p3. P-t-P/HUNT CH '96 and '98 (Bevis-trained for Mr E.E. Williams) r7 w1 (Open) p4 (2 2nds); unseated 1. Useful on ground ranging from firmish to heavy in Ireland, but has run just five times since winning the Ludlow Open of '96 in the fastest time of the day. Blinkered with no improvement on his last two starts and looks finished. *R.N. Bevis — W. Salop.* 334 (O), 1025 (3m10yH), 1128 (Cf).

BUCKS VIEW (IRE) ..10-7.. 11 b.g. Buckskin (FR) — Our View (Our Mirage) 21. Workmanlike. Dam won NH flat and 2m4f Hdle in Ireland. P-t-P '97/9 r7 w4 (inc Open) p3 (2 2nds). Never out of the frame in his nine Points, and is a useful performer, but it is a real pity that we do not see him on a more regular basis. Beat the veteran Bishops Hall cleverly at Eaton Hall, avenging defeat by a stable companion on an earlier visit there, and is smart enough to take his chance in a Hunter Chase. A thorough stayer, responds gamely to pressure (needs to as his trainer can be most persuasive), and best suited by plenty of cut in the ground. *H.R. Hocknell — Cheshire* (Gary Hanmer). 530 (O), 779 (O).

BUDDY GIRIE ..—.. 8 b.g. Lord Bud — Hatsu-Girie (Ascertain USA) fRf. Owner-bred half-brother to Hattie (*qv*). NH May '00 r1 p0 (fell in Hdle: *nt jw, bhnd when fell 4*). Steered an erratic course before falling at halfway on his debut, and the rider then played follow-my-leader past a marker approaching the second fence at Whitwell. *R.W. Swiers — York & Ainsty N.* 696 (OMa), 1003 (OMa).

BUDGHILL ..8-7.. 8 b.g. Gold Dust — Celerity Lady (Lighter) u4534. Robust half-brother to Bedtime Pixie. Looks slow and has not jumped too well to date, but possibly worth persevering with in weak Maidens. *Mrs M. Nicholls — Spooners & W. Dartmoor* (Verity Nicholls). 846 (M), 1519 (CfMa), 1564 (OMa), 1640 (OMa), 1676 (OMa).

BUGLER (U) ..—.. 9 b.g. unknown u. Blew it at the fourth. *Capt G. Chanter — R.A.* 64 (2m4fC).

BUGSY MORAN (IRE) ..9-8.. 11 b.g. Buckskin (FR) — Rusheen's Girl (Dusky Boy) u. Workmanlike rather unfurnished half-brother to Missile Run, and to Irish NH flat winner, Sarah Supreme. NH '97 r1 p1 (very remote last of 3). P-t-P '97 and '99 r9 w1 (Maiden) p4 (2 2nds), and fell 3. Won a bad Maiden unchallenged at Guilsborough in '99, but generally a weak finisher with a tendency to make blunders, and cleared just one fence successfully in 2000. *J.R. Millington — Fernie.* 580 (3mH).

BUKEHORN ..9-1.. 10 b.g. Bold Owl — Milly Kelly (Murrayfield) 36u44. Big strong good-looking fired half-brother to jumping winners, Singlesole, Chichell's Hurst, Ima Delight and Bassenhally (first three Sly-trained). Dam won 2m Hdle for Pam Sly, and grandam, Arctic Festival, fell in Point for her after producing Milly Kelly. NH FLAT Spr '96 r3 p0. NH '98/9 r5 p0. NH Apr/May '00 r4 p0 (6th in Nov Ch: *a bhnd*; unseated in Nov Ch: *trckd ldrs til ld aft 13-nxt, ev ch when ur 3 out*; 4th in Nov HCap Ch: *in tch, hdwy 9, hit 12, no imp aft*; and 4th in Nov Ch *ld, hdd & blun 12, wknd*). An imposing individual who is very well-related, but missed 31 months with leg trouble after April '96. Favourite for what looked to be the simplest of tasks in his Members, but did not get the trip, and connections are struggling to find any distance over which he is effective. *Mrs P.M. Sly — Fitzwilliam.* 769 (M).

BULLENS BAY (IRE) ..10-6§.. 12 b.g. Hallodri (ATA) — Coolgreen Lolly (Blue Chariot) 3p4541r416. Close-coupled plain-faced half-brother to Lollys Patch, and to Irish Pointing winner, Buckshot Roberts. Dam won 4 Irish Points. IRISH P-t-P '93/5 r13 w3 (inc Open) p4; pulled up 1, and refused 1. IRISH NH FLAT r1 p0. NH '95/8 r22 w4 (2m7f-3m3f Hdle) p8; 4th of 5 in only Ch. P-t-P/HUNT CH '97 and '99 r14 w1 (Ladies) p5 (2nds, inc Hunt Ch); unseated 1, refused 1, pulled up 1, and ran out 1. Wildly inconsistent (rather like his partner Fiona Wilson who looks polished one day, but not the next), but a good horse at best, and came with a wet sail to win the first ever Handicap Hunter Chase going away at Newton Abbot. A bargain buy who has done present connections proud, and will almost certainly win again, but predicting when depends solely on his frame of mind. A sketchy jumper of regulation fences, but no longer seems to need to rely on mud for best results. *J. Milton — Ystrad Taf Fechan.* 272 (L), 383 (3mH), 597 (Cf), 877 (L), 1022 (3mH), 1224 (L), 1338 (4m1fH), 1433 (3mH), 1600 (2m5f110yH), 1648 (3mH).

BUMBLE ROCK ..8-12.. 13 ch.m. Corduroy — Spring Gem (unknown) 6. Looked to be a complete no-hoper in his Members, but in the event gave a creditable display, and did not drop out until the final half-mile. *Mrs A. Tate — Worcs.* 1063 (3m2fM).

BUONARROTI ..10-2.. 14 b.g. Ela-Mana-Mou — Amiel (Nonoalco USA) 44. Sturdy half-brother to flat winners, Aerturas (FR) (in USA) and King Of All (IRE) (in Italy). Dam won in Italy. FLAT r8 w1 (14f) p2. NH '91/4 r22 w3 (2m4f-3m Hdles) p6. P-t-P/HUNT CH '95/6 and '98/9 r14 w3 (inc Open) p7 (6 2nds, inc Hunt Ch); pulled up 2. Nearly always gives a good account of himself in Points, but not an easy ride (tends to idle in front), and stands few outings. Suited by mud and stays extremely well, but disappeared in mid-February, and likely to continue to decline if returning. *D.N. Buckett — Hursley Hambledon (Kate Buckett).* 77 (O), 223 (3m2fH).

BURGUNDY BOB (IRE) ..10-6.. 7 gr.g. Roselier (FR) — Katebeaujolais (Politico USA) 1212. Compact half-brother to The Merry Nun (IRE) (*qv*). NH FLAT '99 r2 p0 (tailed off). A useful recruit to Pointing, and cantered home in a very slow Maiden, but later most impressive in a Restricted which was run in the fastest time of the day bar the Ladies. Impressed in his jumping in those victories, but was nothing like as fluent when favourite at Dunthrop, and was already fighting a losing battle when he blundered at the last and was eased. His conqueror was Dawn Invader, who was in the process of running an excellent race until he broke down at Cheltenham next time, so lost nothing in defeat. Should make a lively Novice Hunter Chase prospect if he bounces back to form. *G. Nock — Heythrop (Sue Nock).* 265 (OMa), 458 (R), 791 (R), 1017 (I).

BURKEAN MELODY (IRE) ..9-13.. 10 b.g. Jareer (USA) — Unspoiled (Tina's Pet) p91dp. Sturdy half-brother to flat winner, Sylvan. IRISH FLAT r4 p0. IRISH P-t-P '95/7 r18 w2 (4yo Maiden, and Winners of One) p3; pulled up 5, and fell 3. P-t-P/HUNT CH '98/9 r5 p1 (3rd); pulled up 1, and fell 1. NH '99 (from A.G. Juckes') r2 p0; (fell in 2m Nov Ch: *bhnd, lost tch 7, 5th when fell 2 out*; and 10th in 2m4f110y Nov Sell Hdle: *prom til wknd 5*). Lightly raced in England and was recording his first success since '97 when winning at Chaddesley, but was subsequently disqualified at Portman Square as his pilot Mark Munrowd was not qualified to ride (a very tawdry affair that reflects very badly on the Hunt and its officials). Suited by an easy three miles as he generally fails to stay, and decent ground is essential. Should target his Members again in a bid for compensation in 2001, and hope that no spiteful rivals try to sabotage the bid. Tried tongue-tied. *M.V. Darby — Albrighton Woodland.* 987 (Cf), 1335 (2m4f110yH), 1629 (M), 1674 (I).

BURNTWOOD MELODY ..10-9.. 10 gr.g. Merdon Melody — Marwick (Roan Rocket) 212224. Close-coupled. FLAT r5 p0. NH '94 and '96 (blinkered last 2) r11 p2 (Sells); finished all 4 Chses, beaten 22l minimum. P-t-P/HUNT CH '98/9 r10 w4 (up to Confined) p2 (3rds, last once); failed to finish 4 (ran out 1, on floor 2). Had to endure a curtailed '99 campaign having won four races the previous season, but regained his form with a vengeance in 2000, and showed his liking for some cut in the ground with an impressive defeat of subsequent Hunter Chase winner Mr Freebie at

Southwell. Ensured that Mickthecutaway did not have things all his own way at Leicester, and lost no caste in defeat behind Copper Thistle and Lord Harry subsequently. Finally found the ground too lively when carrying a first-timer safely in his Members. Not very big, but all heart, and deserves to win on a more regular basis — worth another try in Hunter Chases in 2001. *A.P. Garland — Atherstone.* 115 (CCf), 367 (Cf), 462 (2m7f110yH), 1008 (O), 1073 (O), 1414 (M).

BUSHEHR (IRE) ..—.. 9 b.g. Persian Bold — Shejrah (USA) (Northjet) p. Small. IR 7500f, IR 20,000y. FLAT (form for J. Hills; tried blinkered) r11 w1 (10f) p4. NH '95/6 (for S. Coathup, claimed for £9000, tried tongue-tied) r8 p2 (inc 2nd in Sell). Weakened rapidly and pulled up after two miles on his first airing for four years. Former trainer Steve Coatup must often think about the day he claimed him after he finished second, because Martin Pipe nabbed the winner, Make A Stand, for £1000 less and ended up with a Champion Hurdler! *Mrs A.M. Thorpe — Gogerddan.* 35 (Cnr).

BUSMAN (IRE) ..10-3.. 12 ch.g. Be My Guest (USA) — Cistus (Sun Prince) 23p. Small compact half-brother to multiple Hurdles winner, Celcius, and to flat winners, Danegold (IRE) (also successful Hurdler), Bint Albadou (in Ireland — useful) and My Darling (in France). Dam won 6 flat, 6-10f (5 major prizes, including Prix de l'Opera). FLAT (blinkered 1, and tried with tongue-strap, and near-side pricker) r15 w1 (10f) p3. NH '92/4 r14 w2 (2m3f-2m4f Hdles, inc dead-heat, and inc Sell) p6. NH '97/8 r4 w1 (2m3f Fontwell Ch) p0. P-t-P/HUNT CH '95/8 r21 w8 (inc 4 Hunt Chses, 2m3f-3m110y, and 3 Ladies; inc hat-trick '96) p6 (3 2nds; and inc 3 Hunt Chses); fell/unseated 2. Presumably went wrong after three largely disappointing efforts in Handicap company in '98, as he was off the track throughout the following year. Looked set for a successful return to Pointing, but having jumped the last at Llanfrynach in front he was collared on the short run-in by Dawn's Cognac. Finished more than 13 lengths behind the same horse when they next met, and subsequently pulled up on his final appearance at Lydstep. Used to specialise at around 2m4f, but will need watching if connections can get him back on the racecourse in 2001. *K.R. Pearce — Carms.* 481 (L), 836 (L), 1224 (L).

BUSTER BUTTONS ..9-12§.. 9 b.g. Lord Bud — Lady Buttons (New Brig) u15. Compact well-made brother to Bonnie Buttons, and half-brother to Tudor Lord, Basil Grey, Lady Pokey and Wayward Buttons. Dam won 6 Points (inc 4m2f Grimthorpe) and placed 12 for the Jones family. P-t-P '99 r6 p1 (3rd); last, fell/unseated 2, refused 1, and pulled up 1. Reformed by the application of blinkers in 2000, and gained compensation for his Hutton Rudby misfortune when a convincing winner of his Members. Remains an abysmal jumper, and will need to improve that aspect of his makeup if he is to progress. Nigel Tutty was on board his dam when she won her first race back in 1981, and it is great testament to his longevity that he is still booting home winners. *S.G. Jones — Cleveland (Jill Jones).* 627 (OMa), 803 (MMa), 1027 (Cf).

BUSTONI (IRE) ..9-4.. 9 b.g. Bustineto — Sunland Park (Baragoi) pp6. Small workmanlike. IRISH NH FLAT '97 r2 p0. IRISH P-t-P '98/9 r8 w1 (Nov riders Maiden) p3; pulled up 2, and fell 1. A hard-puller who led for at least two miles in both Points for the current yard, but appears to be hopelessly short of stamina, and compounded in a few strides. Taken to post early on his latest outing. *Mrs D.E.H. Turner — Quorn.* 371 (R), 459 (2m4f110yH), 546 (R).

BUTCHERS MINSTREL ..—.. 9 ch.g. Brotherly (USA) — Flash Bunny (Flashback) p. Tall good-topped. Dam, half-sister to Jim Bowie (*qv* '97 Annual), pulled up in a Point. NH '96 (for S. Moore) r1 p0 (pulled up). Broke a blood vessel at Huntingdon in early February, and slithered back into oblivion. *J.R.B. Williams — Teme V. (Mark Jackson).* 151 (3mH).

BUTLER DIDIT ..9-0.. 7 ch.m. Pablond — Hungerdown Lady (New Member) p3. Sturdy compact half-sister to Donald Hawkins. Dam and grandam (Garton Lady) both won a Maiden (latter was also placed 3). Has a proper Pointing pedigree, and her encouraging nine lengths last of three suggests that she should have little trouble emulating mum and gran in a Maiden. The only surprise is that the breeders did not keep her — do they know something we don't? *K.R. Redwood — Lamerton (Kim Matthews).* 254 (CfMa), 655 (OMa).

BUTLER JOHN (IRE) ..10-8.. 12 b.g. The Parson — Corrielek (Menelek) 211112112. Strong good-looking brother to Baptist John (IRE), and to Irish NH flat and jumping winner, Moscow Express (IRE). IRISH NH '94 r7 w1 (2m3f Hdle) p0. NH '95 r6 w1 (2m4f Ch) p1 (2nd). P-t-P '96/9 r28 w20 (inc 11 Opens, Mixed Open, and 3 Ladies) p3 (2nds); fell/unseated 3, and pulled up 1. Incurred his first Pointing defeat since February '97 when no match for Gillan Cove at Milborne St Andrew, but proceeded to notch up another six wins, taking his career tally to 28. A phenomenally speedy galloper, and loves to hear his hooves rattle, but still liable to kick the odd fence into touch, and Neil Harris has sat some dreadful mistakes. Not nearly as fluent in soft ground, and his two latest defeats can be attributed to the underfoot conditions. Blistered at the end of the '98 season, and raced just three times at the back-end of '99, but managed a full campaign in 2000, and will hopefully return for more. A fine tribute to connections. *N. Viney — Dulverton W. (Gerald Dartnall).* 210 (MO), 474 (O), 727 (O), 854 (O), 954 (MO), 1188 (O), 1515 (MO), 1560 (Cf), 1606 (O).

BUTTERWICK KING (IRE) ..9-10.. 9 br.g. Roi Danzig (USA) — Girl On A Swing (High Top) 2p. Big workmanlike hobdayed half-brother to 5 flat winners (2 abroad), including Carbonate (also a successful jumper) and Fragonard. NH FLAT '96 r1 p0. NH '97 r3 p1 (3rd). P-t-P '99 r4 w1 (Maiden) p1 (2nd); and pulled up 2. Found an impressive turn of foot to land an 18-runner Maiden at Bratton Down on the final day of the '99 season, but an infrequent visitor to the racecourse, and suffered another truncated season in 2000. Off the track for 15 weeks between his two starts, and clearly hard to train. Suited by top-of-the-ground conditions, which place less strain on his suspect wind. *Mrs S. Lindley & Messrs Lewis, Little & White — W. Somerset V. (Anna Bucknall)*. 260 (R), 1650 (R).

BUTTON BOY ..9-11.. 9 ch.g. Fearless Action (USA) — Maytide (Vimadee) 23. Half-brother to Shipmate and Swordfish, and to Hurdles winner, Seachange. Dam won 2m6f Ch. P-t-P '98 r3 w1 (Maiden) p1 (3rd). Clearly troubled since a comfortable success at Mollington in March '98 (Novatara and Mr Snowman who filled the places have collectively won eight times since including a Hunter Chase), as he was seeing the racecourse for the first time since when just touched off by another subsequent Hunter Chase winner at Clifton-on-Dunsmore. Might have won had he kept straight in the closing stages, and going right-handed might be essential. A certainty for a Restricted if connections can keep him sound. *P.W.E. Henn — Grafton (Mervyn Loggin)*. 1418 (R), 1626 (3m1f110yH).

BUTTON UP BILL ..9-4.. 8 b.g. Button Bright (USA) — Passadora (Rapid Pass) uup71423. Very small neat. Dam never ran (although she held a Hunters Certificate as a 13-year-old in '98), but is half-sister to 3 nightmares who all refused or ran out for Hugh Thomas, including Bright Road (qv '97 Annual). Grandam, Reed Express ('a little weed') fell in 3 Points for the Thomases (also pulled up 2 for another owner). Great-grandam, Open Road, won 3 Points and placed 5, inc 4 Chses. P-t-P '99 r5 p1 (remote 3rd of 4); last, fell/unseated 2, and pulled up 1. Tailed off in three completions before his success in a three-finisher Maiden on firm at Holnicote, but a well deserved triumph for his small family concern. Not good enough to win a Restricted on the balance of his form, and still needs to brush up his jumping. *J.R. Thomas — Exmoor (Hugh Thomas)*. 105 (OMa), 353 (CfMa), 541 (I), 732 (2m4fOMa), 1373 (OMa), 1467 (R), 1566 (M), 1649 (CCf).

BUTTS CASTLE ..9-0.. 12 b.g. Reving — Celtic Express (Pony Express) p. Very tall rangy half-brother to Bailey Gray (qv). P-t-P '95, '97 and '99 r12 w1 (Maiden) p2 (2nd of 3 twice); last pair 3, and pulled up 6. Reportedly retired after winning at Lifton in '99, but connections clearly had a rethink, though he quickly went back to the old folk's home after pulling up at Milborne St Andrew. Blighted by wind problems throughout his career. Unlikely to do a Sinatra. *Mr & Mrs J.F. Symes — Cotley (John Symes)*. 208 (R).

BUZZ O'THE CROWD ..10-8.. 14 br.g. Sousa — Dotted Swiss (Super Slip) p. Big rangy brother to March Amadeus, and half-brother to Full Tilt. NH '95/6 r6 p2 (28-40/ 3rd in Chses). P-t-P/HUNT CH '93/5 and '97/9 r19 w5 (inc 4 Hunt Chses, 3m-3m2f110y) p7 (4 3rds, inc 3 Hunt Chses); pulled up 3. A useful Hunter Chaser on his day, but has never stood much racing, and appeared to go wrong at Taunton and failed to reappear. A thorough stayer who appreciates mud, and can handle firm, but will need treating with kid gloves if connections can patch him up satisfactorily. *B.J. Williams — Taunton V. (Fiona Walker)*. 581 (3mH).

CABALLUS (USA) ..—§§.. 8 b.g. Danzig Connection (USA) — Rutledge Place (USA) (Caro) pprr. Good-topped attractive half-brother to 4 winners in USA. $62,000y. FLAT (for Lord Huntingdon) r4 p2 (beaten 4-10/, 5 and 7 ran); got loose and bolted second intended start. NH '97/9 (blinkered 1; for Mrs A. Bowlby; wins previously for her sister, Mrs J. Pitman, bought for 5000) r13 w2 (2m-2m1f Hdles) p2 (3rds in Chses, distant once); took no part 3. Consented to show his true ability when a dual winner in soft/heavy, but almost invariably reluctant to race, and will be remembered as a prize pig. Would not set off until the rest had jumped three fences at Kingston Blount, but galloped a lap of the course missing the obstacles, resulting in a caution for Alex Charles-Jones, and a ban on the owner running his charge again. *B. Sarson — Warwicks (Nigel Ridout)*. 919 (2m3f110yH), 1144 (O), 1341 (2m110yH), 1484 (O).

CABBERY ROSE (IRE) ..9-11.. 13 ch.m. Lord Ha Ha — Sailin Top (Sola Topee) p. Lengthy sparsely-made half-sister to 2 Irish Pointing winners, including Amoristic Top. IRISH P-t-P '95/6 r11 w4 (concluded with hat-trick) p3 (2nd after falling once); pulled up 2, and brought down 1. IRISH NH FLAT '93/4 r2 p0. IRISH NH '94 and '96/7 r13 w1 (2m5f Ch) p1 (2nd). NH '96 (still Irish-based) r3 p1 (2nd); fell at 1st once. NH '98 r1 p0 (5th in R.A. Gold Cup). P-t-P/HUNT CH '98/9 r4 p1 (2nd); unseated 1. Steady if unspectacular under Rules, but her appearances have dwindled in the past three years, and disappeared after pulling up on the second weekend of the season in 2000. Usually let down by her lack of acceleration, and can probably be safely ignored if resurfacing. Has been tried in a tongue-strap in the past. *P.L. Southcombe — Cattistock*. 9 (L).

CABILLE (FR) ..9-10.. 9 ch.g. Lesotho (USA) — Ironique (FR) (Riverman USA) p4. Close-coupled hobdayed half-brother to 2 winners over jumps in France (one also successful on flat). IRISH P-t-P '97 r3 p1 (45/ 3rd). NH FLAT '97 r1 p0. NH '98 r8 p2 (last of 3 under once). NH '99 r5 w2 (Maiden and Restricted) p1 (2nd); and fell 2. Error-prone and headstrong under Rules, but found his level in Points, and won two minor races under strong drives from James Owen in '99. Never went a yard on his reappearance, and disappeared after a much improved effort at Kingston Blount in February. Probably has the ability to win again if he can be produced healthy. Wears a cross-noseband. *M.J. Tuckey — Bicester with Whaddon (Herbie Owen)*. 1 (C), 243 (Cf).

CAB ON TARGET ..9-11.. 15 br.g. Strong Gale — Smart Fashion (Carlburg) 8u46. Lengthy brother to Chasing winner, Strong Approach and Irish Hurdles winner, Glenelly Gale, and half-brother to Hurdles winner, Smart Approach (IRE). Dam won an Irish Bumper, and is sister to Everett, and half-sister to numerous winners, including Smart Jack (*qv* '94 Annual). NH FLAT '90 r2 w2 (21 and 22 ran). HUNT CH '97 (for Mr N. Hurst) r4 w2 (2m5f110y-3m1f) p1 (2nd). NH '90/9 r41 w17 (10 Hdles, 2m4f-3m1f, and 7 Chses, 2m4f-3m1f; inc 3 hat-tricks) p16. Famed as a top-class staying hurdler, and returned to racing under Rules after running second in the '97 Cheltenham Foxhunters and Horse & Hound Cup, winning a Cheltenham Handicap in October '98 from none other than Cavalero. Employed as a schoolmaster for Wendy Gibson in 2000, and filled the role admirably, but old age has blunted his speed, and will hopefully no longer be asked to race against horses he would have murdered in his prime. *Miss W. Gibson — Zetland (Ernie Fenwick).* 41 (L), 135 (L), 280 (L), 421 (3m5fL).

CACHE FLEUR (FR) ..10-7.. 15 ch.g. Kashneb (FR) — Blanche Fleur (FR) (Mont Blanc II) 22p121. Lengthy attractive half-brother to 2 French jumping winners. NH FLAT r3 w1 p1 (2nd). NH '90/3 and '94/5 r32 w12 (5 Hdles, 2m3f-2m6f, and 7 Chses, 2m4f-3m5f) p13 (inc 3rd in Ritz Club Ch). P-t-P '98/9 r8 w6 (Ladies, hat-tricks '98 and '99) p2 (2nds). Crowned a magnificent NH career by winning eight Ladies races over three seasons. Thoroughly game in Points and loves to be in the thick of it, but pulled up temporarily lame at Horseheath, and retired after another typically gutsy effort at High Easter. *Mrs G. D'Angibau — Essex & Suffolk.* 95 (L), 319 (L), 414 (L), 827 (L), 1183 (L), 1380 (L).

CADBURY CASTLE ..10-0.. 7 b.m. Midyan (USA) — Orange Hill (High Top) 123f6. Small neat owner-bred half-sister to Jackson Hill, and to 2 flat winners (one in UAE) including Old Provence, and to Harding (jumping winner for Simon Tindall). Dam won 2 2m1f races, inc Cesarewitch. FLAT (for M. Blanshard) r9 p1 (3rd). NH '97/9 (from G. Charles-Jones, bought for 1350) r17 w3 (2m-2m1f Sell Hdles) p4. A speedy little mare who pulls hard, and was at her best in '98, when she won three times from four attempts. Made a good start to her Pointing career when scoring at Charing despite jumping badly right, and then only caught close home by Lily The Lark at Parham (was two lengths ahead at the final fence), but less convincing since, and probably likes to have matters all her own way. Gets the trip surprisingly well considering she is so headstrong, and still only a youngster, so can probably enjoy further successes when able to dominate. *S.P. Tindall — Southdown & Eridge (Jeff Peate).* 289 (Cm), 707 (L), 982 (L), 1107 (L), 1511 (L).

CADDY MAN (IRE) ..10-2.. 12 ch.g. The Parson — Golfers Dream (Carnoustie) 5p3. Strong half-brother to Gunner Stream. Dam won at 5f. IRISH P-t-P '95/8 r12 p6; pulled up 3, and fell/unseated 2 (at last with every chance once). IRISH NH '96/8 r7 w2 (2-3m Chses, inc Hunt) p0. Can go a strong gallop, but does not have a good winning record, and usually looks to struggle to stay three miles. Acts in soft, but presumably has physical problems, as he missed '99, and broke a blood vessel once in 2000. *Dr D.B.A. Silk & D.J. Coldman — Kent & Surrey Bloodhounds (Heather Silk).* 226 (2m4f110yH), 799 (2m4f110yH), 1511 (L).

CADES BAY ..9-7.. 9 b.g. Unfuwain (USA) — Antilla (Averof) 35p7f. Tall rangy half-brother to Eustatia, and to 2 flat winners. Dam, half-sister to very smart flat winner, John French (also a sire), won at 5f. NH FLAT '95 r1 p0. NH '95/7 r5 p2 (3rds, inc when lame final start). P-t-P '99 r2 w1 (Maiden) p0. NH Spr '00 r3 p0 (5th in 2m4f Nov HCap Ch: *pulled hrd, ld, hdd aft 2, pu 8*); pulled up in 3m Nov HCap Ch: *ld to 6, rdn aft, wknd 12, t.o & pu 4 out*; and fell in 2m4f110y Nov HCap Ch: *hld up, bhnd when fell 10*. Whizzed round Ashorne to open his account on firmish ground in '99, but his legs have never stood much racing, and was finished after just two outings in 2000. Rather highly strung (had to be taken to post very gingerly on his final start), and not a true stayer, so the chances of him collecting a Restricted should he resurface are not great. *R.D. Russell — Heythrop (Brenda Russell).* 261 (R), 1335 (2m4f110yH).

CAHERLOW (IRE) ..6-0.. 10 ch.g. Kambalda — Wrens Lass (Wrens Hill) 2cuu. Workmanlike short-backed half-brother to Snaefugl and Coolderry Mist (IRE). Dam won 2m4f Hdle in Ireland. NH FLAT '96/7 (for O. Brennan) r2 p0. NH '97/8 (for J. Mackie, virtually final) r3 p0 (tailed off in 3 Hdles — pulled up 2). Has shown no signs of ability (was 75 lengths last of his only completion in a Point), but evidently thought to possess some, as he was backed down from sixes to 5-2 favourite once. Unseated at the 13th on that occasion, and got no further than the first subsequently, leaving connections none the wiser, but a bit poorer. *Mrs J.E. Goodall — Meynell & S. Staffs.* 528 (OMa), 588 (OMa), 906 (CfMa), 964 (OMa).

CAHORS (IRE) ..10-6.. 8 b.g. Mandalus — Croom River (IRE) (Over The River FR) 33u21. Rangy. P-t-P '98/9 r8 w3 (Maiden, Restricted and Intermediate nov rdrs) p4 (2nds); and refused 1. Carrying far too much condition in early season, but was cherry ripe for his Hunter Chase, debut and duly obliged (veered badly left after the last, and failed to reappear). Has a touch of class and often treated as such by his supporters, and should win more races if his absence does not portend trouble. Wore blinkers at Taunton, but not a sinister character, and has been entrusted to a novice on a couple of occasions. *J.J. Boulter — Portman (Nick Mitchell & John Boulter).* 1 (C), 62 (Cf), 214 (Cf), 325 (Cf), 581 (3mH).

CALIPO BELLO (IRE) ..9-11.. 11 ch.g. Buckskin (FR) — Stradbally Beg (Little Buskins) pp1. Compact attractive half-brother to Temple Tobera and Franwill. Dam won 4&5yo Irish Maiden. NH '94/6 r5 p0. P-t-P '98 r3 p1 (dead-heat 3rd); pulled up 1, and fell 1. Too backward to do himself justice when consistently tailed off under Rules, and very headstrong to boot, but returned from a two year absence to finally confirm the promise when just lasting home at High Easter. Gets worked up before his races, and the top-of-the-ground conditions appeared to help conserve his stamina when successful. Rarely seen, and might struggle to follow up. *D.J. Harding-Jones — Puckeridge (Perry Harding-Jones).* 290 (CMa), 416 (R), 606 (OMa).

CALLEVA STAR (IRE) ..10-5.. 10 b.g. Over The River (FR) — Ask The Madam (Strong Gale) pu222114u4. Workmanlike. Dam won mares Maiden in Ireland. NH '95/9 (for R. Alner, tongue-tied final) r22 w2 (3m2f Chses) p9. Bought Doncaster, Aug for 4400. Tough and consistent and basically very safe (although he tends to jump left), and able to carry Rupert Abrahams safely and give him plenty of fun most weekends. Should have collected his Members, but napped to the boxes (which were repositioned for the next meeting) and was beaten half a length. Gained compensation at Hornby Castle when he took advantage of some zombie-like riding on the runner-up. Lacks acceleration, but keeps going steadily, and should continue to be thereabouts in 2001. *M.D. Abrahams — W. of Yore (Fiona Needham).* 136 (O), 279 (O), 374 (M), 504 (O), 622 (O), 998 (C), 1030 (O), 1327 (O), 1349 (O), 1532 (3m1fH).

CALL HOME (IRE) ..10-7.. 13 b.g. Callernish — Easter Beauty (Raise You Ten) 23u2. Good-bodied quite attractive half-brother to jumping winner, Flashthecash. NH FLAT r2 w2. NH '93/4 and '96/8 r13 w3 (2m6f Hdle, and 2 Chses, 2m3f-3m) p5; fell 3 out when cruising in Hdle once. P-t-P/HUNT CH '96 and '99 r7 w4 (2m6f Hunt Ch and 3 Opens) p2 (2nds); pulled up 1. A useful horse at his best, but his activity has always been restricted (broke a bone in his hock in '95), and now appears to be on the downgrade. Would have obliged on soft ground at Aldington, but Tom Hills dropped a clanger and was collared on the line. Will find similar opportunities few and far between in future. Enjoys being allowed to bowl along in front. *Mrs L. Ferrett — W. Street/Tickham (Tom Hills).* 286 (O), 574 (4mMO), 981 (O), 1171 (O).

CALL ME BERTIE ..9-2.. 8 b.g. Almutanabbi — Call-Me-Sally (Hul A Hul) 5. Small light-framed half-brother to Call-Me-Dinky. Dam was 3rd on flat (also disqualified from 2nd once); and pulled up 3 and unseated in Points for Charlie Fuller. NH '99 r2 p0 (pulled up 1, and fell 1). P-t-P '99 r2 p0 (pulled up 2). Not disgraced in his last two Points, but the Beast of Bodmin makes more appearances, and he is clearly hard to train. Remains worthy of another glance in maiden company, though lack of stamina is a cause for concern. *C.A. Fuller — Brecon & Talybont (Giles Smyly).* 672 (2m4fOMa).

CALL ME DICKINS ..8-8§.. 12 gr.g. Rusticaro (FR) — Bad Start (USA) (Bold Bidder) p4ppp. Tall good-looking half-brother to a French flat winner. FLAT r3 p0 (reluctant at stalls all 3). NH '93 r1 p0 (tailed off last). P-t-P '94/5, '97 and '99 r13 p1 (3rd); failed to finish 9 (refused 1, on floor 3, and carried out 1). Highly temperamental, and remains winless after 22 races. Blinkered more often than not in the last two seasons, and has now acquired a tongue-tie. Not better than last since May '97, and holding on firmly to his squiggle. *Miss E.J. Kessler (Wide Valley Racing) — S. Devon.* 159 (CfMa), 312 (CfMa), 856 (CfMa), 1049 (CfMa), 1390 (OMa).

CALL THE TUNE ..9-10.. 9 b.m. Lancastrian — Wand Of Youth (Mandamus) 472fu545. Small unfurnished. Grandam, Young Ash Leaf, was smart staying Chaser. NH FLAT '98 r2 p0. NH '99 r1 p0. P-t-P '99 r4 p1 (3rd); fell/unseated 3. A moderate jumper, but has twice given perfectly adequate displays, and should be concentrating on Maidens. Has ditched the rider five times in the first mile to date, but managed to jump round Huntingdon on her final start. Has had no less than eight different riders in her Points. *P.J. Lutman — W. Street/Tickham.* 23 (OMa), 131 (OMa), 289 (Cm), 571 (M), 710 (OMa), 825 (R), 1108 (C), 1333 (3mH).

CALVARY HILL ..8-10.. 11 b.g. Karlinsky (USA) — Twilgo (Twilight Alley) ppbp4. Tall rangy trainer-bred brother to Bethany. P-t-P '95 and '98/9 r7 p1 (last of 3); failed to finish 4 (fell/unseated 2). Often shows some speed, but remains a weak finisher, and took 12 races before he managed to beat a rival. Firm ground and a short course look to be the vital requirements if he is ever to spring a surprise. *Mrs W. Doyne-Ditmas — E. Cornwall (Derek Doyne-Ditmas).* 722 (CfMa), 847 (R), 958 (R), 1131 (OMa), 1154 (OMa).

CALYS HALO ..—.. 6 ch.g. Cigar — My-Ninon (Grand Conde FR) p. Rangy owner-bred. Dam is half-sister to Kahala Bay (qv '96 Annual). A real handful on his debut, and pulled hard and raced prominently, but went out like a puff of smoke after a blunder five out. Deemed mad, and promptly retired. *T.E. Short — Bicester with Whaddon (Jenny Pidgeon).* 673 (2m4fOMa).

CAMAN ..9-5.. 14 br.g. Callernish — Chilly For June (Menelek) p44554. Robust half-brother to Face The Climate and Little Gossip. IRISH NH FLAT r2 p0. IRISH NH '91/2 (blinkered 2) r9 p1 (2nd in Ch). IRISH P-t-P '93 r2 w1 (6yo&up Maiden) p0; and pulled up 1. NH '93/5 (blinkered in Sell final) and '98 r8 p3 (Chses). P-t-P/HUNT CH '96/9 r27 w2 (Restricted and Members) p7 (3 3rds, last once); pulled up 3, and unseated 2. Expert in course completion, but usually in his own time, and is becoming elderly. Once better than last in 2000. Shows little zest nowadays, and regained blinkers on his last five starts. *J.A.V. Duell — S. Durham (Sarah Palfreeman)*. 394 (Cf), 804 (Cf), 997 (Cf), 1325 (Cf), 1348 (Cf), 1474 (M).

CAMDEN CARR (IRE) ..—.. 7 b.g. Camden Town — Scrunchie (Selko) pfp. Half-brother to Straight As A Dai (IRE). Bought Tattersalls (Ireland), Aug for 1160. Fat in early season, and has not revealed any stamina so far. *C. Dawson — S. Durham*. 909 (2m4fOMa), 1164 (OMa), 1352 (OMa).

CAMDEN KID (IRE) ..9-2.. 8 ch.g. Camden Town — Blackmiller Lady (Bonne Noel) fbpp2p3. Lengthy attractive. P-t-P '99 r3 p0 (pulled up 3). A hyperactive kid whose two placings have been over 2m4f, but pulls too hard to give himself the chance of staying the full trip. Sweats freely and usually carts two handlers round the paddock (equally volatile after his races). Tried tongue-tied on his last two appearances. Short Maidens are no longer an option and looks sure to struggle in future. *The Valentine Club — Fitzwilliam (Louise Allan)*. 51 (OMa), 233 (OMa), 436 (OMa), 548 (CfMa), 1070 (2m4fOMa), 1420 (OMa), 1589 (2m4fOMa).

CAMDEN LOCH (IRE) ..—.. 6 b.br.g. Camden Town — Poor Elsie (Crash Course) p. Half-brother to Mister RF, and to jumping winner, Blowing Rock (IRE). Not seen until May, when he had a very quiet school for two miles. *D.A. Wales — W. Norfolk*. 1382 (OMa).

CAMERA MAN ..9-13.. 11 ch.g. Scorpio (FR) — Something To Hide (Double-U-Jay) 125. Lengthy owner-bred half-brother to Shaker Maker, and to 2 flat winners, including What A Line (also a successful Hurdler). Dam won 2 12f races and 2m2f-3m and 4 Hdles, 2m5f-3m. NH '95 and '97 r7 w1 (3m Ch) p2 (inc 2nd in Hdle). P-t-P '99 r4 w1 (walkover for Members) p2 (3rds); and pulled up 1. Lightly raced and carries condition, but sprang something of a surprise hen edging out the gambled-on Hylters Chance on the new Chipley Park course on his reappearance. Failed to justify favouritism in a muddling Open at Cothelstone subsequently, and was then off the track for seven weeks until finishing well behind Grimley Gale at Exeter. Suited by top-of-the-ground. Might be able to find another race in 2001. *Mrs P. Shaw — Dulverton W. (Lucy Roberts)*. 143 (C), 637 (O), 1432 (3m1fH).

CAMITROV (FR) ..9-0.. 11 b.g. Sharken (FR) — Emitrovna (FR) (Buisson D'Or) 4p*1*. Compact attractive half-brother to 6 winners in France (including 3 Chasers). Dam won 2 flat and 3 Chses in France. FRENCH FLAT '93/4 r4 w1 (11f). FRENCH NH '94 r5 p4 (3 2nds); and unseated 1 in Chses. NH '94/9 (for Miss H Knight; previously for D. Nicholson; previously for T. Keddy; wins previously for S. Christian) r14 w9 (2m-2m4f Chses, inc £13,000 prize at Punchestown) p5 (inc 3rd in Arkle Ch, earned £8438). Sold Malvern, May for 7000 (to S. Christian). NH Mar '00 r1 w1 (beat Druid's Brook and Macnamarasband (IRE), *9l* and *19l* in Grand Military Gold Cup; *hdwy 5, lft 2nd 15, ld 18, r.o wl*). Fifty-to-one when tailed off and pulled up in an Open in January, but was a revelation after being sent to Nicky Henderson and reappearing six weeks later to gain a £6380 prize at Sandown (25-1). Had been a very classy performer in his youth, but went to pieces under Rules, although it was not his own fault, as he had problems with bursting blood vessels and also missed 12 weeks when he broke a bone in his foot. A remarkable story, not least for Simon Christian, who had trained him for all his three victories to April '95, and presumably hankered after getting him back one way or another. *R.T. Sturgis — Beaufort (-; Nicky Henderson)*. 8 (C), 61 (MO).

CAMOGUE BRIDGE (IRE) ..—.. 10 b.g. Grimesgill (USA) — Linden Dolly (Gulf Pearl) pfup. Medium-sized leggy hobdayed half-brother to Easby Hopes. Dam won 2 Hdles, 2m-2m4f. IRISH NH FLAT '96 r1 p0. IRISH NH '97/8 r8 p0. IRISH P-t-P '96/7 r10 w1 (4&5yo Maiden) p1 (2nd); pulled up 5, and ran out 1. P-t-P '99 (for Messrs Williams, James & R. Mathias) r3 p0 (pulled up 2, and unseated 1). A consistently gormless jumper, and should have a health warning attached. Tried in blinkers once, and has often run tongue-tied. Made all to win in Ireland, but looks devoid of talent nowadays, and presumably flawed. *J.A. Danahar — Kyre*. 336 (R), 392 (R), 669 (R), 1528 (R).

CAMP BANK ..10-9.. 11 b.g. Strong Gale — Rambling Gold (Little Buskins) 314. Tall rangy half-brother to Gold Bits (IRE), and to smart jumping winner and stablemate, Senor El Betrutti (IRE). Dam won NH flat and 2 2m Hdles in Ireland. NH FLAT '95 r3 p1 (2nd). NH '95/8 r10 p1 (3rd of 4 in Ch); last in other Ch. P-t-P '99 r6 w5 (5-timer, inc Mixed and 4m Opens) p1 (3rd). Lightly raced and rather modest under Rules, but quickly rattled off a five-timer in Points concluding with a notable victory in the 4m Heythrop Open. A thorough stayer and taken off his feet on his reappearance at Larkhill, but soon picked up the winning thread in a Mollington stamina test. Presumably met with trouble after finishing fourth in a hot Open at the Farmers Bloodhounds as he failed to reappear, but more victories await if he returns problem free. Usually takes the eye in the paddock, and owes his success in no small measure to superior handling. *G. Nock — Heythrop (Sue Nock)*. 10 (O), 77 (O), 195 (O).

CAMPBELLHILL (IRE) ..8-2.. 9 ch.g. Torus — Gueranne (Green God) pufffup. Lengthy attractive half-brother to NH flat winner, Freelander (IRE). Can show plenty of speed in bad company, but the world's worst jumper, and his mission in life appears to be to exterminate jockeys whose first name begins with M (two demolition attempts apiece on Matthew, Michael and Matt). Ross Garrard escaped on final start, but only by a miracle. Will Portman Square have inflicted a ban on him?

Mr H. Hill — *Mrs M. Sharland* — *Granta H., & Cambridge Univ (Henry Hill).* 87 (OMa), 174 (M), 242 (M), 437 (OMa), 775 (OMa), 1040 (OMa), 1218 (R), 1421 (OMa).

CAMPDEN KITTY ..9-3.. 7 b.m. Henbit (USA) — Catherine Tudor (Tudor Wood) f. Compact half-sister to Allezscally, Tudor Mistress and Wellington Street. Dam, half-sister to Miss Berkeley (*qv* '93 Annual), won 9 Points (inc an Open and 5 Members) and placed 8. NH FLAT '99 r1 p0 (12th of 20). P-t-P '99 r2 p0 (fell 1, and brought down 1). Clearly able, but three attempts over fences have resulted in her coming back riderless (and her supporters with burnt fingers twice), and her confidence must be in tatters. Possibly hurt in the latest tumble, as she failed to reappear. *Miss S. Sadler* — *N. Cotswold (Jim Collett).* 21 (2m4fOMa).

CANAILLOU II (FR) ..9-13.. 11 b.g. Le Riverain (FR) — Julie (FR) (Laniste) pfp32. Tall unfurnished. NH '95/6 r9 w1 (3m1f Ch) p2 (2nds). IRISH NH '96/8 r5 w1 (3m Ch) p0. P-t-P/HUNT CH '99 r4 p1 (3rd). Stays well, but plods badly nowadays, and flattered by his proximity to the winner in his Members. Still inclined to miss the odd fence, and might not be entirely genuine. *Mrs J. Thornton* — *Wheatland (John Downes).* 369 (O), 529 (Cf), 987 (Cf), 1253 (L), 1529 (M).

CANDLE GLOW ..9-9.. 13 ch.m. Capitano — Fused Light (Fury Royal) upf56. Small neat sister to Hurdles winner, Capsize, and half-sister to Wild Illusion, and to Hurdles winner, True Spark. Dam won 2m Hdle. Has had a soft-palate operation. NH '91/3 r12 p1 (2nd of 4). P-t-P/HUNT CH '94/7 and '99 (for Mrs S. Hutchinson) r23 w3 (inc 3m Hunt Ch) p5 (4 3rds); pulled up 5, and fell 1. Made all at high speed to land a double in '96, but frequently empties after little more than two miles, and has failed to score in her last 16 starts. Often takes liberties with the obstacles, and beat just one rival home in 2000. *Mrs L.M. Kemble & Major R.G. Wilson* — *Suffolk (Ruth Hayter).* 29 (Cf), 302 (3Hm), 756 (Cf), 770 (Cf), 1035 (Cnr).

CAN I COME TOO (IRE) ..—§§.. 10 b.g. Aristocracy — Promotor Fidei (Prominer) r. Very tall rangy half-brother to Irish Pointing winners, Sabrita (also a successful Chaser there) and Staffy's Boy. IRISH P-t-P '96 and '98 r4 p0 (4th, pulled up 1, and fell 2 — when leading at last and looking winner once). P-t-P '99 r6 p0 (pulled up 5, and refused 1). The villain of a televised nastie in '99, when Ian Bennett thought the horse capable of jumping from a standstill, and has surely told connections in no uncertain terms that enough is enough. *Mrs M.R. Bennett* — *Badsworth (Ian Bennett).* 283 (OMa).

CANNY CURATE (IRE) ..8-7.. 12 b.g. The Parson — Lisa Martin (Black Minstrel) 2. Very tall. P-t-P '96/7 and '99 r9 r6 p1 (3rd of 4); last pair 2, pulled up 1, unseated 1, and brought down 1. Broke down in '97 and has generally been unable to stay since, but only failed by a neck to peg back the winner in a bad Maiden at Southwell. Sadly finished lame, and at his advanced age a comeback looks most unlikely. *B. Wilberforce* — *Cheshire (Gary Hanmer).* 1076 (OMa).

CANNY'S FORT ..8-12.. 12 ch.m. Fort Nayef — Canny's Tudor (Tudor Cliff) 8p. Tall close-coupled half-sister to Dercanny (dam of Morcan House, *qv*), Candery (dam of Sylcanny, *qv*) and Canny's Character, and to Chasing winners, Canoscan (also a successful Hurdler) and Dercander. Dam pulled up in 2 Maidens for Mr Gibbon, but was subsequently 2nd in a Chase. P-t-P '94 and '96/9 r14 p2; failed to finish 9 (fell/unseated 4). Outstandingly modest over a seven-year spell, and seems destined to remain a maiden. Has never managed more than four outings in a season, and performs like a non-stayer now. *P.F. Gibbon* — *Zetland.* 808 (OMa), 1353 (OMa).

CANTANGO (IRE) ..9-5§.. 11 b.g. Carlingford Castle — Judy Can Dance (Northern Guest USA) 48p2. Good-bodied. P-t-P '96/8 r13 w1 (Maiden) p5 (3 2nds); pulled up 1, fell 2. Resurfaced after a year out of action, but plodded badly in 2000, and showed minimum zest. Almost certainly worth ignoring in future. *W.J. Turcan* — *Fernie (Nick Pomfret).* 119 (CR), 546 (R), 871 (R), 1071 (CR).

CAN'T BE SCRABBLE ..—.. 8 b.g. Gargoor — Scribble Along (Supergrey) fpu. Workmanlike. Dam was 1½ fences last of 3 in a Maiden for Julian Selby (failed to finish in 5 of her other 7 Points). 'Scrabble' is the precise word to describe his current attempts to get to grips with the fences. *J. Selby* — *Tiverton Stag (Linda Blackford).* 1043 (R), 1373 (OMa), 1565 (OMa).

CAPE CRUSADER ..9-0.. 8 b.g. Cruise Missile — Chelworth Countess (Noalto) p36. Tall lengthy light-bodied. P-t-P '98/9 r7 p0 (last pair 3, pulled up 3, and fell 1). Only once better than last but one in ten starts, and beaten 26 lengths on the only occasion that he has made the frame. Unlikely to be given another chance in the current yard, as their inmates are usually competent at worst. *R.G. Makin* — *York & Ainsty S.* 139 (OMa), 380 (OMa), 508 (OMa).

CAPICHE (IRE) ..—.. 12 b.g. Phardante (FR) — Sainthill (St Alphage) f. Rangy half-brother to Sainthills Son and St Robert, and to 2 flat winners, including Knockglas. Dam is sister to top sprinter, Sandford Lad (also a sire). NH FLAT '93 and '95 (for J. Etherington) r4 w1 p1 (2nd). P-t-P '98 r3 p0 (unseated 2, and pulled up 1). NH '99 (for C.L. Popham) r1 p0 (tailed off in Nov Hdle). A fairly decent bumper horse, but has failed to adapt to his new role, and bolted both before and during his latest debacle. Clearly still has an engine, and could be interesting with a strong male rider on board, although plenty of water has gone under the bridge since he last completed. *Mrs D. Little* — *Quantock (Anna Bucknall).* 635 (M).

CAPO CASTANUM ..9-9.. 12 ch.g. Sula Bula — Joscilla (Joshua) 44465. Tall half-brother to Noble Jakey, and to NH flat and jumping winner, Oatis Regrets. Dam, half-sister to Trusty Friend, won 2m6f Hdle. NH FLAT r2 p0. NH '95/9 r18 w1 (3m2f Sell Ch) p3 (2nds, inc 3m HCap Ch). HUNT CH '97 and '99 r4 w1 (3m) p1 (3rd); pulled up 1, and fell 1. Found a poor Hunter Chase at Windsor in '97, but gone in the wind nowadays (tubed), and though still able to bowl along merrily for up to 2m4f he stops quickly. Highly unlikely to achieve much if reappearing. *D.C.G. Gyle-Thompson — Beaufort (Gail Sturgis).* 62 (Cf), 216 (Cnr), 387 (M), 597 (Cf), 750 (O).

CAPSTOWN BAY ..9-8.. 10 b.g. Capitano — Calfstown Maid (Master Buck) 1pp82. Tall good-bodied half-brother to Heather Boy. Dam was unplaced in 14 races, including English/Irish Points. P-t-P '96 and '99 r6 w2 (Maiden and Restricted) p3 (2 2nds); pulled up 1. Has managed an annual success in his three Pointing campaigns (missed '97/8), but has run tongue-tied latterly, and his wind problem has halted his development completely. Still lacks fluency at the fences, but usually fiddles his way out of trouble. In a leading yard, and it will be interesting to see if they persevere with him. *Mrs S.P. Merrick — N. Ledbury (Nicky Sheppard).* 116 (I), 333 (Cf), 474 (O), 611 (C), 1461 (O).

CAPTAIN DUSTY ..—§.. 10 gr.g. Malaspina — Lady Brooklyn (Streak) p. Owner-bred half-brother to Brooklyn Express and Young Tiger. P-t-P '99 r3 p0 (pulled up 2, and refused 1). Fat, unschooled and probably useless. The Leggs are far more successful with their home-bred Arabians, though they too go to the racecourse without an education — they just don't have to worry about jumping fences. *E.J. Legg — Seavington (Miss C. Legg).* 213 (CfMa).

CAPTAIN GEORGE ..9-7.. 8 br.g. Arctic Lord — Bonne Fille (Bonne Noel) p2u. Owner-bred half-brother to Tattlejack (IRE). His five lengths second was a fair effort, and would probably have been in contention at the finish had he not unseated next time. May be able to win a Maiden. Has two paddock handlers. *J.M.I. Evetts — N. Cotswold.* 391 (CfMa), 617 (CMa), 786 (OMa).

CAPTAIN JACK ..—.. 11 b.g. Salse (USA) — Sanctuary (Welsh Pageant) pp. Compact fired half-brother to 4 flat winners, including Durham and Latalomne (USA) (both also a successful Hurdlers), and Sheikh Albadou (top-class sprinter). Dam is an unraced half-sister to useful flat winners, Smuggler and Little Wolf. FLAT '92, '94 and '97/8 (first 4 wins for L. Cumani) r20 w5 (14-16f, inc 4 wins in 5 race spell — been 5 from 6, but short-headed in Ladies previously) p2 (2nds). NH '95/9 (for M. Pipe, bought for 100,000) r8 w1 (3m1f Hdle, 5 ran) p1 (2nd). A useful front-runner over long trips on the flat in his prime, and won a £13,745 prize, and also unsuccessfully contested two Cesarewitchs and a Prix du Cadran. Looked the ideal candidate to become a smart hurdler (Martin Pipe obviously thought so!), but proved bitterly disappointing, and twice went missing for 22 months. Has clearly suffered leg problems, and is an indifferent jumper who was reluctant on his final start under Rules. Wears blinkers. Did not look to be enjoying himself before pulling up in May Confineds, and could be heading for a squiggle if he reappears. *N.J. & Mrs J. Dawe — W. Somerset V. (N. Dawe).* 1371 (Cf), 1554 (O).

CAPTAIN KHEDIVE ..10-6.. 13 ch.g. Deep Run — Wing On (Quayside) ppu241u3. Angular half-brother to Buckley's Court, to NH flat and jumping winner, Crack On, and to Hurdles winner, Richmond Lady. NH FLAT (for P.J. Hobbs) r3 w2 p1 (3rd). NH '94/9 (for N. Twiston-Davies; previously for G. McCourt; 5 wins previously for P. Nicholls; 3 wins previously for P. Hobbs) r39 w8 (3 Hdles, 2m-2m1f Hdles, and 3 Chses, 2m-2m2f) p11; fell/unseated 7 (when clear at last once); ran out 1. NH May '00 r1 p1 (distant 3rd in 2m5f110y HCap Ch: *bhnd, stayed on frm 13, no imp*). Enjoyed plenty of success in his first two yards, but showed temperament very early in his career, and is prone to jump poorly. Normally fails to stay three miles, but surprisingly did so at Pentreclwydau, where he ended a losing sequence of 20 (was ridden by Guy Lewis in the previous success in October '96) and had Gunner Boon six lengths behind him in third place. Often blinkered, although not since his Hunter Chase. Managed to get outbattled by stablemate Archer (that takes some doing!) in his Members, but to his great credit his career earnings total nearly £51,000. Has now broken down. *Mrs J.S. Lewis — Llangibby.* 272 (L), 382 (2m4fH), 599 (L), 817 (M), 991 (L), 1297 (L), 1462 (L).

CAPTAIN MARMALADE ..—.. 12 ch.g. Myjinski (USA) — Lady Seville (Orange Bay) p. Workmanlike brother to flat winner, Ballerina Bay, and half-brother to Jaffa's Boy, and to NH flat winner, The Lady Captain. FLAT r97 w4 (8-16f, inc 2 on (equitrack and one on fibresand) p20; inc Sells. NH '93 and '97/9 (for D. Thom) r15 w1 (2m Amat Sell Hdle) p4 (short-headed once). His five wins include a 23-runner Ladies race and an Amateurs event on the flat, but usually ran well behind, although he could finish strongly on his day. A thinker, but his thoughts on having to make his 113th appearance in a Point would probably be unprintable. *R. Foulds — Puckeridge.* 607 (O).

CAPTAIN OATES ..—.. 8 b.g. Arctic Lord — Captain's Cottage (Relkino) ppp5s. Unfurnished owner-bred. Dam is sister to Captain Teach, and half-sister to 5 other Pointers, including Cottage Joker (qv 2000 Annual). NH FLAT '97 r1 p0. Showed first signs of ability on final start, but usually negatively ridden by a veteran, and it would be interesting to see if more vigorous handling could bring better results. Cleverly named (and the rider probably says 'I may be gone for some time' as he leaves the paddock). *W.A. Bethell — Holderness.* 169 (OMa), 283 (OMa), 399 (OMa), 507 (CMa), 793 (CfMa).

PLATE 29   793 South Wold Confined Maiden 56&7yo: R to L Captain Oates (M. Watson), slipped up, jumps alongside Gentleman Charles (S. Walker), 2nd, and Second Thoughts (W. Wales), 4th, with Aunty Norma (S. Swiers), pu, just visible behind   PHOTO: Roy Parker

CAPTAIN ROSE ..—.. 9 b.g. Soldier Rose — Miss Oxstall's (The Brianstan) pp. Compact well-made owner-bred half-brother to Stormhill Recruit. NH '00 r1 p0 (pulled up in 2m1f Nov Hdle: *t.o ½way, pu 2 out*). Jumped appallingly, and wisely pulled up after a mile when tailed off at Whitwick. *Mrs R. Evans — Croome & W. Warwicks (Charlotte Evans; Richard Evans).* 339 (CfMa).

CARACOL ..10-7.. 12 b.g. Ore — Fit For A King (Royalty) u31p. Tall half-brother to Hurdles winner, Revolt. Dam won 2 2m Hurdles. P-t-p/HUNT CH '95/6 r8 w2 (Maiden and Restricted) p3 (2 3rds); pulled up 2, and ran out 1. NH '96/9 (for J. Neville) r18 w6 (Hdles, 2m1f-2m5f110y) p4 (3 2nds); pulled up 1 and fell 2 Chses. Speedy and won Jimmy Neville six races over hurdles after a Pointing double '94/5, but beat little when trotting up at Hereford, and appeared not to care for the quicker surface when pulled up next time. Probably still has a future in short Hunter Chases if he has not come to any harm. Suited by plenty of cut in the ground. *C.G. Bolton — Gelligaer F. (Tim Jones).* 463 (2mH), 1026 (2m5f110yH), 1157 (2m3fH), 1600 (2m5f110yH).

CARBERY MINISTREL (IRE) ..—§§.. 11 b.g. Black Minstrel — Carbery Star (Kemal FR) pupppp. Tall brother to jumping winner, Jazzman, and half-brother to Castlebay Lad, and to Irish Pointing winners, Drominore and Bens Friend. IRISH P-t-P '95/7 r10 w1 (Maiden) p1 (last of 3); pulled up 2, and unseated 1. Bought Malvern, July for 650. The latest of the abominations to eminate from the Matthews yard (*cf* Bobby Violet and Manalesco). Beat Dublin Hill in heavy in Ireland, but now very reluctant to jump and to gallop properly, and has been ridden in spurs, and blinkered on his last two appearances. Was two fences behind when the jockey eventually gave up at Ludlow. *R. Taberner — Wheatland (Frank Matthews).* 567 (R), 698 (R), 1023 (3mH), 1089 (R), 1321 (Cf), 1408 (Cf).

CARBERY SPIRIT (IRE) ..10-0.. 8 gr.m. Glacial Storm (USA) — Formia Spirit (Pragmatic) f. Sturdy compact half-sister to Flushing Spirit (*qv*). IRISH P-t-P '98 r5 p2 (2nds); pulled up 1. P-t-p '99 r3 w1 (mares Maiden) p0. Made the ideal start at Alnwick, but seen just thrice since, and cleared only one fence successfully in 2000. Might yet be capable of winning again if she has a clean bill of health. *D.A. Whitaker — Fife (Alan & Lucy Normile).* 1118 (R).

CARBONADO ..10-3.. 7 b.g. Anshan — Virevoite (Shareef Dancer USA) 52211p. Workmanlike. NH FLAT '98 r3 p0. NH '98/9 (for T. Tate) r2 p0. Bought Doncaster, May for 1550. Followed two good seconds in which he was beaten a maximum of two lengths with a double (made a noise in the

Restricted, but jumped boldly and came home 25 lengths clear), but unfortunately risked on the firm at Woodford (when 4-7 in his Members), and went home lame, like several others at the meeting. Connections were doing very well with him to that point, but only time will tell whether he can make a recovery. *Mrs M.J. Tuck — Berkeley (H.R. Tuck).* 72 (OMa), 264 (OMa), 471 (OMa), 899 (OMa), 1280 (R), 1489 (M).

CARBURY'S CASE ..—.. 10 b.g. Tigerwood — Kitty Case (Saucy Kit) 5ufp. Workmanlike unfurnished half-brother to National Case. Dam, half-sister to Norman Case (*qv* '92 Annual), was 4th and ran out in Points. Grandam, Final Case, went lame when 2nd in an Adjacent, but previously won 3 flat (5-13f; one at Ostend) and 2 2m Hdles. Twice eliminated with a novice in the first mile, and tailed off twice (last once), and clearly has no potential as a racehorse. *Mrs L.A. Hinchliffe — S. Pembs (Debbie Hamer).* 1225 (OMa), 1456 (OMa), 1616 (R), 1662 (OMa).

CARDENDEN (IRE) ..—.. 13 b.g. Bustomi — Nana (Forlorn River) p. Tall light-framed half-brother to Nathan Blake, and to 2 flat winners (one in Ireland, and one in Hong Kong). Dam won at 5f. NH '92/3 (wins for J. Barclay; previously for Mrs S. Bradburne; used to wear tongue-strap) r47 w2 (2m Chses) p12; inc Sells. Made virtually all when winning twice over two miles (including on firm), but very rarely tackles much further, and last scored in December '96. Had been lame in '95, and may well be so again, having pulled up at halfway in a February Hunter Chase. Has now been pulled up five times, unseated at the first, and run out at the first on his final seven attempts. Once made an amazing journey, when he travelled from Kinneston in Fife to contest a race at Fontwell! *Mrs S. Ruddy — Buccleuch (Michael Ruddy).* 225 (3mH).

CARDINAL BUD (IRE) ..9-7.. 7 br.g. Cardinal Flower — Aglish Belle (IRE) (Buckskin FR) u4uf523. Workmanlike compact. Shows definite signs of ability, but has been a dunderhead in the jumping stakes, and is proving disappointingly slow to score. Came closest when two lengths second behind a lame winner (the third went on to open his account two outings later), and given virtually no chance by the jockey on his previous appearance, which surely warranted a Stewards enquiry. It will be surprising if he does not break his duck eventually. *M.G. Sheppard — Cambs (Josie Sheppard).* 97 (OMa), 290 (OMa), 411 (OMa), 604 (OMa), 844 (OMa), 1290 (OMa), 1513 (OMa).

CARDINAL GAYLE (IRE) ..9-10.. 11 b.g. Cardinal Flower — Bettica (Lord Gayle USA) 54522574. Workmanlike. Dam won 4 Irish flat, 12-14f. NH '94/5 and '97 r12 p5 (inc 2nd, and 3 fences last of 3 in Chses). P-t-P/HUNT CH '98/9 r18 w3 (Maiden, Restricted and Members) p12 (7 2nds); unseated 1. A dependable jumper, but terribly one-paced. The rider lacks the strength to drive him along when he decides to drop the bridle and coast, as he frequently does. Gave his best Pointing display when beating Cahors in '99, but it was no coincidence that J.D. Moore was in the saddle on that occasion. Capable of winning again in minor company, but needs dragging out of his current lethargic state. *Miss A. Findlay, H. Harper & Hon Miss D. Harding — Portman (Louise Alner).* 62 (Cf), 245 (L), 522 (L), 879 (I), 1059 (I), 1203 (I), 1485 (I), 1651 (I).

CARDINALS FOLLY (IRE) ..9-12.. 10 b.g. Lancastrian — Kilclare Lass (Pitpan) 1. Good-topped brother to Kaz Kalem (IRE) (*qv*). IRISH P-t-P '97 r2 p2. IRISH NH '96/8 r3 p0 (inc last, and pulled up 1). Confirmed the promise of his Irish Points when winning a two-finisher Maiden at Chipley Park in early February by the length of the run-in, but finished tired and lame. Apart from '97, has never managed more than one outing in a year, and obviously exceptionally hard to train, which is a pity. *G.G. Lewis — Pentyrch (Louise Latham).* 145 (OMa).

CAREFREE LOVE (IRE) ..8-10.. 7 ch.g. Carefree Dancer (USA) — Eau D'Amour (Tall Noble USA) pf7. Half-brother to Kingofnobles (IRE). Has shown some speed, and should reach the frame if he can produce some stamina in his second season. *C. Dawson — S. Durham.* 501 (2m4fOMa), 624 (OMa), 910 (2m4fOMa).

CARIBBEAN DREAM ..—.. 6 ch.m. Afzal — Lovelek (Golden Love) u. Half-sister to Knight Of Passion (*qv*). Foiled by the first in his Members. Her pedigree is interesting, at least. *H.M. Thomas — V. of Clettwr (Rhydian Jones).* 266 (M).

CARIBOO GOLD (USA) ..10-5.. 12 b.g. Slew O' Gold (USA) — Selket's Treasure (USA) (Gleaming USA) 225f. Strong half-brother to several winners in USA, and to one in Ireland. $175,000y. FLAT (for J. Gosden) r4 p4. NH '93/4 and '96/9 r31 w8 (4 Hdles, 2m-2m5f, and 4 Chses, 3m-3m1f, inc £17,348 prize at Wolverhampton; inc hat-trick '97) p11 (won 3m1f Hdle, but demoted to 2nd once; inc 2nd in '98 Kim Muir). Formerly useful, and has earned almost £67,000 over jumps, but last scored in May '97 and missed two consecutive seasons prior to that. Unable to quicken when favourite on his first two outings of 2000 (completely outpointed by Brambledown once), and tried extreme distances without success latterly. 4m1f at Cheltenham taxed him to the hilt, and turned a somersault at the final fence when attempting to refuse. Wears blinkers, and is not really interested these days. *K.C. Bailey — Pytchley.* 79 (O), 224 (3m2fH), 1024 (3m3f110yH), 1338 (4m1fH).

CARLEY LAD (IRE) ..11-2.. 13 br.g. Crash Course — Leveret (Le Bavard FR) 265314. Lengthy. NH '94/6 and '98/9 (first 3 wins from late G. Richards') r18 w5 (2 3m Hdles, and 3 Chses, 2m5f-3m) p2 (2nds). NH Spr '00 r2 w1 (beat Kings Measure and Master Nova, 3*l* and distance in 3m1f

Wetherby HCap Ch: *hdwy frm ½way, wknd 14, rallied nxt, ld last, stayed on*) p0; and 4th in 3m1f Kelso HCap Ch (*hmpd 13; nd aft*). Reportedly has breathing problems and runs tongue-tied, and is unpredictable, but followed a couple of lacklustre displays (made as series of mistakes once) with an excellent display in the Aintree Foxhunters in which he was very bold and made the running after a mile until headed passing the omitted second last. Remained in cracking form next time, and richly deserved his victory in a £10,062 Chase. Favourite subsequently, but did not seem to be firing on all cylinders, and connections can congratulate themselves on getting so much out of a 12-year-old who has never stood a great deal of racing. *N.B. Mason — Middleton*. 90 (3m1fH), 156 (3mH), 470 (2m4f110yH), 921 (2m6fH).

CARLINARE ..9-9.. 11 b.g. Sousa — Demetria (GER) (Basalt GER) f1. Half-brother to Rosenthal. Dam won 2 races in Germany. P-t-P '97 (for Mr H.R. Hobson) r2 p2. Did not see the racecourse until he was seven and disappeared for two years after a couple of promising placings in East Anglia, but resurfaced north of the border and gained compensation for his defeats when winning a long Maiden at Balcormo Mains. Wears bandages in front and his legs are obviously cause for concern, but his sire's stock tend to develop late in life, and he may well be capable of winning again if he stands the rigours of training. *E. Smith & Miss F. Mason — Fife (Alan & Lucy Normile)*. 718 (CfMa), 1123 (OMa).

CARLTON BRAE ..8-10.. 6 b.m. Primitive Rising (USA) — Carlton Valley (Barolo) fp5. Owner-bred half-sister to Thunderbird (*qv*). Has shown very little so far, but by a good sire of Pointers, and open to improvement. *Mrs F.E. & A.H. Harvey — Puckeridge (Alex Harvey)*. 775 (OMa), 941 (CfMa), 1180 (OMa).

CARNAVEN ..9-12.. 9 b.g. Le Coq D'Or — Carney (New Brig) 14p3fp. Sturdy brother to successful Hurdlers Carnetto, and half-brother to Corby Crown, and to Chasing winner, Billsbrook. Grandam, Boundary Tale, won a Maiden for Bobby Brewis. NH '98 r7 p0 (pulled up 4 inc 2 of 3 Chses — 7th of 8 in the other). NH May '00 (from A.S. Smith's) r1 p0 (pulled up in 3m1f Nov Ch: *w ldrs til wknd 14, t.o & pu last*). Showed his worth when making a successful Pointing debut in his Members, and also staying on well at the finish when third in a Restricted (also at Alnwick), whilst he additionally ran well at Kelso until tiring rapidly to lose two places on the run-in. Never gives the impression of being very fit, and might do substantially better if he followed in the hoof prints of Sunnycliff and was sent to Clive Storey. *R. Brewis — Percy (Rhona Brewis)*. 39 (M), 89 (3m1fH), 301 (2m5fH), 908 (R), 1159 (I).

CARNMONEY (IRE) ..9-8.. 13 gr.g. Torus — Gaelic Lady (Guillaume Tell USA) 5p5. Rangy dipped. IRISH P-t-P '93 r4 p0; pulled up 2, and fell 1. NH '96/7 r11 p0; 5th, 7th, last, pulled up 2 and unseated in Chses. P-t-P '98 r5 w2 (Maiden and Members) p3 (2 3rds). Pretty hopeless under Rules, but found life more to his liking in Points and recorded a double in '98, but less effective after two years off, and disappeared in mid-March in 2000. Presumably has an intermittent problem. *H. Frew — W. Percy (Nick & Kirsty Hargreave)*. 39 (M), 360 (R), 620 (R).

CAROMISU ..9-2.. 8 b.g. Scottish Reel — Muskcat Rambler (Pollerton) f1p3. Unfurnished half-brother to Nanda Devi (*qv*). NH FLAT '98 r2 p0. NH '98 (for J. Mackie) r3 p0. Jumped indifferently, but made nearly all the running to win a 2m4f Maiden at Alpraham under a good strong ride from Brendan Foster, but unimpressive in all his other races, including when partnered by the owner. Wears a tongue-strap. Will surely struggle to follow up. *S.A. Cochrane — Meynell & S. Staffs*. 372 (CfMa), 593 (2m4fOMa), 902 (Cf), 1071 (CR).

CARRAIG-AN-OIR (IRE) ..—.. 12 b.g. Down The Hatch — Dont Rock (Rugged Man) pp. Unfurnished half-brother to Secretrock (IRE), to Chasing winner, Rainbow Castle, and to Hurdles winner, Castlerichardking. Dam won Irish Maiden. IRISH NH FLAT '93/5 r8 w1 (6 ran) p1 (3rd). IRISH NH '93/6 r21 p3 (Hdles). P-t-P/HUNT CH '98 (for Miss T.V. Jenkins) r7 p0; refused 1, pulled up 1, and fell 1. Beat just one rival when last aired in '98, but surprisingly resurfaced in 2000 when pulled up after showing brief early speed twice. Does not stay anything like three miles, and certainly not worth bothering with again. *C. Dix — Curre*. 482 (I), 597 (Cf).

CARRAIG BROL (IRE) ..9-11.. 7 b.g. Cataldi — Davy's Hall (Weavers' Hall) R234. Half-brother to Irish winners, Slaney Bacon (Chasing and Pointing) and Another Contract (Hurdling). IRISH P-t-P '99 r2 p0 (pulled up 2). Speedy enough, but a weak finisher and becoming disappointing, and can be quirky. Ran out on his debut, and jumped badly left at Folkestone, suggesting that a right-handed course is not in his favour. Has every advantage in training and riding, and will probably score if connections stick with him. *T.W. Edmonds — E. Sussex & Romney Marsh (Di Grissell)*. 132 (OMa), 290 (CMa), 576 (OMa), 1537 (2m5fH).

CARR DYKE CASTLE ..—§§.. 7 ch.g. Carlingford Castle — Michele My Belle (Lochnager) Rpppfr. Compact half-brother to Roberts Royal. Dam, half-sister to Rig Steel (*qv* '96 Annual), won 2 Points and was 2nd as a 5-y-o. Despite his tender age he has already shown himself to be thoroughly ungenuine, and aquired blinkers on final start. His dam has certainly bred a couple of holy terrors. *G. Copley — Cottesmore (Tim Tarratt)*. 373 (CfMa), 693 (OMa), 872 (OMa), 1070 (2m4fOMa), 1220 (OMa), 1291 (OMa).

CARRIE'S GIFT ..—.. 7 ch.g. Say Primula — Ale Water (Be Friendly) ufp. Half-brother to Friendly Viking (*qv*). Dam won at 5f (3 ran). Must have schooled badly as he has been blinkered in all his races, and has predictably given the rider a very hard time. Added a near-side pricker on his latest outing. *Mrs M.A. Kendall — Cumberland F.* 188 (OMa), 501 (2m4fOMa), 664 (2m5fOMa).

CARRIG BOY (IRE) ..10-1.. 11 ch.g. Long Pond — Shining Brightly (Giolla Mear) 1. IRISH NH FLAT '96 r2 p0. P-t-P '98/9 r5 w2 (Maiden and Restricted) p2 (2nds); and fell 1. Battled on bravely under pressure to seize his Members in the dying strides, but has never stood much racing and his season was over in an afternoon. Stays really well, and would probably have been Open class had he had the opportunities. *I. Anderson — W. Salop.* 292 (M).

CARSON CITY ..9-8.. 14 ch.g. Carlingford Castle — Even More (Even Money) 4pp. Rangy half-brother to Siobhan's Joy, Coolcotts and Generals Boy, and to 6 winners in Ireland, including Bettys The Boss (IRE) (NH flat and Chasing). Dam won 2m Maiden Hurdle in Ireland. NH FLAT '92 r2 p1 (2nd to stablemate). NH '92/6 r20 w1 (3m4f Hdle) p8 (inc 3 Chses). P-t-P '98/9 r12 p3 (2 2nds); unseated 1, and pulled up 2. Gained the sole win of a generally disappointing career back in '94, but has always needed plenty of cajoling, and displayed minimal interest in proceedings in 2000. Jason Purllant shows plenty of determination, and deserves a similarly minded beast underneath him. *J. Purllant — Cambridge Univ.* 29 (Cf), 92 (Cf), 369 (O).

CASH ACCOUNT ..9-6.. 8 b.g. Lord Bud — Gilzie Bank (New Brig) 2. Leggy unfurnished brother to jumping winner, Banker Count, and half-brother to Banque D'Or, and to Chasing winner, Crosshot. P-t-P '98 r3 p0 (fell/unseated 2, and pulled up 1). Clueless when previously seen, but led for a long way at Mollington, and only gave best in the closing stages. Failed to reappear and obviously stands his racing badly, but worth persevering with if connections are able to. *Mrs V.J.R. Bostock — Atherstone (Roger Harvey).* 790 (OMa).

CASHEL GREEN (IRE) ..9-10.. 10 ch.g. Montelimar (USA) — Mrs McCartney (Pry) p5621u5. Tall. IRISH NH '97 r1 p0 (pulled up in Ch). IRISH NH FLAT '97/8 r3 p0. IRISH P-t-P '98 r4 p1 (2 distances last of 3); pulled up 1. P-t-P/HUNT CH '99 r8 p0 (last pair 3, pulled up 4, and unseated 1). Found an awful race at the 20th attempt (none of the other three finishers have gone on to emulate him), but generally lacking in stamina, and his problems are seemingly wind related as he is frequently tongue-tied. Will find winning opportunities hard to come by in the future. *A. Witcomb — Quorn.* 373 (CfMa), 548 (CfMa), 871 (R), 1220 (OMa), 1269 (OMa), 1530 (2m6fH), 1586 (CN).

CASHEW CHAOS ..9-2.. 9 b.g. Neltino — Blakeney Sound (Blakeney) ppp. Small brother to NH flat and jumping winner, Sounds Like Fun and Hurdles winner, Master Rastus, and half-brother to 2 flat winners (one in Sweden), including Glen Miller. P-t-P '97/8 r7 w1 (deadheat for Maiden) p1 (3rd); pulled up 3. NH Feb/Mar '00 r2 p0 (2m6f Hdle: *mid div, lost plce aft 6, t.o & pu 2 out*; and pulled up in 3m110y Nov Hdle: *bhnd, rdn 7, t.o & pu 9*). Off the track for over 18 months following his Maiden success at Bitterley in '98, but pulled up in all three appearances in 2000, and still looks troubled. Quickly tailed off when tried in blinkers at Hereford, and promptly disappeared. *N. Shutts — Ludlow (Karen Marks).* 925 (2mH).

CASHEW CRISIS (IRE) ..9-6.. 6 b.g. Meneval (USA) — Wish Again (Three Wishes) fu22. Small well-made half-brother to Vicompt De Valmont and Swan's Wish (IRE), to useful jumping winner, Willsford, to Irish Pointing/Hunter Chase and Chasing winner, Neda Charmer, and to an Irish NH flat and Hurdles winner. Sold Tatts (Ireland), Nov for 6607. Very sketchy in his first two races, but gave an improved display when chasing home another Shutts five-year-old in his Members. Backed from 5/2 to 7/4 on a return visit to Bitterley, and should have won, but Mark Rodda did not ride vigorously enough until it was far too late, and got beaten three-quarters of a length. Should soon find compensation. *N. Shutts — Ludlow (Penny Grainger).* 450 (CfMa), 898 (OMa), 986 (M), 1092 (OMa).

CASH MAN (IRE) ..—.. 8 b.g. Mandalus — Cash Discount (Deep Run) p. Smallish close-coupled half-brother to Above Suspicion (IRE), and to Irish Pointing and English Hurdles winner, Cash Box (IRE). P-t-P '98 (for Mr I. Hamilton) r1 w1 (2m4f Maiden). Changed hands for 50,000 gns at Doncaster after winning a short Maiden at Tranwell in '98, but never ran for the purchaser (Paul Nicholls — who paid a barmy price), and suffered irreparable damage on his Pointing debut at Great Trethew. *F.A. Bonsal — Beaufort (Richard Barber).* 164 (R).

CASINO NELL ..—.. 7 gr.m. Neltino — Castelira (Castle) ppfpp. Sturdy half-sister to Mourn Blade, Ten Bob Note, Ernie Fox and Fiery Jack. Dam won Ladies and placed 5 for the late Hunter Rowe (Bridget Hitchcock's father). P-t-P '99 r1 p0 (pulled up). Had shown some ability in Maiden company prior to breaking down at Higham, and being a well-bred mare should have a future in the paddocks if she can't return to the racecourse. Had been tried in a tongue-strap, but it was her Neltino legs that let her down. *D. Nicholls, D. Bailey & Mrs B. Hitchcock — Puckeridge (Alex Harvey).* 23 (OMa), 87 (OMa), 236 (OMa), 1039 (OMa), 1115 (OMa).

PLATE 30   965 Cheshire Forest Open Maiden 56&7yo (Div 1): Cassia Green and the late Mike Worthington, 1st, jump ahead of Bright Reform (C. Barlow), 4th, and Sharp Embrace (J. Burley), 2nd
PHOTO: Peter & Marilyn Sweet

CASSIA GREEN ..9-7.. 7 gr.g. Scallywag — Casa's Star (Top Star) 1. Half-brother to Starlight Fool and My Naughty Nanny. Dam won 2 Points and placed 5 for the Greenways. Grandam, Casa's Image, won a Hunt Ch and 5 Points. Won a very bad youngsters Maiden on firmish at Tabley by 20 lengths, but could do not more than demolish the opposition, and may progress to better things. *Mrs J. Greenway — Cheshire Forest (Reg Crank).* 965 (OMa).

CASTLE ARROW (IRE) ..10-4§.. 8 b.g. Mansooj — Soulful (So Blessed) 545p2u1. Workmanlike half-brother to Irish Pointing winner, Private Yashkan, to an Irish flat winner, and to an Irish Hurdles winner. Dam won at 8f. IRISH P-t-P '97 r1 w1 (4yo Maiden). NH '97/9 r6 p1 (3rd in Hurdle). P-t-P/HUNT CH '99 (for Mr R.M. Stronge) r5 w2 (Restricted and Intermediate) p1 (2nd in Hunt Ch); fell 1. Sold for 10,000 gns after winning a two-finisher Maiden in the slowest time of the day on his Irish Pointing debut in '97 (left clear at the last), and failed to cut much ice under Rules, but has looked more at home between the flags. Present connections enjoy a tilt at the ring, but he managed to let them down on more than one occasion in 2000, and is clearly not to be trusted. Behaves very badly at the start, and has to be led in and taken to post early nowadays, but still capable when everything goes his way, and took advantage of the odds-on favourite's mistake when successful under Julian Pritchard on his final appearance at the John White benefit at Kingston Blount. May win more often now that his confidence has been given a boost, but rarely stays in one yard for very long, and can be given short shrift if his next outing is from a new stable. Blinkered for his most recent success. *N.D. Quesnel — Berks & Bucks (John White).* 243 (Cf), 585 (2m5f110yH), 886 (C), 1145 (L), 1441 (Cnr), 1481 (Cf), 1620 (Cf).

CASTLE BAY (IRE) ..—.. 10 ch.g. Castle Keep — Castle Pearl (Welsh Term) upf. Sturdy. NH FLAT '97 (for L. Lungo) r2 p0. NH '99 (for G.M. Moore) r2 p0. Was an awkward customer, and aquired a tongue-strap at Alnwick, where he took a fatal fall. *Miss C.M. Thompson — Morpeth.* 423 (R), 493 (Cf), 913 (CfMa).

CASTLE CHIEF (IRE) ..9-3.. 12 br.g. Roselier (FR) — Polyxena (FR) (Pretendre) 3p. Rangy half-brother to Amari Prince, and to Irish NH flat winners, Oats A Plenty and Sports Edition (also a successful Hurdler there). IRISH P-t-P '93 r2 p1 (2nd to Faha Gig); and pulled up 1. NH FLAT '94 r2 p1 (2nd of 22). NH '94/6 r6 p1 (2nd in Ch); 4th 5, inc 3 Hdles. P-t-P '99 r2 p0 (unseated 1, and ran out 1). Would be a certainty for a Maiden if he recaptured his best Rules form (second to subsequent Scottish Grand National hero Baronet on his final start over regulation fences), but rarely seen in recent years, and his huge frame needs plenty of scaffolding to keep him in one piece. Deserves a win, but seems to have trouble getting the trip, and becoming advanced in years. *T.R. Gretton — Silverton.* 204 (OMa), 1068 (3m2fOMa).

CASTLE COURT (IRE) ..10-11.. 13 ch.g. Deep Run — Mawbeg Holly (Golden Love) 12p. Big strong brother to One More Run, and to useful NH flat and jumping winner, Dakyns Boy, and half-brother to Irish jumping and English Chasing winner, Holly's Pride (IRE), and Irish NH flat winner Give It Holly. IRISH NH FLAT '93 r4 p2. NH '93/6 r10 w2 (Hdle and Ch, both over 2m5f at Warwicks) p4. HUNT CH '99 r1 p1 (2nd). IRISH NH May '00 r1 p0 (pulled up in Punchestown 3m1f Champion HC: *cl up, 5th 8, wknd nxt, pu 10*). Has always had more than his fair share of ability, and nursed back to form by Charlie Egerton. Recorded his first success since January '96 when edging out Mr Snowman on his reappearance at Ascot, but then failed to give nine pounds to Shekels at Stratford, but that was no disgrace. However, the cotton wool wrapping went back on promptly and he remains incredibly fragile. Won purely on guts and jockeyship at Ascot and his latest partner Vinnie Keane looks to have a bright future ahead of him. *Mrs S.A. Roe — Berks & Bucks (Charlie Egerton).* 919 (2m3f110yH), 1026 (2m5f110yH).

CASTLE FOLLY (IRE) ..10-9.. 9 b.g. Carlingford Castle — Air Plane (Arratos FR) p11321p. Workmanlike good-looking. IRISH P-t-P '98/9 r11 w3 (made all each time, inc Winners of Two, and Adjacent) p3; pulled up 2, and ran out 2. Bought Doncaster, May for 30,000. Quite useful, but his two run-outs in Ireland gave present connections a taste of what might be in store, and he threw away an Open at Kimble by swerving after the final fence when poised to defeat Rectory Garden. Again outbattled by that very game opponent at Lockinge two days later, but has otherwise been in useful form between the flags, although he has been blinkered since an unimpressive victory at Kingston Blount. Did not think much of the bigger fences on his Hunter Chase debut, but is talented enough to score in that sphere if he feels like it. Must have a running rail. Acts on firmish, and is also effective in heavy. *D. & N. Quesnel — Berks & Bucks (John White).* 77 (O), 244 (O), 389 (O), 1144 (O), 1205 (MO), 1621 (O), 1646 (3m4fH).

PLATE 31   389 Beaufort Mens Open: Castle Folly (R. Lawther), 1st, with Lie Detector (J. Gasper), 3rd
PHOTO: Bill Selwyn

CASTLE LYNCH (IRE) ..10-7.. 9 b.m. Castle Keep — Shirowen (Master Owen) f1341131u. Workmanlike half-sister to several winners over jumps, including Midnight Hour (IRE) (in Ireland). NH FLAT '96 r1 p0. NH '97 r3 p0. P-t-P '98/9 r6 w2 (Maiden and Restricted) p1 (2nd); pulled up 2, and unseated 1. Came of age in 2000, and rewarded her connections with four victories including a Wincanton Hunter Chase, but intelligently placed, and faced relatively simple tasks in two of her three Larkhill wins. Quietly fancied for the Ladies Hunter Chase at Stratford on her final start, but lost Pauline Robson a mile from home when going well, and remains inclined to make blunders, particularly over the bigger obstacles. Fired in '98, but generally sound as a bell since, and should win more races, particularly as she has top riders. *Mrs A.M. Kley — Blackmore &*

Sparkford V. (Pauline Tizzard). 10 (O), 63 (I), 262 (MO), 383 (3mH), 685 (2m5fH), 1132 (L), 1339 (2m5fH), 1597 (MO), 1648 (3mH).

CASTLE MANE (IRE) ..12-2.. 9 ch.g. Carlingford Castle — Mantilla Run (Deep Run) 4211. Smallish workmanlike lengthy. IRISH NH '99 r1 w1 (beat Sheltering and Dunaree at Punchestown). P-t-P/HUNT CH '98/9 r8 w8 (inc 2 Hunt Chses, 3m2f-3m2f110y and 2 Opens). The undisputed Champion Hunter Chaser in '99, but lost his unbeaten record on his 2000 reappearance, and found to be suffering from a muscle enzyme deficiency after another defeat in heavy ground at Newbury where uncharacteristic jumping errors sealed his demise. Connections felt it prudent to give the Cheltenham Foxhunters a miss, but he reappeared at the evening meeting there in May where he jumped and galloped inferiors into the ground. Recorded his 11th career success in the (former) Horse & Hound Cup after which the jockey reported that the horse still did not feel fully 100 per cent, and went into summer quarters with rumours rife that he was to join Kim Bailey to challenge for top honours in 2001. Tragically was found with a broken neck in his field at home, and despite every effort to save him had to be put down. Was a phenomenal galloper who would put his head down and battle with real determination, and was a great credit to the training of Caroline Bailey and the riding of Ben Pollock. Might well have gone on to even greater things, but his exploits will live in the memory of all those who witnessed them. C. Dixey — Meynell & S. Staffs (Caroline Bailey). 156 (3mH), 385 (3mH), 1337 (3m2f110yH), 1647 (3m4fH).

PLATE 32   1647 Intrum Justitia (42nd Horse & Hound Cup) Champion HC, Stratford: The brilliant but ill-fated Castle Mane (B. Pollock), 1st, leads Last Option (Mrs F. Needham), 3rd
PHOTO: Brian Armstrong

CASTLE NUTTER ..—.. 7 b.g. Carlingford Castle — Nutcase (Idiot's Delight) p. Small sturdy. Dam (*qv* '99 Annual), won 3 Points and placed 8 after producing Castle Nutter. Sold Ascot, Nov '97 for 2200. Looked unfit and unschooled at Weston Park, and pulled up after a mile when tailed off after a deplorable display of jumping. Mrs C.T. Forber — Saddleworth. 1412 (OMa).

CASTLEROYAL (IRE) ..10-6.. 12 br.g. Royal Fountain — Dicklers Niece (Golden Love) 2p. Big rangy half-brother to Clongeel Lord (IRE). IRISH P-t-P '94 and '96 r7 w2 (7yo&up Maiden and Members) p0; pulled up 1, and fell at last when likely winner. IRISH NH '96 r8 w1 (2m Ch) p3 (inc 2 Hdles, one at Perth, and 2nd in Carlisle Ch). P-t-P/HUNT CH '99 r3 p2 (Hunt Chses, 2nd once). A triple winner in Ireland, but broke down in '96 and took four years to return to the course and appeared to go wrong again at Newcastle. Genuine and a good jumper, but his career must be in jeopardy. B. McNichol — Cumberland F. 662 (O), 917 (3mH).

CASTLE SHELLEY (IRE) ..10-1.. 12 b.g. Carlingford Castle — Briarsfield Lady (Cheval) p543114. Compact attractive. IRISH P-t-P '95/6 r9 w1 (Maiden) p1 (3rd); pulled up 5, and unseated 1. P-t-P

'97 and '99 r13 w1 (Restricted) p3 (2nds, short-headed once, and beaten ¾l); pulled up 4, unseated 2. Successful three times under Rupert Smith in the last two seasons and is a fair performer, but takes a while to run himself fit, and still has a tendency to stop quickly in the manner of a horse who is breaking blood vessels. Becoming much more adept at course completion, and his reliable fencing might enable him to find another minor race. Seems to act on any going. *C.W. Booth — Grafton (Richard Webb).* 263 (I), 543 (I), 749 (Cf), 886 (C), 1243 (Inr), 1441 (Cnr), 1542 (3mH).

CAST THE LINE ..—.. 11 b.g. Pharly (FR) — Off The Reel (USA) (Silent —Screen USA) p. Lengthy well-made half-brother to 2 flat winners, including Chasing winner, Urizen. Dam won 3 10f races. 6600f, 9000y. FLAT (wins for A. Stewart) r16 w3 (10-12f, one on fibresand) p6 (inc 2nd of 35 at Newmarket); Sell final. NH '95/6 (for C. Egerton) r9 w1 (2m1f Hdle) p1 (2nd); pulled up in Sell final. Last scored in October '95, and shuffled off into retirement not long after having developed serious wind trouble (was tubed for his final appearance). Revived for a Members jaunt, but the rider promptly dropped her whip and was scrabbling around in the saddle afterwards. Usually wore headgear in the past, and often tongue-tied. *Mrs E. Thomas — Fitzwilliam.* 769 (M).

CASUAL WATER (IRE) ..9-13.. 10 b.g. Simply Great (FR) — Top Nurse (High Top) 4p3. Narrow compact half-brother to flat winner, Cure The King. IR 3000y. FLAT (first win for M.H.Easterby; 5 more for T. Newcombe, inc hat-trick) r36 w6 (12-15f) p5. NH '94/5 and '97/9 (for V. Dartnall; 3 wins previously for P. Nicholls; 1 win previously for T. Newcombe; 1 win previously for J. White) r20 w5 (3 Hdles, 2m1f-2m2f, and 2 Chses, 2m2f-2m3h) p5; reluctant to race once. The winner of 11 races on sound surfaces, and has career earnings of nearly £60,000, which could have been substantially higher, but for three seconds in '95 when he was beaten half a length or less each time (unlucky twice in contests with a value of more than £10,000 to the winner, including when ridden by Mr F. Grasso Caprioli once). Started to decline under Rules, and jumped badly right on his penultimate appearance. Has since failed to get the trip in Points, and beaten a minimum of 17 lengths. Tried in headgear in the dim and distant past. *T. Hunt — T. Webb — Atherstone (Roger Harvey).* 117 (O), 369 (O), 545 (O).

CATCHATAN (IRE) ..9-8.. 9 b.g. Cataldi — Snowtan (IRE) (Tanfirion) p1. Workmanlike. Sold Doncaster, May for 14,000. Put up an impressive performance for a five-year-old when beating two other finishers (who both went on to score) very easily at Guilsborough. Sure to win again, and might have a bright future. *M.T. & K. Elliot — Heythrop (Ginny Elliot).* 11 (OMa), 1011 (CfMa).

CATCHPHRASE ..9-7.. 11 ch.g. Baron Blakeney — Aldington Miss (Legal Eagle) p85fp33p. Stocky brother to Catchword, and half-brother to Hurdles winner, Aldington Chapple. P-t-P/HUNT CH '97/9 r17 w3 (2m5f Maiden, Club Novices and Members) p1 (3rd); pulled up 7, and fell/unseated 2. Unbeaten when completing in his first season Pointing, but a huge disappointment since, and has now clocked up 20 consecutive defeats over three years. Usually drops the bit after racing prominently for the first couple of miles, and though slightly more motivated by the application of a visor when third twice, their effect seems to have worn off already. *A.A. & Mrs K. Day — Atherstone (Mrs K. Day).* 37 (Cl), 543 (I), 701 (I), 1006 (Cf), 1267 (I), 1414 (M), 1503 (Cf), 538 (CCond).

CATCH THE PIGEON ..—.. 12 b.m. Wonderful Surprise — Cheeky Pigeon (Brave Invader USA) p. Compact owner-bred half-sister to Lord Nick (*qv*). NH FLAT '93 r1 p0. NH '94/5 and '97/9 r20 w1 (2m6f Hdle) p6. Averages little more than two outings per annum, and gained her only success in May '97. Unruly at the start and reluctant to race on her final appearance under Rules, and was pulled up in a very competitive five-runner contest in her only Point. *Mrs R.E. Barr — Cleveland.* 172 (Cm).

CATCHWORD ..10-7.. 10 b.g. Baron Blakeney — Aldington Miss (Legal Eagle) 1113. Compact brother to Catchphrase (*qv*). P-t-P '99 (for Mr A.A. Day) r3 p0 (pulled up 3). Much improved by Andrew Garland in his second season, and rounded off an emphatic hat-trick with victory in a competitive event at Chaddesley in a good time. Stopped in his tracks by a blunder two out when chasing Barna Boy on his Open race debut, but provided he does not follow in the footsteps of his brother looks sure to succeed in that class in 2001. Has two paddock handlers (the legacy of throwing himself to the ground on his '99 debut), but his ability to quicken is not in question and neither, at the moment, is his attitude. *A.P. Garland — Atherstone.* 122 (OMa), 371 (R), 615 (CMod), 1216 (O).

CATECHIST (IRE) ..6-7.. 6 b.g. Cataldi — Emily Bishop (IRE) (The Parson) pR3. Compact half-brother to Irish Pointing winner, Grigori Rusputin. Bought Doncaster, May for 6200. Started at 20-1 thrice, but gave a much improved display when about six lengths third over 2m4f on final start, and may be able to win in 2001. Should not be troubled by the full trip. *Mrs V. Ramm — Cotswold (Jelly Nolan).* 391 (CfMa), 616 (CMa), 673 (2m4fOMa).

CATO (IRE) ..9-4.. 10 b.g. Cataldi — Hidden Virtue (Tanfirion) p. Small close-coupled. IRISH NH FLAT '98 r1 p0 (tailed off). P-t-P '99 r8 w1 (Maiden) p1 (2nd); pulled up 3, and fell 2. All out to justify odds-on favouritism in a poor Maiden at Mordon in '99 (only one of the five other finishers has gone on to score since), and presumably met with a setback following his reappearance as he was not seen again. Used to spring all manner of surprises on Inspector Clouseau, but it would be a real shock if he were to win again. *C.C. Dobson — Braes (Russell Ross).* 807 (R).

CATTON LADY ..9-7.. 11 b.m. Chas Sawyer — Carpenters Gloss (Grange Melody) 323. Tall. Dam, half-sister to Soraway (*qv* '91 Annual), was placed in 2 Maidens for Mrs Dodgson. Grandam, Skyros Lady, won 2 Irish Points and placed 3. NH '96/7 r14 p4 (3rds in Sells, beaten 10½*l* maximum, despite being out of handicap in 3). P-t-P/HUNT CH '98/9 r5 p3 (2 3rds). Placed in six of her last seven Points and few horses would be more deserving of a success, but has had plenty of chances and keeps failing to grasp the nettle. Might strike gold eventually, but will probably frustrate her supporters a few more times before it happens. *Mrs M. Dodgson — Cleveland (Charmaine Raw).* 803 (MMa), 1353 (OMa), 1480 (OMa).

CATWALKER (IRE) ..—.. 10 b.g. Reasonable (FR) — Norse Lady (Viking USA) upp. Tall lengthy brother to Irish flat winner, On The Catwalk, and half-brother to successful Hurdler, Dont Forget Curtis (IRE), and to a winner in USA. IRISH FLAT r14 w1 (5f) p0. IRISH NH '94/5 r11 p2 (3rds). NH '95/8 (sometimes blinkered; for R. Lee, bought for 1500; previously for H. Webb, bought for 2100; debut when sent over by E. O'Grady) r24 p4 (3rds, inc 2 Sell Hdles, and Ch). Gained his sole victory as a two-year-old, and is the loser of 38 races over jumps. Looked to take no interest when failing to get round in Opens after a two year absence. *S.R. Cobden — Farmers Bloodhounds.* 764 (O), 1244 (MO), 1394 (O).

CAUGHT AT DAWN (IRE) ..9-5.. 7 b.g. Supreme Leader — Pharisee (IRE) (Phardante FR) 16. 8200 4-year-old. NH FLAT '99 (from J.J. O'Neill's) r1 p0. Backed from 14s to sixes in a young Maiden at Barbury Castle and duly obliged, but was very unimpressive in the slowest time of the day. Wandered badly in the closing stages and was reluctant to continue after climbing the final fence, and again slowed quickly in the closing stages when 30 lengths sixth in mid-February. Not seen again. Goes a good gallop for a youngster, but may need to be treated with suspicion when he reappears. *J.R. Weston — Worcs (Penny Grainger).* 31 (CMa), 193 (R).

CAULD SIGNAL (IRE) ..—.. 8 b.m. Cataldi — Typhoon Signal (Aristocracy) pfppp. Small light. IRISH NH FLAT '97/9 r5 p0. IRISH NH '98 r8 p0. NH '99 (bought for 850) r1 p0 (pulled up lame). Never even placed from 19 attempts, and maintained her deplorable record in Points. Failed to get further than the fourth fence on two occasions. *G. Richards — Tredegar F.* 105 (OMa), 350 (CfMa), 487 (CfMa), 648 (CfMa), 991 (L).

CAUNDLE ENCORE ..8-12.. 8 gr.m. El Conquistador — Caundle Break (Rugantino) ru3. Strong half-sister to Caundle Steps (*qv*). Whipped round and refused to race on her debut, and unseated at halfway next time, but did rather better when finishing 13 lengths third, and although she never got into contention it was at least a step in the right direction. *P.J. Doggrell — W. Somerset.* 875 (2m4fOMa), 1101 (OMa), 1307 (OMa).

CAUNDLE'S HAND ..8-8.. 10 ch.m. Nearly A Hand — Caundle Break (Rugantino) f2p. Sparely-made half-sister to Caundle Steps (*qv*). P-t-P '98 (for Mrs G. Clist) r2 p0 (unseated 1, and pulled up 1). Thirty lengths second of three in a disaster-strewn Maiden at Bishops Court, but remains a high risk betting proposition as she herself has yet to sort out her faulty jumping. Not without ability, and the penny might drop eventually. *Mr & Mrs R. Partridge — Tiverton (Rose Partridge).* 204 (OMa), 410 (OMa), 738 (OMa).

CAUNDLE STEPS ..9-13§.. 14 b.g. Impecunious — Caundle Break (Rugantino) 3r. Big angular half-sister to Caundle's Hand. Dam is an unraced sister to Plot Lane. Grandam, Trudi Fair, won 6 Points and placed 25 for Peter Doggrell. P-t-P '93/6 and '98/9 r32 w3 (inc Open) p7 (4 2nds, and inc remote last of 2 and of 3); failed to finish 14 (refused 1, and fell/unseated 3). Flattered by an Open success and normally very one-paced, but a steady jumper who likes to dominate — can look ungenuine when things do not go his way. Restricted to just two starts in 2000, and very unlikely to achieve much if he returns for an eighth campaign. Has been tried unsuccessfully in a visor, but not since '95. *P.J. Doggrell — W. Somerset.* 764 (O), 878 (O).

CAVALERO ..12-0.. 12 b.g. Afzal — Jolly Lass (Jolly Me) 2211u1. Tall rangy owner-bred half-brother to Jolly Dick. NH FLAT r2 p1 (2nd at 40-1). NH '95/6 r8 w1 (2m4f Nov Sell Hdle, 20-1, Tote 35-1, 10 ran and 3 finished); pulled up in 3 other Hdles, and pulled up, fell 2 and unseated in Chses. P-t-P/HUNT CH '97/8 r12 w7 (inc 4 Hunt Chses, 2m6f-4m2f110y) p2 (2nds, beaten short-head once, and head once); pulled up 1, and fell 1. NH '98/9 r8 p4 (2 2nds); pulled up 1, fell 1. NH '00 r1 p0 (unseated in Scottish Grand National: *blun & ur* 3). Amazingly improved in '98 and returned from a profitable, but ultimately unsuccessful spell under Rules to Hunter Chasing in 2000 with fairytale results. Produced a burst of speed rarely seen when storming past six rivals up the Cheltenham hill to collect the Foxhunters almost two years after he had won the Aintree version, and put Real Value to the sword again on a return visit the following month. Formerly highly unpredictable, but a true hero now and has amassed £51,206 in prize money from his seven Hunter Chase wins alone. Remains ultra-game, famed for his finish which is often so explosive that Alex Charles-Jones loses the steering for a while, and is still cocky enough to test the might of the birch from time to time. Has helped John Manners attain cult hero status himself, and long may it continue. *H.J. Manners — V.W.H.* 32 (MO), 156 (3mH), 386 (3m1f110yH), 584 (3m2f110yH), 1103 (3m2f110yH).

CAWARRA BOY ..9-0.. 13 b.g. Martinmas — Cawarra Belle (Crimson Beau) 7fppp. Workmanlike compact. NH FLAT '92 (for C. James) r3 p1 (3rd). NH '93/9 (for E. James; wins previously for C. James) r29 w2 (2m-2m1f Hdles) p7 (inc 4 Chses — hung badly right and demoted 2nd after winning once); blinkered last 2, Sell final. Last scored in January '96, and proved to be a waste of time in Points. A remote last on his only completion, and has been totally unable to get the trip. *R.J. Smith — Beaufort.* 5 (Cv&nr), 33 (Cnr), 246 (C), 749 (Cf), 1098 (C).

PLATE 33   583 Christies Foxhunter HC, Cheltenham: Cavalero (A. Charles-Jones), 1st, has very few behind him at the third last, Gillan Cove (R. Young), 6th, on right, will also make remarkable late headway, but Dan's Your Man (P. Cashman), 13th, has run his race

PHOTO: Clare Warwick

CEAD MILE FAILTE ..9-11.. 6 ch.g. Most Welcome — Avionne (Derrylin) 1p. Small sturdy half-brother to Jamies First (IRE). Dam won 8f Clmr; and won 5 Sell Hdles at around 2m for Martin Pipe. FLAT (for R.O'Sullivan; previously for R. Ingram) r11 p1 (3rd). Bought Ascot, Sep '98 for 1050gns. Managed to cling on to a dwindling advantage in a 2m4f Maiden on firmish at Garnons, and was in the process of running another good race when he was pulled up and dismounted in a Restricted. If he was sound he would have prospects in that grade. Pronouncing his name is problematical, but we think it translates as 'A Hundred Thousand Welcomes' (you can certainly see it written on pub walls in Ireland). *Miss J. Fellows — Clifton-on-Teme.* 673 (2m4fOMa), 1460 (R).

CEBU GALE (IRE) ..10-2.. 12 b.g. Strong Gale — Joint Master (Master Owen) p153pf. Tall workmanlike brother to Irish winners, Wintry Shower (Pointing/Chasing) and Wylde Hide (jumping). Dam won 3 Irish Hdles, 2m-2m4f. IRISH NH FLAT '94 r2 p0. IRISH NH '94/5 and '98/9 (worn tongue-strap) r18 p3 (2nd in Hdle and Hunt Ch, and 3rd in Ch). IRISH P-t-P '96/9 r16 w2 (7yo plus Mdn for novice riders, and Winners of Two) p6; pulled up 1, fell 3, and unseated 2. Bought Doncaster, Aug for 600. Did well for a cheapie when picking up an Intermediate at Higham, but had a habit of making blunders, and was unfortunately killed by a crashing fall at Catterick. *R.E. Gray — Cranwell Bloodhounds (Joanna Hughes and Paul Blockley).* 4 (O), 27 (I), 115 (CCf), 301 (2m5fH), 303 (3mH), 465 (3m1fl110yH).

CEDE NULLIS ..10-3§.. 10 b.m. Primitive Rising (USA) — Sweet Mood (Le Johnstan) pp7pppu5f14u. Close-coupled. Dam is sister to Par Kelly (qv '96 Annual). Grandam, Dunreekan, won 3 mediocre Ladies and placed 13 (inc a flat race). P-t-P/HUNT CH '98/9 r9 w1 (Maiden) p1 (2nd); pulled up 6, and ran out 1. A capable mare, but her inconsistencies are seemingly caused by physical flaws (has been tried in a tongue-strap), and also by her mood swings. Sprang a surprise under Laura Eddery at Mordon in late season, but capitulated after looking dangerous at Garthorpe subsequently. A total enigma who can pull hard, but just as likely not to pick up the bridle at all, and has run blinkered (including when successful) in five of her last six appearances. Sure to remain totally unpredictable, and backing her is fraught with risk. *P. Maddison — Middleton.* 48 (Cf), 137 (R), 229 (Cf), 378 (R), 396 (R), 807 (R), 996 (M), 1328 (L), 1350 (L), 1477 (L), 1587 (L), 1648 (3mH).

CEDOR HICKS ..7-12.. 8 ch.m. Seymour Hicks (FR) — Cedor's Daughter (Pallard Court) pp. Very small half-sister to Paper Chipps, Scally's Daughter, Corrie Fearn, Cedor's Son, Made Of Talent and Cedor's Gem. Dam won 7 Hunt Chses, 3m-3m2f (beat Grittar twice), and 3 Points and placed 17 (inc 11 Chses/Hunt Chses). P-t-P '99 r2 p0 (4th of 5, and pulled up 1). Tailed off in all four trips to Garnons in the past two years, but has shown some ability despite looking backward, and almost certainly capable of better if she can be produced fighting fit. Could hardly be better bred for the job, but lacks physical presence, and that together with her inability to stand much racing may conspire against her. *Lady Susan Brooke — Teme V.* 451 (CfMa), 672 (2m4fOMa).

CEFN TIGER ..—.. 6 b.g. Tigerwood — My Bid (Cleon) pp. Dam, half-sister to Uncle Reginald (*qv*), pulled up in 2 Points for Dilwyn Thomas. Pulled up twice in early April, and was dismounted when second favourite in the latest. Shows early pace (impetuous), and might do better if he is unharmed. *D.R. Thomas — Llangeinor.* 835 (OMa), 950 (OMa).

CEFN WOODSMAN ..9-9.. 10 br.g. Tigerwood — Orange Pop (Gimlet) pupuupu42. Compact leggy. Dam refused in 3 of 4 Points (miles last in match after continuing once). Grandam, Orange Pip, was placed in 10 Points. P-t-P '96/9 r26 w1 (Maiden) p9 (7 3rds, last once); pulled up 5, and fell 2. Took 24 outings before he got off the mark, but a steady-jumping plodder, and bought as a schoolmaster by Kate Lovelace (who nevertheless managed to fall off him on four occasions). Did manage to maintain contact with her on last two starts, and should begin the 2001 campaign with confidence restored. Sweated freely on his first two starts with Calamity Kate — clearly knowing what fate awaited her — and will struggle to get his name on the scoresheet again. *D.R. Thomas — Miss K.J. Lovelace — Llangeinor.* 273 (R), 524 (R), 876 (R), 958 (R), 1061 (R), 1309 (R), 1375 (R), 1551 (R), 1616 (R).

CELIAS TWINK ..10-0.. 8 b.m. Buckley — Celia's Halo (Mountain Call) p1. Strong-topped half-sister to Sam's Birthday and Stars. Dam won 10f Sell and 2m Sell Hdle and placed 7, inc 3 remote 3rds in Points for late Sam Thompson. Backward and schooled on her debut, but supported from 14s to sevens when winning a three-finisher Maiden at Newton Bromswold by the best part of a furlong (the only danger ran off the course on the bend approaching two out before continuing). Looks to stay well, and is quite any interesting prospect, but was not seen out again. Her rating is pitched on the high side at present. *Mrs S. Thompson — Pytchley (Tik Saunders).* 121 (OMa), 514 (OMa).

CELTIC ABBEY ..11-5.. 13 b.g. Celtic Cone — Cagaleena (Cagirama) 1. Strong compact smallish owner-bred half-brother to Abbeydore, Dore Bridge and Palm Lady. Dam won 3 Chases (2m-3m1f) for Gerald Powell's father. NH '97/8 r8 p2 (3rds in 2m5f-3m Chses); unseated in '97 and fell in '98 Grand Nationals, and pulled up in Whitbread and Mildmay/Cazalet Chses. P-t-P/HUNT CH '93/7 and '99 r27 w8 (inc 5 Hunt Chses, 2m5f-3m4f, inc '97 Horse & Hound Cup) p9 (6 2nds; inc 6 Hunt Chses); failed to finish 4 (fell 2 — when looking winner of Hunt Ch once). A top-class Hunter Chaser whose career has been blighted by breaking blood vessels latterly. Failed to make the grade when tried Chasing at the very top level and restricted to just one outing in 2000, but slammed Ardstown at Chepstow under a fine attacking ride from Adrian Wintle, and still retains much of his ability. Capable of precision jumping, and best suited by decent ground. *G.J. Powell — S. Herefords.* 683 (3mH).

CELTIC FRIEND (IRE) ..8-7§.. 10 ch.g. Celtic Cone — Pal Alley (Pals Passage) 54p. Small compact half-brother to Irish Hurdles winner, Finbar Furey. P-t-P '97/9 r8 w1 (Maiden) p0 (unseated 2, and pulled up 5). Failed to complete in his first seven races, but amazingly managed to win at Bonvilston when 20-1 and blinkered for the first time on his final start in '99. Beat just one rival in 2000, and tailed off without exception — looked particularly reluctant on his latest appearance. One to avoid if he returns. *Mrs R.M. Thomas — S. Pembs (Owen Thomas).* 836 (L), 1224 (L), 1297 (L).

CELTIC SILVER ..10-3.. 13 gr.g. Celtic Cone — Rockin Berry (Daybrook Lad) ff. Rangy workmanlike brother to Celtic Berry, and half-brother to Reapers Rock and Take Achance On Me. Dam won 2m6f Hunt Ch and 7 Points and placed 13 (inc Chses). NH '94/7 r19 w3 (2m5f-3m1f Chses) p4. P-t-P/HUNT CH '93 and '98/9 r9 w2 (2 4m Mixed Opens) p3 (2 2nds, and inc 3rd in Hunt Ch); pulled up 3. A fair performer under Rules granted top-of-the-ground conditions, and provided rising star Ben Hitchcott with his first winner in the '99 four-miler at Detling, but suffered the first tumble of his career on his return at Tweseldown. Failed to reappear after picking up a serious tendon injury at Larkhill, and has been retired. *P.D. Hitchcott — E. Sussex & Romney Marsh (Di Grissell).* 4 (O), 61 (MO).

CELTIC SPARK ..9-8§.. 13 ch.g. Celtic Cone — Kohinoor Diamond (Roman Warrior) p332p. Small. Dam won 2m Hdle. NH '92/3 (blinkered last 2) r6 p0 (inc Sells). P-t-P '94/6 and '98/9 r30 w12 (inc 3 Opens; hat-trick in '95) p9 (5 2nds; last of 1 once); pulled up 2, and fell/unseated 4. A useful Open horse in his prime, but has suffered leg trouble since the end of the '96 season, and his decline is now on a sharp downward spiral. Has always made mistakes, but his appetite for racing seems to have gone, and downed tools after the last when tried in a visor on his second start in 2000. *M.D. Reed — Chid, Lec & Cowdray (Shirley Reed).* 572 (CfO), 676 (Cf), 826 (O), 1212 (Cf), 1398 (Cf).

CELTIC TOKEN ..9-5.. 12 ch.g. Celtic Cone — Ready Token (SWE) (Record Token) 2f463. Small compact. Dam, half-sister to dam of Kingussie Flower, won on the flat in Sweden, and won 2 Hdles and 2 Chses from 7 starts in England. NH FLAT r2 p0. NH '94/5 r8 p0; Hdles/Chses, failed to finish 4 (fell/unseated 3). P-t-P '96/9 r19 w2 (Maiden and Restricted) p3 (2 2nds); fell/unseated 3, and pulled up 2. A clumsy plodder whose last success dates back to February '98, and has only once been better than last-but-one in his eight most recent outings. Used to front run at a rate of knots, and has always been taken to post early. *Mrs B. Birkmyre — S. & W. Wilts (Sarah Waugh).* 768 (Cf), 1057 (Cf), 1394 (O), 1554 (Cf), 1599 (I).

CELTIC TOWN ..10-0§.. 13 ch.g. Celtic Cone — Booterstown (Master Owen) 21rp22. Sturdy brother to Master Enborne and Bubble And Squeek, and half-brother to Ardstown and Henry Bruce. NH '92/7 r22 w3 (2m5f Hdle, and 2 Chses, 3m-3m2f) p7. P-t-P/HUNT CH '98/9 (for Miss D. Foode & Mr G. Evans) r17 w3 (inc Mixed Open and Ladies) p6 (3 3rds, beaten last once, and inc Hunt Ch); pulled up 2. A thorough stayer and gelled straight away with Peter Kay providing him with his first win at only the second attempt, but incredibly moody, and never went a yard for him on their next two appearances. Filled the runner-up spot on his final two starts when partnered by Julian Pritchard, but beat just one rival home, and is basically ungenuine. Occasionally blinkered. A very dependable jumper, and still of value as a schoolmaster. *Mrs C.L. Goodinson — Portman.* 476 (Cnr), 670 (O), 859 (o), 1015 (4mO), 1192 (O), 1313 (MO).

PLATE 34   962 Cheshire Forest Ladies Open: Celtic Who (Mrs C. Ford), 1st, lands ahead of China Lal (Mrs K. Diggle), 4th   PHOTO: Peter & Marilyn Sweet

CELTIC WHO (IRE) ..10-3.. 10 br.g. Strong Gale — Whosview (Fine Blade USA) 441. Half-brother to Heathview (qv). IRISH NH '96/7 r12 p2 (Chses, beaten 9-15½l). P-t-P '99 r3 w1 (Maiden) p0; last, and fell 1. Failed to get home until the ground dried out and followed up his '99 Maiden win at Tabley with a scrambling success in a Ladies Open on the same course on his final appearance. Probably worth campaigning in sub-3m Hunter Chases on fast ground as he is blessed with more speed than stamina. *Mrs C.P. Lees-Jones — Cheshire (Carrie Ford).* 301 (2m5fH), 904 (L), 962 (L).

CERISIER (IRE) ..8-9.. 8 br.m. Roselier (FR) — Cherry Token (Prince Hansel) 5. Sister to Twobitesothecherry (IRE), and half-sister to Anacoleen and Cherry Orchid, and to Irish Pointing winners, Distant Cherry and Royal Tommy (also English Chasing winner). P-t-P '98/9 (for Mrs V. Embiricos) r3 p1 (remote 3rd of 4); pulled up 1. Incredibly lightly raced and tailed off without exception to date. Has essentially no confidence when confronted by an obstacle and seems a waste of time. *Mrs A.E. Johnson - Thurlow (Tim Bryce).* 605 (OMa).

CERTAIN ANGLE ..9-11.. 12 ch.g. Saxon Farm — Cytisus (Above Suspicion) p336. Good-bodied half-brother to The Throw and Proctors Row, and to jumping winner, Jennie Pat. Dam won 2m Hdle in Ireland. NH FLAT '94 r3 w1 (2m). NH '94/6 r29 w6 (2 Hdles, 2m4f-2m6f, and 4 Chses, 2m6f-3m) p10. P-t-P/HUNT CH '98/9 (for Mr P.C. Browne, Mr G. Gould, Mr J. Rees, Mr G.D. Taylor, Mr S. Dusting, Mr P. Musgrave & Mr J. Hebditch) r14 w5 (Ladies, inc 4-timer '98) p4 (2 2nds, inc a Hunt Ch); pulled up 2, and brought down 1. Enjoyed a fine season in '98 when winning four Ladies Opens (rated 10-6), but his jumping went to pieces the following season, when he appeared to go wrong on his final appearance. Employed as a schoolmaster in the new yard, and gave Edward Chanin some valuable experience, but his decline seems permanent. *Mrs D.M. Chanin — Silverton (N. Chanin).* 727 (O), 852 (Cf), 1047 (Cf), 1304 (Cfnr).

CHACELEY LASS ..—.. 9 b.m. St Columbus — Birds Of A Feather (Warpath) ppu. Sturdy half-sister to Plucky Punter (*qv*). Dam won 12f Sell. NH FLAT '98 (from G. Yardley's) r2 p0 (pulled up final — threw herself down in paddock). Looks a troublesome sort, and her non-completions in Points include five and six-runner races. *D. Wellon — N. Ledbury (Tim Stephenson).* 446 (O), 615 (CMod), 1316 (OMa).

CHADWICK BANK (IRE) ..9-7.. 7 br.g. Actinium (FR) — Beautiful Glen (Furry Glen) 3f2p51. Compact half-brother to Sagaville (IRE) (*qv*). NH FLAT '98 r2 p0. NH '98/9 (for G. McCourt) r6 p1 (3rd in Sell); fell only Ch (blinkered). Inconsistent and was beaten favourite twice in Maidens (let down by his jumping once), but punters finally ignored him at their peril, and he was sent off at a remarkable 33-1 when scoring on dead ground at Dingley. Kept pulling out a bit extra when pressed, but would almost certainly never beat the runner-up (who was hanging) again. Seems likely to remain unpredictable. *Miss R. Murrell & Miss G. Cooper — Bicester with Whaddon (Rebecca Murrell).* 194 (CfMa), 411 (OMa), 605 (OMa), 1021 (2m4fOMa), 1437 (OMa), 1668 (OMa).

CHALCUCHIMA ..8-0§.. 8 gr.g. Reprimand — Ica (Great Nephew) pf2ppp. Smallish close-coupled brother to a winner in France, and half-brother to 9 winners (several abroad), including Aragon (useful on flat). 14,000f, 15,000y. FLAT (for R. Charlton) r5 p0. NH '96/8 (for N. Hawke, bought for 4000) r5 p0 (5th, last, pulled up 2 and unseated — blinkered once; inc 3 Sells). Sold for 2500 and 1650 in '98, and bought Ascot, Nov for 950. Only managed to get round once, when inheriting 40 lengths second at the final fence at Mollington (was very reluctant afterwards, and nearly pulled up approaching the finish). Makes plentiful mistakes, and also has stamina doubts. *Miss H.P.J. Scheffers — O. Berks (Fred Sutherland).* 196 (R), 249 (CfMa), 432 (OMa), 580 (3mH), 1207 (OMa), 1336 (2m4fH).

CHAMPAGNE THUNDER ..8-12.. 9 b.g. Another Hoarwithy — Champagne Peri (The Malster) p3up. Sturdy owner-bred half-brother to Alcofrolic and Cider Man. Dam won 3 Points and 3rd. Grandam, Rockscope, was brought down in a Members. P-t-P '99 (for Mrs D.J. Gaskins) r5 p1 (3rd); fell/unseated 2, ran out 1, and pulled up 1. Error-prone and has suffered one disaster after another to date, and has been no better than last-but-one in his two completions. Tried in a tongue-strap on his final five appearances, and ended the season by going lame. *J. Taylor (The Thunder Club) — Ledbury (John Taylor).* 891 (OMa), 972 (OMa), 1464 (OMa), 1920 (OMa).

CHANCE ENCOUNTER ..9-1.. 11 b.g. Sulaafah (USA) — Bernigra Girl (Royal Match) 46186. Workmanlike plain brother to Ginge, and to Hurdles winner, Allahrakha. Dam won at 6f. NH '95 r6 p0 (useless, inc Sells). P-t-P '98/9 r15 p3 (2 3rds, last once); failed to finish 8 (fell 3, and ran out 1). Took 24 attempts before he finally managed to pass the post in front, but decidedly modest, and none of his victims have yet to go on to boost the form. Already struggling to make an impact in Restricteds, and that trend is likely to continue. At least Jeremy Young can taunt Les Jefford and Paul Flynn that he did what they failed to achieve on Chance Encounter. *C.E. Ash & Miss S.A. Leach — Eggesford (Laura Horsey).* 1095 (R), 1308 (OMa), 1468 (OMa), 1551 (R), 1650 (R).

CHANCELLORS VISION ..9-10.. 8 gr.g. Neltino — Valiant Vision (Brave Invader USA) up1. Leggy unfurnished half-brother to Sleep Walker (*qv*). P-t-P '98 r2 p0 (pulled up 2). Spent two years on the sidelines prior to the 2000 season, and is obviously incredibly hard to keep sound. Would probably have been no worse than third on his reappearance, but appeared to go wrong at Barbury Castle, and finished lame when justifying favouritism subsequently. Obviously has a decent engine, but sadly not the transmission to match. *Mrs A.B. Watts — Weston & Banwell H. (Rose Vickery).* 264 (OMa), 471 (OMa), 888 (OMa).

CHANGE ..9-8.. 7 b.g. North Briton — Karminski (Pitskelly) 24. Small neat half-brother to a winner in Norway. Dam won 3 flat, 13-17f. FLAT (for C. Brittain, who won with the dam) r2 p0. NH '98 (for G. Reed) r3 p0. In the lead after 2m4f in both Maidens, and had two subsequent winners behind him first time out. Takes a lot out of himself by pulling hard, but should score if able to keep going better. *Miss A.S. Ross — Lamerton.* 723 (CfMa), 934 (OMa).

CHAN THE MAN ..—.. 10 b.g. Krisinsky (USA) — Channel Ten (Babu) Rp. Tall half-brother to News Review, Channel Pastime (subsequent Chasing winner) and Channel Island. Dam won 7 Ladies and placed 14. Grandam, Channel View, won 6 Ladies. NH FLAT r2 p0 (ran out on debut). NH '96/9 (for B.J. Llewellyn; previously for M. Pipe; previously for D. Burchell) r14 w1 (2m3f Hereford Nov Ch) p1; pulled up 6. HUNT CH '97 (for Mrs S. Worthington) r1 p0 (4th). Won on only his second start over fences, but became most disappointing under Rules, and even a spell with Martin Pipe bore no fruit. Did not look the type for Pointing as he does not stay three miles, and so it proved. Tried blinkered and tongue-tied in the past. *J.E. Curry — N. Tyne.* 1498 (O), 1578 (O).

CHANTINGO LAD ..9-3.. 10 b.g. Rustingo — Chantry Rose (Ben Novus) 613pppp3. Compact half-brother to Jonivor, an 'abysmal brute', who failed to finish in all his 7 Points. Dam won Maiden and placed 2. P-t-P '97/9 r16 w1 (Maiden) p2 (2nd of 3; and last of 3); pulled up 9, and refused 1. A dependable jumper who has never fallen, but hindered by his lack of stamina, and was left clear two out in his latest victory, having previously taken 14 races to get off the mark. Unsuited by any cut in the ground as it saps his stamina, but will need another large slice of luck to win again. Often wears a tongue-strap. *Mrs S.E. Warman — Llangibby.* 485 (R), 595 (R), 817 (M), 1051 (Cf), 1299 (I), 1401 (Cf), 1449 (I), 1572 (I).

CHAPS ..9-10.. 11 b.g. Buckley — Winnetka (Buckskin FR) p13fp. Tall rangy good-topped. Dam is half-sister to Brimstone Hill (*qv* '96 Annual). Grandam, Trysting Day, won 15 Chses, 2m-3m1f. NH FLAT '96 (for D. Gandolfo) r1 p0. NH '96 and '99 (for Denys Smith, bought for 500; previously for Miss K. George, bought for 1400) r5 p1 (3rd of 4). All out to win a poor Maiden in softish at Witton Castle (wore a pricker on the near-side, and broke a blood vessel), but never got into contention after favourite next time. Hopelessly outclassed in Hunter Chases subsequently, and needs to be searching for far easier opportunities. Makes plenty of mistakes. *D.F. Smith — Hurworth.* 20 (OMa), 133 (CCfMa), 377 (R), 682 (3m3fH), 923 (3m3fH).

CHARACTERISTIC ..—.. 13 b.g. Reformed Character — Far Coriander VII (unknown) pup. Tall rangy fired. P-t-P '95/6 and '98/9 r8 w4 (inc Open) p0; pulled up 1, ran out 3. Unbeaten when completing in Points, but a volatile individual (spooked at the elasticated starting tape on his Hunter Chase debut and dumped Adrian Wintle) who has stood little racing. Tore round Sandon and Tabley under Chris Stockton to record an impressive double in '99 (rated 10-9), and has to go right-handed, but never looked happy in the new yard, and broke down — for the second time — at Weston Park. Has returned to the yard from which he gained all bar one of his successes, and connections are confident of a return. Has very few miles on the clock, and unlikely to make any concessions to age if he gets back on track. *D.H. Godfrey — N. Herefords (Sally Godsall).* 79 (O), 150 (3mH), 294 (O).

CHARDEN ..10-2.. 15 b.g. Touching Wood (USA) — Fighting Lady (Chebs Lad) 5p. Angular close-coupled half-brother to flat winners, Memoria In Eterna and Ultimate Warrior. Dam won 4 flat, 5-7f. FLAT r13 w1 (12f) p3 (2nds). IRISH AMAT FLAT r1 p0. IRISH NH '91/3 (often believed to '92) r31 p4 (inc 3 Chses). IRISH P-t-P '93 r3 p1 (2nd). NH '90, '94, '98/9 r7 p1 (2nd in Ch). P-t-P/HUNT CH '95/6 and '99 r16 w3 (2 Hunt Chses, 3m-3m1f110y Hunt Ch, and Club) p3 (Hunt Chses); unseated 2, and pulled up 1. A horse that will be remembered more for his owner-rider's failings than for his own quite considerable ability. Has twice nipped round Hereford to win Hunter Chases by wide margins, but his talents have usually been mis-directed. Not seen since pulling up in the Cheltenham Foxhunters, and the likelihood of him running to his current rating if he returns seems remote. Has worn headgear in four of his last five starts. *Col R.I. Webb-Bowen — R.A. (Sally Mullins).* 210 (MO), 584 (3m2f110yH).

CHARIOT MAN (IRE) ..9-3.. 9 br.g. Mandalus — Mum's Chariot (Callernish) p5. Small neat. NH '97/8 r7 p2; 5th only Ch (tailed off). P-t-P '99 r4 p1 (2nd); 4th, and pulled up 2. A decent second on his Pointing debut — the three horses behind him have all won since -, but physically flawed and is probably breaking blood vessels on a regular basis. Could win races if his problems could be sorted, but remains very suspect and one to leave alone for betting purposes. *B. Kennedy — Essex F. & U. (Jim Ovel).* 551 (OMa), 606 (OMa).

CHARLES THE THIRD ..8-10.. 9 ch.g. Mr Fluorocarbon — Dunton Lady (Extra) fu. Small compact owner-bred half-brother to Dark Knight (*qv*). P-t-P '98 r1 p0 (refused). Looked astounded by the sight of a fence on his debut and jumped little better on his return from a year off in 2000. Needs to be got fitter to find out if there is any ability lurking within him. *D.H. Roberts — Bicester with Whaddon.* 249 (CfMa), 515 (OMa).

CHARLIEADAMS (IRE) ..9-9.. 11 b.g. Carlingford Castle — Lucy Platter (FR) (Record Token) pf3R2upu3550. Rangy brother to Castle Stephen (IRE) and half-brother to Abbotsham. IRISH NH FLAT '95/6 r4 p0. IRISH NH '96 and '99 r4 p1 (2nd in Hunt Ch; 4th in only similar). IRISH P-t-P '98/9 r8 w2 (7 plus Mdn for novice riders, and Winners of Two) p2; pulled up 2, and fell. An exceptionally impetuous front-runner who invariably carts James Muir, and has made unscheduled trips on four occasions (including when the saddle slipped once, and when an iron snapped once). Has also kept going steadily four times when beaten a maximum of three lengths, and ran particularly well when beaten by half a length second to Parade Racer, and when fourth over 3m2f at Carlisle. Probably substantially better than his rating suggests, and it might be worth Novice Chasing him with a professional aboard. Certainly looks to be rather wasted at present. *J.F.W. Muir — Lauderdale.* 43 (Cf), 110 (O), 186 (O), 362 (O), 419 (Cf), 915 (3m1fH), 975 (O), 1078 (Cf), 1154 (3m2fH), 1345 (2m5fH), 1428 (O), 1445 (3m1fH).

CHARLIE DAZZLE (IRE) ..9-1.. 10 b.g. Supreme Leader — Deep Dazzle (Deep Run) fpf6fR. Small. P-t-P '99 r4 p1 (3rd); and fell/unseated 3. Any ability he has is masked by his inability to clear a fence at speed and he has now crashed in half of his races — before halfway on four occasions. Took charge of a novice in his final start and should have a Government Health Warning stamped on his rump in future. Bonkers and it would be irresponsible to run him again unless he undergoes a complete personality transplant. *J. Ashby — Bilsdale (Fiona Needham).* 281 (OMa), 400 (OMa), 508 (CMa), 1033 (OMa), 1331 (OMa), 1347 (M).

CHARLIE HAWES (IRE) ..9-3.. 12 b.g. Euphemism — Eyecap (King's Ride) 049. Rangy. IRISH P-t-P '96/7 r11 w1 (7 plus Mdn) p2; fell/unseated 4 NH '97/9 (for S. Mellor, bought for 7600 blinkered/visored 3) r15 p0 (inc Sell; inc 5 Chses, inc pulled up 2, and fell). Incredibly lethargic, and certainly needed no assitance from the famed New Forest Strangler to become hopelessly tailed off. A marriage made in heaven. *Miss G.A. Russell — New Forest.* 226 (2m4f110yH), 385 (3mH), 687 (2m6f110yH).

CHARLIE KEAY (IRE) ..9-8.. 9 br.g. Supreme Leader — View Of The Hills (Croghan Hill) 2pu1p. Neat. NH FLAT '97 r1 p0. P-t-P '99 r1 p0 (last). Won a bad Maiden run at a funereal pace in soft ground at Flagg Moor (took over nine minutes!), but had shown a little ability previously, and it was not an unexpected success. Ran unaccountably poorly when pulled up either side of his win and may have an intermittent fault that may account for his lack of outings. Probably needs mud to be seen to advantage, but a watching brief is advised in his quest for Restricted success as the level of his form is below that required to win one. *K. Liscombe & R.P. Hankey — Cheshire Forest (Rob Hankey).* 526 (OMa), 588 (OMa), 964 (OMa), 1251 (OMa), 1411 (R).

CHARLIE'S GIFT ..—.. 8 b.m. Kinglet — Fort Flutter (Beldale Flutter USA) pp. Small neat. P-t-P '99 r3 p0 (fell/unseated 2, and pulled up 1). Failed to get beyond halfway in her debut season and paired with a novice in 2000 when outclassed in Ladies races. Has only contested one Maiden to date, but probably lacks the scope to shoulder the extra weight in them in any case. *Mrs H.L.M. Lockwood-Taylor — N. Cotswold (Florence Lockwood).* 969 (L), 1191 (L).

CHARLIE SMITH ..—.. 6 ch.g. Greensmith — My Pride (Petit Instant) pp. Strong owner-bred half-brother to Lily Lane (qv). Schooling so far, and looks the type to do better in time. *L.C. Bennett — Blackmore & Sparkford V. (Rose Vickery).* 640 (CfMa), 1469 (OMa).

PLATE 35   1025 Jane McAlpine Mem HC, Bangor: Charmers Well (T. Doyle), pu
PHOTO: Colin Turner

CHARLOTTE'S ROSE ..—.. 10 ch.m. Cheyenne Dance (FR) — Thats Char-Lotte (Virginia Boy) uf. Small lengthy owner-bred sister to Cheyenne Pearl, and half-sister to Charlotte Lane. P-t-P '98/9 r6 p0 (last pair 3, fell 2, and pulled up 1). Only once better than last in three completions, and her jumping goes from bad to worse. Has decked some of the craziest kamikaze pilots around, and the good ones simply won't partner her. Tried blinkered once in '99. *I.D.S. Jones — Ystrad Taf Fechan (Shan Farr).* 490 (CfMa), 838 (OMa).

CHARMER'S WELL (IRE) ..10-2.. 13 b.g. Beau Charmeur (FR) — Palmers Well (Proverb) 4p7p*pp*. Tall strong half-brother to Irish NH flat and Hurdles winner, Supreme Gold. Dam is an unraced half-sister to Dromore Castle (*qv* '96 Annual). IRISH P-t-P '93 r4 w1 (Maiden) p1 (3rd); and fell/unseated 2. NH FLAT '94 r2 w1 p0. NH '94/8 r12 w1 (2m5f Hdle) p2 (3rds, inc Ch). HUNT CH '99 r3 w2 (Hunt Chses, 3m1f110y-3m2f) p0; and pulled up 1. NH May '00 r2 p0 (pulled up in HCap Chses: *prom, mist 11, rdn aft, wkng when mist 2 out, pu last*; and *tk keen hld, in tch til pu 10*). Ultimately bitterly disappointing under Rules, but revived by trainer Gary Brown to land a brace of Hunter Chases in '99. Ran well for a long way on his 2000 reappearance, but that race seemingly took its toll, and he was well beaten subsequently. Not a fluent jumper despite having top jockeys throughout his career, and the chances of another winning comeback are slim. *T. Curry — O. Berks (Gary Brown).* 224 (3m2fH), 1025 (3m110yH), 1103 (3m2f110yH).

CHARMING MOSS (IRE) ..—§.. 10 ch.g. Le Moss — Our Charm (Goldhill) 3ppp. Rangy half-brother to Carmelus The Great, and to Irish NH flat and Hurdles winner, Star Service. Dam won mares Maiden, NH flat and 2m2f Ch in Ireland. IRISH P-t-P '97 r2 w1 (5yo plus Maiden) p0; pulled up 1. NH '98/9 (for D. Forster) r5 p1 (21½f 3rd in Ch); 6th of 7, and pulled up 3 in similar. Bought Doncaster, May for 4000. Finished one and a half fences behind Solba when third in an Open, and subsequently exposed as thoroughly ungenuine and a bad jumper. Had tailed himself off by halfway when blinkered on his latest appearance, and is surely not worth bothering with again. *C.J.M. Cottingham — Brocklesby.* 231 (O), 367 (Cf), 797 (R), 1588 (I).

CHARTER ..—.. 10 b.g. Reference Point — Winter Queen (Welsh Pageant) p. Compact brother to Hurdles winner, Tibetan, and half-brother to Marked Card, and to 3 flat winners, including Winter Garden (later a succesful Irish Hurdler) and Safety In Numbers (Smart in England/France), and to NH flat winner, Wintertide. Dam won at 13f in Ireland. FLAT (inc unplaced 2 for J. Naughton) r22 p5. NH FLAT '95/6 (for D. Chappell) r4 w1 p1 (head 2nd). NH '97/8 (for W. Storey) r6 p1 (2nd). Sold Doncaster, Aug for 1100. Missed '99, and obviously has problems, as he disappeared again after one January Point (made mistakes). Has looked ungenuine in the past, and sometimes wears headgear (blinkered at Cottenham). *S.A. Griffiths & S. Fetzer — Suffolk (Neil King).* 18 (I).

CHASING A BID ..—.. 6 b.g. Gildoran — Bride (Remainder Man) rppp. Close-coupled brother to Chasing The Bride (*qv*). Showed no ability, and ultimately acquired a tongue-tie and broke a hind leg at Charlton Horethorne. Nyland Partnership — Blackmore & Sparkford V. (John Dufosee). 57 (OMa), 264 (OMa), 455 (OMa), 955 (OMa).

PLATE 36   *1674 Torrington Farmers Intermediate: Chasing Daisy (J. Snowden), 1st, leads Agile King (Miss C. Tizzard), 4th, three out*
PHOTO: Tim Holt

CHASING DAISY ..10-5.. 9 b.m. Lyphento (USA) — Blue Breeze (USA) (Blue Times USA) 4512221. Workmanlike half-sister to Country Blue and Golf Ball, and to a winner in Sweden. Dam won 5 flat, 12-15f, inc 3 Sells. P-t-P '97/9 r14 w1 (Maiden) p1 (3rd); unseated 3, and pulled up 3. Totally in the doldrums since being left clear to win the first race of her career and had looked consistently like a non-stayer, but turned over a new leaf in 2000, and improved 16 pounds in the ratings. Unlucky to be collared at Trebudannon, and remains suited by an easy three miles on top-of-the-ground. Still rather a live wire, and often mounted on course before being taken to post early, but goes well for Jamie Snowden, and they should be capable of teaming up successfully again. *L. Jenkinson — Blackmore & Sparkford V. (John Dufosee).* 102 (R), 208 (R), 560 (R), 1097 (Inr), 1388 (I), 1554 (Cf), 1674 (I).

CHASING DREAMS ..—.. 10 b.g. St Columbus — Into Song (True Song) p. Tall sparely-made half-brother to Full Song, Missile Man and The Dipstick. Dam won 2m1f Hdle. NH FLAT '97 r1 p0. NH '97/8 (from C. Grant's) r4 p0 (tailed off and pulled up both Chses, mistakes final). Very lightly-raced and useless to date, and was soon struggling when revived briefly in a Maiden. *D. Eccleston & Miss J. Southam — Warwicks.* 618 (CMa).

CHASING THE BRIDE ..11-1.. 8 b.g. Gildoran — Bride (Remainder Man) 3221162. Compact owner-bred brother to Chasing A Bid, and half-brother to Chasing Charlie. Dam won at 12f, and won 2m Hdle at 50-1. P-t-P/HUNT CH '98/9 r12 w6 (inc 4m Mixed Open, Mixed Open and Ladies) p4 (2nds, remote once); fell/unseated 2. A thoroughly likeable seven-year-old who improved again in 2000, and recorded back-to-back Hunter Chase successes at Wincanton and Ascot, but not just an out-and-out stayer as he ran really well in a sub-six minute event on his final appearance. Usually runs in a tongue strap and has had oxygen on standby after the finish. A steady jumper (though still not confident over water), and appears to handle any going. A genuine horse who has been well handled by John Dufosee, and has struck up a good relationship with Michael Miller, so further victories should be a formality. *Mrs S. Hooper — Blackmore & Sparkford V. (John Dufosee).* 34 (MO), 152 (3m1f110yH), 303 (3mH), 467 (3m1f110yH), 800 (3m110yH), 1103 (3m2f110yH), 1433 (3mH).

CHASSAGNE (FR) ..10-4.. 11 br.g. Royal Charter (FR) — Salse Pareille (FR) (Perouges FR) 21s2. Small neat brother to a French Hurdles winner, and half-brother to another. Dam won at 9f in France. NH FLAT '96 r2 p0. P-t-P '98/9 r7 w2 (Maiden and Restricted) p1 (2nd); pulled up 2, and fell 2. A decent performer who could be up to winning Opens if only he could meet the fences in his stride on a more regular basis. May well have accounted for The Crazy Bishop on his reappearance had he pinged the last, and lost all chance on his most recent outing when rooting a fence on the first circuit at Chaddesley. Stands little racing (four outings a season is his maximum), but has a turn of foot when held up, and the booking of a top local rider could make all the difference. His sole victory in 2000 was a walk-over. *Mrs A.R. Piggott — N. Herefords (Sally Sayce).* 987 (Cf), 1274 (I), 1463 (Cf), 1630 (Cf).

CHATERGOLD (IRE) ..10-4.. 9 b.g. Posen (USA) — Fiodoir (Weavers' Hall) 11u26813. Strong half-brother to Irish Hurdles winner, Motility. Dam won 4 12f races in Ireland. NH '96/7 and '98/9 (for A.P Jarvis) r14 p3 (2m5f-3m Chses). P-t-P '98 (for Mr A.P. Turnbull) r5 w2 (Maiden and Restricted) p2 (3rds, last once); and last. Slightly flattered by a Hunter Chase success, but did well on his return to Hunt racing, and owes his upturn in fortunes in no small measure to trainer John White. Tried in a visor under Rules, but exclusively blinkered in 2000, and gives the strong impression that he is reserving a bit for himself — usually has his ears pricked throughout a race. Tough, but no easy ride as he tends to go in fits and starts, and inclined to make errors over big fences. Would have little difficulty picking up a Novices Chase in the Summer months, and best employed in the Hunter Chase arena for financial reasons if nothing else. *C. Shankland — Berks & Bucks (John White).* 219 (CMod), 325 (Cf), 580 (3mH), 685 (2m5fH), 924 (3m1fH), 1334 (3mH), 1535 (2m3fH), 1603 (2m6f110yH).

CHECK THE DECK (IRE) ..—.. 10 b.g. Hollow Hand — Anaglog Dream (Paddy's Stream) pf. Tall half-brother to Irish NH flat and Hurdles winner, Scary Spice. Dam is half-sister to prolific Irish-trained jumping winner, Anaglogs Daughter. IRISH NH FLAT '97 r2 p0. NH '98/9 (for C. Mann) r5 p0 (pulled up both Chses). Bought Doncaster, May for 2000. Only averages two outings a year, and has never got round over fences. Unruly and reluctant to line up and would not jump properly after getting behind on his latest outing, but continued until falling after two miles (unsighted) and injured Barry Kendellen, who soon returned to Ireland and has not been seen since. Later injured in a Summer Hurdle from R. Peacock's yard, and had to be destroyed. *Mrs H.O. Widdicombe — V.W.H. (Sue Widdicombe).* 207 (OMa), 889 (OMa).

CHEEKY POT ..9-3§.. 13 b.g. Petoski — Pato (High Top) p6p7p. Compact well-made half-brother to flat winners, Classic Cliche (IRE) (top class, won St Leger and Dante Stakes in '95 — now siring potential Pointers) and Threatening. Dam won 4 flat, 7-10f. FLAT r30 w2 (8-11f, inc £6209 prize) p5. NH '92/5 r36 w4 (2m-2m4f Hdles, inc Sell) p8; 4th and last only Chses. P-t-P/HUNT CH '96/8 r19 w3 (Ladies) p3 (2 3rds); failed to finish 4 (refused 1, and fell/unseated 2). NH '98 r3 p0 (pulled up 1 in Hdles, inc Sell; pulled up 1. Enjoyed a purple patch Pointing '96/7 when winning three Ladies Opens in a six race spell, but has always been unreliable, and has gone to pot completely nowadays. No better than last in 2000, and has simply given up trying. Wears blinkers, and has been visored. *D.H. Preece — Wheatland (Miss E. Murray).* 860 (L), 991 (L), 1199 (L), 1410 (L), 1525 (L).

CHEROKEE RUN (IRE) ..10-1.. 7 b.g. Commanche Run — Hampton Grange (Boreen FR) 31p3125p. Sturdy half-brother to Our Carol (IRE). Dam is half-sister to Carton (*qv* '99 Annual). P-t-P '99 r3 p0 (pulled up 2, and fell 1). An improved performer since acquiring a tongue-strap, but often a weak finisher and is probably flattered by his current rating. Displayed more courage than the runner-up in both his wins however, and that allied to his reliable jumping should enable him to find another minor race. Blinkered once in '99. *P.T. Cartridge — Worcs (Penny Grainger)*. 30 (CMa), 197 (CfMa), 336 (R), 532 (R), 698 (R), 971 (I), 1356 (I), 1544 (Cf).

CHERRY ALLEY (IRE) ..9-8.. 8 b.m. Persian Mews — Cherry Avenue (King's Ride) f1pp. Lengthy sister to Cherry Tart (IRE), and half-sister to Miss Montgomery (IRE). P-t-P '99 r3 p2; and pulled up 1. Greatly hindered by jumping errors in her first season and fell at the first on her 2000 reappearance, but appreciated the way the Llanfrynach fences parted like the Red Sea (particularly after 11 previous sets of runners had kicked them to pieces), and scored comfortably with three subsequent winners in her wake. Disappointingly pulled up in both attempts in Restricteds since, and a watching brief is advised when she reappears. *Mrs P.E. Holtorp — Golden V. (Angharad Watkins)*. 450 (CfMa), 489 (CfMa), 864 (R), 1228 (R).

CHERRY GOLD ..9-12.. 7 b.g. Rakaposhi King — Merry Cherry (Deep Run) 2124. Workmanlike brother to Cherry Pie (*qv*). P-t-P '99 r2 p2 (2nds). Showed plenty of promise when runner-up in his first three Points, and made no mistake when making all at Lydstep, but has failed to find much off the bridle to date, and has been a beaten favourite in half of his starts. A reliable jumper for a youngster and should win his Restricted, but unlikely to represent much in the way of value. *R.A. Mason — Glamorgan (Evan Williams)*. 1068 (3m2fOMa), 1225 (OMa), 1298 (R), 1615 (R).

CHERRYNUT ..10-4.. 12 b.g. Idiot's Delight — Merry Cherry (Deep Run) 2431. Tall rangy pin-fired half-brother to Cherry Pie (*qv*). NH '95/8 r14 w3 (2m5f — 3m Chses) p3 (remounted after falling once); inc Hdle; refused 1. P-t-P/HUNT CH '94/5 and '99 r15 w10 (inc 2 Hunt Chses, 2m4f110y-3m110y, 2 Opens, and Ladies) p2 (2 2nds, inc a Hunt Ch); pulled up 2. Never scaled the heights that many expected under Rules although he accumulated a highly respectable £25,615, and would have won the '97 Charisma Gold Cup but for climbing the final fence (was pipped on the post by a short head). Enjoyed an outstanding second half of the season in '99, but found himself relocated again in 2000, and never really sparked — faced a simple task when successful. Used to be a very indifferent jumper of big fences, and has never really been able to handle testing ground. More than capable of figuring prominently in Open company again in 2001. Blinkered once in '97. *T.D.B. Barlow — V. of Aylesbury (Lawney Hill)*. 17 (O), 227 (2m5f110yH), 750 (O), 1034 (C).

CHERRY ORCHID ..7-12.. 14 b br.g. Callernish — Cherry Token (Prince Hansel) p7. Tall rangy half-brother to Cerisier (*qv*). IRISH P-t-P '93/8 r2 p2 (distant last of 3 after pulling up once); pulled up 1, fell 2, and carried out 1. IRISH NH '94/5 r5 p0. NH '96/9 (for J. Needham; trained for him latterly by J. Hughes; tried tongue-tied) r11 p2 (distant last and 21l last of 3 in Chses). An ancient maiden who has frequently been tailed off, including in both Points for the present yard (finished 30 lengths behind an unregistered animal in his Members). *P.M. Fletcher — Croome & W. Warwicks, & Worcs (Mickey Harris)*. 194 (CfMa), 1063 (3m2fM).

CHERRY PIE ..—.. 9 b.m. Rakaposhi King — Merry Cherry (Deep Run) fupupp. Workmanlike sister to Cherry Gold, and half-sister to Twelth Man and Cherrynut, to jumping winner, Cherry Dee, and to NH flat and Hurdles winner, Head For The Hills. 4400 4-y-o. NH FLAT '98 (for D. Nicholson) r2 p0. NH '98/9 (for S. Mullins; previously for D. Nicholson) r5 p0 (generally tailed off). Bought Malvern, Oct for 2600. NH Spr '00 r2 p0 (pulled up in 2 Hdles). Much too slow under Rules, but ideally bred for Pointing. The problem is her clueless jumping of fences, which continues to cause many headaches. *Mrs M. Hand & P. Trotman — Lamerton (Mandy Hand)*. 73 (OMa), 158 (CfMa), 409 (OMa), 562 (CfMa).

CHERYL'S LAD (IRE) ..9-10.. 11 b.g. Mister Majestic — Two's Company (Sheshoon) 5u1u4. Tall half-brother to several winners. Dam won 2 French flat, 7-12f. IRISH NH FLAT '94 r3 w2 p1 (3rd). NH '94/8 r21 w7 (4 2m1f Hdles, and 3 Chses, 2m2f-2m4f) p6; one run at Punchestown. P-t-P/HUNT CH '99 r5 p1 (2nd); last pair 3, and pulled up 1. A useful performer under Rules (seven wins alone netted £23,392) when ideally suited by a sub-3m trip on decent ground around a right-handed circuit, but feebly handled by the owner in Points, and his solitary success has been for Daniel Cook in a bad race for his Members. *J.H. Henderson — Granta H., & Belvoir (Henry Hill)*. 83 (Cf), 176 (O), 242 (M), 441 (O), 867 (M).

CHESNUT WOOD ..7-10.. 7 ch.g. Tigerwood — Sally Haven (Haven) 6uu. Brother to Tiger Sally. Dam, half-sister to Lucky Rose (*qv* '94 Annual), won 2 Points and placed 7. Grandam, Trixy, pulled up in a Maiden. Novice ridden, and needs a more experienced partner to sort out his erratic jumping. *Miss H.E. Roberts — Llangeinor*. 949 (OMa), 1055 (CfMa), 1574 (OMa).

CHESTER BEN ..9-13§.. 12 ro.g. Alias Smith (USA) — Saleander (Leander) 24. Rangy brother to smart Irish jumping winner, Jeffell (also won Chasing in England), and half-brother to Salvo and Light The Sky. Dam won a Maiden and placed 3. P-t-P/HUNT CH '95 and '97/9 r16 w1 (Maiden) p7 (4 3rds; and inc 2 Hunt Chses); pulled up 2. Took ages to win his Maiden, but generally lightly raced since, and gives the strong impression that he is not genuine. Carried his head very high when visored and third on his reappearance (months later promoted to second when the winner was disqualified at Portman Square), and has now run up a losing sequence of ten. An expert jumper who has never fallen, but continues to disappoint, and has been retired to go eventing. *M. Barthorpe — S. Wold (Pat Barthorpe).* 585 (2m5f110yH), 1268 (R).

CHEVAL DE MARLY (IRE) ..9-11.. 11 b.g. Roselier (FR) — Woodville Grove (Harwell) p. Workmanlike lengthy half-brother to Windy Ways and Woody Will, and to Hurdles winner, Strong Grove (IRE). Dam won 2m4f mares NH flat in Ireland. P-t-P '99 r3 w1 (Restricted) p1 (2nd); and pulled up 1. Showed an abundance of stamina when successful on his belated racecourse debut at Whitwick, but beat nothing out of the ordinary, and could not cope with the disappointing Aralier Man in a Sandon stamina contest subsequently. May well have suffered a setback on his reappearance (was hanging badly when pulled up three out), as he was not seen out again. Should be treated with caution if he returns. *J.W. Beddoes — N. Salop.* 116 (I).

CHEZ CATALAN ..—.. 10 b.g. Niniski (USA) — Miss Saint-Cloud (Nonoalco USA) fpp. Small well-made brother to Macedonas, to Irish NH flat winner, Scottish Song, and half-brother to flat winner, Chez Jarasse. Dam won 3 flat, 7-10f. FLAT to '98 (best blinkered) r30 w2 (13-15f) p8; inc Sells. NH '94 and '98 r3 p0. P-t-P '99 r2 p0 (pulled up 2). Handicapped in Points by his flat win gained six years ago, but has never been the most resolute of performers and refuses to try at all nowadays. Blinkered on his last four appearances, but not worth bothering with again. *O.R. Dukes — York & Ainsty S.* 997 (Cf), 1542 (3mH), 1591 (3m1fH).

CHIAROSCURO ..9-11§.. 15 b.g. Idiot's Delight — Lampshade (Hot Brandy) 755p. Strong rangy half-brother to Hengist. Dam won 2 Hdles, 2m-3m2f. NH '90/6 r18 w1 (2m4f Hdle) p2 (3rds); no form in 4 Chses. P-t-P/HUNT CH '97/9 r18 w1 (Members) p11 (6 2nds, short-headed once, and last once); unseated 1, and pulled up 1. Inconsistent in Points, but has always had a soft spot for Brampton Bryan, and ran much his best race of the season there when about 12 lengths fifth in a competitive Confined. Blinkered on that occasion, but they failed to galvanise him a second time, and as he showed no zest at all otherwise he can probably be ignored in future. *E.D. Perry — Golden V.* 479 (Cf), 741 (Cf), 862 (Cf), 1463 (Cf).

CHICKABIDDY ..9-2.. 13 b.m. Henbit (USA) — Shoshoni (Ballymoss) 6p3. Small compact half-sister to Macho Man, and to 2 flat winners. Dam won at 10f. NH FLAT '92 r2 p0. NH '92/8 (blinkered once in '95) r55 w8 (6 Hdles, 2m1f-2m4f, the first a Sell; and 2 2m3f Chses) p14. P-t-P '99 r5 p1 (2nd); last pair 2, unseated 1, and ran out 1. A stalwart of the South-West circuit under Rules for many years and owes connections nothing, but all her winning form has been on sound surfaces at up to 2m3f. Only really used as a schoolmistress for Gemma Edwards nowadays. *G.F. Edwards — Devon & Somerset.* 67 (L), 354 (L), 557 (Cf).

CHICODARI ..9-9§.. 9 b.g. Shardari — Chicobin (USA) (J O Tobin USA) p24p81pr. Lengthy half-brother to flat winners, Chicmond and Chilly Breeze. FLAT (for Sir Mark Prescott) r5 w1 (10f) p0. NH '95/7 and '99 (for D. Nicholson) r16 w3 (2m-2m2f) Hdles, promoted from 2nd once) p9 (inc 3 of 4 Chses — 4th in the other). Not short of ability, but has always been ungenuine, and was a reluctant hero when he won his flat race (made all, but hung right). Occasionally jumps left, and was gaining a first success for over four years in his Members. Took no interest in Pointing otherwise (predictably). Frequently blinkered. *Mrs C.J.A. Suthern — N. Cotswold (John Suthern).* 294 (O), 428 (Cf), 702 (Cf), 968 (Cf), 1086 (Cf), 1189 (M), 1416 (O), 1524 (O).

CHIEF ENGINEER ..8-9.. 9 b.g. Wonderful Surprise — Better Try Again (Try My Best USA) pp6up. Light owner-bred half-brother to Country Kizzie. NH June '99 (from T. Carr's) r1 p0 (pulled up — jumped slowly, and tailed off by halfway). Invariably tailed off, and looks most unimpressive. *R. Dalton — Cleveland.* 378 (R), 503 (R), 626 (OMa), 803 (MMa), 1234 (OMa).

CHIEF'S EXAMPLE (USA) ..9-12.. 13 ch.g. Chief's Crown (USA) — Bold Example (USA) (Bold Lad USA) p. Small narrow. P-t-P '99 r1 w1 (Maiden) p3 (2 2nds, of 3 once, and last once). A latecomer to racing who won a two-finisher Maiden on firmish at Holnicote on his final start of '99, but pulled up lame on Edward Chanin's race riding debut at Black Forest Lodge on his reappearance, and has not been seen since. Races tongue-tied, and was blinkered when successful. *Mrs D.M. Chanin — Silverton (Nick Chanin).* 65 (M).

CHIEFTAIN'S CROWN (USA) ..9-12.. 10 ch.g. Chief's Crown (USA) — Simple Taste (USA) (Sharpen Up) pp3f63. Small sturdy half-brother to 5 flat winners abroad (one, Raven Runner, previously won in England). Dam won at 2f in Ireland. FLAT (first 2 for Mrs J. Cecil; subsequently for A. Hide; won for Miss K. George) r14 w1 (10f) p2. NH '95/7 (for R. Simpson; one win previously for T. Hind; hat-trick previously for Miss K. George, bought for 3400; previously for J. White) r14 w4 (2m3f-2m4f Hdles) p2 (2nds). Bought Doncaster, March for 940. The winner of five races including a hat-trick at Plumpton in Spring '96, but was reappearing from a three year absence when showing little in Points prior to his final start (when lucky to inherit third from two ahead of him fell at the final fence). Although the ground would have been against him, he does not seem much of a battler now. Often blinkered on the flat, but only once in a Hurdle. *S.J. Goodchap — N. Ledbury (Emma James).* 481 (L), 751 (L), 1085 (M), 1297 (L), 1410 (L), 1665 (L).

CHILDSWAY ..8-6§.. 13 b.g. Salmon Leap (USA) — Tharita (Thatch USA) 7. Strong half-brother to Madam Doris. NH FLAT r2 p0. NH '94 and '96/7 r10 p0 (last pair 3, pulled up 4, and fell 3). P-t-P/HUNT CH '95/6 and '98/9 r19 w2 (Maiden and Club) p2 (2nds); pulled up 5, fell/unseated 2, and ran out 1. Could have won a stack of races had he been genuine, but usually preferred to spend his time in a state of delinquency, and has run badly for the current yard. Only raced once apiece in the last two years, and beaten more than two fences in the latest. *S.J. Robinson — Zetland.* 134 (I).

CHILI HEIGHTS ..9-6.. 11 gr.g. Chilibang — Highest Tender (Prince Tenderfoot USA) 9. Small compact half-brother to Bali Tender, and to flat winners in Hong Kong, Norway and Malaysia. FLAT r39 w3 (6-7f, inc £6175 prize) p5 (short-headed once). NH '95/7 r10 p1 (31/ last of 3 in Sell); unseated 3rd only Ch. P-t-P '98/9 r10 p1 (3rd); last pair 3, pulled up 4, slipped up 1, and fell 1. Placed just once in three Pointing seasons (for three different yards), and has not surprisingly shown no aptitude for the job. Disappeared after pulling up at Black Forest Lodge in February. Has been tried in blinkers and a visor. *Mrs S.M. Wevill — Lamerton.* 199 (Cf).

CHILL FACTOR ..9-6§.. 11 br.g. Strong Gale — Icy Miss (Random Shot) 31p7u2. Leggy angular half-brother to Chasing winner, Indian Miss. Dam won NH flat, 2 Hdles (2m6f-3m) and 2 2m Chses in Ireland. NH FLAT '96 r3 p1 (3rd). NH '96/7 r7 p1 (3rd). P-t-P/HUNT CH '98/9 r8 p4 (2 3rds); refused 1, unseated 1, and pulled up 1. An ungenuine beast, but manages to hoist his rating a shade higher with each passing season, and finally consented to pass the post in front at Charing. Has been helped by the acquisition of a tongue strap, but again run up the white flag on his final start, and remains one to avoid. Putting a novice on him was an invitation to disaster, and so it proved. Has been tried in blinkers. *Miss P. Wood & W.R. Hacking — E. Sussex & Romney Marsh (Bob Hacking).* 132 (OMa), 290 (CMa), 575 (R), 825 (R), 985 (M), 1104 (R).

CHILLI JO ..8-9.. 9 b.g. Latest Model — Arctic Caper (Pardigras) pp7p7u. Good-bodied brother to Latest Caper. Dam, sister to Mustard, Artic Saffron, and Ground Ginger, and half-sister to Master Pepper and Giant Pepper, won 2 Points and 2nd for Diana Scott. P-t-P '98/9 r6 p0 (pulled up 4, ran out 1, and unseated 1). Finally managed a clear round at the ninth attempt (first-time tongue-tied), but finished stone-bonking last, and seems unable to travel much more than two miles before the staggers set in. A sketchy jumper, and has no prospects. *M. Fooks & P.C. Browne — Minehead H. (Diana Scott).* 203 (R), 881 (OMa), 1095 (R), 1376 (R), 1551 (R), 1640 (OMa).

CHINA GEM (IRE) ..9-8.. 10 b.g. Idiot's Delight — Graeme's Gem (Pry) pp7. Well-made. NH '96/8 (blinkered 1; won from S. Mullins', bought for 3000; previously for C. Brooks) r8 w1 (2m6f Hdle) p1 (2nd); pulled up and fell in Chses (poor jumper). Signed off in '98 with a win on firmish, but had failed to finish on his three preceding outings, and has been last once and pulled up twice since resuming. Ran well up to a point in sub-3m Hunter Chases, but even those trips seem to be beyond him, and it is proving hard to find suitable opportunities. *R.P. Peters — Berks & Bucks (Patrick Chamings).* 460 (2m7f110yH), 802 (2m6fH), 1541 (2m5fH).

CHINA LAL ..9-0.. 9 b.m. Rakaposhi King — Doris Blake (Roscoe Blake) pp4. Very small owner-bred sister to Blacon Point (qv). NH '97 r1 p0. P-t-P '97/9 r14 w1 (Maiden) p6 (3 2nds); unseated 2, and pulled up 3. Deserved her success, but a weak finisher who struggles to stay, and failed to beat a rival home in 2000. Not good enough for short distance Hunter Chases, and may have to rest on her laurels. Has been tried in a near-side pricker. *J.S. Swindells — Cheshire.* 137 (R), 463 (2mH), 962 (L).

CHISM (IRE) ..9-7§.. 10 br.g. Euphemism — Melody Gayle VII (unknown) 2p545656p. Sturdy half-brother to jumping winner, The Full Monty (IRE). P-t-P/HUNT CH '96/9 r22 w7 (inc 2m5f Hunt Ch, and Mixed Open) p8 (4 2nds, inc 6 Hunt Chses); pulled up 3, ran out 1. A useful Pointer to '98, but abhors the thought of hard work, and apart from hanging on to a land a modest 2m5f Wincanton Hunter Chase has declined to put his best foot forward. Left in front when Gunner Welburn departed at the last on his reappearance at Larkhill, and despite Robert Walford's softly softly efforts to nurse him home he was just collared. The local Stewards who should know the horse better relieved the jockey of £100 as they thought he would have done better by trying to drive his reluctant partner's head off. Tried in blinkers (again) and a visor subsequently, but would have none of it, and connections remain totally infuriated by his piggy behaviour. Might reform on his 2001 reappearance, but probably only if an exorcism has taken place in the close season. Has been tried in a tongue-strap. *Mrs J.R. Webber — Portman (Louise Alner).* 10 (O), 152 (3m1f110yH), 262 (MO), 475 (L), 681 (2m4fH), 954 (MO), 1205 (MO), 1532 (3m1fH), 1597 (MO).

CHOC (U) ..—.. 7 gr.g. Zambrano — Cisterle (unknown) 2. Trundled round willingly on Edward Kenny-Herbert's first ride, and finished a long way ahead of a 17-year-old. *Mrs V. Kenny-Herbert — Weston & Banwell H.* 1549 (M).

CHOCOLATE BUTTONS ..9-1.. 12 b.m. Button Bright (USA) — Man Maid (Mandamus) 224p. Compact light owner-bred half-sister to Rum Customer and Little Hen. P-t-P '95/9 r24 w2 (Maiden and Members) p3 (2 2nds; and 4 fences last of 3); withdrawn under orders once, and failed to finish 12 (on floor 6). Not a true stayer, and looked home and hosed at Wadebridge on her reappearance until capitulating on the run-in. Gained her last success courtesy of a walk-over, and will need another slice of luck to reach the winning enclosure again. Has been tried unsuccessfully in blinkers. *J.R. Thomas — Exmoor (Hugh Thomas).* 102 (R), 256 (R), 537 (O), 734 (R).

CHOP-CHOP (IRE) ..—.. 7 b br.g. Be My Native (USA) — Arctic Bavard (Le Bavard FR) pp7p. Neat hobdayed half-brother to jumping winners, Thirty Below (IRE) and Call It A Day (IRE) (smart — earned £212,533). NH FLAT '99 (for S. Sherwood) r1 p0. Bought Doncaster, May for 6800. NH Spr '00 r3 p0 (bhnd in Hdles, pulled up 2 — bbv once). Takes a very fierce hold and shows a lot of early speed, but invariably compounds alarmingly, and surely keeps breaking blood vessels. *A.M. Harvey — Vine & Craven (-; Ralph Beckett).* 21 (2m4fOMa).

CHRIS'S LAD ..—.. 10 b.g. Thowra (FR) — Stockline (Capricorn Line) ppf. Stocky compact. FLAT (wins for B. Meehan, frequently blinkered since 5) r35 w6 (12-18f, inc 26-runner Ladies) p8. NH '94 and '97 (for J. Jenkins; won previously for B. Meehan; debut for R. Hodges) r4 w1 (3m Hdle) p2. Formerly a competent stayer, but choked in his final Hurdle, and was unable to complete the course in Points with a maximum of seven runners when resuming three years later. *R.L. Clifton-Brown — Thurlow (Matthew Gingell).* 417 (Cf), 842 (O), 1034 (C).

CHRISTIEMOUSE ..8-7.. 7 b.m. Milieu — Border Minstrel (Menelek) p2f8. Dam won 2-finisher Maiden (16 started) and placed 15, but could be doggy. Gave her best display when 25 lengths second, but Laura Hislop lost her irons at least twice during the race, and almost came off at the final fence. Worth trying with a more experienced jockey. *P.J. Scott Plummer — Buccleuch.* 113 (OMa), 363 (CfMa), 712 (M), 910 (2m4fOMa).

CHUBBY MORTON ..8-0.. 7 b.g. Rough Stones — Decoyanne (Decoy Boy) 4p. Compact good-bodied half-brother to Cornish Ways (*qv*). Sire, by Blakeney, won 3 flat (12-16f) and 2m Hdle, and left for Norway at the end of his English racing career. P-t-P '99 r3 p0 (pulled up 2, and brought down 1). Aptly named when too backward to break into a gallop in his debut season, but showed an iota of ability when last in a short Maiden at Lanark. Appeared to go wrong at Alnwick subsequently and ominously failed to reappear. *Mr & Mrs J.E. Curry — N. Tyne.* 664 (2m5fOMa), 909 (2m4fOMa).

CHUMMY'S SAGA ..—.. 11 ch.g. Caerleon (USA) — Sagar (Habitat) 6ppp. Rangy half-brother to 6 flat winners (one in France, and one also a successful Hurdler) including Be Warned and Tarawa. Dam won at 11f in France. FLAT (first placing for B. Hills) r8 p2. NH '94/9 (for L. Lungo, bought for 8400, blinkered/visored 4 to '98) r22 w4 (2m5f Hdle, and 3 Chses, 2m1f-2m4f) p3 (2nds, inc 2 Sell Hdles). Formerly effective on firmish and in heavy, but declined latterly under Rules, and was very unconvincing in Points including when novice-ridden twice. A poor jumper, and does not even seem to want to try. *J. Innes — Buccleuch.* 716 (O), 975 (O), 1080 (O), 1428 (O).

CHURCH FIELD (IRE) ..—.. 9 ch.g. Hymns On High — Anacarty (Quayside) ppp3p. Lengthy good-topped. IRISH P-t-P r3 p0 (pulled up 3). NH FLAT '98 r1 p0 (tailed off). NH '98/9 (for C. Popham, blinkered last 2) r3 p0 (pulled up in 3 Hdles). Nearly two fences last once, and pulled up ten times over jumps. Appalling, and it would be no surprise if there was something chronically wrong. *Mr & Mrs C. Atyeo — W. Somerset V. (Carol Atyeo).* 520 (OMa), 739 (OMa), 953 (I), 1102 (OMa), 1565 (OMa).

CHURCH RIDE (IRE) ..9-7.. 12 b.g. King's Ride — Church Brae (The Parson) 3p. Workmanlike lengthy half-brother to Man Of Steel (IRE) (*qv*). P-t-P '94/5 and '97/9 r12 w1 (Maiden) p0; pulled up 4, and on floor 5. An expensive import into the Barber stable in his youth, and picked the pocket of two former stablemates in a sweet success at Charlton Horethorne in '98. Not entirely disgraced on his 2000 reappearance, but stands his racing badly, and his record of four outings in a season seems sure to remain intact. *Mrs G.M. Greenwood — Cotley (Philip Greenwood).* 458 (R), 729 (R).

CICERO'S LAW (IRE) ..8-3.. 8 ch.g. Glacial Storm (USA) — Royal Resemblance (Royal Highway) pp34pp6p. Lengthy unfurnished half-brother to an Irish Hurdles winner. Dam won NH flat and 2 Chses, 2m2f-3m1f, (the latter at Aintree) when Irish-trained. IRISH NH FLAT '97/8 r2 p0. IRISH P-t-P '99 r4 p1 (15l last of 2); pulled up 1, and slipped up 1. Beat only three horses in 2000, but his ten lengths third was an adequate display, and would have been closer had his partner not become unbalanced causing him to hang badly left on the run-in. Did not repeat the form, and the rider gave him no hope of doing so. Sometimes has two paddock handlers. *A.G. Chinery — E. Essex (Paul Chinery).* 24 (OMa), 87 (OMa), 180 (2m4fOMa), 237 (OMa), 441 (OMa), 551 (OMa), 759 (OMa), 1382 (OMa).

CIDER MAN ..9-7.. 6 b.g. Romany Rye — Champagne Peri (The Malster) ff2. Tall home-bred half-brother to Champagne Thunder (*qv*) and Alcofrolic. Dam won 3 Points and 3rd. Grandam, Rockscope, was brought down in a Members. Comes from a successful little stable, and gave an improved display when two lengths second over 2m4f. Will stay the full trip, and it would be surprising if he did not score soon. *R. Bunn — Ledbury (Janet Hughes).* 703 (OMa), 900 (OMa), 1360 (2m4fOMa).

CILL CHUILLINN (IRE) ..9-0.. 13 b.g. Parole — Lady Royal (Sharpen Up) up. Lengthy brother to Sweet Kildare, and to Irish Hurdles winner, Abbeyside Pub. IRISH NH FLAT '93/4 r5 p0. IRISH NH '94 r2 p0. IRISH P-t-P '94 r7 w1 (Maiden, lucky) p2 (3rds); unseated 2. P-t-P '99 (for Lady P. Kirkham) r4 p0 (last pair 2, unseated 1, and pulled up 1). Left clear at the last when successful at Gowran Park in '94, but has proved very moderate since resurfacing in England. Looked badly awry at High Easter, and promptly disappeared. *Miss J.C. Knight — Essex (Mike Jerram).* 179 (R), 610 (R).

CILL CHURNAIN (IRE) ..10-0§§.. 8 b.g. Arctic Cider (USA) — The Dozer (IRE) (Bulldozer) r4r4spp23. Small neat. IRISH P-t-P '98 r2 w1 (4&5yo Maiden) p0; ran out before 2nd on debut. NH '98 r2 p0 (pulled up; and swerved badly right at start and ran out at 1st in Hdles). P-t-P '99 r10 w3 (inc Ladies) p3 (2nds, beaten head once, and neck once); fell/unseated 2, refused 1, and pulled up 1. Remarkably reformed when winning thrice in '99, but has returned to his evil ways, and gave up the moment a struggle loomed in 2000. Usually has to be led in at the start and sometimes gives the impression he is in a going mood by taking a strong hold, but is very ungenuine, and his connections have done incredibly well to extract as much as they have. Presumably not raced in headgear in case he tries something deranged like crossing a river — once did his best to at Worcester. Barking in every sense of the word, but fun to watch as long as his antics don't cause anybody harm. *J.M. Turner — Suffolk.* 129 (O), 287 (L), 414 (L), 512 (L), 677 (L), 1380 (L), 1483 (L), 1587 (L), 1622 (L).

CINNAMON CLUB ..9-0.. 9 b.m. Derrylin — Cinnamon Run (Deep Run) p2. Lengthy half-sister to NH flat winner, Cassia. Dam won Hdle and Ch, both 2m. NH FLAT '97 (for N. Gaselee) r3 p1 (2nd). NH '97/8 (blinkered 2; final for A.P. Jones, claimed by him; won previously for N. Gaselee, who trained the dam) r9 w1 (2m Clmng Hdle) p2. Did not get the trip in Opens, and finished a poor and tired last once (promoted from third). Lightly raced nowadays. *T. Batterbee — Suffolk.* 320 (O), 553 (MO).

CIRCUS COLOURS ..—§§.. 11 b.g. Rainbow Quest (USA) — Circus Plume (High Top) 6prur6rrp. Small close-coupled half-brother to flat winners, Circus Feathers, Circus Light, Barnum Sands and Scarlet Plume. Dam, thoroughly game and genuine, won 4 flat, 7-12f, including '84 Oaks (was also 2nd in Irish Oaks after being given a bad ride by Piggott). FLAT (blinkered 1) r15 w2 (10-12f, inc £6245 prize) p2 (2nds, after hanging left once). NH '94/7 (visored last 2) r27 w4 (2m-2m5f Hdles) p4. P-t-P '98/9 (for Mr K.R. Pearce) r9 w3 (Opens, inc Mixed) p4 (3 2nds); pulled up 1. A well known tail-swisher who revived well to win three Opens in Wales '98/9, but has been nothing but trouble for new connections, and must be near the top of the Portman Square 'soon to be banned list'. Pulled himself up at Southwell and then refused to budge when blinkered at Market Rasen and bolted for two circuits with the rider holding on for grim death when they were removed after having declined the first. Even reunited with the last jockey to win on him at Howick, but refused to race but must surely have used up everyone's patience by now. *E. Haddock & Miss J. Elson — Meynell & S. Staffs (Edmund Haddock).* 118 (L), 368 (L), 442 (L), 566 (L), 598 (O), 670 (O), 903 (O), 1127 (O), 1198 (O).

CITIZEN BAND (IRE) ..9-0.. 13 ch.g. M Double M (USA) — Last Act (Gala Performance USA) ppp4. Workmanlike. Dam won 2 Irish flat, 9-12f. IRISH NH '93 r5 r3 p0. IRISH NH '93 and '95 r8 p0. NH '96 r3 p0. P-t-P '98/9 r8 p3 (2 3rds); last pair 2, on floor 3. Followed six consecutive non-completions with a 37 lengths fourth at Marks Tey, and regularly looks to be carrying too much condition. Seems highly unlikely to win a race. *C.J. Lawson — Essex.* 24 (OMa), 609 (I), 760 (OMa), 942 (CfMa).

CITTADINO ..10-8.. 11 b.g. Good Thyne (USA) — Slave's Bangle (Prince Rheingold) 2111513. Tall rangy half-brother to jumping winner, Gower-Slave, and to Irish Chasing winner, Isle Of Iona. NH FLAT '94/5 (for C. Thornton) r3 w1 p1 (2nd). NH '96/9 (for C. Thornton) r20 w3 (2 Hdles, 2m-2m5f, and 2m4f Ch) p3. Beat Uncle Kenny on his racecourse debut, but became bitterly disappointing latterly under Rules, and only beat three horses in his final seven attempts (never better than last but one). Was much happier in Points and did little wrong, and following a half-length second to the subsequent Hunter Chase winner Donnegale at Brocklesby Park he went on to score at Market Rasen, and at the first three Garthorpe meetings. Was odds-on there on final start, but almost unseated at the third and was never fluent enough after, and in the circumstances did quite well to be only beaten three lengths (additionally, lost a shoe). Goes a terrific gallop, but probably does not like to be headed for long, and gave up rather half-heartedly at Guilsborough. Always prone to a mistake or two. Jill Dawson has done really well to get him motivated again, thus putting herself back into the limelight after some lean years. *C.D. Dawson — Brocklesby (Jill Dawson).* 230 (L), 442 (L), 544 (L), 869 (L), 1007 (L), 1266 (L), 1587 (L).

CITY BUZZ (IRE) ..9-9.. 11 br.g. Phardante (FR) — Tourin Neofa (Teofane) u. Stocky. NH FLAT Nov '94 r1 p0. NH '94/5 r4 p0. P-t-P '96/8 r14 w2 (Maiden and Restricted) p4 (3 3rds, last once); pulled up 1, fell 1, and brought down 1. Inconsistent and best in blinkers previously, but able enough to get competitive against minor opposition, and was poised to take a hand in the finish when unseating his rider on the bend before the second last at Friars Haugh on his reappearance. Missed the '99 season entirely, and was not seen out again in 2000, so obviously has his problems. *S.N. Clark — Fife.* 717 (Cf).

CITY EXPRESS ..—.. 6 ch.g. Rock City — Caroles Express (Scottish Reel) p. Lengthy. Dam won 3 flat, 7-8f, and placed 7;, but failed to finish in 2 Points in '97, and was 11th in a Hdle in '99. NH FLAT '99 (for J. Akehurst) r2 p0 (40 ran in total, and only beat 2). Bought Ascot, June for 1100. Unable to raise a gallop so far, and was tailed off after a mile at Dunthrop. *B. Bebb — Albrighton Woodland (Mark Wellings).* 1019 (2m4fOMa).

CITY RUN (USA) ..8-0.. 9 b.g. Mehmet (USA) — Sable Sham (USA) (Sham USA) ppupp47. Leggy unfurnished half-brother to 2 winners in USA. Dam won at under 5f in USA. Sire was very smart from 8-10f there. FLAT r3 p0. P-t-P '98/9 (for Miss T. Coulson & Mrs C. Hill) r13 p3 (2 3rds, last once); pulled up 3, refused 1, and fell/unseated 3. Has twice run passably under a debutant in his Members, but pathetic otherwise, and failed to beat a rival in 2000. Seems to have difficulty getting the trip. *S. & Mrs T. Holditch — Fitzwilliam (Tracey Holditch).* 23 (OMa), 88 (OMa), 769 (M), 1040 (OMa), 1116 (OMa), 1292 (OMa), 1507 (OMa).

CLARE'S SPRING (IRE) ..—.. 8 ch.g. King Luthier — Do We Know (Derrylin) f. Tall lengthy half-brother to All Greek To Me (IRE), to flat winners, Bo Knows Best (IRE) (also a successful jumper) and Gween, and to a winner in Spain. NH FLAT '97 r1 p0. NH '97/8 (for R. Hodges) r5 p0 (pulled up in both Chses). Useless under Rules, and fell after two miles when returning two years later. *J.M. Bishop — Blackmore & Sparkford V. (Frances Bishop).* 457 (OMa).

CLARET AND BLUE ..9-11.. 7 b.g. Carlingford Castle — Blowing Bubbles (Native Admiral USA) 1p. Good-topped. Dam, half-sister to Kingston Hill Lad (*qv* '92 Annual), won 5 flat (7-8f) as a 4-y-o. Won a weak Maiden at Horseheath decisively, but probably had the excuse of being shin-sore when disappointing next time. Likely to make amends when healthy. *G.T.H. Bailey — Pytchley (Caroline Bailey).* 411 (OMa), 1009 (CR).

CLASSICAL STYLE ..8-8.. 13 b.g. Boreen (FR) — unknown 4. Tall good-looking. P-t-P '99 r1 p0 (pulled up). No racehorse, but got Emma Boone home safely in his Members, and avoided being last by a long way. *Miss E. Boone — W. Norfolk (Amanda Case).* 1285 (M).

CLASSIC CREST (IRE) ..—.. 10 ch.g. Persian Heights — Blunted (Sharpen Up) fp. Plain leggy half-brother to Tramontana (IRE), and to 2 flat winners (one in France). NH FLAT '95 (for G. Moore) r4 p2 (2nds). NH '95/9 (for Miss L. Russell, bought for 3000; won previously for G.M. Moore) r29 w1 (2m6f Hdle) p6 (inc 3 Chses, inc 2nd in Sell); inc 2nd in Sell Hdle. Won on firm in May '96, but later ran up a sequence of six non-completions from eight attempts in the next 12 months. Might have had a chance in his Members, but fell after a mile and brought down a rival, leaving the Alexander boys as the only two still going. Can look reluctant, and wears a visor (has been blinkered in the past). *M.F.B. Nicholson — Fife.* 1117 (MA), 1556 (2m4f110yH).

CLASSIC FAIRY (IRE) ..—.. 9 b.m. Executive Perk — Amy Fairy (The Parson) pp. Well-made. Dam, sister to Clerical Cousin (*qv*), won NH flat, 4 Hdles (2m-2m2f) and 2 Chses (2m-2m4f) in Ireland. NH FLAT '98 (for J. Hughes) r1 p0. Tailed off in her first two races, but showed signs of ability when keeping up for over two miles in a hot Open at Chaddesley. Might be able to surprise in a Maiden, although she appears to have a breathing problem, and usually tongue-tied. *Miss S. Nicholas — United.* 486 (R), 614 (O).

CLASSIC MISTRESS ..9-10.. 7 ch.m. Mystiko (USA) — Boogy Lady (IRE) (Glenstal USA) pf2ub. Smallish unfurnished. P-t-P '99 r4 p0 (last, pulled up 2, and unseated 1). Very novicey in her debut season, but far more clued up in 2000, and would have been runner-up twice but for departing at the last at Cherrybrook once. Still has something to learn about the art of jumping, but should find a race when more fluent. *C. Blank — Dart V. & S. Pool H. (Angharad Watkins).* 159 (CfMa), 855 (CfMa), 1048 (CfMa), 1263 (OMa), 1520 (CfMa).

CLASSIC MS (IRE) ..—.. 10 b.g. Orchestra — High Fi (High Hat) u3pfpp. Tall rangy brother to NH flat winner, Philharmonic (IRE), and half-brother to The Plumley Flyer, to Hurdles winner, End Of Era, to 2 successful Irish Hurdlers, including Highbabs, to Irish jumping winner, Headbanger, and to 2 flat winners abroad and one in Ireland. Looked incredibly slow when a fence last to Spring Wheat in a Members, and has otherwise failed to complete. Sometimes jumps badly, but (amazingly) the owner has one even worse in this department in the shape of Campbellhill. *Mrs M. Sharland — Granta H., & Cambridge Univ (Henry Hill).* 88 (OMa), 174 (M), 242 (M), 774 (OMa), 1039 (OMa), 1219 (OMa).

CLASS OF NINETYTWO (IRE) ..10-1§.. 12 b.g. Lancastrian — Lothian Lassie (Precipice Wood) 1522d223. Good-topped rangy half-brother to Lothian Magic (*qv*). IRISH NH FLAT '93 r5 p0. IRISH NH '93 r3 p0. IRISH P-t-P '95 r5 w3 (up to Winners of One) p1 (2nd); and fell. NH '95/9 (unplaced last 3 for H. Daly; previously for late T. Forster) r13 w5 (3m-3m3f Chses) p3 (inc 3rd in '96 4m NH Ch). A very thorough stayer who made all and kept going steadily to record a ninth career success on his debut in 2000, but that is his only victory since recording a 4-timer to February '96 (subsequently absent for 18 months) and has been dogging it badly since. Tried in blinkers and a visor latterly, and added spurs on final start. Can handle mud, but best ignored after one outing if reappearing at 12. *A. Wynne & M. Williams — Sir W.W. Wynn's (Reg Crank).* 171 (O), 369 (O), 525 (M), 903 (O), 1127 (O), 1253 (L), 1525 (L).

CLAYMORE LAD ..9-8.. 11 b.g. Broadsword (USA) — Cannes Beach (Canadel II) 132pu3. Smallish compact brother to Gilston Lad, and half-brother to Lauderdale Lad (subsequently won Chasing), Cannie's Castle (dam of Queen's Castle), Bright Season, and Dun Law and to Chasing winner, Gilston Lass. Dam was 36l last of 3 in 2m Nov Ch, and was useless in Points (very fiery). Grandam, Bright Beach, won 10 Hunt Chses (inc '68 Cheltenham Foxhunters) and placed 6 (inc Points). Great-grandam, Badger's Beech, won '57 Border Maiden. NH FLAT '96 r1 p0. NH '96/9 (for J. King) r15 p4 (3rds in 3m-3m3f Chses, beaten 29l plus twice). Won a two-finisher Maiden in holding at Mollington (was the slowest race of the day), but has been soundly beaten in Restricteds since. Did give Zoe House a good first ride when second in his Members, but does not usually look to have much appetite for a struggle. *A. Maculan — V.W.H.* 81 (CCfMa), 338 (R), 748 (M), 971 (I), 1206 (R), 1355 (R).

CLAYWALLS ..9-11.. 10 b.g. Meadowbrook — Lady Manello (Mandrake Major) 731. Smallish lengthy. Dam, half-sister to Bavington (*qv*), refused in 2 of 5 Points for Ann Hamilton, but was placed in 2 Hurdles for her. NH '98/9 r3 p0 (4th, 7th and last in Chses). P-t-P '96/7 and '99 r11 w2 (Maiden and Restricted) p4 (neck 2nd; and 3 3rds, last once); pulled up 1. A sound jumper, but very one-paced, and was recording his first success since '97 when making most in his Members. Stays well and handles firmish, but might find one or two too quick for him in more competitive races in future. *I. Hamilton — Tynedale (Ann Hamilton).* 43 (Cf), 108 (I), 418 (M).

C L B JEMILLA ..9-13.. 8 ch.m. Lord Bud — Comarch (Ancient Monro) 421634. Very small sister to Elliott The Butler. Dam, half-sister to Comzan (*qv* '95 Annual), won 9 Points (inc 6 Opens) and placed 23 (inc 3 Hunt Chses) for Pam Wright, and grandam, Compro, won Maiden and placed 7 (inc 3rd in flat race and Sell Hdle) for her. NH FLAT '98 r1 p0 (remote 14th of 15). P-t-P '99 r5 p2. Made the frame on three occasions before winning at Hutton Rudby, but the form has yet to be franked by any of the other six finishers. Microscopic, and will be suited by the lighter weights in Ladies races — beaten 14 lengths into third on her first such venture to date. *Mrs P.P. Wright — Middleton.* 51 (OMa), 437 (OMa), 626 (OMa), 797 (R), 1232 (L), 1351 (CR).

CLEAN SWEEP ..8-3.. 14 br.g. Deep Run — The Charwoman (Menelek) pp. Strong workmanlike half-brother to Cleaning Up and Tidy Up, and to Irish Pointing winners, Maythefifth and Kilbrien Star. P-t-P/HUNT CH '94/9 r18 w2 (Maiden and Members) p5 (4 3rds, last thrice); failed to finish 9 (fell/unseated 3). Finished in front of a remounter when a poor third in his Members in '99, but otherwise a non-finisher in the last two seasons, and gives the impression that he does not stay. Very moderate at best, and has never managed more than four outings per annum, so to have won twice represents something of a triumph. *Mrs G. Drury — O. Surrey & Burstow (Peter Broad).* 575 (R), 1393 (R).

CLEIKUMIN ..8-9.. 8 b.m. Kind Of Hush — Carrapateira (Gunner B) ff. Robust quite attractive home-bred half-sister to Smiths Wynd (*qv*). NH FLAT '99 r3 p0 (50-1 all 3). NH '99 r2 p0 (50-1 both). Probably better than two falls might suggest as she was on the premises for a long way in both, but the crashing cannot be doing her much good, and has not been seen since February. *R. Shiels — Jedforest.* 112 (OMam), 363 (CfMa).

CLERICAL COUSIN (IRE) ..—.. 12 b.g. The Parson — Copp On (Menelek) pp. Tall rangy half-brother to Irish Pointing winners, Try Your Case and Littledrunkgirl, to 2 Irish NH flat winners, including Amy Fairy (also a successful jumper), and to the unraced dam of One Man. IRISH NH FLAT '94 r2 p0. IRISH NH '94 and '96/7 r8 p0 (pulled up in 2 of 3 Chses, broke blood vessel once). NH '97/9 r12 p1 (3rd); pulled twice in Chses. P-t-P '99 r5 p0 (pulled up 2, fell 2, and ran out 1). Generally unfit, prone to be unruly at the start and to do deranged things when he gets going, and has spilt more blood than Dracula, yet still connections race him. Why? *E.W. Froggatt — Meynell & S. Staffs (Jane Froggatt).* 340 (R).

CLIFFORD BAY (IRE) ..9-0.. 7 b.g. Phardante (FR) — Calfstown Night (Bargello) 33. Tall half-brother to jumping winner, Ballygriffin Lad (IRE). Dam is half-sister to Reay Royal (*qv* '92 Annual). 2800 4-y-o. NH '98/9 (for M Hammond) r3 p0. Beaten a length at Higham after being presented with every chance at the last (the eight length leader made a near-catastrophic mistake which caused the rider to lose the irons and the saddle to slip), but finished slowly when favourite and 32 lengths last next time. Gave the impression he could have a problem, and looks suspect. *J.M. Turner — Suffolk.* 1115 (OMa), 1382 (OMa).

CLIFTON MATCH ..8-2.. 9 gr.m. Nicholas Bill — Brave Maiden (Three Legs) 5p. Small good-looking sister to Hurdles winner, Wontcostalotbut, and half-sister to flat and Chasing winner, Clifton Game, and to good jumping winner, Clifton Set. Dam, half-sister to Broughty Pier (*qv* '90 Annual), won 2 flat, 10-12f. NH '95 and '97 (for R. Millman) r2 p0. Bought Ascot, Feb '98 for 1000. Rarely seen, and appears to be useless. *S.D. Whiting — Kent & Surrey Bloodhounds (Jon Casemore).* 1396 (OMa), 1624 (OMa).

CLIMB THE HILL (IRE) ..9-3.. 7 b.g. Dromod Hill — Callady (IRE) (Callernish) 3p. Finished a modest third on his debut, but unconvincing when sent off second favourite two months later. Will possibly do better in time. *T.W. Biddlecombe — O. Berks.* 221 (OMa), 1204 (OMa).

CLINKING ..9-12.. 10 b.g. Glint Of Gold — Kai (Kalamoun) u1f6. Tall half-brother to 4 flat winners (2 abroad — one also successful over jumps), including Kaytiggy and Fabillion. NH FLAT '96/7 (for Mrs A. Perrett; debut for G. Harwood) r4 w1 p0. Sold Ascot, May '98 for 1000. Did not start his career over jumps until he was nine, so in the circumstances it was a good performance to land a Lockinge Intermediate. Wears a cross-noseband, and has pulled too hard and become unsettled since. The first success for Paddy Young, and also took part in a celebrity race at Larkhill with John Manners on top. *N.A. Phillips — O. Berks (Chris Cox).* 248 (R), 1203 (I), 1340 (3m1f110yH), 1481 (Cf).

CLOAK AND DAGGER ..9-5.. 8 b.g. Broadsword (USA) — Night Pry (Pry) p. Dam, half-sister to Kingfisher Blues (*qv* 2000 Annual), won 3 Points consecutively at Siddington and 2nd for Sheena Pilkington, and was previously placed in 4 Irish Points (also won one, but disqualified after failing a dope test). P-t-P '99 r3 w1 (Maiden) p1 (remote 2nd of 3); and pulled up 1. Overcame a last fence mistake to land a woeful Maiden at Garthorpe on the first occasion he had been asked to get competitive, but disappeared after pulling up on the opening day of the 2000 season, and has plenty to prove if he gets the chance to return to action. *Miss S. Pilkington — Berks & Bucks.* 2 (R).

CLONSHIRE CASTLE (IRE) ..9-3§.. 8 b.g. Mazaad — Callula (Crash Course) 4fpf32. Small light half-brother to NH flat and Chasing winner, Luv-U-Frank (IRE), and to Irish NH flat and Hurdles winner, Marian Year. Dam won at 9f in Ireland, and won 2m Hdle there. IRISH P-t-P '98 r2 p1 (2nd); and fell at last, when looking winner. NH FLAT '98 r1 p0. NH '98/9 (for P. Hobbs) r6 p0 (fell in Sell Ch; inc last pair 2 — one a Sell — and pulled up 2 in Hdles). Disappointing. Fell two out when poised to challenge in a Maiden at Bassaleg, and looked the winner, but it may not have been that simple, as he cruised up to the leader approaching the last on his two subsequent attempts, but then found absolutely nil. Could obviously score if he desired, but is taking a very long time about it. Tried tongue-tied. *R.J. Rowsell — Ystrad Taf Fechan.* 268 (CfMa), 350 (CfMa), 1302 (OMa), 1405 (OMa), 1574 (OMa), 1617 (OMa).

CLONTOURA (IRE) ..9-1.. 13 b.g. Salluceva — Clara Novello (Maciver USA) 36. Sturdy. IRISH P-t-P '93/5 r8 w2 p3; fell 2, inc when ½l up at last once. NH '96/8 r9 p1 (2nd in Ch — veered left flat); pulled up 1, fell 1, and dropped down 1. P-t-P '96 and '99 r7 p2 (3rds); pulled up 1, and unseated 1. A fair performer in Irish Points, but has not won since leaving his homeland, and well beaten in his last two Pointing campaigns. Must be getting sick of the sight of Black Forest Lodge. *C. Willis & Mrs J. Browning — Silverton (N. Willis).* 65 (M), 199 (Cf).

CLOUDY CREEK (IRE) ..9-12.. 7 gr.g. Roselier (FR) — Jacob's Creek (IRE) (Buckskin FR) 13. P-t-P '99 r1 p0 (pulled up). Jumped stickily on a solitary fact finding mission in '99, but put up a polished performance to open his account on his reappearance, though the opposition was weak and the only other finisher went lame. Surprisingly failed to cope with Perfect Finisher at Charing subsequently, but probably still weak at present, and was not seen out again in any case. Hails from a good yard, and should improve further with experience. *Dr D.B.A. Silk, G. Addiscote & R. Purkis — Kent & Surrey Bloodhounds (Heather Silk).* 88 (OMa), 285 (CR).

CLUAN GOILL (IRE) ..9-4.. 12 b.g. Borovoe — Okies East (Pauper) p. Tall. IRISH P-t-P '94 and '97/8 r7 p0 (pulled up 3, and fell 1). P-t-P '99 r2 p0 (unseated 1, and pulled up 1). Has displayed an iota of ability during his long drawn out career, but has never contributed to his keep, and does not look likely to. *P. & Mrs S. Richardson — Grafton (P. Richardson).* 754 (CfMa).

COACH (NZ) ..10-4.. 13 b.g. Trubisc (AUS) — Fly (IRE) (Three Legs) 1472112. Tall strong-topped half-brother to Fly Guard (NZ). NZ FLAT '90/5 r23 w4 (8-11f) p6. NZ NH '92 r1 p0 (Hdle). NH '98 r1 p0 (pulled up). P-t-P '99 r7 w1 (Club nov rdrs) p1 (neck 2nd); fell/unseated 4. A fair performer on the flat in his native country, but headstrong and suited by an easy three miles in Points, and has found Larkhill ideal (winner there three times). A bold jumper who does not enjoy riders trying to organise him at the fences, and Paul Keane learnt — the hard way — to let him do his own thing. Looked sure to collect on his Hunter Chase debut at Folkestone, but compounded in the closing stages, and it later transpired that he had burst a blood vessel. Has been retired to the Hampshire hunting fields. *Mrs H.B. Clarke — R.A. (Don Harrington).* 56 (M), 130 (CMod), 325 (Cf), 453 (Cf), 628 (Cf), 768 (Cf), 1541 (2m5fH).

COASTLEY LANE ..—.. 6 b.g. Silver Season — Queenswood Girl (General David) f. Dam, half-sister to Rent Free (*qv* '91 Annual), was placed in 3 Points for David Carr ('provenly moderate'). Grandam, Merry Wood, was 3rd in Restricted. Fell at the third at Lanark. *D. Carr — Haydon (Tim Reed).* 664 (2m5fOMa).

CODDINGTON GIRL ..10-0.. 9 br.m. Green Adventure (USA) — Emancipated (Mansingh USA) pb65214. Plain sparely-made half-sister to Mansun and Coddington Star, and to jumping winner, Superior Finish. NH FLAT r1 p0 (tailed off). P-t-P '99 (for Mr M. Jones) r5 w1 (Maiden) p2 (2nds); pulled up 1, and fell 1. Successful in a three-finisher Maiden at Bitterley in her debut season, but a beaten favourite three times before she landed a Restricted in which she faced a simple task. Often struggles to get the trip (the Brampton Bryan success was run at a crawl as the course had turned into a skidpan), and an easy three miles and top-of-the-ground would appear to be ideal for her. Lacks scope, but seems genuine enough, and may find another minor race. Usually takes the eye in the paddock, but horses of her colour often do. *E.T. Chapman — N. Ledbury (Mike Daniell).* 38 (CR), 340 (R), 392 (R), 612 (CR), 1355 (R), 1548 (R), 1632 (I).

COLD HARBOUR ICICLE (U) ..—.. 10 gr.m. unknown 4. Finished the best part of a mile behind under 50 pounds overweight in his Members. *J. Peace — Badsworth.* 166 (M).

COLD SNAP (IRE) ..9-6.. 8 b.g. Glacial Storm (USA) — Cripton Breeze (Burslem) 2331. Small compact. Dam won twice at Tramore, 9-12f. IRISH P-t-P '99 r2 p0; pulled up 1. NH Oct '99 (for C. Mann) r1 p0 (last). Bought Doncaster, Nov for 3000. Driven out to win one of the worst Maidens of the season (odds-on; took 7min 13s in softish at Maisemore), but had been performing creditably in similar company previously. Consistent and a sensible jumper, and might thereabouts in Restricteds. *A. Wintle — Llangibby (Helen Lewis).* 489 (CfMa), 900 (OMa), 989 (OMa), 1316 (OMa).

COLEBROOK WILLIE ..9-5.. 8 br.g. Dowsing (USA) — A Little Hot (Petong) p4up. Workmanlike. FLAT (tried visored) r4 p0 (inc Sell). NH '96/7 r6 p0 (inc Sells). P-t-P '98/9 r7 w1 (Maiden) p0 (last 2, and pulled up 4). Sprang a surprise — though not to those who punted him from sixes to threes — when winning an awful Maiden at Laleston in '99, but dismounted immediately after the finish, and has frequently stopped in a matter of strides (must have a problem). Never went a yard in blinkers on his reappearance, but then takes the eye in the paddock, and there may be a chance of another miracle if his troubles can be sorted out. Sure to be a fancy price if he does go in again. *N.M. Poacher — Llangeinor.* 1298 (R), 1568 (R), 1659 (R), 1671 (R).

COLEMANS RIVER (IRE) ..8-7.. 10 b.g. Over The River (FR) — Colemans Daughter (Kambalda) p. IRISH NH '98 r1 p0 (pulled up in Ch). IRISH P-t-P '97/8 r9 p1 (distant 3rd); pulled up 4, brought down 2, and fell 1. P-t-P '99 r3 p1 (3rd); pulled up 3. Lightly raced and devoid of talent, but was at least sent off a more realistic price in his latest outing — 50-1. *Miss S. Dutton — Farmers Bloodhounds, & Bicester with Whaddon (Mark Gregory & Miss S. Dutton).* 370 (C).

COLEMORE GREEN ..—.. 8 b.g. Glacial Storm (USA) — Impressive Reward (USA) (Impressive) ppp. Rangy very plain half-brother to Lady Pendragon, and to a French flat and jumping winner. Dam won at 10f. Bought Ascot, July for 2500. His owners seem to have a penchant for big slow boats who either will not or cannot raise a gallop, and they have certainly got themselves a classic to follow Forever Freddy and Here's Humphrey. *J.M. & Mrs V.H.E. Valdes-Scott — Waveney H. (Matthew Gingell).* 97 (OMa), 412 (OMa), 550 (OMa).

COLISNOVA ..—.. 9 ch.m. Ra Nova — Colislace (Coliseum) ffpf. Dam failed to earn a penny in 25 races, including 5 Points (never even finished in them). Grandam, Indian Lace, was last twice and pulled up in Points. Great-grandam, Border Lace, was placed in 8 Ladies. Comes from a family of retards, and does not seem to have a clue about self-preservation. Has fallen by the 11th on three occasions, including when blinkered in the latest. *Mr & Mrs G. Nichol — Jedforest.* 498 (R), 719 (CfMa), 978 (OMa), 1164 (OMa).

COLONEL CARATS ..9-4.. 8 br.g. Golden Heights — Madam Carats (Mandrake Major) 56fu42. Strong workmanlike. Dam is an unraced sister to Carats Major, who won 8 Points and placed 12 for David Applewhite. P-t-P '99 r1 p0 (pulled up). Backward and error-prone in his first six races, but showed much improved form when just touched off in a short Maiden on his final start, and might be capable of winning if he can manage the full trip in 2001. *D. Applewhite — Belvoir.* 436 (OMa), 547 (CfMa), 793 (OMa), 872 (OMa), 1269 (OMa), 1590 (2m4fOMa).

COLONEL FAIRFAX ..8-4§.. 13 gr.g. Alias Smith (USA) — Mistress Meryll (Tower Walk) 8p. Compact half-brother to Miss Portia, to flat winner, Sergeant Meryll, and to a winner abroad. FLAT (tried blinkers/visor) r14 p3 (inc Sell). NH '92/3 r2 p0. P-t-P/HUNT CH '94/9 r45 w1 (Maiden) p6 (3 2nds, last once; and inc last of 3); failed to finish 25 (on floor 8). The veteran of seven consecutive campaigns, but has won just once, and performed dismally in each of the last three seasons. Has worn headgear, and never really enjoyed Pointing. *Mrs N.R. Matthews — Heythrop (Kim Matthews).* 787 (L), 1013 (M).

COLONEL FRAZER (IRE) ..8-7.. 13 b.g. Buckskin (FR) — Tabithat Bay (Laurence O) p. Tall rangy half-brother to Baileys Bridge (IRE). IRISH P-t-P '92 and '94 r8 p1 (3rd); pulled up 6. P-t-P '95/9 r23 w1 (Maiden) p5 (4 3rds, last once); failed to finish 13 (fell 2). Did well to stumble across an awful race in '96, and has beaten just five rivals in 15 starts since. Not a true stayer, and usually forced to pull up. Often blinkered nowadays. *R. Perkins — Tredegar F.* 818 (R).

COLONEL PEDLAR ..—.. 10 b.g. Buzzards Bay — Ginger Dip (Golden Dipper) p. Small close-coupled. Dam, sister to Golden Huntress (*qv* '97 Annual), won 2 Points and 2nd 2 (her only starts in Points). Grandam, Medway Melody, won a Ladies, and won 3 bad Hurdles at around 2m and placed 13. P-t-P '98/9 r3 p0 (pulled up 3). Pulled up in four races over three seasons, and obviously of no account as a racehorse. *Miss M.R. Palmer — Southdown & Eridge (R. Wilkinson).* 710 (OMa).

COLONELS HATCH ..8-7.. 7 ch.g. Gildoran — Toumanova (High Line) fpp1fp. Good-topped half-brother to Henrymyson, to NH flat winner, Good Stuff, and to successful Chaser, Baroncelli. Dam is half-sister to Tamasaga (*qv* '96 Annual). Sold Doncaster, Aug '98 for 2600 (to E. Crow). The fluke winner of a dire 2m4f Maiden at Eyton in which he finished alone, but looked useless otherwise, and this completion proved to be a unique event for him. *J.S. Swindells — Cheshire.* 168 (OMa), 569 (OMa), 906 (CfMa), 1201 (2m4fOMa), 1351 (CR), 1459 (R).

COLONEL WILKIE ..9-2.. 10 b.g. Broadsword (USA) — Peticienne (Mummy's Pet) 7p53. Big strong home-bred half-brother to Batcho Missile (*qv*). P-t-P '97/9 r10 p3 (2 3rds); last pair 6, pulled up 1. A safe jumper (unlike his sibling), but modest in the extreme, and does not appear to get the trip. Looked reluctant at Dunthrop, but should be contesting Maidens in any case. *I.S. Gilbert — Fernie.* 871 (R), 1017 (I), 1268 (R), 1502 (M).

COLOUR OF LIFE ..—.. 11 b.m. Crowning Honors (CAN) — Within A Whisper (Welsh Pageant) pp. Angular sister to Imperial Honors (IRE). FLAT (for C. Elsey at 2) r1 p0 (tailed off last). NH '95/6 (for N. Lampard) r3 p0 (pulled up 3). A complete waste of time in just six outings spread over nine years. *C. Fowlie — Pentyrch (June Marsh).* 601 (CfMa), 745 (R).

COMEDY GAYLE ..—.. 14 b.g. Lir — Follifoot's Folly (Comedy Star USA) ppp. Workmanlike good-quartered half-brother to Melsar and Linton. NH '92 r3 p0. P-t-P/HUNT CH '97/9 r16 w5 (inc 2 Hunt Chses, 2m5f110y-3m) p6 (3 2nds, inc 2 Hunt Chses); unseated 2, and pulled up 2. An ex-eventer and showjumper who embraced Pointing and Hunter Chasing with equal relish winning under the latter code at Newton Abbot and Stratford (rated 10-10), but a pale shadow of himself during an interrupted 2000 season, and looked wrong when pulled up on his final start. None too young and may find making a comeback difficult, but owes connections nothing, and it would be no surprise if he went into honourable retirement. *Miss S. Willcock — Devon & Somerset.* 222 (3m1f110yH), 467 (3m1f110yH), 1374 (MO).

COME ON BOY ..8-8.. 7 ch.g. Henbit (USA) — Miss Reward (Andy Rew) bpp5p. Tall rangy workmanlike. Dam pulled up 3 and fell 2 in Points for Pat Mullen. Grandam, Maquisarde, won a Restricted, but pulled up 3 and unseated 3 in her other Points. His pedigree does not inspire much confidence, and was 35 lengths last on his only completion to date. *Mrs P. Mullen — N. Herefords.* 340 (R), 450 (CfMa), 865 (CfMa), 1092 (OMa), 1635 (OMa).

COMIC TURN ..—.. 12 b.g. Idiot's Delight — Working Away (Workboy) uf. Angular. Dam is an unraced half-sister to Celtic Harry (*qv* '95 Annual). NH FLAT '93 r1 p0 (tailed off). NH '94/5 r2 p0 (tailed off). P-t-P '99 r1 p0 (fell). Partnering him was no laughing matter, as he only cleared ten fences successfully in three Points, and was killed when falling at Chaddesley. *Mrs N. Gretton — N. Cotswold (Tom Gretton).* 1555 (OMa), 1634 (OMa).

COMING THROUGH (IRE) ..10-2§.. 9 ch.g. Le Bavard (FR) — Gay Countess (Master Buck) 3p21. Brother to Irish NH flat winner, Portstewart, and half-brother to jumping winner, Countorus. IRISH P-t-P '97 r2 p0; pulled up 1. P-t-P '98/9 r7 w1 (Maiden) p5 (3 3rds), and pulled up 1. Won a poor Maiden at Eaton Hall on his English debut, but placed seven times in Restricted company before he consented to win again when facing a simple task in his Members. Can be very mulish at the start, and is not one to take too short a price about. Can pick up a Restricted in 2001, but only if he co-operates fully. *D. Pugh — N. Salop (Sheila Crow).* 119 (CR), 532 (R), 782 (R), 1195 (M).

COMMANCHE REBEL (IRE) ..—.. 8 b.g. Commanche Run — Deep Satisfaction (Deep Run) p. Half-brother to Irish NH flat winner, Be My Pleasure. Dam is sister to De Profundis (*qv* 2000 Annual). IRISH P-t-P '98 r1 p0 (fell). IRISH NH FLAT r2 p0. IRISH NH '98 r1 p0 (fell in Hdle). Only jumped three fences before breaking his off-hind at Chaddesley. *The Earl of Bective & G. Cazenove — Golden V. (Giles Smyly).* 616 (CMa).

COMMANCHE SCOUT (IRE) ..—.. 8 ch.g. Commanche Run — Whats In A Name (IRE) (Le Moss) pppp. IRISH NH FLAT '97 r1 p0. IRISH NH '97 and '99 r7 p3 (Hcap Chses, carrying 9.6 max); 7th, last and unseated in Hunt Chses. IRISH P-t-P '98/9 r12 w1 (6 plus Mdn) p6 (inc last of 2, last of 3 after falling, and 3rd of 4); pulled up 3. Sold Doncaster, Aug for 8000. Looked pretty expensive judged on his Irish efforts, and could only keep pulling up in the new yard. Broke a blood vessel at least once, and dismounted on his latest appearance. Seems to be suffering. *P.J. Scott Plummer — Buccleuch (Rhona Elliott).* 359 (Cf), 420 (I), 976 (R), 1366 (I).

COMMASARRIS ..9-13.. 9 gr.g. Joli Wasfi (USA) — Lucy Aura (Free State) 23p. Compact owner-bred half-brother to Rough Aura. Dam, 2nd in Sell Hdle, pulled up in 2 Points ('lumbers along unimpressively'). P-t-P/HUNT CH '97/9 r17 w3 (2m4f Maiden, Restricted and Intermediate) p5 (3 2nds); pulled up 4, fell 2. A keen sort whose rider likes to make the running, but needs to slip the opposition and get clear, as he frequently has nothing to give in the closing stages. Goes well at Charing, but may have suffered a setback there in February, as he failed to reappear. Tends to carry plenty of condition in early season, and it would be interesting to see what results he could produce if attempts were made to hold him up. *Miss M.D.M. Howie — O. Surrey & Burstow.* 25 (Cnr), 127 (Cf), 288 (CMod).

COMMERCIAL ARTIST ..9-12.. 15 b.g. Furry Glen — Blue Suede Shoes (Bargello) 2320rr. Tall brother to Irish NH flat and jumping winner, Mass Appeal, and half-brother to Irish NH flat and jumping winners, Andrea Cova (IRE) and Macallister (IRE). Dam won 14f NH flat and 2m3f Hurdle in Ireland. IRISH NH FLAT '90/1 r3 w1 p1 (3rd). IRISH NH '91/5 r43 w9 (3 Hdles, 2-3m, and 6 Chses, 2m3f-3m1f) p9 (inc 3rds in Cathcart and Hennessy Chses from 6 visits to England). NH '95/9 r18 w1 (3m Ch) p3 (beat one horse in 3 3rds, beaten 22l and distance); refused in first 2 races. HUNT CH '99 (McCain-trained for Mr L.A. Morgan) r4 w1 (3m1f) p0; last 2, and fell 1. A wonderful old campaigner, who was smart in Ireland, and was gaining his first success for three years when taking a modest Cartmel Hunter Chase in '99. Has had to battle against a wind infirmity (has had a soft palate operation, sometimes worn a tongue-strap, and now runs tubed), and not surprisingly appears to have lost the fire in his belly. Surely he has run the last race of a long and most successful career. *D. McCain — Cheshire.* 293 (Cf), 464 (3m110yH), 592 (Cf), 921 (2m6fH), 1253 (L), 1643 (3m2fH).

COMME UNE FLEUR (FR) ..—.. 9 ch.m. Sharpo — Fleur De Ciel (FR) (Kenmare FR) fpppupupp. Lengthy light-framed half-sister to a French flat winner. Dam won at 6f in France. FRENCH FLAT '94/5 r16 w1 (8f) p2 (2nds). First or second in her first three French races, but went steadily downhill after. Consistently dreadful in Points after five years away (never got further than the 14th fence), and is a very risky jumper. Bolted headlong into a hedge and stuck fast after unseating at Howick. Eventually extricated and returned very slowly in the horse ambulance delaying the next race, but evidently not too badly hurt as she was out again just a fortnight later. Stablemate of Teelyna, who achieved six non-completions herself, a serious indictment of connections. *P. Riddick — Gelligaer F.* 34 (MO), 275 (Cf), 479 (Cf), 597 (Cf), 819 (Cf), 1051 (Cf), 1295 (Cf), 1450 (Cf), 1612 (Cf).

COMMUTER COUNTRY ..10-2.. 10 gr.g. Town And Country — Landed Lady (Realm) r141dp6. Workmanlike good-bodied half-brother to Landed Gent and Gennaro. Dam won at 5f. NH FLAT '96 r1 p0. NH '97 r3 p0. P-t-P/HUNT CH '98/9 r12 w6 (inc 2 Confineds) p3 (2nds, fence last once; and inc Hunt Ch); fell 2. Most progressive in '99, and landed a five-timer under Alan Coe (who lost the mount after one ride in 2000), but despite winning a Fakenham Hunter Chase did not quite live up to expectations in 2000. Appeared to go wrong on the firm ground at Higham when odds-on in a three-runner race in March, and dropped away tamely when bidding to emulate his Fakenham exploits a month later. Later disqualified from the Hunter Chase and the owner fined £600, for testing positive to banned substances (traced to a medication being given to another horse in the yard). Good enough to win more races if he returns healthy. Appears to act on any going. Wears a cross-noseband, and has been tried in a nearside pricker. *Mrs P.K.J. Brightwell — Essex & Suffolk.* 130 (CMod), 241 (C), 318 (Cf), 585 (2m5f110yH), 757 (O), 1155 (2m5f110yH).

COMPUTER PICKINGS ..9-5.. 14 b.m. Taufan (USA) — Ricciola (USA) (Stage Door Johnny) p. Lengthy well-made sister to Irish flat and jumping winner, Back Door Johnny. IRISH P-t-P '92/3 r6 w1 (mares Maiden) p1 (2nd); pulled up 3. NH '95 r4 p0. P-t-P '96/9 r14 w1 (Members) p5 (3 3rds); pulled up 2, and unseated 1. Won a three-finisher Members at Witton Castle in '96, and has run well in defeat there on three occasions since, but always has brief campaigns, and pulled up after a mile on her reappearance at her favourite track. Will struggle to gain another deserved success at 14. *F. Crawford — Zetland.* 137 (R).

CONCERTO COLLONGES (FR) ..10-8.. 11 br.g. El Badr — Mariane Collonge (FR) (Cap Martin FR) 423519. Very tall rangy brother or half-brother to 4 winners in France, including useful jumper, Baccarat Collonges. FRENCH NH '95 r3 p0 (pulled up only Chse - blinkered; raced in provinces). P-t-P '97/9 r15 w7 (inc 2 Opens) p5 (4 2nds, beaten short-head once, and last once). A huge strapping horse who looks as though he could jump and gallop all day, and needed every yard of the 3m2f trip to get up near the line when winning a Carlisle Hunter Chase, but surprisingly never got involved at Cheltenham. Enjoyed a vintage '99, but likes mud a commodity he could not really find in 2000, and can win again when conditions are really testing. Jumps for fun, and is a fine ride for Robert Hartley, who has done the steering with aplomb. Do all Hartleys have three initials? *O.R.M. Hartley — Middleton (Annabelle Armitage).* 171 (O), 279 (O), 422 (3m5fO), 999 (4m1fMO), 1154 (3m2fH), 1338 (4m1fH).

CONNEMARA FREEWAY ..—.. 9 br.g. Deltic (USA) — Mandula (Mandamus) p. Big half-brother to Double Lace and Dula Model. NH '99 (from J. Neville's) r1 p0. Attracted market support at Bitterley and made a brief forward move after two miles, but was soon beaten and pulled up (wore bandages). Good to see that Mrs O'Toole has discovered a trainer that she can really empathise with. *Mrs T. O'Toole — Glamorgan (John Thomas).* 994 (OMa).

CONNIE FOLEY ..8-12.. 15 b.g. Floriferous — Get A Bike (Orchardist) pf6. Tall strong. Dam won 2m4f Hdle in Ireland. IRISH P-t-P '92/3 r6 p2 (2nds); pulled up 3, and fell 1. NH '95 r1 p0 (pulled up). P-t-P/HUNT CH '94/5 and '97/9 r27 w1 (Members) p9 (6 3rds, remote twice); failed to finish 11 (on floor 7). Gained his only success in a farcical race at Ashorne in '97 (five of the seven who set out slipped up or ran out, and the saddle went askew on the other finisher), but well beaten in the current yard, and his jumping remains as slipshod as ever. *Miss N.J. Rudge — Farmers Bloodhounds.* 190 (M), 611 (C), 1191 (L).

CONNOR (U) ..—.. 11 b.g. Dixie — Oakley Easter Fun (unknown) u. Two fences adrift when parting with the rider at halfway in his Members. *J. Galbraith — Buccleuch.* 712 (M).

CONNORS ..10-2.. 8 b.g. Persian Mews — Kindly (Tarqogan) 2p. Workmanlike half-brother to Ask Me Kindly (IRE), to jumping winner, Ghia Gneuiagh, to successful Chaser, Fire At Will, and to an Irish NH flat winner. NH FLAT '99 (from E. James') r1 p0. Showed plenty of promise when beaten half a length by Wejem in a Restricted, but sadly suffered injuries which were to claim his life in a Maiden. *Dr P.P. Brown — Berkeley (Dick Baimbridge).* 336 (R), 616 (CMa).

CONQUER (IRE) ..10-4.. 6 b.g. Phardante (FR) — Tullow Performance (Gala Performance USA) 1. Small compact half-brother to jumping winners, Cuilin Bui (in Ireland) and Crank Shaft, to an Irish Hurdles winner, and to Irish NH flat winner, Ardkilly Eclipse. Dam, half-sister to Pride of Tullow (qv '91 Annual), won 2 NH flat and 2 Hdles (2-3m) in Ireland. Bought Doncaster, May for 7000. Spurted clear to win a youngsters Maiden on firmish at Bitterley by an impressive 25 lengths and the same, and reported to have changed hands again to a patron of Henry Daly's yard soon after (presumably for a healthy profit). Looks to be the type who could be speedy enough to score over Hurdles, and should be worth following. *M.G. Rimell — Heythrop.* 989 (OMa).

CONQUER THE KILT ..9-8.. 10 b.g. El Conquistador — Kilton Joy (Sir Nulli) 1u4p3. Lengthy half-brother to Trust The Kilt. Dam was remote 3rd in a Point for Franey Matthews. Grandam, Kilton Dee, was a useless Pointer, but is half-sister to Kilton Jim, who wasn't. Great-grandam, Kilton Hill, won 2m4f Hunt Ch and 5 Points and placed 13. NH FLAT '96/7 r2 p0. NH '97 r4 p0 (last, pulled up 2, and fell at 1st in Hdles). P-t-P '99 r6 p5 (3rds); and unseated 1. Aided and abetted by an official at Milborne St Andrew on his reappearance as it seemed as if he had been beaten the minimum margin by Little Native, but was ajudged to have shared the spoils. Deserved his slice of luck for his previous consistency, but promptly let supporters down on several occasions, and continues to prove disappointing. Prone to errors. Reported to be a weaver and box-walker. *F.G. Matthews — Blackmore & Sparkford V.* 212 (CfMa), 259 (C), 639 (I), 1095 (R), 1280 (R).

D'ESTRUVAL (FR) ..10-6.. 11 b.g. Synefos (USA) — Barbara Conti (ITY) (Teodoro Trivulzio) p. Rangy. FRENCH FLAT r3 p0. FRENCH NH '93/4 r17 w2 (2m1f Chses at Lyons) p6. NH '95/8 r28 w5 (2m4f-2m5f Chses, inc 4-timer '96) p6. P-t-P/HUNT CH '99 r6 w1 (2m4f Hunt Ch) p4 (2 2nds, beaten shorthead once, inc 3 Hunt Chses); and unseated 1. A 2m4f specialist under Rules, and was well ridden by the veteran Terry Smith when lasting home in a Ludlow Hunter Chase over that distance in '99 — his first success for three years. Has struggled with a wind infirmity recently (runs tubed), and failed to reappear after a lifeless display at Warwick in May. Gained all bar one of his English wins on a right-handed track. Visored once under Rules, and was blinkered in France. *T.E.G. Smith — Staff College.* 1447 (2m4fH).

CONTRADICT ..10-2.. 11 b.g. Derring Rose — Contrary Lady (Conwyn) 52p1p. Good-topped half-brother to Bolshie Baron (qv). P-t-P/HUNT CH '96/9 r19 w2 (Maiden and Restricted) p2 (2nds); failed to finish 13 (fell/unseated 5, and ran out 1). Thoroughly inconsistent, but loves a Flete Park mudbath, and recorded his third success under such conditions when responding to Sarah Gaisford's urgings at the Modbury fixture. Contradictory, and had earlier let supporters down under similar conditions, and taking him to Exeter for a firm ground Hunter Chase was pointless. May find another minor race, but will need to be sensibly placed. *Miss S. Gaisford — Dart V. & S. Pool H. (Sarah Waugh).* 310 (I), 651 (M), 1045 (L), 1256 (Inr), 1432 (3m1fH).

COOGEE BILL (IRE) ..9-11.. 7 ch.g. Phardante (FR) — Laois Story (Royal Match) ffp6p. Smallish half-brother to Irish Chasing winner, Macaunta. Dam is half-sister to Win The Match (qv '93 Annual). P-t-P '99 r1 w1 (Maiden). NH Mar/Apr '00 r3 p0 (pulled up in 3m110y Nov Hdle: ur & bolted bef start, bhnd, t.o & pu 2 out; 6th in 3m1f110y Nov Hdle: chsd ldrs, in tch to 8, t.o; and pulled up in 3m Nov Hdle: bhnd, t.o when pu & dismd 2 out). Overcame some hairy jumps to land a touch on his racecourse debut at Chaddesley, but hit the deck on his reappearance, and followed suit in spectacular style at the open ditch in front of the stands at Huntingdon on his Hunter Chase debut. Wisely switched to hurdles after, but further embarrassments followed (dropped the rider and bolted once), and appeared to go wrong at Towcester in April. *G. McCourt — Cotswold V.F.* 16 (R), 151 (3mH).

COOKIE BOY ..9-7.. 10 b.g. Ra Nova — Gypsy Heather (Bivouac) u755p2p. Lengthy half-brother to Border Banker. Dam, half-sister to Border Burg, won 2 Points and placed 5. Grandam, Border Knife, was 3rd in a Maiden. P-t-P '96/8 (for breeder, Mr J.S. Delahooke & Mr A.W. Scott-Harden) r19 w2 (Maiden and Members) p7 (3 2nds); pulled up 5, and fell/unseated 3. Successful once apiece '97/8, but off the course since, and unimproved on his return. Not disgraced in Restricted company, but it looks odds against his winning one, as he lacks any acceleration and occasionally looks short on stamina. Presumably bought as a schoolmaster for Anita Davies, but she gave up the ride after toppling off at Weston Park. *Miss A. Davies — W. Salop (Gordie Edwards).* 292 (M), 567 (R), 589 (R), 864 (R), 1129 (R), 1322 (R), 1411 (R).

COOL CHARACTER (IRE) ..9-8.. 13 b.g. Furry Glen — Raise The Standard (Distinctly USA) 4524p. Workmanlike brother to jumping winner, Change The Act, and half-brother to 2 winners. IRISH NH FLAT '92/3 r4 w1 p1 (2nd). IRISH NH '93/4 r8 w1 (2m Hdle) p4; pulled up only Ch — bbv. NH '94/7 r19 p2 (2nds). P-t-P '98/9 r9 w2 (Members and Confined) p4 (3 3rds, last once; and 2nd of 3). Outstayed Coach to win at Badbury Rings in '99 (rated 10-3), and has provided Tanya Newman with both her successes to date, but only managed to get competitive in his Members in 2000, and proved more one-paced than ever. Not without his problems in the past (has broken blood vessels and has had a wind operation), but has always excelled in the jumping stakes, and makes an ideal ride for a novice. *Miss T. Newman — Seavington.* 67 (L), 211 (Cnr), 519 (M), 768 (Cf), 1432 (3m1fH).

COOL CLOWN ..9-11.. 14 b.g. Idiot's Delight — Fabice (Vonice) 3222up. Leggy angular half-brother to Cool Work (qv). NH FLAT '92 r2 w1 p0; and ran out 1. NH '92/3 and '95/6 r11 w4 (Hdles, 2m5f-3m2f) p4 (2nds); pulled up 6th only Ch. P-t-P '98 r3 p1 (2nd); fell 1. A one time decent mudlark for Martin Pipe, but plagued by injuries, and was returning from another year off in 2000 — had gone wrong on firmish ground at Bratton Down in '98. Provided Ben Trickey with some decent rides when confined to easy surfaces, but beaten a minimum of 15 lengths, and is clearly feeling his age nowadays. Would have been a good Pointer had he been healthy, but unlikely to achieve much if he returns at 14. *B.J. Trickey — Devon & Somerset (Mike Trickey).* 160 (O), 355 (O), 1139 (Cf), 1304 (Cfnr), 1606 (O), 1653 (O).

COOLE ABBEY (IRE) ..11-3.. 9 b.g. Viteric (FR) — Eleanors Joy (Sheer Grit) 1122. Workmanlike compact. IRISH P-t-P '96/7 r6 p2 (just caught when neck 2nd once); pulled up 2, and fell 1. P-t-P/HUNT CH '98/9 r8 w3 (inc 2 Hunt Chses, 2m4f-3m) p3 (2nds in Hunt Chses); fell 1. Hailed as a future star after hammering Martha's Boy at Aintree in his first season Hunter Chasing, but seemed under a cloud for much of '99 and has not stood his racing very well. Won decisevely on his Musselburgh reappearance, but less convincing at Market Rasen, and found disappointingly little in the closing stages in two subsequent defeats. Likes to make the running, and has shown his versatility from between 2m4f and 3m2f on firm or in soft. Will still take all the beating if fully fit in 2001. *Mrs C. Moore — Percy.* 225 (3mH), 586 (3m1fH), 917 (3mH), 1345 (2m5fH).

COOLEST BY PHAR (IRE) ..—.. 9 ch.g. Phardante (FR) — Gemma's Fridge (Frigid Aire) ppp6pp. Plain unfurnished half-brother to Hurdles winner, Cool Dude, and to Irish NH flat and jumping winner, Storm Gem. Dam won NH flat and 2 2m Hdles in Ireland. IR 7000 4-y-o. NH FLAT '97 (debut for M. Sheppard) r2 p0 (swerved and unseated on debut). NH '98/9 (for Mrs P. Ford) r8 p0 (pulled up in 2 of 3 Hdles; last, pulled up 2, and fell/unseated 2 in Chses. A dire contestant who has been a remote last in just two completions from 11 attempts over fences. Wind problems stop him in his tracks — used to wear a tongue-strap, and tubing has brought no relief on his three most recent appearances (added blinkers on the latest). *F. Farrow & Mrs H. Goward — Kyre (Fred Farrow).* 321 (R), 416 (R), 551 (OMa), 844 (OMa), 1116 (OMa), 1292 (OMa).

COOLFLUGH HERO (IRE) ..10-0.. 10 b.g. Torus — Mossy's Niece (Le Bavard FR) 42432. Workmanlike lengthy half-brother to Calmos. IRISH P-t-P '96 r5 p1 (2nd); pulled up 2, and fell 1. P-t-P '97/9 (Crow-trained for Mrs R.H.W. Major) r11 w2 (Maiden and PPORA Restricted) p3 (2 2nds, last once); pulled up 5. A thorough stayer and suited by plenty of cut in the ground, but can be unco-operative, and is finding life in Ladies races rather too demanding. May consent to win another minor race, but don't bank on it. *E.H. Crow — L.E.A. Hopkins — N. Salop (Sheila Crow; Gordie Edwards).* 296 (I), 531 (L), 590 (L), 783 (I), 904 (L).

COOL KEVIN ..9-0.. 8 b.g. Sharkskin Suit (USA) — Cool Snipe (Dynastic) pu6. Small neat. NH FLAT '97 r4 p0. P-t-P '98/9 r7 p1 (2nd); pulled up 1, unseated 3. Hard to sit on in his debut season, and looked an awkward customer when tried in blinkers once (napped to the box-park), but had a couple of subsequent winners behind him when runner-up in '99, and might be capable of a small success himself if his prolonged absence is not a sign of trouble. *Mrs M.A. Kendall — Cumberland F.* 46 (OMa), 187 (OMa), 425 (CfMa).

COOL MILLION ..9-0.. 8 ch.g. Derrylin — Goldaw (Gala Performance USA) pp14. Small light-framed brother to Dunston Trigger, and half-brother to Rolled Gold (qv), and to NH flat and jumping winner,

Bobby Grant. Won a very slowly-run two-finisher youngsters Maiden on firmish at Charlton Horethorne, but evidently greatly flattered by a success, as he was 65 lengths last in a Restricted next time. Michael Miller managed to get him activated, but may be taking the mickey out of the delectable Lucy Bridges. *Mrs H.M. Bridges — Wilton.* 163 (R), 559 (R), 955 (OMa), 1280 (R).

PLATE 37   955 Blackmore & Sparkford Vale Open Maiden 56&7yo (Div 1): Worm's eye view of Cool Million (M. Miller), 1st, landing ahead of Ashloch (S. Kidston), pu   PHOTO: Bill Selwyn

COOL OFF ..—.. 10 b.g. Dubassoff (USA) — Cool Breeze (Windjammer USA) p. Half-brother to Dam The Breeze. Dam, sister to Cool Breeze (*qv* '91 Annual), pulled up in four Points for Gareth Allen. Jumped poorly on his belated debut until pulling up at halfway when tailed off. *G.E. Allen & D. Harris — Pentyrch (Ian Prichard).* 611 (C).

COOLREE (IRE) ..9-11.. 13 b.g. Gianchi — Positron (Free State) ppp4p1p6. Deep-girthed. Dam won at 7f. IRISH P-t-P '92/3 r5 w1 (5yo Mdn) p0; pulled up 2, fell and unseated. IRISH NH FLAT '93 r1 w1 (2m4f). IRISH NH '93 r5 p1 (2nd in Ch). NH '94/9 (from J. King's; wins previously from P. Nicholls') r32 w4 (2m4f-2m5f Chses) p10; broke blood vessel in '95; blinkered once in '97. Normally performs badly these days and is often forced to pull up, but managed to gain a first success for three years in his Members (the dangers conveniently fell by the wayside). Can cope with a sound surface, but is error-prone. Occasionally tongue-tied now. *B.T.R. Weston — Wilton (Mike Clutterbuck).* 35 (Cnr), 61 (MO), 200 (O), 325 (Cf), 474 (O), 762 (M), 1244 (MO), 1339 (2m5fH).

COOL SPELL ..—§.. 8 b.m. Gildoran — Ice Moon (Ballymoss) ppfpu. Lengthy half-sister to Arctic General and Jester's Moon. Dam was 2nd in 2 Points (promoted from 5th once). P-t-P '98 r1 p0 (ran out). A cowardly piece of work to date (has run out once and unseated when trying to do so once), and shows no sign of improvement. Kate Huckfield could not have picked a worse schoolmistress for her race-riding debut, but she seemed to have more control of her mount than some of the others who have ridden her, and after Cool Spell anything else she partners will feel like a stroll in the park. *S. Speller — N. Ledbury (Mike Bevan).* 337 (CfMa), 486 (R), 704 (OMa), 1085 (M), 1278 (OMa).

COOLVAWN LADY (IRE) ..10-9.. 12 b.m. Lancastrian — African Nelly (Pitpan) 22102b1p11p. Plain unfurnished sister to African Bride (IRE), and half-sister to Major Bert (IRE). NH '95, '97 and '99 (for K.A. Morgan; previously for W.R. Halliday; previously for Mrs N. Macauley) r8 p0 (7th, 10th, last, pulled up 4, and fell 1 in Chses). P-t-P/HUNT CH '94 and '96/9 (for Mr W.R. Halliday since '96) r53 w13 (inc 2m3f Hunt Ch, and 9 Opens) p19 (12 2nds, inc 4 Hunt Chses); failed to finish 9 (fell/unseated 4). An amazingly tough mare who took her winning total to 17 during her first season in Wales. Faced some straightforward tasks in Ladies races, but despatched her rivals with clinical efficiency, though once again Hunter Chasing proved beyond her capabilities. An excellent jumper who likes to be in front out of trouble (how ironic that she was brought down at Aintree), and seemed better than ever in the new yard. *D. Brace — Llangeinor.* 1 (C), 272 (L), 346 (L), 584 (3m2f110yH), 644 (Cm), 921 (2m6fH), 946 (L), 1022 (3mH), 1402 (MO), 1570 (MO), 1648 (3mH).

COOL WAGER ..10-2.. 9 br.g. Arctic Lord — Gamblingway (Gambling Debt) 13. Sturdy compact owner-bred half-brother to Gilded Way. Dam, half-sister to The Nations Way, *qv* '94 Annual), was heavily backed when winning a Restricted (her only Point). NH FLAT '98 r1 p0. NH '99 (for R. Buckler) r4 p0. Of no account under Rules, but better in Points, and sustained a steady gallop in the lead throughout the final two miles when scoring at Bratton Down. Subsequently ran well when six lengths third in a warmly-contested Restricted on the same course, and should be able to win in similar company at least. *Miss H. Day — W. Somerset.* 1565 (OMa), 1650 (R).

COOL WEATHER (IRE) ..—§.. 13 b.g. Kemal (FR) — Arctic Tack (Arctic Slave) 4u6. Strong-topped half-brother to Oakprime and Sharp Opinion, to successful Chaser, Pond House (IRE), and to top-class Irish NH flat and jumping winner, Soft Day. NH '94/9 (for N. Hawke; previously for C. Popham, bought for 8200; previously for P. Cheesbrough) r37 p10 (Chses); inc Sells; only ran in 2 Hdles, both in '98. Came closest to scoring under Rules when half a length second, but unreliable and faint-hearted, and a prolific loser who pulled up on his final three attempts. Finished three fences last twice for Brett Parsons in 2000, whilst Peter Thorner (carrying 13st4lb) soon fell off. Hopefully connections will not be bringing any more horses to the races in such a disgraceful state. *P.J. Thorner — Mendip F. (Jo Yates).* 356 (Inr), 731 (M), 957 (CfMa).

COOL WORK ..10-0.. 13 b.g. Teamwork — Fabice (Vonice) u62s. Big half-brother to Cool Clown. Dam won 3 Points and placed 4; her sire Pointed in '82, and her dam, Fab Surprise, failed to finish in 5 Points (ran out/refused 3). P-t-P '96 and '98/9 r15 w1 (Maiden) p3 (2 3rds); pulled up 2, unseated 2, ran out 1, and refused 1. A thorough stayer, but predictably struggling to add to his Flete Park success in which he was left clear at the last, and has failed to add a Restricted in six attempts. A fair second in a Mollington stamina test, but otherwise failed to beat a single another rival in 2000, and makes limited appeal. Can be safely ignored when owner-ridden. *Capt. B.D.A. Ridge — N. Cotswold (Giles Smyly).* 75 (I), 247 (R), 429 (C), 1189 (M).

COOL YULE (IRE) ..10-10.. 13 ch.g. Good Thyne (USA) — Sleigh Lady (Lord Gayle USA) u215. Lengthy attractive hobdayed. IRISH P-t-P '93 and '95/6 r15 w1 (6yo&up Maiden) p5 (beaten head by The Parish Pump once); pulled up 2, and fell/unseated 4 (at last once — would have won). P-t-P/HUNT CH '97/9 r14 w2 (3m2f Hunt Ch and 3m5f Open) p3 (2 3rds); and neck 2nd in Hunt Chses); unseated 1. An out-and-out stayer and has won the last two runnings of the 3m5f Tynedale Open, but something of an enigma, and often needs rousting along from an early stage. Ran blinkered in his latest success, but their effect already seems to have worn off, and a beaten favourite for the third time in his career on his subsequent start. His latest winning pilot Wilson Renwick is outstanding, and looks set for a bright career in the paid ranks. *R.J. Kyle — Jedforest.* 107 (M), 186 (O), 422 (3m5fO), 1160 (O).

COPASTROP ..9-6.. 9 b.g. Deltic (USA) — Erica May (Streak) 232u. Lengthy good-topped owner-bred. Dam is half-sister to 6 Pointers, including Campello Boy (*qv* '90 Annual). P-t-P '99 r2 p0 (ran out 1, and pulled up 1). Lives up to his name in the starting area, but has done little wrong when he gets going, and beaten a maximum of six lengths in his placings. Something of a live wire and has been taken to post early, but should find a race in 2001. *T.B. & Miss K. Stevens — Devon & Somerset (Stuart Stevens).* 562 (CfMa), 728 (R), 1100 (OMa), 1369 (M).

COPPER COIL ..10-2.. 11 ch.g. Undulate (USA) — April Rose (Wollow) p2114u1433. Strong compact. NH FLAT '95 (for A.P. Jones) r2 p0. NH '95/9 (from M. Pitman's; 2 wins previously from M. Pipe's; 1 win previously from R. Buckler's; 1 win previously from W.G.M. Turner's) r37 w4 (2m4f-3m1f Hdles) p9; (inc 26½l 3rd once from 6 Chses; inc 3rd in Sell Hdle). Did not have much of a strike rate under Rules, but absolutely hacked up twice from Martin Pipe's in May '98. Left him after one more run (the owner likes to ring the changes with his trainers), and was becoming disappointing until his attentions were turned to Points. Found two soft opportunities in Military events at Larkhill, and also looked like scoring on the course previously until overwhelmed after the final fence by Bavard Dieu. Inconsistent, but saved his best performance of the year for Dunthrop, where he landed a Confined in game fashion. A sketchy jumper of regulation fences. *R.A. Lloyd — Beaufort (Richard Smith).* 10 (O), 62 (Cf), 259 (C), 456 (C), 631 (MO), 800 (3m110yH), 1016 (Cf), 1134 (Cnr), 1346 (3m1f110yH), 1597 (MO).

COPPER THISTLE (IRE) ..10-13.. 13 b.g. Ovac (ITY) — Phantom Thistle (Deep Run) 1111111121. Workmanlike half-brother to Leinthall Thistle and Crafty Phantom (IRE), to Chasing winner Indulge (IRE), and to Hurdles winner, Chilled (IRE). P-t-P/HUNT CH '93/9 r48 w25 (inc 3m Hunt Ch and 13 Opens; 5-timer in '95, hat-trick and 5-timer in '99) p16 (8 3rds, inc 2 Hunt Chses, and last once); unseated 1, and pulled up 1. The closest thing to a machine running in Points at the moment and churns out identical performances week in week out with metronomic regularity. Has turned Richard Hunnisett from a great enthusiast into an effective pilot, and the combination have made harmonious music on 22 occasions together. Had his run of 13 straight wins halted by Dawn Alert, but only by the minimum margin, having lost the advantage of the inside at a crucial stage on ground firmer than he finds ideal. A brilliant jumper, and fenced immaculately when the impressive winner of the Land Rover Final on his latest appearance (only his second success over the bigger obstacles), and has the heart of a lion. Won races in five different calendar months in 2000, and yet another tribute to the skills of Caroline Bailey. What price another long sequence? *R.S. Hunnisett — Pytchley (Caroline Bailey).* 85 (O), 195 (O), 320 (O), 511 (O), 870 (O), 1008 (O), 1182 (O), 1265 (O), 1381 (O), 1532 (3m1fH).

COPPER THORN ..8-13.. 8 b.m. North Col — Copperclown (Spartan General) p5ppu55. Robust half-sister to Copper Song, Singing Kettle (dam of See More Action, *qv* 2000 Annual), True Tip, Singing Clown, Copper Pan, Copper Bank, Sparkling Clown, Skylark Song and Copper Ridge, and to winning Chaser, True Clown. Dam, half-sister to Priceless Clown (won 5 races in 25 days when rated 11-7 at 6), pulled up in a Point. P-t-P '99 r3 p0 (pulled up 2, and unseated 1). Has shown speed for in excess of two miles on several occasions, but only once better than last to date, and has little respect for the obstacles. Might yet be capable of better, especially if she becomes more streamlined — carries plenty of condition. *Mrs A. Arthers & Mrs C. Boyes — Atherstone (Sam Arthers).* 122 (OMa), 233 (OMa), 548 (CfMa), 906 (CfMa), 1070 (2m4fOMa), 1270 (OMa), 1420 (OMa).

COPPER VALLEY ..9-2.. 8 ch.m. Nearly A Hand — Culm Valley (Port Corsair) u3. Small neat half-sister to Valley's Choice (*qv*). P-t-P '99 r1 p0 (pulled up). Has shown a hint of ability twice (32 lengths last of three on her latest outing), but clearly hard to train, and failed to reappear following two spins at Larkhill in January. *C.J. Down — E. Devon.* 12 (OMa), 58 (OMa).

COPTIC DANCER ..7-7.. 12 b.m. Sayf El Arab (USA) — Copt Hall Royale (Right Tack) pp4pp. Compact half-sister to Royal Pageant and Prospecting, and to 2 flat winners abroad. Dam won 3 flat, 8-10f. P-t-P '96/8 r3 w1 (Maiden) p0; pulled up 2. Emerged just once a year in her first three seasons winning an awful Maiden at Cottenham in '97, but ran — and jumped — like a crab when managing a full campaign in 2000. Can take a strong hold, but looked badly wrong on occasions this season, and clearly troubled. Jumped markedly right-handed when visored on her last two starts. Obviously flattered by a win. *J.J. Greenwood — W. Norfolk.* 416 (R), 554 (R), 773 (R), 1038 (R), 1285 (M).

CORBLEU (IRE) ..9-12.. 11 b.g. Corvaro (USA) — Another Daisy (Major Point) 33f42. Small. Dam is half-sister to Ballybrit (*qv* '99 Annual). NH FLAT '95 r1 p0. NH '95/9 (for S. Bell) r19 w2 (3m Hdle and 2m3f Ch) p5 (inc 3rd in Sell Hdle); ridden by Robert Walford once. Scored twice in '97, but is slow and moderate. A safe jumper who made a competent schoolmaster for Mark Walford, and would certainly have won a bad Open which was run in a very slow time at Dingley had his partner been more experienced (was catching Andrew Sansome after the last, but had let him steal a decisive march). *Mrs G.B. Walford — Middleton (Tim Walford).* 996 (M), 1073 (O), 1151 (O), 1578 (O), 1666 (O).

CORKERS FLAME (IRE) ..9-11.. 10 b.g. Corvaro (USA) — Preflame (Prefairy) p636p. Dam won NH flat and 2 Hdles (2m-2m5f) in Ireland. IRISH NH FLAT '96 r1 p0. IRISH NH '96 r3 p0. IRISH P-t-P '97 r7 w1 (6yo&up Maiden) p3; pulled up 1, and unseated 1. P-t-P '98/9 r4 p1 (last of 2); pulled up 2. Won on top-of-the-ground in Ireland, but lightly raced since, and wasting his time contesting Hunter Chases. Not disgraced at Brampton Bryan, and should be aimed at Restricteds over an easy three miles. *P. Grindey — Saddleworth.* 464 (3m110yH), 861 (C), 1129 (R), 1343 (3m110yH), 1559 (3m110yH).

CORMEEN LORD (IRE) ..10-4.. 12 ch.g. Mister Lord (USA) — Sand-Pit Cross (Pitpan) 623473. Tall half-brother to Ink Flicker (IRE). Dam won an Irish Point. P-t-P '96/9 r16 w4 (inc Confined) p6 (4 3rds); pulled up 1. Romped to an emphatic and unbeaten hat-trick in '97, but disappointing since, and has managed to win just one of his subsequent 13 races. Failed to finish within ten lengths of the winner in any of his 2000 runs, and has developed into a bit of a plodder whose once strong finish seems a thing of the past. Tried in a nearside pricker once. Has few miles on the clock, and might revive if the key to his downturn in fortunes can be found. *J.C. Sharp & Mrs C. Harris — Woodland Pytchley (John Sharp).* 115 (CCf), 288 (CMod), 370 (C), 905 (C), 1006 (Cf), 1381 (O).

CORNER BOY ..10-5.. 14 br.g. Callernish — Rescued (Sir Herbert) 2. Tall strong half-brother to Smoker and Consomme, and to Irish Pointing winner, Brandy Cross (IRE). IRISH P-t-P '93 r3 w2 p0; pulled up 1. NH '93/6 r13 w6 (4 Hdles, 2m4f-3m, inc £8032 prize, and 2 Chses, 3m1f-3m2f) p3 (2nds, beaten head once). P-t-P/HUNT CH '97/9 r10 w5 (Ladies) p3 (2 3rds, inc Hunt Ch); unseated 1. A classy performer over the years, but has never stood much racing (eight of his 13 NH runs came in '94), and failed to reappear after chasing home Imperial Dawn at Southwell. Frequently let down by his jumping, and his tendency to go right-handed seemed more prevelant than ever. Has been retired. *Mrs E.W. Wilson — Brocklesby (Jill Dawson).* 368 (L).

CORNISH FORT ..9-8.. 10 b.m. Shaab — Celtic Fort (Celtic Cone) 2p. Good-bodied. Dam is half-sister to Passenger Flight (*qv* '91 Annual). Grandam, Fort Lodge, won 3 Chses (3m-3m2f), 2 Hunt

Chses and 15 Points and placed 10 for Paul Tylor. P-t-P '99 r4 p2 (2nds); pulled up 1. The subject of sustained market support when runner-up twice in '99 (beaten just half a length once), and punters had their fingers burnt again on her reappearance when Dedalus was in a going mood, but pulled up and dismounted at an early stage at Lifton subsequently and may never gain her just reward. A well-bred mare, and surely has a future in the paddocks if she cannot continue her racing career. *P.A. Tylor — Stevenstone (Keith Cumings).* 857 (CfMa), 1521 (CfMa).

CORNISH HOPE ..—§§.. 7 b.g. Henbit (USA) — Sleepers (Swing Easy USA) pRR. Small. Dam won 6 5f races, one at Cagnes, and including 4-timer at 6 (then Irish-trained, inc 2 wins there). Bought Ascot, June for 1300. Has no steering, and his domination of Sue Young is becoming increasingly pronounced. Has been taken to post early. *K.F. Fisher — E. Cornwall (Robin Linne).* 165 (Cf), 311 (CfMa), 721 (CfMa).

CORNISH WAYS ..—.. 13 b.g. Foolish Ways — Decoyanne (Decoy Boy) ppp. Strong-topped quite attractive half-brother to Master Decoy, Chubby Morton, and to Chasing winner, Cantoris Frater. P-t-P/HUNT CH '93/9 r27 w2 (Maiden and Intermediate) p4 (3 2nds, last once); failed to finish 19 (fell 3). Won once apiece '94 and '96, but has extended his losing sequence to 18, and has only completed once (when last) for the current yard. Ended '96 lame, and stands few outings. Tried in blinkers on his final start, and no longer warrants a rating. *Miss D.L. Penwill — S. Tetcott (F. Penwill).* 1047 (Cf), 1261 (Cf), 1514 (Cf).

COSA FUAIR (IRE) ..9-0.. 11 b.g. Roselier (FR) — Bold And True (Sir Herbert) 3p54. Tall rangy half-brother to Bold Irene (IRE) (*qv*). NH FLAT '95 r1 p0. NH '96/8 r8 p2 (2nd in Hdle, and 3rd in Ch). P-t-P/HUNT CH '99 r5 p0 (4th thrice, 5th, and pulled up 1). Pulls like stink and can go a merry gallop, but has no stamina and continues to prove impossible to place. *Mrs P. Sykes — C. Jarvis — S. Salop (-; Neil King).* 616 (CMa), 906 (CfMa), 1035 (Cnr), 1115 (OMa).

COSY RIDE (IRE) ..7-12§.. 9 b.g. King's Ride — Fortysumthin (IRE) (Forties Field FR) pfuR735. Small sturdy. NH FLAT '96/7 r3 p1 (2nd). NH '98/9 (for N. Twiston-Davies, blinkered last 3) r5 p0; Sells last 2. Bought Malvern, Oct for 800. A bad animal with a wayward streak, and it is surprising anybody agrees to partner him. His least pathetic performance was when 42 lengths third after almost falling at the 12th. Ended his miserable season lame. *J.M.B. Pugh — Llangeinor (Bill Pugh).* 595 (R), 823 (CfMa), 1056 (CfMa), 1454 (OMa), 1615 (R), 1661 (OMa), 1675 (OMa).

COTTAGE LIGHT ..7-7§§.. 13 b.g. Lighter — Flavias Cottage (Marcus Superbus) ppp6. Big strong lengthy half-brother to Cottage Blaze (dam of Blazing Miracle, *qv* 2000 Annual) and Ross Cottage. Dam, half-sister to tragic Cheltenham Gold Cup hero, Tied Cottage, was a useless Pointer — like most of her numerous other relatives. P-t-P/HUNT CH '94/6 and '98/9 (for Mrs S.M. Foale) r16 p2; failed to finish 11 (refused 1, and ran out 1). Ruined a line of ten consecutive 'p's when forced home 66 lengths behind the winner in his Members on his final appearance. Normally blinkered, famously unco-operative, and not worth bothering with again (stable-mate of Caballus, so the owner can certainly pick 'em). *B. Sarson — Warwicks (Nigel Ridout).* 792 (OMa), 1012 (CfMa), 1147 (OMa), 1438 (M).

COTTESMORE ..—.. 10 b.g. Broadsword (USA) — Celestial Bride (Godswalk USA) r. Workmanlike brother to Astra Libra and Saundby Swordsman, to Chasing winner, Guard Of Honour, and to jumping winner Shamana, and half-brother to NH flat and Hurdles winner, Sevso. NH '96/7 (from Mrs A. Johnson) r4 p0 (inc pulled up, and fell). Refused at the fourth with a jockey who was having his first ride. *Miss A.J. Foster — Thurlow.* 1292 (OMa).

COUGAR RUN (IRE) ..10-0.. 10 b brg. Commanche Run — Orra Beg (Dear Gazelle) 2. Big strong half-brother to Golden Gaze. Dam is half-sister to Odysseus (*qv* '97 Annual). NH FLAT '97 r1 p0. NH '98 (blinkered final) r3 p0 (tailed off and pulled up in 3 Chses). Gave a much improved display when chasing home King Torus over 2m4f at Fontwell, but was hanging in the closing stages, and promptly vanished again. Clearly has major problems which will not go away. *Mrs C. Zetter-Wells — Chid, Lec & Cowdray (Lawrence Wells).* 681 (2m4fH).

COULTON ..11-5.. 14 ch.g. Final Straw — Pontevecchio Due (Welsh Pageant) 11116. Strong attractive half-brother to flat winner, Pontevecchio Moda, and to a winner in Germany. Dam won 4 flat, 6-9f. 10,500y. NH FLAT '91 r2 p1 (2nd). NH '91/9 (8 wins for Oliver Sherwood; previously r47 w16 (5 Hdles, 2m-2m4f, and 11 Chses, 2m-2m5f, inc 4-timer in '95) p11; fell/unseated 8. A sensationally successful performer over the years, and has earned a total of £228,249, with the finest hours including the Cathcart Chase, the Martel Aintree Chase and the Desert Orchid Pattern Chase at Wincanton (way back in '93, his then trainer Mick Easterby was predicting that Coulton would be the next Dessie!). Had become a shadow of his former self under Rules, and unplaced eight times since December '97 (had not scored since October '96) prior to his heartwarming renaissance in Hunter Chases. Took his total haul of victories to 20 with four very resolute displays of galloping, but then contested the first ever Handicap, and seemed to have gone over the top when giving a lack-lustre display (was trying to concede 10 pounds or far more all round). Acts on any going and can jump well, but has always been prone to blunders. Does not stay three miles, and invariably kept to the shorter trips now. Had a split tendon operation in

'97, and it says much for his courage that he has eventually managed to battle back. *M.G. St Quinton — V.W.H. (Oliver Sherwood).* 226 (2m4f110yH), 384 (2m3f110yH), 470 (2m4f110yH), 1339 (2m5fH), 1600 (2m5f110yH).

PLATE 38 470 Dick McCreery HC, Sandown: The magnificent Coulton (O. Ellwood), 1st, stands right off at the 4th behind Noyan (Miss L. Horner), 2nd PHOTO: Steven Cargill

COUNSEL ..10-0.. 6 ch.g. Most Welcome — My Polished Corner (IRE) (Tate Gallery USA) uuf11. Good-topped rangy half-brother to flat and Hurdles winner, Safecracker. FLAT (for D. Chapman, bought for 500; previously for K. Burke; previously for C. Brittain; blinkered 1) r25 p3 (2nd, beaten neck once, just caught). His career over obstacles got off to a very bad start when he fell or unseated thrice consecutively (got no further than the 13th), but suddenly seemed to get the message, and won two minor races decisively. Now putting his flat speed to good use, and could be in line for several more successes over the coming years. All will be wishing Alan Walter, who was so cruelly stricken in 2000, a speedy and full recovery. *A. & Mrs J. Walter — Taunton V.H. (Alan Walter).* 106 (OMa), 201 (L), 352 (CfMa), 540 (OMa), 850 (R).

COUNTESS ROSIE ..8-2.. 7 gr.m. Le Solaret (FR) — Sea Countess (Ercolano USA) pp8. Rangy half-sister to In The Van (qv). Bought Doncaster, Nov for 1600. Sixty-five lengths last when completing, and needs to learn to jump much more fluently. *D.F. Smith — Hurworth.* 627 (OMa), 809 (OMa), 1032 (OMa).

COUNT HENRY ..—.. 13 br.g. Country Retreat — Adams Pride (Proud Aly) pp. Dam was poor 3rd in Restricted. Pulled up after less than two miles twice, and is not a racehorse. *Mrs E. Keir — Grafton.* 81 (CCfMa), 197 (CfMa).

COUNT OF FLANDERS (IRE) ..9-13.. 11 b.g. Green Desert (USA) — Marie De Flandre (FR) (Crystal Palace FR) 2f333u. Compact attractive brother to an Italian flat winner, and half-brother to 4 flat winners (one in France), including Sharaf and Red Bordeaux, and Solo Mio (IRE) (also successful in Germany, and in English Hurdle). Dam won 2 French flat at around 10f. 92,000f. FLAT (won for M. Stoute) r4 w1 (10f) p0. NH '96 and 98 (for K. Morgan) r10 w1 (2m2f Sell Hdle) p4 (3rds). A fair galloper who was placed behind some useful performers in Ladies Opens (including Pharare, and Cittadino twice), but finished 26 lengths or more adrift on three other occasions. Deserves a small success, but the problem is that he does not really stay three miles, and is always struggling in the closing stages. *Mrs A.P. Balderstone — Quorn.* 118 (L), 240 (L), 442 (L), 772 (L), 1266 (L), 1417 (L).

COUNTRY BARLE ..9-7.. 13 b.g. Town And Country — Pelant Barle (Prince Barle) f13. Well-made good-looking half-brother to Celtic Barle, The Braughing Baron and Marney Barle. Dam won Maiden and 7 Ladies (inc 2 hat-tricks) and placed 12 for Hugh Hodge. NH FLAT '93 r1 p0. NH

'95 and '98 r4 p0; pulled up 1, and fell 1. P-t-P '97 and '99 r5 p3 (2 3rds); fell/unseated 2. Thoroughly deserved his Horseheath success, but has been a nightmare to train (broke an elbow in '97), and has never managed more than four outings in a year. Prone to make mistakes, but jumped with more care when visored on his last two outings. Will probably struggle in Restricted company if returning. *Mrs I. Hodge — Puckeridge (Hugh Hodge).* 20 (OMa), 97 (OMa), 321 (R).

COUNTRY BUZZARD ..—.. 7 ch.g. Buzzards Bay — Countrypop (Country Retreat) pu. Sturdy owner-bred half-brother to Country Concorde. Dam is half-sister to Sunday Champers. Grandam, Poppywee, won three Points (two Opens) and 3rd twice. Great-grandam, Carnival Candy, won a Maiden and 3rd. NH FLAT '98 (from C.H. Jones') r3 p0. Desperately slow in Bumpers, and looked awful in Points (tailed off and pulled up after two miles; and unseated at the first when blinkered). *R.N. Coles — Heythrop (Ben Lay).* 434 (OMa), 972 (OMa).

COUNTRY CAPTAIN ..9-12.. 8 ch.g. Broadsword (USA) — Royal Chitchat (Le Bavard FR) u. Big strong owner-bred. Dam is half-sister to Simply Joyful (*qv*). P-t-P '99 r3 p1 (2nd); and pulled up 2. Ran well after two quiet schools when runner-up at Bratton Down on his final start in '99, but collapsed onto the ninth fence at Larkhill on his reappearance and sadly expired — Les Jefford was lucky to escape serious injury. *Mrs E.M. Charlton — Cotley (Philip Greenwood).* 57 (OMa).

COUNTRY CONCORDE ..—.. 11 b.g. Ilium — Countrypop (Country Retreat) fp. Compact owner-bred half-brother to Country Buzzard (*qv*). NH FLAT '94 r4 p1 (15/3rd). NH '96 and '98 (from C.H. Jones') r4 p0. Goes missing for about two years at a time, and is useless when he does appear. Remarkably, his record in 2000 mirrored that of Country Buzzard (also trained by Ben Lay), — pulled up after two miles, and fell at the first. *R.N. Coles — Heythrop (Ben Lay).* 249 (CfMa), 388 (I).

COUNTRY GEM ..9-6§§.. 10 b.g. Town And Country — Auto Elegance (Brave Shot) 4r2rr. Tall owner-bred half-brother to Jameswick and Russlers Rob. Dam won at 6f. P-t-P '97/9 r9 p3 (2 3rds, 2 fences last once); pulled up 3. Quickly became cheesed off with racing after a couple of decent placed efforts in '98, and looks for any opportunity to refuse these days. Proved at Lifton that he has the ability to win a race, but surely wrong, and blinkers have made no difference. *W.R. Britton — S. Tetcott.* 1049 (CfMa), 1263 (OMa), 1521 (CfMa), 1642 (M), 1676 (OMa).

COUNTRY LORD ..2-2§§.. 12 ch.g. Town And Country — Nearly A Lady (Nearly A Hand) p575u. Compact good-looking half-brother to Keep On Dreaming. NH FLAT r2 p0. NH '94 and '96 r2 p0 (last, and pulled up 1). P-t-P '95 and '97/9 r18 p1 (3rd); pulled up 5, refused 1, and fell 1. Remarkably inept, but his cries for retirement are still falling on deaf ears, and the bumbling riders clearly get some sort of weird gratification out of forcing him to compete (ridden in spurs in his last three starts). Hates jumping fences and usually clears them with feet to spare. Will hopefully not be seen again. *Mr & Mrs C. Walwin — V.W.H. (Sarah Walwin).* 476 (Cnr), 748 (M), 1207 (OMa), 1284 (OMa), 1493 (OMa).

COUNTRY MADAM ..—.. 10 b.m. Town And Country — Happy Manda (Mandamus) p. Quite attractive. Dam, half-sister to Happy Mannequin (*qv* '87 Season Annual), won 3m Hdle for Ken Nicholas, but failed to finish in 5 of 6 Points (2nd in the exception). Grandam, Happy Chat, won Maiden for his father-in-law. P-t-P '97/8 r4 p1 (2nd); pulled up 3. Not knocked about in her first three starts, but showed distinct signs of ability when runner-up on firmish at Black Forest Lodge in '98, but lamed herself in the process, and despite two years off went wrong again on her reappearance. *K.R.J. Nicholas — Tiverton.* 410 (OMa).

COUNTY BASH ..9-12.. 10 b.m. Shaab — Treloweth Julie (Flandre II) u4ffpp3522. Compact owner-bred. P-t-P '97/9 r12 w1 (Maiden) p1 (2nd); pulled up 2 and fell/unseated 3. Overcame major jumping problems to win easily at Kilworthy in '99, but again had trouble with the fences before finding her form in 2000. Looked to be coasting home in her Members until blundering the rider into orbit at the third last, and fell twice more before she managed to get her eye in. Knocking at the door in Restricteds (beaten a maximum of six lengths when placed in 2000), and her perseverance should pay off eventually. *Mrs W.S. Cook — N. Cornwall.* 99 (M), 203 (R), 255 (R), 536 (R), 852 (Cf), 1042 (R), 1389 (R), 1518 (R), 1608 (R), 1671 (R).

COUNTY DERRY ..9-1§.. 8 b.g. Derrylin — Colonial Princess (Roscoe Blake) pp4pp443u. Workmanlike lengthy. Dam, half-sister to Colonian King (*qv* '97 Annual), won 2 Points and 3rd 2. Grandam, Colonial Queen (always known erroneously as Colonial Queen) won 4 Hunt Chses and 17 Points and 3rd 3, and comes from a tremendous jumping family. P-t-P '99 (for Mr M.G. Sheppard) r1 p0 (pulled up). Not over-taxed in East Anglia when his best effort was over 2m4f at Cottenham, but didn't take to the air when moved to the West Country in March, and looked decidedly reluctant on occasions. Prone to wholesale blunders at present, and probably unsuited by too much give in the ground. Needs to improve in just about every department if he is to succeed. *J.M. Turner — Mrs J. Popham — Suffolk.* 23 (OMa), 88 (OMa), 180 (2m4fOMa), 411 (OMa), 934 (OMa), 1101 (OMa), 1262 (OMa), 1468 (OMa), 1564 (OMa).

COURAGE II (FR) ..—.. 11 b.g. Recif Du Gue (FR) — Scottish Des Isles (FR) (Brilloso FR) pp. Tailed off and pulled up twice. *Mr & Mrs J. Small — Kent & Surrey Bloodhounds (Jon Casemore).* 477 (R), 630 (OMa).

COURIER'S WAY (IRE) ..9-11.. 10 b.g. Riberetto — Coursing Bird (Crash Course) 2ppp. Compact well-made. IRISH P-t-P '96 r3 w1 (4&5yo Maiden) p0; fell 2. P-t-P '97/9 r13 w2 (Restricted and Confined) p2 (2nds, last once); pulled up 3, and unseated 1. Last successful in a two-finisher event on firm at Marks Tey in '99, but after a perfectly respectable reappearance ran like a drain, and a watching brief is advised on his return. Often the victim of errors, and has shown nearly all his form when the ground rides fast. *Mrs C. Kendrick & C. Hills — Essex (Mike Jerram).* 175 (I), 318 (Cf), 609 (I), 824 (Cf).

COURT ALERT ..—.. 6 b.g. Petoski — Banbury Cake (Seaepic USA) p. Owner-bred half-brother to Second Amendment (*qv*). Made a brief forward move after two miles on a May debut, but was soon eased out. Looks sure to do better in time. *Sir Michael Connell — Grafton (Lady Annie Connell).* 1422 (OMa).

COURT AMBER (IRE) ..—§§.. 10 b.g. Cataldi — Fine Cut (Salluceva) pr94urr. Very tall. IRISH NH '96/7 r2 p0 (pulled up in Hdle and Hunt Ch. IRISH P-t-P '97 r5 w1 (6yo Maiden) p1 (2nd); pulled up 2. P-t-P '98/9 r10 w2 (Restricted and Members) p1 (2nd); unseated 2, and pulled up 2. Made the bulk of the running to win two modest events in '99, but has never looked an easy ride, and has turned into a dirty stopper. Would have won at Penshurst but for slamming on the brakes at the second last and Alan Coe was £75 poorer after the Stewards took a dim view of his use of the whip in trying to coax him home. Tries to lose the rider by diving violently right at the fences, and when that does not work he simply digs his toes in. Blinkers seem to have made matters worse, and will be attracting Portman Square's attention if he does not reform quickly. *Mrs C. Cunningham — E. Anglian Bloodhounds (George Cooper).* 27 (I), 96 (I), 543 (I), 1035 (Cnr), 1114 (Cf), 1416 (O), 1510 (O).

COURT MASTER (IRE) ..10-2.. 13 b.g. Bustineto — Moycarkey (Raise You Ten) 5fc10u. Lengthy brother to Chasing winner, Tilden Park, and half-brother to Hymie Bank. IRISH P-t-P '93 r6 w1 (4&5yo Maiden) p4 (very unlucky 2nd once); unseated 1. IRISH NH FLAT '93 r6 p3 (2 2nds). IRISH NH '93 r1 p0. NH '94/8 r32 w1 (2m1f Ch) p16 (inc 3rd in '94 Scottish Champion Hdle). P-t-P/HUNT CH '99 r10 w4 (3 Ladies and Confined) p2 (3rd in Hunt Ch once); unseated 1, ran out 1, and pulled up 1. Basically an under-achiever under Rules, but took to Pointing straight away, and provided David and Lucia Borradaile with four wins between them in '99 as well as giving them a great thrill from the stands when sixth to Elegant Lord in the Aintree Foxhunters. Never seemed quite right in 2000, and gained his only success in a poor three-finisher Open at Badbury Rings — giving Ollie Ellwood a feel before Aintree. Has twice managed to fiddle his way round those big fences, but getting clumsy, and has done nothing for David's confidence in two of their last three attempts. Acts on any going. *D. Borradaile — Cattistock (Lucia Borradaile).* 67 (L), 211 (Cnr), 653 (MO), 764 (O), 921 (2m6fH), 1305 (MO).

COURT THYNE (IRE) ..9-4.. 10 b.g. Good Thyne (USA) — Clonaslee Baby (Konigssee) p3ppp. Plain rangy half-brother to Undertheinfluence and Positive Influence, to Irish NH flat winner, Lackey Hoey, to flat winner, Classical Influence, and to disqualified Hurdles winner, Classical Flame. IRISH P-t-P '97 r4 p0 (pulled up 2, ran out 1, and slipped up 1). P-t-P '98/9 r22 w1 (Maiden) p6 (4 3rds, last twice, 3 fences last once); pulled up 8, fell 3, and slipped up 1. Successful in the final race of the '98 season, but has not finished better than last-but-one in 15 outings since (pulled up in eight), and has generally run as badly as he sometimes looks. Stops quickly on a regular basis, and may be breaking blood vessels. *P.J. Millington — Fernie.* 1073 (O), 1264 (M), 1419 (R), 1502 (M), 1585 (O).

COWANSTOWN PRINCE ..9-8.. 7 ch.g. Derrylin — Craftsmans Made (Jimsun) 321. Smallish brother to NH flat and Hurdles winner, Winston Run, and half-brother to Crafty Gunner, and to Hurdles winners, Orswell Lad (also a successful Chaser), and Shannon Juliette (previously a successful Irish Pointer). IRISH NH '98/9 r7 p0. IRISH NH FLAT (for A.L.T. Moore) r8 p1 (2nd). Has been improving nicely, and followed a promising third with a short head second before he easily landed the odds in soft at Paxford. Jumps well for a beginner, and seems sure to enjoy further successes. Likely to prove to be considerably under-rated. *Mrs S. Bird — Ledbury (Nicky Sheppard).* 391 (CfMa), 899 (OMa), 1194 (OMa).

COWARNE ADVENTURE ..9-2.. 9 ch.g. Green Adventure (USA) — Ticover (Politico USA) p0. Lengthy. Dam was never better than last in 11 Points when trained by Sally Goodsall (over fence 3rd once; was a hopeless non-stayer). P-t-P '97/9 r8 w1 (2m4f Maiden) p2 (2nds); last, and pulled up 4. Looked fitter than previously when winning a 2m4f Maiden in softish at Alpraham in '99, but has never managed more than three outings in a season. Had disappeared by the end of March in 2000, so presumably suffered a setback. Will probably always struggle to stay the full trip in Points. *Mrs S.A. Godsall — N. Herefords.* 336 (R), 684 (2m4fH).

CRAB 'N LOBSTER (IRE) ..8-13.. 11 b.m. Waajib — Storm Crest (Lord Gayle USA) p3p44. Small compact half-sister to 5 flat winners (4 by Daring March, including Ongoing Situation), including Spanish Storm (also a successful Hurdler). Dam won at 5f. FLAT r21 p4 (inc Sell; inc 3rd in Jersey). NH '94/5 r3 p0 (inc Sells). P-t-P '99 r5 p1 (2nd); last, fell/unseated 2, and pulled up 1. Has shown bits and pieces of form, but incredibly moderate, and has trouble staying three miles. At least her wild jumping has improved — and so too her partner, Robert Hodges, and will be hoping to make it 35th time lucky on her 2001 debut. *G. Young — United.* 612 (CR), 858 (M), 995 (OMa), 1465 (OMa), 1634 (OMa).

CRACKER TICKET (IRE) ..—.. 6 b.g. Scenic — Shanliss (Blazing Saddles AUS) pp. Sturdy lengthy. Given a couple of quiet spins in March. *Mrs M. Lewis — Pembs.* 482 (I), 648 (CfMa).

CRACKING CRUMPET ..—.. 10 ch.m. St Columbus — The Dabber (Silly Prices) ppp. Tall rangy owner-bred half-sister to Perfik Lark. Dam, half-sister to If You Say So (*qv*), was placed in 3 Hdles (inc Sells);, but was awful when failing to finish in 3 Points after producing three foals. NH '98/9 (from R. Brotherton's) r4 p0 (last,and pulled up 3). Can show speed for two miles in bad company, but is soon floundering alarmingly, and like so many from the Wellings' yard past and present simply does not get the trip. *H. Bibbey — Albrighton Woodland (Mark Wellings).* 704 (OMa), 995 (OMa), 1629 (M).

CRACKING IDEA (IRE) ..10-6.. 13 b.g. The Parson — Game Sunset (Menelek) p112141. Unfurnished half-brother to Paylins, and to Hurdles winners, Goodtime George (IRE), Sunset Valley and Stormyfairweather (IRE) (also won Chasing — useful). Dam won 2m4f flat and 2 Hdles (2m-2m1f) in Ireland. NH FLAT r3 p1 (2nd). NH '95/6 (blinkered 5) r14 w2 (2m3f Hdle; and 2m4f Ch, 4 ran, after leader unseated 4 out when apparently in command) p3. P-t-P/HUNT CH '97/9 r27 w11 (inc 3m110y Hunt Ch, 5 Opens and 5 Ladies; hat-trick '98 and 4-timer '99) p8 (6 2nds; and inc 4 Hunt Chses); fell/unseated 4, and pulled up 3. A smart little horse who has enjoyed his Pointing, and has benefited greatly from the switch to the lighter weights in Ladies Opens, winning nine such races in the past two seasons. Likes to dominate and can maintain a scorching gallop, but has his off days, particularly if things don't go his way early on. Looks sure to have a big say in Ladies races around Higham in 2001 — also has a soft spot for Charing. Appreciates good or firm ground. *Mrs P.K.J. Brightwell — Essex & Suffolk.* 84 (L), 128 (L), 240 (L), 608 (L), 758 (L), 982 (L), 1113 (L).

CRACK 'N' RUN ..—.. 10 b.g. Golden Heights — Rockspring Amber VII (unknown) pp4pp. Small half-brother to Sonnett (*qv*). Useless. Very poorly bred, and was even beaten 75 lengths in his Members (the runner-up was unregistered, and the third dropped dead). *A. Wear & M. Pennell — N. Staffs (Mark Pennell).* 786 (OMa), 972 (OMa), 1124 (M), 1412 (OMa), 1527 (OMa).

CRACKSMAN ..—.. 8 b.g. Scallywag — Furstin (Furry Glen) ffp. Small neat brother to Spin The Coin and Hurdles winner, First Crack, and half-brother to Hasty Glen and Furdonnaty, and to Hurdles winner, First Bee. Dam won at 8f. NH FLAT '97/8 (from F. Jordon's) r3 p0 (not better than 14th!) NH May '00 r1 p0 (pulled up in 2m3f110y Sell Hdle: *a bhnd, t.o & pu 7*). Fell in two Maidens and lay winded for ten minutes at the last at Eyton (would probably have been pulled up, but apart from the winner who was 12 lengths clear — and he never completed the course otherwise — there was nothing else still going). *D. Pugh — N. Salop.* 593 (2m4fOMa), 1201 (2m4fOMa).

CRADLE MOUNTAIN ..9-8.. 8 b.g. Rakaposhi King — Spartan Daisy (Spartan General) 21. Smallish compact good-bodied half-brother to Horace, Tandem and Floral Reef and to NH flat and Hurdles winner, Give Me An Answer. Dam won 3m1f Nov Hdle and 3 Nov Chses (2m4f-3m2f), and is sister to General Rule (*qv* '93 Annual). Great-grandam, Bright Daisy, won 4 Points (inc a dead-heat) and placed 9. P-t-P '98/9 r6 p0; pulled up 4. Pulled up in four of his first six starts, but had shown some ability, and was the subject of a minor gamble on his reappearance, but got run out of it after the last and had to settle for second. Justified favouritism three weeks later, but the victory was not without a price as he finished lame. *Mrs A. Vaughan-Jones (N. Norfolk Farmers Group) — Dunston H. (Mike Bloom).* 941 (CfMa), 1290 (OMa).

CRAFTBOOK MARCHESA (IRE) ..9-4.. 7 br.m. Un Desperado (FR) — Dushenka (Jalmood USA) upp5p3p2p. Small compact. FLAT '98 r4 p0 (beaten 20*l* plus, last but one twice). NH '98 (for M. Bradley) r1 p0 (pulled up). IRISH P-t-P '99 (bought for 800) r4 p2 (2nds, behind stablemate once); unseated 2. IRISH NH '99 r1 p0. Bought Doncaster, Aug for 600. Performed poorly in her early efforts for the present yard, but did better latterly, and was only beaten about two lengths in two of her four most recent attempts (gave two very feeble displays in between and since). Finished third behind two in a Millington ownership in one of her placings, and the rider put up four pounds overweight in the other, so certainly deserves a change of luck. Might eventually be rewarded. *P.J. Millington — Fernie.* 845 (OMa), 1012 (CfMa), 1040 (OMa), 1290 (OMa), 1422 (OMa), 1504 (CfMa), 1589 (2m4fOMa), 1634 (OMa), 1676 (OMa).

CRAFTY GUNNER ..8-12.. 11 ch.g. Gunner B — Craftsmans Made (Jimsun) 3p4. Strong-topped half-brother to Cowanstown Prince (*qv*). NH FLAT r2 p0. NH Sep '95 and '97 r3 p0 (inc Sell). P-t-P '97 r6 w1 (Maiden) p2 (2nd or 3rd of 4); pulled up 2, and fell 1. Never came off the bridle when winning his Maiden at Tabley in '97 (rated 10-0), but broke down when tried again over hurdles later in the year, and returned in 2000 looking too backward to do himself justice. Prone to sweat up on occasions. *Mrs M. Teague & M. Salmon — Carms (Margery Teague).* 642 (M), 1228 (R), 1548 (R).

CRAFTY PHANTOM (IRE) ..—.. 6 b.m. Warcraft (USA) — Phantom Thistle (Deep Run) f6. Small half-sister to Copper Thistle (IRE) (*qv*). Bought Doncaster, May for 6500. Needs to jump much better and could probably have done with being a bit bigger, but related to a super-star, and chances are she can do better eventually. *Mrs P. Duncan — N. Cotswold (Jelly Nolan).* 471 (OMa), 786 (OMa).

CRAIGDALE ..9-10.. 10 b.g. Mirror Boy — Craigie Way (Palm Track) p5. Small neat owner-bred brother to Reflective Way and half-brother to Lord's Way and Craigies Girl (dam of Read The News, *qv* '98 Annual — also by Mirror Boy). Dam won 5 Points and placed 6, and is half-sister to Jack Sun (*qv*). P-t-P '97/8 r6 p1 (2nd; also disqualified from 3rd once); pulled up 3, and unseated 1. Able to bowl along for around 2m4f, but stops alarmingly, and has yet to finish better than last. His infrequent appearances suggest his health is not what it might be, and has been tried in a tongue-strap. Wayward, and and has been taken to post early. His current rating must be treated with suspicion. *R. Robinson — Dumfries.* 109 (L), 361 (L).

CRAIGHARDIE ..—.. 6 ch.g. Henbit (USA) — Great Chance (General Ironside) p. Half-brother to Great Gale, and to Chasing winner, Saxon Mead. Looked fat and schooled for two miles before pulling up in May. *E. Harvey — Puckeridge (Alex Harvey).* 1382 (OMa).

CRAIGSON ..8-7.. 8 ch.g. Tigerwood — Craig Lass (Rasti FR) 3u3pppp. Small unfurnished. Dam won Maiden and placed 4 for Mrs Hussey, and grandam, Craig Miss, won 4 Points (3 at Howick) and placed 12 for her. P-t-P '98/9 r5 p0 (pulled up 4, and fell 1). Has shown some speed, but struggling to get the trip, and continues to treat the fences with contempt. Twelve attempts at trying and failing to win a Maiden in Wales suggest he ain't much good. *Mrs I.E.M. Hussey — Tredegar F. (Deborah Faulkner).* 488 (CfMa), 746 (CfMa), 1055 (CfMa), 1302 (OMa), 1405 (OMa), 1617 (OMa), 1660 (OMa).

CRANAGH MOSS (IRE) ..9-10.. 12 ch.g. Le Moss — Cranagh Lady (Le Bavard FR) pp61. Tall lengthy brother to Waterloo King, and half-brother to Gigi Beach (IRE) (won Chasing since Pointing) and Gi Gi Brace (IRE). P-t-P '95/9 r18 w1 (Maiden) p5 (3 2nds, last once; and 2 3rds, last once); failed to finish 8 (fell/unseated 5). Has failed to progress since winning his Maiden in '96, and took 17 stabs at trying to land a Restricted before he succeeded under a forceful ride from Steve Blackwell at Bonvilston. Tried hard to avoid winning that day, and has worn headgear more often than not in the last three seasons. Sweats and grinds his teeth in the paddock, and gives the impression that he would rather be somewhere else. Stands little racing (ended '99 lame), and will struggle to win again. *P. Mahoney — Gelligaer F. (Tony Mahoney).* 1054 (R), 1298 (R), 1453 (R), 1615 (R).

CRASHBALLOO (IRE) ..8-13§.. 10 ch.g. Balinger — Crash Approach (Crash Course) 66. Good-topped half-brother to Irish NH flat winner, Adamant Approach. NH '96/8 r9 p1 (2nd); 8th, pulled up 1, and fell 1 in Chses; pulled up in final 2 Hdles. P-t-P/HUNT CH '99 (for Mr J. Wade) r7 p1 (3rd); unseated 1, and pulled up 1. Incredibly slow when ridden by a strong male jockey in '99, but took the opportunity to go even slower with more demure handling in 2000. Takes little interest, and blinkers have failed to goad him into action. *Miss K. Roncoroni — S. Durham.* 1123 (OMa), 1330 (OMa).

CREAM SUPREME (IRE) ..10-4.. 11 gr.g. Supreme Leader — Grandpa's River (Over The River FR) 136123. Rangy half-brother to Irish jumping winner, Beat The Second (IRE). IRISH P-t-P '97 r4 w1 (Members) p0; pulled up 2. P-t-P/HUNT CH '98/9 r13 w5 (inc Mixed Open, and 3 Confineds) p6 (3 2nds); and pulled up 1. Very capable on his day, but has a moody streak, and sometimes refuses to co-operate despite the vigorous urgings of Evil Williams. Can quicken to good effect when inclined, and rarely beaten if he is in contention over the third last. Successful thrice apiece at Bonvilston and Howick. Usually wears headgear, although not in his latest victory. Should push his winning tally towards double figures in 2001. *Mrs J.M. Hegarty — Glamorgan (Evan Williams).* 598 (O), 1065 (3m2fO), 1226 (O), 1451 (MO), 1570 (MO), 1672 (O).

CREDO IS KING (IRE) ..9-11.. 11 b.g. Le Moss — Merendas Sister (Pauper) p4p. Very big strong brother to Tuskar Flop (*qv*). IRISH P-t-P '95/6 r6 w1 (5&6yo Mdn) p2; pulled up 2, and fell 1. NH '96/9 (for P. Webber, visored 1) r10 w2 (2m6f-3m1f Chses) p0. Won three races (two in soft/heavy to February '97), but has been pulled up on seven of his last eight attempts, and there is obviously something desperately wrong with him. The one completion resulted in a 33 lengths fourth in a really warm Open, but will surely not be trained again. *Mrs L. Goedhuis & Mrs R. Deakin — Pytchley (Tik Saunders).* 79 (O), 1008 (O), 1415 (Cf).

CREDON ..9-9§.. 13 b.g. Sunyboy — Credo's Daughter (Credo) rpp42pp. Tall rangy half-brother to Unique New York, to smart jumping winner, King Credo, to successful Hurdler, Have Faith, to Chasing winner, Cresun, and to Irish NH flat winner, Credo Park. Dam won 4 Irish flat, 11-12½f, and won a 1m6f Hdle there, and won 8 English Chases, 2m-3m3f (won another, but disqualified). NH '93/8 (for S. Woodman, visored 1 in '96) r26 w3 (3m2f-3m3f Chses) p5 (inc 2 Hdles). A thorough stayer who had ability, but unreliable and a difficult ride, and was tailed off on his final three attempts under Rules (last scored in April '97). Did not enjoy Pointing at all, and was blinkered twice, including when beaten the length of the run-in by the only other finisher in his Members. Seems likely to be pensioned off. *J. & M. Bryant — Glamorgan (Mags Ree).* 334 (O), 597 (Cf), 742 (O), 821 (MO), 1050 (M), 1295 (Cf), 1451 (MO).

CRESSWELL CHERRY (IRE) ..9-2.. 6 b.m. Camden Town — Cherry Country (Town And Country) p3. Dam is half-sister to Gaelic Cherry (*qv* '96 Annual). Solf Goffs (Ireland), Aug for 1607. Ran in snatches when about 20 lengths third at Bonvilston, but might do better in time. *B. McKay — S. Pembs.* 1223 (2m4fOMa), 1456 (OMa).

CRESSWELL QUAY ..9-12.. 8 ch.g. Bold Fox — Karatina (FR) (Dilettante II) u1p1526. Strong-topped half-brother to Tiger Tina (qv). NH FLAT '98 r2 p0. NH '98 (from P. Bowen's) r5 p0. Can dole out drubbings to poor opponents in West Wales, and came home unchallenged in very soft and on firmish, but is unreliable and can look a difficult ride. Went out like a light when second favourite once, and was beaten favourite on his two most recent outings. Not one to support with any confidence, but has the ability to score again if he feels like it. *B. McKay & M. Cole — S. Pembs (Bruce McKay).* 267 (CfMa), 348 (CfMa), 486 (R), 832 (R), 1022 (3mH), 1221 (M), 1449 (I).

PLATE 39   1672 Torrington Farmers Mens Open: Cream Supreme (E. Williams), 3rd
PHOTO: Brian Armstrong

CRESTED LASS ..—.. 11 b.m. Crested Lark — Flying Pins (Jabs Delight) ppppu. Lengthy. A poor jumper and unenjoyable ride who has been deeply unimpressive when failing to complete. *Mrs S.M. Grindall — Atherstone (Sam Arthers).* 373 (CfMa), 1012 (CfMa), 1076 (OMa), 1269 (OMa), 1414 (M), 1507 (OMa).

CRESTWOOD LAD (USA) ..9-7.. 12 ch.g. Palace Music (USA) — Sweet Ellen (USA) (Vitriolic) 53. Strong good-looking half-brother to 4 flat winners (3 in USA), including smart sprinter, Shuttlecock Corner. Dam won at 6f in USA. FLAT r11 p2 (3rds). NH '92/3 r7 p0 (inc Sells). P-t-P '95 and '97/9 r22 w1 (Maiden) p9 (5 3rds, inc 2 fences last after remounting once; and inc neck 2nd twice); failed to finish 7 (ran out 1, and fell/unseated 3). Was a most deserving winner (placed in nine Maidens before he finally won one), but always hindered by his lack of stamina, and has reportedly been retired. Nearly always used to sweat up, but was capable of jumping his rivals silly. *W.O. Yardley — Worcs (Netty Higgins).* 1551 (R), 1633 (CR).

CREWMAN (IRE) ..9-9.. 8 b.g. Fairy King (USA) — Boat Race (USA) (Seattle Slew USA) p1. Small long-backed dipped brother to Irish flat winner, America's Cup, and half-brother to a winner in Hong Kong. P-t-P '98 (for Mr A.J. Rhead) r1 p0 (pulled up). Given a quiet school on his Pointing debut, and repeated the dose after a season off, but made the long journey to Buckfastleigh worthwhile when bolting up next time. Not seen again and may have suffered another reverse, but the form of the race was franked with both placed horses winning subsequently, and would be of interest in a Restricted if he was produced healthy. *Ms S. Bryan — N. Ledbury (Rachel Bryan).* 339 (CfMa), 656 (OMa).

CREWSKI ..—.. 6 br.g. Newski (USA) — Darlin' Again (Jolly Me) pp. Compact unfurnished owner-bred. Fat and unskilled so far, and had twice pulled up by halfway. *H.J. Manners — Berks & Bucks.* 1021 (2m4fOMa), 1204 (OMa).

CRICKETING ..—.. 9 b.g. Northern Game — Mandikova (Hard Fought) pupRf. Very small. NH FLAT '98 r2 p1 (3rd — promoted from 4th). NH '99 (for T. George, blinkered final) r7 p1 (3rd in Sell). Bought Doncaster, June for 1000. A very hard puller who invariably takes off in the early stages, and the owner only managed to safely negotiate three fences in total from two attempts on him. Does not settle well enough to get the trip (or even to complete the course so far). Usually tongue-tied now. *P. Johnson — Sinnington (Michael Brown).* 282 (OMa), 399 (OMa), 808 (OMa), 1331 (OMa), 1588 (I).

CRIMSON BOW ..8-6.. 11 b.m. Balinger — Crimson Flag (Kinglet) p. Neat sister to Bet A Lot. P-t-P '96/9 r16 w1 (Members) p2 (3rds, of 4, and last); pulled up 4, and fell/unseated 5. Won a two-finisher Members in '99, but extremely moderate, and has never mastered the art of jumping fences at speed. Disappeared after pulling up in the first week of February in 2000 and may well have suffered a setback. *Miss C.R. Thomas — V. of Lune H.* 137 (R).

CROCKED AGAIN (IRE) ..—.. 8 ch.g. Dragon Palace (USA) — Philly-Free (Avocat) ffp40. Half-brother to Finnigan Free. IRISH P-t-P '98 r2 w1 (5yo Mdn, 2 finished) p0; and pulled up. IRISH NH FLAT '98 r3 p3 (2 3rds). IRISH NH '98/9 r2 p1 (2nd in Hdle). NH Apr/May '00 r2 p0 (remote 4th in Nov Hdle: *ld and clr to 5, hdd nxt, wknd, t.o*; and last in 2m1f Sell HCap Hdle: *rr, pulled hrd, rap hdwy to ld 3, hdd nxt, wknd 5, t.o*). Scored in heavy in Ireland, but it must have been a freak result. Wears a cross-noseband and runs much too freely to have any hope of getting the trip now, and crashed in both English Points, including when tired at the last once. Was even stopping in his tracks after little more than 1m4f over Hurdles. *E. Knight — Berks & Bucks (Philippa Chamings; Patrick Chamings).* 38 (CR), 331 (R), 583 (2m5f110yH).

CROFTON LAKE ..—.. 13 ch.g. Alias Smith (USA) — Joyful Star (Rubor) pp. Strong good-looking half-brother to Hurdles winners, Jumbo Star and Jumbo's Dream. Dam, half-sister to Victory Morn (*qv* '90 Annual), won 2-finisher 2m5f Ch at Cartmel for John Dixon. NH FLAT '92/3 r3 p0. NH '93/9 (blinkered once in '96) r35 w1 (3m Hdle) p5 (inc 2nd in Ch); inc pulled up 9, and unseated 2. A remarkably dreary performer in a nine year career. Gained his sole victory in a match on firm in '96 (all out), and there were never more than six runners when he was placed. *Mrs E.M. Dixon — Cumberland F.* 1151 (O), 1365 (O).

CROPREDY LAD ..9-13.. 14 b.g. St Columbus — Lucky Story (Lucky Sovereign) 6p. Tall rangy brother to Lucky Christopher (*qv*). NH '93/7 r20 w1 (3m Ch) p5 (3rds, inc of 4 beaten 48*l* once, and tailed off last twice). P-t-P/HUNT CH '93 and '98/9 r15 w1 (Maiden) p4 (3 2nds, last once; and last of 3); pulled up 5, slipped up 1. A really bold jumper (though twice failed by the big fences at Aintree), but only once successful from 35 attempts since leaving the Tarrys in '93, and looks finished now. Most effective on top-of-the-ground. *A.R. & Mrs S.J. Humphrey — Dunston H. (Sarah Watson).* 92 (Cf), 318 (Cf).

CROSS CANNON ..9-9.. 15 b.g. Kambalda — Cushla (Zabeg) 3237. Tall hobdayed brother to Kushbaloo, and half-brother to Dennis Auburn and Kushdalay (IRE), and to 3 winners in Ireland, including Long March (Pointing). IRISH FLAT r2 p1 (2nd). IRISH NH FLAT '90/1 r4 w2 p1 (3rd). IRISH NH '91/3 r14 w2 (2m Hdle and 2m2f Ch) p7. NH '93/9 (bought for 14,500; 4 wins previously for J.A. Hellens; blinkered 1) r55 w7 (2m1f-2m5f Chses) p20; ran in 3 Sell Hdles latterly. Dropped dead at Hornby Castle. Was an old monkey who would rarely consent to exert himself latterly, but often went well at Sedgefield, where he won five races and was placed ten times, ironically including when runner-up behind a former stablemate in a Hunter Chase. *J. Wade — S. Durham.* 376 (MO), 682 (3m3fH), 805 (O), 1030 (O).

CROSSWELL STAR (IRE) ..8-12.. 10 ch.g. Salluceva — Margaret Hulse (Arctic Chevalier) p7u6. Sturdy good-quartered. P-t-P '96/8 (for Mr A.J. Seddall) r11 w1 (Maiden) p3 (2 3rds, last once); pulled up 4, and fell 1. Produced a power-packed finish to open his account at Cothelstone in '97 (firmish), but has failed to progress since, and beat just one rival home in 2000. Seems quite highly-strung (had two paddock handlers in the previous yard), and usually sweats freely, but his main problem has been his consistently shaky jumping. *M.G. Criddle — Quantock (Brian Forsey).* 1095 (R), 1375 (R), 1467 (R), 1551 (R).

CROWNHILL CROSS ..8-0.. 10 ch.g. Dutch Treat — Royal Cross (Royal Smoke) 6p765p. Lengthy owner-bred. NH '96 r3 p0 (100-1 when tailed off in 2m1f-2m3f Hdles). P-t-P '96/9 r26 w2 (Members) p0; last pair 7, refused 3, pulled up 12, unseated 1, and withdrawn under orders. A safe ride for a novice, but talentless and has never finished in front of more than one rival per race despite winning his Members on two occasions (invariably fails to stay in proper races). His average SP over the last two years is 84-1. May well have gone wrong on his latest appearance. *F.R. Bown — Lamerton (Miss C. Bown).* 101 (L), 165 (Cf), 560 (R), 720 (M), 853 (Inr), 1259 (4mL).

CRUCIAL RUNNER (U) ..6-0.. 13 b.g. Temple Treen — Red Cap Colleen (unknown) p4. Tottered round several fences behind in Members company. *Mrs V. Ollard — Burton, & Holderness (Mark Bennison).* 435 (M), 502 (M).

CRUISE AROUND ..9-0.. 9 b.g. Cruise Missile — New Cherry (New Brig) 745. Brother to Cherry Street and Timeforanother, and half-brother to Hazel Park and Greenacres Rose. Dam was 3rd in a Ladies. P-t-P '98 (for Mr A.R. Trotter) r1 p0 (pulled up). Looked highly temperamental on his debut, and a year off had done nothing for his behaviour, as he threw a tantrum before the start of each of his 2000 debacles. Actually managed to beat a rival on his final appearance and may have some latent ability, but any more brutish behaviour could see him on his bike for good. *S. Ramsay & K. Elgin — Lauderdale.* 424 (R), 497 (R), 719 (CfMa).

CRUISE FREE ..10-3.. 12 b.g. Cruise Missile — Lyons Charity (Impecunious) 5up34. Tall rangy. Grandam, Irish Bounty, won 4 Points. NH FLAT r1 p0 (remote 18th of 19). NH '96 r1 p0 (well tailed off last of 4 in 3m1f Hdle — not fluent). P-t-P/HUNT CH '96/9 r13 w2 (inc Open) p2 (3rds, last once); pulled up 6. Ran abysmally when pulled up thrice in '99, but perked up (clearly buoyed by the exploits of his more illustrious stablemates) in 2000, and ran some fair races without ever looking likely to add to his successes. Did not help himself by missing out on a Maiden and Restricted, but a steady jumper (the last at Barbury is a bit off a bogey fence for Simon Sellars), and might pop up again when he feels like it. *H.J. Manners — V.W.H.* 389 (O), 476 (Cnr), 749 (Cf), 1134 (Cnr), 1340 (3m1f110yH).

CRUNCH TIME (IRE) ..—.. 12 ch.g. Erin's Hope — Grishkin's Bliss (Charlottesville) pp5. Compact half-brother to a Belgian flat winner, and to Irish Hurdles winner, Mollie Wootton (IRE). Dam won at 12f in Ireland. NH FLAT r2 p0 (unruly on debut). NH '94/5 r8 p1 (21/ 3rd in Sell). IRISH NH '96 (for J.T.R. Dreaper) r5 p1 (2nd); Chses, 2m4f-3m1f. P-t-P '97/8 r5 p3 (2 2nds, beaten neck once — appeared to finish 3rd); and pulled up 2. Has verged on a win, but broke down at Weston Park in '98, and now seems of no account. *K. Wynne — Sir W.W. Wynn's.* 569 (OMa), 906 (CfMa), 1197 (OMa).

CUBAN SKIES (IRE) ..8-8.. 11 b.g. Strong Gale — Express Film (Ashmore FR) puuR4. Rangy brother to Irish NH flat winner, Loudy Rowdy (IRE), and half-brother to Gypsy King (IRE). Dam won 2m Hdle in Ireland. IRISH NH FLAT '95 (wore tongue-strap final) r3 p0. NH '97 r2 p1 (31/ last of 3 in 2m1f Nov Ch); and fell 1. P-t-P '97/9 r17 w1 (Maiden) p2 (neck 2nd; and remote last of 3); last pair 5, and failed to finish 9 (fell/unseated 4, and ran out 1). Won a bad Maiden at Paxford in '98, but has always been an unenviable ride, and has failed to complete in seven of his ten starts since. Jumped worse than ever in 2000, but some mugs were still keen to back him in his Members. Has been tried in a tongue strap. *J.L. Barnett — Warwicks (Mrs A. Barnett).* 248 (R), 510 (Cf), 612 (CR), 1192 (O), 1438 (M).

CUCKLINGTON ..9-10§.. 10 b.g. El Conquistador — Belmore (Homeboy) 6p. Tall lengthy. P-t-P '97/9 r17 w1 (Maiden) p4 (2 2nds); failed to finish 7 (fell/unseated 4). Likes to dominate, but not an easy ride, and decent animals easily brush him aside. Failed to reappear after reportedly striking into himself at Black Forest Lodge in March. Clumsy, and will need things to go his way if he is to win again. Wears blinkers. *The Cucklington Club — Blackmore & Sparkford V. (John Dufosee).* 13 (R), 559 (R).

CUMBERLAND YOUTH ..8-10.. 10 b.g. Town And Country — Key Biscayne (Deep Run) p6p6p544r4. Tall good-topped half-brother to Society Member and The Swangler. Dam won an Adjacent, and won 2 Hdles and 5 Chses, all 2m. NH FLAT '96 r1 p0. NH '96/8 (for Miss C. Caroe, frequently blinkered) r19 p1 (distant 3rd of 4); last; pulled up 7 and unseated in Chses; inc pulled up 4 in Hdles; in Sell. Bought Ascot, June for 1000. Appalling under Rules (never less than 33-1), and beaten a minimum of 23 lengths when giving another string of dismal performances in the new yard. Safe enough, but any faint stamina appears to evaporate in the closing stages. *Miss J. Garley — Pytchley.* 20 (OMa), 194 (CfMa), 613 (L), 787 (L), 1018 (OMa), 1421 (OMa), 1530 (2m6fH), 1586 (CN), 1626 (3m1f110yH), 1664 (R).

CURRACLOE ROSE (IRE) ..9-10.. 8 gr.m. Roselier (FR) — Cotton Gale (Strong Gale) pf42uf15. Very small neat sister to Hurdles winner, Absolutely Equiname (IRE). Dam won 2m2f Hdle in Ireland. NH '98 (from C. Morlock's, blinkered final) r5 p0. NH May '00 r1 p0 (31/5th in Nov Hdle: *bhnd, prog 11, nd*). A miniscule mare who cannot afford to tangle with the fences as she found to her cost on three occasions, but possesses plenty of stamina, and certainly deserved her win in a Maiden at Marks Tey (would probably never beat the runner-up again). Had fallen three out with a similar contest apparently at her mercy on her previous outing, and before that had finished a length second once, but it may not be easy to find suitable options for her in future. Looks too slow for Hurdling, but Ladies Opens with an experienced partner might provide some hope. *P.J.H. Rowe — Puckeridge (-; Hugh Collingridge).* 322 (CfMa), 550 (OMa), 604 (OMa), 844 (OMa), 942 (CfMa), 1039 (OMa), 1180 (OMa).

CURTAINSATCHOPWELL (IRE) ..10-1.. 7 b.g. Soviet Lad (USA) — Missquickdecision (IRE) (Master Willie) u4p41u2. Workmanlike. NH FLAT '98 r2 p0. NH '98/9 (for T. Easterby) r7 p1 (2nd). Has a dead mouth and cannot be restrained and establishes some huge leads, so sets off at a great gallop, and frequently burns himself out. Improved as the season progressed, and galloped on strongly throughout the final mile when scoring in a long Maiden on firmish at Dalton Park, and gave another competent display when runner-up to the impressive Master Jock at Wetherby. A very difficult customer who sometimes makes bad mistakes, and Kevin Green has done extremely well to wagon him. Not seen since the end of March, but would have prospects in a Restricted if all went smoothly. *F.S. & Mrs J.M. Newitt — Sinnington (Joanna Newitt).* 169 (OMa), 276 (M), 381 (OMa), 398 (OMa), 508 (CMa), 620 (R), 689 (R).

CUT A NICHE ..9-8.. 11 ch.g. Callernish — Cut And Thrust (Pardal) 376p5. Strong half-brother to Matchplay, Goldtopper and The Proud Pound, to flat winner, Abielle, and to a winner in Holland. Dam won at 8½f. P-t-P '96/9 r15 w3 (Maiden, Restricted and Intermediate) p5 (4 2nds); pulled up 4, and unseated 1. Looked a fair prospect as a youngster, but has only managed an annual success '97/9. Having looked to have turned the corner in '99 (rated 10-2) he reverted to his disappointing self in 2000, when afflicted by a virus and ultimately by sore shins. Frequently lacks fluency, and can look soft. Likely to remain unpredictable in future. *Mrs G. Pidgeon, P. Riddle & R. Kay — Bicester with Whaddon (Jenny Pidgeon).* 241 (C), 476 (Cnr), 883 (Cf), 1394 (O), 1481 (Cf).

CWM BYE ..9-9.. 10 ch.g. Hubbly Bubbly (USA) — To Oneiro (Absalom) 4pf61u. Small compact half-brother to 3 flat winners (one in Norway), including Athenian King and The Institute Boy. Dam won 2 flat, 5-6f. NH FLAT r2 p0. NH '95 and '98 r4 p0. P-t-P '96/7 and '99 r8 w1 (Maiden) p2 (last of 3 once); pulled up 3, and unseated 1. Endured his busiest campaign to date and managed his first success for three years when making all in his three-runner Members, but generally well beaten otherwise, and remains prone to errors. Usually struggles to get the trip, and helped by quick ground, although that places extra strain on his presumably dodgy pins. *Mrs B. Brown — Teme V.* 667 (Cf), 863 (R), 1276 (R), 1463 (Cf), 1543 (M), 1616 (R).

CYBORGO (FR) ..9-12.. 11 b.g. Cyborg (FR) — Quintessence III (FR) (El Condor FR) 3. Sparely-made brother to Hurdles winner, Hors La Loi III (FR). Dam won at 9f in French provinces. FRENCH FLAT r2 p1 (2nd). FRENCH NH '94 r1 p0 (last in Auteuil Hdle, from M. Pipe's). NH '94/9 (for M. Pipe; blinkered 3, tried tongue-tied) r25 w11 (7 Hdles, 2m4f-3m1f, and 4 Chses, 3m-3m3f; inc 5-timer and hat-trick) p4 (2nds); one run Punchestown. Formerly a very game front-runner who has earned £161,557 in this country alone, but last scored in April '97. His biggest triumphs were in the Bonusprint Stayers Hurdle at the Cheltenham Festival value £53,585 (was making his first appearance since runner-up to Dorans Pride in the same race the year before) and the Mumm Mildmay Chase worth £25,568, but pulled up lame in the '98 Gold Cup (and took out See More Business), and has been last twice and pulled up four times including the Grand National since. Was a lovely competitor, and it was sad to see him plodding round Lanark. *S.H. Shirley-Beavan — Jedforest.* 662 (O).

DADDY LONG LEGS ..9-2.. 14 ch.g. Over The River (FR) — Mary Deen (Avocat) pp444u. Tall. IRISH P-t-P '92/3 r7 w2 p3; pulled up 2. IRISH NH FLAT r5 p2. IRISH NH '93/4 and '96 r11 w1 (2m4f Ch) p4 (inc 2 Hdles; short-headed 1). P-t-P '97 r2 w1 (Members) p1 (2nd). Not a bad performer in Ireland and gave Richard Hubbard his first success when landing a two-finisher Members event on firmish at Penshurst in '97, but lost the rider when holding every chance at the second last on a comeback mission three years later. Still willing to try hard, but in the veteran stage nowadays, and is very slow. *R. Hubbard — Mid Surrey F., & O. Surrey, Burstow & W. Kent.* 125 (M), 572 (CfO), 676 (Cf), 827 (L), 1209 (Cnr), 1508 (M).

DAHIYAH (USA) ..—.. 10 b.g. Ogygian (USA) — Sticky Prospect (USA) (Mr Prospector USA) f. Lengthy brother to a winner in USA, and half-brother to 2 others. $100,000y. FLAT to '99 (early runs for W.R. Hern; 3 wins for G.L. Moore, and on for B. Smart; usually visored) r37 w4 (6-7f, 2 on all-weather, and inc 24-runner Sell) p6. NH '95 and '98 (won for D.L. Williams, bought for 6500; one run previously for B. Smart; debut for G.L. Moore, bought for 5200) r11 w1 (2m Sell Hdle) p2 (Chses); pulled up in Czech Hdle in '98. Sold Doncaster, Oct for 1100. A varied and occasionally exotic career ended in death at Market Rasen. *Miss N. Hurn — Fitzwilliam (Katie Thory).* 441 (O).

DAI-NAMIC-STORM (IRE) ..—.. 8 b.m. Glacial Storm (USA) — It Beat All (Laurence O) f. Half-sister to Irish NH flat and Hurdles winner, Kinnegad Girl. Dam won Irish NH flat. Fell after a mile at Erw Lon. *D.A. Rees — Tivyside.* 649 (CfMa).

DAINTY MAN (IRE) ..9-12.. 9 br.g. Cardinal Flower — Web Of Gold (Bustineo) 426p. Neat. IRISH P-t-P '98 r9 w1 (5yo&up Maiden) p4; pulled up 2, and fell 1. P-t-P/HUNT CH '99 r5 w1 (Restricted) p1 (3rd); pulled up 2. Given a great ride by Andrew Dalton when successful on his first attempt in Restricteds in '99, but outclassed subsequently, and consistently gives the impression that he will not go for strong-arm tactics. Often travels well, and probably good enough to win a Confined (far from disgraced at Cheltenham in 2000), but will need things to go his way if he is to be coaxed home. Avoids soft ground. *Miss M.A. De Quincey — Sir W.W. Wynn's (Anne Hewitt).* 564 (I), 861 (C), 1336 (2m4fH), 1558 (3mH).

DAISY (U) ..—.. 10 b.m. Hanoverian stallion — Irish draught mare p. Big rangy. Proceeded in a stately fashion until stopping after two miles to pick the buttercups in her Members. *N.M. Lampard & K. Stewart-Hilliar — Berks & Bucks (Nick Lampard).* 1619 (M).

DAISY FAY ..—.. 6 b.m. Broadsword (USA) — Lily Of The West (True Song) f. Tiny. Dam was 3rd in her only Point for the Mackenzies (was subsequently 2nd in a Hdle), and grandam, Wanchai Lil, won 3 Points and placed 4 (inc 3 flat). Kept hanging left in a 2m4f Maiden in late May, but ran well for two miles before fading and falling heavily three out (was badly winded, but got up eventually). Will need to have a mighty heart to overcome her lack of inches. *Mrs J.H.M. Mackenzie — N. Cotswold.* 1589 (2m4fOMa).

DAISY'S CHOICE ..7-7.. 6 b.m. Tigerwood — Official Lady (Official) p4u8p. Sister to Teigr Pren (*qv*). Very green and a shoddy jumper to date, and was a remote last in both completions. *K.M. Davies — Pembs (Brian Llewellyn).* 267 (CfMa), 648 (CfMa), 834 (OMa), 949 (OMa), 1055 (CfMa).

DALUSMAN (IRE) ..10-2.. 13 b.g. Mandalus — Good Surprise (Maelsheachlainn) u323p2. Sturdy compact half-brother to Tarqogans Surprise, Good Waters and No Rebasse, and to jumping winner, Concert Paper. Dam won a Point and 2m Hdle in Ireland. IRISH HUNT CH '93 r1 p0 (pulled up). NH '96 r1 p0. NH '93 and '95/7 (blinkered 2) r28 w1 (2m5f Ch) p7 (inc 5 Hdles, to 3m4f); inc Sell Hdle. P-t-P '98/9 (for Lady Susan Clark) r10 p6 (5 2nds). Wonderfully consistent, but incredibly difficult to win with, and has clocked up seven placings since his only success which dates back to '96. A safe ride and goes on most surfaces, but frequently becomes disinterested when it comes to a struggle. Gave Nicola Sturgis a good education, but she might have to look elsewhere for winning material. *Miss N. Sturgis — Beaufort (Gail Sturgis).* 218 (L), 335 (L), 390 (L), 751 (L), 1014 (3m5fL), 1191 (L).

DAMAS (FR) ..—§.. 10 b br.g. Video Rock (FR) — Queue De Pie (FR) (Baraban) pppp. Compact attractive half-brother to a French jumping winner, and to a flat winner there. FRENCH NH '95 r10 p4 (3rds). NH '96/9 (for D. McCain; all form previously for M. Pipe, bought for 18,850) r30 w6 (4 Hdles, 2m-2m4f, inc 3 Sells, and 2 Chses, 2m1f-2m5f) p6; refused in '98 Grand National. Bought Doncaster, March for 13,000. Six wins for the maestro included five in '97 (none since), but he typically left nothing for his followers, and was frequently tailed off latterly under Rules. Proved to be an extremely expensive mistake for the new connections, and twice appeared to be limping after he had pulled up. Usually blinkered, and was visored once in the past. Gutless now, though doubtless because of pain. *Mrs B.K. Thomson — Berwicks.* 43 (Cf), 225 (3mH), 359 (Cf), 717 (Cf).

DAMIENS PRIDE (IRE) ..9-8§.. 11 b.g. Bulldozer — Riopoless (Royal And Regal USA) 2pf23223. Compact. IRISH P-t-P '95 r3 p0 (pulled up 2, and refused 1). P-t-P '97/9 (for Mrs K.A. Heywood) r6 w1 (Maiden) p1 (2nd); pulled up 2, refused 1, and ran out 1. Only made three appearances in two years for previous connections following his Maiden victory at Bishops Court in '97, but managed a full season in 2000. Remains an utter villain who has thrown in the towel when holding every chance on at least three occasions (beaten less than a length twice), recently, and should not be touched with a barge-pole by punters. Surely worth a try in headgear as a last resort. *Mrs S.J. Batchelor — Lamerton.* 163 (R), 315 (R), 406 (R), 848 (R), 1043 (R), 1258 (R), 1518 (R), 1639 (R).

DAMIER BLANC (FR) ..—§.. 12 b.g. Damister (USA) — Roche Blanche (FR) (Great Nephew) 7uR37. Lengthy. Dam won at 8f in France. FRENCH FLAT w5 (9-14f, in provinces) p3. FLAT r3 p0. NH '93/5 and '97/8 r29 w4 (2m1f-2m6f Hdles) p5; inc Sell. P-t-P '99 r5 p1 (head 2nd); last pair 2, and pulled up 2. A competent Hurdler at best when the mud was flying, but lost interest latterly under Rules, and simply refuses to try these days — finds three miles rather too far in any case. Frequently wears headgear. Would make a shock winner (100-1 in his latest attempt), and presumably retired. *B.P. Dalton — Thurlow, & Cambs.* 19 (L), 91 (M), 417 (Cf), 549 (Cf), 870 (O).

DANAS ..—.. 8 ch.g. Dawn Johnny (USA) — Dana's Turn (His Turn) p. P-t-P '99 (for Mr C.M.C. Cashmore) r2 p0 (pulled up 2). Well supported in two Maidens in '99, but never gave his supporters reason for optimism, and quickly tailed off on his reappearance for a new yard at Lydstep. Quickly booted out of Chateau Lavis, and clearly has his problems. *J.R. Jones — V. of Clettwr.* 1222 (2m4fOMa).

DANCE ON SIXPENCE ..9-8.. 13 b.g. Lidhame — Burning Ambition (Troy) 3744f. Compact attractive half-brother to flat and Hurdles winner, Her Honour. FLAT (to 8; often blinkered/visored) r42 w3 (5-8f) p7. NH '94/6 r9 p0 (inc Sells). P-t-P '97 r4 w1 (Confined) p3 (2nds, last once). Returned after a three year hiatus, but not better than last-but-one, and finished tailed off when tried in blinkers in his Members. No longer seems to be getting the hint. This form is on good or sound surfaces. *Mrs A.L. Gardiner — E. Essex (Robert Gardiner).* 240 (L), 414 (L), 758 (L), 935 (M), 1114 (Cf).

DANCING BAREFOOT ..8-7.. 12 ch.m. Scallywag — High Venture (High Award) 5upu6. Sturdy. NH FLAT r2 p0 (tailed off 2). NH '96 r4 p0 (Sell final). P-t-P '97 and '99 r7 p1 (3rd of 4); pulled up 3, and unseated 1. Consistently hopeless in the lowest grade, and has no prospects. *Mrs M. Heritage — S. & W. Wilts (Sarah Waugh).* 328 (CfMa), 763 (CfMa), 957 (CfMa), 1555 (OMa), 1598 (OMa).

DANCING PAWS (IRE) ..—.. 6 b.g. Tidaro (USA) — Quayside Charm (Quayside) Strong-topped brother to Chasing winner, Deel Quay (IRE), and half-brother to Irish Pointing winner, Quayfield. Dam won Irish NH flat. Sold Tattersalls May for 3839. Probably just feeling his way when tailed off and pulled up in Maidens. *S.R. Hope — Cheshire (Sue Mullineaux).* 570 (2m4fCfMa), 964 (OMa), 1439 (OMa).

PLATE 40   *1385 South Cornwall Confined: Dancing Ranger (Richard Darke), 1st*
PHOTO: Baths Photographic

DANCING RANGER ..10-3.. 10 b.g. Broadsword (USA) — Elegant Nell (Free State) 3243135. Tall rangy half-brother to Nell's Image and Elegant Wolf. Dam won 2 2m Sell Hdles, and was most unlucky not to complete a hat-trick. NH FLAT '95/6 r3 p0. NH '98 r2 p0 (remote 9th, and pulled up in Hdles). P-t-P '99 r7 w1 (Maiden) p2 (3rds); last 3, and fell 1. A cheap purchase for Pointing, but has done well to win twice and make the frame on six occasions. Not the hardiest stayer and appreciated the less testing conditions at Trebudannon, but not up to Hunter Chase standard, and may live to regret not picking up a Restricted along the way. A sound jumper, and should give connections plenty more fun in 2001. *Mr & Mrs T.D.H. Hughes, Mrs Worth-Grylles, Miss J. Bradford & M. Beer — Lamerton (Pauline & Tony Geering).* 255 (R), 534 (Cf), 720 (M), 1175 (Cf), 1385 (Cf), 1516 (I), 1644 (3m2f110yH).

DANDELION LAD (IRE) ..—§.. 9 ch.g. Phardante (FR) — Jocks Fancy (Patch) p. Heavy-topped. P-t-P '97/9 r6 w1 (Maiden) p0; pulled up 3, and refused 2. Blinkered for the first time when landing a 33-1 shock at Mollington in '98, but it was the only time he has ever produced a clear round, and generally dogs it furiously. Rarely seen (thankfully), and hopelessly tailed off when pulling up in his last two appearances. Never looks fit, and has been tried in spurs. Not worth the hassle again. *K.B. & R.J. Rogers — N. Herefords (Raymond Rogers).* 993 (R).

DANEGELD (IRE) ..10-4§.. 10 b.g. Danehill (USA) — Julip (Track Spare) 522f. Big rangy lop-eared brother to flat winner, Pleasant Memories, and half-brother to 3 flat winners, including Patriarch and My Memoirs. Dam won 2 7f races, and is half-sister to smart flat winner and sire, Tiepolo II. NH FLAT r1 p0. P-t-P/HUNT CH '97/9 r18 w5 (up to Confined) p9 (2nds, inc 2 Hunt Chses); fell 2. Enjoyed an impressive debut season in '97 and is very able, but a hard ride, and would much rather finish second than pass the post in front. Looks after himself, and is most profitably employed in Hunter Chases, though he would need a slice of luck to win one. Sure to continue to frustrate. Usually blinkered nowadays. *Col M.J.F. Sheffield — Hurworth (David Smith).* 151 (3mH), 301 (2m5fH), 469 (3m110yH), 924 (3m1fH).

DANESWELL ..—.. 8 b.g. Seymour Hicks (FR) — Stanton Queen (Most Secret) pfppppb. Plain lengthy brother to Seymours Secret, and half-brother to Scallymay. Dam fell in 2 Points for Mrs Edwards. P-t-P '99 r1 p0 (pulled up). Yet to even look like completing in eight attempts, and has twice looked to pull up unsound. *S.R. Edwards — N. Salop.* 570 (2m4fCfMa), 866 (CfMa), 1068 (3m2fOMa), 1197 (OMa), 1318 (OMa), 1526 (OMa), 1634 (OMa).

DANGER FLYNN (IRE) ..10-1.. 11 b.g. Boreen (FR) — Stramillian (Furry Glen) u3fuu15p. Sturdy. IRISH NH FLAT '95 r1 p0. IRISH NH '94/7 r17 p2 (3rds in Hdles); 5th in Hunt Ch. IRISH P-t-P '97 r5 w1 (Mdn) p4. NH '97/9 (for Mrs P. Sly, bought for 6400) r11 w4 (2 Hdles, 2m7f-3m, and 2

Chses, 2m6f-3m1f; beaten when left clear last once) p2 (caught near finish and beaten neck once). Pulled up on his final start in the previous yard, but that was a rare poor effort for them, and had a good winning record on easy surfaces. Generally very disappointing in the new ownership, and gained his only success at Charing after My Wee Man had hung left after holding a two length advantage at the final fence and was just caught. Visored once, and sometimes sweats badly. The way he falters in the final mile looks suspicious, and the rider has trouble merely staying aboard. Worth trying with a competent jockey. *Miss S.C. Holliday — O. Surrey & Burstow (Ann Blaker).* 128 (L), 245 (L), 307 (L), 827 (L), 982 (L), 1107 (L), 1395 (L), 1511 (L).

DANGEROUS GUEST (IRE) ..10-2§.. 9 b.g. Deploy — Guest List (Be My Guest USA) u12. Strong-topped fired half-brother to 2 flat winners (one in Germany), including Backstabber. Dam won 2 Irish flat, 6-7f. 18,000y. FLAT (for Sir Mark Prescott) r5 w1 (7f, fibresand) p3. NH '98/9 (for J. Old) r6 w1 (2m Hdle) p1 (28*l* 3rd). Bought Doncaster, May for 4000. Has plenty of ability if he can be pursuaded to use it, and was given a fine ride by Tim Mitchell when beating a stablemate in soft at Bishops Court (was reluctant to line up and jumped slowly and did not want to know in the early stages). Definitely best fresh, and won his flat debut, as well as scoring on his first attempt in a Hurdle (overcame a 953 day absence). His legs seem to be consistently troublesome, and appeared to go wrong when finishing half a length second at Buckfastleigh. *A.G. Fear — Cattistock (Richard Barber).* 210 (MO), 403 (Cf), 652 (MO).

DANNICUS ..10-6.. 10 b.g. Derrylin — Kerris Melody (Furry Glen) 2471. Owner-bred half-brother to Kerri-B. NH '96/7 r6 p1 (19*l* 3rd); last and carried out 1 in Chses. P-t-P '99 r5 w2 (Maiden and Restricted) p3 (3rds). Keen and consistent, but looked to have his limitations until tried in a Ladies race for the first time on his final appearance, when battling on gamely to win by a narrow margin. Capable of superb jumping, and his partners are all first class. Was very lightly raced under Rules, and his 2000 season was over by the second week in March, so hopefully not tainted by being injury prone — broke a blood vessel when below par at Lemalla. *D.A. Shone — N. Cotswold (Richard Barber).* 36 (CI), 143 (C), 310 (I), 522 (L).

DANNY DOLITTLE (IRE) ..—.. 8 ch.g. Denel (FR) — Tactique (FR) (Anne's Pretender USA) p. Smallish compact. NH FLAT '98 r3 p0 (tailed off). P-t-P '99 r1 p0 (fell). Impossible to assess at present, but the fact that he has seen the racecourse so infrequently does not augur well. Has been tried in a nearside pricker. *P.C. Pocock — W. Somerset V. (Lynn Jones).* 146 (OMa).

DANNY GALE (IRE) ..8-1.. 10 b.g. Strong Gale — Mary The Rake (On Your Mark) f3ppu. Tall hobdayed. Dam won 3 2m hdles in Ireland. NH FLAT '95 r1 p0. NH '95/7 r9 w1 (2m1f Hdle) p0; inc Sell. P-t-P '99 r2 p1 (3rd); and refused 1. Won at Bangor in '96, but lightly raced and next to useless since. Beaten 29 lengths on his sole completion in 2000, and usually runs out of steam. Remains a consistently poor jumper. *P. Davies — Llangibby.* 479 (Cf), 821 (MO), 1066 (3m2fL), 1297 (L), 1402 (MO).

DAN'S YOUR MAN (IRE) ..10-8.. 9 b.g. Synefos (USA) — Val Lady (FR) (Valdingran) 110ff. Angular half-brother to 4 winners, including in France. IRISH NH FLAT '96/7 r3 w1 p0. IRISH NH '97 and '99 r3 p1 (2nd in Hdle); 4th in Hunt Ch. IRISH P-t-P '98/9 r8 w6 (Opens) p2 (2nds on seasonal debuts, inc behind Elegant Lord). IRISH P-t-P '00 r1 w1 (Killeagh Open by 1½*l* and 50*l*: made all, mist 9, prsd 2 out, stayed on wl). IRISH HUNT CH '00 r3 w1 (beat Spot The Difference, giving 7lb, and Sheltering, giving 19lb, 4½*l* and 1½*l* at Leopardstown: *cl up, ld frm 4, clr 3 out, r.o wl frm last*) p0; fell at Fairyhouse: *trckd ldr til ld 9, fell nxt*; and fell at Punchestown: *disp ld early, lost tch 11, mist 2 out, fell last*. A top-class performer in Ireland, and gained the finest of his nine victories from his first 16 attempts when beating very strong opposition in a Leopardstown Hunter Chase, but jumped badly in the Cheltenham Foxhunters next time, and his fencing has gone to pot since. Revels in mud, but seems to need a return to the smaller obstacles to give him a much-needed confidence booster. Sure to continue difficult to beat, in Points at least. *Mrs C. Cashman — Avondhu (P.F. Cashman, in Ireland).* 584 (3m2f110yH).

DANTE'S GOLD (IRE) ..9-7§.. 10 ch.g. Phardante (FR) — Gold Bank (Over The River FR) u421r3. Big strong-topped. Dam is an unraced sister to Across The Lake. NH FLAT '97 r3 p1 (2nd). NH '98/9 (for C. Egerton; blinkered in Sell final) r4 p0; unseated only CH. Sold Doncaster, May for 800 (to Charlie Egerton). Gave Ryan Bliss his first winner when beating the eternal bridesmaid Springvilla by a neck in a bad Maiden on firmish at Badbury (dwelt at the start but just got up), but probably has more ability than he cares to show, and was reluctant to line up on two subsequent attempts (left once). It may be best to ignore him in future. *R.K. Bliss — Avon V. (Michael Blake).* 33 (Cnr), 208 (R), 328 (CfMa), 763 (CfMa), 1095 (R), 1247 (R).

DARI (IRE) ..—.. 9 ch.g. Be My Native (USA) — Dedham Vale (Dike USA) ppp. Tall rangy brother to Irish flat and Hurdles winner, Native Portrait, and half-brother to Irish Hurdles winner, Dedham Gale (IRE), and to useful Irish jumping winner, Feroda. Dam won at 12f. IRISH NH FLAT '97 r1 p0. IRISH NH '98 r2 p0 (pulled up in 2 Hdles). IRISH P-t-P '98 r4 p1 (21*l* 3rd); pulled up 2, and fell 1. NH '99 r5 p1 3rd in Hdle); pulled up 1. IRISH/HUNT CH '99 r4 p0 (pulled up 2, and fell/unseated 2). Attractively bred and looks the part, but obviously flawed. Ran in a tongue-strap after pulling up when still in contention on his reappearance, so it is presumably a wind related problem. Returned to his fence-bending ways of old on his final start, and should be given a wide berth in future. *B. McNichol — Cumberland F.* 492 (M), 660 (Cf), 1081 (R).

DARING MAGIC ..9-5.. 9 b.m. Daring March — Magic Chat (Le Bavard FR) up. Tall lengthy half-sister to Magic Song. Dam was 3rd in a Restricted for Robert Swiers, but lamed herself next time. NH '97 r1 p0 (pulled up). P-t-P '98 r4 p1 (2nd); pulled up 1. Had shown a little ability, but was killed at Hornby Castle. R.W. Swiers — York & Ainsty N. 283 (OMa), 377 (R).

DARK CHALLENGER (IRE) ..9-11.. 9 b brg. Brush Aside (USA) — Great Aunt Emily (Traditionalist USA) 31281. Tall rangy brother to Market Poseur (IRE), and half-brother to Emily's Niece, Raise A Smile, Kinon-Penny, and Paradise Row (IRE). NH FLAT '96 r1 p0. NH '96/8 (for Mrs J. Pitman) r6 p4 (2 Hdles, and 2nd of 4 and 3rd of 4 in Chses). Bought Ascot, June for 825. Consistent, but none too genuine, and usually blinkered in the present year. Finished alone in a Maiden at Kingston Blount (was nearly a fence ahead when the only other survivor of 12 pulled up exhausted two out), and ran on under pressure to land a Restricted on the same track three months later. Connections have done very well with him, but might find matters more difficult now he is out of Restricteds. *Mrs P.A. White — Berks & Bucks (John White).* 76 (CCfMa), 249 (CfMa), 392 (R), 1146 (R), 1623 (R).

DARK KNIGHT ..10-1.. 8 b.g. Broadsword (USA) — Dunton Lady (Extra) 1pu. Strong brother to Gold Sword, and half-brother to Charles The Third. Dam won Whaddon Members and placed 10 for Mr Roberts. P-t-P '99 r2 p1 (3rd); and pulled up 1. Won an 18-runner Maiden convincingly on his reappearance at Dunthrop, but disappointed next time, and failed to see the track again after becoming entangled in some wire when loose at Kimble. Probably good enough to collect a Restricted when recovered. *D.H. Roberts - Bicester with Whaddon.* 194 (CfMa), 513 (CR), 1146 (R).

DARK RHYTHAM ..10-1.. 12 br.g. True Song — Crozanna (Crozier) 1365u3u. Sparely-made half-brother to St Morwenna, Teapoy, and Tealeaf. Dam, sister to Miss Crozina, and half-sister to Teaplanter (qv '97 Annual), won 4 Points and placed 4. P-t-P/HUNT CH '95/9 r25 w3 (2m4f Maiden and 2 Members) p8 (7 2nds, beaten head once, and neck once); failed to finish 10 (fell/unseated 2). Looked tuned to the minute before bolting up in a good time on his reappearance at Kingston Blount, but has always struggled to stay three miles, and finished his races tamely otherwise. Game enough, and tried hard to give Union Man a race at Garthorpe, but brushed aside before turning for home, and lost second on the flat. Usually held up these days, having previously run from the front. A good ride for the owner (though he managed to topple off on both occasions in 2000), and deserves to find another minor race. *S. Atkins — V. of Aylesbury (Jeff Tredwell).* 247 (R), 388 (I), 785 (I), 1006 (Cf), 1142 (M), 1267 (I), 1487 (M).

DARK VENETIAN ..7-1.. 7 b.m. Gold Dust — Dark Image (Bold As Brass) fpp2. Dam, half-sister to 3 Pointers, including Northern Sensation (qv 2000 Annual), won 2 Points and placed 6 for Mr Down, and grandam, Dark Sensation, won Maiden and 2nd. Great-grandam, also Dark Venetian, won 8 Chses (3m-3m2f), and also won 2m Hdle, but disqualified on technical grounds. Jumped poorly before failing to complete at long odds thrice, and then an exhausted and extremely remote last of two in her Members. It does not look as if she will be bestowing great honour on her forebears. *J. Down — Torrington F. (J. Down & Lisa Smale).* 541 (I), 1519 (CfMa), 1654 (OMa), 1670 (M).

DARREN THE BRAVE ..9-5.. 13 ch.g. Sunyboy — Stey Brae (Malicious) 4p. Rangy half-brother to Chasing winner, Flippance. NH '95 and '97 r8 w1 (3m Ch) p2 (3rds). P-t-P '98/9 r9 p3 (2 3rds); pulled up 3. Very lightly raced under Rules, and well beaten in Points barring a second to Better Future in '98, but has never looked an easy ride, and tends to hang. Pulled up in three starts for present connections, and was lame in the latest. *D. Stephens — S. Cornwall.* 534 (Cf), 652 (MO).

DARZAL ..10-0.. 10 b.g. Afzal — Hi Darlin' (Prince De Galles) p3241 4. Small neat brother to Hizal (qv). P-t-P '98/9 r12 p2; pulled up 5, and on floor 5). NH Jun '00 r1 p0 (4th in 2m110y Nov Ch: outpcd, mist 9, t.o). Much improved in 2000 (previously accident-prone and was becoming disappointing), and finally lost his maiden tag at the 17th attempt when a wide margin scorer on firmish at Larkhill. Still prone to jumping lapses, but could win a Restricted with Alex Charles-Jones up. *H.J. Manners — V.W.H.* 477 (R), 630 (OMa), 1207 (OMa), 1486 (OMa), 1598 (OMa).

DASHMAR ..9-7.. 14 b.g. Rare One — Ballinattin Girl (Laurence O) p67466. Small half-brother to Bobbie's Girl (IRE). NH '93/4 and '95/8 (blinkered/visored 3) r24 w1 (3m Sell Hdle) p2; 6th, last, and pulled up 1 in Chses (not fluent). P-t-P '93, '95 and '99 r12 p5 (4 2nds, of 3 once); pulled up 2, brought down 1, and fell 1. Took an eternity to get off the mark, but well past it now, and not better than last-but-one in his 9 most recent attempts. Has never truly mastered the art of jumping. *Mrs M. Armstrong — Morpeth (Kevin Robson).* 225 (3mH), 494 (L), 661 (L), 974 (L), 1160 (O), 1426 (L).

DAVEY JOHN (IRE) ..8-4.. 10 ch.g. Le Bavard (FR) — Tumble Dream (Tumble Wind USA) ppp5. IRISH P-t-P '98 r1 p0 (fell). IRISH NH FLAT '98 r2 p0. IRISH NH '98 (blinkered) r1 p0 (pulled up in Hdle). P-t-P '99 r3 p0 (5th, pulled up 1, and fell 1). Unsafe and devoid of talent on all known evidence to date. *Mrs E. Jestin — Cumberland (Fergus Jestin).* 363 (CfMa), 811 (I), 1153 (OMa), 1367 (OMa).

DAVID BRUCE (IRE) ..9-6.. 8 ch.g. Camden Town — Quick Romance (Lucky Brief) p25p. Close-coupled half-brother to Caddlestown, to 2 Irish NH flat and Hurdles winners, to NH flat and Hurdles winner, Scoring Pedigree (IRE), to Hurdles winner, Referral Fee, and to successful Irish

Pointer, Those Brown Eyes. Dam won 2m Hdle (3 ran) in Ireland. Irish P-t-P '99 r2 p1 (40*l* last of 3). Bought Ascot, Sep for 680. Headed after a slow jump at the last when beaten three lengths in a youngsters Maiden at Higham, but very disappointing when first or second favourite twice subsequently. Comes from a family of high achievers, but seems to be suffering from some malaise himself. Wore a tongue-strap first time out in 2000. *R.W. Gardiner (Lord Leighton Partnership) — E. Essex (Robert Gardiner)*. 98 (OMa), 237 (OMa), 412 (OMa), 941 (CfMa).

PLATE 41   652 Dart Vale & Haldon Harriers Mixed Open (Div 1): Darren The Brave (D. Stephens), pu, jumps alongside River Swilley (R. Walford), 1st, with Bomba Charger (Richard Darke), 3rd, between horses   PHOTO: Bill Selwyn

DAWN ALERT (IRE) ..10-9.. 12 br.g. Strong Gale — Gamonda (Gala Performance USA) 11116. Unfurnished brother to Peacemaker (IRE), and half-brother to Firewater Station. Dam won at 2m, and won NH flat, 2 Hdles (2m-2m1f) and 2 Chses (2m-2m4f), all in Ireland. IRISH NH FLAT '95 r3 w2 (2m-2m2f) p0. IRISH NH '95/8 (worn blinkers and tongue-strap) r18 w2 (2m Hdle and 2m5f Ch) p7. P-t-P/HUNT CH '99 r9 w2 (Open and Ladies) p1 (remote 2nd); unseated 1, pulled up 1, and brought down 1. A useful performer on good or soundish surfaces, and got the better of Copper Thistle after an epic tussle at High Easter, but appears less effective over regulation fences, and has yet to impress in four Hunter Chase starts. Capable of making the running, and jumped better than usual in 2000, when four different jockeys were successful on him. Sure to win again between the flags. *Mr & Mrs A.G.C. Howland Jackson — Suffolk (Ruth Hayter)*. 885 (L), 1037 (L), 1112 (O), 1381 (O), 1593 (3m2fH).

DAWN CALLER (IRE) ..8-10.. 10 br.g. Derrylin — Raise The Dawn (Rymer) p3. Tall well-made half-brother to successful Hurdlers, Harlequin Chorus and Crocadee (latter also won NH flat), and to NH flat winner, New Dawn. Dam is half-sister to Sands Point (*qv*). IRISH NH FLAT '96 r1 p0. IRISH NH '96 r2 p0. Sold Doncaster, Aug for 600. Broke a blood vessel in his first Irish Hurdle and wore a tongue-strap next time, and then disappeared for four years. Showed speed in Maidens (had warmed up with a spin in a celebrity race for oldies in between) but looked a non-stayer, and finished an exhausted 25*l* 3rd at Umberleigh. *Mrs W. Bradford — E. Cornwall (Pauline & Tony Geering)*. 1641 (OMa), 1675 (OMa).

DAWN INVADER (IRE) ..10-7.. 10 b.g. Fine Blade (USA) — Kova's Daughter (Brave Invader USA) 1211p. Lengthy half-brother to the winners, Multum In Parvo (useful jumper), General Shot (Hurdling) and Freddies Lad (Irish Pointing). NH '96/8 r7 p0 (pulled up 3, and fell 1). P-t-P '97 and '99 (for Mr D.J. Caro) r5 w1 (2m4f Maiden) p1 (remote 3rd); pulled up 2, and fell 1. A regular non-finisher after winning his Maiden at Garnons in '97, but much improved by Nicky Sheppard, and made the bulk of the running when successful three times in 2000. Poised to challenge behind the erratic-fencing Lakefield Rambler coming down the hill at Cheltenham, but broke down at the third last, sadly ruining all the hard work that had gone before. Not always the most fluent of jumpers, but speedy and invariably well handled. *G.F. Smith — Ledbury (Nicky Sheppard)*. 196 (R), 388 (I), 671 (C), 1017 (I), 1340 (3m1f110yH).

DAWN MISSION ..—§.. 9 b.g. Dunbeath (USA) — Bustellina (Busted) uppp. Tall rangy brother to Step Lively, and half-brother to 3 flat winners (one in Hong Kong), including Cumbrian Rhapsody (also a successful Hurdler) and Emmer Green. Dam won at 8f. 2600y. FLAT r8 p2 (10-22/ 3rds). NH '95/8 (blinkered last 9; unplaced last 2 for R. Buckler, bought for 8500; previously for T. Easterby, and for M.H. Easterby) r26 w3 (2 Hdles, 2m-2m6f, and 2m6f Ch) p9 (short-headed once). Sold Wolverhampton, Nov '98 for 4000. Ungenuine and a difficult ride, and can often hang right and has also jumped left. Won his debut over fences, but fell heavily next time, and shattered his confidence (has not got round in six subsequent attempts over the bigger obstacles. Pointing did not cheer him, and although he was only blinkered once he acquired a tongue-strap on final start (February). *Miss J. Lewis — Teme V. (John Tulloch)*. 78 (L), 192 (L), 295 (L), 333 (Cf).

DAWN'S COGNAC (IRE) ..10-8.. 8 b.g. Glacial Storm (USA) — Misty Venture (Foggy Bell) f2111p1b13u. Tall rangy half-brother to Aberaeron Girl (dam of Aaron's Venture and Annascan (*qv* '98 Annual), Mysterious Run (IRE), and to Chasing winner, Super Rapier (IRE). P-t-P '98/9 r6 w2 (Maiden and Restricted) p2 (head 2nd once); and fell 2. Has quickly developed into a useful Ladies horse, but should not be considered invincible, and Pip Jones excelled on him when going right-handed at Llanfrynach — had jumped away to the left on occasions previously. Capable of excellent jumping (though it has looked fragile under pressure in the past), and acts on most ground, though appreciates some cut, and possibly found conditions too quick when third to dead-heaters Hearts Are Wild and Pharare in arguably the best Ladies race of the season at Weston Park. Can be a handful in the paddock, and usually has two attendants. Bit off more than he could chew on his Hunter Chase debut, but worth another chance over the bigger obstacles. *D. Brace — Llangeinor*. 3 (L), 101 (L), 297 (I), 343 (Cf), 481 (L), 743 (L), 836 (L), 1224 (L), 1275 (L), 1410 (L), 1646 (3m4fH).

DAYDREAMER (USA) ..8-11.. 8 b.g. Alleged (USA) — Stardusk (USA) (Stage Door Johnny) u3up2. Strong-topped. Dam 5 races at up to 13f in USA, and is sister to champion turf horse, Johnny D. $85,000y. FLAT (for J. Gosden) r1 p0. NH '97/8 (for G.L. Moore, bought for 1500; previously for R. Buckler, bought for 3000) r5 p2 (9-17/3rds). Shows a little ability in Maidens, but seems to lack stamina or enthusiasm (possibly both), and managed to lose what seemed to be an ideal opportunity on final start. Was very fat in early season. *Mr & Mrs J. Finn-Kelcey — E. Sussex & Romney Marsh (Sara Finn-Kelcey)*. 181 (2m4fOMa), 309 (OMa), 577 (OMa), 985 (M), 1172 (OMa).

DAYTIME DAWN (IRE) ..10-6.. 10 b.g. Rashar (USA) — Ard Clos (Ardoon) 10. Rangy. NH FLAT r2 p0 (last, and fell). NH '96 r5 p0. P-t-P/HUNT CH '97/9 r6 w2 (inc 2m3f Hunt Ch) p0; pulled up 1 and unseated 1. A non-stayer in Points and gets very few chances, but makes the most of them, and recorded his second Hereford Hunter Chase success when outpacing Mr Grimsdale over two miles in April. Always worth a second glance in modest sub-three mile events. *R.N.C. Wale — Pytchley*. 925 (2mH), 1341 (2m110yH).

DEALER BOY (IRE) ..—.. 8 ch.g. Yashgan — Saucy Sally (Dara Monarch) ups. Workmanlike lengthy. P-t-P '98/9 r11 p0 (6th, pulled up 5, fell/unseated 4, and refused 1). NH FLAT '99 (for P.T. Dalton) r2 p0. NH '99 r2 p0. A total disaster area in Points, and even managed to lose the rider between fences on two occasions in 2000. Usually gives the impression of being a non-stayer, and will struggle to find a race. Blinkered on his latest appearance, when launching Lennie Hicks into orbit on the Garnons Big Dipper. *E. Haddock — Meynell & S. Staffs*. 298 (CfMa), 569 (OMa), 673 (2m4fOMa).

DEALER DEL ..8-10.. 7 b.g. Deltic (USA) — No Deal (Sharp Deal) p21. Dam, half-sister to Nice To No (*qv* '98 Annual), pulled up in 2 Points (lame final) for Hazel Leeves, but grandam, Noneed, won 3 Points and placed 3 for her. Did not start until May and looked green, but improved steadily, and won a three-finisher event for the champion in soft at Mounsey Hill Gate. Took a very slow 7min33s and the runner-up was an ungenuine 13-year-old, so will obviously have to find quite a bit more for Restricteds. *Mrs H. Leeves — Minehead H. (Chris Down)*. 1308 (OMa), 1469 (OMa), 1609 (OMa).

DEAN DEIFIR (IRE) ..9-13.. 9 br.g. Mandalus — Fiancee (Royal Match) 41u14. Tall strong half-brother to Knight Hunter (dam of Snowshill Shaker, *qv* 2000 Annual), and Jan's Decision, and to 2 winners abroad. IRISH P-t-P '97/8 r7 p1 (25/ 2nd); pulled up 4, and fell. IRISH NH '98 r1 p0. P-t-P '99 (for Mr & Mrs M. Kemp) r6 w2 (Maiden and Restricted) p2 (¾/ 2nds); 4th, and withdrawn under orders. Adept in minor company, but headstrong, and benefits from the strong handling which was ably supplied by Clive Storey in 2000. Avoided firm ground until this term, but handled it well, and should find another opportunity or two. Wears a cross-noseband, and usually on the verge of eruption in the paddock. *Mrs K. Craggs — College V. & N. Northumberland (Clive Storey)*. 495 (O), 973 (I), 1365 (O), 1498 (O), 1576 (Cf).

DEAR DO ..10-2.. 14 br.g. Swinging Rebel — Earlsgift (Dusky Boy) p534. Tall half-brother to Farm Track. Dam won 5 Points and placed 5. NH FLAT '93 r2 p0. NH '93/8 r41 w7 (2m-2m2f Chses) p20 (inc 3 Hdles). P-t-P '99 r7 w1 (Ladies) p3 (2nd once); pulled up 1. A gift horse to present connections (had won seven Chases mostly around the gaffes for Nicky Henderson previously), and surprisingly had the stamina to land a Ladies Open round Hexham in '99, but failed to reappear after going lame at Lanark in 2000, and may not be able to add to his outstanding completion record. Tried in blinkers under Rules. *J.P. Elliot — Border (Rhona Elliot)*. 185 (L), 359 (Cf), 493 (Cf), 660 (Cf).

DEAR EMILY ..9-10.. 13 b.m. Uncle Pokey — Malmar (Palm Track) p16. Compact unfurnished sister to Smokey Track. NH '95/6 (visored 1) r13 p3 (2 2m4f Hdles, inc Sell, and 2m2f Ch). P-t-P/HUNT CH '95 and '97/9 (for Mrs H.M. Goody in '99) r21 w1 (Maiden) p10 (7 2nds, beaten head once); failed to finish 8 (ran out 1, and on floor 3). Finally won at the 21st attempt, and beaten another 14 times until her wide margin success at Badbury Rings, but has generally preferred to settle for second. A sound jumper and looked after former Jockey Club inmate, Lucy Brack (now at Stratford Racecourse), on her race-riding debut, but finished lame. Maternity soon followed (for Emily, that is), and reported to be in foal to Karinga Bay. *S.J. Claisse — I. of W. (Kate Buckett)*. 331 (R), 767 (R), 1306 (C).

DEBBIE'S DARLING ..—.. 11 b.m. Baron Blakeney — Sunwood (Jimsun) uf. Lengthy half-sister to Ibex (*qv*). NH FLAT '95 (for breeder, M. Pipe) r1 p0. Sold Ascot, Nov '95 for 900, and resold there May '96 for 725. Hampered and unseated at the third on her Pointing debut, but held a slight lead when she fell three out and concussed Sarah Gaisford a week later. Seems to have a little ability, but was not seen again. *Mrs C. Greenslade — S. Devon*. 256 (R), 312 (CfMa).

DEDALUS (FR) ..9-7§.. 6 b.g. Fijar Tango (FR) — Nilmeen (FR) (Right Royal V) 53134. Compact half-brother to useful jumping winner, Champleve (FR), and to a smart French flat winner, and to a successful French chaser. Dam won at 8-10f in France. FRENCH FLAT '98 r2 p0. FRENCH NH '98 r1 p0 (pulled up in Hdle). NH '99 r7 p1 (3rd in Sell Hdle). Able, but usually very reluctant to exert himself, and it was a surprise when he upset the odds-on favourite in holding at Cherrybrook. A careful jumper, but found typically little in subsequent attempts, and connections have done well to extract a win from him. Usually wears headgear, and was tried in a tongue-strap under Rules. *R. Beaton (M. Pipe Racing Club) — Silverton (David Pipe)*. 204 (OMa), 407 (OMa), 857 (CfMa), 1258 (R), 1650 (R).

DEEL QUAY (IRE) ..9-9.. 10 b.g. Tidaro (USA) — Quayside Charm (Quayside) 3c344. Compact sturdy brother to Dancing Paws (IRE) (*qv*). IRISH P-t-P '95 r1 p1 (2nd). NH FLAT '96 r1 p0. NH '96/9 (visored 1) frequently tongue-tied; won for Mrs P. Buckley, bought for 3500; previously for K. Bailey) r17 w1 (3m1f Ch) p5 (pulled up and continued for 3rd once); pulled up in 4 of final 6, inc Sell. Has only fallen once in 22 attempts over fences, but is very slow, and was beaten a minimum of 25 lengths when plodding round in 2000. Has had a soft-palate operation in the past. *M.G. Chatterton — Belvoir*. 443 (Cf), 867 (M), 1072 (Cf), 1216 (O), 1265 (O).

DEEP REFRAIN (IRE) ..9-10.. 11 b.g. Mandalus — Deep Serenade (Deep Run) 2p2pp. Tall sturdy half-brother to Irish NH flat and Hurdles winner, Grange Leader. Dam won 2 NH flat (2m-2m2f) and 2 Hdles (2m-2m1f) in Ireland. IRISH NH FLAT '95/6 r3 p0. IRISH NH '95/6 (tried blinkers) r9 p2 (3rds in Chses). IRISH P-t-P '95 and '97 r7 w3 (to Winners of Two) p2; pulled up and fell. NH '98/9 (for R. Phillips, bought for 13,500) r10 w1 (2m3f Ch — his only Sell) p3; fell last with every chance once (looked held). Bought Doncaster, May for 3000. Won three Irish Points on good or easy ground in '97, but once successful in five other years. Sometimes makes the early running, and kept going steadily when four lengths second to Fawsley Manor, but his other efforts in 2000 were very poor, and it looks as if something is troubling him. Acquired a tongue-strap on his final three appearances, but generally fails to stay three miles. *G.R. Kerr — Pytchley (Caroline Bailey)*. 430 (O), 607 (O), 789 (O), 1005 (M), 1415 (O).

DEEP SONG ..9-6.. 11 ch.g. True Song — Rapagain (Deep Run) u15p. Sparely-made brother to Musical Hit, and half-brother to Bangagin and Rapaboy. NH FLAT '94 r2 p0 (beat one). NH '95 and '97 r5 p1 (last of 3); last 2, and pulled up 2. P-t-P '96 (for Mr P.A. Pritchard) r1 p0 (4th). Utterly useless under Rules, but returned from a three year holiday to land something of a gamble at Newton Bromswold, although only after the Clerk of the Scales had intervened on his supporters behalf. Not disgraced in a slowly-run Restricted at High Easter, but might struggle in that company in future. Owner-rider Carla Thomas made a decent fist of her first season, and should improve if she gets the horsepower. *Miss C.M. Thomas — Oakley (Simon Andrews)*. 20 (OMa), 509 (M), 610 (R), 830 (Cnr).

DEERHUNTER ..9-11.. 10 b br.g. Gunner B — Royal Scarlet (Royal Fountain) 72231. Rangy half-brother to Scarlet Rising, and to NH flat winner, Setatrap. Dam is half-sister to Scarlet Berry (*qv* '99 Annual). NH FLAT '96 (for D. Barker) r2 p0. NH '98/9 (for G. Harker) r2 p0 (tailed off in Hdles — last, and pulled up). Beat Meadowleck by 25 lengths in a very bad eight plus Maiden in soft at Hexham (the contest took 22 seconds longer than any of the other three mile races on the card), but deserved the success, as he had previously given three fair placed displays. Wears bandages and exceptionally lightly raced in the past, but could possibly have credentials in a modest Restricted. *Miss C.A. Blakeborough — Bedale.* 624 (OMa), 694 (OMa), 1031 (M), 1329 (OMa), 1580 (OMa).

DEER PARK LASS (IRE) ..9-13§.. 9 ch.m. Mister Lord (USA) — Adare Flore (IRE) (Fairbairn) p337p22. Rangy unfurnished. IRISH P-t-P '97/8 r13 w1 (5&6yo mares Maiden) p4; pulled up 3, fell 1, refused 1, and brought down 1. IRISH HUNT CH '98 r2 p0 (inc brought down). P-t-P/HUNT CH '99 (for Mr J.R. & Mrs R.A. Schofield) r5 p0 (pulled up 4, and unseated 1). Failed to complete the course and thoroughly temperamental in the previous yard, but slightly more amenable in 2000, and consented to run into the frame on four occasions. Blinkered twice in '99, but not since. More than able enough to win a Restricted, but remains one to beware of. *J. Flint — Holderness (S. Bolton).* 50 (R), 278 (R), 503 (R), 797 (R), 1230 (R), 1577 (R), 1664 (R).

DEFENCE COUNSEL (IRE) ..9-6.. 9 b.g. Darshaan — Maryinsky (USA) (Northern Dancer). 15. Workmanlike half-brother to Major's Law (IRE) (*qv*). NH FLAT '98 (from late G. Richards') r2 p0. Gave Martin Leach a winning first ride in a very slowly-run Members in softish, but made mistakes when beaten 14 lengths in a Restricted. Probably very one-paced, and spends most of his time kept under wraps. *A. Snipe — Blankney (Melvyn Leach).* 366 (M), 546 (R).

DEINKA (IRE) ..8-7.. 12 b.m. Erin's Hope — Monaco Ville (Rheingold) 3. Half-sister to flat and Hurdles winner, Monaco Gold (IRE) (the only one of several siblings to score). IRISH NH FLAT '93 r1 p0. IRISH P-t-P '93 r2 p1 (20*l* 2nd); and fell at 1st. Revived after seven years to give a first-timer some Members race fun, and finished 38 lengths third. *Ms J. Grose — V.W.H.* 748 (M).

DELLONE ..9-6.. 9 b.g. Gunner B — Coire Vannich (Celtic Cone) 4. Strong. Dam won 2 Hdles, 2m-2m1f. NH '97 r1 p0 (refused when tailed off). NH '99 r2 p0 (fell in 2m4f Ch; and 4th in 2m5f Ch). P-t-P '99 r4 p1 (2nd); fell 1. Easily good enough to win a Maiden (looked sure to do so at Andoversford in '99 until his stamina gave out), and beaten little more than three lengths on his reappearance, but failed to return, and presumably met with a setback. Deserves a small success, but is obviously going to remain difficult to place. *M.C. Houghton — Cotswold.* 392 (R).

DEL THE LORRY MAN ..—§§.. 8 ch.g. North Col — Krystle Saint (St Columbus) pupr. Good-topped rangy attractive half-brother to Dels Lad. Dam, half-sister to Smart Rhythm (*qv*), won 2m4f Hunt Ch and 5 Points and placed 8 (inc a Hunt Ch) for Del Wheatley (was extremely flighty). Grandam, Clear Thinking, is half-sister to 7 Pointers. P-t-P '99 r3 p0 (pulled up 3). Madder than Mad Mick the Mad (winner of the 1968 Mr Mad Contest), but as barmy as the jockeys who continue to partner him. In no fit state to be let loose on a racecourse, and hopefully the last has been seen of him. *D.J. Wheatley — Atherstone (Sam Arthers).* 54 (OMa), 123 (OMa), 235 (OMa), 547 (CfMa).

DELWOOD ..—.. 9 br.g. Dancing High — Lorna's Choice (Oats) fp. Tall rangy light half-brother to Tom's Man. Dam was 3rd in Percy Members, and 3rd in dire Hurdles on hard. P-t-P '99 (for Mr C. Dennis & Mrs W. Forster) r2 p0 (pulled up 1, and fell 1). Has fenced atrociously to date, and for the sake of James Ewart's health has hopefully taken redundancy — not seen since the end of February. *Miss V. Burn — Tynedale.* 187 (OMa), 363 (CfMa).

DEMONIAC (FR) ..—.. 10 b.g. Quart De Vin (FR) — Ortie II (FR) (Tourangeau FR) p. Tall half-brother to 2 French jumping winners, including Virbazar (FR). Dam won non-thoroughbreds race on flat in France. IRISH P-t-P '97 r3 w2 (5yo Maiden — tongue tied, and Winners of Two) p1 (2nd). NH '97 (visored 3) r4 p0 (fell in 3 Chses, tongue-tied for the first of them, and pulled up in Hdle). P-t-P '98/9 (for Mr R.J. Rowsell in '99) r5 w2 (Intermediate and Confined) p1 (remote 3rd); pulled up 2. A catastrophe over regulation fences, but won both his starts in '98 (rated 10-2) when still with Martin Pipe, and looked set to become a decent Pointer. Has changed hands twice since, and finished in just one of four races (when last), and seems to have gone in the wind. Has been tried in a tongue-strap. *G.J. Smith — S. Notts.* 48 (Cf).

DENARII (IRE) ..9-5.. 9 ch.m. Denel (FR) — Troubled Course (Crash Course) 1u. Compact good-topped. IRISH P-t-P '97/9 r10 p1 (3rd); pulled up 5. Taken sensibly by Lucy Cowan on her first ride in an elders Maiden at Fakenham, and kept going steadily to beat some desperate opponents with something to spare. Irish form suggests that she is basically slow and moderate. *Mrs A.E. Johnson — Cambs Univ.* 1292 (OMa), 1537 (2m5fH).

DENIM BLUE ..9-9.. 12 ch.g. Mandrake Major — Delphinium (Tin King) 23p4p. Compact half-brother to several winners. Dam won at 6f. FLAT r10 p2. NH '93 r7 p2. P-t-P/HUNT CH '95/8 r17 w3 (inc 2 Hunt Chses, 2m5f-3m1f) p6 (5 2nds); failed to finish 7 (fell/unseated 4 — when in command at last once). Well placed to find two Hunter Chases in '97, but appeared to go wrong on his final start that year, and has been lightly raced and soundly beaten since. Will probably struggle to stage a revival at 12. *Mrs L. Walby — Tynedale (Pauline Robson).* 418 (M), 974 (L), 1150 (L), 1325 (Cf), 1576 (Cf).

DENNETT LOUGH (IRE) ..10-8.. 10 b.g. Torus — Monica's Pet (Sovereign Gleam) 162f253. Rangy good-bodied brother to Irish Hurdles winner, Ardnamona, and half-brother to Moorlough Bay (IRE). Dam won 2m4f Hdle in Ireland. IRISH P-t-P '97 (pulled up). P-t-P/HUNT CH '98/9 r9 w5 (inc PPORA Intermediate and Intermediate) p1 (2nd in Hunt Ch); fell/unseated 2. Unbeaten in his first season for Clive Storey and looked a natural for Hunter Chase success, but revealed as quirky since, and has managed just two placings in that grade. Goes well fresh, but indolent and needs strong handling, and the trainer excelled on him on his reappearance. A thorough stayer and often propelled by his tail, but a risky betting proposition in his usual frame of mind, and very close to a squiggle. *Mrs A.D. Wauchope — College V. & N. Northumberland (Clive Storey)*. 42 (O), 89 (3m1fH), 422 (3m5fO), 1024 (3m3f110yH), 1428 (O), 1445 (3m1fH), 1643 (3m2fH).

DENNEY'S WELL (IRE) ..9-5.. 6 ch.g. Good Thyne (USA) — Julias Well (Golden Love) 1. IRISH P-t-P '99 r4 p0 (7th, and pulled up 3). Enterprisingly handled by Gary Hanmer in a Maiden taking 7min31s in softish at Sandon (17 set off, but only three got round), but was very lucky, as Fanion De Nourry clearly had his measure until the rider eased him prematurely and was pipped on the post. That rival went on to far better things, so it will be interesting to see what Denney's Well can achieve when reappearing. *P.R. Burling — Cheshire (Gary Hanmer)*. 906 (CfMa).

DENNIS ..8-10.. 11 b.g. Crested Lark — Lucky Sandy (St Columbus) pppf. Big strong owner-bred brother to Tarry Awhile, Lucky Crest, Dolly Bloom and Tarry No More. Grandam, Ebony Girl, was 5th, last twice, pulled up 7, and fell 1 in Points. P-t-P '98/9 r5 p0 (5th twice, pulled up 1, and unseated 2). A rare Tarry dud whose consistently poor jumping cost him his life on a Black Saturday for the produce of his dam, as sister Dolly Bloom had died earlier in the day from a heart attack whilst swimming. *G.B. Tarry — Grafton (Jimmy Tarry)*. 1012 (CfMa), 1147 (OMa), 1439 (OMa), 1486 (OMa).

DERE STREET ..9-10.. 7 b.g. Derring Rose — Jed Again (Cagirama) pu1. Half-brother to Mainhope, Peelinick and Callawhope. Dam, half-sister to 4 Pointers including the dam of Fallalaw, was 3rd in a Maiden for Rhona Elliot. Soon tailed off on his debut, but backed from 12s to fours next time, and blundered and unseated at the last when two lengths second and weakening. Disappeared for almost two months, but confirmed the promise when he made almost all the running to score at Whittington. Rather headstrong, but clearly possesses plenty of stamina, and may maintain progress at seven. *Mrs R.L. Elliot & R. Dalgetty — Jedforest (Rhona Elliot)*. 188 (OMa), 363 (CfMa), 1153 (OMa).

DERRING DAN ..—.. 9 b.g. Derring Rose — Kellsboro' Joan (Rymer) pfff. Lengthy plain. P-t-P '99 (for Mr T.R.R. Farr) r3 w1 (Maiden) p1 (2nd); and brought down 1. Won a two-finisher youngsters Maiden on ground that had something for everyone at St Hilary in '99, but suffered three consecutive tumbles with Helen Gray, and their confidence in each other must be impaired. His rider is a danger to herself, and foolishly persevered on an exhausted steed on the latest disaster. *Mrs K.D. Gray — Berwicks*. 111 (R), 358 (M), 424 (R), 663 (R).

DERRYAIR ..10-2.. 8 b.g. Derrylin — Deep Dora (Deep Run) p3821u2. Tall angular owner-bred half-brother to Bit Of An Idiot (*qv*). P-t-P '98/9 r6 w1 (Maiden) p3 (2 2nds); pulled up 2. Did well to score in his debut season, but has not progressed, and often finds little under pressure in the closing stages (has been seen to swish his tail). Given an enterprising ride by James Owen at Guilsborough, and similar tactics might have dealt fruit again — just touched off in his Members when trying to make all. Tends to get wound up in the preliminaries. Just the sort who is susceptible to wind problems. *Mrs D.E.S. Surman — V. of Aylesbury (Herbie Owen)*. 80 (CCfR), 247 (R), 513 (CR), 734 (R), 1009 (CR), 1142 (M), 1487 (M).

DERRYS PREROGATIVE ..8-13.. 11 b.g. Nearly A Hand — Derrycreha Lass (Precipice Wood) 5. Small good-bodied. Dam, half-sister to Boreen Owen (*qv* '99 Annual), won 2m2f Hdle in Ireland, and won 2 2m4f Hdles in England. NH FLAT '94 and '96 r2 p0. NH '96/7 r9 p1 (19l 3rd in Ch); remote 5th of 6 and pulled up 3 in other Chses; inc Sell. P-t-P '99 r5 w1 (Maiden) p1 (3rd); and last 3. Left the lucky winner of a poor Maiden at Chaddesley Corbett in '99, but has always been lightly raced, and exposed as modest in the extreme. Ran well for a long way in a fair Restricted on his reappearance, but was not seen again. *Miss N.J. Rudge — Farmers Bloodhounds*. 193 (R).

DESERT BOOT ..9-7.. 6 gr.g. High Kicker (USA) — Desert Mist (Sharrood USA) f8p62u. Tall rangy. Dam, half-sister to Tremendisto (*qv*), won 2 15f races (inc Sell), and won 5 Hdles, 2m-2m2f. NH FLAT '99 r2 p0 (tailed off both). Mars most of his rounds with plentiful errors, but a four lengths second in his Members was a decent effort for a five-year-old, and would have obvious claims in a Maiden if he repeated the form. Started very slowly and performed erratically before unseating on his latest attempt, and more accomplished riding would be a definite boost. *T.H. Caldwell — Cheshire Forest*. 167 (OMa), 301 (2m5fH), 526 (OMa), 777 (OMa), 959 (M), 1601 (3m2fH).

DESERT CALM (IRE) ..10-1.. 12 br.g. Glow (USA) — Lancette (Double Jump) 4p6*5820*. Compact half-brother to Hurdles winner, Choice Cut (IRE), and to several flat winners, including Darcy's Thatcher and Rasa Penang (both useful). IRISH FLAT '91/5 r45 w4 (7-9f) p8. IRISH NH '94/5 r5 p0. FLAT '96/7 r13 p1 (3rd). NH '96/9 r20 p4 (2 3rds in Hdles; and 2 Chses). HUNT CH '99 r8 w1 (2m3f110y) p3 (2nd once); unseated 1. NH '00 r1 p0 (5th in 2m5f HCap Ch: *hdwy to ld 7, hdd 9, btn 2 out*). Recorded an annual flat success in Ireland '91/4, but less productive over jumps, and was gaining his first victory at the 29th attempt when he snatched the spoils in the final stride of an Ascot 2m3f Hunter Chase in '99. Never so resolute before or since, and his best effort in 2000 was at Towcester, but again he folded tamely in the closing stages. Does not stay three miles and campaigned exclusively at around 2m4f now, but will struggle to add to his tally in future. Has been tried blinkered. *R.N. Fuller — Cheshire (Ginger McCain)*. 153 (2m4f110yH), 382 (2m4fH), 470 (2m4f110yH), 1341 (2m110yH), 1531 (2m110yH), 1600 (2m5f110yH).

DESERT DEVIL ..—.. 9 b.g. Green Desert (USA) — Jolie Pelouse (USA) (Riverman USA) pf. Rangy. NH FLAT '96 r1 p0. NH '96/7 (from R. Allan's; previously from late G. Richards') r2 p0 (tailed off last Hdles). Revived after a three year gap for two outings on different courses at Hexham in late May, but impressed in neither. *N. Park — Border (Kevin Robson)*. 1580 (OMa), 1602 (2m4f110yH).

DESERT RUN (IRE) ..9-0§.. 13 ch.g. Deep Run — Another Dutchess (Master Buck) 43dp465. Tall good-looking brother to Chasing winner, Deep Decision, and half-brother to Sharsman (IRE), and to Chasing winner, Justuce Alone (IRE). IRISH P-t-P '93 r2 w1 (5yo Maiden) p0; pulled up 1. NH '93/7 (blinkered 1) r22 w1 (3m3f Ch) p5 (short-headed once). Pure P-t-P '97/9 r9 p2; last pair 3, pulled up 3, and ran out 1. A safe conveyance who usually plods round for the joint handlers, but has shown little interest for quite some time, and is regularly tailed off these days. Merits retirement. *Miss J. West, B.G. Parsons & M. Heath — Blackmore & Sparkford V. (Jo West & Brett Parsons)*. 257 (L), 405 (L), 653 (MO), 736 (Cnr), 952 (M), 1259 (4mL).

DESERT WALTZ (IRE) ..10-0.. 12 ch.g. Gorytus (USA) — Desert Pet (Petingo) 1p22. Lengthy unfinished half-brother to Chasing winner, Desert Brave (IRE), and to 4 flat winners (2 abroad — one also won jumping in Belgium). Dam won at 12f. IRISH NH FLAT r1 p0. IRISH FLAT r2 p0. IRISH P-t-P '94 r6 p1 (3rd); pulled up 2, and fell 1. P-t-P '95/7 r20 w11 (inc Ladies; hat-trick '95 and 4-timer '96) p8 (2nds); unseated 1. A highly successful Pointer who resurfaced after two seasons absence caused by injury, and though not quite the force of old still managed to hoist his career victories to 12. Retired after chasing home Copper Coil on his favourite track, Larkhill — gained half of his wins there. Could have won Hunter Chases had the fates not conspired against him, but the splendid fact remains that he was never once out of the first two in 22 completions. *H.B. Geddes — Beaufort (Richard Barber)*. 8 (C), 62 (Cf), 259 (C), 456 (C).

DESMOND GOLD (IRE) ..8-7.. 13 b.g. Tumble Gold — Stylish Princess (Prince Tenderfoot USA) 5fpp3. Lengthy half-brother to smart flat winner, Palatial Style. IRISH NH FLAT r1 w1 (6yo&up Maiden) p0; fell/unseated 2. IRISH NH FLAT r2 p0. IRISH NH '93 r1 p0. NH '94/6 (blinkered final) r6 w2 (2m4f-2m7f Hdles) p0. P-t-P/HUNT CH '97/9 r12 w1 (Confined) p4 (3 2nds); pulled up 1, unseated 3, and slipped up 1. Won his Pointing debut, but surprisingly beaten in all 16 ventures since, and has performed woefully in the present yard. Not getting home for previous connections, but performs like a problem horse now, and has failed to beat a rival since '98. *Miss H.E. Roberts — Llangeinor (E. Roberts)*. 1295 (Cf), 1450 (Cf), 1569 (Cf), 1612 (Cf), 1656 (M).

DESPERATE ..10-2.. 13 ch.g. Saxon Farm — Menel Arctic (Menelek) 543432. Strong-topped half-brother to Cwm Arctic. Dam won Irish NH flat. NH '91/6 r29 w7 (6 Hdles, 2m4f-3m3f, the first a Sell; and 3m2f Ch) p5; pulled up in 3 of last 5 attempts. P-t-P/HUNT CH '98/9 r7 w1 (3m Hunt Ch) p4 (2 2nds, inc Hunt Ch, and inc 3rd in Hunt Ch); pulled up 1. Did well to recapture his previous useful NH form in '99, and was gaining his first success since '95 when winning a Chepstow Hunter Chase. Never really going with the same enthusiasm in 2000, and Dickie Barrett was often having to drive his indolent partner along from an early stage. Managed to get into a challenging position on most starts, but the effort to get there usually told, and he was flagging at the finish. Suited by soft ground, but can handle faster conditions. May need to lower his sights in future. *S.E. Bown — Pytchley (Tik Saunders)*. 149 (3mH), 460 (2m7f110yH), 802 (2m6fH), 1025 (3m110yH), 1249 (2m7fH), 1533 (3m1fH).

DESTIN D'ESTRUVAL (FR) ..10-7§.. 10 b.g. Port Etienne (FR) — Vocation (FR) (Toujours Pret USA) 24pf6. Tall. FRENCH FLAT r3 w1 (10f) p1 (3rd). FRENCH NH '94/6 r13 w1 (2m2f Ch) p5 (2nds). NH '96/8 r19 w3 (2m4f-2m5f Chses, lucky once) p6 (inc 2 Hdles — caught near finish in both). NH '99 r1 p0 (4th). HUNT CH '99 r4 w2 (2m4f110y-2m5f110y) p1 (2nd). NH '00 r3 p1 (2nd in 2m4f HCap Ch: *hld up, hdwy 6, outpcd 4 out, rallied app last, stayed on wl*); 4th: *hld up til hdwy 10, wknd 14*; and fell; *hld up in rr, fell 9*). A talented individual, but can look temperamental, and has owed his successes to outstanding riding and training. Twice successful for Alan Dempsey in '99, but Charlie Weaver could not get the same tune out of him. Needs give in the ground and ideally suited by sub-three mile contests. *H.P. Hogarth — York & Ainsty S. (Henrietta Knight)*. 919 (2m3f110yH), 1026 (2m5f110yH).

DETROIT DAVY (IRE) ..10-0.. 10 b.g. Detroit Sam (FR) — Pretty Damsel (Prince Hansel) pu256. Tall strong half-brother to Golden Mac (*qv*). NH FLAT '96 r2 p0 (4ths). NH '96 r1 p0 (last in Hdle). IRISH P-t-P '98 r5 p1 (3rd); last, pulled up 2, and fell 1. P-t-P/HUNT CH '99 r7 w2 (Maiden and Restricted) p2 (2 2nds, inc a Hunt Ch); pulled up 1, and fell 1. An attractive individual who usually gleams in the paddock, and is well suited by soft ground. Incredibly unlucky not to collect a Garnons Intermediate on his second start (Pip Jones was unseated at the penultimate fence with a seemingly unassailable lead), and finished well clear of the third when a well supported second at Buckfastleigh subsequently. Deserves compensation, though usually needs an outing to get fit, and flying too high in Hunter Chases. *G.G. Lewis — Pentyrch (David Oakes)*. 222 (3m1f110yH), 448 (I), 654 (I), 1449 (I), 1644 (3m2f110yH).

DEVIL'S STING (IRE) ..9-3-.. 12 ch.g. Henbit (USA) — Hells Mistress (Skymaster) pp5638p. Tall half-brother to Master Don, to Irish flat and smart English Hurdles winner, Don Valentino, and to flat and Hurdles winner, Scott Bennett. NH '94, '95 and '98 r7 p1 (3rd); pulled up 2, and unseated 1. P-t-P/HUNT CH '96 and '98/9 r10 p1 (2nd); pulled up 7 — broke down final race '96. Handicapped by his inability to stay three miles, and has been plagued by myriad problems. Capable of bowling along for up to 2m4f, but gets not a yard further, and has not proved good enough for sub-three mile races under Rules. *R.C. Harper — Bicester with Whaddon.* 739 (OMa), 972 (OMa), 1207 (OMa), 1423 (OMa), 1486 (OMa), 1598 (OMa), 1668 (OMa).

DEVONSHIRE LAD ..8-11-.. 10 b.g. Sergeant Drummer (USA) — Alice Rairthorn (Romany Air) 3ppup2Rp. Workmanlike lengthy brother to Ive Called Time (*qv*). NH '98 r2 p0 (fell at 1st, and pulled up in Hdles). P-t-P/HUNT CH '96/7 and '99 (Cole-trained for Mr T.G. & Mrs D.B. Lunt) r16 w1 (Maiden) p1 (2nd); pulled up 11, fell/unseated 2, and carried out 1. Broke down one race after opening his account at Vauterhill in '97, and has looked as though something is troubling him since his return in '99 — often stops in a matter of strides, and could well be bursting internally. Gave a passable display when third on his reappearance, but otherwise hopeless and has pulled up in 12 of his last 16 outings. Has been tried blinkered. *Miss D. Cole — Dulverton E.* 102 (R), 202 (I), 728 (R), 958 (R), 1140 (CfR), 1187 (Inr), 1517 (R), 1604 (M).

DFOURSDREAM ..8-12-.. 7 gr.g. Joli Wasfi (USA) — Ruthelen (Pongee) p7. Tall lengthy owner-bred. Dam won a Restricted (a bad race in soft), but failed to finish 8 of 9 other attempts over fences, and showed a distinct lack of enthusiasm. Took on the likes of Well Armed and Slew Man in early season Confineds at Black Forest Lodge, and was very novicey and unsurprisingly completely out of his depth. Maidens will be far more appropriate. *M.J. Gallagher — Tiverton (J. Apps).* 66 (Cf), 199 (Cf).

DIAMOND DUCK ..9-6-.. 9 ch.m. Vital Season — Some Moor (Some Hand) 3142p. Smallish. Dam, half-sister to High Ham Blues (*qv* '97 Annual), won 2 Sell Hdles (2m-2m1f) and 2nd; and was 3rd in a Point for Mr Legg. P-t-P '97/9 (for Mr K.J. Legg & Mr S. Dunevien) r10 p3 (2nd of 3, remote last of 2, and last of 3); pulled up 4. Has looked to be physically defective (often legless in the closing stages) on occasions, but showed improved form in the new yard and enjoyed the undemanding conditions when successful at Cothelstone. A keen sort and usually races prominently, but lacks much scope for improvement, and might have to search long and hard for a suitable Restricted opportunity. Ran in a tongue-strap on one occasion in '99, and has often appeared quite highly strung to boot. *N.J. Case — Taunton V.* 353 (CfMa), 640 (CfMa), 1097 (Inr), 1551 (R), 1639 (R).

DIAMOND LIGHT ..—-.. 14 ch.g. Roman Warrior — Another Jo (Hotfoot) p. Close-coupled. Dam won 2m Sell Hdle. NH '93/4 and '97 r8 p1 (2nd in 2m Nov Ch); pulled up 3 and unseated 2. P-t-P '96 (for Mr V.R. Bishop) r2 p1 (2nd of 3); and last. Hardly bred for Pointing, and resurfaced after a long absence to pull up at Brampton Bryan. His diminutive partner Emma Bryan, who must have robbed several church roofs to get the required amount of lead for her weight cloth, shows considerable promise. *W.J. Bryan - Golden V.* 866 (CfMa).

DIAMOND MARKET ..—-.. 9 gr.g. Absalom — The Victor Girls (Crofthall) ppp. Big half-brother to Moneghetti. FLAT (all placings at 3 for R. Hollinshead; previously for R.J. Price) r16 p3 (7-8½f on Wolverhampton all-weather). NH '97/8 (for J. Spearing; previously for R. Cambidge) r2 p0 (last and pulled up — tailed off both). Useless on his rare appearances over jumps, and even if he did have any ability he would surely not get the trip. *S. McDonald — N. Staffs (Jackie Moule).* 116 (I), 336 (R), 569 (OMa).

DICK'S CABIN ..—-.. 14 br.g. Strong Gale — Lady Park (No Argument) pp. Tall angular brother to Irish Chasing winners, Any Port (also a successful Pointer there) and Pargale. IRISH NH FLAT r7 p1 (2nd to Boro Eight on debut, despite veering badly left); refused to race 1. IRISH NH '93/4 r4 p0. IRISH P-t-P '96 r8 w1 (7yo&up Maiden, after two in front had exited at last) p1 (2nd); pulled up 4. P-t-P/HUNT CH '97/9 r19 w1 (Restricted) p2 (last of 2, and last of 3); failed to finish 13 (fell/unseated 2). Rendered useless by wind problems (ran tubed in '97 and sometimes tongue-tied since), and only once better than last in the current ownership. Should not be embarrassed any longer. *C. & Mrs S.B. Walwin — V.W.H. (Sarah Walwin).* 632 (I), 886 (I).

DICKS DARLIN' ..9-0-.. 8 b.m. My Richard — Hi Darlin' (Prince De Galles) p4pf4. Small compact owner-bred half-sister to Hizal (*qv*). Sire, by Petrizzo, was bred by John Manners, but never ran. NH FLAT '98 r2 p0. NH '99 r5 p0 (tailed off in Hdles, inc Sell). P-t-P '99 r4 p0; last and pulled up 3. NH June '00 r1 p0 (4th in 2m110y Nov Hdle: *jmpd slow 1, sn rr, bhnd when mist 6*). A consistently poor jumper to date, who showed her first signs of ability on final start (still had every chance when coming down five out in a poor Maiden), and might just surprise provided Alex Charles-Jones feels that it is worth the risk. *H.J. Manners — V.W.H.* 630 (CfMa), 753 (CfMa), 1483 (L), 1596 (OMa).

DIDO'S DREAM ..—-.. 8 br.m. Vital Season — Pretty Pantoes (Lepanto GER) fp2p. Owner-bred. Great-grandam, Joyful Tears, failed to finish in 4 of 5 Points, but bred Run To Me (*qv* '90 Annual). P-t-P '99 r2 p0 (unseated 1, and pulled up 1). Error prone and distinctly lacking in talent to date. *P.G. Bevins — Avon V.* 956 (OMa), 1284 (OMa), 1555 (OMa), 1654 (OMa).

DIGITALIS ..—§.. 8 ch.m. Henbit (USA) — Vulpine Lady (Green Shoon) f. Long-backed half-sister to Portknockie, Frosty Lady and Wily Miss. Dam pulled up in 2 Points. P-t-p '99 r4 p0 (pulled up 3, and refused 1). Displayed a little ability in '99, but looks to be another Henbit that has other ideas about racing. Disappeared after a final fence tumble at Thorpe in February, and may have been hurt. *R.L. Burton — S. Salop (Pam Sykes).* 122 (OMa).

DILLON ..9-10.. 11 b.g. Derring Rose — Lucky Gold (Pitpan) p34213. Sturdy. Dam won NH flat and 2 Hdles (2m-2m2f) in Ireland. NH FLAT '94 r2 p0. NH '96 and '98 (form M. Madgwick; previously for M. Channon) r6 p0 (10th of 11 and pulled up in Chses, inc Sell). Bought Malvern, Feb for 1500. Moderate and very one-paced, but found his level in poor Points, and was able to win a Maiden at Lockinge. Held every chance at the final fence in his Members, but faded up the rising ground and appeared to finish lame, which probably means another long spell on the side lines (regularly goes missing for two years at a time). *Mr & Mrs D.J. Forsyth — Warwicks (Fred Hutsby).* 234 (OMa), 515 (OMa), 889 (OMa), 1018 (OMa), 1207 (OMa), 1438 (M).

DILLY MAY DALLY ..—.. 10 ch.m. Don't Dilly Dally — Vulravina (Vulgan) ppp. Small good-topped half-sister to Kula and Mr Pink. P-t-P '97 and '99 (for Mrs S. Hewett in '99) r3 p0 (pulled up 2, and refused 1). Three different owners have all discovered that she is highly unlikely to ever get to the church on time. *Mrs L.T. Spence & B. Duthie — E. Essex (L. Spence).* 844 (OMa), 942 (CfMa), 1040 (OMa).

DINEDOR CHARLIE ..9-12§.. 11 ch.g. Rustigo — Dinedor Lady (Cavo Doro) b73f. Small attractive owner-bred brother to Just Arnold (*qv*). P-t-P '97/9 r12 w1 (Maiden) p2 (3rds, of 4, and remote last); pulled up 4, and fell/unseated 2. Able, and given a good ride by Dai Jones when successful at Howick in '99, but a real villain and always looking for a way out. Needs to poach a reasonable lead and hang on (tactics that almost worked again at Llanfrynach in 2000), as he seems to know instinctively where the line is and hence where to start applying the brakes. Would win a Restricted were he genuine, but not to be trusted as those who have been involved in two uninspired gambles on his '99/00 debuts have found to their cost. Tends to carry plenty of condition. Acquired blinkers on his last two appearances. *R.J. Williams — S. Herefords (Christine Hardinge).* 6 (R), 120 (CR), 483 (R), 596 (R).

DINO'S MISTRAL ..8-4.. 8 b.g. Petong — Marquessa D'Howfen (Pitcairn) p0. Light-framed half-brother to Quessard, to flat winner, Mardessa, and to a successful Hurdler. Dam won at 7f. FLAT (blinkered 1; early runs for breeder, Franny Lee, who won with dam) r18 p0. NH '97/8 (for K. Morgan) r6 p1 (3rd in Sell — very tired when nearly fell last); withdrawn lame start final intended outing. Bought Doncaster, Nov '98 for 1200. A hard player who did not stay two miles over hurdles, and performed without distinction on a brief revival in Points. *W.A. Crozier — Haydon.* 713 (R), 976 (R).

DI'S DREAM ..8-10.. 9 b.m. Buckley — Gillie's Daughter (Hardiran) ppu. Small light half-sister to Wolfie Smith (*qv*). NH '98 r2 p0 (pulled up 2). P-t-P '99 r4 p1 (3rd); and pulled up 3. Beaten 25 lengths on her sole completion, and looks a highly unlikely winner. An excitable mare who has had two paddock handlers, and sweated up. *Miss D. Guilding — N. Ledbury.* 341 (CfMa), 669 (R), 893 (OMa).

DISRESPECT ..—.. 11 b.m. Respect — Miss Sunny (Sunyboy) pppp. Small close-coupled attractive owner-bred half-sister to Tannock Brook, Sunny Meadow and Templand. Dam, sister to Jack Sun (*qv* '99 Annual), pulled up in a Point. P-t-P '96/9 r17 w1 (Maiden) p1 (2nd); failed to finish 9 (unseated 1, and ran out 1). Took five seasons to lose her maiden status, but soundly thrashed in Restricteds since, and soon lagging in the ruck in 2000. Displayed plenty of stamina when successful, but looks most unlikely to repeat the feat. *W.G. Macmillan — Dumfries.* 423 (R), 1162 (R), 1363 (R), 1577 (R).

DISTANT-PORT (IRE) ..10-0§.. 11 b.g. Phardante (FR) — Quayville (Quayside) 41p23p2. Good-bodied half-brother to Happy Higgins, The Dancing Parson and Cloughlea Lad (IRE). NH FLAT r2 p0 (bolted before start on debut). P-t-P '97/9 r19 w2 (Maiden and Restricted) p5 (3rds, inc remote last); failed to finish 6 (ran out 1, refused 1, and on floor 2). Can look a good horse on occasions, but thoroughly inconsistent, and apt to please himself most of the time. Blessed with a turn of foot and usually held up in a bid to utilise it, but has always been a volcanic character, (his half-brother Cloughlea Lad was also potty), and sure to remain unpredictable. Seems to act on any going though his wins have been achieved on ground no quicker than good. *Miss P. Morris & P. Conlon — Croome & W. Warwicks (Trish Morris).* 116 (I), 296 (I), 480 (O), 671 (C), 859 (O), 1087 (MO), 1436 (Cf).

DISTINCTIVE (IRE) ..10-12.. 12 ch.g. Orchestra — Zimuletta (Distinctly USA) 21u12. Robust half-brother to Irish NH flat winner, Zimulante. Dam won 4 Hdles (2m-2m4f) and 2m2f Ch in Ireland. NH FLAT '93 r2 p0. NH '93/9 (for M. Wilkinson) r34 w2 (2m5f-3m Chses, lucky once) p5 (inc 3rd in Hdle). Bought Doncaster, May for 2800. A useful front-runner on his day, but had been unplaced 11 times under Rules since his last win in February '97, and several bad efforts included when he broke a blood vessel once and when finishing distressed once. Perked up in the new yard and scored twice at Chaddesley, once when owner-ridden, and once when partnered by Adrian Wintle in the Dudley Cup. The formerly prestigious Open sunk to a new low in 2000 with just four competitors (the smallest field ever), and two of those were having major sulks, so it was a real no-contest. Ended his season with a valiant second to Coulton over 2m5f at Cheltenham, where he was no match for the winner but well clear of the rest. Likes a little give in the ground. Debbie Jackson is entitled to be delighted with her cheap purchase. *Mrs D.J. Jackson — N. Ledbury.* 449 (L), 611 (C), 860 (L), 1065 (3m2fO), 1339 (2m5fH).

PLATE 42   1065 Worcestershire Mens Open (Lady Dudley Cup): Distinctive (A. Wintle), 1st, jumps the last
                                                                    PHOTO: Bill Selwyn

DIVET HILL ..10-7.. 7 b.g. Milieu — Bargello's Lady (Bargello) 531p1. Home-bred half-brother to Bavington (*qv*). A quick galloper who jumped well and made all when scoring quite impressively on firmish ground at Lockerbie and Mosshouses, but got bogged down in the mud when favourite at Corbridge in between. Looks well above average, and connections have already eschewed a Restricted with him, suggesting that they are confident that he will pay his way in a much better grade. Might be worth noting if he turns up under Rules. Has a promising pilot in the novice Matthew Clayton. *I. Hamilton — Tynedale (Ann Hamilton).* 425 (CfMa), 500 (2m4fOMa), 977 (CfMa), 1162 (R), 1425 (I).

DIVINE INSPIRATION (IRE) ..9-5.. 9 b.g. Torus — Maid Of Florence (Floriferous) 3. Workmanlike. IRISH P-t-P '98 r3 w1 (5&6yo Maiden) p0; pulled up 1. P-t-P/HUNT CH '99 r2 p0 (last, and pulled up 1). Came from out of the clouds to win in Ireland, but has been rather a costly failure since (cost current connections 8500 gns), and either does not stay or will not buckle down, as he has twice capitulated having held every chance at the third last. Clearly not easy to train, and disappeared after flattering to deceive at Black Forest Lodge in March — the place sounds idyllic, but many Pointers never see the light of day again after racing there. *A.J. Paterson — Curre (Sarah George).* 560 (R).

D'NIAL ..8-9.. 9 b.m. Pragmatic — The Ceiriog (Deep Diver) r. Half-sister to Run Of Weld, The Foolish One and The Rent Man. Dam won 4 Hdles, 2m-2m7f, inc Swedish Champion. P-t-P '98 r3 p2 (last of 3 once); pulled up 1. Failed to beat a single rival when placed twice in '98, but missed the following season and was tailed off when declining the open ditch at Erw Lon on her return — joint-favourite! May have suffered a reverse as she was not seen again. *Mrs D.L. Smith-Hooper — Llangeinor.* 270 (CfMa).

DOCKMASTER ..10-3.. 10 b.g. Dominion — Surf Bird (Shareef Dancer USA) p1R51. Small neat half-brother to flat winners, Epic Stand, Baffin Bay and Break The Rules (latter also a successful Hurdler). FLAT (for J. Bethell) r10 p4. NH '94/9 (for Miss K. Milligan, visored 2, worn tongue-strap) r39 w4 (2m-3m4f Hdles, in Sell) p11 (beaten head once); pulled up both Chses. Unreliable, but seemed to enjoy nipping round Higham, and gave Matthew Abrey a winning first ride there as well as being gifted a two-finisher Open on the same course (the only other runner, the 2-7 shot Commuter Country, pulled up). Connections did substantially better with him than might have been expected, as he has had wind problems, and ended his career under Rules lame. Not seen since March. *R.G. Abrey — Suffolk.* 84 (L), 238 (O), 553 (MO), 607 (O), 757 (O).

DOCS DILEMMA (IRE) ..9-13.. 12 br.g. Decent Fellow — Talkative Princess (Prince Regent FR) p. Lengthy half-brother to Manners To Burn. Dam won at 14f (on disqualification in Ireland). IRISH NH FLAT '93/4 r7 p2. IRISH NH '94 r2 p0. NH '94/5 and '97/8 (tried blinkers) r23 w4 (2m1f Hdle, and 3 Chses, 2m7f-3m1f) p9. P-t-P '99 r7 w2 (Ladies) p4 (2 3rds); and 4th. Revived a flagging career when switched to Points in '99 and won two Ladies races under Emma Coveney, but failed to air again after pulling up at Ampton in January 2000. Jumps well and has a penchant for fast ground, but will do well to make another winning comeback at 12, even though opportunities are plentiful in his area. *P. Murphy & Mrs H. Silk — Kent & Surrey Bloodhounds (Heather Silk).* 84 (L).

DOCTOR DUNKLIN (USA) ..9-6.. 12 gr.g. Family Doctor (USA) — Mis Jenifer's Idea (USA) (Capital Idea USA) 4267389. Small. NH FLAT '93 r3 p1 (head 2nd). NH '93/5 and '97/8 (visored once in '95) r21 w1 (2m6f Hdle) p3; last, and pulled up 4 in Chses. P-t-P '99 r6 p1 (last of 2); last 2, and unseated 3. Employed as a schoolmaster in the last two seasons, but has shown little zest, and ran even worse when blinkered on his last two appearances. Gained his solitary success back in '94, and looks certain to have to rest on his laurels. *Mrs V.C. Ward — Belvoir.* 230 (L), 442 (L), 795 (L), 869 (L), 1074 (L), 1155 (2m5f110yH), 1447 (2m4fH).

DOCTOR EDWARD ..—.. 15 gr.g. Ring Bidder — Guilsway (Track Spare) 4. Dam won 2m Hdle. P-t-P '94 (for Mr A. Wynne & Mr D. Manning) r3 p1 (3rd); unseated 1, and pulled up 1. Had enjoyed five seasons in retirement, but reached for the Zimmer frame to provide Sara Stephens with a completion (albeit two fences adrift) in his Members. *Miss S.E. Stephens — Crawley & Horsham.* 711 (M).

DOCTOR-J (IRE) ..9-6.. 11 ch.g. Jareer (USA) — Velvet Breeze (Windjammer USA) &p. Compact half-brother to 2 winners abroad. NH '93/6 and '98/9 (often blinkered; visored 1) r29 w4 (2m-2m1f Sell Hdles) p7; last pair in 2 Chses. P-t-P/HUNT CH '97/8 r14 p3 (2nds, remote of 3 once, and last once); pulled up 1, and fell 1. A fair Selling Hurdler for John White in '94/5, but has run up a losing sequence of 29, and has never shown the remotest sign of being able to stay three miles. Can still take a keen hold, but a waste of time in Points. Has been tried in a tongue-strap. *G. Richards & D. Clunn — Ystrad Taf Fechan.* 479 (Cf), 742 (O).

DO IT ONCE (IRE) ..10-7.. 9 b.g. Strong Gale — Golden Privet (IRE) (Kemal FR) 121. Dam is half-sister to Big Brown Bear (*qv* '88 season Annual). IRISH NH FLAT '97 r1 p0. IRISH NH '97/9, r11 w1 (3m Hunt Ch) p1 (3rd in similar). IRISH P-t-P '99 r3 w1 (7 plus Mdn) p1 (2nd); pulled up 1. Bought Doncaster, Aug for 5000. Showed plenty of determination in the new yard, and upset the hot favourite Rocket Radar at up ton, but could not cope with Well Ted at Paxford in his only defeat. Unusually for a Strong Gale, he has produced all his winning form on easy surfaces, including in heavy. Probably good enough to collect an Open. Wears a tongue-strap. A deserved winner for Michael Keel, who has persevered to improve his riding at long last. *Mrs P. Tollit — Worcs.* 1063 (Cfn), 1190 (Cf), 1358 (Cf).

DO JUSTICE (IRE) ..9-5.. 7 b.g. Bustomi — Kate Just (Mugatpura) 2p. Workmanlike. Dam, half-sister to Nash Brakes (*qv* '97 Annual), won Point and 2m4f Hunt Ch in Ireland; and was placed in 3 Chses (inc a Hunt) in England. Had three subsequent winners behind him when making what looked to be a very promising debut at Alnwick, but clearly went wrong next time, which seems ominous at such an early stage in his career. *E. Fenwick (Gem Partnership) — Zetland (Ernie Fenwick).* 45 (OMa), 381 (OMa).

DOLLY BLOOM ..9-9.. 13 b.m. Crested Lark — Lucky Sandy (St Columbus) p2pf. Tall good-looking sister to Dennis (*qv*). P-t-P '96/9 r24 w3 (Maiden, Restricted and Intermediate) p7 (4 2nds; promoted to 3rd once); pulled up 5, and fell/unseated 2. Well beaten in the current yard (though did give Tash McKim a fair ride when second in her Members), and died from a heart attack whilst swimming on the same day her brother was killed at Kingston Blount. *J. Tredwell — Grafton.* 74 (CCf), 784 (M), 1205 (MO), 1441 (Cnr).

DONA FERENTIS (IRE) ..9-0.. 6 b.m. Homo Sapien — Greek Tan (Pitpan) p. Tall good-topped half-sister to Cornish Twoways (IRE). Sold Tattersalls, Ireland Aug for 8928. Favourite for her debut, but was not pushed once her chance had gone. Looks a scopey individual, and may improve considerably in time. *C.D. Collins — Cottesmore (Caroline Bailey).* 1011 (CfMa).

DONARD SON (IRE) ..9-4.. 10 b.g. Florida Son — Donard Lily (Master Buck) u33. Tall workmanlike half-brother to Irish Pointing winners, Kilmainhamwood and Kav Gan. Dam won mares Maiden in Ireland. IRISH P-t-P '96 r1 p1 (15/2 2nd). Placed in three of just four outings, and has the ability to win a little race, but seems to stand his appearances very badly. Wore a tongue-strap on final start. *D. Merchant — Haydon.* 44 (OMa), 139 (OMa), 914 (OfMa).

DON DU CADRAN (FR) ..9-11.. 12 b.g. Dom Pasquini (FR) — Bel Du Cadran (FR) (Bel Baraka) p32. Tall half-brother to a French flat winner, and to 4 jumping winners there. Dam was a French jumping winner. IRISH P-t-P '94 r1 w1 (4&5yo Maiden). NH '94/7 r11 w3 (2m5f Hdle and 2

Chses, 3m-3m2f) p3. P-t-P '98/9 r7 p3 (3rds; of 4 twice, and last); pulled up 1. First produced in Ireland by Arthur Moore before being sold to the late Tim Forster for whom he won three times including the only two Chases he contested, but has never stood much racing due to several bouts of leg trouble. Placed five times under Charlie Gundry in the last three years, but a weak finisher in Points, and easily brushed aside by decent horses. Has been tried in blinkers. *C.G.S. Gundry — Berkeley.* 597 (Cf), 1311 (Cf), 1489 (M).

DONICKMORE (IRE) ..10-2.. 10 ch.g. Carmelite House (USA) — Sweet Chimes (Orchestra) p11u2210p71. Angular. IRISH NH FLAT '95/6 r5 p1 (3rd). IRISH NH '96/7 and '99 r17 w1 (2m1f Hdle) p1 (3rd in Ch). IRISH P-t-P '96 and '99 r9 w1 (Open) p3; pulled up, carried out, and fell. IRISH P-t-P '00 r9 w4 (beat Another Excuse and An Oon Iss An Owl 3*l* and 8*l* in Muskerry Open: *mist 1, 4th 10, 2nd 3 out, ld last, stayed on*; beat You Know Best and An Oon Iss An Owl 1*l* and 20*l* in United Open: *handy 6, 2nd 4 out, ld nxt, chall 2 out, stayed on*; beat Master Jake and There Tis For Ya 8*l* and 2*l* in Cloyne Open: *7th ½way, mist 9, cl 3rd 4 out, ld last, r.o wl*; and beat Aiseiri and Blazing Crack 12*l* and 4*l* in United Ladies Open: *3rd ½way, ld 5 out, mist 3 out, clr last, r.o wl*) p2 (2 2nds, beaten 6*l* by Brown Paddy in Fermoy Open: *rr, hdwy 7, 2nd 4 out, ld brief 3 out, ev ch til outpcd flat*: and beaten 4*l* by Silver Lake in Lismore Open: *3rd 5 out, 2nd nxt, jnd wnr last, no ex*); pulled up 2, and unseated 1. IRISH HUNT CH '00 r1 p0 (7th at Punchestown Champion HC: *rr, nd, t.o*). Capable of useful performances and won the maximum four Points in Ireland in 2000, but not the best of jumpers, and less convincing in his attempts over the bigger fences. Has scored in heavy and on firm, but tends to run freely, and occasionally has some difficulty lasting the trip on an exacting course. Tried blinkered in the past. *G.J. O'Keeffe — United (in Ireland).* 921 (2m6fH).

DON LUIGI ..9-4§.. 9 b.g. Rakaposhi King — Lorien Lady (Tycoon II) p3p5. Small compact. Dam, sister to Granny's Bay (*qv* '97 Annual), failed to finish in 6 of 7 Points. NH FLAT '96 r1 p0. NH '96 r2 p0 (pulled up in 2 Sell Hdles). P-t-P '99 r9 w1 (Maiden) p1 (last of 2); pulled up 4, and fell 1. Won a bad race at Wadebridge on his first completion over obstacles, but struggling badly in Restricteds since, and has only managed to beat two rivals in his last 10 starts. Ran tongue-tied once in '99 and acquired blinkers in 2000, but looks ungenuine, and probably physically awry. *Mrs J. Perry — Stevenstone (Neil Harris).* 69 (R), 104 (I), 406 (R), 558 (L).

DONNEGALE (IRE) ..10-4.. 9 b.g. Strong Gale — Marys Gift (Monksfield) 3411pf. Smallish workmanlike. Dam won 2 Irish Hdles, 2m-2m3f. NH FLAT '97 r1 p0. NH '97/9 (for T. Tate) r11 w2 (3m2f-3m4f Hdles) p1 (3rd); tailed off and pulled up only Ch — mistakes. Capable of tough performances particularly when stamina is at a premium, and stayed on dourly to beat Cittadino in a Ladies at Brocklesby Park before getting up in the final 50 yards to beat a former stablemate in the Colin Russell Novice Hunter Chase at Catterick (the moral winner was probably the eventual third, who broke a blood vessel). None too keen and was let down by his jumping subsequently, but has the ability to score again in decent company when he feels like it. Normally blinkered, and tried visored on final start. *J. Eddings — Middleton (Tim Walford).* 19 (L), 109 (L), 230 (L), 465 (3m1f110yH), 916 (3m1fH), 1343 (3m110yH).

DON ROYAL ..7-11.. 7 b.g. Rakaposhi King — Donna Farina (Little Buskins) ppppp3. Plain leggy hobdayed brother to Jobsagoodun (*qv*). Bought Doncaster, Aug for 1100. Tailed off and pulled up in his first six races including when about half a mile behind on the first ride for Gemma Harriss (she of the interesting hair — red and black horizontal halves), but acquired blinkers and finished 13 lengths third for her in a really bad Maiden at Dingley which took 14 seconds longer than the other division. Inspires no confidence in the paddock, and would need to improve more than a stone to score. *P.J. Millington — Fernie.* 1006 (Cf), 1070 (2m4fOMa), 1291 (OMa), 1422 (OMa), 1589 (2m4fOMa), 1634 (OMa), 1669 (OMa).

DONSIDE ..8-3.. 13 gr.g. Alias Smith (USA) — Delnadamph (Royal Palace) p. Lengthy half-brother to Peat Stack. NH '95 and '98 r2 p0 (last, and pulled up 1 in Chses). P-t-P/HUNT CH '94/5 and '97/9 r27 w1 (Maiden) p7 (4 2nds); failed to finish 12 (on floor 5, and ran out 1). Won a three-finisher Maiden on firm in '97, but raced and increasingly hopeless since — has not beaten a rival for three years. Visored once in '98, and usually tongue-tied now. Another who failed to emerge from an early trip to Black Forest Lodge in 2000, and looks finished. *N. Burd — E. Devon.* 203 (R).

DON'TCALLMEGEORGE ..—.. 10 b.g. Lighter — Pennulli (Sir Nulli) upp. Sturdy brother to Bright Beacon (*qv*). P-t-P '96 (for Mr H.J. Jarvis) r1 p0 (pulled up). NH FLAT '97 (for J.R. Best) r2 p0. A bad animal whose jumping record speaks for itself, and will hopefully not be seen again. *N. Phillips — O. Berks (Charlie Cox).* 892 (OMa), 1020 (OMa), 1207 (OMa).

DON'T FORGET (IRE) ..—.. 7 ch.m. Boreen (FR) — Regular-Lough (Regular Guy) pppp. Sturdy. Dam won mares Maiden in Ireland. Showed no ability prior to pulling up four times, and may have a breathing problem, as she wore a tongue-tie on her latest appearance. *M.J. Lenihan — Banwen Miners (John Moore).* 596 (R), 835 (OMa), 1302 (OMa), 1496 (OMa).

DON'T LIGHT UP ..9-5§.. 15 b.g. Lighter — Hannah's Bar (Babu) 66. Lengthy fired brother to By Law. Dam won Maiden and placed 2. NH '91/7 r22 w4 (2m5f Hdle, and 3 Chses, 3m1f-3m3f) p7; fell in '97 Grand National. P-t-P '99 (for Miss V.M. Williams) r9 w1 (Confined) p2; 4th, last, unseated 3, and pulled up 1. Gained his first success since '96 when landing a modest Confined at Garnons, but has always needed plenty of stoking, and is usually quick to run up the white flag. Error-prone and Marie Burrough did well to get him round safely (had unseated Frank Windsor-Clive thrice consecutively in '99), but plods badly now and has no interest in proceedings. Regained a visor in 2000, and frequently blinkered previously. *Miss M.D. Burrough — Cotley (Nigel Legg).* 522 (L), 736 (Cnr).

DONT TELL THE WIFE ..10-4.. 15 br.g. Derring Rose — Dame Sue (Mandamus) 411152d. Good-bodied half-brother to Irish NH flat and Hurdles winner, Bawnrock. Dam won 2 12f races, 2 Hdles (2m-2m5f) and 2m Ch. NH FLAT '91 r1 p0. NH '91/7 r54 w8 (2m6f Hdle, 25 ran, and 7 Chses, 2m5f-3m3f) p14 (short-headed once); 5th of 6, pulled up 3, and fell 1 on final 5 attempts. P-t-P '98/9 r14 w8 (inc 2 Ladies) p4 (2 2nds, beaten head once); unseated 1, and ran out 1. A fair money-spinner under Rules, but basically ungenuine, and present connections have done well to rekindle his interest. Ran up a five-timer in the last two months of the '99 season, and again showed his liking for Spring when recording an easy hat-trick in May 2000. Did not care much for the bigger fences at Uttoxeter, and was reported to be suffering with an abscess when beaten for the first time in six visits to Dingley on his final appearance. Always dropped right out and ridden with a lot of confidence by Gemma Hutchinson, but usually in command by the third last, and has not been beaten once he has got to the front in Points. Does not like to be hustled, but still capable of winning again in 2001 if his enthusiasm remains intact. Wore blinkers very occasionally under Rules. *Mrs P.J. Hutchinson — Fernie (Patrick Hutchinson).* 1007 (L), 1417 (L), 1502 (M), 1583 (C), 1593 (3m2fH), 1663 (C).

DORANS JOY (IRE) ..8-8.. 9 b.g. King's Ride — Cacadors Point (Pitpan) 4. Small unfurnished half-brother to Another Point (IRE). IRISH NH FLAT '97 r1 p0. IRISH P-t-P '98 r2 p0 (pulled up 1, and fell 1). NH '98/9 r2 p0 (last, and pulled up, in Hdles). P-t-P '99 (for Mrs R. Arthur) r5 p1 (last of 3); pulled up 2. Invariably on the premises for 2m4f, but stays no further, and has proved too moderate for a Hurdling career. Disappeared after finishing an exhausted 23 lengths fourth of five at Higham in January. *Mrs J.A. Parker — E. Sussex & Romney Marsh (Di Grissell).* 24 (OMa).

DORANSLONE ..—§§.. 8 br.m. Gildoran — Speakalone (Articulate) pp. Small strong home-bred sister to Gillone (qv). P-t-P '99 r4 p0 (pulled up 2, refused 1, and fell 1). Incredibly reluctant in her debut season, and disappeared after pulling up twice in January on her return. Prone to sweat up — a real family trait. *Mrs J.H. Docker — Atherstone.* 7 (OMa), 51 (OMa).

DORGAN ..9-3§.. 10 b.g. Lighter — Lovelyroseofclare (Torus) pppR. Tall strong half-brother to Hurdles winner, Nova Rose, and NH flat winner, Denise's Profiles. Dam won 2 NH flat. IRISH P-t-P '96 r3 p0 (pulled up 1, and unseated 2). IRISH NH '96 r2 p0 (last 2). P-t-P '97/9 r15 w1 (2m4f Maiden) p2; pulled up 8, and fell/unseated 3. Only completed once in his first 13 Points, but amazingly came home in front in a desperate 2m4f Maiden at Southwell. Not surprisingly struggling in Restricteds since, and has revealed the ungenuine side of his psyche on many occasions. Sometimes needs to be led in at the start and often takes a strong hold when he gets rolling, but steadfastly refuses to exert himself when push comes to shove. A non-finisher in 18 of 22 Points. Beyond redemption, and blinkers made no difference once. *Miss A.M. Jepson — S. Notts.* 50 (R), 179 (R), 371 (R), 513 (CfMa).

DOTTY DOLITTLE ..—.. 9 b.m. Rakaposhi King — Flagg Flyer VII (unknown) p2pp. Tiny owner-bred. Finished second in her stone wall Members, but unsurprisingly clambers over regulation fences, and connections are supreme optimists if they think she is a racehorse. *Mrs E. Pearson — High Peak H.* 368 (L), 1250 (NCM), 1412 (OMa), 1523 (C).

DOUBLE INDEMNITY (IRE) ..—.. 8 b.g. Doubletour (USA) — Splendid Pleasure (Dunphy) p. IR 3000y. IRISH FLAT r2 p1 (11½f 3rd of 4). FLAT (for G. Bravery) r2 p0. NH '99 (for L. Barratt) r1 p0 (tailed off and pulled up — not keen). Sold Malvern, Oct for 550. Wore blinkers and made several shoddy jumps before he pulled up at Llanvapley. Looks one to ignore. *C. Staley — Golden V.* 746 (CfMa).

DOUBLE STEAL ..8-7.. 8 b.g. Lord Bud — Halmsgiving (Free State) ppf34. Workmanlike half-brother to Firehalms and Golden Record. NH FLAT '98/9 (for Mrs S. Smith) r3 p0. NH '99 (for P. Eccles) r1 p0 (pulled up in Hdle). Showed a little ability over the Llanfrynach twigs in his first Point, but has been a really inept jumper since, and beaten a minimum of 30 lengths when completing. Would be a most undeserving winner on the form he has shown to date. Blinkered on his last two outings, and added a tongue-tie in the latest. *R. Perkins — Tredegar F.* 491 (CfMa), 900 (OMa), 1223 (2m4fOMa), 1404 (OMa), 1573 (OMa).

DOUBLE TEMPO (IRE) ..—.. 10 b.g. Orchestra — Break Fast (Prince Tenderfoot USA) ppp. Tall workmanlike brother to NH flat winner, Fast Fiddler (IRE). Dam won at 8f in Ireland, and won 2m Hdle there. NH '98/9 (for C. Egerton) r5 w2 (2m4f Hdle, and 2m5f Ch) p1 (3rd). Bought Doncaster, Aug for 3000. Unraced until he was seven, but got his career off to a flying start when scoring on his second and third appearances and earning £6661. Won in soft once, but has appeared to have myriad physical problems and only once able to complete the course in five subsequent attempts (reportedly bled internally on one occasion, and appeared to go temporarily lame in the latest).

Takes a strong hold, but can hang and make mistakes, and is clearly highly suspect. *S.B. Clark — York & Ainsty S.* 280 (L), 505 (L), 1350 (L).

DOUG ENG (IRE) ..9-4.. 8 b.g. King's Ride — Euroville Lady (Light Brigade) 4. Tall workmanlike half-brother to Irish NH flat and Pointing winner, Grasp The Nettle (IRE). Dam won 3m Hdle and 3 Chses (2m4f-3m1f) in Ireland. NH FLAT '97/8 (debut for Mrs J. Pitman) r2 p0. NH '98 (for M. Pitman) r3 p0 (tailed off in Hdles). Bought Doncaster, Aug for 900. Went missing for 18 months after its debut, and has never looked right since. Beaten 32 lengths in a Maiden when returning from another 16 month holiday. *A. Bevan — N. Salop.* 966 (OMa).

DOUJAS ..9-7§.. 11 b.m. Nearly A Hand — Doucement (Cheval) ur3. Small neat half-sister to Delirium and Dr Douski. Dam, half-sister to Quiet Flutter (*qv* '88 Season Annual), won 2 Hdles, 2m-2m2f, and 2m4f Ch, and placed 9 (inc 2 Points). Grandam, Softly Softly, won 3m1f Ch and placed 11 (inc 2 Points). NH FLAT r2 p0. NH '94/5 and '98 r4 p0; pulled up 1. P-t-P/HUNT CH '96 and '98/9 r15 w1 (Maiden) p5 (3 2nds); last pair 2, and failed to finish 7 (refused 1, and fell/unseated 3). In the frame five times since losing her maiden tag, but can be temperamental and her confidence looked shot to pieces whenn virtually falling at Barbury Castle and refusing at Siddington, but came back to run a fair third on her final appearance. Might just find an opening in a poor Restricted one day. *H.J. Manners — V.W.H.* 477 (R), 748 (M), 1135 (R).

DOWNTHEGROUND (IRE) ..9-11.. 8 b.g. Executive Perk — Cainsbridge Queen (Crash Course) uR. Dam, half-sister to Onawing Andaprayer (*qv* '95 Annual), won Irish NH flat (also demoted to 2nd after winning similar), and won 2m6f Hdle in England. IRISH P-t-P '98 r2 p0; pulled up 1. P-t-P '99 r1 w1 (Maiden). The convincing winner of a three-finisher Maiden at Eaton Hall on his only start in '99, but clearly no saint, and his 2000 campaign lasted just two weekends. Looks the sort who would do best for a professional under Rules. *E.H. Crow — N. Salop (Sheila Crow).* 1071 (CR), 1200 (CR).

DOWN THE MINE ..10-0.. 15 b.g. Le Moss — Zauditu (Menelek) 73. Good-bodied half-brother to Grimley Gale (IRE) (*qv*). P-t-P '92/9 r29 w15 (inc 6 Ladies, Mixed Open and Open; hat-trick in '95) p8 (7 2nds); failed to finish 5 (fell 3, and carried out 1). A tremendous servant to Dick Baimbridge over the last seven seasons winning 14 races for him (not bad for a horse that cost 2000gns — the genius of the man!), but four outings a season is his par, and seemed out of sorts in 2000. Never abused by Alison Dare, and his longevity is mainly thanks to her, but honourable retirement must be on the cards. *R.T. Baimbridge — Berkeley.* 34 (MO), 390 (L).

DOWN TO JOE'S (IRE) ..—.. 9 br.g. Be My Native (USA) — Busy Girl (Bustiki) ppppp. Small sparely-made. Dam is sister to Tikitama, and half-sister to Neltama (*qv* '96 Annual). IRISH P-t-P '98 r3 p2 (10-27l 3rds); and pulled up. IRISH NH FLAT '98 r1 p0 (21st of 22). IRISH NH '98 r2 p0 (27th of 28 in Hdle, and pulled up in Ch). Sometimes in contention for as much as 2m4f, but does not appear to stay any further, and drops out rapidly. Makes plentiful mistakes. Dismounted at the fourth on his latest appearance, when pulling up for the sixth consecutive time. *T.D.B. Underwood — Garth & S. Berks.* 250 (CfMa), 329 (CfMa), 679 (OMa), 1624 (OMa), 1662 (OMa).

DOYENNE ..9-11§.. 7 gr.m. Mystiko (USA) — No Chili (Glint Of Gold) 3f33. Small lengthy half-sister to a flat winner in UAE. Dam won at 12f. 17000y. FLAT (for G. Lewis) r9 p1 (3rd); withdrawn once, after unseating and bolting. NH '98/9 (for Mrs D. Haine) r9 w1 (2m4f Hdle — unruly at start) p1 (3rd); inc pulled up 2 and unseated from final 4 attempts. Bought Ascot, June for 2100. Fell at the last at Garnons when five lengths behind up ton Adventure, and has the ability to be a competent Pointer, but ungenuine (often blinkered flat and Hurdling), and declined to exert herself when well beaten subsequently. Not fluent and needed numerous reminders from an early stage on her latest appearance, but there is a chance she might do better if sweetened by a long break. *J. Milton — Ystrad Taf Fechan.* 201 (L), 447 (Cm), 644 (Cm), 1401 (Cf).

DOZMARY POOL ..9-11.. 8 ch.g. Broadsword (USA) — Voolin (Jimmy Reppin) pp2. Strong rangy half-brother to Blakelin and Country Loch, and to Chasing winner, Nicklup. Dam won 3 2m Hdles. P-t-P r2 p0 (pulled up). Nicely bred, but backward to date, and seemingly does not stand his racing well. Finished 30 lengths ahead of a subsequent Hunter Chase winner when second at Eyton, and it will be a surprise if a fit version does not manage to win a Maiden at least in 2001. Named after a stretch of water on Bodmin Moor that is reputed to be the place where Sir Bedivere threw the magical sword Excalibur on the wishes of the dying King Arthur. *Mrs P. Sykes — S. Salop.* 30 (CfMa), 336 (R), 568 (OMa).

DRAGON STOUT ..9-13.. 8 ch.g. Forzando — La Belle Princesse (Royal Match) p54fp1. Tall rangy half-brother to Hurdles winner, Tudor Da Samba. Dam won at 7f in Ireland. P-t-P '98 r5 p1 (½l 2nd); pulled up 2, and brought down 1. Looked an unlucky loser when blundering badly in the lead at the last on his final appearance of '98, but missed the following season, and had to wait until his last appearance of 2000 to finally gain compensation. Can quicken on firmish ground, and should find another opportunity when conditions are right. Often runs in a tongue-strap. *R.T. Dennis — Hurworth (Carol Dennis).* 138 (OMa), 437 (OMa), 625 (OMa), 809 (OMa), 1233 (OMa), 1353 (OMa).

DRAM HURLER (IRE) ..9-13.. 9 ch.g. Buckskin (FR) — Vintage Harvest (Deep Run) u3514. Tall rangy plain half-brother to Riding Crop (IRE) and Vintage Classic (IRE). IRISH NH FLAT '99 r2 p1 (2nd). Bought Doncaster, May for 6000. Backed from 6-1 to half those odds when making the bulk of the running to score at Whittington, and is evidently a very thorough stayer. Beaten 22 lengths in an Intermediate on a return to the track, and looks rather a plodder, but might have a chance in a long Restricted. *D. Smith — S. Durham.* 45 (OMa), 188 (OMa), 423 (R), 816 (OMa), 1152 (I).

PLATE 43   816 Holcombe Harriers Open Maiden: Dram Hurler (R. Morgan), 1st, jumps ahead of Wishing Ash (T. Davidson), fell   PHOTO: Peter & Marilyn Sweet

DREAM HOLIDAY ..—.. 6 b.m. Ski Dancer — Blonde Pryncesse (Pry) p. Half-sister to Pryvate Time (*qv*). Pulled up after two miles on Easter Monday. *E.W. Morris — Pembs.* 1222 (2m4fOMa).

DREAMIN GEORGE (IRE) ..9-4.. 11 b br.g. Mandalus — Galway Grey (Gala Performance USA) p2d12fp. Workmanlike. Dam is half-sister to Pride of Down (*qv* '87 season Annual). IRISH NH FLAT '96/7 r4 p0. IRISH '96/9 r8 p0. Useless in Ireland, but surprisingly improved in his fifth year, and was a first winner for the very ungainly Colin Sherry in a Parham Maiden. Was left clear at the last, but the form was no fluke, as he also performed respectably in two seconds. Subsequently turned a somersault at Folkestone and went crashing under the rails, and unsurprisingly his confidence seemed to be in tatters at Cartmel, where he jumped badly before a blunder caused Tom Doyle to lose his irons and pull up. Could probably score again in minor company if regaining his rhythm. *A. O'Gorman — Kent & Surrey Bloodhounds (Dick McGovern).* 304 (M), 578 (OMa), 710 (OMa), 980 (R), 1537 (2m5fH), 1601 (3m2fH).

DREAMINGTON ROVERS ..6-2.. 7 b.m. Jendali (USA) — Lallax (Laxton) 5. Neat half-sister to Chasing winner, Cheeka. Dam won 2 flat, 7-10f. NH FLAT '98/9 r3 p1 (14*l* 2nd of 6). NH '98/9 (for J.Jenkins) r2 p0; visored in Sell final. Soon tailed off when over two fences behind on her Pointing debut, and suffered the indignity of only finishing four lengths ahead of Jesusa. *D.M. Davies — Carms (Amanda Meakins).* 1222 (2m4fOMa).

DREAMISLE ..8-8.. 7 b.m. Jupiter Island — Musical Dream (Merrymount) pp2. Small neat. Dam, sister to Mountville (*qv* '87 Season Annual), was 3rd in R.A. Members ('jumps wildly as often as not'). P-t-P '99 r2 p0 (pulled up 2). Showed her first signs of ability when second in her Members, but the form amounts to little, and her subsequent prolonged absence is a worry. Needs to improve again to trouble the judge. Has been tried in blinkers. *K. Coe — Essex F. & U.* 87 (OMa), 236 (OMa), 317 (M).

DRIMINAMORE (IRE) ..9-8.. 11 b.g. Buckskin (FR) — Miss Blue Jay (Blue Refrain) uf833. Rangy. IRISH P-t-P '96 r2 p0 (last, and pulled up 1). P-t-P/HUNT CH '97/9 r12 w2 (Maiden and Restricted) p5 (3 3rds); pulled up 1, and fell 1. Well beaten since gaining his latest success in a bad three-finisher Restricted, and remains a weak finisher (has a tendency to break blood vessels). Usually a safe jumper, but had a couple of early season disagreements with Rowena Ramsay, and a third success looks unlikely. *Major General C.A. Ramsay — Berwicks.* 108 (I), 420 (I), 716 (O), 973 (I), 1425 (I).

DRIVING FORCE ..9-0.. 15 ch.g. Be My Native (USA) — Frederika (USA) (The Minstrel CAN) 95p7. Lengthy dipped. IRISH FLAT r15 w1 (8f) p4 (short-headed once). FLAT r2 p0. IRISH NH '90 r4 p1 (3rd). NH '90/5 r55 w13 (5 Hdles, 2m-2m6f, inc 4-timer, 4 on all-weather, and 8 Chses, 2m-2m5f) p17. P-t-P/HUNT CH '97/9 r18 p3 (inc 2 Hunt Chses); fell/unseated 3, and pulled up 1. No more than a safe conveyance for Samantha Hutchings nowadays, and invariably tailed off. The veteran of 92 races, but has never won beyond 2m6f and deserves to be pensioned off. *Mrs A. Brooks — Grafton (Chris Loggin).* 869 (L), 1191 (L), 1417 (L), 1483 (L).

DROMHANA (IRE) ..9-6.. 11 ch.g. Le Bavard (FR) — Honey Come Back (Master Owen) 6p40u6pu. Big workmanlike brother to NH flat and jumping winner, Master Bavard (IRE), and to Irish jumping winner, Rosewood Honey, and half-brother to Hurdles winner, Jakarrdi. Dam won 3 Hdles (2m-2m1f) and 4 Chses (2m-2m4f) in Ireland. IRISH P-t-P '95/6 r9 w4 (inc 2 Opens) p2; pulled up 2, and fell. NH '96/8 r15 w2 (3m-3m2f Chses) p10. P-t-P/HUNT CH '99 (Wormall-trained for Mrs P. Vernon) r6 p2 (2nds in Hunt Chses). Got his English career off to a flying start when successful twice from his first three attempts, but desperately one-paced and beaten in 26 starts since. Normally an expert jumper and presumably re-deployed as a schoolmaster in the latest yard, and Guy Galpin had trouble locating the saddle twice. Regained blinkers on two occasions in 2000. *Mrs P. Harrison — G. Galpin & Mrs J. Dawson — Atherstone (Pam Wormall; Jane Galpin).* 155 (3m4f110yH), 460 (2m7f110yH), 682 (3m3fH), 886 (C), 929 (Cnr), 1134 (Cnr), 1338 (4m1fH), 1471 (Cnr).

DROM ISLAND ..—.. 7 b.m. Jupiter Island — Netherdrom (Netherkelly) p. Workmanlike half-sister to Another Drom. Dam, sister to Dromakelly Lad (*qv '92 Annual*), won 2 Points and placed 3 for Jeff Tredwell. P-t-P '99 r1 p0 (pulled up). In touch at halfway in both her starts and made up significant ground to reach the leaders at Mollington in the latest, but has dropped away rapidly and been pulled up in both. Probably needs to be fitter, but her overall health has to be in question with just an annual appearance for her credit '99/00. *J. Tredwell — Grafton.* 392 (F).

DROMORE DREAM (IRE) ..10-2.. 12 ch.g. Black Minstrel — Vickies Rambler (Wrekin Rambler) 4. Strong lengthy half-brother to Selborne Rambler and Percy Special (IRE). NH '97 r3 p0 (Hdles). P-t-P/HUNT CH '95 and '99 r6 w2 (Maiden and Members) p3 (neck 2nd; and 2 3rds). A good horse when on song, but has rarely been healthy for very long, and managed just a solitary appearance in 2000. Could have been a prolific winning Pointer, but inactivity has dulled his speed, and is very one-paced nowadays. *Mrs J.M. Newitt — Sinnington.* 134 (I).

DRUID MERILL ..9-9.. 7 b.m. Miller's Gilt — Kenton Belle (Hackness) 5f. Compact home-bred. Dam is half-sister to Gay Bergen (*qv '88 Season Annual*). P-t-P '99 r2 p0 (pulled up 2). Showed distinct signs of ability on the first occasion the handbrake was taken off, but took a heavy fall when contesting the lead three out at Stafford Cross, and failed to reappear. Should be up to winning in 2001 if unharmed. *Miss E.J. Kessler — S. Devon (Gordon Chambers).* 722 (CfMa), 933 (OMa).

DRUIDS DREAM ..9-0.. 8 b.m. Pitpan — Canford Abbas (Hasty Word) 3fpp. Lengthy half-sister to The Bold Abbot. P-t-P '99 r2 p0 (pulled up 2). Ran too freely to last home on her reappearance and ran out of gas in dramatic style at Bitterley, but otherwise quickly tailed off in 2000, and probably has a fault. *Mrs G.A. Spencer — Albrighton.* 121 (OMa), 438 (OMa), 990 (OMa), 1527 (OMa).

DRUMAGOLANDS GOLDEN ENVOY (U) ..—.. 8 b.g. Golden Bash — Flower Light (unknown) up. P-t-P '99 (ran as Drumagoland, U) r1 p0 (pulled up). Confined to Members company and runs tongue-tied, but performed surprisingly well when 40-1 at Badbury, and would possibly have surprised the blue-bloods had his owner-rider not toppled through the front door when closing two out. Quickly out of contention otherwise and probably flattered. His stable should have known better than to run him with a different name, and would have been in serious trouble had he actually managed to win. *J. Kwiatkowski — Wilton, & Blackmore & Sparkford V. (John Dufosee).* 762 (M), 952 (M).

DRUMBANES PET ..9-6.. 12 ch.g. Tina's Pet — Confetti Copse (Town And Country) 4up. Workmanlike rangy half-brother to Bunchoffives. IRISH NH '93 r3 p0 (inc last, and pulled up 1). P-t-P '94/9 r15 w1 (Maiden) p3 (3rds); pulled up 6. Exceedingly fragile, and averages less than three outings a season. Needs to concentrate on the worst races open to him and forget about Hunter Chase aspirations. *Mrs C. Lawrence — Eggesford.* 255 (R), 922 (3mH), 928 (MO).

DRUMMOND WARRIOR (IRE) ..9-12.. 12 b.g. Rontino — Speckled Leinster (Prefairy) 4544345. Tall lengthy half-brother to Brave Remark, to 2 Hurdles winners, to a successful Chaser, and to an Irish NH flat winner. Dam won 2 Irish Hdles (1m6f-2m). NH FLAT '94/5 r4 p2 (2nds, one on all weather). NH '95 and '97 r12 w3 (2m1f Hdle, and 2 Chses, 2m-2m5f) p4. P-t-P/HUNT CH '99 r7 p2 (½l 2nd once); pulled up 1, and fell 1. Safe, but unenthusiastic and usually off the bridle soon after halfway. Regularly beaten by wide margins in 2000, and his chances of adding to his tally are diminishing. Anna Burton does well to drive him along, and deserves a more willing partner. *J. Burton — Quorn.* 48 (Cf), 230 (L), 544 (L), 795 (L), 869 (L), 1266 (L), 1415 (Cf).

DRUMSTICK ..10-3.. 15 ch.g. Henbit (USA) — Salustrina (Sallust) 32. Compact good-bodied half-brother to flat winners, Priolina (IRE) (in Ireland), Voila Premiere (IRE), and Ringmaster (IRE), and to a winner in Hong Kong. Dam won 3 7f races in Ireland. FLAT (blinkered 1) r8 p1 (2nd). NH '89/91 and '93/6 r79 w18 (2 Hdles, 2m-2m1f, and 16 Chses, 2m-2m6f, inc 2 hat-tricks) p30. P-t-P/HUNT CH '98/9 r13 p8 (7 3rds, inc 2 Hunt Chses); pulled up 2, unseated 2. A former prolific winner who has collected a remarkable 59 prizes, but not a battler, and has never scored over three miles. Usually takes a keen hold, but easily loses interest, and has only once ever looked like winning any of his 11 Points, when beaten by Lucky Christopher at Kingston Blount after yielding the vital inside on the final bend. Wears a tongue-strap. *P.W.E. Henn — Grafton (Mervyn Loggin).* 1441 (Cnr), 1665 (L).

DRUNKARD'S CORNER ..9-10.. 6 br.m. Tina's Pet — Royal Tycoon (Tycoon II) u217p. Close-coupled sister to flat winners, Tycoon Tina, and half-sister to Tycoon Ted. Dam won 2 2m Hdles, inc a Sell. Bought Malvern, May for 2000. Followed a promising second with quite an impressive win in a younsters Maiden at Didmarton, and was shaping up into a useful performer, but sadly broke a knee and had to be destroyed at Guilsborough. *C.O. King — O. Berks.* 74 (CCf), 220 (OMa), 391 (CfMa), 734 (R), 1009 (CR).

DRY HIGHLINE (IRE) ..10-12.. 9 b.g. Dry Dock — Fandango Girl (Last Fandango) f1u11f. Tall rangy brother to Chasing winner, Gone Ashore (IRE), and to successful Irish Pointer, I'll Remember. IRISH P-t-P '96 and '99 r7 w2 (7yo Maiden, and Winners of One) p2 (2nds); fell 3. IRISH NH FLAT '97/9 r4 p0. IRISH NH '99 r2 p0 (pulled up only Hunt Ch). Bought Doncaster, May for 10,000. An inveterate front runner who can sustain a sensational gallop, and is quite possibly the fastest Pointer in training. Returned the quickest time of the day in all his three victories, including bettering Spring Gale and Dawn Alert who were both carrying a stone less in Ladies company, and has also beaten Tom De Savoie and Rectory Garden when in receipt of weight from both. His claims in a Hunter Chase would clearly be outstanding were it not for his habitual catastrophic errors, which have left riders on the floor in six of thirteen attempts between the flags. Suited by an easy surface and spreadeagles fields, and it might prove profitable to try him over Hurdles. *Mrs C. Villar — Suffolk (Ruth Hayter).* 18 (I), 83 (Cf), 175 (I), 318 (Cf), 884 (O), 1036 (O).

PLATE 44   884 Hampshire Mens Open: Dry Highline (C. Ward-Thomas), 1st, is well clear of L to R Rectory Garden (R. Biddlecombe), 2nd, Golden Gunner (P. Young), pu, and Bally Parson (C. Wadland), pu
PHOTO: Bill Selwyn

DRY HILL LAD ..10-6.. 10 b.g. Cruise Missile — Arctic Lee (Arctic Judge) 38pf. Workmanlike brother to Lady Kay-Lee and Colonel Kay-Lee, and to jumping winner, Over The Pole, and half-brother to

Mayfield Park. Dam won a Maiden and 3rd. NH '96/7 r7 p1 (2nd in Hdle); fell in both Chses. P-t-P/HUNT CH '96 and '99 r13 w2 (inc 3m110y Hunt Ch) p6 (4 2nds, beaten neck once; and inc Hunt Ch); pulled up 1, and fell/unseated 2. Went from Maiden winner to successful Hunter Chaser in '99 and possesses plenty of ability, but not all sweetness and light and prone to make errors. Turned a somersault at Market Rasen, and was not seen subsequently. Faced some stiff tasks in 2000 and found wanting, but might be able to win again if his sights are lowered. *D. Ibbotson — Rockwood H.* 90 (3m1fH), 156 (3mH), 302 (3mH), 586 (3m1fH).

DUAL OR BUST (IRE) ..—.. 10 b.g. Going Broke — Dual's Delight (Dual) pf. Leggy half-brother to Prydel and Harpley Dual (IRE). IRISH P-t-P '96 r2 p1 (2nd); pulled up 1. P-t-P '97 r2 w1 (Maiden) p0; and unseated 1. NH '97/9 (from J.R. Jenkins') r12 w1 (3m Hdle) p3; fell and last twice in 3 Chses. Would have won both Pointing outings in '97 (clear when unseating two out on his debut), and did pretty well over hurdles, but would not face up to regulation fences after a fall at Fakenham, and presumably harmed in his latest spill. Would win more Points if he were 100 per cent, but a watching brief is advised when he returns. *J.S. Ruddy — Enfield Chace (Sue Ruddy).* 85 (O), 238 (O).

DUBLIN HILL (IRE) ..9-9.. 11 b.g. Roselier (FR) — Deep Link (Deep Run) Compact attractive half-brother to Bohola Pete (IRE). Dam was placed 10 times in Ireland, including 2 Points. IRISH NH FLAT r1 p0. IRISH P-t-P '95/6 r8 w1 (Maiden) p1 (3rd); fell/unseated 2, and refused to race 1. IRISH HUNT CH '96 r3 p1 (3rd); pulled up 2. P-t-P '97/8 r11 w1 (Restricted) p1 (2nd); fell/unseated 3, and pulled up 4. Used to be a hot ride, but broke down at Gisburn in '98, and showed nothing in two outings on his return. Unlikely to stage a revival in 2001. *R.H. Knowles — Bilsdale (Fiona Needham).* 505 (L), 1027 (Cf).

DUCHESS OF TUBBER (IRE) ..9-8.. 13 b.m. Buckskin (FR) — Unforgetabubble (Menelek) p35. Leggy workmanlike half-sister to Irish winners, Opryland (jumping) and Bee Seventeen (Pointing). IRISH P-t-P '92/3 r5 w2 p0; pulled up 1, and fell 1. NH '93/5 r16 w3 (3m1f Chses) p2 (3rds). P-t-P/HUNT CH '96/7 and '99 r10 w1 (Ladies) p3 (2 3rds; inc Hunt Ch); pulled up 4. Won a poor Ladies race at Wadebridge in '97 (rated 10-2), but lightly raced and clearly troubled since. May still possess some ability, but overfaced in 2000, and needs to seek out much easier opportunities. Appreciates mud, but can handle quicker conditions. *R.J.S. Linne — E. Cornwall.* 149 (3mH), 314 (L), 922 (3mH).

DUKE OF HADES (IRE) ..—.. 11 ch.g. Duky — Sweet Tarquin (Lucifer USA) p. Smallish plain. IRISH P-t-P '95/6 and '98 r4 w2 (5&6yo Maiden, and Winners of One) p0; fell 2. IRISH NH '96 and '98 r6 p1 (2nd in Hunt Ch); inc 3 Hdles; pulled up in 4m NH Ch at Cheltenham. Won his Irish Points in soft/heavy (the ground was barely raceable once), but has always stood his racing badly, and missed '97 and '99. Led for a long way before weakening rapidly in a February Intermediate, and promptly returned to the darkness from whence he eminated. *R.J. Rowsell — Ystrad Taf Fechan.* 344 (I).

DUKE OF TULLA (IRE) ..—.. 9 b.g. Royal Fountain — Tulla Ross (Tumble Gold) p. Plain lengthy. IRISH P-t-P '97/9 r14 p2 (15l 2nd twice); pulled up 7, brought down, fell 2, and unseated 2. Bought Doncaster, Aug for 1000. Exceptionally moderate (has only completed in two of fifteen attempts), and disappeared after being tailed off in January. *Miss K. Thory — Fitzwilliam.* 24 (OMa).

DULAS BAY ..10-4.. 7 b.g. Selkirk (USA) — Ivory Gull (USA) (Storm Bird CAN) 3. Leggy unfurnished half-brother to 2 flat winners (one in USA), including Mister Kite (later successful over jumps in USA). Dam won at 6f. 11,000y. FLAT r15 p3; inc Sell. NH '97/9 (for M.W. Easterby; often tongue-tied) r11 w1 (2m Hdle) p5; made mistakes in all 4 Chses. Bought Doncaster, Aug for 600. Could hang flat and Hurdling (did so in his only win — made all, but tried to run out early, and was veering on the run-in), but ran well in a Point, when beaten about three lengths with three subsequent winners behind. Has disappointed too often in the past to be considered reliable, but the ability is there if he cares to use it. Only seen in early February. *P.J. Millington — Fernie.* 115 (CCf).

DUNCAHA HERO ..—.. 15 b.g. Golden Love — Arctic Jungle (Arctic Slave) 5. Big strong horse to Golden Arctic, and to Irish Pointing winners, Golden Ice and Ice Warrior, and half-brother to Lovely Clonmoyle (IRE), and to Irish Pointing winner, Artic Highway. IRISH P-t-P '96 r4 p2; pulled up 1. IRISH HUNT CH '96 r1 p0 (last). P-t-P '97 and '99 r6 w1 (Maiden) p2; pulled up 1 and unseated 1. A steady performer, but did not see a racecourse until he was ten and has been incredibly lightly raced since — doubtless excels in other equine arenas. Ran well for a long way on his reappearance at Cottenham, but broke down and promptly went back into hiding. *Miss G.R. Barrow — Pytchley (Neil King).* 16 (R).

DUNETHNA (IRE) ..9-11.. 8 b.g. Phardante (FR) — Portia's Delight (IRE) (The Parson) f3211p. Lengthy quite attractive. IRISH P-t-P '98/9 r2 p2 (inc last of 3 after falling). Bought Doncaster, Aug for 4100. A fair novice who has been improving gradually, and completed a May double in minor events on dead and firmish ground. Soon struggling on his latest appearance, but may have been feeling the effects of a busy time, and could be good enough for Intermediate success in 2001. *Mrs S.E. Edwards — S. Salop (Pam Sykes).* 31 (CMa), 618 (CMa), 865 (CfMa), 1318 (OMa), 1459 (R), 1632 (I).

DUNGANNON LAD ..9-4.. 10 b.g. Skyliner — Sarphele Larches (Gay Fandango USA) f3p52p. Tall. NH FLAT '97 r2 p0 (last once). NH '97 r2 p0 (last 1, and pulled up 1 in Hdles). P-t-P '99 r2 p0 (5th, and pulled up 1). Works himself into a lather before the off, but has slight ability, and a small success would be feasible if he could find some more stamina. A first Pointing ride for Arthur St George who would surely have been more at home on Dragon Stout (or would have stuck a lance through him?). *G. Davies & Miss P. Rogers — S. Herefords (Christine Hardinge).* 341 (CfMa), 451 (CfMa), 602 (CfMa), 995 (OMa), 1093 (OMa), 1278 (OMa).

DUN LAW ..9-5.. 10 b.g. Alias Smith (USA) — Cannes Beach (Canadel II) p3. Stocky half-brother to Claymore Lad (*qv*). Dam was 36*l* last of 3 in 2m Nov Ch for Sheila Dun, and was useless in Points (very fiery). Grandam, Bright Beach, won 10 Hunt Chses (inc '68 Cheltenham Foxhunters) and placed 6 (inc Points) for her. Great-grandam, Badger's Beech, won '57 Border Maiden when ridden by her husband. NH FLAT '96 r2 p0. P-t-P '99 r6 p1 (last of 2); 4th, pulled up 3, and fell 1. Consistently moderate. Must be a Christian as he specialises in looking after young ladies (Gina Hutchinson being the latest), but presumably not thought good enough for the attentions of a strong male jockey. *J.M. Dun — Lauderdale.* 421 (3m5fL), 1424 (M).

DUNLIR ..9-9.. 11 b.g. Lir — Miss Black Glama (Derrylin) 3p5pp6. Very small neat. Dam won 2m1f Sell Hdle. NH FLAT '94 r3 p0. NH '94/9 (for P. Rodford; blinkered once in '95) r38 w1 (2m4f Sell Hdle) p6 (inc 3 Chses). fell/unseated final 3. Error-prone and frequently tailed off under Rules, and was trounced in Points (best effort when 34 lengths third), but at least ended his sequence of crashes. Has made 47 appearances spread over seven years, and his sole victory was gained in a Selling Hurdle on firm in April '95 (lucky, as the leader was carried out by a loose horse at the last). Absent for 11 months after July '98 because of lameness. *Mrs C.M. Hussey — Four Burrow.* 257 (L), 316 (Cf), 725 (L), 1045 (L), 1275 (L), 1514 (Cf).

PLATE 45   1514 Tetcott Confined: L to R Brown Robber (T. Dennis), 2nd, Dunlir (Miss S. Young), 6th, Western Fort (Miss J. Cumings), 4th, Bendor Mark (Mrs M. Hand), pu, and Good King Henry (I. Widdicombe), 7th
                                                      PHOTO: Baths Photograhic

DUNNELLIE ..9-8.. 8 br.m. Dunbeath (USA) — Miss Gallant (Gallo Gallante) p31fp. Compact half-sister to Gallant Oats, Gallants Delight and Gallant Major. Dam won 2m Hdle and 2nd 2, and was 4th in a Point for Christine Johnston. NH FLAT '97 r1 p0. NH '97 r1 p0 (last in Hdle). P-t-P '98/9 r13 w1 (Maiden) p0; pulled up 5, and fell 1. Won a bad Maiden taking 7min 30s in heavy at Lanark in '99, and again showed her liking for a test of stamina when winning her Members (burst in the process), but error prone, and a Restricted success is no formality. Has been tried in a tongue-strap. *Mrs C. Johnston — Cumberland F. (R. Johnston).* 184 (R), 424 (R), 492 (M), 911 (4mMO), 1081 (R).

DUN ROSE ..10-1.. 7 b/br.m. Roscoe Blake — Dun Gay Lass (Rolfe USA) 1112. Dam, sister to Dun Rolfe (*qv* '92 Annual), won 6 Points and 3 Hunt Chses and 2nd 2 (beaten head in '91 Cheltenham Foxhunters or would have completed 10-timer — robbed after the stirrup leather wrenched free of saddle bar) for Mrs Chartres and Phyllis Claxton. NH FLAT '98 r2 p0. NH '99 (from Mrs J. Storey's) r2 p0. Bred from an outstanding mare and has a fair degree of ability herself, and was backed from 6-4 to 4-6 when completing a hat-trick in a Confined at Friars Haugh, but her supporters were very lucky to collect, as the novice rider of first past the post Love Actinium forgot to weigh in. Stays at least 3m2f and can handle cut in the ground, but was no match for Divet Hill on a faster surface at Mosshouses, where she did not help her cause by making a series of mistakes. Should enjoy another good season at seven, and may eventually emulate mother in a Hunter Chase. *Mrs R.M. Chartres — College V. & N. Northumberland (Clive Storey)*. 365 (CfMa), 497 (R), 717 (Cf), 1425 (I).

DUNSFOLD DAZZLER ..9-10.. 9 b.m. Phardante (FR) — Rositary (FR) (Trenel) 33p1pp3. Compact. Dam won 5 Hdles (2m-3m1f) and 4 Chses (2m1f-3m2f), and produced 2 foals including Dunsfold Dazzler before the final 2 victories. P-t-P '99 r5 w1 (Maiden) p2 (2nds); and pulled up 2. Placed in four Restricteds before she came good in a two-finisher slog at St Hilary, but already struggling in better company, and will probably need some luck to win again. Quite fiery, and always has two paddock handlers. *B.R. Hughes — Llangeinor (Mair Hughes)*. 486 (R), 646 (R), 832 (R), 1054 (R), 1227 (I), 1449 (I), 1613 (I).

DUNSTON ACE ..8-8.. 7 b.g. Sizzling Melody — Miss Vaigly Blue (Vaigly Great) b3. Compact. P-t-P '99 r4 p1 (2nd); pulled up 2. Bad tempered, and well beaten in his two placings. Gets about a bit and has turned up in three counties for his six outings, but does not inspire confidence. *T. Walker — Holcombe*. 664 (2m5fOMa), 812 (Cf).

DUNSTON BEN ..—.. 7 b.g. Nomination — Careless Whisper (USA) (Broadway Forli USA) ppp. Sturdy brother to flat winner, Tiddy Oggie. P-t-P '99 (for Mr T. Walker) r2 p0 (2 fences last of 3); and pulled up 1. An awful creature with no redeeming features and not worth keeping in training. *D. Page — Ashford V*. 576 (OMa), 679 (OMa), 984 (OMa).

DUNSTON LADDIE ..—.. 7 b.g. Risk Me (FR) — Merry Kate (Shirley Heights) p. Dam is half-sister to Tuscania (*qv* '97 Annual). Pulled up after two miles in March. *T. Walker — Holcombe*. 689 (R).

DUNSTON SLICK ..8-10.. 8 ch.g. Weld — Havrin Princess (Scallywag) p. Tall unfurnished brother to Princess Scully. NH FLAT '97 r1 p0 (tailed off). P-t-P/HUNT CH '98/9 r8 p1 (3rd); unseated 2, ran out 1, and pulled up 4. A hard puller and has been tried in a nosenet, but only once able to creep round and looks short of stamina. Relatively busy in '99, but otherwise very lightly raced. *T. Walker — Albrighton*. 298 (CfMa).

DUNSTON TRIGGER ..9-2.. 7 ch.g. Derrylin — Goldaw (Gala Performance USA) 3321. Sturdy compact brother to Cool Million (*qv*). P-t-P '99 (for Mr T. Walker) r3 p0 (refused 1, ran out 1, and fell 1). Much improved with competent handling, and justified the odds when 4-6 in a back-end Maiden at Larkhill. Still no world beater, and the form of his win does not equate to much, but clearly head and shoulders above the other Dunston dunces. Will need to improve further if he is to become competitive in Restricteds. *E.W. Dauncey — Blackmore & Sparkford V. (Rose Vickery)*. 472 (OMa), 732 (2m4fOMa), 1241 (OMa), 1596 (OMa).

DURNFORD BAY (IRE) ..9-10.. 8 b.g. Denel (FR) — Chamowen (Master Owen) 421p. Tall workmanlike half-brother to Kissane, and to Irish Hurdles winner, Kemchee. IR 18,000 3-y-o. NH FLAT '98 (debut for Miss H. Knight) r2 p0. NH '98/9 (for N. Twiston-Davies) r6 p0; ran out once. Showed signs of ability in his last two Hurdles, and benefited from a drop to Maidens, winning a youngsters event at Lifton very easily and also achieving two fair placings. Very disappointing when odds-on in a Restricted, but possibly not suited by the soft ground, and may well atone. Has been tongue-tied since his Pointing debut. *E.D. Underhill — Stevenstone (Caroline Egalton)*. 105 (OMa), 1308 (OMa), 1519 (CfMa), 1608 (R).

D V'S DELIGHT ..—.. 10 gr.m. Montreal Boy — Panbel (Dragonara Palace USA) bpp. Half-sister to Master Sleeves. P-t-P '99 r2 p0 (pulled up 2). Showed some speed at Alnwick, but soon tailed off otherwise, and any pretensions she has to becoming a racehorse should be extinguished by now. *G.H.D. Hopes — Cumberland F*. 112 (OMam), 189 (OMam), 719 (CfMa).

DYFFRYN PRINCE (IRE) ..9-10.. 9 ch.g. King Luthier — Solomy (Tyrnavos) pp1425. Compact. P-t-P '98/9 r6 w2 (geldings Maiden and Members) p2; unseated 1, and pulled up 1. Has gained an annual success in his three seasons in Wales for three different trainers, but has two ways of running. Has run tongue-tied, and usually has two handlers in the paddock. Acts on soft ground, but will struggle to maintain his winning record. *H.M. Thomas — V. of Clettwr (Rhydian Jones)*. 38 (CR), 274 (R), 486 (R), 837 (I), 944 (I), 1299 (I).

DYNAMITE DAN (IRE) ..—.. 13 b.g. Ballinamona Boy — Aliceion (Tanfirion) ppppp. Small lengthy half-brother to Irish jumping winner, Cable Beach (IRE), and to Irish NH flat winner, Spatkling Gold. NH FLAT r1 p0. NH '93/4 (tried tongue-tied) r7 p1 (2nd in Hdle). P-t-P '93 and '95/8 r17 w5 (inc PPORA and Intermediate) p2 (2nds); failed to finish 8 (fell/unseated 4). Formerly able when managing to complete, but pulled up in his last six starts, and looked to have something wrong with him in 2000 (forced to miss the previous season). Still inclined to fight the rider, but clearly ailing and unlikely to stop the rot at 13. *B.J. Kennedy — Essex F. & U. (Jim Ovel).* 29 (Cf), 241 (C), 417 (Cf), 607 (O), 756 (Cf).

DYNOUN ..9-10.. 7 b.g. Derrylin — Little Oats (Oats) 1ubp7. Lengthy unfurnished. Dam is half-sister to Gamay and Rose Orchard. IRISH P-t-P '99 r5 p2 (2nds). Bought Ascot, Aug for 6400. The first winner for David Crosse when scoring easily in a Maiden taking 6min55s in softish at Kingston Blount, but it was a poor contest, and has been exposed as very moderate since. Might atone if connections were able to do something about his jumping, which is becoming increasingly shoddy and costing him many lengths. *Mrs P. Perriss & Mrs V. Sceats — Vine & Craven (John Porter).* 250 (CfMa), 392 (R), 791 (R), 940 (R), 1146 (R).

EARL BOON ..9-13.. 13 gr.g. Baron Blakeney — Miss Boon (Road House II) p3. Workmanlike half-brother to Master Boon, Bassinet (dam of Sydney Boon, (qv '99 Annual), Vareck, Celtic Strike, Bartondale, Gunner Boon and Lizzie Boon. Dam was unbeaten in 2 flat (12f), and won 5 Hdles at around 2m and 3 Chses (2m-2m4f) and placed 8. P-t-P/HUNT CH '93/7 and '99 r32 w10 (inc 3 Opens; 4-timer '97) p9 (8 2nds); failed to finish 7 (fell/unseated 2). On the downgrade since being forced to miss the '98 season, but has always earned his corn at Seaborough and presumably worth his weight in gold as a lead horse to the youngsters at home. Capable of superb jumping, but has always been rather one-paced, and owes his successes to sound placing and expert riding. *J.A. Keighley — Taunton V. (Richard Barber).* 735 (MO), 1470 (MO).

EARLY DAWN ..9-6.. 7 ch.m. Rakaposhi King — Early Run (Deep Run) pp3p34. Lengthy half-sister to Ship The Builder and My Nad Knows. P-t-P '99 r1 p1 (3rd). Has made the frame four times, but often too keen for her own good, and struggles to get the trip. Prone to wholesale blunders, and seems moody. Very unruly on her reappearance, and was taken to post early next time. *P. Dowson — Zetland.* 282 (OMa), 380 (OMa), 625 (OMa), 1001 (2m4fOMa), 1324 (M), 1480 (OMa).

EARLY MORNING ..8-7.. 6 ch.g. Cruise Missile — Sparkling Tarqua (Never Die Dancing) pp3. Big rangy brother to Sparkling Missile, and half-brother to Emilys Trust and Muckle Jack. Dam won 7 Chses, 2m-3m2f110y (inc 4-timer), and was 2nd in Grand Annual Ch for Bill James. Looked very slow when 17 lengths last of three, but at least has time on his side. *W. James — Taunton V. (Carroll Gray).* 956 (OMa), 1241 (OMa), 1373 (OMa).

EARLYMORNING LIGHT (IRE) ..10-2.. 12 gr.g. Idiot's Delight — Primrose Wood (Precipice Wood) pp. Lengthy half-brother to jumping winner, Real Tonic. Dam, Whitaker-bred half-sister to Pyjamas (qv '96 Annual), won 2 NH flat, 3 Hdles at around 2m, and 9 Chses, 2-3m. NH FLAT '94 r1 p0. NH '94/7 r22 w6 (2m5f Hdle, and 5 Chses, 2m4f-2m6f) p7. P-t-P/HUNT CH '99 r4 p2; ran out 1. NH May '00 r1 p0 (pulled up in 3m HCap Ch: *hdwy, in tch 9, wknd, pu 14*). A useful two-of-the-ground sub-three mile specialist in his prime, but broke down when winning at Cartmel in '97, and not the same horse since he returned in '99. Restricted to just one appearance in 2000, and sadly looks finished now. *Mrs M. Bowie, A. Nicol & Mrs L. Normile — Fife (Alan & Lucy Normile).* 715 (L).

EASTERS EVE ..5-1.. 16 ch.m. Ginger Boy — Ladeven (Even Money) 1p. Rangy. Dam won 2 Opens and 3rd, and won 2 3m2f Chses for David Evatt. P-t-P '93/4 and '98 r5 p0 (pulled up 4, and fell 1). Failed to complete in five Maidens over a five year period to '98, but resurfaced to provide David Evatt with his 100th winner when left solo from an early stage in her Members. Constantly went right-handed at the fences that day (trying to save a leg?), and broke down when attempting to repeat the dose at Rodmell the following month. Dam of the '96 b.m Lancastrianspring, by Lancastrian. *D.R. Evatt — Southdown & Eridge (Ian Cobb).* 674 (M), 1208 (M).

EASTLANDS HI-LIGHT ..10-5.. 12 ch.g. Saxon Farm — Light O' Love (Lighter) 66p. Small. Dam, half-sister to Eastlands Monkey, won her Members (in '94) and placed 3 for Mr Staveley. P-t-P/HUNT CH '95/9 r31 w2 (Maiden and Intermediate) p16 (11 2nds, beaten head once, inc 4 Hunt Chses; and inc last of 3); failed to finish 6 (unseated 2, and refused 1). Only successful in two of his 34 starts, but has run some excellent races in defeat notably over the bigger fences, and would have been a most deserving winner of a Hunter Chase. Usually needs an outing or two before he hits top form, but sadly finished lame at Sedgefield in April. A real trier who makes up for his lack of gears with sheer determination, but will be doing well to stage a revival at 12. *J.G. Staveley — Liddesdale.* 465 (3m1f110yH), 686 (3m1fH), 923 (3m3fH).

EASTLANDS TWILIGHT ..8-11.. 8 br.g. Le Coq D'Or — Julie Ellis (Kampala) up1. Small home-bred. P-t-P '99 r4 p1 (2nd). A steady jumper for a youngster, and won well at Lanark (the runner-up later followed suit), but looks rather one-paced, and may lack scope. Has already proved he can stay the full trip, and should take a hand in Restricteds if his prolonged absence is not a bad sign. *J.G. Staveley — Liddesdale.* 187 (OMa), 499 (2m4fOMa), 664 (2m5fOMa).

EAU SO SLOE ..8-5.. 10 b.g. Baron Blakeney — Final Attraction (Jalmood USA) ppp335. Big close-coupled half-brother to NH flat winner, Bodfari Cream. NH FLAT '95 r1 p0. NH '96/7 r8 p1 (2nd of 3 in terrible ch); 4th of 5, last, pulled up 1, and fell 2 in other Chses, pulled up in one of 2 Hdles. P-t-P/HUNT CH '99 r8 w1 (Members) p0; last, and pulled up 5. Performed disgracefully in Hunter Chases in '99 until springing a surprise in his very slowly-run Members when with blinkered for the first time. Beaten out of sight in his repeat bid this season, and looks a sorry spectacle. Wears headgear, and was ridden in spurs — poor thing — twice in 2000. Golfer Jesper Parnevik celebrates with a huge cigar after a win; cult figure Frank Matthews lights up his pipe following yet another training disaster (so he gets through loads of rough shag). *F.L. Matthews — Wheatland.* 297 (I), 382 (2m4fH), 896 (P), 1198 (O), 1529 (M), 1630 (Cf).

EBULLIENT EQUINAME (IRE) ..9-12§.. 10 b.g. Zaffaran (USA) — Corvina (Ardoon) ff3342. Tall lengthy. Dam won at 9f in Ireland, and won 2m1f Sell Hdle in England; reportedly also won a race abroad. NH FLAT '95 (for D. Eddy) r4 w2 p2 (3rds). NH '95/9 (2 wins from N. Henderson's, bought for 30,000) r14 w2 (2 Hdles, 2m1f-2m4f) p4 (inc 2nd in Ch). A good Bumper horse, but has generally has been a most expensive failure since leaving Don Eddy. Held every chance but was hard ridden when he fell at the final fence in an Open won by Mister Spectator at Cottenham, but his jumping is always suspect, and he ran in snatches and ultimately dogged it badly in a Confined at Dingley which looked to provide a simple opportunity. Blinkered twice under Rules, and was tongue-tied latterly (has had a wind operation); also absent for 21 months after March '96). Should be ignored as a betting medium if reappearing. *Mrs J. Wilson — Pytchley (Bill Warner).* 327 (O), 771 (O), 868 (Cf), 1005 (M), 1434 (3m110yH), 1503 (Cf).

EDDIE ROMBO ..9-1.. 6 b.g. Aragon — Jolimo (Fortissimo) 3u15. Sturdy half-brother to several winners, including Joli's Great, Jolis Absent, Doc Ryan's and Osric (all flat and Hurdles). Dam won 7 flat, 12-18f. 9000y. FLAT (for N. Tinkler) r7 p0. NH '98/9 (blinkered 2; been tongue-tied) r12 p0 (frequently tailed off, inc Sells). NH June '00 r1 p0 (5th in 2m4f Nov Ch: *bhnd early, mist 2, t.o aft 7*). Useless in 19 races under Rules, but illuminated how dire some Maidens can be when scoring over 2m4f at Whitwell (went eight lengths clear after two out, but idled and only held on by a length). Will need to find plenty more for Restricteds. *R.D.E. Woodhouse — Sinnington.* 167 (OMa), 695 (OMa), 1002 (2m4fOMa).

EDGAR GINK (IRE) ..7.. 7 ch.g. Step Together (USA) — Turbo Run (Deep Run) 2. Half-brother to Turbulent Gale (IRE) and Turbulent Ride (IRE). Sold Tattersalls Ireland, June '98 for 8695. Made a pleasing start when three lengths second at Marks Tey, and should be a natural to win a Maiden. The stable introduced Brackenheath on the same track and sold him for a tidy sum to race with some success under Rules, and perhaps they will be hoping to repeat the feat. *Mrs N.H. Bulgin — Essex F. & U.* 1180 (OMa).

EDGE AHEAD (IRE) ..9-8§.. 11 b.g. Le Bavard (FR) — Blackrath Beauty (Le Tricolore) p264p. Workmanlike lengthy brother to Melroy (IRE), and half-brother to Irish NH flat and jumping winner, Ferrycarrigcrystal. Dam won mares Maiden in Ireland (aged 13!). NH FLAT '97 r1 w1. NH '97/9 (blinkered last 5; for Mrs D. Haine; previously won for her brother, T. Thomson Jones) r9 p1 (3rd in Ch); pulled up other Ch. Won a Bumper on the Southwell all-weather, but regularly tailed off under Rules since, and was reluctant to race on his final appearance. Gave a couple of better displays when making the frame for Emma Coveney, but regained blinkers on his two most recent appearances, and still looks ungenuine and untrustworthy. *Mrs E. Coveney & Mrs E. Taber — O. Surrey, Burstow & W. Kent, & Kent & Surrey Bloodhounds (Emma Coveney).* 162 (I), 304 (M), 574 (4mMO), 707 (L), 983 (Cf).

EDGE OF NIGHT ..9-13.. 12 b.g. Celestial Storm (USA) — Moonlight Fling (Imperial Fling USA) pu5. Very tall rangy. IRISH FLAT r1 p0. IRISH NH FLAT '93/4 r3 w2 p0; one run at Cheltenham Festival. IRISH NH '93/5 r6 p0. NH Mar '97 r1 p0. P-t-P '98 r3 w1 (Members) p2. Stands his racing badly, and now looks unlikely to add to his home win in '98. Was a decent bumper horse for Mick O'Toole, but too big for his own good, and failed to beat a rival in 2000. *Lord Yarborough — Brocklesby (Mark Bennison).* 90 (3m1fH), 229 (Cf), 1216 (O).

EDUCATE ME (IRE) ..8-9.. 10 b.g. Hollow Hand — Widdy (Paddy's Stream) p56p334. Neat half-brother to Irish Pointing winner, Mrs Hushabye (IRE). IRISH P-t-P '96 r5 p1 (3rd); pulled up 2. IRISH NH '95/6 r2 p0 (pulled up only Hunt Ch). P-t-P '97/8 r11 p6 (4 3rds); pulled up 1. Placed nine times in maiden company, but does not stay three miles, and will need to find a bad race in order to get off the mark. A sound jumper who has never fallen, and could probably live up to his name for a beginner. Sometimes wears a tongue-strap. *S. Burley — High Peak H. (Jason Burley).* 437 (OMa), 526 (OMa), 693 (OMa), 906 (CfMa), 1251 (OMa), 1352 (OMa), 1479 (OMa).

EECEL ..—.. 9 ch.g. Remezzo — Stonybridge (Perhapsburg) ppp. Tall lengthy attractive half-brother to Quarry Merchant and Stony Missile. P-t-P '98/9 r7 p0 (pulled up 7). Remarkably consistent, and has now pulled up in all 10 Pointing ventures. It was surprising that a jockey of Adrian Wintle's calibre agreed to partner him, and amazing that he should do so twice. Jumped badly in 2000, and surely wrong. *Mrs M. Howen — Wheatland (Terry Taylor).* 568 (OMa), 778 (OMa), 1412 (OMa).

EFAAD (IRE) ..9-11.. 10 b.g. Shaadi (USA) — Krismas River (Kris) pf5u54. Close-coupled half-brother to an Italian flat winner. Dam won 2 10f races at Dundalk. FLAT r9 p0. NH '94/8 r9 p0 (blinkered in Sell final). P-t-P '99 r4 w1 (Maiden) p0; fell/unseated 2, and pulled up 1. A sloppy jumper of hurdles and learnt the art of fencing the hard way, but finally got his act together at Charm Park in '99. Beaten a minimum of 19 lengths in 2000, and rather flattered by his rating. Still prone to errors, and will need to eradicate them if he is to stand a chance in Restricteds. *S.A. Pinder — York & Ainsty S.* 137 (R), 378 (R), 396 (R), 620 (R), 689 (R), 998 (C).

EFFIE WOOD ..10-0.. 8 br.m. Fearless Action (USA) — Jeanne D'Accord (John De Coombe) 72p22. Small sparely-made half-sister to Woodzee. P-t-P '99 (for Miss P. Cooper) r1 w1 (Maiden). Beat two subsequent winners in a tight finish at Llanvapley on her racecourse debut, but her development has been stunted by her inability to jump consistently well. Lacks the substance to get away with her mistakes, but should collect a Restricted if she can ever produce a fluent round. *Mrs J.M. Porter (Millennium Club)* — *Vine & Craven (John Porter).* 6 (R), 247 (R), 477 (R), 887 (R), 1482 (R).

EGG WELL BOY ..—.. 7 ch.g. Current Edition (IRE) — Rip O'Riley (Levanter) u0. Neat. Dam's 3 efforts in Points included unseated and refused. Grandam, April Lady, won desperate Maiden and 3rd twice (only beat 6 others in 20 attempts). NH FLAT '00 (from D. Burchell's) r1 p0 (12th in 2m110y NH flat: *bhnd final mile, t.o*). Already out of touch when losing the rider at the third at Howick. *J.D. Liley* — *Llangeinor (-; Dai Burchell).* 822 (CfMa).

EGYPT MILL PRINCE ..9-10.. 15 b.g. Deep Run — Just Darina (Three Dons) 6pp24s. Big rangy half-brother to Mikey's Monkey and Flapping Freda (IRE), and to successful Hurdler, Danish Chief. Dam is half-sister to Credit Call. NH '91/6 and '98 r43 w9 (2 2m Hdles, and 7 Chses, 2m-2m4f) p16 (inc 2nd in '93 and '95 Mackesons, and 3rd in '94); pulled up final 3, inc when lame in '96. P-t-P '99 (for Mr S.R. Webb) r2 p1 (2nd); and pulled up 1. A bold jumper and a hard puller who could be very gutsy under Rules, and earned a magnificent £140,522, but pulled up lame on his final appearance of '96 and not the same horse since. Has enjoyed his Pointing, but does not stay three miles, and is very much in the twilight of his career. *Miss A. Maller* — *V.W.H.* 611 (C), 895 (MO), 970 (O), 1440 (MO), 1552 (O), 1631 (MO).

ELEGANT WOLF ..—.. 11 ch.g. Little Wolf — Elegant Nell (Free State) pp. Small light half-brother to Dancing Ranger *(qv)*. P-t-P '99 r8 p0 (pulled up 4, and fell/unseated 4). Remarkably inept, and has made the acquaintance of six jockeys in a dreadful ten race career. Not worth running again. *Mrs S.A. Middleton* — *Eggesford.* 1521 (CfMa), 1565 (OMa).

PLATE 46   997 Middleton Confined: Ella Falls (C. Wilson), 1st, jumps alongside Silent Snipe (W. Burnell), 3rd   PHOTO: John Beasley

ELLA FALLS (IRE) ..10-5.. 6 b.m. Dancing Dissident (USA) — Over Swing (FR) (Saint Cyrien FR) 141u1. Small robust close-coupled half-sister to flat winner, Caudillo. 3100y. FLAT (tried blinkers; for Miss J. Craze; previously placed for D. Nicholls; previously for D. Barron) r19 p1 (3rd). NH '99 r4 p0 (Sells last 2). Gave three fair displays on the flat and one over Hurdles, but they were all first time out, and was never able to sustain the form. Switched to Points after the owner had his permit to train under Rules withdrawn, and won three modest contests impressively, including a Maiden at 25-1 (which form book historians might have taken to be a luscious price on her seasonal reappearance). Seemed to find nil once, and unseated once, but has otherwise kept finding impressive acceleration, and she might well be able to hold her own in much better grade. *J.A. Moore — S. Durham.* 54 (OMa), 440 (R), 620 (R), 815 (Cm), 997 (Cf).

ELLE FLAVADOR ..9-5.. 11 b.m. El Conquistador — Flavirostris (Grisaille) p326518. Lengthy unfurnished half-sister to Mountain-Linnet (*qv*). P-t-P '96/9 (for Miss N.K. Allan in '99; previously for the Watts') r25 w3 (Maiden, Restricted and Intermediate) p8 (5 3rds; and remote 2nd, 2nd of 3, and last of 2); pulled up 6, and unseated 1. A keen sort, but handicapped by her lack of stamina, and usually flagging a long way from the finish. Well below par in '99, but gave some better performances, when returned to the previous owners, although he faced a very simple task when successful. Suited by firm ground. Wears a cross-noseband. *B.R. & Mrs A.B. Watts — Weston & Banwell H. (Rose Vickery).* 161 (L), 357 (Cm), 558 (L), 886 (C), 1237 (Cf), 1549 (M), 1638 (L).

ELLERTON TONY ..9-9.. 9 b.g. Ardar — Ellerton Song (Cree Song) p5fp. Rangy home-bred. Dam is an unraced half-sister to Ellerton Hill (*qv* '98 Annual). Grandam, Kenya Park, won 13 Ladies (inc Middleton 4-miler) and an Open and placed 5 for Thomas Thompson. P-t-P '97/8 r4 w1 (Maiden) p0; pulled up 2, and fell 1. A convincing winner on his first completion in '98, but injured in a fall subsequently, and forced to miss the following season. Returned to action in 2000, but only got round once, when beaten about 20 lengths. Looked to have potential, but clearly still has his problems, and was tried in a tongue-strap in his Members. *T.W. Thompson — Hurworth (Chris Dennis).* 137 (R), 377 (R), 619 (M), 807 (R).

ELL GEE ..9-5.. 11 ch.m. Ra Nova — Evening Song (True Song) 2uu224p. Small. Dam, sister and half-sister to 5 Pointers, including Milled Oats (*qv* 2000 Annual), won 2 Chses (2m-2m4f) for Paul Townsley. NH FLAT r3 p0. NH '96/7 and '99 r10 p0 (last pair 4, fell 2, and pulled up 4). P-t-P/HUNT CH '97/8 (for Mr A.C. Ayres '98) r7 p1 (2nd); fell/unseated 3, and pulled up 2. A long-standing maiden who managed her busiest season to date in 2000, but remains hard to sit on, and appears to find three miles a shade too far. Tried in blinkers latterly under Rules, and may not be very genuine. *P. Townsley — Surrey U. (Pru Townsley).* 578 (OMa), 709 (OMa), 828 (OMa), 1213 (OMa), 1397 (OMa), 1513 (OMa), 1537 (2m5fH).

ELLIEWELLIEWOO ..10-8.. 8 b.m. Syrtos — Ruby's Vision (Balinger) 111p. Tall unfurnished sister to Brockbuster, and half-sister to Hurdles winner, Act Of Faith. Dam is half-sister to Another Sword (*qv* '94 Annual). NH FLAT '97 r1 p0. NH '98/9 (for P. Webber) r6 p1 (15/3rd); pulled up both Chses. Bought Doncaster, Oct for 1600. A costly flop for Webber, but transformed by the genius of Caroline Egalton, and completed a most impressive hat-trick by an aggregate of 50 lengths. Sent off at 4-5 to beat Butler John on her first venture into Open company, but pecked badly and lost her bridle four out, and Les Jefford was soon forced to pull up (the contest was run in an astonishingly fast time, and it is the greatest of pities that she was unable to complete). Very speedy and can find plenty more at the business end, and will certainly be many peoples idea of a banker if she tackles a Novice Hunter Chase. *M. Bryan, D. Jefford, G. Stuart & Mrs C. Egalton — Mid Devon (Caroline Egalton).* 538 (OMa), 729 (R), 953 (I), 1515 (MO).

ELTRYM FLYER ..—.. 9 b.m. Petong — Friendly Glen (Furry Glen) ppp. Half-sister to Armagret. Dam won 2m Hdle and 2m4f Ch. NH '99 (for Miss S. Williamson) r2 p0. Bought Doncaster, Aug for 1300. Not the best of jumpers, and has insufficient stamina for Points. *Mrs P.K.J. Brightwell — Essex & Suffolk.* 88 (OMa), 1040 (OMa), 1115 (OMa).

ELVER SPRING ..9-0.. 8 b.g. Vital Season — Pablena (Pablond) f25p. Brother to Vital To Me. Dam is an unraced sister to Elver Season, and half-sister to Fair Caprice (*qv* '98 Annual). Grandam, Capelena, won 6 Points (inc a dead-heat) and 2 Hunt Chses (3m2f-4m) and placed 14 (inc a Sell Hdle). P-t-P '99 r3 p1 (2nd); unseated 1, and pulled up 1. A disappointment to date (especially to his supporters who have sent him off favourite on four occasions), and surprisingly having trouble getting the trip. Bred to need time, but the patience of connections has surely been taken to the brink. *Mrs H. Dalton & Mrs J. Minton — Wheatland (Andrew Dalton).* 168 (OMa), 298 (CfMa), 790 (OMa), 1068 (3m2fOMa).

ELWILL GLORY (IRE) ..9-6.. 11 b.g. Black Minstrel — Greenfield Glory (Pitpan) 26uuu. Strong lengthy brother to Hugo Henry (IRE) (*qv*). IRISH P-t-P '94/9 r27 w2 (6 plus Maiden, and Winners of One) p3; pulled up 9, fell, and unseated. IRISH NH '96/9 r15 p0 (inc 8th in Hunt Ch). Sold Goffs, Dec for 935. A dual winner on firmish and in heavy in Ireland in '96 (tried in blinkers there), but showed no sign of retaining any ability after finishing 10 lengths second of three on his English debut. Girls fell off him on his three most recent attempts, twice after losing irons. Goes to post poorly. *Miss J. Oakey — Kyre (Martin Oliver).* 533 (I), 667 (Cf), 860 (L), 991 (L), 1066 (3m2fL).

EMERALD ECTASY ..8-11§.. 11 b.m. Green Ruby (USA) — Main Brand (Main Reef) pR4. Small. Dam, tiny, won 8f Sell, but pulled up, fell and unseated in Points. P-t-P '98/9 r7 p0 (ran out 2, fell 1, and pulled up 4). Finally managed a completion at the 10th attempt (finished last), but remains a highly unpleasant ride, and Ian Hambley is not to be envied. Presumably the person who named her could not spell ecstasy (or was on it). *Mrs J. Goudge — S. Cornwall.* 563 (CfMa), 1390 (OMa), 1522 (CfMa).

EMERALD KNIGHT (IRE) ..10-1.. 11 ch.g. Sandalay — Fort Etna (Be Friendly) pp1p. Rangy hollow-backed brother to Sandy Etna (IRE), and to Chasing winner, Sandy Andy, and half-brother to Irish Hurdles winners, Slatt Noble and Blake's Beauty, and to Irish Pointing winners, Barnborough Lad and Youwaitonme. Dam won a 5f race in Ireland. NH '96 r1 p0 (remote 6th of 7 in 2m7f Nov Ch). P-t-P/HUNT CH '95/7 and '99 r15 w3 (inc Open) p6 (4 2nds); pulled up 3. Began his career with a defeat of subsequent Hunter Chase winner The Jogger, but began to look suspect in '97, and was generally disappointing after missing the following season. All out to land his Members in 2000, but added credence to the theory that all was not well when he collapsed and died after pulling up next time. Often visored latterly. Mr & Mrs K. Liscombe — Cheshire Forest (Rob Hankey). 530 (O), 781 (Cf), 959 (M), 1319 (O).

EMPEROR ROSCOE ..—.. 6 b.g. Roscoe Blake — Royal Celt (Celtic Cone) p. Good-topped. Quickly tailed off in a February Maiden. Only an old swinger would remember the original Emperor Roscoe (a pirate of the airways). *A.A. Day — Atherstone.* 122 (OMa).

EMPEROR ROSS (IRE) ..9-9.. 6 b br.g. Roselier (FR) — Gilded Empress (Menelek) f2. Half-brother to Homer's Nod, Double Dose, and Bishops Island, to Irish Hurdles winners, Glen Empress (IRE), and to Irish NH flat winner, Dear Empress. Fell two out when looking poised to make a winning debut at Wetherby, and was 8-11 (heavily backed) on a retrieving mission at Eyton two months later, but came up an above-average Maiden in Fast Lane, and looked to blow up when finishing tired. Should be stronger at six, and a victory is surely just around the corner. *J.R. & Miss L. Hales — Wheatland (Andrew Dalton).* 167 (OMa), 1196 (OMa).

EMSEE-H ..10-2.. 16 br.g. Paddy's Stream — Kincsem (Nelcius) pp41p14pp. Strong brother to Socks Downe, and half-brother to Welsh Consort, to Irish Chasing winner, Over Eager (IRE), to Irish jumping and English Chasing winner, Travelowen, and to Irish Hurdles and English Chasing winner, Travel Over. NH '90/4 (blinkered 1) r49 w8 (2m4f Hdle, and 7 Chses, 2m-2m5f) p17; won 2m4f Ch, but disqualified for carrying wrong weight; short-headed once. P-t-P/HUNT CH '95/9 r34 w6 (inc 4 Ladies) p17 (13 2nds, last twice, inc 2 Hunt Chses, 3m110y-3m7f); pulled up 4. An incredibly tough and honest performer who took his career tally to 16 with a brace of amazingly game wins at Horseheath, but tragically lost his life at High Easter — ironically only fell once throughout his career, at the open ditch in the straight at Sandown in '91, though Steve Smith Eccles did succeed in falling off him at Cheltenham once. Not the classiest horse ever to grace the scene, but had been a marvellous ambassador to the winter game, and a great credit to connections. *J.M. Turner — Suffolk.* 28 (L), 128 (L), 240 (L), 414 (L), 707 (L), 841 (L), 1113 (L), 1266 (L), 1378 (Cf).

ENCIMA DEL RIO (IRE) ..10-0.. 8 ch.g. Over The River (FR) — Spanish Royale (Royal Buck) 23pp2651. Strong length half-brother to Tom Pinch (IRE). Dam won 2m Ch in Ireland. P-t-P '99 (for Mr J.M. Turner) r4 w1 (Maiden) p3 (3rds). A safe jumper and ideal for Ben King to learn on, and a thorough stayer, but would have won more often in 2000 had it not been for the fact that he tends to go through a flat spot in his races (usually at a crucial stage). Managed to time his rally well on his final appearance providing his partner with his first success, and should win again as their proficiency together grows, particularly as he is still eligible for Restricteds. *A.R. & O.W. King — V. of Aylesbury.* 33 (Cnr), 80 (CCfR), 216 (Cnr), 462 (2m7f110yH), 477 (R), 734 (R), 1146 (R), 1487 (M).

ENDEAVOUR (FR) ..—.. 9 b br.g. Video Rock (FR) — Ogigy (FR) (Quart De Vin FR) u. Sturdy compact half-brother to 2 flat winners in French provinces. NH FLAT '96/7 r4 w1 p1 (3rd). NH '98 r3 p0; broke blood vessel in final. Scored in soft in February '97 and may retain some ability, but exceptionally lightly raced, and clearly troubled these days. *M.J. Roberts — E. Sussex & Romney Marsh.* 983 (Cf).

ENERGY MAN ..9-0.. 8 b.g. Hadeer — Cataclysmic (Ela-Mana-Mou) 1p. Compact half-brother to 3 flat winners (two in Holland), including Wannaplantatree. Dam won 2 12f races, and is half-sister to Hardihero (qv '97 Annual). FLAT (first 3 for J. Fanshawe; tried visored) r14 p0. NH '97/8 (for M. Dods, bought for 7500) r3 p0 (tailed off in Sell Hdle). Bought Doncaster, June '98 for 1800. Flattered by winning a dire Maiden at Pentreclywdau (only two of the 11 starters went clear in a grief-stricken contest), and pulled up after an unimpressive display next time. May struggle to achieve much in future. *J. Milton — Ystrad Taf Fechan.* 1301 (OMa), 1400 (R).

ENIGMA BELL ..—.. 8 b.g. Rambo Dancer (CAN) — Skelton (Derrylin) p. Compact attractive brother to flat winner, Charm Dancer, and half-brother to a flat winner. Dam won 2 2-y-o Sells, 7-8f. NH FLAT '97 (for S. Gollings) r1 p0. NH '98/9 (bought for 8000) r4 p0 (8th and pulled up 3 in Hdles). Went missing for 22 months after his debut, and has hardly ever been able to appear since. Almost invariably pulls up when he does. *P.A. Horner-Harker — Hurworth (Sarah Horner-Harker).* 1233 (OMa).

ENSIGN EWART (IRE) ..10-4§.. 10 ch.g. Buckskin (FR) — Clonea Fog (Laurence O) 464285. Tall. NH '98 and '99 r4 p1 (distant 3rd in '99 Grand Military Gold Cup); 4th, 9th, and fell 1. P-t-P/HUNT CH '96/9 r17 w6 (inc 3 Hunt Chses, 3m-3m4f) p7 (6 2nds, beaten short-head once, inc 4 Hunt

Chses); fell 1. Looked a useful staying prospect after winning four races '96/7, but generally disappointing since, and his attitude has looked very suspect on occasions — often the first to come off the bridle in a race. Failed to score for the first time in 2000, and never really going at all on his final two appearances. Usually makes shoals of errors, but keeps his feet well, and has only fallen once — at Sandown. Suited by a long trip in mud, but whether he will revive his flagging career in 2001 is anyone's guess. M.W. Sample — College V. & N. Northumberland (Clive Storey). 155 (3m4f110yH), 422 (3m5fO), 1024 (3m3f110yH), 1120 (O), 1342 (3m1fH), 1591 (3m1fH).

ENVIRONMENTAL LAW ..9-3§.. 10 b.g. Slip Anchor — Dame Margot (USA) (Northern Dancer) 33f. Lengthy sparely-made half-brother to six winners abroad (in such far-flung outposts as Japan, USA, Australia and Denmark). FLAT r1 p0. NH '95/7 r12 p1 (head 2nd); Sell final. P-t-p '98/9 r5 p1 (3rd); pulled up 1, and fell 1. Temperamentally unsound, and was a bad value favourite when falling (beaten at the time) on his final start in a truly insipid event. Has been tried in blinkers. *S. McCormick — Southdown & Eridge (Sally Palmer)*. 578 (OMa), 829 (OMa), 1213 (OMa).

EPSILO DE LA RONCE (FR) ..9-11§.. 9 b br.g. Le Riverain (FR) — India Rosa (FR) (Carnaval) 7f4425. Rangy half-brother to French cross-country winner, Famfoni (FR). Dam won over jumps in France. FRENCH FLAT '95 r1 p0. FRENCH NH '95/8 r21 w8 (2 1m7f Hdles, and 6 Chses, 2m1f-2m3½f) p3 (2nds in Chses). NH '98/9 r7 p1 (2nd in Ch); inc Hdles. Possesses some ability, and finished second in a five-runner Open, but it was a race which nothing wanted to win. Would be good enough to score if he felt like it, but is almost invariably reluctant to exert himself. Sometimes blinkered. *E. Harvey — Puckeridge (Alex Harvey)*. 10 (O), 94 (O), 384 (2m3f110yH), 607 (O), 1288 (O), 1541 (2m5fH).

EQUITY PLAYER ..10-0.. 16 ch.g. Gala Performance (USA) — Eden Dale (Dalesa) 4p4312. Tall brother to Gala-Romance and McDermot (IRE). IRISH P-t-p '89 r3 w1 (4&5yo Open Maiden) p2 (2nds). P-t-P '90, '92/4 (blinkered 1) and '95 (for Mr J.A. Griffiths) r38 w14 (inc 8 Opens, promoted once) p16 (12 2nds, last once); failed to finish 5 (fell/unseated 4). NH '95/8 (for R. Curtis) r19 w5 (3m-3m2f Chses) p6; pulled up 2, and unseated 1. Switched to the professional sphere rather late in life, but made a bright start under Rules when winning three of his first five starts. Gradually lost interest and was only once better than the last pair in his final season, but recorded the 21st success of his career when surprising in a Peper Harow Open. As safe as houses and does well for an oldie, but will find further opportunities scarce. Has been tried unsuccessfully in headgear. *G. Wheatley — T.D.B. Underwood — Garth & S. Berks.* 5 (Cv&nr), 120 (CMod), 706 (Cf), 1246 (Cf), 1394 (O), 1510 (O).

ERBIL (IRE) ..9-10.. 11 b.g. Shardari — Eretna (Golden Fleece USA) 6uu37p4f. Small neat attractive. Dam won at 9f. IRISH FLAT r3 p1 (2nd). FLAT r1 p0. NH '93/4 r9 w2 (2m-2m1f Hdles) p0; inc Sells. P-t-P '98/9 r8 p2 (2nd of 3, and last of 3); pulled up 2, and on floor 2. Last successful back in '94, and although placed in three Ladies Opens since returning from a four year hiatus he consistently fails to stay three miles, and hopes of a victory must be fading. Gave his best display when 10 lengths third to Split Second in a race taking under six minutes at Chaddesley, but failed to beat another rival subsequently. *D.I. Ancil — Grafton (Tricia Mahoney)*. 192 (L), 245 (L), 512 (L), 613 (L), 1007 (L), 1145 (L), 1441 (Cnr), 1531 (2m110yH).

ERIK THE VIKING ..9-4.. 10 b.g. Leading Star — Gay Viking (Wingspread) p3f. Tall good-bodied. Grandam, My Viking, was placed in 2 Maidens for Mr D. Armson in '72. P-t-P '97/8 r6 p2 (2nds); fell/unseated 3. Second twice in '98, behind subsequent Chasing winner Moor Lane once, but missed the following season and restricted to his customary three outings on his return. Again fell victim to the final fence at Sandon, but unlike in '98 was clearly held at the time. Deserves to find a race, but time no longer on his side. *R.J. Armson — Atherstone*. 373 (CfMa), 547 (CfMa), 906 (CfMa).

ERLEMO ..10-3§.. 12 b.g. Mummy's Game — Empress Catherine (Welsh Pageant) 4p. Workmanlike good-bodied brother to flat winner, Kirby Opportunity, and half-brother to 2 flat winners (one on Italy), including Green's Seascape. Dam won at 12f. FLAT r21 p4. NH '92/6 r32 w1 (3m Sell Hdle) p10 (inc 2 3rds in Chses). P-t-P/HUNT CH '97/9 r11 w1 (Confined) p2 (2nds). Lightly raced in Points, and gained his solitary success in a weak race at Garnons. Still capable of decent efforts, and ran really well when 20 lengths last of four to Whatafellow at Weston Park, but ungenuine, and refused to co-operate next time. Sometimes jumps deliberately and used to wear headgear, but only blinkered once '98/00. *Mrs S.F. Tulloch & M.E. Townsend — Teme V. (Sue Tulloch)*. 294 (O), 333 (Cf).

ERNI (FR) ..10-2.. 9 b.g. Un Numide (FR) — Quianoa (FR) (Beaugency FR) 2f12p01. Leggy. NH '96/7 r5 p3. P-t-P '99 r2 p1 (2nd); and last. Clearly not right in '99, but put the record straight this season, though he needed to have his mind made up for him at Dalton Park, and had acquired a visor on his final appearance. An out-and-out stayer (both wins took over seven minutes), and will probably score again when in the mood. *Mr & Mrs W.M. Burnell — Bramham (Wayne Burnell)*. 54 (OMa), 282 (OMa), 507 (CMa), 688 (M), 807 (R), 1445 (3m1fH), 1577 (R).

ESCALATE ..—§.. 7 ch.g. Groom Dancer (USA) — Brosna (USA) (Irish River FR) pr. Small neat half-brother to an Italian flat winner. NH FLAT '98/9 r3 p0. NH '99 (for J.J. O'Neill) r2 p0 (tailed off in Hdles — pulled up 1). A ponderous jumper, and does not want to try. *R. Kendall — Cumberland F.* 44 (OMa), 381 (OMa).

ESERIE DE CORES (USA) ..—.. 11 b.g. Gold Crest (USA) — April Blues (Cure The Blues USA) pp. Very small. IRISH FLAT r1 p0. FLAT (tried blinkers/visor) r12 p1 (3rd in Sell). NH '94 (visored) r4 p1 (26*l* last of 3); inc Sell. P-t-P '95/9 r31 w3 (Maiden, Restricted and Intermediate) p9 (6 2nds); failed to finish 9 (fell/unseated 5). Gleaned three minor events '97/8, but well beaten in the last two seasons, and was tailed off when pulling up twice in 2000. Suited by firmish ground and a short course, but may have suffered a setback. *F.R. & Mrs S.L. Bown — Lamerton (C. Bown).* 165 (Cf), 534 (Cf).

ESKIMO GOLD ..—.. 8 b.m. Gold Dust — Eskimo Slave (New Member) pp. Sparely-made sister to Mudslide, and half-brother to Eskimo Star and Shelly's Sam. Showed a little speed before pulling up in Maidens (when still in touch after two miles on her debut). *A.J. Cottle — Torrington F. (Lisa Smale).* 407 (OMa), 656 (OMa).

EUROGREEN (IRE) ..8-8.. 7 b.g. Eurobus — Lily Green (Green Shoon) 22. Dam is sister to Howaryafxd, and half-sister to Komori (IRE) (*qv* 2000 Annual). IRISH P-t-P '99/00 r5 p0 (pulled up 5). Dramatically improved since pulling up twice in Ireland in early 2000. Beaten a maximum of two lengths in his seconds, and certainly has his name written on a Welsh Maiden if he continues to contest them. *Mrs C.M. Marles — Curre.* 949 (OMa), 1406 (OMa).

EVAN'S COLLIER BOY (IRE) ..10-2.. 8 b.g. Supreme Leader — Little Treat (Miner's Lamp) 11p. P-t-P '98 r3 p1 (2nd); and pulled up 2. Looked a bright prospect despite failing to win in '98, but forced to miss the following season, and failed to reappear after suffering another setback at Llanvapley. Tows his two handlers round the paddock, and maintains a strong gallop, but too strong even for Pip Jones, and won unchallenged twice for Jamie Jukes. Would have claims in a Novice Hunter Chase if he paid the fences more respect. Will hopefully make a full recovery — is expected to resume at the first Cottenham for the third time in 2001. *D. Brace — Llangeinor.* 22 (2m4fOMa), 274 (R), 742 (O).

EVEIES BOY (IRE) ..9-2.. 6 b.g. Shardari — Bloomfield (IRE) (Alzao USA) p21. Tall strong-topped. IRISH FLAT r1 p0. IRISH NH FLAT '99 r2 p0. IRISH NH '99 (blinkered final) r4 p0. Gave one fair display in Ireland when 18 lengths fourth in a Hurdle, but otherwise beat a total of two in six more attempts. Took a while to find his stride in the new yard, but ended his campaign with an easy win over 2m4f at up ton, where he made virtually all. A big sort who may have been weak, and probably open to further improvement. *R. Mathias — Brecon & Talybont.* 478 (M), 1222 (2m4fOMa), 1361 (2m4fOMa).

EVENKEEL (IRE) ..8-7.. 9 b.g. Horage — Corozal (Corvaro USA) ff. Sturdy brother to flat winner, Il Corsair (later successful in Italy), and half-brother to several other winners abroad. Dam won at 10f in Ireland. IRISH NH FLAT '97/8 r8 p1 (2nd). IRISH NH '97/8 r5 p0. NH '99 (for D. Wintle) r3 p0 (blinkered in Sell final). Has not held out much hope in his races to date. Could hardly be more inappropriately named, as an even keel is the one thing he is consistently struggling to maintain. *D.P. Smith — Heythrop (Sarah Kellard-Smith).* 76 (CCfMa), 515 (OMa).

EVER EDDY ..—.. 8 ch.g. North Street — Tandys Tonic (Full Of Beans) pup. Big strong brother to Be Are and Haven. Dam won a Restricted and 2 2m5f Hunt Chses, but failed to finish in her last 6 races (fell/unseated 3). Sire pulled up 5, fell 1 and refused 1 in Points ('hates jumping'). P-t-P '99 r2 p0 (ran out 1, and pulled up 1). Very green in his debut season, and did not reappear until May 2000, but attracted a fair bit of support on one occasion, and clearly someone believes him to have some ability. Has a lot to learn. *Mrs F.H.S. Gilbert — Dart V.H. & S. Pool H. (Stephen Elford).* 1520 (CfMa), 1641 (OMa), 1676 (OMa).

EVERREADY GO ..8-10.. 9 ch.m. K-Battery — Meadowlark (Marmaduke) 3p6. Home-bred half-sister to Larkin Girl. P-t-P '99 r3 p0 (fell/unseated 2, and pulled up 1). Beaten a long way when placed on her reappearance and sent off a surprising favourite next time, but never gave her supporters a moments encouragement, and badly tailed off last subsequently. Makes little appeal as a future winner. *W.M. Aitchison — Border.* 714 (C), 1163 (OMa), 1367 (OMa).

EVERSO IRISH ..9-12.. 12 b.g. Hatim (USA) — Ever So (Mummy's Pet) uuppup. Unfurnished half-brother to flat winner, Ever So Artistic. Dam won 2 6f races. FLAT r14 p1 (3rd of 22 in Sell). NH '92/3 and '95 (tried tongue-tied) r11 p0; fell 3. P-t-P/HUNT CH '95/9 r28 w3 (inc Ladies) p8 (5 2nds, last twice; and last of 3 once); pulled up 5, and fell 2. Won a sub-standard Ladies in '99, but usually fails to get the trip, and hampered by a novice in 2000. Suited by firm ground, and has enjoyed his fair share of good fortune in the past, and seems to have used it up. *D.F. Crockford — Ross H. (Pip Hooley).* 481 (L), 699 (L), 1014 (3m5fL), 1410 (L), 1547 (L), 1673 (L).

EVER SO WINDY ..9-10.. 8 ch.g. Russlers Rod — Samantha Whiskers (Old Lucky) p. Strong-topped half-brother to Baywyn and Harmantic. Dam, half-sister to Campello Boy (*qv* '90 Annual), was 20*l*

2nd in a Point, but failed to finish in 7 of 9 other attempts. P-t-p '99 r6 w2 (Maiden and Members) p1 (last of 3); pulled up 2, and fell 1. Beat a total of two rivals in '99 and ended up with two victories, but ran out of luck at Black Forest Lodge on his return, as he was assured of another success when he went lame approaching the final fence. Failed to reappear, and a breakdown so early in his career in not a good sign. *S.R. Elford — Mid Devon.* 198 (M).

EVE'S TREASURE ..10-3.. 11 ch.m. Bustino — Before Long (Longleat USA) 1. Small light half-sister to Our Martha and Not Mistaken. FLAT r6 p0 (inc Sells). NH '93/5 and '98 r11 p3 (2nds); inc Sell. P-t-P '99 r2 w2 (Members and Club). Maintained her unbeaten record in Points at Market Rasen when making the majority of the running, but promptly disappeared, and is clearly very hard to keep sound. Would be an interesting proposition in a Ladies race around the Lincolnshire circuit if hale and hearty in 2001. *S.W. Campion — Burton.* 47 (C).

EXARCH (USA) ..—.. 12 b.g. His Majesty (USA) — Velvet (USA) (Sir Ivor) p. Strong-topped compact. Dam won a flat race in USA. FLAT r3 p0. NH '93 and '94 r7 w1 (3m Nov Claiming Hdle, 3 ran) p2. P-t-P '97 and '99 r5 p2 (2nd of 3 twice); last 1, pulled up 1, and fell 1. Able when inclined to '97, but in virtual retirement since, and has failed to beat a rival in just three starts '99/00. Often blinkered under Rules, including when successful. *Mrs C. Foster — Essex F. & U.* 317 (M).

EXCISE MAN ..10-3.. 13 ch.g. Import — Super Satin (Lord Of Verona) 811u1122p8. Strong brother to Super Sandy, and half-brother to Satinanda (dam of 4 Pointers, including Satin Flash (*qv*), Super Saga, Super Fountain (subsequently successful under Rules), Washakie and Satin D'Or, and to Chasing winner, Super Tony. Dam was 2nd in Nov Hdle for late Heppy Walton. NH FLAT '92 r1 p0. NH '93/6 and '98/9 r32 w2 (2m-2m4f Hexham Chses) p4. P-t-P/HUNT CH '94 and '98 r13 w2 (inc Confined) p3 (2 2nds); failed to finish 3 (fell/unseated 3). Has successfully mixed Pointing with a career under Rules for several years now, and doubled his previous winning tally with four Open victories 2000 — dead-heated once. Often sweats and gets on his toes, but genuine, and is intelligently handled by Jimmy Walton. Acts on any going. Wears a tongue-strap. *F.T. Walton — Border (Jimmy Walton).* 43 (Cf), 186 (O), 362 (O), 495 (O), 716 (O), 1080 (O), 1160 (O), 1365 (O), 1578 (O), 1643 (3m2fH).

EXE CRACKER ..9-13.. 12 ch.g. Blushing Scribe (USA) — Broken Paws (Busted) 2u1. Sturdy. FLAT (at 5) r3 p0. NH '94/5 r8 w1 (2m1f Hdle) p2 (inc 2nd in Sell). P-t-P '99 r5 p0 (4th, pulled up 2, and fell/unseated 2). Broke down in '95, but nursed back to health after a near four year absence, and rewarded connections with victory in a modest Open at Cothelstone in which Les Jefford's tactical supremacy came into play. Was gaining compensation for an unlucky defeat in his Members where he appeared to be travelling better than the eventual winner when parting company with the rider at the second last. Disappeared before the end of March, so all may not be well. Wears a tongue-strap. *Mrs K. Wood & J. Radford — E. Devon (Chris Down).* 199 (Cf), 401 (M), 637 (O).

EXECUTIVE BLUE (IRE) ..9-3.. 10 b.m. Executive Perk — Perfect Blue (Blue Lightning) pf22. Small light half-sister to Crown Jewel, to Hurdles winner, Velindre, and to Irish Pointing winner, Derryluman. Dam won 2 Hdles (2m-2m4f) in Ireland. P-t-P '98 (for Mrs D. Jackson) r2 p0 (last, and unseated 1). A raving maniac in the previous yard and ridden in the paddock on her reappearance at Tweseldown, but rather more sober after a years absence, though still not on the verge of a win. Would have finished tailed off at Garnons had the leaders not stopped to refuel, and has appeared not to stay herself. *G.C. Barfoot-Saunt — Ledbury.* 7 (OMa), 55 (OMa), 451 (CfMa), 1493 (OMa).

EXECUTIVE OFFICE (IRE) ..9-12.. 8 bl.g. Executive Perk — Lilly's Pride (IRE) (Long Pond) ppr6p523. Lengthy. IRISH P-t-P '98/9 r8 w2 (5&6yo Mdn, and Winners of One) p1 (2nd); unseated, and slipped up. IRISH NH '98/9 (tried tongue-tied) r5 p0 (finished in 2 Hunt Chses). Bought Doncaster, Aug for 8000. Scored twice in Ireland including on firm, but definitely does not get the trip in English Points, and has faded after giving some prominent displays (could have claimed second once, but was 12 lengths down and exhausted when he declined the final fence and unseated). Placed in two Hunter Chases, but the form is meaningless, as he was beaten 26 lengths once, and a distance once. Sometimes sweats up. Finding the right race for him is obviously going to continue to be a struggle. *S.T. Lewis — Cotswold V.F.* 33 (CI), 333 (Cf), 448 (I), 615 (CMod), 897 (I), 1336 (2m4fH), 1534 (3m1f110yH), 1627 (2m5fH).

EXEMPLAR (IRE) ..10-6.. 13 b.g. Carlingford Castle — Mabbots Own (Royal Trip) u433122. Good-bodied. IRISH P-t-P '93/4 r8 w4 (inc 3 Opens) p1 (2nd); unseated 2. IRISH HUNT CH r1 p0 (fell). NH '94/7 r36 w5 (4 Hdles, 2m5f-2m7f, and 2m5f Ch) p11 (inc 3rd in Sell Hdle). P-t-P '98/9 r13 p3 (2 3rds; and 2nd of 3); pulled up 5, and unseated 3. Finally began to gel with Didie Rowell, and justified favouritism in a poor race at Rodmell. Ran much better in defeat on his final start, but has never been an out-and-out stayer, and was collared near the line after holding a six length advantage over the last. Like many by his sire probably saves a bit for himself (was blinkered and spurred twice in '98), but might be capable of another minor success. Acts on any going. *Mrs D. Rowell — Crawley & Horsham.* 215 (C), 305 (Cf), 711 (M), 830 (Cnr), 1209 (Cnr), 1398 (Cf), 1511

(L).

EXMOOR FOREST ..9-5.. 7 b.m. Relief Pitcher — Truelyn (True Song) 25. Unfurnished sister to Westington. Dam pulled up in 2 Points for Mr Jeyes. NH FLAT '98 r1 p0. NH '99 (from Mrs C. Hicks') r1 p0 (pulled up in Hdle). Made no noticeable errors when beaten a maximum of nine lengths in Maidens, and would probably only have to continue in the same vein to collect one eventually. *Mr & Mrs C. Jeyes & Mrs & Mrs C. Winne — Exmoor (Sue Maude).* 874 (2m4fOMa), 1308 (OMa).

EYE OF THE STORM (IRE) ..9-1.. 10 b.g. Strong Gale — Belon Brig (New Brig) p47. Tall rangy. Dam won 3 Chses, 2m4f-3m. NH FLAT '96 r2 p0. NH '98/9 (for J.J. Quinn) r4 p0. Can be headstrong, but stands few outings, and beaten more than 40 lengths when completing in Points. Doubtless has something wrong with him (reportedly bled internally once under Rules). *W. Morley — Derwent (Richard Morley).* 378 (R), 400 (OMa), 627 (OMa).

FABLES GREEN ..—.. 8 b.g. Rolfe (USA) — Cuckmere Grange (Floriana) p. Home-bred half-brother to Mere Class. 25-1 and never troubled the leaders at Detling. *Mrs J. Stuart Evans — Hampshire (John Stuart Evans).* 576 (OMa).

FACTOR TEN (IRE) ..10-2.. 13 b.g. Kemal (FR) — Kissowen (Pitpan) 35425. Tall attractive half-brother to Wise Prince (IRE). NH FLAT '92/3 r3 p1 (3rd). NH '93/7 r20 w6 (2 Hdles, 2m-2m6f, and 4 Chses, 2m5f-3m1f; inc hat-trick '96) p7. P-t-P/HUNT CH '98 r6 w1 (Club nov rdrs) p3 (3 3rds, last once, and inc Hunt Ch); 4th, and unseated 1. In the form of his life in '96 and won four Chases in the space of five months (all on top-of-the-ground), but blighted by broken blood vessels otherwise, though he has seemed to have conquered that problem in the current yard. Returned from a year off in 2000 and can still go a good gallop, but lacks a turn of foot, and was run out of a Huntingdon Hunter Chase in consequence. Appeared not to stay 4m2f on his final start, has been a splendid schoolmaster for James Richardson, who has handled him well. May have to lower his sights if he is to score at 13. *J. Richardson — Cotswold (Susie Richardson).* 1060 (MO), 1306 (C), 1346 (3m1f110yH), 1542 (3mH), 1592 (4m2fH).

FAHA GIG (IRE) ..10-3.. 12 b.m. Hatim (USA) — Hazel Gig (Captain's Gig USA) 4u43522. Small compact half-sister to Ashmore Boy, Jaunty Gig and Small Flame (IRE), to Irish flat winners, Gig Time, to flat winners, Directors' Choice (also a successful Hurdler) and Majik Prince, and to Hurdles winner, Majestic Affair (IRE). Dam won at 12f in Ireland. IRISH NH FLAT '93, '98 r11 p2 (short-headed in Ch, and 3rd in Hdle). IRISH HUNT CH '94, '96 and '98 r8 w2 (in '94) p3. IRISH P-t-P '93/4, '96 and '98 r24 w8 (inc 2 Ladies) p10; fell 1. P-t-P '99 r8 w1 (Members) p4 (3 3rds). Notably tough and genuine when winning ten races in Ireland, but has proved very one-paced in the current yard, though her course completion record remains one to be proud of. Not quick enough for the best Ladies horses, but a suitable mount for a novice, and deserves another success. Suited by a stamina test in soft ground. *B.J. Kennedy — Essex F. & U. (Jim Ovel).* 19 (L), 84 (L), 95 (L), 289 (Cm), 319 (L), 555 (Cnr), 1035 (Cnr).

FAIR ALLY ..9-7.. 11 gr.g. Scallywag — Fair Kitty (Saucy Kit) 54551p5. Tall strong good-looking half-brother to Fair Vicky, Kitsbel, Saxon Fair (won Chasing since Pointing), and Steady Man, and to flat and Hurdles winner, Kitty Come Home. Dam won 8 flat (15-16f), and 5 Hdles (2m-3m1f). NH '96/7 r9 p1 (3rd in Ch); inc last twice, pulled up 2, and fell 2 (with every chance 2 out once). P-t-P '95/6 and '98/9 r15 p6 (2 2nds); pulled up 5, and unseated 1. A typically flighty Scallywag and contrived to lose his first 28 races, but clicked at the first time of asking with Rory Lawther in the plate in a Hackwood Maiden. Pulls hard and usually has two paddock handlers, and jumps well, but has an unreliable temperament, and will find life tough in Restricteds. Has been tried in blinkers and a tongue-strap, and wears a cross-noseband. *Mr & Mrs E.F.B. Monck — Grafton (Jenny Pidgeon).* 23 (OMa), 220 (OMa), 330 (R), 550 (OMa), 889 (OMa), 1206 (R), 1537 (2m5fH).

FAIR CHARMEUR (IRE) ..7-12.. 7 ch.m. Buckskin (FR) — Beau Croft Lass (Beau Charmeur FR) fpfp. Tiny neat. Dam is sister to Knowe Head (*qv* '99 Annual). P-t-P '99 r3 p0 (last, and pulled up 2). Knee high to a grasshopper, finds even Welsh fences insurmountable, and fortunate not to come back riderless on all four starts in 2000. At least she is prepared to have a crack, but unless connections plant her in some potting compost and a miracle occurs she will always be fighting a losing battle. *R.R. Smedley — Tivyside.* 268 (CfMa), 649 (CfMa), 835 (OMa), 1225 (OMa).

FAIR CROSSING ..10-3.. 15 ch.g. Over The River (FR) — Golden Chestnut (Green Shoon) 3374215. Tall workmanlike half-brother to Free To Conker (IRE), to jumping winner, Lucky Master (IRE), to Hurdles winner, Belle Rose (IRE), and to Irish Pointing winners, Gathering Moss and Official Portrait (IRE) (also won Hurdling there). NH FLAT r2 p0. NH '91/2 and '94/5 r13 w2 (2m5f Hdle and 3m3f Ch) p5 (beaten head once). P-t-P/HUNT CH '96/9 r14 w6 (inc 2 Opens) p4 (2nds); pulled up 1. Has done well for a horse with dodgy legs, but could not repeat his fantastic '99 season. Still tries hard, and recorded his ninth career success when lifting a Kingston Blount Confined in which the cumulative age of the first four home was 53. Sure-footed, but very one-paced nowadays, and finding an opening at 15 will prove tough. *M. Emmanuel — V. of Aylesbury*

(Lawney Hill). 244 (O), 461 (2m4f110yH), 749 (Cf), 1144 (O), 1282 (O), 1481 (Cf), 1621 (O).

FAIR EXCHANGE ..10-5.. 8 b.g. Bustino — Sharp Vixen (Laurence O) 11f12. Workmanlike. P-t-P '98/9 r7 w2 (Maiden and Restricted) p3 (2 3rds, last once); last 1, and pulled up 1. Pulled up after a lifeless display at Ampton in January '99, and presumably laid low as he failed to reappear that year, but has bounced back in fine form, and is developing into a useful stayer. Might have run up a four-timer but for falling two out when upsides Noughtosixty once, but jumped and hung right when beaten on his final start and hopefully did not do himself a mischief. Won his three races by an aggregate of 65 lengths, is able to maintain a strong gallop, and jumps well enough to be a worthy contender in a Hunter Chase if all is well in 2001. *Mrs M.G. Sheppard - Cambs.* 91 (M), 288 (CMod), 413 (I), 840 (I), 1378 (Cf).

FAIR FARM BOY ..10-1.. 11 b.g. Oats — Miss Orby (Paddy's Stream) p3p3312. Small compact owner-bred half-brother to Fair Farm Lad. Dam won an Irish Point, and was 3rd in an English Adjacent. P-t-P '98/9 r10 w1 (Maiden) p2; pulled up 4, and fell/unseated 3. Took no time at all to land a bad Maiden, but jumped with reckless abandon in '99, and looked wrong. Discovered some fluency (at times) in 2000 and competently disposed of seven others in a soft ground Restricted at Garthorpe, but reportedly banged a knee when beaten in an awful 4m Open at Dingley on his final start — 4-7fav! Clearly suited by a test of stamina, but has more than moderate under normal conditions. *R.C. Watchorn — Cranwell Bloodhounds.* 173 (R), 371 (R), 589 (R), 905 (C), 1009 (CR), 1268 (R), 1505 (4mmMO).

FAIR FARM LAD ..8-7§.. 9 b.g. Derring Rose — Miss Orby (Paddy's Stream) 256p14. Lengthy owner-bred half-brother to Fair Farm Boy (*qv*). NH '98 r5 p1 (21*l* 3rd). P-t-P '99 (for Mr H. Copley) r4 p0 (pulled up 4). Did his best to throw away Maiden success at Southwell (hung right on the flat, and only just managed to fend off a rival on three legs), and looks a typically moody Derring Rose. Will need to be on his best behaviour to land a Restricted. *W.J. Moore — Belvoir.* 53 (OMa), 124 (OMa), 372 (CfMa), 867 (M), 1076 (OMa), 1218 (R).

FAIR STORM (IRE) ..8-5.. 7 b.g. Glacial Storm (USA) — Mary Gleason (Gleason USA) p. Medium-sized. NH FLAT '98 r1 p0 (pulled up). P-t-P '99 (for Mrs C.N. Burton) r4 p0; pulled up 2. Beaten a minimum of 31 lengths when completing in '99, and shapes like a non-stayer. Disappeared after one outing in March, and may have suffered a setback. Wears a cross-noseband, and has two paddock handlers. *Mr & Mrs M. Ward — Warwicks (M. Ward).* 774 (OMa).

FAIR WIND (IRE) ..10-8.. 9 b.g. Strong Gale — Corcomroe (Busted) 112u. Workmanlike half-brother to Ainlee Road. P-t-P '99 r6 w1 (Maiden) p2 (2nds, beaten short-head once); fell/unseated 3. A progressive horse who put up a good performance to beat River Swilley at Larkhill in the fastest time of the day, and should have won a Ladies race at Littlewindsor subsequently, but the owner — whose return from serious injury has been very welcome and little short of miraculous — could not quite do her mount justice. Seems to handle all surfaces alike, but probably a typical Strong Gale, and has been most successful on top-of-the-ground. Has improved in the jumping department, and would not be out of place in a Novices Hunter Chase. Should continue to do well. *Miss R.J.E. David — Wilton.* 69 (R), 263 (I), 522 (L), 954 (MO).

FAIRY BELL ..—§.. 8 b.m. Silly Prices — Queen Bell (King Sitric) p. Close-coupled attractive sister to Barney Cross, and half-sister to Fourth Bell (dam of French Bell (*qv*), and Hetty Bell). Dam was 3rd of 4 and pulled up 2 in Points for Keith Waters. Grandam, Veronica Bell, won 7 Hunt Chses (inc dead-heat) and placed 9 (inc Hdle). Great-grandam, Viper Bell, won Points. P-t-P '99 r3 p0 (refused 1, ran out 1 and pulled up 1). Fat and clueless to date, but at least connections seem to have got the message, as she quickly disappeared after another poor display at Alnwick in February. *K. Waters — Braes.* 189 (OMam).

FANCY A BUCK ..—.. 6 b.m. Buckley — Fortune's Fancy (Workboy) p. Small half-sister to a flat winner. Grandam, Polly Peachum, was smart sprinter. Burly on a May debut, and blew up quickly at halfway. *Ms Hanna Walsgrove — Quorn (Nick Pomfret).* 1420 (OMa).

FANION DE NOURRY (FR) ..10-8.. 8 ch.g. Bad Conduct (USA) — Ottomane (FR) (Quart De Vin FR) 334216112. Tall rangy. FRENCH NH '97 r6 p0 (Hdle and 5 Chses; fell 3, pulled up 1). NH '98/9 (for T. Caldwell) r9 p0 (ran out 2, inc one of 2 Chses — the other was a Sell). Bought Doncaster, Nov for 2000. A much improved performer since his ability to handle extreme distances was capitalised on, and is now quite useful. Would have won a 7min31s Maiden at Sandon had Jason Merry not eased prematurely (he was fined £50 for losing the race), but only beaten twice in five attempts when well handled by Lenny Hicks subsequently, and looked sure to score over 4m2f at Uttoxeter until he tied up after the last and was just collared by Hatcham Boy. Previously relished the long uphill finish when scoring unchallenged at Towcester, and there should be more victories in store when conditions are favourable. Not the easiest of rides, and connections have done well with him. *E. Haddock — Meynell & S. Staffs.* 436 (OMa), 568 (OMa), 672 (2m4fOMa), 906 (CfMa), 1068 (3m2fOMa), 1200 (CR), 1418 (R), 1533 (3m1fH), 1592 (4m2fH).

FARADAY ..—.. 11 b.g. Electric — Muffet's Gold (Cavo Doro) u874ppp. Strong lengthy half-brother to Dondale Rose, and to a winner in Sweden. NH FLAT r1 p0 (last); withdrawn intended debut (lame in stables). NH '96 (blinkered final) r3 p0 (pulled up in Sell Hdle and Ch, and fell in Ch). P-t-P '97/9 r12 w3 (Maiden, Restricted and Members — hat-trick) p3 (last of 2 once); pulled up 5. Landed a hat-trick on sound surfaces in '97, but beat nothing of note, and has performed dismally in the current yard (fat and useless). Tailed off without exception when completing since his glory days, and only makes up the numbers nowadays. *T.E. Wardall — Atherstone.* 118 (L), 544 (L), 787 (L), 868 (Cf), 1014 (3m5fL), 1414 (M), 1667 (I).

FAREBIT ..9-0.. 7 b.m. Henbit (USA) — Ina's Farewell (Random Shot) 521. Small plain half-sister to Graceland (qv). 5400 4-y-o. NH FLAT '99 (for Jane Storey) r1 p0. Schooled in her first Maiden, finished two lengths second next time, and then won a slowly-run three-finisher contest on firmish at Aspatria. A steady performer who should be able to rate higher, and likely to be thereabouts in Restricteds. *C. Storey — College V. & N. Northumberland.* 45 (OMa), 664 (2m5fOMa), 1368 (OMa).

FAR FOREST ..—§§.. 8 b.g. Rakaposhi King — Ledwyche (Pamroy) prrrp. Strong workmanlike half-brother to Ledwyche Gate and Ledwyche Bank. P-t-P '98/9 r11 p3 (2 2nds, last once; and 3rd of 4); failed to finish 8 (ran out 1, refused 1, and fell/unseated 2). Able, but a real thinker (would be a Dr Jekyll were he human), and it has become second nature for him to stop and have a look at his surroundings rather than do what he was bred to do. Has been partnered by eight different jockeys and made monkeys out of all of them. Wears headgear, but makes Beelzebub look positively angelic these days. Should be banned before he does something deranged and causes someone an injury. The trainer was previously irresponsible enough to run Red Breaker (qv 2000 Annual). *Mrs P.A. Price & Miss J. Evans — Ludlow (Geoff Evans).* 122 (OMa), 337 (CfMa), 569 (OMa), 673 (2m4fOMa), 1196 (OMa).

FAR FROM PERFECT (IRE) ..9-9.. 9 gr.m. Phardante (FR) — Kilistrano (Capistrano) 21. Half-sister to several winners, including in Ireland. Dam won 2 5f races at 2 in Ireland. A late comer to racing (had previously bred a foal), but ran well in two visits to Maisemore, and followed a half length second with a comfortable success in a five-runner affair. The second was unbeaten twice subsequently, and the third broke down with a race at his mercy, so the form looks decent. May be able to score again. *A.J. Williams — Llangibby (Sue Williams).* 891 (OMa), 1315 (OMa).

FAR GLEN (IRE) ..—.. 6 b.g. Phardante (FR) — Asigh Glen (Furry Glen) pp. Brother to Irish Pointing and Chasing winner, Pharbeitfrome. Sold Doncaster, May for 13,000. Tailed off and pulled up after two miles twice (unable to race properly until the rider lent forward and removed his tongue-strap on the second occasion!). *M.H. Ings — Teme V. (Billie Brown).* 990 (OMa), 1277 (OMa).

FARM TALK ..8-2.. 9 ch.g. Palm Track — Kilkenny Gorge (Deep Run) 42p. Small robust. Dam, sister to Ardbrennan (qv), was placed in 3 Points (3rd behind two stablemates in 18-runner race once). NH FLAT '97 r2 p0 (tailed off). NH '97 r1 p0 (pulled up in Hdle). P-t-P '98 r3 p0 (pulled up 2, and fell 1). Showed a modicum of ability though failing to complete in '98, but beaten by a horse that had previously never finished in five outings with favourite at Charm Park, and looks to be having trouble getting the trip. Has an uphill struggle ahead in his search for success. *Mrs S.M. Tennant — Middleton.* 809 (OMa), 1235 (OMa), 1352 (OMa).

FAR SENIOR ..8-12§.. 15 ch.g. Al Sirat (USA) — Ross Lady (Master Buck) p4. Tall rangy half-brother to Who Is He and Kelburne Lad (IRE). IRISH NH FLAT r1 p0. IRISH P-t-P '90 r2 w1 (45&6yo Maiden) p0; unseated 1. IRISH NH '94 r4 w1 (2m4f Hdle) p1 (2nd). NH '90/4 and '95/7 r46 w10 (2m5f Hdle, and 9 Chses, 2m4f-3m2f, inc 4 in 5 race spell; 6 prizes value between £4150 and £10,235 — latter for 2nd in H. and T. Walker Gold Cup) p10; pulled up 1. IRISH NH '95 r1 p0 (unseated in 4m1f Amat race over banks at Punchestown). P-t-P/HUNT CH '95 and '98 (for Miss L. Montgomery in '98) r6 w2 (Open and Mixed Open) p2 (2nds); pulled up 1, and unseated 1. A useful top-of-the-ground Chaser to '96, but of no account since leaving Kim Bailey until winning a brace of Opens for Dick Baimbridge when partnered by Julian Pritchard in '98. Resurfaced in another new yard after a year off, but often looked disinterested in his prime and only went a mile before boredom set in twice. Deserves to spend the rest of his days doing something that befits a senior citizen. *C.R. Millington — Fernie.* 1417 (L), 1502 (M).

FARTHING WOOD ..9-2.. 7 gr.g. Le Coq D'Or — Willow Wood (Precipice Wood) p4. Neat light owner-bred half-brother to Willoughby Moss (qv). Schooled on his debut, but did much better when five lengths fourth next time. Should improve as he strengthens, and is a possible Maiden winner. *Mrs B.K. Thomson — Berwicks.* 1084 (2m4fOMa), 1430 (OMa).

FASGO (IRE) ..10-0.. 6 b.g. Montelimar (USA) — Action Plan (Creative Plan USA) 3143. Dam won 2 Irish Chses, 2m-2m2f. Bought Doncaster, May for 7800. 8-1 when winning an 18-runner Maiden at Larkhill, but has ironically been beaten when favourite or joint-favourite in all his other attempts. Can be novicey, and was badly let down by his jumping for the second time when making four mistakes in the final mile on his latest outing. Has avoided soft ground to date, and evidently thought able to handle firm. Does well to keep completing, and has the potential to be quite useful if becoming fluent. *T.A. Smith — Mendip F. (Richard Barber).* 265 (OMa), 455 (OMa), 734 (R), 1488 (R).

FAST FLOW (IRE) ..8-7.. 9 ch.m. Over The River (FR) — Hi Cal (Callernish) pf4. Very small half-sister to Malenski (IRE). P-t-P '97/9 (for Mr K. Godwin in '99) r7 p1 (3rd); pulled up 5, and brought down 1. Beaten a minimum of 38 lengths in two completions (would have been closer to the winner once but for falling at the last), and does not inspire confidence. Another diddy mare that Amanda Meakins can partner without her feet leaving the ground (*cf* Fair Charmeur). In her fourth ownership in as many years. *D.M. Davies — Carms (Amanda Meakins).* 220 (OMa), 267 (CfMa), 348 (CfMa).

FAST FREEZE ..9-7§.. 15 b.g. Vision (USA) — Gohar (USA) (Barachois CAN) p. Small neat half-brother to Master Of Troy, to Hurdles winner, Tamandu, and to winners in USA and Austria. Dam won 5f Clmr in USA. NH FLAT r1 p0. NH '90/1 and '97 r14 w2 (2m4f Hdles, inc Clmr) p2 (2nds). P-t-P/HUNT CH '92/6 (visored 1) and '99 (for Mr P.H. Richards in '99) r38 w3 (Open and 2 Ladies) p11 (8 3rds, of 4 once, beating remounter, and last twice); failed to finish 12 (fell/unseated 5, and refused 1). Formerly able, but frequently has disappointed, and no better than last in his final seven starts. Looks well past it now. *N.J. Criddle — Tredegar F. (Trevor Haines).* 821 (MO).

FAST LANE (IRE) ..10-0.. 7 b br.g. Montelimar (USA) — Toretta (Torus) 1. Half-brother to Uncle Billy (IRE) (*qv*). IRISH P-t-P '99 r2 p0 (4th 2). Impressive when winning a Maiden on dead ground at Eyton, where he was drawing right away when he made a bad mistake two out. Could have a bright future. His sire is certainly producing some useful novices, with this one and Monty's Tag amongst the best. Potentially seriously under-rated. *D. Manning — N. Salop (Sheila Crow).* 1196 (OMa).

FAST RUN (IRE) ..8-7§.. 13 ch.g. Commanche Run — Starlite Night (USA) (Star De Naskra USA) pp3pfpp. Compact good-topped. Dam won at 7f. FLAT r4 p1 (2nd); inc Sells. NH '91/2 and '94/8 r20 p9 (8 Hdles to 3m2f; 2nd in Ch). P-t-P/HUNT CH '93 and '98/9 r15 w2 (Maiden and Members) p2 (2nds); failed to finish 7 (refused 1, and unseated 1). Gave Michelle Taylor a couple of fair rides at Badbury Rings in 2000 (though one ended in a tumble), but beaten 25 lengths in his latest placing, and still struggles to stay three miles. A regular non-finisher in Points, and normally too faint-hearted to win. *Miss M. Taylor — Portman.* 330 (R), 458 (R), 765 (L), 953 (I), 1058 (M), 1306 (C), 1471 (Cnr).

FATHER ANDY (IRE) ..11-4.. 8 ch.g. Executive Perk — Twinkle Sunset (Deep Run) 5312212f6. Workmanlike. Dam is half-sister to Cracking Idea (IRE) (*qv*). IRISH P-t-P '98/9 r2 w2 (5yo's Mdn and Winners of 2). IRISH NH FLAT '98/9 r5 p2 (just caught when ½l 2nd once). IRISH NH '98/9 r5 p1 (27l 3rd in Hunt Ch). IRISH P-t-P '00 r1 p0 (5th in Lisgoold Open: *mists 2 & 4, 3rd 9-3 out, wknd nxt, nd*). IRISH HUNT CH '00 r7 w2 (beat Fernhill Queen and Round Tower Lass nk and 15l at Clonmel: *mid-div, lft 3rd 2 out, 2nd last, ld cl home*; and beat Very Noble and You Know Best 3l and 2l at Gowran: *6th ½way, 3rd 3 out, ld last, rdn out*) p3 (2 2nds: beaten hd by Idiot's Star at Thurles: *hld up, 3rd 2 out, ld app last, hdd cl home*; beaten 20l by Sheltering at Fairyhouse: *5th when pckd 3, rdn 3 out, 2nd nxt, no imp*; and beaten 4l and dist by Sheltering and Spot The Difference at Fairyhouse: *4th ½way, 3rd 5 out, mist & lost tch 2 out, r.o u.p*); 6th at Punchestown: *mid-div, 5th 10, 4th & rdn 5 out, nd*; and fell 1. A tough Irish performer who is more than competent, but invariably slammed by Sheltering on their frequent meetings, and does not aspire to the top grade yet. Suited by plenty of give in the ground, and his one visit to England resulted in a fine one length second to Lakefield Rambler at Aintree. Would have given the winner an even harder task had he not blundered at the final fence, and it could well pay off to travel him across the Irish Sea again. *Mrs S. McCloy — Limerick (Michael Hourigan, in Ireland).* 924 (3m1fH).

FATHER HENRY (IRE) ..—.. 10 b.g. The Parson — Little Sloop (Balinger) upupp. Compact half-brother to Irish Pointing and Hurdling winner, Dinghy. Dam won at 8f, and won 4 2m Hdles. NH '97/8 (for N. Henderson) r5 p1 (3rd). IRISH NH '98/9 r8 p0. IRISH P-t-P '99 r1 w1 (6yo plus Mdn). NH Apr '00 (for R.H. York) r1 p0 (pulled up in Hdle:*t.o & pu 11*). His Irish victory in heavy appeared to come courtesy of a judging error, and seemed to lose his confidence completely after unseating first time out in 2000. Jumped particularly badly in his final Point. Formerly owned by the Queen Mum. *H.R. Cook — Surrey U. (Chris Elliott).* 6 (R), 13 (R), 239 (R), 305 (Cf).

FATHER'S JOY ..8-12.. 11 b.m. Scottish Reel — Miss Becca (Young Man FR) p732u63p. Small angular. FLAT r1 p0. NH '93/4 and '96 r12 p1 (3rd in Sell, demoted from 2nd). P-t-P '98/9 r25 p1 (last of 3); pulled up 13, fell/unseated 6, and ran out 1. Didn't venture to as many far-flung Pointing outposts as she did in '99, but doesn't stay, still jumps as consistently poorly, and looks destined to remain a maiden. Had managed to complete just 20% of her races for the current yard prior to 2000, but has now hiked that figure up by a staggering 10%. Might win if a meeting was staged at Lourdes. *P.J. Millington — Fernie.* 234 (OMa), 436 (OMa), 679 (OMa), 1012 (CfMa), 1035 (Cnr), 1219 (OMa), 1292 (OMa), 1382 (OMa).

FAWN PRINCE (IRE) ..—.. 8 b.g. Electric — Regent Star (Prince Regent FR) f. Close-coupled half-brother to several winners (including abroad), including Loch Scavaig (IRE) (NH flat and Hurdles), and to Irish Chasing winner, Fairies Cross. Dam won at 7f in Ireland. IRISH FLAT Jun '99 r1 p0. IRISH NH FLAT '97 r2 w1 p0. IRISH NH '97/9 r9 w1 (2m1f Hdle) p1 (3rd); ran in Festival Bumper. Looked competent enough when scoring on firmish and in softish in Ireland, but fell at halfway on his English Pointing debut, and hurt himself (wore a cross-noseband, and looked rather too exuberant). *A. Lochore — W. Norfolk.* 1035 (Cnr).

FAWSLEY MANOR ..10-4.. 11 ch.m. St Columbus — True Manor (True Song) 12313. Tall strong home-bred sister to Magical Manor (*qv*). P-t-P '97/9 r13 w5 (up to Confined) p4 (2nds); ran out 1, and fell/unseated 2. An honest and likeable mare who has thankfully made a full recovery from a nasty incident at Clifton-on-Dunsmore in '99, when she staked herself on the running rail as Jimmy Tarry tried for an non-existent gap on the inner. Made the jump to Open company at the first attempt — albeit in a weak one — and added another for good measure, taking her winning tally to seven from 17 races. Not always fluent and may struggle to raise her rating in future, but gutsy, has few miles on the clock, and should be able to score again. *Viscount Gage & G.B. Tarry — Pytchley (Jimmy Tarry).* 789 (O), 1216 (O), 1416 (O), 1484 (O), 1621 (O).

FEARLESS BERTIE ..9-8.. 10 b.g. Fearless Action (USA) — Rambert (Mandamus) 0. Small neat half-brother to a winner in Denmark. P-t-P '96/8 r7 w1 (2m4f Maiden) p3 (2 2nds); failed to finish 3 (fell/unseated 2). Won a short Maiden at Dingley on his first completion in '97, but off the track since three placings the following season, and managed just one appearance in 2000. Clearly hard to train (three outings in a season is his record), and made no show in the latest. *Miss J. Johnston & S. Miles — Bicester with Whaddon (Joan Johnston).* 871 (R).

FED ON OATS ..—.. 13 b.g. Oats — Fedelm (Celtic Cone) sRp. Strong good-looking half-brother to jumping winner, Mr Mahdlo. NH FLAT '93 r1 p1 (3rd). NH '94 and '97/8 (2 wins from Miss V. Williams'; previously from D. Nicholson's) r15 w3 (2m Hdle, and 2 2m1f Chses) p3; looked winner of 2m Hdle when fell last once. Formerly quite useful when his legs allowed, but was absent for 36 months after going lame in April '94. Last scored in September '97, and has been last once and a non-finisher five times in his six most recent starts. Was not an easy ride for a professional, and is far from ideal for Debbie Powell. *J. Kottler — Clifton-on-Teme (Debbie Powell).* 335 (L), 860 (L), 991 (L).

FEEL THE POWER (IRE) ..9-3$.. 13 b.g. Torus — Donadea (Mugatpura) p4pR. Tall rangy. Dam won 2 Hdles (2m-2m6f) and 2 Chses (2m1f-2m6f) in Ireland. IRISH P-t-P '94 r1 w1 (Adjacent, for non-park winners). NH '94/7 r11 w1 (2m5f Hdle) p8. P-t-P/HUNT CH '99 r3 p1 (3rd); last, and unseated 1. A dual winner in '94, but a typical Torus in that he would find little after travelling well, and has failed to score again since. Broke down in his Members and injured John Maxse when dumping him, and as he had not taken to Pointing seems very unlikely to stage a revival. *Mrs S. Maxse — Hampshire.* 1 (C), 127 (Cf), 325 (Cf), 882 (M).

FELLOW SIOUX ..9-8.. 14 ch.g. Sunley Builds — Sue Lark (Sir Lark) pp8. Tall strong-topped home-bred brother to Just For A Lark, and half-brother to Scallykath, Suantley and Suesultimate, and to Chasing winner, Another Hubblick. Dam won 2 Sell Hdles, 2m1f-2m4f (also won 2m5f HCap, but demoted to 2nd). P-t-P/HUNT CH '93/9 r29 w7 (up to Confined) p4 (2 3rds, last once); failed to finish 12 (fell/unseated 2, ran out 1). Completed his eighth consecutive season in Points in 2000, but has failed to score since '97, and seems to be breaking blood vessels on a regular basis nowadays — and presumably always has been. Wears a near-side pricker to counteract bad hanging problems, but a back number now, and probably not worth running again. Has his quirks, but is a brave horse to have overcome his bleeding problems and win seven races. *T.B. Stevens — Devon & Somerset (Stuart Stevens).* 638 (Cf), 1096 (MO), 1371 (Cf).

FENCING MASTER ..10-5.. 12 b.g. Broadsword (USA) — Adroit (Ritudyr) pu41. Tall rangy half-brother to Right Company (*qv*). NH FLAT '94 r1 p0. NH '94/5 r4 p1 (3rd). P-t-P '98 r4 w2 (Maiden and Restricted) p1 (2nd); and unseated 1. Off the track for three years prior to '98 and missed the next season too, but showed he still retains plenty of ability and enthusiasm when battling on well to beat his four years younger half-brother in testing conditions at Kimble. A free-running sort and still inclined to make mistakes, but has no mileage on the clock for a horse of his age, and can win again if connections can keep him sound. *M.H.D. Barlow — Bicester with Whaddon (Robert Elwell).* 246 (C), 510 (Cf), 785 (I), 1143 (I).

FENNY PRINCE ..—.. 8 b.g. Naskracker (USA) — Zara Express (Pony Express) ppp. Tall. Dam, half-sister to Stainless Steel (*qv* 2000 Annual), was about a fence 3rd in 2 Points for the Sweatlands (failed to finish in 10 of 15 attempts). P-t-P '99 r2 p0 (pulled up 2). Unimpressively bred and has yet to get beyond 2m4f in five attempts. Looks to be heading towards his mother's dismal record. *S.H. Sweatland — E. Devon (Martin Sweatland).* 355 (O), 933 (OMa), 1048 (CfMa).

FERGIE (U) ..—.. 9 ch.m. unknown p. Fat and gingery and unpopular in the market at Charing. Immediately disappeared for another holiday. *R.D. Thomson — Ashford V.* 1109 (M).

FERNHILL BLAZE (IRE) ..9-1.. 8 b.g. High Estate — Bonnie Isle (Pitcairn) pff. Close-coupled half-brother to Island Forest (USA) (subsequent Chasing winner), to Hurdles winner, Tensile (IRE), and to flat winners in France and USA. Dam won 5 flat, 6-8f, and was 2nd in '79 Oaks. FLAT r1 p0 (last — started slowly and soon tailed off). P-t-P '98/9 r2 p1 (3rd); and fell 1. Might have finished third on three occasions but for mishaps at the penultimate obstacle twice. Seems to have trouble getting the trip, and his infrequent visits to the races suggest he is rather fragile. Might yet be capable of springing a surprise. *M.G. Jones — Gelligaer F.* 72 (OMa), 267 (CfMa), 601 (CfMa).

FERN LEADER (IRE) ..9-9.. 11 b.g. Supreme Leader — Mossbrook (Le Moss) 63puf434226. Smallish compact. P-t-P '95/6 (for Mr W.R. Ward) r8 w3 (up to Confined) p0; pulled up 1, and fell 1. NH FLAT Jan '97 (for Mrs A. Swinbank) r1 p0. NH '97/8 (for C. Grant; previously for Mrs A. Swinbank) r20 w2 (2m5f-3m Chses) p9 (inc 7 2nds); (fell/unseated 4). Won three minor Points in impressive fashion in '96 when trained by Chris Grant and picked up two Chases when back in his care, but used to make shoals of errors over big fences, and often beaten in races he should have won. Ran well when second in visors twice in May, but otherwise well beaten for his new connections. Frequently out on his feet in the closing stages under Rules, and an easy three miles is required these days. Often blinkered in the past. *Mrs J. Hughes — Cranwell Bloodhounds (Paul Blockley).* 3 (L), 25 (Cnr), 95 (L), 443 (Cf), 461 (2m4f10yH), 1073 (O), 1209 (Cnr), 1253 (L), 1417 (L), 1550 (Cnr), 1584 (CCond).

FERRYHILL (IRE) ..9-12.. 8 b.g. Over The River (FR) — Eden Valley (Kambalda) 18. Tall strong half-brother to Irish Pointing and Chasing winner, Tremble Valley. Dam won 2 Irish Chses, 2m4f-3m (wore blinkers). NH FLAT Jan '98 r1 p1 (3rd). NH '98/9 (for Miss H. Knight) r3 p0; 6th and brought down in Chses. Sold Malvern, May for 5800. Gifted a Larkhill Maiden after the ten length leader had unseated at the last, but was disappointing next time, and is difficult to evaluate. Looks the part, but yet to run much, and absent since mid-February. *J.J. Boulter — Portman (Nick Mitchell & John Boulter).* 12 (OMa), 208 (R).

FESTIVAL (FR) ..—.. 8 gr.g. Mourtazam — Oseille (FR) (Le Pontet FR) f. Very tall good-looking half-brother to a French flat winner. Dam won 2 10f races in France, and won 3 races over obstacles in the Provinces. NH FLAT '97 r1 p0. NH '98/9 (final for G. McCourt; previously for A.P. Jones) r4 p0; (7th of 8, last and pulled up in Hdles; last in Ch). Bought Ascot, June for 2700. Takes an almighty hold and invariably gallops himself into the ground, and looks a very troublesome sort. Probably difficult to train (was absent for 17 months after his debut, and did not reappear after falling at the 11th in a Point). *C. Kemball — Surrey U.* 790 (OMa).

FETTLE UP ..9-8§.. 13 ch.g. Lyphard's Special (USA) — Fire Risk (Thatch USA) 57. Workmanlike half-brother to flat winner, Pavaka, and to Irish Hurdles winner, Pompier. FLAT r8 p0. NH '91/4 r14 w2 (2m4f-3m Hdles) p4; gained five of six prizes on all-weather. P-t-P/HUNT CH '95/6 and '98/9 r24 w4 (3 Ladies and Members) p8 (5 3rds, last once); fell/unseated 3, and pulled up 3. Successful on six occasions prior to missing the '97 season, but unreliable and beaten 12 times since his resumption. Beat one rival home in two March Confineds, and no longer worthy of consideration. Almost exclusively blinkered over jumps. *Mrs D.R. Brotherton — Middleton (Serena Brotherton).* 394 (Cf), 623 (Cf).

FEVER PITCH ..9-6.. 11 gr.g. Kalaglow — Seragsbee (Sagaro) bu14p. Big strong-topped half-brother to Genuine Reason, and to flat winner, Hi-Aud. NH '94/5 and '99 (for R.J. Hodges; previously for R.G. Frost) r9 p1 (last of 3); last and failed to finish 2 in Chses. P-t-P '97 r5 p2 (last of 3 once); refused 1, and pulled up 1. Switched to racing under Rules because of a lack of stamina, but did not prove good enough, and very lucky to stumble across a poor Maiden at Larkhill — where the runner-up was seemingly out for a jolly — to make it 17th time lucky. Stopped quickly on a return visit, and clearly still does not get the trip properly. *W.G. Gooden, Mrs B. Lock, R. Napper & L. Vernoum — Mendip F. (Brett Parsons & Jo West).* 352 (CfMa), 457 (OMa), 629 (OMa), 1135 (R), 1336 (2m4fH).

FIBREGUIDE TECH ..—.. 18 b.g. Uncle Pokey — Starcat (Avocat) p. Rangy brother to Miss Chatel and Apairtogether, and half-brother to Avostar. NH FLAT r1 p1 (3rd). NH '87 and '95 r7 p0. P-t-P/HUNT CH '88/94 and '97/9 r34 w9 (inc Hunt Ch, and 3 Opens) p10 (9 2nds, inc 3 Hunt Chses, 2m4f-2m6f, and 3rd in Hunt Ch); failed to finish 12 (on floor 8). A smashing old horse who has never stood much racing, and has raced just 12 times in the last eight years, but made a surprise reappearance in 2000 when providing Hannah Kinsey with more experience at Eyton. His Members success in '99 would have been the ideal swansong, but perhaps a return in 2001 is not beyond the realms of possibility. *Mrs T.R. Kinsey — Cheshire Forest.* 1320 (L).

FIDDLERS KNAP ..10-1.. 11 br.g. Queen's Soldier (USA) — Sharp Reef (Milford) 1. Rangy attractive owner-bred. P-t-P '96/7 and '99 r10 w1 (Maiden) p3 (2nds, beaten neck once); pulled up 3, ran out 1, and fell 1. Took longer to win his Maiden than he should have — often the victim of poor placing and riding — and has plenty of ability, but not an easy ride (wears a cross-noseband and often pulls hard), and clearly needs 12 months rest between successes. Recorded a decent time when winning at Black Forest Lodge, and good enough to score in better company if his health permits. *J. Hobbs — N. Cotswold.* 203 (R).

FIDDLER'S LANE ..—§.. 13 b.g. Mart Lane — Alto Sax (Prince De Galles) p. Tall owner-bred brother to Daisy Lane, and half-brother to Sweet Joanna. Dam won Ladies and placed 2 for Pat Kerby (whose leg she broke once). P-t-P '94/6 and '98/9 r15 w1 (Maiden) p0; pulled up 8, ran out 1, and fell/unseated 5. Sprang a major surprise when scoring at 14-1 in '96 (and half-sister Sweet Joanna completed what was probably the most unlikely family double of the year), but has never completed otherwise, and blinkered when the rider bottled out after two miles in the latest attempt. Has only once managed more than two outings in a year ('98), and ended that season lame. Mum was a tad loopy and he has more than followed her example. *Miss P. Kerby — Clifton-on-Teme.* 697 (M).

FIERY JACK ..9-6§.. 8 ch.g. Broadsword (USA) — Castelira (Castle) f3431p73. Leggy half-brother to Casino Nell (qv). P-t-P '98/9 r13 p1 (2nd); pulled up 10, ran out 1. Hopeless when owner-ridden (one completion from nine attempts), but has produced rateable form for Nigel Tutty, and won a three-finisher Maiden at Wetherby on his 18th attempt. Named with feeling (has been troublesome in the preliminaries and had two paddock handlers), and likely to continue to struggle now that he is out of the lowest grade. *R.S. Lochman — York & Ainsty S.* 168 (OMa), 283 (OMa), 399 (OMa), 508 (CMa), 694 (OMa), 1000 (R), 1230 (R), 1351 (CR).

FINAL ANALYSIS (IRE) ..10-1.. 8 b.g. Mister Lord (USA) — Abbey Belle (Kambalda) 2u31p4. Tall half-brother to Irish Pointing winner, Black Abbey. P-t-P '99 r4 w1 (deadheat Maiden) p2 (¾l 2nd once); and fell 1. Looked a shade fortunate to be awarded a share of the spoils at Kingston Blount in '99, but had more than enough in hand to satisfy the judge at Hackwood Park in 2000, where he received a typically strong drive from James Owen. Apt to make the odd blunder (though it usually takes a lot to dislodge his partner), and rarely represents much in the way of value. A weak finisher to date and may be a bit of a softie (blinkered on his final start), so needs treating with caution when he reappears. *M.J. Tuckey — Bicester with Whaddon (Herbie Owen).* 80 (CCfR), 193 (R), 427 (M), 887 (R), 1143 (I), 1485 (I).

PLATE 47   887 Hampshire Restricted: Final Analysis (J. Owen), 1st, lands ahead of Ngala (H. Tett), 4th, with Sunczech (B. Kendellen), 6th, just getting their noses in shot

PHOTO: Bill Selwyn

FINAL BEAT (IRE) ..9-9§.. 12 ch.g. Orchestra — Market Romance (African Sky) 436260. Compact. IRISH NH FLAT '93 r1 p0. IRISH P-t-P '94/5 r8 w1 (45&6yo Maiden, 4 ran) p1 (2nd); pulled up 2, and fell 2. IRISH NH '94 r1 p0. NH '95/7 r20 p8 (Chses). P-t-P '98/9 r10 w3 (2 Restricteds and Intermediate) p6 (5 3rds). Enjoyed something of a renaissance in '99 with three successes (one on a disqualification), but had frequently looked unenthusiastic before, and reverted to his old ways this term. Remarkably safe and has never failed to complete in Points, but the chances of him being goaded back into the winners enclosure seem slim. Has been tried unsuccessfully in blinkers. *C.J. Cundall — Holderness (Mary Sowersby).* 375 (Cf), 504 (O), 691 (O), 997 (Cf), 1327 (O), 1584 (CCond).

FINAL CHANCE ..—.. 7 ch.m. Nader — Milly's Chance (Mljet) uupufup. Robust home-bred half-sister to Millyhenry (*qv*). NH FLAT '99 r2 p0. NH '99 r2 p0 (inc Sell). Whilst Millyhenry carried all before him in 2000, Final Chance tried to trample all beneath her. Was in contention when unseating half a mile from home twice, but there is so far no evidence that she stays three miles, although she should do on breeding. It would be interesting to hear Portman Square's attitude to her record. *L. Tizzard — Blackmore & Sparkford V. (Alan Tizzard).* 410 (OMa), 641 (CfMa), 733 (2m4fOMa), 875 (2m4fOMa), 1102 (OMa), 1241 (OMa), 1468 (OMa).

FINAL OPTION (IRE) ..8-13.. 13 b.g. Quayside — Death Or Glory (Hasdrubal) pp745. Small compact half-brother to Irish jumping winner, Super Dealer (IRE). IRISH NH FLAT r3 p0. IRISH NH '92/4 r9 p0 (inc last pair 4, pulled up 2, and fell 1). IRISH P-t-P '93/4 r18 p5; pulled up 5, and unseated 1. P-t-P/HUNT CH '95/9 r32 w1 (Maiden) p10 (7 2nds); failed to finish 9 (fell/unseated 2). Took no fewer than 62 attempts to get off the mark (23 of them in Welsh Maidens!!), but finally succeeded in a Bonvilston event in '99. Predictably struggling in Restricteds since, and usually finds his rivals travelling a few m.p.h quicker than he can manage. Often blinkered in Ireland. *G.A. Fynn — Tredegar F. (Ian Johnson).* 596 (R), 744 (R), 818 (R), 1403 (I), 1453 (R).

FINAL QUAY ..—§.. 10 b.m. Derring Rose — Final Flirtation (Clear Run) urp. Tiny sister to Final Rose (*qv*). NH '99 (from N. Twiston-Davies) r3 p1 (8½l 3rd at 2m6f); last, and pulled up 1 in Hdles. P-t-P '98/9 r5 p0 (ran out 2, and pulled up 3). An obnoxious dwarf with no steering and the other usual Derring Rose idiosyncrasies. Visored once in '99, and acquired blinkers this term. Pulled up lame at Weston Park, and will hopefully not be returning. *C.J. Hammett — Cotswold (Marcella Bailiss).* 892 (OMa), 972 (OMa), 1413 (OMa).

FINAL ROSE ..9-11.. 11 b.m. Derring Rose — Final Flirtation (Clear Run) u22. Small neat sister to Final Quay. Dam, half-sister to 6 Pointers including Final Answer (dam of Final Cruise, (*qv*), won 4 Points and placed 8 for Mr E.D. Llewellyn. NH '97 r3 p0 (last, and pulled up 2 in Hdles). P-t-P '95/6 and '98/9 r10 w1 (Maiden) p1 (3rd); fell 3, pulled up 5. Speedy, but too frail to survive her jumping errors and often runs out of gas after 2m4f or so. Beaten a minimum of ten lengths in her Restricted completions, but an habitual front-runner who never manages many outings, and will need to improve to win one. *D.H. Llewellyn — S. Pembs.* 837 (I), 947 (R), 1228 (R).

FINE EXAMPLE ..8-12.. 11 b.g. Nearly A Hand — Debbiedamus (Mandamus) p. Small half-brother to Handsome Deb and Mumpsimus. P-t-P '99 r3 p1 (2nd); ran out 1, and pulled up 1. Managed to slip the field once at Flete Park in '99, but capitulated up the hill and was collared in the dying strides. Otherwise on his worst behaviour, and may well have suffered a setback in his most recent attempt. Reported to go bananas if boxed up and has to be hacked to the course each time and stabled overnight. *Mr & Mrs A.J. Jones — Modbury H. (Alan Jones).* 1041 (M).

FINE STALKER (IRE) ..9-12.. 13 ch.g. Stalker — Bellinor (Le Levanstell) f1f. Compact brother to Hurdles winner, Ste-Jen, and half-brother to a winner in Malaysia. Dam won 2 Irish flat, 8-12f. NH '95/6 r5 p2. P-t-P '94 and '98/9 r5 p1 (2nd); fell/unseated 2. Survived one awful mistake when deservedly opening his account at Tweseldown, but seems intent in testing the might of the birch wherever he goes, and usually pays the penalty. Good enough to win in better company, but stands his racing badly, and may have hurt himself in the latest spill. *D.J. Caro — N. Ledbury.* 20 (OMa), 220 (OMa), 336 (R).

FINE TIMES ..9-13.. 7 b.g. Timeless Times (USA) — Marfen (Lochnager) pp4135. Small sturdy brother to flat winner, Ramsey Hope. FLAT (usually visored) r24 p2 (2nd, 5-6f). NH '98 r2 p0 (last, and pulled up 1, inc Sell). P-t-P '99 r2 p0 (fell 2). Well ridden by Matthew Mackley to prevail in a modest Brocklesby Maiden, and has stayed on better since acquiring a tongue-strap. Has to be held up in order to conserve his stamina, but has a feasible chance in Restricteds now that his fencing is up to scratch. *J.M. Robinson — Burton.* 51 (OMa), 181 (2m4fOMa), 439 (OMa), 793 (CfMa), 1287 (R), 1419 (R).

FINGERHILL (IRE) ..9-7.. 12 b.g. Boyne Valley — Diamond Glow (Kalaglow) 3. Tall lengthy half-brother to I've Copped It (IRE) and River Diamond (IRE). IRISH NH FLAT '96 (blinkered) r1 p0. IRISH NH '96 r1 p0 (10th of 11 in Hunt Ch). IRISH P-t-P '93/6 (tried tongue-tied) r29 w4 (inc Open) p10; pulled up 10, and carried out. NH '96 and'98 r9 p2 (Chses, inc ½l 2nd in bad race). Ran seven times as a four year old in Irish Points, and later made seven appearances in two months for the present stable before vanishing for almost two years. Tailed off and pulled up twice when returning in '98, and although he gave a better display when 12 lengths third in his Members after another long absence he is clearly physically wrecked. Error prone and has jumped left, and probably finds three miles just too far. *V. Thompson — Percy.* 39 (M).

FINNIGAN FREE ..10-9.. 11 ch.g. Los Cerrillos (ARG) — Philly-Free (Avocat) 11111. Strong-topped half-brother to Crocked Again (IRE). NH '94/5 and '97/8 (for G.A. Ham; previously for C.T. Nash) r15 p4 (2nds). P-t-P/HUNT CH '96/7 r2 p1 (3rd); and pulled up 2. Was struggling to stay three miles until joining the current yard, since when he has gone from Maiden winner to Hunter Chase hero in the space of five starts. Can take a keen hold, but is more amenable to restraint these days, and forged a potent partnership with Anthony Honeyball on his final four outings. Made the most of the weight concession from Chasing The Bride at Chepstow, but it was still a useful performance, and further victories over regulation fences are very much on the cards. Acts on any going. *Miss S. Rich — V. of Aylesbury (Richard Barber).* 409 (OMa), 734 (R), 930 (I), 1238 (O), 1433 (3mH).

PLATE 48   930 Axe Vale Harriers Intermediate: Finnigan Free (A. Honeyball), 1st, leads Western Fort (Miss J. Cumings), 3rd, five out   PHOTO: Tim Holt

FINNIGAN'S LOT (IRE) ..9-12.. 7 b.g. Lancastrian — Light Bidder (Auction Ring USA) up316. Workmanlike. NH FLAT Nov '98 r1 p0. NH '99 r1 p0. Usually moderate and a weak finisher, but teamed up just the once with Robert Walford, and his galvanic driving enabled him to score in a youngsters Maiden at Lockinge. Unless their partnership is resumed his rating is probably several pounds too high. *E. James — Cotswold V.F.* 284 (2m4fCMa), 471 (OMa), 956 (OMa), 1204 (OMa), 1419 (R).

FINNOW THYNE (IRE) ..10-7.. 11 br.g. Good Thyne (USA) — Mother Cluck (Energist) 113p5. Tall workmanlike half-brother to Race To The Rhythm, and to Irish NH flat winner, Furry Duck (IRE). Dam won 3 Irish flat, 14-16f, including a Bumper and a NH flat. IRISH P-t-P '96/8 r9 p5; pulled up 2, and fell 1. P-t-P '99 (for Mr T.D.B. Underwood) r5 w3 (Maiden, Restricted and PPORA, hat-trick) p1 (3rd); and pulled up 1. Lightly raced in Ireland, but reeled off a hat-trick in minor company for Tim Underwood in '99, and carried on the good work for present connections. Benefited from far superior handling when defeating Satchmo at Folkestone, and certainly had his task made easier at Stratford by Chatergold's last fence blunder, but probably ran his best race in defeat when a close third to Lakefield Rambler at Aintree. Pulled up at Huntingdon when the rider thought erroneously that the horse had been struck into, and possibly found the ground too quick at Chepstow. Well handled by David Dunsdon and his cousin Nick Gifford, and looks sure to win again. *Mrs S. Dunsdon — Crawley & Horsham (Nick Gifford).* 300 (2m5fH), 580 (3mH), 924 (3m1fH), 1335 (2m4f110yH), 1433 (3mH).

FINTONA BOY (IRE) ..10-7.. 12 b.g. Royal Fountain — Clonbanin Vulvic (Kitsos) 461111. Workmanlike. IRISH P-t-P '94/5 r6 w2 (6yo&up Maiden, and Winners of One) p2 (3rds, last once). P-t-P '99 r4 p0 (4th, pulled up 2, and fell 1). Bought out of the bargain basement, but has proved to be a shrewd purchase, winning four minor races on varying ground under Richard Burton. Much improved since being fitted with a tongue-strap, but beat little in his sequence, and may require further skilful placing from Caroline Chadney to win in better class. Likes to help to force the pace, and is capable of jumping very well. *D.P. Tyler — Croome & W. Warwicks (Caroline Chadney).* 333 (Cf), 543 (I), 702 (Cf), 944 (I), 1272 (Cf), 1354 (M).

FIONNUALA (U) ..6-7.. 6 b.m. Lir — Mary Yellan (Shaab) 2. Small. Dam, half-sister to 3 Pointers including, Sunnyrank (*qv* '96 Annual), failed to finish to 6 Points for Yvonne Doyne-Ditmas.

Trudged round Garnons to finish 25 lengths last in a match for her Members. *Mrs Y. & Miss S.R. Doyne-Ditmas — Ross H. (V.W. Jordan).* 444 (M).

FIREMAN ..8-13§.. 9 ch.g. Lighter — Suella (Langton Heath) pu4p. Good-bodied. Dam won a Maiden and 3rd (was very prone to break blood vessels). P-t-P '98/9 r6 p0 (last, pulled up 4, and fell 1). Not better than last in ten starts, and can't or won't raise his game in the final mile or so. Blinkered on his last three appearances, and may well be extracting the proverbial. Invariably has two paddock handlers. *Mrs S.M. Newell — S. Herefords (Christine Hardinge).* 12 (OMa), 122 (OMa), 601 (CfMa), 994 (OMa).

FIRE ON ICE (IRE) ..10-1.. 9 b.g. Sadler's Wells (USA) — Foolish Lady (USA) (Foolish Pleasure USA) 31up. Lengthy half-brother to flat winner, Scottish Jester, and to successful Hurdler, Flintlock. Dam is half-sister to Dancing Brave. FLAT (for M. Stoute) r6 w1 (11f) p2 (3rds). NH '97/8 (for Mrs D. Haine; bought for 1200; tried tongue-tied) r5 p4. Gave some fair displays over Hurdles, and deserved his success in a Higham Confined, where he made a good recovery from a bad mistake two out. Disappeared for three months, and looked backward when reappearing and failing to finish twice. Consistently looks difficult to train, or would doubtless have achieved more. *D. Sibley & Miss S. Turner — Suffolk (Neil King).* 15 (C), 29 (Cf), 1286 (Cf), 1378 (Cf).

FIRST TENOR (IRE) ..9-11.. 7 b.g. Glacial Storm (USA) — Rustic Path (Proverb) 4. Workmanlike. Dam won 2m1f Hdle and 2m6f Ch in Ireland. P-t-P '99 r1 p1 (2nd). Has shown ability in both his Points and had two subsequent winners behind him in the latest, but disappeared after the first day of the season in 2000, and clearly met with a setback. Should win a Maiden at least if he is able to return. *D. Brace — Llangeinor.* 7 (OMa).

PLATE 49   471 Avon Vale Open Maiden 567&8yo (Div 1): L to R Finnigan's Lot (M. Walters), pu, Barton Bog (A. Evans), pu, and Winning Storm Town (Miss S. Talbot), 4th, land ahead of (L to R) Shamrock Lad (D. Dennis), pu, Last Gamble (G. Maundrell), pu, Barton Nic (P. Keane), 1st, and Chancellor's Vision (Miss S. Vickery), pu   PHOTO: Bill Selwyn

FISCAL GALE (IRE) ..—.. 9 b.g. Strong Gale — Dunleer Duchess (Our Mirage) f. Workmanlike. Dam won 2 NH flat and 2 Hdles (2m-2m1f) in Ireland. IRISH NH FLAT '97 r1 p0. IRISH NH '97/9 r9

p1 (3rd in Ch). Bought Doncaster, Aug for 3400. Killed by a crashing fall at Alnwick. Mr & Mrs C. Strang Steel — College V. & N. Northumberland (Clive Storey). 43 (Cf).

FISCAL POLICY ..10-0.. 13 b.g. Politico (USA) — Moschata (Star Moss) 72462733. Tall brother to Imperial Charter, and half-brother to Dalmigavie Lad. Dam won 2m1f Sell Hdle. P-t-p/HUNT CH '93 and '96/9 r32 w6 (inc 3 Opens) p11 (8 2nds, beaten neck once; and inc 3rd in Hunt Ch); failed to finish 8 (unseated 3). A fine servant to the Trotter family for several seasons, but desperately one-paced now, and has to rely on grim determination to get him into the shake up. Suited by a long trip in mud and only just collared by Concerto Collonges at Carlisle over Easter, but still gives the impression that stronger handling would have won him more races. Unsuccessful in his last 19 starts, but remains an armchair ride, and could not be begrudged another win. *A.R. Trotter — Berwicks.* 156 (3mH), 358 (M), 915 (3m1fH), 1024 (3m3f110yH), 1154 (3m2fH), 1342 (3m1fH), 1498 (O), 1578 (O).

FISHERMAN JACK ..9-5.. 6 b.g. Carlingford Castle — Troublewithjack (Sulaafa USA) 31. Plain stocky owner-bred half-brother to Shipley Hill Lad. Beaten about 20 lengths on an encouraging debut, and confirmed the promise when landing a Maiden at Thorpe. Part of a memorable day for Helen Harvey and Matthew Mackley, who were responsible for the last three winners on the card. Looks to stay particularly well for a five year old, and should certainly score again. *Mrs H. Lynch — Quorn (Helen Harvey).* 1012 (CfMa), 1219 (OMa).

FISH QUAY ..—§.. 18 ch.g. Quayside — Winkle (Whistler) p. Tall rangy half-brother to a winner abroad. NH FLAT r3 p2 (2nds). NH '87/91 (blinkered 1 — '88), '94/5 and '97/8 r44 w4 (3 Hdles, 2m-2m4f, and 3m Ch) p10 (inc head and neck 2nds); fell at last when clear once; broke blood vessel once. P-t-P/HUNT CH '92/4 and '96/9 r44 w3 (inc Ladies) p10 (5 2nds, beaten fence once; and inc 2 Hunt Chses); failed to finish 15 (refused 1, ran out 4, and fell 1). Sprang a 25-1 surprise when successful in his Members in '98, but pulled up in the corresponding race twice since. Used to go a breakneck gallop and still quick enough to get to the front, but always a tricky ride and never easy to win with, and is fast catching up with Methuselah. *Mrs K.M. Lamb — Percy.* 907 (M).

FISTRAL FLAME ..9-8.. 7 ch.m. Superlative — Northern Empress (Northfields USA) 343p. Sturdy compact half-sister to Annaben and Prince Tino, to a winner in Belgium, to 5 flat winners (one in Belgium), including Press On Nicky and Press The Bell, and to successful jumper, Easy Buck. FLAT r3 p0. P-t-P '99 r3 p2 (2nds); and fell 1. Usually attracts market support, but exposed as a non-stayer, and appeared to go wrong when still in touch at Mollington on her latest appearance — would doubtless have ground to a halt up the hill in any case. Remains eligible for 2m4f Maidens for one more year, but whether she will be able to take advantage of one is open to question. *A.R. Hunt — Vine & Craven (Sarah Scott).* 22 (2m4fOMa), 284 (2m4fCMa), 471 (OMa), 786 (OMa).

FITNESS FANATIC ..—.. 13 b.g. Nishapour (FR) — Bustling Nelly (Bustino) p. Small half-brother to 4 flat winners (one in Germany) including Busy Flight (very smart) and Silk Degrees (also a successful jumper). FLAT r10 p1 (2nd). NH '92/4 r8 w1 (2m2f Sell Hdle, only run in such company) p1 (2nd to stablemate). P-t-P '99 r2 p0 (unseated 1, and pulled up 1). In virtual retirement since '94, and three Pointing escapades have proved fruitless. *Miss J. Bradley — Crawley & Horsham.* 308 (O).

FIVE O'ONE (IRE) ..—.. 8 b.g. Phardante (FR) — Levi's Star (Levmoss) pp. Workmanlike half-brother to 6 winners in Ireland, including Furry Star and The Golam (both Pointing — former also won NH flat and jumping), Baptismal Fire (NH flat and jumping), and Telltalk and Bitter Harvest (both NH flat — former also won over Hurdles). IRISH NH FLAT '98 r2 p0. Bought Doncaster, May for 3600. Jumped sketchily in both Points, and was weakening rapidly when he pulled up at halfway in the latest. Rarely seen. *S.N. Wilshire — V. of Aylesbury (Lawney Hill).* 514 (OMa), 1142 (M).

FLAMING COLD (IRE) ..9-7.. 7 b.m. Glacial Storm (USA) — Grin And Bear It (Deep Run) p5pp. Workmanlike lengthy. Dam is sister to Tiderunner (*qv*). IRISH P-t-P '99 r2 w2 (5yo mares Maidens — distant 2nd of 4 in the first of them, but later awarded race). Ultimately unbeaten in Ireland (in heavy once; and in a bizarre contest in which her rider and those of the third and fourth were fined £100 apiece for making insufficient effort!), and looked poised to beat Newman's Conquest in a Restricted at Stafford Cross, but could not recover from a bad mistake at the last. Possibly not a true stayer, and was bitterly disappointing otherwise for the new yard. Needs treating with suspicion, as she clambered over the first two fences and was pulled up and dismounted after a mile on her latest outing. *J.H. Burbidge — O. Surrey & Burstow (Ollie Cann).* 315 (R), 931 (R), 1206 (R), 1563 (R).

FLAMING SUNRISE ..9-10.. 10 b.g. Super Sunrise — Young Ash Linn (Deep Run) 1u3p91f. Stocky compact half-brother to Young Moss. Dam won 2m1f Hdle and 3m Ch. Grandam, Young Ash Leaf, won Scottish Grand National. NH '98/9 (for breeder, R. McDonald) r3 p0 (50-1, 66-1 and 200-1). Gave one fair display in the previous ownership, but hardly ever ran until joining the present yard at nine. Promptly won a Maiden for Luke Morgan at Alnwick (beat Sunnycliff, who almost unseated at the last — and in retrospect, may have been lucky to do so), but inconsistently handled by Doreen Calder since. Kept in a prominent position throughout when landing a Restricted at Balcormo to increase his remarkable tally of victories, but too often allowed to run in snatches. Jumped right in his Members, but the race could present a good opportunity for him in 2001 if he can wrest it away from Across The Card. *Miss D.M.M. Calder — Berwicks.* 188 (OMa), 358 (M), 498 (R), 713 (R), 976 (R), 1118 (R), 1425 (I).

FLAPJACK LAD ..9-12§.. 12 b.g. Oats — Reperage (USA) (Key To Content USA) 37024p. Tall half-brother to Heavenly Seven (qv). NH FLAT Dec '93 r2 p1 (2nd). NH '94/9 (for N. Twiston-Davies) r46 w6 (2m1f Hdle, and 5 Chses, 2m4f-3m3f, awarded 1) p13; and withdrawn under orders once. Has a magnificent completion record, and had got round in 34 of 35 attempts including the Aintree Foxhunters prior to pulling up on his latest outing. No battler these days and has accumulated a losing sequence of 18, but was able to give the novice Tom Bishop some valuable experience, including when finishing eight lengths second. *Mrs F.D. Bishop — Blackmore & Sparkford V.* 628 (Cf), 735 (MO), 921 (2m6fH), 1237 (Cf), 1304 (Cfnr), 1432 (3m1fH).

PLATE 50   1118 Fife Restricted: Flaming Sunrise (Miss D. Calder), 1st, leads Mini Cruise (D. Morgan), 2nd, at the second
PHOTO: Alan Mitchell

FLASHING GALE (IRE) ..9-7.. 9 b.g. Strong Gale — Flash 'n' Run (Record Run) p2p. Compact. P-t-P '99 r3 p2. Evidently thought to have a fair amount of ability as he has been nibbled at in the books on more than one occasion, and looked like winning at Duncombe Park, but flagged in the final half furlong, and caught near the line. Sent off favourite at Charm Park next time, and was poised to challenge when pulling up lame two from home. *J.J. Coates — Pendle Forest & Craven (David Coates).* 138 (OMa), 283 (OMa), 400 (OMa).

FLASHLIGHT ..9-0.. 10 ch.g. Lighter — Altun Ha (Morston FR) p68sp. Lengthy unfurnished brother to Frangipane. P-t-P '96/8 r5 w1 (Maiden) p1 (3rd); last, refused 1, and pulled up 1. Galloped on resolutely to win a long youngsters Maiden at Wetherby in '98, but missed the following season, and ran as though something was amiss in 2000. Had previously managed no more than two outings in a season, and his problems appear to have nullified his ability. *A.G. Bonas — Cleveland.* 173 (R), 377 (R), 465 (3m1f110yH), 923 (3m3fH), 1230 (R).

FLASHMAN ..—.. 11 b.g. Flash Of Steel — Proper Madam (Mummy's Pet) pppp. Compact half-brother to Pride Of Kashmir, and to 3 winning sprinters. Dam won 6 flat, 5-6f (5 at minimum trip). FLAT '92/6 and 98 (both wins for B. Llewellyn at 5; previously for F. Lee, tried blinkers) r38 w2 (16-18f)p9. NH '94/5 and '97/9 (for B. Llewellyn, bought for 4200) r13 p2; pulled up in 3 of final 5, inc Sells. Stayed remarkably well on the flat considering he comes from a sprinting family, but does not fire at all these days, and all he can do is pull up. *Mrs L. Crawford — Llangibby (Emma Crawford).* 895 (MO), 1297 (L), 1612 (Cf), 1657 (Cf).

FLEET MILL ..10-3.. 9 b.m. Town And Country — Culm Port (Port Corsair) p114. Good-bodied half-sister to Culm Baron, Nearly At Sea, and Portoski. Dam, sister to Culm Valley (qv '88 Season Annual), won 6 Chses (3m-3m2f), 2 Hunt Chses, and 7 Points and placed 12. Grandam, Copper Plate II, was a useless Pointer, but great-grandam, Fonteray, won 3 Points. P-t-P '98 r4 p0 (pulled up 2, unseated 1 and ran out 1). As green as grass in her debut season, but far more clued up when resuming two years later, and duly bolted up at Cothelstone after an easy reintroduction a fortnight earlier. Confirmed that promise with an equally authoritative success next time, but failed to land a blow on ground quicker than she had encountered before on her final start. From a useful Pointing family, and should be able to win again. *D. Fox-Ledger — Blackmore & Sparkford V. (Penny Cave).* 847 (R), 1101 (OMa), 1309 (R), 1516 (I).

FLICKERING FLAME ..9-0.. 11 ch.g. Lighter — Flimsy Jacky (David Jack) pu43. Leggy workmanlike brother to Flimsy Flame, and half-brother to Flimsy Fortune, Puldavnic, Flimsy Truth (won Chasing since Pointing), and Slick Alice. Dam was placed in 2 of 11 Points (only completed the course twice). P-t-P '98/9 (for Mr R.J. Matthews in '99) r7 w1 (Maiden) p0; and pulled up 6. Won a poor Maiden at Howick in '98 (rated 9-7), but pulled up in his next five starts, and failed to beat a rival in both completions for new connections. Lost a novice girl quickly once, but gave the owner a good ride at Kingston Blount on his final appearance. *M.B. Tillett — Berks & Bucks, & Tedworth (Nick Lampard).* 35 (Cnr), 476 (Cnr), 1279 (M), 1619 (M).

FLIP THE LID (IRE) ..10-3.. 12 b.m. Orchestra — Punters Gold (Yankee Gold) 2. Leggy sister to Irish NH flat winner, Punter's Symphony (IRE). Dam won Irish NH flat. IRISH P-t-P '95 r1 p0 (pulled up). P-t-P '96/7 r8 w5 (inc Open, and inc hat-trick '96) p2 (head 2nd once); pulled up 1. NH '99 r3 r1 (2nd in 2m5f Nov Ch); pulled up 1. A useful Pointer '96/7 with five wins to her credit (rated 10-9), but went lame in the latest and forced off the course for more than two years subsequently. Her latest revival was fleeting, but she did split two useful mares at Wetherby, and even if she does not return to the racecourse as seems likely a career in the paddocks should beckon. *P. Sawney — Cleveland (Jackie Sawney).* 172 (Cm).

FLOCKMASTER (IRE) ..9-13.. 10 ch.g. Accordion — Only A Laugh (Torus) p3pu14p. Robust. P-t-P '97/9 r16 w2 (Maiden and Restricted) p6 (2 2nds); pulled up 5, refused 1, and unseated 1. Has improved marginally from year to year, but only moderate, and seemed lucky when winning at Pentreclwydau (Bel-De-Moor, ridden by Flockmaster's previous pilot Tim Vaughan, looked to be going best when he was knocked out of the saddle by a loose horse after four out). Usually has little in the tank at the end of a race, and is certainly biting off more than he can chew in Hunter Chases. *M.G. Jones — Gelligaer F.* 142 (I), 202 (I), 344 (I), 837 (I), 1299 (I), 1535 (2m3fH), 1644 (3m2f10yH).

FLOOREX CARPETMAN ..8-13.. 6 b.g. Damister (USA) — Charmed I'm Sure (Nicholas Bill) f3. Close-coupled. Dam won 2 2m2f Sell Hdles. NH FLAT '99 (for A. Carroll) r2 p0. Bought Malvern, May for 1250. Flattered by his 12 lengths last in a Maiden, because he only inherited the prize when two in front departed at the final fence. Gives the impression that he may not stay three miles. *P. Richardson — Grafton.* 753 (CfMa), 1010 (CfMa).

FLORUCEVA (IRE) ..10-7.. 11 ch.m. Florida Son — Lluceva Bay (Salluceva) f33. Compact quite attractive. IRISH NH FLAT '96 r1 p0. IRISH P-t-P '95/7 r7 p3; pulled up, and fell/unseated 3. P-t-P/HUNT CH '98/9 (for Mr B. McNichol) r12 w3 (inc 2 Hunt Chses, 2m5f-3m1f) p4 (3 2nds; and inc 3 Hunt Chses); unseated 1, and pulled up 2. A very talented mare who incredibly took five seasons to win a race, but made hay in '99 when three successes included a defeat of Coole Abbey at Sedgefield. Suffered a crashing fall on her debut for new connections at Fakenham (barely cleared the guard-rail), and was slightly disappointing when she reappeared seven weeks later. Usually takes a strong hold and is capable of making all, but it will be interesting to see if James and Richard Tate can get the best out of her when she returns. *T.P. Tate — Bramham.* 227 (2m5f110yH), 916 (3m1fH), 1535 (2m5fH).

FLOWER OF DUNBLANE ..9-7.. 10 ch.m. Ardross — Anita's Choice (Shantung) ppR3p. Good-bodied attractive half-sister to Lady Alice, to Hurdles winner, More Champagne, and to a winner in Hong Kong. Dam won at 12f, and won 2m Hdle. NH '96/8 (blinkered 2) r13 p1 (distant last of 3); pulled up 2, ran out 1 and fell 1. P-t-P '97 and '99 r8 w1 (Maiden) p2 (3rds); pulled up 2, and fell 1. NH May '00 r1 p0 (pulled up in 3m110y Nov Hdle: *wknd 7, t.o aft, pu 8*). Won a bad three-finisher Maiden at Balcormo in her first season Pointing, but predictably struggling in Restricted company since. Reserved her best performance for the Fife track in 2000 when five lengths third on her final start, but still looks an awkward ride. *Mrs J. McGregor — Fife.* 360 (R), 663 (R), 976 (R), 1118 (R).

FLOWING AGAIN ..—.. 6 ch.m. Then Again — Another Relation (Relkino) p. Dam, half-sister to Meldrew (*qv* 2000 Annual), fell in a Point for Richard Barber. Pulled up after 2m4f when fading on an April debut. *R.J. Barber — Taunton V.* 956 (OMa).

FLOWING FORTUNE ..9-7.. 7 b.g. Kenmare (FR) — Green Flower (USA) (Fappiano USA) 75pp24. Sturdy good-looking half-brother to a French flat winner. FLAT (for E. Dunlop) r4 p1 (2nd of 3 in Newmarket Challenge Cup). NH '98 (blinkered 1; pulled up in Sell Final, bought for 6000; previously for H. Daly; previously for late T. Forster, bought for 12,500) r6 p1 (3rd). Generally a very poor performer, but ended the season with a couple of better displays, and was only beaten two and a half lengths when second. Yet to find anything in the closing stages, and has a history of disappointments behind him, but still quite a youngster, and may get there eventually. *S.B. Clark — York & Ainsty S.* 21 (2m4fOMa), 55 (OMa), 282 (OMa), 398 (OMa), 809 (OMa), 1032 (OMa).

FLUSHING SPIRIT (IRE) ..7-0.. 9 ch.m. Henbit (USA) — Formia Spirit (Pragmatic) p. Lengthy sister to Irish Pointing and English Chasing winner, Lough Lein Spirit (IRE), and half-sister to Carbery Spirit (IRE). NH FLAT '97 r2 p1 (3rd). P-t-P '99 r3 p1 (2 fences last of 2); pulled up 1, and fell 1. Well-related, but looks a difficult ride (typical Henbit), and one of umpteen horses that failed to see the light of day after a trip to Black Forest Lodge in 2000 — the early season meeting certainly finds out the crocks. *N. Banks — Quantock (Kay Rees & Polly Curling).* 72 (OMa).

FLUTTERBUD ..10-3.. 9 b.m. Lord Bud — Spartan Flutter (Spartan General) fup1p. Half-sister to Spartan Ranger, Fast Flutter and Raise A Flutter. Dam, half-sister to Sir Wager (*qv* '97 Annual), won 2 Points and 2 Chases, 2m6f-3m. NH '97/8 r5 w1 (2m5f Hdle) p0. P-t-P '99 r3 w1 (Confined) p0; pulled up 1, and fell 1. Twice successful in Points, but has failed to complete otherwise, and remains a very undependable jumper. Looked to have taken Gunner Boon's measure on her reappearance at Erw Lon, but was being overhauled when she came down at the last, and jumped poorly in her next two outings — appeared to resent blinkers and the firm ground once. Succeeded in a war of attrition at St Hilary where her jumping held together well in the bottomless ground, but whether it will do so again is uncertain. *R.A. Mason — Glamorgan (Evan Williams).* 275 (Cf), 343 (Cf), 945 (O), 1051 (Cf), 1612 (Cf).

FLYING ARRANGEMENT ..9-0.. 7 b.m. Bold Arrangement — Soaring Eagles (Piaffer USA) 5p. P-t-P '99 r1 p0 (fell). NH '99 r1 p0 (pulled up). Not wholly disgraced when around 18 lengths last in her Members, but presumably suffered a setback when pulled up after the third on a return visit to Friars Haugh, as she failed to reappear. *Mrs H.O. Graham — Jedforest.* 107 (M), 364 (CfMa).

FLYING FELLOW (IRE) ..—.. 10 b.g. Noalto — Decent Vulgan (Decent Fellow) ppp5. Small close-coupled half-brother to Dunsdon (IRE). IRISH P-t-P '96 r5 p2 (3rds); pulled up 2, and brought down 1. P-t-P '97/8 (for Mr D.J. Little in '99) r10 w2 (inc Open) p3 (2 2nds); pulled up 1, unseated 1, and ran out 1. NH June '00 r1 p0 (5th in 2m5f110y Nov Ch: *ld to 3, wknd 10, t.o*). Disappeared after winning his last two starts in '98, including a two-finisher Ladies, but did not look fully wound up when pulled up thrice for new connections in 2000. Can be impulsive, and usually gets very warm in the preliminaries. *A.J. Chamberlain — V.W.H.* 631 (MO), 968 (Cf), 1481 (Cf).

FLYING IMP ..9-12.. 10 b.g. Faustus (USA) — Quenlyn (Welsh Pageant) 436323. Close-coupled barrelly half-brother to flat winners, Roxby Melody and Heathyards Gem, and to Belgian flat and Hurdles and English jumping winner, Briggs Builders. FLAT r5 p0. NH '95/6 (visored 1) and '98 r8 p0 (debut in Sell). P-t-P/HUNT CH '97/9 r10 w3 (Maiden, Intermediate and Club Restricted) p5 (3 2nds); pulled up 1. Enjoyed his busiest season to date in 2000, but prone to disappoint, and jumped moderately (and often to the right) all year. Has been placed in Open company on four occasions, but yet to look like winning one, and is obviously outclassed in Hunter Chases. Can handle hock deep mud, and avoids anything sounder than good. *A.C. Heal — Blackmore & Sparkford V. (Jane Galpin).* 32 (MO), 223 (3m2fH), 402 (O), 521 (O), 1177 (O), 1282 (O).

FLYING MARIA ..10-8.. 10 gr.m. Neltino — Flying Mistress (Lear Jet) 113u. Lengthy light-framed sister to jumping winner, Flying Instructor. Dam won 5 Chses, 2m-3m2f. P-t-P/HUNT CH '96/9 r21 w4 (Maiden, Restricted, PPORA Mares and Intermediate) p7 (6 2nds, inc 3 Hunt Chses); failed to finish 7 (refused 1, ran out 1, and fell 2). Placed in three sub-3m Hunter Chases before she gained her just reward in most emphatic style on her reappearance at Ludlow. Less impressive at Newton Abbot subsequently, but lost no caste in defeat when trying to give away weight all round at Ascot. Made fewer errors under Les Jefford, and it was not the mares fault that he was unseated when favourite at Cheltenham. Handles most surfaces, but seems more fond of cut in the ground these days, and looks sure to win again when conditions are right. *J.S. Papworth — S. Cornwall.* 382 (2m4fH), 583 (2m5f110yH), 919 (2m3f110yH), 1341 (2m110yH).

FLYING ON ..9-5.. 9 b.g. Wace (USA) — Quick Exit (David Jack) 3p. Tall half-brother to The Artful Rascal and Caldecott, and to NH flat and jumping winner, Kenmore-Speed. Dam, a hard ride, was 3rd in a Maiden, and grandam, Hasty Exit, won Maiden and 5 Ladies (inc dead-heat with Tenor) and placed 17 (inc 3rd in Hdle). NH FLAT '97 r1 p1 (3rd). NH '97/8 r3 p0; pulled up in 2 of 3 Hdles. P-t-P '99 (Wormall-trained for breeder, Mrs D. Whiteman) r2 p0 (pulled up 1, and fell 1). NH Mar '00 r1 p0 (pulled up in Nov Ch: *ld til wknd 4, t.o & pu 11*). Has two gears, flat out and stop, and can engage the former for much of the journey, but sadly it seems not all of it. Has the ability to win a Maiden on an easy track, but gets few opportunities, and clearly hard to keep sound. *Mrs R. Wormall — Atherstone (Pam Wormall; Jill Wormall).*

FOLDING ..9-7.. 10 b.g. Rymer — Dealers Dream (Whistlefield) fpu3p. Unfurnished half-brother to Knap Hand. Grandam, Middle For Diddle, won a Maiden. NH FLAT '97 r1 p0. NH '97/8 r6 p1 (distant 3rd of 4). P-t-P '99 r1 p0 (pulled up). Very headstrong, and too much of a handful for the trainer (though a christian compared to his Free To Conker (*qv*), but seems not to stay three miles in any case, and only finished ahead of those when third at Lockinge. Would need to improve his fencing to win a Maiden even if he could summon up some extra stamina. Wore a tongue-strap on his final three outings. *Mrs E. Young — Farmers Bloodhounds (Mark Hawkins).* 81 (CCfMa), 290 (CMa), 517 (OMa), 1207 (OMa), 1584 (CCond).

FONTAINE AGAIN (IRE) ..9-7§§.. 8 b.g. Lafontaine (USA) — Black Again (Strong Gale) ur5r1. Workmanlike. P-t-P '98/9 r2 p0 (pulled up 1, and ran out 1). Finally got his act together when making virtually all to land a bad Maiden at Bredwardine, but previously very badly behaved and twice gave supporters no run for their money — literally on one occasion. Not to be trusted until he has proved he is a reformed reprobate. *C.J. Hitchings — Kyre (Andy Morgan).* 30 (CMa), 57 (OMa), 565 (O), 1091 (OMa), 1465 (OMa).

FONTAINE FABLES (IRE) ..9-3§.. 11 gr.g. Lafontaine (USA) — Garland Song (My Swanee) 48p5p. Tall half-brother to a flat winner. IRISH FLAT r4 w1 (12f) p2. IRISH NH FLAT '94/5 r7 w1 p2 (3rds); one run at Cheltenham. IRISH NH '95/7 r16 w2 (2 2m Hdles) p5 (inc 2nd in Ch). NH '98/9 (for E. James) r5 p0 (tailed off, inc Sell, and inc 2 Chses — pulled up 1). Won four races in Ireland to May '96, but has consistently dogged it in the last three years, and was invariably remote if completing in Points. Usually blinkered, and tried tongue-tied in previous yards. Safely ignored unless perhaps if he was asked to deputize for Splodge in his Members. *Lord Yarborough — Brocklesby (Mark Bennison).* 47 (C), 115 (CCf), 231 (O), 794 (Cf), 918 (2m4fH).

FOODBROKER STAR (IRE) ..9-10.. 11 gr.g. Roselier (FR) — Stormy Breeze (Little Buskins) p35. Small long-backed half-brother to Stormy Spring, to Hurdles winner, The Cider And Bun, and to 2 winners in Ireland (one NH flat; one Pointing). NH '95/9 (blinkered 3; final 2 for T. Needham, bought for 14,000 — pulled up in Hdle and fell in Ch; wins previously for J. Gifford) r24 w2 (2m1f Hdle-finished 2nd, but hampered and awarded race; and 3m Ch, worth £13,282) p4; ran out 1. Inconsistent at best, but has not scored in 17 attempts since landing a valuable prize at Lingfield in December '96. The Tollit family usually buy proven older horses who retain the ability to win Points, but they could doomed to disappointment with this one. *Mrs C. Banks — Worcs.* 191 (Cf), 449 (L), 590 (L).

FOOLED YOU (USA) ..—.. 7 b.g. Wild Again (USA) — Foolish Miz (USA) (Foolish Pleasure USA) ppp. Small unfurnished half-sister to 4 winners abroad. $100,000y. FLAT (for E. Dunlop) r2 p0. NH '99 (for H. Daly, bought for 8400) r1 p0 (pulled up). Fooled at least two people into wasting massive sums of money on him and continued in deplorable form in Points. Wore a tongue-strap in the final couple. *Mrs B. Abraham & Mrs S. Deacon — Ludlow (Nick Pomfret).* 54 (OMa), 123 (OMa), 872 (OMa).

FORBIDDEN WATERS (IRE) ..10-4§.. 10 b.g. Over The River (FR) — Monalee Stream (Paddy's Stream) 21pp1p. Strong good-looking brother to Irish NH flat and jumping winner, Monalee River, and half-brother to Irish NH flat winner, Lisard River. NH FLAT '96/7 r2 w0. NH '97 r2 w1 (2m4f Hdle) p1 (3rd). P-t-p '99 r6 p1 (2nd); pulled up 2, and fell/unseated 2. Often travels well in his races, but frequently fails to deliver, and finds little for pressure. Did well to defeat Slew Man at Cothelstone where Shirley Vickery's experience and dogged persistence were vital factors, and had enough in the tank to land a poor event at Larkhill subsequently. Best when held up and produced late, and evidently prefers a sound surface. Occasionally blinkered. *R.J. Bullock — Blackmore & Sparkford V. (Rose Vickery).* 354 (L), 636 (L), 851 (L), 1132 (L), 1595 (Cf), 1653 (O).

FOR CHRISTIE (IRE) ..9-4.. 12 ch.g. Lancastrian — Lovenos (Golden Love) p346. Compact good-topped half-brother to NH flat and Hurdles winner, Five Flags (IRE), and to Irish Hurdles winner, Martial Run. Dam won Irish NH flat. P-t-P '94/6 r4 w1 (Maiden) p0; fell/unseated 2. NH '98/9 (for N. Hawke) r5 p1 (2nd); fell 1, and pulled up 1. Was a Holnicote Maiden under Joe Tizzard in '96, but never able to stand much racing, and no longer retains the same level of ability. Capable of bowling along for around 2m4f, but struggling to get home in 2000, and will be hard pushed to land a Restricted. *G. Kierle — R. Bown & J. Hardwell — Taunton V. (Alison Handel).* 583 (2m5f110yH), 1095 (R), 1240 (R), 1518 (R).

FORDSTOWN (IRE) ..10-0§.. 12 ch.g. Le Bavard (FR) — Gortroe Queen (Simbir) 331r17p. Tall half-brother to Parson's Quest and I Is, and to Hurdles winner, Mrs Mayhew (IRE). Dam won 2 flat (2m-2m1f), 3 Hdles (2m-2m1f) and 2 Chses (2m2f-2m4f) in Ireland. IRISH P-t-P '94 r3 w1 (4&5yo Maiden) p1 (3rd); pulled up 1. NH '94/5 (tubed lately) and '98 r11 w1 (poor 2m5f Mdn Ch) p1 (3rd); pulled up 5. P-t-P/HUNT CH '96/9 r33 w4 (inc 3m3f Hunt Ch) p9 (5 2nds, last twice; and inc 4 Hunt Chses); pulled up 2, fell/unseated 3. Remains capable of fair efforts when on a going day, but still inclined to drop the bit and mope round at the back, and not surprisingly failed to take a shine to a return visit to Aintree. Faced a simple task in his Members, but his defeat of a three-legged Mountain Thyne was more meritorious, and ended a sequence of 13 defeats. Stays well and a safe ride, but will need more luck to increase his tally. *J.F. Alexander — Fife (Nick Alexander).* 110 (O), 660 (Cf), 714 (O), 921 (2m6fH), 1117 (M), 1428 (O), 1578 (O).

FOREST FEATHER (IRE) ..10-4.. 13 b.g. Arapahos (FR) — Mistress Boreen (Boreen FR) 317. Compact. IRISH P-t-P '92 r4 w1 (4&5yo Maiden) p0; fell 2. NH '93/8 r34 w3 (2m5f-2m7f Hdles) p12 (short-headed once, and beaten a head once). P-t-P/HUNT CH '99 r7 p2 (3rds); unseated 2. Marked his return to form with a decent third in a fast Chaddesley Confined won by subsequent Dudley Cup winner Distinctive, but then landed a Market Rasen Hunter Chase which was in truth no better than a modest Restricted. Sent off a generous 4-1 that day, but had the race in safe keeping from halfway, and benefited from the presence of David O'Meara in the saddle. Suited by top-of-the-ground and strong handling. *Miss J.E. Mathias — Llangeinor.* 611 (C), 801 (3m1fH), 1433 (3mH).

FOREST FOUNTAIN (IRE) ..10-12.. 10 b.g. Royal Fountain — Forest Gale (Strong Gale) 152b22431. Smallish workmanlike half-brother to Sir Galeforce (IRE), Wishing William (IRE) and Philtre (IRE). IRISH P-t-P '95 r1 p0 (pulled up). P-t-P/HUNT CH '96/7 and '99 r15 w6 (inc 2 Opens, Mixed Open and Ladies) p4 (3 2nds, and inc Hunt Ch); pulled up 4, and fell 1. A useful Open horse who finally achieved his Hunter Chase goal at the 7th attempt, but not before he had frightened his backers by veering left on the run-in. Began his season with a fluent success in a modest Larkhill event, but rather lost his way subsequently, and was a beaten favourite in four successive Opens, though a defeat by Lochnomore was no disgrace. Cut in the ground seems to be his Achilles heel, and he is a much better horse on a sound surface. Jumps and stays well, and always has top riders. Sure to win more good races under the right conditions. *J.D. & Mrs A.M. Callow — Albrighton Woodland (Helen Needham).* 59 (MO), 156 (3mH), 334 (O), 584 (3m2f110yH), 614 (O), 895 (MO), 1087 (MO), 1338 (4m1fH), 1558 (3mH).

FOREST MOSS (IRE) ..—.. 12 b.m. Le Moss — Siege Queen (Tarqogan) f. Small half-sister to jumping winner, Young Tomo (IRE), and to 2 Irish Pointing winners, including Mossy Fortress. Dam is half-sister to Kilknockin (*qv* '94 Annual). NH '98 (from S. Mullins') r3 p0. Revived for four minutes in February until taking a crashing fall at Chipley Park. Spent her early years at stud, and produced a chestnut filly by Bootsman Bains (GER) in '95 — also had a dead filly by him in '94. *J.H. Young — New Forest.* 147 (OMa).

FOREST MUSK (IRE) ..—.. 10 b.g. Strong Gale — Brown Forest (Brave Invader USA) ppppp. Tall rangy roman-nosed half-brother to Knockanoran (IRE), and to Irish Pointing winner, Cookoo Charlie (IRE). IRISH P-t-P '96 r5 p3 (3rds); pulled up 1, and fell 1. NH FLAT '96 r1 p0. NH '96/7 r6 w1 (2m7f Hdle) p1 (2nd); beaten 20*l* plus in 2 Chses. P-t-P '99 (for Mr S.J. Claisse & Mr E.R.J. Finneron) r6 w1 (Members) p0; last 2, fell/unseated 2, and pulled up 1. Wooden-headed with little in the way of brakes and steering, and gave Ian Hambley a torrid time in 2000. Not short on ability, but extracting it has always been fraught with danger, and not worth bothering with again. Now seems to be gone in the wind. Will this evidence convince the South East buffoons who fined Simon Claisse £125 in '99 that their decision was scandalous? *M.D. & P. Ansel — S. Cornwall (Ian Hambley).* 534 (Cf), 727 (O), 854 (O), 1188 (O), 1307 (O).

FORESTRY ..8-9.. 7 b.g. Highest Honor (FR) — Arboretum (IRE) (Green Desert USA) pf4fp. Light-framed. Dam won 2 flat, 6-7f. FLAT (for J. Smyth-Osbourne) r4 p0. NH '98/9 (for M. Wilkinson, bought for 5400) r7 p2 (3rds, Sell final). Sold Ascot, June for 840. His Hurdling form suggested he might be good enough to win a Maiden, but has disappointingly failed to get the trip so far, and is additionally an unreliable jumper. *N. Lowe — Cotswold V.F.* 898 (OMa), 1091 (OMa), 1315 (OMa), 1465 (OMa), 1634 (OMa).

FOREVER DREAMING (IRE) ..10-0.. 10 b.g. Le Moss — On A Dream (Balinger) 5f441p. Compact. P-t-P '97 (for Mrs M. Cooper) r2 w1 (Maiden) p1 (2nd). NH '98/9 (for S. Mellor) r12 p3 (inc 2nd of 3 in 3m2f Nov Ch); pulled up 5. Won a bad Maiden taking 7min 22s in '97, but lost his way under Rules subsequently, and needed a return to Pointing to revive his fortunes. Can finish strongly when inclined and outgunned Iron Pyrites at Maisemore, but needs an extreme test of stamina to bring out the best in him. Visored twice over regulation obstacles, and ran blinkered on his last three starts in 2000. Broke down at Cheltenham and has been retired. *C. Gwin — Heythrop (Mark Rimell).* 13 (R), 80 (CCfR), 261 (R), 612 (CR), 896 (R), 1338 (4m1fH).

FOR JOSH (IRE) ..9-0.. 12 ch.g. Hard Fought — Twice Regal (Royal Prerogative) 5. Compact half-brother to jumping winner, Sireric (IRE) and 2 flat winners (one in Belgium). IRISH NH FLAT '95 r2 p0. IRISH HUNT CH '96 r1 p0 (fell). IRISH P-t-P '95/6 r4 w1 (7yo&up Maiden) p1 (3rd); pulled up 2. NH '97/8 r3 p0 (pulled up in 2 Hdles, and unseated in Ch). P-t-P/HUNT CH '99 r6 p0 (6th, unseated 2, pulled up 2, and brought down 1). Has an appalling completion record for Paul Townsley, but managed to stagger round Charing 56 lengths behind the winner in his latest attempt. May have gone wrong in the process, as he failed to reappear. *P. Townsley — Surrey U. (Pru Townsley).* 126 (R).

FORMAL INVITATION (IRE) ..10-6.. 12 ch.g. Be My Guest (USA) — Clarista (USA) (Riva Ridge USA) f1p24. Tall rangy half-brother to 4 flat winners (one in Germany), including Huntswood and Indhar. Dam is half-sister to Teenoso and Topsy. FLAT r16 w2 (11-12f, inc Sell) p2 (3rds). NH '93 and '96/7 r12 w6 (2 Hdles, 2m-2m1f, and 4 Chses, 2m-2m4f-2m6f; inc a winner '97) p5. P-t-P/HUNT CH '99 r4 p2 (2nds, inc a Hunt Chs), and pulled up 2. A useful sub-3m horse under Rules, and gained his first success over the full trip when successful at Barbury Castle in the first month of the season. Sent off at 14-1 on that occasion having broken the frame of the third last fence at Larkhill when falling there the week before, but jumped impeccably and was in command after Mickthecutaway had taken the cowards way out at the end of the back straight. Failed to cope with Butler John on a return visit, but should still be up to winning in Open company again in 2001. Not suited by too much juice in the ground. *C.B. Smith — Cotswold (David Maybury).* 10 (O), 34 (MO), 154 (3mH), 474 (O), 684 (2m4fH).

FOR PAUL (IRE) ..9-11.. 9 b.g. Legal Circles (USA) — Noble For Stamps (Deep Run) 1. Good-bodied brother to Irish Pointing and English jumping winner, For Cathal (IRE). IRISH P-t-P '97/8 r7 p1 (last of 3 after being waved round final fence); pulled up 3, fell 1, and ran out 1. P-t-P '99 r4 w1 (Maiden) p0; pulled up 2, and ran out 1. Has only completed the course three times in 12 attempts, but successful on the last two occasions, and produced cherry-ripe for his sole outing in 2000. A keen sort and barely stays three miles, but is well served by fast ground. Sure to have the bookies running for cover when he next comes out of hiding. *D. Kelly & A. Woollacott — Stevenstone (Gerald Dartnall).* 1518 (R).

FORTUNE HUNTER (IRE) ..9-7.. 7 ch.g. Lycius (USA) — Cardomine (Dom Racine FR) ppf2up3633313. Medium-sized compact attractive half-brother to flat winner, Douce Maison. 21,000f, 37,000y. FLAT (first 3 for W. Jarvis; visored 1) r4 p0. NH '97/8 (for J. Norton) r7 p2 (neck 2nd once). A hard-puller who often makes mistakes and usually looks irresolute, but stood up well to a gruelling campaign, and finally managed to break his duck at the 12th attempt in a Point. The scene was a six-runner youngsters Maiden on firm at Dingley, in which Millington provided three of the contestants, plus another he had sold to his brother! The race was run at a crawl and took 27seconds longer than the other Maiden, but was enterprisingly dashed into a clear lead at the top of the hill and just maintained a dwindling advantage under wild upright urgings. Has been sold, and the new connections are already planning to run him at the first meeting of 2001! *P.J. Millington — Fernie.* 55 (OMa), 117 (O), 235 (OMa), 373 (CfMa), 411 (OMa), 515 (OMa), 593 (2m4fOMa), 792 (OMa), 1070 (2m4fOMa), 1290 (OMa), 1420 (OMa), 1504 (OMa), 1586 (CN).

FORTUNES LEAP ..6-0.. 9 br.g. Puissance — Lucky Starkist (Lucky Wednesday) pp. Small light-framed half-brother to Hurdles winner, Gunmaker. Dam won 4 flat, 5-7f (the first a Sell). FLAT r8 p0 (inc Sells). NH Nov '95 r1 p0 (pulled up in Sell). P-t-P '97/8 (for Miss C. Jones) r4 p1 (distant last of 3); pulled up 2, fell 1. Can show speed for up to 2m on his rare appearances, but stays no further, and only claimed a prize after stopping for a rest once. *C. Dix — Gelligaer F.* 1300 (OMa), 1455 (OMa).

FOR WILLIAM ..9-13.. 15 b.g. Whistling Deer — Pampered Sue (Pampered King) 3541. Compact half-brother to For Michael, to Irish NH flat and jumping winner, Otahengaue (IRE), and to Irish NH flat winner, Furry King. Dam won at 2m, and won 2 Hdles (2m1f-2m3f), all in Ireland. IRISH NH FLAT '90 r7 w2 p3. IRISH NH '90/3 and '95 r54 w6 (2 Hdles, 2m-2m6f, and 4 Chses, 2m4f-3m3f, including £8280 and £6900 prizes) p15 (2nd in '92 and '93 Kerry Nationals, earned £12,000 in the attempts); blinkered when last in '95 Grand National, after unseating. P-t-P '98/9 r3 p1 (last of 3); pulled up 1, and unseated 1. A fine money-spinner in his homeland, but given some amazingly uncompetitive rides by the owner until Jenny Grant took over on his final start at Peper Harow, where he rallied bravely to pass two rivals on the run-in and hold a third at bay. Will need her regular assistance if he returns unless Maxine Rigg suffers another rush of blood as happened at Aldington, where she led the field to halfway. *Mrs M. Rigg — Southdown & Eridge.* 307 (L), 827 (L), 1170 (L), 1395 (L).

FOSSY BEAR ..10-2.. 9 br.m. Lir — Full Spirit (Bay Spirit) 1u212p. Small neat. Dam, sister to Full Alirt (qv), only finished in one of 16 races (a Hurdle; competed in 14 Points) for the Youngs ('a useless pest, like mother'). P-t-P/HUNT CH '97/9 r12 w1 (Maiden) p1 (head 2nd); pulled up 5, and fell/unseated 3. Given some typically easy rides in her first couple of seasons, but a game little mare who likes to get competitive and has appreciated the opportunity to become so. Battles well for Sue Young, and would have won three times in 2000, but the pilot was outwitted by Les Jefford at Bratton Down. Well suited by plenty of cut in the ground, and found conditions too fast when tried in another Hunter Chase on her final start. Seems certain to win again. *B.R.J. Young, Miss S. Young & Mrs K. Rogers — E. Cornwall (Sue Young).* 157 (M), 256 (R), 728 (R), 849 (R), 1137 (I), 1433 (3mH).

FOUNTAIN BANK (IRE) ..9-8.. 8 b.g. Lafontaine (USA) — Clogrecon Lass (Raise You Ten) p23221. Very small half-brother to Irish winners, Runaway Gold (Pointing), Clogrecon Boy (Hurdling) and Caledonian Bridge (NH flat and Hurdles). Dam won 2m6f Hdle in Ireland. NH FLAT r2 p1 (3rd). NH '98/9 (for J. Spearing, blinkered last 2) r4 p0. Bought Doncaster, Aug for 3800. Normally a weak finisher, but had shown consistency when placed in four consecutive Maidens, and was certainly not scoring out of turn when he took a bad race at Higham. Jumps well for a titch, but will find matters more difficult in future. Wears a visor nowadays. *T. Alexander & R. Barr — Easton H. (Matthew Gingell).* 22 (2m4fOMa), 24 (OMa), 237 (OMa), 604 (OMa), 760 (OMa), 1116 (OMa).

FOUNTAIN GLEN (IRE) ..—.. 9 b.g. Royal Fountain — Glenflo (Flower Robe) fpp. Workmanlike compact. Fell at the first on his belated debut, and jumped poorly before pulling up when tailed off twice subsequently. *D. Shorey — N. Ledbury (Jim Collett).* 612 (CR), 891 (OMa), 1018 (OMa).

FOUNTAIN STREET (IRE) ..9-11.. 8 b.g. Sharp Charter — Maylands (Windjammer USA) fpp3c122. Good-topped. IRISH NH FLAT '98 r1 p0 (remote last). P-t-P '99 r3 p1 (3rd); and pulled up 2. Very unruly in '99 and still inclined to act the goat and pull hard, but has been sorted out by Richard Burton, and rewarded him with victory in a Bitterley Maiden. Beat little with nothing to spare on that occasion, but sent off favourite in both Restricted attempts subsequently, and was beaten a maximum of four lengths. Seems indifferent to ground conditions, but not an out-and-out stayer, and helped by an easy track. *Mrs T.R. Kinsey — Cheshire Forest.* 54 (OMa), 298 (OMa), 570 (2m4fCfMa), 777 (OMa), 906 (CfMa), 1092 (OMa), 1276 (R), 1460 (R).

FOUR NORTH (IRE) ..—.. 10 ch.g. Balinger — Careless Biddy (Laurence O) fp. Lengthy plain half-brother to Attitude Adjuster, Severe Gust (IRE) and Proove Positive (IRE), to Hurdles winner, Shallow Walk, and to a jumping winner in USA. IRISH P-t-P '96/8 r5 p0 (pulled up 5). P-t-P '99 r4 p0 (pulled up 4). A half-brother to the '86 Cheltenham Foxhunters hero, but devoid of talent himself, and extended his inept course completion record to 11 in 2000. Ended '99 lame, and is surely wrong. *R. Douglas — Buccleuch.* 365 (CfMa), 493 (Cf).

FOXLEY LAD ..8-4.. 8 ch.g. Little Wolf — If And When (Balliol) pc. Small. Dam won at 7f, and won 3 Hdles (2m-2m4f, inc 2 Sells) and placed total of 10, including 6 Points for Ray Godwin. P-t-P '98/9 r5 p0; pulled up 3. Lightly raced and has shown nothing tangible yet, but in a yard that does well particularly when the money is down. It might be unwise to put a line through him just yet, even though he has little scope for improvement, and the 2m4f avenue is no longer available to him. Tried in blinkers once in '99. *R. Godwin — N. Ledbury (Jon Rudge).* 673 (2m4fOMa), 1360 (2m4fOMa).

FOXWOOD POLO ..—.. 6 ch.m. Glacial Storm (USA) — Deep Creek (Deep Run) pp. Half-sister to Wishy Washy (IRE). Wishy washy herself to date. *Mrs M.A. Kendall — Cumberland F.* 500 (2m4fOMa), 816 (OMa).

FOXWYN ..7-0.. 9 b.g. Cashwyn — Flaming Fox (Healaugh Fox) p5. Strong-topped compact owner-bred. P-t-P '99 r6 p1 (last of 3); pulled up 4, and unseated 1. Has displayed a little speed, but lacking in the stamina department, and has beaten just one rival in eight starts. *Mrs C. Clift — Beaufort (Nick Bush).* 753 (CfMa), 957 (CfMa).

FOXY BLUE ..9-4.. 16 b.g. Fine Blue — Moxy (unknown) 3. Workmanlike lengthy owner-bred. NH '94 r4 p0 (4th of 5, last, and pulled up 2 in Chses). P-t-P '90/3, '95/6 and '99 r39 w1 (Maiden) p10 (3rds); failed to finish 19 (ran out 2, and unseated 3). Ancient and only unearthed for his Members nowadays. Beaten 38 seconds — around 150 lengths — in the latest renewal. *R. Evans — Cheshire.* 587 (M).

FOXY DAWN ..9-7.. 10 ch.g. Gabitat — Serious Affair (Valiyar) 354bp36517. Sturdy compact. P-t-P '98/9 (for Mr D.G. Alers-Hankey in '99) r7 w2 (Maiden and Restricted) p2 (3rds, last once); fell 1. Had a good record in his first two seasons with two wins and four placings to his credit, but generally disappointing in the new yard, and beat a bad lot when successful at Holnicote. Usually takes the eye in the paddock where he has two handlers, but still not always fluent at the fences, and seems unsuited by too much cut in the ground. *B.A. Sanderson & Mrs K.M. Horsburgh — Tiverton (Mary Horsburgh).* 140 (M), 202 (I), 310 (I), 557 (Cf), 730 (I), 853 (Inr), 1097 (Inr), 1370 (I), 1472 (I), 1638 (L).

PLATE 51   1472 Minehead Harriers & West Somerset Intermediate: L to R Foxy Dawn (D. Alers-Hankey), 1st, from Leejay Luki (A. Honeyball), 2nd   PHOTO: Baths Photograhic

FOXY LASS ..—.. 12 ch.m. Celtic Cone — Hunters Glen (Tiger Shark) ff. Small compact sister to Glen Moselle, and half-sister to Glentime. Dam failed to finish in 3 Points, but grandam, Esca, won a very weak 2m Nov Ch and placed 16 flat/NH (showed no form in Points). NH FLAT '93 r2 p0. NH '93/4 (for breeder, R. Cambidge) r7 p0 (Sells mostly). Consistently useless at a minimum of 33-1 under Rules, and unwisely revived after a six year lapse for two crashes in Points. *M. Moule — Kyre (Jackie Moule).* 861 (C), 1220 (OMa).

FRAGRANT LORD ..9-10.. 12 b.g. Germont — Tiger Feet (Pongee) 44p4fp4. Rangy unfurnished half-brother to Fragrant Fortune. Dam won 2m Nov Hdle and placed 3. P-t-P '96/9 r11 w2 (Members and Restricted) p0; pulled up 4, and fell/unseated 3. Flat to the boards in both successes, and has patently failed to cope with the rise in class since. Proved easy to beat in 2000, and his Corbridge win in '99 may well be his last. Usually lacks fluency, and seems unsuited by a sound surface. *Mrs V. Jackson — Morpeth.* 43 (Cf), 108 (I), 359 (Cf), 420 (I), 717 (Cf), 1366 (I), 1495 (I).

FRANGIPANE ..9-10.. 7 ch.m. Lighter — Altun Ha (Morston FR) 1. Small sister to Flashlight. P-t-P '99 r1 p0 (4th of 5). Showed a spark of ability on her racecourse debut in '99 and positively ran away with a three-finisher Maiden at Weston Park on her return, but presumably met with a setback as she failed to reappear. There seemed no fluke about her victory, and a Restricted should follow soon if she is able to resume in 2001. *A.R.C. Hill — Wheatland (John Downes).* 298 (CfMa).

FRANKIE MONEYBAGS ..—.. 10 b.g. Shaab — Flandell (Flandre II) ubu. Strong rangy. Takes a keen hold and has shown early speed, but yet to complete the course. Favourite once and second favourite once (9-4 in a race containing Black Dante!), but has only emptied the money bags of the bold Wevill supporters. *Mrs S.M. Wevill — Lamerton (Tim Dennis).* 158 (CfMa), 312 (CfMa), 722 (CfMa).

FRANKIE MUCK ..9-7.. 9 ch.g. Gunner B — Muckertoo (Sagaro) sp2f. Small compact brother to jumping winner, Madam Muck, and half-brother to jumping winner, Freddie Muck. Dam is half-sister to smart staying Hurdler, Mrs Muck. NH FLAT '96/7 r4 p0. NH '98/9 r7 p1 (3rd). P-t-P '99 r4 p1 (3rd); last, and fell/unseated 2. Not an easy ride for Charlotte Stucley, and had decked her three times before he broke his back in a fall at Cothelstone. *Miss C.C. Stucley & N.A. Twiston-Davies — Devon & Somerset (David Pipe).* 540 (OMa), 738 (OMa), 880 (OMa), 1099 (OMa).

FRANKIES FLUTTER ..9-6.. 8 b.g. Latest Model — Arctic Cinnamon (Langton Heath) fpp3pfp1. Sturdy attractive. Dam is an unraced half-sister to Emma Pepper (*qv* '95 Annual, who is by Latest Model). P-t-P '99 r1 p0 (pulled up). Had shown some speed but only finished in front of one rival before springing a 14-1 surprise on his final appearance at Lifton. The winning time was very slow, but the runner-up won next time (allegedly) so he might prove to have the scope for Restricted success. *W.C.F. Keat — Eggesford.* 253 (CfMa), 312 (CfMa), 540 (OMa), 656 (OMa), 856 (CfMa), 1173 (M), 1519 (CfMa), 1641 (OMa).

FRANKLINS BEST (IRE) ..10-0.. 8 b.g. Parliament — Dollyliner (Skyliner) 221f6u2. Small light. IRISH NH FLAT '97 r3 p0. IRISH NH '98 r5 p0. P-t-P '99 r6 p2; unseated 2, and pulled up 2. Not winning out of turn at Littlewindsor having been placed in his previous four starts, and ran well enough on his final outing to suggest that a similar event is within his compass. Seems quite a handful and has two paddock handlers, but easy enough to settle in a race, although the odd bad jump tends to get him into trouble. *G.B. Foot — Seavington.* 213 (CfMa), 331 (R), 519 (M), 767 (R), 931 (R), 1240 (R), 1309 (R).

FRANKLY FEAR ..9-6.. 8 b.g. Lyphento (USA) — Frankly New (New Member) 168p43. Workmanlike lengthy. Dam, half-sister to 5 Pointers, including Kings Bill (*qv* '93 Annual), failed to finish in 3 Points. Great-grandam, April Queen, won 6 Points and Liverpool Foxhunters. P-t-P '99 r2 p0 (pulled up 1, and fell 1). Looked to have done plenty of work before his not unexpected Great Trethew victory, but needed to as the race was a real survival of the fittest job taking over seven minutes. Failed to run up to that form again, and it may be that the race bottomed him completely. Worth another chance in Restricted company. *Mrs G.M. Brake & Mrs M. Murray — Eggesford (Laura Horsey).* 158 (CfMa), 315 (R), 728 (R), 1140 (CfR), 1309 (R), 1534 (3m1f110yH).

FRANK NAYLAR ..9-7.. 10 b.g. All Fair — The Deer Hound (Cash And Carry) 3234d. Workmanlike half-brother to After The Fox (jumping winner since Pointing), and Brue Hound Boy, and to Hurdles winner, Daves Delight. Dam lamed herself in the last of 4 unsuccessful Pointing efforts. NH FLAT '95/6 r3 p0. NH '95/7 (for R. Buckler) r3 p0 (pulled up in blinkers final). Beaten under seven lengths in three Maiden placings, but moderate and is finding it difficult to score. Might be suited by a stiff test of stamina, and deserves a little success. Perhaps he should target eight year old plus contests. *Mrs F. Partridge — Blackmore & Sparkford V. (Peter Froud).* 72 (OMa), 207 (OMa), 738 (OMa), 957 (CfMa).

FREDDIE FOX ..9-6.. 15 b.g. Scallywag — Gouly Duff (Party Mink) 325. Big rangy brother to Another Scally and Noble Question. Dam was 2nd in 4 Points (lame final). P-t-P/HUNT CH '91/9 r35 w7 (inc 2m5f Hunt Ch) p13 (6 2nds, last once; and inc 3 Hunt Chses); failed to finish 8 (fell 2). A gallant old veteran who has now raced for 10 consecutive seasons, but has often been held in check by his lack of acceleration. A cumbersome mover and jumper, but very honest, and almost provided Gemma Garton with her first success in a two-finisher 'race' taking well over eight minutes at Flagg. *Mrs A.B. Garton — Cheshire Forest (Tim Garton).* 959 (M), 1252 (Cf), 1408 (Cf).

FREE AND EQUAL (IRE) ..9-2§.. 10 ch.g. Le Bavard (FR) — Huntoon (Gay Fandango USA) p3p44. Small sparely-made half-brother to Irish NH flat winners, The Subbie (also a successful jumper there) and Rearin Sue. IRISH NH FLAT '95/6 r3 p0. IRISH NH '96 r3 p0. IRISH P-t-P '97/8 r7 p2; pulled up 1, and fell 1. P-t-P '99 r6 w1 (Maiden) p1 (last of 3); last 2, and pulled up 2. Amazingly consented to win a dreadful Northaw Maiden in a slow time, but generally a very sour little horse, and would not do a tap when beaten 30 lengths plus in 2000. Tried in spurs. Retired from racing, and now enjoying gentler pastimes (with his rating, he might be a good thing for an egg and spoon race). *D.C. Morgan (Whitestick Partnership) — Cambs (Simon Andrews).* 86 (R), 91 (M), 610 (R), 761 (R), 843 (R).

FREEDOM FIGHTER ..10-5.. 10 b.g. Fearless Action (USA) — Zuleika Hill (Yellow River) 2pfu2p4pp37. Strong workmanlike owner-bred. Dam ran badly in Points at 5 in '78. P-t-P/HUNT CH '98/9 r17 w3 (inc 3m Hunt Ch) p4 (3 3rds, last once); unseated 1, and pulled up 4. Much improved towards the end of '99, but had luck very much on his side in the Interlink Express Restricted Final at Stratford though none since. Runs Stratford better than anywhere else, and had 12 rivals behind him in two placings there in 2000. Sweats profusely and pulls hard, but is suited by an easy three miles, and deserves to find another opening. *Mrs R. Gasson — Farmers Bloodhounds.* 94 (O), 154 (3mH), 302 (3mH), 430 (O), 580 (3mH), 631 (MO), 895 (MO), 1023 (3mH), 1337 (3m2f110yH), 1558 (3mH), 1646 (3m4fH).

FREEMOUNT BOY (IRE) ..8-6.. 8 ch.g. Parliament — Hills Angel (IRE) (Salluceva) 4fp. Half-brother to Very Very Noble (*qv*). IRISH P-t-P '98/9 r3 p0 (pulled up 3). Bought Malvern, May for 1200. Has only completed in one of six races, when beaten 50 lengths. Fell at the first when tried in a tongue-strap. *G.B. Foot — Seavington.* 212 (CfMa), 330 (K), 518 (2m4fOMa).

FREESTYLER (IRE) ..9-11.. 9 b br.g. Phardante (FR) — Financial Burden (Mandalus) 61u3. Tall workmanlike brother to Will Hill (IRE). IRISH P-t-P '97 and '99 r13 w1 (7yo Mdn) p3; pulled up 5, unseated, ran out 2 and refused. IRISH NH FLAT '97/8 r4 p0. IRISH NH '98/9 r5 p0. Bought Doncaster, Aug for 7500. Goes a decent gallop and seems to do his best, but had luck on his side in a Restricted in soft at Southwell, where he was virtually presented with the prize after three well fancied rivals had all bitten the mud. Broke a blood vessel and was all out to hold on, and has given other signs of physical infirmity, having had a soft palate operation in the past. Runs tongue-tied, makes a few errors, and is generally proving to be a weak finisher now. *Mrs B.L. Shaw — United (Gary Hanmer).* 905 (C), 1071 (CR), 1601 (3m2fH), 1667 (I).

FREE TO CONKER (IRE) ..—.. 8 b.g. Executive Perk — Golden Chestnut (Green Shoon) pfpp. Compact half-brother to Fair Crossing (*qv*). 4800 5-y-o. NH FLAT '98 r1 p0. NH '99 (for K. Bailey) r1 p0 (pulled up in Ch). Bought Doncaster, May for 3000. Usually sets off as if the hounds of hell are on his trail, and has no hope of getting round a course whilst he continues to go at such a lunatic early pace. Wears a cross-noseband, and has been taken to post early. *Mrs E. Young — Farmers Bloodhounds (Mark Hawkins).* 31 (CMa), 714 (CCf), 1019 (2m4fOMa), 1204 (OMa).

FRENCH BELL ..—.. 7 b.m. Milieu — Fourth Bell (Royal Fountain) p. Plain. Dam, half-sister to Fairy Bell (*qv*), was 3rd in a Point for Keith Waters. P-t-P '99 r1 p0 (pulled up). Has shown little aptitude in two Maidens ten months apart. *K. Waters — Braes.* 46 (OMa).

FRENCH BUCK (IRE) ..10-6.. 11 br.g. Phardante (FR) — Flying Silver (Master Buck) p2p. Tall rangy half-brother to Rip Van Winkle (*qv*). NH FLAT '94/5 r4 w1 (ridden by Mark Rimell) p1 (3rd). NH '95/7 r12 w1 (2m Hdle) p2 (3rds); 6th, 9th, last and pulled up in Chses. P-t-P/HUNT CH '99 r2 p1 (3rd). Difficult to train and has only once managed more than four outings in a year, but still retains plenty of ability, and almost sprang a 20-1 shock when second to Distinctive at Chaddesley. Suited by an easy three miles, and like many by his sire appreciates a sound surface. Often blinkered under Rules. Broke down at Maisemore, and has been reported dead. *Mrs C.J.M. Scott & partners — Heythrop (Mark Rimell).* 17 (O), 611 (C), 895 (MO).

FRENCHMAN (IRE) ..—.. 9 ch.g. John French — Mistress Anna (Arapaho) fp. Brother to Never Wonder (IRE) (*qv*). Tres vite in the early stages, but has so far gone no more than two miles. Wore a tongue-strap on his debut. *Mrs J.A. Rickett — Cheshire Forest.* 964 (OMa), 1318 (OMa).

FRENCH MELODY (IRE) ..8-4.. 8 ch.g. Le Bavard (FR) — Witchey Witch (IRE) (Le Moss) p4p. Lengthy unfurnished. IRISH P-t-P '99 r5 p0; pulled up 2, and unseated. Continued his bad run of form in the new yard, and was 55 lengths last when completing. Does not seem to get the trip. The trainer has an amazingly awful string. *Mrs C. Lockett — Kyre (Jackie Moule).* 528 (OMa), 588 (OMa), 866 (CfMa).

FRENCH TALE (IRE) ..—.. 10 ch.g. Roselier (FR) — Proverb Lady (Proverb) p. Strong half-brother to Itendra, and to jumping winner, Pariah (IRE). NH '98/9 (from A. Harvey's) r2 p0. Has looked useless when pulling up in just one race apiece in the last three years, and a new (non-racing) home has been found for him. *W.J. Tolhurst — Essex & Suffolk.* 323 (CfMa).

FRESH ICE (IRE) ..10-4.. 11 ch.g. Aristocracy — Quefort (Quayside) 262p. Big strong half-brother to Black Quartz and Highland Minstrel, to Irish Pointing winner, Redmint, and to Irish NH flat winners, Ardnaglug Cross, Tricias Pride and Unarmed (IRE) (latter also won Hurdles there). P-t-P/HUNT CH '96/9 r16 w4 (up to Confined) p6 (4 2nds); pulled up 2, and fell/unseated 3. A steady galloper and capable of decent efforts, but only averages four outings a year, and is clearly not easy to keep on the straight and narrow. Made Copper Thistle dig deep at Garthorpe in April, but ran badly there later in the month, and may well have suffered a recurrence of the broken blood vessel that affected him on one occasion in '99. Could usually be relied upon to demolish one fence per race, but an improved jumper of late, and deserves another success. *D.F. Iveson — Pytchley (Tik Saunders).* 93 (C), 510 (Cf), 870 (O), 1265 (O).

FRESH PRINCE ..10-11.. 13 b.g. Balinger — Lasses Nightshade (Deadly Nightshade) 1p11p. Tall rangy half-brother to True Shade and Nothingtodowithme, and to jumping winner, Spinning Steel. Dam won Maiden and placed 5. P-t-P '95/7 and '99 r16 w7 (inc 3 Opens) p2 (2nds); failed to finish 6 (ran out 1, and fell 1). An awesome looking beast who won the four-year-old Lightweight Hunter Class at the Royal, and is capable of majestic front-running, but has appeared to bleed on occasions, and missed two full months of the season after stopping very quickly on his Hunter Chase debut at Kempton in February. Had earlier romped home in the fastest time of the day at Larkhill and returned to win twice more against vastly inferior rivals, but did not jump with his usual fluency and was pulled up again at Chaddesley subsequently. Has taken his winning tally into double figures, and should collect more races if his problems are only temporary. Acts on top-of-the-ground. *Mrs V. Ramm — Cotswold (Jelly Nolan).* 61 (MO), 303 (3mH), 1440 (MO), 1585 (O), 1631 (MO).

PLATE 52   1585 Melton Hunt Club Mens Open: Fresh Prince (Julian Pritchard), 1st, jumps ahead of Mr Dennehy (David Dennis), 3rd
PHOTO: Bill Selwyn

FRIAR WADDON ..10-3.. 8 b.g. Pablond — Looking Swell (Simbir) up51. Sturdy compact half-brother to Scott Elliott. P-t-P '99 r5 w1 (Maiden) p2; pulled up 1. Had a large band of followers in '99 and justified market support when winning at Kingston St Mary, but most of them had deserted him after failing to beat a rival in his first three outings in 2000, and was a rewarding 6-1 when he popped up again at Holnicote on his final start. The key to him is clearly the ground — must have it as lively as possible. Returned a decent time in his latest success, and might prove good enough to contest Ladies races in 2001. *P.J. Clarke — Devon & Somerset (Keith Cumings).* 330 (R), 404 (I), 1042 (R), 1376 (R).

FRIDAYS CHILD ..8-0.. 9 b.m. Bold Fox — Fassbinder (El-Birillo) p. Lengthy dipped very lean. P-t-P '97 r3 p1 (remote last of 3); pulled up 1, and fell 1. A headstrong sort when last seen and three years absence has not blunted her early speed, but stopped dead at halfway on her reappearance, and clearly either has no stamina whatsoever or a major flaw. *Mr & Mrs K. Kelso — Pembs (Beverley Thomas).* 269 (CfMa).

FRIENDLY VIKING ..8-8.. 11 ch.g. Viking (USA) — Ale Water (Be Friendly) p. Small close-coupled half-brother to Carrie's Gift. Dam won at 5f (3 ran). NH FLAT Jan '94 r1 p0 (tailed off). NH '94 r4 p0 (last 2, and pulled up 2; Sell final). P-t-P/HUNT CH '95/8 r15 w1 (Maiden) p0; failed to finish 11 (ran out 1, refused 1, and fell 1). Last or a non-finisher in all but one of his 20 outings over jumps, the exception being his win in soft at Kilworthy in '98. Obviously troubled since, as he missed the following season, and managed just one appearance in 2000. *Mrs J. Holden-White — E. Cornwall.* 256 (R).

FRIENDS OF BERNARD (IRE) ..9-13.. 11 ch.g. Phardante (FR) — Arctic Shine (Arctic Slave) p1. Angular half-brother to a Chasing winner, to smart Irish jumping winner, Belvederian (won £80,000), and to 3 winning Irish Pointers, including Belgrove Girl (one also a successful jumper). Dam won 3 Hdles and a Ch at around 2m in Ireland. IRISH NH FLAT '95/6 r2 p0 (tailed off). P-t-P '98/9 r17 w1 (Maiden) p4 (3 2nds, beaten head once); last pair 7, fell/unseated 4, and brought down 1. Made most to compensate connections for what appeared to be a judging blunder at Cottenham in '99 when successful at Detling, but his tendency to jump right is still pronounced (trying to save a leg?), and he ominously failed to reappear. An habitual front-runner who is suited by decent ground, and could win again if unharmed. *M.P. Avery, K. Pearce, J. Dance & A. Hill — V. of Aylesbury (Lawney Hill).* 248 (R), 575 (R).

FRISKY-BREEZE ..—§§.. 8 br.m. Newski (USA) — Sunny Breeze (Roi Soleil) upfpu. Light-framed owner-bred half-sister to Breeze-Bloc (qv). P-t-P '99 r5 p0 (refused 1, ran out 1, pulled up 1, and unseated 2). A prize villainess who failed to get beyond the 7th fence in her debut season, and fared little better in 2000. Hurls herself over the fences, and is a most unenviable and unrewarding ride. Ridden into the paddock on two occasions in 2000 (the legacy of rolling over when mounted once in '99), and is always taken to post early. Hopefully connections will have the sense not to run her again. *J.B. Shears — Mid Devon.* 205 (OMa), 855 (CfMa), 934 (OMa), 1641 (OMa), 1676 (OMa).

FROSTY DEAL (IRE) ..9-3.. 9 gr.g. Neltino — Altovise (Black Minstrel) p2. Half-brother to Betontheback. P-t-P '98 r2 p0 (pulled up 2). Went wrong in '98 and lame again after finishing last of two at Ampton — led throughout the final mile, but was already beaten when clouting the last. Neltino strikes again. *A.F.J.J. Moss — Suffolk (Julie Read).* 20 (OMa), 88 (OMa).

FROSTY JO ..8-0.. 7 b.m. Prince Of Peace — Bingley Sharlene (Good Apple) p5ppp. Close-coupled owner-bred sister to Pioneer Pete, and half-sister to Timarisk. NH '98 (from R. Frost's) r3 p0 (remote last, pulled up and fell — all at Newton Abbot). Impetuous and may be a tricky sort like her siblings, and was about 30 lengths last on her only completion. Goes to post early. Might possibly surprise one day. *P. & Mrs M. Haimes & S.R. Elford — Dartmoor (Stephen Elford).* 857 (CfMa), 1372 (OMa), 1469 (OMa), 1640 (OMa), 1675 (OMa).

FROWN ..9-10.. 11 ch.g. Bustino — Highbrow (Shirley Heights) 5fpp425. Sturdy half-brother to Hurdles winner, Doctor Green (FR). Dam won at 8f, and showed some very good placed form subsequently (was a tail-swisher). NH '94/8 r14 w1 (2m4f Hdle) p2 (2nds in Chses); 7th, pulled up 2, and fell 2 in other Chses. P-t-P '99 r1 p0 (pulled up). Won on his jumping debut, but error-prone since (particularly over regulation fences), and has never been able to follow up. Regularly blinkered nowadays, and beaten a minimum of 18 lengths when completing in 2000. Out of his depth in Hunter Chases, and would be more at home if he had his sights lowered. *Mrs A. Thorpe — Gogerddan.* 345 (O), 468 (3m1f110yH), 799 (2m4f110yH), 922 (3mH), 945 (O), 1157 (2m3fH), 1346 (3m1f110yH).

FROZEN DROP ..9-10.. 14 b.g. Le Bavard (FR) — Frozen Ground (Arctic Slave) p4553f233. Compact half-brother to Usario and Arctic Quest, to Hurdles winner, Arctic Ground (IRE), and to Irish Pointing and Chasing winner, Over The Maine (IRE). Dam won 2 Hdles, 2-3m. IRISH P-t-P '92/3 r7 w1 (Maiden) p1 (3rd); pulled up 3, and fell 1. NH '93/8 (visored 1, in '94) r44 w6 (2m7f-3m3f Chses) p23 (inc 3rd in Hdle). P-t-P '99 r2 w1 (Club) p1 (last of 3). A former decent top-of-the-ground Chaser, but was recording his first success since '96 when a game winner at Cotley Farm in '99. Has a long history and very one-paced now, but performed the task of schooling Tom Bishop admirably. *Mrs F.D. Bishop — Blackmore & Sparkford V.* 454 (4mMO), 634 (C), 736 (Cnr), 952 (M), 1057 (Cf), 1134 (Cnr), 1306 (C), 1471 (Cnr), 1550 (Cnr).

PLATE 53   454 Staff College & RMA Draghounds Mixed Open: L to R Frozen Drop (J. Barnes), pu, and Amtrak Express (H. Froud), pu, at the 4th   PHOTO: Brian Armstrong

FRUIT CROP ..8-12.. 8 ch.m. Weld — Fruit Farm (Twiberry) 3ff2fp. Workmanlike owner-bred sister to Harweld (*qv*). P-t-P '99 r1 p0 (pulled up). Handled with kid gloves in her early starts, but suffered two successive falls and has refused to co-operate since. Never went a yard on her final outing following yet another tumble, and surely punters confidence in her in the future will be as lacking as her own confidence at the fences. Wisely shunned by Alastair Crow after the combination cleared just one fence successfully. *E.H. Crow — N. Salop (Sheila Crow).* 181 (2m4fOMa), 593 (2m4fOMa), 964 (OMa), 1125 (OMa), 1318 (OMa), 1413 (OMa).

FRYUP DIGITAL ..—.. 6 ch.g. High Lodge — Comedy Imp (Import) p. Half-brother to Fryup Satellite. Dam, sister or half-sister to 5 Pointers, including Flying Lion (*qv* 2000 Annual), was 3 fences last of 3 in a Members and pulled up twice in Points. Sold Malvern, May '98 for 5200. Looked to be given a quiet time before pulling up on a February debut. *A. Dimmock — Staintondale (Mary Sowersby).* 167 (OMa).

FRYUP SATELLITE ..10-0.. 10 br.g. Leading Star — Comedy Imp (Import) p4. Compact robust owner-bred half-brother to Fryup Digital (*qv*). FLAT (for L. Lloyd-James) r7 p0. NH '95/9 (from Mrs J. Brown's) r29 w1 (2m3f Amat Hdle) p11 (inc 6 Chses, and short-headed in Sell Hdle). Gives creditable displays on occasions, but has only won one race in six years, when scraping home by a head and the same in December '96. Far from disgraced in his second Point, but may have had a setback. *J. Lees — Staintondale (Paul Halder).* 279 (O), 623 (Cf).

FULL ALIRT ..9-12.. 13 ch.m. Lir — Full Tan (Dairialatan) p5p6. Small light sister to Lirsleftover, and half-sister to Full Spirit (dam of Fossy Bear *qv*). Dam, 'a useless pest', pulled up 1, and ran out 1 in Points for Basil Young. NH FLAT r1 p0 (15th of 16). NH '93 r4 p0 (inc last, and fell 2; Sell final). P-t-P/HUNT CH '94/9 r26 w5 (inc 3m Hunt Ch) p10 (5 2nds; and inc 3 Hunt Chses); pulled up 7, and fell/unseated 2. A speedy mare with a useful turn of foot, but without a win since romping home in a Taunton Hunter Chase in '97 (rated 10-3), and well below par in 2000. Has five victories to her credit and unlucky not to have accrued more, but lightly raced in recent years, and will find a revival in fortunes hard to come by at 13. *B.R.J. Young — E. Cornwall (Sue Young).* 581 (3mH), 683 (3mH), 1138 (MO), 1638 (L).

FULL BORE (IRE) ..7-7§.. 9 b.g. Boreen (FR) — Jukebox Katie (Jukebox) ppppp. Stocky. Dam won 2m Sell Hdle. P-t-P '98/9 r8 p2; last pair 2, unseated 2, and pulled up 2. A hard puller in '99 when very prone to errors, but becoming increasingly reluctant and pulls himself up more often than not nowadays. Still an incompetent jumper, and not worth racing again. *T.P. Whales — W. Norfolk.* 88 (OMa), 98 (OMa), 416 (R), 550 (OMa), 1116 (OMa), 1507 (OMa).

FULLOFANCY ..9-10.. 8 ch.m. Interrex (CAN) — Metafan (Last Fandango) fu2. Lengthy owner-bred. Dam is half-sister to Poors Wood (*qv* '98 Annual). NH '97 (from R. Buckler's) r1 p1 (3rd). Was staying on in the closing stages when sixteen lengths third in a Hurdle, but took three years to resurface. Victim of the final fence in her first two Maidens (when second and held once; but when looking the winner in the other), but rather disappointing when runner-up at Lockinge. Should be a good thing to atone in similar grade, particularly as she is now eligible for eight year old plus contests. *Mrs B. Bishop — Portman (Ali Tory).* 733 (2m4fOMa), 933 (OMa), 1204 (OMa).

FULL OF CHAT (IRE) ..9-0.. 12 ch.m. Good Thyne (USA) — Hay Party (Party Mink) ppppuR4u. Small neat half-sister to Jolly Jack (IRE). Dam won 2 Irish Hdles, 2m-2m4f. IRISH P-t-P '93 r1 p1 (3rd). NH '94 and '96 r3 p0; pulled up 1. P-t-P/HUNT CH '95 and '99 r7 w1 (Maiden) p0; fell 2, and pulled up 3. A keen sort and often tries to make the running, but prone to bad errors, and is continually out of her depth in Hunter Chases. May have ruined her chance of Restricted success in the process as time is running out for her. Can get pretty stirred up in the paddock, and has two handlers. *B. McNichol — Cumberland F. (Paul Johnston).* 360 (R), 492 (M), 717 (Cf), 1078 (Cf), 1345 (2m5fH), 1446 (3m1fH), 1602 (2m4f110yH), 1643 (3m2fH).

FULL SCORE (IRE) ..10-4.. 12 b.g. Orchestra — Country Character (Furry Glen) 313. Half-brother to Country Choice, and to Irish NH flat winner, Rural Run (IRE). IRISH NH FLAT r4 p0. IRISH P-t-P '94/5 r7 p1 (2nd); won, but disqualified for interference once; pulled up 3. P-t-P '96/8 (for Mrs J. Webber in '98) r9 w2 (Maiden and Restricted) p4 (3 3rds, distant last after remounting once); unseated 1, and pulled up 2. Has never stood many outings, and ended '98 (his most productive season) lame. Resurfaced after two years convalescence and won his third Point under Julian Pritchard when making all at Andoversford, but unsuited by the soft ground when well held at Paxford subsequently. Runs from the front and is a good jumper, but usually sent off at a false price. *Mrs C. Mackness — N. Cotswold (Jelly Nolan).* 701 (I), 971 (I), 1190 (Cf).

FUNCHEON GALE ..10-0.. 14 b.g. Strong Gale — Funcheon Breeze (Deep Run) p36pp. Deep-girthed. IRISH P-t-P '92/4 r13 w1 (6yo&up Maiden) p4; pulled up 3, slipped up 1, and unseated 1. NH '96/7 r19 w5 (2m6f-3m2f Chses) p5; broke blood vessel once. P-t-P/HUNT CH '95 and '99 r6 p2 (3rds in Hunt Chses); pulled up 3, and fell 1. Tries hard, but without a win since May '97, and finds life too tough in Hunter Chases nowadays. Safely ignored in Points, especially when the trainer is in the saddle. *W.J. Lee - Oxford (Ann Lee).* 919 (2m3f110yH), 1205 (MO), 1357 (MOnr), 1533 (3m1fH), 1647 (3m4fH).

FUNDY (IRE) ..11-0.. 12 b.g. Arapahos (FR) — S T Blue (Bluerullah) p. Half-brother to The Earth Moved (IRE). Dam won 2m mares Hdle in Ireland. IRISH P-t-P '94/6 r10 w2 (inc Winners Of One) p 5 (4 2nds, beaten head in Ladies when bidding for hat-trick on final three starts); pulled up 1. P-t-P '97 and '99 r6 w4 (Ladies) p0; unseated 1, and ran out 1. A very smart Ladies horse, but fragile and off the track for two years after winning twice in '97. Returned to destroy useful opposition in '99, but managed only two outings and disappeared after apparently going wrong at Eyton in March in 2000. Game and a devastating galloper, and it is a crying shame that his career has been blighted by injury. *Mr & Mrs A.J. Brazier — Croome & W. Warwicks (Andrew Dalton).* 566 (L).

FUNNY FARM ..10-0§.. 11 ch.g. Funny Man — Bra Belle (Petit Instant) p63313. Tall rangy angular half-brother to Bare Fisted (*qv*). P-t-P '96/8 r9 w3 (Maiden, Restricted and Intermediate) p1 (2nd); ran out 1, fell 1, brought down 1, and pulled up 1. Went lame when winning his third race of '98 and forced to spend the following season on the sidelines, but still retains ability, and kept galloping for the eight and a half minutes it took to cover four miles of Flete Park in April. Becoming more awkward than ever, and Shirley Vickery twice spent the entire race with both hands on the one rein trying to combat her mount's inclination to hang. Perfectly capable of scoring again, but could not be supported with any confidence. Has been tried in blinkers. *Mrs J. Walter — Devon & Somerset (Alan Walter).* 59 (MO), 262 (MO), 735 (MO), 922 (3mH), 1044 (4mO), 1259 (4mL).

FURIOUS AVENGER ..10-0.. 12 ch.g. True Song — Furious Babs (Fury Royal) p331. Tall rangy half-brother to Furious Retreat. Dam, very temperamental, was placed in 5 Points. P-t-P/HUNT CH '95/6 and '98/9 r11 w1 (Maiden) p2 (3rds, of 4 once); fell 1, pulled up 2. Very lightly raced and backward in his first three seasons, but had a chance to run himself fit in '99, and landed a Garthorpe Maiden (lucky, as the eight-length leader failed to negotiate the final bend). Won on merit in 2000, but the Paxford Restricted he captured was weakly contested, and the favourite did not stay. Not as highly strung as mother, but frequently sweats and has had two paddock handlers. *B.L. Lay — Heythrop.* 248 (R), 429 (C), 971 (I), 1193 (Rn).

FURRY FOX (IRE) ..9-4.. 13 b.g. Furry Glen — Pillow Chat (Le Bavard FR) pp255. Tall half-brother to Irish Pointing winner, Desertmore. NH FLAT r1 p0. NH '96/7 r9 w1 (3m3f Ch) p3. P-t-P '94/5 and

'98/9 (for Mr J. Cumming in '99) r19 w3 (up to Confined) p8 (4 2nds); failed to finish 5 (fell 1). Won three Points to '96, but has run up a losing sequence of 14. Only likely to extend it if he returns, despite what was a decent effort for an old boy at Cursneh Hill. *T. Jewitt — V.W.H.* 895 (MO), 968 (Cf), 1273 (O), 1492 (O), 1631 (MO).

FURSAN (USA) ..10-4.. 8 b.g. Fred Astaire (USA) — Ancient Art (USA) (Tell USA) 61332. Sturdy attractive half-brother to several winners in USA. Dam won 4 races in USA, and was 3rd in Del Mar Oaks. £38,000f, 16,000y. FLAT (for N. Graham) r7 p2. NH '96/7 and Jul '99 (final for R. Phillips; previously for N. Twiston-Davies, bought for 26,000) r3 p0 (inc pulled up 2; 8-11 on debut). Takes a demonic hold and has to be steadied at the start to prevent him from getting to the front and burning himself out, but given a good ride by Paul Phillips after being unruly in the preliminaries when ideally suited by the short track in a youngsters Maiden at Stafford Cross. Normally struggles to stay three miles, but has run well when twice beaten only four lengths in 2m5f Hunter Chases, and well worth persevering with in similar events. Runs tongue-tied. *P. & E. Phillips, P. Reed & S. Berry — Axe V.H. (Paul Phillips).* 732 (2m4fOMa), 934 (OMa), 1140 (CfR), 1444 (2m5fH), 1627 (2m5fH).

GAELIC (IRE) ..—.. 9 b.m. Strong Gale — Carminda (Proverb) pp. Workmanlike half-sister to Irish Hurdles winner, Mydante (IRE). Dam won 4 Points (in an Open). NH FLAT '98 r3 p0 (withdrawn not under starter's orders once). NH '98/9 (for N. Twiston-Davies) r6 w1 (2m4f Sell Hdle) p0. Sold Doncaster, May for 4000. Generally runs badly, and probably has something wrong with him. Wore a tongue-strap and was remote when pulling up after two miles in early season Opens. *Mrs Watkins-Pitchford & Mrs S. Smith-Kellard — Heythrop (Sarah Kellard-Smith).* 77 (O), 195 (O).

GAELIC BLUE ..—.. 11 ch.g. Celtic Cone — Giollaretta (Giolla Mear) fppp. Big strong half-brother to Chasing winner, Greenheart. Dam won 2 Irish Chses, 2m3f-2m4f. NH '96/9 (for Mrs S. Smith) r25 w4 (2m4f-3m1f Chses) p8 (inc 3rd in Hdle); would have completed 4-timer Spring'97 but fell last when 6l clear once. Bought Doncaster, May for 4500. Used to be a decent competitor, but has fallen or unseated in six of 22 Chases, and his jumping has gone to pot completely under Rules latterly (pulled up twice and fell twice on his final four attempts). Continued to perform appallingly for the new year, and has hopefully been retired. Often wears a tongue-strap, and was reluctant to leave the paddock when blinkered for his latest debacle. *Mrs J.F. Fitzgerald — O. Berks.* 59 (MO), 327 (O), 389 (O), 1205 (MO).

GAELIC ROYALE (IRE) ..8-7.. 8 b.m. Welsh Term — Devon Royale (Le Prince) pppf3. Compact half-sister to Storm Man (IRE) (qv). IRISH NH '97 and '99 r3 p1 (21l 3rd in Ch). IRISH NH FLAT '99 r1 p0. IRISH P-t-P '98/9 r7 w1 (5&6yo mares Maiden) p0; pulled up 3, and fell 3. Bought Doncaster, Aug for 3000. Obviously purchased because of her kinship to Storm Man (IRE), but the stable have had no joy with her so far. Not seen since finishing 28 lengths last at Howick on her only completion, and was exceptionally lucky to get the prize after two in front of her had departed two out. *C.W.M. Cornelius — Ystrad Taf Fechan (Shan Farr).* 38 (CR), 273 (R), 347 (R), 485 (R), 596 (R).

GAELIC WARRIOR ..9-5.. 14 b.g. Belfort (FR) — Practicality (Weavers' Hall) pup3up. Tall rangy brother to flat and Chasing winner, Kamart, and half-brother to Saywhen, to 2 winners abroad, and to a successful Hurdler. IRISH NH FLAT r1 p0. IRISH NH '94 r1 p0. NH '95/6 r2 p0 (fell 2). P-t-P/HUNT CH '95/8 r28 w2 (Opens) p9 (4 2nds, beaten neck once; and inc 3rd in Hunt Ch); failed to finish 10 (on floor 4). Scored on his English debut — race took 8min 9s, but beaten in 32 of 33 attempts since and declined sharply in '99. Failed to beat a rival this term and looks finished now. *P.E. Clark — York & Ainsty S. (Liz Clark).* 41 (L), 90 (3m1fH), 170 (L), 506 (Cf), 997 (Cf), 1348 (Cf).

GALANT DES EPEIRES (FR) ..—.. 10 ch.g. Galant Vert (FR) — Marie De Bethisy (FR) (Balidar) f. FRENCH FLAT '94 r4 p2. FRENCH NH '94 r4 w2 (Hdles at Pau and Auteuil, 1m7f-1m7f110y) p1 (2nd); 4th only Ch. IRISH NH '96/7 and '99 r7 p0 (Chses). Strutted his stuff as a youngster in France, but very lightly raced and useless in two other countries. Tongue-tied and fell when struggling in a January Open. *Mrs G.M. Brooke — Bramham.* 17 (O).

GALAROI (IRE) ..9-13.. 12 b.g. Supreme Leader — Bank Rate (Deep Run) p3pR31u3. Tall rangy half-brother to Irish NH flat and jumping winner, Tubberorum. IRISH P-t-P '95 r1 p1 (3rd). P-t-P/HUNT CH '96 and '98 r15 w7 (inc 3 Opens) p2 (2nds); fell/unseated 4. Enjoyed an excellent year in '98 winning four times, but off the track for a year either side and has declined in the interim. Wears a tongue-strap, but seems to be having more problems with his wind and often dropped away meekly in 2000, but superior fencing won him the day at Penshurst. Ridden in spurs, but game and honest and it is a pity his career has suffered so many interruptions. *D.C. Robinson — Mid Surrey F. (Marion Robinson).* 286 (O), 308 (O), 572 (CfO), 678 (O), 706 (Cf), 826 (O), 981 (O), 1210 (O).

GALEAWAY (IRE) ..10-7.. 7 b.g. Strong Gale — Geeaway (Gala Performance USA) 741. Rangy brother to Laura Lugs (IRE) and Bitofamixup (IRE), and half-brother to Azurlordshipleases, and to NH flat winners, Skinaway and Stand Easy (IRE). NH '2000 r1 p0 (7th in 2m4f110y Nov Hdle:

bhnd early, tailed off). Novicey but displayed promise on his first run over fences, and showed the benefit of experience when driven out to score over 3m2f at Folkestone. A scopey sort with plenty of improvement left in him, and could develop into a useful Hunter Chaser. If he is only as half as successful as Bitofamixup it will be a worthy achievement. *M. Roberts — E. Sussex & Romney Marsh.* 1333 (3mH), 1536 (3m2fH).

GALE BLAZER ..8-12.. 8 br.m. Strong Gale — Royal Blaze (Scallywag) u. Rangy unfurnished. Dam is sister to Gray Rosette (*qv* '99 Annual). NH FLAT '97 r1 p0 (well tailed off last). P-t-P '99 r2 p0 (6th, and pulled up 1). Beaten 30 lengths when sixth on her first attempt over the full trip in '99, but failed to survive the first without mishap on her only outing since. *A. Wakeham — Middleton (B.J. Gillies).* 235 (OMa).

GALE TOI (IRE) ..—.. 12 br.g. Strong Gale — Zitas Toi (Chinatown) pfp. Tall workmanlike brother to Ginger Pink and Irish Pointing and Hurdles winner, Gales Way, and half-brother to Irish Pointing winner, Shopwell. Dam won 3 Points in Ireland. IRISH FLAT '95 r1 p1 (3rd). IRISH NH FLAT '93 r5 w2 p1 (3rd). IRISH NH '93/7 r19 w1 (2m Hdle) p6. NH '97/8 r5 w1 (2m Ch) p4 (3rds). P-t-P/HUNT CH '99 r7 w3 (Hunt Chses, 2m110y-2m5f) p0; 4th, 7th, unseated 1, and pulled up 1. In his element when landing three sub-3m Hunter Chases in '99 (rated 10-12), but never going in an interrupted 2000 campaign when clearly not right. Speedy and a bold jumper — though caught out at Bechers this year — and can handle most surfaces adeptly. Might revive in 2001, but a watching brief is advised until he does perk up. *R. Cook — Surrey U. (Chris Elliott).* 61 (MO), 921 (2m6fH), 1531 (2m110yH).

GALLANT EFFORT (IRE) ..8-0§.. 13 b.g. Thatching — Meeting Adjourned (General Assembly USA) p7. Tall rangy. Dam won 2 Irish flat, 8-11f. FLAT (worn eyeshield) r10 p1 (3rd in Sell). NH '91/4 (visored 1) r37 w5 (4 Hdles, 2m2f-2m4f, 3 on all-weather, and 2m5f Ch) p17 (beaten ½/ or less 4). P-t-P '97/9 r24 p6 (3 2nds, last once); pulled up 4, unseated 1. Plods incredibly badly nowadays and was so far behind in his latest start that the rider had to pick his way through the crowd after jumping the last. A safe conveyance for Charles Sclater, but unsuccessful in all his 26 Points and sure to bow out that way. Regained blinkers in 2000. *C. Sclater — S. Dorset (Sarah Clarke).* 561 (O), 736 (Cnr).

GALLANT LORD (IRE) ..9-8.. 12 ch.g. Mister Lord (USA) — Knockantota Star (Gail Star) pp1. Strong-topped brother to jumping winner, Star Of David (IRE). IRISH P-t-P '95 r3 w1 (6 plus unplaced Mdn) p0; slipped up 1. NH '96/7 and '99 (from Mrs L. Jewell's) r6 p0 (pulled up in 2 Hdles, and well tailed off last and pulled up 3 in Chses). Useless when pulling up in seven of his first eight attempts in the present ownership, and had absences of 18 months and 16 months amongst them, but sprang a shock for Ben Hitchcott when dropped to a Restricted at Charing. It was a bad race, but it at least justified having kept him in training for five previously fruitless years. *P.J. Allen — Cambs Univ (Paul McNicholl).* 920 (3mH), 1026 (2m5f110yH), 1104 (R).

GALLANT MAJOR ..9-8.. 9 ch.g. Infantry — Miss Gallant (Gallo Gallante) p33231. Tall rangy owner-bred half-brother to Dunnellie (*qv*). NH FLAT '96 r1 p0. NH '96 and '98 r3 p0. P-t-P '99 r5 p1 (3rd); 4th, 5th, pulled up 1, and fell 1. Generally struggles to get the trip, but could not be begrudged his Aspatria success after four consecutive placings. Had nothing in hand when victorious and aided by the sound surface and Andrew Robson's vigorous urgings. Needs to improve for Restricteds, but has the right attitude and may have the scope to do so. Has been tried in a tongue-strap including unsuccessful. *Mrs C. Johnston — Cumberland F.* 44 (OMa), 114 (OMa), 364 (CfMa), 665 (OMa), 913 (CfMa), 1367 (OMa).

GALLATIN (IRE) ..9-1-.. 8 gr.g. Brush Aside (USA) — Satelite Lady (General Ironside) f. P-t-P '99 r3 p0 (4th, 5th, and pulled up 1). Showed some promise in '99, but sadly killed in a fall at Larkhill in January. *J. Chromiak — Portman (Louise Alner).* 12 (OMa).

GALZIG ..—.. 13 b.g. Alzao (USA) — Idabella (FR) (Carwhite) pp. Close-coupled half-brother to 2 flat winners (one in Hong Kong), including Stapleford Lass. Dam won at 9f in France. IRISH FLAT r8 p0. IRISH NH '91/2 and '94 (blinkered 1) r18 p2 (3rds). IRISH P-t-P '95 r7 w2 (inc 7yoplus Maiden on disqualification) p3; fell 1. P-t-P/HUNT CH '96/9 r17 w2 (Confined and Ladies) p7 (5 2nds: and inc 3 2m5f110y Hunt Chses); pulled up 6. Showed improved form when switched to Ladies races in '98 (rated 10-2), but pulled up in just three starts since changing hands and looks a spent force now. Has often looked a short-runner in the past. *Hon Gerald Maitland-Carew — Lauderdale (Nick & Kirsty Hargreave).* 186 (O), 419 (Cf).

GAMAY ..10-8.. 11 b.g. Rymer — Darling Rose (Darling Boy) u212111. Sparely-made half-brother to Rose Orchard (dam of Nuclear Beach (*qv*). NH '97/8 r9 w1 (3m Nov Hdle) p1 (head 2nd); pulled up 2. P-t-P '95/7 r9 w1 (Maiden) p3 (2 2nds; and 3rd of 4); fell/unseated 2, and ran out 2. Landed a Worcester Novice Hurdle after Pointing in '97 — Bullens Bay (*qv*) was third — and only just collared in a Handicap at Huntingdon later in the season, but had spent a year on the sidelines prior to his return to Hunt racing in 2000. Quickly rediscovered his form and though he found some simple opportunities his defeat of Iranos at Ston Easton was a useful effort. Not an easy ride and suited by exaggerated waiting tactics as he often hangs when in front, but has a turn of foot and handles most surfaces though never risked on anything quicker than good. Will surely be placed to advantage again in the future. *J.J. Boulter — S. Dorset (Nick Mitchell & John Boulter).* 5 (Cv&nr), 34 (MO), 209 (M), 402 (O), 735 (MO), 1177 (O), 1306 (C).

PLATE 54   1306 Cotley Countryside Alliance Club Members 10yo&up: Gamay (N. Mitchell), 1st
PHOTO: Brian Armstrong

GAME DRIVE (IRE) ..—.. 9 b.g. Dancing Brave (USA) — Twixt (Kings Lake USA) fpfpp. Sturdy half-brother to 3 flat winners (2 abroad, including Bon Point — useful in France). Dam won 2 French flat at around 7f. NH FLAT '96 r4 p0. NH '97 (for K. Morgan, tried tongue-tied) r1 p0 (tailed off and pulled up in Hdle). A very dodgy jumper who never completes the course. *Mrs J. Johnson & A. Betts — Quorn (Julie Johnson).* 373 (CfMa), 514 (OMa), 1011 (CfMa), 1220 (OMa), 1420 (OMa).

GAME GUNNER ..8-7.. 9 b.g. Gunner B — The Waiting Game (Cruise Missile) 48. Big heavy-topped. Dam is sister to Snaffles (qv 2000 Annual). Grandam, Suntino, won a Maiden and placed 7 (appallingly ridden, or would have had a stack of wins). Plodded to completion in Maidens, but his better effort was first time out. Looks the type who will be very difficult to get fit, and is possibly worth another chance. *Miss B. Lewis — Warwicks.* 786 (OMa), 1423 (OMa).

G-AND-T ..9-0.. 8 b.m. Gildoran — Littledrunkgirl (Carlingford Castle) p3. Half-sister to Rifleman Johnston. Dam won 2 Irish Points including an Open when ridden by Adrian Maguire and owned by Tockie McKie. P-t-P '99 r3 w1 (dead-heat Maiden) p0; 6th, and fell 1. Adjudged to have dead-heated with Final Analysis at Kingston Blount last year (looked to win outright), but only managed two outings this season with a 16 week gap between them and presumably suffered a setback. Still young enough to atone if 100 per cent in 2001. *Mrs J.M.E. Mann — Warwicks.* 38 (CR), 1442 (R).

GANGSTER ..10-4.. 7 b.g. Gunner B — Moll (Rugantino) 1432. Tall good-topped half-brother to Rymolbreese, Kelly's Court and Sharpside, and to jumping winner, Seabrook Lad. Dam won 2m5f Nov Hdle at 50-1. Made an ideal start when scoring easily at Southwell, and has lost little in defeat since. Twice made the frame behind smart Bill Warner novices (Union Man once, with subsequent Hunter Chase winner Springfield Rex second; and Shoemaker, who only had one and a half lengths to spare), and was possibly unsuited by the very soft ground when third at Kimble. A good jumper for a learner, and should soon be placed to advantage again. *Sir Michael Connell — Pytchley (Caroline Bailey).* 372 (CfMa), 871 (R), 1146 (R), 1419 (R).

GARETHSON (IRE) ..—.. 10 b.g. Cataldi — Tartan Sash (Crofter USA) pp. Tall strong brother to Ballymaloe Boy (IRE). IRISH P-t-P '95/6 r8 w2 (looked beaten both, but twice awarded a dead-heat!) p1 (3rd); pulled up, and fell 2. NH '96/9 (for Miss H. Knight, bought for 30,000) r18 w2 (2m4f-2m6f Chses) p7 (short-headed once). The winner of four races on good or easy surfaces, but generally a major disappointment under Rules, and often let down by his jumping. Carried plenty of condition and did not impress when pulled up in Opens three months apart for the new yard. *A. King — V. of Aylesbury.* 61 (MO), 1205 (MO).

GARNWIN (IRE) ..—.. 11 b.g. Strong Gale — Lisnamandra (Le Bavard FR) pp. Small. Dam is sister to Arctic Bard (*qv* '93 Annual). NH '95/9 (for N. Henderson) r26 w5 (2m4f Hdle, and 4 Chses, 2m4f-2m5f; inc 4-timer) p4 (short-headed once). Formerly suited by firmish ground, but last scored in March '97, and is a very disappointing lacklustre customer these days. Has pulled up six times and fallen once when unplaced on his last 11 outings. Used to have a tendency to idle in front, but now idles throughout, and probably does not feel well. *Mrs S. Messer-Bennetts — N. Cornwall.* 1047 (Cf), 1638 (L).

GARRISON COMMANDER (IRE) ..—.. 12 b.g. Phardante (FR) — Rent A Card (Raise You Ten) *p*0. Strong lengthy brother to Irish NH flat and Hurdles winner, Shanes Hero (IRE), and half-brother to Reydon, to jumping winner, Yorkshire Edition (IRE), and to Irish Hurdles winner, Pair Of Queens. NH '94/6 r7 p3 (inc 2 Chses). HUNT CH '98 (for Mr R. Ogden) r1 w1 (3m1f Hunt Ch) p0. NH Mar '00 r1 p0 (pulled up in 2m4f110y Amat Rdrs HCap Ch: *hld up, hdwy 5, blun & pu 7*). Often looked too tubby under Rules, but appreciated the drop in class when beating none other than Balisteros in a Kelso Hunter Chase on his only appearance in '98. Clearly stricken again since and soon became tailed off when beaten furlongs at Aintree. *P. Townsley — Surrey U.* 921 (2m6fH).

GARRISON FRIENDLY (IRE) ..9-11.. 8 b.g. Buckskin (FR) — Ikeathy (Be Friendly) u43. Smallish workmanlike half-brother to Another Garrison (IRE). Dam won at 5f in Ireland, and won 2m5f Hdle and 3 2m Chses there. IR 22,000 3-y-o. IRISH P-t-P '97 r4 w2 p0; pulled up, and fell at last (might have completed hat-trick). NH '98/9 (for N. Henderson; blinkered final) r11 w1 (3m Ch) p3 (2nds; 2 Hdles, and distant last in Ch). Bought Doncaster, Nov for 11,000. A sketchy jumper of regulation fences and not an easy ride, but showed signs of a return to form when ten lengths under a seven pound penalty in a Confined. Whipped home in unorthodox fashion (earning his partner a caution), and it might be worth trying a competent jockey on him. *N. Wilson — Hampshire (Chris Goulding).* 216 (Cnr), 1282 (O), 1509 (Cf).

GARRYSPILLANE (IRE) ..10-6.. 9 b.g. Royal Fountain — Lucylet (Kinglet) 23113. Workmanlike half-brother to Luciman (IRE) and Pharmistice (IRE), and to Hurdles winner, Supreme Fortune (IRE). Dam won NH flat and 3 Hdles (2m-2m2f). IRISH P-t-P '97 r3 p1 (2nd); unseated 1. IRISH NH '96/7 r2 p0 (inc last in Hunt Ch). P-t-P '98/9 r6 w3 (Club Maiden, Restricted and Intermediate) p2 (2nds); and pulled up 1. Does well from limited opportunities and showed improved form in 2000, but no easy ride and has to be held onto for as long as possible. Looked sure to win on his reappearance, but got to the front too soon and weakened close near the finish and almost suffered a similar fate at Sandon. Had nothing to beat in his Members where blinkers were tried for the first time, but not disgraced behind Lord Harry and a rejuvenated My Nominee (who had finished behind him at Sandon) on his Hunter Chase debut at Bangor subsequently. Usually sent off favourite or thereabouts and might prove good enough to tackle Open company in 2001. *M.T. Mann — Wheatland (Paul Jones).* 529 (Cf), 781 (Cf), 1128 (Cf), 1529 (M), 1559 (3m110yH).

GATCHOU MANS (FR) ..10-4.. 7 gr.g. Royal Charter (FR) — Vindjica Mans (FR) (Quart De Vin FR) u3u223. Sparely-made. FRENCH FLAT '97 r2 p0. FRENCH NH '98/9 r17 w2 (2m4f Ch at Lion d'Angers and 2m6f 110y cross country at Durtal) p1 (3rd). Has begun to run quite well in Ladies Opens after a sticky start, but is no match for the likes of Spring Gale or Imperial Dawn. His stable are often enterprising when placing their charges, and he might be rewarded if they cast their net further afield to avoid the local stars. Certainly deserves a success. *Mr & Mrs A.G.C. Howland Jackson — Suffolk (Ruth Hayter).* 84 (L), 287 (L), 608 (L), 758 (L), 939 (L), 1183 (L).

GAVASKAR (IRE) ..—.. 12 b.g. Indian King (USA) — Sovereign Bloom (Florescence) p. Tall half-brother to 5 winners (2 abroad). Dam won at 6f in Ireland. NH FLAT '93 r1 p0. NH '93/9 (blinkered/visored 5; for Miss S. Baxter; previously for A. Streeter; previously for J. Cullinan, bought for 3200; won previously for G.B. Balding) r29 w1 (2m1f Hdle) p2; inc Sells; very poor in Chses. Sold Doncaster, Nov for 1100. Gained his sole win in May '94, and has followed three consecutive prizes with 22 unplaced efforts. An indifferent jumper and woefully slow, and his outlook is anything but sunny. *S. Halliday — Meynell & S. Staffs.* 781 (Cf).

GAY CAVALIER ..—.. 7 b.g. Almoojid — Indomitable (AP) (Indian King USA) upf. Small very light-framed owner-bred half-brother to Gaysun (Chasing winner since Pointing). Has major jumping and steering problems at present, but comes from the same mould as his gallant little half-brother, and can possibly do better if he ever learns to settle. *R.G. Gay — S. Cornwall (Mike Biddick).* 848 (R), 1049 (CfMa), 1262 (OMa).

GAY RUFFIAN ..—.. 15 b.g. Welsh Term — Alcinea (FR) (Sweet Revenge) pp. Small light-framed half-brother to 2 winners in Hong Kong, including Top News (IRE) (previously successful in Ireland). Dam won 2 5f races. FLAT r16 w1 (13f) p4 (inc 3 Sells, inc short head and neck 2nds). NH '89/95 and '97/8 r55 w11 (6 Hdles, 2m-2m4f, inc £5443 prize, and 5 Chses, 2m-3m2f, inc £5095 prize, inc hat-trick) p14; fell at 7th in '94 Grand National. P-t-P/HUNT CH '96/7 (for Miss C.D. Dyson) r7 p2 (remote last of 3 once); and last pair 5. Made all to gain the last of his 11 wins over jumps in a Uttoxeter Selling Hurdle in April '98, but a beaten favourite there next time and resurfaced over 18 months later to act as schoolmaster to Charlotte Hicks. Only went a maximum of two miles and looks well past his sell by date now. *Miss C. Hicks — Cotswold.* 218 (L), 335 (L).

GEISHA ..—.. 9 b.m. Royal Vulcan — Maycrest (Imperial Fling USA) u. Close-coupled attractive half-sister to 2 flat winners. NH FLAT Feb '97 (for P. Webber) r1 p0. NH '97/8 (for N. Babbage) r3 p0. Sent off favourite for a weak elders Maiden, but parted with the rider when close up after two miles. May have some ability, but getting her to the racecourse seems to present many problems. *Mrs M. Scudamore — Cotswold.* 893 (OMa).

GEMINI MIST ..9-11.. 10 b.m. Ardross — Festive Season (Silly Season) 31R14. Compact owner-bred half-sister to Arctic Revel (*qv*). NH FLAT '95/6 r4 p1 (3rd). NH '96/9 r10 p0; inc Sell; last time, and pulled up 1 in Chses. P-t-P '99 r3 p0 (4th, unseated 1, and slipped up 1). Hopeless under Rules and hindered by a novice in her first season Pointing, but quickly struck up a good relationship with Claire Stretton and finally got home in front at the 19th attempt at Ston Easton. Won again at Kingston St Mary (the jockey making up for a horlicks of a ride in her Members), but will find matters more difficult in future as was demonstrated when 22 lengths last of four in her first Intermediate. Wears blinkers. *Mrs N. Dutfield — Blackmore & Sparkford V., & Axe V.H.* 520 (OMa), 738 (OMa), 926 (M), 1240 (R), 1607 (I).

GEMOLLY (IRE) ..9-11§.. 8 b.m. Be My Native (USA) — Hayhurst (Sandhurst Prince) 21r. Small light-framed half-sister to a winner in Italy. Dam won 2 2m Hdles in Ireland. FLAT r4 p0. NH '97/9 (bought for 700; debut for M. Meade; visored 3) r13 p1 (3rd); inc Sells; inc pulled up 5, and unseated. Stays really well and proved she can do it when she chooses when landing a youngsters Maiden at Hornby Castle under a very good ride from Clive Mulhall, but is often reluctant in the early stages, and needs much driving. A nasty-tempered little cow, and hospitalised the owner when kicking him in the stomach at the start at Dalton Park before declining the first fence. *R.E. Barr — Cleveland (Christine Barr).* 169 (OMa), 379 (OMa), 503 (R).

GENERAL ASSEMBLY (IRE) ..10-1§.. 9 b.g. Pharly (FR) — Hastening (Shirley Heights) 513217. Strong-topped rangy half-brother to flat winners, General Academy (English-trained, but scored in Rome) and Alacrity. Dam, unraced, is from family of Kris and Diesis. IR 26,000y. FLAT (won at 3 for H. Cecil) r14 w1 (13f) p2 (behind Cecil stablemates then!). NH '98/9 (for G. Margarson, bought for 2000, blinkered last 2) r10 p3 (3rds); also 4th thrice. Beat Dato Star by seven lengths when winning on the flat, but has long been a frustrating individual, and rarely consents to do his best. A safe jumper in Points and scored on his merits at Cottenham, but made very heavy weather of landing a five-runner Open at Fakenham, where he looked held until Prince of Saints virtually fell four out. Was 4-6 on that occasion, and beaten at 4-5 previously, so certainly makes his supporters suffer. Nigel Bloom has done very well to coax him to two victories. *P.P. Hall — W. Norfolk.* 17 (O), 176 (O), 320 (O), 771 (O), 1288 (O), 1586 (CN).

GENERAL BRANDY ..9-12.. 15 b.g. Cruise Missile — Brandy's Honour (Hot Brandy) p15. Lengthy unfurnished brother to The Difference. Dam 'hates racing' pulled up 1, refused 1, and unseated 1 in Points. Grandam, Honour Again, pulled up in 2 Points. NH '93/5 r21 w2 (3m Chses) p2. P-t-P/HUNT CH '96/9 r14 w3 (inc Open) p3 (2 3rds); failed to finish 4 (fell/unseated 2). Landed his Members for the third year running following an easy prep race a week before thus winning his fourth race at Hutton Rudby. Far from disgraced for an oldie when around 16 lengths fifth in a Ladies subsequently and few would bet against him winning at the Hurworth for a fifth time in 2001. *E.W. Tuer — Hurworth (Grant Tuer).* 504 (O), 619 (M), 806 (L).

GENERAL GEORGE ..—.. 8 br.g. Contest (USA) — Right Rosy (Riberetto) ppp. Dam, half-sister to Heninski (*qv* '00 Annual), won Maiden and placed 2 '95/6 and '98 (pulled up 3 for Mr Oseman). P-t-P '99 r2 p0 (last, and unseated 1). Has yet to get competitive, but gives the impression that he is struggling to get the trip. Needs to become more amenable to restraint if he is to achieve anything in his third season. *D.J. Oseman — N. Ledbury (Chris Hooley).* 744 (R), 900 (OMa), 1092 (OMa).

GENERAL GIGGS (IRE) ..9-11.. 13 br.g. Sandalay — Cold Sea (Arctic Slave) 48p. Strong compact half-brother to two Irish Pointing/Chasing winners, including Bering Strait. IRISH P-t-P '92/3 r11 w1 (5&6yo Maiden); pulled up 2, and unseated 1. NH '97 r1 p0 (pulled up). P-t-P/HUNT CH '94/5 and '98/9 r21 w2 (inc 2m6f110y Hunt Ch) p6 (5 2nds, and last of 3); fell/unseated 3. Showed greatly improved form to land a 2m6f Hunter Chase at Market Rasen in '95, but spent most of the next two years on the sidelines and was gaining his first success since when providing Emma Smith with her first success in '99. Soundly beaten in the current yard otherwise and appeared to go wrong at Hackwood in April. Usually blinkered. *R.F. Prideaux — S. Dorset.* 209 (MA), 326 (L), 886 (C).

GENERAL JACKIE (IRE) ..9-11.. 11 b.g. Supreme Leader — Carry On Jackie (David Jack) 15. Small compact hobdayed half-brother to Lean Ar Aghaidh and Lean Ort, to Irish Pointing winner, Lean Den Obair, and to an Irish NH flat winner. Dam won 2 5f races and 2m Hdle in Ireland. NH '95/6 r7 p1 (2nd of 3). P-t-P '97/9 r9 p1 (remote 3rd of 4); last, pulled up 6, and unseated 1. Had every chance when almost falling at the last flight of hurdles on his racecourse debut, but hopeless since until stumbling across a feeble Maiden at Rodmell where superior fencing won the day. Recorded a slow time and well held in a Restricted subsequently so a follow up might be a tall order. Wore a hood in '98. *R.V. & R.P.T. Mair — E. Sussex & Romney Marsh (Miss A. McCabe).* 1213 (OMa), 1393 (R).

GENERAL TYPHOON ..9-6.. 10 ch.g. Nearly A Hand — Steel Typhoon (General Ironside) 5u15p. Brother to Tactix (Hurdles winner since Pointing). P-t-P '99 r3 p1 (2nd); 5th, and unseated 1. Rather a late beginner, but made amends for a disappointing effort at Stafford Cross last year when landing an older horses Maiden convincingly at Charlton Horethorne in April. A beaten favourite in a Restricted next time (not for the first time) and needs to gain consistency to figure more prominently in them. Seems suited by top-of-the-ground. *R.J. & Mrs V.A. Tory — S. Dorset (Mary Tory).* 7 (OMa), 261 (R), 957 (CfMa), 1309 (R), 1467 (R).

GENEREUX ..9-3.. 8 ch.g. Generous (IRE) — Flo Russell (USA) (Round Table) 46. Neat smallish half-brother to 8 winners (6 abroad and one in Ireland, including Flow Back (flat) and Machikane Jindaiko (earned £500,000 in Japan). FLAT r1 p0. NH '97 r8 p5 (3rds). P-t-P '98 r1 w1 (Maiden) p0. Looked decidedly ungenuine over hurdles, but clicked at the first time of asking in Points when successful at Black Forest Lodge however there was a sting in the tail as he suffered a setback and was forced to miss the entire '99 season. Ran a fair race on his return, but never going or jumping well next time and his troubles are clearly not sorted yet. Wore a tongue-strap on his latest appearance, but it will take some masterly training from the Seaborough handler to get this one's career back on track. *J.R. Berkley — Cattistock (Richard Barber).* 164 (R), 406 (R).

GENEROUS DEAL (IRE) ..10-2.. 7 ch.g. Generous (IRE) — Honor To Her (USA) (Sir Ivor) ppppp5331. Small sturdy half-brother to 2 French flat winners (one scored later in USA). NH FLAT '98/9 (for Mrs L. Stubbs; too free in blinkers once) r4 p0. His success in a four-runner Bumper in soft rendered him ineligible for Maidens and Restricteds, and consequently took a long time to find his stride in Points, in which he has generally pulled hard and sometimes made too many mistakes. Improved as the season progressed, and the re-application of blinkers helped him to score comfortably at Higham on his final start. It was a weak Confined, but can possibly score again if he finds another. Over-rated on balance. *J.M. Turner — Suffolk.* 27 (I), 96 (I), 175 (I), 288 (CMod), 413 (I), 609 (I), 840 (I), 1017 (I), 1114 (Cf).

GENTLEMAN CHARLES (IRE) ..9-11.. 7 b.g. Jurado (USA) — Asinara (Julio Mariner) pb221. Tall workmanlike half-brother to flat and Hurdles winner Prophits Pride. Dam won 2 Irish NH flat. 10,000 4-y-o. NH FLAT '98/9 r2 p0. NH '99 (for P. Webber) r2 p0. Bought Doncaster, Aug for 5000. In front at the final fence before going down by one length and two lengths in Maiden seconds, and was not scoring out of turn when he lasted home in a youngsters Maiden at Charm Park. Finished tired, and will need to produce a bit more in the closing stages when he upgrades to Restricteds. *Lady Hewitt & Miss E.M. Hewitt — Middleton (Tony Walker).* 167 (OMa), 437 (OMa), 793 (CfMa), 1032 (OMa), 1233 (OMa).

GEORDIES EXPRESS ..9-13.. 9 b.g. Tina's Pet — Maestroes Beauty (Music Maestro) 3fu15. Plain unfurnished. P-t-P '98/9 r7 w1 (Maiden) p2; fell/unseated 3. Won his Maiden by a wide margin, but a consistently careless jumper and would have followed up in a Corbridge Restricted this season but for blundering Andrew Richardson out of the saddle at the final fence. Made amends (in an Open of all things) next time when forcing a dead-heat with Excise Man, but was outclassed in a Carlisle Hunter Chase subsequently. Might win again, but may not raise his rating much higher unless he treats the fences with more respect. *G.T. Bewley — Border.* 111 (R), 360 (R), 424 (R), 716 (O), 1154 (3m2fH).

PLATE 55　　716 Duke of Buccleuch's Mens Open: L to R Geordie's Express (A. Richardson), 1st, just shades Rainbow Times (C. Storey), 3rd, and Excise Man (J. Walton), 1st, but it was a dead-heat at the line
　　　　　　　　　　　　　　　　　　　　　　　　　　　　PHOTO: Alan Mitchell

GEORGE ASHFORD (IRE) ..9-12.. 11 b.g. Ashford (USA) — Running Feud (Prince Tenderfoot USA) p37556. Close-coupled half-brother to Bid For Tools (IRE) (qv). IRISH NH FLAT '94/5 r11 p4. IRISH NH '94/5 r7 w1 (2m2f Hdle) p1. NH '95/7 r18 w2 (2m5f Hdle and 3m1f Ch) p4 (inc 3rd in Sell Hdle). P-t-P '99 r1 p0 (pulled up). Last scored in August '96, but still gives the impression that some ability still lurks within him and ran a half decent race on the only occasion he was blinkered in 2000. Out of his depth in Hunter Chases, but a return to Points with a strong rider and headgear might do the trick. *I. Hooper & P. Johnson — Albrighton (P.R. Johnson).* 529 (Cf), 700 (O), 1086 (Cf), 1128 (Cf), 1293 (3mH), 1592 (4m2fH).

GEORGE DILLINGHAM ..10-8.. 11 b.g. Top Ville — Premier Rose (Sharp Edge) 21*5533*. Tall quite attractive half-brother to Provence and Blanchland, to flat and Hurdles winner, Final Stab (IRE), and to flat winner, Opera Ghost. Dam won 4 flat, 6-7f. FLAT r30 w3 (10-14f) p12 (inc short head, head and neck 2nds). NH '94/5 and '97/8 r10 w2 (2m-2m1f Hdles) p4 (2nds, beaten a head once). P-t-P '99 r3 p2 (remote 3rd of 4 once); and fell 1. NH '00 (for M. Jackson) r4 p3 (3rds); (5th in 2m4f HCap Ch: *mist 6, hdwy 8, wknd frm 3 out*; 5th in 2m3f Nov Ch: *rr, hdwy 11, one pce 3 out*; 3rd in 2m4f110y HCap Ch: *prom, mists 3 & 4, ld 9-11, wknd app 2 out*; and 3rd in 2m110y HCap Ch: *hld up & bhnd, hdwy 7, stayed on frm 3 out*). Quite a useful performer over the years and was still able to win on the flat at eight, but has done very well given few opportunities over obstacles. Loves plenty of cut in the ground and turned the tables on Hersilia when scoring at Eaton Hall. Only just held on that day and three miles has always stretched his stamina to the limit, but is now struggling at the shorter trips under Rules as well. Should be able to score again in Points, but will need to pick the right spot. *Mrs S.P. Gent — N. Ledbury (Annie Downes).* 566 (L), 780 (L).

GEORGETOWN ..9-8.. 10 ch.g. Ballacashtal (CAN) — Wessex Kingdom (Vaigly Great) f54f12p. Tall half-brother to Hurdles winner, Saxon Magic, and to 2 successful sprinters. Dam won at 5f. NH '97/8 (for J. Gifford) r9 p0 (poor Hurdler/Chaser; ran out when saddle slipped 1). A bad animal when trying a range of trips up to 3m3f under Rules, and his early Points were not encouraging, but gave a much improved display when landing an eight year old plus Maiden on firmish at Lifton (had nothing to beat, but apart from Butler John, nothing bettered his time). Disappointing at 8-11 when a length second on a return visit, but possibly did not care for the softer patches, and broke down after negotiating the plough at Umberleigh (one of several casualties there). Brought back in the horse ambulance, but became very distressed later in the day and had to be put down. Mr & Mrs P.G. Atherton — Four Burrow (Caroline Egalton). 106 (OMa), 311 (CfMa), 540 (OMa), 724 (CfMa), 1521 (CfMa), 1639 (R), 1671 (R).

GEORGIE GRACE ..—.. 8 b.g. Easter Topic — Full Of Love (Full Of Hope) ppR. Plain rangy. Dam, half-sister to Amsam (qv '88 Season Annual), won 2m Hdle (33-1 on hard — lucky) and placed 3; subsequently pulled up 1, and fell 1 in Points. P-t-P '98/9 (for Mr I. Johnson) r2 p0 (pulled up 1, and ran out 1). Useless on all known evidence, makes mistakes and has twice taken the cowards way out. *R.J. Andrews & B. Place — Tredegar F. (Deborah Faulkner).* 1093 (OMa), 1404 (OMa), 1455 (OMa).

GEREJ (POL) ..8-9.. 11 ch.g. Unoaprile — Gerda (POL) (Damon POL) pp5. Plain. P-t-P '98/9 r13 w1 (Maiden) p4 (3 2nds; and 3rd of 4); last twice, pulled up 3, and fell/unseated 3. Won a bad Maiden by 20 lengths when very busy in '98, but feeling the strain since and has managed just four appearances in the meantime. Finished early again in 2000 and seems to have problems. *Miss K.L. Thory — Fitzwilliam.* 16 (R), 86 (R), 120 (CfR).

GER'S GIRL (IRE) ..8-7.. 9 b.m. Venetian Gate — Timeless Beauty (Tumble Wind USA) p35p. Small. IRISH NH FLAT r1 p0. IRISH P-t-P '98/9 r7 p0 (pulled up 6, and fell 1). Produced a rateable effort when completing for the first time in a Point at the ninth attempt (nine lengths third of four), but was tailed off last next time, and then broke down in her Members. *D.W. Clark — Essex & Suffolk (Kelly Smith).* 239 (R), 760 (OMa), 941 (OMa), 1110 (M).

GET THE GIST (IRE) ..9-9.. 8 b.g. Ore — Rare Picture (Pollerton) 9212. Unfurnished half-brother to Chasing winner, Romany Creek (IRE). Dam is half-sister to Trim The Web (qv '95 Annual). Had a blatant school on his debut, but has been doing well in feeble company since, and given a typically patient ride by the 'Head Waiter' Paul Hamer when swooping to lead on the run-in in a Bonvilston Maiden on firm there next time, and had previously been beaten only half a length once, so further victories should be assured. *R. Kent — Ystrad Taf Fechan (Debbie Hamer).* 1223 (2m4fOMa), 1302 (OMa), 1457 (OMa), 1615 (R).

GIBRALTAR LADY ..7-7.. 8 ch.m. Gildoran — Gibraltar Girl (True Song) pp7p. Rangy rather unfurnished half-sister to Gibraltar Queen. Dam, half-sister to True Moss (qv '92 Annual), won 3m1f Hunt Ch and 7 Points and placed 10 (inc a Hunt Ch) for John Bailey. Grandam, Malaria, won 3 Ladies (inc 2 matches) and placed 16. P-t-P '99 (for Mr J.T. Bailey) r3 p0 (pulled up 3). Out of a tough and talented mare, but seems intent on running herself into the ground as quickly as possible and has only twice been able to stagger further than two miles. Careers about in splendid isolation until she hits a brickwall and has no chance of staying the full trip in her deluded state. Steve Craddock (who has surely never gone quicker on horseback) could be forgiven for reaching for the valium bottle the next time the owner rings for his services. Often mounted outside the paddock. *Mrs S.M. Wevill — Lamerton.* 311 (CfMa), 583 (2m5f110yH), 720 (M), 857 (CfMa).

GI GI BRACE (IRE) ..—.. 6 ch.m. Castle Keep — Cranagh Lady (Le Bavard FR) f. Angular half-sister to Cranagh Moss (IRE) (*qv*). Bought Tattersalls Ireland Aug, for 1071. Sent off favourite for her debut, but given a very bad ride by a novice until he decked her when tailed off two out. Evidently hurt by the experience. *D. Brace — Tregear F.* 487 (CfMa).

GIKONGORO ..—.. 8 ch.g. Dominion — Sea Charm (Julio Mariner) u. Close-coupled owner-bred half-brother to flat winner, Profilic, and to 2 winners abroad. Dam is half-sister to Bajan Sunshine (*qv* '88 season Annual). NH FLAT '97 (debut from P. Haslam's) r2 p0. Broke down in '97, and unseated three out when struggling on a very brief comeback three years later. *H.A.N. Orde-Powlett — W. of Yore.* 136 (O).

GILDED WAY ..—.. 7 b.g. Gildoran — Gamblingway (Gambling Debt) ufpp. Half-brother to Cool Wager (*qv*). Bought Malvern, Oct for 1700. Held back by consistently bad jumping to date, but did fall in the lead after two miles once, and could possibly achieve something if learning from his errors. *E. Haddock — Meynell & S. Staffs.* 298 (CfMa), 438 (OMa), 1422 (OMa), 1526 (OMa).

GILDORFLAME ..—.. 9 b.m. Gildoran — Regal Flame (Royalty) p. Small. Dam, half-sister to Caradon (*qv* 2000 Annual; also by Gildoran), won NH flat. Only jumped two fences before going lame at Upper Sapey. *Mrs S.L. Bates — Modbury H.* 704 (OMa).

GILDROM ..10-8.. 7 b.g. Gildoran — Drombay (Relkino) 12121. Compact well-made. P-t-P '99 r4 w1 (2m4f Maiden) p2 (2nds); and brought down 1. Looked a bright prospect when winning on his debut in a short Larkhill Maiden and has done well to make the first two in all seven completions since, but continually struggles to see out the trip and seems to need to get clear in the final mile and then hang on. Clocked outstanding times when successful at Didmarton and Guilsborough and would have outstanding claims in a Novice Hunter Chase on an easy track. Kept to ground close to good and benefits from having Mark Rimell in the saddle — and Rory Lawther at Guilsborough. *M.T. & J.K. Elliot — Heythrop (Ginny Elliot).* 14 (R), 219 (CMod), 388 (I), 749 (Cf), 1006 (Cf).

GILLAN COVE (IRE) ..11-3.. 12 b.g. The Parson — Shanban (Shackleton) 116p. Strong brother to Irish/English Chasing winner, Big Ben Dun, and half-brother to Sarpal and Runwellsuzie (who failed to finish in 11 races over fences — ten Points — between them), to Decent Sort (dam of Redmire *qv*), and to an Irish NH flat winner. Dam won an Irish Bumper. NH'94/9 (for R. Alner) r24 w3 (3m1f Hdle, and 2 3m3f Chses) p8 (inc neck 2nd of 24 in 3m Hdle at '96 Cheltenham Festival). IRISH NH May '00 r1 p0 (pulled up in 3m1f HCap Ch: *cl up, disp ld brief 6, 2nd to 12, 4th 5 out, wknd & pu nxt*). Moody and can be a complicated ride, but stays exceptionally well, and is best with some give in the ground. Produced two excellent efforts in Points, notably when beating Butler John and Miss O'Grady at Milborne St Andrew, and then came flying up the hill when under seven lengths sixth in the Foxhunters (had been tailed off six out, and set himself an impossible task; had done something similar at the same meeting four years earlier). Approaching the veteran stage, but does not have too many miles on the clock, and it will be interesting to see what he can achieve in future Irish stamina tests. *M.T. Lockyer & S. Vass — Portman (Susie Old; J.P. Byrne in Ireland).* 210 (MO), 308 (O), 584 (3m2f110yH).

GILLONE ..10-7.. 9 b.g. Gildoran — Speakalone (Articulate) 8u31112. Tall rangy brother to Doranslone, and half-brother to Brownslone, Hobnobber, Bucklelone, Bucks Law and Nelti. Dam won Maiden and last of 3, and grandam, All Alone II, won 16 Points, both for John Docker. P-t-P '98/9 r9 w2 (Club Maiden and Restricted) p1 (2nd); pulled up 2, unseated 1, and ran out 1. Has developed into a useful performer, but something of a character and is always mounted on course and taken to post early in a bid to keep him calm. Always sweats up and often takes a keen hold, but settles much better than he used to and is able to produce a turn of foot at the finish if required. Becoming something of a Garthorpe specialist with three wins and a second to Copper Thistle there. Avoids ground any quicker than good. A sound jumper who has been well handled by Joe Docker (and brother Nick) and would not look out of place in a Hunter Chase in 2001. *J.H. Docker — Atherstone.* 1 (C), 171 (O), 367 (Cf), 543 (I), 868 (Cf), 1072 (Cf), 1265 (O).

GILT AIR ..—.. 7 b.m. Gildoran — Bampton Fair (Free Boy) fp0. Big rangy trainer-bred half-sister to jumping winner, Bay Fair. Grandam, Eyecatcher, was 3rd in Rag Trade's '76 National (Red Rum was 2nd). NH FLAT 2000 (for M. Bosley) r1 p0 (15th of 18: *prom, sn wknd, t.o*). Made an inauspicious start in Maidens, as she took a crashing fall when weakening quickly after two miles on her debut and lay on the floor for several minutes, and then pulled up after almost refusing at the tenth. Wears a tongue-strap, and looks none too keen. *J.F. Long — O. Berks (J. Bosley; M. Bosley).* 57 (OMa), 1019 (2m4fOMa).

GINGER DUCHESS ..—.. 7 ch.m. Roviris — Haselbech (Spartan General) uppf. Half-sister to Sam Pepper, Jack Presto, Peter Presto and I'm A Bute. Dam, ridden by Shan Farr, was 2nd in 2 Points. Grandam, Dark Parting, was 4th in big field for Oakley Maiden on only start. Great-grandam, Dark Rate, won 3 Points. Gave unimpressive displays of jumping, and finally broke a leg at Lydstep. *T.R.R. Farr — Ystrad Taf Fechan (Shan Farr).* 602 (CfMa), 746 (CfMa), 834 (OMa), 1223 (2m4fOMa).

GINGER PUDDING ..9-6.. 8 ch.g. Infantry — Spring Tide (Take A Reef) 433. Very strong-topped compact owner-bred brother to Pudding. P-t-P '98/9 r4 p1 (3rd of 4); pulled up 2, unseated 1.

Hinted at ability in '99 and confirmed that impression this season with two fair placings, but beaten eight lengths minimum and seems to stand his racing badly. Has at least eliminated the blunders from his make-up, but still needs to find more improvement to score. *P. Rackham — W. Norfolk (David Wales).* 123 (OMa), 411 (OMa), 604 (OMa).

GIVE IT A WHIRL ..10-7.. 12 ch.g. Revolutionary (USA) — No Love (Bustiki) f33121p. Lengthy sparely-made brother to Round The Bend. NH '95 r3 p0 (last, and pulled up 2). P-t-P/HUNT CH '96/9 r21 w3 (up to Confined) p6 (4 2nds, of 3 once); fell/unseated 4, and pulled up 4. Enjoyed his most productive season with two wins, but sadly his last as he broke down when going for a Hunter Chase double at Huntingdon and has been retired. Often took a strong hold and occasionally jumped right, but very game on his day and dug deep for Tim Lane at Brocklesby Park to repeat his '99 success. May have been a shade fortunate to land his Hunter Chase as Stormy Words appeared to have matters well in control when stopping dramatically near the finish, but had looked booked for no better than third halfway up the run-in and his perseverance did him great credit. *Mr & Mrs R. Haddow — Cottesmore (Ross Haddow).* 18 (I), 48 (Cf), 116 (I), 229 (Cf), 369 (O), 1334 (3mH), 1542 (3mH).

GIVEMEYOURHAND (IRE) ..8-9§.. 12 ch.g. Parliament — Ottavia Abu (Octavo USA) pup6. Very lean half-brother to Irish flat and English/Irish Hurdles winner, Earp (IRE), and to a winner in Malaysia. Dam won mares Maiden in Ireland. IRISH P-t-P '94/7 r12 w1 (6yo&up Maiden) p4 (2nds); pulled up 5, and fell 1. NH '97/8 r7 p2 (4-11*l* 2nds, last once). HUNT CH '99 r4 p0 (6th, last 2, and pulled up 1). Placed in his first two Novice Chases after winning an Irish Maiden in '96, but fell next time and his form steadily went downhill. Remains eligible for Restricteds, but generally overfaced by running in Hunter Chases. Looks wrong. *F.W.W. Chapman — Border.* 419 (Cf), 908 (R), 1591 (3m1fH), 1602 (2m4f110yH).

GIVRY (IRE) ..9-11.. 11 b.g. Remainder Man — Beyond The Rainbow (Royal Palace) 34p1. Light-framed brother to Quenby Girl (IRE) and to Irish NH flat winner, One More Chance (IRE), and half-brother to Hobournes, and to flat winner, Heemee. NH '97 r6 p0 (4th, pulled up 1, and fell 1 in Chses). P-t-P '95 and '98/9 r9 w1 (Maiden) p1 (3rd); pulled up 3, and fell 2. Generally a disappointing performer, but sprang a 25-1 surprise on his final start when providing Nigel Parker with his first winner at Charlton Horethorne. Wore headgear for the first time in both successes (blinkers in the first, and a visor in the latest). Suited by a sound surface. Tried tongue-tied in the past. *N. & Mrs R.E. Parker — Seavington (Nigel Parker).* 330 (R), 519 (M), 734 (R), 958 (R).

GLACIAL TRIAL (IRE) ..10-5§.. 8 b.m. Glacial Storm (USA) — Protrial (Proverb) fr11. Workmanlike half-brother to Irish Hurdles winner, Nativetrial. Dam won Maiden in Ireland. IRISH P-t-P '98 r3 w1 (5yo mares Maiden) p1 (3rd); and pulled up 1. IRISH NH FLAT '98 r8 r1 p0. P-t-P '99 r2 w1 (Restricted) p0; and unseated 1. A mare of undoubted ability, but quirky and has not gelled with Alastair Crow — failed to complete in three outings together and favourite in the last two, but does go for Michael Worthington and the combination remains unbeaten in three attempts. Probably best when held up for as long as possible as she possesses a tidy turn of foot, but prone to hang and clearly never going to be all sweetness and light. Has shown winning form on all types of ground. Wore headgear on her last two outings which clearly helped, but it remains to be seen whether their effects will be long-lasting. *M.J. Parr — N. Salop (Sheila Crow).* 564 (I), 960 (Cf), 1321 (Cf), 1632 (I).

GLAD ALL OVER ..9-1.. 10 ch.m. Jupiter Island — Midsummer Gladness (Midsummer Night II) 2. Half-sister to Happy Blade. Dam, sister to Barmer Girl (*qv* '90 Annual), won 2m4f Hunt Ch and 8 Points and placed 9. P-t-P '99 r3 p0 (last, pulled up 1, and fell 1). Out of a tough front-running mare, but a late starter herself and has clearly not been easy to train. Disappeared after finishing second in a Maiden at Marks Tey in February in which a subsequent winner trailed home 15 lengths behind her. *D. Hays — Essex F. & U.* 323 (CfMa).

GLADYS ..8-0.. 9 b.m. Gypsy Castle — Dizzy Dora (Rubor) ppp. Lengthy light-framed plain half-sister to Bear Faced. Dam, sister to Barretts Hill (*qv* '87 Season Annual), won 2 Points and placed 4 (inc 2 poor 3rds in Chses) for Zoe Green. P-t-P '99 r6 p0 (last pair 2, and pulled up 4). Hopelessly inept, always tailed off and has only beaten one rival in nine starts. *Miss Z.A. Green — Cumberland.* 365 (CfMa), 978 (CfMa), 1367 (OMa).

GLAISNOCK LAD (IRE) ..10-4.. 9 b.g. Andretti — Owenette (Master Owen) 3f13. Workmanlike half-brother to The Lady's Partner, to Chasing winner, The Nigelstan, to successful Hurdler, Deep In Debt, and to Irish winners, Try Another (jumping) and The Lady's Knight (NH flat and Hurdles). NH '97/9 (for R.H. Alner) r10 w2 (3m-3m1f Chses) p2. P-t-P/HUNT CH '98 (for Mr J. Burley) r5 w3 (inc 2m5f Hunt Ch) p2 (dead-heat for 2nd, and remote 3rd of 4). His two requisites are a right-handed course and top-of-the-ground and a fair performer under such conditions, but gets few opportunities and sometimes looks moody. Quickened readily to win at Larkhill and ran well in one of the hottest Members races of the year on his final start. Blinkered once under Rules. *Mrs R. Rodwell — Blackmore & Sparkford V. (Jane Galpin).* 61 (MO), 210 (MO), 631 (MO), 952 (M).

GLAMDRING ..9-4.. 13 ch.m. Broadsword (USA) — Fairies First (Nulli Secundus) spfpf. Plain sparely-made half-sister to Bilquis. P-t-P '95/6 r7 p0 (fell/unseated 7). An abomination when owner-ridden in previous seasons and still remarkably unsafe, but does possess some speed and was still in front though running on vapour when exiting four out once. Usually looks dreadful in the paddock and acquired blinkers on her final start. May be capable of springing a surprise, but a typical chestnut mare and could not be trusted. *Miss J. Wellings — N. Staffs.* 293 (Cf), 564 (f), 588 (OMa), 864 (R), 960 (Cf).

GLEN CHERRY ..9-13§.. 15 b.g. Furry Glen — Our Cherry (Tarqogan) p24pp2. Tall rangy half-brother to Real Class, to Italian Chasing winner, Deep Runner, (IRE), to an Irish NH flat winner, and to jumping winner, Guinda (IRE). Dam won Bumper and 3m Ch in Ireland. NH '91/4 (blinkered last 5) r18 w4 (2m4f-3m Chses, inc £6937 prize) p4 (inc 3rd in Hdle); led til fell 2 out once; refused 1. P-t-p '95/9 r16 w5 (Mixed Open, Confined and 3 Clubs) p4 (3 2nds; and last of 3); refused 1, and pulled up 4. Farmed some very uncompetitive races to '98, but well beaten since and beat just three others in 2000. A very reliable jumper and can still bowl along in front for a while, but anno domini has got the better of him now. *P.A.D. Scouller — Garth & S. Berks (Nigel Allen).* 219 (CMod), 452 (M), 628 (Cf), 886 (C), 1108 (C), 1595 (Cf).

GLENCLOY (IRE) ..9-5.. 7 ch.g. Nad Elshiba (USA) — Lady Montana (What A Guest) 62p43321. Tall angular. IRISH P-t-P '99 r6 p1 (distant 3rd); pulled up 3, fell and unseated. Bought Malvern, July for 3800. A very poor performer who generally fails to get the trip, but rather surprisingly seemed better suited by front-running tactics when leading throughout the final two miles at High Easter. It looked an awful race, and beaten a minimum of 25 lengths in four of five placings previously, so is obviously going to have to find a great deal more for Restricteds. Gets on his toes, and has two paddock handlers. *B. Clark & Miss C. Lucas — Puckeridge (Mick Clark).* 22 (2m4fOMa), 97 (OMa), 236 (OMa), 516 (OMa), 605 (OMa), 845 (OMa), 1039 (OMa), 1382 (OMa).

GLENDINE (IRE) ..9-5.. 11 b.g. Glenstal (USA) — African Godess (Godswalk USA) 7p08p4p68. Small compact half-brother to Irish NH flat winner, That's The Suss. IRISH HUNT CH '93 r3 p0 (4th, and last 2). IRISH P-t-P '95/6 r13 w1 (6yo&up Maiden) p4; pulled up 3, and unseated 1. NH '97 r5 p2 (3rds in Hdle and Ch); last, pulled up 1, and fell 1 in other Chses. P-t-P '98/9 r6 w1 (Restricted) p1 (2nd); last pair 2, and pulled up 2. Goaded into action by Lawrence Lay once in '98, but indolent and will not go for the owner and tailed off without exception in 2000. Has been tried in blinkers to no avail. *D.P. Smith — Heythrop (Sarah Kellard-Smith).* 63 (I), 191 (Cf), 543 (I), 785 (I), 897 (I), 1013 (M), 1203 (I), 1356 (I), 1485 (I).

GLENELLY (IRE) ..—§.. 8 b.g. Lafontaine (USA) — Vic's Rose (Derring Rose) pR. Dam is half-sister to Applejo (qv '88 season Annual). IRISH P-t-P '98 r1 p0 (disqualified from 4th — no hunters certificate). IRISH NH '98 r2 p0 (pulled up 1). Looks to have an attitude problem, and was never going keenly before he ran out and unseated at the 11th at Corbridge. *Mrs D.B. Johnstone — Berwicks.* 626 (OMa), 1166 (OMa).

GLENPINE (IRE) ..10-5.. 10 b.m. Persian Mews — Ardagh Princess (Proverb) 119. Small close-coupled half-sister to Haveafewmanners (IRE) (qv). IRISH P-t-P '96/8 r14 p5; pulled up 5, and fell 3. IRISH NH '98/9 r8 w1 (3 Hunt Ch) p2 (inc 3rd in Ch). Looked to show improved form when completing a ready double at Hackwood (soft ground once), but was disappointing when finishing a fence last on firm at Wincanton. Had scored on rather similar going in Ireland, so the change of surface may not be a valid excuse. Her stable do well with their few Pointers, and likely to atone when she returns to them. *W. Smith — Hursley Hambledon.* 883 (Cf), 1248 (OMa), 1444 (2m5fH).

GLENSELIER (IRE) ..9-9§.. 12 gr.g. Roselier (FR) — Glentoran Valley (Little Buskins) 2p. Strong attractive fired brother to Irish Pointing and Chasing winner, Sister Rosza (IRE) (subsequently won Chasing in England), and half-brother to Cairneymount. Dam won 5 Irish Points. IRISH P-t-P '95/7 r12 p3; pulled up 5. P-t-P '98/9 (for Mr G. Bruckshaw & Miss L.G. Dalton) r6 w2 (Maiden and Restricted) p1 (3rd of 4); pulled up 1, and unseated 1. Looked doggy when trained by Heather Dalton and she did well to extract two wins from him, but would not go a yard for the new owner in two outings that year. Blinkered in his first three English Points, but not since. *I. Hudson — Oakley.* 509 (M), 1006 (Cf).

GLENVILLE BREEZE (IRE) ..9-4.. 12 b.g. Kambalda — Vina's Last (Royal Buck) p. Compact brother to Major Row and Knockumshin, and half-brother to Call Vina. IRISH NH FLAT r1 p0. IRISH P-t-P '94/6 r12 p1 (3rd); pulled up 6. P-t-P '97/9 r8 w1 (geldings Maiden) p1 (2nd); last pair 2, pulled up 3, and fell 1. Beat Kinnefad King at Lydstep in '99, but has not matched his development since and has beaten just one rival in three attempts since. Suffered his usual fate on his sole appearance in 2000 and seems unlikely to play too prominent a role in the future. *G. Greenhaf — Tredegar F. (Tim Jones).* 832 (R).

GLEVUM ..10-4.. 9 gr.m. Town And Country — Peggy Wig (Counsel) 11111123. Lengthy well-made half-sister to Grey Toupe'e and Platinum Springs, to flat winner, Andi Alja, and to successful Hurdler, Longriver Lady. Dam won 2 Sells, 7-8f. NH FLAT Mar/Apr '97 r2 p0. NH '97/9 (for N. Twiston-Davies) r13 p2 (3rds, inc Ch). Very moderate under Rules, and was a gift to present connections. Did them proud, and benefitted from some excellent placing when completing a six-timer at venues spread from Devon to Cambridgeshire. Also unearthed contests with five or less runners on three occasions, and is ideal for mares contests. Met her match in Slew Man at

Cothelstone (a bad blunder at halfway did not help), but is normally a determined front-runner. Thomas Scudamore shines on her and looks destined to become a big name in future, but he probably received a family wigging after misjudging the pace and galloping her into the ground at Stratford. Makes a few errors but is worth trying again over the bigger obstacles. *Mrs M. Scudamore — Cotswold.* 20 (OMa), 38 (CR), 202 (I), 357 (Cm), 752 (Cm), 967 (M), 1098 (C), 1645 (3mH).

GLOBAL LEGEND ..7-0.. 11 b.g. Oats — Mirthful (Will Somers) 1. Strong compact brother to Irish NH flat and Hurdles winner, Simenon, and half-brother to Jolejester (dam of Oh So Droll *qv*), and Gentle Jester, and to flat and useful Hurdles winner, State Jester. Dam won 3 flat, 9-10f. IRISH NH FLAT '94/5 and '97 r3 p1 (3rd). IRISH NH '95 and '97 r3 p1 (3rd). NH '97/9 (for I. Emmerson, bought for 8600; previously for H. Johnson) r13 p5 (inc 2 Chses). Bought Doncaster, Nov for 3800. Able, but has always been his worst enemy, and did not jump well over regulation fences. Finally came good at the 20th attempt in his seventh year, but it could hardly be called a race, as his sole opponent was a five year old pony making her debut. *R.J. Osborne — Ross H. (Chris Hooley).* 444 (M).

GNEVEGUILLA ..—.. 7 gr.g. Chilibang — Cwm Deri (IRE) (Alzao USA) pp. Tall good-topped half-brother to 2 flat winners (one in Sweden), including Kossolian. IRISH P-t-P '98 r5 w1 (4yo Championship, 3 ran) p0; pulled up 1. P-t-P '99 (for Mrs C. Banks) r3 p0 (pulled up 3). Won a very sub standard race for the Eagle Star Championship in Ireland in '98, but a non-stayer since his arrival in England and has pulled up in all five ventures. Ran in a tongue-strap in '99, but tubed this year and obviously badly wrong in his wind. *Mrs K.M. Price — N. Cotswold (Harry Wheeler).* 886 (C), 1607 (I).

GOAWAYOUTOFTHAT (IRE) ..10-4.. 7 b.g. Carefree Dancer (USA) — Creative Princess (IRE) (Creative Plan USA) 41p. IRISH P-t-P '99 r1 w1 (Confined Mdn). Returned the second fastest time of the 11 races at Maisemore, and was backed to beat Union Man next time, but weakened before three out and soon pulled up. His rating looks plenty high enough, but benefits from the assistance of Julian Pritchard, and may be able to justify it. *Mrs P. Duncan — Ledbury (Jelly Nolan).* 13 (R), 894 (R), 1267 (I).

GODDESS ..8-13.. 7 b.m. River God (USA) — Deaconess (The Parson) 3. Dam, sister to Hurdles winner, Holy Joe, won a Maiden and 2nd. P-t-P '99 r1 p0 (pulled up). Fifteen lengths last of three in an Eaton Hall Maiden on her only start in 2000 and difficult to evaluate at present, but her appearances are strictly rationed and the indication is that she is not easy to train. Might achieve something more tangible if she were able to stand a full campaign. *R.S. Williams — Cheshire.* 527 (OMa).

GOFORITGIRL ..9-0.. 9 b.m. Cruise Missile — Duvessa (Glen Quaich) pffppp. Leggy lengthy half-sister to Karicleigh Man and Karicleigh Boy (won Hurdle since Pointing), and to NH flat winner, Karicleigh Lad. Dam won Torrington Maiden and 2nd for Mr Eveleigh, and subsequently won 2 3m2f Chses. P-t-P '99 r1 p0 (pulled up). Not as awful as her form figures read, but struggles to get the trip and frequently let down by her jumping. Well supported at Bratton Down in May and was going well in second when falling a mile from home and as she receives excellent assistance from the saddle should find a race with some luck in 2001. *E.C. Eveleigh — E. Devon (Chris Down).* 11 (OMa), 738 (OMa), 1565 (OMa), 1654 (OMa), 1675 (OMa).

GOFORITKATE (IRE) ..—.. 8 ch.m. Carefree Dancer (USA) — Kemals Kate (Kemal FR) p. Half-sister to disqualified Irish Pointing winner, Clerhane Rose. IRISH P-t-P '99 r6 p3 (2nds); pulled up, and unseated. Sold Tattersalls Ireland Nov, for 3035. Supported at long odds despite looking backward at Newton Bromswold, but weakened and pulled up three out, and not seen again. Should have a chance in Maidens on her best Irish form, as she was only beaten half a length once. *V.T. Bradshaw — Worcs.* 513 (CR).

GOFORITMRSMULLIGAN (IRE) ..9-3.. 8 b.m. Mandalus — Cherry Dancer (Monksfield) pfp0. Lengthy sister to Irish Pointing and Hurdles winner, Mardon. Dam won Irish NH flat. IRISH P-t-P '98 r4 p1 (2nd); pulled up 1, and fell 1. P-t-P '99 (for Mr J.R. Weston) r9 w1 (Maiden) p2 (2nd of 3 twice); 4th, pulled up 4, and unseated 1. A weak finisher for previous connections, but managed a win in a poor race at Bredwardine. Totally out of control for the owner in 2000, but at least he had the sense to hand over the reins to another on her final start. Can show speed, but not a good jumper and did not look fit enough in the new yard. *P.M. Hall — S. Notts (Nick Pomfret).* 429 (C), 513 (CR), 791 (R), 871 (R).

GOING AROUND ..9-6.. 13 b.g. Baron Blakeney — Elect (New Member) 3p43p37u4. Small angular half-brother to Electress, and to Chasing winner, Parliamentarian (IRE). Dam won Hdle and 3 Chses, all 2m1f. NH FLAT r3 p2. NH '94/6 r11 w3 (2m3f-2m6f Hdles, inc £9400 prize) p2 (2nds); pulled up 3, and fell 1 in Chses. P-t-P '97/9 (for Mr M.H.G. Lang) r17 w2 (Confineds — one on a technical disqualification) p1 (3rd); pulled up 4, and fell/unseated 4. Began the '99 season with a defeat of Fawsley Manor at Kingston Blount, but failed to beat another rival in four subsequent attempts and changed hands after the season. Usually fails to see the trip out and only twice better than last in 2000. An inconsistent jumper, but generally a safe ride for a novice thought April Webb did have a few teething problems with him. *M. Sherington — Easton H. (Matthew Gingell).* 29 (Cf), 151 (3mH), 241 (C), 555 (Cnr), 603 (M), 756 (Cf), 939 (L), 1113 (L), 1288 (O).

GOING SOLO (U) ..—.. 8 b.m. Albutaman — Kincorra (unknown) f. Carried 13st 4lbs and made mistakes before crashing heavily at the fifth in her Members. *Miss E. Morgan — Monmouths.* 740 (M).

GOLDEN GUNNER (IRE) ..—.. 13 ch.g. Mazaad — Sun Gift (Guillaume Tell USA) ppppppp. Small compact well-made half-brother to several winners here and abroad, including flat and Hurdles winners, Gymcrak Cyrano (IRE) and River Wye (IRE) (latter also won Chasing). IR8600f, 17,500y. FLAT (won for M. Tompkins) r8 w1 (12f) p0. NH '91/4 (blinkered last 3; 3 wins for Mrs M. and late M. McCourt, bought for 10,000; 1 win previously for M. Tompkins) r19 w4 (2m Hdles, one on equitrack) p3; one run Enghien. Won five races to October '92, but was an extremely sorry spectacle when making an ill-advised return after a six year absence. Hopelessly short of stamina in Points, and useless in sub-three mile Hunter Chases. Regained blinkers on his final three appearances. *N. Thomas — O. Berks.* 474 (O), 884 (O), 968 (Cf), 1202 (M), 1341 (2m110yH), 1447 (2m4fH).

GOLDEN JESTER ..—..§.. 7 b.m. Gold Dust — Jesstrapaul (Tycoon II) RpRp. Sparely-made owner-bred half-sister to Montimezzo. Dam is half-sister to New Mill House (*qv* '97 Annual). Has very faulty steering, and all over the place when most unpleasant in her races to date. *G.J. Giddy — Torrington F. (Andrew Congdon).* 874 (2m4fOMa), 1390 (OMa), 1519 (CfMa), 1641 (OMa).

GOLDEN KNIGHT ..6-12.. 7 ch.g. Morston's Heir — Nocturnal Reverie (USA) (Assert) p5u. Sturdy owner-bred. Dam won at 12f. Hopelessly tailed off last on his only completion, and his bad jumping is highlighted by the wild wavings of the rider. *G.H. Barber — Essex F. & U.* 180 (2m4fOMa), 317 (M), 604 (OMa).

GOLDEN MAC ..8-7.. 14 ch.g. Court Macsherry — Pretty Damsel (Prince Hansel) 5u8u7u. Lengthy strong-topped half-brother to Idleigh's Comet and Detroit Davy (IRE), to Irish Pointing winner, Western Breeze, and to successful Hurdler, Pretty Gayle. IRISH P-t-P '91/4 r18 w1 (5yo Maiden) p2 (3rds); pulled up 10, and fell 2. P-t-P/HUNT CH '95/7 and '99 (for Hon Mrs A.C. Webb-Carter) r21 w1 (Club) p4 (3 3rds, 4 once, and last twice, inc Hunt Ch); pulled up 6, unseated 1. Produced a sprint finish to gain his first win for four years in '96, but has given the impression he may not be genuine (has hung badly, and blinkered/visored twice in '95). Partnered by beginners '99/00, and limbered up for the latest campaign in Hyde Park. Julian Barnard was widely fancied to fall off every time, so he can congratulate himself on failing to do so in 50 per cent of his attempts. *J. Barnard — E. Sussex & Romney Marsh (Di Grissell).* 25 (Cnr), 130 (CMod), 288 (CMod), 574 (4mMO), 706 (Cf), 830 (Cnr).

GOLDEN SADDLE (USA) ..—.. 7 b.g. Riverman (USA) — Rossard (DEN) (Glacial DEN) pp. Short-backed half-brother to 3 flat winners (2 abroad), including Unusual Heat (useful in Ireland/USA). Dam won 14 flat to 14f in Scandinavia and USA. IRISH FLAT r1 p0. FLAT r10 p0 (inc Sells; tailed off in blinkers final). NH '97/8 r3 p0 (tailed off — 5th of 6, last and pulled up). P-t-P '99 r1 p0 (unseated). Useless over hurdles and appeared not to get the trip when pulled up in both Points this year. *B. Hurst — S. Cornwall.* 933 (OMa), 1519 (CfMa).

GOLDEN SAVANNAH ..10-0.. 11 b.g. Presidium — Golden Pampas (Golden Fleece USA) 432543. Strong hobdayed half-brother to 2 winners abroad (one useful in Spain). FLAT r3 p1 (3rd of 4). NH '93/6 and '98 (blinkered 2) r18 w1 (2m Hdle) p1 (last of 3); pulled up 2, unseated 1. P-t-P/HUNT CH '96 and '98/9 r21 w3 (inc 2 Opens) p8 (3 2nds, ran a Hunt Ch); pulled up 4, ran out 1, and on floor 3. Managed an annual success in his three previous Pointing campaigns and still capable of decent efforts, but unlucky to come up against Blanville in his repeat bid for the V.W.H. Open particularly as the 6ft5in owner-rider was hampered by a slipping saddle in the closing stages. A sound jumper, but generally easy to beat and decent horses have nothing to fear from him. *A. Maculan — V.W.H. (Countess Susie Goess-Saurau).* 79 (O), 217 (O), 750 (O), 970 (O), 1205 (MO), 1357 (MOnr).

GOLDEN SAXON ..8-11.. 8 ch.g. Saxon Farm — Going After Gold (King's Ride) uu4p. Rangy half-brother to Gold Or Bust. Dam, half-sister to Street Trader (*qv*), was entered for Points as an 11yo in '96, but never appeared for what would have been a belated racecourse debut. NH FLAT '98 (for S. Brookshaw) r1 p0. Died when breaking his pelvis at Whittington. *Mrs S.M. Shone — Flint & Denbigh.* 776 (M), 816 (OMa), 1092 (OMa), 1153 (OMa).

GOLDEN SUNSET ..7-6.. 10 ch.m. Karlinsky (USA) — Bally River (River Beau) p6p5pppp. Small plain sister to Bally Sky. P-t-P '99 r6 p0 (last 2, pulled up 3, and unseated 1). Invariably lagging miles behind from an early stage, but managed to finish in front of another rival at the 10th attempt which represents a major feather in her cap as the owner-rider is famously non-competitive. *Miss P.D. Mitchell — E. Cornwall.* 159 (CfMa), 311 (CfMa), 540 (OMa), 721 (CfMa), 853 (Inr), 1043 (R), 1522 (CfMa), 1638 (L).

GOLD'N SHROUD (IRE) ..10-3.. 10 b.g. Shy Groom (USA) — Launch The Raft (Home Guard USA) p2422. Tall strong-topped half-brother to Black Rhombus (IRE). FLAT r8 p0. NH '94/5 and '97 r7 w1 (2m1f Hdle) p3; fell 2 (at last when clear on debut). P-t-P '97/8 r10 w2 (Confineds) p3 (2 2nds, of 3 once); pulled up 3, and unseated 1. Ended the '98 season lame and off the course the following season, but a fair performer on his day and looked to have been primed for the United Confined Hunts race following an easy spin round Chaddesley on his reappearance. Looked sure to win turning for home until his stamina gave out approaching the last and he had to settle for second best. Unsuited by the soft ground next time, but ended the season with two more honourable seconds and deserves to find compensation in 2001. Jumps well and is admirably suited by an easy three miles on top-of-the-ground. *J.W. Delahay — N. Herefords (Sally Pearson).* 611 (C), 862 (Cf), 1272 (Cf), 1463 (Cf), 1597 (MO).

GOLDOAK ..—.. 6 ch.g. Sunley Builds — Indian Election (Sula Bula) up. Good-topped attractive owner-bred half-brother to Black Oak (*qv*). Appalling twice, and only managed to clamber over a total of two obstacles. Gave the impression of never having seen a fence before. *T.E. Pocock — W. Somerset V. (Rosie Pocock).* 1094 (M), 1373 (OMa).

GOLDSTEANE .9-1.. 7 b.m. Gildoran — Banbury Cake (Seaepic USA) pp4p. Small compact home-bred half-sister to Second Amendment (*qv*). NH FLAT Oct '99 r1 p0. Tailed off in all her races to date, including when giving Sam Brodie his first ride and finishing fourth of five in the Bar bore. A safe jumper for a baby, and might possibly be able to go faster in time. *S.J. Connell — Grafton (Lady Annie Connell).* 872 (OMa), 1204 (OMa), 1257 (C), 1486 (OMa).

GOLD TALISMAN ..8-12.. 12 b.m. Scorpio (FR) — Jyponica (Wabash) pp. Tall lengthy well-made sister to Quango King. Dam won 2 Points and placed 11. P-t-P '96/7 and '99 r10 p3 (2 2nds); pulled up 6, and fell 1. Beaten between 11 and 30 lengths in her three placings, but usually pulled up and was tailed off when doing so after two miles twice in 2000. Stands little racing, seems difficult to get fit and will need a bad race in order to get off the mark. *P.T. Hollins — Cheshire (Sue Mullineaux).* 336 (R), 587 (M).

GOLF LAND (IRE) ..9-9.. 9 ch.g. Be My Native (USA) — Just Clara (Camden Town) 1Rp. Compact attractive. NH FLAT '96 r4 p2. NH '96/7 r5 p1 (3rd in Hdle); tailed off last in Sell final. NH '98/9 (for W.G. Reed) r4 p0. P-t-P '98 r2 p1 (2 fences last of 3); and fell 1. A poor jumper of hurdles, but finally got his act together at Friars Haugh where he looked in command when left clear at the last. Used to avoid soft ground under Rules and did not act on it when acquiring a tongue-strap on his final start. Not the easiest of rides and looks rather soft. *W.M. Aitchison — Border.* 718 (CfMa), 976 (R), 1162 (R).

GO NOMADIC ..10-3.. 7 br.g. Nomadic Way (USA) — Dreamago (Sir Mago) p321922. Compact. Dam, half-sister to Sonydee (*qv* '92 Annual), won 2 Points and placed 5 for the Atkinsons. Grandam, Dreamadee, won 14 Points and placed 11 (inc a Hunt Ch). Great-grandam, Sams Dream, won 2m1f Hdle and was 3rd in Ladies. P-t-P '99 r2 p0 (pulled up 2). Green and erratic when pulled up in his first three Points, but the penny soon dropped and dictated terms throughout when successful in a slowly-run 2m4f Maiden at Dalston. Acquired a tongue-strap after disappointing in his first Restricted, but subsequent placed efforts on differing ground at Alnwick and Corbridge suggest he will win in that grade though he needs to brush up his jumping technique. *D.G. Atkinson — Bedale.* 45 (OMa), 169 (OMa), 380 (OMa), 500 (2m4fOMa), 689 (R), 908 (R), 1162 (R).

GOOD FOR A LAUGH ..—.. 8 b.g. Idiot's Delight — Mekhala (Menelek) p. Big leggy workmanlike half-brother to Lady Rerico (dam of Paddy For Paddy *qv*), Kelly Murphy, Great Pokey and Young Brave. Dam won 2m Nov Ch. IRISH NH FLAT '90 r1 p0. IRISH NH '89/93 r26 w5 (2m Hdle, and 3 Chses, 2m1f-2m2f, inc £9750 prize) p9; 4 runs in England. NH '93/4 and '96/7 r24 w5 (2m-2m5f Chses) p8. P-t-P/HUNT CH '98/9 r8 w2 (2m110y Hunt Ch and Members) p1 (2nd); ran out 1, and pulled up 1. An admirable campaigner whose 12 wins and 18 placings netted £62,226 under Rules, and made a remarkable comeback which was fully chronicled in the 1999 Annual, but a non-finisher in three starts over the last two seasons and retirement surely beckons. Often wears a tongue-strap. *D. Walker — Spooners & W. Dartmoor (Mrs N. Walker).* 200 (O).

GOOD FOR A LOAN ..10-4.. 14 b.g. Daring March — Game For A Laugh (Martinmas) ppp611. Well-made good-looking brother to flat and Chasing winner, Allimac Nomis. Dam won 2 flat, 7-8f. FLAT (won for R. Lee; previously for A. Stewart, who trained the dam) r17 w1 (12f) p4 (beaten a head once). NH '90/3, '95 and '97/8 (for R. Lee, bought for 16,000, blinkered last 5) r26 w6 (4 Hdles, 2m-2m4f, and 2 2m Chses; one win equitrack) p5. A veteran who had not scored for five years until he notched a double during five days in May (25-1 at Bredwardine), but has had absences of 31 months and 19 months during that period. Good or preferably firm ground is vital to him, and hung right in the closing stages of both victories, suggesting that he was coming to the end of his tether over three miles. Connections did well to revive him after such a long spell in the doldrums, and remarkably returned the fastest time of the day twice (admittedly Brampton Bryan had turned into a skating rink, and the main aim of the contestants was to avoid slipping up). *M.W. Jones & E. Layton — N. Herefords (Mark Doyle).* 474 (O), 862 (Cf), 988 (O), 1272 (Cf), 1463 (Cf), 1544 (Cf).

GOOD (IRE) ..9-11.. 9 b.g. Persian Heights — Tres Bien (Pitskelly) 414. Compact half-brother to 2 flat winners (one in Italy), including Persian Lord. FLAT (tried blinkered/visored) r12 p0. NH '95/6 r3 p0 (last twice). P-t-P '99 r2 p1 (3rd); and last. Of no account on the flat or over hurdles, but finished quite well when third in a Lanark 2m5f Maiden last year (S B S B By Jove was upsides at the finish) and only had to toddle round to win his Members at Tranwell this term. Usually very much on edge beforehand and has yet to prove his stamina over the full trip. Wore a tongue-strap on his most recent start. *Mrs V. Jackson — Morpeth.* 494 (L), 1077 (M), 1427 (R).

GOOD JOB ..8-9.. 9 b.m. King's Ride — Oh So Ripe (Deep Run) p5pp. Small half-sister to The First One. NH FLAT '97 and '99 (for C. Mann) r4 p1 (3rd); tailed off and pulled up final. Bought Ascot, June for 950. Last but not disgraced on her only completion, and is possibly better than she has been able to show so far. Stoutly bred, but something seemed to be stopping her from getting the trip in 2000 (shin sore?). *Mrs S.K. Edmunds & J.H. Busby — Grafton (Sylvia Edmunds)*. 234 (OMa), 515 (OMa), 1010 (CfMa), 1270 (OMa).

GOOD KING HENRY ..9-8§.. 15 b.g. St Columbus — Cooks' Knife (Perhapsbury) 32674. Good-bodied brother to Angel Fare, and half-brother to Bramley Edge and Bob Grinder. P-t-P/HUNT CH '93/7 (tried blinkered) and '98/9 r37 w3 (inc 3m2f110y Hunt Ch) p8 (inc beaten head in Hunt Ch once; and 4 3rds, last twice, inc 2 Hunt Chses); failed to finish 17 (fell/unseated 4). Retired after eight consecutive seasons of service during which his finest hour was when winning a 3m3f Hunter Chase at Newton Abbot in '98. Generally temperamental and would have achieved more had he been more co-operative, but gave connections plenty of fun and bows out unharmed. *I.J. Widdicombe — Dart V. & S. Pool H.* 651 (M), 1047 (Cf), 1261 (Cf), 1514 (Cf), 1636 (Cf).

GOOD PROFIT ..9-0.. 12 ch.g. Meadowbrook — Night Profit (Carnival Night) 6623p. Strong quite attractive brother to Normans Profit, and half-brother to Gold Profit (dam of Overton Girl *qv*), Poppers Lad, Poppers Girl, Watchknowe Lad, Night Time Girl, Sound Profit and Poppers. Dam pulled up in 3 of 4 races for Billy Young (inc 3 Points). NH FLAT r3 p0. NH '95/6 and '98/9 r10 p1 (distant 2nd of 3); pulled up 3, unseated 1, and only beat Normans Profit once. P-t-P/HUNT CH '96/9 r20 p2 (last of 2 once); fell/unseated 4, and pulled up 8. Managed to double his number of placings over fences in 2000, but still clinging desperately to his maiden status after 36 races of one description or another. Came closest when blinkered for the first time in his Members, but the company was dreary and they were soon dispensed with. Amazingly the subject of a market move on his final start, but not surprisingly let his loopy supporters down. *W.G. Young — Lanarks & Renfrews, & Eglinton.* 113 (OMa), 423 (R), 659 (M), 977 (CfMa), 1123 (OMa).

GOOD THYNE GIRL ..—.. 9 ch.m. Good Thyne (USA) — Kentucky Calling (Pry) pf. Stocky half-sister to Musical Vocation (IRE). Dam, sister to Infielder (*qv* '93 Annual), won 2m1f Sell Hdle (also won similar over 2m, but disqualified) and placed 5; and subsequently no form in 3 Adjacents. 2000 4-y-o. NH FLAT Nov '96 (for Miss H. Knight) r1 p0 NH '99 (from R.E. Fowler's, bought for 1150) r3 p1 (distant last of 3); pulled up final 2. Died in a fall at Barbury Castle. *Miss J. Rees — O. Berks.* 260 (R), 1284 (OMa).

GORSEY BANK (IRE) ..9-8.. 9 b.g. Lancastrian — Yankee's Princess (Yankee Gold) 2u31p. Lengthy workmanlike half-brother to Irish winners, Jumped Bail (flat) and Delphi Lodge (IRE) (NH flat and jumping — useful). Dam won 2 8f races (inc Irish Lincoln) and 3 Hdles at around 2m in Ireland. IRISH P-t-P '98/9 r4 p0 (4th 2, and pulled up 2). Bought Malvern, July for 2100. Ran well on his English debut and again when a close third (unseated when odds-on in between), and gained his reward in a three-finisher Maiden at Bitterley. Tried a Hunter Chase next time, but went mental approaching the first fence, and the jockey had no option but to pull up. Had given no trouble previously, and could be worth respecting in a Restricted provided he does not get any more bees in his bonnet. *E.A. Thomas — N. Herefords.* 341 (CfMa), 617 (CMa), 891 (OMa), 1093 (OMa), 1293 (3mH).

GO UNIVERSAL (IRE) ..9-12.. 13 br.g. Teofane — Lady Dorcet (Condorcet FR) p38p. Good-topped half-brother to successful Hurdler and smart Chaser, Lord Dorcet (IRE) (earned over £100,000). Dam won at 9f in Ireland. NH '93/9 (for N. Chance; 5 wins previously for C. Brooks; 1 win previously for M. Bradstock) r24 w6 (2m4f-2m6f Chses) p5 (inc 3rd in Hdle; beaten head for £23,811 prize in '96 John Hughes, and earned £14,110 with 2nd in '96 Tripleprint Gold Cup); pulled up in '98 Grand National; inc 5-timer, one at Listowel (unseated 2 out when leading in previous race). Formerly smart, and was in cracking form between August and December '95, but has not scored since, and declined badly latterly. Gave one fair display in a Point, but it was very sad to see him pull up lame in his Members. *Miss S. West — Tedworth.* 210 (MO), 327 (O), 687 (2m6f110yH), 1279 (M).

GOVERNOR'S BAY ..—.. 10 gr.g. Governor General — Overseas (Sea Hawk II) pf. Leggy attractive half-brother to Sand Star (*qv*). FLAT to '94 r7 p0 (inc Sells). P-t-P '99 r3 p0 (pulled up 3). Pulls hard for about half a mile, but stops as if shot and there seems more chance of the Pope fathering a child than of him staying three miles. A waste of time and has been tried in blinkers and a tongue-strap. *Mrs A.P. Kelly — Flint & Denbigh (Stephen Kelly).* 1196 (OMa), 1323 (OMa).

GOWENBACKTODUDLEY ..—.. 8 b.m. Al Amead — Maria Slim (Owen Dudley) rpp. Light-framed sister to Slim Chance. Dam won a 2-finisher Maiden for Mr Latham (only beat 7 horses in 15 Points — 4 of them in one race). Jumped appallingly in three Maidens. Has a hideous name, and it is a pity that the opportunity to call her Fat Chance was missed. *J.T. Latham — Llangibby (Tim Jones).* 491 (CfMa), 951 (OMa), 1301 (OMa).

GOWLAUN ..9-2.. 12 b.g. Electric — Tura (Northfields USA) p. Tall half-brother to 4 flat winners (one in Germany), including Routing and Other Club (also successful Hurdlers). Dam won at 7f in Ireland. IRISH NH FLAT r2 w1 p0. NH FLAT r1 p0. P-t-P '97/9 r9 w1 (Members) p0 (last 2, pulled up 5, and unseated 1). Won an uncompetitive Hunt race in a slow time last year, but usually forced to pull up and has never stood his racing well. Pulled up after two miles at Guilsborough on his only appearance in 2000 and looks finished now. *W.J. Moore — Belvoir.* 1006 (Cf).

GRACELAND ..7-7.. 9 ch.m. Buckley — Ina's Farewell (Random Shot) p. Big lengthy half-sister to Our Tommy and Farebit, and to jumping winner, Ardrina. NH FLAT '97 r1 p0. NH '97/8 r3 p0 (10th of 11, and pulled up in Hdles, and remote last in Ch). P-t-P '99 (for Mr I. Baker & Mr K. Boddy) r4 p0 (last, pulled up 2, and unseated 1). Consistently dreadful, but at least she does not strut her stuff very often. Tried tongue-tied under Rules. *N.D. Tutty — Hurworth (Karen Tutty).* 137 (R).

GRADIENT ..9-13.. 11 b.g. Shirley Heights — Grimpola (GER) (Windwurf GER) pf. Lengthy brother to flat winner, Golden Heights, and half-brother to flat winners, Gondolier, Goonda and Gryada. Dam won at 6f and 8f in Germany, including their 1000 Guineas. FLAT r3 p1. P-t-P '99 r1 p0 (pulled up). Beaten half a length at Sandown on his only appearance as a three-year-old and looked sure to win on his Pointing debut six years later, but went lame when in command at the third last. Recovered well enough to race in 2000 and can now lay claim to being one of the unluckiest horses in training having fallen at the last when assured of victory at Cothelstone. Richly deserves compensation. *N.J. Dawe — W. Somerset V.* 957 (CfMa), 1094 (M).

GRAIN HILL ..8-10.. 7 b.m. North Col — New World (St Columbus) 8uufR35. Lengthy workmanlike half-sister to Smart Song (*qv*). P-t-P '99 r1 p0 (fell). Impetuous and error prone to date, but not without ability and might have scored already had she been more amenable to restraint. Blinkered (after ducking out at up ton) and mounted on course in her last two starts. Still eligible for short Maidens so there is still hope and stronger handling could prove beneficial. *J.W. & Mrs N.A. Hedges — Warwicks (Julie Marles).* 21 (2m4fOMa), 30 (CMa), 250 (CfMa), 1019 (2m4fOMa), 1360 (2m4fOMa), 1435 (OMa), 1589 (2m4fOMa).

PLATE 56   338 North Herefordshire Restricted (Div 2): Grand Canyon (A. Wintle), pu, lands ahead of (L to R) J'accuse (S. Currey), pu, Baptist John (A. Phillips), pu, and Hill Sprite (R. Barrett), 5th
PHOTO: John Beasley

GRAND APPLAUSE (IRE) ..—§.. 11 gr.g. Mazaad — Standing Ovation (Godswalk USA) f. Strong compact brother to Irish flat winners, Lady Blayney and Crowded House (IRE) (latter also a successful Hurdler there), and to another in Austria, and half-brother to a flat winner. Dam won at 12f in Ireland. 6000y. FLAT (inc for M. Usher; tried blinkered) r26 p5. NH '93/8 (visored 1; for J.S. Smith, bought for 4100; previously for M. Salaman; previously for M. Muggeridge; won previously for R. Simpson) r21 w1 (2m1f Hdle) p10 (remounted last of 3 once; inc 3 Chses); ran out 1; inc Sells. Ungenuine and a poor jumper, and beaten 20 times over obstacles since winning a six-runner Hurdle in November '93. Crossed the Solent to fall at the water in 2000. *P.E. Legge — I. of W.* 215 (C).

GRAND CANYON (IRE) ..9-8.. 8 b.g. Gallic Heir — Kay Kelly (Pitskelly) pp4243*p*. Tall. IRISH NH FLAT '97 r1 p0. IRISH P-t-P '97/8 r4 w1 (5yo Maiden) p2. NH '98/9 (for P. Eccles, bought for 12,500, blinkered 1) r5 p1 (2nd); pulled up in other Hdle, and last and pulled up 2 in Chses. NH May '00 (for D.J. Wintle) r1 p0 (pulled up in 2m3f110y Sell Hdle: *ld 2-3, rdn 5, wknd 7, t.o & pu 3 out*). Moderate and does not seem to have a trip — fails to stay over three miles, and was five lengths last of two on the only occasion he was beaten less than 15 lengths, and finished 20 lengths fourth in a Hunter Chase in which he made a couple of mistakes and was never near the leaders. Had a famous namesake with a (NZ) suffix, and perhaps there is some justice in his being so mediocre. *J.W. Egan — Teme V. (John Tulloch).* 196 (R), 338 (R), 485 (R), 745 (R), 925 (2mH), 1193 (R).

GRANDPA MAURICE (IRE) ..7-12.. 7 b.g. Astronef — War Ballad (FR) (Green Dancer USA) 55p. Tall half-brother to Irish flat and Hurdles winner, Sense of Value. 750 4-y-o. NH FLAT Jan '99 r1 p0 (tailed off). NH '99 (from R. Baker's) r2 p0 (tailed off when pulled up at 100-1 in both Hdles). Can show a fair bit of speed, but stops as if shot, and was 26 lengths last at best in his completions. Blinkered on his penultimate appearance. Labouring under a wind infirmity, and tubing him appeared to bring him no relief on final start. *Dr Ian R. Shenkin — E. Devon (David Pipe).* 73 (OMa), 352 (CfMa), 562 (CfMa).

GRANGE PRIZE ..8-7.. 15 ch.g. Le Bavard (FR) — Queen's Prize (Random Shot) p479p5p76. Small close-coupled half-brother to NH flat winner, Regal Gem (IRE), and to Irish Hurdles winner, Right'N'Royal. IRISH NH FLAT r5 p0. IRISH NH '91 and '93 r6 p0. IRISH P-t-P '93 r7 p5 (inc remounted last of 2, and last of 3); pulled up 2. P-t-P '94/6 and '98/9 (for Mr R. Greenway) r25 w1 (Maiden) p8 (4 3rds, last twice); failed to finish 3 (unseated 1). A patent safety (made the ideal schoolmaster for both pilots '99/00), but creeps along slower than a hearse and a calendar is usually needed to determine how far he has been beaten nowadays. Blinkered once in '99. *Miss K.J. Henry — Warwicks (Vicki Lay).* 78 (L), 246 (C), 429 (C), 886 (C), 1146 (R), 1438 (M), 1482 (R), 1583 (C), 1623 (R).

GRANGEWICK FLIGHT ..9-9.. 7 b.g. Lighter — Feathery (Le Coq D'Or) 33. Good-topped rangy. Dam is half-sister to Grey Bunny (*qv* '94 Annual). P-t-P '99 r1 p0 (8th). Made a pleasing start in '99 and ran well in an unfit state on his return, but highly untractable before at Newton Bromswold subsequently and failed to reappear. Lost acres of ground through hanging left, but had shown no signs of reluctance before and should win if he behaves in 2001. *Mr & Mrs J.L. Marks — Fitzwilliam.* 233 (OMa), 514 (OMa).

GRANITE'S SURPRISE ..8-0.. 12 ch.g. Wonderful Surprise — Granite's Ghost (Grey Ghost) pp4p. Big strong. P-t-P '98/9 (for Miss F. Hatfield) r7 p2 (2nds, promoted once); 4th, pulled up 3, and unseated 1. Placed twice in '98, but appeared just once the following year when he ran himself into the ground before halfway and tailed off without exception in the new yard. *K. O'Brien — O. Surrey & Burstow.* 291 (CMa), 416 (R), 1172 (OMa), 1513 (OMa).

GRANNIES DELIGHT (IRE) ..8-12.. 8 b.g. Yashgan — Beech Glen (Furry Glen) ppp4. Good-topped lengthy half-brother to Shamron (IRE) (*qv*). P-t-P '99 r3 p0 (last, and pulled up 2). Showed some ability for the first time in his last two outings, but ran out of gas in the closing stages (even when tried over 2m4f) and seems to have a stamina deficiency. Might achieve better results if dropped out especially as short Maidens are no longer an option. *F.K. Baxter — Quorn.* 54 (OMa), 1220 (OMa), 1421 (OMa), 1590 (2m4fOMa).

GRANSTOWN LAKE (IRE) ..9-1.. 10 b.g. Clearly Bust — More Hassel (Torenaga) 7R. Small sturdy. IRISH P-t-P '96 r1 w1 (4&5yo Maiden). NH '97/8 r5 p0 (pulled up in 5 Hdles, inc Sells). P-t-P '99 r5 p0 (pulled up 4, and fell 1). A total crackpot who will tear off uncontrollably if the rider ups anchor. Forced to complete under an iron grip on his reappearance, but got his revenge next time when he failed to take a bend at Cothelstone. Like his dam is more hassle than he is worth. *Mr & Mrs D. Puddy & Mrs A. Tong — W. Somerset V. (Laura Horsey).* 639 (I), 1094 (M).

GRANTS CAROUSE ..8-0.. 14 ch.g. Carlingford Castle — Clashawley (Deep Run) pppp3p. Strong compact half-brother to Irish Pointing and Hurdles winner, Geata Bawn (IRE). IRISH P-t-P '94/6 r14 w1 (6yo&up Maiden) p6; failed to finish 7 (carried out 1, and fell/unseated 2). IRISH NH FLAT r4 p0. NH '98 r1 p0 (tailed off in 3m2f Nov Hdle). P-t-P/HUNT CH '97/9 r13 p1 (2nd of 3); pulled up 4, and unseated 1. Beaten in all 30 starts since winning the 11th of a 13 race card in Ireland back in '94 and only once better than last for the current owner. Regularly stops dead in a matter of strides and usually pulls up. Clumsy, but jumped even worse when blinkered once in 2000 and not worth racing again. *M. Wells — S. Notts.* 120 (CR), 371 (R), 440 (R), 546 (R), 1214 (M), 1268 (R).

GRANVILLE GRILL ..10-7.. 16 b.g. Furry Glen — Glamorous Night (Sir Herbert) p1521. Tall brother to Red Scorpion, and half-brother to Hearsay, Glamorous Guy and King's Courtier (IRE), and to Irish NH flat and jumping winner, Star Cast. IRISH NH FLAT r4 p0. IRISH P-t-P '90 r1 w1 (5&6yo Maiden). IRISH NH '93/3 (blinkered 1) r16 w2 (2m2f-2m5f Chses) p3. P-t-P '94/6 r39 w14 (inc Mixed Open and 3 Opens; 4-timer in '95) p8 (3 3rds, last once); disqualified from 3rd once; failed to finish 14 (unseated 4). A grand old warrior who, like his partner, makes few concessions to age and landed his Members for the third year in succession, and fourth time in all, in 2000. Followed up in a weak Open at Andoversford thus taking his winning tally to 19. A strong galloper who can keep going with great resolution, but jumps left, and taking him on at his own front-running game is the way to beat him. Boils over, and always goes to the start early, but incredibly keen upon the 2001 Beaufort Members would be a fitting race to clock up his 20th career success. Usually needs an outing to put him straight. *E.W. Smith — Beaufort (John Deutsch).* 195 (O), 387 (M), 749 (Cf), 968 (Cf), 1192 (O).

GRAPHIC DESIGNER (IRE) ..9-05.. 12 b.g. Sheer Grit — Kates Princess (Pitpan) pp413. Strong lengthy half-brother to Yeoman Cricketer and Princess Easy, to NH flat winner, Kate O'Kirkham, and to a winner in Belgium. Dam won 2m Hdle in Ireland. NH '95/6 r5 p1 (2nd); remote 7th of 8, pulled up 2, and fell 1 in Chses. P-t-P '97 and '99 r5 p3 (2nd of 3 twice, and last of 3); pulled up 1, and unseated 1. Lightly raced and had looked a non-stayer until happening upon a bad Maiden at Peper Harow which he won unimpressively. Last of three in a Restricted next time and looks odds against scoring in that company. *J.J. Hazeltine — Surrey U.* 220 (OMa), 309 (OMa), 1245 (OMa), 1396 (OMa), 1512 (R).

GRECIAN LARK ..10-4.. 13 b.g. Crested Lark — Grecian Lace (Spartan General) 5425. Good-bodied attractive owner-bred brother to Grecian Star and half-brother to Kingbrook, Fine Lace, Grecian Saint and Bobbin Lace. Dam, sister to Spartan Lace, won Hunter Chase and 4 Points and placed 6 for Bunny Tarry. Grandam, French Lace, won 2 Irish Points at 4, and won 4 Ladies in England. P-t-P/HUNT CH '95/9 r29 w10 (inc 6 Opens, and inc hat-trick '96) p11 (8 2nds; and inc last of 3 once; inc 2 Hunt Chses); pulled up 2, and fell 2. Successful at least once in each of his previous five campaigns, but beaten a minimum of 16 lengths in 2000 and clearly out of sorts, though consistency had never been his strong suit. Blinkered on five occasions in '99 and tried in a tongue-strap once the previous year. Formerly capable of producing a turn of foot when he felt like it, but unpredictable and his decline could be permanent. *J. White & G.B. Tarry — Grafton (Jimmy Tarry).* 148 (3m1fl110yH), 244 (O), 511 (O), 1008 (O).

GRECIAN STAR ..10-8.. 9 b.g. Crested Lark — Grecian Lace (Spartan General) pf1231u. Tarry-bred brother to Grecian Lark (*qv*). P-t-P '99 r3 w2 (Maiden and Club Restricted) p0; and unseated 1. Made the perfect start, but his stable was under a cloud in early 2000 and he never really sparked despite doubling his winning tally. Set an impossible task once, but particularly disappointing when fading quickly at Kimble and his jumping still requires plenty of attention. A strong finisher on his day, but looks to be going down the same avenue as his brother and may need plenty of kidding in the future. Has two handlers. *J. White & G.B. Tarry — Grafton (Jimmy Tarry).* 75 (I), 296 (I), 429 (C), 785 (I), 1143 (I), 1485 (I), 1620 (Cf).

GREEN ANKER ..8-3.. 9 ch.g. Green Adventure (USA) — Ankerdine Belle (Paddy Boy) 3fuufp. Sparely-made owner-bred half-brother to Majic Belle. Dam won 2m Hdle. P-t-P '98/9 r4 p0 (pulled up 3, and unseated 1). Speedy, but well beaten on the only occasion he has jumped a clear round and consistently looks a non-stayer. His half-sister was utterly ungenuine and jumped poorly when failing to win in 17 attempts to '98 and he looks unlikely to enhance the family reputation. *D.J.B. Denny — Devon & Somerset (Mrs P. Horton).* 563 (CfMa), 958 (R), 1241 (OMa), 1307 (OMa), 1468 (OMa), 1565 (OMa).

GREENFIELD MAID (IRE) ..7-0.. 12 ch.m. Red Johnnie — Cuan Maid (Whistling Top) 4p. Small sparely-made half-sister to Ferry Gale. NH FLAT '94 r1 p0 (hampered start, tailed off final 6f). P-t-P/HUNT CH '97/8 (for Mr J.V.C. Davenport) r9 p2 (3rd of 4 twice); last, pulled up 5, and fell 1. A useless non-stayer who lacked fluency to '98 and no better on her belated return. *Miss C. Powell — Golden V.* 490 (CfMa), 995 (OMa).

GREENFINCH (CAN) ..—§.. 10 gr.g. Green Dancer (USA) — Princess Verna (USA) (Al Hattab USA) p2upr. Lengthy half-brother to 2 winners in USA including Hurdles winner, Alcalali (USA) $53,000y. FLAT (tried blinkers; early run for R. Hannon) r11 p0. NH '95 and '97/8 (for B. Murtagh; previously Mrs M. Naughton, bought for 5000) r17 p5 (3 Hdles and 2 Chses; maximum of 5 finishers in 4); ran out on debut; inc Sells. Placed for the sixth time when inheriting second at the final fence at Whittington, but could not be persuaded to complete the course otherwise in 2000, and looks thoroughly ungenuine. Used to wear a visor, and sometimes goes missing for long periods. *R.A. Fisher — Cumberland F.* 492 (M), 816 (OMa), 1153 (OMa), 1154 (3m2fH), 1499 (OMa).

GREENHILL TARE AWAY ..10-4.. 13 b.g. Oats — Burlington Belle (Galivanter) 3u22p. Tall rangy half-brother to flat and useful jumping winner, Mr Moonraker, to jumping winners, Connaught Cracker and Greenhill Raffles, to Hurdles winner, Connaught's Pride, to 5f winner, Greenhill Jazz Time, and to a winner in Italy. NH FLAT '93 r2 p0. NH '94/8 r22 w8 (4 Hdles, 2m6f-3m2f, and 4 3m2f Chses) p3. P-t-P '99 r2 p2. A smart performer under Rules, but unable to score since winning at Chepstow in December '95, and although his fortunes have revived somewhat in Points he appears too one-paced to get his head in front. A thorough stayer, and suited by mud, but only went just over a mile before pulling up in the 4m Grimthorpe Gold Cup and may have suffered a reverse. *Sir Stephen Furness — Zetland (Chris Dennis).* 42 (O), 90 (3m1fH), 376 (MO), 493 (Cf), 999 (4m1fMO).

GREEN LEADER (IRE) ..9-8.. 9 b.m. Lapierre — Green Feathers (IRE) (Supreme Leader) 4. IRISH P-t-P '98 r6 p5; pulled up 1. Plugged on to be beaten between five lengths and 17 lengths in five Irish placings, and only missed second by two heads at Newton Bromswold. Suffering from sore shins since, but a win should be a foregone conclusion if the problem clears. *R. Andrews — Enfield Chace (Simon Andrews).* 515 (OMa).

GREG'S PROFILES ..9-9.. 10 br.g. Strong Gale — The Howlet (New Brig) f. Small close-coupled half-brother to Perdix, and to NH flat and Hurdles winner, Nevermind Hey. Dam won 3 Chses at around 2m. NH FLAT '96 r1 p0. NH '97/8 r10 p0 (inc pulled up in Sell Hdle final). P-t-P '99 r1 p0 (fell). Useless under Rules, but appeared to be going well when capsizing five out in the Badbury Maiden won by the smart Here Comes Henry. Well supported in both his Points and might be worth another chance if he has not come to any harm though his fencing is of course a cause for concern. *M. Moore & Mrs D. Wethered — Berks & Bucks.* 329 (CfMa).

GREVILLE AGAIN (IRE) ..9-12.. 12 ch.g. Phardante (FR) — Maravo (Octavo USA) p3375p. Tall rangy. IRISH P-t-P '94 r2 w1 (5-y-o's Maiden, beat Out The Door) p0. NH '94/5 and '97/8 r13 w2 (3m1f-3m2f) p6 (inc 4 Chses). P-t-P/HUNT CH '99 r7 p3 (inc 3rd of 4 twice); 4th twice, unseated 1, and pulled up 1. Placed in four Opens '99/00, but yet to finish within ten lengths of the winner and has become very one-paced. Appreciates plenty of cut, but risked on firmish at Wolverhampton and ended up lame. Very unlikely to achieve much if he is able to return. *A.G. Wadlow — Wheatland (John Groucott).* 334 (O), 530 (O), 779 (O), 902 (Cf), 1343 (3m10yH), 1523 (C).

GREYBURY STAR (IRE) ..—.. 13 b.g. Roselier (FR) — Diamond Angel (Diamonds Are Trump USA) p. Lengthy half-brother to Smurf (IRE). NH '95 r3 p0 (4th, pulled up 1, and fell 1 in Chses). P-t-P/HUNT CH '93/4 and '97/8 (for Dr D.B.A. Silk, Mr R. Purkis & Mr T. Freeman) r7 w1 (Maiden) p2 (last of 2 once); pulled up 1, and fell 1. Had ability, but rarely runs, and is a hard ride. Regained blinkers in 2000, but disappeared after pulling up once in February and not worth putting back into training. *Mrs H. Silk — Kent & Surrey Bloodhounds.* 241 (C).

GREY DANTE (IRE) ..—.. 10 gr.m. Phardante (FR) — Grey Squirrell (Golden Gorden) p. Sturdy half-sister to Squirrellsdaughter, Grey Gordon (IRE) and Daftasabrush (IRE), and to Irish Pointing and useful English jumping winner, Tug Of Gold. NH FLAT '96 r3 p0 (twice ridden by Sam Beddoes). P-t-P '99 r1 p0 (brought down). Well related, but seems nigh on impossible to train and promptly went back into hiding after pulling up at Thorpe Lodge in February (well supported, but failed to recover from a blunder a mile from home). *J.W. Beddoes — N. Salop.* 123 (OMa).

GREY GOSSIP (IRE) ..9-0.. 10 gr.g. Le Bavard (FR) — Perato (Nishapour FR) 2. Good-topped half-brother to Mandate (IRE). Dam won 2m mares Hdle in Ireland. P-t-P '98 r2 p1 (2nd); and 4th. Not disgraced in his debut season, but forced to miss '99 and restricted to just one start this term. Raced prominently throughout at Market Rasen, but eventually no match for the winner who failed to frank the form subsequently. *G.J. Smith — Cranwell Bloodhounds.* 52 (OMa).

GREY JERRY ..9-5.. 10 gr.g. Kinglet — Orphan Grey (Crash Course) 4523. Tall lengthy half-brother to Blakes Orphan, Kellys Orphan and Tom Boy. Dam won 2m2f Mdn Hdle and placed 3 (inc flat) in Ireland: and won Ladies (under Belinda Cooper) and placed 2. P-t-P '96/8 r10 p2 (2nd of 3 once); last, pulled up 6, and fell 1. Went wrong when the subject of market support at Holnicote in '98, but resurfaced in 2000 to add two more modest placings to his collection. Yet to look like winning and acquired blinkers on his final start. *Sir Richard Cooper — Blackmore & Sparkford V. (Jane Cooper).* 213 (CfMa), 407 (OMa), 739 (OMa), 957 (CfMa).

GREY LODGE ..8-0.. 7 gr.m. Pocketed (USA) — Alchemistress (Grey Ghost) u4. Small neat. Dam, 3rd of 5f, was subsequently a non-finisher in 4 Points for Christine Forber ('pulls so hard she has no hope of staying 3m'). Unseated three out when holding a slight lead in a joke race at Eyton, but was last and one and a half fences behind the winner next time, and could not even beat the abysmal Village Gossip. *Mrs C.T. Forber — Saddleworth.* 1201 (2m4fOMa), 1413 (OMa).

GREY MYSTERY ..9-0.. 7 gr.m. Vouchsafe — Strathdearn (Saritamer USA) 2pp. Tall owner-bred half-sister to Little Earn, and to Hurdles winner, Eager Beaver, Might Move and Madame Ruby. Dam won at 12f, and won 3 Hdles, 2m-2m1f. Had two subsequent winners behind her when three lengths second at Alpraham, but pulled up after bad blunders at the twelve (second favourite) and the seventh (backed from 5-2 to evens) subsequently. Has only tackled 2m4f so far, but there should be a race for her if she is taught to jump properly. Could also do with losing weight. *Mrs J.B. Williams — Cheshire (Sue Mullineaux).* 593 (2m4fOMa), 1070 (2m4fOMa), 1201 (2m4fOMa).

GREY ROCK (IRE) ..9-0.. 10 gr.m. Roselier (FR) — Leallen (Le Bavard FR) u38. Lengthy half-sister to jumping winner, Lord Noelie (IRE). IRISH P-t-P '96 r6 p1 (last of 2); pulled up 5. P-t-P/HUNT CH '97/9 r16 w1 (Maiden) p4 (2 2nds); pulled up 2, and fell/unseated 3. Lost her maiden status in a race taking 8mins 10s, but beaten in 14 Restricteds since usually lacks guidance from above. Eight lengths last of three for Maxine Bremner once this term, but needs the regular assistance of a strong jockey if she is ever to win score again which seems unlikely now. *Mrs B.E. Miller — Cumberland F.* 111 (R), 713 (R), 976 (R).

PLATE 57   326 Hursley Hambledon Ladies Open: Grey Smoke (Miss B. Lloyd), 1st, has the measure of Mizyan (Miss M. Coombe), 2nd   PHOTO: Tim Holt

GREY SMOKE ..10-9.. 11 gr.g. Alias Smith (USA) — Salira (Double Jump) 113s. Tall strong-topped brother to Sally Smith, and half-brother to Saleander, Leara (dam of Barn Elms *qv* '99 Annual), Double Light, Dehra Dun, Regal Estate, Some Fingers and Durham Hornet, and to NH flat and jumping winner, Calira. Dam won 6f Seller at 2yrs. NH FLAT r2 p0. NH '95/8 r14 w3 (3m Chses) p4; pulled up in 3 of final 4 attempts; withdrawn at start after breaking a blood vessel once. P-t-P '95 and '99 r3 w2 (Maiden and Club nov rdrs) p0; and unseated 1. A useful front-runner at best, and has done well to overcome injury — broke a bone in his shoulder in '97 and had three screws fitted — and regain his ability. Successful in his first four Pointing completions including two competitive Ladies races, but found the extra distance and the easier ground against him when third to Rip Van Winkle at Dunthrop. Supremely game, a fine jumper and suited by decent ground. Well handled by Brioney Lloyd and should win again next year. *Lady Vestey — Cotswold.* 326 (L), 475 (L), 1014 (3m5fL), 1631 (MO).

GREY WARRIOR ..9-9.. 8 gr.g. Rolfe (USA) — Statfold Pride (Precipice Wood) u42. Tall good-topped owner-bred half-brother to Statfold Pam, Statfold Supreme and Statfold Solva, and to Chasing winner, Jurassic Classic. Dam won 2 Hdles (2m-2m1f) and 3m Ch. P-t-P '99 r1 p0 (last). Well related, and has shown ability in all three completions, but error prone and ridden in such a way to suggest that stamina may not be his forte. No match for a 12 year old having her 17th start when a well supported favourite at Garthorpe, but still carrying a fair bit of condition and should find a race when produced fighting fit. *P.S. Hewitt — Quorn.* 121 (OMa), 372 (CfMa), 547 (CfMa).

GRIMLEY GALE (IRE) ..11-12.. 12 br.m. Strong Gale — Zauditu (Menelek) u11112. Compact half-sister to Down The Mine, Phardance (IRE) and Zaudante (IRE). P-t-P/HUNT CH '94/9 r31 w22 (inc 6 Hunt Chses, 2m4f-3m4f, 4 Opens, Mixed Open, and 5 Ladies) p3 (2 3rds; and 2nd in Hunt Ch); fell 2. NH Oct '99 r1 p0 (9th in 3m HCap Ch: *bhnd frm 12, t.o*). A top-class Pointer whose attentions have been switched almost exclusively to Hunter Chases in the last two years with equally outstanding results. Unable to get a prep race in before the Cheltenham Foxhunters, but had every chance when blundering Shirley Vickery out of the saddle with a mile to run. Only tasted defeat once when completing, but went down with honours to the ill-fated Castle Mane when trying to defend the Horse & Hound Cup. Undefeated in six visits to Ludlow now and best when the hooves are rattling, but avoids mud which bogs her down. Prone to make one bad blunder per race, but has top riders who are usually capable of keeping their seat. Probably has one more productive season in her before she goes to stud. A long-standing credit to connections. *Mr & Mrs R.M. Phillips — Clifton-on-Teme (Mark Jackson).* 584 (3m2f110yH), 684 (2m4fH), 920 (3mH), 1023 (3mH), 1432 (3m1fH), 1647 (3m4fH).

GROMIT (U) ..—.. 13 b.g. unknown u. Workmanlike. One of two hunters to contest his Members, and both riders were decanted at the third. *F. Crawford — Bedale.* 1031 (M).

GROVE VICTOR (IRE) ..9-4.. 10 ch.g. Abednego — Lobelia's Last (Whistling Deer) puup2u. Strong compact half-brother to Irish NH flat and Hurdles winner, Mick McCann (IRE). IRISH NH FLAT '95 r2 p0. IRISH NH '96 and '98 (blinkered 2) r4 p0 (inc pulled up in Ch). IRISH P-t-P '96 and '98 r9 w1 (6yo&up Maiden) p4 (3rds); pulled up 2. P-t-P '99 (for Mr R. Mathias) r5 p1 (3rd); unseated 2, and pulled up 2. Capable of showing early speed, but a consistently clumsy jumper and frequently returns with an empty saddle — though Philip Andrew needed no provocation to vacate his position twice. No match for the winner in his three-finisher Members and future prospects look bleak. Carrying plenty of unnecessary weight in early season. *Mrs S.V. Andrew — Fitzwilliam (Trevor Marks).* 119 (CR), 179 (R), 371 (R), 546 (R), 769 (M), 871 (R).

GRUNGE (IRE) ..9-10.. 13 b br.g. Crash Course — Hills Of Fashion (Tarqogan) 3ur516. Rangy half-brother to Mount Patrick, to Irish NH flat and Hurdles winner, Owen's Fashion, and to Irish Chasing winner, Hill Of Bargy. IRISH P-t-P '93 r1 w1 (4&5yo Mdn). IRISH NH FLAT '93 r1 w1. NH '94/9 (for D. Murray-Smith; blinkered/visored 2) r22 w2 (3m Hdles at Towcester) p5; pulled up, fell, and refused (continued) in Chses in '95. A weary old plodder who does not have much enthusiasm for the game, but his Members came gift-wrapped, and provided him with a first success for three years. Very unlikely to be good enough for anything better if tried again at thirteen. *Mrs H. Cowell & Mrs S. Nash — Cheshire (Chris Clark).* 77 (O), 293 (Cf), 334 (O), 529 (Cf), 587 (M), 902 (Cf).

GT HAYES POMMARD ..9-7.. 11 b.g. Trampler — Great Hayes Bene (Night Thought) 657u323f3. Very small light half-brother to numerous eventers. P-t-P '95/9 r28 w1 (Members) p5 (4 3rds, of 4 once, and last once); last 3, fell/unseated 12, and pulled up 7. Has made the frame nine times since his shock 50-1 success in '97 and looked unlucky in two visits to Whitwick '99/00 (one of three in line when unseating three out in the latest), but the rider has severe limitations and the horse has generally deserved better. Prone to hang and jump right-handed (has worn an off-side pricker) and was blinkered twice in '99. Usually has two paddock handlers. His day may yet come again. *D. Howells — Avon R.* 6 (R), 33 (Cnr), 75 (I), 340 (R), 485 (R), 1054 (R), 1181 (R), 1615 (R), 1659 (R).

GUARD A DREAM (IRE) ..9-2.. 7 ch.g. Durgam (USA) — Adarenna (FR) (Mill Reef USA) p4f15p. Small light-framed flashy half-brother to a French flat winner, and to successful Irish/English Hurdles winner, Adaramann (IRE). IR 5000y. FLAT (for Mrs M. Reveley at 3) r4 p1 (25 *l* 2nd of 4); inc Sells. Sold Doncaster, Oct '97 for 900, and resold Goffs Ireland, Dec '97 for 396. Showed improved form when winning a Maiden at firmish at Bassaleg, but beaten about 30 lengths in a Restricted there next time, and has looked moderate to date. Will need to find more if he is to score again. *R.J. Rowsell — Ystrad Taf Fechan.* 491 (CfMa), 822 (CfMa), 1300 (OMa), 1404 (OMa), 1568 (R), 1616 (R).

GUEST ALLIANCE (IRE) ..9-4.. 9 ch.g. Zaffaran (USA) — Alhargah (Be My Guest USA) up. Close-coupled good-bodied half-brother to 3 flat winners (one in Italy). FLAT r37 w2 (16f on Lingfield all-weather) p9 (inc 2nd in Sell prior to wins). NH '97/8 r5 w1 (2m3f Hdle) p0. P-t-P '99 r1 p0 (4th). In front when unseating after two miles on his reappearance, but appeared to go wrong at Clifton-on-Dunsmore subsequently. A thorough stayer on the flat, and won a Maiden Hurdle on his jumping debut, but has looked flawed since. *T.E. Wardall — Atherstone.* 1217 (L), 1417 (L).

GUILSBOROUGH GORSE ..9-12.. 6 b.g. Past Glories — Buckby Folly (Netherkelly) p1f4. Half-brother to Sharley Cop. Dam, bred by Sarah York, won 2m4f Hdle when trained for her by Maurice Camacho. Won a Wetherby Maiden taking 7min21s in the manner of a promising young stayer, but has had problems with jumping lapses since. May require some cut in the ground, and could have a decent future when conditions are favourable. *Mrs E.C. York — Middleton (Tim Walford).* 51 (OMa), 169 (OMa), 689 (M), 1000 (R).

GUNERKILLINGHURST ..8-7.. 12 ch.g. Nearly A Hand — Killinghurst Girl VII (unknown) 5ppup3p. Plain owner-bred. Just a souped-up hunter who came to racing as an afterthought, and on the only occasion he finished in front of another horse the judge mistakenly placed him last! The politically correct lobby would surely have something to say about his name. *J. Studd — Blackmore & Sparkford V. (John Dufosee).* 147 (OMa), 309 (OMa), 457 (OMa), 763 (CfMa), 889 (OMa), 1062 (OMa), 1308 (OMa).

GUNMETAL ..9-10.. 6 gr.g. High Lodge — Amber Vale (Warpath) p1p. Close-coupled half-brother to Bright Hour and Vale Of York. Dam won 5 flat, 9-16f. NH FLAT '99 (for J. Wainwright, tongue-tied final) r2 p0. Showed the benefits of an easy introduction when driven out to win a very weak Maiden at Brocklesby Park, but looked below par and ran no sort of a race next time. Absent since early March, and will need to brush up his jumping when he reappears, but probably has some scope for improvement. *P.W. Clifton — Holderness (Mary Sowersby).* 137 (R), 234 (OMa), 440 (R).

GUNNER BOON ..10-7.. 11 b.g. Gunner B — Miss Boon (Road House II) p1131321. Very tall half-brother to Earl Boon (qv). P-t-P/HUNT CH '96/8 r23 w9 (inc 4 Ladies) p8 (7 2nds — robbed by blind judge once); ran out 1, fell/unseated 3, withdrawn under orders once, and disqualified from win once for missing marker. Went wrong in '98, but returned to further enhance his c.v with another four successes. Remarkably consistent and has never failed to reach the frame when completing, but his jumping has let him down in two Hunter Chases and seems unlikely to tackle the bigger fences again in a hurry. A powerful galloper , and capable of making all, but becoming more clumsy and has shown a tendency to dart left-handed at the obstacles. Owes plenty to Pip Jones who copes well with his errors, but sure to win again. Acts on any going though some cut is preferable. *D. Brace — Llangeinor.* 19 (L), 141 (MO), 275 (Cf), 459 (2m4f110yH), 645 (MO), 1297 (L), 1451 (MO), 1658 (MO).

GUNNER B SPECIAL ..9-7.. 8 ch.g. Gunner B — Sola Mia (Tolomeo) 241p. Sturdy compact brother to NH flat winner, Son Of A Gun. Dam won at 6f. FLAT (early runs for R. Bowring) r11 p0. NH '97/8 (from J. Neville's) r7 p0 (regularly tailed off, in Sells). A headstrong front-runner who invariably faded badly flat and Hurdling, (was often tongue-tied and wore headgear), but found lowly Points more suitable, and made all and came home virtually solo in heavy at Pantyderi. Even now he is struggling to get the trip, and was beaten favourite twice, including when pulled up on his latest outing in mid-March. Missed '99, and seems to have had another set back. *B.E.V. Thomas (The Eagle Club) — Tredegar F. (Tim Jones).* 71 (OMa), 204 (OMa), 350 (CfMa), 483 (R).

GUNNERS DAWN ..8-5.. 10 b.m. Rustingo — Gunner Go (Gunner B) p9pp. Small owner-bred. P-t-P '97/9 r7 p2 (3rds, remote last once); pulled up 4, and unseated 1. NH '99 (for Mrs P. Ford) r5 p1 (remote last in Ch); 6th, and pulled up 3 — inc 2 other Chses. Has led for a long way on four occasions in Points, but does not get the trip, and beaten just one rival in his last ten starts. *Mrs S.V. Corbin — N. Herefords.* 332 (M), 483 (R), 866 (CfMa), 1091 (OMa).

PLATE 58   1025 Jane McAlpine Mem HC, Bangor: Gunner Welbur (B. Pollock), 1st, completes a hat-trick
PHOTO: Colin Turner

GUNNER WELBURN ..11-6.. 9 ch.g. Gunner B — Vedra (IRE) (Carlingford Castle) f111f. Big rangy half-brother to Wild Dream. P-t-P/HUNT CH '98/9 r8 w5 (inc 3m1f110y Hunt Ch, inc 4-timer '99) p2 (2nds); and pulled up 1. IRISH NH May '00 r1 p0 (fell in Punchestown Champion HC: *trckd ldrs in 4th, 3rd 8, cl up 4 out, rdn nxt, no imp when fell last*). Developed into a useful stayer in '99 and rounded that season off with a win in the Bowring Intermediate Final at Cheltenham in May, but gave the Festival a miss this year after two comprehensive wins in February — would have won at Larkhill on his reappearance but for falling at the last behind Sheltering who had been beaten by Castle Mane in the corresponding event 12 months earlier. Faced his stiffest task to date when shipped to Punchestown on his final appearance, but was a beaten third when coming to grief at the last behind Sheltering who had been beaten by Castle Mane in the corresponding event 12 months earlier. Suited by a stamina test in mud and is generally a sound jumper, but looks a shade below the standard required to win a Championship event at present. Will find more opportunities, however, and were it to come up soft at Stratford next June would be a worthy successor to his illustrious stable companion. *W.A. Ritson — Pytchley (Caroline Bailey).* 10 (O), 148 (3m1f110yH), 299 (3m2f110yH), 1025 (3m110yH).

GUN RUNNER ..8-9.. 8 ch.g. Gunner B — What's In Store (Captain James) p3. Strong. IRISH NH '98 r2 p0 (tailed off in Hdle, and last in Ch). P-t-P '99 r2 p1 (2nd of 3); and fell 1. Beaten a minimum of 15 lengths in his two placed efforts and surprisingly for a son of Gunner B seems to lack stamina. Mounted on course and taken to post early on his reappearance. *A.C.R. Stubbs — Cheshire.* 298 (CfMa), 570 (2m4fCfMa).

GUY MORNAY ..8-2.. 8 b.g. Feelings (FR) — Wedderburn (Royalty) 3p. Brother to Felt Better, and Hurdles winner, Mary's Feelings, and half-brother to Tindles Bible, and to Irish Pointing and English Chasing winner, Glenbrook D'Or. P-t-P '99 r3 p0 (last, pulled up 1, and fell 1). Taken steadily when completing twice from five starts, but pulled up after an early mistake in his most recent appearance and may well have gone wrong. Probably capable of much better than he has shown to date, but has plenty to prove if he returns. *K. Jackson — Cumberland.* 664 (2m5fOMa), 1368 (OMa).

GWENLLIAN ..—.. 6 gr.m. Deploy — Llwy Bren (Lidhame) p. Half-sister to flat winner, Rushcutter Bay. Tailed off and pulled up at halfway at Chaddesley. Related to a sprinter, and may be in the wrong job. *W.J. Swinnerton — N. Salop (M. Edwards).* 618 (CMa).

GWEN'S A SINGER ..—.. 7 ch.m. Fearless Action (USA) — Air Streak (Air Trooper) p. Leggy half-sister to Up Your Street. Dam, half-sister to Dawn Street (*qv* '91 Annual), won Maiden and placed 4 (inc 2nd in Hdle). P-t-P '99 r2 p0 (pulled up 2). Tailed off and pulled up thrice '99/00, and has yet to go beyond two miles. Jumped poorly on the most recent occasion. *R. Clarke — Bicester with Whaddon.* 514 (OMa).

GYMCRAK GORJOS ..9-11.. 7 b br.m. Rock Hopper — Bit O' May (Mummy's Pet) 61246. Compact robust half-sister to May Runner, and to 2 flat winners (one in Germany), and Summer Express. 7400y. FLAT r11 p2 (2nds). NH '98 (for G. Holmes) r1 p0. Bought Doncaster, Sep '98 for 1000. Enterprisingly handled by David Thomas (on his first winner) when landing much the slowest of the four divisions of the Maiden at Market Rasen. Held on by half a length and the same after nipping through on the inner on the bend approaching the last, but only one of the five behind her scored subsequently, and is finding it difficult to get her head in front again. Jumps well for a beginner, and may be able to find a Restricted eventually. Wore blinkers in the previous yard. *M. Jackson — Middleton (Jinty Monteith).* 235 (OMa), 438 (OMa), 794 (Cf), 996 (M), 1418 (R).

GYMCRAK TIGER (IRE) ..10-4.. 11 b.g. Colmore Row — Gossip (Sharp Edge) 22u3p5. Lengthy good-looking half-brother to Lord Ellangowan (IRE) (*qv*). FLAT (inc win for M.H. Easterby at 2) r14 w2 (6-12f, inc sell at 8) p3. NH '93/8 (for G. Holmes, tried blinkered) r16 w2 (2m1f-2m4f Hdles) p3. Ran very solid races on his first two attempts in 2000 and chased home Trade Dispute and Cool Abbey (Overflowing River and Howayman were the respective thirds), but hampered by a rising faller and unseated when favourite next time, and never recaptured the form afterwards. Pulled up on his final start under Rules, when reappearing from a seven month absence, and missed '99, and may be less than hale and hearty nowadays. Has not won over jumps since November '95, and was tackling fences for the first time at the age of ten. *I.A. Brown — Sinnington.* 155 (3m4f110yH), 586 (3m1fH), 918 (2m4fH), 1030 (O), 1335 (2m4f110yH), 1446 (3m1fH).

GYPSY GERRY ..10-0.. 11 b.g. Sunyboy — La Chunga (Queen's Hussar) 424334. Lengthy unfurnished half-brother to Sagaro Belle and Border Edition, and to flat winner, Woodpecker Boy. IRISH P-t-P '95/6 r7 p2 (about 1/3rds); pulled up 2, fell 1, and ran out 1. P-t-P '97/9 (for Mr C. de P. Berry) r15 w7 (up to Confined) p8 (6 2nds, of 3 twice; and last of 3 once). Well placed to land seven Points in the previous yard, and never failed to make the frame, but prone to disappoint latterly and the new owner-rider could not quite extract his best. A fine jumper, but finds little under pressure and the application of blinkers on his last three appearances made little difference (had previously run unsuccessfully in a visor). *T. Clarkson — Eggesford (Kay Rees & Polly Curling).* 66 (Cf), 165 (Cf), 258 (Cf), 637 (O), 1044 (4mO), 1305 (MO).

GYPSY HAZE ..9-6.. 6 ch.m. Romany Rye — Brilliant Haze VII (unknown) R2R14. Tiny light-framed home-bred half-sister to Kristal Haze (*qv*). The latest in a line of midgets, but all have won, and is remarkably plucky on her day in the circumstances. Very unlucky at Llanvapley when she was just taking up the running when skidding on landing at the final fence, but made amends in a three-finisher Maiden at St Hilary where she ploughed through the heavy ground to score in a slow time. Has locked her jaw and run off the course or virtually done so on her three other outings, but it is probable that she can win again if she stays on the straight and narrow. *Mr & Mrs P. Dando — Pentyrch (Phil Dando).* 648 (CfMa), 746 (CfMa), 834 (OMa), 1055 (CfMa), 1298 (R).

GYPSY LUCK ..10-1.. 12 b.m. Sula Bula — Pine Gypsy (Workboy) 3431. Compact sister to Gypsy Blues, and to jumping winner, Philip's Woody. Dam won 3 Points (including a walk-over) and placed 3. P-t-P/HUNT CH '94/9 r22 w2 (Maiden and Restricted) p9 (6 3rds); pulled up 3, and fell/unseated 4. Emerged from the fog with a clear advantage approaching the last on her final appearance at Bratton Down, but Amanda Bush appeared to doze off and the partnership only just clung on to end a sequence of 11 defeats in which she had made the frame on seven occasions. A proficient jumper, but can look moody and has been ridden in spurs. Usually runs several pounds below her rating. *J.G. Cann — E. Devon (Ollie Cann).* 953 (I), 1203 (I), 1607 (I), 1651 (I).

HACKETTS CROSS (IRE) ..10-2-. 13 b.g. Rusticaro (FR) — Anglesea Market (Sea Hawk II) p. Compact half-brother to 3 flat winners (one in Ireland, also a successful Hurdler; and including one in Belgium), and to an Irish NH flat winner. IRISH FLAT '92/3 r11 w2 (14-16f Amat; also won private sweepstake) p2. IRISH NH FLAT '92/3 r5 w2 (inc dead-heat) p1 (3rd). IRISH NH '92/5 r11 w1 (2m2f Hdle) p4. FLAT '95 r3 p0. NH '95/7 r25 w5 (4 Hdles, 2m1f-2m4f, and 2m6f Ch; won 3 Sells) p10. P-t-P/HUNT CH '99 r3 p1 (3rd); pulled up 1, and fell 1. A prolific prize-winner until breaking down in '97, but has only managed four outings since and disappeared after pulling up at Ludlow in early March. Ran well when third in a Ladies last year, but unlikely to get many more chances. Has never won beyond 2m6f and most effective on sound surfaces which put too much pressure on his fragile legs nowadays. *G.W. Briscoe — W. Salop.* 382 (2m4fH).

HAGON BECK ..10-5-. 8 ch.g. Baron Blakeney — Oxnead (Balinger) 4212. Workmanlike angular Martin-bred. Dam, half-sister to 3 Pointers, including Mr Fudge (*qv*), was last of 3 in a Members and distant 3rd of 4 in a Hurdle. P-t-P '98/9 r3 p0 (last 1, and fell/unseated 2). Ended '98 with a crashing fall and clearly met with trouble after failing to clear one fence successfully last year, but bolted up in his Members this term. Had earlier run well at Garthorpe, but a return visit ended disappointingly as he was found to be lame (again?) after chasing home the unbeaten Union Man. A Restricted would be well within his capabilities if he could be returned sound. *Mrs S. Martin & Mrs J. Stamp — N. Norfolk H., & W. Norfolk (William Wales).* 412 (OMa), 872 (OMa), 1285 (M), 1586 (CN).

HALF EACH ..10-0-. 9 b.m. Weld — Golden Valley (Hotfoot) 5513u. Small neat half-sister to Golden Lark, Only Me, Woolstonwood, See More Castles and Ambersam. Dam pulled up in 3 Points. P-t-P/HUNT CH '97/8 (for Mrs G.B. Walford) r8 w2 (Maiden and Restricted) p0; last pair 2, fell/unseated 2, ran out 1, and pulled up 1. NH '98/9 (for Miss K. Milligan) r7 p0 (pulled up 4, unseated 1, and took no part 1; visored final start). Displayed plenty of stamina when successful twice in '98, but seemed put off by regulation fences and achieved nothing when switched to hurdling. Given a good ride by Lucy Watson when coming from off a strong pace at Brocklesby Park, but found conditions on the lively side subsequently and seems best with some cut in the ground. Suited by the lighter weights in Ladies races and may find another modest opportunity. *Mrs C.A. Watson — Middleton (Tim Walford).* 19 (L), 397 (L), 795 (L), 806 (L), 1364 (L).

HALF MOON SPINNEY ..9-9-. 11 br.g. True Song — Dane Hole (Past Petition) pp. Plain unfurnished brother to Gawcott Wood, and half-brother to Thursby (subsequent Chasing winner), Jack's Barn, Trafford Bridge and Boddington Hill. P-t-P '97/9 r7 w2 (Maiden and Restricted) p1 (2nd); unseated 2, and pulled up 2. Successful once apiece '98/9, but never runs much and failed to reappear after two spins in February this season. Stays well, but avoids firm ground and is virtually impossible to keep right. *M.J. Holliday — Mid Surrey F. (Ann Blaker).* 125 (M), 288 (CMod).

HALHAM TARN (IRE) ..10-2-. 11 b.g. Pennine Walk — Nouniya (Vayrann) 520953. Compact. FLAT (wore eye-shield on all-weather) r18 w2 (10-12f, inc all-weather) p5. NH '98/8 r40 w1 (2m Hdle) p10. P-t-P/HUNT CH '96 and '98/9 (for Miss M. Tufnell) r13 w2 (2 Hunt Chses, 2m110y-2m1f) p5 (4 2nds, last once; and inc 4 Hunt Chses); pulled up 6 and unseated 1. NH Spr '00 r2 p0 (5th in 2m HCap Ch: *hld up, a rr*; and 9th in 2m4f HCap Hdle: *mist 2, handy til ld app 6, hdd app 3 out, lost plce, t.o*). A decent performer at around two miles, but barely stays even that distance and twice beaten in races he looked set to win in 2000. Runs in a tongue-strap more often than not, and clearly finds it impossible to breath properly at the end of his races now. Suited by waiting tactics and always has top riders. *Mrs M.L. Luck — O. Berks (Gary Brown).* 463 (2mH), 921 (2m6fH), 1341 (2m110yH), 1531 (2m110yH).

HALL'S MILL (IRE) ..10-10-. 12 ch.g. Buckskin (FR) — Grainne Geal (General Ironside) 4561. Tall brother to What Chance (IRE), and half-brother to Madam Sioux (IRE), and to Irish Pointing winner, Bayloughbess. IRISH NH '97 r1 p0 (last in Ch). IRISH P-t-P '94 and '96/7 r9 w1 (unplaced Maiden) p1 (last of 2); pulled up 2, and fell 1. P-t-P/HUNT CH '98/9 r10 w4 (inc 2 Confineds) p2 (Hunt Chses); and fell/unseated 4. Unbeaten when completing in English Points, but not as convincing over regulation obstacles until springing a 20-1 surprise at Cheltenham of all places on his most recent appearance. Carried Alex Charles-Jones past three rivals up the famous hill (shades of Cavalero) and snatched the verdict in the shadows of the post. Had been absent for five weeks prior to his victory and had not been getting home in 2000, but clearly 100 per cent at Prestbury Park and will win more races if connections can keep him right though his appearances have dwindled in the last two seasons. Can maintain a strong gallop and has ironed out the majority of his jumping errors, but sticks to left-handed courses nowadays. *Mrs E.H. Irving — S. & W. Wilts (Sarah Waugh).* 154 (3mH), 583 (2m5f110yH), 687 (2m6f110yH), 1336 (2m4fH).

HAL'S PRINCE ..9-12-. 14 b.g. Le Moss — Hal's Pauper (Official) pp1p4. Compact half-brother to Shildon (IRE), and to Irish Pointing and English jumping winner, Superior Risk (IRE). NH FLAT r2 p0. NH '94/5 and '98 (for D. Brace when successful in '98) r10 w1 (2m Nov HCap Ch) p0; fell 3, and pulled up 2. P-t-P '93 and '97/8 (for Mr P. Watts, Mr J. Davies & Mr T.L. Jones) r15 w6 (up to Confined) p2 (2nds); failed to finish 5 (fell/unseated 3). Loves to force the pace, but off the track in '99 and has regressed with age. Often peppers his round with mistakes, but did not have to leave the ground once to provide Pip Jones with her 200th Point-to-Point winner when walking over in his Members. Usually fails to get the trip unless conditions are easy and has probably done enough now. *Mrs P.J. Lee — Tredegar F. (Tim Jones).* 1051 (Cf), 1295 (Cf), 1567 (M), 1569 (Cf), 1657 (Cf).

HAMISH ..9-5.. 7 b.g. Rakaposhi King — Kellamba (Netherkelly) p1pp. Owner-bred. Dam, half-sister to Bertie Boy (*qv* '93 Annual). Grandam, Ambalad ('the incredible hulk'), pulled up in all 4 Points, and ultimately broke down. Great-grandam, Ambatina, won 2 Points and 2nd 2. Great-great-grandam, Amba III, won 21 Points and placed 8. NH Oct '99 (for H.D.Daly) r1 p0 (4th). Got up close home to head the old dog Vulpin De Laugere in a particularly bad Maiden in holding at Eaton Hall, but unimpressive when pulling up thrice otherwise, and was very slow to start once. If he manages to return to form long trips should not bother him. *Mrs J.G. Griffith — Cheshire Forest (Reg Crank).* 570 (2m4fCfMa), 778 (OMa), 963 (R), 1200 (CR).

HAM N'EGGS ..—.. 10 b.g. Robellino (USA) — Rose And The Ring (Welsh Pageant) f. Good-bodied half-brother to Teucer, and to several flat winners, including Next Dance (also successful Hurdler), Lay The Blame, Benjarong, Derryring and Electric Rose. 5600y. FLAT (wins for R. Hannon) r21 w3 (7-8f, inc £7960 prize) p3 (beaten head for £7700 prize once,). NH '96/8 (for M. Hammond, bought for 9800, visored 3) r23 w5 (3 Hdles, 2m-2m2f, and 2 Chses, 2m-2m3f; inc hat-trick '96; one win on a technical disqualification) p7. Enjoyed plenty of success as a youngster, but the wheels have fallen right off now, and crashing after a mile on his only appearance since '98. Has always had a tendency to be error-prone, has hung badly left, and never successful beyond 2m3f. *Mrs L. Barr — Easton H. (Matthew Gingell).* 226 (2m4f110yH).

HANDFAST POINT ..9-9.. 10 b.g. Golden Heights — Typhoo Warning (Broadsword USA) 1p. Lengthy. P-t-p '97/9 r10 p3 (2nds, beaten neck once); pulled up 3, refused 1, and fell/unseated 3. Consistently hindered by the rider in previous seasons, but came with a wet sail to capture a Market Rasen Maiden on his reappearance. Had not stood many outings before and disappeared after appearing to go wrong three weeks later. At least he gained his just reward. *C.J. Vale — Belvoir.* 439 (OMa), 797 (R).

HANDSOME IS (IRE) ..8-2§.. 6 br.m. Mandalus — Brave Ruby (Proverb) ppp2. Dam won mares Maiden in Ireland. Sold Doncaster, May for 4200. Hung badly on her penultimate appearance, and then made favourite for an utterly ghastly three-runner Maiden at Southwell, but threw her head in the air on the flat after going six lengths clear and chucked the race away. Promptly retired from racing, reportedly etching out a new career in gentler equine pursuits. *Mrs S. Harley — Middleton (Tim Walford).* 168 (OMa), 398 (OMa), 696 (OMa), 1075 (OMa).

HANDY BOY ..—.. 6 b.g. Arzanni — Handymouse (Nearly A Hand) up. Dam, sister to 2 Pointers, including Hart Hill Lady (*qv* '94 Annual), won 2m1f Hdle and 2nd 2, and was placed in 2 Points. Pulled up after two miles on what was effectively his only outing (very late to the paddock on his debut, dwelt and threw the rider off after ten yards, quickly remounted, and then chucked him off again). *Mrs K.T. Pilkington — Enfield Chace (Alex Harvey).* 321 (R), 1116 (OMa).

HANGING GROVE (IRE) ..10-0.. 11 b.g. Asir — Churchlands Madam (Proverb) 4dp3. Compact attractive. NH FLAT '95 r3 p0. NH '95/6 and '97/8 r10 w1 (2m1f Sell Hdle) p2. P-t-P '98 r5 p2 (2nds, 3 fences last once); last pair 2, and unseated 1. Still capable of fair efforts as his third to Highway Lad at Kingston St Mary demonstrates, but has never been particularly consistent and his opportunities have become few and far between. His ability to truly stay three miles remains questionable. *J.H. Forbes — Mendip F.* 561 (O), 1098 (O), 1237 (Cf).

HANUKKAH ..9-4§.. 12 b.m. Oats — Badsworth Girl (Arch Sculptor) p331. Small close-coupled. Dam, half-sister to top Chaser, Badsworth Boy, won 2 Hdles, 2m-2m1f (was temperamental). P-t-P '95/9 r29 p5 (2 2nds, of 3 once); failed to finish 14 (on floor 4, and refused to start 1). Beaten at least eight lengths in 17 completions over six seasons prior to her final start where she was left clear at the penultimate fence to come home a clear cut winner at the 33rd attempt. Often difficult in the preliminaries and has been mounted on the course and taken to post early. Failed to reappear after her triumph and will surely have to rest on her laurels. *M.C.D. & P. Ansell & W. Hambley — S. Cornwall (Ian Hambley).* 105 (CfMa), 539 (OMa), 724 (CfMa).

HAPPEN TO MAKE IT (IRE) ..9-12.. 9 br.g. Supreme Leader — Magic User (Deep Run) 4R1. Unfurnished half-brother to Robin Of Loxley (IRE), and to Irish NH flat and Hurdles winner, Flying South. Great-grandam, Surprise Packet, won 1958 Liverpool Foxhunters. IRISH P-t-P '99 r2 p0 (pulled up 2). IRISH NH '99 r3 p1 (dead-heat 3rd in Hdle). Made most until fading quickly after two out on his English debut (well backed), ran out after two miles next time (favourite), but happened to make it third time lucky when making all on firm at Ashorne, where Julian Pritchard had to survive a bad blunder two out. quite speedy in a lowly grade at least, but lightly raced to date, and will hopefully spend more outings than Robin Of Loxley, who never got a chance to reveal his full potential. *Mrs V. Ramm — Cotswold (Jelly Nolan).* 197 (CfMa), 455 (OMa), 1439 (OMa).

HAPPY BLADE ..—.. 8 ch.g. Broadsword (USA) — Midsummer Gladness (Midsummer Night II) fu. Half-brother to Glad All Over (*qv*). Dam won 2m4f Hunt Ch and 8 Points and placed 9. His rider gave some embarrassing displays at Sandon in '99, and unfortunately appears to have got even worse. Fell at the fifth with Happy Blade at Kingston Blount, foolishly remounted and continued two fences behind, but crashed again at the ninth; and toppled off at the 12th at Mollington. *B.G. Durrell — Pytchley.* 249 (CfMa), 792 (OMa).

HAPPY BLAKE ..9-13.. 10 b.g. Blakelight — Happy To Play (Knave To Play) 2ff122. Compact well-made half-brother to Play An Ace (*qv*). NH FLAT Apr '97 r1 p0. NH '98/9 (from Mrs J. Storey's; tried tongue-tie) r7 p1 (3rd). Does not manage many fluent rounds, but was driven out to land a bad Maiden at Stainton, having fallen at the final fence with every chance the time before. Most disappointing on his latest appearance when beaten at 4-7 in a three-runner Restricted, but may have found the ground too firm, and certainly made far too many mistakes. May be able to atone. *Mrs B. Pigg & Mrs C. Todd — Haydon (Clive Storey).* 113 (OMa), 424 (R), 626 (OMa), 809 (OMa), 1326 (R), 1496 (R).

HAPPY CHAPPY ..—.. 8 b.g. Gildoran — Artalinda (Indiaro) p. Compact half-brother to Linger Balinda, Timbo and Indiway. Dam was 3rd in Ladies from 10 Points/Hunt Ch. Tailed off at Rodmell, where he looked backward and made a bad mistake after a mile which caused the rider to lose his irons. *Mrs B. Lewis — Ashford V.* 679 (OMa).

HAPPY MINSTRAL (USA) ..10-2.. 7 b.g. Alleged (USA) — Minstrelete (USA) (Round Table) 14461. Sturdy half-brother to 9 flat winners here and abroad, including Punctilio (useful in Ireland). Dam won at 8f in USA. IR 44,000y. FLAT (for M. Johnston to 3, blinkered final) r9 w1 (8f) p2 (2nds of 3). IRISH NH '98 r4 p1 (3rd). NH '98/9 (blinkered first 3; for Miss J. Baxter; previously for P. Nicholls, bought for 16,000) r8 p3 (inc 3rd in Sell). Bought Malvern, May for 1200. Won as two-year-old, but had looked very poor latterly over Hurdles. A switch to Points stalled his decline, but was lucky to find two simple opportunites — a four-finisher Confined taking seven minutes in soft at Garnons in which the hot favourite Well Ted became exhausted, and a two-finisher Mixed Open in similar conditions at Maisemore where the three length leader fell three out. Seems lazy, and was tried blinkered twice in mid-season. Has good riders. *R.H. Hughes — Kyre (Annie Downes).* 445 (Cf), 670 (O), 987 (Cf), 1086 (Cf), 1313 (MO).

HAPPY TEAM ..9-9.. 8 ch.m. Teamster — Happy Tino (Rugantino) 222fs. Workmanlike home-bred half-sister to Parditino (*qv*). P-t-P '99 r2 p1 (2nd); and pulled up 1. Has been well supported each time she has run, particularly so at Stafford Cross where two mistakes at around the two mile mark proved costly. Looked to have been found the ideal opportunity at Bratton Down in a three-runner affair, but once again Lady Luck was lobbing stones at her and she fell at the third last when holding every chance. Beaten a maximum of five lengths in her four placings and it will only be a matter of time before she gains richly deserved compensation. *Mrs C. Nicholas — Tiverton (Ken Nicholas).* 146 (OMa), 733 (2m4fOMa), 933 (OMa), 1141 (CfMa), 1308 (OMa).

HARBOUR BLAZE (IRE) ..10-1.. 11 ch.g. Lord Ha Ha — Harbour Shuil (Proverb) 32u234u4. Tall rangy. IRISH NH FLAT '96/7 r4 p0 (last once). IRISH NH '97 r2 p0 (Hdles, fell 1). P-t-P '98/9 r13 w2 (Maiden and Restricted) p4 (2 2nds); pulled up 3, and fell 2. Inconsistent due to his faulty jumping, but capable of decent efforts on his day though they are becoming fewer and far between. Failed to build upon his second to Pharlindo at Duncombe Park and not all that far away from a squiggle. Runner-up on the only occasion that he has run in Ladies company and might be worth another spin in such a race. Stays well and does best when there is a fair cut in the ground. *S.B. Clark — York & Ainsty S.* 134 (I), 277 (Cf), 394 (Cf), 692 (I), 804 (Cf), 1027 (Cf), 1348 (Cf), 1478 (I).

HARBOUR ISLAND ..10-6§.. 9 b.g. Rainbow Quest (USA) — Quay Line (High Line) 643p1. Small light half-brother to 6 flat winners (one in Jersey), including Purple Splash (also successful Hurdler) and Coleridge. Dam won 6 flat at 3 (10-15f, inc Park Hill Stakes). FLAT (for M. Stoute) r9 w1 (14f) p2. NH '97/9 (for M. Pipe, bought for 20,000) r12 w1 (2m4f Hdle) p0; 6th to Istabraq in '97 Sun Alliance, but last and pulled up 2 on final 3 attempts. Bought Ascot, July for 700. Bred in the purple, but has given many thoroughly ungenuine displays, and apparently sickened Martin Pipe beyond endurance. Remained very quirky in Points, but was beaten just over a length when third at 25-1 in a Confined, and scored two outings later at 20-1 in similar company in softish at Pentreclwydau, where John Llewellyn made a brilliant recovery from a bad blunder at the last. Never went a yard in an Open previously, and cannot be trusted an inch. Wears blinkers, and has been visored. A triumph for connections, but is just as likely to achieve a double squiggle as he is to reach 10-6. *R. Flint — Llangeinor.* 480 (O), 598 (O), 819 (O), 945 (O), 1295 (Cf).

HARDY WEATHER (IRE) ..9-4.. 12 br.g. Strong Gale — Hardy Colleen (Hardboy) pu. Small compact. IRISH P-t-P '95 r2 w1 (6yo&up Maiden) p0; fell 1. IRISH NH FLAT '95 r1 p1 (2nd). NH '95/8 r10 p5 (3 Hdles, and 2 2nds in Chses). P-t-P '99 r6 p0 (5th, last 2, fell/unseated 2, and pulled up 1). Made most when defeating Fundy by 10 lengths in Ireland, and subsequently put up some good displays under Rules, but has been far less successful as a Pointer, and makes plenty of blunders and does not go well for the owner. Disappeared after two early runs and may well have suffered a setback. *C.J.W. Smyth — O. Berks.* 63 (I), 216 (Cnr).

HARDY WOLF ..—.. 10 ch.g. Little Wolf — Sister Corruption (Bribe) fpppp. Rangy home-bred. P-t-P '97/8 r6 p1 (distant 2nd); 6th, pulled up 3, and refused 1. Went wrong at Bredwardine in '98, and has performed miserably since his return. Looks unwilling under pressure and is a consistently poor jumper. Pulled up and dismounted when risked on firm ground again at Bonvilston and clearly not held in very high regard. Carries plenty of condition. *W.A.P. Layton — S. Herefords (Christine Hardinge).* 995 (OMa), 1277 (OMa), 1455 (OMa), 1624 (OMa), 1661 (OMa).

HARLEIDALUS (IRE) ..9-4.. 7 b.g. Mandalus — Spartan Park (Scorpio FR) p51. Rangy brother to Spartan Breeze. Dam pulled up in 3 Irish races including 2 Points in '97. Grandam is half-sister to Spartan Missile. P-t-P '99 (for Mr W.M. Aitchison) r2 p0 (fell 2). NH Jun '99 r2 p0. Cleared a total of two fences successfully in '99, and is still no easy ride, but fiddled his way round Lockerbie to beat one badly hanging rival and dear old Meadowleck after two confidence boosters in Restricteds. Like many by his sire appreciated the sound underfoot conditions when successful, and may have more scope for improvement. *W.T. Reed — Haydon (Tim Reed).* 40 (R), 184 (R), 978 (CfMa).

HARLEQUIN BOY ..9-0§.. 8 b.g. Roscoe Blake — Gain The Day (Bivouac) ppp1pp. Wormanlike half-brother to Cinders Day. Dam, sister or half-sister to 3 Pointers including Gorse Hunter (*qv* '93 Annual), won 2m4f Ch and 3rd in 2 Hdles; subsequently pulled up in 3 Points. Bought Malvern, May for 2000. Blinkered for the first time when winning a three-finisher youngster Maiden on firmish at Charlton Horethorne, but is ungenuine and regularly jumps left, and has been pulled up in all his other races. Mark Shears did well to get him to score, and it looks very much as if it will prove to be a one-off. Has at least one inveterate gambler amongst his list of owners, and was punted heavily on his first two starts, but it didn't last long and was an unloved 9-1 when successful. *R. Crabb, D. Dodd, R. & Mrs S. Richards & C. Tizzard — Blackmore & Sparkford V. (Pauline Tizzard).* 12 (OMa), 58 (OMa), 213 (OMa), 956 (OMa), 1135 (R), 1309 (R).

HARLEYBURN ..9-8.. 9 b.g. Wonderful Surprise — Miss Anax (Anax) puu332pup. Smallish unfurnished brother to Wattasupriseforus. P-t-P '98/9 r6 p2; pulled up 2, and unseated 1. Affected by a virus in '99, but has always been a weak finisher and still struggling to get home. Almost sprang a 40-1 surprise when beaten a length by Little Brockwell at Corbridge when blinkered for the first time, but a beaten favourite four times subsequently and should not be supported at cramped odds again. Headstrong, and threw a tantrum at the start once and still has trouble catching the rider. *Mrs M.A. Bowie — Buccleuch (Jim Bowie).* 46 (OMa), 114 (OMa), 188 (OMa), 420 (I), 712 (M), 1123 (OMa), 1431 (OMa), 1500 (OMa), 1580 (OMa).

HARPS HALL (IRE) ..9-1.. 7 ch.g. Yashgan — Parsons Glen (IRE) (Glen Quaich) 363p4. Tall. IRISH P-t-P '99 r2 p1 (50*I* last of 3); and pulled up. Bought Doncaster, Aug for 5000. Two placed efforts at Brocklesby Park were reasonable, but otherwise most disappointing, particularly 4-7 for his Members (never went a yard). A very weak finisher at present, and was sweating profusely and jumped deliberately at times when fourth in his latest appearance — would have won the race in the absence of anything owned by a Millington! *Mrs J.A. Youdan — Grove & Rufford.* 234 (OMa), 436 (OMa), 793 (CfMa), 1069 (M), 1504 (CfMa).

HARRY HENBIT (IRE) ..—.. 10 b.g. Henbit (USA) — I'm Grannie (Perspex) ff. Small neat half-brother to Who's In Charge, and to jumping winner, Four Deep (IRE). IRISH NH FLAT '97 r1 p0. IRISH NH '97/8 (tried blinkered) r7 p0. NH '00 r1 p0 (fell in 2m110y Nov Ch: *prom, wknd 5 out, fell nxt*). Lightly raced and has never earned a bean, but his stable have a good record with unlikely material (other than the famous example of Norton's Coin), and he ran well enough for a long way at Hereford to suggest that he might have excellent in a Welsh Maiden. *S.G. Griffiths — Gogerddan.* 468 (3m1f110yH).

HARRY LAWS ..9-9.. 8 b.g. Feelings (FR) — Pohet (Pongee) fp21p. Tall rangy home-bred brother to Naughty Feelings. Dam won 2 Hdles, 2m-2m2f. P-t-P '99 r3 p0 (pulled up 2, and ran out 1). Schooling in his first season, but far more competitive in 2000 and seized the initiative on the run-in after the leader had blundered at the last when successful at Corbridge. Seems a natural front-runner, but has twice stopped quickly as though something was amiss and supporting him in future might be a risky business. Has the scope to improve if all is well. *W.J. Laws — Tynedale.* 425 (CfMa), 719 (CfMa), 913 (CfMa), 1164 (OMa), 1363 (R).

HARRY TARTAR ..9-6.. 10 b.g. Cisto (FR) — Tartar Holly VII (unknown) 635. Plain unfurnished owner-bred brother to Henry Tartar. P-t-P/HUNT CH '96/7 and '99 r15 w1 (Maiden) p2 (2nds); pulled up 5, and fell/unseated 3. Beat little when readily landing an older horses Maiden at Fakenham last year and has predictably struggled in Restricted company since. Becoming indolent, and looks unlikely to figure in competitive races again. *J.D. Parker (The Parker Family) — Waveney H. (Juliet Arthur).* 239 (R), 761 (R), 1111 (R).

HARVEST HOME (IRE) ..8-13§.. 9 b.g. Dromod Hill — Carlys Bank (Saucy Kit) f4. Narrow light. Dam, half-sister to 5 Pointers including Rightsaidfred (*qv* '96 Annual), won a Maiden and 3rd (became a bitter disappointment after winning her debut totally unchallenged). Grandam is Ladybank (*qv* Granville Guest in '98 Annual). P-t-P '97/9 r6 p0 (pulled up 3, refused 1, fell 1, and ran out 1). Lightly raced and a most unpleasant ride to date and Tim Dennis will probably not have been too disappointed that his season was over in the space of a week in 2000. Has been taken to post early and tried in a tongue-strap. *W.P. Harper — Tetcott (Tim Dennis).* 254 (CfMa), 311 (CfMa).

HARVEYSINAHURRY ..9-0.. 8 b.g. Push On — Shylyn (Hay Chas) p2p. Workmanlike brother to Pushlyn and Henrys No Pushover, and to NH flat winner, Sir Gymcrak. Dam, half-sister to Aj's Boy, was last and pulled up 3 in Points. Damsire won 2m2f Ch. NH FLAT '98 (for G. Knight) r1 p0. Four lengths second behind a nine-year-old making her only appearance ever, and the race was further devalued by the two favourites falling. Gave a poor display next time, and cannot be taken seriously yet. *C. Clark & G. Fielding — Dulverton E. (F. Hollis).* 850 (R), 1099 (OMa), 1307 (OMa).

HARWELD ..10-4.. 9 ch.g. Weld — Fruit Farm (Twiberry) 11. Tall rangy owner-bred brother to Fruit Crop, and half-brother to Fruit Of Oak (IRE) and Fruit Field. Dam, half-sister to Farriers Favourite (qv '99 Annual), won 13 Points (inc 5 Ladies and Open) and placed 7. P-t-P '97/9 r5 w1 (2m4f Maiden) p0; fell/unseated 2, refused 1, and pulled up 1. An enigmatic character, but seems back on the straight and narrow (for the time being at least) and was quite impressive in winning two slowly-run races in 2000. Quite a live wire who does not stand much racing, and not averse to digging his toes in when in the mood, but has plenty of ability when he wishes to reveal it and will win again if his current co-operative mood lasts. Not yet the most fluent of jumpers. *E.H. Crow — N. Salop (Sheila Crow).* 120 (CR), 783 (I).

HATCHAM BOY (IRE) ..10-10.. 11 br.g. Roselier (FR) — Auling (Tarqogan) u211112221. Workmanlike. Dam won 2-finisher N Ledbury Members. NH FLAT '95 r1 p1 (2nd). NH '95/8 r16 w2 (2m6f Hdle and 3m Ch) p6; fell/unseated 5, inc Hdle. P-t-P/HUNT CH '99 r10 w2 (Open and Ladies) p7 (4 3rds, of 4 once, and last once, and inc Hunt Ch); and unseated 1. A poor jumper under Rules, and often disappointed, but has proved wonderfully consistent in Points and has never failed to make the frame in 18 completions. Farmed some easy options in Open company, but had to call upon all his reserves of stamina and determination to win a 4m2f Uttoxeter Hunter Chase on his final start. Remains a fiddly jumper and often loses his pitch during the course of a race, but gets excellent assistance from Christian Ward-Thomas and is now prepared to scrape for him. Sure to run up another sequence in 2001, but has a long way to go before he gets close to former stablemate St Gregory's haul. *Mr & Mrs A.G.C. Howland Jackson — Suffolk (Ruth Hayter).* 17 (O), 85 (O), 218 (L), 415 (O), 553 (MO), 842 (O), 938 (3m4fO), 1182 (O), 1532 (3m1fH), 1592 (4m2fH).

HATCH GATE ..—.. 8 gr.g. Lighter — Yankee Silver (Yankee Gold) uppp. Brother to Elmers Marsh and Iron Hill. P-t-P '99 r1 p0 (pulled up). Jumps poorly, and seems devoid of talent. *A.J. & Mrs D.M. Lawes — Chid, Lec & Cowdray (Andrew Lawes).* 130 (CMod), 284 (2m4fCMa), 457 (OMa), 984 (OMa).

HATTERILL RIDGE ..10-2§.. 11 br.g. Rustingo — Nun Owen (Owen Anthony) 23p26. Small unfurnished. Dam, half-sister to Celtic Abbott (qv '95 Annual), won NH flat and 2 Points and 2nd. Grandam, Scottish Nun, won 9 Points and placed 13. P-t-P '96/9 r16 w3 (Members, Restricted and PPORA) p3 (2 2nds); pulled up 7, and fell 1. Won three minor races to '98, but an erratic jumper who can be a hard ride and did well to chase home subsequent dual Hunter Chase winner Lakefield Rambler on his only start last year. Did well to gain another three prizes in 2000, including a third at Stratford, but has avoided winning in his last nine outings despite the assistance of some of the best jockeys in the sport. Has been tried in blinkers and a pricker once. Suited by top-of-the-ground. *Mrs J. Hughes — Ledbury.* 297 (I), 580 (3mH), 1064 (3m2fCf), 1490 (I), 1558 (3mH).

HATTIE ..9-2.. 7 b.m. Sylvan Express — Hatsu-Girie (Ascertain USA) 56. Half-sister to Buddy Girie. Dam, half-sister to Pepper Elder (qv '93 Annual), won 3 Chses, 2m4f-3m3f, for Robert Swiers. P-t-P '99 r3 p0 (last, and pulled up 2). Only once better than last in five starts, and yet to finish within 20 lengths of the winner, but out of a decent mare and has shown a little ability. Getting few opportunities however, and her season was over by mid-March. *R.W. Swiers — York & Ainsty N.* 167 (OMa), 627 (OMa).

HATTON FARM BABE ..10-6.. 10 b.m. Lochnager — Hatton Farm Girl (Humdoleila) 2111. Small neat. Dam, half-sister to Space Gem (qv '92 Annual), was quickly tailed off before pulling up in 3 Points for Susan Norbury in '93. P-t-P/HUNT CH '98/9 r8 w1 (Members) p2 (3rds, of 4 once); fell 1, and pulled up 3. Too strong for the owner in the past, but hit it off immediately with Sue Sharratt who has been able to do her full justice. Won two competitive stamina tests before facing a simple task in her Members on her final outing, and looks the sort who could do well in Ladies races in future. Speedy, but has abundant stamina and is best suited by plenty of cut in the ground. *Mrs S.A. Norbury — N. Staffs.* 532 (R), 589 (R), 902 (Cf), 1124 (M).

HAUGHTON LAD (IRE) ..10-1.. 12 b.g. Drumalis — I'm The Latest (Polyfoto) 12u6u. Unfurnished half-brother to Taufast and Latest Thyne (IRE), and to flat winners, Taupie and Kamaress. Dam won 3 8f races in Ireland. IRISH NH FLAT '93/4 r9 p2 (beaten head once). IRISH FLAT '94 r2 p0; disqualified for not weighing-in once. NH '95/7 r17 p3 (Hdles, 2 2nds; inc Sell); claimed for £6000 final outing. P-t-P '98 r8 w1 (Maiden) p0; last, pulled up 4, and fell 2. Took 31 races to open his account, but beat three subsequent winners easily in the process and it is hard to believe that he failed to beat another rival in '98. Returned from a season on the sidelines and was the chief beneficiary of Pharare's late departure at Garnons, but reverted back to his disappointing ways when substitute riders were employed on his last three starts. Flattered by an Open success, and remains untrustworthy. Avoids ground any softer than good. *Mrs R. Mackness — Cotswold (Jelly Nolan).* 668 (L), 699 (L), 969 (L), 1417 (L), 1561 (MO).

HAUNTING MUSIC (IRE) ..9-6.. 13 b.g. Cataldi — Theme Music (Tudor Music) up52p. Tall rangy good-looking half-brother to Monty's Theme (IRE), to 2 Irish flat winners, and to a successful Pointer there. Dam won at 5f in Ireland. IRISH NH FLAT '94/5 r3 w1 p0. IRISH NH '95 r2 w1 (2m6f Hdle) p1 (2nd). NH '96/8 (wins for Mrs A. Perrett; previously for G. Harwood) r12 w2 (2m5g Chses) p5. Sold Ascot, March for 1500. Did not get the trip in Points, but had been purchased as a schoolmaster for Liz Neyens, and gave her some decent experience, notably when a fair second at Rodmell. Unfortunately died in a bizarre accident at home. Miss E.C.M. Neyens — Grafton (Jenny Pidgeon). 28 (L), 78 (L), 969 (L), 1211 (L), 1417 (L).

HAVE A BREAK ..9-11.. 6 b.g. Most Welcome — Miss Tealeaf (USA) (Lear Fan USA) p4fp21. Lengthy half-brother to Hurdles winner, Mr Jake. FLAT (blinkered last 2) r6 p0. NH '98 (for C. Egerton; blinkered and tongue-tied) r1 p0. Looks a very tricky ride and has taken some sorting out, but followed a one length second with a narrow victory at Kingston Blount, which concluded an incredible day for his trainer (five winners) and Rory Lawther (partnered four of the five). Hung right after the last and could not be straightened, and possibly lucky to keep the prize, as he did not leave Tonrin with much room. It was fortunate that his partner was on such a high, as it took adrenalin, and inspiration to get the horse home. May lack the scope to improve his rating. *N.D. Quesnel — Berks & Bucks (John White).* 249 (CfMa), 328 (CfMa), 754 (CfMa), 1021 (2m4fOMa), 1439 (OMa), 1624 (OMa).

HAVEAFEWMANNERS (IRE) ..10-0.. 11 b.m. Celio Rufo — Ardagh Princess (Proverb) p2pppf3*25*. Compact half-sister to Glenpine (IRE). Dam is an unraced sister to Tophatter (*qv* '95 Annual). IRISH NH '95/7 r9 w1 (2m6f Hdle) p1 (2nd); fell in Hunt Ch. IRISH P-t-P '97 r5 w1 (6&7yo mares Maiden) p1 (last of 3 after jockey had ridden finish a circuit too soon); pulled up 2, and fell 1. NH '98 r4 p0 (bhnd in Hdles; fell 1). P-t-P/HUNT CH '98/9 r9 p3 (2 2nds; and last of 3); fell/unseated 3, pulled up 2, and ran out 1. NH '00 (for P. Eccles) r2 p1 (2nd in 3m2f Nov Ch: *ld til hdd 6, wknd 12, lft in ld 3 out, hdd when fell last, rmtd*; and 5th in 2m5f Nov Ch: *ld, mist & hdd 2, wknd 7, sn t.o*). A confirmed front-runner (wears a kineton and usually pulls very hard), but invariably runs herself into the ground and has yet to last home in 12 Points. Unlucky in her Members in 2000 as Mia Lowndes lost her irons when making a hash of the last and the partnership were collared near the finish, and deserves to win a minor event. Often tongue-tied, and was blinkered once in '98. *G.W. Briscoe — W. Salop.* 35 (Cnr), 292 (M), 862 (Cf), 1025 (3m110yH), 1151 (O), 1254 (O), 1343 (3m110yH).

HAVEN LIGHT ..9-12.. 14 b.g. Flower Robe — Points Review (Major Point) 16p4. Compact. IRISH P-t-P '91/3 r9 w1 (5yo Maiden) p0; last of 3, but disqualified, and failed to finish 3 (fell 1, and ran out 1). IRISH NH FLAT r1 p0. IRISH NH '93 r3 p0. P-t-P/HUNT CH '94/9 r27 w6 (inc Restricted, PPORA and Intermediate) p7 (4 3rds); failed to finish 10 (fell/unseated 3 — when 20*l* clear 2 out once). A grand old servant to the Spencers and has managed an annual success in each of the last six seasons for them (won twice in '99). Picked up his Members for the fourth time in five years on his reappearance, but as in previous seasons has been found wanting in more competitive races subsequently. A superb jumper, but not a true stayer and has found the hilly course at Upper Sapey much to his liking as he can freewheel for much of the last mile before gathering himself for the uphill finish. Best suited by fast ground, but can handle it much softer. Always turned out immaculately. *Mrs J.P. Spencer — Clifton-on-Teme (Kay Spencer).* 697 (M), 988 (O), 1272 (Cf), 1630 (Cf).

HAVE TO THINK ..—§.. 13 b.g. Impecunious — Dusty Run (Deep Run) urpp. Rangy half-brother to NH flat winner, Barbary Falcon. IRISH NH '92/6 r38 w7 (2m Hdle, and 6 Chses, 2m-3m1f) p10 (2nd, and 9 3rds); one run Aintree. NH '96/8 (for P. Nicholls, bought for 28,000) r8 p2. Enjoyed great success on all types of ground in Ireland, but has declined appallingly, and unplaced in his last ten English races. Occasionally blinkered, and has worn a tongue-strap. Did not want to know in Points, and hopefully retired. *J.A.C. Sheppard — Quantock.* 195 (O), 334 (O), 446 (O), 1087 (MO).

HAWAIIAN SAM (IRE) ..9-10.. 11 b.g. Hawaiian Return (USA) — Thomastown Girl (Tekoah) 7p. Big rangy half-brother to Doran's Town Lad. Dam, half-sister to Champion Hurdler, For Auction, won an Irish Bumper and was disqualified after winning another. NH '94/9 (two wins for K. Burke; previously for A. Turnell) r27 w4 (2m Hdle, and 3 Chses, 2m5f-3m1f, 4 ran and 2 finished once) p9. Scored on his final outing in the previous yard (June '99), but soundly beaten in two Sandown Hunter Chases in 2000, including a race in which he should have had a live chance. Made several mistakes on that occasion, and is always prone to errors. Suited by a little cut in the ground. *Brig C.K. Price — O. Berks (Gary Brown).* 226 (2m4f110yH), 469 (3m110yH).

HAY DANCE ..9-6.. 10 b.g. Shareef Dancer (USA) — Hay Reef (Mill Reef USA) p53. Small neat half-brother to 6 flat winners (one in Belgium), and to successful Hurdler, Pharly Reef. Dam, half-sister to Wassi, won at 10f. FLAT '94/5 (for J. Leigh) r8 p0. IRISH FLAT '96 r1 p0. IRISH NH '95/6 (bought for 1500) r5 w1 (2m Hdle) p1 (2nd). NH '96/9 (for P. Hobbs) r13 w4 (2-2m1f Hdles, 5 ran thrice) p4; inc Sell. Bought Ascot, June for 2500. A competent Hurdler at the minimum trip, particularly on firm ground, but fell on three of his final five attempts. Showed plenty of early speed in Ladies Opens, but slowed dramatically and beaten 40 lengths minimum, and the only way he would stay three miles in the back of a horsebox. *Mrs S.J. Ruddle — Waveney H. (John Ibbott)*. 608 (L), 939 (L), 1289 (L).

HAYDENS FIELD ..9-9.. 7 b.g. Bedford (USA) — Releta (Relkino) 1. Small half-brother to Hurdles winner, Reltic, and to Chasing winner, Reluckino. Dam won 4 Points consecutively and placed in 2 Hunt Chses (rated 10-10). P-t-P '99 r2 p0 (last pair twice). Out of a very useful mare who used to gallop her rivals into submission and took a leaf out of her book when building up a huge lead at Black Forest Lodge, but virtually stopped on the approach to three out and did well to wrestle back the initiative in the closing stages. Had no subsequent scorers behind him, and failed to air again, but displayed plenty of speed and whilst quirky looks up to winning again provided he has come to no lasting harm. *Miss H. Lewis — Llangibby*. 207 (OMa).

HAYNE CONDOR ..7-8.. 8 b.g. Northern Game — Holcombe Lass (Baltus) ppf. Strong-topped half-brother to Hayne Lass. Dam won Tiverton Members and placed 5, and grandam, Balius II, won Tiverton Members and 3rd. P-t-P '99 r8 p0 (last, pulled up 4, and fell/unseated 3). Completed on the only occasion Les Jefford has partnered him, but finished a remote last, and has otherwise pulled up through a lack of stamina or got on the floor. *Mrs M.J. Reed — Silverton (Linda Blackford)*. 562 (CfMa), 655 (OMa), 856 (CfMa).

HAZEL REILLY (IRE) ..9-9.. 10 b.m. Mister Lord (USA) — Vickies Gold (Golden Love) 2123p55p. Compact sister to Rambling Lord (IRE), Lord Vick (IRE), Lord Harry (IRE) and Fortune Of Gold (IRE). P-t-P '98/9 r4 p0 (pulled up 3, and fell 1). Failed to complete in her first two seasons, but managed a full campaign for the first time in 2000 and did well in the first half of the season. Rallied gamely to justify favouritism at Duncombe Park and finished strongly in Restricted company on three occasions, but began to struggle when the ground dried up and clearly needs a severe test of stamina. Should win again when conditions are suitable. *J. Mackley — S. Durham (Sarah Dent)*. 133 (CCfMa), 283 (OMa), 396 (R), 797 (R), 1000 (R), 1230 (R), 1349 (O), 1478 (I).

HAZY SEA (IRE) ..10-3.. 9 b.g. Supreme Leader — Sea Castle (Carlingford Castle) p1. Unfurnished. IRISH P-t-P '97/8 r6 w1 (5&6yo Mdn) p2; pulled up 2. IRISH NH '98/9 (blinkered last 3) r11 p0 (inc P-t-P flat; pulled up and unseated in Chses). Bought Doncaster, Aug for 1900. Came with a strong late burst under an efficient ride from Charlie Weaver when shocking the punters at 33-1 at Kimble, but conditions have been barely raceable earlier in the day (two fences were omitted), and a delve back into the Irish form book showed that his only previous victory had been in heavy. Looked quite useful, but now has to prove he can do it when the mud is not flying. An interesting prospect for the owner and her gaggle of Girl Power helpers. *Mrs J. Shirley — Oxford*. 610 (R), 1146 (R).

HEARTS ARE WILD ..10-9.. 14 ch.g. Scallywag — Henry's True Love (Random Shot) 31p11f. Tall deep-bodied half-brother to jumping winner, Sail By The Stars. Dam is half-sister to useful jumping winner, Dublin Express, the dam of top-class jumping winner, Dublin Flyer. NH '91/6 r15 w3 (2m1f Hdle, and 2 2m4f Chses) p3 (2nds). P-t-P '97 and '99 r5 w4 (3 Ladies and Mixed Open, inc hat-trick '99) p1 (2nd). A sprightly teenager who can still go at a pace many of his juniors cannot handle and makes the bulk of the running when successful. Did not see out the extended trip at Dunthrop on ground easier than he likes, but involved in one of the races of the season at Weston Park where he and Pharare winged fence after fence vying for the lead, and in the end the judge could not split them (though it appeared that Hearts Are Wild had just prevailed). Still takes a strong hold at times, and is a very bold jumper, but also a willing battler and there is nothing in his make up that is not truly admirable. Has few miles on the clock and there is no reason to believe he will not have an equally successful season in 2001. Probably needs a run to put him straight. *Miss P. Gundry & T. Nixon — Cotley (John Daniell)*. 101 (L), 558 (L), 1014 (3m5fL), 1410 (L), 1553 (L), 1648 (3mH).

HEATHBURN (IRE) ..9-11.. 8 b.g. Lafontaine (USA) — Taberna Lady (Paddy's Stream) u21f1. Strong-topped. Dam is half-sister to 4 Pointing winners (3 in Ireland), including The Mill Height. IRISH P-t-P '98/9 r12 p7; pulled up 1. Sold Doncaster, May for 7000. Kept knocking on the door in Ireland, and finally delivered after eight placings when collecting a two-finisher Maiden in soft at Cottenham. Seemed to derive confidence, because he fell two out with every chance next time, and then gave his best yet when easily landing a Restricted. A thorough stayer, and might start to win quite regularaly in future. *M. Ward-Thomas — Mr & Mrs A.G.C. Howland-Jackson — Suffolk (Ruth Hayter)*. 259 (C), 550 (OMa), 1040 (OMa), 1181 (R), 1379 (R).

HEATHER LAD ..9-11.. 8 ch.g. Highlands — Ragged Rose (Scallywag) 3u226162. Close-coupled half-brother to Wild Briar. Dam failed to finish in four Points for Mrs Taylor (looked a handful). P-t-P '98/9 r6 p0; pulled up 3, unseated 1. Flattered on several occasions before eventually opening his account at Hornby Castle, but cast in a similar mould to his mother and does not make life easy for David Raw. Seems best when he can be persuaded to settle in behind, but can get rather het up beforehand and has two handlers. A steady jumper, and his reliability should enable him to find another opportunity. *C.B. Taylor — S. Durham*. 133 (CCfMa), 380 (OMa), 624 (OMa), 693 (OMa), 1004 (OMa), 1032 (OMa), 1326 (R), 1474 (M).

HEATHVIEW ..9-6.. 14 b.g. Pitpan — Whosview (Fine Blade USA) pp. Small sturdy half-brother to Far View (IRE), Hey Chief (IRE), Celtic Who (IRE) and Good View (IRE). NH FLAT r2 p2 (3rds). NH '93/6 and '97 r37 w3 (2m2f Hdle, and 2 Chses, 2m1f-2m6f, lucky once) p13; fell/unseated 6 (in lead at last once), and refused 1. P-t-P/HUNT CH '97 and '99 r9 w2 (Members and Confined) p2 (remote 3rd of 4 once; inc Hunt Ch); pulled up 1, and fell 2. Found two simple opportunities in '97, but soft and will not battle when matters get difficult. Well beaten when completing in '99 and looks a spent force now. *Mrs P. Corbett — Tedworth (Philippa Chamings).* 1246 (Cf), 1279 (M).

HEATHYARD'S FLIGHT ..—.. 7 b.g. Statoblest — Jeanne Avril (Music Boy) ppu. Small light half-brother to 3 winners, including useful sprinter, Mary Hinge. Dam won 2 6f races. FLAT r5 p0 (inc Sells). P-t-P '99 r4 p0 (pulled up 3, and unseated 1). Anchored in his first season, but has failed to stay when the handbrake has been let off and unlikely to prove good enough for shorter races under Rules. Still eligible for 2m4f Maidens, but even that trip has looked beyond his stamina limitations to date. *Mrs E. Kulbicki — Curre (Andrew Price).* 672 (2m4fOMa), 747 (CfMa), 925 (2mH).

HEAVENLY BLUES ..9-8.. 9 ch.g. Gods Solution — Pitskelly Blues (Pitskelly) p7. Good-topped lengthy home-bred half-brother to Roxkelly Blues and Super Blues, and to Hurdles winner, Rhythm And Blues. Dam won 6 Points and 3 Chses (2-3m) consecutively prior to breaking down. P-t-P '99 r2 p0 (pulled up 2). Showed up well for a long way in both outings in 2000, but disappeared quickly and gave the impression that three miles is stretching his stamina beyond breaking point. Might be worth one more chance in a Maiden on an easy track. *Mrs L. Spink — Zetland.* 139 (OMa), 377 (R).

HEAVENLY CITIZEN (IRE) ..9-12.. 13 ch.g. Ovac (ITY) — Miss Pushover (Push On) 5u644. Rangy. IRISH NH FLAT r1 p0. IRISH P-t-P '92/3 r17 w2 p8 (looked winner when placed 2nd once); pulled up 4, and fell/unseated 3. IRISH NH '93 r4 w2 (2m6f-3m, one over banks) p0. NH '93/4 and 96/9 r30 w2 (3m2f Chses) p6. P-t-P '95 (for Mr J.L. Gledson) r2 p0 (ran out 1, and pulled up 1). A competent performer in soft under Rules and gained both his English wins at Catterick, but became indolent and has not gone for a novice on his return to Points. Has been tried blinkered and tongue-tied in the past. Can be safely ignored in future. *Miss E. Edminson — Border.* 496 (C), 912 (Cf), 1078 (Cf), 1168 (O), 1501 (M).

HEAVENLY SEVEN ..8-13.. 7 b.m. Buckley — Reperage (USA) (Key To Content USA) pu. Strong-topped rangy home-bred sister to Buckley House, and half-sister to Flapjack Lad. Dam won at 8f in France. P-t-P '99 r6 p1 (2nd of 3); and pulled up 5. Frequently headstrong and an alarming jumper in her debut season, and no better in two early season Maidens on her return. Absent since late January and may have suffered a setback. *Mrs R.F. Knipe — S. Herefords (Robin Knipe).* 22 (2m4fOMa), 58 (OMa).

HECTORS WAY ..9-7.. 10 ch.g. Doctor Wall — Ty-Pren (Precipice Wood) p. Tall parrot-mouthed half-brother to Torc Falls. Dam won a Maiden and placed 7, inc a Hunt Ch. P-t-P '97/8 r5 w1 (Maiden) p2 (3rd of 4, after rejoining once); and pulled up 2. Left clear to win a Maisemore Maiden in '98, but broke down next time and his comeback lasted just one race. Had been lame in '97 and clearly has legs of jelly. *J. Bates — Croome & W. Warwicks (Sarah Bates).* 567 (R).

HEE'S A DANCER ..10-6.. 9 b.g. Rambo Dancer (CAN) — Heemee (On Your Mark) 64326p5. Small compact brother to flat winner, Dancing Rainbow. Dam won 2 5f races, inc a Sell. FLAT r11 p0. NH '95/7 r11 w2 (2m-2m1f) p2 (2nds in Chses). P-t-P/HUNT CH '99 r10 w4 (inc 2m4f Hunt Ch, Mixed Open and Ladies) p3 (2 2nds); and fell/unseated 3. A cheap buy for present connections, but served them well in '99 when four victories included a modest Ludlow Hunter Chase. Could not manage to maintain his strike rate in 2000, but ran well on several occasions, none more so than when third to Grimley Gale back at Ludlow. A good galloper, who is happy to front-run, and effective on most ground (though appreciates some cut), but still liable to careless errors. A reunion with Dai Jones for whom he won three times last year might prove beneficial. *Mr & Mrs R.W.J. Willcox — Llangeinor.* 150 (3mH), 272 (L), 684 (2m4fH), 1293 (3mH), 1341 (2m110yH), 1444 (2m5fH), 1600 (2m5f110yH).

HEHAS ..9-10.. 11 b.g. True Song — Shewill (Evening Trial) 5f74711. Lengthy owner-bred brother to Hemust, Hehad and Shedoes, and half-brother to Shedid (dam of He's A Lad *qv*), Hedoes, She Has and Hesgreen. Dam, half-sister to Hewould, won Maiden and 2nd 4. P-t-P '96 and '98/9 r12 w3 (Maiden, Restricted and Members) p3 (2 2nds; and 3rd of 4); pulled up 1. Enjoyed his busiest season to date in 2000, but had to wait until May before he could find his form. Tends to become outpaced at the vital stage of a race, but has a strong finish when it does eventually kick in and used it do good effect in his Members. Beat little at Larkhill next time , but game and can usually be relied upon to put in a faultless round so another minor race should be on the cards in 2001. Acts on a sound surface. *Mrs E.C. Cockburn — Warwicks.* 63 (I), 191 (Cf), 615 (CMod), 886 (C), 1015 (4mO), 1438 (M), 1599 (I).

HEIR OF GOLD (IRE) ..9-10.. 9 b.g. Air Display (USA) — Golden Owen (Master Owen) 15p. Tall rangy half-brother to Paddy Van Halan, Gaddy Owen and Meigle Street. P-t-P '98/9 r3 p1 (2nd); pulled up 1, and carried out 1. A good second at Brocklesby Park in '99, and went one better this season, but clearly hard to train and pulled up lame at Fakenham in April. A keen sort with a willing attitude, and it will be a pity if he cannot be nursed back to fitness. *M. Barthorpe — S. Wold (Pat Barthorpe).* 233 (OMa), 797 (R), 1287 (R).

HELENA JUSTINA ..9-6.. 8 b.m. Derrylin — Jennie Pat (Rymer) 144. Small half-sister to Hurdles winners, Jennie's Prospect and You're Agoodun. Dam, half-sister to Certain Angle (*qv*), won 5 Hdles (2m2f-3m) and 3 3m Chses in Ireland. Made the perfect start when the easy winner of the slowest of the day at Higham in January, but the only one behind her to score subsequently did not do so until April, and it was an exceptionally lowly contest. Beaten 40 lengths in both attempts since, and may find 12 stone quite an impost. *B.A. Kilpatrick & Mrs G. D'Angibau — Essex & Suffolk (Gi d'Angibau).* 24 (OMa), 126 (R), 554 (R).

HELISMAD ..—.. 6 b.g. Thowra (FR) — Princess Mona (Prince Regent FR) pR. Sturdy half-brother to Hurdles winner, Aramon. Dam won at 8f, and won 2m Hdle. FLAT r3 p0 (tailed off). NH '98 (for M. Haynes) r2 p0 (tailed off and pulled up both). Sold Ascot, March for 500. Useless to date, and has never finished over jumps (ran out at the third on first start). Looked fat in points. *Mrs D.P. Collings — S. Cornwall.* 932 (R), 1391 (OMa).

HELLO ME MAN (IRE) ..10-3.. 13 b.g. Asir — Tide Gate (Dike USA) R331p. Good-bodied half-brother to Liberty Square. IRISH NH FLAT '92 r1 w1. IRISH NH '92 and '94/5 r9 p2 (2nds in Hdles). NH '96/9 (for B. Llewellyn) r25 w3 (2m4f-2m5f Hdles, hat-trick May/June '97, first a Sell) p5 (inc 2 Chses). A tricky customer who gave Kate Crank a horrible time before running out with her in the early stages of his first point, and was generally outclassed in Ladies Opens, but ably assisted by Kathryn Diggle when finding a soft option at Whittington, where a challenger departed at the last when two lengths down and closing. Was gaining a first success since his hat-trick in '97 (when he veered right going to the final obstacle in his middle win), and had occasionally been blinkered in the past. *Mrs N.M. Hugo — Sir W.W. Wynn's.* 590 (L), 780 (L), 960 (Cf), 1150 (L), 1410 (L).

PLATE 59   *1150 Vale of Lune Harriers Greig Middleton Ladies Open: Hello Me Man (Mrs K. Diggle), 1st, is well clear*
PHOTO: Peter & Marilyn Sweet

HEMERO (IRE) ..9-2.. 9 br.g. Henbit (USA) — Garda Spirit (Garda's Revenge USA) p2p36p6p. Tall. Dam won 2m Hdle in Ireland. IRISH NH FLAT r1 p0. IRISH NH '96 r3 p0. IRISH P-t-P '97 r4 p1 (2nd); pulled up 1, and fell and remounted. NH '97/8 r14 p1 (2nd of 3); pulled up 5; inc Sell Hdle. P-t-P '99 r6 w1 (Maiden) p1 (3rd of 4); last pair 3, and pulled up 1. Managed to last home when equipped with a tongue-tie for the first time on his final start last year, but has struggled to stay in better company since and was collared in the final strides of a Restricted at Black Forest Lodge in March. Well beaten otherwise and is not good enough to contest short distance Hunter Chases competitively. A spectacular jumper at times, but his wind trouble (has run tubed under Rules) is the major factor in his performances and is likely to continue to hold him back. *Mrs S.E. Wall —*

Axe V.H. (Philip Greenwood). 208 (R), 559 (R), 633 (R), 926 (M), 1375 (R), 1444 (2m5fH), 1639 (R), 1671 (R).

HENAH HILL ..9-5.. 7 b.g. Skyliner — Allez Stanwick (Goldhill) p44u. Half-brother to Popeshall (*qv*). Beaten between five lengths and ten lengths in his fourths, and was only narrowly beaten for third in both. Possibly needs decent ground, and has done quite enough to suggest that a Maiden victory awaits him soon. *Miss S. Williamson — Zetland.* 624 (OMa), 910 (2m4fOMa), 1330 (OMa), 1480 (OMa).

HENAVOS ..8-2.. 7 b.m. Henbit (USA) — Navos (Tyrnavos) 9uR. Half-sister to Moor Lady (*qv*). Has shown no apptitude for the job so far. *R. Walmsley — Bramham.* 21 (2m4fOMa), 168 (OMa), 439 (OMa).

HENDRA CHIEFTAIN ..—.. 7 ch.g. Shaab — Strumpetus (Bold As Brass) pppp. Unfurnished. Dam won 3 Points and placed 10 for David Congdon (rated 9-0; only fell once in 8 seasons, and 'sometimes able to take advantage of incredibly bad opponents'). Grandam, Crumpetus, was a poor Pointer, but great-grandam, Muffin II, won 2 Points. Uninspired when pulling up four times to date (at the last once, but only went two miles thrice). *D.G. Congdon — Four Burrow (Neil Harris).* 724 (CfMa), 934 (OMa), 1390 (OMa), 1609 (OMa).

HENLEY (U) ..6-0.. 14 b.g. unknown u. P-t-P '96/9 r4 w2 (2m4f King's Troop) p2. Competently handled when winning the King's Troop race '98/9, but the new rider fell off after a mile when in search of the hat-trick. *Capt. H.W. Jelley — R.A.* 64 (2m4fC).

HENPECKED (IRE) ..7-0.. 10 b.g. Henbit (USA) — Desmond Lady (Maculata) fup4. Unfurnished. NH FLAT '96 r2 p1 (3rd). NH '96 (from M. Hammond's) r1 p0; fell in Hdle. Led for about 2m4f before slowing alarmingly to finish hopelessly tailed off last on his only Pointing completion. Looks an unruly sort, and never seems to be fit. *B. Kennedy — Essex F. & U. (Jim Ovel).* 239 (R), 937 (I), 1040 (OMa), 1383 (OMa).

PLATE 60   1492 Berkeley Mens Open: Henry Bruce (Julian Pritchard), 3rd, leads Skip'N'Time (M. Miller), 2nd, and the hidden Smile Pleeze (T. Stephenson), 1st, at the 2nd last

PHOTO: Brian Armstrong

HENRY BRUCE ..10-9.. 9 ch.g. Buckley — Booterstown (Master Owen) f4f13. Good-topped half-brother to Celtic Town (*qv*). NH '98 r1 p0 (pulled up). P-t-P/HUNT CH '98/9 r14 w5 (inc 3m2f Hunt Ch, and inc 4-timer '99) p3 (2 2nds); pulled up 3, and ran out 2. Not as receptive to the Mansell powers of persuasion as he was when enjoying a tremendous season in '99, and gained his solitary 2000 success after Julian Pritchard had picked up the ride following a show of petulance at Towcester when Dave Mansell threw his whip and helmet to the ground after Red Rebel had caused him to fall. Came back refreshed after a mid-season break and recorded much the fastest time of the day at Maisemore and only beaten just over a length when third at the Berkeley subsequently. Stays very well and can handle most surfaces, but most fond of mud. None of the McCurrich horses were at their best in 2000 so a return to winning ways looks on the cards next year though keeping his mind focused will as usual be the key. Wears blinkers. *Mrs S. Cartridge & Miss T.M. McCurrich — Worcs (Theresa McCurrich).* 156 (3mH), 299 (3m2f110yH), 466 (3m1fH), 1311 (Cf), 1492 (O).

HENRY HENBIT ..—.. 6 b.g. Henbit (USA) — Turn Mill (Latest Model) p05. Dam, half-sister to Meadow Lad (*qv* '91 Annual), won 3 Points (including 2 Opens, including '90 Dudley Cup by short head at 20-1) and placed 5 (inc 2 Hunt Chses). Grandam, Ruby Sherry, won a Maiden. NH FLAT May '00 r2 p0 (13th of 18; *a bhnd*; and 5th *chsd ldr to 4f out, wknd nxt*). Novicey in a Maiden, and has looked something of a difficult ride so far. Bred from an interesting mare, but many by Henbit are not the nicest of beings. *Mrs J. Wilson — Pytchley (Bill Warner; Kim Bailey).* 548 (CfMa).

HENRYSON ..—.. 9 bl.g. Henricus (ATA) — Lowton's Nikita VII (unknown) p. Strong owner-bred. Pulled up at halfway on a February debut (looked backward, and made a bad blunder at the fourth). *Miss H. Parr — Mid Devon.* 311 (CfMa).

HENRYS SONG ..9-10.. 11 ch.g. True Song — The Rymer Girl (Rymer) 214. Strong-topped half-brother to Lady Of Verse. Dam is half-sister to Smart Pal (*qv* '99 Annual). Grandam, Smart Bird, failed to finish in 3 Points. P-t-P '98/9 r7 p1 (3rd); last pair 2, fell 2, and pulled up 2. A late developer, but produced improved form in his third season, though out-plodding a twelve-year-old in a race taking 8min 25s is nothing to write home about, and needs to improve on his 14 lengths fourth to take a hand in Restricteds. *T.D.H. Hughes & Messrs Gold, Bowyer, Down & Geering — Lamerton (Pauline & Tony Geering).* 722 (CfMa), 1179 (OMa), 1608 (R).

HENRY TARTAR ..8-13.. 6 ch.g. Cisto (FR) — Tartar Holly VII (unknown) 4. Compact owner-bred brother to Harry Tartar. Made a string of mistakes when 20 lengths last, but persistently tried hard to close between fences, and can win a Maiden when fluent. *J.D. Parker — Waveney H. (Juliet Arthur).* 760 (OMa).

HENSUE ..9-7.. 12 b.g. Henricus (ATA) — Sue Ming VII (Mins Baby) pp. Neat good-bodied owner-bred brother to Miss Ricus, and half-brother to Rapid Rascal. Dam won Dulverton E. Members from 8 attempts. P-t-P '98/9 r50 (for Mrs K.M. Horsburgh) r50 (inc Restricted, PPOA and Intermediate *nov rdrs*) p23 (9 2nds, last thrice); failed to finish 8 (unseated 3). Provided Caroline Prouse with her first winner in '99, but well beaten since and another horse who failed to run again after a trip to Black Forest Lodge in 2000. Previously game and an excellent schoolmaster, but six busy seasons seem to have taken their toll. *H. & Mrs S. Prouse — Eggesford (Sarah Prouse).* 9 (L), 557 (Cf).

HENWYN ..9-9.. 8 b.g. Henbit (USA) — Macusla (Lighter) pup2p. Half-brother to Hurdles winners, Akulite and Minusla. Dam won NH flat, 2 Hdles (2m-2m4f) and 2m Ch. P-t-P '98/9 r4 w1 (2m4f Maiden) p1 (3rd of 4); pulled up 1. Readily justified favouritism in a firm ground 2m4f Maiden at Eyton last year, but has not stayed the full trip since and usually forced to pull up. Ran too badly to be true on occasions and a lack of stamina might not be his only problem. *D.A. Smith — S. Salop (Mandy Bryan).* 567 (R), 612 (CR), 948 (R), 1317 (M), 1632 (I).

HERBERT LODGE (IRE) ..—.. 12 b.g. Montelimar (USA) — Mindyourbusiness (Run The Gantlet USA) p3ppup. Small sturdy brother to Irish NH flat winners, Shannon Oak and Donnybrook Fair. Dam won at 6f in Ireland. IRISH FLAT r5 w2 (16f, one on a disqualification) p1 (2nd). IRISH NH FLAT '93/4 r2 w2. NH '94 and '96/8 r13 w2 (2m1f Hdle and 2m5f Ch) p7 (clear last, but eased and caught near finish in 2m1f Ch once). HUNT CH '99 (for Mr W. Rucker) r1 p0 (pulled up). A fair top-of-the-ground performer under Rules, but could be moody, and has performed abysmally since leaving Kim Bailey. Tried in a tongue-strap twice '99/00, and presumably has a wind problem. *Mrs E. Kulbicki — Curre.* 481 (L), 594 (M), 743 (L), 1295 (Cf), 1401 (Cf), 1504 (Cf).

HERE COMES HENRY ..10-9.. 7 ch.g. Dortino — Epryana (English Prince) 11111. Dam won 2 Sell Hdles, 2m-2m4f, and 2m5f Ch. Sire an unraced son of Bustino. P-t-P '99 r3 p1 (3rd of 4); and pulled up 2. Given an easy time in his debut season, but the gloves certainly came off in 2000 and his rise was impressive, if not quite meteoric. Comfortably won his first two races, but his defeats of Ross Cottage and Khayal either side of a spot of pot-hunting were useful performances, and it will be no surprise to see him line up in a Hunter Chase before too long. Kept to ground close to good, but jumps well for a youngster, and has struck up a useful alliance with Richard Young who handled him well. *A.D. Old — Portman (Susie Old).* 329 (CfMa), 477 (R), 737 (I), 1058 (M), 1305 (MO).

HERE COMES THE SUN ..—.. 7 b.m. Joli Wasfi (USA) — Handy Lane (Nearly A Hand) p. Sturdy compact half-sister to Halsway Lane and Sulaafah Lane. Dam won 3 2m1f Hdle and 2 Chses (2m-2m4f). P-t-P '99 r2 p0 (unseated 1, and pulled up 1). Did not clear one fence in competent style in '99, but looked to have done plenty of work for her reappearance and ran well until weakening in the final half mile though the form is meaningless as the race was run in a time 14 seconds slower than the three-finisher Hunt race. Was not seen again, and may have met with a setback, but worth a second glance if she is able to return. *Miss L.E. Claydon — Quantock (Tim Long).* 352 (CfMa).

HERE COMES TROUBLE ..—.. 10 b.g. Forzando — Rabuba (Connaught) pp. NH'98 (from John Berry's) r p0 (7th and pulled up). Jumped poorly in Maidens, and was diving away to the left before he tried to refuse at the thirteenth and was pulled up in the latest. Doubtless useless. *Miss K.E. Johnston — E. Essex.* 416 (R), 774 (OMa).

PLATE 61　　1305 Cotley Mixed Open: Here Comes Henry (R. Young), 1st, leads Shrewd Thought
(T. Greed), 5th　　　　　　　　　　　　　　　　　　PHOTO: Brian Armstrong

HERE'S HUMPHREY ..—§§.. 12 b.g. Le Moss — Bucketful (Brave Invader USA) p. Big strong rangy. Dam won an Irish NH flat. P-t-P '96 r3 p0 (refused 3). NH '97 (for J. Whyte) r3 p0 (pulled up 3). Has always loathed racing, but surprisingly brought out again after more than two years off and showed his disgust by refusing to put one foot in font of the other without protest. Came under heavy pressure approaching the first, but had managed to pull himself up by the eighth. Wore blinkers and got wound up despite two paddock handlers and promptly disappeared back into the pits (of Hell?). *J.M. & Mrs V.H.E. Valdes-Scott — Waveney H. (Matthew Gingell).* 98 (OMa).

HERSILIA (IRE) ..10-7.. 10 br.m. Mandalus — Milan Pride (Northern Guest USA) f12. Small neat sister to Hurdles winner, Oh So Cosy (IRE) to Irish NH flat and jumping winner, Finchpalm, and to Irish Pointing and jumping winner, Nicholls Cross. IRISH NH FLAT '95 r4 p0. IRISH NH '95/8 (tried blinkered) r37 w2 (2m4f Hdle and 2m Ch) p9. P-t-P '99 r8 w1 (Ladies) p3 (2 3rds, last once); 5th twice, 6th, and pulled up 1. Came from a near impossible position to score at Eyton and has significant ability, but the rider is little more than a passenger and the mare is sometimes content to loiter with her at the back. Allowed George Dillingham to get his revenge at Eaton Hall, but would not have done so had the riders been transposed. Deserves a top-flight pilot. *L.A.E. Hopkins — N. Salop (Gordie Edwards).* 177 (L), 566 (L), 780 (L).

HERZAGOVA (U) ..—.. 11 bl.m. unknown u. Herza no go va at Larkhill (just a mile or so). *Capt. G. Chanter — R.A.* 64 (2m4fC).

HE'S A LAD ..9-3.. 6 ch.g. Broadsword (USA) — Shedid (St Columbus) 2. Lengthy angular. Dam, half-sister to 7 Pointers, including Hehas (*qv*), won 3m2f Hunt Ch and 13 Points (7 Ladies) and placed 25 for Pat Rowe ('a very game wee mare'). Unruly in the paddock before finishing five lengths second at Brocklesby Park. It was the slowest of the three Maidens by 14 seconds, and he and the third failed to reappear, whilst the winner and fourth did not score subsequently. Nevertheless, he is bred from a super mare and could be an exciting long term prospect. *Mrs P. Rowe & C. Bazley — Pytchley (Caroline Bailey).* 235 (OMa).

HESGREEN ..9-0.. 8 br.g. Green Ruby (USA) — Shewill (Evening Trial) pp5p. Very tall lengthy light-framed owner-bred half-brother to Hehas (*qv*). P-t-P '99 r2 p0 (pulled up 2). Aptly named in his first season, but hesanonstayer would be more appropriate now that we have seen more of him. Has run prominently for up to 2m4f, but quickly falls in a heap and has only once managed to complete. Needs to summon up some more stamina if he is to emulate his sibling who has it in abundance. *C. Egan & Mrs E.C. Cockburn — Warwicks (Ann Cockburn).* 194 (CfMa), 1012 (CfMa), 1435 (OMa), 1598 (OMa).

HESSAC (FR) ..9-10.. 6 b.g. Beyssac (FR) — Chic Lilie (FR) (Olmeto) 214. Very small neat. Finished a promising four lengths second to Union Man at Newton Bromswold, and was impressive when streaking clear of two other finishers in very soft conditions at Kimble. Did not seem to give his true running when odds-on and disappointing next time, but could be speedy enough to be worth trying in long distance Hurdles. Only a pony and will have plenty to do without his seven pounds allowance in future, and if he sticks to Points Ladies Opens might be the best option. On that note, hopefully Lorna Collins will make a full recovery from the dreadful injuries she suffered in an accident in 2000. *C.D. Collins — Cottesmore (Caroline Bailey).* 517 (OMa), 1147 (OMa), 1418 (R).

HETTY BELL ..8-6.. 9 gr.m. Say Primula — Queen Bell (King Sitric) uppp3. Sturdy owner-bred half-sister to Fairy Bell (*qv*). P-t-P '97/8 r6 p2 (3rds, last once); pulled up 2, and unseated 1. Showed some ability in '98, but missed '99 through injury and once again produced far too fat to do herself justice this term. Tailed off without exception and barely able to wobble into a gallop on occasions. *K. Waters — Braes.* 1081 (R), 1163 (OMa), 1331 (OMa), 1480 (OMa), 1580 (OMa).

HEY CHIEF (IRE) ..9-6.. 11 br.g. Torus — Whosview (Fine Blade USA) u321p0. Lengthy half-brother to Heathview (*qv*). IRISH P-t-P '96/7 r9 p2 (2nds); pulled up 3, fell/unseated 2, and carried out 1. P-t-P '98/9 r13 p4 (2 2nds); last 5, pulled up 3 and refused 1. Took 25 attempts to get off the mark, but did so with his tail propelling him and is usually a very weak finisher. Has given the impression that he might be bleeding on a regular basis, but tried in blinkers on his reappearance and is probably just as unpromising. A fine jumper, but already labouring in Restricteds and worth opposing in them. Has been tried in a tongue-strap. *Mr & Mrs C. Strang Steel — College V. & N. Northumberland (Clive Storey).* 114 (OMa), 365 (CfMa), 498 (R), 665 (OMa), 976 (R), 1427 (R).

HEY SAM (IRE) ..9-4.. 8 b.g. Samhoi (USA) — Beswick Paper Lady (Giolla Mear) 36454. Very tall. NH FLAT '97 r1 p0. Safe enough, but very slow and looks ungenuine, and acquired blinkers on his last two appearances. Would be an undeserving winner. *J. Wade — S. Durham.* 379 (OMa), 499 (2m4fOMa), 1003 (OMa), 1033 (OMa), 1329 (OMa).

HIBOU ..8-10.. 10 b.g. Jupiter Island — Rare Pleasure (Pitpan) pp. Tall. Dam, half-sister to Smart Jack (*qv* '94 Annual) and Everett, won an Irish Point, and won 2 Hdle (2m4f-2m5f) and 2m5f Ch in England. P-t-P '98 r3 p2; and pulled up 1. Looked to be on the verge of a win in '98, but forced to sit out the following season and pulled up in just two March Maidens this year. Clearly troubled, and time is against him now. *R.T. Dennis — Hurworth (Carol Dennis).* 438 (OMa), 626 (OMa).

HICKEY'S GIN MILL (IRE) ..—.. 7 b.m. Macmillion — Di's Wag (Scallywag) p. Pulled up after two miles when 50-1 at Barbury Castle. *Miss T. Ide — Berkeley (Trevor Ide).* 471 (OMa).

HIDDEN ISLAND ..10-2.. 14 br.g. Derring Rose — Monavalla (Kabale) 43132. Small neat half-brother to Noel Luck, to Irish NH flat winner, Do Us A Favour, and to Irish Hurdles winner, Doonega (IRE). Dam won Irish Maiden. P-t-P '94/5 and '98 r8 w1 (Maiden) p2 (2nds); refused 1, pulled up 1, and fell 1. NH '99 (for Miss S.E. Hall) r2 p0 (5th, and pulled up in Chses). A thorough stayer, but has been dogged by misfortune since winning a Dalston Maiden in '94. Was a certainty for a Restricted on his best form and duly obliged at a rewarding price at Alnwick, but let down by the riders feeble efforts subsequently. Far less quirky than most by his sire and should win again granted strong handling. *Miss E. Robinson — Zetland.* 278 (R), 620 (R), 908 (R), 1027 (Cf), 1324 (M).

HIGHBRIDGE (IRE) ..10-4.. 8 b.g. Lafontaine (USA) — Lichen Lane (Le Moss) 11p. Tall rangy. P-t-P '99 r2 p0 (pulled up 2). NH Jun '99 (from P.D. Evans') r1 p0. An imposing individual who still looks rather weak, but completed a ready double in minor races and had an excuse when disappointing at Cheltenham as he lost a shoe. Not the sort who will stand many races, and kept ground close to good, but still improving and gets excellent assistance from Tony Evans. Well beaten in a sole venture over hurdles in '99, but should continue to rise through the ranks and could still have prospects under Rules. *J.E. Potter — W. Salop (Tracey McTaggart).* 570 (2m4fCfMa), 863 (R), 1336 (2m4fH).

HIGHBURY ..8-11.. 8 b.g. Vague Shot — Wrightway Blues (Majority Blue) f24u6p. Small. Dam won at 5f (3 ran). P-t-P '98/9 r5 p2; and pulled up 3. Placed on three occasions, but has become very disappointing, and easily gets left behind by bigger rivals. Sold to go Pointing in Wales, where his diminutive stature should not be such a disadvantage, and there is surely a Maiden amongst the miriad opportunities for him there. *Mrs P.A. Russell — Middleton.* 45 (OMa), 139 (OMa), 233 (OMa), 399 (OMa), 793 (OMa), 1001 (2m4fOMa).

HIGH EXPECTATIONS (IRE) ..9-12.. 6 ch.g. Over The River (FR) — Andy's Fancy (IRE) (Andretti) 21. Good-topped. NH FLAT '99 r1 p0. Showed plenty of ability when chasing home Manhatton Rainbow at Alnwick (the rider fell off before the start, and almost came adrift again when held at the final fence), and quickened up the hill to land a 7min5s Maiden at softish at Duncombe Park in very decisive fashion. Not seen since February, but gives the impression of being potentially useful, and will be worth watching closely when he reappears. *R. & J. Tate — Bramham.* 46 (OMa), 281 (OMa).

HIGHFURLONG (IRE) ..9-0§.. 11 ch.g. Doulab (USA) — Cheerful Heart (Petingo) 3p45pp. Plain stocky half-brother to Suluk (won 18 of his 22 starts on all-weather at Southwell, and previously successful on the flat in Ireland), to Hurdles winner, Seize The Day (IRE) and to flat winner, Momtaaz. Dam won at 12f in Ireland. P-t-P '97 and '99 r7 p5 (3 2nds); last, and pulled up 1. Placed in six Points, but despite the efforts of several top riders has avoided winning and been becoming even doggier prior to pulling up lame at Clifton-on-Dunsmore in May. Bringing him back would be a waste of time. Has been tried in blinkers. *J. & Mrs N. Oldring, A.C. Kemp & K. Irving — Bicester with Whaddon (Tony Kemp).* 24 (OMa), 76 (CCfMa), 194 (CfMa), 516 (OMa), 1012 (CfMa), 1422 (OMa).

HIGHGATE (U) ..5-12.. 12 b.m. unknown 2. P-t-P '97 and '99 (for Lt C.M.P. Farr) r2 p0 (last, and fell 1). Had clearly been pulling the gun carriage swiftly at home as she was sent off favourite for the King's Troop yawn, but was shot down after the last by Highnoon. *Capt. E.B.J. Botterill — R.A.* 64 (2m4fC).

HIGH GREEN ..9-3.. 9 b.g. Green Adventure (USA) — High Affair (High Line) p. Big rangy home-bred half-brother to Pilot Error and Brave Man. P-t-P '99 r5 w1 (2m5f Maiden) p0; pulled up 3, and fell 1. Won a short Maiden on the only occasion he went clear in '99, but had looked a non-stayer over the full distance and broke down at Garthorpe on his reappearance. Was blinkered when successful. *Mrs P. Badger — N. Ledbury (Caroline Chadney).* 546 (R).

HIGH GUARDIAN ..10-0§.. 12 ch.g. Amerian (USA) — Hypetra (One Little Boy) p413pp3. Tall rangy. Dam unseated in a Point. P-t-P/HUNT CH '95 and '97/9 r25 w7 (inc 4m Mixed Open, 4m2f Open, and Ladies) p7 (4 3rds); pulled up 4, slipped up 1, and fell 1. Remarkably successful in '98 when scoring five times, but increasingly less interested in exerting himself since and only gets involved over marathon trips now. Gained his 2000 success thanks to Julian Pritchard (originally awarded a dead-heat, but got the outright victory in the Stewards room), but incredibly hard work and did not go a yard for a novice once. Has won in blinkers and might revive in them one more time, but don't bank on it. *I.C. Brice — Llangeinor (Tim Jones).* 4 (O), 454 (4mMO), 574 (4mMO), 1015 (4mO), 1338 (4mMO), 1571 (Cnr), 1614 (4mMO).

HIGHLAND MONARCH ..10-4.. 8 b.g. Super Sunrise — Highland Chance (Bronze Hill) 1p12u. Brother to Madame Bella (*qv*). P-t-P '99 r3 w1 (Maiden) p1 (3rd); and last. A decent novice who has only taken two attempts each at capturing a Maiden, Restricted and Confined, and may have extended the sequence but for unseating at the last when holding a narrow advantage in an Intermediate on his final start. Keen, and has made all, but settling better as he gains experience and should continue on the upgrade. Rarely allowed to start at a realistic price and has been sent off favourite on six occasions. *Mrs A.D. Wauchope — College V. & N. Northumberland (Clive Storey).* 111 (R), 359 (Cf), 912 (Cf), 1159 (I), 1366 (I).

HIGHLAND PEARL ..—.. 8 br.m. Loch Pearl — Emersdale Glen (Ceredigion) uppupu. Owner-bred half-sister to Emerald Conquest. Dam won 2 Points and placed 4 (inc last of 3 in Irish Ch). Useless at long odds in her six races to date. Safely negotiated a total of three fences on three occasions, and it was a daft decision if ever there was one to give Suzy May her first ride on her (in the event, she was cast asunder at the second). *C.D. May — S. & W. Wilts (Mrs J. May).* 12 (OMa), 31 (CMa), 145 (OMa), 656 (OMa), 732 (2m4fOMa), 1130 (M).

HIGHLAND SYMPHONY ..8-1.. 7 b.m. Scottish Reel — Florita (Lord Gayle USA) 54p. Small neat half-sister to a winner in Jersey. P-t-P '99 r4 p0 (5th, pulled up 2, and fell 1). Clearly thought to have ability as she has twice been sent off a warm favourite, but has yet to finish within 30 lengths of the winner and still has plenty to learn. *R. Tate — Bilsdale (Fiona Needham).* 1234 (OMa), 1352 (OMa), 1479 (OMa).

HIGH LEARIE ..9-11.. 11 b.g. Petoski — Lady Doubloon (Pieces Of Eight) 7p45. Strong lengthy half-brother to NH flat and jumping winner, Butler's Twitch, to a flat winner, and to a successful Hurdler. NH FLAT '94/5 (for O. Sherwood) r3 p0 (4th thrice). NH '95/9 (for Alex Harvey) r24 w4 (2m2f Hdle, and 3 Chses, 3m-3m2f) p7. Won four races on good or soft ground by making all the running, but seems to become disillusioned if he is headed, and consistently performed as if he were a spent force in 2000. Wears blinkers. *F.E. Harvey — Puckeridge (Alex Harvey).* 17 (O), 223 (3m2fH), 320 (O), 938 (3m4fO).

HIGHMOOR LADY (U) ..—.. 7 b.m. High Lodge — Bryony (unknown) f. Workmanlike hunter type. Fell when tailed off in her Members. *Mrs J. Hopkins — W. of Yore (Eleanor Blane).* 374 (M).

HIGHNOON (U) ..6-0.. 10 b.m. unknown 1. Won the showdown with Highgate from the last to land the King's Troop race, and though we don't know what fate awaits her in 2001, do not forsake her now that you may need her by your side. *Capt. H.W. Jelley — R.A.* 64 (2m4fC).

HIGH PARK LADY (IRE) ..8-12.. 10 br.m. Phardante (FR) — Baranee (My Swanee) pp. Small unfurnished half-sister to Par-Bar (IRE), and to Irish flat and Hurdles winner, Barney Buchlyvie. Dam won at 12f in Ireland, and won 3 2m Hdles (one on a disqualification) there. IRISH P-t-P '96 r5 p1 (2nd); pulled up 3, and fell 1. IRISH NH '96/7 (blinkered 1) r8 p0. P-t-P '98 r4 w1 (Maiden) p1 (3rd); and pulled up 2. NH '98 (for P.R. Chamings) r5 p4 (3 2nds, 2m-2m4f Chses); and refused 1. Placed in two Points (made much of the running on each occasion) after winning a match at Bexhill in '98, but went back into hiding after pulling up twice in February on her return. *T.D.B. Underwood — Garth & S. Berks.* 226 (2m4f110yH), 330 (R).

HIGH STURT ..9-4.. 7 b.m. Petoski — Barge Mistress (Bargello) ppr323. Sparely-made half-sister to Seventh Lock and Postlebury, to Chasing winners, Country Mistress and Vallis Vale, and to successful Hurdler, Barge Boy. P-t-P '99 r4 p0 (pulled up 3, and refused 1). Does possess a little ability, but struggles to stay three miles and not afraid to apply the brakes when things got too tough. Ran her best race yet when partnered by Neil Harris on her final start, but the company was weak and she will need to find a bad race in order to get off the mark. *Miss E. Oram — Blackmore & Sparkford V. (John Dufosee).* 105 (OMa), 933 (OMa), 1131 (OMa), 1390 (OMa), 1596 (OMa), 1654 (OMa).

HIGHTECH TOUCH ..9-10.. 11 b.g. Sunley Builds — Caribs Love (Caliban) 1pu. Strong compact owner-bred. NH '97/8 r8 p1 (2nd). P-t-P '99 r5 p1 (2nd of 3); 4th twice, and fell/unseated 2. Beat 18 others when runner-up in a 2m Hurdle at Warwick in '97, and finally delivered the goods at Badbury Rings, but a disappointing favourite next time and reverted back to being a clumsy jumper on his final start. Has the ability to win a Restricted, but wildly inconsistent and gets few chances. *Mrs J. Stuart Evans — Hampshire (John Stuart Evans).* 328 (CfMa), 575 (R), 1393 (R).

HIGHWAY FIVE (IRE) ..9-12§.. 13 ch.g. Carlingford Castle — Final Triumph (Laurence O) 3453050303. Smallish unfurnished half-brother to Irish Pointing winner, Cottage Gold. IRISH P-t-P '93 r2 p0 (pulled up 2). NH '95 r3 p1 (2nd); pulled up 1. P-t-P/HUNT CH '95 and '97/9 r39 w3 (2 Hunt Chses, 3m110y-3m1f110y, and Ladies) p13 (7 2nds, and inc 5 Hunt Chses); pulled up 7, and fell/unseated 3. Expert at course completion and a fair performer in his time, but amazingly indolent now and usually takes minimal interest in proceedings which is frustrating as his 23 lengths third to Secret Bay at Ludlow on his reappearance was no disgrace. Can be a sketchy jumper although a spill is a rarity and he has jumped round Aintree, but blinkered to no avail in '99, and also ridden in spurs and tried in a tongue-strap. Ridden with great pluck and no little skill by Lorna Brooke who looked very tidy in her first season and deserves a mount to match her own enthusiasm. Plods quicker on decent ground than he does in a bog, but even looks miserable walking round the paddock thesedays and will surely not regain any sparkle at 13. *Lady Susan Brooke — Teme V.* 150 (3mH), 335 (L), 449 (L), 468 (3m1f110yH), 683 (3mH), 860 (L), 1086 (Cf), 1275 (L), 1338 (4m1fH), 1543 (M).

HIGHWAY LAD ..10-4.. 12 b.g. Nearly A Hand — Hilda's Way (Royal Highway) 1ppp18. Unfurnished half-brother to Highway Parade, Highway Jim and Highway Light, and to jumping winner, Highway Express. Dam won 2 Points and placed 3 for Mr White. NH FLAT r2 p0. NH '95 r2 p0. P-t-P '96/7 and '99 r10 w2 (Restricted and Intermediate) p6 (5 2nds, and last of 3); unseated 1. Adept at surprises and followed a 16-1 success in '99 with a 25-1 victory on his return at Larkhill where he outbattled Chism on the run to the line, but ran three lethargic races in succession before first-time blinkers revitalised him at Kingston St Mary. Found the ground too lively at Towcester subsequently and is ideally suited by some cut. Could win again at 12 particularly if he regains his old consistency. *M. White — Cotley (Philip Greenwood).* 10 (O), 149 (3mH), 727 (O), 954 (MO), 1237 (Cf), 1532 (3m1fH).

HIJACKED ..9-9.. 7 b.g. True Song — Scamper (Abwah) u217pp. Workmanlike unfurnished owner-bred half-brother to Sharp Alice. Dam won at 14f, and was unbeaten in 3 Hdles (2-3m). P-t-P '99 r3 p0 (pulled up 3). Taken gently in his early races, but won with some authority at Whitwick and two of his victims have since lost their maiden status. Has proved disappointing in Restricteds to date, but in a decent yard and young enough to atone. Sired a foal before he set out on a Pointing career. *A. Hollingsworth — Worcs.* 22 (2m4fOMa), 122 (OMa), 341 (OMa), 513 (CF), 896 (R), 1355 (R).

HIL LADY ..9-0.. 10 b.m. Arctic Lord — First Attempt (Proverb) p44. Very small stocky. Dam, half-sister to Ryton Guard (qv '98 Annual), won 3 Points (one in Ireland, and 2 Adjacents in Wales) and placed in 12 various. P-t-P/HUNT CH '96/9 r20 w1 (Maiden) p8 (4 3rds, last thrice; and last of 2 twice); and failed to finish 8 (on floor 3). NH Jul '99 (from H. Lavis') r1 p0 (6th in Hdle). Could take a strong hold and often made the running previously, but devoid of speed in 2000, and has beaten only nine horses and a remounter over jumps in 23 races spread over five seasons. Did well to win a race of any description, but unlikely to repeat the feat. *Mr & Mrs M. Sullivan — Pembs (Gary Barber).* 832 (R), 947 (R), 1228 (R).

HILLHEAD (IRE) ..10-2.. 12 br.g. Aristocracy — Serpentine Artiste (Buckskin FR) 921344355. Lengthy attractive half-brother to Irish Pointing winner, Godfreys Cross, and to NH flat winner, Lucy Walters (IRE). IRISH P-t-P '94 r3 w1 (4&5yo Maiden) p0; and pulled up 2. IRISH NH '97 r8 w1 (2m4f Ch) p0. NH '95 and '97/8 r8 p1 (2nd in Ch). P-t-P/HUNT CH '99 r5 p4 (3 2nds, of 3 once; and inc 3rd in Hunt Ch); and pulled up 1. A patent safety (has never fallen), but usually easy to beat and could hardly fail not to win a poor event at Buckfastleigh. Has made the frame in all four Ladies races he has contested and also in both Hunter Chases. *Mrs J. Barran — Blackmore & Sparkford V. (Jane Galpin).* 10 (O), 67 (L), 257 (L), 522 (L), 735 (MO), 1306 (C), 1432 (3m1fH), 1562 (C), 1606 (O).

HILL ISLAND ..10-0.. 14 br.g. Strong Gale — Affordalot (Fordham USA) 3p8p23. Good-bodied half-brother to Manalesco. IRISH NH FLAT r1 p0. IRISH P-t-P '92/3 r8 w1 (6yo&up Maiden) p2; failed to finish 5 (fell 4; 2 out twice — looked certain winner once, and possible winner once). IRISH NH '93 r1 p0. P-t-P/HUNT CH '94/9 (for Mr C.M. Gee) r34 w11 (inc Open; 4-timer in '96) p13 (8 2nds, and inc 3rd in Hunt Ch); failed to finish 7 (fell/unseated 5 — at last when left in lead once). A useful and consistent performer for Colin Gee and has won at least once in the previous five seasons, but afflicted by wind trouble in '98 and has run tubed on occasions since. Beginning to lose his speed, but still game and gave Lucinda Sweeting a couple of good rides in 2000, notably when finishing like a train at Dunthrop on his reappearance. Acquired blinkers on his final start which is something of an insult to a horse whose determination has helped him to win 12 races. *Miss L.J.C. Sweeting — Heythrop*. 192 (L), 454 (4mMO), 510 (Cf), 749 (Cf), 1034 (C), 1481 (Cf).

HILL'S ELECTRIC (IRE) ..—.. 9 br.g. Electric — Turvey (Royal Buck) pp. Strong half-brother to Senior Partner (IRE), and to Irish NH flat winner, Zareba. Dam won 2 Irish Points. NH FLAT '97 r3 p0. P-t-P '98 r1 p0 (pulled up). Showed ability in Bumpers and made a favourable impression on his return to action prior to pulling up in an Intermediate at Weston Park, but went lame when poised to challenge at Eyton and was not seen again. Has undoubtedly got the ability to win races, but a poor jumper and rarely has a clean bill of health. *C.J. Hitchings — Kyre (Mandy Bryan)*. 297 (I), 569 (OMa).

HILL SPRITE ..8-12.. 10 b.m. Lighter — Belsprit Lady (Belfalas) u57. Tall half-sister to Imatoff. Dam won NH flat. NH FLAT '97 r1 p0. P-t-P '99 r5 w1 (Maiden) p2 (3rds, remote last once); and 5th twice. Displayed plenty of stamina when successful in a three-finisher Maiden at Whitwick last year, but takes an age to warm up and has been soundly beaten in Restriteds since. Looked ill at ease on her final appearance in 2000 and may have gone wrong. *R. Styles — N. Herefords (Sally Godsall)*. 75 (I), 338 (R), 483 (R).

HILL TOP FLYER (IRE) ..—.. 8 b.g. Orchestra — Idanna (Hays) ffpspp. P-t-P '98 (for Mr V. Thompson) r2 p0 (pulled up 2). A case of the blind leading the blind to date and is in dire need of competent handling. A schooling session involving Messrs Marsh and Parry would make eventful viewing; assuming they have them which given their mounts racecourse performances seems doubtful. *P. Riddick & T. Marsh — Sinnington (Paul Riddick)*. 1302 (OMa), 1405 (OMa), 1457 (OMa), 1574 (OMa), 1617 (OMa), 1660 (OMa).

HILLWALK ..9-10.. 15 b.g. Croghan Hill — Bell Walks Fancy (Entrechat) 3p. Workmanlike half-brother to jumping winner, Jet Rules (IRE), and to NH Flat and Hurdles winners, Jet Tabs (IRE) and Canasta (IRE) and to successful Irish Hurdler, Dowhatyoulike. IRISH FLAT r2 p1 (3rd). IRISH P-t-P '90 r2 w1 (4-6yo Mdn) p0; and pulled up. IRISH NH FLAT '90/1 r3 w3. IRISH NH '91/2 r5 w1 (2m4f Hdle) p2 (2nds). NH '93/8 (for R. Curtis), blinkered once in '96) r49 w8 (2m5f-3m1f Chses) p10 (inc 3rd in Hdle); lost weight-cloth and disqualified from 2nd once; pulled up in '98 Grand National. Has enjoyed a remarkable level of success in the past, and was scored at least once every year '90/7. Error-prone and inconsistent, and has been pulled up in six of his ten most recent attempts, but did give a respectable display for an oldie when fourteen lengths third in a Confined. It would be a surprise if he turned out again at 15. *A. & Mrs I. Graham — Puckeridge (Alex Harvey)*. 936 (Cf), 1184 (Cf).

HIL'S BLUFF (IRE) ..—.. 6 ch.m. Cardinal Flower — Celtic Lace (Celtic Cone) pu. Sister to Another Bula (IRE) (qv). Has looked backward and given a maximum of two miles to date, and comes from a family who seem to need plenty of time. Wore blinkers in Points, and was looking as if she might justify favouritism when she broke her pelvis at Chipley Park (destroyed). *C. & Mrs H. Bubb — N. Herefords (Richard Mathias)*. 866 (CfMa), 1093 (OMa).

HILTONSTOWN LASS (IRE) ..10-11.. 11 b.m. Denel (FR) — Mount Gawn (Harwell) 32713. Smallish compact. IRISH NH r8 p4 (Hunt Chses); inc Hdles. IRISH P-t-P '95/7 r12 w1 (mares Maiden) p2 (2nds); pulled up 4, fell/unseated 2, slipped up 1. P-t-P/HUNT CH '98/9 (for Mr J.F. Thompson) r13 w5 (inc 4 Hunt Chses, 2m3f110y-3m3f) p4 (4 2nds, inc 3 Hunt Chses); unseated 1. A useful mare and has shown her versatility by scoring on firm ground and in softish, at distances from 2m4f to 3m3f. A disappointment on her return, but returned to form when outspeeding Coole Abbey on one of her favourite hunting grounds, Sedgefield, and always a force to be reckoned with in the weaker Hunter Chases. *Mrs P.A. Watson — Middleton (Tim Walford)*. 172 (Cm), 582 (3m3fH), 921 (2m6fH), 1345 (2m5fH), 1628 (2m4f110yH).

HIZAL ..8-10.. 12 b.g. Afzal — Hi Darlin' (Prince De Galles) 581u. Small compact brother to Darzal and half-brother to Dicks Darlin'. Dam, half-sister to 3 Pointers including Knight Of Love, won 2 Points (promoted from 2nd once), a 2m6f Hdle, and a 2m4f Ch. Grandam, Hi Mia, was 3rd of 4 in Maiden, and remote last of 3 in Nov Ch. NH FLAT r1 p0 (all-weather). NH '94, '95, and '97 r29 w1 (2m4f Ch) p6 (3 2nds, last once); failed to finish 10 (fell/unseated 4, also remounted once); inc Sells. P-t-P/HUNT CH '95/6 and '98/9 r26 w1 (Maiden) p9 (5 3rds, of 4 twice; and inc fence last of 2 once); failed to finish 13 (fell/unseated 4). Aimed as low as possible in the current yard and rewarded connections with a win in their local, but has otherwise only beaten eleven horses in his last 23 attempts. Prone to errors, but was pretty much foot perfect when providing David Hayes with his first success at Marks Tey. *Mr & Mrs A. Willis & A.R. Coe — Essex F. & U. (Keith & Colin Coe)*. 29 (Cf), 127 (Cf), 317 (M), 555 (Cnr).

HOBBY DE BEYSSAC (FR) ..–.. 6 b.m. Beyssac (FR) — Tiliane (FR) (Kilian) fp. Small half-brother to French Hurdles winner, Geneve. FRENCH NH '98/9 r11 p4 (3 3rds); all bar one at Auteuil. *C.M. Batterham — E. Devon (David Pipe).* 57 (OMa), 145 (OMa).

HOBGOBLIN ..–.. 8 ch.g. Fearless Action (USA) — Swallow This (Town Crier) p. Close-coupled owner-bred. Dam is half-sister to Gather No Moss (qv '87 season Annual). Wore a cross-noseband and a martingale at Dunthrop, and was taken to post early and strangled in the race until he pulled up at the 11th (very novicey), and gave the impression of being a hot ride). *P.T. Griffith — Bicester with Whaddon (Herbie Owen).* 1021 (2m4fOMa).

HOBNOB (IRE) ..9-2§.. 8 ch.g. Glacial Storm (USA) — Lepida (Royal Match) 1pp3. Tall half-brother to Poppea (IRE), to Hurdles winner, Juno Away, Irish Pointing and English Hurdles winner, Claudia Electric (IRE) and NH flat and Hurdles winner, Killusty. Dam won 2 2m Hdles in Ireland. P-t-P '98 (for Mr P. Green) r1 p0 (pulled up). NH FLAT Jan '99 r1 p0. NH Mar '99 (from M. Pipe's) r1 p0 (pulled up). Swiftly exited the Pipe yard having added failures in a bumper and a hurdle to an ignominious Pointing debut, but made a winning debut for Tik Saunders in the slowest of four Maidens at Thorpe. Looked decidedly reluctant when tried in a tongue-strap, and the subject of a misdirected gamble in his Members (napped to the box-park on his racecourse debut). One to have reservations about. *Mrs J.A. Saunders — Pytchley.* 123 (OMa), 440 (R), 1005 (M), 1218 (R).

HOLCOMBE HANDSEL ..–.. 10 ch.m. Nearly A Hand — Holcombe Jane (Baltus) pp. Light-framed narrow owner-bred sister to Holcombe Handful, and half-sister to Holcombe Ideal and Kentlands Lad. Dam is an unraced half-sister to 5 Pointers, including Holcombe Bill (qv '96 Annual). Tailed off in both end of season ventures. Not bred for Pointing honours. *J.R. Wescott — Devon & Somerset.* 1564 (OMa), 1676 (OMa).

HOLDING THE FORT (IRE) ..9-6.. 7 b.g. Moscow Society (USA) — Lady Of Desmond (Menelek) 32. Half-brother to Spurious. IRISH P-t-P '99 r3 p0 (last but once twice, and pulled up). Beaten 17 lengths when third (the runner-up scored subsequently) and six lengths when second in Maidens, and it looks perfectly possible that his next effort will result in a win. *I. Anderson — W. Salop.* 865 (CfMa), 1527 (OMa).

HOLD YOUR RANKS ..9-13.. 14 b.g. Ranksborough — Holdmetight (New Brig) f47331. Big rangy half-brother to Hold And Fort and to jumping winner, Holdimclose. Dam failed to finish in 3 Points for Richard Frost, but was later placed in 2 Hdles and a Chase. NH '93/9 r28 w7 (4 Hdles, 2m1f-2m6f, and 3 2m6f Chses) p7 (beaten head once). Has always enjoyed bombing round Newton Abbot, where he has gained all his seven victories, and revels in thick mud. Generally tutoring the beginner Derek McKenna in 2000, but George Welch did the honours when he captured the Bar bore (which looked much more in keeping at its new venue at down-to-earth Flete Park). Must have given the Frost's a lot of pleasure over the year (they bought the dam for a mere 310gns), and they doubtless had a few bob on when he was backed from 5-1 to 9-4 in a contest which was made to measure for him. *Walnut House Partnership — Modbury H. (Nicky Frost).* 165 (Cf), 652 (MO), 852 (Cf), 1041 (M), 1188 (O), 1257 (C).

HOLIDAY TIME (IRE) ..10-2.. 11 b.m. Bustineto — Holiday Voucher (Le Moss) pp74542. Smallish. IRISH P-t-P '95/7 r13 p2 (10-38/ 3rds); pulled up 9, and fell 1. P-t-P '98/9 r7 w1 (Maiden) p2; ran out 1, and pulled up 3. Has stood her racing badly in the past, but enjoyed her busiest season to date in 2000, though never looked like winning. Pulls hard, and usually a weak finisher and flattered by her proximity to Spring Gale on her final appearance. *Mrs I. Hodge — Puckeridge (Hugh Hodge).* 86 (R), 92 (Cf), 285 (CR), 416 (R), 980 (R), 1181 (R), 1289 (L).

HOLIWAY STAR (IRE) ..9-8§§.. 11 b.g. Fools Holme (USA) — Small Is Beautiful (Condorcet FR) p5r. Small compact half-brother to Small Wind, to Hurdles winner, Pie Hatch (IRE), and to Irish flat winners, Run My Beauty and Blue Stocking. IRISH FLAT (tried blinkers) r19 w3 (7-8f) p5. IRISH NH '94/8 r31 w5 (2 Hdles, 2m-2m1f, and 3 Chses, 2m-2m4f) p6 (inc beaten head once, and neck and short head 3rd). NH '98/9 (first 2 for D.L. Williams) r17 p2 (26/ 2nd in Hdle, and 3½/ 2nd in Ch); inc Sells. Had an excellent strike rate in Ireland '94/5, and gained all his eight successes in that period, but is a real little dog now. Undoubtedly retains ability and often threatens to deceive (could have won a 2m1f Chase for present connections in October '99, but carried his head to one side and refused to overtake the leader), and is just as likely to be reluctant to set off nowadays. Virtually refused to participate in his first Point, and would not take one forward step in the latest. *Mrs S. Horner-Harker — Hurworth.* 135 (L), 277 (Cf), 394 (Cf).

HOLLOA AWAY (IRE) ..8-12.. 9 b.g. Red Sunset — Lili Bengam (Welsh Saint) pufu5f. Compact brother to flat winner, Pytchley Night. Dam won at 5f in Ireland. NH FLAT '97 r1 w1. NH '97/8 r5 p1 (3rd in Hdle). P-t-P/HUNT CH '99 r9 p0 (disqualified from 3rd — not weigh-in); and last 2, pulled up 3, and fell 3. Won a 17-runner Worcester Bumper on his racecourse debut, but does not stay much more than two miles, and his jumping goes completely to pot when he gets tired. Can take a strong hold and has been mounted on course and taken to post early. Blinkered in three of his last four appearances, but not worth bothering with again. *W.F. Reid — V.W.H. (Martin Wood).* 388 (I), 600 (I), 748 (M), 971 (I), 1243 (Inr), 1441 (Cnr).

HOLLOW PALM (IRE) ..—.. 10 b.g. Hollow Hand — Meneroyal (Menelek) p. NH FLAT '97 (for L. Lungo) r3 p1 (distant 3rd). Made his first appearance for three years in a Confined, and gave a lot of trouble in the preliminaries and soon became tailed off. *R.L. Morgan — Dumfries.* 419 (Cf).

HOLLOW SOUND (IRE) ..9-4.. 12 ch.m. Orchestra — Bells Hollow (Rarity) ppf. Lengthy workmanlike sister to Banana Boat and Nowladiesandgents (IRE), and to Hurdles winner, Hoh Music (IRE), and half-sister to Banana Boat, and to French Chasing winner, Waregem Prijs. IRISH NH FLAT r1 p0. IRISH NH '94 and '96 r12 p0 (5th, 6th, and fell 2 in Chses). NH '98 r1 p0 (tailed off and pulled up in 3m HCap Ch). P-t-P '97/9 (for Mr T.D. Sproat) r11 w2 (Maiden and Restricted) p3 (2nds); 4th, fell 1, and pulled up 4. Won two poor Points emphatically in '97, but laid low by a virus after and has failed to score in 12 subsequent starts (failed to finish in eight of them). Looked wrong during an interrupted 2000 campaign and retirement is surely the best option. *L. Allsopp — Pentyrch.* 344 (I), 482 (I), 1295 (Cf).

HOLMBY COPSE ..9-8§.. 11 b.g. Neltino — Truella (True Song) 63343625. Strong compact attractive brother to Holmby Mill, and half-brother to True Light. Dam is sister to Tenelord (*qv* '98 Annual). Grandam, Tenella, was 3rd in Hunt Ch for Dick Saunders. P-t-P '96 and '98 (for Mr C.R. Saunders & Mr T.E. Hartgrave) r6 w1 (Club Maiden) p1 (2nd); pulled up 3, and brought down 1. Given the boot by Caroline Bailey after managing just six outings in three years, but completed a full season in 2000 after missing the previous one. An unenviable ride as he pulls hard, but finds little off the bridle and Tony Humphrey has done well on him. Excitable, and has two handlers and is usually taken to post early. *Mr P. Nash — A.R. & Mrs S.J. Humphrey — Kyre, & Farmers Bloodhounds (Sarah Watson).* 119 (CR), 190 (M), 336 (R), 669 (R), 843 (R), 940 (R), 1181 (R), 1287 (R).

HOLY MOSES (IRE) ..7-0.. 7 ch.g. Classic Memory — Much Obliged (Crash Course) pp. Small stocky. P-t-P '99 r3 p0 (last, unseated 1, and pulled up 1. Jumped appallingly on his return and the rider bottled out after taking two fences in haphazard fashion on his subsequent start. How he managed to jump round Wolverhampton last year is beyond belief. *E.J. Cantillon — Thurlow.* 1290 (OMa), 1527 (OMa).

HOLY STING (IRE) ..9-0.. 12 b.g. The Parson — Little Credit (Little Buskins) 4. Strong-topped compact brother to Vatacan Bank and Minister For Fun (IRE), and Irish jumping winner, Ned Of The Hill, and half-brother to Irish Pointing winner, Mum's Eyes. Dam won Irish Maiden. NH FLAT '94 r3 p0. NH '94/8 r21 w3 (2 Hdles, 2m7f-3m Hdle, and 3m3f Ch) p5. HUNT CH '98 (for Mr G. MacEchern) r4 p3 (3rds, of 4 once); and pulled up 1. A fair mudlark under Rules to '96, but frequently blinkered and showed little interest when switched to Hunter Chasing in '98. Returned from a year off for a jolly in his Members and eventually came home 42 lengths behind the winner. *J.A.T. de Giles — V.W.H.* 748 (M).

HOMFRAY (U) ..5-5.. 11 b.g. unknown 3. P-t-P '97/8 r2 p0 (ran out, and unseated). Failed to get beyond the 10th in two previous stabs at the King's Troop race, but performed better under a different rider in 2000 and finished an honourable third. Hopefully his previous partner did not get the hump. *Capt. G. Chanter — R.A. 64 (2m4fC).*

HOMO DORNEY (IRE) ..8-7.. 8 b.m. Homo Sapien — Sheer Dorney (Sheer Grit) cpu3. Compact. Dam is half-sister to Fantus (*qv* '99 Annual). IRISH P-t-P '97 r2 p0 (pulled up 1, and unseated at first). NH '98 r1 p0 (pulled up). P-t-P '99 r1 p0 (pulled up). Finally managed a clear round at the eighth attempt, but had looked unlucky on two occasions earlier in 2000 and does possess a small measure of ability. *Mrs C. Moore — Percy.* 112 (OMam), 363 (CfMa), 1166 (OMa), 1368 (OMa).

HONEYSUCKLE LIL ..9-0.. 11 b.m. Welsh Captain — L'Irondelle (On Your Mark) R7u2. Big strong. NH FLAT '96 r2 p0. NH '96 r1 p0 (last in Hdle — tailed off halfway). P-t-P '99 r1 p0 (pulled up). Showed her first signs of ability on her third start in 2000 when unseating at the penultimate fence whilst lying a close fourth in a slow Maiden at Market Rasen. Grossly flattered by her proximity to the eased down winner in her Members, but is at least managing to get Tim Gardham into the action. *Mrs V. Gardham — Holderness.* 116 (I), 235 (OMa), 438 (OMa), 502 (M).

HOOKY'S TREAT ..9-7.. 10 b.m. Dutch Treat — Hookah Girl (Hubble Bubble) 321s3f. Sparely-made. P-t-P/HUNT CH '97/8 r17 p2 (3 3rds, last twice); fell/unseated 2, and pulled up 1. Gained her success in fortuitous circumstances as the leader was 15 lengths clear when slipping up on the flat after four out, but had made the frame on nine previous occasions so it was not undeserved. Suffered the same fate as Senso in her next race and was outclassed in the Hunter Chase. Only modest, but reliable and a steady jumper and should keep plugging way in Restricteds. *Mrs H.O. Graham — Jedforest.* 44 (OMa), 107 (M), 364 (CfMa), 497 (R), 911 (4mMO), 1154 (3m2fH).

HOPEFUL EARL (IRE) ..8-12.. 10 ch.g. Mister Lord (USA) — Bay Star (Pimpernels Tune) pu3p. Big rangy. IRISH P-t-P '98 r8 p3; pulled up 2, and unseated 2. A slow and cumbersome creature who was 17 lengths last on his only English completion, and appeared to breakdown badly next time. *Mrs S. Horner-Harker — Hurworth.* 400 (OMa), 507 (CMa), 695 (OMa), 1032 (OMa).

HOPEFULL DRUMMER ..9-8.. 12 b.g. Sergeant Drummer (USA) — Hopeful Leigh (Flandre II) f. Strong brother to Drummers Hope. Dam pulled up in 2 Points as a 14-y-o in '90 when trained by Debbie Cole. NH FLAT r2 p0 (21st of 22, and pulled up 1). P-t-P '94/7 r10 w3 (Maiden, Members and Restricted) p1 (2nd); pulled up 3, and fell 1. Reappeared after missing two full seasons, but was not without his supporters at Lifton and was the best backed horse in the race. Survived a blunder at the fourth, but not another five fences later. Had a willing attitude in the past, but never able to run much and promptly went back into obscurity. *W. Westacott — Dulverton E. (Neil Harris)*. 1637 (O).

HOPE'S DELIGHT (IRE) ..—§.. 13 b.g. Mister Lord (USA) — Cooliney Queen (General Ironside) p3pprp. Compact well-made. IRISH P-t-P '94 and '96/7 r7 w2 (7 plus unplaced Mdn, 5 ran and 3 finished, and Winners of One) p0; pulled up first 4 starts. IRISH NH '97 r3 p0 (Chses). A poor jumper who was annoyed at having his retirement interrupted, and gave feeble displays of slow and moderate jumping. 30 lengths last on his only completion, and blinkered to no avail on his latest attempt. *D.S. Frankland — Grafton*. 510 (Cf), 784 (M), 1016 (Cf), 1144 (O), 1436 (Cf), 1481 (Cf).

HOPIES DELIGHT ..9-13.. 8 gr.g. Genuine Gift (CAN) — Georgias Fancy (Montreal Boy) 8. Compact. Dam is an unraced sister to 4 Pointers, including McNay, and half-sister to another. P-t-P/HUNT CH '98/9 r13 w1 (2m4f Maiden) p3 (2nds): refused 1, fell/unseated 3, and pulled up 1. Won a bad Maiden as a five-year-old, but has performed well in Restricteds since and still just about held every chance when parting company with the rider at the last in the latest. Remounted to complete, but returned lame and failed to reappear. Deserves compensation. *G.H.D. Hopes — Cumberland F.* 184 (R).

HORTON ..8-8.. 11 ch.g. Rafolon (FR) — Salmonway Song (Salmonway Spirit) p57pp34. Strong. P-t-P '97/9 r15 p0 (last pair 3, pulled up 8, and on floor 4). Rarely looks fit and the usual veteran rider is remarkably uncompetitive. Only once better than last in each of the last two seasons and is splendidly hopeless. Often mounted on the course and taken to post early. *Mrs C.M. Spurgeon — S. Cornwall (Stephen Parkin)*. 158 (CfMa), 563 (CfMa), 932 (R), 1048 (CfMa), 1263 (OMa), 1384 (M), 1521 (CfMa).

HORTON-CUM-PEEL (IRE) ..10-1.. 10 b.g. Swan's Rock — Lady Beecham (Laurence O) puf3f. Lengthy well-made half-brother to Staigue Fort (IRE) (qv). P-t-P '98 r3 w1 (Maiden) p0; 7th, and fell 1. NH Jun '00 r1 p0 (fell in 3m Nov Ch: *chsd ldr, ld 3, hdd 6, fell 12*). Landed a touch on his debut in a long and slowly-run Maiden at Whittington, but presumably went wrong subsequently as he missed the entire '99 season. Let down by his jumping on his return, but would be much more at home in Restricteds. *Mrs T.R. Kinsey — Cheshire Forest.* 811 (I), 959 (M), 1343 (3m110yH), 1601 (3m2fH).

HORUS (IRE) ..10-3.. 6 b.g. Teenoso (USA) — Jennie's First (Idiot's Delight) p1114. Compact attractive owner-bred half-brother to Nortonthorpe-Rose and Hollyhock. Clearly known to be quite useful as the opportunity to pick-up a Maiden was ignored, and collected a ready hat-trick without having to beat much (there were only three in his Open, and one of those failed to get round). Acts well in soft, but had his colours lowered by Black Dante in heavy at Bratton Down, where he was heavily eased on the long run-in once his chance had gone. Not seen again, but is potentially considerably under-rated, and it will be interesting to see what he achieves in competitive contests in less testing going. Hollyhock has not yet achieved anything under Rules, but Horus might be a different proposition. *B.A. Kilpatrick — Taunton V.H. (David Pipe)*. 11 (OMa), 255 (R), 404 (I), 878 (O), 1138 (MO).

HOSTETLER ..9-13§.. 12 ch.g. Fit To Fight (USA) — Diana's Bow (Great Nephew) u556512. Smallish strong-topped half-brother to flat winner, Bespoken and to Hurdles winner, So Keen. IRISH FLAT r3 p0. IRISH NH '92/3 r10 w1 (2m Hdle) p1 (3rd). IRISH NH '93/5 r19 p2 (Chses); inc Sell Hdles. P-t-P '96/9 r25 w1 (Club) p6 (4 3rds, remote once, and last once); pulled up 2, and fell/unseated 2. A safe conveyance, but had gone 18 races without a win until springing a 16-1 surprise at Dingley where he showed far more resolution than the runner-up. Tailed off without exception otherwise in 2000 and usually plods badly. Occasionally blinkered under Rules. *Mrs S. Norris — Pytchley (Jenny Garley)*. 192 (L), 431 (L), 787 (L), 1007 (L), 1296 (L), 1503 (Cf), 1663 (Co).

HOT CHOCOHOLIC ..—.. 12 b.g. Hotfoot — Silver Stone (Derrylin) 9. Brother to Abbey Curve, and to flat winner, Gypsey Pop. Fat in an Intermediate, but forced to continue although two fences behind and exhausted, and collapsed and died afterwards (a truly ignorant piece of riding by Lisa Spence). *Mrs L.T. Spence — E. Essex.* 609 (I).

HOT'N SPROUTY ..—.. 7 ch.m. Current Edition (IRE) — Hot Hander (Nearly A Hand) p. Dam won 2 Hdles, 2m-2m5f, and placed 3, but failed to beat another horse in 7 Points for Pip Jones (2nd once; 'very bad jumping of fences has long been her trademark'). Grandam, Fiery Sol, pulled up thrice and fell in Points after producing Hot Handed. Made mistakes before pulling up on an April debut. The owner has reportedly given up the thrills of Welsh Pointing to go and live in Canberra, the most boring city on earth. Bet she'll be back for 2001. *Miss P. Jones — Tredegar F. (Tim Jones)*. 950 (OMa).

HOTSCENT (IRE) ..9-4.. 10 br.m. Creative Plan (USA) — North Rose VII (unknown) fR6u4. Lengthy sparely-made sister to Artistic Plan (IRE). IRISH P-t-P '96 r3 p1 (25l 2nd); pulled up 1, and fell 1. IRISH NH FLAT '97 r1 p0. IRISH NH '96/7 r6 p0. P-t-P '98/9 r10 w1 (Maiden) p4 (3 3rds); pulled up 4. Looked sure to be involved in the finish of her Members, but ducked out at the third last (alongside the box-park) when holding a narrow lead. Well beaten otherwise and has not formed a harmonious relationship with Clare Wilberforce. Acquired blinkers on her final start. Has looked a short-runner in the past. *Mrs B.L. Shaw — United (Gary Hanmer).* 118 (L), 858 (M), 963 (R), 1253 (L), 1528 (R).

HOTTENTOT ..—.. 8 ch.m. Sula Bula — Hot 'n Scopey (Hot Brandy) fu. Compact half-sister to Chasing winner, Luke Warm, and successful Hurdles winner, Hot 'N Saucy. Dam, rated 10-8, won 2 Points including a Ladies, in which she sprinted clear of Mendip Express and Prince Milborne. Grandam, Horoscope, won 4 Hunt Chses (2m6f-3m3f) and 9 Ladies and placed 17 (inc 10 Hunt Chses). Great-grandam, Pure Chance, won 4 Ladies and 3rd twice. NH FLAT Feb '99 r1 p0. NH '99 (for J. Old) r2 p0; tailed off both Hdles. Fell at the seventh and unseated at the third in Maidens. Comes from a line of patrician ladies, and what a pity that the-common-as-muck Sula Bula was allowed to infiltrate the family. *Mrs S. Horton & S. Jarrett — Beaufort (Joanna Bush).* 673 (2m4fOMa), 1361 (2m4fOMa).

HOT TODDY (IRE) ..8-1.. 6 b.g. Glacial Storm (USA) — Technical Merit (Gala Performance USA) 7. Sturdy half-brother to Well Bank and Percy Pit. Dam won 2m6f Sell Hdle. Sold Tattersalls, Ireland June for 35,714. Sent off joint-favourite for a May Maiden, but looked in need of the outing and was allowed to coast home in a remote last. Cost a small fortune, although her siblings both earned nil points for Technical Merit. *Miss H.J. Hinckley — Wheatland (John Groucott).* 1465 (OMa).

HOUSELOPE BECK ..10-2.. 11 ch.g. Meadowbrook — Hallo Cheeky (Flatbush) 4f43Rp. Lengthy quite attractive owner-bred brother to Houselope Brook, and half-brother to Sandedge and Houselope Spring. Dam won 9f Sell, and won 3 Sell Hdles, 2m-2m4f (raced latterly for Mr White). NH '98 r1 p0 (8th of 9). P-t-P/HUNT CH '95/9 r21 w2 (Maiden and Ladies) p3; failed to finish 7 (fell/unseated 4). Won on his racecourse debut, but only once more in 27 subsequent attempts and twice fell victim to bad luck in 2000. Was upsides the winner and travelling the better when capsizing at the last at Alnwick and had every chance when running out at the fourth last in a Ladies race won by Balisteros at Aspatria later in the season. Stays well and deserves to find another opening, but clumsy and even managed to collide with the running rail on the way to the start once. *Mrs F.V. White — Haydon.* 41 (L), 183 (CCf), 421 (3m5fL), 975 (O), 1364 (L), 1579 (L).

HOUSE OF OASIS (IRE) ..—.. 10 b.g. Dancing Lights (USA) — Weaver's Fool (Weavers' Hall) pfp. Small neat half-brother to Lisnavaragh, and to Irish NH flat and English jumping winner, Castlevennon. IRISH NH FLAT '97 r1 p0. IRISH P-t-P '98/9 r7 p1 (3rd); pulled up 4, and fell. Sold Doncaster, Aug for 800. Appeared to make a promising Irish debut, but went the wrong way after, and it is a rare occasion when he even completes the course. Punters can desert him with confidence. *Mrs M. Armstrong — Morpeth (Kevin Robson).* 188 (OMa), 497 (R), 665 (OMa).

HOWAYMAN ..10-10.. 11 b.g. Faustus (USA) — Our Mable (Posse USA) 35Rp. Compact good-topped half-brother to a winner abroad. P-t-P/HUNT CH '95/9 r30 w17 (inc 10 Hunt Chses, 2m4f110y-3m1f, and 2 Opens; inc hat-tricks '96 and '98) p8 (5 2nds, beaten neck twice; and inc 6 Hunt Chses); pulled up 2, and fell 2. NH Aut '99 (from M. Todhunter's) r4 w1 (2m6f110y Ch) p1 (3rd). An excellent performer with a superb strike rate, but was becoming increasingly lazy in '99 and suffered his first blank season in 2000. Seemed in need of the race on his reappearance, and ran well in the Aintree Foxhunters despite a few mistakes, but cocked his jaw and took the wrong course at Hexham next time and managed to rip off both hind shoes when running below par at Stratford subsequently. Did not seem quite right all year and may well revive after a break. Stays three miles, but equally if not more effective over shorter trips and appreciates a sound surface. Wears blinkers. *Mrs A. Waggott — Dumfries (Kate Anderson).* 586 (3m1fH), 921 (2m6fH), 1446 (3m1fH), 1648 (3mH).

HOW BURN ..9-12.. 8 b.g. Meadowbrook — Kinkell (Netherkelly) 3b. Tall good-bodied owner-bred. P-t-P '99 r5 w1 (Members) p0; last pair 2, and pulled up 2. Landed a few bets when comfortably landing his Members in '99, and a decent third in a Restricted on his reappearance, but brought down at halfway next time and failed to reappear. Looks to have the ability to win again if none the worse for his spill. *Mrs V. Jackson — Morpeth.* 184 (R), 360 (R).

HOW FRIENDLY ..8-8.. 11 ch.g. Gabitat — Bucks Fizz Music (Be Friendly) 9p17p5. Compact. NH FLAT r1 p0 (tailed off). NH '97 (from D. Duggan's) r1 p0 (fell). P-t-P/HUNT CH '95/8 r23 w3 (up to Confined) p9 (7 3rds, of 3 once, and last twice); failed to finish 8 (fell/unseated 3). Won three Points on firm to '97, but had performed dismally for present connections until he rallied to head the favourite near the finish in his Members this year. Reverted to type subsequently and was soon labouring in Hunter Chase company at Folkestone. Often failed to get the trip in the past. *Mrs B. Ansell — W. Street/Tickham.* 127 (Cf), 288 (CMod), 571 (M), 824 (Cf), 1394 (O), 1540 (2m5fH).

HOWLING JACK ..—.. 8 ch.g. Little Wolf — Jack's Love (Grey Love) p. Half-brother to Malvern Lad (qv). Sold Malvern, May '98 for 2000, but returned. Tailed off by halfway by mid-January, and not seen again. *Viscountess Boyne & J. Downes — Wheatland (John Downes).* 21 (2m4fOMa).

HOWSHAM ..—.. 7 br.m. Lyphento (USA) — Mystic Love (He Loves Me) p. P-t-P '99 r1 p0 (fell). Led for two miles before falling on her racecourse debut, but made no show prior to pulling up on her return and promptly disappeared. *T.W. Midgley — Saltersgate F. (Paul Midgley).* 169 (OMa).

HOWSYOURLUCK (IRE) ..9-9.. 10 b.g. Carlingford Castle — Lilardia (Taufan USA) p12p3pp. Sturdy half-brother to Hurdles winner, Tenbit (IRE). Dam won at 12f. IRISH NH FLAT '97 r1 p0. IRISH P-t-P '96 and '98 r5 p1 (20*l* 3rd in unplaced Maiden); pulled up 2, and fell 1. P-t-P '99 r5 p0; disqualified from Maiden win (had missed marker); fell 2, slipped up 1, and pulled up 1. Gained compensation for losing a race last year when landing a gamble at Erw Lon, and only just touched off in desperate conditions at Pantyderi in his first Restricted, but disappointing since and acquired a visor on his last two starts. Keen, and usually helps force the pace, but has little respect for the fences and may have developed a wind problem as he ran in a tongue-strap on his final outing. Looks worth opposing in future as his weaknesses seem to be increasing. *G. Austin — Banwen Miners (John Moore).* 20 (OMa), 268 (CfMa), 347 (R), 486 (R), 1228 (R), 1298 (R), 1616 (R).

PLATE 62   268 Vale of Clettwr Confined Maiden (Div 2): L to R Weaver Square (and the mightily moustachioed M. Parry), ur, and Howsyourluck (T. Vaughan), 1st, jump together

PHOTO: Bill Selwyn

HUGO HENRY (IRE) ..9-6.. 10 br.g. Black Minstrel — Greenfield Glory (Pitpan) ppp2. Compact unfurnished brother to Irish Pointing winner, Elwill Glory (IRE). Dam won mares Maiden in Ireland. IRISH P-t-P '95 and '97/8 r16 w1 (6yo Maiden) p2; pulled up 8, and fell 1. P-t-P '99 (for Miss J. Balmer) r3 p0 (pulled up 3). A well backed favourite when winning in Ireland in '97, but a consistently poor jumper who usually pulls too hard for his own good. Marginally improved in the new yard, but the form of his second at Brampton Bryan should not be taken literally as the race was run just prior to the rest of the meeting being abandoned due to the dangerously slippery ground. Rather highly strung and has been mounted on the course. Wears a tongue-strap nowadays. *D. Hardwick — Teme V. (Steve Flook).* 1089 (R), 1276 (R), 1459 (R), 1548 (R).

HUMARA (IRE) ..8-7.. 9 b.m. Astronef — Estivalia (Persian Bold) uu4ppf3u. Workmanlike half-sister to 3 flat winners, including Gippeswyck Lady and Arcevia. NH FLAT Dec '98 r1 p0 (tailed off). NH '98/9 r3 p0 (last pair 2, and pulled up in Hdles). Gives the occasional adequate display and might have finished second on her latest outing had the saddle not slipped causing the rider to be decanted after the last, but also performs appallingly on occasions, as she did when two fences last of three in a Members. A very clumsy jumper who rarely gets round, but it is possible that she might surprise one day. *G.F. Edwards — Devon & Somerset.* 146 (OMa), 206 (OMa), 352 (CfMa), 562 (CfMa), 739 (OMa), 1102 (OMa), 1369 (M), 1469 (OMa).

HUMPHREY ..8-7.. 10 ch.g. Lighter — Woodbury Lane (Sir Nulli) upp. Tall powerful. Dam is an unraced half-sister to 4 lightly-raced Newell Pointers, including Rose Lawn (qv '93 Annual). Grandam, Brumelle, was 4th in a Point and failed to finish 8 for Mr Newell. P-t-P '97 and '99 r4 p1 (2nd); pulled up 3. Ran tubed when a poor second in a very slow Maiden at Bitterley in '99, and when failing to complete thrice this year. Rendered useless by his disability. *Mrs S.M. Newell — Croome & W. Warwicks.* 337 (CfMa), 893 (OMa), 1354 (M).

HUNTSBYDALE ..10-1§.. 13 b.m. Relkino — Bowery Babe (Tantivy) p4R1p. Close-coupled owner-bred half-sister to Bowery Boy and Maison Rouge. Dam won 2 2m4f Chses in Ireland. NH FLAT '94 r1 p0. P-t-P '94, '96 and '98/9 r12 p4 (3 2nds, of 3 once); pulled up 5, and fell/unseated 2. Incredibly lightly raced over the years and had looked sure to end her career as a maiden, but grasped the mettle in the nick of time at Garthorpe (where she won very easily) as she broke down there next time. Had been most exasperating as she had thrown away a golden opportunity in '98, but deserved to get off the mark despite her sometimes petulant behaviour. *J.R. Knight — Belvoir (Jane Knight).* 54 (OMa), 234 (OMa), 439 (OMa), 547 (CfMa), 867 (M).

HURRICANE ANDREW (IRE) ..9-9.. 13 ch.g. Hawaiian Return (USA) — Viable (Nagami) 414. Compact good-bodied half-brother to Hurricane Sarah, and to Irish NH flat and Hurdles winner, Nimble Wind. NH '92, '95/7 and '99 r14 w2 (3m-3m1f Chses) p2. P-t-P/HUNT CH '94/5 and '99 (for Mr J.A. Moore) r8 w4 (up to Confined, inc hat-trick) p1 (last of 3); pulled up 3. Won four of his first seven Points, and had a fair degree of success as a front-runner under Rules, but pulled up on his only two starts in '99 and looked finished. Nursed back to health by Richard Price and won a poor three-runner Open at Brampton Bryan where Nick Oliver pinched the race from the favourite's grasp in the last strides (and let the judge know just in case he wasn't sure). Very nervously handled by Vicki Price having her first ride on his final start and his future career looks to be as a schoolmaster. *R.J. Price — S. Durham.* 1273 (O), 1545 (O), 1631 (MO).

HURRICANE BLAKE ..9-12§.. 13 b.g. Blakeney — Nibelunga (Miami Springs) 245p. Good-topped half-brother to Hurdles winner, Go-Go-Power-Ranger, and to NH flat winner, Festive Lassie. Dam won at 9f in USA. NH FLAT Mar '92 r2 w1 (on fibresand) p0. NH '92/5, '97 and '99 (3 wins for M. Pipe; previously for C. Popham, bought for 18,000; previously for G. Grissell, 4 wins, bought for 12,000; one win previously for D. Cantillon) r28 w7 (3 Hdles, 2m6f-2m7f, and 4 Chses, 3m-3m3f) p8. By no means lacking in ability, but usually reluctant these days, requires much driving, and makes a plethora of slow jumps. Needs good or firm ground, and would not race properly in 2000 after a respectable eight lengths second to Gunner Welburn first time out. Produced super-fit by maestro Pipe to overcome a 20 month absence when unbeaten in three outings in July/August '97, but a non-scorer since enduring a further 25 month lapse. Normally blinkered. *A.G. Fear — Quantock (Laura Horsey).* 148 (3m1f110yH), 386 (3m1f110yH), 680 (3m1fH), 1096 (MO).

HYA PRIM ..9-3.. 10 ch.g. Say Primula — Rilin (Ribston) 4pfu. Good-bodied brother to Sayonara and half-brother to Dakeem. NH FLAT '95/6 r3 p0. NH '96/9 (blinkered 1; for C. Grant; previously for breeder N. Chamberlain) r21 p2 (3rd in self Hdle, and 2nd in Ch); fell in w of 9 Chses. Sold Doncaster, Aug for 500 (to S. Grant). A very disappointing loser of 28 races. His two and a half length second in a 2m4f Chase in March '98 should have given him outstanding claims in a Maiden, but continued to frustrate any remaining hopeful supporters after finishing 11 lengths fourth on his debut. May have something wrong with him. *T. Grant & Miss N. Veasey — S. Notts (Robert Mackley).* 20 (OMa), 233 (OMa), 373 (CfMa), 798 (OMa).

HYDRO (IRE) ..8-6.. 10 b.g. Electric — Loughanmore (Bargello) 6. Workmanlike half-brother to Irish Pointing and Chasing winner, Celia's Joy, to Irish Hurdles winner, Lady Letitia, and to the superstar Wayward Lad (won 6 Hdles and 22 Chses and £277,255). NH FLAT Apr '96 r1 p1 (2nd). NH '96/9 (for M. Hammond) r6 p2 (3rd in Hdle, and very remote last in Ch); tailed off all 4 Chses (pulled up 2). Bought Doncaster, May for 2300. Most disappointing since his debut and averaged less than two outings per annum over five years, and was given away by the Daltons after it transpired that he had a major problem with broken blood vessels. *J.N. Dalton — Albrighton (Andrew Dalton).* 233 (OMa).

HYLTERS CHANCE (IRE) ..10-0.. 10 ch.g. Zaffaran (USA) — Stickey Stream (Paddy's Stream) 2fp27R253. Sturdy compact. NH FLAT '95 r1 p0. NH '96/8 (for P. Hobbs, blinkered /visored 2) r16 w2 (3m Hdle, and awarded 3m Ch as winner lost weight-cloth) p2 (short-headed once, and beaten neck once). Ran as well as could have been expected in his three seconds including behind Mizyan and Millyhenry, and came closest to success first time out, when he was caught near the finish by Camera Man at Chipley Park. A reliable jumper (although he gave Joanna Buck a fall on her first ride), but can look moody, and persuading him to score is proving to be a difficult task. Regained a visor on his final three appearances. *P.C. Browne, J. Hebditch, P. Musgrave, J. Rees & G.D. Taylor — Taunton V. (Kay Rees & Polly Curling).* 143 (C), 354 (L), 454 (4mMO), 653 (MO), 927 (Cf), 1374 (MO), 1470 (MO), 1638 (L), 1673 (L).

IBERIAN (IRE) ..9-7.. 8 b.m. Riberetto — Liosemer Rose (Normandy) pp5pp. Strong-topped. IRISH P-t-P '98/9 r8 w1 (5&6yo mares Maiden) p3 (3rds); pulled up, and fell. IRISH HUNT CH '99 r1 p0 (fell). Doubtless purchased because she shares the sire of Tomcappagh, who would be a favourite in the yard, but has so far been most disappointing and although she can go a good gallop for 2m4f she invariably compounds rapidly. Given five quick runs in early season, but has been absent since February. Her Irish victory was gained in heavy. *J.P.C. Wall — E. Sussex & Romney Marsh (Sarah Wall).* 14 (R), 86 (R), 178 (Cm), 289 (Cm), 306 (R).

IBEX ..10-5.. 7 b.g. Gunner B — Sunwood (Jimsun) c1ff. Good-bodied half-brother to Debbie's Darling. Dam won 2 Hdles (2m1f-2m3f) for Martin Pipe. P-t-P '99 r7 w2 (Maiden and Club Restricted) p2 (2nds); unseated 1, ran out 1, and pulled up 1. Had not looked an easy, but possessed plenty of speed and won by much the quickest 12st time of the day at Wadebridge.

Made the long journey to Weston Park to contest a hot Open in his next race, but was under pressure when making his exit five out and tragically met his end after another crash two months later. *M.C. Pipe — Taunton V.H. (David Pipe).* 63 (I), 104 (I), 294 (O), 1096 (MO).

ICANTSAY (IRE) ..9-1.. 11 b.g. Carlingford Castle — Another Ann (Torenaga) 673up. Small light-framed. IRISH P-t-P '96/7 r9 p1 (3rd); pulled up 4. P-t-P '98/9 (for Mrs J.B.W. Morrison) r5 p1 (3rd of 4); pulled up 3, and unseated 1. Not better than last-but-one in 10 English Points and looks to be another Carlingford Castle with little zest. Can be safely ignored if he reappears. *Miss J.B.W. Monteith — Middleton.* 54 (OMa), 277 (Cf), 400 (OMa), 696 (OMa), 999 (4m1fMO).

ICENFRIENDLY (IRE) ..9-13.. 8 b.g. Lancastrian — No Ice (Laurence O) R1p3p. Tall workmanlike. Dam won 4&5yo Maiden and 2m2f Ch in Ireland. P-t-P '98/9 r4 w1 (Maiden) p1 (2nd); last, and pulled up 1. Disappeared after the first week in February '99, but looked a horse to follow. Made heavy weather of landing his Restricted (appeared to finish unsound) and proved a major disappointment subsequently. Dismounted after pulling up at Llanfrynach in March and obviously has an intermittent fault. Still likely to win races if connections can sort him out. *D. Brace — Llangeinor.* 2 (R), 102 (R), 296 (I), 344 (I), 482 (I).

ICE N' SLICE (IRE) ..—.. 9 gr.m. Homo Sapien — Fairytale-Ending (Sweet Story) up. Small narrow half-sister to Chip'n'Run. P-t-P '98/9 r3 p0 (pulled up 2, and brought down 1). Yet to finish in five races over three seasons, and has not proved that she gets three miles. *Miss P.J. Cornes — S. Salop (Jon Cornes).* 568 (OMa), 865 (CfMa).

ICKFORD OKEY ..10-6.. 9 b.g. Broadsword (USA) — Running Kiss (Deep Run) pp. Tall rangy brother to Sharp Embrace. NH FLAT '97 r2 p0. NH '97/8 r3 p0. P-t-P '99 r5 w3 (inc Open) p1 (2nd); and unseated 1. Too immature to do himself justice under Rules, but improved rapidly throughout '99 and ended up with a defeat of Lochnagrain in a Mollington Open. Pulled up at the two opening meets of the season in 2000 and failed to reappear. Bandaged in front at Larkhill and it is hoped that his legs have not begun to give way under his considerable frame. Has shown form on varying ground, but must be treated with caution if he returns. *P.J. & K.D. Morgan — V. of Aylesbury (Sue Harbour).* 4 (O), 10 (O).

IDLEWILD (IRE) ..9-6§§.. 6 br.g. Phardante (FR) — Delia Murphy (Golden Love) up523p. Angular unattractive. Dam, sister to Easter Frolic, won 4 Irish Chses, 2m-2m4f (promoted from 2nd once; also demoted to 2nd in another). Sold Goffs, Ireland June for 3571. Eliminated in the first half mile on his first two appearances and jumped badly and was promptly tailed off when hunting round for last next time. Subsequently proved himself to be a rogue of the first order, and threw away three races he was poised to win. Short-headed at Garnons after hanging right and trying to pull up on the run-in (swerved left just after the post and chucked Scott Joynes off), veered left and slowed badly after leading at the final fence when six and a half lengths third there, and then cruised through to join the winner two out but pulled himself up on the final bend at Andoversford (blinkered). Unbelievably frustrating, and it is tempting to invent a triple squiggle just for him. *Mrs V. Ramm — Ledbury (Nicky Sheppard).* 12 (OMa), 60 (OMa), 122 (OMa), 450 (CfMa), 672 (2m4fOMa), 972 (OMa).

I DONT BELIEVE IT (IRE) ..—.. 8 b.g. Actinium (FR) — Billeragh Fountain (IRE) (Royal Fountain) pp. Dam is half-sister to Lover Bill (qv '95 Annual). IRISH P-t-P '99 r2 p0 (pulled up, and slipped up). IRISH NH '99 r1 p0 (tailed off and pulled up in Ch). Pulled up after two miles maximum on consecutive Saturdays in February to maintain his record of non-completions. *E.S. Wilkins & C.J. Williams — S. Pembs (L.J. Wilkins).* 268 (CfMa), 349 (CfMa).

I DON'T THINK SO ..—§§.. 10 b.m. Mas Media — Misdevious (USA) (Alleged USA) up. Tall leggy half-sister to flat winner, Mogin, and to 3 flat winners abroad. NH '96 r3 p0 (beat one). P-t-P '99 r6 p1 (remote 2nd); last, fell/unseated 2, refused 1, and pulled up 1. Beaten the length of the Cottenham run-in on his Pointing debut, but has failed to beat a rival since and has become highly reluctant now. Has dug her toes in at the start in her last four races and refused to budge until the others had gone out of sight in the latest. Acquired blinkers in 2000, but a rocket would have been more appropriate. Must be on the verge of a ban. *N.J. Pewter — E. Essex.* 178 (Cm), 239 (R).

I DO THE JOKES (IRE) ..—.. 11 b.g. Buckskin (FR) — Leannan (Callernish) p. Tall. NH FLAT Mar '95 (for J. Gifford) r1 p0. NH '97/9 (for J. Gifford; previously for T. Casey) r8 p0; (finished in all 3 Chses). Bought Ascot, June for 500. Seems hard to train (was absent for 31 months after his debut), and has never raised a smile in his life. *K.D. Giles — W. Street/Tickham.* 126 (R).

IFAFA BEACH (IRE) ..—§.. 9 b.g. Le Moss — Greenpeace (Master Owen) pp. Half-brother to NH flat and Hurdles winner, Dissington Dene, and to Irish Hurdles winner, Siochain (IRE), and to an Irish NH flat winner. Dam won Irish NH flat. NH FLAT '97 r2 p0 (tailed off both). P-t-P '99 r4 p0 (unseated 2, and pulled up 2). Well-related, but does everything with increased reluctance and must be a physical wreck. Not worth the bother again, and overfaced almost every time he goes racing. *K. Hunter — V. of Lune H.* 494 (L), 813 (L).

IFS AND BUTS ..—.. 6 ch.m. Nicholas Bill — Porto Irene (Porto Bello) p. Small owner-bred half-sister to Vic's Girl (qv). Potentially as appalling as the other homebreds introduced by Donald Tucker in 2000 (Jug of Wine and Vic's Girl). *D.C. Tucker — S. & W. Wilts (M.T. Aylesbury).* 1130 (M).

IF YOU SAY SO ..10-0§.. 15 ch.g. Say Primula — Vinovia (Ribston) p26. Sturdy goose-rumped brother to Chasing winner, I'm The Man, and half-brother to The Dabber (dam of Cracking Crumpet *qv*), and What A Miss. NH '91/2, '93/5 and '98 r19 w2 (2m7f-3m Hdles) p4 (inc 3rd in Ch). P-t-P/HUNT CH '96 and '98/9 r11 p2; failed to finish 7 (fell/unseated 4, and refused 1). Able, but highly temperamental and allowed Rosa's Revenge to overtake him near the finish after doing much of the donkey work at Flete Park. Could have won on a more regular basis had he not been such a thinker. Has never stood much racing and five outings in a year is his p.b. *K.F. Ellis — S. Devon.* 1044 (4mO), 1261 (Cf), 1432 (3m1fH).

I HAVEN'T A BUCK (IRE) ..10-2.. 13 ch.g. Buckskin (FR) — Lovely Colour (Shantung) p4ppp. Tall rangy half-brother to Irish Bumper and useful English jumping winner, I Haventalight, to Irish NH flat and Hurdles winner, Lovely Run, and to successful Hurdler, Villa Recos. Dam won 2 2m flat. IRISH P-t-P '94/6 r12 w2 (6yo&up Maiden, and Winners Of One) p4 (2nds); fell/unseated 2 (at last once — unlucky), and pulled up 1. IRISH NH '95/6 r2 p0 (6th of 7 in Ch, and fell in Hunt Ch). NH '99 r1 p0 (pulled up). P-t-P/HUNT CH '97/9 r7 w2 (inc Open) p3 (2 2nds; and 3rd in Hunt Ch); and pulled up 3. A fair performer at his best, but has always been very lightly raced and looks faulty at times. Pulled up apparently lame twice at Weston Park this year, and reappeared not long after on both occasions. Still able to bowl along in front and far from disgraced when around 14 lengths fourth in a Stratford Hunter Chase, but rather loses interest if headed and was visored on his latest appearance. Usually avoids ground any firmer than good. *J. Balmer & I. Anderson — W. Salop (Ian Anderson).* 294 (O), 580 (3mH), 1336 (2m4fH), 1409 (O), 1557 (3m1fH).

ILANDRA (IRE) ..7-10.. 9 b.m. Roi Danzig (USA) — Island Goddess (Godswalk USA) pppfp4p. Lengthy half-sister to Lyford Cay (IRE). IRISH FLAT r6 p2. FLAT r23 p3 (inc 19*l* 3rd in Sell). NH '95/8 (blinkered 1) r9 p0 (Sells latterly). P-t-P '99 r3 p0 (last pair 2, and pulled up 1). A truly dreadful animal who has contested 48 races of one description or another without the slightest sniff of a victory, and beaten a total of 161 lengths in her three Pointing completions. Can show early speed, but jumps badly and must be awry. *Mrs A.E. Leonard — N. Cotswold (Alan Peachey).* 36 (Cl), 194 (CfmA), 370 (C), 753 (CfmA), 995 (OMa), 1284 (OMa), 1420 (OMa).

I LIKE THE DEAL ..9-7.. 10 b.m. Lighter — Skidmore (Paddy's Stream) 3u33p. Lengthy. Dam disgraced herself in 4 Points (pulled up 2, and refused 2). P-t-P '96/9 r13 w1 (Maiden) p2; pulled up 5, fell 1, and ran out 1. Won a Maiden in '98 after a real threat had fallen three out, but can look ungenuine and a hard ride to boot. Generally improved in 2000 thanks to Champion handling, and could win a Restricted if she chose to, but even Les Jefford could not curb her tendency to hang and jump right on her final start. *B.M. Ayre — Dulverton E.* 931 (R), 1140 (CfR), 1518 (R), 1604 (M), 1651 (I).

ILLINEYLAD (IRE) ..10-1.. 7 b.g. Whitehall Bridge — Illiney Girl (Lochnager) 24f12. Robust half-brother to flat winner, Quick Stel, and to successful Hurdler, Lady Magnum (IRE). Dam won 3 flat, 5-6f, the first a Sell. IRISH FLAT r3 p0. FLAT (visored) r1 p0. NH '98 r5 p0 (inc 3 Sells). P-t-P '99 r3 w2 (Maiden and Restricted) p0; and slipped up 1. Has won three minor Points (the last two simple tasks at Bassaley) but has his limitations and needs to improve further in order to play more than just a supporting role in Confined company. May possess a little more scope and can always rely on plenty of assistance from the saddle. Acts on top-of-the-ground. Has been tried in a visor under Rules. *Mrs N.S. Sharpe — S. Herefords.* 482 (I), 741 (Cf), 988 (O), 1403 (I), 1544 (Cf).

I'M CONVINCED ..8-13.. 7 b.g. Petoski — Childhay (Roi Soleil) 42. Owner-bred half-brother to Childhay Chocolate (Chasing winner since Pointing) and Childhay Millie, and to jumping winner, Sursum Corda. Twenty-five lengths last on his debut (second favourite), and 32 lengths last of four next time (demoted fourth close home, officially placed third, and subsequently promoted; favourite). Shows some speed, but needs to find some stamina. *T.C. & M.M. Frost — Berkeley (Richard Barber).* 874 (2m4fOMa), 1062 (OMa).

I'M FOXY ..8-8.. 10 b.m. Joligeneration — Tinker's Quest (Romany Air) p3f. Good-bodied half-sister to Soeur Marie (*qv*). P-t-P '97 (for Mrs A. Frank) r5 p0 (5th, and ran out 1). Went awol for two years after an undistinguished season in '97, but slightly improved for the break and managed to make the frame (despite finishing last) when beaten 25 lengths at Bishopsleigh. Not impressing as a likely future winner. Wears blinkers. *Mrs C.A. Mock — Tiverton Stag.* 849 (R), 1179 (OMa), 1468 (OMa).

IMPENNY ..9-5.. 8 br.m. Impecunious — My Molly (Averof) 51. Unfurnished owner-bred half-sister to Chalvey Grove. NH FLAT '98 (for M. Bradley) r2 p0. NH '99 (for Mrs. C. Hicks) r2 p0 (last and fell in Hdles). Provided Mark Wall with his first success in a Maiden on firmish at Mollington in March, but although eight others finished only one of them scored subsequently (Barton Bog, who had hated the ground). Lightly raced, and may turn out to be very moderate. *G. Ivall — Ross H. (John White).* 471 (OMa), 790 (OMa).

IMPERATIVE ..9-10.. 9 b.g. Impecunious — Sprightly Miss (Master Spiritus) fff2. Lengthy sparely-made half-brother to Master Bertie. Dam won 2 Points and placed 5 for Roger Jowett. P-t-P '98/9 r8 p2 (3rd of 4 once); last pair 2, ran out 1, fell 1, and pulled up 2. Largely disappointing in '99, and looked a non-stayer, but stamina doubts pale into insignificance when compared with his erratic jumping in 2000. Hit the deck three times in quick succession, but only beaten half a length in a seven minute Maiden at Parham and clearly has the ability to win a race. Absent since the end of February and may have suffered a reverse. *Dr R. Jowett — Wilton.* 11 (OMa), 62 (Cf), 220 (OMa), 309 (OMa).

IMPERIAL DAWN (IRE) ..10-8§.. 9 gr.g. Roselier (FR) — Sister Cecelia (Trombone) 1R11221. Unfurnished half-brother to Irish Pointing and English Hurdles winner, Fuzzy Logic (IRE). Dam is an unraced half-sister to False Note. IRISH NH '97/8 r10 p0. IRISH P-t-P '97 and '99 r12 w3 (inc winners of Two) p5; pulled up 3. Bought Doncaster, Aug for 13,000. A very funny customer. Would be unbeatable in Ladies Opens if he always produced the excellent form which enabled him to beat subsequent Hunter Chase scorers Ardstown and Donnygale at Cottenham on his English debut, but sometimes down tools in a race, and either picks up too late or not at all. Coaxed to victory at Newton Bromswold where Lily The Lark finished third, but it was typical of his inconsistency when he allowed her to beat him at Guilsborough, which represented a turn around of 20 lengths. Lisa Rowe does fairly well with him on balance, but punters are always liable to end up with burned fingers, and may continue in a similar vein in 2001. *C. Bazley & Mrs P. Rowe — Pytchley (Caroline Bailey).* 19 (L), 230 (L), 368 (L), 512 (L), 772 (L), 1007 (L), 1183 (L).

IMPERIAL HONORS (IRE) ..8-11.. 10 ch.g. Crowning Honors (CAN) — Within A Whisper (Welsh Pageant) p4. Smallish brother to Colour Of Life. NH FLAT '96 r3 p0. NH '96/7 r6 p0; pulled up 2. P-t-P '98 (for Miss Z.L. Urquhart & Mr S. Coady) r2 p0 (pulled up 2). Useless on all known form, and beaten most of the length of the home straight when last in his Members. Was reluctant to start in his last two outings over hurdles, and jumps fences moderately. *Miss Z.L. Urquhart — Avon V. (Nick Lampard).* 247 (R), 473 (M).

IMPERIAL LINE (IRE) ..9-9.. 7 ch.g. Mac's Imp (USA) — Ellaline (Corvaro USA) pf32u2. Lengthy good-bodied half-brother to 2 flat winners (one in Germany, and the other, Mobile Miss (IRE), in Ireland). Dam won at 7f in Ireland. FLAT (tried blinkered) r10 p0. NH '98 r2 p0. P-t-P '99 r2 p0 (last, and unseated 1). Very impetuous and has trouble lasting home, but beaten no more than nine lengths in his three placed efforts and should be able to find a weak race in 2001 if some extra stamina is forthcoming. His home course at Stainton will afford him one of the best opportunities to get three miles. *P. Cowey — Cleveland (Tina Jackson).* 168 (OMa), 507 (CMa), 694 (OMa), 803 (MMa), 1032 (OMa), 1233 (OMa).

IMPERIAL TOKAY (USA) ..—.. 11 gr.g. Caro — Chaudennay (USA) (Assert) ppp. Lengthy. Dam won 12f Cheshire Oaks. FLAT (first 4 for B. Hills) r5 p0. NH '94 (for A. Forbes, bought for 1100, visored first 2) r3 p0. Utterly useless, and has pulled up in all six outings over jumps. Left on the rack for six years, but did not mature in to a pleasing vintage. *A.N. & Miss E.C. Brown — Quorn (Miss E.C. Brown).* 1076 (OMa), 1220 (OMa), 1421 (OMa).

IMPETUOSITY (IRE) ..8-9.. 7 ch.m. Imp Society (USA) — Catherine Clare (Sallust) 3. Lengthy half-brother to 3 flat winners (2 in Ireland, including Three Musketeers), including Bozeman. Dam won 3 Irish flat, 8-12f. 57000f, 3200y. FLAT (for C. Thornton at 3) r4 p0 (Sell Hual). NH'99 (from S. Cole's, bought for 1300) r3 p0 (tailed off). Gave a first indication of having some ability when seven lengths third at Lifton (the runner-up scored next time), and might possibly manage a win eventually. *R.C. Smith — Torrington F.* 1520 (CfMa).

IMPS WAY ..8-13.. 6 br.m. Nomadic Way (USA) — Dalton's Delight (Wonderful Surprise) pp35. Small. Sister to Implicity Suzie (qv '97 Annual), had a hunter's certificate in '99 but failed to appear. Finished 19 lengths last of three in her Members, but the race was run at a crawl, and will need to find some speed to figure prominently in Maidens. Given her age, that is not an impossibility. *Mrs T. Corrigan-Clark — Derwent.* 169 (OMa), 283 (OMa), 393 (M), 625 (OMa).

IM STRUGGLING ..9-4.. 6 b.g. Totem (USA) — Vanda The Second (Primitive Rising USA) uupuf1. Neat owner-bred. Dam is half-sister to Rhy-Bye (qv '93 Annual). Was certainly living up to his name when partnered by the amazingly incompetent Kevin Lupton on his first four starts (managed to cling on to him for two miles once, but went one mile or less on three other occasions). Gave Gordon Markham a fall on their first outing together, but then survived more irratic jumping to beat one other finisher in a four-runner Maiden on firm at Corbridge (the outsider of the party; left in front when the one length leader unseated three out). May prove to be grossly flattered by winning. *M.A. Humphreys — Farndale.* 281 (OMa), 381 (OMa), 503 (R), 627 (OMa), 1352 (OMa), 1499 (OMa).

INCBRUSH ..9-6.. 7 b.g. Brush Aside (USA) — Incamelia (St Columbus) pu. Good-topped. Dam won 2m5f Hdle and 4 Chses (3m-3m2f) for the Hendersons. Grandam, Indamelia, won at 5f, and won 7 Hdles(2m-3m); won another which was declared void) and 3 Chses (2m4f-2m6f) and 5 Hunt Chses (2m4f-3m2f) and 2 points, and placed total of 21 for late John Thorne (Diana Henderson's father). Great-grandam, Barton's Sister, won 2m Ch for him. Soon tailed off when given a blatant school on his debut, but reappeared at Guilsborough a week later and was coming with what looked to be a winning run when he hit the falling Syrpiro and unseated after the last. Comes from an outstanding family who go back into the mists of time, and compensation surely awaits. *Mrs D.A. Henderson — Warwicks (Nigel Ridout).* 872 (OMa), 1010 (CfMa).

INCH CROSS (IRE) ..10-5.. 10 b.g. Supreme Leader — Glenaveel (Furry Glen) 143u4. Big rangy hobdayed half-brother to Chasing winner, Inch Way, (IRE). IRISH P-t-P '96/7 r10 w3 (inc 2 Opens) p2 (pulled up 3, and fell 2. P-t-P '98/9 r8 p1 (3rd); pulled up 2, and unseated 1. Carried too much condition in the previous yard (was with Nick Pomfret) but made streamlined by Caroline Bailey and produced the goods at the first time of asking for her and landed a few shrewd bets in the process. Both the second and third that day gained their revenge on him when they next met at Brocklesby Park, where the ground had more cut in it, and though he has won in soft ground in Ireland a sound surface seems far more suitable. Almost lost Richard Hunnisett on the flat at Thorpe, but succeeded at Garthorpe where he was in the process a running well behind Gillone. Not beaten at all far on his Hunter Chase debut (Give It A Whirl 2 — Inch Cross 1) and should continue to play a good supporting role to Copper Thistle for the owner. His wind trouble (is hobdayed and has run tongue-tied) no longer seems a problem to him. *R.S. Hunnisett — Pytchley (Caroline Bailey).* 48 (Cf), 115 (CCf), 229 (Cf), 868 (Cf), 1334 (3mH).

INCH FOUNTAIN (IRE) ..—.. 10 br.g. Royal Fountain — The Priory (Oats) 114p. Tall half-brother to Priory Rose. IRISH P-t-P '95 r1 w1 (4yo Maiden). P-t-P '96/8 r4 w1 (Restricted) p2 (2nds); and pulled up 1. Talked of in glowing terms after winning his first two Points, but only ventured to the racecourse three more times in the next two seasons and was absent for the entire '99 campaign. Quickly made up for lost time with an impressive early season double, but a major flop at Eaton Hall subsequently and ran as though something was amiss when pulled up at Sandon. Clearly very talented (worth 10-7 when on song) but mystery surrounds his well being as it always has. Needs some cut in the ground, but does not seem to be able to handle a bog. *M.J. Parr - N. Salop (Sheila Crow).* 75 (I), 370 (C), 529 (Cf), 1128 (Cf).

INDEFENCE (IRE) ..10-7.. 10 b.g. Conquering Hero (USA) — Cathryn's Song (Prince Tenderfoot USA) 31. Sturdy half-brother to prolific flat winners, Katy's Lad, Stairway To Heaven and Westbridge Lad (amassed 25 victories between them). 1400y. FLAT (for M. Channon, wins at 2, visored last 2) r15 w2 (7f, one on fibresand) p7 (short-headed once). NH '95/6 and '98 (for Mrs J. Pitman) r13 w4 (2m-2m5f Hdles, in '96 Supreme Nov Hdle at Cheltenham Festival worth £45,247 when 25-1); inc hat-trick to '96) p2. Sold Ascot, Sep '98 for 5000. A former classy performer in the mud, and beat 26 rivals when attaining his greatest triumph, but has suffered two absences of 22 months since, and his legs are exceptionally fragile. Gave a competent display in his first Point and then collected a notable scalp when the only horse to beat Rip Van Winkle in 2000, but sadly lamed himself in the process. Another resurrection could be too much to hope for. *Mrs P. Tollit — Worcs (Pip Hooley).* 481 (L), 860 (L).

INDIAN KNIGHT ..9-10.. 16 b.g. Kinglet — Indian Whistle (Rugantino) 23u. Strong good-looking brother to Indian Rose (dam of Rose Garden *qv*), and half-brother to Indian Eagle, Indian Major, Indian Debt, Indian Officer, Indian Trooper, Indian Minor and Gladys Emmanuel (Chasing winner since Pointing). Dam won 4 2m Hdles and 2nd (only ran 6 times). P-t-P/HUNT CH '91/9 r47 w9 (4 Opens; and inc walk-over for Confined) p12 (8 2nds, last once; and inc 2 Hunt Chses); failed to finish 14 (fell/unseated 6, and ran out 2). On the scene for ten consecutive seasons now, and deserves a medal for his longevity, but on a long losing sequence (beaten 13 times since April '97) and basically too old for the job now. Has enjoyed a chequered career, but with many memorable highlights, and surely his gold manger awaits. *C.A. Green — S. & W. Wilts.* 764 (O), 1130 (M), 1595 (Cf).

INDIAN MILLER ..8-7.. 10 ch.g. Gildoran — Milltown Lady (Deep Run) pfffpu. Strong. NH '98 (for J.A.B. Old) r1 p0 (tailed off in Hdle). Has shown signs of ability, and frequently gives a prominent showing, but makes one bad mistake per race (usually when tiring) and ends up on the floor. Has been tried tongue-tied. *M.S. Green — S. & W. Wilts (Jane Green).* 6 (R), 212 (CfMa), 329 (CfMa), 409 (OMa), 881 (OMa), 957 (CfMa).

INDIAN MUSE ..8-4.. 6 b.m. Commanche Run — Mountain Muse (Sunyboy) 3p4p. Sturdy. Dam is half-sister to Simply Joyful (*qv* 2000 Annual). Yet to get seriously involved in a race, and was last beaten 35 lengths and 40 lengths in her completions. *Mr & Mrs P.S. Awdry — Blackmore & Sparkford V. (John Dufosee).* 408 (OMa), 733 (2m4fOMa), 880 (OMa), 1100 (OMa).

INFORAPOP ..9-13.. 6 b.g. Greensmith — Panda Pops (Cornuto) p221. Smallish compact attractive half-brother to Badger Beer (*qv*). Has shown plenty of early promise, but proved to be intractable in the closing stages and gave away possible winning chances when second at Holnicote (was almost unrideable after two out, having made numerous bad jumps), and gave himself too much to do and was again hanging in the closing stages at Lifton. Nick Mitchell made more use of him at Umberleigh, and came to the last with a useful lead, but looked to be just run out of it by Sea Spirit on the line. The rider's body language suggested he knew he had been beaten, but the Judge thought otherwise and gave him the nod. Was not winning out of turn, and may prove to be one of the better winners of the Torrington Maiden. *S.M. Philpot — Blackmore & Sparkford V. (John Dufosee).* 934 (OMa), 1372 (OMa), 1641 (OMa), 1676 (OMa).

INGLEBRIG LAD ..9-1.. 8 b.g. Primitive Rising (USA) — Inglebrig (New Brig) 2p. Owner-bred brother to Inglerise, and half-brother to Carlton Lad and Inglebrook. Caught close home in a weak 2m4f Maiden at Dalston (had been 20 lengths clear four out, and was still six lengths ahead at the last but napped and surrendered the advantage), but faded in the holding ground at Corbridge and although being left second two out Clive Storey elected to pull him up immediately. Worth trying again on better going. *Mrs F. Deans — Eglinton.* 501 (2m4fOMa), 1166 (OMa).

INGLEBY JACK ..9-1.. 8 ch.g. Broadsword (USA) — Days Gorse (Nearcottage Pearl) p. Strong half-brother to Captain Pineapple. Dam, tiny sister to Hays Wood (*qv* '87 Season Annual), won 4 Points (3 Ladies) and placed 12 (inc 2 Hunt Chses). Grandam, Gambrita, won a Maiden and placed 4.

P-t-P '98/9 r5 p1 (3rd of 4); pulled up 2, and fell 1. Able to bowl along for up to 2m4f, but weakens alarmingly particularly in testing conditions, and beaten 55 lengths in his sole placing. Stopped dead after making a mistake at the 14th at Wetherby on his return and was not able to reappear. *Mrs D. Frank — Hurworth (Paul Frank).* 168 (OMa).

INGLERISE .10-0.. 6 br.m. Primitive Rising (USA) — Inglebrig (New Brig) u31. Sister to Inglebrig Lad (*qv*). Unseated at the first on her debut, but came from well off the pace to finish a promising 16 lengths third at Tabley. Maintained her rapid improvement when cantering home on the bit on firmish at Wolverhampton, and is starting to look a useful prospect. Should be worth following at six. *D. Williams — Cheshire (Gary Hanmer).* 570 (2m4fCfMa), 964 (OMa), 1527 (OMa).

INLIGHT ..—.. 8 b.g. Lir — Cruise Lady (Cruise Missile) f. Wiry pony. Dam, half-sister to The Copper Key (*qv* '98 Annual), was 2 fences last and pulled up 5 in Points. Unimpressive in the paddock and fell at the third in a February Maiden. *W.M. Smith — E. Cornwall.* 159 (CfMa).

INNISHFEA (IRE) ..9-9.. 9 b.m. Duky — Amach An Doras (Tumble Wind USA) 452p. Rangy good-looking. IRISH NH '97 r2 p0 (17th of 18, and pulled up). IRISH P-t-P '97/9 r17 w1 (6 plus mares Maiden) p3; pulled up 4, brought down, fell 2, and unseated. A hard puller who is usually very prominent for at least 2m4f, but proving disappointing, and was beaten favourite twice in Restricteds. Had every chance when one length second once, but found nothing, and is either short of determination or stamina (possibly both). *G.D. Brickell — Ross H. (Pip Hooley).* 297 (I), 485 (R), 698 (R), 992 (R).

INNS OF COURT ..—.. 8 ch.g. Infantry — Deviji (Mansingh USA) pp. Rangy good-topped. P-t-P '99 r3 p0 (pulled up 3). Backward and given a quiet time in his debut season, but capitulated after leading for two miles at High Easter this term and was not seen again. Kept jumping to the left on the fast surface and may have done himself a mischief. *M.J. Jerram — Essex.* 22 (2m4fOMa), 605 (OMa).

IN PLACE (USA) ..9-10.. 13 b.g. Roberto (USA) — Placer Queen (Habitat) 4pp. Neat attractive half-brother to flat and Hurdles winner, Above The Cut (USA), and to flat winner, Invisible Halo. Dam won at up to 10f in Canada. FLAT r3 p0. NH '91 r2 p0. P-t-P/HUNT CH '93/4 and '98/9 r23 w2 (Restricted and Members) p5 (3 2nds, of 3 once); pulled up 8, and unseated 1. Won two minor races (one a match for his Members) in '99, but usually fails to get the trip and has been pulled up in five of his nine subsequent starts. Sometimes gets on his toes and has two handlers, and occasionally sent to post early. Has a tendency to jump to his left. *G. Whisker — Farmers Bloodhounds (Rebecca Murrell).* 190 (M), 302 (3mH), 511 (O).

INSIDEOUT ..10-6.. 8 b.g. Macmillion — Parijoun (Manado) 421f. Tall good-bodied half-brother to Persian Lion, and to flat winners, Caspian Morn and Caspian Gold. FLAT r4 p0. P-t-P/HUNT CH '98/9 r13 w3 (Maiden, Restricted and Intermediate) p1 (3rd in Hunt Ch); fell 2, slipped up 1. Looked a decent prospect when winning his last two starts in '98, but had fallen in his opening two ventures and jumped erratically throughout the following season. Had been fencing with more aplomb in 2000 and finished strongly to win a Dalton Park Confined in March, but fell four out when going well at Hutton Rudby a week later and tragically broke his neck. *A. Jackson — Cleveland (Lynne Ward).* 135 (L), 375 (Cf), 506 (Cf), 623 (Cf).

INSULATE ..9-13.. 11 ch.m. Sula Bula — Penny Catcher (Barolo) 65p. Rangy half-sister to Fixed Penalty. Dam, bad-legged, failed to finish in 4 of 5 Points for Stephen March. Grandam, Forepenny Lass, failed to finish in 7 points. Great-grandam, Fair Clyde, was distant 2nd in Maiden after pulling up. P-t-P '96/7 and '99 r9 w1 (PPORA Mares) p2; fell/unseated 4, pulled up 1. Won a two-finisher Mares event at Marks Tey in testing conditions in '99 three years after finishing a length second on the same course, but stands her racing badly and made no show in just three outings this year. Used to jump poorly, but her lack of acceleration has been her real cross to bare. *S. March — E. Essex.* 178 (Cm), 320 (O), 574 (4mMO).

IN THE FUTURE (IRE) ..8-11.. 10 b.m. Phardante (FR) — Chief Dilke (Saulingo) p97. Light-framed sister to Fiddler's Leap (IRE), and to 4 winners, including Clowater Lady (IRE) (Irish NH flat and Irish/English Hurdles) and Holdforth (Hurdles). Dam won at 6f, and later won 3 flat and over Hurdles in Belgium. IRISH P-t-P '96 r4 p1 (last of 2); last, and pulled up 2. NH FLAT '96 r1 p0. P-t-P '99 r3 p0 (5th twice, and pulled up 1). Stone-bonking last in five of her six Pointing completions and possesses precious little ability. Appears unable to stay three miles. *P. Spittle — N. Cotswold (Alan Peachey).* 336 (R), 749 (Cf), 1422 (OMa).

IN THE VAN ..9-2.. 9 b.g. Bedford (USA) — Sea Countess (Ercolano USA) u6323. Lengthy half-brother to Sober Island and Countess Rosie. NH FLAT '97/8 r4 p2 (2nds). NH '98/9 (for Mrs D. Haine; blinkered 1, often tongue-tied) r8 p0; last, pulled up and brought down in Chses (poor jumper). Sold Doncaster, May for 1500. Just caught on his racecourse debut, but very disappointing ever since, and still a Maiden after 17 attempts. Can go a decent gallop, but a very weak finisher who does not get the trip, possibly because of physical disabilities (has broken blood vessels in the past). Quite amusingly named. *Mrs S. Morley — Derwent (Richard Morley).* 53 (OMa), 281 (OMa), 399 (OMa), 625 (OMa), 809 (OMa).

INTREPID GAL ..—.. 6 b.m. Terimon — Padrigal (Paddy's Stream) fp. Small. Dam, half-sister to Karannsu (*qv* '92 Annual), won 2 Hunt Chses (2m6f-3m1f) and 7 Points (inc 2 Opens and a Ladies) and placed 6 (was 2nd once for Mr Cheatle, after producing Interpid Gal). NH FLAT Oct '99 r1 p0. NH Oct '99 r1 p0 (jumped slowly and pulled up in Hdle). Mother was tough and likeable, but gives no impression of enjoying the game herself so far, and clambered over the fences until pulling up at halfway when tailed off on her latest attempt. *J.N. Cheatle — Cottesmore (Nick Pomfret)*. 51 (OMa), 181 (2m4fOMa).

IRANOS (FR) ..10-2.. 9 b.g. Labus (FR) — Misvaria (FR) (On My Way USA) f115212f. Lengthy brother to useful French jumping winner, Artemus. NH FLAT '96/7 r4 w2 p0. NH '97/9 On M. Pipe) r11 w2 (Hdles, 2m4f-2m5f) p3 (2nds, inc of 3 in Ch); pulled up and unseated (with every chance 3 out) in other Chses, ran Sell. Wears blinkers and is easily outbattled by decent competitors, but has the ability to score if matters are not too difficult, and luckily found three suitable opportunities when there were five runners or less in 2000 (including a match). Scored once on firmish when Tim Mitchell's jockeyship was the telling factor, but is ideally suited by a great deal of mud. Not the most natural of jumpers. *Mrs P.B. Browne — Taunton V.H. (David Pipe)*. 10 (O), 100 (O), 252 (O), 402 (O), 735 (MO), 1139 (Cf), 1374 (MO), 1560 (Cf).

IRISH BRUSH (IRE) ..—.. 7 b.m. Brush Aside (USA) — Deep Cailin (Deep Run) fppp. Well-made. Dam half-sister to Pongo Waring (qv). Takes a keen hold and has twice led in the middle stages of her races, but compounds quickly, and yet to get round including in a four-runner event in heavy on final start. *Mrs I.E. Penfold & Mrs L. Gregory — Quantock (Tim Long)*. 640 (CfMa), 1469 (OMa), 1564 (OMa), 1655 (OMa).

IRISH BUZZ (IRE) ..9-6.. 9 b.g. Satco (FR) — Brisbee (Prince Bee) pfp. Leggy. IRISH NH FLAT '96 r3 p0. IRISH NH '96 r2 p0. NH '96/8 r5 p0 (pulled up final 3). P-t-P '99 (for Mr W.I. Owens) r8 w1 (Maiden) p3 (2 3rds); last, pulled up 2, and fell 1. Overcame some erratic early season jumping to land a Cursneh Hill Maiden and a fair second in his first Restricted, but made a late start for new connections in 2000 and failed to complete in three starts. Gets very on edge before his races and was late into the paddock on his reappearance in a bid to keep him calm. *Mrs J. Clifford — Avon V.* 1206 (R), 1280 (R), 1671 (R).

IRISHEYESARESMILIN (IRE) ..10-5.. 7 br.g. John French — Laugh Away (Furry Glen) 1221. Compact. Dam, half-sister to Sea Scamp (qv '96 Annual), won at 2m in Ireland. P-t-P '99 r3 w2 (Maiden and Members) p0; and last. Looked another potential Bailey world-beater after disposing of the opposition in his final two races in '99, but has not really confirmed that opinion this year. Won unchallenged on his reappearance, but finished very tired, and went down narrowly when odds-on in his next two races, though his defeat by Gillone at Garthorpe was no disgrace. Fended off Lottie The Lotus in game style in his Members subsequently and there is a lot to like about his attitude, but his performances are workmanlike and lack real class. Connections would doubtless have been horrified to know that their charge would be beaten by a rival eight years his senior at the start of the campaign, but they still have a fair tool to go to war with next year and more successes seem assured. Has only once encountered ground softer than good. *Mrs A. Scotney — Pytchley (Caroline Bailey)*. 50 (R), 191 (Cf), 543 (I), 1005 (M).

IRISH KINSMAN ..8-3.. 8 b.g. Distant Relative — Inesdela (Wolver Hollow) 6u7. Workmanlike half-brother to an Irish flat winner. FLAT (early runs for P. Walwyn) r11 p0. NH '96/7 (for G. Yardley) r4 p0 (tailed off, inc Sell final). Useless in all his 18 races. Tried blinkered flat and Hurdling. *Miss S. Dutton & M. Gregory — Bicester with Whaddon*. 672 (2m4fOMa), 872 (OMa), 1590 (2m4fOMa).

IRON BUCK ..—.. 8 gr.g. Buckley — Rusty To Reign (General Ironside) pfp. Rangy brother to Rusty Buck (qv). Travelled from Devon to Yorkshire to Herefordshire, only to give clueless displays of jumping each time. *B. Davies — N. Ledbury*. 73 (OMa), 167 (OMa), 337 (CfMa).

IRON PYRITES ..10-0.. 8 b.m. Blaze O'Gold (USA) — All Our Yesterdays (Jimsun) 1211. Big rangy owner-bred half-sister to Lady Mouse (qv '99 Annual). Dam won 2 Hdles, 2m3f-2m7f. A determined and likeable mare who is always striving hard at the end of her races, and enjoyed a fine debut season in minor company. Can handle easy under foot conditions, but not always especially fluent, and was jumping as if she did not care for the firmer ground on final start. Her attitude should enable her to hold her own in better grade, and may have a chance in Opens eventually. *Miss A.E. Greenow — Golden V. (Steve Lloyd & Angharad Watkins)*. 491 (CfMa), 896 (R), 1088 (R), 1458 (M).

I SAY DANCER (IRE) ..9-0.. 8 b.m. Distinctly North (USA) — Lady Marigot (Lord Gayle USA) 3562u7. Small half-sister to 3 flat winners (one abroad, and one in Ireland). Dam won at 10f in Ireland. FLAT r1 p0 (tailed off). NH '96/7 r3 p0 (last 2, and pulled up — tailed off, inc Sell). P-t-P '99 r6 p0 (last, pulled up 4, and unseated 1). Stays much better than she used to, but only moderate and has a tendency to boil over in the preliminaries. Not beaten far on her reappearance, but the time was slow and well held since including when the subject of a gamble on her final start. Prone to make mistakes and lacks the substance to shrug them off. *Miss T. Hammond & R. Goodwin — Border (Tina Hammond)*. 426 (CfMa), 626 (OMa), 808 (OMa), 977 (CfMa), 1165 (OMa), 1430 (OMa).

ISHEREAL (IRE) ..9-11.. 10 gr.g. Carlingford Castle — Boreenace (Boreen FR) pc16. Small stocky. P-t-P '97/9 r12 p4 (3rds); pulled up 3, and on floor 3. Placed four times in the past and seemed to be lacking motivation, but did nothing wrong when winning at Tabley, though King Paddy was poised to challenge until ducking out at the last. Well beaten subsequently and remains one not to place too much faith in. *Mrs B. Smith — Cheshire (Steve Griffiths)*. 569 (OMa), 906 (CfMa), 964 (OMa), 1528 (R).

ISHMA (IRE) ..9-12§.. 10 b.g. Kambalda — Scat-Cat (Furry Glen) 832u3u831. Close-coupled brother to NH flat and jumping winner, Bramblehill Duke (IRE). NH '96/7 (blinkered final '96) r8 p0 (pulled up 8, inc Sell Hdle, and jumped badly in both Chses). P-t-P/HUNT CH '97/9 r26 w1 (Maiden) p10 (5 2nds, last thrice; and inc last of 3 once); failed to finish 10 (on floor 2, refused 1, and ran out 1). Won a bad race in '97, and disqualified from another for taking the wrong course the following year, but performed dismally last term when his season was over in February. Perked up on three trips to Charing in 2000 and won the last of them, his Members, after leading throughout the final circuit. The owner-rider is of little assistance and the combination can usually be safely ignored. Invariably blinkered. *D. Page — Ashford V.* 25 (Cnr), 126 (R), 285 (CR), 306 (R), 416 (R), 675 (CR), 825 (R), 980 (R), 1109 (M).

ISLAND ECHO (IRE) ..10-6.. 10 b.g. Black Minstrel — Bavards Best (Le Bavard FR) 27132. Tall attractive. IRISH P-t-P '96/7 r10 w1 (Maiden) p5; pulled up 3. P-t-P '98 r5 w1 (PPORA Restricted) p2 (3rds); disqualified from 4th once — not weigh in; and unseated 1. Missed a year after winning at Wetherby in '98, but has come back an improved performer and was well handled by James Tate when landing a 2m4f Hunter Chase at Huntingdon, but the jockey must have thought he was perched on Pegasus in two subsequent races and gave his mount far too much to do on each occasion. Has many worthy attributes and deserves a more tactically aware pilot. *T.P. Tate — Bramham.* 384 (2m3f110yH), 687 (2m6f110yH), 1335 (2m4f110yH), 1447 (2m4fH), 1591 (3m1fH).

ISLAND GIFT ..—.. 8 ch.m. Jupiter Island — Lynemore (Nearly A Hand) fp. Half-sister to Starting Again. Dam, half-sister to North Bannister (qv '96 Annual), won NH flat, 3 2m Hdles, and 2 Chses (2m6f-3m); latterly for late Tim Forster. NH '98/9 (for late T. Forster; debut for R. Dickin) r2 p0. Has only managed four outings in three years, and fell at the second once and tailed off in the other three. *M.P. Wiggin — Ludlow (Geoff Evans).* 220 (OMa), 704 (OMa).

ISLAND VISION (IRE) ..10-4.. 11 b.g. Vision (USA) — Verandah (Jaazeiro USA) 3132u. Strong-topped brother to flat and Hurdles winner, Kinlet Vision, and half-brother to Hurdles winner, Bella With A Zee. Dam won 8f race in Ireland. IRISH FLAT r22 w3 (11-13f) p9. IRISH NH '93/5 r11 w1 (2m4f Hdle) p3 — also won 2m Hdle, but subsequently disqualified. NH '96/9 (for J.O'Shea, bought for 14,000) r15 w1 (2m Hdle) p3; also won 2m Hdle, but subsequently disqualified; inc Sells. Sold Doncaster, Nov for 500. Did not start until late April in 2000, but enjoyed a reasonable season, and gained his first success for four years when giving Joanna Hughes her first winner in a poor five-runner Ladies at Rodmell. One-paced nowadays, but has gained all his six successes over the years on firmish ground. Often wears headgear in the previous yard. Connections extracted victory from another cheapie (Cebu Gale), and they certainly lack nothing in enthusiasm, as Fern Leader who also performed at Rodmell, turned up to compete at Flagg Moor the following day! The guiding light behind the operation seems to be Hughes' boyfriend Paul Blockley, a former professional jockey and trainer until he disappeared from the scene. *R.E. Gray & Mrs J. Hughes — Cranwell Bloodhounds (Joanna Hughes).* 1113 (L), 1201 (L), 1380 (L), 1525 (L), 1587 (L).

ITALIAN MAN (IRE) ..8-11.. 13 b.g. Don Orazio — Via Del Tabacco (Ballymoss) p5. Workmanlike fired half-brother to Irish NH flat and smart English Hurdles winner, Vicario Di Bray (ITY), and to 3 winners in Italy. Dam won 2 races in Italy. IRISH P-t-P '93/4 r4 p3; pulled up 1. NH '95/6 r6 p0 (5th, last pair 3, pulled up 1, and fell 1 in Chses). P-t-P '97 and '99 r4 w1 (Maiden) p2 (2nds); unseated 1. Made all to win a good Maiden in '97, but restricted to just three outings since and seems a case of a good horse with bad legs. Nibbled at in the market and not wholly disgraced on his latest appearance, but the odds are well and truly stacked against him now. *J.A.C. Sheppard — Quantock.* 734 (R), 1089 (R).

ITANI ..—.. 9 b.g. Tuam — Kenn Towy Streak (Streak) fp. Compact brother to Fruitation. NH '97 (for M. Wilkinson) r2 p0 (tailed off and pulled up 2). Useless on his rare appearances. *Miss S. Wesley — Grafton.* 250 (CfMa), 514 (OMa).

ITA'S FELLOW (IRE) ..9-13.. 13 ch.g. Decent Fellow — Castle Ita (Midland Gayle) uu125p. Lengthy light half-brother to Bannagh Mor (IRE) (qv). P-t-P/HUNT CH '95/9 r18 w8 (inc Open; hat-trick '97) p4 (head 2nd; and 3 3rds, last once); refused 1, and on floor 3. Has an excellent record in Points, with nine wins and five places from 21 attempts, but has not always gelled with Michael Prince (who has fallen off him thrice) and Sue Sharratt (who won on Hatton Farm Babe that same afternoon) was aboard in his latest success. Beaten at odds-on next time, and the experiment was not repeated. Did not look at all keen when tried in a visor once in 2000 and looks moody nowadays. Stays well, but will be hard pressed to win again unless Miss Sharratt is invited back. *R. Prince — Meynell & S. Staffs.* 334 (O), 529 (Cf), 592 (Cf), 901 (M), 960 (Cf), 1128 (Cf).

ITS A HANDFULL ..8-13.. 8 b.g. Itsu (USA) — Star Part (West Partisan) 1ppp. Tiny. Dam, half-sister to Starember Lad and Newstarsky (qv '98 Annual), won 2-finisher Maiden and 3rd twice for Joe

Price. P-t-P '98/9 r9 p0; failed to finish 7 (unseated 1, refused 1, and ran out 1). Only once better than last in his first nine starts, but the fact that he was sent off as short as 3-1 tells how bad a race it was that he won on his reappearance at Llanfrynach. None of his victims have since gone on to score and his subsequent efforts in Restricteds have been uninspiring. Lacks scope. *J.J.E. Price — Llangibby.* 488 (CfMa), 818 (R), 1054 (R), 1460 (R).

ITSARCHIE ..9-6.. 8 ch.g. Itsu (USA) — Panto Girl (Lepanto GER) pppp21. Tall rangy roach-backed owner-bred brother to Itspantotime (*qv*). P-t-P '99 r1 p0 (pulled up). Pulled up in his first five starts, but had shown an iota of ability before becoming the subject of a gamble on his penultimate outing. Those who were on each-way came out smiling as he went down by under a length in the fastest of four Maidens, but he went one better when a warm favourite on a return visit to Bonvilston subsequently though it was only in the last hundred yards that he wore down the long-time leader. Has scope for improvement, but family history suggests that he will not find it easy in better company. *J. Jones — Gelligaer F.* 269 (CfMa), 490 (CfMa), 898 (OMa), 1055 (CfMa), 1456 (OMa), 1618 (OMa).

IT'S BEYOND BELIEF (IRE) ..9-9.. 7 b.g. Supreme Leader — Rossacurra (Deep Run) 2. Half-brother to Irish Pointing winner, Alamillo, and to a jumping winner in Switzerland. P-t-P '99 r2 p1 (3rd); and fell 1. Caught out by the bogey fence at Didmarton on his debut in '99 after surviving two earlier mistakes but subsequently off the track for two months and proved a disappointing favourite at Bratton Down. Failed to reappear after filling the runner-up berth at Larkhill in January this season. Compounded quickly after jumping the second last and would have been a modest third but for the clear leader unseating at the last. Has the undoubted ability to win, but seems prone to mishap. *J. Keighley & P.K. Barber — Blackmore & Sparkford V. (Richard Barber).* 12 (OMa).

PLATE 63   1568 Tredegar Farmers Restricted: R to L Baron Itsu (P. Sheldrake), 1st, jumps with Itscinders (J. Jukes), 3rd, with Welsh Warrior (T. Vaughan), 2nd, close behind

PHOTO: John Mullen

ITSCINDERS ..9-8.. 11 br.m. Itsu (USA) — Ambley Wood (Honour Bound) ppp23f2p. Small owner-bred sister to Itscountryman, and half-sister to J J Tomas, Miss Foxglove (dam of Itsdigitalis *qv*), and Lady Forrester. Dam won 2 Points and placed 7 (including 2nd of 3 in Nov Hdle, and bad 3rd in Nov Ch). P-t-P '98/9 r8 w1 (Maiden) p1 (last of 3); pulled up 3, and fell 2. Won a bad Maiden at Bassaleg having failed to complete in her first two races (typical) but beaten in 12 Restricteds since and only seems able to show form in poor races on firm ground. Mistimed her challenge when second at Bonvilston, but capitulated when ridden close to the pace next time and seems quite content in frustrating her supporters. *J. Jones — Gelligaer F.* 274 (R), 483 (R), 1054 (R), 1453 (R), 1568 (R), 1615 (R), 1659 (R), 1671 (R).

ITSDIGITALIS ..—.. 8 b.m. Itsu (USA) — Miss Foxglove (Tom Noddy) p. Dam, a very small half-sister to

Itscinders (*qv*), was very remote 3rd in 2 Maidens (beat one horse). Gradam, Ambley wood, won 2 Points and placed 7 (inc Hdle and Ch). Made a short-lived forward move after two miles on a mid-May debut, but weakened rapidly and was soon tailed off. Looked backward, so it mightjust be worth getting her fit and lowering her to Maidens. *C.W. Banwell — Ystrad Taf Fechan.* 1450 (Cf).

ITSFORU ..10-3.. 9 b.g. Itsu (USA) — Game Trust (National Trust) p3p. Strong compact half-brother to Bankit. Dam won 6 Points and 2 Hunt Chses (2m4f-2m6f) and placed 12 for late Colin Nash, and Itsforu is named in his memory. P-t-P '98/9 r10 w2 (Maiden and Restricted) p4 (3 2nds, last once); pulled up 1, and fell/unseated 3. Incredibly unlucky despite winning twice in his first two seasons, but did not reappear until the third week in April this year and looked out of sorts in three Hunter Chases. Often the victim of errors previously, but jumped regulation obstacles soundly. Good enough to win more Points if his career can be resurrected. *Mrs S. Nash — O. Berks (Jane Fitzgerald).* 1103 (3m2f110yH), 1340 (3m1f110yH), 1627 (2m5fH).

ITSFREDDIE ..9-5.. 9 ch.g. Itsu (USA) — Pensham's Lawyer (Spanish Lawyer) p2pp1. Light owner-bred brother to Itswillie (*qv*). P-t-P '99 r2 p0 (pulled up 2). Displayed his first signs of ability when just edged out in a poor Maiden at Llanfrynach, but went one better in an equally weak event at Chaddesley on his final appearance. Seems willing under pressure, but will need to improve further when raised in class. *J. Jones — Gelligaer F.* 267 (CfMa), 487 (CfMa), 891 (OMa), 1056 (CfMa), 1634 (OMa).

ITS GRAND ..9-12§.. 12 b.g. Sula Bula — Light Of Zion (Pieces Of Eight) fR272. Sturdy half-brother to Artful Arthur and New Problem. NH FLAT '93 r2 p0. NH '93/8 (2 wins for W. Turner; previously for P. Richens; 2 wins previously for M. Bradley; previously for R. Manning, his breeder — owned by him subsequently) r36 w4 (2m4f-3m2f Sell Hdles) p7; inc 5 Chses. Ungenuine and did not like regulation fences, and reverted to Hurdling for his final 11 attempts. Predictably proved to be a difficult ride for the enthusiastic veteran owner, and performances for her included a fall and a run out, but she did better when coaxing him in to second at Bratton Down (very poor contest, apart from the winner). Gave his best display for Rory Lawther when chasing home Glenpine at Hackwood, but ran in snatches, and was never really co-operating. Blinkered subsequently (had worn headgear twice in the past). Effective in soft, but has not consented to score since November '97. *Mrs J.V. Wilkinson — S. & W. Wilts.* 201 (L), 405 (L), 883 (Cf), 1562 (C), 1652 (L).

IT'S HIMSELF ..11-2.. 9 b.g. Rakaposhi King — Coole Pilate (Celtic Cone) 1174. Rangy brother to Chasing winner, Cherokee Chief, and half-brother to Irish Pointing/jumping and English Hurdles winner, Lyreen Wonder. Dam is half-sister to Bear Claw (*qv> 2000 Annual*). IRISH NH '96/7 r4 p0. IRISH P-t-P '98/9 r3 w2 (inc Open) p0; pulled up. IRISH P-t-P '00 r1 w1 (beat Over To Bens and Very Adaptable 1½l and 12l in Carlow Farmers Open: *ld at mod pce, hdd 9, 3rd 2 out, chall last, qcknd wl*). Does not run much, but given a masterful ride by Tony Martin when ploughing through the heavy ground at Haydock to be such doubty rivals as Cavalero and Castle Mane (it would certainly have been a different story had thosde two been at their best). Runs tongue-tied, and made many mistakes in all three visits to England. Gained his four victories consecutively, spread over three years, and will add plenty more if able to appear more regularly. *P.M. Barrett — Kildare (Tony Martin, in Ireland).* 156 (3mH), 584 (3m2f110yH), 924 (3m1fH).

ITSJAYEMM ..—.. 9 b.g. Itsu (USA) — Panto Girl (Lepanto GER) pp. Neat attractive owner-bred brother to Itspantonine (*qv*). P-t-P '98 r1 p0 (pulled up). Backward, and has yet to go beyond two miles to date. Seems difficult to train. *J. Jones - Gelligaer F.* 350 (CfMa), 602 (CfMa).

ITS MURPHY MAN ..—.. 12 ch.g. Itsu (USA) — Gaie Pretense (FR) (Pretendre) fpppppp. Tall strong-topped half-brother to Hurdles winner, Rubins Boy. Dam won at 12f in France. P-t-P/HUNT CH '95/8 r16 w1 (Members) p2 (3rds); pulled up 8, unseated 2. Won a bad four-runner event run at a crawl in '97, but does not stay at normal racing speed and has pulled up in 10 of his subsequent 15 starts. Blinkered on his debut, but not since. *Mrs E. Keir — Grafton.* 75 (I), 243 (Cf), 428 (Cf), 510 (Cf), 1016 (Cf), 1190 (Cf), 1436 (Cf).

IT'S NOT MY FAULT (IRE) ..9-10§.. 13 b.g. Red Sunset — Glas Y Dorlan (Sexton Blake) 522pp52p1. Small close-coupled. Dam won 2 flat, 11-12f. FLAT r7 p0. NH '91, '92/4 and '95/7 r43 w4 (2m5f-2m6f Sell Hdles, inc dead-heat; one on all-weather, and 2m7f Ch) p20. P-t-P '97 and '99 (for Mr P.D. Jones & Mr P. Trotman) r14 w1 (Members) p7 (2 2nds); pulled up 1. Won under Rules after a consistent and successful season Pointing in '97, and reportedly retired in '99, but returned and kept busy in 2000. Only managed to beat three rivals all year, but collected four prizes. A notoriously difficult ride with a tendency to hang left, but looks after himself and has never returned with an empty saddle. Occasionally blinkered flat and hurdling. *P.D. Jones — R. Sheehan — P.D. Jones — Dart V. & S. Pool H., & Torrington F. (Peter Jones).* 66 (Cf), 103 (Cf), 251 (M), 651 (M), 1047 (Cf), 1257 (C), 1387 (O), 1606 (O), 1670 (M).

PLATE 64   924 Martell Reserve Nov HC, Aintree: Irish invader It's Himself (A.J. Martin), 4th, is well behind early on   PHOTO: Steven Cargill

IT'SNOTSIMPLE (IRE) ..10-2.. 9 b.m. Homo Sapien — Perpetue (Proverb) pp1p. Good-bodied half-sister to Irish NH flat and Chasing winner, Lucky Bust. IRISH NH FLAT '97 r2 p0. IRISH P-t-P '96/7 r3 w1 (2 finisher 5yo Maiden) p1 (2nd in match); and pulled up 1. NH '97/8 r7 p0 (last and pulled up 3 in Hdles, inc Sell; and 4th of 5, last, and pulled up in Chses). P-t-P '99 r9 w3 (Members, Intermediate nov rdrs and Confined) p4 (2nds); pulled up 1. Transformed by a switch to Points in '99 and claimed seven prizes, but appeared to suffer a minor setback after her reappearance this term and was subsequently off the course for seven weeks. Returned to form, and landed a touch in the process, when winning at Lifton, but ended the season on another low. Likes to help force the pace, but not at home in holding ground and can probably win again when conditions are right. *Mrs S. Messer-Bennetts — N. Cornwall.* 257 (L), 1046 (Cm), 1636 (Cf), 1652 (L).

ITSPANTOTIME ..9-0.. 11 b.m. Itsu (USA) — Panto Girl (Lepanto GER) pbfp4p. Small sister to Itsjayemm and Itsarchie. Dam, half-sister to Day Express (*qv* '93 Annual), was distant 3rd in a Restricted for John Jones. P-t-P '97/9 r11 w1 (Maiden) p3 (inc last of 2); pulled up 2. Made the frame seven times consecutively before winning an insipid race at Bonvilston in '99, but predictably struggling in Restricteds since and generally tends to lack stamina. *J. Jones — Gelligaer F.* 347 (R), 595 (R), 896 (R), 1054 (R), 1448 (M), 1672 (O).

ITSSTORMINGNORMA ..9-9$.. 11 b.m. Itsu (USA) — Norman Currency (Normandy) 2pp. Small neat owner-bred. Dam was placed in 3 Points. Grandam, Pennyworth, won 3 Points and placed 4. Great-grandam, Island Beauty, won Curre Maiden. P-t-P '95/9 r18 w1 (Maiden) p6 (3 3rds); pulled up 5, and refused 1. Took four seasons and 12 races to get off the mark, and provided Jason Cook with his first winner, but whereas his career has begun to take off hers has bottomed out, and whilst she has filled the runners-up berth in each of her last three completions she has remained a short-runner with an ungenuine nature. *J. Jones — Gelligaer F.* 1572 (I), 1613 (I), 1674 (I).

ITSTHEJONESBOY ..8-13.. 11 ch.g. Itsu (USA) — Maella (FR) (Traffic) 1p. Strong-topped owner-bred brother to Myitsu, and half-brother to Rogamaja, Miss Daffodil (dam of Tomolly *qv* '00 Annual), and Marshall Boldella, to successful Hurdler, Senior Steward, and to a flat winner. Dam won over Hurdles in France. P-t-P '97/9 r9 p2 (2nds); pulled up 4, and fell 1. Tubed after just three races, but a genuine soul and valiantly made all for a deserved success in a bad Bassaleg Maiden run in a slow time on his reappearance. Would struggle to find a worse race, and ran out of steam after just two miles next time. *J. Jones — Gelligaer F.* 1574 (OMa), 1616 (R).

ITSWILLIE ..9-5.. 10 ch.g. Itsu (USA) — Pensham's Lawyer (Spanish Lawyer) 32. Owner-bred brother to Itspenshams and Itsfreddie, and half-brother to Model Lawyer, Pensham's Pride and Officially Pensham. Dam is an unraced half-sister to Pensham's Son. Grandam, Pensham, won 44 Points and a Maiden Hunt Ch and placed 26. P-t-P '99 r3 p0 (pulled up 2, and unseated 1). Showed some aptitude despite failing to complete in his debut season, and ran well despite looking unfit on his reappearance. Made no impression on the easy winner from three out at Howick next time and failed to reappear, but could go one better if he was produced fighting fit. *J. Jones — Gelligaer F.* 349 (CfMa), 601 (CfMa).

ITS WORTH A BOB ..9-2.. 9 b.g. Gildoran — Rolling Dice (Balinger) 3. Lengthy half-brother to Top Trump, and to Chasing winner, Pitchthedice. Dam, half-sister to Risk A Bet (*qv* '93 Annual), ran in 4 Points (unseated at the last when clear once) and subsequently won 2m4f Ch and placed 3 for Angie Murray. NH '98 r1 p0 (pulled up). P-t-P '99 r1 p0 (slipped up). Showed promise on his Pointing debut last year, and again went into many notebooks as a likely future winner when 29 lengths third to Union Man at Newton Bromswold, but sadly seems nigh on impossible to train and failed to reappear. *Mrs A.M. Murray — V. of Aylesbury.* 517 (OMa).

IVANS DREAM ..—.. 7 gr.g. Silver Owl — Karaka (Good Times ITY) p. Sturdy owner-bred half-brother to Miltown Castle. Given a school by the champion in mid-May. *J.S. Papworth — S. Cornwall.* 1520 (CfMa).

IVEAGH LAD ..9-10.. 15 br.g. Irish Star — Lady McQuaid (Mick McQuaid) 4. Strong compact half-brother to Cottage Counsel (IRE). IRISH NH FLAT '90 and '92 r3 p0. IRISH NH '91/2 r4 p0 (swerved and unseated in Ch). IRISH P-t-P '92 r2 w1 (4yo plus Maiden) p0; fell when challenging 2 out. NH '92 r4 p4 (last of 3 once and 3rd of 4 thrice in Chses — beaten 27l minimum). P-t-P/HUNT CH '93/6 and '98 r21 w4 (inc 2 Hunt Chses, 3m1f-3m3f) p5 (3 2nds, inc Hunt Ch); failed to finish 5 (fell 2). Ran the opposition ragged in four wins '93/5, but only able to manage five outings since and broke down (again?) at Stainton on his reappearance. Was a habitual front-runner who used to pull like a train , but has surely come to the end of the line now. *P. Sawney - Cleveland (Jackie Sawney).* 805 (O).

IVE CALLED TIME ..10-0.. 13 b.g. Sergeant Drummer (USA) — Alice Rairthorn (Romany Air) 53uu. Small workmanlike brother to Devonshire Lad, and half-brother to Alice Woodlark (dam of Alice Sunrise *qv*), and Alice Passthorn (dam of Bogey Man *qv*). Dam won Members and placed 6 (inc 2 Hdles, one a Sell). NH FLAT '92 r1 p0. NH '94/5 r6 p2 (2nds of 3 and of 4 in Chses); inc Sell Hdle. P-t-P/HUNT CH '96/9 r23 w4 (up to Confined) p11 (8 2nds, last once; and inc 3rd in Hunt Ch); failed to finish 7 (unseated 1). A triple winner in '96, and revived after a spell in the doldrums last year, but becoming elderly and beat just one rival in 2000. His jumping has deteriorated in recent times and can be hard to sit on. Occasionally tongue-tied in the last two years and his wind is clearly not what it used to be. *Mrs M. De Burgh & Capt. G. Chanter — Devon & Somerset (Sue Maude).* 143 (C), 259 (C), 557 (Cf), 1471 (Cnr).

IVESTON (IRE) ..8-7.. 7 b.m. Yashgan — The Magpie Bush (Jasmine Star) 4p. Tall rangy. P-t-P '99 r2 p0 (unseated, and pulled up). Beaten more than 20 lengths when last on her reappearance and as in the previous season disappeared after failing to complete in a 2m4f event at Dalston in March. *R.A. Ross — Braes.* 112 (OMam), 501 (2m4fOMa).

IVORS BOY ..—§§.. 8 b.g. Rushmere — Scotch Dawn (Jock Scot) Rpp. Half-brother to Scotch Missile and Scotch Law. Dam won 2 Points and placed 8. Grandam, Angelic Dawn, won a Ladies. Has twice failed to get further than a mile, and looks a lunatic. His breeder usually has no products — no wonder he got shot of this one. Acquired an off-side pricker on final start. *Miss S. Jakeway — Curre, & S. Cornwall.* 595 (R), 900 (OMa), 1316 (OMa).

IVY BOY (IRE) ..10-1.. 11 ch.g. Riot Helmet — Ivy Run (Arapaho) p8. Lengthy half-brother to Irish Pointing winner, Ivy Breeze. Dam, half-sister to Tremayne (*qv* '94 Annual), won mares Maiden in Ireland. IRISH P-t-P '94 r2 w1 (4yo Maiden) p0; pulled up. IRISH NH FLAT '95/6 r5 p3 (2nds, short-headed once). IRISH NH '96 r2 p2 (3rds, beaten 2 short heads once). NH '96 and '98/9 (for C. Mann, bought for 10,000) r5 w2 (2m5f-3m Chses) p0. Bought Doncaster, May for 2000. Beat the smart Village King when capturing a £5168 prize in a three-runner Chase at Newbury in November '98 but has only managed four unproductive outings since. Had also been absent for 23 months after December '96, and is clearly exceptionally hard to train, which is a pity, because he gives the impression of still retaining some ability. Likes soft ground, and might surprise in a Point if his legs were up to it. *A.J. Thomas — Kyre (Richard Morley).* 153 (2m4f110yH), 683 (3mH).

JABIRU (IRE) ..8-2.. 8 b br.g. Lafontaine (USA) — Country Glen (Furry Glen) 13pf22. Strong-topped rangy half-brother to Irish Hurdles winner, Sandra Louise. NH FLAT '97/8 r3 p1 (2nd). NH '98/9 (for P. Hobbs) r5 p2 (22-33l3rds in Hdles). Bought Doncaster, May for 5500. His National Hunt form looked to give him very strong claims in a Maiden, and he duly obliged at the first time of asking at the rewarding odds of 7-1 at Black Forest Lodge. Beat Morris Piper, and was just ahead of him when he fell at the last at Stafford Cross subsequently, but looked very vulnerable, and has been something of a disappointment when well-backed in Restricteds so far. Already placed in three, and will surely capture one before too much longer. Gives the impression of not being able to gallop properly in heavy ground, and a dryer season might help. Made too many mistakes when tried in a Hunter Chase. *Mrs K.M. Horsburgh — Tiverton.* 204 (OMa), 315 (R), 583 (2m5f110yH), 932 (R), 1140 (CfR), 1376 (R).

J'ACCUSE (IRE) ..10-0.. 11 ch.g. Torus — Glens Princess (Prince Hansel) p4u4pu1p. Big strong-topped half-brother to Le Meille (IRE), and to Irish jumping and English Chasing winner, Papillon (IRE). Dam won 2m Hdle and 2 Chses (2m-2m4f) in Ireland. NH FLAT '95/6 r3 p0. NH '96 r3 p1 (3rd). P-t-P '98 r4 w1 (Members) p2 (2nds); and unseated 1. Looked sure to win at Llanvapley until Fiona Wilson fell off at the last, but made amends at Pentreclwydau subsequently. Error prone and lacks consistency, but his efforts are all the more valiant because he slipped both rear tendons off his hocks in '98. A cheap purchase and connections have done well to nurse him through his problems. *Mrs E. Kulbicki — Curre.* 338 (R), 595 (R), 744 (R), 1089 (R), 1200 (CR), 1276 (R), 1298 (R), 1449 (I).

JAC DEL PRINCE ..9-11.. 11 b.g. Teofane — Star Shell (Queen's Hussar) p8p. Lengthy half-brother to Royal Mountbrowne (*qv*). NH FLAT '95 r2 p0. NH '95/8 r14 p4 (2nds in 3m3f Chses); refused final. P-t-P '99 r7 w1 (Maiden) p5 (2nds); and pulled up 1. Did well to win at Witton Castle last year, and collected five other prizes, but desperately one-paced and looked badly out of sorts in 2000. Likes to front run and is a good ride for a novice, but a watching brief is advised if he returns. *R. Walker — W. of Yore.* 620 (R), 689 (R), 1028 (R).

JACK BOOTS ..—.. 10 gr.g. Baron Blakeney — Miss Bootsie (Casino Boy) Rpfpf. Leggy angular flea-bitten. Dam was 2nd in 2 Points (would have won a deplorable Maiden on hard, but slipped up). NH '95 and '98 (for R.J. Hodges) r3 p0 (last, pulled up 1, and fell 1). P-t-P '98 (for Mr & Mrs R.J. House) r5 w1 (Maiden) p1 (3rd); 4th, ran out 1, and pulled up 1. Won a bad Maiden for Geoff Barfoot-Saunt in '98, but a hard ride and has been too much of a handful for Jonathan Phillips on his return. Ran and jumped as well as he looked throughout 2000 and acquired a visor on his final appearance. *D.T. Phillips — Quantock.* 948 (R), 1228 (R), 1298 (R), 1452 (R), 1659 (R).

JACK CRUISE ..8-13.. 9 b.g. Cruise Missile — Creole Bay (Kind Of Hush) pp33f. Small compact. Dam won 2 Points and placed 9 (inc a flat and 4 Hdles for David Barrington). P-t-P '98/9 r9 p1 (2nd); last, pulled up 4, and fell/unseated 3. Not without ability, and only beaten a length in a Bitterley Maiden last year, but only seems to stay 2m4f maximum and beaten out of sight in both placings in 2000. Does not appear anywhere near good enough for short distance Hunter Chases and will prove difficult to place. *Mrs D.J. Barrington — Radnor & W. Herefords (Antony Woods).* 450 (CfMa), 491 (CfMa), 1271 (M), 1464 (OMa), 1627 (2m5fH).

JACK DORY (IRE) ..—.. 9 b.g. Lapierre — Gentle Lass (Cardinal Flower) pp. Lengthy quite attractive half-brother to Irish NH flat winner, Shean Hill. IR13,000 4-y-o. IRISH NH FLAT '96/7 r3 p0. IRISH P-t-P '97 r3 p1 (2nd); last, and unseated. NH '97/9 r10 p1 (last of 2 on debut). Beaten a neck by Bramble Hill Duke in Ireland, but has now been pulled up in his seven most recent attempts (a Hurdle, four Chases and two Points), and there is surely something grotesquely wrong with him. Hopefully not going to be asked to compete again. *J.G. Bradburne — Fife.* 914 (CfMa), 1118 (R).

JACK FLASH ..8-12.. 7 ch.g. Primitive Rising (USA) — Moss Pink (USA) (Levmoss) 37. Unfurnished half-brother to Mr Murdock and Just Nelly, to successful Hurdlers, Kalamoss, Abigail's Dream (also succesful on flat) and Fanny Robin, and to 2 flat winners, including Ben's Surprise. NH FLAT '98/9 (for S. Kettlewell; visored final) r3 p0. Bought Doncaster, May for 5000. Beaten 25 lengths or more in early season youngsters Maidens, but showed a little ability. Athletically bred, but could do with jumping better, and is not standing his racing very well to date. *Mrs A.N. Jenkins — Wheatland (Andrew Dalton).* 31 (CMa), 169 (OMa).

JACKPAT (IRE) ..7-8.. 9 b.g. Brush Aside (USA) — Chatty Lady (Over The River FR) 5. IRISH P-t-P '98/9 r3 p0; pulled up 1. Bought Malvern, Sep for 3600. 63 lengths last at Larkhill in February. According to the sales catalogue, he was given 'three extremely quiet runs' in Ireland (there's honesty for you!). *Miss J. Oakey — Worcs (Theresa McCurrich).* 265 (Oma).

JACKS DREAM ..—.. 7 b.m. Thethingaboutitis (USA) — Double Dose (Al Sirat USA) pp. Dam, half-sister to Bishops Island (*qv* 2000 Annual), failed to finish in 9 of 10 Points for Corrina Hirst (inc fell/unseated 4, and refused/ran out 4 'suffers from a double does of dogginess'). Looked novicey before pulling up in Maidens. *Mrs C. Hirst — Saddleworth.* 1201 (2m4fOMa), 1526 (OMa).

JACKSON HILL ..9-12.. 8 b.g. Priolo (USA) — Orange Hill (High Top) 4. Good-bodied half-brother to Cadbury Castle (*qv*). 55,000y. FLAT (for R. Charlton) r5 w3 (7-10f) p0. Was establishing a splendid record on the flat until he split a pastern on the gallops, and was making his first appearance for three years when 15 lengths fourth in his Members. Used to be ridden by Tim Sprake, who had been establishing himself as a leading flat jockey until a mundane trip to the paper shop wrecked his life and career. *J. Sprake — Blackmore & Sparkford V.* 952 (M).

JACKSON'S HOLE ..10-8.. 8 b.g. Brush Aside (USA) — Jack's The Girl (IRE) (Supreme Leader) 11121. Workmanlike robust. IR 34,000 3-y-o. NH FLAT Spr '98 r2 p0. NH '98/9 (for P. Nicholls) r4 p0. Bought Doncaster, May for 1450. Originally very expensive, but a hard puller and weak finisher when useless for Nichols, and looked a careless jumper. Kept impressing and finding a turn of foot in Points, and would have been unbeaten but for a dozily over-confident ride from David Easterby at Dalton Park, was two lengths clear and going well when not fluent at the last, where he allowed himself to get out jockeyed by Lyn Ward on Inside Out (went down by a length at 2-5; had beaten the pair by six lengths on their previous outing). Not seen since mid-March, but his willing attitude and accelleration would make him look a natural for a Novice Hunter Chase. Ironically, might be worth about 34,000gns now! *Miss S. Fenwick & Mrs S.E. Mason — Middleton (Ian Mason).* 51 (OMa), 278 (R), 375 (Cf), 506 (Cf), 623 (Cf).

JACK SUN ..—.. 11 br.g. Sunyboy — Miss Craigie (New Brig) pp. Small brother to Miss Sunny (dam of Tannock Brook, *qv*), and half-brother to Craigie Way, Collingwood Craig, Shiona Anne and Royal Surprise, and to Chasing winners, Brownhill Lass and Mr Coggy. Dam, half-sister to Craigie Castle and Skud, won 3m Amat Hdle and 3 Hunt Chses and 5 Points, and grandam, Thanet Belle, won Hunt Ch and 4 Opens. P-t-P '96/8 r7 w1 (Maiden) p2 (2nds, beaten neck once); pulled up 2, and fell/unseated 2. The only one of five starters to go clear at Clyst St Mary in '97 (took 7min 45s) but has never stood much racing and broke down at on his reappearance at Tweseldown the following year. Resurfaced to pull up twice in 2000, and looks highly unlikely to stage a revival. *J.E. Snowden — Blackmore & Sparkford V. (John Dufosee).* 456 (C), 952 (M).

JACK THE TD (IRE) ..10-3.. 12 b.g. Rochebrun (FR) — Lily Of Dunmoon (Prince Regent FR) 4pup4. Tall rangy half-brother to Ruben James (IRE). IRISH P-t-P '94 r1 p0. NH '94/7 r9 p1 (distant 3rd); inc Sell Hdle; distant 4th and unseated in Chses - not jump well in either. P-t-P/HUNT CH '97/9 r20 w4 (inc 2m6f Hunt Ch) p5 (4 2nds, inc 2 Hunt Chses); pulled up 2, and fell/unseated 2. NH Apr '00 r2 p0 (blinkered when pulled up in 2m1f110y Nov Ch: *chsd ldr til aft 6, wknd, t.o & pu 4 out*; and 4th in 2m Nov HCap Hdle: *ld 2-3, ld 5 til aft nxt, wknd 3 out*). In the form of his life in '98 winning four races including a poor Towcester Hunter Chase under owner John Cornwall, but beaten 13 times consecutively since and faded quickly out of contention this year, including two short cuts under Rules. Prone to make errors, and sometimes runs in snatches. Acquired blinkers in 2000 and something seems to be wrong. *J.R. Cornwall — Belvoir.* 26 (O), 94 (O), 545 (O).

JACOB'S WIFE ..10-4.. 11 gr.m. Baron Blakeney — Vido (Vimadee) 21f4. Tall light-framed half-sister to Royal Owendo, Woodmanton and Crested Flame. Dam won 6 Chses (2-3m) and placed 10. NH '94/8 r22 w4 (2m Hdle, and 3 Chses, 2m-2m5f) p4 (inc 2 heads 3rd). P-t-P '99 r5 w2 (Confineds) p3 (3rd of 4 twice). A fair performer granted a sound surface and has done well despite rather limited opportunities in Points. Faced a straightforward task when successful at Tabley and may well have followed up but for falling when going well in the lead three out at Wolverhampton next time. Can be unreliable however, and found nothing off the bridle in her first and last starts, and needs treating with a certain amount of caution. Sure to remain unpredictable. *R.J. French — N. Salop (Sheila Crow).* 178 (Cm), 961 (O), 1524 (O), 1645 (3mH).

JALCANTO ..10-8.. 11 ch.g. Jalmood (USA) — Bella Canto (Crooner) 3412. Tall rangy half-brother to 5 flat winners (one in Belgium), including Tingle Bell (also a successful Hurdler). Dam won 4 flat, 8-10f. FLAT '92/6 r26 w2 (8-16f, inc Sell) p6. NH '94/8 r15 w4 (2m1f-2m6f Hdles, inc hat-trick '95) p5 (inc 2nd in Ch); pulled up 2, and unseated 1 in other Chses. P-t-P '99 (for Mr J. Rudge) r3 w2 (Open and Mixed Open) p1 (2nd). Landed a well engineered touch at Cothelstone last year and looked the most likely winner of a Catterick Hunter Chase jumping the last on his reappearance, but was overhauled by two rivals in the final 50 yards. Went clear after the fall of Jacob's Wife to win at Dunstall Park after a mid-season break, but no match for Barna Boy at Chaddesley subsequently. Goes best fresh and avoids cut in the ground so his campaigns are usually brief. Should win again when conditions are right. *T.M. Hayes — N. Ledbury (Jon Rudge).* 465 (3m1f110yH), 614 (O), 1524 (O), 1631 (MO).

JAMBO BWANA ..—.. 8 ch.g. Henbit (USA) — Four Friends (Quayside) pp. Sturdy. Dam won NH flat (won another, but demoted to 2nd), a 2m Hdle, and 4 Chses (2m3f-3m) in Ireland. NH FLAT Nov '97 r2 p0. NH '98/9 (for N. Henderson; previously for late G. Richards) r4 p0. Bought Doncaster, May for 1000. Yet to give any indication of merit. Unlike most Millington horses, he was out of action after two runs to mid-February. *P.J. Millington — Fernie.* 51 (OMa), 167 (OMa).

JAMES ISAAC (IRE) ..—.. 7 b.g. Andretti — Tourney's Girl (Yankee Gold) 1. Lengthy half-brother to Nasayer (IRE) (*qv*). IRISH NH FLAT '98 r3 p0. NH June/Aug '99 (for G.M. Moore; blinkered first 2) r4 p2 (3rds); Sell final. Beaten a maximum of seven lengths at up to 2m1f in Hurdling thirds in the previous year, but did not look very enthusiastic. Unearthed an extremely moderate youngsters Maiden on firmish at Bitterley on his Pointing debut, and jumped left and made all to come home 20 lengths clear, but nothing behind him has scored since. It will be interesting to see what he produces if something takes him on. *R. Mathias — Brecon & Talybont (Christine Hardinge).* 990 (OMa).

JAMES PIGG ..9-10§.. 14 b.g. Lord Ha Ha — Bank Strike (Even Money) p2p734p. Lengthy quite attractive half-brother to Pay Freeze, to Irish Pointing winners, Serbelle and Treelagh, and to successful Irish Hurdler, Rahealty. IRISH NH FLAT '92 r2 p0. IRISH NH '92/4 r25 w3 (2m4f Hdle, and 2 Chses, 2m-2m5f) p5. NH '95/8 r28 w7 (2m3f-3m2f Chses, inc hat-trick '95) p5 (short-headed once). P-t-P '99 (for Mr M.J. Colenutt) r4 w1 (Ladies — on a disqualification) p1 (2nd); 4th, and pulled up 1. Adept at picking up prize-money in small fields under Rules, but basically not that genuine and his only Pointing success in 11 outings was gained courtesy of Portman Square. Came closest to another when flattering in his two-finisher Members, but otherwise well beaten in 2000.

Suited by top-of-the-ground and usually not prepared to try very hard when conditions are testing. *M.J. & Mrs C. Gray — Taunton V. (Carroll Gray)*. 638 (Cf), 1236 (M), 1304 (Cfnr), 1371 (Cf), 1552 (O), 1637 (O), 1652 (L).

JAMES THE FIRST ..9-11§.. 13 ch.g. Wolver Heights — Juliette Mariner (Welsh Pageant) f6*0816*. Strong-topped lengthy fired half-brother to Catch The Cross. NH FLAT '92 r4 w1 (on all-weather) p1 (2nd). NH '92/7 and '99 r49 w12 (4 Hdles, 2m-2m1f, and 9 Chses, 2m-2m4f; inc hat-trick) p13. P-t-P/HUNT CH '98/9 r5 w1 (Open) p2 (Hunt Chses, 2nd once); pulled up 1, and unseated 1. NH '00 r4 w1 (2m110y Sell Hdle: *hdwy & prom 4, ld 6, mist last, all out*) p0 (12th in 2m5f Sell HCap Hdle: *chsd ldrs, drvn along, wknd 3 out*; 8th in 2m5f110y Sell HCap Hdle: *chsd ldrs til lost plce 7*; and 6th in 2m1f110y Sell Hdle: *sis, bhnd, hdwy app 3 out, sn rdn & btn*). Formerly useful when allowed to dominate (worth 10-9), and goes well when fresh, but very moody and restricted to just three outings in the last two years. His jumping has become a major cause for concern and clearly has his physical problems too. Has been tried in blinkers. *E.W. Tuer — Hurworth*. 384 (2m3f110yH), 622 (O).

JAMIES FIRST (IRE) ..9-9.. 8 ch.g. Commanche Run — Avionne (Derrylin) ufp8uf1f31. Neat plain half-brother to Cead Mile Failte. Dam won at 8f, and subsequently won 5 Sell Hdles at around 2m for Martin Pipe. NH '96/7 (for R. Ingram) r3 p0 (tailed off). An exceptionally tricky customer who has an appalling record with three jockeys (particularly Lisa Parrott, who has been unseated or fallen by half way in three of four attempts, and who should not be allowed on him again), but transformed by David Dunsdon, who has extracted two victories and a third. Lucky in a Maiden at Penshurst when the eight length leader departed at the last, but should have scored at Peper Harow, where he took the bend before two out too sharply and lost all momentum and had to settle for five lengths third. At least it enabled him to collect a Restricted, which he did easily when returning to Penshurst (only four ran). Quite speedy, and can probably win again for his favourite. *Mrs F. & Miss L. Ashfield — Surrey U. (Sarah Dawson)*. 6 (R), 14 (R), 60 (OMa), 218 (L), 307 (L), 707 (L), 828 (OMa), 1243 (Inr), 1398 (Cf), 1512 (R).

JAPODENE ..10-5.. 13 b.m. Uncle Pokey — Another Denetop (Another River) f6321222. Lengthy light-framed. Dam won 2 Hdles, 2m2f-3m, inc Sell. NH '95 r3 p0 (last, and pulled up 2; Sell final). P-t-P/HUNT CH '97/9 r18 w5 (inc 4 Ladies) p4 (2 2nds); pulled up 2, and fell 1. Very lightly raced prior to '98, but has blossomed since and her convincing Stainton success this year was her sixth in total. Speedy and rarely fails to complete, but tends to get outstayed in competitive races and run out of it on the flat in four of her last five outings. *J. Mackley — S. Durham (Sarah Dent)*. 19 (L), 135 (L), 397 (L), 621 (L), 806 (L), 1328 (L), 1350 (L), 1477 (L).

JASILU ..10-1.. 11 ch.m. Faustus (USA) — Mosso (Ercolano USA) 6p. Strong half-sister to flat winner, Mossy Rose. Dam won 2 6f races. FLAT (at 2) r3 p0 (inc Sells). NH '96/7 r8 w3 (2m5f – 3m Chses) p2 (3rds); pulled up 3. P-t-P/HUNT CH '95/6 and '99 r22 w3 (inc 3m2f Hunt Ch) p7 (3 2nds; and inc 3rd in Hunt Ch); pulled up 6 and unseated 1. Did well to win six races to '97, but has always had a moody streak, and her enthusiasm has not returned since leaving Kim Bailey. Has finished ahead of just four rivals for present connections and gives the impression that she is breaking blood vessels as she often stops very quickly. Used to wear blinkers, and regained them on her final start. *A.G. Lay — V. of Aylesbury (Lynne Redman)*. 511 (O), 687 (2m6f110yH).

JASPER (U) ..—.. 6 ch.g. unknown — unknown. Stone-bonking last in his Members — by more than half a mile. *B. Wollham — Sir W.W. Wynn's*. 525 (M).

JAVAMAN ..8-0.. 9 b.g. Homo Sapien — Brownhill Lass (Sunyboy) uu7u. Compact. Dam, sister to Jack Sun, and half-sister to Royal Surprise (qv), won 4 Chses, 2m-3m (3 at Ayr). NH FLAT Nov/Dec '98 r2 p0. NH '99 (for R. Goldie, who raced the dam) r3 p0. Can show speed, but is too headstrong, and was beaten 65 lengths on the only occasion he completed. Has unseated three times, but not his fault when the saddle slipped at the last once, and also got as far as two out once. Tends to be fractious in the preliminaries. Might just spring a surprise if he decided to behave himself. *W. Wilson — V. of Lune H.* 498 (R), 811 (I), 1153 (OMa), 1368 (OMa).

JAVELIN COOL (IRE) ..9-9.. 10 gr.g. Roselier (FR) — Wonderful Lilly (Prince Hansel) 425. Strong compact brother to Hurdles winner, Valigan (IRE), and half-brother to Poets Corner (IRE), and to Hurdles winner, Wonderfull Polly (IRE). Dam won 2 NH flat, a 12f race, and 3 Hdles (2m-2m4f) in Ireland. NH '96/8 r13 p1 (3rd of 4); ran badly in 7 Chses, pulled up 3, and unseated 1. P-t-P/HUNT CH '99 (for Mrs L.M. Kemble) r7 w1 (Maiden) p1 (3rd of 4); last pair 2, and pulled up 3. Blinkered when successful in a two-finisher Maiden at High Easter last year, but disappeared after three quick runs in the first half of this season and may have gone wrong. Not disgraced behind Ardeal on his reappearance, but has not looked much of a battler and usually fades tamely. *Miss S.M. Jenkins — Thurlow, & Cambs (Neil King)*. 86 (R), 91 (M), 239 (R).

JAYAREJAY ..—.. 9 b.g. Newski (USA) — Pailin (Blue Refrain) f. Looked a very wild ride before crashing at the fifth at Howick. *R. Hares — Berkeley (R. Tuck)*. 822 (CfMa).

JAZETASON ..8-0.. 9 ch.g. Jazetas — Tachyline (Tachypous) ppppu5R6. Tall lengthy half-brother to Joli Hardy. Dam is half-sister to Grand Hussar (qv '87 season Annual). P-t-P '98/9 r10 p0 (unseated

3, ran out 1, and pulled up 6). Utterly awful with more vices than you can shake a stick it and putting a novice girl on him beggared belief. Finally managed a completion at the 16th attempt, but finished tailed off last as he did again on his final appearance. Looks bonkers and performed no better in blinkers twice, but a strong pilot could probably sort him out (not that one would consent to sit on him now). *Mrs E.A. Shaddick — W. Somerset V. (Sally Barnett).* 352 (CfMa), 640 (CfMa), 881 (OMa), 957 (CfMa), 1094 (M), 1101 (OMa), 1469 (OMa), 1564 (OMa).

JAZZ TRACK (IRE) ..—§.. 7 b.g. Sadler's Wells (USA) — Minnie Hauk (USA) (Sir Ivor) pp. Compact good-bodied brother to useful English/French flat winner, Chief Contender, and to flat winner, Tafrah, and half-brother to 5 winners (4 in Ireland or abroad; and one a successful Hurdler). Dam won 2 Irish flat, 7-8f. FLAT (won for P. Chapple-Hyam) r8 w1 (16f) p3. NH '97/9 (for M. Pipe, bought for 28,000) r11 w1 (3m2f Hdle) p2 (2nds, short-headed once). Bought Ascot, July for 1500. Won his penultimate race for Pipe, but did not look enthusiastic despite having a simple task. Soon hated Pointing, and climbed the fences and tailed off and pulled up by half way when last seen in January. Wears a tongue-strap and blinkers (also tried in a visor previously), and ran tubed once on the flat. There seems to be no way of alleviating his suffering, and must be ignored. *O.R. Dukes — York & Ainsty S.* 17 (O), 42 (O).

JEEPERS (IRE) ..9-6.. 10 gr.g. Nearly A Nose (USA) — Broker Aems (The Go-Between) 25236155. Good-bodied half-brother to What Will Tom Say (IRE). Dam won a flat race in Austria. IRISH P-t-P '96/7 r2 w1 (6yo Maiden) p1 (3rd). NH '97/8 r7 p0 (pulled up in 2 of 4 Hdles; and pulled up 1, and fell/unseated 2 in Chses). P-t-P '99 r6 w1 (Restricted) p1 (3rd); 6th, and pulled up 3. Won his Restricted at Wadebridge, but has not come close to landing an Intermediate yet (11 lengths fifth at Lifton being his best effort), and usually fails to stay. Made all to beat a bad lot in his Members and provide Derek McKenna with his inaugural success in the process, but will be hard pressed to add to his haul. *Mrs H.D. Power — S. Cornwall.* 104 (I), 258 (Cf), 541 (I), 730 (I), 930 (I), 1384 (M), 1516 (I), 1637 (I).

JELALI (IRE) ..9-10.. 8 b.g. Last Tycoon — Lautreamont (Auction Ring USA) 4. Lengthy half-brother to a winner in Japan. Dam won 2 French flat, 9-11f. IR 8500f, 18,000y. FLAT r10 p1 (11/3rd). NH '96/9 (for D. Murray-Smith — often tongue-tied; blinkered final) r10 w1 (2m3f Hdle) p1 (3rd); remote 5th, pulled up, and fell in Chses; Sell Hdle final. Won his Hurdling debut in December '96, but pulled up on his next two appearances, and then went missing for 23 months. Never any good since returning, and presumably impeded by a wind defect. Did as well as could have been hoped when 20 lengths fourth to Lord Harry in an Open, but failed to reappear. *Miss T.S. McPartland — N. Salop (Gordie Edwards).* 565 (OMa).

JENTAR EQUILIBRA (IRE) ..9-8.. 9 b.m. Miner's Lamp — Cora Gold (Goldhill) p21. Good-topped half-sister to Hurdles winner, West Monkton, and to Irish Pointing winners, By Golly and Spancilhill Melody. Dam is half-sister to Andros Gale (*qv* '99). NH FLAT Mar '98 r1 p0. NH '98 (for R.J. Price) r1 p0 (Sell). Bought Malvern, May '98 for 2000. Gave encouragement on her Pointing debut, and then followed a ten length second on firmish at Bratton Down with a comfortable success there in heavy. Forged clear after a blunder at the last, and looks a thorough stayer. Should at least be up to Restricted success. *P.J. Quinn & A. Fear — Quantock (Laura Horsey).* 957 (CfMa), 1565 (OMa), 1654 (OMa).

JESTASTAR ..9-11.. 10 b.g. Jester — Mickley Spacetrail (Space King) p13. Close-coupled brother to Noble Star. Dam, half-sister to Mickley Treasure (*qv* '95 Annual), pulled up in 2 Points. P-t-P/HUNT CH '96/9 r10 p2 (last of 3 once); pulled up 5, and fell/unseated 2. Incredibly lightly raced and failed to complete in his first seven races spread over four seasons, but much improved in the second half of last season and finally got off the mark at Larkhill after the likely winner had unseated at the last. Not disgraced in a Hackwood Restricted subsequently, but whether he will get enough opportunities to win one is debatable. *Mrs J.M. Bush & Mrs S. Garside — Beaufort (Joanna Bush).* 204 (OMa), 630 (OMa), 887 (R).

JESUSA ..6-0§§.. 7 b.m. Kalaglow — Chadensike (Taufan USA) ruppup4u64ppp. Small plain half-sister to flat winner, Mr Frosty. Dam won 3 7f races. P-t-P '99 r1 p0 (refused). A total shambles. Cleared a total of three fences in her first three Points and has gone from bad to appalling since. Cannot gallop or jump properly, but continually forced on by jockeys who are old enough to know better. Beaten a total of seven fences in three completions and was so far adrift in the latest that the runners for the next were about to be mounted when she tottered in. Has no intentions of becoming a racehorse and connections should take the hint. Ran in a tongue-strap on one occasion. At least she makes Sea Search look good. *K.W. Johnson & Partners — Llandeilo F. (C.R. Johnson; Gerry Maloney).* 268 (CfMa), 350 (CfMa), 487 (CfMa), 649 (CfMa), 745 (R), 834 (OMa), 943 (M), 1055 (CfMa), 1222 (2m4fOMa), 1300 (OMa), 1454 (OMa), 1618 (OMa), 1660 (OMa).

JEVINGTON (IRE) ..—.. 9 b.g. Mandalus — Hyde's Pride (Proverb) u. Workmanlike brother to B Fifty Two (IRE), and to Irish Pointing and Chasing winner, Mandy Browne. IR 17,000 4-y-o. NH FLAT Dec '97 r1 p0. NH '98/9 (for I. Williams, blinkered final) r4 p0 (pulled up in 4 Hdles). IRISH NH FLAT '99 r4 p1 (2nd). IRISH NH '99 r2 p1; unseated at 3rd only Ch. Bought Doncaster, Aug for 1300. A poor performer on the evidence to date. Was still in contention when he unseated at the 14th in a mid-February Maiden, but his jumping had been far from faultless. *Mrs D. Cornelius — Ystrad Taf Fechan (Shan Farr).* 270 (CfMa).

JIGTIME ..11-3.. 12 b.m. Scottish Reel — Travel Again (Derrylin) f3. Lengthy. P-t-P/HUNT CH '95/8 r12 w9 (inc 7·Hunt Chses, 3m1f-3m4f) p1 (distant 3rd of 4 in Hunt Ch); fell 1. NH '97/8 r2 w1 (3m1f Kelso Ch) p0; and fell 1. A magnificent mare who went from Maiden winner to a classy Hunter Chaser in the blink of an eye. Loved Kelso and gained five of her wins there, but clearly amiss when favourite for the '98 Horse & Hound Cup as she was to spend the next 18 months on the sidelines. Fell on her comeback at Alnwick, but looked to have retained most if not all of her ability when finishing a creditable 13 lengths third to It's Himself and Cavalero at Haydock. Tragedy lurked around the corner however, and she collapsed and died soon after the finish. Never really got the opportunity to prove her greatness (fell four out when still going well in the '98 Cheltenham Foxhunters), but not just the Scots will mourn her passing. J.W. Hughes & W. Darling — Buccleuch (Bill Hughes). 42 (O), 156 (3mH).

JILLY WIG (IRE) ..10-6.. 9 b.m. Strong Gale — Music Interpreter (Kampala) 2p. Sister to Litening Conductor, and half-sister to NH flat winner, Mr Collins. Dam won 3 flat (14-16f) and 2m1f Hdle in Ireland. P-t-P '97/9 r5 w2 (Maiden and Restricted) p3 (2 2nds). Talented but fragile, and has been restricted to just seven appearances in four seasons. Confirmed herself a smart prospect when disposing of Gunner Welburn in '99, and made a pleasing comeback when a ring-rusty second at Barbury Castle. Surprisingly risked on firm ground at Woodford and never looked happy before Julian Pritchard pulled her up after three out. The subsequent Stewards Enquiry was told that the mare kept changing her legs and that she was eased out to avoid possible injury. Hopefully will have come to no lasting harm and will be able to race again. Capable of superb jumping. *Count & Countess Goess-Saurau — V.W.H. (Countess Susie Goess-Saurau).* 1283 (I), 1490 (I).

PLATE 65   1490 Berkeley Intermediate: Jilly Wig (Julian Pritchard), pu, takes a chunk of the fence
PHOTO: Brian Armstrong

JIMMY THE ONE (NZ) ..9-5.. 7 b.g. First Norman (USA) — Marossa (NZ) (Marceau AUS) p21f. Robust compact. NH FLAT '99 (for A. Hobbs) r2 p0. Followed a 15 length second with a win in a three-finisher youngsters Maiden at Buckfastleigh, but it was the slowest race of the day by far. Last and struggling when he fell in a Restricted two months later, and currently has plenty to prove in that grade. *Mrs Y. Watson & H.S. Channon — Lamerton (Yvonne Watson & Jo Channon).* 162 (I), 254 (CfMa), 655 (OMa), 1563 (R).

JIMS FLOSSY ..—.. 7 ch.m. Gildoran — Flo-Jo (DEN) (Pelton Lad) p. Dam is half-sister to Good Seoul (*qv* '96 Annual). Well behind when pulling up after a blunder at the fourth at Garnons. *J.A. Danahar — Worcs.* 672 (2m4fOMa).

JOAO PASSOS (IRE) ..—.. 7 b.g. Phardante (FR) — Double Token (Furry Glen) f. Dam won 2m5f Hdle in Ireland. Sold Tattersalls Ireland Aug '98 for 5217. A long way behind when he fell at the sixth at Barbury Castle in January, and not sighted since. *Mrs S. Humphreys — Cattistock (Richard Barber).* 38 (CR).

JO BLOGGS (IRE) ..8-9.. 8 b.g. Jurado (USA) — Miss Teresa (Dusky Boy) 6pp. Half-brother to Mini Orchestra (IRE). IRISH P-t-P '99 r11 p1 (fence late of 3); pulled up 4, unseated, brought down and ran out. Useless in Ireland, and faded badly after leading early in his first two English outings. Acquired a tongue-strap in the latest, and seemed to hate it, because he was immediately struggling, and was jumping violently left and nearly going through the wings from the third until eventually pulled up at the fifteenth. Obviously has problems. *P. Tipples — E. Sussex & Romney Marsh (Di Grissell).* 131 (OMa), 829 (OMa), 984 (OMa).

JOBSAGOODUN ..9-9.. 10 b.g. Rakaposhi King — Donna Farina (Little Buskins) 2134. Tall brother to Don Royal, and to jumping winner Mountain Path. Dam, half-sister to Farina Stream (*qv* '94 Annual), won Hdle and 5 Chses (4 consecutively), all at 2m. NH FLAT Mar '96 r1 p0. NH '96/9 (for N. Henderson) r8 p1 (2nd in Ch); pulled up in other 2 Chses, inc when lame final-favourite). Bought Malvern, July for 1700. His second in a Chase was a decent effort, and started his Pointing career with a good effort behind Glevum, so was certainly not scoring out of turn when he captured a weak Maiden at Black Forest Lodge. Not disgraced behind useful winners in Restricteds subsequently, but has been absent since early March, which raises suspicions about his fragile legs (was only able to appear once apiece in '98 and '99). *W.O. Yardley (Four Crickets Partnership) — Worcs (Netty Higgins).* 20 (OMa), 72 (OMa), 196 (R), 458 (R).

JOCK ..—.. 9 b.g. Scottish Reel — Northern Lady (The Brianstan) 5pup. Sturdy half-brother to Lady's Pet and to flat winner, De Rigeur. Dam won 3 2-y-o races, 5-6f. NH '97 (for Miss S. Williamson) r1 p0 (tailed off and pulled up). Unpromising. Nearly fell at the final fence when hopelessly tailed off last on his only completion, and went no more than a mile in two of three subsequent attempts (threw the rider at the start and continued two fences behind once; and unseated in the paddock once). *T. Walker — Holcombe.* 234 (OMa), 526 (OMa), 665 (OMa), 777 (OMa).

JOE SMOKE ..9-1.. 8 gr.g. Palm Track — Ask Jean (Ascertain USA) fpp250p. Plain rangy. Dam, half-sister to 5 Pointers including the dam of Dear Jean (*qv* '99 Annual), won 5 Points and placed 7 (including 2nd in a Hunt Ch) for Mary Sowersby's late father, and grandam, Fort Jean, ran in 3 Points for him. P-t-P '98/9 (for Mr M.E. Sowersby) r4 p0 (ran out 1, fell 1, and pulled up 2). NH '00 r2 p0 (11th in 2m4f110y Nov Hdle: *chsd ldrs til lost plce 6, sn bhnd*; and pulled up in 3m2f Nov Ch: *bhnd til pu 5*). A length second in a very slow Whitwell Maiden (the rider wanted to object to the winner, but did not include the necessary deposit), but consistently hopeless otherwise and has not been an easy ride. Usually fails to stay and looks an unlikely future winner. *P.W. Clifton — Holderness (Mary Sowersby).* 169 (OMa), 233 (OMa), 400 (OMa), 1003 (OMa), 1032 (OMa).

JOESOWNBELLE ..—.. 9 b.m. Bell Ringer — Maggy Marsh VII (unknown) p. Tailed off in a May Maiden (reared and unseated in the paddock). *Mrs J. Bodley — Tredegar F. (K. Bodley).* 1454 (OMa).

JOHNNY COOL ..8-6.. 11 gr.g. Dawn Johnny (USA) — Artic Rain (Gaberdine) 6fp5. Strong rangy. Dam won 2 Points at Lincoln and placed 2. P-t-P/HUNT CH '98/9 r6 p1 (3rd); pulled up 4. Pulls hard and can tank along for up to 2m4f, but does a yard further and is nowhere near good enough for short Hunter Chases. Decked by the rider when out on his feet on one occasion (a day when the normally sensible Mark Hewitt left his brain in the changing room). Gained his placing in a very slow race, but connections have now resorted to blinkers and the last chance saloon beckons. *R.E. Gray — Cranwell Bloodhounds (Joanna Hughes).* 23 (OMa), 124 (OMa), 384 (2m3f110yH), 759 (OMa).

JOHNNY MU (IRE) ..—.. 9 ch.g. Executive Perk — Australite (Realm) p. Tall plain rangy half-brother to No Inhibitions. IRISH P-t-P '98 r2 p0 (tailed off both, pulled up 1). P-t-P '99 r1 p0 (pulled up). Pulled up on a day when Kevin Needham continually took the scenic route round Newton Bromswold. Led for 2m4f, but stopped quickly and looks devoid of stamina and stands his racing badly. *J.L. Marks — Fitzwilliam.* 515 (OMa).

JOHN ROBIN ..8-13.. 9 b.g. Green Adventure (USA) — Pamaris (Pamroy) p2p24. Angular sparely-made half-brother to Hod Wood. NH '98 r1 p0 (tailed off in 2m Sell Hdle). P-t-P '97/9 (for Mr N. Shutts) r14 p5 (4 2nds, of 3 twice); pulled up 3, and fell 3. Continually flatters, but does not truly stay three miles and is a consistently weak finisher. Highly strung, and usually sweats excessively and has to be taken to post early or else he goes ballistic in the paddock. Worth opposing even if the task looks simple in future. *S.H. Sweetland — E. Devon (Martin Sweetland).* 145 (OMa), 253 (CfMa), 401 (M), 1178 (OMa), 1641 (OMa).

JOHN'S RIGHT (IRE) ..9-8.. 10 b.g. Buckskin (FR) — Tree-By-Tu (Laurence O) p. Sturdy compact brother to Irish Pointing winner, Silent Sneeze. IRISH NH '96/7 r4 p0 (pulled up only Ch). IRISH P-t-P '95/7 r18 w1 (5yo Maiden) p6; pulled up 4, and unseated 1. P-t-P '99 (for Mrs E.A. Birt-Llewellin) r5 w1 (Restricted) p2 (3rd of 4 once); and pulled up 2. Won a modest event in a slow time at Lydstep last year (the runner-up managed to get left 20 lengths), but well held otherwise and failed to return unscathed from a return trip in 2000. Appears unlikely to achieve a third success. *H. Havard — Tivyside (Paul Davies).* 1227 (I).

JOHNSTONS BUCK (IRE) ..—§.. 12 b.g. Buckskin (FR) — Another Crash (Crash Course) f. Rangy. Dam is half-sister to Glen Fintaig (*qv* '94 Annual). IRISH NH '93/4 r5 p1 (2nd). IRISH NH FLAT '94 r1 p0. NH '95/7 (for B. Curley) r4 w1 (2m7f Hdle, 5 ran) p0; inc Sell. Bought Doncaster, May '97 for 4800. Won a five-runner Hurdle in soft in March '96, but twice virtually refused to race under Rules. Finally returned to the course after a three year absence, with a predictably bad result (unruly in the paddock, slowly away, and fell at the twelvth). *T.D. Marlow — Cheshire.* 961 (O).

JOHN TUFTY ..9-9.. 10 ch.g. Vin St Benet — Raffles Virginia (Whistling Deer) 4p665f259. Compact. FLAT r5 p0. NH '94/9 (for G. Prodromou; won previously for J. Pearce) r35 w1 (2m1f Sell Hdle) p7 (inc 2 of 13 Chses). Gave four respectable displays in 2000, but is an extremely moderate competitor, and hopelessly easy to beat in Hunter Chases, in which his partner Rachel Illman (works for John Bridger, and often wins best turned out prizes) is very novicey. Frequently wore headgear latterly under Rules. Lucky when winning his first ever Hurdle (the leader fell two out), and has since accumulated a losing sequence of 43, which the owner tried to end by declaring him for a Maiden at Kingston Blount, but he was foiled when a phone call to the guru of Hinton Martell confirmed that he was ineligible! *K.J. Walls — Dunston H.* 15 (C), 83 (Cf), 151 (3mH), 681 (2m4fH), 802 (2m6fH), 1026 (2m5f110yH), 1344 (3m2fH), 1542 (3mH), 1648 (3mH).

JOINT ACCOUNT ..10-13.. 11 ch.g. Sayyaf — Dancing Clara (Billion USA) pf1. Lengthy. NH FLAT r2 p0. NH '98 r1 p0 (4th in 2m6f Nov HCap Ch). P-t-P/HUNT CH '96/9 r25 w7 (inc 3 Hunt Chses, 2m5f-3m1f) p9 (7 2nds; inc 4 Hunt Chses); failed to finish 8 (fell/unseated 6). A consistently useful Hunter Chaser, but remains a clumsy jumper and never seems to learn from his mistakes. Pulls hard under restraint, but not many horses can go with him when Fiona Needham lets out an inch of rein and pulverised second division opposition on his final appearance at Sedgefield. Should win again providing he doesn't try to take too many bundles of birch with him. Acts on top-of-the-ground and less effective on a slower surface. *K. Needham — Bilsdale (Fiona Needham).* 225 (3mH), 384 (2m3f110yH), 923 (3m3fH).

JOJO (IRE) ..9-12§.. 11 ch.g. Buckskin (FR) — Autumn Queen (Menelek) 1321p7p. Workmanlike lengthy half-brother to Chasing winner, Murt's Man (IRE), to Hurdles winners, Snowy Autumn and Mickeen, and to Irish Hurdles winner, Ahead Of The Posse. NH '95/8 r12 w1 (2m4f hdle) p2 (3rds, inc Ch). P-t-P '99 r5 w1 (Members) p1 (last of 3); 4th, and pulled up 2. Able, but a real villain and rising star Ben Hitchcott has excelled on him several times. Frequently makes the running, but liable to down tools without warning and did his best to throw away certain victory on his reappearance at Charing. Kidded home at Bexhill subsequently, but ran particularly sourly after. Likely to revive when fresh, but probably not for very long. Usually avoids firm ground. Wears blinkers. *Mrs J. Grist — E. Sussex & Romney Marsh (Di Grissell).* 130 (CMod), 305 (Cf), 824 (Cf), 983 (Cf), 1108 (C), 1398 (Cf), 1510 (O).

JO JOS BEST FRIEND ..9-13.. 7 b.m. Little Wolf — Snitton (Rymer) 142183. Unfurnished half-sister to Snitton South and Snitton Salvo. Dam, temperamental half-sister to Snitton Stream (*qv* '98 Annual), was placed in 2 Points. P-t-P '99 r5 w1 (Maiden) p3 (2 2nds, last once); and unseated 1. Scored readily on her reappearance at Tweseldown, but went missing for 10 weeks and was subsequently given too much to do at Lydstep once, but made amends on a return visit. Did not take to regulation fences at Cheltenham on her Hunter Chase debut, and probably found the ground too lively when a disappointing odds-on favourite on her final outing. Looks capable of winning in Confined company in 2001 and could raise her rating by a few more pounds. *P.S. Payne & Mrs P. Davies — Gelligaer F. (John Moore).* 2 (R), 600 (I), 837 (I), 1227 (I), 1336 (2m4fH), 1448 (M).

JOLI EAU ..8-0.. 10 b.g. Joligeneration — Chetsford Water (Sir Lark) pp. Tall workmanlike half-brother to Sir Joleigh. Dam is half-sister to Champagne Bar (*qv* '92 Annual). Grandam, Champagne Suzy, won 9 Points and placed 13. P-t-p '99 r5 p0 (last pair 2, pulled up 2, and fell 1). Showed speed for 2m4f at Cherrybrook once last year, but yet to finish in the same parish as the winner, and looked decidedly ungenuine in a brief 2000 campaign. Blinkered on his final start when (100-1 in an Open) the rider was cautioned for galloping on past the fences after pulling up after a mile. *N.E. Lethbridge & Mrs V.S. Long — S. Devon (Simon Partridge).* 70 (OMa), 210 (MO).

JOLIE ROSLIN ..9-4.. 7 gr.m. Joli Wasfi (USA) — Robina (Royben) 2p1. Rangy. Dam, half-sister to Rodden Brook, was placed in 2 Points and the Cattistock Buchanon (remember them?) for Hilary Tutte, who bred her (the only horse she beat in 9 Points was a fatty carting 14 stone). Novicey in her first two races including when outclassed in a match for her Members (jumped slowly and to the left several times), but did better when winning a very slow and muddling youngsters Maiden on firm at Holnicote. Evidently getting the hang of things, and may progress sufficiently for Restricteds. *Mrs H. Tutte — Cattistock.* 873 (M), 1240 (R), 1372 (OMa).

JOLIFAST ..—.. 7 gr.g. Joligeneration — Fast Market (Petong) pu. Tall. Dam won 10f Sell. Looked to be given an easy time when second favourite on his debut, and unseated at the third on his only subsequent attempt. *Mrs S.J. Evans — Devon & Somerset (Mike Trickey).* 563 (CfMa), 956 (OMa).

JOLIFICATION ..9-11.. 10 b.g. Joli Wasfi (USA) — Lillylee Lady (USA) (Shecky Greene USA) u1p1fp. Tall half-brother to Cheren Lady and Royal Sweep. A late arrival from the world of eventing, but made the most of a very simple task when winning a very slowly run two-finisher elders Maiden in soft at Ston Easton. Wore blinkers in all his subsequent races, a more meritorious victory when he put his jumping skills to good use in a Restricted at Cothelstone, where he started at 14-1 after some shrewdies had taken 20s. Fell at the second next time, and jumped very slowly and did not want to know on his latest attempt (possibly disliked the firm ground). Related to a couple of very bad animals, and connections may have achieved a remarkable feat in extracting two victories from him. *J. Cridland, G. Taylor, Miss J. Hardy & D. Thomas — Taunton V. (John Honeyball).* 455 (OMa), 739 (OMa), 876 (R), 1095 (R), 1283 (I), 1370 (I).

JOLI HARDY ..9-3.. 8 gr.m. Joli Wasfi (USA) — Tachyline (Tachypous) p. Workmanlike half-sister to Jazetason (*qv*). P-t-P '99 (for Mr G. Craig) r2 p1 (2nd); and 4th. Trained by Richard Barber in her debut season when she finished a promising second in a 7min 10s Maiden at Bishops Court, but only able to stand one race in 2000 when pulled up at Larkhill in January. In a good yard, and young enough to atone if her problems can be solved. *G. Taylor, J. Hardy, J. Cridland & D. Thomas — Taunton V. (John Honeyball).* 11 (OMa).

JOLIROSE ..—.. 6 b.m. Joligeneration — Rose Red City (Relkino) pp. Close-coupled owner-bred half-sister to Willet Wizard. Dam, half-sister to jumping winner, Legal Right (USA), was on the floor in 3 of 4 Points (pulled up in the other). A rank outsider when schooling for 2m and 2m4f in Restricteds. *D.G. Stephens — W. Somerset.* 560 (R), 847 (R).

JOLITAN ..—.. 6 b.g. Joligeneration — Tanber Lass (New Member) pp. Dam, half-sister to 3 Pointers including Good For Business (*qv* '97 Annual), won 5 points (4 in '91) and placed 7). Grandam, Santan, won Maiden and 3rd 2. Twice pulled up after 2m4f. *E.B.A. Evans — Devon & Somerset (Mike Trickey).* 1102 (OMa), 1308 (OMa).

JOLLY JACK (IRE) ..10-2.. 10 b.g. Jolly Jake (NZ) — Hay Party (Party Mink) u. Smallish compact half-brother to Full Of Chat (IRE) (*qv*). P-t-P/HUNT CH '99 r5 w1 (Intermediate) p1 (2nd of 3); and pulled up 3. Beat modest rivals impressively in a Maisemore Intermediate on softish last year, but has failed to complete in three outings since (rider thought horse lame when pulled up once) and only cleared two fences successfully in 2000. A late starter, and already seems to have hit a snag. May be able to put his disappointments behind him if it again next year. *S.T. Lewis — Cotswold V.F.* 17 (O).

JOLLY MINSTER ..9-12.. 7 b.g. Minster Son — Dash Cascade (Absalom) 2f632. Smallish compact half-brother to a winner in Turkey. NHY FLAT Spr '98 r2 p0. NH '98/9 (from Mrs M Reveley's) r6 p2. Very disappointing. Has made the frame on nine occasions, but still struggling vainly to win a humble Maiden. Does not seem to stay too well, and came closest to success at Witton Castle (which can sometimes favour short-runners) when beaten half a length on his latest attempt. Can surely break his duck eventually. *D.G. Atkinson — Bedale.* 398 (OMa), 627 (OMa), 910 (2m4fOMa), 1001 (2m4fOMa), 1329 (OMa).

JOLSON ..9-7.. 10 ch.g. Black Minstrel — Pearly Lady (Tycoon II) 2. Compact quite attractive. NH FLAT '97 r1 p0. NH '98/9 r5 p0 (inc last, and pulled up 3, inc Ch). P-t-P '99 r4 p2 (3rds, of 4 once); and pulled up 2. Stands little racing, and a weak finisher, but good enough to win a Maiden on his best form. Belied his starting price in his Members this year and was still in front jumping the last, but could not raise his game on the run-in. Probably flattered in a steadily run race, but deserves to score one day. *R. Barwell — Tiverton.* 140 (M).

JORIDI LE FORIGE (IRE) ..9-6§.. 10 b.g. Seclude (USA) — Rose Deer (Whistling Deer) pp14. Tall half-brother to Irish Hurdles and English jumping winner, Dr Bones (IRE), and to flat and Hurdles winner, Stoned Imaculate (IRE). IRISH NH '96/7 r5 p1 (15*l> 3rd of 27*). NH '98 r4 p2 (7-20l 3rds in 3m2f Chses). Shut up shop quickly in his races under Rules, and demoted to Points to become a rare competitor for Ferdie Murphy in that sphere. Ungenuine, and generally trounced, but was an exceptionally luck and undeserving winner of the first running of his Members in which he would have finished third had not catastrophies occurred to the two leaders in the home straight. Sometimes blinkered, including on his final outing. Got Ben Orde-Powlett off the mark, to revive memories of his father Harry's exploits on such as The Froddler last century. *F. Murphy — W. of Yore.* 54 (OMa), 173 (R), 374 (M), 503 (R).

JOSAMERIC ..9-2.. 7 b.g. River God (USA) — Scale Model (Latest Model) p44. Good-topped. Dam, sister to Turn Mill (*qv* '93 Annual), won 2m4f Ch for Joe Roper (competed without success for a further 4 seasons). NH FLAT '99 (from C. Jackson's; previously from D. Duggan's) r3 p0 (last 2, and pulled up; started very slowly once). Badly tailed off in Maidens, and is currently useless. Has had two paddock handlers. *J. Roper — N. Ledbury (Tim Stephenson).* 72 (OMa), 899 (OMa), 989 (OMa).

JOSH'S CHOICE (IRE) ..—.. 6 ch.g. Tremblant — Normandy Lady (Normandy) ppp. Tall rangy half-brother to Irish Pointing winner, Gerrymander. Tailed off and pulled up thrice. Favourite for his debut, but Simon Sporborg made not the slightest attempt to put him in the race, and the Stewards could at least have slapped him about the head with a dead haddock to appease the punters. *H.D. Hill & C.H. Sporborg — Puckeridge (Christopher Sporborg).* 97 (OMa), 412 (OMa), 774 (OMa).

JOSS BAY ..—.. 9 ch.g. Nearly A Hand — Maranzi (Jimmy Reppin) up. Tall narrow. Dam won 2m4f Hdle and 6 Chses, 2m-2m4f (4 at Worcester). 5000 4-u-o. NH '97 and '99 (for T. Tate) r5 p0. Bought Doncaster, May for 500. An excitable sort who stands very few races, and gives the impression there is something wrong with him. A disastrous jumper of fences who only got as far as the fourth in one of his Points, and fell at the first in his only Chase and galloped headlong in to two of his opponents when running loose and killed them both. (And yet another guide in the resulting shemozzle). *G.E. Davidson — Cumberland.* 420 (I), 497 (R).

JO'S WEDDING ..9-6.. 10 ch.g. Newski (USA) — Meant (Menelek) RpRfpf. Sturdy owner-bred. Dam, half-sister to Malya Mal (*qv* '93 Annual), won 4 Points (up to Adjacent) and placed 5. NH FLAT '97/8 (from R. Millman's) r2 p0 (pulled hard; hung left once). A confirmed bolter who performs as if he is on a suicide mission, and gave Sarah Gaisford a terrible time on his first three outings (got no further than half way before disasters occurred). Acquired Leslie Jefford (just the once) and fell at the fifteenth when in a huge lead, but then pulled up by Nick Mitchell when still second after two miles (had made several mistakes), and fell at the last with James Young at Mounsey Hill Gate when he had a farcical race in the bag (none of the contestants went clear). A message to riders is clear — accept an invitation to Jo's Wedding and you may end up at your own funeral. *Mrs J.C. Edwards — Dartmoor (-; David Pipe).* 158 (CfMa), 254 (CfMa), 654 (I), 1263 (OMa), 1521 (CfMa), 1610 (OMa).

JOYFUL HERO ..9-9.. 11 b.m. War Hero — Joy Travel (Ete Indien USA) uup5. Small compact half-sister to Warner For Sport and Boraston. Dam won NH flat, 4 Hdles (2m-2m4f) and 2m4f Ch in Ireland. P-t-P '96/9 r18 w1 (Club Maiden) p5 (last of 2, and 4 3rds); also disqualified from 2nd once — not weigh-in; pulled up 7, and fell 1. Surprisingly improved when winning on firmish at Charing in '98, but has subsequently been beaten a minimum of 15 lengths in six outings. Does not handle cut in the ground, and usually fails to stay. *R.T. Dench — Ashford V.* 127 (Cf), 285 (CfM), 416 (R), 573 (CfL).

JR-KAY (IRE) ..10-2.. 11 ch.g. Tremblant — Promising Very VII (unknown) 342p. Tall good-bodied quite attractive half-brother to Sarvo (IRE), and to Hurdles winner, Kleineleaba (IRE). IRISH P-t-P '95 r4 w1 (4&5yo Maiden) p0; pulled up 2. P-t-P/HUNT CH '96 and '99 r9 w4 (inc 3m2f Hunt Ch, and Open) p1 (3rd of 4); pulled up 1 and fell 2. Unbeaten when standing up in '96, but unfortunately disappeared for three years though produced a similar level of ability on his return including a defeat of Concerto Collonges. A thorough stayer but has become very one-paced and made mistakes on his latest start. Would doubtless have won many staying Chases under Rules had he not spent so much time in the wilderness. *N.W.A. Bannister — Pendle Forest & Craven (Annabelle Armitage).* 171 (O), 279 (O), 495 (O), 686 (3m1fH).

JUDICIAL FIELD (IRE) ..10-1.. 12 b.g. Law Society (USA) — Bold Meadows (Persian Bold) p2. Lengthy brother to Irish flat winner, Rahal, and half-brother to flat winners, Field Of Vision (IRE) (also won over Hurdles), Boristova and Strawberry Beds (last pair in Ireland). Dam won 2 Irish flat, 7-12f. IRISH FLAT r19 w4 (7-12f, inc £7020 prize) p7. IRISH NH '92/4 r17 w2 (2m Hdles) p6; 2 runs Cheltenham. FLAT '96 r3 p0. NH '94/8 r28 w4 (2m3f-2m6f Chses) p14. P-t-P '99 r4 w1 (Open) p0; last pair 2, and ran out 1. A prolific prize-winner over the years, but ran badly in his last seven races under Rules and present connections have done well to rekindle his interest. Won a weak Open at Tranwell last year, but finished lame after chasing home Rainbow Times at Friars Haugh and may well have reached the end of the line. Usually blinkered. *G.R. Moscrop — Border.* 42 (O), 110 (O).

JUDICIAL QUEEN ..9-10.. 12 b.m. First Footman — Injudicious (Quorum) p2pu12. Smallish compact half-sister to Tudor Beacon and Judicious Captain (won Chasing since Pointing), and to Chasing winner, Light Sentence. Dam won at 8f. P-t-P '98/9 r11 p2; last 2, pulled up 5, slipped up 1, and refused 1. A latecomer to Pointing, and has usually failed to get the trip, but found a weak opportunity on firm at Ashorne and grasped it under a good ride from Alex Charles-Jones. Seemed under a cloud when performing dismally in '99, but her success was a deserved one, though a follow up will prove difficult. *A.J. & Mrs J.M. Owen — Bicester with Whaddon (Rachel Matheson).* 617 (CMa), 845 (OMa), 1020 (OMa), 1207 (OMa), 1435 (OMa), 1594 (R).

JUDITH JONES ..—.. 7 b.m Nader — Shotaway (Cruise Missile) pp. Very small neat. Dam, half-sister to Out Of Line (*qv* '98 Annual), 'off her trolley', was an abomination in Points for Keith Kerley. Grandam, Hold The Line, won an Irish Point and placed 2, inc when 3rd in W. Kent Members. Pulled up twice at Black Forest Lodge (made mistakes on her debut, and went lame next time). *K.G. Kerley — Portman.* 72 (OMa), 207 (OMa).

JUG OF WINE ..5-6.. 9 b.m. Nicholas Bill — Fill The Jug (Derrylin) fup4pp3f. Small unfurnished. Dam won 6f Sell and placed 13, inc 7 Hdles. A woefully inept creature, and was about two fences last when she crept to completion twice. Tailed off when asked to jump the last at Umberleigh and fell pole-axed on the other side. Should not have been racing. *D.C. Tucker — S. & W. Wilts (M.T. Aylesbury).* 407 (OMa), 763 (CfMa), 876 (R), 1099 (OMa), 1131 (OMa), 1370 (I), 1555 (OMa), 1675 (OMa).

JUINEVERA (IRE) ..—.. 6 b.m Tenby — Atlantic Dream (USA) (Muscovite USA) ff. Half-brother to flat winner, Storiths. Dam won at 6f in Ireland. IRISH FLAT r9 p1 (3rd). FLAT (tried blinkers) r3 p0. NH

'99 r1 p0 (tailed off and pulled up — mistakes). An untalented jumper to date, who has fallen in both Maidens, but was close-up when departing four out in the latest (Tom Oates rose to his feet, but was promptly knocked down by another horse and injured). *J.S. Haldane — College V. & N. Northumberland.* 500 (2m4fOMa), 664 (2m5fOMa).

JUKE BOX BILLY (IRE) ..9-12.. 13 ch.g. Kemal (FR) — Friendly Circle (Crash Course) 433546. Stocky. Dam, half-sister to Meentiagh Glen (*qv* '93 Annual), won Irish NH flat. NH '93/9 (2 wins from Mrs J. Brown's, bought for 10,000; one win previously for P. Monteith; one win previously for H. Johnson) r40 w4 (2m4f Hdle, and 3 Chses, 2m5f-3m, 3 and 5 ran final two) p10; ran out once in '94. Won four races on good or firmish to March '98, and arguably unlucky on three other occasions (either fell, or blundered his chance away), but apart from a 12 lengths third to Whatafellow in an Open he was totally lacking in verve in 2000. Can still be clumsy, and was hopelessly tailed off in three Hunter Chases, in which he was tongue-tied (had a tie-back operation in '94). *J.H. Hewitt — Sinnington (Vicky Parvin).* 231 (O), 395 (O), 691 (O), 917 (3mH), 1446 (3m1fH), 1628 (2m4f110yH).

JUKINO ..9-8.. 11 ch.m. Relkino — Royal Snip (Royal Highway) 25. Many by Relkino combine ability with bad legs, and she appears to be no exception. Performed creditably twice at Cothelstone, but seemed to be lamed by the firm ground when about 10 lengths fourth in an Intermediate. *A.J. Oldham — W. Somerset.* 351 (M), 639 (I).

JULIES JOY (IRE) ..8-13.. 10 ch.m. Le Moss — Iron Star (General Ironside) 331p5. Small light-framed sister to Irish Pointing winner, She Devil, and to Chasing winner, Steel Moss (IRE), and half-sister to The Hucklebuck. IRISH P-t-P '97/8 r6 p1 (2nd); pulled up 4, and fell 1. P-t-P '99 (for Mr P. Riddick) r4 p2 (3rds, remote of 4 once); pulled up 1, and fell 1. Has always shown the speed required to win, but a remarkably crooked jumper and her tendency to go right-handed at the fences is more pronounced than ever. Placed four times before she finally got off the mark at Howick where she forfeited ground at every fence but battled her way back into contention and was upsides Marnies Song when she took her rival out at the last fence with another right-handed swipe. Already labouring in better company and will struggle to find another opportunity. *C.J. Penycate — Tredegar F. (Ian Johnson).* 489 (CfMa), 602 (CfMa), 823 (CfMa), 1054 (R), 1400 (R).

JUPITER LORD ..—.. 10 b.g. Jupiter Island — Angelic Appeal (Star Appeal) pp. Half-brother to Not Quite White, and flat to winner, Just Mine. P-t-P '99 r2 p0 (refused 1, and pulled up 1). Has twice attempted to stop at the first fence(succeeded once), but showed some improvement in an elder horses Maiden at Balcormo Mains when he held every chance until making a mistake two out. Failed to reappear so we are none the wiser as to whether the penny has dropped or not, though races don't come much worse. *S.J. Leadbetter — College V. & N. Northumberland.* 913 (CfMa), 1123 (OMa).

JUST A DIAMOND ..9-2.. 8 ch.m. Primitive Rising (USA) — Just Diamonds (Laurence O) 1. Half-sister to Kellys Diamond and Just Johnie. Dam, half-sister to Force Of Destiny (*qv* '87 Season Annual), was placed in 2 Points for Di Walton. Slogged through the holding ground to make a winning debut in a youngsters Maiden at Corbridge, but the opposition evaporated in the closing stages, and she was eventually left to come home alone. Has the right type of pedigree for Pointing, and will hopefully be kept busier in future. *Mrs D. Walton — W. Percy.* 1166 (OMa).

JUST ARNOLD ..—.. 12 ch.g. Rustingo — Dinedor Lady (Cavo Doro) fp. Small sturdy brother to Dinedor Charlie and Rusty Ringo. Looked backward and did not impress when finally reaching the racecourse as an 11-year-old. *Mrs S.M. Mason — S. Herefords (Christine Hardinge).* 490 (CfMa), 744 (R).

JUST A SINGLE (IRE) ..8-8.. 10 b.g. Adbass (USA) — Sniggy (Belfort FR) ppppppfp. Small close-coupled half-brother to Single Man (IRE). FLAT (blinkered 2) r8 p0. NH '95/6 r2 p0 (last and pulled up — tailed off in Sells). P-t-P '97/8 (for Mr M.J. & Mrs C. Brown) r4 p1 (2nd); pulled up 1, and ran out 1. Has speed, but tainted by lunacy and twelve months on the sidelines have not improved matters. A market springer at Dalton Park (so not all the asylum places are filled yet), but capitulated after flattering with a mile to run and remains a hard and unrewarding ride. Wears a tongue-strap and has been tried in blinkers. *A. Morris — Sinnington.* 137 (R), 399 (OMa), 507 (CMa), 625 (OMa), 809 (OMa), 1330 (OMa), 1352 (OMa), 1479 (OMa).

JUST BERT (IRE) ..10-4.. 11 b.g. Kambalda — Cappagh Flier (Lock Diamond) 11f31347. Small brother to Diamond Flier (IRE). P-t-P/HUNT CH '95/9 r24 w7 (inc 3m Hunt Ch, and Ladies match) p7 (5 2nds); fell/unseated 6. A tough stayer who has gained a prize in 19 of 25 completions and enjoyed his most productive season to date in 2000. Returned to Ladies races after a two year gap and immediately hit form with victory over Dawn's Cognac and Hearts Are Wild at Wadebridge in a sparkling time. Notched up two more wins against much inferior opposition, but less effective in Hunter Chases where diminutive stature counts against him. Prone to make the odd blunder, but usually jumps well and can handle all types of ground, but goes best with some cut. One of only six horses for whom two Hunters Certificates were registered. Unless it was just another of Weatherbys mistakes it was a complete waste of money as the horse never ran outside Open company. *Mrs S. Alford — N. Cornwall, & Eggesford (Mike Biddick).* 101 (L), 390 (L), 680 (3m1fH), 851 (L), 1386 (L), 1561 (MO), 1593 (3m2fH), 1648 (3mH).

PLATE 66   *1386 South Cornwall Ladies Open: Just Bert (Miss T. Cave), 1st*

PHOTO: Baths Photograhic

JUST BRUCE ..10-0.. 12 ch.g. Hotfoot — Selborne Lass (Deep Run) p3p67. Small neat attractive owner-bred brother to Wonky and The Whole Lot, and half-brother to Sutton Lass and Colonel Arthur. Dam won 2m Sell Hdle. NH '94/9 r39 w3 (2m-2m4f Chses) p9. P-t-P '94 r2 p0; unseated 1, and pulled up 1. Rarely attempted three miles under Rules, where all three of his wins came on right-handed courses, so it has been no surprise that stamina has been his undoing since reverting back to Points. Still a keen-going sort, and gave Louise White an exhilarating ride on her debut at Brocklesby Park, but well beaten otherwise. Tried in blinkers once under Rules. Usually sweats excessively. Best on top-of-the-ground though has won in soft. *A.M. Heath — Cambs (Libby Heath).* 441 (O), 795 (L), 921 (2m6fH), 1265 (O), 1417 (L).

JUST CHARLIE ..10-0.. 12 b.g. Bustino — Derring Miss (Derrylin) 5p52f. Smallish workmanlike half-brother to flat winner, Blazing Red (in Austria). Dam won at 6f. NH FLAT r1 p0. NH '93/4 and '96 r5 p1 (dead-heat for 2nd in Ch). P-t-P '94/7 and '99 r32 w11 (inc Open) p10 (6 2nds); failed to finish 6 (fell/unseated 2). A useful Pointer on undemanding courses to '97 when he enjoyed six victories, but missed the following season and has won just once in ten starts since. Has made all successfully, but David Easterby usually likes to play a waiting game though his partner appears too one-paced to quicken into contention nowadays. Declining steadily and will find matters even tougher in future. *Mrs S.E. Mason — Middleton (Ian Mason).* 48 (Cf), 277 (Cf), 622 (O), 805 (O), 1231 (O).

JUST CHICA ..9-6.. 10 gr.g. Siberian Express (USA) — Lightening Reef (Bon Sang FR) 2p. Lengthy light-framed. P-t-P '97/8 r3 p1 (3rd); 4th, and pulled up 1. Has given encouragement in all three completions, but stands his racing badly and carried too much condition in 2000. Would be a deserving winner, but getting him to the races in peak fitness seems an impossibility. *R.G. Abrey — Suffolk.* 551 (OMa), 775 (OMa).

JUST DESTINY (IRE) ..8-7.. 11 ch.g. Strong Statement (USA) — Blackwater Rose VII (unknown) 4. P-t-P '98 (for Mr C.P. Hobbs) r3 p0 (pulled up 2, and unseated 1). Might have succeeded on only his second racecourse appearance as he was finishing to good effect when baulked at the final fence in an Andoversford Maiden, but pulled up lame when sent off favourite in his next outing and could only plod round to finish a remote last in his Members when resurfacing two years later. *G. Lockwood — N. Cotswold (Florence Lockwood).* 1189 (M).

JUST FELIX ..8-7.. 11 b.g. Feelings (FR) — Salvage Girl (Military) pp. Compact half-brother to Seriously Smart. P-t-P '99 r2 p0 (6th, and pulled up 1). Soon remote in two April Maidens last year, but far more frisky in 2000 and for about two miles in both starts. Weakened dramatically and pulled up twice and will need to adopt a calmer attitude if he is to achieve anything tangible. *Mrs P.C. Stirling — Lauderdale.* 1163 (OMa), 1431 (OMa).

JUST FOR A REASON ..—.. 9 b.g. Siberian Express (USA) — Artaius Rose (FR) (Artaius USA) p. Compact half-brother to Warren Boy. 8400 2-y-o. FLAT r5 p0. NH '96/8 (sometimes blinkered/visored; for A. and R. Jukes, claimed for £5000; won previously for D. Murray-Smith) r27 w1 (2m Clmng Hdle) p6 (inc 28/3rd of 4 in Ch); mostly Sells. Won in February '96, and beaten in all 26 outings since. Pulled up in five of the final seven, and is useless and apparently ungenuine these days. *M.A. Lloyd — Albrighton Woodland.* 862 (Cf).

JUST HOPING ..9-12.. 8 b.g. Primitive Rising (USA) — Happy Penny (Tower Joy) p. Small neat. Dam is sister to Primitive Penny, and half-relative to Rabble Rouser (*qv* '98 Annual). Grandam, Penny Pink, won a Restricted at 5. Ran and jumped well for 2m4f in a Restricted on a January debut, and looked promising, but has not been seen since. Would be interesting in a Maiden if he reappears. *Lady Susan Watson — Middleton.* 40 (R).

JUST JACK ..9-5.. 15 br.g. Ovac (ITY) — Precision Chopper (Menelek) 8pp6u34. Compact brother to Luke's The Bizz (IRE), and half-brother to Mistress Tara, and to Irish jumping and English Chasing winner, The Outback Way (IRE). IRISH P-t-P '94 r1 p0. P-t-P/HUNT CH '91/9 r47 w5 (inc 2m5f110y Hunt Ch, and Open) p5 (2nds, last once); failed to finish 16 (fell/unseated 10, and ran out 1). A grand servant to Peter Jonason over ten consecutive seasons, but very much a back number in the last three (despite an unchallenged Cottenham success in '99) and used as a schoolmaster for daughter Fiona in 2000. Looked after her in the main, but beat just one rival in four completions and goes as slowly as befits a senior citizen nowadays. *P. Jonason — Cambs.* 15 (C), 91 (M), 240 (L), 608 (L), 758 (L), 1034 (C), 1289 (L).

JUST LIKE MADGE ..10-7.. 10 ch.m. Cruise Missile — Madge Spartan (Spartan General) 63f1231. Tall rangy sister to Miss Isle, Cruising Madge and Miss Madge, and half-sister to True Spartan, Little Holly, Manor Park Crumpet and Southern-Radar. Dam won 6 Points and 3m2f Hunt Ch and placed 7. P-t-P '96/9 r10 w4 (up to Confined) p2; pulled up 2, and fell/unseated 2. A reformed character in '99, but more highly strung than a Stradivarius (typical chestnut mare) and has proved a very hard tactical ride since. Tends to lose her pitch with about a mile to run and finds herself with too much ground to make up particularly on courses where stamina does not come into play. Gained her first victory away from her beloved Mollington (adores the place even more than a certain Pointing guru and has won six times there) when scoring at Garthorpe on her final outing. Sweats excessively and is usually mounted outside the paddock and taken to post early. Blinkered once in '96. Sure to win again, but no longer represents value (beaten favourite four times in 2000) and likely to remain an enigma. *S.J. Woolley, E.E. Ecclestone & D. Turner — Grafton (Jimmy Tarry).* 74 (CCf), 291 (F), 428 (Cf), 784 (M), 1006 (Cf), 1415 (Cf), 1584 (CCond).

JUST MAI-BEE ..8-10.. 9 gr.g. Chilibang — Just Maisy (Broadsword USA) upbp5. Small. Dam, half-sister to Bengers Moor (*qv* '98 Annual), was 2nd in 6 Points '93/6. NH FLAT '98 r1 p0 (pulled up). P-t-P/HUNT CH '97/9 r19 p2 (3rds, of 4 once); last pair 5, and failed to finish 12 (unseated 1, and refused 1). Has contested 25 races and only beaten four horses and only once better than last in his last nine outings. Pulled up and dismounted twice in 2000 and must give his partners the impression that something is drastically wrong. *B. Hurst — S. Cornwall.* 558 (L), 654 (I), 1262 (OMa), 1522 (CfMa), 1641 (OMa).

JUST MARMALADE ..9-11§.. 12 ch.g. Noalto — Kitty Come Home (Monsanto FR) 578p72631. Tall lengthy brother to Stray Harmony (won Chasing since Pointing — unbelievably lucky, *qv* The H'Penny Marvel) and Stray Return, and half-brother to Nearly An Eye (prolific Chasing winner since Pointing until fatally injured), Coiled Spring (successful Hurdler after Pointing) and Kitty Returns. Dam won at 14f, and won 2m1f Hdle. NH FLAT r2 p1 (3rd). NH '94/5 and '98 r8 p1 (3rd in 3m Ch). P-t-P/HUNT CH '96/9 r21 w2 (Maiden and Restricted) p5 (3 3rds, last once); pulled up 3, and on floor 2. Beaten in 25 races since winning twice in '96, but awarded his Members on a technicality thus providing Jane Williams with her first winner. A safe jumper, but quick to lose interest nowadays and can be safely ignored in competitive races. Usually awash with sweat in the paddock. *Mrs A.D. Williams — Albrighton Woodland.* 192 (L), 333 (Cf), 615 (CMod), 904 (L), 1014 (3m5fL), 1126 (L), 1358 (Cf), 1523 (Cf), 1629 (M).

JUST MIGHT ..—.. 10 b.g. Amerian (USA) — Just Musk (Rose Knight) u. Half-brother to Idol Knight and Cabernet. Dam won 2 very weak Points and placed 8 (inc 3rd in 3m4f Hunt Ch); final placing for Linda Lamyman. Floundered over the first two fences and got rid of his rider at the third in his Members, so we were deprived of the chance to see if he was as incredibly slow as his siblings. *Mrs L. Lamyman — Belvoir.* 867 (M).

JUST NED ..9-1.. 10 b.g. Gunner B — Heckley Loch (Lochnager) 57fp5. Leggy brother to Hurdles winner, Surprise Gunner. Dam completed hat-trick in 2m Hdles, the first a Sell. NH FLAT '97 r3 p0. NH '97 and Spr '99 r4 p0. P-t-P '98 (for Mr R.W. Brydon) r3 p1 (fence 3rd of 4); 4th, and 6th. Confined to Chases in 2000 and jumped moderately and tailed off without exception when completing. A lightly raced maiden and seems likely to remain one. *P.J. Douglas — College V. & N. Northumberland (Swannee Haldane).* 301 (2m5fH), 465 (3m1f110yH), 918 (2m4fH), 1445 (3m1fH), 1556 (2m4f110yH).

JUST ONE QUESTION (IRE) ..10-4.. 11 b.g. Torus — Stormy Night (Deep Run) 212p. Tall rangy half-brother to Hurdles winner, If And But (IRE). IRISH NH FLAT '95/6 r4 w1. NH '97/8 r9 p2 (2nd in

Hdle and Ch). P-t-P '99 (for Mrs T.C. Clemence) r4 w1 (Members) p2 (2nd of 3 once); and pulled up 1. Survived a multitude of minor errors when landing a gamble in his Members last year, but generally a weak finisher and had come to the end of his tether when recording his third career success at Horseheath in February. Has brief campaigns and usually avoids sound surfaces. Wears a tongue-strap. *Mrs K. Pilkington — Enfield Chace.* 27 (I), 96 (I), 241 (C), 572 (CfO).

JUST OZ (U) ..—.. 10 ch.g. unknown 4. Huge hunter. P-t-P '99 r1 p0 (last of 4). Carried 15 pounds less than he did 12 months ago when achieving exactly the same result in his Members so perhaps the good doctor's diet was in vain. *Dr L. Free — Chid, Lec & Cowdray (Miss J. Lodge).* 304 (M).

JUST REUBEN (IRE) ..7-7.. 6 gr.g. Roselier (FR) — Sharp Mama VII (unknown) 7pR75fp. Brother to Plessey Rose Lee (IRE). Beaten a minimum of 58 lengths with a total of one horse behind him when he managed to complete, and it would be most surprising if Louise Alner could be bothered with him again (despite their sire, his sister had no aspirations to being a racehorse either). *A. Trowbridge — Portman (Louise Alner).* 7 (OMa), 212 (CfMa), 328 (CfMa), 455 (OMa), 733 (2m4fOMa), 955 (OMa), 1131 (OMa).

JUST RUFFLED ..—.. 12 b.g. Rough Lad — Deep Harmony (White Hart Lane) ppppupp. Workmanlike. P-t-P '97 (for Mrs P.A. Hooper) r1 p0 (refused). Immediately tailed off and toiled by the fourth in his Members three years ago and clearly not overjoyed at being brought back to Pointing. Useless on all known evidence and pulled up when the rider thought he had gone lame in his latest foray. Has been tried in blinkers. *Miss P.A. Williams — S. Pembs (Owen Thomas).* 267 (CfMa), 347 (M), 486 (R), 650 (CfMa), 1221 (M), 1225 (OMa), 1300 (OMa).

JUST SUPREME (IRE) ..—.. 10 b.g. Supreme Leader — Just Ginger (The Parson) p. Dam is sister to Pat Cullen (*qv* '99 Annual). IRISH NH FLAT '97 r1 p0. IRISH NH '96/7 and '99 r8 p0 (8th and fell in Hunt Chses; pulled up, fell and unseated in Chses). IRISH P-t-P '97/9 r7 w1 (7 plus unplaced Mdn) p2; pulled up, and fell 2. Had a very poor jumping record in Ireland, but managed to win one of the contests they kindly put on for total duffers (at least they make good selling Points!) Pulled up when struggling in a February Restricted for the new yard. *Tudor Lodge Partners — S. Pembs (Keith & Linda Goldsworthy).* 273 (R).

JUST TAKETHE MICKY ..10-0.. 11 b.g. Gay Meadow — Oujarater (Adropejo) 453. Compact brother to Kirby Moorside, and half-brother to Lightcliffe Lady, Little Wenlock, Tough Minded and Shalma. Dam won 5 Hdles at around 2m. P-t-P '96/7 and '99 r9 w1 (Maiden) p0; last 2, pulled up 4, and fell 2. Made most to land much the slowest of three Maidens at Witton Castle last year, but beaten a minimum of 20 lengths during an interrupted 2000 campaign. Jumped straighter than usual this year (usually dives right-handed) but one-paced and stands little racing. *Lady Susan Watson — Middleton.* 137 (R), 1000 (R), 1230 (R).

JUST THE BUSINESS ..9-5.. 8 b.g. Golden Heights — Hockers Lane (Sunyboy) 442218. Leggy compact. Dam, half-sister to Bill Cornwall (*qv* '94 Annual), was placed twice at Aldington (4 years apart) for Peter Bull. NH FLAT '98/9 (from Miss A. Newton-Smith's r2 p0). A fair galloper, but was hard ridden from two out when winning a 2m4f Maiden at Charing by 12 lengths, and has otherwise given the impression of failing to get the trip (had been six lengths clear at the penultimate the time before, but jumped the last slowly and was caught on the run-in). Usually blinkered nowadays. Will need to find more for Restricteds. *P.A. Bull — Ashford V. (Liz Howes).* 21 (2m4fOMa), 304 (OMa), 411 (OMa), 576 (OMa), 1105 (2m4fOMa), 1335 (2m4f110yH).

JUST TRY ME (IRE) ..—.. 7 b.g. Darshaan — Just Society (USA) (Devil's Bag USA) pufup0. Compact. Dam won 2 Irish flat, 5-6f (dead heated once, but subsequently awarded race outright). IRISH FLAT (tried blinkers) r8 p1 (8f) p1 (2nd). IRISH NH '98/9 r4 p0. NH May '00 (from G. Moore's) r2 p0 (pulled up in 2m Nov Hdle: *hld up, headway 5, wknd 3 out, pu nxt*; and last in 2m2f HCap Hdle: *a bhnd*). Diabolical, but he and Phillip Hall have established their own little piece of history, having parted company in three races at Rodmell — and there have only been two meetings! One wobbly was at the second fence in a match with a 15-year-old; on another occasion, he galloped loose for three circuits (that's not much more than going round Larkhill once). Usually wears a tongue-strap. *Mr & Mrs J.J. Patty — Southdown & Eridge (Mrs J. Patty).* 305 (Cf), 674 (M), 676 (Cf), 1212 (Cf).

JYMJAM JOHNNY (IRE) ..10-3§.. 12 b.g. Torus — Inventus (Pitpan) 24. Tall. NH FLAT Apr '93 r1 p0. NH '93/9 (blinkered/visored 4; 3 wins for J.J. O'Neill; one win previously for J. Akehurst) r35 w4 (2 Hdles, 2m1f-2m2f, and 2 Chses, 2m5f-2m6f) p10 (beaten head once). All his four wins under Rules were gained on easy surfaces and made most of the running in three of them, but is a monkey who must not be touched with the whip. Should have made fitness and freshness tell first time out at Alnwick, but was beaten half a length by Dennett Lough after being given a totally uninspired ride by James Tate, and vanished after a February Hunter Chase in which he gave up the ghost after a couple of mistakes. *Dr M.P. Tate — Middleton (Tim Walford).* 42 (O), 90 (3m1fH).

KALAJO ..9-9.. 11 b.g. Kala Shikari — Greenacres Joy (Tycoon II) p. Well-made compact. Dam won 5 Hdles, 2m-2m4f, inc 4 Sells. NH FLAT r1 p0 (well tailed off last). P-t-P '95/6 (for Mr M.J. McGovern) r15 w2 (2m4f Maiden, and Members) p4 (2 2nds, remote last after refusing once); pulled up 5, and fell 1. NH '97/8 (for B. Mactaggart when successful & L. Lungo latterly) r15 w3 (hat-trick in 3m-3m1f Chses) p2. Went through a purple patch under Rules winning three Chases in less than three weeks, but lost his way after leaving Bruce Mactaggart and became incredibly error-prone. His Pointing comeback was brief, and he was not seen out again after pulling up apparently lame at Lanark in March. Was lame at the end of the '96 season so the omens are not good. Has winning form on firm and in soft. Wears a tongue-strap on occasions. *D.J. Dixon — Cumberland F. 662* (O).

KANDLES-KORNER ..8-13.. 7 b.g. Gold Dust — My Kizzy (The Ditton) 1p. Brother to Rice Point (*qv*). P-t-P '99 r1 p0 (5th). Had no subsequent winners behind when taking a slow Barbury Castle event in dead ground on her reappearance and disappointingly pulled up in her first Restricted. Connections were obviously keen to use the services of the former champion jockey, and justified market support in the Maiden, so she may have further improvement in her. *W.R. Thomas — Glamorgan (Judith Tudor).* 472 (OMa), 863 (R).

KANJO OLDA ..9-0.. 11 gr.m. Scallywag — Devine Lady (The Parson) 5p. Strong-topped powerful half-sister to Green King, and to 3 winners (one in Italy), including Go Forum (flat and Hurdles). Dam won 2 Irish flat, 9-12f. P-t-P '96/9 r8 w1 (Maiden) p1 (last of 3); disqualified from 3rd once — not weigh-in; last, unseated 1, and pulled up 3. Won her Maiden at Thorpe in a remarkably quick time, but has never stood many races and that was her lot in '99. Usually too burly to do herself justice and failed to beat a rival in just two starts this term. Used to pull hard, and can still lay handy for up to 2m4f, but soon tires and will be hard pushed to win again. *Mr & Mrs M.A. Lloyd — Wheatland (Frank Matthews).* 698 (R), 1200 (CR).

KANONA ..10-0.. 10 ch.g. Gunner B — Pugilistic (Hard Fought) pf. Leggy unfurnished brother to NH flat winner, Northern Fusilier, and to Hurdles winner, Gunner Marc. NH FLAT '95 r2 p0. NH '95/6 r3 p1 (last of 3). P-t-P '99 r7 w1 (Maiden) p4 (2 3rds, of 4 once); 8th, and pulled up 1. Made all to get off the mark at Whitwell last year, and unlucky in his penultimate start as he floundered in a patch of false ground approaching the last when only beaten one and a half lengths. May have been hurt when taking an early fall at Charm Park in March as he failed to reappear. *J.M. Walker — Hurworth (David Smith).* 137 (R), 396 (R).

KARABURAN ..10-2.. 7 b.g. Shareef Dancer (USA) — Kalmia (Miller's Mate) p71511313. Small lengthy half-brother to NH flat winner, Il Cavaliere, and to Irish NH flat and Hurdles winner, Kahoutek. Dam won at 10f in France. NH '97/8 r10 w1 (2m4f Hdle) p0 inc Sells. P-t-P/HUNT CH '99 r7 w1 (Ladies) p3 (2 3rds, of 4 once); 4th, last, and pulled up 1. Wore headgear and could look ungenuine under Rules, but has taken on a new lease of life in Points and won four Opens in the last 14 months. Far more consistent than he used to be, but still not a natural jumper and Fiona Wilson has done well on him. Not disgraced behind Balisteros on his final start and worth persevering with in Hunter Chases. Acts on any going. *J. Milton — Ystrad Taf Fechan.* 34 (MO), 222 (3m1f110yH), 335 (L), 481 (L), 599 (L), 821 (MO), 1066 (3m2fL), 1399 (M), 1593 (3m2fH).

KARAR (IRE) ..9-8§.. 11 b.g. Shardari — Karaferya (USA) (Green Dancer USA) 6. Robust half-brother to Irish NH flat winner, Karakam. Dam won 2 10f races (one at Nottingham; and one quite valuable prize at Phoenix Park). IRISH FLAT r3 w1 (12f) p0. FLAT r1 p0. NH '93/8 r43 w6 (5 Hdles, 2m6f-3m2f, and 2m5f Ch) p13; finished in all 11 Chses. P-t-P '99 r5 p0 (5th, 6th, and pulled up 3). A decent staying handicap hurdler on his day, but much less effective over fences and did not take to Pointing in '99 when looking increasingly reluctant. Collapsed and died after finishing last in a Marks Tey Open on his reappearance. *Mrs J.K. Marriage — Essex (Simon Marriage).* 320 (O).

KARLIN'S QUEST ..9-4.. 10 b.g. Karlinsky (USA) — Lost Valley (Perdu) ppp. Small stocky half-brother to Hurdles winner, Nagobelia. Dam won 5f Seller, and won 2 2m Sell Hdles. NH FLAT r1 p0 (tailed off). NH '98 r2 p0 (55½l last, and unseated in 2m1f-2m4f Hdles. P-t-P/HUNT CH '97/9 r14 w1 (Maiden) p4 (3 3rds); failed to finish 9 (ran out 1, carried 1, fell 2). Took 11 attempts before he lost his maiden status last year, but has proved to be an error-prone weak finisher otherwise and has failed to finish in six subsequent outings. Sure to continue to struggle in Restricteds. *S.C. Horn — Lamerton.* 203 (R), 558 (L), 1518 (R).

KATJACK (IRE) ..—.. 8 br.g. Detroit Sam (FR) — Elmley Gayle (Midland Gayle) ufp90. Small close-coupled. Dam is half-sister to Nevada Gold (*qv*). NH FLAT '99 r2 p0. NH '99 (been tongue-tied) r3 p0; (all runs Hexham). NH '00 r3 p0 (pulled up in 2m6f110y Nov Hdle: *bhnd, t.o and pulled up 2 out*; 9th in 2m4f110y Nov Hdle: *prom to 7, sn lost plce*; and 10th in 3m Nov Hdle: *started slow, a bhnd*). Made catastrophic mistakes and departed at around halfway in both Points. Later broke down badly, and not expected to be saved. *J.L. Brown — Haydon.* 187 (OMa), 360 (R).

KAYS-LASS ..9-9.. 8 b.m. Lyphento (USA) — Reckless Rat (Pamroy) 23pp. Tall strong. Dam won 2 Points and placed 4 for Mr Hole, but pulled up in 7 of her final 9 attempts. Grandam, Lady Keene, pulled up in a Point. P-t-P '99 r4 w1 (Maiden) p0; and pulled up 3. Finished four lengths second, but awarded an Erw Lon Maiden as the winner had missed a marker and gone the wrong side of the finishing posts on her only completion last year. Beaten a minimum of 12 lengths in her two placings in Restricteds in 2000, but only went a mile before pulling up in her last two starts and looks wrong. Tends to get herself worked up in the paddock and has two handlers. *J. Hole — Gelligaer F. (Lisa Day).* 647 (R), 818 (R), 1453 (R), 1623 (R).

KAZ KALEM (IRE) ..9-2.. 9 b.g. Lancastrian — Kilclare Lass (Pitpan) 34. Unfurnished brother to Cardinals Folly (IRE), and half-brother to Irish Pointing winner, Kilclare Hill. NH FLAT '97 r3 p0. NH '98/9 (for P. Hobbs) r3 p0. Bought Doncaster, Aug for 700. Beaten five lengths in both Points, but was a disappointing favourite in a weak Maiden, and would not be good enough to win on that sort of form. Only able to average two outings per annum. Wears a cross-noseband and bandages. *R. Vickers — Cumberland F.* 492 (M), 665 (OMa).

PLATE 67   599 Curre Ladies Open: R to L Karaburan (Miss F. Wilson), 1st, and Warren Boy (Miss P. Jones), 2nd   PHOTO: Alun Sedgmore

KEEP A SECRET ..10-0.. 10 b.g. Moor House — Potterway (Velvet Prince) f68231f. Rangy unfurnished half-brother to Primitive Way and The Dust Buster. Dam, sister to 3 Pointers, won 3m3f Hunt Ch and 6 Points and placed 8 for the Atkinsons. P-t-P '97/9 r15 w2 (Maiden and Members) p2 (2nds); pulled up 5, ran out 1, and unseated 1. Out of luck in five Restricteds since winning a bad Maiden at Hutton Rudby in '99, but struck gold in his first Intermediate in testing conditions at Corbridge this year having previously failed to retain his crown in his Members. Usually dropped out to conserve his stamina and was produced at just the right time by Peter Atkinson in his latest success. Still not a sure-footed conveyance and a return visit to Corbridge ended at the first fence. May have shot himself in the foot as far as gaining a fourth victory is concerned. *D.G. Atkinson — Bedale.* 173 (R), 279 (O), 396 (R), 804 (Cf), 1031 (M), 1159 (I), 1498 (O).

KEEP CLEAR (IRE) ..—.. 11 b.g. Clearly Bust — Keep Dancing (Lord Gayle USA) pp. Brother to NH flat and English Chasing winner, Dancetillyoudrop (IRE). IRISH NH FLAT '94 r6 w1 p1 (3rd). IRISH NH '95/8 r24 w1 (2m Hdle) p3 (inc 3rd in Ch). NH '98/9 (for C. Grant, bought for 6000, blinkered 1) r5 p1 (33/ 3rd of 4 in Ch). Bought Doncaster, Aug for 1800. Last one in '95, and is very lightly raced and of no account these days. Error-prone over bigger fences. *R. Hancox & K. Gallagher — N. Ledbury (R. Hancox).* 895 (MO), 1358 (Cf).

KELDAN STAR (IRE) ..—.. 7 b.g. Top Of The World — Kylemore Abbess (Monksfield) ppppu5. Tall rangy. Dam won 2m Hdle in Ireland. Gave a string of desparate displays, and was about two fences last with the rider out of sync when finally achieving a completion. *B.A. Hall — Gelligaer F. (M.G. Jones).* 145 (OMa), 270 (CfMa), 489 (CfMa), 601 (CfMa), 1197 (OMa), 1464 (OMa).

KELLY CANYON ..—.. 9 ch.g. Good Thyne (USA) — Kitty Castle (Rubor) p. Home-bred half-brother to Cornkitty and Corncastle. Grandam, Mee, won 5 Points (4 Ladies) and 2nd 2. Great-grandam, Lazy Jane, won 6 Points. Tailed off in early February. Descended from a line which has been in the Thomson family for aeons, but they seem to be running out of steam now. *D. & A.M. Thomson — Buccleuch.* 113 (OMa).

KELLY'S ISLAND ..—.. 11 br.m. Jupiter Island — Kelly's Maid (Netherkelly) ff. Good-topped close-coupled sister to Maida Hill, and half-sister to Kellytino. Dam is sister to Kelly's Honor. Grandam,

Maid Of Honour II, won 2 Points and 3rd 2. Capsized twice in February Maidens. *G. Copley — Cottesmore (Tim Tarratt).* 124 (OMa), 234 (OMa).

KELLY'S ORIGINAL ..10-2.. 13 b.g. Netherkelly — The Beginning (Goldhill) 6313p. Workmanlike half-brother to Itsgoneoff, Cosmic Flash, Island Beat and New Hope. Dam won 4 Sell Hdles, 2m-2m1f (also disqualified from similar for carrying incorrect weight). P-t-P/HUNT CH '93/6 and '98/9 r29 w5 (inc 2 Confineds) p17 (8 3rds, last twice; and inc 2 Hunt Chses); failed to finish 6 (fell/unseated 2). Successful on four occasions in '98, and unlucky to be caught near the finish in a Huntingdon Hunter Chase in which he tried to take the penultimate fence with him, but drew a blank against more exalted opposition the following year and his 2000 victory at Marks Tey ended a losing sequence of 11. Used to tire in the closing stages and is once again becoming a weak finisher. Prefers a sound surface to mud. *Mrs W.J. Tolhurst — Essex & Suffolk.* 607 (O), 841 (L), 936 (Cf), 1114 (Cf), 1334 (3mH).

KEMILLER (IRE) ..9-0.. 11 b.g. King's Ride — Icy Gal (Frigid Aire) ppp. Lengthy workmanlike half-brother to Rag Bolt (IRE). NH FLAT '95 r1 p0. NH '95/6 r5 p1 (3rd). P-t-P '98/9 r9 w1 (Maiden) p0; pulled up 4, and fell 2. Well ridden by Fred Hutsby when successful in an elder horses Maiden at Woodford in '99, but consistently fails to stay and four subsequent races have all resulted in him being pulled up. Usually sweats excessively beforehand. *M.R. Rollett — N. Cotswold.* 612 (CR), 894 (R), 1418 (R).

KENDOR PASS (IRE) ..9-12.. 13 b.g. Hard Fought — Proceeding (Monsanto FR) 5624s. Compact attractive half-brother to jumping winner, Uk Hygeine (IRE). Dam won 3 flat, 10-12f, inc Sell. IRISH FLAT '95/6 r8 p1 (2nd); pulled up 6, and ran out 1. P-t-P '96/7 r19 w1 (Maiden) p8 (5 3rds); unseated 3, and pulled up 1. Won what turned out to be a bad Maiden at Hutton Rudby in '97, but well beaten since apart from two respectable seconds in his local '99/00. An expert jumper and has never fallen at a fence though the previous owner used to fall off occasionally. *Mrs N.C. Wilson — Middleton.* 442 (L), 621 (L), 996 (M), 1328 (L), 1350 (L).

KENILWORTH LAD ..9-13.. 13 br.g. Ring Bidder — Lucky Joker (Cawston's Clown) p21. Small compact brother to Bidders Clown. Dam won at 7f. NH FLAT '92 r2 w2 (1m4f-2m). NH '93/5 and '97 r21 w5 (3 Hdles, 2m6f-3m) p12 (inc 2 Chses). P-t-P/HUNT CH '98/9 r13 p4 (3 3rds, last once); failed to finish 6 (fell/unseated 2, and brought down 1). Unbeaten in two Bumpers and was a good staying Hurdler at best, but beaten 22 times since his last success in '94 until stumbling across a feeble Ladies race at Thorpe in which he was the only one to go clear on his final outing. Often let his supporters down under Rules and usually settles for a place at best now. *W.J. Moore — Belvoir.* 869 (L), 1074 (L), 1217 (L).

KENNY DAVIS (IRE) ..10-3.. 8 b.g. Mazaad — Very Seldom (Rarity) 231b1u. Small light half-brother to 3 flat winners, including Euro Sceptic and Jimmy The Skunk. FLAT r2 p0. P-t-P-type '98/9 r11 p2 (2nds, fence last once); last, pulled up 3, fell/unseated 4, and ran out 1. Greatly incapacitated by the rider in previous seasons, but has learnt to adapt to the unorthodox happenings above and has developed into a promising performer. Won his Restricted in the fastest 12st times of the day (clocked an identical time as Cache Fleur recorded in the Ladies) and arguably unlucky in Open company on his final start as he was finishing to good effect when unseating at the penultimate fence. Possesses a tidy turn of foot (needs to as the pilot often sits well out of his ground) and will gain compensation in a similar race soon. Would raise his rating by several more pounds if he was partnered by a top jockey. *Miss M. Askew — Stevenstone (Paul Blagg).* 131 (OMa), 284 (2m4fCMa), 412 (OMa), 657 (R), 825 (R), 1394 (O).

KENTLANDS LAD ..—.. 6 ch.g. Triune — Holcombe Jane (Baltus) up. Half-brother to Holcombe Handsel (*qv*). Only got as far as the first on his debut, and pulled up after 2m3f next time. *M.R. Lavis — Taunton V. (Carroll Gray).* 204 (OMa), 656 (OMa).

KENTUCKY GOLD (IRE) ..9-8§.. 12 b.g. Le Bavard (FR) — Darjoy (Darantus) 9f5u42746. Big strong good-looking brother to Irish NH flat and jumping winner, Dis Fiove, and Hurdles winner, Do Be Have (IRE), and half-brother to jumping winners, Tennessee Twist (IRE), and Royal Athlete (won '95 Grand National). NH FLAT '95 r2 p0. NH '95/9 r17 p2 (3m½f-3m2f Chses). P-t-P/HUNT CH '98 r6 w4 (inc 3m1f Hunt Ch, and inc hat-trick) p2 (3rds, inc Hunt Ch). NH Apr '00 r2 p0 (7th in 3m HCap Ch: *bhnd til drvn 5, t.o 11*: and 4th in 3m2f Nov HCap Ch: *ld til hdd aft 3 out, wknd*). Appeared useless under Rules, but immensely improved by a switch to Pointing in '99 and gained his fourth victory of the season in a Hexham Maiden Hunter Chase. Whatever shocked him into action last year was missing this, and he looked remarkably sour, particularly on his last three starts. May have lost his confidence as a result of a first fence fall at Plumpton, but certainly one to treat with caution when he returns. Suited by a test of stamina when on song. *J. Halewood — Cheshire (Mark Williamson).* 89 (3m1fH), 223 (3m2fH), 334 (O), 383 (3m4H), 579 (3m2fH), 587 (M), 1342 (3m1fH).

KERRISDALE ..9-10.. 9 b.m. Arctic Lord — Good Way (Good Apple) p5321f. Workmanlike half-sister to The Way North (*qv*). NH '97/9 (for P. Beaumont) r9 p0 (inc pulled up 2, and fell). Had no difficulty capturing her Members, but generally extremely one-paced, and is probably going to struggle now a Maiden is no longer an option. Had previously finished an official three quarters of a length second in that company, but appeared to have deserved a dead-heat. Normally a reliable jumper, but fell at the third and broke David Thomas's collar-bone on final start. Runs tongue-tied. *First Past The Post RC (R.P. Watts) — Staintondale (Annabelle Armitage).* 234 (OMa), 399 (OMa), 798 (OMa), 808 (OMa), 1229 (M), 1351 (CR).

KERRY GOLD MINE ..9-13.. 8 ch.g. Blaze O'Gold (USA) — Kerry Maid (Maestoso) 1u2. Strong Price-bred brother to Kerry Power Major, and half-brother to Kerry Soldier Blue. Dam was a useless Pointer for Margaret Price. Owned by D. Brace latterly. Made much of running in the final mile when successful on his debut at Chippley Park, but twice beaten at even money since (unseated at the sixth once, and beaten a length by Secret Beauty once). Absent since mid-March, but should be good enough to atone in a Restricted when fit. *R. Price — D. Brace — Brecon & Talybont (David Gibbs; -).* 146 (OMa), 347 (R), 646 (R).

KERRY SOLDIER BLUE ..10-7.. 12 gr.g. Fine Blue — Kerry Maid (Maestoso) 111224. Smallish lengthy good-topped half-brother to Kerry Gold Mine (*qv*). P-t-P/HUNT CH '96/9 r14 w6 (up to Confined) p4 (3 2nds, last once; and 3rd in Hunt Ch); pulled up 4. A very game front-running Pointer and followed up his '99 four-timer with a hat-trick this year. Has not enjoyed the same success in Hunter Chases, but has twice led over the last at Cheltenham only to be run out of it up the hill and deserves to win over the bigger obstacles. Jumps well and responds gamely to pressure which has been ably supplied by Pip Jones in all his wins, but tends to get bogged down in very soft ground. Usually needs an outing to put him spot on. *R.W.A. Price — Brecon & Talybont.* 295 (L), 478 (M), 895 (MO), 1022 (3mH), 1336 (2m4fH), 1558 (3mH).

KESZAM ..9-10.. 9 b.m. Zambrano — Flying Kestrel (Weatherbird) 473. Lengthy. Dam only beat a hunter in 13 Points for Jeff Fear (failed to finish 11 — refused 4). P-t-P '98/9 r10 w1 (Maiden) p3 (2nds, of 3 once); ran out 2, pulled up 3 and fell 1. Proved unpredictable and a hard ride in '99, but won her maiden in softish at Bratton Down and might have followed up immediately in a Restricted at Umberleigh but for a last fence blunder. Ran well when just over seven lengths third in a Cothelstone Intermediate on firm ground in March, but failed to reappear and may have suffered a setback. *J.E. Fear — Weston & Banwell H.* 330 (R), 406 (R), 639 (I).

PLATE 68   1231 Staintondale Mens Open: Key Debate and Guy Brewer, 1st, get in close but jump well
PHOTO: Roy Parker

KEY DEBATE ..11-4.. 9 b.g. Gildoran — Key To Heaven (Lucifer USA) 121111. Compact half-brother to Keyword and Key Issue. An amazing novice. Won five races by an aggregate of more than 100 lengths (and it could have been a lot more), and goes a sensational gallop to keep spreadeagling the opposition. Certainly no angel and is walked to the start by Gill Walford to prevent him from bubbling over too much, but has made a man of Guy Brewer, who did brilliantly to survive an earthquake of a mistake at the third from home at Huntington. Capable of fine leaping, but does not meet every fence in his stride, although generally becoming less risky than he was. Broke a blood vessel once, but otherwise uncatchable, and the manner in which he stormed away with two Hunter Chases suggest that plenty more victories await under Rules. Has had a chequered career, as the breeders apparently found him to be unmanageable, whilst he later had a spell with Jenny Pigeon, when a broken pelvis was diagnosed. *Mrs M. Cooper — Middleton (Tim Walford).* 55 (OMa), 232 (R), 797 (R), 1231 (O), 1333 (3mH), 1446 (3m1fH).

KHALIDI (IRE) ..9-10.. 12 b.g. Shernazar — Khaiyla (Mill Reef USA) 64412. Small neat attractive half-brother to Irish flat winners, Khalyani and Khayrawani (IRE) (latter also a smart Hurdler — won at Aintree and Cheltenham on English forays in '99), and to a French flat winner. IRISH FLAT '91/2 r7 w2 (10-12f) p2. FLAT '93 and '95 r4 p1 (3rd). NH '93/9 (for D. Gandolfo; blinkered 1 — too free; broke blood vessel once in '94) r36 w7 (5 Hdles, 2m-2m5f, and 2 2m2f Chses) p9. Formerly competent and won nine races on ground close to good. But unplaced in his final nine attempts under Rules, and has lost interest. A safe conveyance for the newcomer Malvina MacGregor in Ladies Opens, and won a match at Barbury Castle after his rival had fallen at the final fence when 20 lengths clear, but soundly trounced when not better than a poor last otherwise, including in another match. *Miss M.I. MacGregor — S. Dorset.* 475 (L), 636 (L), 885 (L), 1281 (L), 1553 (L).

KHANDYS SLAVE (IRE) ..9-0.. 13 ch.m. Le Johnstan — Snow Sweet (Arctic Slave) pp. Compact half-sister to Snowy Run and Arctic Red. Dam won an Irish Bumper. P-t-P '94/7 r11 w1 (Maiden) p2 (2nds, remote once); pulled up 6. Pulled up in six of her first eight outings, but appreciated the (then) short course at Bonvilston when taking just 5min 37s to win her Maiden in '97. Missing from action since until pulling up on both appearances this year. Presumably at stud in the interim, and no longer of account as a racehorse. *K.M. Stanworth — Tredegar F.* 744 (R), 1054 (R).

KHATIR (CAN) ..9-9§.. 10 gr.g. Alwasmi (USA) — Perfect Poppy (Poppy Jay) p2p7. Well-made good-looking half-brother to a winner in USA. Dam won 10 races. $50,000y. FLAT (for D. Morley) r12 w2 (10-15f) p3 (3rds). NH '94/7 (for M. Pipe, bought for 17,000) r22 w3 (2m1f-2m4f Hdles) p4. Started his Hurdling career in a blaze of glory and scored at Cheltenham, Newbury and Haydock and finished second to Anzum from his first four attempts, but last scored in November '94, and beaten 22 times since. Only appeared once in '97, missed the next two years, and gave just one respectable display when reviving (three lengths second in an Open, in which he started at 25-1 and ran in snatches). Decended to Sellers latterly for Pipe, but never asked to tackle fences in the past, and has long been ungenuine. Wears blinkers, and tried visored and with a tongue-tie in the past. *P. Swift & I. Bennett — Rockwood H. (P. Swift).* 796 (O), 961 (O), 1293 (3mH), 1666 (O).

KHAYAL (USA) ..10-7.. 7 b.g. Green Dancer (USA) — Look Who's Dancing (USA) (Affirmed USA) p12. Good-bodied. Dam won 3 races up to 9f in USA. FLAT r1 p0. NH '97/8 r7 p2. P-t-P '99 r4 w4 (Maiden, Restricted, Mixed Open and Intermediate — 4-timer) p0. Often found little when push came to shove flat and hurdling, but beyond reproach in Points last year and went through the season unbeaten. Looked burly on his return and blew up with three to jump, but failed to reappear for seven weeks. Backed as though defeat was out of the question at Stafford Cross and had the race in safe keeping soon after taking up the running with two to jump, but let supporters down on his final start though time may tell he was facing an impossible task. Well handled by the champion jockey, and seems certain to win again granted the opportunities. Has yet to encounter extremes of going in Points. Visored once over hurdles. *G.J. Cossey — Taunton V. (Carroll Gray).* 200 (O), 928 (MO), 1305 (MO).

KIDLAW ..9-9.. 13 b.g. Good Times (ITY) — Bedfellow (Crepello) 635. Big rangy half-brother to 4 winners (one in Italy), including Bedhead (flat) and Great Law (Hurdles). Dam won 2 flat, 6-8f, and is half-sister to Polygamy (Oaks) and One Over Parr (Cheshire Oaks). NH '91/3, '95 and '97/8 r19 w3 (2 2m1f Hdles, and 2m5f Ch) p7. P-t-P '95 and '99 r11 w2 (Confined and Members) p2 (2nds, remote once, and of 3 once); last 3, fell 2, and pulled up 2. Fell in his first two Points, but capable of superb jumping and frequently with the pace until weakening in the final mile. Revived well for enough present connections to land his Members in '99 at a sweltering 33-1, but a huge hulk of a horse and his size has always placed a great strain on his legs which gave way again on his final start at Tabley. *J.S.E. Turner — Sir W.W. Wynn's.* 293 (Cf), 525 (M), 961 (O).

KILGOBBIN (IRE) ..9-10.. 10 ch.g. Kambalda — Paldamask (Native Prince) p. Strong compact half-brother to Ballyshiel. Dam won 6 5f races in Ireland. IRISH P-t-P '95/6 r4 p0; pulled up 1, and fell 1. P-t-P '97/9 r14 w2 (Maiden and Restricted) p9 (4 2nds, of 3 once); fell/unseated 2. Took 15 races to get off the mark and regularly looked a non-stayer, but won successive races in '99 when much improved. Managed just one outing in 2000 when pulled up at Howick and may have suffered a setback. Unlikely to have the opposition quaking in their boots if he returns. *O.J. Stephens — Llangibby (David Stephens).* 597 (Cf).

KILLATTY PLAYER (IRE) ..10-7.. 11 b.m. The Noble Player (USA) — Tiefland (Right Tack) R2b331351. Compact workmanlike half-sister to Caro Wood, Mighty Murphy and Parsons Choice (IRE), and to Irish flat winner, Haulboulder. IRISH P-t-P '95/6 r12 w1 (6yo&up mares Maiden) p3; pulled up 3, and fell 1. P-t-P/HUNT '97/9 r21 w3 (inc Ladies) p11 (8 3rds, last twice; and inc Hunt Ch); pulled up 3, and fell/unseated 2. A capable mare on her day, but can be extremely moody and a hard ride. However, returned her best stats yet in 2000 and forged a winning alliance with Mouse

Barlow after Candy Thomas had hit the ground twice in unusual circumstances. Often gets outpaced and loses interest in mid-race, but a thorough stayer and will pick up the bit again if inclined. Suited by some cut in the ground, but can handle firmish. Will probably win again against the lesser Ladies horses, but should be regarded as a risky betting medium. *I. Anderson — W. Salop.* 295 (L), 447 (Cm), 566 (L), 904 (L), 991 (L), 1066 (3m2fL), 1199 (L), 1410 (L), 1525 (L).

KILLERTON CLOVER ..8-12.. 8 ch.m. High Season — Winning Clover (Winden) 85. Small neat half-sister to Lucky Clover. Dam (*qv* '88 Season Annual), won Maiden and placed 6 (inc 4 Chses) for Derrick Llewellyn, and comes from the family of Clobracken Lad (*qv*). P-t-P '99 r3 p1 (last of 3); last, and pulled up 1. Flattered, but not entirely disgraced when last of three on her debut in '99 and showed plenty of speed in her most recent outing, but has only beaten one rival in her career to date and is looking rather fragile. *D.G.L. Llewellin — E. Devon.* 72 (OMa), 254 (CfMa).

KILLESHIN ..—.. 15 bl.g. Al Sirat (USA) — Spin Off (Wrekin Rambler) pp. Tall rather lightly-made half-brother to 2 Irish Hurdles winners (one also won NH flat). Dam won at 9f in Ireland. NH FLAT r1 p0. NH '90/2 and '94/8 r38 w2 (4m1f-4m2f Chses) p4; 7th & 6th (after remounting) in '97/8 Grand Nationals. HUNT CH '94 r4 w3 (2m3f-2m6f) p0; and pulled up 1. The '94 Aintree Foxhunters hero, and added another big race to his repertoire when successful in the £22,561 Tote Eider Chase at Newcastle two years later, but fell into the handicappers grip subsequently and has not won since. A sorry sight when soon tailed off on his return, and has been retired. Used to get so far behind that he seemed most likely to be pulled up, but could produce devastating acceleration, and will long be remembered for it. *H.J. Manners — V.W.H.* 10 (O), 35 (Cnr).

PLATE 69   1151 Vale of Lune Harriers Land Rover Mens Open: Kilminfoyle (P. Robson), 2nd, but walk the competition for most equipment on a horse's head

PHOTO: Peter & Marilyn Sweet

KILMINFOYLE ..9-13.. 14 b.g. Furry Glen — Loreto Lady (Brave Invader USA) uuf72p. Tall rangy brother to Furry Loch. NH FLAT r1 p0. NH '93/4 r12 w2 (3m1f Chses) p3 (Hdles). P-t-P/HUNT CH '96/7 and '99 r10 w1 (Ladies) p3 (2 3rds); pulled up 2, and fell/unseated 2. A very thorough stayer, but has won only once since present connections shelled out 8600gns for him in '95 and his current losing sequence now stands at 12. Decked Paul Robson in his first three outings in 2000, but almost made up for his misdemeanours at Whittington. Beginning to look ungenuine in any case and unlikely to redress the balance at 14. *Mrs S.H. Shirley-Beavan — Jedforest (Simon Shirley-Beavan).* 43 (Cf), 110 (O), 362 (O), 493 (Cf), 1151 (O), 1365 (O).

KILMINGTON (IRE) ..10-3.. 12 gr.g. Roselier (FR) — Hope You're Lucky (Quayside) 424r224. Small with large chestnut splodges. Brother to Hurdles winner, Lucky Ross (IRE). NH '94/5 and 96/9 r23 w5 (2m6f Hdles, and 3 3m-3m2f Chses) p5. P-t-P '96 r2 p1 (2nd); and fell. Returned to Josh Gifford after a short spell Pointing in '96 and did well from limited opportunities when forcing the pace. A safe if somewhat deliberate jumper, but becoming quirky, particularly at the start, and has been led in since refusing to race at Taunton. Finds little under pressure, and though he has the ability to win Points it seems unwise to trust him far. Acts on any going. *H.T. Pelham — S. & W. Wilts (Jane Galpin).* 262 (MO), 383 (3mH), 581 (3mH), 886 (C), 954 (MO), 1133 (O), 1337 (3m2f110yH).

KILTONGA ..—.. 14 b.g. Indian King (USA) — Miss Teto (African Sky) p. Unfurnished half-brother to Irish Hurdles winner, Bailenagun (IRE), and to Irish flat winner, Khareedah. IRISH FLAT '89/90 r8 p1 (3rd of 4). IRISH NH '90/1 r8 p1 (2nd). NH '91/4 r18 w1 (2m1f Sell Hdle) p0; pulled up 10, inc last 4 starts. P-t-P '95/6 and '98 (for Miss L.J. Horsey) r11 p2 (3rds, of 4 once, and last once); last pair 4, pulled up 3, and unseated 1. Tubed when last successful in '92, but has achieved little in Points and partnered by veteran novice Paul Anderson when tailed off in his Members '98 and 2000. *P. Anderson — Quantock, & W. Somerset V.* 1094 (M).

KIMBER HILL LAD ..—§.. 8 ch.g. Jester — Good Appeal (Star Appeal) p. Tall unfurnished. Dam, half-sister to For A Lark (*qv* '95 Annual), won a Maiden in '96 (also placed 5). NH FLAT r1 p0 (tailed off). P-t-P '99 r2 p0 (refused 1, and pulled up 1). Supported at big prices on his Pointing debut, but jumped appallingly until refusing after 1m4f, and has since been pulled up twice at Wadebridge. Absent since February and seems to have problems. *Mrs W. Murphy — N. Cornwall (Colin Heard).* 99 (M).

KIMBROSS ..9-7§.. 10 ch.g. Ardross — Kate Kimberley (Sparkler) p4344. Rangy half-brother to Hurdles winners, Sparkling Yasmin and Robara (latter also won Chasing). NH FLAT r3 p0. P-t-P '97 and '99 r10 w1 (Maiden) p1 (2nd); last pair 3, pulled up 4, and unseated 1. Got off the mark in a bad Maiden in testing ground at Umberleigh in '99, but struggling in Restricteds since and usually finds nothing in the closing stages. Sent off favourite for a poor event at Cherrybrook, but even the best efforts of Les Jefford could not coax him home. Visored on his final start, but never went a yard and is best ignored in future. *Mrs J. Robshaw & F. Hollis — Dulverton E. (Freddie Hollis).* 315 (R), 403 (Cf), 848 (R), 1042 (R), 1140 (CfR).

KINCORA (IRE) ..10-0.. 10 b.g. King Persian — Miss Noora (Ahonoora) 3251244. Smallish. Dam won 2 Irish flat, 8-10f. IRISH NH '96 r6 p0. IRISH P-t-P '96/8 r10 p4; pulled up 3. P-t-P/HUNT CH '99 r6 w2 (Club Maiden and Restricted) p2 (2nds); 4th, and unseated 1. Consistent in minor races, and jumps particularly well, but lacks a turn of foot and is suited by forcing tactics. Outclassed in Hunter Chases, but might find a weak Ladies Open in Kent. Has run tongue-tied in the past. *Mrs L. Stock — W. Street/Tickham.* 27 (I), 128 (L), 300 (2m5fH), 573 (CfL), 827 (L), 1155 (2m5f110yH), 1536 (3m2fH).

KIND OF CHIC ..—.. 10 ch.m. Kind Of Hush — Arras Style (Nicholas Bill) fpppf. Small compact home-bred half-sister to Arras-Tina. P-t-P '97 (for Mrs S.E. Mason) r2 w1 (Maiden) p1 (2nd of 3). Won a bad youngster Maiden at Charm Park in '97 (rated 9-3) but promptly disappeared for two whole years and has performed with a total lack of talent since her return. Failed to get beyond two miles in 2000 and looks badly wrong. Has been tried in a tongue-strap. *D.A. Kinsella — Hurworth.* 797 (R), 1230 (R), 1326 (R), 1351 (CfR), 1475 (R).

KIND PRINCE ..9-1.. 9 b.g. Kind Of Hush — Silent Princess (King Of Spain) 17pp. Small compact Harris-bred. Dam won 2 24mf Sell Hdles at Southwell. FLAT (for J.A. Harris) r4 p0. NH '95/6 and '98/9 (blinkered 3; final for R. Whitaker; won previously for M. Bielby; previously for S. Harris) r16 w1 (2m Sell Hdles) p2. NH Spr '00 (for J.L. Harris) r3 p0 (7th in 3m1f110y Nov HCap Ch: *keen, ld 3-12, wknd and eased*; pulled up in 2m4f Nov HCap Ch: *mist 5, bhnd, rdn 7, t.o and pulled up 11*; and pulled up in 2m5f220y HCap Hdle: *ld to 4, rdn & wknd, t.o and pulled up last*). Had little difficulty shrugging aside the favourite when a one-ride for Shaun Harris in his Members, but that race always looks as if it deserves to be scrapped, and is hopelessly outclassed under Rules. Takes a keen hold. Once went missing for 30 months. *S.A. Harris — Badsworth (-; J. Harris).* 166 (M).

KING CURAN (USA) ..—§.. 10 b.g. Lear Fan (USA) — Runaway Lady (USA) (Caucasus USA) pfr. Small brother to a winner in USA, and half-brother to another. Dam won 2 flat at up to 9f in USA. $40,000y. FLAT (2 wins for D. Haydn-Jones; 3 wins previously for A. Bailey, claimed for £9000; 3 wins previously for M. Bell) r44 w8 (7-10f) p4. NH '96/9 (final for A. Jukes, bought for 650; won previously for P. Bowen, bought for 6500; debut for A. Bailey) r11 w1 (2m3f Hdle) p0. Bought Ascot, June for 900. Often wore headgear in the past and was inconsistent, and did not score on the flat after '96 (although he added a desperate Selling Hurdle in October '97). But could be a good battler on his day, and was particularly well served by sound surfaces. Hates every moment now and obviously has something badly wrong with him, and it was horrible to see him so humbled in his Members (two fences adrift when finally refusing at the 11th). Should be prevented from appearing again. *R.J.A. Willis — O. Berks (F. Sutherland).* 789 (O), 1026 (2m5f110yH), 1202 (M).

KINGENNIE ..10-3.. 8 b.m. Dunbeath (USA) — Loch Brandy (Harwell) 33. Tall workmanlike half-sister to jumping winner, Linlathen. Dam won 3m3f Hunt Ch and 4 Points and placed 14 (inc a Hdle) for Mrs Niven (was Peter Niven's first winner in '83). P-t-P '98 r1 p0. NH FLAT Nov '98 r1 p0. NH '98/9 (for Mrs M. Reveley) r5 w1 (2m4f Nov Hdle) p1 (3rd). Sent off at 33-1 for her hurdling debut, but belied those odds and won convincingly. Could not repeat that form in just four more starts, and returned to Pointing in 2000. Beaten 11 and 26 lengths when third in Ladies races at Friars Haugh in February, but failed to reappear. Has the ability to do well between the flags, but stands her racing badly. Acts in soft ground. *Mrs J.A. Niven — Fife.* 109 (L), 361 (L).

KING FLY ..9-11.. 11 ch.g. Saxon Farm — Deep Goddess (Deep Run) 2. Strong half-brother to Irish Hurdles winner, Borrismore Flash (IRE). NH '97 r6 p1 (2nd). P-t-P/HUNT CH '96 and '98/9 r13 w1 (Maiden) p5 (3 2nds, dead-heated once; inc 3rd in Hunt Ch); pulled up 5, and on floor 2. Won his Maiden in the fastest time of the day back in '98, but has never stood much racing and clearly went wrong when pulled up twice in the space of three days last year. Usually takes a keen hold but fails to last home and did just that when second to a horse four years his senior in his Members on his only outing in 2000. *P.A. Horner-Harker — Hurworth (Sarah Horner-Harker).* 619 (M).

KING HAB (IRE) ..8-5.. 9 b.g. King Of Clubs — Habanna (Habitat) f. Lengthy half-brother to Blue Bourbon and Tring Park, to Irish Hurdles winner, Clanfluther, and to 5 flat winners (including in Ireland and Italy), including Grove Aries. Dam won 2 2-y-o's in Ireland, 5-6f. IRISH NH FLAT '96 r3 p0. P-t-P '99 (for Mr B.J. Kelly) r3 p1 (2nd of 3); and pulled up 2. NH Jul '99 r1 p0 (pulled up). Never started at more than 2-1 (favourite twice) in '99, but compounded quickly in all three outings after making the bulk of the running and clearly has severe stamina limitations. Fell in the first mile on his return at Larkhill, and may have been hurt as he failed to reappear. *Mrs F.M. Vigar — Pembs (Lucy Pinney).* 455 (OMa).

KING HIGH ..—§.. 14 b.g. Shirley Heights — Regal Twin (USA) (Majestic Prince USA) rur. Well-made good-looking half-brother to several winners. Dam won at 8f. FLAT r7 w1 (18f) p2 (2nds). NH '91 and '97 r2 p1 (3rd). P-t-P/HUNT CH '97 (for Mrs L. Wrighton) r2 p1 (3rd in Hunt Ch); and pulled up 1. Unreliable on the flat, but did win a three-horse race at 1-28 (!). Made a fair comeback in a Folkestone Hunter Chase after a five year lapse in '97, but pulled himself next time, and immediately made his feelings perfectly clear when revived again in 2000. Still has ability, but should not be touched with a barge pole. *Mrs Y. Bryce — Cambs Univ (Tim Bryce).* 771 (O), 936 (Cf), 1184 (Cf).

KINGLASSIE ..—.. 7 b.m. Rakaposhi King — Lillies Brig (New Brig) pfp. Light-framed half-sister to jumping winner, Solsgirth. Dam, half-sister to Kinneston (*qv* '95 Annual), won a Hunt Ch (on a disqualification) and 2 Points and placed 9 (inc 3 Chses). Grandam, Dysie Mary, was 3rd in Maiden. NH FLAT '99 (for J. Barclay) r1 p0 (last). Bought Doncaster, Aug for 1500. Kicked out of the nest by her breeders after just one outing, and gave the impression of being the worst horse in David Pipe's yard in 2000. *N. Burd — Taunton V.H. (David Pipe).* 72 (OMa), 205 (OMa), 353 (CfMa).

KING OF CAIRO ..8-10.. 13 ch.g. Sunyboy — Queen Of The Nile (Hittite Glory) ppuppp2p. Compact well-made half-brother to Mr Goonhilly and Thecabbageflinger, to flat winner, Burnditch Girl and to Hurdles winner, Among Islands. P-t-P/HUNT CH '94/5 and '97/9 (for Mr C. Smith) r19 w1 (Maiden) p1 (2nd); last pair 3, pulled up 9, and fell/unseated 5. Won a Maiden in soft at Kilworthy in '98, but has only managed to complete once from 13 subsequent outings and can be safely ignored. Makes plenty of mistakes and usually carries plenty of condition. *Miss R. Hatheson & Mrs M.C.D. Ansell — S. Cornwall (Ian Hambley).* 164 (R), 315 (R), 728 (R), 850 (R), 1043 (R), 1258 (R), 1384 (M), 1518 (R).

KING OF CLARE (IRE) ..10-5.. 9 b.g. King's Ride — Renewal (Dual) 3p. Workmanlike. IRISH P-t-P '97/8 r7 w1 (5yo&up unplaced Maiden) p1 (lucky 2nd of 3); pulled up 2. P-t-P/HUNT CH '99 r6 w1 (Restricted) p3 (2 2nds; and remote last of 3); 6th, and fell 1. A shock 33-1 winner on his English debut, proved that no fluke when an excellent second to a subsequent Hunter Chase winner on his next start. Began 2000 with another decent placed effort when third at Mollington, but failed to reappear after pulling up at Dunthrop in February and may have gone wrong. Would have prospects in a soft ground Intermediate if he could prove his fitness first. *D.J. Murphy — Warwicks.* 75 (I), 191 (Cf).

KINGOFNOBLES (IRE) ..9-8§.. 12 ch.g. King Persian — Eau D'Amour (Tall Noble USA) 942. Big strong half-brother to Carefree Love (IRE). IRISH P-t-P '94 r5 p1 (3rd); pulled up 3, and unseated 1. P-t-P/HUNT CH '95/8 r17 w1 (Maiden) p7 (6 2nds, last once); pulled up 4, and unseated 1. Won his Maiden cheekily in '95, but has not consented to put his best hoof forward since and has filled the runners-up berth on six occasions since. Beaten 20 lengths in the latest when last in his Members and may have suffered a recurrence of the problems that kept him of the track in '99 as he failed to reappear. Ran and jumped well when fourth in a Dunthrop Restricted previously, and still possesses the ability to win one, but could not be trusted with the housekeeping money at any cost. Usually has two handlers, and has been tried in blinkers. *K.B. Rogers — N. Herefords (Raymond Rogers).* 33 (Cnr), 193 (R), 332 (M).

KING PADDY (IRE) ..9-9.. 9 b.g. King's Ride — Nebechal (Native Bazaar) 5R762. P-t-P '97 (for Mrs S.A. Evans) r2 p0 (pulled up 2). NH '97/9 (for Mrs S.M. Johnson) r10 p2; pulled up 3 inc only Chse. Only beaten half a length in a 2m4f Novice Hurdle at Wetherby in '98 (had 16 others in his wake) and would be a Maiden certainty on that form, but has twice run out when races were there for the taking and clearly cannot be trusted. Seems to handle all types of going. Runs tongue-tied. *R.C. Bevan — N. Salop.* 293 (Cf), 568 (OMa), 583 (2m5f110yH), 964 (OMa), 1195 (R).

PLATE 70   639 Quantock Staghounds Intermediate: Kingsbridge (L. Jefford), 1st

PHOTO: Brian Armstrong

KINGSBRIDGE (IRE) ..10-2.. 7 b.g. Cataldi — Rockport Rosa (IRE) (Roselier FR) 3131214. Small light, NH FLAT '98 r1 p0. Sold Ascot, May for 2800, but rturned to Martin Pipe. A free-running little horse who can look a trappy ride, but consistently good jockeyship has enabled him to complete the course in all seven attempts and win three of them. Has made mistakes and shown a tendency to hang left, and was probably lucky in his Members, where he was only left with a former Pipe veteran to beat after a live danger had fallen four out. Acts on firm, and seemed unsuited by very soft on his latest outing. Invariably looks well, and should be particularly worth noting in early season in 2001 — will appreciate the underfoot conditions at Black Forest Lodge. *M.C. Pipe — Taunton V.H. (David Pipe).* 146 (OMa), 353 (CfMa), 536 (R), 639 (I), 927 (Cf), 1236 (M), 1652 (L).

KINGS CHOIR ..9-2§.. 9 ch.g. Kinglet — Singing Story (True Song) 63253235. Strong lengthy brother to Second Story. Dam, sister or half-sister to 5 Pointers, including Fixby's Song (qv '94 Annual), was placed in 4 Points for Mrs Prosser (had a bad temperament). Grandam, Fixby Story, won 2 Points and 3rd 3. P-t-P '97/9 r11 p3 (2 2nds, of 3 once); refused 1, unseated 1, and pulled up 3. In the money eight times, but still clinging desperately to his maiden status after 19 attempts and is crying out for strong handling. Came from out of the clouds twice in 2000 having been allowed to drop right out of contention and whilst he does nothing to help the rider a strong pilot would at least be able to galvanise him earlier. *Mrs R. Prosser — Atherstone (Sam Arthers).* 121 (OMa), 372 (CfMa), 433 (OMa), 786 (OMa), 906 (CfMa), 1010 (CfMa), 1125 (OMa), 1414 (M).

KING'S COURTIER (IRE) ..9-9.. 12 b.g. King's Ride — Glamorous Night (Sir Herbert) 3pp. Tall angular half-brother to Granville Grill (qv). NH FLAT '94 and '95 r3 p0. NH '95/7 r14 p1 (3rd in Ch); 6th, pulled up 1, and fell 1 in other Chses. P-t-P/HUNT CH '98/9 r7 w1 (Maiden) p3 (2nd once); fell 1, brought down 1. Pathetic under Rules, but won at the first time of asking in Points when Chasing The Bride was his nearest pursuer. Generally disappointing since and has not looked the stoutest of stayers, but pulled up after no more than two miles in his last two outings and seems wrong. Blinkered in the latest. *Sir Richard Hardy & C.L. Tizzard — Blackmore & Sparkford V. (Pauline Tizzard).* 657 (R), 958 (R), 1095 (R).

KINGS CUP ..7-8.. 11 b.g. Palm Track — Queens Cup (Kadir Cup) ff4. Small angular scrawny home-bred. Dam was last thrice, pulled up 10, fell/unseated 6, refused 2 and ran out in Points ('as useless now as she was on her debut, and has a kamikaze pilot'). P-t-P '99 r1 p0 (pulled up). Speedy, but excitable and becoming as adept at crash landing as his mother was. Led for a long way on his final outing and does actually possess some ability, but must calm down if he is to make something of it. *Mrs S. Morley — Staintondale.* 1004 (OMa), 1028 (R), 1234 (OMa).

KINGS LANE ..9-12.. 12 b.g. Majestic Streak — Gala Lane (Gala Performance USA) 4f6u2. Compact
unfurnished half-brother to Liffey Lane (*qv*), and to jumping winner, Coqui Lane. NH FLAT Spr '94
(for G.R. Dun) r3 p0. NH '96/9 r28 w2 (2m5f-3m4f Hdles, inc Amat Sell at 33-1) p7 (6 3rds, inc
5 Chses); broke blood vessel 1. A funny customer who has never been consistent, and is not an
easy ride, but only failed by a head to gain a first success for three years when Michael Dun
partnered him in his Members (five pounds overweight unfortunately proved to be a crucial factor
in his defeat). Can be remarkably clumsy for such an experienced campaigner. *J.M. Dun —
Lauderdale.* 110 (O), 419 (Cf), 717 (Cf), 916 (3m1fH), 1424 (M).

KING'S MANDATE (IRE) ..9-3.. 12 br.g. Mandalus — Shady Lucia (Pollerton) 24. Strong-topped half-
brother to Irish NH flat winner, Sheer Pleasure. Dam is half-sister to Strong Suspicion (*qv* '97
Annual). IRISH P-t-P '94 r1 p0 (pulled up). IRISH NH FLAT '95 r1 p0. IRISH NH '96 r7 p1 (3rd);
fell in both Chses. P-t-P '99 r3 p2 (2nd of 3, and 3rd of 4); and pulled up 1. Carrying too much
condition in '99, but looked spot on for his Ampton reappearance and travelled like the winner
throughout the final mile until flagging in the final 100 yards. Disappointed subsequently and was
not seen again, but would probably appreciate less of a stamina test and may still manage a
success at 12 if healthy. *J.S. Ruddy — Enfield Chace.* 87 (OMa), 239 (R).

KING'S RESPONSE (IRE) ..10-3.. 9 br.g. King's Ride — Kiltannon (Dalsaan) p. Workmanlike. IRISH
P-t-P '97 r1 p0 (pulled up). P-t-P '99 r4 w2 (Maiden and Restricted) p1 (2nd); and pulled up 1.
Turned two poor races into processions in '99 and looked a useful novice, but clearly very fragile
(missed '98 and pulled up and dismounted on his '99 reappearance) and only saw the racecourse
once this year when pulled up in a Wadebridge Intermediate. Led for 2m3f, but kept jumping
right-handed and even though second place was assured Pip Jones felt it prudent to pull him up.
An exuberant galloper who pulls hard, and it will be a great pity if his problems cannot be put
right. *D. Brace — Llangeinor.* 104 (I).

KINGSTHORPE ..10-0.. 13 ch.g. Brotherly (USA) — Miss Kewmill (Billion USA) 3u34p. Small light
brother to Brother Harold and Rising Sap. NH FLAT r1 p0 (pulled up). NH '92/4 r7 p0 (inc last,
pulled up 2, and fell 2; Sell final). P-t-P/HUNT CH '96/9 r21 w2 (inc 3m Hunt Ch) p4 (3 2nds);
pulled up 6, fell/unseated 2, and ran out 1. Flattered by a Hunter Chase success in '98, and has not
looked like winning in eight subsequent ventures. Usually struggles to stay three miles and his best
form has been on sound surfaces. Getting old and will find success even more harder to come by
in future. *M. Jones — Ledbury (Mike Daniell).* 667 (Cf), 890 (M), 1358 (Cf), 1463 (Cf), 1630 (Cf).

KINGS TOKEN ..9-8.. 11 b.g. Rakaposhi King — Pro-Token (Proverb) 2p3539upp5. Good-topped.
Dam, half-sister to Run Token (*qv* '96 Annual), won a Maiden and 3rd 3. P-t-P/HUNT CH '96/9 r25
w2 (Maiden and Members) p7 (4 3rds, last once; inc Hunt Ch); pulled up 7, and fell/unseated 2. NH
'00 (from J. Walton's) r2 p0 (pulled up in 2m4f110y Mdn Ch: *bhnd; outpcd frm 6, pu 12*; and 5th in
3m Nov Ch: *in tch, chfd 4 out, sn btn*). Has managed to win two minor races, but lacks consistency
and has a tendency to get left a long way behind. Made a valiant bid to make all at Alnwick on his
reappearance (as he had done when successful there in '99) but was fighting a losing battle from two
out and had to settle for second best. Will need some luck if he is to score in Restricted company,
but likely to play a prominent role in Hunt races again in 2001. *F.T. Walton — Border, & W. Percy
(Jimmy Walton).* 39 (M), 184 (R), 360 (R), 498 (R), 1162 (R), 1427 (R), 1501 (M), 1577 (R).

KING TORUS (IRE) ..10-11§.. 11 b.g. Torus — Kam A Dusk (Kambalda) 51612. Workmanlike
compact. IRISH P-t-P '95/6 r8 w1 (Adjacent) p3. NH '98/9 r3 p2 (3rds in 3m-3m1f HCap Chses).
P-t-P/HUNT CH '97/9 r17 w9 (inc 4 Hunt Chses, 2m5f-3m) p7 (4 2nds; and inc 4 Hunt Chses).
NH '00 r1 p0 (6th in 2m6f110y HCap Ch: *prom; ld 5-8, ld aft nxt til hdd 11, outpcd frm 4 out,
wknd 2 out*). Completed a seven-times '97/8, but a big disappointment when drawing a blank last
year, and looked decidedly unwilling to exert himself when hard work loomed. Bounced back to
form when front-running tactics were re-employed at Fontwell and Wincanton this year, but
reverted to his evil ways at Newton Abbot and downed tools when looking home and hosed.
Appreciates top-of-the-ground and speedy enough to be at home over sub-3m trips, but has to be
treated with extreme suspicion and is a very risky betting medium now. *N. Viney — Dulverton W.
(Victor Dartnall).* 384 (2m3f110yH), 681 (2m4fH), 1444 (2m5fH), 1600 (2m5f110yH).

KING TUDOR ..9-0.. 8 br.g. Lir — Veronica Ann (Henbit USA) up22p. Small neat owner-bred. Dam,
temperamental, won at 12f. P-t-P '98/9 r12 p0 (last pair 3, pulled up 7, and fell/unseated 2). Failed
to complete in his first nine attempts, but has improved and at least made the frame twice in 2000.
Not yet looking good enough to win however, and will need to search for a bad race in order to
get off the mark. *F.R. & Mrs S.L. Bown — Lamerton (Miss C. Bown).* 106 (OMa), 159 (CfMa), 538
(OMa), 721 (CfMa), 857 (CfMa).

KINLOGH GALE (IRE) ..9-4.. 13 b.g. Strong Gale — Kinlogh Maid (Random Shot) pppp56. Tall rangy
half-brother to Irish Pointing winner, Bucks Maid. Dam won an Irish Point. IRISH P-t-P '94 r2 p0
(pulled up 1, and unseated 1). NH '94, '95, '97 and '98 r16 p8 (2m6f-3m3f Chses). P-t-P/HUNT
CH '96/9 r13 w2 (Maiden and Restricted) p4 (2 2nds); pulled up 2, and fell 1. Won two minor

Points in '97, but has laboured badly in the current ownership and rarely completes now. Usually blinkered and has been tried in a tongue-strap. *D.H. Bennett — Beaufort.* 263 (I), 953 (I), 1098 (C), 1306 (C), 1550 (Cnr), 1651 (I).

KINNEFAD KING (IRE) ..10-5.. 10 b.g. King Luthier — Willie Pat (Pitpan) 111u12. Sturdy half-brother to Mighty Haggis and Scale Down (IRE). IRISH P-t-P '97 r6 p0 (last, pulled up 4, and fell 1). P-t-P '98/9 r12 w2 (Maiden and Restricted) p5 (4 2nds, beaten head once); pulled up 3, and unseated 1. A much improved horse since acquiring a tongue-strap and has forged a useful partnership with Christian Williams, but has his quirks (tried to duck out in appalling conditions at Pantyderi) and has to be produced as late as possible. Unlucky not to have gone through 2000 unbeaten as he was not quite dead and buried when unseating at St Hilary and failed to recover from another last fence blunder when beaten half a length by Mr Dow Jones on his final start. Good enough to have a crack at Hunter Chases, but whether he will like the bigger fences is another matter. *R.A. Jones — Glamorgan (Robert Williams).* 344 (I), 643 (Cf), 741 (Cf), 1051 (Cf), 1226 (O), 1296 (O).

KINSALE FLORALE (IRE) ..—§§.. 8 b.m. Supreme Leader — Glittering Steel (Golden Love) urpR. Neat half-sister to Oflaherty's Babe (IRE). IRISH P-t-P '98/9 r13 p0 (inc pulled up 5, refused 2, ran out 1, and left). P-t-P '99 r2 p1 (last of 3); and unseated 1. A particularly nasty piece of work. Would have won on her English debut but downed tools in a big way after jumping the last with a three length cushion and has shown minimum interest in proceedings since. Has ability and was leading when running out with a mile to cover on her final start, but thoroughly temperamental and has become liable to plant herself at the start. Often taken to post early, but shows no sign of reforming. *Miss J. Oakey — Worcs.* 1201 (2m4fOMa), 1277 (OMa), 1413 (OMa), 1526 (OMa).

KIRKHARLE (IRE) ..9-0.. 7 b.g. Commanche Run — Dardy Daughter (Side Track) 5. Close-coupled. Dam is half-sister to Festival Light (*qv* '99 Annual). P-t-P '99 r2 p2 (3rds). Shaped with encouragement as a five-year-old, but restricted to just one outing in 2000 and has obviously had his problems (his stable was stricken with a virus in '99). Young enough to atone when served with a clean bill of health. *I. Hamilton — Tynedale (Ann Hamilton).* 113 (OMa).

KISSAIR (IRE) ..10-6.. 10 b.g. Most Welcome — Salonniere (FR) (Bikala) 24. Compact sparely-made half-brother to Red River Rose and Braveheart. Dam won at 10f. 8000f, 16000y. FLAt (for G. Lewis) r16 w4 (10f) p1 (2nd). NH '95/7 and '99 (for N. Henderson; hat-trick previously for M. Pipe; blinkered 1) r16 w4 (3 Hdles, 2m-2m1f, and 2m2f Ch) p5. Won four races on the flat in '94 including a £6,072 prize, and added another £56,248 when sent jumping, with his finest hour being gained in the £36,098 Triumph Hurdle. Formerly able to front-run to good effect, but unpredictable, and has only scored once since Cheltenham '95, in a four-runner Bangor Chase in '99. Only able to make five appearances since March '97, but gave a splendid display when seven lengths second to Whatafellow in a fast run Open on his debut Point. Disappointing and eased next time, and vanished again. When on song he revels in mud. *Miss N.E.M. Atkinson — Bicester with Whaddon.* 294 (O), 545 (O).

KITES HARDWICKE ..9-11.. 14 b.g. Sunyboy — Kitty Stobling (Goldhill) 5p816p7. Strong-topped lengthy. Dam was short-headed in a Point. IRISH NH FLAT r7 p1 (2nd). IRISH P-t-P '92 r2 w1 (4&5yo Maiden) p0. IRISH NH '93/4 (blinkered 1) r12 p2 (3rds in Chses). P-t-P/HUNT CH '95/7 r18 w2 (Restricted and dead-heat for Club Ladies) p6 (4 2nds; 3rd of 4, and last of 3); failed to finish 6 (unseated 5). Stays well, and used to go a decent clip, but plods badly now under feeble handling (the regular rider spends more energy chewing gum than he does driving his mount along) and his latest success was in a bad slowly-run Open in a bog in which the odds-on jolly unseated after two miles. *P. Sheppard & Mrs C. Behrens — Grafton (Simon Gilmore).* 35 (Cnr), 93 (C), 191 (Cf), 430 (O), 750 (O), 1265 (O), 1532 (3m1fH).

KNAP HAND ..—.. 6 b.g. Nicholas Bill — Dealers Dream (Whistlefield) ppuRf. Good-bodied owner-bred half-brother to Folding (*qv*). Showed a hint of ability once, but looks a difficult ride, and it would be a good idea to get an experienced jockey to sort him out before he turns into a mini-Hitler. *D.V. Gardner — Silverton (Lucy Gardner).* 563 (CfMa), 857 (CfMa), 1391 (OMa), 1609 (OMa), 1675 (OMa).

KNIGHT OF PASSION ..11-0.. 9 b.g. Arctic Lord — Lovelek (Golden Love) 1f28. Small plain half-brother to Caribbean Dream. Dam, half-sister to Minstrels Joy (IRE) (*qv* '97 Annual), won 4 minor Points (maximum of 4 finishers) and placed 3 (inc an Irish Hdl). P-t-P/HUNT CH '97/9 r14 w7 (inc 3m1f Hunt Ch; and inc hat-trick '99) p2 (3rds, inc Hunt Ch); pulled up 2, and fell 1. Has done remarkably well for a diddy and has won his six of his last seven Points, but prone to blunders and ideally could have done with being an inch or two bigger. What he lacks in stature he makes up for in guts and ran the race of his life in the Cheltenham Foxhunters where he raced in the leading line until fading and blundering at the last. Sadly dismounted after the finish and was not seen out again. Loves to make the running and would remain invincible in Ladies races if he were able to return to them. Acts in soft. *R.K. Crabb — Cotley (Pauline Tizzard).* 9 (L), 156 (3mH), 299 (3m2f110yH), 584 (3m2f110yH).

KNOCKFIARNE MAGIC (IRE) ..9-2.. 9 b.g. Buzzards Bay — Daisy Star (Star Appeal) 3. Half-brother to NH flat and Hurdles winner, Northern Star. Dam is half-sister to Blakeneys Gift (*qv* '96 Annual). Not given a hard time after fading on his belated debut in a non-Rules runners Maiden, and could be worth trying again. *S.D. Williams — Cheshire (A. Williams).* 1318 (OMa).

KNOCK IT BACK (IRE) ..9-12.. 9 ch.g. Down The Hatch — Lady Hapsburg (Perhapsburg) fp. Tall angular brother to Kings Hatch, and half-brother to Irish Hurdles winner, Tom Kenny. IRISH P-t-P '97 r2 w1 (5yo&up Maiden) p1 (3rd). IRISH NH '97/8 r8 w1 (2m4f Hdle) p0; finished in all 3 Chses. P-t-P '99 r3 p2 (3rds, distant last after remounting once); and last. An excitable sort who pulls hard and seems unable to stay much beyond 2m4f. Pulled up quickly soon after halfway at Sandon on his most recent outing and has presumably suffered a setback. *Mrs M.R. Lea — Cheshire (Gary Hanmer).* 461 (2m4f110yH), 902 (Cf).

KNOCKNASHANE (IRE) ..—.. 11 b.g. Glow (USA) — Ashken (Artaius USA) rp. Compact. Dam won 2 9f races in Ireland. IRISH P-t-P '95 r1 p0 (fell). IRISH NH FLAT '96 r1 p0. Emerged from hibernation to manage two outings in eight days in March, but never looked like finishing in either, and is clearly useless. Amazingly, was sent off second favourite in the first of them. *D. Timmis — W. Salop.* 528 (OMa), 588 (OMa).

KNOCK STAR (IRE) ..9-7.. 10 gr.g. Celio Rufo — Star Of Monroe (Derring Rose) 221p6u5. Sturdy compact. IRISH P-t-P '95 r2 p0; pulled up 1. NH '97/9 (blinkered 2, often tongue-tied; for G. Charles-Jones; previously for C. Kellett; previously for T. Bill; previously for R. Champion) r23 p3 (inc 2nd of 20 and 3rd in Sells); remote 5th twice, pulled up 2 and fell in Chses. Bought Malvern, Oct for 1800. A very poor jumper who did not enjoy himself over Regulation fences, and made his final 16 appearances under Rules over Hurdles. Coped better in Points and often made the running, and lasted home at Kilworthy to give Simon Partridge (33) his first success. Has shown bits and pieces of form otherwise, and was one length ahead when he unseated two out in a Restricted, but was looking a sitting duck for Team Captain. Might unearth another lowly opportunity. *Miss E.A. Baverstock & S.G. Partridge — S. Devon (Simon Partridge).* 409 (OMa), 556 (M), 721 (CfMa), 1042 (R), 1376 (R), 1563 (R), 1639 (R).

KNOCKTHOMAS (IRE) ..10-5.. 12 gr.g. Good Thyne (USA) — Fortuity (Fortino II) f. Lengthy half-brother to Flying Shuttle (dam of Powder Monkey *qv* '96 Annual), to flat and Hurdles winner, Twice Lucky, and to Irish winners, Cutarue (flat) and Break The Bank (flat and Hurdles), also to Irish Hurdles winner, Forty One. Dam won 2 Irish Hurdles, 1m6f-2m2f. IRISH NH FLAT '95 r1 p0. IRISH NH '95/6 r8 w1 (3m Hdle) p0; 6th only Ch, previously pulled up with broken blood vessels in final 2 Hdles. P-t-P '98 r1 w1 (Open) p0. Won a modest three-finisher Open at Garnons on his Pointing debut in '98, but has never stood much racing and had been on the sidelines until reappearing at Whitwick this year. Had every chance when falling after two miles, but promptly disappeared again and is clearly a useful horse with myriad problems. *D. Pugh — Gelligaer F.* 334 (O).

KOATHARY (USA) ..9-11.. 10 b.g. Capote (USA) — Jeffo (USA) (Ridan) u44. Lengthy half-brother to 5 winners in USA, and to another in France. Dam won 3 races at up to 9f in USA. FLAT (wins for G. Cottrell, bought for 12,000; previously for M. Stoute) r27 w3 (8-9f) p4 (neck 2nd once — just caught). NH '97/9 (final run in Sell for K. Clutterbuck; previously for A. Harvey, bought for 20,000, sometimes blinkered) r15 p1 (18¼l 3rd on debut); pulled up 2 and unseated in Chses. A useful flat performer in '96 when he completed a hat-trick on firmish at Goodwood twice and at Sandown, but has been a consistent tail of woe since his attentions were turned to jumping. Looked as if he might finally going to achieve something when he moved menacingly per 2m4f in his last two Points, but compounded rapidly in both, and clearly does not get the trip. *H.R. Hobson — Puckeridge.* 756 (Cf), 842 (O), 936 (Cf).

KOPAIN ..8-9.. 11 b.g. Idiot's Delight — Saroan Meed (Midsummer Night II) fp33p. Workmanlike half-brother to Royal George (IRE). Dam won 2m2f Hdle. IRISH NH FLAT '95 and '97 r4 p1 (3rd). IRISH NH '96/7 r9 p1 (2nd in Hdle). NH '99 (for L. Wells) r1 p0. Sold Doncaster, June for 1300. Looked short of stamina when third in two Maidens (both runners-up are very old hands in that sphere), and seems to have recurring leg problems (missed '98, ran once in '99, and pulled up quickly and dismounted on his most recent attempt). *G. Richards — Ystrad Taf Fechan (David Gibbs).* 71 (OMa), 268 (CfMa), 490 (CfMa), 822 (CfMa), 951 (OMa).

KOTA TINGGI ..9-7.. 10 b.m. Tragic Role (USA) — Sea Siesta (Vaigly Great) 332. Sister to Hurdles winner, Theme Arena. P-t-P '99 r2 p1 (2nd); and pulled up 1. Survived countless errors when a fast-finishing second at Bitterley in her belated debut season, and has made the frame each time since, but does not seem to stay too well when ridden up with the pace. Jumped much better in 2000 and may yet pay a deserved visit to the winners enclosure. *Mrs C.A. Inglesant — Ludlow (Rupert Inglesant).* 1092 (OMa), 1196 (OMa), 1318 (OMa).

KRALINGEN ..9-13.. 9 ch.m. Move Off — Elitist (Keren) u46. Compact goose-rumped half-sister to Broken English (*qv*). FLAT r11 p0. NH '95/8 r22 w1 (3m Sell Hdle) p5 (inc 3rd beaten 23-27l in 2 Chses). P-t-P/HUNT CH '99 r4 p0 (4th, last pair 2, and pulled up 1). A confirmed front-runner who made all to spring a 33-1 surprise at Musselburgh in '98, but has since run up a sequence of 15 defeats. Not wholly disgraced in Ladies races this year, but still some way off winning one. May be best going right-handed. Has been tried in blinkers. *Miss T. Hammond — Border.* 621 (L), 806 (L), 1079 (L).

KRISTAL HAZE ..10-1.. 9 b.m. Krisinsky (USA) — Brilliant Haze VII (unknown) 32p317b1p3. Sturdy home-bred half-sister to Pearly Haze and Gypsy Haze. P-t-P '97/9 r22 w3 (Maiden, Restricted and PPORA Mares) p7 (4 3rds, of 4 twice); pulled up 9, and ran out 1. Has done well to register at least one success in each of her four Pointing campaigns, but lacks consistency and can jump sketchily though she has never fallen. Appeared not to stay when tried over 4m, but should be able to win again in minor company. Seems indifferent to ground conditions. Has been tried in blinkers. *P. & Mrs K. Dando — Pentyrch (Phil Dando).* 37 (CI), 344 (I), 600 (I), 741 (Cf), 837 (I), 1336 (2m4fH), 1450 (Cf), 1611 (M), 1614 (4mMO), 1657 (Cf).

KYARRA ..9-0.. 7 b.m. Northern State (USA) — Vocalist (Crooner) p2. Stocky. Dam, half-sister to Thornden (*qv* '92 Annual), won 3 flat, 5-8f, and performed creditably in 1000 Guineas and Irish 1000 Guineas. Presented with the opportunity of a lifetime in a Maiden at Hackwood which took 24 seconds longer than the other division, and made most of the running and looked in command when left four lengths clear at the last, but unfortunately connections had sent her to the races looking like a tub of lard, and she blew up and was just overhauled by a lame rival. *Mrs S.J. Coupe — Bicester with Whaddon.* 618 (CMa), 888 (OMa).

KYRE MOSS ..—§.. 6 ch.g. Le Moss — Lullaby Baby (Kind Of Hush) ppR. Plain rangy half-brother to Brooksong. Dam won 2 12f races (inc Sell) and 2m Sell Hdle. Bought Malvern, Oct for 700. NH FLAT Sept '99 (for P James) r1 p0 (fat, unable to raise a gallop after 6f, and soon well tailed off). Remarkably cumbersome, and is not remotely interested in racing. *Miss A.J. Morris — Ystrad Taf Fechan (Nick Jones).* 1055 (CfMa), 1399 (M), 1455 (OMa).

LABULA BAY ..10-0.. 7 b.g. Sula Bula — Lady Barunbe (Deep Run) 412. Tall. NH FLAT '98/9 r2 p0. NH '98/9 (for C. Popham, blinkered final) r3 p0 (last and pulled up 2 in Hdles). Bought Malvern, July for 2700. Invariably tailed off under Rules, but found Pointing easier, and readily won a Maiden at Charing in the slowest time of the day. Had nothing to beat, but his one length second in a Restricted nearly three months later was a creditable effort, and he might be able to do one better in that grade. *H.R. Cook — Staff College (Chris Elliott).* 30 (CMa), 132 (OMa), 1247 (R).

LADY ALICE ..9-4.. 7 b.m. Green Adventure (USA) — Anita's Choice (Shantung) p2224. Small half-sister to Flower Of Dunblane (*qv*). NH FLAT Spr '99 r2 p0. NH '99 (from Miss L. Russell's) r3 p0 (8th of 9 and pulled up 2 in Hdles). Was far too slow to keep up under Rules, but another to benefit from the huge plunge into Maidens, and has been reasonably consistent but a weak finisher. Only beaten half a length once, but was a disappointing favourite next time, and absent since early April. It might be an idea to try her over 2m4f when she returns. *Mrs J. Provan — Fife.* 46 (OMa), 112 (OMam), 364 (CfMa), 719 (CfMa), 977 (CfMa).

LADY BUCKLAND ..9-6.. 8 b.m. Gildoran — Four M's (Majestic Maharaj) pp4. Lengthy light. Dam, half-sister to 3 Pointers, won 2 2-finisher Points and 2nd. P-t-P '98/9 r4 w1 (Maiden) p1 (neck 2nd); unseated 1, and pulled up 1. Stuck on well to justify favouritism at Llanfrynach in '99, and only just beaten in her first Restricted, but does not stand her racing well and looked out of sorts in 2000 when consistently dropping out of contention after two miles. Worth another chance if she is able to return. *N.B. Jones — Llangibby (Tim Jones).* 6 (R), 69 (R), 273 (R).

LADY CLIFFORD ..—.. 7 b.m. Rolfe (USA) — Come On Clover (Oats) pf. Compact unfurnished owner-bred half-sister to Buckaroo (*qv*). All dressed up with no where to go when Brampton Bryan was abandoned on her intended debut (had been at the course waiting for about six hours!), but showed a tiny trace of ability before tailing off and pulling up at Bonvilston. *J. Bowen — S. Herefords (Michael Hammond).* 1617 (OMa), 1676 (OMa).

LADY DOT (IRE) ..9-11.. 8 ch.m. Mister Lord (USA) — Anvil Chorus (Levanter) u2s. Sister to Kilfinny Cross (IRE), and half-brother to Chasing winners, Act In Time (IRE) and Victory Anthem. P-t-P '99 r3 w1 (Maiden) p0; unseated 1, and pulled up 1. Made most to score unchallenged at Eyton last year, but set far too much to do when second to a subsequent Hunter Chase winner on a return visit this year, though she was flattered by the winning margin. Has failed to complete otherwise, but should gain compensation in a Restricted. *K.J. Mitchell — N. Salop (Sheila Crow).* 963 (R), 1200 (CR), 1322 (R).

LADY EMERALD ..10-4.. 11 ch.m. St Columbus — Lucky Diamond (Eborneezer) 6363pf. Lengthy Goodwin-bred sister to Miss Solitaire and Dromain. Dam was placed thrice in 11 Points. Grandam, Lady Barbara II, failed to finish in 3 Points. P-t-P '98/9 r6 w1 (Maiden) p2 (2nds); pulled up 1, and fell 2. Won a modest 18-runner Maiden on firmish at Ashorne in '98, but has so far failed to add to her account despite some fair efforts. Twice beaten less than a length the following season, but took a while to find her form in 2000 and reserved her best effort when tried in a Ladies race for the first time on her final start. Would have finished a good second to Mr Custard but for tipping up at the last and deserves some form of compensation though her fencing still needs tidying up. *Mrs M. Goodwin & G.B. Tarry — Grafton (Jimmy Tarry).* 248 (R), 791 (R), 1146 (R), 1482 (R), 1623 (R), 1665 (L).

LADY GOODWIN ..—.. 7 b.m. Baron Blakeney — Servalan (Souvran) p. Light-framed owner-bred sister to Larry (*qv*). novicey in last until she pulled up after two miles on a May debut. *R.H. York — Staff College.* 1393 (R).

LADY KILTON ..9-5.. 11 b.m. Welsh Captain — Kilton Jill (Adropejo) p5f. Compact home-bred half-sister to Lord Kilton (*qv*). P-t-P '97/9 r8 w1 (Maiden) p0 (last pair 2, pulled up 4, and unseated 1). Stumbled across a bad Maiden at Dunthrop in '99, but predictably struggling in Restricteds since including when favourite next time and when the subject of market support on her final outing this year. Even her staunchest supporters will concede that she is only very moderate. Absent since March and may have hurt herself in her spill. *Mrs D. Cowley — Pytchley.* 196 (R), 336 (R), 429 (C).

LADYLANDS ..9-8.. 8 b.m. Lord Bud — Pretty Lass (Workboy) 216p6. Compact half-sister to Father's Gift, Ledburian and Newton Wold. Dam won 2 Chses, 2-3m. NH '97 r2 p0 (pulled up 2). P-t-P '99 r6 p2 (last of 3 once); last pair 2, and pulled up 2. Placed in three Maidens over the full trip before she won one over 2m4f, and has improved, but already finding life hard in Restricteds and running her in a Hunter Chase was pure fantasy. Often makes the running, but does not seem the stoutest of stayers and less forcing tactics might help. *Mrs S.E. Raw — S. Durham (Colin Taylor).* 695 (OMa), 909 (2m4fOMa), 1028 (R), 1154 (3m2fH), 1475 (R).

LADY LIR ..9-11.. 12 ch.m. Lir — Kimberley Ann (St Columbus) 4f. Very small neat Young-bred sister to The Kimbler (*qv*). NH FLAT r3 p0. NH '94/5 r5 p0 (inc last pair twice, and pulled up 1). P-t-P/HUNT CH '96/9 r25 w2 (Maiden and 4m Ladies) p5 (3 2nds, inc Hunt Ch); pulled up 12, and fell 1. Beaten 17 times after losing her maiden status until winning a four-mile Ladies race at Flete Park last year, and has always lacked consistency, but frequently overfaced and clearly appreciated the severe test of stamina. Presumably incapacitated by her fall at Lemalla this year as she failed to reappear. *M.D. Rusden — E. Cornwall.* 201 (L), 314 (L).

LADY MANA MOU (IRE) ..—.. 8 b.m. Heavenly Manna — Lady Mordred (Sir Mordred) pf. Dam is half-sister to The Parish Pump (*qv*). IRISH P-t-P '98 r2 p0; pulled up 1. Sold Doncaster, Aug '98 for 2100. Went a maximum of two miles when a long shot in Maidens. *Mrs J. Hughes — Cranwell Bloodhounds.* 872 (OMa), 1070 (2m4fOMa).

LADY MURRHILL (IRE) ..8-0.. 6 b.m. King Luthier — Tuney Lady (Boreen FR) f44f. Compact. Dam is half-sister to Staigue Fort (*qv*). Sold Tattersalls Ireland Aug '98 for 391. A remote last in both completions, including when remounting after unseating at the final obstacle when a fence behind. Needs an intensive course of schooling before she reappears. *F.G. Murray — Pembs (Graham Lavis).* 1222 (2m4fOMa), 1302 (OMa), 1617 (OMa), 1660 (OMa).

LADY NEVADA (IRE) ..9-4.. 8 ch.m. Mister Lord (USA) — Nevada Lady (Trimmingham) 5p4f1. Half-sister to Maltese Cross (IRE) (*qv*). Lengthy half-sister to Maltese Cross and Teme Willow. IRISH P-t-P '99 r6 p3; pulled up, fell and unseated. Useless in four attempts for Sarah Hopkins (tailed off when completing), but instantly profited from the acquisition of Simon Prior on final start, and won a bad Maiden taking 7min49s in heavy at Sandon. Looked very backward in early season. Will need to find more for Restricteds, even when strongly handled. *L.A.E. Hopkins — W. Salop (Gordie Edwards).* 180 (2m4fOMa), 298 (CfMa), 570 (2m4fOMa), 906 (CfMa), 1125 (CfMa).

LADY OF VERSE ..7-12§.. 9 b.m. Lord Bud — The Rymer Girl (Rymer) fp5pp. Half-sister to Henrys Song (*qv*). P-t-P '98/9 r7 p1 (last of 3); last, ran out 2, and pulled up 3. Consistently dreadful and has yet to beat a rival in 12 Points. A poor jumper, and fell heavily when tried in blinkers. *B. Neaves — W. Street/Tickham.* 131 (OMa), 289 (Cm), 571 (M), 828 (OMa), 1397 (OMa).

LADY PALAMON (IRE) ..8-0.. 7 b br.m. Montelimar (USA) — Actress Mandy (IRE) (Mandalus) 37p. Lengthy sister to Irish Pointing winner, Oh Me Oh Moigh. IR 6000 4-y-o. NH FLAT Jan '99 r1 p0. NH '99 (for P. Eccles) r1 p0 (pulled up in Hdle). Sold Ascot, May for 1200. Very poor to date, and the best she has achieved is a 25 length third (tired quickly in the final half-mile). *R. Perkins — Tredegar F.* 487 (CfMa), 602 (CfMa), 1405 (OMa).

LADY PING ..—.. 8 ch.m. Crested Lark — Chess Queen (Cisto FR) p. Small. Dam, owner-bred, was last twice, pulled up 3, and fell/unseated 3 in Points ('soon gets tailed off, and is a gormless jumper' — ran until '95). P-t-P '99 r2 p0 (pulled up 2). Error-prone, has pulled up in all three attempts to date, and only went two miles in the latest. Has inherited all of mums least endearing qualities. *H.M. Shakespeare — Monmouths.* 989 (OMa).

LADY'S PET ..—.. 10 b.g. Tina's Pet — Northern Lady (The Brianstan) p. Workmanlike half-brother to Jock (*qv*). NH FLAT '97 (for Miss S. Williamson) r1 p0. Glimpsed briefly at Eyton, where he pulled up after two miles when tailed off. *T. Walker — Holcombe.* 1197 (OMa).

LA EMNI (IRE) ..9-6.. 10 b.g. Supreme Leader — Shuil Alainn (Levanter) pu14p. Very tall half-brother to 6 winners in Ireland, incuding 3 Points (one also a successful Chaser). Dam won NH flat and

2m Hdle in Ireland (also won 2m5f Hdle, but disqualified). IRISH P-t-p '97 r3 p0; pulled up 1. Sold Doncaster, Aug '97 for 800. Gave mother a seventh individual winner when finishing alone for Steve Charlton in his Members, but was lucky, as Pause For Thought thought to pause at the final fence when two lengths clear and fell fatally. Slow otherwise, and did not get on well with the owner in their two attempts together. *M.B. Mawhinney — Bilsdale*. 1032 (OMa), 1234 (OMa), 1347 (M), 1475 (R), 1577 (R).

LA KABYLE (FR) ..9-12.. 7 b.m. Bikala — La Psalette (Kashmir II) 783314. Lengthy half-sister to Pointing winner, Mad Princess, and to flat winner, Mister Mat (sire of Mister Banjo). FRENCH FLAT '97/8 r4 p0. FRENCH NH '97/8 r10 w3 (2 Hdles, 2m-2m1f110y and 2m1f110y Ch; all claimers at Enghein). Extremely hot-headed and finds it difficult to get the trip because she pulls so hard, but finished a creditable third in a Confined, and settled her best yet for Adrian Wintle when scoring in similar company at Garnons. Prone to errors, and probably best on top of the ground. Absorbed the foal from her first pregnancy, and was due to visit Classic Cliche after the season. *Mrs S. Knipe — S. Herefords (Robin Knipe)*. 32 (MO), 178 (Cm), 333 (Cf), 445 (Cf), 667 (Cf), 920 (3mH).

LAKEFIELD RAMBLER (IRE) ..11-5.. 9 b.g. Lafontaine (USA) — Debonair Dolly (Cidrax FR) 114113. Big strong half-brother to Irish Pointing winners, Lakefield Leader (subsequent successful English Hurdler) and Popeye The Guy. Dam won 2 Irish NH flat. IRISH P-t-P '97 r1 p1 (last of 3). IRISH NH '97/8 r5 p0 (inc 13th of 14 and fell in Chses). P-t-P '99 r5 w3 (Maiden, Restricted and Intermediate) p1 (3rd of 4); and unseated 1. Ended '99 in excellent fettle, but improved again this season and now has the strength to match his frame. Made his Hunter Chase debut in the showpiece at Cheltenham, and led the field until coming down the hill for the final time, but still had every chance jumping the last and was only four and a half lengths adrift of the winner at the line. A tenacious front-runner who can maintain a blistering gallop, but can be too bold for his own good at the fences and was lucky to get away with a plethora of errors when successful on a return trip to Prestbury Park. Disappointed when favourite for the John Corbet subsequently, but it may have been a case of one race too many and he looks sure to take plenty of pegging back in the future. Bravely and skilfully ridden by Polly Gundry, who sits his mistakes well. A class act and handles any going. *A.J. Powell — Beaufort (Richard Barber)*. 161 (L), 314 (L), 584 (3m2f110yH), 924 (3m1fH), 1340 (3m1f110yH), 1646 (3m4fH).

LAKE MISSION ..10-0.. 16 b.g. Blakeney — Missed Blessing (So Blessed) 27. Smallish compact robust half-brother to 4 flat winners, including Unblest (smart; also sire). Dam won 2 flat, 6-8f (was useful). FLAT r6 w1 (12f) p1 (3rd). NH '89/96 r34 w6 (2m Hdle, and 5 Chses, 2m4f-2m5f) p9 (beaten a head twice, including by Panto Prince in £7616 race, after hanging left). P-t-P '97/8 (for Mr C.T. Nash) r7 w2 (inc Ladies) p5 (3 2nds). A smart sub-3m Chaser in his prime and has done remarkably well to glean eight prizes in Points, particularly as he is rather fragile. Returned from a twelve month absence to finish an honourable second to Rip Van Winkle at Dunthrop, but missed the frame for the first time in Points when tailed off last at Newton Bromswold and his career spanning 11 years may have run its course. *Mrs A. Jefferis — Bicester with Whaddon*. 192 (L), 512 (L).

LAKE OF LOUGHREA (IRE) ..9-12§.. 11 ch.g. Kings Lake (USA) — Polynesian Charm (USA) (What A Pleasure USA) 3444. Good-topped lengthy half-brothr to 9 flat winners (4 in USA), including August (also a successful Hurdler) and Koraloona. IRISH FLAT r19 w3 (12-14f, one at Laytown) p2 (2nds). IRISH P-t-P '93/4 r11 w2 (2m1f-2m4f Hdles) p3 (2nds, beaten head once). NH '95/9 (for J. Mackie; wins previously for K. Bailey, bought for 17,000) r34 w3 (2m-2m4f Chses) p10 (inc 2nd in 2 Sell Hdles, short-headed once; also beaten head once). Bought Ascot, July for 3100. Notched eight wins on a beach or good or firm ground in his youth, but has become most exasperating, and beaten in all 28 attempts since his last success in May '96. Maddeningly, he has made the frame in 19, but often temperamental, and can be error-prone. Given a succession of awful rides by the Southern version of Noel Wilson in Points — immediately lost touch and made no attempt to close when 45 lengths last of three; sent in to a clear lead and galloped into the ground when he should have held a favourite's chance in his Members; and fined £50 for misuse of the whip. *N. Wilson — Hampshire (Chris Goulding)*. 678 (O), 882 (W), 1246 (Cf), 1541 (2m5fH).

LAKESIDE LAD ..10-2.. 9 b.g. St Columbus — Beyond The Trimm (Trimmingham) puf33u4p. Tall. NH FLAT r1 p0. NH '96 r1 p0 (Nov Sell Hdle — unruly and kicked stablemate at start, and refused to race). P-t-P/HUNT CH '97/9 (for Mr A. Wright) r11 w1 (Maiden) p3 (2 2nds, inc Hunt Ch); pulled up 1, brought down 1, and fell/unseated 3. NH '99 (for T. Wall) r3 p3 (2 2nds, 3m-3m2f Chses). NH Mar '00 r1 p0 (fell in R.A. Gold Cup: *chsd wnr, wknd 12, 5th when fell last*). Won his Maiden at Bitterley in '98 and has since plied his trade almost exclusively over regulation fences. Gave two respectable displays when third twice to Grimley Gale at Ludlow in April, but would surely benefit from a switch back to Pointing where there is still eligible for Restricteds. Can be hard to sit on, and has been tried in blinkers. *R.D. Griffiths — Kyre (Steve Griffiths)*. 303 (3mH), 580 (3mH), 920 (3mH), 1023 (3mH), 1343 (3m110yH), 1533 (3m1fH), 1646 (3m4fH).

LA MAJA (IRE) ..9-7§.. 12 b.m. Lafontaine (USA) — Eiger Sanctions (St Alphage) pupu. Smallish compact sister to Irish/Hong Kong flat winner, Tax Plan, and half-sister to an Irish flat winner. IRISH FLAT '93 r2 p0. IRISH NH FLAT '93/5 r6 p0. IRISH NH '95 r1 p0. IRISH P-t-P '96 r6 w1 (mares Maiden) p2; pulled up 1, and fell 2. P-t-P/HUNT CH '97/8 (for Mrs N.C. Wilson) r10 p1 (2nd in Hunt Ch); last 2, fell/unseated 2, refused 1, and pulled up 2. A hard and unrewarding ride even before she went wrong in February '98, and unchanged on her return in 2000. Only once better than last in her ten most recent attempts and has become very error-prone. *Miss J.E. Foster — Pendle Forest & Craven.* 1028 (R), 1152 (I), 1328 (L), 1478 (I).

LA MON DERE (IRE) ..9-9§.. 10 b.g. Lafontaine (USA) — Brown Foam (Horage) pp43. Rangy brother to Sarenacare (IRE). IRISH P-t-P '96 r6 w1 p2 (2nds); pulled up 2. NH '97 r4 p0 (8th of 9 and last in Hdles, and 2 fences last and pulled up in Chses — pulled off all 4). P-t-P '98/9 r7 w1 (Intermediate) p1 (2nd); last 2, and unseated 1. All out when capturing an Intermediate in '98, but most disappointing since and looks thoroughly ungenuine. Has only beaten three rivals home in his last eight starts and has performed with an equal lack of enthusiasm in headgear. Acquired a tongue-strap on his last three appearances. *J. Mahon & A. Knight — Croome & W. Warwicks (Jim Mahon).* 191 (Cf), 749 (Cf), 1016 (Cf), 1354 (Mo).

LANCASHIRE LEGEND ..—.. 8 gr.g. Belfort (FR) — Peters Pet Girl (Norwick USA) f. Workmanlike brother to flat winner, A Million Watts. 4200f, 10,000y. FLAT '99 (for M. Brisbourne; previously for N. Littmoden; previously for J.A. Harris; won previously for S. Dow; tried in headgear) r51 w1 (7f) p10; inc Sells. Bought Malvern, Oct for 600. A busy body who has done best on all-weather surfaces, but gained his only success on equitrack in '96. Had a tendency to carry his head high and sometimes found little. Soon departed when making an unimpressive start to his new career. *Mrs E. Coombes — N. Ledbury (Mike Bevan).* 895 (MO).

LANCASTER BOY (IRE) ..9-4.. 10 b.g. Lancastrian — Solar Sky (Mandalus) ppp3. Very tall angular half-brother to NH flat winner, Passing Cloud (IRE). P-t-P '99 r2 p0 (pulled up 2). Can go a good clip for about 2m4f, but beaten 27 lengths when third on his only completion at Marks Tey and simply does not stay. May have a physical defect as he stops with such rapidity. *Mrs M.J. Thorogood — Essex (Chris Thorogood).* 322 (CfMa), 551 (OMa), 760 (OMa), 942 (CfMa).

LANKRIDGE ..10-9.. 11 b.g. Alzao (USA) — Free Dance (FR) (Green Dancer USA) 2. Small close-coupled attractive half-brother to 5 flat winners, including Freestone (also a successful Hurdler) and Free Mover. Dam won 2 9f races in France. FLAT r10 p1 (3rd). NH '96 r4 w2 (2m-2m2f Hdles) p1 (3rd). P-t-P '98/9 r3 w2 (Open and Mixed Open) p0. Given to the Shaws after developing leg trouble, and nursed back to fitness to win two Opens at Holnicote '98/9. Made his Hunter Chase debut at Exeter this term and ran well, though no match for the winner, but was promptly put back into his cotton wool wrapping for another year. Connections find themselves in a catch 22 situation as he requires firmish ground, but his fragile legs cannot take much strain, hence his infrequent appearances. Always looks magnificent in the paddock and has sent the Master of The Chase into a state of ecstasy in the past — if riding a National winner does it for Mick Fitzgerald just looking at Lankridge does it for our Tel. Tried blinkered over Hurdles and visored in his first Point. *P. & Mrs F. Shaw — Cattistock.* 680 (3m1fH).

LARDANTE (IRE) ..9-3.. 8 b br.g. Phardante (FR) — Larry's Law (IRE) (Law Society USA) 624. IRISH P-t-P '99 r2 p0 (pulled up 2). Had no chance with the easy winner when eight lengths second at Witton Castle, where he was backed from 16-1 to 3-1, and performed poorly when about 15 lengths last on firm next time. Moderate to date. *Miss A. Stephenson — V. of Lune H.* 1153 (OMa), 1331 (OMa), 1500 (OMa).

LA RIVIERA (IRE) ..10-9.. 9 ch.g. Over The River (FR) — La Gloriosa (Ardross) 1211. Good-bodied half-brother to Irish NH flat and Hurdles winner, Princess Gloria (IRE). NH '96/9 (from A. Charlton's) r16 w2 (2m1f-2m3f Chses) p3 (inc 3rd in Hdle). Only averages four outings a year, but proved a useful recruit to Ladies Opens, and only Balisteros was able to beat him. Had earlier defeated that doubty rival on the same course (Alnwick) where he came from too far back, and subsequently showed a good turn of foot to twice go clear of Japodene on the run-in. Would surely have strong claims in a Hunter chase. *J. Hogg — N. Tyne (Pauline Robson).* 41 (L), 185 (L), 621 (L), 1328 (L).

LARKIN ABOUT ..—.. 6 ch.g. Crested Lark — Auntie Dora (Idiot's Delight) p. Dam is sister to Bit Of An Idiot (qv). Bought Malvern, July for 5000. Looked to be going well when he pulled up lame at the 11th on an unfortunate debut. *G. Treglown (Larkin Lads Partnership) — N. Ledbury (Teresa Spearing).* 1091 (OMa).

LARKSHILL (IRE) ..9-5.. 10 b.g. Phardante (FR) — Fairy Hollow (Furry Glen) p4p4. Lengthy brother to The Hollow (IRE) (qv). NH FLAT Nov '96 r2 p0. NH '96/9 (for J. Fitzgerald; tongue-tied) r17 w1 (2m5f Sell Hdle, only such, 25-1) p1 (2nd); poor Chser (mistakes; ran out 1). Bought Doncaster, May for 1500. Hopelessly outclassed in Opens. Wore a tongue-strap in the first of them, and it was declared and not fitted next time, when he finished last after breaking a blood vessel. *T.H.J. Bannister - Pendle Forest & Craven (Christine Billington).* 691 (O), 814 (O), 1151 (O), 1476 (O).

LARRY ..9-8.. 6 b.g. Baron Blakeney — Servalan (Souvran) f5234. Unfurnished brother to Lady Goodwin, and half-brother to Psamead and Valander. Dam pulled up in 2 Points for Ray York, but grandam, Goodwin Lady, won 3 Points at Tweseldown for him. NH FLAT Spr '99 r2 p0. NH '99 r1 p0 (pulled up in Hdle). Short-headed by the only other finisher at Parham, but a disappointing favourite twice subsequently. Performed fairly well for a five-year-old, and that overdue success should not be too long in coming. *R.H. York — Staff College.* 60 (OMa), 457 (OMa), 709 (OMa), 984 (OMa), 1397 (OMa).

PLATE 71   457 Staff College & RMA Sandhurst Draghounds Open Maiden (Div 2): L to R at the first, Stormhill Warrior (R. Emmett), 6th, Summer Pudding (J. Young), pu, Summer Haven (F. Brennan), 2nd, Larry (P. York), 5th, and Paul (Miss L. Collins), 4th   PHOTO: Tim Holt

LARRY THE LAMB ..9-12.. 16 ch.g. St Columbus — Florence Eliza (Floriana) 2255. Very small light-framed half-brother to Sporting Lark, Lily The Lark, Lottie The Lotus and Lennie The Lord. Grandam, Estoile, was placed in 4 Hunt Chses and 3 Points. P-t-P '92/9 (for Mrs G. D'Angibau) r44 w12 (inc Mixed Open, and 6 Ladies; inc hat-trick '96) p22 (16 2nds, last once); fell/unseated 7, slipped up 1. An admirably consistent performer over nine consecutive seasons (it could be as many as 11, but the Tarry home-breds usually spend their formative years dossing about in the field) and 39 completions include 12 wins and 24 placings. Declining steadily, but remains lion-hearted and provided Victoria Hayter with some much needed experience. *Miss V.E. Hayter — Suffolk (Ruth Hayter).* 841 (L), 1113 (L), 1380 (L), 1483 (L).

LAST GAMBLE ..—.. 9 b.g. Deltic (USA) — Rare Game (Raise You Ten) ppp. Stocky compact half-brother to Arnold's Hill, New Game, All The Trumps, Bright Lady, Silver Game and Silver Hill. Dam was pulled up in 2 Points for Mervyn Fear. P-t-P '99 r2 p0 (unseated 1, and pulled up 1). Has shown some speed to halfway, but still carrying plenty of condition on his final start in 2000 and has never been fully fit. Has already developed a tendency to jump right-handed. *R.M. Fear — Avon V.* 329 (CfMa), 471 (OMa), 889 (OMa).

LASTOFTHE LITTLES ..—.. 9 b.g. Lighter — Little Nun (Crozier) up. Big strong half-brother to Hills Little One. Dam was unplaced in 5 Points (the final for Clive Hitchings), but is half-sister to 5 Pointers (4 winners), including Little Bilsham and Little Battle. Grandam, Little Burger, won 4 Points and placed 14. P-t-P '97 and '99 r4 p0 (pulled up 2, unseated 2). Has displayed a modicum of ability, but never runs much, has yet to finish and is rather too big for his own good. *C.J. Hitchings — Kyre.* 341 (CfMa), 618 (CMa).

LAST OPTION ..11-11.. 9 br.g. Primitive Rising (USA) — Saint Motunde (Tyrant USA) 1f2.33. Stocky compact half-brother to 2 flat winners, including Saint Navarro, and to Hurdles winner, Lord Of

The Land. Dam won 6 flat, 6-8f, inc 4-timer at 8. NH '99 r1 p1 (2nd in 3m HCap Ch). P-t-P/HUNT CH '97/9 r18 w8 (inc 4 Hunt Chses, 3m1f-3m4f; inc hat-trick '98) p6 (4 2nds; and inc 4 Hunt Chses); last, fell/unseated 2, ran out 1, and pulled up 1. IRISH NH '00 r1 p1 (dist 3rd to Sheltering in Cox's Cash & Carry Champion HC at Punchestown: *mid-div, 7th ½way, rem 4th & rdn 2 out, kpt on u.p*). A top class Hunter Chaser and emerged with great credit after going in search of the top prizes in '99 (third in the Cheltenham Foxhunters and runner-up in the Horse & Hound Cup). Did not reappear until April in 2000 so Cheltenham was off the agenda, and bit the dust at the first in the Liverpool Foxhunters, but posted another good effort in the Horse & Hound Cup when third to Castle Mane and Grimley Gale on his final appearance. Possesses speed and stamina, but not always fluent and seemed more error-prone than usual this term. Kept to ground close to good and appears not to like it too soft. Usually takes the eye in the paddock. Should be winning on a more regular basis if he can manage a full campaign in 2001. *R. Tate — Bilsdale*. 802 (2m6fH), 921 (2m6fH), 1024 (3m3f110yH), 1647 (3m4fH).

LATE ENCOUNTER ..10-2.. 10 ch.g. Ra Nova — Kadelian (Rustingo) 2ppupp. Tall. Dam won 2m Hdle. NH FLAT '96 r2 p0. NH '96/7 and '98/9 r12 w1 (2m6f HCap Hdle) p2 (inc 2nd in HCap Ch); also withdrawn once. P-t-P/HUNT CH '98 r10 w3 (inc 2m3f Hunt Ch) p4 (3rds, of 4 twice, and inc 2 Hunt Chses); fell 2, and refused 1. Reverted to hurdling after landing a Hereford Hunter Chase in '98, and made most to win a 2m6f event at Newton Abbot later in the year. Ran well when chasing home Bells Life at Bangor on his reappearance, but things went rapidly downhill after and he never went a yard in five subsequent outings. Blinkers brought no improvement once, and must be shunned until he shows more vigour. Withdrawn at the start once in '99 as he was found to have bled on the way to post and it is possible that he has been afflicted again. *S.R. Brown — Monmouths*. 153 (2m4f110yH), 382 (2m4fH), 581 (3mH), 742 (O), 1026 (2m5f110yH), 1600 (2m5f110yH).

LATEST THYNE (IRE) ..9-4§.. 11 br.g. Good Thyne (USA) — I'm The Latest (Polyfoto) p0pp. Workmanlike half-brother to Haughton Lad (IRE) (*qv*). IRISH NH FLAT '94 r3 p2 (2nds). NH '95/7 r8 w1 (2m5f Ch) p1 (3rd in Hdle). P-t-P '99 (for Mr M.P. Wiggin) r6 p3 (last of 2; and 3 2nds, of 4 once); fell/unseated 2, and refused 1. Won on his final start under Rules in '97, but has been a big disappointment in Points and looks to have a major problem. Managed three placings in '99, but did not look keen in any of them and only able to complete once this year. Struggles to stay three miles in any case and is best left well alone. Blinkered once in '99, and tried in a visor on one occasion in 2000. *C.R. Elliot & R.J. Brereton — Ludlow (Geoff Evans)*. 895 (MO), 1086 (Cf), 1199 (L), 1338 (4m1fH).

LA TORMENTA (IRE) ..9-3.. 8 b.m. Glacial Storm (USA) — Green Gale (Strong Gale) 5up2. Small light-framed hobdayed half-sister to Live Wire (IRE). P-t-P '98/9 r5 p1 (pulled up 3, and ran out 1. NH '99 (from Miss D. Cole's) r6 p0 (6th, pulled up 4, and fell 1; inc 2 Chses). Has made much of the running when second twice, and only beaten a half lengths in the latest, but the form amounts to little and she has been constantly hampered by wind problems (was tubed as a five-year-old). Deserves a small success, but poor opposition, firmish ground and an easy track will be essential requirements. *Mrs M. Cook — Dulverton E*. 146 (OMa), 540 (OMa), 956 (OMa), 1391 (OMa).

LA TOSCA ..—.. 7 b.m. Teenoso (USA) — Rostra (Legal Eagle) p. Half-sister to Suny Rose. Dam, half-sister to Blessed Oliver (*qv*), won 2 2m Hdles, and 7 Chses, 2m-2m4f. Not on song for a March debut. *W. Wood — Heythrop (Jon Trice-Rolph)*. 754 (CfMa).

LATZIO ..—.. 8 b.m. Arrasas (USA) — Remould (Reform) fp. Small half-sister to 4 flat winners (3 abroad). Dam won at 5f. FLAT (for B. Pearce to 3, tried blinkers) r13 p2 (3rds at 5-12f, of 4 beaten 25 *l* in latter, and beaten 1¼ *l* in Sell previously). Looked a useless non-stayer when going less than two miles twice. Gets on her toes and has two paddock handlers, and wears a cross-noseband and pulls hard. *N. Smith — Oxford (Di Grissell)*. 785 (I), 1147 (OMa).

LAUDATION (IRE) ..8-5.. 9 ch.g. Bold Arrangement — Hooray Lady (Ahonoora) 5. Rangy smallish. Dam won 6 8f races. FLAT r4 p0. NH '95 r1 p0 (last — not jump well and badly tailed off). P-t-P '97 (Hamer-trained for Mr R.A. Mason) and '98 r9 p3 (2nds of 3, remote twice); and pulled up 6. Capitulated after jumping the second last in front at Erw Lon this season and was eventually beaten more than the length of the run-in. Missed the '99 season and clearly hard to train these days, but very modest and racegoers are not missing much. *R.J. Hamer — Llangeinor*. 650 (CfMa).

LAUGHING FONTAINE (IRE) ..9-10.. 11 b.g. Lafontaine (USA) — Graig Island (Furry Glen) p4pup. Smallish lengthy. IRISH NH FLAT '96 r15 r1 p0 (pulled up). IRISH NH '96 r3 p0. NH '96/9 (been tongue-tied; won for K. Bailey; previously for F. Murphy) r16 w1 (3m Ch, 4 ran) p1 (2nd in Hdle); banned for 30 days under non-triers Rule on final start for Ferdy Murphy. Sold Doncaster, May for 1700, and resold there in Aug for 500. Broke a fetlock and destroyed at High Easter. Was 15 lengths last on the only occasion he managed to complete in a Point. *Miss K. Thory & Mrs M. Hoffman — Fitzwilliam (Katie Thory)*. 19 (L), 28 (L), 368 (L), 442 (L), 608 (L).

LAURAS CONQUEST ..8-0.. 9 b.g. El Conquistador — Laura's Dream (Royal Blend) pp4. Tall brother to Elly's Dream. Very soundly beaten to date, and was 36 lengths fourth when completing. *S. Hicks & Mrs I.R. Cook — Pembs (E.W. Morris).* 831 (M), 1616 (R), 1662 (OMa).

LAUREL SEEKER (USA) ..9-7.. 7 b.g. Mining (USA) — L'On Vite (USA) (Secretariat USA) 3p4. Small neat half-brother to a winner abroad. $42,000y, 10,000 2-y-o. FLAT r7 w1 (12f, equitrack) p1 (3rd). NH '97/9 (from P. Hobbs', bought for 3400, blinkered 2, tongue-tied; pulled up debut for Mrs A. Perrett) r12 w1 (2m1f Hdle) p6 (5 2nds); poor 5th in only Ch. Faced tough tasks in Opens, in which he is probably struggling to get the trip. Sometimes profuses. If he did manage to stay he might be better suited by Ladies company. *J. Tudor — Llangeinor.* 945 (O), 1296 (O), 1402 (MO).

LAUREN'S LAD ..—.. 6 ch.g. Tachyon Park — Glory Isle (Hittite Glory) ppp. Sturdy half-brother to 3 flat winners (2 abroad), and to successful All Weather Hurdles and jumping winner, Blasket Hero. Dam won a 9f. 5200y. FLAT (often blinkered; including for Lady Herries; won previously for G. Lewis at 2) r14 w1 (7f Nursery, 16 ran) p1 (2nd). NH '98/9 (for B. Llewellyn, bought for 6500, blinkered 1) r6 p1 (distant and lucky 3rd of 4); Sells last 3. Unpromising, looked a difficult ride over Hurdles, and his flat win means he is up against it in Points. Invariably pulls up, and was 100-1 in the latest. *A. Fear — Berkeley (Mike Harding).* 1096 (MO), 1489 (M), 1606 (O).

LAVALIGHT ..9-12§.. 14 b.g. Lighter — Laval (Cheval) 4p23. Workmanlike half-brother to Lavair, and to the winners, Lively Lily (Hurdles), Nova Champ (Chasing) and Lapiaffe (flat and jumping). Dam won 2m3f Nov Hdle. NH FLAT r1 p0. NH '91/7 (blinkered 1) r41 w2 (2m1f-2m6f Hdles) p3; inc Sells; failed to finish 6 (fell/unseated 4). P-t-P/HUNT CH '96/9 (for Mr R.I. Lane & Miss L. Johnson) r18 w1 (Confined) p5 (4 3rds; inc last in 2m3f Hunt Ch); ran out 1, and pulled up 4. Sprang a 20-1 surprise when winning a three-finisher Confined last year, but pulls hard and usually fails to stay and that success ended a 46 race drought. Beaten a minimum of 15 lengths in 2000 and another shock at 14 looks highly improbable. Occasionally blinkered, but not since '98. *Mrs T.C. Leahy (The Leahy Family) — Blackmore & Sparkford V. (John Dufosee).* 653 (MO), 927 (Cf), 1471 (Cnr), 1595 (Cf).

LAW DESIGNER (IRE) ..8-4.. 9 ch.g. Architect (USA) — Femme Gendarme (USA) (Policeman FR) p. Small sturdy compact half-brother to flat winner, Joseph's Wine. Dam won at up to 9f in USA. NH '97 r2 p0 (well tailed off last twice, inc Sell). P-t-P '99 r3 p0 (4th, 5th, and pulled up 1). 24 lengths fourth once in '99, but tailed off otherwise and looked most unco-operative on his only appearance in 2000. Ran tongue-tied last year and looks awry. *Miss N. Kent & L.C. Maultby — Burton (Nicole Kent).* 435 (M).

LAWSONS LADY ..—.. 10 ch.m. Zaffaran (USA) — The Ladystee (Brave Shot) p. Lengthy home-bred. P-t-P '98 r2 p0 (pulled up 2). Looked most unpleasant in '98 (was withdrawn on her final intended appearance after becoming unruly in the paddock, had thrown herself to the floor there in her previous race) and in an equally unresponsive mood on her belated return. Taken to post early in the latest debacle and jumped badly until pulling before halfway. *W.L. Thomas — Kyre.* 600 (I).

LAYBACK ..—.. 10 ch.g. Brotherly (USA) — Casual Kate (Don Enrico USA) Rp. Small angular half-brother to So Easy. Dam pulled up in 2 Points for Mrs Weaver, as did her dam, Kate The Great. Jumped badly and soon tailed off before running out and unseating after 2m4f on his belated debut. Pedigree alone should ensure that he is useless. *J.W.E. Weaver — Clifton-on-Teme.* 341 (CfMa), 704 (OMa).

LAZY ACRES (IRE) ..9-1.. 12 ch.g. Lord Ha Ha — Fanny Brave (Brave Invader USA) pp4pp. Sturdy compact. IRISH P-t-P '94 and '96/7 r9 p2; pulled up 6. P-t-P '99 (for Mr R.J. Lamb) r8 p2 (2nds, of 3 once); unseated 3, and pulled up 3. Showed an iota of promise when second in three and four-finisher Maidens last year, but has never looked an easy ride and the new owner could not galvanise him into action at all. Has become very anti-social at the start and frequently gives away acres of ground there. Usually taken to post early. *Ms A. Counsell — Cambs Univ (Chris Lawson).* 936 (Cf), 1040 (OMa), 1180 (OMa), 1382 (OMa), 1486 (OMa).

LEAD STORY (IRE) ..10-7.. 8 br.g. Lead On Time (USA) — Mashmoon (USA) (Habitat) p5521221. Strong-topped compact half-brother to flat and Hurdles winner, Talathath (FR), and to Irish flat winner, Gold Braisim. Dam won 2 flat, 6-8f. FLAT r4 p0. NH '97/8 r5 p0. P-t-P '99 r4 w2 (Maiden and Restricted) p1 (head 2nd of 3); and 4th. Left a favourable impression when signing off his debut season with a double, but took a while to find his form in 2000. Just held on to land his Members on the first occasion Tabitha Cave had partnered him and extended her unbeaten record on him when easily taking a Newton Abbot Hunter Chase on their final appearance. Travels and jumps well and can handle very soft ground, but probably appreciates a much less testing surface and a flat track also seems ideal. Would take a lot of beating in Ladies races if connections decided on that route. *Mrs M. Trueman — Modbury H. (Gordon Chambers).* 162 (I), 404 (I), 654 (I), 730 (I), 1041 (M), 1256 (Inr), 1535 (2m3fH), 1644 (3m2f110yH).

LEAMLARA ROSE (IRE) ..9-7.. 10 b.m. Le Moss — Clash Boreen (Arapaho) p. Tall rangy half-sister to Maxxum Express (IRE). IRISH P-t-P '96/7 r6 p1 (25l 2nd); pulled up 4. P-t-P '98/9 r6 w1 (Maiden) p0; pulled up 4. Had been struggling to get home, but appreciated the better ground when landing a Maiden at Ashorne last year. Only seen once in 2000 when pulled up at Larkhill in February and has clearly met with a setback. *Mrs P.A. Wallis — N. Ledbury (Pip Hooley).* 260 (R).

LEAP FROG ..9-9.. 10 ch.g. Gildoran — Caer-Gai (Royal Palace) 62pp4. Tall rangy half-brother to Powys. Dam, half-sister to Caergwrle (1000 Guineas) won at 8f (won another similar, but disqualified). NH FLAT '96 r2 p0. NH '96/8 r7 p2 (3rds, inc Ch); pulled up in other Ch. P-t-P '99 r4 w2 (Maiden and Restricted) p0; 4th, and pulled up 1. Appeared to have stamina limitations last year, but returned from a mid-season break to win twice with some authority in May. Ran out of gas up the hill at Mollington on his second start in 2000 and got the staggers in all his three subsequent races at around the 2m5f mark and it would come as no surprise to find that he has a wind problem. Gets worked up in the paddock and usually goes to post early. *Countess Goess-Saurau & S. Compton — V.W.H. (Countess Susie Goess-Saurau).* 1 (C), 74 (CCf), 263 (I), 561 (O), 1370 (I).

LEAVE IT BE (IRE) ..9-11.. 12 br.g. Supreme Leader — Royal Escort (Royal Highway) fp. Compact half-brother to No Escort and Royal Survivor. IRISH P-t-P '94/6 r14 w2 (4&5yo Maiden and Open; also disqualified from Winners of Two — prohibited substances) p4; pulled up 3, fell 3, and brought down 1. IRISH HUNT CH '96 and '98 r4 p1 (3rd); 5th, pulled up 1, and unseated 1. P-t-P '99 r2 p0 (4th, and pulled up 1). A fair Pointer in Ireland, but clearly has his problems now and for the second season running only managed two outings and disappeared early. Backed at long odds on his 2000 debut, but fell before they had gone a mile, and ran as though something was seriously amiss when soon tailed off next time. *Mrs E.H. Irving — S. & W. Wilts (Sarah Waugh).* 34 (MO), 383 (3mH).

LE CABRO D'OR ..9-9§.. 7 b.g. Gildoran — Deirdre's Choice (Golden Love) 2R17. Lengthy unfurnished half-brother to Select Sam, Judy Line, Brooms Bell and Scarlett O'Hara. Dam won an Irish Point, and was subsequently 4th and pulled up for Christopher Sporborg. Grandam, Deirdre's Joy, won Bumper, 2 Hdles (2m-2m1f) and 4 Points in Ireland. P-t-P '99 r1 p0 (4th). Won very easily albeit in a slow time at Marks Tey, but a most unenviable ride and will cock his jaw without provocation and career off the track at right angles. Very highly strung and has two handlers and usually takes a fierce hold, but it seems connections may have given up on him after his latest deranged act performed whilst in command of a Restricted at Garthorpe. Would be a mountainous challenge for however takes him on, but just the sort of barmpot Dick Baimbridge could sort out. *Mrs C.H. Sporborg — Puckeridge (Christopher Sporborg).* 22 (2m4fOma), 181 (2m4fOMa), 322 (CfMa), 546 (R).

LEDBURIAN ..9-12.. 11 br.g. Primitive Rising (USA) — Pretty Lass (Workboy) 2331. Big strong half-brother to Ladylands (qv). NH FLAT '96 r1 p0. NH '97 and '99 (from A.G. Hobbs') r7 p0 (pulled up in Hdle; and pulled up 4, and unseated 1 in Chses — reluctant to race and jumped very slowly once). P-t-P '98 (for Mrs Y. Allsop) r2 w1 (Maiden) p0; and 6th. Cut no ice in two outings under Rules in '99 after winning an elders Maiden in soft at Bitterley the previous year, but new connections have done well with him and he justified favouritism with little to spare in a Novice riders event at Cherrybrook on his final start. Generally much more enthusiastic than he was under Rules, but very one-paced and needs plenty of driving. Appreciates plenty of cut in the ground as it helps to slow the others down. *H.S. Channon — Spooners & W. Dartmoor, & E. Cornwall, & Lamerton (Yvonne Watson & Jo Channon).* 157 (M), 406 (R), 720 (M), 853 (Inr).

LEDWYCHE GATE ..9-11§.. 14 b.g. Roscoe Blake — Ledwyche (Pamroy) p7. Big strong half-brother to Far Forest (qv). P-t-P/HUNT CH '92/3 and '95/9 r31 w8 (inc 3m2f Hunt Ch) p7 (5 2nds, short-headed once, and inc 2 Hunt Chses); failed to finish 12 (fell/unseated 4). Successful three times in his Members in previous seasons, and clearly loves running in the direction of his stables which are located adjacent to the course at Bitterley, but has always been an enigmatic character and seems to have taken the hump completely now. Can be a determined front-runner, but needs stoking up and is usually very hit and miss at the fences and dogged it furiously after losing the lead in both 2000 outings. Wears blinkers. Will be hard pushed to stage a revival at 14. *L. Evans — Ludlow (Geoff Evans).* 986 (M), 1592 (4m2fH).

LEEJAY LUKI ..9-6.. 11 ch.g. Farajullah — Subook (Salmon Leap USA) p62uf. Lengthy. P-t-P '97/9 r10 w2 (Maiden and Restricted) p1 (3rd of 4); pulled up 2, and on floor 2). Stayed on dourly to lead in the final 100 yards of two minor races in May '98, but evidently not right when making just one appearance the following year and only managed one decent effort in 2000. Looked as though he might peg the winner back at Holnicote in May, but several jumping errors took their toll in the closing stages and he went down by two lengths. Has begun to jump in a very haphazard manner and came back riderless in both subsequent ventures which included a heavy fall for himself on his latest appearance. Stays well and tries hard, but only moderate and will struggle to win again. Has two handlers in the paddock. *Mrs S.K. Notley — Taunton V.* 953 (I), 1371 (Cf), 1472 (I), 1607 (I), 1674 (I).

LEGAL ARTIST (IRE) ..9-13.. 11 b.g. Tate Gallery (USA) — Dowdstown Miss (Wolver Hollow) 43. Compact half-brother to Bitofabuzz (IRE), and to 3 winners in USA. Dam, half-sister to Strong Gale, won twice at up to 12f in USA. 15,000f, 12,000y. FLAT r16 w3 (11-12f, one on equitrack) p3 (beaten head once). NH '93/9 (for Miss C. Johnsey, bought for 9000; 2 wins previously for N. Graham) r32 w5 (2 Hdles, 2m1f-2m2f, and 3 Chses, 2m4f-3m) p6; fell 2 out once or would have completed hat-trick; pulled up 5 of final 7 attempts. Enjoyed an above-average rate of success until September '97, but has clearly had major problems since. Needs good or firmish ground, but quickly dismounted on his most recent outing, and has obviously had another setback. *Miss J. Congdon & Miss S. Garnett — Torrington F. (Andrew Congdon).* 101 (L), 636 (L).

LEGAL PETITION ..9-5.. 7 b.m. Petoski — Legal Aid (Legal Eagle) 3. Tall half-sister to Legal Vision and Legal Affair. Dam won 3 Chses at around 2m for Mr Hill. NH FLAT '98 (from G. Cottrell's) r2 p0. Her six lengths third for the champion on firm looked encouraging, but is getting very little opportunity to prove herself. *P.R. Hill — E. Devon (Chris Down).* 640 (CfMa).

PLATE 72   1479 South Durham Open Maiden (Div 1): Leg Beforum (S. Swiers), 1st

PHOTO: Roy Parker

LEG BEFORUM (IRE) ..9-10.. 7 b.g. Distinctly North (USA) — Paulines Girl (Hello Gorgeous USA) 24Rf21. Very small unfurnished half-brother to Irish Pointing and Hurdles winner, Lisdoylelady (IRE). IR1300f, IR4400y, 3800 2-y-o. FLAT (for L. Montague-Hall; debut for G.L. Moore) r12 p2. NH '97/8 (for Miss S. Williamson, bought for 2200; previously for M. Sowersby, bought for 3200) r6 p0 (inc pulled up 2, and unseated at first). Ran reasonably in his two seconds, and gained a deserved wide margin success on firm at Mordon. Beat little and took a long time to get off the mark, and may struggle in competitive company, as he is only a pony. Tried in headgear in previous yards. *J. Mackley — S. Durham (Sarah Dent).* 627 (OMa), 808 (OMa), 1003 (OMa), 1329 (OMa), 1352 (OMa), 1479 (OMa).

LEGGIES LEGACY ..8-4.. 10 b.g. Jupiter Island — Hit The Line (Saulingo) pru. Small owner-bred half-brother to Flashing Silks. Dam won at 6f. NH FLAT '97 r1 p0. P-t-P '98/9 r2 p1 (3rd); and pulled up 1. Beaten a shade over five lengths when third in a bad Maiden at Peper Harow on his only appearance last year, but clearly thought to be lacking in stamina as he ran twice in sub-3m Hunter Chases in 2000. In no state to do himself justice on his return and obviously frightened himself to death as he has been most reluctant to leave terra firma since. Probably mentally scarred for good. *A.G. Russell — Southdown & Eridge.* 300 (2m5fH), 578 (OMa), 1540 (2m5fH).

LE MEILLE (IRE) ..—.. 12 ch.g. Le Bavard (FR) — Glens Princess (Prince Hansel) p. Rangy unfurnished half-brother to J'Accuse (IRE)(*qv*), and to Irish jumping and English Chasing winner, Papillon (IRE). NH FLAT Spr '94 r2 p1 (3rd). NH '94/7 (one win for K. Burke; previously for A. Jarvis) r18 w3 (2m5f-3m3f Chses) p6 (inc 3rd in Hdle); broke blood vessel once. Won three Chases on good or firmish ground, but sometimes suffered with his jumping. Broke down badly in '97, and was a brief revival as a patch up job when backed from 33s to 10s and pulling up in a Confined. *Mrs C.J.A. Suthern — N. Cotswold (John Suthern).* 191 (Cf).

LEONARD'S DREAM ..—.. 9 b.m. Latest Model — Midinette (Midsummer Night II) pp. Sparely-made sister to Blue Night and Summer Moon. Dam won 2m Hdle; but failed to finish in 5 of 8 Points. P-t-P '99 r1 p0 (pulled up). Showed a bit of speed on her reappearance, but jumped poorly on much quicker terrain next time and does not look very inspiring. *Mrs E. Scott — Minehead H.* 1138 (MO), 1468 (OMa).

LEON GARCIA (IRE) ..10-0.. 8 b.m. Asir — Philosophical (Welsh Chanter) 1. Sister to NH flat and Hurdles winner, John Bush (IRE). Dam won 3 Sells, 8-10f, and 2m Hdle. IRISH NH '98 r2 p0. IRISH P-t-P '97/9 r10 w1 (5&6yo mares Mdn) p6. IRISH NH '98 r2 p0. Regularly finishes thereabouts in Points, and was gaining her second success in very soft ground when scoring on her English debut at Cursneh Hill. Did not beat much but seemed to have plenty in hand, and it is conceivable that she is under-rated. *Miss J. Oakey — Worcs.* 1276 (R).

LETHEM GHOST ..—.. 6 ro.m. Scorpio (FR) — Strawberry Split (Anax) b. Dam, half-sister to 3 Pointers, including Silver Shilling (*qv* '97 Annual), won 2m Sell Hdle, and later fell and unseated in Points. Bought Doncaster, May for 2000. Brought down at the first at Friars Haugh. *T. Butt — Border.* 719 (CfMa).

LETS TWIST AGAIN (IRE) ..9-12§.. 11 ch.g. Glenstal (USA) — Gorgeous Twist (Hello Gorgeous USA) ppu5up42f. Small good-bodied. IRISH FLAT '92 r4 p0. IRISH NH '93 r1 p0. IRISH P-t-P '96 r9 p3 (3rds — slipped on bend and unseated and remounted once, or would have won); pulled up 4. P-t-P/HUNT CH '97/8 (for Mrs S. Bird) r14 w4 (up to Confined, inc hat-trick) p8 (4 2nds, last once); pulled up 1. NH '98/9 (from M. Sheppard's; blinkered 3) r11 w1 (3m2f Nov Chse) p1 (2nd); pulled 2, fell 1. A fair if somewhat moody top-of-the-ground front-runner for the Sheppards, but became totally disinterested in racing halfway through '99 and plodded miserably on his return to Points. Killed in a fall at Marks Tey in April. *N.J. King — Suffolk.* 95 (L), 177 (L), 319 (L), 414 (L), 608 (L), 772 (L), 939 (L), 1037 (L), 1183 (L).

LE VIENNA (IRE) ..8-5.. 12 b.g. Le Bavard (FR) — Northern Push (Push On) ppp23p. Big rangy brother to Northern Yarn (IRE), and half-brother to jumping winner, Cokenny Boy, and to successful Hurdler, West Bay. IRISH P-t-P '94/5 r6 p1 (22½l 3rd); 6th of 7, and pulled up 4. P-t-P '96/9 r32 p5 (4 2nds, of 3 twice, and 3rd of 4); pulled up 11, and brought down 1. A big cumbersome boat who is still trawling the depths of Welsh Maidens after five seasons. Lumbered to two more placings in 2000, and produced his best display for David Stephens, but though he has the virtue of being a safe ride, he will require a desperate race to score. Has worn a tongue-strap in the past, and sometimes blinkered. *S.G. Currey — Curre.* 338 (R), 485 (R), 594 (M), 822 (CfMa), 949 (OMa), 1194 (OMa).

LEWESDON COUNTESS ..8-12.. 8 b.m. Say Primula — Lewesdon View (Dubassoff USA) ufpf6732. Compact half-sister to NH flat winner, Lewesdon Manor. Dam, half-sister to Bivdown (*qv* '87 Season Annual), suffered from leg trouble, but won 2 Points three years apart and placed 5 for Terry Beadle. P-t-P '99 r2 p0 (pulled up 2). An equine bulldozer in her first six races, but finally beginning to respect the fences and a small win now seems conceivable. Will however find fewer worse Maidens than the two she was placed in and needs to continue to improve to win one. *T.R. Beadle — Bedale.* 189 (OMam), 379 (OMa), 501 (2m4fOMa), 1235 (OMa), 1352 (OMa), 1480 (OMa), 1582 (2m4fOMa), 1669 (OMa).

LEWESDON MANOR ..9-10.. 10 b.g. Broadsword (USA) — Lewesdon View (Dubassoff USA) 12. Workmanlike good-bodied half-brother to Lewesdon Countess (*qv*). NH FLAT '97 r3 w1 p0. NH '98/9 (from P. Webber's; tongue-tied final) r5 p2 (3rds in Chses, only beat a rejoiner, and beaten 38l plus, and 2 distances). Won a bumper in soft on his racecourse debut, but lacked fluency and achieved nothing subsequently. Better off in Points and justified favouritism in his Members, and might be up to landing a Restricted, but does not get many chances. *J.G. Phillips — V.W.H.* 748 (M), 1203 (I).

LEWIS ..9-10.. 10 b.g. Wonderful Surprise — Gas Lighter (Lighter) p38. Compact. Dam was 2nd in Maiden for Tina Jackson (on the floor in 5 of 8 other attempts). P-t-P '98/9 r9 p2 (2nds of 3); last pair 3, pulled up 2, and fell 2. Placed in three races, but has only had six horses finish behind him in 12 starts, and usually struggles to get the trip. Blinkered in both of his final two starts '99/00. Might last home one day, but an easy track will be essential. *H.L. Thompson — Cleveland (Tina Jackson).* 282 (OMa), 378 (R), 508 (CMa).

LIBIDO ..9-0.. 6 b.g. Good Thyne (USA) — Country Mistress (Town And Country) 1. Dam, half-sister to High Sturt (qv), won bad 5-runner 2m1f Ch for Count Konrad Goess-Saurau. Attracted market support on his debut in a youngsters Maiden on firm at Woodford, and duly disposed of two rivals in the slowest time of the day. Should improve further. The sight of the Count striding around his estates in his lederhosen might arouse the odd few, and who wouldn't exercise Libido if Susie asked?. *Countess S. Goess-Saurau — V.W.H.* 1494 (CfMa).

PLATE 73   1494 Berkeley 56&7yo: Libido (Miss P. Gundry), 1st, after the 2nd last
PHOTO: Brian Armstrong

LIE DETECTOR ..10-6.. 13 b.g. Nearly A Hand — Rose Ravine (Deep Run) p5393p. Tall strong half-brother to Cardinal Red, and to NH flat and Hurdles winners, Admiral Rose and Frosty Canyon. Dam, smart, won 7 Hdles, 2m-3m1f, including a highly controversial success at Cheltenham Festival. NH FLAT '93 r1 p0. NH '93/6 r19 w4 (2m7f Hdle and 3 Chses, 3m-3m1f) p6. P-t-P/HUNT CH '98/9 r10 w2 (Opens) p3 (last of 2; and 2 3rds inc Hunt Ch); pulled up 1, and fell 1. Fairly distinguished at his best under Rules, and revived well in the current ownership to win two Opens in '99, but rather disappointing this season and failed to finish within 15 lengths of the winner in four completions. Used to stay well, but finished weakly in 2000 and may not have been right as he was never going well on his final start. Becoming elderly and might struggle to regain his old ability at 13. *Dr R. Gasper — Warwicks (Jon Trice-Rolph).* 59 (MO), 195 (O), 389 (O), 683 (3mH), 895 (MO), 970 (O).

LIFE OF A STAR (IRE) ..8-7.. 8 b.g. Strong Gale — Nellie's Dream (Over The River FR) pp4pp. Good-topped lengthy hobdayed half-brother to Irish NH flat and Hurdles winner, Impulsive Dream (IRE) and Kev's Lass. IRISH P-t-P '99 r3 p0 (last 2, and pulled up). Sold Doncaster, May for 1000. Weakened quickly up the final hill when 17 lengths fourth on his only completion, and consistently fails to get the trip. Bred to stay, and is presumably being stopped by wind problems. *Miss A. Hardy & D.K. Everard - Essex (David Everard).* 411 (OMa), 610 (R), 844 (OMa), 1180 (OMa), 1383 (OMa).

LIFFEY LANE ..8-9.. 9 b.g. Respect — Gala Lane (Gala Performance USA) pp6p. Small compact half-brother to Kings Lane (qv). NH '98 r1 p0 (last, and pulled up 2 — well tailed off all 3). P-t-P '99 r6 p1 (2nd); 5th, 6th, pulled up 2, and fell 1. Beaten 10 lengths when second in his Members last year, but a hot-head and stands little chance of staying three miles unless he learns to settle. Usually manages to get to the front at some stage in his races, but guaranteed to be running on vapour in the last half-mile. Gets on his toes in the paddock and has had two handlers. *Mrs K. Weir & Mrs S. Thompson — Border.* 114 (OMa), 365 (CfMa), 719 (CfMa), 1032 (OMa).

LIFT THE LATCH (IRE) ..—.. 9 b.g. Strong Gale — Pallastown Run (Deep Run) pp. Big good-topped half-brother to Palladante (IRE). NH FLAT '97 r1 p0. NH '97 r1 p0. P-t-P '99 r2 p0 (pulled up 2).

Looks the part, but has pulled up in all four Points and simply cannot breath properly (has had a tie-back and soft palate operations). Wore a tongue-strap once in '99. *A.D. Peachey & Mrs J. Holloway — N. Cotswold (Alan Peachey).* 191 (Cf), 371 (R).

LIGHTENING STEEL ..—.. 10 gr.g. Sulaafah (USA) — Wotusay (Lighter) 3ppp. Tall lengthy. Dam half-sister to Young Pretender (*qv* '88 season Annual), pulled up in a Point in '93 (jumped badly, and immediately tailed-off). NH FLAT Spr '97 r2 p0. NH '97/8 (for D. Caro) r3 p0 (last and pulled up 2 in Hdles). Sold Malvern, May for 1350. About a fence behind the winner when third of four on his only completion, and jumped badly on his two most recent attempts (and to the left in the latest). Performs as if there is something badly wrong with him. *P. Morris — Albrighton.* 569 (OMa), 1093 (OMa), 1196 (OMa), 1413 (OMa).

LIGHTER LORD ..9-0.. 10 b.g. Lighter — Lady Vulmid (Sir Lark) 3cpp4. Attractive unfurnished. Dam is sister to Bonanza Boy. P-t-P '97 (for Mr R.C. Pudd) r1 p1 (2nd). NH '99 r2 p0 (6th and pulled up in Chses; blinkered 1). Twenty lengths second in a Lydstep Maiden on firm in '97, and 15 lengths third on his 2000 reappearance, but failed to finish when favourite twice (carried out in melee once, and rider pulled up thinking horse unsound once) and looks nothing out of the ordinary on his infrequent appearances. *Miss H. Day — W. Somerset.* 207 (OMa), 352 (CfMa), 409 (OMa), 847 (R), 1100 (OMa).

LIGHT THE SKY ..8-6.. 8 b.g. Lighter — Saleander (Leander) 37p3p46. Half-brother to Chester Ben (*qv*). P-t-P '99 r5 p1 (2nd); 4th twice, 7th, and fell 1. Capable of prominent showings, but a weak finisher, and the closest he has come to winning was when two lengths second to a horse that had failed to complete the course in four previous starts at Garthorpe last year. A safe jumper, but finds nothing under pressure and beginning to appear ungenuine. *W.J. Turcan — Fernie (Nick Pomfret).* 21 (2m4fOMa), 124 (OMa), 548 (CfMa), 872 (OMa), 1219 (OMa), 1421 (OMa), 1590 (2m4fOMa).

LILLIEPLANT (IRE) ..9-12.. 9 b.m. Aristocracy — Canute Princess (Torenaga) 11p. Angular. P-t-P '97/9 r7 p2; pulled up 2, and fell/unseated 2. Placed twice at Howick '98/9, and finally came good there twice in 2000, but not before she had given her supporters heart failure at the start. Played up badly on both occasions, but once she had got to the front was as good as gold and won unchallenged by an aggregate of 35 lengths. Disappointed when odds-on at Bassaleg subsequently where she again whipped round at the start, but has the ability to win again if she channels it in the right direction. Always goes to post early. Has a multitude of followers and it seems that more money changes hands over her than at the turnstiles of the Millennium Dome. *A.J. Plant — Curre (Lyndon Williams).* 602 (CfMa), 818 (R), 1403 (I).

LILLIES BUTTLER ..8-4.. 7 ch.m. Gildoran — Ananda (Majestic Maharaj) p32p. Workmanlike half-sister to Rosanda. Dam is half-sister to Sea Vale (*qv* '94 Annual). Bought Doncaster, Aug for 500. Achieved two remote placings with one horse behind her in youngsters Maidens taking a minimum of 7min12s but never looked remotely like winning in either, and all she has proved is that she can keep going through corn in heavy or holding ground. Second favourite of 16 on her final start, but was immediately taken off her feet, and did not seem to appreciate the 'normal' surface. *Ms C. Griffiths — Llangeinor (S. Jones).* 348 (CfMa), 747 (CfMa), 1055 (CfMa), 1302 (OMa).

LILLOOET (IRE) ..9-11§.. 10 br.m. Yashgan — Rashee Lady (Avocat) pp32fp. Unfurnished lengthy sister to Irish Pointing winner, Touch Of Autumn. IRISH NH '96 r1 p0. IRISH P-t-P '96 and '98 r9 p4 (2nds); pulled up 2, and fell 1. P-t-P '99 r7 w1 (Maiden) p3 (2nd of 3; and 2 3rds, last once); and pulled up 3. Made heavy weather of winning a bad Maiden in testing ground at Heathfield last year, and is basically ungenuine, but plenty of ability and only went down by the minimum margin in a Horseheath Restricted this year. Was upsides the winner when departing at the penultimate fence at Littlewindsor subsequently and would be deserving of compensation if she were not such a total bow-wow. Only goes for Chris Gordon, but even he has to don spurs, whilst the blinkers she wears are not there to make a fashion statement. *R. & M. Fielder — Chid, Lec & Cowdray (Ray Fielder).* 14 (R), 86 (R), 304 (M), 416 (R), 524 (R), 876 (R).

LILY BROWN ..—.. 6 br.m. Sula Bula — Lily Mab (Prince Mab FR) p. Home-bred half-sister to Hurdles winners. Tipping The Line, Barton Ward (both also successful in NH flat) and Barton Bill. Dam won at 12f, and won 2 2m Hdles. Pulled up soon after making a couple of mistakes in mid-March. *Mrs L. Harrington — Avon V. (Don Harrington).* 472 (OMa).

LILY LANE ..8-1.. 9 ch.g. Town And Country — My Pride (Petit Instant) 4f3pp. Rangy half-brother to Medway Boy, Sula Pride, Prides Delight and Charlie Smith. Dam failed to finish in 5 Points for Mr Bennett. P-t-P '97 r2 p0 (last, and pulled up 1). Resurfaced after a lengthy absence in 2000, but only beat one rival and tended to make mistakes. May not stay three miles and was pulled up when still holding third place on his final appearance. Seems quite excitable and often gets very warm and has two handlers. *L.C. Bennett — Blackmore & Sparkford V. (Rose Vickery).* 472 (OMa), 738 (OMa), 1359 (OMa), 1598 (OMa), 1609 (OMa).

LILY THE LARK ..10-7.. 13 b.m. Crested Lark — Florence Eliza (Floriana) 3pbR1311115. Small close-coupled attractive half-sister to Larry The Lamb (qv). P-t-P/HUNT CH '95/9 r29 w10 (inc 7 Ladies and Club Ladies; 4-timer in '98) p10 (7 3rds, inc Hunt Ch); fell/unseated 2, and pulled up 2. In top form in '98 winning six times, but turned very sour last year after Heather Irving got injured and clearly did not take to Hunter Chasing. Had her moments again in 2000, but generally a rejuvenated mare since 'mummy' has been back in the plate and picked up another five Ladies races. Becoming a hard ride however, and frequently drops the bridle and loses her pitch, but very determined when she is galvanised into action and few can resist her rallies. Usually avoids anything firmer than good. Sweated up uncharacteristically when disappointing on her final start and may have gone over the top, but sure to add to her tally if she returns in the right mood in 2001. *Miss H.M. Irving, F. East & A. Hartgrove — Farmers Bloodhounds (Heather Irving).* 3 (L), 78 (L), 118 (L), 192 (L), 307 (L), 512 (L), 707 (L), 1007 (L), 1145 (L), 1253 (L), 1417 (L).

PLATE 74   3 Thames Valley Club Ladies Open: Lily The Lark (Miss H. Irving), 3rd, lands ahead of Bel Lane (Miss C. Spearing), 5th   PHOTO: Brian Armstrong

LIMITED LIABILITY ..9-12.. 11 b.g. Bustino — Fine Asset (Hot Spark) f3u443p3. Workmanlike hobdayed half-brother to Gilded Omen, and to 2 flat winners, including Faultless Speech. 5400y. FLAT r4 p0. NH '94,'96 and '98 (for P. Webber; debut in oldies flat for Sir M. Prescott) r6 w1 (2m2f Mdn Hdle) p1 (31/3rd after numerous mistakes in Ch). Gained his only victory on firmish on June '96, and never came close to a victory in Points until he finished three lengths third on final start. Takes a very strong hold, and bolted before the race when tried in blinkers once. Misses alternate years and looked badly wrong on his penultimate appearance under Rules, so at least new connections did well to more than equal his previous total of outings. *B. & Mrs P.A. Twinn — E. Essex (Paula Twinn).* 25 (Cnr), 84 (L), 240 (L), 319 (L), 549 (Cf), 608 (L), 935 (M), 1184 (Cf).

LIMOSA ..9-7.. 10 b.m. Jalmood (USA) — Larive (Blakeney) 73657. Sturdy half-sister to Miss Madelon (qv). FLAT (for F. Johnson Houghton) r17 w1 (15f) p3. NH '96/8 (won for Mrs L. Richards; previously for Mrs P. Robeson) r14 w1 (2m4f Hdle) p2; inc Sell; last 2 and pulled up 2 in Chses. Sold Ascot, May for 500. All out to win a bad Hurdle on firm in August '96, but subsequently disappointing, and was blinkered on her last three starts. Proved to be a careful jumper in Points, and gave one fair display when three and a half lengths third, but beaten out of sight otherwise, and does not seem to want to try. *Mrs M. Garner — Oakley.* 511 (O), 788 (Cf), 1006 (Cf), 1381 (O), 1481 (Cf).

LINDALIGHTER ..9-8.. 11 bl.m. Lighter — Linda's Wish (Harvest Spirit) ppppp4p. Neat light. Dam was 20/2nd in a Point. NH '95 r2 p0 (Hdles). P-t-P/HUNT CH '95/7 r18 w1 (Maiden) p6 (3 2nds, of 3 once); fell 5, and pulled up 4. Took 18 attempts to get off the mark, and basically does not stay three miles, but only beaten 10 lengths when fourth in a Restricted on her penultimate start in 2000 and still possesses ability. Usually chalked up at a fancy price however, and it would be a shock result were she to oblige again. *M.F. Howard — Worcs (Sue Hancox).* 612 (CR), 698 (R), 992 (R), 1193 (R), 1411 (R), 1460 (R), 1630 (Cf).

LINDON RUN ..9-12.. 12 b.g. Cruise Missile — Trial Run (Deep Run) pp4d42393. Big strong rangy brother to May Run, and half-brother to Scot's Run, Hartford Gent, Political Belle and Political Bill. P-t-P/HUNT CH '95/9 r20 w2 (2m4f Maiden, and Restricted) p3 (2 2nds; and last of 3); failed to finish 9 (on floor 4). A dual winner at Tranwell '96/7, but does not stay well and failed to beat a rival in '99. Beaten a minimum of 11 in his three placings this year, and has been consistently outclassed in sub-3m Hunter Chases. Wears a tongue-strap. *Mrs O. Donaldson — Morpeth (Kevin Robson).* 183 (CCf), 420 (I), 496 (C), 917 (3mH), 1121 (I), 1366 (I), 1445 (3m1fH), 1602 (2m4fH10yH).

LINGCOOL ..7-12.. 11 b.m. Uncle Pokey — Cooling (Tycoon II) up7. Workmanlike half-sister to Doc Lodge and Dunblair, and to 2 flat winners, including Lucky Blue (also won Hurdling). Dam won 3 flat, 10-13f. NH FLAT r1 p0. NH '94 r2 p0 (last 1, and pulled up 1). P-t-P '95/8 r19 w1 (Maiden) p4 (3 3rds); failed to finish 14 (unseated 3). Made all to win at Mordon in '97 (rated 9-9) but a regular non-finisher before and since, and would have failed to beat a rival on her return but for the rider not driving her past Mountain Lion in the shadows of the post in her Members. Used to wear blinkers, but did not in 2000. *R. Morley — Derwent, & Middleton.* 393 (M), 689 (R), 996 (M).

LINGERING LAUGHTER (IRE) ..9-3.. 10 ch.g. Balinger — Merry Mirth (Menelek) *pu.* Compact brother to Neily Joe (IRE) and NH flat winner, Happy Hussar (IRE), and half-brother to Irish Chasing winner, Slaney Fayre (IRE), to Irish Hurdles winners, Cock Cockburn and General Norman, and to Irish NH flat winners, Arctic River (IRE) and Sheer Mirth. Dam won 2m2f Hdle in Ireland. NH FLAT '96 r1 p0. P-t-P '98 (for Mr J. Neville) r1 w1 (Maiden) p0. NH Feb '00 r1 p0 (pulled up in 3m2f Nov Chse: *hld up, 6th when mist 11, wknd app 4 out, t.o when pu 3 out*). Won a poor three-finisher Tweseldown Maiden on firmish in '98, but stands his racing badly and only surfaces every other year. Failed to negotiate the third at Ascot on his Hunter Chase debut and promptly disappeared. *A.J. Williams — Tredegar F.* 800 (3m110yH).

LINGHAM LADY ..9-4.. 8 b.m. Lord Bud — Old Mill Lady (Royal Goblin) 34fp. Half-sister to Lingham Magic. Dam won 2 Sell Hdles and Nov Ch (all 2m); subsequently showed no form for Joe Swiers, inc Hunt Chses. P-t-P '99 r1 p0 (pulled up). Caught the eye on her first two starts this term particularly when a fast-finishing fourth at Wetherby, but was held by the winner when capsizing at the penultimate fence in her Members. Disappointed back in Maiden company subsequently, but may have been out for a confidence booster and she should be able to open her account in 2001. *J.E. Swiers — W. of Yore.* 51 (OMa), 167 (OMa), 374 (M), 1032 (OMa).

LINK COPPER ..9-11.. 12 ch.g. Whistlefield — Letitica (Deep Run) pf32p. Compact good-bodied owner-bred half-brother to Lets Go Polly, and to jumping winner, Lets Be Frank. NH '92/4 r4 p0 (last, and pulled up 3, inc both Chses). P-t-P/HUNT CH '94/9 r34 w7 (inc 3 Confineds) p12 (8 2nds, inc Hunt Ch); also disqualified from 2nd after testing positive in Hunt Ch; pulled up 9, slipped up 1, and fell 1. Has a great history of physical problems so his achievements have been particularly meritorious, but has not won since completing a four-timer in '98 and his losing run now stands at 14. Only managed to beat one rival in 2000 and seems to be on the downgrade. Usually a safe jumper, but his fall at Black Forest Lodge left Sarah Jackson in a serious condition from which she is thankfully progressing. Suited by a sound surface. *Mrs E.J. Taplin — Devon & Somerset.* 354 (L), 557 (Cf), 1096 (MO), 1369 (M), 1473 (Cf).

LINLATHEN ..10-3.. 11 ch.g. Move Off — Loch Brandy (Harwell) 221f34. Compact good-bodied half-brother to Kingennie (*qv*). NH FLAT '94 r2 p0. NH '94/8 r22 w5 (4 Hdles, 2m-2m7f, inc hat-trick, and 3m Ch) p9. P-t-P/HUNT CH '99 r8 p4 (4 2nds, inc 2 Hunt Chses); 5th, fell/unseated 2, and brought down 1. A fair performer under Rules, and should have a much better record in Points than he possesses, but feebly handled on more than one occasion last year and it was not surprising that Guy Brewer could extract a win out of him on their only appearance together. Usually ridden from off the pace, but is very one-paced and cannot quicken in the manner the usual rider expects, and has become prone to making the odd serious error. Acts on all but extremes of going. *Mrs A. Bell — Belvoir.* 48 (Cf), 229 (Cf), 794 (Cf), 1443 (3mH), 1542 (3mH), 1603 (2m6f110yH).

LINTON ..8-11.. 11 b.m. St David — Follifoot's Folly (Comedy Star USA) pp42ppp. Workmanlike owner-bred half-sister to Comedy Gayle (*qv*). P-t-P '97 and '99 r7 p0 (5th twice, and pulled up 5). Made the frame for the first time in her career when runner-up in much the slowest race of the day at Cherrybrook, but pulled up in 10 of her other 13 starts and is no racehorse. *Miss J.F. Diggory — E. Cornwall.* 157 (M), 312 (CfMa), 721 (CfMa), 855 (CfMa), 1049 (CfMa), 1522 (CfMa), 1641 (OMa).

LIRKIMALONG ..—.. 8 ch.g. Lir — Kimberley Ann (St Columbus) ppp. Compact unfurnished home-bred brother to The Kimbler (*qv*). Lurking at the back when 25-1 or more in Restricteds, but it will be absolutely no surprise (especially to the stewards, who will not have noticed anything) if he romps to victory when the brakes are let off in a Maiden. Has two paddock handlers, and has been taken to post early. *B.R.J. Young — E. Cornwall (Sue Young)*. 163 (R), 315 (R), 729 (R).

LIRSLEFTOVER ..9-12.. 9 ch.g. Lir — Full Tan (Dairialatan) 3p15p. Small neat attractive Young-bred brother to Full Alirt (*qv*). P-t-P '98/9 r9 w2 (Maiden and Intermediate) p0 (4th of 5, pulled up 5, and unseated 1). Pulled up thrice consecutively between winning on his first and last starts in '99 and landed a touch at Flete Park this year having pulled up after jumping just seven fences when favourite at Kilworthy three weeks earlier. Had been the subject of a Stewards Enquiry in '99 so the local boys deemed it unnecessary to have the pilot in again. A typically excitable Young scruffbag and has two paddock handlers. Sure to remain as unpredictable as the trainer wishes, but bound to win again sooner or later. *B.R.J. Young, Miss S. Young & Mrs K. Rogers — E. Cornwall (Sue Young)*. 258 (Cf), 726 (Cf), 1047 (Cf), 1261 (Cf), 1605 (L).

LISALEEN WREN (IRE) ..4-0.. 12 br.g. The Parson — Kitty Wren (Warpath) p1. Sturdy. Dam, sister to Copgrove (*qv* '93 Annual), and sister or half-sister to 10 other winners, won at 12f, and won 4 2m Hdles (all 5 wins in Sells). IRISH P-t-P '94 r3 p0 (last 2, and ran out). IRISH NH FLAT '94 r1 p0. NH '95 and '97 (often blinkered/visored; for G. Woodward; previously for S. Norton) r9 p2 (2nd in Hdle, and 24l 3rd in Ch); pulled up 3 inc final 2, inc Sell Hdle. Bought Doncaster, May for 1000. A woeful creature who goes missing for years on end, and was the least deserving winner of the season when he crawled round Aldington after being left alone at the eighth in a match. Finally got Gusieppe Gigantesco (40) off the mark, but he could have completed the course quicker if he had been pushed round in a supermarket by Kevin Tork. *G.G. Gigantesco — O. Surrey & Burstow*. 825 (R), 1168 (R).

LISTENUP LORD ..—.. 6 b.g. Arctic Lord — Charty Lass (Le Bavard FR) pp. Tiny brother to Maid To Talk. Dam is sister to Dawn Alert, and half-sister to Peacemaker (*qv*). Bought Malvern, July 1250. Broke a hind leg at Pentreclwydau. *E.D. Perry — Golden V.* 746 (CfMa), 1302 (OMa).

LITTLE BROCKWELL (IRE) ..10-7.. 8 ch.m. Nestor — Tacovaon (Avocat) 1p11. Lengthy sister to Hurdles winner, Grey Abbey (IRE). P-t-P '98/9 r5 w2 (Maiden and Restricted) p0; fell 1. Unbeaten when completing '99/00, and has quickly developed into a useful performer under Pauline Robson's care, but showed the flipside of her nature at Tranwell (had reared over in the paddock on her reappearance) and seems typically chestnut mare-ish. Made the jump to Open company with ease on her final start, but only after Luke Morgan had survived a last fence blunder, and if she can keep her temper in check should enjoy more success, though she has yet to beat a seriously good animal yet. Has two handlers. Wears a tongue-strap. *W.E. & Mrs L. Philipson — Braes (Pauline Robson)*. 420 (I), 1078 (Cf), 1158 (M), 1365 (O).

LITTLE BROWN BEAR (IRE) ..9-13.. 7 br.g. Strong Gale — Gladtogetit (Green Shoon) 2. Small neat half-brother to Swincombe (IRE). Dam, sister to Green Sheen (IRE) (*qv* 2000 Annual), won mares Maiden and NH Flat in Ireland, and won 3 Chses (2m6f-3m) in England. P-t-P '99 r1 p1 (2nd). Has finished in front of three subsequent winners with runner-up in Maidens '99/00, and looks a cast iron future winner himself, but seems incredibly fragile and has needed 12 months to recover between outings. Could not be better bred and will hopefully be able to stand a full campaign in 2001. *G.B. Barlow — Cheshire Forest*. 966 (OMa).

LITTLE BUCK (IRE) ..10-11.. 13 b.g. Buckskin (FR) — Little Quince (Laurence O) 1106f. Neat sparely-made. IRISH FLAT '95 r1 p0. IRISH NH FLAT r18 w2 (2m2f) p4 (3 2nds). IRISH NH '95/6 r9 w2 (2 Hdles, 2m2f-2m4f) p5 (2nds). NH '96/7 r4 p2 (2nds, inc only Ch, beaten distance after clear leader fell last, and of 3 of 3 in Hdle). Produced fighting fit to overcome a three year absence when scoring in good style at Plumpton and Kempton, but competed at the highest level afterwards. Took part in both Foxhunters and not discredited when beaten 20 lengths at Aintree, and then fell four out when looking second best in the race won by Castle Mane at Cheltenham (not fluent and jumped right). Has looked untrustworthy and found little on occasions in the past, but certainly revels in this mud. His talented partner Keith Culligan certainly deserves more chances, whilst Lawrence Wells had already demonstrated his skills at readying one first time out when Ordacta captured a £7052 Hurdle at Kempton after 311 days off. *Mrs C. Zetter-Wells — Chid, Lec & Cowdray (Lawrence Wells)*. 223 (3m2fH), 303 (3mH), 584 (3m2f110yH), 921 (2m6fH), 1337 (3m2f110yH).

LITTLE BUSTER ..—.. 10 gr.g. Baron Blakeney — Bealsmead (Rugantino) ppp. Brother to Three B's (*qv*). NH '99 (for J. Panvert) r2 p0 (tailed off and pulled up twice in 4 days). Sold Ascot, May for 2000. The latest in a long line of beastly Bealsmead's, and could not even plod to completion in a farce in which none of the eight contestants went clear. *Mrs D. Little — Vine & Craven (Anna Bucknall)*. 849 (R), 1101 (OMa), 1610 (OMa).

LITTLE CRUMPLIN ..10-2.. 9 b.g. Pablond — Speckyfoureyes (Blue Cashmere) 3. Lengthy hobdayed. Dam won NH flat and 2 2m4f Hdles. NH FLAT '96/7 r2 p1 (3rd). NH '97/8 r3 p0. P-t-P '99 r7 w1 (Maiden) p3 (3rds); last pair 2, and fell 1. Seemed to appreciate the easy three miles when scooting home at Larkhill in '99, and might have captured a Restricted at the first time of asking but for falling two out when holding a narrow lead at Kingston Blount subsequently, but disappeared after just one outing in 2000 and presumably went wrong. Was third in a hot Larkhill Restricted won by River Swilley having led going into the last, and compensation awaits if he is able to return. *M.J. Tuckey & M.J. Owen — Bicester with Whaddon (Herbie Owen).* 13 (R).

LITTLE FARMER ..—.. 7 b.g. Little Wolf — Sea Farmer (Cantab) bp. Half-brother to Pretty Boy George (*qv*). Sold Doncaster, Jan for 2000. Brought down at the second on his debut, and then bolted one and a half circuits of Detling before contesting the race and pulling up at the 11th. Phillip Hall certainly agrees to ride some loads of rubbish (eg Just Try Me), and 35 minutes later Leggies Legacy refused at the third with him. *C. Hall — Southdown & Eridge (Suzanne Hall).* 309 (OMa), 577 (OMa).

LITTLE NATIVE (IRE) ..10-0.. 6 b.br.g. Be My Native (USA) — Royal Character (Reformed Character) 1u. Workmanlike half-brother to Bit Of A Character (*qv*). Bought Doncaster, May for 27,000. Got off to a bright start when officially dead-heating with Conquer The Kilt in a Milborne St Andrew Maiden (our man on line gave him the nod by a short head; the stewards inflicted a £50 fine on Tim Mitchell for excessive use of the whip), and was tracking the leaders when he unseated Polly Gundry four out in a Restricted two months later. Would doubtless have had no chance with another five-year-old Abbots Court, but looks a promising novice in his own right, and likely to score again soon. *P.K. Barber & J.A. Keighley — Blackmore & Sparkford V. (Richard Barber).* 212 (CfMa), 1135 (R).

LITTLE-NIPPER ..—.. 16 ch.g. Derrylin — Emily Kent (Royal Palace) p. Rangy goose-rumped half-brother to Loddon Lad, to jumping winner, Emily's Star, and to Hurdles winner, Buzzi Boy. NH FLAT '89 r2 w1 p0. NH '89/90, '92/3 and '97 r17 w2 (2m Hdle and 2m5f Ch) p3. P-t-P '98 (for Mr D.C. Bostock') r1 p0 (fell). A fair performer under Rules the best part of a decade ago, and rumoured to have been retired after falling in his first Point in '98, but returned to put up before halfway in a Cartmel Hunter Chase for new connections this year. Has made more comebacks than ol' blue eyes himself, but surely his pension book has been called for now. *S. Currie — Pendle Forest & Craven.* 1643 (3m2fH).

LITTLE RIVER PLACE ..—.. 8 ch.g. Master Willie — Be Spartan (Spartan General) p. Strong-topped owner-bred half-brother to Rowan Heights, and to the winners, Easby Joker (NH flat and jumping), Pennethorpe Place (NH flat) and Baron Safeguard (Hurdles). NH '98 (from G.B. Balding's) r2 p0 (tailed off 2 — pulled up 1). Weakened quickly after making a lot of the running at Detling, and appears hard to train. *Sir Christopher Wates — E. Sussex & Romney Marsh (Di Grissell).* 759 (OMa).

LITTLE SANTA (IRE) ..10-3.. 9 b.m. Little Bighorn — Santa's Gold (Tumble Gold) 2upp22. Lengthy. IRISH P-t-P '97 r4 p0 (4th, pulled up 2, and brought down 1). P-t-P '98/9 r13 w2 (Maiden and PPORA Mares) p5 (4 2nds, beaten neck once); unseated 2, pulled up 1, and ran out 1. Took 14 races to get off the mark, but came good in a bad Maiden at Corbridge and followed up with victory in a PPORA mares race at Mosshouses in '99. Again proved aggravating in 2000 when runner-up three more times, beaten under two lengths twice, and was pulled up apparently unsound for the second time in two years at Friars Haugh. An improved performer, but becoming quirkier (reluctant to start once) and is not an easy ride. Sometimes wears a tongue-strap. *Mrs D. Davidson — Percy (Nick & Kirsty Hargreave).* 361 (L), 621 (L), 715 (L), 1079 (L), 1429 (Cm), 1495 (I).

LITTLE STAR ..9-8.. 8 ch.m. Le Moss — Mickley Vulstar (Sea Moss) pp2f. Small plain half-sister to Instabene, Guild Street, Mickleover and Abbey Moss. Dam, half-sister to 8 Pointers, won a Members and 3rd. Her 20 lengths second represented a much improved effort, but unfortunately broke a shoulder at Brampton Bryan next time. *Miss B. Hyde — N. Herefords (Sally Godsall).* 332 (M), 484 (R), 616 (CMa), 865 (CfMa).

LITTLE VERA ..9-11.. 6 b.m. Carlingford Castle — Bonnyhill Lass (Royal Fountain) 1. Plain. Dam, is half-sister to Fell Mist (*qv* '99 Annual), was 2nd in a Maiden for Charmaine Raw ('seems very moody'). NH FLAT June '99 (from C. Grant's) r1 p0. Backed from 20s to 7s and whoed a little ability in her Bumper, and made a winning start in Points despite hanging left on the run-in in a Maiden in softish at Witton Castle. May have scope for further improvement. *H. Raw — Hurworth (Charmaine Raw).* 1330 (OMa).

LITTLE VERALYN ..9-1.. 6 b.m. Good Thyne (USA) — The Little Bag (True Song) p3. Small. Dam won 8 Points (inc an Open) and hat-trick for Mrs Jarvis) and placed 6, and grandam, Ruakura, won 6 Points (3 in Ireland) and placed 12. novicey on her debut, but did a lot better when five lengths third in a very slowly-run Maiden next time. Descended from a good line, and it will be disappointing if she does not land a Maiden at least at six. *Dr D.B.A. Silk & H. Jarvis — Kent & Surrey Bloodhounds (Heather Silk).* 98 (OMa), 291 (CMa).

LIVE WIRE (IRE) ..9-9.. 10 b.g. Electric — Green Gale (Strong Gale) 13436. Sturdy half-brother to La Tormenta (IRE). P-t-P/HUNT CH '96/9 (for Mr C.C. Trietline) r14 w1 (Maiden) p2; pulled up 5, and unseated 1. Won a bad Maiden at Upper Sapey, but failed to progress in the previous yard, and beaten 12 times consecutively over four seasons until Caroline Bailey got her hands on him. Won at 20-1 on his first attempt for her, but failed to reproduce that form again in four subsequent starts. A safe ride for Gregor Kerr, but can be guaranteed to lose his pitch as soon as the tempo increases before staying on again when it is too late and it is for that reason that he is suited by a stiff uphill finish. Basically disappointing, and will continue to be one of the stables lesser lights for as long as he resides there. *Dr G.R. Kerr — Farmers Bloodhounds (Caroline Bailey).* 74 (CCf), 428 (Cf), 609 (I), 1006 (Cf), 1267 (I).

LLAN CROSS LADY (IRE) ..—.. 9 b.m. Jeu De Paille (FR) — Nan's Mill (Milford) 3f. Tall. P-t-P '98 r3 p0 (pulled up 3). NH '98 r1 p0 (pulled up). Showed speed for up to 2m2f when last seen, but appeared to stay not a yard further, and again set out as though the devil himself was in pursuit on her return. Not a novice ride (out of control on her reappearance and crashed when leading a week later), but even experienced pilots had trouble anchoring her previously, and seems very unlikely to achieve much in Points. *D.L. Evans — Pembs (Gary Barber).* 1052 (L), 1224 (L).

LOCAL CUSTOMER ..8-6.. 16 b.g. Le Bavard (FR) — Penny Bar (Bargello) 5546. Tall lengthy hobdayed brother to Irish Pointing winner, Aegean Pearl. IRISH NH '90 r1 p0. IRISH P-t-P '91 r3 w1 (5yo&up Maiden) p2 (2nds). NH '91/2 (blinkered 6) and '93/5 r24 w4 (2m4f-3m2f Chses) p7. P-t-P/HUNT CH '93 and '97/9 r23 w2 (Opens) p4 (2nd in Hunt Ch; and 3 3rds; also disqualified from 2nd for not weighing-in once); refused 1, unseated 2, and pulled up 5. Sweetened to great effect in '93, but a sorry sight since and plods amazingly slowly nowadays. Hopelessly tailed off last in five outings for Sue Matthews and should humiliated no more. *Miss S.E. Matthews — Pembs.* 1224 (L), 1402 (MO), 1571 (Cnr), 1658 (MO).

LOC A LUA (IRE) ..9-7.. 9 b.g. Rising — Alchymya (Cosmo) 2f. Tall rangy. Dam won mares Maiden in Ireland. IRISH NH '97 r1 p0. Gave what looked to be a promising display when five lengths second to Philtre at Whitwick on his first appearance for three years, but fell at halfway when favourite next time, and promptly vanished again. Takes a keen hold, and jumped to the right once, so may have been trying to save a leg. *D. Carroll — Teme V. (John Tulloch).* 339 (CfMa), 491 (CfMa).

LOCH ASH ..9-7.. 8 b.g. Lochnager — Seeker's Sister (Ashmore FR) up2p4. Good-bodied plain half-brother to Sister Lark (*qv*). P-t-P '98/9 r5 p0 (pulled up 4, and fell 1). A strong-pulling non-stayer, but persuaded to complete for the first time in eight outings by Mark Jackson when second in his Members where he jumped the last upsides the winner only to go down by a length. Flattered by the bare form and was a bad value favourite on his final start where he had run himself into the ground by the third last and finished tailed off. Appears on the verge of exploding in the paddock and has two handlers. *R.M. Phillips & P. Nash — Mr & Mrs R.M. Phillips — Clifton-on-Teme (Annie Downes).* 527 (OMa), 673 (2m4fOMa), 697 (OMa), 989 (OMa), 1466 (OMa).

LOCHCHOIRE ..—.. 8 b.g. Lochnager — Shemust (Deadly Nightshade) pp. Tall lengthy half-brother to Shecould. Dam is half-sister to 8 Pointers, including Castle Of May (*qv* '94 Annual). NH FLAT '99 r1 p0 (16th). P-t-P '99 (for Mr D.V. Gardner) r3 p0 (pulled up 2, and ran out 1). NH Jun '99 r1 p0 (pulled up at 6th). Has only once gone beyond two miles to date, has yet to finish and it seems unlikely that he will stay much further. Taken to post early on his reappearance. *M.D. Jones — Llangibby.* 392 (R), 479 (Cf).

LOCHNAGRAIN (IRE) ..10-8.. 13 b.g. Strong Gale — Mountain Sedge (Goldhill) 1. Small half-brother to Ronans Birthday and Wild Argosy, and to jumping winner, Mountain Mear. Dam won a 12f flat race and 2 2m Hdles in Ireland. NH FLAT '93 and '94 r3 w1 p0. NH '94/8 r28 w8 (4 Hdles, 2m-3m1f, and 4 Chses, 2m1f-3m1f; inc hat-trick) p14. P-t-P/HUNT CH '98/9 r13 w5 (2m6f Hunt Ch, 3 Opens and Mixed Open, inc 4-timer '99) p4 (3 3rds, and of once); pulled up 1, brought down 1, and fell 1. A useful performer under Rules, but often failed to deliver as much as he promised, and found Pointing right up his street. Won Opens effortlessly in '99, and made the switch back to regulation fences in some style when landing a Hereford Hunter Chase this year, though the opposition was not particularly strong. Failed to reappear and may have suffered a setback. Can be sketchy over big fences (though jumped well in the main at Hereford) but can produce a turn of foot particularly on a sound surface. Has had a soft-palate operation, and formerly tried in a tongue-strap. *Mrs S. Dunsdon — Surrey U. (Nick Gifford).* 468 (3m1f110yH).

LOCH NA KEAL ..9-9.. 9 b.m. Weldnaas (USA) — Keyanloch (Lochnager) p57. Light-framed half-sister to flat winner, Porte Belloch. Dam, half-sister to Key Diver (*qv* '99 Annual), won 2m Hdle. NH FLAT '96 (first 3 for C.T. Nash) r4 p1 (2nd). NH '96/8 (won from C. Morlock's) r10 w1 (2m5f Hdle, 6 ran and 3 finished) p2; pulled up final 3, Chses last 2. Contested the lead at the 14th in both Points, but failed to get the trip, and was last when completing in her Members. Tried a shorter Hunter Chase, but was outclassed. Generally lightly raced, and gained her only success on firmish in May '97. *Mr & Mrs S. Kimber — O. Berks (Mrs J. Kimber).* 736 (Cnr), 1202 (M), 1444 (2m5fH).

LOCHNOMORE ..10-9.. 8 br.g. Lochnager — Chocolate Ripple (Hasty Word) f1f114. Workmanlike. Grandam, Gay Ripple, failed to finish in 2 Points. P-t-P '98/9 r6 w2 (Maiden and

Restricted) p3 (2nds, beaten head once); and unseated 1. Followed three seconds in which he was beaten a maximum of two lengths with a stylish double in '99, and has maintained his climb up the ratings this season. Unbeaten in his last five Pointing completions, he was most impressive in his annihilation of Mickthecutaway in the fastest time of the day at Bitterley, but his fast low style of fencing has so far got him into trouble over the bigger obstacles. Fell at the first when racecourse on his Hunter Chase debut and was still in with a fighting chance until a last fence blunder ended his hopes on his final outing at Cheltenham. Raced almost exclusively on soft ground until this season, but has coped admirably on a much quicker surface. Has top riders at his disposal, Richard Burton being the latest. A keen sort, not surprisingly considering his sire, and unlikely to appreciate a severe test of stamina, but will hopefully get another chance to prove his worth over regulation fences in 2001. *Mrs J. Thornton — Wheatland (John Downes)*. 18 (I), 175 (I), 580 (3mH), 614 (O), 988 (O), 1336 (2m4fH).

LOCKETT'S LAMP (IRE) ..8-2.. 8 b.g. Miner's Lamp — Comeragh Breeze (Beau Chapeau) f2. Tall strong. P-t-P '98 r2 p0 (last, and fell 1). Well held in both completions to date, but was performing off the back of a fall each time and might be capable of better. Clearly hard to train though, and his jumping requires attention. *Mrs D.E. Farmer — Blackmore & Sparkford V. (Jane Galpin)*. 12 (OMa), 408 (OMa).

LOFTUS LAD (IRE) ..9-13§.. 13 b.g. Le Bavard (FR) — Maeves Invader (Brave Invader USA) pcp. Tall lengthy. IRISH P-t-P '93/6 r21 w3 (inc Open) p7 (2nds); pulled up 3, and refused. IRISH NH '94 and '96/8 (tried blinkered) r28 w2 (2m6f Chses) p4; inc 5th in Hunt Ch. P-t-P '99 (for Mr T.D.B. Underwood) r5 p2 (3rds); 4th, and pulled up 2. Won fives races in Ireland to '96, but beaten in his 30 most recent attempts, and has failed to complete in his last five racecourse appearances. Quite well supported when carried out by a loose horse in his Members, but unlikely to achieve much outside of Hunt class in future. *J. Read — Hursley Hambledon (Kate Buckett)*. 130 (CMod), 324 (M), 453 (CF).

LOFTY DEED (USA) ..—.. 11 b.g. Shadeed (USA) — Soar Aloft (USA) (Avatar USA) fr. Leggy half-brother to 5 winners in USA. FLAT r15 p3 (all at 2; inc 2 Sells, short-headed once). NH '94/9 r36 w1 (2m Sell Hdle) p6; ran poorly 2 Chses. P-t-P '99 (for Mr G.M. Thomson & Mrs C. Hicks) r6 p3 (2 3rds, of 4 once); refused 2, and pulled up 1. Raced almost exclusively in Selling Hurdles under Rules, and won one at Leicester back in '95, but has never been very keen and beaten in his last 40 races. Failed to clear one fence successfully in 2000, indeed, foiled by the first fence in his last four Points, and should not be asked to race in them again. Often blinkered in the past. *M. Howell — Worcs.* 1064 (3m2fCf), 1436 (Cf).

LOGICAL FUN ..8-4§.. 13 b.g. Nishapour (FR) — Thimblerigger (Sharpen Up) prr. Short-legged sturdy half-brother to Cleavers Gate, to flat winner, Mister Baileys (top-class, won '94 2000 Guineas), and to 3 winners abroad, including Skimbleshanks (in Canada) and Dearly Dancing (Germany). Dam won at 10f. IRISH FLAT '90 r4 p1 (3rd). IRISH NH FLAT '92 r3 w1 (on sands at Laytown) p2 (2nds, short-headed once). IRISH NH '92 r6 w1 (2m Hdle) p4. FLAT r1 p0. NH '92/3 (lame final) r7 p1 (3rd). P-t-P/HUNT CH '96/9 r20 p5 (3 2nds); pulled up 8, and unseated 1. A winner on a beach and in a bog to '92, and has five decne Pointing placings to his name, but performed abysmally in '99, and even worse this time around. Regained blinkers on his final start, and must be ailing. How he would love to trade places with his sibling, enjoying the delights of the blueblooded girls at the Vinery Stud in Kentucky. *L. Brennan — Cheshire Forest.* 781 (Cf), 903 (O), 1198 (O).

LONESOME TRAVELLER (NZ) ..9-10.. 12 b.g. Danzatore (CAN) — Honey Doll (Rheingold) 4. Tall strong half-brother to 2 winners in USA. P-t-P/HUNT CH '95/6 and '98/9 (for Mr & Mrs R. Hand) r39 w4 (inc Confined) p15 (9 2nds, last once); pulled up 2, and fell 1. NH Summer '99 (from D.C. Turner's) r2 p0 (pulled up 2). An expert jumper, but has made the frame on 22 occasions, but indolent and requires plenty of rousting to keep his mind on the job. Got little help from the saddle on his reappearance and was only too pleased to lope along near the back. Suited by long trips in mud, and hates firm ground. Absent since January. *M. Stevens — Aldenham H.* 85 (O).

LONGMORE (IRE) ..9-12.. 9 br.g. Miner's Lamp — Gambell And Dream (Warpath) f143. Half-brother to Chasing winner, Black Statement (IRE). IRISH P-t-P '96 and '98/9 r18 w2 (4&5yos Mdn, and Winners of One) p2 (2nds); pulled up 8, and fell. Sold Doncaster, May for 10,000. Ploughed through the heavy ground when landing an Intermediate taking nearly seven minutes at Great Trethew (River Swilley was holding a slight advantage but exhausted when he declined the final fence, leaving only two to get round), but disappointing when beaten more than 25 lengths subsequently (favourite once). Might find another easy opportunity, but pulled up in almost 50 per cent of his Irish Points, and is clearly nothing special, by Barber standards at least. *J.G. Phillips — Cattistock (Richard Barber)*. 37 (CI), 162 (I), 521 (O), 1133 (O).

LONGSTONE BOY (IRE) ..10-6.. 9 br.g. Mazaad — Inger-Lea (Record Run) 331u. Workmanlike. Dam won 2m4f Sell Hdle. NH FLAT '97 r1 p0. P-t-P '98/9 r4 w2 (Maiden and Restricted) p0; pulled up 1, and unseated 1. Swooped late in typical Paul Hamer style when successful twice in '99, and added his Members this season, but found the ground too lively otherwise in 2000 and on the one occasion he got genuinely soft ground his habit of belting fences caused his undoing. Should take a soft ground Intermediate at the very least in 2001. *E.R. Clough & Mrs D. Harris — S. Pembs (Debbie Hamer).* 600 (I), 837 (I), 1221 (M), 1613 (I).

PLATE 75   1221 South Pembrokeshire Hunt Members: Cresswell Quay (G. Lewis), 2nd, and Longstone Boy (P. Hamer), 1st, are none too tidy at a very rare beastie — a Welsh permanent wooden jump
PHOTO: Alun Sedgemore

LOOK IN THE MIRROR ..10-9.. 10 b.g. Rakaposhi King — Moaning Jenny (Privy Seal) u2f432112. Lengthy angular half-brother to NH flat winner, Steady Eddy. NH FLAT '96 r2 p0. NH '97/8 r14 w1 (3m2f Sell Hdle) p3 (2nds). P-t-P '99 r11 w3 (2 Ladies and PPORA) p2 (3rds, remote once); 4th twice, 5th, and unseated 3. A gift horse to present connections, who have done extremely well to extract five wins from an animal previously prone to be very moody. Looked sure to win on his debut in Hunter Chases when rounding the final turn at Hereford with a clear lead, but compounded on the run to the judge (the last fence was omitted) and was collared in the final furlong. Fell three out when in total command at Mollington next time, but gained compensation when making all at Hereford subsequently. A reformed character who clearly appreciates the presence of a girl in the saddle and capable of jumping boldly in the lead throughout. Sure to win again if maintaining his consistent new found enthusiasm. *C. Hammett — Cotswold (Fergal O'Brien).* 79 (O), 222 (3m1f110yH), 787 (L), 860 (L), 1087 (MO), 1266 (L), 1346 (3m1f110yH), 1605 (L), 1648 (3mH).

LOOK SHARPE ..9-6§.. 10 b.g. Looking Glass — Washburn Flyer (Owen Dudley) pRfp. Unfurnished. NH FLAT r2 p1 (24l 2nd). P-t-P '97/9 r11 p3 (2nds, of 3 once); on floor 4, and pulled up 1. Undoubtedly has the ability to win a little race, but a Jeykll and Hyde character and thesedays the former is nowhere to be seen. Pulls like stink, treats the fences with no respect, and often difficult to steer, but otherwise a real Christian apart from when he's terrorising the others at the start. Has been taken to post early. *T.S. Sharpe — York & Ainsty S.* 798 (OMa), 1003 (OMa), 1331 (OMa), 1628 (2m4f110yH).

LOOKS LIKE REIGN ..—.. 7 b.g. Royal Vulcan — Spy The Ark (Arkan) ppfpff. Small close-coupled unfurnished. Dam, 'has no potential', pulled up in 3 Points for the Masons. A wild jumper and hard puller who is an exceptionally unpleasant ride, and sometimes goes to post early (has unseated in the paddock, and also at the start). Broke a blood vessel on his debut. Remote when senselessly presented at the final fence at Garthorpe, where he took a crashing fall — another brainless piece of riding by the gnarled veteran Andy Tutton, who was similarly dim on Stable Girl at Guilsborough. Should not be allowed to compete whilst in such a state. *J.R. & Miss S. Mason — Pytchley (John Mason).* 94 (O), 431 (L), 1021 (2m4fOMa), 1421 (OMa), 1437 (OMa), 1590 (2m4fOMa).

LOOK WHO'S CALLING (IRE) ..—.. 8 b.g. Al Hareb (USA) — House Call (Artaius USA) ppp. Big half-brother to flat winners, Look Who's Here and Munguy (both later also successful abroad). FLAT (for B. McMahon, tried in blinkers) r21 p5 (beaten 9*l* plus final 3, inc Sell). Sold Doncaster, Nov for 600. Inconsistent and had steering problems on the flat, and has so far shown no aptitude for Pointing (pulled up thrice, including with a slipped saddle once). *Miss L. Llewellyn & V. Hughes — Llangeinor (Lisa Llewellyn).* 349 (CfMa), 455 (OMa), 950 (OMa).

LORD CHAMBERLAIN ..8-5.. 8 b.g. Be My Chief (USA) — Metaphysique (FR) (Law Society USA) ppfr. Tall half-brother to flat winner, Philosophic. Dam won at 10f in France. P-t-P '99 r1 p1 (3rd). NH FLAT Summer '99 (from H. Lavis') r2 p0. Thirty-one lengths third on his only Pointing appearance in '99, but an unmitigated disaster this year and refused when tried in blinkers on his final start. Got wedged in the fence, but was extricated, and may need some confidence therapy before he reappears. *J.R. Jones — V. of Clettwr.* 30 (CMa), 270 (CfMa), 834 (OMa), 951 (OMa).

LORD ELLANGOWAN (IRE) ..9-6.. 8 ch.g. Astronef — Gossip (Sharp Edge) pff5f142. Compact brother to flat winner, Celestial Rumour and half-brother to Gymcrak Tiger (IRE), and to 2 winners (one in Malaysia). 5600y, 4800 2-y-o. FLAT r16 p2 (2nds on equitrack in '96, beaten head once). NH '96/8 (for R. Ingram, blinkered last 4) r5 p0. Not better than 55 lengths last in his first five Points (fell in three of them), but then acquired David Dunsdon, and beat the only other finisher by a short head in a Maiden on firmish at Parham. Still only capable of modest form, but in a weak area, which may enable him to score again. His new partner also transformed former stablemate Jamies First, and his unusual talent coupled with excellent connections (cousin to Nick Gifford) should ensure that he goes far. *Mr & Mrs S.J. & Miss S.A. Dawson — Surrey U. (Sarah Dawson).* 5 (Cv&nr), 10 (O), 63 (I), 221 (OMa), 309 (OMa), 709 (OMa), 1104 (R), 1392 (M).

PLATE 76   *1392 Surrey Union Hunt Members: Lord Ellangowan (D. Dunsdon), 2nd, lands ahead of Time Enough (P. Townsley), 3rd, and Bit Of An Idiot (D. Slattery), 1st*

PHOTO: John Beasley

LORD GEORGE ..9-13.. 9 ch.g. Lord Bud — Mini Gazette (London Gazette) p66p33. Small sparely-made half-brother to St Amour and Rough Edge. P-t-P '97/9 r17 w1 (Maiden) p4 (3 2nds, of 3 once); pulled up 6, and fell 1. Finally managed to hit the target at the 17th attempt, but struggles to stay when conditions are testing and only struck form when the ground dried up in May this season. Beaten eight-and-a-half and six lengths when third in races taking only just over six minutes on his last two starts and might strike it lucky under similar conditions in 2001. Ran too freely when tried in blinkers once. *D.G. Atkinson — Bedale.* 137 (R), 278 (R), 620 (R), 807 (R), 1348 (Cf), 1475 (R).

LORD HARRY (IRE) ..11-7.. 9 b.g. Mister Lord (USA) — Vickies Gold (Golden Love) 111111. Big lengthy brother to Hazel Reilly (IRE) (*qv*). IRISH P-t-P '96/7 r7 w3 (up to Winners of Two) p3 (3rds); and fell 1. P-t-P/HUNT CH '98/9 r9 w5 (inc 3 Confineds and Open) p3 (2 3rds, inc Hunt Ch; and head 2nd in Hunt Ch). A useful Pointer before the start of the 2000 season, but had flopped when taking on class opponents, so his resurgence as a potential star was good to see. Readily rattled off an Open four-timer and then Alastair Crow made up for his '98 Bangor faux-pas when landing a richly deserved success in the North West Area Championship Final in May. Saved his most impressive performance for last when quickening to the front turning for home he dished out an authoritative beating to Balisteros in the John Corbet Cup at Stratford with Lakefield Rambler et al trailing 30 lengths and more behind. A resolute galloper who is blessed with a turn of foot and makes no noticeable jumping errors. Deserves the opportunity to have a crack at the premier races in 2001, and good enough to aim at the top staying Handicaps. *M.J. Parr — N. Salop (Sheila Crow)*. 369 (O), 565 (O), 903 (O), 1073 (O), 1559 (3m110yH), 1646 (3m4fH).

PLATE 77   1646 Weatherbys John Corbet Champion Nov HC, Stratford: The superb Lord Harry (A. Crow), 1st, leads Balisteros (Miss J. Wormall), 2nd, at the second last

PHOTO: Brian Armstrong

LORDINTHESKY (IRE) ..10-2.. 10 ch.g. Mister Lord (USA) — Deirdre Elizabeth (Salluceva) 23725p. Sturdy half-brother to Banteer Bet (IRE) (*qv*). IRISH NH FLAT '98 r1 p0. IRISH NH '98 r1 p0 (cross-country ch). IRISH P-t-P '96/7 and '99 r11 w1 (4&5yo Mdn) p4 (3rds); pulled up 2, and unseated. Bought Malvern, Oct for 3200. Gave decent displays when beaten a maximum of 11 lengths in three Pointing placings, but was outclassed in Hunter Chases. Failed to recover from a bad mistake at Ludlow, and was subsequently destroyed. Mrs A. Price — Teme V. 340 (R), 479 (Cf), 683 (3mH), 863 (R), 1023 (3mH), 1293 (3mH).

LORD KILTON ..9-0.. 13 ch.g. Crested Lark — Kilton Jill (Adropejo) pp. Small half-brother to Lady Kilton. Dam won 2 Points and 3rd 2 (one win for Bob Cowley). Grandam, Kilton Hill, won 2m4f Hunt Ch and 5 Points and placed 13. P-t-P/HUNT CH '93/9 r14 w1 (2m4f110y Hunt Ch) p1 (2nd); failed to finish 11 (unseated 2, and ran out 1). The incredibly lucky winner of a farcical two runner Warwick Hunter Chase in '97, but hardly ever runs and has pulled up in just four outings since. Never going keenly on his latest appearance and will surely not be asked to turn out again in 2001. *Mrs D. Cowley — Pytchley*. 1192 (O), 1585 (O).

LORD KNOX (IRE) ..10-3.. 11 ch.g. Tale Quale — Lady Knox (Dalsaan) 33p71pp2. Big strong. IRISH P-t-P '96 r6 p0; pulled up 3. P-t-P/HUNT CH '97/9 r17 w2 (Maiden and Restricted) p3 (3rds, of 4 once); pulled up 4, and fell 2. Successful in both of his first two completions, but usually takes a fierce hold and fails to stay, and had run up 16 successive defeats prior to his latest victory in an uncompetitive four-runner Hunt race. Ran well in a sub-3m Hunter Chase on his final start, but those behind him were truly awful, and he will rarely find such a weak race again. Avoids ground any softer than good. Blinkered once in '98. *B.G. Clark — Puckeridge.* 18 (I), 92 (Cf), 510 (Cf), 609 (I), 839 (M), 937 (I), 1381 (O), 1540 (2m5fH).

LORD LARD (IRE) ..7-11.. 7 b.g. Lord Americo — Shuil Ard (Quayside) fp3pp. Small neat half-brother to Native Isle (IRE) *(qv).* Has only managed to plod to completion once so far, when 65 lengths last. *M.H. Weston — Worcs.* 337 (CfMa), 528 (OMa), 898 (OMa), 1068 (3m2fOMa), 1360 (2m4fOMa).

LORD LEVI (IRE) ..10-6.. 11 ch.g. Mister Lord (USA) — Puntabela (Way Up North) p1p34. Good-topped. IRISH P-t-p '95 and '98 r9 w1 (7yo&up Maiden) p1 (3rd); pulled up 3, and fell/unseated 2. P-t-P '99 r4 p1 (last of 3); 6th, 8th, and pulled up 1. Disqualified by the local Stewards after winning a three-finisher Restricted at Lanark, but subsequently reinstated on appeal by the Jockey Club Disciplinary Committee. Much improved by the acquisition of Wilson Renwick on his last two starts, but hit the front too soon at Kelso and then overdid the waiting tactics at Hexham. Previously a headstrong sort who struggled to get the trip, but more amenable to restraint now and deserves compensation over the bigger fences. *Mrs L.A. Ogilvie — Lanarks & Renfrews.* 360 (R), 663 (R), 915 (3m1fH), 1342 (3m1fH), 1445 (3m1fH).

LORD NICK ..10-1.. 11 b.g. Silly Prices — Cheeky Pigeon (Brave Invader USA) p22. Small neat trainer-bred half-brother to Catch The Pigeon. Dam, half-sister to Lion Hill *(qv* '88 Season Annual), was entered for Points as a 15-year-old in '97, but failed to appear. NH FLAT '96 r2 p0 (always behind). NH '96 r1 p0. P-t-P '98 (for Mrs C. Barr & Mrs P. Cartmell) r2 w1 (Maiden) p0; and 5th. Won his Maiden on firm ground at Mordon in '99, and twice beaten four lengths in Restricteds this year, but very sparingly raced to date and has only managed eight outings in five years. Not very big to be humping 12st and might be worth a spin in Ladies company. *Mrs R.E. Barr — Cleveland (Christine Barr).* 689 (R), 807 (R), 1475 (R).

LORD NORTH (IRE) ..—.. 6 b.g. Master Lord (USA) — Mrs Hegarty (Decent Fellow) p. Dam is half-sister to Ballyhannon *(qv).* Sold Doncaster, May for 22,000. Hinted at ability before pulling up at Maisemore (in a race won by a horse who cost 1550gns). *J. Wright — Croome & W. Warwicks (Gabe Mahon).* 899 (OMa).

LORD OF THE RINGS ..9-6.. 9 b.g. Arctic Lord — Sister Of Gold (The Parson) 92f4pu. Small neat brother to Twotensforafive, and half-brother to Irish NH flat and Hurdles winner, Cardinal Mark. NH FLAT '97 r3 p0. NH '97/8 r10 p3; Sells last 2. P-t-P '99 (for Mr J.M. Turner) r6 w1 (Maiden) p2 (3rds, of 4 once); 6th, and pulled up 2. Lacked resolve in the previous yard and confirmed that impression in 2000. Brushed aside in a poor Ladies at Bishops Court, and never went a yard in his last two appearances. The antithesis of stablemate Millyhenry, but at least riding him keeps Charlotte Tizzards' feet (and occasionally all of her) on the ground. *A. Tizzard — Blackmore & Sparkford V.* 208 (R), 405 (L), 636 (L), 879 (I), 1061 (R), 1376 (R).

LORD RYMAX ..—.. 9 b.g. Rymer — Heron's Mirage (Grey Mirage) pp. Big rangy owner-bred half-brother to Red Oassis *(qv).* P-t-P '99 r1 p0 (pulled up). Kept in touch for 2m2f on his final start, but looked an awkward cus previously and a racecourse appearance is a rarity. Appears to be rather highly strung. *Mrs J.Z. Munday — Ludlow (Geoff Evans).* 339 (CfMa), 669 (R).

LORD SPIDER ..9-9.. 9 b.g. Town And Country — Lolly Spider (Rugantino) pfp. Big strong half-brother to Express Spider, Majestic Spider, Country Spider, Baroness Spider, Handy Spider, Conkerdor and Spiderdore. Dam, half-sister to Crane Fly and cousin to Romany Biscuit, was 3rd twice in Points. Grandam, Brown Spider, won 8 Points and a Cheltenham Hunter Chase and placed 8, and great-grandam, Miss Muffet IV, won 3 Points. P-t-P '97 and '99 r2 p1 (2nd) and unseated 1. Only able to appear twice in the previous three seasons, but sent off odds-on on his latest outing only to disappoint once more. From a very successful family, and in a knowledgeable yard, but seems impossible to train properly and is a talent gone down the drain. *J.G. Cann — E. Devon (Ollie Cann).* 260 (R), 401 (M), 739 (OMa).

LORD TORRIDON (IRE) ..—.. 8 b.g. Torus — Minizen Lass (Hittite Glory) ff. Dam won 6 flat, 6-7f, inc 5-timer at 3. Gave lady riders torrid times when crashing in Maidens (in the lead at the 11th, and at the second). *A. Hamilton — Jedforest.* 188 (OMa), 1153 (OMa).

L'ORPHELIN ..9-1.. 6 ch.g. Gildoran — Balula (Balinger) f36. Lengthy attractive owner-bred. Dam is half-sister to Wodehouse *(qv* '98 Annual). Could do with jumping better, but ran reasonably well when completing (including in a competitive Maiden on latest start), and should improve sufficiently to score soon. *Mrs J.E.B. Pope & Friends — Blackmore & Sparkford V. (Pauline Tizzard).* 732 (2m4fOMa), 874 (2m4fOMa), 1131 (OMa).

LOSTYNDYKE (IRE) ..9-7.. 11 b.g. Aristocracy — Kylebrack Wood VII (unknown) f. Tall half-brother to Odonnell Abu (IRE). IRISH P-t-P '95/7 r6 p1 (20f 3rd); pulled up 2, and fell 1. NH '98 r1 p0 (pulled up in 3m Ch). P-t-P/HUNT CH '98/9 r15 w1 (Maiden) p3 (2 2nds, ½l last once; and 3rd of 4); last 5, pulled up 4, ran out 1, and fell 1. A regular weak finisher whose only success to date came in a three-finisher Maiden at Howick taking 7min 15s in '98. Presumably hurt as a result of his Erw Lon tumble in February as he failed to reappear. *N. Criddle & M. & K. Glastonbury — Pentyrch (Ian Prichard).* 273 (R).

LOST YOUR MARBLES (IRE) ..9-0.. 8 b.m. Mandalus — Greensted Lady (Great Nephew) 41pupup5pu. Sturdy half-sister to flat and Chasing winner, Mr Poppleton. Dam won 2 flat, 12-14f. NH FLAT '98 r2 p0. NH '98 r1 p0 (pulled up in Hdle). P-t-P '99 r5 p1 (3rd of 4); pulled up 3, and fell 1. Won a poor youngsters Maiden at Larkhill in the opening month of the season, but only managed one more completion from eight subsequent starts when last tailed off last at Flete Park. Ran well for a substitute rider at Badbury Rings on one occasion in which she would have been a very respectable second to The Earth Moved but for unseating at the last. Gets in a stew before the race and has two handlers, but might be able to pick up a Restricted when conditions aren't too testing in 2001. *J.H. Mead — R.A.* 11 (OMa), 60 (OMa), 260 (R), 330 (R), 536 (R), 633 (R), 729 (R), 1043 (R), 1135 (R), 1536 (3m2fH).

LOTHIAN COMMODORE ..9-4.. 11 gr.g. Alias Smith (USA) — Lothian Lightning (Lighter) p. Big lengthy brother to Lothian Pilot, Lothian Lily and Chasing winner, Lothian Commander, and half-brother to Officer Lothian. HUNT CH '97 r1 p0 (5th). NH '96/7 and '99 (from N.G. Richards' in '99) r6 p0 (pulled up 5). Only able to complete the course twice from eight outings over a five-year period and obviously has a major physical flaw. *D.A. Whitaker — Fife (Alan & Lucy Normile).* 44 (OMa).

LOTHIAN MAGIC (IRE) ..9-0.. 10 ch.m. Florida Son — Lothian Lassie (Precipice Wood) 4. Tall half-sister to Precipice Run, and Class Of Ninetytwo (IRE), and to Irish NH flat and Hurdles winner, Lothian Buckskin. IRISH P-t-P '96/8 r13 w1 (5yo&up mares Maiden) p4; pulled up 5, and fell 1. P-t-P '99 (for Mr & Mrs C. Strang Steel) r8 p0 (4th, 6th, last pair 3, pulled up 2, and unseated 1). Won a three-finisher soft ground Maiden taking 7min 4s in Ireland in '97, but exposed as moderate in Restricteds last year. Almost immediately off the bridle on her reappearance in 2000, but plodded on to finish 20 lengths last of four. Failed to emerge again and may have gone wrong. *P. Stevens — V.W.H. (Sue Widdicombe).* 340 (R).

LOTTERY TICKET (IRE) ..9-11.. 12 b.g. The Parson — Beauty Run (Deep Run) 645777435 5u. Rangy unfurnished. Dam won Irish NH flat. NH FLAT Spr '95 r4 w1 p2 (2nds). NH '95/9 (one win for T. George; previously for J. Edwards; blinkered 1) r23 w1 (3m2f Ch, 4 ran and 3 finished) p7; pulled up 3 of final 4. Bought Malvern, May for 2100. Often let down by his jumping under Rules, but it was a fine feat to manage to complete the course in all ten Opens. Lazy and a hard ride, and tried in spurs. Often in contention for a long way, but simple to beat, and is done for as soon as the owner gets tired and begins to flop wildly in the saddle. *S.J. Robinson — Zetland.* 42 (O), 136 (O), 376 (MO), 422 (3m5fO), 622 (O), 716 (O), 1030 (O), 1327 (O), 1476 (O), 1578 (O), 1643 (3m2fH).

LOTTIE THE LOTUS ..10-3.. 12 ch.m. Crested Lark — Florence Eliza (Floriana) f22232. Strong home-bred half-sister to Larry The Lamb (*qv*). P-t-P '97/9 (for Mr, Mrs B. Smith & Mr G.B. Tarry) r8 w2 (Maiden and Restricted) p4 (2 2nds); and fell/unseated 2. A typical Tarry ride, but not as successful as she should be and has had her challenge mis-timed on at least five occasions in the past two seasons as well as letting two Kingston Blount events slip away through jumping errors. A beaten favourite five times in her career and punters certainly play with fire when investing on her. Often sweats and never takes the eye, but a tough mare with a turn of foot and deserves to win on a more regular basis in 2001. Acts on any going. *S. Watts & G.B. Tarry — Pytchley (Jimmy Tarry).* 243 (Cf), 510 (Cf), 788 (Cf), 1005 (M), 1215 (Cm), 1481 (Cf).

LOUGH NEAGH (IRE) ..8-6.. 11 b.g. Il Pontevecchio — Hanseletta (Prince Hansel) 3p3f3spp. Small unfurnished. Dam won Irish Maiden. P-t-P '99 r5 p2 (3rd of 4 once); last 2, and pulled up 1. Very modest and let slip a golden opportunity when Paul Sheldrake (who was riding like a whirling dervish on crack) managed to get himself unseated at the last when upsides the winner in a bad Pentreclwydau Maiden. Has only beaten three rivals in his 13 starts and often jumps badly. Tried in blinkers on his final start, but never picked up the bridle, and will struggle to secure a win. *B. Warfield — Pembs (Gary Barber).* 348 (CfMa), 650 (CfMa), 1056 (CfMa), 1225 (OMa), 1301 (OMa), 1456 (OMa), 1615 (OMa), 1661 (OMa).

LOUIS RENEE (IRE) ..—.. 10 ch.g. Cardinal Flower — Moon Lock (Lock And Load USA) uu. Tall rangy attractive brother to Irish Pointing winner, Dunmoon Lady, and half-brother to Irish Pointing winners, Tourig Lady (also won Chasing there) and Moon Lock Rose. NH FLAT '96/7 r2 p0. NH '98 (for W. McKenzie-Coles) r3 p0 (48/ 5th and pulled up 2 in Hdles). Twice got rid of Ben Woodhouse in the first mile, and fell again when loose once. Has always stood his racing exceptionally badly. *R.D.E. Woodhouse — Sinnington.* 276 (M), 394 (Cf).

LOUP ROUGE ..—.. 7 ch.m. Little Wolf — All Risks (Pitcairn) p. Small half-sister to Master Pan (*qv*). Bought Malvern, Oct for 1000. Connections had obviously done no preparatory work before taking her to Garnons, where she looked fat, started slowly, jumped badly and was hopelessly tailed off until pulled up after a mile. *V.W. Jordan — Ross H.* 450 (CfMa).

LOVE ACTINIUM (IRE) ..10-1.. 10 b.m. Actinium (FR) — Flashing Gaze (Ashmore FR) 15f1d. Compact quite attractive. NH '95 r2 p0. IRISH P-t-P '96 r2 p0 (mares Maiden) p1 (2nd); pulled up 4, and fell/unseated 2 (with every chance at last). NH '98 r1 p0 (pulled up in 3m Hdle). P-t-P/HUNT CH '97/9 r8 p2 (2nds); pulled up 1, and fell/unseated 3. An unlucky mare in previous seasons, and thoroughly deserved her Restricted success at Friars Haugh on her return, but only a sadist would have enjoyed her next appearance there. Fell at the first in her Members, but declared to run again around three hours later in the Confined which she duly won cleverly, however the sting in the tail came when Craig Niblo forgot to weigh-in, and connections were left to curse their ill luck once more. Compensation awaits. *E.J. Jamieson & D.I. McComb — Buccleuch (David McComb)*. 360 (R), 493 (Cf), 712 (M), 717 (Cf).

LOVELY LYNSEY (IRE) ..9-13.. 9 b.m. Buckskin (FR) — Wessex Habit (Monksfield) 53. Smallish attractive. Dam is half-sister to Vintage Lad (*qv* '97 Annual). IRISH NH FLAT '96/7 r4 p0. IRISH NH '97/8 (worn blinkers) r12 p2 (2nd in Hdle, and 3rd in Ch). P-t-P '99 (for Mr R. Mathias) r3 w2 (Maiden and Restricted) p0; and unseated 1. Well supported when winning two minor Points last year, but her season lasted just two weekends in 2000 and she appeared to finish unsound at Bexhill. Seems to lack the necessary scope to win again. *J.S.S. Hollins — Ashford V. (Gill Gladders)*. 824 (Cf), 983 (Cf).

LOXLEY-LAD ..9-9.. 9 gr.g. Zambrano — Loxley Air (Romany Air) p1pp35p. Lengthy half-brother to Gipsy Rew. Dam won Maiden and placed 4 for Mr Cox. P-t-P '99 (for Mr Mathias) r3 w2 (Maiden and 1). Schooled in erratic fashion last back-end, but not without ability and sprang a 33-1 shock on his first completion at Holnicote. Looked like repeating the dose at a later meeting there, but went down narrowly in a modest Restricted. Seems rather one-paced, but a steady jumper now and might be able to win again. Tried in a visor on his final outing in '99 and often tongue-tied this year. *G.P. Cox — Taunton V. (Carroll Gray)*. 207 (OMa), 352 (CfMa), 406 (R), 876 (R), 1375 (R), 1608 (R), 1650 (R).

PLATE 78　　352 West Somerset & Minehead Harriers Confined Maiden (Div 1): Loxley-Lad (G. Richards), 1st, jumps alongside Spirito (Jeremy Young), 2nd　　PHOTO: Brian Armstrong

LUCAS COURT ..9-7.. 15 b.g. Henbit (USA) — Boudoir (Klairon) p42. Angular short-backed half-brother to 2 flat winners, including Gayle's Pride (IRE) (in Austria). Dam won 2 flat, 6-8f. IRISH FLAT '88/9 r3 p1 (3rd). IRISH NH '89/93 (frequently blinkered) r38 w2 (2m4f Hdle and 2m Ch) p10. NH '94 r1 p0. P-t-P/HUNT CH '96 and '98/9 r14 p5 (3 2nds and last of 3 twice); pulled up 3, and unseated 1. A dual Irish winner in soft to '91, but has not scored since and failed to beat a rival in 2000. Regained blinkers in his Members, but ran poorly, and clearly not to be trusted in his old age. *S. Garrott — Ashford V.* 983 (Cf), 1109 (M), 1167 (CMod).

LUCKASHAN (IRE) ..9-13.. 6 b.g. Wakashan — Run Of Luck (Lucky Brief) 1f4p. Small compact half-brother to Hurdles winner, Over The Odds (IRE). Dam is half-sister to Boycott (*qv* '97 Annual) and Eliogarty. Sold Tattersalls Ireland Aug, for 3571. Made a winning start in a bad Maiden at Newton Bromswold (runner-up was the desperate Yodeller Bill), but let down by his jumping since. Seems to have plenty of stamina for a five-year-old, but tied up dramatically in the very soft ground at Kimble, and after going three lengths clear between the last two fences he stopped to nothing on the flat. Will need to be more confident at the obstacles if he is to realise his potential. *C.D. Collins — Cottesmore (Caroline Bailey).* 515 (OMa), 1009 (CR), 1146 (R), 1586 (CN).

LUCKY CHRISTOPHER ..10-0.. 16 b.g. St Columbus — Lucky Story (Lucky Sovereign) u233324. Compact good-bodied brother to Cropredy Lad and Larks Tail. P-t-P/HUNT CH '90/1 and '94/9 (for Mr B. & Mrs A. Smith & Mr G.B. Tarry) r52 w25 (inc 3m2f Hunt Ch, and 10 Opens; 6-timer in '95, 5-timer in '96 and '97) p16 (6 3rds, last once, and inc a Hunt Ch); failed to finish 9 (ran out 1, and fell/unseated 4). An extremely game old horse with an outstanding strike rate (has failed to win a prize in just 13 of 59 races) but this year was the first time he had failed to register a Pointing victory since his winning run began in '94. Still willing to try, but age has dulled his speed and no longer able to finish with his usual flourish. Has been a great credit to connections and would still make someone an ideal schoolmaster. *Mrs M. Goodwin & G.B. Tarry — Grafton (Jimmy Tarry).* 245 (L), 431 (L), 787 (L), 1145 (L), 1483 (L), 1622 (L), 1665 (L).

LUCKY COOMBE ..8-6.. 10 br.g. Newski (USA) — Fleeting Victoria (Vicky Joe) pp. Brother to Passing Comment, and half-brother to Moorcross and Tangle Trial. P-t-P '99 r6 p0 (pulled up 2, fell/unseated 4). Three lengths clear when unseating at the last at Kilworthy last year, but still seeking his first completion, and looked decidedly unenthusiastic when on his return (favourite once!!). Only managed two outings in March, and may have suffered a setback. *M.D. Wilkins — Spooners & W. Dartmoor (Mike Biddick).* 539 (OMa), 658 (R).

LUCKY JIM ..9-5.. 9 b.g. Faustus (USA) — Lola Black (FR) (Relkino) 15. Big half-brother to Hurdles winners, Thornton Gate (useful; also successful on flat) and Royal Crest. Dam won at 10f in France. P-t-P '98 r4 p1 (3rd); pulled up 2, and unseated 1. Beaten less than four lengths in his first completion, but had to wait 25 months before getting another chance and duly opened his account in the fastest of four Bonvilston Maidens this May. Failed to justify market support on his Restricted debut a week later when 30 lengths last at Bratton Down and needs to improve to figure in them in 2001. *Miss K. Lovelace — S. Dorset.* 1456 (OMa), 1563 (R).

LUCKY JOE (IRE) ..9-5.. 8 br.g. Denel (FR) — Breezy Dawn (Kemal FR) p1. Small. Dam won 2m6f Hdle in Ireland. IRISH P-t-P '98 r4 p0 (pulled up 3, and slipped up 1). P-t-P '99 (for Mr P.J. Millington) r6 w1 (Maiden) p1 (3rd); 5th, fell/unseated 2, and pulled up 1. Won a poor Maiden in soft at Mollington last year, and initiated a field day for trainer John White when landing his Members after a nine-week break on his latest appearance. Has beaten nothing of note, lacks scope and will struggle to find another opportunity. *C. Harris — Berks & Bucks (John White).* 791 (R), 1619 (M).

LUCKY TANNER ..10-2.. 10 b.g. Silly Prices — Go Gipsy (Move Off) 15641. Compact. NH FLAT r3 p0. NH '96/7 r4 p0 (3 Hdles, inc last once, and pulled up 1; and fell first in Ch). P-t-P '98/9 r6 w1 (Maiden) p1 (3rd); pulled up 1. Has made the most of his limited opportunities and connections can congratulate themselves on having got three races out of a cheap Henrietta Knight chuck-out. Stays on well and both his 2000 success were achieved in races were he looked to have no earthly chance with a mile to run. Already outclassed in Ladies races so will prove difficult to place successfully in future. *Miss J. Young, A. & Mrs P. Archer, S. Wheeler & Miss B. Willis — Tedworth (Jenny Young).* 331 (R), 475 (L), 749 (Cf), 1014 (3m5fL), 1279 (M).

LUCKY THURSDAY ..9-0.. 11 b.g. Sousa — Horwood Spirit (Sir Lark) fppup. Small. Dam, sister to Lucky Friday and Kelpie Way, was in a Point for Andrew Congdon, but failed to finish in her other 7 attempts (refused or ran out 3). Grandam, Kelpie Spirit, won a Maiden and placed 3. P-t-P '96 and '99 r13 w2 (Members — 2 finished, and Restricted) p1 (3rd); fell/unseated 3, and pulled up 7. Has only managed to complete in three of his 18 races, and it seems nothing short of miraculous that he has won two of them, but has had only three others behind him and is remarkably moderate. Kept jumping markedly left-handed in 2000, and only went a mile or so before pulling up on his final appearance so may have a problem. An unsafe conveyance, and usually blinkered. *A.W. Congdon — Torrington F.* 104 (I), 561 (O), 1097 (Inr), 1472 (I), 1516 (I).

LUFAH WOOD ..—.. 8 b.g. Sulaafah (USA) — Marty's Round (Martinmas) p. Angular. Tailed off and pulled up after 2m4f in a January Maiden. *Miss J. Wright — Quantock (Laura Horsey).* 70 (OMa).

LUKE SKYWALKER ..9-3.. 10 b.g. Leading Star — Princess Kadir (Kadir Cup) pp. Owner-bred half-brother to Current Prince. P-t-P '98 (for Miss A. Vos) r1 p0 (4th). Showed a modicum of ability on his debut in '98, but none on his return and clearly does not feel the force. Raced in Kent, Dorset and Leicestershire in his three outings — was he transported by the Millennium Falcon? *J. Richardson — Cotswold (Susan Richardson).* 330 (R), 543 (I).

LUKE THE DUKE (IRE) ..9-4.. 8 ch.g. Invited (USA) — Christy's Arrow (Mon Capitaine) p7. Half-brother to Monarrow (IRE). Dam is sister or half-sister to 3 Pointers, and to Cheltenham Gold Cup hero, Captain Christy. IRISH NH '97/8 r13 p1 (27½f 3rd in Ch); finished 3 and fell in Hunt Chses. IRISH P-t-P '99 r2 w1 (5yo Mdn) p0; and fell. Bought Doncaster, Nov '98 for 5000. Struggled at long odds twice in Hunter Chases. Scored in soft in Ireland, but only moderate, and needs to seek out much easier options now. Seems to have become difficult to train, and missed several potential engagements in 2000. *R. Donald Brown — O. Berks (Gary Brown).* 223 (2mH), 925 (2mH).

LULAGH-B ..9-9.. 10 ch.m. Gunner B — Lulagh Bird (Weathercock) pR2p. Dam, very unsound, was 3rd in 2 Points for Mr Barnes (promoted from 4th once). Grandam, Killulagh II, failed to finish in

4 Points. P-t-P '98 r1 p0 (pulled up). Showed some promise before running out at Wetherby, and only just pipped on the post in her next race having jumped the last with a five length advantage, but never going on her final appearance and may have suffered a recurrence of the problem that kept her off the track in '99. *N. & Mrs G. Barnes — Middleton.* 400 (OMa), 696 (OMa), 1004 (OMa), 1329 (OMa).

LUMBACK LADY ..9-12.. 11 b.m. State Diplomacy (USA) — Jalome (Uncle Pokey) 21. Compact robust. NH '96/9 (for B. Mactaggart; worn tongue-strap) r23 p6 (to 2m1f); 4th 6; unplaced 2 Sells. Sold Doncaster, June for 1000. Deserved a win over Hurdles, but was inconsistent and disappointing, and could pull hard. Finally able to claim a modest reward in an elders Maiden at Erw Lon when partnered by Pip Jones (connections were evidently working on the 'if you can't beat them join them' theory, because she had previously beaten their charge by one and a half fences by Gunner B special, but not seen since. *G.C.K. Hughes, M. Davis & H. Ceredig — Llangeinor (Gavin Hughes).* 350 (CfMa), 650 (CfMa).

LUNAR DANCER ..8-11.. 9 b.g. Dancing High — Pauper Moon (Pauper) u40. Lengthy attractive. Dam won 2m1f Hdle. NH FLAT '97 (won debut for A. Charlton) r2 w1 p1 (3rd). NH '97/8 (for P. Dalton, bought for 37,000) r5 p0; pulled up in one of 2 Hdles, and last and pulled up 2 in Chses. Finished tailed-off last for Barry Logan once, but Ben Durrell (see also Happy Blade) threw himself off at the third at Cottenham, having almost done so at the first two fences, and then completed at Newton Bromswold, where he set off 15 lengths behind the rest and was always tailed-off with his mount always finishing full of running. Durrell clearly has no clue what he is doing either in or out of the saddle, because last year he ran a flat winner in a Maiden and in 2000 he ran a Bumper winner in a Restricted!! *B.G. Durrell — Pytchley.* 175 (I), 371 (R), 510 (Cf).

LUNEY RIVER ..9-5.. 12 b.m. Idiot's Delight — Perfect Saint (St Paddy) 3u4u471p1p. Rangy half-sister to Tregony. NH '98 r1 p0 (6th in 2m110y Ch). P-t-P '95, '97 and '99 (for Mrs A.V. Morris & Mr R.C. Tonks) r22 p1 (3rd of 4); fell/unseated 6, and pulled up 9. Usually takes a keen hold, but has been much more amenable to restraint in the last two seasons and finally able to get home in front at the 30th time of asking at Cherrybrook. Followed up in a truly dreadful two-finisher Intermediate for which she was odds-on, but the elation was short-lived as she appeared to finish lame on her final outing. Has proved simple to beat in competitive races, but at least provided Lucy Gardner with her first winners. Blinkered twice in '98, but no since. *Dartmoor Pixies Racing Club — Silverton (Lucy Gardner).* 71 (OMa), 146 (OMa), 202 (I), 257 (L), 562 (CfMa), 725 (L), 856 (CfMa), 1045 (L), 1187 (Inr), 1386 (L).

PLATE 79　　1187 Four Burrow Intermediate (Nov Rdrs): L to R the field are together at the last, Luney River (Miss L. Gardner), 1st, and Devonshire Lad (A. Ede), 2nd PHOTO: Baths Photograhic

LUSTY LIGHT ..10-0.. 15 b.g. Strong Gale — Pale Maid (Rise'n Shine II) p1. Workmanlike brother to jumping winner, Wink Gulliver, and half-brother to Carved Opal, and to a hurdles winner, an Irish flat winner, and a winner in Belgium. Dam won at 6f. NH '91/6 r33 w10 (2 Hdles, 2m-2m6f, and 8 Chses, 2m4f-3m4f; inc 5-timer in '94) p8; refused 1 in '94; fell at 1st in '95 Grand National, and 16th of 17 in '96. P-t-P/HUNT CH '99 (for Mr B.R.H. Burrough & Mr W.J. Tolhurst) r6 w1 (Open) p2 (3rd in Hunt Ch once); and 4th thrice. A cracking Chaser on good ground for Jenny Pitman in his prime, and skilfully nursed back after three years of inactivity to beat Forest Fountain in a Cottenham Open last year. Failed to return to the level of that form again in '99, but showed his well-being when disposing of vastly inferior opposition in his Members this year where he was blinkered for the first time. *W.J. Tolhurst — Essex & Suffolk.* 238 (O), 1110 (M).

LUVLY BUBBLY ..9-4.. 13 b.g. Carlingford Castle — Mill Shine (Milan) p74pup16. Small close-coupled attractive half-brother to Easy Breezy, S B S By Jove, Easy Perks and to NH flat and Hurdles winners, Konvekta Control and Oh So Bright. Dam won NH flat and 2 Hdles (2m-2m4f), in Ireland. NH '93/4 r3 p0 (tailed off in last pair thrice). P-t-P '96/9 r23 w2 (PPORA Maiden and Members) p7 (5 2nds, remote last once); unseated 2, and pulled up 5. Successful in his Members '99/00, but only had five opponents last year and none this. Tailed off last in a Restricted an hour after his latest triumph and though safe labours badly now. Has been tried in blinkers. *C. Hall — Haydon.* 40 (R), 184 (R), 423 (R), 497 (R), 973 (I), 1363 (R), 1575 (M), 1577 (R).

LYDFORD CASTLE ..9-12.. 7 b.g. Thornberry (USA) — Our Generator (Starch Reduced) 21p3. Compact well-made half-brother to Our Brook. Dam was 3rd in 2 Points as a 13-year-old. NH '98 r1 p0 (tailed off). P-t-P '99 r4 p3 (2 2nds); and fell 1. Gained a deserved success in a heavy ground Lemalla Maiden, but seemed to encounter problems on his next outing and finished apparently unsound when next reappearing some ten weeks later. Beaten less than a length in his first Restricted and should easily gain compensation in one if he is passed fit in 2001. *R. & E. Jarman & Mrs B. Fuller — Lamerton (John Squire).* 159 (CfMa), 311 (CfMa), 404 (I), 1517 (R).

LYFORD CAY (IRE) ..9-3§.. 11 b.g. Waajib — Island Goddess (Godswalk USA) p. Smallish close-coupled half-brother to Ilandra (IRE). FLAT r20 w1 (7f) p3 (2 2nds). NH '93/4 and '96/7 r10 p1 (3rd); pulled up 3, and fell 2. P-t-P '95/6 and '98/9 r12 p2 (last of 3 once); fell/unseated 4, and pulled up 5. Abhors Pointing as much as his sibling and jumped with his head in the air in his latest attempt. Has only managed three completion from 15 starts over fences and not worth bothering with again. Often wore headgear under Rules. *Miss L.J. Grattan — Buccleuch.* 41 (L).

LYNPHORD GIRL ..9-9§§.. 10 ch.m. Lyphento (USA) — Woodlands Angel (Levanter) 6up21. Tall angular owner-bred. NH FLAT r2 p0. P-t-P '97/9 r11 w1 (Maiden) p2; 4th, pulled up 2, unseated 2, slipped up 1, and ran out 2. In her third year in as many years, but posted her second success when defeating the odds-on jolly in a Lifton restricted on her final start. Not always as co-operative though and can be a thoroughly obnoxious ride with a tendency to hang and pull herself up. Appreciated being re-united with Tigger Barnes, who can rib a certain former champion jockey about his shortcomings on the mare in '99. Sure to remain unpredictable in future, but will struggle all the same. *A. & Mrs J.A. Cayford — Mendip F. (Caroline Keevil).* 560 (R), 1135 (R), 1376 (R), 1467 (R), 1639 (R).

LYNX MARINE (IRE) ..—.. 10 ch.g. Bold Marina — Theresa Marie VII (unknown) f. IRISH P-t-P '96 r1 p0 (refused at 2nd). IRISH NH FLAT '96 r3 p0. IRISH NH '97 r2 p0. Killed by a crashing fall at Wetherby. *P. Swift — Grove & Rufford (K. Frost).* 173 (R).

LYRICAL SEAL ..9-11.. 11 b.m. Dubassoff (USA) — Sea-Rosemary (Seaepic USA) 57341. Very small neat home-bred. NH FLAT r3 p0. NH '95/6 (often blinkered) r10 p2 (30 lengths 3rd, and distant last of 3 in Chses); last once, and pulled up 2 in other Chses; 6th, last, and pulled up 3 in Hdles. P-t-P '97/9 r11 w1 (Maiden) p3 (3rd of 4 twice); last pair 6, and unseated 1. A safe ride, but had managed no more than a modest Maiden success before landing a 16-runner Hereford Hunter Chase on her final appearance. Sent off at 25-1, but got the run of the race, and seemed to gel with Philip York who was partnering her for the first time. Will struggle to carry her penalty in future, but once again it advertised the talents of her trainer. Wears blinkers. *Mrs J. Dening — S. & W. Wilts (Sarah Waugh).* 6 (R), 208 (R), 767 (R), 958 (R), 1626 (3m1f110yH).

MACAMORE STAR ..9-5.. 15 b.g. Callernish — Lucy Ladybird (Menelek) pp9. Brother to Double U-A. IRISH NH FLAT '92/3 r3 w1 p1. IRISH NH '92/5 r18 w1 (2m Ch) p4. P-t-P/HUNT CH '98 (for Mr A.J. Baillie) r5 p0 (last pair 2, pulled up 2, and ran out 1). A dual winner in heavy in Ireland to '94, but impaired by leg trouble since (has also broken blood vessels) and well beaten when on the comeback trail (again) in 2000. Tried in a tongue-strap in '98, and gives the impression of not being able to breath properly as well. *Mr & Mrs M.A. Connors — Albrighton (M.A. Connors).* 461 (2m4f110yH), 862 (Cf), 1086 (Cf).

MACFIN (IRE) ..10-0.. 8 b.g. Brevet — Lough Sholin (Kemal FR) 2p352u4. Good-topped. Dam won 2m2f Irish NH flat. IRISH P-t-P '98 r4 w1 (5&6yo Maiden) p0; pulled up 2. P-t-P '99 r3 p0 (6th, unseated 1, and pulled up 1). Tries hard, and can produce a strong finishing kick, but always manages to get himself detached from the leaders and never close enough to put it to good use. Deserves to win a Restricted; needs to find one on a long track when the ground rides quick. *T.M. Fowler — Fitzwilliam (Louise Allan).* 50 (R), 440 (R), 544 (L), 869 (L), 1009 (CR), 1218 (R), 1419 (R).

MACKABEE (IRE) ..10-2§.. 12 b.g. Supreme Leader — Donegal Queen (Quayside) p2. Compact half-brother to Irish NH flat and Hurdles winner, May Sunset (IRE) and to Irish Hurdles winner, Some Bright Spark. NH FLAT r2 p0. NH '94/5 (blinkered 1) r5 p0. P-t-P '96/9 r24 w3 (Restricted and 2 Members) p8 (5 2nds); fell/unseated 3, and pulled up 6. Beat Kerry Soldier Blue in his Members in '98, but generally disappointing in the last two seasons when becoming rather lightly raced. Had been pulled up in five of his previous seven outings prior to a fair second to an old adversary at Weston Park, but promptly disappeared before his questionable enthusiasm could be checked up on again. Often blinkered since '98. *Miss E. Murray — Albrighton.* 116 (I), 295 (L).

MACKOY (IRE) ..9-9.. 8 b.g. Riverhead (USA) — Urdite (FR) (Concertino FR) pp35425. Good-topped half-brother to Hurdles winner, Thunderpoint (IRE), and to a French flat and jumping winner. IRISH P-t-P '98/9 r10 w1 (Mdn) p0; pulled up 7. Bought Malvern, July for 3400. A very safe jumper, but moderate and simple to beat, and dead-heated with a 14-year-old who was still eligible for Restricteds when coming closest to success (three and a half lengths third). His lack of stamina means he will need a bad race to score. *B. Dowling — Puckeridge.* 96 (I), 416 (R), 610 (R), 940 (R), 1038 (R), 1379 (R), 1584 (CCond).

MAC'S BLADE (USA) ..—.. 9 ch.g. Imp Society (USA) — Safety Razor (USA) (Blade USA) pppppppf. Strong compact half-brother to 2 winners in USA. Dam won twice in USA. P-t-P '97/9 r16 w1 (Club Maiden) p3 (last of 2; 3rd of 4, and last of 3); failed to finish 10 (on floor 5, and refused 1). Fortunate to collect a Dalton Park Maiden on his final outing in '99, and previously a poor jumper, but looked as though he had been pulled in straight from the field on his first three appearances, and ran accordingly. No better in four subsequent starts and is surely badly wrong (has a weird hind leg action). Unimproved by blinkers and a tongue-strap. *M.J. Brown — Sinnington.* 276 (M), 377 (R), 396 (R), 503 (R), 807 (R), 1326 (R), 1348 (Cf).

MAC'S VIEW (IRE) ..8-13.. 7 b.g. Tidaro (USA) — Sweet View (King's Ride) f5. Bought Tattersalls Ireland Aug, for 2232. Fell at the seventh on his debut, but then a plunge from 10-1 to 2-1 joint-favourite at Eastingwold. Weakened rapidly from three out to finish a tired 34 lengths fifth, and no conclusions can be drawn about him yet. *C. Dawson — S. Durham.* 1002 (2m4fOMa), 1353 (OMa).

MADAM DORIS ..—.. 8 b.m. Then Again — Tharita (Thatch USA) pp. Lengthy home-bred half-sister to Childsway. Made little show when an outsider in Maidens. *Miss K. Tripp — Weston & Banwell H.* 472 (OMa), 1102 (OMa).

MADAME BELLA ..9-2.. 9 b.m. Super Sunrise — Highland Chance (Bronze Hill) 9pp. Very small light-framed sister to Highland Monarch, and half-sister to Highland Chart. Dam pulled up in 3 of 4 Points. Grandam, Maeve, won 19 Ladies and walked over for Members and placed 11 (only out of first 3 thrice in Points) for Mabel Bell. P-t-P '98/9 r8 w1 (Maiden) p1 (3rd); fell 3, and pulled up 1. Gained compensation for a last fence fall at Aspatria when winning a firm ground Corbridge Maiden a week later on her final start in '98, but only lightly raced and well beaten since. Pulled up with something amiss at Lanark this March and not seen again. *Mrs M. Bell — Lauderdale (Joan Hollands).* 111 (I), 421 (3m5fL), 661 (L).

MADAME DEFARGE ..9-7.. 10 br.m. Vital Season — La Tricoteuse (Le Tricolore) 674ppu. Stocky half-sister to Gay Muse, and to Irish Hurdles winner, Bal O'Yarn. P-t-P r8 w1 (Maiden) p3 (2 3rds, last once); pulled up 1 and unseated 1. Stood her busiest, but least successful campaign in 2000 and now seems to be labouring under a wind infirmity as she ran fitted with a tongue-strap on her last four starts. Shaped like a thorough stayer when landing a Corbridge Maiden in '99, but needs to prove her fitness if she reappears. *Mrs C.M. Leech — Tynedale (Nick & Kirsty Hargreave).* 184 (R), 360 (R), 418 (M), 713 (R), 1162 (R), 1496 (R).

MADAME LA CLAIRE ..9-12.. 8 ch.m. Superlative — Tyrian Princess (Comedy Star USA) 231. Small compact. Dam won 7f Sell. P-t-P '99 r7 p4 (3 2nds; and 3rd of 4); last, unseated 1, and pulled up 1. A most deserving winner following six consecutive placings, but her Wetherby victory was tinged with sadness as she had broken down in the process. Game and a thorough stayer, and if she cannot race again will hopefully pass on those attributes to her offspring. *C.M. Dalton & Miss A.M. Rees — York & Ainsty S. (Chris Dalton).* 55 (OMa), 168 (OMa), 695 (OMa).

MADAM ROSE (IRE) ..9-6.. 11 br.m. Cardinal Flower — Misquested (Lord Ha Ha) p23pu2p. Sparely-made half-sister to Irish Hurdles winner, Fort Deely (IRE). NH FLAT '94 and '95 r2 p0. NH '95/7 r12 p1 (2nd of 3 in dire Ch — beaten distance after being badly hampered by loose horse at last); last twice, after unseating once, and unseated in other Chses. P-t-P/HUNT CH '98/9 r16 p4 (2nd of 3 once; and last of 3 twice); pulled up 7. Very speedy, but does not stay three miles and continues to flatter only to deceive. Usually wears a cross-noseband (ran in a Belgian gag at least once in 2000) and has been tried tongue-tied. Placed in four Maidens, and deserves a success, but still no nearer to achieving one after 37 attempts. *Mrs L. Glanville & Mrs D. Hartnell — Axe V.H. (Lee Glanville).* 67 (L), 206 (OMa), 559 (R), 880 (OMa), 1555 (OMa), 1598 (OMa), 1676 (OMa).

MADAM SIOUX (IRE) ..10-2.. 8 b.m. Commanche Run — Grainne Geal (General Ironside) 32f. Sparely-made half-sister to Hall's Mill (IRE) (qv). IRISH P-t-P '97/9 r10 w2 (5 plus mares Mdn, and Winners of One) p3; pulled up 1. Finished a gallant runner-up on the second of her three visits to

Wincanton, but unfortunately fell at the first and broke a leg next time. *A.J. Heywood — Tetcott (Tim Dennis).* 152 (3m1f110yH), 467 (3m1f110yH), 685 (2m5fH).

MADEMIST JAZ ..—.. 8 ch.m. Lord Bud — Mademist Susie (French Vine) p. Half-sister to Chasing winner, Mademist Sam. Dam, half-sister to 5 Pointers including Royal Pocket (*qv*), won 8 Points and 2 Hunt Chses and placed 8 (inc 5 Hunt Chses) for Mr Hill before breaking down. Grandam, Giner Fury, pulled up and unseated in Points. Tailed off and pulled up after two miles in early March. Has an ideal pedigree, and it would have certainly been interesting to have seen more of her. *M.J. Hill — Hurworth.* 436 (OMa).

MAES GWYN DREAMER ..8-12.. 11 b.g. Dreams To Reality (USA) — Fairlina (Quality Fair) pppp. Compact half-brother to Maesgwyn Bach, Maesgwyn Star (4th in the '95 High Peak cross-country race), Maes Gwyn Eto, Maes Gwyn, Bally Fair II and Maes Gwyn Lad. P-t-P '96/7 and '99 r8 p1 (remote 3rd of 4); pulled up 4, and fell 2. Beaten over 20 lengths in two completions from 12 attempts, and performed like a horse with a physical handicap in 2000. Stopped very quickly on his reappearance and went no further than two miles otherwise. *Mrs M. Teague & M. Salmon — Carms.* 480 (O), 650 (CfMa), 838 (OMa), 1225 (OMa).

MAGGIES BROTHER ..10-0.. 8 b.g. Brotherly (USA) — Sallisses (Pamroy) 1133p3f. Workmanlike owner-bred half-brother to Rusty Fellow (*qv*). P-t-P '98/9 r8 w1 (Club Maiden) p1 (3rd); last, pulled up 4, and unseated 1. Has scored on his seasonal reappearance '99/00, and followed up in a 15-runner Confined at Whitwick this year, but remains a hard ride and usually goes in fits and starts. Gained more consistency in 2000, and should certainly be able to win again, but has to date looked well below Hunter Chase standard. An improved jumper and has proved himself to be equally effective at courses other than Chaddesley. Stays well and best suited by some cut in the ground. *Mrs G.M. Shail — Ledbury (Roy Shail).* 193 (R), 333 (Cf), 615 (CMod), 897 (I), 1336 (2m4fH), 1356 (I), 1626 (3m1f110yH).

MAGGIE SIMPSON ..8-12.. 8 ch.m. Say Primula — Little Mittens (Little Buskins) p. Small owner-bred half-sister to Nite Sprite (*qv*). P-t-P '99 r3 p0 (last, and pulled up 2). Not entirely disgraced when 25 lengths fourth once in '99, but pulled up otherwise and managed just one outing in March this year. Doh! *R.E. Barr — Cleveland.* 507 (CMa).

MAGICAL MANOR ..9-4.. 12 ch.m. St Columbus — True Manor (True Song) pp12. Compact well-made sister to Fawsley Manor and Kilworth Manor. Dam, sister and half-sister to 3 Tarry Pointers including Sunshine Manor (*qv* '98 Annual), failed to stay in 6 Points for Bunny Tarry (failed to finish 4). P-t-P '97/9 r9 p2 (3rds); 5th of 6, fell/unseated 2, and pulled up 4. Very lightly raced and only able to manage an annual completion '97/9, but blessed by good fortune in 2000 when left clear at the last by the departure of two rivals at Guilsborough. Recorded the slowest time of three divisions of the Maiden that day and beaten 30 lengths in her first Restricted so will need to find some improvement to win one which at her advanced age seems most unlikely. *J. White & G.B. Tarry — Grafton (Jimmy Tarry).* 514 (OMa), 790 (OMa), 1010 (CfMa), 1218 (R).

MAGICAL POITIN (IRE) ..9-7.. 8 ch.m. Magical Strike (USA) — Poitin Still (Royal Match) fp4434up1. Compact. IRISH NH FLAT '93 r2 p0. P-t-P '99 r5 p1 (3rd); 5th, pulled up 2, and unseated 1. Gets exhausted over the full trip, but 2m4f just about right and won over that trip on her final start (her last ever chance over that trip). An excitable mare, but unless she can summon up some extra stamina reserves will find Restricteds no laughing matter. *Mrs S. Ruddy — Buccleuch (Michael Ruddy).* 112 (OMam), 189 (OMam), 499 (2m4fOMam), 712 (M), 909 (2m4fOMa), 1084 (2m4fOMa), 1330 (OMa), 1556 (2m4f110yH), 1581 (2m4fOMam).

MAGIC CALLER (IRE) ..—.. 11 b.g. Callernish — Brecaun Lady (Push On) p4pp. Good-bodied. IRISH P-t-P '95/6 r6 p0 (pulled up 5). Nearly two fences last in his Members, and is incapable of raising a gallop. Has now been pulled up in eight of ten attempts. *E.H. Shillabeer & Miss D. Wilson — Spooners & W. Dartmoor (Miss D. Wilson).* 407 (OMa), 846 (M), 1048 (CfMa), 1263 (OMa).

MAGICMAN ..—.. 6 b.g. Nomadic Way (USA) — Wizard Of Was (Anax) pp. Dam, placed in 5 Hdles, would have won 2m4f Ladies event but for swerving badly left near the finish. Pulled up twice, three months apart (lost his action temporarily after a mile in the latest). *J.W. Nellis — Middleton (Tim Walford).* 22 (2m4fOMa), 1002 (2m4fOMa).

MAGIC MOLE ..—.. 9 b.m. Sulaafah (USA) — Kite's Nest (Nicholas Bill) p. Small light owner-bred. P-t-P '97/8 r2 w1 (Members) p1 (3rd). Won her Members on her racecourse debut in '97, but disappeared after creditable third in a Restricted twelve months later and pulled up back at Badbury Rings on her comeback. Had ability, but clearly not able to stand up to the rigours of training. *R.J. Hill — Wilton (Minette Batters).* 762 (M).

MAGNI MOMENTI ..—.. 6 b.m. King's Signet (USA) — Halka (Daring March) uuRp96. Compact half-sister to 2 flat winners, incuding Chasing winner, Nuclear Express. 6000y. FLAT r14 p3 (6-10f, inc Sell). NH (for S. Moore) r2 p0 (beaten 35l plus). Sold Ascot, Nov for 700. NH May '2000 (for Mrs P. Ford) r2 p0; (9th in 2m3f110y Nov Hdle: *rr, t.o 8*; and 6th in 2m110y Hdle: *prom til blun 3 out*). Gave scary displays of running and jumping for four different jockeys in Points, and was badly outclassed even in the lowest grade over Hurdles. her partners will be hoping that they do not become momentomories. *G.W. D'Arcy — Ross H. (Pip Hooley)*. 341 (CfMa), 672 (2m4fOMa), 898 (OMa), 1019 (2m4fOMa).

MAGNUS MAXIMUS ..8-13.. 9 b.g. Takachiho — L'Oraz (Ile De Bourbon USA) p4. Rangy. Grandam, Oraza, won German 1000 Guineas and Oaks. NH FLAT '97 r3 p0. NH '98 (for Mrs Sue Lamyman) r1 p0 (tailed off last in Sell). Rarely makes it to the arena, but both Maiden efforts were respectable, particularly a five lengths fourth. A little extra stamina should enable him to get off the mark, if the opportunity arises. *S. & Mrs L. Lamyman — Blankney (Lynda Lamyman)*. 233 (OMa), 438 (OMa).

MAGS SUPER TOI (IRE) ..9-13.. 12 b.g. Supreme Leader — Mags Toi (Prince Hansel) p1p. Very small. Dam won 2 Irish Points, and is half-sister to Perspex Way (qv '90 Annual). IRISH P-t-P '94 and '96 r10 w2 (6yo&up Maiden, and Winners of One) p2 (3rds); pulled up 4. IRISH NH '94 and '96/7 r15 w1 (3m Hdle) p1 (2nd). P-t-P '99 r4 p1 (2nd); 4th, pulled up 1, and fell 1. A fair performer on a sound surface in Ireland, but was recording his first win for three years when successful in his Members. Usually fails to get home in more competitive races, and must find 12st7lb a real impost. *W. Kathrens & A. Jenkins — Curre (Lyndon Williams)*. 480 (O), 594 (M), 1051 (Cf).

MAID O'TULLY (IRE) ..9-10.. 10 ch.m. Abednego — The Bay O'Tully (Treasure Bay) 415u433. Lengthy unfurnished. IRISH NH '97 r1 p0. IRISH P-t-P '96/7 r8 p3; pulled up 2, and fell/unseated 3. P-t-P '98/9 (for Mr A. Witcomb) r9 p0 (last 2, and pulled up 7). Not better than last in the previous two yards, but much improved in 2000 and came out best in a slow motion finish on soft ground at Garnons. Not wholly disgraced on a return visit when conditions were much quicker and would not need to improve much to win a run-of-the-mill Restricted in 2001, though her rating has probably peaked. *O.T. Lloyd — Golden V. (Joli Smith)*. 205 (OMa), 450 (CfMa), 669 (R), 863 (R), 993 (R), 1276 (R), 1458 (M).

MAIL SHOT (IRE) ..8-8.. 6 b.g. Maledetto (IRE) — Pallachine (FR) (Lichine USA) p6. Close-coupled half-brother to a winner in Malaysia. FLAT (for S. Dow) r11 p2 (beaten 5-8½l). NH '99 (bought for 3300) r1 p0 (pulled up). A very hard puller who has shown plenty of early speed, but weakened quickly to 30 lengths last when completing, and will need to settle much better if he is to get the trip. *Mrs E.H. Heath — Cambs*. 797 (R), 1421 (OMa).

MAINLIER ..9-3.. 8 gr.g. Roselier (FR) — Maintown (Remainder Man) pf2p. Close-coupled half-brother to Main Missile. Dam won 2m1f Sell Hdle and 2 2m Chses when trained for Gerald Spencer by Martin Pipe. NH FLAT Nov '98 r1 p0. NH '99 (from M. Pipe's) r2 p1 (2nd). Disappointing and a weak finisher, and consistently lets his supporters down (often starts at short odds). 20 lengths second on his only completion, but probably just about good enough to score if a simple opportunity arose. *G.M. Spencer - N. Ledbury*. 31 (CMa), 265 (OMa), 990 (OMa), 1197 (OMa).

MAINVALLEY QUEEN (IRE) ..—.. 10 b.m. Jolly Jake (NZ) — Hilly-Acre (Wrens Hill) p. Narrow unfurnished. IRISH P-t-P '98 r7 p1 (2nd); last, pulled up 3, and unseated 2. IRISH NH FLAT '98 r1 p0. IRISH NH '98 r1 p0 (pulled up lame in Hdle). Seems to be a non-stayer, and made mistakes on her English debut. It looks as if her legs may have let her down again. *Mrs M. Bourne — Atherstone (Roger Harvey)*. 121 (OMa).

MAI POINT ..9-10.. 8 b.m. Blakeney — Quilpee Mai (Pee Mai) 71p16. Small neat half-sister to Just Patrimony, Kelly's Eye, Just Maisy (dam of Just Mai-Bee qv), Bengers Moor (subsequent Chasing winner) and Newick Park. Dam won at 11½f, and was placed 8, including 2 Points for David Claydon. P-t-P '99 (for Mr D.L. Claydon) r3 p1 (3rd of 4); 4th, and pulled up 1. Stepped up on a fairly encouraging debut season to win twice at Higham in 2000 justifying favouritism both times. Failed to cope when upped in class on her final start, but may not have seen out the trip and can probably win again on an easy course. Pulled up at Ampton as the jockey thought (mistakenly) that the horse had gone lame. A good jumper, but has yet to race on ground much softer than good. *Mrs P.A. Twinn — E. Essex*. 178 (Cm), 237 (OMa), 554 (R), 761 (R), 937 (I).

MAJESTIC QUEEN ..—.. 14 b.m. Morston's Heir — Royal Guest (Guest Of Honour) u. Lengthy sister to Majestic Heir and Royal Vintage. Grandam, Presume II, won Maiden for George Barber. NH '94 r2 p0. Jumped very irratically and soon tailed off before unseating at halfway on her first appearance for six years. Presumably has the marshmallow legs which are the inheritance of virtually everything sired by Morston's Heir. *G.H. Barber — Essex F. & U.* 175 (I).

MAJOR BUGLER (IRE) ..9-9.. 12 b.g. Thatching — Bugle Sound (Bustino) 2448. Tall lengthy brother to Irish flat winner, Sound Of Victory, and half-brother to 2 Irish flat winners (one disqualified), and to successful Hurdlers, Dari Sound and Docklands Limo. Dam won at 10f, and is half-sister to See You Then (thrice Champion Hurdler) and Dubian (placed in 2 Oaks, and dam of 1000 Guineas winner, Sayyedati). FLAT r13 w2 (10-12f, £6223 and £9474 prizes) p4 (short-headed once). NH '92/6 r19 w2 (2m1f Hdles, inc £6375) p4 (earned £8480 when 2nd once, and £6217 when 3rd in Triumph); sent to Ireland once. P-t-P '97 (for Mr M. Kerr-Dineen & Mr H. Chisholm) r2 p1 (2nd); and pulled up 1. Not far below top-class over hurdles in his hey-day, but mostly hopeless in his last three seasons under Rules, and plods reluctantly now. Looks after number one, but lightly raced and of little account in Points. *H. Chisholm — Beaufort (Mrs C. Chisholm)*. 246 (C), 389 (O), 671 (C), 968 (Cf).

MAJORITY MAJOR (IRE) ..10-6.. 12 b.g. Cheval — La Perla (Majority Blue) 5pu31311. Strong half-brother to Jupiter Express, Night Pearl, Snowy Pearl, Kingstown Joy and No Takers, to Irish Pointing winners, Holbrook and Dawstown, to Irish NH flat winner, Real Pearl, and to a winner in Belgium. Dam won 3 flat, 5-7f. NH '93/4 and '96/9 (unplaced last for J. Wade; previously for P. Cheesbrough; first 2 for late W.A. Stephenson) r34 w3 (3m3f Hdle, and 2 Chses, 3m-3m5f) p9; pulled up 3 of final 4, Sell final. Looks a real character, and Trevor Glass has to work exceptionally hard on him. Was performing badly until he had a remarkable change of heart at Sedgefield and captured a Hunter Chase at 20-1, but proved his inconsistency over the same track and trip when 14 lengths behind the runner-up Brownrath King next time (had previously beaten him a distance!). Blinkered twice subsequently, and got the better of a dual with Blyth Brook in an Open before pot-hunting his Members at 1-3. Has never fallen, but often makes mistakes, and unseated at Wetherby. Was lame in '94 and then absent for 17 months, and had not scored under Rules since December '97, so connections did really well to get him motivated again. Suited by extreme distances, and has scored three times over 3m3f or further at Sedgefield. *Miss M.D. Myco — S. Durham.* 42 (O), 110 (O), 171 (O), 496 (C), 682 (3m3fH), 923 (3m3fH), 1327 (O), 1474 (M).

MAJOR LOOK (NZ) ..—.. 13 gr.g. Jiggs Alarm (USA) — War Belle (NZ) (War Hawk) p. Tall strong rangy. NEW ZEALAND FLAT '94 w1 (10f). HUNT CH '95 (for Mrs H.J. Clarke) r2 w1 (2m5f) p1 (2nd). NH '96/7 (for S.A. Brookshaw) r5 p1 (3rd of 4 in 2m4f Ch); pulled up 2. Ridden by his former trainer when running out the decisive winner of a Uttoxeter Hunter Chase in May '95 and looked set for a bright career, but never able to reproduce that form again and had been off the course for the best part of three years with leg trouble prior to his 2000 comeback. Only went a mile and a half before he pulled up at Wetherby and it transpired that he had broken down again. *Mrs T.R. Kinsey — Cheshire Forest.* 690 (L).

MAJOR MAN (IRE) ..—.. 11 ch.g. Le Moss — Carradyne Touch (Gleason USA) p. Lengthy rather unfurnished. IRISH P-t-P '96 r5 w1 (Maiden for novice riders) p2; pulled up 1. P-t-P '97/8 r6 w1 (Restricted) p0 (5th, fell/unseated 3, and pulled up 1). Showed some acceleration when successful at Wadebridge in March '98 (recorded a time only two seconds slower than his then stablemate Butler John 35 minutes later), but has clearly had his problems since and was appearing on a racecourse for the first time since when breaking down at Ampton in January. *N. Wrighton — E. Anglian Bloodhounds (George Cooper).* 83 (Cf).

MAJOR'S LAW (IRE) ..10-3.. 12 b.g. Law Society (USA) — Maryinsky (USA) (Northern Dancer) p216b. Small well-made brother to a flat winner, La Sky, and half-brother to Defence Counsel (IRE) and to 4 flat winners (3 abroad), including Legal Case (useful). Dam won 2 races at up to 9f in USA. 42,000y. FLAT '92 and '98 (won for C. Brittain) r20 w1 (6f) p5. NH '92/9 (hat-trick for R. Simpson; previously for T. Hind; one win previously for J. White; one win for Miss R. Patman; one win previously for I. Campbell, bought for 16,500) r32 w6 (2m-2m7f Hdles, inc Sell; inc hat-trick '97/8, inc 3 and 5 ran) p10 (beaten head once); poor 6th of 7 only Ch ('95). Has broken blood vessels. Bought Doncaster, Mar for 700. Quirky and unpredictable, but loves mud, and followed a neck second in an Open in which he was carrying a seven pound penalty with a remarkable victory over two miles at Leicester, where he lost his pitch in the home straight but rallied gamely on the flat to snatch the prize from the grasp of the flagging Halham Tarn. Showed no zest in two subsequent attempts, and made mistakes on his latest appearance. A bargain buy for new connections, and has now won for six different trainers. His form book comments include the bizarre and mysterious 'not clear run on inside when avoided race goer approaching two out'! *H.G. & D. Owen — Bicester with Whaddon (Herbie Owen).* 77 (O), 244 (O), 463 (2mH), 919 (2m3f110yH), 1155 (2m5f110yH).

MAJOR TOM (IRE) ..10-0.. 7 ch.g. Mister Lord (USA) — Crash Street (Crash Course) 240. Rangy. NH FLAT '98 r3 p3 (3rd). P-t-P/HUNT CH '99 r3 w2 (Maiden and PPORA Restricted) p1 (3rd in Hunt Ch). Unbeaten in Points in '99, and looked likely to develop into a decent Hunter Chaser, but things have not gone to plan since at Catterick on his reappearance (subsequently missing for eight weeks). Young enough to make up for lost time and could still prove useful in the years ahead if he can stand up to training. *T.P. Tate — Bramham.* 465 (3m1f110yH), 1342 (3m1fH), 1445 (3m1fH).

MAKE UP YOUR MIND (IRE) ..8-11.. 9 b.g. Little Bighorn — Our Decision (Hawaiian Return USA) 6. Dam is sister to Hawaiian Prince (*qv* '98 Annual). IRISH P-t-P '97/8 r8 p1 (2nd); last, pulled up 5, and fell. IRISH NH FLAT '98 r3 p0. IRISH NH '99 r1 p0. Weakened quickly when nearly 30 lengths last at Maisemore. Appears to lack stamina, as he seemed to have won Irish Point in the bag until he compounded and was just caught close home (the only time he has been placed from 13 attempts). *R. Hancox — N. Ledbury.* 891 (OMa).

MAKIN' DOO (IRE) ..10-6.. 11 ch.g. Black Minstrel — Ariannrun (Deep Run) 333p4. Rangy good-bodied half-brother to Hurdles winners, Valerios King (IRE) and Shore Party (IRE) (latter also won Chasing). P-t-P/HUNT CH '96/9 r18 w6 (inc 2 Opens; disqualified from another — carried wrong weight; and inc hat-trick '97) p4 (3 3rds); pulled up 3, and brought down 1. A useful staying Pointer on his day, and finally put his best foot forward in a Hunter Chase when beaten less than a length at Kelso, but as in previous seasons his form tailed off and was a disappointing favourite at Carlisle on his final start. Totally outclassed in the Cheltenham Foxhunters, and probably needs to return to the easier options available in Points to win again. At least his confidence will receive a much needed boost after suffering seven straight defeats. Worth a try in blinkers. *R.G. Makin — York & Ainsty S.* 17 (O), 89 (3m1fH), 302 (3mH), 584 (3m2f110yH), 1154 (2mfH).

MALE ORDER (IRE) ..—.. 7 b.g. Mandalus — Deep Lass (Deep Run) fp. Workmanlike half-brother to Smitten Not Bitten (IRE), and to Irish Pointing and Hurdles winner, Very Adaptable. Did not look to be going well when he fell at the 11th on his debut, but was sent off favourite or second-favourite in both attempts, so evidently thought to have some ability. Proved too head strong at Lockerbie and was pulled up at the 15th, and apparently very green so far. *R.A. Bartlett — Fife.* 364 (CfMa), 977 (CfMa).

MALIHABAD (IRE) ..10-0.. 12 ch.g. Shahrastani (USA) — Mill River (FR) (Mill Reef USA) 273dp3f3. Rangy strong-topped half-brother to several winners. Dam won at 11f in France. IRISH NH FLAT '93 r2 w1 p0. IRISH NH '93/4 r9 w1 (2m Hdle) p0. FLAT r3 p0. NH '95 and '97/8 r18 p3 (3rd in Sell Hdle); and 2 Chses. P-t-P '99 r2 w1 (Ladies) p0; and 6th. A lucky winner in '99 when the clear leader unseated at the last, but refused to exert himself after his reappearance at Milborne St Andrew and acquired blinkers on his last two outings. Not a fluent jumper and can probably be ignored in future, and certainly after a race or two. Broke a blood vessel once under Rules and may not push himself too hard for fear of doing so again. Later disqualified from the third at Wincanton for testing positive to a banned substance, and his owner fined £600. The source was Equipalazone, a medication being given by the vet to another horse in his yard. *G.F. Gingell — Blackmore & Sparkford V. (Jane Galpin).* 214 (Cf), 326 (L), 467 (3m1f110yH), 685 (2m5fH), 885 (L), 1132 (L), 1374 (MO).

MALTBY'S CHARLIE ..—.. 7 b.g. Infantry — Charlton Athletic (Bustino) pp. Workmanlike half-brother to Teeton Nishaball and Sunley Spring. Pulled up lame at halfway at Hackwood, to become the latest in a long line of bad-legged horses sired by Infantry. *Mr & Mrs J. Rawding & G. Smith — Bicester with Whaddon (M. Smith).* 604 (OMa), 889 (OMa).

MALTBY SON ..10-6.. 9 b.g. Infantry — Top Soprano (High Top) ppbp21u. Compact brother to Soldier's Song, and half-brother to Jack Ramsey, Big Country and Fortunes Wood, to flat and jumping winner, Setter Country, to NH flat and useful jumping winner, Linton Rocks, and to successful Hurdler, Sovereigns Sound. Dam won at 5f. P-t-P '97/9 r10 w3 (inc Open) p4 (2nds); last, and unseated 1. At his busiest in 2000, and kept up his annual success when responding to Lawney Hills' hard driving in a Ladies event at Garthorpe where the long odds-on jolly lost a shoe. Only managed one other completion when runner-up at Kingston Blount where he was the subject of plenty of market support. Jumps well, but often fades quickly and has been tried in a tongue-strap. An unsafe betting medium, but could win another modest Ladies event on an easy track. *T.A. Ellis & Mrs R.A. Smith — V. of Aylesbury (Rebecca Smith).* 17 (O), 78 (L), 227 (2m5f110yH), 1007 (L), 1483 (L), 1587 (L), 1648 (3mH).

MALTESE CROSS (IRE) ..9-0§.. 12 br.g. Supreme Leader — Nevada Lady (Trimmingham) pfrp. Compact good-topped lop-eared half-brother to Teme Willow (IRE) and Lady Nevada (IRE). IRISH NH FLAT '93 r2 p0 (last twice). IRISH HUNT CH '97 r1 p0 (pulled up). IRISH P-t-P '94/5 and '97 r16 p2; pulled up 6, fell 2, and ran out 3. P-t-P '99 (for E.H. Crow) r5 w1 (Maiden) p0; pulled up 2, and unseated 1. Easily justified favouritism on his 22nd appearance, but the race was run in 7min 31s and took little winning. Failed to complete for new connections, and even he could not keep going in the arduous conditions at Flagg when a place was going begging. Exposed as very moderate, getting old, and unlikely to win again. *Mrs J. Cardwell — Cheshire Forest (Ralph Hirons).* 173 (R), 959 (M), 1252 (Cf), 1343 (3m110yH).

MALVERN LAD ..8-7.. 11 ch.g. Lighter — Jack's Love (Grey Love) p. Lengthy angular half-brother to Ryming Jack, Flight Of Love and Howling Jack. Grandam, Gay Girl, won 2 Points, and bred the smart Pointer, Warsprite Girl. P-t-P '96 and '99 r5 p0 (last, pulled up 3, and fell 1). Has looked ill-prepared in most of his races, and his results are predictably poor. Pulls hard, but jumps badly, and on the one occasion he managed a clear round was beaten 50 lengths into last place. Hard to train, and not worth bothering with any more. *T.F.G. Marks — Fitzwilliam.* 97 (OMa).

MANALESCO (IRE) ..—.. 12 b.g. Anita's Prince — Affordalot (Fordham USA) pp. Small close-coupled half-brother to Hill Island. IRISH FLAT '91/2 r7 p2 (3rds). IRISH NH '92/5 r11 p0. IRISH P-t-P '95 and '98 r4 w1 (Mdn) p0: pulled up all 3 in '98 (dismounted final). Bought Malvern, July for 450. Appalling in the inevitable Matthews tradition, and was already a fence behind when pulling up after two miles at Warwick (100-1, and totally unfit). *Mrs L. Danton — Wheatland (Frank Matthews).* 148 (3m1f110yH), 293 (Cf).

MANAMOUR ..9-10.. 14 br.g. Mandalus — Fifi L'Amour (Fair Turn) fp75pp. Big workmanlike lop-eared brother to Mantastic (IRE), and to Irish NH flat and Hurdles winner, Fidalus. IRISH NH FLAT r6 p0. IRISH NH '92/3 r2 p0 (fell in Ch). IRISH P-t-P '93 r5 w1 (5yo plus Maiden) p2. P-t-P '94 (for Mr G. Samuel) r7 p2 (2nds, of 3 once). NH '95/9 (for R. Lee) r25 w5 (2m-2m3f Chses) p4. A fair Handicap Chaser at under 2m4f on firmish ground for Richard Lee to '97, but well beaten in his last six races under Rules and basically too old to do himself justice any more. Suffered his first fall in England on his reappearance which resulted in Robert Cooper breaking his wrist and almost put the same rider on the floor when making a dreadful mistake on his final start. Was always best going right-handed, but deserves to be allowed to draw his pension now. *V.Y. Gethin — N. Herefords.* 32 (MO), 61 (MO), 150 (3mH), 382 (2m4fH), 859 (O), 1157 (2m3fH).

MANDALADY (IRE) ..8-2.. 8 br.m. Mandalus — Coppenagh Girl (Kambalda) f5pfpppp. Small close-coupled. Dam won NH flat, 2 Hdles (2m-2m2f) and 2m2f Ch (only one of 3 to go clear) in Ireland. NH FLAT '97 r1 p0 (last). NH '97/8 r2 p0 (pulled up in 2 Hdles). P-t-P '99 r5 p0 (last, pulled up 3, and fell 1). Has shown some speed, but tried in a tongue-strap at an early stage in her career and now gone in the wind completely as she was tubed on her penultimate appearance. Has yet to beat a rival in 16 attempts and unlikely to better that statistic. *J.D. Brownrigg — I. of W. (Philip Legge).* 220 (OMa), 264 (OMa), 328 (CfMa), 433 (OMa), 710 (OMa), 829 (OMa), 1131 (OMa), 1245 (OMa).

MANDALAY MAN (IRE) ..9-0.. 8 br.g. Mandalus — Nice Little Earner (Warpath) fup3p275u. Lengthy unfurnished. Grandam, Tartan Eve, won 7 Ladies and placed 15 (inc a Ch). NH FLAT '98 r1 p0 (tailed off). P-t-P '99 (for Mr D. Millard) r3 p2; and pulled up 1. Sent packing by Richard Barber after just one season, and labouring under three different pilots in 2000. Jumps poorly and does not seem to stay despite strenuous efforts to hold him up, and will require a truly insipid contest to open his account. Has been tried in blinkers. *P.J. Millington — Fernie.* 52 (OMa), 168 (OMa), 372 (CfMa), 412 (OMa), 516 (OMa), 1291 (OMa), 1423 (OMa), 1504 (CfMa), 1590 (2m4fOMa).

MANDELA SQUARE ..—.. 7 b.g. Henbit (USA) — Miss Berkeley (Park Lane) sp. Strong-topped. Dam, half-sister to Catherine Tudor (*qv* '88 Season Annual), was unplaced in 11 Points for the Worthingtons ('devoid of stamina, and apart from a fifth is one step up from rubbish, as the only horse she has ever beaten is Dusty Bin'). P-t-P '99 r1 p0 (pulled up). Unattractively bred, and has looked more liable to do something deranged in the paddock than something spectacular on the racecourse to date. Has run and jumped in an erratic fashion so far. *Mrs J.M. Worthington — Sir W.W. Wynn's.* 964 (OMa), 1412 (OMa).

MANDIKA ..—.. 13 b.g. Flash Of Steel — Bushti Music (Bustino) pf. Compact attractive half-brother to Storm Drum, and to flat winners, Kingsley, Bourbon Jack and Deceit The Second. FLAT r5 p1 (3rd). NH '91/3 and '98/9 r13 w3 (2 2m6f Hdles, and 2m4f Ch) p0. P-t-P '95 r4 w2 (Opens) p0; pulled up 1, and fell 1. Appears at spasmodic intervals, but last successful in '93, and predictably made no impact (except on the landing side of the third fence in the back straight at Sedgefield) on his return. *S.I. Pittendrigh — Braes.* 419 (Cf), 923 (3m3fH).

MANDRIL (IRE) ..9-5.. 10 b.g. Mandalus — Open Your Eyes (Beau Charmeur FR) 1u442. Strong attractive half-brother to Rovac (*qv*). IRISH P-t-P '97 r1 p1 (3rd). P-t-P '98/9 (for Mrs D.E.H. Turner) r7 p1 (3rd); on floor 3, and pulled up 1.NH '99 (for C.R. Egerton) r2 p1 (3rd). A lightly raced non-stayer in the previous yard, and has not proved good enough in sub-3m event under Rules, but led throughout the final mile on his reappearance at Market Rasen and won untroubled, albeit in much the slowest time of the day. Not surprisingly failed to get home in two Charm Park events subsequently and needs to ply his trade on the easiest tracks he can find. *J. Byrne — Staintondale.* 53 (OMa), 301 (2m5fH), 396 (R), 918 (2m4fH), 1229 (M).

MANDY ..8-0.. 9 ch.m. Nader — Marley Brandy (Hot Brandy) 55. Sturdy owner-bred. Finished a poor last twice, but looked very unfit, so she would wouldn't she. *G.W. Giddings — S. & W. Wilts.* 472 (OMa), 888 (OMa).

MANHATTAN RAINBOW (IRE) ..10-10.. 10 b.g. Mandalus — Clara Girl (Fine Blade USA) 112011. Unfurnished half-brother to Pantara Prince (IRE) (*qv*). IRISH NH FLAT '97 r1 p0. IRISH NH '98 r1 p0 (pulled up in Hunt Ch). IRISH P-t-P '98 r5 p1 (3rd); pulled up 1, and fell. NH '98/9 (from Mrs S. Bradburne's, visored last 2) r11 p5 (Chses, beaton 7-33ℓ). Remarkably failed to score until his fourth year, but promptly got off the mark at the surprisingly generous odds of 7-1 (backed from 10s) when dropped to a Maiden. Immediately upgraded to Hunter Chases and gave three very gallant displays when unbeaten at Kelso, and had to fight particularly hard in the latest, as he was headed two out and looked beaten after the novice David Da Silva lost an iron at the last, but rallied to lead again in the final 150 yards. His partner was extremely untidy but splendidly aggressive, and he could be a name to note if developing some finesse. Also scored twice under very powerful drives from Wilson Renwick, strong and stylish in amateur events and now carving out what should be a profitable career as a professional. Manhattan Rainbow suffered his only defeats when runner-up to Coole Abbey and when take to Cheltenham on December 27, and his willing attitude would stand him in excellent stead if he returned to Novice Chasing. *Mrs C.J. Kerr — Lauderdale (Joan Hollands).* 46 (OMa), 89 (3m1fH), 225 (3mH), 584 (3m2f110yH), 916 (3m1fH), 1342 (3m1fH).

MANNA BRAVE (IRE) ..10-1.. 7 b.g. Commanche Run — Manna Rose (Bonne Noel) 211p. Workmanlike lengthy half-brother to Easy Life (IRE), and to Irish Pointing and Chasing winner, Drop The Act (IRE). NH FLAT Spr '98 r2 p0. NH '98/9 (from A. Harvey's; been tongue-tied) r5 p0 (pulled up Hnal 4). Hopeless under Rules, but was getting his act together nicely in Points, and completed a ready double in modest contests. A thorough stayer, but unfortunately pulled up lame when bidding for a hat-trick. *W.J. Tolhurst — Essex & Suffolk.* 180 (2m4fOMa), 236 (OMa), 554 (R), 937 (I).

MANNAGAR (IRE) ..6-9.. 9 ch.g. Irish River (FR) — Meadow Glen Lady (USA) (Believe It USA) ppfu. Strong lengthy half-brother to Madiyan (USA), and to Irish flat winners, Madaraka (USA) and Madaniyya (USA), and to a winner in Italy. Dam won at 6f in USA. IRISH FLAT '95 r2 p0. FLAT r5 p0 (tailed off; tried blinkers). NH '96/7 r3 p0. P-t-P '98 r1 p0 (last). Only once better than last in eight starts over obstacles and reported to have finished distressed on that occasion. Resurfaced after a season off, but could barely muster a gallop and is obviously a complete physical wreck. *D. Page — Easton H.* 179 (R), 323 (CfMa), 551 (OMa), 603 (M).

MAN OF ANTRIM (IRE) ..—.. 7 b.g. Mandalus — Thistletopper (Le Bavard FR) p. Small neat brother to Keeper's Call (IRE). IRISH P-t-P '99 r2 w1 (5yo Geldings Mdn) p1 (2nd). Looked a useful novice in Ireland where he scored on firmish, but suffered a reverse in a February Restricted for the new yard. *M.R. Smith — E. Sussex & Romney Marsh (Sara Hickman).* 179 (R).

MAN OF MYSTERY ..10-1.. 15 b.g. Torus — Queens Folly (King's Bench) 3. Big rangy brother to NH flat winner, Lovelyroseofclare, and half-brother to Spend Easy, and to Irish Chasing winner, Fatal Hesitation. Dam won 3 2m Hdles. NH FLAT r2 p0. NH '91/6 r39 w7 (2m5f Hdle, and 6 Chses, 2m3f-3m1f, inc hat-trick at Hereford, and earned £11,079 in 2-finisher Aintree race) p7. P-t-P '97/9 r25 w3 (Ladies) p7 (5 3rds; last of 2 once); pulled up 8. An habitual front-runner and has made all when successful in three poor Ladies Opens '97/9, but easily passed by decent campaigners and managed just one appearance in 2000 when beaten 31 lengths at Detling. No more than a safe conveyance for an inexperienced rider nowadays. Thrice blinkered and tried in a near-side pricker under Rules. *Mrs S.A. Sansom — O. Surrey & Burstow (Ann Blaker).* 573 (CfL).

MAN OF STEELE (IRE) ..9-12.. 8 b.g. Ala Hounak — Church Brae (The Parson) u15333. Workmanlike good-bodied brother to Steel Brae (IRE) and Vals Castle (IRE), and half-brother to Church Ride (IRE), and to Irish Pointing winner, Island Harriet (IRE). IRISH P-t-P '97/8 r5 w1 (4yo Maiden) p1 (promoted from 4th to 3rd); pulled up 1. P-t-P/HUNT CH '99 r8 w2 (Restricted and Intermediate) p3 (2 2nds, inc beaten neck in Hunt Ch); last pair 2, and fell 1. A dual winner in '99, and consistently thereabouts when completing, but finding it hard to cope outside of Confined company which is disappointing as he finished in front of (an admittedly below-par) Lord Harry when second in a Uttoxeter Hunter Chase last year. Kept to ground close to good. One-paced, but genuine and should find another opportunity if sensibly placed, though stronger handling would help. *Hon Miss D. Harding — Portman (Louise Alner).* 9 (L), 214 (Cf), 326 (L), 631 (MO), 800 (3m110yH), 1557 (3m1fH).

PLATE 80   327 Hursley Hambledon Land Rover Mens Open: R to L Aintgottime (R. Lawther), 2nd, and Man Of The Match (B. Kendellen), 4th, lead from Go Universal (N. Mitchell), 3rd, and Northern Kingdom (J. Diment), pu
PHOTO: Tim Holt

MAN OF THE MATCH ..9-12.. 11 b.g. Vital Season — Kate The Shrew (Comedy Star USA) 42f. Tall strong brother to Summers Pride and Summerbridge. Dam failed to finish in four of five Points. NH

'97/8 r13 p6 (3rd in Hdle; and inc 5 Chses). P-t-P '99 r10 w3 (Maiden, Restricted and Members) p2; 5th, pulled up 2, unseated 1, and brought down 1. Inconsistent and often looked work-shy under Rules, but found Pointing more to his liking and enjoyed a good season in '99 particularly when fitted with blinkers. Not disgraced on his debut in Open company on his return nor when chasing home Village Copper in the fastest time of the day at Ampton (both times without headgear), but probably found the ground too testing next time and failed to reappear. Hopefully not going to become as susceptible to injury as the owners husband but cut a hind leg on his final appearance, and may have run his last race. *Mrs E. Pearce — Grafton (Jenny Pidgeon).* 327 (O), 552 (I), 1016 (Cf).

MANOR RHYME ..8-11§.. 14 b.g. Le Bavard (FR) — Scotch And Ice (Balinger) 4p5pp. Very tall rangy half-brother to NH flat and Chasing winner, Frys No Fool. IRISH NH '93/4 r8 p0. IRISH P-t-P '92/4 r12 w1 (6yo&up Maiden) p0; pulled up 8. NH '94/7 r25 w1 (3m1f Ch) p9. P-t-P '99 r8 w1 (Club nov rdrs) p1 (3rd); 4th, last 2, pulled up 2, and unseated 1. Sprang a 40-1 shock when winning without coming off the bridle at Cothelstone last year, but amazingly inconsistent and had been well beaten prior to returning to Cothelstone this year where he was destroyed after sustaining an injury in the very race he had won twelve months earlier. *Mrs N. Gretton — Silverton (Tom Gretton).* 199 (Cf), 403 (Cf), 557 (Cf), 1015 (4mO), 1550 (Cnr).

MANVULANE (IRE) ..—.. 11 b.g. Mandalus — La Vulane (Laurence O) u. Tall workmanlike. NH FLAT Spr '95 r2 p0. NH '95/9 (visored 3 to '97) r14 w1 (2m2f Ch) p5 (inc 3 Hdles). Finally scored in softish on his 15th attempt under Rules (lost touch halfway, jumped right and made a mistake at the last, but led under pressure near the finish), but has never managed more than four outings in a year, and unseated after two miles when trailing badly in his only Point. *Mrs C.J. Black — Cheshire Forest (Reg Crank).* 566 (L).

MAQUILLEUX ..8-11.. 8 ch.g. Gildoran — Marque De Soleil (Sunyboy) p2p. Strong half-brother to Marquis Of Bedford (*qv*). Made most until caught after the last when three lengths second at Barbury Castle, and was in front four out next time, but tired quickly and pulled up (struck into himself). Both races too around seven minutes, and might well be able to last home on a less demanding track. *Ms K. Crocker — N. Cotswold (Giles Smyly).* 197 (CfMa), 472 (OMa), 1068 (3m2fOMa).

MARAUDER (IRE) ..—§§.. 8 b.g. Yashgan — Sweet Slievenamon (Arctic Slave) pff. Workmanlike lengthy half-brother to Carrigaline Lad, Deep Chance and Spur Bay, to Irish Hurdles winner, Cormac's Lass, and to Chasing winner, Tremplin (IRE). 9000 5-y-o. NH FLAT Nov '98 (for N. Hawke) r1 p0. NH '99 (bought for 2000; previously for S. Mullins) r4 p0 (last 2 and pulled up 2 in Hdles). Wears blinkers, and is bad ride and thoroughly ungenuine to boot. *Mrs A. Price — Teme V.* 450 (CfMa), 673 (2m4fOMa), 989 (OMa).

MARCHING MARQUIS (IRE) ..10-13.. 10 b.g. Aristocracy — Lady Go Marching (USA) (Go Marching USA) 12. Big rangy brother to Stanmore (IRE), and half-brother to 4 Italian flat winners (one also successful over jumps there). Dam won 3 races at up to 9f in USA. NH FLAT '96 r2 w1 p1 (2nd). NH '96/7 r6 w1 (2m5f Hdle) p2; clear when unseated at last once. HUNT CH '99 r5 w2 (2m4f110y) p2; and pulled up 1. NH Mar '00 r1 p1 (2nd in 3m1f Amat rdrs HCap Ch: *ld 5, mist 2 out, sn hdd & btn*). A useful Hunter Chaser when conditions aren't testing and won his third race on the bounce when his reappearance, but has been plagued by injury over the years and that was the last we saw of him in 2000. More than capable of winning again, but Gary Brown will need to don his Florence Nightingale costume in order to keep him in one piece. Well handled by the promising Tom Gibney again at Newbury. *R. Donald Brown — O. Berks (Gary Brown).* 154 (3mH).

MARISOL (IRE) ..9-10.. 8 b.m. Mujtahid (USA) — Stanerra's Star (Shadeed USA) 11p1. Leggy light-framed half-sister to a flat winner in Italy. Grandam, Stanerra, won 7 flat inc Japan Cup, and earned £299,754 (having cost 5000gns), but never bred a winner. FLAT r11 p2. NH FLAT '97/8 r2 p0. NH '98/9 (for P. Montieth) r4 p1 (2nd); inc Sell. Bought Doncaster, Aug for 1400. Outclassed in a Hunter Chase, but did very well to maintain an unbeaten record in minor Points, in which she showed a willing attitude when put under pressure. Has useful riders, but they have to be determined with her, and there was possibly an element of luck in the Maiden success (a close second when left clear at the last). Acts on firm, happy to make the running, and can probably find other opportunities. *J. Parfitt — Gelligaer F. (Lisa Day).* 1222 (2m4fOMa), 1448 (M), 1535 (2m3fH), 1659 (R).

MARIUS (IRE) ..10-4.. 11 b.g. Cyrano De Bergerac — Nesreen (The Parson) 52123. Small compact. Dam won 2 flat (14-16f) and 2m Hdle in Ireland. IR 4300y. FLAt (for B. Hills) r14 w3 (7½-9f) p1 (3rd). NH '94/8 (from J. Gifford's) r29 w4 (3 Hdles, 2m1f-2m2f, and 2m3f Ch) p10; 4th 9. Lucky when winning a Chase in November '97, but lacked confidence under Rules subsequently, and found nil on occasions. Revived in Points and enjoyed himself in Ladies Opens, and outstayed Monkey Ago up the testing final hill at Duncombe Park, but twice had to settle for placing behind that rival, including when half a length second having been checked at an earlier stage at Witton Castle. All his eight wins have been gained on easy surfaces, and was a particularly precocious two-year-old, when he scored thrice. His completion record over jumps is outstanding, because he has only failed to get round in one of 34 attempts (when pulled up). Had a slight setback and absent after March. *Mrs P.A. Russell (The Marius Partnership) — Middleton.* 41 (L), 135 (L), 280 (L), 397 (L), 690 (L).

MARKET POSEUR (IRE) ..—.. 7 b.g. Brush Aside (USA) — Great Aunt Emily (Traditionalist USA) p. Brother to Dark Challenger (IRE) (*qv*). Sold Tattersalls Ireland Aug, '98 for 9565. Pulled up two out on a May debut, but may be capable of better in time. *Mrs J.D. Dillon — Rockwood H. (Stephen Wiles).* 1330 (OMa).

MARKET SPRINGER (IRE) ..10-2.. 10 gr.g. Roselier (FR) — An Carthanach (Good Thyne USA) 323u. Tall. NH FLAT '97 r2 p0. NH '98 r6 p1 (distant 2nd in Ch, only 2 went clear — the pair who had been clear both fell, and one remounted); pulled up 1, and fell 2 in other Chses. P-t-p '99 r3 w1 (Maiden) p0; and unseated 2. Stayed on well to win at Llanfrynach in '99, and again ran his best race of the season there in 2000. Only failed by a neck to peg back the winner who recorded one of the fastest times of the day and should have little difficulty in winning a similar race next year. Sometimes has problems catching Bethan Williams, but generally an improved jumper. May not appreciate a sound surface. *Mrs M. Williams & Mrs C.M. Marles — Curre (Lyndon Williams).* 69 (R), 484 (R), 894 (R), 1400 (R).

MARKHAM LAD ..—.. 11 b.g. Revolutionary (USA) — Markham Lady (Athens Wood) R. Strong owner-bred half-brother to former Pritchard Pointer Markham Lad ('careers around like a lunatic' 'should never be on a racecourse'). NH FLAT r1 p0 (17th of 18 — tailed off halfway). P-t-P '97/9 r15 p1 (last of 3); failed to finish 14 (on floor 7, and refused 2). Plays havoc with whoever throws his leg across him and should have been banned long ago. Disgracefully, has only finished in one of 16 Points when hopelessly tailed off last of three in '97. *D. Pritchard — Badsworth.* 506 (Cf).

MARNIES SONG ..8-0.. 8 ch.m. Little Wolf — Marnie's Girl (Crooner) p4pfp6u3pp. Angular half-sister to Balcraig Boy, Marnie's Refrain and Mischievous Girl. P-t-P '99 r5 p0 (pulled up 4, and unseated 1). Denied a possible win at Howick when she was knocked into the middle of next week at the final fence by the eventual winner, but judged on her other efforts there is no guarantee that she would have consented to crosss the line in front and cannot be considered unlucky. Jumps poorly and finds nothing of the bridle. Wears blinkers. *M. Roberts & A. Hall — Ystrad Taf Fechan (David Gibbs).* 269 (CfMa), 488 (CfMa), 746 (CfMa), 823 (CfMa), 1312 (Cm), 1406 (OMa), 1456 (OMa), 1618 (OMa), 1645 (3mH), 1660 (OMa).

MARQUIS (U) ..—.. a b.g. unknown 3. One and a half fences third in his Members, but gave the jockey a safe first ride. *Mrs H. Hillard — Berkeley.* 1489 (M).

MARQUIS OF BEDFORD ..9-0.. 7 ch.g. Bedford (USA) — Marque De Soleil (Sunyboy) p5. Good-topped home-bred half-brother to Maquilleux. Dam is half-sister to Miss Martlet (*qv* '95 Annual). Grandam, Foot Mark, pulled up in 2 Points. P-t-P '99 r1 p0 (unseated). Unseated three out when holding every chance on his only start in '99, but only managed two early season appearances this year and weakened after 2m2f both times. Needs to improve his jumping, and reported to be havinf a soft-palate operation to improve his wind. *Mrs P.K. Smyly — N. Cotswold (Giles Smyly).* 122 (OMa), 391 (CfMa).

MARSDEN ..—.. 7 b.g. Lochearnhead (USA) — Fishing Smack (Bustiki) p. Dam won 2 2m Sell Hdles and placed 13 (inc 6 Chses) for late Barry Byford, and subsequently won a Confined and placed 2 for him before breaking down. P-t-P '99 r1 p0 (pulled up). Twice in touch for two miles '99/00, but eventually tailed off when pulling up in both outings and seems hard to train. *Mrs R. Byford — E. Anglian Bloodhounds (Bruce Andrews).* 237 (OMa).

MARTHA LEADER (IRE) ..9-5§.. 9 b.g. Supreme Leader — Madame Martha (Carlingford Castle) 18f. Small wiry brother to Martha's Boy (IRE) (*qv*). IRISH P-t-P '98 r4 p0 (tailed off and pulled up 4). P-t-P '99 r4 p2 (2nds of 3); 6th, and refused 1. Nowhere near as talented as his big brother, but came good on his third visit to Charing when successful in much the slowest time of the day. Has looked to be lacking in both stamina and resolution in the past and a well beaten last on his first attempt in Restricteds. *D.C. Robinson — Mid Surrey F.* 291 (CfMa), 575 (R), 825 (R).

MARTHA'S BOY (IRE) ..11-3.. 10 b.g. Supreme Leader — Madame Martha (Carlingford Castle) f. Angular workmanlike brother to Martha Leader (IRE), and half-brother to Irish Pointing winner, Minstrel Madame. IRISH P-t-P '96 r2 p0 (pulled up 1, and fell 1). P-t-P/HUNT CH '97/8 r9 w5 (inc 3 Hunt Chses, 3m-3m1f) p0 (pulled up 1, and fell/unseated 3). A disaster in his first five attempts, but underwent a dramatic transformation in '98 when completing a five-timer with the minimum of fuss. Gained the last three of those wins in the Hunter Chase arena, including a £7253 prize at Aintree, and looked a potential star, but pulled up lame at Folkestone and forced to miss the following season. Made his comeback on home territory at Rodmell, but fought the rider until crashing after only a mile and was not seen again. Possesses a remarkable turn of foot and it will be a crying shame if he never gets another chance to use it. *D.C. Robinson — Mid Surrey F. (Marion Robinson).* 1212 (Cf).

MARWOODS MANDATE (IRE) ..9-1.. 7 b.g. Top Of The World — Futurum Lady VII (unknown) pf33p. Tall rangy half-brother to Knockreigh Cross (IRE) and Seldom Seen (IRE). NH FLAT '98 (for P.

Eccles) r2 p0. Placed in two Maidens, but there has to be doubts about his stamina, and it was a pretty pathetic effort when he let the 13-year-old Vulpin De Laugere overtake him on the run-in once. Will struggle to score on that sort or showing. *G.W. Swinbank — W. Salop.* 292 (M), 593 (2m4fOMa), 778 (OMa), 1153 (OMa), 1323 (OMa).

MASKED MARTIN ..8-13.. 10 b.g. Bustino — Mardi Gras Belle (USA) (Masked Dancer USA) p3pp. Lengthy. FLAT r4 p0 (tailed off). NH '95/7 r8 p0 (inc last pair 2 and pulled up in Hdles; last twice, pulled up 1, and fell 1 in Chses). P-t-P '98/9 (for Mr A.L. Watts) r6 p1 (2nd); 5th, and pulled up 4. Thirty lengths second of four once in '99, but bettered that when around six lengths third at Kilworthy this year, though the time was exceptionally slow. Usually pulls up and looks a most unlikely winner. Has been tried in blinkers under Rules. *Mr & Mrs D. Beasley & C. Baker — Lamerton (Mrs D. Beasley).* 657 (R), 721 (CfMa), 1370 (I), 1521 (CfMa).

MASTER BANKER ..9-2.. 7 b.g. Golden Heights — Miss Bali Ha'i (Balinger) pp34. Workmanlike. Dam was 6th and pulled up 3 in Points. Grandam, General Outlook, won 2 Points (one on a disqualification) and placed 4. Great-grandam, Steal-A-Look, won a Maiden. Great-great-grandam, Icy Steel, won 11 Points. P-t-P '99 r1 p0 (pulled up). A funny creature, who now arrives mounted in the paddock, but showed his first sign of ability when four lengths third in the slowest of four Maidens at Clifton-on-Dunsmore in May. Might have finished closer but for spinning wide off the final bend when holding a clear advantage. Poor jumping has masked his (not considerable) talent otherwise, but a fluent round would give him a chance of landing a run-of-the-mill event. *Mrs C. Page, Mrs D. Pritchard & T. Goodman — Warwicks (John Pritchard).* 900 (OMa), 1147 (OMa), 1421 (OMa), 1435 (OMa).

MASTER BOSTON (IRE) ..10-10.. 13 gr.g. Soughaan (USA) — Ballinoe Lass (Captain James) 61. Good-topped half-brother to Swing To The Left (IRE) and My Secret (IRE). NH '93/9 (blinkered once in '97) r63 w9 (3 Hdles, 2m4f-2m6f, and 6 2m5f Chses) p16 (after remounting once). A grand servant on good or easy surfaces in his prime, but was ending a losing sequence of 26 which dated back to January '96 (when he completed a four-timer; lucky once, and possibly lucky once) when landing a Fakenham Hunter Chase. Was scoring for the ninth time over his specialist trip of about 2m6f, but certainly helped by the opposition blundering their chances away, including three of his seven rivals who were eliminated in an early melee. Not seen again, but the triumph (which was a first success under Rules for Ben Woodhouse) hoisted his career earnings to £56,949. Can often be a sketchy jumper himself. *M.K. Oldham — Sinnington (Bob Woodhouse).* 90 (3m1fH), 227 (2m5f110yH).

MASTER BUCKLEY ..9-5.. 11 b.g. Buckley — Ivy Hill (Cantab) pppp1. Workmanlike half-brother to Cheeky Skiver, Ivanter, Red Rondo, Cantantivy, The Stoat and Hygga Bank. Dam won a Maiden, but failed to finish in 11 of 14 other attempts. NH FLAT r1 p0. P-t-P '96/9 r17 w2 (Maiden and Restricted) p5 (4 3rds, remote of 4 once); failed to finish 7 (fell/unseated 2). Pulled up four times under Charlie White in 2000, but had the temerity to beat him when he chose to partner a much better fancied stablemate on his final appearance in a weak race at Bratton Down. Handles well and firmish, but has the typical Buckley streak of temperament and strong handling is clearly essential. *S. Redwood — Tiverton Stag (Tessa White).* 654 (I), 853 (Inr), 1370 (I), 1472 (I), 1649 (CCf).

MASTER CHUZZLEWIT (IRE) ..9-8-.. 10 b.g. Rontino — Quatemala (Welsh Saint) 73p. Strong half-brother to Crafty Copper, and to Irish NH flat and jumping winner, Coqualla. Dam won 2 Irish 3-y-o's, 5-6f. IRISH P-t-P '96 r4 p1 (3rd); pulled up, and fell. IRISH NH FLAT '96/7 r5 p2. IRISH NH '95 and '97/8 r6 p0. NH '99 (for S. Griffiths; tongue-tied) r5 w1 (2m1f Ch) p1 (2nd). Won a four-runner Chase in heavy at 33-1 for previous connections (*qv* Harry Henbit), but flashed his tail when 16 lengths third in an Open and does not seem to have much ability left, like many of his stablemates was under the cloud of a virus in 2000. *Miss D. Stone & T.L. Greig — Grafton (Jenny Pidgeon).* 25 (Cnr), 789 (O), 1073 (O).

MASTER COMEDY ..9-5.. 17 b.g. Comedy Star (USA) — Romardia (Romulus) 52p. Compact owner-bred half-brother to Martineau, and to winners at home and in France. Dam won at 7f. FLAT r6 p0. NH '87/98 r68 w3 (2m2f-3m3f Chses, 33-1 latest) p14 (short-headed once; inc 3rd in Hdle); inc Sells. P-t-P '99 r5 p0 (4th, last 3, and ran out 1). Used to be a popular part of the furniture at Fontwell, where he made 20 of his final 52 appearances under Rules, and gained all his victories at the track. Wears blinkers. A gallant old veteran and it was sad to see him end his career when breaking down badly at Hackwood Park. *Miss J. Wilkinson — Hursley Hambledon (Vincent Simpson).* 216 (Cnr), 324 (M), 884 (O).

MASTER CROOK ..—.. 9 ch.g. Leifson's Colony VII — Golden Starfish (Porto Bello) u. Half-brother to Midas Man. Dam, half-sister to Fishing Season (*qv* '96 Annual), failed to finish in 2 Points. Already a long way behind the leader when he dumped the rider at the fourth in a February Maiden. *Dr A. Crookston — Lanarks & Renfrews.* 365 (CfMa).

MASTER HYDE (USA) ..9-8.. 12 gr.g. Trempolino (USA) — Sandspur (USA) (Al Hattab USA) 5uup.

Leggy half-brother to several winners in USA. FLAT (to 10; 3 wins for P. Mitchell; tried in headgear) r54 w5 (7-12f, 3 on equitrack) p12 (short headed once). NH '94/9 (3 wins for J. Goldie; previously for R. Allan; 2 wins previously for W. Storey, bought for 4000) r37 w5 (2m-2m7f Hdles) p8 (inc 2 3rds in Sells); inc 4 Chses. NH '00 r1 p0 (pulled up in 2m4f110y HCap Hdle: *bhnd, hmpd & lost plce 6, eff aft nxt, sn bhnd & eased, pu 2 out*).Has done more than his share of winning in the past and gained ten victories (all on sound surfaces or equitrack), but a sketchy jumper and often ungenuine. Deeply frustrating these days as he travels supremely easily but will not a thing when let down, and has established a losing sequence of 17. The new owner James Brown (not to be confused with the Godfather of soul) showed a major lack of talent when falling off at the first and at the second in his two attempts. *J.M. Brown — Eglinton.* 110 (O), 716 (O), 975 (O).

MASTER JOCK ..10-10.. 7 ch.g. Scottish Reel — Mistress Corrado (New Member) 1. Half-brother to Master Will. Dam, sister to Members Rights, pulled up in 2 Points for Peter Burke. Grandam, Mistress Rights, was bad 3rd and fell twice in Points. Great-grandam, Flaming Fiddler, was a poor Pointer. P-t-P '99 r2 w1 (2m4f Maiden) p1 (2nd). Beat two young duffers without breaking sweat at Southwell last year, but looked potentially useful in doing so and produced an impressive performance when following up in a Wetherby Restricted on his only outing in 2000. Declined the fast gallop set by the eventual runner-up, but picked him up easily at the second last and won in the fastest 12st7lb time of the day. Gary Hanmer spent most of the run-in wrestling him to a walk and as he failed to reappear there is the suspicion that he went wrong, but will hopefully be able to stand a full campaign in 2001 and is worth following. *P.S. Burke — Wheatland (Paul Jones).* 689 (R).

MASTER JOEY ..—§.. 11 b.g. Blakeney — Grafitti Gal (USA) (Pronto) 5. Small half-brother to 2 winners in USA. Dam won at up to 11f in USA. Grandam, Graffiti, was one of best fillies of her generation in USA. IRISH NH FLAT '94 and '96 r4 w1 p0. IRISH NH '95 and '97 r10 p1 (3rd in Hdle). P-t-P '98/9 (for Mrs J. Yeomans) r3 p0 (pulled up 3). Remounted after falling five out in his Members, but was tailed off at the time and has looked wrong since crossing the Irish Sea. Tried in blinkers and spurs on his final outing in '99, and connections did not bother to register him for anything more than Hunt Members races in 2000. *M. Perry — Berkeley.* 1489 (M).

MASTER KIWI (NZ) ..8-12.. 14 b.g. Bagwis (AUS) — Veela (NZ) (Oakville) p273454p. Workmanlike hobdayed. NH FLAT r3 p0. NH '94 and '96 r3 p0 (pulled up in Chses). P-t-P/HUNT CH '96 and '98/9 r18 w3 (Maiden, Restricted and Members) p1 (last of 3); 4th, last pair 7, pulled up 4, unseated 1, and ran out 1. Awarded his Members after the first past the post had missed a marker last year, and was ending a three year drought, but did not enjoy the same luck in 2000 and was only once better than last when completing. Ungenuine and loves to take things easy under Tessa Hayes. Often taken to post early and mounted on the course. *F. & Mrs J. Hayes — Dulverton E., & Tiverton Staghounds (Mrs J.A. Hayes).* 1097 (Inr), 1136 (M), 1370 (I), 1472 (I), 1560 (Cf), 1604 (M), 1649 (CCf), 1674 (I).

MASTER OF TROY ..8-12.. 13 b.g. Trojan Fen — Gohar (USA) (Barachois CAN) 232. Strong compact one-eyed half-brother to Fast Freeze (*qv*). FLAT r6 w1 (14f) p0. NH '91/5 and '97 (blinkered/visored 3) r38 w4 (2m-2m4f Hdles) p9; finished well beaten in 5 Chses. P-t-P/HUNT CH '99 r6 w5 (3m2f Hunt Ch, and 4 Ladies — 5-timer) p1 (3rd). Bought for less money than some spend at a car-boot sale, but proved a tremendous bargain in '99 winning four Ladies races and the Greig Middleton final at Warwick. The McCurrich yard was never firing in 2000 and he finished whacked after both his Hunter Chases, after a roughed off after an excellent second to Split Second at Chaddesley in mid-March. Has a history of leg trouble, but could quicken impressively when required and will hopefully be able to stage a revival in 2001. *Miss T. McCurrich — Worcs.* 223 (3m2fH), 385 (3mH), 613 (L).

MASTER PAGE ..—.. 7 br.g. Tudor Diver — Pansy Potter (Blue And Grey) pp. Tall half-brother to Rumbleinthejungle. Bought Malvern, May for 2100. Bred to be remarkably slow, and certainly looks it so far. *Mrs M.J. Thorogood — Essex (Chris Thorogood).* 1181 (R), 1377 (M).

MASTER PAN ..8-8.. 8 b.g. Pitpan — All Risks (Pitcairn) pp3. Tall strong owner-bred half-brother to Delightfilly and Loup Rouge, and to a winner in Austria. Dam won at 8f. P-t-P '99 r3 p0 (pulled up 2, and brought down 1). Still carrying plenty of condition when 23 lengths third of four in testing conditions at Flete Park on his final outing, but looks painfully slow and that has been his only completion to date. *I. Foale — Dart V. & S. Pool H. (Ralph Hirons).* 730 (I), 1049 (CfMa), 1262 (OMa).

MASTER ROCKY ..9-10.. 9 b.g. Jumbo Hirt (USA) — Dunlean (Leander) pf. Owner-bred half-brother to Vaigly Grey and Miss Dunbay. P-t-P '99 r1 w1 (Maiden) p0. Overcame his apparent inexperience to win at Mosshouses on his racecourse debut, but did not look right when pulling up on his reappearance and was a beaten fourth when falling at the last on his Hunter Chase debut subsequently. Not disgraced at Carlisle against vastly more experienced rivals and will take some beating in a Restricted if all is well in 2001. *P.J. McDonald — Haydon (Tim Reed).* 714 (C), 1154 (3m2fH).

MASTER WELDER ..9-1.. 9 ch.g. Weld — Scally Jenks (Scallywag) fp3p. Tall half-brother to The Pedlar,

Scally Hicks, and Scallywace. Grandam, Acuity, won Hunt Ch (left lucky 2nd, and later awarded race on technicality) and Maiden and placed 6 for Ken Edwards. P-t-P '98 r5 w1 (deadheat Maiden) p1 (½l 2nd); pulled up 2, and ran out 1. Hung left and presumably went wrong when awarded a dead-heat on his final appearance in '98 (looked to finish second) as he was forced to miss the following season in its entirety. Visored on his return, but his only piece of form when five and a half lengths last of three in his Members, and failed to reappear after striking into himself at Eyton next time. Wilful, and needs strong handling to curb his errant tendencies. *K.C.G. Edwards — Ludlow (Geoff Evans).* 612 (CR), 744 (R), 986 (M), 1200 (CR).

MASTER WILL ..9-6.. 6 ch.g. Rakaposhi King — Mistress Corrado (New Member) 22. Small owner-bred alf-brother to Master Jock (*qv*). Showed plenty of promise despite running very green on his debut (the stewards made themselves look total buffoons by calling Gary Hanmer before them, and one can only wonder if they are holding a witch-hunt against that talented rider), and again let down by inexperience when odds-on next time. Challenged on the bit after three out, but hung left on the bend between the last two fences, and was unrideable until rallying on the run-in to be beaten three quarters of a length. Sure to go one better soon, and may develop into a decent performer. *P.S. Burke — Wheatland (Paul Jones).* 1526 (OMa), 1668 (OMa).

MAUDETTE (IRE) ..8-11.. 6 b.m. Phardante (FR) — Doucha Girl (Sheer Grit) 5f9. Workmanlike half-sister to Carolstyle (IRE). Bought Doncaster, May for 9000. NH FLAT May '00 r1 p0; (9th in 2m1f NH flat: *in tch til rdn 3f out*). Showed some ability in her second Point (fell two out when second and ridden), and may do better if returned to Maidens. *T.H. Caldwell — Cheshire Forest.* 778 (OMa), 965 (OMa).

MAXIMIZE (IRE) ..9-12.. 7 b.g. Mandalus — Lone Run (Kemal FR) 1. Bought Doncaster, May '98 for 10,000. Comes from a yard who are best known for their eventers, and already the winner in pre-novice in that sphere. Gave a fluent display when landing a poor Maiden at Friars Haugh with his head in his chest in February, and could be an interesting contender if returned to Points. *Lady Vestey — Buccleuch (Ian Stark).* 114 (OMa).

MAXIMUS (IRE) ..9-12.. 6 br.g. Un Desperado (FR) — Fais Vite (USA) (Sharpen Up) u1. Half-brother to 2 flat winners (one in France), including Bo Knows Nigel. Odd-on when unseating at halfway on his debut, but atoned with a smooth winning display at Penshurst (favourite again). Clearly a decent prospect, and should be worth watching with interest. *A. Cowing & B. Cockerell — E. Sussex & Romney Marsh (Di Grissell).* 1105 (2m4fOMa), 1513 (OMa).

MAYBRIDGE LADY ..9-12.. 8 ch.m. Lighter — Shadow Play (Busted) 17pp. Tall sister to Sail On By, and half-sister to Arran View, and to flat and Hurdles winner, My Buddy. NH FLAT '97 r3 p1 (3rd). NH '97 r2 p0. P-t-P '99 r1 p0 (pulled up). Landed a touch on her reappearance when comfortably landing a modest Maiden at Chipley Park, but out of luck since and pulled up lame on the firm ground at Holnicote on her latest outing. *Mrs J.F. Deithrick — Eggesford (Kay Rees & Polly Curling).* 147 (OMa), 728 (R), 850 (R), 1376 (R).

MAYFAIR MONARCH ..8-1.. 6 ch.g. King's Signet (USA) — Mayfair Cecilia (Brotherly USA) 4fpf. A speedy sort, but has twice fallen in the lead after about two miles, and was 38 lengths fourth on the only occasion he saw a race to the conclusion (and pecked very badly two out on that occasion). His beginner-rider is unable to teach him anything, and it would surely be worth getting him an experienced partner before more damage is done. *Mr & Mrs P.E. Froud — Blackmore & Sparkford V. (Peter Froud).* 265 (OMa), 640 (CfMa), 733 (2m4fOMa), 1099 (OMa).

MAYHEM ..9-0.. 9 br.m. Sergeant Drummer (USA) — Cinbar (Cintrist) p3u3f. Robust sister to Avin Fun Bar and Barrette, and half-sister to Iron Bar and Sinbad's Secret. Dam won a Hunt Ch and 16 Points and placed 19 (inc Hunt Ch). Grandam, Evens Bar, won 3 Hunt Chses and 5 Points and placed 4 (inc 3 Hunt Chses) for Anne Frank. P-t-P '98/9 (for Mrs C.A. Mock & Mrs A. Frank) r5 p1 (2nd); pulled up 3, and ran out 1. Beaten between three and 34 lengths in her three placings, and nearly became the unworthy recipient of a success at Mounsey Hill Gate on her final start, but having seen the two leaders foiled by the final fence she too was too exhausted to get over it successfully. Might get even luckier one day. *G.J. & Mrs C.A. Mock — Tiverton Stag (Claire Mock).* 932 (R), 1136 (M), 1469 (OMa), 1564 (OMa), 1610 (OMa).

MAY ROSE ..8-8.. 11 ch.m. Ayres Rock — Misty Morn III (Mount Sherwood) u5. Small sparely-made half-sister to Mopsons Cross and Rolling Wave. Dam pulled up in Point in '95. NH FLAT '96 r1 p0 (tailed off). P-t-P '99 r2 p0 (ran out 1, and pulled up 1). A hard-pulling erratic jumper, but showed some semblance of sanity for Julian Pritchard on her final outing when around 24 lengths fifth at Chaddesley. Wears a cross-noseband and has worn a martingale. *D. Amies — N. Ledbury (John Rudge).* 1527 (OMa), 1634 (OMa).

MCLOUGHLIN (IRE) ..9-0§.. 12 ch.g. Orchestra — Boyne Bridge (Brave Invader USA) p3p55p. Workmanlike fired. NH '97/8 r7 p0 (last twice, pulled up 3, and unseated 2 in Chses). P-t-P '94/5 and '99 r14 p3 (2 2nds, remote last once, and last of 3); pulled up 6, refused 1, carried out 1, and fell/unseated 2. Gave his best ever display when around two lengths second in a Chaddesley Maiden in '99, but next to useless in 19 others races and wasting his time in Hunter Chases in which he does not have the remotest chance. Has never jumped fences with much relish. *P. Senter — N. Ledbury.* 893 (OMa), 1020 (OMa), 1023 (3mH), 1340 (3m1f110yH), 1527 (OMa), 1668 (OMa).

MEADOWBANK ..10-3.. 7 b.g. Meadowbrook — Polypodium (Politico USA) f11. Tall half-brother to Petrea (*qv*). NH '99 (for M.W. Easterby) r3 p0. Looked an above-average novice in two early season wins (showed plenty of stamina, and galloped on strongly), but not seen since the beginning of March. Should be guaranteed further successes if he does not have a problem. *Major M. Watson — Middleton (David Easterby).* 167 (OMa), 282 (OMa), 396 (R).

PLATE 81   396 Derwent Restricted: Meadowbank (M. Watson), 1st, leads Scruton (D. Easterby), 3rd, and Normins Hussar (G. Brewer), fell, Hazel Reilly (D. Thomas), 3rd, Tracey Town (Miss Rachel Clark), 7th, and Cede Nullis (S. Brisby), pu.   PHOTO: Roy Parker

MEADOWLECK ..8-10.. 12 b.m. Meadowbrook — Leckywil (Menelek) p7376pp2. Small lengthy light-framed half-sister to Miss Jedd. Dam was 2nd in 2 Maidens for Billy Young. NH FLAT '94 r4 p0 (Debut from P. Monteith's; refused to race once). NH '94/9 (blinkered once in '96) r69 p3 (3rds, inc Sell); well tailed off last, pulled up and fell in Chses. Owned by an incurable optimist who has kept her in training for seven years, during which time she has accumulated 81 defeats and a mere five placings. Often front-runs for a way, but has littered her career with numerous mistakes. Wears a tongue-strap these days. Twice managed to totter her way to pittances in Points, but was 13 lengths last of three and 25 lengths second of four (after inheriting that position at the final fence in the latter). *W.G. Young — Lanarks & Renfrews.* 363 (CfMa), 665 (OMa), 978 (CfMa), 1123 (OMa), 1430 (OMa), 1445 (3m1fH), 1500 (OMa), 1580 (OMa).

MEAT LOAF (IRE) ..8-7§.. 7 gr.g. Mandalus — Only Flower (Warpath) p4ppr. Unfurnished. Dam, sister to Copgrave (*qv* '93 Annual), won 14f flat, 2m2f Hdle and 2m6f Ch in Ireland. Started at a ludicrous 3-1 or less in all his races, but was five lengths fourth in an appalling contest on the only occasion he completed the course (very green and vering around). His namesake must weigh about 20 stone, but he could still probably run faster. *G. Dalziel (The Valley View Partnership) — Blackmore & Sparkford V. (John Dufosee).* 629 (OMa), 888 (OMa), 1062 (OMa), 1555 (OMa), 1675 (OMa).

MECCA PRINCE (IRE) ..9-10.. 6 ch.g. Shalford (IRE) — Fashion Parade (Mount Hagen FR) 1p4352. Close-coupled half-brother to 3 flat winners (one in Ireland, and one in Holland). 9500 2-y-o. NH

'98/9 (for R. Whitaker, blinkered 1) r5 p0. Bought Ascot, May for 820. A first winner for 16-year-old James Tudor in a three-finisher Maiden in soft at Erw Lon, and has generally performed reasonably in Restricteds since. Not difficult to beat in them and his rating may have peaked, but might be able to score again eventually. *J. Tudor — Llangeinor.* 269 (CfMa), 745 (R), 818 (R), 947 (R), 1298 (R), 1452 (R).

PLATE 82   269 Vale of Clettwr Confined Maiden (Div 3): Mecca Prince (James Tudor), 1st, nearside jumps the ditch with Bright Beacon (E. Williams), 3rd (the woodwork forming the ditch is not much lower than the fence!)   PHOTO: Bill Selwyn

MEDIA LUZ ..—§§.. 7 b.m. Weld — Hung Over (Smackover) pupp. Small. Dam, half-sister to Inhurst (qv '99 Annual). P-t-P '99 r5 p0 (unseated 3, and refused 2). Remarkable inept and has been eliminated before halfway seven times to date. Got as far as the third last for a competent rider once, but whether he will agree to partner her again is doubtful. *Mrs J. Smale — Torrington F. (Lisa Smale).* 255 (R), 408 (OMa), 536 (R), 656 (OMa).

MEDIAS MAID ..—§.. 11 b.m. Mas Media — Silleys Maid (Continuation) p. Lengthy light-framed owner-bred half-sister to 2 flat winners. Dam won 5 flat, 5-6f. NH '94 and '97 r6 p0 (last pair 5, and pulled up 1). P-t-P '96/9 r20 w1 (Maiden) p2 (2nds); last pair 6, ran out 1, fell/unseated 2, and pulled up 8. Stumbled across a weak Maiden on firm at Bratton Down in '96, but not so lucky in 18 subsequent attempts and not better than last since '97. Actually led for a while on her belated reappearance, but capitulated and remains a slovenly jumper. Blinkered once in '97. *R.T. Grant — Tiverton Stag.* 1671 (R).

MEFEIN BOY (IRE) ..9-9.. 8 br.g. Royal Fountain — Aelia Paetina (Buckskin FR) p17393p5. Small. IRISH NH '98 r3 p0. P-t-P '99 r7 p3 (2 2nds); 4th, last, pulled up 1, and fell 1. Showed improved form when tried in headgear in '99, but ran without it when presented with a Hornby Castle Maiden in which the unassailable leaders' rider was unseated after a leather broke on the run-in. Gave his best display in Restricteds on the same course, but looks soft and remains a sketchy jumper. Has been tried in a tongue-strap. *Mrs J.W. Furness — Hurworth.* 133 (CCfMa), 380 (OMa), 503 (R), 689 (R), 871 (R), 1028 (R), 1230 (R), 1475 (R).

MEL (IRE) ..9-13.. 11 ch.g. Millfontaine — Nataf (Whistling Deer) 482321. Lengthy. Dam won Maiden in Ireland. IRISH P-t-P '95 r1 p1 (2nd). NH '95/7 r13 p4 (3 Sell Hdles, 2m5f-3m3f, and 15l 3rd in Ch); 8th, last twice, and pulled up in other Chses. P-t-P '98 r7 p4 (2 2nds; and 3rd of 4 twice); 4th, unseated 1, and pulled up 1. A deserved winner following 12 assorted placings, but very one-paced and likely to prove a push-over in half decent Restricteds. Has the virtue of been a safe jumper and has never fallen, but even his reliability is unlikely to make up for his shortcomings. Tongue-tied latterly under Rules. *Miss M.K. Eames — Cotley (Philip Greenwood).* 455 (OMa), 725 (L), 957 (CfMa), 1131 (OMa), 1303 (M), 1564 (OMa).

MELNIK ..10-12.. 10 ch.g. Nashwan (USA) — Melodist (USA) (The Minstrel CAN) 1. Robust compact attractive half-brother to Irish flat and English jumping winner, Song Of The Sword. Dam won 3 flat (8-12f, Italian Oaks, a dead-heat with Diminuendo for Irish Oaks, and one in England). FLAT r5 p2 (beaten 8-9l). NH '94/5, '96/7 r14 w3 (2m2f-2m4f Hdles, inc £10,942 prize at Cheltenham; and 2m3f Ch) p4. P-t-P/HUNT CH '98 r5 w4 (Ladies — 4-timer inc walkover) p1 (head 2nd in Hunt Ch). Bred to win a Derby, but has had to settle for somewhat smaller fare, though his Pointing achievements have been exemplary. Unbeaten in five Ladies Opens, but clearly very hard to train nowadays (missed '99) and only managed one pulverising defeat of two inferiors this year before connections had to call time. Has thoroughly enjoyed winging little fences in Points, though much of the credit of his rejuvenation must go to Carrie Ford who has handled him with great skill. Needs good or easy surfaces. Worth trying in another Hunter Chase if he is able to return in 2001 as he has nothing to prove in Points. *M. Silcock & F. Taylor — W. Salop (Carrie Ford).* 531 (L).

MELODY PRINCESS ..10-0.. 8 b.m. Ardross — Letteressie (Alias Smith USA) 4ppR421u. Small unimpressive-looking. NH FLAT '98 r2 p0. NH '98 r3 p0 (tailed off Hdles, inc Sell). P-t-P '99 (for Mr J.A. Atkin) r5 w1 (Maiden) p2 (2nd of 3 once); 7th, and unseated 1. Carried home by Tim Lane when opening her account at Guilsborough last year, but struggled in Restricteds this year until galvanised by Dominic Alers-Hankey in late-season. Inconsistent and only goes for strong pilots, and will need to raise her standards again to compete successfully in future. *Mrs C. Oram & A. Wilkins — V.W.H. (Danielle Olding).* 247 (R), 392 (R), 748 (M), 887 (R), 1206 (R), 1375 (R), 1608 (R), 1651 (I).

MELROY (IRE) ..8-6.. 10 b.g. Le Bavard (FR) — Blackrath Beauty (Le Tricolore) 2p. Close-coupled brother to Edge Ahead (IRE) (qv). NH FLAT May '96 (for Mrs M. Jones) r1 p0. NH '98 (for T. Haynes) r2 p0. Sold Ascot, Aug for 700. Left a lucky second two out in a bad Maiden, and although not entirely disgraced, he hardly ever runs, and was tailed off when pulled up at halfway next time. *Mrs W. Doyne-Ditmas — E. Cornwall.* 724 (CfMa), 1565 (OMa).

MEMBERS CRUISE ..10-2.. 11 ch.g. Cruise Missile — Members Joy (New Member) p. Compact half-brother to Members Imp. Dam pulled up in 2 Points for Mr Smith. Grandam, Joytina, was a useless Pointer/Chaser for him. P-t-P '96/7 and '99 r10 w3 (Maiden, Restricted and Intermediate) p3 (3rds, of 4 once); fell/unseated 3. A fair performer in minor company '98/9 and hasn't run a bad race during that period, but has never stood many outings and disappeared after pulling up at Mollington on his 2000 debut. Chased home Jilly Wig and Gunner Welburn in '99, and sure to win again if he returns in good health, but has been prone to the odd blunder. *E.W. Smith — Beaufort (John Deutsch).* 77 (O).

MENALDI (IRE) ..9-9.. 11 b.g. Meneval (USA) — Top Riggin (Jupiter Pluvius) 241p4u. Sturdy compact. NH '96/9 (blinkered 1; for J. Wade; previously for P. Cheesbrough) 25 p4 (inc 2nd in Ch); inc Sell Ch. Very disappointing under Rules, and was unplaced in his last 11 attempts. Finally broke his duck on his 28th outing in a Maiden at Hutton Rudby, but decidedly moderate in Restricteds since, and flattered by having found an opportunity at last. *Miss M.D. Myco — Miss K. Roncoroni — S. Durham.* 44 (OMa), 113 (OMa), 624 (OMa), 713 (R), 1326 (R), 1475 (R).

MENDIP PRINCE (IRE) ..9-7.. 11 b.g. King's Ride — Atlantic Hope (Brave Invader USA) 4p44726. Compact well-made tired brother to NH flat and Chasing winner, Warfield Lad (IRE), and half-brother to Juranstan and Opus Winwood (IRE), and to Irish Pointing and Chasing winner, Brian's Delight (IRE). NH FLAT '94/5 r3 w1 p0. NH '96/7 r5 p1 (3rd in Hdle); 4th only Ch (mistakes). P-t-P '98/9 (for Mrs C.J. Bibbey) r5 p3 (3rds, of 4 once); pulled up 1, and fell 1. Occasionally flatters, but has never won over jumps, and the closest he came in 2000 was when three-quarters of a length second of three finishers in his Members. Usually gives the impression that he finds three miles too far. Hampered and fell at the first when tried in blinkers once in the previous yard. *Mrs J. M. Porter — Vine & Craven (John Porter).* 1 (C), 36 (Cl), 215 (C), 388 (I), 937 (I), 1242 (M), 1395 (L).

MENDIP SON ..10-1.. 11 b.g. Hallgate — Silver Surprise (Son Of Silver) p2ppp73. Compact light. Dam won at 10f, and won 2m1f Hdle. NH FLAT r1 p0. NH '94/5 (visored final) and '97 r6 p2 (2nds). P-t-P '96/7 and '99 r14 w2 (Maiden and Restricted) p3 (2nds); pulled up 7, and ran out 1. Reformed when successful once apiece in '97 and '99, but finished weakly in 2000 having led at some stage in most of his races and has become disappointing once again. Suited by a sound surface. Wears blinkers. *Mrs H.E. Rees — Cattistock.* 63 (I), 211 (Cnr), 356 (Inr), 736 (Cnr), 953 (I), 1134 (Cnr), 1535 (2m3fH).

MERE CLASS ..9-2.. 15 b.g. Class Distinction — Cuckmere Grange (Floriana) 3. Big strong home-bred half-brother to Fables Green. NH FLAT r1 p0. NH '91 and '92/6 r20 w5 (2m4f-3m2f Chses, inc hat-trick) p5; pulled up in 3 of final 4 attempts. P-t-P '92 and '98/9 r7 w2 (2m5f Maiden and Restricted) p1 (2nd); pulled up 1, brought down 1, and fell 1. Useful to '93 winning seven races, but pulled up in four of his last six starts under Rules and has only managed five outings in the last three years. Brought down at halfway on Dawn Powell's first ride in '99, but guided her round Hackwood Park safely this year when a poor third in his Members. Could have gone a long way had circumstances allowed. *Mrs J. Stuart Evans — Hampshire (John Stuart Evans).* 882 (M).

MERELY MORTAL ..9-0.. 10 b.g. Rolfe (USA) — Lagskona (Be Friendly) 644. Strong compact. NH FLAT '95/6 r4 p0. NH '96/8 r6 p0 (inc Sells). P-t-P '99 r4 p1 (2nd); 4th, and pulled up 2. Able to show speed for around two miles, but soon weakens and remains prone to errors. Not better than last-but-one in five completions and will need to be very lucky to win. *Mrs J. Owen — Flint & Denbigh.* 297 (I), 526 (OMa), 778 (OMa).

MERGER MANIA ..9-11.. 9 b.g. Precocious — Scrummage (Workboy) 24uuR2p51. Small close-coupled. Dam won 3 flat, 7-8f. FLAT r2 p0 (tailed off last 2, inc Sell). NH '96 r2 p0 (last after dwelling, and pulled up — mistakes both). P-t-P/HUNT CH '97/8 r13 w2 (Maiden and Restricted) p1 (3rd); pulled up 2, fell 1, and ran out 2. Mixes a fair degree of ability with a large dose of hair-raising lunacy. Often hurtles off in an uncontrollable manner and has scared the living daylights out of ten jockeys who have made his acquaintance in Points. Would have won a Ludlow Hunter Chase in '98 but for crashing at the second last fence and late errors cost him dear on his comeback at Whitwick after a season off. Spent much of the rest of the season thinking of new ways to dislodge his partners and has perfected the art of jumping violently right-handed whilst still keeping his feet. Walked over for his latest success, but would win competitive races if only his brain was not so addled. Wears a cross-noseband and has been tried in blinkers. *W.I. Owens — Radnor & W. Herefords (Steve Flook).* 333 (Cf), 479 (Cf), 684 (2m4fH), 862 (Cf), 987 (Cf), 1086 (Cf), 1271 (M), 1346 (3m1f110yH), 1463 (Cf), 1546 (I).

MERINO WALTZ (USA) ..9-7.. 15 b.g. Nijinsky (CAN) — Bethamane (USA) (Wajima USA) p. Big lengthy. IRISH NH FLAT '90 r4 w1 p0. P-t-P/HUNT CH '95/6 and '98/9 r12 p4 (2 3rds, inc Hunt Ch); unseated 2, and pulled up 2. Had some good form to his credit over jumps in the past, but has never won over obstacles from limited opportunities. Tailed off after two miles in a Hereford Hunter Chase in May on his return and is in virtual retirement now. *Mrs S.Y. Farthing — Monmouths.* 1346 (3m1f110yH).

MERLYNS CHOICE ..9-10§.. 17 b.g. Ovac (ITY) — Liffey's Choice (Little Buskins) 8. Small lengthy brother to Kaim Park, and half-brother to River Mandate and Mammy's Choice (IRE) (subsequently won Chasing), to NH flat and jumping winner, Special Account, to Irish Pointing and Chasing winner, Friday Thirteenth (IRE), and to Irish NH flat winner, Rio Grande. Dam won 2m Irish Hurdle. IRISH NH FLAT r7 p0. IRISH P-t-P '90 r4 w2 p1 (3rd). IRISH NH '88 and '90/4 (blinkered 3) r29 w3 (2m6f-3m Hdles, and 3m4f Ch) p6. P-t-P '95/9 r40 w2 (inc Confined) p17 (9 3rds, last thrice); failed to finish 6 (unseated 1). Outstanding at course completion, but has declined alarmingly since winning three races in Ireland and often tails himself up or runs in snatches now. Chose the former on his return when furlongs last in a Ladies at Alpraham and was not seen again. Did well to win at 15, but starting to show signs of wear and tear. Not blinkered since '96. *A.D. Woodward — S. Notts.* 590 (L).

MERRIE JAR (IRE) ..10-1.. 7 b.g. Jareer (USA) — Merrie Moment (IRE) (Taufan USA) p1311. Compact half-brother to flat winner, Sassy. IRISH FLAT r1 p0. IRISH Nh '97 and '99 r6 p0. Fairly speedy, but makes plenty of mistakes at present, and was 30 lengths third at 1-2 once. A dual winner in minor company at Erw Lon (once on firm), but has not raced since early April, although he did turn up to collect his members (it looked as if it might turn out to be a walk-over when Tim Vaughan's name was seen to be against all the five entries on the racecard!). Would have prospect in Intermediates if he brushed up his jumping. *H.B. Ward — Banwen Miners (John Moore).* 146 (OMa), 648 (CfMa), 832 (R), 947 (R), 1294 (M).

MERRY SHOT (IRE) ..—.. 9 b.g. Cataldi — Borgina (Boreen FR) p2pp. Strong. IR 6800 4-y-o. NH FLAT Dec '97 r2 w1 p0. NH '98/9 (last on final for M. Pitman; previously for Mrs J. Pitman; blinkered 4) r10 p3 (2nds in Chses); pulled up 5. Bought Ascot, Sep for 4400. A maiden over jumps and has always been inconsistent, but worth 10-2 on his creditable second in a six-runner Mixed Open. Generally performs as if there is something badly wrong with him, and reverted to hopeless efforts subsequently. *C.A. Green — S. & W. Wilts.* 263 (I), 631 (MO), 1133 (O), 1444 (2m5fH).

MESLING ..9-2.. 9 ch.g. Alias Smith (USA) — Polly's Hand (Nearly A Hand) pp652u22. Close-coupled. Dam 'lurched from one crisis to the next' when failing to finish in 5 Points for Mrs Anderson (lame final). Grandam, Polly Scarlet, won Restricted and Adjacent (finished alone in match after refusing) and placed 9. P-t-P '99 r4 p1 (2nd of 3); last pair 2, and pulled up 1. Runner-up four times '99/00, but a weak finisher and has only had four others behind him on those occasions. Not helped by his consistently inaccurate jumping and will need a bad race to score. Can be quite a handful in the paddock. *C. Anderson — Border.* 188 (OMa), 497 (R), 718 (CfMa), 914 (CfMa), 1082 (CMa), 1164 (OMa), 1368 (OMa), 1499 (OMa).

METRO FASHION (IRE) ..9-3§.. 10 ch.g. Carlingford Castle — Good Resemblance (Kemal FR) p2p4p00. Lengthy unfurnished. IRISH NH FLAT '97 r1 p0. IRISH P-t-P '97 r5 p2 (2nds); pulled up, and unseated 2. NH '97 (for O. O'Neill) r1 p0. NH '00 r2 p0 (12th in 2m Nov Hdle: *chsd ldrs to 4, bhnd when carried lft 2 out*; and 11th in 2m4f Hdle: *chsd ldrs, mist 4, sn lost plce, t.o*). Finished three-quarters of a length second to weak moment in Ireland, but that was long ago, and they have certainly followed vastly different paths since. Definitely has the ability to win a Maiden and was five lengths second once, but very disappointing and looked ungenuine subsequently, and must not be trusted. *J.A. Atkin — Pytchley (T.J. Atkin)*. 373 (CfMa), 548 (CfMa), 703 (OMa), 1012 (CfMa), 1422 (OMa).

MEZZO PRINCESS ..8-12.. 9 b.m. Remezzo — Kam Tsin Princess (Prince Regent FR) pp1. Light-framed. Dam won 2m Hdle. P-t-P '99 r4 p1 (3rd of 4); last, pulled up 1, and fell 1. Beaten almost 30 lengths when third of four in a 2m4f Maiden on her final outing in '99, and looked likely to need a miracle to register a success. How apt that she should get one on All Fools Day 2000 when the recipient of a walkover for her Members. Usually pulls hard, and has no prospects in Restricteds. *T. Walker — Holcombe*. 569 (OMa), 694 (OMa), 810 (M).

MIA FORT ..8-9.. 8 ch.m. Bold Fort — Mia Xandra (Nearly A Hand) ppfp62. Small. Dam was 8th of 9, pulled up 4 and fell 2 in Points for Edward McGuinness. P-t-P '99 r1 p0 (pulled up). A consistently poor jumper, but produced her first rateable effort when second in a bad Laleston Maiden on her final start. Unimpressive looking and rarely looks fully wound up. *E.A. McGuinness — Gelligaer F. (M.G. Jones)*. 73 (OMa), 206 (OMa), 1201 (2m4fOMa), 1302 (OMa), 1465 (OMa), 1660 (OMa).

MICK MACKIE (IRE) ..9-13.. 8 b.g. Glacial Storm (USA) — Telamonia (Ballymoss) 31. Medium-sized attractive half-brother to Fergal's Delight, to Irish Pointing and jumping winner, Olivers Glen, and to a NH flat winner. IRISH P-t-P '98/9 r5 p3 (2nds, beaten neck once); pulled up, and carried out. IRISH NH '99 r4 p2 (3rds in Chses). Showed plenty of promise in Ireland, and came up against a subsequent Hunter Chase winner in a Maiden when favourite and third on his English debut. Made no mistake with a ready 15 length success next time, and a Restricted at least should be a doddle for him. May reach the ten stone range before long. *Mrs V. Ramm & Mrs C. Mackness — Cotswold (Jelly Nolan)*. 1068 (3m2fOMa), 1422 (OMa).

MICK MAN (IRE) ..9-0.. 10 b.g. Electric — Belle Chanel (Moyrath Jet) ppp24. Sturdy compact half-brother to Stormy Fashion. Dam won 2m5f NH flat, a Point, a 2m Hdle, and 2 Chses, 2m-2m4f, in Ireland. IRISH NH '96/7 r8 w1 (3m Hdle) p1 (3rd); fell at 3rd and at 1st in Chses. Scored in heavy in Ireland, but was emerging from three years in hiding when failing to beat another horse in the new yard. Left a poor second time out in an Open, and continued with the rider flailing around and administering needless reminders, and then finished almost two fences adrift in his Members. A sorry sight. *S.J. Robinson — Zetland*. 496 (C), 623 (Cf), 998 (C), 1080 (O), 1324 (M).

MICKTHECUTAWAY (IRE) ..10-6.. 9 b.g. Rontino — Le-Mu-Co (Varano) R211222. Tall lengthy half-brother to Irish Genius (IRE). IRISH P-t-P '97/8 r9 w2 (Hunt, and Winners of 2) p1 (3rd); pulled up 2, and fell/unseated 3 (at last with every chance once). IRISH NH '97/8 r5 p2 (Hunt Chses). P-t-P/HUNT CH '99 r6 w3 (inc Open) p3 (2 3rds, inc Hunt Ch). A useful Pointer on his day, but not an easy ride and has an ungenuine streak. Clocked the fastest time of the day when beating Forest Fountain at Whitwick and dominated an uncompetitive Leicester Hunter Chase subsequently, but a beaten favourite twice since and given an untypically foolish ride by Andrew Dalton at Flagg where he restarted after pulling up three out to claim a very remote second. Stays well and best suited by forcing tactics and plenty of cut in the ground, but can be clumsy at the fences. Best to return to his best when fresh. *Mr & Mrs A.J. Brazier — Wheatland (Andrew Dalton)*. 34 (MO), 117 (O), 334 (O), 462 (2m7f110yH), 988 (O), 1087 (MO), 1254 (O).

MICRO MISSILE ..—.. 15 ch.m. Cruise Missile — Ribmis (Simbir) p. MARLBOROUGH CUP '95 p1 p0 (fell). P-t-P '95 (for Mrs C. Wells) r1 p0 (fell). Wisely took five years off (at stud?) after two spills in '95, but pulled up after keeping in touch to halfway at Charlton Horethorne in April and promptly disappeared. *A.J. Powell — Beaufort*. 957 (CfMa).

MIDNIGHT DYNAMITE ..—.. 7 br.g. Lochearnhead (USA) — Dune Rider (USA) (Cresta Rider USA) pppp. Lengthy unfurnished. Tailed off and pulled up in Maidens, and appears to be the latest in a long line of Chinnery loonies. Deprived of another outing when he threw the rider going to the start at Horseheath, and disappeared over the horizon (pity they found him eventually). *A. Chinnery — E. Essex (Paul Chinery)*. 550 (OMa), 605 (OMa), 941 (CfMa), 1115 (OMa).

MIDNIGHT ROYAL ..—.. 6 b.m. Prince Daniel (USA) — Dontella's Girl (Royal Clipper) p. Owner-bred. Dam, sister or half-sister to 4 Pointers, won 2 Points and 3rd twice. Popped up in May to go 2m2f in a Maiden. *N.J. Pewter — Suffolk*. 1383 (OMa).

MIDNIGHT SERVICE (IRE) ..9-11§.. 12 b.g. The Parson — Stringfellows (Laurence O) 15155. Big strong. Dam won Irish NH flat. IRISH NH '94 r1 p0. IRISH P-t-P '96 (blinkered 1) r2 p0; pulled up 1. P-t-P/HUNT CH '97/9 r20 w2 (Restricted and Intermediate) p9 (5 3rds, inc Hunt Ch); pulled up 3. Capable of spirited efforts as he showed when beating Burntwood Melody at Thorpe on his reappearance, but thoroughly inconsistent and often loses interest. Wears blinkers and needs plenty of cajoling, but Robert Barrett does a good job on him and has been in the saddle in his last three victories. An expert jumper who has never fallen. *T.R. Newton — Pytchley (Tik Saunders)*. 115 (CCf), 229 (Cf), 441 (O), 1416 (O), 1532 (3m1fH).

MIDSUMMER GLEN (IRE) ..10-8.. 8 b.g. Glenstal (USA) — Right Then (No Argument) 22221323. Strong. IRISH NH '98 r2 p0. IRISH NH FLAT '98/9 r3 p0. IRISH P-t-P '99 r4 w1 (6 plus Mdn) p1 (2nd); pulled up, and brought down. Bought Doncaster, Aug for 4600. Ran a string of good races in throughout the season and was beaten three quarters of a length or less when second thrice (errors at the final fence cost him vital ground on two occasions; and failed by a head to beat Balisteros at Kelso, where Maxim Bremners wild urgings on the run-in earned a four day ban), so richly deserved his success in a Maiden Hunter Chase on the same course. Lucky to meet such feeble opposition, as the three behind him did not manage a victory in 2000 from a total of 24 attempts. Subsequently outclassed behind top opposition at Eyre before returning to Kelso to give another fine display behind the course specialist Manhatton Rainbow, but looked a bit weary and never got going when favourite there on final start. Tough and normally admirably consistent, and deserves to win more often. *Mrs R.P. Darling — Buccleuch (Bill Hughes).* 43 (Cf), 359 (Cf), 660 (Cf), 686 (3m1fH), 915 (3m1fH), 1024 (3m3f110yH), 1342 (3m1fH), 1591 (3m1fH).

MIGHTY MERC ..9-9.. 13 ch.g. Shaab — Cornish Saffron (Spitsbergen) pppfu. Plain rangy angular. NH FLAT r1 p0. NH '95 and '97/8 r14 w1 (3m1f Ch) p3 (3rds, beaten 20 lengths plus, and last twice); fell three out when clear once; pulled up 2. P-t-P '94, '97 and '99 (for Mr M. Broad) r12 w1 (Club Maiden) p0; pulled up 7. In surprisingly good nick on a sound surface under Rules in '97, but woeful in his last 15 appearances and has managed just four completions. Has never been a fluent jumper and acquired a tongue-strap on his last three starts. Clearly badly wrong in his wind and not worth running again. *Miss S.K. Cosgrove — Cambs (Michael Burman).* 17 (O), 83 (Cf), 94 (O), 177 (L), 770 (Cf).

MIGHTY MONARCH (IRE) ..8-7.. 8 b.g. King's Ride — Foxy Jane (Pollerton) ffpp5. Workmanlike. Sold Doncaster, May for 900. A hard puller who has shown early speed twice, but got his campaign off on a bad footing with a couple of falls, and was 32 lengths fifth when he eventually managed to get round. Had an absence of over two months in mid-season. *P.J. Millington — Fernie.* 54 (OMa), 169 (OMa), 373 (CfMa), 412 (OMa), 1507 (OMa).

MIGHTY MOSS (IRE) ..11-7.. 10 b.g. Moscow Society (USA) — Derry Girl (Rarity) 1151. Rangy half-brother to Irish NH flat and Hurdles winner, Castlekelly River (IRE), and Irish Hurdles winner, Bannow Bay (IRE). IRISH NH FLAT '96 r1 p1 (3rd). NH FLAT '95/6 r4 w2 p2. NH '96/8 (from D. Nicholson's) r10 w3 (Hdles, 2m4f-3m1f) p6 (5 2nds). A brilliant performer at the top level, and had earned £57,492 to '98, and never missed the frame including three visits to the Cheltenham Festival, where he was third in the Bumper, one length second to Istabraq in the Royal Sun Alliance, and fourth in the Bonus Print Stayers Hurdle. Only averages four runs a year and missed '99, but returned in tip-top shape to toy with inferior opposition at Huntingdon twice, and then favourite for his major target the Cheltenham Foxhunters, but did not get the most inspired of rides and was beaten just over six lengths. Made no mistake on his final outing at Eyre, where he relished the 3m3f 110y trip. Only risked or good or easy surfaces and has made the odd mistake since switching to fences, but never looks like falling, and can deal with most opponents without coming off the bridle. Very much a family concern despite being in a professional yard, and it might easily prove to be second time lucky in the Foxhunters of 2001. *K. Hutsby — Warwicks (Alan King).* 151 (3mH), 302 (3mH), 584 (3m2f110yH), 1024 (3m3f110yH).

MIGHTY RISING ..8-13.. 6 b.g. Primitive Rising (USA) — Mighty Miss (Doc Marten) 35f4p. Compact attractive. Dam, half-sister to First Trick (qv '94 Annual), won 2 Points and placed 4 to '94. Failed to progress after an apparently encouraging six lengths third in a non-Rules Maiden on his debut, and only two horses have finished behind him so far. Jumps well enough, and might possibly do better at six. *P.W. Clifton — Holderness (Mary Sowersby).* 138 (OMa), 282 (OMa), 436 (OMa), 1001 (2m4fOMa), 1233 (OMa).

MIGHTY WIZARD ..—.. 11 br.g. Doc Marten — Powder Horn (Scottish Rifle) p. Half-brother to Powder Prim. Dam won 2m Sell Hdle, 5 Chses (2m4f-3m3f) and an Open and placed total of 15 (inc a flat), principally for Jackie Barr. P-t-P '96 and '98 r2 p0 (4th, and pulled up 1). Casts his magic bi-annually, but clearly reading from the wrong spellbook, and pulled up lame after jumping just three fences on his latest sojourn. Out of a useful mare, but never seems destined to emulate her achievements. *J.O. Barr — Cleveland (Jackie Barr).* 626 (OMa).

MIGSY MALONE ..8-10.. 6 b.m. Afzal — The Dizzy Mole (IRE) (Salluceva) p7p. Tall strong-topped home-bred. Given three quick runs in May, and showed speed in the final two. Looks the type to have scope for improvement, but there is something of a question mark regarding her stamina at present. *Mrs M.A. Jukes — V. of Clettwr (Beverley Thomas).* 1302 (OMa), 1457 (OMa), 1617 (OMa).

MIKE'S DREAM ..9-7.. 9 b.g. Motivate — Carreg Goch (Kala Shikari) 2pp22u1f. Lengthy half-brother to Rachel's Boy. NH FLAT '97 r1 p0 (last). P-t-P '99 r1 p1 (3rd of 4). A deserved winner of a bad Maiden at Bassaleg after several praiseworthy efforts earlier in the season, but constantly thwarted by his inability to jump accurately at speed and tipped up when giving a good account of himself in his first Restricted subsequently. Greater fluency should enable him to win again in modest company. Seems indifferent to ground conditions. *S. Jones — Llangeinor.* 70 (OMa), 204 (OMa), 484 (R), 838 (OMa), 1056 (CfMa), 1302 (OMa), 1573 (OMa), 1615 (R).

MILITARY DREAMER ..—.. 9 b.g. Lightning Dealer — Bubbly Isle (Military) ppp. Half-brother to All Change. P-t-P '99 r1 p0 (pulled up). Looked short on stamina when pulled up in his first three Points and broke down in the fourth. *Mrs K.R. Blackwell — Grafton (Richard Webb).* 193 (R), 1207 (OMa), 1439 (OMa).

MILITARY MAN ..10-3.. 11 ch.g. Broadsword (USA) — Pearl Bride (Spartan General) 221p3225. Plain compact brother to Rolleston Blade and Cumberland Gap. P-t-P/HUNT CH '95 and '97/9 r29 w2 (Maiden and Restricted) p11 (7 2nds, last once); fell/unseated 5, and pulled up 5. Posted two decent early season efforts when runner-up at Barbury Castle and Weston Park, but usually a weak finisher who lacks resolve and was out on his feet when the fortuitous winner of a Garnons Intermediate subsequently. Was going strongly in the lead when the rider steered him the wrong side of a marker less than a mile from home on his first venture into Ladies company, but well beaten when odds-on in his Members and remains an unreliable betting proposition. Acts on any going. *A.W. Argent — Albrighton Woodland (Penny Grainger).* 35 (Cnr), 296 (I), 448 (I), 920 (3mH), 1086 (Cf), 1357 (MOnr), 1547 (L), 1629 (M).

MILLBANK HONEY ..8-9.. 11 ch.m. Headin' Up — Lucky Broxted (Broxted) pfpRp. Sturdy. P-t-P '98 r6 p3 (inc 3rd of 4 twice); pulled up 2, and unseated 1. Beaten a minimum of eight lengths when placed in three bad Welsh Maidens in '98 (finished 30 lengths behind Final Option when favourite once) and failed to go more than two miles without mishap on her return. Taking her to Cheltenham was an act of lunacy. *Miss J. Fowler — Pembs.* 1056 (CfMa), 1225 (OMa), 1336 (2m4fH), 1454 (OMa), 1535 (2m3fH).

MILL COPSE DILEMMA ..—.. 10 b.m. Its Without Doubt VII — Cara Kitt VII (unknown) f. 50-1 and fell at the fifth when already struggling on an unpromising debut. *J. Bowen — Tedworth.* 458 (R).

MILLCROFT REGATTA (IRE) ..9-0§.. 9 br.g. Miner's Lamp — Stradbally Bay (Shackleton) ur85. Strong-topped half-brother to Irish Hurdles winner, Goodnight Irene. NH '96/9 (for R. Alner, blinkered final) r12 p4 (Chses). Disappointing under Rules, and even more so in Points, in which he should theoretically have had a decent chance. Probably ungenuine, and has a novice partner in Robert McKenzie Johnston, who was very shaky to start with but seems to be coping better. Only averages four outings a year. *R.A. McKenzie Johnston — Portman (Ali Tory).* 212 (CfMa), 409 (OMa), 520 (OMa), 738 (OMa).

MILL O'THE RAGS (IRE) ..10-2.. 12 b.g. Strong Gale — Lady Rag (Ragapan) ups3Rf54. Close-coupled. NH '94/7 r23 w6 (3 Hdles, 2m-2m1f, and 3 Chses, 2m1f-2m5f) p4 (2nds); last once and pulled up 3 from 4 attempts Autumn '97 (blinkered final). P-t-P/HUNT CH '98/9 (for Mrs E. Clark, Mr R. Ames, Mr R. Oliver-Smith & Mrs A.J. McVay) r17 w3 (2m4f110y Hunt Ch, Open and Ladies) p6 (5 2nds, and inc 3 Hunt Chses); fell 1, pulled up 4. Revived by the current yard after going to pieces latterly under Rules and provided Ann-Marie Hayes with her first winner at Cottenham last year. Unlucky on consecutive Saturdays in March this term with the same rider on board, particularly so at Higham where the combination had made stealthy headway to join the odds-on Cracking Idea when falling two out. Resents being hit these days, but might just win again with softly-softly tactics. Needs good or firm ground. *R. Ames & Mrs E. Clarke — Suffolk (Neil King).* 28 (L), 82 (M), 177 (L), 238 (O), 608 (L), 758 (L), 1113 (L), 1380 (L).

MILLSTOCK ..9-1.. 11 b.m. Interrex (CAN) — Millingdale (Tumble Wind USA) 4p83. Small neat half-sister to a flat winner, to flat and prolific jumping winner, Norstock, and to Chasing winners, Corpus and Out Of Stock. NH FLAT r1 p0. NH '94/5 r5 p0 (5th, last twice, pulled up 1, and fell 1; inc Sell). P-t-P '97/8 r10 p2 (2nds, of 3 once); last pair 2, pulled up 5, and fell 1. At stud since recording two modest placings in '98, but well beaten on her return and looks unlikely to gain what would be a deserved success. The owner-rider appeared rustier than the horse after 12 months out of the saddle, and promptly fell off trying to mount. To add injury to insult, she then broke a bone in her leg and was on crutches as Geoff Barfoot-Saunt deputised at Ashorne. He could manage no better than last, so the intrepid Natasha was back in the saddle only three weeks later (after just the one vault, presumably), and completed her busiest ever season with six rides. *Miss N.J. Stallard — Cotswold V.F.* 617 (CMa), 994 (OMa), 1435 (OMa), 1635 (OMa).

MILLYHENRY ..11-0.. 10 b.g. White Prince (USA) — Milly's Chance (Mljet) 1u311111114. Workmanlike lengthy half-brother to Final Chance. Dam, sister or half-sister to 4 Tizzard Pointers, including Venn Boy (*qv* '00 Annual), was 3rd in 2 Points for them, Grandam, Ace Chance, a disappointing tail-swisher, was placed in 7 Points and a Chase for them. P-t-P/HUNT CH '97/9 r16 w5 (up to Confined) p3 (2 2nds, of 3 once); last 2, fell/unseated 3 (looked unlucky once), and pulled up 3. A steady performer in his first two campaigns, but much improved last year and again in 2000. Clicked with Charlotte Tizzard from the moment he provided her with her first success on her race-riding debut at Barbury Castle and by the end of the season they had accumulated another six wins together (Tabitha Cave successfully deputised at Cothelstone once). Faced some very simple tasks, but his defeat of Mizyan and Just Bert was a useful effort, though firmly put in his place by Castle Mane and co. in the Horse & Hound Cup on his final outing. Looked a picture throughout the season and, but for two blunders in February, jumped immaculately as well. Suited by top-of-the-ground, but can handle it softer. Will be hard pressed to match his achievements in 2001, but sure to give things his all and is a credit to connections. *L.G. Tizzard — Blackmore & Sparkford V. (Pauline Tizzard).* 35 (Cnr), 211 (Cnr), 354 (L), 523 (Cnr), 638 (Cf), 952 (M), 1096 (MO), 1304 (Cfnr), 1470 (MO), 1561 (MO), 1647 (3m4fH).

PLATE 83   952 Blackmore & Sparkford Vale Hunt Members: Millyhenry (Miss C. Tizzard), 1st
PHOTO: Baths Photograhic

MILLY LE MOSS (IRE) ..9-9.. 12 b.m. Le Moss — Trianqo (Tarqogan) 2pp. Small compact half-sister to jumping winners, Stupid Cupid and Run Up The Flag. Dam won 2 Irish Points. NH FLAT '94/5 r2 p0. NH '94/8 r17 p0 (Sell final). P-t-P '99 r6 w1 (Maiden - 2 finished) p1 (3rd of 4); and pulled up 4. Lost touch at halfway in a Pantyderi Maiden in soft last year, but kept plodding on, and finally rewarded when the clear leader departed two out. Had the same scenario in front on her on her reappearance at Erw Lon, but this time the leader kept his feet and she came home a poor second. Pulled up in two subsequent attempts (saddle slipped once) and looks too slow to become seriously involved in Restricteds. *J. Nicholas — Ystrad Taf Fechan.* 274 (R), 486 (R), 1054 (R).

MILTOWN CASTLE ..—§§.. 8 ch.g. Prince Of Peace — Karaka (Good Times ITY) pfpRRRR. Tall home-bred half-brother to Ivans Dream. An appalling brute who did not get beyond halfway on six occasions, including when running out for four different jockeys latterly (the stupidity of putting the very inexperienced Louise Jackson on him once incurred the wrath of the stewards, as she could easily have caused an horrendous accident when losing control). How many more misdemeanours will be allowed before he is banned? *Mrs P. Papworth — S. Cornwall (John Papworth).* 253 (CfMa), 540 (OMa), 721 (CfMa), 934 (OMa), 1391 (OMa), 1519 (CfMa), 1641 (OMa).

MINDEN ROSE ..10-4.. 8 b.m. Lord Bud — Two Travellers (Deep Run) 1. Sturdy sister to Romany Run and Be Upstanding. P-t-P '99 r3 w1 (Maiden) p1 (3rd of 4); and brought down 1. Romped her Maiden in '99, and barely out of second gear when following up in a Restricted on her reappearance at Alnwick in January, but not seen since and may have suffered a setback. Will hopefully be fit to face a full campaign in 2001 as she looks a potentially useful prospect. *P. Maddison — Middleton.* 40 (R).

MINELLA DERBY (IRE) ..9-10.. 11 br.g. Sexton Blake — Black-Crash (Crash Course) 647547. Unfurnished half-brother to Just Whisper, to Irish NH flat and Hurdles winners, Total Confusion and Wither Or Which (IRE) (won Festival Bumper at Cheltenham), and to a German jumping winner. Dam is half-sister to Black Monkey (*qv* '92 Annual). IRISH NH FLAT '96 r1 w1. NH '96/9 (for P. Nicholls, bought for 45,000) r9 w1 (2m5f Hdle) p2 (2nds in Chses, just caught once); ran out with every chance in Hdle; blinkered in Sell Ch once (favourite, but made mistakes). Bought Doncaster, May for 4000. NH May 2000 r3 p0 (5th in 2m2f110y Claiming Hdle: *rr til late hdwy*; 4th in 3m Amat HCap Hdle: *hld up in rr, hdwy 8, one pce nxt*; and 7th in 2m6f HCap Hdle: *rr, hrd rdn 9, 3rd when blun last, nt rec*). Generally a fiasco for Nicholls after winning his debut in November '96, and was absent for 21 months after February '97 (had leg problems). Tends to make shoals of errors and did not enjoy himself in Hunter Chases (blinkered in the first of them), but did better when reverting to Hurdles, and might yet be up to winning a Seller. Trys a wide range of distances, but discovering the correct one seems to be very difficult. *Mrs S. Buckland — O. Berks (Gary Brown).* 583 (2m5f110yH), 919 (2m3f110yH), 1155 (2m5f110yH).

MINELLA GOLD (IRE) ..10-3.. 12 b.g. The Parson — Slieveglagh Queen (Proverb) 1u3432d6. Tall rangy. IRISH NH FLAT '95 r4 w1 p3. IRISH NH '95/9 (tried blinkered) r21 w3 (Hdles, 2m-2m4f) p6 (for L. Lungo). NH '99 (for L. Lungo) r2 p1 (3rd in Ch). Beat Tea Box on his debut for the new stable at Alnwick, looked lucky, as Houselope Beck seemed to being going the best when he fell at the last), but did not fair nearly as well as that rival subsequently, and has become disappointing. Regularaly makes the frame, but either cannot or will not find much in the closing stages, and his best chance of scoring again would probably be if he stuck to Intermediates. Can handle soft ground, but went four years between victories. *Mrs W.M. Scott — Buccleuch.* 183 (CCf), 362 (O), 582 (3m3fH), 916 (3m1fH), 1078 (Cf), 1159 (I), 1428 (O).

MINELLA SILVER (IRE) ..—.. 8 gr.g. Roselier (FR) — Mrs Minella (Deep Run) f. IRISH NH '98 r1 p0. IRISH P-t-P '98/9 r 5 w2 (5&6yo Mdn, and poor Open — 4 ran and 2 finished) p1 (last of 3). Bought Doncaster, May for 33,000. A dual winner in heavy in Ireland, and made favourite for a Mixed Open in January, in which he appeared to be galloping with tremendous dash when he fell in a ten length lead at the 11th. Looked a useful prospect (a tentative 10-11, but evidently did himself a mischief, and failed to reappear. *Miss H.J. Hinckley — Heythrop (Mark Rimell).* 34 (MO).

PLATE 84   40 West Percy Restricted: Minden Rose (C. Mulhall), 1st, is in command at the last
PHOTO: Alan Mitchell

MINER'S BILL (IRE) ..10-3.. 10 br.g. Miner's Lamp — Lady Tarsel (Tarqogan) fu11. Smallish compact half-brother to Murberry (IRE) (*qv*). NH FLAT Nov/Dec '97 r2 p1 (neck 2nd). NH '98 (for J. King) r3 p2 (½l 2nd in 2m5f Hdle). Bought Ascot, Dec '98 for 500. Showed plenty of ability under Rules, but obviously had a problem when he was sold so cheaply, and new connections seem to have done very well to guide him back to health. Fell or unseated with Tabitha Cave twice (in a slight lead two out and going well once), but subsequently unbeaten for Lesley Jefford, even though he missed out on a Maiden. Has not been seen since early April, but is perfectly capable of scoring again if sound in 2001. *Mrs P.A. Cave — Blackmore & Sparkford V.* 315 (R), 410 (OMa), 728 (R), 879 (I).

MINE'S A GIN (IRE) ..10-6.. 10 gr.g. Roselier (FR) — Cathedral Street (Boreen Beag) 624111. Tall rangy brother to smart jumping winner, Montroe (IRE). P-t-P '96/9 (for Mrs J.M. Cumings) r20 w5 (inc 2 Ladies) p5 (3 2nds, last once); pulled up 7. Pulled up on his first three outings of '96 and '97, but rather more successful since and has won six of his last nine Points. Looked out of sorts when tailed off at Stafford Cross in April, but returned six weeks later to notch his second career hat-trick. Acts on any going and usually a fantastic jumper. Sure to win again in Ladies company with the assistance of Jo Cumings. *A.J. & R. Dunsford — Devon & Somerset (Keith Cumings).* 326 (L), 725 (L), 928 (MO), 1369 (M), 1562 (C), 1652 (L).

MING ..—.. 9 b.m. Dixi (BEL) — Wilstrap Lady (Le Bavard FR) p. Dam only beat one horse in 8 Points (non-finisher in 6), when 31/ 3rd. In front when making a mistake four out in his Members, but promptly dropped right out. *Mrs J. Theker — Blankney (Margaret Morris).* 366 (M).

MINIBELLE ..9-7.. 9 br.m. Macmillion — Pokey's Belle (Uncle Pokey) p. Small half-sister to Derrybelle. Dam is half-sister to Beau Seigneur (*qv* '95 Annual). NH FLAT '97 r3 p0. NH '97 r2 p0 (8th, and pulled up in Hdles — tailed off both). NH '99 r6 p0. P-t-P '99 r1 w1 (Maiden) p0. Produced after the last when successful in a poor Maiden at Bassaleg in '99, but exposed as moderate under Rules both before and since, and generally fails to stay a true three miles. Made favourite for her Pointing return, but was one of the many horses who could not go through the Llanvapley version of the Somme battlefields and ground to halt at the end of the back straight second time round. Would be more profitably employed in Selling Hurdles which she has yet to try. *D.L. Williams — Glamorgan (Beverley Moore-Williams).* 744 (R).

MINI CRUISE ..10-1.. 11 ch.g. Cruise Missile — Mini Pie (Dike USA) 57pp4p3211. Good-bodied lengthy half-brother to Hurdles winner, Mac's Gift. Dam dead-heated for 8f race. NH '95/6 r5 p0. P-t-P '97/9 r12 w1 (Maiden) p7 (3 3rds, of 4 once, and last once); pulled up 3. Successful three times in May '99/00, and given enterprising rides by Luke Morgan in the two most recent, though the opposition was modest, and but for Michael Dun's overweight would have been beaten at 1-2 in his Members. Not a true stayer and needs to get clear, but an accurate jumper who has never fallen and might stumble across another weak opportunity when conditions are right. *Miss J. Fisher — Lauderdale.* 40 (R), 111 (R), 360 (R), 424 (R), 498 (R), 663 (R), 976 (R), 1118 (R), 1424 (M), 1496 (R).

MININO (IRE) ..9-8.. 8 ch.g. Glacial Storm (USA) — Haughty-Ha (Lord Ha Ha) f45f13. Tall rangy. Dam won 2 Points in Ireland, and grandam, Hovering, won 4 Points there. IRISH P-t-P '98 (for Barry Kennedy) r5 p3; fell 1. IRISH NH '98/9 r4 p0 (6th twice, last and pulled up in Chses). IRISH NH FLAT '99 r1 p0. Slow to register a victory, but finally made it at the 15th attempt when scraping home by a head in a bad Maiden at Cottenham. A weak finisher, and may struggle in Restricteds, blinkered on his last three outings. *B.J. Kennedy — Essex F. & U. (Jim Ovell).* 16 (R), 98 (OMa), 284 (2m4fCMa), 411 (OMa), 775 (OMa), 1038 (R).

MINOR KEY (IRE) ..8-12.. 11 b.g. Orchestra — Maid Of Moyode (Giolla Mear) u5pp. Small light-framed half-brother to Chasing winner, The Moor (IRE). Dam won an Irish Point, and won 3 Chses (2m-2m4f) in England. IRISH NH FLAT '94 r1 p0. IRISH P-t-P '94 and '96 r6 w2 (6 plus Mdn, and Winners of Two) p1 (3rd), fell, and unseated. NH '96/7 (for J. Jenkins) r11 p4 (7/ 3rd and distant 3rd of 4 in Hdles, and 27/ last of 2 and distant 3rd of 4 in Chses); inc pulled up 5, and fell 2. Very poor since leaving Ireland, and was 40 lengths behind on the only occasion he managed to complete in the latest yard. Wore a tongue-strap on his first two attempts. Missed '95 and '98/9. And disappeared again in mid-March. *Mrs R. Pilkington — Enfield Chace.* 93 (C), 288 (CMod), 574 (4mMO), 609 (I).

MINSTER ECHO ..—.. 6 ch.m. Minster Son — Fair Echo (Quality Fair) Rppp. Half-sister to Bold Echo. Prone to bad mistakes, and has been a distinctly hairy ride so far. *J.A. Featherstone — Staintondale (Mary Sowersby).* 437 (OMa), 627 (OMa), 1002 (2m4fOMa), 1234 (OMa).

MINSTER STAR ..7-12.. 7 ch.m. Minster Son — Star Of The Sea (Absalom) 3p. Unfurnished. 1000y. FLAT r6 p1 (10/3rd). NH '97 (from J. Spearing's) r1 p1 (3rd of 4 — jumped very poorly). Her three thirds have been unimpressive displays, and crawled up the final hill at Mollington when beaten 43 lengths in the latest (left second and almost refused at the last, stopped on the flat, but continued and nearly caught the reluctant runner-up. *R.S. & A. Rainbow — N. Cotswold.* 432 (OMa), 703 (OMa).

MINSTREL FIRE (IRE) ..—.. 13 ch.g. Black Minstrel — Duhallow Hazel (Major Point) pupp. Half-brother to Pat Cullen. IRISH NH FLAT '92/3 r7 p1 (3rd). IRISH NH '93/7 r36 w3 (2m Hdle and 2 2m1f Chses) p10. IRISH P-t-P '99 r8 p0 (pulled up 7, and unseated). A triple winner in Ireland to '95, but has gone to pieces alarmingly, and even the Rowsells have been unable to work the oracle with him. Has never completed the course in 12 Points, and unseated Zoe Livermore on her first ride in his Members. Generally looks to have a problem which stops him in his tracks. Has virtually no tail. *R.J. Rowsell — Ystrad Taf Fechan.* 1052 (L), 1399 (M), 1451 (MO), 1571 (Cnr).

MINSTREL'S QUAY (IRE) ..9-8§.. 10 ch.g. Black Minstrel — Quayside Lady (Quayside) u47. IRISH P-t-P '96/7 r16 w1 (Maiden) p2; failed to finish 8 (fell/unseated 4 and ran out 1). IRISH NH '97 r1 p0 (pulled up in Ch). P-t-P '98/9 (for Mr D.E. Edwards) r8 w1 (Restricted) p0; fell/unseated 2, and pulled up 4. Survived two mistakes, including a particularly bad one at the last, where two challenging rivals departed, when successful at Eyton in '99, but well beaten in three Intermediates for new connections this March. Often awkward and a frequent non-finisher in the past, and has been tried in blinkers. *R.J. Brown — Vine & Craven (Caroline Gordon).* 388 (I), 632 (I), 785 (I).

MINTY'S FOLLY (IRE) ..—.. 11 ch.g. Fools Holme (USA) — Sugarbird (Star Appeal) pp. Tall good-looking half-brother to 4 flat winners, including Sapieha (Horris Hill Stakes), Long Siege and Hurdles winners, Dajraan (IRE) (smart in France) and Serious Danger (IRE). Dam won at 5f. NH FLAT Spr '94 r2 p0. NH '94/5 (for D. Nicholson) r4 p1 (2nd); pulled up in Ch final. Ground to a halt after about a mile twice when revived after a five year absence. Was tubed on his last appearance under Rules, and wore blinkers in the Hunter Chase. It would be amazing if he ever ran again. Presumably named with great feeling. *S. Lycett — Cotswold.* 197 (CfMa), 463 (2mH).

MIORBHAIL ..9-6.. 10 br.g. Wonderful Surprise — Florrie Palmer (Deadly Nightshade) f44. Compact half-brother to Another Formula and Florries Daughter. Dam, half-sister to H And K Wager (*qv* '91 Annual), 3rd in Ch, won 3 Points and placed 2 for Mrs Gray. P-t-P '98 r4 w1 (Maiden) p1 (2nd); pulled up 1, and brought down 1. Off the track for 12 months since winning on firmish at Witton Castle in '98, and managed just three outings in 2000. Takes a strong hold, but was in the process of running a decent race when falling five out on his reappearance at Market Rasen, and could win a modest Restricted if all went according to plan. Does not appear to handle softer surfaces. *Mrs F.M. Gray — Middleton (Tim Walford).* 50 (R), 378 (I), and 442 (L).

MIRROR MELODY ..8-7.. 12 b.m. Mirror Boy — Celia (Grange Melody) ppp. Robust. Dam won 2 Points and placed 5 for Robert Robinson (inc last of 3 in Ch; also promoted to 3rd in Irish Ch). P-t-P '94/5 and '97/8 r7 p5 (4 3rds); pulled up 2. Made the frame on a regular basis in the past, but a racecourse appearance has always been a rarity and no longer looks like breaking her duck. A weak finisher, and acquired a tongue-strap when generally outclassed in 2000. *R. Robinson — Dumfries.* 421 (3m5fL), 661 (L), 1082 (CMa).

MISBLAIZE ..—.. 7 br.m. Positive Statement (USA) — Pleasure Bid (Mon Plaisir) pf. Small close-coupled home-bred half-sister to Uncle Reginald (*qv*). Backward and very novicey when going a maximum of two miles to date, and was a remote last when falling heavily at the twelfth at Kingston Blount. *Mrs R. Hurley — Warwicks.* 1147 (OMa), 1486 (OMa).

MISCHIEVOUS ANDY (IRE) ..9-7§.. 12 b.g. Andy Rew — Sindy's Sister (Fidalgo) 4454. Compact rather unfurnished brother to 3 Irish flat winners, including Brother Will (also prolific jumping winner). IRISH P-t-P '95 and '97 r8 w1 (6yo&up Maiden) p3 (last of 3 after being carried out, continuing and refusing once); pulled up 2. IRISH NH FLAT '95 r1 p1 (3rd). IRISH NH '96/7 r8 p1; fell only Hunt Ch. P-t-P/HUNT CH '98/9 (for Mr A.J. Balmer) r14 w1 (Restricted) p3 (2 3rds; and neck 2nd); last pair 3, fell/unseated 2, and pulled up 5. A thorough stayer, but was lucky when winning his Restricted at 20-1 as the runner-up was having to fend off an equine version of Jaws in the home straight, and has shown minimal interest since. Has been tried in blinkers. *Mr J. & Miss A. Pigg — Tynedale.* 912 (Cf), 973 (I), 1159 (I), 1425 (I).

MISMETALLIC ..8-12.. 10 ch.m. True Song — Misprite (Master Stephen) p4. Unfurnished sister to Billsley, and half-sister to Northsprite. Dam won 2 Points and placed 10. Grandam, Lily Pond II, was close 3rd in 2 Adjacents. P-t-P '97/9 r8 w1 (Maiden) p1 (3rd); last, and fell/unseated 4, and pulled up 1. A clumsy jumper, but not devoid of ability and beat 14 others when successful in softish at Newton Bromswold in '98. Has been hard to train since, and has had to endure two interrupted campaigns. Bowled along in the lead for 2m3f on her last outing, but stopped very quickly and may have encountered yet more trouble. *C. & Mrs T. Cowper — Warwicks (Tracey Cowper).* 196 (R), 1442 (R).

MISS ACCOUNTS (IRE) ..9-13.. 10 gr.m. Roselier (FR) — Tara Weed (Tarqogan) p534785. Small sister to Irish Hurdles winner, Tara Sound, and half-sister to Man's Best Friend. P-t-P '97 and '99 r12 w2 (PPORA Maiden and Ladies) p4 (3 2nds; and remote 3rd); fell/unseated 3, and pulled up 1. Unpredictable, and has done little since making all at Whittington last year. Suited by a severe test of stamina, but seemed under a cloud for the entire season, and even threw a wobbler on the way to post on her final appearance. May revive if connections can solve the puzzle. *R.P. Watts — Staintondale (Annabelle Armitage).* 280 (L), 421 (3m5fL), 494 (L), 690 (L), 999 (4m1fMO), 1343 (3m110yH), 1579 (L).

MISS BLUE ..8-12.. 6 b.m. Weld — Gadabout (Galivanter) 3. owner-bred half-sister to Red Spice (*qv*). Backward in her Members, but got round eventually to finish last and a fence behind. *R.A. & Mrs A. Owen — Flint & Denbigh.* 776 (Mem).

MISS BUBBLES (IRE) ..9-7.. 7 b.m. Conquering Hero (USA) — Alitos Choice (Baptism) p. Half-sister to 2 flat winners (one abroad), including Winners Choice. P-t-P '99 r3 w1 (Members) p0; 5th, and pulled up 1. The outsider when winning a match for her Members in '99, but trailed until pulling up at the 11th with a slipped saddle on her reappearance in February and was not seen again. *P. Diggle — Dumfries.* 111 (R).

MISS CAITLIN (IRE) ..9-5.. 7 b.m. Over The River (FR) — Kraydel (Northern Guest USA) pp3. Very small light half-sister to At The Acorn (IRE). Dam won 2 12f races in Ireland. IRISH P-t-P '99 r1 p0 (pulled up). Bought Doncaster, May for 500. Nothing to look at, but gave a much improved display when 27 lengths third at Hampton, where she was in front of the subsequent dual winner Heathburn over the final two fences. Not seen since (mid-March), but a Maiden success is possible when fit. *P.J. Millington — Fernie.* 232 (R), 372 (CfMa), 550 (OMa).

MISSED CALL (IRE) ..9-10.. 9 b.g. Phardante (FR) — Una's Run (Deep Run) fp1222. Workmanlike rangy. NH FLAT '97 r3 p1 (2nd). NH '97/9 (for M. Tompkins) r10 p4 (inc distant last of 3 in one of 2 Chses); Sell Hdle final. Bought Ascot, June for 3400. Presented with a virtual gift in a two-finisher elders Maiden at Maisemore, but often deeply frustrating when accumulating eight placings otherwise. Would have registered four seconds in Points but for falling at the last once, and keeps getting run out of it in the closing stages (had no proven stamina under Rules). In the lead two out on all three of his most recent appearances (favourite twice), but even top riders could not keep him in front until the post, and especially maddening when 1-2 in a match. *A. Tranter (1471 Racing Club) — Albrighton Woodland (Mark Wellings).* 337 (CfMa), 703 (OMa), 893 (OMa), 1088 (R), 1314 (R), 1459 (R).

MISS GALE (IRE) ..9-5.. 8 br.m. Strong Gale — Derrygold (Derrylin) 1. Strong sister to NH flat winner, Strong Mint (IRE), and half-sister to flat winner, Emsleys Choice. Dam won 3 flat, 6-7f, and won 2m Hdle (previously refused to race in her last 3 appearances on the flat). NH FLAT '99 r1 p0 (fell). P-t-P '99 r1 p0 (last). Beat nothing of note at Cursneh Hill, but her attitude was commendable and will surely appreciate much better going. Has only managed three outings in an 18 month period, and clearly hard to train, but has plenty of scope for improvement and it would be no surprise if she were to blossom one day. *R.M. & Mrs M. Phillips — Clifton-on-Teme (Annie Downes).* 1277 (OMa).

MISS GLORIA ..—§.. 7 b.m. Past Glories — Miss Broadfields (Bivouac) fuppp. Unfurnished half-sister to Political Field. Dam, sister or half-sister to 5 Pointers, including, Yankee Rhythm (*qv* '95 Annual), won a bad Maiden and 3rd for Ron Watson. An unenviable ride and looks a proper madam, and fell victim of the sixth fence on three occasions (jumped violently right there and almost unseated when nearing the horseboxes in the latest — 100-1 and blinkered). Not the first of her family to be tainted by dementia. *R.G. Watson — Holderness (Mary Sowersby).* 169 (OMa), 283 (OMa), 379 (OMa), 507 (CMa), 625 (OMa).

MISS HOITY TOITY ..8-13.. 9 b.m. St Columbus — Classey (Dubassoff USA) uf3pp4. Small neat light owner-bred sister to Bit Of A Snob (successful Hurdler since Pointing). The latest harem scarem Tarry eight-year-old homebred to be pulled in from the field, and looked as wild as many of her predecessors. Gave one decent display when 12 lengths third, but beaten favourite twice since, and misdemeanours in races so far include unseating when trying to refuse, falling, pulling very hard, and running very wide on more than one occasion. Also dynamite in the paddock (has two handlers) and lashed out with both barrels at Jimmy's niece's horse at Ashorne, but Lucy had the last laugh when Shortcut Shorty was 28 lengths clear of Miss Hoity Toity when he scored at Dingley. Perhaps she energies will be channeled to better use one day. *R. Morris & G.B. Tarry — Grafton (Jimmy Tarry).* 433 (OMa), 792 (OMa), 1219 (OMa), 1435 (OMa), 1624 (OMa), 1669 (OMa).

MISSION LORD (IRE) ..8-7.. 7 b.g. Mac's Imp (USA) — Amber Giotto (Wolverlife) ups442p. Good-topped. Dam won 5 Irish flat, 8-10f. IRISH FLAT r4 p0 (last of 4). Beaten at least 35 lengths in his first two completions and was then an exhausted eight lengths last of two, and proved a most unworthy favourite on his final outing, where he made mistakes and was tailed off and pulled up after 2m4f. A bad animal who has shown no signs of possessing any stamina to date. *M.J. Spuffard & F. Goldsworthy — S. Pembs.* 649 (CfMa), 744 (R), 835 (OMa), 950 (OMa), 1222 (2m4fOMa), 1455 (OMa), 1660 (OMa).

MISS JONES ..8-5.. 9 gr.m. Alias Smith (USA) — Upholder (Young Generation) pp7. P-t-P '99 r3 p0 (pulled up 3). Pulls hard, and an erratic jumper to boot, but not better than last six starts to date. Clearly needs Rigsby to chivvy her along when she feels like she's had enough. *Mrs A. Huggins — Bilsdale (Paul Frank).* 138 (OMa), 399 (OMa), 626 (OMa).

MISS MADELON ..9-12.. 9 gr.m. Absalom — Larive (Blakeney) p. Strong half-sister to Limosa, and to flat and jumping winners, Rapid Mover and Mister Blake, and to Hurdles winner, Bisquet-De-Bouche. Dam won at 12f. FLAT r7 p0 (inc Sells). NH '95 r2 p0. P-t-P '97 and '99 (for Mrs J.C. Cooper) r5 w1 (Maiden) p2 (3rds); and pulled up 3. Made all and quickened readily to win a youngsters Maiden on firm at Stainton as a five-year-old, but has stood her racing badly, and looked wrong when tailed off and pulled up after less than two miles on her reappearance for new connections. *Mrs S. Roxburgh — Vine & Craven (John Porter).* 477 (R).

MISSMASS ..9-0.. 8 b.m. Then Again — Massawa (FR) (Tennyson FR) 55f. Workmanlike lengthy sister to Hurdles winner, Poetic Fancy. NH '98/9 (for D. Wintle; previously for J. Smith) r8 p1 (match for Ch); 6th in other Ch; inc Sells. Consistently poor, and never shows any resolution. Presented with an amazing freak opportunity to earn a £4133 prize at Worcester in September '99 after the withdrawal of the three market leaders because of the firm ground turned a Chase into a match, but she spurned the gift and surrendered tamely to a rival twice her age. *Miss S. Sadler — N. Cotswold (Jim Collett).* 22 (2m4fOMa), 673 (2m4fOMa), 1194 (OMa).

MISS MOLLY ..—.. 8 b.m. Arzanni — Another Molly (Choral Society) fp. Leggy sister to NH flat and Hurdles winner, Lady Marlow, and half-sister to Celtic Reg. Dam won at 2m in Ireland. NH FLAT '99 r1 p0. NH '99 r1 p0 (pulled up in 2m4f Nov Hdle). P-t-P '99 (for Mrs C.M. Brown) r1 p0 (pulled up). Added to her miserable completion record when failing to get round in two March maidens and has been absent since. *D. Tyler — N. Ledbury (Caroline Chadney).* 472 (OMa), 672 (2m4fOMa).

MISS MOUSE ..9-4.. 9 br.m. Arctic Lord — Gypsy's Barn Rat (Balliol) f34f. Very small light-framed home-bred half-sister to flat winner Gipsy Princess. Dam won 3 Sells, 7-8f. NH FLAT '97 (for P. Mooney) r2 p0. NH '97/8 (from K. Cornerford's) r5 p0. A scrawny mare who comes out worst in tussles with the fences, and spoiled every Point with at least one serious blunder (also jumped right once). Finished seven lengths third on her best effort (evens favourite), but lacks scope for improvement. *A.H. Scott — Essex & Suffolk (Ruth Hayter).* 179 (R), 322 (CfMa), 606 (OMa), 889 (OMa).

MISS MUCKLEY ..—.. 9 b.m. Buckley — Flea Pit (Sir Lark) p. Strong-topped compact sister to Bucks Flea, and half-sister to Bushfire Moon, to Irish flat and English jumping winner, Mrs Peopleater, and to a winner in Belgium. P-t-P '99 r3 p0 (7th, pulled up 1, and fell 1). Signed off in '99 with a crashing eighth fence fall at Bratton Down having been backed from 7-1 to half those odds, but went lame on her reappearance at Black Forest Lodge. *M.F. Harding — Berkeley.* 204 (OMa).

MISS O'GRADY (IRE) ..10-11.. 9 ch.m. Over The River (FR) — Polar Mistress (IRE) (Strong Gale) p311u. Lengthy sister to Mabel's Memory (IRE). P-t-P/HUNT CH '98/9 r10 w6 (inc 2m5f Hunt Ch and Mixed Open, inc 5-timer '99) p2 (2nds); and pulled up 2. In tremendous heart in '99 winning her last five starts including a very gutsy effort in a 2m5f Cheltenham Hunter Chase. Broke a blood vessel on her reappearance at Barbury Castle when a well supported favourite and seemed unwilling to let herself down next time, perhaps fearing a similar occurrence, but bounced back to form with two subsequent Open wins. Got no further than the eighth in the Cheltenham Foxhunters and has not been seen again. A classy mare with a willing attitude, but has burst on three occasions '98/00 and hopefully it will not have a lasting effect on her physche. Acts on any going. *Mrs J.M. Miller — Portman (Louise Alner).* 32 (MO), 210 (MO), 327 (O), 402 (O), 584 (3m2f110yH).

MISS ONDEE (FR) ..9-10.. 7 b.m. Dress Parade — Lady Caroline (FR) (Hasty Tudor USA) 2pp6. Small light-framed. FRENCH FLAT '96/7 r12 w1 (1m5f110y claimer at Longchamp) p2. NH '97/9 (blinkered 4 early runs; unplaced last 6 for Karen Marks, bought out of Sell for 6800; previously for M. Pipe, claimed for 12,300) r28 w6 (2m-2m2f Hdles, inc 3 Sells) p9; unseated in final 2 of 4 Chses, when trying to refuse once. NH Mar 2000 r1 p0 (6th in 2m1f Claiming Hdle: *chsd ldrs to 5, lost tch, t.o*). The master magician miraculously conjured six wins out of her, but mere mortals have no hope of pursuading her to put her best foot forward, and was 20 lengths second of three on the only occasion she consented to complete in a Point. Tends to jump slowly and reluctantly, and there would not seem to be much sense in persevering with her. *N. Shutts — Worcs (Penny Grainger).* 49 (C), 447 (CM), 668 (L).

MISS PENNYHILL (IRE) ..9-11.. 8 b.m. Conquering Hero (USA) — Teodosia (Ashmore FR) u54pf5131. Lengthy light half-sister to Irish flat winner, Tinerana Law. IRISH FLAT r5 w1 (13f Clmr) p0. IRISH NH '96/7 r16 w1 (2m Hdle) p3. NH '97/9 r16 w1 (2m3f Ch) p5. NH '00 r6 w2 (3m1f110y HCap Ch: *ld, clr 13-16, clr agn 2 out, kpt on*; and 3m1f110y HCap Ch: *ld 1 & agn 3, drew clr frm 14, stayed on*) p1 (3rd in 3m1f HCap Ch: *ld to 10, mist 2 out*); and (*pulled up in 2m6f110y HCap Ch; outpcd halfway, pu 4 out*; fell in 3m1f110y HCap Ch: *ld 2-8, ld 10-3 out, 2nd when fell out*; and 5th in 2m110y HCap Ch: *ld when mist 4, hdd 3 out, sn btn*). Inconsistent and moody (often blinkered/visored to '99), and it has been safe to disregard her everywhere apart from at Hereford, where she is a completely changed animal. Has galloped round the course with great exuberance for all three English wins, as well as finishing second in a 16-runner race, and falling when chasing the leader three out. Always liable to make a few mistakes. Probably worth a stone more at her favourite venue. *A. Sadik — N. Ledbury.* 150 (3mH), 222 (3m1f110yH), 681 (2m4fH).

MISS PHARLY ..—.. 7 b.m. Pharly (FR) — Pleasant Land (Green Dancer USA) f. Small neat. Sold Ascot, July for 500. Green and sketchy in the rear until she took a crashing fall four out at Whitwick, and not seen again. *W.I. Owens — Radnor & W. Herefords (Steve Flook).* 339 (CfMa).

MISS PILKINGTON ..8-6.. 8 ch.m. Green Adventure (USA) — Penny's Affair (Chingnu) pp43. Small half-sister to All Things Nice (*qv*). A poor last in both completions, and does not impress at present. *Mrs M.R. Daniell — Ledbury (Mike Daniell).* 78 (L), 391 (CfMa), 1361 (2m4fOMa), 1494 (CfMa).

MISS PINK ..—.. 7 gr.m. Arzanni — Ewe Lamb (Free State) upp. Lengthy good-topped. Dam won at 5f; and subsequently won 2 2m Hdles at Huntingdon for Pam Sly. NH FLAT Spr '98 r2 p0. NH '98 r2 p0. A sad disappointment since finishing an apparently promising fourth of 22 in a Bumper on her debut, and her jumping when failing to complete in Maidens varied from poor to abysmal. *Mrs P.M. Sly — Fitzwilliam.* 52 (OMa), 180 (2m4fOMa), 439 (OMa).

MISS PORTCELLO ..10-5.. 8 b.m. Bybicello — Port Mallaig (Royal Fountain) p123p2. Small narrow. P-t-P '98/9 r6 w1 (Maiden) p1 (3rd of 4); (unseated 3, and pulled up 1). Took the fat end of eight minutes when winning at Lockerbie in '99 and showed the benefit of a pipeopener the previous month when winning a Restricted in gutsy style at Friars Haugh this year. Beaten six lengths or less when placed in better company since and might just be good enough to win a Ladies race in 2001 (is certainly suited by the lesser weights in them). Acts in soft and may not care too much for a sound surface. *W.F. Jeffrey — Lauderdale (Joan Hollands).* 111 (R), 713 (R), 1078 (Cf), 1161 (L), 1364 (L), 1576 (Cf).

MISTER AUDI (IRE) ..10-6.. 9 br.g. Good Thyne (USA) — Symphony Orchestra (Orchestra) 3p221322. Close-coupled half-brother to Butlers Cross (IRE), and to Irish Pointing and Hurdles winner, The Boylerman. IR 10,000 4-y-o. IRISH NH FLAT '96/7 r4 p0. IRISH NH FLAT '96/7 r7 p0 (finished in both Hunt Chses). IRISH P-t-P '98 r3 w1 (Adjacent Mdn) p1 (3rd). NH '99 (for M. Hammond) r1 p0 (6th in Ch). Appeared to show improved form towards the end of the season, but has only once scored on his merits from 23 attempts, as he was presented with a Restricted on firm at Horseheath after Ar Aghaidh Abhaile had made a bee line for the horseboxes and thrown the race away on the run-in. Later beaten a head by Sense Of Adventure after a good tussle and chased home Grecian Star, and may justify his currently rather suspect rating if Andrew Sansome can get him to do his best. *J.M. Turner — Suffolk.* 2 (R), 86 (R), 554 (R), 610 (R), 843 (R), 1155 (2m5f110yH), 1286 (Cf), 1485 (I).

MISTER CHIPS ..9-3.. 10 b.g. Macmillion — Nikali (Siliconn) 2f52. Compact good-bodied half-brother to Tammy's Choice and Nikaroo, and to jumping winner, Mister Feathers. NH FLAT '96/7 r2 p0. NH '97/9 (for J. King, blinkered last 2) r10 p0 (inc 4 Chses). Bought Ascot, June for 2200. Feeble under Rules, and costly to follow in Maidens, in which he invariably started at 4-1 or less. Weakens rapidly in the closing stages, and clearly does not quite get the trip, and has not been seen since finishing four lengths second of three in Rodmell in mid-March. *Mrs C.L. Taylor — Ashford V.* 132 (OMa), 290 (CMa), 578 (OMa), 679 (OMa).

MISTER DEEP (IRE) ..9-13.. 7 b.g. Mister Lord (USA) — Deep Pond (IRE) (Long Pond) p2. Gave a much improved display on his second outing when four lengths second in early March, but immediately disappeared (as did the third). Looks capable of winning a Maiden at least when returning. *G. Keirle — Portman (Louise Alner).* 212 (CfMa), 455 (OMa).

MISTER HORATIO ..10-6.. 11 b.g. Derring Rose — Miss Horatio (Spartan General) 1223f7. Strong good-looking. Dam won 3m Hdle. P-t-P/HUNT CH '95/7 and '99 r24 w7 (inc 3m110y Hunt Chse and 2 Opens) p9 (2nds, inc 4 Hunt Chses); fell/unseated 2. Won six times in his first three seasons, but ended '97 lame and forced to miss the following year. Has not been as prolific since and has looked decidedly irresolute on several occasions, getting beaten when winning seemed certain. Hoisted the white flag in the closing stages on his reappearance at Erw Lon, but had enough in hand to hold on, and fell in a heap after the last in a Bangor Hunter Chase subsequently having looked assured of victory turning for home. Ran with his tongue tied down in two of his remaining races, but that did not appear to resolve his problem which if wind related might get sorted in the closed season. If, however Derring Rose syndrome is to blame, no amount of veterinary assistance will help. A watching brief is strongly advised when he returns. *W.D. Lewis — Pembs.* 271 (O), 464 (3m110yH), 687 (2m6f110yH), 1022 (3mH), 1339 (2m5fH), 1443 (3mH).

MISTER JAY DAY ..9-8.. 11 b.g. Domitor (USA) — Habille ..(On Your Mark) 4u423p. Tiny home-bred. NH FLAT r1 p0 (tailed off). P-t-P '96/9 r18 w2 (Maiden and Members) p5 (4 3rds); pulled up 8, and fell 3. No bigger than a pony, and has done well to win two races at Bonvilston '97/8, but struggling to get out of Restricteds, and sometimes looks less than enthusiastic. Beaten no more than two and a half lengths when placed twice at his favourite course in May, and may well strike lucky again there in 2001. *W.J. Day — Gelligaer F. (Lisa Day).* 486 (R), 931 (R), 1400 (R), 1448 (M), 1616 (R), 1671 (R).

MISTER MAIN MAN (IRE) ..9-12.. 13 ch.g. Remainder Man — Mainstown Belle (Peacock FR) puu. Strong workmanlike. P-t-P/HUNT CH '93/4 and '96/8 r19 w6 (inc 3m2f Hunt Ch, Mixed Open; inc hat-trick '94) p9 (6 2nds, inc Hunt Ch); pulled up 1, and brought down 1. Not the same horse since breaking down after an impressive hat-trick in '94, and is becoming lightly raced. Not seen since Simon Sporborg leapt out of the saddle at Horseheath in the first week of March. Was he hoping to offer girlfriend Jo Slack some assistance after she had flown through the air from Damier Blanc a split-second earlier? Formerly game and a reliable jumper, but seems in decline now. *Sir Chippendale Keswick — Puckeridge (Christopher Sporborg).* 83 (Cf), 259 (C), 417 (Cf).

MISTER MCGASKILL ..9-9.. 12 ch.g. Itsu (USA) — Deep Depression (Weathercock) pp. Lengthy quite attractive half-brother to Miss Hokee Pokee and The Weatherman. Dam was 3rd in 4 Points. P-t-P '96/8 r11 w1 (Maiden) p3 (2 2nds); last, pulled up 5, and fell 1. The only one of nine starters to go clear in a Margam Maiden in '96, but has never managed more than four outings in a season and has been pulled up in more than half of his races. Dislikes firm ground and not particularly keen on the Llanvapley cornfield either. *Mrs E.A. Thomas — Glamorgan.* 741 (Cf), 894 (R).

MISTER MOSS (IRE) ..10-3.. 8 b.g. Don Tristan (USA) — Lindas Statement (IRE) (Strong Statement USA) p13. Good-topped brother to Irish Pointing winner, Thison. IRISH P-t-P '98 r4 p0 (last twice, pulled up 1, and fell 1). P-t-P '99 (for Mr M.A. Lloyd & Mrs A. Goodwin) r1 w1 (Maiden) p0. Made all to land a touch on his only appearance in '99, and again the subject of a gamble on his reappearance, but this time the bookies had cause to breath a sigh of relief as he capitulated after three out having looked to be going really well just moments before. Took seven weeks to recover, but promptly landed a Restricted at Tabley, where stamina does not come into play, before running third in a Dunstall Park Open. Clearly very speedy, but his stamina seems virtually non-existent and will be difficult to place unless he proves to be good enough for sub-3m Hunter Chases. *Mr & Mrs M. Fenton — Cheshire (Gary Hamner).* 296 (I), 963 (R), 1524 (O).

PLATE 85   *963 Cheshire Forest Restricted: Mister Moss (G. Hamner), 1st, is an easy winner*
                                                        PHOTO: Peter & Marilyn Sweet

MISTER PIMPERNEL (IRE) ..8-12.. 7 b.g. Pimpernels Tune — Kilmurry Queen (IRE) (Mister Lord USA) pp3p. Small compact. Dam, sister to Earthmover, won mares Maiden in Ireland. P-t-P '99 (for Mr G.L. Edwards & Mr L.A.E. Hopkins) r2 p0 (pulled up 1, and fell 1). A poor jumper to date, and beaten 23 lengths in his sole completion. Only went a mile before pulling up on his final start and may have gone wrong. *G.L. Edwards & L.A.E. Hopkins — N. Salop (Gordie Edwards).* 593 (2m4fOMa), 965 (2m4fOMa).

MISTER RIVER (IRE) ..9-11.. 10 ch.g. Over The River (FR) — Miss Redmarshall (Most Secret) pf4p3pp. Tall half-brother to Sequestrator and Miss Monty (IRE), and to 2 flat winners, including Graniton Bay. Dam won 6 flat, 5-6f (inc 2 Sells; also disqualified from another win) and placed 10. NH FLAT Spr '97 r1 p0. NH '98 (for D. Elsworth) r3 p0 (pulled up in 2 of 3 Hdles). Bought Malvern, Feb for 800. Ungenuine and often blinkered latterly, and only completed the course in three of ten attempts over jumps, but had an elders Maiden on firm at Woodford at his mercy until he pulled up lame two out. Missed 20 months after his Bumper and another 14 months prior to 2000, which looks an extremely bad omen for the future. *A.J. Whiting — Berkeley (Kevin Whiting).* 260 (R), 457 (OMa), 738 (OMa), 972 (OMa), 1315 (OMa), 1336 (2m4fH), 1493 (OMa).

MISTER SOFTIE (IRE) ..10-5.. 6 ch.g. Priolo (USA) — Bold Strike (FR) (Bold Lad USA) 41115f41. Smallish half-brother to Extra Stout (IRE), and to 9 winners (6 abroad), including a successful Hurdler. Dam won 3 races at around 8f in France. IRISH P-t-P '99 r2 p0 (pulled up, and brought down). IRISH P-t-P '00 r3 w2 (deadheat with Headtheball beating Mountgarry dd-ht and 10*l* in Ashford Maiden: *2nd to 7, 3rd 9, 2nd & chall 2 out, outj last, rallied to dead heat on line*; and beat Once In A While and Satco Prince 5*l* and 10*l* in Dundalk Winners of 2: *2nd ½way, ld 10, clr*

3 out, stayed on wl) p0; and 4th in Tyrella Maiden: (*rr, prog ½way, 4th 3 out*) IRISH HUNT CH '00 r4 w2 (beat Mr Merc and Shepperdon 7*l* and 9*l* at Downpatrick: *4th when mist 9, 2nd & rdn 4 out, ld 2 out, stayed on wl*; and beat (after disqualification of original winner, Fernhill Queen) Nellie Gale and Ballvalogue 11*l* and 2*l* at Killarney: *mid-div, 3rd 4 out, rdn nxt, 2nd last, fin 2nd, promoted*); 4th at Punchestown: *rr, 8th 2 out, lft dist 4th at last*; and fell 1. A progressive performer in Ireland where he has scored on firmish and in heavy, but made too many errors on his only visit to England. Has done extremely well for a youngster, but favoured by Lady Luck, as he was awarded his Maiden outright after a dead-heater tested positive, and gained one of his Hunter Chases after the first past the post had been stood down for weighing-in fractionally over one pound light. Likely to improve further with more fluent jumping, and could have prospects in Handicaps eventually. *D.J. Reddan — Ward U. (Tony Martin, in Ireland).* 924 (3m1fH).

MISTER SPECTATOR (IRE) ..10-5.. 12 br.g. Mandalus — Focal Point (Hawaiian Sound USA) p1uup. Tall. NH FLAT r1 p0. NH '94 r1 p0 (tailed off last). P-t-P/HUNT CH '95/8 r11 w3 (hat-trick '97, inc Open) p1 (2nd in Hunt Ch); failed to finish 7 (fell 4, and ran out 1). A habitual front-runner, and usually wins or fails to finish, with the latter now gaining supremacy. Has always been very hard to keep sound, but useful when right and led a modest field a merry dance in his latest victory at Cottenham. Shed the rider twice subsequently, and dropped away very tamely when pulled up in a very strongly run Huntingdon Hunter Chase in which even he could not get to the front. Has to go right-handed. Connections can congratulate themselves on getting him back to somewhere near his best even if it was fleeting. *P. Hughes — E. Sussex & Romney Marsh (Alison Hickman).* 130 (CMod), 771 (O), 981 (O), 1036 (O), 1335 (2m4f110yH).

MISTER TRICK (IRE) ..10-6.. 11 br.g. Roselier (FR) — Fly Fuss (Little Buskins) 24331. Workmanlike compact half-brother to 2 Hurdles winners, including Belle Busk (IRE) (also a successful Chaser). NH '95/9 (for L. Lungo) r23 w3 (3m-3m5f Chses) p4 (inc head 2nd over 4m1f). Sold Doncaster, May for 5000. Inconsistent and does not always co-operate, and had become disappointing latterly under Rules, but redeemed himself on occasions in Points. Comes into his own when stamina is at a premium, and beat Hatcham Boy by four lengths in a 3m4f Open at Marks Tey, but had finished 16 lengths adrift of that rival on their previous meeting over a normal trip. Future plans should include all the longest opportunities available. *K. Williams & H. Lascelles — Pytchley (Neil King).* 320 (O), 510 (Cf), 607 (O), 842 (O), 938 (3m4fO).

MISTI HUNTER (IRE) ..10-5.. 12 gr.g. Roselier (FR) — Lovely Stranger (Le Bavard FR) 3u3432424. Compact unfurnished half-brother to Irish NH flat and Hurdles winner, Dramatic Dame (IRE), and to Irish Pointing winner, Lovely Hand. Dam won 2m Hdle in Ireland. NH FLAT r1 p0. NH '94/5 and '96 r16 w2 (3m1f Chses) p5 (inc 3 Hdles, the first a Sell). P-t-P/HUNT CH '97 and '99 r14 w1 (Open) p6 (3 3rds, last once; and laqst of 2 once); pulled up 3. Formerly useful on a sound surface, but very one-paced nowadays, and has accumulated 10 placings since his last success in '97. Used to give trouble in the preliminaries and still occasionally led round at the start, but his record of having never lost a rider is no more after Rachel Clark fell off him at Duncombe Park. *Mrs D. Ibbotson — York & Ainsty S. (Liz Clark).* 135 (L), 277 (Cf), 505 (L), 794 (Cf), 998 (C), 1232 (L), 1585 (O), 1603 (2m6f110yH), 1648 (3mH).

MITCHELLS BEST ..9-4.. 15 br.g. True Song — Emmalina (Doubtless II) p664. Big strong half-brother to Sideliner. Dam pulled up and unseated in Points. NH '97 r2 p0 (pulled up in Chses). P-t-P/HUNT CH '91/7 and '99 r46 w4 (Maiden, 2 Members and Restricted — lucky) p17 (7 2nds, beaten neck once); failed to finish 9 (on floor 2). A patent safety, but has never really delivered what he first promised back in '91 and has only managed to win once since '93. Incredibly slow these days, but always looks a picture and lass Sharon Smith can be guaranteed the best turned out prize. *A. Hollingsworth — Worcs.* 18 (I), 333 (Cf), 987 (Cf), 1063 (3m2fM).

MIZYAN (IRE) ..10-6.. 13 b.g. Melyno — Maid Of Erin (USA) (Irish River FR) 321211122. Rangy angular half-brother to flat winners, Erin Bird (subsequently smart in Italy) and Fighting Temeraire (in Austria). FLAT to '98 (blinkered 2) r42 w4 (12-14f, 2 on all-weather) p12. NH '92/7 r25 w4 (2m-2m4f, 3 on Southwell all-weather) p11. P-t-P '99 r7 w4 (Ladies, inc hat-trick) p3 (2 2nds; and 3rd of 4). Rejuvenated since his move to Seaborough, and has not failed to make the frame in 16 Opens winning half of them. Not invincible, and was no match for Millyhenry at Bratton Down, but hard to beat in second class Ladies Opens. Capable of superb jumping, but always likely to miss one fence out and Polly Gundry has to have her wits about her when it happens. Acts on any going. *P. Maltby — Taunton V. (Richard Barber).* 32 (MO), 326 (L), 653 (MO), 851 (L), 1060 (MO), 1239 (L), 1374 (MO), 1561 (MO), 1605 (L).

MODEL AGENT ..—.. 6 b.m. Gildoran — Springaleak (Lafontaine USA) p. Dam won NH flat, 4 Hdles (2m-2m4f) and 6 Chses (2m4f-3m2f), and merited a Timeform essay (as talented but quirky). Sold Malvern, May for 2300. Looked fairly hair-raising before pulled up at halfway when tailed off in mid-April. Her parents were very Bloomsbury (talented but dotty), and it will be interesting to see which way their love child swings. *J.P. Price — Radnor & W. Herefords (Clive Davies).* 1093 (OMa).

MOLLYCARRSBREKFAST ..9-8.. 6 b.g. Presidium — Imperial Flame (Imperial Lantern) f21. Tiny. Dam is half-sister to Hurdles winner, Swift. NH FLAT '99 (for W.G.M. Turner) r2 p0 (tailed off 2 — hung left final). Rescued from the slaughterhouse just before he looked destined to become a hound's breakfast, and repaid this act of great kindness by winning a Maiden at Cothelstone, having previously finished a creditable four lengths second. Speedy, but does not look the easiest of rides. Miniscule, and if he manages to succeed in a Restricted he will probably need to switch to Ladies Opens afterwards. *D. Ridge — Quantock (Sarah Robinson)*. 255 (R), 640 (CfMa), 1100 (OMa).

MONEGHETTI ..8-0.. 10 ch.g. Faustus (USA) — The Victor Girls (Crofthall) 3p. Strong-topped half-brother to Diamond Market. FLAT (visored final) r22 w2 (7-8f, both all-weather) p5 (Sell final). NH '95/6 r3 p0 (remote 4th, and pulled up 2). P-t-P '99 r6 p0 (pulled up 4, and fell/unseated 2). Managed his first Pointing completion on his reappearance, but was a remote last of three, and does not stay a yard beyond two miles. Prone to blunders in '99, and had disappeared by the first week in February this time around. *P.G. Harvey — Albrighton (Annie Spencer)*. 49 (C), 117 (O).

MONERE ..—.. 9 ch.g. Infantry — Kimble Lady (Averof) ppp. Big rangy. P-t-P '98/9 r7 w1 (Maiden) p1 (2nd); pulled up 3, and unseated 1. Had eight finishers behind him when winning at Higham last year (rated 9-5), but pulled up in all four outings since, and acquired blinkers on his latest two appearances. Did not emerge until late-April in 2000 and has presumably had some problem. *G.I. Cooper — E. Anglian Bloodhounds*. 1181 (R), 1379 (R), 1512 (R).

MONEY DON'T MATTER ..9-12.. 9 br.m. Arctic Lord — Raheny (Sir Herbert) 54p. Small lengthy half-sister to Frau Kitz, to an Irish Chasing winner, and to an Irish NH flat winner. P-t-P '97/9 r15 w2 (2m4f Maiden, and Restricted) p1 (3rd of 4); failed to finish 8 (fell/unseated 2, and ran out 1). Improved as the result of a soft-palate operation and the application of a tongue-strap in '99, and won a slow Restricted convincingly at Bredwardine, but suffered an interrupted 2000 campaign and only managed three starts. Not disgraced when completing, but still below the level required to win an Intermediate and does not seem to stay too well. *S.W. Rudge — N. Ledbury (Jon Rudge)*. 615 (CMod), 1356 (I), 1632 (I).

MONKEY AGO ..10-6.. 14 b.g. Black Minstrel — Arctic Sue (Arctic Slave) 11221. Smallish compact brother to Frozen Minstrel, and half-brother to Arctic Menelek, Group Hat and Arcticaldi (IRE), to Chasing winners, Pan Arctic and Oriental Boy (IRE), to successful jumper, Kamal Siddiqi, and to 2 Irish Pointing winners, including Ballycar Lass. IRISH NH FLAT '92/3 r8 w1 p3. NH '94/5 r7 p2 (3rds). IRISH NH '93/4 and '96/7 r31 w4 (2m Hdle and 3 Chses, 2m4f-3m, inc £12,900 prize) p5 (short-headed once); unplaced last 6 runs when returned from England. P-t-P '98/9 (for Mrs S.E. Mason) r16 w5 (inc 2 Opens, and Ladies) p6 (3 2nds); pulled up 1, and fell/unseated 2. Lost his way under Rules, but a remarkably consistent Pointer and has struck up an excellent rapport with Jo Foster. Not out of the first two in seven outings together (including two in the previous ownership) they combined to win three more Ladies Opens in 2000. A splendid jumper who can front run to great effect and best suited by a test of stamina. Has made no concessions to age and there is no reason to believe that he will in 2001. *Miss J.E. Foster — Pendle Forest & Craven*. 135 (L), 170 (L), 280 (L), 505 (L), 690 (L).

MONKS SOHAM (IRE) ..9-10.. 13 b.g. The Parson — Kadaga (Linacre) 211. Good-topped half-brother to Cherryhill Beauty. Dam won 2m5f Maiden Hdle in Ireland. NH FLAT Mar '94 (for F. Murphy) r1 p0. NH '94/9 (pulled up in blinkers once; for late G. Hubbard; trained for him on debut by F. Murphy) r25 w3 (2m4f-2m6f Chses, 4,5 and 6 ran) p8 (inc 4 Hdles); fell last with every chance once. Comes from a stable who do well with limited material, and they managed to unearth three races with six runners or less for their veteran. No match for Struggles Glory at Charing, and jumped stickily and was never going well in his Members, but kept going stoutly to catch the tired leader approaching the last. Again well served by his battling qualities at Aldington, but was very lucky to pip Call Home by a short head, as Tom Hills failed to ride out after being six lengths clear coming to the final fence (fined £115). *J.D. Parker (The Parker Family) — Waveney H. (Juliet Arthur)*. 129 (O), 755 (M), 1171 (O).

MONTECOT (FR) ..9-12.. 12 b.g. Le Riverain (FR) — Pour Ta Pomme (FR) (Stratege USA) 63u2. Good-looking compact half-brother to 2 Pointing winners in France (including high-class Hurdler Le Bambois). FRENCH NH '92/6 r40 w1 (2m5f110y HCap Ch at Auteuil) p9. NH '97/8 (pulled up final for Lady Connell; previously trained for her by S. Mellor) r11 p3; no form in 3 Chses. Beaten a neck by Young Kenny on his English debut with Destin D'Estruval ahead third and Boots Madden 15 lengths away in fourth, but ran twice more in the next ten days, and this lunacy appeared to wreck him. Pulled up on alternate outings in four of his final seven starts, and has broken blood vessels as well as looking lame once. A change of stable and a switch to Points appeared to bring some improvement, and would have been placed three times consecutively but for unseating at the last once, but has no acccelleration these days, and was beaten favourite in his Members. Also contested a Celebrities race on the flat at Ascot. *Mrs R.R.M. Berry — O. Berks*. 75 (I), 243 (Cf), 476 (Cmr), 1202 (M).

MONTEPULCIANO (IRE) ..9-0§§.. 7 b.g. Mandalus — Sparkling Mary (Kambalda) rpr32. Big rangy. Dam is half-sister to Across The Lake (*qv* '98 Annual). Sold Doncaster, May '98 for 12,000. Must have looked very imposing in the Sales ring, but has proved to be a lot of money down the drain so far. Refused at the first once, jumped very slowly and to the right once, and would not start once from his first three outings, and then got round in doggy fashion for two 15 length placings (last; and of four when amazingly sent off favourite). Doubtless has the ability to score, but his villianous tendencies are very deeply ingrained at present. Presumably Liebfraumilch was already taken when it came to naming him. *J.J. Boulter — Portman (Nick Mitchell & John Boulter).* 213 (CfMa), 407 (OMa), 732 (2m4fOMa), 875 (2m4fOMa), 1262 (OMa).

MONTYS TAG (IRE) ..10-4.. 8 b.g. Montelimar (USA) — Herbal Lady (Good Thyne USA) 11. Workmanlike rangy hobdayed. Dam won 2m2f NH flat in Ireland. NH FLAT '99 (from Mrs P Sly's) r1 p1 (3rd). Stayed on well when nine lengths third of 20 in a Bumper, and confirmed the promise when making a lot of the running and galloping on strongly for an easy double in minor company. Can handle heavy and looks an out-and-out stayer, and it would be no surprise if he were to run well in a long Novice Hunter Chase. *M.W. Gore — Enfield Chace (Simon Andrews).* 98 (OMa), 321 (R).

MONTY'S THEME (IRE) ..9-10.. 7 b br.g. Montelimar (USA) — Theme Music (Tudor Music) 1p3. Tall workmanlike half-brother to Haunting Music (IRE) (qv). Bought Doncaster, May '98 for 17,000. Had no difficulty outstaying Prah Sands in a three-finisher youngsters Maiden at Larkhill, but beaten favourite twice since (not helped by a couple of slow jumps once; and ten lengths third behind a stablemate). May turn out to be better than he has shown recently. *J.A. Keighley — Blackmore & Sparkford V. (Richard Barber).* 58 (OMa), 458 (R), 1061 (R).

PLATE 86   *458 Staff College & RMA Draghounds Restrcited: Monty's Theme (Miss P. Gundry), pu,*
PHOTO: Brian Armstrong

MOOBAKKR (USA) ..10-2.. 10 b.g. Mr Prospector (USA) — Without Feathers (USA) (Brave Shot) p. Smallish compact half-brother to 2 winners in USA. Dam won 12 races in USA, inc Group One Monmouth Oaks. IRISH FLAT r5 w1 (10f) p0. NH '94/8 r37 w5 (2m2f-3m Hdles, inc Sell) p9 (inc 2nd in 2 Chses). HUNT CH '99 r2 p1 (2nd in Hunt Ch); and 4th. Very disappointing latterly under Rules, but looked to have regained his enthusiasm when joining David Ingle in '99 only for him to go wrong on his reappearance this year. Was very busy until '97, and clearing suffering the effects now. Has been tried tongue-tied. *D.E. Ingle — S. Wold.* 586 (3m1fH).

MOODY'S STAR ..9-3.. 6 b.m. Arzanni — Streber (Scorpio FR) u. Grandam, Mount Avenue, won 2m2f Hdle and placed 2 in Ireland, but failed to finish in all 4 Points for Stewart Pike. Would probably have finished a remote second had she not dumped Shirley Vickery approaching three out at Holnicote, and should be worth another look when returning. *S. Pike — E. Devon.* 353 (CfMa).

MOONDYNE ..8-2.. 7 ch.m. Le Moss — Border Cherry (Deep Run) 3. Very small light half-sister to Border Light. Extremely dosy in the paddock before finishing 15 lengths third at Bredwardine, but may get closer to the leaders when she is more alert. *Mrs D. Joyce — Golden V.* 1466 (OMa).

MOON ISLAND ..—§.. 7 b.m. Jupiter Island — Wild Moon (Belfalas) puppppp. Strong. Dam won Maiden and Restricted for Vera Steggles. NH FLAT '99 (from J. King's) r2 p0 (tailed off last 2).

Unseated at the fourth once, and tailed off in every other race she has contested. Shows an extremely poor attitude, and there is conceivably something wrong with her. *Mrs V. Steggles — Grafton (Simon Gilmore)*. 30 (CMa), 76 (CCfMa), 250 (CfMa), 1021 (2m4fOMa), 1420 (OMa), 1507 (OMa).

MOON RISING ..9-10.. 9 b.g. Primitive Rising (USA) — Saucy Moon (Saucy Kit) rppp2f2. Brother to Oxendale, and half-brother to Sun N Moon and Moonlight Cruise. Dam won 2 2m Chses. P-t-P '99 r1 p0 (fell). Disastrous in his first three Points, but much improved since a couple of confidence-boosters and looks to be on the verge of a win. Beaten one length and four lengths when twice a runner-up in Maidens at Penshurst and was travelling well when falling at Peper Harow in between. Should get off the mark in 2001. *R. Dench — Ashford V.* 127 (Cf), 413 (I), 575 (R), 705 (R), 829 (OMa), 1397 (OMa), 1513 (OMa).

MOONSTONE (IRE) ..10-1.. 6 b.m. Statoblest — Opening Day (Day Is Done) 334. Small light-framed half-sister to 3 flat winners (one in Italy), including Norwegian Blue and Evanro. Dam won at 8f in Ireland. IR 7000y. FLAT (for A. Jarvis; tried visored) r23 w1 (7f) p1 (2nd). NH '98/9 (for B. Baugh) r9 p3 (2nd of 16 in Clmr, and 2 Sells). Inconsistent, and her win in a muddling affair on the flat made life difficult for her in Points, but gave very creditable displays when making the frame each time. Deserved to score, but has been reported dead. *Mrs M.L. Trow (A. & H. Partners) — Worcs (Theresa McCurrich)*. 178 (Cm), 566 (L), 1086 (Cf).

MOON TIGER ..10-0.. 8 b.g. Tigerwood — Moon Haven (Brave Simon) p23321343. Small. Dam, sister to Cefn Andy (*qv* '90 Annual), pulled up 4 in '94, grandam, Cefn Inver, pulled up 7 and fell/unseated 2, and great-grandam, Exinver, was placed 9; all Pointed for Dilwyn Thomas. NH FLAT '97 r1 p0 (16th of 17). NH '97 r1 p0 (tailed off and pulled up in Hdle). P-t-P '98/9 r14 w3 (Maiden, Restricted and Intermediate) p2 (2nds); pulled up 3, fell 1. A consistent Pointer in his grade, and outbattled Anorak in his latest success at Erw Lon, but one-paced and usually has to settle for a place. A steady if unspectacular jumper, but all heart and deserves his successes. Probably acts on any going. *D.R. Thomas — Llangeinor (John Moore)*. 271 (O), 343 (Cf), 480 (O), 643 (Cf), 833 (O), 945 (O), 1226 (O), 1296 (O), 1451 (MO).

MOORE'S MELODIES (IRE) ..9-10.. 10 br.g. Orchestra — Markree Castle (Pitpan) 1. Big heavy-topped half-brother to Hurdles winners, Swift Conveyance (IRE) and Phar Better (IRE). Dam won 2m4f Hdle and 2m2f Ch in Ireland. IRISH NH '96/8 r9 w1 (2m4f Ch) p0. P-t-P/HUNT CH '99 (for Mr T. Alexander & Mrs D.M. Hall) r7 p1 (2nd of 3); 4th, 8th, pulled up 3, and fell 1. Began his Pointing career by falling three times in one race (twice when loose!) and remains a sketchy jumper, but managed to justify favouritism in his Members on his only start in 2000. Faced some stiff tasks in '99, and likely to have to do so again outside of his local in future. Has been tried in blinkers. *T. Alexander — Easton H. (Matthew Gingell)*. 603 (M).

MOOR LADY ..9-0.. 8 b.m. Primitive Rising (USA) — Navos (Tyrnavos) 4p7pfp5. Compact rather unfurnished sister to Moor Lane, and to Hurdles winner, Little Serena, and half-sister to Henavos. Dam won 2m Hdle for John Walmsley. P-t-P '98/9 r6 w1 (Maiden) p3 (2nd of 3; and 2 3rds, of 4 once); pulled up 1. Successful in a three-finisher Maiden at Brocklesby Park last year, and bred to stay really well, but doesn't, presumably due to a wind problem as she was fitted with a tongue-strap on her most recent start. Runs out of steam after about 2m3f maximum, and unless her afflictions can be fixed will never supplement her gains. *R. Walmsley — Bramham.* 16 (R), 173 (R), 440 (R), 1028 (R), 1230 (R), 1326 (R), 1351 (CR).

MOORLAND ABBOT ..7-10.. 13 b.g. Lir — Moorland Heath VII (unknown) p5p6pp. Small brother to Moorland Rose, and half-brother to Moorland Highflyer. P-t-P '93/6 and '98/9 r38 w1 (Maiden) p8 (5 2nds, after remounting twice, last once; and last of 3 once); failed to finish 6 (fell/unseated 3, and refused 2). Produced a gutsy effort when winning a 7min 30s Maiden at Flete Park in '93, but beaten 40 times otherwise, and the rider still rarely lets him break into a fully-fledged gallop. Last nine times when completing since returning from lameness in '98, and sometimes in danger of being lapped. *Miss P.D. Mitchell — E. Cornwall.* 315 (R), 534 (Cf), 726 (Cf), 848 (R), 1045 (L), 1259 (4mL).

MOORLAND ROSE ..9-0.. 6 br.m. Lir — Moorland Heath VII (unknown) rp53p68. Small stocky sister to Moorland Abbot (*qv*). Yet to finish better than a moderate last but one, and usually contests contests in which she does not have an earthly, but has looked perfectly willing since refusals on her debut, and it would be no surprise if she won a Maiden provided a competent rider was allowed aboard. *Miss P.D. Mitchell — E. Cornwall.* 157 (M), 730 (I), 855 (CfMa), 1048 (CfMa), 1187 (Inr), 1256 (Inr), 1514 (Cf).

MORCAN HOUSE ..8-7.. 9 b.g. Moor House — Dercanny (Derek H) ppf7. Workmanlike plain half-brother to Hurdles winner, Sylcan Express. Dam, half-sister to Canny's Fort (*qv*), was 2nd in an Adjacent and a Hunt Ch, and placed in a Hdle and 2 Chses for the Gibbons. Grandam, Canny's Tudor, pulled up in 2 Maidens for them. P-t-P '99 r4 p0 (pulled up 3, and fell 1). Looks to have difficulty getting the trip (like his sibling) and has only managed one tailed off completion to date. Seems liable to fall if not pulled up quickly enough when he gets tired. *P.F. Gibbon — Zetland.* 139 (OMa), 400 (OMa), 693 (OMa), 1032 (OMa).

MORCHARD MILLY ..9-6.. 14 br.m. Remezzo — Border Gem (Border Chief) 7. Small owner-bred half-sister to Morchard Gem. Dam won 6 Hdles, 2m-3m2f. NH '91/2 and '97/8 r8 p2 (3rds in 3m3f Nov Chses); pulled up 3, and fell 1. P-t-P/HUNT CH '93/9 r50 w1 (Members) p20 (8 2nds, 2 fences last after running out once; and inc last of 3); failed to finish 17 (unseated 5, ran out 3). Successful in just one of her 52 races, and has never possessed the battling qualities of her dam. Only beat two horses when completing in '99, and finished lame when badly tailed off last on her reappearance. Used to wear a near-side pricker and is sometimes blinkered. *R.T. Grant — Tiverton Stag.* 930 (I).

MORE FUN (USA) ..—.. 8 b.g. Sanglamore (USA) — Arewehavingfunyet (USA) (Sham USA) 4pp. Small half-brother to 4 winners in France. Dam won 5 races at 2 in USA. FRENCH FLAT '95/6 (from Criquette Head's) r2 w1 (8f) p1 (½l 2nd). NH '99 (bought for 6200) r4 p0 (distant 4th, and pulled up 3). Rated 9-11 after finishing 24 lengths fourth in a Confined (became very tired in the closing stages and lost two positions on the run-in), but has pulled up in five of six other attempts for present connections, and surely has something badly wrong with him. *M.C. Banks — Cambs.* 92 (Cf), 318 (Cf), 1114 (Cf).

MORE JOY ..9-11.. 13 b.g. Lighter — Caubeen (Scottish Rifle) 14ppp. Workmanlike brother to Hickory Hollow, and half-brother to Red Lane. Dam won 2m Hdle (also demoted to 2nd after wining similar), and was placed in 8 Points and a Hdle. IRISH NH FLAT '94 r1 p0. IRISH NH '94 r4 p0 (inc 2 Chses). NH '95/7 (blinkered 1) r20 p2 (short-headed once). P-t-P/HUNT CH '95 and '98/9 r10 p4 (2 2nds; and inc 2 Hunt Chses); pulled up 2, and ran out 1. Only able to run once apiece '98/9, but finally ended a frustrating run of 35 defeats when winning beating 12 others in an Alnwick Maiden run in the slowest time of the day on his reappearance. Suffers with his legs and looked unsound next time and failed to cope with regulation fences subsequently. Unlikely to get many more chances at lifting a Restricted. *E. Luke — Braes.* 45 (OMa), 184 (R), 301 (2m5fH), 686 (3m1fH), 1577 (R).

MORE METTLE ..9-4.. 7 ch.g. Sanglamore (USA) — Mettlesome (Lomond USA) ppp5p. Strong-topped half-brother to flat winners, Sea Mark and Im Let Alone. Dam won 3 French flat races. Sold Doncaster, Jan '97 for 750. Was in the process of giving his first respectable display when he broke a leg between the final two fences at Dingley. Mr & Mrs C. Pike & A. Adams — Grafton (Simon Gilmore). 514 (OMa), 754 (CfMa), 1012 (CfMa), 1422 (OMa), 1504 (CfMa).

MORE PEOPLE (IRE) ..9-12.. 9 br.g. Phardante (FR) — Stay As You Are (Buckskin FR) 1f23. Compact half-brother to useful jumping winner, Stormtracker (IRE) and to Chasing winner, Gale Force (IRE). Dam is half-sister to General Highway (qv '97 Annual). IRISH P-t-P '97 r2 p1 (3rd); and pulled up. IRISH NH '99 (blinkered) r13 p1 (3rd); fell at first and unseated in Chses; broke blood vessel once. Bought Ascot, Nov for 3000. The Baimbridge/Pritchard connection ensured that he was sent off favourite or second favourite in all his Points, but was unable to follow up a success in a Maiden in firmish at Chaddesley, where he jumped left. Performances in Restricteds suggest that he will win one. *Mrs L.L. Garrett — Berkeley (Dick Baimbridge).* 618 (CMa), 896 (R), 1488 (R), 1608 (R).

MORGAN'S ROSE ..9-0.. 10 b.m. Morgans Choice — Roses In May (Mummy's Game) pp55. Small. Dam won 2 Points and placed 2 '93/7. P-t-P '99 r7 p0 (pulled up 4, fell/unseated 2, and ran out 1). Generally just another useless monstrosity from the Smale yard, but her respectable 10 lengths fifth in a Lifton Restricted (though totally unfathomable) would make her a possibility in a Maiden. Aptly became the last horse to complete the course in 2000 when tailed off at Umberleigh which is probably a more accurate reflection of her ability. *Mrs J. Smale — Torrington F. (Lisa Smale).* 538 (OMa), 931 (R), 1517 (R), 1676 (OMa).

MORNAY DES GARNES (FR) ..8-1.. 12 ch.g. Quart De Vin (FR) — Eclatante (Tourangeau FR) b2. Rangy half-brother to 4 winners in France. Dam won 2 French flat races. Dam won 2 French flat races. NH '94/6 r5 p2 (3rds); pulled up 1. IRISH NH '94/6 r4 p0 (fell only Hunt Ch). P-t-P '98/9 r7 p1 (remote last of 3); (5th of 6, pulled up 3, and unseated 2). Succeeded in another Members completion in 2000, but still gets wound up in the preliminaries, and has otherwise failed to finish in nine Points for present connections. Carrying plenty of conditionin 2000, and seemingly not trained like a racehorse anymore. *Mrs D.J. Scantlebury — Morpeth.* 719 (CfMa), 1077 (Ma).

MORNDER ROMANY ..9-0.. 11 ch.g. Little Wolf — Runder Morn (Articulate) f. Sparely-made. Dam, sister or half-sister to 3 Pointers, was a useless non-stayer in 10 Points for Miss Mills (could go a good gallop for 2m4f, but ultimately only beat one horse). P-t-P '98 r2 p2 (2nds, remote of 3 once). Looked a non-stayer when last seen in '98, and has obviously had training problems since and made it to the track just once this year when falling at the two mile mark at Weston Park. Very unlikely to make up for lost time should he get another chance. *Miss W.D.M. Mills — N. Ledbury (R. Oliver).* 1412 (OMa).

MORPH ..9-8.. 7 gr.g. Baron Blakeney — Amber Marsh (Arctic Kanda) ff2. Tall owner-bred brother to Noah (qv). NH FLAT '98/9 r2 p0 (tailed off — pulled up debut). Fell at Higham (when a close second at the 12th and at Detling (when four lengths clear and with the race apparently in the bag two out — lay winded for 15 minutes), but recovered to just fail at Mollington, where he still had five lengths to find at the last. Deserves a change of fortune after a rotten season, and it would be very surprising if he did not collect a Maiden with a fluent round. *R.H. York — Staff College.* 236 (OMa), 577 (OMa), 792 (OMa).

MORRIS PIPER ..10-4.. 8 b.g. Long Leave — Miss Cone (Celtic Cone) 52131rp2. Small unfurnished home-bred half-brother to Mister Cone. Dam, half-sister to Still In Business (*qv*), won 2 Points and 3rd. Grandam, Mill Miss, won Ladies (beat rejoiner in freak contest) and 3rd. P-t-P '98/9 r9 p4 (2 2nds); last pair 3, and pulled up 2. An improved stayer since the acquisition of a tongue-strap and enjoyed much his most successful season to date in 2000, but seems quite highly strung and declined to jump off once when odds-on at Holnicote. Benefits greatly from the presence of Leslie Jefford in the saddle and likely to win again for him. A sound jumper, and regulation fences hold no fears for him, but rarely represents value and usually avoids ground with cut in. *I.W. Farley — E. Devon (Monique Pike)*. 21 (2m4fOMa), 204 (OMa), 563 (CfMa), 685 (2m5fH), 932 (R), 1370 (I), 1535 (2m3fH), 1674 (I).

MOSCOW SQUEAKER (IRE) ..9-2§.. 8 ch.g. Moscow Society (USA) — Topeka (Allangrange) 443p. Very light-framed half-brother to Waycross, and to Irish Pointing winner, Runeka. Dam won 2m4f NH flat in Ireland, and won 2m Hdle and 4 Chses (2m4f-3m6f) in England. IRISH P-t-P '97 r1 p0 (pulled up). P-t-P '99 (for Miss J. Oakey) r3 p0 (fell/unseated 2, and pulled up 1). Most reluctant in his first English season, and though rather better behaved equally unsuccessful in his second and ended the season lame when sent off joint-favourite at Eyton. Not beaten at all far in his completions and might be capable of a small success if he co-operates and comes sound again. Twice blinkered in '99. *Mrs V. Ramm — Worcs (Miss T. Nolan)*. 618 (CMa), 900 (OMa), 1197 (OMa), 1634 (OMa).

MO'S KELIRO ..9-6.. 9 b.m. Lir — Bossy Cleo (Proud Challenge) p6p. Small unfurnished owner-bred half-sister to Its A Doddle and Poppy Cleo. Dam won E. Cornwall Members and 3rd. P-t-P/HUNT CH '97/9 r16 w1 (Members) p3 (2 2nds, of 3 once; and last of 3); failed to finish 6 (fell/unseated 2, ran out 2). Very modest, and took 16 races to get off the mark, but missed the chance of Maiden success and has been found wanting in better class. Absent since mid-March. *C. Fowlie — Pentyrch (Mrs J. Marsh)*. 218 (L), 483 (R), 644 (Cm).

MOSS HARVEY ..9-12.. 6 ch.g. Le Moss — Wings Ground (Murrayfield) 31. Lengthy unfurnished owner-bred half-brother to Domhnall Beag and Rare Flutter. Dam, half-sister to Blessed Oliver (*qv*), won 2 2m Hdles and 2 Chses, 2m-2m4f. Showed promise on his debut, and confirmed it with rather an impressive success over 2m4f in softish at Garthorpe. Produced a strong late rattle, and it is possible he will prove too good for Pointing in due course. One to note. *J.R. Salter — Wheatland (Paul Jones)*. 1422 (OMa), 1589 (2m4fOMa).

MOSSIDE ..9-2§.. 12 ch.g. Le Moss — Eight Of Diamonds (Silent Spring) 7pup34p. Small neat half-brother to Laurie-O, and to Chasing winners, Scarlet Dymond and Celtic Diamond. NH '95 r2 p0 (tailed off and pulled up 2). P-t-P/HUNT CH '96/9 r29 w1 (Maiden) p9 (4 2nds); pulled up 10, and unseated 2. Won a bad Maiden by the narrowest of margins in '96, but increasingly reluctant to exert himself since and is a waste time now. The merits of running him in Hunters Chases are mystifying. Occasionally blinkered in the past. *B.W. Gillbard — Dulverton E. (Debbie Cole)*. 729 (R), 922 (3mH), 1176 (R), 1433 (3mH), 1560 (Cf), 1604 (M), 1650 (R).

MOSTA (IRE) ..9-0.. 8 b.m. Moscow Society (USA) — Shenley Annabella (Thatching) 34343. Neat half-sister to Irish winners, Regit (NH flat) and Hakkinen (IRE) (jumping). IRISH NH FLAT '97 r1 p0. IRISH NH '97/8 r7 p0. IRISH P-t-P '98 r4 p1 (2nd); pulled up 1, and fell 1. P-t-P/HUNT CH '99 r4 w1 (Maiden) p1 (2nd of 3); and last twice. Needed some divine intervention to get off the mark (the two length leader, who still clings to Maiden status, stumbled and fell at the last), but predictably struggling in a higher grade and beat a minimum of 26 lengths in three Restricteds since. The strange subject of a gamble on his second appearance in 2000. *Mrs H. Norman — Mid Surrey F.* 125 (M), 289 (Cm), 675 (CR), 830 (Cfm), 1104 (R).

MOSTYN ..10-3.. 10 ch.g. Astral Master — Temple Rock (Melody Rock) 3u54102. Good-topped compact home-bred. Dam was a useless Pointer (pulled up in 5 of 7 Points). P-t-P/HUNT CH '96/9 r21 w3 (Maiden, Restricted and Intermediate) p6 (3 2nds; and last of 3); pulled up 4, and fell 1. A steady jumper in Points, and usually makes the bulk of the running when successful, but flattered by an Open win in which the favourite misbehaved. Often gives the impression that he finds three miles too far, but has found regulation fences too demanding when tackling sub-3m Hunter Chases. Given an enterprising ride by Adrian Wintle when slipping the field for a long while over four miles on his final start, but had nothing in the locker when the winner collared him at the last. Wins infrequently, but specialises in surprises and discounted at your peril. *R.J. Weaver — Berkeley (John Tuck)*. 200 (O), 389 (O), 561 (O), 968 (Cf), 1133 (O), 1336 (2m4fH), 1614 (4mMO).

MOTU TAPU ..8-7.. 8 b.g. Nicholas Bill — Tabareek (Jaazeiro USA) 7up. Angular. Dam won 5 Hdles, 2m-2m6f. NH FLAT July '99 (for N. Twiston-Davies) r1 p0. Sold Malvern, Oct for 400. Looked like finishing about ten lengths second until he unseated at the last at Lydstep, but pulled up and dismounted when well adrift next time, and it could be that he does not have the best of legs. *T.J. Harries — V. of Clettwr (Miss B. Jones)*. 949 (OMa), 1223 (2m4fOMa), 1465 (OMa).

MOUNTAIN-LINNET ..—.. 14 b.g. Vital Season — Flavirostris (Grisaille) upuupuppp. Small short-backed owner-bred brother to Stone-Falcon and Most Vital, and half-brother to Elle Flavador. P-t-P '95/7 (for Major R.P. Thorman) r16 w1 (Maiden) p3 (2 2nds, last once); failed to finish 7 (fell 3).

A modest, but hard-working beast when last appearing, but not the safest of jumpers and the new owner has needed no provocation to plop out of the saddle on three occasions, negotiating just three fences successfully in the process. Pulls up when lady-ridden and never belies his often huge starting prices now. *A. Corrie — Seavington (Mrs C. Worsdale).* 639 (I), 876 (R), 953 (I), 1097 (Inr), 1176 (R), 1304 (Cfnr), 1375 (R), 1608 (R), 1673 (L).

MOUNTAIN LION ..7-10.. 9 ch.g. Move Off — Sheer Panache (Fury Royal) 8. Compact brother to Move In Style, and half-brother to Prime Style (*qv*). P-t-P '99 (for Mr R.F.L. Clark) r4 p0 (pulled up 4). Clueless and fenced appallingly in '99, but at least managed to get round for Tamara Hall when tailed off last in his Members this year (not registered to run in anything else). More of a goat than a lion so far. *Miss T. Hall — Middleton.* 996 (M).

MOUNTAIN TAE (IRE) ..9-0§.. 9 ch.g. Over The River (FR) — Woodside Run (IRE) (Deep Run) ppbRf24us. Unfurnished. IRISH NH FLAT '99 r1 p0. IRISH NH '98/9 r3 p0 (last 2 and fell in Hdles). IRISH P-t-P '99 r1 p0 (pulled up). Bought Malvern, May for 2000. Twice partnered by Phillip York and almost refused and fell at the last when eight lengths clear at Detling and was a two length runner-up at Hackwood on those occasions, but has otherwise been partnered by the owner Richard Green, who is a dreadful encumbrance. Baffles the poor horse with his inept attempts to present him at an obstacle, and was a fence behind on their only completion together. Allowing him to participate in a Hunter Chase was outrageous. *R.M. Green — Vine & Craven (John Porter).* 11 (OMa), 38 (CR), 457 (OMa), 710 (OMa), 828 (OMa), 1245 (OMa), 1396 (OMa), 1537 (2m5fH), 1624 (OMa).

MOUNTAIN THYNE (IRE) ..9-12.. 8 br.g. Good Thyne (USA) — Vanhalensdarling (Green Shoon) 212. Dam won 3 Irish Points under brilliant rides from Adrian Maguire in '91. P-t-P '99 r4 w1 (Maiden) p2 (2nds); and 4th. Runner-up in three Restricteds (favourite each time) before he succeeded in winning one at Corbridge, but absent since finishing lame at his home venue in March. An improved jumper, but rather one-paced, and the fact that a leg has given way so early in his career does not bode well. *Mrs R.L. Elliot & Mrs C. Scott-Plummer — Jedforest (Rhona Elliot).* 111 (R), 423 (R), 714 (C).

MOUNT FABER ..9-8.. 11 b.g. Headin' Up — Wise Lady (Law Of The Wise) 267482. Lengthy half-brother to Iculookin'. Dam won 3 Points and 2m4f Hunt Ch and placed 9. NH FLAT r2 p0. P-t-P '96/9 r21 w1 (Maiden) p8 (5 2nds); pulled up 5. Blinkered for the first time when winning at Hornby Castle in '96, but looked reluctant passing the boxes after two out and repeated the trick when in command on his reappearance at Balcormo Mains, and managed to get beat. Turns it in on a regular basis and is a very frustrating dog as he could be decent if only he were prepared to try. Placed eight times since his victory and must be shunned. *R.G. Watson — Bramham (Philip Watson).* 377 (R), 503 (R), 689 (R), 1028 (R), 1230 (R), 1351 (ZR).

MOUNT GAY ..9-8.. 8 b.g. Montelimar (USA) — Candlebright (Lighter) 41. Tall lengthy. Dam, half-sister to Wake Up Luv (*qv*), won 5 Hdles at around 2m and 5 Chses (2m4f-2m6f) for the Whitakers. Grandam, Arctic Ander, won 4 Chses, 2m-2m4f. P-t-P '99 r2 p1 (2nd); and fell 1. Not quite as volatile as he was in his debut season, but takes a strong hold and had soon pulled his way to the front when a convincing winner at Balcormo Mains. Stand little racing, but his jumping has improved and should have the scope for Restricteds at least. *Mrs D.A. Whitaker — Fife (Alan & Lucy Normile).* 46 (OMa), 1122 (OMa).

MOUNT KEEN ..8-7.. 9 b.g. Takachiho — Make A Bee Line (Prince Bee) p4. Small neat roman-nosed. NH '96 r1 p0 (pulled up). P-t-P '98 (for Mr A.T. & Mr J. Goldsworthy) r4 p1 (remote last of 3); 4th, pulled up 1, and fell 1. Seems to stay no more than 2m4f, and made no impact after a year off. Has been taken to post early. *D. Stephens — S. Cornwall.* 562 (CfMa), 722 (CfMa).

MOVE A MINUTE (USA) ..—.. 12 b.g. Al Nasr (FR) — Call Me Goddess (USA) (Prince John) uu. Well-made attractive half-brother to 5 flat winners (4 abroad, including Smuggly — smart in France, and Asl — useful in Italy). Dam won 3 flat at up to 8f in USA. $30,000y. FLAT (for D. Elsworth) r7 p1 (short-headed on debut). NH '93/4 (for J. Gifford) r8 w1 (2m Hdle) p0. Sold Ascot, Feb '95 for 1300. Determined to move at a mile a minute when seeing the light of day again after six years, and was a furlong ahead when departing at halfway in a Members. Strangled successfully by Julian Pritchard next time, only for him to get dumped at the sixth. Terrifying. *Mrs K. Scott — Exmoor (Peter Scott).* 1566 (M), 1606 (O).

MOVE THE CLOUDS ..9-5§§.. 7 gr.m. Environment Friend — Che Gambe (USA) (Lyphard USA) cr. Tall light half-sister to 2 flat winners (one in Spain), including Walk That Walk. Dam won at 6f in USA. FLAT (blinkered 1) r9 p1 (3rd). P-t-P '99 r3 p1 (2nd after refusing); pulled up 1, and fell 1. A real madam who can be dangerous if she arrives in the paddock (has been known not to) and downed tools big time when holding every chance at Bassaleg last year. Carried out by an incompetent on her return, but refused to race next time and it seems connections have lost patience with her and who can blame them. *J.J.V. Phillips — Tredegar F.* 349 (CfMa), 602 (CfMa).

MR BALOO ..—.. 7 b.g. Petoski — Miss Bunce (Mummy's Game) ppr. Good-bodied owner-bred. Dam is sister to Torenaga's Triumph (*qv* '94 Annual). Unpromising efforts so far suggest that he does not get the trip. *Mrs J.M. Prendergast — S. & W. Wilts (Sarah Waugh).* 655 (OMa), 955 (OMa), 1360 (2m4fOMa).

MR BEN GUNN ..9-12§.. 9 ch.g. Newski (USA) — Long John Silvia (Celtic Cone) 2df338. Smallish. Dam failed to finish in 3 Points, but grandam, Hidden Treasure, won 2m4f Ch and 5 Points and placed total of 10. P-t-P '99 r5 w1 (Maiden) p1 (2nd); 5th, and ran out 2. An extremely awkward customer in his early appearances and still far from angelic. Usually forfeits ground at the start, and makes mistakes, but has managed three fair placings since his '99 success at Dunthrop, and will probably consent to win a Restricted one day. Often taken to post early, but pulls hard and finishes tamely. Avoids left-handed tracks. *M.A. Tylor — Heythrop (Lucinda Sweeting)*. 260 (R), 458 (R), 513 (CR), 785 (I), 1014 (3m5fL).

PLATE 87   *1122 Fife Open Maiden 56&7yo: Mount Gay (L. Morgan), 1st, lead at the last*
PHOTO: Alan Mitchell

MR BOSSMAN (IRE) ..9-12.. 8 b.g. Jolly Jake (NZ) — Imperial Greeting (Be My Guest USA) p251. Workmanlike well-made. IRISH NH FLAT '97 r1 p0. IRISH NH '97/8 (tried blinkered) r5 p0. Only contested two Maidens, but ran well when chasing Polar King home at Wetherby, and confirmed the promise in a modest event at Hutton Rudby. May be good enough for Restricteds, but does not stand many outings, and did not reappear after the success in mid-March. *Mrs H.M. Woods — Zetland (Peter Woods)*. 40 (R), 168 (OMa), 420 (I), 625 (OMa).

MR BRANIGAN (IRE) ..10-13.. 11 b.g. Cataldi — Silver Doll (Sovereign Gleam) 1p. Workmanlike good-topped half-brother to Crash Bar and Penalty Double, to Irish Hurdles and English Chasing winner, Dalkey Sound, and to Irish NH flat and Hurdles winner, Silver Gypsey. Dam won 3 flat (14-16f) and 3 Hdles (2m2f-2m4f) in Ireland. P-t-P/HUNT CH '95/9 r14 w6 (inc 2 Hunt Chses, 3m-3m1f) p3 (2 2nds, beaten neck once); failed to finish 5 (fell/unseated 4). Unbeaten when completing in Hunter Chases '98/00, and possesses substantial ability, but has appalling legs and connections had no option, but to call it a day after he went wrong again at Leicester in March. Stayed well and possessed a useful turn of foot which would have carried him to many more successes had he been dealt a better hand. *W. Roe — Pytchley (Caroline Bailey)*. 90 (3m1fH), 460 (2m7f110yH).

MR BUMBLE ..—.. 7 gr.g. Blow The Whistle — MCA Lucky Star (Lucky Wednesday) p. Small compact half-brother to Beyond The Stars (*qv*). Anything but a busy bee when backward on his debut at Flete Park, but in a knowledgeable yard, and he might do better when asked to try. *Mrs S. Messer-Bennetts — N. Cornwall*. 1262 (OMa).

MR BUREAUCRAT (NZ) ..—.. 12 b.g. Markella (FR) — Katex (NZ) (Ex Officio AUS) p. Big lengthy half-brother to a winner in New Zealand. NZ w6 flat (up to 8f). NH '95/7 r10 w1 (2m Hdle) p0; jumped badly in 2 Chses — pulled up 1, and unseated 1. P-t-P/HUNT CH '98 (for Mr S.J. Stearn) r5 p3 (2nd of 3; and 2 3rds, of 4 once); last, and pulled up 1. Disappeared for a season after three placed efforts in '98, and appeared to go wrong immediately on his belated return. A hard puller, but regularly prone to dive right at the fences and was probably trying to save a leg. Worth 10-4 at best, but very suspect now. *I.R. Bennett — Badsworth.* 1327 (O).

MR CUSTARD ..10-6.. 9 b.g. Newski (USA) — May Owen (Master Owen) 632123321. Tall strong-topped roman-nosed. Dam was a bad Pointer. P-t-P '98/9 r10 w3 (Maiden, Members and Intermediate) p3 (2 2nds); last, pulled up 1, and fell/unseated 2. Regularly in the money, and performs to a consistent level, but might have achieved more in 2000 had he received stronger handling. Won two Ladies races including a narrow defeat of Newton Point at Siddington, but Lucinda Sweeting has been unable to do her mount justice when push comes to shove particularly over regulation fences. Can maintain a strong if one-paced gallop, but sticks his head out willingly and deserves to win again. Sweats profusely, and prone to make the odd error though jumps well on balance. *M.A. Tylor — Heythrop (Lucinda Sweeting).* 191 (Cf), 453 (Cf), 512 (L), 751 (L), 969 (L), 1335 (2m4f110yH), 1443 (3mH), 1558 (3mH), 1665 (L).

PLATE 88   751 V W H Ladies Open: Mr Custard (Miss L. Sweeting), 1st   PHOTO: Bill Selwyn

MR DENNEHY (IRE) ..10-5.. 12 ch.g. Callernish — Down By The River (Over The River FR) ppu131. Rangy half-brother to Chasing winner, Broadwater Boy (IRE). Dam won 4&5yo Maiden in Ireland. IRISH P-t-P '96 r6 p1 (19/ 3rd); pulled up 2, and fell 2. P-t-P '97/9 (for Mr J. Morris, Mr N. Walker & Mr R. Chalkley) r17 w4 (up to Confined) p2; fell/unseated 5, slipped up 1, and pulled up 5. Can bowl along merrily on a sound surface, and has gained three of his last four wins at Chaddesley (rather fortunate in the latest as Bishops Hall had taken his measure when falling at the last), but seems happier going right-handed and landed a touch when successful at Ashorne in May. Less erratic at the fences than he used to be, but still makes the odd mistake and broke a blood vessel at least once in 2000 (has probably done it before). Suited by an easy three miles and may find another easy opportunity at 12. *N. Walker — Worcs (Rob Summers).* 785 (I), 925 (2mH), 1335 (2m4f110yH), 1436 (Cf), 1585 (O), 1630 (Cf).

MR DICK ..10-9.. 11 gr.g. Absalom — Red Spider (Red God) 212. Small light-framed half-brother to Blushing Spy and Gordon, and to the winners, Volcanoes Spark (flat), and Golden Fox and Vanart (both Hurdling), Abu Kadra (flat and jumping), and Little Red Spider (NH flat). Dam won at 8f in Ireland. NH FLAT r1 p0. NH '94/5 r6 p1 (2nd). P-t-P/HUNT CH '96/9 r21 w10 (inc 4 Opens) p5 (2nds); pulled up 1, and fell 1. Has needed his seasonal reappearance '99/00, but otherwise unbeaten in his last six Points until suffering defeat at the hands of Solba at Brocklesby Park. Subsequently found to be lame and has not been seen since. Has beaten subsequently successful Hunter Chasers, but his two ventures into that grade have been disappointing and the likelihood of him returning to them seems slim. Broke the course record at Whitwell-on-the-Hill last year and recorded the fastest time of the day in his latest win despite having nothing to gallop with over the final six furlongs. Suited by top-of-the-ground. Will hopefully be able to make a speedy recovery. *Mrs J.C. Cooper — Middleton.* 395 (O), 504 (O), 796 (O).

MR DOW JONES (IRE) ..10-7.. 9 b.g. The Bart (USA) — Roseowen (Derring Rose) 2p302222133. Small sparely-made. IRISH P-t-P '98 r3 w1 (6yo Maiden) p1 (2nd). IRISH NH FLAT '98 r1 p0 (wore tongue-strap). P-t-P/HUNT CH '99 r8 w4 (inc 3m Hunt Ch, and Open) p1 (2nd); fell/unseated 3. Enjoyed a fruitful year in '99, when remaining upright, but generally disappointing this year and needed a slice of luck to score an unimpressive success at Pentreclywdau. Lacks the stature to cope with errors that have become his trademark, and may have won a Stratford Hunter Chase on his final outing had he not clouted the penultimate fence. Twice runner-up in Ladies races, including over 3m5f at Dunthrop, and looks sure to succeed in that type of event on a regular basis particularly if his jumping becomes more assured. Can handle mud, but seems to travel better on a less testing surface. *Mrs L.A. Goldsworthy — S. Pembs (Keith & Linda Goldsworthy).* 149 (3mH), 299 (3m2f110yH), 383 (3mH), 584 (3m2f110yH), 645 (MO), 836 (L), 1014 (3m5fL), 1226 (O), 1296 (O), 1600 (2m5f110yH), 1648 (3mH).

MR DRAKE (IRE) ..9-12.. 11 b.g. Salluceva — Salambos (Doon) 9. Strong-topped half-brother to Comhampton, to Chasing winner, Mackinnon, and to 2 Hurdling winners. P-t-P '96/9 r9 w2 (Club Maiden, and Restricted) p2 (last of 2 once); pulled up 4, and unseated 1. Has never stood much racing and finished lame when winning the second of two races in determined fashion in '98. Only managed one outing the following season and lame again after his reappearance at Chaddesley. *J.W. Powell — Ledbury (John Taylor).* 615 (CMod).

MR EDGAR (IRE) ..—.. 10 b.g. Over The River (FR) — Cyn Alley (The Parson) p. Compact half-brother to Peachy Beach (IRE), and to Irish Pointing winner, I Can Imagine. NH '95/6 and '98/9 (r. J. Gifford) r7 w1 (2m3f Hdle) p2 (2nds, inc beaten 18l in Ch). Bought Ascot, June for 1100. Carried his head awkwardly but still managed to beat the very wayward Dacelo (who threw the race away) in a Hurdle on firmish in October '96, but seems almost impossible to keep sound, and has only managed eight outings in six years. Tailed off after a mile in January when spotted briefly in a Point. *R.M. Bluck — N. Cotswold.* 61 (MO).

MR EGLANTINE ..8-3.. 9 ch.g. Mr Fluorocarbon — Sweet Rosa (Absalom) 3r. Big rangy. NH '96 and '98 r8 p0 (pulled up 4, inc final 3; inc Sell). P-t-P '99 (for Mr J. Flint) r6 p0 (5th, last, pulled up 2, and fell 2). Ables along in a very cumbersome manner and beaten a minimum of 29 lengths in his three completions. Made his feelings on Pointing pretty clear on his final start and has never enjoyed jumping. *S.R. Bolton — Holderness.* 502 (M), 798 (OMa).

MR FITZ (IRE) ..9-0.. 8 b.g. Andretti — Lisalway Lass (Wolverlife) f1u6. Unfurnished half-brother to Chasing winner, Stop The Waller (IRE). NH FLAT '98/9 (first 2 for P. Hedger) r3 p0. NH '99 (from Mrs A. Perrett's) r2 p0. Did nothing wrong when winning a youngsters Maiden on firmish at Detling (a first success for Mick Sheridan, 31), but it seems to have been a fluke, as he never won a yard when favourite or second favourite in two subsequent ventures. Drops himself right out, and was very slowly away before plodding home a fence behind the rest at Rodmell. *Mrs A.J. & Miss J. Gadd — Chid, Lec & Cowdray (R. Gadd).* 304 (M), 576 (OMa), 705 (R), 1209 (Cnr).

MR FIVE WOOD (IRE) ..9-9.. 13 ch.g. Denel (FR) — Beau Lady (Beau Chapeau) pp33. Very tall strong half-brother to Irish Pointing winner, Dancing At Laharn (IRE), and to NH flat winner, Harris Croft Star (IRE). Dam won a NH flat, 4 Hdles (2m-2m6f) and 3m Ch in Ireland. IRISH NH '93/5 and '97 (been blinkered) r22 w5 (4 Hdles, 2m4f-2m6f, and 2m4f Ch; inc 3 wins at Down Royal, and one at Ayr) p4 (3rds; one at Perth). P-t-P '99 (for Mr P.M. Hall) r6 p2 (2nds); last pair 2, unseated 1, and pulled up 1. Feebly handled in his first English season, but has been on the decline since leaving his homeland and beaten a minimum of 15 lengths when completing for the new owner. Appeared to pull up lame at Guilsborough, but was back in action three weeks later. *J. Purllant — Cambs Univ.* 770 (Cf), 1008 (O), 1286 (Cf), 1505 (4mMO).

MR FREEBIE (DEN) ..10-10.. 11 b.g. Viking (USA) — Sirenivo (USA) (Sir Ivor) 132122. Strong half-brother to Sirundy, to flat winner, Sunley Sinner, and to succesful Hurdler, Basic Fun. Dam won 3 10f races (was useful). P-t-P '97 and '99 r7 w2 (2m5f Maiden, and Restricted) p0; last pair 2, and pulled up 3. An improving sort who shot up the ratings in 2000, and has developed into a useful stayer. Ran a shocker by his recent standards when beaten at odds-on at Southwell (never going well or jumping well), but bounced back with a game victory at Towcester and only beaten inches by Overflowing River over 4m1f at Cheltenham on his final appearance. Speedy enough to win round Cottenham, but stamina appears to be his forte and can handle most surfaces except perhaps sticky. Usually held up, and can get some way out of his ground. Gets on well with Nibby Bloom and has helped put trainer David Ingle on the map. *Mrs R.L. Banks — S. Wold (David Ingle).* 18 (I), 151 (3mH), 367 (Cf), 466 (3m1fH), 999 (4m1fMO), 1338 (4m1fH).

MR FREEMAN (IRE) ..9-2§.. 10 br.g. Actinium (FR) — Mameen's Gift (Boreen FR) up078. Tall half-brother to Irish Pointing winner, Marillo. IRISH NH FLAT '97 (blinkered final) r2 p0. IRISH P-t-P '96/7 r7 w1 (Maiden) p3; ran out 1, and fell 1 (in slight lead at last, but looking held). P-t-P '98/9 r14 w1 (Restricted) p2; unseated 3, and pulled up 2. Beaten 13 times since the surprise 16-1 winner of a Dingley Maiden in '98, and is a thoroughly work-shy beast with no zest for racing whatsoever. Usually one of the first to come off the bridle, but does nothing to assist his partners and headgear has made little difference. Only once better than last-but-one in his last 10 starts, and clearly not up for redemption. *R.A. Jeffery & Mrs M. Jackson — Grafton (Simon Gilmore).* 75 (I), 296 (I), 510 (Cf), 788 (Cf), 1203 (I).

MR FUDGE ..9-3.. 14 gr.g. Broadsword (USA) — Blades (Supreme Sovereign) p3f. Very tall half-brother to Oakgrove, Not So Sharp and Oxnead (dam of Hagon Beck (*qv*)) and Tailormade. NH FLAT r3 p1 (3rd). NH '93 and '95/9 (for M.E. Sowersby latterly) r21 w2 (2m1f-2m3f Chses) p4. P-t-P/HUNT CH '94/5 (for Mr P.W. Clifton) r9 w3 (inc 2m4f Hunt Ch) p3 (3rds in Hunt Chses); fell 3 (when a fence ahead at the last once). Formerly a fair front-running sub-3m handicapper, but a light of other days now and beaten nine lengths when last of three in his Members on his only completion this year. Used to make shoals of mistakes under Rules and proved on his final start that he is too old to learn the error of his ways. Has been tried in blinkers. *P. Lentelink - Lanarks & Renfrews, & Eglinton.* 493 (Cf), 659 (M), 975 (O).

MR GOLIGHTLY ..9-9.. 14 b.g. Lighter — Go Gently (New Member) 43734646u. Strong-topped half-brother to Picador and Cotapaxi (latter won Chasing since Pointing). Grandam, Softly Softly, was 2nd in 2 Points, and won 3m Nov Ch and placed 9 for late Toby Cobden. P-t-P/HUNT CH '93/7 and '99 r25 w7 (inc 5 Hunt Chses, 2m3f110y-3m, inc hat-trick '95) p9 (5 2nds, beaten head in Hunt Ch once, and neck once, and of 3 once); failed to finish 5 (fell/unseated 2, and ran out 1). A lovely old horse, and formerly a near top-clas Hunter Chaser (rated 11-2 at best), but a sorry sight since pulling up on his only outing of '97 and his performances in 2000 were lamentable. Often let down by his lady riders partners and the current one continually flops onto him in a most ungainly fashion. Running him again over regulation fences would be heartless and has hopefully already begun his retirement. *Mrs B.I. Cobden — Seavington (Jane Reed).* 9 (L), 153 (2m4f110yH), 303 (3mH), 519 (M), 725 (L), 922 (3mH), 1174 (L), 1305 (MO), 1648 (3mH).

MR GREENGRASS ..—.. 7 ch.g. Green Adventure (USA) — Amethea (True Song) p. Tall workmanlike half-brother to Rusty Flame (*qv*). Bought Malvern, May for 1800. Mr Green as Grass at Guilsborough. Looks the part on one hand, and has an unattractive pedigree on the other. *D.J. Harding-Jones — Puckeridge (Perry Harding-Jones).* 1009 (CR).

MR GRIMSDALE (IRE) ..10-8.. 9 ch.g. Grimesgill (USA) — Lady Rose Walk (Sir Herbert) 2u218. Medium-sized good-looking. IRISH NH FLAT r1 p0. IRISH P-t-P '98 r1 p0 (last). P-t-P '99 (for Col S.R. Allen) r5 w1 (Club) p1 (distant last of 3); 4th, pulled up 1, and fell 1. Much improved for strong-handling in 2000, and showed a battling attitude when forced home by Tom Scudamore at Uttoxeter, but appeared not to care for the quicker surface next time. Possesses more speed than stamina and should continue to pay his way in sub-3m Hunter Chases. *A.J. Chambers — Heythrop (Martin Tate).* 18 (I), 580 (3mH), 925 (2mH), 1249 (2m7fH), 1558 (3mH).

MR HATCHET (IRE) ..—.. 10 ch.g. Executive Perk — Aubretia (USA) (Hatchet Man USA) f. Leggy brother to Irish Hurdles winner, See More Perks (IRE), and half-brother to Irish/English Hurdles winner, Welsh lad (IRE) and to flat winner, Charming Gift. Dam won at 7f. NH FLAT r2 p0 (17*l* 4th, and distant 4th after virtually bolting). NH '99 r2 p1 (2nd); and ran out 1. An excitable sort with a tendency to pull hard in the past, but resurfaced after two seasons missing only to break a hind leg at Mollington. *A. Hollingsworth — Worcs.* 75 (I).

MR HOOK ..9-10.. 9 b.g. Primitive Rising (USA) — Miss Puck (Tepukei) u31pp6u. Strong brother to Miss Fly, and half-brother to Mr Norm and Reivers Way. Dam only beat one rival in 7 Points for Bill Brown (showed unpleasant tendencies). P-t-P '97/9 r15 p3 (remote last of 2; and 2 3rds last once); pulled up 5, fell 1, and brought down 1. Placed three times prior to his shock success, but had looked totally awry and was sent off the 50-1 rank outsider in a field of 11. Would not have won had Young Ardross not broken down and predictably struggling in better company since. Regained blinkers on one occasion in 2000, but jumped worse than usual and spurs certainly did nothing to make him go quicker. Blew his chance of Maiden success and looks unlikely to receive another gift from the Gods. *W. Brown — Sinnington (Ian Brown).* 55 (OMa), 276 (M), 378 (R), 506 (Cf), 804 (Cf), 1027 (Cf), 1349 (O).

MR JERVIS (IRE) ..9-8.. 12 b.g. M Double M (USA) — Amorosa (GER) (Frontal) 2216f. Good-topped half-brother to a winner in Germany. NH '93/6 and '98/9 (for J. Gifford) r17 w1 (2m3f Ch) p7 (inc 5 Hdles); one run at Punchestown. Rather slow and suffers with his legs (has been absent for spells of 18 months and 24 months in the past), but usually a safe jumper, and was scoring for the second time in soft when he provided Tory Tremlett with her first winner in a dire four-runner two-finisher Ladies at Bishops Court. Disappeared after taking a crashing fall at Stafford Cross. *Miss V.M. Tremlett — Silverton (Paul Hopgood).* 65 (M), 257 (L), 405 (L), 725 (L), 929 (Cnr).

MR KETTLESTONE ..9-6.. 8 ch.g. Gildoran — Nosey's Daughter (Song) p. Sweeting-bred half-brother to Sun Setting, and to Hurdles winner, Cool Runner. P-t-P '99 (for Mr J. Tyndall & Mr P.A. Deal) r5 p1 (3rd); 6th, fell 2, and ran out 1. A real handful. Overheats in the preliminaries despite the presence of two paddock handlers and has proved a very tricky ride to date. Out of control for the trainer in '99, and disappeared after pulling up at Barbury Castle in the first month of the season this year. Has the ability to win a race if all is well though lack of stamina is another problem he has to overcome. *C. Sweeting & J. Tyndall — Heythrop (Lucinda Sweeting).* 31 (CMa).

MR KEVERNAIR ..9-4.. 11 b.g. High Season — Mena Gold (Golden Passenger) p3p5. Tall strong. Dam is an unraced sister or half-sister to 3 Pointers. Grandam, Mena Lodge, won 3 Points and 3rd twice, and great-grandam, Fort Lodge, won 3 Chses, 2 Hunt Chses and 15 Points and placed 10. P-t-P '97/8 r6 w1 (Maiden) p0; and pulled up 5. Won an elders Maiden taking 7min 11s at Lemalla on his only completion '97/8, but off the track since and well beaten on his return. Pulls hard, and taken to post early after an unruly display on his reappearance during which he broke a blood vessel. *A.J. Scrimgeour — Dulverton W. (Lucy Roberts).* 256 (R), 523 (Cnr), 728 (R), 1095 (R).

MR MAD ..9-12§.. 13 b.g. Good Times (ITY) — Mistress Bowen (Owen Anthony) p13p24fp. Compact brother to Good Holidays, and half-brother to Goewin, and to a winner abroad. FLAT r7 p0 (inc Sell). NH '92 r2 p0 (tailed off 2, pulled up 1). P-t-P/HUNT CH '93/4 and '96/9 r28 w4 (inc Intermediate) p11 (6 3rds, last once); pulled up 6, and fell 2. A competent performer in minor company, but usually visored nowadays (occasionally blinkered) and sometimes looks none too keen. Landed his third victory at Erw Lon when successful in his Members, and nearly made in three at Lydstep when narrowly beaten by Bullens Bay subsequently. Not a particularly fluent jumper, but suited by soft ground. *G. Phillips — Carms (Debbie Hamer).* 272 (L), 642 (M), 833 (O), 1051 (Cf), 1224 (L), 1295 (Cf), 1450 (Cf), 1612 (Cf).

MR MAGGET (IRE) ..10-2.. 9 gr.g. Salluceva — Linda Dudley (Owen Dudley) 2p1114. Close-coupled well-made. IRISH NH FLAT '96/7 r4 p0. IRISH NH '96/9 r12 p2 (2nd in Hdle and Ch). Bought Goffs, Aug for 1205. Bought by the current yard for Caroline Fryer, but she could not cope with him when favourite at Ampton, and the ride was subsequently entrusted to Nigel Bloom, who experience won the day. Immediately notched a hat-trick in minor company, which included a match for an Intermediate. Has plenty of stamina, and acts on firm and probably on soft. Those who call him Mr Maggot will soon be taught the error of their ways by Hyacinth Bouquet-Bloom. *R. Mathias — R.P & Miss C. Fryer — Brecon & Talybont (-; Mike Bloom).* 273 (R), 550 (OMa), 760 (OMa), 940 (R), 1185 (I), 1381 (O).

MR MAGNETIC (IRE) ..—.. 10 b.g. Point North — Miss Ironside (General Ironside) uuuR. Strong compact. IRISH NH FLAT '96/7 r6 w1 (2m4f) p0. IRISH NH '97/9 r12 w1 (3m2f Ch) p4 (inc 2 Hdles). Won a four-runner three-finisher Chase in April '98, and later finished one and a half lengths third over 3m6f, but was blinkered in a Hurdle on his final outing under Rules. Could be let down by his jumping, and seems to have had a problem with gurgling. Partnered by the beginner Domonic Harvey in Points, and he fell off three times (would have finished a poor second of three once) and ran out after a mile. The supremely stylish performances of the former professional in the family have evidently not rubbed off on him yet — or have they?. *D.T. Harvey — Devon & Somerset.* 141 (MO), 355 (O), 557 (Cf), 653 (MO).

MR MARK (IRE) ..9-5.. 9 b.g. Buckskin (FR) — Lady Karola (Lord Gayle USA) 35353p. Dam won at 12f in Ireland. IRISH NH FLAT '97 r1 p0. IRISH NH '97/9 r13 p0 (disqualified from 3rd once); pulled up in Hunt Ch. IRISH P-t-P '99 r6 w1 (7 plus Mdn) p2; fell 1. Bought Doncaster, May for 4200. Scored in soft in Ireland, and managed three thirds in Restricteds for the new yard, but beaten a minimum of 14 lengths, and went down hill badly after giving his best display first time out. Pulled up at halfway on his latest and feeblest attempt yet. *L. Brennan — Cheshire Forest (Reg Crank).* 173 (R), 532 (R), 782 (R), 1129 (R), 1322 (R), 1528 (R).

MR MATCHIT (IRE) ..—.. 9 b.g. Mandalus — Twitchit (Crash Course) upp. Small neat half-brother to Bi Then (IRE). Dam won Irish NH flat. IRISH NH '96 r1 p0 (last). IRISH P-t-P '96 r2 p0; fell 1. NH '98 (for Miss L. Russell, bought for 2900) r3 p1 (distant 2nd of 3 in Hdle). A hard puller who did not stay in Irish Points, and a reluctant and useless Hurdler in Scotland in '98. Invariably stands his racing badly. The new owner needs no provocation to fall off. *I. Hudson — Oakley.* 97 (OMa), 197 (CfMa), 512 (L).

MR MAX (IRE) ..9-11.. 8 b.g. Parliament — Aria (Saintly Song) 214. Compact half-brother to flat winner, African Opera, and to successful Irish Hurdler, Same As That. Dam won 2 Irish flat, 10-12f. NH FLAT '98 r2 p0. P-t-P '99 r2 p1 (3rd); and 5th. A Maiden certainty following two decent efforts in better class last year, and duly obliged at Dunthrop, but appeared not to relish the faster conditions when subsequently tailed off in a Larkhill Restricted for which he was sent off favourite. Broke a cannon bone two years ago so his performances are even more meritorious, and can win again if his connections calculated risk has not backfired on some more. *N.D. Edden — N. Cotswold (Sally Caton).* 900 (OMa), 1020 (OMa), 1594 (R).

MR MCCARNEY (IRE) ..10-1.. 9 ch.g. Cardinal Flower — Villawood (Quayside) fp1. Tall strong-topped. Dam won Point and 2m Hdle in Ireland. IRISH P-tP '98 r4 w2 (5&6yo Mdn, and Winners of Two) p0; pulled up 2. NH '98 (for P. Nicholls) r2 p0 (tailed off last of 4 in Chses). A dual winner in soft in Ireland, but went to pieces when changing hands later in the year. Blundered his way out of the race by the 10th in his first two outings in 2000 (tongue-tied on his debut), but sprang a 20-1 surprise in a long Confined at Charm Park in early March under a vigorous ride from Wayne Burnell. The form looks very suspect, as the first four home were covered by three lengths, and his victims did not win a race between them all year. Absent since. *Mrs A.J. Addyman — Bramham.* 277 (Cf), 375 (Cf), 394 (Cf).

MR MCQUAKER ..—.. 8 b.g. Past Glories — Mary McQuaker (Acer) ff. Unfurnished half-brother to Grey Ace, Jilly Grey and Politicians Prayer and to Hurdles winner, Elegant Mary. Dam won at 8f, and won 3 2m2f Hdles at Cartmel. Fell at the 10th and at the seventh, but might have the potential to do better if he can ever master the fences. *I. Hamilton — Tynedale (Ann Hamilton).* 718 (CfMa), 1084 (2m4fOMa).

MR MOTIVATOR ..9-8.. 11 b.g. Rolfe (USA) — National Clover (National Trust) ff334p761pu. Tall heavy-topped half-brother to Four Leaf Clover, Welsh Clover and Scottish Clover, and to NH flat and top-class jumping winner, Go Ballistic. Dam, '84 Grand Marnier winner, won 27 Points, inc 24 Ladies and an Open, and placed 20. Grandam, Clover Bud, won Welsh Grand National and 6 other Cases (3-4m) and 9 Points. NH FLAT '96 r1 p0. NH '96/7 r5 p0 (2 Hdles — last, and pulled up 1; and 3 Chses — 7th of 8, and fell/unseated 2). P-t-P '98 r6 w2 (Maiden and Club Novices) p3 (2 2nds); and fell 1. Ended '99 in good heart, but crash landed twice on his return in January and generally overfaced subsequently. Landed a 2m4f Warwick Hunter Chase in May under a positive ride from Frank Windsor-Clive, but fatally injured at Stratford the following month after making a string of blunders. V.Y. Gethin — N. Herefords. 34 (MO), 59 (MO), 148 (3m1f110yH), 226 (2m4f110yH), 469 (3m110yH), 683 (3mH), 897 (I), 925 (2mH), 1447 (2m4fH), 1600 (2m5f110yH), 1647 (3m4fH).

MR NORM ..7-9.. 7 ch.g. Nomadic Way (USA) — Miss Puck (Tepukei) Rfupf44p. Small compact owner-bred half-brother to Mr Hook (qv). P-t-P '99 r2 p0 (fell/unseated 2). Only once better than last in 10 Pointing escapades, and poor jumping and running out of steam are certainly the norm for him. Will need improve radically in all spheres to stand a chance of winning. *W. Brown — Sinnington (Ian Brown).* 139 (OMa), 283 (OMa), 398 (OMa), 808 (OMa), 1001 (2m4fOMa), 1033 (OMa), 1235 (OMa), 1352 (OMa).

MR PEOPLES (IRE) ..8-8.. 9 ch.g. Noalto — People (Al Sirat USA) p5fp. Tall strong-topped half-brother to Irish Chasing winner, Russian Gale, and Hurdles winner, Mywend's (IRE). IRISH P-t-P '96/7 r4 p1 (2nd); pulled up 3; tried tongue-tied. P-t-P/HUNT CH '98/9 r6 p2 (3rds, last once); pulled up 4. Has the looks, but an impetuous front-runner who does not stay three miles, and can be guaranteed to finish exhausted if he manages to complete. Has been tried tongue-tied and obviously defective. *K. Liscombe — Cheshire Forest.* 527 (OMa), 777 (OMa), 964 (OMa), 1323 (OMa).

MR PISTACHIO (IRE) ..9-12.. 6 b.g. Royal Fountain — Knockananig (Pitpan) 11f. Workmanlike half-brother to Irish pointing winner, Lurgoe. His intended debut developed into high drama when he went into a bucking bronco act on the way to the start at Garnons, and threw Alan Phillips (who was airlifted to hospital whilst the ghouls looked on, but luckily not seriously hurt as had originally been feared), but gave no problems and created a decent impression subsequently. Completed a double in holding and on firm, but had almost nothing to beat (the runner-up in his Members was another Shutts five-year-old), and of the 17 other events at the two meetings only one slower time was recorded. Could do no more than score decisively, and a Restricted at least should be his for the taking. *N. Shutts — Ludlow (Penny Grainger).* 527 (OMa), 986 (M), 1129 (R).

MR PRIMETIME (IRE) ..10-6§.. 11 b.g. Phardante (FR) — Bavette (Le Bavard FR) 7822. Strong rangy half-brother to Irish Pointing winner, Pharanged, and to Irish Chasing winner, Eddie. NH FLAT r1 p0. NH '95/6 r13 w1 (2m2f Ch) p3 (inc 3rd in Hdle). P-t-P '97 and '99 r8 p4 (2 3rds, last once; and inc neck 2nd); unseated 1, and refused 1. Won an awful firm ground Chase by a wide margin in '96, but has only averaged four outings a year in three Pointing seasons since and has yet to add to his score. Jumped dreadfully for the trainer on his Hunter chase debut after which Nick Bannister regained the ride. Chirped up after a deplorable effort at Duncombe Park to finish second in two Confineds (beaten a length and a half maximum) and could easily win Points were he genuine. Absent since mid-March and always to be treated with suspicion. *N.W.A. Bannister — Middleton (Annabelle Armitage).* 155 (3m4f110yH), 277 (Cf), 394 (Cf), 623 (Cf).

MR ROBSTEE ..9-4.. 10 b.g. Pragmatic — Miss Northwick (Remezzo) 232pp. Small unfurnished owner-bred. P-t-P '96 and '98/9 r11 p2 (3rds, last once); pulled up 5, refused 1, and brought down 1. Beaten a minimum of 12 lengths when placed in his first three starts this year (blew up on the first two occasions), but reverted back to his hopeless former self subsequently and may have gone wrong at Kingston Blount. Suited by an easy three miles and a sound surface, but a win still seems unlikely. *P.H. King — V.W.H.* 147 (OMa), 629 (OMa), 753 (CfMa), 1131 (OMa), 1486 (OMa).

MRS DRUMMOND (IRE) ..—.. 8 br.m. Dromod Hill — Dear France (USA) (Affirmed USA) puup. Compact. FLAT (early runs for A. Jarvis) r8 p1 (3rd in amat); inc Sells. NH '97 r4 p1 (3rd in Sell). P-t-P '98 r3 p0 (5th, pulled up 1, and fell 1). Looked temperamental over hurdles and has appeared ill sorted to Pointing. Acquired blinkers on her fourth and final outing in the space of a month, but pulled up quickly after two miles and has presumably suffered a setback. *P. Armitage — Sinnington (Michael Brown).* 137 (R), 168 (OMa), 276 (M), 381 (OMa).

MRS DUF ..9-3.. 7 b.m. Teenoso (USA) — Hatherley (Deep Run) 2. Sister to Peasedown Tofana (*qv*). Came charging past five of her rivals from three out in a 2m4f Maiden at Ston Easton, but could not get near the very easy winner. Her sister notched a double at seven, and must have an outstanding chance of emulating her. *Mrs S. Alner — Portman (Louise Alner).* 732 (2m4fOMa).

MR SMUDGE ..9-13.. 9 ch.g. Fearless Action (USA) — Amerian County (Amerian USA) 3f3123p. Compact owner-bred brother to Fraction. P-t-P '98 r4 w1 (Maiden) p2 (2nd of 3, and last of 2); and fell 1. Created a favourable impression in '98, and a year off has clearly not affected his development too much. Far from disgraced when placed at Didmarton and Siddington before outstaying the runner-up in his Members, and responded gamely to Andy Martins' liberal use of the whip when third to Copper Thistle in the Land Rover final at Towcester (the rider picked up a six day ban for his efforts) subsequently. One-paced, but genuine and should be able to win again providing he is sensibly placed. *C. & Mrs F. Marriott — Heythrop (Fran Marriott).* 392 (R), 477 (R), 749 (Cf), 1013 (M), 1416 (O), 1532 (3m1fH), 1646 (3m4fH).

MR SNOWMAN ..10-11.. 9 b.g. Lightning Dealer — Evintime (Hot Brandy) 11221. Tall strong half-brother to Arble March (*qv*). P-t-P '98/9 r6 w2 (Maiden and Intermediate) p3 (2 2nds, beaten head once); pulled up 1. Has developed into a useful performer under the intelligent handling of his trainer, and has not missed the frame in ten completions. Took to Hunter Chasing like a duck to water, and unlucky not to win three as Vinny Keane would have outridden many professionals in getting Castle Court home at Ascot. Acts on any going and possesses both speed and stamina. Found Fakenham too sharp, but a much improved jumper, and looks destined for many more successes. *Mrs T.J. Hill & S.N. Wilshire — V. of Aylesbury (Lawney Hill).* 243 (Cf), 459 (2m4f110yH), 919 (2m3f110yH), 1155 (2m5f110yH), 1530 (2m6fH).

MR SPECK ..—.. 9 b.g. Henbit (USA) — Erroll's Elite (Saulingo) p. Half-brother to Jane's Feelings. NH '98 r2 p0 (tailed off and pulled both Chses). Led until weakening rapidly after two miles on a rare outing in early February. *D.W. Barker — Bedale (Grant Tuer).* 133 (CCfMa).

MRS SHERMAN ..8-10.. 6 b.m. Derrylin — Temporary Affair (Mandalus) 56u. Robust attractive good-sized half-sister to Royal Fling. Dam won Tanatside Maiden and 2nd 2. Tailed off last twice when looking to need the outings, and then fell at halfway. She and sis are not cutting much of a dash at present. *Mrs L. Williamson — Cheshire (Mark Williamson).* 570 (2m4fCfMa), 966 (OMa), 1201 (2m4fOMa).

MR STACKHOUSE (IRE) ..9-5.. 10 gr.g. Step Together (USA) — Best Dressed (Pumps USA) RprR. Very tall rangy half-brother to Beau Dandy. P-t-P '99 r4 p0 (last, pulled up 2, and ran out 1). Built like a brick outhouse, but even less manoeuvrable and has the added problem of being unable to stay three miles. Must be one of the biggest horses in training (his mother must have been a giraffe who was rogered by a Chieftain tank) and is able to step over the fences, but blinkers have failed to curb his wayward tendencies and likely to attract the attentions of Portman Square before too long. *J. Taylor, C. Kelland & A. Grimmit — Ledbury (John Taylor).* 618 (CMa), 866 (CfMa), 1018 (OMa), 1405 (OMa).

MRS WUMPKINS (IRE) ..9-5.. 10 b.m. Phardante (FR) — Mr Jersey (Crash Course) u. Workmanlike lengthy half-sister to Irish Hurdles winner, Clara's Dream and Irish NH flat winner, Accountancy Native. P-t-P '96/7 (for Mr D. Brace) r11 w1 (Maiden) p2 (2nds, beaten head once); pulled up 6, and unseated 1. NH '99 (for Denys Smith) r3 p0 (fell and pulled up 2 in Chses). Won and pulled up six times in her debut season, and failed to cope with regulation fences three years later. Disappeared after unseating early on at Cottenham in January and clearly has her problems. *D.F. Smith — Hurworth.* 938 (R).

MR TUCKER ..8-1.. 9 b.g. Toirdealbhach — Felicity Fair (Quality Fair) pp. Smallish workmanlike owner-bred. Sire was a decent Chaser at best, and won as a 13-year-old. P-t-P '99 r2 p0 (6th, and pulled up 1). Kept up for a shade over two miles in both 2000 outings, but promptly beat a hasty retreat and pulled up. Beaten 60 lengths on his sole completion and getting few opportunities to better himself. Has two handlers. *I. Gilbert — Fernie.* 1270 (OMa), 1502 (M).

MUCKLE JACK ..9-5.. 11 ch.g. Nearly A Hand — Sparkling Tarqua (Never Die Dancing) 424233. Tall narrow half-brother to Early Morning (*qv*). P-t-P '96 and '98 r3 p0 (5th, last, and ran out 1). Capable of producing a prominent display in minor company, but a weak finisher to date, and the presence of blinkers when favourite at Eyton suggests he is not putting his best foot forward. Often the subject of market support, but even his staunchest followers will be starting to despair soon. *Mrs S.P. Gent — Curre (Christine Hardinge).* 450 (CfMa), 594 (M), 995 (OMa), 1091 (OMa), 1323 (OMa), 1624 (OMa).

MUDAHIM ..9-13.. 15 b.g. Shareef Dancer (USA) — Mariska (FR) (Tanerko) 2. Strong good-looking brother to an Irish flat winner, and half-brother to 5 winners (2 abroad). FLAT (for D. Wintle) r1 p0. NH FLAT Spr '90 r3 w1 p2 (3rds). NH '90/9 (blinkered 3; unplaced 3 for P. Hobbs; won 2 previously for Mrs J Pitman, bought for 26,000; previously for C. Broad) r44 w12 (5 Hdles, 2m-3m, and 7 Chses, 2m4f-3m5f) p10 (inc 3rd at Punchestown once); unseated at 6th (Bechers) in Grand National final start. A fabulously successful campaigner who earned £195,484, with his greatest triumph being in the '97 Irish Grand National (£62,700), in which he just defied two pounds overweight to get up in the final stride — the photo finish print shocked the punters who had backed Amble Speedy at 1-8 to get the verdict. Other top victories were in the '97 Racing Post Chase (£30,380) and the '95 Cleeve Hurdle (£25,120) but looked very unhappy and was reluctant to race when asked to tackle the Grand National fences at 13. Revived (wisely?) to give Vicky Simpson a good ride round in his Members, in which he was backed from 10s to 5s but could not cope with a one-eyed tubed rival. Connoisseurs of the absurd will be fascinated to learn that he won the Bumper in which Quixall Crossett (finished last) made his debut! *T. Adams — Buccleuch.* 712 (M).

MUDDLED MONK ..—.. 8 b.g. Fearless Action (USA) — Elizas Pet (Entanglement) p. Strong-topped owner-bred. Dam is half-sister to 4 Pointers, including Eliza's Toddy (*qv* '91 Annual). Grandam, Eliza III, won an Open Moderate and placed 2. P-t-P '99 r3 p0 (pulled up 3). Went a maximum of two miles in '99, but pulled up after half that distance on his return and having failed to reappear must have gone wrong. *P.J.H. Wills — Heythrop.* 249 (CfMa).

MUDSLIDE ..9-12.. 7 b.g. Gold Dust — Eskimo Slave (New Member) 15. Tall rangy brother to Eskimo Gold (*qv*). P-t-P '99 r6 p0 (fell/unseated 5, and pulled up 1). Inordinately clumsy in his first season when decking three different pilots, but big enough to step over the fences and produced a clear round to win easily at Ston Easton on his reappearance. Reverted to type next time and had to survive two fence-bending errors in order to finish a poor fifth and has not been seen since. *Mrs M.E. Paterson — Taunton V. (Richard Barber).* 733 (2m4fOMa), 932 (R).

MUFFLED MIST ..—.. 10 b.m. Ayyabaan — Keep Fighting (Baltus) p. Neat half-sister to Gerwyn, Battling Psyche, and The Clinker. P-t-P '97 (for Mrs M. Borthwick) r1 p0 (pulled up). NH '98 (for A.C. Whillans) r2 p0 (fell and pulled up in Chses). Maintained her remarkable non-completion record when pulled up at Larkhill on her belated return. Formerly the perpetrator of deranged acts in Wales and Scotland and tried to demolish the paddock at Larkhill for good measure. *R.T. Sturgis — Glamorgan (Gail Sturgis).* 261 (R).

MULLINGAR (IRE) ..9-8.. 12 b.g. Orchestra — Bramble Rose (Pals Passage) p5p344p546. Tall rather unfurnished half-brother to Connaught Cleaners and Bramble King. NH FLAT '94 r3 p0. NH '94/7 r12 w1 (3m Ch) p1 (3rd). P-t-P/HUNT CH '98/9 r15 p4 (3 3rds, of 4 twice; and 2nd of 3); pulled up 1. A careful jumper who can be relied upon to complete, and still able to give the odd reasonable display, but one-paced and has not won since March '95. Gets on his toes in the preliminaries, but often needs rousting along at an early stage, and sure to remain exasperating in future. Has been tried in blinkers. *Mrs S. Bell — Tynedale.* 41 (L), 109 (L), 185 (L), 362 (O), 422 (3m5fO), 716 (O), 917 (3mH), 1030 (O), 1498 (O), 1591 (3m1fH).

MUNTAFI ..9-4§.. 10 b.g. Unfuwain (USA) — Princess Sucree (USA) (Roberto USA) 53p3p6p. Neat half-brother to 5 winners (2 in USA), including useful Burooj. FLAT r9 w1 (12f) p1 (2nd). NH '94/7 r16 w2 (2m-2m1f Hdles) p2. P-t-P/HUNT CH '99 r6 w3 (2 Hunt Chses, 3m-3m1f110y, and Open) p1 (3rd); and pulled up 2. Successfully revived by current connections in '99, when a dual Hunter Chase winner, but totally out of sorts this year, and seems a very moody individual. Future performances clearly depend on what side of the bed he gets out of in the morning. Acts in soft ground and had avoided a sound surface over jumps until acquiring blinkers on his final start. *S.T. Lewis — Cotswold V.F.* 32 (MO), 79 (O), 334 (O), 446 (O), 1103 (3m2f110yH), 1340 (3m1f110yH), 1432 (3m1fH).

MURBERRY (IRE) ..9-10.. 11 br.m. Strong Statement (USA) — Lady Tarsel (Tarqogan) 574272. Sturdy quite attractive half-sister to Miner's Bill (IRE), to Irish Pointing winners, Curracloe Star and Calogan (latter also won All Weather Hurdles). IRISH P-t-P '95 r5 w1 (mares Maiden) p1 (2nd); pulled up 1, and fell/unseated 2. P-t-P '96 (for Mr M.E. Pinto) r3 w1 (PPORA Restricted) p1 (2nd); and last. NH '96/9 (for Mrs I. McKie) r11 p5; pulled up in blinkers final start. Placed five times under Rules without ever looking liable to win, and a return to Points did nothing, but confirm her as a safe conveyance. Rated 10-5 when winning at Parham in '96, but has looked woefully one-paced since. *M.H.D. Barlow — Bicester with Whaddon (Miss S. Firmin).* 18 (I), 191 (Cf), 427 (M), 752 (Cm), 1203 (I), 1436 (Cf).

MURPHYS MANDARIN ..9-7.. 8 ch.g. Right Regent — Shavegreen Holly VII (unknown) p. P-t-P '99 r6 p4 (2nd of 3 twice; and 2 3rds); and fell 2. Unlucky not to fill the runners-up spot on four occasions in his debut season (actually appeared to finish in that position once, but the judge disagreed), but pulled up lame when still in contention on his reappearance at Chipley Park. Not a fluent jumper, and may not get the chance to hone his art. *Miss J. Pimblett — Mendip F. (Richard Barber).* 146 (OMa).

MURPHYS WAY ..10-0.. 12 br.m. Ardross — Choir (High Top) 1242. Very tall rangy half-sister to prolific flat and jumping winner, Celestial Choir (earned over £150,000 for Les Eyre), to Hurdles winner, Whitley Grange Boy and to flat winner, Choral Sundown. NH FLAT '93 r3 w1 p0. FLAT '93 and '95 (for breeder, L. Eyre; tried visored, and worn near-side pricker) r11 p2 (2nds). Scored on her debut in '93, and gained a first success since when beating a terrible Rogues Gallery in an Open at Eyton (six ran, but was the only contestant who had any oomph about her at all). Showed the performance to be no fluke subsequently, and was rather unlucky over 3m2f at Cartmel, where she jumped the final fence seven lengths clear but was overhauled in the final 100 yards of the longest run-in in the country. Did extremely well considering she had never jumped obstacles in public until she was 11, and it is not impossible that she could yet capture a Hunter Chase if tried in the again. Spent some of her missing years at stud. *Mrs C. Hirst — Saddleworth.* 1198 (O), 1319 (O), 1559 (3m110yH), 1643 (3m2fH).

MURTON HEIGHTS ..10-4.. 11 ch.g. Primitive Rising (USA) — Cornetta (Cornuto) 1p. Lengthy brother to Rye Head and High Intake, and half-brother to Miley Pike and Douglas Ridge. Dam was last, pulled up 2, and fell 1 in Points for Karen Tutty. NH FLAT r1 p0. P-t-P/HUNT CH '95, '97 and '99 r7 w2 (Maiden and Restricted) p0; pulled up 2, and unseated 1. Looked in need of the run, but stayed on strongly to defeat Concerto Collonges on his reappearance, but has been desperately hard to train (seven outings in five seasons prior to 2000) and sadly broke down yet again at Wetherby in March. Would have been a useful performer if he'd had the wheels to match his engine. *N.D. Tutty — Hurworth (Karen Tutty).* 279 (O), 691 (O).

MUSICAL HIT ..9-0.. 10 ch.g. True Song — Rapagain (Deep Run) p23441. Good-bodied lengthy home-bred brother to Deep Song (*qv*). NH FLAT '95/6 r4 p1 (3rd). NH '96/7 r11 p1 (3rd of 4 in Ch — beaten one and a half fences after many mistakes); pulled up 7, inc 3 Hdles. P-t-P '98 (for Mrs R.G.D. Hurley & Mrs E. Wharton) r3 p2 (2nd of 3, and last of 3); and 6th. Often blinkered latterly under Rules, and had looked none too keen on occasions, but found an awful elders Maiden at up ton and made the most of the opportunity. Will find life a real struggle when raised in class. *Mrs E.M. Wharton — Warwicks (Charlie Wadland).* 197 (CfMa), 434 (OMa), 786 (OMa), 1068 (3m2fOMa), 1270 (OMa), 1359 (OMa).

MUSIC CLASS (IRE) ..8-8.. 10 ch.g. Orchestra — Tacova (Avocat) 7446p456. Small sturdy half-brother to Tacoment. Dam won 2m Nov Sell Hdle and 2m1f Sell Ch. NH '96/9 (blinkered 5; for R. Baker, bought for 1650; previously for C. Brooks) r18 p1 (21⅂ 3rd); inc Sells; last in only Ch (tailed off ½way). A very experienced but woeful Maiden, and was beaten a minimum of 21 lengths with a total of three horses behind him in 2000. Blinkered once. Surely has a major problem. *B.P. Jones — Berks & Bucks (John Gallagher).* 76 (CCfMa), 207 (OMa), 329 (CfMa), 462 (2m7f110yH), 738 (OMa), 1020 (OMa), 1194 (OMa), 1530 (2m6fH).

MUSKORA (IRE) ..10-1§.. 12 b.g. Muscatite — Singing Wren (Julio Mariner) f6. Workmanlike lengthy half-brother to Hazel Crest. NH FLAT r1 p0. NH '93/6 r34 w14 (10 Hdles, 2m-2m4f, and 4 Chses, 2m-2m5f) p8. P-t-P/HUNT CH '97/9 r10 w6 (Ladies, inc hat-trick '97) p1 (2nd); refused 1, and fell 1. A most prolific winner, and a tremendous galloper who won his first five Ladies Opens, but a notoriously funny customer who sulks if things do not go his way. Normally goes well fresh, but fell at the third on his return and downed tools as soon as he was headed on his most recent start. Used to love Worcester, and still has a soft spot for Friars Haugh and if he does stage another revival it will probably happen on the banks of the Tweed. Suited by top-of-the-ground. *Mrs F. Percy-Davis — Jedforest (Simon Shirley-Beavan).* 361 (L), 806 (L).

MUSTANG MOLLY ..9-11.. 9 br.m. Soldier Rose — Mindblowing (Convolvulus) p523. Small. Dam, half-sister to Tom The Light (*qv* '93 Annual), pulled up in a Point at 13 for Andy Martin. P-t-P '98/9 r5 p2 (last of 3 once); pulled up 3. Placed in four of her last six starts, but a hard pulling front-runner who seems unable to stay the full trip and is well below the required standard in sub-3m Hunter Chases. Deserves a small success and may get lucky on a short course one day. *Mr & Mrs A.J. Martin — Heythrop.* 585 (2m5f110yH), 799 (2m4f110yH), 1422 (OMa), 1676 (OMa).

MUTUAL MEMORIES ..7-2.. 13 b.g. Relkino — Mindblowing (Pongee) b. Strong compact half-brother to Hey Bingo and Dunston Reel. Dam won at 5f. NH FLAT r2 p0. NH '94/6 r7 p1 (3rd); fell only Ch. P-t-P/HUNT CH '97 and '99 r10 w1 (Maiden) p2 (2 3rds; and inc Hunt Ch); pulled up 5. Lifeless and useless '99/00, and over a fence behind in last in just two completions from six attempts, but much-loved by his owner Raymond Burrow, and was able to give the near-50 year old a safe first ride round in his Members. *Miss C. Norman & R. Burrow — Tiverton Staghounds.* 1136 (M).

MY BEST MAN ..9-12§.. 14 br.g. True Song — Eventime (Hot Brandy) p2pR. Small unfurnished owner-bred half-brother to Arble March (qv). P-t-P/HUNT CH '92/3 and '95/9 r32 w7 (inc 2 Opens, and Ladies) p9 (7 2nds, beaten neck once; inc Hunt Ch); failed to finish 9 (fell/unseated 5). A thorough stayer and on good terms with himself to '99, but started to look decidedly awkward last season and has become most untrustworthy now. Hung left in his latest victory, and then hung badly right next time and cocked his jaw and ran out on his latest appearance. Has been a good servant, but clearly fed up nowadays and seems set in his ways. Wears blinkers. *A. Hill — V. of Aylesbury.* 319 (L), 1145 (L), 1395 (L), 1622 (L).

MY CLEAN SWEEP (IRE) ..10-1.. 7 br.g. Brush Aside (USA) — My Only Hope (Brave Invader USA) 361. Half-brother to Lingering Hope (IRE) and Strong Hope (IRE), and to Irish Pointing winner, Different Chief (IRE). Dam won Irish NH flat. P-t-P '99 r4 w1 (Maiden) p1 (2nd of 3); and pulled up 2. Did well to win at five and made a promising reappearance when two lengths third to Glevum in an 18-runner Restricted at Barbury Castle. Only able to run twice more this year, but captured a less than competitive event at Littlewindsor where he was left well clear two out. May have the scope to maintain his progress in 2001. *B.N. Lock & C.W.W. Dupont — Cattistock (Richard Barber).* 38 (CR), 208 (R), 524 (R).

MY FRIEND BILLY (IRE) ..9-9.. 9 ch.g. Yashgan — Super Boreen (Boreen FR) 410. Small close-coupled half-brother to Keefis Baby (IRE). NH FLAT '97 r1 p0. NH '97/8 r5 p0 (pulled up 2 in Hdles; 11th of 12, pulled up, and fell at last when distant 3rd in Chses). P-t-P '99 r10 p4 (2 2nds); last pair 4, and unseated 2. Just held on to win a poor Maiden at Mollington, but was not winning out of turn after four previous placings. Often error-prone and short of stamina before so to win on such a stiff track was surprising. Has little scope for improvement, and tailed off on his first crack at Restricteds. Has been tried in a visor. *W.T. Winter — Atherstone (Sarah Phizacklea).* 121 (OMa), 792 (OMa), 871 (R).

MY HAPPY LORD ..7-11.. 10 b.g. Arctic Lord — Happy Tino (Rugantino) pf6. Workmanlike plain home-bred half-brother to Parditino (qv). P-t-P '98/9 r4 p0 (pulled up 3, and fell 1). Appeared to show improvement when tongue-tied for the first time on her second outing this season, but beaten around 27 lengths when last subsequently and seems incredibly moderate. Rarely gets the chance to prove otherwise and three outings in a season in his record. *Mrs K.R.J. Nicholas — Tiverton (Ken Nicholas).* 147 (OMa), 353 (CfMa), 562 (CfMa).

MY JESS ..—.. 7 b.m. Jester — Miss Levantine (Levanter) fppf. Lengthy half-sister to Forty Winks. Dam won 2 Members and placed 3, and is half-sister to 6 Pointers, including Eagle Tavern (qv '93 Annual). P-t-P '99 r4 p0 (pulled up 3, and refused 1). Has shown some speed, but does not stay and if she has not been mentally scarred after her second near-death experience it will be a minor miracle. A chap called Cottle used to run a circus and she might be better off performing in one. *A.J. Cottle — Torrington F.* 535 (L), 655 (OMa), 857 (CfMa), 1520 (CfMa).

MYLES OF MOSS (IRE) ..9-4.. 11 gr.m. Le Moss — Willshego (Welsh Captain) p53443p. Half-sister to Janice Price (IRE), and to Irish NH flat winner, Fenagh Express (IRE). IRISH P-t-P '95 r2 p2 (beaten 11-15*l*). NH '99 r2 p0 (Mdn Hdles; pulled up 1). P-t-P '99 r2 p0; 4th twice. Often thereabouts in modest Points, but does not appear to stay three miles, and has not proved anywhere near good enough when dropped in trip. Beaten three lengths or less when third twice in 2000, and may strike lucky one day. *Mrs L.A. Ogilvie — Lanarks & Renfrews.* 112 (OMam), 365 (CfMa), 665 (OMa), 718 (CfMa), 1123 (OMa), 1430 (OMa), 1556 (2m4f110yH).

MY NAD KNOWS ..9-7§§.. 8 b.g. Derrylin — Early Run (Deep Run) 44rr. Strong-topped lengthy half-brother to Early Dawn (qv). NH '97/8 r4 p0 (8th, last, pulled up 1, and fell 1; Sell final). P-t-P '99 r3 w1 (Maiden) p0; and pulled up 2. Won a poor Maiden taking 7min 18s in testing conditions last year, but not better than last in four outings since, and has taken it upon himself to misbehave at the start now. Refused to set off at all at up ton and declined the first after dwelling badly subsequently. *Mrs M. Baimbridge — Ledbury (A. Graham).* 896 (R), 1193 (R), 1355 (R), 1548 (R).

MY NOMINEE ..10-9.. 13 b.g. Nomination — Salala (Connaught) p434u2224. Lengthy light-framed half-brother to My Moona and Terrington, and to a winner abroad. Dam won at 7f. FLAT (hung left twice, and tried in a near-side pricker next time) r7 w1 (7f, awarded race after finishing 2nd) p0. P-t-P/HUNT CH '93/9 r61 w12 (inc 8 Hunt Chses, 2m4f110y-3m110y, and 3 Opens, and inc 4-timer, and hat-trick) p20 (11 2nds; inc 7 Hunt Chses); failed to finish 12 (fell/unseated 4). A useful Hunter Chaser when in the mood, but usually prefers to hide his ability and has contrived to lose his last 26 races. Unlucky on occasions in 2000 and had Lee Stephens knocked out of the saddle by a loose horse when going well with only two to jump at Tabley. Strung three seconds together subsequently, including a very respectable effort behind Lord

Harry on his favourite track, Bangor, where he has won four times in the past. Likes to dominate, but sulks if he is taken on and finding a race for him at 13 will be no easy task. Wears blinkers. *D.E. Nicholls — N. Salop.* 153 (2m4f110yH), 293 (Cf), 565 (O), 781 (Cf), 960 (Cf), 1128 (Cf), 1408 (Cf), 1559 (3m110yH), 1628 (2m4f110yH).

MY PRIDES WAY ..9-5.. 12 b.m. Prince Of Peace — My Always (Kalimnos) 33211. Workmanlike sister to Neil's Way, and half-sister to NH flat and Hurdles winner, Gods Squad. Dam won 3m2f Ch. Grandam, Myway, won 37 Points. P-t-P '95/9 r19 p5 (3 2nds, of 3 once; last of 3, and 3rd of 4); pulled up 4, and fell/unseated 5. Made all and kept on steadily to record her first success after six years trying, and having got the taste promptly did the same again in her Members where Donna Penwill was celebrating her first success. Very moderate, but tries hard and deserved her momemts of glory. Will find Restricteds far more competitive. *Mrs D.M. Penwill — S. Tetcott (Freddie Penwill).* 723 (CfMa), 857 (CfMa), 1049 (CfMa), 1262 (OMa), 1642 (M).

MY SAM ..9-7.. 6 ch.m. Minster Son — Samonia (Rolfe USA) p25p. Compact unfurnished owner-bred sister to Son Of Sam, and half-sister to Political Sam and Priceless Sam. Dam fell in only Point, but won 3 Hdles, 2m-2m4f, and a Sell for Mr Barker. Had looked a certain future winner when one length second at Hornby Castle, but unfortunately broke a leg at Mordon. *J.W. Barker — Hurworth (Lynne Ward).* 619 (M), 1033 (OMa), 1233 (OMa), 1480 (OMa).

MY SHOUT ..—.. 9 b.g. Nicholas Bill — Ruth's River (Young Man FR) 3122pp. Tall half-brother to Newzealandfudge. Dam is sister to My Young Man (*qv* '98 Annual). P-t-P '97/9 (for Mrs T.H. Regis) r13 w7 (inc 3 Opens, inc 6-timer '99) p2 (2nds, remote once); pulled up 3, and fell 1. Transformed by the acquisition of Ben Pollock in '99, and went through the year unbeaten — rated 10-10 -, but only managed one unimpressive Higham success this year and looked wrong when pulling up in his final two outings. Had disappointed on his reappearance, and though far from disgraced when failing to give five pounds to Mighty Moss at Huntingdon his eclipse by Mr Snowman at Leicester was less encouraging. Can look rather excitable, but never travelling with his usual zest at any stage in 2000, and clearly not right. Will hopefully get the chance to prove himself all over again next year. Only risked on good or easy surfaces. *Mrs D.P.G. Flory — Pytchley (Caroline Bailey).* 4 (O), 26 (O), 151 (3mH), 459 (2m4fH), 800 (3m110yH), 1144 (O).

MY SISTER LUCY ..10-4.. 11 b.m. Farajullah — Woven Gold (No Lute FR) pp522. Small. FLAT r8 p0. NH '93/6 (occasionally blinkered/visored; for Miss K. Whitehouse; previously for Mrs A. Knight; won previously for A. Jarvis) r21 w1 (2m1f Sell Hdle) p2 (2nds). Gained her sole vitory in October '93 and has had absences of 18 months and four years since, but ran amazingly well when two lengths second in a Confined when Kahlil Burke partnered her. The owner was back on board when she finished 20 lengths second in her Members, but the greatest misfortune was to come up against the spriteliest 17-year-old in the country. Sadly, she finished lame. *I. Hooper — Albrighton.* 294 (O), 702 (Cf), 988 (O), 1086 (Cf), 1407 (M).

MY SON TOM ..—.. 12 b.g. My Dad Tom (USA) — Narinne (Undulate USA) pp. Leggy half-brother to Millyford Bridge. NH FLAT Oct '95 r1 p0. NH '96 (for J. Long) r1 p0 (pulled up in Hdle — jumped badly). Pulled up after two miles twice. Well down to the owner's normal standard. *Mrs G. Drury — O. Surrey & Burstow (Peter Broad).* 291 (CMa), 825 (R).

MYSTERY ARISTOCRAT (IRE) ..9-8.. 11 b.g. Aristocracy — Mystery Of Life (Wolverlife) pu22225u5. IRISH '96 and '98 r10 w1 (Maiden) p3 (2nds, beaten neck twice, and 1½l). P-t-P '99 (for Mr B.N. Lock & Mr C.W.W. Dupont) r8 w2 (Restricted and Intermediate nov rdrs) p3 (2 3rds); 4th, pulled up 1, and fell 1. Won twice for novice riders in '99 (one of them being Paul Flynn so he doesn't really count), and despite four successive placings in mid-season wouldn't really extend himself for Rupert Tory and let his backers down on several occasions as he had done the previous year. Can jump well, but lost his partner twice after blunders in 2000, and can probably be ignored unless both horse and rider suddenly decide to get serious. *N.J & Mrs M.A. Tory - S. Dorset (Monica Tory).* 61 (MO), 209 (M), 389 (O), 523 (Cnr), 766 (Cnr), 878 (O), 1134 (Cnr), 1304 (Cfnr), 1484 (O).

MYSTERY BELLE ..9-1.. 11 gr.m. Baron Blakeney — Bredon Belle (Conwyn) pp. Small light-framed half-sister to Belle Fiore and Belle Chapelle. Dam pulled up 1, and refused 1 in Points for Mrs Newell. Grandam, Castle Belle, won Moderate and 2nd from only 3 starts. Great-grandam, Cotswold Belle, was a good Ladies horse. P-t-P '95/6 and '98/9 r8 p2 (2nds, of 3 once); last 1, pulled up 4, and fell 1. Stands little racing, and struggles to get the trip when she does make a rare trip to the races. Must be impossible to train as she was very fat on her reappearance. *Mrs S.M. Newell — S. Herefords (Christine Hardinge).* 491 (CfMa), 891 (OMa).

MYSTICAL MUSIC ..9-2.. 8 br.m. Silly Prices — Mystic Music (Hansel's Nephew) f1p. Dam, half-sister to 3 Pointers including Mystic Major (*qv* '00 Annual), won 13 Hunt Chses, inc 2 Horse and Hound Cups, 2m4f-3m2f, and 7 Points inc 4 Opens, and placed 9 (inc 6 2nds in Hunt Chses). Grandam, Mystic Mintet, won 3 Points and placed 3. Came with a late rattle to beat three bad rivals (non of whom scored subsequently) over 2m4f on dead ground at Dalston in March, where she made ten lengths on the run-in, but was a disappointing favourite on a firmer surface subsequently. Revived memories of her lovely mother who ended with a rating of 11-12 and a comment 'her supreme brilliance will long be remembered', but is only pony-sized herself, which will naturally be a handicap. It could be interesting to see how she handles Ladies Opens. *S. Scott — Buccleuch (Bill Hughes)*. 113 (OMa), 501 (2m4fOMa), 973 (I).

MYSTIC LEGACY ..—.. 12 b.m. Pragmatic — Mystic Queen (Golden Vision) p. Half-sister to Mystic Manna. P-t-P '99 r3 p0 (pulled up 2, and fell 1). A late starter, and seems to have no aptitude for racing whatsoever. *Miss C.A.B. Allsopp — O. Berks (Rachel Matheson)*. 260 (R).

MYSTIC MOMENT (IRE) ..8-0.. 10 ch.m. Entitled — Rusty Goddess (Hard Fought) p6u. Small neat half-sister to flat winner, Impy Fox. Dam won at 10f in Ireland. IRISH P-t-P '97 r4 w2 (5yo&up mares Maiden and mares Open) p1 (3rd); and pulled up 1. P-t-P '98/9 (for Mr J.J. Boulter) r5 p1 (3rd); fell 2, and pulled up 1. Showed plenty of speed, though little stamina, in the previous yard, but the current owner-rider seems remarkably uncompetitive and was soon tailed off thrice in 2000. *Miss S.E. Lane — Portman*. 211 (Cnr), 523 (Cnr), 1304 (Cfnr).

MYSTIC WARRIOR (USA) ..9-0.. 6 b.g. Majestic Light (USA) — Phoenix Sunshine (USA) (Encino USA) fp33. Good-topped half-brother to a winner in USA. Dam won 9 races and $226,889 in USA. NH FLAT July '99 (for P. Webber) r1 p0. Bought Doncaster, Aug for 1700. Went less than two miles in his first two Points, but showed improved form when about ten lengths third twice subsequently, including when last in an Open (unruly and finally had to be mounted outside the paddock). Quickly dismounted on final start, but should go close in a Maiden if all remains well. *N. & Mrs J. Elliott — Dart V. & S. Pool H. (Gordon Chambers)*. 728 (R), 1042 (R), 1260 (O), 1519 (CfMa).

MYTTON'S CHOICE (IRE) ..10-0.. 10 b.g. Nordance (USA) — Classic Choice (Patch) 3341. Compact brother to a winner in Italy, and half-brother to 3 winners (one abroad), including flat and Hurdles winner, Palisander (IRE). IR 2500f, 6000y. FLAT (blinkered 3) r11 p0. NH '94/8 (2 spells for A. Bailey); won in middle for D. Nicholson) r18 w4 (2m-2m1f Hdles) p6 (demoted to 2nd after winning once; beaten head once); ran out and unseated on debut. Can hang right and be unruly (looks a bit nutty), but has done well on balance over jumps, particularly as he has had absences of 23 months and 21 months before returning in 2000. In a Catch 22 situation because he needs good or ideally firm surfaces, but his legs will no longer tolerate them, and unfortunately finished lame when landing a bad Open at Whittington (his first victory since October '96). *P.H. Morris & Miss J. Francis — W. Salop (Peter Morris)*. 292 (M), 529 (Cf), 592 (Cf), 1151 (O).

PLATE 89   1151 Vale of Lune Harriers Land Rover Mens Open: Myttons Choice (C. Barlow), 1st, Charlie looks a little under-horsed   PHOTO: Peter & Marilyn Sweet

MY WEE MAN (IRE) ..10-7.. 10 b.g. Carlingford Castle — Pollerun Slave (Pollerton) 121. Very small compact. NH FLAT '97 r1 p0. NH '98 r2 p1 (3½l 2nd of 3 in Ch). P-t-P '97 and '99 (for Mr & Mrs W. Rucker) r5 w3 (2m4f Maiden, Restricted and Intermediate) p1 (last of 2); and last. Aptly named, but has plenty of heart and has made the transition to Ladies races very successfully. Denied by a head when caught close home at Charing, but staged a late rally of his own when winning by a neck at Penshurst subsequently. Does not stand much racing, but should be hard to beat in Ladies races in Kent next year. *Miss J. Wickens — Worcs.* 982 (L), 1107 (L), 1511 (L).

MY YOUNG PET ..9-3.. 12 ch.g. Young Man (FR) — Tierna's Pet (Laurence O) 55. Half-brother to Run Pet Run, Silly Pet (won Chasing since Pointing) and Tierna's Respect. Dam failed to finish in 3 Points. NH '97 r1 p0 (pulled in Hdle). P-t-P '95 and '99 r5 p1 (3rd of 4); last, pulled up 2, and unseated 1. Useless in his first six races (beaten two fences on two occasions), but remarkably improved on his final start, albeit in the lowest grade, and at least he can say he finished in front of Meadowleck. Mind you most of the equine world have managed to do that so perhaps he should keep it under his hat. *J. Manclark — Buccleuch.* 712 (M), 1123 (OMa).

NADJATI (USA) ..10-6.. 12 ch.g. Assert — Najidiya (USA) (Riverman USA) u332. Lengthy unfurnished half-brother to Hurdles winners, Clean Edge (USA) and Nannaka. IRISH FLAT '91/2 r4 w1 (12f) p2 (3rds). NH '93/7 r31 w5 (4 Hdles, 2m-2m1f, and 2m4f Ch) p9. P-t-P/HUNT CH '98/9 r13 w7 (inc 2 Hunt Chses, 3m2f-3m2f110y, and 4 Opens; inc 5-timer '99) p5 (4 2nds, last once). Able if rather faint-hearted under Rules, and in his first season Pointing, beyond reproach last year when a five-timer included Hunter Chases at Folkestone and Fontwell. Again proved his lack of bottle during an interrupted campaign in 2000, but probably needed the outing when bidding for a repeat bid at Folkestone. Has gained all but one of his 13 wins on a sound surface. Often wore headgear under Rules, but has never been blinkered in Points (contrary to previous reports). Quite likely to encounter more easy options next year, and will win if he's in the mood. *C.S. Hall — Southdown & Eridge (Suzanne Hall).* 129 (O), 286 (O), 1538 (3m2fH), 1625 (3m2f110yH).

NAGARA SOUND ..8-12.. 10 b.g. Lochnager — Safe 'n' Sound (Good Investment USA) 43. Workmanlike compact half-brother to Casino Sand and to Hurdles winner, Nova Lad. Dam won 2m 3-y-o Sell Hdle. NH FLAT '95 r3 p1 (2nd). NH '95/8 (for breeder, B. Preece) r14 p1 (3rd in Hdle); pulled up in Sell Ch final. Has always been exceptionally short of ability, and was gaining a first placing for four years when a fence last of three in his Members. Seems to be edging into virtual retirement. *G.L. Edwards — N. Salop.* 964 (OMa), 1195 (M).

NAME OF OUR FATHER ..9-12.. 8 b.g. Northern Baby (CAN) — Ten Hail Marys (USA) (Halo USA) p3242. Small neat well-made half-brother to Irish Hurdles winner, Tasik Chini (USA). Dam won at 9f in USA. FLAT (inc for M. Featherston-Godley, bought for 12,000; inc 2nd previously for J. Gosden) r11 p1 (2nd). NH '96/9 (for P. Bowen) r32 w8 (7 Hdles, 2m-3m, and 3m Ch) p15; also 4th, and fell in lead 3 out once. Cost Peter Bowen 2700gns and went on to earn £38,026 over jumps, and six wins during an excellent year in '97 included a hat-trick and an amazing acrobatic feat by Richard Johnson after the saddle had slipped at Cartmel once. Nothing like as successful when registering just one victory since, but made a most amiable schoolmaster for Emma Bryan, and beaten a maximum of seven lengths in three placings. Acts on any going, but has had a hectic time for one who is still a comparative youngster, and does not find anything in the closing stages now. *W.J. Bryan — Golden V.* 743 (L), 860 (L), 1066 (3m2fL), 1275 (L), 1458 (M).

NAMRON (IRE) ..8-9.. 8 br.g. Strong Gale — Rigton Angle (Sit In The Corner USA) p2p21p. Unfurnished. IRISH NH '98/9 r8 p0 (inc 5 Chses — 6th, last 2, and pulled up 2). Goes a decent gallop and often makes the running, but has a major wind problem, and beaten 15 lengths with just one horse behind him in his seconds. Acquired a tube on his final three appearances and surprisingly kept going for the only time when landing a Maiden on firmish at Holnicote in the slowest time of the day, but did his usual trick of compounding rapidly when adding a tongue-tie next time. Clearly not out of the woods yet. *W. Rayner, S. Durnford, J. Sluggett & D. Carey — Quantock (Kay Rees & Polly Curling).* 71 (OMa), 955 (OMa), 1101 (OMa), 1373 (OMa), 1469 (OMa), 1608 (R).

NANDA DEVI ..9-2.. 10 b.g. Scorpio (FR) — Muskcat Rambler (Pollerton) 2p48p. Enormous rangy half-brother to Bridgnorth Lass and Caromisu, to Hurdles winner, Ess El Ar, and to NH flat winner, The Angel Leek. P-t-P '97/8 (for Mr J. Knowles) r4 p1 (3rd); pulled up 1, and fell 2. Disappeared for 12 months after a crashing fall at Marks Tey in '98, but returned to act as schoolmaster to David Maxwell and Holly Campbell this year. Inherited last of two in his Members, and made some late headway though eventually well beaten in a Garthorpe Restricted, but otherwise tailed off and has surely been too big for his own good. *S. Hill — Granta H., & Cottesmore (Henry Hill).* 242 (M), 438 (OMa), 542 (M), 871 (R), 1035 (Cnr).

NASAYER (IRE) ..9-8.. 11 b.g. Asir — Tourney's Girl (Yankee Gold) pR3f3225. Workmanlike good-topped half-brother to James Isaac (IRE), to Irish Chasing winner, Feeling Grand and to Irish

Pointong winner, Davy Bustin. NH '94/8 (for N. Mason) r11 p3 (inc 3rd in Ch). Looked a Maiden certainty on his best form under Rules, but has been consistently disappointing, although he has managed four placings and was only beaten one length in the latest. Deserves to score, but seems to be rather let down by his rider, who is far from rythmical. Has gone missing for periods of 24 months and 15 months in the past. *Mrs M.R. & Miss H. Dunning — Cranwell Bloodhounds (Miss H. Dunning).* 234 (OMa), 439 (OMa), 507 (CMa), 798 (OMa), 1004 (OMa), 1269 (OMa), 1507 (OMa), 1603 (2m6f110yH).

PLATE 90 401 East Devon Hunt Members: L to R Native Alliance (Miss O. Green), 1st, and Exe Cracker (L. Jefford), ur, are ahead, but can you spot John Robin (M. Sweetland), pu, and Lord Spider (M. Miller), fell, behind? PHOTO: Brian Armstrong

NATIVE ALLIANCE (IRE) ..9-13.. 12 ch.g. Be My Native (USA) — Chelsea Charmer (Ballymore) p1u. Compact good-looking brother to Irish Hurdles winner, Chelsea Native, and half-brother to a winner in USA. Dam, half-sister to Musroora (qv '96 Annual), won at 8f in Ireland. IR 14,500 4-y-o. NH FLAT '94 r1 w1. NH '94/5 r7 w1 (2m6f Hdle) p3; final run at Cheltenham Festival. Most impressive in his only Bumper, but did not achieve nearly as much as was doubtless expected subsequently. Had a very hard race on his penultimate appearance (five lengths clear at the last, but beaten three quarters of a length), and then signed off at the Cheltenham Festival in '95. Resumed to win for the third time in mud when finishing alone in his Members, but was probably lucky, as Exe Cracker was level and apparently going better when he unseated two out. Has obviously had his demons. *M.C. Pipe — E. Devon (David Pipe).* 161 (L), 401 (M), 736 (Cnr).

NATIVE CANNON (IRE) ..9-8.. 8 b.g. Be My Native (USA) — Plamas (Tumble Wind USA) 31. Hobdayed. IRISH P-t-P '97 and '99 r3 p1 (2nd — unruly paddock, and reluctant to start and lost 30l; won 4-y-o Mdn, but disqualified for interference at last. IRISH NH '97/9 (worn tongue-strap) r10 p0; 10th of 11 only Ch; whipped round and started slowly once. Bought Doncaster, Aug for 2500. Has been temperamental and disappointing in the past, but performed reasonably when 22 lengths third on his English debut, and for a Sheila Crow horse ridden by Brendon Foster he started at a remarkably generous 10-1 when finally scoring in his fourth year at Wolverhampton. May have a chance in Restricteds. *R.J. French — N. Salop (Sheila Crow).* 966 (OMa), 1526 (OMa).

NATIVE COVE (IRE) ..10-1.. 9 b.g. Be My Native (USA) — Down All The Coves (Athenius) p51242f0. Compact good-bodied half-brother to Buckaneer Bay and Supreme Spirit (IRE). IRISH P-t-P '97 r4 p3; disqualified from 3rd once (not weigh-in). P-t-P/HUNT CH '98 r9 w2 (Maiden and Restricted) p2 (last of 3 once); pulled up 1. Won two minor Points by wide margins at Eyton in '98, but subsequently off the track for 12 months. Only managed to secure his Members this year, but gave two decent displays in Hunter Chases, when second to Grimley Gale on her favourite stamping ground and when falling whilst poised to challenge three out at Hereford (a race he could have won as it turned out). Partnered by Sue Sharratt on his final start, and might be up to winning a second division Ladies race for her in 2001. *E. Haddock — Meynell & S. Staffs.* 367 (Cf), 564 (I), 901 (M), 1023 (3mH), 1416 (O), 1524 (O), 1626 (3m1f110yH), 1648 (3mH).

NATIVE DAWN (IRE) ..8-9.. 8 ch.g. Be My Native (USA) — Twilight Dawn (Deep Run) pfpp25p. Leggy half-brother to Irish Pointing winner, Dawn Hunt. IRISH P-t-P '98 r2 p1 (3rd); and pulled up. NH FLAT (for O. Brennan, bought for 1700) r1 p0. A headstrong individual who invariably led until halfway in his last five races, but is strangled by wind trouble, stops alarmingly. Achieved a rare completion but as usual failed to get home when 12 lengths second over 2m4f, and as that distance is no longer an option there does not seem to be any sense in persevering with him. Has had a soft palate operation, tried in a tongue-strap, and tubed on his latest appearance. *Mrs P. Cook & Mrs A. Blaker — Surrey U. (Ann Blaker).* 11 (OMa), 131 (OMa), 284 (2m4fCMa), 709 (OMa), 1105 (2m4fOMa), 1397 (OMa), 1513 (OMa).

NATIVE ISLE (IRE) ..9-8.. 9 ch.g. Be My Native (USA) — Shuil Ard (Quayside) 23. Small half-brother to Lord Lard (IRE), and to Hurdles winner, Knayton Prospect. P-t-P '97 and '99 r3 w1 (2m4f Maiden) p0; 4th, and pulled up 1. Arguably unlucky on his seasonal reappearance at Kingston Blount as he was three lengths clear and apparently in control when a diabolical blunder all but stopped him in his tracks. Stands his racing badly and was not seen out again for another seven weeks when third at Bitterley. Yet to confirm that he truly stays three miles, but should win a Restricted if he does. *D.J. Caro — N. Ledbury.* 248 (R), 993 (R).

NATIVE RAIN (IRE) ..—.. 6 b.g. Jurado (USA) — Bold Lyndsey (Be My Native USA) ppp. Lengthy. Dam won 2 Irish Hdles, 2m-2m2f. Proceeded extremely slowly before pulling up in the first two miles when tailed off on the first rides for Elizabeth Lea. *Miss E.S. Lea — Cheshire.* 587 (M), 778 (OMa), 965 (OMa).

NATIVE RAMBLER (IRE) ..10-3.. 11 ch.g. Le Bavard (FR) — Native Shot (Random Shot) pp751. Tall rangy. Dam won Irish NH flat. NH FLAT r1 p0. NH '95/6 and '98 r9 p1 (3rd in 3m Ch); (10th of 11, and pulled up 2 in Hdles, and 4th twice, last, pulled up 2 and fell 1 in Chses). P-t-P/HUNT CH '97/9 (for Mrs A. Price) r12 w1 (Maiden) p4 (3rds, last once, and inc 2 Hunt Chses); pulled up 2, and fell 1. Out of his depth Hunter Chasing in '99, and well beaten under the owner in his first four attempts this season, but much improved under Scott Joynes at Dingley when just holding on in a fair Restricted. Usually sweats and races freely, and his rating has almost certainly peaked. Wears a cross-noseband. *Miss C.E. Stafford — N. Cotswold (Sarah Stafford).* 1311 (Cf), 1417 (L), 1460 (R), 1623 (R), 1664 (R).

NATIVE VENTURE (IRE) ..10-4.. 13 b.g. Noalto — Aiguiere (FR) (Native Guile USA) 32p. Smallish half-brother to Irish NH flat and Irish/English Hurdles winner, Go Now, and to Irish Hurdles winner, Cormac Lady. Dam reportedly won 7 races in France. IRISH NH '92/6 r23 w3 (2m4f-3m Chses, inc 2 Hunt Chses) p2. IRISH P-t-P '94 and '96 r6 w3 p1 (2nd); pulled up 1. NH '97/8 r12 p5 (inc 2nd in Sell). P-t-P '99 r8 w6 (Ladies, 2 hat-tricks) p2 (2nds). Nursed back to grand form by Emma Coveney in '99 after a while in the doldrums, but a beaten favourite three times in 2000 when his season was cut short in mid-March. Blew up on his reappearance, but seemingly had no excuses when outgunned by Lily The Lark at Parham. Has a history of leg trouble and the lively ground at Detling may have caused his problems as he failed to reappear. Stays well and suited by plenty of cut in the ground. *Mrs E. Coveney — O. Surrey & Burstow.* 177 (L), 307 (L), 573 (CfL).

NATTICO (IRE) ..8-12.. 10 ch.g. Buckskin (FR) — Lady Pauper (IRE) (Le Moss) 764pu. Lengthy unfurnished half-brother to Nouvalari (IRE), and to Irish Pointing winner, Anne's Farewell. IRISH NH '97/8 r7 p0. IRISH P-t-P '97/9 r25 w1 (5 plus Mdn, novice rideres, appeared to win by shorthead but awarded dead-heat) p4; pulled up 9, fell and unseated. Beaten at least 25 lengths in his first four runs for the new yard (jumped right once), but His Buddaha offered him salvation in a Restricted at Aldington, in which his only opponent was a donkey partnered by a 40-year-old who had never ridden a winner. Sent off at 1-4, he jinked left at the eighth and Sarah Gladders toppled out of the saddle. *D. Rolfe — Ashford V. (Gill Gladders).* 127 (Cf), 285 (CR), 675 (CR), 1104 (R), 1168 (R).

NAUGHTY FEELINGS ..8-7.. 7 b.g. Feelings (FR) — Pohet (Pongee) p6f. Big strong home-bred brother to Harry Laws (qv). NH FLAT '98 r1 p0. NH '98 (from W. McKeown's) r2 p0. An indifferent jumper who has soon been struggling in Maidens to date. His brother scraped a win at seven after dismal early displays, so perhaps he needs a bit more time himself. *W.J. Laws — Tynedale.* 426 (CfMa), 909 (2m4fOMa), 1084 (2m4fMa).

NAUTICAL LAD ..9-13.. 6 b.g. Crested Lark — Spanish Mermaid (Julio Mariner) f21. Dam is half-sister to Second Attempt (qv '95 Annual). Fell at the first on his debut, but then caught near the finish and beaten a neck by a stablemate in his Members. Continued his upward trend in a youngsters Maiden at Garthorpe, where he held on gamely after being left in the lead two out (the departure of Nick Docker proving advantageous to Jo Docker). A progressive five-year-old, and looks sure to increase his tally over the years. *D. Jones & Messrs Barclay, Brandrick, Hubbard & West — Cottesmore (Tim Tarratt).* 373 (CfMa), 542 (M), 872 (OMa).

NAWRIK (IRE) ..9-5.. 12 ch.g. Orchestra — Rustic Rose (Rusticaro FR) pp4p. Smallish half-brother to Irish Pointing winner, Burren Beauty (IRE). IRISH NH FLAT '93 r3 p2 (3rds). IRISH NH '93 r3 p1 (3rd). NH '93/5 r21 w3 (3m1f Chses) p4 (inc 2 Hdles). P-t-P '96 and '98 (for Mr & Mrs J.K. Petherer) r10 p2 (2nds, of 3 once); pulled up 3. Once a fair staying chaser, and gave one useful display in Points when second to Cavalero in '98, but has obviously had major problems and only once went more than 2m3f in 2000 when tailed off at Littlewindsor. Puts no effort into his performances now and looks finished. Has been tried in blinkers. *M. Garner — M. Flynn — Oakley.* 17 (O), 74 (CCf), 523 (Cnr), 736 (Cnr).

NEARLY A BEAU ..10-2.. 10 b.g. Nearly A Hand — Lucibella (Comedy Star USA) 5p. Rangy brother to Jeremy Spider, and half-brother to Copper Dart and Copper Rose Hill. Dam was placed in 2 Points (unraced 3rd of 4, and promoted from last to distant 2nd of 3). P-t-P '98/9 (for Mr M. Weir) r5 w1 (Maiden) p1 (3rd); pulled up 2. In a different yard for each of his three Pointing campaigns, and stands few races. Looked a thorough stayer when successful at Bratton Down last year, but weakened alarmingly in both outings in 2000, and like most of his trainers string was clearly under the weather. Worth another chance. *N. Shutts — Worcs (Theresa McCurrich).* 75 (I), 179 (R).

NEARLY A JESTER ..—.. 10 ch.g. Nearly A Hand — Jerpoint Jessy (Tula Rocket) upf. Unfurnished brother to Hurdles winner, Gentleman Jim. Dam, sister to Tula Point (*qv* '88 Season Annual), won 2m5f Hdle. A late starter who was backed form 10s to 5s on his final appearance (probably punters getting desperate to find something to win such a dire contest), but was let down by his jumping again and fell four out when 12 lengths behind the leader. Had been very slowly away on his previous outing. *A.J.H. Hallows — Vine & Craven (Alex Hales).* 249 (CfMa), 630 (OMa), 1062 (OMa).

NEARLY ALL RIGHT ..8-12.. 12 ch.g. Nearly A Hand — Solhoon (Tycoon II) 5p5pp. Compact quite attractive half-brother to Miss Drury and Taisie Touch, and to Hurdles winners, Solerof and Kingswood Resopal. Dam won 2 Sells, 6-7f. NH '97 r3 p0 (last, pulled up 1, and fell 1 in Hdles). P-t-P '94/6 (blinkered 1) and '98/9 r24 w1 (Maiden) p5 (3 2nds, last once); pulled up 11, and fell 3. A real reprobate until he turned nine, and won at Stallenge Thorne in '98, but hopeless in his last 14 starts (beaten 20 lengths minimum in just four completions) and pulled up very lame on his final outing. Raised his rating by 104 pounds after a season off in '97, but heading in the opposite direction just as quickly now. *S. Redwood — Tiverton Stag (Tessa White).* 144 (R), 315 (R), 560 (R), 1140 (CfR), 1376 (R).

NEARLY FAIR ..9-9.. 10 ch.m. Nearly A Hand — Fair Cone (Celtic Cone) p435p. Small lengthy owner-bred. Dam, half-sister to Straight Brandy (*qv* '97 Annual), won a Maiden and placed 3. Grandam, Fair Spirit, won a Maiden and a 2m Ch and placed total of 5. P-t-P '97 and '99 r9 w1 (Maiden) p2 (Remote 2nd of 3 once); 4th, pulled up 4, and fell 1. Outslogged an exhausted rival to win at Flete Park last year, but far too slow to get involved otherwise and beaten upwards of 15 lengths when completing in 2000. Wears bandages in front, and has stood few outings. *Mrs S.M. Trump — Silverton.* 164 (R), 315 (R), 524 (R), 728 (R), 1043 (R).

NEED MORE PRACTICE ..9-12§.. 8 b.g. Never So Bold — Princess Sunshine (Busted) 46u1r1. Lengthy well-made half-brother to Sunlight Express, and to NH flat and Hurdles winner, Nirvana Prince. NH FLAT '98 (for B. Preece) r2 p0. Can look quirky and does not seem to be the easiest of rides, but has useful partners, and is improving. Won two of his last three attempts and edged right on the run-in at Bitterley in the latest, where he had refused to set off the time before. Wears a tongue-tie. Has beaten little so far, but may be up to Intermediates. *J.D.W. Chilton & Mrs D. Davies — S. Salop (Pam Sykes).* 31 (CMa), 338 (R), 526 (OMa), 866 (CfMa), 993 (R), 1089 (R).

NEEDWOOD NEPTUNE ..9-10§.. 11 b.g. Rolfe (USA) — Needwood Nymph (Bold Owl) 955pppp71. Small sturdy. Dam won 3 flat, 12-13f. NH '94 r2 p0 (4th and pulled up in Sells). P-t-P '96/9 r15 w2 (Maiden and Intermediate) p5 (4 3rds; and neck 2nd); pulled up 1, fell/unseated 2, and brought down 1. A miserable spectacle who usually performs with minimum zest, but goaded into life by Andrew Sansome on his final appearances '99/00 when successful at Dingley, including an appalling Open which was run in a time one second slower than a division of the Maiden. Utterly lifeless when owner-ridden, and is usually visored and ridden in spurs. Will doubtless be trained with June 3rd in mind next year. *P.A. Bennett — Atherstone (D. Lowe).* 115 (CCf), 367 (Cf), 545 (O), 1008 (O), 1128 (Cf), 1265 (O), 1416 (O), 1584 (CCond), 1666 (O).

NEELISAGIN (IRE) ..9-7.. 10 b.g. Wylfa — Mystrique (Streak) 4p5093. Plain angular half-brother to Jellique. IRISH P-t-P '96 r6 p0 (inc last, pulled up 3, and fell 1). P-t-P '97 and '99 r16 w2 (Maiden and Club Novices) p7 (5 3rds, of 4 once, and last twice); refused 1, and pulled up 2. An admirable jumper, and deserved his successes in '99, but otherwise hopelessly easy to beat and only once better than tailed off this year. Often races in a tongue-strap, and seems troubled nowadays. *W.J. Turcan - Fernie (Nick Pomfret).* 25 (Cnr), 116 (I), 175 (I), 543 (I), 785 (I), 1035 (Cnr).

NELLS DELIGHT ..8-12.. 10 b.m. Idiot's Delight — Coolek (Menelek) pu3. Small sister to Castle Tyrant, and half-brother to Blue Beat and Man Of Ice, and to jumping winner, Cool Gunner. Dam won 2 Points and placed twice. P-t-P '97/9 r10 p1 (2nd); pulled up 5, and fell 3. Beaten between three and 25 lengths when managing to complete, but seems further away from a win than ever. Acquired blinkers in 2000, remains a poor jumper, and is definitely of no account. *S. Clark — Bedale.* 399 (OMa), 627 (OMa), 1003 (OMa).

NELSUN ..9-5.. 7 gr.g. Neltino — Sunday School (Joshua) p2p. Dam won 11 Points (inc 6 Opens) and placed 16 (inc 2 Hunt Chses), but was disastrous for Mrs Macfarlane after being purchased for 12,000 (failed to finish in 3 of 4 attempts, and broke down on final start). Started favourite twice (purely because of the Bailey connections), but the best he could manage was a 25 length second. Quite possibly capable of better, but it has to be worrying that he is bred by a stallion who gets many who cannot stand training and out of a mare who went lame. *Mrs F. Macfarlane — Pytchley (Caroline Bailey).* 194 (CfMa), 412 (OMa), 872 (OMa).

NELTI ..—.. 10 br.g. Neltino — Speakalone (Articulate) p. Sturdy compact owner-bred half-brother to Gillone (*qv*). P-t-P '98 r4 p0 (pulled up 3, and fell 1). Went no further than two miles on four occasions in '98, and failed to emerge again after figuring prominently for two thirds of the journey on his belated reappearance. Well-bred, but seems impossible to train. *Mrs J.H. Docker — Atherstone.* 373 (CfMa).

NETHERBROOK LAD ..8-11.. 9 ch.g. Vouchsafe — Netherbrook Lass (Netherkelly) p3p. Plain lengthy half-brother to Broadbrook Lass. Dam is an unraced homebred half-sister to 5 Pointers, including Dunsbrook Lad (*qv* '96 Annual). Grandam, Dunsbrook Lass, won 8 Points (inc 4m and 4m4f Opens) and 2nd 4. Great-grandam, Dunsmore Lass, won 4 Points for the Ings family. P-t-P '98/9 r8 w1 (Maiden) p1 (2nd); pulled up 5. Won a bad three-finisher Maiden in '98, but has looked wrong since, and not better than last in seven subsequent races. Rarely looks fit these days, and acquired a tongue-tie on his latest start. Absent since March. *M.H. Ings — Teme V. (Billie Brown).* 340 (R), 448 (I), 486 (R).

NETHER GOBIONS ..10-8.. 15 br.g. Netherkelly — Madame De Luce (Don't Look) 111p. Stocky compact. Dam, sister to Dialling Code (*qv* '91 Annual), pulled up in 3 Points. P-t-P '92/9 r46 w17 (inc 13 Opens, inc hat-trick '98) p7 (3 2nds); failed to finish 14 (on floor 6). Trained to perfection by Dick Baimbridge, and has now amassed 19 wins in 34 starts for him. Loves to bowl along in front, and not many can match him for speed though thesedays few turn up to take him on and the last time he beat a double-figure field was on his final reappearance in '98. Gets low at the fences, but Julian Pritchard excels on him and it was surprising to see Alison Dare renew her association on his final start for the first time since falling with him at Badbury Rings in '95. Almost as good as ever at 14, and it would be nice to see him notch his 20th success for Dick in 2001. *Late P. Clutterbuck — Berkeley (Dick Baimbridge).* 700 (O), 970 (O), 1461 (O), 1605 (L).

NEVA-AGREE ..9-11.. 9 ch.g. St Columbus — Nee-Argee (Rymer) 7p61266. Compact good-bodied. Dam, half-sister to Simply Joyful (*qv* '00 Annual), won a Maiden (at her 28th attempt) in '96 and placed 3 for Carole Ikin. P-t-P '99 r5 w1 (2m4f Maiden) p0; 4th, and fell 3. Capable of fair efforts on his day, but moody and lacking in consistency. Has gained both successes at Garthorpe under Richard Armson, but appears unable to handle cut in the ground. A much more accurate jumper than he used to be, but still not totally foot-perfect, and acquired a visor on his final appearance. *P.J. & Mrs C. Ikin — Fernie (Carol Ikin).* 119 (CR), 232 (R), 440 (R), 546 (R), 801 (3m1fH), 1415 (Cf), 1588 (I).

NEVADA GOLD ..10-6.. 15 ch.g. Kemal (FR) — French Note (Eton Rambler) 4123. Tall rangy half-brother to East River and Black Book, to Hurdles winner, Bolaney Girl (IRE), and to Irish Pointing winner, Serious Note. NH '91/8 r44 w6 (2m Hdle and 5 Chses, 2m5f-3m) p14. P-t-P/HUNT CH '98/9 r12 w2 (Confined and Club) p5 (3 2nds); ran out 1, and pulled up 1. Used to come from off the pace under Rules, but adopts forcing tactics theses days, and has achieved decent results in the current yard since a disastrous beginning in '98. Won for Ray Rogers at up ton and the partnership should have doubled up at Brampton Bryan next time, but despite jumping his rivals silly was run out of it near the finish. Made much of the running in a 4m2f Uttoxeter Hunter Chase on his final appearance and gives the impression that if his enthusiasm remains intact he could win again at 15. Suited by a sound surface. Has been tried in blinkers. *D. Yeomans — Kyre (Annie Downes).* 861 (C), 1357 (MOnr), 1545 (O), 1592 (4m2fH).

NEVER ON TIME ..—.. 7 b.g. Nader — Eurolady (Kafu) p. Owner-bred. Soon behind on his debut. *J.H. Forbes — Mendip F.* 874 (2m4fOMa).

NEVER WONDER (IRE) ..10-0.. 6 b.g. John French — Mistress Anna (Arapaho) u3c13. Tall good-looking brother to Frenchman (IRE), and half-brother to General Delight. A fair five-year-old, and won a three-finisher Maiden at Wetherby, where those who had backed him at 4-7 had to survive a scare when he was hampered by loose horses at the last and the rider lost an iron. Forced out at the penultimate when closing on his previous appearance, and had been very novicey but given perhaps his best display when five lengths third earlier. Could be a useful prospect, and it might be worth getting one of the top local amateurs to partner him in future. *Mrs M. Dickinson — Bramham (Richard & James Tate).* 168 (OMa), 282 (OMa), 398 (OMa), 696 (OMa), 1000 (R).

NEWBY END (IRE) ..10-1.. 7 br.g. Over The River (FR) — Comeallye (Kambalda) u5u221128. Lengthy well-made brother to Kenmare River (IRE), and half-brother to Sandy King (IRE). NH FLAT '98 r3 p1 (2nd). NH '98/9 (from M. Madgwick's, blinkered final) r9 p3. Partnered by a novice in early season and unseated him in two of four attempts, but has generally been most consistent since Dan Dennis took over, and completed a double after rivals who had apparently been going better left him in the lead (particularly fortunate in a two-finisher Open at Penshurst). Sometimes looks plenty game enough, but can appear reluctant on other occasions. Missed out on a Maiden, but was able to collect second in a very weak Hunter Chase, in which he started favourite but did not find much in the closing stages. Can possibly score on his merits in 2001. *J.D. Brownrigg — I. of W. (Philip Legge).* 265 (OMa), 325 (Cf), 706 (Cf), 825 (R), 1131 (OMa), 1247 (R), 1510 (O), 1537 (2m5fH), 1646 (3m4fH).

NEWCHURCH LAD ..9-0.. 10 gr.g. Motivate — Miss Rem's Girl VII (unknown) ppfp2p. Lengthy unfurnished. Dam fell in her Members for Mr Remnant in '96. P-t-P '97/9 r6 p0 (pulled up 3, refused 1, and fell/unseated 2). A consistently dreadful jumper from day one, but finally managed a completion when four lengths second of three finishers in a bad Maiden at Maisemore this year. Had looked likely to play a hand in the finish of a Howick event previously, but crashed out at the second last when holding every chance and there is a slight possibility that he could find an opening one day. *L.J. Remnant — Curre.* 482 (I), 601 (CfMa), 823 (CfMa), 1056 (CfMa), 1316 (OMa), 1405 (OMa).

NEW HOPE ..8-12.. 8 b.m. Neltino — The Beginning (Goldhill) 54. Small neat half-sister to Kelly's Original (qv). P-t-P '99 r4 p1 (last of 3); 4th, unseated 1, and pulled up 1. Beaten between 21 and 35 lengths in four completions '99/00, but her Neltino legs have already given way as she was lame at Thorpe in February and has not been seen since. *Mrs M. Bellamy — Woodland Pytchley.* 54 (OMa), 124 (OMa).

NEWICK PARK ..8-11.. 6 gr.g. Chilibang — Quilpee Mai (Pee Mai) u3u7. Half-brother to Mai Point (qv). NH Jun '00 r1 w1 (2m1f10y Mdn Hdle: *chsd ldrs, rdn 7, r.o to ld nr fin*). A tricky customer in Points and twice jinked and unseated and was 21 lengths last on his only completion. Favourite twice, but if his supporters retained any faith they were in for a delightful surprise when he left previous efforts way behind him to score at Folkestone. Will doubtless continue over Hurdles for the forseeable future. Had he remained Pointing, we would have predicted a lack of stamina. *M. Childs & N. Scotland — E. Sussex & Romney Marsh (Di Grissell).* 577 (OMa), 828 (OMa), 1383 (OMa).

NEW LIZARD ..—.. 7 ch.m. Rubicund — Bowtina (Rugantino) f. Owner-bred half-sister to Princess Bowtina and Captain Flashard. Dam is half-sister to 4 Pointers, including Pantomime Bell (qv '91 Annual). Her only appearance resulted in a March tumble. *C.P. Hobbs — N. Cotswold.* 568 (OMa).

NEWLYN ..—.. 8 b.g. Newski (USA) — Lynaberack (Ardross) pppp. Lengthy well-made owner-bred. Generally novice-ridden, and tailed off and pulled up four times to date. Dismounted in the latest. *R.G. Andrews — Silverton (Gordon Chambers).* 315 (R), 729 (R), 856 (CfMa), 1262 (OMa).

NEWMAN'S CONQUEST ..10-6.. 9 ch.m. El Conquistador — Newman's Girl (New Member) fp21f311. Small. Dam won 6 Points and placed 12 for the Dibbens, and grandam, Heather Mandy, won a Moderate and placed 8 for them. P-t-P '97/9 r11 w1 (Members) p3 (2 2nds); fell/unseated 5, and pulled up 1. Beat a rival who subsequently dropped dead in a match for her Members in '98, but a nightmare jumper since until acquiring Nick Mitchell on her last two starts. Has to go right-handed (wore an off-side pricker on her debut) but a speedy mare when the fences don't get in her way and looks sure to win again now that her confidence has finally been restored. Often taken to post early and has been tried in blinkers. *Mrs A.M. Reed & Miss C. Dibben — Blackmore & Sparkford V. (John Dufosee).* 2 (R), 458 (R), 633 (R), 931 (R), 1134 (Cnr), 1256 (Inr), 1516 (I), 1637 (O).

NEWT ..—.. 7 ch.m. Noble Imp — Daring Liz (Dairialatan) p. Small neat home-bred half-sister to Reptile Princess, Lizzy Gecko and Yealm Oyster. Dam, half-sister to Lizzie The Twig, won Maiden and placed 5. Grandam, Lizzy The Lizard, won 8 Points and placed 4m National Hunt Ch and placed 10 (inc 2 Hdles, and 2nd in National Hunt Ch). Inevitably unable to keep up when 200-1 in a hot Mixed Open, but at least her jumping looked competent until she pulled up after two miles. *D. Doyne-Ditmas — E. Cornwall.* 1561 (MO).

NEWTON POINT ..10-7.. 12 b.g. Blakeney — Assertive (USA) (Assert) 12212. Lengthy good-looking. 6800f. FLAT r13 w2 (14-16f) p2 (3rds). NH '93/6 and '98 (from S. Earle's; 4 wins previously from D. Nicholson's; 4 wins previously for T. George, bought for 6800; one win previously for G. Pritchard-Gordon) r36 w9 (8 Hdles, 2m1f-3m1f, and 3m1f Ch) p13 (beaten head once). Very genuine at best and ran up a sequence of four wins from five attempts to May '96, but had failed to score under Rules since, and missed '96 and '99. Jumping exploits alone earned him £52,958, and made an excellent schoolmaster for the newcomer Belinda Keighley, who handled him competently for two wins and three seconds behind Mr Custard, Glevum and Henry Bruce (beaten a maximum of four lengths). Lacked fluency over regulation fences, and had landed four Hurdles since his only Chasing success. Stays forever, but used to need plenty of driving (occasionally blinkered in the past). Probably prefers the softly softly touch now, and looked a bit moody on his final start. *Mrs E.W. Pegna — Cotswold (Dolly Maude).* 476 (Cnr), 751 (L), 967 (M), 1134 (Cnr), 1311 (Cf).

NEWTOWN RAMBLER (IRE) ..9-8.. 11 br.g. Step Together (USA) — Knocknahour Windy VII (unknown) p4f. Tall brother to Irish Chasing winner, Corrigeen Rambler (IRE). IRISH P-t-P '96 r2 p0 (pulled up 2). P-t-P '97/9 (for Mr W.K. Hooper & Mrs G. Pidgeon) r10 w1 (Members) p0; 5th, pulled up 6, and fell/unseated 2. Successful on the only occasion he completed from six starts in '98, and usually shows early dash before compounding rapidly, but stands his racing badly and off the track for 15 weeks prior to his latest outing. Looks the part in the paddock, but clearly isn't. Primarily used as a team-chaser and hunter by his adoring trainer. *Mrs G. Pidgeon — Farmers Bloodhounds (Jenny Pidgeon).* 2 (R), 27 (I), 1393 (R).

NEWTOWN ROSIE (IRE) ..10-2.. 12 gr.m. Roselier (FR) — Sicilian Princess (Sicilian Prince) pp22. Half-sister to Random Place and Prince Ceva, and to jumping winner, Cuthill Hope (IRE). Dam won 3 Irish Points and placed 4. IRISH p-t-P '94/6 r11 w3 (up to Winners of 2) p1 (2nd); pulled up, fell 2 and ran out. NH '96/7 (for Mrs A. Johnson, bought for 16,000) r5 p1 (28/ 3rd of 4 in Ch). Has had a chequered career. A triple winner in mud in Irish Points, and would have won her English debut but for falling at the last and letting in Father Sky in a five-runner affair (remounted). Proved to be an exceptionally expensive purchase and rarely seen after going lame and breaking a blood vessel in the same race in November '96, but staged a minor rally in the new yard, and finished a creditable second twice including behind Struggles Glory at Plumpton. Not the most fluent of jumpers, and is getting old. *Mrs M.A. Prince — E. Sussex & Romney Marsh (Sara Hickman).* 223 (3m2fH), 305 (Cf), 414 (L), 579 (3m2fH).

NEW YORKER (USA) ..8-5.. 6 ch.g. Gilded Time (USA) — Doris's Secret (USA) (Nikoli) pp769p. Compact half-brother to 4 winners in USA (including Bee El Tee and Certam De May). Dam won up to 7f in USA. Sold Tattersalls Ireland, July '98 for 9000. Has never beaten another horse, and looks a very troubled child. Wore a tongue-strap after his debut, and equipped with headgear on his four most recent fattings. Pulled up and dismounted in the latest. *N. Shutts — Ludlow (Karen Marks).* 169 (OMa), 451 (CfMa), 672 (2m4fOMa), 865 (CfMa), 925 (2mH), 1093 (OMa).

NGALA (IRE) ..8-7.. 10 b.m. Colonel Godfrey (USA) — La Danse (Le Moss) pppr437p. Small light half-sister to Irish Pointing winner, Le Bann. IRISH NH '96 and '98 r3 p0. IRISH P—t-P '96/9 r23 w1 (Hunt) p6; pulled up 10, and unseated. Bought Doncaster, May for 2500. Sometimes blinkered in Ireland where she signed off with a win in a bad race, and is a painfully slow creature who apart from when ten lengths fourth was never within 30 lengths of a success in the new yard. Proved perfectly safe for two young Tetts to start on, but they now need something a lot quicker to get them competitive. *C.C. Tett — Vine & Craven (John Porter).* 3 (L), 35 (Cnr), 331 (R), 477 (R), 887 (R), 1242 (M), 1393 (R), 1551 (R).

PLATE 91   1606 Dulverton East Mens Open: From far away and long ago, Nibble and George Cooper enjoy a break in deepest Somerset   PHOTO: Brian Armstrong

NIBBLE ..10-5.. 13 b.g. Nicholas Bill — Sigh (Highland Melody) p4221u114. Very small brother to jumping winner, Frankus, and to a winner in Hong Kong. Dam won at 8f. P-t-P '96/9 (for Mr G.I. Cooper) r16 w2 (Maiden and Restricted) p4 (3 3rds, last twice); fell/unseated 5, and pulled up 1. Won two of his first three Points, but had suffered 17 defeats before going to post at High Easter in March when he managed to end his run of ill luck. Dumped George Cooper at an early stage next time, but bounced back to record a further two victories, coming from off the pace both times and being produced to win his race at the second last. His problem was one of a lack of confidence at the fences, and is still prone to make mistakes, but weathers them much better now and can win again as he has few miles on the clock for a veteran. Acts on any going. *Ms C. Cunningham — E. Anglian Bloodhounds (Matt Hazell)*. 83 (Cf), 175 (I), 318 (Cf), 413 (I), 609 (I), 936 (Cf), 1184 (Cf), 1378 (Cf), 1606 (O).

NICK'S WAY ..—.. 7 ch.g. Nicholas Bill — Perspex Way (Perspex) pp. Tall angular half-brother to Regent's Way and Arctic Way. Dam, half-sister to Pitway (*qv* '87 Season Annual), won 8 Points (the first in Ireland) and placed 8. Looked green, but went at least 2m4f in both attempts, and may do better as he matures. *Mrs T. White — Dulverton E.* 559 (R), 1042 (R).

NICK THE BISCUIT ..9-11.. 10 b.g. Nicholas Bill — Maryland Cookie (USA) (Bold Hour) 952. Small sturdy close-coupled half-brother to Sweet On Willie (USA), to flat winners, Amber Cookie and Maryland Willie, and to flat and Hurdles winner, Master Charlie. FLAT r13 p3 (2 on all-weather). NH '94 and '96 r6 p2 (Sells). P-t-P '97/9 (for Mrs H.M. Knott) r16 w3 (Maiden, Restricted and Intermediate) p5 (2 2nds, beaten short head once; and inc last of 3 twice); pulled up 3. Inconsistent and unpredictable, but had managed an annual success in his three previous Pointing campaigns, including when landing a gamble at Wolverhampton in '98. Can look defective and missed eight weeks of the season following his reappearance, and never looked like winning on his return. Acts on a sound surface. Visored over hurdles, and has been tried tongue-tied. *G. Pollard — Albrighton Woodland (Jon Rudge)*. 611 (C), 1525 (L), 1629 (M).

NICKYS PERIL ..9-12.. 9 ch.m. Nicholas Bill — Priceless Peril (Silly Prices) 1p23. Small angular half-sister to Major Peril. Dam, half-sister to Paddy's Peril, won 2m4f Hdle and placed 5 (inc an Open and a Hunt Ch), but was basically insane. NH FLAT '97 r2 p0. P-t-P '98/9 r4 p1 (3rd); fell/unseated 2, and pulled up 1. Finally able to fulfil the promise of previous efforts when winning a two-finisher Maiden at Alnwick on her reappearance, but stopped quickly after making mistakes next time and has not quite got home in stamina tests since. Finds seven minute races too demanding a test, but should be able to find another opportunity. Manages very few outings. *J.S. Haldane — College V. & N. Northumberland*. 189 (OMam), 423 (R), 1081 (R), 1577 (R).

PLATE 92   532 Sir W.W. Wynn's Restricted: Night Irene (G. Hanmer), 1st, is ahead of Analystic (C. Stockton), pu, and Cherokee Run (M. Keel), 3rd   PHOTO: Peter & Marilyn Sweet

NIGHT IRENE (IRE) ..10-8.. 7 b.m. Rontino — Killbally Castle (IRE) (Over The River FR) 11. Dam is half-sister to Frozen Drop (*qv* 2000 Annual). IRISH P-t-P '99 r3 w1 (5&6yo mares Mdn); and fell (at last, when close 2nd but beaten). The most impressive winner of three races in mud, and the only horse to better her time has been Weak Moment, who was engaged in a battle to beat Bucks View at Eaton Hall whereas she was romping to a 25 length success. Suffered from oxygen deficiency after that race, and was given six weeks to recover from any possible ill effects. An exciting prospect who looks a natural for Hunter or Novice Chases, and lucky Mike Parr to have this one as second string to Lord Harry. *M.J. Parr — N. Salop (Paul Jones).* 532 (R), 1215 (Cm).

NIGHT RIOT (IRE) ..—.. 9 b.g. Riot Helmet — Evening Bun (Baragoi) p. Compact brother to Evening Rush, and jumping winner, Donnybrook (IRE), and half-brother to Irish Pointing winner, Straw Again. Soon labouring in a January Maiden. *K. James — Morpeth.* 44 (OMa).

NIGHT TIME ..9-10.. 9 b.g. Night Shift (USA) — Gathering Place (USA) (Hawaii) 535. Compact half-brother to 2 winners in USA. Dam won in USA. 31,000f. FLAT (inc for R. Hannon) r22 p4. NH '95/9 (for R. Baker; previously for S. Howe; one win previously for A. Hobbs; previously for F. Jordan; one win previously for A. Streeter, bought for 700; previously for O. Sherwood) r38 w2 (2m-2m1f Hdles, inc Sell) p8 (beaten head once); 23*l* 4th, brought down at first, and pulled up at 4th in Chses. Kept busy over the years, but has not scored since May '97 (when ridden by his current partner Gordon Shenkin, then a conditional), and unplaced on his final 15 attempts under Rules. Has broken blood vessels and been tongue-tied, and does not find things easy, but there is a slim chance that he might pick up a Point if he put his mind to it. *Mrs C. Wonnacott — Dartmoor.* 1041 (M), 1385 (Cf), 1514 (Cf).

NIGHT WIND ..10-0.. 14 b.g. Strong Gale — Kylogue Lady (London Gazette) pp. Tall angular. Dam won Bumper, 3 Hdles (2m-2m5f) and 3 Chses (2m4f-3m) in Ireland. NH '92/5 (broke blood vessel 1) r13 w3 (2 Hdles, 2m-2m1f, and 2m Ch) p3. P-t-P '96/9 r22 w5 (Ladies) p12 (9 2nds; and inc last of 3 once); fell 3, pulled up 1. A consistently useful Ladies horse on a sound surface in the previous four seasons, but clearly under the weather in 2000, and did not get his ground when he was able to compete. Jumps and stays well, and notably game, but finding another opportunity at 14 will not be easy especially if he is having to cope with a problem. *Mrs P. Tollit — Worcs (Pip Hooley).* 1066 (3m2fL), 1191 (L).

NILOUFER ..9-8.. 10 br.m. Nader — Latanett (Dairialatan) 1. Good-bodied half-sister to Some Action, Stephleys Girl, Oil Be Damned and Inky. Had done nothing more than invigorating than hunting before she arrived at Cothelstone as a nine-year-old debutante (the top age allowed in that particular contest), but sprang a surprise after the two favourites had come to grief (one literally). It looked an exceptionally bad race and she may be over-rated, but full marks to her for trying. *D. & Mrs C. Hobbs — S. & W. Wilts (Sally Kirkpatrick).* 1099 (OMa).

NINETEENOFIVE (IRE) ..7-12.. 9 b.g. Lancastrian — Coalauct (Crash Course) fp4pf. Light-framed half-brother to Irish winners, Lady Clarina (Pointing) and Ballybrown Flash (Hurdles). IRISH P-t-P '97/8 r8 p1 (45*l* last of 3); last, pulled up 5 and unseated. NH Aut '99 (for R. Williams) r2 p0 (beat Marauder when 9th of 10 in Hdle, and pulled up in Ch). Has contested 15 races but only ever finished in front of three horses, and two of those have never bettered last over jumps themselves! Very unruly at the start first time out in 2000, and taken to post early on his next appearance. *R.D. Griffiths — Kyre (Steve Griffiths).* 337 (CfMa), 486 (R), 865 (CfMa), 995 (OMa), 1323 (OMa).

NISBET ..9-3.. 7 b.g. Lithgie-Brig — Drummond Lass (Peacock FR) pf3. Very small close-coupled half-brother to Bold Navigator and Moreflash. Dam won 4 Points (including an Open) and placed 7 (including 2ns in a Hunt Ch). Sire only finished in one of 6 races, including 4 Points (*qv* '95 Annual), but his dam won bad 2m4f Hdle and a Members and placed 4. P-t-P '99 r3 p1 (2nd) and pulled up 2. Had three subsequent winners behind him when half a length second at Mosshouses in his debut season, and beaten just three lengths in his final outing this year. Could have done with being an inch or two bigger. Absent since early March, but should find an opportunity in 2001. *Mrs A. Rutherford — Lauderdale.* 45 (OMa), 114 (OMa), 425 (CfMa).

NISHKINA ..9-7.. 13 b.g. Nishapour (FR) — Varishkina (Derring-Do) p26532R4. Angular. Dam won 2 flat, 7-8½f (one on disqualification). FLAT (blinkered 1) r8 p3 (inc Sells). NH '91/3 (blinkered 2) r20 w5 (2m-2m2f Hdles, inc 4-timer in 3-y-o's; the first a Sell) p9 (inc 4 Chses). P-t-P/HUNT CH '94/9 r40 w5 (inc 2 Confineds) p11 (8 2nds); failed to finish 12 (on floor 7). Had managed an annual success in five of his previous six campaigns, including his Members for the last three years, but could not enhance either of those records in 2000. Got outspeeded in his local after setting a ridiculously slow pace (the race took 57 seconds longer than the next slowest on the card) and was well beaten in competitive events subsequently. Declines to exert himself nowadays and has been tried in blinkers to no avail, and visored on his last three starts. *C.J. Cundall — Derwent (Mary Sowersby).* 171 (O), 393 (M), 623 (Cf), 805 (O), 1231 (O), 1349 (O), 1583 (C), 1666 (O).

NISHVAMITRA ..9-4.. 11 gr.g. Nishapour (FR) — Red Nanda (Status Seeker) pp31. Tall workmanlike half-brother to Nanda Moon, to flat winner, Amron Lad, and to a winner in Spain. Dam won 2 Irish flat, 7-12f, including dead-heat. NH FLAT r4 w1 p1 (3rd); 4th 2. NH '95 r4 p2. P-t-P '96 and '99 r5 p2 (remote 2nd; and remote 3rd of 4); last, and pulled up 2. Beaten a minimum of 33 lengths in his four Pointing completions (including when apparently finishing lame at Tabley this year) prior to winning his Members, and looks most unlikely to add to his tally in more competitive races. *A.D. Woodward — S. Notts.* 115 (CCf), 543 (I), 961 (O), 1214 (M).

NOAH ..10-6.. 6 ch.g. Baron Blakeney — Amber Marsh (Arctic Kanda) 211f. Tall unfurnished brother to Morph. Dam ran in just 8 racesa to 13, including 2 Points for Ray York. NH FLAT '99 r2 p0 (tailed off). No match for The Red Boy on his Pointing debut, but to the probable surprise of many onlookers that day he went on to produce by far the more solid form subsequently. Completed a ready double and was impressive in the Restricted, and apparently unlucky not to complete the hat-trick when falling at the last with a slight advantage at an Intermediate (some of Morph's bad luck rubbing off on him). Highly rated for a five-year-old, and may be able to justify the mark as he rises in class. Already possesses plenty of stamina, and can act in softish. *R.H. York — Staff College.* 21 (2m4fOMa), 131 (OMa), 306 (R), 632 (I).

NOBLE HYMN ..10-4.. 8 br.g. Arctic Lord — Soraway (Choral Society) 112. Tall. Dam, half-sister to Carpenters Gloss (qv '88 Season Annual), won 2 Points (including 2-finisher Maiden on hard) and 3rd 3, and grandam, Skyros Lady, won 2 Irish Points and placed 3. IR 11,000 3-y-o. NH FLAT '98 r2 p1 (3rd). NH '99 (for H. Johnson, tongue-tied final) r4 p0. Bought Doncaster, Nov for 4000. Poor under Rules, but showed determination for hard fought victories in minor Points, and rallied close home to snatch a Restricted at Whitwell (wore a tongue-strap) sent off at 4-7 in an Intermediate, but was 12 lengths second and did not appear to relish the firm ground or short course. Can probably benefit from his assciation with Clive Mulhall again. *Miss G.M. Featherstone — York & Ainsty S.* 399 (OMa), 1000 (R), 1478 (I).

NOBLE STAR ..9-4.. 9 b.g. Jester — Mickley Spacetrail (Space King) 13p. Workmanlike brother to Jestastar (qv). P-t-P '97/9 r8 p1 (2nd); last, pulled up 4, and fell 2. Stands his racing badly, and usually fails to get home, but unearthed an ideal opportunity at Black Forest Lodge and handed the race after the leader took the last at a snails pace (in the hand only had an inch or two to spare after flagging up the run-in). Will be difficult to place in future as he is not good enough for sub-3m events. *Mrs J.M. Bush, S. Garside, K. Adcock & S. Horton — Beaufort (Joanna Bush).* 70 (OMa), 633 (R), 1616 (R).

NODDADANTE (IRE) ..10-5.. 11 b.g. Phardante (FR) — Loughcopple (Over The River FR) 31. Tall. NH '96/8 r16 w1 (2m6f Sell Hdle) p0; 5th, pulled up, fell 2 and unseated in Chses. P-t-P '99 r8 p0 (last 2, and fell/unseated 6). Has returned with an empty saddle in nine of his 13 outings over fences, including six Points last year, but still retains ability and was gaining his first success since March '97 when winning a Littlewindsor Open in which he made no noticeable errors under a patient ride from Nick Mitchell. Can win again if he retains competent handling. *N.R. Mitchell — S. Dorset.* 209 (M), 521 (O).

NODFORMS INFERNO ..9-4S.. 12 b.g. Idiot's Delight — River Linnet (Forlorn River) pp4pp. Leggy half-brother to Time To Sing. Dam won at 12f on a disqualification; and fell in a Point in '95. NH FLAT r2 p0. NH '94/6 r4 p0. P-t-P '97 and '99 (for Miss S.E. Lawrence & Mr R.G. Turvey) r9 w1 (Members) p2 (last of 2 twice); ran out 1, pulled up 2, and fell 2. Takes a demonic hold, and usually burns himself out, but amazingly fortunate to succeed in his Members last year when the three horses in front of him were involved in a schmozzle on the bend after three out. Led for a maximum of two miles in 2000, and subsequently destroyed after pulling up at Cothelstone. *R.G. Turvey & G. Guppy — Quantock (Kay Rees & Polly Curling).* 69 (R), 356 (Inr), 560 (R), 848 (R), 1095 (R).

NO DOZING (IRE) ..8-11.. 12 b.g. Bulldozer — Miss Pet Tina (Choral Society) 8f. Leggy half-brother to Tena Lass, and to jumping winner, Georgic. IRISH NH FLAT '93/4 r5 p1 (2nd). IRISH NH '94 r5 p0. NH '94 r2 p0. P-t-P '97/9 r8 p0; pulled up 2, fell/unseated 2, and refused 1. Stands very few outings and has put no heart into his performances since suffering a crashing fall on firm ground at Badbury Rings in '98. Ridden in spurs in his last three attempts. *J. Byrne — Avon V.* 33 (Cnr), 196 (R).

NO ESCAPE ..7-12.. 8 b.g. Escapism (USA) — Laki Lady (Frankincense) ppppp5. Tall lengthy. P-t-P '99 r1 p0 (unseated). Failed to survive the first on his racecourse debut, and still generally clueless when it comes to jumping, but managed to navigate his way to a completion on his final start when 59 lengths last of five in a poor Bassaleg maiden. Shows no aptitude for Pointing. Tongue-tied on his latest appearance. Has two handlers. *Mr & Mrs K.A. Williams — Gelligaer F. (K.A. Williams).* 489 (CfMa), 746 (CfMa), 823 (CfMa), 1055 (CfMa), 1300 (OMa), 1404 (OMa).

NO FIDDLING (IRE) ..—§.. 10 br.g. Glenstal (USA) — Gradille (Home Guard USA) p21130pp. Rangy half-brother to 3 Irish flat winners, including Canadian Patriot, and to another in Belgium. Dam, half-sister to Gravity Force (qv '93 Annual), won 2 flat, 6-7f. IRISH FLAT p1 (2nd). NH '95/9 (blinkered/visored 2 in '97; 2 wins for G. McCourt; previously for M. Wilkinson) r18 w3 (2m7f Hdle, and 2 Chses, 2m5f-3m) p4. Bought Doncaster, Mar for 1800. Had a well-deserved reputation as a monkey under Rules, but acts well in soft and has plenty of ability on his day, and was motivated by Christian Williams (pretty good, but not yet as good as he thinks he is) in a two-finisher Open and a Chepstow Hunter Chase. Came home unchallenged in both, and then ran perfectly well when third behind two hot pots at Cheltenham, but dogged it when favourite for a 23-runner event over 4m1f on the course next time prior to pulling up at 4-7 in a Point (the rider's explanation was that he had 'displaced his shoulder'). Sent hotfoot to the sales, and must have appalled his new connections when he refused to do a tap at Stratford (perhaps they should have glanced in a looseleaf first). Has aspired to 11-1, but could turn out to be a real turkey in future. *S. Fisher & R. Jones — N. Shutts — Glamorgan (Robert Williams; Karen Marks).* 343 (Cf), 597 (Cf), 742 (O), 1022 (3mH), 1103 (3m2f110yH), 1338 (4m1fH), 1614 (4mMO), 1648 (3mH).

NO LOSS ..10-6.. 7 b.g. Ardross — Lady Geneva (Royalty) 211. Sturdy owner-bred brother to NH flat and jumping winner, Arkley Royal, and half-brother to NH flat winners, Swiss Tune (in Ireland) and Buck's Palace (also a successful Hurdler). P-t-P '99 r2 p1 (2nd); and pulled up 1. A promising second in two of his first three Points, but obviously did himself a mischief on his reappearance this year and was subsequently off the track for 17 weeks. Returned in great shape however and justified favouritism as an odds-on shot should in both wins on contrasting ground. Has plenty of scope, will have learnt a lot, and looks a horse with a bright future. Must be followed. Wears a cross-noseband. *S. Pike — E. Devon.* 11 (OMa), 1464 (OMa), 1650 (R).

NOMOREMISSNICEGIRL ..9-2.. 7 b.m. Gold Dust — Tintern Memory (Cruise Missile) R2p. Narrow half-sister to Tinterndrummergirl. P-t-P '99 (for Mr D. Stephens) r2 p0 (last, and pulled up 1). Showed her first sign of ability when 25 lengths last of two finishers at Lydstep, but still yet to beat a rival in just five starts. Might achieve something more tangible in 2001. *Mrs S.A. Turner — Gelligaer F.* 601 (CfMa), 835 (OMa), 1222 (2m4fOMa).

NO MORE NICE GUY (IRE) ..10-4.. 12 b.g. Remainder Man — Vaguely Decent (Decent Fellow) 2313334132. Strong. NH FLAT r2 p0. P-t-P/HUNT CH '95/6 and '98/9 r22 w2 (Maidens) p10 (5 2nds; and inc last or 3 twice, after remounting once); pulled up 4, and ran out 1. NH '99 r2 p0 (tailed off in Nov Chses). Gave some commendable displays when out of luck in '99, but on even better terms with himself this year, and won two and three-finisher events at Buckfastleigh and Trebudannon. Stays well, and suited by some cut in the ground, though can handle much faster conditions and has managed to jump round in his last 17 races (has never fallen). Sometimes looks a difficult ride, and has been seen to hang (tried in an of-side pricker) but Mandy Hand does well on him, and another minor success is not inconceivable. *Mrs M.E. Turner — Dartmoor (Dennis Turner).* 69 (R), 203 (R), 256 (R), 310 (I), 558 (L), 726 (Cf), 1041 (M), 1388 (I), 1644 (3m2f110yH), 1673 (L).

NO NEED FOR ALARM ..8-5.. 6 ch.m. Romany Rye — Sunley Words (Sunley Builds) fp5R. Good-bodied. Pulls hard and has been a very difficult ride, and was 30 lengths last on her only completion (amazingly sent off favourite). Has twice made an exit at the fifth, when the saddle slipped once, and when she ran off the course with Polly Gundry once. May prove to have some ability, but at present looks temperamental, possibly due to having some Sunley Builds in her pedigree. *P.J. Quinn — Eggesford (Richard Barber).* 159 (CfMa), 254 (CfMa), 518 (2m4fOMa), 1241 (OMa).

NONEOFYOURBUSINESS (IRE) ..7-5.. 10 b.m. Sallucéva — Roriston Queen (Furry Glen) puupp3. Strong-topped. IRISH P-t-P '95/6 r9 p1 (2nd); pulled up 6, and fell/unseated 2. P-t-P '97 and '99 r7 w1 (Members) p0; last, and pulled up 5. Won a dire race for his Members on jockeyship in '97, but missed the following year and has performed deplorably since. Occasionally wears a tongue-strap, and acquired blinkers in 2000. Sometimes jumps left, but never looks keen, and must have something horribly wrong with her. *Miss T. Hammond & J. Dobson — Border.* 420 (I), 1081 (R), 1162 (R), 1326 (R), 1363 (R), 1501 (M).

NO PAIN NO GAIN (IRE) ..—.. 13 ch.g. Orchestra — Clarrie (Ballyciptic) p. Tall good-looking brother to Hurdles winners, Top Note (IRE) (also won NH flat) and All Talk No Action, and half-brother to 3 Irish NH flat winners. Dam won 2m Hdle in Ireland. NH '94/8 (blinkered 1; final for C. Parker; 4 wins previously for J. Gifford; 3 wins previously for B. Curley) r29 w7 (4 Hdles, 2m-2m5f, and 3 Chses, 2m-2m5f) p8 (2nd in Sell on debut, did not run in Sell agn; inc 1¼l 2nd in Ch after falling 5 out — rider lost whip — and remounting); fell 2 out when disputing lead once. Bought Doncaster, Aug for 500. Used to be a good performer on easy surfaces at up to 2m5f, but has clearly become virtually impossible to train, and only twice seen since '97. Tailed off and pulled up in an Open in a brief reappearance. *J. Murphy — Lanarks & Renfrews.* 110 (O).

NO PROBLEM JAC ..9-6.. 8 b.m. Safawan — Out On A Flyer (Comedy Star USA) fppu5ppfp. Small neat sister to Solway Saffy. Dam won at 6f; and subsequently won 2 Sell Hdles (2m-2m1f, 3 and 5 ran) on hard for David Harrison. NH FLAT '97 r2 p0. NH '98 r2 p0 (last, and pulled up 1 in Hdles). P-t-P/HUNT CH '99 r7 w1 (2m4f Maiden) p0; 5th, and pulled up 5. Generally useless and often looks troubled, but did manage to win a 2m4f Maiden at Hexham in '99. A total disaster since, and has failed to get round in nine subsequent starts and tailed off last when he did. Often pulls hard, but makes countless jumping errors and runs out of breath in a matter of seconds. Wears a tongue-strap, and acquired blinkers in 2000. *D.A. Harrison — Cumberland (Mrs M.E. Haughan).* 111 (R), 494 (L), 661 (L), 815 (Cm), 974 (L), 1079 (L), 1118 (R), 1362 (M), 1556 (2m4f110yH).

NO QUIBBLE ..—.. 7 b.m. Belfort (FR) — Spartiquick (Spartan General) p. Half-sister to Broad Statement (*qv*). Very well-related and connections may have been cherishing high hopes for six years, so it must have been a real dampener when she went lame on her debut and had to be collected by the horse ambulance. *J.M. Castle — Bicester with Whaddon (Richard Mathias).* 672 (2m4fOMa).

NO QUITTING (IRE) ..10-2§.. 11 b.g. Sheer Grit — Curraheen Quiz (Quisling) r7. Sturdy. Dam won an Irish Maiden. P-t-P/HUNT CH '95/6 and '99 r7 w3 (inc 2m5f110y Hunt Ch) p0 (refused 1, fell 1, and pulled up 2). Proved himself a useful sort when gamely winning a Fakenham Hunter Chase last year, but has been plagued by knee problems and has never managed more than three outings in a season. Stopped quickly, and promptly failed to live up to his name, on his reappearance and failed to return after making no show at High Easter subsequently and looks troubled. Bought as a hunter after failing to finish twice in '95, and connections have done well to extract three wins from a horse thought to be useless for racing purposes. *M.A. Kemp — Suffolk.* 94 (O), 607 (O).

NORDIC SPREE (IRE) ..10-0.. 9 b.g. Nordico (USA) — Moonsilk (Solinus) 2p323. Compact well-made half-brother to 5 flat winners (one in Italy, and one Night Spell, in Ireland), including Moonax (IRE) ('94 St Leger, and £425,779), and Moon River. IR 10,000y. IRISH FLAT r4 p0. IRISH NH '95 r3 p0. FLAT r1 p0. NH '96/9 (for K. Vincent; won previously for G.L. Moore; debut for C. Moore) r28 w1 (2m5f Hdle) p9 (inc 5 Chses). Brilliantly ridden by A.P. McCoy when winning a five-runner Hurdle in soft, and also when finishing second at three quarters of a length or less twice, but unplaced on his final eight attempts under Rules, and often looks ungenuine. Gave some fair displays on occasions in 2000, and the best of them was when a close second behind a 25-1 shot for Rilly Goschen in a muddling Ladies. Might be worth trying in similar company again. Regularly wears headgear, and added a tongue-strap on final start. *M. Clarke — N. Benstead — S. & W. Wilts (Philippa Chamings; Richard Parker).* 461 (2m4f110yH), 883 (Cf), 1171 (O), 1395 (L), 1541 (2m5fH).

NORMANDY DUKE (NZ) ..9-0§.. 9 ch.g. First Norman (USA) — Royal Step (NZ) (Ring Round The Moon) pppp. Tall strong half-brother to 3 flat winners in the Antipodes. NH FLAT '96 r2 p0. NH '97/8 r4 p0. P-t-P '99 (for Mr P.J. Millington) r13 p2; last pair 3, pulled up 5, and fell/unseated 3. Subjected to a gruelling campaign in '99, and has looked thoroughly jaded since his arrival in the North. Prone to make bad blunders, and is an utter rogue not worth bothering with again. Tried in a visor on one occasion last year. *Mrs K. Hargreave — W. Percy.* 46 (OMa), 976 (R), 1163 (OMa), 1430 (OMa).

NORMANSTOWN (U) ..—.. 14 bl.g. unknown p. Only went a mile in his Members, having been unruly at the start prior to dwelling. *Mrs C. Tett — Vine & Craven.* 1242 (M).

NORMAN WARRIOR ..9-9.. 12 gr.g. Petong — Petulengra (Mummy's Pet) p57p. Compact well-made half-brother to Hurdles winner, Witchway North. Dam won 2 flat, 5-6f. FLAT r24 w4 (8f, inc 2 Sells) p1 (3rd). NH '93 and '95 r9 p0 (inc Sell). P-t-P '99 (for Mr E. Wonnacott) r6 p3 (2nd of 3 twice); 4th, and pulled up 2. A decent miler on the flat, but did not take to hurdling, and has positively detested Pointing. Will not entertain the idea of hard work now and hopelessly tailed off in both completions this year. Regained blinkers in 2000. *J.A. Danahar — Kyre (Suzanne Hall).* 333 (Cf), 390 (L), 969 (L), 1313 (MO).

NORMAN WAY ..—§§.. 6 b.g. Nomadic Way (USA) — Skycap Lady (Derek H) prcfrp. Close-coupled half-brother to Captain Primitive and Blazing Times. Dam, sister or half-sister to 3 Pointers, was placed in 3 Points for John Cornforth (unlucky not to have won). Grandam, Skyvan, won 5 Irish Points. Already remarkably ungenuine, and will pull himself up at the drop of a hat. Connections soon ousted the dreadful Blazing Times, and they will surely despatch this one just as quickly. *J. Cornforth — York & Ainsty N.* 167 (OMa), 379 (OMa), 506 (Cf), 695 (OMa), 1001 (2m4fOMa), 1033 (OMa).

NORMINS HUSSAR (IRE) ..9-8.. 9 b.g. Glacial Storm (USA) — Little Slip (Super Slip) f6p. Compact unfurnished. IRISH NH '97 (blinkered 1) r6 p0 (pulled up only Ch). IRISH NH FLAT '97 r1 p0. P-t-P '99 r5 w1 (Maiden) p0; last, and fell/unseated 3. Produced an error-free round when winning a long Maiden in soft ground at Hutton Rudby last year, but mostly victim to careless mistakes otherwise and has come back riderless in half his Points. Not without ability, but needs intensive re-schooling if he is to make use of it. *Mrs M. Dodgson — Cleveland (Charmaine Raw).* 396 (R), 807 (R), 1000 (R).

NORTH COAST GIRL ..—.. 8 b.m. Birthright — Miss Mollington (Seaepic USA) uppp. Tiny. P-t-P '98/9 r10 p1 (2 fences last of 3); pulled up 7, and fell 2. Hindered by her lack of inches, and has only staggered to one completion in 14 outings when she beaten so far that search parties were being organised before she eventually hoved into view. Actually attracted some money on her reappearance, but it had gone west by the time they had reached halfway. *T. Long — Four Burrow (Stephen Long).* 1186 (M), 1389 (R), 1520 (CfMa), 1641 (OMa).

NORTHERN BLUFF ..10-7.. 11 b.g. Precocious — Mainmast (Bustino) p4432u. Workmanlike half-brother to flat winners, Instantaneous and Progression (won '94 Czech Derby). FLAT (visored latterly) r8 p2 (3rds). NH '94/5 (blinkered final) r3 p0. P-t-P/HUNT CH '96/9 r23 w6 (5-timer inc 2m5f Hunt Ch '96) p6 (5 2nds); pulled up 5, and fell 2 (at last with every chance once). Rattled off a five-timer in his first season, including a cheeky success over 2m5f at Uttoxeter, but has clearly had his problems since and often a very weak finisher over three miles. Has the speed for short distance Hunter Chases though, and gave a good account of himself when chasing home Shafi at Cheltenham, but can ruin his chances with costly blunders. *J. Deutsch (Bluffers Partnership) —*

Beaufort (John Deutsch). 79 (O), 463 (2mH), 750 (O), 1016 (Cf), 1341 (2m110yH), 1531 (2m110yH).

NORTHERN KINGDOM (USA) ..9-10.. 12 b.g. Graustark — Wonder Mar (USA) (Fire Dancer USA) 5p3. Sturdy half-brother to a winner in USA. Dam won 2 flat at around 8f in USA. $30,000f, $50,000y. FLAT (for S. Norton; not look keen in visor one) r12 w1 (12f Amat) p5. NH '96 (for K. Bailey) r1 p0. Looked promising when six lengths fourth on his Hurdling debut, but promptly went missing for four years, and faced difficult tasks in Points on his return. Not disgraced when nine lengths third in his Members, and conceivably worth trying again at 12. His sole success was gained in a five-runner race on fibresand in '92, but did have the distinction of having the future Champion Hurdler Alderbrook behind him in third! *J.C. Soden — O. Berks (John Bosley).* 5 (Cv&nr), 327 (O), 1202 (M).

NORTHERN PRINCE ..—.. 8 br.g. North Col — Chestertons Choice (Country Retreat) p. Workmanlike owner-bred half-brother to Chesterton Song and True Choice. Dam is half-sister to Motor Bike Man (*qv* '93 Annual). Kept up for a couple of miles before tailing off on an adequate debut at Chaddesley. *P. Thorne — Warwicks.* 618 (CMa).

NORTHERN YARN (IRE) ..9-8.. 8 b.g. Le Bavard (FR) — Northern Push (Push On) p14pp3p. Strong-topped brother to Le Vienna (IRE) (*qv*). NH FLAT '98 r1 p0. NH '98 r1 p0 (pulled up in Hdle). P-t-P '99 r5 w1 (Maiden) p1 (3rd of 4); 4th twice, and pulled up 1. Won a bad Maiden at Kimble in '99, but a shade lucky to follow up in a Kingston Blount Restricted this year as the clear leader made a bad blunder two out when in control. Well beaten otherwise, and although he is bred to stay well he frequently doesn't and may have an underlying fault. Needs to improve a great deal for Intermediates. *B. & Mrs L. Bedford & Mrs J. Bedford — V. of Aylesbury (Sally Skier).* 80 (CCfR), 248 (R), 428 (Cf), 749 (Cf), 802 (2m6fH), 1203 (I), 1485 (I).

NORTH NEWCOMBE ..8-6.. 7 br.g. Northern Game — Irina Newcombe (Langton Heath) p2pu2. Sparely-made owner-bred. Finished 40 lengths last of two and six lengths second of three in Maidens run at a crawl in heavy at Bratton Down, and there is currently no evidence to suggest that he is anything other than very slow. Will possibly be able to find a little extra in his second season. *Mrs M.A. Hall — Devon & Somerset (Jeremy Scott).* 563 (CfMa), 1141 (CfMa), 1520 (CfMa), 1609 (OMa), 1655 (OMa).

NORTHSPRITE ..9-5.. 7 b.g. North Col — Misprite (Master Stephen) 3. Owner-bred half-brother to Mismetallic (*qv*). Dropped from 10-1 to 3-1 when making his debut in an Open (the bookies trying to con the bank holiday crowd?), and in the event did very well to get within two lengths of Granville Grill. It was the slowest race of the day and the form could be suspect, but it would certainly be most interesting to have another look at him in a Maiden. Could well be under-rated. *Mrs A.P. Bird — Warwicks (Julie Marles).* 1192 (O).

NOSMO KING (IRE) ..9-9.. 10 b.g. Nordico (USA) — Selenis (Huntercombe) 9645u. Small neat half-brother to Hurdles winner, Ataman. Dam won 3 flat, 5-6f. FLAT r8 p1 (3rd of 5 in 5f Sell). NH '94/7 (blinkered 2) r13 p1 (3rd); virtually refused when unseating on debut; Sells latterly. P-t-P/HUNT CH '98/9 r16 w2 (Maiden and Ladies) p6 (4 3rds, last once); pulled up 1, fell/unseated 3, and brought down 1. Won a Ladies in very testing conditions at Lanark last year, but rarely runs up to that sort of form (the runner-up went on to land a hat-trick subsequently) and only once better than last in 2000. Regained blinkers this year, but to no avail, and one to avoid in his current apathy. *Mrs M.A. Kendall — Cumberland F.* 41 (L), 376 (MO), 492 (M), 661 (L), 813 (L).

NOSSI BE ..10-2.. 12 b.g. Just A Monarch — Beau Wonder (Veiled Wonder USA) 5p31. Small compact owner-bred half-brother to Handsome Ned and Zaroydle. P-t-P '96 and '98/9 r10 w4 (Maiden, Restricted, Members and Intermediate) p3 (2 3rds); pulled up 2. Has an excellent wins to runs ratio, and is a splendidly willing little horse, but has never managed more than four outings in a season and avoids sound surfaces. Faced a simple task in his latest success when making all in a two-runner Confined. Stays well, and is an expert jumper. *Mrs T. Arthur — E. Sussex & Romney Marsh (Juliet Arthur).* 127 (Cf), 288 (CMod), 824 (Cf), 1169 (Cf).

NOSY PARKER (IRE) ..8-6.. 7 b.g. Nearly A Nose (USA) — Splendidly Gay (Lord Gayle USA) ppu35p. Sturdy half-brother to 2 flat winners (one in Ireland). Dam won 2 flat, 10-14f; subsequently won 2m Hdle in Ireland. NH FLAT '98 r1 p0. Capable of prominent displays, but not a particularly good jumper and has no stamina. Finished last twice, but beaten about 30 lengths in both, and there does not appear to be any hope of improvement. Tried in a tongue-strap. *A.H. Harvey — Puckeridge.* 97 (OMa), 237 (OMa), 577 (OMa), 839 (M), 1291 (OMa), 1596 (OMa).

NOT FOR PROFIT (IRE) ..—§.. 9 b.g. Tremblant — Skebawn (Super Slip) ppupupRp. Small plain. IRISH NH FLAT '98 r2 p0 (12th of 13, and pulled up). IRISH P-t-P '97/9 r12 w1 (6 plus Mdn) p1 (2nd); pulled up 9, and unseated. Bought Malvern, July for 1500. Left to collect an Irish Maiden in heavy after the probable winner had fallen two out, but it was obviously a miracle, as he has failed to complete in 18 of 19 other attempts. Devoid of stamina (probably because of wind trouble — wears a tongue-strap), and also looks ungenuine (blinkered thrice in 2000). Almost catapulted Fiona Wilson into a tree when crashing through the wing at Bassaleg (at least she didn't drown in the pond), and ended his appalling season by pulling up lame. *P. Morgan — Llynfi V.* 38 (CR), 274 (R), 347 (R), 485 (R), 745 (R), 1054 (R), 1400 (R), 1568 (R).

NOTHING TO FEAR ..9-0.. 13 b.g. Day Is Done — Pembridge (Master Sing) 3557u. Tiny half-brother to Masters Nephew. Dam won Maiden and placed 3, and subsequently 3rd in Ladies. P-t-P '94, '96 and '98 r10 w2 (Maiden and Members) p3 (3rd of 4 twice, beaten 2 fences once); pulled up 1, ran out 1, and fell/unseated 2. Won two poor races '98/9, but employed as a schoolmaster in the latest season and filled the role adequately whilst beating just one rival. Unseated Joanna Buck when tried in blinkers on his final start. *Miss A.S. White — W. Somerset (Chris White)*. 351 (R), 523 (Cnr), 1473 (Cf), 1650 (R), 1671 (R).

NOTHINGTOTELLME (IRE) ..10-1.. 10 gr.g. Roselier (FR) — Tower Road (Polaroid) 4. Smallish sparely-made half-brother to Aughnacloy Rose (qv). P-t-P '96/8 r5 w1 (Maiden) p3 (2 2nds, dead-heat once; and 3rd of 4); pulled up 1. A good horse that has endured all kinds of problems and a racecourse appearance is a rarity these days. Looked a useful staying prospect when narrowly beaten in a fast time at Lockerbie in '99, and shaped encouragingly on his Hunter Chase debut on his sole appearance this year, but promptly went back into hiding, and will seemingly never be able to show his true ability. Would be a certainty for a Restricted at the very least if he could manage another outing. *R.A. Bartlett — Fife (Gillian Kerr)*. 686 (3m1fH).

NOTHING VENTURED ..10-3.. 12 b.g. Sonnen Gold — Dream Venture (Giolla Mear) 21p. Medium-sized compact. Dam won 2m1f Sell Hdle. P-t-P/HUNT CH '96/8 r15 w7 (inc 2 Opens) p5 (2nds, inc Hunt Ch); last, fell 1, and pulled up 1. An ex-eventer who has developed into a splendid Pointer, but missed the '99 season and did not need to be at his best to land his Members on his return. Suited by top-of-the-ground and front-running tactics, but clearly has his problems now and failed to reappear following a disappointing performance at Bangor. *A. Beedles & Countess Susie Goess-Saurau — S. Salop (Alistair Beedles)*. 565 (O), 1317 (M), 1559 (3m110yH).

NO TIME TO WAIT ..8-7.. 10 b.g. Dubassoff (USA) — Flopsy Mopsy (Full Of Hope) p55. Unfurnished brother to Chasing winner, Dubelle. NH FLAT '97 r2 p0. NH '99 r2 p0. P-t-P '98/9 r8 p0 (last 3, unseated 3, and pulled up 2). Can be headstrong and has worn a martingale, and has patently failed to stay three miles to date. Used to jump badly, but has at least improved in that respect. *Mrs J.M. Jones — Pendle Forest & Craven (Jo Foster)*. 1033 (OMa), 1330 (OMa), 1479 (OMa).

NOT MY LINE ..9-7.. 12 gr.g. Entre Nous — Uno Navarro (Raga Navarro ITY) p68. Sturdy compact half-brother to Irish Hurdles winner, Aye Surely. IRISH NH FLAT r4 p0. IRISH NH '93/4 r10 p4. IRISH P-t-P '93/4 r4 w1 (5yo Maiden) p2; pulled up 1. P-t-P/HUNT CH '95/7 r10 w2 (Hunt Chses, 2m110y-2m5f110y) p1 (2nd); pulled up 1, and fell 1. NH '98/9 r4 w1 (2m Hcap Ch) p0; pulled up 2. A specialist at distances short of three miles, and won a Towcester Handicap over the minimum trip in '98 after a successful Hunter Chase campaign the year before. Not always the most fluent of jumpers and made errors when well below his best on his return. Will be hard pressed to stage a revival. Suited by plenty of cut in the ground. *W.F. Caudwell — O. Berks (Matt Hazell)*. 153 (2m4f110yH), 461 (2m4f110yH), 684 (2m4fH).

NOTOOBIG ..9-5.. 9 b.g. Lafontaine (USA) — Sugar Owl (Bold Owl) 444. Tall half-brother to a flat winner. NH '97/9 (1st three for P. Cheesbrough) r6 p0 (tailed off in both Chses — last, and pulled up). Notooquick under Rules at odds of between 50-1 and 200-1, but plodded round safely in Points when beaten between ten lengths and 26 lengths in his fourths. Would need a bad race to score. *J. Wade — S. Durham*. 424 (R), 627 (OMa), 1004 (OMa).

NOT SO PRIM ..10-4.. 9 b.m. Primitive Rising (USA) — Sobriquet (Roan Rocket) p121. Sturdy attractive owner-bred. NH FLAT r1 p0 (furlongs last). P-t-P '97/8 r7 p0 (4th, fell/unseated 2, and pulled up 4). Carrying too much condition when failing to get the trip in the past, but much more streamlined in 2000 and reaped the rewards. Remains impetuous, but prepared to battle gamely, and it was a shame that she ended the season lame. Missed the '99 campaign so her rehabilitation may take some time. *Mrs D. Ibbotson — York & Ainsty S. (David Ibbotson)*. 507 (CMa), 798 (OMa), 1000 (R), 1326 (R).

NOT YET DECENT (IRE) ..—.. 8 gr.g. Decent Fellow — Yet (Last Fandango) uppp. Dam won at 10f. Showed no ability when failing to finish at odds of 16-1 upwards in Maidens. *T.J.C. Seegar — O. Surrey & Burstow (Andrew Irvine)*. 829 (OMa), 984 (OMa), 1396 (OMa), 1513 (OMa).

NOUGHTOSIXTY (IRE) ..10-7.. 9 b.g. Brevet — Arch Hall (Harwell) 1p112. Workmanlike lengthy. P-t-P '99 (for Mr M.J. Bloom) r1 w1 (Maiden). Won his first two Points in gutsy fashion, but a disappointing favourite when pulled up after making mistakes on his Intermediate debut and may not have enjoyed the holding ground. Got back on track with a brace of wins in March, including an impressive piece of front-running at Newton Bromswold, and was not disgraced when finding Gillone too good on his favourite stomping ground subsequently. A strong galloper with a determined attitude, and may prove good enough to upgrade successfully to Hunter Chases in 2001 though he may require decent ground. *Mrs F.M. Reynolds, Mrs C. Gibbs & Mrs L. Arkwright — Pytchley (Caroline Bailey)*. 6 (R), 75 (I), 413 (I), 510 (Cf), 868 (Cf).

NOUVALARI (IRE) ..9-5.. 9 b.g. Arokar (FR) — Lady Pauper (IRE) (Le Moss) fpp3. Half-brother to Nattico (IRE). P-t-P (for Mr N.W. Padfield) r3 w1 (Maiden) p0; pulled up 1, and fell 1. Won on firmish at Horseheath at the first attempt, but missed the '99 season and performed like a physical wreck in the new yard. Prone to diabolical mistakes, and must be given a wide berth until his health improves. *N. Shutts — Ludlow (Karen Marks)*. 173 (R), 445 (Cf), 863 (R), 1548 (R).

NOVA NITA ..10-5.. 11 b.m. Ra Nova — Jovenita (High Top) 1212p25. Small unfurnished half-sister to Joven Top, to Chasing winner, Tough Cookie, and to a winner in Belgium. NH FLAT r2 p0. P-t-P '96/7 and '99 r10 w4 (up to Intermediate) p5 (4 2nds); and fell 1. A consistent little mare who has contested 16 Points, winning six (lucky once), and finishing runner-up seven times. Has appreciated the extra weight off her back in Ladies races, and not disgraced on her Hunter Chase debut at Stratford on her final outing. Stays well, and can handle any going. Should combine with Valerie Jackson to win again. Successful on four occasions at Friars Haugh. *R. Black — Dumfries (Kate Anderson).* 361 (L), 661 (L), 974 (L), 1079 (L), 1426 (L), 1579 (L), 1648 (3mH).

NOVASUN ..8-12.. 11 ch.g. Sunley Builds — Owenova (Owen Anthony) pppp425. Sturdy half-brother to Rushenova. Dam won 2 Points and last of 3 twice for John Elliott. Grandam, Astra Nova, won 6 Points and placed 11. NH FLAT r2 p0 (tailed off both). P-t-P '97/9 r9 p1 (last of 3); last, pulled up 5, and fell 2. Capable of a bold showing for up to 2m4f on occasions, and might have been unlucky not to have been awarded a dead-heat when officially short-headed at Mollington in March, but will get fewer easier options. Can lack fluency, and has been tried in blinkers. *J.W. Elliott — S. & W. Wilts (Sarah Waugh).* 2 (R), 13 (R), 213 (CfMa), 455 (OMa), 520 (OMa), 786 (OMa), 1020 (OMa).

PLATE 93   1020 Heythrop Open Maiden 6yo&up (Div 2): Novasun (P. York), 5th, and Weldsun (J. Trice-Rolph), P, jump ahead of (L to R) True Hustler (F. Hutsby), pu, and Teachers Pet (Miss L. Sweeting), ref
　　　　　　　　　　　　　　　　　　　　　　　　　　　　　　　　　　　PHOTO: John Beasley

NOVATARA ..10-3.. 9 ch.g. Ra Nova — Asphaltara (Scallywag) 320. Compact well-made owner-bred half-brother to Nethertara, Asphaltino and Tombola. Dam was 5th, and pulled up 1 in Points for the late Tom Regis. P-t-P '97/9 (for Mrs T.H. Regis) r12 w3 (Maiden, Restricted and Intermediate) p4 (3 2nds); pulled up 4, and ran out 1. In good form for Caroline Bailey in minor Points last year, but jumped regulation fences appallingly for his new yard, and did remarkably well in the circumstances to finish as close as he did to Chasing The Bride at Ascot. Needs an overhaul in that department if Hunter Chasing is on the agenda in 2001, but should again be a force to be reckoned with in Points. Stays well and appreciates plenty of cut in the ground. *P.C.E. Woods — O. Berks (Gary Brown).* 300 (2m5fH), 800 (3m110yH), 1338 (4m1fH).

NOWHISKI ..10-0.. 13 b.g. Petoski — Be Faithful (Val De Loir) ppp1. Workmanlike half-brother to several winners, including Top Wing and Cleonte (both flat). Dam won at 7f. FLAT (visored final) r7 p0. NH '91/2 r11 w1 (2m2f Sell Hdle) p3 (3rds). P-t-P/HUNT CH '96/7 and '99 r13 w3 (hat-trick in Ladies) p2 (2nd in Hunt Ch; and last of 3); pulled up 5, and unseated 1. Pulled up in his previous six attempts, but beat a far more interesting stablemate when bowing out in his Members this year. Landed a hat-trick on sound surfaces in '96, but had been plagued by leg and sinus problems ever since and it was good to see him in such a spirited mood again. *C. Morris & T. Tarratt — Cottesmore (Tim Tarratt).* 118 (L), 230 (L), 463 (2mH), 542 (M).

NOW WE KNOW (IRE) ..10-9.. 13 ch.g. Denel (FR) — Struell Course (Green Shoon) 1up. Tall attractive brother to Antica Roma (IRE). IRISH P-t-P '93/4 r4 p1 (2nd). P-t-P '95 (for Mr M.J. Drake, Mr T. Doxsey & Mr R. Herbert) r4 w3 (Maiden, and 2 Restricteds — hat-trick) p1 (2nd). NH '95/9 (for M. Sheppard) r21 w3 (3m6f Hcap Ch, and two 2m2f Hdles) p6. NH May '00 r1 p0 (pulled up in 3m6f HCap Ch: bhnd, blun 1, t.o 14, pu 4 out). A useful Pointer in '95, but never really warmed to regulation fences and gained his best results under Rules over the smaller obstacles. Returned to the amateur sphere in triumph at Hereford where Julian Pritchard gave him a superb ride, but his old jumping frailties were exposed on a return trip when favourite for an amateur race. Has done well to win seven times, but could have achieved more had he been a more natural jumper. Suited by plenty of cut in the ground. *M.J. Drake — Ledbury (Nicky Sheppard).* 222 (3m1f110yH), 468 (3m1f110yH).

NOYAN ..10-10.. 11 ch.g. Northern Baby (CAN) — Istiska (FR) (Irish River FR) f2p21 1217. Compact half-brother to Zeniska, to flat and Hurdles winner, Terdad (USA), to an Irish flat winner, to 2 French flat and jumping winners, and to a winner in USA. 9000f. FLAT (tried blinkers/visor; 2 wins for L. Lungo; hat-trick previously for M. Bell) r 27 w5 (7-13f; 2 on all-weather) p3; one run at Velieferdi in Turkey. NH '94/9 (for K. Ryan; 4 wins previously for R. Fahey; previously for D. Nicholls; 3 wins previously for L. Lungo, bought for 14,000) r30 w7 (3 Hdles, 2m-2m4f, and 4 Chses, 2m-3m1f) p7 (short headed once). Bought Doncaster, Aug for 10,000. NH Mar '00 r1 w1 (3m11oy Royal Artillery Gold Cup: jw, made all, unchall). A fabulous competitor over the years, and five wins on the flat included a £12,135 prize. Has since earned £75,862 under Rules (recouped his purchase price for current connections) but had not scored since his finest hour in April '97, when he beat Bobbyjo in the Heineken Gold Cup value £37,200 at Punchestown. Left Richard Fahey soon after, and appeared to decline badly in the next year, but his fortunes revived again in 2000, and he gave some cracking displays on the prevailing fast surfaces (has never scored in soft). Can jump magnificently, and has done much better since being allowed to stride along in front. Particularly well handled by Lucy Horner, who became the first woman to ride the winner of the Royal Artillery Gold Cup at Sandown since its inception in 1867. His next best success was at Exeter, but could not cope with Grimley Gale there, and also had to give best to Coulton at Sandown. A credit to the new owner, but even more so to himself. *R. Cook — Surrey U. (Chris Elliott).* 4 (O), 59 (MO), 152 (3m1f110yH), 470 (2m4f110yH), 680 (3m1fH), 1432 (3m1fH), 1538 (3m2fH), 1600 (2m5f110yH).

NUCLEAR BEACH ..—.. 6 b.g. Henbit (USA) — Rose Orchard (Rouser) p. Tall rangy. Dam, half-sister to Gamay, won 2 Points and placed 7 (inc a Hunt Ch). Bought Doncaster, Aug for 3300. Very novicey and never got involved in a most uncompetitive Members (backed from twos to threes despite looking very backward). *The Beach Boys Partnership — Cambs Univ (Matthew Gingell).* 174 (M).

NUNS CONE ..10-2§§.. 13 ch.g. Celtic Cone — Nunswalk (The Parson) p2p. Small neat brother to Nunson, and half-brother to Mariners Walk and Nuns Best Friend, and to Hurdles winners, Nuns Royal and Nuns Jewel. Dam won Sell Hdle and Ch, both 2m. NH FLAT '93 r3 p0. NH '94/8 r21 w3 (2m1f-3m Hdles) p3 (inc Sell). P-t-P '99 (for Mrs H. Walsgrove) r6 p0 (pulled up 5, and unseated 1). Won for three different trainers when a former frequent front-runner, but never tried over fences under Rules, and has not approved of the obstacles in Points. Gave up as soon as a struggle loomed when a remote second at Garthorpe this year, and pulled up lame at Dingley next time. *Miss M.E. Crowden — Woodland Pytchley (D. Lane).* 1503 (Cf), 1583 (C), 1665 (L).

NURSERY STORY ..—.. 13 ch.g. Ayyabaan — Sharp Story (Sharpen Up) ppu. Tiny half-brother to Sunny Story and Noddy's Story. NH FLAT '94 r2 p0. NH '95 r2 p0 (tailed off in Hdle and when last in Ch). P-t-P '93/4 and '96 (for Mr A. Aldridge) r9 p1 (last of 3); failed to finish 8 (fell/unseated 2). Revived unsuccessfully after going AWOL for three seasons, and appeared to be lame at Guilsborough on her middle run. Used to virtually bolt in the lead, but age has dulled his impetuosity. *Mrs L. Gibbon — Essex & Suffolk.* 761 (R), 1009 (CR), 1115 (OMa).

NUTTY SOLERA ..9-0§.. 11 ch.g. Henbit (USA) — Friendly Cherry (Bargello) pp956. Tall rangy. Dam failed to finish in 6 Points (consistently unwilling, and did not earn a bean in 25 races over 7 years). IRISH P-t-P '96 r4 w1 (6yo&up Maiden) p1 (2nd); pulled up 2. IRISH NH FLAT '96 r1 w1. NH FLAT '96 r3 p2. NH '97/8 r11 p2; 6th and pulled up 2 in Chses. P-t-P '99 r3 p0 (pulled up 3). Looked potentially useful when winning twice in Ireland in '96, but a major disappointment since his exportation and has frequently appeared ungenuine. Flattered by his 14 lengths fifth at Bitterley as the race was run at a crawl, and finished stone last in his Members subsequently. *W.G. & Mrs S. Jordan — Albrighton Woodland (Mark Wellings).* 296 (I), 615 (CMod), 862 (Cf), 1090 (I), 1629 (M).

OAK HOUSE ..—.. 9 ch.g. Revlow — Hana Bako (Duke Of Ragusa) pp. Tall lengthy attractive. P-t-P '99 r2 p0 (pulled up 3). Looks the business, but has never shown the slightest interest in five Points, and failed to reappear following another ungenuine performance at Cottenham in February. *Mrs P. King — Suffolk (Julie Read).* 87 (OMa), 179 (R).

OAKLANDS BILLY ..9-7.. 12 b.g. Silly Prices — Fishermans Lass (Articulate) p3f. Sturdy close-coupled half-brother to Carole's Delight and Mamica (Chasing winner since Pointing), and to Hurdles winner, Royal Invader. Dam failed to finish in 10 Points (fell/unseated 3). NH '97 r2 p0 (5th of 6, and pulled up 1 in Chses). P-t-P/HUNT CH '98/9 r7 p1 (last of 2); failed to finish 4, fell 1, and brought down 1. A habitual front-runner, but does not stay, and has only ever managed two Pointing completions. Prone to make mistakes and stands few outings. *R.G. Russ — Cleveland.* 1329 (OMa), 1353 (OMa), 1480 (OMa).

OAKLANDS JIMMY ..—.. 7 b.g. Primitive Rising (USA) — Sovereign Gal (Sovereign King) ppp. A rank outsider when pulled up in Maidens, and could be bent on emulating his dam's unenviable record. *R.G. Russ — Cleveland.* 803 (MMa), 1330 (OMa), 1479 (OMa).

OAKLANDS MILLIE (IRE) ..9-0.. 8 b.m. Millfontaine — Milpe (Milan) pup36p. Narrow. P-t-P '98 r1 p0 (pulled up). Has displayed a little speed, but beaten out of sight when completing, and is by no means a safe conveyance. Lacks scope for improvement. *P. Williamson — Hurworth.* 138 (OMa), 281 (OMa), 399 (OMa), 619 (M), 1032 (OMa), 1480 (OMa).

OAKLANDS WOLF ..9-4.. 10 b.g. Little Wolf — Savage Sally (Owen Anthony) 4p. Small neat brother to Little Sal, and half-brother to Savage Oak. Dam won 4 Points and placed 2. NH '98 (from J. Neville's) r4 p0 (inc 11th of 12, and pulled up 2). 15 lengths fourth in a Maiden with a subsequent dual winner just behind him, but has obviously had problems, and broke down next time. *K.M. Stanworth — Tredegar F. (Tim Jones).* 72 (OMa), 205 (OMa).

OAT COUTURE ..10-1.. 13 b.g. Oats — Marjoemin (Import) uf544u. Tall workmanlike half-brother to Give It Laldy. Dam dead-heated for Maiden and placed 4 (ran to '91). NH FLAT '94 r1 p0. NH '94/7 and '99 (for L. Lungo; often blinkered and tongue-tied latterly) r27 w6 (4 Hdles, 2m6f, and 2 Chses, 2m-2m5f) p6 (2nds, beaten neck twice). Not very easy to train and had two absences of more than a year under Rules, but a decent performer at his best, and was good enough to win his final start in '99. Inconsistent and has never been a reliable jumper, and got the novice Shelley Johnstone into some trouble in Points, but was two lengths down and staying on when coming to grief at the final fence in the latest. One-paced these days and must have mud. Did not do badly when completing, but would make it difficult to score if returning at 13. *Miss S. Johnstone — Buccleuch.* 109 (L), 361 (L), 494 (L), 661 (L), 1079 (L), 1150 (L).

OBELOS (USA) ..—.. 10 ch.g. Diesis — Fair Sousanne (Busted) pp. Angular brother to flat winner, Gisarne (won Lupe Stakes), and half-brother to 4 flat winners, including Incisive, Belhomme and Admiral's Inn. FLAT (tried visored; one win for Miss S. Wilton, bought for 9000; one win previously for Mrs J. Cecil) r24 w2 (10f, 19 ran once) p5. NH '97/8 (for R. Frost; previously for Miss S. Wilton) r8 p2 (Sells). Produced a smart performance on the flat when three quarters of a length second to Pasternac in a valuable 20-runner race at York, but has suffered pain (missed '94 with a cracked pelvis and lame in '95), and generally untrustworthy. A weak finisher over Hurdles and was once a distant second to Miss Ondee (*qv*), and his two attempts in Points were far from encouraging. *Mrs A. Ray — Dart V. & S. Pool H. (Mags Ree).* 599 (L), 895 (MO).

PLATE 94   *1142 Vale of Aylesbury Hunt Members: Oboedire (D. Barlow), 1st*

PHOTO: Brian Armstrong

OBOEDIRE (IRE) ..10-0.. 8 br.g. Royal Fountain — Another Pride (Golden Love) 151. Tall half-brother to Irish NH flat, Pointing and Chasing winner, Master McCartan, and to Irish Pointing winners, Fools With Horses and Lancastrian Pride (died notching his fourth consecutive win, including 2 Chses).

Dam, half-sister to Bocock's Pride (qv '98 Annual), won 2 Points, a Hunt Ch, and a 3m Ch in Ireland. P-t-P '99 r3 w1 (Maiden) p0; unseated 1, and pulled up 1. Has won three modest races in resolute fashion, but yet to beat anything of note and has already proved that he needs quite a severe test of stamina to be effective. Jumps soundly, and should have the scope to progress as he is raised in class. Acts in soft. *T.D.B. Barlow — V. of Aylesbury (Lawney Hill).* 80 (CCfR), 785 (I), 1142 (M).

OFFICE HOURS ..9-2.. 9 b.g. Danehill (USA) — Charmina (FR) (Nonoalco USA) 2. Compact brother to flat winner, Great Child, and half-brother to 4 flat winners (3 abroad). Dam won at 8f in France. 12,500y. FLAT (placings for C. Cyzer; tried blinkered) r24 p5. NH '96/9 (for R. Lee, bought for 4200; previously for R. Baker, bought for 825; previously for W.G.M. Turner) r14 p1 (2½f 3rd in Sell); inc pulled up 4 and fell 2; last and fell 2 in Chses. Bought Doncaster. Nov for 3200. Showed ability in one Selling Hurdle, but much more often gave the impression of having something wrong with him, and occasionally tongue-tied. Backed down to favourite in his Members, and a 15 length second behind a fair performer suggested he might be capable of winning a Maiden, but was not seen again. *Miss B.M. Neal — Burton (Tony Walker).* 435 (M).

OFFLEY LUCIELASTIC ..9-8.. 8 b.m. Tromeros — Village Pride (Quality Fair) ff451. Leggy unfurnished owner-bred sister to Offley Thomas, and half-sister to First Touch. P-t-P '98/9 r6 w1 (Maiden) p3 (2 2nds; and 3rd of 4); 6th, and pulled up 1. Failed to make the anticipated improvement in her third season due mainly to her early season jumping lapses. Justified favouritism in a poor Flagg Confined on her final start, but forfeited the chance of a Restricted success in the process. Might be able to hold her own in more competitive races now that her fencing is more assured. *Miss J.L. Hartley — N. Salop (Richard Hollinshead).* 173 (R), 371 (R), 532 (R), 905 (C), 1252 (Cf).

OFFLEY THOMAS ..—.. 7 b.g. Tromeros — Village Pride (Quality Fair) p. Owner-bred brother to Offley Lucielastic (qv). Appeared to have a setback on his debut, but it is possible that he can achieve something when returning. *Miss J.L. Hartley & R. Wycherley — N. Salop (Richard Hollinshead).* 569 (OMa).

OFFSHORE (IRE) ..8-11.. 8 b.g. Over The River (FR) — Parson's Princess (The Parson) p4p. Lengthy unfurnished half-brother to Irish NH flat winner, Indalo. NH FLAT '98 (for J. Gifford) r3 p1 (3rd); and 4th 2. Showed some ability when beaten between five lengths and 22 lengths in Bumpers, and was sent off favourite for a Maiden, but made mistakes and was beaten about 20 lengths. Appears to be very hard to train, because he then disappeared for almost four months before looking to go lame. *F.R. Jackson — O. Surrey & Burstow.* 17 (O), 60 (OMa), 1508 (M).

OFF THE CUFF (IRE) ..—.. 8 b.g. Brush Aside (USA) — Woodford Dawn (Deep Run) upp. Small unimpressive. Dam won Irish NH flat. P-t-P '99 (for Mr R. Ogden) r3 w1 (Maiden) p0; and pulled up 2. Won the fastest of three division of a Bratton Down Maiden last year, but off the track for ten weeks following his second appearance in 2000, and broke down irreparably at Holnicote on his return. *H.B. Geddes — Beaufort (Richard Barber).* 260 (R), 458 (R), 1467 (R).

OFLAHERTY'S BABE (IRE) ..10-1.. 12 b.g. Arapahos (FR) — Glittering Steel (Golden Love) 3bf2. Robust attractive half-brother to Kinsale Florale (IRE). IRISH P-t-P '93/4 r15 w1 (Confined Maiden for novice riders) p3; pulled up 3, and fell/unseated 6. P-t-P '95/6 and '98/9 r17 w3 (up to Confined) p3 (2 2nds; 3 once); pulled up 5, and fell 2. Forced to endure as many lows as highs in his five competitive seasons in England, and in the form if his life when successful twice last year, but finished lame after attempting to make all in his Members and has been retired. *D.J. Harding-Jones — Puckeridge (Perry Harding-Jones).* 83 (Cf), 223 (3m2fH), 318 (Cf), 549 (Cf).

O'FLAHERTY'S (IRE) ..9-7.. 9 ch.g. Balinger — Deise Lady (Le Bavard FR) 21. Tall workmanlike. Dam won Irish Point. IRISH P-t-P '98 r4 p2 (2nds); fell 2 (when 2nd at last once). IRISH HUNT CH '98 r1 p0. P-t-P '99 r2 p1 (2nd of 3); and unseated 1. Runner-up in four of his first six Points, but eventually came good in the slowest time of the day at Upper Sapey on his latest outing. No world-beater, and might struggle in Restricteds particularly if his astute yard are not prepared to offer him board and lodgings any more. Usually starts at a false price. *Mrs H. Dalton — Wheatland (Andrew Dalton).* 439 (OMa), 703 (OMa).

OH SO DROLL ..9-0.. 7 b.g. Teenoso (USA) — Jolejester (Relkino) 2f. Dam, half-sister to Global Legend (qv), pulled up in a Point, but previously won a NH flat and 3rd 2 (inc a flat race). P-t-P '99 r1 p0 (fell). Runner-up to a potentially decent animal at Eyton on his reappearance, but on the floor in both his other Points (at the first in the latest) and getting few opportunities to practice his art. In a top yard and ought to be able to win in his third season. *R.L. Burton & N. Fielding - S. Salop (Andrew Dalton).* 570 (2m4fCfMa), 866 (CfMa).

OH SO TRENDY ..—.. 12 gr.g. Baron Blakeney — Trentishoe (Romany Air) u. Half-brother to Trendy Lady. Dam won 3m2f Hunt Ch and 6 Points and 2nd 4 (inc 2 Hunt Chses) for Gail Harrison, and won 2 HCap Chses (3m1f-3m2f) and placed 4 from late F. Walwyn's. P-t-P '99 (for Miss G.M.A. Harrison) r2 p0 (pulled up 2). Out of a splendid mare, but a latecomer to racing, and does not seem to be taking it very seriously. Only went 1m2f before ditching the rider in his latest attempt. *R.J. Alford — Taunton V.H.* 1241 (OMa).

OISIN DUBH (IRE) ..9-12.. 12 b.g. Supreme Leader — Gaoth Na Bride (Strong Gale) uu21. Workmanlike half-brother to Ar Aghaidh Abhaile (IRE) (*qv*). IRISH P-t-p '94/5 r9 p2; pulled up 2, and on floor 3. IRISH NH FLAT '96 r1 p0. P-t-P/HUNT CH '97/9 r8 p1 (3rd); pulled up 6, and fell 1. Lightly raced and often overfaced in previous years, but sensibly campaigned in 2000 and rewarded the faithful when successful in a poor Maiden at Peper Harow on his final appearance. Usually takes a keen hold, and peppers his round with mistakes, but jumped and settled perfectly well for Emma Coveney, and might be able to find a weak Restricted in 2001. *K. Tork — O. Surrey & Burstow.* 679 (OMa), 709 (OMa), 828 (OMa), 1397 (OMa).

OKEFORD (IRE) ..10-2.. 7 b.g. Rakaposhi King — Sheer Water (Vital Season) u211. Compact sturdy. Dam won 8 Points (concluded with 4-timer in Ladies) and 2nd for Robert Alner (was rated 10-8). NH FLAT '99 r1 p0. NH '99 (from R. Alner's) r1 p0. Attractively bred, but had looked backward in his early races, although he was heavily supported in his two Pointing defeats. Got into the groove subsequently, and was starting to look quite useful when he unfortunately broke down on the firmish ground at Kingston Blount. A watching brief will be required if he returns. *Mrs B. Tarlo — Portman (Louise Alner).* 30 (CMa), 329 (CfMa), 874 (2m4fOMa), 1482 (R).

OLD HARRY'S WIFE ..9-2.. 11 b.m. Idiot's Delight — Blakesware Gift (Dominion) fp5u53p. Workmanlike lengthy. Dam won at 12f, and won 2m Hdle (both Sells). P-t-P '96/9 r20 w1 (Maiden) p4 (3 2nds, last once; and 2 fences 3rd of 4); pulled up 5, and fell/unseated 2. Did eventually break her duck in a two-finisher Maiden in '98, but finding life increasingly difficult in Restricteds since. Still not a fluent jumper, but her main failing is a lack of stamina, and consistently on the retreat well before the finish theses days. *Mrs J.E. Purdie — Portman.* 63 (I), 260 (R), 734 (R), 958 (R), 1135 (R), 1467 (R), 1639 (R).

OLE GUNNAR (IRE) ..9-5§.. 9 b.g. Le Bavard (FR) — Rareitess (Rarity) fbrpp221. IRISH P-t-p '98 r1 p1 (2nd). P-t-P '99 r3 p0 (4th, pulled up 1, and fell 1). Lost his confidence completely after two early season tumbles (not his fault once), but it eventually returned and despite Mark Wilesmiths' best efforts to fall off at the last secured his Maiden at Weston Park on his final outing. Had been set too much to do in his previous two starts, but produced at just the right time when successful. Has his quirks, and is by no means an easy ride, but may consent to win again one day, though highly unlikely to be as prolific as his namesake. Wears a cross-noseband. *M.C. Wilesmith — Ledbury (Emma Wilesmith).* 339 (CfMa), 477 (R), 629 (OMa), 790 (OMa), 893 (OMa), 994 (OMa), 1194 (OMa), 1412 (OMa).

OLIVE BASKET ..9-7.. 10 b.m. Neltino — Casket (Pannier) 9p133. Smallish compact half-sister to Le Sac and Sacket. Dam won 5 Ladies (including dead-heat) and placed 3. P-t-P '96/9 r16 w1 (Maiden) p2 (3rds); pulled up 6, and fell/unseated 2. Won a Maiden first time out in '98, but not very big and helped by the lighter weights available in Ladies races since. Flattered by winning one however, as it was a poor race on firmish that fell her way, and has been trounced twice since. Has gained both victories at Badbury Rings, and prefers the usual sound surface there. *P.L. Southcombe — Cattistock.* 326 (L), 636 (L), 765 (L), 969 (L), 1239 (L).

OLLARDALE (IRE) ..9-12.. 13 b.g. Abednego — Kauai-Ka-Zum (Kauai King) 7. Strong rangy half-brother to Irish NH flat and jumping winner, Shanaghey West. P-t-P/HUNT CH '95/9 r19 w6 (up to Confined) p6 (3 3rds, of 4 once, and last once); pulled up 6, and fell 1. A useful Pointer on his day, but frequently irresolute and not quite the same since he ended the '98 season lame. Gifted his latest success in a match for his Members last year when his rival declined to try, and only managed one outing in 2000. Not disgraced when around 12 lengths seventh at Brampton Bryan, but has never stood much racing and clearly more hard to train than ever now. Wears blinkers. *W.S. Littleworth — Golden V.* 862 (Cf).

OLYMPIAN ..9-12.. 14 ch.g. High Line — Elysian (Northfields USA) p2. Close-coupled half-brother to 4 flat winners, including Arcady. Dam won at 6f, and comes from an excellent family. FLAT (for P. Walwyn) r6 p1 (3rd). NH '90/8 (owned by Jimmy Neville, 2 wins when trained by him; one win previously from M. Piper; 4 wins previously from T. McGovern's) r52 w10 (9 Hdles, 2m-3m, and 2m5f Ch; 2 hat-tricks) p 13. A former grand front-runner at best, but has not scored since November '96, and is moody and was running badly latterly under Rules. Only tried four Chases and did not really adapt to them, and his final 14 outings were out of Hurdles. All his form has been on good or firm ground, but had a peak of brilliance in '93, when he captured the Coral Cup and the Imperial Cup which netted him a £50,000 bonus which added to his £104,748 in prize money makes for an outstanding achievement. Normally wears headgear and must have found Pointing pretty prosaic, but his 20 length second in a Confined (well-backed) was an adequate display for a 13-year-old. *Mrs S. Williams — Llangibby.* 895 (MO), 1612 (Cf).

OMAR'S ODYSSEY (IRE) ..9-3.. 6 ch.g. Sharifabad (IRE) — Tales Of Homer (Home Guard USA) 4145. Small half-brother to 2 flat winners in Ireland, including Teresian Girl, and to another in Holland. 5000 2-y-o. FLAT (often blinkered/visored) r14 p0. NH '99 (for P. Mitchell) r1 p0. Sold Ascot, Sep for 975. Showed ability for the first time when beating bad rivals in a 2m4f Maiden at Lydstep, but his attitude has looked rather questionable since, and was travelling strongly for a long way but found nothing off the bridle once. May find three miles stretching his stamina. Possibly worth another chance at six. *M. Spuffard & Mrs F. Goldsworthy — S. Pembs.* 270 (CfMa), 1223 (2m4fOMa), 1452 (R), 1615 (R).

OMIDJOY (IRE) ..9-0.. 11 ch.m. Nishapour (FR) — Fancy Finish (Final Straw) pp2. Very small neat. FLAT r13 p4 (short-headed once; 1-5 when 12/2nd to Electrolyte in 4-horse race once). NH '93/6 r34 w1 (2m4f Sell Hdle) p18 (beaten head once; inc 22/ last of 3 in Ch). P-t-P '97 and '99 (for Mrs L. Wrighton) r10 p2 (2nds, last once); last pair 4, pulled up 3, and unseated 1. A prolific loser whose only success from 59 starts came in a five-runner Plumpton Selling Hurdle in '95. Of no account in Points in which she never puts her best foot forward, and beaten a fence when second in her Members this year. Usually sports blinkers. *Mrs L. Gibbon — Essex & Suffolk.* 549 (Cf), 1007 (L), 1110 (M).

ONCE IS ENOUGH ..—.. 6 b.m. Broadsword (USA) — Yellow Iris (Le Bavard FR) pp. Small half-sister to Irish Trooper, and to NH flat and Hurdles winner, Connaught Crusader. Bought Malvern, July '98 for 1200. Looked to be carrying too much condition when tailed off and pulled up twice. *A Simpson — S. Pembs (Billie Brown).* 672 (2m4fOMa), 989 (OMa).

ONE BOY ..9-12.. 9 gr.g. Scallywag — Saucy Eater (Saucy Kit) ff15fp. Big attractive brother to Favourite Song, Als Diner and Rule Out The Rest, and half-brother to Hannah Millie Mick and Long Melford. Dam won 7 Hdles, 2m-3m1f. NH FLAT '95 r1 p0 (tailed off). NH '97 r1 p0 (pulled up in Hdle). P-t-P '98/9 (for Mrs K.T. Pilkington) r4 w1 (2m4f Maiden) p1 (3rd); fell 2. A typical Scallywag with aggressive tendencies, but successfully anchored by Anthony Honeyball when gaining his latest success. Fell in five of his last eight races, including when the first race-ride for Owyn Nelmes, so it was sadly ironic that he should meet his end in such innocuous circumstances. Used to wear over-reach boots so presumably struck into himself at Umberleigh. *K.A. & O. Nelmes — S. Dorset (Ken Nelmes).* 927 (Cf), 1057 (Cf), 1467 (R), 1562 (C), 1651 (I), 1674 (I).

ONEFORTHEFROG (IRE) ..—§.. 8 ch.g. Good Thyne (USA) — Deep Black (Deep Run) prp. Big rangy. NH FLAT '98 r1 p0. NH '99 (for C. Egerton) r2 p0 (pulled up both Hdles). Completely useless on his few outings to date, and was very slowly away at Lockinge and jumped right before refusing at the fourth. *Miss A. Hughes — V.W.H.* 754 (CfMa), 1204 (OMa), 1610 (OMa).

ONEFORWILLIE ..9-7.. 8 b.g. Rakaposhi King — Upham Reunion (Paridel) 6ppp5. Lengthy workmanlike brother to NH flat and jumping winner, Royal Event, and half-brother to Lamorna Bay, Upham Queen, Homeward Step and Union Leader. Dam, half-sister to 5 winners under Rules, including Master Upham, pulled up 3 and unseated in Points, and pulled up in a Hurdle. P-t-P '98 (for Mr D.A. Smith) r2 p0 (pulled up 2). NH '98/9 (for P. Bowen) r8 w1 (2m4f Hdle) p1. NH Jun '00 (from P. Bowen's) r1 p0 (5th in 2m110y Nov Ch: *pulled hrd, ld 1-3, lost plce 7, t.o).* Won a bad novice hurdle on firmish at Worcester after pulling up in two Maiden Points in '98, but only once better than tailed off in seven other outings, and quickly relegated to Pointing once more. Does not stay three miles, and is outclassed in Open company. Has been tried tongue-tied. *I.R. Snowden — Blackmore & Sparkford V. (John Dufosee).* 68 (O), 262 (MO), 561 (O), 768 (Cf).

ONE MANS LEGACY ..8-13.. 8 b.m. One Man Band — Storm Foot (Import) fp2p. Tall rangy owner-bred half-sister to Strewth (*qv*). Sire, by Formidable (USA), won 2 flat, 6-7f. P-t-P '99 r3 p0 (last, and pulled up 2). Seven lengths second in a short Upton Maiden, but exposed as moderate and seems unable to stay in races over the full trip. If she has the ability to win a race her current connections will extract it, but at present that does not seem likely. *Mrs C. Chadney — Croome & W. Warwicks.* 673 (2m4fOMa), 990 (OMa), 1361 (2m4fOMa), 1527 (OMa).

ONE MORE BILL ..8-7§.. 11 b.g. Silly Prices — Another Treat (Derring-Do) pp. Small strong-topped hobdayed half-brother to You Cheeky, and to 5 flat winners (one in France), including Forest Fantasy and Another Thrill (also successful Hurdler). Dam won 2 flat (10-12f) and placed 3. NH FLAT '95 r3 p1 (2nd of 4). NH '95 and '96 r3 p0. P-t-P '98/9 r9 p1 (last of 3); 4th, last, pulled up 1, ran out 1, and fell 1. Not wholly disgraced in his first season Pointing, but has shown more temperament than ability since. Acquired a visor in 2000, but without improvement and looks a complete waste of time. Has looked short on stamina so running him in a 3m2f Hunter Chase was not a bright idea. *G.C. Evans — W. Street/Tickham.* 578 (OMa), 1536 (3m2fH).

ONE MORE MAN (IRE) ..7-9.. 10 b.g. Remainder Man — Pampered Sally (Paddy's Stream) p7. Workmanlike half-brother to Societys Stream (IRE). IRISH P-t-P '95 r1 p0 (fell). NH '96/8 (blinkered 1) r9 p0 (6 Chses, inc last pair 2, pulled up 2, and unseated 1). P-t-P '99 (for Mr N. Wilson) r3 p1 (last of 3); unseated 1, and pulled up 1. Chronic under Rules, and not much better in Points, though conceivably better than the owner made him look in his latest outing when soon hopelessly tailed off. *C.P. Goulding — Hampshire.* 309 (OMa), 1396 (OMa).

ONE OF THE NATIVES (IRE) ..10-1.. 7 b.g. Be My Native (USA) — Take Me Home (Amoristic USA) 32121. Compact half-brother to NH flat winner, Festive Teak (IRE), and to an Irish Pointing winner. Dam won NH flat, 2m4f Hdle and 2m Ch in Ireland. NH FLAT '99 (from D. Nicholson's) r2 p0. Jumps well for a novice, and has kept improving in minor company. Twice showed a tendency to hang left, and would probably have won a Restricted at Stafford Cross had Tim Mitchell not put his shoulder out and been unable to assist him all the way up the home straight (this early April race was the last of the season for his unfortunate jockey). Well-related, and might develop into an Open contender in time. *D. Mercer — Miss J. Pimblett & Mrs J. Eager — Cattistock (Richard Barber).* 11 (OMa), 57 (OMa), 264 (OMa), 931 (R), 1061 (R).

ONESEVENFOUR (IRE) ..9-6.. 12 ch.g. Jamesmead — Granny Grumble (Politico USA) p. Big roman-nosed brother to Burrells Wharf (IRE), and half-brother to Irish Pointing and English jumping winner, Gratomi (IRE). Dam won Irish NH flat. NH FLAT '95 r1 p0. NH '95/6 r5 p2 (2m5f Chses). P-t-P/HUNT CH '99 r3 p0 (4th, 8th, and fell 1). Disappointing under Rules, and though able to bomb along merrily for about 2m4f in Points soon capitulates and is surely running under a physical disability. Broke a blood vessel once in '95, and has probably done so on other occasions. *J.R. Wilson — Cheshire (Colin Taylor).* 568 (OMa).

ON MERIT ..9-4.. 7 b.g. Terimon — Onika (Great Nephew) f22up2. Strong. Dam won 2 8f races. 4800y. FLAT r1 p0 (refused to enter stalls next intended start). NH '98 (for breeder, S. Gollings) r3 p0 (ran out once). Bought Doncaster, Sep for 500. An unruly type in the previous yard, but seems to have calmed down with age, and his seconds in Maidens have been adequate efforts. Normally makes the running, but can suffer from jumping lapses, and is easy to mow down in the closing stages even at 2m4f. Does not like firm ground. May manage to hang on whilst the shorter trip is still an option at seven, although punters may have deserted him by then (beaten favourite in his three most recent attempts). *G. & Mrs W. Nichol — Jedforest.* 364 (CfMa), 499 (2m4fOMa), 718 (CfMa), 1166 (OMa), 1367 (OMa), 1582 (2m4fOMa).

ON TARGET ..9-4.. 9 b.g. Cruise Missile — Phantom Folly (Master Spiritus) 32316. Sturdy. Dam pulled up in 5 Points (was tailed off by halfway in all her races). P-t-P '98/9 r7 p0 (5th, last, pulled up 3, and fell 2). Improved with better jumping, but struggling to get the trip, and only able to hit the bullseye in a poor Higham Maiden on firm. Heavily punted at Thorpe earlier in the season so at least his supporters gained compensation, but will continue to toil in better company. *Mr & Mrs S.R.W. Howlett — Dunston H. (Mike Bloom).* 23 (OMa), 121 (OMa), 239 (R), 759 (OMa), 1111 (R).

ON THE BEER (IRE) ..6-11.. 13 b.g. Kemal (FR) — Mad For Her Beer (Proverb) u7ppp. Tall rangy half-brother to Lyme Gold (IRE), and to Irish Pointing/Chasing winner, What Thing (IRE). IRISH P-t-P '94 r4 w1 (6yo plus Maiden, promoted from 2nd after being crossed) p1 (last of 2); pulled up 2. P-t-P/HUNT CH '95/6 (for Mr H.D. Hill & Mr C.M. Sporborg) r11 w2 (Intermediate and Confined) p6 (5 2nds, of 3 once, and inc Hunt Ch); fell 2. NH Apr '96 r1 p0. A consistent if rather one-paced performer when last seen in '96, but labouring under a beginner rider when tailed off on five occasions this year. Presumably a scheduled hobdaying operation in '96 did not work satisfactorily. *Mr & Mrs M. Bailey — Essex F. & U. (Jim Ovel).* 317 (M), 572 (CfO), 756 (Cf), 1035 (Cnr), 1381 (O).

ON THE BONE ..9-3.. 9 b.m. Lyphento (USA) — Lydia Languish (Hotfoot) 4c. Dam, half-sister to Kerry Orchid (*qv* '99 Annual), won 6f Sell. Subject of some market support when 30 lengths fourth on her belated debut, but was carried out by a loose horse after a mile next time. *K. Smith — Atherstone (Roger Harvey).* 547 (CfMa), 906 (CfMa).

ON THE FLY ..10-0.. 10 b.g. Bustino — My Greatest Star (Great Nephew) 2p1p. Sturdy compact half-brother to a winner in Italy. NH FLAT r4 p0. NH '96 r1 p0. P-t-P/HUNT CH '97 and '99 (for Mr Brown & Mr P.J. Teasdale) r18 w4 (up to Confined) p5 (3 2nds, last once); last, pulled up 5, and fell/unseated 3. Developed into a decent Pointer in '99, winning unextended on three occasions, but looked less successful in the Hunter Chase arena where his jumping is still a cause for concern. That said, actually ended up winning the Fakenham race at Portman Square when the winner tested positive. Can go a strong gallop, but probably needs to get clear, as he seems quite a weak finisher, and has yet to prove himself in competitive company. Wears a tongue-strap. *M.J. Brown — Sinnington.* 136 (O), 375 (Cf), 585 (2m5f110yH), 801 (3m1fH).

OPERA FAN (IRE) ..10-10.. 9 b.g. Taufan (USA) — Shannon Lady (Monsanto FR) p12p. Lengthy good-bodied half-brother to Area Girl, Pommes Frites and Fervent Fan (all 2-y-o winners, at 5-6f). FLAT r16 p3. NH '95/8 r16 w4 (2m Hdles, last 3 Sells) p2 (2nds). P-t-P '99 r7 w5 (Ladies, inc 4-timer) p0; unseated 1, and ran out 1. Unbeaten when completing in Ladies races '99/00, but connections quite rightly took the step to raise him in class this year and their decision was not met with much luck. Put up a good performance when runner-up to subsequent Cheltenham Foxhunters hero Cavalero at Warwick, but whilst he was basking in glory at Prestbury Park, Opera Fan was hobbling back to the unsaddling area having been pulled up lame at the last. Not as fluent over big fences as he is in Points, and may have to return to the smaller obstacles if he is able to resume in 2001. Usually makes all when successful, but game and can fight back if required as he did at Erw Lon in his latest win. Suited by plenty of cut in the ground. *Miss L. Llewellyn & V.J. Hughes — Llangeinor (Lisa Llewellyn).* 149 (3mH), 272 (L), 386 (3m1f110yH), 584 (3m2f110yH).

OPERA FESTIVAL (IRE) ..8-7.. 11 ch.g. Buckskin (FR) — Glencairn Belle (Golden Love) 23. Medium-sized quite attractive. Dam is half-sister to James Pigg (*qv*). IRISH P-t-P '95 r4 p2; pulled up, and ran out. NH '96 and '98 (for R. Baker; blinkered 2) r8 p1 (2nd); pulled up 5. Bought Malvern, Feb for 400. Was absent for 26 months after May '96, but later able to give one bold display when second in a 3m3f Chase when blinkered for the first time. Ungenuine, and tailed off and pulled up twice subsequently before disappearing for another 16 months. Slumped to Maidens and was 20 lengths second and 42 lengths third (favourite), and continues to look disinterested and suspect. The furthest journey she made from the previous yard was to the sales ring, because she had seven excursions to Newton Abbot and one to Exeter! *D. Stephens — S. Cornwall.* 540 (OMa), 724 (CfMa).

OPTIMISM REIGNS (IRE) ..—.. 10 b.g. Euphemism — Ellis Town (Camden Town) 4ppppp. Tall rangy half-brother to Irish flat, NH flat and jumping winner, Rathbawn Prince (IRE). IRISH NH FLAT '96 r4 w1 (2m2f) p1 (2nd). NH '97/9 (for M. Jefferson; previously for N. Chance) r5 p1 (2nd); remote 4th of 5, fell and unseated in Chses. Bought Doncaster, May for 2800. Second in a Hurdle when 11-8 on his English debut, and fourth at 4-5 next time, and pessimism has reigned ever since. Can be a bad jumper, and followed a 38 lengths fourth with a string of appalling displays in Points (blinkered once, and wore a tongue-strap once). *S.B. Clark — York & Ainsty S.* 18 (I), 134 (I), 370 (C), 506 (Cf), 999 (4m1fMO), 1348 (Cf).

ORDOG MOR (IRE) ..—.. 12 ch.g. Boreen (FR) — Minorette (Miralgo) p. Compact stocky half-brother to Observe and Espy, and to 4 winners in Ireland, Strong Dilemma (IRE) (Chasing), Minorettes Girl (NH flat, and smart Hurdler), and to Irish NH flat and Hurdles winners, Guess Twice and Sub-Editor. Dam won at 8f in France, and won 6 jump races in France and Italy. IRISH NH FLAT '95/3 r7 p3 (3rds). NH '95/9 (for M. Meagher, visored last 2) r30 w7 (3 Hdles, 2m7f-3m1f, and 4 Chses, 2m5f-3m1f; inc hat-trick in June/July '96) p7; would have won only Sell on debut, but ran out at last when leading. Sold Doncaster, Oct for 2000. Could jump well and bowl along merrily on firm ground when a competent front-runner in his prime, but had lost his form, and made a sad start for the new yard when dropping dead at Balcormo. T. Bell — Fife (Alan & Lucy Normile). 1119 (L).

ORPHAN OLLY ..—.. 11 b.g. Relkino — Austrian Maid (Faberge II) p. Half-brother to Oh To Be, Porchester Run, Jordanstown Prince and Little Tristram (dam of Pulpits Edge *qv*), and to Irish NH flat, Pointing and Chasing winner, Cranlome. Dam won a Bumper and placed 10 (inc 7 Hdles) in Ireland. P-t-P '96/7 r10 w2 (Maiden and Restricted) p3 (fence last of 2; and 2 3rds, last once); fell/unseated 4, and pulled up 1. NH '99 r2 p0 (last and pulled up in Nov Hdles). Won two minor Points in convincing fashion in '97, but ran badly on his final appearance that year and obviously went wrong as he was forced to miss most of the following two years. Never recovered from being hampered by a loose horse on his return, but failed to reappear and a big question mark surrounds his well being once again. Prone to errors. *R.H. York — Staff College.* 18 (I).

ORSWELLTHATENSWELL ..10-6§.. 10 b.g. Ballacashtal (CAN) — A'Dhahirah (Beldale Flutter USA) 53234314. Lengthy dipped half-brother to NH flat and flat winner, Row Ree, and to 2 winners in Sweden. NH FLAT '97 r2 w1 (2m1f) p0. NH '97/8 r9 p0; blinkered and refused to race only Ch. P-t-P/HUNT CH '99 r7 w1 (Confined) p5 (4 3rds, remote last once, and inc Hunt Ch); and 6th. NH Jun '00 r1 p0 (4th in 2m5f Nov Ch: *ld 2-7, mist 9, t.o aft*). Won a six-runner Bumper on his debut, but reported to be a nasty piece of work, and bolts out hunting and at exercise. Superb at self-preservation, but usually declines to try, and has been beaten in races more genuine horses would have won easily. Made most, and survived one bad mistake when winning a 2m4f Wetherby Hunter Chase on his final start, once again admiring trainer Fiona Needhams' prowess at handling awkward gits. Perfectly capable of winning again, but best supported with someone else's money. *R. Tate — Bilsdale (Fiona Needham).* 134 (I), 623 (Cf), 795 (L), 1328 (L), 1350 (L), 1478 (I), 1628 (2m4f110yH).

ORTON HOUSE ..9-0§.. 14 b.g. Silly Prices — Who's Free (Sit In The Corner USA) 66245. Sparely-made brother to Who's Silly Now. Dam, pony-sized, won 4 Hdles, 2-3m, and 3m Ch and placed 18 (inc 3 flat), but was unplaced in 7 Points and a Hunt Ch at 5. NH '91/5 r10 p1 (3rd); 7th only Ch — mistakes. P-t-P/HUNT CH '96/9 r32 w4 (inc Open) p5 (4 3rds, inc of 4, and last); pulled up 7, refused 1, and fell/unseated 2. Safe, but slow and has become increasingly doggy in recent years. Outbattled when favourite for a repeat success in his Members, and well beaten in more competitive races. Blinkered once in '98, and has worn a tongue-strap occasionally since. *Mrs A.P. Kelly — Flint & Denbigh (Stephen Kelly).* 171 (O), 565 (O), 776 (M), 960 (Cf), 1523 (C).

OSGATHORPE ..9-0.. 14 ch.g. Dunbeath (USA) — Darlingka (Darling Boy) 4p. Rangy unfurnished hobdayed half-brother to Kashkiss, and to 4 flat winners (2 abroad), including Idolized and Stylish Darling. Dam won 2 12f races. FLAT (blinkered/visored 2) r28 w1 (7f) p4; ran in Sells latterly. NH '91/7 r11 w1 (2m1f Hdle) p3 (2nd in 2 Chses; inc Sell). P-t-P/HUNT CH '94/9 (for Mrs F.M. Reynolds, Mrs C. Gibbs & Mrs L. Arkwright) r38 w6 (5 Ladies and Mixed Open) p7 (4 2nds, beaten head once, and inc Hunt Ch); failed to finish 14 (on floor 5). Inconsistent and unreliable until transformed in '97, but has gone rapidly downhill since and even a spell with Caroline Bailey has failed to ignite him. Plods badly, but at least he remains a pretty safe conveyance. Absent since March. Blinkered once in '99, and has been tried in a tongue-strap. *Mr & Mrs M.A. Bailiss — Fernie (Mark Bailiss).* 443 (Cf), 770 (Cf).

O SO BOSSY ..10-2.. 11 ch.g. Sousa — Bubbling Spirit (Hubble Bubble) pu122f14. Tall plain owner-bred half-brother to Horwood Drummer. Dam, half-sister to 4 Pointers, including Lucky Friday, won 5 Points (one on a disqualification) and placed 4 for Andrew Congdon. Grandam, Kelpie

Spirit, won a Maiden and placed 3. P-t-P '97/9 r9 w1 (Maiden) p3 (2 2nds, of 3 once); last pair 3, and fell/unseated 3. Only able to appear once apiece '97/8, but far more sociable since and has a fairly decent record in minor events. Revels in mud, and won twice for Jenny Congdon under such conditions this year when making the bulk of the running. An inconsistent jumper, particularly over big fences, but a late developer and may improve again at 11. *A.W. Congdon — Torrington F.* 69 (R), 202 (I), 310 (I), 535 (L), 852 (Cf), 1023 (3mH), 1175 (Cf), 1644 (3m2f110yH).

OSSIE DALE (IRE) ..9-12.. 8 ch.g. Balinger — Brickey Shalow (Cheval) fp31. Rangy. IRISH P-t-P '99 r4 p0 (fell twice, unseated, and brought down). Unseated at the start and then fell at the second on his Irish debut to set the pattern which continued in Britain with a fifth consecutive grounding. Pulled up after a bad blunder four out next time, almost got it right at last when making all until unseating at the final fence at Lydstep when 15 lengths clear (remounted), and finally made it eighth time lucky when never headed on firm at Erw Lon. It was a notably bad Maiden, and more will be required for Restricteds. *Mrs J. Mathias — S. Pembs.* 31 (CMa), 348 (CfMa), 834 (OMa), 950 (OMa).

OTTER RIVER ..—.. 12 ch.g. Celtic Cone — Ottery News (Pony Express) ppppp. Lengthy rather unfurnished half-brother to Tipton Times, Precis, Tony's Croney and Playing Away. Dam won 5 Hunt Chses (2m1f-3m2f, inc '81 Horse and Hound Cup), 4 Points, 3 Hdles (2m-3m1f) and 5 Chses (2m5f-3m2f, won another, but disqualified to 2nd) and placed total of 19 (inc 5 Hunt Chses and, '81/2 Whitbreads) for Oliver Carter. Grandam, Stenquill, won 9 Hdles (2m-2m4f) and 6 Chses (2-3m) and placed 10. NH '98/9 r7 p1 (distant 3rd); ran out 1, pulled up 2, and fell 2. P-t-P/HUNT CH '95, '97/8 (for Mr O.J. Carter) r8 p0 (6th, fell/unseated 5 and pulled up 2). Bred from a superb and remarkably consistent mare, but the antithesis of mum, and surely labouring under some grotesque disability. Very slow to get fit in 2000, but showed some speed at Bitterley only to stop dead in a matter of strides and is not worth bothering with again. *Miss R. Cooper — S. Cornwall (Paul Morris).* 588 (OMa), 792 (OMa), 864 (R), 994 (OMa), 1527 (OMa).

OUR EDDIE ..—.. 12 ch.g. Gabitat — Ragusa Girl (Morston FR) upppu3p. Tall. FLAT r53 w5 (10f, inc Sell) p10. NH '92. '97 and '99 (unplaced final 5 for R. Williams; previously for K. Wingrove, bought for 1900; previously for breeder, B. Gubby) r15 p2 (Sells — beaten 6l by stablemate after saddle slipped once); last and pulled up in Chses. Those with long memories will recall his decent performances at Lingfield, where he gained all his victories (four in '94 and one in '96; three on the equitrack). A total wreck in the current yard, and 12 attempts have yielded three lasts and nine non-completions. Finished 53 seconds after the winner and distressed once, and Kahlil Burke was in his dimwit mode, and had clearly forgotten that a month before he earned a suspension of one week for failing to pull up a tired horse when out of contention. Formerly wore headgear, and sometimes has a tongue-strap now. The owner runs many under permit, although a look through the formbook at the performances of such as This One, Nineteenofive, Coal To Diamonds, Officianado, Staceys Choice, Shana Coole and Desert Kingdom would make any normal trainer shudder. *R. Williams — Gelligaer F.* 599 (L), 743 (L), 821 (MO), 1026 (2m5f110yH), 1157 (2m3fH), 1461 (O), 1626 (3m1f110yH).

OUR HARRY ..10-1.. 11 b.g. White Mill — Swn-Y-Mor VII (unknown) p1. Rangy workmanlike owner-bred. P-t-P '98/9 r6 w1 (Maiden) p2; pulled up 2. Won a two-finisher Maiden in very arduous conditions at Pantyderi in '98, and made most to land a 19-runner restricted at Lydstep on his latest appearance, but clearly hard to train and has never managed more than three outings in a season. Jumps well, and has a commendable attitude, and might prove good enough for an Intermediate. *G.H. James — Carms (Vicky Teale).* 832 (R), 1228 (R).

OUR MAN FLIN (IRE) ..9-8.. 8 br.g. Mandalus — Flinging (Good Times ITY) 231. Tall workmanlike. Dam is half-sister to 3 Pointers, including Brimstone Hill (*qv* '96 Annual). NH FLAT '97 (for Dr D. Chesney) r3 p1 (3rd). NH '98/9 (for Mrs A. Johnson, bought for 10,000, hooded and blinkered final 5; previously for Dr D. Chesney) r9 p1 (3rd in Sell Hdle); finished tailed off in both Chses. An expensive failure under Rules, but Maidens were more suitable, and won at Marks Tey under a good ride from Andrew Sansome. Had been fitted with a tongue-tie in his two previous attempts, and was favourite when three lengths third at Cottenham, where Daniel Cook was fined £50 and severely cautioned for incorrect use of the whip and marking the horse. It would be surprising if he had any improvement in him. *M.F. Rogerson — Thurlow (Tim Bryce).* 236 (OMa), 775 (OMa), 942 (CfMa).

OUR MAN NED (IRE) ..—.. 7 ch.g. Un Desperado (FR) — Tasmania Star (Captain James) pp. Hobdayed half-brother to NH flat and jumping winner, Slingsby (IRE), and to a winner in Italy. Dam won 2-y-o race in Italy. Sold Doncaster, Nov '98 for 550, and resold later. Pulled up at the 14th in Maidens (after a bad mistake at the 13th in the latest). *R. Cook — Staff College (Chris Elliott).* 290 (CMa), 576 (OMa).

OUR WIZZER (IRE) ..9-4.. 12 ch.g. Bulldozer — Straffan Lady (Ballyciptic) pu56u. Plain angular. NH '93/4 and '95/6 r10 p1 (2nd in match for Ch); fell/unseated 3. P-t-P/HUNT CH '95 and '98/9 (for Mr B.S. Heath) r18 w3 (up to Confined) p4 (3 2nds, of 4 once); pulled up 4, fell/unseated 2, and slipped up 1. A decent galloper who won three minor Points to '98, but declined sharply the following year, and no longer of any account. Can prove hard to sit on and the new owner ended up on the floor twice at Badbury Rings this year. Wears a cross-noseband. *C.R. Whittaker — S. & W. Wilts (Sarah Waugh).* 211 (Cnr), 325 (Cf), 453 (Cf), 639 (I), 766 (Cnr).

OUT BY NIGHT (IRE) ..9-9.. 10 b.g. Phardante (FR) — Love And Idleness (Malinowski USA) ppbp42. Strong attractive half-brother to Irish NH flat, Pointing jumping winner, Deejaydee (IRE). NH FLAT '95 r1 p0. NH '96 and '98/9 (for G.M. Moore) r17 p4 (Chses); fell/unseated 6. Bought Doncaster, May for 5600. Disappointing and a poor jumper under Rules, but his best form had suggested that a Maiden would be easy meat for him. Showed plenty of speed in them, and was sometimes held up and sometimes ridden from the front, but the end result was always the same — he simply could not get the trip. Deserves to score, but it would probably require some kind of fluke for him to do so. *I.R. Mann — V. of Aylesbury (Lawney Hill).* 20 (OMa), 197 (CfMa), 1039 (OMa), 1147 (OMa), 1422 (OMa), 1486 (OMa).

OUT OF ACTONS (IRE) ..9-3.. 10 b.g. Convinced — More Incentive (Kampala) p4234u22. Strong-topped. IRISH P-t-P '97/8 r5 p3 (15*l* and distant 2nd, and 2¾*l* last of 3). P-t-P '99 r5 p0 (pulled up 5). Pulled up after a maximum of two miles in his debut English season, but does possess some ability and should have won a bad elders Maiden at High Easter this year, but the owner-rider was incapable of riding a finish and went down by a head (a sneeze or even a cough might have been enough). After two more close calls it seemed Craig Jarvis must have bought himself an Equiciser so vigorously was he was throwing himself about the saddle on his final start. Another close second resulted, but had he not put up five pounds of overweight this could easily have gone the other way. Neil King has done a really good job in getting the horse healthy, and both deserve better. Insulted by blinkers, and tried in a tongue-strap in the past. *C. Jarvis — Suffolk (Neil King).* 88 (OMa), 323 (CfMa), 606 (OMa), 759 (OMa), 941 (CfMa), 1040 (OMa), 1292 (OMa), 1382 (OMa).

OUT OF THE BLUE ..9-3.. 9 b.m. Lochnager — Expletive (Shiny Tenth) up9p24454. Small good-quartered. Dam won 7 flat, 5-12f (the first a Sell); won 3 at Leicester aged 7). FLAT r1 p0. NH '96/8 r18 p1 (3rd); Sells latterly; brought down first only Ch (an infamous occasion, as Carl Llewellyn refused to take the ride after a brouhaha about her alleged lack of jumping ability, which was disputed by a kamikazi Pointing jockey who had 'schooled' her). P-t-P '99 r5 w1 (Maiden) p1 (3rd; also disqualified from 3rd once — not weigh-in); pulled up 1, and fell 1. Narrowly beaten in a slowly-run race for her Members, but does not stay three miles at normal speed, and was lucky to stumble across a race in '99 when the jockey gave her a most enterprising ride. *E.P. Parkes — United.* 119 (CR), 338 (R), 567 (R), 615 (CMod), 858 (M), 992 (R), 1411 (R), 1528 (R), 1633 (CR).

OUT ON THE TOWN ..9-7§.. 11 ch.m. Town And Country — Bank House Lodge (Funny Man) pRp2pppp. Small half-sister to Stormhill Banker. P-t-P '97/9 r17 w1 (Maiden) p2 (3rd of 4 once); pulled up 8, fell 1, and refused 2. Usually fails to stay and is forced to pull up, but incredibly unlucky at Erw Lon this year when she went the wrong side of a doll between the final two fences when seemingly in command of a bad four-runner Restricted. Beaten ten lengths on her next trip there, but has now run up 20 defeats since her Maiden success in '97 and the sequence looks set to be extended should she return. *K. James — Glamorgan.* 485 (R), 647 (R), 818 (R), 948 (R), 1089 (R), 1228 (R), 1400 (R), 1452 (R).

OUTRAGEOUS AFFAIR ..9-7.. 9 b.m. Idiot's Delight — Lac Royale (Lochnager) 4316p4p. Workmanlike half-sister to Hurdles winner, Jimmy The Gillie. Dam won 2 Hdles, 2m-2m1f. NH FLAT '97 r3 p0. NH '97/8 r9 p0 (last twice, and pulled up 1 in Chses). P-t-P '99 r5 p2 (3rds of 4; also disqualified from 3rd once — not weigh-in); last, and pulled up 1. Looked a non-stayer in '99, but made up a phenomenal amount of ground when third at Alpraham this term and provided Rachael Reynolds with her first success at Brampton Bryan in their next outing. Outclassed since, but her nearest victim that day had since won a Restricted, and there is a possibility that she may emulate him one day, particularly as the rider grows in confidence. *Miss R.S. Reynolds — Kyre.* 449 (L), 588 (OMa), 865 (CfMa), 1014 (3m5fL), 1411 (R), 1614 (4mMO), 1671 (R).

OUTSIDE THE RAIN (IRE) ..—.. 9 b.m. Glacial Storm (USA) — Rose Of Solway (Derring Rose) pupuup. Sturdy compact half-sister to Skinsey Finnegan (IRE). P-t-P '99 (for Mr S.W. Macfarlane) r3 p0 (unseated 2, and pulled up 1). Inept jumping masks what ability she may possess, and has ditched Tom Macfarlane on five occasions '99/00. Might be improved by stronger handling. *Marchioness of Blandford — N. Norfolk H.* 24 (OMa), 98 (OMa), 606 (OMa), 1020 (OMa), 1312 (Cm), 1523 (C).

OVERFLOWING RIVER (IRE) ..10-12.. 12 ch.g. Over The River (FR) — Side Wink (Quayside) 35131. Lengthy brother to Micklegate Run (IRE), and half-brother to Lochinvar Lord. IRISH P-t-P '93 r1 p0 (pulled up). NH '94/8 r16 w4 (3m1f-3m5f Chses) p3. P-t-P/HUNT CH '99 r3 w2 (4m1f Hunt Ch, and 4m Mixed Open) p0; and 6th. A useful top-of-the-ground Chaser when he can find extreme distances, and was successful in his repeat bid for the four-miler at Cheltenhams' May evening fixture, where Trevor Glass literally picked him up and carried him past Mr Freebie in the last stride. Had previously failed to win back-to-back Grimthorpe Gold Cups, but time may tell that he was taking on a very useful tool in Prominent. Vulnerable at a bare three miles, and does not manage many races, but thoroughly game and is a credit to connections. *J. Wade — S. Durham.* 155 (3m4f110yH), 422 (3m5fO), 582 (3m3fH), 999 (4m1fMO), 1338 (4m1fH).

OVER IN McGANNS (IRE) ..9-3.. 11 b.g. Carlingford Castle — Vodka And Soda (Niels) p5. Unfurnished. IRISH P-t-P '94 and '96 r5 p2 (3rds, after falling at last once); pulled up 1, and brought down 1. P-t-P '99 r6 p0 (last 2, pulled up 3, and unseated 1). Only once better than last in eight Points, and looks another disinterested Carlingford Castle. Benefits from professional handling, but seems not to stay and presumably not thought good enough to take under Rules. *D. Smith — S. Durham.* 282 (OMa), 624 (OMa).

PLATE 95   1338 Winning Post at Cheltenham HC, Cheltenham: Overflowing River (T. Glass), 1st, is pressed by Mr Freebie (N. Bloom), 2nd, at the last   PHOTO: Brian Armstrong

OVER THE BARROW (IRE) ..9-3.. 11 b.g. Over The River (FR) — Twice As Fluffy (Pollerton) ppp. Small compact brother to Irish Pointing winner, Up The Slaney and to NH flat winner, Twice As Good (IRE). IRISH P-t-P '96/8 r17 w1 (7&8yo Maiden) p3; pulled up 8, slipped up 2, and fell 1. P-t-P/HUNT CH '99 (for Miss D. Ross & Miss E.M. Davison) r3 p0 (5th, last, and pulled up 1). Had a poor completion record in Ireland, but seems defective now, and was dismounted after pulling up on his reappearance and lame without question on his latest. *Miss E.M. Davison — Fernie.* 1009 (CR), 1071 (CR), 1419 (R).

OVER THE HILL (IRE) ..10-9§.. 9 b.g. Over The River (FR) — Joint Equity (Callernish) 2pup3f. Workmanlike lengthy. IRISH P-t-P '97 r3 p0 (pulled up 3). P-t-P/HUNT CH '98/9 r5 w1 (3m2f Hunt Ch) p0; fell 2, and pulled up 2. Had failed to complete in his first seven races, but landed a bad Cartmel Hunter Chase without any problem on his final appearance in '99. Flattered on his reappearance this year, but ran a stinker when sent off favourite at Hereford next time and now looks thoroughly ungenuine. Benefits from the presence of top riders, but even the likes of Armytage and Scudamore cannot work with such doggy ammunition. Might be worth one last try in blinkers. A consistently poor jumper. *C.N. Nimmo — Bicester with Whaddon.* 89 (3m1fH), 222 (3m1f110yH), 686 (3m1fH), 1024 (3m3f110yH), 1530 (2m6fH), 1643 (3m2fH).

OVER THE MASTER (IRE) ..10-2.. 9 ch.g. Over The River (FR) — Covette (Master Owen) u3. Tall rangy half-brother to Who-Have-I. NH '97/8 r4 p0 (fell 2, inc only Ch). P-t-P '99 (for Mr P.J. Millington) r9 w2 (Maiden and Confined; also disqualified once — tested positive) p1 (3rd); 4th twice, pulled up 2, and fell 1. Won three times under Patrick Millington last year, but had some hard races, and disappeared after a promising third at Dunthrop in mid-February this year. A thorough stayer suited by plenty of cut in the ground, and will hopefully be able to make a full recovery from what ever has kept him on the sidelines. *Mrs R.G. Samworth — Cottesmore, & V. of Aylesbury (Lawney Hill).* 74 (CCf), 191 (Cf).

OVERTON GIRL ..—.. 10 b.m. Germont — Gold Profit (Rubor) pf. Sturdy half-sister to Singing Profit. Dam, half-sister to Normans Profit, was 3rd in 3 Hdles for Billy Young (remained a Maiden after 42 chances, including Points/Hunt Chses). Grandam, Night Profit, pulled up in 3 of 4 races (including 3 Points) for him. NH '99 r1 p0 (pulled up in Sell — fat, and soon tailed off). It would be a huge surprise if she was anything other than useless. *W.G. Young — Lanarks & Renfrews.* 498 (R), 1118 (R).

OXENDALE ..10-4.. 8 ch.g. Primitive Rising (USA) — Saucy Moon (Saucy Kit) ff1u2. Brother to Moon Rising (qv). P-t-P '98/9 r3 p2 (last of 2 once); and unseated 1. Put two falls behind him when successful at Bexhill, but lost the rider at the first next time, and needs to adopt a calmer disposition if he is to maintain his improvement. Has two handlers, and gets stirred up in the preliminaries, and proceeds to take a strong hold in the race which usually means he is running out of gas in the closing stages. Could win plenty more races in his Area, if he goes the right way. *Mrs S. Dench — Ashford V. (Roy Dench).* 577 (OMa), 710 (OMa), 984 (OMa), 1104 (R), 1393 (R).

OZZIE JONES ..10-7.. 10 b.g. Formidable (USA) — Distant Relation (Great Nephew) 12. Close-coupled. Dam won at 11f in France, and won a flat race and 4 Hdles in Jersey. FLAT r22 w1 (12f Sell) p4. NH '94/6 and '98/9 r34 w7 (inc 5 3m-3m2f Hcap Chses) p8. P-t-P/HUNT CH '97/8 r9 w6 (5 Ladies and Members — hat-tricks '97 & '98) p2 (2nds in Hunt Chses); and ran out 1. Enjoyed a fantastically successful spell under Rules from June '98 to October '99 winning six times and only once failing to reach the frame from 15 starts. Reverted to Hunter Chases in 2000, and made short work of the opposition on his reappearance at Ludlow, but could not manage to give seven pounds to Look In The Mirror at Hereford just five days later. Has proved a real bargain for Keith Pearce, who has handled him well, and gets excellent assistance from daughter Lucy. Has plenty of miles on the clock, and may not have time on his side, but should win again on the sound surfaces he prefers. Has been tried in blinkers. *K.R. Pearce — Carms.* 1293 (3mH), 1346 (3m1f110yH).

PABLOWMORE ..10-4.. 11 b.g. Pablond — Carrowmore (Crozier) 56. Tall workmanlike brother to Whinstone Mill and half-brother to Kerryair. P-t-P/HUNT CH '96/9 r16 w7 (inc 2 Opens) p5 (2 2nds); pulled up 2. A splendidly consistent Pointer who has won seven times and only missed the frame twice in 15 attempts, but tailed off in both Hunter Chase ventures this February, and has presumably hit trouble. Has a fair turn of foot, and likes mud, but has tended not to jump regulation fences with the same accuracy as those in Points. Will need treating with a certain amount of caution when he reappears. *R.W. Green — W. Percy.* 225 (3mH), 301 (2m5fH).

PLATE 96   656 Dart Vale & Haldon Harriers Open Maiden 56&7yo (Div 2): Pachakutec (R. Woollacott), pu, lands clear of L to R Wise Examiner (Richard Darke), 2nd, Black Dante (A. Charles-Jones), fell, Crewman (M. Munrowd), 1st, and Frankies Flutter (D. Doyne-Ditmas), 3rd
PHOTO: Bill Selwyn

PACHAKUTEC (IRE) ..—.. 8 b.g. Cataldi — Kiri's Return (Hawaiian Return USA) pppp. Rangy half-brother to Kiri's Rose (IRE). P-t-P '99 r1 p0 (pulled up). Made little impact in his first four outings, but was still in front having made most of the running when breaking down irreparably at Buckfastleigh. *Lady Earle — Tiverton.* 69 (R), 146 (OMa), 254 (CfMa), 656 (OMa).

PACKITIN PARKY ..—.. 8 b.g. Rakaposhi King — Divine Affair (IRE) (The Parson) pp. Strong-topped brother to NH flat winner, Concert Pianist. NH FLAT '97 r1 p0. NH '97/9 (for D. McCain) r11 p1 (3rd in Sell — would have been 39lb better off with winner in a HCap!); tailed off last only Ch. Bought Malvern, Oct for 1500. Not seen until mid-May and then given a couple of easy runs in Maidens, but there is a chance that he might be capable of surprising when fitter. *Miss E.A. Cork — E. Cornwall.* 1520 (CfMa), 1609 (OMa).

PACO'S BOY ..9-5.. 16 b.g. Good Thyne (USA) — Jeremique (Sunny Way) 6. Lengthy good-looking windsucker. Half-brother to Chasing winner, Jemaro (IRE). Dam won at 2m in Ireland. NH FLAT r3 w1 (2m2f) p1 (3rd). NH '89/94 and '98 r36 w6 (2 Hdles, 2m4f-2m6f, and 4 Chses, 2m4f-3m1f) p12 (earned £5364 when 2nd in Kim Muir). P-t-P/HUNT CH '95/7 and '99 r26 w5 (inc 2 Opens, and hat-trick in '95) p9 (2nd of 3, and last of 2; and 7 3rds, last thrice); pulled up 2. Highly inconsistent over the years, but remarkably safe, and can be praised for 28 consecutive completions. Lightly raced and very moderate now, but still of use as a schoolmaster, and gave a good account of himself for a long way under a novice on his only appearance in 2000. Often wore headgear in the past. *R.H. York — Surrey U.* 5 (Cv&nr).

PADDINGTON BEAR (U) ..—.. 7 b.g. Charlie Fox — unknown 4. Tootled round four fences behind the rest in his Members. *Mrs S. Stafford — United.* 858 (M).

PADDY CASEY (IRE) ..—.§.. 9 ch.g. Le Bavard (FR) — Rozmeen (FR) (Relko) pRr. Half-brother to Mister Point and to Irish NH flat Pointing and Hurdles winner, Crossfarnogue (IRE). Dam won 3 races at around 11f in French provinces. IRISH P-t-P '97/9 r11 w1 (7 plus Mdn) p1 (26/3rd); pulled up 6 (inc final 3) and fell. Bought Doncaster, May for 800. Never had more than a little ability, and six consecutive non-completions indicate that he has gone at the game completely. *K. Tork — Surrey U., & O. Surrey, Burstow & W. Kent.* 705 (R), 1210 (O), 1508 (M).

PADDY CLYDE (IRE) ..—.. 8 b.g. Royal Fountain — Thats Irish (Furry Glen) pp. Workmanlike half-brother to Joctor Don (IRE). IR 20,000 4-y-o. NH FLAT '99 (for P. Webber; tried tongue-tied) r2 p0 (last and pulled up). Sold Doncaster, May for 3400. Originally cost a mint, but has only performed like a horse with problems to date. *P.M. Webb — O. Surrey & Burstow (Ann Blaker).* 131 (OMa), 576 (OMa).

PADDY FOR PADDY ..10-1.. 7 b.g. Mandalus — Lady Rerico (Pamroy) 42212. Workmanlike brother to Irish jumping winner, Tyndarius (IRE), and half-brother to Crown Royale. Dam, half-sister to Good For A Laugh (*qv*), won Restricted and 3rd. P-t-P '99 r1 w1 (Maiden). Made a very pleasing start to his career last year, and has done little wrong since, but lacks a change of gear, and is very much an out-and-out stayer. Not entirely convincing in his defeat of Wise Prince at Brampton, but that rival boosted the form subsequently, and he would have appreciated much more cut in the ground. Supported as if defeat was not an option on his final appearance, but the shortened Eyton circuit was not ideal for him, and the winner is no mug. A likeable sort who can be expected to win on a more regular basis in 2001, particularly if he gets the right conditions. *Mrs J. Thornton — Wheatland (John Downes).* 38 (CR), 371 (R), 612 (CR), 864 (R), 1321 (Cf).

PADDY MAGUIRE (IRE) ..8-12.. 8 b.g. Mazaad — Knocknagow (Buckskin FR) p334. Lengthy. P-t-P '98 (for Mr F. Jestin) r4 w1 (Maiden) p0; 4th, ran out 1, and pulled up 1. NH '98/9 (for L. Lungo) r8 p1. Did well to win as a five-year-old, but subsequently disappointed over hurdles, and did not look wholly genuine at times. Well beaten after completing in Restricteds in 2000, and was sharper in blinkers than without, but needs to improve a great deal to win one, and does not appear to have the necessary resolve. Winning a race taking 7min 57s as a baby has clearly left its mark. *A.W. Argent — Ludlow (Penny Grainger).* 445 (Cf), 669 (R), 992 (R), 1067 (3m2fR).

PAIR OF JACKS (IRE) ..9-1.. 11 ch.g. Music Boy — Lobbino (Bustino) p7563p. Lengthy half-brother to 2 flat winners (one in France), including Lobinda. FLAT to '98 r54 w1 (6f) p9 (short-headed twice). NH '94/9 r48 w6 (2m-2m1f Hdles, the first a Sell) p17 (inc 3 Chses). P-t-P '99 r4 p0 (last, and pulled up 3). An amazingly busy performer who has now made 110 appearances, but last scored in November '96, and as his prime requisites are firm ground and two miles, it is not surprising that he has only once finished better than last in Points. Wears blinkers. *Miss J. Wickens — Kent & Surrey Bloodhounds.* 286 (O), 573 (CfL), 758 (L), 827 (L), 1211 (L), 1509 (Cf).

PALACE KING (IRE) ..9-5.. 12 ch.g. Great Eastern — Fancy Girl (Mon Capitaine) p4. Rangy. IRISH NH FLAT '93 r1 p0 (last). IRISH NH '94 r1 p0 (tailed off and pulled up in Ch). IRISH P-t-P '94 r8 p0 (last, pulled up 5, and fell/unseated 2). P-t-P '95/9 (for Mrs P. Strawbridge) r34 w2 (Members) p4 (3 3rds, of 4 once and last twice); fell/unseated 4, and pulled up 9. Won his Members in '95 and '97, but shows the minimum enthusiasm now, and has managed to avoid success in no fewer than 25 Restricteds. Novice ridden in 2000, and quickly became tailed off. Has been tried in a tongue-strap in the past. *M.J. Wheeler — Cotley.* 356 (Inr), 559 (R).

PALACE PARADE (USA) ..10-3.. 11 ch.g. Cure The Blues (USA) — Parasail (USA) (In Reality) 1u14141. Sturdy quite attractive brother to a winner in USA, and half-brother to several other winners there. Dam won in USA. IRISH FLAT r3 p0. FLAT (for R. Millman) r7 p0. NH '94/9 (won from A. Hobbs'; 2 spells previously for T. Newcombe; previously for G. Ham; previously for N.

Ayliffe; previously for Mrs N. Dutfield) r33 w1 (2m7f Sell Hdle, 22 ran) p4; tailed off last only Ch. Only once successful in 43 attempts from seven previous yards, and gave atrocious displays on his last five appearances. Inconsistent in 2000, but Colin Heard got an excellent tune out of him, and they won on four of five attempts together. Put the icing on the cake for the new connections (who enjoyed a good year all round), when scoring at Fontwell, and there should be further successes to come when his favourite is aboard. Blinkered on five occasions in the past. *H.S. Channon — Lamerton, & Spooners & W. Dartmoor (Yvonne Watson & Jo Channon)*. 103 (Cf), 257 (L), 534 (Cf), 680 (3m1fH), 846 (M), 1471 (Cnr), 1625 (3m2f110yH).

PALLADIUM BOY ..—.. 11 b.g. Supreme Leader — Dear Jem (Dragonara Palace USA) uf. Tall half-brother to Dear Miff, to NH flat and Hurdles winner, Colossus Of Roads, to successful Irish Pointer, Nancy Hanks, and to a flat winner in Sweden. Dam won at 5f. NH FLAT '95/6 r4 p0. NH '96/8 (wins for M. Pipe; previously for Mrs J. Retter) r16 w2 (Hdle & Ch, both 2m4f) p3 (2nd in Sell Ch final). Sold Doncaster, May for 1000. Originally very disappointing, and Martin Pipe did well to get a couple wins out of him. Inconsistent at best, and has become lightly raced. Had a short but disastrous spell in Points, and absent since taking a crashing fall at Pantyderi in February. *Miss G. Roberts — Ystrad Taf Fechan (Robert Rowsell)*. 272 (L), 346 (L).

PLATE 97   351 West Somerset & Minehead Harriers Hunt Members: Pallingham Lad (S. Kidston), 1st, at the last
PHOTO: Brian Armstrong

PALLINGHAM LAD (IRE) ..9-9.. 11 b.g. Torenaga — Star Mill (Milan) 2163pu33. Compact half-brother to Irish jumping winner, Desert Lord, and to Irish Pointing and Chasing winner, Hannies Girl (IRE). NH FLAT r1 p0. NH '95 and '96 r2 p0 (inc Sell). P-t-P '97/8 r5 w1 (Maiden) p2 (3rd of 4 once); fell/unseated 2. Broke down one race after finishing alone at Great Trethew in '98, and could not compete last year, but made his comeback a successful one when winning his Members in which the odds-on favourite unseated after a mile. Has run passably in Restricteds for which he is still qualified, and might be able to win one eventually. Races tongue-tied nowadays, and tried once in blinkers this year. *P.C. Pocock & Mrs L. Jones — W. Somerset V. (Lynn Jones)*. 144 (R), 351 (M), 728 (R), 876 (R), 1043 (R), 1140 (CfR), 1376 (R), 1563 (R).

PALMED OFF ..9-2.. 10 b.m. Palm Track — Alpro (Count Albany) r. Smallish half-sister to Midge and Fingal. Dam, half-sister to 5 Pointers, won Maiden and placed 10. Grandam, Prophet's Star, won 4 flat and 4 NH in Ireland, and won Badsworth Ladies. P-t-P '97/8 r4 p1 (last of 3); 5th, ran out 1, and fell 1. Displayed a modicum of ability in '98, but failed to reappear last year, and was tailed off when refusing on her only outing in 2000. Absent since February, and clearly troubled. *R.T. Dennis — Hurworth (Carol Dennis)*. 133 (CCfMa).

PALM GOLD ..—.. 9 br.m. Palm Track — Golden Chorus (Golden Mallard) pupp8p. Compact well-made owner-bred sister to Pashby Wood, and half-sister to Another Chant. Dam, half-sister to Final

Chant (*qv* '96 Annual), pulled up in 2 Points for David Brydon. Looks very slow, and was beaten 33 lengths on the only occasion she managed to plug to completion. *D.A.D. Brydon — Staintondale, & Derwent.* 377 (R), 393 (M), 620 (R), 809 (OMa), 1033 (OMa), 1229 (M).

PANCHO'S TANGO (IRE) ..—.. 11 b.g. Arapahos (FR) — Pike Review (Dawn Review) p. Tall rangy. IRISH P-t-p '97 r3 w2 (inc Open) p0; pulled up 1. IRISH NH '97/8 r17 w4 (2m-2m4f Chses) p2 (2nds, inc Hunt Ch; beaten head once). NH '99 r3 p0. Unplaced on his nine most recent attempts, and tailed off in all four for present connections. Ground to a halt in a few strides in the latest, and something clearly went badly wrong. Formerly a useful mud lark, particularly in '97, when he won five races. Also successful at the meeting where he landed his Maiden were Brush Me Up, Lough Lein Spirit, Clonroche Slave, Torduff Express, Claudia Electric and Buckshee, all of whom made varying degrees of impact over here subsequently. *N. Shutts — Ludlow (Karen Marks).* 149 (3mH).

PANDA SHANDY ..9-0.. 13 b.m. Nearly A Hand — Panda Pops (Cornuto) 065p7p. Small compact sister to Nearly A Pop, and half-sister to Badger Beer (*qv*). P-t-P/HUNT CH '93/8 (for Mrs S. Woodhouse) r14 w6 (inc Open and Mixed Open) p2 (last of 2, and last of 3); last, fell 4, and pulled up 1. A gutsy little mare in her prime, and prior to breaking down in '98 had won six of her 13 starts, but a shadow of her former self since her return, and failed to beat a single rival in 2000. Gave Hugo Froud his first rides, but was bullied into completion at Ascot (after receiving a two day ban for dropping his hands at Plumpton) and it was a shame to see such a gallant mare treated in such a way. Deserves retirement or a partner who will treat her with some respect. *P.E. Froud — Blackmore & Sparkford V. (John Dufosee).* 33 (Cnr), 327 (O), 579 (3m2fH), 736 (Cnr), 919 (2m3f110yH), 1248 (Cm).

PANGERAN (USA) ..10-9.. 9 ch.g. Forty Niner (USA) — Smart Heiress (USA) (Vaguely Noble) 643u11u31. Good-bodied half-brother to 4 winners of 36 races in USA. Dam won 6 races and $154,999 there. FRENCH FLAT r2 p0. FLAT r1 p0. NH '96/7 and '98 r14 p5 (3 2nds, beaten head once; and inc last of 3 once). P-t-P/HUNT CH '98/9 r9 w3 (inc 2m5f Hunt Ch; also disqualified once for taking wrong course) p4 (3 2nds, beaten head once); and 4th. A much improved performer in the current yard, and has now matched his dams tally of wins, though not quite her prize-money. Usually takes a keen grip, and is suited by an easy three miles or more preferably shorter trips, and can maintain a strong gallop provided the ground is not too testing. Remains an erratic jumper, but Neil King has on the whole proved very difficult to shift, and the combination can look forward to more success in the future, providing he is able to dominate proceedings. *Mrs A.J. McVay & R.Oliver Smith — Suffolk (Neil King).* 17 (O), 151 (3mH), 227 (2m5f110yH), 460 (2m7f110yH), 756 (Cf), 1036 (O), 1156 (3m110yH), 1536 (3m2fH), 1627 (2m5fH).

PANICKED (IRE) ..—.. 11 ch.g. Parliament — Grange Kova (Allangrange) p. Rangy brother to Irish Hurdles winner, I Have You Now, and half-brother to Polecroft. IRISH NH FLAT '96 r2 p1 (3rd). IRISH NH '96 and '98 (blinkered final) r3 w1 (2m Hdle) p0. Clearly exceptionally hard to train, and has pulled up in just three outings since '96. *Miss S. Wallin — Bicester with Whaddon.* 885 (L).

PANTARA PRINCE (IRE) ..9-12§.. 12 b.g Ovac (ITY) — Clara Girl (Fine Blade USA) 3p. Lengthy quite attractive half-brother to Manhattan Rainbow (IRE). Dam won a Bumper in Ireland. IRISH P-t-p '94/5 r9 w1 (6yo&up Maiden) p3 (inc neck and ½l 2nds); pulled up 3. NH '96/7 r8 p4 (Chses). P-t-P/HUNT CH '96 and '98/9 (for Mr R.S. Hunnisett) r14 w1 (Restricted) p6 (2 2nds, inc Hunt Ch); refused 1 and pulled up 1. Generally one-paced and disappointing in England, and six starts from Caroline Bailey's yard yielded just a single placing last year, but has looked soft on occasions, and managed just two outings for another new yard in 2000. Ran prominently for a long way in the Heythrop 4-miler on his latest start, but the way he capitulated suggests he has a problem, and will do well to achieve anything positive in future. *A.D. Sansome — Grafton (Mervyn Loggin).* 771 (O), 1015 (4mO).

PAPARAZZO ..9-7§.. 10 b.g. Posen (USA) — Royale Warning (USA) (Sir Ivor) p3. Tall rangy half-brother to 3 flat winners (one in Ireland and 2 abroad — one prolific in USA). Dam won 2000f. FLAT (for J. Bethell) r1 p0. NH '95/9 (blinkered 1; for W. Jenks, bought for 12,000; all form bar one placing previously for G.M. Moore) r26 w1 (2m1f Ch) p7 (short-headed once; just caught when beaten ½l once). Sold Doncaster, Nov for 5400. Only once successful from 29 attempts in a long career, when driven right out to win a very bad race at Hexham Chase in October '97. Inconsistent and ungenuine, and would surely have little hope of getting the trip in Points (tailed off in both, including when 70 lengths last). *C.J.B. Barlow — S. Jones — Cheshire (Chris Clark; -).* 177 (L), 531 (L).

PAPERBACK WRITER ..9-2§.. 9 b.m. Efisio — Penset (Red Sunset) 4p54424. Robust half-sister to Hurdles winner, Fleur De Tal. NH FLAT '98 r1 p0. NH '98/9 r7 p0 (pulled up 5, inc only Ch). Takes care not to fall, and was one length second in an insipid contest on firm at Corbridge, but performed appallingly when 75 lengths last next time (50 lengths behind Meadowlec — what an insult). Only twice better than last in a Point, and is regularly reluctant to take any interest. Often visored, and went much worse when spurred on her final appearance. *F.V. White — Percy (George White).* 39 (M), 625 (OMa), 913 (CfMa), 1082 (CMa), 1429 (Cm), 1500 (OMa), 1580 (OMa).

PARADE RACER ..10-7.. 10 b.g. Derring Rose — Dusky Damsel (Sahib) 11134. Lengthy half-brother to Dark Comic, Duskey Comic, Country Damsel and Panto Lady. Dam won at 6f, and completed a hat-trick in 2m1f Newton Abbot Nov Hdles. NH FLAT '95/6 r2 p0. NH '96/9 (for P. Murphy) r17 w1 (2m5f Hdle) p3 (inc 39/3rd in Ch). Bought Doncaster, May for 1100. A poor performer in the previous yard, but did not owe them anything, because he landed a major gamble in a Seller on his only success in January '97. Has had a wind operation and was purchased for peanuts, but really took to Pointing, and notched a decisive hat-trick, beating Midsummer Glen on his first two outings. Well handled by Andrew Richardson on those occasions, but still got outridden in the final 100 yards at Kelso, and still finished less than two lengths behind Balisteros who beat Midsummer Glen by a head. Lack lustre on final start, but should again produce decent efforts when returning fresh. *T. Butt — Border.* 43 (Cf), 359 (Cf), 419 (Cf), 686 (3m1fH), 1365 (O).

PARADISE ROW (IRE) ..9-1.. 11 b.g. Gunner B — Great Aunt Emily (Traditionalist USA) 53. Workmanlike lengthy half-brother to Dark Challenger (IRE) (qv). NH '94/5 r6 p2. P-t-P '96 r3 p3 (2 2nds). Jumped poorly, and looked ungenuine when tried in blinkers over hurdles, but has made the frame in four of his five Points despite spending three seasons on the sidelines. Beaten a minimum of 19 lengths in 2000 when prominent for a long way in both outings at Garthorpe, but cannot or will not dig deep when the going gets tough, and looks an unlikely winner. *Mrs J.A. Youdan — Grove & Rufford.* 547 (CfMa), 1269 (OMa).

PARDITINO ..9-13.. 13 b.g. Pardigras — Happy Tino (Rugantino) p134454. Compact brother to Happy Padre, and half-brother to Mantinolas, Happy News, My Happy Lord and Happy Team. Grandam, Happy Chat, won Maiden and 3 Chses (2-3m; ridden by Ken Nicholas in 2). P-t-P '94/9 r37 w9 (inc 2 Opens) p11 (6 2nds); pulled up 7, refused 1, and unseated 3. Christened the winners enclosure at Chipley Park when providing Julie Nicholas with her first success in his Members, but no more than an honest plodder now, and otherwise beaten a minimum of 15 lengths in 2000. Does however reflect great credit on connections, and has now taken his score into double figures whilst remaining a patent safety. Acts on any going. *Mrs C. Nicholas — Tiverton (Ken Nicholas).* 35 (Cnr), 140 (M), 403 (Cf), 638 (Cf), 929 (Cnr), 1098 (C), 1237 (Cf).

PARIS OF TROY ..—.. 13 b.h. Trojan Fen — Little Loch Broom (Reform) p. Compact good-looking half-brother to flat winners, Homeland, Fawzi, Soft Currency and Musaahim. FLAT r15 w2 (8-10f) p2. NH '92 r11 w6 (2m-2m6f Hdles, unbeaten in last 4; inc one on all-weather) p1 (2nd). P-t-P '96 r1 p0 (pulled up). A highly successful front-runner on all surfaces to '92, and led Stephens Pet a merry dance for 2m4f at up ton four years later, but pulled up lame on that occasion, and was seeing the racecourse for the first time since when pulled up at Mounsey Hill Gate this year. Presumably has his thoughts cast in a more carnal direction these days. *Miss L.A. Price — N. Cotswold (Harry Wheeler).* 1605 (L).

PARLIAMENT HOUSE (IRE) ..9-3.. 11 ch.g. Parliament — Sabie Star (Hardgreen USA) pp. Sturdy. Dam won 2m2f Hdle in Ireland. IRISH P-t-P '94 r2 p0 (pulled up 1, and fell 1). P-t-P '99 r5 p2 (3rds); pulled up 2, and fell 1. Had been off the course for five years prior to his four lengths third to subsequent hurdling winner Thebwlboy at Bassaleg last year, but appeared to go wrong there next time, and pulled up and dismounted once again on his 2000 reappearance. Clearly has to have a sound surface, but his legs have never been able to take the strain. *Mrs J.E. Tamplin — Tredegar F. (N. Tamplin).* 650 (CfMa), 822 (CfMa).

PARMAN (IRE) ..10-3.. 10 b.g. Zaffaran (USA) — Wild Civil (Be Friendly) f44561. Strong. Dam won Irish Maiden. IRISH P-t-P '96/9 r20 w3 (inc 4m Open, and novice riders Open) p5; pulled up 5, unseated 3, fell, and ran out. Sold Doncaster, May for 10,000. Looked a doubtful stayer in his first three Irish campaigns, but suddenly blossomed in '99, and won three of his final four attempts and also second to Longmore (qv). Irish connections wisely sold him expensively whilst he was flushed with success, and has been a reasonably competent but one-paced performer in England. Only able to pick up his Members, but it was not his fault that he was unintelligently placed — revels in mud in which there was plenty in 2000, but did all his racing on ground close to good. *R.H. Dalgety — O. Berks (Caroline Gordon).* 195 (O), 453 (Cf), 476 (Cnr), 883 (Cf), 968 (Cf), 1202 (M).

PARSONS SECRET ..8-0.. 7 b.m. Derrylin — Thevicarsdaughter (The Parson) ppu3pp. Tall workmanlike sister to Securon Lady. Bought Malvern, May for 1050. Finished 11 lengths third once, but generally deplorable and went no more than two miles in four of five other attempts. Hung badly for an inexperienced rider once. *S. Jones — Llangeinor.* 147 (OMa), 206 (OMa), 350 (CfMa), 746 (CfMa), 1300 (OMa), 1574 (OMa).

PARSON'S WAY ..10-1.. 14 b.g. The Parson — Daithis Coleen (Carnival Night) ppp2p. Tall lengthy brother to Manassass and Le Piccolage, and to Irish jumping winner, An Parson Beag, and half-brother to Sea Clipper (IRE), and to Irish Pointing winner, Wind Flute. NH FLAT r1 p0. NH '93/5 r19 w1 (2m6f Amat HCap Ch) p1 (2nd); inc pulled up 9 Chses. P-t-P/HUNT CH '96/9 (for Mrs D. Rowell) r24 w3 (Opens) p11 (6 2nds, last twice; and inc last of 3 twice); pulled up 5, refused 1, and fell 1. Still able if he can dominate, but has never been prepared to battle, and downed tools after looking sure to win at Rodmell under Chris Gordon this year. Did not go a yard for the new owner twice in early season, but put up a more prominent display on his final start until appearing to go wrong. Not to be trusted again even if the opportunity seems simple. Usually blinkered, and also tried visored in 2000. *S. Fisher — Mid Surrey F. (Ann Blaker).* 125 (M), 216 (Cnr), 308 (O), 676 (Cf), 830 (Cnr).

PARTY ELEPHANT ..7-0.. 12 b.m. Politico (USA) — Princess Davinia (Saintly Song) 79. Home-bred. Perhaps predictably for a playful Pachyderm, she was about a fence behind when finishing last twice. *Miss F. Hartley — Sinnington (Vicky Parvin).* 693 (OMa), 1004 (OMa).

PASHBY WOOD ..8-6.. 8 b.m. Palm Track — Golden Chorus (Golden Mallard) pfpppp2f. Compact well-made home-bred sister to Palm Gold (qv). A sporting enterprise, but unfortunately is as slow as her sister and not quite as safe. Finished five lengths second in a non-placed Maiden on her only completion, but you cannot sink any lower than that. *D.A.D. Brydon — Staintondale.* 506 (Cf), 623 (Cf), 696 (OMa), 804 (Cf), 1032 (OMa), 1234 (OMa), 1352 (OMa).

PATRINGTON BOY ..8-5.. 8 b.g. Sayf El Arab (USA) — Gunnard (Gunner B) bpp. Good-topped half-brother to Prince Of Plusha, to Hurdles winner, Hot Breeze, and to 2 flat winners. Dam won 2 Sells, 8-10f. FLAT r1 p0 (Sell). NH '97 r2 p0. P-t-P '99 (for Mrs D.E.H. Turner) r3 p0 (5th, and last 2). Only once better than last in six Points, and failed to complete in the new year this year. Not bred to stay, and so it has proved. *R. Shelton — Belvoir (Robert Mackley).* 235 (OMa), 547 (CfMa), 695 (OMa).

PATRIO (IRE) ..9-0.. 8 b.m. Polish Patriot (USA) — Fleetwood Fancy (Taufan USA) Rp4rp53. Small neat half-sister to 4 flat winners (2 abroad), including Elly Fleetwood (IRE) and Western Fleet (USA). Dam won at 5f in Ireland, and later won twice at up to 9f in USA. FLAT r10 p0 (inc Sells). P-t-P/HUNT CH '98/9 r10 p0 (last 2, pulled up 6, and unseated 2). Has shown speed, but can be hard to control, and has only once finished better than last when 18 lengths third on her most recent outing. Struggles to get the trip, and would be a most surprising winner. Missed a marker without retracing on her 2000 reappearance, but James Cole successfully evaded censure. *P. Spry — Spooners & W. Dartmoor (J. Cole).* 158 (CfMa), 539 (OMa), 724 (CfMa), 846 (M), 1048 (CfMa), 1520 (CfMa), 1641 (OMa).

PAUL (IRE) ..9-3.. 9 b.g. Lapierre — Miss Philomena (Raise You Ten) 7345. Small half-brother to Irish Pointing winner, Raise A Trick. IRISH NH FLAT '96 r6 p1 (12/3rd of 5). P-t-P '98/9 (for Mr L. Streeton) r15 p9 (7 2nds, last thrice); pulled up 1, fell/unseated 2. A competent jumper, but desperately easy to beat, and has failed to score in 22 starts over jumps. Ridden by Lorna Collins, daughter of Chris, in her last seven outings, but apart from a decent staying-on third at Tweseldown this year has not looked likely to get her off the mark. *C.D. Collins — V. of Aylesbury.* 33 (Cnr), 220 (OMa), 457 (OMa), 634 (C).

PAUSE FOR THOUGHT ..9-9.. 8 b.g. Bairn (USA) — Mill D'Art (Artaius USA) pff. Leggy light-bodied half-brother to Hurdles winner, Familiar Art, and to a flat winner in Norway. NH FLAT '97 r3 p0. NH '97/8 r10 p1 (2nd in Sell). P-t-P '99 r2 p1 (2nd); and pulled up 1. Looked sure to better his second place at Easingwold last year, when jumping the last with a two length lead in his Members, but sadly suffered a fatal fall. *R. Tate — Bilsdale.* 379 (OMa), 624 (OMa), 1347 (M).

PEACEMAKER (IRE) ..9-11.. 9 br.g. Strong Gale — Gamonda (Gala Performance USA) 31pp43. Rangy brother to Dawn Alert (qv). NH FLAT '97 r2 p0. NH '98/9 (for Mrs D. Haine, blinkered final, tried tongue-tied) r8 p1 (distant 3rd in Ch). Sold Doncaster, Nov for 5500. Hopelessly below standard under Rules, and had a problem with gurgling, but the less frenetic pace in Points seems to suit him. All out to win a three-finisher Maiden at Ampton, but has also performed reasonably when making the frame and beaten about 12 lengths thrice, including behind a hot pair in the latest. A steady jumper, and should find a Restricted. *J.R. Cornwall — Belvoir.* 20 (OMa), 87 (OMa), 151 (3mH), 371 (R), 546 (R), 871 (R).

PEAFIELD (IRE) ..10-1.. 12 b.g. Torus — La'bavette (Le Bavard FR) 533f12. Lengthy brother to Strong Character, and to Irish NH flat winner, Kilkenny Castle. IRISH NH '95/7 r17 p3 (Chses). IRISH NH FLAT '97 r1 p0. IRISH P-t-P '93/5 and '97 r19 w1 (4&5yo Maiden) p6; pulled up 5 and fell 1. P-t-P '98/9 r12 w2 (Confineds) p7 (5 2nds, of 3 once; and 2 3rds, last once); pulled up 1. Consistent in a modest grade, but often fails to deliver more than he promises, and only Philip York has been able to coax him home in this country. Usually a very safe jumper, but can be deliberate especially on ground that is quicker than he prefers. Slipped a tendon off a hock in '99, but showed no ill effects this year, and probably still good enough to win in the South East at 12. *T.D.B. Underwood & A. Parrish — Garth & S. Berks (Tim Underwood).* 676 (Cf), 883 (Cf), 1108 (C), 1398 (Cf), 1509 (Cf), 1620 (Cf).

PEANUTS PET ..9-6.. 16 b.g. Tina's Pet — Sinzinbra (Royal Palace) 2u24543. Small neat half-brother to Cumbrian Way and Cashew King, and to smart jumping winners, Mr Snugfit (2nd in Grand National) and Young Snugfit (also successful on flat), to winning Hurdlers, Half Brother (also succesful Chaser), Snuggle (also winner on flat) and Snugfit's Image, and to flat winner, Superb Singer. Dam won 2 flat; (7-10f). FLAT r14 w2 (16f) p2 (inc last of 3). NH '89/95 r54 w9 (6 Hdles, 2m-2m5f, and 3 Chses, 2m-2m1f) p13; earned £62,706. P-t-P '96/9 r38 w9 (inc 7 Opens; hat-trick '97) p21 (16 2nds, beaten short head once, and head once; and inc last of 3 once); pulled up 2. An incredibly tough little horse under all codes, and now retired with an outstanding record of 20 wins and 39 placings from a total of 113 starts. Had become very one-paced, and failed to score for the first time in five Pointing seasons in 2000, but remained heroically game to the end, and still held every chance at the last in his Members on his final appearance. A remarkably safe ride in Points, and only once lost a rider when hampered by a faller. *D.R. Barnard — Essex.* 84 (L), 177 (L), 417 (Cf), 608 (L), 841 (L), 1037 (L), 1377 (M).

PEARLY HAZE ..9-13.. 8 b.m. Zero Watt (USA) — Brilliant Haze VII (unknown) p52. Very small neat home-bred half-sister to Kristal Haze (qv). P-t-P '98 (for Mr P. & Mrs K. Dando) r4 w3 (Maiden, Restricted and Members) p0; and fell 1. NH '98 (for T.H. Caldwell) r2 p0. Only tiny, but created a very favourable impression when going unbeaten through '98 when completing, but two outings over hurdles was all she could manage under Rules, and presumably met with a setback. Not disgraced on her comeback in 2000, but clearly not going to be the prolific winner she looked like becoming in Wales. Still capable of winning races if the state of her health improves. *A.R. & Mrs S.J. Humphrey — Dunston H. (Sarah Watson).* 770 (Cf), 937 (l), 1114 (Cf).

PEARLY LOCH ..—.. 9 b.m. Lochnager — Pearly Dream (Rymer) p. Small very light-framed. NH FLAT '98 r2 p0 (hampered and fell on debut). P-t-P '99 r1 p0 (unseated). Dogged by ill luck throughout her short career (knocked over on her debut, and claimed by the first on her only appearance last year) and was destroyed after severing a tendon at Larkhill. *Mrs R. Jowett — Wilton.* 455 (OMa).

PEARLY'S SONG ..9-2.. 9 gr.g. True Song — Pearly's Orphan (Precipice Wood) 3pf. Very tall rangy half-brother to Baron's Pearl and to Chasing winner, Pearl Epee. Gave a plucky display and showed some promise when 12 lengths third on his debut, but did not seem to care for the firmer ground and was tailed off by halfway next time. Would probably have finished a modest second had he not fallen three out on his final attempt. Absent since the end of March, but would be a very interesting prospect in a Maiden in soft if the trainer decided to ride him. *Miss S.L. Bailey — Bilsdale (Fiona Needham).* 281 (OMa), 625 (OMa), 798 (OMa).

PEAR TREE PERCY ..9-3.. 8 ch.g. Broadsword (USA) — Howanever (Buckskin FR) p5p. Half-brother to Stick Or Bust. Dam, 'little more than a pony', was 5th and fell in Points; previously won 2-finisher mares Maiden and 2nd 2 (inc NH flat) in Ireland. P-t-P '99 r4 w1 (Maiden) p0; fell 2, and pulled up 1. Hit the deck in two of his first three starts, but won a long Gisburn Maiden on his final appearance last year, and looked to have turned the corner. Only once managed to cover more than two miles in 2000, when tailed off at Tabley, and seems under a cloud at present. Has plenty to prove when he returns. *K. Liscombe — Cheshire Forest.* 782 (R), 963 (R), 1322 (R).

PEASEDOWN TOFANA ..9-12.. 8 b.m. Teenoso (USA) — Hatherley (Deep Run) 2u11. Workmanlike sister to Mrs Duf. Dam is half-sister to Cool Bandit (qv '99 Annual). NH FLAT '98 r2 p0. NH '98/9 (from R. Alner's) r3 p1 (distant 3rd). Gave competent displays in her three Pointing completions, and registered a double in minor company without much fuss. Will probably continue to be thereabouts when she meets the next rise in class. *Sir Richard Sutton — Portman (Louise Alner).* 407 (OMa), 732 (2m4fOMa), 881 (OMa), 1206 (R).

PEATSVILLE (IRE) ..8-9.. 9 b.g. Ela-Mana-Mou — Windy Cheyenne (USA) (Tumble Wind USA) ppp. Big half-brother to several winners, most of them at 2yrs. Dam won 5 sprints in USA. NH FLAT r5 p0. NH '96 r2 p1 (distant last of 2 — 3 ran); and pulled up 1. P-t-P/HUNT CH '98/9 r7 p0 (last 2, pulled up 4, and refused 1). Last in both Pointing completions from ten attempts, and proved beyond doubt on his final appearance that he is never going to stay three miles even on firm ground. *M.P. Allen — Warwicks.* 517 (OMa), 891 (OMa), 1438 (M).

PEBBLE BEACH (IRE) ..9-10.. 11 gr.g. Roselier (FR) — Indian Idol (Indian Ruler USA) 25746. Light-framed half-brother to Irish NH flat and Pointing winner, Dunhill Idol. NH FLAT '94/5 r4 p0. NH '95/9 (for G.M. Moore) r23 w2 (Hdle and Ch, both 3m1f) p7 (beaten a head by the eased Master Kit once). Unplaced in his last eight outings under Rules and only appeared once in '99, but seemed to have turned a corner when he gave a fine display at Alnwick and finished four lengths second to La Riveria with a number of decent performers notably Balisteros behind him. Nothing like as convincing subsequently, and was particularly disappointing when last and favourite for his Members. Wears a tongue-strap. Has not scored since October '97. *T.R. Beadle — Bedale.* 41 (L), 185 (L), 384 (2m3f110yH), 1031 (M), 1643 (3m2fH).

PEE-O-TEMPA ..—.. 9 br.m. Good Times (ITY) — More And More (Tudor Diver) p. Unfurnished. P-t-P '98/9 r3 p0 (pulled up 2, and fell 1). Bled not for the first time on her reappearance, and connections wisely decided to call it a day there and then. Has been retired. *T. Hartgrove — Pytchley (Caroline Bailey).* 51 (OMa).

PENACTION ..8-9.. 7 b.m. Fearless Action (USA) — Pentino (Rugantino) p3. Small. Dam, sister to Rugy, and half-sister to 2 more Pointers, won 2 Points and placed 15 (inc 8 Hunt Chses); failed to score for Robin Rainbow latterly. P-t-P '99 r3 p0 (last, unseated 1, and pulled up 1). Lightly raced, but the early indications are that she does not stay. Beaten around 35 lengths when last twice, and has also made jumping errors. Uninspiring. *R.S. & A. Rainbow — N. Cotswold.* 618 (CMa), 704 (OMa).

PENAWORD ..—.. 8 b.g. Broadsword (USA) — Pensun (Jimsun) pfpp. Small owner-bred half-brother to Rolpen (qv). P-t-P '99 r1 p0 (pulled up). Yet to go more than 2m4f, and has looked backward and error prone to date. *R.G. Weaving — Warwicks (John Pritchard).* 249 (CfMa), 898 (OMa), 1011 (CfMa), 1194 (OMa).

PENDIL'S DREAM ..8-9.. 7 b.m. Handsome Sailor — Pendil's Niece (Roscoe Blake) pff4. Small narrow. Dam, sister or half-sister to 7 Pointers, including Reuter (qv), won 3 Points (inc PPOA) and placedr 3. Yet to show any ability or stamina, and was a fence behind on her only completion, but it remains possible that she might do better eventually. *R. Edwards — Cheshire.* 526 (OMa), 588 (OMa), 966 (OMa), 1412 (OMa).

PENDRAGON ..9-10.. 9 b.g. Bold Fox — Celtic Royale (Celtic Cone) f521f24. Rangy. P-t-P '98 r3 p0 (last pair 2, and pulled up 1). Has improved following a years inactivity, and easily justified favouritism at Littlewindsor, and might have given Shobrooke Mill something to think about had he not fallen at Bratton Down next time. Ran and jumped poorly when visored for the first time and novice-ridden in his Members subsequently, but the prevailing sound surface was probably the most significant factor, and ideally wants plenty of cut. *Mr & Mrs N. Faulks — Exmoor.* 352 (CfMa), 455 (OMa), 738 (OMa), 880 (OMa), 1140 (CfR), 1280 (K), 1566 (M).

PENNCALER (IRE) ..9-8§.. 11 ch.g. Callernish — Pennyland (Le Bavard FR) 14. Tall rangy half-brother to Irish Pointing winners, Penny Bride and Roseland. Dam won 4&5yo Maiden and 2m2f Ch In Ireland. NH FLAT '95 r2 p0. NH '95/8 r17 p5 (2 3rds in Hdles; and 3 Chses); tried to run out and refused once. P-t-P '99 r2 p2 (3rds, of 4 once). Thoroughly ungenuine when often blinkered under Rules, but has plenty of ability, and finally used some of it when winning a long Maiden at Mollington. Jumped the last with a seven length advantage, but was stopping all the way up the hill and had only two in hand at the line. Finished even slower on much better ground on a return trip three weeks later, and may have gone wrong in the process as he was dismounted after the line and failed to reappear. *M. Emmanuel (Emmanuel Family) — V. of Aylesbury (Lawney Hill).* 433 (OMa), 791 (R).

PENNINE VIEW ..10-3.. 14 ch.g. Slim Jim — Salvia (Salvo) 832. Compact owner-bred half-brother to flat and Hurdles winner, Broad View. P-t-P/HUNT CH '93/7 and '99 r25 w4 (up to Confined) p9 (4 2nds; and inc 2 3rds in Hunt Chses); failed to finish 8 (fell/unseated 3, and ran out 1). A thorough stayer, and returned to something like his best this year after looking wrong in '99, but has never found winning easy, and could not quite justify significant market support when a decent second at Aspatria on his final start. Jumps soundly, but wears bandages in front, and tends to hang badly left as though he is saving a leg. *J.J. Dixon — Cumberland F.* 661 (L), 1149 (Cf), 1366 (I).

PENNY APPEAL ..—§§.. 7 ch.m. Clantime — Petroc Concert (Tina's Pet) rpupp. Small sister to a winner in Norway. NH FLAT '98 r2 p0 (last, and pulled up 1 with slipped saddle). FLAT r2 p0. P-t-P '99 r4 p0 (pulled up 2, unseated 1 and ran out 1). Came to Pointing immediately after contesting a race over five furlongs, and still believes she is a sprinter. Possesses two gears, flat-out and stop, but hates being restrained, and shows a complete lack of respect for the fences. A waste of space, and hopefully connections will have the good sense not to inflict her upon us again. *C. Skelton — Brecon & Talybont (Jackie Skelton).* 448 (I), 478 (M), 673 (2m4fOMa), 900 (OMa), 1360 (2m4fOMa).

PENNYMAN (IRE) ..9-5.. 11 b.g. Mandalus — Maggie's Penny (Woodville II) p374. Dam won a Point and a Hunt Ch in Ireland. P-t-P '96 r1 p0 (pulled up). Not beaten that far when tried on a sound surface in his last two starts, and might just be able to win a small race, but has not appeared to stay in more testing conditions. Disappeared without trace for three seasons prior to 2000, and has clearly had his problems. *C. Dawson — S. Durham.* 497 (R), 626 (OMa), 808 (OMa), 1367 (OMa).

PENNYS BOY ..—.. 9 b.g. White Prince (USA) — Windfall Penny (Blast) upfpp. Plain unfurnished brother to Penny's Prince (qv). P-t-P '98 (for Mr J. Sprake) r1 p0 (pulled up). A very poor jumper, and shows no sign of enjoying himself. Ran just once in two years for his breeder, and clearly has a major problem. *Mrs N. Gretton — N. Cotswold (Tom Gretton).* 410 (OMa), 753 (CfMa), 892 (OMa), 995 (OMa), 1189 (M).

PENNY'S PRINCE ..9-12.. 11 b.g. White Prince (USA) — Windfall Penny (Blast) ppp. Very light-framed plain brother to Pennys Boy. Dam won 4 Points (the last of them for the Sprakes) and placed 12 (inc a Sell Hdle). P-t-P '96 and '98/9 r17 w3 (Maiden, Restricted and Intermediate) p1 (3rd); pulled up 2, and fell/unseated 6. A dual winner in '99, but also suffered four spills, and it seems that he no longer enjoys being an equine crash-test dummy, and looked decidedly irresolute on his latest appearance. Scored on firm and in softish, but the worm has clearly turned, and it would be unwise to trust him again until his confidence returns if at all. *J. Sprake — Blackmore & Sparkford V.* 210 (MO), 521 (O), 1133 (O).

PENNYWISE ..10-3.. 8 br.m. Lepanto (GER) — Stubbin Moor (Kinglet) f1p55943. Smallish light-framed half-sister to jumping winner, Edgemoor Prince, and successful Chaser, Captain Stockford. Grandam, Pennyless, won 8 Points (7 Adjacents) and placed 8, and won 2 Hdles and a Chase (all 2m). NH FLAT '97/8 r3 w1 (2m2f) p2. NH '98/9 (for Miss V. Williams) r2 p0; 5th, and unseated in Hdles. NH '00 (from M. Sowersby's) r5 p1 (3rd in 3m Nov Hdle: *ld to 9, rdn & wknd 2 out*; 5th in 3m Nov Hdle: *pulled hrd, chsd wnr frm 3 out, wknd*; 5th in 2m4f110y Nov HCap Hdle: *cl up, ld 4-3 out, one pce*; 9th in 2m5f110y HCap Hdle: *chsd ldrs, ld 6, hdd nxt, wknd 3 out*; and 4th in 2m HCap Hdle: *prom, ld app 2 out, hdd bef last, no ex*). Won her racecourse debut and scored again three years later when making all and surviving errors in a five-runner Confined at Market Rasen, but is far from a natural over fences, and made numerous mistakes in a Hunter Chase there. Reasonably speedy, but difficult to place successfully, as she does not the sufficient quality for average Hurdles. A drop to Sellers would increase her prospects. *P. Clifton — Holderness (Mary Sowersby; Mike Sowersby).* 277 (Cf), 443 (Cf), 586 (3m1fH).

PENROSE LAD (NZ) ..9-5.. 11 b.g. Captain Jason (NZ) — Salimah (NZ) (Double Nearco CAN) p105p. Workmanlike. NH FLAT '96 r2 p0. NH '96/8 (for P. Webber; previously for D. Nicholson) r15 p7; fell in both Chses, with slight advantage 2 out once. Gave plenty of respectable displays under Rules and certainly could not be begrudged his victory in a Maiden at Garthorpe (the second and third retain that status), but current connections inexplicably bought themselves a two miler to go Pointing, and he has been tailed off with just one horse behind him in three attempts since. Does not look like achieving anything in future. *W. Tellwright — Quorn (Di Turner).* 93 (C), 548 (CfMa), 871 (R), 1009 (CR), 1411 (R).

PENTHOUSE MINSTREL ..8-7.. 7 b br.g. Seven Hearts — Pentameron (Heres) ppp3. Unfurnished. Made a small step in the right direction when about six lengths last in a bad Maiden, but still has far to go. Has two paddock handlers, and not always too fluent. *P.D.J. Litston — Mendip F. (Nikki Stevens).* 520 (OMa), 732 (2m4fOMa), 933 (OMa), 1609 (OMa).

PEOVER EYE ..—.. 6 ch.g. Milieu — Gusty Brook (Meadowbrook) upuup. Big strong. Dam is half-sister to Speakers Corner and Eve Pet. Inordinately clumsy at present, and has got rid of partners before halfway on three occasions. Peover and Beover are both English hamlets whose names rhyme if pronounced correctly — bet even Carol Vorderman couldn't spell both correctly! *Mrs C.M. Brown — Cheshire Forest (Ralph Hirons).* 593 (2m4fOMa), 964 (OMa), 1251 (OMa), 1439 (OMa), 1527 (OMa).

PERAMBULATE (NZ) ..10-1.. 9 br.g. Oregon (USA) — French Flavour (NZ) (Zamazaan FR) 4624p. Strong rangy half-brother to a winner in Malaysia. P-t-P '97/8 r7 w2 (Maiden and Confined) p1 (3rd); pulled up 3, and unseated 1. Looked potentially useful when unbeaten in '97, but a major disappointment when not better than tailed off the following year, and spent '99 on the sidelines. Looked as though he might be on the way back after three reasonable efforts on his belated return, but reverted to type in his last two outings, and clearly still ailing. Appears to dislike a sound surface, but his problems lie deeper than that. *W.A. Ritson — Sir W.W. Wynn's (Mrs T. Ritson).* 862 (Cf), 1090 (I), 1152 (I), 1321 (Cf), 1523 (C).

PERCY ARMS ..—.. 10 b.g. Cree Song — Condec (Swing Easy USA) Rp. P-t-P '99 r3 p0 (pulled up 2, and fell 1). Seems to have lost all confidence following a Peper Harow fall last year, and did not have a cut at the fences at all in 2000. *R. Parker - Surrey U.* 309 (OMa), 578 (OMa).

PERCY MEDLICOTT ..9-13.. 8 ch.g. Baron Blakeney — Grafton Maisey (Jimsun) 22233. Strong lengthy half-brother to Shy Lizzie. P-t-P '98/9 r10 w1 (Maiden) p1 (3rd); failed to finish 6 (unseated 2, ran out 2). Made a successful reappearance in '99, but has misbehaved badly since, and even the presence of the former champion in the saddle has not been enough to persuade him to co-operate. Placed in his last four Restricteds, and undoubtedly has the ability to win one, but wholly untrustworthy at present, and should be avoided. Never went a yard when blinkered thrice last year, and has not worn them since. *Mr & Mrs P. Needham — Albrighton Woodland (Helen Needham).* 120 (CR), 261 (R), 669 (R), 864 (R), 1629 (M).

PERCY SMOLLETT ..13-5.. 13 br.g. Oats — Misty Sunset (Le Bavard FR) 22f24. Tall workmanlike half-brother to Henry Cone, and to NH flat winners, Silver Sunset and Wilmott's Fancy (latter also won Hurdles). Dam, half-sister to Sunset Run (*qv* '98 Annual), won 2m4f Hdle for Mr Murray. NH FLAT '92 r1 p0. NH '92/7 and '99 (6 wins from D. Nicholson's; previously from J. McConnochie's) r24 w8 (2m4f Hdle, and 7 Chses, 2m1f-3m) p7; one run at Fairyhouse (pulled up lame). His career earnings under Rules stand at £61,902, and was at his peak when winning six races and second once in a seven race spell for Nicholson '94/6. Has suffered with his legs, and only appeared once after March '97. Made a good start to Pointing when chasing home Knight Of Passion and Bankhead, but subsequently disappointed badly when twice failing at odds-on in Points and when last of two in a Hunter Chase. Has shown a tendency to hang and only ever successful on right-handed tracks, principally when there has been plenty of mud. Always a laid back individual, and old age is probably making him more indolent. *R.G. Murray — Ludlow (Geoff Evans).* 9 (L), 78 (L), 219 (CMod), 466 (3m1fH), 780 (L).

PERDIX ..—.. 6 b.m. Broadsword (USA) — The Howlet (New Brig) ppfpfp6p. Very small half-sister to Greg's Profiles (*qv*). Remarkably inept so far. Jumped badly left in her first three races, and was 65 lengths last on her only completion. Had a hectic time as a five-year-old, and it would be no surprise if connections were now fed up with her. *Mrs C.A. Coward — York & Ainsty S.* 53 (OMa), 139 (OMa), 282 (OMa), 379 (OMa), 398 (OMa), 507 (CMa), 625 (OMa), 1233 (OMa).

PERFECT FINISHER ..10-3.. 10 b.g. Captain Maverick (USA) — Miss Eutopia (Dunphy) p21p6p6fp. Lengthy workmanlike. NH '94 r1 p0 (tailed off). P-t-P '98/9 r10 w1 (Maiden) p1 (3rd); 7th, last, unseated 1, and pulled up 5. Given to Mark Hawkins after breaking down in '94, and having been given plenty of time to recover has won twice for him despite not looking the ideal novice ride. Sweats excessively, and can be impetuous, but tries hard, and might have won twice more in 2000, but thwarted by Amy Melvins' lack of experience at Dunthrop, and fell three out when going strongly in the lead at Maisemore on his penultimate start. Does not seem to stay too well at times, but his willing attitude should stand him in good stead in future, and his Members looks an ideal target in 2001. *M.A. Hawkins — Farmers Bloodhounds.* 36 (CI), 190 (M), 285 (CR), 543 (I), 897 (I), 1006 (Cf), 1203 (I), 1313 (MO), 1416 (O).

PERFECT LIGHT ..10-4.. 12 b.g. Salmon Leap (USA) — Sheer Gold (Yankee Gold) fpp. Tall half-brother to Hays Lodge. Dam won 2 Irish flat, 12-16f, and won 4 Hurdles, 2m4f-3m (was useful). FLAT r7 p0. NH '92/6 r6 p2; 4th only Ch. P-t-P '97/8 (for Mr V.Y. Gethin & Miss F. Stone) r9 w6 (inc 2 Opens, one 3m2f; inc hat-trick '98) p1 (2nd); and fell/unseated 2. IRISH P-t-P/HUNT CH '99 (for E. Bolger) r3 p1 (30*l* last of 3). IRISH NH '99 r3 p0. A hard-puller who soon establishes a clear lead, and only Solba managed to get the better of him when completing '97/8, but less successful in Ireland the following year when his only piece of form was a poor third behind Dixon Varner. Was getting the staggers when he came down at the final open ditch in his Members on his return to English Points, and dropped out tamely when pulled up subsequently, and presumably has some fault now. Tends to jump right, and has always been rather hit and miss, but will long be remembered for jumping Solba ragged in the '98 Dudley Cup. Wears a cross-noseband. *C.J. Hitchings — N. Herefords (Annie Downes).* 332 (M), 530 (O), 859 (O).

PLATE 98   *9 Army Ladies Open: L to R Percy Smollett (Miss S. Vickery), 2nd, and Silver Sleeve (Miss L. Bridges), pu, jump ahead of Mr Golightly (Mrs J. Reed), ref, between horses and Tomcappagh (Miss J. Grant), 3rd, early in the race*   PHOTO: Brian Armstrong

PERFECT MINSTREL (IRE) ..10-2.. 10 b.g. Black Minstrel — Ashford Doll (Pitcairn) 121. Workmanlike compact. Dam won at 12f in Ireland. NH '96 r1 p0 (tailed off last). P-t-P '98 r4 w1 (Maiden) p0; last, pulled up 1, and fell 1. Stronger physically since his last campaign, and coped well with the heavy ground at Mollington on his comeback, but better suited by a sounder surface and comfortably landed a five-runner Restricted on firm at Ashorne on his final appearance. Ran his best race in 2000 in defeat behind Burgundy Bob, and a reproduction would see him home in an Intermediate next year. Wears a cross-noseband. *Mrs V. McKie — Bicester with Whaddon.* 427 (M), 791 (R), 1442 (R).

PERHAPS (USA) ..10-2.. 10 b.m. Lord Avie (USA) — Allegedly Flashing (USA) (Alleged USA) 3. Workmanlike lengthy half-sister to 2 winners in USA. FLAT r5 p0. NH '95/6 r10 w2 (2m2f Hdle and 2m2f Ch) p5. P-t-P/HUNT CH '97/9 (for Mrs C. Banks & Mrs P. Tollit) r10 w2 (Opens) p1 (2nd); pulled up 2, and brought down 1. Unable to stand a full campaign until she was eight, but moody and unreliable and probably aided by being sparingly raced. Won a 7min 17s Open in softish in '99, but sent back to her owners after a promising comeback this year, and presumably a career as a broodmare beckons. *Mrs C. Banks — Worcs (Evan Williams).* 143 (C).

PERKING ..8-4.. 8 b.g. Kinglet — Persue (Perhapsburg) 5ppp. Robust close-coupled brother to Purslet (*qv*). P-t-P '99 r5 p0 (pulled up 4, and fell 1). Has shown some speed, but a short-runner to date, and has not been an entirely convincing jumper. Could do with being fitter, but probably well below average ability anyway. *B.J. Vine, T. Trigg & Miss C. Weller — Avon V. (Claire Weller).* 60 (OMa), 264 (OMa), 732 (2m4fOMa), 1021 (2m4fOMa).

PERRIPAGE ..8-12.. 10 ch.g. Nearly A Hand — Perrimay (Levanter) pupppupR. Half-brother to Sulason. Dam, 'the Miss Havisham of racing', was placed in 7 Points for Richard Miller. Grandam, Neat Perry, won 11 Points and RA Gold Cup and placed 11. P-t-P '97/9 (for Mr R.N. Miller) r13 w1 (Maiden) p2 (neck 2nd of 3, and 3rd of 4); pulled up 4, fell/unseated 2, and refused 1. The winner of a two-finisher Maiden at Larkhill in '99, but unmotivated before the application of blinkers, and has taken the rise out of the inexperienced rider in the new yard. Thrice eliminated inside the first mile, and has quickly lost interest otherwise, and a visor has made no difference. Needs sorting out by a strong pilot, but probably beyond salvation now. *Mrs S. Sansom & P. Rhodes — O. Surrey & Burstow (Ann Blaker).* 126 (R), 285 (CR), 306 (R), 575 (R), 825 (R), 1104 (R), 1393 (R), 1508 (M).

PERSEVERANCE ..9-2.. 15 b.g. Pardigras — Perplexity (Pony Express) p54. Plain owner-bred half-brother to Sure Goer, Miss Pernickity and Blackdown Beauty. Dam is half-sister to Permit (*qv* '98 Annual). P-t-P '92/9 r29 w2 (Maiden and Club Restricted) p4 (2 3rds, last once); failed to finish 16 (unseated 3). Capable on his day, but has always lacked consistency, and gained his last win back in '96. Lightly raced, and of little account since, and well beaten under novice girls in 2000. Wears a cross-noseband, and often taken to post early. *D.H. Bennett — Beaufort.* 749 (Cf), 1097 (Inr), 1243 (Inr).

PERSEVERE ..—.. 7 b.m. Pursuit Of Love — Seastream (USA) (Alleged USA) p. Small. 8000y. FLAT (visored 3, inc Sell; for G. Roe, bought for 3500; previously for Lord Huntingdon) r12 p1 (3rd on debut); refused to race final; unseated and bolted before start once previously. Sold Ascot, Nov '98 for 500. Looked a nutter on the flat and was described by Timeform as 'one to leave alone', and subsequently advertised in the sales catalogue as 'a girl's ride' (charming). Made most until the 12th in a Maiden, but was tailed off a couple of fences later, and thankfully not seen again. *Miss S. Dutton & J. Gregory — Farmers Bloodhounds.* 617 (CMa).

PERSIAN BOY (IRE) ..9-12.. 9 b.g. Brush Aside (USA) — Bargara (Bargello) pp34112543p. Compact good-looking half-brother to Patrickswell, Mister Joule (IRE) and Battle Royal (IRE), to Hurdles winner, Mossgard, and to Irish jumping winners, Cahervillahow (smart) and Bosphorus (also won NH flat), and to successful Irish Hurdler. IR 55,000 4-y-o. NH '97/8 (for O. Sherwood) r8 p0 (pulled up 4, inc both Chses). Bought Ascot, March for 1100. All out when winning a Maiden in his garden at Ampton, and well placed to follow up two weeks later in a Restricted at Parham (bad contests, with three finishers in both), but his obvious lack of stamina always catches him out in competitive company. Pulls keenly and regularly races up with the pace, but the final half mile is a constant problem for him. Has had a 'modified ahern operation' (answers to that one on the back of a postcard please!). *J.M. Turner — Suffolk.* 6 (R), 131 (OMa), 290 (OMa), 322 (CfMa), 551 (OMa), 705 (R), 937 (I), 1155 (2m5f110yH), 1267 (I), 1537 (2m5fH), 1667 (I).

PERSIAN BUTTERFLY ..9-11.. 9 b.m. Dancing Dissident (USA) — Butterfly Kiss (Beldale Flutter USA) 4p184. Small half-sister to Hurdles winner, Suivez. Dam won at 12f. FLAT (visored 1) r14 p0. NH '96/8 r25 w1 (2m1f Sell Hdle) p5 (inc 3rd in Ch). P-t-P/HUNT CH '99 r6 p2; last pair 2, and fell 2. Only able to win one of her first 47 races, and had struggled to stay three miles in Points, but aided by a sound surface and the fall of the likely winner, landed a Ladies at Mollington. Well beaten otherwise in 2000, and is probably flattered by an Open success. Expends a lot of nervous energy through excessive sweating in the preliminaries. *S. Astaire — Bicester with Whaddon (Chris Loggin).* 3 (L), 475 (L), 787 (L), 1417 (L), 1483 (L).

PERSIAN DAWN ..9-5.. 8 br.m. Anshan — Visible Form (Formidable USA) p2p17. Close-coupled attractive half-sister to Russian Vision, to 4 flat winners (one in Germany), including Azeb and Living Image, to successful Hurdler, Spofforth, and to Irish flat and Hurdles winner, Gift Token. Dam won 2 flat, 6-10f. 4200f, 12,500y. FLAT (early runs for Major D. Chappell) r11 p1 (8/ 3rd). NH '96/9 (blinkered 1; from R. Frost's, bought for 700; previously for R. Phillips) r13 p2; mostly Sells. Left clear after the likely winner had unseated at the last in a youngsters Maiden at Stafford Cross, but was idly ridden, and only just held off the rallying champion by half a length. Consistently exposed as extremely moderate otherwise, and finished lame when failing to land a gamble next time. *R. John — Eggesford.* 146 (OMa), 205 (OMa), 725 (L), 933 (OMa), 1517 (R).

PERSIAN MYSTIC (IRE) ..10-4.. 9 ch.g. Bold Arrangement — Bombalurina (Pharly FR) pp21. Compact half-brother to an Irish flat winner. Dam is half-sister to Cornamona (*qv* '97 Annual). IRISH FLAT r19 w1 (9f) p4 (short-headed once). IRISH NH '96 r12 w1 (2m Hdle) p4. NH '97/9 (for D. Wintle, twice blinkered, tongue-tied final) r18 p6 (inc 2 Sells); led 'til fell last once (looked winner). Able, but constantly disappointing, and was gaining only his third success from 53 attempts when he won his Members. Made a few slow jumps, but proved to be in a slightly better mood than Anorak, who had beaten him convincingly on their two previous meetings. Might decide to run up to his current rating again, but it generally needs taking with a bucket of salt. *Mrs J. Howells — Llangeinor (William Howells).* 741 (Cf), 1295 (Cf), 1450 (Cf), 1656 (M).

PERSIAN RAIDER ..—.. 12 gr.g. Whistlefield — Go Persian (Persian Plan AUS) fppp. Rangy. Old and mystified, and does not have the faintest idea of how to jump properly. Bred from a mare who slogged away fruitlessly for six seasons over Hurdles. *Miss M.L. Hawkings — Taunton V.H.* 641 (CfMa), 953 (I), 1370 (I), 1467 (R).

PERSIAN SWORD ..—.. 15 b.g. Broadsword (USA) — Sorraia (El Ruedo) uuup. Tall brother to Silver Madam, and half-brother to Langston and Two Gents. NH '89/91, '93/5 and '97/8 (for D. Nicholson) r36 w4 (2 Hdles and 2 Chses, all 2m) p5. Gained the last of his four wins (all in mud) in November '93, and has not even been placed since January '95. A sketchy jumper of regulation fences, and made an ill-advised return in Ladies Opens, in which Paul Swindin fell off in all three attempts. Tried in spurs, and blinkered on his two most recent outings. *Mrs J. Marles — Warwicks.* 191 (Cf), 368 (L), 512 (L), 895 (MO).

PERSIAN VIEW (IRE) ..9-11§§.. 11 ch.g. Persian Bold — Recapture (Sassafras FR) p3. Sturdy compact brother to 2 flat winners (one abroad), and half-brother to 3 others (2 abroad, one also successful over jumps in Italy). IRISH FLAT r2 w1 (12f, on sands at Laytown) p0. IRISH NH FLAT '94 r6 p2 (2nds). NH '94/7 and '99 (for N. Babbage, bought for 1600; wins previously for K. Bailey, bought for 7200; tongue-tied final) r22 w5 (2 Hdles, 2m6f-3m3f, and 3 Chses, 3m-3m2f) p6. Bought Malvern, Sep for 1400. Gained the most recent of his wins when thrice successful between September and November '97, but is a famously temperamental animal, and has refused to race twice, and frequently been reluctant to do so. Claimed in the sales catalogue to have 'no vices' (these booklets often contain more romance than Mills and Boon), and was soon up to his old tricks again in Points, finishing 25 lengths third at Howick after whipping round and setting off a fence behind the rest. Seems hard to train these days. *W.H. Pugh — Llangeinor.* 480 (O), 598 (O).

PERSONAL GUARANTEE ..—.. 6 b. Broadsword (USA) — Sun Goddess (FR) (Deep Roots) pp. Small half-sister to jumping winner, Oban. Dam won 2 French flat, 10-12f. Pulled up in early season Maidens (very novicey and tailed off after a mile on her debut, having veered and made a slow start). *M.J. Brown — York & Ainsty S.* 380 (OMa), 398 (OMa).

PERSONA PRIDE ..—..§§.. 7 gr.g. St Enodoc — Le Jour Fortune (Twilight Alley) pp. Lengthy brother to Petite Fortune. Dam, 3rd in Hdle, won 9 Points (inc 4 Ladies) and placed 6 (inc 2 3rds in Hunt Chses) for Percy Priday. Remarkably quick to develop a dislike for racing, and virtually pulls himself up as soon as he feels he has done enough. *P. Priday — Radnor & W. Herefords (Richard Mathias).* 667 (Cf), 1466 (OMa).

PETER POINTER ..—.. 13 br.g. Relkino — Housemistress (New Member) R. Small brother to Hurdles winner, Chain Line, and half-brother to Rons Venture. Dam won 2 Hunt Chses and 14 Points (13 Ladies, 3m-3m3f) and placed 11 (inc a Hdle). NH FLAT '93 r2 p0. NH '94, '96 and '99 r6 p1 (3rd in 2m Claiming Hdle). P-t-P '97/8 r4 p0 (last pair 2, and pulled up 2). Out of a very tough mare who was a prolific winner, but of no account himself even in the lowest grade, and seemed tainted by madness. Destroyed after breaking a hind leg sustained in a run out at Bredwardine. *A.J. Williams — Llangibby (Sue Williams).* 1462 (L).

PETREA ..8-9.. 6 b.m. St Ninian — Polypodium (Politico USA) 57. Small compact owner-bred half-sister to Meadowbank, and to NH flat winner, Black Secret. Dam is half-sister to 5 Pointers, including Good For A Laugh (qv). Poured from a completely different mould to Meadowbank, and faded tamely when a disappointing favourite on her second attempt, but has certainly done enough to justify hopes that she will produce more at six. *Mrs E.C. York — Middleton (Tim Walford).* 439 (OMa), 793 (CfMa).

PEYTON JONES ..9-10.. 8 b.g. Presidium — York Street (USA) (Diamond Shoal) 5p15. Sturdy half-brother to Hurdles winner, Coochie. NH '96 and '98 r4 p0 (last twice, and pulled up 2 — tailed off all 4). P-t-P '99 (for Mr M. Biddick) r6 w1 (Maiden) p1 (3rd of 4); 6th, pulled up 2, and fell 1. Well supported on occasions in both Pointing yards, but seemingly on able to show his ability on a sound surface, and supplemented his '99 Maiden success with a ready win at Cothelstone this year. Not a stout stayer, but should find another easy opportunity when the ground rides fast. *R. Willis (M & W Partnership) — Portman (Richard Miller).* 69 (R), 331 (R), 1551 (R), 1651 (I).

PHAEDAIR ..9-8.. 11 b.g. Strong Gale — Festive Season (Silly Season) pu055. Big strong half-brother to Arctic Revel (qv). NH '95/6 r6 p1 (distant 3rd in Ch); 5th of 6, last, pulled up 1, and unseated 1 in Chses, and pulled up in Hdle (unseated before start and bolted). P-t-P '97/8 r6 w2 (Maiden and Restricted) p0; 4th, and fell/unseated 3. Once talented, but totally insane, and has gone AWOL from the preliminaries on four occasions. Successful in two of his three completions '98/9, but well below par in 2000, and will be looking at a ban if his pre-race behaviour does not improve soon. Always taken to post early, but withdrawn from his intended reappearance at Hereford after he bucked Jamie Diment and bolted a circuit and a half. Jockeys, you have been warned. *Mrs P. Gordon, Mrs A. Godey & P. Webb — O. Surrey & Burstow, & Mid Surrey F. (F.E. Sutherland).* 789 (O), 1205 (MO), 1341 (2m110yH), 1447 (2m4fH), 1530 (2m6fH).

PHANTOM SLIPPER ..8-0.. 11 gr.g. Pragmatic — Tender Soul (Prince Tenderfoot USA) pp. Tall rangy brother to Longford, and half-brother to Hurdles winner, Ardoon Prince. P-t-P/HUNT CH '96 and '98/9 r13 p3 (2nd of 3; and 2 3rds, last once); last pair 2, pulled up 4, unseated 1, and ran out 2. Made the frame on four occasions '98/9 after disastrous beginnings, but only able to beat some of the South Easts' worst performers which quickly puts his level of ability into context. Pulled up in both outings this year, and acquired blinkers in the first of them. Would make a surprising and highly undeserving winner. *L.J. Bowman & T. Warr — Kent & Surrey Bloodhounds (Sarah Warr).* 829 (OMa), 984 (OMa).

PHARARE (IRE) ..10-11.. 11 ch.g. Phardante (FR) — Shakie Lady (Tug Of War) 111u11. Small well-made. NH FLAT '94 r1 p0. NH '94/7 r30 w4 (2m-3m2f Hdles) p8 (inc 2 Chses). P.t-P '99 r6 w6 (Ladies, 6-timer). A fabulously talented Ladies horse who has been adjudged unbeaten in his 11 completions (would have won the other but the trainer fell off at the last). Capable of spread-eagling the field from an early start, but can sit in behind and quickens as soon as Caroline Spearing lets out an inch of rein, usually with about a mile to run. Involved in one of the races of the season at Weston Park on his penultimate start where he appeared to have been pipped on the post by Hearts Are Wild, the pair having fought tooth and nail for supremacy throughout the final mile. The judge however could not split them and honours were officially even. Acts on any going, but a left-handed track seems essential, and has not been asked to race in a clockwise direction in Points. Will remain hard to beat in 2001. *Mrs M. Williams — N. Ledbury (Caroline Spearing).* 118 (L), 245 (L), 397 (L), 668 (L), 1410 (L), 1483 (L).

PHAR AWAY CRUISE ..—.. 8 b.m. Phardante (FR) — Indian Cruise (Cruise Missile) ppp. Sparely-made. Dam won 2m5f Ch and last of 2; and was placed in 2 Points after producing Phar Away Cruise ('may barely stay 3m'). Grandam, Indian Diva, won 3 Hunt Chses (2m4f-3m2f) and 5 Points and placed 8 (inc 2 Hunt Chses and HCap). P.t-P '99 r2 p0 (pulled up 2). Showed speed before stopping quickly after two miles at Clifton-on-Dunsmore, but dreadful otherwise, and has pulled up in all five starts. Has acquired an off-side pricker. *Mrs D. Cowley — Pytchley.* 514 (OMa), 1423 (OMa), 1589 (2m4fOMa).

PHAR FROM CHANCE ..10-1.. 6 ch.g. Phardante (FR) — Chancer's Last (Foggy Bell) 21. Home-bred half-brother to Spaceage Gold (qv). Weakened and headed close home after looking in command between the last two at Charing, but kept going strongly for a 12 lengths success when confirming the promise in another 2m4f Maiden at Stoneaston. Likely to stay three miles, and looks a very pleasing prospect who should be worth following. *Count K. Goess-Saurau — V.W.H.* 284 (2m4fCMa), 732 (2m4fOMa).

PHARLINDO (IRE) ..10-4§.. 10 b.g. Phardante (FR) — Linda Martin (Furry Glen) 1pfuff. Compact half-brother to Linda's Prince (IRE). Dam won Irish NH flat. IRISH NH '95/6 (blinkered final) r9 p0. P.t-P '97/9 r14 w3 (Maiden, Restricted and Intermediate) p3 (2nds); failed to finish 8 (ran out 3, and fell/unseated 4). A useful Pointer when all goes well, but takes a fierce hold, hangs violently right-handed, and often takes the fences by the roots. Recorded his fourth career victory, and second at Duncombe Park, when making a successful reappearance, but could not get round in five subsequent attempts, and his vices get worse instead of better. Ridden with nerves of steel (and maybe several valium) by Fiona Needham. Wears a cross-noseband, and an off-side pricker. *Mrs J.W. Furness — Hurworth.* 277 (Cf), 375 (Cf), 506 (Cf), 816 (Cf), 997 (Cf), 1266 (L).

PHAR LORD (IRE) ..9-2.. 7 br.g. Phardante (FR) — Buckskin Lady (Buckskin FR) 1p. Tall half-brother to Chasing winner, Grundon (IRE). Sold Malvern, Oct for 1850. Made a winning start in mid-February at Black Forest Lodge, but was opposed by a bunch saddoes who still never won anything. Faded in the final half mile of a Restricted and not seen again, but might proved to be under-rated in that grade if he reappears. *D.C.J. Skinner — Berkeley (Mike Harding).* 206 (OMa), 477 (R).

PHARMISTICE (IRE) ..10-5.. 10 b.g. Phardante (FR) — Lucylet (Kinglet) 312214. Tall attractive half-brother to Garryspillane (IRE) (qv). NH FLAT '96 r3 p0. NH '96/8 r6 w2 (2m7f Hdles) p1 (2nd); 4th and 8th in Chses. P.t-P '99 r5 w1 (Members) p1 (2nd); 4th, and unseated 2. Won twice and second over hurdles at Kelso '96/7, and had the right credentials to make a useful Pointer, but an excitable sort who takes a strong hold, and it took Nicola Stirling a little while to master him, and become secure. The pair now make a formidable partnership particularly on a sound surface, and whilst his three Pointing successes have come in two and three-finisher affairs his three placings behind Balisteros in 2000 have been equally useful efforts. A sound jumper, and should win again if he can avoid the aforementioned on a more regular basis in 2001. Has two handlers, and wears a cross-noseband. *Mrs P.C. Stirling — Lauderdale.* 421 (3m5fL), 715 (L), 1161 (L), 1426 (L), 1447 (L), 1579 (L).

PHARNISKEY (IRE) ..—.. 10 b.g. Phardante (FR) — Mahon Falls (Proverb) ffuu. Dam won mares Maiden in Ireland. IRISH P.t-P '97/9 r6 w1 (7 plus Maiden) p3; pulled up 1. Sold Doncaster, May for 8000. Looked expensive for a rising nine-year-old who had only averaged two outings per annum in Ireland, but if he had any ability he certainly masked it with his alarming jumping. One displayed verged on earning him rating, but it looked as if survival was uppermost in Ollie Elwood's mind (very wise of him) on his latest attempt, but he got dumped yet again, making the wisdom of possibly persevering for another season ponderable. *J. Studd — S. & W. Wilts (Sarah Waugh).* 958 (R), 1135 (R), 1280 (R), 1594 (R).

PHARPEN (IRE) ..9-9.. 7 b.g. Phardante (FR) — Penthouse Pearl (Green Shoon) f6p1. Strong. Dam won NH flat and 2m Hdle in Ireland. P.t-P '99 r2 p1 (2nd of 3); and unseated 1. Took rather longer to open his account than expected (though schooled blatantly once after a fall at Weston Park on his reappearance) but easily waltzed home by a wide margin in a poor Maiden at Bredwardine on his first start, and looks to possess enough scope for Restricteds at least next year. Looks a typical Phardante, and unlikely to be seen to advantage on an easy surface. *Mrs C. Robinson — Albrighton.* 298 (CfMa), 616 (CMa), 989 (OMa), 1466 (OMa).

PHARSILK (IRE) ..9-8.. 12 ch.g. Phardante (FR) — Boule De Soie (The Parson) pp. Strong good-looking half-brother to Most Rich (IRE). IRISH NH '94/6 (blinkered once) r16 w1 (2m Ch) p3 (inc 3rd in Hdle; 2nd in 2 Chses, short-headed once). NH '97 r2 p1 (2nd); and pulled up 1. P-t-P/HUNT CH '99 r3 p0 (4th, and fell/unseated 2). Gained his only success over the minimum trip at Down Royal in '96, but a confirmed tearaway who cannot sustain his gallop over further, and has failed to finish in all three Points '99/00. Has never stood much racing, and his appearances in the last four years have been strictly rationed. *A. Read — S. Dorset (Ken Nelmes).* 209 (M), 383 (3mH).

PHARSTAR (IRE) ..10-1.. 10 b.g. Phardante (FR) — Winter Fox (Martinmas) pp1. Rangy half-brother to Winter Gale (IRE), to jumping winner, Belstone Fox, to NH flat winner, Leinthall Fox, and to Irish flat and Hurdles winner, Sylvia Fox. IRISH NH FLAT '96 r2 p2 (3rds). NH '98 (for N. Henderson) r2 p0 (fell only Ch, when well clear at the 6th). Bought Doncaster, May for 2000. Showed David Easterby at his best when winning much the fastest of the three Maidens at Hutton Rudby, and made all, but settled well in front, when equipped with a drop noseband and a twisted snaffle, but had bolted at a suicidal pace and failed to get round on three previous attempts over fences. Has stood his racing extremely, and getting a victory out of him was surely a triumph for connections. *Mrs A.M. Easterby — Middleton (David Easterby).* 54 (OMa), 399 (OMa), 627 (OMa).

PHARTOOMANNY (IRE) ..8-10.. 11 b.m. Phardante (FR) — Deep Whistle (Deep Run) u76s6p. Sister to Irish Pointing winner, Dantes Whistle. IRISH P-t-P '97 r5 w1 (6 plus mares Mdn) p0; pulled up, and fell 2. NH '97 (for B. Mactaggart, bought for 4300) r1 p0. Safe enough, but has no ability these days, and beaten a minimum of 36 lengths with a total of three behind her if completing in 2000. Tried in a tongue-strap once. *Mrs C. Fox & Mrs F.D.A. Snowden — Tiverton (Sarah Kittow).* 164 (R), 315 (R), 729 (R), 1045 (L), 1309 (R), 1467 (R).

PHAR TOP (IRE) ..—.. 6 b.m. Phardante (FR) — Topping Out (Kampala) f. Good-topped. Dam is half-sister to Secret Four (*qv*). Fell after a mile in late May. Better bred than many Welsh maidens (her dam was placed in two flat and five Hurdles in Ireland), and should do better in time. *Mrs H. Gibbon — Pembs (Graham Lavis).* 1617 (OMa).

PHILELWYN (IRE) ..9-9.. 10 br.m. Strong Gale — Miss Kamsy (Kambalda) 516. Unfurnished half-sister to Irish NH flat and Hurdles winner, Ross Moff (IRE) (also won English Hurdles). Dam won 2m4f Hdle. P-t-P '96/8 (for Mr P.E. Griffiths & Mr E. Parkes) r15 p5 (3 2nds, of 3 once; and inc last of 3 once); pulled up 7, and fell/unseated 3. Gained her success at the 17th attempt, but it was much deserved after five placings, and four years of trying. Did not stay well enough to be considered seriously in Restricteds, but looked to have considerable potential as a broodmare, but believed to have succumbed to a rare illness in the Summer. *E.P. Parkes — United (Richard Wilding).* 121 (OMa), 337 (CfMa), 612 (CR).

PHILTRE (IRE) ..10-11.. 7 b.g. Phardante (FR) — Forest Gale (Strong Gale) 1122p. Smallish unfurnished half-brother to Forest Fountain (IRE) (*qv*). P-t-P '99 r3 p2 (2nds, short head of 3 once); and fell 1. Showed plenty of ability as a five-year-old, and soon made his mark in 2000, making most to win at Whitwick and Chaddesley. Found the vastly more experienced Strong Chairman just too good next time, and will rarely meet a horse of the calibre of Key Debate again. Probably found the trip too far for him at this stage in his career when pulled up in the John Corbet on his final appearance, but is confidently expected to do well in 2001. Not particularly robust, but a good mover, and is bred to be suited by top-of-the-ground. *J.D. & Mrs A.M. Callow — Albrighton Woodland (Helen Needham).* 339 (CfMa), 612 (CR), 1064 (3m2fCf), 1333 (3mH), 1646 (3m4fH).

PICARD (IRE) ..9-8.. 8 b.g. Durgam (USA) — Miners Society (Miner's Lamp) 2u4u. Small sturdy. IRISH FLAT r10 p1 (2nd). IRISH NH '97 r1 p0 (last). NH '98 r2 p0 (fell 1, and unseated 1 in Chses). P-t-P '99 r5 w1 (Maiden) p0; last, fell/unseated 2, and pulled up 1. Made all and survived a blunder to win a two-finisher Maiden on firmish last year, but has not gelled with a novice rider in 2000, and his jumping remains chancy. Beaten less than five lengths when regaining blinkers at Cherrybrook, and retained them in his next outing where he was making the best of his way home when parting company with Linda Hawkins at the 14th at Holnicote (the fence where he almost threw Maiden victory away 12 months previous). Good enough to win an average Restricted if he co-operated, but his enthusiasm can also be called into question. Has been tried tongue-tied. *A. & Mrs J. Walter — Taunton V.H. (Alan Walter).* 356 (Inr), 560 (R), 853 (Inr), 1375 (R).

PICCADILLY WOOD ..—§.. 7 gr.g. Newski (USA) — Dark Acre (Peacock FR) pppRu2p. Small lengthy. Dam won 3 minor Points and placed 8 for Jason Warner (previously 3rd once in Ireland). Deeply inadequate in both running and jumping, and was never in the contest when 20 lengths last of two on his only completion. Additionally temperamental, and the rider opted out at the final fence in a match for his Members, having almost been refused with three out. *J.S. Warner — Cotswold V.F.* 147 (OMa), 341 (CfMa), 486 (R), 602 (CfMa), 899 (OMa), 1019 (2m4fOMa), 1310 (M).

PICCOLINA ..—.. 9 ch.m. Phardante (FR) — Highland Chain (Furry Glen) p. Angular. Dam won 2m5f Hdle. NH '97 (for R. Phillips) r2 p0 (tailed off). Made a rare appearance when showing speed for two miles in a Confined (66-1), but soon weakened and pulled up. *Ms Rebecca Howard — Cranwell Bloodhounds (T. Howard).* 868 (Cf).

PICK-N-CRUISE ..9-12.. 9 b.m. Cruise Missile — Pickled Tink (Tickled Pink) p1u. Small light-framed half-sister to Wolf Hunter and Chalet Pierre. Dam, 3rd in an Open, was previously awarded 3m3f HCap Hdle. NH FLAT '97 r1 p0. NH '97/8 r5 p0 (9th of 10, last, and pulled up 3 in Hdles). P-t-P '97 and '99 r5 p0 (fell 2, ran out 1, and pulled up 2). Looked crackers in previous years, and still prone to dive off on a tangent, but successfully wagonned by David Stephens at Trebudannon to land a three-finisher Maiden on firm. Pulls hard, and has been taken to post early, and still could not be supported with any confidence. Wears a cross-noseband. *G. Andrew — S. Cornwall.* 849 (R), 1390 (OMa), 1518 (R).

PIGEON HILL BUCK (IRE) ..8-9.. 10 b.g. Satco (FR) — Like A Dove (Ahonoora) ppu. Light-framed. IRISH NH FLAT '95/6 r4 p0. IRISH NH '96 r2 p0. IRISH P-t-P '97/8 r8 p2 (3rds, last once); pulled up 5, and fell 1. P-t-P '99 r1 p0 (5th). Placed twice at Tallanstown '97/8, and only beaten three lengths once, but has shown a distinct lack of stamina and jumping prowess since his move to Wales. Only once better than last in Points, and does not look likely to better his record by much in future. *D. Pugh - Gelligaer F.* 1068 (3m2fOMa), 1301 (OMa), 1435 (OMa).

PILLAGING PICT ..9-4.. 6 ch.g. Primitive Rising (USA) — Carat Stick (Gold Rod) 2. Home-bred half-brother to Price Of Gold (qv). Entered on numerous occasions and even got to the track without running at least twice, but it was late May before he made his debut over 2m4f in soft, and finished a promising five lengths second. Looks a banker to score in similar company, and might turn out to be useful in time. *F.T. Walton — Border.* 1581 (2m4fOMa).

PILLMERE LAD ..9-8.. 11 b.g. Karlinsky (USA) — La Jolie Fille (Go Blue) 2d1fp. Tall rangy owner-bred half-brother to Kingsmill Imp, Easter Again (dam of Tamar Lily qv), Tamar Lass and Kingsmill Quay. Dam, half-sister to Transmitter (raced for David Du Plessis until he was 19), won a Maiden and 2nd 2 for him. P-t-P '95/6 r3 p0 (pulled up 2, and fell 1). Managed a completion at the fourth attempt following a four year hiatus, though immediately disqualified when the rider forgot to weigh-in, but Amanda Barnett made no such aberration next time after winning a Flete Park Maiden in 7min 12s. Fell heavily on a return visit, and does not seem to have improved his jumping technique whilst out of action. Stays well, and handles very soft ground, but unlikely to prove quick enough for Restricteds under normal conditions. *Miss J. du Plessis — E. Cornwall.* 157 (M), 1048 (CfMa), 1258 (R), 1639 (R).

PILMUR GOLD ..—.. 6 b.m. Tumble Gold — Pilmuir Abba VII (unknown) fp. Fell at halfway and injured Ashley Turnbull in her Members, and 100-1 and hopelessly outclassed in a Confined next time. Boringly named considering all that Abba potential (Abba dabba don't?). Got any others? *W.D. Parker — Jedforest.* 107 (M), 493 (Cf).

PILTDOWN LADY ..7-0.. 8 gr.m. Arctic Lord — Houston Belle (Milford) pp3pp4. Small light-framed half-sister to Edward Bear. Dam, half-sister to Twice Knightly (qv '98 Annual), won 3 2m Hdles. NH July '99 (for J. Smyth-Osbourne) r1 p0 (tailed off). A hopeless last in both completions (over a fence adrift in the latest), and either needs the rider to get stuck into her or is one of the slowest horses around. Even Piltdown Man had more life in him. *Marchioness Blandford — Heythrop (Becky Blandford).* 792 (OMa), 1021 (2m4fOMa), 1316 (OMa), 1435 (OMa), 1526 (OMa), 1596 (OMa).

PIMBERLEY PLACE (IRE) ..—§§.. 13 b.g. Spanish Place (USA) — Pimberley Shades (Pollerton) fp. Lengthy angular brother to Irish Hurdles winner, Outrigger (IRE). Dam is half-sister to Paul (qv). IRISH NH FLAT '93/4 r5 w1 (2m2f) p4 (3 3rds). IRISH NH '94/5 r13 w3 (Hdles, 2m-2m2f) p1; ran out once, and took no part at Aintree once. NH '95/9 r25 w3 (2m2f-3m Chses) p7; refused once, and refused to race 5. Could go a great gallop and pull very hard in his youth, and was quirky but talented until he became irredeemably sour. Blinkered prior to 2000, and tried in spurs, has given hugely temperamental displays in all his last nine outings, and if connections were not thoroughly sick of him before Hunter Chasing they must be now. *A.J. Cresser — Heythrop (Nigel Twiston-Davies).* 802 (2m6fH), 1026 (2m5f110yH).

PIMS GUNNER (IRE) ..9-8.. 13 b.g. Montelimar (USA) — My Sweetie (Bleep-Bleep) 0. Small half-brother to a flat winner, a successful Hurdler, and an Irish flat and Hurdles winner. FLAT r12 w2 (6-11f) p1 (2nd). NH '91/8 r62 w7 (2 2m Hdles, one on all-weather, and 5 Chses, 2m4f-3m2f) p24. P-t-P '99 (for Miss H. Walsgrove) r4 p1 (remote 3rd); 5th, last, and pulled up 1. A prolific winner in the past, but last successful in '95, and lightly raced and generally tailed off in the last three years. Often tongue-tied. *Mrs C.P. Lees — Woodland Pytchley.* 510 (Cf).

PINOCCIO ..9-8§.. 14 b.g. Full Of Hope — White Oaks (Galivanter) 3pp. Lengthy unfurnished. Dam was useless, including in 3 Points (2 fences last, pulled up 1, and fell 1) for Mr K. O'Brien. NH '96/7 r9 p3 (2nd of 3 in only Hdle; and remote last of 3 in 2 Chses); pulled up 4. P-t-P/HUNT CH '93 (blinkered/visored 2), '95 and '98/9 r18 w2 (Maiden and Restricted) p3 (3rds, inc distant of 4 in Hunt Ch); pulled up 6, and unseated 2. Twice a winner, six years apart, at Peper Harow, but basically ungenuine, and frequently overfaced. Often owner-ridden at several pounds overweight, and sometimes mounted outside the paddock and taken to post early. *D.C. O'Brien — Ashford V.* 579 (3m2fH), 824 (Cf), 1398 (Cf).

PINOULI ..9-8.. 7 b.m. Jupiter Island — Poppy's Pride (Uncle Pokey) up41pup. Compact good-topped half-sister to NH flat winner, Poppy's Dream. 7700 4-y-o. NH FLAT '98/9 (for Mrs D. Haine) r2 p0. Sold Doncaster, May for 1250. Made most and survived a blunder at the last when winning what looked to be an above-average youngsters Maiden on firmish at Tabley, but none of her other form to date is remotely comparable, and sometimes suffers jumping lapses. Possibly capable of surprising again. *D.E. Nicholls — N. Salop.* 297 (I), 568 (OMa), 777 (OMa), 966 (OMa), 1129 (R), 1411 (R), 1528 (R).

PLATE 99   966 Cheshire Forest Open Maiden 56&7yo (Div 2): Pinouli (J.R. Barlow), 1st
PHOTO: Peter & Marilyn Sweet

PIPISTRELLA ..—.. 8 b.m. Teenoso (USA) — Batease (Quiet Fling USA) p. Half-sister to Specialarrangement (IRE), Spalease and Jack's Nephew. Dam, half-sister to Sheer Jest, was 3rd in a Hdle, and won 2 Points and 2nd for Judy Wilson and Bill Warner. Blundered badly and broke her shoulder on a tragic debut at Market Rasen. *Mrs J. Wilson — Pytchley (Bill Warner).* 438 (OMa).

PIXIE IN PURPLE (IRE) ..—.. 10 ch.g. Executive Perk — Glint Of Baron (Glint Of Gold) pp. Small lengthy dip-backed. P-t-P '96/7 (for Mr D.E. Stephens & Mrs C. Ransom) r5 w1 (Maiden) p0; last, pulled up 1, fell 1, and ran out 1. Quite impressive when winning a late season Maiden at Lifton in '96, but needed 11 weeks off to recover from a fall the following year, and ended the season lame. Made his belated comeback in 2000, but could only manage two outings, and sadly seems impossible to keep sound for any length of time. *D. Stephens — S. Cornwall.* 729 (R), 1389 (R).

PLAY ALONE (IRE) ..9-0.. 6 b.m. Mandalus — Solo Player (Blue Refrain) pf. Sister to jumping winner, Soloman (IRE), and half-sister to a flat and jumping winner in Switzerland. Bought Doncaster, May for 5000. Backed from tens to fours in her second Maiden and was tracking the leaders, when she fell heavily five out. Possibly worth noting in similar company if unscathed. *D. Wales & S. Woods — W. Norfolk (David Wales).* 942 (CfMa), 1116 (OMa).

PLAY AN ACE ..8-0.. 8 b.g. Hello Handsome — Happy To Play (Knave To Play) 3pp. Owner-bred brother to Happy Handsome, and half-brother to Happy Blake. Dam won Members and match for Restricted and placed 3 for the former Miss Pigg. 25 lengths third in gruelling conditions on his debut, but has looked very slow and made the odd mistake since. *Mrs C.J. Todd — Haydon (Melanie Blakey).* 1165 (OMa), 1330 (OMa), 1500 (OMa).

PLAYING AWAY ..—.. 6 ch.m. Northern Game — Ottery News (Pony Express) fp. Small half-sister to Otter River (qv). NH Mar '00 r1 p0 (pulled up in 2m6f Mdn Hdle: *a bhnd, pu 6*). Fell at halfway when a close last in her Members, which was won by a horse who had made his previous appearance at the Cheltenham Fesitival (o.k., so it had been five years earlier and he had finished

16th). Carrying condition to date, but would possibly have a chance in Maidens if fitter. *O.J. Carter — E. Devon*. 401 (M).

PLAYING FOR MONEY ..—.. 7 ch.m. On Side — Kings Money (King Morgan) fpp. Lengthy. Dam, sister or half-sister to 3 Wakeham Pointers, was placed in 5 lowly Points for them. Performed irratically before failing to finish in Maidens. Has two paddock handlers. *Mrs A.P. Wakeham — Dartmoor (Gordon Chambers)*. 253 (CfMa), 723 (CfMa), 874 (2m4fOMa).

PLAYING THE FOOL ..10-1.. 11 b.m. Idiot's Delight — Celtic Blade (Celtic Cone) 13. Small half-sister to First Harvest, Cut The Corn and Swashbuckle. NH '97/8 r3 p0 (last in Hdle; last after jumping badly, and pulled up in Chses). P-t-P '95/7 and '99 r15 w1 (Maiden) p3 (2 2nds; and 3rd of 4); failed to finish 8 (fell/unseated 3). Given a supremely confident ride by Sergio Gordon-Watson when successful at Garnons on her reappearance, but generally shapes like a non-stayer, and dropped away quickly in more testing ground at Maisemore on her only subsequent start. Never runs much, and her rating could be rather suspect as she normally aspires to about seven pounds less. *C.J. Bennett — Ledbury*. 669 (R), 890 (M).

PLAY IT DOWN ..—.. 7 ch.m. Thethingaboutitis (USA) — Pipe Down (Maris Piper) f. Dam, owner-bred, was a fun ride for Lady B with a remote last of 2 and of 3 twice in the Tedworth Members. Dwelt and steered a very wide course before departing at the fourth in her Members. *Lady Barbara Kwiatkowska — Tedworth*. 1279 (M).

PLAYLORD ..9-12.. 8 b.g. Arctic Lord — Show Rose (Coliseum) 624f1f2. Rangy half-brother to Impale and One For The Moon. Dam won 2m4f Hdle and 2m Ch. NH FLAT '98 r2 p1 (3rd). NH '98/9 (pulled up final for J. Cullinan; previously for G. McCourt) r7 p1 (2nd); 36f 4th of 5 only Ch. A fair galloper, but has often been disappointing, and is not an ideal betting medium because of his tendency to break blood vessels. Made virtually all and able to keep going strongly when winning a 2m4f Maiden in soft at Southwell, and a couple of his other efforts have been respectable, when falling in a slight lead two out once, and when one length second in his Members. Certainly good enough to win a Restricted on a day he is not afflicted. *J.H. Docker & Mrs S. Buckler — Atherstone (John Docker)*. 169 (OMa), 372 (CfMa), 548 (CfMa), 872 (OMa), 1070 (2m4fOMa), 1268 (R), 1414 (M).

PLAYMORE (IRE) ..10-2.. 10 ch.g. Ore — Playactress (Trimmingham) ppp. Tall rangy. IRISH NH FLAT '97 (blinkered 1) r2 p0. IRISH P-t-P '97/8 r10 p0 (last but one twice, pulled up 5, and fell 3). P-t-P/HUNT CH '99 (for Mr O.P.J. Meli, Mr W. Farnell & Mrs G.M. Summers) r5 w2 (Maiden and Members) p1 (3rd); slipped up 1, and pulled up 1. Much improved by present connection in '99, and was desperately unlucky in the Interlink Final at Stratford, where he slipped up rounding the final bend when in no danger. Clearly awry in 2000, and has developed a tendency to hang badly left which cost him a place at Newton Bromswold when David Dennis could not get him round the final turn. Needs watching when he returns. *Mrs G.M. Summers — Croome & W. Warwicks (Rob Summers)*. 260 (R), 513 (CR), 687 (2m6f110yH).

PLAY POKER (IRE) ..10-4.. 13 ch.g. Buckskin (FR) — Trulos (Three Dons) f1f4p41p. Strong brother to Cherokee Dancer. P-t-P/HUNT CH '94/9 r30 w10 (inc 5 Ladies, hat-tricks '98 and '99) p6 (4 2nds); pulled up 6, and on floor 6. A prolific winner in recent years, but seemed to encounter problems in 2000, and was twice dismounted after disappointing performances apparently unsound. Fell in four of his first ten Points, and once again had trouble negotiating the fences, giving Alison Dare (who broke her collarbone) and Leslie Jefford nasty tumbles in the early part of the season. Took his winning tally to 12 with comfortable Open wins at Black Forest Lodge and Cothelstone, but had acquired blinkers by the time of his latest success, and ran badly in them when a well supported favourite on his final start. Something of an enigma at present, and seems to be turning into quite a hypochondriac. Ideally suited by a sound surface. *Mrs S.L. Hobbs, J. Rees, S. Dusting & W. Shields — Taunton V. (Kay Rees & Polly Curling)*. 67 (L), 201 (L), 355 (O), 558 (L), 1096 (MO), 1371 (Cf), 1552 (O), 1672 (O).

PLAY THE KING (IRE) ..10-0.. 8 b br.g. Royal Fountain — Arrogant Miss (King's Ride) u3. IRISH P-t-P '98 r1 p1 (3rd). IRISH NH FLAT '98/9 r2 p0. IRISH NH '99 (trained by E. Hales) r2 p0. Most unlucky on his English début when blundering and unseating at the last in a ten length lead at Larkhill, but presumably did not give his true running when favourite and 20 lengths third next time. Not seen since mid-February, and his stable appeared to be under a cloud, but deserves compensation when fit. *Miss R. Snow — Miss C. Mason — Vine & Craven (Alex Hales)*. 12 (OMa), 250 (CfMa).

PLEASE CALL (IRE) ..9-6.. 12 b.g. Flair Path — Javana (Levanter) u4fp1. Small compact. IRISH NH FLAT '93/4 r5 p1 (3rd). IRISH NH '93/4 r3 p0. NH '96/7 r3 p1 (1¼l 2nd in Sell). P-t-P '98/9 r9 w1 (Maiden) p2 (2nds, beaten head once); fell/unseated 2. A lightly raced performer who often lacks fluency, but has done well to make the frame in all his Pointing completions, and win on two occasions. Gained his latest success in a close three-finisher event on firm at Dingley, but lamed himself in the process. Benefited from the experienced Tom Illsley in the saddle as he seemed to have little chance until galvanised in the closing stages, and many believed the judge called it wrong. *Mrs M. Upstone —*

Bicester with Whaddon. 196 (R), 513 (CR), 791 (R), 1418 (R), 1506 (R).

PLUCKY PUNTER ..9-3.. 13 b.g. Idiot's Delight — Birds Of A Feather (Warpath) 3fup. Small compact attractive half-brother to Chaceley Lass. Dam won 12f Sell. NH '92/3 and '94/5 r12 p4 (inc only 2 Chses). P-t-P/HUNT CH '96/9 r18 w2 (Maiden and Restricted) p6 (4 3rds, last twice); last 2, pulled up 5, ran out 1, and refused 1. Made all to record a double on sound surfaces in '97, but a headstrong sort and usually fails to stay, and has been soundly beaten in his last 17 outings. Teamed with a novice on three occasions in 2000, but has never appeared particularly safe over fences, and the combination only came back in one piece once. Wears a tongue-strap and a cross-noseband, and has been tried unsuccessfully in blinkers. *J.R. Jones — V. of Clettwr.* 266 (M), 643 (Cf), 837 (I), 944 (I).

PLUNDER BAY (USA) ..—.. 10 b.g. Cutlass (USA) — La Ninouchka (USA) (Bombay Duck USA) ff. Strong compact half-brother to 3 flat winners (2 abroad), including Silver Wisp (3rd in '92 Derby). Dam won 3 flat in USA. $30,000y. FLAT (for G. Lewis) r12 w1 (7f) p0. NH '94/9 (blinkered once in '96; for N. Henderson; one win previously for D. Nicholson) r29 w5 (2 Hdles, 2m-2m5f, and 3 Chses, 2m1f-2m5f) p5. Bought Doncaster, May for 1200. Took a crashing fall at the second at Thorpe and the nine following races were severely delayed by the arrival of the air ambulance and (when the rider reached the hospital all she wanted to do was to have a fag!), and then forced to jumped the final obstacle at Southwell although remote and exhausted, and got stuck on top and paid for his partner's folly with his life. *K.A. Morgan — Cranwell Bloodhounds (Fiona Hatfield).* 115 (CCf), 368 (L).

POACHER'S PADDY (IRE) ..—.. 6 b.m. Jurado (USA) — Ross Maid (Random Shot) ppp. Half-sister to Corsewall Point (IRE), and to Irish Pointing winner, Fire Street. In touch for at least two miles on her last two attempts, but needs to find some stamina. *N. Poacher — Llangeinor.* 747 (CfMa), 949 (OMa), 1618 (OMa).

PO CAP EEL ..9-9.. 11 b.m. Uncle Pokey — Hejera (Cantab) u4p2. Workmanlike good-topped sister to Plat Reany and Pebble Rock, and to Hurdles winner, Men Of Yorkshire, and half-sister to Political Diamond and Brookthorpe. NH FLAT r1 p0 (pulled up). NH '97/8 r2 p0 (5th of 6, and pulled up 1 in Chses). P-t-P '96/7 and '99 r6 p1 (head and neck 3rd); last thrice, and pulled up 2. Stands her racing badly, but without ability, and has made the frame more often than not. Not ridden with much enterprise until her final appearance in 2000, but Hannah Kinsey has been improving steadily and won't be long in opening her account. Wears a cross-noseband. *Mrs T.R. Kinsey — Cheshire Forest.* 52 (OMa), 120 (CR), 296 (I), 569 (OMa).

POCKET OSCAR ..8-5.. 7 ch.g. Pocketed (USA) — Little Anthem (True Song) p4. Dam is half-sister to 3 Pointers, including General Rule (*qv* '93 Annual), won 2 appalling Points for Christine Forber and placed 10 (inc 2 NH flat and Hdle) ('can be a proper madam'). Grandam, Bright Daisy, won 4 Points (inc dead-heat) and placed 7. Sire comes from a very good family, but his 3 wins in 2m Hdles for John Jenkins included a Seller. Soon struggling to keep up before finishing 38 lengths last in a non-Rules runner Maiden. *Mrs C.T. Forber — Saddleworth.* 965 (OMa), 1318 (OMa).

POETS CORNER ..8-2.. 7 b.g. Mandalus — Wonderful Lilly (Prince Hansel) pf. Workmanlike half-brother to Javelin Cool (IRE) (*qv*). Gave a couple of very ponderous displays of jumping, and was soon stuck in the Dunthrop mud before he eventually fell at the final fence when plodding on in the battle for a remote third. *M. Kehoe — N. Herefords (Fiona Kehoe).* 515 (OMa), 1019 (2m4fOMa).

POET'S SONG (IRE) ..9-7.. 9 br.g. Accordion — Kilgarve Lady (Tender King) ffpp5p. Lengthy light-framed. NH FLAT '98 r2 p0. NH '98 r1 p0 (pulled up in Hdle when about 3 flights behind). P-t-P '99 r5 w1 (Maiden) p2 (2nds, remote of 3 once); unseated 1, and pulled up 1. Landed a Llanvapley Maiden on his first jumping completion in '99, but fenced remarkably badly this year, and only managed to get round once when 20 lengths last at up ton. The form of his win remains inconclusive, and could not be supported with any confidence in future. *M.G. Jones — Gelligaer F. (M. Jones).* 69 (R), 559 (R), 596 (R), 832 (R), 1355 (R), 1488 (R).

POINTED REMARK (IRE) ..—.. 10 ch.g. Exactly Sharp (USA) — King's Chase (King's Leap) p. Rangy fired half-brother to 7 winners (3 abroad; 3 subsequently won abroad). NH FLAT '95/7 r4 w1 p2 (3rds). NH '99 (for N. Henderson) r2 p0; remote 9th of 10 and pulled up in Hdles. Bought Ascot, June for 1000. Won in May '96, but has only achieved seven outings in his life, and obviously plagued by terrible legs. Made a fleeting reappearance when tailed off in January. *Mrs C. Hardinge — S. Herefords.* 37 (Cl).

POLAR ANA (IRE) ..9-11.. 12 b.m. Pollerton — O Ana (Laurence O) 453337. Sturdy good-looking. P-t-P/HUNT CH '95/8 r28 w6 (inc 4 Ladies; hat-trick '97) p14 (7 2nds, of 3 thrice; and 7 3rds, last thrice, inc Hunt Ch); failed to finish 4 (fell/unseated 2). Has made the frame on 26 occasions, and been successful six times, but absent in '99, and no longer as good as she was. Usually dropped out in the rear, but not quick enough to peg the leaders back on a sound surface, and ran her best races in 2000 when there was some cut in the ground. Has a fabulous completion record, but will have to target easier options if she is to win again. *Mrs P.A. McIntyre — Ashford V. (Gill Gladders).* 573 (CfL), 707 (L), 827 (L), 1107 (L), 1170 (L), 1511 (L).

POLAR KING (IRE) ..10-6.. 8 b.g. Glacial Storm (USA) — Our Little Lamb (Prince Regent FR) 1f112. Compact good-looking half-brother to Chasing winner, The Bushkeeper (IRE). NH FLAT '97 r3 p1 (2nd). NH '97/9 (for C. Thornton) r10 p4 (¾l 2nd, caught 50yds out in 3m2f Hdle once). A poor jumper of Hurdles and has suffered from the occasional blunder in Points, but proved to be a decent novice who can find some extra in the closing stages. Reappearing only five days after a win when he was beaten at 2-5 at Easingwold, where he never looked to be going well and made a bad mistake at the ninth, and David Easterby was fined £125 for excessive use of the whip. Stays at least 3m2f, and may have the scope for Opens. *I. Bray — Middleton (David Easterby).* 168 (OMa), 378 (R), 503 (R), 1325 (Cf), 1348 (Cf).

PLATE 100   503 Holderness Restricted: Polar King (D. Easterby), 1st, holds off a challenge from Yornoangel (R. Clark), 2nd
PHOTO: Roy Parker

POLITICAL BILL ..9-5.. 10 ch.g. Politico (USA) — Trial Run (Deep Run) pp. Sturdy lengthy brother to Political Belle, and half-brother to Lindon Run (qv). NH '96/7 r2 p0. P-t-P '99 r4 p1 (2nd of 3); 4th twice, and fell 1. A steady jumper, and looked likely to be suited by a severe test of stamina after several not unpromising efforts last year, but clearly under a cloud in 2000 when his season lasted less than a week. Has led at some stage in five of his six Points, and may still be able to win a small race if his problems can be sorted. *Mrs J.R. Middleton — Morpeth.* 364 (CfMa), 423 (R).

POLITINA ..—.. 7 b.m. Neltino — Fair Policy (Politico USA) p. Dam, home-bred, is sister to Present Policy (qv '91 Annual), won a Maiden and 2nd for the Turcans. Bacward when tailed off on a May debut. *W.J. Turcan — Fernie (Nick Pomfret).* 1423 (OMa).

POLKA ..—.. 6 b.g. Slip Anchor — Peace Dance (Bikala) u. Sparely-made. FLAT (for C. Thornton) r4 p0 (tailed off). Bought Doncaster, May for 1100. May have had problems on the flat (has had a tie-back operation), and got no further than the first fence in his Members. *P.T. Norman — Quantock.* 635 (M).

POLLY BUCKRUM ..9-5.. 6 gr.m. Buckley — Decorum (Quorum) bp. Strong home-bred half-sister to The Rum Mariner (qv). Brought down at the first on her debut, but showed promise until weakening and making a mistake which caused the rider to become unbalanced three out next time (was soon pulled up, and Rob Hodges was lucky to escape censure, as she could have easily have been placed). Could be interesting in a Maiden if competently handled. *Mrs C.M. Rogers — Radnor & W. Herefords (Clive Davies).* 866 (CfMa), 990 (OMa).

POLLY GUNNER ..—.. 8 ch.m. Gunner B — Emifive (Kind Of Hush) pp. Big strong. Dam won Maiden, and was 2nd in Hdle. P-t-P '98/9 r2 p0 (pulled up 2). Pulled up four times over a three year period, and seems defective. *R.J. Brown — Vine & Craven (Caroline Gordon).* 1284 (OMa), 1513 (OMa).

POLLY LIVE WIRE ..9-7.. 7 b.m. El Conquistador — Flash Wire (Flatbush) pf233f3d21pfp. Tiny. Dam, half-sister to Bronwire (*qv* '94 Annual), pulled up in 2 Points. Grandam, Wire In, fell in 3 Points. P-t-P '99 r4 p0 (4th, pulled up 2, and fell 1). Knocked at the door for so long in Maidens that Patrick Millington clearly got bored, and decided a four-mile Open was the best way to get off the mark, and so it proved when successful in a truly awful event at Dingley. Knee-high to a grasshopper, and must find jumping fences a real struggle, but very plucky and has developed her own style of getting through them. Kept on the go from January to June, and clearly hardy, but will hopefully not suffer the after effects like her former stablemate Verity Valentine did in 2000 after a similarly hectic campaign last year. Would benefit from a switch to Ladies races. Usually dropped out behind and wears a citation to help the owner anchor her. *P.J. Millington — Fernie.* 87 (OMa), 551 (OMa), 696 (OMa), 844 (OMa), 1011 (CfMa), 1039 (OMa), 1291 (OMa), 1421 (OMa), 1505 (4mMO), 1586 (CN), 1646 (3m4fH), 1666 (O).

POLLY MAID ..—.. 12 ch.m. Politico (USA) — Weather Maid (Weathercock) p. Home-bred half-sister to Maid Mandarin and Sand Track. Dam, a maiden after 8 seasons, was 2nd in 3 Points (failed to finish 16). P-t-P '99 r2 p0 (ran out 1, and pulled up 1). A late starter who has shown brief early speed, but yet to go beyond two miles, and looks unpromising. *Mrs S. Morley — Staintondale.* 1229 (M).

POLLY'S LADY ..8-6.. 11 ch.m. Mirror Boy — Terrona Lady (unknown) u0p. Small stocky owner-bred half-sister to Boyup Brook. P-t-P '97/9 r7 w1 (Maiden) p2; 9th, and last pair 3. A narrow winner at Mosshouses last year, and had managed to complete in all her starts '97/9, but only succeeded once in 2000, and taken off her feet on sound surfaces in her last two starts. Tends to get rather geed up in the preliminaries, and does not stand many outings. *J. John Paterson — Jedforest.* 713 (R), 976 (R), 1427 (R).

POLLY WATT ..—.. 7 b.m. Zero Watt (USA) — Menefort Castle (Menelek) p. Half-sister to Menefort. Dam won 2 Irish Points (one on a disqualification) and placed 5 (inc a Hunt Ch); and won a Restricted for Alan Williams. Gave a horrible display of jumping before clambering over the fifth and immediately giving up on a late May debut. *A.J. Williams — Llangibby (we Williams).* 1618 (OMa).

POLO KIT (IRE) ..—.. 10 b.g. Trempolino (USA) — Nikitina (Nijinsky CAN) pp. Compact half-brother to several winners (including in Ireland and France), including Inchtina (flat). Dam won at 10f in Ireland. 14,500f, 30,000y. FLAT won for J. Fanshawe; visored once) r13 w1 (14f) p2. NH '96 and '98/9 (first 2 for R. O'Sullivan, bought for 14,000) r5 p0 (5th and pulled up 3 in Hdles, inc Sell, and unseated at first when attempting to refuse in a Ch). All his flat form was at three, and terrible in the next yard after being sold expensively. Prominent for two miles in both Ladies Opens, but appeared unable to get the trip and dropped right out. Seems troubled. *G. Richards — Tredegar F. (Nicky Sharpe).* 743 (L), 946 (L).

PONGO WARING (IRE) ..10-1.. 12 b.g. Strong Gale — Super Cailin (Brave Invader USA) 684353. Compact fired (in '96) brother to Chasing winner, Finkle Street (IRE), and half-brother to at least 3 winners over jumps. NH FLAT '94 r2 p0. NH '94/8 r17 w6 (2 2m4f Hdles, and 4 Chses, 2m3f-2m7f) p3. P-t-P '99 r3 w1 (Ladies) p1 (2nd); and unseated 1. A useful sub-3m performer on a sound surface under Rules, and still retains the ability to run well in Points, but found himself out of his depth in Hunter Chases. Third in a hot Ladies at Guilsborough, where Don't Tell The Wife and Cittadino finished behind him, and filled the same position behind the first mentioned on his final appearance at Clifton-on-Dunsmore. Has done well to overcome all manner of physical problems, but has become one-paced and will not find winning opportunities easy to come by in future. A very proficient jumper, and has never fallen. *Miss S.A. Loggin — Bicester with Whaddon (Mervyn Loggin).* 78 (L), 226 (2m4f110yH), 687 (2m6f110yH), 1007 (L), 1332 (3mH), 1417 (L).

PONTABULA ..10-2.. 11 b.g. Sula Bula — Lady Penstone (Jimsun) 63p43. Compact unimpressive-looking. NH FLAT r1 p0. NH '94/5 (blinkered final) r6 p2 (Sells). P-t-P/HUNT CH '96 and '98/9 r14 w6 (inc 2 Hunt Chses, 2m4f110y-2m5f, and Open) p4 (2nds, inc 2 Hunt Chses, distant last once); last, pulled up 1, and fell 2. Battled on bravely to win six of his last nine races to '98, but struggling with his wind since, and now finds trouble. Remains ultra-game, but three miles is too far for him these days, and his best effort in 2000 came over 2m4f when third to King Torus at Fontwell. Acts on any going. *H.J. Manners — V.W.H.* 34 (MO), 149 (3mH), 299 (3m2f110yH), 474 (O), 681 (2m4fH).

PONTOON BRIDGE ..9-12.. 14 ch.g. Carlingford Castle — Lumax (Maximilian) pup43. Rangy half-brother to Irish NH flat and Hurdles winner, Ring Four, and to NH flat and Hurdles winner, Macy (IRE). Dam won Norwegian Oaks, and won a Hdle there. NH FLAT '92 r1 w1. NH '92/4 and '96/7 r17 w5 (3 Hdles, 2m1f-2m2f, and 2 2m5f Chses) p4. P-t-P/HUNT CH '98/9 r7 p1 (2nd in Hunt Ch); unseated 1, and pulled up 1. A very successful front-runner at best, but only effective to 2m5f, and even the Easingwold circuit was too long for him on his latest appearance. Has begun to make lots of mistakes in Hunter Chases, but no longer effective in that arena, and his inability to stay three miles makes his winning chances negligible in future. Prefers a sound surface, and does not usually stand many outings. Tried blinkered once in 2000. *J.S. Swindells — Cheshire*. 226 (2m4f110yH), 384 (2m3f110yH), 684 (2m4fH), 1199 (L), 1350 (L).

PLATE 101   1350 Bilsdale Ladies Open: Pontoon Bridge (Mrs K. Diggle), 3rd, leads Temple Garth (Miss F. Hartley), 1st, and Vital Issue (Miss J. Foster), 5th, at the last.   PHOTO: Roy Parker

POPESHALL ..10-4.. 14 b.g. Mufrij — Allez Stanwick (Goldhill) 412. Neat quite attractive home-bred half-brother to Willie Butt, Go Silly, Stanwick Fort, Stanwick Hall and Henah Hill. Dam won 7f Sell, 4 Hdles (2m-2m4f, inc walk-over for Sell) and a Ladies. P-t-P/HUNT CH '92/5 (for Mr T.W. Williamson) r13 w5 (inc 3 Hunt Chses, 2m4f-3m1f) p3 (2 2nds; and inc 2 Hunt Chses); failed to finish 3 (unseated 1, and carried out 1). NH '96/8 (for Miss S. Williamson) r8 w1 (2m7f HCap Chse) p2 (2nds); unseated 1, and pulled up 1. A former decent top-of-the-ground performer whose best efforts were at under three miles, and new connections have done well to revive him after a lengthy absence. Possibly fortunate to have won at Ampton as the runner-up broke down, but his defeat by Pangeran next time was no disgrace for a veteran. Has never stood many outings. *Mrs P.K.J. Brightwell — Essex & Suffolk*. 83 (Cf), 549 (Cf), 756 (Cf).

POPPERS ..—.. 8 ch.g. Germont — Night Profit (Carnival Night) ppbpf9p. Owner-bred half-brother to Good Profit (*qv*). NH '00 r2 p0 (9th in 2m Sell Hdle: *sn bhnd, t.o halfway*; and pulled up in 2m4f110y Nov Hdle: *ld to 2, lost plce qckly, wl bhnd when pu 7*). Seems to be incredibly unfit, and can only go for about a mile before he blows up big time and is reduced to a waddle. *W.G. Young — Lanarks & Renfrews*. 364 (CfMa), 499 (2m4fOMa), 664 (2m5fOMa), 718 (CfMa), 1122 (OMa).

POPPYCOCK (IRE) ..—.. 7 b.m. Regular Guy — Costenetta (IRE) (Runnett) p. Small. Bought Doncaster, May for 800. Already tailed off when he nearly fell at the tenth and was promptly pulled up in February. *P.J. Sanderson — Kyre (Fiona Needham)*. 341 (CfMa).

PORTERS LODGE ..8-12.. 8 b.g. Balliol — Parabems (Swing Easy USA) 2423. Half-brother to flat winner, Swinging Lady. Dam won 3 flat, 5-6f. P-t-P '98/9 r6 p2 (remote 3rd of 4 once); pulled up 4. In the frame in his last six starts, but has had a maximum of two finishers behind him, and does not stay three miles. Will need plenty of luck if he is ever to get off the mark. *R. John — Eggesford*. 145 (OMa), 563 (CfMa), 1519 (CfMa), 1655 (OMa).

PORT VALENSKA (IRE) ..8-7§.. 8 b.g. Roi Danzig (USA) — Silvera (Ribero) u47p7. Small half-brother to several winners. Dam won at 8f. NH FLAT '97 r1 p0. NH '97 (often blinkered/visored; for John Harris; previously for Mrs J. Conway; previously for J.L. Harris) r13 p1 (3rd in Sell). A reluctant maiden who is easy to trounce in the poorest company, and probably not worth bothering with again. *R.D.E. Woodhouse — Sinnington*. 169 (OMa), 281 (OMa), 508 (CMa), 694 (OMa), 1004 (OMa).

POSH SPICE (IRE) ..10-6.. 10 b.m. Neshad (USA) — Escalado (Homing) 322. Strong-topped attractive half-sister to 2 flat winners (one in Ireland, including Darling Dianne). NH FLAT '97 r1 p1 (3rd). NH '97/8 r5 w2 (2m4f-2m7f Hdles) p0. P-t-P '99 r3 w1 (PPORA Mares) p0; pulled up 1, and fell 1. Won both her handicaps over hurdles in '98 and her opening Point the following year, but has never managed more than four outings in a year, and appears difficult to train. Well held in her first two outings in 2000, but ran better for Ben Hitchcott on her Hunter Chase debut when chasing home African Warrior in the Mares Final at Stratford, and should be able to win again. Wore a tongue-strap on her reappearance this year. *R. Cook — Surrey U. (Chris Elliott).* 572 (CfO), 1248 (Cm), 1645 (3mH).

POSSIBLE PARDON (NZ) ..10-2.. 7 b.g. Iades (FR) — Wonderful Excuse (NZ) (Alibhai NZ) 24231213. Good-topped. P-t-p '99 (for Mr Pike & Mr I. Zaid) r4 w1 (Maiden) p2 (2nd of 3; and remote 3rd); and pulled up 1. A thorough stayer, but needed blinkers and Nick Mitchell to sharpen him up in 2000. Tends to jumps sketchily at times, but has the virtue of being able to handle all types of going, and almost certain to win more races. Might be worth trying over four miles in 2001. Has two handlers in the paddock. *B.H. Pike — Blackmore & Sparkford V. (John Dufosee).* 6 (R), 144 (R), 306 (R), 477 (R), 876 (R), 953 (I), 1283 (I), 1653 (O).

PLATE 102   1283 Tedworth Intermediate: Possible Pardon (N. Mitchell), 1st, in splendid isolation
PHOTO: Brian Armstrong

POSTAGE STAMP ..9-12.. 14 ch.g. The Noble Player (USA) — Takealetter (Wolver Hollow) 6p*u*. Good-topped. FLAT r25 w2 (11-16f, one on all-weather) p7. NH '91/6 r19 w7 (4 Hdles, 2m2f-2m6f, and 3 Chses, 2m3f-2m4f; inc hat-trick) p2. HUNT CH '98 r2 p2 (2nds). NH Apr '00 (from F. Murphy's) r1 p0 (unseated in 3m HCap Ch: *rr til ur 10*). A smart performer on a sound surface at best, and has earned £47,188 over jumps alone, but very lightly raced in recent years, and has always shown a propensity to jump and hang to his right. Resurfaced to aid Ben Orde-Powletts' development, but no longer possesses even half of his former ability. *P.J. O'Donnell — W. of Yore (Harry Orde-Powlett).* 277 (Cf), 504 (O).

POUCHER (IRE) ..9-12.. 11 b.g. Dock Leaf — Jacqueline Grey (Torus) p634. Close-coupled. IRISH NH '94/5 r11 w1 (2m Hdle) p5. NH '96/8 r11 w2 (2m6f-3m2f Chses) p3. P-t-P '99 (for Mrs A.L. Wood & Mr M.P. Wiggin) r5 w1 (Club nov rdrs) p2; last, and pulled up 1. Error-prone under Rules when successful in two Chases on easy surfaces though took to Pointing straight away last year when winning on his debut at Chaddesley, but remains remarkably clumsy, and has made countless errors in his eight subsequent starts. Beaten a minimum of 33 lengths in 2000, and has become most disappointing. Suited by lashings of mud. Wears a cross-noseband. *G.C. Evans (The Barker Family) — Ludlow (Geoff Evans).* 222 (3m1f110yH), 335 (L), 743 (L), 1357 (MOnr).

POWER UNIT ..9-4.. 6 ch.g. Risk Me (FR) — Hazel Bee (Starch Reduced) Rp3u1. Dam, half-sister to Hazel Mill (*qv* '93 Annual), won at 6f. A keen sort who can look a handful, but made most and outbattled a reluctant opponent to take a youngsters Maiden in soft at Bonvilston. Had show some ability the time before, and likely to improve his rating at six (will need to for Restricteds). *C.A. Hanbury & M. Honey — Ystrad Taf Fechan (Debbie Hamer)*. 648 (CfMa), 834 (OMa), 1222 (2m4fOMa), 1455 (OMa), 1617 (OMa).

POYNDER PARK (IRE) ..10-4.. 10 b.g. Mandalus — So Deep (Deep Run) 5p2121pp. Lengthy workmanlike half-brother to So Phar So Good. Dam fell when exhausted on her belated debut in a Point as an 11-year-old in '95. Grandam, Bit Of A Wit, won 3m2f Hunt Ch and 7 Points and placed 8. P-t-P '97/9 r9 w2 (Maiden and Restricted) p2; 4th twice, pulled up 2, and fell 1. At his best when stamina is at a premium, and has done well to win four times under Luke Morgan '99/00, but ended the season with two dismal efforts in Hunter Chases on differing ground, and may not be brave enough over big fences. Consistent in Points once he has had an outing, and should put his main attributes to good use again in 2001 though has been seen to hang, and it may not be wise to trust him implicitly. *Mrs V.A. Stevenson — Dumfries (Yda Morgan)*. 43 (Cf), 183 (CCf), 420 (I), 660 (Cf), 1030 (O), 1121 (I), 1445 (3m1fH), 1601 (3m2fH).

PLATE 103   1102 West Somerset Vale Open Maiden (Div 2, Part 2): The imposing Prah Sands (J. Young), 1st, opens his account   PHOTO: Baths Photograhic

PRAH SANDS ..10-4.. 8 b.g. Henbit (USA) — Minor Furlong (Native Bazaar) 32281p22. Big rangy half-brother to Mini Furlong, Abitbizarre and Countrywide Lad, and to Chasing winner, The Carrot Man. Dam, a twin, is an unraced half-sister to Miss Furlong (dam of Pillow Spin, (*qv* '97 Annual). P-t-P '99 r5 p2 (2nds, last once); pulled up 2, and fell 1. A really imposing individual, and a bold leaper who goes a good lick, but has taken a while to develop the strength to match his frame. Still does not appear to be an out-and-out stayer, especially when conditions are testing. Landed a three-finisher Maiden at Cothelstone by a wide margin, but was run out of two Restricteds at the much more testing Bratton Down subsequently. Sold after the season to Colin Tizzard to run under Rules, and it will be fascinating to see how he fares. *Mrs G.M. Brake — Quantock (Laura Horsey)*. 12 (OMa), 58 (OMa), 457 (OMa), 583 (2m5f110yH), 1102 (OMa), 1258 (R), 1563 (R), 1650 (R).

PREMIER FIRST (IRE) ..9-0.. 12 br.g. Good Thyne (USA) — Bowerina (Daring Display) USA) p435p776. Sturdy half-brother to Hurdles winner, Noble Athlete (IRE). Dam won at 10f in Ireland. NH FLAT '95 r1 p0. NH '95/6 r11 p1 (2nd in Ch). P-t-P/HUNT CH '98/9 r21 w1 (Maiden) p6 (3rds, dead-heated once, of 4 twice, and last once); pulled up 2, and fell 1. Amazingly slow, and took 28 attempts before he got off the mark, but has failed to beat a rival in eight of his 11 subsequent completions. Remains adept at getting round, which is handy because all Pewter pilots have an in-built aversion to pulling up, and has only failed to finish in five of 41 appearances. Wears a cross-noseband, and regained blinkers on his last two starts following several moody displays. *N.J. Pewter — Suffolk.* 17 (O), 82 (M), 179 (R), 555 (Cnr), 610 (R), 1035 (Cnr), 1287 (R), 1540 (2m5fH).

PREMPTED ..—.. 7 ch.g. Crested Lark — Prevada (Soldier Rose) p. Half-brother to Flycatcher. Dam won 2m5f Maiden from only 2 starts for Jim Mahon, and grandam, Trovada, pulled up in all 3 Points as a 5-y-o for him (ultimately lame). May have some ability, but not seen after an apparently encouraging display in mid-March, which could be worrying as he comes from a family who are as fragile as bone china. *Mrs B. Graham & J. Mahon — Croome & W. Warwicks.* 568 (OMa).

PRESELI HEATHER ..9-0.. 7 b.m. Ski Dancer — Jacqueline (Harvest Sun) 3. Strong-topped sister to Preseli Dip, and half-sister to Preseli View. Dam won 6 Points (inc a walkover) and placed 5 for Mr Lewis (found simple opportunities, inc 4 Members). P-t-P '99 (for Mr W.D. Lewis) r5 p2 (last of 3 twice); 4th, and pulled up 2. Has struggled into the frame in her last four starts, but only beat two rivals in the process, and disappeared after finishing 28 lengths behind the winner in the latest this March. Makes a few errors, and will have to do a great deal better to win. *Mrs I. Goode — Gelligaer F.* 601 (CfMa).

PRESTIGE LORD (IRE) ..10-2.. 9 b.g. Lord Americo — Fiona's Wish (Wishing Star) p5. Strong good-looking brother to Ashburton Lord (IRE), and half-brother to Irish Pointing winner, Northern Fiona. IRISH P-t-P '97 r3 w1 (5yo Maiden) p0; fell 1. P-t-P '98 r3 w1 (PPORA) p1 (3rd); and fell 1. Made one heart-stopping blunder when successful at Newton Bromswold in '98, but unable to race the following year, and made just two late-season appearances in 2000. Jumped badly before pulling up at Garthorpe, but showed he retains some ability when 15 lengths fifth to Glacial Trial subsequently. A headstrong sort who goes to post early, and still good enough to win races if his problems could be resolved. *C.R.R. Sweeting & P.A. Deal — Heythrop (Lucinda Sweeting).* 1588 (I), 1632 (I).

PRESUMING ED (IRE) ..9-10.. 8 b.g. Nordico (USA) — Top Knot (High Top) 3f13. Strong. Dam won 3 Irish flat, 12-16f. FLAT r3 p0. P-t-P '98 r3 p1 (neck 2nd); ran out 1, and pulled up 1. Not without ability, but prone to hang and jump violently left-handed, and has now acquired a near-side pricker. Quite a strong galloper, and usually helps force the pace, but equally liable to hit the fences when he's not taking them crookedly. Won his Maiden easily, but will always be a challenge. Missed '99, and has been sparingly raced otherwise. *Mrs J.S. Lewis — Llangibby.* 273 (R), 673 (2m4foOMa), 822 (CfMa), 1088 (R).

PRETORIA DANCER ..10-4§.. 9 b.g. Dancing Brave (USA) — Pretoria (Habitat) 346232. Small good-bodied brother to French Chasing/English jumping winner, Aardwolf, and half-brother to Hurdles winner, Pontevedra (IRE), to NH flat winner, Waterburg (IRE), and to flat winner, Nassma (IRE). Dam won 2 flat, 7-10f, including Listed race in Rome. FLAT r7 w1 (14f) p0. NH '96 r5 p2 (21-25l 3rds, to 3m3f). P-t-P '98 r12 w1 (Members) p4 (2nds, of 3 once, and last once); pulled up 2, unseated 1. Failed to beat a rival in his first three attempts under Fergal O'Brien, but beaten a maximum of two and a half lengths when runner-up twice in their last three appearances, and with a bit more resolution might have added to his '98 Andoversford success. Best if allowed to dominate, but he's not a natural jumper, and wears headgear. *Mrs C. Mackness — Cotswold (Jelly Nolan).* 967 (M), 1311 (Cf), 1416 (O), 1523 (C), 1606 (O), 1672 (O).

PRETTY BOY GEORGE ..8-8.. 12 ch.g. St Columbus — Sea Farmer (Cantab) 704. Lengthy half-brother to Classic Bart, Tubb Corner and Little Farmer. Dam failed to finish in 3 races inc 2 NH flat! NH FLAT '93 r1 p0. NH '94/5 (for K. Clutterbuck) r8 p0 (last, pulled up and unseated in Chses). Can go an enthusiastic gallop until about halfway, but dropped right out to finish a remote last, and is not a racehorse. *C.C. Bealby — Quorn.* 547 (CfMa), 871 (R), 1264 (M).

PRICELESS SAM ..9-12.. 10 b.m. Silly Prices — Samonia (Rolfe USA) 5. Sparely-made owner-bred half-sister to My Sam (*qv*). NH FLAT r1 p0. P-t-P '96 and '98 r5 w1 (Maiden) p2 (2nds); 4th, and pulled up 1. Broke down in '96, and suffered another setback after winning easily at Witton Castle two years later, but made it back to the racecourse this year. Failed to recover from an early blunder when 28 lengths last at Wetherby, and promptly vanished again. A good mare, but with brittle legs, and will no doubt have to rest on her laurels and take up maternal duties. *J.W. Barker — Hurworth (Lynne Ward).* 137 (R).

PRICE OF GOLD ..—.. 11 b.m. Silly Prices — Carat Stick (Gold Rod) f. Small half-sister to Pillaging Pict. Dam, half-sister to Ram The Thor (*qv* '90 Annual), won NH flat and 4 Hdles (2m1f-3m1f) for the Waltons. NH FLAT '94/5 r3 p0. NH '95 (for F. Walton) r1 p0 (remote last in Hdle). Fell at halfway when making a surprise reappearance in her Members (a contest in which fences rather than lengths separated the five finishers). *Mrs S. Scott — Border.* 1501 (M).

PRIDE OF KASHMIR ..9-12.. 8 gr.g. Petong — Proper Madam (Mummy's Pet) 44. Neat brother to 5f winner, Osomental, and half-brother to Flashman, and several other winners (mainly sprinters). Dam won 6 flat, 5-6f. FLAT (for P. Harris) r18 p3 (beaten a head once). NH '97/9 (for P. Hobbs) r20 w5 (4 Hdles, 2m1f-2m5f, inc hat-trick '97, and 2m5f Ch) p3. A difficult ride who has hung on occasions in the past, and tried in headgear, but was game at best, and gained all his successes on good or principally firmish ground. Disappointing since winning his Chasing debut and looks to have needed sweetening, but a two lengths fourth at Peper Harow suggested that he may be on the way back. Cary Ford seemed willing to drive to the ends of the earth to partner him twice, which suggests that she too has faith. *E.F.B. & Mrs J. Monck — Grafton (Jenny Pidgeon).* 326 (L), 1395 (L).

PRIDEWOOD GOLDING ..9-13.. 14 ch.g. Soldier Rose — Quick Reply (Tarqogan) 12. Small compact half-brother to Pridewood Target, and to Hurdles winner, Pridewood Fuggle. Dam won an Irish Point; and won 2m3f Hdle and 2m Ch in England; and pulled up in a Point on her final appearance. NH FLAT r2 p0. NH '92/3, '94 and '98 r20 p3 (2 2nds, inc 2m4f110y HCap Ch). P-t-P/HUNT CH '97/9 r17 w1 (Maiden) p3 (head 2nd; and 2 3rds); pulled up 5, and fell/unseated 2. Had won only once from 39 attempts prior to 2000, but nursed back to form in the current yard, and landed a three-finisher Restricted on his reappearance. Not disgraced behind Wise Prince subsequently, and despite his advancing years might be able to win again. Acts on any going. A triumph for Emma James, who had real difficulty in obtaining her Riders Certificate this year, but proved all the doubters wrong with her most productive season for some time. *E.A. Thomas — Miss E. James — N. Herefords (Emma James).* 1616 (R), 1667 (I).

PRIESTTHORN (IRE) ..9-10.. 6 b.g. Denel (FR) — Pollys Flake (Will Somers) 1. Half-brother to Searcher, Classsical Pop and Chasing winner, Smith's Band (IRE), and to Irish Hurdles winner, Bells Bridge. Dam won 2m2f flat and 3 Hdles (2m-2m2f) in Ireland. Made it look easy when beating two subsequent non-scorers at Littlewindsor, and should eventually prove himself to be competent in competitive company. Part of a great day at the office for Louise Alner, who trained the winners of three of the four available Maidens. *H. Wellstead — Portman (Louise Alner).* 875 (2m4fOMa).

PRIME COURSE (IRE) ..10-2.. 12 b.g. Crash Course — Prime Mistress (Skymaster) 142212p. Big strong brother to Irish NH flat and Hurdles winner, Beglawella, and half-brother to Irish NH flat winner, Osmo, and Irish NH flat and Chasing winner, Kings Hill. NH FLAT r2 p0 (tailed off 2). NH '95 r1 p0. P-t-P/HUNT CH '96/9 r20 w4 (inc Open) p6 (2 2nds, last once; and 4 3rds, of 4 once, and remote last once); pulled up 7, and fell/unseated 2. Has had to endure sore shins throughout his career which invite him to jump markedly left-handed at times, but has maintained steady improvement in the last two years, and ran his best race to date when dead-heating with High Guardian over four miles at Detling. Lost his share of the race in the Stewards room, and connections were unable to retrieve matters at the subsequent appeal at Portman Square. Gained compensation with an easy win in a three-finisher Open at Rodmell, but his affliction reared its head again when forced to pull up on his final appearance. Does well on balance, but has never had more than three finisher in his wake when successful, and could never be supported with much confidence. Has been tried in a visor. *E.J. Farrant — Mid Surrey F. (Anne Farrant).* 125 (M), 300 (2m5fH), 574 (4mMO), 826 (O), 1210 (O), 1394 (O), 1510 (O).

PRIMELLE ..—.. 10 ro.m. Say Primula — Flavelle (Lucky Sovereign) pp. Dam was useless in 5 flat and 13 Hurdles; and in 11 Points spread over 4 seasons for Mrs Harris (only completed twice — last once). Just as slow as her pedigree suggested she would be. *W.B. Harris — Hurworth (Fiona Needham).* 138 (OMa), 436 (OMa).

PRIMERO (IRE) ..10-5.. 7 b.g. Lycius (USA) — Pipitina (Bustino) 3144f31. Tall rangy hobdayed half-brother to a German flat winner. Dam won 2 flat, 15-16f. FLAT (blinkered final) r5 p0 (beat one). NH '97/9 (for P.F. Nicholls latterly) r6 p1 (3rd in 2m6f Nov Chse); pulled up 4 inc when blinkered twice, and unseated 1. P-t-P '99 r5 w1 (Maiden) p3 (2 2nds); and fell 1. A fair performer when all goes well, but prone to diabolical blunders, and Anthony Honeyball performed wonders when getting him home at Cothelstone on his final appearance in 2000. Admirably consistent considering his breathing problems, but usually avoids cut in the ground, and has done all his winning on a sound surface. Should be able to find a similar opening in future. Wears a tongue-strap. *Mrs M. Emery — Taunton V. (John Honeyball).* 144 (R), 658 (R), 927 (Cf), 1059 (I), 1236 (M), 1473 (Cf), 1554 (Cf).

PRIME STYLE ..10-4.. 12 ch.g. Say Primula — Sheer Panache (Fury Royal) p1ffp211p. Owner-bred brother to Sheer Prejudice, and half-brother to Move In Style and Mountain Lion. P-t-P '95 and '97 r7 w2 (Maiden and Members) p0; fell/unseated 3. NH '99 (for J.H. Johnson) r5 p0. Won twice on a sound surface in '95, but evidently went wrong, and was showing his first piece of form since when a fair fourth over hurdles at Market Rasen in June '99. Showed no ill effects when returning to Pointing in 2000, and was well handled by Chris Gibbon when successful on three occasions. Takes a strong hold, and usually establishes a long lead and makes all, but can be clumsy, and did not quite see out the trip when tried over four miles once. Has done really well for an old crock, and with few miles on the clock can win again. Acts on a sound surface, and can handle softish. Wears a cross-noseband. *N. Manners — Zetland (Chris Gibbon).* 134 (I), 377 (R), 504 (O), 623 (Cf), 911 (4mMO), 1027 (Cf), 1324 (M), 1348 (Cf), 1588 (I).

PRIMITIVE CHARLES ..9-10.. 8 b.g. Primitive Rising (USA) — Clairet (Sagaro) pp31p47. Small neat. Dam was 2nd in Hdle; and won 2 Points and 3rd for Mr Clark. NH FLAT '98 r1 p0 (5th). P-t-P '98/9 r6 w1 (2m4f Maiden) p2 (3rds, of 4 once); pulled up 1. NH Jun '00 r1 p0 (7th in 2m7f110y

Nov Ch: *a bhnd, t.o*). Beat Lochnomore and Pangeran when successful over 2m4f at Cottenham on his reappearance last year, but missed the next two months of the season, and has proved a major disappointment since. Came from well off the pace and produced very late to win his Members in 2000, but soundly thrashed otherwise, and must surely have a problem. Donned blinkers in his last five outings. *J.F. Thompson — Bedale (Tim Walford).* 50 (R), 173 (R), 807 (R), 1031 (M), 1335 (2m4f110yH), 1577 (R).

PRIMITIVE KING ..9-13.. 9 b.g. Primitive Rising (USA) — Middlestone Queen (Tumble Wind USA) 235pp. Small. Dam won 2 Hdles at around 2m. P-t-P '97/9 r12 w4 (up to Confined) p1 (last of 3); fell/unseated 2, and pulled up 2. A fair performer when passing the post first in five of his 12 starts '97/9, but consistently disappointing this year despite having a favourites chance on two occasions. Remains prone to the odd bad error, and did not stay when tried over four miles. Still relatively inexperienced, and might be able to bounce back to form in 2001. *Mr & Mrs M.D. Reed — Chid, Lec & Cowdray (Shirley Reed).* 130 (CMod), 288 (CMod), 574 (4mMO), 1108 (C), 1395 (L).

PRIMITIVE MAN ..10-4.. 11 b.g. Primitive Rising (USA) — Tiemandee (Mandrake Major) 221bp. Tall trainer-bred half-brother to Hurdles winner, Manwell. NH FLAT '96 r3 p0. NH '96/7 (for breeder, B. Temple) r2 p0. Made a fine start to his Pointing career with a one length second to Jackson's Hole and a two length defeat by Prominent, and then beat two potential useful long-term prospects in a very slowly-run Maiden at Brocklesby Park. Beaten favourite in two subsequent attempts, and presumably went wrong when weakening quickly and pulling up in the latest. Has always been liable to disappear for huge periods, which is a pity, because he is a resolute sort whose full resources remain untapped. *Mrs J. Dwyer — Middleton (Bruce Temple).* 51 (OMa), 134 (I), 235 (OMa), 396 (R), 440 (R).

PLATE 104   377 West of Yore Restricted (Div 1): Prime Style (C. Gibbon), 1st, jumps ahead of L to R Yornoangel (R. Clark), ur, and Heavenly Blues (C. Wilson), 7th   PHOTO: Bill Selwyn

PRIMITIVE SATIN ..—.. 6 ch.g. Primitive Rising (USA) — Satinanda (Leander) p. Half-brother to With Respect (*qv*). A fence behind when pulling up at halfway at Mosshouses, but may not always go so slowly. *F.T. Walton — Border.* 1430 (OMa).

PRIMITIVE STREAK ..10-3.. 10 b.g. Primitive Rising (USA) — Purple Streak (Majestic Streak) pp3232. Tall half-brother to Strike Camp. P-t-P '97 (for Mr J.L. Gledson) r2 p1 (2nd); and unseated 1. NH '97/9 (for R.J. Hodges) r14 w2 (2m1f-2m3f HCap Chses) p4; fell/unseated 2. Showed promise in two Maiden Points in '97, and subsequently won two soft ground Chases, but was never tried over three miles under Rules, and has proved a weak finisher on his return to Pointing. Capable of jumping extra well, but wears a tongue-strap, and finds it impossible to raise his game in the final half-mile. Might be worth trying in sub-3m Hunter Chases with a strong jockey. *M.D. Abrahams — Bilsdale (Fiona Needham).* 376 (MO), 796 (O), 870 (O), 1231 (O), 1325 (Cf), 1476 (O).

PRIMITIVE WAY ..9-13.. 9 b.g. Primitive Rising (USA) — Potterway (Velvet Prince) pf. Compact attractive owner-bred half-brother to Keep A Secret (*qv*). P-t-P '97/8 (for Mr D.G. Atkinson) r9 w3 (Maiden, Restricted and Members) p2 (short head 2nd once); pulled up 1. Recorded a hat-trick in minor races in '98, but off the track the following season, and disappeared after a second fence fall at Alnwick in February on his return. Was a thorough stayer who jumped particularly well as a six-year-old, but clearly in the wars at present. _The Hon Gerald Maitland-Carew — Lauderdale (Julia Furness)._ 43 (Cf), 183 (CCf).

PRIMROSE HILL ..—§§.. 8 b.m. Lord David S (USA) — Country Carnival (Town And Country) prrr. Compact half-sister to Hurdles winner, Primitive Heart. Dam won 2 8f races inc Sell, and won 2m Hdle. NH '98 (for H. Alexander) r5 p0 (inc pulled up 3, and ran out; inc Sells). Refuses adamantly to indulge in any form of exertion, and merely content to follow the primrose path of dalliance. On the verge of a ban. _D.W. Wilsher & Mr Seymour — Cambs Univ (Stephen Wilsher)._ 15 (C), 174 (M), 323 (CfMa), 551 (OMa).

PRIMULAS DAUGHTER ..—.. 7 b.m. Say Primula — Niel's Crystal (Indiaro) pppp. Angular. Dam won 8min 20s Members on her debut at 5, and was 3rd on her only subsequent venture. Grandam, half-sister to Matchboard, won 3 Points (disqualified from another) and placed 7. Bought Malvern, Feb for 3000. Jumped adequately and showed a little speed, but had become remote by the time she pulled up in all four attempts. _Mrs V. Palmer — Mid Surrey F. (Sarah Palmer)._ 24 (OMa), 289 (Cm), 432 (OMa), 984 (OMa).

PRINCE BALTASAR ..—.. 12 ch.g. Claude Monet (USA) — Farababy (FR) (Faraway Son USA) p5. Rangy half-brother to flat and Hurdles winner, Leven Baby, and to a winner in Argentina. Dam won 2 7f races in France. NH '94/5 and '97 r13 p1 (3rd in Ch); last, pulled up 1, and fell 1 in other Chses; inc pulled up 4 in Hdles. P-t-P '99 r1 p0 (pulled up). Beaten less than eight lengths when third of four in a 2m5f Maiden Chase on his final appearance under Rules in '97, but has only once managed more than two outings in a year, and has been tailed off in all three Pointing ventures. _C. Lawson — Middleton._ 798 (OMa), 1352 (OMa).

PRINCE BUCK (IRE) ..10-10.. 11 b.g. Buckskin (FR) — Rechime (Prince Regent FR) 2151f3. Big strong. P-t-P/HUNT CH '96/7 r7 w3 (inc 3m2f Hunt Ch) p1 (last of 2); fell 1, ran out 1. NH '97/8 r5 w2 (3m1f Chses) p0. A smart performer who has made the bulk of the running in his four wins over regulation fences on easy surfaces. Gave four pounds and a 12 length beating to Chasing The Bride in the latest, but disappointed at Fontwell next time, and seemed to prove beyond doubt that he finds 3m2f as far as he wants to go when well beaten on his final start. A keen front-runner and a sound jumper, and it would make far more economic sense to run him in handicaps than Hunter Chases in future. _M.J. Roberts — E. Sussex & Romney Marsh._ 26 (O), 152 (3m1f110yH), 299 (3m2f110yH), 708 (O), 1106 (O), 1539 (3m7fH).

PRINCE ITSU ..—§.. 13 b.g. Itsu (USA) — Beige Princess (French Beige) pp. Half-brother to Hurdles winner, Kharab Bibi. P-t-P '95/9 r8 w1 (Maiden) p0; last, pulled up 3, ran out 2, and fell 1. Highly strung, and has only ever managed 10 races over six seasons. Exclusively aired in May/June in the last two years, and has failed to complete in four of his five starts since winning much the slowest race of the afternoon at Maisemore in '97. Usually takes a very strong hold, and once jumped a hedge alongside a fence at Howick. _J. Jones — Gelligaer F._ 1633 (CR), 1659 (R).

PRINCE MOSHAR ..9-5§.. 7 b.g. Primitive Rising (USA) — Mostimus (Doulab USA) p8uprp. Attractive rather unfurnished. Dam won at 5f. P-t-P '99 r5 w1 (2m4f Maiden) p0; pulled up 3, and unseated 1. Won a poor 2m4f Maiden at Tranwell last year, but has otherwise looked a touch loopy, and has failed to complete in seven of his eight starts since. Thoroughly misbehaved in 2000, and should be left well alone. Often mounted outside the paddock and taken to post early. _J. Carr — S. Durham._ 689 (R), 807 (R), 1162 (R), 1326 (R), 1474 (M), 1577 (R).

PRINCE OF PERILS ..9-6.. 7 b.g. Lord Bud — Kumari Peril (Rebel Prince) 51. Sturdy half-brother to Hurdles winner, Scottish Peril. Dam is half-sister to Border Peri (*qv* '91 Annual). 3100 4-y-o. NH FLAT r1 p0 (last, 300-1, and tailed off). Reappeared from a ten week absence to win a 2m4f Maiden in soft at Hexham, but it remains to be seen whether he will be able to make a successful transition to Restricteds. At least the full trip should not be a problem. _J.S. Haldane — College V. & N. Northumberland._ 499 (2m4fOMa), 1582 (2m4fOMa).

PRINCE OF SAINTS (IRE) ..10-1§.. 10 ch.g. Boyne Valley — Sandy's Daughter (Raise You Ten) pp2p31243341p. Good-topped attractive half-brother to Indian Lore (IRE), and to disqualified Irish Pointing winner, Pauls Birthday. Grandam, Sandy Sprite, broke down when 5l 5th in Specify's Grand National, having led over the final fence. NH FLAT '95 r1 p0. NH '96/9 (for M. Hammond) r18 w5 (2m Chses) p2. Capable of fair efforts on his going days, but will readily let himself get outbattle, as he showed when throwing away a race at Horseheath in which he should have beaten Hatcham Boy. Unable to score in his local Area, but taken with success to Rodmell (where he unearthed a bad four-runner race) and Kingston Blount (where he went four lengths clear after two out, but idled and was all out to stave off a 15-year-old). Acts on any ground and has a good completion record, but did not seem fit enough to get the trip in early season, and his best performances under Rules were at Catterick, where he nipped round the sharp track for four victories. Usually blinkered, and needs things to go his own way. *J.M. Turner — Suffolk.* 26 (O), 94 (O), 238 (O), 417 (Cf), 511 (O), 678 (O), 842 (O), 981 (O), 1156 (3m110yH), 1288 (O), 1511 (L), 1622 (L), 1665 (L).

PRINCESS LU (IRE) ..9-7.. 11 b.g. Nordance (USA) — Beaulieu (Red God) pff6. Workmanlike. Dam won at 9f in Ireland. IRISH NH FLAT '94 r2 p0. IRISH NH '94/6 r15 w1 (2m Ch) p0. P-t-P '97/8 r8 p1 (3rd of 4); pulled up 4. Won a three-runner Chase at Tramore in '95, but has only once earned a prize in 28 other races, and had the misfortune to be partnered by two of the least able jockeys in 2000. Sometimes runs prominently, but error-prone, and clearly finds three miles too far. A gelding despite his name. *M.G. Jones — Gelligaer F.* 382 (2m4fH), 741 (Cf), 895 (MO), 1492 (O).

PRINCESS SCULLY ..—.. 6 b.m. Weld — Havrin Princess (Scallywag) pu. Small compact sister to Dunston Slick. A war-torn veteran after just three visits to the races. Cut an ear badly in the lorry in the car park at Garthorpe and had to be withdrawn (still standing with her head hung down dejectedly a long time after the mishap), and crashed through the rails when galloping loose next time and had to be collected in the horse ambulance. *P. Morris — Albrighton.* 1091 (OMa), 1668 (OMa).

PRINCE TEETON ..—§.. 12 b.g. Prince Of Peace — Princess Teeton (Dairialatan) pp. Tall workmanlike. Dam, half-sister to Vulgarion and 3 other Pointers, and originally a show-jumper, was 20*l* 2nd of 3 in a Ladies for Mrs Richards. NH FLAT '93 r2 p0. NH '94/6 (from R. Buckler's) r10 w3 (2m6f Hdles) p0; pulled up lame only Ch. Notched a hat-trick in '95, but things went badly wrong for him afterwards, and fell at the third on his only appearance of '96. Hated every moment and did not even reach halfway on a brief revival in Points (blinkered in the latest). *R. & Mrs S.H. Richards — Blackmore & Sparkford V. (Pauline Tizzard).* 8 (C), 141 (MO).

PRINCIPAL PROFILE ..—.. 7 b.m. Skyliner — Fille De Phaeton (Sun Prince) f. Small neat half-sister to Harry Covert, Phaetons Glory and Hansom Marshal, to jumping winner, Toad Along, to successful Hurdler, Emsboy, and to a winner in Belgium. NH FLAT Jul '99 r1 p0. Has been hopelessly tailed off in a Bumper and fallen at the third in a Maiden to date. *Miss K. George — Oxford Draghounds.* 1245 (OMa).

PRIORY PIPER ..9-10.. 12 b.g. Maris Piper — Priory Girl (Rugantino) pp91457. Unfurnished. FLAT r2 p0 (Sells). NH '93/6 r24 p4 (3 3rds in Sell Hdles, beaten 22*l* plus, and 2nd in Ch); inc pulled up 2 and fell/unseated 3 in 7 other Chses. P-t-P/HUNT CH '97/9 r21 w3 (up to Confined) p4 (3 2nds, beaten once); pulled up 3, and fell/unseated 4. Specialises in winning when least expected, and has gone in at odds of 6-1, 25-1 and 10-1 in his last three victories, but best known for his ability to kick birch into the middle of next week whilst still remaining upright. Usually runs from the front, and can maintain a strong gallop, but consistency has never been his greatest asset. Goes well for Lenny Hicks, and may be able to win another small race. *C.W. Evans — Pytchley (Roger Harvey).* 116 (I), 296 (I), 510 (Cf), 788 (Cf), 1005 (M), 1334 (3mH), 1415 (Cf).

PRIVATE JET (IRE) ..10-2.. 12 b.g. Dara Monarch — Torriglia (USA) (Nijinsky CAN) pp451p. Light-framed brother to flat winner, Gabitti (IRE), and half-brother to 3 winners abroad. NH FLAT r3 p0. NH '93/4 (blinkered 1) r10 p2 (2nds, inc Sell); tailed off last twice and fell 1 in Chses. P-t-P/HUNT CH '95/9 r25 w1 (2m4f110y Hunt Ch) p8 (4 2nds; inc 4 Hunt Chses); pulled up 5, and fell/unseated 3. Usually fails to get the trip in Points, but successfully anchored by Richard Clark when landing a touch on the easy Stainton circuit this year. Has become a poor jumper of regulation fences, and only went a mile before pulling up at Sedgefield on his latest appearance, but has gained fair results in sub-3m Hunter Chses in the past. Wears a cross-noseband, occasionally blinkered, and has been tried tongue-tied. *P.H. Sanders — Sinnington (Ian Brown).* 153 (2m4f110yH), 384 (2m3f110yH), 504 (O), 621 (L), 805 (O), 923 (3m3fH).

PROBLEMATIC ..8-11.. 9 b.g. Gargoor — Bridle Way VII (unknown) p. Tall good-bodied. P-t-P '98/9 r3 p1 (2nd of 3); and last twice. Finished very tired when 25 lengths second of three only his only outing in '99, and looked fit when pulling up after making a blunder at the 13th on his reappearance at Chipley Park. Failed to return, and sadly appears prophetically named. *A.J. Chamberlain — V.W.H.* 145 (OMa).

PRO BONO (IRE) ..10-7.. 11 ch.g. Tale Quale — Quality Suite (Prince Hansel) 65472f. Smallish dipped half-brother to Spanish Fly (IRE). IRISH NH FLAT '94 r2 p0. IRISH NH '94/5 r12 w1 (2m Hdle) p3 (inc head 2nd in Ch); 4th, fell 1, and ran out 1 in other Chses. NH '98/9 r5 p1 (3rd); pulled up 1. P-t-P/HUNT CH '96/9 r17 w4 (Hunt Chses, 2m110y-2m5f110y) p7 (4 3rds; all Hunt Chses); fell/unseated 4, and pulled up 4. A speedy and quite useful performer who has become a specialist at 2m6f or less, but cannot usually resist trying to uproot at least one fence per race. Has been ridden to victory in his last two races by Noel Fehily and Seamus Durack, and his latest regular partner Marcus Foley looks well above average. Does not win as often as he should due to his jumping, but could still pop up in 2001. Tried tongue-tied in '98. *W.F. Caudwell — O. Berks (Matt Hazell).* 384 (2m3f110yH), 687 (2m6f110yH), 1026 (2m5f110yH), 1341 (2m110yH), 1434 (3m110yH), 1628 (2m4f110yH).

PROCOL'S BOY ..—.. 6 b.g. Meadowbrook — Brown Bee III (Marcus Superbus) pp. Brother to River Bee, and half-brother to Zam Bee (*qv*). Given two schooling runs in eight days, and may eventually show the benefits of this quiet introduction. *P.M. Hodges — Holderness (Tony Walker)*. 1234 (OMa), 1329 (OMa).

PROFESSOR LONGHAIR ..9-0.. 14 br.g. Strong Gale — Orient Conquest (Dual) 466666. Workmanlike half-brother to Irish Pointing winner, Nephin Far (IRE), and to Irish NH flat winner, Posture Quay (IRE). Dam won 2 Irish Hdles, 2m-2m2f. NH FLAT r1 p0. NH '94 r4 p0 (last, and pulled up 3). P-t-P/HUNT CH '95/9 (for Mrs F.A. Martin) r38 w6 (inc 2 Hunt Chses, 3m1f110y-3m2f, and 3 Ladies) p11 (6 3rds, inc 2 Hunt Chses); pulled up 2, ran out 1, and fell/unseated 4. Highly regarded as a schoolmaster when winning three times in '97, but has become increasingly unwilling in the current yard, and Peter Bennett has been unable to instil any zip into his recent performances. Used to jump well, but even that aspect of his game has gone to pot, and looks fed up to the back teeth nowadays. Would undoubtedly perk up for a change of rider. Twice insulted by blinkers in '99. *P.A. Bennett — Atherstone (D. Lowe)*. 789 (O), 870 (O), 1414 (M), 1523 (C), 1583 (C), 1666 (O).

PROFESSOR PAGE (IRE) ..9-5.. 11 b.g. Spanish Place (USA) — Knight's Princess (Menelek) R3pR. Small half-brother to Morgan. NH FLAT '95 r2 p2 (3rds). NH '95 and '97/8 (blinkered/visored 3) r17 w2 (3m1f-3m2f Chses, inc match, very lucky, rival remounted; and remote 2nd when left clear 3 out in the other!) p8 inc 3rd in Hdle; also 3rd after remounting — 10*l* clear when unseated at last). P-t-P '99 r6 p2 (last of 2 once); last 2, ran out 1, and pulled up 1. Remarkably lucky when successful under Rules, but has not enjoyed Pointing, and spends his time looking to run out nowadays. Highly unlikely to reform, and should be avoided at all costs. *M. Coates — Southdown & Eridge (Jeff Peate)*. 128 (L), 677 (L), 827 (L), 1212 (Cf).

PROFESSOR STRONG (IRE) ..7-11.. 13 b br.g. Strong Gale — Chapter Four (Shackleton) f5. Enormous rangy half-brother to Book Of Kells, Writer's Quay and Fiction Writer, to jumping winner, Scribbler, to Chasing winner, Page Of Gold, and to Irish NH flat and jumping winner, Sarsfield The Man (IRE). Dam won 2m4f Hdle in Ireland. IRISH NH '94/6 r18 w3 (3m1f Chses) p3) promoted from 5th once). NH '97/8 (for A. Forbes, bought for 1600; previously for P. Nicholls) r8 p2 (3rds, distant once); pulled up 3, and fell 2. A gigantic animal who produced some decent efforts in Ireland, and ended his career there when earning a £9675 prize, but made errors in his first two English yards, and has fallen on exceptionally hard times now. Performed appallingly in 2000, including when blinkered at Taunton. Missed one intended outing as the horsebox broke down on the way to the track. *M.A. Hill — Wheatland*. 922 (3mH), 1529 (M).

PROFILER (IRE) ..—.. 10 b.g. Rontino — Ash Copse (Golden Love) p0u. Big strong home-bred half-brother to Roscoe's Gemma. Dam was placed in 2 Points. Grandam, My Mela, won 3 Irish Points, and is half-sister to The Dikler. P-t-P '96 and '99 r3 p0 (pulled up 3). NH Summer '00 (from Mrs V Ward's) r2 p0 (10th in 2m HCap Hdle: *ld til hdd 5, wkng when blun 3 out, eased*; and unseated in 2m Nov Ch: *bhnd, hmpd 3, blun & ur 2 out*). More elusive than a Blue Moon, and can be guaranteed to pull up when he does appear. *H.L. Thompson — Cleveland (Tina Jackson)*. 1033 (OMa).

PROLOGUE (IRE) ..9-7.. 10 b.g. Mandalus — Advance Notice (Le Bavard FR) 243. Tall brother to Auchendolly (IRE). IRISH P-t-P '96 r1 p0 (pulled up). IRISH NH FLAT '96 r1 p0. IRISH NH '96/7 r4 p0. P-t-P '98/9 r10 w1 (Maiden) p3 (2 3rds, last once); pulled up 2, and fell 2. Has failed to progress following his Maiden success in '98, and having been tried in a visor the following year looked decidedly reluctant (albeit in a state of exhaustion) when beaten at Flagg on his reappearance in 2000. Beaten the best part of 10 lengths when returned to Restricteds on his final start, and will struggle to win one in future. *R.P. Hankey — Cheshire Forest*. 1255 (C), 1408 (Cf), 1528 (R).

PROMINENT ..10-12.. 7 b.g. Primo Dominie — Mary Bankes (USA) (Northern Baby CAN) 13111. Good-topped lengthy half-brother to flat winner, Mild Rebuke. FLAT r10 p1 (3rd). P-t-P '99 r4 w2 (Maiden and Restricted) p0; last, and unseated 1. Bred to travel incredibly quickly for less than a mile, but has developed into a smart staying Pointer, and his victory in the Grimthorpe was an outstanding performance for a six-year-old. Not disgraced on his Hunter Chase debut when outspeeded over the last three fences by Coole Abbey, and has been partnered by David Easterby since giving rise to speculation that he could have a future under Rules with father Mick. Suited by some cut in the ground. *M.J. Brown — York & Ainsty S.* 134 (I), 225 (3mH), 376 (MO), 395 (O), 999 (4m1fMO).

PROPER CHARLIE ..9-9.. 8 b.g. Broadsword (USA) — Highgate Lady (Rubor) up42. Compact good-topped. Dam, half-sister to Highgate Amber (*qv* '92 Annual), won 21 Points (18 Ladies) and placed 10 (never missed the frame in her 36 completions; last 18 wins for Joey Newton). Bred from an utterly delightful mare and showed plenty of promise himself, but a strong stuffy sort, and gives the impression he has not yet been fit enough. Rather unlucky over a probably inadequate 2m4f on final start, as he was five lengths clear two out, but jumped the last slowly and could not quicken when overtaken by the potentially useful Moss Harvey on the run-in. It will be surprising and disappointing if he does not win races and rate a lot higher in his second campaign. *J.R. Newton — Belvoir*. 1011 (CfMa), 1196 (OMa), 1423 (OMa), 1589 (2m4fOMa).

PROPHET'S THUMB (IRE) ..9-8.. 12 b.g. Arapahos (FR) — Smack On (Reformed Character) p4. Very small close-coupled. IRISH NH '93/4 r3 p0. IRISH P-t-P '93 and '93/7 (tried blinkers) r20 p4 (beaten head once after weakening alarmingly on flat having looked in control); pulled up 4, fell 2 and unseated 1. P-t-p '98/9 (for Miss A. Holland & Mr A. Gunther) r12 w2 (Maiden and Intermediate nov rdrs) p3 (2 3rds); pulled up 4. A sound jumper for one so diminutive, but took 27 attempts to get off the mark, and has only managed one success in 10 outings since. A good ride for a novice, but Tessa Good only partnered him once in 2000 when 19 lengths fourth of five in his Members. Acts on a sound surface. *Mrs S. Good — O. Berks.* 968 (Cf), 1202 (M).

PROUD FOUNTAIN (IRE) ..9-11.. 8 br.g. Royal Fountain — Proud Polly (IRE) (Pollerton) 5. IRISH P-t-P '99 r6 p2 (8l and distant 3rds, last once); pulled up 4. P-t-P/HUNT CH '99 (for Mrs S. Scott) r5 w1 (Maiden) p2; last, and pulled up 1. Ended '99 with a narrow success at Mosshouses, having been thrust unsuccessfully into the Hunter Chase arena previously, but only able to appear once for new connections this year when a fair fifth at Newton Bromswold. Quietly fancied, and may be able to recover losses if able to return in 2001. *S.N. Wilshire — V. of Aylesbury.* 513 (CR).

PRUDENT MINER (IRE) ..9-0.. 10 b.g. Miner's Lamp — Prudent Birdie (Lucifer USA) pp65u5up7p. Strong-topped brother to Irish Pointing winner, Miners Dance. IRISH NH FLAT '98 r1 p0. IRISH P-t-P '98/9 r7 w1 (7yo Mdn) p3 (inc last of 2 and last of 3); pulled up 1. NH Mar '00 r1 p0 (pulled up in 3m110y Amat Rdrs Ch: *a bhnd, t.o*). Looked moderate in Ireland, but did manage a success in holding, and it is just conceivable that he retains some ability. Has no hope of showing it with the overweight Robert Skinner, who flops around in the saddle like a rag doll. Invariably remote if managing to complete in 2000, and the only time a rival was behind him was at Sandown, when he beat one who had continued after pulling up for a rest. *R.C. Skinner - Brecon & Talybont (Linda Blackford).* 406 (R), 853 (Inr), 929 (Cnr), 1137 (I), 1176 (R), 1376 (R), 1563 (R), 1651 (I), 1671 (R).

PRU'S PROFILES (IRE) ..—.. 10 b.g. Tale Quale — Hazy Hill (Goldhill) f. Neat workmanlike half-brother to All Weather Hurdles winner, Chapel Hill (IRE), and to Irish NH flat and Pointing winner, Hazy Rose. 28,000 4yo. NH FLAT '95/6 (for N. Twiston-Davies) r2 p0. NH '96 and '98 r4 p1 (3rd); fell only Ch. Proved to be an extremely hairy ride on his debut over fences, and crashed at the first and injured a leg when reappearing two years later. Subsequently gained notoriety in the 'collusive bidders' case (see Racing Post of March 10 for full details), in which damages of £51,480 were awarded against the Curragh Bloodstock Agency, whilst humiliated trainers Paul Webber and Oliver Sherwood were each fined £4000 for acting 'in a manner prejudicial to the good reputation of horse racing. *Miss K. George — Oxford.* 148 (3m1f110yH).

PRUSSIAN STEEL (IRE) ..9-8.. 10 gr.g. Torus — Lady Barnaby (Young Barnaby) pu22us. Tall workmanlike. NH FLAT Feb '97 r1 p0. NH '97/8 (for Miss V. Wiliams; previously for M. Bradstock) r4 p1 (21l 3rd). Sold Malvern, July for 2200. Made the frame in three of just four attempts for previous yards, and his third was gained in a fair race. Goes missing for very long periods, and it was ironic that when he at last managed a full campaign the gods kept conspiring against him. Two exits were not his fault (baulked once, and slipped up once), and also stumbled and unseated when catching the leader once, whilst he was twice second at a maximum of two lengths at Littlewindsor including when short-headed by Basil. Thoroughly deserves a change of luck. *Mrs J. McCullough — Axe V.H. (Philip Greenwood).* 213 (CfMa), 409 (OMa), 520 (OMa), 881 (OMa), 1308 (OMa), 1565 (OMa).

PRYVATE TIME ..8-4.. 7 b.m. Still Time Left — Blonde Pryncesse (Pry) p25p. Half-sister to Dream Holiday, and to Hurdles winner, Landsker Pryde. Dam, sister to Diggory Delvet (*qv* '91 Annual), won 2 weak W. Wales Ladies and placed 2. Her fence last of two to Roger is hardly going to set her on the road to glory, but only young, and to borrow from her sire, there's still time left. *E.W. Morris — Pembs.* 834 (OMa), 951 (OMa), 1223 (2m4fOMa), 1404 (OMa).

PULHAM DOWNE ..9-4.. 6 ch.g. Baron Blakeney — Dame Nellie (Dominion) p3. Half-brother to Hurdles winners, Con Tricks and St John's Hill. Dam won at 7f. Showed a little promise when a fence last of three at Lockinge. Is his trainer going to jump up and down and wave her knickers in the air if this one wins? *N.R. Freak, C. Kendall, S. Wadey & A. Tory — Portman (Ali Tory).* 880 (OMa), 1204 (OMa).

PULKERRY (IRE) ..8-10.. 11 ch.g. King Luthier — Kylemore Abbey (Junius USA) cf4. Strong-topped lengthy half-brother to Hurdles winner, Rhoman Coin (IRE). Dam is half-sister to Prince Jakatom (*qv* '94 Annual). IRISH NH FLAT '96 r1 p1 (2nd). NH '98 (for P. Winkworth) r2 p0. Favourite when second for an Irish Bumper in '96, but has only totaled five outings since (and was carried out at the third in one of them), and his 35 lengths last does not auger well for the future. *Miss A. Agnew — Warwicks (Andy Martin).* 972 (OMa), 1435 (OMa), 1624 (OMa).

PULL ON ..9-2.. 7 bay g. Push On — The Manson Flyer (Green Shoon) f1. Tall rangy. Dam is half-sister to Parsoness (*qv* '93 Annual). NH FLAT Summer '99 r2 p0. NH '99 r1 p0 (pulled up in Hdle). An eye-catching individual who appeared to be in the process of running a decent race when he fell after two miles in his first Point, and duly beat the only other finisher Mission Lord on firm at Bonvilston, but both looked at full stretch in the closing stages, and the form is worthless. Tends to hang left, and wears a near-side pricker. Will possibly be able to mature into a more meaningful performer eventually. *W.J. Evans — Pembs (Mary Evans).* 1302 (OMa), 1455 (OMa).

PULPITS EDGE ..—.. 10 b.g. Broadsword (USA) — Little Tristram (Kinglet) uup. Small neat. Dam, half-sister to Orphan Olly (*qv*), failed to finish in 4 Points ('schooling her might help'). P-t-P '99 r1 p0 (pulled up). Eliminated by the fourth fence twice in 2000, and soon lagging when pulled up on his final appearance. Looks hopeless, but might be able to go quicker if his cross-noseband were removed. *Mrs J. Wilcox — Ludlow.* 339 (CfMa), 865 (CfMa), 994 (OMa).

PUNNETT'S TOWN ..—§.. 11 br.m. Sulaafah (USA) — Queen's Bronze (King's Troop) Rr. Light-framed half-sister to Hurdles winner, Brent Riverside. P-t-P '97/9 r5 p0 (ran out 4, and pulled up 1). An abomination who has at long last been banned. Will hopefully not breed clones of herself if she goes to stud. *Mrs L.P. Baker — Coakham Bloodhounds.* 85 (O), 221 (OMa).

PUNTERS OVERHEAD (IRE) ..10-9.. 13 b.g. Black Minstrel — Boyne Saint (Saint Crespin III) p. Sparely-made half-brother to several winners, including abroad. Dam won 3 races in Ireland. NH FLAT '94 r2 w1 p0. NH '94/6 (blinkered 1) r11 w1 (2m6f Ch) p6. P-t-P '99 r2 w2 (Open and Ladies). A former useful though injury prone performer who was nursed back to health by the team at Seaborough to win both his Points in '99, but did not reappear after January, and broke down after just one fence on his 2000 debut. Would probably have achieved many more successes had he been sounder. *Mrs E. Hutchinson — Taunton V. (Richard Barber).* 152 (3m1f110yH).

PURE AIR ..9-7.. 9 b.g. Derrylin — Pure Poetry (Elegant Air) p516p. Smallish unfurnished. IRISH P-t-P '97 r4 w1 (5yo Mdn) p0; last, pulled up and took no part. NH '97/9 (for Mrs C. Hicks, bought for 3600, blinkered once) r11 p0 (inc pulled up 4 in Hdles, inc Sells; pulled up and fell 2 in Chses). Bought Malvern, Oct for 400. Not better than tailed off last in four of his five Irish Points, but rather miraculously managed to snatch a short head verdict from the only other to go clear in a Restricted in the clotting mud at Pantyderi. His Irish success was also freaky, as the 12 length winner was disqualified when it was discovered that he was a four-year-old! Never less than 40-1 in the previous yard under Rules, and has had a tie-back operation, so the latest connections did well to extract a success from their cheapie. Appeared to go lame on firm on final start. *M.J. Spuffard & F. Goldsworthy — S. Pembs.* 38 (CR), 273 (R), 347 (R), 837 (I), 944 (I).

PURE GRIT (IRE) ..—.. 11 b.g. Sheer Grit — Shuil Eile (Deep Run) p. Workmanlike half-brother to Chasing winner, Lisdante (IRE), to 3 winners in Ireland, including Shuil Ar Aghaidh (NH flat and useful staying Hurdler) and Rawhide (very useful staying jumper). Dam, dam to Why Forget, and half-sister to Rhu Na Haven (*qv* '98 Annual), won NH flat and 2 Hdles (2m-2m4f) in Ireland. IRISH NH FLAT '95/6 r3 p1 (3rd). IRISH NH '97 r1 p0 (pulled up in Hdle). P-t-P '99 (for Mr S. Rammel) r1 p0 (pulled up). Attractively bred, and showed ability when third in a Limerick Bumper in '96, but has pulled up apparently lame in both English Points, and seems to have a bleak future. *Mrs B.L. Shaw — United (Gary Hanmer).* 1668 (OMa).

PURSLET ..8-11.. 10 b.m. Kinglet — Persue (Perhapsburg) 73p. Small neat sister to Perking, and half-sister to Sunymanor, Perboy and Perjoy. Dam won Maiden and placed 8. Grandam, Astwood Susie, failed to finish in 8 Points, but great-grandam, Davy's Sweetheart, won 10 Points. P-t-P '98/9 r9 p5 (4 3rds, of 4 once, and last once); pulled up 3, and fell 1. Has made the frame in six of her last eight Points, and beaten less than three lengths thrice, but a weak finisher, and sidelined with a tendon problem after three early runs in 2000. Deserves to win a little race if able to return, but is leaving it rather late. Wears a cross-noseband. *Miss N.J. Stallard — Cotswold V.F.* 72 (OMa), 206 (OMa), 341 (CfMa).

PUSHOVER (FR) ..9-0.. 9 b.g. Dowsing (USA) — Pushoff (USA) (Sauce Boat USA) ppp. Small neat half-brother to Irish flat winner, Champagne 'N Roses. Dam won at 5f (looked temperamental). P-t-P '98/9 r6 w1 (Maiden) p0; refused 1, and pulled up 4. Won a poor Maiden on his only completion in '99, but pulled up after a maximum of 2m4f in 2000, and that performance looks to be a flash in the pan. *J. Pearson — N. Herefords.* 332 (M), 612 (CR), 864 (R).

PYR FOUR ..10-3.. 14 b.g. Strong Gale — Distant Castle (Deep Run) 4. Tall rangy brother to Broomhill Duker (IRE), to Irish Pointing winner, Reen-O-Foil, and to Irish Hurdles winner, Storming Ahead, and half-brother to Moss Castle. Dam won a Point, a NH flat, 3 Hdles, 2m1f-3m, and 2 Chses, 2m4f-2m5f, in Ireland. IRISH NH FLAT '92/3 r2 p0. IRISH NH '92/6 r20 w3 (2m1f Hdle, and 2 Chses, 2m2f-2m6f) p2 (2nds, beaten head once). NH '97 (for G. McCourt) r4 p3. A triple winner in Ireland in '95, and revived after a three year absence to give Ben Pauling an excellent first ride at Larkhill (only beaten 13 lengths in a contest in which the first three all went on to land Hunter Chases), but heartbreakingly dropped dead a few minutes later. *H.C. Pauling — Heythrop.* 59 (MO).

QU'APPELLE ..9-0.. 8 ch.g. Teamster — Gay Rhythm (Quiet Fling USA) p23p4. Close-coupled. Dam, sister to Gay Rhythm (*qv* '91 Annual), won a Restricted on hard and placed 4 (inc a Hunt Ch) for the Tills, but was generally completely unable to stay 3m. NH '97 r2 p0 (tailed off both). P-t-P '99 r1 p0 (fell). Seems cast in the same mould as mother, and is unable to get the trip at present. Beaten a minimum of 12 lengths when making the frame, but only had one rival behind him, and the option of short Maidens is no longer available to connections. With firm ground, bad opposition, and an easy course if he is ever to open his account. *R.H. & C.M. Till — Wilton (Linda Syckelmoore).* 71 (OMa), 518 (2m4fOMa), 762 (M), 1245 (OMa), 1468 (OMa).

PLATE 105   44 West Percy Open Maiden (Div 1): Quarterstaff (C. Wilson), 1st, has it sewn up at the brand new second last   PHOTO: Alan Mitchell

QUARTERSTAFF ..10-7.. 7 b.g. Charmer — Quaranta (Hotfoot) 11136. Close-coupled brother to flat and jumping winner, Quango and Irish flat and jumping winner, Quinze, and half-brother to several winners, including Quinlan Terry (Cambridgeshire). Dam won at 5f. 9500y. FLAT (for Mrs A. Swinbank, blinkered final; previously for C. Wall) r9 p1 (3rd in Sell). Disappointing on the flat, but proved to be a different kettle of fish when sent Pointing, and showed plenty of speed and some acceleration to notch a ready hat-trick in minor company. Sent all the way to Cheltenham for his Hunter Chase debut over 2m4f, and finished a creditable third in a 20-runner event, but could not recover from a bad blunder three out when favourite for the Heart next time. Needs to jump the bigger fences better, but will win over them when he does. *Mrs J. Wilson — Zetland.* 44 (OMa), 184 (R), 692 (I), 1336 (2m4fH), 1445 (3m1fH).

QUEEN BIDDY (IRE) ..10-2.. 9 b.m. King's Ride — Hopeful Biddy (Deep Run) 1421f3. Workmanlike lengthy half-sister to The Right Attitude (IRE) (*qv*). IRISH P-t-P '97 r2 p1 (3rd beaten 23 lengths after two ahead had fallen at last); and fell 1. P-t-P '98/9 (for Mr P. Sawney) r5 p0 (4th, pulled up 3, and unseated 1). Took some time to eradicate the jumping errors that were holding her back, but struck at the first time of asking for new connections, and landed some tidy bets in the process. Soon staked her claim in Restricteds, and was upsides the winner when departing at the second last in a Balcormo Mains Intermediate. Unfortunately succumbed after the season to a most unusual 'knotted' gut. *D.J. Simpson — College V. & N. Northumberland (Clive Storey).* 112 (OMam), 360 (R), 620 (R), 807 (R), 1121 (I), 1495 (I).

QUEENOFTHEMOUNTAIN ..—.. 9 b.m. Motivate — Levotesse (Levmoss) p. Small angular owner-bred half-sister to Mountain Slave, Journo's Joy and She Wood She. Dam, half-sister to Who's Next (*qv*), was placed in 3 Sell Hdles; and broke down in a Point for Mrs Howells. P-t-P '98 r1 p0 (refused). Went a lot further than she did when last sighted, but soon labouring in the rear at Erw Lon, and was pulled up after 2m4f. Two outings in three seasons does not bode well for her future. *Mrs J. Howells — Llangeinor.* 950 (OMa).

QUEEN'S AWARD (IRE) ..—.. 12 ch.g. Bishop Of Orange — Demelza Carne (Woodville II) pp. Tall angular half-brother to Hurdy. NH FLAT '93 r1 p0. P-t-P '99 (for Mr J. Bowen & Miss L. Wonnacott) r2 p0 (pulled up 2). A fair staying handicap hurdler in the past, but never took to regulation fences, and has shown no spark when pulled up in all four Pointing ventures. Stands his racing badly now, and seems very unlikely to make an impact at 12. *Miss L. Wonnacott — Tetcott.* 165 (Cf), 727 (O).

QUEENS CURATE ..—.. 14 b.m. Bustineto — Bright Gail (Levanter) p. Long-backed half-sister to a flat winner. IRISH P-t-P '93 r3 p1 (3rd); pulled up 1. IRISH NH FLAT '91 r1 p1 (3rd). IRISH NH

'91 r5 p0. NH '93/9 r13 p2 (3rds in Chses, beaten 15l, and distance); pulled up 8, inc first 3 and final 3; inc Sell. a waste of time. Frequently becomes tailed off early, and jumped right in her Point. Not placed since '94, was lame in '97 and probably also in '95, and has pulled up once annually for the past four years. *Mrs E.B. Scott — Quantock.* 389 (O).

QUEEN'S EQUA ..8-13.. 11 b.m. Queen's Soldier (USA) — Equa (Cheval) p2f. Sturdy half-sister to Captain Equaty and Equatime. Dam was 30*l* 2nd in Gelligaer Members, and failed to finish in 3 other Points. P-t-P '96/8 r16 p2 (3rds, last once); last, pulled up 9, and fell 1. A long-standing maiden, who broke a leg when tipping up at the fourth in the last of three Welsh Maidens in May when blinkered for the first time. *Miss S.R. Major — Llangeinor.* 1300 (OMa), 1405 (OMa), 1573 (OMa).

QUEENS TOKEN ..—.. 8 b.m. Rakaposhi King — Kins Token (Relkino) pp. Half-sister to Kingussie Flower. P-t-P '99 r2 p0 (pulled up 2). Yet to go more than 2m4f, and looks a hard to train non-stayer. *M.H.D. Barlow & Miss S. Firmin — Bicester with Whaddon (Robert Elwell).* 194 (CfMa), 516 (OMa).

QUESTIONAIRE ..10-0.. 8 b.m. Northern State (USA) — Broken Melody (Busted) 5234f. Small sturdy half-sister to 3 flat winners (one in Denmark), including Bold Melody (also a successful Hurdler) and Fanfold. FLAT r2 p0. P-t-P '98/9 r9 w2 (Maiden and Restricted) p3 (2 2nds, of 3 once); and pulled up 4. A ready winner twice in May '99, but has failed to upgrade successfully, and made more errors than usual in 2000. Numbered Kinnefad King amongst her victims last year, and it would be unwise to write her off just yet. Once started 11-2 favourite for a 15-runner Welsh Maiden — beat that for value. Has a large question mark-shaped blaze, hence her name? *C.C. Morgan — Tredegar F. (David Stephens).* 388 (I), 600 (I), 820 (Cm), 1098 (C), 1312 (Cm).

PLATE 106   820 Llangibby PPORA Club Members Mares: Its blazingly obvious how Questionaire got his name
PHOTO: Harry Armstrong

QUICK RESPONSE (IRE) ..9-0.. 8 gr.g. Roselier (FR) — Deceptive Response (Furry Glen) upbppff. Small sparely-made brother to Irish Pointing winner, Parabellum. IRISH P-t-P '99 r4 p0 (pulled up 4). Bought Malvern, Oct for 3000. Has shown some speed, but never enough stamina. Twice failed to get round in one day for the unheard of Melanie Norledge at Barbury Castle (was hanging right when he gave up at the final fence on the second attempt), and later fell with her in his Members. Despite never having got round in nine attempts connections then decided that Cheltenham was the place to be, and after surviving a blunder at the third he duly fell four out when a 66-1 shot. Possibly not as bad as he appears, but would need far more competent management to prove it. *M. Harris — N. Cotswold (Mark Rimell; -).* 31 (CMa), 36 (CI), 194 (CfMa), 471 (OMa), 1020 (OMa), 1189 (M), 1336 (2m4fH).

QUICK SUCCESSION (IRE) ..8-9.. 8 b.g. King's Ride — Tony's Lass (Document) p4p. Good-bodied compact half-brother to Hawaiian Venture, to prolific Irish NH flat and jumping winner, Random

Prince, and to Irish NH flat and Hurdles winner, Maradyke Bridge. 14,500 4yo. NH FLAT Spr '98 r2 p0. NH '99 (for N. Gaselee) r1 p0 (tailed off in hdle). Bought Ascot, June for 840. Jumped right in his first Point, 20 lengths fourth after a bad blunder three out in the second, and then disappeared following a lifeless display in early March. *J. Trice-Rolph — Heythrop.* 76 (CCfMa), 250 (CfMa), 391 (CfMa).

QUIET CONFIDENCE (IRE) ..10-1.. 11 b.m. Pennine Walk — Northern Wisdom (Northfields USA) 7. Small lengthy angular half-sister to 4 flat winners, including Blue Grit. IRISH FLAT '93 r6 p0. NH '94 r3 p0 (last 2 and unseated, inc Sells — very reluctant once). P-t-P/HUNT CH '95/8 (for Mrs S.E. Kerley & Mr S. Stickland) r16 w5 (inc 3m Hunt Ch) p5 (4 2nds, inc 3 Hunt Chses); pulled up 1, and unseated 2. A speedy mare who has made most in five wins on good or firm, but has always had light campaigns, and failed to reappear after finishing a remote last at Black Forest Lodge in January. Missed the '99 season, and clearly feeling the effects of her penchant for a sound surface. *Mrs S. Kerley — Portman (Keith Kerley).* 67 (L).

QUIET MISTRESS ..9-10§.. 11 b.m. Kind Of Hush — Miss Acrow (Comedy Star USA) 466p3p. Good-bodied sister to flat and Hurdles winner, Quiet Miss, and half-sister to Acrow Line and Acrow Lord (successful Hurdlers — latter also won on flat). NH '94, and '95/7 (blinkered last 4) r17 w2 (2m4f-2m5f Sell Hdles) p6 (inc 2 2nds in Chses). P-t-P '98 (for Mr W.A. Bethell) r7 w1 (match for Members) p3 (3rds, last twice); 4th, last, and pulled up 1. Beat a showjumper who kept refusing in a match for her Members in '98, but not until she had stopped twice herself, and is renowned for her moody behaviour. No less disinterested after a year off, and beaten a minimum of 19 lengths, but generally tailed off, and regained blinkers on her last two starts. *Mrs L. Latchford — Burton (Margaret Morris).* 435 (M), 794 (Cf), 868 (Cf), 1215 (Cm), 1349 (O), 1584 (CCond).

QUITE A MISS ..9-6.. 11 b.m. True Song — Nitty's Girl (Spartan General) pp2p. Sturdy compact half-sister to Sam The Sloth. Dam won 2 Ladies and placed 6 for Chris Loggin. P-t-P '96/9 r9 w1 (Maiden) p3 (2 3rds, of 4 once); 5th, pulled up 3, and fell 1. Took advantage of the antics of her rivals to score at Mollington in '97, but often overfaced since, and ran badly in 2000 except for a modest second in a four-runner Restricted on firm at Ashorne. Has never managed more than four outings in a season. *C.W. Loggin & R. West — Bicester with Whaddon (Chris Loggin).* 969 (L), 1145 (L), 1442 (R), 1664 (R).

QUIT THE CREEK ..9-9.. 8 b.m. Then Again — Have Form (Haveroid) 213. Small light half-sister to flat winner, Shikari's Son. P-t-P '99 r2 p0 (pulled up 2). Given an easy time on her reappearance, and reaped the benefit next time when landing a 17-runner youngsters Maiden at Maisemore in softish. Beaten 11 lengths in her first Restricted on a much quicker surface, but had two subsequent winners behind when successful, and it will be a surprise if she cannot win again. Not bred to, but seems to have plenty of stamina. *H. Price — Llangibby (Rachel Price).* 629 (OMa), 900 (OMa), 1411 (R).

QUIXOTRY ..9-0.. 10 ro.g. Risk Me (FR) — Grey Charter (Runnymede) 2f7. Small light half-brother to a winner in Scandinavia. FLAT r4 p0. NH '95 and '97 r6 p0 (Sells latterly). P-t-P '99 r2 p1 (2nd); and pulled up 1. Twice a runner-up '99/00, but sprint bred, and does not stay three miles. Not surprisingly found the Alpraham too testing on his reappearance, but faded tamely on the much easier Chaddesley circuit when sent off joint-favourite on his final start. Pulls hard, and wears a cross-noseband. *Miss S. Hogbin — Meynell & S. Staffs.* 588 (OMa), 901 (M), 1634 (OMa).

RADIO DAYS (IRE) ..9-10.. 10 ch.g. Boreen (FR) — Sensible Sue (Orchestra) pp64p. Stocky. IRISH P-t-P '96 r1 p0 (pulled up). P-t-P/HUNT CH '97/9 (for Mr T.D. Sproat) r13 w6 (inc 2 Opens) p2 (2nds); pulled up 1, and fell 2. Unbeaten in his first five races, and was worth 10-7 and useful at best, but has slipped into a state of lethargy in the last two seasons, and even a change of scenery has failed to buck the trend. Only once better than last in 2000, and did not reach halfway on his final appearance. Looks badly wrong, and can be dismissed quickly unless a cure can be found. *A. Tizzard & P. Foot — Blackmore & Sparkford V. (Alan Tizzard).* 59 (MO), 403 (Cf), 877 (L), 1060 (MO), 1305 (MO).

RAFTER ..9-11.. 9 b.g. Enryco Mieo — Spangle (Pongee) 4112. Smallish unfurnished. A fence last on his belated debut, but sprang a 20-1 surprise in a Marks Tey Maiden, where he ran on gallantly to catch the leader in the final 100 yards. Completed a quick double in a Cottenham Restricted, but was very lucky as the ten length leader unseated at the last, and then no match for the easy winner of his Members. Gave Chris Carman a most enjoyable season, but will have more to do in competitive events in future. *C. Carman — N. Norfolk H., & W. Norfolk.* 775 (OMa), 941 (CfMa), 1038 (R), 1285 (M).

RAG BOLT (IRE) ..8-9.. 8 b.g. Brush Aside (USA) — Icy Gal (Frigid Aire) 4pR3. Half-brother to Kemiller (IRE). IRISH P-t-P '98 r1 p0. IRISH NH FLAT '98 r1 p0. IRISH NH '98 r1 p0; pulled up in Ch. Beaten more than 30 lengths in both completions when returning from a two year absence, and gives the impression that there is probably something wrong with him. *N.W. Padfield — Enfield Chace.* 132 (OMa), 412 (OMa), 604 (OMa), 941 (CfMa).

RAINBOW LEGACY .—.. 9 b.g. Sulaafah (USA) — Star Alert (Red Alert) p. Half-brother to Venus Saga (dam of Albert Woods (*qv*), and Sagaro Sun. Tailed off and pulled up after two miles when hopelessly outclassed in a Confined. *Mrs G. Drury — O. Surrey & Burstow (Peter Broad).* 572 (CfO).

RAINBOW TIMES (IRE) ..10-3.. 8 b.m. Jareer (USA) — Princess The Great (USA) (Alleged USA) 1243213. Small neat. Dam won 12f flat and 3 2m Hdles in Ireland. IRISH NH FLAT '97 (blinkered) r1 p0. IRISH NH '97 (blinkered final) r5 p0. P-t-P/HUNT CH '98/9 r10 w4 (up to Confined) p4 (3 2nds, last once); unseated 1. A useful mare on her day, and has amassed six wins since crossing the Irish Sea, but not as reliable as her record suggests, and has been turned over when favourite no fewer than eight times in three years. A thorough stayer, and suited by easy ground, but future performances depend entirely on her frame of mind. Has the make and shape of a Ladies horse, but has never been tried in one though Valerie Jackson did partner her when she was trained by the Andersons. Occasionally blinkered. *Mrs J.M. Lancaster — College V. & N. Northumberland (Clive Storey).* 110 (O), 362 (O), 582 (3m3fH), 716 (O), 975 (O), 1160 (O), 1429 (Cm).

RAINBOW WALK (IRE) ..10-2.. 11 ch.g. Rainbow Quest (USA) — Widows Walk (Habitat) 505u304. Good-looking lengthy half-brother to flat winner, Sadler's Walk. Grandam, On The House, won 1000 Guineas. FLAT r13 w2 (10-12f, Lingfield all-weather) p2 (3rds). NH '95/6 r12 p4 (inc 2nd in Ch); inc Sell; pulled up other Ch. P-t-P '98 r10 w1 (Ladies) p2 (2nd of 3 once); 4th twice, 6th twice, and last thrice. Bred to win a classic, but fractured a pedal bone as a two-year-old and could only aspire to win on the equitrack, and cut little ice under National Hunt Rules. Won a bad five-runner Ladies at Chaddesley in '98, but unable to appear the following season, and remains a weak finisher judged on his 2000 efforts. Ran his best race of the season when fourth at Clifton-on-Dunsmore on his final outing, but was only two lengths of second having made much of the running. Had cleared a staggering 255 fences without mishap until unseating Anna Burton at Guilsborough, but the rider surely needs some fresh blood if she is to score again as both he and Drummond Warrior seem past their best. *J. Burton — Quorn.* 118 (L), 226 (2m4f110yH), 613 (L), 1007 (L), 1191 (L), 1341 (2m110yH), 1417 (L).

RAINCHECK ..10-0§.. 10 b.g. Mtoto — Lashing (USA) (Storm Bird CAN) 4. Good-bodied compact half-brother to flat winner, Straw Thatch. Dam, $450,000y, won 2 flat, 6-8f. FLAT r4 p0 (last twice). NH '95/7 (blinkered 1) and '99 r15 p2 (2nds in Chses); last, pulled up 4, fell/unseated 3, and left in other Chses, and last, pulled up 2, and fell 1 in Hdles. P-t-P/HUNT CH '97/9 r6 w2 (inc 2m5f Hunt Ch) p1 (3rd); pulled up 2. Quite useful at around 2m5f when he decides to co-operate, and completed a double in his first two starts of '98, but disappointing since, and had been pulled up in three successive races prior to finishing last on his only outing this year. Ran well until his stamina gave out at Higham, and still possesses some ability, but evidently almost impossible to train. Usually jumps left-handed, and is frequently tongue-tied. *Mrs G. Worsley — O. Surrey & Burstow.* 238 (O).

RAINING STAIRS (IRE) ..9-2.. 10 b.g. Orchestra — Strong Gale Lass (Strong Gale) p77p5. Tall rangy. NH FLAT '96 r1 p0. NH '96/8 r10 p1 (2nd); inc 5th and pulled up 2 in Chses. P-t-P '99 r4 w1 (Maiden) p0; 5th, fell 1, and brought down 1. Showed plenty of stamina to win a weak elders Maiden at Maisemore last year, but often gurgled when disappointing under Rules, and back-pedalled after no more than two miles when only once better than last in 2000. *J. Trice-Rolph — Heythrop.* 13 (R), 193 (R), 392 (R), 749 (Cf), 1013 (M).

RAIN STREET (IRE) ..—.. 10 ch.g. Phardante (FR) — Two In A Million (Rarity) fpp. Strong compact half-brother to Don't Tell Judy (IRE). Dam won at 8f in Ireland. Fell at the 11th on his debut aged nine, and looked most unpromising when tailed off by halfway twice subsequently. *A. Nicholls — Sinnington (Susan Nicholls).* 283 (OMa), 378 (R), 624 (OMa).

RAISE AND GAIN (IRE) ..10-0.. 10 ch.g. Rising — Bellus Mandy (IRE) (Mandalus) p11. Rangy. Dam is half-sister to Lord Geldof (qv '88 Season Annual). NH FLAT '95 (blinkered) r2 p0 (for N. Twiston-Davies). NH '99 r2 p0 (remote 6th and pulled up in Hdles). Making only the sixth appearance of his career when backed from tens to fives and landing an elders Maiden at Maisemore (had jumped left when tailed off in his previous Point), and the form worked out really well as the next three home all went on to score. Showed an ability to handle firm ground when following up in game fashion at Weston Park, but said to have a breathing problem, and may now need a wind operation. Was absent for no less than 40 months after December '95, and connections have done well to get him going at last. *I.K. Johnson — Radnor & W. Herefords (Sue Johnson).* 617 (CMa), 891 (OMa), 1411 (R).

RAKAPOSHI RYME (IRE) ..9-8.. 8 ch.m. Rakaposhi King — Muffet's Spider (Rymer) fpp. Compact good-bodied half-sister to Mighty Strong. P-t-P '99 (for Mr P. Kennen) r2 w1 (Maiden) p0; and last. Looked promising when winning a Bratton Down Maiden on just her second start, but a bitter disappointment since, and has been let down by her jumping. Absent for ten weeks after falling on her reappearance, but made countless errors when tried in blinkers at Bishopsleigh. Might appreciate better ground than she encountered in 2000, and still young enough to atone. *Mrs J. Scott — S. Devon.* 164 (R), 1176 (R), 1608 (R).

RALLEGIO ..9-9.. 12 b.g. Alleging (USA) — Radigo (Ragstone) u3533. Small strong-topped half-brother to Hurdles winner, Nouvelle Cuisine. Dam won 2 10f races. NH FLAT Spr '93 r2 p0. NH '94 and '96/7 (for P. Monteith) r38 w5 (3 Hdles, 2m-2m1f, and 2 Chses, 2m-2m1f) p12 (inc 3 Sell Hdles). Was at his best between January and March '97 when he won three of his four attempts, and formerly best in soft, but has never scored beyond 2m1f, and probably struggles to stay three miles. Beaten 16 lengths on the only occasion he was able to avoid Balisteros in Ladies Opens, and finished last three times in a four race spell, being beaten between a fence and two fences twice. Deserves three cheers for his excellent completion record, having got round in 42 of 45 outings over jumps. *B. White — Jedforest (Anne Combe).* 494 (L), 661 (L), 1079 (L), 1119 (L), 1364 (L).

RAMBLING MICK (IRE) ..—.. 8 b.g. Detroit Sam (FR) — Rambling Moss (Le Moss) p. NH June '99 r1 p0. Tailed off and pulled up after mistakes in a Hurdle and a Maiden to date (had two paddock handlers and on his toes in the latest). *D. Carr — Haydon.* 977 (CfMa).

RAPHAEL BODINE (IRE) ..9-3.. 12 b.g. Crash Course — Noelbonne Femme (Bonne Noel) u96R. Tall plain half-brother to Young Nimrod (*qv*). IRISH NH FLAT '94/5 r4 p2 (short head and neck 2nds). IRISH NH '94 r1 p0. NH '95/7 r7 w1 (2m1f Hdle) p2; pulled up 3. Can pull hard and show early speed, but obviously has a problem, and was tailed off with one horse behind him when completing in Hunter Chases. Tried in a tongue-strap. Won in April '96, went missing for 17 months soon after, and appeared to be lame when his career ground to a halt again in '97. *Miss V.M. Williams — S. Herefords.* 151 (3mH), 384 (2m3f110yH), 463 (2mH), 895 (MO).

RAPID LINER ..9-0.. 8 b.g. Skyliner — Stellaris (Star Appeal) 424. Workmanlike compact half-brother to Ashdren, and to flat winners Celestine and Blue Radiance. 4200f, 8600y. FLAT (early runs for A. Harrison) r12 p0. NH '96/7 and '99 (from R. Baker's, bought for 500, blinkered latterly; debut for H. Oliver) r15 p1 (distant 3rd — tailed off halfway); inc Sells. Useless and a very poor jumper when regularly tailed off in the worst company over Hurdles, but appeared to give a surprisingly improved display when 33-1 and snatching eight lengths second over 2m4f at Dunthrop. Made favourite but was beaten 25 lengths next time, and it looks almost certain that the effort was a flash in the pan. *B.P. Jones — Berks & Bucks (John Gallagher).* 733 (2m4fOMa), 1021 (2m4fOMa), 1360 (2m4fOMa).

PLATE 107   *891 Ledbury Open Maiden (Div 1): Raise And Gain (R. Burton), 1st, just leads Gorsey Bank (R. Cooper), 3rd, and grey Far From Perfect (A. Wintle), 2nd, at the last*

                             PHOTO: Tim Holt

RAPID RASCAL ..8-4.. 16 b.g. Rapid Pass — Sue Ming VII (Mins Baby) p7f. Sturdy half-brother to Hensue (*qv*). P-t-P '90/8 (for Mr W.H. Pugh) r80 w6 (inc Open and 2 Ladies) p20 (12 2nds, last once; and 8 3rds, last twice); failed to finish 28 (on floor 10, and ran out 1). NH Mar '00 r1 p0 (7th in 3m2f110y Ch: *a bhnd, t.o*). Competed in nine successive seasons to '98, and was a real front-runner at best, but only ever capable of beating modest opposition. Broke a hind leg at Howick. *Miss L. Horner — Tredegar F. (Beverley Moore-Williams).* 743 (L), 819 (Cf).

RAP UP FAST (USA) ..9-8.. 12 b.g. Eskimo (USA) — Naomi's Flash (USA) (Ray Jeter USA) 3p. Leggy light-framed. Dam won 29 races at up to 7f in USA. FLAT r7 p0. NH '92/3 (blinkered 3) r12 p1 (3rd); inc last pair 4, pulled up 3, and fell 2; inc Sells. P-t-P/HUNT CH '94/9 r18 w2 (Maiden and Restricted) p3 (3rds, last once); pulled up 4, and fell 1. A lightly raced minnow by Baimbridge standards, but still improved by more than a stone for his move to Berkeley. Pulls hard, and can lack fluency, and Alison Dare usually keeps her distance. Appeared to suffer a reverse on his latest outing. The real mystery is why Dick has entertained such a modest beast for so long. *R.T. Baimbridge — Berkeley.* 668 (L), 1632 (I).

RARE BETTY ..7-10.. 8 b.m. Oedipus Complex — Duckbill (Nicholas Bill) 2. Sturdy sister to The Wriggler, and half-sister to Meeshak James. Dam is half-sister to Daring Duck (*qv* '00 Annual). Kept Splodge company for 2m4f in a Members match, but got tired in the home straight. *Mrs C.M. Sanderson — Brocklesby.* 228 (M).

RASCALETTO ..9-0.. 14 b.m. Scallywag — Happy Returns (Saucy Kit) p8. Strong owner-bred half-sister to Dancing Returns and Sutton Lighter. Dam, half-sister to Rousing Fortune, won '79 BMW Final Hunt Ch and 8 Ladies. NH FLAT '93 r1 p0. P-t-P '93/5 and '98 (for Mr M.J. Whiteman & Mr E. Turner) r23 w1 (Maiden) p4 (2 3rds, of 4 once); failed to finish 16 (ran out 1, brought down 1, and fell/unseated 8). Used not to lack speed, but could be wayward, and was a desperate jumper. Won an elders Maiden on firm at Bitterley in '95, but absent in '99, and failed to beat a rival in two May outings on her return. From a family of barmpots, and no doubt likely to perpetuate the line further. *E. Turner — Ludlow.* 1459 (R), 1632 (I).

RASCALLY ..9-13.. 11 gr.m. Scallywag — Blue Gift (Hasty Word) 44. Rangy sister to Lillybrook and Scally Blue. Dam, half-sister to 5 Pointers including Mr Mellors, was 3rd in 2 Maidens. NH FLAT r1 p0. NH '95/9 r20 w5 (2m4f-2m6f Hcap Hdles) p3. P-t-P '97 r1 p0 (pulled up). A fair hurdler on her day with a penchant for Hexham (made the frame at five successive fixtures there during '96 including two wins) but lightly raced since being beaten at odds-on there in '97. Finished lame after winning the last of her hurdles in '99, but ran two adequate races in 2000 (eight weeks apart) and may still have a prominent role to play in Points if she could stand up to it. *J. Townson — Pendle Forest & Craven (Sue Smith).* 465 (3m1f110yH), 1335 (2m4f110yH).

RASH-GALE (IRE) ..9-2.. 8 ch.m. Rashar (USA) — Ross Gale (Strong Gale) 17u. Well-made. Dam won NH flat and 2m6f Hdle in Ireland. IRISH P-t-P '98 r5 p0; pulled up 2, and fell. IRISH NH FLAT '98 r3 p0. IRISH NH '98 r1 p0. Appeared to be a non-stayer in Ireland and did nothing to dispel that theory when 30 lengths last and unseating in her two most recent English Points, but previously left the miraculous winner of one of the farcical Maidens which crop up from time to time from Garnons. Was plodding along in a remote third in the soft ground coming to three out, but the two in front literally ground to a halt, leaving her clear at the last to score in a time 18 seconds slower than the other division. *M.J. Jackson — Kyre (Annie Downes).* 451 (CfMa), 669 (R), 1089 (R).

RASTA MAN ..10-1.. 13 b.g. Ore — Bellino (Andrea Mantegna) pp35412323. Workmanlike. Dam won 3m Hdle. NH FLAT r2 p0. NH '93/4 r6 p3 (inc 2 Sells). P-t-P/HUNT CH '95 and '97/9 r28 w10 (inc Open; and inc hat-trick in '98) p11 (6 2nds, of 3 once; and inc 3rd of 4 twice, inc Hunt Ch); fell/unseated 2. Does well in minor races, and maintained his record of having won at least once in each of his Pointing campaigns when recording his 11th success in his Members for which he was well backed. Stays extreme distances, and has made the frame in all four attempts over four miles, and acquired a tongue-strap in 2000, and not as consistent as he used to be. Acts on any going, but relishes mud. *K.C. & J.C. Heard — Eggesford (John Heard).* 160 (O), 316 (Cf), 653 (MO), 852 (Cf), 1044 (4mO), 1173 (M), 1259 (4mL), 1514 (Cf), 1560 (Cf), 1637 (O).

RATHKEAL (IRE) ..8-7§.. 10 gr.g. Roselier (FR) — Fandango Lady (Last Fandango) 5pp6. Smallish workmanlike. NH FLAT '96 r2 p0. NH '96/8 r11 p0 (inc pulled up in 4 of 7 Chses). P-t-P '99 (for Mr J.M. Turner) r8 w1 (Maiden) p3 (3rds, of 4 once); last 2, and pulled up 3. Blinkered for the first time when all out to win a weak Maiden at Marks Tey last year, but tailed off without exception in 2000, and failed to beat a rival. Has never impressed with his attitude, and there seems little chance of him ever doing so. Ran without headgear this year. *J.T. Ibbott — Waveney H.* 761 (R), 940 (R), 1111 (R), 1379 (R).

RAVE-ON-HADLEY (IRE) ..10-0.. 11 b.g. Commanche Run — Fleet Fact (Known Fact USA) 133. Small neat. FLAT r22 w1 (10f, all-weather) p1 (2nd, beaten head in Sell). NH '95 and '98 r11 p3 (Sell). P-t-P '99 r2 w2 (Open and Confined). A bargain buy for present connections, who has done well in Wales winning his first three Points, and not failing to make the frame. Takes a keen grip, and usually makes all when successful, but disappointed when taken on at Bassaleg, and could never get to the front on his final appearance. Has stood little racing over jumps, and absent for nine weeks between his first two starts in 2000, but needs a sound surface, and is clearly not easy to train. Has been taken to post early. *Mrs C.A. Williams & R. Weston — Glamorgan (Evan Williams).* 597 (Cf), 1569 (Cf), 1658 (MO).

REACH FOR GLORY ..9-6.. 12 b.g. Reach — Carlton Glory (Blakeney) 7. Very small neat half-brother to flat winner, Molly Music, and to a winner in Norway. FLAT r39 w3 (11-16f, inc 2 Sells) p11; also won in Jersey in '94. NH '93/8 r35 w3 (2m1f-2m5f Hdles, inc 2 Sells) p10; beaten in match at Les Landes. P-t-P '99 (for Mr G. Richards) r4 p0 (pulled up 2, and pulled up 2. In the form of his life in the Summer of '95 when successful in three of four Hurdles, but has gone downhill since, and without a win in his last 21 attempts. Yet to beat a rival in five Points, but has never intimated that he stays three miles. Sometimes wore headgear in the past. *Miss P. Swindin — Warwicks (Julie Marles).* 613 (L).

REAL PROGRESS (IRE) ..10-1.. 13 ch.g. Ashford (USA) — Dulcet Dido (Dike USA) 0p83. Good-bodied quite attractive half-brother to Irish NH flat winner, No Shouting, to a winner in Hong Kong, and to Irish Pointing winner, Screen Printer. IRISH P-t-P '92 r4 w2 (4-y-o Maiden and 4-y-o Winners of Two) p1 (3rd); and pulled up. NH FLAT '92 r1 p0. NH '92/6 r34 w8 (2m Hdle, and 7 Chses, 2m4f-3m4f) p11 (short-headed once). HUNT CH '98 (for Mr A. Stennett) r4 p2 (3rds) 4th, and pulled up 1. A star Chaser in the '94/5 season, but out of sorts since missing '97, and has shown minimum enthusiasm in the latest yard. Absent in '99, and stands little racing nowadays. Blinkered once in '96, and regained then on his most recent appearance. *D.J. Renney — Heythrop (Mrs D.J. Renney).* 510 (Cf), 968 (Cf), 1583 (C), 1631 (MO).

REAL VALUE (IRE) ..11-6.. 10 b.g. Matching Pair — Silent Verb (Proverb) f1112f2p. Sparely-made. Dam won 56&7yo mares Maiden in Ireland. IRISH P-t-P '97 r2 p0 (pulled up 2). P-t-P '98/9 r10 w8 (up to Confined) p0; and fell 2. Unbeaten in his first 11 completions, and it took Cavalero a herculean effort to lower his colours in the Cheltenham Foxhunters having led the field from the top of the hill until the last hundred yards. Suffered a more comprehensive defeat to the Manners horse at more advantageous terms on a return trip to Prestbury Park the following month, but it was particularly disappointing to see him risked in a nothing event at Folkestone where he looked ill at ease throughout until pulled up with four to jump. Hopefully has come to no lasting harm, and will be back to tackle the showpiece events next year for which he looks the ideal successor. A thoroughly genuine sort, but sometimes too keen for his own good, and both his falls in 2000 came at open ditches. Acts on firmish, but much prefers an easy surface. *A. Cowing & B. Cockerell — E. Sussex & Romney Marsh (Di Grissell).* 17 (O), 94 (O), 286 (O), 385 (3mH), 584 (3m2f110yH), 924 (3m1fH), 1103 (3m2f110yH), 1344 (3m2fH).

REBEL KING ..9-8.. 11 b.g. Doc Marten — Cape Farewell (Record Run) p33p. Good-bodied half-brother to Hurdles winner, Caulker, and to flat winner, Cledeschamps. Dam won 2m Hdle. NH '93/9 (for M. Barnes) r65 w3 (2m2f Hdle, and 2 Chses, 2m1f-2m5f) p24; inc Sells; refused once. Won three races on good or firmish ground to June '97, but has been doggy since, and was unplaced on his last 13 attempts under Rules. Looked no more enthusiastic in Points, and was beaten between 16 lengths and 32 lengths when plodding into thirds of four at Whittington. *Miss A. Wilson — V. of Lune H.* 493 (Cf), 814 (O), 1148 (M), 1365 (O).

PLATE 108   5 Thames Valley Club Club Members 7yo&up (Vet & Nov Rdrs): L to R Cawarra Boy (M. Walters), 7th, Royal Arctic (J. Oldring), 2nd, and Rectory Garden (R. Biddlecombe), 1st, head the field   PHOTO: Bill Selwyn

RECTORY GARDEN (IRE) ..10-10.. 12 b.g. The Parson — Peace Run (Deep Run) 11123211. Rangy half-brother to Brave Edwin (IRE), and to Hurdles winner, Highland Way (IRE). NH FLAT Dec '93 r1 p0. NH '94/9 (for H. Daly, wins previously for late T. Forster; blinkered 1) r29 w8 (2m Hdle, and 7 Chses,

2m5f-3m2f) p15. Introduced Robert Biddlecombe to the sport in 2000, and is the best Pointer he will ever ride. Utterly genuine and consistent (what an insult when he was blinkered once under Rules!), and after unseating at the final flight on his jumping debut he has never failed to get round in 36 subsequent outings. Needs good ground or mud, and although he was an erratic jumper when younger he is now brilliant in that department, and seems to meet virtually every fence on the perfect stride. Generally contested the fastest race of the day, and arguably unlucky not to have gone through the season unbeaten — his partner's lack of experience caused him to misjudge the pace in the Coronation Cup and at Hackwood, and he was also lucky that his mount took him to the front at the right time at Kimble. Must have brought connections great joy, although nothing could have topped Edredon Bleu in the Queen Mother Champion Chase. *T.W. Biddlecombe — O. Berks.* 5 (Cv&nr), 32 (MO), 217 (O), 262 (MO), 454 (4mMO), 884 (O), 1144 (O), 1205 (MO).

RED CHANNEL (IRE) ..9-3.. 11 b.g. Import — Winscarlet North (Garland Knight) pp4p5. Smallish unfurnished half-brother to Irish Chasing winner, Lotto Lolly, and to a jumping winner in Belgium. FLAT r2 p0. NH '95/6 r8 p0 (inc pulled up 3 in Hdles; 4th, and 6th in Chses, not jump well once, and inc Sell). P-t-P/HUNT CH '97/9 (for Mr A. Hickman & Mr N. Smith) r11 w3 (2m4f Maiden, Restricted and Intermediate) p3 (2 3rds, last once); 4th, pulled up 2, and fell/unseated 2. A very hard puller who carries his head between his knees, and has made most to win three bad races on sound surfaces '97/8, but suffered an interrupted season in '99, and rarely got involved when beating just one rival in 2000. Stays an easy three miles, but lacks fluency, and would appreciate stronger handling than he received from an inexperienced girl this year. *L. & Miss P. Bryan-Brown — E. Sussex & Romney Marsh (Sara Hickman).* 28 (L), 128 (L), 677 (L), 985 (M), 1209 (Cnr).

RED FOX (U) ..—.. 11 ch.g. Young Golden — unknown 2. Faded rapidly in the final mile of his Members, and finished one and a half fences last of two. *Mrs J. Lancaster — Dumfries.* 979 (M).

RED FRIDAY ..—.. 8 ch.g. Le Moss — Elegant Nell (Free State) p. Half-brother to Dancing Ranger (qv). Sold malvern, Oct '98 for 750. Pulled up after two miles when backward and struggling in January, and not seen again. *Mrs K. Pickering — Brocklesby.* 15 (C).

RED LEO (USA) ..—.. 8 b.g. Crafty Prospector (USA) — Lucky Brook (USA) (What Luck USA) ppp. Lengthy hobdayed half-brother to 3 flat winners (2 in USA), including Spot Prize. Dam won 4 flat at up to 7f in USA. FLAT r1 p0. P-t-P '99 (for Mr, Mrs Knight & Mr G. Martin) r1 p0 (pulled up). Takes a hard hold, and has shown speed to halfway, but does not stay, and has been pulled up in all four appearances. Ended the season lame, and has already had problems with his wind. *Mr & Mrs Knight, G. Martin & M. King — Cotswold (G. Martin).* 247 (R), 472 (OMa), 1413 (OMa).

REDMIRE ..9-0.. 7 b.m. Nomadic Way (USA) — Decent Sort (Decent Fellow) 468p4f. Small plain unfurnished. Dam, half-sister to 3 Pointers including, Gillan Cove (IRE) (qv), who failed to complete the course in 11 races over fences between them, won Maiden and 3rd twice, but pulled up in all 4 attempts after her win. P-t-P '99 r4 p1 (last of 3); 4th, 5th, and fell 1. Usually manages to complete despite the odd error, but only once within 20 lengths of the winner at the finish, and does not appear to stay three miles. Needs to make real improvement from six to seven to get into the shake up in 2001. *A. Pennock — Staintondale.* 169 (OMa), 282 (OMa), 627 (OMa), 1001 (2m4fOMa), 1233 (OMa), 1352 (OMa).

RED NECK ..10-5.. 10 ch.g. Nishapour (FR) — Roda Haxan (Huntercombe) 1p41. Angular half-brother to a flat winner. FLAT r7 p0 (inc Sell). P-t-P '97 r2 p0 (pulled up 2). NH '97 (for P. Bowen) r7 w1 (2m4f Hdle) p2. Wore a tongue-strap for the first time over jumps when winning a 2m4f Maiden Hurdle at Worcester in July '97, but had been off the course since later that year until returning to Points in 2000. Won two minor events convincingly, but less effective in Hunter Chases, and formed part of a good year for Tim Vaughan. Used to prefer a sound surface, but avoids anything quicker than good nowadays, and coped well with soft ground at Bonvilston. Races with plenty of enthusiasm, and can surely win more Points if not too highly tried. Wears a cross-noseband in addition to being tongue-tied. *Mrs C.E. Goldsworthy — Tredegar F. (John Moore).* 479 (Cf), 1022 (3mH), 1341 (2m110yH), 1612 (Cf).

RED OASSIS ..10-6.. 10 ch.g. Rymer — Heron's Mirage (Grey Mirage) 11. Small owner-bred brother to Silver Sumal and Lord Rymax and half-brother to Quick Vision, Heron's Jake, Heron's Sam and Vision Of Light. NH FLAT '97 r2 p0 (last once). NH '97 r2 p0 (remote 8th of 9 and fell at first in Hdles). P-t-P '98/9 r5 p1 (3rd); pulled up 1, and fell/unseated 3. Much improved by the move to Andrew Dalton, and twice won readily under his guidance. Beat nothing of note, and the winning times were not special, but showed the ability to handle differing ground, and now that his confidence is sky-high might be capable of upgrading successfully. Four outings in a year in his record. *Mrs J.Z. Munday — Ludlow (Andrew Dalton).* 704 (OMa), 992 (R).

REDORAN ..8-3.. 10 b.m. Gildoran — Red Spirit (Starch Reduced) p4. Tall lengthy half-sister to Slip Haven. Dam won 6 Points (was disqualified once) and placed 7. P-t-P '96/7 and '99 (for Mr T.G. Morgan) r11 p3 (2 2nds, last once; and last of 3); pulled up 5, and fell/unseated 3. Placed in all three of her starts in '97, but has shown little since missing the following season, and although only beaten around eight lengths on her latest appearance the presence of Le Vienna in the placings shows how bad the form is. Stands her racing badly, and her 2000 season was over in the space of a week. *D.J. & Mrs R.R. Richards — S. Pembs.* 838 (OMa), 949 (OMa).

RED PARADE (NZ) ..10-2.. 13 b.g. Church Parade — Infra Ray (NZ) (Attalas) 4543. Small compact. NH FLAT '93/4 (for D.H. Barons) r4 w1 p1 (3rd). NH '95/7 and '99 (for n. Hawke, blinkered final; one win previously for Mrs J. Renfree-Barons) r12 w1 (2m4f Hdle) p5 (inc 3 3rds in Chses); last, pulled up 4 inc Sell Ch, and unseated 1 on final 6 attempts. A dual winner in soft/heavy to January '95, and there were 21 and 24 runners in those contests. Absent for 25 months after February '97, and went to pieces completely under Rules latterly, but showed signs of a mini-revival in 2000. Not disgraced when completing the course behind such luminaries as Gillan Cove, Lochnagrain, Butler John and Black Dante, and there is a chance that he could yet surprise if returned at 13 to seek out much easier options. *M. Thomas & W. Tilley — G. Keirle & S. Jarrett — M. Thomas & B. White — Taunton V. (Alison Handel).* 210 (MO), 468 (3m1f110yH), 954 (MO), 1138 (MO).

RED REBEL ..10-5.. 9 gr.g. Scallywag — Little Red Flower (Blakeney) 1surp21. Compact. P-t-P/HUNT CH '97/9 r14 w4 (inc 3m2f Hunt Ch) p3 (2 2nds); ran out 1, pulled up 1, and fell 3. The impressive winner of four races including a weak Hunter Chase '97/8, but appeared to suffer a reverse following a promising reappearance last year, and has shown little resolution since. Made most to win two three-finisher affairs in 2000, but much less convincing in competitive races, and steadfastly refused to go by Just Like Madge at Garthorpe. Stays exceptionally well, and has shown form on firmish and in soft ground, but his tendency to jump right-handed has become more pronounced (ask Dave Mansell about it) and presumably has a fault. Likely to remain something of an enigma. *Mrs M.E. Moody — Pytchley (Caroline Bailey).* 49 (Cf), 117 (O), 227 (2m5f110yH), 466 (3m1fH), 1415 (Cf), 1584 (CCond), 1663 (C).

RED SPARK ..9-4.. 9 ch.g. Electric — Sarah Carter (Reesh) fpr. Dam won at 5f. P-t-P '99 r1 p0 (last). Seems to have trouble getting the trip, and was tiring in a poor second when declining the last on his final appearance at Maisemore. Needs to develop some more stamina, but as there is little in his pedigree that might be a tall order. Wears a cross-noseband. *Mrs A.D. Hope — N. Cotswold (Mrs S. Walker).* 194 (CfMa), 618 (CMa), 892 (OMa).

RED SPECTACLE (IRE) ..10-6.. 9 b.g. Red Sunset — Buz Kashi (Bold Lad IRE) 13115. Small neat half-brother to flat winners, Golden Memories, Kash Juwain and Jehol. Dam won 2 flat, 6-8f (also won 8f Coronation Stakes at Royal Ascot, but disqualified — robbed by the Stewards). FLAT (allform 1) r30 w3 (9-14f, one on all-weather) p8. NH '95/6 r3 w1 (2m6f Hdle) p0. P-t-P/HUNT CH '98/9 r12 p5 (2 2nds); pulled up 1, and fell/unseated 2. Made all in three of his four wins under Rules, but had failed to show much sparkle in his first two seasons Pointing. Redressed the balance in 2000 with three Open race successes under Nigel Tutty, but none of them took much winning, and was eclipsed against better animals on his final start. Missed 12 weeks of the season, and in the circumstances did remarkably well. Blinkered once in '99. *J.D. Jemmeson — W. of Yore.* 136 (O), 1327 (O), 1349 (O), 1476 (O), 1628 (2m4f110yH).

RED SPICE ..9-0.. 9 ch.g. Green Adventure (USA) — Gadabout (Galivanter) bbu4u23p. Lengthy well-made owner-bred half-brother to Suny Sorell, Blown Flutter, Black Rock and Miss Blue. Dam is half-sister to Spartan Flutter (dam of Spartan Ranger, *qv* '95 Annual). P-t-P '98 r4 p2 (3rd of 4 once); last, and pulled up 1. Hung right on the run-in when second on his final appearance in '98, and presumably went wrong as he missed the following year. Very much out of luck in early 2000, but ran well in a long Maiden at Whittington only to let supporters down when joint-favourite for a weak race next time. Seems to favour going right-handed, and often jumps in that direction. *R.A. Owen — Flint & Denbigh.* 173 (R), 296 (I), 569 (OMa), 616 (CMa), 964 (OMa), 1153 (OMa), 1465 (OMa), 1559 (3m110yH).

REESHLOCH ..9-11.. 12 b.g. Reesh — Abalone (Abwah) 5. Strong-topped half-brother to 4 flat winners, including Lonely Street. NH '94/9 (for A. Turnell) r24 w1 (2m Hdle) p3 (inc 2 2nds in Chses). Bought Doncaster, May for 500. Made virtually all to score in heavy in January '95, but has not even been placed since November '96, and was absent for 19 months after March '97. Occasionally blinkered under Rules, and was pulled up in his final two attempts. Had jumping problems on occasions, and fell or unseated four times in Chases. Ran well for 2m4f in his only Point, but seems to come with a lot of physical and emotional baggage these days. *B.J. Llewellyn — Gelligaer F.* 479 (Cf).

REFLECTIVE WAY ..7-12.. 8 ch.m. Mirror Boy — Craigie Way (Palm Track) 7pp. Lengthy owner-bred sister to Craigdale (*qv*). A fence behind from four out when last on her only completion, and was tongue-tied and looked as if she had something wrong with her on her latest appearance. *R. Robinson — Dumfries.* 499 (2m4fOMa), 778 (OMa), 1084 (2m4fOMa).

REGAL AURA (IRE) ..—.. 11 ch.g. Glow (USA) — Dignified Air (FR) (Wolver Hollow) p. Small well-made half-brother to Ullswater, to Irish flat winner, Proud Titania (IRE), and to Italian flat winners, Partenopeo (IRE) and Speziee (IRE). Dam won at 6f. Approx 11,000y (in France). FLAT (allform for G. Harwood at 2; worn headgear) r19 w1 (7f) p3. NH '93/9 (bought for 5100; previously 3 wins for G.M. Moore, bought for 7600) r29 w7 (3 Hdles, 2m-2m2f, and 4 Chses, 2m5f) p6 (beaten head once). A successful Hurdler who went on to prove himself to be a game front-runner at best over fences at Plumpton, where he gained all his four victories, but seems to have major problems with broken blood vessels these days, and has perhaps been retired. *D.C. O'Brien — Ashford V.* 830 (Cnr).

REGAL BAY ..9-12.. 11 b.g. Scorpio (FR) — Pendle Princess (Broxted) pp. Sturdy brother to Pendil's Pleasure, Regal Shadow and Zodiac Prince. Dam, half-sister to Pendil's Joy, won a Maiden (also last, pulled up 2, and fell/unseated 3 — was tubed latterly). P.t-P '96/9 r18 w4 (up to Intermediate) p4 (2 2nds; and inc last of 3 once); pulled up 5. Did well to win four modest races '97/8, but gave the impression all was not right last year, and pulled up lame on his reappearance. Resurfaced four weeks later, but lost touch quickly after two miles and was pulled up soon after. Acts on firmish, but clearly troubled. *D.A. Wales — W. Norfolk.* 936 (Cf), 1378 (Cf).

REGAL BRIDE ..—.. 7 b.m. Alhaatmi — Regal Ranee (Indian Ruler) f. Workmanlike lengthy owner-bred half-sister to Regal Role (*qv*). Fat and clueless at Thorpe in February, and was soon well tailed off before taking a crashing fall at the sixth. *R.D. Chandler — Belvoir.* 115 (CCf).

REGAL ROLE ..—.. 8 b.m. Rolfe (USA) — Regal Ranee (Indian Ruler) pup. Lengthy workmanlike owner-bred half-sister to Singh Song and Regal Bride. Dam won Maiden and placed 4. P-t-P '99 r5 p0 (pulled up 4, and unseated 1). Very error-prone when failing to get round in her first season (only reached halfway twice) and failed to reappear after apparently going lame at Thorpe Loge this February. Singh Song was a notable non-stayer, and her performances to date also suggest a lack of stamina. *R. Chandler — Belvoir.* 22 (24mfOMa), 52 (OMa), 122 (OMa).

REGAL WOLF ..9-0.. 8 ch.g. Little Wolf — Sovereign Maiden (Nearly A Hand) p4puR315p. Lengthy unfurnished. Dam was second in a Maiden, but grandam, Sovereign Piece, failed to finish in 2 Points. P-t-P '98/9 (for Mrs S. Condry & Mrs P. Dod) r12 p4 (2 2nds, of 3 once); pulled up 3, refused 1, and fell 1. A satisfactory jumper, but inclined to be moody, and took 19 attempts to lose his maiden tag. Did so when equipped with blinkers on the first occasion Godfrey Maundrell had partnered him, but the opposition was truly feeble, and his uninspiring efforts in Restricteds do not bode well for the future. *Mrs S. Condry — Blackmore & Sparkford V. (John Dufosee).* 11 (OMa), 106 (OMa), 212 (CfMa), 763 (CfMa), 889 (OMa), 1101 (OMa), 1245 (OMa), 1389 (R), 1551 (R).

REGAR (IRE) ..9-0.. 9 b.g. Buckskin (FR) — Pass Thurn (Trimmingham) p4. Dam, half-sister to Davalbury (*qv* '2000 Annual), won 2 IRISH NH flat. IRISH NH FLAT P-t-P '97 r1 p0 (pulled up). IRISH NH FLAT '98 r1 p0. IRISH NH '97/8 r4 p0. NH '99 (for I. Ferguson in Ireland; blinkered final) r2 p0 (both at Musselburgh). Scraped a lowly rating when 15 lengths fourth at Alnwick, where he was in contention until hitting two out and weakening quickly and walking up the run-in, but looks a typical Buckskin in that he does not stand many outings. *B. McNichol — Cumberland F.* 663 (R), 914 (CfMa).

REGENCY COTTAGE ..9-10.. 11 b.g. Relkino — Sunny Cottage (Sunyboy) p. Lengthy attractive half-brother to Hoofer Syd, and to a French jumping winner. P-t-P '97 and '99 r8 w2 (Maiden and Restricted) p3 (2 2nds, last once); 4th, and pulled up 2. An ex-eventer who has been rather fortunate to win two minor Points considering his lack of stamina, and his fragility. Missed '98, was pulled up and dismounted on his final appearance last year, and stood just one outing in 2000. His jumping seems to be the only thing that is sound about him. *D.A. Wales — W. Norfolk.* 413 (I).

REG'S ROCKET ..8-5.. 9 b.g. Rustingo — Lunar Monarch (Lone Star) u55. Plain chunky owner-bred half-brother to Blucanoo. Dam won Maiden and 3rd 4. P-t-P '98/9 r7 p2 (remote last of 3 once); pulled up 4. Does possess some ability, and gave prominent displays in his last two appearances, but does not stand many outings, and has struggled to get the trip. Will need a hard race to score. *P. Havard — N. Herefords.* 332 (M), 617 (CMa), 865 (CfMa).

REIGN DANCE ..10-0.. 10 ch.g. Kinglet — Gay Criselle (Decoy Boy) f. Tall rangy attractive half-brother to Hurdles winner, Versatility. Dam won 2m4f Hdle. P-t-P/HUNT CH '96/9 r12 w2 (inc 2m4f110y Hunt Ch) p2 (3rds, inc Hunt Ch); pulled up 6. Trotted up in two three-finisher 2m4f events in '98, but has never been easy to train, and averages less than three outings a season. Remains unproven over the full trip in Points as he failed to reappear following a fall on the opening day of the season, and its back to the drawing board as far as connections are concerned. *Mrs D.H. McCarthy & Mrs S. Horsman — O. Surrey & Burstow (Christine McCarthy).* 4 (O).

REITERATE ..9-10.. 8 b.m. Then Again — Indubitable (Sharpo) 1. Smallish sturdy half-sister to flat winner, Cugina. Dam won at 10f. FLAT r6 p0. NH '97/8 r3 p0. P-t-P '99 r4 p1 (2nd); last, and pulled up 2. Useless under Rules, and gave her first creditable display when second in her final Point in '99, and bounded round Black Forest Lodge for an easy victory in February. Unfortunately broke down in the process, but Helen Bridges did well to extract a win from a mare who only cost 500 guineas. *Mrs H.M. Bridges — Wilton.* 205 (OMa).

RELOCATE (IRE) ..9-1.. 8 b.g. Supreme Leader — Kakala (Bargello) 3p. Half-brother to Alpine Castle (IRE) (*qv*). IRISH P-t-P '99 r4 p0 (6th, and pulled up 3). Showed some ability for the first time and had a subsequent winner behind him when just over 12 lengths third in a 2m4f Maiden at Charing, but possibly did not get the trip next time. If Tim Underwood hangs on to him it may transpire that he was keeping something up his sleeve. *T.D.B. Underwood & A. Parrish — Garth & S. Berks (Tim Underwood).* 1105 (2m4fOMa), 1513 (OMa).

REMEMBER EQUINAME ..—.. 6 gr.m. Belfort (FR) — Easby Mosella (Le Moss) pu. Small. Dam, half-sister to Real Gent (*qv* '98 Annual). pulled up 3 and fell in Maidens. 700 2yo. NH FLAT '99 (for

D. Eddy, blinkered final) r3 p0 (tailed off 2, and refused to race). Bought Doncaster, May for 2100. There has been some good Equinames to line Don Eddy's pockets in the past, but this one looks to be a best forgotten Equiname. *J. Burley & G. Jones — High Peak H. (Jason Burley).* 1527 (OMa), 1589 (2m4fOMa).

REMEMBER RIDEMORE (IRE) ..9-8.. 8 ch.g. Classic Memory — Stoney Broke (Pauper) 31p2. Tall rangy angular half-brother to Irish Pointing and English Chasing winner, Stoney Burke (IRE). Dam won an Irish 4 & 5-y-o's Maiden. P-t-P '98 r2 p1 (2nd of 3); and pulled up 1. Missed the '99 season following a bout of lameness, but looked in good shape throughout 2000, and easily won a three-finisher Maiden at Bishops Court. Beaten by a potentially useful sort on his final appearance, and should be able to emulate him in a Restricted in 2001. A big and rather one-paced individual, and may not be able to stand many outings. *A. & Mrs J. Barron — Cattistock (Richard Barber).* 213 (CfMa), 408 (OMa), 524 (R), 1135 (R).

REMILAN (IRE) ..9-12.. 10 b.g. Remainder Man — Alice Milan (Milan) 3p2d823454. Big strong good-looking. P-t-P/HUNT CH '96/9 r22 w7 (inc 2 Opens) p8 (5 2nds; and inc last of 3; and inc 4 Hunt Chses); pulled up 3, and fell 1. An excellent jumper, and generally on good terms with himself when successful seven times '98/9, but has lost interest completely and often refuses to race properly now. Often gets on his toes, and sweats up in the preliminaries, but that's as far as his enthusiasm goes, and despite Andrew Sansomes continued ministrations is best left well alone. Usually blinkered. *J.M. Turner — Suffolk.* 82 (M), 320 (O), 553 (MO), 607 (O), 708 (O), 938 (3m4fO), 1484 (O), 1539 (3m7fH), 1621 (O).

RENARDINE BOY (IRE) ..—.. 8 ch.g. Carlingford Castle — Lady Hiltop (Prince Hansel) pp. Good-topped half-brother to several winners, (including in ireland), including Springholm (jumping) and Do Rightly (IRE) (Chasing). NH FLAT '98 r2 p0. NH '98/9 (final for M. Pitman; previously for Mrs J. Pitman, blinkered once) r7 p2. Sold Ascot, Nov for 575. Gave two fair displays over 3m-3m2f in Hurdles, including a 12 length second in July '99 on his final attempt. Earned £675 that evening but was virtually given away for less subsequently, and Pointing displays suggest there are problems. Would be a Maiden certainty if he could be revived. *B. Hurst — S. Cornwall.* 928 (MO), 1263 (OMa).

REPEAT OFFER ..—§.. 9 b.g. Then Again — Bloffa (Derrylin) pp. Workmanlike. Dam won at 6f. NH FLAT '96/8 r4 w1 p2. NH '98/9 (for Mrs L. Jewell, bought for 2600; previously for P. Cundell, who won with the dam) r8 p4 (inc 3rd in Sell). Sold Doncaster, Nov for 1500. Quite a competitive sort until he was asked to jump obstacles, but it has been down hill all the way since then. Jumped slowly and was most reluctant until pulled up after a mile when tailed off in his second Point, and it will be surprising if he was ever trained again. *D.F. Smith — Hurworth.* 171 (O), 376 (MO).

RESKUE LINE ..—.. 11 ro.g. Respect — Kiku (Faberge II) p. Good-bodied half-brother to Royal Top and Turbo Chief. P-t-P '96/8 (for Mr A. Shaw) r6 p1 (3rd); pulled up 4, fell 1. Incredibly busy by his standards with four appearances in '98, but needed the following year off to recover, and returned only to underline how moderate he is. Twenty lengths third in his Members is likely to be his best lifetime performance. *Miss R.J. Ellis — Bedale (Carol Dennis).* 400 (Oma).

RESOURCE (IRE) ..—.. 8 ch.g. Simply Great (FR) — Melarka (Dara Monarch) pp. Tall strong half-brother to Irish NH flat winner, Kingfisher Flyer (IRE). Dam won at 8f in Ireland. NH FLAT Nov '98 r1 p0. NH '99 (for J. Old) r2 p0 (tailed off in Hdles). Bought Ascot, June for 2000. Rarely seen, and misbehaved at the start and lost 30 lengths when dwelling on his final outing. This Resource already looks exhausted. *Mrs E. Coleman — Lamerton (Pauline and Tony Gearing).* 105 (OMa), 724 (CfMa).

RESTLESS NATIVE (IRE) ..9-5.. 7 b.m. Be My Native (USA) — Tartan Thistle (Ovac ITY) 632. Half-sister to Autumn Flame (IRE). IRISH P-t-P '99 r2 p0 (last and pulled up). Sold Doncaster, Aug for 3400. Beaten at least 17 lengths in Maidens and only had one horse behind her when placed, but it may be possible to find a little pace for her eventually. *R.J. Francome — Beaufort (Sylvia Francome).* 520 (OMa), 881 (OMa), 1102 (OMa).

REUTER ..8-0§.. 13 b.g. Scorpio (FR) — Pendella (Pendragon) ppp3p. Tall lengthy fired brother to Pendil's Delight and Chasing winner, Stephen's Brae, and half-brother to Pendlewood, Pendleton, Pendle Princess (dam of Regal Bay (qv), Pendil's Niece (dam of Pendil's Dream (qv), Pendil's Pride, Pendil's Joy and Pendil's Nephew. Dam is sister to '70s jumping superstar, Pendil. IRISH NH FLAT '93 r1 p0. IRISH NH '96 r5 w1 (2m4f Ch) p0. NH '98 r2 p0 (4th, and pulled up 1 in HCap Chses, 2m5f-3m1f). P-t-P/HUNT CH '98/9 r5 p1 (2nd of 3); pulled up 3, and fell 1. Gained his only success at Sligo in '96, but has been a nightmare to train, and enjoyed his busiest campaign since this year. Clearly in no mood to put his battered legs through more pain, and has become very unwilling. Tried in headgear in 2000, but only managed a poor third in his Members, and not worth keeping in training. *R.A. Barr — Easton H. (Matthew Gingell).* 26 (O), 94 (O), 241 (C), 603 (M), 771 (O).

REVE DE VALSE (USA) ..8-7.. 14 ch.g. Conquistador Cielo (USA) — Dancing Vaguely (USA) (Vaguely Noble) p5p6u4. Rangy half-brother to Daphnis (USA), and to 2 flat winners. Dam won 2 12f races in France. Grandam, Dancing Maid, won 3 top races in France including Prix d'Essai des Pouliches and Prix Vermeille, and was short-headed by Fair Salinia in the '78 Oaks. FRENCH FLAT '89/90 r7 p2 (2nds). FRENCH NH '90 r3 p1 (2nd in Hdle). FLAT r2 p0. NH '90/9 (tried visored in '91; 3 wins for R. Johnson; previously for Denys Smith, bought for 8200) r66 w10 (7 Hdles, 2m-2m2f, inc Sell, and 3 Chses, 2m-2m2f, inc Sell) p17. Useful when completing a five-timer '90/1, but successes have been thin on the ground since, and last scored in September '97. Has accumulated a losing sequence of 22 subsequently, and was useless and generally fences behind in Points. Blinkered once, and regularly wears a tongue-strap. Not enjoying himself, and hopefully pensioned off. *Miss V. Burn & Mrs D. Hopkins — Tynedale.* 361 (L), 418 (M), 717 (Cf), 912 (Cf), 1079 (L), 1161 (L).

REVING-ALICE ..—.. 6 b.m. Revlow — Miss Burgundy (Gambling Debt) f. Unfurnished. Fell after 2m2f in mid-March. *P.O.J. Hosgood — Silverton.* 562 (CfMa).

REXY BOY ..—.. 14 b.g. Dunbeath (USA) — Coca (Levmoss) pp. Strong-topped lengthy half-brother to Tudor Fun, to Hurdles winner, Farfields Prince, and to 5 flat winners (2 abroad, and one in Ireland), including Greenwich Papillon and Greenwich Bambi. FLAT (tried blinkers/visor) r33 w2 (12-16f) p5. NH '91/5 (visored 2) r20 w2 (2m4f Hdles) p0; Sell final. P-t-P '96 and '98 (for Mr B. & Mr N. King) r8 w1 (Members) p3 (2 2nds); pulled up 1, ran out 1, and brought down 1. NH '98 (from R. Lee's) r2 p1 (3rd in 3m2f110y Nov Ch). Unreliable flat and hurdling, and gained his only Pointing success in a three-finisher Members where he started odds-on. Clearly hard to train in recent years, and jumped poorly when pulled up twice in 2000. Looks finished. *Mrs J. Webster — Warwicks (Ann Cockburn).* 614 (O), 1006 (Cf).

RHYME AND CHIME ..9-13.. 10 b.g. Rymer — Belle Deirdrie (Mandamus) 3p2up. Small. Dam failed to finish in 3 Points. P-t-P '96/9 r12 w1 (Maiden) p1 (2nd); last 3, fell/unseated 4, and pulled up 3. A diabolical jumper, and a hard ride in his first three seasons, but tamed by Tigger Barnes when successful at Bishops Court last year. Remains a chancy jumper, and has yet to look like winning a Restricted, and not seen since pulling up after barely two miles at Ston Easton in March. *E.W.A. Dauncey — Blackmore & Sparkford V. (Rose Vickery).* 6 (R), 163 (R), 406 (R), 477 (R), 734 (R).

RIBINGTON ..9-9.. 12 b.g. Riberetto — By Midnight (By Rights) 2pu3. Big strong half-brother to Midingo, Celtic William, Midnight Sailor and Farriana. Dam, half-sister to Ciders Nephew, was 3rd of 4 from 7 Points (failed to finish 5) for Mr Layton. Grandam, Indifari, was useless Pointer/Hurdler. Great-grandam, also called Farriana, won 7 Points when ridden by Mr Layton. P-t-P/HUNT CH '95 and '97/9 (for Mr W.S. Layton) r21 w1 (Members) p3 (2 2nds, last once); failed to finish 13 (fell 2). Won a farcical Members run in 8min 21s in '97, but generally a weak and regular non-finisher. Ran his best race for some time on his 2000 reappearance, but even the Pipe/Scudamore combination could not turn this base metal into gold. Blinkered thrice in '99. *N. Burd — Radnor & W. Herefords (David Pipe).* 560 (R), 734 (R), 1095 (R), 1671 (R).

RICE POINT ..9-12.. 8 b.g. Gold Dust — My Kizzy (The Ditton) pp643. Rangy well-made owner-bred brother to Kandles-Korner, and half-brother to Tarka Country and Tarka Trail. Dam walked over for Stevenstone Members and was placed in 3 Points for John Squire (distant last of 3 after unseating once — would have won), Grandam, Top Of The Pops II (dam of Pop Song), won 2-finisher Stevenstone Members and placed 7 for him. P-t-P '98/9 r3 w1 (Maiden) p0; pulled up 1, and fell 1. Won an uncompetitive Maiden at Great Trethew in '98, but pulled up on his only outing the following year, and a very weak finisher in 2000 when generally encountering easy surfaces. Jumped the last just in front, but weakened to finish seven lengths fourth at Kilworthy, and fizzled away to nothing in a race taking only just over six minutes on his final appearance. His size suggests he may have a wind problem, but won on a sound surface, and it may be prudent to avoid testing conditions. Wears a cross-noseband. *J. Squire — Stevenstone.* 165 (Cf), 315 (R), 541 (I), 728 (R), 932 (R).

RICHES TO RAGS (IRE) ..9-2§.. 11 ch.g. Castle Keep — Merry Buskins (Little Buskins) 2. Leggy light-framed. Dam, half-sister to Valley So Deep (*qv* '92 Annual), won 2m4f Ch in Ireland. NH FLAT Spr '96 r2 p0. NH '97/8 and Aut '99 (for A. Carroll); previously for J. Spearing; previously for D. Nicholson) r12 p3 (2 2nds, betaen head once, and distant 3rd); inc Sell; jumped erratically before falling only Ch. Presumably not lame for the first time when he hobble home a seven length second on firm at Bonvilston, as he has suffered two long absences in the past. Should have achieved a lot more than he has done, but notoriously ungenuine, and often wore headgear under Rules. *A.J. Thomas — Kyre Bloodhounds.* 1454 (OMa).

RICH TRADITION (IRE) ..—.. 13 b.g. Torus — Dawn Of Spring VII (unknown) p. Tall half-brother to Abbey Venture, and to Irish Pointing winner, The Vendor. Dam won 4 Irish Points, including South County Dublin Members thrice. IRISH NH FLAT '93 r3 w2 (2m1f-2m2f) p0. IRISH NH '92/5 and '97/8 r31 w3 (2 Hdles, 2m4f-3m, and 2m6f Ch) p6. IRISH P-t-P '98 r4 p1 (2nd); pulled up 2. P-t-P '99 (for Mr C.W. Mellard) r2 p0 (last, and pulled up 1). A very successful mudlark in Ireland, and won five races there '93/5, but unable to score since, and tailed off in all three English Points including when 100-1 in the latest. *A. Witcomb — Quorn.* 367 (Cf).

RICKSHAW ..—.. 8 gr.g. My Richard — Jolly Girl (Jolly Me) pp. Half-brother to Colourful Boy and Bungle. Dam is sister to Spambruco. Grandam, Colourful Girl, failed to finish in 3 Points. A safe conveyance, but goes so slowly that the rider would probably do better to get off and push. *P.W. Sellars — V.W.H. (Simon Sellars).* 196 (R), 248 (R).

RIEVERS WAY ..—.. 6 br.g. Nomadic Way (USA) — Miss Puck (Tepukei) up. Owner-bred half-brother to Mr Hook (*qv*). Made an unimpressive start, and was unruly in the paddock and difficult to mount before the rider fell off after a mile on his debut. *W. Brown — Sinnington (Ian Brown)*. 809 (OMa), 1233 (OMa).

RIGHT COMPANY ..10-4.. 8 b.g. Infantry — Adroit (Ritudyr) 421s2. Tall workmanlike half-brother to Cut Above Average, Mr Trumpeter and Fencing Master. Dam was a useless Pointer for Jim Cunningham. Grandam, Detroit, was placed in 7 Points/Hunter Chases for him, and bred the Hunter Chase winners, Armoured Car and Bannamoor. P-t-p '99 r4 w1 (Maiden) p0; with twice, and fell 1. Shows a most determined attitude, and his two wins have been dour struggles at Newton Bromswold, but lacks acceleration, and did not seem to be firing on all cylinders at times this year. Broke a blood vessel when favourite on his final outing in '99, and punters have fielded against him since. Sure to win again, but may not be able to raise his rating much higher. Has two handlers, and avoided sound surfaces in 2000. *J.A. Cunningham — Bicester with Whaddon (Caroline Bailey)*. 2 (R), 196 (R), 513 (Cf), 1006 (Cf), 1143 (I).

RIGHT RON RUN ..8-8.. 9 b.g. Primitive Rising (USA) — Sheshells (Zino) 0ppf8. Small wiry. Dam won 2m Hdle on hard, but broke down next time. NH FLAT '97 r1 p0. P-t-P/HUNT CH '98/9 r11 p2; 5th, last pair 3, fell/unseated 2, and pulled up 3. Capable of tanking along for up to 2m4f, but does not stay a yard further, and seems to be in decline already. Acquired a visor on his final two starts, but seemingly more in hope than expectation, and obtained the same dire results. *C.C. Pounder — Bedale (Trevor Pounder)*. 627 (OMa), 693 (OMa), 1330 (OMa), 1352 (OMa), 1480 (OMa).

RIMPTON BOY ..9-3.. 6 gr.g. Interrex (CAN) — Ardelle Grey (Ardross) 13. Neat home-bred. Dam won 7f Sell at 2, and was later successful in Switzerland. Darted clear to make a winning debut over 2m4f at Littlewindsor (5-1; a stablemate at shorter odds finished 15 lengths third), but appeared to get exhausted in more testing ground over a longer trip when backed from 5-2 to evens and finishing 19 lengths third in a Restricted. If he has sufficient stamina he could rate several pounds higher at six. *Mrs E. Hutchinson — Taunton V. (Richard Barber)*. 518 (2m4fOMa), 849 (R).

RIO SANTO (IRE) ..—.. 6 b.g. Alphabatim (USA) — Skimpan (Pitpan) p. Half-brother to jumping winner, Skipcarl (IRE). Dam, half-sister to Mossy Mill (*qv* '91 Annual), won 2 Irish Points. Tailed off and pulled up after two miles at Mollington (looked unfit, and gave a very immature display of jumping). *W.J. Turcan — Fernie (Nick Pomfret)*. 786 (OMa).

RIOT LADY (IRE) ..—.. 10 b.m. Riot Helmet — Golden Eily (Golden Love) up. Small sturdy. IRISH P-t-P '95/6 r6 p3; pulled up 2, and fell 1. P-t-P '97/9 r7 p1 (3rd); pulled up 4. Has made the frame on six occasions, but moderate and has yet to prove she stays three miles. Pulled up in seven of her 15 starts, and lame in the latest. *Miss K.E. Crank — Cheshire Forest*. 959 (M), 1413 (OMa).

RIPARIUS (USA) ..10-8.. 10 b.g. Riverman (USA) — Sweet Simone (FR) (Green Dancer USA) 121331. Sturdy brother to a useful French/USA flat winner, and half-brother to 4 flat winners (2 abroad), including Cinnamon Rose (in Ireland) and The Sandfly. 55,000y. FLAT (for H. Candy) r24 w3 (12f) p6 (3rds). NH '97/9 (for P. Webber) r20 w4 (2 Hdles, 2m-2m1f, and 2 2m5f Chses) p8; pulled up 2 of final 3 attempts. Bought Doncaster, Aug for 9200. Possesses plenty of ability, but seemed to become jaded both flat and National Hunt and tried in blinkers on the odd occasion. Looked perfectly amenable in Ladies Opens and enjoyed a good season, but it would have been a lot better but for the mighty presence of Balisteros, who was too good for him in their first three encounters. Finally able to exact a rather surprising revenge at Hexham, where the soft ground and long trip were right up his alley. Connections of 'Seve' were quick to press their claim that he was unfit because he had not raced for two weeks! Very consistent, and should again be hard to beat when he can avoid the marauding scot. *Mrs S. Atkinson (The Star Group) — Morpeth (Pauline Robson)*. 109 (L), 494 (L), 661 (L), 1079 (L), 1426 (L), 1579 (L).

RIPPING YARN (IRE) ..—.. 8 b.g. Brush Aside (USA) — Ask The Missus (IRE) (Carlingford Castle) p. Stocky half-brother to French Buck in Irish Pointing winner, She Insists. Tailed off and pulled up after two miles at Didmarton. *Ms R.M. Wardall — O. Berks*. 391 (CfMa).

RIP VAN WINKLE ..10-8.. 14 br.g. Le Bavard (FR) — Flying Silver (Master Buck) 11211. Lengthy half-brother to French Buck (IRE). Dam won 3m mares Hdle (promoted from 2nd after being hampered) and 2m1f Ch in Ireland. IRISH NH FLAT '92 r3 p0. IRISH NH '92 r2 p0. IRISH P-t-P '93/4 r9 w1 (Maiden) p1 (2nd); pulled up 3, and fell 2. P-t-P '95/9 r21 w14 (inc 2 Opens and 9 Ladies; inc 5-timer '97, and hat-tricks '96 and '98) p3 (2nds); ran out 1, and fell 2. Almost invincible '96/8, but a beaten favourite on three occasions last year when generally out of sorts. Belied his age, to bounce back in great shape in 2000, and seemed even better than ever as he took his winning tally to 19. Not as quick as he used to be and takes quite a while to warm to his task in competitive races, and could not get to grips with Indefence at Brampton Bryan, but found the 3m5f trip ideal at Dunthrop where Alison Dare was at her vintage best on him. Capable of brilliant jumping, and never abused. Testament to the skill of his connections, and will hopefully grace the scene for a while longer. *Dr P.P. Brown — Berkeley (Dick Baimbridge)*. 192 (L), 699 (L), 860 (L), 1014 (3m5fL), 1462 (L).

RISE TO IT (IRE) ..9-11.. 9 ch.g. Rising — Ballinamona Karen (Tepukei) 51p25. Tall workmanlike. IRISH P-t-P '97/9 r8 w1 (Mdn) p4; pulled up 3. Beat the alleged hotpot The Red Boy at Cottenham, where he jumped better than his rival in the closing stages, but was a bitterly disappointing favourite at 4-7 and evens when thrashed out of sight in five and three-runner Intermediates in holding Eaton Hall. Had scored in heavy in Ireland, so the ground was surely not an excuse. Can be unruly in the preliminaries. There looks to be something troubling him, and best watched until a solution is found. *M.J. Parr — N. Salop (Paul Jones).* 38 (CR), 179 (R), 533 (I), 783 (I), 1335 (2m4f110yH).

RISING DAWN (IRE) ..—.. 9 ch.g. Rising — Bawnard Lady (Ragapan) upfppp. Good-topped. Dam won 2m Hdle in Ireland. NH FLAT '97 (for Mrs A. Swinbank) r1 p0. Bought Doncaster, May for 700. Gave bad displays of running and jumping in his sixth non-completions. Soon went lame on final start. *P.J. Millington — Fernie.* 37 (CI), 121 (OMa), 369 (O), 437 (OMa), 1292 (OMa), 1421 (OMa).

RISING SAP ..10-1.. 11 ch.g. Brotherly (USA) — Miss Kewmill (Billion USA) 2f23p13. Big strong brother to Kingsthorpe (*qv*). P-t-P/HUNT CH '96/7 r6 w1 (Maiden) p1 (2nd); last, and pulled up 3. NH '97 r2 p0; pulled up 1. Won a poor Maiden at Chaddesley in '96, but quickly rushed into Hunter Chases the following season and performed dismally. Presumably went wrong as he had not been seen for three years until resurfacing in 2000, but managed to beat a renowned rogue when tried in blinkers for the first time, and collected four other prizes. One-paced, and has his fair share of temperament, but stays well, and handles a sound surface. Rather highly strung, and tends to boil over in the preliminaries, and has two handlers. *J.D. Downes — Wheatland.* 16 (R), 179 (R), 564 (I), 863 (R), 1200 (CR), 1523 (C), 1632 (I).

RISKY DEE ..9-13.. 12 b.g. Risk Me (FR) — Linn O' Dee (King Of Spain) u. Tall rangy brother to Hintertux. Dam won 3 5f races. NH '95/8 r15 p2 (3rds in Chses); fell 1. P-t-P/HUNT CH '94/6 and '98/9 r18 w3 (inc 2m5f Hunt Ch) p2 (2nds in 2m5f Hunt Chses); pulled up 4, and fell/unseated 4. Speedy when managing an annual success '94/6, but below par since until perking up on his solitary appearance last year. Jumped just one fence without mishap in 2000, and it remains to be seen if his enthusiasm remains intact. Suited by a sound surface. *R. Morley — Middleton.* 996 (M).

RIVER BLOOM ..9-9.. 8 ch.m. Fearless Action (USA) — Welton Rose (Bivouac) 2pp. Owner-bred. P-t-P '99 r3 p0 (pulled up 2, and ran out 1). Carried plenty of condition when second to an exhausted rival in a slow Maiden at Barbury Castle on her reappearance, but pulled up lame when moving up to challenge with four to jump at Mollington subsequently, and has not been seen since. Has shown more than enough ability to win a small race if connections can get her right. *Mrs R. Gasson — Farmers Bloodhounds.* 31 (CMa), 74 (CCf), 432 (OMa).

RIVER CARRON (IRE) ..—.. 9 b.g. Baba Karam — Sooner Or Later (Sheshoon) ufpff. Good-bodied half-brother to Sooner Still and Underwychwood (IRE), and to several winners, including in Ireland. A kamikaze performer who pressed the self-destruct button once too often at Lifton. *A.J. Scrimgeour — Devon & Somerset (Keith Cumings).* 353 (CfMa), 729 (R), 847 (R), 1610 (OMa), 1640 (OMa).

RIVERDALE HENRY (U) ..—.. 9 ch.g. Ballysimon — Riverdale Sal (unknown) 4. Carried 15st 10lbs in his Members and proved just too macho for Bruce (14st 6lb) as they wobbled thrillingly up the run-in. *W.H. Walker — S. Notts.* 1214 (M).

RIVER FERDINAND (IRE) ..9-0.. 9 ch.g. Over The River (FR) — Augustaeliza (IRE) (Callernish) uppu0u. Rangy angular brother to Irish Pointing winner, Ashie's Friend (IRE). IRISH P-t-P '98 r2 p0 (pulled up 2). P-t-P '99 (for Mrs C. Egalton) r3 w1 (Maiden) p1 (2nd); and last. Won much the slowest of four Maidens at Wadebridge on his English debut, and made the frame in his first two Restricteds, but soon given the boot by Caroline Egalton, and has failed to beat a rival since. Makes countless blunders, and performs as though he has something badly wrong with him. Ducked out through the wing on his latest outing, and should be avoided until he shows signs of a revival. *Mrs S.V. Andrew — K.J. Walls — Fitzwilliam (Trevor Marks).* 239 (R), 440 (R), 546 (R), 871 (R), 1558 (3mH), 1622 (L).

RIVER GALA (IRE) ..9-5§.. 11 ch.g. Over The River (FR) — Silver Gala (Gala Performance USA) 3334p. Tall rangy brother to Over And Under (IRE), and Irish Chasing winner, Nervous Kate, and half-brother to Irish NH flat and Hurdles winner, Lancastrians Dream. IRISH P-t-P '95 r6 w1 (4&5yo Mdn) p2; pulled up 1. NH '96/9 (from R. Hodges) r12 p5 (Chses). Proved extremely easy to beat when third in three Restricteds (last twice), and seems to combine a lack of both stamina and generosity. Blinkered on his three most recent attempts. It would be surprising if his stable could be bothered with him again. *Mrs S.J. Maltby — Taunton V. (Richard Barber).* 14 (R), 163 (R), 331 (R), 657 (R), 850 (R).

RIVERLORD ..—.. 7 b.g. River God (USA) — Sultry (Sula Bula) ppb. Half-brother to Annie's Scally. Dam sister or half-sister to 3 Pointers, including Sustaining (*qv* '97 Annual), pulled up in 2 Points. NH FLAT '98 (for G. Ham) r2 p0 (tailed off both). An excitable sort who is taken to post early, and gives every indication of being useless. *G. Little — Berks & Bucks (Nick Lampard).* 30 (CMa), 221 (OMa), 471 (OMa).

RIVER MANDATE ..10-2.. 14 b br.g. Mandalus — Liffey's Choice (Little Buskins) u1u. Tall brother to Mammy's Choice (IRE) and half-brother to Merlyns Choice (*qv*). IRISH NH FLAT '93 r1 p1 (2nd). IRISH NH '92 r2 p0. NH '93/4 and '96/8 (no 5st T. Forster; blinkered/visored 4) r22 w7 (2m4f-3m1f Vhses) p10; pulled up in '97 Grand National. Won five races consecutively to November '96 (was absent for 23 months before the last of them), and gained his most recent success under Rules in January '98 when given a brilliant ride by Paul Carbery. Had wonderful sequence when he made the frame 17 times consecutively, and only one of those was a fourth, but is deliberate jumper and can be lazy. Capable of staying on stoutly, and Tessa Clark did well to galvanise him in a Ladies at Whittington where he snatched a short head verdict on the line, but proved awkward for Flora Barnett, who got tipped off at the third in both attempts. *C. Barnett — Miss F.A. Barnett — Sir W.W. Wynn's.* 525 (M), 813 (L), 1199 (L).

RIVER MOY ..9-0.. 7 b.m. River God (USA) — Moya's Star (Top Star) p76. Small half-sister to Moya's Girl, Moya's Tip Top, Churchill Star and Moya's Son. Dam won 7 Points consecutively and 2nd 4 for Mr Owen. Finished taile off last in both completions. *K.R. Owen — Flint & Denbigh.* 528 (OMa), 777 (OMa), 960 (Cf).

RIVER OF GOLD (IRE) ..9-9.. 7 b.g. Ikdam — Minnies River (IRE) (Over The River FR) 13. IRISH P-t-P '99 r5 p1 (2nd); pulled up, and unseated. Bought Doncaster, Aug for 4500. NH Mar '00 (for B. Mactaggart) r1 p1 (3rd in 3m110y Nov Hdle: *chsd ldrs, ev ch last, no ex*). Won a Maiden at Friars Haugh in decisive fashion, and then showed himself speedy enough to overcome mistakes when a respectable third in a Hurdle. Looks as if he might have a future in Novice Chases eventually. *J.W. Hughes - Buccleuch.* 113 (OMa).

RIVER RISING ..9-2.. 7 br.g. Primitive Rising (USA) — Dragons Daughter (Mandrake Major) pfp. Good-topped owner-bred. Dam is half-sister to Stilltodo (qv '99 Annual). Fell three out when holding a small lead at Hornby Castle, and possibly having a confidence restorer next time. May find compensation in his second campaign. *W.R. Wilson — Zetland (Jim Wilson).* 187 (OMa), 379 (OMa), 1001 (2m4fOMa).

RIVER ROOM ..10-8.. 11 ch.g. Gunner B — Final Melody (Final Straw) p. Strong-topped attractive brother to Chasing winner, Sunuvugun. Dam is an unraced half-sister to Champion Hurdler, Royal Gait (previously champion stayer in France and Spain). NH FLAT '94 r2 p0. NH '95/6 and '98 r13 w3 (2m4f-2m6f Hdles) p1 (2nd). P-t-P '99 r4 w2 (Mixed Opens) p0; and last twice. A game performer at best under Rules, and returned to winning for in '99, after two remarkably quiet pipeopeners. Landed a gamble on both occasions in Bassaleg Opens, but the whole escapade left a sour taste as the Welsh Stewards (typically) took no action. Never going well on his return at Howick, and after pulling up it transpired he had broken down behind. Acts on a sound surface. Blinkered latterly under Rules. *R.J. Rowsell — Ystrad Taf Fechan.* 821 (MO).

PLATE 109   1428 Lauderdale Mens Open: L to R Riverside Run (J. Walton), 1st, leads Dennett Lough (C. Storey), 2nd, Charlieadams (J. Muir), 6th, and Todcrag (T. Scott), 3rd, at the last
PHOTO: Alan Mitchell

RIVERSIDE RUN (IRE) ..10-5.. 8 b.g. Commanche Run — Annamoss (Le Moss) p1f435417. Lengthy. IRISH P-t-P '98 r2 p1 (2nd); and pulled up 1. P-t-P '99 r7 w1 (Maiden) p2; 4th twice, and pulled up 2. A steady performer, and has made the frame in 11 of 13 completions, but lacks acceleration, and is not entirely foot-perfect. Graduated to Open success when teamed with Jimmy Walton for the first time at Mosshouses, but has made too many errors in Hunter Chases to date. Tends to get on his toes, and can pull and has been pulled up with a slipped saddle on three occasions. Has done his winning on a sound surface. *R. Miller-Bakewell — Percy*. 40 (R), 108 (I), 186 (O), 493 (Cf), 622 (O), 918 (2m4fH), 1120 (O), 1428 (O), 1445 (3m1fH).

RIVERSTOWN LAD ..9-7.. 14 b.g. Touching Wood (USA) — Malija (FR) (Malicious) 3. Compact well-made half-brother to 4 flat winners (3 in Italy). Dam won middle distance races in France and Ireland. IRISH FLAT r11 p1 (3rd). IRISH NH '90/4, '96 and '98/9 (blinkered once in '99) r53 w1 (2m6f Hdle) p10 (inc 3 Chses). IRISH P-t-P '98/9 r7 p3; pulled up 1. Outpaced throughout when finishing 50 lengths third at Higham (inherited that position at the penultimate). The veteran of 72 outings, but his sole victory was gained in heavy way back in '92. *Mrs J. Hughes — Cranwell Bloodhounds*. 758 (L).

RIVER SURPRISE (IRE) ..9-1.. 8 b.g. Over The River (FR) — Reelin Surprise (Royal Match) pp4p. Sturdy brother to Irish Pointing winner, Reelin River. Dam won 2m2f Hdle in Ireland. IRISH P-t-P '98 r2 p1 (22l 3rd); and pulled up. Bought Doncaster, May for 1200. Showed a trace of ability despite mistakes when five lengths fourth in a Maiden, but never going well next time, and does not give the impression of being particularly sound. *Miss K. Thory — Fitzwilliam*. 23 (OMa), 1116 (OMa), 1290 (OMa), 1423 (OMa).

RIVER SWILLEY (IRE) ..10-4§.. 8 ch.g. Over The River (FR) — Orient Moonbeam (Deep Run) 1r215r. Tall heavy-topped. P-t-P '99 r3 w1 (Maiden) p1 (2nd); and 4th. Game and genuine on his day, but a funny customer, and often tends to jump in a slovenly manner and has twice refused (once when exhausted). Quickened readily under a good ride from Robert Walford to defeat The Earth Moved in his Restricted, but much less convincing otherwise, and may have an intermittent fault. Has the scope to do well if he goes the right way and his problems can be sorted, and could not be in much better hands. *H. Wellstead — Portman (Louise Alner)*. 13 (R), 162 (I), 263 (I), 652 (MO), 954 (MO), 1133 (O).

ROBBIE BEE ..10-0.. 11 b.g. Robellino (USA) — Calgary (Run The Gantlet USA) r. Small neat half-brother to Calicon, and to 2 flat winners (one in Italy). FLAT r3 p0. NH '94 r1 p0 (tailed off). P-t-P/HUNT CH '98/9 r9 w1 (Restricted) p3 (2 2nds, inc Hunt Ch); last pair 2, and unseated 1. Returned at 50-1 when opening his Pointing account on his debut in '98, but lightly raced and just unable to cope with the stiffer tasks since. Looked sure to add to his gains eventually, but sadly broke down on his 2000 reappearance. *Mrs A.L. Tory — Portman*. 162 (I).

ROBERO ..9-10.. 10 b.g. Robellino (USA) — Copt Hall Princess (Crowned Prince USA) 3p5p. Strong smallish half-brother to Chasing winner, High Mood, and to 4 flat winners (2 in Italy), including Prince Merandi (also a successful Hurdler) and Dovedon Lady. Dam won at 7f. FLAT r12 p3. NH '95/6 r11 p3 (inc 20l 3rd in O5); fell only other Ch; inc Sell Hdle. P-t-P '99/9 r11 w2 (Maiden and Restricted) p5 (2 2nds, of 3 once); pulled up 1. Well ridden by Julian Pritchard to gain an annual success '97/8, but out of sorts since, and has been unimproved by the application of a tongue-strap. Appeared to go wrong on his latest appearance when pulled up after two bad mistakes in the first mile. Wore headgear under Rules. *T. Hayes — N. Ledbury (Jon Rudge)*. 564 (I), 701 (I), 1357 (MOnr), 1632 (I).

ROBERT'S TOY (IRE) ..9-7.. 10 b.g. Salt Dome (USA) — Zazu (Cure The Blues USA) 74p8. Compact light hlaf-brother to Irish flat winner, Ben Ruff. IRISH FLAT r8 w1 (10f) p1 (3rd). IRISH NH '94 r2 p0. NH '95/9 (for G. Ham, bought out of Sell for £2500; wins previously for M. Pipe) r45 w9 (6 Hdles, 2m-2m3f, the last 2 Sells, and 3 Chses, 2m-2m2f) p15 (short-headed once, and beaten neck once). NH Apr '00 (from Miss D. Cole's) r1 p0 (8th in 2m1f HCap Hdle: *prom til wknd 5*). Yet another in the long line of horses who win a stack for Martin Pipe and then achieve very little for subsequent trainers. A confirmed pace setter, who invariably made the bulk of the running when scoring, but a sketchy jumper, and definitely has insufficient stamina for Points, in which he could not finish better than last. Frequently blinkered. Acts in softish or on firm, and is still showing speed, but needs to return to Sellers at up to 2m3f. *L.W. Wickett — Stevenstone (Neil Harris)*. 68 (O), 252 (O), 653 (MO).

ROBERT THE RASCAL ..9-0§.. 8 ch.g. Scottish Reel — Midnight Mary (Celtic Cone) p2pp7. Dam won 2m Sell Hdle when ridden by John Carden. P-t-P '99 r1 p0 (refused). Showed his first signs of ability when runner-up in holding ground at Eaton Hall, but did not appear to care for a sound surface when favourite at Tabley next time, and not surprisingly beaten out of sight on his Hunter Chase debut. The two horses who finished immediately behind at Eaton Hall have since won so in theory he ought to follow their example, but his suspect temperament might not allow him to do so. *C. James — Saddleworth*. 527 (OMa), 777 (OMa), 965 (OMa), 1125 (OMa), 1343 (3m110yH).

ROB MINE (IRE) ..10-7.. 9 b.g. Roselier (FR) — Noddi Fliw (Jasmine Star) 1f62. Tall brother to Noddis Dilemma (IRE), and to Irish Hurdles winner, Rosie Lil (IRE). IRISH NH '96 r3 p0 (only beat 2, in big fields). P-t-P/HUNT CH '98 r6 w4 (inc Open, inc hat-trick) p1 (2nd in Hunt Ch); and unseated 1. Only defeated once when completing in Points, but has proved expensive to follow in Hunter

Chases. Out of action for a season after winning four times in '98, but looked to have returned every bit as good when trouncing 14 rivals on the opening day of the season. Ridden too aggressively in the testing conditions when taking a tired fall at the last at Chepstow, but had no apparent excuses when tailed off next time, and has been absent since mid-March. A strong galloper, but may not stay too well in soft ground, and does not appear easy to train. *Sir Chippendale Keswick & C.H. Sporborg — Puckeridge (Christopher Sporborg).* 4 (O), 149 (3mH), 303 (3mH), 545 (O).

ROBSAND (IRE) ..9-9.. 12 b.g. Sandalay — Remindful (Bargello) pp555. Compact brother to The Big Fella (IRE) (*qv*). IRISH P-t-P '94 r3 w1 (5 plus Mdn) p0; pulled up 2. NH '94/8 (for G.B. Balding, bought for 19,000, visored 2 and tried tongue-tied) r19 p6 (beaten 20*l* plus in4, inc 4m NH Ch). Sold Ascot, March for 700. Won his Irish Point in very soft, but was a consistently expensive failure during five years with Balding. Has broken blood vessels in the past, and only a weary plodder in Points, but splendidly safe (has never fallen in his life and normally completes), and might yet suit a beginner. His legion of fans (or to be more accurate, his many ancient anoraks) were thrilled to see that Tony Shaw had jocked himself up on the racecard at Garthorpe, as they had thrilled to his exploits whilst in their prams, but evidently the former Miss Bodger had put her foot down and he did not participate. *A.L. Shaw — N. Cotswold.* 1016 (Cf), 1492 (O), 1585 (O), 1597 (MO), 1664 (R).

ROCKET RADAR ..10-6.. 10 b.g. Vouchsafe — Courtney Pennant (Angus) 442. Tall lop-eared half-brother to Pyro Pennant and Stonemoss. P-t-P/HUNT CH '96/9 r12 w4 (inc 2m7f110y Hunt Ch, and inc hat-trick '97) p5 (2 2nds, last once); pulled up 1. Completed an impressive hat-trick against modest opposition when unbeaten in '97, but has not been easy to train since, and averages just three outings per annum. Battled his way to a Hunter Chase success at Worcester last year, but suffered another interrupted campaign in 2000, and was absent for 10 weeks following his reappearance. Looked sure to collect his fifth victory when coasting in a clear lead with two to jump on his latest outing at Upton, but was overwhelmed by Do It Once in the final 50 yards. A likeable individual, who rarely makes an error, and thoroughly deserves to win again. *Mrs J. Hughes — Ledbury.* 302 (3mH), 1293 (3mH), 1358 (Cf).

ROCK ON BUD (IRE) ..9-5.. 10 ch.g. Glow (USA) — Addabub (Manado) pp74. Half-brother to 2 flat winners who went on to add 15 victories abroad between them. Dam won at 10f in Ireland, and won 2m Hdle there. IRISH NH FLAT '95/6 r6 p0. IRISH NH '97 and '99 r4 p0 (unseated in Hunt Ch; last and pulled up 2 in Chses). IRISH P-t-P '97/9 r15 w1 (7 plus Mdn) p7; pulled up 5 (inc all 4 starts '99), and brought down. Sold Doncaster, Aug for 800. Exceptionally disappointing in Ireland, and the runner-up when he gained his victory was the dreaded Free And Equal (*qv*). Did a little better in the new yard, but is one-paced and very easy to beat, and may have a job to get the trip. Normally wears a tongue-strap. *Mrs M. Armstrong — Morpeth (Kevin Robson).* 663 (R), 918 (2m4fH), 976 (R), 1118 (R).

ROCKVILLE PIKE (IRE) ..9-8.. 9 b.g. Glenstal (USA) — Sound Pet (Runnett) ppppp0. Smallish quite attractive. FLAT (visored latterly) r18 w2 (5-7f, inc Sell) p1 (3rd). NH '97/8 r8 p0; fell 2, pulled up 1. P-t-P '98 r5 p1 (2nd); 4th, slipped up 1, pulled up 1, and fell 1. Precocious enough to run at Royal Ascot as a two-year-old, but finds Pointing rather demeaning, and patently fails to stay in any case. A clumsy jumper, and nowhere near good enough for sub-3m Hunter Chases. Acquired blinkers on his final start. Wears a cross-noseband. *F. Faulkner — N. Ledbury (A. Graham).* 294 (O), 474 (O), 684 (2m4fH), 895 (MO), 1311 (Cf), 1341 (2m110yH).

ROCKY PARK ..—.. 15 ch.g. Derrylin — Songe D'Inde (Sheshoon) u. Lengthy brother to Hurdles winner, Derechef, and half-brother to a French flat winner. Dam is a middle distance winner in France. NH FLAT '91 (for C.G. Roach) r1 p0. NH '91/9 (for G.B. Balding) r30 w2 (2m2f Hdle and 2m5f Ch) p13. A dual winner in soft to November '94, but has twice been absent for spells of 19 months since. Makes frequent errors, and his poor jumping came back to haunt him yet again when he unseated at Bishops Court. *D.C. Emmett — Tiverton.* 403 (Cf).

RODNEY TROTTER ..—.. 7 b.g. True Song — Silver Thorn (Record Run) p. Owner-bred. Dam won 2m4f Sell Hdle. Pulled up at Upton. Surprising the owner didn't decide to call him Neddy Seagoon. *B. Eccles — N. Cotswold (Giles Smyly).* 1361 (2m4fOMa).

ROGER (IRE) ..9-13.. 9 ch.g. Magical Strike (USA) — Saint Simbir (Simbir) 41p2. Plain sturdy half-brother to Moving Force, and to Irish Hurdles winners, Barnageera Boy (IRE) (also successful Chaser there, and in England) and Bobstar Danver (IRE). Dam won at 9f in Ireland. P-t-P/HUNT CH '97/9 r17 p5 (3rds, of 4 thrice); pulled up 4, fell/unseated 6, and refused 1. Incompetently handled in his first two seasons, but has finally turned the corner in the current yard, and has gained a prize in six of his nine starts for them. Virtually solo in the last mile when finally breaking his duck at Erw Lon, but only failed by the minimum margin to follow up at Bassaleg on his final appearance, and a reproduction would see him win a Restricted in 2001. Acts on a sound surface, and struggles to stay when conditions are more testing. *Mrs D.C. Faulkner — Tredegar F.* 602 (CfMa), 951 (OMa), 1298 (R), 1400 (R).

ROLCAP ..9-10.. 9 b.g. Rolfe (USA) — Bright Bonnet (Spartan General) 21ppp2p. Sturdy owner-bred. P-t-P '98/9 r6 p2; pulled up 4. Made the frame on three consecutive occasions before he opened his account in a bog at Mollington, but has quickly turned very sour. Tried in blinkers after a lifeless display at Newton Bromswold, but was pulled up after a bad mistake and they were quickly dispensed with. Ran in snatches when narrowly beaten in his Members, and virtually pulled himself up on his final start, and looks one to avoid at all costs. *R.G. Weaving — Warwicks (John Pritchard)*. 250 (CfMa), 432 (OMa), 513 (CR), 894 (R), 1419 (R), 1438 (M), 1586 (CN).

ROLFES DELIGHT ..10-9.. 9 b.g. Rolfe (USA) — Idiot's Run (Idiot's Delight) 116. P-tP/HUNT CH '99 r4 w1 (2m4f Maiden) p0; 4th, 5th, and unseated 1. Comfortably landed a 2m4f Maiden at Eyton in '99, and followed up on the course on his belated reappearance this year when clocking the fastest time of the day. Dominated proceedings throughout the final circuit when taking a competitive looking Bangor Hunter Chase subsequently, but could not reproduce that form on a return visit. Fast improving until his disappointing finale, and providing he stays sound, should win plenty more races in the years ahead. *G.L. Edwards — W. Salop*. 1200 (CR), 1343 (3m110yH), 1559 (3m110yH).

ROLIER (IRE) ..9-7.. 11 gr.g. Roselier (FR) — Countess Tudor (Beau Tudor) R5p. Lengthy. IRISH NH FLAT '94 and '96 r2 p0. IRISH P-t-P '94/6 r12 p4; pulled up 4, and fell/unseated 2. P-t-P '97/8 (for Mr T.A.B. Fineone Partnership) r12 w8 (up to Confined; inc 4-timer '98) p1 (head 2nd); pulled up 1, unseated 1, and ran out 1. A splendidly tough Pointer when with the Daltons, and only tasted defeat once in nine completions, but pulled up lame in his first Open and forced to spend the '99 season on the sidelines. Looked a shadow of his former self in the new yard, and pulled up and dismounted after less than a mile on his final start. Clearly still troubled. Pity. *Mrs D.M. Wells-Kendrew — Flint & Denbigh (Stephen Kelly)*. 781 (Cf), 1073 (O), 1319 (O).

ROLLED GOLD ..—.. 12 b.g. Rymer — Goldaw (Gala Performance USA) p. Strong-quartered half-brother to Cool Million (*qv*). NH FLAT Spr '95 r2 p1 (neck 2nd). NH '97/7 (wins for Miss V. Williams; previously for M. Pipe) r7 w2 (3m1f Chses) p0. Ended his career under Rules with a double in bad contests, but was very lucky that the ten length leader unseated at the last once. Went missing for three years, only to pull up on the briefest of revivals. *Miss J.M. Green — Ludlow (Penny Grainger)*. 333 (Cf).

ROLL WITH IT (IRE) ..10-3.. 8 b.g. Royal Fountain — Deirdre Elizabeth (Salluceva) 11f20. Workmanlike half-brother to Banteer Bet (IRE) (*qv*). IRISH P-t-P '97/9 r7 w1 (5yo Mdn) p2 (2nds, inc dead-heat); fell 2. IRISH NH FLAT '98/9 r7 p1 (2nd). IRISH NH '98/9 r8 p2 (2 3rds in Hdles, inc dead-heat). NH May '00 r2 p1 (2nd in 3m Nov Hdle: *chsd wnr & mist 6, rdn 9, ev ch til wknd 3 out*; and 10th in 2m4f HCap Hdle: *hld up, mist 8, lost tch*). A thorough stayer who can handle heavy ground, and strode to a confident double in Points prior to falling at the fourth. Has shown ability on occasions over Hurdles, but the bigger obstacles are more his game, and could probably finish thereabouts in novices Chases. *I. Anderson — W. Salop*. 338 (R), 482 (I), 592 (Cf).

ROLPEN ..9-9.. 9 b.g. Rolfe (USA) — Pensun (Jimsun) ppp8p. Small close-coupled well-made owner-bred half-brother to Penlet, Penly, Tinsun and Penaword. Dam is half-sister to 4 Pointers, including Rugy. P-t-P '98/9 r9 w1 (Maiden) p1 (3rd); pulled up 3, and fell/unseated 3. Won a modest Maiden decisively at Clifton-on-Dunsmore on his final outing in '99, but in common with several of his stablemates this year, never looked happy, and there must have been a problem in the yard. Tailed off in each of his five appearances, and raced with great reluctance on his final start. *R.G. Weaving — Warwicks (John Pritchard)*. 612 (CR), 1009 (CR), 1146 (R), 1415 (Cf), 1584 (CCond).

ROLY POLY (IRE) ..9-9.. 8 b.g. Phardante (FR) — Turkish Sultana (IRE) (Kemal FR) 14316. Sturdy close-coupled. IRISH NH FLAT '97/8 r4 p0. IRISH NH '97/9 (tried blinkered) r14 p1 (2nd). Bought Doncaster, May for 1500. Proved suited by a drop to Points, and reserved his best efforts for Thorpe, where he won two minor contests by a very easy aggregate of 40 lengths. A sound jumper, and should be able to score again. *A.W. Speck — Belvoir (Helen Harvey)*. 121 (OMa), 797 (R), 867 (M), 1218 (R), 1586 (CN).

ROLY PRIOR ..9-10.. 12 b.g. Celtic Cone — Moonduster (Sparkler) 52354. Small half-brother to Zoot Money, and to a German flat winner. Dam won at 2m. NH FLAT r3 p0. NH '94/5 r5 p1 (3rd). P-t-P/HUNT CH '96/9 r25 w9 (inc 7 Ladies, and Club Ladies; 5-timer in '98) p7 (5 2nds, beaten head once); pulled up 1, and fell/unseated 4. Not much more than a pony, and improved greatly for the switch to Ladies races in '97, and even more so for his move to the current yard a year later. Bitterly disappointing since, and has been looking as if he is enjoying himself. Only once beaten less than 20 lengths in 2000, and not seen since finishing a remote fourth to Persian Butterfly at Mollington in March. Worth 10-8 at best, but will be a real challenge to get him back anywhere neat that at 12. Suited by an easy surface. *Mrs R.G. Samworth — V. of Aylesbury (Lawney Hill)*. 78 (L), 245 (L), 431 (L), 544 (L), 787 (L).

ROMALITA ..9-6.. 11 b.g. Robellino (USA) — Princess Zita (Manado) 33p5p43. Compact good-bodied brother to a French flat winner, and half-brother to 4 flat winners (one in Brazil), including Russian Sable. Dam won at 7f. 10,500y. FLAT '98 (to '98; blinkered/visored 2) r51 w1 (14f Sell) p11 (short-headed once). NH '93/8 (final for C. Popham, bought for 700; previously for M. Blanchard, blinkered 3 in '96) r21 p7; Sells final 2. Safe enough, but simply does not stay three miles, and beaten a minimum of 20 lengths in Points. Has accumulated 21 placings over the years, but can look a difficult ride, but despite some decent efforts he has lost 78 of 79 races (the exception was in '95). *Miss D. Cole — S. Smale — Dulverton E., & Tiverton Staghounds (-; Neil Harris).* 252 (O), 313 (O), 537 (O), 652 (MO), 954 (MO), 1136 (M), 1387 (O).

ROMAN GALE (IRE) ..10-2.. 12 br.g. Strong Gale — Verenda (Roman Gift) 4pp3f11p. Rangy angular half-brother to 4 winners in Ireland, including Manver (IRE) (Pointing; subsequently won English Hurdle), Carenda (Pointing), and Marenda (Hurdles). IRISH P-t-P '94/7 r12 w2 (Mdn, and Winners of One) p4; pulled up 3, and fell 2 (in lead at last once — would have won). Developed leg trouble in Ireland and reportedly purchased for £800, and looked rusty when returning from a three year absence. Later partnered by a complete beginner (who did not do too badly), but it was the association with Andrew Price which really paid off in May, when he landed an Intermediate in which the first four were covered by less than a length (16-1) and a Confined (5-1). Can gallop strongly on firm, and may continue to do well on that surface if able to stand the strain. *R.J. Rowsell — Ystrad Taf Fechan.* 482 (I), 741 (Cf), 1051 (Cf), 1299 (I), 1399 (M), 1449 (I), 1569 (Cf), 1626 (3m1f110yH).

ROMAN ROMANY ..9-8.. 12 ch.g. Sir Patrick — Roman Lass (Roi Soleil) p84. Sturdy lengthy. Grandam (Romenda), great-grandam (Vallenda) and great-great-grandam (Sleepy Valley) were all Pointing winners. NH FLAT r1 p0. NH '93 r2 p0. P-t-P/HUNT CH '97/8 (for Mrs D. Bevan) r8 w2 (Maiden and Club Restricted) p0; fell/unseated 2, and pulled up 3. Made all to win two bad races in '97, but quirky, often jumps away to the right, and has clearly been difficult to train. Not wholly disgraced in 2000, but ultimately beaten along way, and will struggle to win again. Wears a cross-noseband. *R. Staley — Golden V.* 615 (CMod), 862 (Cf), 1458 (M).

ROMANTIC NATIVE (IRE) ..9-7.. 7 b.g. Be My Native (USA) — Gay Seeker (Status Seeker) In. Brother to Irish Hurdles winner, My Native Girl, and half-brother to The Bull Blackman (IRE). Dam won 2m mares Mdn Hdle in Ireland. Sold Doncaster, Aug for 3400. Unsurprisingly only able to manage a remote third to Key Debate in a remarkably fast Maiden at Market Rasen, but franked the form in a contest which proceeded at a far more sedate pace taking 7min 38s in softish at Wetherby. Looks quite promising, and can hopefully manage a busier second campaign. *R.J. Marley — Middleton.* 55 (OMa), 167 (OMa).

ROMANY CHAT ..9-9.. 9 b.g. Backchat (USA) — Ranee's Song (True Song) p2234p2124. Good-topped. Dam was useless in Hurdles and a Point (pulled up) for Roger Gasson. Grandam, Indian Ranee, won 4 Points and placed 5 (inc 3rd in Hunt Ch). P-t-P '99 r5 p0 (4th, 6th, pulled up 2, and unseated 1). An excitable fellow who takes a strong hold, and has found it difficult to last the full trip. Twice run out of it on the run-in before just prevailing on firm ground at Ashorne, and was a most deserving winner. Gave a good account in his first Restricted, and superior reliability should enable him to win one eventually. Sometimes makes mistakes, but has never fallen, and benefits from the presence of Andy Martin in the saddle. Has two handlers. *Mrs R. Gasson - Warwicks.* 12 (OMa), 76 (CCfMa), 197 (CfMa), 433 (OMa), 630 (OMa), 891 (OMa), 1020 (OMa), 1437 (OMa), 1623 (R), 1667 (I).

RON MIEL (IRE) ..8-0.. 7 b.g. Brush Aside (USA) — Try Le Reste (IRE) (Le Moss) p6. Strong-topped lengthy. Dam is half-sister to Ryton Guard (qv '98 Annual). IRISH P-t-P '99 r5 p0 (last, pulled up 3 and unseated). Did not start until late May, and has still not beaten another horse in seven attempts. *Miss J. Meredith — Kyre Bloodhounds (Paul Senter).* 1634 (OMa), 1669 (OMa).

RON ON THE RUN (IRE) ..9-4§.. 11 b.g. Wassl — Celestial Path (Godswalk USA) 4524. Compact attractive half-brother to 4 winners, including Karazan (flat) and Aslan (IRE) (NH flat and Hurdles). Dam won 4 Irish flat, 5-7f. NH FLAT '94/5 r4 p2 (3rds). NH '95/7 r8 p2. P-t-P '99 r5 p3 (2 2nds); pulled up 1, and fell 1. In the frame in six of seven completions (remounted once) but a consistently bad jumper, and totally lacking in resolution. Looked to have been handed a Market Rasen Maiden on a plate when left five lengths clear at the last, but hoisted the white flag on the run-in, and surrendered his advantage close home. Has the ability to win, but gutless, and must be avoided. Wears blinkers. *Mrs J. Dwyer — Middleton (Bruce Temple).* 53 (OMa), 281 (OMa), 436 (OMa), 508 (CMa).

ROOTSMAN (IRE) ..9-11.. 11 b.g. Glenstal (USA) — Modena (Sassafras FR) 5555ps. Compact half-brother to Crofter's Cline, and to 2 flat winners (one in Ireland). IRISH NH '93 r2 p0. IRISH NH '94 and '95 r12 p1 (21¼/ 3rd). P-t-P '97/9 r12 w3 (up to Confined) p6 (2 2nds, of 3 once; and 4 3rds); pulled up 1. Earned a prize in nine of his first 10 Points, but becoming ever more deeply frustrating, and his temperament seems to have got the better of him for the present. Can quicken, and looked dangerous when moving up to challenge at Bitterley this year, but hung fire under pressure, and subsequently tried once in a visor. Usually needs an outing or two to get fit, but could still win races if he applied himself better. Suited by some cut in the ground. *Mrs S.E. de Courcy-Parry — N. Ledbury (Tim Stephenson).* 68 (O), 667 (Cf), 861 (C), 1086 (Cf), 1311 (Cf), 1463 (Cf).

ROSALEE ROYALE ..9-5.. 9 ch.m. Out Of Hand — Miss Ark Royal (Broadsword USA) 32. Lengthy. Dam won 2m2f Sell Hdle. P-t-P (blinkered 1) r6 p0 (inc last 4, and unseated; inc Sells). NH FLAT '96 r2 p0. NH '96/7 r2 p0 (6th, and last in Sells). P-t-P '98/9 r8 p4 (2nd of 3, and 3 3rds, of 4 twice, and last once); fell 3, and pulled up 1. Began her career believing she was auditioning for a part in the re-make of Ben Hur, but has done better since, and has run into the placings in her last six starts. Yet to look like winning however, and has become lightly raced, but tries hard, and deserves to find a small race. *Mrs S. Kittow — Tiverton.* 147 (OMa), 1101 (OMa).

ROSA'S REVENGE ..10-4.. 13 br.m. Pony Express — Royal Brief (Eberneezer) p111. Small good-bodied. Dam won Maiden and placed 6. Grandam, Caragama, won Maiden and placed 5. P-t-P '95/9 r27 w4 (up to Confined) p12 (6 2nds, last once); pulled up 5, brought down 1, and unseated 1. Disappointingly unenthusiastic in her first two seasons and required blinkers to get off the mark, but has blossomed and only once out of the frame in 15 completions since '98. Can front run to good effect, but twice came from behind in 2000, and has been superbly handled by Leslie Jefford in six successes. Loves mud, and has finally done away with headgear, but still liable to get fruity in the paddock and has been taken to post early. Can win again at 13. *G.W. Johnson — Dartmoor (Lucy Johnson).* 316 (Cf), 852 (Cf), 1046 (Cm), 1261 (Cf).

ROSCOE BURN ..9-9.. 9 ch.g. Meadowbrook — Rosecko (White Speck) 34145. Tall rangy owner-bred. P-t-P '98/9 r7 p1 (2nd); last pair 2, pulled up 3, and fell 1. Has taken time to fill his frame, but goes a fair gallop, and had two subsequent scorers on his heels when successful at Alnwick. Not entirely disgraced in Restricteds, and should be able to win one eventually though a sound surface seems essential. *Mrs D.B. Johnstone — Berwicks.* 113 (OMa), 624 (OMa), 913 (CfMa), 976 (R), 1427 (R).

ROSCOES DINKY ..9-0.. 14 br.m. Roscoe Blake — Minibus (John Splendid) fp3. Small sister to Roscoe Spate, and half-sister to Hurdles winner, Draw The Line. Dam won at 6f. FLAT (inc when blinkered in Sell) r5 p0. NH '90/1 (blinkered final) r4 p0 (last, pulled up 2, and fell 1; inc Sell). P-t-P/HUNT CH '92/4 and '99 r17 w1 (Maiden) p2 (2nds); pulled up 4, fell 2. Returned from a five-year sabbatical to open her account at Bredwardine last year, but has often failed to get the trip, and lacks the substance to shrug off her frequent blunders. Failed to beat a rival in 2000, and looks too old now. *Mrs A. Turner — S. Herefords (P. Turner).* 340 (R), 448 (L), 666 (M).

ROSCOLVIN (IRE) ..9-10.. 9 b.g. Prince Rupert (FR) — Chepstow House (USA) (Northern Baby CAN) pp. Strong half-brother to a jumping winner in USA. IRISH FLAT '95 r3 p1 (2nd). IRISH NH '95/6 (blinkered final) r6 p1 (2nd). P-t-P/HUNT CH '97/9 r15 w3 (Maiden, Restricted and Intermediate) p3 (3rds, last once, and inc Hunt Ch); pulled up 5. Three times a winner at Cottenham, and unlucky when falling and remounting there in '97, but pulled up in five of his last seven starts and shows little relish for a struggle these days. Acts on firm, but sometimes jumps stickily, and seems to have something at fault. *Miss J. King — Suffolk (Julie Read).* 1156 (3m110yH), 1381 (O).

ROSE GARDEN ..10-1.. 12 b.m. Pragmatic — Indian Rose (Kinglet) 5. Tall rangy half-sister to Chasing winner, Glindigo (IRE). Dam, sister to Indian Knight (*qv*), was 3rd in her Members for Pat Pocock in '90. P-t-P '95 r1 p1 (remote 3rd of 4). NH '96/9 r9 w1 (2m5f HCap Chse) p2. Won a Wincanton Chase on the first occasion he encountered a sound surface, but has never managed more than four outings in a year, and is clearly hard to train. Looked in need of the run on his Hunter Chase debut, and not disgraced in finishing around 15 off the winner, but failed to reappear. Has never gone beyond 2m7f, and was tailed off on that occasion. *T.E. Pocock — W. Somerset V.* 685 (2m5fH).

ROSE KING ..9-12.. 14 b.g. King's Ride — Choral Rose (Blue Refrain) 2pup2. Tall rangy. NH FLAT r1 p1 (2nd). NH '93/4 and '97 r10 w2 (2m1f Hdle and 3m Ch) p2 (3rds, of 4 once). P-t-P/HUNT CH '96 and '98/9 r9 w2 (Members) p2; pulled up 1, and brought down 1. Very lightly raced, and never fulfilled his potential under Rules, and has only ever managed to win two Members races in 13 Pointing ventures. Headed close home when bidding for a third at Detling on his reappearance, but easily held in more competitive events, and remains prone to blunders. Busier than ever '99/00, but the pity is he's too old to make use of his injury free state. *T.R. Hills — W. Street/Tickham.* 571 (M), 824 (Cf), 1167 (CMod), 1394 (O), 1509 (Cf).

ROSEWOOD LADY (IRE) ..—.. 6 b.m. Maledetto (IRE) — Thrill Seeker (IRE) (Treasure Kay) up. Smallish sparely-made. 3600 2yo. FLAT (for K. Burke, sometimes visored) r13 w1 (6f Sell) p4. Bought Ascot, Nov '98 for 925. Came extremely close to registering three wins on the flat (beaten half a length, but would have won in another couple of strides, and just caught when short-headed once), but faced an impossible task behind Butler John in a Mixed Open on her debut over jumps (150-1), and struggling when unseating after a mile). Ridden by Kahlil Burke at Torrington (no relation, presumably, to the horse's former trainer), and as if two Burkes weren't enough, several more backed her down to 9-4 for the three-runner Members. Predictably she was the first to cry enough, and seems a very unlikely winner at three miles (her sire is also responsible for Mail Shot, *qv*). *R. Smith — Torrington F.* 1515 (MO), 1670 (M).

ROSMARINO ..9-12.. 11 br.g. Persian Bold — No More Rosies (Warpath) 13663. Smallish compact brother to Tam O'Shanter, and to flat and jumping winner, Eau De Cologne, and half-brother to the winners, Beachy Head (flat and jumping), Only A Rose (Hurdling), and All In The Mind (flat). Dam won at 10f, and is half-sister to 8 winners, including John Splendid (also sire) and Mount Athos (3rd in Derby). FLAT r14 w1 (13f) p1 (3rd). NH '95/7 r2 p2; inc pulled up 2, and fell 1. P-t-P '99 r4 w1 (PPORA) p2 (2nds); and fell 1. Does not stand much racing, but goes well fresh, and produced fighting fit when landing a touch on his reappearance this year. Survived an objection from the rider of the second after leaning on him going to the last, but could not reproduce that effort in four subsequent starts. A thorough stayer, and suited by soft ground, but not the bravest when it comes to a battle. *Miss R. Howell & M. McCaull — Wheatland (Andrew Dalton).* 293 (Cf), 402 (O), 529 (Cf), 1015 (4mO), 1128 (Cf).

ROSSALEEN ..10-1.. 10 b.m. Ardross — Tawny Silk (Little Buskins) pu1321. Leggy unfurnished. Dam won mares Maiden in Ireland (also disqualified from similar after omitting a fence). NH '99 (for breeder, Miss H. Day) r1 p0. Virtually unraced until she was nine, and the Shaws have done well with her. One-paced under normal conditions, but comes into her own over extreme trips in mud, and after a 20-1 success at Bishops Court she later landed a Restricted taking over eight minutes at Bishopsleigh. Blinkered in her third and fourth Points, but not since. *Mrs J.L. Kelly — Cattistock (Fiona & Peter Shaw).* 69 (R), 255 (R), 410 (OMa), 734 (R), 1046 (Cm), 1176 (R).

ROSS COTTAGE ..10-2.. 9 b.g. Hyrossi — Flavias Cottage (Marcus Superbus) 222. Smallish close-coupled half-brother to Cottage Light *(qv)*. Sire won a Maiden and 2nd 5. P-t-P '98/9 r9 w2 (2m4f Maiden, and Restricted) p4 (2 2nds); pulled up 1, and fell/unseated 2. A useful Pointer who has never failed to make the frame when completing, but has had the misfortune to lock horns with the some useful novices recently, and deserves to add to his tally. Lacks a turn of foot, and is suited by forcing tactics. Has shown form in soft and on firmish, but prefers the former. *P.R., J.P. & A.J. Bateman — Quantock (Tim Long).* 63 (I), 404 (I), 737 (I).

ROSSELL ISLAND (IRE) ..10-0.. 10 br.g. Strong Gale — Fraoch Ban (Deep Run) 12f. Workmanlike half-brother to Irish Hurdles winner, Jo Peeks. Dam won Irish NH flat, but demoted to 2nd for causing interference. NH FLAT Mar '66 r1 p0. NH '96/9 (for Mrs J. Pitman) r17 w2 (2m Hdle and 2m1f Ch) p3; has broken blood vessels. Bought Ascot, June for 5600. Won twice at Towcester and was also a fast-finishing second there, and added an Open in which only two finished at Holnicote before disappointing badly at 1-2 in similar company. Fitted with blinkers when he led the calvary charge of 26 to the first fence in the Aintree Foxhunters, and took a fatal fall. *M.C. Pipe — Taunton V.H. (David Pipe).* 355 (O), 537 (O), 921 (2m6fH).

ROUNDABOUT ..—.. 8 b.m. Henbit (USA) — Rouse About (Rouser) ppf. Small light. Dam, half-sister to 3 Pointers, including Bahama (qv '92 Annual), won 2 Points and placed 5 for John Swinnerton (was bred by him). P-t-P '99 r6 p0 (pulled up 3, and fell 3). On the deck four times before reaching halfway to date. Her jumping certainly hasn't gone full circle yet, and remains a wild and unrewarding ride. *W.J. Swinnerton — N. Salop.* 298 (CfMa), 568 (OMa), 965 (OMa).

ROUND THE BEND ..9-10.. 9 b.g. Revolutionary (USA) — No Love (Bustiki) 35p221. Close-coupled brother to Give It A Whirl. An enthusiastic galloper like his brother, but tends to be too free, and was beaten 20 lengths or more in his first two placings. Got a lot closer when two lengths second at Thorpe, and ended the season leading throughout the final two miles and keeping on gallantly at Clifton-on-Dunsmore. Excitable, but Give It A Whirl was best at 11, so there must be hope of further improvement as he matures. *Mrs S. Allan & P.S. Phazey — Fitzwilliam (Louise Allan).* 52 (OMa), 235 (OMa), 439 (OMa), 1011 (CfMa), 1219 (OMa), 1423 (OMa).

ROVAC ..7-8.. 14 b.g. Ovac (ITY) — Open Your Eyes (Beau Charmeur FR) 5. Strong compact half-brother to Mandril (IRE) and Bonny Rigg (IRE), and to Irish Pointing winner, Mordella Lass (IRE). IRISH P-t-P '94 r2 p1 (2nd); and pulled up 1. P-t-P '97/9 r7 p1 (2nd); pulled up 1, and fell/unseated 2. Had the ability to win a small race, but has never managed more than four outings in a year, and approaches 14 with a mere 10 starts under his belt. At least Jonathon Fryer completed the course safely on him in his Members albeit fences adrift of the winner. *Mrs G. & Mrs J. Fryer — W. Norfolk (Jonathon Fryer).* 1285 (M).

ROVING REBEL ..—.. 14 b.g. Prince Of Peace — Proven Gypsy (Ampney Prince) pppf. Small sturdy owner-bred half-brother to Roving Bandit, Roving Vagabond and Roving Gypsy. P-t-P '93/8 r14 w1 (Maiden) p2 (3rds); failed to finish 11 (fell/unseated 3). Only ever able to complete three times, but made one count when successful at Bishops Court in '94. Stands his racing badly, and broke down in '98, but can still shift a bit, and carted Caroline Prouse at high speed until crashing after two miles in his latest outing. Occasionally blinkered. *Mrs A.P. Wakeham — Dartmoor (H. Wakeham).* 161 (L), 314 (L), 729 (R), 929 (Cnr).

ROWLING SEA (IRE) ..—.. 7 b.g. Toca Madera — Push Over Lass (Wolverlife) upp. Suffered a fatal injury at Erw Lon. *R.W.J. & S.M. Willcox — Llangeinor (R.W.J. Willcox).* 747 (CfMa), 822 (CfMa), 950 (OMa).

ROYAL ACTION ..9-8.. 8 b.g. Royal Academy (USA) — Ivor's Honey (Sir Ivor) u5fup63. Compact half-brother to Tolmin, to flat winners, Honeybird, Artaius Mead and Stiffelio (IRE), and to a winner in France. Dam won at 10f in Ireland. 24,000y. FLAT (ran badly when blinkered) r15 w4 (8-10f, all on all-weather) p3 (beaten head once). NH '96/8 (won for O. Sherwood; previously for J. Banks) r7 w1 (2m3f Hdle, 3 ran) p4. Won five races '96/7 including four consecutively on the flat (made virtually all twice), but has been an awkward on plenty of occasions over jumps, and was once withdrawn after unseating and crashing through the rails and injuring Jamie Osborne in the process. Reappeared in Points after a 25 month absence during which he had a lot problems at home with broken blood vessels, and showed on occasions that he retains ability, but Paul Chinery was certainly not the best man for him, and the teaming produced some very hair-raising displays. It would be interesting to see what a Nigel Bloom or a Simon Andrews could produce. *A.G. Chinery — E. Essex (Paul Chinery).* 756 (Cf), 842 (O), 935 (M), 1114 (Cf), 1378 (Cf), 1585 (O), 1666 (O).

ROYAL ARCTIC (IRE) ..9-12§.. 11 ch.g. Sandalay — Remindful (Bargello) 2p5*728p*. Rangy brother to The Big Fella (IRE) (*qv*). IRISH P-t-P '96/7 r8 w2 (7 plus Mdn, and Winners of Two) p3; pulled up, fell and unseated. NH '97/9 (for S. Mellor, bought for 15,000, visored 2) r19 w2 (2m5f Hdles) p4; finished in all 3 Chses. Bought Doncaster, May for 900. NH Spr '00 (from Miss H. Irving's) r4 p1 (2nd in 3m1f HCap Ch: *hld up, drvn 6, outpcd 8, stayed on, nt rch wnr*); 7th in 3m2f Amat rdrs HCap Ch: *chsd ldrs til wknd 8*; 8th in 3m2f Nov HCap Ch: *outpcd and bhnd frm ½way*; and pulled up 1. Has no problems slogging through mud and could have won a lot more races had he so desired, but a very sour performer who needs much kidding, and rarely consented to race properly in 2000. Wears blinkers nowadays. On the credit side, he was very cheap and did earn £1184 when taking second on the run-in at Towcester, where he was 40-1 and ten pounds out of the handicap (had contested an amateurs Chase the time before, but his porky partner put up a ludicrous 21 pounds overweight, which was hardly fair to any betting loonies who might have supported him each way in a field of eight at 66-1). *A.C. Kemp, K. Rolls & D. Tomkins — Farmers Bloodhounds (Tony Kemp).* 5 (Cv&nr), 25 (Cnr), 154 (3mH).

ROYAL BANKER (IRE) ..9-10.. 11 b.g. Roselier (FR) — Dottie's Wasp (Tarqogan) 3514. Workmanlike compact. NH '96/7 (blinkered 2) r6 p1 (23*l* 2nd of 3 in Ch); last, pulled up 1, and fell/unseated in other Chses. P-t-P/HUNT CH '98/9 r5 w1 (Maiden) p3 (2 2nds; and inc 2 Hunt Chses). A dual winner in soft ground at Horseheath, and is a thorough stayer, but has never been keen on over exertion, and frequently declines to put it all in. Does not stand his racing well, and can never be supported with confidence. *A.W.K. Merriam — Easton H. (Jean Merriam).* 93 (C), 285 (CR), 416 (R), 552 (I).

ROYAL CHARGER (IRE) ..8-8.. 9 b.g. Euphemism — Royal Brigade (Light Brigade) bpp3. Very tall half-brother to Premier Brigade (2nd in a Point in '91). Dam was 2nd in 3 Irish Points. P-t-P '97/9 (for Mr H. Atkinson) r9 p1 (3rd); pulled up 6, and brought down 1. A gawky individual, and has yet to finish closer than 13 lengths behind the winner, but exposed as an ungenuine non-stayer now. Rather highly strung, and blinkered to no avail on his latest outing. *D. Winter — Cranwell Bloodhounds (Carol Ikin).* 372 (CfMa), 798 (OMa), 1420 (OMa), 1522 (CfMa).

ROYAL CHIP ..9-5.. 9 gr.g. Rakaposhi King — Up Cooke (Deep Run) 3pp321p. Unfurnished. dam won 3 Hdles and 2 Chses, all around 2m. NH FLAT Mar '97 r1 p0. NH '99 (for breeder, Miss K. Milligan) r2 p0. Bought Doncaster, Oct for 1600. Collapsed in a heap because of wind problems in his early Points, but tubing him brought relief on his last three outings, and followed a one length second with a win in a bad Maiden at Lifton. Tailed off and pulled up on his latest appearance, and is probably going to struggle to achieve much in competitive company. *J.F. Weldhen — Four Burrow.* 73 (OMa), 312 (CfMa), 855 (CfMa), 1186 (M), 1390 (OMa), 1522 (CfMa), 1639 (R).

ROYAL DEW (IRE) ..9-11.. 8 br.g. Royal Fountain — Ardglass Mist (Black Minstrel) pp1. Workmanlike compact. NH '98 r2 p0. P-t-P '99 (for Mrs S.L. Barber) r5 p2; last 2, and unseated 1. Placed twice for the Dalton in '99, but required blinkers to keep his mind on the job, and did not seem very keen. Visored when pulled up twice in the new yard, but the headgear was left off when successful at Parham where the Stewards held an enquiry into his improved performance. David Evatts explanation that the horse had suffered with his teeth was certainly novel, and duly accepted. Beat no subsequent winners, and even if he keeps his regular dental appointments further success may not be forthcoming. *D.B. Evatt —Southdown & Eridge (Ian Cobb).* 57 (OMa), 221 (OMa), 309 (OMa).

ROYAL ESTATE ..10-8.. 8 b.g. Rakaposhi King — Country Seat (Paddy's Stream) p2f1331. Good-topped. Dam is half-sister to 6 winners, including Legal Emperor (*qv* '92 Annual). P-t-P '99 r1 w1 (Maiden). A shade fortunate to win on his racecourse debut, and enjoyed similar luck to '99 when successful again at Siddington this year, but there was a lot to like about his Hunter Chase debut at Huntingdon subsequently. Despite making numerous errors he still had every chance at the last, and stuck on well to be edged out in a three-way photo. Won a two-finisher event in the fastest time of the day on his final outing and did not appear inconvenienced by the firm ground. Has developed into a decent performer, and improved fluency can win in better class. *Hon. Hon. Mrs T. Stopford-Sackville — Heythrop (Tim Holland-Martin).* 63 (I), 193 (R), 477 (R), 749 (Cf), 968 (Cf), 1334 (3mH).

ROYAL FLING ..—§.. 7 b.m. Rakaposhi King — Temporary Affair (Mandalus) pprpp. Small half-sister to Mrs Sherman (*qv*). A remarkably reluctant youngster, and had already lost touch when she refused at the seventh and dumped the rider on the fence in the worst race she will ever contest (a three-runner Maiden). Her next fling will probably be as far as Lady Susan can throw her. *Susan Lady Barlow — Cheshire (Sue Mullineaux).* 588 (OMa), 816 (OMa), 1075 (OMa), 1153 (OMa), 1367 (OMa).

ROYAL GEORGE (IRE) ..8-2.. 7 b.g. Mandalus — Saroan Meed (Midsummer Night II) f2. Sturdy half-brother Kopain (IRE) (*qv*). Fell at the second on his debut, and then finished 30 lengths second in a Maiden in which half of the contestants were missing when the stretch of plough cam round for the final time. *R.T. Baker — Radnor & W. Herefords (Clare Walker).* 489 (CfMa), 747 (CfMa).

ROYAL LEADER (IRE) ..—.. 10 b.g. Supreme Leader — Ribble Rabble (Deep Run) p. dam is half-sister to Massingham (*qv* '93 Annual). IRISH NH FLAT '97 r1 p0. IRISH NH '97/8 (wore blinkers and tongue-strap once) r8 p0 (fell only Ch). IRISH P-t-P '96/7 and '99 r9 w1 (6 plus Mdn, beaten ½l, but judge awarded dead-heat) p2; pulled up 4, and fell 2. Broke a shoulder and destroyed at Chaddesley. Miss J. Meredith — N. Ledbury (Paul Senter). 615 (CMod).

ROYAL MOUNTBROWNE ..10-0.. 13 b.g. Royal Vulcan — Star Shell (Queen's Hussar) 1624534. Tall rangy brother to Vulcan Star, and half-brother to Jac Del Prince. IRISH P-t-P '92/3 r5 w2 p2 (2nds); and fell. IRISH NH FLAT '92/3 r3 p1 (short-head 2nd). IRISH NH '93/7 r38 w10 (2m4f Hdle, and 9 Chses, 2m2f-3m) p9; ran once apiece at Ayr and Cheltenham. NH '97/9 (for Miss M. Rowland) r12 p3 (22-32*l* 3rds). Sold Doncaster, June for 800. Achieved some excellent results in Ireland, and his career earnings under Rules stand at £82,522. A confirmed mud-lover who was at his peak in '96 when five wins included three Graded races including £12,900 and £22,750 prizes. The latter was at Punchestown, where the remainder of the field was comprised of Merry Gale, Time For A Run, Imperial Call, Klairon Davis and Life Of A Lord, but had accumulated 17 subsequent defeats until he broke the sequence on his debut for the new yard in a Ladies at Black Forest Lodge. Takes a keen hold and gallops up with the pace, but has always been prone to blunder, and also makes some slow jumps now. Often tongue-tied, although not in 2000. Has achieved veteran status and become easy to beat again, but David Gibbs and Emily Jones did well to revitalise him the once. *D.C. Gibbs — Ystrad Taf Fechan*. 67 (L), 226 (2m4f110yH), 382 (2m4fH), 481 (L), 919 (2m3f110yH), 1157 (2m3fH), 1447 (2m4fH).

ROYAL ORCHARD ..9-7.. 11 ch.g. Regal Steel — Windfall VI (Master Owen) ppu34fpf5. Close-coupled well-made half-brother to Prince Pippin, Old Applejack, Crunch, Great Granny Smith (dam of Bramley *qv*), Roxby Toffee Apple, Scrumpy Country, Miss Crabapple, Russett King and Apple Anthem. Dam won 2 Points and placed 8 (inc a Hunt Ch) for Fran Marriott. P-t-P '97/9 r14 w1 (Club Maiden) p4 (3 2nds); 7th, last pair 3, pulled up 4, and fell 1. Consented to put his best foot forward in '99 when in addition to a Mollington success he collected four placings, but never went a yard this year, and blinkered with no improvement on his last two appearances. Presumably ailing as his jumping went to pot as well. Usually slow to get fit, and should be shunned until he shows signs of a revival. *C. Marriott — Heythrop (Fran Marriott)*. 13 (R), 80 (CCfR), 196 (R), 246 (C), 429 (C), 791 (R), 1146 (R), 1419 (R), 1482 (R).

ROYAL POCKET ..—.. 15 ch.m. True Song — Ginger Fury (Fury Royal) p. Well-made sister to Face The Music, and half-sister to Mademist Susie (dam of Mademist Jaz *qv*), Gingerfield, Royal Balinger and The Ginger Broad. Dam pulled up and unseated in Points. P-t-P '92 and '94 (for Mr I.P. Crane) r8 w1 (Maiden) p1 (½l 2nd); pulled up 3, and fell/unseated 2. Won a youngsters Maiden at Garthorpe in '92, but went wrong later in the season, and only able to run three times since. Not surprising quickly tailed off when backward on her very belated return. *Mrs H. Lynch — Quorn (Helen Harvey)*. 903 (O).

ROYAL RAVEN (IRE) ..9-1.. 10 b.g. Castle Keep — Decent Dame (Decent Fellow) 7. Strong half-brother to Chasing winner, Glitter Isle (IRE) and to NH flat and Hurdles winner, Mentmore Towers (IRE). NH FLAT '96 r2 p1 (2nd). NH '97/7 and '99 (for J. Gifford) r11 w1 (2m4f Hdle) p2 (inc 3rd in Ch). Bought Ascot, June for 3200. Scored on firmish at Ascot in November '99 (only six ran), but clearly hard to train (once missing for 23 months), and left Pointing in a flap after one outing in January. *D.L. Gill, K. Biltoo & D. Kogan — Essex (David Gill)*. 15 (C).

ROYAL RUPERT ..9-2.. 14 ro.g. Royal Match — Bidula (Manacle) 32u3324. Angular unfurnished half-brother to Familiar Friend, and to flat winners, Friends For Ever (also a successful Hurdler) and Sulastar, and to a winner in Austria. NH FLAT r1 p0. FLAT r1 p0. NH '91/2 r7 p1 (3rd); pulled up 4; inc Sells. P-t-P/HUNT CH '94/6 and '98/9 r26 w1 (Maiden) p6 (4 2nds; and last of 3 twice); unseated 5, pulled up 1, and slipped up 1. Only successful once in 32 Points, and usually prefers to settle for a place of which he has gleaned 11. A safe jumper, though the owner is prone to fall off, but always finishes his races weakly, and likely to have to settle for a single success. *N. Benstead — Kent & Surrey Bloodhounds (Richard Parker)*. 36 (Cl), 126 (R), 285 (CR), 306 (R), 575 (R), 705 (R), 980 (R).

ROYAL SEASON ..9-3.. 9 ch.g. Vital Season — Royal Buskins (White Prince USA) up. Dam, sister to Princess Buskins (*qv*), won 12 Points (inc 6 Opens, one 4m; and 4-timer) and 2nd 7. P-t-P '98/9 r3 p0; 7th, pulled up 1, and unseated 1. Has a great pedigree, but the breeder soon got shot of him, and has failed to get round in four attempts for the current yard. Prominent when unseating twice '99/00, but absent since February this year, and clearly troubled. *Mrs D. Rowell — Kent & Surrey Bloodhounds*. 209 (OMa), 309 (OMa).

ROYAL SEGOS ..8-0.. 14 b.g. High Line — Segos (Runnymede) p4pp. Tall workmanlike brother to Highland Bounty, and half-brother to Wilkins and a flat winner. Dam won at 8f. NH FLAT r2 p0. NH '91 and '93/6 r16 p4 (Hdle and 3 Chses). P-t-P/HUNT CH '97/8 (for Mr A.J. Baillie) r12 w2 (Maiden and Restricted) p1 (2nd in Hunt Ch); pulled up 1, ran out 1, and unseated 1. Began his Pointing career with a double, but steadily went downhill, and plods badly now. Made a safe conveyance for Stuart Shaw, but failed to beat a rival when tailed off on each occasion in 2000. *S. Shaw — Meynell & S. Staffs*. 592 (Cf), 901 (M), 1128 (Cf), 1267 (I).

ROYAL SILK ..—.. 8 b.g. Brotherly (USA) — Surplus Silk (Redundant) Rp. Leggy unfurnished. Dam pulled up 2 and fell in Points. If he has ever been schooled it was certainly not apparent, and ran out at the fourth, and pulled up at the sixth after starting slowly, jumping very badly, and quickly becoming well tailed off. A severe warning to connections from the stewards would not have gone amiss. *Mrs E. Weaver — Clifton-on-Teme.* 865 (CfMa), 1412 (OMa).

ROYAL SURPRISE ..9-10.. 14 b.g. Royal Fountain — Miss Craigie (New Brig) upp36432. Workmanlike short-backed half-brother to Jack Sun (*qv*). NH '92/4 and (blinkered last 3) r15 p4 (3rds, distant last once). P-t-P/HUNT CH '95/6 and '98/9 (for Mrs S. Hook, Mrs Spence & Mrs Small) r28 w2 (Maiden and Restricted) p11 (7 2nds, inc Hunt Ch); unseated 2, and pulled up 3. A secure jumper, but desperately one-paced, and placed nine times as often as he wins. Made the ideal schoolmaster for Louise Ingram, and gave her a couple of decent rides, but beaten a minimum of 16 lengths in 2000, and it would be surprising if he could win again. *Mrs A. & Miss L. Ingram — E. Essex (Louise Ingram).* 95 (L), 240 (L), 319 (L), 552 (I), 609 (I), 840 (I), 935 (M), 1185 (I).

ROYAL SWEEP ..—§§.. 12 b.g. Swing Easy (USA) — Lillylee Lady (USA) (Shecky Greene USA) u4. Half-brother to Jolification (*qv*). P-t-P '97 r5 p0 (refused 2, fell/unseated 2, and ran out 1). NH '98/9 (for Dr P. Pritchard) r7 p0; inc pulled up 4, fell 2. Sent off no shorter than 100-1 in seven outings under Rules, and failed to finish in all four Chases (at least the trainer who also rode him could administer first-aid to himself) including a spill at a water-jump. Got round without mishap for the first time over fences in his Members, but was hopelessly tailed off, and even an unregistered hunter sped past him on the run-in. *E.H. Lord — Berkeley.* 892 (OMa), 1489 (M).

RUBEN JAMES (IRE) ..8-4.. 9 b.g. Jolly Jake (NZ) — Lily Of Dunmoon (Prince Regent FR) pppp6. Half-brother to Jack The Td (IRE). IRISH P-t-P '97/9 r10 p2 (inc 38f 3rd); pulled up 3, and fell. Bought Ascot, June for 3000. Blinkered on his last two attempts and finally got round when beaten about 25 lengths, but tends to stop quickly, suggesting that there is something badly wrong with him. *Mr & Mrs J.F. Symes — Cotley (John Symes).* 213 (CfMa), 540 (OMa), 738 (OMa), 880 (OMa), 1100 (OMa).

RUBIAN PRINCESS ..7-0.. 6 b.m. Kinglet — Once Bitten (Brave Invader USA) 874. Half-sister to Carrick Lanes, Miss Vagabond and Cautious Leader, and to NH flat winner, Celtic Park. Dam won 2m1f Sell Hdle. Bought Malvern, May for 2800. A long way behind and with just one horse in her wake so far, but at least managed to negotiate 56 fences without mishap, and there will certainly be plenty of worse Welsh maidens around in 2001. *E.J. Pearse — Curre (Steve Lloyd).* 1223 (2m4fOMa), 1406 (OMa), 1618 (OMa).

PLATE 110   1136 Tiverton Staghounds Hunt Members: Ru Bidding (R. Emmett), pu, is ahead of Another Bula (Miss S. Robinson), 5th, with Master Kiwi (G. Richards), 2nd, and the partly hidden Valnau (C. White), 1st, in close attendance   PHOTO: Tim Holt

RU BIDDING ..—.. 7 br.m. Teamster — Sdenka Princess (Prince De Galles) pppp. Appeared to be of no account when tailed off and pulled up at odds of 33-1 upwards. *Mrs D. Sampson — Tiverton Stag (Sarah Kittow)*. 255 (R), 563 (CfMa), 1136 (M), 1307 (OMa).

RUBON PRINCE (IRE) ..10-0.. 10 ch.g. Kambalda — Oh Clare (Laurence O) 1S0. Small neat half-brother to River Clare. NH FLAT Sept '97 r2 p0. NH '97/9 r27 p10 (inc 8 Chses); 4th 6. NH Mar '00 r1 p0 (11th in 4m Amat rdrs Ch: *lost tch ½way, t.o*). Slow and error-prone under Rules, but had so much experience and so many placings behind him that he was virtually certain to be good enough to score in minor Points, and although he missed out on the opportunity of a Maiden he kept going steadily to collect a Restricted in softish at Wetherby. Much more gainfully employed in Chases, where he can plod round to collect a couple of hundred pounds merely for finishing a remote fourth. *N.B. Mason — Middleton*. 173 (R), 375 (Cf).

RUBY ROSA ..—.. 9 b.m. Idiot's Delight — Whey (Sallust) p. Small neat. Dam won at 5f. NH FLAT '97 r2 p0. NH '97/8 r3 p0. P-t-P '99 r3 p0 (5th, and pulled up 2). Showed some speed in all her starts in '99, but appears not to stay, and only managed to visit the racecourse once this year when tried in a visor. *Miss A. Barnett — Ludlow (Geoff Evans)*. 891 (OMa).

RUDDY MARVEL LASS ..9-0.. 8 ch.m. Gunner B — Corbitt Coins (Deep Run) pp. Rangy half-sister to Emerald Queen and Derring Run. Dam won a 3m1f Hdle, but was demoted to 2nd after beating Bonanza Boy a short head. P-t-P '99 r6 p2 (3rds, of 4 once); 8th, fell/unseated 2, and pulled up 1. Bred to stay all day, but has shown little stamina on the evidence to date, and her best performance came over 2m4f last year. Exhausted when pulled up twice after showing speed for two miles in 2000, and stops so quickly that she must be faulty. Absent since February. *T. Evans — Enfield Chace*. 98 (OMa), 322 (CfMa).

RUECASTLE ..8-11.. 13 b.g. Politico (USA) — Topazolite (Hessonite) 5. Smallish workmanlike. Dam was a poor Pointer. NH '95 and '98/9 r10 p0 (pulled up 2, and fell 1). P-t-P '96/9 (for Mr W.G. Reed) r11 w1 (Maiden) p1 (remote 3rd of 4); pulled up 4, and fell 1. Survived mistakes at the final three fences when making all at Tranwell in '96, but has only beaten three rivals in 16 other races over fences, and remains very moderate and lightly raced. *Miss J. Hutchinson — Haydon*. 1602 (2m4f110yH).

RUE DE FORT ..8-6§.. 13 gr.g. Belfort (FR) — Royal Huntress (Royal Avenue) pprp3. Tall light-bodied half-brother to Chasing Gold, to flat and jumping winner, Royal Craftsman, and to Hurdles winner, Just Hush. Dam won 2 Hdles, 2m2f-2m6f. FLAT r5 p0. NH '92 r2 p0 (tailed off both, inc Sell). P-t-P/HUNT CH '94/5 and '97/9 r20 w1 (Maiden) p6 (5 2nds); pulled up 11. Made most when successful for the only time in '94, but has always struggled to see out the trip, and managed relatively few outings due to leg trouble. Remains quite speedy, and often has to be taken to post early, but does not stay much beyond two miles now, and only beat Final Option in 2000. *Mrs M. Teague — Carms*. 347 (R), 483 (R), 642 (M), 832 (R), 1078 (Cf).

RUFF ACCOUNT ..8-0.. 14 b.g. Ruffo (USA) — Dutch Account VII (unknown) 6. Compact owner-bred. P-t-P '95/7 r12 w2 (Maiden and Members) p2 (3rds); pulled up 5. Showed the benefit of a soft-palate operation when winning twice in '96, but ailing again when only able to run five times since, and only resurfaced to give Emma Brader some experience in 2000. *R.G. Brader — Middleton*. 996 (M).

RULE OUT THE REST ..9-13.. 10 ch.g. Scallywag — Saucy Eater (Saucy Kit) 2p. Tall strong-topped attractive brother to One Boy (*qv*). NH FLAT '95/6 (for T. Tate) r3 p0. NH '96/7 and Sep '99 (bought for 1700) r8 w1 (2m6f Hdle) p1 (3rd). Won a five-runner three-finisher Hurdle on firmish in October '96, but has managed a mere seven outings since. Finished 20 lengths second in a sub-standard Open at Market Rasen, and was hopelessly outclassed in the Land Rover Final two months later. Should be looking for the simplest opportunities. *Mrs S. Horner-Harker — Hurworth*. 441 (O), 1532 (3m1fH).

RUM REBEL ..10-2.. 10 br.g. Silly Prices — Rebrona (Rebel Prince) 3824. Strong-topped scopey homebred brother to Billy Buoyant. Dam, half-sister to Sarona Smith (*qv* '00 Annual), won 2 Points (slowly-run affairs, on jockeyship), but was tailed out last or pulled up in all but one of her 14 other races. NH FLAT r3 p0. NH '96 r1 p0 (pulled up). P-t-P '97/9 r9 r4 p2 (Maiden and Restricted) p0 (last, pulled up 3, and unseated 1). Twice successful on easy ground last season when there was no plausible reason behind his inconsistent performances, but failed to oblige when the money was down in 2000, and twice beaten when significantly supported. Also punted from 8s to 3s once when unseating in '98, and has certainly become a good friend to the Northern bookies. Stays well, but seems quite excitable, and gets few opportunities. *F.T. Walton — Border (Jimmy Walton)*. 183 (CCf), 493 (Cf), 717 (Cf), 1078 (Cf).

RUN FOR THE MILL ..9-9.. 9 b.g. Primitive Rising (USA) — Brydonna (Good Times ITY) u165up. Strong compact. NH FLAT '96/7 r3 p0. NH '97/8 r6 p2 (3rds). P-t-P '99 r4 p2 (2nds, of 3 once); and fell/unseated 2. Highly excitable, and takes a fierce hold, but benefited from the incredibly slow gallop set in his Members when sprinting clear in the closing stages. Does not stay under normal circumstances, and Michael Morley sometimes forgets to slip the reins and falls off. Has been mounted outside the paddock, and taken to post early. Wears a cross-noseband. *R. Morley — Derwent.* 51 (OMa), 393 (M), 689 (R), 807 (R), 1028 (R), 1230 (R).

RUNNING FRAU ..9-13.. 14 ch.m. Deep Run — Suzi Hegi (Mon Capitaine) p5p. Lengthy unfurnished half-sister to Short Circuit (IRE), and to Irish Pointing winner, Smokey Lonesome; and is dam of Irish Pointing winner, Lord Kilpatrick (IRE). Dam won 2 Irish Points. IRISH P-t-P '91/3 r8 w1 (Maiden) p0; pulled up 2, and fell/unseated 4. P-t-P '96/9 (for late Sir Sanderson Temple) r29 w2 (Clubs) p4 (3 3rds, last once); unseated 5, refused 1, and pulled up 2. Previously capable, but a difficult tactical ride, and suffered from feeble handling in Points until '99. Soon labouring in the new yard, and never looked likely to produce the strong finish she once had in her armoury. *K. Thomas — V. of Lune H.* 533 (I), 1152 (I), 1366 (I).

RUNNING FREE (IRE) ..9-12.. 7 b.g. Waajib — Selchis (Main Reef) f45. Workmanlike half-brother to Irish NH flat and flat winner, Cochis Run. IR 6800f, 13,000y. FLAT (for M. Featherston-Godley) r17 w2 (12-14f, inc Sell) p2. NH '98 (for K. Bailey, bought for 13,000) r5 p0. Sold Doncaster, Nov '98 for 500. Showed good speed in all three Points, but rapidly ran out of steam when beaten about 16 lengths in the final two, and currently seems to find it impossible to get the trip. Matters are complicated for him by his flat wins in '97. Sometimes wore headgear in previous starts. Very lightly raced now, and absent since mid-March. *J.A. Moore — S. Durham.* 49 (C), 186 (O), 623 (Cf).

RUNNING MUTE ..9-11.. 7 b.g. Roscoe Blake — Rose Albertine (Record Token) 45532. Home-bred half-brother to Tinafoil. Has impressed in his jumping for a novice, and came closest to success when one length third. A disappointing favourite next time, but possibly found the ground too firm. It is rather surprising that he has not scored already, but is surely going to do so before much longer. *J.E.M. Vestey — Jedforest (Simon Shirley-Beavan).* 363 (CfMa), 500 (2m4fOMa), 1153 (OMa), 1367 (OMa), 1480 (OMa).

RUN TO THE GLEN ..—.. 6 b.m. Bold Fox — Glen Maye (Maystreak) pR2p. Half-sister to Maybeiwood. Dam won 2 Members matches and placed 3 for the Bartons, and previously won 3 2m Sell Hdles (one on a technical disqualification) and placed 10 (inc 3rd in flat race and Ch). Has not gone any sort of gallop so far, and was two fences behind after two miles at Lydstep, but kept tottering on, and was eventually rewarded with second after multiple defections. *Mrs M.E. Barton — Pembs.* 348 (CfMa), 649 (CfMa), 834 (OMa), 951 (OMa).

RUN WITH JOY (IRE) ..8-4.. 10 b.g. Sharrood (USA) — Durun (Run The Gantlet USA) p3u. Lengthy brother to flat winner, Durunroo, and half-brother to Durbo, to flat and jumping winner, Dwadme, and to 4 winners (one abroad). Dam won 3 flat, 10-12f. Grandam, Duboff, won 11 flat, 7-10f, inc Sun Chariot Stakes and Child Stakes. FLAT r4 p0. NH '95 (blinkered 1) and '97 r12 p3 (2nd in Mdn Hdle, and 3rds in Chses); inc Sells. P-t-P '96 and '98/9 r11 p0 (last 4, pulled up 6, and slipped up 1). Capable of running prominently, but does not stay anywhere near three miles, and has never beaten a rival in 14 Points. Busy in his first season over hurdles, but has only once managed more than four outings in a year otherwise. *J.H. Berwick — S. Devon (Mrs S. Berwick).* 406 (R), 556 (M), 929 (Cnr).

RUPERT (U) ..—.. 8 b.g. Rupertino — Purple Lady (unknown) u. A hunter taking on two racehorses who included What A Hand in his Members, and the bookies offering of 10-1 was a swindle. *D. Line — Staff College.* 592 (M).

RUPERTS CHOICE (IRE) ..10-4.. 9 ch.g. Phardante (FR) — Miss Nancy (Giolla Mear) 51133p71. Workmanlike half-brother to The Peeler (IRE). P-t-P/HUNT CH '97/9 r11 w5 (inc 3m Hunt Ch) p2 (2nds); last pair 2, pulled up 1, unseated 1. NH Mar '00 r1 p1 (3rd in 3m110y Ch: *hdwy 12, poor 2nd 2 out, blun last, lost 2nd run-in*). A useful novice when completing a courageous five-timer in '98, but fully awry last year in common with many of his stablemates. Returned to form with the aid of blinkers in 2000, and responded to a particularly vigorous ride from Alex Harvey when successful over 3m7f at Folkestone on his final appearance. Suited by a sound surface, and much less effective with cut in the ground. Sure to win again, but still prone to get left behind, and sometimes declines to pick up the bridle so strong handling is essential. *H.D. Hill & C.H. Sporborg — Puckeridge (Christopher Sporborg).* 10 (O), 92 (Cf), 262 (MO), 415 (O), 938 (3m4fO), 1338 (4m1fH), 1539 (3m7fH).

RUPERT'S PRINCESS (IRE) ..—§.. 9 b.m. Prince Rupert (FR) — Llanelli (Welsh Saint) ppp0. Sturdy half-sister to a winner in Sweden. IR 14,000y. FLAT r19 w1 (5f) p5 (2nds, Sell final). NH '96 r4 p0 (8th, last, and pulled up 2, inc Sells). NH Apr '00 r2 p0 (pulled up in 2m1f Nov Hdle: *prom, drvn 3, sn lost tch, t.o & pu 3 out*; and 10th in 2m3f Amat HCap Hdle: *t.o frm 4*). A slow and reluctant jumper who soon tailed herself off in Points before pulling up after a mile in both. Won on her racecourse debut and was second in her next four outings (to a maximum of 6f), but sometimes tried blinkered subsequently. It is impossible to fathom out why anybody could be bothered to race her in 2000, particularly in Hurdles. *Miss L.K. Hilder — V.W.H. (Ted Haynes).* 1016 (Cf), 1205 (MO).

RURAL GOSSIP ..—.. 8 ch.g. Henbit (USA) — Rose Dally (Le Bavard FR) puf. Owner-bred. A hard ride at present, and did not get further than halfway without mishap. *Mrs J.M. Worthington — Sir W.W. Wynn's.* 906 (CfMa), 1196 (OMa), 1526 (OMa).

RUSHAWAY ..—.. 10 b.g. Robellino (USA) — Brush Away (Ahonoora) 4ppRp. Small half-brother to 4 winners, including Hurdles winners, Formidable Partner, Go Tally-Ho and Mr Vincent (latter two also won on flat). FLAT (for R. Hannon) r5 p1 (8/ 3rd). NH '95 and '97 (for Miss C. Johnsey) r3 p2 (2nds, inc of 4 beaten a distance). Has always looked very hard to train, and ended a thoroughly miserable season in Points by pulling up lame at Lifton (was collected by the horse ambulance). *H.W. Ford & S. Searle — Torrington F. (Andrew Congdon).* 147 (OMa), 407 (OMa), 559 (R), 1099 (OMa), 1521 (CfMa).

RUSHENOVA ..8-0.. 8 br.g. Rushmere — Owenova (Owen Anthony) rs. Small owner-bred half-brother to Novasun (*qv*). P-t-P '98/9 r10 p0 (last, pulled up 8, and fell 1). An appalling beast who has only got round once (when 39 lengths last) in 12 Points, and shows no sign of reforming. Absent since slipping up on the flat at Parham in February. *J.W. Elliott — Surrey U. (Richard Parker).* 131 (OMa), 309 (OMa).

RUSHES LANE ..8-5.. 7 b.g. Gargoor — Star Of Parnassus (Star Appeal) 65. Strong compact half-brother to Star Traveller (won Chasing since Pointing). Sire, by Kris, only managed 3 unplaced outings on the flat for Neville Callaghan (Claiming class), and looked unsound. P-t-P '99 r4 p0 (last, pulled up 2, and refused 1). Wobbled to his third consecutive completion on his final start, when amazingly punted from 33s to 16-1, but beaten a minimum of 35 lengths, and his only chance of success is to become an equine version of Vanessa Feltz. *Mrs P. O'Connor — Fernie (Liz Powell).* 123 (OMa), 372 (CfMa).

RUSHING AGAIN ..10-3.. 6 br.g. Rushmere — Saunders Grove (IRE) (Sunyboy) p1. Dam pulled up in a Point in '98. Grandam, Beeches View, was 3rd in 4 Points, and is half-sister to 4 Pointers, including Rushing Wild (*qv* '93 Annual). Pulled up at halfway on his debut at Larkhill, but returned there seven weeks later to win a 17-runner Maiden which threw up three subsequent scorers from the five who finished behind. Backed from eights to threes and did the job well, and may have scope for plenty more improvement. *J.A. Keighley — Blackmore & Sparkford V. (Richard Barber).* 455 (OMa), 1131 (OMa).

RUSH 'N TEAR ..10-1.. 10 b.g. Rushmere — May Singer (Record Run) p2p. Sturdy compact. Dam is an unraced half-sister to Moze Tidy (*qv* '98 Annual), who is also by Rushmere. Grandam, Church Belle, won Farmers race and 3m Hdle and placed total of 5 for Mrs W. Hawkins. P-t-P/HUNT CH '98/9 r6 p2 (last of 2; and 3rd in Hunt Ch); last pair 2, and fell/unseated 2. Has made the frame in all five completions, and is quite speedy, but can be erratic at the fences, and stands very few outings. Gives the impression that three miles is stretching his stamina, but would be better off in Maidens (has only contested three). *Mrs A.A. Hawkins — Crawley & Horsham.* 309 (OMa), 711 (M), 800 (3m110yH).

PLATE 111   647 Carmarthenshire Restricted (Div 2): Rusnetto (G. Lewis), 1st, leads from Out On The Town (James Tudor), ran out   PHOTO: Alun Sedgmore

RUSNETTO (IRE) ..10-4.. 11 br.g. Torus — Moynetto (Bustineto) 13p24211. Workmanlike brother to Irish NH flat winner, Blazing Arrow. IRISH P-t-P '96 and '99 r8 w1 (6 plus Mdn) p2 (3rds); pulled up 3. NH '98 (for R. Alner, Irish owned) r2 p1 (3rd in Ch — blinkered). Began his latest campaign with a somewhat unconvincing victory in a two-finisher Restricted in which the two length leader ran the wrong side of a Hurdle approaching the last, and then experienced something of a lull, but really blossomed in May, and after failing by a head to hold Roman Gale he completed a double at the last two meetings in the Welsh Area. Wears a visor and can sometimes look as if he needs a lot of pursuading, and connections did well with him. Acts on any going. *Mrs C.L. Rogers — Carms (Debbie Hamer).* 647 (R), 944 (I), 1053 (O), 1227 (I), 1299 (I), 1449 (I), 1613 (I), 1657 (O).

RUSSIAN CASTLE (IRE) ..10-0§.. 12 b.g. Carlingford Castle — Pampered Russian (Deep Run) p5p35. Workmanlike compact brother to Chasing winner, Castle Red (IRE). NH '93/8 r40 w4 (3m3f-3m6f Chses, 3 at Sedgefield) p15 (inc 7 Hdles). P-t-P '99 (for Mr E.H. Crow) r1 p0 (refused). Stays forever, and had a perfectly respectable record under Rules, but only once better than last in Points, and gives the impression that something is wrong with him. Not disgraced when third at Whittington where the long track and sound surface were ideal, and still inclined to pull hard, but Alan McKay seemed unable to control him fully. Could yet surprise in a poor race when conditions are right. *Mrs L. Williamson — Flint & Denbigh.* 530 (O), 779 (O), 961 (O), 1151 (O), 1409 (O).

RUSSIAN PRINCE (IRE) ..8-12.. 6 b.g. Soviet Lad (USA) — Sweet Goodbye (Petorius) 49f. Lengthy unfurnished half-brother to 2 flat winners (one in Belgium), including Stolen Kiss. NH FLAT Spr '99 r3 p0. NH '99 (for J. Curtis) r1 p0 (tailed off in Hdle). Made one bad error per race in Maidens, and although he has show some speed he cannot be trusted until the jumping errors are sorted out. *S.R. Bolton — Holderness.* 507 (CMa), 793 (CfMa), 1235 (OMa).

RUSTIC GENT (IRE) ..9-0§.. 13 gr.g. Rusticaro (FR) — Namur (Amber Rama USA) 7pp. Lengthy half-brother to a French jumping winner, and to two successful Hurdlers, including Out Of Range. IRISH NH FLAT '92/3 r2 p0. IRISH NH '92/3 r9 w1 (2m Ch) p1 (3rd). NH '93/9 r419 w3 (2m Chses, inc Sell) p4; pulled up 3. P-t-P/HUNT CH '98/9 r10 p1 (remote last of 3); last 2, pulled up 5, refused 1, and unseated 1. Gained his only success over the minimum trip, but does not stay in Points, and has yet to beat a rival in nine attempts. Jumps slowly, and shows no zest any more, and not worth bothering with again. Often wore headgear in the past. *S.T. Lewis — Cotswold V.F.* 667 (Cf), 895 (MO), 968 (Cf).

RUSTIC REVELRY ..10-5.. 8 b.g. Afzal — Country Festival (Town And Country) 513f4f1R1216. Lengthy unfurnished. Dam, half-sister to Gemini Mist (*qv*), won 2 Points and 3rd (ran to '96). Grandam, Festive Season, won 5 Points and 2nd 2. NH FLAT '98 r3 p0. NH '98 r3 p0. P-t-P/HUNT CH '99 r7 w2 (2m4f Maiden and Restricted) p2 (2nds, of 3 once); last pair 3. Kept incredibly busy in 2000, and was on the go from January to June, but maintained his form remarkably well, and rewarded connections with four wins. Very speedy, and suited by an easy three miles in Points, but ideally suited by a shorter trip in Hunter Chases, and won a weak event over 2m5f at Folkestone on his penultimate start. Remains rather an erratic jumper, but with increased fluency should be able to win again. Tried once in blinkers this year, but fell at the second. *R.H. York — Staff College.* 1 (C), 31 (CI), 130 (CMod), 300 (2m5fH), 459 (2m4f110yH), 634 (C), 785 (I), 981 (O), 1108 (C), 1335 (2m4f110yH), 1540 (2m5fH), 1646 (3m4fH).

RUSTY BLADE ..9-0.. 12 b.g. Broadsword (USA) — Sea Sand (Sousa) 0787. Close-coupled brother to jumping winner, Triggerfish. NH '93/5 and '97/8 r30 w4 (3m Chses, inc £7025 prize; 50-1 once) p7 (5 3rds, beaten short head and neck once). HUNT CH '97 (for Mrs M.I. Nisbet) r2 p1 (3rd in Hunt Ch); and pulled up 1. NH Mar '00 r1 p0 (8th in 3m4f Amat rdrs HCap Ch: *chsd ldrs to ½way, bhnd when blun 13*). A decent top of the ground Chaser in Scotland to '98, but declined rapidly this year, and was only able to beat one rival. Used to enjoy racing at Scone Palace, and won five prizes there. Often needed driving along from an early stage and blinkered latterly under Rules, and regained them on his final start. *Mrs A.F. Tullie — Berwicks (Swannee Haldane).* 89 (3m1fH), 225 (3mH), 686 (3m1fH).

RUSTY BRIDGE ..10-6.. 14 b.g. Rustingo — Bridge Ash (Normandy) 42416. Well-made half-brother to jumping winner and stablemate, Derring Bridge. Dam won 4 Hdles, 2m4f-3m, and 6 Chses, 2m-4m4f, and placed 15 (also disqualified from 2nd in Open) for Ivor Johnson. NH '94/6 and '99 r19 p4 (3rds). P-t-P/HUNT CH '92/9 r62 w7 (inc 5 Hunt Chses, 3m-4m2f110y) p27 (Hunt Chses to 4m3f; 12 2nds); failed to finish 7 (on floor 4). Amazingly tough when making 59 appearances '94/7, but raced much more sparingly since, and was gaining his first success for three years when making most in the Heythrop our-miler. Usually sets off at the head of affairs, and regularly drops the bit and loses his place, but Richard Burton did not allow him that luxury at Dunthrop, and the old horse gamely answered his every call. Treats sub-4m events as sprints, and half of his wins have come over marathon trips. A grand performer who has never fallen despite crossing somewhere in the region of 1500 fences, and his latest success was one of the seasons highlights. A credit to connections. *I.K. Johnson — Radnor & W. Herefords (Sue Johnson).* 222 (3m1f110yH), 468 (3m1f110yH), 683 (3mH), 1015 (4mO), 1338 (4m1fH).

RUSTY BUCK ..10-1.. 9 b.g. Buckley — Rusty To Reign (General Ironside) u51p14. Compact quite attractive brother to Iron Buck, and half-brother to Scraptastic and Rusty King. Dam was 2nd in 2 Points. P-t-P '98/9 r11 w2 (Maiden and Members) p2 (last of 3 once); last 2, fell 1, and pulled up 4. Ended '99 with a wide margin double, and added two more wins to his tally this year, but often a law unto himself, and only goes when he wants to. Yet to win anything more grand than a Restricted, and may not be able, or willing, to raise his rating. A thorough stayer, and suited by plenty of cut in the ground, but future performances depend entirely on his mood. *Mr & Mrs C.M. Burleigh — Radnor & W. Herefords (Clive Davies).* 336 (R), 483 (R), 745 (R), 987 (Cf), 1271 (M), 1449 (I).

RUSTY FELLOW ..10-4.. 8 b.g. Rustingo — Sallisses (Pamroy) 43p1254. Plain lengthy half-brother to Maggies Brother and Sallioko. Dam won a Point and a 3m1f Hunt Ch and placed total of 7 for late Ray Shail. P-t-P/HUNT CH '95/9 r31 w3 (Maiden, Restricted and Intermediate) p10 (5 2nds, distant once; and inc distant 3rd twice; and inc 2 Hunt Chses); failed to finish 12 (refused 3, and on floor 7). An out-and-out-stayer who has to be driven along from pillar to post, but despite not winning anything better than an Intermediate has given some excellent displays in much better company '99/00. Got involved in a rare set-to with Rusty Bridge in the Heythrop four-miler, and it was a pity that one of them had to lose, but he could not quite match his rival on the run to the final fence. Has never jumped fluently, and in the circumstances has done well to complete as often as he has, but worth persevering with over regulation fences in the hope that one day he might get lucky. Has been ridden in spurs. *Mrs G.M. Shail — Ledbury (Roy Shail).* 149 (3mH), 386 (3m1f110yH), 683 (3mH), 890 (M), 1015 (4mO), 1338 (4m1fH), 1592 (4m2fH).

RUSTY FLAME ..9-5.. 8 ch.g. Rustingo — Amethea (True Song) 47fpp. Leggy light-framed half-brother to Mr Greengrass. Dam, very temperamental, won Maiden and placed 4 (inc 2 Hdles and Ch). NH FLAT '98 r1 p0 (well tailed off). NH '98 r1 p0 (pulled up in Hdle). P-t-P '99 r5 p0 (pulled up 3, and fell/unseated 2). Often makes the running, but usually fails to stay, and on the one occasion he was still galloping with any purpose in the closing stages he fell when his Members looked in the bag. Well supported when a chance ride for Julian Pritchard on his final start, but dropped out quickly having led for two miles. Clearly handles cornfields, but has yet to show a preference on normal terrain. *Mrs C.M. Collins — Monmouths (Reg Brown).* 337 (CfMa), 491 (CfMa), 740 (M), 925 (2mH), 1093 (OMa).

RUSTY KING ..—.. 7 ch.g. Rakaposhi King — Rusty To Reign (General Ironside) Rp. Owner-bred half-brother to Rusty Buck (*qv*). Has made mistakes and looks very green so far, but gives the impression that he can probably win a Maiden eventually if gaining competent handling. *Mr & Mrs C.M. Burleigh — Radnor & W. Herefords (Clive Davies).* 865 (CfMa), 1091 (OMa).

RUTH'S BOY (IRE) ..10-2.. 12 br.g. Lord Ha Ha — Club Belle (Al Sirat USA) 2. Leggy unfurnished. NH FLAT r1 p0. NH '94/5 & '97/9 r23 w2 (2m5f-3m1f Plumpton Chses) p8 (inc 6 2nds). P-t-P '96/7 (for late Mr T.A. Forster) r12 w2 (Maiden and Restricted) p5 (4 2nds); pulled up 1, fell 2. Won nine prizes under Rules on sound surfaces for Alex Johnson after Pointing '96/7, but was no world-beater, and did all his winning at Plumpton. No match for Noyan at Folkestone on his only appearance this year, but retains much of his ability, and could still win Points in 2001. A bold jumper, but lacks any acceleration. *Mrs A.E. Johnson — Thurlow.* 1538 (3m2fH).

RYDER CUP (IRE) ..9-12.. 9 b.g. Orchestra — Vaghe Stelle (ITY) (Looking For) p3p14p3. Tall workmanlike. IRISH P-t-P '96 r3 w1 (4-y-o Maiden) p0; fell 1. NH '97 r3 p2 (2nds, 12-15l over 2m4f-3m). P-t-P '98 r6 w1 (Restricted) p0; pulled up 4, and fell 1. Only able to complete the course once in his first season in English Points when successful at Larkhill, but forced to miss the following year, and apart from another modest win on Salisbury Plain has performed like a horse with a problem on his return. Returned at 20-1 in his latest win which was a fair reflection of his chance, and likely to be a similar price if he goes in again. *G.C. Maundrell — Tedworth (Claire Weller).* 36 (Cl), 96 (I), 263 (I), 453 (Cf), 737 (I), 883 (Cf), 1279 (M).

RYDERS WELLS ..9-7§.. 14 gr.g. Warpath — The Lathkill (Clear River) 37pp7. Compact half-brother to Will Do My Best and Rufus Boy. Dam won 4 Points and placed 3 (inc 2nd in 2 Hdles) for Teddy Astley-Arlington. P-t-P/HUNT CH '93/9 r43 w4 (up to Confined) p12 (7 2nds, inc Hunt Ch); failed to finish 19 (on floor 6). Usually comes off the bridle on the way to post these days, and despite Simon Walkers' best efforts shows absolutely no zest when under way. Has dogged it in his last 16 attempts, and seems unlikely to change his ways at 14. Wears blinkers. *E.F. Astley-Arlington — Blankney (Margaret Morris).* 47 (Cl), 115 (CCf), 229 (Cf), 796 (O), 1434 (3m110yH).

RYE RUM (IRE) ..8-12.. 10 br.g. Strong Gale — Eimers Pet (Paddy's Stream) 6f5b360. Very small neat half-brother to NH flat winner, Valhalla (IRE). NH FLAT '96 r1 p0 (19th of 20). NH '96/9 r11 p2 (1st 2nd); pulled up 10. P-t-P '98 r6 p3 (2 2nds); last 2, and pulled up 1. Ran in headgear when pulled up in 10 of 12 outings under Rules, but has managed to get into the money on five occasions, and does possess some ability. Frequently given very negative rides in Points, and out of his depth in Hunter Chases, but could oblige in Maiden company providing stamina is not at a premium. *J.W.F. Aynsley — W. Percy.* 45 (OMa), 363 (CfMa), 424 (R), 719 (CfMa), 1163 (OMa), 1345 (2m5fH), 1445 (3m1fH).

RYMEROLE ..—.. 11 ch.g. Rymer — Hayburnwyke (Pretty Form) pp. Big owner-bred half-brother to Roscoe Boy, Herman Blake, Conbrook, Layedback Jack and Naughty Nellie. P-t-P '96/8 (for Mr C.D. Dawson) r4 p1 (2nd of 3); and pulled up 3. 20 lengths second of three over 2m5f on his racecourse debut in '96, but pulled up in just five outings since, and seems physically disabled. *Lord Yarborough — Brocklesby (Mark Bennison).* 798 (OMa), 1220 (OMa).

RYMING CUPLET ..—.. 16 b.g. Rymer — Leisure Bay (Jock Scot) pp. Workmanlike hobdayed half-brother to Ekaytee (dam of Vercheny *qv*) and Celtic Leisure. Dam, placed in 3 flat, won 2m Nov Hdle and placed 4 for Gerald Tanner. P-t-P/HUNT CH '91/7 (for Mr G. Tanner) r38 w16 (inc 5 Hunt Chses, 2m5f-3m2f, Ladies, and 4 Opens, and inc 4-timer '93, and hat-trick '94) p10 (6 2nds, of 3 twice and inc 3 3rds in Hunt Chses); failed to finish 9 (fell 1). A useful performer '92/6 when successful on 15 occasions, but never looked happy when winning just one of six appearances the following year, and presumably only brought out of retirement to give Ben Trickey more experience in 2000. *Mrs E.C. Trickey — Devon & Somerset (Mike Trickey).* 727 (O), 929 (Cnr).

RYMIN THYNE ..8-12.. 12 ch.g. Good Thyne (USA) — Mrs Popple (Deep Run) p436. Good-bodied half-brother to Irish Pointing winner, No One's Perfect. P-t-P/HUNT CH '95/6 and '98/9 (for Mr R.J. Myram) r8 w1 (Maiden) p3 (2 2nds, last once, and last of 3); and pulled up 4. Won gamely at Howick in '98, and probably could have achieved a lot more, but has stood very few outings, and 2000 was his busiest season to date. Made errors under Dave Mansell once, but beaten little more than three lengths at Bonvilston subsequently, and is still prepared to try. Deserves another success, but age might defy him. *G. Roberts — Monmouths (Shirley Farthing).* 683 (3mH), 864 (R), 1453 (R), 1615 (R).

SABRE KING ..10-5.. 13 ch.g. Broadsword (USA) — King's Lavender (King's Troop) r4u2p1. Strong half-brother to Finkin (dam of Chabby Thoughts *qv* '99 Annual), Two Kings and Kintino. Dam won Maiden and 3rd for Jeff Tredwell. P-t-P '94/8 r19 w3 (Maiden, Restricted and PPORA Intermediate) p4 (3 2nds); failed to finish 12 (fell/unseated 4, and carried out 1). A funny old horse who on his day is still capable of maintaining a strong gallop, but has become cantankerous and just as likely to dig his toes in and not start at all. Finished well clear of the rest when a highly creditable seond to Cittadino at Garthorpe, and battled willingly for Tash McKim to get up near the finish to beat Ardeal on a return visit. Only able to stand light campaigns, and ended '98 lame, so connections have done really well to get him back in such fine shape. Wears blinkers. *J. Tredwell — Grafton.* 216 (Cnr), 218 (L), 512 (L), 869 (L), 1415 (Cf), 1588 (I).

SACRIFICE ..9-9.. 6 b.g. Arctic Lord — Kellyann (Jellaby) 5p1. Dam, half-sister to Enchanted Man (*qv* '98 Annual), won 2m1f Hdle and 3m Ch. Performed creditably on his debut, but could not justify favouritism next time. Possibly suited by the reduction in trip when making amends over 2m4f at up ton, and has done well to score as a five-year-old. Should be stronger at six, and likely to be thereabouts in Restricteds. *M.J. Cornish & D. Jones — Quantock (Tim Long).* 732 (2m4fOMa), 955 (OMa), 1360 (2m4fOMa).

SAFARA ..—.. 7 b.g. Safawan — Avahra (Sahib) pppp. Good-bodied half-brother to Petencore, and to 6 flat winners, including Ruckley (also a successful Hurdler) and Cumbrian Melody, and to a winner in Belgium. Dam won 3 5f races (also won at 6f, but disqualified). NH FLAT '99 (for W. Jenks) r1 p0 (tailed off). Sold Doncaster, Nov for 650. Useless to date, and not a fluent jumper. *R.G. Chapman — Four Burrow.* 724 (CfMa), 850 (R), 1186 (M), 1391 (OMa).

SAFE COTTAGE ..—..§.. 9 b.g. Vouchsafe — Poppet's Cottage (Kinglet) pp7p. Light-framed. Dam, half-sister to Crescent Cottage (*qv* '88 Season Annual) pulled up 7 and unseated in Points for the Cowleys. P-t-P '99 r1 p0 (pulled up). Tailed off in all five attempts, and only once able to finish when last at Mollington. Displays minimum enthusiasm and has no redeeming characteristics. *Mrs D. Cowley — Pytchley (D. Cowley).* 250 (CfMa), 517 (OMa), 786 (OMa), 1420 (OMa).

SAFETY (USA) ..9-10.. 14 b.g. Topsider (USA) — Flare Pass (USA) (Buckpasser) ppfp. Sturdy compact half-brother to several winners here and abroad. FLAT r17 w2 (9-16f, one on all-weather) p1 (2nd); had busiest season at 9. NH '90/6 and '98 r48 w14 (13 Hdles, 2m-2m1f, inc hat-trick, and 2m Ch; inc 3 Sells) p15. P-t-P/HUNT CH '98/9 (for Mrs P.A. White) r9 w3 (2 Members, and Club Nov Rdrs) p2 (2nd in Hunt Ch once); last pair 2, pulled up 1, and fell 1. Formerly a fabulous servant to John White, but a quirky character who needs to dictate, and already seems to be falling apart at the seams as he broke a blood vessel at least once in 2000. Appreciates a sound surface, and an easy three miles. Wears blinkers. Unlikely to stage a revival at 14. *G. Wright & Mrs S.E. Busby — Farmers Bloodhounds (Sue Busby).* 561 (O), 766 (Cnr), 1035 (Cnr), 1441 (Cnr).

SAFFRON FLAME (IRE) ..9-8§.. 11 b.g. Sandalay — Tip The Gold (Harwell) p5664p. Good-bodied attractive half-brother to Trespasser (IRE) and The Other Eye (IRE). P-t-P/HUNT CH '95/9 (for Mr R.J. Rowsell) r18 w4 (up to Intermediate) p7 (4 2nds, of 3 once, and last in Hunt Ch once); pulled up 1, and unseated 1. Won three times in '96, and looked set to graduate to better things, but a grave disappointment since and has only managed to add one more win to his tally from 17 starts. Used as a schoolmaster in the two most recent seasons, and was quite content to plod round at his own pace under Nicola Rudge in 2000. Regained blinkers when ridiculously taken to Stratford on his final appearance. *Mrs A. Rudge — Farmers Bloodhounds (Nicola Rudge).* 195 (O), 335 (L), 613 (L), 860 (L), 1066 (3m2fL), 1443 (3mH).

SAFFRON MOSS ..10-3.. 11 ch.g. Le Moss — Saffron's Daughter (Prince Hansel) 6fpf526p15814. Compact rather light brother to Hurdles winner, Tartan Moss (IRE), and half-brother to Sister Gale and Wolfie's Daughter, and to Hurdles winner, So Pink (IRE) (in Ireland, also won NH flat there). Dam won 3m1f Ch. NH FLAT r2 p0 (40 ran — beat one). P-t-P/HUNT CH '95/9 r37 w3 (inc 3m Hunt Ch, and Open) p11 (6 2nds, last once; and last of 3 twice; inc Hunt Ch); failed to finish 12 (fell/unseated 5, and ran out 1). An out-and-out stayer, and not fazed by deep going, and has thoroughly enjoyed the eccentric conditions available at St Hilary in the past two seasons. Rather indolent these days, but gets on well with Jamie Jukes and galloped on resolutely for the 8min 45s duration of the Pentyrch 4-miler in his latest success. Prone to blunders, and usually manages to get on the floor once a year (didn't in '99 so made up for it in 2000), but generally fiddles his way out of trouble. Has been tried in blinkers unsuccessfully. *T.R.R. Farr — Ystrad Taf Fechan (Shan Farr).* 33 (Cnr), 149 (3mH), 271 (O), 345 (O), 598 (O), 742 (O), 833 (O), 1022 (3mH), 1053 (O), 1226 (O), 1592 (4m2fH), 1614 (4mMO), 1672 (O).

PLATE 112   1672 Torrington Farmers Mens Open: Saffron Moss (J. Jukes), 4th, lands just ahead of Amtrak Express (H. Froud), ur, and Villains Brief (M. Shears), pu   PHOTO: Brian Armstrong

SAGAVILLE (IRE) ..9-9.. 11 b.g. Mister Lord (USA) — Beautiful Glen (Furry Glen) pupf1pp. Workmanlike rangy brother to Beautiful Day (IRE), and half-brother to Chadwick Bank (IRE). NH '96 r3 p0 (last and pulled up in Hdles, and unseated in Ch). P-t-P '97/9 r15 w1 (Maiden) p6 (4 3rds); pulled up 3, and fell 1. Made up to win a long Maiden in holding ground at Flete Park in '98, but took 11 attempts before he found a Restricted on his only completion this year. Usually lacks motivation, and has become error-prone, and will struggle to win again. Seemingly only goes for Sam Holdsworth. *Mr & Mrs R.H. Pedrick — Dart V. & S. Pool H. (Gordon Chambers).* 69 (R), 251 (M), 315 (R), 651 (M), 848 (R), 1044 (4mO), 1516 (I).

SAIL ON BY ..—.. 7 b.m. Lighter — Shadow Play (Busted) pup. Plain sparely-made sister to Maybridge Lady (*qv*). Hinted at ability in her first two attempts, and is probably better than her current form figures might suggest. Worth bearing in mind for a Maiden. *Miss E. Inman — Cottesmore (Tim Tarratt).* 793 (CfMa), 1070 (2m4fOMa), 1290 (OMa).

SAILOR JIM ..9-12.. 14 gr.g. Scallywag — Madge Hill (Spartan General) 77p433458. Tall lengthy brother to Scally Hill and half-brother to Carat Of Gold. Dam won 2 Points and placed 6. Grandam, Alice Roe, won 3 Points in Ireland; and won 9 Ladies and placed 8. NH FLAT '92 r1 p0. NH '92 and '94/7 r29 w4 (2m4f-2m5f Chses) p10. P-t-P/HUNT CH '92/4 and '98/9 r15 w2 (inc 2m4f110y Hunt Ch) p2 (inc Hunt Ch); failed to finish 9 (fell/unseated 3). NH '00 (from P.

Dalton's) r6 p2 (3rds at 2m4f: *ld to 2, outpcd 9, stayed on frm 4 out, nt chall,* and 3m2f: *ld to 2, wknd last*); and 7th in 2m4f110y Ch: *hmpd 2, hdwy 4, ld 8-11, wknd 3 out, t.o*; 7th in 2m4f110y Ch: *ld to 2, mist 6, t.o*; pulled up in 3m Ch: *blun 2, t.o & pu 5*; and 4th in 2m4f110y Ch: *prom, ld 10-4 out, t.o aft*). A former useful front-runner at around 2m4f, but not the force of old since returning to the amateur code, and only once better than last in his latest eight starts. Blinkered once in '99. *W. Tellwright — Meynell & S. Staffs.* 1249 (2m7fH), 1443 (3mH), 1603 (2m6f110yH).

SAINT BENE'T (IRE) ..9-12§.. 13 b.g. Glenstal (USA) — Basilea (FR) (Frere Basile FR) 8p. Small neat half-brother to 2 French flat winners, including Labbasea (IRE). FLAT r22 w1 (9f Clmr) p4. NH '92/5, '97 and '99 r23 w2 (2m-2m1f Sell Hdles) p5. NEWMARKET TOWN PLATE '94 r1 p0 (8th). P-t-P/HUNT CH '94/7 (for Mr G. Prodromou) r25 w2 (inc Open — promoted) p7 (5 2nds, of 3 once; inc 4 Hunt Chses); pulled up 5. Able, when inclined, but lightly raced in recent years, and in no mood to put his best foot forward in 2000 when tailed off last on his only completion. Wears blinkers or a visor. Absent since January, and it would be a miracle were he to consent to try again. *K.J. Walls — Dunston H.* 17 (O), 85 (O).

SAINT JOSEPH ..10-10.. 11 ch.g. Lir — Kimberley Ann (St Columbus) 31114. Small close-coupled home-bred brother to The Kimbler (*qv*). NH '99 r4 p1 (2nd). P-t-P/HUNT CH '96/9 r18 w2 (inc Open) p5 (3 2nds, inc 2 Hunt Chses); pulled up 6, and fell 1. The flagship of Sue Young's scruffy academy. Usually comes from another county when successful, and sensibly declined the frenetic early pace when winning twice at Taunton this year, but has his limitations and could never get to grips with the likes of Cavalero at Cheltenham subsequently. Revels in soft ground, rarely makes a mistake, and is a thoroughly genuine stayer. Broke a blood vessel in '96, and lame once in '99, but has never missed a season and is remarkably durable. Should continue to do well under the right conditions. *B.R.J. Young, Miss S. Young & Mrs K. Rogers — E. Cornwall (Sue Young).* 161 (L), 383 (3mH), 851 (L), 922 (3mH), 1103 (3m2f110yH).

SALES DODGER (IRE) ..8-2-.. 8 gr.g. Celio Rufo — Lynn Grange (Northern Guest USA) pp54p. Robust. Dam is half-sister to Ponentino (*qv* '94 Annual). IRISH NH '98 r0 (often blinkered) r9 p0. IRISH NH FLAT '99 r1 p0. Bought Malvern, Sep for 1250. Last, pulled up twice and fell at the first on his final four attempts in Ireland, and continued to be in deplorable form in Points, in which he was beaten a minimum of 27 lengths and only had one horse behind him. Can show early speed only to slow alarmingly, and it is not worth persevering with him on current evidence. *Mrs J.P. Spencer — Clifton-on-Teme (Kay Spencer).* 900 (OMa), 1092 (OMa), 1360 (2m4fOMa), 1464 (OMa), 1635 (OMa).

SALFORD QUAY (IRE) ..8-10.. 8 b.g. King's Ride — Super Lane (Mart Lane) p41us. Tall rangy half-sister to Irish Pointing winner, Littlealaddin. IRISH FLAT Nov/Dec '97 13n 3yo. NH FLAT '98/9 (for Mrs J. Pitman) r3 p0. NH '98/9 (for Miss H. Knight) r2 p0. Bought Malvern, May for 4000. Given board and lodgings by the two Goddesses of Lambourn in his time, but the stable cat could have probably run faster. Only had to proceed at a funereal pace to collect a two-finisher Members on firm after the 40 length leader had fallen at the 13th. Beaten 47 lengths in a Maiden the time before, and that sums him up. *Mrs E.J. Richards, Mrs E. Tucker & Mrs H. Blum — Quantock (Tim Long).* 72 (OMa), 407 (OMa), 635 (M), 931 (R), 1095 (R).

SALLIOKO ..8-8.. 7 ch.m. Mioko (FR) — Sallisses (Pamroy) pup3. Sparely-made compact home-bred half-sister to Rusty Fellow (*qv*). P-t-P '99 r1 p1 (3rd of 4). Beaten a miniumum of 27 lengths in her two placings, and needs to improve her jumping, but inmates from her stable are notoriously slow to find their form and she may yet prove capable of troubling the judge. Her dam took 16 races to get off the mark, but won a Cheltenham Hunter Chase two outings later. *Mrs G.M. Shail — Ledbury (Roy Shail).* 341 (CfMa), 618 (CMa), 899 (OMa), 1361 (2m4fOMa).

SALLY ROD (IRE) ..—.. 8 gr.m. Phardante (FR) — Hi Dixie (IRE) (Bob Back USA) p. Dam won 7 plus Maiden in Ireland in '97. IRISH FLAT '99 r3 p0. IRISH NH '99 r1 p0 (last — soon tailed off after bad mistake early). Bought Doncaster, Aug for 950. Appeared to have an immediate set back in February, as she only took two obstacles before pulling up. *B.R. Hughes — Llangeinor.* 350 (CfMa).

SALLY SCALLY ..10-3.. 9 ch.m. Scallywag — Petite Cone (Celtic Cone) f58u11. Small neat. Dam is half-sister to Young Mariner (*qv*). NH FLAT '99 r3 p1 (3rd). NH '97/9 (for Miss I. Foustok; previously for R. Champion; previously for A. Hobbs) r14 p1; pulled up all 3 Chses (blinkerd once). Her two placed efforts under Rules were decent, but showed nothing else, although her last two trainers were hardly winner-producing factories. Has a tendency to pull too hard, and it took a while for her new owner to master her, but quite impressive and showed a turn of foot when registering a firm ground double at the end of the season. Looks the type who could adapt to Ladies Opens with success. *H.L. Thompson — Cleveland (Tina Jackson).* 695 (OMa), 809 (OMa), 1004 (OMa), 1329 (OMa), 1352 (OMa), 1475 (R).

SALLY'S TWINS ..9-11.. 8 b.m. Dowsing (USA) — Bird Of Love (Ela-Mana-Mou) fp51. Rangy. FLAT r8 p1 (15l 3rd). NH '96/8 r7 p2 (3rds, inc dead-heat). P-t-P '99 r5 w2 (Maiden and

Restricted) p2 (3rds); and fell 1. Twice successful in her debut season (once thanks to the winning jockey walking straight into the changing rooms), but took some time to recover from a fall on her reappearance this year, and her sole success was in a very slowly-run Intermediate at Bitterley. Prefers some cut in the ground, but usually ridden for a turn of foot, and will probably win again now her confidence has returned. Sometimes sweats up, and worth opposing when she does. Wears a cross-noseband. *Mrs L.P. Vaughan — S. Herefords (Willie Hayes).* 447 (Cm), 615 (CMod), 987 (Cf), 1090 (I).

SALMON MEAD (IRE) ..9-7.. 12 b.g. Lancastrian — New Brook (Paddy's Stream) ppp46p2p. Tall rangy half-brother to Irish Pointing winner, Killenagh Moss. P-t-P '94/9 r45 w9 (inc Ladies) p14 (6 2nds, last once; and inc last of 3 twice); failed to finish 17 (fell/unseated 5). Well placed to win eight times in the previous yard, but much less successful since, and his role has become one of schoolmaster recently. Almost broke a losing sequence of 20 in his Members, but Nicola Barnes tired long before he did, and the combination were collared near the finish. Wears blinkers, and usually takes no more than just a passing interest these days. *Mrs J.K. Marriage (The Marriage Family) — Essex (Simon Marriage).* 92 (Cf), 574 (4mmMO), 756 (Cf), 841 (L), 939 (L), 1113 (L), 1377 (M), 1536 (3m2fH).

SALMON POUTCHER ..10-2.. 12 ch.m. Brando — Heythrop VII (unknown) 1. Lengthy owner-bred. P-t-P/HUNT CH '96/9 r12 w2 (Maiden and Intermediate) p2 (2nds); pulled up 6. Has only once managed more than two outings in a season, but a fair Pointer on her day and beat Gildrom in a competitive Intermediate at Siddington last year. A rare outside ride for Alison Dare when making all to land a gamble in her Members on her only outing in 2000 after the only danger had broken down four out. Acts on a sound surface. *Mrs J.L. Phelps — Berkeley.* 1489 (M).

PLATE 113　　1489 Berkeley Hunt Members: Salmon Poutcher (Miss A. Dare), 1st, makes all, a rare outside ride for the former Champion　　　　　　　PHOTO: Brian Armstrong

SALTIS (IRE) ..9-11.. 9 ch.g. Salt Dome (USA) — Mrs Tittlemouse (Nonoalco USA) 33. Lengthy unfurnished brother to flat winner, Mohican Brave, and half-brother to 5 flat winners (one in Italy), including King Rat. FLAT (for D. Arbuthnot) r19 p3 (3rds at 2). NH '96/8 (for A. Forbes, bought for 2100; debut for Mrs P. Grainger; bought for 1800) r18 p6 (5 3rds, inc Sell); inc 4 Chses (fell once). Has toyed with a vast range of opportunities and accumulated 11 placings along the way, but still to win after 39 attempts, and clearly enjoys hanging on to Maiden status. Was beaten ten lengths and 29 lengths in Pointing thirds, and may have hit a snag in early March (has been absent for quite long periods in the past). *Mrs J. Galpin — Blackmore & Sparkford V.* 212 (CfMa), 455 (OMa).

SAM (U) ..—.. 10 b.g. unknown 3. Massive heavyweight hunter. Completed a one-two-three for Mike Biddick in his Members, but literally finished a mile behind the lucky winner. *M. Biddick — N. Cornwall.* 99 (M).

PLATE 114   99 North Cornwall Hunt Members: L to R all hunting dress and hairy heels, father
Mike Biddick on Sam, 3rd, jumps alongside Whitelegs and son Tom, 2nd

PHOTO: Baths Photographic

SAME DIFFERENCE (IRE) ..9-2§.. 13 b.g. Seymour Hicks (FR) — Santa Fe (GER) (Orsini) 346up23. Workmanlike unfurnished half-brother to an Irish NH flat winner, and to 8 winners in Germany. IRISH NH FLAT '92/4 r10 p3. IRISH NH '93/4 r9 p0. NH '94/6 and '97 r21 w3 (2m5f Hdle, and 2 Chses, 2m5f-3m) p4 (inc 2nd in Sell Ch); pulled up 1. P-t-P '97/9 r18 w1 (Open) p9 (7 3rds, last thrice); pulled up 2, and unseated 1. An ultra-safe plodder these days, and frequently takes no interest in proceedings, but his course completion record is a worthy one, and he has never fallen. Robbed of a victory by a stablemate in his Members, which would have ended a 19 race drought, but ultimately well beaten otherwise, and has regained the blinkers he used to wear in Ireland. *Mrs M.E. Barton — Llandeilo F.* 275 (Cf), 343 (Cf), 479 (Cf), 643 (Cf), 742 (O), 943 (M), 1224 (L).

SAM QUALE (IRE) ..9-12.. 9 ch.g. Tale Quale — Samanthabrownthorn (Mandalus) 24317. Sturdy attractive. IRISH P-t-P '96/7 r9 p4; pulled up 3, and fell 1. P-t-P '98/9 (for late Capt. T.A. Forster) r7 w1 (Maiden) p5 (2 2nds; and 3 3rds, remote last once); pulled up 1. Of no account in Ireland, but won his only outing in '98, and looked significantly improved. Has, however, struggled somewhat since, and usually done for a turn of foot, but appreciated the drop back into Restricteds when finishing strongly to win at Bredwardine. Only good enough for a bit part in Ladies races to date, and may be better employed elsewhere. *M.P. Wiggin — Ludlow (Geoff Evans).* 218 (L), 613 (L), 699 (L), 1460 (R), 1632 (I).

SAMS DAY (IRE) ..10-0.. 7 b.g. Samhoi (USA) — Daras Day (Arapahos FR) 1. Dam won Irish Maiden. IRISH P-t-P '99 r5 p1 (3rd); pulled up 2. Showed promise in Ireland, and confirmed it in a slowly-run Maiden at Eyton. Hard held when taking up the running after the last under a very cheeky ride from Brendon Foster, and it looks as if he could develop into a useful performer. One to watch. *G. Samuel — N. Salop (Sheila Crow).* 1197 (OMa).

SAM THE SLOTH ..—.. 9 ch.m. Mr Fluorocarbon — Nitty's Girl (Spartan General) pp. Owner-bred half-sister to Quite A Miss (*qv*). Remote when pulled up at the 11th in both attempts. Of course it would only be silly superstition to suppose that a horse with sloth in the name could not go on to equine greatness. *Miss S.J. Johnson — Bicester with Whaddon.* 785 (I), 1269 (OMa).

SAND HUTTON (IRE) ..8-0.. 10 ch.g. Interrex (CAN) — All Fine (Fine Blade USA) 5 0. Tall rangy. P-t-P '98/9 (for Mrs A.M. Easterby) r3 w1 (Maiden) p0; 4th, and pulled up 1. NH '99 (for J.W. Curtis) r2 p0 (pulled up 2). NH May '00 (from T. McGovern's) r1 p0 (11th in 2m5f Nov Sell Hdle: *ld to 5,* *wknd*). Looked potentially interesting when winning the fastest of three divisions of a Duncombe Park Maiden last year, but pulled up in his next three starts (rider thought he had burst once) and given a dreadful ride on his only outing this year. Thrashed throughout the final mile by Colin Sherry, despite being totally out of contention, and the jockey was lucky to get away with just a £125 fine. Clearly troubled physically, and probably mentally as well now. *A. O'Gorman — Holderness, & Kent & Surrey Bloodhounds.* 981 (O).

SANDI DEVIL ..9-0.. 10 ch.g. Devil To Play — Kandilove (Kabale) ppp8p0p. Leggy light-framed owner-bred brother to The Devils Kandi. P-t-P/HUNT CH '97/9 r15 p1 (2nd); pulled up 8, and fell 1. Can bowl along for up to two miles in Points, but stops rapidly, and the fact that he has regained blinkers on a regular basis suggests it is not just through lack of stamina. Only once better than last in final 15 outings and is a complete dud. *Mrs S.J. Smith — Meynell & S. Staffs.* 116 (I), 297 (I), 384 (2m3f110yH), 925 (2mH), 1157 (2m3fH), 1447 (2m4fH), 1668 (OMa).

S AND O P ..—.. 7 b.g. Arctic Lord — Beringa Bee (Sunley Builds) fp. Narrow light half-brother to Bee-A-Scally. Dam is sister to Builder Boy (*qv* '98 Annual). NH FLAT '98/9 r3 p0. NH '99 (for M.C. Pipe) r1 p0 (fell in Hdle). Pulled very hard and led for a way in both Points, but looks to have no stamina, and is unpromising. *Mr & Mrs M.A. Lloyd & A. Goodwin — United (Mel Lloyd).* 570 (2m4fCfMa), 1412 (OMa).

SANDS OF GOLD (IRE) ..9-12§.. 13 ch.g. Le Moss — Twice Lucky (Condorcet FR) u7. Angular sparely-made brother to Irish Pointing and jumping winner, Merciful Hour, and half-brother to Lucky Landing (IRE), and to Irish Chasing winner, Bit On The Hide. Dam won 2 flat, 8-12f, inc Sell, and won 2m Hdle. IRISH P-t-P '93 r2 p0 (pulled up 2). P-t-P/HUNT CH '94/5, '97 and '99 (for Mr B. Badham) r14 w2 (inc 3m2f Hunt Ch) p5 (3 2nds, inc 2 Hunt Chses); pulled up 1. Missed the '96 and '98 seasons, and won a 3m2f Cartmel Hunter Chase in the intervening year, but has never run or jumped willingly, and soon tailed off on his latest appearance at Cheltenham. Dumped the owner at an early stage in his Members previously, which is a race he has more chance of winning than the others he has contested recently. Blinkered in '99, and visored in his most recent attempt. *T. Pickett — Easton H. (Matthew Gingell).* 603 (M), 1339 (2m5fH).

SANDS POINT ..9-6§.. 11 b.g. Rakaposhi King — Jacqueline Jane (David Jack) fup13p. Tall half-brother to Straight Leader and Walton Thorns, and to jumping winner, Silver Wind. NH FLAT '94 r1 p0. NH '94/5 and '97/8 r23 p3 (inc 2nd in Sell; and 3rd in Ch); disqualified from head 2nd for irresponsible riding (hung badly right on bend and caused havoc). P-t-P '99 (for Mrs S. Popham) r6 p2 (3rds, remote of 4 once); and 4th 4. Proved slightly less ungenuine than the runner-up when finally getting off the mark at the 34th attempt in a slow-motion two-finisher Maiden at Southwell. Will never be gifted such an opportunity again, but at least he grasped it. Usually blinkered in the previous yard, but dispensed with them in 2000. *A.F. Budge — Belvoir (Mrs P. Visick).* 373 (CfMa), 798 (OMa), 867 (M), 1075 (OMa), 1268 (R), 1533 (3m1fH).

SAND STAR ..—§.. 9 b.m. Lugana Beach — Overseas (Sea Hawk II) pp. Sturdy close-coupled half-sister to Governor's, Harbour Bazaar and to flat and Hurdles winner, Rocky Bay, and to 4 flat winners, including Turtle Bay, Swallow Bay and Atlantic Bay. FLAT r25 w2 (7f all-weather) p7; started very slowly twice. P-t-P '98/9 r11 p1 (3rd); 4th, pulled up 7, and fell/unseated 2. Aptly named in view of her all-weather successes, but an appalling waste of time in Points, and pulled up lame in the latest. Devoid of stamina and enthusiasm, and blinkered twice to no avail. *M.I. Eynon — S. Pembs (Owen Thomas).* 272 (L), 481 (L).

SAND TRACK ..7-11.. 11 ch.g. Palm Track — Weather Maid (Weathercock) fp3p. Small very light home-bred half-brother to Polly Maid (*qv*). P-t-P '99 r2 p0 (5th, and ran out 1). A hyperactive pocket-size pest, and has ruled himself out before halfway in half of his races to date. Thirty lengths third at Charm Park, but needs to improve dramatically to stand any sort of chance in future, and lacks the scope to do so. *Mrs S. Morley — Staintondale.* 1003 (OMa), 1032 (OMa), 1235 (OMa), 1479 (OMa).

SANDY FLOSS (IRE) ..—.. 8 b.g. Green Desert (USA) — Mill On The Floss (Mill Reef USA) pp. Good-topped brother to flat winner, Hatta's Mill, and half-brother to several flat winners, including Yeltsin, Milly Ha Ha and Milly Of The Valley. Dam won 2 flat, 7-12f, and comes from an excellent family. FLAT (inc for R. Buckler, bought for 16,000; previously for H. Cecil) r13 p4. NH '97 and Aug '99 (for P. Hedger; previously for J. King) r2 p1 (22/3rd). Bred for flat glory, but has long been a major disappointment. Pulled up after 2m4f in both Maidens, including when surprisingly sent off favourite for the first of them. Could be mulish at the stalls when inconsistent on the flat, and revived memories of his dam, who refused to enter the traps in the Oakes. *M. Stephenson — N. Ledbury.* 900 (OMa), 990 (OMa).

SANSNIP ..9-1§.. 11 b.g. Impecunious — Sansem (New Member) 7. Tall rangy brother to Santim, and half-brother to Final Express and Rusty Spinner. Dam is an unraced sister or half-sister to 4 Pointers, including Sanber and Withen Wood. P-t-P '97/9 r13 w1 (Maiden) p1 (3rd); fell/unseated 5, ran out 1, and pulled up 3. Needed a jockey of the calibre of Paul Flynn to coax him home at Cothelstone in '98, but a recalcitrant beast otherwise, and has done nothing worthwhile either before or since. Dismounted after the post on his belated comeback, and failed to reappear. *B. Hurst — S. Cornwall.* 1516 (I).

SANTA BARBARA (IRE) ..9-8.. 10 b.m. Henbit (USA) — Fiery Rose (Boreen FR) 26p. Strong-topped half-sister to Joe White and Wholestone (IRE). Dam won an Irish NH flat. NH FLAT '96 r2 p0. NH '97/8 r4 p0. P-t-P '99 r4 p3 (2 2nds; and last of 3); and 6th. Beaten between one-and-a-half and 16 lengths when placed in four Maidens '99/00, and has held every chance at the penultimate fence in three of them, but has failed to raise her game when required, and looks a typically unentusiastic Henbit. Twice a beaten favourite, and punters should look elsewhere. *J.A.V. Duell — S. Durham (Sarah Palfreeman).* 399 (OMa), 1000 (R), 1480 (OMa).

SANTIM ..—.. 10 b.g. Impecunious — Sansem (New Member) p. Owner-bred brother to Sansnip (qv). P-t-P '98/9 r5 p0 (6th, unseated 2, and pulled up 2). Useless on his rare appearances, and jumped appallingly when soon tailed off on his only outing in 2000. *G.W. Giddings — S. & W. Wilts.* 957 (CfMa).

SARCOID (IRE) ..9-10.. 11 ch.g. Saronicos — Pretty Bonnet (Carlburg) 35. Lengthy. Dam won 3m Hdle in Ireland. IRISH P-t-P '96/7 r6 w1 (Maiden) p4; pulled up 1. P-t-P '98/9 r3 w1 (Restricted) p2 (2nds). Stand his racing exceptionally badly, but won on his English debut in the manner of a good horse, and followed that with two seconds beaten a maximum of five lengths. Given precious little chance by a novice girl on his 2000 reappearance, but never going when reunited with Gary Hanmer a week later, and promptly disappeared. Needs treating with caution when he returns. *S.P. Rammell — Cheshire (Gary Hanmer).* 1126 (L), 1267 (I).

SARENACARE (IRE) ..8-2.. 9 b.g. Lafontaine (USA) — Brown Foam (Horage) p334. Workmanlike brother to La Mon Dere (IRE). NH FLAT '96 r2 p0. NH '97/8 (for S. Dow; previously for R. Frost; previously for P. Hobbs) r5 p0 (finished in both Chses). Did not jump well when one and a half lengths third in an abysmal Maiden run at a crawl at Hackwood, but generally tailed off under Rules, and in all his three other Points (was last twice, and a fence behind in his Members). Looks to have something badly wrong with him, and acquired a tongue-strap on his last two starts. *Mrs J.M. Gumbley — Surrey U. (Pam Tetley).* 290 (CMa), 710 (OMa), 888 (OMa), 1392 (M).

SARONICA-R ..8-7.. 11 b.m. Rolfe (USA) — Pattaya Girl (Comedy Star USA) ppppfpp. Small close-coupled well-made. P-t-P '96/9 r15 w1 (Members) p0; pulled up 6, and fell/unseated 3. Not better than last in eight starts since getting up close home to win her Members last year, and is surely going to have to rest on her laurels. Rarely got beyond the two-mile mark in 2000, and remains a poor jumper. Has two handlers, and usually gets very warm in the preliminaries. *L.J. Remnant — Curre.* 484 (R), 744 (R), 818 (R), 1054 (R), 1400 (R), 1568 (R), 1616 (R).

SASSY STREET (IRE) ..10-1.. 8 b.g. Danehill (USA) — Sassy Lane (Sassafras FR) 43124. Tall half-brother to a flat winner in USA and to another in Italy, and to an Italian jumping winner. Dam won 2 French flat, 10-12f, inc at Nantes. FLAT r6 p0. NH '97 r4 p0 (7th, last, and pulled up 2, inc Sell). P-t-P '99 r3 p0 (fell/unseated 2, and refused 1). Disastrous in '99, but far more composed this year, and adjudged to have won outright at Stainton where he appeared to have dead-heated, but looked unlucky on his first attempt in a Restricted when beaten a length at Witton Castle having been comprehensively outridden in the closing stages. Should gain compensation, and could improve further with stronger handling. *D.A. Wood — Bilsdale.* 282 (OMa), 438 (OMa), 808 (OMa), 1028 (R), 1230 (R).

SATCHMO (IRE) ..11-6.. 9 b.g. Satco (FR) — Taradale (Torus) 121u2. Big rangy. IRISH P-t-P '98/9 (for Gavin Wragg) r9 w2 (6yo Maiden, and Open) p2 (2nds); pulled up, and fell 2. IRISH NH May '00 r1 p1 (2nd in 3m1f Hunt Ch: *cl up, dspl bl brief 4 out, rdn 2 out, u.p when blun last, nt rec*). A magnificent looking creature who was unsurprisingly sent off favourite for his English debut at Folkestone, but beaten six lengths after Gavin Wragg (who did not partner him to either Irish success) had been at his most appalling. Had joined the winner going smoothly when Wragg nearly fell off three out and lost an iron, and stayed on pluckily despite not being ridden at the home straight. Had three different jockeys subsequently and was very impressive for Ben Hitchcott at Sandown, where he bettered the time of the Novices Handicap Chase by six seconds (and was carrying 15 pounds more than that winner), but gave Julian Pritchard a torrid time at Aintree before the partnership was severed at the fourth. Gained his best prize of the season when taken to Punchestown where he earned £3800 for a distant second, but that was over 3m1f, and his performances to date suggest that shorter trips are possibly more suitable. Providing he can forget his unfortunate experience of the Mildmay fences he would look an outstanding claimant to the Foxhunters there. *G.J.D. Wragg — E. Sussex & Romney Marsh (Di Grissell).* 127 (Cf), 300 (2m5fH), 799 (2m4f110yH), 924 (3m1fH).

SATCO SUPREME (IRE) ..8-4.. 10 b.g. Satco (FR) — Supreme Song (Supreme Sovereign) u643. Rangy half-brother to 4 flat winners (2 in Ireland, and one apiece in Germany and Spain). IRISH P-t-P '96 r2 p0 (pulled up at halfway in both). P-t-P '98/9 (for Mr P. Mahoney) r10 p0 (last pair 2, pulled up 6, and fell/unseated 2). Has twice figured prominently for a long way in poor Maidens at Bassaleg '99/00, but exposed as modest in the extreme and rarely looks to be putting much heart into his efforts. Does not stay three miles. Thrice blinkered. *N.J. Edwards — Gelligaer F.* 601 (CfMa), 1456 (OMa), 1574 (OMa), 1662 (OMa).

SATELLITE EXPRESS (IRE) ..—§.. 8 b.g. Henbit (USA) — Waffling (Lomond USA) ppppp. Rangy unfurnished crib-biter. NH FLAT '97 r2 p0 (hung left closing stages both). P-t-P '98 (for Mrs E.

Sharp) r3 p0 (last, and pulled up 2). A real villain who hangs like a gate, and pulled himself up after a mile when clear on his final appearance. Blinkered twice in 2000, but not worth racing again. *P. Hughes — E. Sussex & Romney Marsh (Alison Hickman).* 131 (OMa), 284 (2m4fCMa), 775 (OMa), 1105 (2m4fOMa), 1172 (OMa).

PLATE 115   799 *Ubique HC, Sandown: Satchmo (B. Hitchcott), 1st, bolts up*

PHOTO: Steven Cargill

SATIN FLASH ..—.. 7 b.m. Dancing High — Satinanda (Leander) p. Home-bred half-sister to With Respect (*qv*). NH '99 r2 p0. Presumably went wrong when pulling up and dismounting in February. *F.T. Walton — Border (Jimmy Walton).* 112 (OMam).

SATORI ..—.. 8 gr.g. Thethingaboutitis (USA) — Version (Sir Lark) 5p. Small light-framed. 66 lengths last on his debut, and proved a most unworthy favourite next time, as he could only proceed irratically in the rear until pulling up. Only ran in January. *Mrs J.M. Cragg — Four Burrow (David Pipe).* 14 (R), 70 (OMa).

SAUCY'S WOLF ..9-7.. 11 ch.g. Little Wolf — Barton Sauce (Saucy Kit) 33f3u333p. Compact half-brother to Barton Rose (*qv*). NH FLAT r3 p0. NH '96/7 r4 p0 (pulled up 2, fell at first, and ran out and unseated on bend in Chses, final a Sell). P-t-P '96 and '98/9 r21 p4 (2 2nds); pulled up 7, carried out 1, and fell/unseated 4. In the money on ten occasions, but only once beaten less than six lengths, retains Maiden status despite 37 chances. Has frequently given the impression that he could win if he wanted to, and acquired blinkers twice in the latest campaign. Remains a sketchy jumper at times. *E.M. & Mrs D.T. Treneer — Dartmoor.* 158 (CfMa), 253 (CfMa), 410 (OMa), 562 (CfMa), 658 (R), 856 (CfMa), 1049 (CfMa), 1257 (C), 1522 (CfMa).

SAUNDBY SWORDSMAN ..—.. 6 b.g. Broadsword (USA) — Celestial Bride (Godswalk USA) u. Brother to Astra Libra and Cottesmore (*qv*). Dropping out after early speed when he unseated at the 11th at Southwell. *Mrs J.A. Youdan — Grove & Rufford.* 372 (CfMa).

SAUSALITO ..8-7.. 8 b.m. Lighter — Saucy Sprite (Balliol) p6. Half-sister to Sebastopol (*qv*). Bought Doncaster, Aug '98 for 4000. novicey in two February Maidens, and was 46 lengths last in the latest. *R. Hand — Lamerton.* 204 (OMa), 254 (CfMa).

SAVUTI (IRE) ..9-9.. 12 ch.g. Amoristic (USA) — Aprils Choice (Never Slip) ppp5p84p. Rangy brother to Irish Pointing winner, Delightful Choice. Dam is half-sister to Ballinvelig (*qv* '92 Annual). IRISH P-t-P '94 r1 p0. IRISH NH FLAT '94 and '96 r2 p0. IRISH NH '96/7 r10 w3 (2m1f Hdle, and 2 Chses, 2m1f-2m4f) p1 (2nd). NH '95 and '97/9 r11 p1 (last of 3 in Ch after 2 bad mistakes). HUNT CH '99 (for Mrs S. Buckland) r5 p0 (4th, last, and pulled up 3). Not without ability in Ireland, but pulls hard, and drops out tamely after 1m4f maximum nowadays, and surely has something amiss. Acquired a tongue-strap in 2000, and given his size has probably gone in the wind. Often taken to post early in an attempt to stop him running away. Occasionally blinkered. *D. Jenkins & M.*

Davies — Gogerddan (Mrs A.M. Thorpe). 34 (MO), 153 (2m4f110yH), 684 (2m4fH), 945 (O), 1053 (O), 1447 (2m4fH), 1570 (MO), 1658 (MO).

SAXON FAIR ..10-2.. 12 ch.g. Saxon Farm — Fair Kitty (Saucy Kit) 4p. Sparely-made compact half-brother to Fair Ally (qv). NH '92/3 and '97 r7 w1 (2m5f Ch) p0. P-t-P '94/6 and '99 r18 w6 (inc Open) p7 (5 2nds, of 3 once); failed to finish 5 (fell 1). Formerly a useful front-runner, and was gifted an Open at Flagg in '99 when the only one to go clear, but very hard to train these days, and carried plenty of condition when well beaten this year. Struggles with his legs but for which he would still be winning races, and unlikely to make much of an impact in future. *J.D. Lomas — United.* 334 (O), 903 (O).

SAXON MOSS ..8-13.. 7 ch.g. Le Moss — Saxon Gift (Saxon Farm) ppp46. Strong-topped brother to Monsieur Mossiman. Dam is half-sister to Dear Do (qv). Grandam, Earlsgift won 5 Points and placed 5. Jumps well enough, but a weak finisher at present, and only one horse has finished behind him. Possibly worth trying again. *G.J. Smith — S. Notts.* 398 (OMa), 694 (OMa), 966 (OMa), 1251 (OMa), 1422 (OMa).

SAXON QUEEN ..9-10.. 7 b.m. Lord Bud — Saxon Slave (Be Friendly) 2231p. Small unfurnished half-sister to Singing Sam. Dam won 2 Chses, 2m4f-3m. P-t-P '99 r2 p1 (2nd of 3); and pulled up 1. Took rather longer to win her Maiden than anticipated, and cost favourite backers dear on three occasions before she gained an unimpressive success at Pentreclwydau where she benefited from an aggressive ride from her trainer. Appeared not to relish the firm ground on her final start, and whilst she should win a Restricted lacks the scope for too much improvement. Does not seem to stay very well. *R.A. Mason — Glamorgan (Evan Williams).* 268 (CfMa), 349 (CfMa), 1091 (OMa), 1300 (OMa), 1452 (R).

SAYONARA ..—.. 8 ch.g. Say Primula — Rilin (Ribston) u. Lengthy brother to Hya Prim (qv). NH FLAT '97/8 r2 p0. NH '98/9 r7, for H. Johnson, bought for 4500; previously for breeder, N. Chamberlain) r7 p2 (3rds, inc distant last). Sold Doncaster, June for 4600. Has always been a poor jumper, and followed errors with an unseat at halfway in a Maiden. Bolted going to the start once under Rules, and is a headstrong individual who has worn a nose-net. It does not take long for his owners to wave him farewell. *Mrs P.K.J. Brightwell — Essex & Suffolk.* 411 (OMa).

SAY SADIE ..—.. 8 gr.m. Say Primula — Ellaron (Abwah) up. Owner-bred sister to Say Charlie and Say Daphne. A messy jumper who was soon struggling twice in May. *C. Dawson — S. Durham.* 1474 (M), 1581 (2m4fOMa).

SAYWHEN ..10-3.. 9 br.g. Say Primula — Practicality (Weavers' Hall) 336143. Strong-topped ugly half-brother to Gaelic Warrior, to flat and Chasing winner, Kamart, to 2 winners abroad, and to a successful Hurdler. P-t-P '99 r7 w1 (Maiden) p2 (2nd of 3, and last of 3); last, pulled up 2, and unseated 1. A remarkably clumsy clot, but managed to produce an error-free round for a change when winning at Bitterley this year. Usually manages to meet most fences out of sync, and has found little under pressure, but his two most recent outings suggest that he will pay his way in minor races in 2001. Can run from the front, and best suited by top-of-the-ground. *Mrs A. Price — Teme V.* 484 (R), 671 (C), 862 (Cf), 993 (R), 1090 (I), 1463 (Cf).

S B S BY JOVE ..10-5.. 8 ch.g. Jupiter Island — Mill Shine (Milan) 11. Light attractive half-brother to Luvly Bubbly (qv). P-t-P '99 (for Mr D.D. Stewart) r4 p0 (4th, fell/unseated 2, and pulled up 1). Came to Edward Retter with an appalling reputation ('has a future in catering'), having proved to be utterly bonkers o'er the border, but has undergone a remarkable transformation, and waltzed home in two February outings under Alex Charles-Jones. Very much on edge in both, but proved amenable to restraint, and jumped impeccably, and if his delinquent days are truly a thing of the past will go on to better things. His next appearance is eagerly awaited. *E. Retter — Dartmoor.* 106 (OMa), 260 (R).

SCALLY HILL ..9-2§.. 10 gr.m. Scallywag — Madge Hill (Spartan General) 85p. Big strong sister to Sailor Jim (qv). P-t-P '96/9 r15 w1 (Maiden) p5 (4 2nds, beaten 2 fences once; and last of 3); pulled up 5, and fell 1. Most disappointing, and has been tailed off in four Restricteds since capturing a bad three-finisher Maiden at Weston Park last year. Usually attempts to make the running, but expends plenty of nervous energy in the preliminaries, and carries too much condition. Will have to get very lucky again to supplement his gains. *Mr & Mrs P. Johnson — W. Salop.* 589 (R), 782 (R), 1129 (R).

SCALLY LANE ..8-10.. 9 b.m. Scallywag — Farthing Lane (Tamerlane) 5. Lengthy. 26 lengths last on a belated debut in February, and was mounted on the course and seemed to be a typical Scallywag. *Mrs J. Dennis — Tetcott (C. Cox).* 106 (OMa).

SCALLYMAY ..9-4.. 10 gr.m. Scallywag — Stanton Queen (Most Secret) uppppppp. Big strong-topped rangy half-sister to Daneswell (qv). P-t-P/HUNT CH '98/9 r10 w1 (Maiden) p1 (3rd); (pulled up 4, fell/unseated 3, and ran out 1). A hair-raising ride, but finally came good in a three-finisher Maiden at Bratton Down last year. Took nine attempts to even get round, and has reverted to non-completion mode once again. Pulls hard, can be difficult to steer, and occasionally jumps right, and only once managed to go further than two miles in 2000. It would be a miracle were she to win again. Has been tried tongue-tied. *S.R. Edwards — N. Salop.* 247 (LA), 567 (R), 782 (R), 1322 (R), 1528 (R), 1632 (I), 1664 (R).

SCARBA ..9-12.. 13 b.g. Skyliner — Looking For Gold (Goldfella) u3p. Tall deep-girthed. Dam, half-sister to Outgunned (*qv* '93 Annual), won 2m1f Sell Hdle. Grandam, Out Late, was placed in 3 Points (inc when demoted 2nd after winning Maiden). Great-grandam, Colindin, won 4 flat (5-8f), 3 2m Hdles, and 5 Points (inc 4 Ladies). FLAT r6 p1 (2nd). NH '93/8 r39 w3 (2m-3m Hdles) p11. P-t-P '99 r4 w1 (Confined) p2; and last. Successful on his fencing debut at Hackwood Park last year, and has since posted several decent placed efforts, but pulled up lame in the race he had won 12 months previously on his final start. Stays well, and suited by plenty of give in the ground, but will not be easy to nurse back to winning ways at 13. *Miss J. Barton, D. Boneham & J. Campbell — Bicester with Whaddon (Jayne Barton).* 510 (Cf), 634 (C), 883 (Cf).

SCARLET LETCH ..10-0.. 13 br.m. Zambrano — Scarlet Letch (New Brig) ppp. Light-framed half-sister to Scarlet Coon, and to jumping winner, Scarlet Terror. Dam won 10 Chses (3m-4m1f) and placed 10. NH '92/3 and '94/5 r9 p1 (distant last of 3 — tailed off halfway); 5th, and last pair 3 in Chses. P-t-P/HUNT CH '96/8 r13 w4 (inc 2 Intermediates — one 3m6f, inc hat-trick '97) p5 (3 3rds, inc Hunt Ch); pulled up 1. A very consistent mare, and had not missed the frame in 11 consecutive starts prior to pulling up lame at Weston Park in '98. Missed the following season, and despite looking a picture has yet to get much beyond halfway in three Points and is clearly still troubled. Pulled up and dismounted after jumping just four fences at the Brecon, and stopped very quickly on her next outing some seven weeks later, and sadly looks finished. *P.J. Sanderson — Kyre (Sheila Crow).* 334 (O), 480 (O), 1273 (O).

PLATE 116　　260 United Services Restricted (Div 1): The reformed S B S By Jove (A. Charles-Jones), 1st, storms past Lilliput　　　　　　　PHOTO: Brian Armstrong

SCARLET RAMBLER ..—.. 12 ch.g. Blakeney Point — Rambling Rolls (Silver Cloud) u. Compact (with huge white face) half-brother to Middleton Tiny, Middleton Percy and Throw Bridge. NH FLAT Spr '94 r3 p0. NH '94/5 and '97/9 (for R. Frost, bought for 1400; one run previously for R. Stronge, bought for 800; won previously for Miss H. Knight; previously for N. Twiston-Davies) r20 w1 (2m3f Hdle) p2 (3rds, inc Ch — of 4, beaten 46l); inc Sells. Won a bad Hurdle on firmish in September '97, but has only ever been a very poor performer. The best thing about him was his completion record (got round in 21 out of his first 22 attempts), so it was an irony when he unseated Robert Bateman in his Members, and the mishap necessitated the summoning of the air ambulance. *R.N. Bateman — Dart V. & S. Pool H. (Andrew Congdon).* 651 (M).

SCARLETT O'HARA ..10-5.. 9 b.m. Ardross — Deirdre's Choice (Golden Love) 113up. Big lengthy workmanlike half-sister to Le Cabro D'Or (*qv*). P-t-P '97/8 (for Mr C.H. Sporborg & Sir Chips Keswick) r9 w4 (up to Intermediate) p1 (2nd); 5th, refused 1, fell 1, and brought down 1. Went missing for a year after winning four times in '98, but quickly picked up the winning thread at with an early season double at Cottenham. Disappointed when favourite at Marks Tey next time, when the ground was very heavy, and again when bidding for her fourth success at Cottenham subsequently, but has never looked happy on a sound surface, and ended the season by going lame. Can quicken in minor company, and is usually ridden for speed, but sometimes take liberties with the fences, and may well be out of action for another 12 months. *C.H. Sporborg — Puckeridge*. 15 (C), 178 (Cm), 318 (Cf), 770 (Cf), 936 (Cf).

SCHISANDRA ..9-2.. 7 b.m. Petong — Volcalmeh (Lidhame) puu4f6. Half-sister to Hurdles winner, Lady Felix. Dam won at 7f. FLAT r6 p0 (inc Sell). P-t-P '99 r4 p0 (unseated 3, and pulled up 1). A candidate for the worst jumper in the country, though still getting precious little help from above, and has returned Blagg-less in six of her ten outings. Almost fell in one of her completions, and has not surprisingly failed to beat a rival. Should not be allowed to compete in such a clueless state. *Miss M.D.M. Howie — O. Surrey & Burstow*. 132 (OMa), 289 (Cm), 828 (OMa), 984 (OMa), 1105 (2m4fOMa), 1513 (OMa).

SCHLEPP (IRE) ..—.. 9 b.m. Good Thyne (USA) — Julia's Pauper (Pauper) p. Half-sister to Cherrygayle (IRE). IRISH P-t-P '97 and '99 r17 w1 (6yo plus mares Mdn) p6; pulled up 6, and fell. Bred a colt by John French in '98. Sold Doncaster, May for 3000. Ended a long sequence of disappointments in Ireland when winning her final Point there, but must have been awstruck by the opposition in a Great Trethew Ladies, as two went on to capture two Hunter Chases apiece and the other landed a four mile Open. *G. Maddigan, Mr & Mrs Fisher, F. Parry — Lamerton (Pauline & Tony Geering)*. 161 (L).

SCHOLAR GREEN ..—§.. 9 b.g. Green Adventure (USA) — Quelle Chemise (Night Shift USA) pp. Good-bodied lengthy. Dam is half-sister to Quarterstaff (*qv*). NH FLAT Nov/Dec '96 r3 p0. NH '97 and '99 (for G. Yardley; very reluctant in blinkers final start) r4 p0. A useless dog, and has now been pulled up five times consecutively. *Miss H. Tainton — N. Ledbury*. 995 (OMa), 1092 (OMa).

SCOTTISH CLOVER ..8-3.. 8 ch.m. Scottish Reel — National Clover (National Trust) 1ppp. Strong owner-bred half-sister to Mr Motivator (*qv*). P-t-P '99 r1 p0 (pulled up). Just held on to win a bad Maiden in the slowest time of the day at Llanfrynach, but none of her victims have gone on to boost the form and has herself been unable to complete the course in three subsequent starts. From a remarkably successful family, and may yet prove her success was no fluke as she has looked to be carrying plenty of condition to date. *M.H. Ings — Teme V. (Billie Brown)*. 490 (CfMa), 864 (R), 1276 (R), 1460 (R).

SCOTTISH SPIRIT ..—.. 10 b.m. Lochnager — Witch Brandy (Hot Brandy) u. Sold Doncaster, May for 700. It would be surprising if she was anything other than hopeless. *R.F. Wright — W. Street/Tickham (Miss S. Fraser)*. 132 (OMa).

SCRABO VIEW (IRE) ..10-0.. 13 ch.g. Denel (FR) — Patricias Choice (Laurence O) 84u1u. Tall half-brother to Irish Hurdles winner, Sharri Dee. IRISH NH FLAT '93 r1 p1 (3rd). NH '93/7 (often blinkered) r36 w5 (3 Hdles, 2m1f-3m1f, first 2 Sells; and 2 Chses, 3m1f-3m2f) p10. P-t-P '99 r5 p0 (last pair 4, and unseated 1). Generally well beaten in Points, but a thorough stayer and made the most of a relatively weak opportunity in a 4-mile Open at Alnwick where he showed more resolve than the favourite. Had not won for the best part of four years and the likelihood is that he will struggle to do so again outside of his Members which he would probably have won in '99 but for unseating in a match. Suited by a sound surface. *Miss S.M. Ward — Braes of Derwent*. 135 (L), 376 (MO), 621 (L), 911 (4mMO), 1029 (L).

SCRAPTASTIC ..9-9.. 10 ch.g. Scallywag — Rusty To Reign (General Ironside) 4223. Strong attractive half-brother to Rusty Buck (*qv*). Dam was 2nd in 2 Points. P-t-P/HUNT CH '97 r5 p0 (6th, pulled up 2, and fell 2). NH '98/9 (for P. Beaumont) r4 p1 (2nd). Impetuous and a weak finisher to date (like his dam), but jumps well and should have little difficulty opening his account. May require an easy track and a sound surface, and if Nick Bell could adopt Linlathen-style tactics, that would certainly help. Wears a cross-noseband. *Mrs A. Bell — Belvoir*. 54 (OMa), 234 (OMa), 438 (OMa), 548 (CfMa).

SCRUTON ..9-11.. 7 b.g. Cruise Missile — My Martina (My Swallow) 41237. Very big strong half-brother to Malvern Cantina. Dam won 3 Points and placed 7 (inc 3rd in Hdle). P-t-P '99 r3 p0 (4th, 5th, and pulled up 1). Improved by the acquisition of David Easterby, and just held on to land a Witton Castle Maiden, but not an easy ride as waiting tactics were overdone at Wetherby next time, and has tended to fade when ridden up with the pace. Jumps soundly now after very erratic beginnings, and should prove reliable enough to win a Restricted. A massive individual, and may not have reached his physical peak yet. *R. Coward — York & Ainsty S. (Cherry Coward)*. 55 (OMa), 138 (OMa), 173 (R), 396 (R), 1326 (R).

SCUD MISSILE (IRE) ..—.. 10 b.g. Persian Heights — Desert Bluebell (Kalaglow) 4pu. Close-coupled hobdayed half-brother to 4 flat winners (one in Italy), including Roses In The Snow, Distant Mirage and Taylil. 14,500y. FLAT (early runs for F. Johnson Houghton; tried tongue-tied) r10 p1 (3rd). NH '95/9 (for late M. Heaton-Ellis, bought for 4000; one win previously for P. Payne; 2 wins previously for G. Johnson Houghton, bought for 4200) r20 w3 (2m4f-2m7f Hdles) p8 (inc 3rd in Sell); finished remote in 2 Chses. Won braced races on good or firm ground to April '97, but only able to manage one outing apiece '98 and '99. Outclassed in Opens when switching to Points, and if there is any future hope for him it would be in a Members. *S.J. Goodings — Avon V. (J. Clifford).* 637 (O), 1205 (MO), 1282 (O).

SEABRIGHT SUNSET ..—.. 7 b br.g. Skyliner — Seabright Smile (Pitpan) up. Lengthy half-brother to Seabright Saga. Dam won 2 Hdles, 2-3m, for Dr Parry. Showed no immediate promise in modest company. *Dr L.G. Parry — Cumberland (Fergus Jestin).* 1083 (2m4fOMa), 1362 (M).

SEA JAY SON ..9-3.. 10 b.g. Tampa Bay — Annes Nimp (Noble Imp) 423. Workmanlike lengthy. dam, 'little better than useless', was placed in Sell Hdle and in 2 Points (had a total of 3 behind her when gaining the prizes). Not disgraced for a horse who seems to have come to racing as an afterthought, and was very unlucky to meet a rival of the calibre of Palace Parade when second in his Members. Shows plenty of early tow, but looks to have a problem getting the trip, and beaten a minimum of 17 lengths so far. *Major W.L.S. Lane — Spooners & W. Dartmoor (Mandy Hand).* 71 (OMa), 846 (M), 1521 (CfMa).

SEAMAC ..8-9.. 10 b.g. Macmillion — Space Lace (Space King) 2. Dam pulled up in 5 of 7 Points for the Fowlers, but grandam, Sealace, won 17 Points (13 Adjacents) and placed 12 for them. Finished 30 lengths second on his debut aged nine, but has a lot to live down to, as his grandams representatives have continued to lose all their 45 Points! *T. Fowler — Worcs (Theresa McCurrich).* 892 (OMa).

SEA PATROL ..9-4§.. 14 b.g. Shirley Heights — Boathouse (Habitat) r5. Unfurnished lengthy half-brother to flat winners, Dry Dock (useful; also sire) and River Patrol. Dam won 2 flat, 7-8f, and is half-sister to 8 winners, including Bireme (Oaks) and Balinger (also sire). NH FLAT r3 p2. NH '93/4 and '96/7 r14 w2 (2m6f Hdle and 2m4f Nov Ch) p3 (3rd in Sell Hdle and 2 Chses, Sell final). P-t-P '97/9 r10 w1 (Members) p0; failed to finish 7 (unseated 2, and ran out 1). Was an awkward customer under Rules, and has proved a wholly unsuitable mount for Dick Pike to try to open his account on. Pulled himself up on all three outings last year, and declined the first open ditch in his Members on his return, but managed his first completion since '97 on his final appearance. His reluctance was presumably due to a physical fault as he collapsed and died after crossing the line at Cursneh Hill. Wore blinkers, and had been tried in a tongue-strap. *J.R. Pike — S. Herefords.* 666 (M), 1272 (Cf).

SEA SEARCH ..8-8.. 14 ch.g. Deep Run — Gift Seeker (Status Seeker) ppf2pp4ppppp6pps. Big powerful half-brother to Chasing winner, Shopaholic (IRE), and to Irish Hurdles winner, Supplicate. Dam won 1m4f Bumper and 2m1f Hdle in Ireland. NH FLAT r1 p0. NH '92/3 and '96 r6 p0. P-t-P/HUNT Ch '94/7 and '99 r32 w2 (Maiden and Members) p7 (4 2nds, last after running out twice in match; and 3 3rds, remote last once); failed to finish 19 (ran out 1, and fell/unseated 3). One of the busiest performers of the season, but an absolute disgrace, and only managed to beat three rivals all year — unbelievably two of them went on to win three races between them later on. Usually looks as though he has been pulled straight in out the field, and sometimes barely able to raise a gallop. Appeared to finish lame at Bassaleg in May, but ran a further five times. A wretched creature to behold nowadays, and having suffered wind and leg problems in the past deserves retirement. *C.R. Johnson — Llandeilo F.* 273 (R), 347 (R), 483 (R), 595 (R), 646 (R), 744 (R), 832 (R), 943 (M), 1022 (3mH), 1298 (R), 1400 (R), 1452 (R), 1568 (R), 1615 (R), 1632 (I), 1659 (R).

SEA SPIRIT ..9-13.. 9 gr.m. Nearly A Hand — Uncornered (USA) (Silver Series USA) fp4f422. Compact owner-bred half-sister to Polly's Corner. P-t-P '97/8 r3 p0 (unseated 1, and pulled up 2). Went wrong after just three appearances and forced to sit out the '99 season, but managed a full campaign in 2000, and very unlucky not to have at least got a share of the spoils in the final race of the season. Appeared to have poked her head in front right on the line, but the judge thought otherwise and gave the verdict to the well-backed favourite. Thoroughly deserves compensation, and should get it in 2001. Appears not to handle testing conditions. *Mrs E.M. Elliot — Dart V. & S. Pool H. (Emma Kelley).* 538 (OMa), 728 (R), 857 (CfMa), 1100 (OMa), 1565 (OMa), 1640 (OMa), 1519 (CfMa).

SEA URCHIN ..9-12.. 8 b.g. Scallywag — Sailor's Shanty (Dubassoff USA) 1f12. Neat. Dam, home-bred half-sister to Davy's Lad (*qv* '98 Annual), was placed in 5 Points for Mr Philips. Grandam, Colisfare, won 3 Points at the Lanark and Renfrew and placed 12. Great-grandam, Fanfare III, won a Point and placed 4. P-t-P '99 r1 p0 (pulled up). Seems even more highly strung than many by his sire, but has an equal amount of ability and quickly moved through the ranks in the early months of the season. Presumably stumped up by the prevailing firm ground at Black Forest Lodge in March as he went missing for nine weeks and may just have needed the run when failing by two lengths to concede 5lbs to Newman's Conquest at Lifton. Possesses a decent turn of foot, and sure to win again if his temperament can continue to be harnessed effectively. Usually arrives mounted in the paddock, and is taken to post early. Wears a cross-noseband. *J.H. Philips — Western (Hendrick Wiegersma).* 73 (OMa), 203 (R), 559 (R), 1516 (I).

SEBASTOPOL ..10-3.. 12 b.g. Royal Match — Saucy Sprite (Balliol) 23p2. Small good-bodied half-brother to Sausalito. Dam won 2m Sell Hdle. NH FLAT r3 w1 (all-weather) p1 (3rd). NH '94/6 and '98 r13 p1 (2nd); 9th, last, and pulled up in Chses. P-t-P '97 and '99 r14 w3 (2 Members and Intermediate) p1 (3rd); pulled up 4, and unseated 1. Has become consistent at a modest level, and usually makes the running, but not an out-and-out stayer and is generally easy to beat. Tries hard, and rarely makes a mistake, and might be able to notch another win at 12. Suited by a sound surface. *Mrs M. Murphy — Ystrad Taf Fechan (Nick Jones).* 479 (Cf), 597 (Cf), 821 (MO), 946 (L).

SECOND AMENDMENT ..9-5.. 8 b.m. Jupiter Island — Banbury Cake (Seapic USA) 136. Good-bodied compact half-sister to Broad Steane, Larkross, Goldsteane and Court Alert. Dam won 6 Points and placed 13. NH FLAT '97/8 r3 p0. P-t-P '99 r6 p1 (3rd of 4); fell 3, and pulled up 2. NH Oct '99 r3 p0 (Sell Hdles). A dreadful jumper last year, but landed a bit of a touch on her reappearance when getting up in the last stride to win a poor Maiden at Mollington. Only managed to beat one rival in two subsequent outings, and despite being stoutly-bred seems to have stamina limitations. Will need to improve at least 7lbs for Resticteds. *Mrs L. Gregory — Grafton (Lady Annie Connell).* 786 (OMa), 1206 (R), 1482 (R).

SECOND BITE ..—.. 8 b.m. Gildoran — Cherry Morello (Bargello) c. Home-bred sister to Mazzard, and half-sister to Acetylene (qv). Carried out approaching the fourth on a most unfortunate debut, and was injured when a loose horse rammed her into a lorry. *Mrs L. Treloggen — Weston & Banwell H. (Ron Treloggen).* 352 (CfMa).

SECOND STORY ..—.. 8 ch.m. Kinglet — Singing Story (True Song) pp. Tall lengthy owner-bred sister to Kings Choir (qv). Nothing like fit enough when pulled up in Maidens, and jumped very stickily on her debut. *Mrs R. Prosser — Atherstone (Sam Arthers).* 124 (OMa), 515 (OMa).

SECOND THOUGHTS ..9-4.. 7 b.m. Derrylin — Dunsilly Bell (London Bells CAN) ff34p. Unfurnished half-sister to jumping winner, Dragon King. NH '99 (for B. Llewellyn) r1 p0 (last). Bought Ascot, June for 3600. A tricky ride who can be headstrong, but only beaten between six lengths and 12 lengths when completing, and made most until fading two out once. Should win a little race when settling. Might prefer firmer ground than she has met so far. *W.A. & Mrs A. Wales — W. Norfolk (William Wales).* 23 (OMa), 237 (OMa), 437 (OMa), 793 (CfMa), 1291 (OMa).

SECRET ALLIANCE (IRE) ..9-8.. 9 b.g. Royal Fountain — Hardy Polly (Pollerton) p62f5. Workmanlike unfurnished half-brother to Nun So Game. P-t-P '98/9 (for Mr E.H. Crow) r6 w1 (Maiden) p1 (3rd); 5th, refused 1, and fell/unseated 2. Won unchallenged at Eyton last year, but lacks consistency, and again only managed one decent effort in 2000 when chasing home Mister Moss at Tabley. Often takes a keen hold, and rarely sees the trip out, and can make mistakes as well. Will be hard pressed to win a Restricted unless significant improvement is forthcoming. *P.C. & Mrs S.E. Handley — N. Salop (Sheila Crow).* 371 (R), 589 (R), 963 (R), 1129 (R), 1200 (CR).

PLATE 117   461 Clinton Racing-Away Racing No Tax Sherwood Rangers Yeomanry HC, Leicester: Secret Bay (B. Pollock), 1st, at the second last   PHOTO: Brian Armstrong

SECRET BAY ..11-6.. 12 b.g. Zambrano — Secret Storm (Secret Ace) 11112. Strong compact half-brother to Aces High and Wee Macgregor. Dam is sister to Whistling Thorn. P-t-P/HUNT CH '97/9 (for Mr S.P. Dent) r14 w8 (inc 4 Hunt Chses, 2m7f-3m1f, and Open; inc walk-over and 5-timer in '97) p5 (3 2nds; and inc 2 Hunt Chses). An ex-eventer who bounced back to his best in the new yard, and quickly reeled off a short-price hat-trick in Hunter Chases, but despite jumping in his usual impeccable way found himself with too much ground to make up when favourite for the Aintree Foxhunters and crossed the line nine lengths adrift of Bells Life. Clocked an extraordinarily fast time when demolishing inferiors at Cottenham on his return, but beat little of consequence subsequently, and has always been found out by the top performers. A strong galloper, who meets the fences with pin-point accuracy everytime, and though he can handle an easy surface much prefers it on top. Well placed by Caroline Bailey, and seems certain to win more races for the owner whose first horse he is. *Mrs J.A. Bowen — Pytchley (Caroline Bailey).* 17 (O), 150 (3mH), 461 (2m4f110yH), 687 (2m6f110yH), 921 (2m6fH).

SECRET BEAUTY (IRE) ..9-7.. 7 ch.m. Arcane (USA) — Height Of Elegance (Shirley Heights) 1p1p136p. Plain lengthy half-sister to a flat winner in Germany, and to another in Italy. Dam won at 11f in French Provinces. IR 3800y. NH '97/9 (for N. Babbage) r5 p2. A specialist on home ground at Erw Lon where she has scored in soft and on good and firm, and kept on gamely for each of the victories, but gets low marks for consistency. Enjoyed a splendid first season, but it will be surprising if she can emulate it. *H.J. Barton — Llandeilo F.* 270 (CfMa), 484 (R), 646 (R), 837 (I), 943 (M), 1227 (I), 1299 (I), 1613 (I).

SECRET CAN'T SAY (IRE) ..9-11.. 7 b.m. Jurado (USA) — Jims Cousin (Jimsun) 2211ppfp. Workmanlike half-sister to Irish jumping winner, Rahanine Melody (IRE) (4-timer in '98 concluded by 3 visits to Scotland and Wales). P-t-P '99 r2 p1 (3rd of 4); and pulled up 1. Has gained her prizes when a maximum of four have completed, and followed two seconds at Erw Lon with a wide-margin double (very lucky once). Failed to complete in her last four starts, but was in the process of running a big race when tipping up at Bonvilston, and had almost certainly done enough for the season when taken to Hereford on her final outing where she figured prominently for a long way. Still only a youngster and likely to revive in 2001. *Mrs L.A. Goldsworthy — S. Pembs (Keith & Linda Goldsworthy).* 269 (CfMa), 648 (CfMa), 834 (OMa), 948 (R), 1227 (I), 1403 (I), 1613 (I), 1626 (3m1f110yH).

SECRET FOUR ..9-3.. 15 b.g. My Top — Secret Top (African Sky) 4p94u4. Small close-coupled half-brother to NH flat and jumping winner, Dictum (IRE), and to 2 Irish flat winners, including Let It Ride (IRE) (also a successful Hurdler there). IRISH FLAT '88/9 r20 w1 (8f — £7800 race at 2) p7. IRISH NH '90 r1 p0. FLAT (blinkered last 2) r9 p3 (just caught in short head and neck 2nds). NH '90/2 and '94/6 r41 w8 (2m2f-2m5f Hdles, inc Clmr) p14. P-t-P/HUNT CH '97/9 r15 w5 (Ladies, inc hat-trick) p5 (3 2nds). A useful hurdler when winning five times in the '90/1 season, but considerably less successful since bouncing back to form with four victories in Ladies Opens in '97. Deteriorated conseiderably when only once better than last in 2000, and has been retired. *Miss K. Langdell — Silverton (David Pipe).* 314 (L), 558 (L), 725 (L), 851 (L), 1174 (L), 1259 (4mL).

SECRET MUSIC ..8-7§.. 10 b.g. Southern Music — Secret Rebel (Rebel Prince) p4. Small sturdy brother to Rebel Tom, and half-brother to Florabalda. Dam won Maiden and placed 4. P-t-P '96/8 r15 p4 (2 2nds, remote last once; and inc last of 3); failed to finish 9 (fell/unseated 4, and refused 1). Only once beaten less than 30 lengths in 17 starts, and has frequently looked a highly unpleasant ride. Missed the '99 season, and seems hard to train nowadays. Fell when blinkered once in '97. *D. Parravani - Waveney H. (John Ibbott).* 942 (CfMa), 1507 (OMa).

SECRETROCK (IRE) ..9-2.. 8 b brg. Jolly Jake (NZ) — Dont Rock (Rugged Man) 1p. Half-brother to Carraig-An-Oir (IRE) (qv). IRISH P-t-P '99 r6 p0; pulled up 2, carried out, and fell. IRISH NH FLAT '99 r1 p0. Much improved on Irish efforts when landing a youngsters Maiden which contained fields of corn at Llanvapley, and beat the other two finishers by 30 lengths, but the form looks worthless. Faded in the closing stages of a Restricted (joint-favourite), and has something to prove in that grade. *Miss S. Hyde & Miss K. Guard — Radnor & W. Herefords (Richard Mathias).* 747 (CfMa), 992 (R).

SECRET STREAMS (IRE) ..10-0.. 7 br.g. Over The River (FR) — Brigette's Secret (Good Thyne USA) 122. P-t-P '99 r1 p1 (2nd). Showed a fair turn of foot when successful at Tweseldown, and looked certain to win again before the end of the season, but had the misfortune to encounter Ardeal next time, and dismounted after the finish on what turned out to be his final appearance at Cottenham. Speedier than most by his sire, and looks a sure thing for a Restricted at the very least in 2001, assuming he's fit enough to return. *C.H. Sporborg & Sir Chippendale Keswick — Puckeridge (Christopher Sporborg).* 7 (OMa), 86 (R), 773 (R).

SECRET TRUTH ..9-13.. 12 ch.m. Nestor — Another Nitty (Country Retreat) ppp24p5. Strong good-looking half-sister to Trinity Song and Wayward Mischief. Dam won Restricted and 2m CH and placed 8. Grandam, Nitty, won 4 Points and placed 8 (disqualified once). P-t-P/HUNT CH '96/9 r24 w2 (Maiden and PPORA) p7 (4 3rds, of 4 once, and inc 2 Hunt Chses); pulled up 10, and unseated 1. A volatile mare who is hard to restrain, and gets on her toes, sweats profusely, and has two handlers. Unable to score since winning twice in '98, and is a consistently weak finisher, but beaten less than five lengths at Stratford this season, and is still capable of the odd good effort. Seems best on a sound surface nowadays. *Mr & Mrs A.J. Martin — Heythrop (Andy Martin).* 195 (O), 897 (I), 1026 (2m5f110yH), 1312 (Cm), 1443 (3mH), 1645 (3mH), 1674 (I).

SECURON LADY ..9-9.. 10 b.m. Derrylin — Thevicarsdaughter (The Parson) 62. Compact sister to Parsons Secret. NH FLAT '96 and '97 r2 p0. P-t-P '98/9 r16 w2 (Maiden and Members) p5 (3rds, of 4 twice and last once); pulled up 2, refused 1, and fell/unseated 4. Has won a couple of modest event taking 6min 44s plus, but yet to look like adding to her score after 14 attempts in Restricteds, and often mars her rounds with erratic jumping. Fortunate to inherit a prize in her latest venture, and has been absent since March. Has been mulish at the start in the past. *M.J. O'Connor — Mendip F. (Caroline Keevil).* 144 (R), 524 (R).

SEE ME SHINE ..9-10.. 10 b.m. Lighter — See My Style (Irish Love) 74. Rangy. Dam won an Irish NH flat, and won 2m4f Hdle in England; also won 4 Points for Jennifer Snell; placed total of 9. NH FLAT '95 and '96 r2 p0. P-t-P '98 r2 w1 (Maiden) p0; and 4th. Won a long and slowly-run Maiden at Wolverhampton in '98, but evidently difficult to train since (missed '99) and failed to reappear after a trip to Black Forest Lodge in the opening month of the season. Has the ability to win a Restricted, but whether she will get another chance is the question. *Mrs H.A. Snell & P. Haslam-Fox — S. Herefords (Christine Hardinge).* 13 (R), 69 (R).

SEE MORE ACTION ..9-6§§.. 9 ch.g. Seymour Hicks (FR) — Singing Kettle (True Song) 52f4. Small sturdy flashy. Dam, sister to 6 Pointers, including Sparkling Clown (*qv* '00 Annual), won a Maiden and placed 2, but only completed in one of 10 attempts after her success (last 6 starts for Stephen Adams). NH FLAT r3 p0. NH '98 r1 p0 (pulled up in Hdle). P-t-P '97 and '99 r8 p2 (3rds, of 4 once); ran out 3, and pulled up 3. A hard-puller who invariably makes the early running, but a weak finisher, and beaten a minimum of 13 lengths in three placed efforts '99/00. Used to have defective steering, but appears to have undergone successful wheel-balancing though he is still inclined to jump to the right. Favourite on his final start which indicates how bad a race it was, but punters would be best advised to give him the swerve. Blinkered once in '97, but ran out. *R. Edwards — N. Salop.* 1196 (OMa), 1323 (OMa), 1527 (OMa), 1635 (OMa).

SEE MORE SENSE ..10-8.. 7 br.g. Seymour Hicks (FR) — Flower Of Tintern (Free State) 12. Tall rangy. Dam, half-sister to Agassi's Ace (*qv*), won 2 8f races, and 2 2m Hdles. Bought Doncaster, May '98 for 21,000. Bypassed a Maiden when making a winning debut in Restricted company at Milborne St Andrew, where he jumped right and was dismounted after the finish. Not seen again for two months, and when he did reappear he had the great misfortune to come up against Millyhenry, who was in the middle of completing his eight-timer. Favourite to beat him and only failed by one and a half lengths to do so, and it looked a splendid effort for a novice. By the sire of See More Indians, and has the makings of a quality performer. *P.K. Barber — Blackmore & Sparkford V. (Richard Barber).* 208 (R), 952 (M).

PLATE 118   208 South Dorset Restricted: See More Sense (T. Mitchell), 1st, follows out-of-shot Aberfoyle Park (R. Walford), 2nd, ahead of My Clean Sweep (Miss P. Gundry), 6th, and Dante's Gold (R. Bliss), 4th   PHOTO: Brian Armstrong

SEETHROUGH ..8-10.. 7 gr.m. Scallywag — Designer (Celtic Cone) p. Half-sister to First Design, Master Mariner, and Miss Match, and to jumping winner, Follow De Call. P-t-P '99 r1 p1 (3rd).

Performed creditably despite looking very much in need of the run when seven lengths third on her racecourse debut last year, but presumably laid low after her reappearance at Howick. Will hopefully be able to stand a full season in 2001, but the early omens are not encouraging. *Mrs G.E. Jones — Kyre (Roy Shail).* 596 (R).

SEEWARDY (U) ..—.. 6 ch.g. Gold Dust — Little To Look At (unknown) p. Small unfurnished. Soon tailed off in his Members. *R.A. Barr & M.J. Gingell — Easton H. (Matthew Gingell).* 603 (M).

SEE YOU ALWAYS (IRE) ..8-7.. 11 b.g. Royal Fountain — Lohunda Park (Malinowski USA) 3p4. Robust compact brother to Irish Pointing winners, Ballylemon (IRE) (also a successful Hurdler there) and Starlight Fountain, and half-brother to Pats Minstrel. NH FLAT '95 r1 p0. NH '95/7 r16 w1 (2m Sell Hdle) p0; bad efforts in 6 Chses. P-t-P '98/9 r9 p3 (last of 2; and 2 3rds of 4); 5th, last pair 3, and pulled up 2. Won a bad Towcester Selling Hurdle on firm in '95 (25-1 outsider in a field of five), but remarkably unsuccessful since, and has failed to beat a rival in the last two seasons despite being sent off favourite twice. More than a fence behind in his Members, and plods badly now. Has not fallen in 18 attempts over fences (unseated once), but often lacks fluency. *Mrs P. Robertson — V. of Lune H.* 813 (L), 962 (L), 1148 (M).

SELDOM SEEN (IRE) ..—.. 10 ch.g. Le Moss — Futurum Lady VII (unknown) uup. Half-brother to Marwoods Mandate (IRE) (qv). NH FLAT '96 r1 p0 (last — tailed off halfway). Seldom Seen was seldom seen until a mishap at Aspatria which meant he will never be seen again. *J.L. Brown — Haydon.* 713 (R), 1330 (OMa), 1367 (OMa).

SEMLIKI ..8-7.. 8 b.g. Nearly A Hand — River Culm (Royal Salmon) p3p. Tall half-brother to Broadway Swinger (qv). P-t-P '99 r2 p0 (pulled up 2). Taken steadily in his early races, but made errors and looked short of stamina when the gloves came off on his last two appearances at Garthorpe. Weak and lightly raced to date, and may be capable of better as he matures. *Mrs C. Cooke — Cottesmore.* 97 (OMa), 542 (M), 872 (OMa).

SENIOR PARTNER (IRE) ..9-5.. 7 b.g. Arapahos (FR) — Turvey (Royal Buck) 231. Tall workmanlike half-brother to Hill's Electric (IRE) (qv). IRISH NH '98/9 r5 p0. Sold Goffs Ireland, Aug for 1517. 20 lengths second (inherited that position two out) and 40 lengths third (favourite; lost a few lengths when nearly carried out after 2m2f), and left to finish solo in a youngsters Maiden at Detling in which the four length leader fell two out. Almost declined the final fence, and may have problems, because he has not been seen since mid-March. Would need to be perkier for Restricteds. *N.W. Padfield — Enfield Chace.* 181 (2m4fOMa), 323 (CfMa), 577 (OMa).

SENORA D'OR ..9-9.. 11 br.m. Le Coq D'Or — Eustacia Vye (Viking Chief) u4ppf. Plain unfurnished. NH '96 r2 p1 (3rd). P-t-P '96 and '98 r6 w2 (Maiden, and incredibly lucky in Restricted) p0; 5th, last, and pulled up 2. Successful twice on firmish in '96, but only able to appear bi-annually since, and well beaten on her only completion in 2000. Still retains some ability, but extracting it is nigh on impossible, and has become rather error-prone. *Mrs A. Rutherford — Lauderdale.* 359 (Cf), 419 (Cf), 714 (C), 915 (3m1fH), 1425 (I).

SENSE OF ADVENTURE ..10-7.. 8 ch.g. Lord Bud — Mistral Magic (Crofter USA) 11. Lengthy good-bodied half-brother to Tom The Tank. Well-backed and showed a handy turn of foot when making a most satisfactory debut in a Cottenham Restricted, and then had to pull out all the stops in a Fakenham Confined, but eventually prevailed by a rather cheeky head under a fine ride from Nigel Bloom. Gave his supporters a scare when ballooning some of the fences and dropping back to be last after a mile, but seemed to conquer his nerves as the race progressed, and showed plenty of pluck in the end. Registered the fastest time of the day by five seconds, and might be worth following all the way to Novice Hunter Chases eventually. *H.B. Hodge — Puckeridge.* 773 (R), 1286 (Cf).

SENSO (IRE) ..10-4.. 10 b.g. Persian Heights — Flosshilde (Rheingold) R3s31pf1p. Close-coupled workmanlike half-brother to Lost Art and Tara Boy, to Hurdles winner, Golden Path (IRE), and to 2 flat winners, including Franco Bacetti (in Italy). ITALIAN FLAT r3 p1 (2nd). FLAT (at 4/5) r2 p0 (Sell final). NH '95/6 r7 p0 (inc Sells). P-t-P '97 (for Mr R. Green) r3 p0 (last 2, and unseated 1). Developed a tendency to surrender tamely in the previous yard after mingling with Italian juveniles, but has successfully jumped ship since a lengthy absence, and provided Caroline Cox with her first winners in 2000. Stays surprisingly well, but a somewhat perilous jumper, and may have gone wrong when pulled up and dismounted on his final start. Can be wilful at times, but in a good yard, and might be persuaded to win again if fit next year. *Mrs P.M. Shirley-Beavan & Miss C. Cox — Jedforest (Simon Shirley-Beavan).* 46 (OMa), 107 (M), 364 (CfMa), 497 (R), 719 (CfMa), 976 (R), 1081 (R), 1162 (R), 1366 (I).

SEOD RIOGA (IRE) ..10-6.. 12 br.g. Down The Hatch — Jackie's Pet (Strong Gale) 2212. Rangy half-brother to Stillorgan Park (IRE), and to Irish Pointing winner, Carry On Brendan (IRE). IRISH P-t-P '93/4 r4 w3 (inc Open) p1 (3rd). NH '94/8 r27 w5 (2 Hdles, 2m5f-3m1f, and 3 Chses, 2m1f-3m1f) p7. P-t-P '99 r5 w1 (Open) p4 (2nds, of 3 once). A former decent performer under Rules who has been a wonderful servant for Simon Tindall, and has not been out of the first two in nine Points. Incredibly unlucky to bump into the likes of Real Value (twice), Struggles Glory, Satchmo and Blanville, so his victories have been thoroughly deserved. Acts on any going, and still speedy enough to dominate a race taking only just over six minutes, so can surely look forward to more success, with a bit of luck, in 2001. *S.P. Tindall — Southdown & Eridge (Jeff Peate)*. 127 (Cf), 305 (Cf), 572 (CfO), 981 (O).

SERENZE (IRE) ..9-8.. 8 b.g. Jolly Jake (NZ) — Strong Language (Formidable USA) 4p. Close-coupled half-brother to NH flat winner, Patriarch (IRE). Dam won 2 flat, 10-13f (inc a Sell), and won a 2m2f Sell Hdle. IRISH P-t-P '98 r7 p3; pulled up 1. P-t-P '99 r5 w1 (Maiden) p1 (last of 2); pulled up 2, and ran out 1. Made all to beat two racecourse debutantes at Eyton last year, and a length last of two in his first Restricted, but managed just two appearances in 2000 and made little impression. Four times a beaten favourite in England, and punters should take the hint. *W.D. Edwards — N. Salop (Sheila Crow)*. 963 (R), 1411 (R).

SERGEANT MILLER ..—.. 7 gr.g. Rustingo — Ernie's Pride (Fleece) ppp. Rangy. P-t-P '99 r1 p0 (pulled up). Inordinately cumbersome in running and jumping to date, and has carried an awful lot of condition. Might be capable of better if weight-watchers get hold of him, but don't bet on it. *Mrs J.L. Games — Golden V. (Joli Smith)*. 341 (CfMa), 451 (CfMa), 487 (CfMa).

SERIOUSLY SMART ..8-7.. 8 b.m. Primitive Rising (USA) — Salvage Girl (Military) p. Small compact sturdy half-sister to Just Felix. P-t-P '99 (for Mr J.G. Cann) r3 p0 (5th, and pulled up 2). Very green in her debut season, and only saw the racecourse once in 2000, when pulled up at Larkhill in February. Might be capable of better if she stands up to regular racing. *T. Hamlin — E. Devon (Ollie Cann)*. 264 (OMa).

SETTING SAIL ..9-4.. 7 b.m. Yachtsman (USA) — Water Eaton Gal (Legal Eagle) 23342. Microscopic half-sister to New Flame, Up And Running and The Other Half. Dam won 2 2m Sell Hdles. P-t-P '99 (for Mr M. Smalley) r1 p1 (3rd). A steady jumper for a youngster, and has made the frame in all six appearances, but must find even 11st 9lbs a real struggle and now that she has gained some experience might be worth throwing straight into Ladies races next year. Hung left-handed throughout her latest outing, so much so that Valerie Jackson's saddle slipped as she tried to counteract it, and may have been feeling the ground. *Mrs T.M. Gibson — Tynedale*. 189 (OMam), 363 (CfMa), 418 (M), 719 (CfMa), 978 (CfMa).

SEVEN FOUR SEVEN ..10-1.. 10 b.m. Jumbo Hirt (USA) — Star Of The Ocean (Callernish) 23. Lengthy unfurnished. NH FLAT '97 r2 p0 (last twice). NH '97 r1 p0 (last in Hdle). P-t-P '98/9 r10 w3 (2m4f Maiden, Restricted and PPORA Mares) p2 (2nds, of 3 once); 4th of 5, fell/unseated 2, and pulled up 2. An odd mare who is far from plain sailing, but has gained a prize in seven of her 12 Points, and provided Kevin Rosier with two-thirds of his winners. Only managed two outings in 2000, and returned lame on the last occasion. A thorough stayer, but can be very grumpy, and the latest setback will not have helped improve matters. *K. Rosier — Pendle Forest & Craven*. 998 (C), 1152 (I).

SEVENTH SYMPHONY (IRE) ..9-4.. 11 b.g. Orchestra — Trudy Belle (Furry Glen) pp3sp. Lengthy unfurnished hobbasy brother to Andy Burnett (IRE). IRISH P-t-P '96 and '99 r8 w1 (Maiden, novice riders) p1 (last of 3); pulled up 4, and fell 2. IRISH NH FLAT r1 p0. IRISH NH '98/9 r5 p1 (22l 3rd in Hunt Ch); pulled up other Hunt Ch. Sold Doncaster, Aug for 500. Scored in very soft on his only appearance of '96, but beaten in all 18 attempts since, and 12 lengths third on his only completion for the new yard. Sometimes wears a tongue-strap, and wind problems are presumably the reason why he struggles to get home. *Miss D. Edwards — Tredegar F. (Tim Jones)*. 744 (R), 947 (R), 1452 (R), 1659 (R), 1671 (R).

SEVERN MAGIC ..9-13.. 8 b.m. Buckley — La Margarite (Bonne Noel) 1. Half-sister to Pamela's Lad. Dam won 2m6f Hdle in '88. P-t-P '99 r2 p0 (fell 2). Fell in both her '99 starts, and a clear round appeared to be Adrian Wintle's only goal on her reappearance at Mollington, but the rider still had a double handful jumping the third last, and the mare made up all of 15 lengths to pass five rivals and win going away. Clearly talented, but suffered a setback and was unable to run again. Hopefully will not turn out to be as awkward as some by her sire, and worth watching closely when she returns. *C. Bosley & Mr & Mrs R. Vaughan — O. Berks (Matt Hazell)*. 76 (CCfMa).

SEYMOUR'S DOUBLE ..10-3.. 10 b.g. Seymour Hicks (FR) — Ida Spider (Ben Novus) 232212. Small neat half-brother to Henry Spider, Ardent Spy and Spy's Delight, to NH flat and useful jumping winner, Ida's Delight, to jumping winner, Sikera Spy, and to winning Hurdler, Comedy Spy. NH FLAT '96 r2 p0. NH '96 r3 p0. P-t-P '99 r5 w1 (Maiden) p0; fell 3, and pulled up 1. Headstrong, and something of an equine stuntman at the fences in his first season, but has improved appreciably in both respects, and enjoyed the lesser weight on his back when popped into Ladies company on his two most recent starts. Landed a gamble in the first of them, but his victim Sun Surfer narrowly gained his revenge when they met again on the same course a week later. Usually held up for a late challenge, and should put his consistency to good use again in 2001. *Viscountess Boyne & J. Downes — Wheatland (John Downes)*. 37 (CI), 296 (I), 567 (R), 992 (R), 1199 (L), 1320 (L).

SHADOWGRAFF ..8-13.. 11 b.m. Scorpio (FR) — Panatate (Panco) p3pp3. Strong-topped half-sister to Shadow Walker and Pay The Fine. Grandam, Agitate, won 2 2m Chses and 3 Ladies and placed total of 10 (9 2nds). P-t-P '96 and '99 r10 w1 (Maiden) p0; pulled up 2, and fell 2. NH '99 r1 p0 (pulled up). Won a bad three-finisher Maiden at Dingley at the tenth attempt last year, and not disgraced when third in two seven minute Restricteds in 2000, but well beaten otherwise, and usually carries too much condition. *A. Hollingsworth — Worcs.* 78 (L), 193 (R), 336 (R), 894 (R), 1067 (3m2fR).

SHADY EXCHANGE (IRE) ..9-0.. 6 b.g. Le Bavard (FR) — Torus Light (Torus) up. Brother to Irish Hurdles winner, Mayo Magic. Appeared twice at Mollington, and made most for two miles and was still 25 lengths second when he pulled up rapidly at the last in the latest. Ran very promisingly, and will not have to do much better to win a Maiden, if allowed to complete the course. *T.L. Greig — Grafton (Jenny Pidgeon).* 76 (CCfMa), 432 (OMa).

SHAFI (IRE) ..10-9.. 10 b.g. Reference Point — Azyaa (Kris) p2232412. Small neat half-brother to flat winners, Hadith, Yarob, Mukhatab and Ihtiraz. Dam won at 8f. FLAT r8 w1 (11f) p3. DUBAI FLAT '95 and '97 w4 (10-12f). NH '98 r3 p0 (4th, last and pulled up 1). P-t-P '99 (for Mr M.C. Pipe) r2 w2 (Opens). A decent animal on the level, and put his flat-race speed to good use when winning two Opens at Black Forest Lodge last year, but has found three miles too far in better company since, and appreciated the drop in distance when running away with a 22-runner Cheltenham Hunter Chase over the minimum trip on his penultimate start. Ridden by Mark Trott for the first time on that occasion and jumped much more fluently for him than for his previous partner. Speedy and pulls hard, but sure to play a prominent role in sub-3m events next year, and could prove impossible to beat over the minimum trip. Unsuited by an easy surface. *G. Byard — Radnor & W. Herefords (Steve Flook).* 34 (MO), 150 (3mH), 226 (2m4f110yH), 460 (2m7f110yH), 920 (3mH), 1023 (3mH), 1341 (2m110yH), 1447 (2m4fH).

SHAKE FIVE (IRE) ..10-0.. 10 br.g. Tremblant — Five Swallows (Crash Course) p33. Lengthy half-brother to Irish Pointing winner, Glenard Lad. P-t-P '96/9 r24 w12 (inc 7 Opens) p9 (6 2nds, of 3 once; and inc 3rd of 4 once). An incredibly tough campaigner who has gained a prize in 23 of 27 races, and reeled off an eight-timer in as soon as blinkers were fitted in '98, but it has been doom and gloom since and has been unable to score in his last eight races, and severed a tendon in the latest. Used to battle bravely, and was suited by going right-handed. *Mrs C.H. Sporborg — Puckeridge (Christopher Sporborg).* 17 (O), 85 (O), 176 (O).

SHAMELESS LADY ..9-5.. 11 b.m. Bold Owl — Spartan's Girl (Spartan General) p3425pp. Lengthy windsucker. Sister to successful Chaser, Bold Spartan, and to Hurdles winner, Roys Dilemma, and half-sister to Carl's Choice, Queen Of Sparta, Mrs Teasdale, Busters Sister and Spartan Joker. Dam won W. Pytchley Members and 3rd. NH FLAT r3 p0. NH '94/6 r7 p0 (last, and unseated 1 in Chses). P-t-P '97 and '99 r9 w1 (Maiden) p0; pulled up 2, and fell/unseated 2. Won a bad Maiden at Flete Park on her final appearance in '97, but beaten 12 times since returning from a year on the sidelines, and beaten a minimum of 15 lengths when completing in 2000. A steady jumper, but very moderate, and will continue to struggle in Restricteds. *R.C. & Mrs M. Darke — Dart V. & S. Pool H. (Caroline Keevil).* 163 (R), 251 (M), 406 (R), 658 (R), 849 (R), 1258 (R), 1517 (R).

SHAMROCK LAD ..9-2.. 8 br.g. Impecunious — Flame Lady (Tudor Flame) 4pf. Dam, half-sister to Master Nobby (qv '87 Season Annual), won a Club Maiden for David Dando ('looks a doubtful stayer'). Grandam, Nobore, was last of 3 in a Maiden. Has a poor pedigree, and was beaten 47 lengths on his only completion. *D.J. Dando — Beaufort.* 264 (OMa), 471 (OMa), 630 (OMa).

SHAMRON (IRE) ..9-13.. 11 b.m. Torus — Beech Glen (Furry Glen) 53. Lengthy half-sister to Grannies Delight (IRE), and to Irish NH flat winner, Tuesday (IRE). IRISH NH '97 r5 p2 (Chses). IRISH P-t-P '95/8 r13 w1 (5yo&up mares Maiden) p2 (2nds). P-t-P '99 r6 p4 (3 2nds); and pulled up 2. Beaten seven lengths or less on four occasions for present connections, and often gives the impression that she is going to deliver, but finds nothing off the bridle and is becoming most frustrating. Not to be trusted an inch in future. Has been tried in a tongue-strap in Ireland. *J.S.S. Hollins — Ashford V. (Gill Gladders).* 575 (R), 825 (R).

SHANAVOGH ..10-10.. 10 b.g. Idiot's Delight — Honeybuzzard (FR) (Sea Hawk II) 2p11. Workmanlike angular half-brother to 5 winners (including abroad), including Jopanini (Hurdles). Dam won at 10f in Ireland. IRISH P-t-P '95 r2 p1 (last of 3); and pulled up. NH FLAT Nov '95 r1 p0. NH '95/9 (for G.M. Moore) r18 w4 (3 Hdles, 2m4f-2m5f, and 2m5f Ch) p9 (fell and remounted once); fell 2 or would probably have won 2m Ch once. Bought Doncaster, Aug for 22,000. A consistent sort who would have made the frame 14 times consecutively under Rules but for falling once (was in the first three on 12 occasions), but did not seem to be at his best in his early points. Concluded with an emphatic double two months apart, and recorded quick times in both. Can maintain a determined domination in the final mile, and will be difficult to beat in Opens in this sort of form. *R.S. Hunnisett — Pytchley (Caroline Bailey).* 231 (O), 369 (O), 545 (O), 1416 (O).

SHANBALLYMORE (IRE) ..9-12.. 12 b.g. Teofane — Greenhall Madam (Lucifer USA) f7f61159. Smallish compact. NH '96 r1 p0. P-t-P/HUNT CH '95/6 (for Mrs W.J.N. Tilley & Mrs J.R. Parr) r9 w1 (2m4f Maiden) p4 (3 2nds, of 3 once). Managed nine successive completions in his first two seasons, but took a while to get his eye in after such a lengthy absence, and ended up on the floor in two of his first three starts this year. Stayed on well to gain two narrow wins in modest company on differing surfaces subsequently, but had his limitations exposed in more competitive races on his last two appearances. One-paced, and will always be up against it in future. *Mrs D. Gray Williams — Flint & Denbigh.* 90 (3m1fH), 171 (O), 293 (Cf), 567 (R), 776 (M), 812 (Cf), 1151 (O), 1343 (3m110yH).

SHANNONS CHARM ..—.. 10 b.m. Michael's Revenge — Ottilia (Tudor Flame) p. Good-bodied. Made a belated racecourse debut in June and zoomed into a clear lead which had taken him 25 lengths ahead by the eighth, but stopped to nothing when headed at the 11th and pulled up at the next. *Miss F. Wilkins — Portman (Donna Sargent).* 1654 (OMa).

SHARED-INTEREST ..9-4.. 7 ch.m. Interrex (CAN) — La Campagnola (Hubble Bubble) 1. Angular. NH FLAT '99 (from G. Knight's) r1 p0 (tailed off). The comfortable 33-1 winner at a Maiden at Kingston St Mary (50s was available in places), but it was a bad race, and will have a lot more to do in Restricteds. *D.J. Adams — Taunton V. (Alison Handel).* 1241 (OMa).

SHARETON ..9-13.. 10 br.g. Lighter — Share (Khalkis) f12f. Brother to Share A Light, and half-brother to Gosh. Dam won Bumper and 2m Hdle in Ireland and won 3 2m Hdles in England. P-t-P '99 r3 p1 (2nd); and pulled up 2. Finally confirmed the promise of his Pointing debut with an unchallenged win in a slowly-run Maiden at Cothelstone, but consistently bad jumping continues to halt his development. Would romp a Restricted if ever he produced another clear round, but clearly much work needs to be done before he reappears, and has yet to prove that he can gallop for an end-to-end three miles. *J.H. Green & B.E. Perrett — Blackmore & Sparkford V. (Rose Vickery).* 213 (CfMa), 641 (CfMa), 1095 (R), 1309 (R).

SHARIAKANNDI (FR) ..9-7§.. 9 b.g. Lashkari — Shapaara (Rheingold) 5pp. Tall brother to a French flat winner, and half-brother to 2 others. Dam is half-sister to Shergar. NH FLAT '96 (first two for D. Eddy) r4 p1 (2nd). NH '97/8 (for J. King, bought for 6500, blinkered final) r12 w1 (2m7f Hdle) p1 (3rd). Has always been a difficult ride who needs plenty of driving, and refused to co-operate after his Pointing debut. Blinkered next time, to no avail. Missed '99 and not seen after February 2000, and would need a complete change of heart to achieve anything in future. *H.B. Geddes — Taunton V. (Richard Barber).* 34 (MO), 160 (O), 327 (O).

SHARIMAGE (IRE) ..10-6.. 10 ch.g. Luxury Image — Even Fort (Even Money) 333. Plain angular half-brother to Irish NH flat, Hurdles and pointing winner, Fort Invader. Dam won Bumper and 3 Hdles (2m-2m5f) in Ireland. IRISH P-t-P '96/7 r7 w3 (awarded 4&5yo Mdn by stewards; and 2 Winners of Two) p1 (2nd); slipped up, and fell. IRISH NH '97/9 r21 w2 (Hunt Chses) p5 (Chses). Bought Doncaster, Aug for 7200. Beaten about 12 lengths on each outing in the new yard and invariably ran well, but came up against remarkably hot opponents. Met Whatafellow and Mick The Cutaway at Thorpe where he jumped deliberatley in th early stages, tried to give the subsequent Hunter Chase winners Lord Harry and Give It A Whirl seven pounds at Southwell, and then one-paced behind Keltic Abbey and Ardstown (also both receiving weight) in a Chepstow Hunter Chase. Has scored on firmish, but mud is ideal, and probably additionally well suited by a test of stamina. Certainly deserves a success in 2001. *Mrs C. Mackness — Ledbury (Nicky Sheppard).* 117 (O), 369 (O), 683 (3mH).

SHARPAMAN ..9-8.. 6 b.g. Mandalus — Sharp Glance (IRE) (Deep Run) 2p. Half-brother to Hurdles winner, Digup St Edmunds. Bought Doncaster, May for 5000. Beaten a head by the only other finisher in holding at Corbridge, but looked the winner until he blundered at the final fence. Suffered another costly jumping lapse next time when doing the splits at the 14th and immediately pulling up, and is difficult to evaluate, but could be promising if becoming fluent. *S.H. Shirley-Beavan — Jedforest.* 1164 (OMa), 1479 (OMa).

SHARP EMBRACE ..9-8.. 8 ch.g. Broadsword (USA) — Running Kiss (Deep Run) p7u244. Small light-framed brother to Ickford Okey. NH FLAT '97 r1 p0. NH '97/8 r12 p2 (3rd in Hdle, and 2nd in Ch); pulled up and fell other Chses; inc Sells. P-t-P '99 r3 p1 (3rd of 4); and unseated 2. A catastrophe when over-ridden, but has produced rateable form under Jason Burley, though needs to improve on a 20 lengths second at Tabley to warrant close inspection in a Maiden. Often wore headgear under Rules and seems to lack resolve. *Miss S. Rodman — High Peak H.* 280 (L), 590 (L), 906 (CfMa), 965 (OMa), 1125 (OMa), 1323 (OMa).

SHARP SEAL ..—.. 7 b.g. Broadsword (USA) — Little Beaver (Privy Seal) f. Half-brother to B For Business (qv). Sold Ascot, Sept '98 for 4200. Soon tailed off on his debut, and came to grief when they jumped the water for the second time. *J.D. Brownrigg — I. of W. (Philip Legge).* 215 (C).

SHARP THYNE (IRE) ..10-3.. 11 b.g. Good Thyne (USA) — Cornamucla (Lucky Guy) p6432343. Attractive good-bodied half-brother to The Major General and Tied For Time (IRE), and to Irish Hurdles winner, Ballinderry Glen. Dam won a NH flat race and a Point in Ireland. IRISH P-t-P '95 r2 w1 (5yo Maiden) p0; pulled up 1. IRISH NH FLAT r1 p0. NH '97/9 (for P.J. Hobbs) r12 w2 (3m-3m2f Hdles) p2; pulled up 3. P-t-P '97 (for late Mrs R.L. Matson) r1 p0 (pulled up). A fair if somewhat indolent hurdler for Phillip Hobbs, but too soft for steeplechasing and was pulled up in two of three attempts over the bigger obstacles. Reserved a fair bit for himself on his return to pointing in 2000, and could not be persuaded to win for love nor money. Usually races prominently, but too much of a rogue to place any faith in despite his undoubted ability. Wears blinkers. Suited by a sound surface. *B. Meikle (Sharp Thyne Society) — Border.* 41 (L), 109 (L), 361 (L), 715 (L), 974 (L), 1150 (L), 1426 (L), 1497 (L).

SHARSMAN (IRE) ..10-5.. 11 b.g. Callernish — Another Dutchess (Master Buck) 212. Compact half-brother to Desert Run (IRE) *(qv)*. P-t-P '95/7 and '99 r8 w3 (up to Confined) p4 (3 2nds, of 3 once); pulled up 2, and fell 3. A likeable sort, but his racecourse appearances have been strictly rationed and avoids ground any firmer than good. Recorded his fourth career success when pegging back Three Saints at Eaton Hall, but a beaten favourite either side, though only beaten a maximum of two and a half lengths. Stays well, and would have solid claims in Open company next year. *A.R. Trott — N. Salop (Sheila Crow).* 116 (I), 781 (Cf), 905 (C).

SHAY GAP (IRE) ..10-1.. 8 br.g. Yashgan — Anavore (Darantus) u13. Half-brother to Irish NH flat and jumping winner, King Of The Glen. NH FLAT '98 r2 p0. P-t-P '99 r8 w2 p0 (4th, 6th, and pulled up 1). Successful on the second of three March appearances, when three subsequent winners trailed in behind, and subsequently had the best view of the Lord Levi/Wills Perk incident at Lanark when finishing a close third in his first Restricted. Had tried to duck out on his return and needed to have his mind made up for him at Dalston, but it would be surprising if he was not able to win again. Yet to encounter ground quicker than good. Wears a cross-noseband. *M.H. Walton — Border (Clive Storey).* 426 (CfMa), 499 (2m4fOMa), 663 (R).

SHEDOES ..9-3.. 12 ch.m. Troy Song — Shewill (Evening Trial) 4. Lengthy good-quartered owner-bred sister to Hehas *(qv)*. P-t-P '94, '97 and '99 r11 p4 (2 2nds of 3); (last, pulled up 5, and fell 1). Enjoyed her most productive year to date in '99, when beaten between six-and-a-half and 20 lengths in four placings, but appeared just once this year when 13 lengths fourth at Ashorne. Could have won races in her youth, but was never fit enough, and too old now. *Mrs E.C. Cockburn — Warwicks.* 1437 (OMa).

SHEELIN LAD (IRE) ..—.. 13 ch.g. Orchestra — Aryumad (Goldhill) ppp. Big strong-topped half-brother to Whistling Rufus (IRE) *(qv)*. IRISH P-t-P '94 r3 w2 (6 plus Mdn, and Winners of One) p1 (2nd). IRISH NH '92/3 r4 p0. NH '94/7 and '99 (bought for 12,500; one win previously for L. Lungo, bought for 21,000) r18 w3 (3m-3m2f Chses, inc £8520 prize) p6. Stays extra well and has accumulated five wins on ground ranging from firmish to heavy, but on the go for nine years (with a couple of breaks of 16 and 18 months), and looked a spent force when carrying a great deal of condition in 2000. *Mrs T.J. McInnes Skinner — Belvoir (Chris Vale).* 794 (Cf), 867 (M), 1415 (Cf).

SHEEPHAVEN ..9-6.. 17 b.g. Relkino — Suffolk Broads (Moulton) 155. Tall rangy brother to a Hurdles winner. IRISH NH FLAT '89/90 r2 p0. IRISH NH '90 r3 p2 (Hdles). NH '90/1, '93/5 and '97 (pulled up final for D. Nicholson; 3 wins previously for T. Casey; previously for T. Etherington) r25 w4 (3m-3m4f) p5 (beaten head once); clear when fell last once. Wore blinkers under Rules and had only appeared once since '95, and resuming at 16 looked highly optimistic, but proved that dreams can come true when left in the lead at the final fence in his Members. Gave Delmi Davies his first success in the process after a few seasons trying. Unsurprisingly badly outclassed in Opens afterwards. *Mrs M.M.J. Davies — V. of Clettwr.* 266 (M), 645 (MO), 833 (O).

SHEHAB (IRE) ..—.. 8 b.g. Persian Bold — Fenjaan (Trojan Fen) ppfpp. Good-bodied half-brother to flat winner, Shocker, and to a winner in Dubai. Dam won 4 8f races consecutively. FLAT (won for W. Haggas) r4 w1 (10f) p1 (2nd). NH '97 (for P. Hedger); claimed for £18,000 after flat win) r2 w1 (2m2f Hdle) p1 (3rd). Bought Ascot, Nov for 500. A hard puller who usually showed plenty of early speed for five different jockeys in Points, but gallops himself into the ground, and 2m2f is the upper limit of his stamina. *K. Richards — Llangeinor.* 141 (MO), 275 (Cf), 345 (O), 480 (O), 598 (O).

SHEKELS (IRE) ..10-10.. 10 ch.g. Orchestra — Rare Currency (Rarity) 14. Strong lengthy good-looking. NH FLAT '96 r3 p1 (3rd), NH '97/9 (for S. Sherwood, blinkered final 2; wins previously for C. Brooks) r16 w4 (2m Hdle, and 3 Chses, 2m4f-2m5f) p3. Bought Doncaster, May for 9000. Made all in each of his four wins for Charlie Brooks, but seemed to become jaded. Not lacking in ability and was racing over his ideal distance of 2m6f when he scored first time out in a 16-runner field, but did not appear to take much interest when favourite next time, and the rider picked up a five day ban for easing prematurely and losing third place. Has been operated on for a soft palate. Showed at Stratford that it is not vital that he leads throughout. *Mrs S. Dunsdon — Surrey U. (Nick Gifford).* 1026 (2m5f110yH), 1332 (3mH).

SHELTERING (IRE) ..—.. 9 b.g. Strong Gale — Lady Brenda (Crash Course) 1131f1. Lengthy. IRISH P-t-P '99 r1 w1 (7 plus Mdn). IRISH NH '97 and '99 r6 w4 (2m6f-3m1f Hunt Chses) p1 (2nd to Castle Mane at Punchestown); inc Hdle. IRISH P-t-P '00 r1 w1 (beat The Noble Rouge and Another Excuse 4*l* and 5*l* in Lisgoold Open: *made all, went clr aft 2 out, eased flat, easy*). IRISH HUNT CH '00 r4 w3 (beat Spot Thedifference and Father Andy 4*l* and dist at Fairyhouse: *3rd til 2nd ½way, lft in ld 13, clr 5 out, r.o frm last*; beat Father Andy and Millbrook Warrior 20*l* and 7*l* at Fairyhouse: *trckd ldrs, cl 2nd 4 out, ld nxt, sn drew clr*; and beat Satchmo and Last Option dist and 5*l* at Punchestown: *made all, mist 2 out, wl clr last*) p1 (3rd, beaten 4½*l* and 1½*l* by Dan's Your Man and Spot Thedifference at Leopardstown: *ld early, 2nd 4, rdn 3 out, no ex*). Top of the Irish tree for the last two seasons, and confirmed his position there when landing the Champion Hunters Chase at Punchestown, in which he had been runner-up to Castle Mane the previous year. His only other defeat '99/00 was when trying to concede 19 pounds to Dan's Your Man at Leopardstown, but like so many of his visiting compatriots in 2000 was let down by his jumping on an English foray, and having missed the break in the Cheltenham Foxhunters he fenced indifferently until exiting at the fifth. Revels in heavy ground (rather surprisingly for a Strong Gale), and is notably speedy and genuine. With a fluent round he could easily pose a potent threat at the Cheltenham Festival in 2001. Wears a tongue-strap. *Mrs S. Catherwood — Tipperary (Edward O'Grady).* 584 (3m2f110yH).

PLATE 119   584 Christies Foxhunters HC, Cheltenham: *Fancied Irishman Sheltering* (P. Fenton), fell, strides to post   PHOTO: Brian Armstrong

SHENOSO ..—.. 6 b.m. Teenoso (USA) — Mossy Morning (Le Moss) ppp. A completely useless five-year-old who has been tubed since her debut, and acquired a visor in her Members, in which she was two fences adrift when eventually pulling up. *Mr & Mrs E. Graham — Dumfries.* 425 (CfMa), 664 (2m5fOMa), 979 (M).

SHE WOOD SHE ..—.. 8 bl.m. Tigerwood — Levotesse (Levmoss) pp. Small light-framed half-sister to Queenofthemountain (qv). P-t-P '99 (for Mr D.L. Gibbs & Mr G. Richards) r7 p0 (pulled up 6, and unseated 1). Eliminated in the first two miles on six occasions, and remains a consistently poor jumper. Lacks the substance to survive her errors and is consequently useless. *Mrs C.J. Enser — Lamerton.* 100 (O), 933 (OMa).

SHILLELAGH OAK ..9-6.. 11 ch.g. Nishapour (FR) — Sweet Ecstasy (Rarity) 08p. Tall rangy half-brother to a winner in Belgium. Dam won 3 flat, 6-12f. IRISH NH FLAT '95 r5 p2 (3rds). IRISH NH '95/6 r2 p0. IRISH P-t-P '96/7 r10 w1 (7 plus Mdn) p3; pulled up 4. NH '97/8 and Aut '99 (for J. O'Shea, bought for 8100; visored 1) r9 p1. Scored by a head in heavy in Ireland when gaining his only victory, and was short-headed in a Chase on his English debut, but has never managed a placing since. Has a history of breaking blood vessels which will not go away. *C.E. Moir — Cotswold (Pat Hayes).* 1336 (2m4fH), 1444 (2m5fH), 1608 (R).

SHINE A LITTLE (IRE) ..9-0.. 8 ch.g. Little Wolf — Green Shine (Green Shoon) p3. Lengthy half-brother to Erins Return. Dam was 20l last of 3 in a Restricted at 13 (her only season to race). IRISH P-t-P '98 r1 p0 (remote 4th). P-t-P '99 r4 p0 (pulled up 4). Has shown speed for up to two miles, but never appears fit and was beaten more than a fence in her latest outing. Off the track for nine weeks between her last two starts in '99, and her season had ended by mid-February this time. *P.J. Jonason — Cambs.* 21 (2m4fOMa), 236 (OMa).

SHINGLE BEACH (IRE) ..9-12.. 9 b.g. Electric — Crazy Rose (FR) (Son Of Silver) 2822. Big strong half-brother to 2 French Hurdling winners. IRISH P-t-P '98/9 r10 w1 (7 plus Mdn) p3; pulled up 4, and fell. Bought Doncaster, Aug for 2000. Very moderate in Ireland, and had been a poor third when the two leaders fell two and presented him with a Maiden. Looked promising although slightly flattered by his proximity to Minden Rose on his English debut, but dogged in in a Hunter Chase next time, and has been blinkered since. Not disgraced in another Restricted, but was made favourite for a four mile Mixed Open (a conspicuously uncompetitive affair) and was no match for the outsider of the party. There is a victory to be wrenched out of him if he can be persuaded to give of his best. *Miss E.M. & Mrs M. Shirley-Beava424 — Jedforest (Simon Shirley-Beavan).* 40 (R), 89 (3m1fH), 424 (R), 911 (4mMO).

SHINING LEADER (IRE) ..9-3.. 10 b.g. Supreme Leader — Shining Run (Deep Run) 1. Half-brother to Irish Hurdles winner, Brambleshine. Dam, half-sister to Friends of Bernard (*qv*), won mares Maiden in Ireland. IRISH P-t-P '97/9 r8 p2 (3rds); pulled up 4, and fell. Never able to run much and jumped right on his English debut at Higham, but made virtually all and was eight lengths clear when he hit the last and Harry Fowler lost his irons and the saddle slipped but just managed to get him home under frenetic driving. It would have been rotten luck had he been caught, but even unchallenged success would have left him with more to find for Restricteds. *R.W. Gardiner (Lord Leighton Partnership) — E. Essex (Robert Gardiner).* 1115 (OMa).

SHIPS DECANTER (IRE) ..10-6.. 9 b/br.g. Lafontaine (USA) — Proven Right (Kemal FR) 4113. Rangy brother to Irish Pointing winner, Moral Justice. IRISH P-t-P '98/9 r3 w1 (6yo Mdn) p0. IRISH NH '98/9 r8 p2 (Hunt Chses); Pulled up both Chses. IRISH P-t-P '00 r2 w1 (after original winner disqualified) beat Bart Eile and Supreme Decision 40*l* and 6*l* in Punchestown Adjacent Winners of 1: *trckd ldrs, 3rd 3 out, fin 2nd, promoted*; and 4th in Comber Winners of 2; *prog to mid div ½way, stayed on.* Only an average contestant in Ireland and was awarded his Adjacent in 2000 as the first past the post carried the incorrect weight, but found a very soft opportunity at Sandown when triumphing under the Northumbrian export Bas Nicholl. Turned out there again the following day, but had a far more difficult task, and plodded home a poor third. Currently looks flattered by a Hunter Chase success. Wears blinkers and a tongue-strap. *J.S.R. Nicholl — Kildare (Tony Martin, in Ireland).* 469 (3m110yH), 470 (2m4f110yH).

SHOBROOKE MILL ..10-6.. 8 ch.g. Shaab — Jubilee Leigh (Hubble Bubble) 2pu21. Gigantic rangy half-brother to Creedy Valley. Grandam, Hanago Leigh, was distant last of 3 in Eggesford Members for Sarah Prouse. P-t-P '99 r6 w1 (Maiden) p1 (2nd); last, fell 2, and brought down 1. On the upgrade now that a regular rider has been secured, but still prone to errors despite being big enough to step over the fences. His Maiden victory was gained in just over six minutes, but has strengthened up considerably since, and handled the testing conditions well on his final start which was run in 7min 15s. A Restricted success is lost forever, but the likelihood is that he will soon advance to Opens. Can take a strong hold and wears a cross-noseband. *H. & Mrs S. Prouse — Eggesford (Sarah Prouse).* 14 (R), 261 (R), 580 (3mH), 729 (R), 1140 (CfR).

PLATE 120   1140 Tiverton Staghounds Confined Restricted: Shobrooke Mill (A. Charles-Jones), 1st, leads the about-to-fall Pendragon (N. Mitchell), Fursan (P. Phillips), 3rd, is somewhere there as well
PHOTO: Tim Holt

SHOEMAKER (IRE) ..10-5.. 7 b.g. Good Thyne (USA) — Kalanshoe (Random Shot) 11. Tall half-brother to Prince Ronan (IRE) and to successful Hurdler, Strong Paladin (IRE). Dam won 2m2f NH flat in Ireland. Chased home by the eternal maiden Father's Joy at Guilsborough, but it was a smooth and impressive performance, and confirmed the impression in a better contest at Clifton-on-Dunsmore. It looks as if he will prove smart, and connections must be looking forward to 2001 with relish as they also have care of the other top novice in the Area, Union Man. *Mr & Mrs W.J. Warner — Mrs J. Wilson — Pytchley (Bill Warner).* 1012 (CfMa), 1419 (R).

SHOON WIND ..10-5.. 18 b.g. Green Shoon — Gone (Whistling Wind) 1. Tall lengthy brother to Green Tops, Gone's Girl and Syd Green (IRE), and half-brother to Tipping Along (IRE), to Irish Pointing winner, Port And White, to Hurdles winner, Jazz Duke, and NH flat winner, Perfect Pal (IRE). Dam won 2m4f Hdle in Ireland. NH '87/94 (visored 1) r45 w10 (2 Hdles, 2m-3m1f, and 8 Chses, 2m4f-3m1f) p12 (short-headed for £9910 prize); fell 2 out when leading in £8545 race. P-t-P '95/9 r21 w11 (inc 3 Opens) p8 (4 2nds, last once; and 4 3rds, last once); fell 1. Without doubt the fleetest 17-year-old in the country, and recorded the 22nd success of his long and illustrious career when jogging round to collect his Members on his sole appearance in 2000. Only once missed the frame in 22 Points when an uncharacteristic faller at Dingley in '96, and has had one of the most admirable lives imaginable. If he has run his last race then we wish him a long and enjoyable retirement. *J.N. Dalton — Albrighton.* 1407 (M).

SHORTCUT SHORTY ..9-2.. 9 b.g. Winter Words — My Hostess (Gabitat) p5p1. Good-topped lengthy. Jumped very poorly and hopelessly tailed off (last once) when given no guidance by a novice on his first three starts, but made nearly all and plugged on steadily to win a Dingley Maiden on dead ground when Charlie Wadland took over. His time was the slowest of the day by 13 seconds or far more, but at least he tried, which is more than could ever have been said of his dam who was very mulish and had an aversion to starting stalls. *Miss L.S. Goodwin & S. Shepherd — Bicester with Whaddon.* 1435 (OMa), 1486 (OMa), 1624 (OMa), 1669 (OMa).

SHOTLEY AGAIN ..9-9.. 11 b.g. Then Again — Sweet Candice (African Sky) 2. Strong-topped half-brother to 2 flat winners. Dam won at 5f, and is half-sister to Cluga Gurm (qv '91 Annual). 2500f, 1500y, 5000 2-y-o. FLAT r31 w2 (7f, the first a Sell) p4. NH '95/6 (for N. Bycroft) r2 p0. Sold Doncaster, Nov '96 for 500. A dual flat winner to '94 (in soft once), but had been off the course for four years before reappearing to finish a game six lengths second in his Members. It looked as if he might have been capable of landing a minor Point, but promptly scuttled back into hiding. *M. Holmes — Axe V.H.* 926 (M).

SHOULDHAVESAIDNO (IRE) ..8-5.. 10 br.m. Orchestra — Corbal-Lis (Tumble Gold) ps54pp. Small. NH '97 and '99 (for R. Simpson; previously for T. Hind) r3 p0 (pulled up in 2 Hdles, and fell in Ch). Bought Doncaster, March for 680. Generally unable to complete in Points, and beaten 33 lengths plus with only one behind her when she did get round. Herbie Owen purchased two out of Rod Simpson's yard at the same Doncaster sale, but whilst this one was a dud the other (Major's Law) cost only 20gns more and later collected a Hunter Chase? *Mr & Mrs E. Cardew — Bicester with Whaddon (Herbie Owen).* 20 (OMa), 81 (CCfMa), 250 (CfMa), 434 (OMa), 738 (OMa), 1147 (OMa).

SHREWD THOUGHT (USA) ..9-12.. 10 ch.g. Lyphard's Wish (FR) — Tamed Shrew (USA) (Sir Ivor) 4pp15. Tall strong half-brother to a winner in USA. Dam won a flat race in USA. NH FLAT r2 p0. NH '95/6 r5 p0. P-t-P/HUNT CH '97/9 (for Mrs E.J. Coleman, Mrs C. Ball, Mr & Mrs D. Fisher) r11 w3 (Maiden, Restricted and Members) p2 (3rd of 4 once); pulled up 2, and fell/unseated 2. Would almost certainly have completed an unbeaten hat-trick in '97 but for falling in his Members, but pulled up on his only outing the following season, and has never really recovered his old zip since. Made all in his first three wins, but took up the running as late as the final fence when successful in his three-finisher Members this year. Occasionally awkward at the start in the previous yard, and is not the most fluent of jumpers at times, and likely to prove frustrating in future. *J.M. Salter — Axe V.H. (Philip Greenwood).* 63 (I), 214 (Cf), 730 (I), 926 (M), 1305 (MO).

SHRIMBELLE ..—.. 18 b.m. Shrivenham — Bella IX (Conwyn) 3. Plain. Dam ran in 4 Points for Mr Fear (last 2, and pulled up 2). P-t-P '89/92 and '94/5 r30 p4 (3 3rds, last once); failed to finish 17 (refused 5, and fell/unseated 4). A long-standing maiden, and returned after missing the previous four seasons to plod home 45 lengths behind the winner in her Members. Not a bad effort for an oldie, but to put it into context an unregistered hunter was 30 lengths in front of her. *J.E. Fear — Weston & Banwell H.* 1549 (M).

SHROPSHIRE GALE (IRE) ..—.. 10 b.g. Strong Gale — Willow Fashion (Quayside) u. Workmanlike. NH FLAT Spr '97 (for S. Brookshaw) r3 p1 (2nd). NH '98 (for P. Hobbs) r1 p0; pulled up in Hdle. Bought Doncaster, May '98 for 900. Making only the fifth appearance of his life when backed from 12-1 to half those odds in a January Maiden, but unseated after two miles when close up. Almost certainly had ability, but training him has been one long never-ending nightmare. *D. Ibbotson — Rockwood H.* 51 (OMa).

SHUIL'S STAR (IRE) ..10-9.. 10 b.g. Henbit (USA) — Shuil Run (Deep Run) 4264. Workmanlike. P-t-P/HUNT CH '96/9 r18 w5 (inc 2 Opens) p6 (4 2nds, of 3 once, and last once; and 3rd of 4 once, inc Hunt Ch); pulled up 2. Won four of his first seven races, but cursed by broken blood vessels since, and has managed just one success (from a 15-year-old and a bad maiden) from his last 15 starts. Goes well fresh, and returned to his best when around 17 lengths fourth to Bells Life in the Aintree Foxhunters and when runner-up to Lakefield Rambler at Cheltenham, but disappointed on ground faster than he cares for at Chepstow, and subsequently beaten a long way in the John Corbet Cup. Sometimes makes mistakes, and the overriding impression is that he will need to return to Points in order to win again. Best suited by plenty of cut in the ground. Twice blinkered in '99. *R.A. Mason — Glamorgan (Evan Williams).* 921 (2m6fH), 1340 (3m1f110yH), 1433 (3mH), 1646 (3m4fH).

SHULA ..—.. 8 b.m. Dutch Treat — Last In Line (Dynastic) p. Lengthy owner-bred. Dam, 'very slow and moderate', was placed in 4 Points. Grandam, Late For Tea, won 8 Points and placed 13. P-t-P '99 r3 p0 (pulled up 3). Pulled up at around the two mile mark thrice, and once got as far as the second last. If only she were as talented as her mother. *B.T. & T.M. Joyce — Fitzwilliam (Sally Kandalaft).* 372 (CfMa).

SIBOR STAR ..9-13.. 7 b.g. Man Among Men (IRE) — My Ratbag (Main Reef) 331. Rangy owner-bred. Dam, half-sister to Free Hand (*qv* '91 Annual), won 10f Claimer. FLAT r5 p0 (inc Sells). NH '98 (from D. Burchell's) r7 p1 (3rd); Sell final. A well-beaten third but performed reasonably in his first two Points, but appeared to give a much improved display when making virtually all and finishing full of running at Bitterley. Only had two behind him, but was much the quickest of the three Maiden divisions, and it would be surprising if he could not win a Welsh Restricted at least. *T. Price — Brecon & Talybont.* 478 (M), 899 (OMa), 1091 (OMa).

SIDE BAR ..8-12.. 11 b.g. Mummy's Game — Joli's Girl (Mansingh USA) p8pp3p. Small compact half-brother to flat winner, Joli's Princess. Dam won at 9f. FLAT to '98 r28 w2 (13-14f Sells, one on all-weather) p4. NH '93/8 r22 w2 (2m2f Sell Hdles) p3 (inc 2 Chses, beaten 28-33l). P-t-P '99 r6 p0 (5th twice, pulled up 3, and unseated 1). Won four sellers which included two Hurdles at the end of '94, but unreliable, and does not stay three miles. Usually wears headgear, and runs tongue-tied, but has only beaten three rivals in 12 Points, and shows no sign of enjoying himself any more. *D.T. Phillips — Llangeinor.* 480 (O), 643 (Cf), 819 (Cf), 1051 (Cf), 1571 (Cnr), 1658 (MO).

SIDELINER ..9-8.. 13 ch.g. Green Shoon — Emmalina (Doubtless II) 5ppp7. Compact half-brother to Mitchells Pride (*qv*). NH '97 r2 p0 (last and pulled up in Chses — tailed off both). P-t-P '93, '95/7 and '99 r26 w1 (Club Maiden) p6 (4 3rds); pulled up 10, and fell 2. Won a poor Maiden in '95, and is a competent jumper, but has met with defeat in 19 Restricteds since and has been exposed as incredibly easy to beat. Gave his best display for some time when nine lengths fifth in a decent race on his 2000 reappearance, but could not produce that level of ability again, and is wasting his time in Hunter Chases. *A. Hollingsworth — Worcs.* 191 (Cf), 338 (R), 993 (R), 1338 (4m1fH), 1558 (3mH).

SIDNEY STREET ..7-0.. 8 b.g. Palm Track — Pricket Walk (Amboise) ppff3pp9. Small brother to Palm Walk. Dam is an unraced half-sister to 6 Pointers, including the dam of Dear Jean (*qv* '99 Annual). NH '97 (for M. Sowersby) r2 p0 (last and pulled up). Sold Doncaster, Nov '97 for 1700. Can take a strong hold if he feels like it, but invariably tails himself off, and has never beaten another horse on his rare completions. Not only useless, but also bad tempered and an irratic jumper, and normally wears headgear and equipped with a tongue-strap twice. Potentially lethal when the inept Robert Barr decides to partner him. *R. Sharington — Easton H. (Matthew Gingell).* 21 (2m4fOMa), 23 (OMa), 181 (2m4fOMa), 605 (OMa), 774 (OMa), 1039 (OMa), 1290 (OMa), 1590 (2m4fOMa).

SIGMA WIRELESS (IRE) ..7-8.. 12 b.g. Henbit (USA) — Canelle (Sassafras FR) 3. Tall half-brother to Philpride and Martin Thomas. IRISH NH FLAT '94 and '96 r6 w1 p1 (2nd). IRISH NH '95/6 r27 p3 (2nd). NH '96 (blinkered 4; for T. Etherington, bought for 6000; wins previously for late T. Forster, bought for 6800) r 22 w3 (2 Hdles, 2m4f-2m7f, and 3m Ch) p8. Jumped slowly when winning a terrible three-finisher Chase, and then his final 11 attempts under Rules were all over Hurdles. Seems to be in virtual retirement now, but was odds-on on a brief reappearance in his Members, in which he did not look to enjoy himself and faded to finish a poor last. *Mrs M. Morris — Blankney.* 386 (M).

SIGN ..10-4.. 12 gr.g. Sharrood (USA) — Polly Packer (Reform) 42. Tall owner-bred half-brother to Topper Two, to flat and Hurdles winners, up ton Park (raced by Philip Newton) and Regal Reform, and to flat winner, Sun Street. NH FLAT '92 r1 p1 (2nd). P-t-P '95 and '97/9 r13 w5 (inc 2 Intermediates) p3 (2nds); pulled up 1, and fell 1. A useful Pointer on his day, but very fragile, and averages less than three outings a year. Successful in five of his first eight starts, but without a win since '97, and has had the misfortune to cross swords with the likes of King Torus and My Shout when they were at their peak. Jumps well, and usually races up with the pace, but rather a weak finisher and only once beaten less than ten lengths in the last two campaigns. Has only ever won going right-handed. *P. Newton — Cambs (Libby Newton).* 1286 (Cf), 1484 (O).

SILENT SNIPE ..9-10.. 8 ch.g. Jendali (USA) — Sasol (Bustino) fp13p. Rangy unfurnished half-brother to Dawn Secret. Driven into the lead after the last when winning a long and weak Maiden on patchy ground at Wetherby, but met some far tougher opponents subsequently. Would certainly be more at home in Restricteds at present. Gained his name after a wind operation which has left him unable to whinny. *Mrs D. Ibbotson — York & Ainsty S. (David Ibbotson).* 437 (OMa), 508 (CMa), 693 (OMa), 997 (Cf), 1588 (I).

SILK OATS ..8-8.. 11 ch.m. Oats — Celtic Silk (Celtic Cone) pp5p. Sturdy attractive half-sister to Young Ardross and Mister-B. Dam is an unraced half-sister to Master Donnington (*qv* '99 Annual). P-t-P '96/9 r9 p1 (2nd); last 2, ran out 1, and pulled up 5. Not without ability, and was 10 lengths second once in '98, but has stood her racing badly, and is prone to make mistakes. Seems likely to end her career a maiden. Wears a cross-noseband. *M.S. Wilesmith — Ledbury (Emma Wilesmith).* 221 (OMa), 337 (CfMa), 1465 (OMa), 1598 (OMa).

SILK VESTMENTS ..9-12.. 9 b br.m. Rakaposhi King — Preachers Popsy (The Parson) 3p3uR5. Very small unimpressive-looking half-sister to NH flat winner, Scarlet Poppy. Dam is half-sister to Kilruddery (*qv* '92 Annual). NH FLAT '98 r3 p2. NH '98/9 (for Miss V. Williams) r10 w1 (2m5f Hdle) p6 (3 2nds). Lucky when winning her Hurdle as a rival led but made a mistake at the last and the rider lost his irons, but possibly rather unfortunate when a neck second once, as she was slightly hampered. Tiny to have tackled regulation fences and made scores of errors or slow jumps so it was something of a miracle that she achieved four completions and three placings, although beaten 11 lengths or much more. Contesting the lead when she blundered at the final fence before finishing two lengths third to Hatcham Boy in her first Ladies, but disappointing and did not recapture that form subsequently, and Didie Rowell got no further than the fourth on her last two attempts. At least she chose the right one when partnering Exemplar at Penshurst subsequently, where Silk Vestments was 12 lengths adrift. Possibly struggles to stay three miles. Tried tongue-tied once over Hurdles. *J. Rowell — Kent & Surrey Bloodhounds (Didie Rowell).* 218 (L), 307 (L), 707 (L), 1211 (L), 1395 (L), 1511 (L).

SILLY BOY ..—.. 6 ch.g. Crested Lark — Sutton Lass (Politico USA) pppp. Dam, sister or half-sister to 4 Pointers including Just Bruce (*qv*), won Maiden and 2nd 2 over 5 seasons (inc '97) for Mr Harper ('does not truly get the trip'). Remote when pulled up each time, but yet to tackle a Maiden. Has two paddock handlers, and sweated up once. *H.C. Harper — Bicester with Whaddon (R. Harper).* 428 (Cf), 669 (R), 971 (I), 1418 (R).

SILVERDALESURESHOT ..10-8.. 9 b.g. Wace (USA) — Upshot (Marcus Superbus) 41422315. Compact. Dam, 'a horror' who 'frequently proves uncontrollable' beat one horse when placed in 3 Points (last of 2 after falling once) for Mrs Evans. P-t-P/HUNT CH '98/9 r9 w5 (inc 3m110y Hunt Ch; ind inc 4-timer '99) p3 (2 2nds; and 3rd in Hunt Ch); and unseated 1. A progressive type in '99, when successful four times, and has done well in the main this year, but one or two negative idiosyncrasies have become apparent, and was twice beaten at odds-on. Won well despite hanging left on the run-in at Bangor in March, but a similar manoeuvre cost him the race at Uttoxeter subsequently, and has tended to run in snatches. Gained his most recent success in a three runner Hereford event which took little winning, but proved disappointing on his final start when a never nearer fifth at Cartmel after again running in fits and starts. Sometimes makes mistakes or jumps slowly and might be worth trying in headgear in a bid to keep him focused at all times. It would be a pity if his temperament overwhelmed him as he had appeared thoroughly resloute, and will hopefully put matters straight in 2001. Appears to handle any going. *Mrs P. Evans — W. Salop.* 150 (3mH), 464 (3m110yH), 779 (O), 1025 (3m110yH), 1249 (2m7fH), 1293 (3mH), 1534 (3m1f110yH), 1643 (3m2fH).

SILVER ELLIE ..—.. 9 ch.m. Precious Metal — Red Squaw (Tribal Chief) pp. Half-sister to Red Rambo and Tribal Solace. Unattractively bred, and probably has no racing potential. *J.D. Telfer — Liddesdale.* 973 (I), 1330 (OMa).

SILVERFORT LAD (IRE) ..9-10§.. 12 gr.g. Roselier (FR) — Sweet Run (Deep Run) 4p2p235. Compact. IRISH NH '94 r3 p0. IRISH P-t-P '95 r3 w1 (5yo&up Maiden) p1 (2nd). IRISH HUNT CH '95 r1 w1 (2m6f). NH '95/7 and '99 (last run for Mrs D. Thomas) r11 w2 (3m-3m3f Chses) p2; tried to run out 1. P-t-P/HUNT CH '99 (for Mr G. Taylor, Mr J. Cridland, Mr D. Thomas & Mr J. Honeyball) r9 p3 (2nd of 3; and 2 3rds, remote last once); 5th, last 2, pulled up 2, and fell 1. Made most when successful twice under Rules as a novice, and has adopted similar tactics when making the frame in seven Points, but ungenuine and downs tools immediately once headed nowadays. Occasionally blinkered, and has had three different sets of owners in just two seasons. Suited by some ease in the ground. *D. Griffiths — Glamorgan (Robert Williams).* 345 (O), 598 (O), 1053 (O), 1451 (MO), 1571 (Cnr), 1612 (Cf), 1657 (Cf).

SILVER HILL ..9-5.. 11 b.m. Pragmatic — Rare Game (Raise You Ten) fp6pfu364. Workmanlike lengthy half-sister to Last Gamble (*qv*). NH '97 r2 p0 (pulled up 1, and fell 1 in Chses — tailed off both). P-t-P '98/9 r11 w1 (Maiden) p5 (4 2nds, of 3 once, and last once; and last of 3); pulled up 4. Followed four consecutive seconds with a Larkhill success in her début season, but has been found wanting in better company and beaten 14 times since. Makes plenty of errors, and twice ended up on the floor when exhausted at Badbury Rings. Blinkered twice in '99. *M.P. Fear — Avon V.* 330 (R), 473 (M), 634 (C), 886 (C), 1061 (R), 1134 (Cnr), 1243 (Inr), 1393 (R), 1550 (Cnr).

SILVERINO ..—.. 15 gr.g. Relkino — Silver Tips (High Top) r. Big rangy angular brother to a flat winner in Italy, and half-brother to a flat winner, and to a successful Hurdler. Dam won 3 flat, 7-8f. NH '90/8 (for G. Knight; one win previously for P. Rodford; previously for S. Earle, bought for 4000; 2 wins previously for G.L. and C. Moore) r46 w4 (2m6f Hdle, and 3 Chses, 3m-3m3f) p11. Won four races principally in thick mud to March '97, but frequently wore headgear, and was ungenuine and required plenty of driving. Looked awful when slumping round the paddock in his Members (was examined by the vet), and he and Samantha Kennard appeared to hate the idea of a race in equal measure. *Miss S. Kennard — Axe V.H. (G. Kennard).* 926 (M).

SILVER JOY ..—.. 6 b.m. Silver Kite (USA) — Oh My Joy (Grundy) pfp. Smallish lengthy half-sister to Hurdles winner, Steam On. Dam, half-sister to Byroc Boy (*qv* '90 Annual), won at 10f, and won 2m2f Hdle (both Sells). FLAT (for K. McAuliffe, tried blinkered/visored) r10 p0 (inc Sell). NH '98 (for R. Stronge, bought for 700) r1 p0 (tailed off and pulled up). Bought Ascot, Sep '98 for 750. Performed poorly in 14 various races to date, and Julian Pritchard could not get any extra response out of her when he accepted the ride on final start. Possibly only stays about 1m4f. *M.G. Jones — Gelligaer F.* 747 (CfMa), 835 (OMa), 1361 (2m4fOMa).

SILVER MAN ..9-12.. 7 gr.g. Silver Owl — What An Experiance (Chance Meeting) pp22. Compact half-brother to Susies Prince, Prince Warrior and Fabbl Approved. Dam, half-sister to Spambruco (*qv* '96 Annual), a non-stayer was 3rd in a Maiden (failed to finish in 8 of 12 other attempts) for Dennis Turner. Grandam, Colourful Girl, failed to finish in 3 Points. P-t-P '99 r4 w1 (Maiden) p0; 4th, 7th, and pulled up 1. A shade fortunate when successful in a two-finisher Maiden on softish at Lemalla last year as a likely danger exited two out. Suffered an interrupted campaign in 2000, but only beaten a length-and-a-half maximum in two end-of-season Restricteds and should be able to go one better in due course. A sound jumper, but appears unsuited by a severe test of stamina. *Mrs M.E. Turner — Dartmoor (Dennis Turner).* 255 (R), 406 (R), 1389 (R), 1517 (R).

SILVER SLEEVE (IRE) ..9-1§.. 9 b.g. Taufan (USA) — Sable Coated (Caerleon USA) pu6pp2u726. Workmanlike. FLAT r10 p0. NH '95/6 r15 w1 (2m3f Hdle) p4 (inc 3rd in Sell). P-t-P '99 r5 p3 (2 2nds); and last 2. Gained his only win at Stratford in July '96, and has made the placings on seven occasions since, but missed the whole of '97 and '98. Never looked like winning in 2000, but always seems likely to wave goodbye to Lucy Bridges, and succeeded on two occasions. Regained blinkers in 2000, and his enthusiasm does not match that of his partner. Never tried beyond 2m6f under Rules, and usually fails to stay in Points. *Miss L.H. & Mrs H.M. Bridges — Wilton (Helen Bridges).* 9 (L), 35 (Cnr), 325 (Cf), 454 (4mMO), 636 (L), 762 (M), 929 (Cnr), 1057 (Cf), 1174 (L), 1483 (L).

SILVER STANDARD ..9-3.. 11 b.g. Jupiter Island — One Half Silver (CAN) (Plugged Nickle USA) 60. Neat half-brother to 3 flat winners (one in Ireland, and one in France), including Petarga. 3500y. FLAT (for J.W. Watts) r11 w1 (7f, 4 ran) p1 (2nd). NH '93/8 (final 5 for H. Daly; wins previously for late T. Forster, bought for 7800) r40 w6 (2m2f-2m7f Hdles) p2 (inc 2 Chses, 51/3rd once). Won seven races on good ground or in mud to October '97, but has always been a very poor jumper, and even fell four times over Hurdles. Missed '99 and did not resume for the new yard until mid-May, and was predictably let down by his fencing in Hunter Chases. Retains speed, and could be substantially under-rated if he tried Pointing and appreciated the smaller obstacles. *K.R. Pearce — Carms.* 1443 (4mH), 1592 (4m2fH).

SILVER SUMAL ..8-11.. 12 gr.g. Rymer — Heron's Mirage (Grey Mirage) 548f. Tall rangy owner-bred brother to Red Oassis (*qv*). NH FLAT Aut '93 (for C. Broad) r2 p0. NH '96 and '98 (for J. O'Shea; previously for H. Oliver) r7 p0 (inc Sell; pulled up lame only Ch). NH May '00 r2 p0 (8th in 2m1f110y HCap Ch: *in tch, rdn app 7, wknd 4 out*; and fell in 2m5f110y Nov Ch: *in tch, blun 7, wknd 11, fell 4 out*). Began his career way back in '93, but plagued by bouts of leg trouble, and has suffered absences of 27 months, 30 months and 15 months since. Can be headstrong and wears a cross-noseband and has had two handlers, and led after two miles until caught two out and fading rapidly in an elders Maiden, but clearly does not quite get the trip Pointing, and is way below standard under Rules. *Mrs J.Z. Munday — Ludlow (Andrew Dalton).* 568 (OMa), 994 (OMa).

SIMMIE ..—.. 16 b.g. Buckskin (FR) — Miss Dunbrody (Le Prince) p. Workmanlike half-brother to Prince Torus, and to Irish NH flat winner Lady Occupier. Dam won Irish NH flat. NH '90/2 (for late G. Hubbard, and when trained for him by F. Murphy) r12 p2 (3rds); pulled up both Chses. Dormant for eoans but revived to take care of Lucinda Barrett-Nobbs in his Members, and may have enjoyed chit-chatting with Monks Soham about the good old days they spent together at Jeff Hubbard's. *Mrs N. Barrett-Nobbs - Waveney H.* 755 (M).

SIMPLE ARITHMETIC ..10-2.. 13 ch.g. Southern Music — Graphics Eska (Jimmy Reppin) 41p2. Strong good-looking half-brother to Hurdles winner, Arithmetic. Dam, half-sister to Tartan Tyrant (*qv* '93 Annual), won 2m4f Hdle. NH FLAT '92/3 r3 w1 p0. NH '94/6 and '98/9 (for K. Bailey, bought for 9000, blinkered last 2) r15 w2 (2m1f Hdles) p5 (inc 3 3rds in Chses). A smart novice in softish/heavy who failed to progress, but only because his problems multiplied, and bad legs kept him out of action for periods of 19 and 24 months. Fell or unseated in three of nine attempts over regulation fences, and had not scored since December '94, but proved ideal for learners in Points, and apart from giving Bradley Cole his first success (at Milborne St Andrew) he was also a creditable 20 lengths the better of Markus Goess-Saurau. Robbed of greater glories by his infirmities, and another victory at 12 was certainly a plus. *M. Goess-Saurau — V.W.H. (Countess Susie Goess-Saurau).* 34 (MO), 211 (Cnr), 308 (O), 1134 (Cnr).

SIMPLY A STAR (IRE) ..9-10.. 11 ch.g. Simply Great (FR) — Burren Star (Hardgreen USA) *up*. Light-framed. FLAT r3 p0. DUTCH FLAT w1 (9f). BELGIAN FLAT r3 w1 (9f). NH '96 r1 p0. P-t-P '96/9 r18 w1 (Confined) p5 (4 3rds); pulled up 5, and fell/unseated 4. NH Mar '00 (from Alan Armstrong's) r1 p0 (unseated in 3m110y Ch: *bhnd, t.o frm 12, blun & ur 17*). Showed plenty of ability when successful in '96, but a bitter disappointment since, and has tended to race ungenuine. Lightly raced in recent seasons, and managed just the one appearance in 2000 when tailed off and pulled up in the Grimthorpe, a race he was third in the previous year. Often blinkered, and safely ignored now. *Major M. Watson — Meynell & S. Staffs (Alan Armstrong; -)*. 999 (4m1fMO).

SIMPLY SUSIE ..9-0.. 8 ch.m. Sula Bula — Ma-Bellona (Sweet Revenge) u3. Half-sister to High Hopes. P-t-P '99 r6 w1 (Members) p3 (2 3rds, of 4 once and last once); 4th, and 8th. Won a bad race for her Members in testing ground last year, but subsequently disappointed on a quicker surface, including when beaten at odds-on once. Got jarred up whilst running loose on her reappearance, and roughed off after finishing a remote third when well supported in her Members. Still has it all to prove in Restricteds. *Mrs L. Harrington — Avon V. (Don Harrington)*. 38 (CR), 473 (M).

SINBAD'S SECRET ..9-1.. 10 br.g. Joligeneration — Cinbar (Cintrist) 6. Close-coupled attractive half-brother to Mayhem (*qv*). P-t-P '99 (for Mr D.R. Brotherton) r2 p0 (unseated 1, and pulled up 1). Had a curtailed season in '99, and managed just the one appearance this year, but did show some ability when 17 lengths sixth at Hutton Rudby, and might be worth another look in 2001. *J.O. Barr — Cleveland (Jackie Barr)*. 624 (OMa).

SINCH ..—.. 6 ch.m. Inchinor — Swinging Gold (Swing Easy USA) p2p. Workmanlike lengthy half-sister to 3 flat winners (one in Swewden), including So So and Spinechiller. Dam won 2 5f races. 3400y. FLAT (for D. Barron) r4 p0. Bought Doncaster, Nov '98 for 800. Showed no merit in Maidens, and was floundering a long way behind Little Brockwell in a match for her Members until she unseated at the last and remounted. Not a fluent jumper as yet. *B. Stonehouse — Braes*. 1084 (2m4fOMa), 1158 (M), 1368 (OMa).

SING CHERRY RIPE ..8-10.. 11 b.m. Bustability — Sian Melody VII (unknown) 6434324. Small owner-bred half-sister to Black Dan. P-t-P '99 r5 p1 (3rd); and last 4. Her completion record is exemplary, but does not tell the whole story as her jumping can be sketchy and was certainly a contributory factor in her two-and-a-half length defeat at Bonvilston. Never remotely involved in a finish otherwise and does not inspire as a future winner. *Mrs A. James — Pembs*. 650 (CfMa), 831 (M), 950 (OMa), 1225 (OMa), 1300 (OMa), 1457 (OMa), 1661 (OMa).

SINGLE MAN (NZ) ..9-7.. 13 gr.g. Isle Of Man (NZ) — Tolaga Bay (NZ) (Tiber) 6p6u569. Tall workmanlike freeze-marked. NZ FLAT '97/8 r4 p1 (2nd). NZ NH '97/8 r14 w2 (2m4f Chses) p1 (3rd). P-t-P/HUNT CH '99 (for Mr J.C. Tuck) r4 p1 (2nd); 12th, and pulled up 2. NH '99 r2 p0 (pulled up 2). Supported from 50s to 14s when second at Larkhill in '99, but never remotely involved this year, and only once better than last in five comletions. Does not appear to stay three miles, and acquired headgear in 2000. *Miss T.O. Blazey — Blackmore & Sparkford V. (Jo West & Brett Parsons)*. 62 (Cf), 214 (Cf), 354 (L), 523 (Cnr), 1304 (Cfnr), 1471 (Cnr), 1562 (C).

SIP OF BRANDY (IRE) ..10-3§.. 8 ch.g. Sharp Charter — Manhattan Brandy (Frankincense) pf2p71034. Narrow half-brother to April's Baby (won bad Chase after Pointing), to Irish Hurdles winner, Jimmy's Brandy, and to prolific Irish winner, Captain Brandy (NH flat, jumping and Pointing). IRISH P-t-P '97/8 r11 w1 (5yo&up unplaced Maiden) p1 (3rd); pulled up 2, and fell 2. P-t-P/HUNT CH '99 r13 w1 (Intermediate) p2 (2nds, of 3 once); 4th, last pair 4, pulled up 4, and fell 1. A thorough stayer, but indolent and needs plenty of drving, and has gained both Welsh successes under strong male riders at Lydstep. Often makes mistakes, but usually keeps his feet and carried a novice girl round successfully on his last two starts. Only beaten around six lengths at Pentreclwydau, and his physique suggests the weights in Ladies races will suit him better than having to hump 12st plus. Blinkered on a regular basis in '99, but not since. *Mrs L.A. Goldsworthy — S. Pembs (Keith & Linda Goldsworthy)*. 3 (L), 35 (Cnr), 275 (Cf), 467 (3m1f110yH), 643 (Cf), 833 (O), 1015 (4mO), 1221 (M), 1297 (L).

SIRE DE BRUMETZ (FR) ..—.. 6 b.g. Nashamaa — La Beaumont (FR) (Hellios USA) fpp5. Smallish unfurnished. Last and a fence behind when he achieved a completion, and will need a miracle to become a racehorse if this is the best he can offer. *N.J. Pewter — Suffolk*. 180 (2m4fOMa), 237 (OMa), 551 (OMa), 604 (OMa).

SIR FROSTY ..9-13.. 8 b.g. Arctic Lord — Snowy Autumn (Deep Run) 25p1135. Workmanlike owner-bred. Dam won 2m6f Hdle. P-t-P '98/9 r7 w1 (Maiden) p4 (3 3rds, beaten short head and neck once, and last once); 4th, and fell 1. Took rather longer to open his account than might have been expected, and remains liable to disappoint especially when the emphasis is on stamina. A reliable jumper, and appreciates some cut in the ground. Should be able to find another opportunity, but may not aspire to the heights that once looked attainable. Has worn a tongue-strap when successful. *Mr & Mrs J.F. Tucker — Quantock (Kay Rees & Polly Curling)*. 38 (CR), 164 (R), 458 (R), 847 (R), 1097 (Inr), 1304 (Cfnr), 1471 (Cnr).

SIR GEORGE CHUFFY (IRE) ..9-4.. 13 b.g. Welsh Term — Grand Legacy (Relko) u6. Compact good-looking brother to a winner in Italy. FLAT r6 p2 (3rds). P-t-P/HUNT CH '93/6 and '98 (for Mr H.A. Shone) r12 w1 (2m4f Maiden) p3 (2 3rds); failed to finish 7 (unseated 1, and ran out 1). Won over 2m4f in holding in '95, but manages remarkably few outings, and does not truly stay three miles. Resurfaced after another spell on the sidelines to act as schoolmaster to Michelle Mullineaux who fell off him once, but managed to complete when incredibly remote throughout at Alpraham. *M. Mullineaux — Cheshire.* 368 (L), 590 (L).

SIR RUSCOTT (IRE) ..—.. 7 b.g. Mister Lord (USA) — Clash Moss (Le Moss) pp. Dam won 6 plus Maiden in Ireland (also failed to finish 19; pulled up in all 5 attempts after victory). Sold Doncaster, June for 950. Tailed off in Maidens on following Saturdays in March, and jumped abysmally and went less than a mile in the latest. Subsequently entered for a Bumper, but failed to appear. *Mrs Y. Ruscoe & D. Scott — York & Ainsty S.* 398 (OMa), 507 (CMa).

SIR WILLIAM ..—.. 7 ch.g. Karlinsky (USA) — Charmezzo (Remezzo) p. Sturdy owner-bred brother to Ashdown Boy (*qv*). A typical Bond beginner when fat and novicey in a Maiden, but the family usually get there eventually, and if he emulates Ashdown Boy his day will come in 2004. *L. Bond — Stevenstone (Pen Bond).* 1610 (OMa).

SIR WYNHAM ..10-3.. 12 b.g. Shrivenham — Miss Rosewyn (Wynkell) 36f8511. Sparely-made brother to Station Rank and Sandford Orcas, and to Chasing winner, Master South Lad, and half-brother to Rosebergen. An ex-eventer who showed plenty of speed when partnered by Ollie Ellwood, but then had an unconvincing spell for the beginner John Case until transformed on the firm ground at Cothelstone and Larkhill on consecutive May Wednesdays. Blitzed round in the lead throughout in both, and few jockeys can have enjoyed such wide margin victories on their first successes (by two fences, and by 30 lengths!). Can be unruly and has thrown the rider in the paddock and mounted outside and taken to post early on final start. His times suggest that he would be good enough to score again in minor company if conditions were right. *N.J. Case — Blackmore & Sparkford V.* 7 (OMa), 63 (I), 213 (CfMa), 455 (OMa), 1131 (OMa), 1555 (OMa), 1594 (R).

SISTER JIM ..—§.. 11 b.m. Oats — Midnight Pansy (Deadly Nightshade) ppRpsRpr. Small compact half-sister to Rocky Balboa, and several winners, including Jimsintime, Jimbalou and Taxi Lad (all successful Hurdlers). NH FLAT '95/6 r3 p0 (54 ran and beat just 4!). NH '96 and '98 (from R.J. Price's, blinkered final) r6 p0 (last, pulled up 4, and fell in Hdles). Has never given one display which is better than utterly appalling, and it is unbelievable that anybody wants to waste time and money taking her to the races. Generally very poorly handled and is prone to run out. Regained blinkers on three most recent appearances. Very late to the paddock and to the start once. The owner should be looking out for a letter from Portman Square. *B. Davies — N. Ledbury.* 703 (OMa), 892 (OMa), 1404 (OMa), 1464 (OMa), 1573 (OMa), 1634 (OMa), 1662 (OMa), 1675 (OMa).

SISTER KIT (IRE) ..9-9.. 8 b.m. Glacial Storm (USA) — Good Holidays (Good Times ITY) 1. Dam, sister to Mr Mad (*qv*), was placed in 2 sprints, and won 3 Points and placed 5 (lame in '92, and reappeared '95/6). FLAT (inc for B. Paling) r11 p1 (16/ 3rd of 5). NH '98 (for B. Llewellyn) r1 p0 (tailed off). Left to beat one other finisher after the narrow leader had unseated at the last in a muddy Maiden at Cursneh Hill. Reportedly bowing out on this belated victory to go to stud. *D. Brace - Llangeinor.* 1278 (OMa).

SISTER LARK ..9-5.. 12 ch.m. True Song — Seeker's Sister (Ashmore FR) p4p74p46p. Compact well-made half-sister to Solars Sister and Loch Ash. Dam, half-sister to Corporal Cruiser (*qv* '93 Annual), won 2 Irish Points. P-t-P/HUNT CH '94/9 r48 w2 (Maiden and Restricted) p14 (9 2nds, inc 2 Hunt Chses); failed to finish 16 (ran out 1, and on floor 4). A prolific loser, and has only succeeded twice in 57 attempts spread over seven years. Jumps safely, but only once better than last in 2000, and seems to have slipped into an irretrievable decline. Thrice visored prior to '99. *N.B. Jones — Llangeinor (Paul Haskins).* 10 (O), 68 (O), 344 (I), 580 (3mH), 644 (Cm), 837 (I), 944 (I), 1023 (3mH), 1613 (I).

SISTER SUE ..—.. 9 b.m. Brotherly (USA) — Mistys Motive (Motivate) pp5p. Small lengthy. P-t-P '99 r5 p0 (last, fell 2, ran out 1, and pulled up 1). Has an unappealing pedigree and has proved to be devoid of talent. Yet to beat a rival in nine starts, and shows a rank lack of enthusiasm. Wears a cross-noseband. *J.W.E. Weaver — Clifton-on-Teme.* 703 (OMa), 995 (OMa), 1466 (OMa), 1635 (OMa).

SISTER SWING ..—.. 6 br.m. Arctic Lord — Seal Marine (Harwell) p. Workmanlike sister to Penguin and No Trouble, and half-sister to Sweet Manatte, My Main Man and Merlin's Lad (Chasing winner since Pointing). Dam, half-sister to South Sunrise (*qv* '96 Annual), won 3m2f Hunt Ch and 6 Points and 2nd 2. Given a gentle introduction in a Restricted, and there may well be better to come from this attractively bred mare. *Sealmarine Partnership — Dulverton W. (Keith Cumings).* 728 (R).

SIX CLERKS (IRE) ..10-3§.. 8 b.g. Shadeed (USA) — Skidmore Girl (USA) (Vaguely Noble) f3fp. Small compact well-made half-brother to a winner in Italy. 17,000f, 12,000y. FLAT (tried blinkers) r15 p5. NH '96/9 (bought for 6600; won previously for J. Fitzgerald, blinkered 1) r23 w1 (2m Hdle) p9 (inc 2 Chses); inc Sell Hdles final 6. Would probably have finished third in his first two Hunter Chases but for falling at the last at Newbury, and his one and a half length defeat by Cooltan and Island Echo was a very good effort (kept on well under pressure to make six lengths from the final fence), but disappointing since, and has long been ungenuine. Beaten on 51 occasions, and struggled home at 4-9 in February '97 on the only occasion he stuck his head in front when it mattered. *W.J. Odell — Heythrop (Mrs S.M. Odell).* 154 (3mH), 384 (2m3f110yH), 580 (3mH), 687 (2m6f110yH).

SIXTH SENSE (IRE) ..9-1.. 7 b.g. Be My Native (USA) — Fallen Glass (Shack USA) pu233. Workmanlike. IRISH P-t-P '99 r3 p0 (last, pulled up and fell). Bought Doncaster, May for 2000. Placed in three Maidens and gave a creditable display when second, but a disappointing favourite twice since, and lacked fluency on his final start. Does not seem to be progressing in the right direction at present. *H.R. Hobson — Puckeridge.* 7 (OMa), 839 (M), 942 (CfMa), 1180 (OMa), 1291 (OMa).

SKEOUGH (IRE) ..—.. 13 br.g. Tanfirion — Birchwood (Fordham USA) p. Small compact well-made half-brother to Irish NH flat and Hurdles winner, Native Dara (IRE). Dam won 2m flat in Ireland. IRISH FLAT '90 and '93 r6 p0. IRISH NH FLAT '92/3 r7 w1 (2m1f) p2 (3rds). IRISH NH '93 r2 w1 (2m Hdle) p0; 7th and 8th in Chses. NH '93/5 and '96 r11 p2 (3rds in Hdles). P-t-P '98/9 (for Mrs R. Wilson) r5 p0 (pulled up 4, and fell 1). Has shown no form for six years, is embarrassingly poor in Points, and presumably consigned to the equine dustbin after another hopeless performance at Dunthrop. Sometimes wears a tongue-strap, and presumably gagging for breath. *Mrs G.V. MacKay-Russell — Pytchley.* 195 (O).

SKINSEY FINNEGAN (IRE) ..9-9.. 7 b.g. Fresh Breeze (USA) — Rose Of Solway (Derring Rose) pppp34p. Small neat half-brother to Outside The Rain (IRE). IRISH P-t-P '98 r2 p0; pulled up 1. P-t-P '99 r4 w1 (Maiden) p0; and pulled up 3. Finished tired when the wide-margin winner of a seven-minute Maiden at Horseheath last year, but is far from being a stayer and usually forced to pull up through exhaustion. Needs to concentrate on easy tracks like Cottenham, but has no chance of winning again for as long as he continues to pull like a train. *B. Kennedy — Essex F. & U. (Jim Ovel).* 86 (R), 96 (I), 321 (R), 416 (R), 773 (R), 940 (R), 1379 (R).

SKIP'N'TIME ..10-10.. 11 b.g. Idiot's Delight — Skipton Bridge (Harwell) 420522. Workmanlike. P-t-P/HUNT CH '95/6 and '98/9 r16 w7 (inc 2 Hunt Chses, 3m11f110y and Mixed Open, inc 4-timer '99) p7 (6 2nds, last once, inc Hunt Ch; and 3rd in Hunt Ch); pulled up 1, and unseated 1. Developed into a useful Hunter Chaser last year, but has never been entirely straightforward, and managed to get beaten when sent odds favourite on four occasions in 2000 (odds-on in three). Usually ridden from behind, and has to be produced as late as possible, but twice beaten less than a length this year, and on both occasions left the impression that he should have won. Quirkier than ever, but still very able, and it would be unwise to write off his chances of further success over regulation fences too soon. Does not go for the whip, but can quicken, and acts on most surfaces. *M.S. Rose — Portman (Richard Miller).* 61 (MO), 154 (MO), 584 (3m2f110yH), 735 (MO), 1337 (3m2f110yH), 1492 (O).

SKIRMISHING ..7-5.. 8 b.g. Infantry — Miss Barle (Prince Barle) 4. Half-brother to Miss Simitar. Dam won 3 Points and placed 2 for Dudley Moore, and grandam, Miss Queensway, won a Point and placed 16 various (last 4 for Dudley Moore). Ran rather better in his Members than 38 lengths fourth might suggest, but is a once-raced eight-year-old by Infantry, whose stock are notorius for standing few outings. *T.W. & Mrs K.A. Moore — Essex F. & U. (Tim Moore).* 317 (M).

SKOMAR ODDY ..10-4.. 8 b.g. Nearly A Hand — Dale Road (Le Tricolore) 2. Brother to Merry Morn, and half-brother to Portfield Fair (dam of Some Grey *qv*), Avenue Royal and Jack Sound, and to April Airs (dam of Handsome Harvey and Royal Barge). Dam was 2nd in 3 Points (beaten distance, of 3, and last) for Ted and Brenda Harries. P-t-P '99 r2 w2 (Maiden and Restricted). Produced late in the day to win both his starts in '99, and looked sure to pick Mister Horatio off on his reappearance at Erw Lon, but Jamie Jukes sat remarkably still on the run-in and the combination went down narrowly. As it turned out the horse returned lame, and the jockey was naturally trying to nurse him home. Looked as though he would prove to be every bit as good as Jack Sound, who won 15 races for connections, and will hopefully make a speedy recovery. *Mr & Mrs E.L. Harries — Pembs (Bert Lavis).* 271 (O).

SLAVE'S CHOICE ..—.. 8 b.g. Arctic Lord — Panning (Pitpan) p. Tall. Dam is half-sister to Future King (*qv* 2000 Annual). NH '97/8 (from H. Johnson's) r3 p0 (pulled up 3). Rarely runs, and useless and always pulls up when he does. *T.W. Ellwood — Zetland (Chris Dennis).* 46 (OMa).

SLEDMERE (IRE) ..8-7.. 6 ch.g. Shalford (IRE) — Jazirah (Main Reef) p2p8. Strong-topped compact half-brother to flat winner, Finsbury Flyer. Dam is half-sister to The Engineer (*qv* '99 Annual). 12,500 2yo. FLAT (for N. Tinkler at 2) r3 P0 (inc last). NH May '00 r1 p0 (8th in 2m6f Mdn Hdle: *disp ld to 7, rdn & lost plce*). Eliminated in bizarre circumstances on his Pointing debut after George Moscrop had been hit on the head by the falling Billy Burn at the second and later plummeted to the ground after pulling up when probably unconscious, but attracted market support when partnered by Thomas Scott subsequently. Did not impress in either, and finished a fence behind Buckaroo in his Members after inheriting second at the 13th. Looks a very stuffy individual, and was still carrying plenty of condition in the Hurdle. *G.R. Moscrop — Border.* 1431 (OMa), 1501 (M), 1581 (2m4fOMa).

SLEEP WALKER ..9-8.. 9 b.m. Kinglet — Valiant Vision (Brave Invader USA) ur. Half-sister to Sun Visor and Chancellors Vision. Grandam, Sweet Dreams, won Irish Grand National. P-t-P '99 (for Mr P.H. Neal) r2 w1 (Maiden) p0; and pulled up 1. Won a two-finisher Maiden which developed into a sprint on testing ground at Newton Bromswold on her debut, but yet to manage a clear round in Restricteds, and was exhausted when applying the brakes after a circuit at Mollington on her latest appearance. A victory has been a bonus, as she badly damaged a hind tendon as a three-year-old, and later bred a foal, but needs treating with caution if she returns. *Lord Willoughby de Broke — Warwicks (P. Neal).* 6 (R), 80 (CCfR).

SLEEPY BOY ..7-13.. 8 br.g. Zero Watt (USA) — Furnace Lass VII (unknown) u8. Unfurnished half-brother to Nigel's Boy. FLAT r3 p0 (beat one; tailed off last in Sells final 2). NH '96 (for W. Storey) r1 p0. Unseated after a mile and tailed off last in Maidens, and evidently still very dozy despite four years in bed. *G.W. Jones — Pentyrch.* 602 (CfMa), 1457 (OMa).

SLEIPNIR ..—.. 8 br.g. Executive Perk — Sindur (Rolfe USA) pff8. Tall owner-bred. Dam is sister and half-sister to 2 useless Pointers. NH FLAT Feb '98 r1 p0 (tailed off last). NH '99 (from Gardie Grissell's) r2 p0 (last and pulled up in Hdles). Looks a donkey, and fell after two miles twice when partnered by Ben Hitcott. Subsequently given an atrocious ride by Colin Sherry (who was spoken to by the stewards) at Peper Harow, where he jumped appallingly but was forced to plough on although tailed off in the final mile and virtually fell at the final obstacle when about three fences behind. *Mrs J. Grist — E. Sussex & Romney Marsh (Di Grissell).* 131 (OMa), 284 (2m4fCMa), 679 (OMa), 1396 (OMa).

SLEW MAN (FR) ..10-8.. 10 b.g. Baby Turk — Slew Of Fortune (USA) (Seattle Slew USA) 2111211121. Small attractive half-brother to a French flat winner. FRENCH FLAT r17 w4 (7-10f Clmrs) p7. NH '94/7 r11 w1 (2m Hdle) p3. P-t-P '99 r6 w2 (Opens) p2 (2nds, last once); and unseated 2. Lost the rider in his first two Points (unlucky once), but has not missed the first two in 14 starts since, and looks smart when pitched against inferior opposition. Possesses a useful turn of foot and can usually ridden with utmost confidence, but has not proved reliable enough in a battle to be considered a totally safe betting medium, and has been beaten when odds-on on four occasions '99/00. Well handled by Olivia Green in five of his victories, and has had capable deputies in Messrs Farrant, Jefford and Scudamore on the other occasions. Has amassed 14 wins already, and despite not always looking the most natural jumper looks certain to add to his total in 2001. Acts on most surfaces, but may not appreciate holding ground. *B.A. Kilpatrick — E. Devon (David Pipe).* 68 (O), 199 (Cf), 354 (L), 535 (L), 636 (L), 877 (L), 929 (Cnr), 1098 (C), 1238 (O), 1371 (Cf).

PLATE 121   354 West Somerset & Minehead Harriers Ladies Open: L to R Slew Man (Miss O. Green), 1st, leads Forbidden Waters (Miss S. Vickery), 2nd, at the last fence

PHOTO: Baths Photographic

SLIABH FOY (IRE) ..9-13.. 8 b.g. Electric — Lily Gale (IRE) (Strong Gale) uuupu414. Compact half-brother to Lynnes Daniella (IRE). IRISH P-t-P '98/9 r7 p1 (16f 3rd); pulled up, fell 2, and ran out (impeded). IRISH NH '99 (worn tongue-strap) r4 p0. Given some exceptionally tentative rides by the beginner Fraser Marshall when he came within inches of falling off six times in as many attempts, but he persevered gamely, and was rewarded with success in a dire Maiden in soft at Aldington. It clearly did wonders for his confidence, because a six lengths fourth in a Restricted was a huge improvement, and suggests that he may be able to marshal Fraser into the winner's enclosure again. *Mr & Mrs F. Marshall — E. Sussex & Romney Marsh (Di Grissell).* 291 (CMa), 577 (OMa), 679 (OMa), 709 (OMa), 985 (M), 1105 (2m4fOMa), 1172 (OMa), 1393 (R).

SLIGHTLY SPECIAL (IRE) ..9-6§.. 9 ch.g. Digamist (USA) — Tunguska (Busted) ppp5u. Lengthy half-brother to Challenger Row (IRE), to flat winners, Trooping and Tango, and to an Irish Hurdles winner. Dam won at 10f. IRISH FLAT r11 p1 (2nd). IRISH NH '95 r2 p0. FLAT r8 p0. NH '96/8 (visored final 2) r25 w1 (2m Hdle) p8 (inc 3 Sells). P-t-P '99 (for Mr T. Hopkins) r7 p0 (last 3, unseated 3, and pulled up 1). Won a poor Novices Hurdle in June '97, but has loathed Pointing, and not better than 20 lengths last in four completions. Capable of phenomenally bad jumping, and Adrian Wintle wisely pulled him up after trying to demolish three fences at Bitterley once. Wears blinkers. *N. Lowe — Cotswold V.F.* 895 (MO), 1087 (MO), 1313 (MO), 1462 (L), 1622 (L).

SLIP AWAY ..9-10.. 8 gr.g. Jumbo Hirt (USA) — Au Pair (Runnymede) Rp5. Compact attractive owner-bred half-brother to flat and prolific Chasing winner, Yangtse-Kiang. Dam is half-sister to Grey Bunny (*qv* '94 Annual). NH FLAT '97 r2 p0. P-t-P/HUNT CH '98/9 r8 w2 (Members and Restricted) p2 (3rds, deadheat once); pulled up 1, and ran out 1. A thorough stayer, and has twice kept going gamely to win narrowly at Dalston, but has also gone out through the wing twice, and acquired blinkers on his latest appearance. Did not reappear until mid-April this year, and by the time he had got mind and body in order the ground had gone against him so a more profitable year should be enjoyed in 2001. Unlike his sibling seems suited by a soft surface. *Mrs D.A. Harrison — Cumberland (Mrs M.E. Haughan).* 1080 (O), 1121 (I), 1366 (I).

SLIP HAVEN ..—.. 9 b.m. Rakaposhi King — Red Spirit (Starch Reduced) fppp. Small plain half-sister to Redoran (*qv*). P-t-P '98/9 r5 p0 (pulled up 2, and fell/unseated 3). Hopelessly inept, and those responsible for her odds being reduced from 20s to 3s at Laleston have surely been rounded up and returned to their institutions by now. Has never mastered the art of jumping, and though able to show brief speed has never intimated that she would be able to gallop for three miles. So far seven jockeys have accepted the ride, but only two have been potty enough to come back for more — and Andrew Price should know better. Wears a cross-noseband, and has sported a martingale. *R. Moulds — Gelligaer F. (F.H. Williams).* 1295 (Cf), 1401 (Cf), 1661 (OMa), 1675 (OMa).

SLIPPEN-ON ..—.. 9 ch.g. General Surprise — Slipperstone VII (unknown) pp. Tall well-made. P-t-P '98 r2 p0 (pulled up 2). Tailed off and pulled up in all four outings, and looks no more than a hunter. *P.W. Glover — Torrington F.* 1308 (OMa), 1522 (CfMa).

SLOBADAM ..8-10.. 8 ch.g. Blow The Whistle — Cheeky Monkey (Shiny Tenth) 6p295. Small neat half-brother to Cheeky Chimp. Dam won 2 poor Points at Lincoln for Milsom Robinson prior to going lame. Sire, by Music Maestro, was a bad flat maiden for Ron Sheather. P-t-P '99 r5 p0 (pulled up 4, and fell 1). Generally unfit, and a poor jumper when failing to beat a rival in his first seven starts, and beaten six lengths when second in a joke Maiden taking 9min 1s at Flagg subsequently. Does not seem to stay, and unimproved by a tongue-strap on his final three outings. *M. Robinson — Burton.* 435 (M), 872 (OMa), 1251 (OMa), 1480 (OMa), 1590 (2m4fOMa).

SLUBBERDEGULLIAN ..—§§.. 8 b.g. Criminal Law — Sheild Maiden VII (unknown) cRR. Lengthy good-topped. A total lunatic who went less than a mile each time, and is completely unrideable. The stewards should banish him to Bedlam. *G. Beibly — Taunton V.* 352 (CfMa), 641 (CfMa), 1371 (Cf).

SMACKWATER JACK (IRE) ..9-12.. 8 ch.g. Montelimar (USA) — Liberties (Don) 1u. Half-brother to Its The Bidder (IRE). P-t-P '99 r2 w1 (2m4f Maiden) p0; and pulled up 1. Scored easily on his final outing last year, and added to his account on his reappearance in 2000, winning a stamina test at Great Trethew. Faced his stiffest task to date on his next outing when pitched against Gildrom and Dawn Invader at Didmarton, but was found wanting, and was a beaten third when succumbing to his third noticeable mistake at the last. Failed to reappear, and may have suffered a setback, but in a leading yard, and sure to recover losses. *H.J. Irish — Portman (Louise Alner).* 163 (R), 388 (I).

SMART ORANGE (IRE) ..9-12.. 7 ch.g. Phardante (FR) — Kylogue's Delight (Strong Gale) p3p533. Hobdayed brother to Irish Pointing winner, Kyleogue King. P-t-P '99 r1 w1 (Maiden). Hung right when winning a poor and slowly-run Maiden at Bitterley on his racecourse debut, and has jumped in that direction ever since. Swallowed his tongue on his reappearance and ran with it tied down subsequently, but disappointing on balance, and his best effort was when eight-and-a-half lengths third at Kingston Blount. Young enough to atone, but can only race in one direction, and appears unable to cope with cut in the ground. Has had a soft-palate operation and his wind is clearly a major problem. *Miss H.J. Hinckley — Heythrop (Mark Rimell).* 38 (CR), 260 (R), 1355 (R), 1588 (I), 1623 (R), 1664 (R).

SMART RHYTHM ..10-4.. 13 ch.m. True Song — Clear Thinking (Articulate) 5p7243. Lengthy owner-bred sister to Smart Beat, and half-sister to Laura Norder, Shoot Off and Krystle Saint (dam of Dels Lad and Del The Lorry Man *qv*). Dam is half-sister to 7 Pointers. P-t-P '93 and '95/9 r23 w2 (Maiden and PPORA Restricted) p5 (4 2nds; and 3rd of 4); pulled up 7, fell 1, and refused 1. At her busiest in 2000, but despite two respectable front-running displays at Garthorpe never really looked likely to add to her previous wins. Basically ungenuine, and would often tail herself off in the past, but Richard Armson has done well to cajole her to put her best foot forward recently, and might just get the better of her again. *R.H. Woodward — Belvoir (Helen Harvey).* 116 (I), 296 (I), 543 (I), 867 (M), 1215 (Cm), 1584 (CCond).

SMART SONG ..9-12.. 10 b.g. True Song — New World (St Columbus) 76r. Unfurnished hobdayed half-brother to Grain Hill. Dam, half-sister to 3 Pointers, won 2 Points and placed 3. Grandam, Bright Daisy, won 4 Points (including a dead-heat) and placed 7. P-t-P '96/9 r9 w1 (Maiden) p2 (remote 2nd of 3 once); last, and pulled up 4. NH '99 (from O. O'Neill's) r5 w1 (2m5f110y Nov Ch) p1 (3rd); pulled up 2. Won a bad Maiden at Whitwick on his '98 reappearance, but has never got the trip very well, and three outings in a season is his max. Hunter Chasing exclusively in 2000, but was completely outclassed, and an imminent return to Points seems logical. *G.F. Hammond — S. Herefords (Michael Hammond).* 684 (2m4fH), 1293 (3mH), 1443 (3mH).

SMART TEACHER (USA) ..9-5.. 11 br.g. Smarten (USA) — Finality (USA) (In Reality) f5pp. Sturdy half-brother to 4 winners in USA. Dam won 2 races in USA. FLAT (tried visored) r19 w2 (8f) p2 (short-headed once); inc Sells. NH '95 r3 p0 (last twice, and pulled up 1). P-t-P/HUNT CH '96/9 (for Mrs J. Coates & Mrs N.R. Matthews) r9 p0 (4th, last, pulled up 6, and unseated 1). Very headstrong, and won twice on sound surfaces at Beverley in his youth, but a waste of time in Points in which he does not get the trip. Led to post early on his penultimate start, but appeared not to like being chaperoned and threw a wobbler causing him to be left 20 lengths, and the ploy was not repeated. Wears a cross-noseband. *Mrs N.R. Matthews — Heythrop (Kim Matthews).* 428 (Cf), 788 (Cf), 1016 (Cf), 1481 (Cf).

SMIDDY LAD ..9-7.. 10 ch.g. Crofthall — Carrapateira (Gunner B) fu533f. Good-topped owner-bred half-brother to Smiths Wynd (*qv*). NH FLAT '95/6 r2 p0. NH '97/9 (2 runs in '98 from C. Fairhurst's) r15 p2; fell only Ch. Not placed under Rules since '97, and very disappointing and tongue-tied latterly (has also broken blood vessels). Ran well for a long way on several occasions in 2000 and deserves a success, but has a very poor jumping record over fences, and is further handicapped by an inability to stay more than 2m6f. *R. Shiels — Jedforest.* 45 (OMa), 113 (OMa), 465 (3m1f110yH), 915 (3m1fH), 1123 (OMa), 1431 (OMa).

PLATE 122   36 Point-to-Point Owners & Riders Club PPORA Club Members Intermediate (Div 1): Smile Pleeze (T. Stephenson), 1st, leads Dannicus (A. Honeyball), 2nd, at the last

PHOTO: Tim Holt

SMILE PLEEZE (IRE) ..10-7.. 9 b.g. Naheez (USA) — Harkin Park (Pollerton) 1255115. Workmanlike compact. Dam is half-sister to 7 winners, including Fame The Spur (*qv* '93 Annual). NH FLAT '97 r1 p0. NH '97 r4 p0. P-t-P '98/9 (for Mr I.R. Snowden) r15 w2 (Maiden and Restricted) p6 (4 3rds, last once); pulled up 3, and fell/unseated 2. Exposed as moderate and not particularly trustworthy in the previous yard, but much improved by a change in scenery, and won thrice in 2000 producing a hitherto unseen burst of acceleration on two occasions. Set off joint-favourite in the Heythrop four-miler, but never threatened to give the yard a third success in the race in the last five years, and probably needs a sound surface to produce his best. Has formed a good relationship with Tim Stephenson, who allows his mount to lope round well off the pace before galvanising him into action, something he had to do earlier than usual in their latest success. Sure to be aimed at the main stamina tests next year, and if he maintains the same level of enthusiasm as he showed this year should do well. *Miss S. Troughton — Ledbury (Mike Daniell).* 36 (CI), 195 (O), 614 (O), 1015 (4mO), 1319 (O), 1492 (O), 1646 (3m4fH).

SMITHS WYND ..9-2.. 9 gr.g. Alias Smith (USA) — Carrapateira (Gunner B) 463. Tall owner-bred half-brother to Smiddy Lad and Cleikumin, and to jumping winner, Pink Gin. Dam is half-sister to New Years Eve (*qv* '91 Annual). P-t-P '98 r2 p0 (unseated 1, and pulled up 1). NH '99 r4 p1 (3rd); pulled up 2, and fell. Made mistakes when tried over regulation obstacles, and looked an uncertain stayer when beaten a minimum of 18 lengths in Maidens. The vagaries of breeding are no better illustrated than by his dams progeny, three of which appear not to stay, whilst the other stays longer than the mother-in-law. *R. Shiels — Jedforest.* 44 (OMa), 225 (3mH), 718 (CfMa).

SMOOTH SILK (IRE) ..—.. 8 ch.g. Over The River (FR) — Centralspires Best (Nishapour FR) pppRup. IRISH P-t-P '99 r2 p0 (pulled up 2). Bought Malvern, Oct for 800. Disappointing, never finishes, and did not even go two miles on four occasions in the present yard. *D. Page — Ashford V.* 290 (CMa), 507 (OMa), 829 (OMa), 1109 (M), 1172 (OMa), 1397 (OMa).

SMUDGES SEASON ..7-6.. 9 b.m. Vital Season — La Marquesa (Lepanto GER) ppp4. Small half-sister to Watercombe Cracker and Heel Kracker. A badly bred little mare who has not yet worked out how to jump properly, and was over a fence behind when she managed a completion. Takes her name from the large grey smudge on her flank. *D.C. Emmett (The Emmett Family) — Tiverton (Gerald Emmett).* 848 (R), 929 (Cnr), 1178 (OMa), 1469 (OMa).

SMURF (IRE) ..9-9.. 7 b.g. Eurobus — Diamond Angel (Diamonds Are Trump USA) 1f. Very big strong half-brother to Greybury Star (IRE). Going best when the only danger left him well clear in a 2m4f Maiden at Cottenham, but beat very little, and fell when toiling in the ruck next time. Probably had an excuse, and it would be interesting to see this really imposing individual again. *Mr & Mrs S. Murphy, M. Clarke & Mrs M. Ruff — Suffolk (Neil King).* 181 (2m4fOMa), 610 (R).

SNAPPER ..10-7.. 10 b.g. Gunner B — Fortalice (Saucy Kit) 41335. Small owner-bred half-brother to Fortinas Flyer, Fort Alicia, and Auntie Alice. Dam, half-sister to Birling Jack, was 3rd in a Maiden (looked temperamental). P-t-P/HUNT CH '96/9 r18 w4 (inc 2m4f110y Hunt Ch and Ladies) p6 (4 3rds, of 4 once); fell 2. Much improved in '99 when two victories included a 2m4f Perth Hunter Chase, but basically a thorough stayer who revels in mud. Took a three-finisher Open at Lanark this year, but although he has become expert at course completion he remains a sketchy jumper and errors combined with the lack of suitable ground made him far less effective over regulation fences in 2000. Should win again when conditions are right, but liable to run several pounds below his rating otherwise. *R.H. Black — Fife (Jane Dawson).* 225 (3mH), 662 (O), 917 (3mH), 1120 (O), 1342 (3m1fH).

SNITTON SALVO ..—§§.. 6 b.g. Cruise Missile — Snitton (Rymer) prrf. Brother to Snitton South, and half-brother to Jo Jos Best Friend (*qv*). Dam, temperamental, was placed in 2 Points for Capt. Lumsden. The owner is certainly developing a talent for breeding and racing appalling rubbish (his last performer was Far Forest, (*qv*). *Capt. J.M.G. Lumsden — Ludlow (Geoff Evans).* 527 (OMa), 745 (R), 777 (OMa), 1318 (OMa).

SNITTON SOUTH ..8-13.. 8 b.g. Cruise Missile — Snitton (Rymer) p644. Brother to Snitton Salvo, and half-brother to Jo Jos Best Friend (*qv*). A poor jumper in early season, and although he seemed to derive some benefit from tubing for the first time when 11 lengths fourth his next effort was very feeble. May prefer firmish ground, but probably does not have the scope to be anything better than moderate. *F.T. Walton — Border.* 364 (CfMa), 714 (C), 913 (CfMa), 1582 (2m4fOMa).

SNOOTY ESKIMO (IRE) ..9-8.. 9 ch.g. Aristocracy — Over The Arctic (Over The River FR) 0pp4. Tall lengthy half-brother to NH flat and Hurdles winner, Itsonlyme (IRE). Dam, half-sister to Speriamo (*qv* '88 Season Annual), won 2 Irish Points. IR 12,000 4yo. NH FLAT '96/7 r4 p0. NH '97/9 r14 p1 (27l 2nd); pulled up 5; inc in one of 3 Chses. Has made 22 appearances in five years, but only managed one placing. Most inconsistent, and although he is sometimes in front after 2m4f over fences he invariably compounds alarmingly in the manner of a non-stayer. *A. Fraser — College V. & N. Northumberland (Swanee Haldane).* 89 (3m1fH), 301 (2m5fH), 1556 (2m4f110yH), 1591 (3m1fH).

SNOWBOY (IRE) ..9-5.. 9 br.g. Celio Rufo — Laurestown Rose (Derring Rose) p53434. Compact well-made. Dam is an unraced half-sister to Greenwood Lad (*qv* '88 Season Annual). NH FLAT

'97 r2 p0. NH '97/9 (for R. Lee) r10 p2 (12-14*l* 3rds in Chses). Bought Malvern, Sep for 6000. Proving to be very disappointing. Made the frame four times consecutively, but beaten a minimum of eight lengths, and is always wilting in the closing stages. Tongue-tied in his first Point, and jumped indifferently in the latest. His chief problem is that he does not quite stay three miles. *Mrs J.M. Bailey — R.A.* 12 (OMa), 616 (CMa), 958 (R), 1131 (OMa), 1437 (OMa), 1598 (OMa).

SNOW CLOUD ..8-1.. 7 b.m. Today And Tomorrow — Fancy Pages (Touch Paper) 3r. Unfurnished sister to a flat winner. Dam won 2 5f Sells. 2500f. FLAT (for breedere, D. O'Brien) r1 p0 (remote last). Bought Ascot, Nov '98 for 500. Jumped irratically in the lead in both Points, and although she kept going slowly to complete in her Members she galloped herself into the ground in a Maiden and was tailed off and crawling when refusing at the 14th (the owner-rider should have been fined for failing to pull up). Plenty speedy enough and it might be worth trying an experienced jockey on her. *Miss I.G. Tompsett — Llandeilo F.* 943 (M), 1301 (OMa).

SNOWSHILL HARVEST (IRE) ..9-0.. 10 b.g. Strong Gale — Slave-Lady (Menelek) ffp6652. Tall half-brother to Bala Boy, and to 2 Irish Pointing winners, Mount Alto Lady, and Splendid Melody (IRE) (also a successful English Hurdler). 23,000 4yo. NH '96/9 (for A. Turnell) r9 p0 (5th of 6, last, pulled up 3 and fell in Chses). Sold Doncaster, May for 2200. A fearful jumper, and fell once with Tim Mitchell (broke his collarbone — the last thing that he needed) and twice with Polly Gundry, and subsequently sold on the course at Larkhill. Has been breaking blood vessels, but at least managed to complete for the new stable, albeit a long way behind. Driven all the way to the line when a poor second at Torrington, and snow in harvest is more likely than Don Harrington getting a win from him. *H.B. Geddes — Mrs E. Harrington — Taunton V. (Richard Barber; Don Harrington).* 213 (CfMa), 457 (OMa), 629 (OMa), 889 (OMa), 1207 (OMa), 1527 (OMa), 1598 (OMa), 1675 (OMa).

SOCIAL VISION (IRE) ..8-7.. 11 b.g. Parliament — Elegant Miss (Prince Tenderfoot USA) p36. Neat. FLAT (visored 2) r5 p0 (debut in Sell). P-t-P '95/9 r11 p2 (2nds); last 3, and pulled up 6. Began Pointing with a yard that used to specialise in cheap buys off the flat, but chucked out after three seasons with precious little to show and has performed dismally in the current yard. Rarely runs and has never appeared to stay three miles. Visored once in '98. *Mrs G.V. MacKay-Russell (Harbury Partnership) — Pytchley (Mark Cowley).* 340 (R), 792 (OMa), 1194 (OMa).

SOCK HOP (IRE) ..—.. 10 b.g. Radical — Odd Sox (FR) (Main Reef) pp. Sturdy close-coupled. IRISH P-t-P '97 r2 p0 (pulled up 2). Sold Malvern, May '97 for 1200. Pulled back briefly in Maidens, but had stopped rapidly before halfway in both, and it would be no surprise to learn that he was a bleeder. *P. Smith — Warwicks.* 516 (OMa), 1011 (CfMa).

SOEUR MARIE ..—.. 7 b.m. Sergeant Drummer (USA) — Tinker's Quest (Romany Air) u. Sister to Tinker Tailor and Dinkies Quest, and half-sister to I'm Foxy. Dam won 9 Points and placed 14 (became very mulish latterly). Unseated Jo Cummings at the second at Wadebridge, and reportedly injured whilst running loose. *Miss S. Holroyd — E. Devon.* 106 (OMa).

SO FRANK ..9-2.. 8 b.g. North Col — Summers Fern (Celtic Cone) pff23. Compact unfurnished. Dam, 'devoid of stamina', was 30*l* 3rd in a Maiden for Rob Summers. P-t-P '99 r2 p1 (2nd); and pulled up 1. Twice beaten in races he has looked likely to win, and a lack of stamina has been to blame both times. Collared in the last strides over 2m4f at Garthorpe in '99, and beaten a length at Ashorne this year after being produced with what appeared to be a perfectly timed run. Deserves compensation, though short Maidens will no longer be an option, and cut in the ground saps his strength. Not yet a fluent jumper. *B.R. & Mrs G. Summers — Worcs.* 264 (OMa), 515 (OMa), 1021 (2m4fOMa), 1437 (OMa), 1590 (2m4fOMa).

SOLBA (USA) ..10-7§.. 12 b.g. Solford (USA) — Papaba (Patch) u1p112. Strong lengthy half-brother to 3 winners in USA. Dam won 2 flat in USA. IRISH FLAT '93/4 r7 w1 (16f) p2 (short-headed once). IRISH NH FLAT '93/4 r5 p2 (2nds). IRISH NH '93/5 r16 w4 (2m-2m5f Hdles) p4 (short-headed once, and beaten head once). NH '95/7 r19 w4 (2m4f-3m1f Chses, inc hat-trick) p6. P-t-P '98/9 (for Mrs S.L. Barber) r12 w9 (8 Opens, and 3m4f Mixed Open, 6-timer '98) p2; ran out 1. A talented performer under Rules, but became jaded, and has followed a similar script, though to a lesser degree in Points. Skilfully sweetened to land a six-timer in '98, and took the Dudley Cup the following year, but interspersed were two thoroughly moody efforts, and again contrived to get beaten twice when odds-on in 2000. Dumped the trainer at the first on his reappearance, and was outclassed in the Cheltenham Foxhunters, but returned to Points to land his second Open of the year at Brocklesby Park, and followed up at Brampton Bryan. Sent off a warm favourite for what appeared to be a below strength renewal of the Dudley Cup on his final start, but jumped deliberately several times and was easily disposed of by Desperate after the writing was on the wall fully a mile from home. Has now won 21 races, mostly on an easy surface, and combines high talent with tantrums, but the latter are becoming more prevalent, and should no longer be feared as he once was. Blinkered twice in '98. *A.J. Brazier & Mrs S.P. Smith — Wheatland (Andrew Dalton).* 171 (O), 231 (O), 584 (3m2f110yH), 796 (O), 859 (O), 1065 (3m2fO).

SOLDIER'S SONG ..—.. 8 b.m. Infantry — Top Soprano (High Top) p. Sturdy sister to Maltby Son (*qv*). FLAT r3 p0. NH '98 (from R. Hodges') r2 p0. Tailed off in all three attempts to date. Missed '99, and her lack of outings suggests that she could be yet another victim of Infantry legs. *Lt Col & Mrs E.L. Stocker — Blackmore & Sparkford V. (Penny Cave).* 934 (OMa).

SOLEIL D'ETE ..8-1.. 9 b.m. Vital Season — Trade Only (Andrea Mantegna) 5p. Small ewe-necked. NH Aut '99 (from R. Hodges') r2 p0. A remote last once and tailed off and pulled up thrice, and clearly as bad as she looks. *N.J. Hoare — Blackmore & Sparkford V. (John Dufosee).* 70 (OMa), 409 (OMa).

SOLO GENT ..10-8§.. 12 br.g. Le Bavard (FR) — Go-It-Alone (Linacre) 83322911p. Tall rangy. Dam won at 5f, and is half-sister to Royal Irish (*qv* 2000 Annual). NH FLAT Aut '93 r2 p0. NH '93/9 (blinkered once in '96, been tongue-tied; final from G. McCourt's; previously from Anthony Jones') r46 w7 (2m6f Hdle, and 6 Chses, 2m5f-3m7f) p12. An extraordinary character. Would be a superstar if racing was centralised at Huntingdon, where he has won seven times and also finished second to Mighty Moss, but nothing like such a determined battler elsewhere. Even managed to get beaten in his members, although that was the first time he had raced on a left-handed track over fences since '96 (tends to jump right). Suited by good or sound surfaces. Occasionally blinkered/visored in 2000, and partnered by the talented Tom Doyle in both victories. Stays extreme distances, but downed tools early when tried over four miles at Dunthrop. Can only be trusted to run up to his rating at Huntingdon, where the sight of the horse boxes at the end of the home straight encourages him into a very determined forward surge. *A.A. King — Avon V. (Anthony Jones).* 10 (O), 59 (MO), 224 (3m2fH), 302 (3mH), 473 (M), 1015 (4mO), 1332 (3mH), 1542 (3mH), 1625 (3m2f110yH).

SOLOMANS SISTER ..10-0.. 11 ch.m. Lir — Cornish Princess (True Code) 12112923. Well-made sister to Prince Soloman. Dam won5 Points and 3m2f Hunt Ch prior to winning 4m1f Brooke Bond Oxo Chase for George Turner. P-t-P '98/9 r7 p3 (2 2nds, last once); pulled up 2, unseated 1, and ran out 1. Cast aside her previously rogueish behaviour in 2000 when winning three times in the space of four weeks in the first half of the season, and showed a particular fondness for a muddy surface. Went off the boil latterly, but finally lived up to her breeding, and repaid her followers with interest. Has faced stiff tasks in both the Ladies races she has contested to date, but should hold her own if she manages to avoid the local stars next year, and retains her enthusiasm. *Mrs S.E. Turner — Lamerton (George Turner; Pauline & Tony Geering).* 159 (CfMa), 255 (R), 315 (R), 541 (I), 720 (M), 852 (Cf), 1386 (L), 1605 (L).

SOLOMONS MINES (IRE) ..9-2.. 13 b.g. Miner's Lamp — Crookhaven (Arctic Slave) ppp. Workmanlike brother to Hurdles winner, Dysart O'Dea (IRE), and half-sister to Waterhay, and to Irish NH flat and Hurdles winner, Lauraven. IRISH NH FLAT '93 r1 p0. P-t-P '99 (for Miss C. Goatley) r4 p2 (3rd of 4 once); unseated 1, and pulled up 1. Resurfaced after a five year hiatus in '99, and ran a fair race for an inexperienced veteran when runner-up at Siddington, and may still have some ability, but soon tailed off for a beginner in 2000. Wears a cross-noseband. *B.T. Stewart-Brown — Vine & Craven (Caroline Goatley).* 260 (R), 477 (R), 818 (R).

SOLO TRIP ..—.. 7 b.m. Henbit (USA) — Jane's Daughter (Pitpan) ppp. Big sister to Trigger Castle, and half-sister to Tulane, River Don (Chasing winner since Pointing) and Grindalythe, and to jumping winner, Mister Muddyways. Bought Doncaster, May '98 for 5800. Had a very negative first season when tailed off and pulled up after about two miles thrice. *J. Studd — S. & W. Wilts (Sarah Waugh).* 656 (OMa), 955 (OMa), 1131 (OMa).

SOLWAY COASTER ..9-8.. 8 b.g. Jumbo Hirt (USA) — Lady Mag (Silver Season) p. Small lightly-made owner-bred half-brother to Hurdles winner, Solway Rose. P-t-P '98/9 r4 p1 (2nd of 3); pulled up 3. Wore blinkers for the first time when ten lengths second of three in a 2m5f Maiden at Lanark in '99, but pulled up in his four other outings, including his only start this year. Went lame at Aspatria in 2000, by which time he had acquired a tongue-strap. Has ability, but clearly a whole host of problems too. *Mrs D.A. Harrison — Cumberland.* 1362 (M).

SOLWAY DONAL (IRE) ..9-4.. 8 b.m. Celio Rufo — Knockaville (Crozier) f1fp. Workmanlike half-sister to 3 winners over jumps, including Henrietta Howard (IRE) (NH flat and Hurdles). NH FLAT Oct '99 (from J.J. O'Neill's) r1 p0. Fell in her first Maiden, but overcame a mistake at the last when winning a three-finisher contest by 25 lengths at Alnwick. Seemed unnerved by the bigger obstacles when shooting up in class to Hunter Chases, and almost came to grief in both visits to Sedgefield. Would be more at home in Restricteds for the time being. *D.A. Harrison — Cumberland (Mrs M.E. Haughan).* 112 (OMam), 187 (OMa), 301 (2m5fH), 682 (3m3fH).

SOLWAY SAFFY ..9-1.. 6 b.m. Safawan — Out On A Flyer (Comedy Star USA) pp33p. Small light sister to No Problem Jac (*qv*). Managed to plug into a couple of unimpressive thirds, but was very tired when beating one home over 2m4f, and then a fence behind in last. usually tongue-tied, and may be handicapped by a breathing problem. *D.A. Harrison — Cumberland.* 46 (OMa), 114 (OMa), 1084 (2m4fOMa), 1122 (OMa), 1582 (2m4fOMa).

SOLWAYSANDS ..8-9.. 11 b.g. Germont — Castle Pound (Majestic Streak) p610. Strong workmanlike half-brother to Mhuc Mara. Dam is half-sister to Secret Brae. Grandam, Fezanmac, was 4th of 5, and pulled up 3 in Points. Great-grandam, Coup D'Hazard, was 4th in 2 Maidens. P-t-P/HUNT CH '95/9 r22 w3 (Maiden and 2 Members) p6 (4 2nds); pulled up 6, and unseated 1. Won three modest races on firm '96/7, but out of sorts since, and could hardly fail not to win his Members for the third time this year after the favourite had run out at the fifth leaving him to cope with a tubed five-year-old (who eventually pulled up) and an unregistered hunter. Well beaten in Restricteds, and acquired blinkers in 2000. *K. Little — Dumfries.* 184 (R), 424 (R), 979 (M), 1427 (R).

SOLWAY SPICE ..—.. 6 b.m. Minster Son — Spicey Cut (Cut Above) pppf. Small light-framed owner-bred half-sister to Hurdles winner, Solway Breeze (IRE). Has struggled badly in her outings to date. *D.A. Harrison — Cumberland (Mrs M.E. Haughan).* 909 (2m4fOMa), 977 (CfMa), 1083 (2m4fOMa), 1368 (OMa).

SOME GREY ..—.. 9 gr.m. Scallywag — Portfield Fair (Gold Rod) pp5. Sturdy good-quartered. Dam, half-sister to Skomar Shody (qv), won 2 points and placed 9 for Ted harries, and grandam, Dale Road, was 2nd in 3 Points for him. NH Aut '99 (from P. Bowen's) r3 p0 (broke blood vessel on debut). Can pull hard and look a difficult ride (typical Scallywag), but has become tailed off in all her races, including when about two fences last in a Maiden in which she jumped slowly (was crawling in the final quarter mile and should have been pulled up). Not worth racing again. *E.L. Harries — Pembs (Graham Lavis).* 486 (R), 1225 (OMa), 1662 (OMa).

SOME TOURIST (IRE) ..10-0.. 13 b.g. Torus — Noellespir (Bargello) 411241R. Strong-topped half-brother to jumping winner, Ambleside (IRE). Dam won mares Maiden in Ireland. IRISH P-t-P '94/6 r16 w1 (Maiden) p3 (3rds); pulled up 6. P-t-P/HUNT CH '97/9 r14 w4 (Restricted, 2 Members, and Club nov rdrs) p2; pulled up 3. A thorough stayer, but able to farm some dire contests in his area over the past three seasons, and has been successful in two two-finisher events and finished alone once. Jumps well, and appreciates mud, but can sometimes look indolent and tried spurred on his final appearance in '99. A fine ride for both Bensteads, and will probably score again when conditions are right. *N. Benstead — Kent & Surrey Bloodhounds (Richard Parker).* 33 (Cnr), 216 (Cnr), 304 (M), 830 (Cnr), 983 (Cf), 1167 (CMod), 1398 (Cf).

SOME-TOY ..10-0.. 15 ch.g. Arkan — Cedar Of Galaxy (Bauble) 6p. Tall rangy half-brother to Wadebridge Fair. P-t-P/HUNT CH '92/4 and '96/9 r33 w12 (inc 3 Hunt Chses, 2m5f-3m1f110y, 2 Ladies, and Open) p7 (4 2nds, and inc 3 Hunt Chses); failed to finish 8 (on floor 6). A smart Pointer to '96 and won eight of ten completed attempts, but has often seemed under a cloud since, and failed to score for the first time in eight seasons in 2000. Game, and could handle extremes of going, but sometimes clumsy, and though only beaten around 15 lengths on his return in a Cherrybrook Confined appears to have entered the twilight of his career. *J. Squire — Stevenstone.* 852 (Cf), 1514 (O).

SONNENSKI ..—.. 9 ch.g. Newski (USA) — Jade 'n Amber (Sonnen Gold) p. Strong. Dam is half-sister to Bolt The gate (qv '88 Season Annual). Backward and novice ridden in his Members, and tailed off after a mile. *Miss J.A. Weeks — E. Cornwall.* 157 (M).

SON OF COURAGE ..8-2.. 8 br.g. Straight Knight — Fort Courage (Cash And Carry) p. Owner-bred half-brother to Fortitude Star. Dam won 3 Points (hat-trick) and 3rd 3 for Mr Smale. P-t-P '99 r1 p0 (4th). Backed from 10s to a quarter of those odds on his racecourse debut, and not wholly disgraced, but did not reappear for almost 12 months and pulled up after 2m4f when he did. The subject of market support again at Lifton, and clearly someone is convinced of his ability, but has back-pedalled after a maximum of two miles to date. Went to post early on his latest appearance. *M.G. Smale — Lamerton.* 1519 (CfMa).

SON OF IRIS ..8-12.. 13 br.g. Strong Gale — Sprats Hill (Deep Run) p45. Small workmanlike half-brother to Dunbrody Abbey. Dam won 2 3m Chses, and placed total of 8 (inc 2 English and one Irish Point). NH FLAT '93 r3 p1 (2nd). NH '93/9 (for Mrs M. Reveley) r35 w8 (2m6f Hdle, and 7 Chses, 2m5f-3m1f, inc 4-timer in '97) p6; ran out on debut; unseated in lead at last once (vulnerable). Formerly a good competitor, but has reportedly broken blood vessels and ran badly in his final three outings under Rules. Did not enjoy Pointing, and was a remote last in both completions (blinkered in the latest). *W.T. Fagg & Miss L. Parr — E. Essex.* 607 (O), 771 (O), 935 (M).

SON OF SAM ..9-13.. 7 b.g. Minster Son — Samonia (Rolfe USA) 1. Leggy light-framed brother to My Sam (qv). NH FLAT '98 (from C. Grant's) r2 p0. Romped the quickest of the three youngsters Maidens at Hornby Castle in February, despite having no real pursuers in the final half mile (only two got round). Seemed unfancied at 20-1, but clearly stays extra well, and would look interesting in a Restricted if resuming. *Mrs S.M. Barker — Hurworth.* 381 (OMa).

SOON COME (USA) ..8-11§.. 9 ch.g. Bering — Charmer (FR) (Crystal Palace FR) R. Tall rangy half-brother to 2 French flat winners, and to a successful Hurdler there. Dam won at 8f in France. NH FLAT '97 r1 p0. NH '97 r1 p0. IRISH NH FLAT '97 r1 p0. IRISH NH '97 r2 p0 (last in both Hdles). P-t-P '99 r7 p1 (2nd); last pair 2, pulled up 3, and fell 1. Takes a fierce hold and refuses to settle, but does possess some ability and only beaten around five lengths in two Maidens in '99. Finds nothing when let down however, and his reputation received another knock when he went through the wing of the fourth on his belated comeback at Lifton. *Mr J. Bowen & Miss L. Wonnacott — Cranwell Bloodhounds (Linda Wonnacott).* 1516 (I).

SO PEACEFUL ..9-0.. 7 b.m. Prince Of Peace — Indian Election (Sula Bula) 3. Compact owner-bred half-sister to Black Oak (*qv*). Not seen since making a reasonable debut when 35 lengths third in February. *T.E. Pocock — W. Somerset V. (Sarah Robinson).* 205 (OMa).

SOUDEN LYRIC ..—.. 8 b.g. Tumble Gold — Palmy (USA) (Buckfinder USA) pf. Home-bred. Dam is half-sister to 4 Pointers, including, Midfielder (*qv* '98 Annual). Has not impressed in his running or jumping to date. *G.T. Bewley — Border.* 425 (CfMa), 718 (CfMa).

SOUNDS STRONG (IRE) ..10-6.. 12 br.g. Strong Gale — Jazz Bavard (Le Bavard FR) 223u21u. Tall workmanlike half-brother to Chasing winner, Glendoe (IRE). IRISH P-t-P '93/4 r2 w1 (5yo Maiden) p0; and pulled up 1. NH '94/8 r15 w3 (3m-3m1f Chses) p4 (2nds, short-headed once, and beaten neck by Strath Royal once). NH '99 r1 p0 (7th). P-t-P '99 r5 w1 (Open) p2 (2nds); 4th, and pulled up 1. Formerly a useful if rather lightly raced performer under Rules, but could be accident prone and fell in three of his last five appearances. Lucky to pick up a Whittington Open last year, after the winner was disqualified for not carrying a penalty, but was not blessed with such good fortune there this year as he would have won at the first meeting had the rider been more forceful with him. Won his first race on merit since December '96 when Ranald Morgan guided him home in a Kelso Hunter Chase on his penultimate start, and the likelihood of further success is enhanced if he retains strong handling. A thorough stayer, but lacks a turn of foot, and no longer suited to waiting tactics. Acts on all, but extremes of going. *N.W.A. Bannister — Pendle Forest & Craven (Annabelle Armitage).* 496 (C), 812 (Cf), 1025 (3m110yH), 1149 (Cf), 1446 (3m1fH), 1591 (3m1fH), 1643 (3m2fH).

SOUTHERN CROSS ..9-11§.. 9 ch.g. Buckley — Muznah (Royal And Regal USA) 5pu. Strong-topped half-brother to 5 Hurdling winners, including Anzum (smart), Jazilah (useful; also successful on flat) and Nahar (useful); the other pair including Formal Affair, both also won on flat. Dam won 2 flat, 7-8f. NH FLAT '96 r4 w1 p1 (3rd). NH '97/8 (for M.W. Easterby, blinkered last 5(r16 p4. IRISH NH '98/9 (bought for 2800) r3 p0 (inc 2 Chses). Not short of ability, but was irresolute when beaten about six lengths in his first Point, and has always been an awkward customer who has contrived never to score from 18 attempts over jumps. Blinkered in 2000 and became less keen with each outing, and extracting a success will be a realy challenge for connections. Often irratice at the fences. *R.J. Rowsell — Ystrad Taf Fechan.* 819 (Cf), 1051 (Cf), 1299 (I).

SOUTHERN FLIGHT ..10-0.. 12 b.g. Southern Music — Fly Blackie (Dear Gazelle) 4pp. Tall workmanlike half-brother to Chase That Dream. Dam, 3rd in Nov Hdle, pulled up in 3 Points. P-t-P/HUNT CH '95/9 r18 w5 (up to Confined) p3 (2 2nds); pulled up 4, slipped up 1, and fell/unseated 2. Never beaten when completing the course '95/6, and looked like developing into a useful mudlark, but only managed one full season in the next three, and has presumably been blighted by breaking blood vessels on a regular basis. Only managed three outings in 2000, and definitely cursed by his problem on one occasion and in all probability in the others as well. Could not be supported with any confidence in future. *Mrs J. Cumings & P.J. Clarke — Devon & Somerset (Keith Cumings).* 161 (L), 403 (Cf), 653 (MO).

SOUTHERN NIGHTS ..—.. 11 ch.g. Ra Nova — Southern Bird (Shiny Tenth) pp. Lengthy brother to Southerncrosspatch. Dam won 2m Hdle in France. NH FLAT '95 r1 p0. NH '96/7 (wins for K. Bailey; debut for Mrs P. Sly) r7 w2 (2m5f-3m Hdles) p2 (2nds); pulled up lame final. Won twice at Towcester November/December '96, but has always had very dodgy legs (was absent for 19 months after his racecourse debut), and could only pull up twice when resuming after a three year gap. *Mr & Mrs A. Varey — Vine & Craven (Alan Varey).* 1242 (M), 1357 (MOnr).

SOUTHERN RIDGE ..—.. 10 b.g. Indian Ridge — Southern Sky (Comedy Star USA) p. Compact well-made half-brother to flat winner, Southern Dominion, and to successful Hurdlers, Southern-Be-George and Southern Chief. Dam won 4 7f races (3 at Goodwood). FLAT (early runs for C. Horgan; previously for D. Elsworth) r15 w1 (6f) p0. NH '95/6 and '98 (won from R. Frost's; previously for R. Baker; previously for W.G.M. Turner) r15 w1 (2m1f Hdle) p2 (2nds); pulled up final. Won a 19-runner race at Newbury as a two-year-old, and scored over Hurdles in September '96, but has clearly been exceptionally difficult to train since, and looks to be a spent force. *N.J. Holdsworth — Dartmoor.* 201 (L).

SOUTHERN TARGET ..—.. 8 ch.g. Cruise Missile — Tuftess (Spartan General) pp. Dam is half-sister to 5 Pointers, including True Dowry (*qv* '94 Annual). Carryig plenty of condition when given a couple of quiet runs in May. *G.I. Cooper — East Anglian Bloodhounds (C. Cunningham).* 1422 (OMa), 1513 (OMa).

SOUTH WESTERLY (IRE) ..10-2.. 13 br.g. Strong Gale — Kilclogher Lass (Deep Run) pp. Wormanlike rangy. IRISH NH FLAT '93 r2 p0. IRISH NH '93/4 r4 p0. NH '94/6 r16 w5 (3m-3m4f Hdles) p4. P-t-P '98/9 (for Mr W.H. Strawson) r6 w1 (Club Conditional) p1 (3rd); 6th, pulled up 2, and fell 1. NH '99 (from Mrs M. reveley's) r3 p1 (2nd); pulled up 1, unseated 1. A useful staying Hurdler when winning five races consecutively on good or sound surfaces in '95, but was gaining his first success when carried home by Simon Walker in a close finish at Garthorpe on his final appearance last year. Pulled up in both outings for new connections in 2000, and needs treating with suspicion if he returns. *Miss E. Bywater — Quorn.* 545 (O), 794 (Cf).

SOVEREIGNS MATCH ..10-1.. 13 b.g. Royal Match — Sovereign's Folly (Sovereign Bill) pp12p1p3.

Strong compact half-brother to Hurdles winner, Kings Folly. NH FLAT r2 p0. NH '93 and '97 r4 p3 (3rds, distant last on all-weather once; inc 2 Chses). P-t-P/HUNT CH '95/8 r14 w1 (Maiden) p3 (2 2nds; inc Hunt Ch); pulled up 8. A competent jumper, but has a history of breaking blood vessels, and was lame in '96 and missed the '99 season so connections have done well to revive him. Recorded two easy victories under Matthew Mackley, but seems to go lame intermittently these days and it is clearly in the back of his mind as he often refuses to over-exert himself. Acquired blinkers on his final start, and wore a tongue-strap when winning at Easingwold. Suited by a sound surface. *J.M. Robinson — Burton.* 47 (C), 232 (R), 435 (M), 546 (R), 801 (3m1fH), 1351 (CR), 1478 (I), 1583 (C).

PLATE 123   1351 Bilsdale Dodson & Horrell PPORA Club Members Restricted: Sovereigns Match (M. Mackley), 1st, is clear of Mount Faber (S. Charlton), 2nd   PHOTO: Roy Parker

SOVEREIGN SPRAY (IRE) ..9-9.. 11 b.g. Celio Rufo — Countess Spray (Even Say) p22p5. Workmanlike half-brother to Irish Pointing, NH flat and Hurdles winner, Ballagh Countess. NH '94/5 r5 p0. P-t-P '96/9 r14 w6 (up to Confined) p2 (2nds, head of 3 once, and last once); pulled up 3, slippewd up 1, and fell 1. Had a good record in minor events prior to 2000, but always sparingly raced, and failed to win for the first time in five seasons. Appreciates mud, but could never find it this year, and his rating dipped by nine pounds. Decidedly unhappy on his last two appearances, but may well be able to stage a revival if conditions are more suitable next year. Has been pulled up in four of five seasonal debuts. *S.P. Tindall — Southdown & Eridge (Jeff Peate).* 288 (CMod), 706 (Cf), 983 (Cf), 1108 (C), 1509 (Cf).

SOVIET SIP ..9-3.. 6 ch.g. Presidium — Sip Of Orange (Celtic Cone) 1p. Half-brother to Jaffa, and to Hurdles winner, Orange Imp. Dam won 6 Hdles, 2m-3m1f. All out when making a winning debut in a two-finisher Maiden in soft at Erw Lon (the slowest of the four divisions, and was all out to get home), but never going well when returning there a month later. Possibly capable of atoning. *Mrs J. Mathias — S. Pembs.* 267 (CfMa), 646 (R).

SPACEAGE GOLD ..—.. 12 b.g. Sunyboy — Chancer's Last (Foggy Bell) pppp2p. Strong-topped attractive half-brother to Chancy Oats, Splint, Tricky Trevor and Phar From Chance. Dam won 4 Chses, 2m-2m4f. NH FLAT '95 r2 p0. NH '95/8 r16 w1 (3m2f Hdle) p3; remote 4th of 5, and pulled up 1 in Chses. P-t-P '99 (for Mr P.A. Rackham) r1 p0 (pulled up). All out to win a four-runner Hurdle on firmish at Cheltenham in '96, but very lightly raced since, and looked very miserable when managing only one remote completion in Points. Visored on his last four starts. T. Phillips & Mrs S. Platt — Dunston H. (Tim Phillips). 92 (Cf), 176 (O), 770 (Cf), 936 (Cf), 1106 (O), 1333 (3mH).

SPACE CAPPA ..9-12.. 13 br.g. Capitano — Space Speaker (Space King) p31p43. Lengthy workmanlike brother to Space Molly. P-t-P/HUNT CH '94/6 r12 w3 (inc 3m Hunt Ch) p3 (2 2nds);

failed to finish 6 (fell/unseated 2). NH '97/9 r14 p6; pulled up 4. Made the bulk of the running when successful in three races including a Taunton Hunter Chase in a five race spell '95/6, but appeared to go wrong at Liverpool and failed to score when sent under Rules. Justified favouritism in a modest Ladies taking 8min 15s at Bishopsleigh this year, but well held under less testing conditions, and tailed off and pulled up in both Hunter Chases. Not the force he once was, but still able to plough through deep mud, and worth bearing in mind should similar conditions prevail in 2001. *D.G. Stephens — W. Somerset (Vicky Stephens).* 922 (3mH), 1045 (L), 1174 (L), 1346 (3m1f110yH), 1605 (L), 1652 (L).

SPACE HOPPER (IRE) ..8-2.. 6 ch.g. Mister Lord (USA) — Kilmalooda Lass (Prince Rheingold) 8. Tall well-made. dam is half-sister to Queen's Award (*qv* Annual). Bought Doncaster, Aug '98 for 6200. novicey on a late-May debut, but looks the type who might have scope for improvement. *N.D. Edden — N. Cotswold.* 1590 (2m4fOMa).

SPANISH JEST ..8-4.. 10 b.g. Jester — Donnacelli (Don Carlos) pp3pu4. Strong-topped compact half-brother to Modina April. P-t-p '97 and '99 r7 p0 (pulled up 5, fell/unseated 2). Highly excitable, and usually runs from the front, but has yet to finish in front of a rival, and seems to have severe stamina limitations. Will need a bad race to score. Has two handlers. *Mrs M.D. Burrough — Seavington.* 331 (R), 519 (M), 763 (CfMa), 932 (R), 1062 (OMa), 1640 (OMa).

SPANISH RIVER ..9-3.. 10 ro.g. El Conquistador — Swanee Girl (My Swanee) 3pu61. Lengthy unfurnished. Dam won a Restricted and third for Sarah-Jane Baxter. NH FLAT '96/7 r2 p0 (prominent for over a mile in both). NH '97 r1 p0 (fell at first in Ch). P-t-P '97 and '99 r5 p1 (last of 3); pulled up 4. Made all to get himself and jockey Guy Weatherley off the mark in a slow Maiden at Badbury Rings, but had the luxury of a 15 length advantage throughout the final mile after his nearest rival had exited, and usually fails to stay. A sketchy jumper who favours going left-handed, and will be difficult to place successfully again. *Mrs S.J. Baxter — R.A.* 328 (CfMa), 477 (R), 763 (CfMa), 889 (OMa), 1062 (OMa).

SPAREBIT ..9-4.. 7 b.m. Henbit (USA) — Sparticone (Celtic Cone) 34p26. Small attractive owner-bred half-sister to Oliver Himself and Sharp Madam. Dam won a Hunt Ch and 10 Points and placed 7 for Judy Wilson. Great-grandam, Alice Roe, won 3 Irish and 3 English Points. P-t-p '99 r3 p0 (pulled up 2, and unseated 1). Only once went further than 1m2f in her first season, but much more competitive in 2000, and had every chance when five lengths second at Clifton-on-Dunsmore. Proved disappointing at Garthorpe subsequently, and whilst her dam was game and genuine, she may take her lead from her sire, whose offspring are often anything but. *Mrs J. Wilson — Pytchley (Bill Warner).* 53 (OMa), 181 (2m4fOMa), 436 (OMa), 1423 (OMa), 1589 (2m4fOMa).

SPARE ON ..8-0.. 9 b.m. Zambrano — Sunnyside (Doulab USA) p2p. Small neat home-bred. Ten lengths last of two behind a weary plodder in her Members, and does not look to have much to recommend her. *R.A. Ford (Ball Boy Partners) — Quantock (Mrs Penny Burnell).* 403 (Cf), 635 (M), 881 (OMa).

SPARKLING CASCADE (IRE) ..9-4.. 9 b.m. Royal Fountain — Yukon Law (Goldhill) 1pp. Small plain unfurnished. P-t-p '99 (for Mr P. Bertram) r5 p1 (2nd); 6th, and pulled up 3. Maintained her steady improvement from last year to win a stamina test at Flete Park on her reappearance where Leslie Jefford forced her head in front in the last strides, but subsequently pulled up in the closing stages of two Restricteds. Very lean on her return, and may not stand much racing. *M.G. Tootell — Tiverton (Sarah Kittow).* 1049 (CfMa), 1258 (R), 1563 (R).

SPARKLING ELVER ..—.. 6 ch.m. Gran Alba (USA) — Elver Season (Vital Season) p. Dam, half-sister to 6 Pointers, including Three Potato Four (*qv*), won 3 Hunt Chses, 2m4f-3m1f (hat-trick) and 11 Points (inc 6-timer, and 7 Opens) and placed 7. Grandam, Capelina, was 3rd in Sell Hdle, and won 6 Points (inc dead-heat) and 2 Hunt Chses (3m2f-4m) and placed 13 for late John Cork. From a great winner-producing family, and made some of the running for two miles on a pleasing debut at Cotley Farm. Could be worth bearing in mind for a Maiden success. *Mrs S. Cork — E. Devon (Chris Down).* 1308 (OMa).

SPARKLING GIFT (IRE) ..9-7.. 8 b.m. Naheez (USA) — Northern Gift (Northern Guest USA) fp22. Compact sister to Irish jumping winner, Dazzling Guest, and half-sister to Nelloes Pet (IRE), and to NH flat and Hurdles winner, North Tyne (IRE). Showed a degree in promise in all her races, and ended the season with a half length second. Needs to find a little extra stamina, but should win a Maiden when she does. *Mrs P. Robertson — V. of Lune H. (Sarah Robertson).* 380 (OMa), 778 (OMa), 1148 (M), 1367 (OMa).

SPARKLING SECRET ..8-10.. 6 ch.g. Tina's Pet — Sparkling Hock (Hot Spark) pp4. Dam is half-sister to Perang Percy (*qv* '96 Annual). 1000 2yo. FLAT (for C. Murray) r1 p0 (last in Sell). Bought Doncaster, Aug '97 for 750. Made mistakes on his debut, but has shown a modicum of promise since, and got round for the first time when 15 lengths last. Should be worth trying again at six. *Mr & Mrs J.F. Symes — Taunton V. (John Symes).* 874 (2m4fOMa), 1102 (OMa), 1307 (OMa).

SPARTAN GOLD ..—.. 7 b.m. Headin' Up — Spartan Native (Native Bazaar) pp. Workmanlike unfurnished half-sister to Natal and Raka King. P-t-P '99 r3 p0 (pulled up 3). Showed some ability when not knocked about in her first season, but pulled up after two miles twice in 2000, and is no further down the line than when she started. *P.J. Allen — N. Ledbury.* 450 (CfMa), 900 (OMa).

SPARTANS LAST ..—.. 6 ch.m. Prince Of Peace — Spartan Mariner (Spartan General) ppp. Rangy owner-bred half-sister to Spartans Winney (*qv*). Looks very green and something of a handful, but clearly only schooling so far, and has made just one appearance in a Maiden. The progeny of her sire often improve after a poor start, and she certainly should not be written off yet. *P.D. Rogers — Dartmoor (P.D. Rogers).* 66 (Cf), 162 (I), 721 (CfMa).

SPARTANS WINNEY ..9-8.. 8 ch.m. Nearly A Hand — Spartan Mariner (Spartan General) 54. Tiny neat sister to Sparties Image and half-sister to Spartans Dina and Spartans Last. Dam won 9 Points and placed 12 for David Rogers. P-t-p '98/9 r10 w1 (Maiden) p0 (4th, last pair 4, pulled up 2, and fell/unseated 2). Won a three-finisher Maiden in testing conditions at Bishops Court in '99, but beaten a minimum of 13 lengths in four Restricteds since, and lacks scope for improvement. Only a dot, and would prefer the lesser weights in Ladies races. Seems hard to train and has only once managed an uninterrupted campaign. *P.D. Rogers — Dartmoor.* 102 (R), 932 (R).

SPARTIES IMAGE ..7-8.. 7 ch.m. Nearly A Hand — Spartan Mariner (Spartan General) pp6. Small lengthy unfurnished owner-bred sister to Spartans Winney (*qv*). P-t-P '99 r1 p0 (last). Tailed off last in both completions, but has been both physically and mentally backward to date, and may be capable of better in due course. *P.D. Rogers — Dartmoor.* 72 (OMa), 159 (CfMa), 855 (CfMa).

SPEARHEAD AGAIN (IRE) ..9-12.. 12 b.g. Strong Gale — Affordthe Queen (Pitpan) p535. Well-made brother to NH flat and jumping winner, Queen Of Spades (IRE), and half-brother to Dolly Sparks (IRE). Dam is an unraced half-sister to Dark Dawn (*qv* 2000 Annual). NH FLAT '93/4 r2 p0. NH '93/7 (visored once in '96; won for Miss V. Williams; previously for late K. Bridgwater; previously for S. Christian) r15 w1 (2m5f Ch) p4 (3rds, inc Hdle); fell 2 out when disputing lead once (looked unlucky). Gained his sole success in a very bad Chase on firmish, and has been error-prone over fences. Showed speed for a long way when resuming in Points after a three year absence, when connections plunged on him from two to 4-6 in his Members, but consistently lacked the stamina for the job. *J. Rudge — N. Ledbury.* 1085 (M), 1358 (Cf), 1630 (Cf), 1672 (O).

SPECK ..9-6.. 12 ch.g. Telsmoss — Dorothy Jane (He Loves Me) 57fp. Leggy plain half-brother to Morchard Mill. Yet to finish better than last, but did fall when still holding a slight lead three out on his penultimate appearance. Disappointed next time, and although he is a keen free-running sort there is as yet no clear evidence that he stays three miles. Aptly named, as he is a mass of speckily splodges. *Miss C. Derryman — Seavington.* 519 (M), 1308 (OMa), 1564 (OMa), 1609 (OMa).

SPECKLES (IRE) ..—.. 7 b.m. Brush Aside (USA) — Daring Duchess (Brave Invader USA) pb. NH FLAT '98 (for K. Ryan) r2 p0. Evidently did not impress connections with her attitude in her first Maiden, as she acquired blinkers when brought down next time. *P. Diggle — Dumfries.* 363 (CfMa), 664 (2m5fOMa).

SPECTACULAR VIEW (IRE) ..9-10.. 6 b.g. Scenic — La Petruschka (Ballad Rock) pp51b6. Compact quite attractive half-brother to Elite Force (IRE), and to a winner in Czech Republic. Ran out the very easy winner of a Maiden on firm at Morden, but that is his only positive sign of ability to date. Finished tailed off in a Restricted later, and sound ground may be the key to him, as he has appeared to flounder in holding. Worth another chance when conditions seem to be in his favour. *C. Dawson — S. Durham.* 807 (R), 1166 (OMa), 1430 (OMa), 1480 (OMa), 1627 (2m5fH), 1664 (R).

SPECTRE ..9-5.. 10 b.g. Respect — Spring-Ann (Workboy) f3p16. Tall rangy. NH FLAT '96 (for J.K.M. Oliver) r2 p0. Went eventing after two spins on the flat, but presumably too keen for that sphere judging by his Pointing escapades. Closing quickly on the principals and left well clear at the second last when opening his account at Cottenham, but his first appearance in Restricteds was a particularly tame effort. A hard-puller and probably does not stay that well, but an imposing sort, and should find another opening. *A.J. Papworth — Dunston H. (Mike Bloom).* 24 (OMa), 122 (OMa), 770 (Cf), 1039 (OMa), 1287 (R).

SPECULATIVE ..—.. 7 b.g. Suave Dancer (USA) — Gull Nook (Mill Reef USA) f. Half-brother to several winners, including Pentire (yop-class on flat). Dam won 2 flat, 11-12f (beat the dam of Sandy Floss, *qv*, in the '86 Ribblesdale Stakes). Grandam is half-sister to Shirley Heights. 10,000 2yo. FLAT r7 p0 (inc Sells). NH '97 (for W. Storey) r3 p0 (9th of 10, last, and pulled up; mistakes). Exceedingly disappointing in the previous years, and took a crashing fall at the third in his only Point. *K.A. & Mrs R.A. Hicks — Portman (Rose Hicks).* 875 (2m4fOMa).

SPEECH BUBBLE (IRE) ..8-13.. 9 br.m. Bowling Pin — Shikanne (Spin Of A Coin) u. Small. P-t-P '98/9 (for Mrs C. Handel) r6 p0 (4th, 9th, and pulled up 4). Unimpressive in both looks and achievement to date, and her best effort was when 13 lengths fourth in a Holnicote maiden on firm in '99. Has had few chances to improve on that since, and shed the rider when in the rear after two miles on her only start this year. *Mrs L. Roberts — Dulverton E. (Miss G. Doig).* 1099 (OMa).

SPEEDY SNAPS PRIDE ..—.. 9 gr.g. Hallgate — Pineapple's Pride (John De Coombe) ppp. Sturdy half-brother to flat winner, Pineapple Prince. dam won at 5f. FLAT (won for P. Cundell; one run for J>A> Harris) r34 w1 (7f Sell) p9. NH '97 (for J>C> Poulton; debut for P. Cundell) r4 p0 (mostly Sells). Bought Malvern, Feb for 1600. Managed to scrape a win by a short head in '96, but was fat and barely able to raise a gallop in Points. Often blinkered in the past. *Mrs F. Ferneyhough & N. Page — Cambs Univ (Nick Page).* 174 (M), 318 (Cf), 770 (Cf).

SPIDERDORE ..8-7.. 7 b.g. El Conquistador — Lolly Spider (Rugantino) p5. Brother to Conkerdore, and half-brother to Lord Spider (*qv*). Bought Ascot, June for 3700. Finished nearly 40 lengths last when completing, but is a big sort who is verging on 17hh, and surely not strong enough to do himself justice yet. On the debit side, the similarly large Lord Spider (now nine) has never got round since he was a five-year-old. *M. Hehoe & A. Chorlton — Bicester with Whaddon (Fiona Kehoe).* 517 (OMa), 872 (OMa).

SPIKE BARNES ..—.. 6 b.g. Bedford (USA) — Ballintava (Better By Far) f. Dam failed to finish in 12 Points for Mr Ross (fell/unseated 3, and refused 2; 'a real donkey...why on earth bother with her?'). Foiled by the first at Hackwood. *D.A.N. Ross - Grafton.* 1245 (OMa).

SPIN LIGHTLY (IRE) ..—.. 10 br.g. Spin Of A Coin — Lady Lightly (Nepotism) p. Big strong-topped rangy. P-t-P '98/9 r7 p0 (pulled up 6, and fell 1). Maintained his remarkable record by pulling up in his Members and displayed signs of temperament to boot. Has never once looked fit, and wobbles to his usual fate of non-completion every time. *W. Murdoch — Belvoir.* 867 (M).

SPIRITO ..8-8.. 6 b.g. Mystiko (USA) — Classic Beam (Cut Above) p24p. Smallish good-looking half-brother to 2 flat winners (one in Germany), including Classic Line. 7500y. FLAT (for Lord Huntingdon; tried visored) r5 p0. NH '98 (bought for 2200) r1 p0 (tailed off). Collected a lowly rating when finishing half a length second at Holnicote, but only had dead wood behind him, and was beaten 20 lengths next time. Missed '99, and came to rather an abrupt end in March in 2000. *M.R. Churches — Mendip F.* 147 (OMa), 352 (CfMa), 518 (2m4fOMa), 733 (2m4fOMa).

SPIRIT OF LIFE ..9-0.. 8 b.m. Nearly A Hand — Spirit Of Youth (Kind Of Hush) fupp1. Small neat. P-t-P '98 r2 p0 (pulled up 2). Jumped badly on her return, but helped by the lack of fences (only 13 were jumped due to the state of the ground) when winning a two-finisher Maiden taking 8min 20s than a habitual loser at Bishopsleigh. Will have to improve immensely for Restricteds, and lacks scope. *F.R. Bown — Lamerton (Miss C. Bown).* 312 (CfMa), 540 (OMa), 724 (CfMa), 857 (CfMa), 1178 (OMa).

SPIRIT PRINCE ..9-4.. 9 b.g. White Prince (USA) — Anascend (Ascendant) ppR2242. Strong. Dam won 2 Points (lucky when finishing alone in Members once) and placed 9 (inc flat). P-t-P '97 (for Miss C.M. Voyce) r4 p0 (last, pulled up 2, and unseated 1). Missed the '98/9 seasons entirely, and despite the almost exclusive services of Julian Pritchard has managed to avoid winning on his return. A real hot-head, who gets on his toes and sweats excessively, and usually jumps markedly right-handed. Beaten between five and 20 lengths with runner-up in Maidens, but last in two of those and only had one rival behind in the other, and simply does not stay. Tried to run out to the box-park at the Brecon, and is one to avoid at all costs. *P.B. Miles — N. Herefords.* 341 (CfMa), 392 (R), 484 (R), 704 (OMa), 893 (OMa), 972 (OMa), 1278 (OMa).

SPLIT SECOND ..10-6.. 12 b.g. Damister (USA) — Moment In Time (Without Fear FR) 321111. Workmanlike half-brother to flat winners, Make Time and Superenfer. Dam won 2 7f races. FLAT (tried visored) r6 p0. NH '92/4 (blinkered 1; tried tongue-strap) r11 p4 (short-headed once; inc 3rd of 4 in Ch); unseated only other Ch. P-t-P '95/9 r16 w13 (inc 11 Ladies, one a match; hat-trick '98) p2; and 4th. A smart Ladies horse, who although vulnerable on his seasonal debut, has only tasted defeat in five of 22 Points. Enjoyed his busiest season to date in 2000, during which he acquired a near-side pricker, but did not need to be at his best most of the time, and met nothing of significance during his four-timer. Can handle soft ground, but much prefers a sound surface. Always looks and jumps well, and possesses a decent turn of foot, but most of the locals run a mile when they see him, and rarely goes off at a working mans price. Should run up another sequence if all goes his way in 2001, but the chinks in his armour are there to be exploited. *Mrs P.J. Willis — Berkeley (Dick Baimbridge).* 326 (L), 475 (L), 613 (L), 991 (L), 1191 (L), 1491 (L).

SPLODGE ..10-2.. 10 b.g. Oedipus Complex — Gardella (Garnered) 12p. Big. Dam, sister to Medway Gauntlet (*qv* '90 Annual), was quickly tailed off twice in Brocklesby Members (3rd once). Turned out to have been the value bet of the season when 4-6 to beat an unraced hunter in his Members, as he kept on gamely to chase Key Debate home (again at Brocklesby Park) with five previous winners well behind him. Made mistakes when tailed off in the Grimthorpe, but is a game sort who should go well when returning to home territory in 2001. *Earl of Yarborough — S. Wold, & Brocklesby (Mark Bennison).* 228 (M), 797 (R), 999 (4m1fMO).

SPORTING CHANCE ..9-7.. 9 ch.g. Ikdam — Tumbling Ego (Abednego) p. Sparely-made. Dam is half-sister to Parsons Brig (*qv* '99 Annual). NH FLAT '97 r1 p0. NH '97/8 r4 p0. P-t-P '99 r3 w1 (Maiden) p0; and pulled up 2. Tailed off without exception under Rules, but landed a gamble when winning a conspicuously bad Maiden at Lifton last year. Pulled up in both Restricteds since, and failed to return after a solitary appearance at Black Forest Lodge this year. *H.S. Channon — Lamerton (Jo Channon & Yvonne Watson).* 69 (R).

SPOT ON MILLIE ..—.. 6 gr.m. Weld — Damsong (Petong) ppf. Small light. Bought Doncaster, Nov for 1000. Yet to show any ability, and was winded when she fell at Bonvilston. *J.W. Tudor — Llangeinor.* 268 (CfMa), 648 (CfMa), 1455 (OMa).

SPOT THE DIFFERENCE (IRE) ..10-8.. 8 b.g. Lafontaine (USA) — Spotted Choice (Callernish) 228. Tall. Dam is half-sister to Double Tricks (*qv* '95 Annual). IRISH P-t-P '98 r3 w1 (5&6yo Mdn) p0; pulled up 1. IRISH NH '98/9 r4 w1 (3m Hunt Ch) p1 (2nd in 4m NH Ch); pulled up and fell at first in Chses. IRISH HUNT CH '00 r2 p2 (2nds, beaten *4l* by Sheltering at Fairyhouse: *ww, 7th ½way, 2nd 5 out, rdn & ev ch 2 out, no ex*; and beaten *4½l* by Dan's Your Man at Leopardstown: *trckd ldrs, 3rd & rdn 3 out, no imp til r.o frm last*). Sparingly raced, but has some useful form to his credit, and ran well in both attempts in Ireland in 2000. In contention after a blunder at the third (the Chair) at Aintree, and not seen again. Handles soft ground, but possibly finds four miles a shade too far. Can surely return to winning ways if fit in 2001. *J.P. McManus — Scarteen (Enda Bolger, in Ireland)*. 921 (2m6fH).

SPOT THE MUSIC (IRE) ..—.. 7 b.m. Orchestra — Precious Petra (Bing II) upp. Small sturdy half-sister to Yours Truly (IRE), and to 2 Hurdles winners, including Delpiombo (also successful on flat). Dam won 6f Seller. P-t-P '99 r3 p0 (pulled up 3). Has blundered round aimlessly in six Maidens to date, without looking likely to improve. *A.R. Trotter — Berwicks.* 112 (OMam), 365 (CfMa), 718 (CfMa).

SPRINGFIELD PRINCE (IRE) ..—§.. 8 b.g. Phardante (FR) — Springfield Music (Black Minstrel) pp. Tall. Tailed off and pulled up twice, and looks reluctant to try. *Mrs S. Bell — Morpeth.* 913 (CfMa), 1082 (CMa).

SPRINGFIELD REX ..10-9.. 10 ch.g. Oedipus Complex — Scarlet Coon (Tycoon II) 2p2u11. Leggy light-framed brother to Springfield Pet. Dam won 3 Points (and disqualified from another) and 2nd 3 for Margaret Pinney. Grandam, Scarlet Letch, won 10 Chses, 3m-4m1f. P-t-P '97 and '99 (for Mrs C.W. Pinney & Mr P. Walker) r9 w1 (Maiden) p2 (3rds); 4th, pulled up 2, fell 2, and brought down 1. Disappointing in early season 2000, but posted his best effort to date when runner-up to the unbeaten Union Man at Garthorpe following a six week break, and won decisively on his last two appearances including on his Hunter Chase debut at Aintree. Well ridden by Fiona Needham, and should continue to prosper as long as he remains healthy. *D. Ingle, Mrs C.W. Pinney & P. Webster — S. Wold (David Ingle).* 47 (C), 232 (R), 871 (R), 1071 (CR), 1232 (L), 1557 (3m1fH).

SPRING GALE (IRE) ..10-11.. 10 b.g. Strong Gale — Orospring (Tesoro Mio) 31111u112. Workmanlike lengthy. NH FLAT '96 (for S. Sherwood) r2 p1 (3rd). NH '96/9 (for O. Sherwood) r23 w5 (3 Hdles, 2m4f-2m7f, and 2 Chses, 2m4f-2m6f) p12. Possesses plenty of ability, but ungenuine when often blinkered latterly under Rules, and the Turner's did a great job of sweetening him in 2000. Can still look quirky particularly at the start, but Zoe Turner has really got to grips with him, and possibly unlucky not to complete a seven-timer, as he unseated two out when two lengths second at 2-5 at Cottenham (Dawn Alert, who went on to score, was a distance behind him in the Greig Middleton Final). His confidence was riding high when he made a successful transition to Hunter Chases at Fakenham, and then lost absolutely nothing in defeat behind Balisteros at Uttoxeter. Acts on extremes of going, and is a clever jumper. It could be difficult to prevent him from running up another sequence in 2001. *J.M. Turner — Suffolk.* 95 (L), 177 (L), 319 (L), 608 (L), 939 (L), 1037 (L), 1289 (L), 1434 (3m110yH), 1593 (3m2fH).

SPRINGHILL QUAY (IRE) ..9-13.. 12 br.g. Quayside — Home Rejoicing (Carlburg) p3pp. Tall good-bodied. NH '96/7 r3 p0 (4th, and pulled up 2). P-t-P/HUNT CH '95 and '98/9 r15 w3 (Maiden, Restricted and Intermediate) p4 (3 2nds); last pair 2, pulled up 3, ran out 1, and brought down 2. Looked a good prospect when winning his Maiden in '95, but sorely troubled since, and connections did well to bring him back for two wins last year. Never remotely involved in 2000, and only able to appear once in each of the first four months of the season. Not the most fluent of jumpers, but has yet to lose a rider through his own mistakes. *S.B. Clark — York & Ainsty S.* 48 (Cf), 277 (Cf), 506 (Cf), 999 (4m1fMO).

SPRING MARATHON (USA) ..9-11.. 11 b.g. Topsider (USA) — April Run (Run The Gantlet USA) 2p43u2p. Tall good-bodied half-brother to 2 Irish Flat winners. Dam won 8 flat (10½-13½f), including Prix Vermeille, Turf Classic (twice), and Washington D.C. International, and made the frame in the Japan Cup and 2 Arc's (was trained in France by Francois Boutin). IRISH FLAT r1 p0. FLAT r3 p0. NH '93/5 and '97/9 r29 w5 (4 2m1f-3m2f Hdles & 3m2f Chse) p6; taken to Ireland once; blinkered last two outings. P-t-P '97 (for Mrs N. Dutfield) r3 w2 (Opens) p0; and pulled up 1. A fair staying Hurdler under Rules, but never as convincing over fences, and has not excelled since his return to Points. At his best with plenty of cut in the ground, but not an easy ride, and needs plenty of driving to keep him interested. Beaten a mimimum of eight lengths in 2000, and showed a general lack of zest, but never encountered the soft ground that he prefers. *Miss E.C. Tory — S. Dorset (Mary Tory).* 209 (M), 326 (L), 390 (L), 877 (L), 927 (Cf), 1132 (L), 1470 (MO).

SPRINGVILLA (IRE) ..9-9.. 13 b.g. Invited (USA) — Rooske Loraine (Vulgan) p22p. Small neat half-brother to Irish Pointing winner, Mr Turpin. Dam won 4 Irish Hdles, 2m-2m5f. IRISH P-t-P '93/4 (tried in blinkers) r8 p1 (2nd); pulled up 4, and fell 1. P-t-P '95/7 and '99 r10 p3 (2nds, last once); 5th, and fell/unseated 6. Formerly a nightmare ride, and came back riderless in six of his first eight English Points, but a much safer conveyance since, and instead his followers have had to endure the sight of him finishing second in his last five completions. His main problem is a lack of stamina, and only caught in the dying strides at Badbury Rings this year, and though he thoroughly deserves a success the cards always seem to be stacked against him. Suited by top-of-the-ground. *C.A. Green — S. & W. Wilts.* 260 (R), 630 (OMa), 763 (CfMa), 1131 (OMa).

SPRING WHEAT ..9-9.. 9 b.m. Nicholas Bill — Florista (Oats) 41p1. Small stocky. P-t-P '98/9 r6 p2 (3rds, last once); last, pulled up 2, and fell 1. Has improved with the acquisition of a tongue-strap, and jumped safely when successful in her Members, but her High Easter Restricted success was a surprise particularly as it came just six days after a most uninspiring performance at Garthorpe. Passed four rivals in unorthodox fashion (Catherine Tuke received a caution for her use of the whip) from the third last, and snatched the verdict close home. The form of the race looks suspect however, as the runner-up is a renowned weak-finisher, and the third, just three lengths behind, was a 14-year-old. Looks sure to struggle in future. *Miss C. Tuke — Thurlow, & Cambs, & Cambridge University.* 91 (M), 174 (M), 546 (R), 610 (R).

SPRINTFAYRE ..—.. 13 b.g. Magnolia Lad — Headliner (Pampered King) p. Angular half-brother to Head Of Defence, and to a winner in Belgium. NH FLAT '93/4 (first two for R. Simpson) r3 w1 p0. NH '94/9 (2 wins for J. Long; previously for Mrs M. Long) r24 w2 (Hdles, 2m-2m3f, inc Sell) p2; ran out 2. Scored on his debut in '93 and added two more wins plus two placings in '96, but has gained no other prizes. In the unlikely event of a return at 13 he seems sure to prove useless. *Mrs A.G. Drury — O. Surrey & Burstow (Peter Broad).* 1394 (O).

SPRUCE ..9-11.. 8 ch.m. Buckley — Mossberry Fair (Mossberry) 32423. Lengthy half-sister to flat and jumping winner, Pegasus Bay. Dam won 4 2m Hdles. NH FLAT '98/4 Hdles. NH '99 r2 p0 (last, and pulled up in Hdles). P-t-P '99 (for Mrs H.O. Graham) r7 w1 (Maiden) p0; 6th, last, pulled up 1, fell/unseated 3. Won a two-finisher Maiden at Friars Haugh in testing conditions last year, and has since posted some sound efforts in more competitive company, but not helped by the new riders inexperience, and would have won at Lemalla with stronger handling. Error-prone in the previous year, but much improved in that respect now. Deserves compensation, and should get it as the pilot gains experience. A thorough stayer, and appreciates plenty of cut. *Mrs R. Fell — Dartmoor.* 164 (R), 315 (R), 536 (R), 726 (Cf), 850 (R).

SPUFFINGTON ..9-8.. 13 b.g. Sula Bula — Pita (Raffingora) 855p5p34. Tall strong-topped. NH '93/8 r29 w4 (2m1f Hdle and 3 Chses, 2m4f-2m5f) p14; unseated in '97 Grand National. P-t-P/HUNT CH '98/9 (for Mr W.J. Turcan) r8 p3 (2 3rds, inc Hunt Ch); last, and pulled up 2. Enjoyed a purple patch of four wins and four placings from eight starts during the 12 months from March '94, but hopelessly easy to beat since, and tailed off without exception in his schoolmaster role in 2000. As safe as houses, but does not pass trees very quickly nowadays, and is a desperate plodder. Blinkered once in '99. *P.P. Hall — W. Norfolk (Tim Bryce).* 19 (L), 92 (Cf), 318 (Cf), 770 (Cf), 868 (Cf), 1184 (Cf), 1285 (M), 1583 (C).

SPUMANTE ..9-12.. 9 ch.g. Executive Man — Midler (Comedy Star USA) 4fp11. Lengthy half-brother to Spittal Beck. Dam won at 7-11½f in Italy. FLAT r10 p3. NH '96 r7 p2. P-t-P '98/9 r5 p2 (2nds, of 3 once); 4th, pulled up 1, and fell 1. Very much a non-stayer in the past, and still struggles to get the trip when conditions are testing, but struck twice in quick succession when the ground dried out in May, and won with a bit in hand both times. Has to come from off the pace to conserve his stamina, but has struck up a good relationship with Gary Hanmer, and may be able to win another minor event. *F.G. Poingdestre (Les Bush, Garry & Danny Partnership) — W. Salop (Peter Morris).* 122 (OMa), 527 (OMa), 1196 (OMa), 1413 (OMa), 1528 (R).

SQUADDIE ..9-13.. 9 ch.g. Infantry — Mendelita (King's Company) fp21f322up. Small lengthy brother to Company Commander. Dam won 3 Hdles and 3 Chses, all 2m. NH FLAT '97 r4 p3 (2 3rds). NH '98 (unplaced last 2 for M. Hammond, bought for 6800; previously for P. Payne) r9 p1 (3rd). Consistent when he avoids falling or unseating, and beaten less than three lengths in four placings (behind a Millington horse once), but finds little in the closing stages, and possibly barely gets the trip. Enterprisingly handled by Andrew Sansome when scoring unchallenged at Ampton, and was virtually solo when he got tired two out and barely clambered over the last. Showed himself to be a rare firebrand on that occasion, and was ridden from the stable yard to the paddock by Zoe Turner, and when he got there he proved awkward and knocked over his handler. Not a fun person to live with, but has the ability to land another modest contest. Changed stables, and his arrival in the Millington yard in June did little for his chances, though he may well feel more at home there. *J.M. Turner — P.J. Millington — Suffolk.* 20 (OMa), 87 (OMa), 291 (CMa), 550 (OMa), 773 (R), 940 (R), 1111 (R), 1287 (R), 1664 (R), 1674 (I).

SQUARE ONE (IRE) ..9-12.. 7 b.m. Mandalus — Deep Dollar (Deep Run) 211p. Small neat sister to Hurdles winner, One More Dime (IRE), and half-sister to Hurdles winners, Cash For Questions (IRE) and Madame President (IRE). P-t-P '99 r1 p0 (4th). Caught near the line on her reappearance, but made up five lengths from the last to land a Market Rasen Maiden, and subsequently justified favouritism in her Members. Disappointed in her first Restricted, but the rider looked very under-horsed, and she appeared not to appreciate the much softer surface. Lacks scope, but jumps soundly and has shown a willing attitude, and may be quick enough to move into Ladies races in 2001. *Mrs C. Price — Belvoir (Chris Bealby).* 167 (OMa), 436 (OMa), 867 (M), 1268 (R).

SQUERREY ..—.. 10 ch.g. Royal Vulcan — Dark Rosheen (Rushmere) u. Strong. Dam, sister and half-sister to 6 Pointers, pulled up after a mile in a Maiden for Mrs Betts. Grandam, Proviso, won 2 Points and 2nd twice for her. NH Apr '96 r1 p0 (tailed off and pulled up — green). P-t-P '97 r2 p0 (refused 1, and pulled up 1). Broke down at Penshurst in '97, and was paying his first visit to the racecourse since when ditching the rider before halfway at Charing. Has shown no aptitude so far, and clearly remains troubled. *Mrs T.C. Betts — Ashford V.* 291 (CMa).

STABLE GIRL ..—.. 7 b.m. Baron Blakeney — Blazing Manor (True Song) pp9r. Small unfurnished owner-bred half-sister to Tanborough (*qv*). Tailed off in Maidens, and jumped slowly throughout the final mile when a fence last once. It was sad to see the former grafter Andy Tutton handling her so ineptly. *M.R. Keith — Pytchley.* 249 (CfMa), 514 (OMa), 790 (OMa), 1010 (CfMa).

STAIGUE FORT (IRE) ..9-13.. 13 b.g. Torus — Lady Beecham (Laurence O) u424u. Tall rangy good-looking half-brother to Horton-Cum-Peel (IRE), and to Irish Pointing winner, Aine's Antics. Dam completed a hat-trick in Irish Points. IRISH P-t-P '93 r6 p0; pulled up 3. NH '93 and '95/6 r12 w2 (3m-3m3f Chses) p5. P-t-P/HUNT CH '95 and '97/9 (for Mr T.R.P.S. Norton) r22 w2 (Maiden and Open) p9 (5 3rds, inc Hunt Ch); pulled up 1, fell 1, and slipped up 1 (would have won). Formerly best when able to dominate over a long trip on firm, and a sound jumper so predictably did well in his role as schoolmaster to Victoria Stubbs. Almost benefitted from the withdrawal of Balisteros at the Holcombe, but despite jumping his rivals silly was short-headed on the line. Failed to get seriously involved otherwise, and his lack of acceleration will probably condemn him to further defeats in future. *P. Stubbs — Cheshire (Reg Crank).* 170 (L), 566 (L), 813 (L), 1150 (L), 1525 (L).

STALBRIDGE GOLD ..9-7.. 12 ch.m. Vital Season — Abridged (Nearly A Hand) 35p8. Leggy plain Dufosee-bred half-sister to Stalbridge Return and Stalbridge Bill. NH FLAT '95 r1 p0. NH '95 r1 p0 (tailed off last in 2m1f Nov Ch — mistakes). P-t-P/HUNT CH '94/9 (for Mr C.J. Barnes) r33 w6 (inc 2 Confineds) p12 (8 2nds, inc Hunt Ch); pulled up 11. Won six times '96/8, but has often appeared ungenerous, and has filled the runner-up berth on eight occasions, at two lengths or less in seven. Employed as a schoolmistress in the latest season, and filled the role competently without ever looking like taking Jason Ferguson to the winners enclosure. Blinkered once in '99, and previously tried in a near-side pricker. *Mr & Mrs D.G.R. Ferguson — Blackmore & Sparkford V. (John Dufosee).* 100 (O), 327 (O), 476 (Cnr), 886 (C).

STANMORE (IRE) ..10-7.. 9 b.g. Aristocracy — Lady Go Marching (USA) (Go Marching USA) 2361. Compact attrctive brother to Marching Marquis (IRE) (*qv*). NH FLAT '96/7 r3 p0. NH '97/9 (blinkered 2; one win for S. Sherwood; previously for C. Brooks) r18 w4 (2m4f Hdle. and 3 Chses, 2m4f-2m6f) p5. Bought Doncaster, May for 14,000. Not a bargain, but ran well when chasing home Grimley Gale at Ludlow in his first Hunt Chase, and redeemed a reputation which was beginning to sag again when he scored from weak opposition at Market Rasen. Confined to short cuts, but gives the impression that these duties could be within his scope nowadays. Sometimes performs as if he has an intermittent fault. *S.E. Bown — Pytchley (Tik Saunders).* 684 (2m4fH), 799 (2m4f110yH), 1447 (2m4fH), 1603 (2m6f110yH).

STANWICK HALL ..8-13.. 9 b.g. Poetic Justice — Allez Stanwick (Goldhill) ffp9puu7f. Workmanlike lengthy half-brother to Popeshall (*qv*). NH FLAT '97 (for Miss S. Williamson) r1 p0. Bought Doncaster, Aug for 950. Possibly has more ability than he has shown, but certainly possesses a rare capacity for parting with his jockeys. His members proved a disaster for the trainer, who saddled three of the four contestants, but none of them got round. *K. Needham — Bilsdale (Fiona Needham).* 52 (OMa), 399 (OMa), 439 (OMa), 627 (OMa), 809 (OMa), 1033 (OMa), 1235 (OMa), 1329 (OMa), 1347 (M).

STAR CHANGES ..10-2.. 8 b.g. Derrylin — Sweet Linda (Saucy Kit) 35313d22. Smallish compact half-brother to Troubadour Boy and Spirit Of Success. Dam won Members and placed 7. NH FLAT '98 r1 p0. P-t-P '98/9 r10 w1 (Maiden) p3 (2 3rds, of 4 once); pulled up 5. Made all to jusify favouritism in a slowly-run three-finisher Maiden at Bredwardine in '99, and has maintained a consistent level of ability since. Placed in three Restricteds before he finally captured one at Eyton, and should win his next Intermediate if the same pattern is followed. Can stay on strongly, and better behaved at the start than he used to be. Wore blinkers once in '99. *A. Hollingsworth — Worcs.* 16 (R), 119 (CR), 248 (R), 567 (R), 897 (I), 1090 (I), 1356 (I).

STAR CHASER ..9-12.. 10 b.g. Rustingo — Star Nello (Remainder) f3p63114. Strong-topped brother to Supatingo, and half-brother to Star Cruiser and Master Tom. Dam won 3m3f Jeep-Christie final at Chepstow and 2 Points and placed 12 (inc a Hunt Ch) for Adrian Watkins. P-t-P '98/9 r9 w1 (Maiden) p3 (2 3rds, of 4 once); last pair 2, and pulled up 3. Took ten races to get off the mark, and is nothing special, but a competent performer on a sound surface, and won two poor races convincingly in May. Much less effective on soft ground, and pulled up in his Members at odds-on this year when conditions were testing. May be able to seek out another weak race at the back-end in 2001. *A.V. Watkins — Monmouths.* 340 (R), 595 (R), 740 (M), 818 (R), 1400 (R), 1452 (R), 1572 (I), 1612 (Cf).

STAR DESIGN (IRE) ..9-5.. 7 b.g. Jupiter Island — Gippeswyck Lady (Pas De Seul) Rppf. Brother to Star Island (IRE). Sold Tattersalls (Ireland), Nov '98 for 1304. Missed a marker early once, made mistakes once, and weakened quickly after 2m4f once. *C. Dawson — S. Durham.* 1003 (OMa), 1163 (OMa), 1431 (OMa), 1582 (2m4fOMa).

STAR GENERAL ..—.. 8 br.g. Rock City — Bright-One (Electric) p. Rangy hobdayed half-brother to Hurdles winners, Mill-Dot and Albrighton (also successful on flat). Dam won 2 2m Hdles. 1300 5yo. NH FLAT '99 (for T. George) r2 p0 (tailed off). Bought Malvern, Sep for 900. Looked a hot ride before pulling up when tailed off in a Maiden (taken to post early, and pulled hard). *Mrs F.J. Walker & J. Pepper — Taunton V.* 732 (2m4fOMa).

STAR ISLAND ..8-10.. 8 b.g. Jupiter Island — Gippeswyck Lady (Pas De Seul) 4p3p1p. Strong-topped brother to Star Design (IRE). Dam won 3 flat, 14-18f, and was sent to Thailand after breeding 2 foals here. NH FLAT '97 (for D. Elsworth) r2 p0. Sold Ascot, Feb '97 for 1000, and resold Malvern, Oct '98 for 1800. Took a while to get off the mark, but finally succeeded in a poor contest at Bassaleg. Seems to have weaknesses in both the stamina and jumping departments, and will need to improve a fair amount if he is to follow up in a Restricted. *H.L. Davies — Llangibby.* 489 (CfMa), 747 (CfMa), 823 (CfMa), 1300 (CMa), 1406 (OMa), 1452 (R).

STARLIGHT FOOL ..10-0.. 12 b.g. Idiot's Delight — Casa's Star (Top Star) 13p4. Sturdy half-brother to My Naughty Nanny and Cassia Green. Dam won 2 Points and placed 5. Grandam, Casa's Image, won a Hunt Ch and 5 Points. NH FLAT '94 r1 p0. NH '95/7 r8 p0 (pulled up 1, and fell 1 in Chses). P-t-P '98/9 r4 w1 (Maiden) p2 (2nds). Stands few outings, but goes well fresh, and won a three-finisher Restricted in which Key Debate bled at Brocklesby Park on his reappearance. Looked on bad terms with himself at Garthorpe subsequently, and may have a few problems of his own. Certainly worth a cursory look on his 2001 debut, but can probably be disregarded after. *Mr & Mrs S.E. Bown — Pytchley (Tik Saunders).* 232 (R), 585 (2m5f110yH), 1267 (I), 1415 (Cf).

STAR MARSHALL (IRE) ..—.. 9 b.g. Bustomi — Marshallstown (Callernish) ff. Dam won NH flat and 2m Hdle in Ireland. IRISH NH '98 r6 p0 (last and fell at 2m in Chses). Kept up his bad jumping record when falling at the eighth in both Maidens (wore blinkers and a cross-noseband in the first of them, and was in front when departing). *Miss A. Sedgwick — Heythrop (Scott Joynes).* 81 (CCfMa), 753 (CfMa).

STARMONT ..8-0.. 9 br.g. Sulaafah (USA) — Kiki Star (Some Hand) ppp. Rangy half-brother to What A Hand, and to jumping winner, Miss Marigold. Dam won 3 Sells, 10-12f. P-t-P '98/9 r14 p1 (last of 3); last, pulled up 9, and fell/unseated 3. Can bowl along for about 2m4f, but cannot or will not sustain his effort, and not better than last in 17 attempts. Usually gets worked up in the preliminaries, and is mounted on course and taken to post early. Acquired blinkers on his last two appearances, and looks a real no-hoper. *Mrs S. Cocks — Silverton (Linda Blackford).* 65 (M), 145 (OMa), 539 (OMa).

STARPATH (NZ) ..10-4.. 9 ch.g. Starjo (NZ) — Centa Belle (NZ) (Centurius) 451912. Big rangy. NZ FLAT '97 r3 w1 (10½f) p0. NX NH '97/9 r12 w1 (2½c) p3 (3rds). A good jumper who proved at Ston Easton that Robert Biddlecombe does not need Rectory Garden alone to partner a winner, and later gave a plucky display over four miles in a Ladies at Flete Park, where he rallied to regain the advantage of looking beaten. Rather disappointing when 20 lengths second next time, but it would be surprising if he could not score again. Might be the right type to try in Novices Chases. *J.J. Boulter — Portman (Nick Mitchell & John Boulter).* 211 (Cnr), 454 (4mMO), 736 (Cnr), 1014 (3m5fL), 1259 (4mL), 1653 (O).

STARTING AGAIN ..9-10.. 7 b.g. Petoski — Lynemore (Nearly A Hand) p4. Workmanlike half-brother to Island Gift (qv). NH FLAT '98 (for breeder, late T. Forster) r1 w1. Missed '99 and was pulled up and dismounted in his first Point, but gave a reasonable display when 15 lengths fourth a week later. Has presumably suffered another of his setbacks since. *M.P. Wiggin — Ludlow (Geoff Evans).* 615 (CMod), 701 (I).

STATE MEDLAR ..—.. 10 ro.g. Pragmatic — Lizzie The Twig (Precipice Wood) cp. Half-brother to Raise A Loan, to Chasing winner, Our Ghillie, and to Hurdles winner, Crazy Crusader. Dam, half-sister to the dam of Reptile Princess (qv '00 Annual), was 2nd in an Adjacent. P-t-P '97 r1 p0 (ran out). Disappeared for two years following his not wholly unpromising debut, but was carried out in a melee on his return, and tailed off and pulled up after 2m2f next time. Hard to enthuse about his winning prospects at ten. *Mrs R.J. Horton — Devon & Somerset.* 352 (CfMa), 388 (I).

ST ATHANS LAD ..9-0.. 16 b.g. Crooner — Greasby Girl (John Splendid) uppu. Lengthy brother to Conductive. FLAT r6 p0. NH '88/90, '92/4, and '96/7 r47 w12 (2m-2m3f Chses, inc 5-timer) p17 (inc 7 Hdles); ran out and fell at Waregem once ('94); ran out once; and virtually refused to race final 4 attempts (completely sickened once). P-t-P '98 (for Mr E.H. Crow) r2 p0 (last, and pulled up 1). An amazingly quirky old horse who has only ever won once away from his beloved Fontwell, but has not scored sine '94, and spends most of his time doing daft things at the start these days. Did not get on with Brian Seddon, but Filippo Giuliani's Latin tones clearly worked the oracle on his latest appearance, and the combination would probably have been a poor second at Eyton but for parting company at the fourth last. Needs a sound surface, but the likelihood of him consenting to win again is very remote. Used to wear headgear, but ran au natural in 2000. *Mrs L. Williamson — Flint & Denbigh.* 776 (M), 961 (O), 1149 (Cf), 1198 (O).

STAY LUCKY (NZ) ..10-4§.. 12 b.g. Sir Sydney (NZ) — Against The Odds (NZ) (Harbor Prince USA) 83353p. Workmanlike brother to a winner in New Zealand, and half-brother to another. NZ FLAT w4. NZ NH w1 (Ch). NH '96/9 (for N. Henderson, blinkered 3) r9 p4 (2nd in Hdle, and 3 Chses); one run Punchestown. Sold Doncaster, May for 4000. A decent performer in New Zealand who was presumably sold for a tidy sum subsequently, but has never managed to score since leaving the Antipodes, and lost his confidence over fences in the previous yard. Still prone to errors, and although he managed three modest thirds in Hunter Chases he never looked likely to get seriously involved, and his enthusiasm for the task is fairly negligible. Has Julian Pritchard to drive him, and might be happier if dropped to Points. *J.G. Phillips — V.W.H. (Jim Wilson).* 303 (3mH), 469 (3m110yH), 687 (2m6f110yH), 1103 (3m2f110yH), 1332 (3mH), 1592 (4m2fH).

STEEL BRAE (IRE) ..—§.. 9 br.m. Ala Hounak — Church Brae (The Parson) p. Sister to Man Of Steele (IRE) (qv). 2000 5yo. NH FLAT '98 r2 p0. NH '98 (for N. Waggott) r1 p0 (pulled up in Hdle). Looked very mulish in a Maiden, and made a couple of bad blunders before veering left and pulling herself up after two miles. *J.E. Curry — N. Tyne.* 665 (OMa).

STEEL GEM (IRE) ..9-12.. 12 b.g. Flash Of Steel — Ferjima's Gem (USA) (Wajima USA) ppp. Light-framed half-brother to a star performer in Venezuela. IRISH FLAT r11 p2. IRISH NH '93/5 r10 p5. NH '95/7 r7 p2. P-t-P/HUNT CH '99 r3 w1 (Maiden) p1 (3rd in Hunt Ch); and 5th. Did well to win at long last in '99 considering he has spent so much time on the sidelines, but managed only three outings in early season this year, and may well have gone wrong again. Required oxygen after his Sandon success, and having finished lame on at least two occasions in the past cannot be described as lacking in guts. Tried blinkered in Ireland. *R. Packer — Llangibby (D. Thomas).* 2 (R), 219 (CMod), 336 (R).

STEEL MY SONG ..9-6.. 9 ch.m. Regal Steel — My Music (Sole Mio USA) p4418p. Small quite attractive owner-bred half-sister to Jackson Blue, Great Gusto, Marsh's Law and Reel Rascal. P-t-P '98/9 r5 p2 (2nd of 3 once); pulled up 3. Made the frame on four occasions before her deserved Clifton-on-Dunsmore success in which she held on tenaciously having jumped the last with a four length advantage. Well held since, and needs to improve considerably for Restricteds. Usually held up well off the pace, and has stamina limitations. *Miss D.B. Stanhope — Woodland Pytchley.* 55 (OMa), 759 (OMa), 845 (OMa), 1421 (OMa), 1421 (OMa), 1584 (CCond), 1664 (R).

STEEL RIGG (IRE) ..10-3.. 9 ch.g. Lancastrian — Cute Play (Salluceva) 67u63u3172. Compact half-brother to Cheater (IRE), to jumping winner, Gysart (IRE), to Irish Pointing winner, Crooked Answer, and to NH flat winner, Tribal Dancer (IRE). Dam is half-sister to high-class Irish Hurdler/useful Chaser, Straight Row. NH FLAT '98 r3 p1 (2nd); 4th, and 9th. NH '98/9 r5 w1 (2m4f Nov Hdle) p1 (distant 3rd). P-t-P '98 r2 p0; pulled up 1, and fell 1. NH May '00 r1 p1 (2nd in 3m Nov Ch: *ld 4-5, ld 15-nxt, outpcd app last*). Displayed plenty of stamina when springing a 33-1 surprise in a Hexham Novice Hurdle last year, and returned to the Northumberland venue to record his first Pointing triumph in 2000. Much less effective when conditions are not so testing, and has tended to make mistakes, but granted another arduous test, should be able to make his presence felt again. *I. Hamilton — Tynedale (Ann Hamilton).* 41 (L), 135 (L), 421 (3m5fL), 661 (L), 918 (2m4fH), 1080 (O), 1160 (O), 1578 (O), 1643 (3m2fH).

STELLAR FORCE (IRE) ..10-0.. 10 br.g. Strong Gale — Glenroe Star (Furry Glen) p6. Workmanlike. Dam won mares NH flat in Ireland. NH FLAT '96 r1 p0. NH '96/7 r4 p0 (last, and pulled up 2 in Hdles; and fell in Ch). P-t-P/HUNT CH '98/9 r8 w2 (Maiden and Confined) p1 (2nd); unseated 2, and pulled up 3. Landed two minor Points in '98, but only able to manage four outings since, and has looked out of sorts. Failed to beat a rival when seen twice this February, and has never really been clearly not in order. Stays well when on song, and wears a cross-noseband. *Mrs J. Horner — Hurworth (Sarah Horner Harker).* 134 (I), 375 (Cf).

STEP LIVELY ..9-11.. 7 ch.m. Dunbeath (USA) — Bustellina (Busted) 21. Small compact sister to Dawn Mission, and half-sister to 3 flat winners (one in Hong Kong), including Cumbrian Rhapsody (also a successful Hurdler) and Emmer Green. Dam won at 8f. P-t-P '99 r2 p1 (2nd of 3); and fell 1. Displayed a nifty turn of foot when successful in a youngsters Maiden at Charm Park, having been ridden with great confidence, and looks capable of winning a Retsricted at the very least, next year. Absent since early March. *Mrs J.C. Cooper — Middleton.* 233 (OMa), 398 (OMa).

STEP QUICK (IRE) ..9-3.. 7 ch.g. All Haste (USA) — Little Steps (Step Together USA) p3f5. Tall rangy. P-t-P '99 r4 p0 (9th, and pulled up 3). NH FLAT Oct '99 (from P. Bowen's) r2 p0. Failed to land a blow when six-and-a-half lengths third on the easy Chaddesley circuit, but struggles to get the trip, especially when conditions are testing, and lay winded for several minutes after a last fence fall when favourite at Upper Sapey next time. Needs to find some extra stamina if he is ever going to get off the mark. *D.A. Smith — S. Salop (Mandy Bryan).* 570 (2m4fCfMa), 617 (CMa), 704 (OMa), 966 (OMa).

ST HELIER ..9-2.. 6 b.m. Gildoran — Belhelvie (Mart Lane) p3f. Small. Dam, half-sister to 3 Pointers, including Celtic Sport (*qv* '98 Annual), won Maiden and 2 Restricteds (desperately unlucky in another as the saddle-cloth fell off within spitting distance of the post) and placed 4 for Owen Stephens. Grandam, Bell-Amys, won 2m Sell Hdle, and won Hunt Ch and 5 points (4 Ladies) and placed 6 (mostly for Mr Stephens). Never put in the race on her first two appearances, but was doing sterling late work when it was too late at Cothelstone, where she finished about 14 lengths third. Sent off favourite next time, but blundered badly at the seventh and fell three fences later. A fluent round will surely enable her to emulate mum and gran soon. Hopefully schooling her in public is a thing of the past. *O.J. Stephens — Llangibby (David Stephens)*. 899 (OMa), 1100 (OMa), 1456 (OMa).

STICK OR BUST ..—.. 6 b.g. Bustino — Howanever (Buckskin FR) pu. Lengthy attractive half-brother to Pear Tree Percy (qv). Sold Doncaster, Nov for 1900. Went less than two miles in Maidens, but might be able to do better eventually. *R. Green — Suffolk (Julie Read)*. 774 (OMa), 1290 (OMa).

STILL IN BUSINESS ..10-5.. 13 b.g. Don Enrico (USA) — Mill Miss (Typhoon) puuu1. Lengthy brother to Miss Enrico and Stillmore Business, and half-brother to Miss Cone (dam of Mister Cone and Morris Piper qv) and Anythingyoulike. Dam won Ladies (beat rejoiner in freak contest) and 3rd. P-t-P/HUNT CH '93/9 (for Mr R.G. Williams) r40 w15 (inc 2 Hunt Chses, 2m5f-3m Hunt Ch, 4 Opens and 2 Mixed Opens; 4-timer in '95, hat-trick in '98) p9 (5 2nds, and inc last of 3 once; inc 4 Hunt Chses); failed to finish 10 (fell/unseated 5). A smart Pointer when winning 12 of 19 attempts '95/8, but much less effective over regulation fences, and sold out of the Barber yard at the end of the '99 season during which he had given the impression of being a bleeder. Had difficulty catching the new owner-rider on occasions this year, but despite the uninspiring form figures successfully justified favouritism in his Members on his final appearance. Future performances depend entirely on how much Andrew Ayers improves in the saddle. Suited by a sound surface. *A. Ayers — E. Essex (Robert Gardiner)*. 92 (Cf), 176 (O), 607 (O), 756 (Cf), 935 (M).

STILLMORE BUSINESS ..10-3.. 10 ch.g. Don Enrico (USA) — Mill Miss (Typhoon) 532141p214d. Workmanlike brother to Still In Business (qv). P-t-P '96/9 r20 w3 (Maiden, Restricted and Intermediate) p6 (5 3rds, of 4 twice, and last once); pulled up 4, and on floor 6. No great shakes, but has been well placed to win six times in his career, and is ideally suited by a sound surface though he has won in soft ground. Still inclined to make clumsy mistakes, and no longer effective on a long track, but maintains a steady rating, and should find another weak opportunity when conditions are right. *R.G. Williams — Taunton V. (Richard Barber)*. 59 (MO), 214 (Cf), 403 (Cf), 634 (C), 877 (L), 927 (Cf), 1237 (Cf), 1371 (Cf), 1473 (Cf), 1562 (C).

PLATE 124   1371 Devon & Somerset Staghounds Confined: Stillmore Business (Miss P. Gundry), 2nd, jumps boldly ahead of A Few Dollars More (G. Maundrell), 5th   PHOTO: Brian Armstrong

STILLORGAN PARK (IRE) ..—.. 11 b.g. Supreme Leader — Jackie's Pet (Strong Gale) p. Tall workmanlike half-brother to Seod Rioga (IRE) (qv). IRISH P-t-P '96 r5 w1 (6 plus Mdn) p1 (last of 2); pulled up, and unseated. IRISH NH '97/9 (blinkered last 2) r9 p1 (2nd in Ch). Lightly raced and rarely shows much form, and if he does retain any ability it would be seen to more advantage in a Restricted rather than against the likes of Lochnamore in an Open. *K.R. Ford — Brecon & Talybont.* 988 (O).

STINGING BEE ..9-8.. 10 b.g. Respect — Regal Bee (Royal Fountain) 145. Tall rangy. Dam, half-sister to Zam Bee (qv 2000 Annual), won 2m4f Hdle. Grandam, Brown Bee III, won 2m Hdle and placed 2, and won an Open. NH '96/8 (for G. Reed) r15 p1 (19l 3rd in Ch). Very poor under Rules, but able to plod to a 25 length victory in a Maiden in softish at Southwell after 14 of the 16 who set out had fallen by the wayside. 20-1 that day, but did not do too badly when fifth in a hot Restricted, and needs to concentrate on that class. *Mrs A. Bell — Belvoir.* 373 (CfMa), 462 (2m7f110yH), 871 (R).

STONEBROKE (IRE) ..9-0.. 9 ch.g. Broken Hearted — Fairy Gull (Hawaiian Return USA) p4533. Rangy. IRISH NH FLAT '98 r2 p0 (tailed off). IRISH P-t-P '99 r10 p1 (last of 3); pulled up 5, fell, and unseated. Dire in Irish Points (only beat one horse), but slightly better in the new yard, and was only beaten half a length when last of three in a Restricted (made nearly all until collared on the run-in). Normally fails to get the trip, and was beaten 20 lengths on the same course next time. *Mr & Mrs T. George — Pytchley (Jenny Garley).* 75 (I), 550 (OMa), 1012 (CfMa), 1506 (R), 1668 (OMa).

STONEHILL PROSPECT ..—.. 7 b.m. Lightning Dealer — Ditchling Beacon (High Line) pp. Small light-framed half-sister to King Neon, Herhorse, Cook's Flyer, Kickles Lass and jumping winner, Sandy's Beacon. Some of her siblings have been much better than average, but is rather a weed herself as well as being by an inferior sire, and she jumped appallingly on her debut. *Messrs G. Alderman, Bliss, North & Robinson — Bicester with Whaddon (Fiona Kehoe).* 516 (OMa), 1204 (OMa).

STONEMOSS ..—§.. 9 b.m. Le Moss — Courtney Pennant (Angus) r. Half-sister to Rocket Radar (qv). P-t-P '99 r2 p0 (ran out 2). A wild ride to date, and declined the first after a slow start on her sole appearance in 2000. Will hopefully not emerge again. *G.H. Wagstaff — Tredegar F.* 745 (R).

STONEY RIVER (IRE) ..10-6.. 7 b.g. Riverhead (USA) — Another Space (Brave Invader USA) 1112u. Half-brother to Paddy Burke (IRE). IRISH P-t-P '99 r2 p0 (pulled up 2). Made a fine start to his English career with a hat-trick for Robert Walford, and made a noise but only failed by a head to complete the four-timer for a substitute. Thought worthy of a trip to Aintree for his first Hunter Chase, and sent off favourite, but was second and held when he blundered and unseated at the last. Needs to be more accurate over the bigger fences, but should certainly be able to score over them provided his gurgling does not worsen. *C.W.W. Dupont & B.N. Lock — Portman (Louise Alner).* 213 (CfMa), 261 (R), 654 (I), 1057 (Cf), 1557 (3m1fH).

STONEY VALLEY ..9-10.. 11 b.g. Caerleon (USA) — Startino (Bustino) pp925. Compact good-looking half-brother to NH flat winner, Double Star, and jumping winner, Advance East, and to a winner in Germany. Dam won 3 flat, 8-12f (hat-trick). FLAT r15 w2 (10f) p0. NH '94/7 r17 w4 (2m-2m1f Hdles) p5. P-t-P/HUNT CH '98/9 r5 w3 (hat-trick, inc 2m5f110y Hunt Ch) p1 (3rd); pulled up 1. A terrific performer on his day, but lame after his final Hurdling success in '95, and had not won since until landing the '98 hat-trick which concluded in a Fakenham Hunter Chase. Seemed to go wrong again on his only start last year, and despite bowling along for a fair way on three occasions in 2000 failed to beat a rival, and looks finished now. Wore a visor on his return to Points this year. *B. Dowling — Easton H. (Matthew Gingell).* 227 (2m5f110yH), 384 (2m3f110yH), 607 (O), 757 (O), 936 (Cf).

STORIES BOLD ..9-2.. 10 b.g. Newski (USA) — Stories Belle (Poetic Justice) p5. Good-bodied. Dam is half-sister to Stories Gold (qv '90 Annual). P-t-P '99 r6 p3 (2 3rds, of 4 once); pulled up 2, and unseated 1. Beaten a minimum of eight lengths in three staying-on placing in '99, but finished early after two trips to Black Forest Lodge this year. Looked to have the ability for a small win, but his enforced absence is obviously a worry. *Mrs J. Parsons — Dartmoor.* 71 (OMa), 199 (Cf).

STORM ALIVE (IRE) ..10-6.. 10 b.g. Electric — Gaileen (Boreen FR) p8211p2. Compact well-made half-brother to Irish NH flat winner, Tale Gail (IRE), and to Irish Pointing winner, Roseen (IRE). Dam won 2m Hdle in Ireland. P-t-P/HUNT CH '96/9 r13 w1 (2m4f Maiden) p3 (2 2nds); last pair 3, pulled up 5 and unseated 1. Appeared healthier than usual this year, and connections were rewarded with two successes and two decent placings. Recorded the fastest time of the day at Tranwell, and his effort behind Balisteros at Aspatria subsequently suggests he may continue his renaissance in Ladies races next year. A sound jumper, with improved stamina, and it would be surprising if he could not win again. *Mrs V. Jackson — Morpeth.* 40 (R), 111 (R), 423 (R), 498 (R), 1078 (Cf), 1154 (3m2fH), 1364 (L).

STORM DRUM ..9-6§.. 12 ch.g. Celestial Storm (USA) — Bushti Music (Bustino) p4u. Good-bodied compact half-brother to Mandika (qv). FLAT r10 w1 (12f) p1 (3rd). NH '93/6 r35 w4 (2m-3m1f Hdles) p10; Sells latterly; remote last and fell in Chses. P-t-P '98/9 r8 w2 (Members) p2 (3rds). An able, but ungenuine top-of-the-ground Hurdler who never had the bottle for fences, and had accumulated 19 successive defeats before winning his Members in '98. Repeated the success last year, but seemingly has no intentions of doing so again, and failed to beat a rival in 2000. Usually blinkered. *K.D. Giles & Mrs H. Silk — W. Street/Tickham (Kevin Giles).* 824 (Cf), 1107 (L), 1398 (Cf).

STORMHILL DAYDREAM ..8-10.. 7 b.m. Buckley — In A Dream (Caruso) pup25. Compact workmanlike half-sister to Celtic Sage, Foolish Fantasy and Stormhill Pilgrim, and to Hurdles winner, War Well (FR). P-t-P '99 r1 p0 (pulled up). As green as grass on her racecourse debut, but gained plenty of experience in a short time in 2000. Tailed off each time to date, but inherited second at Pentreclwydau after most of her rivals perished in a strongly-run race. Looked unenthusiastic when popped a question that day, and needs to improve greatly to manage a win. *Mrs H.E.L. Williams — S. Pembs (Charlotte Williams).* 834 (OMa), 951 (OMa), 1225 (OMa), 1301 (OMa), 1456 (OMa).

STORMHILL FARMER ..9-5.. 9 b.g. Vouchsafe — Farmer's Fun (Broadsword USA) p54754. Tall. P-t-P '98/9 r12 p3 (2 2nds, beaten head once); fell/unseated 5. Beaten a head at Horseheath in '99 when four subsequent winners finished behind him, but unable to reproduce that form in any of his subsequent nine attempts, and performs as if he has something amiss. Often on the premises for as much as 2m4f, but stops quickly and may be affected by a wind problem. *N. Warner — Croome & W. Warwicks.* 98 (OMa), 247 (R), 437 (OMa), 790 (OMa), 891 (OMa), 1354 (M).

STORMHILL RECRUIT ..9-8.. 11 b.g. Welsh Captain — Miss Oxstall's (The Brianstan) p227p72. Strong-topped lengthy brother to Captain Rose. P-t-P '95/9 r23 w2 (Maiden and Intermediate) p7 (5 2nds, 3 once, and last once); fell/unseated 3, and pulled up 6. Has two wins to his credit, but becoming frustratingly adept at finishing second, and has twice been beaten less than a length. Capable of forcing the tempo, and usually a good jumper, but his resolution has to be called into question now, particularly after being turned over at odds-on in his three-runner Members this year. Sometimes looks defective, but seems to act on any going. *Mrs A. Price — Teme V.* 333 (Cf), 446 (O), 670 (O), 861 (C), 987 (Cf), 1272 (Cf), 1543 (M).

STORMHILL SOLDIER ..8-6.. 8 b.g. Welsh Captain — Port'n Lemon (Hot Brandy) 4pp. Compact good-topped brother to Stormhill Warrior (qv). NH '99 r1 p0 (pulled up in 2m6f110y Hdle). P-t-P '99 r1 p0 (pulled up). Not unattractively bred, but tailed off in all five outings to date, and dismounted on his final start. Does not jump fluently. *R.J. Matthews — Oxford (Mrs A.M. Thorpe).* 792 (OMa), 1147 (OMa), 1486 (OMa).

STORMHILL WARRIOR ..9-0.. 10 b.g. Welsh Captain — Port'n Lemon (Hot Brandy) 546. Leggy quite attractive brother to Captain's Port and Stormhill Soldier, and half-brother to Little Lemon, Neat Spirit and Saffron Spirit. Dam won 3m Ch; and won 3 Ladies and placed 4 (inc 2 Hunt Chses). NH '97 and '98 r2 p0 (pulled up in Chses). P-t-P '98 r4 p1 (3rd); 4th, 5th, and pulled up 1. Missed the '99 season following a bout of lameness the previous year, but well beaten on his return, and has yet to finish within 15 lengths of the winner. Partnered by diabetic jockey Roy Emmett, but does not look likely to provide him with a winner. *Mrs A.M. Batchelor — Tiverton (Julian Batchelor).* 140 (M), 254 (CfMa), 457 (OMa).

STORM MAN (IRE) ..10-3.. 9 br.g. Glacial Storm (USA) — Devon Royale (Le Prince) pp45222372. Stocky half-brother to Rinanna Bay and Gaelic Royale (IRE), and to Hurdles winner, Prince Sandrovitch (IRE). Dam won 2m Hdle and 2m Ch in Ireland. IRISH NH FLAT '96/8 r5 p0. IRISH P-t-P '97/8 r4 w1 (Maiden) p0; pulled up 2, and fell 1. P-t-P '99 r11 w1 (Restricted) p2 (2nds); 5th, last pair 2, and pulled up 5. Tries hard, but a weak finisher due to a wind infirmity, and has accrued seven placings against one win since crossing the Irish Sea. Beaten less than five lengths on four occasions, and deserves to add another win to his c.v. Suited by a sound surface. Occasionally tongue-tied. *C.W.M. Cornelius — Ystrad Taf Fechan (Shan Farr).* 344 (I), 600 (I), 743 (L), 837 (I), 1052 (L), 1299 (I), 1403 (I), 1449 (I), 1593 (3m2fH), 1657 (Cf).

STORMY SESSION ..10-2.. 11 b.g. Celestial Storm (USA) — No Jazz (Jaazeiro USA) 746. Workmanlike half-brother to A Suitable Girl (qv). NH FLAT '94 (for B.M. Temple) r2 p0. NH '94, '97 and '99 (won for P. Nicholls; previously for N. Twiston-Davies, bought for 8000) r18 w1 (2m6f Ch) p 6 (inc 2nd in Hdle). Gives the odd fair display, including when fourth in his only Point (was also beaten half a length or less thrice under Rules), but wears headgear and has a poor winning record. Injured a tendon and was absent for 29 months after September '94, missed a further 16 months after December '97, and vanished once more after mid-March in 2000. *J. Alexander — Fife (N.W. Alexander).* 89 (3m1fH), 359 (Cf), 582 (3m3fH).

STORMY WORDS ..10-3.. 8 b.m. Strong Gale — Spandulay (USA) (Arts And Letters USA) u1422. Sturdy half-sister to Dismissal (IRE). Dam won 5 Ladies and placed 6 (inc a Hunt Ch and a Hdle) for Judy Wilson to '94. P-t-P '98 r3 w1 (2m4f Maiden) p0; pulled up 1, and fell 1. Quickened to win a 2m4f Maiden at Eyton in '98, but subsequently suffered a setback when favourite for a Restricted and forced to spend the following season on the sidelines. Ran out a convincing winner at Market Rasen this March, but contrived to get beaten in her next three outings and has developed into a very quirky character indeed. Hung badly left at Cottenham and the other way at Dunthrop, but her piece de resistance came at Huntingdon where she had a Hunter Chase at her mercy until suddenly applying the brakes in the shadows of the post. Has to be dropped out and be produced with a late run, and has undoubted ability, but could not be supported with any confidence at present. *Mrs J. Wilson — Pytchley (Bill Warner).* 179 (R), 440 (R), 770 (Cf), 1016 (Cf), 1334 (3mH).

STRAIGHT BARON ..8-10§.. 8 gr.g. Baron Blakeney — Straight Gin (Ginger Boy) pp3. Half-brother to Straight Touch. Dam, sister to Cool Ginger and half-sister to Kaloore (*qv* '98 Annual), won 2m2f Hdle and 2m4f Ch for Mr Taylor. P-t-p '99 r2 p0 (ran out 1, and pulled up 1). In front with around half a mile to run in each of his 2000 appearances, but has so far wilted out of contention, and beaten nine lengths in his solitary completion. May be capable of better if learning to become more settled. *A.J. Taylor — Southdown & Eridge.* 7 (OMa), 710 (OMa), 1172 (OMa).

STRAPPED FOR CASH ..9-2.. 10 b.m. Impecunious — Mistress Rights (Master Spiritus) 3. Half-sister to Members Rights and Mistress Corrado (dam of Master Will and Master Jock *qv*). Dam was bad 3rd and fell 2 in Points. Grandam, Flaming Fiddler, was a poor Pointer. Beaten fractionally over a length on her belated debut at Bitterley, where it looked as if she would justify a market plunge when landing three lengths clear at the final fence. Appeared to cling on to second (from a horse who scored subsequently), and deserves to find compensation. *Mrs Z. Hammond — S. Herefords (Michael Hammond).* 994 (OMa).

STRATHMORE LODGE ..9-12.. 12 b.m. Skyliner — Coliemore (Coliseum) f352142p. Tall rangy half-sister to Mount Ephraim and Man Of Moreef, to jumping winners, Ardlussa Bay, Dubious Jake and More Distinct (also successful NH flat), and to Hurdles winner, Moreof A Gunner. Dam won NH flat race and 2m Hurdle. NH FLAT '93 r3 p2 (3rds). NH '94/8 r12 w2 (2m5f-2m6f Hdles, 40-1 once); pulled up only Ch. P-t-p/HUNT CH '99 (for Miss B. Oliver & Mr M. Armstrong) r5 p2 (2 2nds, inc a Hunt Ch); 4th, unseated 1, and pulled up 1. A sketchy jumper in Hunter Chases, but has made the frame on five occasions '99/00, and is best employed picking up place money there rather than doing the rounds in Points. Very game on her day, but one-paced, and decent horses have nothing to fear from her. Acts on any going. *Miss B. Oliver — Tynedale (Kevin Robson).* 419 (Cf), 495 (O), 686 (3m1fH), 918 (2m4fH), 1429 (Cm), 1556 (2m4f110yH), 1628 (2m4f110yH), 1645 (3mH).

STRATUS ..—.. 11 gr.g. Then Again — Splash Of Red (Scallywag) p. Workmanlike half-brother to jumping winner, Miami Splash. NH '96 and '98 (for R. Alner; debut for S. Earle) r3 p1 (2nd of 3 in Ch); pulled up other Ch. Bought Malvern, May '98 for 4000. Attracted support in the ring and showed speed for two miles in January, but merely getting him to the track always poses huge problems, and immediately vanished again. Not a good jumper. *B.P. Jones — Berks & Bucks (John Gallagher).* 33 (Cnr).

STRAWBERRY BLOSSOM ..9-7.. 7 ro.m. Baron Blakeney — Katchum (Jimsun) 35. Owner-bred. Jumped round safely in May Maidens on consecutive weekends, and showed some promise. Over-rated at present, but should live up to the mark in her second season. *R.H. York — Staff College.* 1396 (OMa), 1513 (OMa).

STRAWBERRY HILL (IRE) ..8-11.. 7 b.g. Lancastrian — Tudor Lady (Green Shoon) 7. Half-brother to Ardscud (*qv*). P-t-p '99 (for Mr P.F. & Mrs B. Nicholls) r2 p0 (pulled up 1, and fell 1). Got loose before the start when favourite on his racecourse debut last year, and pulled up when well supported next time. Again backed as though defeat was out of the question on his reappearance, but faded in the last half-mile to trail in some 31 lengths behind the winner. Clearly thought to have some ability, but a big let down to date, and may have a fault. *E. Gutner & M. Krysztofiak — Taunton V. (Richard Barber).* 520 (OMa).

STREET KID ..9-0.. 13 b.g. Teenoso (USA) — Chalkey Road (Relko) 286. Small neat half-brother to Irish Hurdles winner, Lauravin (IRE). Dam won 3 flat, 12-13f. NH FLAT '92 r2 p0. NH '92, '93, '95 and '98 r10 w2 (2m-2m6f Hdles, 50-1 once) p3 (2nds); pulled up 1. P-t-p/HUNT CH '98/9 r8 w1 (Members) p1 (3rd); last pair 3, pulled up 2, and fell 1. Remarkably lightly raced and tried in a tongue-strap under Rules, but apart from winning his Members in '99, has not appeared to stay three miles. Finished a creditable runner-up in a modest event on his reappearance this year, but did not get home on a softer surface subsequently, and only of use as a schoolmaster nowadays. *G.P.P. Stewart — Vine & Craven (Philippa Chamings).* 628 (Cf), 1134 (Cnr), 1398 (Cf).

STREET TRADER (IRE) ..—.. 11 ch.g. Import — Mancha Lady (Milan) fp. Good-bodied half-brother to Kings Reward and Irish Pointing winner, Sweldon. IRISH P-t-p '95 r1 p0. NH '97/8 (from T. Casey's) r3 p0 (last and pulled up 2 in Chses). A slovenly jumper who seems to be almost untrainable, and not seen after a couple of atrocious displays in January (fell at the first once). *A.J.S. Palmer — Mid Surrey F. (Sarah Palmer).* 520 (OMa).

STRETCHIT ..9-9.. 11 b.g. Full Extent (USA) — Snippet (Ragstone) 3255u242. Lengthy sparely-made half-brother to Snappit, Ring Me Back and Snippetoff and to jumping winner, The Eens. NH '95/6 (tried blinkers/visor) r10 p1 (distant 2nd in 3m4f Sell); fell only Ch. P-t-P/HUNT CH '97/9 (for Mr L. & Miss T. McCurrich) r21 w4 (inc Ladies, inc hat-trick '98) p11 (9 2nds; inc 2 Hunt Chses, and inc 3rd in Hunt Ch); fell/unseated 2. Much improved when completing a game hat-trick in '98, and far from disgraced in better company last year, but in common with many of Theresa McCurrich's inmates never sparked after his seasonal reappearance in 2000, and was reduced to acting as a schoolmaster on his last four starts. Had avoided firm ground in Points until the current campaign, though showed no real signs of disliking it. Stays extremely well, and will hopefully be able to end his run of defeats which now stands at 15 in 2001. *C. & Miss T. McCurrich — Mrs N.J. Bird — Worcs (Theresa McCurrich).* 78 (L), 177 (L), 383 (3mH), 611 (C), 991 (L), 1063 (3m2fM), 1191 (L), 1491 (L).

STREWTH ..9-9.. 7 b.g. Cruise Missile — Storm Foot (Import) *90*p9. Very big half-brother to One Mans Legacy, and to Irish NH flat and Hurdles winner, Toureen Girl. P-t-P '99 r2 p0 (refused 1, and pulled up 1). NH '00 r2 p0 (tailed off in 2m3f-2m5f Nov Hdles). Threw an elephantine strop in the paddock on his debut, but has looked better behaved though devoid of talent since his move to a professional yard. Needs to jump better if he to remain over regulation obstacles. *Mrs J.K. Peutherer — O. Berks (Henrietta Knight).* 802 (2m6fH), 1336 (2m4fH).

STRICTLY HARD ..7-11.. 7 b.m. Reprimand — Formidable Dancer (Formidable USA) 8p. Leggy unfurnished half-sister to 3 flat winners (2 abroad), including Fighter Squadron. 1900f, 3800y. FLAT (for G. Bravery) r5 p0. NH '98 (for E. Storey, bought for 600) r1 p0 (tailed off and pulled up). Gradually sinking to lower depths, and was last on the occasion of her completion in a Point. *Miss A. Combe — Jedforest.* 500 (2m4fOMa), 910 (2m4fOMa).

STRIDE TO GLORY (IRE) ..9-9.. 10 b.g. Superpower — Damira (FR) (Pharly FR) 26u134p. Small stocky half-brother to 3 flat winners abroad. P-t-P '96/9 r19 w2 (Maiden and Restricted) p1 (3rd); fell/unseated 4, and pulled up 2. Often unco-operative in the past, and only managed two outings in February for present connections last year, but made all to win a modest Confined at Stainton as soon as blinkers were reapplied in 2000. Only once better than last otherwise, and their galvanic effects soon wore off. Can probably be safely disregarded in future. *Mrs H.M. Arnold — Cleveland.* 170 (L), 394 (Cf), 692 (I), 804 (Cf), 1029 (L), 1232 (L), 1350 (L).

STRIKE ACCORD (IRE) ..—§.. 7 br.g. Accordion — Ritual Girl (Ballad Rock) upur. Sparely-made brother to Hurdles winner, Song For Jess (IRE). Dam won at 11f in Ireland. NH FLAT '98 (from M. Muggeridge's) r1 p0. Rapidly going from bad to worse, and was not even prepared to try on his latest attempt. *A. Rybak — O. Berks (Charlie Cox).* 472 (OMa), 630 (OMa), 900 (OMa), 1019 (2m4fOMa).

STRONACROIBH ..9-0.. 8 b.g. Respect — Cool Date (Arctic Slave) ffpp. Half-brother to Park Slave, Cool Fountain and Zam's Slave (subsequent jumping winner), and to Irish NH flat and Hurdles winner, Fountain Slave. P-t-P '99 r3 p0 (pulled up 2, and unseated 1). Rather excitable to date, and has been unable to complete in all seven starts, but has shown some speed and might improve if he could be persuaded to calm down, and pay more attention to the fences. Unworthy of support at present, but at least that means punters don't have to try and pronounce his name. *Mrs V.J. Gilmour — Fife.* 365 (CfMa), 718 (CfMa), 910 (2m4fOMa), 1122 (OMa).

STRONG ACCOUNT (IRE) ..8-7.. 12 ch.g. Strong Statement (USA) — Clare's Hansel (Prince Hansel) 6p53p. Small compact flashy half-brother to Admiral Ironside and Rayman (IRE), and to Irish Pointing winners, Streaming Along, Deer Clare and Gerry And Tom. NH '94/5 r3 p0. P-t-P '96/9 (for Mr A.J. Mobley) r13 p6 (4 2nds, and last once; and 2 3rds, last once); failed to finish 4 (unseated 2, and ran out 1). Placed on six occasions '97/8, and remains capable of showing speed for as much as 2m4f, but then his stamina packs up, and failed to beat a rival in 2000. The previous yard gave up on him eventually, and having been tried unsuccessfully in a tongue-strap this year, his new connections are faced with an uphill battle. *R.K. Sealey — Worcs.* 197 (CfMa), 567 (R), 618 (CMa), 892 (OMa), 1063 (3m2fM).

STRONGALONG (IRE) ..9-10.. 11 b.g. Strong Gale — Cailin Cainnteach (Le Bavard FR) 3677fp. Stocky compact. Dam won Irish NH flat. NH '95/8 r27 p5 (4 Chses, neck 2nd once; 3rd in only Hdle). P-t-P '99 r9 w5 (inc Ladies) p1 (3rd); 4th twice, and unseated 1. Clumsy and incredibly one-paced under Rules, but much improved by a switch to Points last year, and won five times for Kate Roncoroni. A huge disappointment in 2000, however, and only managed to finish better than last on one occasion. Pulled up and dismounted on his final when third prize was seemingly assured, and might well have succumbed to the prevailing firm ground. Not many Pointers, begin their season in Kent, and end it via Berwickshire in Durham. Clearly not right at present, and will need watching when he returns. *Miss K.B. Roncoroni — O. Berks, & Jedforest.* 128 (L), 218 (L), 421 (3m5fL), 621 (L), 717 (Cf), 1477 (L).

STRONG AMBITION (IRE) ..9-9.. 10 b.m. Strong Gale — Maigue Side Rena (General Ironside) 45. IRISH NH FLAT '97/8 r2 p0. IRISH NH '97/8 r3 p0 (unplaced in Hunt Ch). IRISH P-t-P '97/8 r13 p5; pulled up 4, and fell 1. P-t-P '99 (for Mr M.J. Tuckey & Mr J. Owen) r3 w2 (Maiden and Members) p1 (2nd). Won on her first appearance for present connections in '99, but off the track for eight weeks between her last two outings, and had disappeared by the end of February this year. Has been well supported in both her wins, and probably has the ability to take a Restricted, but obviously under a cloud at present, and best watched when she returns. *M.J. Tuckey — Bicester with Whaddon (Herbie Owen).* 6 (R), 248 (R).

STRONG CHAIRMAN (IRE) ..10-6.. 10 br.g. Strong Gale — The Furnituremaker (Mandalus) 3456p123. Tall roman-nosed brother to Chasing winner, Strong Cabinet (IRE). P-t-P '96/7 (for Mr J.A. Keighley) r8 w6 (inc 3 Opens, inc undefeated 5-timer '97) p1 (3rd); and unseated 1. NH '97/9 (for P.F. Nicholls) r8 w1 (3m Nov Chse) p2 (2nds); 15th in '99 Grand National on final start. A smart six-year-old when unbeaten in five Points, but did not carry the form into racing under Rules, and his only win came in a two-finisher Chase at Newbury. Sprang a 20-1 surprise at Chaddesley in April on his return to Pointing, but generally disappointing, and may not be the most courageous horse ever to have looked through a bridle. Always turned out looking a picture, like his stablemates, and has helped with Sam Waley-Cohen's education, but his outlook on racing needs to change if he is to get his career back on track. *R. Waley-Cohen — Warwicks.* 5 (Cv&nr), 148 (3m1f110yH), 302 (3mH), 454 (4mMO), 614 (O), 1064 (3m2fCf), 1144 (O), 1337 (3m2f110yH).

PLATE 125   1064 Worcestershire Confined: Strong Chairman (S. Waley-Cohen), 1st, leads Philtre (Julian Pritchard), 2nd, as Wejem (A. Dalton), falls at the last   PHOTO: Bill Selwyn

STRONG DEBATE (IRE) ..9-2.. 9 b.g. Strong Gale — Miss Le Bavard (Le Bavard FR) p6Ru. Dam, half-sister to Ballyneety (*qv* '94 Annual), won NH flat, 3 flat (14-16f) and 3 Hdles (2m-2m4f) in Ireland. IRISH NH FLAT '98 r2 p0. Bought Doncaster, Oct '98 for 1800. Bred from a useful mare and can show early speed, but was last on his only completion, and there is doubtless something wrong with him. The can be unruly in the preliminaries. *Dr A. Crookston — Lanarks & Renfrews, & Eglinton (Neil Crookston).* 659 (M), 908 (R), 978 (CfMa), 1123 (OMa).

STRONG FOCUS (IRE) ..8-13.. 9 b.g. Strong Gale — Scotch News (London Gazette) p. Good-bodied half-brother to Old Father Time, to Irish Pointing winner, Barchester, and to NH flat winner, Andero. Dam is an unraced sister to Willie Wumpkins. IRISH NH '97 r1 p0 (105*l* last). P-t-P '99 r9 p0 (5th, last 5, pulled up 2, and refused 1). A steady jumper, but very slow, and beaten more than 20 lengths in five of six completions in which he has finished in front of just two rivals. Disappeared after pulling up at Friars Haugh in February. *N.G. Crookston — Lanarks & Renfrews.* 113 (OMa).

STRONG MEDICINE ..10-1.. 14 b.g. Strong Gale — In The Forest (Crowded Room) 1126. Strong lengthy half-brother to Pitpan's Glory and Adage. NH FLAT '92 r2 p0. NH '92/8 r42 w12 (5 Hdles, 2m-2m7f, and 7 Chses, 2m4f-3m1f; inc hat-trick '94) p11; one run unseated at 2nd and twice refused at 3rd in 3 consecutive Chses in '93. P-t-P/HUNT CH '99 r6 w1 (Open) p2; 4th, 5th, and 7th. A hard-pulling front-runner who was a prolific winner until November '96, but had run up a losing sequence of 16 until galvanised by first time blinkers when landing an Open at Cottenham last year. Made an immediate impact with Emma Coveney in the saddle on his return, but does not hold his form for any period of time, and proved a disappointing favourite on his last two starts. Quirky, and usually jumps right-handed whilst being prone to hang left, and needs to dominate. Suited by a sound surface. May revive when fresh even at 14. *Dr D.B.A. & Mrs H. Silk — Kent & Surrey Bloodhounds (Heather Silk).* 28 (L), 772 (L), 885 (L), 1541 (2m5fH).

PLATE 126   *885 Hampshire Ladies Open: Strong Medicine (Mrs E. Coveney), 2nd*
PHOTO: Bill Selwyn

STRONG MISSION (IRE) ..9-5.. 10 b.g. br.g. Strong Gale — Churchtown Mist (Modern Dancer) u5423. Tall workmanlike hobdayed. Dam is half-sister to Bad Trade (qv '96 Annual). IRISH NH FLAT '97 r1 p1 (3rd). NH '98/9 (for B. Mactaggart) r8 p1 (distant last of 3 in Ch); 7th of 8, last, pulled up and fell 2 in other Chses. Sold Doncaster, Sep for 1700. A very headstrong sort who often makes blunders, but was in front three out or later when beaten six lengths and costing his owners a winner at Sandon previously was an insufficient penalty. Deserves to hang for a victory, but it is clearly going to be struggle. *S. Halliday — Mrs A.P. Kelly — Flint & Denbigh (-; Stephen Kelly).* 776 (M), 964 (OMa), 1197 (OMa), 1412 (OMa), 1527 (OMa).

STRONG STUFF (IRE) ..9-12.. 11 b.g. Strong Gale — Must Rain (Raincheck) 24ppfu42. Small compact half-brother to The Next Night, Muskin and to Irish Pointing, NH flat and Hurdles winner, Ask Pat. Dam won 3 Irish Points. IRISH P-t-P '95/6 r5 w1 (6 plus Mdn) p2 (2nds); pulled up 1. NH '96/9 (for M. Pitman; won previously for K. Bailey, bought for 19,000) r5 w1 (3m3f Ch) p2 (3rds, inc last). Only managed five outings in four years under Rules, and probably lucky when scoring, as the prolific winner Galatasori Jane fell at the last with every chance. Has suffered from a plethora of physical problems, including fracturing his nose (!) when falling at the first in a Chase, and also gurgled under Rules (tried tongue-tied once in 2000). Looked very reluctant in one Point and blinkered in the next two, but unseated at the second and fell, so the experiment was not repeated. Finally gave a commendable display when two lengths second at 25-1, but chances are it was a one-off. *J.B. Shears — Mid Devon.* 198 (M), 313 (O), 402 (O), 852 (Cf), 928 (MO), 1261 (Cf), 1515 (MO), 1636 (Cf).

STRUGGLES GLORY (IRE) ..11-2.. 10 b.g. Kamehameha (USA) — Another Struggle (Cheval) 141f1. Workmanlike half-brother to Irish Pointing winner, All A Struggle (IRE). IRISH P-t-P '96 r2 p2. P-t-P/HUNT CH '97 and '99 r8 w6 (5-timer inc 2 Hunt Chses, 3m-3m110y) p2 (2nds in Hunt Chses). Straight out of the top-drawer, and is unbeaten in six English Points, but let down by the veteran owner-rider's lack of oomph in Hunter Chases, and failed to survive the first when tackling the big fences at Aintree this year. Usually helps to force the pace and can maintain a remorseless gallop that very few can live with. Deserves to win a big prize, but will probably never get the chance to prove himself under professional guidance. Acts on any going, but particularly fond of a sound surface. *D.C. Robinson — Mid Surrey F.* 129 (O), 303 (3mH), 579 (3m2fH), 921 (2m6fH), 1106 (O).

STYGIAN STAR (IRE) ..9-9.. 8 ch.m. Over The River (FR) — Star Attention (Northfields USA) 6f22. Small light attractive half-sister to I'm A Miss, Star Tracker and Star Mover, and to Hurdles winner, Primrose Star. Dam won 2 flat, 5-6f. NH FLAT '99 (from Miss K. Milligan's) r2 p0. Showed fair speed in Maidens and was second twice in May, but folded quickly in the closing stages of both, and may be a short-runner. Will possibly be able to last home in similar company on an easy track. *Mrs J. Smethurst — S. Durham.* 500 (2m4fOMa), 909 (2m4fOMa), 1330 (OMa), 1479 (OMa).

SUBA LIN ..9-9.. 12 b.m. Sula Bula — Tula Lin (Tula Rocket) 3p1p. Small light-framed. Dam, half-sister to 3 Pointers, failed to finish in 11 Points for Mrs Atyeo (revived briefly as a 16-year-old in '92). P-t-P '95/7 r13 p1 (last of 3); 4th, last 2, pulled up 7, unseated 1, and refused 1. Broke down in '97, and had been off the course since then until her return in 2000. Did not beat a rival this year, but left solo to win her Members after the clear leader had crashed heavily at the last. Her prospects in Restricteds can only be described as dim, but at least her connections decision to bring her back into training was vindicated. *A. & Mrs C. Atyeo — W. Somerset V. (Carol Atyeo).* 641 (CfMa), 880 (OMa), 1094 (M), 1563 (R).

SUDDEN SALLY (IRE) ..10-5.. 10 b.m. Bustomi — Donnabimba (Don ITY) 4. Smallish compact half-sister to 2 flat winners (one in Belgium). P-t-P/HUNT CH '97/9 r17 w2 (inc Ladies) p1 (last of 3); pulled up 4, and fell/unseated 4. An excitable mare who often gets in a tizz before her races, and has been taken to post early, but very speedy, and showed dramatic improvement last year. Won twice on softish, including a Ladies at 25-1, but disappeared after finishing 20 lengths fourth to Balisteros on her 2000 reappearance, and her rating could be suspect. *J.W. Hughes — Buccleuch.* 185 (L).

SUGAR LOVE ..—.. 11 b.m. Tout Ensemble — Black Love (Windjammer USA) f. Small compact owner-bred. Fell at halfway in February. Certainly not a racehorse, so it was surprising to see him turn up for a Celebrities flat event at Plumpton. *J. Berry Jessop — Essex.* 323 (CfMa).

SUGAR MILL ..—.. 11 b.g. Slip Anchor — Great Tom (Great Nephew) pp. Workmanlike half-brother to Admiral Villeneuve (*qv*). NH FLAT '94/5 r3 w1 p1 (3rd). FLAT '95/7 (for Mrs M. Reveley) r16 w5 (12-15f) p5 (short-headed once, beaten neck once). Often outpaced in the early stages of his flat races, but could gallop on with great gusto, and had a fine strike rate until he disappeared after winning his only start of '97. It was tragic to find that Kevin Tork had got hold of him for Pointing, and broke down with Colin Sherry (who also lamed the other Tork runner that afternoon, and also disgraced himself when continuing for far too long on Sleipnir, *qv*) at Rodmell, where he got loose in the paddock and bloodied the nose of a woman who tried to catch him before being mounted at the boxes and taken to post early. *K. Tork — O. Surrey & Burstow.* 983 (Cf), 1212 (Cf).

SUGI ..9-0.. 12 b.g. Oats — Ledee (Le Bavard FR) 4f44. Small half-brother to Grey Scally and to Hurdles winners, Springfield Rhyme and Springfield Scally (latter also won NH flat). IRISH NH FLAT r1 p1 (3rd). P-t-P/HUNT CH '96/9 r13 w1 (Maiden) p4 (2 2nds); fell/unseated 2, and ran out 1. Won a 3m4f Maiden in sticky ground in '97, but does not get into gear quickly enough over regular trips, and does not manage many outings. Just the sort who might appreciate a trip to somewhere really demanding like Flagg Moor, though time is passing by and has gone 11 races since his win. *Mrs S. Guild & I. Wynne — Sir W.W. Wynn's.* 338 (R), 589 (R), 1129 (R), 1322 (R).

SULA SPIRIT ..8-0.. 7 b.m. Sula Bula — Gaelic Spirit (Master Spiritus) 5u. Lengthy unfurnished herring-gutted. 55 lengths last on her debut, and unseated when fading next time. It will be a challenge for David Pipe to get this one to shine. *K. & Mrs E. Oliver — Dartmoor (David Pipe).* 934 (OMa), 1262 (OMa).

SULPHUR SPRINGS (IRE) ..8-10.. 9 ch.g. Don't Forget Me — Short Wave (FR) 1u16. Compact half-brother to useful French Chaser Sandcreek. FRENCH FLAT '95 r5 w1 (1m2f at Evry) p2 (2nds). FRENCH NH '96/9 r21 p8 (inc 3rd in '99 French Grand National). NH Mar '00 (from M. Pipe's) r1 p0 (6th in 4m National Hunt Ch: *outpcd frm halfway*). A strong and determined galloper who twice won in the fastest time of the day at Tweseldown (equal with Hatcham Boy in the Ladies once), but was struggling from four out until he unseated at the last at Larkhill in between. Wore a tongue-strap on his two most recent appearances. Looks useful, and we bet that Martin Pipe would like to get his mitts on him to team with A.P. McCoy in Chases! *P.A.D. Scouller — Garth & S. Berks (John Perry; Martin Pipe).* 1 (C), 62 (Cf), 215 (C).

SULTAN OF SWING ..—.. 12 b.g. Idiot's Delight — Tropical Swing (Swing Easy USA) pfpuuRp. Tall rangy hobdayed half-brother to Solar Swing. IRISH NH FLAT (blinkered final) r3 p0. IRISH P-t-P '95/6 r5 p1 (2nd); pulled up 2, and fell 1. P-t-P '97 (for Mr H.B. Geddes) r5 w2 (Maiden and Restricted) p2 (last of 2; and last of 3); and pulled up 1. Won twice when Barber-trained in '97, but used to hang badly and has been tried in a near-side pricker. Resurfaced after three years off, but a complete disaster in the current yard, and never went beyond two miles in seven starts. A physical wreck with all the vices imaginable, and acquired a visor in his last three calamities. *Mrs M.B. Stephens — E. Kent.* 27 (I), 130 (CMod), 288 (CMod), 572 (CfO), 824 (Cf), 1344 (3m2fH), 1509 (Cf).

SUMMERBRIDGE ..—§.. 8 b.g. Vital Season — Kate The Shrew (Comedy Star USA) p. Workmanlike brother to Man Of The Match (qv). P-t-P '99 r5 p0 (pulled up 3, and ran out 2). Often untractable in his first season, and failed to reappear after pulling up at Chipley Park in early February 2000. Has given no grounds for optimism in his short career to date. *P. Thorman — Cotley (Kay Rees & Polly Curling).* 145 (OMa).

SUMMER HAVEN ..9-2§.. 12 b.m. Nearly A Hand — Wild Corn (Cornuto) p33pp2. Compact unfurnished. Dam won NH flat and 3 2m Hdles (disqualified after winning another). NH '96/7 r14 p1 (2nd in 3m Hdle); bolted and withdrawn after unseating at start on intended debut; well tailed off last in only two Chases. P-t-P '95 and '98/9 r16 p3 (2 2nds; and 3rd of 4); pulled up 6, refused 2, unseated 2, and ran out 1. Placed in three Maidens, and her Members twice '99/00, and has revealed enough ability to win, but a maddening mare who is always looking for a way to refuse. Made her intentions perfectly clear on her reappearance when attempting to stop and breasting the first open ditch at Tweseldown, and even Lawrence Lay has failed to persuade her to score. Must be shunned at all costs if she returns. *M.J. Rawlins — Berks & Bucks (Mrs T. Rawlins).* 220 (OMa), 457 (OMa), 753 (CfMa), 1131 (OMa), 1346 (3m1f110yH), 1619 (M).

SUMMERHOUSE ..8-5.. 7 ch.m. Sunley Builds — Sherdon Hutch (New Member) p. Small. Dam was placed in 6 Points and a Hunt Ch for Chris Boumphrey. P-t-P '99 (Mr & Mrs C. Boumphrey & Mr & Mrs A. Jones) r3 p0 (last pair 2, and unseated 1). Not overtaxed in her debut season, but a trip to Black Forest Lodge was the last we saw of her in 2000. Prone to wholesale blunders, and has to prove her fitness when she returns. *S.R. Elford — Mid Devon.* 207 (OMa).

SUMMER PUDDING ..9-4.. 8 ch.m. Vital Season — Lady Magenta (Rolfe USA) ppppf. Lengthy owner-bred half-sister to Travelling Jack. P-t-P '99 r2 p0 (fell/unseated 2). Too keen for her own good to date, and spends much of her time dashing off in an uncontrollable manner. Jumped appallingly in her first season, but though that aspect of her make-up still requires attention, it is her lack of steering that is of prime concern now. Rarely allowed to start at a sensible price, and has flummoxed both the reigning and former champion jockeys. Has only once been tried left-handed, and got no further than the third before making an unscheduled crash-landing. Clearly has the ability to win, but the queue of available (and willing) partners is a dwindling one. *Mr & Mrs R.P. Thompson — Cotley (Pauline Tizzard).* 264 (OMa), 457 (OMa), 655 (OMa), 733 (2m4fOMa), 875 (2m4fOMa), 1101 (OMa).

SUMMIT ..9-5.. 10 b.g. Salse (USA) — Reltop (High Top) 3ff. Big strong-topped half-brother to several winners, including Just David (Chester Cup) and Kenilworth Dancer (Hurdles) Dam won at 12f. 33,000gy. FLAT (for R. Hannon to '94; one run for Mrs J Pitman in '95, bought for 8500) r8 w2 (10-12f) p3 (inc short head and neck 3rd in Queen's Vase). NH '97/8 (for Miss C. Johnsey) r3 p0. A decent middle-distance performer on the flat in his youth, but has had hardly any jumping experience, so it was surprising to see him run so well when one length third in a Confined (might have scored had the rider pushed him along sooner). Highly perilous when taking crashing falls at the seventh and at the first subsequently, and it may be hard to find a jockey prepared to risk a plunge from the Summit in future. *D. Hooper — Torrington F. (Andrew Congdon).* 66 (Cf), 653 (MO), 928 (MO).

SUNCZECH (IRE) ..8-4.. 11 b.m. Sunyboy — Miss Prague (Mon Capitaine) p6f. Light-framed half-sister to Velka (qv). IRISH P-t-P '95/7 r10 p5; pulled up 4. P-t-P/HUNT CH '98/9 (for Mr T. Waters) r7 w1 (Maiden) p2; pulled up 3, and fell 1. Made the frame on six occasions before she gained her just reward at Charing on her reappearance last year, but reported to have been a complete nightmare at home in the previous yard, and has failed to beat a rival since. Has looked incredibly reluctant since falling at Folkestone in '99, so another spill on her latest outing could be the final straw. *S.C. Clark, Mrs C. Kavanagh & D. Jefferys — V. of Aylesbury (Lynne Redman).* 247 (R), 887 (R), 1206 (R).

SUN LARK ..9-0.. 7 b.g. Crested Lark — Sunylyn (Sunyboy) 24d. Tall half-brother to Salcantay and Uncle Norman. Dam sister to Elmboy, and half-sister to Aj's Boy (qv '98 Annual), won 2 2m4f Hunt Chses and 5 Points and placed 7. Showed he has ability when ten lengths second on his debut, but faded in the heavy ground when a disappointing favourite next time, and disqualified from 25 lengths fourth after Michael Miller failed to weigh in (fined £40). May be able to score on better going, but it was a pity he needed tubing before he'd even ran. *Mrs K. Wilson — S. Dorset (Rose Vickery).* 1307 (OMa), 1654 (OMa).

SUNLEY SPRING ..—.. 8 br.g. Dowsing (USA) — Charlton Athletic (Bustino) fRp. Home-bred half-brother to Maltby's Charlie (qv). Still contesting the lead when he fell heavily two out and was winded on his debut, but took charge and ran out early next time, and then pulled up in the closing stages. Might possibly achieve something if he could be persuaded to calm down. *J.B. Sunley — Surrey U. (Di Grissell).* 984 (OMa), 1397 (OMa), 1513 (OMa).

SUNNYCLIFF ..10-6.. 8 b.g. Dancing High — Nicolini (Nicholas Bill) 27111. Tall. Dam, bred by Bobby Brewis, won 3 flat for him, 10-12f. Coming on a treat, and although he is still prone to be novicey in the closing stages he completed a ready-hat-trick with rather an impressive victory at Perth. Wore a tongue-strap on his first two attempts, but has disgarded since. Speedy enough to win at 2m4f, but the full trip evidently poses no problems. Looks to have needed time, and may do even better at eight. Bobby Brewis (who still rides out) partnered Whinstone Hill to win an Aintree Foxhunters, and perhaps he harbours dreams that Sunnycliff can carry his colours to a triumph there again nearly half a century later. *R. Brewis — College V. & N. Northumberland (Clive Storey).* 188 (OMa), 425 (CfMa), 910 (2m4fOMa), 1427 (R), 1556 (2m4f110yH).

SUN OF CHANCE ..9-10.. 17 b.g. Sunyboy — Chance A Look (Don't Look) f6372p. Small light owner-bred brother to Osceola, and half-brother to Treble Chance and Looking, to jumping winner, Relative Chance, and to Hurdles winner, Sundiata. Dam won 7 Chases, 2m-3m1f. NH FLAT r2 p0. NH '90 r1 p0. P-t-P/HUNT CH '93/9 r37 w6 (inc Open) p13 (6 3rds, last once); failed to finish 11 (fell/unseated 5). A tough little horse on his day, and has done well to accumulate six wins and 15 placings, but showing his age in the last couple of seasons, and generally beaten out of sight when completing in 2000. Looks about ready for retirement. *Miss M. Ree — Glamorgan.* 446 (O), 741 (Cf), 1053 (O), 1297 (L), 1402 (MO), 1570 (MO).

SUNRISE SENSATION ..10-5.. 8 ch.g. Super Sunrise — Gilzie's Touch (Feelings FR) 42f. Lengthy. NH FLAT Jan/Feb '97 r2 p0. NH '97/9 (for breeder, R. McDonald) r12 w1 (2m1f Hdle) p1 (3rd); last only Ch. Sold Doncaster, Aug for 4000. Was running well in Points, but sadly broke a leg when apparently about to get outspeeded by Prominent at Hornby Castle. *C.H.A. Denny — York & Ainsty N. (Annabelle Armitage).* 42 (O), 171 (O), 376 (MO).

SUN SURFER (FR) ..10-4.. 13 ch.g. R B Chesne — Sweet Cashmere (FR) (Kashmir II) 3u45221f. Tall attractive half-brother to Hurdles winner, Sailep (FR) and to several flat winners in France and elsewhere. Dam, middle distance winner in France. Approx £22,000y in France. FRENCH FLAT '90/1 r6 w2 (1m1f55y and 1m2f) p1 (3rd). FLAT (for H. Cecil at 2) r3 p2 (3rds); final run in France. NH '93/6 and '98/9 (blinkered once in '95; for H. Daly; previously for late T. Forster) r33 w7 (2m-2m6f Hdles, inc hat-trick) p11 (inc 2 2nds in Chses — ran over hurdles all 20 subsequent attempts). Chiefly known as a mudlark when earning over £50,000 in a long career, but was a sticky jumper of regulation fences, and took some time to find his stride in Points (additionally, he did not seem to like Andrew Dalton much twice). Did better once headgear was fitted, and gained a first success for four years when beating Seymour's Double by three quarters of a length at Eyton (revenge for a half length defeat on the same track the time before). Has certainly done more than his bit in the past, and probably does not believe in over-exertion now. *Mrs L.A. Windsor & Mrs M.J. Woodhams — Albrighton (Andrew Dalton).* 230 (L), 442 (L), 530 (O), 902 (Cf), 991 (L), 1199 (L), 1320 (L), 1525 (L).

SUPERCHARMER ..10-3.. 7 ch.g. Charmer — Surpassing (Superlative) pp16f. Close-coupled well-made brother to a winner in Italy. Dam won at 7f. FLAT r18 p2 (3rds). NH '97 r2 p0 (beat one, inc Sell). P-t-P '99 r5 w2 (2m4f Maiden and Restricted) p1 (3rd of 4); last, and unseated 1. An ex-sprinter who won on both his first two completions in '99, but ran out twice in one race when tried left-handed, and ended the season lame. Took a while to find his form this year, and could only succeed in a four runner Intermediate at Corbridge. Speedy, but has to go right-handed, and cannot handle cut in the ground, but was in the process of running a fair race on his first attempt in a Ladies when falling at the last on his final appearance, and may be able to make his mark in that sphere in 2001. Wore blinkers once over hurdles. *M.A. Humphreys — Farndale.* 279 (O), 504 (O), 1495 (I), 1603 (2m6f110yH), 1665 (L).

SUPERIOR WEAPON (IRE) ..10-3.. 7 b.g. Riverhead (USA) — Ballytrustan Maid (IRE) (Orchestra) 712. Close-coupled. P-t-P '99 r1 p0 (ran out). Ran out and jumped a wall on his debut in '99, and is clearly never going to be straightforward, but has a high cruising speed, and made all to beat one other finisher in a time 14 seconds quicker than the second division of a 2m4f Maiden at Tranwell. Has yet to prove himself over the full trip, and gives the impression that he will always struggle to do so, but could quite conceivably prove good enough for sub-3m Hunter Chases. *I. Hamilton — Tynedale (Ann Hamilton).* 45 (OMa), 1083 (2m4fOMa), 1427 (R).

SUPERMISTER ..8-8.. 8 b.g. Damister (USA) — Superfina (USA) (Fluorescent Light USA) pppp7. Small neat half-brother to Hurdles winner, Josifina. FLAT (tried blinkers) r9 p0. NH '96 r1 p0 (pulled up). P-t-P '98 r1 p0 (pulled up). A useless non-stayer, often hindered by the rider in Points, and finished lame on his Hunter Chase debut. Has tried every facet of the sport, and proved equally inept in all, and not worth bothering with again. *Mrs S. Davies — Albrighton (Paul Morris).* 568 (OMa), 990 (OMa), 1201 (2m4fOMa), 1323 (OMa), 1531 (2m110yH).

SUPER ROOSTER ..9-5.. 7 gr.g. Superlative — Mummy's Chick (Mummy's Pet) ppRp. Very tall rangy half-brother to Jim Cantle. Dam won at 5f. NH FLAT '98 r2 p0. P-t-P '99 r3 p1 (3rd); unseated 1, and pulled up 1. Has ability, but often unmanageable on the course, and pulled up lame when sent off co-favourite on his most recent appearance. Too keen, and probably too big for his own good. Has been taken to post early. *R. House & Family — Quantock (Tim Long).* 73 (OMa), 353 (CfMa), 518 (2m4fOMa), 733 (2m4fOMa).

SUPER SAFFRON ..9-0.. 11 b.m. Pollerton — Sagora (Sagaro) b3. Big rangy half-sister to Marwenna and to Irish winners, The Silver Rolls (Pointing) and Dee Ell (NH flat and jumping). NH FLAT '95 and '97 r2 p1 (3rd). NH '97/9 (for B. Smart) r7 p2 (3rd in Hdle, and jumped left when last of 2 in Ch); pulled up at 4th after rider lost irons in other Ch. Sold Doncaster, May for 4000. Led into two out at Kimble, but faded rapidly in the testing ground and finished a very tired 37 lengths last. 'Would easily win a Maiden at best, but clearly suffers a stream of training troubles'. _Mr & Mrs A. Varey — Vine & Craven (Alan Varey)._ 754 (CfMa), 1147 (OMa).

SUPER TROUPER (IRE) ..—.. 8 b.g. Electric — Cora Domhain (Deep Run) R. IRISH P-t-P '99 r4 p0 (pulled up 2, fell, and ran out). More party pooper than Super Trouper, and was ducking out for the second time in his short career when he ran past the sixth at Clifton-on-Dunsmore. _Mrs A. Grist — Farmers Bloodhounds (Andrew Wheeler)._ 1421 (OMa).

SUPREME DREAM (IRE) ..9-7.. 12 b.m. Supreme Leader — Rock Solid (Hardboy) 48u6u. Small sister to Hurdles winner, Envopakleada (IRE), and half-sister to Tudor Lodge. P-t-P '94/9 r35 w4 (inc 2 Ladies) p8 (5 3rds, last once); failed to finish 11 (ran out 2, and fell/unseated 8). Moody, but capable on her day, and held her form well until ending the '99 season lame. Tailed off without exception in three completions this year, and seems to have gone to pot completely. Used to get the owner-rider into all sorts of trouble, and she still has not lost the knack of falling off. Could aspire to 10-5 when on a going day, but will do well to stage a comeback at 12. _Mrs P.E. Adams — Pytchley._ 431 (L), 869 (L), 1005 (M), 1266 (L), 1533 (3m1fH).

SURPRISE VIEW ..—.. 9 b.m. Picture Post — Tilloujo (Ovac ITY) p. Small plain owner-bred. Sire, by Polyfoto, was a useless 2-y-o for Mick Easterby in '76 (ran in a Seller). P-t-P '97/9 r10 p0 (6th, last, pulled up 5, unseated 2, and ran out 1). Bred to be useless, and has not failed to disappoint. Can show speed for up to 2m4f, but stays no further, and has only managed an annual appearance '99/00. _Mrs S. Gibson — Sinnington (Bill Brown)._ 138 (OMa).

SUSIES MELODY (IRE) ..9-12.. 10 ch.g. Carlingford Castle — Stardust Melody (Pas De Seul) p2156. Plain angular lengthy. P-t-P '96 and '98/9 (for Mr D.S. Dennis) r11 w1 (Maiden) p5 (3 2nds); unseated 1. Deserved his Maiden win following five placed efforts, but generally a weak finisher, and has needed to seek out firm ground opportunities on easy courses since. Did just that when successful in a three-finisher Restricted at Larkhill, but the chances of a repeat look slim. Acquired a tongue-strap in 2000. _Miss A.M. Reed — I. of W. (Kate Buckett)._ 215 (C), 330 (R), 633 (R), 953 (I), 1485 (I).

SUTTON LIGHTER ..9-0.. 11 b.g. Lighter — Happy Returns (Saucy Kit) pR3p. Leggy quite attractive owner-bred half-brother to Rascaletto (_qv_). P-t-P '96 r4 p0 (pulled up 4). Resurfaced four years after his debut season, but remains scatter-brained (like his sibling), and the only piece of form to his name is a passable eight lengths third at Brampton Bryan. Usually too excitable to produce the goods, has two handlers, and is taken to post early. Pulls hard, and wears a cross-noseband. _E. Turner — Ludlow._ 568 (OMa), 703 (OMa), 866 (CfMa), 1018 (OMa).

SWAN'S WISH (IRE) ..8-5§.. 12 ch.g. Swan's Rock — Wish Again (Three Wishes) pppRfu6p. Small lightly-made half-brother to Cashew Crisis (IRE) (_qv_). IRISH P-t-P '94, '96 and '98 r9 w3 (consecutively, inc Open) p3; pulled up, and unseated. IRISH HUNT CH '98 r1 p0. A triple winner in yielding ground in Ireland, and is beautifully bred, but lacks the substance of his relatives, and is a very pale imitation of them now. Has always been error-prone, and useless with novices in his final five Points (40 lengths last on his only completion). Looks temperamental, and was blinkered once. _R. Rowsell — Mrs J. Hughes — R. Rowsell — Ystrad Taf Fechan._ 275 (Cf), 343 (Cf), 1254 (O), 1399 (M), 1571 (Cnr), 1612 (Cf), 1657 (Cf), 1672 (O).

SWEET TALKER (IRE) ..9-8.. 9 b.g. Le Bavard (FR) — Vultellobar (Bargello) pp31fpp. Leggy half-brother to Erin's Bar (IRE) (Chasing winner since Pointing). NH FLAT '96 r1 p0 (withdrawn after unseating and bolting before start on intended debut). NH '97 r1 p0 (pulled up in Hdle). P-t-P '98 r1 p0 (pulled up). Well supported when successful in a truly awful Maiden run in a slow time at Cottenham, but uninspiring otherwise, and pulled up lame when joint-favourite for an equally bad event on his final appearance at Dingley. _A. & Mrs C. Aldridge — Thurlow (Neville King)._ 175 (I), 323 (CfMa), 606 (OMa), 774 (OMa), 1038 (R), 1287 (R), 1506 (R).

SWEET WILLIAM ..8-9.. 11 b.g. Soldier Rose — Kandy Belle (Hot Brandy) 2. Compact half-brother to Kandyson. Dam, half-sister to 2 Pointers, won 2m 3-y-o Hdle for Philip Allingham, and grandam, Sunny Belle, won 2m Sell Hdle for him in '70 (was bred by him). NH FLAT '96 r1 p0. P-t-P '98 (for Mr P.B. Allingham) r6 p4 (2 2nds, last once; 2 3rds, last once); last, and pulled up 1. Beaten between 10 and 50 lengths when placed on four occasions in '98, but missed the following season, and threw away a winning opportunity at High Easter on his return by hanging badly right on the run-in. Beaten half-a-length by the inappropriately named Always Trying, and may have gone wrong in the process as he failed to reappear. _Mrs K. Pilkington — Enfield Chace._ 1383 (OMa).

SWIFTLY SUPREME (IRE) ..—.. 8 b.m. Supreme Leader — Malozza Brig (New Brig) p3. Half-sister to Swiss Comfort (IRE). Dam, sister to Jimmy Brig (_qv_ '92 Annual), was distant 3rd in a Point (only ran twice). NH FLAT '97/8 (debut for E.M. Caine) r4 p0. NH '99 (from T. Cuthbert's) r1 p0. Can be headstrong early, but rapidly runs out of steam once the race starts in earnest, and had a patient judge to thank for her third at Whittington (tailed off when unseating two out, but eventually remounted). *G.E. Davidson — Cumberland.* 426 (CfMa), 815 (Cm).

SWIFT VENTURE (IRE) ..10-2.. 9 b.g. Meneval (USA) — Golden Seekers (Manado) f212p3u1. Compact brother to jumping winner, Goldenswift (IRE) and half-brother to Irish Chasing winner, Jolly John. NH FLAT Jan '98 r1 p0 (very fat). NH '98/9 r3 p0 (last, and pulled up in Hdles, and pulled up in Ch). Useless under Rules and looked beyond redemption, but much improved by a change of yard, and won two races gamely on firmish whilst his two seconds included behind a subsequent Hunter Chase scorer. Can show some acceleration at best, and capable of scoring again, although it is a pity the chance of a Maiden was forfeited. *A.G. & Mrs Y. Masters — Dartmoor (A. Masters).* 254 (CfMa), 311 (CfMa), 657 (R), 930 (I), 1047 (Cf), 1261 (Cf), 1388 (I), 1514 (Cf).

SWINCOMBE (IRE) ..9-12.. 6 b.g. Good Thyne (USA) — Gladtogetit (Green Shoon) pp1. Good-topped owner-bred half-brother to Little Brown Bear (IRE) (*qv*). Pulled up in his first two Maidens and was sent off at 50-1 for a 16-runner event at Cotley Farm, but came with a steady run to pass five horses from three out and lead after the last. Can collect a Restricted at least before long, and may be a decent stayer in the making. *T.J. Whitley — Dart V. & S. Pool H. (Emma Kelley).* 856 (CfMa), 1048 (CfMa), 1308 (OMa).

SWINGING SIXTIES (IRE) ..9-13.. 10 b.g. Fairy King (USA) — La Bella Fontana (Lafontaine USA) r62. Good-topped brother to Revoque (joint-top rated 2-year-old of '96), and half-brother to Hurdles winner, Barsal. FLAT (tried blinkered/visored) r20 w2 (8-10f) p4; one run at Baden-Baden. NH '95/7 r7 p1 (3rd in Sell). P-t-P '99 r3 p0 (fell 2, and pulled up 1). Gave more prominent displays than in his first season, and produced a decent effort when second to Karaburan at Howick, but not a true stayer, and has not stood much racing since his days on the level. Found dead in his field after season. *Mrs D.L. Smith-Hooper — Llangeinor.* 271 (O), 561 (O), 821 (MO).

SYD GREEN (IRE) ..10-3.. 13 b.g. Green Shoon — Gone (Whistling Wind) ff. Lengthy unfurnished brother to Shoon Wind (*qv*). NH FLAT r1 p0 (tailed off). NH '93 r2 p0 (last and slipped up — tailed off both). P-t-P/HUNT CH '94/9 r18 w5 (inc 3m1f Hunt Ch) p6 (4 2nds, inc 2 Hunt Chses; and inc 3rd in Hunt Ch); fell/unseated 3, and pulled up 3. Vastly improved in '96 when sent Hunter Chasing, but injured a shoulder in a fall 12 months later, and generally not the same horse since. Possesses abundant stamina, but can pull hard, and is not the easiest of rides, and Simon Walker has done well on him. Booked for places when tipping up in the closing stages twice in 2000, almost fell at an earlier stage on his final appearances, and seems to have spent much of his career in the wars. Training him has required the patience of Job, and must be incredibly frustrating. *P.M. Hodges — Holderness (Tony Walker).* 794 (Cf), 1476 (O).

SYLCANNY ..9-4.. 7 ch.m. Sylvan Express — Candery (Derek H) 373. Medium-sized quite attractive. Dam, half-sister to Canny's Fort (*qv*), failed to finish in 2 Points for the Gibbons, as did grandam, Canny's Tudor, who was subsequently 2nd in a Ch. Beaten at least 27 lengths so far, but at least her jumping has improved since a very shaky display on her debut. May be able to get involved in some finishes in her second season. *P.F. Gibbon — Zetland.* 696 (OMa), 1033 (OMa), 1479 (OMa).

SYRPIRO ..9-5.. 7 b.g. Syrtos — Piropo (Impecunious) ppup. Lengthy well-made. Yet to finish including when favourite and second favourite, but gave one creditable display at Guilsborough where he blundered and unseated at the last when just in front when looking vulnerable (knocked his challenger out of the contest, leaving the prize to a bad 11-year-old). Disappointing next time, but may be able to atone if he can dispel some doubts about his stamina. *Sir Michael Connell — Pytchley (Caroline Bailey).* 373 (CfMa), 514 (OMa), 1010 (CfMa), 1589 (2m4fOMa).

TABRIZ ..10-0.. 8 b.m. Persian Heights — Faisalah (Gay Mecene USA) 753. Compact half-sister to flat winners, Nadwaty and Bint Nadia. FLAT (for J. Bethell, tried blinkered/visored) r17 w1 (8f) p6. NH '97/9 (for Mrs P. Avison, bought for 3800) r11 w1 (2m1f Sell Hdle) p3. Regularly troublesome in the preliminaries (withdrawn once on the flat after bolting, and was mounted at the saddling boxes before landing a Selling Hurdle), and sometimes goes to post early, so in the circumstances Angela Thompson did well to master her for three completions. Jumps proficiently, but a weak finisher, and was no match for Marius and Monkey Ago (who reversed positions) on her last two attempts. Absent since February. *Miss A.M. Thompson — Zetland (Chris Dennis).* 41 (L), 135 (L), 280 (L).

TABULA RASA ..8-12.. 7 gr.g. Good Times (ITY) — Rosevean (Abergwiffy) fpuu. Compact. Only writing letters on the Tabula Rasa so far, and is a most unenviable ride, but showed speed before departing on his last two attempts, and there is a chance he might surprise if ever managing to go clear. *Mrs R.B. Denny — Tedworth (Claire Weller).* 206 (OMa), 407 (OMa), 655 (OMa), 1361 (2m4fOMa).

TAILORMADE ..—.. 9 ch.g. Broadsword (USA) — Blades (Supreme Sovereign) pp. Tall lengthy brother to Mr Fudge (*qv*). 8200 4yo. NH FLAT Jan '97 r1 p0. NH '97/8 (for H. Daly; previously for late T. Forster) r3 p0 (11th of 12, pulled up and fell in Hdles). Can look a hard ride, and never better than tailed off in just six appearances spread over four years. *A.P. Bealby — Grove & Rufford.* 234 (OMa), 868 (Cf).

TAKE ACHANCE ON ME ..8-9.. 9 b.g. Arctic Lord — Rockin Berry (Daybrook Lad) fp22. Big rangy half-brother to Celtic Silver (*qv*). P-t-P '97/9 (for Mr B. Davies) r5 p2 (last of 3 once); last, and pulled up 2. Very well-related, but very moderate indeed himself, and has been beaten a minimum of 20 lengths when runner-up in three Maidens '99/00. A big slow boat who does not seem to stay very well, and will find it very difficult to uphold the family honour. *J. Ruck — Kyre (Steve Griffiths).* 893 (OMa), 1068 (3m2fOMa), 1359 (OMa), 1466 (OMa).

TAKE A FLYER (IRE) ..—§§.. 11 b.g. Air Display (USA) — Venus Of Stretham (Tower Walk) pR5. Workmanlike half-brother to a successful Hurdler, and to a winner in Belgium. Dam won 10 flat, 5-10f. IR 1100f, IR 1350y. FLAT r5 p0. NH '94/8 (for R. Hodges; sometimes blinkered) r32 w4 (2m1f-2m2f Hdles, Sells last 2, one on all-weather) p3; fell both Chses. Bought Ascot, Sep '98 for 10050. A reasonable Hurdler in a lowly grade until his last win in April '96, but only appeared once in '98 and missed '99. Has a deplorable record now, and has been 43 lengths last, pulled up six times, fallen twice and run out on his two most recent attempts. Thoroughly mulish in Points, and did not even want to set off in them. *J.F. Lawrence — E. Anglian Bloodhounds.* 936 (Cf), 1112 (O), 1378 (Cf).

TAKE A RIGHT ..—.. 9 b.g. Skyliner — Miss Colenca (Petong) pup. Small close-coupled half-brother to flat winner, Napoleon's Return. FLAT r1 p1 (distant last of 3 — 66-1 and fat). NH '96 r3 p0 (last pair two, and pulled up). P-t-P '97 and '99 r5 p0 (pulled up 5). Yet to even look like finishing in Points, and appears devoid of any stamina. Seems quite highly strung, and has had two handlers. Wears a cross-noseband. *Mrs J.A. Cornes — S. Salop (Jon Cornes).* 569 (OMa), 866 (CfMa), 995 (OMa).

TAKE IT EASY (IRE) ..—§.. 9 ch.g. Orchestra — Permanent Lady (The Parson) pppp. Rangy workmanlike. NH FLAT '97/8 r2 p0. NH '98 r1 p0 (fell in Hdle); blinkered on final intended start, but bolted and unseated. P-t-P '99 (for Mr J.M. Turner) r5 p0 (pulled up 5). A non-finisher in ten starts over jumps, and shows absolutely no interest whatsoever. Blinkered once in '99, but his problems seem physical, and he was heard making an awful racket at High Easter this year. Will surely not appear on a racecourse again. *D. Parravani — Waveney H. (John Ibbott).* 551 (OMa), 606 (OMa), 755 (M), 1115 (OMa).

TAKE MY SIDE (IRE) ..—.. 9 b.g. Be My Native (USA) — Fight For It (Strong Gale) 2uu. Tall workmanlike brother to Irish NH flat and jumping winner, The Bongo Man (IRE) and Irish NH flat winner, Leopard Rock (IRE). IRISH P-t-P '97 r2 w1 (4&5yo Mdn) p0; and pulled up. NH FLAT Oct '97 r1 p0. NH '97/9 r14 w1 (2m4f Hdle, 25-1) p4 (3rds in Chses). The shock winner of a Hurdle in heavy, but seems to have mental and physical problems, blinkered in Points, and was 40 lengths second to Gillan Cove in the first of them, but jumped poorly when favourite in two subsequent attempts, and was going nowhere when he unseated three out in the latest. Was tried tongue-tied under Rules. His 10-3 rating is suspended for the time being at least. *M. Roberts — E. Sussex & Romney Marsh.* 308 (O), 572 (CfO), 826 (O).

TAKE THE BRUSH (IRE) ..8-13.. 7 b.m. Brush Aside (USA) — Ballywilliam Girl (Royal Match) pp51up. Workmanlike. IR 1800 3yo. IRISH P-t-P '98 r2 p2 (2nds). NH '99 (for C. Kellett) r1 p0 (well tailed off 7th of 8). Bought Doncaster, May for 5500. Gave five bad displays in the new yard and only had Piccadilly Wood behind her all year, but at least that was good enough for her to land a 2m4f Maiden at Dunthrop, where Rory Lawther was far too canny to lie up with the suicidal pace of the leaders in a contest in which eight failed to get round. The best one can say of her otherwise is that she does not stay three miles. *N.D. Quesnel — V. of Aylesbury (Karen Lawther).* 81 (CCfMa), 250 (CfMa), 753 (CfMa), 1019 (2m4fOMa), 1393 (R), 1487 (M).

TAKE THE BUCKSKIN ..10-3.. 14 b.g. Buckskin (FR) — Honeyburn (Straight Rule) r22p. Tall rangy hobdayed (before his debut) half-brother to NH flat and Hurdles winner, Uncle Keeny (IRE). Dam comes from excellent jumping family, which includes such as Deep Sensation, The Benign Bishop and Chandigar. NH FLAT '93 r1 w1 (on all-weather). NH '93/8 r16 w2 (2 3m1f Hdles) p9 (inc 2 Chses). P-t-P '99 (for Mr C. Foster & Mr A.M. Crosby) r4 p2; 4th, and pulled up 1. Went to pieces latterly under Rules, but would be capable of winning Points if his wind were up to it. Usually in contention until the closing stages, but a weak finisher, and though only beaten a maximum of nine lengths in four placings '99/00, behind such as My Shout and Gillone, his problems appear to be getting worse, and was pulled up after only two miles in his Members on his final start. Wears a tongue-strap. *Mrs M. Bissill — Mrs H. Lynch — Quorn (Robert Crosby; Helen Harvey).* 170 (L), 690 (L), 1072 (Cf), 1264 (M).

TAKE THE RISK ..—.. 7 b.m. Risk Me (FR) — Spanish Beauty (Torus) pu. Dam, half-sister to La Plume (*qv* '95 Annual), won an Adjacent in Ireland, and was subsequently 3rd in an English Point. Bought Malvern, Oct '98 for 800. Looked novicey when going two miles or less in Maidens. *Mrs D. Jackson & F.E. Cook — S. Cornwall (Mrs D. Jackson).* 538 (OMa), 1009 (CfMa).

TAKE TWO ..9-8.. 13 b.g. Jupiter Island — Dancing Daughter (Dance In Time CAN) p3uR. Small neat half-brother to Hurdles winner, Rake Hey, and to 3 flat winners, including Melodys Daughter and Gone To Pot. Dam won at 14f. FLAT (blinkered 2 in '91) r20 w3 (8f) p3. NH '94, '95 and '96 r21 w8 (7 Hdles, 2m-2m1f, and 2m5f Ch; inc 3 Sells; also disqualified from 2m Sell Hdle — prohibited substances; 2 wins on all-weather; hat-trick first 3 starts) p4. P-t-P '98/9 (for Miss J.E. Foster) r20 w2 (inc Confined) p5 (4 3rds, of 4 once; and last of 2); fell/unseated 3, and brought down 1. A fairly prolific winner in the past, but has only managed to capture two of his 24 Points, and the new owner-rider has not been able to control one side of him. Untried over fences until he was ten, and after two falls in his last five starts of '99 this was not the time to put a learner on him. Tried in blinkers once in '99, when he also acquired a tongue-strap. *S.A. Pinder — York & Ainsty S.* 48 (Cf), 136 (O), 171 (O), 376 (MO).

TALE BRIDGE (IRE) ..9-12.. 8 b.g. Tale Quale — Loobagh Bridge (River Beauty) p322. Compact brother to Tell Tale (*qv*). NH FLAT '98 r1 p0. NH '98 r3 p0. P-t-P '99 (for Miss S. Lunn) r4 w1 (Maiden) p0; 5th, last, and pulled up 1. Easily won a Maiden designed for bad animals at Charm Park last year, and having changed hands has improved steadily, and gave his best display yet in a Restricted on his final appearance. Seems unsuited by easy surfaces, but should prove good enough to win a run-of-the-mill event in 2001. *Miss A. Lakin — Cheshire.* 782 (R), 963 (R), 1150 (L), 1411 (R).

TALKALOT (IRE) ..9-5.. 10 ch.g. Le Bavard (FR) — Miss Breta VII (unknown) ppp17. Rangy half-brother to 3 Irish NH flat winners, including Mobile Man and Slaney Lamb (both also successful jumpers). Dam won Irish NH flat. IRISH NH FLAT '96/7 r6 p3 (3rds, inc dead-heat). IRISH NH '97 r3 p0. NH '98 (for M. Sheppard, bought for 5000). Sold Ascot, Mar for 600. Showed speed but appeared to pull much too hard for Fred Hutsby in his first three Points, but Adrian Wintle managed to anchor him at Bitterley, where he kept going steadily to win an elders Maiden on firmish. Beat conspicuously bad rivals and was a poor last next time, and connections can consider themselves to have done well to extract a victory. Wears a cross-noseband. *A.G. Brown — N. Ledbury (Gerald Spencer).* 146 (OMa), 337 (CMa), 616 (CMa), 995 (OMa), 1200 (CR).

TALLAGE (FR) ..9-12.. 9 gr.g. Hours After (USA) — Suetagar (Zino) pr. Dam won at 10f in France. FRENCH FLAT/NH r26 w1 (1m7f Hdle at Enghien) p10 (inc over fences), won another Hdle on a disqualification, but lost it again on a reversal. P-t-P '98 r4 p2 (last of 3 once); pulled up 1, and fell 1. Had ability, and only beaten a length in a Parham Confined in '98, but disappeared for 12 months subsequently, and has run badly on his return. May well need mud in abundance, and could be worth bearing in mind were the Sandhurst area to flood in 2001, though the owner would need to be more positive on him. *P.A.D. Scouller — Garth & S. Berks (Nigel Allen).* 983 (Cf), 1398 (Cf).

TAMALLY ..—.. 11 b.g. Scallywag — Tamtine (Immortal Knight) p. Very big. Dam, half-sister to My John Charlott (*qv* '88 Season Annual), won Atherstone Members (beat Lone Soldier) and 2nd. Made a belated attempt to try to emulate mother, but could only lumber along for two miles before giving up. *Mrs J. Manicom — Atherstone.* 1414 (M).

TAMAR LILY ..9-8.. 7 b.m. Lir — Easter Again (Shaab) pp. Compact. Dam, sister or half-sister to 4 du Plessis Pointers including Kingsmill Quay (*qv* '99 Annual), was 2nd in a Point for them. NH '98 r1 p0 (fell when tailed off in Hdle); unruly and withdrawn after saddle slipped on intended debut. P-t-P '99 r3 w1 (Members) p0; unseated 1, and refused 1. Looks a handful, but has won on the only occasion she has completed to date when 33-1 and making all in her Members last year. Led for 2m4f in both 2000 starts prior to pulling up, but her season lasted just a fortnight, and is obviously not easy to train. Has two handlers, and wears a cross-noseband. *Miss J. du Plessis — E. Cornwall.* 847 (R), 1043 (R).

TANBOROUGH ..—.. 8 ch.g. Crested Lark — Blazing Manor (True Song) p. Half-brother to Manor's Maid and Stable Girl. Dam, sister and half-sister to 3 Pointers, including Fury Manor, was 2nd in a Maiden for Mark Keith (broke down when poised to score on final appearance). Tailed off and pulled up after two miles in January. *M.R. Keith — Pytchley.* 79 (O).

TANGLE BARON ..9-2§.. 13 gr.g. Baron Blakeney — Spartangle (Spartan General) p3. Strong rangy half-brother to Tangle Jim, Tangle Kelly and Tangle Touch. P-t-P/HUNT CH '94/9 r43 w7 (up to Confined) p13 (7 2nds, beaten neck twice); disqualified from Intermediate win — rider failed to weigh-in; failed to finish 10 (on floor 4, and ran out 1). Won at least once per season during his first five campaigns, but has never been very reliable, and has always required a sound surface. Beaten at least 20 lengths when completing '99/00, and a remote last in his Members in the latest. *A.R. & J.J. Tanner — S. Salop (Russell Teague).* 862 (Cf), 1317 (M).

TANGLEFOOT TIPPLE ..9-6.. 10 b.g. Buckskin (FR) — Portodamus (Porto Bello) 26. Lengthy unfurnished half-brother to Lady Porto, and to Hurdles winner, Caldamus. NH FLAT '96/7 r3 p2 (2nds). NH '97 r2 p0. P-t-P '99 r4 p1 (2nd of 3); pulled up 2, and fell 1. Beaten a head after hanging left inside the final furlong on his racecourse debut, and again on his 2000 reappearance, but has let his supporters down badly when favourite on three other occasions, and presumably has something wrong with him. Absent since February. *Mrs J.E. Purdie — Portman.* 105 (OMa), 328 (CfMa).

TANGO'S DELIGHT ..—.. 13 b.g. Idiot's Delight — Lucky Tango (Tangle) ppup. Very tall rangy half-brother to Vivaque, Nearly A Tango and Twocantango, and to jumping winner, Kariwak. NH FLAT '93/4 r3 p1 (2nd). NH '94/9 (for R. Baker, bought for 6600; won previously for D. Elsworth) r37 w1 (2m2f Sell Ch) p4 (inc Sell Hdle); ran out once. Got up close-home when winning a Selling Chase in May '96, but has performed abysmally in his 13 most recent attempts, and pulled up in six of them. Hopefully there are no plans to bring him back for further embarrassments. *B.P. Jones — Berks & Bucks (John Gallagher)*. 74 (CCf), 200 (O), 736 (Cnr), 1531 (2m110yH).

TAN HILL SPARKY ..—.. 10 b.m. Leading Star — Carrickmoleen (Bargello) fp3fp. Tall rangy. Dam won 3 Points and 2nd 4 (inc a Ch) in Ireland; but pulled up 3 times and refused when in W. Norfolk country. P-t-P '98/9 r6 p0 (pulled up 6). Failed to finish her first eight races, and beaten furlongs when she finally succeeded, but carries far too much condition, and was still looking porky on her final outing in 2000. Has never jumped with any accuracy. *Mrs A. Holman — W. Norfolk.* 238 (O), 938 (3m4fO), 1112 (O), 1292 (OMa), 1584 (CCond).

TANTARA LODGE (IRE) ..9-0.. 10 b.g. Import — Fashion Blade (Tanfirion) ppp. Stocky compact. NH '96/7 r4 p1 (2nd). P-t-P '98/9 r8 w1 (Maiden) p1 (3rd of 4); 5th, 6th, pulled up 3, and unseated 1. Has no stamina, and gained his win in fluke circumstances when the clear leader pulled herself up after the last. Tailed off without exception since, and made mistakes when tried over 2m4f at Ludlow. Blinkered twice last year, and tried in a visor in 2000. Has been tried tongue-tied. *C. & Mrs S.J. Jones - Albrighton Woodland (Mark Wellings).* 567 (R), 684 (2m4fH), 896 (R).

TARGET TIME ..9-4.. 11 b.m. Faustus (USA) — Alicia Markova (Habat) p6up6. Workmanlike lengthy half-sister to 5 flat winners, (one in Malaysia), including Sharp Consul (IRE), and Internal Affair. FLAT (blinkered 1) r4 p0 (all at Haydock). P-t-P/HUNT CH '96/9 r17 w1 (Maiden) p5 (3 3rds); fell/unseated 5, and pulled up 4. A lethal jumper when partnered by two incompetents in '96, and gained her win in a walk-over, but only once beaten less than 30 lengths in the last two seasons, and the chances of her winning a competitive race are receding rapidly. Thrice blinkered in '96, and visored in her last two appearances. *B. Neaves — W. Street/Tickham.* 25 (Cnr), 126 (R), 285 (CR), 574 (4mMO), 825 (R).

TARIAN (USA) ..7-8.. 9 b.g. Lyphard (USA) — Chain Fern (USA) (Blushing Groom FR) Rppp5puup. Very small plain half-brother to flat winners, Dayville and Woodwardia. Dam is an unraced sister to Al Bahathri. FLAT r9 p1 (5/2nd of 17). NH '97 r3 p1 (3rd). P-t-P '98/9 r9 p0 pulled up 6, and fell 1. Utterly hopeless in Points, and 47 lengths last in his only completion, but not helped by inept riding performances latterly, nor by his lack of inches. Often slowly away recently, and has been tried in blinkers. Seems tainted by lunacy, and hopefully will not run again. *K. Richards — Llangeinor.* 348 (CfMa), 485 (R), 595 (R), 823 (CfMa), 950 (OMa), 1056 (CfMa), 1404 (OMa), 1454 (OMa), 1574 (OMa).

TARJUMAAN (USA) ..—.. 10 b.br.g. Private Account (USA) — Etoile D'Amore (USA) (The Minstrel CAN) fppup. Workmanlike half-brother to successful Hurdler, Loving Omen, and to 3 flat winners in USA. Dam won at 7f. NH FLAT Feb '95 (for R. O'Sullivan) r1 p0 (24th of 25). NH '95 (for John Berry) r1 p0 (pulled up in Hdle). Does not has an ADO ability, and it will be no surprise to learn that there was something badly wrong with him. *C.P. Vanhien — Quorn.* 517 (OMa), 1011 (CfMa), 1264 (M), 1423 (OMa), 1586 (On).

TARRY AWHILE ..9-7§.. 15 ch.g. Crested Lark — Lucky Sandy (St Columbus) prppr. Very big strong brother to Dennis (qv). P-t-P/HUNT CH '92/8 (for Sir Michael Connell) r38 w2 (Maiden and Restricted) p10 (8 2nds); failed to finish 16 (fell/unseated 3, refused 2, carried out 1, and ran out 1). Placed on two occasions '95/8, but has only consented to win once since '93, and did not take kindly to being brought back after a year on the sidelines. Used to mistime his challenge to perfection, but never allowed himself the opportunity in 2000 and dogged it furiously long before the finish. Blinkered once in '97. A truly maddening beast, and surely won't be put into training again. *G.B. Tarry — Pytchley, & Grafton (Jimmy Tarry).* 428 (Cf), 784 (M), 1005 (M), 1485 (I), 1663 (C).

TARTHOOTH (IRE) ..10-7.. 10 ch.g. Bob Back (USA) — Zoly (USA) (Val De L'Orne FR) 422f421. Sturdy brother to Hurdles winner, Love You Madly (IRE) and an Irish flat winner, and half-brother to successful Hurdler, Battleplan. Dam won a flat race in Belgium. IR 5200f, IR 7200y. FLAT '93/5 (for J. Benstead) r15 w3 (13-17f) p3. IRISH FLAT '96 r2 p1 (3rd). IRISH NH '96/9 r25 w4 (3 Hdles, 2m4f-3m, and 3m Ch; inc hat trick '96) p14. Bought Doncaster, May for 20,000. Was very expensive for a horse who had only scored once since '96, and proved disappointing in Points, although he did finally manage to score when beating a 14-year-old in an Open at Barbury Castle. Chased home the likes of Camp Bank, Rectory Garden and Blanville, so the success was not undeserved. Normally blinkered, and possibly best when able to dominate in the mud. Has done best for Godfrey Maundrel, who gets him jumping fluently. *C.C. Bennett — Vine & Craven (John Porter).* 4 (O), 77 (O), 217 (O), 454 (4mMO), 884 (O), 1244 (MO), 1282 (O).

TAURA'S RASCAL ..—.. 12 b.g. Scallywag — Centaura (Centaurus) p. Massive brother to Border Barley (qv). P-t-P/HUNT CH '95/7 (for Mr F.J. Brennan) r9 w3 (2m4f Maiden, Restricted and Intermediate nov rdrs) p2 (3rd in Hunt Ch once); pulled up 1, and fell 2 (looked winner once). Won twice on firmish in '97, but not built to appreciate such surfaces, and spent the next two years on the sidelines. Looked and ran as though in need of the race on his return, but did not surface again, and it would appear his massive frame has got the better of him. *Miss S.L. Holt — O. Berks (Barry Brennan).* 453 (Cf).

when he fell at the second at Perth and was left with terrible injuries. *N.H. Oliver — N. Ledbury.* 539 (OMa), 1400 (R).

TEAL BAY ..9-13.. 9 b.m. Scallywag — Centaura (Centaurus) u1p. Compact home-bred sister to Border Barley (*qv*). NH FLAT Mar '97 r1 p0. NH '98/9 (from S. Brookshaw's) r6 p2 (10-17*l* 3rds, 2m5f-3m2f). Showed some promise over Hurdles, and able to confirm it under a good patient ride from David Barlow in a Maiden on the long Alpraham track (was settled off the pace whilst a lunatic pair dashed well clear). A very thorough stayer, but averages less than three outings per annum, and it was discouraging to see her pulled up and dismounted at Bitterley. *P.A. Jones — W. Salop.* 568 (OMa), 588 (OMa), 992 (R).

TEAM CAPTAIN ..10-0.. 7 ch.g. Teamster — Silly Sausage (Silly Answer) fu211. Lengthy unfurnished. Dam was placed in 4 races, inc 3rd in 2 Points (final for Peter Hickman) ('good enough to win, but clearly very hard to train'). NH FLAT '99 (from P. Hobbs) r1 p0. Foiled by errors in his first two Points, but has not stopped improving since, and although he only won a poor Maiden in a slow time at Cotley Farm his Restricted success was a considerably more meritorious effort. Gradually working his way up the handicap, and might be able to make the grade in Opens eventually. *P.J. Hickman — E. Devon (Chris Down).* 457 (OMa), 733 (2m4fOMa), 934 (OMa), 1307 (OMa), 1563 (R).

TEDSTONE FOX ..8-8.. 9 b.g. Bold Fox — Royal Wren (Blast) 42pf3p2s2. Neat. Dam won 3 Hdles, 2m-3m. P-t-P '97/9 r15 p1 (last of 3); last pair 2, pulled up 8, and fell/unseated 4. Improved in his fourth season, but did not have much of a record previously, and still lacks basic stamina. Takes a strong hold, and his partners have allowed him to build up a huge lead on occasions, but has compounded every time, and has only once finished within ten lengths of the winner. Has finally become much more fluent, and will probably win a bad race eventually. *Mrs E. Weaver — Clifton-on-Teme (J.W. Weaver).* 146 (OMa), 337 (CfMa), 451 (CfMa), 618 (CMa), 697 (M), 925 (2mH), 1464 (OMa), 1634 (OMa), 1662 (OMa).

TEELYNA ..—.. 9 b.m. Teenoso (USA) — Lynda-B (Strong Gale) uppppp. Tall light-framed. Gave three abysmal displays of jumping for Gwin Marsh (including when blinkered once), and twice stopped rapidly after two miles when gaining more competent jockeys subsequently. Has a serious attitude problem, but may be breaking blood vessels as well. *P. Riddick — Gelligaer F. (Vicky Hanks).* 38 (CR), 145 (OMa), 269 (CfMa), 488 (CfMa), 602 (CfMa), 1092 (OMa).

PLATE 128   1673 Torrington Farmers Ladies Open: Tee Tee Too and Emma James, 1st, are clear at the last   PHOTO: Baths Photographic

TEE TEE TOO (IRE) ..10-4.. 9 ch.g. Hatim (USA) — Scottish Welcome (Be My Guest USA) 2421. Small stocky half-brother to 3 winners in Italy, IR 1400f, IR 4800y. FLAT (inc for Miss K. Milligan; won previously for P. Haslam) r32 w1 (6f fibresand) p7. NH '95/9 (for C. Jackson; previously for F.

Jordon; previously for A. Carroll, bought for 2600; debut for A. Harrison) r26 p3 (3rds, inc Sell Hdle and Ch). A tail-swisher, and his form was nothing to write home about, just one victory from 58 attempts, until he went Pointing. Did little wrong in 2000, and beaten a maximum of nine lengths in his four attempts. Ran well enough when chasing home Dawn's Cognac and Rip Van Winkle, and had a much easier task when winning at Umberleigh. Occasionally blinkered in the past, to no avail. Should find another race. *Miss S. Jackson — N. Ledbury (Emma James).* 1275 (L), 1358 (Cf), 1462 (L), 1673 (L).

TEETON BUILDS ..9-7.. 9 ch.g. Sunley Builds — Sunday Champers (True Song) 1p2555p. Big rangy. Dam won 3 Points and placed 4 (inc a Hunt Ch) for Joan Tice. Grandam, Poppywee, won 3 Points (2 Opens) and 3rd twice. Great-grandam, Carnival Candy, won a Maiden and 3rd. P-t-P '98/9 r5 w2 (Maiden and Restricted) p1 (2nd); pulled up 1, and fell 1. Successful three times in a four race span '98/00, but lucky in the middle success, and proved disappointing after scoring on his reappearance this year. Generally labouring in the final mile in 2000, and may not have been right as he had seen the trip out well previously, but ominously blinkered on his latest appearance. Never happy when risked on firm ground on his final outing, and it was no surprise that he came back unsound. Wears over-reach boots. *Mrs J.M. Tice — Pytchley.* 93 (C), 286 (O), 415 (O), 510 (Cf), 870 (O), 1265 (O), 1440 (MO).

TEETON HEAVENS ..9-9.. 10 b.m. Sunley Builds — Angels Are Near (Floriferous) 1f3. Workmanlike owner-bred. P-t-P '97/8 (for Mrs J.M. Tice) r8 w1 (Maiden) p1 (2nd); last pair 3, pulled up 1 and unseated 2. Won in her debut season for Ben Pollock, but all at sea under a novice girl in '98, and absent since until resurfacing for new connections this year. Beat a bunch of old dears in her Members with the minimum of fuss, but fell early next time, and finished very tired when a poor last of three finishers back at Hackwood Park. Ran tongue-tied at Badbury Rings, and possibly lacks the stamina to cope with soft ground. Clearly not easy to train, but might have a chance in Restricteds. *M.D.P. & Mrs J. Butler — Hampshire (Kate Buckett).* 882 (M), 1061 (R), 1248 (Cm).

TEETON TANGO ..—.. 10 ch.m. Sunley Builds — Kemalkan (Kemal FR) p. Dam is half-sister to Fleckefjord (IRE) (qv 2000 Annual). Met a horrible fate at Bonvilston, where she broke down on both forelegs. *Mrs M. Brice — Llangeinor.* 1456 (OMa).

TEIGR PREN ..9-0.. 10 b.g. Tigerwood — Official Lady (Official) 5u55f3p. Tall lengthy brother to Daisy's Choice. Dam, half-sister to Kerstin's Choice (qv '98 Annual), was last of 3 in a Maiden. P-t-P/HUNT CH '97/9 r20 w2 (Maiden and Restricted) p8 (7 3rds, of 4 twice, and last thrice); pulled up 5, and fell 1. Successful in two minor races '98/9, and can slog through the most arduous conditions, but only once better than last in 2000, and usually out on his feet when completing. Used to jump badly, but generally safe these days, and should not have been presented at the fence where he unseated at Pantyderi as he was too exhausted. It would be a surprise if he could trouble the judge outside of Members races in the future. *K.M. Davies — Pembs (Brian Llewellyn).* 275 (Cf), 343 (Cf), 482 (I), 843 (M), 944 (I), 1051 (Cf), 1227 (I).

TEJAQUE ..—.. 6 b.m. Lord Of Arabia — Devil's Gold (Goldfella) b. Brought down after two miles when apparently being given a quiet time on her debut. *B.W. Farthing — Monmouths (Shirley Farthing).* 1455 (OMa).

TEKROC (IRE) ..—.. 10 b.g. Executive Perk — Power Supply (Paddy's Stream) pp. IRISH P-t-p '97/8 r8 p1 (3rd); pulled up 4, and fell 2. Pulled up in his last four races, and appears to break blood vessels with monotonous regularity. Fell two outings back, and prematurely killed off by the Irish Formbook (not that we haven't been guilty of 'reports of his death are greatly exaggerated' comments ourselves!). *Mr & Mrs W. Miller, C McKenzie, K. Landells — Cumberland.* 365 (CfMa), 914 (CfMa).

TELIMAR (IRE) ..9-1.. 7 b.g. Montelimar (USA) — Running Pet (Deep Run) f42. Finished fast and only missed second place by a length in a very good 2m4f Maiden at Ston Easton (the three behind him all went on to score), but surely did not give his true running when beaten by a bad animal next time. His stable had a year to forget in 2000, and if fortunes change he should soon be off the mark. Potentially considerably under-rated. *I.M. Ham & S.M. Francis — Weston & Banwell H. (Ron Treloggen).* 353 (CfMa), 732 (2m4fOMa), 956 (OMa).

TELLAPORKY ..9-5.. 12 b.g. Bold Fort — Ab Dabh (Spanish Gold) u4pp4fp. Smallish. NH '96/9 (for R. Simpson latterly) r15 p5 (inc sellers, and 2 Chses); visored final start. HUNT CH '97 (for Mr T. Hind) r7 p1 (3rd); 4th thrice, last pair 2, and unseated 1. A modest front-running Maiden under Rules, but rarely gives a respectable display any longer, and has become very inaccurate at the obstacles. Failed to stay up the Mollington hill on the only occasion he avoided last in 2000, but put Emma Owen in hospital when crashing at Larkhill subsequently. Wears a cross-noseband, and applied blinkers on two occasions this year. *Mr & Mrs E. Cardew — Mrs J. & Miss E.L. Owen — Bicester with Whaddon (Herbie Owen).* 20 (OMa), 76 (CfMa), 150 (3mH), 300 (2m5fH), 309 (OMa), 630 (OMa), 739 (OMa).

TELLHERPATIT (IRE) ..9-8.. 8 ch.m. Torus — Lady Sese (Kampala) f. Light-framed. Dam is an unraced half-sister to smart jumping winner, Bertone. NH FLAT '97 r1 p0. NH '98/9 r2 p0 (10th in 2m110y Hdle, and pulled up 1). P-t-P '99 (for Mrs J.M. Storey) r2 p0 (4th, and pulled up 1). A hard-puller who runs herself into the ground, and having quickly established a huge lead was being rapidly overhauled when falling heavily just after halfway on her belated reappearance. Putting an inexperienced girl up was tantamount to disaster, and should be running in Maidens with a strong pilot. *Mrs S. Stafford — Morpeth.* 1665 (L).

TELL TALE (IRE) ..9-13.. 9 b.g. Tale Quale — Loobagh Bridge (River Beauty) fp435. Small compact brother to Tale Bridge (IRE) and half-brother to Irish winners, Break Away Bridge (NH flat) and Must Stay (Pointing). P-t-P '97/9 r9 w2 (Maiden and Restricted) p1 (2nd); last pair 2, and pulled up 4. A thorough stayer, and has gained both his wins by wide margins at Marks Tey including a defeat of Village Copper in the latest, but one-paced and seemingly cannot handle soft ground. Gave his best display of the season when third at High Easter, but has basically failed to progress in 2000, and will probably require some luck to win again. *Mrs M.E. Latham — Essex F. & U. (Nicola Bulgin).* 175 (I), 574 (4mMO), 937 (I), 1378 (Cf), 1485 (I).

TELUK (IRE) ..—§.. 10 ch.g. Sula Bula — Little Union (Prince Regent FR) pRpppp. Good-bodied. NH FLAT '96 r1 p0. NH "96/9 (for Mrs J. Pitman) r4 p1 (27f); pulled up 3rd only Ch. Bought Ascot, June for 775. NH Apr '00 r1 p0 pulled up in 2m Sell Hdle: *t.o 4, pu 6*. Rarely seen in the previous yard (amazing that that La Pitman put up with him for so long), and is ungenuine and gave a string of abysmal displays in 2000. Surely the last has been seen of him. *J.W. Whyte — Waveney H.* 23 (OMa), 239 (R), 551 (OMa), 755 (M), 941 (CfMa).

TEME WILLOW (IRE) ..9-3.. 10 ch.g. Henbit (USA) — Nevada Lady (Trimmingham) 4525pp. Sturdy compact half-brother to Maltese Cross (IRE) (*qv*). P-t-P '98/9 r4 w1 (Maiden) p0 (pulled up 3). Pulled up in his first three races, but won a poor Maiden in authoritative style at Bitterley last year, and gave prominent displays in Restricteds in the first half of this season. Went down by three lengths at Llanvapley where the rider objected unsuccessfully to the winner on the grounds of hitting his mount across the face with his whip, but his form tailed off subsequently, and is probably best fresh. Did not appear to appreciate the firm ground on his final start. Being by Henbit there is always a chance that his temperament will get the better of him. *Dr J.G. Garman & Mrs S.E. Vaughan — Teme V. (Michael Hammond).* 173 (R), 392 (R), 744 (R), 992 (R), 1200 (CR), 1411 (R).

TEMPLE GARTH ..10-4.. 12 b.g. Baron Blakeney — Future Chance (Hopeful Venture) 443p5131. Strong workmanlike half-brother to 2 flat winners (one in Italy). Dam won at 11f. NH '93/7 and '98 r37 w7 (4 Hdles, 2m5f-3m2f, inc Sell, and 3 Chses, 3m-3m1f) p7. P-t-P/HUNT CH '98/9 r13 w1 (Ladies) p5 (3 2nds, inc Hunt Ch; inc last of 3 once); pulled up 1. Provided Freya Hartley with her first winner last year, but the combination seemed rather out of kilter in 2000, and it was not until May that he showed his true form. Developed a turn of foot at the age of ten, and produced it at just the right time when successful at Easingwold (the fastest track in the country) where he whizzed past four rivals from the second last. Went to Cartmel on his final start to line up in a Hunter Chase where he was sent off at 33-1, but under a splendid drive from Guy Brewer, he gamely responded to secure the prize in the final 100 yards. Normally an expert jumper who is suited by a sound surface, and can win again when conditions are right. *Miss F. Hartley — Sinnington.* 397 (L), 505 (L), 621 (L), 1029 (L), 1232 (L), 1350 (L), 1477 (L), 1643 (3m2fH).

TEMPLERAINEY (IRE) ..9-10§.. 13 b.g. Welsh Term — Saharan (Tarboosh USA) p. Tall rangy. IRISH NH FLAT '92/3 r4 w1 p3. IRISH AMAT FLAT '93 r2 p1 (3rd). NH '93/4 and '95 r14 w1 (2m Hdle) p2 (3rds); 5th, last, pulled up 2, and fell 2 in Chses. P-t-P '97/9 r8 w1 (Confined) p2; 4th, refused 1, slipped up 1, and pulled up 2. Finished a good second in a very slowly run event at Chaddesley Corbett on his last appearance in '99, but has long suffered wind problems (has been tried tubed) and pulled up before halfway on his only outing this year in which he wore a tongue-strap. Only gets three miles when conditions are not testing, but it is hard to envisage him winning again. *J.J. Smith — Beaufort.* 1016 (Cf).

TEMPLEROAN PRINCE ..9-10.. 14 b.g. Buckskin (FR) — Good Credentials (Take A Reef) 4ppp6. Tall rangy brother to Irish Pointing winner, Impeccable Buck (IRE) and half-brother to Irish NH flat and Hurdles winner, Ioder Wan (IRE). Dam won at 9f in Ireland, and won 2m Hdle there. IRISH FLAT r4 p2. IRISH NH FLAT '92 r4 w1 p0. IRISH NH '92/8 r48 w2 (Hdles, 2m2f-3m) p8 (inc 3rd in Ch); one run Cheltenham. P-t-P '99 (for Mrs C.M. Lucas, Mr & Mrs W. Clark) r5 p2 (2nds); 6th, and pulled up 2. Last won a race in '93, and seems to be labouring under a wind problem nowadays. Received a succession of early reminders in his first three outings this year, but all to no avail, and only once got past the two-mile mark in contention. Wears a tongue-strap. *Mrs C.M. Lucas — Warwicks (M. Lucas).* 74 (CCf), 191 (Cf), 428 (Cf), 1016 (Cf), 1190 (Cf).

TEN BOB NOTE ..9-11.. 12 b.g. True Song — Castelira (Castle) 542f. Big rangy half-brother to Casino Nell (*qv*). P-t-P '97/8 r5 w1 (Maiden) p2 (3rd of 4 once); unseated 1, and refused 1. An excitable character who has to be taken to post early, and takes a strong hold when under way, but usually struggles to see the trip out, and threw away a good opportunity when tipping up at Hackwood Park in his latest outing. Never runs much, and missed eight weeks of the season between his final two appearances this year. Wears blinkers. *J.J. Smith — Beaufort (Richard Smith).* 2 (R), 196 (R), 338 (R), 1247 (R).

PLATE 129   2 Thames Valley Club Retricted (Div 2): L to R Ten Bob Note (M. Walters), 5th, Mister Audi (A. Sansome), 3rd, and Jo Jos Best Friend (T. Vaughan), 1st   PHOTO: Bill Selwyn

TENELLA'S LAST ..9-9.. 13 ch.m. Broadsword (USA) — Tenella (Wrekin Rambler) u6sup3p. Light-framed half-sister to Tenesaint, Tenesong and Rambling Song (all subsequent Chasing winners), and to Tenecount, Songella and Tenelord. Dam was 3rd in Hunt Ch. P-t-P/HUNT CH '94/6 and '98/9 r29 w2 (Maiden and Members) p8 (5 2nds, last once; and inc last of 3); failed to finish 9 (fell/unseated 6). Gained her last success in her Members in '98, but can look reluctant, and has run up a sequence of 17 defeats since. Stays well, but can be error-prone, and beaten a minimum of 15 lengths when completing this year. Schooling a novice for the most part in 2000, and her best display was for Ranald Morgan, but remains a poor performer in Restricteds, and will struggle to find another opening. *Mrs Y.H. Morgan — Tynedale.* 418 (M), 976 (R), 1081 (R), 1152 (I), 1162 (R), 1363 (R), 1577 (R).

TENOR BET (IRE) ..9-6.. 8 ch.g. Noalto — Gem Princess (Little Buskins) 733. Half-brother to Irish NH flat and Hurdles winner, The Grey Mare. IRISH NH '98/9 (blinkered once) r5 p0 (inc last pair 3, and pulled up). Sold Goffs, Aug for 1339. Useless in Ireland, but did a little better when dropped to Maidens in the new yard, and beaten between six lengths and 11 lengths in his third. There may have been a total of 13 finished behind, but only one of those went on to score, and he had previously finished ahead of him. Jumps safely, but clearly no better than moderate, and was hanging left on his latest appearance. *Mrs J. Stewart — Hurworth (Charmaine Raw).* 439 (OMa), 627 (OMa), 808 (OMa).

TEN PAST ELEVEN (IRE) ..8-9.. 9 b.m. Mandalus — Philis's Friend (Le Moss) 3p. Workmanlike lengthy. IRISH P-t-P '97/8 r6 p1 (40*l* last of 3 in unplaced Maiden); pulled up 3, and fell 1. P-t-P '99 r6 w1 (Maiden) p1 (last of 3); and pulled up 4. Gained her win in a diabolical Maiden at Pentreclwydau, but otherwise not better than last, and had to be destroyed after breaking a fetlock at Erw Lon. Used to wear a tongue-strap. *Mrs L. Meyrick & Miss C. Williams — S. Pembs.* 347 (R), 644 (Cm).

TERRANO STAR (IRE) ..8-9.. 10 ch.g. Phardante (FR) — Sovereign Sox (Don) 447. Very tall rangy brother to Nissan Star (IRE). IRISH P-t-P '95/6 r7 w1 (Maiden) p1 (last of 2); pulled up 1, carried out 1, unseated 1, and ran out 1. NH FLAT '96 r1 p0. NH '96 r1 p0 (fell in Ch). P-t-P '99 r5 p1 (last of 3); pulled up 3, and fell 1. A forlorn looking beast, who rarely looks well, and usually much too fat to do himself justice. Runs tubed nowadays, and has not beaten a rival over jumps since making all to win his Irish Maiden in '96. Remains a clumsy jumper. *E. Rhodes — V. of Clettwr.* 266 (M), 344 (I), 482 (I).

TEST OF LOYALTY ..9-0.. 7 b.g. Niniski (USA) — River Chimes (Forlorn River) 535322u3. Light-framed half-brother to Rapid Chimes, to useful sprinter, Absent Chimes, and to jumping winner, Dancing River. NH '99 r1 (13th of 15 in 2m Hdle). P-t-P '99 r2 p0; 4th twice. Has a commendable completion record, but not surprisingly in view of his pedigree struggles to stay even over 2m4f. Has given his best displays on a sound surface, and was still in front when unseating Andrew Robson at the third last in what turned out to be a two-finisher Maiden at Corbridge on his penultimate outing. Will probably find an opening eventually, but life will get even tougher if he does. *F.V. White — Percy.* 46 (OMa), 501 (2m4fOMa), 718 (CfMa), 910 (2m4fOMa), 1084 (2m4fOMa), 1430 (OMa), 1499 (OMa), 1581 (2m4fOMa).

TEXAN BABY (BEL) ..10-3.. 12 b.g. Baby Turk — Texan Rose (FR) (Margouillat FR) 132. Tall rangy brother to a French flat winner, and half-brother to another, and to a winner in Belgium. Dam won 2 12f races and a Hdle in France. NH FLAT '93 r4 w1 p1 (2nd). NH '93/8 (for N. Twiston-Davies) r19 w2 (Hdles, 2m6f-3m2f) p10 (inc 8 Chses). Sold Doncaster, may '98 for 4000. Absent in '99, and was breaking a losing sequence of 20 which stretched back to December '93 when he jumped right but made all to win an Open unchallenged at Wadebridge. Landed a punt from 14-1 to 6-1, and proved it was no fluke with fair placed efforts behind Butler John and Slew Man subsequently. Has always been error-prone (and sometimes not keen either), and difficult for Kevin Sheppard to handle, so he did well to get him round in all three attempts. *K. Sheppard — Aldenham H. (John Papworth).* 537 (O), 727 (O), 929 (Cnr).

THANK U JIM ..9-13.. 13 b.g. Bootsman Bains (GER) — Oregano (Track Spare) ppp. Close-coupled robust owner-bred half-brother to River Ramble. P-t-P/HUNT CH '93/5 and '97/9 r24 w6 (inc 3m Hunt Ch, and 4 Ladies) p5 (2nds); pulled up 7, and fell/unseated 3. A strong galloper at best, but appeared to suffer a training setback in '98, and has only managed one completion since. Dropped out quickly after two miles in each of his 2000 appearances, and may have something amiss. Gets on well with Tina Jackson despite the occasional faux pas, but connections will be doing well to get him back to anywhere near his best at 13. *Mrs G. Sunter — Cleveland.* 422 (3m5fO), 690 (L), 1350 (L).

THATL DO ..—.. 7 b.m. Afzal — Skalmey (Scorpio FR) pp. Very small light-framed. Dam pulled up in 3 Points for the Warners. NH '99 r2 p0 (pulled up in Hdles). P-t-P '99 r1 p0 (slipped up). Yet to display any ability over jumps, and tailed off and pulled up after 2m3f twice this year. Lacks scope, and seems doomed to failure. *C.H. Warner — Pembs.* 31 (CMa), 644 (Cm).

THAT OLD FEELING (IRE) ..9-12.. 9 b.g. Waajib — Swift Reply (He Loves Me) 64ff. Small neat half-brother to Countercheck (IRE), to Irish Hurdles winner, Ministerial Model (IRE) and to a winner in Italy. Dam won at 12f in Ireland, and is half-sister to Quick Reaction (qv '95 Annual). FLAT (won for R. Hannon at 2 — all form for him; also for D. Chapman, bought for 2000) r18 w1 (8f) p2 (2nds); inc Sells. NH '95/7 and '99 (for G. Kelly; previously for J. White, bought for 26,000) r9 p0; pulled up final 3; Sell final. Dreadful for Jerry Kelly, but far from disgraced on most occasions in Points, although he was handicapped by bad jumping and by having to compete in Opens. Was still in contention when he made a bad blunder three out at Hornby Castle, and fell two out when second but held by Polar King at Witton Castle, where he was just in front of stablemate Vital Issue at the time. Tried blinkered in the past and in a visor on his most recent outing, and was normally tongue-tied in Points. Has the ability to spring a surprise if all went smoothly. *M.J. Brown — Sinnington.* 1030 (O), 1231 (O), 1325 (Cf), 1349 (O).

THATS DEDICATION (IRE) ..10-3.. 9 b.g. Zaffaran (USA) — Bridevalley (Deep Run) 2133u2p. Tall rangy. IRISH P-t-P '97 r1 p1 (½l 2nd to a subsequent Irish NH flat winner). P-t-P/HUNT CH '98 r9 w3 (Restricted, Members and Confined) p3 (2 2nds); and 4th thrice. Consistent in minor company, and has done well to win five races, but has benefited from some weak races, irresolute opposition and sensible placing. A sound jumper, and suited by a long trip in soft ground, but risked on a much sounder surface in the second half of the season, and appeared to go wrong at Folkestone. Always takes the eye in the paddock. Ridden in spurs, and acquired a tongue-strap in 2000. *D.C. Robinson — Mid Surrey F. (Marion Robinson).* 125 (M), 288 (CMod), 305 (Cf), 462 (2m7f110yH), 676 (Cf), 708 (O), 1108 (C), 1536 (3m2fH).

THATSFOREEL ..9-13.. 8 b.g. Scottish Reel — That Space (Space King) 1. Lengthy good-bodied home-bred brother to Hurdles winner, Cuillin Caper, and half-brother to Wrekin Lad, Piu Moto, Space Voyager, Freight King, Spacious Sovereign, Miswiskers and Safeasthat. P-t-P '98/9 r6 w2 (2m4f Maiden, and 3m2f Restricted) p2; 8th, and pulled up 1. Changed hands for a small fortune after winning twice when in the care of Heather Dalton in '98, but a major disappointment last year, and restricted to just one appearance in 2000. At least he made it a winning one, albeit by a scrambling neck at Eyton, but his health is clearly a major cause for concern. *C.J. Hitchings — Kyre (Andy Morgan).* 564 (I).

THEAIRYMAN (IRE) ..—.. 12 ch.g. Roselier (FR) — Turnpike Lass (Indigenous) up. Smallish compact half-brother to Irish Pointing and Chasing winner, Ted Said. Dam won unplaced Novice Point in Ireland. IRISH P-t-P '94 and '96/7 r14 w1 (Maiden) p0; pulled up 9, brought down 1, and fell/unseated 2. P-t-P/HUNT CH '98/9 (for Mr R.E. Evans) r3 w1 (Restricted) p0; pulled up 1 and unseated 2. Won gamely in mud on his Welsh debut, and can be effective at a lowly level, but only able to run four times since, and two of those were on the same day this year. Worth 9-13 at best, but clearly ailing, and may not get another chance to prove himself. *H.W. Lavis — Pembs.* 831 (M), 837 (I).

THE ALLEYCAT (IRE) ..10-6.. 10 b.g. Tidaro (USA) — Allitess (Mugatpura) 1p01u. Tall good-looking half-brother to Short List, Fiftysevenchannels (IRE) (both subsequent Chasing winners), Allezmoss and Mrs Blobby (IRE). Dam won 2 Irish NH flat. P-t-P '97/9 (for Mrs P.M. Shirley-Beavan & Mr J. Scott) r14 w3 (up to Confined) p8 (2nds, of 3 once); 4th of 5, and pulled up 2. Splendidly consistent in his first three seasons, and began 2000 with a ready success in his Members despite almost failing to negotiate the turn for home, but ran badly in holding ground next time and never went a yard on a perfect surface on his Hunter Chase debut subsequently. Redeemed himself with victory at rewarding odds at Morpeth next time, but his jumping of regulation fences got him into trouble again at Kelso, and Paul Robson was sent into orbit after a monumental blunder when leading five out. On the upgrade, and certain to win again if able to avoid errors, but a sound surface seems vital. Tried in a tongue-strap once in '98. *Mrs P.M. Shirley-Beavan — Jedforest (Simon Shirley-Beavan).* 107 (M), 1159 (I), 1335 (2m4f110yH), 1478 (I), 1591 (3m1fH).

THE ARCHDEACON (IRE) ..10-0.. 8 b.g. Mandalus — Best Of Kin (Pry) 1144. Lengthy half-brother to The Rural Dean (IRE) (qv). IRISH P-t-P '98 r6 p0 (pulled up 2, fell/unseated 2, brought down 1, and ran out 1). P-t-P '99 (for Mr P. Conlon & Miss P. Morris) r3 w1 (Maiden) p0; and fell 2. NH '99 (from D. Wintle's) r2 p0 (tailed off in Hdles). Seemed unable to avoid deep ground when failing to complete in Ireland, and is much happier on a livelier surface. Made an impressive return to action at Llanfrynach, before dishing out a four length beating to his sibling in a long Maisemore Intermediate, but again appeared not to handle the more testing ground on his last two appearances. Usually held up, and delivered late. Jumps quite well now considering his earlier disasters, and should be able to win again in the right conditions. *Miss P. Morris — Croome & W. Warwicks.* 485 (R), 897 (I), 1064 (3m2fCf), 1190 (Cf).

THE ARKLE BAR (IRE) ..7-8.. 8 b.g. Glacial Storm (USA) — Lucky Mistake (Averof) p3p. Close-coupled. Dam won 7f Sell, and won 4 Hdles (inc a Sell) and a Ch at around 2m. IRISH NH FLAT '98 r2 p0. IRISH NH '97/9 r5 p0; fell only Hunt Ch). IRISH P-t-P '99 r6 p4; fell 1. 33 lengths last on his only completion in 2000, but never seemed to be fit enough, and did not jump well first time out. *B.J. Kennedy — Essex F. & U. (Jim Ovel).* 88 (OMa), 317 (Mn), 760 (OMa).

THE BANDON CAR (IRE) ..9-6.. 8 b.g. Royal Fountain — Celia's Pride (Buckskin FR) 155474. Small light-framed. IRISH P-t-P '97 r1 p0 (fell). P-t-P '98/9 r5 p0 (refused 3, and fell 2). Had failed to complete in his previous six attempts, yet started a mere 5-1 on his reappearance in a 12-runner Maiden at Lemalla which he won by a wide margin having been left clear three out. Failed to land a gamble in his Members next time, and disappointed again when the subject of market support in a Flete Park Restricted subsequently. A thorough stayer who can handle deep mud, but has not impressed with his attitude either before or since winning, and remains liable to jumping errors. *Mr & Mrs R. Jones — Lamerton.* 312 (CfMa), 720 (M), 848 (R), 1256 (Inr), 1518 (R), 1639 (R).

THE BEE'S CASTLE (IRE) ..—.. 9 b.g. Carlingford Castle — Winterwood (Bargello) pfppu. Small lengthy half-brother to La Cotinga, Bavard Bay and Saville Beg, to jumping winner, Palosanto (IRE), to Irish Pointing and English Chasing winner, Try Next Door, and to Irish NH flat winner, Roborough. Has struggled alarmingly in both running and jumping, and is clearly the black sheep of the family. *E. Spain & P.J. Ikin — Fernie (Carol Ikin).* 235 (OMa), 437 (OMa), 905 (C), 1010 (CfMa), 1219 (OMa).

THEBETSONMARY ..9-13.. 8 gr.m. Le Solaret (FR) — Tom's Little Bet (Scallywag) 114. Rangy. Dam, half-sister to Tom's Little Will (qv '95 Annual), won 2m6f Hdle. Made a bright start to her career when easily winning a Maiden in heavy and when battling to a game neck victory in a Restricted, but a shade disappointing when 27 lengths last in her Members. Jumps well for a beginner, and can probably atone. *Mrs J. Mathias — S. Pembs.* 349 (CfMa), 484 (R), 1221 (M).

THE BIG FELLA (IRE) ..10-1.. 10 ch.g. Sandalay — Remindful (Bargello) 92. Big strong brother to Robsand (IRE) and Royal Arctic (IRE), and half-brother to The Caumrue (IRE). IRISH P-t-P '97/8 r9 w1 (7yo&up geldings Maiden) p4; pulled up 3. IRISH HUNT CH '98 r1 p0 (pulled up). P-t-P/HUNT CH '99 r7 w2 (Restricted and Intermediate) p1 (3rd); 4th, 5th, 6th, and pulled up 1. Won two severe stamina tests in '99, but only able to appear twice this February, and may have encountered trouble. Wore a visor for the first time when not discredited behind Inch Fountain on his most recent outing. Suited by deep ground. *R. Griffiths (The Big Fellas Partnership) — W. Salop (Peter Morris).* 156 (3mH), 370 (C).

THE BIG LAD (IRE) ..9-12.. 8 b.g. Montelimar (USA) — Amelioras Daughter (General Ironside) f4u431. Big rangy half-brother to Irish NH flat winner, Katie Fairy. Dam won 3 2m2f Hdles in Ireland. NH '98 (for T. McGovern) r1 p0 (pulled up). Sold Doncaster, March for 2200. Twice victim of clumsy errors and is basically a plodder, but was still too quick for the opposition in a weak Maiden at Clifton-on-Dunsmore (the eight length runner-up had finished a head in front of him on their previous encounter). Can probably pound on at his own pace for a long time, and may find a Restricted. *G.J. Smith — Quorn.* 400 (OMa), 593 (2m4fOMa), 696 (OMa), 1021 (2m4fOMa), 1270 (OMa), 1420 (OMa).

THE BISHOPS SISTER (IRE) ..9-5.. 9 b.m. Yashgan — Fatal Hesitation (Torus) p64. Small neat. Dam won 3 Irish Chses, 2-3m. IRISH P-t-P '97/8 r8 p0; pulled up 5, and fell/unseated 2. P-t-P '99 (for

Mr R. Mathias & Miss K. Guard) r5 w1 (Maiden) p1 (2nd); last, pulled up 1, and fell 1. Found it almost impossible to complete the course in Ireland, but showed improved form last year, and won a slowly-run Maiden at Bexhill on her penultimate outing. Had looked to have a stamina deficiency previously, and not better than last when tailed off three times in February this year. Seems to have suffered a setback. *Mr & Mrs P.V.M. Egan — Ashford V. (Gill Gladders).* 130 (CMod), 289 (Cm), 306 (R).

THE BOILER WHITE (IRE) ..9-3§.. 13 ch.g. Deep Run — Cill Dara (Lord Gayle USA) 5u045p. Leggy compact chaser who ran well in NH flat and jumping winner, Gimme Five, and half-brother to 2 Irish flat winners. Dam won 7 Irish flat, 10-16f, inc Irish Cesarewitch twice. IRISH NH '92/3 r2 p0. IRISH P-t-P '94 r2 w1 (6 plus Maiden) p1 (2nd). NH '94/6 r22 w4 (2 Hdles, 2m4f-2m6f, and 2 Chses, 2m4f-3m3f) p5 (pulled up before continuing for 2nd after numerous mistakes once). P-t-P/HUNT CH '97/8 r12 w1 (Ladies) p2; 7th, last pair 2, pulled up 2, and unseated 1. A former useful performer, but became disenchanted with racing a long while ago, and had gone two years without a win until beating a bad lot at Thorpe in '97. Ended the following season lame, and failed to beat a rival when exclusively tailed off on his comeback this year. Has been tried in headgear under Rules. *E.W. Froggatt — Meynell & S. Staffs (P. Froggatt).* 566 (L), 905 (C), 1086 (Cf), 1126 (L), 1253 (L), 1525 (L).

THE BOLD ABBOT ..9-12.. 11 b.g. Derring Rose — Canford Abbas (Hasty Word) 55524uuu443. Unfurnished half-brother to Druids Dream. NH FLAT r1 po (tailed off). NH '95 r2 p0 (pulled up 1). P-t-P '96/9 r31 w6 (up to Confined) p10 (8 2nds, beaten neck once, and last once); pulled up 2, and on floor 6. Has won five times for present connections, and proved a great ride for Sarah West, but rather below par in 2000, and only once beaten less than ten lengths when a fine five and three quarter lengths fourth to Last Option at Towcester. Subsequently got rid of the rider three times in succession, and can be clumsy, but his lack of consistency is now his main failing. *Miss S. West & J. Barnes — Mendip F. (Sarah West).* 101 (L), 354 (L), 581 (3mH), 731 (M), 802 (2m6fH), 1014 (3m5fL), 1237 (Cf), 1340 (3m1f110yH), 1473 (Cf), 1554 (Cf), 1625 (3m2f110yH).

THE BOMBERS MOON ..8-13.. 8 br.g. Lord Bud — Oakington (Henry The Seventh) 6R5. Tall strong home-bred half-brother to Hurricane Gilbert. NH FLAT '97 r2 p0 (tailed off). P-t-P '98 r2 p0 (fell 1, and brought down 1). NH '98 r2 p0 (pulled up 2). Sweats freely, and takes a strong hold, but shows a distinct lack of stamina, and beaten a minimum of 18 lengths to date. Has been weak and immature, and might be able to stay on better in future. *Mrs E.H. Heath — Cambs.* 438 (OMa), 1270 (OMa), 1423 (OMa).

THE BOREE LOG ..—.. 10 ch.g. Revolutionary (USA) — Morse Princess (Communication) ppp. Lengthy. P-t-P '99 r3 p0 (fell/unseated 2, and pulled up 1). Pulls hard for a mile, but compounds rapidly, and has yet to go more than two miles without mishap. At least the owner has decided to put himself through the mill again after last years experiences. *A. Davis — Quorn.* 55 (OMa), 1010 (CfMa), 1437 (OMa).

THE BUTCHER BOY ..9-11.. 8 ch.g. Broadsword (USA) — Annie'll Do (Horage) p322. Lengthy. Grandam, Anaglogs Daughter, was top-class Irish Chaser. IRISH NH FLAT '98 r1 p0. IRISH NH '97/8 r3 p0. Bought Doncaster, May for 2800. Tried to set the pace but made a string of alarming errors when favourite for his Pointing debut, and kept under an iron grip by David Easterby subsequently (to an embarrassing degree at Hornby Castle), but still failed to find any kind of rhythm at the obstacles and beaten a minimum of eight lengths. Disappeared after mid-March. Sent off at odd-on on his two most recent appearances, and those who have continued to throw money at him will hope he has gone for the chop. *Mrs P.A. Russell — Middleton.* 53 (OMa), 137 (R), 381 (OMa), 508 (CMa).

THECABBAGEFLINGER ..8-0.. 9 b.g. Puget (USA) — Queen Of The Nile (Hittite Glory) uupfp3. Workmanlike half-brother to King Of Cairo and Mr Goonhilly, to flat winner, Burnditch Girl, and to successful Hurdler, Among Islands. NH '99 (for P. Eccles) r1 p0 (pulled up in Sell). Bought Malvern, July for 850. Went a mile or less when Young Flinger in three Maidens (got rid of the JJ and RR varities), and is a hard puller, but seemed to concentrate better when fitted with blinkers on his last two starts, and inherited 30 length third at the final fence at Holnicote. Whoever named him surely consigned him to a life of mediocrity. *T. Wheeler — Quantock (Laura Horsey).* 11 (OMa), 212 (CfMa), 520 (OMa), 1099 (OMa), 1263 (OMa), 1469 (OMa).

THE CAFFLER (IRE) ..9-11.. 11 b.g. Mandalus — Creagh (Sky Boy) 33u334p. Big strong attractive. IRISH P-t-P '95/6 r4 w1 (5yo&up Maiden) p0; pulled up 2. P-t-P/HUNT CH '97/9 r15 w1 (Restricted) p5 (4 2nds); and fell/unseated 3. A winner on firm and in yielding, but a weak finisher, and has been unable to score in his last 18 attempts. Beaten a minimum of 12 lengths in 2000, and though his jumping remains competent his chances of winning again are remote. Has always been remarkably hyperactive in the preliminaries, and now gets taken to post early. *Major General C.A. Ramsay — Berwicks.* 43 (Cf), 358 (M), 714 (C), 912 (Cf), 1121 (I), 1366 (I), 1576 (Cf).

THE CAPTAIN'S WISH ..9-11.. 10 ch.g. Infantry — The Lady's Wish (Three Wishes) f4466. Tall rangy. NH FLAT Nov '95 r1 p0. NH '96/8 (for D. Nicholson) r12 w1 (2m1f Hdle) p5 (inc 2 Chses); 4th

4, including when demoted from 3rd once. Gave several good displays under Rules and won in May '96, but was absent for 20 months after March '97, and revived in Hunter Chases after another 16 months off. Not only suffers from Infantry legs (apparently), but additionally dibilitated by a major wind problem. Ran tubed in 2000, and also had a tongue-strap on his first three outings. Beaten a minimum of 20 lengths (when last at Ascot), but would probably have been a competent performer had he not been handicapped. *M. Chamberlain — Bicester with Whaddon (Gary Brown)*. 685 (2m5fH), 799 (2m4f110yH), 800 (3m110yH), 1335 (2m4f110yH), 1444 (2m5fH).

THE CHAIN GANG ..8-11.. 8 b.g. Baron Blakeney — Delvin Princess (Aglojo) 6. Owner-bred half-brother to Prinzal. P-t-P '99 r3 p0 (unseated 2, and pulled up 1). A poor jumper in his first season, but made no noticeable errors and kept up for 2m4f in a decent Maiden at Didmarton on his return. Was not seen again, but in a yard which seems to be going places, and might be worth keeping an eye on if he returns. *P.C. Froud — O. Berks (Matt Hazell)*. 391 (CfMa).

THE CORINTHIAN (U) ..8-5.. 10 b.g. Fire Rocket — Cathy's Clown (unknown) 5. A Greek who came bearing no gifts in his Members. *Miss E. Hancock — Sir W.W. Wynn's*. 525 (M).

THE CRAZY BISHOP (IRE) ..10-10§.. 13 b.g. The Parson — Pixelated (Mon Capitaine) 6u45r111. Rangy half-brother to Hold Your Horses (IRE), to jumping winner, Candy Tuft, and to Irish Pointing winner Buck Related. IRISH NH FLAT '92/3 r7 w2 p3 (2nds). IRISH NH '93 and '95/8 (often worn blinkers and tongue-strap) r35 w5 (2m Hdle, and 4 Chses, 2m-2m5f) p7; ran out 1. IRISH P-t-P '99 r6 w3 (Opens) p3 (2 2nds; and head and 25l 3rd). HUNT CH '99 (for Mrs D.E. Quinn) r1 p0. A prolific winner in Ireland, but took a while to gel with Ben Shaw, and his supporters did their money on two occasions when he was backed from tens to threes. Made amends on his last three starts, and landed a touch at Bitterley in the process, but has his quirks, and the rider sometimes does not carry a whip. Likes to help force the pace, and can handle any going. Ben Shaw did well after a shaky start, and should continue to progress under the watchful eye of the Daltons. *Mrs C. Shaw — Wheatland (Andrew Dalton)*. 32 (MO), 294 (O), 369 (O), 476 (Cnr), 702 (Cf), 987 (Cf), 1087 (MO), 1273 (O).

PLATE 130   1303 Cotley Hunt Members: The Criosra (Miss T. Newman), 1st, leads Mel (Miss K. Eames), 2nd, at the last   PHOTO: Brian Armstrong

THE CRIOSRA (IRE) ..9-12.. 12 gr.g. Carlingford Castle — Whisky Path (Warpath) 3143. IRISH NH FLAT '93 r1 p0. IRISH NH '93/4 r7 p0 (4th, last and pulled up in Chses — tailed off all three). IRISH P-t-P '93 and '96 r5 w1 (Maiden) p1 (3rd); pulled up 1. P-t-P '97/9 r14 w1 (Members) p5 (3 2nds); unseated 2, and pulled up 2. Ended a long losing run when winning his three-finisher Members in '99, and readily maintained his grip on the race this year, but very one-paced in competitive races, and was a most undeserving favourite at Larkhill subsequently. Jumps safely, and can handle most types of going. Has been tried in blinkers, but not since '98. *Miss N.J. Grant — Cotley (Christine Derryman).* 654 (I), 1303 (M), 1599 (I), 1651 (I).

THE CROOKED OAK ..10-1.. 9 ch.g. Fearless Action (USA) — Life Goes On (Pharly FR) pu11515. Workmanlike quite attractive. Dam is half-sister to Smart Performer (*qv* '95 Annual). NH FLAT '96 (debut for L. Cottrell) r3 p1 (2nd). NH '97/8 (from late J. Birkett's; previously for N. Twiston-Davies) r9 p2 (3rds in Chses, beaten 19-33*l*, inc Sell). Basically outclassed under Rules including in Hunter Chases, but is unbeaten in minor Points for the much improved Gareth Thomas. Completed a double in holding ground at Eaton Hall (two finished in the Maiden), and made light of a simple task in his Members. Stays very well, and seems suited by smaller fences. Can score again. *K. Thomas — V. of Lune H. (Stuart Currie).* 155 (3m4f110yH), 384 (2m3f110yH), 528 (OMa), 782 (R), 1025 (3m110yH), 1148 (M), 1559 (3m110yH).

THE CROPPY BOY ..10-2.. 9 b.g. Arctic Lord — Deep Cut (Deep Run) f1p1. Angular half-brother to Son Of A Gunner. NH FLAT '96/7 r4 p0. NH '97/9 (for J. Neville) r5 p0. A keen sort who likes to try and make all, and succeeded in poor contests in softish at Maisemore and on firm at Woodford. Jumped to the left in both, and faded after mistakes in between. Sweats up and has acquired two paddock handlers, and unseated in the preliminaries and went over a fence loose on another occasion. Never stands many outings, but is quick enough to score again. *Mrs N.S. Sharpe — S. Herefords.* 744 (R), 892 (OMa), 1088 (R), 1488 (R).

PLATE 131   1488 Berkeley Restricted: The Croppy Boy (A. Wintle), 1st, leads L to R partially obscured Poet's Song (T. Stephenson), pu, Ashmead Rambler (Miss A. Bush), 4th, Fasgo (Miss P. Gundry), 3rd, and More People (Julian Pritchard), 2nd   PHOTO: Bill Selwyn

THE DANCING PARSON ..—.. 14 b.m. The Parson — Quayville (Quayside) pp. Small close-coupled half-sister to Distant-Port (IRE) (*qv*). IRISH NH FLAT r4 p0. IRISH NH '93 r1 p0 (pulled up in cross-country Ch). IRISH P-t-P '92/4 (usually blinkered) r24 w5 (inc hat-trick; inc Open) p10; pulled up 3, and fell/unseated 4. P-t-P '95/7 r5 p0; 4th, 5th, 7th, 8th, and pulled up 1. A regular prize winner in Ireland, but only able to appear seven times in six years for present connections, and has pulled up in her last three. Regained blinkers at Garnons. *T.B. Brown — Cotswold V.F. (Geoff Barfoot-Saunt).* 357 (Cm), 447 (Cm).

THE DEVILS KANDI ..8-5.. 12 b.g. Devil To Play — Kandilove (Kabale) p. Tall lengthy owner-bred brother to Sandi Devil. P-t-P '98/9 r3 p1 (remote last of 3); and pulled up 2. Made a late start to his Pointing career, and has made just four half-hearted appearances in three years. Yet to beat a rival, and is simply not a racehorse. *Mrs S.J. Smith — Meynell & S. Staffs.* 1526 (OMa).

THE DUST BUSTER ..8-10.. 8 ch.g. Primitive Rising (USA) — Potterway (Velvet Prince) ppuf5ru. Tall lengthy brother to Primitive Way, and half-brother to Keep A Secret (*qv*). P-t-P '99 r6 p0 (last, pulled up 4, and fell 1). A slovenly jumper, and has only beaten one rival in 13 starts, but often given some very negative rides, and seems only to happy to lope round at the back. It would be interesting to see if he really is as bad as his record suggests, and putting a strong jockey up might be quite revealing. *A.R. Trotter — Berwicks.* 114 (OMa), 363 (CfMa), 501 (2m4fOMa), 664 (2m5fOMa), 909 (2m4fOMa), 1083 (2m4fOMa), 1500 (OMa).

THE DYKE LOUPER ..9-4.. 8 br.m. Beau Ideal — Batty Betty (Royal Fountain) fp223. Small light. Dam, half-sister to 3 Pointers, including Madame Beck (*qv* '99 Annual), won Maiden and placed 5 (inc a Ch) for the Threadgalls. Grandam, My Mimosa, won 5 Points and placed 13 (inc 2 Hunt Chses). P-t-P '99 r4 p1 (short-head 2nd); 4th twice, and pulled up 1. Unlucky to be short-headed at Corbridge last year when Sandy Forster dropped her hands, but beaten a minimum of eight lengths in 2000, and has not progressed. Still inclined to make mistakes, and does not get the trip when conditions are testing. *J. Threadgall — Lauderdale.* 425 (CfMa), 719 (CfMa), 1083 (2m4fOMa), 1163 (OMa), 1431 (OMa).

THE EARLY BIRD ..—.. 10 b.m. Bold Owl — Monsoon (Royal Palace) p. Half-sister to Hurdles winner, Willy Willy. Dam won 2m6f Hdle. P-t-P '96 r3 p0 (pulled up 3). NH FLAT '96 r1 p0. NH '98 (for P. Monteith) r3 p0 (inc last and pulled up in Chses). Figured prominently for 2m3f at Alnwick, but ultimately pulled up, and was not seen again. Appears most infrequently, and has yet to show any concrete form. *Mrs V. Nyberg — Lauderdale.* 189 (OMam).

THE EARTH MOVED (IRE) ..10-2.. 7 b.g. Brush Aside (USA) — S T Blue (Bluerullah) 2f1. Half-brother to Fundy (IRE) (*qv*). P-t-P '99 r4 w1 (Maiden) p2; and pulled up 1. A beaten favourite on three occasions since losing his maiden tag, but given an ultra-confident ride by Anthony Honeyball when successful at Badbury Rings on his latest appearance, and looks to have a bright future ahead though both his campaigns have finished quite early to date. Appears to have eradicated most of his jumping errors, and the latest clear round should have boosted his confidence further. *R.M. Penny — Mendip F. (Richard Barber).* 13 (R), 144 (R), 330 (R).

THE FINAL OPTIMIST ..—.. 7 b.m. North Col — Wildly Optimistic (Hard Fact) pp. Big owner-bred half-sister to Truly Optimistic (*qv*). Has made far too many mistakes when tailed off to date, and the owner must be finally optimistic that she has run out of hopelessly pessimistic horses (the four children of Wildy Optimistic have contested a total of 33 Points and lost the lot). *Mrs R.C. Hayward — Warwicks.* 1067 (3m2fR), 1194 (OMa).

THE FIRST ONE ..9-7.. 8 ch.g. Henbit (USA) — Oh So Ripe (Deep Run) bf324. Tall rangy half-brother to Good Job. P-t-P '99 r1 p0 (pulled up). Almost out for the count following two trips to Larkhill, but managed three completions subsequently though his supporters were much the poorer twice. Beaten between six and 15 lengths when placed, but has proved a weak finisher, and the appearance of his sire in his pedigree rings a tiny warning bell. Has the ability to win if he is willing to oblige. *Mrs B.M. Longman — Blackmore & Sparkford V. (Richard Barber).* 12 (OMa), 60 (OMa), 518 (2m4fOMa), 875 (2m4fOMa), 1308 (OMa).

THE FLUTER ..—.. 10 ch.g. Cruise Missile — Queenlet Ella (Kinglet) upr. Dam was placed in 2 Points; but pulled up in 5 of 5 attempts when joining Mr Gladwin in '92. P-t-P '97 (for Mr W.E.O. Gladwin) r1 p0 (6th). Shown a hint of ability on his debut, but none when picking up his career three years later under a novice who even managed to fall off between fences once. *I.F. Harbour — V. of Aylesbury (Sue Harbour).* 249 (CfMa), 433 (OMa), 514 (OMa).

THE FLYING DRAGON ..—.. 7 b.m. Cruise Missile — Dragon Lass (Cheval) p. Stocky sister to Woodram Lass and Stede Quarter, and half-sister to jumping winner, Bonnie Dundee. Dam, 3rd in Hdle, fell in her only Point. Her lack of experience was plain when she only went a mile at Peper Harow. *R.T. Dench — Ashford V.* 1396 (OMa).

THE FLYING PHANTOM ..9-11.. 10 gr.g. Sharrood (USA) — Miss Flossa (FR) (Big John FR) 3. Lengthy unfurnished. 5400 2yo. FLAT r32 w2 (7-14f) p12; one run at Longchamp. NH '97 (for M. Tompkins) r4 w1 (2m Hdle) p1 (23*l* 3rd of 5). Successful on his Hurdling debut, but came a crashing fall in the Supreme Novices at the Cheltenham Festival next time, and no good since. Made a brief resumption after three years on the side-lines, and was not disgraced when 24 lengths last in an Open, but possibly failed to get the trip. His earlier connections suffered from delusions of grandeur, and although he never scored on the flat after '94 he competed in the Derby (was 20th), The Chester Cup, and The Cesarewitch of '97 in which he was last of 31. A grey horse with half a brown nose (but that's not where the saying comes from). *Mrs F. Denniff — Grove & Rufford.* 441 (O).

THE FROSTY FOX (IRE) ..9-7.. 10 gr.g. King Luthier — No Breeze (Strong Gale) 2u35u331. Lengthy. P-t-P '97/8 r7 p4 (3 2nds); pulled up 1, and fell/unseated 2. Five times a beaten favourite, and placed on eight occasions before he finally got off the mark in the penultimate race of the season, but might have been fortunate as his nearest pursuer broke down approaching the last. Races prominently, but missed the '99 season, and has become a weak finisher since. Remains prone to errors, and needs to improve to make any impact in Restricteds. Has two handlers. *Mrs L.A. Syckelmoore — Wilton.* 73 (CfMa), 213 (CfMa), 329 (CfMa), 520 (OMa), 881 (OMa), 1308 (OMa), 1598 (OMa), 1675 (OMa).

THE GADFLY ..9-12.. 9 br.g. Welsh Captain — Spartan Imp (Spartan General) 832431. Workmanlike half-brother to Spartan Dancer. NH FLAT '97 r1 p0 (136/ last). NH '97/8 r6 p0 (7th of 8, last 4 times, and pulled up in Hdles). P-t-P '99 r1 p0 (pulled up). Useless under Rules, but has found his level in weak Points, and dominated an elders Maiden at Laleston on his most recent appearance. Wore blinkers and had the benefit of Jamie Jukes for the first time this year, but recorded a faster time than the Restricted winner, and would have prospects in that type of race himself in 2001. *D.L. Evans — Pembs (Graham Lavis).* 483 (R), 831 (M), 1300 (OMa), 1454 (OMa), 1615 (R), 1661 (OMa).

THE GLOW (IRE) ..9-8.. 13 b.g. Glow (USA) — Full Choke (Shirley Heights) 9pp3pp24. Compact good-looking half-brother to a flat winner in Italy. Dam won at 2m2f. NH FLAT '92 r2 p1 (3rd). NH '92/7 (blinkered 3) r25 w4 (2m4f Hdle, and 3 Chses, 2m4f-2m5f) p9; twice refused at final fence at Kempton, when clear once. P-t-P '99 r6 w2 (Confineds) p1 (2nd); 4th, and fell 2. A useful performer in his youth, and present connections did well to revive his fortunes last year, but most disappointing in 2000, and when he found a race bad enough to get into contention he appeared to shirk the issue. Regained blinkers in his last two outings, and looks to have had enough. *Miss J. Goddard — W. Street/Tickham (Trevor Crawford).* 130 (CMod), 238 (O), 305 (Cf), 571 (M), 706 (Cf), 830 (Cnr), 1169 (Cf), 1398 (Cf).

THE GREEN FOOL ..10-2.. 14 ch.g. Southern Music — Random Thatch (Random Shot) 7332p3. Lengthy good-bodied half-brother to Coolreny (IRE) and Randomar (IRE). IRISH NH FLAT '91 r3 p1 (3rd). NH '91/6 and '98/9 r51 w5 (4 Hdles, 2-3m, and 2m5f Ch) p14. P-t-P/HUNT CH '96 and '98/9 (for Mr V. Thompson) r9 p3 (3rds, last twice); fell/unseated 2, and pulled up 3. Genuine and did well until going lame at Sedgefield in '95, and has always taken care at the obstacles so it was no surprise he would prove to be an ideal mount for an inexperienced rider. Carried Harry Humble into the frame on four occasions, but very one-paced nowadays, and decent horses have nothing to fear. Worth training with his Members in mind next year as he would have skated this years renewal. Wears a cross-noseband, and has been tried in blinkers. *H.W. Humble — Percy.* 359 (Cf), 419 (Cf), 717 (Cf), 912 (Cf), 1078 (Cf), 1446 (3m1fH).

THE GREENKEEPER (IRE) ..—.. 8 b.g. Beau Sher — Hurricane Hattie (Strong Gale) ppp. Sturdy. P-t-P '98 (for Mr S.G. Edwards) r1 p0 (pulled up). NH '99 (for P.J. Hobbs) r1 p0 (pulled up). Not without ability, and can take a strong hold, but seems to have a hole in him somewhere, and finds it impossible to complete the course. *Mrs N.G. Smyth — Exmoor (Lucy Roberts).* 147 (OMa), 730 (I), 956 (OMa).

THE GREY BAY ..8-4.. 9 gr.m. Totem (USA) — Tenez La Corde (Boco USA) pp0u. Strong sister to Hurdles winner, Totem Fole. Dam, half-sister to Prewelli (qv '96 Annual), was 4th, and pulled up (broke down) in Points. NH '99 (for Mrs M. Reveley) r7 p0 (inc Sells). A disappointing favourite in her final Hurdle, and has been unable to redeem herself at long odds in Points. Jumped poorly once. *Mrs V.B. Munro — Cleveland (Graham Russ).* 137 (R), 375 (Cf), 627 (OMa), 803 (MMa).

THE GREY FRIAR ..—.. 12 gr.g. Pragmatic — Misty Lough (Deep Run) p. Tall half-brother to Howard bred The Handsome Friar (qv). NH FLAT Nov '95 r2 p1 (3rd). NH '96 (from Miss H. Knight's) r5 p2 (2nds). Leading when he broke a leg after two miles at Buckfastleigh. M.J. Howard — S. & W. Wilts (Sarah Waugh). 658 (R).

THE GREY SHADOW ..—.. 9 gr.g. Zambrano — Kara Star (Whistlewood) p. Half-brother to Don't Argue. Dam was placed in 2 Points. Emerged from the shadows at eight and hinted at ability, but proved a ghostly presence and not seen again. *M. Edwards — W. Somerset (C. White).* 738 (OMa).

THE HANDSOME FRIAR ..—.. 10 b.g. Nearly A Hand — Misty Lough (Deep Run) pp. Owner-bred half-brother to Blakeneys Run (dam of Russells Runner, qv '00 Annual), The Grey Friar and Mister Tinker. P-t-P '98/9 r5 p1 (remote last of 3); unseated 1, and pulled up 3. Tubed before he ever ran, and wears a tongue-strap, but still useless, and regularly tailed off after showing early speed. Not worth the bother again. *M.J. Howard — S. & W. Wilts (Sarah Waugh).* 1131 (OMa), 1468 (OMa).

THE HAPPY MONARCH (IRE) ..9-7.. 9 gr.g. Roselier (FR) — Larrys Glen (Laurence O) 321uu5. Rangy half-brother to Villains Brief (IRE) (qv). NH FLAT Nov '97 r1 p0. NH '98/9 (for Mrs A. Bowlby; previously for Mrs J. Pitman) r6 p1 (distant last of 3 in Ch); pulled up, fell and unseated in other Chses. Sold Ascot, June for 3000. Consistently bad under Rules, was beaten about 20 lengths in his first two Maidens, but found a suitable opportunity at Whitwell, where he got up near the finish to snatch a Maiden by a head. Clumsy since, and may find it rather a struggle to collect a Restricted. *R. Tate — Bilsdale.* 54 (OMa), 798 (OMa), 1004 (OMa), 1028 (R), 1230 (R), 1326 (R).

THE HATCHER (NZ) ..9-12.. 13 br.g. Captain Jason (NZ) — Pulka (NZ) (North Pole) 556168. Tall rangy. NH FLAT Oct '94 r1 p0. NH '94/5 and '98/9 (blinkered 3; for D. Gandolfo; previously for N. Hawke; won previously for Mrs J. Renfree-Barons, when owned by Mrs Hatcher) r12 w1 (2m6f Hdle) p2 (Chses); broke blood vessel final. Won on his Hurdling debut in December '94, but later went missing for three years, and has obviously had a few physical problems. Jumps safely in Points, and sprang a shock when 25-1 in a Confined at Mollington (the opposition appeared to flounder in the heavy ground), but a plodder who only had a total of four behind him otherwise.

Gave the impression of hating firmish ground once. *R.J. & Mrs B.A. House — V. of Aylesbury (Sue Harbour).* 4 (O), 74 (CCf), 243 (Cf), 428 (Cf), 788 (Cf), 1015 (4mO).

THE HAZEL HARRIER (IRE) ..9-12.. 8 ch.g. Denel (FR) — Golden Echo (Golden Love) p51u54fu6. Plain lengthy. Dam won 2m4f Ch in Ireland. P-t-P '98/9 r7 p2 (2nds); 6th, pulled up 2, unseated 1, and brought down 1. NH FLAT '99 r2 p0. Moderate and a particularly shoddy jumper, but good enough to outspeed three other finishers to win his Members. Beaten 17 lengths in his best effort since, but his kamikaze style of jumping would be enough to make most jockeys emigrate. Tried blinkered on his penultimate appearance, but only reached the fifth; a blindfold would probably have better results. *A.J. Lockwood — Sinnington.* 137 (R), 169 (OMa), 276 (M), 397 (L), 505 (L), 689 (R), 1000 (R), 1326 (R), 1348 (Cf).

THE HERBIVORE (IRE) ..—§.. 12 b.g. Lancastrian — Lean Over (Over The River FR) 2rpr9. Big strong. NH FLAT Feb '95 r1 p0. NH '95/8 r9 p3 (3rds in Chses); inc pulled up 4, and refused. NH Jun '00 r1 p0 (9th in 2m7f110y Nov Hdle: *a bhnd, t.o 9*). Should be a theoretical certainty for a Maiden and had two subsequent scorers behind him when he was eight lengths second to a decent animal at Higham, but is far too keen to refuse, and did so when 4-5 and a close third but beaten at the final fence next time. Sometimes tongue-tied, and blinkered on his three most recent appearances. No longer warrants a rating. *M.J. Roberts — E. Sussex & Romney Marsh.* 23 (OMa), 709 (OMa), 984 (OMa), 1104 (R).

THE HOBBIT (IRE) ..10-6.. 8 ch.g. Mister Lord (USA) — Sustentation (The Parson) 611233. Tall rangy. P-t-P '98/9 r8 w3 (Maiden, Restricted and Intermediate) p2 (3rds); pulled up 2, fell 1. An out-and-out stayer with a good record when he completes, and relished the testing conditions when winning back-to-back Opens in February. Looked dangerous at the last when tried over four miles at Larkhill, but has been unco-operative in the past, and did not find as much as anticipated on the run-in. Showed he could handle much faster ground on his Hunter Chase debut which was run in under six minutes, but would have appreciated more of a stamina test, and worth persevering with over regulation fences as he is safe if sometimes slow over the obstacles. Did not appear to enjoy being blinkered once in '99. *Mrs S. Humphreys — Cattistock (Richard Barber).* 10 (O), 160 (O), 313 (O), 454 (4mMO), 954 (MO), 1433 (3mH).

THE HOLLOW (IRE) ..8-4§.. 11 b.m. Phardante (FR) — Fairy Hollow (Furry Glen) p65. Workmanlike sister to Larkshill (IRE). IRISH P-t-P '94 r1 p0. NH '94 r1 p0. P-t-P '96/8 r10 p0 (5th twice, 6th, pulled up 5, refused 1, and fell 1). Missed '95 and '99, and has looked suspect since falling five out when holding every chance on her Pointing debut. Blinkered once in '98. *Miss A. Barnett — Ludlow (Geoff Evans).* 528 (OMa), 1197 (OMa), 1669 (OMa).

THE HONEST POACHER (IRE) ..9-9.. 11 b.g. Saronicos — Shanaway (Moss Court) 5p. Tall half-brother to El Bae, and to Irish NH flat winners, Brush The Flag (IRE), and Take Me Home (latter also won jumping). Dam won 2 Irish Points. P-t-P '95 and '97 (for Mr F.M. Green) r2 w1 (Maiden); and fell 1. NH '99 (for H.D. Daly) r4 p1 (2nd in 3m1f Chse); fell, pulled up and last. Never saw a two-finisher Maiden at Llanvapley under a certain R. Johnson on his debut, but never saw a racecourse in '96 or '98, and though not disgraced on his comeback this year was subsequently pulled up in similar company. Had the ability to be a decent performer, but not the constitution to go with it. *Mrs S. Guild — Sir W.W. Wynn's (Pat Powley).* 567 (R), 864 (R).

THE H'PENNY MARVEL (IRE) ..9-7.. 11 br.g. Sexton Blake — Casacello (Punchinello) 3. Good-topped lengthy like half-brother to Casabuck, Lucycello and Ri-Na-Rithann, to Irish Pointing and smart jumping winner, Wolf Of Badenoch, and to Irish NH flat and Hurdles winner, Mars Playfair. Dam won a Bumper and 2 Hdles (2m-2m2f and placed 13 in Ireland. IRISH P-t-P '97 r4 w1 (5yo&up unplaced Maiden) p0; pulled up 1, and fell 1. NH '97 r3 w1 (3m Nov Ch) p0; pulled up 1, and fell 1. P-t-P/HUNT CH '98/9 (for Mr S.G.B. Morrison) r5 p0 (4th, and last 4). Amazingly lucky when winning at Worceseter in '97, but except for being a steady jumper has little going for him, and has been tailed off in all five Points, from a very early stage in the latest. Has never scored more than four outings in a season. Blinkered once in '98. *G.G. Tawell — Oakley.* 509 (M).

THE HUSSEY'S KING (IRE) ..10-1.. 7 b.g. King's Ride — Deep Rouge (Deep Run) 1. Sold Tattersalls (Ireland), Nov '98 for 7826. Sent off favourite for a 16-runner Maiden at Witton Castle, and survived a bad mistake three out to justify the support when getting up near the line. The fastest of the three divisions by ten seconds, and it will be interesting to see him again. *Mrs J.D. Dillon — Rockwood H. (Stephen Wiles).* 1329 (OMa).

THE ISLANDER ..8-8§.. 8 b.g. Derrylin — Lindisfarne Rose (Deep Run) 4p2p. Tall strong. 15,500 4yo. NH FLAT '98 r3 p0. NH '98/9 (for G.B. Balding) r4 p0 (pulled up only Ch). Sold Malvern, May for 3000. Regularay tailed off at long odds under Rules, and did not look keen in the chase. Not fluent in Points, and although he plodded into the frame twice he continues to look disinterested. *R. Barrow & Mrs J. Long — Quantock (Tim Long).* 70 (OMa), 207 (OMa), 641 (CfMa), 934 (OMa).

THE KILLALOE RUN ..9-5.. 10 ch.m. Insan (USA) — Thatchville (Thatch USA) 565. Workmanlike lengthy home-bred half-sister to a flat winner, and to successful Hurdler, Prince Palacio. Dam won 2 flat, 5-6f. NH FLAT '95 r2 p1 (2nd). NH '96 (for M. Jefferson) r2 p0. Beaten favourite on no few than three occasions under Rules (at 8-11 on final start), and kept hanging left when second in a Bumper. Resumed four years later to plug round safely in Points, but beaten a minimum of ten lengths, and is clearly very moderate. *Miss L. Carr — Braes.* 808 (OMa), 1230 (R), 1329 (OMa).

THE KIMBLER ..10-1.. 13 ch.g. Lir — Kimberley Ann (St Columbus) 3p. Very small light-framed Young-bred brother to Belitlir, Lady Lir, Saint Joseph and Lirkimalong. Dam, half-sister to Harringworth and 6 other Pointers, was placed in 3 very poor Points (last after remounting once). Grandam, Dark Parting, was 4th in big field for Oakley Maiden on only start. Great-grandam, Dark Rate, won 3 Points. NH '93 and '94 r3 p0 (fell/unseated at first in Hdle and Ch, and pulled up in Hdle). P-t-P '93/9 r26 w4 (inc 2 Confineds) p11 (7 2nds; and remote 3rd once); failed to finish 8 (unseated 2, and carried out 1). A game battler on his day, and finished with a rare flourish when almost snatching a modest second on his belated reappearance, but does not appear to be the soundest horse in training, and has stood on average just three outings in each of the last six years. Last won in '97, and seems to be running on borrowed time. *B.R.J. & Miss S. Young — E. Cornwall (Sue Young).* 1174 (L), 1636 (Cf).

THE LAST MISTRESS ..9-8.. 14 b.m. Mandalus — Slinky Persin (Jupiter Pluvius) p5443p. Light sparely-made half-sister to Irish jumping winner, Kinky Lady. Dam won 2 flat (10f-12f) and 2m Hdle in Ireland. IRISH NH FLAT '91 r2 p0. IRISH NH '91/2 r13 p2 (2nds in Hdle — beaten neck, rider lost irons, and Ch). NH '93, '96 and '98 r6 p0. P-t-P/HUNT CH '94/8 r23 w3 (up to Intermediate) p9 (6 3rds; inc 2 Hunt Chses); pulled up 7. A fair performer on a sound surface at best, but badly out of form in '98, and only once beaten less than 20 lengths on her return when last in a slowly-run Members. Has been tried in a tongue-strap, and sometimes goes to post early. Usually has short campaigns, and will be pushed to get into the shake-up at 14. *J.J.E. Price — Llangibby.* 479 (Cf), 597 (Cf), 817 (M), 1053 (O), 1402 (MO), 1492 (O).

THE LAST SHOUT (IRE) ..9-0.. 8 b.g. Yashgan — Apia Sunshine (Simbir) pppppp25. Lengthy workmanlike. Dam won 3 Irish flat, 12-16f. IRISH NH '98 r1 p0. IRISH P-t-P '98/9 r9 p3; pulled up 5. Bought Doncaster, Aug for 1400. Can show early speed, but a poor jumper, and has been pulled up on no fewer than 12 occasions. Often stops very rapidly, so is either ungenuine or (probably more likely) breaking blood vessels. Blinkered on his sixth most recent appearances. Did manage to end the season with a couple of completions at Dingley, but could not get Dont Tell The Wife to break sweat, and the efforts are meaningless. *P.J. Millington — Fernie.* 122 (OMa), 234 (OMa), 372 (CfMa), 411 (OMa), 514 (OMa), 588 (OMa), 790 (OMa), 1502 (M), 1668 (OMa).

THE LEGEND OF ZEB ..9-3.. 11 gr.g. Remezzo — Chorley Seven Springs VII (unknown) 2. Big rangy. P-t-P '99 (for Mr M.A. Connors) r4 p1 (last of 2); 4th, and unseated 2. Out of control when owner-ridden, but has done better for Sue Sharratt, and jumped boldly in the lead for a long way at Eaton Hall on his only appearance in 2000. Takes a strong hold, and probably does not stay three miles, but could probably win a small race especially if he had a regular go at it. *Miss J.L. East & T. Peake — W. Salop.* 527 (OMa).

THE MARMALADE CAT ..8-3.. 12 ch.g. Escapism (USA) — Garrison Girl (Queen's Hussar) 2. NH '93 and '96 r3 p0; carried out, pulled up and fell. P-t-P '98 (ran as Marmalade Cat, U) r1 p1 (2nd). Has jumped impeccably when twice runner-up in his Members, but the owner has been comprehensively outridden in the closing stages on both occasions. *P. Browse — Easton H. (Neil King).* 603 (M).

THE MERRY NUN (IRE) ..—.. 12 ch.m. Lancastrian — Katebeaujolais (Politico USA) p. Rangy attractive half-sister to Loslomos (IRE) and Burgundy Bob (IRE), and to Irish NH flat winner, River Of Wine. NH FLAT r1 p0. NH '96 r1 p0 (pulled up). P-t-P '97/8 r4 p0 (pulled up 2, and fell/unseated 2). Maintained her miserable non-completion record over jumps when pulling up at Mollington in January. Two outings a year is a hectic schedule for her. *Miss S.A. Loggin — Bicester with Whaddon (Mervyn Loggin).* 76 (CCfMa).

THE MILLMASTER (IRE) ..9-3.. 10 b.g. Mister Lord (USA) — Rolling Mill (Hardboy) 54f263. Tall lengthy. NH '96/7 r9 p0 (pulled up in 2 of 4 Chses). P-t-P/HUNT CH '98/9 r11 w1 (Maiden) p3 (2 2nds); last pair 3, unseated 1, and pulled up 1. Made all and scored unchallenged when blinkered for the first time at Ampton in '98, but usually capitulates, and only able to manage three placings in modest Restricteds since. Changes yards on a regular basis, but usually has two paddock handlers. *M. Keane — Puckeridge (Mick Clark).* 27 (I), 96 (I), 687 (2m6f110yH), 1038 (R), 1333 (3mH), 1379 (R).

THE MINISTER (IRE) ..10-5.. 12 br.g. Black Minstrel — Miss Hi-Land (Tyrant USA) p1522. Lengthy brother to Hurdles winner, Burgundy Boy. Dam won at 8f in Ireland. IRISH P-t-P '93 r3 p0 (4th, pulled up, and unseated). NH '93/8 r12 w2 (2m-2m5f Chses) p0; pulled up 5. P-t-P/HUNT CH '99 r6 w1 (Ladies) p1 (2nd); 4th, fell/unseated 2, and pulled up 1. Successful twice in Ladies races on sound surfaces '99/00, but can be remarkably clumsy at the fences and jumped appallingly when odds-on at Brocklesby Park this year. Never ran very often under Rules, but has been more prolific in the current yard, and could win again when conditions are right providing his erratic fencing holds up. *H.L. Thompson — Cleveland (Tina Jackson).* 280 (L), 505 (L), 795 (L), 806 (L), 1029 (L).

THE NAUGHTY VICAR ..8-7§.. 11 ch.g. The Parson — Kylogue Daisy (Little Buskins) 629. Tall good-bodied brother to Chasing winner, Parsons Boy, and half-brother to Loose Wheels, to jumping winner, General Command (IRE), and to Irish NH flat and English Hurdles winner, Farmer's Cross. NH FLAT '95 r1 p0. NH '95/7 r4 p0 (invariably tailed off). P-t-P '99 (for Mr P. Riddick) r14 p4 (3 2nds); 4th, last pair 3, pulled up 4, unseated 1, and ran out 1. Remarkably busy in '99, but confined to just one outing in each of the first three months of this year, and could not manage to finish within 30 lengths of the winner. Has shirked a struggle in the past, and is led in now having forfeited ground at the start on many occasions previously. Aptly named, and only divine intervention will enable this crafty cleric to score. Often blinkered. *Mrs R. Pocock — Taunton V. (Carroll Gray).* 72 (OMa), 353 (CfMa), 520 (OMa).

THE NOBLE REBEL (IRE) ..8-0.. 10 b.g. Welsh Term — Bell Of St Mark (Belfalas) u74637p. Workmanlike. IRISH P-t-P '98/9 r5 p1 (3rd); pulled up 1. IRISH NH FLAT '97/8 r3 p0. IRISH NH '97 and '99 (blinkered final) r9 p1 (50l 3rd); 12th of 13, pulled up and fell in Chses. A very experienced maiden who has consistently shown himself to be devoid of ability, and not better than last in 2000. Was beaten about one and a half fences on the couple of occasions he made the frame. *D. Ward (The Rebellers) — Staintondale (Andrew Pennock).* 51 (OMa), 281 (OMa), 798 (OMa), 809 (OMa), 1229 (M), 1353 (OMa), 1580 (OMa).

PLATE 132   798 South Wold Open Maiden 8yo&up: Not So Prim (S. Swiers), 1st, leads The Way North (N. Kent), ur, The Noble Rebel (A. Pennock), 4th, and the grey Pearly's Song (K. Needham), fell, another 'The' The Happy Monarch (Mrs F. Needham), 2nd, is just visible behind

PHOTO: Roy Parker

THE OTHER EYE (IRE) ..8-13.. 8 br.g. Looking For — Tip The Gold (Harwell) p45. Lengthy unfurnished half-brother to Saffron Flame (IRE) (*qv*). IRISH NH FLAT '98/9 r3 p0. Bought Doncaster, May for 5000. Moderate so far and beaten about 20 lengths when completing, but did at least have more behind him than in front on his final start. Not seen since March. *M. Jackson — Middleton (Jinty Monteith).* 168 (OMa), 436 (OMa), 793 (CfMa).

THE OTHER HALF ..9-12.. 9 ch.g. Alias Smith (USA) — Water Eaton Gal (Legal Eagle) 35u142. Tall strong-topped half-brother to Setting Sail (*qv*). NH FLAT '98 r2 p0. NH '98/9 r3 p0 (for L. Lungo, blinkered 2) r13 p3 (inc distant 3rd in Ch); pulled up and fell in other Chses. Made the most of an easy opportunity when winning a bad Maiden in soft at Tranwell, and can finish thereabouts in weak company, but basically ungenuine. Regained blinkers on his four most recent outings. May be pursuaded to collect a Restricted if he does not work too hard. *Mrs G. Robinson — Morpeth (Pauline Robson).* 45 (OMa), 188 (OMa), 719 (CfMa), 1082 (CMa), 1162 (R), 1363 (R).

THE PARISH PUMP (IRE) ..10-2.. 13 br.g. Bustineto — Ladies Gazette (London Gazette) 30p. Smallish lengthy fired half-brother to Our Boreen and Artists Gazette, and to an Irish Chasing winner. Dam won 2m Hdle in Ireland. IRISH NH FLAT r2 p0. IRISH NH '92's r8 p2 (inc 3rd in 4m1f La Touche Cup); 4th and fell in Hunt Chses. IRISH P-t-P '92 and '95/6 r6 w3 p2. P-t-P/HUNT CH '97 and '99 r7 w5 (inc 3m1f Hunt Ch and 2 Opens) p0; and fell/unseated 2. Unbeaten when completing in two previous campaigns for Carrie Ford, but turned over at 1-3 on his reappearance, and was never going well prior to pulling up at Flagg Moor on his final start. Requires constant nursing and soft ground because of his frail legs, but clearly not right in 2000. A determined front-runner with bags of stamina at best, but will test connections skill to the full if a comeback is planned. *R. Burgess — W. Salop (Carrie Ford).* 590 (L), 921 (2m6fH), 1253 (L).

THE PARLOUR MAID ..9-2.. 7 ch.m. St Ninian — Super Sue (Lochnager) pp1. Half-sister to Hurdles winner, Super Nomad. Dam is sister to Lochnaver (qv '98 Annual), and half-sister to 6 other Pointers. Great-grandam, Society Queen, won a Point. Bought Doncaster, Aug '98 for 800. Punters considered her inferior to four rivals in a bad youngsters Maiden at Corbridge, but she proved keen to serve and ploughed through the holding ground to score in a time of 7min20s. The runner-up was so exhausted he could hardly complete the course and the form is meaningless, but still a baby, and may be able to prove herself in a proper contest. *T.W. Scott — Border.* 713 (R), 977 (CfMa), 1165 (OMa).

THE PEELER (IRE) ..9-8.. 8 b.g. Orchestra — Miss Nancy (Giolla Mear) 21. Half-brother to Ruperts Choice (IRE). IR 25,000 3yo. NH '99 (for L. Lungo) r2 p0. Sold Doncaster, May for 2600. Lightly raced so far, but followed an encouraging second with a win in a Maiden at Alnwick, in which he profited from the strong riding of Wilson Renwick. Looks a competent jumper, and should at least have place prospects in Restricteds. *R.J. Kyle — Jedforest.* 425 (CfMa), 914 (CfMa).

THE PORTSOY LOON ..9-7§.. 14 b.g. Miami Springs — Glittering Gem (Silly Season) pp. Tall. NH FLAT r2 p0. NH '92/5 r13 w1 (3m Ch) p0. P-t-P/HUNT CH '96/9 r14 p10 (4 2nds; and inc 3rd of 4 once, and last of 3 twice); last 1, and pulled up 3. Once able, but a total scutter, and avoids hard work whenever a struggle looms. Placed in 10 of his 16 Points, but his outings have dwindled to a trickle in recent years, and was never going well in 2000. Regained blinkers on his final start. Went lame in '99, and a runner at 14 seems odds against. *M.W. Baker — Coakham Bloodhounds (Mrs L.P. Baker).* 983 (Cf), 1167 (CMod).

THE QUAKERS WAKE (IRE) ..8-6.. 9 b.g. Henbit (USA) — La Croisette (Nishapour FR) prp56. Smallish well-made half-brother to Irish NH flat and English Hurdles winner, Caoimseach (IRE), to flat winner, Ivory's Of Radlett, and to Irish Hurdles winners, Father Michael and Follow The Leader (latter also won Irish NH flat). IRISH P-t-P '99 r5 p1 (16/3rd); pulled up 4. Can show a little speed, but does not stay and gets very tired, and was beaten at least 25 lengths with just one behind him in 2000. Not worth training again on the evidence to hand. *P.H. Morris & M. Tomlinson — W. Salop (Peter Morris).* 371 (R), 569 (OMa), 1323 (OMa), 1412 (OMa), 1634 (OMa).

THEREANDBACK (IRE) ..9-1§.. 8 ch.g. Camden Town — Difficult Forecast (Rheingold) 3. Tall rangy brother to Irish NH flat winner, Kentish Town. P-t-P '98/9 (for Mr T.R. Beadle) r5 w1 (Maiden) p0; pulled up 2, and fell/unseated 2. Looked promising when successful as a five-year-old, but ended '98 lame, and has managed just two appearances since. Went in fits and starts at Thorpe Lodge, but still had every chance at the second last only to down tools dramatically. There seems every chance that he has not got over his problems, mentally if not physically. *F.K. Baxter — Quorn.* 120 (CR).

THERE BE DEMONS (USA) ..—.. 6 b.g. Devil's Bag (USA) — Krisalya (Kris) p. Strong half-brother to flat winners, Egoli, Crystal Cavern and Comic Hill. Dam won over 10f. 35,000y. FLAT (for G. Wragg) r3 p0. Finished five and a half lengths fourth to the Smart Diktate at Newmarket, but was last in bandages on his final flat outing. Took a strong hold and jumped badly in the early stages of a Maiden, and ran very green until pulling up with a broken blood vessel. Might have been useful, but his name appears to say it all. *Mrs A. Hays — Thurlow (Neil King).* 1291 (OMa).

THE RED BOY (IRE) ..10-4.. 7 ch.g. Boyne Valley — River Regent (Over The River FR) 124. Workmanlike. Looked smart when quickening impressively in a 2m4f Maiden at Cottenham on his debut, but outjumped consistently in the closing stages by Rise To It when two lengths second there next time, and had an 11 week break before he reappeared for a disappointing fourth. Was the first winner for Kevin Edmunds (32), but he has not really shone in his handling of the horse since, and it would be interesting to see if Simon Sporborg could turn the tide. Stays on gallantly in the closing stages, has a lot of potential if he returns to his best. *C.H. Sporborg — Puckeridge.* 21 (2m4fOMa), 179 (R), 1287 (R).

THEREWEARETHEN (USA) ..9-8.. 8 ch.g. Danzig Connection (USA) — Up To Juliet (USA) (First Balcony) 572p. Sturdy compact half-brother to 7 winners of 48 races in USA. Dam won 8 races and $220,660 in USA. P-t-P '98/9 (for Mrs S.J. Watson) r4 w2 (Maiden and Members) p0; last 1, and pulled up 1. Got his career off to a flying start when successful in two modest events at Lydstep, but dismal in four of five attempts for current connections, and only seems to go when there is mud up to his knees. Still has the ability to land a Restricted, but a wet Spring will be vital to his requirements. Strong handling also seems a must. *A.R. & Mrs S.J. Humphrey — Dunston H. (Sarah Watson).* 86 (R), 239 (R), 321 (R), 416 (R).

THE RIGHT ATTITUDE (IRE) ..9-10.. 11 b.g. Lancastrian — Hopeful Biddy (Deep Run) 153. Tall rangy angular brother to Irish Pointing winner, Mrs Giggs, and half-brother to Inspector Morse and Queen Biddy (IRE). IRISH NH FLAT '95/7 r4 p0. IRISH P-t-P '97 r2 p1 (3rd); and pulled up. P-t-P '98 (for Mr D.J. & Mrs C.B. Clapham) r5 w1 (Maiden) p2 (2nds, of 3 once); and pulled up 2. NH '98 (for D.G. Duggan) r1 (pulled up). Clumsy and a weak finisher in '98, but made no errors and stuck on best of all when narrowly winning a slow Restricted at Didmarton under a strong ride from Adrian Wintle. Stayed on too late when third in a very slowly-run event at Bitterley subsequently, but has prospects in similar company in 2001. Suited by waiting tactics. Wears a cross-noseband. *C.S. Packer & Miss V. Hanks — Curre (Vicky Hanks).* 392 (R), 600 (I), 1090 (I).

THE RISING BUCK (IRE) ..7-9.. 9 b.g. Buckskin (FR) — Najdowski (Deep Run) p. IRISH P-t-P '97/8 r7 p2; pulled up 4. IRISH NH '98 r1 p0 (last in Ch). P-t-P '99 r4 p1 (remote last of 3); last 1, refused 1, and pulled up 1. Showed some ability in Ireland, but yet to beat a rival in this country, and only emerged for his Members in 2000. Jumps safely, but appears not to stay, and presumably has a major fault. *L.A.E. Hopkins — N. Salop.* 1195 (M).

THE RUM MARINER ..9-13.. 14 gr.g. Julio Mariner — Decorum (Quorum) 1p4s1u5. Tall half-brother to Cursneh Decor, Rethgil, Darleyfordbay, Tot Of Rum and Polly Buckrum. Dam won 2 Points and placed 3 for Alan Rogers. IRISH P-t-P '95/6 r2 p0. P-t-P/HUNT CH '94/9 r40 w8 (inc 3 Confineds; hat-trick '95) p12 (9 2nds; inc 3 Hunt Chses); failed to finish 16 (fell/unseated 4). A fair Pointer on his day, and perked up for the liaison with Richard Mathias and Candy Thomas to push his winning tally into double figures in 2000. Often needed a race in the previous yard, but fought back from what looked a hopeless position to win going away on his reappearance, and followed up at Brampton Bryan on his second appearance of the day in a two-finisher Ladies. Likes to force the pace, and capable of jumping well, but just as likely to take a fence by the roots. Suited by a right-handed track, and is effective on extremes of going. A likeable old horse despite all his foibles, and it was good to see him back in the winners enclosure at 13. *T.A. Rogers — Radnor & W. Herefords (Richard Mathias).* 862 (Cf), 987 (Cf), 1343 (3m110yH), 1544 (Cf), 1547 (L), 1626 (3m1f110yH), 1665 (L).

THE RURAL DEAN (IRE) ..10-1.. 10 ch.g. Good Thyne (USA) — Best Of Kin (Pry) p1u22c. Lengthy brother to NH flat and Hurdles winner, Exterior Profiles, and half-brother to The Archdeacon (IRE), and to Irish Pointing and English Chasing winner, The Reverend Bert. Dam won a Maiden in Ireland. IRISH NH FLAT '96 r3 p0. IRISH NH '96 r2 p0 (16th of 17 and pulled up in Hdles). IRISH P-t-P '97 r1 w1 (5&6yo unplaced Mdn). Won an Irish Maiden in their sixth, they only jumped 11 fences(!), and scored again a Llanfrynach just two outings but three years later. Put up a game display, as he did when chasing home his half-brother The Archdeacon at Maisemore, but is sometimes let down by his jumping. May be able to register another success with a fluent round. *A.K. Leigh — Llangibby.* 273 (R), 483 (R), 741 (Cf), 897 (I), 1051 (Cf), 1299 (I).

THE SECRET GREY ..9-1.. 10 gr.g. Rakaposhi King — Locketts Lane (Mandamus) 5f32. Lengthy well-made half-brother to Lockrymer (fell in both his Points) and Laurel Park (destroyed in his only Point). Dam is half-sister to 5 Pointers. NH FLAT '96 r2 p0. NH '96/8 (blinkered 3) r14 p4 (Chses to 2m2f). P-t-P '99 (for Mr A.J. Morley) r3 p1 (3rd); last, and pulled up 1. Placed on seven occasions, but rarely tried at much beyond the minimum trip under Rules, and patently does not stay in Points. Has been lightly raced in recent years. *K. Coe — Essex F. & U.* 24 (OMa), 131 (OMa), 551 (OMa), 759 (OMa).

THE SHY PADRE (IRE) ..9-4.. 12 br.g. The Parson — Kenodon (Menelek) p22u2up5. Tall rangy unfurnished brother to Hurdles winner, Capincur Eile, and half-brother to Irish Pointing and jumping winner, Florida Light. NH FLAT '94 r3 p1 (2nd). NH '95/8 (visored once; for I. Semple; previously for M. Pitman, bought for 3800; previously for Mrs J. Pitman; previously for R. Lee) r17 p5 (3 Hdles, and 2 Chses). Certainly shy of winning, and is now the veteran of 28 defeats. Placed on nine occasions and beaten six lengths and five lengths in seconds in Points, but does not seem to have the will to get his head in front at the right moment. Occasionally dwelt with under Rules, and virtually refused to race once (was performing badly latterly). Might yet get there at 12, and it could be an idea to concentrate solely on elders Maidens. *J.D. Townson — Pendle Forest & Craven.* 171 (O), 278 (R), 400 (OMa), 816 (OMa), 964 (OMa), 1154 (3m2fH), 1343 (3m110yH), 1480 (OMa).

THE STUFFED PUFFIN (IRE) ..9-6.. 9 b.g. Cataldi — Proud Fairy (Prefairy) 586u7p3. Smallish compact half-brother to a Hurdles winner, to NH flat winner, Belsprit Lady (dam of Imatoff, *qv* 2000 Annual), and to successful Irish Pointer, Queen Boadicea. NH FLAT '96/7 r3 p0. NH '97 r6 p0. P-t-P '98/9 (for Mr W.E. Wilde) r6 w1 (2m5f Maiden) p1 (2nd); pulled up 3, and fell 1. Maintained a tremendous gallop when winning a 2m5f Maiden at up ton last year, but could not see out the full distance, and the new yard has been at pains to hold him up. Ran in a nosenet on his first two starts this year, but remains a non-stayer, and his best effort came in a race taking little more than six minutes on his final appearance. Dick Baimbridge excels with other peoples cast-offs, but it rarely works the other way.

Has broken a blood vessel on at least one occasion. Wears a cross-noseband. *C. Brake — Taunton V.H.* 559 (R), 729 (R), 932 (R), 1061 (R), 1309 (R), 1467 (R), 1551 (R).

THE TIDE RACE ..8-8.. 13 b.m. Politico (USA) — Brox Treasure (Broxted) 2. Sister to Just Donald, and half-sister to Chasing winner, Jay'm. Great-grandam, Hunter's Cairn, won 2 Points. P-t-P '97 and '99 r5 p0 (6th, pulled up 3, and ran out 1). Incredibly slow, and easily brushed aside by Bucket Of Gold in her Members. Did not race until she was nine, and an outing has always been a rarity. *G.H. Dook — Grove & Rufford (Tony Walker).* 1069 (M).

THE UGLY DUCKLING ..9-8.. 11 br.g. Lir — Dule Darkie (Bay Spirit) 33314344f. Small sparely-made. Dam only finished in one of seven Points, when 35 lengths third of four. P-t-P '96/7 r17 p9 (3 2nds, of 3 twice and last once; 6 3rds, of 4 thrice); pulled up 3, unseated 1, and ran out 1. Placed nine times '96/7, then disappeared for three years, but came back in a flurry of eiderdown to break his duck at Kilworthy. Usually makes some of the running, but remains a weak finisher, and may have to get used to making the frame in Restricteds for the time being. Jumps well, and his second fence fall on his most recent start was most uncharacteristic. *K.C. & J.C. Heard — Eggesford (Pauline & Tony Geering).* 159 (CfMa), 311 (CfMa), 538 (OMa), 723 (CfMa), 849 (R), 1042 (R), 1176 (R), 1389 (R), 1517 (R).

THE UGLY GUNNER ..9-3.. 8 b.g. Gunner B — My Aisling (John De Coombe) p253u3. Strong short-backed half-brother to Agile King (*qv*). NH FLAT Jan '99 r2 p0 (tailed off). NH '99 (for D. McCain) r6 p0 (tailed off in Sell, and when last in Ch). Bought Malvern, July for 2000. Has benefitted from a drop to Maidens, and could possibly have lasted home had he not unseated at the final fence at Cursneh Hill, but is regularly a weak finisher who has become disappointing (was backed from 14s to 9-2 once, and joint-favourite next time). His stable were out of form after their triumphant year in 1999, and perhaps he can score if their fortunes revive in 2001. *L. & Miss T. McCurrich — Worcs (Theresa McCurrich).* 264 (OMa), 703 (OMa), 1068 (3m2fOMa), 1194 (OMa), 1278 (OMa), 1565 (OMa).

THE WAY NORTH ..8-9.. 12 b.g. Northern Game — Good Way (Good Apple) ppp. Good-topped owner-bred half-brother to Kerrisdale, to Hurdles winner, Aban Way, and to Chasing winner, My Skiway. Dam is half-sister to dam of My Prides Way (*qv*). P-t-P '96 and '98/9 r9 p1 (3rd); pulled up 3, unseated 1, and ran out 1. Has shown a little ability, but never runs much, and tailed off and pulled up thrice in 2000. Ran tubed in '98, but not since, and has no realistic chance of winning. *Mrs A.C. Wakeham — Middleton (B.J. Gillies).* 399 (OMa), 798 (OMa), 1032 (OMa).

THE WHOLE HOG (IRE) ..10-4.. 12 b.g. Cataldi — Beeston (Our Babu) 3563. Good-topped half-brother to NH flat and jumping winner, Esha Ness, and to 3 winners over jumps in Ireland. Dam won at 6f in England, and won 2m2f Hdle in Ireland. IRISH NH '94/5 r2 p0. NH '95/8 r19 w5 (2m7f-3m3f Chses) p4 (inc 2nd in Sell before wins). HUNT CH '99 r1 p0 (pulled up). Formerly a fair staying Chaser who went to pot in '98, but staged something of a comeback in 2000, and ran passably on three occasions. Needs a sound surface, but often a sketchy jumper of regulation fences, and has run tongue-tied '99/00. Might still win a Point, but remains too suspect to place much faith in. *G.W. Briscoe — W. Salop.* 33 (Cnr), 150 (3mH), 302 (3mH), 1409 (O).

THINKABOUTTHAT (IRE) ..9-0.. 12 br.g. Roselier (FR) — Rossian (Silent Spring) 5pp554. Workmanlike brother to Touring-Turtle (IRE) and Hurdles winner, Rosey Boy (IRE) and half-brother to Golden Croft. IRISH P-t-P '94/6 r9 p0; pulled up 5, and fell 1. P-t-P/HUNT CH '97/9 r23 w2 (Maiden and Restricted) p6 (3 2nds; and inc last of 3 twice); pulled up 3, and unseated 3. Was James Muir's first winner back in '97, but hopeless since the middle of the following season, and only once better than last '99/00. Always went best fresh, and soon trained off. Still front runs for up to 2m4f, but soon gives up the ghost, and is not worth putting back into training again. *J.F.W. Muir — Lauderdale.* 108 (I), 183 (CCf), 660 (Cf), 714 (C), 973 (I), 1424 (M).

THINKERS EFFORT (IRE) ..—.. 8 b.g. Glacial Storm (USA) — Fiona's Waltz (General Ironside) p. IRISH P-t-P '98/9 r5 w2 (Adjacent Mdn, and Winners of two) r1 (3rd); pulled up 1. NH '99 (from H. Daly's) r1 w1 (2m7f Hdle). Very effective in mud and had a 50 per cent winning record to '99, so it was rather a surprise to see him returning to Points in 2000. Apparently had an immediate setback in January. *G. Myers & E. Fowler — Worcs (Martin Oliver).* 34 (MO).

THINKING TWICE (USA) ..10-1.. 12 ch.g. Kris — Good Thinking (USA) (Raja Baba USA) fu4R2243. Smallish sturdy fired half-brother to 2 winners in Ireland. Dam won at 7f in Ireland. FLAT r13 w2 (7-12f, inc £5299 at Newmarket) p3 (3rds). NH '92/3 and '95/7 r22 w4 (2m-2m5f Hdles; one at Punchestown) p5 (inc 3rd of 4 only Ch). P-t-P/HUNT CH '98/9 r9 w2 (Ladies) p2; last 2, pulled up 1, and unseated 2. Highly talented as a youngster and won more than £50,000 over Hurdles alone, but unfortunately went doggy, and acquired blinkers latterly. Has slight stringhalt and required a tie-back operation in his youth, but still capable of fair efforts in Points providing he goes right-handed. Becoming clumsy over big fences, and ought to give Hunter Chasing a miss. Unlucky to clash with Slew Man and Well Armed in April, but gave them both a race, and could still pick up a weak Ladies race if the opportunity arose in 2001. *J. Chaffey (The Thinking Partnership) — Silverton (Gordon Chambers).* 152 (3m1f110yH), 383 (3mH), 402 (O), 725 (L), 877 (L), 1045 (L), 1444 (2m5fH), 1638 (L).

THINK POSITIVE (IRE) ..10-1§.. 9 b.g. Black Minstrel — Royal Bonnet (Beau Chapeau) 213. Brother to an Irish jumping winner, and half-brother to Chasing winner, General James, to Irish Chasing winner, All In The Game (IRE), and to Irish NH flat winner, Closutton Express (IRE). Dam is an unraced half-sister to Cheltenham Gold Cup winner, Davy Lad. P-t-P '98/9 r8 w1 (Maiden) p1 (2nd); 5th, unseated 1, and pulled up 4. Returned from a nine week absence to record his second soft ground success, but an appallingly a fortnight later, and seems unable to string two decent performances together. A thorough stayer, but moody with it, and cannot be relied upon to produce anything like his rating. *G.C. Maundrell — Berks & Bucks (Claire Weller)*. 164 (R), 1042 (R), 1283 (I).

THIRKLEBY SKEENA ..8-10.. 10 br.m. Marching On — Thirkleby Kate VII (Bivouac) pu. Workmanlike half-sister to Dubalea and Lasting Charm. NH '97/8 r7 p0 (inc Sell). P-t-P '99 r2 p1 (2nd of 3); and last. Can go a good gallop, and finished in front of a subsequent winner when second at Hutton Rudby in '99, but does not appear to stay three miles, and her 2000 campaign was over in February. Stands her racing badly, and may have a problem. *P.J. Dennis — Hurworth*. 133 (CCfMa), 282 (OMa).

THIS IS MY LIFE (IRE) ..10-0.. 12 ch.g. General View — Bluemore (Morston FR) 6. Lengthy half-brother to 4 flat winners (2 in Ireland, including Another Flyer, and one in Spain). IRISH FLAT '92/5 r22 w2 (10-16f) p4 (2nds, inc dead-heat). IRISH NH '93 and '95 r4 w1 (2m Hdle) p0. NH '97/9 (2 wins for Miss K. Milligan, bought for 5000; 2 wins previously for C. Brooks) r22 w4 (2m-2m2f Chses) p4. Sold Doncaster, Nov for 500. The winner of seven races on good or firmish ground, and able to score as recently as July '99 when he collected a £4241 prize. Only beaten a head in a race worth £3764 the previous month, so it was obvious that something had gone alarmingly wrong when the latest connections were able to pick him up for a mere 500gns. Stood one outing and not disgraced, but the ground at up to 2m2f was probably too far, and now the wheels seem to have come off good and proper. Formerly tongue-tied, and has been a very erractic jumper who fell or unseated six times, and was famously 'schooled' by Richard Guest at Perth (he threw his jockey's licence at the stewards, but has since rescinded the decision, and great success has followed). *R. Bailey — Aldenham H.* 684 (2m4fH).

THISTLEKICKER (IRE) ..—.. 9 b.g. Mandalus — Miss Ranova (Giacometti) fp3. Small light-framed brother to Greatest Friend (IRE). Dam is half-sister to Jody's Boy (*qv* '95 Annual) and Ra Nova. NH FLAT '98 (first two for M. Bradstock) r3 p0. NH '98 (for N. Hawke) r3 p0 (Sells); ran out at first once. Sold Doncaster, Nov '98 for 1000, and resold Ascot, Feb for 1450. NH May '00 (from D. Thomson's) r2 p1 (3rd in 2m2f Nov Hdle: *mists in rr, hdwy 3 out, one pce last*; and pulled up in 2m4f110y Mdn Hdle: *a bhnd, t.o & pu 2 out*). Regularly tailed off, and fell three out and winded in his only Point, but showed ability for the first time every when third at 50-1 in a Hurdle. Seems likely to stick to them, but will need to prove that it was not a fluke. *Mrs J. McGregor — S. Durham*. 973 (I).

THOMAS CROWN (IRE) ..9-10.. 9 b.g. Last Tycoon — Upward Trend (Salmon Leap USA) up2p4p. Compact half-brother to Hurdles winner, Mellow Master. dam won 5 Irish flat, 8-10f (4 listed races and a Group 3, when smart at 3). FLAT (wore tongue-strap; for N. Walker; previously bought for R. Hannon) r8 p0. NH '97/9 (visored 1; wins for D. Williams; previously for M. Bosley, bought for 650) r27 w2 (Hdle and Ch, both 2m6f) p11 (inc 6 Sells prior to wins; pulled up at Waregem and Pardubice. NEWMARKET TOWN PLATE '99 p1 (3rd). Can still show flashes of ability and was 15 lengths second in a bad Ladies at Badbury, but sometimes jumps right and may have trouble staying, although it could be just the veteran rider running out of puff. Occasionally wears a tongue-strap. *Mrs J.V. Wilkinson — Portman*. 67 (L), 522 (L), 765 (L), 885 (L), 1622 (L), 1673 (L).

THORNBIRD ..9-2.. 7 b.m. Thornberry (USA) — Some Value (Some Hand) ppp. Workmanlike. Dam is half-sister to Merrington and Holsworthy. Pulled up in Maidens, and could do with jumping better. *D. Bluett — N. Cornwall (Karen Heard)*. 158 (CfMa), 539 (OMa), 1565 (OMa).

THOR'S PHANTOM ..9-4.. 8 ch.g. Weldnaas (USA) — La Carlotta (Ela-Mana-Mou) pf3. Sturdy. Day-bred brother to Hurdles winner, Fastini Gold. FLAT r4 p0. NH '97 (from M. Usher's) r1 p0. Rather headstrong at present, but has shown some ability, and fell three out when leading narrowly at Dunthrop. The horse who claimed eight lengths second that day was 15 lengths behind him when he finished ten lengths third over 2m4f at up ton, and he may be able to score provided he can stay the extra half mile. *Miss D.J. Day & Mrs J. Cartwright — Heythrop (Fran Marriott)*. 194 (CfMa), 1021 (2m4fOMa), 1360 (2m4fOMa).

THREE B'S ..—.. 11 b.m. Baron Blakeney — Bealsmead (Rugantino) p. Sister to Little Buster and half-sister to Captain Beal, Lady Beal and Miss Beal. Dam won Maiden and placed 6 for Mrs Drury ('very moderate indeed, and often tailed off since winning a very bad race in '79'). Grandam, Bibbernette, was poor last of 3 in Maiden (also disqualified from 3rd once). P-t-P '97 r1 p1 (last of 3). Beaten out of sight when making her debut in '97, and emerged from her prolonged spell of inactivity to pull up after 1m2f at Penshurst. Born to be useless, and has lived up to expectations. *Mrs G. Drury — O. Surrey & Burstow (Peter Broad)*. 828 (OMa).

THREE MONROES (IRE) ..8-13.. 8 ch.g. Boreen (FR) — Superfine (Tiepolo II) ppuup4222. Lengthy. IRISH P-t-P '98/9 r7 p2; pulled up 4, and ran out. IRISH NH FLAT '99 r1 p0. Bought Doncaster, Aug for 2400. Did not gel with Mark Munrowd and was tailed off last when finally achieving a completion at the sixth attempt, but has done a bit better for Tim Stephenson when beaten a maximum of 12 lengths in three seconds. Invariably had every chance half a mile out or later in them, but is a very weak finisher, and may still have a mountain to climb if he is to score. Frequently attracted hefty market support in Ireland, where he was equally frustrating. *Miss E. Tweed — N. Ledbury (Mike Bevan).* 21 (2m4fOMa), 55 (OMa), 123 (OMa), 341 (CfMa), 616 (CMa), 990 (OMa), 1085 (M), 1277 (OMa), 1413 (OMa).

THREE OF CLUBS (IRE) ..9-7.. 12 b.g. Roselier (FR) — Calyx Pit (Pitpan) p. Tall good-looking half-brother to Hurdles winner, Henry Vill (IRE), and to Irish Pointing winner, The Moderator. NH FLAT '93 r1 p0. NH '94/5 r7 p3 (15/ 2nd in Hdle, and 25-19/ 3rds in Chses). P-t-P/HUNT CH '99 (for Mr R.W. Dilliway) r5 w1 (Maiden) p0; pulled up 2, and fell 2. Showed ability under Rules, and won a Maiden at Ampton in impressive style, but has performed like a physical wreck otherwise, and failed to complete in Points. Only managed one outing in the new yard, and seems permanently flawed. *D.F. Donegan — Mid Surrey F. (Miss V. Park).* 980 (R).

THREE POTATO FOUR ..10-7.. 14 b.g. Pablond — Capelona (Mon Fetiche) 1172. Heavy-topped quite attractive brother to Ime Not Bitter and Fair Caprice, and half-brother to Celtic Capri, Elvercone, Elver Season (dam of Sparkling Elver *qv*) and Elver Panto, and to Hurdles winner, Capeli Cone. Dam, 3rd in Nov Hdle, won 6 Points (inc dead-heat) and 2 Hunt Chses (3m2f-4m) and placed 13. NH '98 r3 p0 (2m7f110y-3m3f Chses). P-t-P/HUNT CH '93/6 and '98/9 r21 w4 (inc Open) p14 (8 3rds, inc 4 Hunt Chses); pulled up 2, and fell 1. Rather one-paced, but a most reliable jumper, and has gained a prize in all but one of 22 completions. Won two Ladies races taking well over seven minutes convincingly before running poorly at Bangor, but put up his best effort to date in the Fraser Cup at Cartmel on his final appearance when chasing home Whatafellow (had been two lengths in '98, and 14 lengths third last year). Better than ever in 2000, and there seems no reason why he cannot win again at 14. *Sir John Barlow — Cheshire.* 590 (L), 904 (L), 1559 (3m110yH), 1601 (3m2fH).

THREE SAINTS (IRE) ..10-3.. 12 b.g. Rising — Oh Dora (Even Money) 3122. Rangy half-brother to an Irish NH flat winner. Dam won 2m Hdle in Ireland. IRISH NH FLAT '95 r2 p1. NH '95/9 (blinkered last 4; for H. Daly; won previously for late T. Forster) r12 w1 (2m5f Ch) p2 (inc 3rd in Hdle). Finished in front of Mulligan when three quarters of a length second in an Irish Bumper, and won a Chase in heavy March '96, but was absent for 21 months after February '97, and gave poor displays under Rules subsequently (pulled up in two of his final three outings). Returned to form in Points, and was suited by the long trip and holding ground when beating another ex-Forster horse in his Members, and also performed very creditably in all three placings. One-paced, and four outings constitutes a busy year for him. *W.G. Dutton — Sir W.W. Wynn's.* 334 (O), 525 (M), 781 (Cf), 1149 (Cf).

THUNDERBIRD ..—.. 9 b.m. Funny Man — Carlton Valley (Barolo) puu. Rangy half-sister to Carlton Brae. Dam, half-sister to Chatterley, Prince Carlton, Carlton Bridge, Seventh Valley and Royal Battle, won Maiden and placed 5 (raced latterly for Alex Harvey). Grandam, Non Such Valley, fell in 3 Points. NH FLAT Feb '97 r1 p0. NH '97/8 (for A. Harvey) r4 p0 (inc pulled up 2 and fell at first in Hdles). Has come to a Thunderbird stop in six of seven attempts over jumps, and although she was just in front when losing the rider approaching five out in the latest (bandaged) she immediately disappeared again. *H.R. Hobson — Puckeridge.* 20 (OMa), 97 (OMa), 606 (OMa).

THURLES PICKPOCKET (IRE) ..10-4.. 10 b.g. Hollow Hand — Sugar Lady (Dalsaan) 11323. Tall rangy half-brother to Irish NH flat winner, Monksaan (IRE). P-t-P '96/9 r13 w3 (Maiden, Members and Restricted) p6 (5 2nds, remote last once); last, pulled up 2, and fell/unseated 3. Has improved for the switch to Ladies races, and won twice in the space of a week, responding to Sam Hodge's urgings to get the better of Cache Fleur on the second occasion. Finished behind that rival on ground softer than ideal when third to Spring Gale subsequently, but was not disgraced behind Cittadino at Garthorpe. Consistent in second-class Opens, and has made the frame in all 15 completions and could improve further if he became more fluent. *Miss J.S. Stevens — E. Anglian Bloodhounds (George Cooper).* 84 (L), 95 (L), 319 (L), 546 (L), 939 (L).

TIBS EVE (IRE) ..8-9.. 10 b.g. Buckskin (FR) — Laurenca (Laurence O) 538p. Workmanlike brother to Whats Your Problem and Ballilaurenka (IRE), and to Irish Pointing winner, Glenabow, and half-brother to NH flat winner, Commanche Law (IRE). P-t-P '98 r3 p1 (3rd); unseated 1, and pulled up 1. Beaten 12 and 20 lengths when third in Maidens two years apart, and has twice been sent off favourite, but stands his racing badly and has tended to make far too many mistakes. Soon tailed off under a debutant carrying 21 pounds overweight on his final appearance, and cried enough before halfway. *J.D. & A.M. Callow — Albrighton Woodland.* 337 (CfMa), 526 (OMa), 790 (OMa), 1629 (M).

TICKERTY'S GIFT ..9-7§.. 11 b.g. Formidable (USA) — Handy Dancer (Green God) 953pp0. Small half-brother to Roll A Dollar, and to 6 flat winners, including Karinga Bay (smart), Mersey Beat (also a successful Hurdler) and Hardy Dancer. Dam won 3 10f races. FLAT (first win for R. Hannon) r21 w2 (10-11f) p0. NH '94/9 (for G.L. Moore) r43 w9 (2m1f-2m3f Hdles) p12. NH May '00 (from G. Brown's) r2 p0 (pulled up in 2m6f110y HCap Hdle: *ld til pu & dism 6*; and last in 2m HCap Hdle: *ld 2-5, wknd qckly, t.o*). Had a love affair with Lingfield where he gained one flat success and all his nine Hurdling victories (made all in five; one on firmish, but the vast majority in mud) and was also a neck second there, but highly unsuccessful on other tracks. Jumped poorly and did not enjoy himself at all in Hunter Chases, and was 40 lengths last of three when gaining his only prize. Often wears headgear. Reverted to the smaller obstacles latterly, but the virtual demise of jumping at 'lovely leafy' has totally scuppered him. *M.A. Styles — O. Berks (Gary Brown).* 226 (2m4f110yH), 461 (2m4f110yH), 801 (3m1fH), 1026 (2m5f110yH).

TICKET TO THE MOON ..10-5.. 11 b.m. Pollerton — Spring Rocket (Harwell) 33f. Small neat half-sister to Bomber Command. Dam won 2 Points (after remounting in Members once) and 2nd twice, and won 3 Chses (3m-3m2f, very lucky once) and 2nd thrice. P-t-P/HUNT CH '95/9 r19 w6 (inc 2m5f110y Hunt Ch and Open) p12 (4 2nds, inc 3 Hunt Chses; and inc last of 3 once); pulled up 1. A splendidly genuine and consistent mare who has made the frame in all 20 completions including five Hunter Chases. Has never won first time out, and blew up in the closing stages on her reappearance at Hereford, but looked straight enough when third at Kilworthy next time having had every chance jumping the last. Looked to have sustained a life threatening injury when suffering the first fall of her career at Taunton subsequently, and it is hoped she can be saved even if it means an end to her racing days. Has always been lightly raced, and generally searches for soft ground. *Mrs J. Scott — S. Devon.* 222 (3m1f110yH), 725 (L), 922 (3mH).

TICKLE THE TILLER (IRE) ..9-0.. 8 b.m. Strong Gale — Balancing Act (Balinger) p. Tall half-sister to jumping winner, Door To Door (IRE). Dam is an unraced half-sister to Granville Again and Morley Street, and is out of Matchboard, a fine Pointer/Chaser for Bill Shand-Kydd. NH FLAT '99 (from P. Webber's) r2 p0. Favourite for a February Maiden, but jumped badly early and although she got into contention at the 14th he soon weakened and pulled up after nearly stopping at the penultimate. Appears to have had a setback. *W. Shand Kydd — Bicester with Whaddon (Fiona Kehoe).* 98 (OMa).

TIDAL REEF (IRE) ..10-1§.. 9 br.g. Tidaro (USA) — Windsor Reef (Take A Reef) p1114. Small neat attractive half-brother to Crobeg. Dam won 2 Irish NH flat. P-t-P '97/9 r15 p0; failed to finish 11 (refused 1 and fell/unseated 2). Incredibly moderate, and a non-stayer in his first three seasons, but enjoyed the very steady pace set in both his first two successes, and found the 2m5f trip ideal when winning a more competitive event at Folkestone on his Hunter Chase debut. Not an easy ride in that he can be lazy and tends to jump right, but generally on his best behaviour in 2000. Will not find success so easy to come by in future. Blinkered twice in '98. *R. Fielder — Chid, Lec & Cowdray.* 220 (OMa), 679 (OMa), 980 (R), 1537 (2m5fH), 1625 (3m2f110yH).

TIDARO FAIRY (IRE) ..9-13.. 10 b.g. Tidaro (USA) — Green Fairy (Green Shoon) 4p. Small close-coupled. IRISH P-t-P '97/8 r16 p1 (25l last of 3); pulled up 8, and fell 1. IRISH NH FLAT '98 r1 p0. P-t-P '99 (for Mr M.D. Eddery & Mr D. Jack) r9 w1 (Maiden) p6 (4 3rds, of 4 twice); 4th, and pulled up 1. Made all when opening his account at Wetherby last year, and showed his liking for a distance of ground when runner-up in the 4m Grimthorpe Gold Cup, but appeared to finish lame, and has been pulled up in two of his three subsequent outings. Only able to run twice for new connections in 2000, and looks suspect now. *A. Bowling — V. of Lune H.* 812 (Cf), 1149 (Cf).

TIDERUNNER (IRE) ..9-5.. 13 b.g. Deep Run — Boherdeel (Boreen FR) pp26u5. Compact half-brother to Scotton Banks (IRE). NH '93/4 r3 p0. P-t-P '95 and '97/9 r16 w4 (up to Intermediate) p2; pulled up 5. Extremely lightly raced until he was nine, but flattered by his hat-trick in '98, and has been soundly beaten since. Only once better than last in 2000, and gained his latest placing only after remounting. Often takes little interest these days, and has acquired blinkers. *Mrs M. Morris — Blankney.* 48 (Cf), 796 (O), 1217 (L), 1350 (L), 1503 (Cf), 1583 (C).

TIED FOR TIME (IRE) ..10-4.. 9 b.g. Montelimar (USA) — Cornamucla (Lucky Guy) p1. Tall half-brother to Sharp Thyne (qv). NH FLAT '97/8 r2 p0. NH '98 r2 p0 (last and pulled up in Hdles). P-t-P '99 (for Miss L. Robertson & Mrs H. Greenshield) r4 w1 (Maiden) p0; ran out 1, pulled up 1, and brought down 1. Only able to complete twice in Points, but has won narrowly on both occasions. Gained his latest success in a time equal to that recorded by Balisteros in the following event, and probably has the scope to win again, but stands his racing badly and seems to require a sound surface. *M. Jackson — Middleton (Tony Walker).* 1000 (R), 1028 (R).

TIERNA'S RESPECT ..9-8.. 9 b.g. Respect — Tierna's Pet (Laurence O) f4. Tall half-brother to My Young Pet (qv). P-t-P '98/9 (for Mrs J.K. Peutherer) r7 p3 (2 2nds, beaten neck once); last, and pulled up 3. Came close to winning when runner-up twice in '99, and travels well out of his area in search of easy options, but does not stay, and his season was over by mid February in 2000. Usually takes the eye in the paddock, but twice a beaten favourite last year, and got no further than the first when well supported on his reappearance. *J.R. Sutcliffe — Albrighton Woodland (Mark Wellings).* 87 (OMa), 221 (OMa).

TIGER BELL ..—.. 8 b.g. Tigerwood — Bribella (Bribe) pfpuf. Tiny angular. Dam, sister to Captain Rondo (*qv* '91 Annual), 'game but slow', won Maiden and placed 5. P-t-P '99 r1 p0 (fell). Foiled by the fences in the first mile on four occasions to date, and has yet to go more than 2m3f. No bigger than a pony, and finds even Welsh fences insurmountable. *Miss H.E. Roberts — Llangeinor (E. Roberts).* 146 (OMa), 270 (CfMa), 346 (L), 595 (R), 649 (CfMa).

TIGER KING ..9-2.. 8 b.g. Rakaposhi King — Woodford Lady (Mandalus) 4fp51. Sturdy. P-t-P '99 r2 p1 (2nd of 3); and refused 1. Speedy, but a very erratic jumper, and nearly threw away his Maiden success by hanging left on the run-in. Beat no subsequent winners in a very slow time, and would have had to survive an objection from the runner-up had Steve Charlton not mislaid his wallet. Needs to improve in all departments for Restricteds, but credit to Clive Mulhall for getting a win out of such an unenviable ride. *P. Sadler — Rockwood H. (Stephen Wiles).* 138 (OMa), 380 (OMa), 400 (OMa), 910 (2m4fOMa), 1003 (OMa).

TIGER LORD ..9-10.. 10 br.g. Tigerwood — Roushane (Rustingo) 6362122p4pp. Small unfurnished brother to All For Tack. P-t-P/HUNT CH '96/9 r19 w1 (Maiden) p3 (2 3rds); pulled up 10. Beat a bad lot at Howick in '98, but incredibly lucky in his latest success there as he was booked for a poor third until the two leaders both fell independently at the second last. Tries hard, and often makes the running, but lacks scope, and will probably require more good fortune if he is to win again. Never went a yard when tried in a visor, and the experiment was not repeated. Wears a cross-noseband. *W.J. Day — Gelligaer F. (Lisa Day).* 69 (R), 274 (R), 336 (R), 485 (R), 596 (R), 741 (Cf), 819 (Cf), 1022 (3mH), 1227 (I), 1403 (I), 1449 (I).

TIGER PAWS (IRE) ..9-13.. 11 b.m. Carlingford Castle — Miss Tarbow (Tarqogan) p03. Small half-sister to Deep Tarbow. P-t-P '95/6 and '98 (for Mr S.R. & Mrs M. Hope) r7 w1 (Maiden) p1 (3rd); 4th, refused 1, pulled up 1, and fell 2. NH '99 (for P.R. Webber) r5 p1 (neck 2nd in 2m4f Selling HCap Chse); last, 6th and unseated 2. Won comfortably at Eaton Hall in '98, but did not really take to regulation fences, and quickly descended to sellers. Retains some ability, and stayed on when 15 lengths third in a long Restricted at Alpraham, but has never stood her racing particularly well and gets few chances. *Mrs C.M. Brown — Cheshire Forest (Ralph Hirons).* 172 (Cm), 567 (R), 589 (R).

TIGERSUN ..8-7.. 7 b.g. Tigerwood — Sunfly (Sunyboy) pp1p. Small light. Dam, sister or half-sister to 3 Pointers, including Tumbril (*qv* '97 Annual), won Maiden and Restricted and placed 5 for Dilwyn Thomas. Pulled up in his first two races (when still just in touch after two miles on his debut — it looked a clear case of schooling in public, but no questions were asked but benefitted from the gentle introduction when winning an eight-finisher Maiden on firm at Erw Lon. Kept on gamely, but the opposition was basically pathetic. Outclassed in his Members, but could be stronger and better in his second campaign. *D.R. Thomas — Llangeinor.* 480 (O), 596 (R), 949 (OMa), 1656 (M).

TIGER TINA ..10-0.. 10 b.m. Tigerwood — Karatina (FR) (Dilettante II) 271p. Leggy angular half-sister to Yukon Tina, Sunny Bakara, Karazona, Young William, Karabique, Karaffi, Cleddau King and Cresswell Quay. Dam reportedly won jumping in Jersey. P-t-P '99 r1 w1 (Maiden) p1 (2nd); ran out 1, fell/unseated 2, and pulled up 1. Impressive in two soft ground wins, but ended 2000 on a disappointing note when pulled up at Garnons, and suspicion surrounds her well-being. Less erratic than she was, and has gained both her wins for Anthony Evans by coming from behind. Will win again if all is well. Wears a cross-noseband. *Miss M. Bayliss — Cotswold.* 75 (I), 218 (L), 273 (R), 447 (Cm).

TIGHTER BUDGET (USA) ..9-9.. 14 b.g. Desert Wine (USA) — Silver Ice (USA) (Icecapade USA) 4u383p. Tall strong-topped half-brother to 2 winners in USA. Dam won 14 flat at up to 8f in USA (earned $271,825). NH '90 and '93/8 (for Mrs D. Sayer; previously for her mother, Mrs E. Slack; unplaced first 3 for late W.A. Stephenson) r55 w9 (4 Hdles, 2m-2m7f and 5 Chses, 2m5f-3m1f) p20. Sold Doncaster, Aug for 1800. Nine victories under Rules, four apiece at Hexham and Kelso, and a hat-trick by an aggregate of more than 60 lengths in September/October '96. Much better on firmish than other surfaces, but has jumped and hung right, and likes things his own way. Has always been best when able to blaze a trail, and although he set off in great style in his races at 13 he quickly gave up once collared. A real character, and has clearly decided to pension himself off. *Mrs P.J. Hutchinson — Fernie (Patrick Hutchinson).* 177 (L), 303 (3mH), 770 (Cf), 1006 (Cf), 1037 (L), 1334 (3mH).

TILLEYS ORCHID ..—.. 7 b.m. Little Wolf — Bittleys Hand (Nearly A Hand) f. Small. Dam, half-sister to Tom Furze (*qv*), was last (bar a rejoiner once) or a non-finisher in 25 of 26 Points for the Cookleys ('the rider suffers from perpetual inertia'). Great-grandam, Orchid Moor, won 14 Ladies (also disqualified once) and 2nd thrice, but broke down while completing a 10-timer. Fat in a late May Maiden, and fell after a mile when already toiling in the ruck. Looks to be another Cooksley incompetent. *A. Cooksley — Weston & Banwell H.* 1640 (OMa).

TILT TECH FLYER ..9-9.. 16 b.g. Windjammer (USA) — Queen Kate (Queen's Hussar) p640. Tall half-brother to McCallun and Johnny-K (IRE), to Irish Pointing winner, All-Together, and to NH flat winner, Smiles Better. Dam won 8f Sell. FLAT r24 w3 (8f) p4 (3rds). NH '89/91, '92/4 and '96/7 r34 w5 (2m-2m1f Hdles, last 2 Sells) p4; remote 6th of 7 only Ch ('94). P-t-P/HUNT CH '98/9 r3 w1 (Ladies) p0; 5th, and pulled up 1. A successful hurdler when there was cut in the ground, but won his Pointing debut on firmish, and produced his best effort since on similar terrain when beaten less than two lengths at Howick. Retains plenty of ability for a 15-year-old, but stands little racing now, and acquired a tongue-strap in 2000. Suited by forcing tactics. *J. Milton — Ystrad Taf Fechan.* 275 (Cf), 643 (Cf), 819 (Cf), 921 (2m6fH).

TIMARISK ..8-8.. 10 b.g. Newski (USA) — Bingley Sharlene (Good Apple) puu. Tall half-brother to Frosty Jo (*qv*). P-t-P '98/9 (for Mr & Mrs A.C. Raymond) r6 p0 (7th, slipped up 1, and pulled up 4). An excitable sort who pulls hard, and does not stay the trip in Points, but does not have the ability to compete successfully in sub-3m Hunter Chases in which he is a poor jumper. Seems destined to fail. Wears a cross-noseband, and has been taken to post early. *Mrs R.E. Parker — Seavington (Nigel Parker).* 685 (2m5fH), 925 (2mH), 1341 (2m110yH).

TIMBER TOP (IRE) ..8-6.. 8 b.g. Supreme Leader — Modelligo Wood (IRE) (Ragapan) p3p3. Small workmanlike. P-t-P '99 (for Mr M.J. Trickey) r2 p0 (pulled up 2). Beaten two lengths when third in a Maiden run 13 seconds slower than any other race on the card at Holnicote, but struggling to get the trip otherwise, and lacks fluency. A well-backed favourite on his final outing, but needs to improve significantly on what he has achieved so far to win. *Mrs P. Elgar & Mrs P. Watson — Devon & Somerset (Mike Trickey).* 146 (OMa), 352 (CfMa), 1100 (OMa), 1241 (OMa).

TIMBER WOLF (IRE) ..9-1.. 8 b.g. Little Wolf — Larchwood (Precipice Wood) 4pppp. Small light-framed. Dam, half-sister to 4 Clark Pointers, including She's No Nun (*qv* '95 Annual), won 2m6f Hdle and 2 Chses (2m4f-2m5f) for her. P-t-P '98/9 r8 w1 (Maiden) p2 (3rds, last once); pulled up 3, and fell 1. Kept on under some vigorous persuasion from Nick Mitchell when successful in a bad Maiden at Larkhill in '99, but only able to complete in one Restricted since, and has completely lost his confidence since taking a heavy fall at the scene of his victory. Permanently under a cloud at present. *Mr & Mrs Z.S. Clark — Blackmore & Sparkford V. (John Dufosee).* 14 (R), 261 (R), 406 (R), 524 (R), 1247 (R).

TIME ENOUGH (IRE) ..9-12.. 12 ch.g. Callernish — Easter Gazette (London Gazette) u54234. Compact. IRISH P-t-P '93 r1 w1 (4yo Maiden). NH '93/6 and '98 r26 w4 (2m4f-3m1f Chses) p6 (inc 3rd in Hdle). P-t-P/HUNT CH '99 r5 w1 (Members) p2 (2nd in Hunt Ch once); 4th, and pulled up 1. Won five races on differing ground to '96, but revived in modest Points after a spell in the doldrums, but beaten at odds-on when blinkered for the first time in his Members this year, and is very easy to overcome now. Used to make plenty of mistakes over regulation fences, and is still far from fluent. Needs to concentrate on the easiest options available in future, and give Hunter Chases a swerve. *P. Townsley — Surrey U. (Pru Townsley).* 154 (3mH), 224 (3m2fH), 461 (2m4f110yH), 572 (CfO), 1392 (M), 1538 (3m2fH).

TIMEFORANOTHER ..—.. 8 b.m. Cruise Missile — New Cherry (New Brig) uu. Tall sister to Cruise Around (*qv*). A very shoddy jumper who blundered Fiona Needham out of the saddle on consecutive Sundays in February. *G.D. Benson — Bilsdale (Fiona Needham).* 282 (OMa), 381 (OMa).

TIME TO SHARE (IRE) ..9-7.. 7 b.g. Mandalus — Grand Glancer (Pas De Seul) upp. P-t-P '99 r4 w1 (Maiden) p0; and pulled up 3. Left clear after the last by the hanging runner-up when winning a Maiden at Bonvilston last year, but has failed to complete in six other attempts. Unlucky when unseating at the last with a narrow advantage in his Members on his reappearance, but never remotely involved in two Restricteds. Seems best when there is cut in the ground, but beginning to look incredibly modest at best. *I. Thomas & G. Lewis — Tredegar F., & V. of Clettwr (Tim Jones).* 266 (M), 484 (R), 832 (R).

TIMMY TUFF (IRE) ..—§.. 10 b.g. Torenaga — Aprolon Lady (Mon Capitaine) upup. Lengthy unfurnished half-brother to It's The Wind, Hold Hard, Many A Slip and Duke Of Aprolon, and to Irish Pointing winners, Ballyhindon, Three Shares and Ileclash. Dam dead-heated for Irish Maiden. IRISH P-t-P '96/7 r10 p2 (3rds); pulled up 4, and fell 1. P-t-P '99 r5 p1 (2nd); last 2, refused 1, and pulled up 1. 5 lengths second once in '99, but has failed to finish in his last six appearances, and still apt to dig his toes in at the start. Can show speed, but usually on the retreat after no more than two miles, and looks most untrustworthy. *K.R. Yeates & D.C. Swordy — Radnor & W. Herefords.* 488 (CfMa), 865 (CfMa), 994 (OMa), 1092 (OMa).

TIMOTHY GEORGE (IRE) ..8-8.. 7 b.g. Don't Forget Me — Ward Of Court (IRE) (Law Society USA) ppp3635p4. Small. FLAT r5 p0. NH '97/8 r7 p0 (inc Sells). P-t-P '99 (for Mr P.J. Millington) r8 p1 (2nd); last 2, and pulled up 5. Has made the frame in five Maidens on sound surfaces, but does not stay three miles, and is ungenuine in addition. Sometimes makes mistakes, and should be avoided at all costs. Visored once last year, and acquired blinkers and a tongue-strap in 2000. *Mrs T. Renwick — Fernie (Miss S. Renwick).* 436 (OMa), 903 (O), 1270 (OMa), 1383 (OMa), 1507 (OMa), 1596 (OMa), 1668 (OMa), 1675 (OMa).

TIN CUP ..9-3§.. 9 b.g. Broadsword (USA) — Osmium (Petong) f56pp. Workmanlike half-brother to No Morals. IRISH NH FLAT '97 r1 p0 (tailed off last). P-t-P '98/9 r8 p1 (3rd of 4); 6th, pulled up

5, and fell 1. Continued his uninspiring run of performances in 2000, but appears to have a stamina deficiency, and has been tried in headgear. There seems no rhyme nor reason to his choice of engagements, but would find life a whole lot easier if he concentrated solely on Maidens. *J.N.R. Billinge — Fife.* 420 (I), 717 (Cf), 918 (2m4fH), 1024 (3m3f110yH), 1123 (OMa).

TINDLES BIBLE ..9-11.. 9 b.g. Le Coq D'Or — Wedderburn (Royalty) 3. Robust brother to Irish Pointing and English Chasing winner, Glenbrook D'or, and half-brother to Guy Mornay (*qv*). NH '97/8 (from M. Todhunter's) r4 p3 (2nds). Showed plenty of ability over Hurdles including when second in a 21-runner race, and started favourite for a Maiden, but was outpaced in the closing stages and finished seven lengths third. Clearly very hard to train, but would be a certainty for a Maiden at best. Presumably his name is a gross mis-spelling of William Tyndale, who produced the first English-language in 1526. *K. Jackson — Cumberland (Elizabeth Jestin).* 1081 (R).

TINY ..8-1.. 6 ch.m. Romany Rye — Goodbye Roscoe (Roscoe Blake) 575p. Neat attractive. Dam won 2 Points and placed 7 (inc a Ch) for Joanne Hegarty. Did well to achieve three consecutive completions at five, but her jumping went awry on final start. Should make the frame in some Maidens if regaining fluency in 2001. *Mrs J.M. Hegarty — Glamorgan (Evan Williams).* 949 (OMa), 1223 (2m4fOMa), 1454 (OMa), 1574 (OMa).

TIOTAO (IRE) ..—.. 11 b.g. Burslem — Linbel (Linacre) f5. Workmanlike half-brother to Lord Chanticleer, and to 6 winners, including Neblin (useful flat and Hurdling). Dam won at 9f in Ireland. NH FLAT '96 r1 p0. NH '96/7 and '99 (for R. Baker, bought for 2100; previously for Mrs L. Jewell; previously for C. Parker) r20 p2 (inc 2nd in Sell); ran out once; last and pulled up 2 in Chses; failed to finish in 6 of final 7 attempts. Concluded an appalling sequence when finishing about two fences last, and is now reported to be dead. *B.P. Jones — Berks & Bucks (John Gallagher).* 37 (Cl), 205 (OMa).

TIPPING AWAY (IRE) ..—.. 9 ch.g. Phardante (FR) — Gaelic Sport (Pollerton) pup. Brother to Sun Strand, and half-brother to Slaney hotpot (both Irish NH flat winners). IRISH NH FLAT '97 r1 p0. IRISH NH '97 r3 p0. IRISH P-t-P '97 and '99 r4 w1 (4&5yo Mdn) p0; pulled up 2. Got up close home to win his Irish Pointing debut, but lightly raced since, and there seems to be something badly wrong with him. Unseated after a mile when tried in blinkers in his Members. *Lady P. Kirkham — Grove & Rufford (D. Reynolds).* 871 (R), 1069 (M), 1218 (R).

TIPSY LAIRD (IRE) ..8-10.. 7 b.g. Un Desperado (FR) — Ever Mine (Mount Hagen FR) pf. Half-brother to Amazing Man (IRE). IRISH P-t-P '98 r1 p0 (pulled up). IRISH NH FLAT '98 r1 p0 (last). P-t-P '99 r1 w1 (2m4f Maiden). Disqualified after finishing alone at Lanark last year because the rider was not qualified, but was unable to gain compensation in 2000. A well backed favourite when pulled up and dismounted on his reappearance in a 2m5f Maiden back at Lanark, and fell heavily three out when tiring subsequently. A free-going sort, but finished exhausted in his win, and seems unable to stay much beyond 2m4f. *R.A. Bartlett — Fife.* 664 (2m5fOMa), 914 (CfMa).

TIRLEY MISSILE ..10-2.. 15 ch.g. Cruise Missile — Tic-On-Rose (Celtic Cone) 42451. Rangy unfurnished half-brother to Rose Of Macmillion and Derring Tirley. Dam won 2m mares Nov Hdle. Grandam, Tudor Tirley, won 4 Points and 2m3f Hunt Ch for Mr Smith. NH '94/5 and '97 r9 p3 (1¾l 2nd in Ch; inc 2 Hdles, inc 1½l 2nd). P-t-P/HUNT CH '92/4 and '99 r12 w3 (Maiden, Members and PPORA Restricted) p2 (inc 3rd of 4 in 2m5f Hunt Ch); fell/unseated 4, and ran out 1. Has done well to farm his Members since returning to Pointing, and gave some other fair displays in 2000, but remains an erratic jumper, and is far too old to change his ways. Has gained all his wins going left-handed including three at Maisemore, but has always jumped in the other direction, and has never been able to stand regular racing. *D.E.S. Smith — Cotswold V.F.* 75 (I), 448 (I), 615 (CMod), 897 (I), 1310 (M).

TITAN THAI (IRE) ..10-3.. 12 b.g. Supreme Leader — Thai Nang (Tap On Wood) 55. Lengthy plain half-brother to NH flat winners, Kilcarne Bay (IRE) and Fenagh Flyer (latter in Ireland), and to Irish Hurdles winners, Thai Electric and Colonial Sunset. NH '94 and '97/9 (visored 2) r26 w3 (2m5f-3m2f Chses, no chance when left clear once — probably 4th best!) p7 (inc 2nd in Sell; and inc 3rd in 2 Hdles). Gained the latest of his three Chasing successes in a Seller in June '99, but has often been let down by his jumping, and was beaten between 25 lengths and 30 lengths in February Hunter Chases. Not seen since (was absent for 36 months after October '94, but scored on his very belated reappearance). Usually wears headgear, and tried tongue-tied. Has broken blood vessels in the past. *N.B. Mason — Middleton.* 89 (3m1fH), 155 (3m4f110yH).

TITUS ANDRONICUS ..9-13.. 14 b.g. Oats — Lavilla (Tycoon II) p1p253. Strong attractive half-brother to Sceptical, to Hurdles winners, Hawthorn Hill Lad and Mister Half-Chance, to an Irish Pointing winner, and to an Irish NH flat winner. NH '92/4 and '95/6 r26 w1 (2m3f Ch) p10. P-t-P/HUNT CH '98/9 r17 w9 (inc Open, Mixed Open and Ladies; inc 5-timer '98) p5 (2nds); last pair 2, and pulled up 1. Transformed by Heather Irving when successful in seven of nine outings in '98, but in decline since, and only just managed to hang on in his Members this year. Surrendered an eight length advantage turning for home at Mollington subsequently, and no longer has the heart for a struggle. A sketchy jumper in the last two years, and must be approaching retirement soon.

Mrs K. Irving, Mrs N. Oldring & A. Kemp — Farmers Bloodhounds (Tony Kemp). 79 (O), 190 (M), 308 (O), 787 (L), 1014 (3m5fL), 1254 (O).

T'NIGHTSTHENIGHT ..9-1.. 7 b.g. Scallywag — Misty Sky (Hot Brandy) r. Big strong brother to Cloud Cover, and half-brother to Beinn Mohr. Dam won 3 Points and placed 4 (inc Nov Hdle). P-t-P '99 r1 p0 (fell). In the process of running a fair race until capsizing at the last on his debut, but collapsed through exhaustion after running well to three out on his reappearance, and has not been seen since. Keen, but seems to have a stamina problem, and is not having much fun at present. A watching brief is advised if he returns. *C.J.B. Barlow — Cheshire (Chris Clark).* 180 (2m4fOMa).

TOARLITE (IRE) ..10-0.. 10 b.g. Euphemism — Autolite (Energist) p442p. Rangy half-brother to Irish Pointing winner, Show Me The Light. Dam won mares Maiden in Ireland. IRISH P-t-P '97/8 r9 w3 (7yo&up Maiden, Confined and Adjacent) p0; pulled up 4. P-t-P '99 r7 w1 (Open) p1 (fence last of 2); last, and pulled up 4. Had a useful record in mud across the Irish Sea, and scored in similar conditions at Lanark last year, but was very lucky as the clear leader departed at the last. Finished lame on two occasions after his win, and never going with much enthusiasm in 2000 before breaking down at Cartmel. Tried in blinkers in '99, and wore a visor on his last three appearances. *A.R. Trotter — Berwicks.* 90 (3m1fH), 358 (M), 1349 (O), 1498 (O), 1601 (3m2fH).

TOBIAS (IRE) ..—§.. 6 b.g. Erdelistan (FR) — Ann's Penny (Cidrax FR) ur. Lengthy. Dam won mares Mdn in Ireland. Shed Mark Munrowd at the first on his debut, and then acquired Julian Pritchard, who he threw over the second fence when refusing (undaunted, his partner clambered back aboard, but was hurtled through the air on the take off side after another stop at the third). Will require banning unless he has a complete change of heart. *T. Hayes — N. Ledbury (John Rudge).* 1526 (OMa), 1668 (OMa).

TODCRAG ..10-7.. 12 b.g. Feelings (FR) — Redetwig (Carlton Grange) 53. Very small compact brother to Rede Rebel, and half-brother to Redesbeg, Geordies Brig, Redediver and Down The Drive. Dam, pony-sized, won a Maiden and placed 6 for Thomas Scott. P-t-P/HUNT CH '94/8 r21 w12 (inc 6 Opens 3m-3m5f, inc 5-timer '96, and 4-timer '98) p6 (2nds, last twice); fell 1. Incredibly brave for a wee might, and his 22 Pointing attempts have yielded 12 wins and seven placings, but knocked about badly by a fall on his debut over regulation fences, and forced to miss the '99 season. Looked as though in need of his reappearance, but showed he retains much of his ability, and all of his tenacity when a close third at Mosshouses, and could still win Points if returned next year. Stays well, and acts on any going. *Mrs M. Scott — Border.* 1078 (Cf), 1428 (O).

TODD (USA) ..9-7.. 10 b.g. Theatrical — Boldara (Alydar USA) p. Compact half-brother to 2 French flat winners, and to a winner in USA. Dam won 7 races and $143,009 in USA (was best at around 8f). IRISH FLAT r6 p1 (2nd). FLAT '95/6 (tried blinkered) r12 w1 (10f, all-weather) p0. NH '96/8 r8 p1 (2nd); inc Sell; 9th and fell 1 in Chses. P-t-P '99 (for Mr A.H. Harvey) r5 p1 (3rd of 4); last, pulled up 2, and fell 1. Placed on his hurdling debut, but has been very disappointing over jumps since, and has only beaten one rival in six Points. An indifferent jumper, and managed just one appearance for new connections in 2000. Has been tried in a tongue-strap. *D.C. Weaving — Seavington.* 954 (MO).

TOD'S BROTHER ..9-9.. 7 b.g. Gildoran — Versina (Leander) pp1. Big rangy owner-bred half-brother to Tom's Influence (qv). Taken quietly until pulled up after two miles in his first two Maidens, and still looked to be carrying condition in a youngsters event in softish at Fakenham, but sympathetically handled by Nigel Bloom to spring a 20-1 surprise. Beat very little but accomplished the task in good style, and seems sure to have scope for further improvement. *Mrs A.W.K. Merriam — Easton H.* 515 (OMa), 1040 (OMa), 1291 (OMa).

TOFINO SWELL ..—.. 9 b.m. Primitive Rising (USA) — Celtic Sands (Celtic Cone) ppf0. Small sturdy. Dam, half-sister to 4 Pointers, including No Woed (qv '98 Annual), won 2m1f Amat Mdn Hdle. Grandam, Rapena, was bad 3rd of 4 in Restricted (after hanging all the way), and fell or refused in 5 of her other 11 Points. 13,500 5yo. NH FLAT Summer '98 r2 p0 (slipped up once). NH '98/9 (tried tongue-tied) r13 p1 (3rd); inc Sells; unseated at first only Ch. NH '00 r1 p0 (14th in 2m1f Nov Hdle: *in tch ½way, sn bhnd*). Gave fair displays in three Hurdles May/June '99, but went much too fast in the early stages of both Points, and galloped herself into the ground. Tackled regulation fences for the second time in a Hunter Chase, and again came to grief at the first. An excitable little mare, and has taken to post early, and mounted on the course. Finding the key to her is proving to be most elusive. *Mrs H.O. Graham — Jedforest.* 112 (OMam), 361 (L), 918 (2m4fH).

TOLEPA (IRE) ..—.. 8 b.m. Contract Law (USA) — Our Investment (Crofter USA) fpppp. Leggy sister to a French flat winner. Dam won 7f race in Ireland. FLAT r9 p0. NH '97 (for J.J. O'Neill) r1 p0 (Sell). Bought Ascot, Aug '97 for 825. Charges off at a lunatic gallop with the hapless Lee Tibbatts, and invariably establishes a long lead in the early stages, but is never going to the get the trip whilst she continues to bolt, and there can be absolutely no fun whatsoever in riding her. *Mrs S.A. Brown - Cotley (Gordon Herrod).* 407 (OMa), 518 (2m4fOMa), 875 (2m4fOMa), 934 (OMa), 1373 (OMa).

TOMCAPPAGH (IRE) ..10-4.. 10 b.g. Riberetto — Shuil Suas (Menelek) 3pf5.5p. Big half-brother to Ballinacourty. Dam won an Irish NH flat. P-t-P/HUNT CH '96/9 r15 w2 (inc 2m5f Hunt Ch) p5 (3

3rds, of 4 once; and 2 2nds; inc 4 Hunt Chses); pulled up 5, and fell 1. NH '00 r2 p0 (5th in 2m5f Nov Ch: *a bhnd*; and pulled up in 3m HCap Ch: *mists 3 & 7, bhnd when pu 4 out*). Kept going gamely to win a 2m5f Maiden Hunter Chase in softish at Folkestone last year, but disappeared in mid-March, and has performed dismally since his return. Generally lightly raced, and avoids firm ground, but absent since February, and clearly has his problems. Not the most fluent jumper of regulation fences. *Mrs S. Wall — Kent & Surrey Bloodhounds.* 9 (L), 59 (MO), 154 (3mH), 303 (3mH).

TOM DE SAVOIE (IRE) ..10-8.. 8 br.g. War Hero — Black Pilot (Linacre) 2f11312. Tall workmanlike half-brother to Barton Bulldozer (IRE). P-t-P '98/9 r8 w4 (up to Confined) p1 (2nd); pulled up 1, and fell 2. A useful seven-year-old, and has won nearly half his races, but less impressive in 2000 than he was 12 months ago, and his jumping remains untidy. Let his supporters down twice before opening his account this year, and made heavy weather of accounting for Torus Spa on his Hunter Chase debut, but no match for either Copper Thistle or Mr Snowman either side. Has the advantage of being in one of the best yards, and will surely win again, but looked a bit reluctant when winning once in '99, and his attitude is once again giving cause for concern. Kept to ground close to good. *W.G.N. Barber — W. Norfolk (Caroline Bailey).* 83 (Cf), 175 (I), 417 (Cf), 607 (O), 1008 (O), 1156 (3m110yH), 1530 (2m6fH).

TOM FURZE ..9-10.. 14 b.g. Sula Bula — Bittleys Wood (Straight Lad) p. Strong half-brother to La Belle Helene and Bittleys Hand (dam of Tilleys Orchid *qv*). Dam was 3rd of 27 to Corbiere in a NH flat race on her only appearance. Grandam, Orchid Moor, won 14 Ladies (also disqualified once) and second thrice — broke down when completing a 10-timer. NH '93 r2 p1 (3rd). P-t-P/HUNT CH '94/9 r12 w3 (2m5f Hunt Ch, an Open, and awarded a Restricted) p4 (2 2nds, last twice, beaten neck once); pulled up 4, and unseated 1. A good galloper on sound surfaces, but barely gets the trip in Points, and has never managed to stand more than four outings in a season. Formerly placed to great effect, and would have won two 2m5f Hunter Chases but for the legendary Warwick fiasco in '97, but pulled up in three of his last five races and looks finished now. *Mrs K. Buckett — Hursley Hambledon.* 62 (Cf).

TOM KIRBY ..—.. 9 b.g. Wonderful Surprise — Sister Sam (Pamroy) p. Strong lengthy. Dam (*qv* '91 Annual) won a Restricted and placed 7 (inc 2 Hunt Chses) for Tim Smith. P-t-P '98/9 r4 p0 (ran out 1, and pulled up 3). Has shown a distinct lack of enthusiasm when failing to complete five times, and produced his worst display yet in 2000. *T.D. Smith — Farndale (N.C. Smith).* 626 (OMa).

TOMMYKNOCKER ..8-6.. 9 ch.g. Woodman (USA) — Repercutionist (USA) (Beaudelaire USA) 52pr42pp. Close-coupled half-brother to jumping winner, Northern Drums. Dam won 2 French flat, 5-7f. FLAT r13 p0. NH '95/6 r4 p0 (inc 3 Sells). P-t-P '97/9 r18 p3 (2 3rds, of 4 once); failed to finish 8 (refused 1, and brought down 1). Has participated in no fewer than 25 Welsh Maidens without success, but proved that there are worse performers out there when second twice in 2000, and went down by less than a length in the latest. Usually lacks resolution when he does find a race bad enough to get involved in, and has run dismally on the two occasions he has been sent off favourite. Tried blinkered flat and hurdling. *Mrs D.C. & T. Faulkner — Tredegar F. (Deborah Faulkner).* 491 (CfMa), 602 (CfMa), 949 (OMa), 1301 (OMa), 1406 (OMa), 1574 (OMa), 1616 (R), 1662 (OMa).

TOMMY O'DWYER (IRE) ..10-2.. 12 b.g. Black Minstrel — Collective (Pragmatic) p. Unfurnished. P-t-P '95/7 and '99 r15 w1 (Club Maiden) p5 (3 3rds, of 4 once); fell/unseated 3, and pulled up 3. Showed no lack of stamina when winning a 7min 34s Maiden in softish in '96, but very lightly raced and has faced some stiff tasks since. Missed '98 because of lameness, but showed good form against the likes of Split Second last year, and would still win a Restricted if able to reproduce that effort. Absent since his sole 2000 appearance in February. *A.K. Pritchard — V. of Aylesbury (Lawney Hill).* 179 (R).

TOMMYS WEBB (IRE) ..10-7.. 13 b.g. Asir — Coleman Lass (Pry) 2pp. Smallish workmanlike. IRISH P-t-P '94/5 r5 p1 (3rd); pulled up 3. HUNT CH '97 r1 p0 (4th). NH '98 r1 p1 (20l 3rd in 2m4f Clmng Hdle). HUNT CH '99 r3 w1 (2m5f110y) p1 (2nd); and 5th. Has only ever contested sub-3m events in England, but made his mark when successful over 2m5f at Fakenham on his reappearance last year, and not disgraced behind Master Boston in the 2000 renewal. Obviously a decent animal, but his racecourse appearances have been strictly rationed, and he was pulled up and dismounted on his latest start. *A. Hartgrove — Bicester with Whaddon (Chris Nimmo).* 227 (2m5f110yH), 687 (2m6f110yH), 1026 (2m5f110yH).

TOM PINCH (IRE) ..—.. 12 b.g. Mandalus — Spanish Royale (Royal Buck) pbp4. Compact good-topped half-brother to Encima Del Rio (IRE) (*qv*). IRISH P-t-P '95 r3 w1 (6plus Mdn) p1 (3rd); and ran out when challenging 2 out. NH '96/9 (final from J. Mackie's — very unlucky, as well clear when blundered 2 out and saddle slipped, and jumped slowly and unseated at last; previously for G.B. Balding) r12 w1 (3m Sell Ch, sold for 6800) p5 (inc Hdle). NH Apr '00 r1 p0 (4th in 2m4f HCap Ch: *rr, blun 10*). Beat Master Kit in an Irish Point and has given a number of decent displays since, but seemed unsuitable for the new owner/rider, as he pulled too hard and was difficult to control. Acts on firm, and ran a much better race for Andrew Sansom when tongue-tied at Fakenham, and would probably be an interesting bet if he could find another Selling Chase. *J.R. Cornwall — Belvoir.* 17 (O), 117 (O), 1025 (3m110yH).

TOMS CHOICE (IRE) ..9-6.. 12 gr.g. Mandalus — Prior Engagement (Push On) 86p. Big strong. NH
'97/9 r6 p1 (3rd in 2m Chse). P-t-p '95/7 (for Mr M.F. Harding) r6 p3 (2 2nds; and 3rd of 4); pulled
up 1, and unseated 1. Made the frame on four occasions before going lame in '97, but never stayed
a yard beyond 2m3f, and appeared to suffer a heart attack when expiring in the early stages at
Didmarton in March. Blinkered on that fateful day. *J.C. Tuck — Beaufort.* 63 (I), 211 (Cnr), 387 (M).

TOM'S INFLUENCE ..9-6.. 9 br.m. Pitpan — Versina (Leander) 5p1pp. Tall rangy half-sister to
Coppinger's Cave, Trewornan Bridge and Tod's Brother. Dam won 2 Points and placed 2.
Grandam, Verosina, won 2 Hunt Chses (2m4f-3m) and 4 Points and placed 7. P-t-p '99 r2 p0
(refused 1, and pulled up 1). Not better than tailed off last until winning a bad three-finisher
Maiden at Penshurst, and has rapidly run out of steam after 2m4f in Restricteds since. Gives the
impression that she may have developed a fault. *R. & Mrs P. Cranney — Waveney H. (Juliet
Arthur).* 132 (OMa), 290 (CMa), 829 (OMa), 980 (R), 1287 (R).

TOM'S LAD ..—.. 8 gr.g. Scallywag — Menquilla (Menelek) f. Sturdy half-brother to Larquill. Dam
won 4 Chses, 2m3f-3m (the first 3 in Ireland) and placed 9 (inc 2 Points, one in Ireland). NH '98
r1 p0 (pulled up). May have ability, but clearly hard to train, and not seen since he fell when
pressing the leaders first on January. *Sir Michael Connell — Grafton.* 23 (OMa).

TOM'S MAN ..9-7.. 7 ch.g. Milieu — Lorna's Choice (Oats) 222pp. Close-coupled half-brother to
Delwood (qv). NH FLAT '98 r2 p0. NH '98 r2 p0. Tried 2m4f for the first time and was only beaten
a neck when collecting his third consecutive Hunter, but stopped to nothing in the tacky ground
next time, and then badly outclassed in a Hunter Chase. May be able to score on a firmer surface,
but wears a tongue-strap, and is a weak finisher. *F.V. White — Percy (George White).* 114 (OMa),
379 (OMa), 909 (2m4fOMa), 1083 (2m4fOMa), 1556 (2m4f110yH).

TOM SNOUT (IRE) ..10-4§.. 13 b.g. Kambalda — Nesford (Walshford) 2p3. Tall good-looking half-
brother to Malvernian and Ballyea Boy (IRE), to NH flat winner and Chasing winner, Tom's River
(IRE), to Irish Pointing winners, Summer Blade and Winters Hill (also jumping winner there), and to
all-weather Hurdles winner, Proverbs Girl. Dam won 2m Hdle in Ireland. IRISH NH FLAT '92/3 r4
p1 (3rd). IRISH '92 and '94 r3 w1 (4&5yo Maiden) p2 (3rds). IRISH NH '94/5 r8 w1 (3m Hdle)
p2 (3rds, inc Ch). P-t-p '96, and '98/9 r19 w4 (inc Open and 2 Ladies) p6 (4 2nds, of 3 once); pulled
up 1, fell/unseated 3, slipped up 1, and refused 1. Capable of useful efforts, and should have won
more than his current haul, but has appeared temperamentally unsound on occasions. Went clear
turning for home on his reappearance at Tweseldown, but was worn down by Balisteros in the final
50 yards and regained blinkers on his next outing. Can handle any going, but remains in an unco-
operative frame of mind, and absent since appearing to finish lame at Cothelstone in March. *J.
Scammell — Blackmore & Sparkford V. (Rose Vickery).* 3 (L), 210 (MO), 638 (Cf).

TOM'S PRIZE ..9-13.. 6 ch.g. Gunner B — Pandora's Prize (Royal Vulcan) 2212u. Unfurnished. Dam,
sister to Bear's Flight (qv '98 Annual), and half-sister to Half Sharp, was bought by Pam Joynes after
winning 2m4f Sell Hdle. NH '98/9 (from T. Wall's) r4 p0. Made light of a simple task in a
youngsters Maiden at Maisemore, and gave some bold displays of jumping when second thrice.
Goes a good gallop (headstrong), but barely stays the trip, and tends to be run out of it in the
closing stages even at 2m4f. There is nothing wrong with his attitude, and if he strengthens and
finds some extra stamina at six he might score quite regularly. *Mrs P.M. Joynes — Heythrop (Scott
Joynes).* 124 (OMa), 672 (2m4fOMa), 898 (OMa), 1013 (W), 1335 (2m4f110yH).

TOM'S SURPRISE ..8-10.. 8 ch.g. Jendali (USA) — Porto Louise (Porto Bello) p6460426. Plain lengthy
owner-bred half-brother to Gonalston Percy. Dam won 2 2m Sell Hdles, the second for Frank Jackson.
NH '97 r1 p0 (distant last). P-t-p '98/9 r8 p1 (2nd); last 4, and pulled up 3. A competent jumper, and
twice runner-up in feeble contests at Thorpe, but usually carrying far too much condition to do himself
justice, and needs to be made fitter. *F.S. Jackson — S. Notts (R.J. Jackson).* 54 (OMa), 124 (OMa), 235
(OMa), 439 (OMa), 793 (CfMa), 1070 (2m4fOMa), 1214 (W), 1434 (3m110yH).

TONI'S TIGER ..—.. 7 b.g. Shere Khan — Miss Jay-Are (Bunny Boy) ppp. Comes from a stable
renowned for running disgracefully useless horses, and combined with Bang On Target and Sultan
Of Swing to amass a total of 16 non-completions from as many attempts in 2000. *Mrs M.B.
Stephens — E. Kent.* 577 (OMa), 829 (OMa), 1105 (2m4fOMa).

TONRIN ..9-6.. 9 b.g. General Wade — Hot Tramp (Country Retreat) f53p2. Smallish. Dam won 4
Hdles at around 2m (the first a Sell), and revived for 4 outings aged 14 after missing the 6 previous
seasons. NH FLAT '97 r1 p0 (pulled himself up). NH '97 r2 p0 (pulled up in Hdles). P-t-p '99 r6
p1 (2nd); 4th, pulled up 1, and fell/unseated 2. A crackpot in previous yards, and remains a most
unrewarding ride as he often acts the goat at the start, but then charges off uncontrollably. Just
touched off on his final start in which both he and the winner were desperate not to cross the line
in front, but usually fails to stay, and will get fewer easier opportunities. Walked to post once in a
bid to settle his nerves. *D. Walker — Staff College.* 679 (OMa), 889 (OMa), 1397 (OMa), 1540
(2m5fH), 1624 (OMa).

TONY'S CRONEY ..—.. 8 ch.g. Tout Ensemble — Ottery News (Pony Express) pup. Sturdy half-
brother to Otter River (qv). Looked a difficult ride and acquired blinkers at Bratton Down, where

he severed a tendon and had to be destroyed. O.J. Carter - E. Devon. 1307 (OMa), 1626 (3m1f110yH), 1654 (OMa).

TONY'S TIME ..8-11.. 7 b.g. Tina's Pet — Time Warp (Town And Country) p31. Tall good-bodied half-brother to Hurdles winner, Time For A Flutter. Dam, sister to Norse Country (*qv* '95 Annual), 3rd on flat, pulled up and fell in Points 5 years later. P-t-p '99 r1 p0 (pulled up). Left well clear by the fall of the odds-on favourite at the third last when winning a two-finisher Maiden in testing conditions at Bratton Down, and the jury remains out on him until he has had a chance to prove his stamina in a competitive race. *Mrs S. Faulks — Exmoor.* 204 (OMa), 733 (2m4fOMa), 1141 (CfMa).

TOOK A CHANCE (IRE) ..8-5.. 9 b.g. Lancastrian — Shady Miss (Mandamus) f6p. Tall workmanlike. Dam won Maiden and placed 3, and comes from a good jumping family. P-t-p '98 (for late Capt. T.A. Forster) r4 p1 (2nd); pulled up 2, and unseated 1. NH FLAT '98 r1 p0. NH '99 (for T. Keddy) r3 p0 (pulled up 3). A modest jumper who has shown speed for a maximum of two miles since his six length second in '98, and beaten 42 lengths in his only other completion over jumps. *W.E. Castrey — N. Herefords (Sally Sayce).* 332 (M), 602 (CfMa), 995 (OMa).

TOO PHAR TO TOUCH ..—.. 6 br.m. Wace (USA) — Carew Mill (Hubble Bubble) p. Dam, half-sister to Phar Too Touchy (*qv* '98 Annual), was lat of 2 and 3rd of 4 (fence behind in both) in Maidens for the Spuffards. Seemed very green and pulled up after a couple of errors at consecutive fences in mid-May. *M.J. Spuffard & F. Goldsworthy — S. Pembs.* 1457 (OMa).

TOOTH PICK (IRE) ..9-12.. 11 b.g. Milk Of The Barley — Kentstown Girl (Prince Tenderfoot USA) 2614up. Brother to Irish flat/Hurdles and English Chasing winner, Sam Vaughan (IRE), and half-brother to Irish Hurdles winner, Explain This (IRE), and to an Irish flat and Hurdles winner. IRISH NH FLAT '95 r1 p0. IRISH NH '95 r7 p1 (3rd). IRISH P-t-P '97 r5 p3. P-t-P '98/9 (for Mr T.D.B. Underwood & Mr C. Shankland) r20 w6 (up to Confined) p7 (2nds, last once); pulled up 5, and unseated 1. Poor in Ireland, but scored six times for Tim Underwood '98/9 including three at Kingston Blount, and could produce a turn of foot when in the mood. Just touched off on his debut for new connections, but split Sulphur Springs and Village Copper, and quickened to win a slowly-run Confined at Parham subsequently. Disappointed on his final three appearances, and not seen since a particularly poor effort at Peper Harow. Reported not to like being in front for too long, and to have burst a blood vessel once in '99. Could conceivably win again if he chose to. Has been tried in blinkers. *H.J. Hawksfield — Chid, Lec & Cowdray (Richard Parker).* 215 (C), 572 (CfO), 706 (Cf), 824 (Cf), 1212 (Cf), 1394 (O).

TOP DESIGNER (IRE) ..9-2.. 8 ch.g. Simply Great (FR) — Exemplary Fashion (Master Owen) 224p. Leggy angular half-brother to Floating River (IRE). NH FLAT '98 r1 p1 (15*l* 3rd). P-t-P '99 (for late Capt. T.A. Forster) r1 p1 (3rd). Made the frame in his first five races, but acquired a tongue-tie on his second start in 2000, and his performances have got worse instead of better. Good enough to win a race, and so far two of those who have finished behind have since done so, but clearly has a problem. Sent off favourite on three occasions in Points, and a well-backed second-favourite on his final appearance, but punters should proceed with great caution as far as he is concerned in future. *M.P. Wiggin — Ludlow (Geoff Evans).* 221 (OMa), 618 (CMa), 703 (OMa), 990 (OMa).

TOPICAL TIP (IRE) ..9-11.. 12 b.g. Tip Moss (FR) — Sami (FR) (Sukawa FR) 25p1. Well-made half-brother to Chasing winner, Philatelic (IRE). Dam, sister to Prince Wo (winner of Prix La Barka), won 3 flat and 2 Hdles in France. IRISH P-t-P r1 w1 (4yo Mdn). IRISH NH '94/6 and '98 r25 w2 (2m3f-2m5f Chses) p7 (inc 3rd at Cheltenham in '95). Won three races in Ireland to '96, but 11th of 12 and pulled up twice on his only appearances in the next three years, and was blinkered in the latest. Staged a mini-revival in the new yard, and just held on to land his Members, but is only moderate these days. *A. Hales (Merrylegs Racing Club) — Vine & Craven (Alex Hales).* 670 (O), 895 (MO), 1015 (4mO), 1242 (M).

TOP OF THE RANGE (IRE) ..—.. 12 ch.g. Quayside — Dersina (Deep Run) u. Dam won an Irish Maiden. IRISH P-t-P '94/5 r12 p6; pulled up 3, and fell at last when probable winner. P-t-P '96/7 r6 w1 (Maiden — 2 finished) p1 (3rd); pulled up 3. NH '99 (for P.W. d'Arcy) r1 p0 (pulled up). Gained a deserved success at High Easter in '96, but clearly troubled since, and pulled himself up on his only outing under Rules three years later. Only managed to clear one fence successfully in 2000 before he disappeared back into hiding. *Mr & Mrs P.C. Cornwell — Suffolk.* 416 (R).

TOP TOY (IRE) ..9-11.. 7 b.g. Strong Gale — Hansel's Lady (IRE) (The Parson) 2f2. Small. Beaten favourite in all three Maidens, but was unlucky at Market Rasen where he fell in the clear lead at the last, and then caught a tartar when thrashed by Conquer at Bitterley. Seems sure to find compensation in similar company very soon. *J.R. & Miss L. Hales — Wheatland (Andrew Dalton).* 138 (OMa), 436 (OMa), 989 (OMa).

TOP TRUMP ..9-5.. 10 b.m. Neltino — Rolling Dice (Balinger) 5. Rangy half-sister to Its Worth A Bob (*qv*). P-t-P '96 and '98/9 r9 p1 (3rd of 4); 7th, and pulled up 7. Ran well for a long way when 17 lengths fifth in a long Maiden at Mollington on her reappearance, and could probably have won a race by now had she been sensibly placed, but has only once managed more than two outings in a season, and clearly suffers the frailties of so many by Neltino. *Mrs L. Redman & M. Thomas — V. of Aylesbury (Lynne Redman).* 76 (CCfMa).

TORUS SPA (IRE) ..10-6.. 10 ch.g. Torus — Deep Spa (Deep Run) p462234. Rangy. IRISH P-t-P '96 r2 p1 (left 25*l* by two departures at last); and unseated 1. NH '97/8 r5 w1 (3m1f Amat Sell Ch, despite rider dropping whip a circuit from home, wore a tongue-tie) p2 (2nds, of 3 beaten 26*l* in Hdle, and last in Ch). P-t-P/HUNT CH '99 r7 w2 (Open and Confined) p3 (2 2nds, inc a Hunt Ch); 5th, and pulled up 1. A hard puller who can go a strong gallop, but ideally has to dominate, and usually downs tools once he has been headed. Won twice for Andrew Sansome in '99, but gained his best results for Emma Coveney this year, and ran well at Fakenham for the second year running when chasing home Tom De Savoie in April. Tried with waiting tactics subsequently, but could never land a blow, and just as likely to frustrate in future. Acts on top of the ground. *J.M. Turner — Suffolk.* 85 (O), 176 (O), 869 (L), 982 (L), 1156 (3m110yH), 1434 (3m110yH), 1539 (3m7fH).

TOSAWI'S GIRL (IRE) ..—.. 10 b.m. Commanche Run — Madeira Lady (On Your Mark) pp. Close-coupled half-sister to Hurdles winner, Up The Clarets (IRE). IRISH FLAT '94 r2 p0. P-t-P '97/9 r8 p0 (last, pulled up 4, and fell/unseated 3). 34 lengths last on the only occasion she has completed over jumps, and usually tears off before capitulating, but quickly tailed off in both 2000 appearances, and seems badly wrong. Blinkered twice in '98. *Mrs A.P. Kelly — Flint & Denbigh (Stephen Kelly).* 588 (OMa), 780 (L).

TOTAL RELIEF ..9-10.. 6 b.g. Relief Pitcher — Totally Tiddly (French Vine) 631. Half-brother to Extraspecial Brew and Country Brew. Dam won Maiden and placed 8. Grandam, Baba-Loo, was a useless Pointer. All over the place on his debut, but proved to be a quick learner, and followed a 15 length third in a bad race with an easy success in a Maiden in softish at Witton Castle. Showed a decent turn of foot which should stand him in good stead in a Restricted at least. *Mrs B. Till — Sinnington.* 1002 (2m4fOMa), 1234 (OMa), 1331 (OMa).

TOUCH OF WINTER ..—.. 15 br.g. Strong Gale — Ballyhoura Lady (Green Shoon) pp. Workmanlike half-brother to Irish Pointing and English Chasing winner, Grand Scenery (IRE), and to Irish NH flat and Hurdles and English Chasing winner, Duhallow Ladge. Dam won a NH flat, 3 Hdles (2m5f-3m), and 4 Chses (2m6f-3m) in Ireland (including a 5-timer). IRISH P-t-P '90 r1 p1 (2nd). NH '91/5 (blinkered) r32 w3 (2m4f Hdle on all-weather, and 2 2m7f Chses) p5. P-t-P/HUNT CH '96/7 and '99 r16 w2 (Open and Members) p5 (3 2nds; and last of 3 twice); pulled up 4, and unseated 2. Showed much improved form when dividing Moving Earth and Charlie Strong at Charlton Horethorne last year, but appeared to finish lame, and has been pulled up in just four starts since. Previously sadly unpredictable, but woeful in 2000, and finished. *M.W. Kwiatkowski — Tedworth (Caroline Keevil).* 1096 (MO), 1279 (M).

TOUGH DECISION ..8-9.. 8 b.g. Dixi (BEL) — Mistress Foy (Freeby Boy) 48p. P-t-P '99 r3 p1 (3rd of 4); unseated 1, and pulled up 1. Beaten a minimum of 20 lengths when completing, and beginning to look defective after a faintly promising start. Wears a cross-noseband. *Mrs J.M. Reynard — Bedale.* 379 (OMa), 624 (OMa), 694 (OMa).

TOURING-TURTLE (IRE) ..9-5.. 9 gr.g. Roselier (FR) — Rossian (Silent Spring) 66563. Angular brother to Thinkaboutthat (IRE) (*qv*). IRISH P-t-P '96/8 r17 w1 (2m6f Hdle) p5. NH '98 and Sep '99 (for M. Muggeridge) r4 p0 (pulled up 4, inc 2 Chses). NH Jun '00 r1 p1 (30½*l* 3rd in 2m5f110y Nov Ch: *rdn & wknd 11*). Won an Irish Hurdle on firmish in '97, but was awful in his first English yard, and beaten a minimum of 30 lengths when jumping round in weary fashion in Points in 2000. Beaten a similar distance on his first attempt for Colin Tizzard, but did give the impression that he might be on the way back towards finding some slightly better form. *Mrs H.M. Goody — Hursley Hambledon (Kate Buckett; Colin Tizzard).* 127 (Cf), 453 (Cf), 628 (Cf), 824 (Cf).

TOYTOWN KING (IRE) ..—.. 12 b.g. Royal Fountain — Lucky Pace (Lucky Brief) 34. Workmanlike half-brother to Lucky Helmet, to Irish Pointing winner, Brief Pace, and to NH flat and Hurdles winner, Andrews Minstrel. IRISH P-t-P '93 and '96/7 r16 p2; pulled up 7, and fell 2. P-t-P '98/9 r3 p1 (2nd of 3); pulled up 1, and unseated 1. Beaten 21 times over nine years, and only serves to provide Russell Betts with some fun in his Members now. Tailed off from halfway in both attempts in 2000, but at least the owner kept the partnership intact. *R. Betts — West Street/Tickham, & V. of Aylesbury.* 1142 (M), 1487 (M).

TRACEYTOWN (IRE) ..9-6.. 9 ch.m. Lancastrian — Knockarone Star (Paddy's Stream) 1754ppf. Sturdy half-sister to What About That (IRE). IRISH P-t-P '97 r2 p2 (2nd of 3 and 3rd of 4 in mares Mdns). NH FLAT '98 r1 p0. NH '98/9 (for G.B. Balding) r5 p0 (generally tailed off). Bought Doncaster, May for 2600. Useless under Rules, but a return to Points after a three year absence from them enabled her to score in a Maiden on firmish at Market Rasen, in which she provided Rachel Clark with her first winner. A safe enough ride, but has proved decidedly moderate since. Was reluctant on her latest appearance, and fell two out when tailed off and tired (should have been pulled up). Lacks scope. *R.D. Jones — York & Ainsty S. (Liz Clark).* 52 (OMa), 396 (R), 503 (R), 807 (R), 1000 (R), 1230 (R), 1351 (CR).

TRACK O' PROFIT (IRE) ..10-3.. 9 ch.g. Kambalda — Teazle (Quayside) p2242. Lengthy half-brother to Irish Pointing winner, Loury The Louse, and to Super Franky (won 6 in Ireland in '99, inc NH flat, Hdles and Chse). IRISH P-t-P '97/9 r14 w2 (5yo plus Maiden, and Confined Open) p4 (2nds); last, pulled up 3, fell 3, and brought down 1. IRISH NH FLAT '98 r1 p0. IRISH NH '98 r1 p1 (3rd in Hdle). NH Aut '99 (for C. Popham, bought for 2000) r8 p3 (Chses, inc distant last of 3 in Sell). Won two Irish Points in mud (including a defeat of Cebu Gale), but has found it impossible to score since. Can cope with a wide range of distances, and is a handy sort to have for jumping round the West Country circuits, as he can often pick up a decent place prize without ever threatening to get his head in front. Would have a better chance of scoring between the flags, but it makes far more sense to keep him over the tracks o' profit. *R.J.S. Linne — E. Cornwall.* 162 (I), 310 (I), 583 (2m5f110yH), 1432 (3m1fH), 1644 (3m2f110yH).

TRADE DISPUTE (IRE) ..11-7.. 9 ro.g. Ela-Mana-Mou — Safety Feature (Be My Guest USA) 1f31. Smallish compact half-brother to Irish flat winners, Trade Survivor and Out'N'About (IRE) (also successful Hurdler), and to Irish NH flat winner, Arms Ban (IRE). IRISH FLAT '95/6 and '98 (blinkered when winning Ulster Cesarewitch) r14 w2 (2m-2m2f) p1 (2nd). IRISH NH '95/6 r5 w3 (2m Hdles) p0. P-t-P/HUNT CH '99 r6 w4 (3 Hunt Chses, 3m1f-3m4f110y, and Open, inc hat-trick) p1 (3rd of 4 in Hunt Ch); and unseated 1. NH Feb '00 r1 p0 (fell in 3m3f Sedgefield HCap Chse: *hld up, stdy hdwy ½way, ld 14, blun nxt, 20l clr when fell last*). A crack Hunter Chaser whose only defeats in eight completions over fences have come following a bad blunder at Huntingdon, and when two lengths third to Cavalero in the Cheltenham Foxhunters. Barely out of a canter to win at Catterick and Newcastle either side, and would have strong claims in useful handicap company, but sometimes makes diabolical errors, and failed to survive one on his debut in such a race when invincible at Sedgefield. Formerly a useful performer in Ireland, and connections have done a sterling job to produce him in such fine shape. Stays extremely well, handles any going, and will hopefully return for another crack at the Prestbury Park feature. *G. Tuer — Hurworth (Edwin Tuer).* 155 (3m4f110yH), 584 (3m2f110yH), 917 (3mH).

TRADE HILL SHALAMAR (U) ..8-0.. 11 ch.g. unknown 5. A fat hunter who was amazingly sent off favourite to beat four thoroughbreds in his Members, but ran as he looked and plodded home a remote last. *A. Bealby — Cottesmore.* 542 (M).

TRAIN LOVER (NZ) ..9-8.. 11 br.g. Beau Zephyr (AUS) — Belle Rail (NZ) (Man The Rail USA) pf. Big strong ex-team chaser. P-t-P '98 r3 w1 (Maiden) p1 (2nd); and 6th. Did well to make a winning debut at Market Rasen, but has clearly been hard to train since, and having missed '99 could only appear twice in April this season. Sent off favourite for his Members, but was beaten when falling a mile from home. Has plenty to prove when he returns. *G.J. Smith — Quorn, & S. Notts.* 963 (R), 1214 (M).

TRANQUIL LORD (IRE) ..9-7.. 13 b.g. Le Moss — Sedate (Green Shoon) 45pp4up. Compact rather light half-brother to Irish Pointing winner, Generalanaesthetic. IRISH P-t-P '93/5 r13 p3 (inc last of 3; and head 2nd — deserved a dead-heat); pulled up 5, ran out 1, fell when in command at last once, and slipped up 1. P-t-P '96/7 and '99 r12 w1 (Maiden) p5 (4 2nds); pulled up 4, and unseated 2. Deserved his '96 success following six placings, but broke down the following season, and has looked all at sea since. Shows snippets of form, but beaten a minimum of 20 lengths in 2000, and rarely looks happy any more. *D.P. Smith — Heythrop (Sarah Kellard-Smith).* 80 (CCfR), 429 (C), 513 (CR), 863 (R), 1355 (R), 1482 (R), 1623 (R).

TRAVEL BY LAND ..9-10.. 7 b.g. Landyap (USA) — Travel Myth (Bairn USA) 14441p. Lengthy half-brother to flat winner, Lasham. NH FLAT Apr '99 r1 p0 (well tailed off and virtually pulled up). NH '99 (for M. Pipe) r2 p0 (pulled up in one of 2 Hdles). Lady ridden in Points, and was a first success for Olivia Green when coming home a mile ahead (literally) of the Biddick duo of hunters in his Members, in which he was lucky as the clear leader unseated three out. Missed out on a Maiden opportunity, but benefitted from an intelligent ride from Tabitha Cave when saving vital ground on one of the bends at Trebudannon and rather stealing a Restricted. Acts on firm ground and is a good jumper, but does not usually aspire to quite such a high rating. *M. Biddick — N. Cornwall.* 99 (M), 541 (I), 850 (R), 1043 (R), 1389 (R), 1636 (Cf).

TRAVELLING JACK ..—.. 6 ch.g. Lyphento (USA) — Lady Magenta (Rolfe USA) fpf. Lengthy half-brother to Summer Pudding. Makes some appalling errors and can jump violently to the right, and is currently as troublesome as Summer Pudding (qv). Hopelessly tailed off and crawling from the 13th until he fell four fences later at Bratton Down, and James Young should have been censured for this thoroughly idiotic piece of riding. *M. Rowe — Eggesford (Laura Horsey).* 253 (CfMa), 722

(CfMa), 1564 (OMa).

TRAVEL SAFELY (IRE) ..9-9.. 7 ch.g. Over The River (FR) — Missfethard-On-Sea (Deep Run) 234p1p2pp. Compact. Dam is half-sister to Senior Partner (qv). IRISH P-t-P '99 r3 p0 (pulled up 3). Sold Doncaster, May for 2000. Was wildly inconsistent and visored twice latterly, but did manage to give connections some fun including a win in a two-finisher youngsters Maiden at Lydstep as well as acheiving a close last of two twice before he died at Bassaleg. R.J. Evans — Ystrad Taf Fechan. 267 (CfMa), 350 (CfMa), 491 (CfMa), 602 (CfMa), 835 (OMa), 1298 (R), 1399 (M), 1452 (R), 1568 (R).

TREMENDISTO ..10-2.. 11 b.g. Petoski — Misty Halo (High Top) 443p27. Tall rangy half-brother to flat and Hurdles winners, Heritage (also a successful Chaser — cost 120,000 gns) and Desert Mist, and to flat winners, Rock Face, Finlaggan and Shifting Mist. Dam won 21 flat, 8-18f (one on Isle of Man). 2000y. FLAT (to '99) r31 p8. NH FLAT Oct '94 (for Capt J. Wilson) r1 p1 (2nd). NH '96/9 (very free in blinkers once; 2 wins from T. Wall's; previously for D. McCain) r20 w3 (2m1f Hdles, inc Sell) p5; fell 2nd only Ch. Did not inherit the great courage of his dam, and is a really quirky character who refused to race on five occasions over Hurdles including on his final three appearances. Much better in Points since being reluctant to line up and dwelling on his debut in them, and often pulls hard once he has set off (wears a cross-noseband), but does not have enough stamina for three miles, and beaten 14 lengths plus if completing. It is a pity he does not stay, because he came no where near to achieving the expected double squiggle. D.P. Constable — N. Salop (Mrs J. Wall). 480 (O), 859 (O), 988 (O), 1087 (MO), 1409 (O), 1603 (2m6f110yH).

TREVVEETHAN (IRE) ..9-5.. 12 ch.g. On Your Mark — Carrick Slaney (Red God) p4. Good-bodied fired half-brother to an Italian flat winner, and to an Irish Hurdles winner. FLAT r4 p0 (inc Sell). NH '92/6 (visored 1) r19 p6 (inc 2 Sells). P-t-P/HUNT CH '97/9 (for Mr G. & Mrs K. Smyly) r15 w4 (Maiden, 2 Members and PPORA) p4 (2 3rds, last once); last pair 3, pulled up 1, and on floor 3. Has managed to gain an annual success in the present yard '97/9, but has not been easy to train, and broke a blood vessel once last year. Only appeared twice in 2000, and had nine weeks off in between, but tailed off both times, and will do well to regain his form at 12. An edgy sort who usually sweats excessively. N. Sutton & Mrs R. Lane — N. Cotswold (Giles Smyly). 476 (Cnr), 1523 (C).

T REX (U) ..—.. 7 b.g. unknown R. Martin Weston was evidently hoping to strike gold at his home meeting where he ran Lord Lard and T Rex, but the former pulled up, whilst the latter ducked past the first with 'Marge' Keel. M.H. Weston — Croome & W. Warwicks. 1354 (M).

TRIAL AND ERROR ..8-12.. 9 b.g. Oedipus Complex — Martell Lady (Petit Pretendre) 3. Small compact. Dam won her Members and placed 5 (inc a Hdle) for Sheila Mollett. P-t-P '99 r1 p0 (fell). By the same sire as his more illustrious stablemate Ways And Means, and like her has stood little racing, but there the comparison ends, and beaten 25 lengths when third in his Members this year. Might be capable of better if he could appear more often. Mrs S.A. Mollett — Burton. 435 (M).

TRICKY TREVOR (IRE) ..9-12.. 8 b br.g. Arctic Lord — Chancer's Last (Foggy Bell) p2u23R13. Lengthy good-bodied half-brother to Spaceage Gold (qv). NH FLAT '98 r3 p2. NH '98 (for K. Bailey, blinkered last 2) r7 p1 (2nd in Hdle); 5th and fell in Chses. Bought Doncaster, Aug for 4600. Would have gained a fourth placing under Rules had he not stumbled and fallen after the last when a close second in a Hurdle in July '99, so it was remarkable that he could not win a Maiden until his seventh attempt. Beaten favourite on four occasions including when desperately unlucky at Hornby Castle, where he was unassailable when a leather broke and he decanted his partner on the run-in, but finally gained compensation on the same track despite wavering around in the closing stages. A Tricky Trevor indeed and swishes his tail violently, and was twice out-ridden in very respectable seconds and Holly Delahooke also went the wrong side of a marker once. Clearly has plenty of ability, and it would be interesting to see what a leading male jockey could make of him. J.S. Delahooke — Zetland. 45 (OMa), 282 (OMa), 380 (OMa), 507 (CMa), 816 (OMa), 1003 (OMa), 1033 (OMa), 1326 (R).

TRIFAST LAD ..9-11.. 16 ch.g. Scallywag — Cilla (Highland Melody) 35622. Tall rangy. P-t-P/HUNT CH '92/3 and '95/9 r24 w8 (inc 3 Hunt Chses, 2m4f110y-3m110y, and 2 Opens) p10 (9 2nds; and inc 4 Hunt Chses); pulled up 1, and fell 1. Unbeaten in Points '92/3 and also won over timber fences at Barbury Castle in '96, but best remembered for collecting three Hunter Chases as a 12-year-old. Still prepared to try, and gave Lesley Baker some good rides, but woefully one-paced and was overwhelmed by another veteran in his Members. A patent safety, and will be fondly remembered if 2000 was his swansong. M. & Mrs S. Roberts — E. Sussex & Romney Marsh, & Coakham Bloodhounds (Mike Roberts). 216 (Cnr), 305 (Cf), 573 (CfL), 985 (M), 1170 (L).

TRIGGER CASTLE ..9-4.. 6 b.m. Henbit (USA) — Jane's Daughter (Pitpan) p3. Sister to Solo Trip (qv). Bought Doncaster, May for 4600. Green at present, but ran a tidy race when about eight lengths third at Witton Castle, and would have been closer but for a bad mistake three out. Looks destined for a Maiden success at least. S. Birkinshaw — Middleton (Tony Walker). 1235 (OMa), 1331 (OMa).

PLATE 133   1027 Bedale Confined: Triple Eaves (C. Mulhall), 1st   PHOTO: Roy Parker

TRIPLE EAVES ..10-5.. 10 ch.g. Exorbitant — Torlonia (Royal Palace) 1443d16u. Sparely-made angular half-brother to Gissmo, and to flat winner, Izitallworthit. NH '96 r1 p0 (tailed off — not jump well). P-t-P '98/9 r11 w1 (Maiden) p3 (2 2nds); fell/unseated 3. A decent Pointer on his day, but inconsistent in both running and jumping, and lucky not to come back riderless in both Hunter Chase ventures. Gets excellent assistance from Clive Mulhall, and might be able to win in Open company in 2001. Can take a strong hold, and wears a cross-noseband. *R.G. Makin — York & Ainsty S.* 137 (R), 229 (Cf), 543 (I), 811 (I), 1027 (Cf), 1334 (3mH), 1601 (3m2fH).

TRIVIAL (IRE) ..10-5.. 9 b.m. Rakaposhi King — Miss Rubbish (Rubor) 5221u1. Small close-coupled attractive owner-bred half-sister to Little Idiot. Dam was 2nd in 2 Maidens for Tim Brockbank, and subsequently won 4 Chses (2m4f-3m) and placed 4 (inc 3rd in a Hdle, and Scottish Grand National) for him. P-t-P '98/9 r9 w2 (2m4f Maiden, and Members) p0; 4th, pulled up 3, refused 1, and fell 2. A hard ride who has looked reluctant, but much improved in 2000, and recorded much the fastest time of the day when successful at Whittington. Might have followed up at the next meeting there, but ejected the rider when upsides at the penultimate, but made amends when capturing her Members for the second year running subsequently. Has won on firmish, and in softish, but has shown a tendency to jump away to the left. Should win again as long as her enthusiasm holds. Wears a cross-noseband. *J.T. Brockbank — Cumberland.* 360 (R), 497 (R), 713 (R), 811 (I), 1149 (Cf), 1362 (M).

TROJAN LOVE (IRE) ..—.. 8 b.m. Cyrano De Bergerac — Love Of Paris (Trojan Fen) pf. Small sturdy. NH FLAT '97 (for S. Griffiths) r1 p0 (remote last). Bought Ascot, June for 2000. Gave unimpressive displays when only reaching halfway. *Mr & Mrs T.M. Bagley — Essex (Terry Bagley).* 321 (R), 550 (OMa).

TROOPER PIPPIN ..—.. 9 b.g. Sergeant Drummer (USA) — Zipwitch (Brianston Zipper) uup. Good-bodied brother to Batman. Dam was a useless Pointer for Mrs Rising. P-t-P '98 r1 p0 (pulled up). Unseated Alex Ede twice in the first mile, and then schooled for two miles at Buckfastleigh. Unpromising on the evidence to date. *Mrs R.P. Rising — Silverton (Gordon Chambers).* 65 (M), 163 (R), 254 (CfMa).

TROPNEVAD ..9-3§.. 13 ch.g. Alias Smith (USA) — Confident Girl (Quorum) f018rpp3p2p. Small robust half-brother to 4 winning Hurdlers, including Natural Ability (in Ireland — also won NH flat there), Ashfield Boy and Gone With The Vet (also won NH flat). NH FLAT r3 p0. NH '93/6 r17 p3 (3rds, inc Sell, and distant last; and 15*l* 3rd of 4 in Ch); 5th, last and unseated 1 in other Chses. P-t-P '97/9 (for Mr A.S. Nelson) r7 p3 (2 3rds, of 4 once). Took 30 races to get off the mark, and had his task made easier when his main danger departed two out in his two-finisher Members.

Unlikely to receive another gift so soon. Ungenuine, and has had a different owner in three of his four Pointing campaigns, but the present one seems to have a soft spot for him. Wears blinkers, and usually makes mistakes. *A.S. Nelson — N.P. & J.L. Williams — College V. & N. Northumberland.* 46 (OMa), 89 (3m1fH), 182 (M), 359 (Cf), 713 (R), 911 (4mmMO), 1078 (Cf), 1159 (I), 1427 (R), 1497 (L), 1579 (L).

TRUDYS BIRTHDAY (U) ..—.. a gr.m. Mistake — Control 5. Finally lumbered to completion in her Members, in which she was a first ride for the veteran Michael MacGregor, who was bent on celebrating his wife Trudy's birthday in style. Put off and refused at halfway, and later pulled up for a picnic before eventually continuing. By mistake out of control just about sums it up. *M.J. MacGregor — Border (Teresa Gibson).* 1501 (M).

PLATE 134   811 Holcombe Harriers Intermediate: Trivial (R. Morgan), 1st, is ahead of Allrite Bonny Lass (L. Morgan), 2nd   PHOTO: Peter & Marilyn Sweet

TRUE CHIMES ..9-8.. 10 ch.g. True Song — Ballytina (Rugantino) u4537p. Very tall strong half-brother to Ballyaction. Dam, sister or half-sister to 4 Pointers, including Ashford Ditton, was 3rd in a Maiden for Ena Cardew. NH '96 r1 p0. P-t-P/HUNT CH '97/9 r12 w2 (2m4f Maiden, and Restricted) p3 (2 3rds, inc Hunt Ch); pulled up 1, and fell/unseated 3. Takes a keen hold, and regularly gives a prominent display, but prone to errors, and usually runs out of stamina. Has made the frame in two Hunter Chases, and ran well for a long way at Leicester on his most recent attempt, and would be worth trying again over sub-3m trips as his Pointing exploits are getting him nowhere. Wears a cross-noseband. *A. & Mrs E.V. Cardew — Bicester with Whaddon (Herbie Owen).* 63 (I), 191 (Cf), 462 (2m7f110yH), 632 (I), 886 (C), 1017 (I).

TRUE FORTUNE ..9-12.. 11 b.g. True Song — Cost A Fortune (Silver Cloud) 425184. Compact. Dam won a Maiden and placed 4 (3 in Ireland). P-t-P/HUNT CH '95/8 (for Mr D.J. Miller) r13 w5 (inc 2m7f110y Hunt Ch, and Open) p4 (3 2nds, inc 3 Hunt Chses); fell/unseated 3, and pulled up 1. NH '98/9 (for V. Dartnall) r7 w1 (3m2f HCap Chse) p2 (2nds). A thorough stayer and suited by soft ground, but needed the aid of blinkers to win his second race over regulation fences, and looked very one-paced on his return to Points in 2000. Managed to win his Members on totally unsuitable ground, but no match for Bit Of A Citizen when odds-on at Pantyderi previously, and was well beaten in his last two appearances. Much slower to come to hand in the new yard, and seems to have lost his zip. *G. Barber — Pembs (Mark Barber).* 35 (Cnr), 345 (O), 670 (O), 831 (M), 1022 (3mH), 1226 (O).

TRUE FRED ..9-2§.. 12 ch.g. True Song — Silver Spartan (Spartan General) fpppp4up. Small strong brother to Spartan Chief and Silver Skylark, and to Hurdles winner, Competitive Bid, and half-brother to The Grim Reaper. NH '94 and '97 r3 p1 (last of 3 in Hdle). P-t-P '94 and '96/9 (for Mrs A. Price) r22 w1 (Members) p4 (2nd of 3; and 3 3rds, last once); pulled up 8, and fell/unseated 5. Won a bad and slowly-run three-finisher Members in '96, but has a history of leg trouble, and steadfastly refuses to exert himself now. Had seven different pilots in 2000 (Richard Burton was rewarded with an extra go after getting him round at Upper Sapey) but regularly visored/blinkered with no effect, and is fast becoming a waste of time. *R.J. Brereton — Ludlow (Geoff Evans).* 13 (R), 75 (I), 120 (CR), 196 (R), 484 (R), 698 (R), 1548 (R), 1664 (R).

TRUE HUSTLER ..9-6.. 8 ch.g. True Song — Spartan Clown (Spartan General) 22ppf2fu. Workmanlike owner-bred brother to Wheel Tapper, Tapalong (dam of Ryans Star *qv* 2000 Annual), Silver Fig, True Sparkle and Thornton Flyer, and to Chasing winner, Clown Around. Dam won 2m Nov Ch, but failed to finish in 4 Hunt Chses. P-t-P '99 r3 p0 (4th, and pulled up 2). Usually thereabouts, but finds differing ways of retaining his Maiden status, and his latest blunder broke Fred Hutsby's arm. Has finished in front of three subsequent winners when placed in Maidens, but pulls hard, makes too many mistakes, and cannot or will not find anything in the closing stages. Should find an opening eventually, but unlikely to achieve much more. Blinkered on his last four appearances. *H. Hutsby — Warwicks (Fred Hutsby).* 30 (CMa), 194 (CfMa), 433 (OMa), 1020 (OMa), 1204 (OMa), 1435 (OMa), 1624 (OMa), 1675 (OMa).

TRUE STEEL ..10-6.. 15 b.g. Deep Run — Aran Tour (Arapaho) 14.5. Tall lengthy half-brother to Cool Dawn (IRE) (won '98 Cheltenham Gold Cup after Pointing), and to Hurdles winner, Rye Crossing (IRE). NH '90/3 and '96 r7 p2 (2nds, inc R.A. Gold Cup); ran Sell. P-t-P/HUNT CH '94 and '96/9 r17 w4 (inc 2m4f110y Hunt Ch; and inc hat-trick '94) p6 (4 2nds, inc 3 Hunt Chses; and last of 3); pulled up 3, and fell 1. NH Mar '00 r1 p0 (5th in 3m110y R.A Gold Cup: *chsd ldrs til wknd 12*). Usually runs at Sandown, and has made 10 of his last 14 appearances there. Used to have a fine turn of foot, and showed his retains plenty of ability when produced late to beat Irisheyesaresmilin in a fast time at Dunthrop. Has very brittle legs, and stands few outings, but Jon Trice-Rolph can be rightly proud of his achievements with a horse who can be a hot ride and often has to be mounted on course. *J.C. Trice-Rolph — Heythrop.* 191 (Cf), 470 (2m4f110yH).

TRUEWAY TWO ..8-8.. 8 br.m. True Song — Portway (Pardigras) p. Dam, half-sister to 2 Pointers, including The Nations Way (*qv* '94 Annual), only completed in 2 of 8 Points for the Russells. P-t-P '99 r4 p0 (5th, and pulled up 3). Has twice shown ability when reaching the last before pulling up, but only appeared once in 2000, and may have suffered a setback. *R.D. Russell — Heythrop.* 194 (CfMa).

TRULY OPTIMISTIC ..8-12.. 12 b.m. True Song — Wildly Optimistic (Hard Fact) 34p6. Well-made owner-bred sister to Totally Optimistic, and half-sister to Very Cavalier and The Final Optimist. P-t-P '95/9 r17 p2 (2nds); last 2, pulled up 9, and fell 1. Her best effort was when five lengths second in '99, but has had 21 chances to lose her maiden status, and usually fails to stay. Even the most optimistic have begun to get pessimistic about her winning. Seems quite highly strung, and regularly sweats and gets on her toes. *Mrs R.C. Hayward — Warwicks.* 516 (OMa), 790 (OMa), 1018 (OMa), 1435 (OMa).

TUATH DEUCHAINNE ..8-7.. 8 b.g. Brooksway Oats (IRE) — Easter Trial VII (unknown) pp4p. Tall plain owner-bred. P-t-P '99 r2 p0 (pulled up 2, and unseated 1). Has shown speed to halfway twice, but badly tailed off in his only completion, and is no racehorse. Commentators the length and breadth of Britain will be hoping he does not venture to their neck of the woods in future. *Miss R. Pask — Belvoir.* 24 (OMa), 124 (OMa), 168 (OMa), 372 (CfMa).

TUBB CORNER ..8-3.. 9 ch.g. Mr Fluorocarbon — Sea Farmer (Cantab) pp4. Small sturdy half-brother to Pretty Boy George (*qv*). A late starter who looked a hot-head on his debut, and was beaten 25 lengths when achieving a completion. *Mrs S.M. Trump — Silverton.* 310 (I), 730 (I), 855 (CfMa).

TUBBER ROADS (IRE) ..10-6.. 8 b.g. Un Desperado (FR) — Node (Deep Run) 1343138. Close-coupled. IRISH P-t-P r1 p1 (2nd). IRISH NH FLAT '98 r8 r2 (3rd in race for Pointers). Gave a very promising display in his Irish Point, but was out of action in '99. Returned to take a 2m4f Maiden at the first time of asking for the new yard, but did not quite get the trip when third in a Restricted, and it was a wise move to switch him to shorter Hunter Chases. Two miles may be a shade inadequate and got much too far behind before finishing third at Hereford, but 2m6f is eminently suitable, and gave a fine forcing display to beat Mr Snowman at Fakenham (appreciated the track far better than his rival). Probably disliked the firmish ground on final start, but should certainly find other opportunities at his preferred trip when underfoot conditions are easier. *W.F. Caudwell — O. Berks (Matt Hazell).* 284 (2m4fCMa), 440 (R), 685 (2m5fH), 925 (2mH), 1155 (2m5f110yH), 1341 (2m110yH), 1600 (2m5f110yH).

TUDOR FELLOW (IRE) ..—.. 12 ch.g. Decent Fellow — Canadian Tudor (Tudor Music) ppp. Small sparely-made. IRISH P-t-P '93/4 r8 w2 (4&5yo Maiden, and Hunt) p0; pulled up 1. NH '94/9 r28 p7 (Chses); inc Sells. HUNT CH '99 (for Mr N.J. Fogg) r1 p1 (2nd). Won two two-finisher Points taking well over seven minutes in Ireland in '94, but most frustrating since, and looked and performed as if he were about to drop dead at any moment in 2000. Wore a tongue-strap on his reappearance, and is in no fit state to be on a racecourse. *M. Wells — S. Notts.* 116 (I), 229 (Cf), 1073 (O).

TUDOR FLIGHT ..9-2.. 10 b.m. Forzando — Tudor Pilgrim (Welsh Pageant) 2pp42. Compact half-sister to flat and Hurdles winner, Gloriana. Dam won at 7f. FLAT (visored 1) r16 p3; Sell final. NH '95/6 r7 p3 (inc 2 Sells). P-t-P '97/9 (for Mr I.A. Brown) r18 p5 (4 2nds); failed to finish 12 (fell/unseated 5, and ran out 1). Does not lack speed, and beaten a maximum of seven lengths in six of her placings, but struggles to get the trip, and remains prone to make mistakes. Deserves to find a race, but is leaving things a little late. Wears a cross-noseband. *Mrs S.A. Turner — Gelligaer F.* 490 (CfMa), 704 (OMa), 994 (OMa), 1404 (OMa), 1573 (OMa).

TUDOR LODGE (IRE) ..10-2.. 8 ch.m. Glacial Storm (USA) — Rock Solid (Hardboy) ufp2u13f. Small compact half-sister to Supreme Dream (IRE) (qv). P-t-P '98/9 (for Mrs J. Mathias) r6 w3 (Mares Maiden, Restricted and Intermediate — hat-trick) p1 (last of 3); pulled up 1, and unseated 1. A progressive mare in '99, but it took a while for Sarah Swindells to get to grips with her this year, and has found fences in the North and West somewhat stiffer than what she was used to in Wales. Most determined when she puts in a clear round, appreciates plenty of cut, and could win on a more regular basis in future. *J.S. Swindells — Cheshire.* 135 (L), 170 (L), 566 (L), 590 (L), 904 (L), 1074 (L), 1462 (L), 1601 (3m2fH).

TUFREE ..—.. 8 b.g. Broadsword (USA) — Fanta's Girl (Barbaro) p. Owner-bred half-brother to Hurdles winner, Tuwun. Dam, half-sister to Official Souvenir (qv '93 Annual) and 5 other Pointers including Sir Bryn, won Maiden and placed 4. Grandam, Present Fantasy, was unplaced in Points. Showed speed to halfway in a Maiden, but had become tailed off when he pulled up after 2m4f. *Mrs E.A.G. Crossley Cooke — O. Berks (Philip Greenwood).* 220 (OMa).

TUMLIN OOT (IRE) ..10-5.. 12 b.g. Amazing Bust — Tumlin Brig (New Brig) 3p21. Tall strong half-brother to Parsons Brig, and to Hurdles winner, Brownside Brig (unsuccessful in his first 3 races, when trained by Swannee Haldane). NH '95/6 r7 p0 (pulled up 2, and fell in Chses). HUNT CH '97/8 (for Mr J.S. Haldane) r8 w1 (Maiden) p2; pulled up 5. Should have won in a driving finish at Newton Bromswold, but Mike Lurcock's technique has not yet evolved to be as good as that of Ben Pollock, and made ample amends when justifying favouritism at Cottenham subsequently. Used to jump poorly over regulation fences, but has found the smaller obstacles in Points no problem, and should be able to win again as he has very few miles on the clock. Stays well. *M. Lurcock — Fitzwilliam.* 86 (R), 440 (R), 513 (CR), 1035 (Cnr).

TURNING TRIX ..9-13.. 14 b.g. Buckskin (FR) — Merry Run (Deep Run) 1p343. Rangy unfurnished brother to NH flat and Hurdles winner, Hideabound (IRE), and half-brother to Wrens Trix. NH FLAT '92 (for S. Sherwood) r1 w1. NH '93/8 (for D. Nicholson; 1 win previously for S. Sherwood) r25 w5 (Chses, 2m4f-3m) p7 (inc 2 Hdles); 13th in '97 Grand National. Won five Chases including a £7100 prize between January '95 and March '97, but only appeared twice in '98 and missed '99. A gift to Rebecca Curtis, and gave her a dream first ride when winning a Novice Jockeys event at Barbury Castle (just held on), but was not quick enough for more competitive events subsequently. Error-prone over regulation fences, but splendidly safe in Points. *Miss R. Curtis — Tivyside.* 33 (Cnr), 272 (L), 645 (MO), 836 (L), 946 (L).

TURN UP THE HEAT ..—.. 7 ch.g. Prince Of Peace — Trewithien (Air Trooper) u. Compact. Dam won 3 Hdles at around 2m, and is half-sister to 4 Pointers, including Trecometti (qv '98 Annual). NH FLAT '98/9 r2 p0 (tailed off). NH '99 (for N. Hawke) r1 p0 (tailed off in Hdle). Awful under Rules when only one horse finished behind him, and lost contact with Orlando Jackson at the first in a Maiden. *O.T. Jackson — Taunton V.* 409 (OMa).

TURRILL HOUSE ..—.. 9 b.m. Charmer — Megabucks (Buckskin FR) p. Lengthy. Dam won 4 flat (10-12f) and 3 Hdles at around 2m (inc £13,500 prize), all in Ireland at 4. FLAT r12 w1 (2m fibresand) p1 (3rd). NH '96/9 (for W. Musson) r18 w4 (2m-2m5f Hdles, the first a Sell) p4. More than competent when it was required in the previous yard, and gained her first success in a Selling Hurdle in which she started favourite, having earned the comment 'never put in the race' on her previous attempt in similar company the time before. Was quick enough to open her flat account as a seven-year-old, and although she did not look an easy ride on her Pointing debut the ability is still there if she can be persuaded to settle and jump better. *J.R. Weston — Worcs.* 447 (Cm).

TURSAL (IRE) ..9-4§.. 12 b.g. Fine Blade (USA) — Turlough Pet (Retieme) u1p5u7. Big strong. NH FLAT '95 r2 p0. NH '95/7 r7 p1 (3rd); ran out in Sell; also pulled up, and fell 2. P-t-P '99 r5 w1 (Maiden) p1 (2nd of 3); 5th, 8th, and refused 1. Took 7min 30s to win his Maiden in '99, and the best part of seven minutes to wrap up his Members this year when partnered on both occasions by the owner. Made mistakes in the latter, and has seen the back of Andrew Crookston twice either side, and could not be supported with any confidence in a Restricted. *A.R. Campbell — Lanarks & Renfrews, & Eglinton.* 359 (Cf), 659 (M), 717 (Cf), 976 (R), 1118 (R), 1427 (R).

TUSKAR FLOP ..10-3.. 14 b.g. Le Moss — Merendas Sister (Pauper) 1222p. Attractive good-bodied brother to General Moss and Credo Is King (IRE), and half-brother to Sweet Merenda (IRE). IRISH NH FLAT '94 r1 p0. IRISH NH '94 r2 p0. IRISH P-t-P '95 and '97 r11 w4 (inc 2 4-runner Opens) p1 (2nd); pulled up 3 and fell 1. P-t-P '98/9 (for late Capt. T.A. Forster) r13 w3 (Opens) p5 (3 2nds, last once; 2 3rds, of 4, and last once); last 1, pulled up 2, unseated 1, and ran out 1. Won four Points in Ireland in '97, and has now equalled that feat in this country, but needs a sound surface to produce his best. Whizzed round Black Forest Lodge in under six minutes to defeat Well Armed on his reappearance, but then saw the backsides of three useful performers, and found the ground too testing on his final appearance. Retains his ability well for a veteran, and could yet win again when conditions are right. Broke a blood vessel once in '99. *Mr & Mrs M.J. Trickey — Devon & Somerset (Mike Trickey).* 561 (O), 727 (O), 928 (MO), 1096 (MO), 1238 (O).

TWEED BRIG ..9-1.. 9 b.g. Meadowbrook — Starry Brig (New Brig) 5R. Dam won 5 Points (4 Ladies, inc hat-trick) and placed 10 for Graham Macmillan. P-t-P '98 r1 p0 (unseated). Not beaten far on his reappearance though the race was run at a very slow pace, and it may flatter him, but worth another chance in Maidens. Had tried to stop on his debut, and clearly has other miscreant tendencies as he hung violently left until ducking out at the fifth when odds-on his Members subsequently. *W.G. Macmillan — Dumfries.* 665 (OMa), 979 (M).

TWILIGHT TOM ..9-12.. 12 ro.g. Pragmatic — Starlight Beauty (Scallywag) 412pu4. Lengthy owner-bred half-brother to Celestial Stream, Bonny Beau and Dark Delight. Dam, an unraced sister to Willy Wagtail, is out of Grange Gipsy, who won 2 Hdles (2m4f-3m1f) and 3m1f Ch for the Williams family. P-t-P/HUNT CH '96/9 r12 w4 (inc 2 Confineds) p1 (2nd); pulled up 6, and fell 1. A fair Pointer on his day, and can be ultra game, but holds his form for only a couple of outings, and apart from landing a gamble at Garnons did nothing to write home about in 2000. Usually needs an outing to get fit, and is suited by soft ground though he can handle a much quicker surface. *L.J. Williams — Curre.* 271 (O), 446 (O), 743 (L), 1022 (3mH), 1402 (MO), 1451 (MO).

TWO OF DIAMONDS ..—.. 7 b.g. Mr Fluorocarbon — Shelleys Rocky Gem (Kemal FR) pp. Plain good-topped. Backward when tailed off and pulled up after 2m4f in early season Maidens. *R.F.L. Clark — Middleton (Caroline Clark).* 235 (OMa), 398 (OMa).

TWOPINTSAHALFONE (IRE) ..9-4.. 9 b.g. Arctic Cider (USA) — Leave Me Here (Le Moss) 43f2. IRISH NH '99 r3 p0. Made the frame in three Maidens, but proved very easy to beat, and was 20 lengths second in first time blinkers on his latest attempt. Evidently going to struggle to score, even with weak opportunities in abundance. *Mrs E.A.B. Llewellin — Pembs (Graham Lavis).* 349 (CfMa), 650 (CfMa), 838 (OMa), 1225 (OMa).

TWOTENSFORAFIVE ..9-8.. 8 b.g. Arctic Lord — Sister Of Gold (The Parson) 21p. Compact brother to Lord Of The Rings (*qv*). IRISH NH '98/9 (blinkered final) r15 p2. Generally disappointing in Ireland, but had been placed in two handicap Hurdles at around three miles, and found Welsh Points easier. Produced a good effort when one length second to Kerry Soldier Blue in his Members, and then won a Maiden easily on firmish at Howick, but let his supporters down when 4-6 in a Restricted. Can score in that company if returning to form. *R. Mathias, S. & G. Williams & A. James — Brecon & Talybont (Richard Mathias).* 478 (M), 601 (CfMa), 1228 (R).

TYNDRUM GOLD ..9-4.. 11 br.g. Sonnen Gold — Firwood (Touching Wood USA) 4p555p64. Tall rangy half-brother to Arthur Henry. NH FLAT r1 p0. NH '95 and 97/9 r17 p2 (3rds). P-t-P '96 (for Mr J.L. Holdroyd) r6 p0 (4th, and pulled up 5). Often jumped hurdles badly, and never ran over fences under Rules, but has shown no great relish for them in Points. Usually off the bridle from the word go, and regained blinkers on his last four starts. A long-standing maiden and clearly wishes to remain one. *Mrs A.J. Lockwood — Sinnington.* 377 (R), 399 (OMa), 508 (CMa), 693 (OMa), 1004 (OMa), 1032 (OMa), 1329 (OMa), 1353 (OMa).

TYPICAL WOMAN (IRE) ..8-0.. 10 b.m. Executive Perk — Beau Jo (Joshua) 5fp. Small compact half-sister to Welsh Legion, and to Irish Pointing winner, Master Julian. Dam won NH flat, 2m2f flat, and 4 Hdles, 2m-2m4f, all in Ireland. P-t-P '97 r2 p0 (unseated 1, and pulled up 1). NH FLAT '97 r1 p0. NH '98 (for P.J. Hobbs) r2 p1 (3rd). Beaten less than eight lengths when third over hurdles at Worcester in '98, but has only managed one completion in five Pointing excursions, and seems hard to train. Led for a long way on her reappearance, but subsequently off the track for 10 weeks, and needs to improve considerably to be worthy of consideration. *A.H. & E.P.S. Bulled — Devon & Somerset.* 562 (CfMa), 1565 (OMa), 1654 (OMa).

UBU VAL (FR) ..10-3.. 15 b.g. Kashneb (FR) — Lady Val (FR) (Credit Man) 16*8*. Robust. NH FLAT r1 p0. NH '92 and '95/8 r10 w2 (3m-3m2f Chses) p2; pulled up and last 2 on final 3 attempts. P-t-P/HUNT CH '93/5 and '98 r20 w7 (inc 2 Opens) p11 (8 2nds); unseated 1. NH Apr '00 r1 p0 (blinkered when last in Chse: *in itch to 11*). An expert jumper who used to be able to produce a sprint finish over extreme distances in mud, but only able to keep on at the one pace in recent years during which he has been lightly raced. Took his winning tally into double figures with an easy success in his Members, and gave a bold showing for a long way in the Grimthorpe where he was blinkered for the first time. Retains much of his enthusiasm and there's no reason to suggest he will not be back to win again at Dalton Park in 2001. *W.A. Bethell — Holderness.* 502 (M), 999 (4m1fMO).

UCKERBY LAD ..9-12.. 10 b.g. Tobin Lad (USA) — Chomolonga (High Top) p6p2p6p. Good-bodied workmanlike. FLAT (blinkered 2) r10 p2 (8-11f, one on all-weather); inc Sell. NH '94, '95 and '97 r3 p0 (last twice, and pulled up 1). P-t-P '96 and '98/9 r16 w3 (up to Confined) p4 (2 2nds; and last of 3 twice); last pair 3, pulled up 3, and fell 3. Lightly raced, and of little account over jumps until gaining three wins and four placings '98/9, and proved to be most game. Somewhat error-prone before Colin Heard took over the reins, but a disappointment when taking on better class opposition in 2000, and managed just one placed effort when a modest second of three in an 8min event at Bishopsleigh. Needs to give Opens and Hunter Chases a swerve and concentrate on the easiest options available in Points in future. *Mrs Y. Watson, K. Champion & P. Rattenbury — Lamerton (Yvonne Watson & Jo Channon).* 258 (Cf), 310 (I), 402 (O), 1175 (Cf), 1433 (3mH), 1562 (C), 1644 (3m2f110yH).

UK EUROLAD ..9-11.. 9 b.g. Say Primula — Maleiha (Martinmas) 4p22p. Tall workmanlike. P-t-P '98/9 r6 p1 (fence last of 2); pulled up 4, and fell 1. Improved with increased stamina levels in 2000, but still not enough for him to register his first success, though he came agonisingly close when totally unfancied at Bexhill. Failed to justify favouritism next time when the ground was probably not quick enough, and beat a hasty retreat after a blunder before halfway on his subsequent Hunter Chase debut. Will probably find a simple option before much longer on one of the easier tracks. Pulls hard, and wears a cross-noseband. *Miss C. Larkins — W. Street/Tickham.* 291 (CMa), 578 (OMa), 984 (OMa), 1396 (OMa), 1537 (2m5fH).

ULVICK STAR (IRE) ..10-7§.. 9 b.g. Lord Americo — She's Approaching (Ragapan) uu13. Compact attractive half-brother to Dont Tell Harry (IRE). NH FLAT '97 r1 p0. P-t-P '98/9 (for Mrs J. Read) r6 w1 (Maiden) p1 (2nd); pulled up 1, and fell/unseated 3. Has ineffective brakes, and sometimes ignores the fences, but has undoubted ability, and proved too resolute for the placed horses when making most at Higham in his latest success. Found the fences too demanding on his Hunter Chase debut, but it was a good effort nonetheless, and the horse immediately behind him subsequently won in that sphere. Very much a brown-trousers ride, but good enough to win many more Points if he can be persuaded to settle better. *Mrs P. King — Suffolk (Julie Read).* 773 (R), 1038 (R), 1111 (R), 1333 (3mH).

UNCLE ADA (IRE) ..—.. 6 ch.g. Phardante (FR) — Park Belle (IRE) (Strong Gale) ppu. Dam is half-sister to Pits Delight (qv '96 Annual). Ada Doom when bringing cold comfort to connections so far. *Mrs C. Robinson — Albrighton.* 570 (2m4fCfMa), 990 (OMa), 1323 (OMa).

UNCLE BILLY (IRE) ..9-0.. 8 br.g. Lafontaine (USA) — Toretta (Torus) 1p2. Half-brother to Fast lane (IRE). Dam won 4 Irish Hdles, 2m-2m5f. P-t-P '99 r2 p0 (last, and unseated 1). Improved by the application of blinkers in 2000, but the form of his Mollington success, where his case still looked hopeless jumping the last, is nothing special. Achieved more when second at Chaddesley, but does not look an easy ride, and makes far too many silly errors. Does nothing, but stay, and will need an extreme test to win again. *M. Levene — N. Cotswold (Giles Smyly).* 434 (OMa), 791 (R), 1067 (3m2fR).

UNCLE BUCK (IRE) ..9-6.. 8 b.g. Buckskin (FR) — River Glen (Furry Glen) 2p1p. Workmanlike good-topped. Dam is half-sister to Greenwood Lad (qv '88 Season Annual). P-t-P '98 r1 p0 (pulled up). Made most when successful in a four-finisher Maiden on firm at Horseheath, but does not appear to have the strongest constitution, and had been pulled up the time before when the rider thought he had gone lame. Missed the '99 season, and sparingly raced this year, so may not get many opportunities in the future. *M.G. Sheppard — Cambs (Josie Sheppard).* 98 (OMa), 322 (CfMa), 845 (OMa), 1379 (R).

UNCLE DEN ..9-2.. 11 b.g. Uncle Pokey — Meggies Dene (Apollo Eight) fp246p. Robust half-brother to Little Greyside and Ramstar. Dam won 2m1f Hdle and 3 Chses, 2-3m. P-t-P '98/9 r11 p2 (fence 2nd once); unseated 5, and pulled up 4. Not the safest conveyance in the world, and usually gets left well behind when owner-ridden, but seems modest in any case, and put to the sword despite competent handling in Hunter Chases on his final two starts. Might stand a chance in Maidens with a strong jockey. *I. Hudson — Oakley.* 243 (Cf), 516 (OMa), 889 (OMa), 1207 (OMa), 1537 (2m5fH), 1628 (2m4f110yH).

UNCLE JAMES (IRE) ..8-13.. 10 br.g. Young Man (FR) — Hampsruth (Sea Hawk II) pp5p. Good-bodied brother to Cliffalda and My Young Man. P-t-P '97/8 r5 p2 (2nds); 4th, and unseated 1. Not beaten far when second twice in '97, but suffered a setback the following year, and missed the '99 season. Made no show on his return, and threw in the towel when blinkered on his most recent appearance. Has always struggled with his health, and has had enough now. *C.W. White — Dulverton E. (Tina White).* 728 (R), 847 (R), 1100 (OMa), 1468 (OMa).

UNCLE REGINALD ..9-8.. 8 b.g. Chauve Souris — Pleasure Bid (Mon Plaisir) 23. Workmanlike unfurnished half-brother to My Bid (dam of Cefn Tiger qv), Charlie's Nephew, Bidore and Misblaize. Dam, half-sister to Charlie Potheen, won 2m Nov Hdle. Grandam, Irish Biddy, won 6 Points for Bronwen Hurley's father. Sire (whose name is French for a bat — of the belfry variety), by Beldale Flutter (USA), won at 12f for Geoff Wragg, but also gave plenty of good placed displays, including 2nd in the Ebor. P-t-P '99 r6 p1 (2nd); 4th thrice, ran out 1, and pulled up 1. Desperately unlucky on his final appearance in '99, as he was eight lengths clear when he stumbled and the rider lost control on the approach to the straight at Garthorpe, but presumably hit trouble in 2000 when his season was over in February. One-paced, but deserves compensation on his return. *Mrs R. Hurley — Warwicks (B. Hurley).* 81 (CCfMa), 197 (CfMa).

UNCLE TOM ..9-9.. 10 b.g. Scallywag — Reebok (Scottish Rifle) 41p. Tall. Dam won Hunt Ch and Maiden and placed 7 (inc last of 3 in Ch). Grandam, Gypsy Way, was 2nd in Members, and won 2 Sell Hdles, 2m-2m3f. P-t-P '97 r1 p0 (pulled up). Taken steadily on his first two outings, but kept going well enough to open his account at Bitterley, where Robert Cooper was the difference between winning and losing. Recorded the slowest time of the day by far, and needs to improve to stand a chance in Restricteds. *Mrs M.P. Marfell — Radnor & W. Herefords (Ian Johnson).* 567 (R), 994 (OMa), 1355 (R).

UNCLE TOM COBLEY (U) ..—.. a ch.g. unknown u. A pony who only negotiated two fences safely in his Members. No wonder they wanted Tom Pearce's grey mare. *Miss L. Pounder — Bedale.* 1031 (M).

UNDER MILK WOOD ..8-7.. 9 b.g. Still Time Left — Springaliance (Reliance II) fuu7p. Very small. Dam won 2m Sell Hdle. P-t-P '98/9 r6 w1 (Maiden) p0 (last, pulled up 3, and unseated 1). Found a unique opportunity in which to open his account on his first completion at St Hilary in '99, but has failed to beat a rival in six starts since. Error-prone, and shapes like a non-stayer. Wears a cross-noseband. *Mrs G. Pritchard — Ystrad Taf Fechan.* 484 (R), 818 (R), 1453 (R), 1568 (R), 1616 (R).

UNDER THE CARPET (IRE) ..—.. 9 b.g. Brush Aside (USA) — Grenache (Menelek) pp. Robust half-brother to Hurdles winner, Nine O Three (IRE). IR 15,000 4yo. NH FLAT '98 (from J. Old's) r1 p0. Appears to be a physical mess, and gave feeble displays when starting at 4-1 or less in Maidens. *W.E. Sturt — Hursley Hambledon (Kate Buckett).* 328 (CfMa), 828 (OMa).

PLATE 135   1586 Melton Hunt Club Members Novices: Union Man (S. Morris), 1st, completes an unbeaten season   PHOTO: Bill Selwyn

UNION MAN ..10-12.. 8 ch.g. Teamster — Cobusino (Bustino) 1111. Tall rangy. NH FLAT '98 (from N. Gaselee's) r1 p0. A powerful galloper who demolished the opposition in a most impressive four-timer, and nothing has managed to make a race of it with him so far. The opponent who did best was Springfield Rex, and he went on to score at Aintree, so the potential of Union Man is clearly boundless. Took a few liberties with the fences when completing his hat-trick at Garthorpe, and perhaps needs to tackle the bigger obstacles fairly soon if he is not to become too sloppy. Only risked on good or easy surfaces. Ably assisted by Stewart Morris, whose star was in the ascendant in 2000 after a lean spell which followed him being Champion Novice Rider. *P. Newton — Pytchley (Bill Warner).* 517 (OMa), 871 (R), 1267 (I), 1586 (CN).

UNION STATION (IRE) ..—§.. 9 b.g. Homo Sapien — Way Ahead (Sovereign Path) pfppup. Strong-topped lengthy half-brother to flat winner, Quietly Impressive. Dam won at 8f. NH FLAT Nov '98 r1 p0 (14th of 15). NH '98/9 (for N. Hawke, tried tongue-tied) r4 p0 (last after dwelling and pulled up 3 in Hdles — after trying to pull up and running wide after 2nd once). A hard ride who can be depended upon to give an abysmal display, and the very ungainly Brett Parsons is only an added handicap. Should never be on a racecourse. *B.G. Parsons — Blackmore & Sparkford V. (Brett Parsons & Jo West).* 68 (O), 211 (Cnr), 521 (O), 929 (Cnr), 1098 (C), 1237 (Cf).

UNOR (FR) ..9-6.. 15 b.g. Pot D'Or (FR) — Fyrole II (FR) (Le Tyrol) p5. Tall light-framed. NH '90/2 and '94/6 r15 w2 (2m5f-3m Chses) p3 (2 3rds, of 4, and last in Chses); pulled up 3, and fell 1. P-t-P/HUNT CH '93/5 and '98/9 r15 w4 (inc 2 Hunt Chses, 2m4f110y-3m) p2 (3rds in Hunt Chses); pulled up 4, and fell 1. Formerly a standing dish at Perth where he has won four times, but held together by more bandages than The Mummy these days and his fragility has restricted his racecourse appearances to a bare minimum in recent years. Wears a tongue-strap. *Miss H.B. Hamilton — Lauderdale.* 717 (Cf), 912 (Cf).

UNREQUITED LOVE (IRE) ..—.. 7 ch.g. Broken Hearted — Belle Savenay (Coquelin USA) pp. Tall well-made half-brother to jumping winner, Water Font (IRE). NH FLAT Jan '99 r1 p0 (tailed off). NH '99 r1 p0 (tailed off in Hdle). Made mistakes prior to pulling up when struggling in Maidens. *N. Shutts — Ludlow (Karen Marks).* 450 (CfMa), 1092 (OMa).

UP AND OVER (IRE) ..9-7§.. 10 b.g. Henbit (USA) — Tell-Em-All (Le Bavard FR) 5b57p. Rangy. IRISH P-t-P '98 r5 w1 (6 plus Mdn) p0; pulled up, and fell. NH '98/9 (from Mrs J. Brown's; previously from R. Tate's) r10 p2 (Chses). Placed twice at up to 3m3f in Chases and also fell two out when second and beaten once, but made too many mistakes. Showed no enthusiasm at all in 2000 (another ungenuine Henbit?), and was tailed off when blinkered on his latest attempt. *Mrs J.M. Jones — Pendle Forest & Craven (Jo Foster).* 173 (R), 396 (R), 440 (R), 1028 (R), 1232 (L).

UPANOFF ..8-12.. 10 br.m. Dubassoff (USA) — Upham Jubilee (Murrayfield) pf64p. Compact half-sister to Sybillabee and Hand Over Fist. Dam won Maiden and 2nd 2 (inc Hunt Ch). Grandam, Bright Eyes, was unplaced in Points, but won 3 flat, 8-10f. P-t-P '98/9 r6 p0 (5th, and pulled up 5). Occasionally shows glimpses of ability, but has only ever finished in front of two rivals, and usually fails to get the trip. Not a fluent jumper, and has never completed in Maiden company. *H.C. Pauling — Heythrop.* 194 (CfMa), 250 (CfMa), 429 (C), 752 (Cm), 1020 (OMa).

UP THE ROAD (IRE) ..8-10.. 9 b.g. Beau Sher — Killanny Bridge (Hallez FR) pppp5. Plain short-backed half-brother to Irish Pointing and English jumping winner, Down The Road, and to an Irish NH flat winner. IRISH P-t-P '97 r3 p0 (pulled up 2, and ran out 1). P-t-P '98/9 (for Mr P.J. Millington) r8 p0 (unseated 2, and pulled up 6). Stoutly bred, but runs like an arthritic camel, and only once able to complete the course when 35 lengths last in his Members. Often immediately tailed off, and must have something very badly wrong with him. *Miss S.E. Tacy — Fernie.* 548 (CfMa), 1012 (CfMa), 1217 (L), 1417 (L), 1502 (M).

UPTON ADVENTURE ..10-4.. 8 br.m. Green Adventure (USA) — Country Rise (Country Retreat) f1b1211. Workmanlike. Dam, half-sister to Little Rise (*qv* '95 Annual), failed to finish in 9 of 10 points for Peter Corbett, but grandam, Dido's Hill, won Maiden and 3rd 4 for him. P-t-P '99 r6 w1 (Maiden) p2 (2nds, of 3 once); 4th, and fell/unseated 2. A likeable mare who has made the frame in all her completions, and has been well placed to win five times. Stays particularly well, and her latest defeat can be attributed to the fact the race was run in under six minutes, but can quicken, and has been well handled by Scott Joynes since he took over the reins. Liable to the odd jumping lapse, but basically sound, and seems to handle all surfaces the same. Carries little in the way of condition, but tough and genuine and should hold her own when upgraded. *P.J. Corbett — Ledbury (Nicky Sheppard).* 14 (R), 119 (CR), 296 (I), 447 (Cm), 615 (CMod), 861 (C), 1312 (Cm).

UPTON ORBIT ..—§.. 12 b.g. Riberetto — Well Starched (Starch Reduced) 0pu9p. Small light. Dam won Restricted and 2nd. P-t-P/HUNT CH '94/6 and '98/9 r21 w1 (Maiden) p4 (2 2nds); failed to finish 12 (refused 2, fell/unseated 3). Appeared to finish lame on his reappearance, and tailed off in his four subsequent outings. Was capable of fair efforts when in the mood, but next to useless since returning from an absence in '98. *T.P. Hitchman — Warwicks (John Pritchard).* 615 (CMod), 1009 (CR), 1438 (M), 1584 (CCond), 1664 (R).

UP YOUR STREET ..8-7.. 6 b.m. Petoski — Air Streak (Air Trooper) f23p3p. Small compact half-sister to Gwen's A Singer (*qv*). Sold Malvern, Oct for 1800. Placed in three Maidens, but was last in two of them, and invariably beaten 20 lengths or slightly more. Favourite on two occasions, but has only shown exceptionally limited ability so far. Perhaps connections will decide that the best place for her is down the road. *F.J. Ayres & T.L. Jones — Tredegar F. (Tim Jones).* 489 (CfMa), 1223 (2m4fOMa), 1277 (OMa), 1455 (OMa), 1660 (OMa), 1676 (OMa).

URON V (FR) ..9-13.. 15 b.g. Cap Martin (FR) — Jolivette (FR) (Laniste) 2p2f4p. Small neat half-brother to 4 French flat winners (2 also won Chasing). NH '90/8 (2 wins from Mrs M. Jones'; previously from C. Wall's, bought for 8600; 5 wins previously for Mrs M. Reveley; 2 wins previously for M. Hammond) r40 w9 (4 Hdles, 2m4f-3m1f, and 5 Chses, 3m-3m2f) p16 (short-headed once, and beaten head once); ran out once. Has amassed a goodly number of prizes over the years, and gave his best display in a Point first time out when three lengths second to Strong Medicine (the greater experience of Emma Coveney told against Tory Hayter), but never performed as well subsequently, and was flattered to get within eight lengths of Cracking Idea. Long in the tooth, and unsurprisingly he often decides to take things easily now. *Mrs E.M. Bousquet-Payne — E. Essex (Ruth Hayter).* 28 (L), 128 (L), 240 (L), 319 (L), 414 (L), 1037 (L).

US FOUR (IRE) ..10-4.. 11 b.g. Mandalus — Rock Plant (Ovac ITY) 3012. Small close-coupled. IRISH NH FLAT '95/7 r9 p1 (2nd). IRISH NH '96/7 r8 p1 (3rd in Hdle). P-t-P/HUNT CH '99 r2 p0 (5th twice). Did not stay three miles when tried in a Point in '99, but credit to connections for persevering with him in sub-3m Hunter Chases, and he came good at 20-1 under a good ride from Stuart Morris over the minimum trip at Towcester. Appeared not to relish a struggle at Hexham next time, and is definitely one to have reservations about. Acts on a sound surface. Wears blinkers. *C.N. Nimmo — Bicester with Whaddon.* 463 (2MH), 1341 (2m110yH), 1531 (2m110yH), 1602 (2m4f110yH).

VAGUE IDEA ..10-3.. 8 gr.g. Tout Ensemble — Roodle Doodle (Rugantino) R11. Lengthy deep-girthed. Dam, half-sister to 8 Pointers, including Otter Mill (*qv* '97 Annual), won 2m4f Ch and 4 Points (inc 2 Ladies) and placed total of 8 for Oliver Carter. Grandam, Jolly Music, won 2m Hdle for him. The only Pointer to score twice in June, and followed up a success in a Maiden in heavy at Bratton Down (5-2 an outsider of four) with a victory in a 16-runner Restricted on firmish with arable at Umberleigh (16-1). A strong finisher, and looks the best prospect the octogenarian owner has had for a long time. Partnered by Kahlil Burke, who has undergone an amazing transformation. Previously he appeared to be brain dead and was most notable for persevering on exhausted horses who should have been pulled up, but he then rode a 33-1 winner at Garthorpe and a 66-1 scorer over Hurdles at Hexham (both for trainers who are rarely associated with victories), and he now appears to be stylish and polished and full of elan, and very much one to note. *O.J. Carter — E. Devon.* 1308 (OMa), 1655 (OMa), 1671 (R).

VALENTINE KING (IRE) ..8-9.. 8 b.g. Over The River (FR) — Pitpan Lass (Pitpan) p. Strong good-looking half-brother to Darkbrook, and to Irish Pointing winner, Supersonia. Dam won 3 Irish Points. P-t-P '99 r3 p1 (last of 3); last, and pulled up 1. Finished exhausted when 28 lengths last of three in '99, and disappeared after the opening day of the season this year. Looks to have something at fault with him. *Mrs D.H. McCarthy & P. Dealy — O. Surrey & Burstow (Christine McCarthy).* 7 (OMa).

VALE OF OAK ..9-1.. 10 b.m. Meadowbrook — Farm Consultation (Farm Walk) 8f. Small neat half-sister to Redchester, Fruit Farm (dam of 4 Pointers inc Fruit Crop *qv*), Farmers Glory, and Farriers Favourite, to NH flat and Chasing winner, Proud Con, to jumping winner, Heart Of Oak, and to the dam of Farriers Fantasy (*qv* '98 Annual). Dam is an unraced half-sister to King Con, Red Account, et al. NH FLAT '96 r1 p0. P-t-P '97/8 r3 w1 (Maiden) p0; and last twice. Fortunate when winning at Didmarton in '97, but has been seen only three times since, and failed to beat a rival in two completions. Heavily bandaged in front, and clearly a bad-legged mare. Has two handlers. *Miss S.J. Crew — V.W.H.* 392 (R), 818 (R).

VALIANT WARRIOR ..10-10.. 13 br.g. Valiyar — Jouvencelle (Rusticaro FR) 52f. Compact half-brother to flat and smart jumping winner, Land Afar, to a flat winner, and to successful Hurdlers, Picket Piece and Hatta Breeze. 16,000gy. FLAT (all form for H. Candy at 3) r18 w1 (12f) p2 (beaten head once). NH '92/8 (blinkered once in '92; wins for M. Hammond, bought for 4100; previously for D. Nicholson) r37 w10 (2m5f Hdle, and 9 Chses, 2m4f-3m) p12; 10th in '97 Grand National; inc Celebs flat; refused once. Seemed ungenuine in his youth and had a tendency to hang badly right, but later reformed and proved to be very tough and genuine and a grand servant to Micky Hammond. Career earnings over jumps amount to £64,742 including a £10,942 prize, and looked sure to add a Leicester Hunter Chase to his list of triumphs, but found little when ridden on the run-in and was overwhelmed by the storming dash of Ardstown. Fell at the first in the Aintree Foxhunters, and perhaps retirement beckons. His trainer, a former Hammond employee, has now joined the professional ranks himself. *P. Sellars — W. of Yore (Jedd O'Keefe).* 90 (3m1fH), 460 (2m7f110yH), 921 (2m6fH).

VALIBUS (FR) ..9-9.. 16 b.g. Labus (FR) — Valgrinette (FR) (Valdingran FR) p4. Small compact good-looking. P-t-P '91/2 and '94/9 r33 w10 (inc 2 Opens and 6 Confineds) p3 (inc 3rd of 4 twice); failed to finish 19 (refused 2, and ran out 1). Strangely inconsistent in the past, and has ten victories to his credit, but has failed to complete twice as often. Well held in his last two completions at Kingston Blount '99/00, and seems very unlikely to trouble the judge at 16. Suited by a sound surface. *P.A.D. Scouller — Garth & S. Berks (Nigel Allen).* 572 (CfO), 1481 (Cf).

VALLEY HOPPER ..9-7.. 6 b.g. Rock Hopper — Polly Verry (Politico USA) 242. Dam, sister or half-sister to 2 Pointers including, Fils Du Parc (*qv* '96 Annual), won Ladies and placed 9 (inc 3rd in Hunt Ch). Grandam, Merry Leap, won 2 2m Sell Hdles and 2 Points and placed total of 3. Tired from three out and fell at the last in his Members (remounted), and tried 2m4f Maidens subsequently, but gave the impression that a return to the full trip would not worry him at six. Should win, because he could hardly have been expected to cope with Sunnycliff but nevertheless performed creditably when four lengths second, again at Alnwick. *C. Storey — College V. & N. Northumberland.* 182 (M), 500 (2m4fOMa), 910 (2m4fOMa).

VALLEY'S CHOICE ..9-11.. 12 ch.m. Morgans Choice — Culm Valley (Port Corsair) p2225p. Smallish half-sister to Village Copper, Copper Valley and Atoski. Dam, sister and half-sister to 3 Pointers, won a 2m1f Hdle, 2 Chses (3m1f-3m2f) and 6 Points and placed total of 7. NH FLAT r1 p0 (beaten about 2*l* for 2nd). NH '95/6 r6 p0 (inc Sells). P-t-p '97/9 r17 w4 (up to Confined) p7 (4 2nds); pulled up 1, and fell 1. Successful twice apiece in '97 and '99, and has proved a valuable schoolmistress to Charlie White, who has handled her well recently. Very one-paced these days, and suited by mud, but appeared to go wrong on her final appearance when pulled up and dismounted at Mounsey Hill Gate. *Mrs A.C. Martin & Mrs J. Keatley — Eggesford (Tessa White).* 162 (I), 258 (Cf), 557 (Cf), 1173 (M), 1256 (Inr), 1607 (I).

VALNAU (FR) ..10-1§.. 14 b.g. Grandchant (FR) — Matale (FR) (Danoso) p132. Neat. NH FLAT r3 p1 (¾*l* 3rd). NH '93/4 and '97 r6 p0 (inc 4 Chses, inc Sell, fell 1). P-t-P/HUNT CH '94 and '98/9 r9 w4 (up to Confined) p4 (3 2nds). Won both his Points by an aggregate of 55 lengths in '94, and still possesses a fair measure of ability, but has never been able to stand much racing. Only twice out of the money in Points, and recorded his fifth success when defying the elements at Bratton Down in game fashion. Suited by mud, avoids anything firmer than good, and stays very well, but not an easy ride, and Charlie White did well to survive a bad blunder and keep him going in appalling conditions in his Members. Blinkered to '97, and has been seen to hang left, and jump right. *S. Redwood — Tiverton Stag (Tessa White).* 727 (O), 1136 (M), 1177 (O), 1649 (CCf).

VALS CASTLE (IRE) ..9-8.. 7 b.m. Ala Hounak — Church Brae (The Parson) Ruup1f4. Small neat sister to Man Of Steele (IRE) (*qv*). P-t-P '99 r1 p0 (pulled up). Too much of a handful for Ruth Clark, but Grant Tuer only needed one sighter before he got his eye in, and the combination clicked at Charm Park. Beat no subsequent winners in the slowest time of the day, and although it was a resounding success more will be required in Restricteds. More consistent jumping would also aid her cause. *S. Clark — Bedale.* 625 (OMa), 695 (OMa), 1002 (2m4fOMa), 1033 (OMa), 1235 (OMa), 1326 (R), 1348 (Cf).

VANSELL ..9-13.. 10 b.m. Rambo Dancer (CAN) — Firmiter (Royal Palace) 452p. Leggy light. NH FLAT '96 r1 p0. NH '96 r1 p0. P-t-P '98/9 r16 w3 (Maiden, Members and Restricted) p3 (3rds); pulled up 4, and on floor 3. Successful three times at the end of the season '98/9, and comes into her own on a sound surface, but does not seem to stay when conditions are more testing, and ended 2000 by going lame at Bratton Down. Landed a touch in her last victory, but the odds are stacked against her now. Tends to get very warm in the preliminaries, and has two handlers. *Mrs J. McCullough — Axe V.H. (Philip Greenwood).* 654 (I), 927 (Cf), 1370 (I), 1562 (C).

VEILED DANCER (IRE) ..9-4.. 8 b.m. Shareef Dancer (USA) — Fatal Distraction (Formidable USA) 221. Compact good-bodied half-sister to a winner in Sweden. FLAT (for J. Dunlop) r6 p1 (8*l* 3rd). NH '97/9 (from R. Frost's, bought for 3000, ridden by Sam Holdsworth) r10 p1 (2nd of 4); pulled up 4 (inc final 3) and fell; inc Sells. Not good enough for the flat or Hurdling, but more at ease in lowly Points, and followed a couple of decent seconds with a comfortable success at Lifton. Her jumping is generally steady, and may have a chance in Restricteds. *N.J. Holdsworth — Dartmoor.* 563 (CfMa), 1520 (CfMa), 1640 (OMa).

VELKA ..9-8.. 12 br.m. Uncle Pokey — Miss Prague (Mon Capitaine) up2p2234. Tall workmanlike sister to Uncle's Emma, and half-sister to Sunczech (IRE). Dam won an Irish Point, and an English Restricted. IRISH NH '94 r1 p0. IRISH P-t-P '94 r5 p1 (3rd - promoted from 4th); pulled up 1, and unseated 1. NH '95 r5 p1 (29*l* 3rd in Ch); fell first other Ch. P-t-P/HUNT CH '96/9 (for Mr R.V. & Mr R.P. Mair) r17 w4 (inc Ladies) p7 (6 2nds, inc Hunt Ch); pulled up 2, and fell 2. Successful in each of her previous four campaigns, but despite holding every chance at the last on three occasions in 2000 could not maintain her record. Usually helps force the pace, but barely stays three miles, and needs to get clear nowadays to stand a chance of hanging on. Genuine, and prefers a sound surface, but will not find winning any easier in future. *Mr & Mrs H. Ellison — Ashford V. (Sara Hickman).* 28 (L), 128 (L), 677 (L), 882 (L), 1109 (M), 1209 (Cnr), 1395 (L), 1540 (2m5fH).

VELLATOR (IRE) ..9-11.. 9 b.g. Petoski — Improperty (Law Society USA) 1. Unfurnished half-brother to flat winners, Portite Sophie and Wildmoor. NH FLAT Nov/Dec '97 r2 p0. NH '98 r2 p0 (pulled up and ran out in Hdles). Showed slight ability under Rules, and had a rare opportunity to prove himself when landing a Maiden at Black Forest Lodge in January. The second and third went on to score, but immediately returned to the sidelines himself. *A.J.K. & Mrs P.A. Dunn — Minehead H.* 71 (OMa).

VENDOON (IRE) ..9-0.. 11 b.g. Sanchi Steeple — Lovely Venture (He Loves Me) f7u06. Small half-brother to Irish flat winner, Model Dancer. IRISH NH FLAT '94 r2 w2. NH '95/9 (for P. Bowen; previously for late M. Heaton-Ellis) r8 p0 (pulled up 4, inc both Chses; inc Sell Hdle). NH May '00 r2 p0 (12th in 2m3f Mdn Ch: *sn t.o*; and 6th in 2m110y Nov Ch: *hmpd & blun 5, sn bhnd*). His Irish connections must have thought they were on to something (and perhaps they were when they went to the sales) after he had landed 18 and 20-runner Bumpers in the mud, but has been bitterly disappointing since, and was only able to appear once apiece '98/9. Useless for yet another yard in 2000, and his jumping is exceptionally poor. Tried tongue-tied once, and blinkered once. His three remote lasts included on consecutive days in May. *Mrs F. Jansen — O. Berks (Gary Brown).* 300 (2m5fH), 463 (2mH), 681 (2m4fH).

VENN OTTERY ..—.. 6 b.g. Access Ski — Tom's Comedy (Comedy Star USA) p. Dam is half-sister to Tom's Little Will (*qv* '95 Annual). Faced an impossible task on his debut, and pulled up at the tenth when tailed off at Newton Abbot. *O.J. Carter - E. Devon.* 583 (2m5f110yH).

VERCHENY ..8-3.. 6 b.m. Petoski — Ekaytee (Levanter) 5. Dam, half-sister to Ryming Cuplet (*qv*), won 6 Points (5 Ladies) and placed 21 (inc 6 Hdles) for Gerald Tanner (who bred her). Tailed off last in February. Comes from a family of prolific winners, so will certainly be worth another look when she returns. *G. Tanner — Taunton V. (Richard Barber).* 212 (CfMa).

VERDE LUNA ..9-13.. 9 b.g. Green Desert (USA) — Mamaluna (USA) (Roberto USA) 3p0f. Small close-coupled half-brother to flat winner, Maroulla (IRE). Dam won 3 flat, 8-10f, inc Nassau Stakes. FLAT r13 p3. NH '95/8 r33 w3 (2 Hdles, 2m1f-2m4f, and 2m5f Ch) p11. NH '99 r1 p0 (9th in 2m3f HCap Ch). HUNT CH '99 (for Mr R.J. Smith) r2 w1 (2m3f) p1 (head 2nd). Adept at picking up prize money under Rules, but does not stay beyond 2m4f, so running him over three miles on three occasions in 2000 seemed rather odd. Wore a visor this year, has previously been blinkered, and has looked temperamental, but still remains capable of good efforts when conditions are right. Acts on a sound surface. *J. Parfitt — Gelligaer F. (Lisa Day).* 928 (MO), 1432 (3m1fH), 1600 (2m5f110yH), 1672 (O).

VERDI EDITION ..—.. 7 ch.g. Current Edition (IRE) — Lady Verdi (USA) (Monteverdi) pp. Good-topped attractive owner-bred. Dam won at 12f. NH FLAT Spr '98 (debut for K. Burke; second run for R. Juckes) r2 p0. NH '99 (from K. Burke's) r2 p0. Gambled on in both his races, but broke a leg at Laleston. *F.H. Williams — Gelligaer F.* 1454 (OMa), 1660 (OMa).

VERITY VALENTINE (IRE) ..10-1.. 8 b.m. King's Ride — More Than Words (Proverb) 2p. Workmanlike lop-eared half-sister to 3 Irish Pointing winners, including Polly The Dolly and Golly Miss Molly, and to a jumping winner in USA. Dam won Irish Maiden. NH FLAT '98 r2 p0 (4th once). NH '98 r4 p1 (Hdles, 15l 3rd); Sell final. P-t-P '99 (for Mr P.J. Millington) r12 w1 (Maiden) p5 (4 2nds, 2 fences last once after remounting); 6th, last pair 3, ran out 1, and pulled up 1. Kept incredibly busy during a gruelling '99 campaign, and may have suffered the backlash in 2000, as she was only able to run twice. Hopelessly outclassed behind Satchmo at Sandown, where she continually jumped away to her left, and dropped out very tamely at Chepstow subsequently as if something had gone amiss. Very game on her day, and has become more fluent with practice, and may be able to bounce back after a rest. Acts on any going. *A.J. Le Jeune — O. Berks (Gary Brown).* 799 (2m4f110yH), 1433 (3mH).

VERNHAM WOOD ..9-0.. 12 b.g. Electric — Bois Le Duc (Kalydon) p34. Rangy half-brother to Daring Duck and to 2 flat winners. P-t-P '95, '97 and '99 r5 p1 (3rd of 4); pulled up 2, and fell 2. Hardly ever runs, though much busier now than he used to be, and managed two seasons back-to-back for the first time, but never reveals enough stamina, and faded quickly after holding every chance three out twice in 2000. *Lt Col L.W. & Mrs P.H.K. McNaught — Dumfries (Kevin Anderson).* 364 (CfMa), 1082 (CMa), 1431 (OMa).

VERSICIUM (FR) ..9-12.. 7 ch.g. Mister Sicy (FR) — Verdurine (FR) (General Holme USA) 31u4p. Rangy. FRENCH FLAT '96/8 r9 p1 (2nd). FRENCH NH '97/8 r8 p4 (3 2nds, inc only Ch). Came up against SBS By Jove in his first Maiden, but had little difficulty landing an easier contest in softish at Buckfastleigh. Rather disappointing since, and was lit up by first time blinkers and ran much too freely in a Confined, but was still five lengths second (although very tired) when he pulled up at the last. Does not look an easy ride and always starts at a short price, and although he should easily collect a Restricted punters are unlikely to get rich. *Mrs S. Ling (Arthur White Partnership) — E. Devon (David Pipe).* 106 (OMa), 254 (CfMa), 734 (R), 876 (R), 1047 (Cf).

VERTICAL AIR ..9-4.. 8 b.g. Pablond — Joyful's Girl (White Prince USA) 3. Leggy lengthy brother to Passing Fair. Grandam, Joyful Tears, failed to finish in 4 of 5 Points. NH FLAT '97/8 r2 p0. NH '98 r8 p1 (3rd). Backed from 10-1 to 3-1 in a youngsters Maiden in February, but weakened to finish last of three. Beaten about 20 lengths, but only missed second by half a length, and could probably win a Maiden if trouble free. Hung badly right and jumped right once under Rules. *D. McCain — Cheshire.* 298 (CfMa).

VERULAM (IRE) ..10-0.. 8 b br.g. Marju (IRE) — Hot Curry (USA) (Sharpen Up) 22p. Small neat half-brother to flat winners, Jingoist and Marchant Ming (IRE) (latter also a successful Hurdler). Dam won at 8f in USA. IR 13,000y. FLAT (first 4 for J. Toller) r3 p0. NH '96/7 (for J. Jenkins, bought for 12,000) r8 w1 (2m1f Hdle) p1 (2nd); pulled up lame final. Second and first (on firm in August '96) in four-runner contests from his first two attempts over Hurdles, but achieved nothing subsequently before breaking down. Revived after three years and gave a couple of forcing displays before having to give best in the closing stages when second twice, and would perhaps last home with less weight on his back in a Ladies Open if remaining sound. *Mrs M. Mitchell — Ledbury (Nicky Sheppard).* 667 (Cf), 890 (M), 1463 (Cf).

VERY DARING ..9-12.. 11 b.g. Derring Rose — La Verite (Vitiges FR) p6. Small stocky. Dam won 2m Ch. P-t-P/HUNT CH '95/8 (for Miss S. Sharratt) r27 w2 (inc Ladies) p5 (4 3rds, last once; inc Hunt Ch); pulled up 5, and on floor 3. Has managed two wins, but lacks consistency, and easy to beat in competitive races. Very busy in his younger days, but managed just two outings in 2000, and showed little zest in either. Missed '99, and ran only once in '96, and may have an intermittent problem. *Miss R. Booth — Farmers Bloodhounds.* 904 (L), 1627 (2m5fH).

VERYVEL (CZE) ..9-12.. 10 b.g. Paico — Vernea (CZE) (Negresco) p243p. Compact good-bodied. NH '94/8 r26 w3 (2 2m Hdles, and 2m4f Ch) p6; inc Sell. P-t-P/HUNT CH '99 (for Mr G. Lewis & Mr J.J.V. Phillips) r9 w5 (inc 3m5f Ladies) p3 (2 3rds, of 4 once); and pulled up 1. Had accumulated 13 defeats since his last win under Rules until switched to Pointing with excellent results in '99, but has always been prone to mood swings, and generally refused to exert himself in the new yard. Likes to dominate, but beaten a minimum of 20 lengths in 2000, and gave up the ghost at a very early stage on his final start. This years exploits make Tim and Pip Jones's efforts last year look even more remarkable. Visored twice over hurdles. Acts on any going. *M.A. Kemp — Worcs.* 415 (O), 678 (O), 938 (3m4fO), 1182 (O), 1288 (O).

VERY VERY NOBLE (IRE) ..—.. 7 ch.g. Aristocracy — Hills Angel (Salluceva) 112f. Big half-brother to Freemount Boy. Dam is half-sister to Sunny Mount (*qv 2000 Annual*). IRISH P-t-P '99 r2 p1 (last of 2 — ineptly ridden); and fell. IRISH P-t-P '00 r1 w1 (beat Ban Beag and Our Century dist and dist in Comber Geldings Maiden: *ld/disp, lft wl clr 5 out, 2l ld last*). IRISH HUNT CH '00 r2 w1 (beat High Star and Mahankhali short-head and 15l at Downpatrick: *ld, drvn along 2 out, hdd last, rallied u.p to ld line*) p1 (2nd, beaten 3l by Father Andy at Gowran: *prom, 3rd ½way, 2nd 5 out, ld app 3 out, rdn nxt, hdd last, no ex flat*). Maturing nicely, and followed a Maiden win with a good success on his debut in a Hunter Chase. Pulled rather too hard next time, and then only got as far as the fourth before crashing out at Aintree. A good prospect who seems sure to win more than his share in future. *Mrs P. Brown — Iveagh (J.J. Lambe, in Ireland).* 924 (3m1fH).

VIA DEL QUATRO (IRE) ..9-8§.. 9 b.m. Posen (USA) — Gulistan (Sharpen Up) 3643up445. Strong-topped lengthy half-sister to Parkbhride, to flat winner, Are You Guilty, and to a winner in Italy. IRISH FLAT r4 p0. IRISH P-t-P '96/7 r7 w1 (5yo mares Mdn) p4; pulled up 1. NH '97/9 (for S. Mullins) r22 w2 (3m3f Chses) p8. Bought Malvern, July for 6500. Made all to win twice on sound surfaces at Fontwell, but is an exceptionally lazy mare who is always happy to dog it, and only had one horse behind her in nine Points. Normally wears headgear. Best left alone. *M.J. O'Connor — Mendip F. (Caroline Keevil).* 141 (MO), 210 (MO), 357 (Cm), 731 (M), 954 (MO), 1096 (MO), 1374 (MO), 1470 (MO), 1552 (O).

PLATE 136   678 Southdown & Eridge Mens Open: L to R Galaroi (D. Robinson), ran out, jumps alongside Veryvel (D. Kemp), 2nd, and Lake Of Loughrea (N. Wilson), 3rd

PHOTO: John Beasley

VIARDOT (IRE) ..10-1§.. 12 b.g. Sadler's Wells (USA) — Vive La Reine (Vienna) p37p1715. Close-coupled lengthy half-brother to Louviers, and to 4 flat winners (including in France and USA), including very smart R B Chesne. Dam, sister to Vaguely Noble, won at 12f in France. FLAT r18 w3 (10-12f) p4 (very unlucky when head 2nd once). NH '93/7 r18 w6 (2m1f-2m6f Hdles) p5. P-t-p/HUNT CH '98/9 r15 w1 (Confined) p5 (4 3rds); pulled up 2, and fell/unseated 2. Lacks consistency, and can look a hard ride, but can handle mud up to his withers, and revelled in the bog-like conditions at Llanvapley and St Hilary this year. Went kindly for Gemma Roberts, who proved there is more than one way to skin a rabbit and that strong-arm tactics are not necessarily best for an old thinker like him. Sure to prove hard to fathom when he returns, but was much slower to get fit than usual this year. *R.J. Rowsell — Ystrad Taf Fechan.* 271 (O), 345 (O), 481 (L), 597 (Cf), 743 (L), 1022 (3mH), 1052 (L), 1297 (L).

VICOSA (IRE) ..9-12.. 12 gr.g. General View — Mesena (Pals Passage) 5145. Compact half-brother to Viascorit, to Chasing winner, Master Gleason, and to Irish NH flat and Hurdles winner, Reneagh. IRISH FLAT r25 w2 (9-10f) p5. IRISH NH '93/4 r14 w3 (2m Hdles) p3. NH '94/9 (blinkered/visored 4, inc one win in '94/5; all wins for R. Alner; previously for S. Gollings) r29 w4 (2m-3m1f Chses) p10; refused once. Bought Doncaster, May for 4100. Performed poorly latterly under Rules, and generally not much better in Points, but remarkably managed to beat Weak Moment (1-3) in a four-runner Open at Whittington, where he rallied under pressure to lead after the last. All his best efforts are on sound surfaces, and can congratulate himself on an excellent completion record in this country (has got round in 31 of 33 attempts). *H.A. Shone — Cheshire (Sue Mullineaux).* 691 (O), 814 (O), 1151 (O), 1365 (O).

VIC'S GIRL ..—§§.. 7 b.m. Jester — Porto Irene (Porto Bello) uuRppR. Leggy compact owner-bred half-sister to Ifs And Buts. Dam is half-sister to Sheer Water (*qv* '92 Annual). A hard puller and wild jumper who has a pronounced steering defect, and went a mile or less on four occasions before disasters occurred. Connections are happy to put inexperienced pilots on her, which seems thoroughly reprehensible. *D.C. Tucker — S. & W. Wilts (M.T. Aylesbury).* 518 (2m4fOMa), 628 (Cf), 874 (2m4fOMa), 1102 (OMa), 1284 (OMa), 1372 (OMa).

VICTORIA'S BOY (IRE) ..10-12.. 8 b.g. Denel (FR) — Cloghroe Lady (Hardboy) 41211. Compact. IRISH P-t-P '97 r3 p2 (2nds, last once); and fell 1. IRISH NH FLAT '97 r1 p0. IRISH NH '98 r2 p0 (last in Hdle and Hunt Ch). P-t-P/HUNT CH '99 (for Mr P. Spencer) r7 w1 (Maiden) p3 (2nd of 2; and 2 3rds, last once); 4th, 9th, and pulled up 1. Generally disappointing in '99, and looked set for another similar season after his reappearance, but rejuvenated by a nine-week break, and turned in some vastly improved efforts once the ground had dried up. Always to the fore in the Heart of All England at Hexham, a race he had finished tailed off in 12 months earlier, he ran out a six length winner, and now that the key to him has been found can look forward to more success. Jumps well. *D.J. Dickson — Middleton (Tim Walford).* 111 (R), 996 (M), 1230 (R), 1363 (R), 1445 (3m1fH).

VIKING ART ..9-7.. 8 ch.m. Broadsword (USA) — Celtic Burn (Celtic Cone) 4u. Lengthy. NH FLAT '98 r2 p0. NH '98 r1 p0. P-t-P '99 r1 p0 (unseated). Has shown plenty of ability in three January Maidens '99/00, but has been error-prone, and looked a surprisingly weak finisher to date. Clearly up to winning a race, but seems hard to train. *R.H. York — Staff College.* 22 (2m4fOMa), 58 (OMa).

VIKING FLAME ..10-2.. 12 ch.m. Viking (USA) — Olympic Loser (Sassafras FR) 1up31. Small light. Dam, half-sister to Busted, won 2 14f races. P-t-P '94/5 and '97/9 r17 w2 (Maiden and Members) p5 (4 3rds, of 4 once, and last once); pulled up 4 and unseated 2. Successful in both her starts in '98, but below par last year, only to bounce back in 2000. Won the slowest of ten races at Whitwick on her reappearance and rounded the season off with a more praiseworthy success at up ton. Responds to pressure gamely on her day, but can look disinterested at other times, and seems typically chestnut mare-ish. Suited by some cut in the ground, and strong handling. Formerly very lightly raced, but has managed more outings in the last two years than in the previous four put together. *R.C.H. Hall — V.W.H. (Joanna Bush).* 340 (R), 476 (Cnr), 971 (I), 1312 (Cm), 1356 (I).

VIKING LILY (IRE) ..—.. 7 ch.m. Yashgan — Powis Lass (Buckskin FR) p. IRISH P-t-P '99 r1 w1 (5yo mares Mdn). Sold Doncaster, May for 5000. A lucky winner in Ireland as the two length leader fell two out and badly hampered the closest pursuer, and was making only her second appearance when she pulled up after 2m4f in February. Seems to have had a setback. *J. Rowell — Kent & Surrey Bloodhounds (Didie Rowell).* 306 (R).

VILLAGE COPPER ..10-5.. 9 b.g. Town And Country — Culm Valley (Port Corsair) 1131127. Sturdy half-brother to Valley's Choice (*qv*). P-t-P '97/9 r11 w1 (2m4f Maiden) p7 (6 2nds, beaten head once); last pair 2, and pulled up 1. Placed seven times compared to one win in his first three seasons, but far more prolific in 2000, and has developed into quite a useful top-of-the-ground Pointer. Quite highly strung, and has two handlers, but a strong galloper, and can quicken if necessary. Got struck into, and has a shoe ripped off on his penultimate start, and never going well on his Hunter Chase debut subsequently. Usually preceded by his reputation, and had been sent off favourite in 11 of his last 14 races. A safe jumper, and best served by a flat right-handed track like Cottenham where he has won three times. *Mr & Mrs A.G.C. Howland Jackson — Suffolk (Ruth Hayter).* 16 (R), 82 (M), 215 (C), 552 (I), 770 (Cf), 936 (Cf), 1334 (3mH).

VILLAGE GOSSIP ..8-7.. 8 b.m. Henbit (USA) — Tattle (St Paddy) 5Rppp5p3p. Small compact half-sister to flat and Hurdles winner, Charlafrivola, and to 3 winners abroad. NH FLAT '98 r2 p0 (tailed off both). P-t-P '99 r7 p0 (pulled up 5, unseated 1, and ran out 1). Often on the engine for as much as 2m4f, but headstrong and wilful, and stays no further. Has beaten two rivals in 16 races over jumps, and not likely to enhance her record in the future. *J. Foster — Albrighton (Annie Spencer)*. 51 (OMa), 124 (OMa), 298 (CfMa), 439 (OMa), 570 (2m4fCfMa), 989 (OMa), 1323 (OMa), 1413 (OMa), 1526 (OMa).

VILLAINS BRIEF (IRE) ..9-8.. 12 b.g. Torus — Larrys Glen (Laurence O) p8u2pup4p. Compact well-made half-brother to The Happy Monarch. Dam won Irish NH flat. NH FLAT r1 p0. NH '94/6 r11 p1 (2nd); inc Sell; last once, and fell 1 in Chses. P-t-P '97/9 r24 w3 (up to Intermediate) p5 (3 2nds, beaten head once, and remote of 3 once); ran out 1, unseated 3, and pulled up 4. Won three times under Rory Lawther in his first season Pointing, but has regularly taken the mickey out of Jan Kwiatkowski since, and has adroitly stretched his losing sequence to 26. A safe jumper, but has lost the rider on five occasions, and usually beaten wide margins when completing now. Normally blinkered, and previously tried visored. *Mrs S. Kwiatkowski — S. & W. Wilts (John Dufosee)*. 453 (Cf), 561 (O), 766 (Cnr), 1130 (M), 1306 (C), 1471 (Cnr), 1550 (Cnr), 1595 (Cf), 1672 (O).

VIMCHASE ..8-11.. 15 ch.g. Slim Jim — Vimys Pet (Lord Nelson FR) 5w04p. Lengthy. Dam won 2 NH flat, 2m-2m2f. NH FLAT r3 p1 (2nd). NH '90/2 (visored 1) r14 p0 (jumped poorly in 5 Chses — inc last, and fell). P-t-P '94 (blinkered 1) and '97 r14 w1 (Maiden) p5 (4 3rds, of 4 once, and last once); last 3, pulled up 1, and fell/unseated 4. Appears once in every three seasons nowadays, and beaten a minimum of 37 lengths when completing 4 times. Withdrawn at the start once as he was found to be lame. See you in 2003. *B.G. Duke — Burton*. 435 (M), 797 (R), 871 (R), 1072 (Cf), 1267 (I).

VINTAGE CHOICE (IRE) ..9-8.. 9 b.g. Brush Aside (USA) — Shady Jumbo (Callernish) pp3p. Tall rangy. IRISH P-t-P '97 r3 p3 (promoted from 4th to 3rd once). P-t-P/HUNT CH '98 (for Mr I.A. Balding) r3 w1 (Maiden) p1 (distant 3rd of 4 in Hunt Ch); and pulled up 1. Won on firmish at Market Rasen in '98, but jumped poorly otherwise, and clearly awry since. Had accumulated plenty of fat during his time on the sidelines, and carried an awful lot of condition in 2000 when tailed off and pulled up on each occasion (restarted and finished a remote last once). Not a natural jumper, and must be labouring under a physical disability. *F.S. Jackson — S. Notts (R.J. Jackson)*. 50 (R), 120 (CR), 232 (R), 871 (R).

VITAL HESITATION ..9-7.. 9 br.m. Vital Season — Jim's Darleen (Jimsun) fu6Rp3p. Small. Dam extremely moderate, won Maiden and placed 9 (inc a Ch). P-t-P '98/9 r8 p3 (2 2nds, of 3 once); pulled up 2, and fell 1. Knocking at the door with three placings in '99, but has not progressed, and remains a weak finisher with a propensity to make errors. Hindered by the rider to a large extent in 2000, but even Alex Charles-Jones could not work the oracle when a market springer on her penultimate start, and a small success still seems only a remote possibility. *M.H. Wood & J. Nicholas — V.W.H. (Martin Wood)*. 194 (CfMa), 392 (R), 455 (OMa), 752 (Cm), 1245 (OMa), 1439 (OMa), 1598 (OMa).

VITAL ISSUE (IRE) ..10-9.. 9 b br.g. Electric — Dreamello (Bargello) uu25f21. Compact half-brother to Irish Pointing winners, Tidal Moon and Toberella, and to 2 Irish NH flat winners (one also a successful Hurdler there, the other also a successful Pointer there). Dam is half-sister to Bright Dream (qv '90 Annual). IRISH P-t-P '97 r1 w1 (5yo Mdn). IRISH NH FLAT '97 r1 w1. NH FLAT Nov '97 r1 p0. NH '98 (for J.J. O'Neill) r3 w1 (3m1f Hdle) p1 (2nd); and 4th. Bought Doncaster, Nov '98 for 1800. Sold to Anne Duchess of Westminster after being unbeaten twice in Ireland, and scored for her in a Hurdle in heavy, but apparently went wrong in '98, and purchased cheaply subsequently. Unable to score in Points and fell or unseated before halfway in three of them, and although he gave good displays when chasing home Polar King and Fresh Prince it was still a huge shock when he beat a competitive field in the 18-runner Horse and Hound Ladies Hunter Chase at Stratford (33-1, Tote 91-1). Came with a strong run under Jo Foster to lead soon after the last, and there looked to be no fluke about it. Could probably win a Novices Chase on this sort of form. *P.S. Johnson — Sinnington (Michael Brown)*. 277 (Cf), 395 (O), 1325 (Cf), 1350 (L), 1476 (O), 1585 (O), 1648 (3mH).

VITAL SHOT ..8-6.. 12 b.m. Vital Season — Skilla (Mexico III) p. Sister to Hurdles winner, Dexterous Lady, and half-sister to jumping winner, Miramare, and to 2 flat winners (and another who was disqualified). Dam won at 11f in France. P-t-P '94/7 r12 w2 (Maiden and Restricted) p0; pulled up 7. Made most to land a poor Maiden in '96, and gifted a walk-over the following year, but her revival after two years off lasted just one day. Presumably busy with maternal duties in between. *Mrs R. Baldwin & M. Hillier — Beaufort (Ruth Baldwin)*. 3 (L).

VITAMAN (IRE) ..—.. 12 b.g. King's Ride — Sea Cygnet (Menelek) p6pp. Small good-bodied. NH FLAT Apr '94 r1 w1. NH '96/8 (unplaced final for I. Williams; previously for Mrs J. Pitman) r10 w2 (2 Hdles, 2m4f-2m5f) p0; unseated once Ch. Formerly game when fit, but has a long history of major training problems, and was unable to achieve anything in Points, in which he broke a blood vessel at least once. *J.S. Warner — Cotswold V.F.* 49 (C), 143 (C), 333 (Cf), 597 (Cf).

VULGAN PRINCE ..9-0.. 13 b.g. Scorpio (FR) — Burton Princess (Prince Barle) 1d54. Good-topped lengthy brother to Prince's Gift and Janejolawrieclaire, and half-brother to Brenda Blake (dam of Inspector Blake (qv '00 Annual), Blakes Bay and Spring Rhyme. Dam was placed in 3 Points.

Grandam, Burton's Best, won 2 Irish Points. P-t-P '95/9 r13 w2 (Maiden and Members) p5 (3 3rds); pulled up 3, and unseated 1. Stands his racing badly, and has only once managed more than four outings in a season, and averages less than three. Ran his best race yet for preconnection when making a successful reappearance in his Members where he was backed from 4s to 5-2, but Richard Barrett's weight-cloth had gone awol during the running of the race, and disqualification was inevitable. Could not reproduce the Newton Bromswold run in better company subsequently, and a Restricted success now seems most unlikely. *M. Garner — Oakley.* 509 (M), 791 (R), 1379 (R).

VULPIN DE LAUGERE (FR) ..8-7§.. 14 b.g. Olmeto — Quisling II (FR) (Trenel) 2R4226ppp24. Tall compact. NH FLAT '93 r1 p0. NH '93/6 r14 p5 (2m4f-3m Chses). IRISH NH '96/7 r4 p1 (2nd). P-t-P/HUNT CH '98/9 (for Mrs R. Cambray) r9 p1 (3rd); pulled up 5. Amazingly ungenuine, and managed to get the better of Messrs Burton and Pritchard in 2000 after they both probably thought that they would win on him. Can maintain a steady gallop for as long as it suits, but knows exactly when to apply the brakes, and not surprisingly made mincemeat of the new owner-rider. An arrant rogue, who hangs at will, and not to be trusted a millimetre. Wears blinkers. *Miss A.J. Sykes — C. Jarvis — United (Pam Sykes; Neil King).* 123 (OMa), 339 (CfMa), 569 (OMa), 778 (OMa), 995 (OMa), 1180 (OMa), 1287 (R), 1383 (OMa), 1583 (C), 1609 (OMa), 1668 (OMa).

WAISU ..—.. 10 b.m. Baron Blakeney — Hawaian Eagle (Pony Express) pppp. Small light dipped. P-t-P '99 (for Mrs M. Sharland & Mr H. Hill) r7 p0 (last, pulled up 3, and fell/unseated 3). A consistently bad jumper who was badly tailed off last in her only completion. Would be better off in Maidens, but barely good enough for them. Apparently his name is an acronym for 'why am I so ugly', but 'why am I so useless' would have been more accurate. *H. Hill — Cambs Univ.* 178 (Cm), 773 (R), 1215 (Cm), 1418 (R).

WAKE UP LUV ..—.. 16 ch.g. Some Hand — Arctic Ander (Leander) p. Lengthy half-brother to Jimmy Shand, to jumping winner, Candlebright, Chasing winner, Relkander, and to succesful Hurdler, Scilly Cay. Dam won 4 Chses, 2m-2m4f. IRISH NH FLAT '90 r5 p2 (3rds). IRISH NH '91/4 (blinkered 1) r41 w4 (2m4f-2m6f Chses) p8. IRISH NH '95 r1 p0. NH '96 and '99 r4 p1 (25l 3rd of 4); pulled up 2, and fell 1. P-t-P/HUNT CH '97/9 r17 w1 (Ladies) p4 (3 3rds, inc Hunt Chses); pulled up 6, and on floor 2. Gained his latest success when making all to win a four-runner Ladies on firm at Howick in '97, but has had to endure all kinds of physical setbacks (lame on at least four occasion in Ireland, and has broken blood vessels) and basically too old now. Pulled up at Hereford in February, and absent since. *R. Williams — Gelligaer F.* 222 (3m1f-11o0yH).

WALKERS POINT ..9-0.. 15 b.g. Le Moss — Saltee Star (Arapaho) uup. Workmanlike lengthy half-brother to On The Other Hand and to Hurdles winner, Jervaulx (IRE). IRISH NH FLAT '92 r4 w1 p2 (3rds). IRISH NH '92 r4 p0. IRISH P-t-P '92 r1 p0 (pulled up). NH '93 and '94 r4 p0 (last 3, and pulled up — tailed off all 4). P-t-P/HUNT CH '95/8 r25 w6 (inc 2 Confineds, inc hat-trick '95); also disqualified from Intermediate win) p6 (4 2nds); pulled up 4, and fell/unseated 2. A good Pointer at a modest level when Devon-based, but hindered by some inept riding since '97, and his latest partner to fall off needed no provocation. Absent since February, and does not appear to be enjoying himself any longer. *C.W. Loggin & S. Astaire — Bicester with Whaddon (Chris Loggin).* 5 (Cv&nr), 35 (Cnr), 215 (C).

WALLS COURT ..9-6.. 14 ch.g. Cardinal Flower — Anega (Run The Gantlet USA) p. Tall good-bodied attractive half-brother to Irish/English NH flat winner, Quadco (IRE). NH FLAT r1 p0. IRISH P-t-P '92 r6 p2 (2nds); fell 4. IRISH NH '92/4 r14 p5 (3rd in Chses); fell/unseated 3. NH '94/5 and '96/7 r28 w2 (2m4f-2m5f Chses) p11. P-t-P/HUNT CH '95 and '99 (for Mr P. McKie) r10 p5 (3 2nds of 3; 2 3rds); pulled up 2. A bold-jumping front-runner in his prime, but amazingly took 37 attempts to get off the mark, and his career tally of two wins from 60 starts is a poor return for a horse who had so much ability. Managed just one outing in 2000, and looks finished now. Regularly blinkered in the past. *F.M. Barton — Holcombe (Tony Walker).* 565 (O).

WALTON STREET ..8-7.. 8 b.g. Jester — May Reef (IRE) (Simply Great FR) pp5ppu. Sparely-made. Dam won 2 2-y-o races, 5-6f, inc a Sell. P-t-P '99 (for Mr C. Smith) r3 p0 (pulled up 2, and fell 1). 26 lengths last on his sole completion, but a remarkably bad jumper, and it is a miracle that he has only fallen once. Runs on his nerves, and usually spent by the two-mile mark at the latest. *Miss J.F. Diggory — E. Cornwall.* 310 (I), 654 (I), 723 (CfMa), 857 (CfMa), 1519 (CfMa), 1640 (OMa).

WANDERING WILD ..8-9.. 6 ch.m. Nomadic Way (USA) — Wild Child (Grey Ghost) pp91. Sturdy. Dam, sister or half-sister to 3 Pointers, including, Bugley (*qv* '98 Annual), won 2m4f Hunt Ch on technicality and 6 Points (inc an Open) and placed 9 (inc a Hunt Ch) for Stuart Fletcher, and grandam, Girl Sunday, won 2 Points and placed 2 for him. Very green in early season and schooled in public on three occasions, but got her act together in a non-placed Maiden at Charm Park. It was a poor contest by definition, but clearly on an upward curve, and perhaps she will develop into a decent Ladies horse in time. *H.S. Fletcher (Lasun Friends) — Cleveland (Lynne Ward).* 379 (OMa), 626 (OMa), 1033 (OMa), 1234 (OMa).

WANSTEAD (IRE) ..9-11.. 9 ch.g. Be My Native (USA) — All The Same (Cajun) f194. Narrow half-brother to 3 winners abroad. IRISH FLAT r4 p1 (3rd). IRISH NH '95 r2 p2 (2nds). FLAT r1 p0. NH '95/8 r23 p7; inc Sell. P-t-P '99 r3 w1 (Maiden) p1 (½l 2nd); and 4th. Not a battler when beaten in all 30 attempts flat and hurdling, but won his maiden at the first attempt, and held on by the narrowest of margins to supplement a Restricted this year. Well held when raised in class, and may have reached the pinnacle of his ability. Tried in headgear and a tongue-tie under Rules, and has broken a blood vessel. *H. Morgan & D. Francis — Carms (Emma Jones).* 1298 (R), 1400 (R), 1558 (3mH), 1613 (I).

WARDY HILL ..—§.. 10 b.m. Lighter — Royal Seal (Privy Seal) rupp. Workmanlike. P-t-P '97/8 r6 p0 (last, fell/unseated 2, and pulled up 3). Utterly abominable, and it must be some kind of punishment for the novice girls who frequently get the leg up to partner her. Ridden under an iron grip in her last two starts, but looks incapable of better when unleashed. *D.J.E. Scott — Cambs Univ.* 174 (M), 241 (C), 322 (CfMa), 606 (OMa).

WARNER FOR SPORT ..7-0.. 12 b.g. Mandalus — Joy Travel (Ete Indien USA) ppp. Workmanlike half-brother to Joyful Hero (*qv*). NH FLAT r1 p0. NH '94/5 r4 p0 (8th, last twice, and unseated 1). P-t-P '96/7 (for Mr W.J. Brown, Mr R.O. & Mrs I.J. Bishop) r5 p0 (last, unseated 1, and pulled up 3). Hopeless on the rare occasions he has made it to the racecourse, and presumably labouring under a physical disability. Gets on his toes and has two handlers in the preliminaries, but shows little sign of life once under way. *Mrs I.J. Bishop & W. Sweeney — Puckeridge (Alex Harvey).* 179 (R), 416 (R), 578 (OMa).

WARNER'S SPORTS ..—.. 12 b.g. Strong Gale — Cala Conta (Deep Run) pp. Tall half-brother to The Four Glens, and to jumping winners, Point Made and Warner For Winners. Dam won Irish Hdle. P-t-P '95 (for Mr T. Warner) r2 p1 (3rd); and pulled up 1. NH '95/9 (for P.J. Hobbs) r12 w3 (hat-trick in 3m-3m2f HCap Chses) p0; pulled up 5. Successful in three Chases in '96 having got himself leniently handicapped, but having badly right in the latest and never looked the same again, quickly descending into selling class. Soon had a novice in trouble this year, and barely reached halfway in just two outings. Tried in a tongue-strap on his final outing under Rules, and seems troubled. *Mrs C.J. Kershaw — College V. & N. Northumberland.* 495 (O), 1078 (Cf).

WARNING BOARD ..—.. 10 b.g. Bairn (USA) — Candle In The Wind (Thatching) fup. Workmanlike half-brother to flat and Hurdles winner, Distant Storm, and to a winner in Sweden. Dam won at 6f. NH FLAT '97/8 r2 p0. NH '98 r1 p0 (last in Hdle). P-t-P '99 r2 p0 (ran out 1, and fell 1). A nervy individual who has yet to look like completing in Points. Enough to put John Berwick off race-riding for good. *G.C. Stanton — Mid Devon (Mrs S. Berwick).* 723 (CfMa), 1517 (R), 1641 (OMa).

WARREN BOY ..10-1.. 11 b.g. Hotfoot — Artaius Rose (FR) (Artaius USA) 32p2p4230pp. Small close-coupled attractive half-brother to Just For A Reason. P-t-P/HUNT CH '95/9 r32 w10 (inc 2m110y Hunt Ch and 3 Ladies; 4-timer '98) p4 (3 2nds, of 3 once); pulled up 9, and fell/unseated 3. NH '99 (from J. Neville's) r1 p0 (tailed off in Hdle). Invariably makes all if successful, and has an excellent record, but unable to score in 2000, and usually ended up very leg weary. Pulled up by Pip Jones at Ludlow fearing injury (two-day ban for interference was subsequently quashed) but was clearly lame at Umberleigh on his final appearance. Acts on any going, but a sound surface is most appreciated. Will do well to comeback to form at 11. *F.J. Ayres — Tredegar F. (Tim Jones).* 67 (L), 201 (L), 382 (2m4fH), 599 (L), 742 (O), 833 (O), 1401 (Cf), 1570 (MO), 1600 (2m5f110yH), 1658 (MO), 1673 (L).

WARRIOR BARD (IRE) ..10-0.. 11 ch.g. Black Minstrel — Enco's War (Tug Of War) 3. Compact. IRISH P-t-P '94 r1 p1 (3rd). NH FLAT r1 p0. NH '94/5 r4 p0 (pulled up 3 — needed oxygen once). P-t-P '96/8 r6 w4 (inc Intermediate) p0; and fell 2. Unbeaten in four English Pointing completions '96/7, but has proved a nightmare to train, and has only once stood more than one race in a season. Absent in '99, but attracted plenty of support on his comeback, and having raced keenly established a long advantage with a mile to run, but blew up after a mistake four out, and finished a well beaten third. Could have been very useful had he been problem free. *Mr & Mrs R. Puddick — Beaufort.* 387 (M).

WAR WHOOP ..7-0.. 9 ch.g. Mandrake Major — Mohican (Great Nephew) 3. Small close-coupled brother to NH flat winner, Herbalist, and half-brother to flat winner, Colonel Custer. Dam won at 12f. NH FLAT Spr '96 (for C. Thornton) r4 w1 p1 (3rd). NH '96/9 (for Miss L. Russell, bought for 10,000; 1 win previously for C. Thornton) r25 w2 (2m6f Hdle and 3m2f Ch) p5 (3 2nds); inc Sell Hdle. Sold Doncaster, Nov for 1600. The winner of three bad races on firmish, but had a sequence when he pulled up four times from five attempts in '97, and was also pulled up in five of six outings in '99. Did not impress when 35 lengths last in his Members, in which he was quickly dismounted after the finish and lashing out with a hind leg, and is little better than useless now. *T. Walker — Albrighton.* 1407 (M).

WATACON ..—§.. 9 ch.g. Zero Watt (USA) — Clontarf (Derrylin) rp5fR. Workmanlike. Takes a ferocious grip and is an extremely hairy ride, but shows plenty of speed, and might be able to win if only it was harnessed better. Last on his only completion, and misdemeanours include veering right at the start and being left, and running straight on at a bend after a mile and leaving the course. *M.J. Brown — Sinnington.* 277 (Cf), 281 (OMa), 378 (R), 400 (OMa), 1033 (OMa).

WATCHIT LAD ..9-7.. 11 b.g. El-Birillo — Watch Lady (Home Guard USA) p524p363. Compact good-bodied half-brother to a flat winner, and to jumping winner, Pit Pony. P-t-P/HUNT CH '96/7 and '99 r15 w3 (inc 2 Confineds) p2 (3rds, of 4 once); pulled up 2, and fell/unseated 5. Thrown in at the deep end, and struggled originally, but more sensibly placed in '99, and won three minor races. Likes to force the pace, but seems to have developed a problem, and was tried in a tongue-strap in 2000. Ran well when beaten just over two lengths at Cursneh Hill, but regularly lost a handy position this year, and his ability to produce an end-to-end gallop seems to have deserted him. A poor jumper of regulation fences, and has yet to beat a rival in six Hunter Chases. Acts on any going, but a watching brief is advised when he returns. *Mrs A. Price — Teme V.* 294 (O), 480 (O), 859 (O), 988 (O), 1087 (MO), 1273 (O), 1346 (3m1f110yH), 1545 (O).

WATCHYOURBACK (NZ) ..9-1.. 7 ch.g. Watchman (NZ) — English Lass (NZ) (English Harbour) p3. Compact quite attractive. Pulled up at halfway on his debut (unseated at the start and galloped up and down a hedge before being caught), but showed some promise when 22 lengths third at Wolverhampton. It could have been a hot Maiden for mid-May, and seems likely to improve with experience. *N.H. Oliver — N. Ledbury.* 1406 (OMa), 1526 (OMa).

WATTS THE POINT (IRE) ..—.. 8 b.g. Electric — Killinure Point (Smooth Stepper) p. Brother to Faha Point (IRE). Dam won 2 Irish Points. NH FLAT '98/9 (for D. Duggan) r2 p0. NH '99 (for T. George) r2 p0 (pulled up both Hdles). Tailed off in all five races, and presumably went wrong when pulling up at halfway in the latest (an uninspired gamble from 12s-6s). *Mrs G.M. Summers — Croome & W. Warwicks (Rob Summers).* 792 (OMa).

WAYS AND MEANS ..10-5.. 14 b.m. Oedipus Complex — Snow Mountain (Mountain Call) 432. Small neat sister to Snow Charm. Dam won 2 2m Hdles and placed 5 (inc 2 flat); and won 5 Points and placed 10 (inc 2 Hunt Chses) for Sheila Mollett. NH FLAT r1 p0. P-t-P '92/9 r27 w6 (3 Members, Restricted and 2 Confineds) p11 (7 2nds, last once); failed to finish 4 (fell 2). A game little mare who makes the most of her opportunities, and has accumulated six wins, and 13 placings in nine consecutive Pointing campaigns. Without a win since '97, but not through lack of trying, and has been unlucky to come up against the likes of Hurricane Linda and Night Irene at Thorpe Lodge '99/00. Has gained four of her wins at Market Rasen, and thoroughly deserves another. *Mrs S.A. Mollett — Burton.* 622 (O), 794 (Cf), 1215 (Cm).

WAYWARD BUTTONS ..9-3.. 7 b.g. Nomadic Way (USA) — Lady Buttons (New Brig) 4p. Workmanlike half-brother to Buster Buttons (qv). Showed signs of ability in both Maidens, and should have scope for improvement in the second campaign, although he has not been seen since February. Was sent off at a ludicrous 4-5 on his debut, but not pushed when beaten, and finished 11 lengths last. *A. Scott-Harden — Zetland (Chris Dennis).* 139 (CCfMa), 379 (OMa).

WAYWARD MISCHIEF ..—.. 9 ch.m. Royal Vulcan — Another Nitty (Country Retreat) p. Half-sister to Secret Truth (qv). Dam and grandam both raced for Chris Loggin. Pulled up after two miles in March. *Miss S. Dawson — Surrey U.* 706 (Cf).

WAYWARD SPREE ..—.. 7 b.m. Teenoso (USA) — Garvenish (Balinger) p. Small compact. Dam is half-sister to Phil's Dream (qv '97 Annual). Novicey on her debut in late May, and was tailed off and pulled up after 2m4f. *Mrs G. Greenwood — Cotley (Philip Greenwood).* 1565 (OMa).

WEAK MOMENT (IRE) ..10-8.. 11 gr.g. Roselier (FR) — Hazy Valley (Golden Love) 3112p1. Small rangy light. IRISH P-t-P '96/7 r6 w1 (5yo&up Maiden) p5. P-t-P '98/9 r8 w4 (inc 2 Confineds) p3 (2 2nds, beaten a head once; and 3rd of 4); and last 1. A thorough stayer who remains on the upgrade, but has in truth been well placed, and has only once beaten more than three other finishers in seven wins. Reported sustained an over-reach when pulled up in the Heythrop four-miler, but can be moody, and is vulnerable when there isn't plenty of cut in the ground. Has been slow to mature, and yet to prove himself in a truly competitive race, but will hopefully get the opportunity to do so in 2001. *I. & Mrs N.S. Hollows — N. Salop (Sheila Crow).* 293 (Cf), 530 (O), 591 (O), 814 (O), 1015 (4mO), 1254 (O).

WEAVER SQUARE (IRE) ..—.. 12 b.g. Torus — Canute Villa (Hardicanute) upp. Tall rangy half-brother to 6 winners of 34 races in Ireland, including Galevilla Express (flat and jumping) and Crehelp Express (Hurdles). IRISH NH FLAT '95/7 r3 p0. IRISH NH '95/7 r4 p1 (last of 3). NH '97/9 (blinkered 2; final 3 for J. Neville; previously for P. Eccles, bought for 3800) r12 p1 (3rd); pulled up 8, inc 5 Chses; inc Sells. An appalling veteran who normally pulls up hard, and surely has something chronically wrong with him. *G. Jones — Pentyrch.* 268 (CfMa), 484 (R), 650 (CfMa).

WEDNESDAYS AUCTION (IRE) ..9-10.. 13 b.g. Mazaad — Happy Always (Lucky Wednesday) pup51. Small short-backed half-brother to Irish flat winner, Tender Always. FLAT r9 w1 (9f) p0. NH

'93/5 r13 p2 (2nds, inc Sell); 7th, last twice, and fell 1 in Chses. P-t-P/HUNT CH '97/9 (for Mrs M. Rigg) r13 w1 (Ladies) p2 (2 2nds, inc a Hunt Ch); unseated 2, and pulled up 4. The lucky winner of a Ladies race in '99 when generally ridden with a lack of enterprise, but a safe conveyance, and recorded his third win when just out-plodding the only other finisher in his slowly-run Members in 2000. Has received two gifts in two years, and unlikely to benefit from another, though in his area anything is possible. Has been tried in headgear under Rules. *Mrs C. Andrews — Southdown & Eridge (Jeff Peate).* 128 (L), 307 (L), 830 (Cnr), 982 (L), 1208 (M).

WEEJUMPAWUD ..10-6.. 11 b.m. Jumbo Hirt (USA) — Weewumpawud (King Log) p1425. Small neat half-sister to Wudimp. Dam was placed in 2 Points; subsequently won 3 Chses (2-3m) and placed 5 for Joseph Storey. NH '97 r4 p0 (fell first only Ch). P-t-p/HUNT CH '96 and '98/9 r17 w5 (inc 2 Ladies) p3 (2nd of 3; and 2 3rds, of 4 once); pulled up 4. An inveterate front-runner, but rarely leaves herself with anything for the business end, and is vulnerable against strong-finishers. Dominated proceedings when successful at Hutton Rudby, and ran her best race yet in Hunter Chases when second in the Heart at Hexham, but suited by a sound surface and the rain softened ground at Cartmel sapped her strength when tailed off on her final start. Jumps well, and would be hard to beat if switched back to Ladies races in 2001. *C. Storey — College V. & N. Northumberland.* 419 (Cf), 622 (O), 1345 (2m5fH), 1445 (3m1fH), 1601 (3m2fH).

WEE KELPIE ..8-7.. 8 b.m. Roscoe Blake — Celtic View (Celtic Cone) 6ppp. P-t-P '98 (for Mr A. Woods) r1 p0 (unseated). Foiled by the first on her debut, and unable to beat a rival on her comeback two years later. Showed some speed for the first time on her latest appearance, but looks unpromising. *Mrs D.J. Barrington — Radnor & W. Herefords (Antony Woods).* 673 (2m4fOMa), 990 (OMa), 1277 (OMa), 1634 (OMa).

WEJEM (IRE) ..10-3.. 12 gr.g. Roselier (FR) — Steal On (General Ironside) 111f. Robust half-brother to Another Man (IRE) (*qv*). IRISH P-t-P '93 and '96/7 r8 w1 (7 plus Mdn) p2 (2nds); pulled up 3. IRISH NH FLAT '93 r2 p0. IRISH NH '93/5 and '97/8 (blinkered final 2) r15 p2 (3rds in Hdle and Hunt Ch). NH '98 (for J.R. Turner) r3 p1 (3rd in Ch); inc Sell Ch. Sold Doncaster, May '98 for 4400. A modest competitor in previous yards, and only once successful from 28 attempts to '98. Surprisingly able to notch a hat-trick in 2000, and benefited from the strong riding of Andrew Dalton, as he was all out to hold on twice. Seems to need easy surfaces and can handle extreme distances, but one-paced, and reaped the benefits of being in a top yard. *Mrs H. Dalton & Mrs B. Hickinbottom — Wheatland (Andrew Dalton).* 336 (R), 533 (I), 905 (C), 1064 (3m2fCf).

PLATE 137   533 Sir W.W. Wynn's Intermediate: Wejem (A. Dalton), 1st

PHOTO: Peter & Marilyn Sweet

WELDSON ..—.. 9 ch.g. Weld — Linpac Belle (Steel Heart) ppp. Tall half-brother to Belle Of Steel. P-t-P '98/9 r4 p0 (pulled up 3, carried out 1). Sets off with good intentions, but yet to go more than a couple of miles, and obviously has a major fault. Acquired a tongue-strap on his final start. *C.M. Clarke — N. Cotswold (Jon Trice-Rolph).* 891 (OMa), 1020 (OMa), 1189 (M).

PLATE 138   1189 North Cotswold Hunt Members: Weldson (J. Trice-Rolph), pu, jumps alongside Quick Response (Miss M. Norledge), fell   PHOTO: John Beasley

WELL ARMED (IRE) ..10-6§.. 10 b.g. Moscow Society (USA) — Sales Centre (Deep Run) 11121u113p. Small light half-brother to Irish Pointing/Chasing winner, Stroll Home (IRE). IRISH P-t-P '96 r2 w1 (4&5yo Maiden) p0. IRISH NH FLAT '96 r2 p1 (3rd). IRISH NH '96 r1 p0. NH '97/8 r9 p2 (3rd in Hdle, and 1¼l 2nd in Ch). P-t-P/HUNT CH '99 r9 w5 (inc 2 Opens, inc 4-timer) p3 (2 2nds; and last of 3); and unseated 1. A useful Pointer who has been ridden to victory by seven different riders, but despite possessing a touch of class wears blinkers and can be extremely moody. Usually held up, and ridden for a turn of foot, and has won five times at Black Forest Lodge, but remains a risky proposition over regulation fences. Rarely sent off at attractive odds, and has been 4-5 or shorter in eight of his wins due mainly to the Pipe factor. Prefers some cut in the ground, and likely to run up another sequence when fresh. *Mrs L. Sharpe & D. Williams — D. Williams — Dart V. & S. Pool H. (David Pipe; -).* 66 (Cf), 200 (O), 251 (M), 561 (O), 651 (M), 922 (3mH), 1045 (L), 1260 (O), 1515 (MO), 1673 (L).

WELL ARRANGED (IRE) ..9-13.. 10 ch.g. Bold Arrangement — Eurynome (Be My Guest USA) 3p. Lengthy dipped brother to flat winner, Summer Wind (IRE). Dam won at 10f in France. IRISH FLAT '94 r5 p2. FLAT (blinkered 2 latterly) r15 w2 (14-15f, one on all-weather) p1 (3rd). NH '95/6 r5 p3 (2nds). P-t-P/HUNT CH '98/9 r13 w1 (Ladies) p3 (2 3rds, of 4 once, and last once); fell/unseated 2. Can pull hard, and usually sets off prominently, but struggles to get the trip these days, and having been tried in a tongue-strap in the past may have developed a problem with his wind. Unable to score since a useful win at Sandon in '98, and only managed two appearances in 2000. *Mrs A.M. Brindley — Atherstone (Roger Harvey).* 295 (L), 1007 (L).

WELL I NEVER ..9-9.. 7 ch.g. Henbit (USA) — Arachova (High Line) p3f432. Unfurnished half-brother to a winner in Sweden. Dam won at 12f. NH FLAT '98/9 r3 p0. Sold Doncaster, Aug for 950. Ran and jumped poorly on his first four starts, but improved when Lenny Hicks took over for the final two. Has mingled with winners, and finished half a length ahead of The Big Lad over 2m4f at Dunthrop, but was eight lengths second to him at Clifton-on-Dunsmore. Twenty lengths third in that race was the Millington runner Fortune Hunter, who went on to score subsequently, so he should be able to get off the mark provided he finds some extra stamina. *P.J. Millington — Mrs J. Hunt — Fernie (-; Roger Harvey).* 30 (CMa), 123 (OMa), 233 (OMa), 693 (OMa), 1021 (2m4fOMa), 1420 (OMa).

WELL MATCHED ..9-11.. 6 b.g. Weldnaas (USA) — Mandrian (Mandamus) 4d1. Half-brother to Autonomous, Mildame and Annyban, to successful Hurdlers, Handy Lass (also won on flat), Matchless (also won NH flat), and Santo Boy, and to flat winner, Manful. Dam won 2 flat, 8-12f. Related to a host of winners, and quickly made his mark with a ready success in soft at Garthorpe. Looks a bright prospect, and should be worth following in future. *A. Armstrong (Well Matched Group) — Cranwell Bloodhounds.* 872 (OMa), 1270 (OMa).

PLATE 139   *1673 Torrington Farmers Ladies Open: Evens favourite, Well Armed (Miss O. Green) has pulled up, and joint National Ladies Champion Novice Rider Olivia said she'd eat her hat if it didn't win*   PHOTO: Brian Armstrong

WELL TED (IRE) ..10-9.. 9 ch.g. Carlingford Castle — Pollyfane (Pollerton) 34u11. Good-topped. IRISH P-t-P '97 r3 w1 (4&5yo Maiden, looked lucky) p1 (head 2nd); and fell at 1st. IRISH NH FLAT '97 r4 p0. IRISH NH '97 r2 p0. P-t-P '99 r4 w2 (Restricted and Intermediate) p0; and unseated 1. Finished very tired in his first two outings this year, but very unlucky at Siddington where victory seemed assured until a last fence blunder, and twice won readily in April. Usually confidently ridden from off the pace, and can finish quite strongly, but remains liable to jumping lapses. Defeated subsequent Chasing winner Ad Hoc in '99, and should prove more than good enough to win Opens in 2001. Suited by a soft surface. *G.J. Fisher, D. Gallivan, L.P. Riley & M. Seabourne — Berkeley (Dick Baimbridge).* 294 (O), 445 (Cf), 749 (Cf), 968 (Cf), 1190 (Cf).

WELSH WARRIOR ..9-11.. 8 b.g. Librate — Mayo Melody (Highland Melody) ffu12c. Tall lengthy half-brother to Fathers Footprints and to Chasing winner, Stardust Roc. FLAT '98 r4 p0 (inc 2 Sells). NH '98 (for M. Bradley) r1 p0 (pulled up). Erratic jumping was his literal downfall in his first three Points, but had shown speed, and was contesting the lead when he departed at the final fence at Bassaleg. Comfortably beat a lame villian at Bonvilston on firm next time, but then unable to cope with Baran Itsu (who had been left to score at Bassaleg) when they had a re-match. Quick enough to go one better in a Restricted, but is still making far too many errors. *S.A. James — Banwen Miners (John Moore).* 4 (O), 1301 (OMa), 1405 (OMa), 1454 (OMa), 1568 (R), 1659 (R).

WE MOVE EARTH ..10-4.. 7 b.g. Scallywag — Mistress Seymour (Seymour Hicks FR) 1f11p. Tall rangy. P-t-P '99 r2 p1 (2nd of 3); and fell 1. The impressive winner of three minor Points, but has developed a tendency to jump right-handed, and sadly pulled up lame when holding every chance on his Hunter Chase debut at Cheltenham. Yet to beat a worthy opponent, but his fencing whilst not being straight has been accurate, and his demeanour is far more laid back than many by his sire. Will hopefully make a speedy recovery, and prove himself in better class, but the fact that a leg has given way at such an early stage in his career is not a positive sign. *R.M. Penny — Mendip F. (Richard Barber).* 30 (CMa), 331 (R), 406 (R), 731 (M), 1336 (2m4fH).

WESLEYS CHOICE ..—.. 12 b.g. Cruise Missile — Valley Mist (Perhapsburg) f. Rangy brother to Cruise Valley and Happy Valley, and half-brother to Rising Mist and Come On Valley. Dam won 5 Points and placed 6 (also disqualified from 2nd once), Grandam, Lady Charlotte, won 3 Points and placed 6. P-t-P '98 (for Mr C. Rush) r3 p0 (last, pulled up 1, and fell 1). Demolished the fourth fence at Cherrybrook before capsizing four fences later on his only appearance in 2000. Beaten fields on his only completion two years ago, and is as slow as a boat. *Mrs M.M. Smith — E. Cornwall.* 856 (CfMa).

WEST ASHRIDGE ..—.. 6 ch.m. No Evil — Classical Chimes (Los Cerrillos ARG) pp. Good-bodied. Dam fell or unseated in all 3 Points (got no further than eighth fence). Pulled up in the final mile twice, and quickly dismounted in the latest. *D.T. Hooper — Torrington F. (Andrew Congdon).* 106 (OMa), 1263 (OMa).

WESTCOUNTRY LAD ..10-4.. 11 b.g. General Surprise — Charmezzo (Remezzo) 11p10. Big rangy owner-bred half-brother to Ashdown Boy (*qv*). P-t-P/HUNT CH '96/7 and '99 r12 w2 (Maiden and Restricted) p4 (2 3rds, of 4 once); unseated 1, and pulled up 1. A thorough stayer who is not afraid of hard work, but has taken a while to mature physically, and produced much improved form in 2000. Can plough through the deepest mud, and won two two-finisher events in testing conditions before defeating Butler John in waterlogged ground at Trebudannon; the meeting was abandoned not long after he had pipped the favourite on the line, and landed a few nice bets. A sound jumper in Points, but despite his size is much less assured in Hunter Chases, and has been unable to cope in that sphere to date. His genuine nature, and ability to gallop all day should enable him to win more stamina tests. *L. Bond — Stevenstone (Pen Bond).* 165 (Cf), 316 (Cf), 680 (3m1fH), 1188 (O), 1338 (4m1fH).

WESTER LAD ..9-0.. 12 b.g. Germont — Lawsuitlaw (Cagirama) 4. Strong brother to Gemma Law and Lethem Laird. P-t-P '95, '97 and '99 r5 p0 (4th twice, pulled up 1, and fell/unseated 2). Only emerged bi-annually until this year, but has only managed one outing apiece in his last three campaigns, and went back into hiding after a respectable fourth at Alnwick in February. Had a subsequent winner immediately behind him, and probably would have won a few races in the past had he been able to compete. *T. Butt — Border.* 188 (OMa).

WESTERN FORT (IRE) ..10-2.. 11 ch.g. Saher — Moon Away (Mount Hagen FR) 22123343. Big strong. IRISH P-t-P '96 r6 p0 (remote 6th, pulled up 4, and fell 1). IRISH NH FLAT '96 r1 p0 (remote 13th of 14). P-t-P '97/9 r19 w2 (Maiden and Restricted) p6 (4 3rds, of 4 once, and last once); pulled up 5. Successful on three occasions at Black Forest Lodge '98/00, but generally finds winning difficult, and often finds nothing in the closing stages. Has made the frame in his last 16 completions, and his consistency and sound jumping should continue to stand him in good stead, and worth noting at his favourite track again in 2001. Acts on a sound surface, and avoids genuinely soft ground. *R.G. Westacott — Devon & Somerset (Keith Cumings).* 66 (Cf), 202 (I), 557 (Cf), 639 (I), 930 (I), 1310 (I), 1514 (Cf), 1674 (I).

WESTERN PEARL (IRE) ..7-5.. 13 gr.g. Sarab — Legs And Things (Three Legs) 45. Sturdy half-brother to flat and Hurdles winner, Coquillage, to Irish NH flat winner, Forget Us Not, to French flat winner, Madrileno (IRE), and to a winner in Spain. Dam won 2 6f races in Ireland. IRISH NH FLAT r1 p0. P-t-P '94/7 (for Mrs P.J. Price) r9 p2 (2nds, remote last once); last pair 2, pulled up 3, and fell/unseated 2. Unable to run much due to bad legs in the past, and was emerging from a three year absence when finishing last in both outings this year. Had the ability to win, and would have done so in a bad Maiden at Bitterley in '95 but for unseating at the last, but only able to travel at slow speeds now. *R.J. Cotton — S. Herefords.* 487 (CfMa), 994 (OMa).

WESTHALL JONSTAN (IRE) ..8-7.. 7 b.g. Supreme Leader — Dara Moss (IRE) (Le Moss) pppp5. Workmanlike. Dam is half-sister to The Boiler White (*qv*). Sold Doncaster, May for 1000. Has become very tired in most of his races, and gives the impression that he is not nearly fit enough. Possibly not as bad as he has appeared to date. *J. Carr — S. Durham.* 624 (OMa), 808 (OMa), 1084 (2m4fOMa), 1163 (OMa), 1331 (OMa).

WESTINGTON ..—.. 8 b.g. Relief Pitcher — Truelyn (True Song) p. Workmanlike lengthy brother to Exmoor Forest (*qv*). Pulled up after 2m4f on an exploratory outing in mid-May. *Miss C.V. Hart — N. Cotswold (Helen Hart).* 1459 (R).

WEST LUTTON ..8-10.. 9 b.g. Scorpio (FR) — Crammond Brig (New Brig) ppp. Workmanlike half-brother to Hutcel Brig, Risky Bid and Hutcel Bell, and to jumping winner, Easthorpe. Dam won 2 NH flat and 3 Hdles, 2m-3m1f. NH FLAT '97 r1 p0. NH '97 and '98 r4 p0; pulled up 2. P-t-P '97/9 (for Mr R.D.E. Woodhouse) r10 p0; 6th twice, fell/unseated 5, and pulled up 1. Often the victim of appalling jumping in the past, but lack of stamina now appears to be his chief problem. Gets about quite a bit, and has had a different owner in each of his Pointing campaigns, but seems troubled, and would be better off in Maidens. *S. Letters — O. Berks (Chris Cox).* 36 (CI), 734 (R), 896 (R).

WESTWINDS ..10-7.. 9 b.g. Vital Season — April's Crook (Crozier) 31. Home-bred brother to Avril Showers (*qv*). P-t-P '98/9 (for Mr R. & Mrs N. Atkinson) r8 w1 (Maiden) p4 (3 3rds, of 4, and last);

pulled up 2, and brought down 1. Well-related, and typically late maturing, and recorded the fastest three mile time of the day when beating Burgundy Bob at Larkhill, but the only disappointing thing about him is that he was unable to reappear. A good jumper, and is suited by top of the ground. Well ridden by Miranda Coombe, and will surely win again if getting the green light for 2001. Wears a cross-noseband. *Mrs N.M. Coombe — Cattistock (Wib Coombe).* 208 (R), 458 (R).

WEYCROFT VALLEY ..8-4.. 10 b.m. North Street — Kitty's Copes (Persian Plan AUS) 43bp44. Good-topped rangy. Grandam, Flippity Mist, failed to finish in 2 Points for Gordon Herrod in '81. P-t-P '97/9 r10 p1 (last of 3); last 3, pulled up 5, and fell 1. Last to stagger home in eight completions, and has yet to beat a rival. Can show speed for up to 2m4f, but the tank quickly empties, and has to get through the last half mile on vapour. Most jockeys would pull her up, but Lee Tibbatts has a complete at all costs attitude to Pointing. *G. Herrod — Cotley.* 206 (OMa), 410 (OMa), 738 (OMa), 957 (CfMa), 1241 (OMa), 1303 (M).

WHATACHARLIE ..8-7.. 7 b.g. Nicholas Bill — Zulu Dancer (Sula Bula) ffpppp. Brother to Frumerty. Dam is half-sister to Panto Lady (*qv* '99 Annual). P-t-P '99 r3 p0 (last, unseated 1, and pulled up 1). Not without ability, and afflicted by appalling wind, and has had three operations on it to date. Generally jumps well, and often on the premises with half a mile to run, but quickly struggles for breath, and was on the verge of collapse when he fell at Barbury Castle in January; subsequently down for several minutes. Tubing, and a tie-back op have failed, but connections are hoping a soft-palate operation will prove effective, and capable of winning if it does. *Mrs L. Harrington — Avon V. (Don Harrington).* 11 (OMa), 31 (CMa), 131 (OMa), 264 (OMa), 391 (CfMa), 472 (CMa).

WHAT A COINCIDENCE ..—.. 8 b.m. Daring March — Coincidence Girl (Manacle) p. Close-coupled half-sister to Another Islay (*qv*). Met a grisly fate when she broke both forelegs on the flat at Alnwick. *Miss L.J. Grattan — Buccleuch.* 44 (OMa).

WHATAFELLOW (IRE) ..10-12.. 11 ch.g. Arapahos (FR) — Dara's March (March Parade) 1191f11p. Good-bodied brother to Irish Pointing winners, Ardmore Princess and Ourownfellow (IRE) (subsequently a successful English jumper), and half-brother to Bishop Town Boy. Dam won 3 Irish Points and placed 7. IRISH P-t-P '94/5 r7 w1 (4yo Maiden on disqualification) p2 (3rds); pulled up 2. P-t-P/HUNT CH '96/9 r26 w12 (inc 3 Opens, inc 5-timer '99) p9 (4 2nds); fell 2 (would have won once). A top-class Pointer who is now well on the way to 20 victories, and has scored on ground ranging from very soft to firm. Has been greatly improved since the application of blinkers in mid '98, but gained his first Hunter Chase success at Cartmel without them. Usually loiters in the rear for the first part of the race, but once Alistair Crow kicks him into overdrive few rivals can go with him, and is often in command fully a mile from home. Tough, but can become disillusioned, and found life too arduous when taking on the best at Cheltenham and Stratford, but at least connections were prepared to have a crack at the top prizes this year. *G. Samuel — N. Salop (Sheila Crow).* 117 (O), 294 (O), 584 (3m2f110yH), 691 (O), 1025 (3m110yH), 1409 (O), 1601 (3m2fH), 1647 (3m4fH).

WHAT A FIDDLER (IRE) ..10-7.. 8 ch.g. Orchestra — Crowenstown Miss (Over The River FR) 111. Leggy lengthy. Dam is half-sister to Captain Bravado (*qv* 2000 Annual). NH FLAT Mar '97 r1 p1 (2nd). NH '97/8 r6 p3 (2nd in Hdle, placed in 2 Chses). Has not raced much, but was able to prove himself a useful novice in Points, and his victory in an 18-runner Restricted at Charm Park was given a big boost when the four length second Victoria's Boy landed a Hunter Chase. His previous wins meant little (the Members was a match), but consistently shows a turn of foot, and deserves a chance over the bigger obstacles again. *R. & J. Tate — Bramham.* 400 (OMa), 688 (M), 1230 (R).

WHAT A HAND ..10-0.. 13 ch.g. Nearly A Hand — Kiki Star (Some Hand) p211. Tall good-bodied half-brother to jumping winner, Miss Marigold. Dam won 4 Sells, 10-12f. IRISH P-t-P '97 r1 w1 (United Open). IRISH HUNT CH '97 r3 w2 p0; and fell 1. P-t-P/HUNT CH '94/7 (for Mr F.A. Bonsal) r13 w9 (inc 3 Hunt Chses 3m–3m2f110y, Mixed Open and Open; hat-trick in '96) p0; and failed to finish 5 (fell/unseated 4). NH '97/8 r6 p2 (2nds); fell 1st in '98 Grand National. IRISH NH '98/9 (for E.M. O'Sullivan) r6 p0. A smart performer in his time, and although disappointing on his second spell in Ireland, and nowhere near as good as he once was did well to win two uncompetitive races in 2000. Six races under Paul Nicholls in the '97/8 season failed to result in a win, and ended in ignominious circumstances at Aintree, and of four career falls three have occurred at the first fence. Acts in mud, and avoids firm ground. Has been tried in blinkers. *T.D.B. Underwood — Garth & S. Berks.* 127 (Cf), 243 (Cf), 452 (M), 1246 (Cf).

WHATAMONKEY ..8-11.. 8 gr.g. Thethingaboutitis (USA) — Shrood Biddy (Sharrood USA) pp4. Half-brother to Wizadora. Dam is half-sister to Sunlight Express (*qv* '94 Annual). Tailed off by the fifth twice (jumped deliberately once), but did better when 32 lengths last in what looked to be a hot Maiden. The present rider is no help, but it would be interesting to see what Kahlil Burke (who has ridden a winner for the stable) could make of him. *P. Morris — Albrighton.* 866 (CfMa), 1318 (OMa), 1526 (OMa).

WHAT'S YOUR STORY (IRE) ..—.. 12 ch.g. The Parson — Lolos Run VII (unknown) f. Tall half-brother to jumping winner, Killula Chief. Dam, won Maiden in Ireland. NH FLAT Spr '94 (for D,

Nicholson) r3 w1 p0. NH '95/8 (for P. Webber; 1 wins previously for D. Nicholson) r18 w3 (3 Hdles, 2m6f-3m1f) p7 (inc 3rd in Ch); 4th and fell in other Chses (in lead 2 out once — looked winner); intimidated and ran out once. Tended to jump badly under Rules, and made his final nine appearances over Hurdles. Fell after a mile and broke a leg at Thorpe, which was very sad for the novice Emma Marley. *Miss E.J. Marley — N. Ledbury.* 118 (L).

WHAT THE HECK (IRE) ..9-11.. 9 b.g. Mister Lord (USA) — Arianrhod (L'Homme Arme) 74. Big rangy brother to Hurdles winners, Ariadler (IRE) and Lord Pat (IRE). NH '97/8 r6 p0 (unseated in 2 of 4 Hdles — saddle slipped once, and hampered once; and last and pulled up in Chses). P-t-P/HUNT CH '99 r6 w2 (2m4f Maiden, and Members) p0; last, unseated 2, and pulled up 1. Won two minor races in '99, but only able to appear twice this season and has clearly hit a snag. Only beaten 15 lengths in a fair Restricted at Hutton Rudby, and should be capable of winning one if healthy in 2001. Has not appeared to be the stoutest of stayers to date. *Miss M.D. Myco — S. Durham.* 301 (2m5fH), 620 (R).

WHERESBOB ..—§§.. 7 ch.g. Jumbo Hirt (USA) — Cathys Clown (Moray Mink) RppR. Strong-topped owner-bred. An evil sort who changed partners for every race, but none of them could steer him as far as halfway. *Mrs M. Robinson — Cumberland F.* 381 (OMa), 499 (2m4fOMa), 664 (2m5fOMa), 978 (CfMa).

WHERE'S SAM (IRE) ..9-7.. 11 b.g. Torenaga — Rosy Dawn (Rushmere) fp35375. Good-bodied. IRISH P-t-P '97/9 r20 w2 (7 plus Mdn, and Ladies — left in lead last, lucky) p9; pulled up 6 and fell 2. Bought Malvern, July for 2500. Much improved by a change of yard when scoring twice in Ireland in '99, but could not sustain the form in the latest stable, and apart from a decent effort when eight lengths third he was unable to beat another horse. Faced stiff tasks on occasions, and should be concentrating on Confineds. *J.M. Bowen, B. Edwards & Mrs L. Grylls — Tetcott (Linda Wonnacott).* 103 (Cf), 252 (O), 534 (Cf), 726 (Cf), 854 (O), 1432 (3m1fH), 1535 (2m3fH).

WHINHOLME LASS (IRE) ..—.. 9 b.m. Mister Lord (USA) — Deep Down (Deep Run) ppup. Small half-sister to London Run and Deep Bit (IRE), to good flat and Hurdles winner, Pearl Run, to Irish Pointing winner, Curraghtown, and to Irish Hurdles winner, Suffolk Bells. P-t-P '98 (for Mr F. Kirby) r2 p0 (pulled up 1, and fell 1). NH '98 r1 p0 (pulled up). Yet to complete in seven starts over jumps, and does not inspire confidence. Wears a cross-noseband. *Miss J.M. Barrable — E. Devon (D. Llewellin).* 849 (R), 1048 (CfMa), 1263 (OMa), 1518 (R).

WHIPPERS DELIGHT (IRE) ..10-6.. 13 ch.g. King Persian — Crashing Juno (Crash Course) 12p. Rather unfurnished half-brother to jumping winner, Macroom, to Hurdles winner, Precious Juno (IRE), and to a winner in Norway. 800y. FLAT (blinkered 1; for D. Barron; wins previously for J. Berry) r14 w2 (7f Sells at 2) p1 (3rd). NH '91/9 (from G. Charles-Jones; bought for 2000) r75 w10 (6 Hdles, 2m-2m2f, and 4 Chses, 2m-3m1f) p28; ran out 1. A good servant who cost current connections 2000 guineas and went on to earn them £43,815 under Rules, and despite being inconsistent and prone to bad patches he has on balance given a great deal of fun. Needs good ground or mud, and is a confirmed front-runner who made all to land a competitive four-runner Ladies at Charing, but sadly broke down when 1-3 on a firmish surface at Rodmell. *S.P. Tindall — Southdown & Eridge (Jeff Peate).* 287 (L), 573 (CfL), 1211 (L).

WHISKEY GALORE ..9-0.. 8 b.g. Lighter — Moonbreaker (Twilight Alley) 3435. Half-brother to Tycoon Moon (dam of The Commentator *qv* '00 Annual), Linlithgow Palace and Rawyards Brig. P-t-P '99 (for Mrs J. McGregor & Mrs D. Thomson) r4 p1 (remote last of 2); pulled up 2, and fell 1. Has made the frame in four Maidens, but yet to finish within 10 lengths of the winner, and looks some way short of the required standard at present. Wears a cross-noseband, and does not seem blessed with limitless stamina. *Mrs J. McGregor — Fife.* 187 (OMa), 365 (CfMa), 719 (CfMa), 977 (CfMa).

WHISPERING PINES (NZ) ..10-10.. 9 b.g. Cache Of Gold (USA) — Woodhill (NZ) (Zamazaan FR) f. Strong. P-t-P '99 r6 w2 (inc Open) p3 (2 2nds); and fell 1. Won two Opens on testing ground in '99, and looked a progressive sort, but lamed himself when falling at Tweseldown on his return, and was unable to reappear. Appeared not to stay four miles once, but had no trouble over 3m2f, and will hopefully make a full recovery. *J.J. Boulter — S. Dorset (Nick Mitchell).* 4 (O).

WHISPERING STEEL ..9-13.. 15 b.g. Furry Glen — Shady Grove (Deep Run) 63pb. Strong workmanlike brother to Irish Pointing/jumping winner, Knox Court, and half-brother to Priesthill (IRE). NH '91/8 (blinkered 2 to '95) r35 w11 (2 Hdles, 2m-2m1f, and 9 Chses, 2m4f-3m1f) p7. P-t-P '99 (for Mrs D. Reid & Miss L. Whitaker) r2 p0 (7th, and pulled up 1). A former useful Chaser, but often error-prone, and failed to complete the course in his final season under Rules. Gave one decent display in Points when third at Friars Haugh, but otherwise lacking in interest, and failed to reappear after being brought down in April. Usually bandaged on his off-hind. *Mrs L. Normile & Mrs D. Reid — Fife (Alan & Lucy Normile).* 110 (O), 359 (Cf), 717 (Cf), 1117 (M).

WHISTLING BUCK (IRE) ..10-1§.. 13 br.g. Whistling Deer — Buck Ends (Master Buck) 315p62. Tall. Dam won 2 2m Hdles at Down Royal (4 and 5 ran). NH FLAT '92 r4 w1 p1 (3rd). NH '93 and '95/8 r32 w1 (2m4f Hdle) p5 (inc 3rd in Sell Ch). P-t-P/HUNT CH '99 (for Mr B.J. Llewellyn) r7 p1 (2nd); last pair 4, and pulled up 2. Came from a seemingly impossible position to record his first success for four years at Llanfrynach, but often looks ungenuine, and frequently has to be driven along from an early stage. Well ridden by Jamie Jukes when winning, and might have obliged on their final appearance together had he taken the last with more conviction. Wears a tongue-strap, and has been tried in headgear. Acts on any going. *P. Morgan — Llynfi V.* 271 (O), 480 (O), 643 (Cf), 1022 (3mH), 1297 (L), 1569 (Cf).

WHISTLING JAKE (IRE) ..10-3.. 10 b.g. Jolly Jake (NZ) — Hibiscus (Green Shoon) 3. Tall rangy. NH FLAT '97 r1 p1 (33*l* 3rd). P-t-P '99 r1 w1 (Maiden). Scored unchallenged in a race taking 7m 44s on his Pointing debut, but only able to appear once since, and was given a most unenterprising ride by Alastair Crow. Looks a scopey individual, and clearly talented, but obviously has his problems which are exacerbated by his huge frame. *C. & Mrs S.J. Edwards — N. Salop (Sheila Crow).* 592 (Cf).

WHISTLING RUFUS (IRE) ..9-9.. 9 gr.g. Celio Rufo — Aryumad (Goldhill) 6p1f2. Tall half-brother to Sheelin Lad (IRE), and to Irish Pointing winner, Oldtown Girl. 8200 4yo. NH FLAT Mar '97 r1 p0. NH '97/9 (for N. Twiston-Davies; blinkered once) r6 p1 (3rd). Has been a very disappointing competitor, but was left clear four out to win a bad Maiden at Siddington (the other four to finish have still not opened their accounts, and looked unlikely to do so). Faded quickly in the final half mile of his three other Points and clearly struggles to get the trip, but was not keen when tried over a shorter distance at Stratford. Has had perennial leg problems, and retired afterdamaging a hind suspensory. *Mrs C.M. Scott (Argomad Partnership) — Heythrop (Mark Rimell).* 76 (CCfMa), 568 (OMa), 753 (CfMa), 1026 (2m5f110yH), 1193 (R).

WHISTLING SONG ..—.. 6 ch.m. True Song — Sancal (Whistlefield) pp. Sister to I'm Joking. Remote when pulled up at the fourteenth twice (fractious in the paddock on her debut). *Mrs C.M. Weaver & J.P. Thorne — Heythrop (Jon Trice-Rolph).* 792 (OMa), 972 (OMa).

WHITBY ..9-12.. 13 b.g. Little Wolf — Amy Belle (Town And Country) p. Tall. IRISH P-t-P '92/3 r10 w1 (Maiden) p2; pulled up 6, inc all 4 prior to 9-2 win! IRISH NH '94/6 r23 w1 (2m4f Ch) p0. P-t-P/HUNT CH '98/9 r10 w1 (3m1f Hunt Ch) p3 (2 3rds, last once, and inc Hunt Ch); unseated 1, and refused 2. Produced a rare burst of speed on the run-in to capture a Market Rasen Hunter Chase last year, but has preferred to remain anonymous in most of his other 43 starts, and failed to emerge after taking on some top class opposition in a Haydock mud-bath in February. Could have scored more frequently if he had not been so weak-willed. *D.J. Hardman — Pendle Forest & Craven (Christine Billington).* 156 (3mH).

WHITEGATES WILLIE ..10-5.. 9 b.g. Buckskin (FR) — Whitegates Lady (Le Coq D'Or) 1p1p. Compact half-brother to Hurdles winners, Whitegate's Son and Whitegatesprincess (IRE). Dam, sister to Ardesee (qv '98 Annual), won 2 2m4f Hdles. NH FLAT '96 r3 p0. NH '96/8 r13 p4 (Chses, to 2m5f). P-t-P/HUNT CH '99 (for Mrs J.C.M. Wood) r3 p0 (5th, and pulled up 2). Formerly a disappointing non-stayer, but vastly improved by Gary Hanmer, and won two races convincingly including a 7min 33s Restricted in testing ground at Sandon. Earlier landed a massive plunge at Thorpe Lodge, but found Hunter Chase company too demanding on his final appearance. Used to make the running, but accepts restraint with no bother now, and can be expected to win again in his class. Has been tried tongue-tied. Another triumph for his trainer. *D. Manning — Cheshire (Gary Hanmer).* 124 (OMa), 782 (R), 1129 (R), 1343 (3m110yH).

WHITELEGS (U) ..—.. 10 ch.m. Golden Heather — Lonesome (unknown) 2. Heavyweight hunter. Tom Biddick's first ride, and just managed to pass dad on the run-in (both carried 14 stone seven pounds), but literally a mile behind another from the stable. *M. Biddick — N. Cornwall.* 99 (M).

WHITE SMOKE (IRE) ..9-6§.. 9 ch.g. Carlingford Castle — Gaye Diane (Down The Hatch) 591pf86. Good-bodied half-brother to Irish NH flat winner, Hollow Gold. IRISH P-t-P '98 r4 w1 (5 plus Mdn) p0; pulled up 1. IRISH NH FLAT '97 r2 p0. IRISH NH '99 r4 p0. NH '98 (from T. McGovern's, bought for 13,000) r1 p0 (pulled up). Won a dire Irish Maiden in soft, and gave Russell Ross his first success in a five-runner Restricted on firmish at Rodmell, but it seems to have been something of a miracle, because he was not better than a remote last in six other Points in 2000. Did nothing wrong when scoring, but has since given the impression of being ungenuine. Travelled far and wide for his racing, including visits to Leicestershire and Somerset. *Mrs S. Rowe — Crawley & Horsham.* 416 (R), 546 (R), 675 (CR), 953 (I), 1212 (Cf), 1398 (Cf), 1509 (Cf).

WHITE WILLOW ..8-2.. 12 b.g. Touching Wood (USA) — Dimant Blanche (USA) (Gummo USA) 4. Small brother to White Diamond, and half-brother to a winner in Germany. Dam won at 5f. FLAT (to '97; first 2 for B. Hanbury — 2nd twice) r36 w4 (11-14f, one on fibresand) p12 (beaten head once, and neck once). NH '93/7 (for T. Wall; wins previously for Mrs M. Reveley) r29 w5 (2m-2m2f Hdles) p10 (one relegated 2nd for interference after winning 2m2f Hdle). Second to Viardot (qv) on his racecourse debut, and went on to gain nine victories on varying ground to December '96, but has always been moody, and regularly wears headgear. Plodded round unenthusiastically for a poor fourth in his Members, and like Sugar Mill, another who did well in their prime for Mary Reveley, has fallen on desperately hard times now. *F.L. Matthews — Wheatland.* 1529 (M).

WHO IS EQUINAME (IRE) ..10-6.. 11 b.g. Bob Back (USA) — Instanter (Morston FR) pp341. Workmanlike half-brother to 3 Hurdles winners, (2 in Ireland, including Done Instantly, also successful flat/NH flat and Chasing there), and Noble Insight. Dam won 2m Hdle in Ireland. NH FLAT '94 (for D. Eddy) r4 p3 (2 2nds). NH '94/5 and '97 in Henderson's; bought for 41,000) r15 w3 (2m Hdle, and 2 Chses, 2m6f-3m) p5 (3rd once at Punchestown). Would have won three of his final four starts under Rules but for falling in the lead two out once (in a farcical contest at Worcester in which only one went clear), but absent since scoring on his final outing in December '97. Best in blinkers and regained them after pulling up in his first two Points, and gained a hard fought half length success in a Confined at Clifton-on-Dunsmore, but does not always look too willing these days. Has been an expensive failure on balance, and the new yard did well to shake off the cobwebs and extract a belated victory. *Mrs J. Wilson — Pytchley (Bill Warner).* 10 (O), 85 (O), 510 (Cf), 1006 (Cf), 1415 (Cf).

WHO'S NEXT ..10-1§.. 13 b.g. Oats — Kaotesse (Djakao FR) 25. Lengthy unfurnished half-brother to Levotesse (dam of 4 Pointers including She Wood She *qv*), and Easy Kao, and to Hurdles winner, Blue Disc. NH FLAT r2 w1 (all-weather, 4 ran) p0. NH '92 and '96 r7 p3 (3rd in Hdle; and 2 Chses); pulled up 1. P-t-P/HUNT CH '94/6 and '98 r11 w4 (inc 2m5f110y Hunt Ch) p3 (2 3rds). Capable of useful efforts, but reported to suffer with bad corns, and disappeared for more than two years after winning at Marks Tey in '98. Ran well when second there on his comeback, but has never been predictable, and dropped out tamely under pressure next time. Has been tried in blinkers in the past. *H.R. Hobson — Puckeridge.* 1184 (Cf), 1286 (Cf).

WHO'S THE MAN ..—.. 7 gr.g. Arzanni — Tommys Dream (Le Bavard FR) p. Dam, half-sister to Paddy's Glen (*qv* '87 Season Annual), won Irish NH flat and 4 English Hdles (2m-3m1f). Showed speed to halfway before fading and pulling up at the last in a May Maiden. *N.M.L. Ewart — Cumberland F.* 1329 (OMa).

WHO'S YOUR MAN (IRE) ..9-7.. 11 br.g. Strong Statement (USA) — Pennies River (Over The River FR) 3p2p49. Tall strong half-brother to Irish NH flat winner, Wyn Waw Soon (IRE), and Irish Hurdles winner, Lord Penny. IRISH P-t-P '94/6 r13 p3; pulled up 7, and fell/unseated 2. P-t-P/HUNT CH '97/9 (for Mr P.H. Morris) r17 w2 (Maiden and Members) p6 (2 2nds, last once); pulled up 6. A fair galloper, and usually runs prominently, but a weak finisher who finds nothing off the bridle. Only beat three rivals in 2000, and needs to concentrate on the weakest opportunities available. Acts on any going. Visored once in '98. *Mrs J.E Symonds — S. Herefords (Nicky Sharpe).* 340 (R), 484 (R), 666 (M), 818 (R), 1157 (2m3fH), 1592 (4m2fH).

WIBBLEY WOBBLEY ..10-3.. 9 b.g. Arctic Lord — Burrow Star (Four Burrow) u111231. Workmanlike lengthy owner-bred. Dam won 5 minor Points (3 as a 12-year-old) and 2nd. P-t-P '98/9 (for Mrs C. Rowcliffe) r8 p3 (2 2nds, beaten short head once); pulled up 1, ran out 2, and fell/unseated 2. Frightening in his first season , but much improved since joining Keith Cumings, and has gone from strength to strength since being robbed by the judge at Wadebridge last year. Won four races by an aggregate of 95 lengths, and time may tell his defeat by Black Dante at Bratton Down was his best effort to date as a bright future under Rules is predicted for his vanquisher. Acts on any going, but reported to need a left-handed track. Gets excellent assistance from Jo Cumings, and sure to upgrade successfully in 2001. *R. Davies — Dulverton W. (Keith Cumings).* 105 (OMa), 407 (OMa), 536 (R), 730 (I), 1138 (MO), 1305 (MO), 1566 (M).

WILD BRIAR ..8-8.. 6 ch.m. Green Adventure (USA) — Ragged Rose (Scallywag) p4s. Home-bred half-sister to Heather Lad (*qv*). Finished a tired 12 lengths fourth after late mistakes in a 2m4f contest, but tailed off when failing to finish twice. Will need to improve a fair amount to get seriously involved. *C.B. Taylor — S. Durham.* 626 (OMa), 1002 (2m4fOMa), 1329 (OMa).

WILD BUCK (IRE) ..9-7§.. 10 b.g. Buckskin (FR) — Free For Ever (Little Buskins) 6. Tall brother to Chasing winner, Abercromby Chief. Dam won 2m5f NH flat in Ireland. IRISH NH '96 r3 p0. IRISH P-t-P '97/8 r6 w1 (7yo&up Maiden) p1 (3rd). P-t-P/HUNT CH '99 r8 p1 (remote 3rd of 4); last pair 2, pulled up 3, and unseated 1. NH Oct '99 (from K. Bailey's) r1 p0 (pulled up). Won one of six Points in Ireland, but has shown no enthusiasm whatsoever in the current yard, and the application of blinkers twice in '99 made no difference. Disappeared after another uninspiring effort on the opening day of the season this year. *J. Perriss & L. Attrill — Vine & Craven (John Porter).* 2 (R).

WILD DREAM ..—.. 6 b.m. Derrylin — Vedra (IRE) (Carlingford Castle) u. Compact well-made half-sister to Gunner Welburn. Sold Doncaster, May for 3000. Did not get far before shedding Shirley Vickery on her debut, but related to a star performer and comes from a most successful yard, so will certainly merit consideration when she reappears. *S.L. Pike — E. Devon.* 1131 (OMa).

WILD EDRIC ..9-7.. 9 b.g. Weld — Paper Lady (Document) p831. Dam won 2 Points and placed 8 for Lucy McFarlane; was previously 2nd in an Irish Hdle, and in an English Maiden. P-t-P '97/8 r3 w1 (Maiden) p1 (3rd); pulled up 1. Looked to be on the upgrade when winning at Brampton Bryan in '98, but clearly not easy to train, and has improved for missing the following season. Appeared to be finding his feet when third at Upper Sapey, but all out to justify odds-on favouritism in his Members, and the speed he showed two years ago seems to have deserted him. *Mrs R.M. McFarlane — United (Lucy McFarlane).* 336 (R), 567 (R), 698 (R), 858 (M).

WILD OSCAR (IRE) ..—.. 7 ch.g. Toca Madera — Hawkmoontwosixnine (Viking USA) p. Sold Goffs Ireland, Aug '97 for 1980. Became tailed off after some indifferent jumping on his debut. *M. Edwards — W. Somerset (C. White).* 733 (2m4fOMa).

WILLCHRIS ..10-0.. 14 b.g. Fidel — Culkeern (Master Buck) pp. Small brother to Slievenamaddy. IRISH P-t-P '92/4 r17 w2 (unplaced Maiden and Winners of Two) p5; pulled up 4, slipped up 2, and fell 2. IRISH NH '93/7 r26 w3 (2m3f-2m5f Chses, hat-trick '95, one win Perth) p2 (3rd after falling once). NH '98/9 r8 w1 (3m2f110y HCap Ch) p3 (2 3rds); unseated 1. P-t-P/HUNT CH '98/9 r6 w3 (2 Confineds and Mixed Open) p0; 4th, slipped up 1, and pulled up 1. Staged a notable revival in '98 when winning four times including a handicap at Newton Abbot, but lightly raced and only able to complete the course once since. Likes to dominate, and invariably makes most when successful, but finding another opportunity at 14 will be a hard chore. Goes to post early. *P. Riddick — Gelligaer F.* 271 (O), 480 (O).

PLATE 140   1305 Cotley Mixed Open: Rory Davies' Wibbley Wobbley and Jo Cumings, 3rd, take the last, Jo became Mrs Davies during the summer   PHOTO: Brian Armstrong

WILLET WIZARD ..—.. 8 ch.g. Jester — Rose Red City (Relkino) p. Big rangy owner-bred half-brother to Jolirose (*qv*). NH FLAT '97/8 r2 p0 (tailed off both). NH '99 (tongue-tied) r4 p0 (last 2 and pulled up 2 in Hdles). Lightly raced and useless so far, and was far too fat when he unsurprisingly blew up in a Maiden. *D.G. Stephens — Devon & Somerset (Vicky Stephens).* 934 (OMa).

WILL HILL (IRE) ..9-12.. 6 b.g. Phardante (FR) — Financial Burden (Mandalus) u1. Brother to Freestyler (IRE). Prominent when unseating after two miles on his debut, and confirmed the promise when winning a weak youngsters Maiden at High Easter with a great deal to spare (despite jumping right in the final mile). The stable are in need of new blood as some some of the old favourites have fallen by the wayside, and Will Hill could fill the bill. *H.D. Hill & C.H. Sporborg — Puckeridge (Christopher Sporborg).* 323 (CfMa), 605 (OMa).

WILLIE B BRAVE (IRE) ..9-7.. 10 b.g. Buckskin (FR) — Ranamacken (Sexton Blake) u6455. Tall. IRISH P-t-P '96/7 r8 w2 (5&6 Mdn, and Winners of One) p1 (2nd); pulled up 2, and fell 2. NH '98/9 (for R. Phillips, blinkered last 2) r6 p0 (inc beaten head, and fell last in Sell; pulled up only Ch). Sold Ascot, May for 1500. Best with cut in the ground in Ireland, but has never progressed, and generally lightly raced. Tended to jump slowly when proceeding in a ponderous fashion in 2000, and seems to lack zest. *Mrs C. Lawrence — Eggesford.* 142 (I), 383 (3mH), 726 (Cf), 930 (I), 1138 (MO).

WILLIE MAKEIT (IRE) ..10-3.. 11 b.g. Coquelin (USA) — Turbina (Tudor Melody) 05p4. Sturdy compact half-brother to an Irish Hurdles winner. IRISH P-t-P '94/5 r7 w2 (5yo&up Maiden and Adjacent) p3. IRISH NH FLAT '94 r2 p0. IRISH NH '94 (blinkered final) r3 p0. NH '95/7 and '99 r20 w3 (2m-2m5f Chses, inc 3 and 5 ran; hat-trick) p5. P-t-P/HUNT CH '98/9 r10 w1 (2m6f110y Hunt Ch) p4 (3 2nds, last once; and remote last of 3); pulled up 1 and fell 1. Struggles to stay in

Points, and is more profitably employed in sub-3m Hunter Chases on a sound surface. Won over 2m6f at Market Rasen last year, and gave his best display since when eight lengths fourth in the inaugural Handicap Hunter Chase at Newton Abbot on his latest appearance. Probably not very genuine, and has been tried in blinkers. *N.M. Tory (The Not So Blonde Partnership) — Portman (Ali Tory).* 326 (L), 684 (2m4fH), 1060 (MO), 1600 (2m5f110yH).

WILLOUGHBY MOSS ..8-11.. 9 b.g. Le Moss — Willow Wood (Precipice Wood) p. Tall rangy light-bodied half-brother to Farthing Wood. Dam, half-sister to Phanjo (*qv* '90 Annual), won 2 Points and 2nd (to Flying Ace) for Billie Thomson. P-t-P '99 r3 p0 (4th, last, and pulled up 1). Well supported, and was travelling on the heels of the leaders when pulled up lame with four to jump at Alnwick on his reappearance. Has looked rather excitable, and lacking in stamina to date, and this latest setback could prove curtains. *Mrs B.K. Thomson — Berwicks.* 914 (CfMa).

WILLOWS JAYBE ..—.. 8 ch.m. So Careful — Willows Account (Stetchworth Lad) pp. Half-sister to Willows Casino and Willows Engagement. Dam won a Maiden and 3rd 2 for Gwyn Brace (also failed to finish 7 — refused 2). Grandam, Contra Account, was placed in 3 flat and 2 Hurdles, and won a Maiden and 2nd 3 (was ungenuine). Pulled up in Maidens, including after being virtually carried out and brought to a standstill before the second on her debut. *G. & Miss J. Brace — Llangeinor (Jayne Brace).* 834 (OMa), 1361 (2m4fOMa).

WILLSAN ..—.. 11 ch.g. Nearly A Hand — Sanber (New Member) pp. Stocky compact. Dam won 6 Hunt Chses (3m-3m2f) and 4 Points and placed 9 for Raymond Winslade. P-t-P '96/7 (for Mr R. Winslade) r2 p1 (2nd of 3); and pulled up 1. NH '98 (for R.H. Alner) r2 p0 (fell and pulled up in Chses). Can go a good gallop, but physically flawed, and ran tubed and tongue-tied on his latest appearance. His career has been blighted with problems as he broke a blood vessel in '96, and could surely have won races had he been more fortunate. *J. Honeyball — Taunton V.* 147 (OMa), 560 (R).

WILLS PERK (IRE) ..10-4.. 6 ch.m. Executive Perk — Brandy Hill Girl (Green Shoon) 12. Bought Doncaster, Aug for 6000. Won a Maiden on good to soft at Friars Haugh by 25 lengths after Dere Street had unseated at the last when held, and was odds-on to follow up at Lanark, but failed by a neck to reach Lord Levi. Objected successfully 'for taking my ground after the last' and supporters collected at 8-11, but those who had backed Lord Levi at 20-1 were robbed by the stewards, as the decision was later reversed at Portman Square. Obviously an above-average novice, and she could develop into a useful performer. *T.R. Oates — Dumfries (Kate Anderson).* 363 (CfMa), 663 (R).

WILLY WEE (IRE) ..—.. 10 b.g. Orchestra — Viacandella (Cantab) p55. Half-brother to 5 winners in Ireland (4 by Fidel), including Lyntim and Eddie Wee (both NH flat and jumping), and Helynsar (flat and Hurdles). Dam won 3 Irish Points. IRISH P-t-P '96/7 and '99 r8 w1 (6yo Mdn) p4; pulled up, and fell. IRISH NH FLAT '97 r1 p0. IRISH NH '97 and '99 r5 p2 (15/ 2nd — several runners took wrong course, and 16/ 3rd of 4 in Hunt Ch). Bought Doncaster, Aug for 1000. Shut up shop at an alarming rate after about two miles in 2000, and was the best part of two fences behind when last twice. Surely suffering badly. *R.V. Westwood — Fife.* 301 (2m5fH), 495 (O), 660 (Cf).

WILY MISS ..—§.. 7 b.m. Teenoso (USA) — Vulpine Lady (Green Shoon) rpppu. Small compact half-sister to Digitalis (*qv*). Dam pulled up in 2 Points for Den Probin. NH FLAT '99 (from M. Mullineaux's) r1 p0. A poor jumper who gave a string of deplorable displays, and is clearly ungenuine. Blinkered to no avail on her two most recent outings. *D.A. Probin — Cheshire (Susan Mullineaux).* 593 (2m4fOMa), 694 (OMa), 966 (OMa), 1323 (OMa), 1526 (OMa).

WIND AND STARS ..—.. 9 b.m. Lighter — Spartella (Spartan General) ppr. Half-sister to Woodlands Genhire, Woodlandsfor Power, Mountfosse, and Spartans Conquest. Dam won 7 Hunt Chses, 2m6f-3m2f, and 3 Points and placed 8 for the Barnetts. Attractively bred and consistently shows early speed, but falls into a black hole, and gives the impression that there is something wrong with her. *J.L. Barnett — Warwicks (Mrs I. Barnett).* 704 (OMa), 995 (OMa), 1359 (OMa).

WINDSOCKS (U) ..—.. 16 b.g. unknown p. Blown away by thoroughbreds in his Members. *R. Skinner — Eggesford.* 1173 (M).

WINDYWAY ..7-0.. 9 b.m. North Street — Winceyweather (Amerian USA) ufp5p. Showed a smidgen of ability before crashing out in her first two races, but Lee Tibbatts must have had a terrifying season riding mares for Gordon Herrod (see also Tolepa). Seems to have no idea about how to jump properly at present. *G. Herrod — Cotley.* 880 (OMa), 1099 (OMa), 1308 (OMa), 1469 (OMa), 1610 (OMa).

WINK AND WHISPER ..9-2.. 6 b.m. Gunner B — Lady Hannah (Daring March) 23u. Workmanlike unfurnished owner-bred. Dam is half-sister to Progressive (*qv* '95 Annual). Ran well when beaten a maximum of five lengths in three-finisher maidens, but did not look likely to justify favouritism when she unseated three out at Holnicote. Still looks very green, but it would be a big surprise if she failed to win a race or two at six. *R.J. & Mrs V.A. Tory — S. Dorset (Mary Tory).* 655 (OMa), 933 (OMa), 1372 (OMa).

WINNING TOWN ..9-8.. 8 ch.g. Jester — Lurex Girl (Camden Town) 441226. Very small quite attractive. Dam won 2 2m races. NH FLAT '97 r2 p0. NH '98 r3 p0. P-t-P '99 r5 p3 (2nds); 5th, and unseated 1. Made the frame on five successive occasions before finally gaining a deserved win over 2m4f at Garnons where he rallied to snatch the spoils close home. Not an easy ride over the full trip as he often fails to stay, and Sophie Talbot overdid the waiting tactics at Howick subsequently. Sometimes takes a strong hold, and wears a cross-noseband. Suited by a sound surface. *Miss S.H. Talbot — Albrighton Woodland.* 341 (CfMa), 471 (OMa), 672 (2m4fOMa), 818 (R), 993 (R), 1460 (R).

WINSOME WALLACE (IRE) ..9-8.. 7 ch.g. Montelimar (USA) — Gleann Ard (Deep Run) 5. Half-brother to Irish NH flat winner, Knockaroo (IRE). Dam won Irish NH flat. Only 4-1 when making his debut in a Hunter Chase at Aintree (the appearance of Venetia Williams in training brackets was the all-important factor), but his jumping went to pieces after a blunder at halfway, and he finished tailed off last. The owner has Donallach Mor in the same yard, and will doubtless be hoping that the oracle is worked again. *C.J. Sample — College V. & N. Northumberland (Venetia Williams).* 1557 (3m1fH).

WINTER BELLE (USA) ..9-12.. 13 b.g. Sportin' Life (USA) — Belle O'Reason (USA) (Hail To Reason) pp32p. Strong half-brother to 9 winners in USA, Japan and France. Dam won 7 races in USA. IRISH FLAT r12 w5 (12-16f) p1 (3rd). IRISH NH FLAT '92/3 r4 w2 p2 (3rds, one at Cheltenham). IRISH NH '93/6 r19 w2 (2 Hdles, 2m2f-2m4f) p6 (inc beaten a head in Ch by Klairon Davies, and short-headed once); final run at Worcester (8-11, 3 ran, unseated). NH '96/8 r8 w2 (3m2f Chses at Catterick) p2 (2nds); pulled up in Grand National and Whitbread on final starts. P-t-P/HUNT CH '99 r6 w2 (Opens) p2 (last of 3 once); 4th, and unseated 1. A prolific scorer over the years, but wily, and resents it when his partner becomes animated. Ran well when allowed to dominate this year, but sulked in between, and did not care for the sound surface on his final appearance. An expert jumper, but will do well to extend his winning tally at 13. *J.M. Shepherd-Cross — Grafton (Jenny Pidgeon).* 77 (O), 244 (O), 474 (O), 886 (C), 1484 (O).

WINTER BREEZE ..9-10.. 14 b.g. Strong Gale — Ballyreidy Star (Mon Capitaine) p. Small close-coupled half-brother to All Brains, and to Irish Pointing winner, Ballyreidy Silver. Dam won an Irish Maiden. IRISH P-t-P '96 r8 p0 (4th of 5, last, pulled up 4, unseated 1, and slipped up 1). NH '98 and '99 r7 w1 (2m5f110y Nov Ch) p2; 4th twice, and pulled up 2. P-t-P/HUNT CH '97/9 r10 (for Mrs M. Tory) r14 w3 (Maiden, Restricted and Club nov rdrs) p4 (3 3rds, last once); pulled up 2, fell/unseated 3, and slipped up 1. A poor performer in Ireland, but has done well to win four races since arriving in England, and a soft-palate operation after the '97 season was beneficial. Only able to run four times in the last two years, and has not completed. Unsuited by the surface on his debut for new connections in 2000, and has always appreciated an easy three miles on top of the ground. Very unlikely to stage a revival. *Mrs J.Z. Munday — Ludlow (Martin Evans).* 699 (L).

WINTER GAME (IRE) ..—.. 8 b.g. Glacial Storm (USA) — Polar Bee (Gunner B) f. Half-brother to Tex Mex (IRE) and Bathurst (IRE), and to Irish Pointing winner, Macklette. Dam won 3 Irish flat, 14-16f (inc 2 NH flat). IRISH P-t-P '98 r6 w1 (5 plus Mdn, novice riders — awarded dead-heat, but looked short-headed) p0; pulled up 2 and unseated 2. NH '98/9 (for H. Daly, bought for 12,500) r3 p0 (10th of 11 and pulled up in Hdles; last in Ch). Bought Malvern, May for 1600. Not disgraced in his Members, in which he fell at the final fence when 10 lengths last of four, but has been extremely lightly raced since he was sold expensively into the previous yard, and presumably has problems. *R. Strachan — Ludlow.* 986 (M).

WINTERS COTTAGE (IRE) ..9-10.. 13 ch.g. Sandalay — Hilltown Yvonne (Avocat) pp. Lengthy light. IRISH P-t-P '93 r1 p0 (pulled up). NH '94/5 (visored 2) r6 p1 (2nd of 13 in 2m Hdle). P-t-P/HUNT CH '94, '96 and '98/9 (for Mr M.A., Mr J.H. Lloyd & Mr A. Goodwin) r18 w4 (Maiden, 2 Members, and PPORA Restricted) p3 (2 2nds; and 3rd of 4); pulled up 6, and fell 2. NH '99 r4 p3 (2nds). A fair performer on a sound surface, and did well to win three of eight Points '98/9, but struggles to stay in competitive races, and faded quickly in both attempts this year. Remains eligible for Intermediates, and his shrewd trainer could surely place him to advantage in one as he still retains a fair measure of ability. Tried in a visor on his latest appearance. *P.D. Evans — S. Herefords.* 294 (O), 1338 (4m1fHt).

WINTERS TALE (IRE) ..9-13.. 8 b.m. Glacial Storm (USA) — Perfect Nightmare (Lucifer USA) p17. Sturdy. Dam is half-sister to Davids Tower (qv '93 Annual). P-t-P '99 r3 w1 (Maiden) p2 (last of 2, and 3rd of 4). Recorded the slowest time on the card when winning at Guilsborough in '99, and was unimpressive in taking an uncompetitive race at Kingston Blount this year. A poor jumper, and likely to struggle in better company. *C. Gee — V. of Aylesbury (Lawney Hill).* 196 (R), 246 (C), 510 (Cf).

WINWARD ..8-2§.. 9 b.g. Lafontaine (USA) — Crackingham (Trimmingham) p4pp5fp. Very tall. P-t-P/HUNT CH '98/9 r11 p0 (6th, last 3, pulled up 6, and unseated 1). A big unathletic type who has lumbered round slowly and reluctantly to date. Running him in Hunter Chases is a complete waste of time. Wears blinkers, and acquired a tongue-strap on his latest outing. *R.F. Wright — W. Street/Tickham (Miss S. Fraser).* 126 (R), 571 (M), 825 (R), 1039 (OMa), 1104 (R), 1333 (3mH), 1536 (3m2fH).

WISE EXAMINER (IRE) ..9-2.. 8 b.g. Homo Sapien — Fountains Glory (IRE) (Royal Fountain) pp3233f31p. Tall rangy hobdayed. IRISH P-t-P '98 r3 p2 (6/ 2nd of 3, and 35/ 3rd of 4). IRISH NH FLAT '99 r1 p0. IRISH NH '97/9 r5 p0 (finished in all 4 Chses). Bought Malvern, Sep for 2100. A decent galloper who certainly deserved his success following seven placed efforts, but moderate and barely able to get the trip, and it was not until his eighteenth attempt that he managed to last home on the short sharp Lifton track. Will struggle to find another opportunity. Becoming fractious in the preliminaries, and bolted and unseated leaving the paddock on his most recent start. *E. Wonnacott — Spooners & W. Dartmoor (Pauline & Tony Geering)*. 12 (OMa), 205 (OMa), 540 (OMa), 656 (OMa), 846 (M), 934 (OMa), 1178 (OMa), 1372 (OMa), 1520 (CfMa), 1639 (R).

WISE POINT (IRE) ..8-7.. 10 b.g. Abednego — Corely Point (Cantab) pppR2p. Strong-topped. P-t-P '97/8 r6 p0 (ran out 1, unseated 1, and pulled up 4). Inherited a remote second at Cottenham on his only completed start, and remains a wholly unsuitable mount for his inexperienced partner. More disasters are likely should they team up again in 2001. Wears a cross-noseband. *R.H. Lush — E. Anglian Bloodhounds*. 241 (C), 322 (CfMa), 416 (R), 606 (OMa), 1040 (OMa), 1383 (OMa).

WISE PRINCE (IRE) ..10-2.. 9 b.g. Denel (FR) — Kissowen (Pitpan) 211. Half-brother to Factor Ten (IRE). IRISH P-t-P '98 r1 p1 (30/ 3rd). P-t-P '99 r4 w1 (Maiden) p3 (2 2nds). Has done well to make the frame in all his races, and whilst he has not looked an easy ride (wears a citation, and Alastair Crow avoids him) he seems to be on the upgrade, and has got on well with Lee Stephens. Yet to take a notable scalp, but stays well, and the likelihood of further wins is great though he gets few opportunities. *D. Rogers — N. Salop (Sheila Crow)*. 864 (R), 1355 (R), 1667 (I).

WISHING ASH (IRE) ..9-11.. 8 ch.g. Yashgan — Velvet's Wish (Three Wishes) 7fp. Half-brother to Charmers Wish, and to Irish Pointing winners, Mitchelstown River and Star Of The Ocean. Dam won 4&5yo Irish Maiden. P-t-P '99 r2 p0 (pulled up 1, and fell 1). Not beaten far in one of the most congested finishes of the season on his reappearance, and would have been second in a long Maiden at Whittington, but pulled up lame when joint-favourite at Aspatria subsequently, and failed to emerge again. Clearly has the ability to win if he can be got right. *F. Jestin — Cumberland*. 500 (2m4fOMa), 816 (OMa), 1368 (OMa).

WISHING WILLIAM (IRE) ..10-8.. 9 b.g. Riot Helmet — Forest Gale (Strong Gale) 24133. Lengthy half-brother to Forest Fountain (IRE) (qv). IRISH P-t-P '96/7 r3 w1 (5yo Mdn) p0. NH FLAT Mar '97 r1 p0. NH '97/9 (for Miss H. Knight) r10 w4 (2m5f-3m2f Chses) p2. Never runs very much, but is game and consistent and a most reliable jumper, and was gaining his sixth success when providing Sam Waley-Cohen with his first winner at Mollington. Also only beaten five lengths when placed behind Rob Mine, Copper Thistle and Lochnomore, and did as well as could been hoped against all of them. Likes good or easy surfaces and has no problem getting the trip, and it would be worth trying him in Hunter Chases. *R. Waley-Cohen — Warwicks*. 4 (O), 17 (O), 79 (O), 195 (O), 614 (O).

WITCHES PROMISE ..8-7.. 11 b.m. Cruise Missile — Gregani (The Brianstan) p. P-t-P '96 (for Mrs K. Lawther) r1 p1 (distant last of 3). Showed promise despite finishing a remote third on her debut, but had to wait four years for her next outing, and promptly disappeared after pulling up on the opening day of the season. *M.A. Sharpley & N.J. Pitcher — V. of Aylesbury (Karen Lawther)*. 7 (OMa).

WITHOUT THE AGENT (IRE) ..8-6.. 8 b.g. Krayyan — La Tortue (Lafontaine USA) p1ppp. Tall rangy. Dam is half-sister to Rich Remorse (qv '88 Season Annual). Great-grandam, Kerolite, was placed in 2 Maidens. P-t-P '99 r1 p0 (pulled up). All out to win a bad Maiden in a slow time at Llanfrynach, and has failed to complete in five other starts. A most cumbersome jumper, and has not looked to be enjoying himself since his success. Has it all to do in Restricteds. *J.P. Price — Radnor & W. Herefords (Clive Davies)*. 337 (CfMa), 487 (CfMa), 744 (R), 992 (R), 1276 (R).

WITH RESPECT ..9-0.. 10 ch.g. Respect — Satinanda (Leander) 6pp6p. Strong stocky half-brother to Target Taken, Satin Flash and Primitive Satin. Dam, half-sister to Washakie (qv '99 Annual), won at 5f, and was placed in 7 Points/Hunt Chses for late Heppy Walton ('probably ungenuine and not worth trusting, and still a maiden over jumps despite 35 chances'). NH '97 r1 p0 (pulled up in 2m5f Nov Hdle). P-t-P '97/9 (for Mr & Mrs F.T. Walton) r17 w4 (Maiden, 2 Members and Restricted) p4 (3 2nds; and 3rd of 4); pulled up 4. Successful four times on varying ground in May '98/9, but beat little, and not better than last since teaming up with Diane Crole. Negatively ridden, and soon tailed off on several occasions, and the rider needs to get a grip, and quickly. *M. Emmerson — Percy*. 39 (M), 108 (I), 183 (CCf), 419 (Cf), 714 (C).

WITKOWSKI (IRE) ..9-12.. 9 ch.g. Zaffaran (USA) — Tibo Hine (Scorpio FR) 2. P-t-P '98/9 r3 w1 (Maiden) p0; 4th, and fell 1. Pulls hard, and rarely comes out of hiding, but a capable sort when he does emerge, and landed a gamble in impressive style at Wetherby last year. Rather disappointing on his only start in 2000 when runner-up in what looked a poor race at Garthorpe, but well worth keeping an eye on if he returns next year. *Mr & Mrs C.M. Witt — W. Salop (Gary Hanmer)*. 1268 (R).

PLATE 141   562 South Devon Confined Maiden (Div 1): Witney O'Grady (Richard Darke), 1st, leads Saucy's Wolf (Jeremy Young), 3rd, at the last open ditch   PHOTO: Tim Holt

WITNEY O'GRADY (IRE) ..8-10.. 8 ch.g. Ring Of Ford — C B M Girl (Diamonds Are Trump USA) p1. Workmanlike lengthy half-brother to Ask In Time (IRE) (*qv*). NH FLAT '97/8 r2 p0. P-t-P '99 r6 p0 (last pair 2, pulled up 3, and brought down 1). A poor jumper, and only beat one rival despite the market speaking in favour of him twice in '99, but made no noticeable errors when winning a slow Maiden on firm at Black Forest Lodge on his latest outing. Sent off at 4-1 having been available at sevens, and someone clearly knew the real level of his ability. Needs to improve further for Restricteds. Absent since March. *T. Winzer — Silverton (Gordon Chambers).* 204 (OMa), 562 (CfMa).

WIXOE WONDER (IRE) ..9-7§.. 11 ch.g. Hatim (USA) — Jumana (Windjammer USA) pp8p7. Sturdy attractive half-brother to 2 flat and Hurdles winners (one in Ireland). NH '95/9 (for M. Bradstock) r30 w1 (2m4f Ch) p6 (inc 2 Hdles; inc 24*l* 2nd in Sell Ch); inc pulled up 8 and fell 2. Won a five-runner Chase in May '97, but the loser of his other 34 races. Tends to bowl along in front for a mile or two, but ungenuine (frequently blinkered in the previous yard; also tried tongue-tied), and finds three miles too far. Tried shorter trips in Hunter Chases, but soon gave up when hard work loomed. *Mrs C. Hicks — Cotswold.* 10 (O), 217 (O), 384 (2m3f110yH), 970 (O), 1447 (2m4fH).

WIZADORA ..9-5.. 6 gr.m. Safawan — Shrood Biddy (Sharrood USA) ppp14. Leggy light-framed half-sister to What A Monkey (*qv*). NH FLAT Mar '99 r1 p0. NH '99 (from A. Carroll's, tried tongue-tied; previously from I. Williams') r7 p0 (inc Sells final 2). Generally awful in her first ten races over jumps, and was pulled up in seven of them, including when blinkered and running far too freely in her first three outings of 2000. A revelation when they were taken off and she was ridden with restraint by Kahlil Burke over 2m4f at Garthorpe, and after being dashed eight lengths clear approaching two out she was just able to last home by a head (tiring, but held together in fine style) to spring a 33-1 shock. Does not have any prospect of staying three miles, and if she has any hope in future it might be over the minimum trip in Selling Hurdles. *Mrs S. Davies — Albrighton (Paul Morris).* 1201 (2m4fOMa), 1323 (OMa), 1531 (2m110yH), 1590 (2m4fOMa), 1627 (2m5fH).

WOLFGANG AMADEUS (U) ..—.. 14 b.g. unknown 5. P-t-P '98 r1 p0 (unseated). Decked the owner on his debut in '98, but despite being banana-bound (he had to consume two to make the weight as he had insufficient lead) Russell Dobney maintained the partnership, and waltzed home 95 lengths behind the winner in his Members. *R. Dobney — N. Staffs.* 1124 (M).

WOLFIE'S DAUGHTER ..7-12§.. 8 b.m. Little Wolf — Saffron's Daughter (Prince Hansel) u. Small neat half-sister to Saffron's Daughter (*qv*). NH '98/9 (for Mrs S.M. Farr) r9 p2 (remote last of 3 twice); fell/unseated 2, and pulled up 5. Too insubstantial to survive her customary bloomers, and failed to reappear after losing Mark Wall at Barbury Castle in March. A flighty pony, and stands little chance against great big chasing types in Points. Has been tried in blinkers. *N. Warner — Croome & W. Warwicks. 472 (OMa).*

WOLFIE SMITH ..9-8.. 11 b.g. Little Wolf — Gillie's Daughter (Hardiran) uu826pp. Small half-brother to Di's Dream. Dam won 2 Points and placed 4. Grandam, Gillie's Girl, is half-sister to Master Tammy and Touch Of Tammy, pulled up 1, and fell 1 in Points, but won an Amat Mdn Hdle. P-t-P '96/9 r15 w1 (Maiden) p7 (4 3rds; and inc 2nd of 3 once); pulled up 5. Wore blinkers for the first time when successful for Julian Pritchard in '99, but most unenthusiastic and Wendy Houldey has been unable to goad him to any effect since. Jumps ponderously, and was lucky to beat a rival when sporting no headgear in 2000. *Mrs J. Houldey — Ledbury (Wendy Houldey).* 193 (R), 338 (R), 476 (Cnr), 668 (L), 969 (L), 1088 (R), 1280 (R).

WONASTOW ..9-9.. 10 ch.g. Insan (USA) — Persian Express (Persian Bold) 6p313up. Sturdy half-brother to flat and Hurdles winners, Elite Justice and In Truth (also a successful Chaser), and to Hurdles winner, Sports View. P-t-P '99 r5 p2 (2nd of 3; and last of 3); last, unseated 1, and ran out 1. Made the frame in three Maidens prior to his Members success, but usually a weak finisher, and needs to search for the easiest opportunities in Restricteds rather than tackle Hunter Chases. His hind joints must touch the ground when he is on the move, and it is a miracle that he can gallop as well as he does. *S. Turner — S. Herefords.* 7 (OMa), 339 (CfMa), 450 (CfMa), 666 (M), 1089 (R), 1355 (R), 1433 (3mH).

WONFORD BOY ..10-0.. 7 b.g. Gildoran — Kathleen Callaghan (John French) p421. Good-bodied half-brother to Irish Hurdles winner, Midas Touch. P-t-P '99 r3 w1 (Maiden) p1 (3rd of 4); and fell 1. Displayed remarkable stamina for a five-year-old when winning at Bishops Court on his debut, but thwarted by some diabolical jumping since, and the course builder at Cherrybrook, must have felt like sending his connections the bill for the damage he has inflicted upon the last fence there in the past two years. Finally won his Restricted at Holnicote, and has now shown ability on extremes of going, but may not be as stout a stayer as was first thought. *M.A.F. & Mrs B.M. Searle & R. Money — Dulverton W. (Lucy Roberts).* 406 (R), 729 (R), 847 (R), 1375 (R).

WOOD BUZZARD ..9-2.. 9 b.g. Buzzards Bay — Woody Isle (Precipice Wood) fru22p3. Good-bodied brother to Bay Hobnob. Dam won 2 Points and placed 4 for Alex Mason. Made a bad start to his career, but did better in Maidens when Edward Walker took over, and placed in all three attempts for him. Came close to success at Barbury Castle, where he was favourite and a neck second after blundering badly two out and then not getting much room in the final 100 yards, but this was his golden chance, and has been a weak finisher otherwise. *A.J. Mason — J. De Giles — V.W.H.* 197 (CfMa), 433 (OMa), 754 (CfMa), 972 (OMa), 1284 (OMa), 1537 (2m5fH), 1634 (OMa).

WOODFORD AGAIN ..—.. 9 ch.m. Then Again — Polly Phil (Balidar) p. Workmanlike unfurnished. Dam is half-sister to Songworth (qv '88 Season Annual). NH '99 (from Miss K. Milligan's) r5 p0 (last and pulled up — tailed off halfway both). Useless in her three outings to date. *Mrs J. Smethurst — S. Durham.* 809 (OMa).

WOODLAND KING (IRE) ..9-9.. 9 b.g. King's Ride — Bilma (IRE) (Glenstal USA) 222214. Good-topped half-brother to a winner in Holland. IRISH NH '98/9 r11 p2 (Chses). Bought Ascot, Feb for 3200. A very safe jumper who invariably makes the frame in Points, but the Brecon qualification kept him in Restricteds for much of the season, and when he did finally get off the mark it was disappointingly hard for him (would have had a great deal to do had Joe's Wedding not fallen in a huge lead, and then looked vulnerable when the only other runner still going declined the last). Has finished runner-up to some fair competitors, and at his best he would have strong claims to a Restricted. *R. & Mrs M. Hand & D. Little — Brecon & Talybont (Mandy Hand).* 539 (OMa), 657 (R), 850 (R), 932 (R), 1263 (OMa), 1518 (R).

WOODLANDS STAR ..—.. 7 b.g. Petoski — Woodland View (Precipice Wood) r00. Compact half-brother to Hawanafa, to Irish Pointing and English Hurdles winner, Bann View (IRE), and to successful Hurdler, Clash Of Cymbals. Dam won 2 Irish Hdles (2m-2m4f), and won 2 Hdles (2m4f-2m6f) and 2 2m4f Chses In England. NH FLAT '99 r1 p0 (tailed off last). NH FLAT Apr '00 r2 p0 (12th in 2m: *a bhnd*; and 11th in 2m1f: *jnd ldrs 5f out, wknd 3f out*). Looked the stuff of nightmares in a Maiden, and tore off in a clear lead paying no regard to the fences until he refused and chucked the rider off at the sixth. *Mrs P. Harrison — Atherstone (Pam Wormall; George Reed).* 235 (OMa).

WOODYS WIDGET ..8-1.. 6 b.m. Rislan (USA) — Woodland Firefly (Mins Baby) pfp4. Dam won 2 Points (4-finisher contests at Wadebridge — very unlucky not to add another) and placed 8 (appeared to win once — farcical contest) for Mr Willis. Headstrong and usually makes the early running (was still in front but tiring when she pulled up five out in a bad four-runner Maiden in heavy once), but has a tendency to keep jumping violently left, and was a fence behind on her only competitor. Perhaps a strong male jockey could sort her out. *M. Willis, R. Smith & Mrs S. Box — S. Tetcott (Kathryn Baily).* 159 (CfMa), 538 (OMa), 1179 (OMa), 1520 (R).

WORTHY MEMORIES ..9-10.. 12 b.m. Don't Forget Me — Intrinsic (Troy) p222. Rangy unfurnished. FLAT r6 p0. NH '93 and '97/8 r10 p1 (3rd in Hdle); pulled up 2, unseated 1. P-t-P/HUNT CH '96 and '99 r9 p1 (last of 3); last, pulled up 6, and unseated 1. Much improved by the move to Ruth

Hayter, but still struggling to get the trip, and came closest to her ultimate goal when beaten a head at Cottenham in March. Still inclined to run herself into the ground, and remains error-prone over big fences. Might get lucky on a short course one day. *Mrs E.M. Bousquet-Payne — E. Essex (Ruth Hayter).* 585 (2m5f110yH), 775 (OMa), 935 (M), 1116 (OMa).

WOTANITE ..—.. 11 b.g. Nesselrode (USA) — Melinite (Milesian) pfpppp. Big strong owner-bred brother to Nesselnite, and half-brother to Early Nite and Wildnite. NH FLAT '96 r2 p0 (tailed off). NH '96 r1 p0 (tailed off in Ch — not jump well). P-t-P/HUNT CH '98/9 r8 w1 (Maiden) p0; pulled up 6. Held on to win a bad race on hard at Chaddesley in '98, but has failed to finish in nine outings since, and often appears not to stay. Looked to have lost all confidence following a fall at Dunthrop, but worse was to come as he ended the season lame at Ashorne. *I. & M. Potter — N. Cotswold (Mrs S. Walker).* 119 (CR), 196 (R), 546 (R), 896 (R), 1442 (R).

WOT NO CASH ..9-8.. 9 gr.g. Ballacashtal (CAN) — Madame Non (My Swanee) up5pf53. Lengthy. P-t-P/HUNT CH '97/9 r16 w1 (2m4f Maiden) p1 (3rd); 6th, pulled up 10, and fell/unseated 3. Does not stay three miles, and given a good ride by Rory Lawther when successful over 2m4f at Garthorpe in '99, but error-prone and outclassed in sub-3m Hunter Chases, and will struggle to follow up. *R.C. Harper — Bicester with Whaddon.* 192 (L), 248 (R), 463 (2mH), 919 (2m3f110yH), 1335 (2m4f110yH), 1531 (2m110yH), 1594 (R).

WOTSTHEPROBLEM ..—§.. 9 b.g. Rymer — Alfie's Own (New Brig) pp. Rangy well-made. NH FLAT '97/8 r3 p0. NH '98/9 (for Mrs M. Reveley) r2 p0. Bought Doncaster, May for 4000. The problem is that he is a dog, and additionally one who is not often able to leave his kennel. *C.J.M. Cottingham — Brocklesby.* 798 (OMa), 1584 (CCond).

WRENBURY FARMER ..9-3.. 11 ch.g. Say Primula — Willow Path (Farm Walk) ppp6. Workmanlike half-brother to jumping winner, Back Before Dark, and to successful Hurdler, Back Before Dawn. P-t-P/HUNT CH '96/9 (for Mr P.J. Pitt & Mr B. Evans) r13 w1 (Maiden) p1 (2nd); last pair 2, refused 1, fell 1, and pulled up 5, and disqualified from 4th for not weighing-in. NH '99 (from D. Grissell's) r1 p0. Well placed to find such a bad race when successful at Bitterley in '99, but dismal in seven starts since, and tailed off without exception this year. Usually gets worked up before a race, but shows little interest once under way, and remains a sketchy jumper. A waste of time in Hunter Chases. *P.J. Pitt — Kyre (Steve Griffiths).* 701 (I), 993 (R), 1293 (3mH), 1531 (2m110yH).

WRENS ISLAND (IRE) ..9-10.. 7 br.g. Yashgan — Tipiton (Balboa) f4133. Very big strong. Dam is half-sister to Polly Hampton (*qv* '94 Annual). IRISH P-t-P '99 r2 p0; pulled up once. A giant-sized individual who did well for a six year old, and won a Maiden by 25 lengths at Newton Bromswold. Would have scored on his English debut at Dunthrop, but fell two out when leading. A disappointing favourite there for his Members on first start, but the outing was his second in nine days and may well have come too quickly for him. Should improve sufficiently to reach the ten stone range in 2000, and can certainly score again. *C.M. Gee — Heythrop (Lucinda Sweeting).* 194 (CfMa), 391 (CfMa), 516 (OMa), 896 (R), 1013 (M).

WUDIMP ..10-2.. 12 b.g. Import — Weewumpawud (King Log) 42p. Sturdy good-looking half-brother to Weejumpawud (*qv*). NH '97/8 r15 p5. P-t-P/HUNT CH '94/6 and '99 r15 w8 (inc 3 Hunt Chses, 3m-3m1f110y, and 2 Opens; and inc hat-tricks in '95 and '96) p4 (2nds, inc 2 Hunt Chses). A former high-class performer who ran up a sequence of seven wins and two seconds from nine attempts '95/6, but disappeared for seven weeks after capturing a £7107 prize, and never really as effective since. Fortunate to make a winning comeback in '99 as he was beaten when Royal Stream broke down two out, and only able to make three quick appearances in May this year. Not disgraced behind Steel Rigg at Hexham, but tailed off in a Cartmel Hunter Chase just 10 days later, and will be hard pressed to revive memories of former glories in future. *Mrs K. Craggs — College V. & N. Northumberland (Clive Storey).* 1428 (O), 1578 (O), 1643 (3m2fH).

WYLUP ..9-4.. 9 ch.g. Dancing High — Easter Jane (Palm Track) p7p7p3pp. Tall half-brother to Aristodemus. P-t-P '99 r3 p1 (3rd of 4); 4th of 5, and pulled up 1. A safe jumper, but desperately slow, and failed to beat a rival when completing in 2000. Ended the season by going lame at Hexham. *H. Tulip — Percy.* 39 (M), 188 (OMa), 364 (CfMa), 423 (R), 717 (Cf), 907 (M), 1081 (R), 1162 (R), 1445 (3m1fH).

YANTO ..9-6.. 6 b.g. Cruise Missile — Stockton Slave (Bivouac) fp2p. Smallish compact. Dam sister or half-sister to 3 Pointers, including, Cool Distinction (*qv* '93 Annual), won 8 Points (inc an Open) and placed 7 ('game and consistant...and does not often miss the first 3'). Certainly bred to stay, but yet to prove he does so, and faded in all three attempts at three miles. Rallied after becoming outpcd when only failing by half a length over 2m4f at Garnons, and it will be disappointing if he is not rewarded over a similar trip at six. may improve further if he can get the trip better. *J.D. Callow — Albrighton Woodland (Helen Callow).* 58 (OMa), 341 (CfMa), 673 (2m4fOMa), 866 (CfMa).

YASGOURRA (IRE) ..8-0.. 10 ch.m. Yashgan — Kangourra (Saher) 4pp. Lengthy. IRISH FLAT r1 p0. IRISH P-t-P '95/6 r10 p1 (3rd); pulled up 3, fell 1, and carried out 1. P-t-P '97 and '99 r7 p1 (distant last of 3); pulled up 5, and fell 1. Flattered once or twice in Ireland, but exposed as a modest jumper with an inability to stay three miles. Only able to complete once without mishap since her exportation, and appeared to go wrong on her latest start. *P. Morris — Albrighton.* 517 (OMa), 865 (CfMa), 1407 (M).

YASHWELL (IRE) ..8-7.. 7 b.g. Yashgan — Shesadream (Green Shoon) 45p. Dam won NH flat in Ireland. Beaten over 30 lengths when completing, and has not improved on an apparently encouraging debut. Kept jumping to the right on his two most recent outings (backed from 10s-4s in the latest), and will need sorting out before he returns. *M.G. Sheppard — Cambs.* 605 (OMa), 942 (CfMa), 1383 (OMa).

YODELLER BILL ..8-7.. 10 ch.g. Nicholas Bill — Over The Mountain (Over The River FR) f5632R6p7bp. Tall. Dam is half-sister to Top The Bid (*qv* '98 Annual). Grandam, Funicular, won 2-finisher Maiden in Ireland. P-t-P '97/9 r15 p3 (2nds); ran out 2, unseated 2, and pulled up 2. Beaten five lengths or less in five Maiden placings, but a desperately weak finisher now and barely in motion when crossing the line three-and-a-half lengths behind the winner once at Mollington. Not a fluent jumper, and gives the impression that he does not try very hard, but considering his physical faults that is no surprise. Has been tried in blinkers, a tongue-strap, and spurs, but only once better than last-but-one in the current ownership. *P. Sheppard — Grafton (Simon Gilmore).* 81 (CCfMa), 197 (CfMa), 250 (CfMa), 434 (OMa), 515 (OMa), 784 (M), 1020 (OMa), 1270 (OMa), 1598 (OMa), 1626 (3m1f110yH), 1669 (OMa).

YORNONANGEL ..9-8.. 12 b.g. Lochnager — Angel Dust (Pitskelly) 32u62745pp. Workmanlike. Dam won 2m Hdle. P-t-P/HUNT CH '95/6 and '98/9 r20 w1 (Maiden) p6 (5 3rds, inc Hunt Ch; and remote last of 2); ran out 1, on floor 6, and pulled up 3. Placed in five of the six maidens which preceded his win, but only once beaten less than 12 lengths in 20 starts since, and presumably has a problem because although he used to stay well enough he certainly does not do so now. An erratic jumper, and has never been worthy of his place in Hunter Chases in which he has never finished better than last-but-one. *I.A. Brown — Sinnington.* 50 (R), 276 (M), 377 (R), 396 (R), 503 (R), 807 (R), 923 (3m3fH), 1028 (R), 1230 (R), 1345 (2m5fH).

YOU CAN QUOTE ME (IRE) ..9-12.. 8 ch.g. Executive Perk — Seawise (Dominion) 6321. Lightly-made attractive. P-t-P '99 (for Mr M.A. Johnson) r3 p0 (4th, pulled up 1, and fell 1). Successful at the seventh attempt, but previously very error-prone, and beaten a minimum of 17 lengths when making the frame. Yet to try his hand in Restricted company, and needs to improve on balance, but might be worth watching when laid out for another race at High Easter; fell when favourite for a Maiden there in '99, and joint market leader this year. *A.H. Harvey (The Wickham Partnership) — Puckeridge (Alex Harvey).* 21 (2m4fOMa), 98 (OMa), 322 (OMa), 604 (OMa).

YOUCAT (IRE) ..9-10.. 12 b.g. Yashgan — Vera Van Fleet (Cracksman) pp4p. Rangy workmanlike half-brother to Hurdles winner, Salacity, to Irish jumping winner, Third Agenda (IRE), and to Irish flat winner, The East Anglian. IRISH NH FLAT '94 r4 p0. IRISH HUNT CH '95 r1 p0 (fell). IRISH P-t-P '95/6 r4 w2 (inc Winners Of One) p1 (2nd). P-t-P '97/8 r12 w1 (Confined) p6 (2 2nds, last once; and 4 3rds, of 4 once, and last once); last pair 2, and pulled up 2. A strong galloper at best, but not the same horse since pulling up on firm ground at Cottenham in '97 when 2-7 in a four horse Intermediate. Almost completely lacking in zest in 2000, and unimproved when regaining blinkers on his last two appearances. *I. De Burgh Marsh — Puckeridge (Mike Bloom).* 609 (I), 1017 (I), 1114 (Cf), 1378 (Cf).

YOU MAKE ME LAUGH (IRE) ..10-2.. 9 ch.g. Doubletour (USA) — Bold Sea Reef (Main Reef) u13pp. Rangy brother to Irish flat and Hurdles winner, Leggagh Lady, and half-brother to Irish Pointing winner, Amarach. Dam is half-sister to Yuppy Girl (*qv* 2000 Annual). IRISH FLAT '98 r5 p0. IRISH NH FLAT '96/7 r9 w1 p1 (2nd). IRISH NH '97/9 r11 w1 (2m Hdle) p0; last, pulled up and fell in Chses. Bought Doncaster, Aug for 3400 (1000gns of which was later refunded, as compensation for his being a bad weaver). A triple winner on good or firmish ground, and held on under pressure to score at Howick, but Harbour Island (who finished third) turned the form around to the tune of eight lengths when they met next time at Pentreclywdau. Sometimes disappointing and has failed to finish more often than not over fences, and is not an ideal betting medium. *R.A. Mason — Glamorgan (Evan Williams).* 741 (Cf), 819 (Cf), 1295 (Cf), 1401 (Cf), 1657 (Cf).

YOUMEANDHIM (IRE) ..9-2.. 9 b.g. Balinger — November Bloom (Camden Town) u3Rp2. Sturdy compact. Dam won at 13f in ireland. IRISH P-t-P '98/9 r11 p1 (50*l* 2nd); pulled up 5, and fell 3 (when 2*l* ahead 2 out once). IRISH NH FLAT '99 r1 p0. IRISH NH '99 r1 p0. Threw away a good winning opportunity for the second time when blundering badly and unseating at the final fence when holding a slight advantage at Larkhill, and remains a most disappointing maiden who has squandered 18 opportunities. Taken to Wales for a final chance to atone, but was thrashed by 30 lengths after making numerous mistakes. His own worst enemy, but probably also finds it hard to get the trip. *T.D.B. Underwood — Garth & S. Berks.* 630 (OMa), 1245 (OMa), 1397 (OMa), 1624 (OMa), 1661 (OMa).

YOUNG ARDROSS ..10-3.. 10 b.g. Ardross — Celtic Silk (Celtic Cone) 2u2. Workmanlike rangy half-brother to Silk Oats (*qv*). NH FLAT '96 r1 p0. NH '96/8 r5 p0. P-t-P '99 r3 w1 (Maiden) p1 (2nd); and pulled up 1. Of no account over hurdles, but much happier in Points, and opened his account at Charm Park in '99. Had finished feelingly the time before, and hung when successful, so it cannot be a complete surprise that a leg would give way eventually. That scenario occurred when holding a clear lead on the run-in at Hornby Castle this year, and it was a great shame that he could not at least bow out with another win. Last years comment "could probably collect a Restricted if sound" makes prophetic reading now. *R. Tate — Bilsdale.* 137 (R), 173 (R), 378 (R).

YOUNG GENERAL ..9-5§.. 7 ch.g. Scottish Reel — Make A Signal (Royal Gunner USA) p2pr3. Compact hobdayed brother to flat and Hurdles winner, General Chase, and half-brother to 4 winners (2 abroad), including Surefoot Sillars (Hurdles) and Make A Stand (flat and Hurdles — Champion Hurdler in '97). NH FLAT '98 (for M. Pipe) r3 w1 p1 (3rd, beaten head and short head — just caught). Bought Ascot, Sep '98 for 850. Looked a difficult ride and very indolent in Bumpers, and was all out when scoring, and has jumped indifferently and shown no interest in Pointing. Finished a fence last of two behind a stablemate, and was a very remote third of four on his other completion. Wears blinkers. Looks unlikely to do any better. *J. French & D. Shone — Cattistock (Richard Barber).* 63 (I), 162 (I), 404 (I), 654 (I), 879 (I).

YOUNG IN HEART ..—.. 13 b.m. Hello Handsome — No Sharing (Young Generation) r. Half-sister to Shares Of Gold. Young in heart but old in body, and zimmered towards the first and chickened out in a Confined. *Mr & Mrs H.J. Franklin — Farmers Bloodhounds (H. Franklin).* 968 (Cf).

YOUNG LUCKY ..—.. 10 b.g. Alleging (USA) — By Chance (Le Johnstan) pp. Close-coupled. Dam won 2 6f races. FLAT r9 p1 (9*l* 2nd in Sell). NH '96 r5 p1 (2nd in Sell — blinkered). P-t-P '99 (for Mr D. & Mr M. Staddon) r3 p0 (pulled up 3). Twice runner-up in the worst grade under Rules, but devoid of ability in Points, and has pulled up in all four attempts, jumping badly, and only just avoiding a refusal in the latest. The names Herrod and Tibbatts are becoming synonymous with really poor performances, and this one, Weycroft Valley, Windyway and Tolepa contested 18 races between them in 2000 without beating another horse! *Miss D.J. Curtis — Cotley (Gordon Herrod).* 204 (OMa), 409 (OMa).

YOUNG MANNY ..9-10§.. 10 ch.g. Executive Man — Ashmo (Ashmore FR) 2642pp23u5. Small lengthy half-brother to Flemings Fleur, and to Irish NH flat winner, Flemings Footman. Dam was a useless Pointer for Alan Jessop. NH FLAT '95/7 r3 p0. P-t-P '98/9 r15 w3 (Maiden, Restricted and Intermediate) p4 (2 2nds); fell/unseated 3, ran out 1, and pulled up 4. Usually tries to make the running, but is remarkably faint-hearted, and after consenting to win all in all three completions during '98 has run up 18 consecutive defeats. Capable of jumping well, but just as likely to make silly errors. A reproduction of his Pentreclwydau second, where Gunner Boon finished behind would be good enough to win many races in Wales, but he is too inconsistent to be trusted. Might be worth a try in headgear. *H.J. Barton — Pembs.* 346 (L), 481 (L), 645 (MO), 831 (M), 946 (L), 1226 (O), 1297 (L), 1450 (Cf), 1612 (Cf), 1658 (MO).

PLATE 142   481 Brecon & Talybont Ladies Open: Young Manny (Mrs B. Lewis), 6th, jumps just ahead of Sand Star (Miss J. Gill), pu
PHOTO: John Beasley

YOUNG MARINER ..8-7.. 14 b.g. Julio Mariner — Petite Mandy (Mandamus) 2puuu56. Light-framed half-brother to Mandys Special, Mandys Hero, Noble Wolf and Cool Mandy. Dam won 3 Hunt Chses and 9 Points (inc '81 Dudley Cup) and placed 4 (inc Hunt Ch). NH FLAT r1 p0 (tailed off). P-t-P/HUNT CH '95 and '98/9 (for Mr J.R. Jones) r13 w1 (Maiden) p2 (3rds, of 4 once); pulled up 4, unseated 1. Won a Maiden in '98 having disappeared for two years previously, but woeful since and apart from seasonal debuts at Erw Lon '99/00 has failed to beat a rival. Gave the owner a sound first ride, but his enthusiasm quickly waned. Blinkered once in '98. *J.W. Edwards — V. of Clettwr (Rhydian Jones).* 266 (M), 347 (R), 486 (R), 647 (R), 832 (R), 1228 (R), 1298 (R).

YOUNG NIMROD ..10-3.. 14 b.g. Boreen (FR) — Noelbonne Femme (Bonne Noel) s21018. Very tall half-brother to Raphael Bodine (IRE). IRISH P-t-P '94 r5 w2 (7yo&up Maiden, and Winners Of One) p2; pulled up 1. IRISH NH '94/5 r10 w1 (2m4f Ch) p2; 7th in Hunt Ch; one run at Cheltenham. P-t-P/HUNT CH '97/9 (for Mr G.J.D. Wragg) r19 w2 (inc Open) p3 (2 3rds); pulled up 4, and fell/unseated 5. A strong galloper at best, but has consistently under-achieved when partnered by the previous owner, and showed that even as a teenager he is capable of winning Hunter Chases with competent handling. Was second best on merit in the '97 Aintree Foxhunters, and has jumped round on three consecutive occasions since including with Coral Grissell in the most recent. Suited by an easy, or preferably, sub-3m journey, and top-of-the-ground. Wears a tongue-strap. *G. Gowlett & Mrs A. Bailey — E. Sussex & Romney Marsh (Di Grissell).* 128 (L), 287 (L), 677 (L), 921 (2m6fH), 1541 (2m5fH), 1648 (3mH).

YOUNG RAB ..9-8.. 6 b.g. Nomadic Way (USA) — Penny Pink (Spartan General) 223. Sturdy neat half-brother to Broken Brae, Rabble Rouser, and Primitive Penny (subsequent Chasing winner). Dam won a Restricted at 5. NH FLAT Oct '99 r2 p0 (tailed off both). NH '99 (from G. Kelly's) r1 p0 (pulled up in Hdle). Getting round for three placings as a five year old was no mean feat, but his jumping was not up to scratch on final start, and also needs to find some extra in the closing stages. Beaten favourite on his two most recent attempts, and tongue-tied in the latest. Clearly has an above-average chance of scoring at six. *M.J. Brown — York & Ainsty S.* 626 (OMa), 1001 (2m4fOMa), 1032 (OMa).

YOUNG SAFFY ..—§.. 8 ch.g. Safawan — Miss Pisces (Salmon Leap USA) ppfrp. Brother to Berties Landing and half-brother to Blue Marlin and to NH flat winner, Suffolk Girl. Dam won at 7f. FLAT r4 p0. NH '97 (for Mrs M. Reveley) r1 p1 (3f/3rd). A pathetically inadequate Pointer, and refused when blinkers were fitted once. *A. Pennock — Staintondale.* 167 (OMa), 625 (OMa), 808 (OMa), 1070 (2m4fOMa), 1229 (M).

YOU SAID IT (IRE) ..10-0.. 12 b.g. Pollerton — Key Of The Bar (Bahrain) p223. IRISH P-t-P '94 and '97 r7 w1 (7 plus Maiden) p1 (2nd); pulled up 3. P-t-P '98 r1 w1 (Intermediate). Partnered by Richie Forristal when making all to land a touch on his English debut at Tweseldown in April '98, but has never stood much racing, and made his next appearance this February. Still retains ability, and only just failed to make most in his Members before finishing a close third in a weak Open at Peper Harow. Would probably have been a decent performer had the fates been kinder. *C. Munro — Tedworth (John Pierce).* 325 (Cf), 1060 (MO), 1279 (M), 1394 (O).

ZAFAN (IRE) ..9-9.. 6 ch.g. Zafonic (USA) — Anjuli (Northfields USA) p1. Big rangy half-brother to 3 flat winners, including the splendid Kooyonga (won Coronation Cup and 2nd in 1000 Guineas in '91). Sold Tattersalls (Ireland), July for 7500. Given a blatant school when running a very promising race on his debut, and was eased out when still going strongly, but despite running green he made no mistake in landing the odds in a Dingley Maiden. Looks a really progressive type with bags of scope, and perhaps it will prove to be shades of Alpine Gale, who has proved to be a star under Rules for the yard since she graced the Pointing scene at venues such as Northaw. *D.E. Cantillon — Suffolk.* 1287 (R), 1507 (ONa).

ZAISAN (IRE) ..9-2.. 8 b.g. Executive Perk — Belace (Belfalas) 342. Workmanlike. Dam is half-sister to Vultoro (*qv* '00 Annual). NH '97/8 r11 p2; pulled up only Ch. P-t-P '99 r3 p2 (fence 2nd once); and fell 1. Has made the frame on five occasions in Points, but only once beaten less than 18 lengths, and appears to be getting worse rather than better. Twice made favourite courtesy of his superior handling, but has proved a major let-down to supporters, and may not be very genuine. *Mrs M.C. Sweeney — Crawley & Horsham (Nick Gifford).* 131 (OMa), 576 (OMa), 710 (OMa).

ZAM BAM ..—§§.. 6 b.m. Zambrano — Cisterce (Impecunious) RR. Lengthy plain. Dam won PPOA novice riders (bad race, 25-1) and 2nd. Bought Malvern, Oct for 1200. A Lurcock cock-up in May maidens, in which she ran out at the third and at the first (eliminated Patrick Millington in the process). Zam Bam no thankyou mam. *M. Lurcock — Devon & Somerset.* 1507 (OMa), 1590 (2m4fOMa).

ZAM BEE ..9-9.. 15 gr.g. Zambrano — Brown Bee III (Marcus Superbus) 45. Lengthy brother to Moss Bee, and half-brother to River Bee and Procol's Boy, to Chasing winner, Brook Bee, and to successful jumper, Regal Bee. Dam won 2m Hdle and placed 2, and won an Open. NH '90/4 r54 w5 (2m4f-3m2f Chses) p16 (beaten head once). P-t-P/HUNT CH '96/9 r21 w3 (inc Open, also disqualified from Confined win — missed fence!) p13 (8 2nds, and inc 8 Hunt Chses, once beaten head by Sheer Jest, giving 14 pounds). A magnificent old horse whose completion record makes outstanding reading, but very one-paced since '96, and has managed just one success compared to nine placings. Looked a shadow of his former self in 2000, and was soon taken off his feet when beaten 34 lengths in his Members. Owes connections nothing, and now might be as good a time as any to call it a day. *Mrs A. Bell — Belvoir.* 367 (Cf), 867 (M).

ZARZA ..—§.. 8 b.m. El Conquistador — Upham Georgie Girl VII (unknown) f. Small owner-bred. P-t-P '99 r2 p0 (refused 1, and pulled up 1). Looked to be on a suicide mission on her sole appearance in 2000 as she tore up to the first fence at full-throttle, but made no attempt to clear it and crashed to the ground. Jumped with increased reluctance last year, and was blinkered on her return. It would be crazy to run her again, presuming she survived. *Mrs D. Buckett — Hursley Hambledon.* 247 (R).

ZINGIBAR ..10-2.. 9 b.g. Caerleon (USA) — Duende (High Top) 2s. Strong-topped compact half-brother to flat winners, Mr Bombastique (IRE) (also a successful Hurdler) and The Deep. Dam won at 6f. FLAT r10 w1 (7f) p1 (3rd). NH '95/9 (for M. Bradley, bought for 3800; unplaced debut for B. Hills) r45 w6 (4 Hdles, 2m-2m7f, and 2 Chses, 2m7f-3m2f) p13 (inc 3rd in Sell in '96; short-headed once, and beaten head once). Untrustworthy and can be very reluctant, but has plenty of ability if he decides to try, and gave a fair display when four lengths second in a novice riders Point. Slipped up on the skating rink at Brampton Bryan two months later, but still a comparitive youngster for one who is so experienced, and there could be a race in him if he decides to co-operate. Regularly wears headgear. *Miss J. Houldey — Berkeley.* 736 (Cnr), 1547 (L).

ZODIAC PRINCE ..10-0.. 9 b.g. Scorpio (FR) — Pendle Princess (Broxted) 31. Lengthy unfurnished half-brother to Regal Bay (*qv*). P-t-P '97/8 r7 w2 (Maiden and Members) p3 (2 2nds; and 3rd of 4); pulled up 1, and fell 1. A progressive youngster until disappearing in '99, and clearly retains much of his ability. Beaten by lack of a previous outing when a creditable third in his Members, but outmanoeuvred his sole rival at Maisemore subsequently. Prone to make the odd error, but should be able to hold his own in better company if able to manage a full season in 2001. *Mrs C. Banks & R.H. Philips — Worcs (Charlotte Banks).* 1063 (3m2fM), 1314 (R).

ZVORNIK ..9-5§.. 14 ch.g. Thatching — Cairi Bai (Sallust) p. Plain sturdy. Dam won at 9f in Ireland. IRISH FLAT r8 w1 (7f) p1 (2nd); also demoted to 4th from 2nd once. IRISH NH '90/8 r37 w4 (2 2m Hdles, and 2 2m4f Chses) p8. P-t-P '99 (for Mr R.R. Bainbridge) r7 p0 (4th, last 2, pulled up 2, refused 1, and fell 1). Won a 26-runner race at The Curragh as a two-year-old, and later added four victories over jumps, but antiquated and disinterested now, and pulled up after two miles on his first and to date only appearance for new connections. Blinkered once in '99. *Mrs D. Topping — Cranwell Bloodhounds.* 1253 (L).

Point-to-Point Secretaries Association

CHAIRMAN: *Libby Gilman,*
Coppice Farmhouse, Church Lane, Glaston,
Oakham, Rutland, Leics LE15 9BN
(Tel: 01572 823476)

VICE-CHAIRMAN: *Philip Scouller, Esq,*
Bottom House, Bix, Henley-on-Thames,
Oxon. RG9 6DF (Tel: 01491 574776;
Office 01189 874311; Fax: 01491 577749)

SECRETARY: *Lucy Brack,*
c/o Stratford Racecourse Co. Ltd,
The Racecourse, Luddington Road,
Stratford-on-Avon, Warwickshire. CV37 9SE
(Tel & Fax: 01789 267949;
Mobile 07771 518258; Evening: 01367 850598)

DEVON & CORNWALL

Chairman: *Peter Wakeham, Esq,*
Torne House, Rattery, South Brent, Devon.
TQ10 9LQ (Tel: 01364 643252).

Secretary: *Frank Yeo, Esq,*
Moortown Farm, Tavistock, Devon. PL19 9JZ
(Mobile: 07071 880201).

*Programme Secretary: Max Hawkins, Esq,
Hunters Lodge, Newton St Cyres, Exeter,
Devon. EX5 5BS (Tel: 01392 851275;
Mobile: 07974 656252).

EAST ANGLIA

Chairman: *Andrew Merriam, Esq,*
Oak Lawn House, Rye, Suffolk. IP23 7NN
(Tel: 01379 870362).

*Hon Secretary: William Barber, Esq,
Barn Cottage, Sedgeford, Hunstanton,
Norfolk PE36 5LL (Tel: 01485 570983;
Mobile 07831 535424).

MIDLANDS (Lincoln, Northants & Notts)

Chairman: *Joey Newton, Esq,*
Hall Farm, Stonesby, Melton Mowbray,
Leics LE14 4PY (Tel: 01664 464259;
Mobile 07785 291915).

ADDRESSES FOR AREA SCHEDULES
Each Schedule gives full details of every
meeting and race planned for 2001 in each
Area. They may be obtained by sending an
A5 stamped, self-addressed envelope to those
marked * below.

PLEASE NOTE that the following Areas have
Combined Schedules covering all the
constituent Areas:

i)   West Midlands, South Wales and West Wales

ii) Midlands and Yorkshire

iii) South Midlands and Sandhurst

*Hon Secretary: Mrs Karen Pickering,
Hill Garth Farm, Ulceby, North Lincs
DN39 6TT (Tel: 01469 588192).

NORTHERN (Northumberland, Scotland)

Chairman: *Peter Elliot, Esq,*
The Yett, Hownam, Kelso, Roxburghshire.
TD5 8AW (Tel: 01573 440268)

*Hon Secretary: Tony Hogarth, Esq,
Mosshouses, Galashiels, Selkirkshire. TD1 2PG
(Tel: 01896 860242; Fax: 01896 860295).

NORTH WEST (Shropshire, Cheshire)

Chairman: *Roger Everall, Esq,*
Shrawardine Castle, Shrawardine, Shrewsbury,
Shropshire. SY4 1AJ (Tel: 01743 850253).

*Hon Secretary: John Wilson, Esq,
The Riddings, Tushingham, Whitchurch,
Shropshire SY13 4QL (Tel: 01948 664977;
Office: 01514 327818; Mobile: 07831 262321).

SANDHURST (Surrey, Hampshire & Isle of Wight)

Chairman: *Philip Scouller, Esq,*
Bottom House, Bix, Oxon. RG9 6DF
(Tel: 01491 574776; Office: 01189 874311).

Secretary: *Toby Ward, Esq,*
Church Farm, East Woodhay, Newbury, Berks.
RG20 0AL (Tel: 01635 255098, 01734 332391).

*Schedules: *Lucy Brack*,
Bouthrop Stables, Eastleach Martin, Glos.
GL7 3NW (Tel & Fax: 01367 850598;
Work: 01789 267949; Mobile 07771 518258).

SOUTH EAST (Kent, Sussex, Surrey)

Chairman: *Christopher Hall, Esq,*
Great Danegate, Eridge Green, Tunbridge
Wells, Kent. TN3 9HU (Tel: 01892 515121).

Hon Secretary: *John Hickman, Esq,*
Romney House, Ashford Market, Monument
Way, Orbital Park, Ashford, Kent. TN24 0HB
(Tel: 01233 502222; Fax: 01233 502211).

*Schedules: *Nicky Featherstone*,
28 Exeter Close, Tonbridge, Kent. TN10 4NT
(Tel: 01732 353518; Fax: 01732 506182).

SOUTH MIDLANDS (Warwicks, Oxon, Berks, Bucks)

Chairman: *Chris Marriott, Esq,*
Hull Farm, Chipping Norton, Oxon. OX7 5QF
(Tel: 01608 642616).

*Hon Secretary: *Lucy Brack*,
Bouthrop Stables, Eastleach Martin, Glos.
GL7 3NW (Tel & Fax: 01367 850598;
Work: 01789 267949; Mobile 07771 518258).

SOUTH WALES & MONMOUTHSHIRE

Chairman: *T.R.R. Farr, Esq,*
Bwllfa Farm, Gelli, Pentre. CF41 7NY
(Tel: 01443 435060).

Hon. Secretary: *Colin Cross, Esq,*
67 Van Road, Caerphilly, CF83 1LA
(Tel: 02920 866453; Office: 01189 874311;
Fax: 01491 577749).

*Schedules: *Cynthia Higgon*,
Newton Hall, Crundale, Haverfordwest,
Pembrokeshire. SA62 4EB
(Tel & Fax: 01437 731239).

WELSH BORDER COUNTIES

Chairman: *Frank Morgan, Esq,*
38 South Street, Leominster, Hereford. HR6 8JG
(Tel: 01568 611166; Fax: 01568 611802).

*Hon Secretary: *Dick Pike, Esq,*
The Priory, Kilpeck, Hereford. HR2 9DN
(Tel: 01981 570366).

WESSEX (Somerset, Dorset, Wilts)

Chairman: *Roly Ford, Esq,*
Fire Beacon, Little Quantock, Taunton,
Somerset. TA4 4AP (Tel: 01984 618605).

*Hon Secretary: *Franey Matthews, Esq,*
Peak Ashes, Penselwood, Wincanton,
Somerset. BA9 8LY (Tel & Fax: 01747 840412).

WEST MIDLANDS (Glos, Worcs & Warwicks)

Chairman: *Bill Bush, Esq,*
Old Manor House, West Littleton, Chippenham,
Wiltshire. SN14 8JE (Tel: 01225 891683).

Hon Secretary: *Robert Killen, Esq,*
Littlemead, Tortworth, Wootton-Under-Edge,
Glos. GL12 8HJ (Tel: 01454 261764;
Fax: 01677 425508).

*Schedules: *Cynthia Higgon*,
Newton Hall, Crundale, Haverfordwest,
Pembrokeshire. SA62 4EB
(Tel & Fax: 01437 731239).

WEST WALES

Chairman: *D.L. Reed, Esq,*
Trevayne Farm, Saundersfoot, Pembrokeshire.
SA69 9DL (Tel: 01834 813402).

*Hon Secretary: *Cynthia Higgon*,*
Newton Hall, Crundale, Haverfordwest,
Pembrokeshire. SA62 8HJ
(Tel & Fax: 01437 731239).

YORKSHIRE

Chairman: *J.W. Furness, Esq,*
Manor House, Kirkby Knowle, Thirsk,
North Yorkshire. TO7 2JQ (Tel: 01845 537321).

Hon Secretary: *Sarah Stebbing*,
Mustard Field House, Burneston, North
Yorkshire. DL8 2JD (Tel: 01677 424424).

*Schedules: *T. Bannister, Esq,*
Coniston Hall, Coniston Cold, Skipton,
North Yorkshire. (Tel: 01756 748136).

Point-to-Point Secretaries 2001

*The following is a list of the Secretaries, addresses and telephone numbers
for all the Point-to-Points scheduled in 2001*

Albrighton: Mrs M. Tomkinson, Oulton Farm, Norbury, Staffs. ST20 0PS
(Tel: Stafford [01785] 284223, home; Stafford [01785] 213366, office).

Albrighton Woodland: Mrs J.G. Hancox, Farley Farm, Farley Lane, Romsley, Halesowen,
West Midlands. B62 0LN (Tel: Romsley [01562] 710292, home; [01299] 826111, office).

Aldenham Harriers: Mrs J. Lewin, Gibraltar Farm, London Road, Luton, Bedfordshire. LU1 4LE
(Tel: Luton [01582] 420137)

Army: Mrs B. Mitcheson, King's Hill Cottage, Netheravon, Salisbury, Wiltshire. SP4 9PL
(Tel: Bulford Camp [01980] 670285)

Ashford Valley: H. Ellison, Esq, 35 Littleford, Smarden, Ashford, Kent. TN27 8NL
(Tel: Smarden [01233] 770594, home; Ashford [01233] 629255, office).

Atherstone: Miss F. Vero, Bosworth Mill, Carlton, nr Nuneaton, Warks. CV13 0DA
(Tel: Market Bosworth [01455] 290712 + fax, home; [01455] 290438 office).

Avon Vale: R. Prior, Esq, Lodge Farm, Monkton Farleigh, Bradford-on-Avon, Wiltshire. BA15 2QH
(Tel: Box [01225] 743679, home; Wootton Bassett [01793] 852451, office).

Axe Vale Harriers: Mrs L. Glanville, 8 The Drive, Bicton, East Budleigh, Budleigh Salterton, Devon.
EX9 7BH (Tel: Colaton Raleigh [01395] 567941).

Badsworth: Mrs J. Buckley, Esq, Throstle Cottage, Aketon, Pontefract, W. Yorks. WF7 6HR
(Tel: Pontefract [01977] 706145).

Banwen Miners: Mrs V. James, 36 Drummau Road, Birchgrove, Swansea. SA7 9QA
(Tel: Swansea [01792] 523652).

Beaufort: Mrs C. Clift, Ebbdown Farm, North Wraxall, Chippenham, Wilts. SN14 7AT
(Tel: Chippenham [01225] 891293 + fax).

Bedale: Mrs G. Furness, Manor Farm, Kirby Knowle, Thirsk, N. Yorks. YO7 2JQ
(Tel: Upsall [01845] 537321).

Belvoir: M. Chatterton, Esq, Merrivale Farm, Plungar, Notts. NG13 0JE
(Tel: Harby [01949] 860267).

Berkeley: C.J.M. Walker, Esq, The Chase, Ashmead, Cam, Dursley, Glos. GL11 5EN
(Tel: Dursley [01453] 543572).

Berks & Bucks Drag: N. Quesnel, Esq, Blandys Farm, Blandys Lane, Upper Basildon, Reading,
Berkshire. RG8 8PH
(Tel: Upper Basildon [01491] 671214, home; High Wycombe [01494] 511778, work).

Berwickshire: D.R. Brown, Esq, Easter Henderside, Kelso, Roxburghshire. TD5 7QA (Tel: Kelso
[01573] 224485 + fax).

Bicester with Whaddon Chase (Kingston Blount): Mrs K. Dalton, 83 Station Road, Quainton,
Bucks. HP2 2BT (Tel: Quainton [01296] 655623).

Bicester with Whaddon Chase (Mollington): Miss H. Gosling, Bell Cottage, Stratton Audley,
Bicester, Oxon. OX6 9BQ (Tel: Stratton Audley [01869] 277748.

Bilsdale: Mrs F. Needham, Hesketh Grange, Boltby, Thirsk, N Yorks. YO7 2HU
(Tel: Upsall [01845] 537375).

Blackmore & Sparkford Vale: Mrs C. Hinks, Lower Nyland Farm, Gillingham, Dorset. SP8 5SG
(Tel: Templecombe [01963] 370260, home; [01963] 370892, office fax).

Blankney: Mrs F. Denniff, Manor Farm, Darlton, Newark, Notts. NG22 0TH
(Tel: Dunham-on-Trent [01777] 228724).

Border: Mrs S. Corbett, Girsonfield, Otterburn, Northumberland. NE19 1NT
(Tel: Otterburn [01830] 520771).

Braes of Derwent: Mrs Annette Stenner, Beda Lodge, Hookergate Lane, High Spen, Rowlandsgill,
Tyne and Wear. NE39 2AF (Tel: Rowlands Gill [01207] 544476 + fax).

Bramham Moor: Mrs A. Dalby, Standerton, Wetherby Road, Long Marston, nr York. YO2 7NE
(Tel: Rufforth [01904] 738323).

Brecon and Talybont: D. Jones-Powell, Esq, Glanafon, Fennifach, Brecon, Powys. LD3 9PH
(Tel: Brecon [01874] 623531, home; Grogarry [01871] 622106, office).

Brocklesby: Miss J. Burt, Grange Cottage, Riby, nr Grimsby, Lins. DN37 8NT
(Tel: Roxton [01469] 560266 + fax, home; [01469] 561122, office).

Buccleuch: Mrs V. Scott-Watson, Easter Softlaw, Kelso, Roxburghshire. Scotland. TD5 8BJ
(Tel: Kelso [01573] 224641).

Burton: Miss B. Neal, Sandbeck, Wressle, Brigg, North Lincolnshire. DN20 0BN
(Tel: Brigg [01652] 654168, home; Brigg [01652] 653107, office).

Cambridgeshire: P.A. Thelwall, Esq, 2 Morden Road, Papworth Everard, Cambridgeshire. CB3 8UN (Tel: Papworth St Agnes [01480] 830801).

Cambridgeshire Harriers Hunt Club: Mrs C. Tebbs, c/o The Manor, Horningsea, Cambs. CB5 9JE (Tel: Waterbeach [01223] 860291 + fax).

Cambridge University Drag: Mrs C.B. Scott, The Green, Wardy Hill, Ely, Cambs. CB6 2DE (Tel: Ely [01353] 777876, home; Ely [01353] 741485, office).

Carmarthenshire: Mrs V.J. Teal, Bannister Farm, Laugharne, Carmarthen, Dyfed. SA33 4RS (Tel: Laugharne [01994] 427396 + fax).

Cattistock: P.L. Southcombe, Esq, Hewingbere Cottage, North Perrott, Crewkerne, Somerset. TA18 7TG (Tel: Corscombe [01935] 891721 + fax, home; Martock [01935] 823567, office).

Cheshire: Miss M. Lakin, Whitegates, Main Road, Worleston, Nantwich, Cheshire. CW5 6AN (Tel: [07831] 443626 mobile; Macclesfield [01625] 664141 + fax, office).

Cheshire Forest: Miss Penny Weston, 20 Eaton Road, Tarporley, Cheshire. CW6 0BP (Tel: Tarporley [01829] 732018, home; [01244] 320747, office).

Chiddingfold, Leconfield & Cowdray: Mrs D. Patterson, Crossways Cottage, Newpound Lane, Wisborough Green, West Sussex. RH14 0EF (Tel: Wisborough Green [01403] 700326).

Cleveland: Mrs J. Sunter, Great Isle Farm, Rushyford, Ferryhill, Co. Durham. DL17 0LQ (Tel: Rushyford [01388] 720282)

Clifton-on-Teme: Mrs J. Berry, The Saplings, Apple Cross, Stoke Bliss, Tenbury Wells, Worcs. WR15 8RZ (Tel: Kyre [01885] 410368).

College Valley & North Northumberland: Miss V.J. Peet, Sunilaws, Cornhill-on-Tweed, Northumberland. TD12 4RO (Tel: Mindrum [01890] 882475 + fax).

Cotley: N. Ransford, Esq, Silver Birches, Blackpool Corner, Axminster, Devon. EX13 5UH (Tel: Hawkchurch [01297] 678285, home; [01295] 443150 (mornings), office).

Cotswold: Mrs G. Abbatt, Spring House, Langley Hill Farm, Winchcombe, Glos. GL54 5AA (Tel: Winchcombe [01242] 604376 + fax).

Cotswold Vale Farmers: Ms J. Denton, Bury Court Cottage, Rodley, Westbury-on-Severn, Glos. GL14 1RD (Tel: Westbury-on-Severn [01452] 760644).

Cottesmore: Miss E. Inman, Grange Cottage, Tickencote, Stamford, Lincs. PE9 4AE (Tel: Stamford [01780] 753770, home; Stamford [01780] 752131, office).

Countryside Alliance: D. Miller, Esq, 12 Foley Way, Haverfordwest, Pwmbrokeshire. SA61 1BX (Tel: Haverfordwest [01437] 762828).

Crawley & Horsham: Mrs S.J. Gibson, 9 Heath Close, Mannings Heath, Horsham, West Sussex. RH13 6EE (Tel: Horsham [01403] 263454).

Croome & W. Warwickshire: Mrs V.J. Hopkins, Fern Cottage, Russell Street, Great Comberton, nr Pershore, Worcs. WR10 3DT (Tel: Elmley Castle [01386] 710224 + fax).

Cumberland: Mrs C. Fitzgerald, Corbett Nook, Oulton, Wigton, Cumbria. CA7 0NR (Tel: Wigton [01697] 344415).

Cumberland Farmers: Gillian Blamira, Mid Whinnow, Thursby, Carlisle. CA5 6QL (Tel: Raughton Head [01697] 345144).

Curre: Miss S. Kent, 4 Somerset Cottages, St Anns Street, Chepstow, Gwent. (Tel: Shirenewton [01291] 628249).

Dartmoor: Ms R. McCarthy, Orchard House, Ringmore, Kingsbridge, Devon. TQ7 4HJ. (Tel: Bigbury-on-Sea [01548] 810738 + fax).

Dart Vale & Haldon Harriers: Ms S. Yeoman, 6 Mounthill Cottages, Cummings Cross, Liverton, Newton Abbot, Devon. TQ12 6JG (Tel: Bickington [01626] 821442).

Derwent: D. Poole, Esq, Headon Lodge, Wydale, Brompton-by-Sawdon, Scarborough, North Yorks. YO13 9DG (Tel: West Ayton [01723] 859328 home; West Ayton [01723] 850202 + fax, office).

Devon & Somerset Staghounds: Mrs T. White, Benshayes Farm, Benshayes, Bampton, Tiverton, Somerset. TA4 4NU. (Tel: Bampton [01398] 331441).

Duke of Beaufort's: see Beaufort

Duke of Buccleuch's: see Buccleuch

Dulverton (East): Mrs J.A. Hayes, Sheepwash Farm, Molland, South Molton, Devon. EX36 3NN (Tel: Bishops Nympton [01769] 550276 + fax).

Dulverton (West): Miss Clare Wright, Maycott, High Bullen, North Molton, South Moulton, Devon. EX36 3JW (Tel: Brayford [01598] 740112 + fax).

Dumfriesshire: L. Wilson, Esq, Devorgilla, New Abbey, Dumfriesshire. DG2 8BY (Tel: New Abbey [01387] 850245, home; Castle Douglas [01556] 504030, office).

Dunston Harriers: Ms J. Howlett, Kirk Hall, Rocklands, Attleborough, Norwich, Norfolk. NR17 1XN (Tel: Caston [01953] 483154 + fax).

East Cornwall (Great Trethew): D. Doyne-Ditmas, Esq, Cardeast Farmhouse, Cardinham, Bodmin, Cornwall. PL30 4BY (Tel: Cardinham [01208] 821758 + fax).

East Cornwall (Lemalla): D. Doyne-Ditmas, Esq, Cardeast Farmhouse, Cardinham, Bodmin, Cornwall. PL30 4BY (Tel: Cardinham [01208] 821758 + fax).

East Devon: Mrs L. Parker, Oaklee, Harp Lane, Aylesbeare, Exeter, Devon. EX5 2JL (Tel: Woodbury [01395] 232216).

East Essex: Mrs L. Hayes, Ivy Lodge, Frating, Colchester, Essex. CO7 7HW (Tel: Great Bentley [01206] 250207).

East Kent: R. Wilsher, Esq, Stocklands Farm, Stone Hill, Sellindge, Kent. TN25 6EJ. (Tel: Sellindge [01303] 812380).

Easton Harriers: Mrs J. Baxter, The Alders, Potters Street, Theberton, Leiston, Suffolk. IP16 4RL (Tel: Leiston [01728] 831790).

East Sussex & Romney Marsh: Mrs A. West, Tower Hill Farm, Battle, East Sussex. TN33 0HW (Tel: Battle [01424] 773053 + fax).

Eggesford: Mrs V. Quick, Birch Farm, Coldridge, Crediton, Devon. EX17 6BG (Tel: Crediton [01363] 83216 + fax).

Eglinton: Alex Fergusson, Esq, c/o Stewart Gilmour, 24 Beresford Terrace, Ayr. KA7 2EE (Tel: [07850] 609037, mobile; Ayr [01292] 266768, office).

Enfield Chace: J.R.E. Pirie, Esq, Videne, Hawkshead Road, Little Heath, Potters Bar, Herts. EN6 1LX (Tel: Potters Bar [01707] 654157).

Essex: Mrs J. Marriage, Bedfords Farm, Good Easter, Chelmsford, Essex. CM14 4SQ (Tel: Good Easter [01245] 231353).

Essex & Suffolk: Sally Greenlees, High Pale, Bures, Suffolk. CO8 5JP (Tel: Bures [01787] 228575).

Essex Farmers & Union (February): W.J. Tolhurst, Esq, Langham Hall, Langham, Colchester, Essex. CO4 5PS (Tel: Dedham [01206] 322110, home, Chelmsford [01245] 495111, office).

Essex Farmers & Union (Easter): Dudley Moore, Esq, Park Gate Farm, Layer Marney, Colchester, Essex. (Tel: Tiptree [01621] 815470, home; [01245] 352577, office).

Exmoor: R.R. Watson, Esq, Bremley, Molland, South Moulton, Devon. EX35 6NX (Tel; Anstey Mills [01398] 341347 + fax)

Farmers Draghounds: Mrs S. Busby, Dairy House, Bambury Road, Ettington, Stratford upon Avon, Warwicks. CV37 7SR. Tel: Ettington [01789] 740839 + fax).

Fernie: Mrs J. Jackson, Othorpe, Hallaton Road, Slawstone, Market Harborough, Leics. LE16 7UA (Tel: Hallaton [01858] 555383 + fax, home; Hallaton [01858] 435970, office).

Fife: J. Gilmour, Esq, Balcormo Mains, Leven, Fife. KY8 5QF (Tel: Upper Largo [01333] 360229, home; Upper Largo [01333] 360540, office fax).

Fitzwilliam: M.W. Peggs, Esq, The Priory, Gorefield, nr Wisbech, Cambridgeshire. PE13 4PJ (Tel: Newton [01945] 870388 + fax).

Flint & Denbigh: B. Shone, Esq, Ty Isa, Caerwys, Mold, Flintshire. CH7 5BQ (Tel: Caerwys [01352] 720595).

Four Burrow: D.G. Congdon, Esq, Higher Hendra, Wendron, Helston, Cornwall. TR13 0NR (Tel: Constantine [01326] 340368 + fax).

14 Regiment Royal Artillery: M. Redfern, Esq, 14 Regiment RA, Larkhill, Salisbury, Wilts. SP4 8QT (Tel: Durrington Walls [01980] 594860, home; Durrington Walls [01980] 675437, office).

Gelligaer Farmers: Mrs S.A. Turner, Pant-y-Gwreiddyn Farm, Hollybush, Blackwood, Gwent. NP2 0SA (Tel: Blackwood [01495] 224925, home; Blackwood [01495] 243243, office).

Glamorgan: P.L. Thomas, Esq, Bryn Glas, Aberthin, Cowbridge, Vale of Glamorgan. CF71 7HB (Tel: Cowbridge [01446] 774310, home; Llantrisant [01443] 223653, office).

Golden Valley: Will Benbough, Esq, New Barn Cottage, Clyro, Hereford. HR3 5SG (Tel: Hay-on-Wye [01497] 820710).

Grafton: Miss J. Pidgeon, Astwell Castle Farmhouse, Helmdon, Brackley, Northants. NN13 5QU (Tel: [07831] 316020 mobile).

Granta Harriers: G. Gowlett, 16 Mill Lane, Linton, Cambs. CB1 6JY (Tel: Linton [01223] 893458, home; Linton [01223] 893737, office).

Grove & Rufford: B. Gee, Esq, Highfield Bungalow, Greenway, Carlton in Lindrick, Worksop, Notts. S81 9EX (Tel: North Carlton [01909] 730306, home; Mosborough [0114] 248 3631, office).

Hampshire: Mrs Caroline Moore, Rings Green Cottage, Froxfield, Petersfield, Hants. GU32 1EA (Tel: Hawkley [01730] 827378).

Harborough Hunts Club: A.N. Stewart, Esq, Coplow Lodge Farmhouse, Tilton Lane, Billesdon, Leics. LE7 9DS (Tel: Billesdon [0116] 259 6292).

Harkaway Club: Mrs J.G. Hancox, Farley Farm, Farley Lane, Romsley, Halesowen, West Midlands. B62 0LN (Tel: Romsley [01562] 710292, home; Stourport [01299] 826111, office).

Haydon: Ms Kate Carr, Shortmoor Farm, Wark, Hexham, Northumberland. NE48 3PA (Tel: Slaley [01434] 681270).

Heythrop: C.J.W. Marriott, Esq, Hill Farm, Chipping Norton, Oxon. OX7 5QF (Tel: Chipping Norton [01608] 642616, home; Faringdon [01367] 242422, office).

High Peak Harriers: Mr & Mrs J. Walsh, Aspindle House, Heathcote, Hartington, Derbyshire.
SK17 0AY (Tel: Hartington [01298] 84738 + fax, home; [01509] 232296, office).

Holcombe Harriers: S.P. Knight, Esq, Lower House Farm, 565 Chorley New Road, Lostock, Bolton,
Lancs. BL6 4JU (Tel: Doffcocker [01204] 847574 + fax).

Holderness: Mrs S. Jackson, The Cottage, Warley Cross, Bridlington Road, Brandesburton, Driffield,
West Yorkshire. YO25 8EW (Tel: Beeford [01262] 488170).

Hursley Hambledon: Capt. A.R. Barnden, Forest Farm, Newtown, Fareham, Hants. PO17 6LL
(Tel: Wickham [01329] 833374).

Hurworth: Miss Gillian Lee, 36 Coronation Crescent, Yarm, Cleveland. TS15 9EA
(Tel: Middlesbrough [01642] 897748, home; Durham [0191] 386 5997, office).

Jedforest: Mrs H. Mactaggart, Greendale, Hawick, Roxburghshire. TD9 7LH
(Tel: Hawick [01450] 372086 + fax).

Lamerton: Mrs B.J. Fuller, Smithsons Farm, Kelly, Lifton, Devon. PL16 0HL
(Tel: Chillaton [01822] 860253).

Lanarks & Renfrews: Douglas J.G. McPhail, Esq, Moore Park, Cardross, Argyll. G82 5HD.
(Tel: Cardross [01389] 841649, home; Glasgow City Centre [0141] 226 1067, work).

Lauderdale: A. Hogarth, Esq, Mosshouses, Galashiels, Selkirk. TD1 2PG
(Tel: Blainsea [01896] 860242).

Ledbury: Mrs V. Grundy, Keepers Cottage, Howlers Heath, Chace End, Bromesberrow, Ledbury,
Herefordshire. HR8 1SE
(Tel: Bromesberrow [01531] 650646, home; Bromesberrow [01531] 632302 (emergency only)
office).

Lincolnshire United Hunts Club: Miss E. Forman, The Orchard, 19 East End, Kirmington, Ulceby,
North Lincs. DN39 6Y5 (Tel: Barnetby [01652] 688799).

Llandeilo Farmers: Mrs S. Bell, Derwen Deg, Capel Isaac, Llandeilo, Carmarthenshire. SA19 7AD.
(Tel: Dryslwyn [01558] 668257, home; Llandeilo [01558] 823435, work).

Llangeinor: Mrs J. Tudor, Dolwerdd, Coychurch Road, Pencoed, Bridgend, Mid Glamorgan.
CF35 5LP (Tel: Pencoed [01656] 861076, home; Pencoed [01656] 653111, office).

Llangibby: Mrs Joan Williams, Oakdene, Tyr Winch Road, Old St Mellons, Cardiff,
South Glamorgan. CF3 9UX (Tel: Cardiff [029] 2079 0218).

Ludlow: R.M. Knowles, Esq, Shear Farm, Nash, Ludlow, Shropshire. SY8 3AZ
(Tel: Cleehillstone [01584] 890260.

Melton Hunt Club: Mrs S. Hudson, The Old Inn, Waltham-on-the-Wolds, Melton Mowbray, Leics.
LE14 4AH (Tel: Waltham-on-the-Wolds [01664] 464312 + fax).

Mendip Farmers: T. Killen, Esq, Upper Lodge Farm, Ston Easton, Bath, Avon. BA3 4DH
(Tel: Chewton Mendip [01761] 241319, home; Wells [01749] 679777 (work).

Meynell & South Staffs: J.R. Fairclough, Esq, Home Farm, School Lane, Hints, nr Tamworth, Staffs.
B78 3DW (Tel: Shenstone [01543] 480984).

Mid Devon: Miss A.T. Boyden, Denshams Cottage, Chagford, Newton Abbot, Devon. TQ13 8HH
(Tel: Chagford [01647] 433264).

Middleton: C. Hill, Esq, Garden Cottage, Thornton Park, Thornton-Le-Street, Thirsk, North Yorkshire.
YO7 4DW (Tel: Topcliffe [01845] 574156).

Midlands Area Club: Mrs M. Cherry-Downes, Quince Cottage, Thorpe, Newark, Notts. NG23 5PX.
(Tel: East Stoke [01636] 525221).

Mid Surrey Farmers Draghounds: Mrs J. Donegan, Chart Stud Farm, Heverham Road, Kemsing,
Sevenoaks, Kent. TN15 6NE (Tel: Seal [01732] 761451).

Minehead Harriers & West Somerset: Mrs S.C. Doggrell, Toomer Farm, Henstridge, Templecombe,
Somerset. BA8 0PH (Tel: Milborne Port [01963] 250237 + fax).

Modbury Harriers: Ms R. McCarthy, Orchard House, Ringmore, Kingsbridge, Devon. TQ7 4HJ.
(Tel: Bigbury-on-Sea [01548] 810738 + fax).

Monmouthshire: Mrs E. Egerton, The Stable, Treveddw Farm, Llanvihangel Crucorney,
nr Abergavenny, Monmouth. NP7 7PE
(Tel: Gobion [01873] 890448, home; Gobion [01873] 854308, office).

Morpeth: Jane Peters, Temple Thornton, Northside, Morpeth, Northumberland. NE61 3SP
(Tel: Hartburn [01670] 772385).

New Forest: M. Rabbetts, Esq, Ibsley Grange, Ringwood, Hants. BH24 3PR
(Tel: Ringwood [01425] 472092).

North Cornwall: Mrs E. Lobb, Burwyn, Ruthern Bridge, Bodmin, Cornwall. PL30 5LY
(Tel: Lanivet [01208] 831410 + fax).

North Cotswold: Mrs N. Gretton, Middle Bouts Farm, Bouts Lane, Inkberrow, Worcs. WR7 4HP
(Tel: Inkberrow [01386] 792240; Inkberrow [01386] 792472, fax).

North Herefordshire: F.J.A. Morgan, Esq, 38 South Street, Leominster, Herefordshire. HR6 8JG
(Tel: Kingsland [01568] 708248, home; Leominster [01568] 611166, office).

North Ledbury: Mrs P.A. Wallis, Bandini, Cradley, nr Malvern, Worcs. WR13 5NF
(Tel: Ridgeway Cross [01886] 880355 + fax).
North Norfolk Harriers: Mrs T. Hayward, Heydon, Norwich, Norfolk. NR11 6RE
(Tel: [07778] 755168 mobile).
North Shropshire: Mrs L. Dickin, Aston Farm, Aston, Wellington, Shropshire. TF6 5AE
(Tel: Uppington [01952] 740259 + fax).
North Staffordshire: Miss C.A. Whittles, Little Heath Green Cottage, Arminton,
nr Market Drayton, Shropshire. TFG 2PW
(Tel: Market Drayton [01630] 653087, home; Newcastle [01782] 715555, office).
North West Hunts Club: Mrs L. Walker, Ercall Park, High Ercall, Telford, Shropshire. TF6 6AU
(Tel: High Ercall [01952] 770625).
Oakley: Major Jonn Benjamin, 17 Maple Gardens, Riseley, Bedford. MK44 1DQ
(Tel: Riseley [01234] 708566 + fax).
Old Berkshire: Mrs P. Deal, Sunny Cottage, Bishopstone, Swindon, Wilts. SN6 8PW
(Tel: Wanborough [01793] 790459).
Old Raby Hunt Club: Ms S.E. Town, Park View, Forcett, Richmond, North Yorkshire.
(Tel: East Layton [01325] 718259).
Old Surrey Burstow & West Kent: Miss I. Dubron, 2 Caxton Place, Court Lane, Hadlow, Tonbridge,
Kent. TN11 0JU (Tel: Hadlow [01732] 850007).
Old Surrey Burstow & West Kent: Miss C. Holliday, Dormer Cottage, Sandy Lane, Crawley Down,
Sussex. RH10 4HS (Tel: Copthorne [01342] 712216 + fax).
Oxford University Hunt Club: Mrs A. Lear, Trinders, Bleddington, nr Chipping Norton, Oxfordshire.
OX7 6UX (Tel: Kingham [01608] 659371).
Pembrokeshire: Mr & Mrs D. Roach, 19 St Brides View Road, Roch, Haverfordwest, Dyfed.
SA62 6AZ (Tel: Camrose [01437] 710643).
Pendle Forest & Craven: T. Laxton, Esq, New Page Fold Farm, Cross Lane, Waddington, Clitheroe,
Lancs. BB7 3JH (Tel: Clitheroe [01200] 443566 + fax).
Pentyrch: Mrs K. Dando, Springfield Court, Kingsland Lane, Peterston-super-Ely, Cardiff. CF5 6LG
(Tel: Peterston-super-Ely [01446] 760012).
Percy: G.F. White, Esq, 6 Market Street, Alnwick, Northumberland. NE66 1TL
(Tel: Longhougton [01665] 577430, home; Alnwick [01665] 603231, office).
Point-to-Point Owners Club: Mrs D.A. Harte, 10 Leyfields Crescent, Warwick. CV34 6BA
(Tel: Warwick [01926] 775569).
Portman: Mrs J.M. Abbott, Springhead Farm, Fontmell Magna, Shaftesbury, Dorset. SP7 ONU
(Tel: Fontmell Magna [01747] 811209).
Puckeridge: Miss J.A. Hodge, Quinbury Farm Cottage, Hay Street, Braughing, Ware, Herts.
SG11 2RE (Tel: Puckeridge [01920] 822994).
Pytchley: Miss J. Henderson, Toys Yard, Gold Street, Clipston, Market Harborough, Leics. LE16 9RR
(Tel: Clipston [01858] 525340 + fax).
Quantock Staghounds: B. Bartlett, Esq, Adscombe Farm, Over Stowey, Bridgewater, Somerset.
TA5 1HN (Tel: Nether Stowey [01278] 732260, home; Williton [01984] 632040, work).
Quorn: Mrs L. Murfitt, Manor Cottage, West Leake, nr Loughborough, Leics. LE12 5RF
(Tel: East Leake [01509] 853792 + fax, home; Loughborough [01509] 267721, office).
Radnor & West Herefords: Christine Rogers, Cornhill Cop, Leominster, Herefordshire.
HR6 9DA (Tel: Leominster [01568] 612324).
Ross Harriers: Mrs V. Lock, Chantry Farm, Perrystone, Ross-on-Wye, Herefordshire. HR9 7QU
(Tel: Upton Bishop [01989] 780255).
Royal Artillery: Major C. Lincoln-Jones, Springfield House, New Road, Instow, Bideford, Devon.
EX39 4LN (Tel: Instow [01271] 860057, home; Instow [01271] 861179, work).
Seavington: G. Rendell, Esq, 2 Myrtle Close, Beaminster, Dorset. DT8 3BW
(Tel: Beaminster [01308] 863779).
Silverton: G.T. Chambers, Esq, Higher Wallaford Farm, Buckfastleigh, Devon. TQ11 0HQ
(Tel: Buckfastleigh [01364] 642755, home; Ashburton [01364] 652304, office).
Sinnington: Mrs M. Rooke, Manor Farm, Stonegrave, York. YO62 4LJ
(Tel: Hovingham [01653] 628255).
Sir W.W. Wynn's: C. Dominic, Esq, Brazenhill Lodge, Haughton, Staffordshire. ST18 9JT
(Tel: Bradley [01785] 780323, home; Bridgnorth [01746] 761444, work).
South & West Wilts: P. Forshaw, Esq, New Barn House, Ansty, Salisbury, Wilts. SP3 5PX
(Tel & Fax: Donhead [01747] 828338).
South Cornwall: Mary Cutlack, Menawink, Lanlivery, Bodmin, Cornwall. PL30 5DD
(Tel: Lostwithiel [01208] 872820, home; Lostwithiel [01208] 872278, work).
South Devon: J. Greatrex, Esq, Higher Lydgate Farm, Postbridge, Yelverton, Devon. PL20 6TS
(Tel: Postbridge [01822] 880274 + fax).

South Dorset: T. Atkinson, Esq, 2 The Stables, Clyffe House, Tincleton, Dorchester, Dorset.
DT2 8QR (Tel: Puddletown [01305] 848684 + fax).

Southdown & Eridge (both meetings): N. Wilson, Esq, The Moorings, Pages Hill, Heatherfield,
East Susex. TN21 0UU (Tel: Heathfield [01435] 867666).

South Durham: Mrs S. Dent, Middle Swainston Farm, Wynyard, Wolviston, Cleveland. TS22 5NP
(Tel: Sedgefield [01740] 622871).

South East Hunts Club: Mrs S. Addington-Smith, Lagham Lodge Farm, Tandridge Lane, Lingfield,
Surrey. RH7 6LW (Tel: South Godstone [01342] 892084 + fax).

South Herefordshire: G. Snell, Esq, Lower Lulham, Madley, Hereford. HR2 9JJ
(Tel: Madley [01981] 250253, home; Madley [01981] 251211, fax).

South Midlands Hunt Club: Mrs Susan Busby, Dairy House, Bambury Road, Ettington,
Stratford upon Avon, Warwicks. CV37 7SR (Tel: Ettington [01789] 740839 + fax).

South Nottinghamshire: Miss A. Jepson, Lansic Cottages, Post Office Yard, Hoveringham, Notts.
NG14 7JR (Tel: Lowdham [01159] 664188, home; Lowdham [01159] 555500, office).

South Pembrokeshire: Mrs P. Mathias, Shipping Hill Farm, Manorbier, Tenby, Pembrokeshire.
SA70 8LE (Tel: Manorbier [01834] 871667 + fax).

South Pool Harriers: Ms S. Yeoman, 6 Mounthill Cottages, Cummings Cross, Liverton, Newton
Abbot, Devon. TQ12 6JG (Tel: Bickington [01626] 821442).

South Shropshire: Judy Barton, Lower Vessons, Habberley, Pontesbury, Shropshire. SY5 0SQ
(Tel: Cross Houses [01743] 791077 + fax, home; Cross Houses [01743] 791122, office).

South Tetcott: Mrs Dee Priest, Lakes, Halsdon Cross, Holsworthy, Devon. EX22 6NZ
(Tel: Milton Damerel [01409] 253304).

South Wold: D. Ingle, Esq, The Old Post Office, Main Road, Benniworth, Market Rasen,
Lincolnshire. LN8 6JH (Tel: Burgh-on-Bain [01507] 313476).

Spooners & West Dartmoor: Frank Yeo, Esq, Moortown, Tavistock, Devon. PL19 9JZ
(Tel: Tavistock [01822] 613327, home; Tavistock [01822] 614491, work).

Staff College & R.M.A. Sandhurst Drag: Miss C. Elliott, Step Cottage, Oakhanger, Borden,
Hampshire. GU35 9JB (Tel: Bordon [01420] 475088 + fax).

Staintondale: Mrs W.P. Osborne, Hunt Cottage, Staintondale, nr Scarborough, N. Yorks. YO13 0EL
(Tel: Cloughton [01723] 871017).

Stevenstone: Mrs J.M. Wickett, Hill Farm, Shebbear, Beaworthy, Devon. EX21 5ST
(Tel: Shebbear [01409] 281370 + fax).

Suffolk: B.R. King, Esq, Woods Farm, Fersfield, Diss, Norfolk. IP22 2BL
(Tel: Bressingham [01379] 687302, home; Norwich [01603] 628911, office).

Surrey Union: A. Ayres, Esq, Oakhill, Enton, Milford, Surrey. GU8 5AN
(Tel: Godalming [01483] 417032).

Tanatside: Jean Gow, Wern Sebon, Llanrhaeddr, Oswestry, Shropshire. SY10 0BU
(Tel: [07711] 180427 mobile).

Taunton Vale: Mrs F. Walker, Greenway Farm, North Newton, Bridgewater, Somerset. TA7 0DS
(Tel: North Petherton [01278] 663801 + fax).

Tedworth: R. Denny, Kinwardstone Farm, Burbage, Marlborough, Wilts. SN8 3BU
(Tel & Fax: Burbage [01672] 810668 + fax).

Teme Valley: Ms P. Duggan, Little Folly, Eardisland, nr Leominster, Herefordshire. HR6 9BS
(Tel: Pembridge [01544] 388258).

Tetcott: Mrs J. Dennis, Thorne Farm, Stratton, Bude, Cornwall. EX23 OLU
(Tel: Bude [01288] 352849 + fax).

Thurlow: R.J. Claydon, Bovills Hall, Gazeley, Newmarket, Suffolk. CB8 9RE
(Tel: Ousden [01638] 750235).

Tickham: see **West Street-Tickham**

Tiverton: K.V. Granger, Esq, Grange Lodge, Broadhembury, Honiton, Devon. EX14 0LS
(Tel: Broadhembury [01404] 841223).

Tiverton Staghounds: Mrs C.A. Mock, Bircham Farm, Burrington, Umberleigh, Devon. EX37 9JW
(Tel: Ashreigney [01769] 520203 + fax).

Tivyside: Mr & Mrs W.D. Lewis, Pantycaws Stud Farm, Efailwen, Clynderwen, Dyfed. SA66 7XD
(Tel: Hebron [01994] 419272).

Torrington Farmers: Mrs J. Symons, Hall House, Beaford, Winkleigh, Devon. EX19 8NS
(Tel: Beaford [01805] 603649); and Mrs K. Yeo, North Church Farm, Yarnscombe,
nr Barnstaple. EX31 3LW

Tredegar Farmers: C. Cross, Esq, 67 Van Road, Caerphilly, Wales. CF83 1LA
(Tel: Caerphilly [029] 2086 6453).

Tweseldown Club: Angela Cooper, Common Cottage, Becksteddle, Alton, Hants. GU34 3PR
(Tel: Tisted [01420] 588551).

Tynedale: Miss A. Pigg, Lodge Farm, Prudhoe, Northumberland. NE42 6ED
(Tel: Prudoe [01661] 832356, home; Corbridge [01434] 633100, office).

United Pack: Miss J. Brereton, Chapel Cottage, Twitchen, Craven Arms, Shropshire. SY7 0HN
(Tel: Little Brampton [01588] 660391).

United Services: Major J. Stadward, Stanoc, HQ DRA, Larkhill, Wilts.
(Tel: Durrington Walls [01980] 6595579, home; 01980 675664, office).

Vale of Aylesbury (Easter): Mrs J. Jackson, Hanger Farm, Fingest, nr Heneley, Oxon. RG9 6BQ
(Tel: Lane End [01494] 881321).

Vale of Aylesbury (May): Mrs A. South, The Old Mill, Nether Winchendon, Aylesbury,
Buckinghamshire. HP18 0DY (Tel: Haddenham [01844] 292875).

Vale of Clettwr: Mr & Mrs P. Lewis, Tyssul Stud, Cwnbuad, Carmarthenshire, Wales. SA33 6AT
(Tel: Stoke Climsland [01559] 371282).

Vale of Lune Harriers: K. Thomas, Esq, Murray Holme, Roadhead, Bewcastle, Carlisle. CA6 6PJ
(Tel: Roadhead [01697] 748157, home; Preston [01772] 258087, work).

V.W.H.: Miss S.J. Crew, 2 Mill Piece, Ewen, Cirencester, Glos. GL7 6BT
(Tel: Kemble [01285] 770167, home; Marlborough [01672] 511700, office).

Vine & Craven: Mrs C. Hill, The Kennels, Hannington, Tadley, Hants. RG26 5TX
(Tel: Kingsclere [01635] 298282).

Warwickshire: Mrs A. Cockburn, Glebe Farm, Shuckburgh, Daventry, Northants. NN11 6DX
(Tel: Daventry [01327] 702677).

Waveney Harriers: J.W. Whyte, Esq, Becks Green Farm, Ilketshall St Andrew, Beccles, Suffolk.
NR34 8NB (Tel: Bungay [01986] 781221, home; [01986] 781406, office + fax).

Western: R.A. Baker, Esq, The Barn, Treen Farm. Gurnards Head, Zennor, St Ives, Cornwall.
TR26 3DE (Tel: St Ives [01736] 798747).

West Norfolk: Adam Case, Esq, Croft House, Harpley, King's Lynn, Norfolk, PE31 6TU
(Tel: Great Massingham [01485] 520079, home; King's Lynn [01553] 691691, office).

West of Yore: H. Orde-Powlett, Esq, Wensley Hall, Wensley, Leyburn, N. Yorks. DL8 4HN
(Tel: Leyburn [01969] 623674, home; Leyburn [01969] 623981, office).

Weston & Banwell Harriers: J. Fear, Esq, Manor Farm, Southwick, Mark, Highbridge, Somerset.
TA9 4LH (Tel: Burnham-on-Sea [01278] 783261 + fax).

West Percy: R.M. Landale, Esq, c/o Messrs. John Sale & Partners, 18-20 Glendale Road, Wooler,
Northumberland. NE71 6DW (Tel: Wooler [01668] 217226, home; [01668] 281611 or 281041, office).

West Somerset Vale: Mrs M.G.J. Brake, Mill House, Stogursey, Bridgwater, Somerset. TA5 1TG
(Tel: Nether Stowey [01278] 732556).

West Somerset & Minehead Harriers: Mrs S. Doggrell, Toomer Farm, Henstridge, Templecombe,
Somerset. TA5 1TG (Tel: Milborne Port [01963] 250237 + fax).

West Street-Tickham (March): P. Mercer, Esq, 16 Sasson Close, Larkfield, Aylesford, Kent.
ME20 6UZ (Tel: West Molling [01732] 848046, home; Inner London [020] 7917 4873, work).

West Street-Tickham (May): Sara Sansom, Highfield, 8 Church Hill, Shepherds Well, Dover, Kent.
CT15 7NR (Tel: Shepherds Well [01304] 830056).

Wheatland: Mrs A. Wadlow, The Croft, Morville, Bridgnorth, Shropshire. WV16 4RG
(Tel: Morville [01746] 714205 + fax).

Wilton: M. Elgar, Esq, Slate Cottage, Homington, Salisbury, Wilts. SP5 4NQ
(Tel: Coombe Bissett [01722] 718368, home; Salisbury [01722] 320449, office).

Woodland Pytchley: Miss K. Reynolds, Cowthick Cottage, 1 Kettering Road, Weldon,
Northamptonshire. NN17 3JF (Tel: Corby [01536] 264779, home; Bourne [01778] 424381, work).

Worcestershire: Mrs M. Trow, Tudor Cottage, Rushock, Droitwich, Worcs. WR9 0NP
(Tel: Cutnall Green [01299] 851647).

York & Ainsty: Mrs L. Clark, Red House Farm, Husthwaite, York. YO6 3SH
(Tel: Easingwold [01347] 822581).

Ystrad Taf Fechan: G.R. Dunn, Esq, 7 Gethin Road, Treorchy, Mid Glamorgan. CF2 6SE
(Tel: Treorchy [01443] 773775).

Zetland: E. Fenwick, Esq, Park View, Forcett, Richmond, North Yorkshire. DL11 7SQ
(Tel: East Layton [01325] 718259).

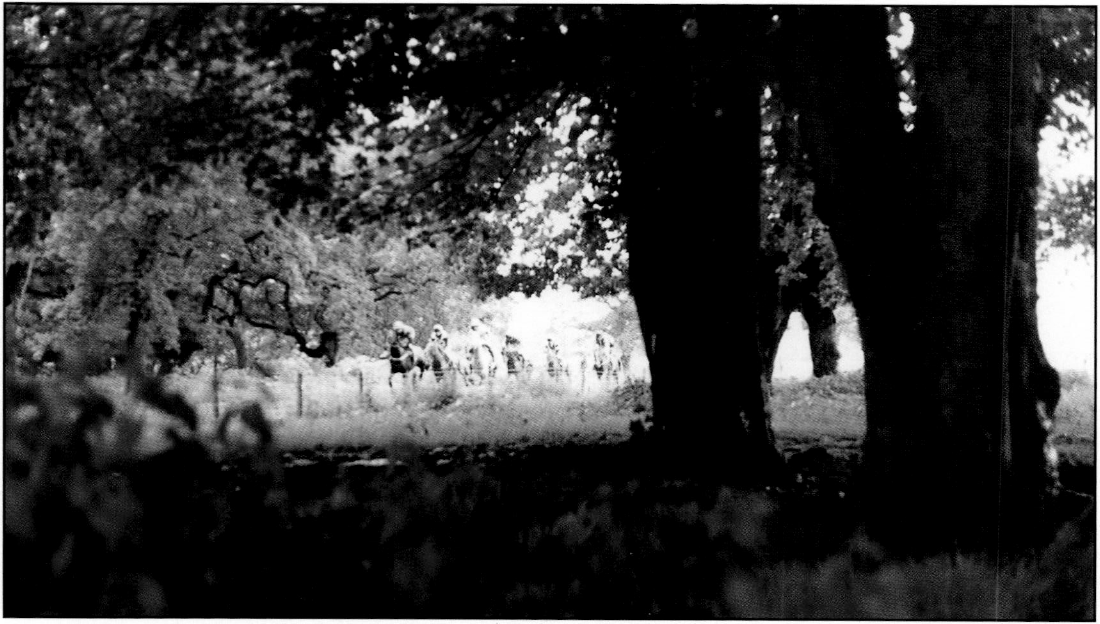

PLATE 143 1657 Llangeinor Confined: Storm Man and Jamie Jukes take the field through deepest South Wales PHOTO: Kathleen Mullen

PLATE 144   407 East Devon Open Maiden (Div 1): The field run behind the trees at the end of the back straight at Bishops Court

PHOTO: Brian Armstrong

PLATE 145 1616 Pentyrch Restricted (Div 2): On the home turn are L to R Itsthejonesboy (J. Jukes), Howsyourluck (T. Vaughan), and Cwm Bye (M. Hammond), ahead of Saronica-R (J. Price), Noble Star (S. Bush), Mister Jay Day (A. Price), Tommyknocker (T. Faulkner), Cefn Woodsman (Miss K. Lovelace), the almost

PLATE 146   214 South Dorset Confined: Leaning to the bend Man Of Steele (Miss D. Harding) leads L to R Malikhad (Miss A. Goschen) and Badger Beer (N. Mitchell), with the barely visible Avril Showers (R. Atkinson) on rails ahead of Stillmore Business (T. Mitchell), Arabian (M. Green) and Cahors (S. Best)

PHOTO: Bill Selwyn

PLATE 147 414 Thurlow Greig Middleton Ladies Open: L to R Lets Twist Again (Miss A. Stennett) jumps ahead of Dance On Sixpence (Mrs S. Hodge) and Cache Fleur (Mrs G. D'Angibau)
PHOTO: John Beasley

PLATE 148 1119 Fife Greig Middleton Ladies Open: *Horse of the year Balisteros and Jill Wormall win their seventh race*

PHOTO: Tim Holt

PLATE 149   1504 Fernie Confined Maiden 56&7yo: A commentator's nightmare of orange and blue, Mandalay Man (R. Armson) and Balmoral Spring (T. Lane), lead L to R Fortune Hunter (P. Millington), the partially obscured More Mettle (J. Diment), Craftbook Marchesa (Miss A. Burton) and Harps Hall (M. Chatterton)

PLATE 150   652 Dart Vale & Haldon Harriers Mixed Open (Div 1): L to R River Swilley (R. Walford) and Dangerous Guest (Miss P. Gundry) are flat to the boards
PHOTO: Bill Selwyn

PLATE 151   72 Silverton Open Maiden (Div 2): L to R Jobsagoodun (M. Yardley), Bonny Rigg (D.Jones), the partially obscured Judith Jones (Miss D. Stafford), Oaklands Wolf (Miss P. Jones), Kinglassie (T. Mitchell) and Carbonado (Miss P. Gundry) take an early fence

PHOTO: Bill Selwyn

PLATE 152   1671 Torrington Farmers Restricted: Down the field in the Capt. Tim Forster Memorial race, L to R Seventh Symphony (J. Cook), Mister Jay Day (A. Price), and Medius Maid (M. Woodward) jump just ahead of Ribington (Miss O. Green) and Hemero (A. Honeyball)   PHOTO: Brian Armstrong

PLATE 153   357 West Somerset & Minehead Harriers PPORA Club Members Mares: Glevum wins again, but Tom Scudamore's expression shows it was no easy task to master Avril Showers and the slightly less young. Robert Atkinson

PHOTO: Mark Johnston

PLATE 154 1426 Lauderdale Ladies Open: Synchronised at the second are L to R Pharmistice (Miss N. Stirling), Sharp Thyne (Mrs K. Hargreave) and Nova Nita (Mrs V. Jackson)
PHOTO: Alan Mitchell

PLATE 155   584 Christies Foxhunter HC, Cheltenham: Ladies Champion Rider Polly Gundry and Lakefield Rambler lead them a merry dance ahead of L to R
Real Value (B. Hitchcott), Knight Of Passion (Miss P. Jones) and Grimley Gale, (Miss S. Vickery)

PHOTO: Brian Armstrong

PLATE 156   878 Cattistock Mens Open: Mens Champion Les Jefford and Horus complete a hat-trick

PHOTO: Brian Armstrong

THE BAILEYS HORSE FEEDS STAKES

The Racing Range

Baileys Racing Range has been developed using fully researched and proven formulae that balance optimum energy, protein, vitamin and mineral levels for racehorses in training. Their unrivalled consistency of quality ensures horses hold their form and recover quickly for maximum performance. Baileys' products are available throughout the UK and Europe as well as the Middle East and Far East. Working closely with Buckeye Equine Nutrition of Ohio, USA since 1989 ensures Baileys benefits from access to the latest American research when formulating and improving their comprehensive range of products.

1 BAILEYS RACEHORSE MIX . . . . No. 10   20kg

High Energy - High Oil - Fully Balanced
Protein 13% . . . .   **Digestible Energy 14MJ/kg**

A palatable, high energy mix formulated for use as the sole concentrate ration for horses in training and at peak fitness.
A true favourite sure to run and run.

2 BAILEYS RACEHORSE CUBES . . . . No. 11   20kg

High Energy - Highly Digestible - Fully Balanced
Protein 13% . . . .   **Digestible Energy 13.5MJ/kg**

Contains a blend of highly digestible ingredients, allowing for ease of absorption and utilisation of the nutrients to provide a feed that meets the nutritional demands of the horse in training.
Plenty of experience and a proven track record.

3 BAILEYS OAT BALANCER MIX 20kg

High Energy - Concentrated - Versatile
Protein 18% . . . .   **Digestible Energy 14MJ/kg**

A palatable, molassed, high energy mix formulated to be fed with oats to horses in hard work.
Runs best alongside Oats from the same stable.

4 BAILEYS NATIONAL HUNT MIX . . . . No. 16   20kg

Fully Balanced - With Oats - Contains Yeast Culture
Protein 13% . . . .   **Digestible Energy 12.5MJ/kg**

Yeast is proven to benefit gut function and increase efficiency of fibre digestion, so this mix is ideal for horses receiving large volumes of concentrate feed daily, travelling regularly and under stress.
A relative newcomer to the Baileys stable but proving popular and getting results.

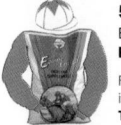

5 BUCKEYE EQUINE ENERGY 6kg   20kg

Energy Dense - Supplementary Feed   BUCKEYE
Protein 12% . . . .   **Digestible Energy 24MJ/kg**

For improving stamina and endurance. Allows the energy density of the ration to be increased without significantly increasing the volume of feed.
The one to watch for staying power - keeps working all the way to the line.

If you want winners, pick Baileys!

Baileys Horse Feeds   Telephone: 01371 850247

w w w . b a i l e y s h o r s e f e e d s . c o . u k

Point-to-Point Courses

All Point-to-Point races are supposed to be run over a mininmum of three miles. Actual distances are not given for each course unless they are known to be well in excess of the minimum.

SF: 2000 Safety Factor *	**J:** Jumps in race
LH or RH: Left or Right-handed	**T:** Approx average race time**
circs: Circuits of course per race	**od:** open ditches
F: Fences on course	**wj:** water jumps
Riders: Leading Riders in the last five years	**(1947):** Year opened***

*   *Lower Safety Factors are normally for Maidens and the other for other races; when more than two Safety Factors are given the middle figures generally refer to Restricteds; special instances are listed; figures in brackets are for 2m4f Maidens.*

**   *Times are an average of all races in the last five years (excluding two-runner contests and any that had fences omitted).*

***   *Pre-war dates shown are the earliest found (unfortunately early returns are vague and incomplete).*

We would welcome any further information or personal reminiscences of early courses.

Changes notified for the coming season are incorporated, but these descriptions are of the courses as used in 2000 and may, therefore, include some that are now defunct.

ALDINGTON, Kent. (1950)
South of A20 and M20, 6m SE of Ashford (Exit 10 or 11, M20).
Meetings: East Kent; West Street-Tickham (May).
SF: 16-20. LH 2 circs. 9F; 19J; 2od (6/15). T: 6min 53.3s.
Slightly undulating galloping course; downhill bend after 1st can be slippery when wet; quick-draining clay and chalk soil, can be hard in dry years, and heavy along bottom of track when wet; 9(18)th is a drop fence. Plentiful car parking, but one exit (uphill) can cause problems. Good viewing from hillside car parks and centre of course.
Riders: *T. Hills 5, Mrs E. Coveney 4, C. Gordon 4, P. Hacking 3, K. Giles 3, D. Parker 3, T. McCarthy 2, A. Welsh 2, A. Hickman 2.*

ALNWICK, Northumberland. (1949)
3m NE of Alnwick (signposted from A1).
Meetings: West Percy; Percy (4m Mixed Open); College Valley & North Northumberland.
SF: 18-22 (18). LH 2 circs. 9F. (2m4f): 15J; 1od (9). T: 5min 29.0s. (3m): 18J; 2od (3/12). T: 6min 35.4s. (4m): 24J; 2od (9/18). T: 8min 58.6s.
Gently undulating course; fairly sharp; usually true ground with good going on old turf; mixture of permanent and portable fences. Permanent wooden changing room, weighing room, etc. Access to car parks good, but exit can be difficult if wet; on steep hill so check handbrake and engage reverse; excellent viewing from there, but come prepared for the bitter winds which can blow from visible North Sea. Ideal for early season meetings as this pocket of land rarely gets frosty. Wonderful setting.
Riders: *A. Parker 11, J. Walton 9, C. Storey 8, M. Bradburne 6, N. Wilson 5, Miss P. Robson 5, A. Robson 4, T. Scott 3, C. Wilson 3.*

ALPRAHAM, Cheshire. (1959*)
3m SE of Tarporley, nr A51.
Meeting: Cheshire.
SF: 18-22 (18). RH 2¼ circs. 8F. (3m): 18J; 2od (3/11). T: 7min 33.1s. (2m4f): 14J; 1od (7). T: 5min 31.5s.
A slightly undulating rectangular stayers course — races are approx 3m4f; can become holding when wet especially in dip between last two fences. Drop fence 4(12) causes problems — course

narrow at that point; sharp bend after 8(16)th; permanent fences well built. Good car parking, but exit is often slow. All fences in view from centre of course — binoculars hardly necessary, but the dip before last fence and crowds on inside of run-in mar closing stages. Facilities very compact. Big fields a rarity as track is so testing. A proper old-fashioned Point-to-Point, and turnout winner was announced as 'the best dressed horse'.

Riders: *A. Crow 7, C. Barlow 5, D. Barlow 4, C. Stockton 4, S. Prior 2, Miss S. Sharratt 2.*

* A course at Alpraham existed pre-WWII

AMPTON, Suffolk. (1971)
4m N of Bury St Edmunds, nr A134.
Meetings: Suffolk; Dunston Harriers.
SF: 15 (Novice Riders)-19. RH 2¾ circs. 7F; 20J; 2od (7/14). T: 6min 45.2s.
Compact and undulating course; not for those of doubtful stamina; two quite acute bends, but fairly easy to negotiate and three uphill fences; ground cuts up on bends. Good car parking, only 100 yards off main road and wide gate avoids congestion, but cars parked inside course hamper view. Re-siting of the paddock, plus the provision of a separate and well-fenced unsaddling enclosure, has greatly improved crowd safety. Attracts low quality horses with good reason. Suffolk meeting announcer is still unclear and not very good.

Riders: *S. Sporborg 9, C. Ward-Thomas 9, N. Bloom 5, A. Coe 5, A. Sansome 4, P. Taiano 3, N. King 3, Miss G. Chown 3.*

ANDOVERSFORD, Glos. (1960)
6m SE Cheltenham, nr junc of A40 and A436. (Exit 11A, M5).
Meeting: Cotswold.
SF: 18-20 (Members)-23. RH 2 circs. 9F; 19J; 2od (4/13). T: 6min 27.2s.
Undulating course with uphill finish; downhill fences in back straight can cause problems; going often firm and short runners can score; fences are well-built; facilities compact. Good car parking, but exit often slow. Viewing reasonable, but it is impossible to see all the course from one place. Track kept in very good order. Strong betting market. Cars now parked both inside and outside course.

Riders: *Julian Pritchard 8, Miss A. Dare 6, J. Deutsch 3, T. Scudamore 2, T. Jones 2, M. Harris 2, E. Williams 2.*

ASHORNE, Warwicks. (1985)
4m S of Warwick between B4097 and B4100. (Exit 13 M40).
Meeting: Warwickshire.
SF: 18-20 (Nov rdrs and Restricted)-25. RH 2¼ circs. 8F; 18J; 2od (4/12). T: 6min 23.5s.
Course rectangular, slightly undulating, uphill finish; dip between 3rd(11th) and 4(12)th; sharp bend after straight. Portable fences small. Car parking good with one wide entry/exit. Plenty of trees, but viewing fair from top end. A good course for spectators, but the hedge in front of the fence after the winning post needs regular trimming before meetings. Now well established and attracts good fields. The number board is poorly sited.

Riders: *Julian Pritchard 4, J. Trice-Rolph 3, Miss S. Duckett 2, C. Wadland 2.*

ASPATRIA, Cumbria. (1991)
At Heathfield, nr A596, 1½ miles NE of Aspatria, between Carlisle and Maryport.
Meeting: Cumberland
SF: 18-21. LH 2¼ circs. 8F; 19J; 2od (5/13). T: 6min 31.9s.
Well-built fences; fairly stiff uphill run after 3rd; viewing from main spectator area hampered by hedges, crops and undulations. Best viewing involves a long walk to top of hill in main car park. Long home straight. Very attractive setting with Solway Firth in background and overlooked by Skiddaw in distance, yet another jewel in the crown of the Northern Area.

Riders: *T. Scott 4, Miss P. Robson 4, R. Morgan 3, J. Walton 3, Mrs V. Jackson 2, A. Parker 2.*

BADBURY RINGS, Dorset. (1949)
4m NW of Wimborne on B3082 (local beauty spot owned by National Trust).
Meetings: Portman; Wilton; Hursley Hambledon.
SF: 16-18. LH 1¾ circs. 10F; 19J; 2od (3/13). T: 6min 22.1s.
Course is rectangular and undulating with three sharp bends round the edge of one large (100 acre) enclosure; uphill to last bend and sharply downhill from last; good turf covering on quick drying chalk gives perfect going in early season, can get very firm later; well-built portable fences can be tricky on run from back straight; used to suit short-runners, but less markedly after changes of recent years; plastic running rails on all bends. Car parking handy to paddock etc, and there is a cheaper park handy to the course, but only one exit. Viewing is superb from the hillside, but start is out of sight from rails. The number board set up on an old trailer is the worst in the area.
Riders: *Miss A. Goschen 8, Miss P. Gundry 5, Miss M. Hill 5, D. Dennis 4, A. Honeyball 4, T. Mitchell 3, R. Nuttall 3.*

BALCORMO MAINS, Fife. (1907)
3m N of Leven between A915 and A916.
Meeting: Fife.
SF: 18-20. RH 2¼ circs. 8F; 18J; 2od (8/16). T: 7min 19.9s.
Superb wide oval galloping course; home and back straights level, but ground falls and rises in between; fences portable; ideal for good jumping stayers. Permanent shed used for weighing room, changing, etc. Car parks adjacent to course with good access. Viewing is excellent from many locations — best on inside of course. The crowds cheer every time the horses come past; most of the student population of St Andrews turn up and behave amusingly (or outrageously according to your viewpoint). A grand spot for racing — a visit is thoroughly recommended. Inconsistency in going is beginning to cause considerable concern.
Riders: *A. Parker 4, Mrs V. Jackson 3, C. Storey 3, R. Morgan 2, R. Hale 2, Miss S. Forster 2, M. Bradburne 2, L. Morgan 2, J. Alexander 2.*

BARBURY CASTLE, Wilts. (1992*)
3m NW of Marlborough. Main entrance off Marlborough to Broad Hinton road. (10m from Exits 15 & 16, M4).
Meetings: Tedworth, Avon Vale; Point-to-Point Owners & Riders Club.
SF: 18 (PPORC Novice Riders)-20. LH 2¼ circs. 8F; 18J; 2od (6/14). T: 6min 46.3s.
Set miles from road in natural amphitheatre; a gently undulating oblong course; superb downland grass, uphill from before 2 out; fences well-built; on chalk so almost inevitably firm after April, but gives perfect going in early season. Viewing is superb with the whole course visible from selected spots. Car parking satisfactory with access/exit via long hard track (but it still costs £5 to walk in to the greedier meetings). Permanent building for weighing room, changing facilities etc. Paddock superb. An outstanding venue, and the PPORC meeting is a must.
Riders: *Miss A. Dare 6, Miss P. Curling 4, M. Wilesmith 4, J. Jukes 4, G. Maundrell 4, T. Lacey 3, Miss P. Gundry 3, Miss J. Cumings 3, Miss A. Goschen 3, A. Charles-Jones 3.*
* Was used as a Point-to-Point course from 1953-62

BASSALEG, Gwent. (1998*)
1m W of Newport. 1m from Exits 27 or 28, M4.
Meetings: Ystrad Taf Fechan; Tredegar Farmers.
SF: 18-20. RH 2¼ circs. 8F; 19J; 2od (6/14). T: 6min 25.5s.
Course layout revised yet again in 2000. Very undulating, uphill after invisible fence 2(10/18) with sharp bend before 5(13)th and through wooded dell and past ponds; downhill from 7(15)th to more gradual bend by start. Last fence moved closer to the winning post in 2000, leaving a long run to the last, and a short run-in; downhill fence 8(16) repositioned for second meeting after one rider was fortunate not to be catapulted into a tree when her mount ran out! Facilities compact, but finish miles from spectators. Badly signposted from M4. Now defunct with Hunts decamping to Rhydygwern.

Riders (all layouts): *Miss P. Jones 10, E. Williams 7, D. Jones 7, J. Tudor 6, C. Williams 6, J. Jukes 5, A. Price 4, J. Cook 3.*
* There had been three previous courses hereabouts, the most recent closed in 1997, before that a different line was used until 1984

BEXHILL, E. Sussex. (1986)
½m N of town at Buckholt Farm, Sidley, just off A269.
Meeting: East Sussex & Romney Marsh.
SF: 16-20. RH 2⅓ circs. 8F; 18J; 2od (6/14). **T:** 6min 50.3s.
Course is an undulating long narrow oval, with bends at both ends on higher ground, fences inviting, but soft; very testing track — times indicate over 3 miles; steep run-in of about 150 yards. Car parking fair. Viewing excellent from top car park. The early date was again a success, and should become permanent.
Riders: *P. York 3, P. Hacking 3, T. Hills 2, Miss S. Gladders 2, C. Gordon 2.*

PLATE 157   67 Silverton Greig Middleton Ladies Open: Royal Mountbrowne (Miss E. Jones), 1st, passes the winning post at Black Forest Lodge ahead of Hillhead (Miss S. Sharratt), 2nd
PHOTO: Bill Selwyn

BISHOPS COURT, Devon. (1979)
½m SW of Ottery St Mary (Exit 29, M5).
Meeting: East Devon.
SF: 17-18-20. LH 2⅔ circs. 7F; 19J; 2od (7/14). **T:** 6min 33.3s.
Flat and rather sharp Linley course, drainage not good; portable fences with big bellies; compact facilities; one of the best courses in the area. Excellent viewing and binoculars not essential. Entrance and exits to car parks good; alternative hard exit when wet. Autocratically ruled by Oliver Carter, but he deserves thanks for keeping this charming venue afloat which was rewarded with 10 races at the latest meeting.
Riders: *T. Mitchell 9, N. Harris 5, Miss J. Cumings 4, M. Miller 4, L. Jefford 4, J. Creighton 4, A. Farrant 4, T. Greed 3, Miss S. Vickery 3, Miss L. Blackford 3, K. Heard 3, J. Tizzard 3, G. Penfold 3.*

BISHOPSLEIGH, Devon. (1964*)
12m W of Tiverton. 1m S of Thelbridge Barton off B3042. (Exits 27 or 31 M5).
Meeting: Eggesford.
SF: 14-16. RH 3 circs. 7F; 21J; 3od (3/10/17). T: 7min 25.5s.
Course is undulating and oval in shape, now all grass and completely redesigned in recent years. Fences portable and soft. Car parking in centre of course satisfactory, but single entrance/exit. Plantation in centre of course makes viewing extremely difficult, but best on outside of course near winning post. Judges stand right on line. Very weak betting market due to proliferation of Bank Holiday fixtures in the area.
Riders: *Miss J. Cumings 4, L. Jefford 4, P. Scholfield 2, K. Heard 2.*
*** A course existed at Bishopsleigh prior to 1939**

BITTERLEY, Salop. (1969)
4m NE of Ludlow, nr A4117.
Meetings: Ludlow; North Ledbury.
SF: 18 (Ladies)-20. LH 2¼ circs. 8F; 18J; 2od (7/15). T: 6min 21.8s.
Short but galloping, basically flat course with gradual uphill finish from 3 out; fences small but hard, and not to be hurdled; last fence very narrow. Access good to car parks and alternative exit along old railway if wet. Viewing excellent from large bank near finish — all fences visible. Delightful setting.
Riders: *A. Phillips 6, R. Burton 5, M. Rimell 5, T. Stephenson 4, R. Bevis 4, A. Dalton 4, R. Cooper 3, Miss A. Dare 2, M. Wilesmith 2, J. Jukes 2, D. Mansell 2, B. Shaw 2, A. Wintle 2.*

PLATE 158   1453 Gelligaer Restricted (Div 2): The field are in the finishing chute and a rope blocks the route out into the country; note the superb covering of grass
PHOTO: Kathleen Mullen

BLACK FOREST LODGE, Devon. (1997)
5m S of Exeter, nr B3381 between A380 and Starcross. Only 6m off end of M5.
Meetings: Silverton; Mid Devon; South Devon.
SF: 16-18. RH 2¼ circs. 8F; 19J; 2od (6/14). T: 6min 19.6s.
Course is oval and undulating, all grass with some tight bends including into home straight. Open

ditch permanent, all other fences portable. Car parking satisfactory. Viewing very good from hill overlooking final fence. Ground firms up alarmingly in dry weather, but they are trying hard to improve the surface, with positive results. Organisation and announcements still could be improved eg no distances or times announced until halfway through the Silverton meeting.
Riders: *Miss J. Cumings 8, D. Alers-Hankey 8, N. Harris 6, L. Jefford 6, A. Farrant 5, T. Scudamore 4, T. Greed 4, A. Holdsworth 4.*

BONVILSTON, Glam. (1997)
4m W of Cardiff, nr A48 (5m from Exit 33, M4).
Meetings: Pentyrch; Gelligaer Farmers.
SF: 16-18. RH 2½ circs (3m). 7F; 18J; 2od (5/12). T: 6min 17.7s. (4m): 24J; 3od (4/11/18).
T: 8min 12.8s.
Very undulating course — good covering of grass; steady uphill climb from 4 out to finish; long downhill run from 5(12)th to 7(14)th followed by sharp bend (mind the pylons), the bends after 6/13 proved trappy at the Gelligaer meeting in 2000. Finish is on a separate chute. Small fences well-built, but easily jumped. Viewing good; all fences clearly visible if you choose your spot carefully. Entrance on a hard track past farm buildings. Might become testing in a wet year.
Riders: *E. Williams 11, J. Jukes 7, Miss P. Jones 5, P. Hamer 4, D. Jones 4, A. Price 3, T. Vaughan 2, S. Shinton 2, Miss C. Thomas 2, Miss A. Meakins 2, G. Richards 2, G. Barfoot-Saunt 2, C. Williams 2.*

BRAMPTON BRYAN, Hereford & Worcs. (1929)
11m W of Ludlow, nr A4113.
Meetings: Teme Valley; United.
SF: 18-20. RH 2¼ circs. 8F; 19J; 2od (7/15). T: 7min 02.1s.
Virtually flat galloping course of 3m1f, with sharp and sometimes slippery bends at end of straights; course extended in direction of river; can be watered when necessary. Good access and exits to car parks. Viewing very fair, and vastly improved from the old days when the only good perch was on a cattle trough. Picturesque setting and charming old-fashioned atmosphere. Frequently attracts plenty of runners. A long way from anywhere. Rearranged Teme Valley meeting in 2000 was held on a surface more suited to Torvill and Dean and racing was abandoned prior to the Maidens.
Riders: *A. Dalton 11, S. Blackwell 6, Miss C. Thomas 5, T. Stephenson 4, R. Bevis 3, P. Hanly 3, Miss E. James 3, M. Worthington 3, G. Hanmer 3.*

BRATTON DOWN, Devon. (1955*)
Alongside A399. 11m N of South Molton 3m S of Blackmoor Gate.
Meetings: Dulverton West; Exmoor; Tiverton Staghounds.
SF: 16 (Restricted)-18. LH 2⅓ circs. 8F. 19J; 2od (8/16). T: 6min 24.1s.
Undulating course on side of hill; sharp turns into and out of home straight can be very slippery; long uphill finish and results of many races change after last fence; going usually good on old moorland turf; fences small and flimsy. Plenty of parking space, but only one entrance/exit. Facilities include a large paddock and a permanent changing room for male jockeys. Viewing, improved in recent years, is good from inside course, but last fence and run-in obscured by crowd. Grand view of Exmoor (but obscured by low cloud, mist and rain for all meetings in 2000), course is over 1000 feet above sea level, and grazed by sheep, with the resulting hazards for unsuspecting racegoers.
Riders: *T. Mitchell 15, N. Harris 9, L. Jefford 8, Miss J. Cumings 6, Miss S. Vickery 4, Miss L. Blackford 3, Miss A. Dare 3, I. Widdicombe 3, C. Heard 3, A. Charles-Jones 3.*
***A course existed at Bratton Down before WWII**

BREDWARDINE, Hereford & Worcs. (1947)
7m E of Hay-on-Wye, on B4352, 2m off A438.
Meeting: Golden Valley.
SF: 18 (Ladies)-20-22. RH 2½ circs. 8F; 18J; 2od (5/12). T: 6min 42.1s.
Flat oval galloping riverside track, with one rather sharp bend; start is in chute off main track and first fence jumped once only. Car parking on hillside, access and exit reasonable. Viewing quite

good, all except first fence (jumped only once) are in view from hill by open ditch, though finish then head on. Beautiful setting. Meeting moved to May in '92 and a great success since, thanks in no small measure to the watering system which has produced very good ground.
Riders: *Julian Pritchard 5, A. Dalton 5, S. Lloyd 3, Miss A. Dare 3, D. Mansell 3, D. Jones 3, A. Phillips 3, J. Tudor 2, A. Wintle 2.*

BROCKLESBY PARK, Lincs. (1958)
Nr A18 10m W of Grimsby (5m E of Exit 5, M180).
Meetings: Brocklesby; South Wold.
SF: 18 (Ladies)-20 (Confined)-22. LH 2¼ circs. 8F; 18J; 2od (6/14). T: 6min 25.8s.
Mainly flat course, but uphill from 100 yards before 2nd(10/18th) to finish; long run (about ½m) between 7(15)th and 8(16)th; fences are a work of art, well-built and irregularly spaced. Hard road up to course; well-sited car parks. Viewing good from car parks and inside course. Course is a fair test and form usually reliable. Bookies very fair. The Judge's stand is now on inside of course, 50 yards back from line, and the rail on landing side of 2nd(10/16th) fences deflecting loose horses has been extended to give additional protection for spectators. Very accessible for Yorkshire horses, and races should be framed to attract them. Entry to course, through a Triumphal Arch, sets the stage for a proper old-fashioned lovable Point-to-Point. Clock on stable block built around 1722 by John Harrison of 'Longitude' fame.
Riders: *S. Walker 6, Mrs F. Needham 5, B. Pollock 5, T. Lane 4, S. Swiers 4, S.R. Andrews 3, Miss H. Irving 3, S. Charlton 2, K. Green 2, G. Brewer 2, Capt S.J. Robinson 2, A. Dalton 2.*

BUCKFASTLEIGH, Devon. (1998*)
On A38 at Dean Court Farm. ½m S of town.
Meetings: South Pool Harriers; Dart Vale & Haldon Harriers.
SF: 16-18. RH 2½ circs. 7F; 19J; 2od (7/14). T: 6min 30.6s.
Roughly triangular undulating sharp course on sloping ground alongside A38; revised in 2000, and now has four fences in line adjacent to main road with three fences in home straight. Excellent viewing and access no problem. Has attracted good size fields since re-opening. Old grandstand not currently in use, but is to be restored eventually.
Riders: *Richard Darke 7, L. Jefford 6, T. Greed 2, T. Dennis 2, R. Walford 2, I. Widdicombe 2, C. Heard 2, A. Farrant 2.*
*** There was a NH course here from 1883 until 1960; used as Point-to-Point venue from 1963 to 1977.**

CHADDESLEY CORBETT, Hereford & Worcs. (1925)
Next to A448 midway between Bromsgove and Kidderminster (Exit 4 or 5, M5).
Meetings: Harkaway Club, Worcestershire; Albrighton Woodland.
SF: 18-23 (Moderate)-25. LH 2 circs. (Worcs.) 8F; 20J; 2od (6/14). T: 6min 57.7s. (Others) 8F; 18J; 2od (4/12). T: 6min 19.5s.
Fairly flat track; easy 3 miles, extended for Worcestershire meeting. One sharp bend on course and open ditch can cause problems; winners usually well there by 3 out; fences well-made, all portable except third (on Worcs layout) and 6th (ditch). Good access to car parks, and downhill exits which can be slow. Viewing is good from all parts of course, but some foliage can get in the way. Big fields and crowds. Strong betting market. Poorly maintained for a busy course.
Riders: *Julian Pritchard 16, A. Dalton 14, T. Stephenson 5, Miss A. Dare 4, M. Worthington 4, M. Harris 4, A. Wintle 4, A. Crow 4.*

CHARING, Kent. (1929)
12m E of Maidstone. Nr A20 and M20.
Meetings: Ashford Valley; Mid Surrey Farmers Draghounds; South East Hunts Club.
SF: 18 (Mares)-23 (16). LH 2⅓ circs. 8F. (3m): 19J; 2od (4/12). T: 6min 35.2s. (2m4f): 15J; 1od (8). T: 5min 17.0s.
Course is undulating and suits stayers; quick-draining chalk based pasture land is seldom heavy; fences firm and well-built mixture of portable and permanent; downhill fences sometimes taken

too fast; fence 2 was resited following a fatal injury in '97 and is now much nearer to the first producing a much longer run to the last fence. Car parking is good with well-made access/exit tracks. Viewing is good especially from inside course. Minimal walking to all facilities.
Riders: *P. Hacking 10, P. Bull 7, D. Robinson 7, T. Hills 6, P. York 6, Miss S. Gladders 5, A. Hickman 4, Stuart Robinson 3, Mrs B. Sillars 3, Miss J. Grant 3, A. Welsh 3.*

CHARLTON HORETHORNE, Somerset. (1995)
Off B3145, 3m NE of Sherborne.
Meeting: Blackmore & Sparkford Vale.
SF: 18 (Restricted)-20. RH 2¼ circs. 8F. 18J; 2od (3/11). T: 6min 50.4s.
Oval course on slope on top of downs; downhill to finish. Portable fences previously rightly castigated in 1999 are now much improved. Car parking good with good access and exit. Facilities compact and reasonable viewing from centre of course. Attracts good size fields and quality horses. A well-organised and efficiently run meeting, but the extortionate car parking charges caused letters to the racing press from disgruntled racegoers in 2000. A fair course, but lacks character.
Riders: *J. Tizzard 7, Miss S. Vickery 6, T. Mitchell 3, L. Jefford 3, M. Felton 2, J. Jukes 2.*

CHARM PARK, N. Yorks. (1949)
Nr Wykeham, off A170, 6m SW of Scarborough.
Meetings: Derwent; Staintondale.
SF: 18-20-24. LH 2⅛ circs. 9F; 19J; 2od (5/14). T: 6min 44.9s.
Course is flat and races are 3m1f; mostly well drained, but can be sticky near 3rd(12th) fence; fences softish, but rather upright; going usually good for March meeting, but sometimes firm for second meeting; popular with owners of inexperienced horses; races often won from behind. An exposed spot so wrap up well. Satisfactory access and exits to car parks and handy to facilities. Viewing superb for the agile from top of old railway embankment, but binoculars necessary to see fences at far end of course, and low sun can also be a problem (including for horses).
Riders: *S. Swiers 8, Mrs F. Needham 7, C. Mulhall 7, D. Easterby 6, S. Charlton 3, R. Edwards 3, G. Brewer 3, C. Cundall 3.*

CHERRYBROOK, Devon. (1986)
2m N of Tavistock nr A386.
Meeting: Spooners & West Dartmoor.
SF: 15-18. LH 2½ circs. 7F; 18J; 2od (5/12). T: 6min 18.9s.
Course is undulating with sharp descent after winning post and testing uphill finish; sharp bend after 5(12)th and 7(14)th; mixture of portable and narrow permanent fences, most well-constructed, but open ditch is upright and above regulation height. Separate entrance and exit to car parks. Viewing reasonable, best near winning post. Judges stand right on line. Commentator head on to finish. Bookies fair. Adjacent to Kilworthy (*qv*), and shares two fences with it — 2 and 7 here being 6 and 7 next door.
Riders: *N. Harris 4, Miss S. Young 4, P. Scholfield 3, Miss S. Vickery 3, L. Jefford 3, C. Heard 3, Mrs M. Hand 2, Miss L. Blackford 2, K. Heard 2.*

CHIPLEY PARK, Somerset. (2000)
3m NE of Wellington, on B3187 (Junc 26 M5)
Meeting: Tiverton.
SF:16-18. RH 2½ circs. 7F; 18J; 2od (7/14). T: 6min 23.5s.
Undulating very open oval course on side of slope; first fence (8/15th) followed by long sweeping bend into home straight; slight dog leg after third fence (10/17th); inner favoured after two out; 120yd uphill run in. Quick-draining, but when wet contours can wash mud onto course after home bend. Large permanent building that can be used by officials and riders. Car park is handy to tarred entrance from nearby main road (no problems getting in or out). Very good viewing, but annoyingly spectators are instructed not to stand on the inside of the course — which is probably the best spot. A good addition to the Area's courses.
Riders: *Miss P. Jones 2.*

CLIFTON-ON-DUNSMORE, Warwicks. (1953)
Next to A5, 3m NW of M1 junc 18, 2m E of Rugby.
Meeting: Atherstone.
SF: 18-20. LH 2¼ circs. 8F; 19J; 2od (7/15). T: 6min 12.4s.
Old Rugby racecourse; gently undulating with start and finish on uphill part of the course; going usually good even when very dry; bend after 4 (12)th sometimes slippery when wet or after watering; fences very small, but hard; 7(15)th causes problems; not a course for a novice jumper. Easy access and exit for vehicles. Activities of private car park on adjoining land have led to entry charge for spectators rather than cars. Viewing is fair from inside of course, but can be obstructed by cars; good general view from outside at top end of course. Watering possible. Attracts large crowds.
Riders: S. Morris 3, R. Hunnisett 3, L. Hicks 3, Mrs J. Dawson 2, Miss H. Phizacklea 2, Miss G. Hutchinson 2, K. Needham 2, B. Pollock 2.

CORBRIDGE, Northumberland. (1920)
3m N of town, off A68 on B6318.
Meetings: Tynedale (3m5f Mens & Ladies Opens); Border; Braes of Derwent.
SF: 17-18-20. RH 2 circs. 9F. (3m): 18J; 2od (3/12). T: 6min 28.0s. (3m5f): 22J; 2od (7/16). T: 7min 52.5s.
Undulating stayers course with three fairly sharp bends; last two fences and finish uphill. Old turf on clay gives good galloping surface; fences well made. Viewing is best on inside of track near commentator's tower. Access to car parks over ridge and furrow field; hardcore exit road. Permanent facilities. Has a variety of SF's for each meeting.
Riders: T. Scott 9, C. Storey 7, Miss P. Robson 6, Mrs V. Jackson 5, J. Walton 5, Mrs K. Hargreave 3, J. Ewart 3, A. Parker 3.

COTHELSTONE, Somerset. (1996)
2m NE of Bishops Lydeard off A358. (Exit 25, M5).
Meetings: Quantock Staghounds; Weston & Banwell Harriers; West Somerset Vale.
SF: 16 (Novice Riders)-18. LH 2½ circs. 7F; 19J; 3od (3/10/17). T: 6min 26.3s.
Almost flat triangular very sharp Linley course; slightly uphill from 3rd(10/17th) to 4(11/18)th; very gently downhill from next. Fences portable and quite well built. Car parking satisfactory. Best viewing from centre of course, but usually planted with crops and spectators are warned off. Finishing post is lined up with the sole oak tree in the home straight (what is the Judge frightened of?). Facilities compact. A very picturesque course set under the Quantock Hills, but compacted sub-soil makes it difficult to provide decent going.
Riders: Miss S. Vickery 9, J. Tizzard 7, R. Treloggen 6, Miss P. Curling 4, J. Creighton 4, G. Barfoot-Saunt 4, T. Mitchell 3, Miss T. Cave 3, Miss P. Gundry 3, Miss L. Blackford 3, M. Miller 3, L. Jefford 3.

COTLEY FARM, Somerset. (1953)
2m SW of Chard, 1½ miles off A30 — signposted from western end of Chard.
Meeting: Cotley.
SF: 17 (Novice Riders)-20. LH 1¾ circs. 9F; 18J; 2od (4/13). T: 6min 38.0s.
Undulating galloping stayers course with precipitous dip after 9 which can be very heavy in wet, with steep climb and sharp turn before next; downhill from 5(14)th with rising ground coming to last; all fences are portable and well-built and regulation height; masses of chestnut paling around the finish/paddock. Plenty of room in car parks, but access/exit can be slow through long winding lanes. Tolerable viewing though 5(14)th and approach to last difficult to see. Four painted milk churns decorate the centre of the paddock.
Riders: Miss T. Cave 3, L. Jefford 3, T. Mitchell 2, R. Atkinson 2, N. Mitchell 2.

COTTENHAM, Cambs. (1931)
4m N of Cambridge nr B1049. (Exit 14, M11).
Meetings: Cambridgeshire Harriers Hunt Club; Cambridge University United Hunts Club; Fitzwilliam; Cambridge University Draghounds.

SF: 18-22-23-25 (16) RH 2¼ circs. 9F; (3m) 19J; 2od (4/13). T: 6min 16.4s. (2m4f) 15J; 1od (9). **T: 4min 55.5s.**

Totally flat oval course; fences well-built and maintained throughout season; three fairly sharp bends suits front runners; open ditch can cause problems when fields are large; old NH course – small grandstand (half of which is supposed to be reserved) still in use. The box park seems to prove very attractive to ungenuine horses who like to hang in there. Car parking very good though large crowds can lead to queues. A variety of SF's apply for each meeting. Excellent viewing from grandstand and banks by paddocks and last fence. Very popular meetings, superbly organised.
Riders: *S. Sporborg 11, S.R. Andrews 9, N. Bloom 9, Miss L. Rowe 9, N. King 6, T. Lane 5, C. Ward-Thomas 5, T. Marks 4, A. Hill 4.*

CURSNEH HILL, Herefords. (1979)
1m W of Leominster nr A44.
Meeting: Radnor & West Herefords.
SF: 16-18. LH 2½ circs. 8F; 18J; 2od (6/13). T: 6min 20.2s.
Very sharp undulating course with short run-in; start and first fence are in chute in centre of course; suits handy horses and winners usually lead before final bend; sharp bends can cause plenty of slipping. Can get very firm and has facilities for watering when necessary. Car parking good; access and exits satisfactory. Good viewing from high bank.
Riders: *Julian Pritchard 4, T. Stephenson 3, Miss S. Vickery 3, S. Lloyd 2, S. Blackwell 2, R. Burton 2, Miss P. Jones 2, Miss A. Dare 2, A. Wintle 2.*

DALSTON, Cumbria. (1927 — at least)
4m SW of Carlisle on B5299. (Exit 42, M6).
Meeting: Cumberland Farmers.
SF: 18-21-23 (18). RH 2¼ circs. 8F; (2m4f) 15J; 2od (3/11). T: 5min 39.7s. (3m) 18J; 2od (6/14). **T: 6min 33.4s.**
Flat course; one of the easiest of northern tracks although galloping nature means horses are unable to get breather; fences (portable) are soft and cause few problems. Good viewing from hillside car park and from centre of course. Single access road gets more rutted each year and is a tight squeeze for horseboxes, and exit through narrow gateway from hillside car park needs improving. Big fields and races are invariably divided. Judges trailer is too near the line. Fences very small and flimsy and well below standard, and badly need replacing. The very narrow gateway after the third fence could make for potential danger on a course with a high safety factor.
Riders: *Miss P. Robson 7, C. Storey 7, R. Morgan 4, A. Parker 4, P. Craggs 3, T. Morrison 2, R. Ford 2, Miss D. Laidlaw 2, K. Rosier 2, J. Ewart 2.*

DALTON PARK, Yorks. (1954)
5m NW of Beverley nr B1248. (Exit 38, M62).
Meeting: Holderness.
SF: 18-20-22. RH 2½ circs. 8F; 20J; 2od (6/14). T: 7min 15.1s.
Course slightly undulating; races are 3m1f; going usually soft and sometimes heavy; fences (portable except open ditch) tend to be small and soft. Horses must be well there and on inside by 2 out to have a chance on short run-in; stamina essential. Satisfactory car parking and exit downhill. Good viewing if prepared to keep on the move — best in centre toward start. Judges stand is right against line. Superb parkland setting.
Riders: *D. Easterby 4, S. Walker 3, R. Hartley 2, Miss T. Jackson 2, Miss S. Brotherson 2.*

DETLING, Kent. (1973)
2m E of Maidstone nr A249, 1m N of village (Exit 7, M20, Exit 5, M2).
Meeting: West Street-Tickham (March).
SF: 18-24. LH 2¼ circs. 9F. (3m): 21J; 2 od (7/16). T: 6min 20.1s. (4m): 28J; 3od (7/16/25). **T: 8min 27.6s.**
Fairly flat oval course with easy bends; now four fences in back straight; long and slightly uphill run-in suits fast finishing stayers; can be holding despite underlying chalk, but gets hard in dry

spells; fences large and firm, but inviting. Fences 1 and 9 are omitted on final circuit of grandiosely titled 4m Kent Grand National. Good access, but exit is down one road and very slow. Viewing best from centre of course, and it is possible to get close to the action, but crowds ruin sight of finish which rather defeats the object. Vigilant stewards. The Hunt committee try very hard to put on a good meeting (unlike most of the others in the Area).
Riders: T. Hills 4, P. Bull 3, Mrs E. Coveney 3, D. Robinson 3, C. Gordon 3, S.R. Andrews 2, P. Hacking 2, B. Hitchcott 2.

DIDMARTON, Glos. (1956)
Nr A433, 6m SW of Tetbury (8m NE of Exit 18, M4).
Meeting: Beaufort.
SF: 18-25. LH 1¾ circs. 10F; 18J; 3od (3/9/13). T: 6min 21.1s.
Undulating course on hillside; downhill from 3rd(13th), uphill from 9; sweeping bends; fences are well made; well drained; a deservedly popular well-organised meeting and bookies generous; exemplary number board. The downhill 8 (last) fence can cause problems. Good car parking, but be early to avoid queue. Excellent viewing from most parts though back straight difficult in bad weather. Can usually be relied on to attract large top-class fields.
Riders: T. Mitchell 5, Miss P. Gundry 3, J. Deutsch 3, Miss P. Curling 2, M. Rimell 2, A. Wintle 2, A. Charles-Jones 2.

DINGLEY, Northants. (1931*)
3m E of Market Harborough, nr A427.
Meetings: Fernie; Woodland Pytchley; Harborough Hunts Club.
SF: 16-18-20-22 (16). RH 2¼ circs. 8F. (3m): 18J; 2od (7/15). T: 6min 39.5s. (2m5f); 16J; 2od (5/13). T: 5min 45.0s. (4m); 24J; 3od (5/13/21).T:8min 47.0s.
Slightly undulating and in places very narrow course in valley bottom; fences smaller and softer than previously since '95 and water jump removed. Fence 6(14)th and 8(16)th portable, bend by start can be tricky when wet. Has a variety of SFs for each meeting. Some permanent buildings; parking on steep hillside; good access, but exit difficult in wet weather. Excellent viewing from natural grandstand. Minimal walking to see everything. Extortionate £15 minimum car park. Watering possible and is ideal for May/June racing. Woodland Pytchley meeting was abandoned in 2000 — many were still arriving well into the afternoon after the very late decision.
Riders: A. Sansome 8, Miss G. Hutchinson 5, B. Pollock 5, T. Lane 4, Julian Pritchard 4, J. Docker 4, Mrs J. Dawson 3, Miss H. Irving 3, A. Charles-Jones 3.
* Used to be a bona-fide venue

DUNCOMBE PARK, Yorks. (1975)
½m SW of Helmsley off A170 12m E of Thirsk
Meeting: Sinnington.
SF: 18-22-25. RH 2 circs. 9F; 18J; 2od (4/13). T: 6min 41.5s.
Course is undulating with sharp bend before stiff 350 yard uphill run; fences portable and well-built; going often good despite early date. Single access/exit — some queues. Viewing good, but finish head on from main spectator area; try centre of course. Completely revamped two years ago, and all the fences on the downhill back straight were removed. This meant that the fence which used to be five out became two out (!), so there is now an incredibly long run to the last, but it is much safer than before, and was very well received by the riders.
Riders: Miss A. Deniel 3, D. Easterby 3, S. Swiers 2, N. Tutty 2, Mrs F. Needham 2, Miss V. Russell 2, M. Watson 2.

DUNTHROP, Oxon. (1983)
2m NE Chipping Norton at junc of A34 & A361.
Meetings: Heythrop; Farmers Bloodhounds.
SF: 18-20 (Farmers Restricted)-22 (Heythrop other races)-25 (Farmers other races) (18). RH 2 circs. 9F. (3m2f); 18J; 2od (4/13). T: 7min 06.6s. (3m5f) 21J; 2od (7/16). T: 8min 17.5s. (4m); 23J; 2od (9/18). T: 8min 42.0s. (2m4f); 14J; 1od (9). T: 5min 23.4s.

Well-drained 3m2f mostly flat course, but uphill from start till after 2nd fence and quite steeply downhill to last, suiting front runners; the six island fences are portable; run-in 300 yards. Car parking good. Viewing satisfactory if you can select your spot. Bookies numerous and odds fair. Heythrop racecard does not contain details of trainers which is a major omission.

Riders: *Miss A. Dare 5, Julian Pritchard 5, A. Charles-Jones 5, J. Trice-Rolph 4, Miss P. Jones 3, Miss H. Irving 3, A. Martin 3, T. Howse 2, S. Joynes 2, R. Lawther 2, R. Hunnisett 2, Mrs K. Sunderland 2, Miss S. Vickery 2, Miss L. Sweeting 2, J. Jukes 2, A. Phillips 2, A. Hill 2.*

EASINGWOLD, Yorks. (1965*)
14m NW of York, nr A19.
Meetings: York & Ainsty; Bilsdale.
SF: 18 (Club races)-23. LH 2¼ circs. 8F; 18J; 2od (3/11). T: 6min 06.0s.
Slightly undulating course with sharp bends, particularly that before the penultimate; uphill finish; fences variable; suits non-stayers; can be slippery on turns. Car parking satisfactory in very long grass; downhill exit. Viewing good, although far side near river partially out of sight — best from top of hill above car park. York & Ainsty abandoned in '99 and 2000 (waterlogged).
Riders: *Mrs F. Needham 4, C. Mulhall 4, R. Tate 3, D. Easterby 3, S. Swiers 2, S. Charlton 2, R. Walmsley 2, P. Atkinson 2, N. Tutty 2, Mrs S. Grant 2, Mrs L. Ward 2.*
* Racing took place on a course at Easingwold before WWII

EATON HALL, Cheshire. (1963)
4m S of Chester, nr A483 and A55.
Meetings: Sir W.W. Wynn's; Flint & Denbigh.
SF: 18-22. RH 2¼ circs. 8F; (3m): 18J; 2od (7/14). T: 6min 37.1s.
Flat galloping 3m2f course with long straights; fences big and well-made — open ditch and next plain fence can cause problems; ground usually very soft in early season when races can take over 7mins, so stamina essential; very firm later on. Course had to be much modified for both meetings in 2000 due to a waterlogged area — almost 3 times round a shorter circuit with 2 fences omitted, start and first fence in shute. This layout my become permanent. Cars park on hard surface — old airfield runways. Viewing best from small bank between paddock and finishing straight unless crowd is large, then try inside course between last two fences. The culling of trees has proved useful. Rather a dull course, but partially redeemed by the view of a beautiful red sandstone church which is where they bury the Grosvenors, and breed Classic winners.
Riders: *A. Crow 15, Mrs C. Ford 8, R. Burton 5, G. Hanmer 5, Miss A. Dare 4, M. Worthington 4, C. Barlow 4, R. Owen 3, D. Barlow 3, A. Dalton 3.*

ERW LON, Carms. (1979)
13m N of Carmarthen on B4336.
Meetings: Vale of Clettwr; Llandeilo Farmers, Carmarthenshire.
SF: 15-18. LH 2⅓ circs. 8F; 18J; 2od (6/14). T: 6min 23.3s.
Oval mainly flat galloping course on mountain grazing land with easy bends; start in shute; downhill from 9(17)th; fences well-made and well-sited; rarely becomes deep, can be sticky. Easy access and separate exit. Poor viewing — be prepared to move around; best in centre of course, 4(12)th fence obscured by horse boxes. It has been suggested that the course would be better if the finish was moved. By having the finish on top of the hill a view of the race unfolding in its final stages would be possible for racegoers and the commentator. Forget winter woollies at peril, very exposed and weather can be diabolical. Set Welsh season in motion in mid-February.
Riders: *Miss P. Jones 26, J. Jukes 26, E. Williams 9, M. Lewis 7, A. Price 6, T. Vaughan 4, P. Williams 4, P. Hamer 4, Miss L. Pearce 4, Miss A. Meakins 4, G. Lewis 4, D. Jones 4.*

EYTON-ON-SEVERN, Salop. (1923)
7m SE of Shrewsbury, nr B4380 via A5 and M54 (Exit 7).
Meetings: North Shropshire; South Shropshire; Tanatside.
**SF: 18-21. LH 1⅓ circs. 13F. (3m): 18J; 2od (6/12). T: 6min 25.6s. (2m4f): 14J; 2od (2/8).
T: 5min 16.6s.**

Very flat galloping course; fences fairly soft with final 3 close together; well drained alongside river. Access to car parks satisfactory, but exit always slow. Excellent view from hill, but horses very distant at far end of course. Shares with Larkhill the distinction (and therefore the added cost) of having most individual fences. A superb course; has been in use for many a year and will hopefully continue to flourish.
Riders: *A. Crow 11, R. Burton 8, A. Dalton 7, G. Hamner 6, M. Worthington 5, J. Cornes 5, A. Beedles 5, D. Barlow 4, C. Barlow 4.*

FAKENHAM, Norfolk. (1978)
2m SW of town.
Meeting: West Norfolk.
SF: 15-18. LH 3 circs. 6F; 18J; 3od (4/10/16), 3 wj (2/8/14). T: 6min 35.5s.
Undulating one mile circuit on outside of NH steeplechase course with horses always on the turn, but good sweeping bends never cause problems; winners usually well there at least a mile out. Portable fences. Watering system available if required, and going regularly close to perfect. Race course car parks; excellent viewing, horses never far away. Not like other NH tracks has a fair pointing atmosphere.
Riders: *W. Wales 5, N. Bloom 5, A. Sansome 4, T. Lane 2, S.R. Andrews 2, N. King 2, Miss Z. Turner 2, A. Coe 2.*

FLAGG MOOR, Derbys. (1892)
On A515, 6m SE Buxton, 15m NW Ashbourne.
Meeting: High Peak Harriers.
SF: 18-20. LH 2 circs. 9F. (3m4f): 18J; 2od (3/12). T: 7min 43.2s.
Very testing well-drained course of 3m4f encircling two farms and crossing four roads; long (half a mile) uphill pull from end of back straight; fences big, but not hard (are of indeterminate number — the racecard map features two sixth fences — and the fourth it shows doesn't exist at all!). Judges stand is still right against ropes. Ground became very testing for both horses and spectators following overnight rain in 2000, and Maiden took over 9mins. Is the only course in the country with the benefit of a toilet in the unsaddling enclosure. Viewing good from bank, but back straight partly obscured; very exposed and open to elements — wrap up well. Satisfactory car parking, but some delay entering. A dramatic and unique place, and the highest in the country at over 1100ft.
Riders: *A. Crow 4, S. Prior 2, R. Ford 2, Miss S. Rodman 2, G. Hamner 2.*

FLETE PARK, Devon. (1980)
Off A379 10m E of Plymouth, leave A38 at Ivybridge via A3121.
Meetings: Dartmoor (4m Mens Open); Modbury Harriers (4m Ladies)
SF: 16-20. RH 2¼ circs. 8F. (3m): 20J; 2od (7/15). T: 7min 03.3s. (4m): 25J; 3od (4/12/20). T: 8min 23.3s.
Hilly demanding course with a sharp bend and long downhill run to 3rd(11/19th) fence; dog-leg onto 140 yard run-in and sharp bend out of finishing straight and uphill through start; very short run-in. Steep downhill entrance to car parks, but separate firm and level exits. Facilities compact though a fair step to changing rooms in cricket pavilion! (course goes round the pitch which is smaller than most bowling greens). Reasonable viewing from high ground overlooking run-in, but one or two fences obscured by trees. Very pleasant setting, once home of top amateur rider the late Lord Mildmay of Flete. A well maintained track — organisers always try to provide decent ground. The decision to move the Pegasus Club race to the Modbury Harriers meeting in 2000 proved a surprising success.
Riders: *L. Jefford 10, Richard Darke 8, K. Heard 6, T. Greed 5, Miss S. Gaisford 5, Mrs M. Hand 4, Miss S. Young 3, T. Dennis 2, Miss T. Cave 2, Miss R. Francis 2, Miss J. Cumings 2, I. Widdicombe 2, A. Farrant 2.*

FRIARS HAUGH, Borders. (1953)
Just W of Kelso, nr A699.
Meetings: Berwickshire; Duke of Buccleuch's; Jedforest.

SF: 16-20 (Intermediate)-23. LH 2⅓ circs. 9F; 18J; 2od (5/12). T: 6min 42.0s.
Course is 3m2f mostly flat with one uphill climb; inviting island fences all well constructed; ground drains well and going usually good even in February; races are run at fast pace. Finish and fences 17 and 18 in seperate chute up centre. Car parking good with easy access. Most of action visible from centre of course. Loose horses sometimes go for a dip in the nearby River Tweed. Finish can now be viewed satisfactorily from best vantage point. Very well organised meetings, but charged £5 per head admission in 2000.
Riders: *C. Storey 18, A. Parker 11, Miss P. Robson 9, P. Craggs 7, Miss S. Forster 6, M. Bradburne 6, T. Oates 5, R. Shiels 5.*

GARNONS, Herefords & Worcs. (1984 — RH in 1st year).
8m W of Hereford, just off A438 (Exit 4, M50).
Meetings: Ross Harriers; South Herefordshire.
SF: 16-18 (Ladies)-20 (16). LH 2½ circs. 7F. (3m): 18J: 2od (7/14). T: 6min 45.2s. (2m4f): 15J; 2od (4/11). T: 5min 37.2s.
Very undulating and very sharp; portable fences stiff. Separate entrance and exit to car parks.
Viewing used to be good, and could be again if the judicious use of a chainsaw was employed, but management seem to have a cynical attitude towards their public. Access on steep grass slope can be very slippery when wet, and narrow gateway very hazardous then, but owner's private driveway may be used. Picturesque, but it palls unless you like trees, trees and more trees. Rather susceptible to waterlogging.
Riders: *C. Storey 18, A. Parker 11, Miss P. Robson 9, P. Craggs 7, Miss S. Forster 6, M. Bradburne 6, T. Oates 5, R. Shiels 5.*

PLATE 159   159 East Cornwall Confined Maiden (Div 2): Past the winning post on the first circuit at Great Trethew
PHOTO: Tim Holt

GARTHORPE, Leics. (1955)
6m E of Melton Mowbray on B676, 7m from A1.
Meetings: Cottesmore; Belvoir; Quorn; Melton Hunt Club.

**SF: 18 (Ladies except Melton)-20 (Melton Ladies)-24 (18). RH 2¼ circs. 8F; (3m): 18J; 2od (3/11).
T: 6min 26.8s. (2m4f): 15J; 1od (8). 5min 22.2s.**

Rectangular well-drained course, the undulations having been levelled and downhill stretches
have been drained. Fences big and well constructed. Much recent attention has been given to
fence building and presentation, but they still need jumping. It is reported that the open ditch
has been widened as well as the pen fences. Run-in slopes to outside; watering system available;
can be slippery if wet. Good access and exit to car parks. More cars will be able to park in 2001
nearer the front following drainage work. Good view from car park on outside of straight. Plan to
have extra toilets and viewing area for disabled in 2001. Judge's stand ideally sited. SF's vary for
each meeting,, but 24 for majority of races at Melton Hunt Club is ludicrous. The inside of
fences 1-4 and 18 are usually dolled off and are kept for the Melton meeting. Strong betting
market at Melton meeting.
Riders: *S. Morris 8, B. Pollock 8, J. Docker 7, R. Armson 6, Mrs J. Dawson 5, Mrs F. Needham 5,
Julian Pritchard 5, A. Sansome 5.*

GREAT TRETHEW, Cornwall. (1986)
1m S of A38; 3m SE of Liskeard.
Meeting: East Cornwall.
SF: 16-18. RH 2½ circs. 7F; 19J; 2od (7/14). T: 6min 33.2s.

Course is a very hilly elongated oval with long straights and two sharp bends; long galloping run
from 6(13)th downhill through start; a deep cleft bisects the course; uphill finish. Run-in very short
— less than 100 yards. Fences (all portable) are in straights, and well-built. Car park in centre of
course can be slippery; separate box park. Viewing good from finishing area though run back to
start out of sight. The South Cornwall had to be abandoned here in 2000 because of waterlogging,
and was switched to Trebudannon — they will remain there in 2001.
Riders: *T. Mitchell 8, Miss P. Curling 8, N. Harris 6, Miss S. Young 5, L. Jefford 5, Miss T. Cave 4,
R. White 3, K. Heard 3, J. Tizzard 3, A. Farrant 3.*

GUILSBOROUGH, Northants. (1951)
Nr A50, 10m NW of Northampton (Exit 18 M1, or via A50 from A14).
Meeting: Pytchley.
SF: 18 (Restricted)-20. LH 2½ circs. 8F; 19J; 2od (7/15). T: 6min 38.3s.

Flat course with 2 long straights and 2 sharp bends which can be slippery when wet; long run to
first, short run-in; finishing line set at an angle, favouring horses on inside; fences very well built
and inviting — 5(13)th portable. Watering possible. Usually masses of runners. Good access to
and exit from car parks (on steep hill), but exit difficult in wet. The cutting down of trees and
hedges has greatly improved viewing in back straight, although fence 8(16)th is still hard to see.
Rural and pleasant.
Riders: *T. Lane 5, B. Pollock 5, S. Morris 4, R. Lawther 3, Miss H. Irving 3, A. Sansome 3, J. Docker 2.*

HACKWOOD PARK, Hants. (1952)
2m SE Basingstoke, signposted from A339 Alton road (Exit 6, M3).
Meetings: Hampshire; Vine & Craven.
SF: 16-18-20. LH 2¾ circs. 7F; 18J; 2od (5/12). T: 6min 28s.

Course on a slope with downhill back straight and uphill finish; very sharp, but by no means easy;
fences permanent, attractively presented, but now rather soft; a much improved venue since
management changed, but limitations of site sadly always apparent. Commentator stands in a high
scaffolding tower which would be ideal for all spectators to take advantage of limited viewing
facilities. Car entry satisfactory, but exit very slow particularly on Bank Holiday.
Riders: *G. Maundrell 4, Miss A. Goschen 3, J. Owen 3, J. Jukes 3, C. Vigors 3, A. James 3,
R. White 2, R. Forristal 2, P. York 2, P. Scouller 2, Miss M. Hill 2, M. Gorman 2, J. Barnes 2,
D. Dennis 2.*

HEXHAM, Northumberland. (1995)
1m SW of town between B6305 & B6306 on NH racecourse.
Meeting: Haydon.
SF: 18(Restricted)-20 (15). LH 2¼ circs. 8F; (3m): 19J; 2od (5/13). T: 7min 22.5s. (2m4f): 14J; 1od (8). T: 5min 38.4s.
Gently undulating course on inside of racecourse; All fences completely rebuilt prior to latest meeting. Last fence resited and run in extended to 200 yds. Good viewing in fine setting, but finish distant and atmosphere inevitably lacking. Wonderful for NH racing — a useless venue for Pointing. Doubts still remain about the going, which is never going to be ideal and has suffered from extremes in short history of course. £5 per head admission charge in 2000.
Riders: T. Scott 3, Miss P. Robson 3, Miss C. Hall 2, J. Walton 2.

HIGHAM, Essex. (1958)
8m NE of Colchester via A12 and B1068.
Meetings: Essex & Suffolk; North Norfolk Harriers; Granta Harriers; Waveney Harriers.
SF: 17-22. LH 2½ circs. 8F; 19J; 2od (6/14). T: 6min 23.7s.
Flat very tight circuit suits front runners; sandy soil usually gives good going even in early season; fences are easier than they used to be. Bookies poor. Flat car parking and no problems, but arrive early to avoid some delay at entrance. Best viewing from centre of course, though finish difficult from there. Gents toilets rudimentary — one of the facilities has a further hazard of a sharp twigged bush growing in an unfortunate position which could prove troublesome to the unwary.
Riders: A. Sansome 8, S. Sporborg 6, A. Hickman 6, A. Coe 6, S.R. Andrews 5, N. King 5, N. Bloom 5, D. Parker 5.

HIGH EASTER, Essex. (1992*)
8m NW of Chelmsford nr A1060 (Exit 8, M11).
Meetings: Essex; Easton Harriers.
SF: 15-20-22. LH 2 circs. 9F; 19J; 2od (4/13). T: 6min 43.4s.
Undulating roughly kidney shaped course with fairly stiff climb to 2 out, downhill stretch and slight drop on fence 4(13)th; well-built inviting portable fences. Back straight on ancient water meadows so will probably always have softer going than higher ground in finishing straight. Turn into back straight now eased. Fences in back straight moved to outside of track and now taken in form of gentle arc and being nearer brook have best of going. Viewing greatly improved by construction of mound on outside of course. All jumps now visible though finish is head on. Pleasant rural setting. Positions of paddock and bookies/tote transposed to good effect. Entrance/exit rather slow as course is in the middle of a maze of country lanes. Compact facilities. Weak betting market. Form guide for Easton Harriers meeting in 2000 was very poor.
Riders: S. Sporborg 4, N. Bloom 4, A. Coe 4, W. Wales 3, R. Gill 3, A. Harvey 3, Mrs L. Gibbon 2, Miss Z. Turner 2, Miss L. Hollis 2, G. Cooper 2, C. Ward-Thomas 2, A. Sansome 2.
* Essex held a meeting at Great Hassels in 1886, within view of present site

HOLNICOTE, Som. (1997*)
Near A39, 3m W of Minehead, 2m E of Porlock.
Meetings: Devon & Somerset Staghounds; Minehead Harriers & West Somerset; West Somerset & Minehead Harriers.
SF: 16-18. RH 2½ circs. 7F; 19J; 3od (3/10/17). T: 6min 41.0s.
Slightly undulating, all grass, tear drop shaped course a few hundred yards from original course. Course is downhill into back straight and slightly uphill from approaching 3rd(10/17th) through finish. Fences (portable) firm and up to height, but 2nd(9/16th) very narrow. Compacted sub-soil. Viewing adequate (good if right spot picked), but hindered by tents and trees. Car parking satisfactory. Facilities compact, but Judge's box right against ropes. Very scenic, on slopes of Exmoor National Park under Dunkery Beacon. A spectacular rainbow remained over the course for virtually the whole of the West Somerset meeting in 2000.
Riders: Miss P. Gundry 7, T. Mitchell 6, Miss J. Cumings 4, J. Tizzard 4, A. Honeyball 4, T. Scudamore 3, Miss S. Vickery 3, I. Dowrick 3.
The original Holnicote course, opened in 1948, was a a few hundred yards away

HORNBY CASTLE, Yorks. (1947)
3m W of A1, S of Catterick.
Meetings: Bedale; West of Yore.
SF: 18-20-25. LH 2¼ circs. 8F; 18J; 2od (3/11). T: 6min 44.3s.
Undulating stayers course; ridge and furrow now removed; fences well-built. Car parking flat, plenty of room. All fences visible from centre of course, but run to 6th fence out of sight, and finish rather distant. PA system not clear at better vantage points. Very weak betting market (needs fresh blood urgently), West of Yore meeting chose their own bookmakers in 2000, which was an interesting move. Judges stand far too close to the line. Horseboxes positioned on the bend entering the final straight caused too many problems, and it is planned to resite them in 2001. Scenic setting with the cute castle perched on a hill.
Riders: *S. Walker 3, S. Swiers 3, Mrs F. Needham 3, D. Easterby 3, C. Mulhall 3, P. Atkinson 2, N. Smith 2, Miss T. Jackson 2, M. Sowersby 2, L. McGrath 2.*

HORSEHEATH, Cambs. (1972)
4m W of Haverhill on A604. (Exits 9 or 10, M11).
Meetings: Cambridgeshire; Puckeridge; Thurlow.
SF: 18-25. RH 1¾ circs. 10F; 18J; 2od (3/12). T: 6min 37.7s.
Undulating galloping course of over three miles; start in chute; uphill finish; fences well built; 1st and 10th jumped only once, 6th (taken downhill) causes most problems; chalk subsoil drains well, but gets very holding in back straight. Plenty of room for parking, but crowds large so arrive early to avoid queue. Viewing very good, but pick vantage point for best sight of finish. Dries out fast in the absence of rain and a pathetic track in a dry year — definitely a course which should be exploited in early season. Has a little fun fair for the children.
Riders: *S. Sporborg 19, S.R. Andrews 7, P. Taiano 7, N. Bloom 5, A. Sansome 5, W. Wales 4, Miss Z. Turner 4, Miss L. Rowe 4.*

HOWICK, Gwent. (1952)
2m W of Chepstow on B4293. (Exit 2, M48).
Meetings: Curre; Llangibby.
SF: 16-18 (Ladies)-20. LH 1¾ circs. 9F; 18J; 2od (3/12). T: 6min 44.4s.
Undulating almost triangular course with one sharp and two sweeping bends; the course layout was changed in 2000 with the open ditch being resited and an additional portable fence (6/15)th being inserted; others are permanent and quite stiff. Fence 2(11) is situated on crest of hill and is quite small; fences 4(13) & 5(14) at far end of course fall away and vary in height by nearly two feet from one side of course to the other. The new layout proved quite successful and may be retained. Spacious, but unorganised car parking, and exit can be slow through the farm. Viewing fair from the hill, but finish in a chute could not be worse sited. Signposting poor from M48. Unpretentious and very friendly atmosphere.
Riders: *E. Williams 11, A. Price 10, Miss P. Jones 6, J. Jukes 6, D. Jones 5, P. Williams 4, D. Stephens (Wales) 4, Miss F. Wilson 3, J. Price 3, G. Lewis 3.*

HUTTON RUDBY, Yorks. (1997*)
4m W of Stokesley between A19 and A172.
Meeting: Hurworth.
SF: 18-20-23. LH 2¾ circs. 8F; 20J; 2od (8/15). T: 6min 31.4s.
Sharp, undulating kidney-shaped course of almost three circuits; start is in a chute with first fence jumped once. Some fences are skimpy. Number-board poor and needs improving. Viewing is good from many points, including near the start. A very attractive setting, more like a Hunter Trial course at the moment.
Riders: *G. Tuer 5, S. Swiers 3, Mrs F. Needham 3, P. Atkinson 2, Mrs L. Ward 2, D. Easterby 2.*
*Hurworth raced on a course also in Skutterskelfe Park, Hutton Rudby from 1957-1984

KILWORTHY, Devon. (1925)
1m N of Tavistock, 1m W of A386.
Meeting: Lamerton.
SF: 16-20-21. LH 2½ circs. 8F; 18J; 2od (3/11). T: 6min 36.6s.
Flat rectangular galloping stayers course with mostly sweeping bends and 4 fences along each side; very stiff uphill finish up chute. Fences well-built (qv Cherrybrook). Excellent old turf. Essential to maintain correct racing line over last four fences. Judges stand is badly positioned right on the line. Hard track access to car parks, but single entrance/exit causes delays. Viewing improved since spectators have been allowed to use natural grandstand, though fence 7(15) is still difficult to see.
Riders: *L. Jefford 7, Miss J. Cumings 4, R. Woollacott 2, P. Scholfield 2, Mrs M. Hand 2, Miss T. Cave 2, M. Miller 2, K. Heard 2, I. Hambley 2, David Dennis 2, C. Heard 2, A. Farrant 2.*

KIMBLE, Bucks. (1912)
5m S of Aylesbury on B4009. 6m from A41.
Meeting: Vale of Aylesbury (Easter).
SF: 18-22. LH 2¼ circs. 9F; 19J; 2od (7/16) 2wj (6/15). T: 6min 48.8s.
Flat stayers course of '3m1f and about 38yds'; portable island fences of average size and build. Car parks have downhill exits; huge crowd at Easter meeting so allow plenty of time. Good viewing, but restricted by parked cars. Strong betting market. Judges stand very near line. Water jump omitted due to heavy ground in 2000. A nice touch is the starter mounted on a stately steed. An officious car park attendant was guarding the reserved parking spaces (soon told his fortune by one of the editors!).
Riders: *R. Lawther 3, Mrs T. Hill 3, A. Barlow 3, T. Illsley 2, M. Emmanuel 2, B. Pollock 2, A. Hill 2.*

KINGSTON BLOUNT, Oxon. (1971)
8m NW of High Wycombe (Exits 5 or 6, M40).
Meetings: Vale of Aylesbury (May); Oxford University Hunt Club; Bicester with Whaddon Chase (April); Berks & Bucks Draghounds.
SF: 18-20-24. LH 2¼ circs. 8F; 18J; 2od (5/13). T: 6min 32.2s.
Undulating course; steep climb after 5(13)th and downhill again before 6(14)th; can be firm due to chalk soil, but sticky in wet weather — water drains off chalk ridge above course; watering system available and can be a boon in May. Very spacious paddock now more conveniently sited than in the past. Car parking good with downhill exit, but can be slippery in wet weather. Good viewing from slope above finish, but it's a long walk. Wagon kindly provided for press, though its position mean few (mostly not press) make use of it (if it was moved into line with the finish it would be packed).
Riders: *J. Tarry 12, R. Lawther 9, Mrs T. Hill 7, R. Sweeting 6, Miss C. Spearing 5, L. Lay 5, T. Underwood 4, J. Owen 4, D. Dennis 4.*

KINGSTON ST MARY, Som. (1987)
3m N of Taunton, off A361. (Exit 25, M5).
Meeting: Taunton Vale Hunts.
SF: 17-20. RH 2¼ circs. 8F; 18J; 2od (5/13). T: 6min 35.2s.
Very undulating course; steep climb after 5(13)th and downhill from 7(15)th; portable fences. Car parking, exits and entrances good. Good grass covering. Viewing only adequate; hedge bisecting course should be cut down, and start is out of sight (official times are guesswork and action disappears from view at vital stage two out). Tends to be packed full of Easter 'hoorays'. Bookies sparse and poor value.
Riders: *T. Mitchell 4, Miss S. Vickery 4, Miss P. Gundry 4, N. Mitchell 2, Miss P. Curling 2, B. O'Doherty 2, A. Honeyball 2.*

LALESTON, Mid-Glam. (1998)
Nr A48 2½m W of Bridgend, 3m from Exit 37, M4
Meeting: Llangeinor.
SF: 15-20. LH 3 circs. 6F; 19J; 3od (4/10/16). T: 6min 35.1s.

Small tight oval course; area cleared through a small wood surfaced with wood chips. Paddock on opposite side of a busy road and many drivers were unhappy at being kept waiting for the streams of spectators crossing onto the course (even a fire engine had to wait!); situation is made worse by car drivers trying to enter through the pedestrian gate, but a separate exit/entrance has been made for horses to cross the road — all very dangerous. Whole of course in view from the paddock side of the road so long as you are tall enough to see over the hedge! Car parking was well manned by numerous attendants in fluorescent marshal's jackets and the arguments of the previous year seemed non-existent.

Riders: *T. Vaughan 5, E. Williams 5, J. Jukes 3, P. Hamer 2, Miss P. Jones 2, M. Lewis 2.*

LANARK, Strathclyde (1995*)
½m SE of town nr A73 & A70, 6m from M74.
Meetings: Eglinton; Lanarkshire & Renfrewshire.
SF: 18-22 (16). RH 2½ circs. 8F; (3m): 18J. 2od (6/13) T: 6min 57.2s. (2m5f): 15J.2od (3/10)
T: 6min 07.2s.
Oval perfectly flat course on old flat track, two straights connected by one long sweeping bend with a sharper one at the opposite end. Portable fences. Grandstand and some other buildings survive, but are crumbling and in a dismal state. Viewing good. Strong betting market. Races usually off late and winning distances rarely announced. Electronic number board. Shabby, with piles of rubbish here and there, needs a good clean up and a lick of paint. The concrete posts in course boundary fence could be a potential danger. Dog owners need providing with pooper scoopers to remove extra hazards for racegoers and jockeys alike. Popular with owners, but poorly supported and has as much atmosphere as a morgue. Lanarkshire and Renfrewshire meeting was abandoned in 2000 after parts of the course were churned up by the local riding club!
Riders: *A. Parker 7, A. Robson 6, R. Morgan 4, P. Craggs 4, C. Storey 4, T. Morrison 3, R. Ford 3, Mrs V. Jackson 3, K. Anderson 3.*
*Lanark was in use as a flat course until 1977

LARKHILL, Wilts. (1947)
5m NW of Amesbury, 10m N of Salisbury, nr A303, A345 and A360.
Meetings: United Services; Royal Artillery; South & West Wilts; New Forest; Army; Staff College & RMA Draghounds; 14th Regiment Royal Artillery.
SF: 18 (Novice riders and 4m Open)-25 (18) RH 1⅓ circs. 13F (3m): 18J; 3od (3/16 & 11). T: 6min 20.9s. (4m): 22J; 4od (2/15 & 7/20). T: 8min 18.2s. (2m4f): 15J; 2od (8/13). T: 5min 46.5s.
Roughly triangular undulating galloping course; stiff climb to the 13th can catch out the non-stayer. Portable fences; chalk soil can be firm in late season, but gives good going even in the wettest weather; permanent buildings; bookies plentiful and generous. Car parking excellent; entrance and exit no problem; entrance/exit road avoiding armed guards. Excellent viewing from most parts though horses get rather distant and disappear briefly between 8 and 9, and for longer on run to 13, but the view of the last mile is second to none. The Coronation Cup has been reduced to one division only since '95, but is still very competitive. A running rail from the last will be introduced in 2001, and the railings along the straight are to be replaced. The only 2m4f race run at the course is now the King's Troop race. Has two meetings in January, and you need to wrap up well — no wind-break between here and Marlborough Downs almost 20 miles away.
Riders: *T. Mitchell 15, M. Miller 14, Miss S. Vickery 11, Miss P. Curling 10, O. Ellwood 9, Miss A. Goschen 8, Julian Pritchard 8, Miss P. Gundry 7, J. Moore 6, A. Charles-Jones 6, R. Walford 5, D. Alers-Hankey 5, Miss D. Stafford 4, L. Jefford 4, J. Tizzard 4, P. Pritchard 3, J. Jukes 3, G. Maundrell 3, D. Dennis 3.*

LEMALLA, Cornwall. (1961)
at Lewannick, on B3257, nr A30, 6m SW of Launceston.
Meeting: East Cornwall.
SF: 16-19. RH: 3½ circs. 6F; 19J; 3od (4/10/16). T: 6min 58.1s.
Sharp undulating oval Linley course, has had several layouts, but currently course runs behind the buildings, so the sharp bend after the ditch has been eased, but other two are right angled; three

portable fences; siting of paddock now much improved; single entrance, but separate box parking; downhill exit available. Viewing poor. The Bolventor Harriers have gone for ever and Lemalla remains — who said black magic works.

Riders: *L. Jefford 5, N. Harris 4, Miss J. Cumings 3, A. Farrant 3, R. Woollacott 2, Mrs M. Hand 2, Miss S. Young 2, Miss P. Gundry 2, Miss P. Curling 2, K. Heard 2, I. Dowrick 2, C. Heard 2, A. Honeyball 2.*

LIFTON, Devon (1993)
3m E of Launceston, N of A30.
Meetings: Tetcott; South Tetcott.
SF: 15-17. RH: 2⅔ circs. 7F; 20J; 2od (7/14). T: 6min 11.0s.
Virtually flat roughly triangular course, but with slight rise coming back towards the spectators. Facilities compact. Good viewing, except for run to 2 out, best on inside of course near finish. Going patchy, and prone to waterlogging; wood chippings used to cover bare areas where former LSWR main line embankment removed. Very pleasant setting, and deservedly popular with owners and spectators — the Withered Arm flourishing again.

Riders: *N. Harris 7, Miss J. Cumings 7, L. Jefford 7, A. Farrant 6, T. Cole 3, Richard Darke 3, Miss T. Cave 3, Miss S. Young 3, Miss K. Baily 3, A. Holdsworth 3.*

LITTLEWINDSOR, Dorset (1993)
3m S of Crewkerne nr A3066. (16m from Exit 25, M5).
Meetings: Cattistock; Seavington.
SF: 16 (Novice Riders)-18 (16). RH: 2½ circs. 7F; (3m): 19J; 3 od (3/10/17). T: 6min 37.8s. (2m4f): 16J; 2od (7/14). T: 5min 33.2s.
Roughly rectangular undulating Linley course; stiff climb from 2nd (9/16); downhill from 6 (13). All portable fences, well made; uphill climb to the finish is taken three times; very testing when soft, but surprisingly easy at other times. Car parking, entrances and exits very good; no problems even when very wet. Viewing fine — best from inside course near finish, or from natural bank overlooking course. Facilities compact. Beautiful views. Fields tend to be on the small side, but attracts quality horses and not just from the Barber stable next door. Both meetings feature a 2m4f Maiden. Number board is exemplary and is a standard which other courses in the area should aim to follow.

Riders: *T. Mitchell 8, N. Mitchell 6, R. Atkinson 5, Miss P. Curling 5, Miss P. Gundry 4, A. Honeyball 4, P. Henley 3, M. Miller 3, J. Moore 3.*

LLANFRYNACH, Brecon. (1963)
3m SE of Brecon off B4558, 2m off A40.
Meeting: Brecon and Talybont.
SF: 15-18 (Members and Ladies)-20. RH 2¾ circs. 8F; 18J; 2od (6/13). T: 6min 38.8s.
Course is flat and twisty — each race involves 10 bends (2 sharp); start is in fairly long separate chute and first fence jumped only once; can withstand torrential rain although going is usually soft/heavy; early season meeting finds out the unfit horses — many non-finishers; huge fields and nine or more races since '86. Good number board and generally well organised. They performed marvels in getting off 14 races (!) in 2000. The announcer does not give out the jockeys' names, but rants on about the Countryside Alliance — probably alienating many of the undecided with his hectoring tones. Awful fences — you can see through them. Viewing reasonable from natural bank. Car parking good, but single access/exit gets treacherous (best leave the Jaguar at home and bring an amphibious vehicle). Attempted to charge grooms travelling in the lorries £5 entry in 2000, but plan thwarted by a trainer who threatened to run over the gatemen unless they got out of his way. Beautiful setting.

Riders: *Miss P. Jones 11, D. Jones 7, S. Lloyd 4, J. Jukes 4, T. Weale 2, S. Shinton 2, S. Blackwell 2, M.P. Jones 2, J. Price 2, G. Lewis 2, E. Williams 2, D. Stephens (Wales) 2, A. Crow 2.*

LLANVAPLEY, Gwent. (1953)
4m E of Abergavenny, nr B4233. 4m from A40.

Meeting: Monmouthshire.
SF: 16-18 (Ladies)-20. LH 2½ circs. 7F; 18J; 2od (6/13). T: 6min 48.5s.
Course is flat and twisty though two bends long and sweeping; short downhill run-in; scenic setting
if you ignore the massive pylons. Car parking satisfactory; two entrances/exits. Viewing very good
from hillside, but copse between 1st(8/15th) and 2nd(9/16th) obscures part of course. The latest
meeting had a cornfield between fences 1 and 2 (8/15 and 9/16) and this produced a quagmire
through which the horses could barely stagger — reminiscent of St Hilary.
Riders: *A. Price 5, S. Blackwell 4, Miss P. Jones 4, J. Price 3, E. Williams 3, P. Williams 2,*
P. Hamer 2, C. Williams 2, B. Potts 2.

LOCKERBIE, Dumfries. (1923)
At Roberthill, 2m W of Lockerbie, alongside A709.
Meeting: Dumfriesshire.
SF: 18-22. RH 2 circs. 9F; 19J; 2od (5/14). T: 7min 29.5s.
Course is flat 3m3f; plenty of good galloping stretches; fences portable now fairly soft. Viewing is
good from bank and car park. Truly grand, and makes every course south of the Border look
cramped. The servants of the gentry no longer dispense drinks, but plenty of 'boot parties' so there
should be no need to go thirsty. No place for a short-runner.
Riders: *R. Morgan 5, Mrs V. Jackson 4, K. Anderson 4, T. Scott 3, Miss P. Robson 3, C. Storey 3.*

LOCKINGE, Oxon. (1953)
2m SE of Wantage on B4494 (8m NW Exit 13, M4).
Meeting: Old Berkshire.
SF: 18-25. LH 2 circs. 9F; 18J; 2od (7/16). T: 6min 32.7s.
Undulating galloping oval course; old downland turf on chalk can get firm, but usually gives good
going for the Easter Monday fixture; fences of average height and build. A long run in from the last
has not yet produced the anticipated close finishes since the reduction of jumps. Many spectators
walk the course beforehand armed with drinks and dogs! Car parking good on steep slope (engage
handbrake and reverse); always a very large crowd so long queues on access and exit; follow signs
if coming from south. Viewing excellent from hillside with superb view of start and finish. Excellent
betting market. A well organised meeting.
Riders: *F. Hutsby 3, R. Dalgety 2, M. Miller 2, A. Charles-Jones 2.*

LYDSTEP, Dyfed. (1948)
3m SW of Tenby, nr A4139.
Meetings: South Pembrokeshire; Pembrokeshire.
SF: 15-16-18 (15/16). LH 2½ circs. 8F; (3m): 19J; 2od (6/14). T: 6min 29.5s. (2m4f) 16J;
2od (3/11). T: 5min 15.0s.
Course is slightly undulating and almost square; two particularly tight bends; does not suit big
long-striding horses; two fences are downhill and can cause errors; sandy soil drains well. Car
parking ample; access/exit takes two lanes of traffic. Excellent viewing if the right spot is chosen.
Pembrokeshire has a lower SF for both maidens.
Riders: *J. Jukes 16, Miss P. Jones 12, D. Jones 11, E. Williams 6, Miss L. Pearce 4, M. Lewis 4,*
P. Hamer 3, J. Keen 3, G. Lewis 3, C. Williams 3.

MAISEMORE PARK, Glos. (1982)
Nr A417, 3m NW of Gloucester (Exit 11, M5).
Meetings: Ledbury; Cotswold Vale Farmers.
SF: 16-23. LH 2½ circs. 7F. (3m): 18J; 2od (7/14). T: 6min 52.2s.
Totally flat, oval course bounded on two sides by River Severn. Now six metal fences. Last two
fences re-sited in 2000 with a slightly longer run-in. Car park access is difficult in wet and bumpy
when hard. Viewing frustrating, trees at foot of hill obscure the vital part of the race. Well worth
maintaining properly.
Riders: *Julian Pritchard 17, Miss A. Dare 9, A. Wintle 9, T. Stephenson 6, Miss P. Jones 4,*
M. Rimell 3, M. Harris 3, S. Lloyd 3, S. Joynes 2, J. Jukes 2, G. Barfoot-Saunt 2.

MARKET RASEN, Lincs. (1992)
1m E of town on S side of A631 (Point-to-Point entrance is off Legsby road).
Meetings: Lincolnshire United Hunts Club; Burton.
SF: 16 (Restricteds)-18-20 (Opens and PPORC only). LH 2½ circs. 7F; 18J; 2od (5/12).
T: 6min 41.0s.
Mainly flat left-handed course inside right-hand NH circuit. Situation makes for tight bends —
uphill bend at far end of course is unavoidably narrow; tight last bend after penultimate makes it
desirable to be in contention on inside. Well-built inviting portable fences. Grass coverage,
particularly at top of hill approaching fence 7 could still be better. The second last is to be moved
further up the hill for 2001 which should make it ride better. Viewing excellent from NH stands and
facilities first class. Watering possible and every effort made to provide the best going and viewing
on the day. It was good to note that the harsh criticism levelled at the Burton meeting in '99 was
taken on board, but the number board is still poor.
Riders: *P. Gee 7, S. Swiers 6, N. Kent 5, Mrs J. Dawson 4, K. Green 4, S. Brisby 3, N. Tutty 3,
S. Walker 2, S. Campion 2, P. Millington 2, N. Wilson 2, Mrs M. Morris 2, Julian Pritchard 2,
G. Smith 2, G. Hanmer 2, D. Easterby 2, A. Pennock 2, A. Hill 2.*

MARKS TEY, Essex. (1952)
5m W of Colchester, at junc of A12 & A120.
Meetings: East Essex; Essex Farmers & Union (February & April).
SF: 18-25. LH 1¾ circs. 10F. (3m) 20J; 2od (3/13) T: 6min 57.1s. (3m4f) 21J; 2od (4/14)
T: 7min 35.5s.
Galloping slightly undulating course with uphill finish; one sharp bend; under all conditions it is a
true stayers course and when wet becomes holding and a severe test of stamina; soon becomes
hard in a dry spell; fences rebuilt and fair and inviting. Good course for maidens. Car parking
excellent; plenty of room. Viewing best from bank near paddock and much improved by thinning
and trimming of hedges and trees, but 5(15)th still hidden. Bad bookies. New smaller paddock for
2000 though apparently not to everyone's taste. Bookies and trade stands resited which gives a
clearer view of start, but area around bookies is a morass when wet. Unattractive setting, but going
much improved recently.
Riders: *A. Sansome 11, A. Coe 11, G. Cooper 8, S.R. Andrews 7, N. Bloom 7, S. Sporborg 5,
Miss L. Rowe 5, W. Wales 4, T. Moore 4, T. Bulgin 4, R. Hunnisett 4.*

MILBORNE ST ANDREW, Dorset. (1991)
Nr A354 ½m SE of village, midway between Blandford and Dorchester.
Meeting: South Dorset.
SF: 18-20. LH 2½ circs. 8F; 19J; 2od (7/15). T: 6min 25.2s.
Undulating roughly triangular Linley course, all grass on chalk downland; downhill from start to
after 2nd, then uphill to last and through finish, downhill again from 6th to 7th (open ditch). All
fences portable and very well-built, and all have plastic wings. Viewing moderate — best from
inside course near winning post or from slope near bookies; thinning out the copse in the middle
of the course to allow for at least a partial view of the start and all the fences in that straight would
be a major improvement. Car parking satisfactory, now two entrances/exits.
Riders: *T. Mitchell 3, Miss P. Curling 3, R. Young 2, R. Nuttall 2, N. Mitchell 2, Miss E. Tory 2,
Miss A. Goschen 2, J. Moore 2.*

MOLLINGTON, Oxon. (1972)
On A423, 5m N of Banbury. Nr M40.
Meetings: Grafton; Bicester with Whaddon Chase (March); South Midlands Area Hunt Club.
SF: 18-20-25. RH 2¼ circs. 8F; 18J; 2od (7/15). T: 6min 40.6s.
Wide undulating galloping track with four long sweeping bends and stiff uphill finish; portable
fences very small; fields tend to be large and of good quality. Car parking good; uphill exits, but no
problems. Viewing above average, whole of circuit in view until the runners disappear behind a
house on outside of the track between the last two fences. Compact facilities. A model course,
although huge crowds at Sunday meetings now make moving around freely rather difficult.

Riders: *J. Tarry 16, Miss H. Irving 5, R. Sweeting 4, M. Rimell 4, F. Hutsby 4, A. Martin 4, R. Lawther 3, Miss S. Vickery 3, Julian Pritchard 3, J. Trice-Rolph 3, C. Wadland 3.*

MORDON, Durham. (1990)
Nr A1 (M), 4 miles S. of Sedgefield, 1 mile N of Great Stainton.
Meetings: South Durham.
SF: 18-20-22. LH: 2½ circs. 8F; 19J; 2od (5/13). T: 6min 27.5s.
Undulating roughly rectangular course — uphill from 8(16)th to 9(17)th and very long downhill run from 2nd(11/18th) to 3rd(12/19th). All fences portable. Facilities compact and near finish and viewing reasonable from that area, but start out of sight and trees obscure 8(16)th. Good, prompt announcements. Hard road entrance. Very exposed and windswept (and dust blowing around) so wrap up well. Poor betting market. Lacks charm.
Riders: *N. Wilson 8, Mrs S. Grant 6, C. Mulhall 3, T. Glass 3, S. Swiers 2, R. Edwards 2, Mrs F. Needham 2.*

MOSSHOUSES, Borders. (1948)
4m NE of Galashiels between A7 and A68.
Meeting: Lauderdale.
SF: 18-20 (Mares)-22. LH 2¼ circs. 8F; 19J; 2od (5/13). T: 6min 35.6s.
Hilly course with very steep climb after fence 5(13) and sharp bend after 8(16). Suits good jumping stayers; fences big and well-built; one drop fence jumped twice. Good access and exits. Perfect viewing from large natural grandstand and finish still obscured by trailer! Well attended and popular meeting with added bonus that if weather is inclement racing can be watched from the car park. Entrance charge of £5 per person.
Riders: *C. Storey 5, W. Kerr 3, R. Morgan 3, A. Parker 3, Miss N. Stirling 2, Miss L. Bradburne 2, Miss A. Bowie 2, M. Bradburne 2, L. Morgan 2.*

MOUNSEY HILL GATE, Som. (1984)
4m N. of Dulverton nr B3323. (Exit 27, M5 via A373 & A396).
Meeting: Dulverton East.
SF: 16-18. RH 2¾ circs. 7F; 20J; 2od (7/14). T: 6min 52.1s.
Oval slightly undulating course with sharp bends; all portable fences. Viewing hopeless. Cars and horse boxes now park on outside of course, handy to paddock etc. Layout changed frequently, but will never be any good for spectators. Two commentators necessary to give spectators any idea of the pattern of the races. Paying customers dwindling year by year — the discerning West Country public will not pay good money to see nothing.
Riders: *N. Harris 4, L. Jefford 4, R. Treloggen 3, Miss A. Dare 3, T. Mitchell 2, Miss S. Young 2, G. Barfoot-Saunt 2, D. Alers-Hankey 2, C. White 2.*

NEWTON BROMSWOLD, Northants. (1953)
3m SE of Rushden, 2m E of A6. (Exit 15, M1).
Meeting: Oakley.
SF: 18-25. RH 2¼ circs. 9F; 19J; 2od (6/15). T: 7min 01.7s.
Testing, undulating course of about 3m2f with uphill finish from penultimate. Fences 1, 2 & 7 are portable, but all are on the big side and extremely well-built; permanent facilities. Plenty of room for parking and two exits. Viewing very good. Deservedly popular (and therefore profitable) with spectators and owners. Threatened with the axe, but has been reprieved. Staged an Open Maiden in last three years; attracted three divisions in first year and four in second and third; a welcome step, as the previous organisation seemed hell-bent on discouraging runners at a course which is ideal for young horses.
Riders: *B. Pollock 8, R. Barrett 3, T. Illsley 2, S. Morris 2, R. Sweeting 2, R. Lawther 2, Mrs T. Hill 2, Miss L. Sweeting 2, Miss L. Rowe 2, Miss H. Irving 2.*

NORTHAW, Herts. (1968*)
2m NE of Potters Bar off A121 (Exit 24, M25).

Meeting: Enfield Chace.
SF: 15 (Members)-18 (Maiden)-20. LH 2½ circs. 8F; 19J; 2od (7/15). T: 6min 18.2s.
Oval, undulating course; quite sharp incline on bend approaching 6(14)th and a steep camber between 4(12) and 6(14). Fences quite soft (four metal-framed), are smallest in Area (particularly the last). Viewing best from far side of track near 6 (14), but it is difficult to hear the commentator on inside of the course. Used to be well under three miles, but the start was moved back to include an extra fence and times indicate the distance is now well up to requirement. Car parking satisfactory, but large crowd can cause delays. Officials transported to start in a smart horse-drawn carriage. Continues to be a garden furniture and barbecue salesman's paradise, and most patrons are not remotely interested in the racing, but are happy to cheer any horse they see on the course, including those which have long since pulled up! Paddock too small for bank holiday crowd; number board poor — no details given of blinkers, overweights, etc and not announced. Race card a disgrace at £2. Remarkably rural setting considering proximity to Central London. Might be even more successful as a mid-week evening fixture. A fun spot, but racing is usually dire.
Riders: *M. Gingell 3, T. MacFarlane 2, S. Sporborg 2, Miss L. Rowe 2.*
* Various Hunts raced on a course at Northaw before World War 1 and between Wars.

PANTYDERI, Dyfed. (1989)
5m S of Cardigan, off B4332 to W of junc with A478.
Meeting: Tivyside.
SF: 15-18. LH 2¼ circs. 8F; 19J; 2od (8/16). T: 6min 18.3s.
Undulating pear-shaped course of less than three miles; portable fences. Horses race uphill to farthest point and downhill back to spectators; can become very heavy (for horses and spectators) at early season meetings. Judge stands on back of a car very near line. Best viewing from bank on outside of course near finish, but 5(13)th not visible. Access along rough stone road; parking can be distant from action when course is boggy — when ground is firm enough parking is on inside of course closer to action. A cold windy (and for 2000 an additional bonus of horizontal rain) spot on hillside, but scenic, and delightfully informal atmosphere. There are better toilets in most Third World countries and long overdue a visit by SPECS (Society of Prevention of Enduring Cruelty to Spectators) who would undoubtedly close it down straight away.
Riders: *Miss P. Jones 13, D. Jones 9, J. Jukes 7, E. Williams 7, J. Keen 5, T. Vaughan 2, P. Hamer 2, Miss F. Wilson 2, M. Lewis 2, J. Tudor 2, J. Price 2, G. Lewis 2, A. Price 2.*

PARHAM, Sussex. (1953)
Nr A283, 4m SE of Pulborough, 1m W of Storrington.
Meetings: Crawley & Horsham; Chiddingfold, Leconfield & Cowdray.
SF: 16-24. RH 2¼ circs. 8F; 18J; 2od (4/12). T: 6min 59.8s.
Slightly undulating oval stayers course of 3m2f; slight rise before post; 4 well-built portable fences. Can be taxing in early season. Car access and exits good. Viewing good, most of course can be seen from hill above finish. Bookies very competitive.
Riders: *P. Hacking 8, J. Van Praagh 4, Miss C. Benstead 3, D. Dunsdon 3, T. Hills 2, P. York 2, Miss S. Gladders 2, Miss J. Grant 2, Miss H. Irving 2, Miss C. Grissell 2, J. Hawksfield 2, H. Dunlop 2, D. Robinson 2, C. Gordon 2, B. Hitchcott 2, A. Welsh 2, A. Hickman 2.*

PAXFORD, Glos. (1997)
2m E of Chipping Campden between B4035 and B4479.
Meeting: North Cotswold.
SF: 18-20-22. LH 2 circs. 8F; 18J; 2od (6/14). T: 6min 27.2s.
Level roughly oval shaped course, but with slight downhill run to fence 3(11) and uphill after 8(16)th; start is at entrance to home straight; short run-in. Horses need to be in contention at the third last to maintain position while negotiating bend into home straight. Viewing is excellent from bank alongside finishing straight. Facilities compact with paddock adjacent to course. Permanent building now provides accommodation for changing rooms, declarations office, sponsor's reception area, etc, all under one roof. Wide downhill entrance and no problems despite bumper crowd.
Riders: *Julian Pritchard 7, E. Walker 4, Miss A. Dare 3, A. Martin 2.*

PENSHURST, Kent. (1977)
3m SW of Penshurst, W of B2188, well sign-posted. (12m Exit 5, M25).
Meetings: Old Surrey & Burstow and West Kent (April and May)
SF: 18-20. LH 2½ circs. 7F; 18J; 2od (6/13). T: 6min 55.7s.
Undulating roughly rectangular course with testing uphill finish; two sharp bends into and out of
bottom straight (can be slippery); portable fences small and soft; only one sited in finishing straight;
drains well except on lower stretches which can be heavy. No car parking problems. Viewing poor
(best spot is very distant from finish) and start and finish difficult to see.
Riders: *P. Hacking 5, Mrs E. Coveney 5, Miss S. Gladders 5, T. Hills 3, P. York 3, P. Bull 3,
D. Dunsdon 3, T. Underwood 2, Stuart Robinson 2, P. Blagg 2, Miss C. Holliday 2, Matt Jones 2,
D. Robinson 2, D. Page 2, D. Dennis 2, C. Gordon 2, A. Warr 2.*

*PLATE 160   1297 Banwen Miners Ladies Open: The ladies have their numbered places for the
toilet queue at Pantreclwydau (the four numbers on the right are presumably the current
occupants); the numberboard man goes through the motions*   PHOTO: Catriona Edwards

PENTRECLWYDAU, West Glamorgan. (1999)
Nr A465, midway between Neath and Merthyr Tydfil.
Meeting: Banwen Miners.
SF: 16-19. LH 2 circs. 7F; 18J; od (7/14). T: 6min 25.3s.
Flat galloping course which continues to meet with approval from most owners and trainers,
though the facilities for spectators are not ideal. Viewing is reasonable although not helped by
hedges and trees. The course has a boggy patch between 2 out and the final fence. Plenty of
runners and has the scope to be a useful addition to the Welsh scene. Parking now more central,
but the toilets remain a total disgrace. There were a mere 10 Portaloos for a huge crowd, and as in
'99 by the end of the day any available hedge was used. The lady announcer started promisingly
with a charming welcome in Welsh, but her subsequent announcements were hopelessly inept.
There still remain many problems to be addressed before the 2001 renewal.
Riders: *T. Vaughan 4, J. Jukes 4, J. Keen 2, E. Williams 2.*

PEPER HAROW, Surrey. (1950)
Nr A3, 3m W of Godalming, 6m SW of Guildford. (15m from Exit 10, M25).
Meeting: Surrey Union.
SF: 16-18. LH 2½ circs. 8F; 18J; 2od (8/14). T: 6min 54.8s.
Flat very sharp course; horses always on turn; start and finish up centre of course; very sharp bend
causes horses to slow into finishing straight; fences well-made; going can vary greatly across
course. Ample car parking; access very good, exit very slow as no longer directly on to A3. Viewing
now worse than ever being obstructed by addition of a funfair inside course between fences
3(9/15) and 4(10/16). Stewards on a bus and consequently fences 5(11) and 6(12) are not visible.
Commentator has hydraulic hoist, but cannot see fence 6(12). Numberboard is now on edge of
plantation and fenced off from public so eliminating risk of injury. Attracts huge crowd of people-
watchers to whom racing is totally inconsequential (and often they're about right).
Riders: *T. Underwood 3, P. Bull 3, Miss J. Grant 3, P. Scouller 2, M. Gorman 2, D. Robinson 2,
D. Dunsdon 2, C. Gordon 2.*

RODMELL, East Sussex. (2000)
3m S of Lewes, off A27
Meetings: Southdown & Eridge (both meetings)
SF: 15 (Novice Riders)-17. LH 3 circs. 7F; 19J; 3od (6/12/18). T:6min 33.2s.
Undulating course just one mile round, very sharp bend leaving home straight; fairly stiff climb to
the last; good grass cover and could become an ice rink if wet. Fences small, but solid and well-
birched. Poor viewing from car park in the centre of course — marginally improved for the second
meeting — and much better from bank alongside back straight; no need for binoculars. A lovely
downland setting with excellent panoramic views of Lewes Castle and the surrounding countryside.
Entrance is down a narrow lane and through the farmyard, so exit can be slow.
Riders: *C. Gordon 2.*

SANDON, Staffs. (1982)
4m SE of Stone, nr A51. (Exit 14, M6).
Meetings: North Staffordshire; Meynell & South Staffordshire.
SF: 18-20 (Ladies)-22. RH 2¾ circs. 7F; 19J; 2od (6/13). T: 7min 09.9s.
Oval slightly undulating course; one sharp bend; portable fences of average size and build; attracts
good fields. Course was turned round to right-handed three years ago though the start and finish
remained in their old positions; the now uphill finish has done away with the old tricky downhill
last fence. Car parking good, but queues on exit. Viewing excellent from embankment along side of
course, apart from some foliage.
Riders: *A. Crow 9, G. Hanmer 6, A. Dalton 5, C. Stockton 4, Miss S. Sharratt 3, Miss S. Baxter 3,
S. Prior 2, R. Burton 2, Mrs M. Barlow 2, M. Prince 2, L. Stephens 2, C. Barlow 2.*

SIDDINGTON, Wilts. (1934*)
2m S of Cirencester, nr A419. (20m from Exit 13, M5 & Exit 15, M4).
Meeting: Vale of White Horse.
SF: 18-25. LH 2 circs. 10F; 18J; 2od (3/13). T: 6min 09.3s.
Tough almost flat course; several drop fences; last in back straight (after 14th) causes most
problems whilst final fences catches out tired horses; going often soft. Car parking good; entry/exit
no problem. Viewing is good from most parts of course, but finish some way away from best area.
Riders: *M. Rimell 3, S. Bush 2, Miss A. Dare 2, Julian Pritchard 2, J. Deutsch 2, E. Walker 2.*
* The Royal Agricultural College raced on a course at Siddington before World War 1

SOUTHWELL, Notts. (1994)
2m SE of town via private approach road from A612, handy to A1 and M1, or by rail to Rolleston
station which adjoins the course.
Meetings: Blankney, Grove & Rufford.
**SF: 17-18 (17) LH 2½ circs. 7F; (3m): 18J; 2od (5/12). T: 6min 52.1s. (2m4f): 15J; 2od (2/9).
T: 5min 49.0s.**

On NH turf course which is dead flat, regular oval. Fences are well-built and sited, and fair, but more demanding than many in the area, particularly the open ditch. Viewing unimpaired. Car parking available on all-weather track in front of the stands. All racecourse facilities available. Runners plentiful. Course now defunct with both Hunts moving to a new course at Nottingham.
Riders: S. Walker 9, G. Hanmer 6, A. Dalton 6, A. Crow 5, N. Wilson 4, P. Gee 3, Mrs J. Dawson 3, Julian Pritchard 3.

PLATE 161　　The paddock at Stafford Cross: The runners parade for the Mixed Open (Race 928); the course curves sharply behind the tents　　　　　　　　　　　　PHOTO: Tim Holt

STAFFORD CROSS, Devon. (1966*)
3m W of Seaton, nr A3052. (Exit 30, M5).
Meeting: Axe Vale Harriers.
SF: 15 (Novice Riders)-17. RH 2⅓ circs. 8F; 18J; 2od (3/11). T: 6min 07.3s.
Flat and sharp, but easy course favouring speed merchants (races often run flat out all the way); Fences now stiffer and up to regulation height. Good level car parks; easy access and exit. Viewing moderate (much better if you can somehow get off the ground!), best from slightly higher ground near 4/12th, but start and run to penultimate out of sight, as is top bend behind tents. Times indicate a short track.
Riders: L. Jefford 4, T. Mitchell 3, Miss P. Gundry 3, Miss P. Curling 2, Miss J. Cumings 2, J. Tizzard 2, A. Honeyball 2.
*Earlier course (opened 1947) was on seaward side of main road

STAINTON, Cleveland. (1995)
4m SW of Middlesborough at junction of A19 and A174, entrance off A174.
Meeting: Cleveland.
SF: 18-20. RH. 2¾ circs. 7F; 20J; 2od (7/14). T: 6min 17.3s.
Gently undulating sharp course on patchy ground. Portable fences. Facilities including paddock inside the course, and fairly good viewing from opposite finish, but commentary almost inaudible from there. Electronic number board — but then racegoers at some major venues have to put up

with their inadequacies. Judge's stand too near line making his job more difficult.

Riders: *S. Swiers 4, N. Wilson 2, N. Tutty 2, N. Smith 2, Mrs L. Ward 2, Miss R. Clark 2, C. Storey 2.*

ST HILARY, Glamorgan. (1970)
2m SE of Cowbridge, nr A48. (5m Exit 34, M4).
Meeting: Glamorgan.
SF: 15-20. RH 2¼ circs. 8F; 19J; 2od (5/13). T: 6min 49.5s.

Flat sharp course; bend near finish and short run-in does not favour late finisher; fences badly in decline, include one drop fence (jumped twice). Car parking satisfactory, exits get congested. Viewing excellent from hill overlooking course, but some of the action rather distant. State of going is extremely unpredictable — stretches of firm and bottomless in '99. An archetypal Welsh course, and exists courtesy of the local farmer, who charges no rent for racing over his land, but it is working farm so there are growing crops and a long stretch of plough in the back straight. Watch the horse's jaws drop in horror as they enter it, and the blessed relief when they finally emerge. Quite extraordinary. It couldn't last, and the last meeting was held here in 2000, and is now defunct.

Riders: *Miss P. Jones 4, J. Jukes 4, C. Williams 3, R. Jones 2, N. Jones 2, J. Price 2, D. Hughes 2.*

STON EASTON, Somerset. (1999)
8m N of Shepton Mallet, alongside A37.
Meeting: Mendip Farmers.
SF: 16-18 (14). RH 2½ circs. 7F; (3m) 18J; 2od (6/13). T: 6min 37.5s. (2m4f) 15J;2od (3/10). T: 5min 15.3s.

Fairly sharp undulating course with reverse bend between fences 2(9/16) and 3(10/17), uphill through finish and downhill through starting area and back straight. Fences portable, but proved flimsy and very easy to break in 2000 — one race had no less than four jumps missing! Car parking satisfactory, but viewing is not good — a little reminiscent of the old Nedge course — it being impossible to see the last two fences and run-in once more than three people arrive (a great pity as atmosphere very friendly and attracts big crowd, top horses and good fields).

Riders: *Miss P. Gundry 5, S. Stronge 2, A. Honeyball 2.*

TABLEY, Cheshire. (1997)
1½m W of Knutsford between A556 and M6 (use Exit 19).
Meeting: Cheshire Forest.
SF: 18-22. RH 2¾ circs. 7F; 19J; 2od (6/13). T: 6min 26.1s.

Flat, sharpish rectangular course about ½m from old course at Sudlow Farm; all portable fences, those in back straight come close together, then long run between 3rd and 4th; run-in is 130yds. Access/exit OK. Viewing poor (too flat) — best in centre. Very large crowd causes congestion around betting ring which is too close to paddock. Lovely setting in parkland in front of Tabley Hall, the Palladian mansion which was the seat of the Leicester family for 700 years.

Riders: *C. Stockton 5, Mrs C. Ford 3, R. Burton 2, J.R. Barlow 2, G. Hanmer 2, D. Coates 2.*

THORPE LODGE, Notts. (1976)
4m SW of Newark-on-Trent, nr A46. 5m from A1.
Meetings: South Notts; Midlands Area Club.
SF: 16-18 (Ladies)-20. LH 2½ circs. 7F; 19J; 2od (6/13). T: 6min 47.6s.

Flat almost square course; providing a fair test, but first bend is sharp and horses often slip. Action has been taken to correct outward slope on bend after penultimate. Gap between 17th and 18th fences can be long, but positioning of latter may vary by 100 yards; winners usually in contention 3 out. All portable fences, firm and consistent. Car parking good, one entrance/exit, but traffic flows well. Viewing excellent from slope overlooking finishing straight. Good betting market even on Bank Holiday.

Riders: S. Walker 6, M. Mackley 4, Julian Pritchard 4, G. Hanmer 4, Miss C. Spearing 3, B. Foster 3, R. Barrett 2, R. Armson 2, P. Gee 2, M. Hewitt 2, J. Turcan 2, J. Tarry 2, D. Crossland 2, A. Woodward 2.

TRANWELL, Northumberland. (1967)
3m SW of Morpeth, nr B6524. Handy to A1.
Meeting: Morpeth.
SF: 18-22. LH 2 circs. 9F; (3m) 18J; 2od (7/16). T: 6min 21.4s. (2m4f) 15J; 2od (4/13).
T: 5min 26.0s.
Mainly flat galloping course with slight uphill finish. Good covering of grass. Excellent car parking on runways of old airfield; good access and exits. Good viewing from bank in centre of course, but finish cannot be judged from there. Judges stand right against the line. 180 yard run-in. The weather was incredibly dreary and dismal in 2000 and the commentator matched the mood perfectly.
Riders: Mrs V. Jackson 7, Miss P. Robson 5, T. Scott 4, P. Craggs 4, J. Walton 4, N. Wilson 3, C. Storey 3, R. Morgan 2, P. Johnson 2, Miss N. Stirling 2, Miss D. Laidlaw 2, Miss C. Hall 2.

TREBUDANNON, Cornwall. (2000)
5m E of Newquay, nr A39
Meetings: Four Burrow; South Cornwall (transferred from Great Trethew)
SF: 14-16. LH 2¾ circs. 7F; 20J (for South Cornwall); 3od (4/11/18). T: 6min 13.5s.
Fairly flat course with slight rise towards final bend; all portable jumps. Compact layout, with paddock bigger than at Cheltenham! Excellent viewing from hillside overlooking home straight. Opening Four Burrow meeting was abandoned after just three races due to waterlogged course. Designed to have eight fences and 19 jumps, but no races at the first meeting had more than 16 jumps because of the state of the ground (details given above relate to the later meeting). The most westerly course in England.
Riders: Miss T. Cave 2.

TWESELDOWN, Hants. (1949*)
3m W of Aldershot, 6m from M3 (Exit 4 or 5).
Meetings: Tweseldown Club; Thames Valley Club.
SF: 18-20 (Novice Riders)-22 (Club Members)-24. RH 2 circs. 9F; 19J; 2od (7/16) 2wj (5/14).
T: 6min 32.2s.
Gently undulating triangular course; uphill bend to last tests stamina when soft, but short-runners often win on good or firm; fences exemplary; sandy soil drains well, but can be wet at bottom near water jump; some old racecourse facilities including stables still available. Car parking excellent, access and exits good. Best viewing from central hill, but must keep on the move; trees and shrubs obscure much of racing, but view of last 2 fences and finish is excellent from stand (but other 10 furlongs totally invisible from there). Scheduled to hold a solitary meeting in 2001 — a far cry from the six meetings of just a few years ago!
Riders: S. Sporborg 4, P. Scouller 4, A. Wintle 4, R. Nuttall 3, J. Maxse 3, C. Bennett 3, B. Pollock 3, T. Underwood 2, T. McCarthy 2, S. Blackwell 2, R. Wakley 2, R. Forristal 2, R. Biddlecombe 2, Mrs A. Rucker 2, Miss P. Jones 2, Miss M. Hill 2, Miss A. Goschen 2, J. Connell 2, D. Dennis 2, A. Charles-Jones 2.
Tweseldown was a NH course from 1884 until 1932 and then the venue of several bona fide military meetings until they were absorbed into Point-to-Pointing in 1949

UMBERLEIGH, Devon. (1971)
Off the A377 at Chapelton, 5m SE Barnstaple.
Meeting: Torrington Farmers.
SF: 18 (Restricted)-20. LH 2¾ circs. 6F; 18J; 3od (4/10/16). T: 6min 30.7s.
Sharp course mostly on side of hill; first 4 fences close together on valley floor; 3rd is higher on landing side; stiff uphill climb after ditch to 5(11/17)th; long downhill run through finish and back to start takes it toll when ground is fast. Judges stand right on line. Facilities compact. Single

entrance/exit from narrow lane; most cars parked on inside of course. Viewing just about adequate from central hill, but necessary to move from one side to the other to see all action; panoramic view of last and run-in. Stages the season's finale and has an end of term atmosphere encouraged by the canned music played over the loudspeaker.
Riders: *Miss P. Curling 2, M. Miller 2, L. Jefford 2, C. Heard 2.*

UPPER SAPEY, Hereford & Worcs. (1984)
At Wolferlow, 6m N of Bromyard nr B4203 (15m W of Exits 5 & 6, M5).
Meeting: Clifton-on-Teme.
SF: 18-20-22. RH 2¼ circs. 8F; 18J; 2od (4/12). T: 6min 26.9s.
Very hilly course; long uphill climb from 3rd(11th) to 6(14)th and then sharp descent to 9(17)th; followed by sharp turn into home straight. Car parking and viewing satisfactory. Compact facilities. Racing is regularly of a low standard. Lacks atmosphere.
Riders: *Julian Pritchard 8, Miss A. Dare 6, A. Dalton 5, T. Stephenson 3, H. Wheeler 3, C. Stockton 2, A. Wintle 2.*

UPTON-ON-SEVERN, Worcs. (1909)
Nr the A38, 8m S of Worcester, handy to M5 & M50 (Exit 1).
Meeting: Croome and W. Warwicks.
SF: 18-22-25 (18). RH 1¾ circs. 10F. (3m) 18J; 2od (6/16). T: 6min 36.8s. (2m5f) 15J; 2od (3/13). T: 5min 21.0s.
Flat testing galloping riverside track; suits stayers; has a couple of sharp bends and vital to take a good line; firm, but well-sloped fences can catch out poor jumpers; sometimes soft patches even when rest is good to firm; improved almost beyond recognition in recent years with much work having been done to improve viewing and drainage. Parking is plentiful and easy; good entry and exits with proper roads on course. Viewing excellent from hill overlooking finish or from centre of course. Strong betting market.
Riders: *Julian Pritchard 13, M. Jackson 4, M. Harris 3, D. Mansell 3, T. Stephenson 2, S. Bush 2, R. Burton 2, Miss A. Dare 2, M. Rimell 2, H. Wheeler 2, A. Wintle 2, A. Phillips 2.*

VAUTERHILL, Devon (1995)
2m SW of Umberleigh, 10m S of Barnstaple, nr B3217.
Meeting: Stevenstone.
SF: 16-18. RH 2½ circs. 7F; 19J; 3od (3/10/17). T: 6min 48.3s.
Mainly flat, kidney shaped course; on the turn much of the way with left hand deviation immediately after start; slightly uphill run-in of only 135 yards. Portable fences. Run-throughs can become boggy in wet conditions. Single entrance/exit. Good viewing from a number of vantage points, compact layout. Signposted locally, but be prepared for a few miles of country lane — course is situated on quite exposed high ground with very scenic views of North Devon countryside. The course is contained within two separate fields, so the going can be variable.
Riders: *G. Penfold 5, N. Harris 3, Miss P. Curling 3, Miss J. Cumings 2, C. Heard 2, A. Holdsworth 2.*

WADEBRIDGE, Cornwall. (1986)
At Royal Cornwall Showground. 1m W of town nr A39.
Meetings: Western; North Cornwall.
SF: 14-16. LH 2½ circs. 8F; 18J; 2od (5/12). T: 6min 24.5s.
Dumbell-shaped course set on panoramic slope at edge of showground. First fence jumped only once from starting chute (adjacent to cemetery!). First six fences all on uphill gradient, long downhill run between fences 7 and 8. Last 2 fences and run-in are uphill. Has a section where the horses run across sand. Fences portable and quite soft. Course very well drained. Access, exit and car parking excellent. Viewing reasonable. Showground facilities. Bookies in large barn which can also serve as paddock in rough weather.

Riders: *L. Jefford 15, N. Harris 12, A. Farrant 9, Miss J. Cumings 8, J. Young 6, Miss S. Young 5, C. Heard 4, T. Mitchell 3, Miss P. Curling 3, Miss L. Blackford 3, J. Creighton 3, D. Stephens (Devon) 3.*

WESTON PARK, Shropshire. (1983)
4m NE of Shifnal, nr A5 and A41. (Exit 12, M6, or Exit 3, M54).
Meetings: Albrighton; West Shropshire.
SF: 18-22. LH 2¼ circs. 7F; 18J; 2od (5/12). T: 6min 54.8s.
Course is basically flat on old parkland; uphill climb after ditch and gentle descent to back straight; three permanent and four portable fences; short run-in and races usually decided by time last fence is reached. Entrance and exit to car parks on hard road so no problems even in the worst weather. Best viewing from inside of track opposite winning post. It is very leafy by the time the Albrighton stage their meeting.
Riders: *A. Crow 15, A. Dalton 12, R. Burton 5, G. Hanmer 3, T. Stephenson 2, R. Bevis 2, Miss P. Jones 2, Miss A. Dare 2, M. Worthington 2, J. Tarry 2, D. Barlow 2.*

WETHERBY, Yorks. (1972)
On NH course, nr A1 junc with A661 & A58.
Meetings: Bramham Moor; Badsworth.
SF: 18-20-22. LH 2¼ circs. 8F; 18J; 2od (4/12). T: 7min 13.2s.
Stayers course of 3m2f on inside of NH course; long pull up slightly rising ground on 250 yard run-in; does not drain well and ground can be rough when firm in late season; fences average size and build; NH course facilities available. Car parking very good — no problems. Excellent viewing from grandstand. Lacks a true Pointing atmosphere.
Riders: *S. Swiers 6, C. Mulhall 5, J. Tate 4, A. Dalton 4, R. Walmsley 3, Miss A. Deniel 3, A. Rebori 3, S. Walker 2, Richard Tate 2, R. Walford 2, R. Hartley 2, N. Wilson 2, N. Smith 2, Mrs F. Needham 2, Miss J. Priest 2, Miss J. Foster 2, G. Tuer 2, G. Hanmer 2, G. Brewer 2, D. Easterby 2, C. Wilson 2, C. Stockton 2.*

WHITTINGTON, Lancs. (1936)
2m SW of Kirkby Lonsdale on B6254, 8m from M6 (Exits 35 and 36).
Meetings: Vale of Lune; Holcombe Harriers.
SF: 18-23. LH 2¼ circs. 8F; 18J; 2od (8/16). T: 7min 02.9s.
Flat very testing 3m2f course on water meadows; 5(13)th fence has higher ground on landing side and causes problems, but very well-built fences; sharp bend after last on 300 yard run-in; going often good; attracts novice horses and riders though experienced jockeys have advantage. Car parking good; hard road access, downhill exit. Beautiful setting. Viewing excellent from steep bank above run-in though horses do go rather far away.
Riders: *Mrs C. Ford 8, R. Ford 7, D. Barlow 6, R. Bevis 3, N. Wilson 3, N. Bannister 3, Miss P. Robson 3, D. Coates 3.*

WHITWELL-ON-THE-HILL, Yorks. (1927)
Alongside A64, 6m SW of Malton, 10m NE of York.
Meeting: Middleton.
SF: 18-23-25 (18). RH 2 circs. 9F. (3m): 18J; 2od (2/11). T: 6min 29.5s. (2m4f): 15J; 1od (8). T: 5min 26.6s. (4m): 24J; 2od (8/17). T: 8min 50.3s.
Good galloping 3m1f out-and-out stayers course, mainly flat, but uphill to last fence; two sharp bends, one before last; the clay soil can become very heavy although much work has been done recently to improve drainage. Car parking good, exit downhill, but over rough ground. Viewing is excellent from adjacent slopes. Grimthorpe Cup is now a Mixed Open. Safety Factor high considering the tight bend before last.
Riders: *C. Mulhall 4, S. Swiers 3, N. Smith 3, T. Glass 2, P. Atkinson 2, N. Tutty 2, G. Brewer 2, D. Easterby 2.*

WHITWICK MANOR, Herefords. (1951)
At Newtown, 8m NE of Hereford nr junc of A417 and A4103. (Exit 2, M50).
Meeting: North Herefords.
SF: 18-24. LH 2 circs. 8F; 18J; 2od (7/15). T: 6min 51.6s.
Undulating stayers course; early season and always popular meeting; going can be heavy; fences
easy; huge fields. Only one access/exit so long queues. Good viewing from hill overlooking
paddock although trees obscure the action from four out until approaching two out. Wellies vital,
paddock and bookies area can become a morass. The most popular course in the country (certainly
with owners) and regularly tops the chart with its number of runners. Very well-organised.
Riders: *Julian Pritchard 10, A. Wintle 5, Miss A. Dare 4, A. Dalton 4, T. Stephenson 2,
Miss C. Spearing 2, M. Harris 2, D. Mansell 2, D. Barlow 2.*

WITTON CASTLE, Co. Durham. (1984)
5m W of Bishop Auckland nr A68, 12 miles from A1 (M).
Meetings: Zetland; Old Raby Hunt Club.
SF: 18-20-25. RH 2½ circs. 7F; 19J; 2od (6/13). T: 6min 21.6s.
Course is level, all grass, set in grounds of Witton Castle, runs around the lakes; good galloping
course. Car parking satisfactory; viewing excellent from bank below paddock. Going is often near
to good in May, and the atmosphere is friendly and informal.
Riders: *S. Swiers 10, Mrs F. Needham 4, D. Easterby 4, C. Mulhall 4, R. Tate 3, N. Tutty 3,
Miss P. Robson 3, S. Walker 2, N. Wilson 2, N. Smith 2, Mrs S. Grant 2, Miss A. Deniel 2,
L. McGrath 2, C. Wilson 2, C. Gibbon 2.*

WOLVERHAMPTON, Staffs. (1996)
On Racecourse 1m N of town, off A449.
Meeting: Wheatland.
SF: 16-18. LH 2⅔ circs. 7F; 19J; 3od (3/9/15). T: 6min 48.9s.
Flat elongated triangular course on turf outside of all-weather racecourse. First three fences close
together, first jumped only once. Full racecourse facilities except no number board so difficult to
obtain details of runners and riders. Slightly better atmosphere than at some other Point-to-Point
meetings on racecourses due to proximity of course to stands. Car parking permitted on all-
weather track.
Riders: *G. Hanmer 7, A. Crow 7, D. Barlow 3, C. Barlow 3, R. Burton 2, Miss S. Vickery 2,
Miss S. Baxter 2, Miss C. Burgess 2, C. Stockton 2.*

WOODFORD, Glos. (1946)
Nr A38, 15m N of Bristol (3m from exit 14, M5).
Meeting: Berkeley.
SF: 18-20-22. LH 2 circs. 10F; 19J; 2od (5/14). T: 6min 40.3s.
Course is flat, in water meadows; has one right-hand bend after 5th; seldom harder than good to
firm for late April/early May meeting so usually plenty of runners; and good quality; sharp bend
after 10th can be a problem; run-throughs at fences are narrow. Strong betting market. Panoramic
viewing from hill though horses disappear after 5(14)th and the next fence is out of sight; finish is
head-on which rather defeats the object. Hedges have been allowed to grow as part of Countryside
Stewardship Scheme and this has not improved matters, and generally does not look as good as it
did. Why not move the tents, bookies, etc to the sloping ground across the stream to the left of the
finish? It must be done!
Riders: *T. Mitchell 6, Miss A. Dare 6, Miss P. Gundry 3, T. Stephenson 2, A. Wintle 2.*

Champion Sires
* includes a deadheat

**Point-to-Points
and Hunter Chases**

1960	Trappeur II	18
1961	Domaha	23
1962	Whiteway	26
1963	Whiteway	20
1964	Whiteway*	25
1965	Whiteway	31
1966	Whiteway	34
1967	Vulgan	21
1968	Exodus	22
1969	Exodus	20
	Vulgan	20
1970	Spiritus	24
1971	Spiritus	27
1972	Fortina	20

1973	Rose Knight	21
	Vulgan	21
1974	Fortina	21
	Romany Air	21
1975	Even Money	25
1976	Indian Ruler	19
1977	Spartan General	39
1978	Spartan General	43
1979	Spartan General	68
1980	Spartan General	34
1981	Spartan General	39
1982	Spartan General	29
1983	Spartan General	43
1984	Spartan General	30
1985	Spartan General	28
1986	Spartan General	32

1987	Menelek	24
1988	Deep Run	27
1989	New Member	28
1990	New Member	23
1991	Pony Express	30
1992	New Member	25
1993	Sunyboy	32
1994	Celtic Cone	34
1995	Strong Gale	32
1996	Strong Gale	33

Point-to-Points only

1997	Strong Gale	58
1998	Strong Gale	35
1999	Strong Gale	60
2000	Phardante (FR)*	38

Leading Point-to-Point Sires 2000
* includes a deadheat

1 PHARDANTE (FR) *38
b. 1982 (Pharly FR - Pallante)
- died in 1998

Pharare (IRE)	5
Black Dante (IRE)	2
Dunethna (IRE)	2
Pharmistice (IRE)	2
Philtre (IRE)	2
Roly Poly (IRE)	2
Ruperts Choice (IRE)	2
Ardnut	1
Azzante (IRE)	1
Ballyharry (IRE)	1
Bonny Rigg (IRE)	1
Brodante King (IRE)	1
Conquer (IRE)	1
Dante's Gold (IRE)	1
Distant-Port (IRE)	1
Dunsfold Dazzler	1
Far From Perfect (IRE)	1
Freestyler (IRE)	1
Friends Of Bernard (IRE)	1
Missed Call (IRE)	1
More People (IRE)	1
Noddadante (IRE)	1
Phar From Chance	1
Phar Lord (IRE)	1

Pharlindo (IRE)	1
Pharpen (IRE)	1
Pharstar (IRE)	1
Will Hill (IRE)	1

2 ROSELIER (FR) 35
gr. 1973 (Misti IV - Peace Rose)
- died in 1998

Hatcham Boy (IRE)	4
Imperial Dawn (IRE)	4
Mine's A Gin (IRE)	3
Weak Moment (IRE)	3
Wejem (IRE)	3
Aly Daley (IRE)	2
Bankhead (IRE)	2
Billie's Mate (IRE)	2
Bright Approach (IRE)	2
Burgundy Bob (IRE)	2
Archer (IRE)	1
Barton Bog (IRE)	1
Cloudy Creek (IRE)	1
Curracloe Rose (IRE)	1
Mister Trick (IRE)	1
Rob Mine (IRE)	1
Royal Banker (IRE)	1
The Happy Monarch (IRE)	1

3 STRONG GALE **34**
br. 1975 (Lord Gayle (USA) f Sterntau)
- died in 1994
Spring Gale (IRE) 5
Dawn Alert (IRE)..4
Belvento (IRE) 3
Do It Once (IRE)..2
Fair Wind (IRE) 2
Roman Gale (IRE) 2
Strong Medicine 2
Ballyhannon (IRE) 1
Camp Bank 1
Cebu Gale (IRE)...1
Celtic Who (IRE)..1
Chill Factor 1
Donnegale (IRE) 1
Lusty Light 1
Miss Gale (IRE)..1
Namron (IRE)..1
Peacemaker (IRE).......................................1
Philelwyn (IRE)..1
Rossell Island (IRE) 1
Stormy Words 1
Strong Chairman (IRE)................................1

4 THE PARSON **26**
b. 1968 (Aureole - Bracey Bridge)
- died in 1990
Butler John (IRE) 6
Rectory Garden (IRE) 5
Cracking Idea (IRE) 4
The Crazy Bishop (IRE) 3
Gillan Cove (IRE)..2
Midnight Service (IRE) 2
Monks Soham (IRE)....................................2
Lisaleen Wren (IRE) 1
Minella Gold (IRE)......................................1

5 CARLINGFORD CASTLE **24**
ch. 1980 (Le Bavard FR - Rachel Ruysch) -
stands at Walton Fields Stud, Church Lane,
Grimston, Melton Mowbray, Leics. LE14
3BY. (Tel: 01664 812298)
Castle Folly (IRE) 3
Bally Wirral (IRE) 2
Castle Shelley (IRE).....................................2
My Wee Man (IRE) 2
Well Ted (IRE) 2
Alpine Castle (IRE)......................................1
Arfer Mole (IRE) 1
Big Seamus (IRE) 1
Claret And Blue..1
Exemplar (IRE) 1
Fisherman Jack 1
Howsyourluck (IRE) 1
Ishereal (IRE)...1
Little Vera 1
Luvly Bubbly 1
Susies Melody (IRE) 1
The Criosra (IRE) 1
White Smoke (IRE) 1

6 ARCTIC LORD **20**
b/br. 1980 (Lord Gayle USA - Arctic
Chimes) - stands at Anngrove Stud,
Mountmellick, Co Laois, Ireland
Wibbley Wobbley..4
Ball In The Net...3
Noble Hymn 2
Sir Frosty 2
The Croppy Boy 2
Cool Wager 1
Kerrisdale..1
Knight Of Passion 1
Playlord 1
Sacrifice..1
Tricky Trevor (IRE) 1
Twotensforafive 1

7 MANDALUS **19**
b/br. 1974 (Mandamus - Laminate)
- died in 1997
Dean Deifir (IRE) 2
Poynder Park (IRE) 2
Square One (IRE) 2
The Archdeacon (IRE) 2
Dreamin George (IRE)..................................1
Harleidalus (IRE) 1
Hersilia (IRE)..1
Lost Your Marbles (IRE) 1
Mandril (IRE)...1
Manhattan Rainbow (IRE)............................1
Maximize (IRE) 1
Mister Spectator (IRE) 1
Our Man Flin (IRE) 1
Paddy For Paddy (IRE) 1
River Mandate..1

7 OVER THE RIVER (FR) **19**
ch. 1974 (Luthier - Medenine FR)
- stands at Garryrichard Stud, Foulksmills,
Co. Wexford, Ireland
La Riviera (IRE)...3
Calleva Star (IRE)..2
Forbidden Waters (IRE) 2
Miss O'Grady (IRE) 2
Newby End (IRE) 2
River Swilley (IRE) 2
Encima Del Rio (IRE) 1
Fair Crossing 1
Ferryhill (IRE) 1
High Expectations (IRE)...............................1
Secret Streams (IRE) 1
Travel Safely (IRE) 1

7 ROYAL FOUNTAIN 19
br. 1977 (Royalty - Fountain)
*- stands at Romany Stud, Kirkley West
Thorn, Ponteland, Newcastle-upon-Tyne,
Northumberland. NE2 0AG.*
(Tel: 01661 825439)
Fintona Boy (IRE) 4
Garryspillane (IRE) 2
Inch Fountain (IRE) 2
Mr Pistachio (IRE) 2
Oboedire (IRE) 2
Roll With It (IRE) 1
Forest Fountain (IRE) 1
Mefein Boy (IRE) 1
Royal Dew (IRE) 1
Sparkling Cascade (IRE) 1
The Bandon Car (IRE) 1

7 SCALLYWAG* 19
gr. 1973 (Sea Hawk II - Scammell)
- died in 1995
Hearts Are Wild...3
We Move Earth..3
Red Rebel 2
Sally Scally 2
Sea Urchin 2
Arthur Henry..1
Bridge Man 1
Cassia Green...1
Fair Ally 1
One Boy 1
Teal Bay 1
Uncle Tom 1

11 SUPREME LEADER..........................18
*b. 1982 (Bustino - Princess Zena) - stands
at Grange Stud, Fermoy, Co Cork, Ireland*
Cream Supreme (IRE)..................................2
Evan's Collier Boy (IRE)...............................2
Absent Citizen (IRE)....................................1
Baby Whale (IRE) 1
Caught At Dawn (IRE).................................1
Charlie Keay (IRE).......................................1
Galaroi (IRE) 1
General Jackie (IRE).....................................1
Happen To Make It (IRE) 1
Hazy Sea (IRE) 1
Inch Cross (IRE)1
La Emni (IRE)..1
Mags Super Toi (IRE)...................................1
Martha Leader (IRE)....................................1
Oisin Dubh (IRE) 1
Shining Leader (IRE)....................................1

12 GLACIAL STORM (USA) 17
b. 1985 (Arctic Tern USA - Hortensia FR)
*- stands at The Beeches, Tallow,
Co Waterford, Ireland.*
Dawn's Cognac (IRE) 5
Polar King (IRE) 3
Glacial Trial (IRE) 2
Cold Snap (IRE) 1
Hobnob (IRE) 1
Mick Mackie (IRE) 1
Minino (IRE)...1
Sister Kit (IRE) 1
Tudor Lodge (IRE) 1
Winters Tale (IRE) 1

13 LE BAVARD (FR)..............................16
ch. 1970 (Devon III - Lueur Doree)
- died in 1995
Rip Van Winkle 4
Ardbei (IRE)..2
Fordstown (IRE) 2
Bachelor-Carrasco (IRE) 1
Bavard Dieu (IRE) 1
Coming Through (IRE).................................1
Native Rambler (IRE) 1
Northern Yarn (IRE) 1
Ole Gunnar (IRE)...1
Sweet Talker (IRE) 1
Talkalot (IRE)..1

14 TOWN AND COUNTRY...................15
b. 1974 (Town Crier - First Huntress)
- died in 1991
Glevum..6
Village Copper 4
Fleet Mill 3
Badger Beer 1
Commuter Country 1
Country Barle 1

15 GILDORAN.....................................14
*b. 1980 (Rheingold - Durtal - stands at
Conduit Farm Stud, Churchill, Oxon.
OX7 6NH. (Tel: 01608 658274)*
Gildrom 3
Gillone 3
Key Debate 3
Ambersam 1
Colonels Hatch 1
Le Cabro D'Or 1
Tod's Brother..1
Wonford Boy..1

15 MISTER LORD (USA)..............14
b. 1979 (Sir Ivor - Forest Friend)
- stands at Clongeel Stud, Boherbue,
Mallow, Co. Cork, Ireland
Lord Harry (IRE)................................4
The Hobbit (IRE)...............................2
Alstack (IRE)......................................1
Ard Na Carrig (IRE)...........................1
Final Analysis (IRE)...........................1
Gallant Lord (IRE).............................1
Hazel Reilly (IRE)...............................1
Lady Nevada (IRE).............................1
Lord Levi (IRE)...................................1
Sagaville (IRE)....................................1

15 RAKAPOSHI KING..............14
b. 1982 (Bustino - Supper Time) - stands at
Shade Oak Stud, Bagley, Ellesmere,
Shropshire. SY12 9BY (Tel: 01939 270516)
Okeford (IRE)....................................2
Royal Estate......................................2
Trivial (IRE)..2
Cherry Gold......................................1
Cradle Mountain..............................1
Hamish..1
Jobsagoodun.....................................1
Look In The Mirror............................1
Royal Chip...1
Sands Point.......................................1
Tiger King..1

18 ARDROSS..............................13
b. 1976 (Run The Gantlet USA
- Le Melody) - died in 1994
Ardeal...3
Gemini Mist.......................................2
No Loss..2
Rossaleen..2
Scarlett O'Hara..................................2
Melody Princess.................................1
Murphys Way.....................................1

18 BARON BLAKENEY................13
gr. 1977 (Blakeney - Teleflora)
- stands at Sapperton House Stud, Tallow,
Co Waterford, Ireland
Catchword..3
Brown Robber...................................2
Noah..2
Arble March.......................................1
Baron Allfours...................................1
Bolshie Baron....................................1
Hagon Beck.......................................1
Jacob's Wife.......................................1
Temple Garth.....................................1

18 BUCKSKIN (FR)....................13
b. 1973 (Yelapa (FR) - Bete A Bon Dieu)
- died in 1995
Jojo...2
Play Poker (IRE).................................2
Whitegates Willie...............................2
Bucket Of Gold..................................1
Bucks View (IRE)...............................1
Calipo Bello (IRE)..............................1
Dram Hurler (IRE)..............................1
Prince Buck (IRE)...............................1
Turning Trix..1
Uncle Buck (IRE)................................1

18 GOOD THYNE (USA)............13
b. 1977 (Herbager - Foreseer USA)
- stands at Glenview Stud, Fermoy, Co.
Cork, Ireland. (Tel: 00 353 25 36322)
Cittadino...4
Shoemaker (IRE)................................2
Cool Yule (IRE)..................................1
Denney's Well (IRE)............................1
Libido..1
Mister Audi (IRE)...............................1
Mountain Thyne (IRE)........................1
Swincombe (IRE)...............................1
The Rural Dean (IRE).........................1

18 TORUS...................................13
b. 1976 (Ribero - Lighted Lamp USA)
- died in 1998
Rusnetto (IRE.....................................)3
Some Tourist (IRE).............................3
Barna Boy (IRE).................................2
Dennett Lough (IRE)..........................1
Hey Chief (IRE)..................................1
J'accuse (IRE).....................................1
Just One Question (IRE).....................1
Peafield (IRE).....................................1

23 BAD CONDUCT (USA)..........12
b. 1983 (Stalwart USA - White Lie)
- at stud in France
Balisteros (FR)....................................10
Fanion De Nourry (FR).......................2

23 BRUSH ASIDE (USA)............12
b. 1986 (Alleged USA - Top Twig)
- died in 1993
Jackson's Hole....................................4
Dark Challenger (IRE.........................)2
Persian Boy (IRE)...............................2
Ballyblack (IRE)..................................1
My Clean Sweep (IRE).......................1
Take The Brush (IRE)..........................1
The Earth Moved (IRE).......................1

23 DERRING ROSE 12
b. 1975 (Derring-Do - Bandi Rosa FR)
- died in 1997
Dont Tell The Wife...................................3
Parade Racer 3
Contradict..1
Dere Street 1
Dillon..1
Fair Farm Lad 1
Hidden Island 1
Mister Horatio...1

23 LANCASTRIAN 12
b. 1977 (Reform - Rosalie II)
- died in 1999
Coolvawn Lady (IRE)...............................4
Cardinals Folly (IRE) 1
Class Of Ninetytwo (IRE).........................1
Finnigan's Lot (IRE) 1
Gorsey Bank (IRE) 1
Icenfriendly (IRE)....................................1
Steel Rigg (IRE).......................................1
The Right Attitude (IRE)...........................1
Traceytown (IRE) 1

23 PRIMITIVE RISING (USA) 12
b. 1984 (Raise A Man USA - Periquito
USA) - stands at Louella Stud, Bardon
Grange, Hugglescote, Leics. LE6 2ST.
(Tel: 01530 813357)
Not So Prim 2
Cede Nullis 1
Inglerise..1
Just A Diamond 1
Ledburian...1
Mr Hook 1
Murton Heights 1
Oxendale 1
Primitive Charles 1
Primitive Man 1
Run For The Mill 1

28 BROADSWORD (USA) 1
b. 1977 (Ack Ack USA - Cutting USA)
- died in 2000
Achill Sound 2
Appley Dapply 1
Claymore Lad...1
Dancing Ranger 1
Dark Knight 1
Fencing Master 1
Fiery Jack 1
Lewesdon Manor 1
Military Man 1
Sabre King 1

28 IDIOT'S DELIGHT............................11
b. 1970 (Silly Season - Dolphinet)
- died in 1991
Bit Of An Idiot 2
Luney River 2
Shanavogh 2
Blank Cheque 1
Cherrynut...1
Outrageous Affair 1
Playing The Fool 1
Starlight Fool 1

30 BE MY NATIVE (USA) *10
b/br. 1979 (Our Native USA
- Witchy Woman USA) - died in 1997
One Of The Natives (IRE)..........................2
Gemolly (IRE)..1
Golf Land (IRE)..1
Little Native (IRE).....................................1
Native Alliance (IRE).................................1
Native Cannon (IRE) 1
Native Cove (IRE) 1
Romantic Native (IRE)..............................1
Wanstead (IRE)..1

30 DENEL (FR) 10
ch. 1979 (Devon III - Vernal FR)
- stands at Liatris Stud, Tullytubbert Road,
Moneyreagh, Co. Down
(Tel: 01232 448047)
Victoria's Boy (IRE)..................................2
Wise Prince (IRE).....................................2
Denarii (IRE) 1
Durnford Bay (IRE) 1
Lucky Joe (IRE) 1
Priestthorn (IRE) 1
Scrabo View (IRE) 1
The Hazel Harrier (IRE).............................1

30 GUNNER B 10
ch. 1974 (Royal Gunner
- Sweet Councillor) stands at Shade Oak
Stud, Bagley, Ellesmere, Salop. SY12 9BY.
(Tel: 01939 270235)
Gunner Boon 4
Deerhunter...1
Gangster 1
Gunner B Special 1
Ibex 1
Snapper 1
Tom's Prize 1

30 LAFONTAINE (USA) **10**
b. 1977 (Sham USA - Valya)
- stands in Ireland
Heathburn (IRE)..2
Highbridge (IRE)..2
Lakefield Rambler (IRE)..............................2
Fontaine Again (IRE) 1
Fountain Bank (IRE) 1
Jabiru (IRE)..1
Uncle Billy (IRE)...1

30 LIR **10**
b/br. 1977 (Lord Gayle USA - Mag USA) -
stands at Hilltown Farm, St Neot, Liskeard,
Cornwall. PL14 6PT.
Solomans Sister 3
Fossy Bear 2
Across The Card 1
Belitlir 1
Lirsleftover 1
Saint Joseph 1
The Ugly Duckling 1

30 MEADOWBROOK **10**
b. 1981 (Mill Reef USA - Hurlingham)
- stands at West Kington Stud, Church
Farm, West Kington, Chippenham, Wilts.
SN14 7Je. (Tel: 01249 782050)
Bow Tie...3
Meadowbank 2
Blyth Brook 1
Boris Brook 1
Boyup Brook 1
Claywalls 1
Roscoe Burn...1

30 MONTELIMAR (USA) **10**
b. 1981 (Alleged USA
- L'Extravagante CAN) - died in 1997
Montys Tag (IRE)..2
Cashel Green (IRE) 1
Fasgo (IRE) 1
Fast Lane (IRE)...1
Monty's Theme (IRE) 1
Mount Gay...1
Smackwater Jack (IRE)................................1
The Big Lad (IRE)...1
Tied For Time (IRE) 1

30 ORCHESTRA **10**
ch. 1974 (Tudor Music - Golden Moss)
- died in 1996
What A Fiddler (IRE)....................................3
Distinctive (IRE)...2
Brewery Lane (IRE)......................................1
Full Score (IRE)..1
Moore's Melodies (IRE) 1
Ryder Cup (IRE)...1
The Peeler (IRE)...1

30 OVAC (ITY) **10**
b. 1973 (Furibondo - Oratch)
- died in 1992
Copper Thistle (IRE) 8
Aeolian...1
Ann's Ambition..1

Sires of Point-to-Point Winners in 2000

* includes a deadheat

Abednego 1
Absalom 1
Accordion 1
Actinium (FR) 2
Afzal.................................5
Air Display (USA) 1
Air Trooper 1
Ala Hounak 2
Alias Smith (USA) 8
Alleged (USA) 2
Always Fair (USA) 1
Amazing Bust 3
Amerian (USA) 1
Andretti 3
Anshan 3
Aragon 1
Arapahos (FR) 5
Arcane (USA) 3
Arctic Lord 20
Ardross 13
Aristocracy 3
Asir.................................2
Astral Master 1
Astronef 1
Ayyabaan 2

Baby Turk 8
Backchat (USA) 1
Bad Conduct (USA) 12
Baldhu Cavalier.................1
Balinger...........................6
Ballacashtal (CAN) 1
Baron Blakeney 13
Bay Spirit.........................1
Be My Guest (USA) 1
Be My Native (USA)*........10
Bedford (USA) 1
Beyssac (FR) 1
Bikala 1
Black Minstrel 8
Blakelight 1
Blakeney 4
Blaze O'Gold (USA)...........5
Bluebird (USA) 1
Blushing Scribe (USA) 1
Bob Back (USA) 2
Bold Arrangement 1
Bold Fox 3
Boreen (FR) 2

Boyne Valley 3
Brando 1
Brevet 3
Broadsword (USA)............11
Brotherly (USA) 5
Brush Aside (USA) 12
Buckley 8
Buckskin (FR)...................13
Bustineto 1
Bustino 4
Button Bright (USA) 1
Bybicello..........................1

Caerleon (USA) 2
Callernish 4
Capitano 2
Captain Jason (NZ) 2
Captain Maverick (USA) 1
Cardinal Flower.................1
Carefree Dancer (USA) 1
Carlingford Castle............24
Castle Keep 3
Cataldi.............................5
Celio Rufo 4
Celtic Cone 1
Chaparly (FR) 2
Charmer 4
Cheval.............................2
Classic Memory.................1
Commanche Run...............9
Conquering Hero (USA) 1
Crash Course....................3
Crested Lark 8
Cruise Missile....................9
Cure The Blues (USA) 3
Cyrano De Bergerac 1

Damister (USA) 4
Dance Floor (USA) 1
Dancing Dissident (USA)....4
Dancing High.....................2
Danehill (USA) 1
Dara Monarch 1
Daring March 2
Darshaan..........................1
Decent Fellow 2
Deep Run.........................2
Deltic (USA) 1
Denel (FR) 10

Deploy 1
Derring Rose 12
Derrylin............................9
Distinctly North (USA)........1
Dominion..........................2
Don Enrico (USA)..............4
Don Tristan (USA)..............1
Don't Forget Me 2
Dortino............................5
Doubletour (USA)..............1
Down The Hatch 1
Dowsing (USA)..................1
Drumalis 1
Dry Dock 3
Dunbeath (USA) 2
Durgam (USA)...................1
Dutch Treat.......................1

El Conquistador* 7
Electric.............................4
Enryco Mieo......................2
Escapism (USA) 2
Eurobus 1
Executive Man...................2
Executive Perk 3
Exodal (USA) 3
Exorbitant.........................2

Fairy King (USA) 1
Faustus (USA) 1
Fearless Action (USA) 4
Feelings (FR) 1
Fijar Tango (FR)..................1
Fine Blade (USA) 4
Fine Blue 3
First Footman.....................1
First Norman (USA) 1
Fit To Fight (USA)...............1
Flair Path 1
Flower Robe......................1
Foolish Pleasure (USA) 1
Forty Niner (USA)..............2
Forzando 1
Fred Astaire (USA) 1
Funny Man 1
Furry Glen 2

Gabitat 2
Gala Performance (USA).....1

Parliament	2
Past Glories	1
Persian Bold	1
Persian Heights	3
Persian Mews	3
Petoski	4
Phardante (FR)*	38
Pharly (FR)	2
Pimpernels Tune	1
Pitpan	1
Pony Express	3
Posen (USA)	2
Pot D'Or (FR)	3
Pragmatic	1
Precocious	1
Presidium	3
Primitive Rising (USA)	12
Primo Dominie	4
Prince Of Peace	2
Push On	1
Queen's Soldier (USA)	1
R B Chesne	1
Ra Nova	2
Rainbow Quest (USA)	1
Rakaposhi King	14
Ranksborough	1
Rashar (USA)	1
Red Sunset	4
Regal Steel	1
Relief Pitcher	1
Relkino	2
Remainder Man	3
Remezzo	1
Respect	2
Revolutionary (USA)	2
Ring Bidder	1
Ring Of Ford	1
Riot Helmet	1
Rising	4
Risk Me (FR)	1
Riverhead (USA)	6
Riverman (USA)	3
Rock Hopper	1
Rolfe (USA)	3
Roman Empire	2
Romany Rye	1
Rontino	3
Roscoe Blake	4
Roselier (FR)	35
Royal Charter (FR)	1
Royal Fountain	19
Royal Match	2

Royal Vulcan	1
Rushmere	1
Rustingo	5
Rymer	6
Sadler's Wells (USA)	3
Safawan	2
Saher	1
Salluceva	5
Samhoi (USA)	1
Sandalay	1
Satco (FR)	1
Say Primula	5
Scallywag*	19
Scenic	1
Scorpio (FR)	3
Scottish Reel	4
Seclude (USA)	1
Seymour Hicks (FR)	2
Shaab	2
Shalford (IRE)	1
Shardari	2
Shareef Dancer (USA)	5
Sharifabad (IRE)	1
Sharp Charter	2
Sheer Grit	1
Shernazar	1
Shrivenham	2
Silly Prices	3
Skyliner	1
Soldier Rose	1
Solford (USA)	3
Sonnen Gold	1
Sousa	6
Southern Music	1
Soviet Lad (USA)	1
St Columbus	4
St Ninian	1
Stalker	1
Starjo (NZ)	2
State Diplomacy (USA)	1
Storm Bird (CAN)	3
Strong Gale	34
Sula Bula	3
Sulaafah (USA)	1
Sunley Builds	3
Sunyboy	1
Super Sunrise	4
Superlative	1
Superpower	1
Supreme Leader	18
Syrtos	3
Tale Quale	2

Taufan (USA)	1
Teamster	6
Teenoso (USA)	6
Teofane	2
The Bart (USA)	1
The Noble Player (USA)	2
The Parson	26
Then Again	2
Thornberry (USA)	1
Tidaro (USA)	4
Tigerwood	4
Timeless Times (USA)	1
Tina's Pet*	3
Tip Moss (FR)	1
Top Ville	1
Torenaga	1
Torus	13
Totem (USA)	1
Tout Ensemble	2
Town And Country	15
Trojan Fen	2
Tromeros	1
Trubisc (AUS)	3
True Song	9
Un Desperado (FR)	2
Un Numide (FR)	2
Uncle Pokey	2
Undulate (USA)	3
unknown	1
Viking (USA)	3
Vision (USA)	1
Vital Season	4
Waajib	3
Wakashan	1
War Hero	2
Weld	4
Weldnaas (USA)	1
Welsh Captain	1
Welsh Saint	1
Whistling Deer	2
White Mill	1
White Prince (USA)	8
Whitehall Bridge	1
Winter Words	1
Yashgan	3
Zaffaran (USA)	3
Zafonic (USA)	1
Zambrano	3

Champion Point-to-Point Riders

	GENTLEMEN			LADIES	
1946	A. Grantham	6	1946	Miss I. Croxon	4
	H. May	6		Miss K. Tatham-Warter	4
	T. Southern	6	1947	Miss A. Covell	5
	R. Turner	6		Miss M. Coke	5
1947	W. How	14	1948	Miss K. Tatham-Warter	4
1948	Maj P. Rawlings	11		Miss J. Brutton	4
1949	Maj G. Cunard	20	1949	Miss K. Tatham-Warter	7
1950	A. Hill	19	1950	Miss D. Brooke	8
1951	Maj G. Cunard	12	1951	Miss P. Rushton	9
1952	Maj G. Cunard	15	1952	Miss G. Moore	8
1953	Maj G. Cunard	13	1953	Miss G. Moore	9
1954	F. Ryall	13	1954	Miss J. Renfree	7
	J. Trevisick	13	1955	Miss J. Renfree	13
1955	J. Everitt	15	1956	Miss J. Renfree	11
1956	E. Greenway	12	1957	Mrs S. French	8
	F. Mathias	12		Miss J. Renfree	8
1957	Maj R. Ingall	14	1958	Miss D. Guilding	8
1958	R. Edwards	12		Miss J. Renfree	8
	N. Williams	12	1959	Mrs D. Coaker (nee Brooke)	12
1959	D. Wales	16	1960	Miss P. Tollit (nee Rushton)	9
1960	R. Edwards	14	1961	Miss F. Robarts	10
	F. Ryall	14	1962	Mrs P. Tollit (nee Rushton)	9
1961	J. Daniell	16	1963	Miss S. Rimell*	5
1962	A.E. Hill	12	1964	Mrs P. Tollit (nee Rushton)	10
1963	Maj G. Cunard	15	1965	Mrs P. Tollit (nee Rushton)	15
1964	Maj G. Cunard	22	1966	Miss U. Brander-Dunbar	10
1965	D. Tatlow	18	1967	Mrs P. Hinch	11
1966	D. Tatlow	25	1968	Miss S. Aston	15
1967	D. Tatlow	24	1969	Miss J. Turner	14
1968	D. Tatlow	18	1970	Miss S. Aston	14
1969	M. Bloom	19	1971	Miss S. Aston	14
1970	D. Turner	19	1972	Miss S. Aston	15
1971	R. Davies	29		Mrs P. Tollit (nee Rushton)	15
1972	R. Miller	21	1973	Mrs M. Forrest	17
1973	R. Miller	23	1974	Mrs J. Bothway (nee Turner)	20
1974	D. Turner	26	1975	Mrs J. Bothway (nee Turner)	17
1975	D. Turner	24	1976	Mrs J. Bothway (nee Turner)	17
1976	D. Turner	22	1977	Mrs J. Shepherd (nee Turner)	17
1977	D. Turner	29	1978	Mrs R. White	11
1978	J. Bryan	32	1979	Miss P. Fisher	10
1979	D. Turner	17	1980	Miss L. King	14
1980	I. McKie	20	1981	Miss L. King	14
	D. Turner	20	1982	Miss J. Pidgeon	18
1981	I. McKie	18	1983	Miss J. Pidgeon	18
1982	P. Greenall	24	1984	Miss M. Lingard	13
1983	J. Llewellyn	19		Miss J. Pidgeon	13
1984	D. Turner	20**	1985	Miss J. Pidgeon	18
	P. Greenall	19	1986	Miss A. Dare	19
1985	P. Greenall	23	1987	Miss A. Dare	17
1986	P. Greenall	28	1988	Mrs J. Litston	16
1987	M. Felton	26	1989	Miss L. Crow	15
1988	P. Scholfield	37	1990	Miss A. Dare	20
1989	M. Felton	26	1991	Miss A. Dare	26
1990	M. Felton	27	1992	Miss A. Dare	21
1991	J. Farthing	26	1993	Miss P. Curling	25
1992	R. Alner	31	1994	Miss P. Curling	35
1993	A. Crow	22	1995	Miss P. Curling	40
1994	N. Bloom	22	1996	Miss A. Dare	31
1995	A. Crow	30	1997	Miss S. Vickery	30
1996	J. Jukes	34	1998	Miss P. Jones	30
1997	Julian Pritchard	37	1999	Miss P. Jones	25
1998	A. Dalton	33	2000	Miss P. Gundry	30
	Julian Pritchard	33			
1999	Julian Pritchard	44			
2000	L. Jefford	42			

* 11 Ladies each had 5 winners - Miss Rimell had
the most 2nds
** included 2 walk-overs (one by arrangement)

Leading Post-War Point-to-Point Riders

Leading riders since the war in order of total winning rides.
(Accuracy is limited by the inadequacy of early records and wishful thinking)
* still race riding

David Turner	343	Charlie Macmillan	101
Alison Dare*	280	Kevin Anderson	100
John Llewellyn	270	Roy Edwards	100
Guy Cunard	268	Bob Woolley	99
Julian Pritchard*	242	George Barber	97
Michael Felton	225	Simon Crank	97
Polly Curling	220	Bob Davies	97
Frank Ryall	218	Dick Hunt	97
Grant Cann	217	Tim Moore	97
Robert Alner	211	David Stephens (Wales)*	97
Pip Jones*	200	Linda Blackford	96
Jimmy Tarry*	194	Stuart Jeanes	95
Richard Miller	178	Bertie Hill	94
Philip Scholfield	178	David Gibson	91
John Daniell	175	Fred Mathias	91
Josie Sheppard	173	Nick Bush	90
Alastair Crow*	186	Gary Hanmer*	90
Tim Mitchell*	185	William Wales*	90
Jamie Jukes*	181	Harry Wheeler	90
Pat Tollit	171	Tim Holland-Martin	89
Robert Hacking	170	Godfrey Maundrell*	88
Simon Andrews*	169	Jon Trice-Rolph*	85
John Sharp*	167	Robert Chugg	84
Peter Greenall	160	Damien Duggan	84
Ron Treloggen	157	Neil Harris*	84
Nigel Bloom*	151	Clive Storey*	84
Steve Brookshaw	148	Graham Macmillan	83
Paul Hacking*	148	Harry Elliott	82
Mike Bloom	145	Pip Fisher	82
Sue Horton	145	Richard Shepherd	82
Tim Rooney*	144	Alistair Ulyet	81
Paul Hamer*	142	Alistair Charlton	80
Bertie Hill	136	Fizz Chown	80
Roger Guilding	135	John Dufosee	79
David Tatlow	133	John Hickman	79
Andrew Dalton*	130	Andrew Parker*	79
Peter Craggs*	129	Noel Wilson*	79
Jill Dawson*	129	Malcolm Arthers	78
Tim Jones	129	Andrew Berry	78
Evan Williams*	129	R. Bloomfield	78
Shirley Vickery*	127	Nick Mitchell*	78
Jenny Pidgeon	126	Paul Taiano*	78
Justin Farthing	124	Henry Cowell	77
Michael Williams (Wales)	124	Tim McCarthy*	77
Mandy Hand*	121	Michael Miller*	77
Les Jefford*	121	Jimmy Frost	76
Dai Jones*	121	John Docker	75
Sheilagh French	119	Tom Greed*	75
Jo Davies*	117	Joe Price*	75
Chris Down	116	Mike Sowersby	75
Philip Scouller*	116	Bill Bryan	74
John Bryan	115	R. Cowell	74
Andrew Sansome*	114	Mary Crouch	74
Lucy Gibbon*	113	David Kinsella	74
Robin Greenway	113	Tommy Philby	74
Bill Jones	113	Ben Pollock*	74
Ian McKie	112	Simon Sporborg*	74
Pauline Robson*	111	George Turner	74
George Cooper*	110	Jonathan Tudor	73
Nigel Tutty*	110	Doreen Calder*	72
David Wales	110	Polly Gundry*	72
Tim Wilkin	109	Shan Morgan	72
Joey Newton	107	Philip Mathias	71
Dick Spencer	107	Bruce Warren	71
Robin Tate	107+	Bill Foulkes	70
Stephen Swiers*	104	Rupert Nuttall	70
Michael Williams (Devon)	103	Hunter Rowe	70
Tim Stephenson*	102		

Leading Riders 2000
Point-to-Point

GENTLEMEN

* winning Hunter Chase Rider 2000

Jockey	1st	2nd	3rd	Career Wins	Jockey	1st	2nd	3rd	Career Wins
L. Jefford *	42	19	9	121	J. Cook	8	2	10	10
Julian Pritchard *	28	29	18	242	J. Walton	7	11	6	65
J. Jukes *	23	17	8	181	J. Tarry	7	9	9	194
G. Hanmer	23	10	10	90	S. Joynes	7	9	3	12
C. Storey	21	18	7	84	M. Miller *	7	6	9	77
R. Burton *	20	16	11	63	C. Heard *	7	6	5	37
N. Mitchell *	19	16	9	78	G. Maundrell	7	5	4	88
N. Bloom *	18	11	7	151	N. Tutty	7	4	5	110
A. Dalton *	17	13	8	130	B. Foster	7	2	3	13
E. Williams	16	10	10	129	A. Evans	7	0	2	59
A. Crow *	16	10	4	186	C. Gordon *	6	13	3	67
R. Lawther	16	6	4	61	C. White	6	10	4	8
A. Wintle *	15	13	5	56	Richard Darke	6	9	12	41
T. Vaughan	14	11	10	24	S. Blackwell *	6	9	6	44
A. Honeyball *	14	8	10	29	S. Swiers *	6	6	2	104
T. Mitchell	14	5	10	185	B. Hitchcott *	6	4	2	10
C. Williams *	13	12	9	21	R. Biddlecombe	6	3	1	6
B. Pollock *	13	9	1	74	D. Dunsdon *	6	2	4	11
A. Price	13	7	7	51	M. Clayton	6	1	4	6
D. Alers-Hankey	12	14	7	31	S. Charlton	5	7	2	23
C. Ward-Thomas	12	6	1	41	A. Harvey *	5	6	4	17
R. Walford *	12	6	0	19	M. Rimell	5	6	3	33
A. Sansome	11	18	7	114	R. Armson	5	5	9	21
T. Stephenson	11	15	16	102	A. Robson	5	5	9	35
D. Easterby	11	6	2	34	A. Coe	5	4	10	45
D. Barlow	11	5	6	66	N. King *	5	4	5	31
T. Scudamore *	11	4	1	16	S.R. Andrews	5	3	5	169
R. Morgan *	11	3	5	30	W. Burnell	5	3	4	21
R. Hunnisett *	11	2	1	24	P. Hamer	5	3	3	142
A. Charles-Jones *	10	9	8	49	P. Taiano	5	3	2	78
C. Mulhall	10	7	8	42	S. Prior *	5	3	1	16
P. York *	9	14	10	30	S. Bush	5	2	4	40
R. Woollacott	9	9	17	12	R. Barrett *	5	2	3	14
R. Young	9	7	1	15	D. Robinson *	5	2	3	34
S. Sporborg	9	5	6	74	D. Dennis *	5	2	2	23
S. Morris *	9	5	4	25	J. Docker	5	2	0	24
M. Mackley	9	3	5	13	P. Scouller *	5	2	0	116
G. Brewer *	9	3	2	14	C. Wilson	5	1	1	37
L. Morgan *	8	7	3	14	A. Richardson	5	0	4	6
N. Harris	8	6	7	84	A. Hickman	5	0	3	53
M. Worthington	8	4	4	28					

LADIES

Jockey	1st	2nd	3rd	Career Wins
Miss P. Gundry *	30	12	11	72
Miss P. Jones	23	14	8	200
Miss P. Robson *	21	10	6	111
Miss J. Cumings	12	6	7	117
Miss T. Cave *	9	3	2	62
Miss A. Dare	8	2	3	280
Miss Z. Turner *	8	0	0	27
Mrs M. Hand	7	14	8	121
Miss C. Thomas	7	5	3	52
Miss O. Green	7	4	5	7
Miss L. Rowe	7	3	1	64
Miss C. Tizzard	7	3	1	7
Miss C. Spearing	7	2	1	27
Miss S. Young *	6	10	4	44
Mrs V. Jackson	6	7	4	45
Mrs G. d'Angibau	6	4	0	50
Miss F. Wilson *	6	1	5	11
Mrs F. Needham *	5	7	5	63
Mrs C. Ford	5	4	9	46
Miss L. Sweeting *	5	4	7	13
Miss H. Irving	5	1	2	45
Miss S. Vickery *	4	9	8	127
Miss M. Bremner	4	6	7	7
Miss S. Sharratt	4	4	2	16
Miss C. Grissell *	4	3	6	9
Miss J. Grant	4	3	3	19
Mrs J. Dawson	4	2	1	129
Mrs M. Barlow	4	0	3	7
Miss J. Wormall *	4	0	1	23
Mrs E. Coveney	3	6	4	33
Miss L. Allan	3	5	5	8
Miss T. Jackson	3	5	3	14
Miss E. Jones	3	3	1	11
Miss J. Congdon	3	2	2	5
Miss J. Foster *	3	2	0	7
Miss G. Hutchinson	3	0	2	11

HUNTER CHASES

* winning Point-to-Point Rider 2000

Jockey	1st	2nd	3rd	Career Wins
B. Pollock **	7	4	0	43
R. Burton **	6	5	2	13
G. Brewer **	5	0	0	5
B. Hitchcott **	4	3	4	4
A. Charles-Jones **	4	1	2	14
Mrs F. Needham **	4	1	1	16
D. Dunsdon **	4	0	1	4
W. Renwick **	3	6	3	3
F Windsor Clive **	3	3	1	4
Julian Pritchard **	3	2	4	19
P. York **	3	2	0	5
T. Glass **	3	0	2	4
M. Bradburne **	3	0	1	14
T. Doyle	3	0	1	3
A. Crow **	3	0	0	4
F. Hutsby **	3	0	0	5
M. Miller **	2	5	1	12
S. Morris **	2	2	1	3
Mrs T. Hill **	2	2	0	4
J. Jukes **	2	2	0	23
Miss J. Wormall **	2	2	0	2
Miss S. Young **	2	2	0	3
D. O'Meara	2	1	1	3
Miss S. Vickery **	2	1	1	16
K. Culligan	2	1	0	2
Miss L. Horner	2	1	0	2
Miss P. Gundry **	2	0	4	8
L. Jefford **	2	0	2	5
Mrs B. Sillars	2	0	1	3
G. Tuer **	2	0	1	4

Winning & Placed Point-to-Point Riders 2000

*Winning Hunter Chase Rider 2000
Cross-country races in italic

Rider	Rides	Wins	Winning and Placed Rides
T. Abbott	3	0	35^3, 211^3.
R. Abrahams	15	2	374^2, 504^2, 622^2, 870^3, (998), (1030), 1231^2, 1325^2, 1476^2.
M. Abrey	4	2	(238), (757).
D. Alers-Hankey	62	12	8^2, (71), (73), 140^3, 143^2, (198), (204), 207^3, (259), 260^2, 265^2, 352^3, (456), (559), (561), 653^2, 727^2, 928^2, (1016), 1096^2, 1138^3, 1140^2, 1240^2, 1241^3, 1375^2, 1376^2, 1470^2, (1472), 1516^2, (1565), 1597^3, (1608), 1650^3.
J. Alexander	11	2	110^3, 660^3, (714), (1117).
M. Alexander	1	0	1117^2.
Miss K. Allan	6	1	353^3, (640), 1551^2.
Miss L. Allan	28	3	50^2, 542^3, 544^3, 758^3, (769), 1009^2, 1011^2, 1074^2, (1217), 1219^2, 1418^3, (1423), 1589^3.
E. Andrewes	6	1	(1270).
Mrs C. Andrews	5	1	(1208).
S.R. Andrews	55	5	91^3, (98), 181^2, (233), (321), 323^3, (577), (578), 607^2, 609^3, 941^3, 942^3, 1036^2.
G. Armitage	4	0	909^3.
Miss A. Armitage	7	0	494^3.
R. Armson	50	5	49^3, 53^3, 115^2, (122), (367), (371), 412^3, (546), 547^3, (615), 867^2, 1008^2, 1073^2, 1216^3, 1291^2, 1414^2, 1503^3, 1507^3, 1584^3.
Mrs H. Arnold	7	1	170^2, (804), 1029^3.
R. Arnold	7	0	410^2.
P. Atkinson	27	2	169^3, 380^2, 398^2, 493^2, (500), 804^2, 908^2, 1001^3, 1031^3, (1159), 1162^2, 1329^2, 1348^3, 1475^3.
R. Atkinson	8	1	357^2, 521^2, (873), 927^3, 1238^3, 1306^3, 1552^2.
J. Attrill	1	1	(64).
A. Ayers	5	1	(935).
Mrs L. Baker	5	0	216^3, 985^2, 1170^2.
N. Bannister	8	0	171^3, 394^2, 495^2, 496^2, 623^2, 812^2.
M. Barber	14	1	(831).
G. Barfoot-Saunt	82	4	(206), 451^2, (635), 641^2, 898^2, 1019^2, 1099^3, (1190), 1273^2, (1360), 1493^2, 1494^2.
A. Barker	5	0	266^3.
A. Barlow	5	1	(1143).
C. Barlow	42	2	77^3, 292^3, 370^2, 529^3, 533^3, 570^3, (587), 591^2, 593^2, (1151).
D. Barlow	45	11	17^2, (80), 191^3, (193), (246), (292), (333), (338), (482), (575), (588), 750^3, 865^3, 866^2, 897^3, (1034), (1142), 1356^3, 1361^3, 1484^2, 1486^2, 1527^2.
J.R. Barlow	31	3	121^3, (810), 812^3, (964), (966), 1148^3, 1407^3.
Mrs M. Barlow	11	4	531^3, (590), (904), 991^3, (1066), 1199^3, (1525).
M. Barnard	7	0	769^3.
Miss H. Barnard	7	0	84^2, 417^2, 1377^3.
J. Barnes	70	3	61^3, 141^3, 212^3, 408^2, 455^3, 521^3, 524^2, 628^3, (631), 731^3, (888), 952^3, 954^2, 956^2, 1133^2, 1177^2, 1282^3, 1374^3, 1467^2, 1555^2, (1639), 1653^3.
Miss N. Barnes	5	0	1377^2.
Miss A. Barnett	17	1	(1048).
R. Barr	6	0	603^3.
R. Barrett *	45	5	93^2, (115), (123), (232), (441), (514), 788^3, 870^2, 1218^3, 1422^3.
Miss R. Barrow	19	0	816^2.
Miss M. Bartlett	7	0	594^3.
A. Bateman	24	1	63^2, 404^2, 639^3, 737^2, (1097), 1304^3.
L. Bates	12	1	133^2, (283), 396^2, 399^2, 627^2, 797^3.
A. Bealby	16	3	(86), (172), 443^2, 691^2, (1264), 1265^3, 1588^2.
Miss S. Beddoes	2	1	1199^2, (1320).

Mrs J. Butler..............4   0   324³, 882².
Miss D. Calder............6   1   498³, (1118).
A. Campbell 3   1   (659).
S. Campion..................1   1   (47).
R. Carey.......................6   0   1198³.
C. Carman 4   2   (941), (1038), 1285².
M. Carter 4   0   1087³.
J. Case 5   2   (1555), (1594).
Miss T. Cave * 36   9   (164), 314², (638), 725³, (1041), (1101), (1308), (1309), (1386),
                                       (1389), (1549), 1561³, 1640³, 1676².

E. Chanin...................6   0   852³, 1047³.
G. Chanter..................4   0   259³.
A. Charles-Jones *.....80 10   6², 14², 22³, 32², 60², 74², (106), (260), 264³, (290), 306², 309²,
                                       471³, 472³, 477³, 633², (722), 729², (954), (1099), (1138), (1140),
                                       1205³, (1435), 1439³, 1594², (1598).

S. Charlton................53   5   51², 134², 138³, (234), (235), 377², 436², (443), 1003², (1229),
                                       1235², (1347), 1349³, 1351².
M. Chatterton 13   0   234³, 443³, 793³, 1072³, 1269³.
P. Chinery 17   0   180³, 1666³.
S. Claisse 6   1   (767).
Miss R. Clark 30   1   134³, 277², 397³, 692³, 804³, (806), 809², 1477².
Miss Rachel Clark 18   1   (52), 135³, 505³, 506³, 998³, 1232².
Miss T. Clark 13   0   525³, 813³, 962², 1152², (1199), 1253³, 1320².
R. Clark 31   2   50³, 276², 277³, (378), 503², (805), 1003³, 1030³.
B. Clarke.....................4   0   (211).
T. Clarkson..................6   0   165², 637³, 1044³.
M. Clayton...............34   6   108³, (418), 500³, 975³, (977), (1083), 1160³, (1425), 1427²,
                                       (1480), (1578).

F Windsor Clive * 18   1   445³, 450³, 491², 666³, (673), 1089³, 1093³.
D. Coates.....................8   1   283², 375³, 960², (1149), 1365³.
S. Cochrane 2   0   1071³.
A. Cockerill 2   0   430³.
A. Coe 64   5   18³, 92³, 97², 551³, 605³, 759², 760³, 773³, (775), (839), 845³,
                                       1038³, 1039², (1110), 1112³, 1114³, (1116), 1185², (1382).
J. Cole.......................12   0   1641³.
T. Cole.......................14   3   (312), 1390², (1522), (1641).
Miss L. Collins 4   0   220³.
Miss J. Congdon........18   3   66³, (310), 535², 636³, 852³, (1175), (1670).
D. Cook 32   2   236², (242), 549³, 553², 775³, 844², (1180), 1184².
J. Cook.......................55   8   (207), 478³, (740), 741³, 746², (837), 899³, (1055), 1090³, (1091),
                                       1406³, 1411³, 1453³, 1454², 1456³, (1571), (1572), (1611), 1657³,
                                       1660³.

Miss K. Cook 12   0   102³, 1560³.
Miss M. Coombe 3   1   326², (458).
G. Cooper..................24   3   318², 413², (609), 761², 843², 940², 1111³, (1184), (1378).
R. Cooper 28   3   340², 341², 479³, 484³, 612³, 891³, (993), (994), (1093), 1271³.
R. Cope *...................43   2   7², 194³, (372), 1146³, 1419², 1594³, (1668).
J. Cornwall................13   1   20³, (87), 871³.
Mrs E. Coveney.........33   3   (28), 95³, 177³, 304², 307², (772), 885², 982², 1104², 1289³,
                                       (1397), 1511³, 1587².

Miss L. Cowan 1   1   (1292).
A. Cowie 1   0   748³.
M. Cowley................26   0   792³, 1442³.
P. Cowley..................25   3   (57), 77², 247², (248), 250³, 578³, 670², (1242), 1393³.
Mrs C. Cox 8   2   107³, 497³, (719), (1162).
S. Craddock 17   1   157², 406³, 534³, (853), 854³.
D. Crosse 19   1   211², (250), 887², 1060², 1279², 1394³, 1482².
A. Crow * 46   16   (75), 116², (117), 119³, 176², 178², 293³, (294), (369), (370), (530),
                                       (565), (591), 592³, (691), 779², (781), 782², (783), 814², (903),
                                       905², (961), 963², 966³, (1073), 1127², (1408), (1409), 1633².

Miss J. Cumings........46   12   66², (101), (201), 202², (407), (536), (557), 639², 725², (730), 851³,
                                       857², 930³, (1045), 1138², 1305³, (1369), 1370³, (1376), 1515³,
                                       (1562), (1566), (1652), 1673³, 1674³.

C. Cundall	14	0	393², 504³, 997², 1231³, 1349².
S. Currey	5	0	949³.
Miss R. Curtis	5	1	(33), 645³, 946³.
Mrs G. d'Angibau	13	6	95², (128), (240), 319², 608², (758), (827), (1113), 1183², (1380).
R. Dalgety	6	1	(1202).
A. Dalton *	70	17	16², 31³, 37², 138², (139), (293), 333³, (334), (336), 371², 402³, (437), 439², (533), 611³, 617³, 618², (703), (704), 796³, (859), 861², (905), 988², 989², 990³, (992), 1065², (1067), 1087², 1128³, 1254², 1317², 1323³, (1407), (1463), (1466), (1544).
Miss A. Dare	16	8	326³, 390³, 475², (613), 668³, (699), 860², (991), (1014), (1191), (1462), (1489), (1491).
Richard Darke	64	6	251³, 252³, 255³, 311², 534², 540³, (562), 652³, 656², (657), 658², 722², 730², 930², 934³, 970², 1048², 1175³, (1179), 1260³, 1261³, (1385), (1514), 1516³, 1519³, (1520), 1675³.
A. Davenhill	5	0	1124³.
Miss R. David	1	0	522².
T. Davidson	40	2	(187), 501², 659², 664³, 815³, 977³, 1081², 1121², 1362³, 1366³, 1577³, 1580², (1582).
D. Davies	4	1	(266).
J. Davies	14	0	625³, 696³, 1324³, 1479³.
Mrs J. Dawson	8	4	230², 368², (442), (544), (869), (1266), 1587³.
Miss H. Delahooke	12	2	282², 507², 816³, (908), 1027³, (1033), 1324², 1326³.
Miss A. Deniel	24	1	(276), 621², 1028³, 1328², 1350².
T. Denniff	3	1	441³, (1069).
D. Dennis *	42	5	330², (633), (824), (882), 1131², 1246³, (1247), 1248³, (1510).
David Dennis	29	2	65³, 145², 146², 205², (556), 733², (1436), 1519², 1520³, 1521², 1585³.
T. Dennis	41	2	163², (258), (720), 723², 848², 1043³, 1258², 1514², 1518², 1522², 1636³, 1639³, 1642².
C. Denny	9	0	171².
J. Deutsch	7	2	(387), 968², (1192).
Mrs K. Diggle	11	1	587², 780³, 960³, (1150), 1350³.
J. Dillon	1	0	1502³.
J. Diment	44	9	79², (391), 432², 434³, 889³, 1202³, 1206², 1423³, 1506³, 1668³.
J. Docker	16	5	167², (436), 542², (543), (867), (868), 872³.
N. Docker	12	2	372², (1070), (1072), 1265², 1414².
J. Downes	10	1	965³, 1195³, 1200², (1323).
D. Doyne-Ditmas	15	0	312³, 656³, 724².
M. Dun	1	0	1424².
D. Dunsdon *	21	6	131³, (221), 676³, (709), 710², (711), 826³, (828), 1392², (1393), 1398³, (1512).
Miss C. Dyson	5	2	(192), (1063).
Miss M. Eames	6	1	957², 1131³, 1303², (1564).
D. Easterby	39	11	(51), 137³, (138), (168), 173², (278), (375), (376), 381², (395), 396³, (503), 506², 508², (623), (627), 805², (999), 1348².
Miss L. Eddery	4	1	(1477).
A. Ede	25	3	100², (105), 316², (726), 1187², (1387), 1515².
K. Edmunds	12	1	(21), 179², 1106².
J. Edwards	3	0	266².
Miss G. Edwards	10	0	557³, 1369³.
Miss C. Elkington	4	0	366², 1217².
Miss P. Ellison	12	0	677³, 1109², 1209², 1395³.
O. Ellwood *	18	4	7³, (8), 259², 456², (762), (764), (1130).
M. Emmanuel	8	2	244³, (433), 1282², (1481).
R. Emmett	21	1	(205), 1256², 1555³.
A. Evans	28	7	(273), (570), 673³, (749), (863), (866), 968³, (1018), (1490).
H. Evans	12	0	596³.
D. Evatt	5	2	(309), (674).
J. Ewart	15	1	112³, (426), 492³, 1331².
T. Faulkner	15	0	274², 602², 1571².
Miss B. Fear	9	0	1243³.
Mrs S. Fell	5	0	164³, 315², 726², 850³.

J. Ferguson ....5 **0** 100³, 1471².

D. Flavin ....9 **1** (328).

Miss K. Fletcher ....1 **0** 166³.

N. Fogg ....1 **1** (1250).

Mrs C. Ford ....31 **5** 19³, 41³, (185), 230³, (526), (531), 566³, 590³, 592², (780), (962), 963³, 966², 1149³, 1150², 1255³, 1320³, 1411².

B. Foster ....22 **7** (120), 181³, 371³, 528², (569), (593), 905³, 1125², (1196), (1197), (1254), (1526).

Miss J. Foster * ....23 **3** (135), (170), 280², 505², (690).

R. Fowler ....20 **3** 88², 237², (1111), (1115), (1507).

P. Frank ....10 **0** 1353³.

M. Frith ....2 **1** (409).

Miss J. Froggatt ....13 **1** 901³, (1255).

H. Froud ....20 **1** 72³, 207², 738³, (1550), 1637².

Miss C. Fryer ....10 **1** 15², 175³, (555), 770², 937³.

Miss S. Gaisford ....11 **1** 651³, (1256).

J. Gallagher ....15 **0** 1021².

T. Gardham ....5 **0** 502².

Miss L. Gardner ....24 **2** 71³, (856), (1187), 1389³, 1608², 1671².

S. Garrott ....3 **0** 1167².

Miss G. Garton ....3 **0** 959³, 1252².

J. Gasper ....13 **0** 389³, 895³.

A St George ....23 **0** 451³, 821², 1093³, 1354².

C. Gibbon ....8 **3** (377), 1027², (1324), (1348).

G. Gigantesco ....3 **1** (1168).

C. Gilbert ....1 **0** 64³.

R. Gill ....7 **1** (1377).

M. Gingell ....36 **1** 24², 29³, 237³, (603), 604², 605², 610³, 756³, 757², 760², 774³.

Miss S. Gladders ....21 **0** 825³, 827³, 983³, 1107³, 1109³, 1170³.

T. Glass * ....45 **3** 44², 168², 376³, 379³, 496³, (625), 626³, 805³, 914³, 999³, (1327), (1474).

M. Goess-Saurau ....1 **0** 1134².

Miss R. Goodwin ......12 **0** 431², 787³, 1145³, 1483³, 1622².

C. Gordon * ....46 **6** (125), 127², 304³, 305², 416², (572), 574², 676², (679), 706², 826², 828², (980), 981², 983², 1104³, 1105², (1210), 1394², (1396), 1512³, 1624².

S. Gordon-Watson ......2 **1** (669), 890³.

M. Gorman ....28 **0** 215³, 711², 1108³, 1397³.

Miss A. Goschen ....26 **2** 214², (257), 518², 522³, 762³, 885³, 1095³, 1101³, 1246², (1248), 1395².

Miss E. Graham ....5 **0** 442², 1074³.

S. Graham ....23 **0** 858².

M. Grange ....13 **0** 174³, 769².

Miss J. Grant ....24 **4** 9³, (287), (289), 573², 677³, 707³, 982³, 1212², (1395), (1398).

T. Greed ....46 **3** (65), 147³, 160², 254³, 313², 520², 524³, 723³, 854², 857³, 881², (926), 1049², 1101², 1141², (1262), 1303³, 1370².

K. Green ....15 **1** 380³, 435³, (508), 689², 794³, 1070², 1215².

M. Green ....16 **0** 763², 764², 768³, 1130³.

Miss O. Green ....32 **7** (99), (354), 356³, (401), (535), 538², 563³, 636², 733³, 735², (877), (929), (1371), 1604³, 1605², 1671³.

T. Greenway ....9 **0** 1528³.

E. Gretton ....11 **0** 204³, 703², 1565³.

A. Gribbin ....10 **0** 589³, 772².

Miss C. Grissell * ......23 **4** 28³, 84³, (237), 287², 414³, 608³, (677), (761), (885), 939², 1183³, 1184³, 1380².

Miss H. Grissell ....6 **2** (985), (1170).

C. Gundry ....4 **0** 1311³, 1489².

Miss P. Gundry * ....97 **30** 13², (30), 32³, 38³, 101³, (161), 162², 263³, 265³, 284², (314), (390), (455), (518), (522), (524), (558), 632², (634), 652², (653), (731), (732), (733), 737³, 849³, 851², 881³, 952², (1057), (1059), (1060), 1061³, 1062², 1102², (1131), (1132), (1236), (1239), (1259), (1280), 1283², 1371², (1374), (1410), 1470³, (1473), 1488³, (1494), (1553), 1561², (1597), (1638).

Miss T. Habgood 15	1	427², (787), 1146², 1419³.
P. Hacking 2	0	130², 288³.
M. Haigh 8	0	1235³.
P. Halder..................11	0	276³.
Miss C. Hall..............20	1	(1575).
P. Hall.....................28	1	286³, 1208², 1210², (1213).
I. Hambley................25	1	312³, 539³, (724), 1384².
P. Hamer..................26	5	(642), 833³, 837³, (1221), 1222³, 1302², 1449², (1457), 1615², (1617), (1657).
Mrs A. Hamilton 18	0	109², 185³, 420³, 661³, 712³, 715², 1119², 1123².
M. Hammond 17	1	744², 994³, (1543).
Mrs M. Hand 49	7	69², (159), 203³, 255², (256), 310³, 314³, (315), 539², (541), 558³, 657², 720², (725), 726³, 846², 850², 932², 1259², (1263), 1385², 1386³, (1388), 1389², 1517², 1521³, 1605³, 1640³, 1673².
G. Hanmer 68	23	(124), (179), 526³, (527), 529², 530², (532), (617), (689), (779), 781³, 782³, (858), 862³, (906), (963), 964³, (986), 1064³, (1071), 1076², (1127), (1128), (1129), (1215), 1268², 1318³, 1321², (1322), (1361), 1408³, 1412², (1413), 1524³, 1526², (1527), (1528), (1529), 1588³, (1589), 1632³, 1667³, 1668².
Miss D. Harding 12	1	(214), 631³, 879², 1059².
Mrs K. Hargreave......26	0	361³, 1429², 1495², 1497³.
M. Harris 12	2	(701), 1063³, (1314), 1437², 1466², 1590³.
Miss G. Harris...........3	0	1669³.
N. Harris..................51	8	104³, 210², 313³, (474), 655³, (727), 846³, 849², (854), (1141), (1186), 1188², 1387³, 1388³, 1391², (1515), (1518), (1560), 1606², 1654³, 1655².
S. Harris....................1	1	(166).
Miss T. Harrison 4	0	476³, 736³, 929³.
Miss F. Hartley 11	1	621³, (1350), 1477³.
R. Hartley *................4	0	279², 422³.
A. Harvey *..............59	5	27², (96), 98³, (180), 241², 322², (323), 575², (604), 839³, 936³, (1181), 1288², 1378³, 1383².
Miss F. Hatfield..........4	0	442³, 772³.
M. Hawkins 15	1	(285).
Miss L. Hawkins 5	0	356².
J. Hawksfield 8	1	215², (706).
D. Hayes.....................4	0	(317).
Miss T. Hayes.............4	0	1472³.
Miss T. Hayter 10	0	28², 240², 841², 1113².
J. Hayward................16	0	831³, 1264³, 1300², 1615³.
C. Heard * 54	7	(103), 106², (143), 159², (253), 254², (311), (534), 536², 637², (655), 720³, 729³, (846), 932³, 1175², 1176³, 1517³.
K. Heard 9	1	847², (1375).
Miss J. Hedley..........17	0	44³, 911³.
M. Hewitt 36	4	(27), 439³, 547², 755³, 790², 1112², (1216), 1220², (1269), (1631).
A. Hickman 25	0	(23), 26³, (239), (286), (571), 710³, 888³, (1105).
Mrs S. Hickman 4	1	414², (1212).
P. Hickman 25	1	(771).
L. Hicks *.................52	4	120³, 436³, 545³, 588², (788), (901), 1021³, (1068), (1418), 1420², 1524².
Mrs T. Hill * 14	2	(243), 245², 841³, 1145², 1483², 1487³, (1587).
W. Hill......................2	2	(298), (1523).
T. Hills 15	0	286², 571², 574³, 984², 1171², 1396², 1509².
Miss L. Hislop...........15	0	363², 1119³, 1364³.
B. Hitchcott *...........38	6	23², 26², (94), (130), 305³, 308², 576³, (708), 824², (983), (1104), (1513).
J. Hobbs....................2	1	(203).
Mrs S. Hodge...........20	2	(84), (95), 240³, 319³, 544², 939³, 1180³, 1289².
R. Hodges................35	1	(450), 858³, 1276³, 1458³, 1529³.
M. Holdforth.............6	3	(126), (324), (632).
A. Holdsworth 12	2	563², (848), 1041², 1049³, 1520², (1640).
Miss J. Hollands........11	1	(713), 1078², 1161³, 1497², 1576².

Miss C. Holliday 11	**1**	245³, (1107).
A. Honeyball *..........84	**14**	36², 58³, (329), (330), 403², 518³, 559², (629), (658), (734), (739), 873², 875², 879³, 880³, 926³, (930), 954³, 957³, (1061), (1095), 1133³, 1135², (1238), (1372), (1467), 1468², 1472², 1473³, (1554), 1562³, (1563).
I. Hooper 6	**0**	700³, 1407².
Miss S. Hopkins 11	**1**	531², (566), 780², 783³, 904².
Mrs S. Horner-Harker..1	**0**	619².
Miss J. Houldey 4	**0**	736².
Miss W. Houldey 6	**0**	668².
D. Howells 9	**0**	485³, 1054², 1181³, 1659³.
Miss Z. Howse............1	**0**	748².
I. Hudson...................8	**0**	509², 889².
S. Huggan 6	**1**	(718).
D. Hughes 27	**2**	486³, 646³, (949), (1054), 1451³, 1613³.
Miss J. Hughes...........4	**0**	1221³.
Mrs J. Hughes 17	**1**	25³, 118², 1113³, 1209³, (1211), 1266³, 1380³, 1417², 1525², 1550².
S. Hughes 13	**1**	492³, (979).
H. Humble 12	**0**	419³, 717³, 907³, 912³.
T. Humphrey..............7	**0**	843³, 1181².
Miss D. Humphreys 1	**0**	64².
R. Hunnisett *...........17	**11**	(48), (85), (195), 229³, 231², (320), (511), (545), (870), (1008), (1182), (1265), 1381², (1416).
Miss G. Hutchinson 9	**3**	770³, 1037³, (1417), (1502), (1583).
Miss Gina Hutchinson 1	**0**	1424³.
F. Hutsby *................39	**3**	30², 141², 190³, 194², (427), 515³, 517³, 552², 789³, 791², 1018², (1207), 1435², 1438³, (1442).
T. Illsley 23	**2**	514², 752², (844), 1147², 1203³, (1506).
R. Inglesant...............4	**0**	1092³, 1196³, 1318².
Miss L. Ingram 7	**0**	552³, 935³.
Miss H. Irving 15	**5**	3³, (307), 512³, (707), 787², (1007), (1145), (1253).
M. Jackson 2	**0**	697².
Miss L. Jackson 6	**0**	1186³.
Miss T. Jackson 33	**3**	281², 378³, (505), 692³, 694³, 803², 806², 1029², 1233², (1352), (1475).
Mrs D. Jackson............3	**1**	449², (611).
Mrs V. Jackson...........47	**6**	184³, (361), 363³, 418³, 423², (425), (498), 661², (974), 976², 978², (1077), (1078), 1079², 1082³, 1364², 1579².
S. Jackson 2	**0**	293², 298³.
Miss E. James...........12	**2**	1085³, 1275², 1462², (1616), 1665³, 1667², (1673).
C. Jarvis 15	**0**	606², 759³, 1292², 1382², 1609².
L. Jefford * 121	**42**	(10), 38², 199², 204², 206², (251), (252), (254), (255), (404), 407³, (538), (540), 541³, 559³, (563), (637), (639), 640³, (651), (728), (729), 848³, (852), 856², (857), 876², (878), (879), 927², (928), 931³, (932), 933², 934², (953), 955², (1043), (1044), (1046), (1049), 1095², (1098), (1137), (1139), (1237), 1238², 1240³, 1241², 1258³, (1260), (1261), 1305², (1307), 1308², 1374², (1464), (1517), 1518³, (1519), (1521), (1595), (1596), 1598², (1607), (1609), 1639², (1650), (1672), 1674².
D. Jewett...................25	**1**	495³, 662², 1081³, 1366², (1429).
Miss C. Jiggins 3	**1**	(25).
I. Johnson 16	**1**	489³, 602³, (823), 1662³.
P. Johnson 12	**1**	379², 426², 500², (1084), 1500³.
Miss F. Jonason 9	**0**	236³, 1034³.
Adam Jones 7	**0**	103², 251², 1387².
D. Jones 41	**3**	70³, 72², (267), 268³, 343², 345³, (349), 350², 480³, 482², 483³, (484), 486², 488², 600³.
Miss E. Jones.............20	**3**	(67), 270³, (449), 666², (834), 836², 1281².

Miss P. Jones 76	23	1², (9), 67³, 71², 101², (102), (141), (146), 201², 272², (275), (295), (297), (342), (343), 344³, (346), (350), (478), (481), 599², 643², 644², (645), 646², (650), (836), (838), (895), (946), 987³, 991², 1014², 1223², (1275), 1277³, (1278), 1297³, 1401², (1402), 1410³, 1451², 1453², 1457³, (1567).
W. Jordan....................2	0	444².
S. Joynes 46	7	(34), (119), 124², 193², 261³, (447), 450², 474², 615², 667³, 672², (861), (898), 1013², 1193³, (1312), 1409², 1461², (1664).
J. Jukes * 125	23	(22), 142³, (144), 147², 271², (274), 345², 348², 349³, (480), 487², 598², (600), 601², 650³, (747), 834³, (893), (948), (950), (990), 1016³, (1017), (1051), (1053), 1088², 1090², 1225³, 1226², (1296), 1301², (1400), 1404³, 1453², 1456², 1568³, 1569², (1570), 1572², (1574), (1614), (1618), (1630), (1634), 1657², (1658), 1659², (1661).
P. Kay..........................4	1	476², (670).
P. Keane.....................17	3	453², (471), 473³, (628), (768), 958³, 1437³.
M. Keel......................39	3	30³, 35², (197), 532³, (698), 892², 971², 972³, 1190², 1194³, 1357², (1358).
J. Keen 57	4	267², 350³, 595², (835), 838³, 951², (1228), 1300³, (1301), (1302), 1399², 1401³, 1403³, 1574³, 1617².
Mrs B. Keighley 5	2	(476), 751², 967², (1134), 1311².
Miss S. Kelly 5	0	613³, 1441³, 1665².
S. Kelly 4	0	776².
D. Kemp 15	0	82², 92², 610³, 678², 1182³.
B. Kendellen 19	1	(56), 241³.
E. Kenny-Herbert 1	0	1549².
N. Kent 37	1	231³, 232³, 961², (1075), 1214², 1268³.
G. Kerr......................10	1	(74), 428³, 430², 789², 1006³.
S. Kidston 40	1	104², 144², (351), 541², 721³, 730³, 876³, 1096³, 1097³, 1369².
B. King........................9	1	33², 80³, 477², (1487).
N. King * 39	5	15³, (29), 91², (181), 238³, 289³, 320², 321², 607³, (756), 842³, (938), (1036), 1114².
P. Kinsella 11	0	619³.
Miss H. Kinsey............7	0	569².
W. Kinsey 5	0	1198².
J. Kwiatkowski 10	0	1130².
Mrs J. Lancaster 1	0	979².
T. Lane * 62	3	48³, 116³, (174), (229), 369², (547), 548², 942², 1038², 1270², 1291³, 1379³, 1436², 1504², 1583², 1589², 1590².
R. Langley....................7	0	752³.
R. Lawther 59	16	76³, (219), (244), (247), (249), (325), 327², 388³, (389), 392², (428), 609², 883², (889), (937), (1006), (1011), (1019), 1144³, 1205², 1267³, 1439², (1619), (1621), (1623), (1624).
L. Lay........................19	1	367³, 429³, 753³, 971³, (1193), 1619².
M. Leach 1	1	(366).
M. Legge.....................9	1	(1284), 1512².
P. Lentelink 3	0	659³.
G. Lewis 44	3	269², 275², (348), 479², 597³, 642³, 645², (647), 648², (832), 835², 944³, 947², 1221², 1227², 1228².
M. Lewis....................25	4	(270), (271), 601³, 642², (646), 831², 834², (943), 1227³, 1450³.
Mrs B. Lewis..............10	0	275³, 346², 943², 1224³, 1297².
J. Liley 6	0	596².
A. Lillingston 10	0	1242², 1245³.
J.L. Llewellyn 17	1	490³, 819³, 822³, (1295).
Miss B. Lloyd 4	2	(326), (475), 1014³.
S. Lloyd 32	4	341³, 448³, (489), (491), 896², (1088), 1089², (1458), 1459³, 1465².
Miss K. Lovelace.......10	0	(1456), 1616².
G. Lowe.......................1	1	(776).
Miss M. Lowndes........3	0	33³, 292².
D. Luff 11	1	641³, (1094), 1102³.
M. Lurcock 11	1	86³, 513², (1035), 1116³.
G. Lush......................6	0	1040².

B. Lusted.................28 **2** (182), 422², (622), 910², 1083², 1084³, 1118³, 1159³, 1163²,
                                     1165³, 1431³.

T. Macfarlane............15 **0** 1316³.
Miss M. MacGregor....5   **1** (1281), 1553².
M. Mackley 58 **9** (121), (435), (542), 546², (793), 867³, 1009³, 1012³, (1218), (1219),
                                     (1220), 1251², (1268), 1287³, (1351), 1505², 1583³.

J. Mactaggart.............2 **0** 662³, 911².
A. Maculan ....15 **1** (81), 217³, 338³, 750², 1355³, 1357³.
P. Maitland-Carew 6   **0** 1427³.
Miss S. Major.............7 **0** 1405², 1656³.
G. Maloney 9   **1** (347).
D. Mansell 86 **3** 49², 178³, (332), 333², 337², 445², 564³, 702², 866³, (890), 988³,
                                     1015², (1524), 1631².

G. Markham *..........24   **2** 626², 1001², 1032³, 1325², (1495), (1499), 1585².
C. Marriott................2 **0** 246³.
F. Marshall..............8   **1** (1172).
A. Martin 60 **3** 31², 75³, 76², 94², 197², 392³, 433³, 629², 749³, (900), (1013),
                                     1020², 1192³, 1312², 1360³, 1416², 1422², (1437), 1442³, 1623²,
                                     1676³.

G. Maundrell 45   **7** 62², 96³, (142), 164², 387², (453), (473), 634², 886², (1042), 1244²,
                                     (1245), 1279³, (1282), 1283³, 1554³.

J. Maxse.....................9 **0** 767³.
D. Maxwell................2 **0** 242².
P. McAllister ....11 **0** 87², 175².
Mrs C. McCarthy 2   **0** 1622³.
Miss T. McCurrich......3   **0** 78³, 177², 613².
L. McGrath ....24 **2** (173), (381), 1033³, 1330³.
D. McKenna ....11 **1** 1041³, 1188³, (1384), 1391³, 1522³.
B. McKim...............14   **0** 81², 197³.
Miss N. McKim.........22   **1** 220², 784², 869², 1007³, 1417³, (1588).
J. Mead ....8 **1** (60).
Miss A. Meakins 32   **0** 1050², 1402².
Miss A. Melvin...........1   **0** 190².
J. Merry.....................17 **0** 568³, 906², 1527³.
Miss T. Messer-Bennetts5   **1** (1636).
Miss C. Metcalfe......13   **0** 426³, 977², 1501³.
A. Michael................9   **0** 351², 635².
M. Miller *...............58 **7** 34³, 63³, 73², 210³, (263), (327), 329³, (402), (955), 1058², 1204²,
                                     1207², 1280³, 1308³, 1376³, 1492², (1551), 1562², 1563³, 1598³,
                                     (1604), (1675).

P. Millington 83 **3** 115³, 119², 123³, 124³, 440², 550³, 554³, 593³, 675², 696², 844³,
                                     1011³, 1070³, 1264², (1287), 1290³, 1383³, 1420³, 1421², (1504),
                                     (1505), 1506², 1634².

Miss D. Mitchell 21   **0** 1048³.
N. Mitchell *.............86 **19** 1³, (12), 34², 60³, 62³, (69), 105², (147), (209), 325², 327³, 331³,
                                     402², (519), (520), (521), 629³, 654², (735), 738², (847), 875³,
                                     (876), (880), 953², (1177), 1262², (1280²), (1283), (1306), 1309²,
                                     (1370), 1372², 1373², 1467³, (1469), (1516), 1595³, 1596², 1636²,
                                     (1637), 1641², 1653², (1676).

T. Mitchell 47 **14** 11³, 12², 14³, 57², (58), (66), 68², (100), (104), 105³, 106³, 146³,
                                     (160), (162), 163³, (208), 209³, (212), 213³, 214³, (264), (313),
                                     (403), 404³, (406), (408), 454², (927), 931³.

L. Morgan * 65 **8** 112², (188), 362³, 364², 420², (660), 719², 811², (815), 976³,
                                     1030², (1121), (1122), (1365), (1424), (1496), 1500², 1576³.

R. Morgan *.............55   **11** 113³, 187³, 188³, (424), (495), 497², (712), 713², 719³, (811), (816),
                                     (913), (975), (978), 1118², (1120), (1123), (1362), 1363³.

M. Morley................24 **1** (393), 399³, 625², 809³, 1234².
Mrs R. Morris...........10 **1** 722³, 855³, (1391).
P. Morris ....19 **0** 569³.
S. Morris * 48 **9** 294², (440), 510³, (517), 868³, (871), 1005³, (1012), 1016², 1206³,
                                     (1267), (1415), 1418², (1419), (1421), 1423², 1503², (1586).

T. Morrison ....14 **1** 108², (664), 973².

J. Muir 14	**0**	186³, 419².
C. Mulhall 51	**10**	17³, (40), 55³, (137), (167), 168³, 169², 172³, 377³, (379), 393³, (399), 435², 546³, (695), (1000), (1003), (1027), 1033², (1329), 1353², 1475², 1478², 1480³, 1577².
M. Munrowd 34	**1**	490², (656), 1630³.
K. Needham 25	**1**	233³, 281³, 514³, (808), 1028².
Mrs F. Needham *.....61	**5**	47², 54³, (133), 137², (277), 378², 437², 623³, (626), 689³, 795², 798², 871², (1004), (1232), 1328³, 1478³.
P. Needham 1	**0**	1629³.
Miss M. Neill 3	**0**	107², 493³.
Miss T. Newman 11	**1**	519², 654³, 877², 1045², (1303), 1638³, 1651³.
Miss E. Neyens 5	**1**	1211².
C. Niblo....................7	**0**	718².
R. Nichol 7	**0**	815², 978³.
Miss J. Nicholas 7	**1**	(140), 403³.
Miss A. Nolan 3	**1**	(668), 699².
Miss K. Norris 7	**1**	(1503), 1663².
H. Norton 3	**0**	914².
F. O'Brien 6	**0**	967³, 1523², 1606³, 1672².
Miss G. O'Callaghan ..3	**0**	1126³.
B. O'Doherty 27	**1**	739², 874², (1241), 1468³, 1609³.
J. O'Rourke................9	**0**	763³.
T. Oates 35	**3**	114², (363), 499², 663², (1153), (1163), 1582².
J. Oldring 15	**2**	5², 24³, (190), (786), 1207³, 1254².
N. Oliver 20	**2**	(539), 1526³, (1545).
B. Orde-Powlett 7	**1**	(374).
J. Owen *..................45	**3**	13³, 80², (194), 244², 247³, 427³, 632³, 634³, 734³, (887), (1009), 1487².
R. Owen 19	**1**	776³, (812), 1153², 1465³.
D. Page 15	**1**	126³, 285², 416³, 980³, (1109).
R. Page......................1	**0**	174².
D. Parker.................15	**4**	129², (755), 761³, 824³, (829), (1169), (1171).
N. Parker...................4	**1**	330³, (958).
S. Parkin....................6	**0**	1384³.
M. Parry..................15	**0**	1571³.
S. Partridge................8	**1**	409², 556², (721).
Miss R. Pask 8	**1**	(1076).
Miss L. Pearce *........19	**1**	481², (649), 832², 836³.
A. Pennock 20	**0**	1229³.
Miss D. Penwill..........1	**1**	(1642).
T. Peoples 2	**0**	289².
G. Perkins 13	**1**	(1660).
W. Pewter 5	**0**	179³.
A. Phillips 25	**3**	(31), 248², 296², (448), (1085), 1086³, 1358³.
P. Phillips...................8	**1**	926², (934), 1140³.
Miss H. Phizacklea 7	**1**	368³, (1414).
Miss S. Phizacklea 12	**1**	(792).
A. Pickering 13	**0**	507³, 1004³, 1269², 1507².
P. Picton-Warlow 1	**0**	1566³.
S. Pinder....................5	**0**	136³.
M. Polley 8	**0**	1110².
B. Pollock *..............39	**13**	4³, (6), (17), (26), (49), (50), 191², 196², 235², (411), 412², (413), (510), (513), (515), 517², 543², 868², (1005), 1143², (1147), 1584², (1663).
M. Portman................7	**1**	387³, (748), 1203².
Miss D. Powell............1	**0**	882³.
K. Prendergast..........13	**1**	(134), 136².
A. Price....................82	**13**	(220), 273³, (446), (487), (594), (595), (602), 741², 745², (817), (818), 820², (822), 823³, 948³, 949², (951), 1088³, 1225², 1298³, (1404), 1406², (1449), (1449), (1569), 1572³, 1616³.
J. Price 61	**3**	(483), (488), 742², 897², 987³, 1051², (1274), 1402³, 1466³, 1630², 1661³.

Miss A. Price............11   2   (529), 743[3], 813[3], 902[3], (960), 1148[2], 1367[2].
Miss J. Priest 7   0   295[2].
M. Prince 5   0   901[2].
S. Prior * 32   5   527[3], (777), (814), 902[2], (1125), 1129[2], (1251), (1252), 1362[2].
J.I. Pritchard............16   1   250[2], (432), 1421[3], 1438[2].
Julian Pritchard * 140   28   10[3], (59), (61), (77), (116), 117[3], 120[2], 123[2], (196), 261[2], 262[3],
(265), 294[3], 297[2], 334[2], 336[2], (339), 340[3], 369[3], 388[2], 391[3], 458[2],
(472), (574), (612), 614[2], (618), 667[2], 669[2], (671), 672[3], 673[2], 698[2],
(700), 701[3], 704[2], (791), 864[3], 890[2], 893[2], (894), 895[2], 899[2], (968),
(970), (971), 1015[3], 1017[2], (1021), 1064[2], 1067[3], 1068[3], 1190[3],
1192[2], (1194), 1278[2], (1310), (1311), 1313[2], 1314[2], 1356[2], 1358[2],
(1422), (1439), (1440), 1459[2], 1460[3], (1461), 1488[2], 1492[3], 1570[3],
(1585), 1608[3], (1620), 1629[2].

P. Pritchard 12   2   200[3], 264[2], 471[2], 560[3], (899), (1133).
Miss C. Prouse...........8   0   853[3].
J. Purllant..................7   0   1286[3], 1505[3].
Miss I. Rabone............4   0   1063[2], 1491[2].
Miss R. Ramsay........11   0   43[3], 358[3], 421[2], 912[3], 1425[3].
W. Ramsay..................4   1   (358), 973[3], 1121[3].
D. Raw 16   2   133[3], 624[2], 693[2], 695[2], (909), (1032), 1474[2].
Mrs J. Reed 10   0   519[3].
D. Reid 3   0   665[3].
D. Renney 4   0   1631[3].
W. Renwick *...........19   4   46[3], 186[2], (189), (360), (422), 425[2], (914), 1430[3].
Miss R. Reynolds 14   1   588[3], (865), 1464[2], 1662[2].
J. Rice........................6   0   1675[2].
G. Richards...............44   1   (352), 353[2], 1099[2], 1136[2], 1236[2], 1373[3], 1375[2], 1469[2], 1552[3].
A. Richardson 27   5   (43), 111[3], (359), (419), 438[3], 714[3], (716), 1580[3], (1581).
J. Richardson 11   1   (766), 970[3], 1060[3], 1486[3].
D. Ridge 3   0   640[2].
Mrs M. Rigg................2   0   307[3].
M. Rimell..................35   5   (14), 18[2], 219[2], 260[3], (388), 611[2], 749[2], (753), 894[2], (896), (989),
1193[2], 1623[3], 1664[3].

Miss G. Roberts 4   2   (743), (1052).
D. Robinson *...........17   5   125[2], (129), (305), 308[3], (676), 706[3], (826), (1106), 1108[2], 1210[3].
Miss S. Robinson......19   1   205[3], (1100), 1564[2], 1654[2].
S.J. Robinson 23   0   1002[3], 1080[2], 1476[3].
Stuart Robinson 4   0   (291).
A. Robson................39   5   (39), (108), 110[2], 114[3], 364[3], 424[3], (492), 501[3], 622[3], (663), 665[2],
908[3], 909[2], 910[3], 913[3], 1084[2], (1367), 1430[2], 1581[3].
Miss P. Robson * 59   21   (3), 40[2], (41), 45[3], (109), 111[2], 183[2], 185[2], 189[2], (230), 418[2], (420),
(421), (423), 424[2], (493), 494[2], (496), 620[3], (621), (661), 974[3],
(1029), 1079[3], (1081), (1082), (1152), (1158), (1161), 1164[2],
(1328), 1342[2], (1364), 1367[3], 1426[3], (1576), (1579).

P. Robson.................11   2   (107), 1151[2], 1368[3], (1478).
M. Rodda..................48   1   533[2], 898[3], 986[2], 1020[3], 1092[2], 1197[3], (1276), 1548[3].
Miss S. Rodman..........4   0   *1250[3]*
R. Rogers....................6   1   332[2], (1357), 1545[2].
Miss K. Roncoroni 11   1   128[3], (624).
Miss L. Rope..............2   0   628[2].
K. Rosier 2   0   998[2], 1152[3].
R. Ross.......................7   1   (675).
Miss L. Rowe 14   7   (19), (218), 287[3], (368), (512), 758[2], (770), 772[2], 1007[2], (1037),
(1183).
Miss S. Rowe 7   0   1551[3].
Mrs D. Rowell...........12   1   218[3], 707[3], 711[3], 830[3], (1209), 1398[2], 1511[2].
Miss V. Russell 5   1   135[2], (280), 397[2], 690[3].
Miss S. Samworth 4   0   431[3].
Miss A. Sansom 9   0   573[3].

A. Sansome............114　11　　2³, 82³, (93), 132³, 238², (284), 290³, 291², 415², 440³, 511³, 549²,
(550), (551), 554², 610², (678), 679³, (705), 708², 771³, 774², 775²,
840³, 842², (843), 845², 935², 937², 938³, 940³, (942), 1017³,
1111², (1114), 1115³, 1116², 1286², 1287², 1288³, 1292³, 1382³,
(1383), 1485², 1596³, (1666).

Miss C. Savell ....3　0　　41².
M. Scales ....10　0　　1464³.
G. Scantlebury............1　0　　1077².
T. Scott.....................35　3　　718³, 913², 1123³, (1164), (1165), (1366), 1428³, 1480², 1501².
P. Scouller * ....16　5　　(1), (215), 452², (750), (981), (1244), 1595².
T. Scudamore * ....35　11　　(20), (38), (199), (200), (202), (353), (355), (357), 536³, 537², 560²,
561³, (752), (967), (972), 1098³.
R. Sealey...................5　0　　892³.
S. Sellars ....15　0　　1134³, 1135³.
J. Sharp ....5　0　　288², 370³.
Miss S. Sharratt ....16　4　　67², 527², 532², (589), (592), (902), 962³, (1124), 1253², 1525³.
B. Shaw ....8　3　　(987), (1087), (1273).
P. Shaw ....8　2　　208³, (410), 734³, 1046², (1176).
M. Shears..................35　2　　198², 408³, 633², 874³, (931), (956), 1256³.
P. Sheldrake ....47　3　　270², 348³, (486), 487³, 648³, 944², 1051³, 1056³, 1301³, (1405),
(1568).
G. Shenkin.................6　0　　1385³.
R. Shepherd-Cross .....5　0　　474³, 886².
K. Sheppard...............9　1　　(537), 727³, 929², 1039³.
P. Sheppard...............12　1　　(430), 515².
M. Sheridan ....4　1　　(576).
D. Sherlock...............38　1　　173³, 587², 782³, (1201), 1255², 1322³.
C. Sherry..................8　1　　(710), 980².
D Da Silva * ....3　1　　(46).
Miss V. Simpson ....1　0　　712².
V. Simpson................3　0　　324².
G. Skone..................15　1　　(833), 950², 1223³.
D. Slattery................18　2　　705³, (830), 1243², (1392).
M. Smethurst ....9　0　　1163³, 1330², 1474³, 1479².
G. Smith ....13　1　　52², 1270³, (1420).
R. Smith...................13　2　　784³, 1010³, (1243), (1441).
W. Smith..................16　0　　855².
J. Snowden ....46　2　　325³, (560), 764³, 767², 1059³, 1062³, 1097², 1307³, 1388², 1390³,
1554², (1674).
Miss W. Southcombe ..9　1　　(765), 969³, 1239³, 1638².
Miss C. Spearing........14　7　　(78), (118), (245), 335², (397), (431), 566², (1410), (1483), 1485³.
Miss T. Spearing........13　1　　701², 861³, 1267², 1272², 1354².
S. Sporborg..............37　9　　(4), (7), (15), 22², 29², 83³, 85³, 86², (92), 176³, (178), (262), 318³,
(322), 415³, 543³, 545², (605), (606), 773².
N. Squires..................1　0　　366³.
Mrs E. Staines...........12　0　　118³, 1189².
Miss N. Stallard..........6　0　　206³, 1635³.
P Strang Steel............12　1　　365³, 498², (665).
Miss H. Steele............1　0　　1285³.
Miss A. Stennett.........12　0　　1037².
D. Stephens (Devon).19　1　　540², 658³, 724³, 1186², (1390).
D. Stephens (Wales)..33　2　　595³, 600², 817³, (819), 820³, 822², 823², 1053³, 1100³, 1316²,
1400³, (1452), 1454³.
L. Stephens ....29　4　　864², 1128², (1195), (1200), 1323², (1355), (1667).
Miss V. Stephens ....7　1　　1045³, (1174), 1652³.
T. Stephenson ....111　11　　16³, (36), 122², 193³, 195², 248³, (296), 337³, 339³, (341), 448²,
(485), (564), 615³, 616², 669³, 671², 697³, 700², 702³, 703³, 859³,
(897), 992³, 993³, 995³, 1085², 1277², 1315², 1355², 1359², 1360²,
1412³, 1413², 1436², (1465), 1492³, (1493), 1494³, (1548), (1633),
1635².
Miss T. Stevens...........7　0　　950³, 1052³, 1457².
Miss N. Stirling...........8　2　　421³, (715), 1161², 1426³, (1497).

Rider	Rides	Wins	Entries
Mrs L. Stock	13	1	27^3, 128^2, (573), 827^2.
C. Stockton	25	3	(171), 525^2, 526^2, 589^2, (697), 778^3, (959).
J. Stonehouse	3	0	1158^2.
C. Storey	76	21	(42), (110), (111), (112), 113^2, (114), 182^2, 184^2, 188^2, 362^2, (365), 423^3, (497), (499), 620^2, 624^3, 663^2, 664^2, 714^2, 716^3, (717), (807), (809), (910), (912), (973), 975^2, (976), 1120^2, 1122^3, 1159^2, (1160), 1165^2, 1326^2, 1327^2, (1368), 1425^2, (1427), 1428^2, 1429^3, (1430), (1431), 1495^3, 1496^2, (1498), 1578^2.
Miss C. Stretton	5	2	520^3, (738), (1240).
Miss V. Stubbs	5	0	813^2.
Miss C. Stucley	13	0	75^2, 880^2.
Miss N. Sturgis	5	0	335^3, 390^2, 751^3, 1191^2.
Miss V. Sturgis	8	1	(62), 216^2.
Miss L. Sweeting *	30	5	192^3, 453^3, 512^2, 513^3, (516), (751), 785^3, 896^3, 969^2, 1013^3, 1034^2, 1266^2, 1481^3, (1486), (1605), (1665).
M. Sweetland	29	0	253^2, 1136^3, 1178^2, 1179^3, 1564^3, 1670^2.
S. Swiers *	51	6	42^3, 51^3, 233^2, 376^2, 395^2, (398), (504), 796^2, (798), 1000^2, (1325), (1326), 1352^2, (1479).
Miss S. Swindells	7	1	590^2, (1074), 1462^3.
P. Taiano	25	5	(24), (91), 98^2, (288), (840), (845), 1290^2, 1378^2, 1381^3, 1513^3.
Miss S. Talbot	13	2	(672), 817^2, 818^2, 993^2, (1297), 1547^2.
J. Tanner	1	0	1317^3.
J. Tarry	46	7	297^3, (429), 510^2, 511^2, (784), 785^2, 788^2, (789), 791^3, 1005^2, 1006^2, (1010), 1143^2, 1215^3, 1216^3, 1218^2, 1219^3, 1415^3, 1416^3, 1481^2, 1482^3, (1484), (1485), (1584), 1621^3.
J. Tate *	8	2	42^2, (281), 282^3, (696), 1000^3.
R. Tate	4	3	46^2, (400), (688), (1230).
G. Tawell	1	0	509^3.
Miss M. Taylor	7	0	765^3.
W. Tellwright	7	1	(548).
H. Tett	6	0	1242^3.
D. Thomas	33	3	55^2, 278^3, 398^3, 400^3, (438), 502^3, 503^3, 794^2, 798^3, 808^2, 1002^2, 1233^3, 1664^2.
G. Thomas	15	3	(528), (782), 814^3, (1148).
H. Thomas	12	1	102^2, 256^2, (1373), 1566^2, 1649^3.
Miss C. Thomas	27	7	218^2, (272), 273^2, 447^2, 478^2, 481^3, 699^3, (860), (862), 904^3, (1126), 1224^2, (1460), (1547), (1613).
Miss Carla Thomas	10	1	(509).
M. Thompson	1	0	39^3.
Miss A. Thompson	4	0	280^3.
G. Thorne	7	0	1299^3.
L. Tibbatts	26	0	410^3.
Mrs S. Tideswell	1	0	1124^2.
M. Tillett	2	0	1619^3.
Miss C. Tizzard	31	7	(35), 354^3, 405^2, (523), (952), (1096), 1239^2, (1304), (1470), (1561), 1599^2.
Miss I. Tompsett	2	0	943^3.
Miss E. Tory	13	1	209^2, 877^3, 933^3, (957), 1132^2.
R. Tory	9	0	389^2, 523^2, 766^2, 878^2.
P. Townsley	9	0	572^2, 578^2, 1213^2, 1392^3, 1397^2.
J. Townson	7	0	278^2, 400^2, 964^2.
Miss V. Tremlett	5	1	65^2, 257^2, (405).
M. Treneer	1	0	1257^3.
J. Trice-Rolph	32	1	8^3, 74^3, (191), 753^2.
B. Trickey	8	0	160^3, 355^2, 1139^2, 1304^2.
M. Trott *	16	1	491^3, 1271^2, 1413^3, (1546), 1548^2.
H. Trotter	7	0	358^2, 1498^3.
R. Trotter	9	0	1498^2, 1578^3.
James Tudor	29	1	(269), 945^3, 947^3, 948^2, 1452^2, 1618^3, 1656^2.
G. Tuer *	13	3	(619), 693^3, 694^2, 1031^2, (1235), 1329^3, (1580).
Miss C. Tuffin	7	1	61^2, 161^2, (454).
Miss C. Tuke	2	1	(610).

C. Williams * ....74 13 271³, 343³, (344), 480², 488³, 597², (643), (644), 647², (741), (742), 818³, 819², (820), 821³, 945², (1050), 1053², 1055³, (1056), (1222), (1223), (1226), 1295², 1296², 1303³, 1400², (1401), 1404², (1450), 1455², 1573³, 1574², 1613³.

E. Williams ....78 16 37³, 143³, (145), 268², 269³, 344², (345), 349², 483², (567), (597), (598), (601), 1065³, 1068², 1091³, 1222², (1225), 1295³, 1296³, 1298², (1299), (1300), (1403), (1406), (1448), (1451), (1453), (1455), 1569³, 1570², 1618², 1658³, (1659), 1660², 1672³.

Miss B. Williams ....15 0 69³, 484², 743², 894³.

Miss C. Williams ....9 0 347³, 1052², 1299², 1403², 1449³.

Miss J. Williams ....9 1 1126², 1523³, (1629).

N. Wilson (Hants) ......6 0 678³, 1509³.

C. Wilson ....31 5 (44), 45², (184), 279³, (692), (997), (1353).

Miss F. Wilson * ....32 6 201³, 272³, (335), (599), 644³, (821), 946², 1066³, (1224), (1298), (1399), 1617³.

Mrs N. Wilson ....5 0 996².

N. Wilson ....23 1 139³, 394³, 627³, 808³, (1330).

A. Wintle * ....93 15 (76), 79³, (337), 339², 391², (392), (444), 446³, 482³, 489², (616), (666), (667), 862², 891², (892), 900³, 989³, 990², (995), (1065), (1090), (1313), (1315), (1316), 1415², 1463², (1488), 1490², 1544², 1597², 1612², 1614².

B. Woodhouse * ....10 1 167³, (1002).

A. Woodward ....6 1 961³, (1214).

M. Woodward...........16 1 523³, (1178).

R. Woollacott............85 9 68³, 140², 144³, 159³, (165), 199³, 203², 311³, 315³, (316), 458³, 537³, 538³, 562², 653³, 721², (723), 728³, 847³, 853², (855), (933), 1042³, 1100², (1188), 1372³, 1514³, (1552), 1560², 1565², 1604², 1637³, (1649), (1654), 1655³.

Miss J. Wormall * ....5 4 (494), (1079), (1119), (1426), 1579³.

M. Worthington ....52 8 (54), 334³, (525), 567³, (620), (778), 781², (965), 1149², 1153³, 1197², (1321), 1409³, 1528², (1632), (1635).

G. Wragg ....1 1 (127).

I. Wynne ....13 1 (568), 1200³, 1321³.

M. Yardley..................6 1 20², (72), 196³, 1633³.

P. York * ....77 9 2², 21², (37), 59², 130³, (131), (132), (306), (452), 572³, 709², (785), 786², 792², 829³, 883³, 884³, 984³, 1105³, (1108), 1244³, 1245², (1246), 1247², 1248², 1396³, 1484³, (1509), 1510², 1620², 1621², 1658², 1661².

J. Young.....................47 3 12³, 58², (158), 457², (1102), 1261², (1468), 1469³, 1549³, 1563², 1650².

Jeremy Young ....33 0 56², 73³, 158³, 252², 253³, 352², 562³, 657³, 856³, 958².

Miss G. Young.............5 2 (331), (1279).

Miss S. Young * ....48 6 (157), 158², 161³, 257³, 258³, 310², 728², (849), (851), 1042², 1043², (1047), 1137², 1174³, 1176², 1179², (1258), 1607², (1610), 1651².

P. Young ....25 1 221³, 1147³, (1203), 1284³, 1315³, 1493³.

R. Young ....32 9 (210), 213², (308), 407², 455², (477), 630², 631², 655², (737), (875), (881), 1057², (1058), 1204³, (1206), (1305).

Winning & Placed
Hunter Chase Riders 2000

Winning Point-to-Point Rider 2000

Rider	No of Rides	No of Wins	Winning and Placed Rides
D. Alers-Hankey *	6	0	469^3.
R. Armson *	3	0	462^2, 801^2.
M. Armytage *	8	1	89^2, 463^3, (915), 1530^3, 1591^3.
N. Bannister	2	0	1025^3.
D. Barlow *	9	0	386^3, 1601^2.
J. Barnes *	9	0	223^3, 383^2, 1432^3.
R. Barrett *	14	1	585^3, 684^2, 799^3, 802^3, 1249^3, 1533^2, (1603).
N. Bell *	4	0	1542^3.
S. Blackwell *	7	1	(1157).
N. Bloom *	3	1	151^3, (466), 1338^2.
C. Bonner	3	0	460^2.
M. Bradburne *	8	3	156^3, (225), (226), (384).
Miss M. Bremner *	6	0	686^2, 1024^3, 1342^2.
G. Brewer *	8	5	(465), (1333), (1445), (1446), (1643).
J. Burley *	2	0	1643^2.
R. Burton *	28	6	(464), 468^2, (920), (1023), 1025^2, 1249^2, (1339), (1432), (1534), 1559^2, 1593^2, 1601^3, 1647^2.
S. Bush *	2	0	224^3.
Miss T. Cave *	3	1	(1644).
A. Charles-Jones *	23	4	149^3, 156^2, (386), (584), 681^3, (1103), (1336).
R. Clark *	9	0	155^2, 586^2.
M. Clayton *	4	0	918^3.
F Windsor Clive *	19	3	(149), 299^3, (460), 683^2, 922^2, (1447), 1538^2.
A. Coe *	4	0	1540^2.
R. Cooper *	9	0	920^3, 1023^3.
R. Cope *	4	1	(299), 1530^2.
Mrs E. Coveney *	4	0	1155^3, 1156^2.
A. Crow *	6	3	(1559), (1601), (1646).
K. Culligan *	6	2	(223), (303), 681^2.
A. Dalton *	5	1	(462).
Richard Darke *	1	0	1535^2.
D. Dennis *	12	1	150^3, 467^2, 468^3, 685^2, (1535), 1537^2.
T. Dennis *	6	0	1523^2, 5811^2.
J. Diment *	7	0	224^2.
R. Douro *	1	0	1603^2.
T. Doyle	13	3	(586), 801^3, (1332), (1542).
D. Dunsdon *	11	4	(300), (468), (580), 924^3, (1026).
K. Edmunds *	2	0	1536^2.
G. Elliott	1	0	924^2.
O. Ellwood *	4	1	(470).
M. Emmanuel *	1	0	461^3.
A. Evans *	8	0	1334^3.
D. Flavin *	7	0	802^2, 1332^2, 1533^3.
P. Flynn *	1	1	(153).
M. Foley	15	1	463^2, 925^3, (1155), 1341^3, 1434^2.
Miss S. Forster	3	0	917^3, 1445^2.

Miss J. Foster * 1	1	(1648).
R. Fowler * 4	0	1333^3.
T. Gibney.................23	1	(154), 300^3, 799^2, 800^2, 1531^3.
T. Glass * 6	3	155^3, (582), (682), 923^3, (1338).
C. Gordon *.................4	1	(1537).
M. Gorman..................5	0	581^3.
Miss A. Goschen *......6	0	1541^3.
Miss C. Grissell *........4	1	(1541).
Miss P. Gundry *........12	2	154^3, (924), 1339^3, (1340), 1535^3, 1646^3.
P. Hall *.....................4	0	1538^3, 1625^2.
Mrs M. Hand * 2	0	1644^3.
G. Hanmer *................5	0	1559^3.
Miss D. Harding *........2	0	800^3, 1557^3.
M. Harris * 5	0	1539^2, 1627^3.
R. Hartley 2	1	(1154).
A. Harvey * 5	1	(1539).
C. Heard * 5	1	(1625).
M. Hewitt * 6	0	301^3.
A. Hickman * 5	0	579^2.
L. Hicks * 5	1	1023^2, (1533), 1592^2.
Mrs T. Hill * 5	2	(459), 919^2, 1155^2, (1530).
B. Hitchcott *.............17	4	(152), (385), 579^3, 584^2, (799), 1026^3, 1103^2, (1536), 1539^3, 1603^3, 1645^2.
A. Honeyball * 5	1	(1433).
Miss L. Horner.............5	2	470^2, (1538), (1645).
H. Humble 2	0	1446^3.
R. Hunnisett *.............2	1	(1532).
F. Hutsby *...................6	3	(151), (302), (1024).
Miss R. Illman............8	0	1344^2.
S. Jackson 1	0	464^3.
L. Jefford *...................9	2	(382), (583), 685^3, 919^3.
D. Jewett * 8	0	1628^2.
Miss E. Jones *............7	0	382^2, 1157^3, 1293^2.
Miss P. Jones * 11	0	299^2, 459^3, 1336^2.
J. Jukes * 14	2	(681), 1341^2, (1444), 1600^2.
P. Keane *...................1	0	1541^2.
V. Keane 6	1	461^2, (919), 1026^2.
M. Keel * 5	0	1534^2.
N. Kent * 8	0	90^3.
N. King * 8	1	227^3, 1536^3, (1627).
T. Lane * 8	1	585^2, (1334).
L. Lay * 4	0	227^2.
M. Lewis * 5	0	464^2, 687^2, 1022^3.
P. Maitland-Carew 4	0	915^2.
D. Mansell * 13	0	150^2, 226^2, 460^3, 465^3, 920^2.
G. Markham *..............2	1	(585).
A. Martin * 13	0	580^2, 1532^3, 1558^3.
A.J. Martin...................3	1	(156).
Miss T. McCurrich........3	0	223^2, 385^3.
L. McGrath * 6	0	90^2, 921^3.
M. Miller *.................12	2	152^2, 154^2, 303^2, (467), (800), 922^3, 1337^2, 1433^2.
N. Mitchell *...............4	1	(581), 1433^3, 1444^2.
L. Morgan *.................3	1	(1556).
R. Morgan *...............10	1	1445^3, 1446^2, (1591).
S. Morris * 11	2	(925), 1334^2, (1531), 1602^2, 1626^3.
J. Muir 4	0	1154^3.
C. Mulhall *...............14	0	89^3, 302^3, 582^2.
Mrs F. Needham * 12	4	(802), (923), 1024^2, (1557), (1628), 1647^3.
J. Nicholl 2	1	(469), 470^3.
Miss A. Nolan *...........1	0	222^2.

D. O'Meara 13	2	149^2, 383^3, (801), (921).
T. Oates * 4	0	586^3.
J. Owen * 12	1	(463).
Miss L. Pearce *.........7	1	(1293), 1346^2, 1648^3.
P. Phillips *.................2	0	1444^3, 1627^2.
B. Pollock * 17	7	(90), (148), (150), 151^3, 385^2, 459^3, (461), (687), 921^2, (1025), (1647).
K. Prendergast *...........1	0	225^3.
S. Prior *.....................3	1	(1343).
Julian Pritchard * 25	3	(222), 580^3, 683^3, 687^3, 1022^2, 1332^3, 1333^2, (1337), (1558).
P. Pritchard * 1	0	1157^2.
Mrs J. Reed 4	0	153^3.
W. Renwick * 16	3	(89), 225^2, (301), 582^3, 682^2, 915^3, (916), 917^3, 918^2, 1342^3, 1345^2, 1531^2.
A. Richardson * 1	0	686^3.
J. Richardson *............6	0	1443^2, 1542^2.
D. Robinson *..............5	1	462^3, (579).
Miss P. Robson *.........7	1	1556^3, (1602).
A. Sansome *..............19	0	382^3, 1156^3, 1434^3, 1537^3, 1557^2.
P. Scouller *.................1	1	(1443).
T. Scudamore * 21	1	148^3, 226^3, 925^2, (1249), 1293^3, 1346^3, 1645^3.
P. Shaw * 2	0	680^2.
Mrs B. Sillars 4	2	(224), 303^3, (1344).
D Da Silva * 1	1	(1342).
J. Snowden *................2	0	583^3.
Miss W. Southcombe * 4	0	467^3.
C. Storey * 10	0	1556^2, 1643^3.
Miss L. Sweeting * 5	1	1335^3, (1346), 1443^3, 1558^2, 1648^2.
S. Swiers * 4	1	(918).
J. Tate * 9	1	384^2, 465^2, 916^3, (1335), 1345^3, 1447^3, 1591^2.
C Ward Thomas 1	1	(1592).
M. Trott * 4	1	(1341), 1447^2.
R. Trotter.....................7	0	1154^2.
G. Tuer * 4	2	(155), 584^3, (917).
Miss C. Tuffin * 1	0	680^3.
D.I. Turner 1	0	302^2.
Miss Z. Turner * 2	1	(1434), 1593^2.
N. Tutty *.....................6	0	682^3, 923^2.
Miss S. Vickery *..........8	2	222^3, 466^2, (684), (685).
W. Wales * 1	1	(1156).
S. Waley-Cohen * 3	0	1337^3.
R. Walford * 9	1	(1345), 1628^3.
C. Ward-Thomas *.........5	0	301^2, 469^2, 1532^2.
Miss S. West 4	0	1625^3.
C. White * 1	0	1626^2.
C. Williams *...............13	1	386^2, 684^3, (1022), 1103^3, 1343^2, 1600^3.
E. Williams *.................6	0	1340^2.
C. Wilson *...................7	0	1336^3, 1602^3.
Miss F. Wilson *............9	1	1593^3, (1600).
A. Wintle * 18	1	153^2, 384^3, (683), 1338^3, 1339^2, 1340^3.
B. Woodhouse * 2	1	(227).
Miss J. Wormall *..........8	2	(686), 916^2, (1593), 1646^2.
M. Worthington * 4	0	1343^3.
G. Wragg * 1	0	300^2.
P. York * 13	3	(680), 1335^3, 1432^2, (1540), (1626).
J. Young *.....................7	0	148^2, 1534^3.
Jeremy Young...............6	0	1540^3.
Miss S. Young *...........10	2	(383), 583^2, (922), 1644^2.

The Busiest Riders in 2000

Point-to-Points				Rider	Hunter Chases			
Total	1st	2nd	3rd		Total	1st	2nd	3rd
140	**28**	**29**	**18**	Julian Pritchard	25	3	2	4
125	23	17	8	J. Jukes	14	2	2	0
121	42	19	9	L. Jefford	9	2	0	2
114	11	18	17	A. Sansome	19	0	1	4
111	11	15	16	T. Stephenson	0	0	0	0
97	30	12	11	Miss P. Gundry	12	2	0	4
97	20	16	11	R. Burton	28	6	5	2
93	15	13	5	A. Wintle	18	1	2	3
91	14	11	10	T. Vaughan	0	0	0	0
86	19	16	9	N. Mitchell	4	1	1	1
86	3	7	4	D. Mansell	13	0	3	2
85	9	9	17	R. Woollacott	0	0	0	0
84	14	8	10	A. Honeyball	5	1	0	0
83	3	8	12	P. Millington	0	0	0	0
82	13	7	7	A. Price	0	0	0	0
82	4	7	1	G. Barfoot-Saunt	0	0	0	0
80	10	9	8	A. Charles-Jones	23	4	1	2
78	16	10	10	E. Williams	6	0	1	0
77	9	14	10	P. York	13	3	2	0
76	23	14	8	Miss P. Jones	11	0	2	1
76	21	18	7	C. Storey	10	0	1	1
74	13	12	9	C. Williams	13	1	2	3
73	18	11	7	N. Bloom	3	1	1	1
70	17	13	8	A. Dalton	5	1	0	0
70	3	8	11	J. Barnes	9	0	1	2
68	23	10	10	G. Hanmer	5	0	0	1
65	8	7	3	L. Morgan	3	1	0	0
64	5	4	10	A. Coe	4	0	1	0
64	6	9	12	Richard Darke	1	0	0	0
62	12	14	7	D. Alers-Hankey	6	0	0	1
62	3	10	4	T. Lane	8	1	1	0
61	3	5	3	J. Price	0	0	0	0
61	5	7	5	Mrs F. Needham	12	4	1	1
60	3	11	7	A. Martin	13	0	1	2
60	6	9	6	S. Blackwell	7	1	0	0
59	21	10	6	Miss P. Robson	7	1	0	1
59	16	6	4	R. Lawther	0	0	0	0
59	5	6	4	A. Harvey	5	1	0	0
58	7	6	9	M. Miller	12	2	5	1
58	9	3	5	M. Mackley	0	0	0	0
57	4	5	6	J. Keen	0	0	0	0

55	11	3	5	R. Morgan	10	1	1	1
55	5	3	5	S.R. Andrews	0	0	0	0
55	8	2	10	J. Cook	0	0	0	0
54	7	6	5	C. Heard	5	1	0	0
53	5	7	2	S. Charlton	0	0	0	0
53	7	11	6	J. Walton	0	0	0	0
52	4	3	4	L. Hicks	5	1	2	0
52	8	4	4	M. Worthington	4	0	0	1
51	10	7	8	C. Mulhall	14	0	1	2
51	6	6	2	S. Swiers	4	1	0	0
51	8	6	7	N. Harris	0	0	0	0
50	5	5	9	R. Armson	3	0	2	0
49	7	14	8	Mrs M. Hand	2	0	0	1
49	4	2	3	C. Wadland	0	0	0	0
48	1	3	4	M. Rodda	0	0	0	0
48	6	10	4	Miss S. Young	10	2	2	0
48	9	5	4	S. Morris	11	2	2	1
47	14	5	10	T. Mitchell	0	0	0	0
47	3	2	6	P. Sheldrake	0	0	0	0
47	3	5	3	J. Young	7	0	1	1
47	6	7	4	Mrs V. Jackson	0	0	0	0
46	16	10	4	A. Crow	6	3	0	0
46	12	6	7	Miss J. Cumings	0	0	0	0
46	2	4	6	J. Snowden	2	0	0	1
46	3	9	6	T. Greed	0	0	0	0
46	4	9	8	Miss S. Vickery	8	2	1	1
46	6	13	3	C. Gordon	4	1	0	0
46	7	9	3	S. Joynes	0	0	0	0
46	7	9	9	J. Tarry	0	0	0	0
45	11	5	6	D. Barlow	9	0	1	1
45	3	2	7	T. Glass	6	3	0	2
45	3	4	5	J. Owen	12	1	0	0
45	5	2	3	R. Barrett	14	1	2	4
45	7	5	4	G. Maundrell	0	0	0	0
44	1	3	6	J. Diment	7	0	1	0
44	1	5	3	G. Richards	0	0	0	0
44	2	7	2	E. Walker	0	0	0	0
44	3	10	3	G. Lewis	0	0	0	0
43	2	2	3	R. Cope	4	1	1	0
43	7	4	5	N. Tutty	6	0	1	1
42	2	3	5	C. Barlow	0	0	0	0
42	5	2	2	D. Dennis	12	1	3	2
42	6	10	4	C. White	1	0	1	0
41	2	8	3	T. Dennis	6	0	1	1
41	3	6	6	D. Jones	0	0	0	0
40	1	4	5	S. Kidston	0	0	0	0
40	2	5	6	T. Davidson	0	0	0	0

Point-to-Point Owners & Riders Association

PRESIDENT: Jim Mahon, Bishopton Hill House, Bishopton, Stratford-on-Avon, Warwicks. CV37 0RG (Tel: 01789 299029)

VICE PRESIDENT: Percy Tory, Crab Farm, Shapwick, Blandford, Dorset. DT11 9JL (Tel: 01258 857206; Fax: 01258 857513)

CHAIRMAN: Richard Russell, Church Farm, Farthingstone, nr Towcester, Nothants. NN12 8HE (Tel: 01327 361208; Office Tel/Fax 01327 361394)

VICE-CHAIRMAN: Simon Claisse, Bouthrop Stables, Eastleach Martin, Gloucestershire. GL7 3NW (Tel & Fax: 01367 850598; Mobile 07785 293966)

SECRETARY: Jeanette Dawson, Horton Court, Westbere Lane, Westbere, Canterbury, Kent. CT2 0JH (Tel: 01227 713080; Fax 01227 713088)

Area Representatives

SOUTH EAST: Tony Alcock, The Willows, Brook, Ashford, Kent. TN25 5PD (Tel & Fax: 01233 812613)

SANDHURST: Simon Claisse, Bouthrop Stables, Eastleach Martin, Glos. (Tel & Fax: 01367 850598; Mobile 07785 293966)

WESSEX: Jeremy Barber, Peckmore Farm, Henley, Crewkerne, Somerset. TA18 8PQ (Tel: 01460 74943) and Leonard Vickery, Knowle End, South Barrow, Yeovil, Somerset. BA22 7LN (Tel: 01963 440043)

DEVON & CORNWALL: Keith Cumings, Eastwood, Bishops Nympton, South Molton, N. Devon. EX36 4PB (Tel: 01769 550528)

WEST WALES: Cynthia Higgon, Newton Hall, Crundale, Haverfordwest, Dyfed SA62 4EB (Tel & Fax: 01437 731239)

SOUTH WALES: Julie Tamplin, Cefn Llwyd Farm, Senghenydd, Abertridwr, Caerphilly, Mid Glamorgan. CF8 2HW (Tel: 01222 830278)

WELSH BORDERS: Graham Saveker, 26 Cotswold Drive, Kings Acre, Hereford. HR4 0TG (Tel & Fax: (01432 343655)

WEST MIDLANDS: Bill Bush, Old Manor House, West Littleton, Chippenham, Wilts. SN14 8JE (Tel: 01225 891683)

SOUTH MIDLANDS: Christopher Loggin, Gaydons, Hinton-in-the-Hedges, Northants. NN13 5NF (Tel: 01869 810594)

EAST ANGLIA: Pat Rowe, Curles Manor, Clavering, Saffron Walden, Essex. CB11 4PW Tel: 01799 550283)

MIDLANDS: John Docker, Rookery Farm, Northbrook Road, Coundon, nr Coventry, Warwicks. CV6 2AJ (Tel: 01203 332036)

NORTH WEST: Tim Garton, White Barn Farm, Slade Lane, Over Alderley, nr Macclesfield, Cheshire. SK10 4SF (Tel: 01625 584543)

NORTHERN: Gus Minto, Gilson, Spylaw Park, Kelso, Borders. TD5 8DS (Tel: 01573 223162)

YORKSHIRE: Tom Bannister, Coniston Cold, Skipton N. Yorks. BD23 4EB (Tel: 01756 748136; Fax 01756 749551; Home: 01729 830206)

Jockeys Representatives

NORTHERN: Simon Whitaker, 2 Scarcroft Hall Cottage, Thorner Lane, Scarcroft, Leeds. LS14 3AQ (Tel: 01132 892265 daytime; 01132 892341 evenings)

SOUTHERN: Grant Cann, Newlands, Cullompton, Devon. EX15 1QQ (Tel: 01884 32284)

Horse & Hound Leading Horse

Grand Marnier National Owners Championship

1970	Barty	Mr A. Gordon-Watson	10 Wins
1971	Golden Batman	Mr C.M.C. Hancock	8 Wins
1972	Pensham	Mrs H.P. Rushton	11 Wins
1973	Master Vesuvius	Mr J.M. Turner	11Wins
1974	Boy Bumble	Mr J.M. Turner	12Wins
1975	Even Harmony	Mr J.M. Turner	11 Wins
1976	Hardcastle	Mr J.M. Turner	9 Wins
1977	Hardcastle	Mr J.M. Turner	11 Wins
1978	Little Fleur	Mr R. Wynn	12Wins
1979	Hargan	Mr P. Tylor	10 Wins
1980	Florida King	Mr T. Hunnable	8 Wins
1981	Nostradamus	Mr J. Sumner	9 Wins
1982	MacKelly	Mr R. Bulgin	8 Wins
1983	Seine Bay	Mrs B. Perry	8 Wins
1984	National Clover	Mr D.G.L. Llewellin	9 Wins
1985	Brigadier Mouse	Mrs C. Foote-Forster	9 Wins
1986	Sweet Diana	Mr C.D. Dawson	9 Wins
1987	Mantinolas	Mrs K.R.J. Nicholas	8 Wins
1988	Stanwick Lad	Mr T.F.G. Marks	10 Wins
1989	For A Lark	Mr J.F. Weldhen	10 Wins

Daily Telegraph Leading Horse

1990	Timber Tool	W.J. Evans	11 Wins
1991	Fort Hall	Mrs L. Wadham	10 Wins
1992	Brunico	Mrs R.J. Mansell	12 Wins
1993	Melton Park	Mr A.J. Papworth	12 Wins

Grand Marnier National Owners Championship

1994	Melton Park	Mr A.J. Papworth	7 Wins
1995	Handsome Harvey	Mr & Mrs E.L. Harries	10 Wins
1996	Phar Too Touchy	Miss R.A. Francis	10 Wins
1997	Butler John (IRE)	Mr N. Viney	10 Wins
1998	St Gregory	Mr & Mrs A. Howland Jackson	9 Wins

Horse & Hound Leading Horse

1999	Copper Thistle	Mr R. Hunnisett	10 Wins
2000	Balisteros (FR)	Mrs B. Thomson	10 Wins

Leading Point-to-Point Owners 2000

1. **MR D. BRACE**..............................17
   Dawn's Cognac (IRE).......................5
   Coolvawn Lady (IRE).......................4
   Gunner Boon......................................4
   Evan's Collier Boy (IRE)...................2
   Icenfriendly (IRE)...............................1
   Sister Kit (IRE)....................................1

2. **MR J.M. TURNER**.........................14
   Spring Gale (IRE)...............................5
   Emsee-H..2
   Persian Boy (IRE)...............................2
   Prince Of Saints (IRE)........................2
   Always Trying 1
   Generous Deal (IRE)...........................1
   Mister Audi (IRE)................................1
   Squaddie...1

2. **MR & MRS A.G.C. HOWLAND
   JACKSON**..14
   Dawn Alert (IRE)...............................4
   Hatcham Boy (IRE)............................4
   Village Copper....................................4
   Heathburn (IRE)..................................2

4. **MR M.J. PARR**...............................11
   Lord Harry (IRE).................................4
   Glacial Trial (IRE)...............................2
   Inch Fountain (IRE) 2
   Night Irene (IRE)................................2
   Rise To It (IRE)....................................1

4. **MR R.S. HUNNISETT**....................11
   Copper Thistle (IRE) 8
   Shanavogh 2
   Inch Cross (IRE)..................................1

4. **MR B.A. KILPATRICK**...................11
   Slew Man (FR)....................................7
   Horus (IRE)..3
   Helena Justina*....................................1
   *with Mrs G. D'Angibau

7. **MRS B.K. THOMSON**.....................10
   Balisteros (FR)....................................10

8. **MR L.G. TIZZARD**............................8
   Millyhenry...8

9. **MR J.J. BOULTER**.............................7
   Gamay...4
   Starpath (NZ).......................................2
   Ferryhill (IRE).....................................1

9. **MRS J. WILSON** 7
   Quarterstaff..3
   Barna Boy (IRE)..................................2
   Shoemaker (IRE)*...............................1
   Stormy Words......................................1
   Who Is Equiname (IRE)......................1
   *also won for Mr & Mrs W.J. Warner

11. **MR D.C. ROBINSON** 6
    Struggles Glory (IRE).........................2
    Thats Dedication (IRE) 2
    Galaroi (IRE) 1
    Martha Leader (IRE)...........................1

11. **MR G. SAMUEL**................................6
    Whatafellow (IRE)...............................4
    Bishops Hall 1
    Sams Day (IRE) 1

11. **MR J. MILTON**..................................6
    Karaburan..4
    Bullens Bay (IRE)................................1
    Energy Man 1

11. **MR M.C. PIPE**...................................6
    Kingsbridge (IRE)...............................3
    Ibex...1
    Native Alliance (IRE).........................1
    Rossell Island (IRE)............................1

11. **MRS L. SHARPE & MR D. WILLIAMS**....6
    Well Armed (IRE)*..............................6

11. **MRS M. SCUDAMORE**......................6
    Glevum..6

11. **MRS P.K.J. BRIGHTWELL** 6
    Cracking Idea (IRE)............................4
    Commuter Country 1
    Popeshall 1

11. **MR N. VINEY**....................................6
    Butler John (IRE)................................6

11. **MR R.A. MASON**...............................6
    Absent Citizen (IRE)...........................1
    Bit Of A Citizen (IRE).........................1
    Cherry Gold...1
    Flutterbud 1
    Saxon Queen 1
    You Make Me Laugh (IRE)..................1

Point-to-Point Statistics 2000

Type of Races	Weight	Runners	Races	Average
Club Members*	12st7lb	48	8	6.00
	12st	215	25	8.60
Club Members (Nov Rdrs)	12st7lb	33	3	11.00
	12st	165	16	10.31
Club Members (Vet & Nov Rdrs)	12st	11	1	11.00
Club Members Conditional	12st7lb	16	1	16.00
Club Members Confined	12st7lb	14	1	14.00
	12st	28	3	9.33
Club Members Confined Restricted	12st...10	1		10.00
Club Members Intermediate	12st	21	2	10.50
Club Members Mares	12st	87	14	6.21
Club Members Moderate	12st	59	5	11.80
Club Members Novices	12st7lb	11	1	11.00
Club Members, 2m4f	12st7lb	8	1	8.00
Club Members Subtotal		**726**	**82**	**8.98**
Confined	12st7lb	109	15	7.27
	12st	1181	123	9.60
Confined (Nov Rdrs)	12st7lb	12	1	12.00
Confined Ladies	11st	9	1	9.00
Confined Mens	12st	15	1	15.00
Confined Restricted	12st	10	1	10.00
Confined, 3m2f	12st	7	1	7.00
Confineds Subtotal		**1343**	**143**	**9.39**
Hunt	12st7lb	543	103	5.327
	12st	312	63	4.95
Hunt (Cross Country), 3m4f	12st7lb	5	1	5.00
Hunt, 3m2f	12st	8	1	8.00
Hunt Members Subtotal		**868**	**168**	**5.18**
Intermediate	12st7lb	12	2	6.00
	12st	746	87	8.57
Intermediate (Nov Rdrs)	12st	43	6	7.17
Intermediates Subtotal		**801**	**95**	**8.43**
Ladies Open	11st	1144	154	7.43
Ladies Open, 3m2f	11st	7	1	7.00
Ladies Open, 3m5f	11st	26	2	13.00
Ladies Open, 4m	11st	7	1	7.00
Ladies Opens Subtotal		**1184**	**158**	**7.49**
Mens Open	12st7lb	424	58	7.31
	12st	705	97	7.27
Mens Open, 3m2f	12st7lb	4	1	4.00
Mens Open, 3m4f	12st7lb	7	1	7.00
Mens Open, 3m5f	12st	8	1	8.00
Mens Open, 4m	12st7lb	24	2	12.00
Mens Opens Subtotal		**1172**	**160**	**7.33**

Most Popular Meetings

Brecon & Talybont	*Llanfrynach*	159 runners
North Herefordshire	*Whitwick Manor*	141 runners
Ledbury	*Maisemore Park*	126 runners
Atherstone	*Clifton-on-Dunsmore*	125 runners
Point-to-Point Owners & Riders Club	*Barbury Castle)*	*125 runners*
Midlands Area Club	Thorpe Lodge	116 runners
Cambridgeshire Harriers Hunt Club	*Cottenham*	115 runners
Ludlow	*Bitterley*	115 runners
Lamerton	*Kilworthy*	113 runners
Spooners & West Dartmoor	*Cherrybrook*	108 runners
Heythrop	*Dunthrop*	107 runners
Oakley	*Newton Bromswold*	107 runners
Farmers Bloodhounds	*Dunthrop*	106 runners
Hurworth	*Hutton Rudby*	105 runners
Harkaway Club	*Chaddesley Corbett*	100 runners

Not Quite-So-Popular Events

Four Burrow*	*Trebudannon*	15 runners
East Kent	*Aldington*	21 runners
High Peak Harriers	*Flagg Moor*	30 runners
Southdown & Eridge	*Rodmell*	30 runners
Cotswold Vale Farmers	*Maisemore Park*	33 runners
Eggesford	*Bishopsleigh*	33 runners
Essex Farmers & Union	*Marks Tey*	33 runners
Tiverton Staghounds	*Bratton Down*	33 runners
Southdown & Eridge	*Rodmell*	34 runners

*abandoned with four races remaining

Most Races

Brecon & Talybont	*Llanfrynach*	14 races
Spooners & West Dartmoor	*Cherrybrook*	12 races
Lamerton	*Kilworthy*	11 races
Ledbury	*Maisemore Park*	11 races
Atherstone	*Clifton-on-Dunsmore*	10 races
Cumberland Farmers	*Dalston*	10 races
East Devon	*Bishops Court*	10 races
Gelligaer Farmers	*Bonvilston*	10 races
Ludlow	*Bitterley*	10 races
Mid Devon	*Black Forest Lodge*	10 races
Midlands Area Club	*Thorpe Lodge*	10 races
North Herefordshire	*Whitwick Manor*	10 races
Vale of Clettwr	*Erw Lon*	10 races

Least Races

Four Burrow	*Trebudannon*	3 races

Biggest Cavalry Charges

Ledbury Mixed Open	*Maisemore Park*	23 runners
Cambridgeshire Harriers Hunt Club Mens Open	*Cottenham*	21 runners
Army Land Rover Mens Open	*Larkhill*	20 runners
Old Raby Hunt Club Restricted	*Witton Castle*	20 runners
Oakley Confined	*Newton Bromswold*	20 runners
Belvoir Restricted	*Garthorpe*	20 runners

Walkovers

Tivyside Hunt Members	*Pantyderi*
Holcombe Harriers Members	*Whittington*
Radnor & West Herefordshire Intermediate	*Cursneh Hill*
Banwen Miners Hunt Members	*Pentreclwydau*
Teme Valley Intermediate	*Brampton Bryan*
Tredegar Farmers Hunt Members	*Bassaleg*
Haydon Hunt Members	*Hexham*
Pentyrch Hunt Members	*Bonvilston*

Analysis of Runners

4455 Hunters Certificates were registered in 2000 (counting once only the six animals for whom two Certificates were allowed to be lodged - an unnecessary complication), but including the eight Certicates which were subsequently revoked. Whichever method of counting is employed this was a new record figure. 40 unregistered horses (including those in the High Peak Cross-Country race) were among the 3909 horses that actually ran in Point-to-Points. A breakdown shows that 2984 (76.3%) were geldings, 923 (23.6%) were mares and 2 (0.05%) were entire; these figures hardly ever vary by more than 1%.

Local Stewards Enquiries

There were 135 enquiries held by Stewards of Meetings. They can be broken down as follows

Reason for enquiry	No of Enquiries	Percentage
Running and Riding	27	20.0
Misuse of Whip	20	14.8
Failure to Weigh-in/not draw Weight	19	14.1
No Medical Record Book	11	8.15
Interference	10	7.41
Passport Irregularities	10	7.41
Taking Wrong Course	8	5.93
Miscellaneous	7	5.19
Not Reporting to Doctor	5	3.70
Reckless Riding	4	2.96
Withdrawal	3	2.22
Failure to Ride Out	3	2.22
Rider Behaviour	3	2.22
Horse Unruly	2	1.48
Schooling in Public	1	0.74
Failure to Parade/Late in Ring	1	0.74
Horse Ineligible	1	0.74

The Jockey Club Veterinary Field Force examined 575 passports at 29 meetings; 179 horses were tested (128 urine and 51 blood samples), there were no positive results.

Entries

The total number of entries made (excluding those for abandoned meetings) was 33,483 compared to last season's 34,304. The 13 abandoned meetings accounted for a further 1730 entries - four of these were later held with new entries.

Most Entries in an Undivided Race

Entries were made for 1562 races in 2000 (including 79 races at abandoned meetings). The most entries in races not divided at close of entries were

Ludlow Restricted...*Bitterley*	60 entries
Derwent Open Maiden 7yo&up.................................*Charm Park*	59 entries
Wheatland Open Maiden..................................*Wolverhampton*	59 entries
Ystrad Taf Fechan Restricted ....*Bassaleg*	55 entries
Croome & West Warwickshire Restricted...............*Upton-on-Severn*	54 entries
Atherstone Restricted ....*Clifton-on-Dunsmore*	54 entries
Meynell & South Staffs Confined Maiden ....*Sandon*	53 entries
Quorn Open Maiden..*Garthorpe*	53 entries
Albrighton Restricted ....*Weston Park*	53 entries

The Least Entries were for:

Brocklesby Hunt Members...................................*Brocklesby Park*	3 entries
Holcombe Harriers Members......................................*Whittington*	3 entries
Haydon Hunt Members ....*Hexham*	3 entries
Royal Artillery Hunt Members ....*Larkhill*	4 entries
College Valley & North Northumberland Hunt Members ....*Alnwick*	4 entries
Tivyside Hunt Members ....*Pantyderi*	4 entries
Monmouthshire Hunt Members......................................*Llanvapley*	4 entries
Cattistock Hunt Members...*Littlewindsor*	4 entries
Dartmoor PPORA Club Members Mares ....*Flete Park*	4 entries
South Tetcott Hunt Members ....*Lifton*	4 entries

The average was 22.6 entries per race.

Most Entries for A Meeting

Entries were made for 214 different meetings (including those abandoned, even if later rearranged). The following received the most entries:

Brecon & Talybont ....*Llanfrynach*	314 entries
Heythrop...*Dunthrop*	290 entries
Ludlow ....*Bitterley*	283 entries
Ledbury ....*Maisemore Park*	276 entries
United...*Brampton Bryan*	274 entries
North Herefordshire.................................*Whitwick Manor*	271 entries
Harkaway Club.................................*Chaddesley Corbett*	267 entries

Fewest entries for a Meeting

Southdown & Eridge ....*Rodmell*	67 entries
North Cornwall ....*Wadebridge*	81 entries
South Cornwall ....*Trebudannon*	90 entries
Ashford Valley ....*Charing*	91 entries
Dunston Harriers ....*Ampton*	96 entries
Four Burrow...*Trebudannon*	97 entries
South Cornwall..*Great Trethew*	98 entries

The average was 165 entries per meeting.

Entries by Horse

4198 individual horses were entered in Point-to-Points in 2000 (including abandoned meetings). The most entered horses was entered 51 times; the complete breakdown is

Number of Times Entered	Number of Horses	Percentage
1-4	1239	29.51%
5-10	1648	39.26%
11-14	680	16.20%
15-19	434	10.34%
20-24	131	3.12%
25-29	45	1.07%
30-34	14	0.33%
35-39	4	0.10%
40-49	1	0.02%
50-100	2	0.05%
TOTAL	4198	

The average was 8.41 entries per horse.

Most Entered Horses

Owner	Horse	Times Entered
Mr D. Brace's	DAWN'S COGNAC (IRE)	51 entries
Mr D. Brace's	COOLVAWN LADY (IRE)	50 entries
Mr D. Brace's	GUNNER BOON	47 entries
The Fennington Friend's	HYLTERS CHANCE (IRE)	39 entries
Mrs L.A. Windsor & Mrs M.J. Woodhams'	SUN SURFER (FR)	39 entries
Mr J. Eaton's	AQUA STAR (IRE)	38 entries
Mrs N.F. Williams'	BANKHEAD (IRE)	35 entries
Mrs C.A. Williams & R. Weston's	RAVE-ON-HADLEY (IRE)	34 entries
Mr J. Jones'	ITSCINDERS	33 entries
D.J. Renney's	REAL PROGRESS (IRE)	33 entries
Mr T.R.R. Farr's	SAFFRON MOSS	33 entries
Mr A.G. Wadlow's	GREVILLE AGAIN (IRE)	32 entries
Mr C. Shaw's	THE CRAZY BISHOP (IRE)	32 entries
Mr J.S. Delahooke's	TRICKY TREVOR (IRE)	32 entries

Most Entered Horses which Never Ran

Owner	Horse	Times Entered
Mr T.R. Hills'	RETAIL RUNNER	13 entries
Mrs E.A. Webber's	MAGNETIC REEL	10 entries
Mr H.W. Lavis'	DERRING DOVE	9 entries
Mr J. Jones'	ITSVELVET	8 entries
Mr J. Burns'	SOSO GOLD	8 entries
Mr R.E. Barr's	BAILEYS BRIDGE (IRE)	7 entries
Mr N. Lilley's	COMMANDER CONN	7 entries
Mr A. Varey's	DUKES MEADOW (IRE)	7 entries
Mr M.J. Arnold's	MISTER BROCK	7 entries
Mr T.R. Hills'	SOUND STATEMENT (IRE)	7 entries

Point-to-Point Runners Analysis 2000

includes cross-country race

Fate	Total	Percentage
1	1540	11.02
2	1512	10.82
3	1398	10.00
4	1115	7.98
5	773	5.53
6	473	3.38
7	259	1.85
8	117	0.83
9	46	0.33
0(10-15)	35	0.25
1 disq	3	0.02
2 disq	9	0.06
3 disq	5	0.04
4 disq	8	0.01
Finishers Sub Total	7293	52.17
Pulled Up	4435	31.73
Unseated Rider	934	6.68
Fell	889	6.36
Ran Out	159	1.14
Refused/Took No Part	149	2.07
Brought Down	54	0.39
Slipped Up	42	0.30
Carried Out	22	0.16
Withdrawn under Orders	1	0.01
Non-Finishers Sub Total	6685	47.83
TOTAL	**13978**	

Annual Statistics

Year	POINT-TO-POINTS				HUNTER CHASES			OVERALL		
	Pt-to-Pt Meetings	Races	Total Runners	Average per Race	Hunter Chases	Total Runners	Average per Race	Horses Competing	Total Runners	Average per Race
1965	194	1024	7624	7.44	89	772	8.67	2153	8396	7.54
1966	185	995	8528	8.57	80	739	9.23	2262	9267	8.62
1967	192	1028	9002	8.75	81	724	8.93	2353	9726	8.77
1968	183	1004	8546	8.48	97	910	9.38	2344	9456	8.58
1969	180	986	8635	8.75	84	761	9.05	2450	9396	8.78
1970	190	1049	9804	9.34	88	873	9.69	2536	10,677	9.39
1971	182	1008	8994	8.92	101	953	9.43	2463	9947	8.96
1972	182	1022	9706	9.50	100	1049	10.49	2556	10,755	9.58
1973	184	1044	8825	8.45	125	1226	9.81	2528	10,051	8.60
1974	178	1036	9545	9.21	116	1169	10.08	2720	10,714	9.30
1975	166	1010	10932	10.82	115	1242	10.80	2860	12,174	10.82
1976	183	1067	9186	8.61	129	1294	10.03	2824	10,480	8.76
1977	179	1086	10709	9.86	126	1370	10.87	2923	12,079	9.97
1978	169	1062	11514	10.84	118	1382	11.71	3086	12,896	10.93
1979	168	1058	11021	10.45	111	1208	10.88	2933	12,229	10.46
1980	177	1110	10647	9.59	128	1415	11.05	3218	12,062	9.74
1981	179	1180	12487	10.58	122	1428	11.70	3264	13,915	10.69
*1982	184	1182	12148	10.28	144	1576	10.94	3395	13,724	10.35
*1983	172	1150	12553	10.92	120	1428	11.90	3352	13,981	11.09
*1984	188	1237	11791	9.53	138	1504	10.90	3398	13,295	9.67
*1985	175	1164	12301	10.57	121	1375	11.36	3454	13,676	10.64
1986	176	1191	12304	10.33	98	1200	12.24	3341	13,504	10.48
*1987	190	1237	11708	9.46	122	1176	9.64	3333	12,884	9.48
*1988	193	1269	12427	9.79	124	1252	10.10	3399	13,679	9.82
1989	189	1282	12429	9.69	135	1289	9.54	3508	13,718	9.68
*1990	196	1279	10546	8.24	124	1098	8.85	3446	11,644	8.30
1991	195	1293	11613	8.98	127	1343	10.57	3499	12,956	9.12
*1992	202	1401	12659	9.04	133	1396	10.50	3577	14,055	9.16
*1993	199	1425	13086	9.18	143	1336	9.34	3765	14,422	9.20
1994	202	1485	14117	9.51	133	1268	9.53	3869	15,385	9.51
1995	203	1492	12815	8.57	137	1311	9.57	3790	14,126	8.67
1996	207	1520	13430	8.86	130	1271	9.77	3818	14,701	8.91
1997	205	1473	11706	7.95	141	1256	8.91	3680	12,970	8.04
1998	193	1451	12464	8.59	135	1229	9.10	3758	13,693	8.63
1999	198	1538	14007	9.11	129	1352	10.48	4005	15,353	9.21
2000	201	1537	13978	9.09	139	1422	10.23	4027	15,400	9.19

* All cross-country races excluded

Horses, Runners and Winners in 2000 by Sex and Age

AGE	5	6	7	8	9	10	11	12	13	14	15	16	17	18	aged	TOTAL
GELDINGS																
How many Raced	148	300	4607	475	471	378	321	214	118	66	22	5	3	1	2	2984
How often they Won	54	153	203	234	187	151	141	93	37	18	6	1	1	0	2	1279
How often they Ran	399	1002	1701	1807	1747	1484	1173	841	466	209	75	14	3	1	2	10,924
Percentage Wins/Runs	13.5	15.3	11.9	12.9	10.7	10.2	12.0	11.1	7.90	8.60	8.00	7.10	33.3	0.00	0.00	11.7
MARES																
How many Raced	96	169	190	156	126	87	59	21	13	2	1	0	1	0	2	923
How often they Won	10	30	67	68	35	17	21	11	0	0	1	0	0	0	2	260
How often they Ran	240	520	650	548	406	348	217	78	38	2	2	0	1	0	2	3052
Percentage Wins/Runs	4.20	5.80	10.3	12.4	8.60	4.90	9.70	14.1	0.00	0.00	50.0	0.00	0.00	0.00	0.00	8.52
ENTRIES																
How many Raced	0	0	1	0	0	0	0	1	0	0	0	0	0	0	0	2
How often they Won	0	0	1	0	0	0	0	0	0	0	0	0	0	0	0	1
How often they Ran	0	0	1	0	0	0	0	1	0	0	0	0	0	0	0	2
Percentage Wins/Runs	0.00	0.00	100	0.00	0.00	0.00	0.00	0.00	0.00	0.00	0.00	0.00	0.00	0.00	0.00	50.0
TOTAL																
How many Raced	244	469	651	631	597	465	380	236	131	68	23	5	4	1	4	3909
How often they Won	64	183	271	302	222	168	162	104	37	18	7	1	1	0	0	1540
How often they Ran	639	1522	2352	2355	2153	1832	1390	920	504	211	77	14	4	1	4	13,978
Percentage Wins/Runs	10.00	12.0	11.5	12.8	10.3	9.20	11.7	11.3	7.30	8.50	9.10	7.10	25.0	0.00	0.00	10.0

2000 Sales

Adams Gold	600 gns	H.R.J. Nelmes	Ascot, Jul
Always Trying	3600 gns	S. Horner-Harker	Doncaster, May
Amber Spark (IRE)	600 gns	Paul Senter	Ascot, Mar
Anotherhandyman	10,500 gns	Harvey Smith	Doncaster, May
Ardbei (IRE)	1900 gns	G.W. Thomas	Malvern, May
Arleneseoin (IRE)	8000 gns	Sarah Dunsdon	Ascot, Jun
Arthur Henry	2000 gns	Cash	Doncaster, Aug
Azzante (IRE)	15,000 gns	Robert Stronge	Doncaster, Aug
Ballad (IRE)	6700 gns	F.E. Harvey	Doncaster, Aug
Ballydesmond (IRE)	2000 gns	P.A. Bennett	Doncaster, May
Barneys Gold (IRE)	1100 gns	B.B.A.	Doncaster, Aug
Basil Street (IRE)	2200 gns	David Smalley Bloodstock	Malvern, May
Bitofabuzz (IRE)	1100 gns	A. Witcomb	Malvern, May
Blackchesters	14,000 gns	I.S. Naylor	Doncaster, Aug
Borrow Mine (IRE)	1200 gns	D. Marriott	Doncaster, May
Brewery Lane (IRE)	300 gns	Cash	Ascot, Sep
Bridge Man	1100 gns	Cash	Malvern, May
Bright Reform (IRE)	800 gns	K. Walls	Doncaster, May
Bright Reform (IRE)	420 gns	Dr Karen Sanderson	Ascot, Sep
Brodante King (IRE)	5500 gns	Colin Tizzard	Doncaster, May
Burntwood Melody	10,500 gns	David Smyly Bloodstock	Doncaster, Aug
Cabille (FR)	500 gns	H. Owen	Ascot, Jun
Camitrov (FR)	8000 gns	Cash	Doncaster, May
Caromisu	2000 gns	Miss T. McCurrich	Doncaster, May
Cashew Crisis (IRE)	15,000 gns	R. Barber	Doncaster, May
Catchatan (IRE)	37,000 gns	Bullard Bloodstock	Doncaster, May
Celtic Town	2400 gns	L. Goodinson	Malvern, Feb
Cerisier (IRE)	2400 gns	British Bloodstock Agency	Ascot, Jul
Chaps	850 gns	J. Conway	Ascot, Jul
Charlie Keay (IRE)	5000 gns	Miss J. Du Plessis	Malvern, Oct
Cherry Pie	2100 gns	Cash	Ascot, Jun
Chop-Chop (IRE)	1800 gns	R. Hand	Doncaster, May
Chummy's Saga	500 gns	Cash	Doncaster, Aug
Clifford Bay (IRE)	4000 gns	P. Stirling	Doncaster, May
Climb The Hill (IRE)	1300 gns	Cash	Malvern, May
Cold Snap (IRE)	5000 gns	Cash	Ascot, Jun
Coolest By Phar (IRE)	450 gns	Lee Lawrence	Ascot, Jun
Cosa Fuair (IRE)	450 gns	F. Sutherland	Ascot, Jun
Counsel	21,000 gns	J. Tuck	Doncaster, May
Countess Rosie	1500 gns	Cash	Ascot, Jul
County Derry	1800 gns	Chris Popham	Ascot, Mar
Crocked Again (IRE)	1400 gns	S.E. Rich	Ascot, Jul
Dancing Ranger	3200 gns	M. Robertson-Young	Ascot, Jul
Dark Challenger (IRE)	2100 gns	J. Weldhen	Ascot, Jul
Deep Refrain (IRE)	480 gns	D. Parravani	Ascot, Jun
Destin D'Estruval (FR)	10,000 gns	Cash	Doncaster, May
Don Royal	3000 gns	Chris Popham	Ascot, Sep
Don Royal	4500 gns	R. Hacking	Ascot, Jul
Down To Joe's (IRE)	1400 gns	R.T. Bainbridge	Ascot, Jul
Drom Island	950 gns	Graham Richards	Malvern, May
Dulas Bay	2000 gns	Cash	Doncaster, Mar
Dunston Ace	2000 gns	Barry Leavy	Malvern, May
Dunston Laddie	800 gns	C. Nenaditch	Malvern, May
Edgar Gink (IRE)	20,000 gns	Aiden Murphy	Doncaster, Aug

Edge Of Night	1100 gns	F.D. Small & Co	Ascot, Jun
Ella Falls (IRE)	26,000 gns	Heather Dalton	Doncaster, May
Elver Spring	1000 gns	Cash	Doncaster, May
Epsilo De La Ronce (FR)	1750 gns	S. Flook	Ascot, Jul
Eveies Boy (IRE)	7200 gns	Cash	Doncaster, Aug
Fair Storm (IRE)	2000 gns	M. & W. Ward	Ascot, Feb
Fern Leader (IRE)	3200 gns	Linda Blackford	Malvern, May
Flying Fellow (IRE)	300 gns	Cash	Ascot, Sep
Fontaine Fables (IRE)	1400 gns	M. Robertson-Young	Ascot, Jun
Foodbroker Star (IRE)	2900 gns	Cash	Ascot, Jun
Fortune Hunter (IRE)	5000 gns	M.J. Norman	Doncaster, May
Foxy Dawn	3300 gns	T.F. Greengrow	Ascot, Sep
Furry Fox (IRE)	1250 gns	T. Jewitt	Ascot, Feb
Gemolly (IRE)	4400 gns	Cash	Ascot, Aug
General George	3100 gns	Dr Karen Sanderson	Ascot, Sep
Genereux	500 gns	Cash	Malvern, Oct
Generous Deal (IRE)	2200 gns	John Gallagher	Doncaster, Aug
Glenelly (IRE)	6000 gns	Elizabeth Johnstone	Malvern, Feb
Global Legend	800 gns	Cash	Ascot, Jun
Goforitkate (IRE)	6000 gns	V. Bradshaw	Malvern, Feb
Grand Canyon	1800 gns	Mrs V. Shirley	Doncaster, Jul
Guard A Dream (IRE)	1000 gns	Mrs K. Mundy	Ascot, Jul
Hamish	5400 gns	F.E. Harvey	Doncaster, Aug
High Expectations (IRE)	8500 gns	Cash	Doncaster, Aug
High Learie	2500 gns	Mrs D. Grissell	Ascot, Jul
High Park Lady (IRE)	1500 gns	Cash	Ascot, Jul
Hill Top Flyer (IRE)	520 gns	Cash	Ascot, Mar
Howling Jack	400 gns	Cash	Malvern, Oct
Howsyourluck (IRE)	1400 gns	Miss Bywater	Malvern, May
Hurricane Andrew (IRE)	1200 gns	Cash	Malvern, Feb
Hya Prim	500 gns	K. Peckham	Ascot, Aug
I'm Convinced	3500 gns	P. Sykes	Doncaster, May
Jack Boots	1350 gns	D. Phillips	Ascot, Feb
Joe Smoke	2300 gns	G.T. Sunter	Doncaster, Aug
John's Right (IRE)	950 gns	J. Rosseff	Ascot, Sep
Jymjam Johnny (IRE)	1000 gns	Dr M. Tate	Doncaster, Aug
Keep A Secret	1400 gns	Richard Barber	Doncaster, Aug
King Hab (IRE)	1000 gns	F. Vigar	Malvern, Feb
Kings Token	2500 gns	A.E. Stubbs & Son	Doncaster, Aug
Ladylands	2500 gns	M. Hill	Doncaster, May
Leon Garcia (IRE)	6400 gns	Cash	Malvern, May
Lily The Lark	6600 gns	Poplars Farm Stud	Malvern, May
Linlathen	9000 gns	Cash	Doncaster, Aug
Little Buster	600 gns	Mrs D. Little	Malvern, Feb
Little Crumplin	2200 gns	Richard Green	Ascot, Mar
Little Native (IRE)	14,000 gns	Lord Tyrone	Doncaster, May
Longmore (IRE)	3000 gns	P. Andrew	Doncaster, May
Magical Poitin (IRE)	3200 gns	Tim Finch	Doncaster, May
Melnik	6100 gns	Cash	Doncaster, May
Mezzo Princess	1000 gns	M. Strattford	Malvern, May
Mick Man (IRE)	3800 gns	S. Robinson	Malvern, Feb
Miss Caitlin (IRE)	1800 gns	Anthony Stroud Bloodstock	Ascot, Jul
Mister Trick (IRE)	2500 gns	Cash	Malvern, Feb
Model Agent	750 gns	D.C. Homewood	Ascot, Jun
Mr Freeman (IRE)	1400 gns	Paddy Farrell	Ascot, Jun
Mr Freeman (IRE)	550 gns	L. Simpson	Malvern, Oct
Mr Magget (IRE)	4400 gns	Cash	Ascot, Feb

Name	Price	Buyer	Sale
Mr Magget (IRE)	4500 gns	N. Warner	Ascot, Jun
My Wee Man (IRE)	2500 gns	Cash	Malvern, Feb
Namron (IRE)	450 gns	R. Hacking	Ascot, Jul
Native Cannon (IRE)	4000 gns	Robin Barwell	Doncaster, Aug
Netherbrook Lad	800 gns	Cash	Malvern, May
Never Wonder (IRE)	20,000 gns	Mark Bradstock	Doncaster, May
No Fiddling (IRE)	8200 gns	Karen Marks	Malvern, May
Nordic Spree (IRE)	5800 gns	Nigel Benstead	Ascot, Mar
Nouvalari (IRE)	500 gns	L. Thomas	Doncaster, Aug
Novatara	6000 gns	BBA (private sale)	Doncaster, Jul
Obelos (USA)	1050 gns	A. Ray	Malvern, Feb
O'flaherty's (IRE)	4400 gns	J. Potter	Doncaster, May
Oneforwillie	850 gns	Cash	Ascot, Apr
Oneforwillie	350 gns	Cash	Ascot, Oct
Ossie Dale (IRE)	2000 gns	Jamie Gray	Malvern, May
Our Man Flin (IRE)	7200 gns	Mrs Ann Price	Ascot, Jul
Paddy Casey (IRE)	1100 gns	Jenny Pidgeon	Ascot, Jul
Paddy Maguire (IRE)	2000 gns	S. & S. Murray	Doncaster, Aug
Pear Tree Percy	3100 gns	Miss S. Horner-Harker	Malvern, Oct
Pebble Beach (IRE)	2400 gns	M.J. Roberts	Doncaster, Aug
Perdix	2400 gns	Gerry Cully	Doncaster, Aug
Perhaps (USA)	1400 gns	Jimmy Byrne Bloodstock	Ascot, Jun
Peyton Jones	4500 gns	Cash	Ascot, Sep
Phaedair	2300 gns	Bob Hacking	Ascot, Feb
Polar King (IRE)	9000 gns	Fred Sutherland	Malvern, Oct
Port Valenska (IRE)	1300 gns	Peter Southcombe	Ascot, Jun
Prah Sands	14,000 gns	Mrs J. Vick	Ascot, Jun
Primitive Charles	2600 gns	C. Tizzard	Doncaster, Aug
Primitive Satin	6000 gns	Cash	Doncaster, Aug
Prince Buck (IRE)	10,000 gns	Robin Tate (private)	Doncaster, Aug
Prudent Miner (IRE)	2700 gns	David Dunsdon	Malvern, Feb
Pull On	6000 gns	J. Skinner	Ascot, Jun
Pure Air	1000 gns	Cash	Malvern, Oct
Pushover (FR)	1000 gns	J. Taylor	Malvern, Oct
Quick Succession (IRE)	550 gns	M.V. Shipley	Ascot, Oct
Rhyme And Chime	750 gns	Cash	Malvern, Oct
Rich Tradition (IRE)	750 gns	J. Holloway	Ascot, Apr
River Gala (IRE)	500 gns	D. Edens	Malvern, Oct
Roman Gale (IRE)	1100 gns	R. Page	Ascot, Jul
Romantic Native (IRE)	10,000 gns	Miss W.J. Bower	Doncaster, Mar
Romantic Native (IRE)	15,000 gns	R. Scholey (private)	Doncaster, Aug
Royal Arctic (IRE)	1600 gns	Richard Fahey	Malvern, May
Running Free (IRE)	4300 gns	John Worth	Doncaster, May
Run To The Glen	2600 gns	Jimmy Byrne Bloodstock	Malvern, May
Rusnetto (IRE)	2600 gns	Miss Sue Troughton	Ascot, Jul
Sally's Twins	8000 gns	Cash	Doncaster, May
Sayonara	1200 gns	Linda Tate Bloodstock	Ascot, Jun
Secretrock (IRE)	1400 gns	M. Gingell	Malvern, May
Shingle Beach (IRE)	2400 gns	S. Jelbert	Doncaster, May
Silver Standard	1000 gns	Cash	Malvern, Oct
Sixth Sense (IRE)	2800 gns	J. Willsmere	Doncaster, May
Sixth Sense (IRE)	350 gns	K. Walls	Ascot, Sep
Snapper	14,000 gns	H. Merrimen	Doncaster, May
Soon Come (USA)	680 gns	Cash	Ascot, Apr
Southern Cross	700 gns	Wonnacott	Malvern, May
Spiderdore	2000 gns	Mike Stephenson	Ascot, Sep
Squaddie	1200 gns	D. Stevenson	Doncaster, May
		Cash	

Stanwick Hall	460 gns	S. Evans	Ascot, Jul
Star Design (IRE)	4000 gns	Graham Leonard	Ascot, Jun
Starmont	1000 gns	T. Donnelly	Malvern, May
Stillorgan Park (IRE)	2200 gns	P. Ford	Malvern, Feb
Stormhill Recruit	900 gns	Mrs F. Walker	Malvern, Oct
Strewth	4500 gns	H. Witcomb	Malvern, May
Strong Ambition (IRE)	1200 gns	Mrs J.M. Newitt	Doncaster, May
Super Trouper (IRE)	1200 gns	Julie Wheeler	Ascot, Mar
Tangle Baron	900 gns	P. Emery	Malvern, May
Tantara Lodge (IRE)	800 gns	K.D. Giles	Ascot, Jul
Tarthooth (IRE)	12,500 gns	B.B.A.	Doncaster, Aug
Tee Tee Too (IRE)	4800 gns	Caroline Mackness	Malvern, Oct
Tell Tale (IRE)	4000 gns	Cash	Doncaster, Aug
Teme Willow (IRE)	1500 gns	Sorrel Price	Ascot, Sep
The Happy Monarch (IRE)	5000 gns	Alan Hill	Ascot, Jul
The Rural Dean (IRE)	5000 gns	M. Bloom	Ascot, Jun
The Whole Hog (IRE)	2000 gns	James Cookson	Doncaster, Aug
Thistlekicker (IRE)	1450 gns	Bob Woodhouse Bloodstock	Ascot, Feb
Tighter Budget	500 gns	Tina Hammond	Doncaster, Jul
Timmy Tuff (IRE)	400 gns	Mr Darby	Malvern, Oct
Topical Tip (IRE)	2000 gns	D. Wales	Doncaster, May
Top Toy (IRE)	11,500 gns	Cash	Doncaster, May
Touring-Turtle (IRE)	1300 gns	C. Tizzard	Ascot, Apr
Tropnevad	600 gns	J. Price	Doncaster, Jul
Verulam (IRE)	1850 gns	Mrs R. Hurley	Malvern, Oct
Veryvel (CZE)	9200 gns	M. Kemp	Malvern, Feb
What A Fiddler (IRE)	5000 gns	Cash	Doncaster, Aug
Whinholme Lass (IRE)	1300 gns	D. Llewellyn	Malvern, Feb
Winters Tale (IRE)	3400 gns	Edward Daly Bloodstock	Malvern, May
Wise Examiner (IRE)	5000 gns	Cash	Ascot, Jul
Woodland King (IRE)	3200 gns	R. Hand	Ascot, Feb
Wrenbury Farmer	800 gns	Mr Chapman	Malvern, May
Young General	900 gns	J. Beswick	Malvern, Oct

Leading Sales Prices in 2000

Catchatan (IRE)	37,000 gns	Doncaster, May
Ella Falls (IRE)	26,000 gns	Doncaster, May
Counsel	21,000 gns	Doncaster, May
Edgar Gink (IRE)	20,000 gns	Doncaster, Aug
Never Wonder (IRE)	20,000 gns	Doncaster, May
Azzante (IRE)	15,000 gns	Doncaster, Aug
Cashew Crisis (IRE)	15,000 gns	Doncaster, Aug
Romantic Native (IRE)	15,000 gns	Doncaster, Aug
Blackchesters	14,000 gns	Doncaster, Aug
Little Native (IRE)	14,000 gns	Doncaster, May
Prah Sands	14,000 gns	Ascot, Jun
Snapper	14,000 gns	Doncaster, May
Tarthooth (IRE)	12,500 gns	Doncaster, Aug
Top Toy (IRE)	11,500 gns	Doncaster, May
Anotherhandyman	10,500 gns	Doncaster, May
Burntwood Melody	10,500 gns	Doncaster, Aug
Destin D'Estruval (FR)	10,000 gns	Doncaster, May
Prince Buck (IRE)	10,000 gns	Doncaster, Aug
Romantic Native (IRE)	10,000 gns	Doncaster, Mar

Top of the Handicap

1959	Whinstone Hill	12-7	R. Brewis	Percy
1960	Whinstone Hill	12-7	R. Brewis	Percy
1961	Pride of Ivanhoe	12-10	S.T. Hewitt	Atherstone
1962	Pride of Ivanhoe	12-10	S.T. Hewitt	Atherstone
1963	Freddie	12-7	R. Tweedie	Duke of Buccleugh's
1964	Freddie	12-8	R. Tweedie	Duke of Buccleugh's
1965	Baulking Green	12-2	J. Reade	Old Berkshire
1966	Baulking Green	12-0	J. Reade	Old Berkshire
1967	Baulking Green	12-0	J. Reade	Old Berkshire
	Cham	12-0	Mrs C. Radclyffe	Old Berkshire
1968	Titus Oates	12-7	C.D. Collins	Zetland
1969	What A Myth	12-8	Lady Weir	Quorn
1970	Battle Royal II	11-13	Lord Mostyn	Flint & Denbigh
1971	Grey Sombrero	12-1	W.F. Caudwell	Old Berkshire
1972	Credit Call	12-2	C.D. Collins	Quorn
1973	Hilbirio	12-0	C.D. Collins	Quorn
1974	Hilbirio	12-0	C.D. Collins	Quorn
1975	Forest Rock	11-12	P.C.R. Wates	Chiddingfold, Lec & Cowdray
1976	Otter Way	12-8	O.J. Carter	East Devon
1977	Long Lane	11-8	R.J. Shepherd	Cotswold
	Remigio	11-8	Mrs G.M. Paterson	Old Surrey & Burstow
1978	Spartan Missile	12-0	M.J. Thorne	Warwickshire
1979	Spartan Missile	13-0	M.J. Thorne	Warwickshire
1980	Spartan Missile	13-0	M.J. Thorne	Warwickshire
1981	Spartan Missile	12-7	M.J. Thorne	Warwickshire
1982	Grittar	12-0	F.H. Gilman	Cottesmore
1983	Eliogarty	11-10	Miss C. Beasley	Meath
1984	Venture to Cognac	11-10	N.E.C. Sherwood	East Essex
1985	Further Thought	11-9	Mrs V. Vanden Bergh	East Sussex & R. Marsh
	Royal Judgement	11-9	Lady Rootes	East Sussex & R. Marsh
1986	Border Burg	11-12	J.S. Delahooke	Whaddon Chase
1987	Border Burg	11-8	J.S. Delahooke	Bicester with Whaddon Chase
1988	Certain Light	11-11	Mrs J. Campbell	Tickham
1989	Call Collect	12-0	J. Clements	Sinnington
1990	Call Collect	12-0	J. Clements	Sinnington
1991	Mystic Music	11-12	Mrs H. Forster	Dumfriesshire
1992	Rushing Wild	11-7	J.A. Keighley	Blackmore & Sparkford Vale
	Teaplanter	11-7	R.G. Russell	Pytchley
1993	Double Silk	12-0	R.C. Wilkins	Mendip Farmers
1994	Double Silk	12-0	R.C. Wilkins	Mendip Farmers
1995	Fantus	11-8	J.A. Keighley	Blackmore & Sparkford Vale
1996	Elegant Lord (IRE)	12-1	J.P. McManus	Scarteen
1997	Fantus	11-12	J.A. Keighley	Blackmore & Sparkford Vale
1998	Earthmover (IRE)	12-7	R.M. Penny	Cattistock
1999	Castle Mane (IRE)	12-4	C.R Dixey	Meynell & S. Staffs
2000	Castle Mane (IRE)	12-2	C.R Dixey	Meynell & S. Staffs

Performance of the Handicap in the 2000 Hunter Chases

139 Hunter Chases were run in 2000. Of these 131 were won by rated horses (the remainder were won by new horses – mostly ex-NH performers – prior to publication of their ratings). 82 of the 131 winners (62%) came from the top two of the Handicap.

The best priced top-rated winners (Tote dividends in brackets) were:

383	Saint Joseph	10-1	(£11.90)	680	Noyan	7-2	(£3.20)
1556	Sunnycliff	4-1	(£4.20)	382	Flying Maria	7-1	(£6.10)
1645	African Warrior	8-1	(£9.90)	1592	Hatcham Boy (IRE)	100-30	(£3.30)jt
468	Lochnagrain (IRE)	4-1	(£3.50)jt	463	Major's Law (IRE)	4-1	(£4.70)
1341	Shafi (IRE)	8-1	(£7.00)jt	1644	Lead Story (IRE)	11-4	(£3.00)

The best second top-rated winners were:

303	Little Buck (IRE)	10-1	(£9.80)	922	Saint Joseph	5-1	(£5.50)
685	Castle Lynch (IRE)	5-1	(£6.90)	1536	Galeaway (IRE)	6-1	(£6.90)jt
149	Ardstown	10-1	(£8.60)	1558	Forest Fountain (IRE)	9-2	(£5.50)jt
154	Marching Marquis (IRE)	5-1	(£5.90)	1346	Look In The Mirror	11-2	(£6.90)
924	Lakefield Rambler (IRE)	6-1	(£9.40)	925	Daytime Dawn (IRE)	9-2	(£4.60)

Backing the two top-rated (inc joints) in either order on the Tote Exacta produced the following:

1536	Galeaway (IRE) & Ballydesmond (IRE)	£139.70
382	Flying Maria & Royal Mountbrowne	£52.80
1558	Forest Fountain (IRE) & Mr Custard	£38.10
1346	Look In The Mirror & Ozzie Jones	£23.90
680	Noyan & Lankridge	£21.80
1644	Lead Story (IRE) & Track O' Profit (IRE)	£21.60TE

Backing the two top-rated (inc joints) in either order as a Computer Straight Forecast reversed produced:

1536	Galeaway (IRE) & Ballydesmond (IRE)	£110.43
382	Flying Maria & Royal Mountbrowne	£38.95
1558	Forest Fountain (IRE) & Mr Custard	£32.86
680	Noyan & Lankridge	£19.86
463	Major's Law (IRE) & Halham Tarn (IRE)	£18.72

Most Prolific Winners 2000
* also winning Point-to-Pointer in 2000
** also winning Hunter Chaser in 2000

Point-to-Points

Balisteros (FR)** 10
Copper Thistle (IRE)** 8
Millyhenry.............................8
Slew Man (FR) 7
Butler John (IRE) 6
Glevum.................................6
Well Armed (IRE) 6
Dawn's Cognac (IRE) 5
Here Comes Henry................5
Lily The Lark 5
Pharare (IRE)........................5
Rectory Garden (IRE) 5
Spring Gale (IRE)** 5
Allrite Pet 4
Cittadino 4
Coolvawn Lady (IRE) 4
Cracking Idea (IRE) 4
Dawn Alert (IRE) 4
Excise Man 4
Finnigan Free** 4
Fintona Boy (IRE) 4
Gamay 4
Gunner Boon 4
Hatcham Boy (IRE)**............4
Imperial Dawn (IRE) 4
Jackson's Hole 4
Karaburan.............................4
Kinnefad King (IRE)..............4
Lord Harry (IRE)** 4
Mizyan (IRE) 4
Prominent.............................4
Rip Van Winkle 4
Split Second 4
Union Man............................4
Upton Adventure 4
Village Copper 4
Whatafellow (IRE)**.............4
Wibbley Wobbley 4
African Warrior** 3
Anorak (USA) 3
Ardeal 3
Ball In The Net 3
Belarus (IRE).........................3
Bells Wood 3
Belvento (IRE)......................3
Blanville (FR)**.....................3

Bow Tie 3
Brave Noddy (IRE) 3
Castle Folly (IRE)..................3
Castle Lynch (IRE)**.............3
Catchword............................3
Coach (NZ)...........................3
Copper Coil...........................3
Dawn Invader (IRE)..............3
Dont Tell The Wife................3
Dry Highline (IRE) 3
Dun Rose 3
Ella Falls (IRE) 3
Elliewelliewoo......................3
Fair Exchange 3
Fresh Prince 3
Gildrom................................3
Gillone 3
Hatton Farm Babe 3
Hearts Are Wild....................3
Horus (IRE) 3
Iranos (FR) 3
Iron Pyrites 3
Just Bert (IRE).......................3
Kerry Soldier Blue 3
Key Debate** 3
Kingsbridge (IRE) 3
La Riviera (IRE) 3
Little Brockwell (IRE) 3
Lochnomore..........................3
Marisol (IRE) 3
Merrie Jar (IRE).....................3
Mine's A Gin (IRE) 3
Monkey Ago..........................3
Mr Magget (IRE)...................3
Nether Gobions.....................3
Newman's Conquest..............3
Nibble 3
Noughtosixty (IRE)...............3
Palace Parade (USA)**..........3
Parade Racer 3
Polar King (IRE).....................3
Prime Style 3
Quarterstaff 3
Red Spectacle (IRE)...............3
Riparius (USA) 3
Rosa's Revenge.....................3
Rusnetto (IRE).......................3
Rustic Revelry**....................3
Secret Beauty (IRE) 3

Smile Pleeze (IRE)................3
Solba (USA)..........................3
Solomans Sister 3
Some Tourist (IRE)................3
Stillmore Business 3
Stoney River (IRE) 3
The Crazy Bishop (IRE) 3
The Crooked Oak 3
We Move Earth.....................3
Weak Moment (IRE)..............3
Wejem (IRE) 3
Westcountry Lad 3

Hunter Chasers

Coulton 4
Grimley Gale (IRE) 4
Balisteros (FR)* 3
Cavalero 3
Gunner Welburn 3
Manhattan Rainbow (IRE)* .3
Mighty Moss (IRE).................3
Secret Bay* 3
Ardstown 2
Bells Life (IRE) 2
Brambledown (IRE)...............2
Castle Mane (IRE) 2
Chasing The Bride 2
Coole Abbey (IRE) 2
Finnow Thyne (IRE)...............2
Flying Maria 2
Key Debate* 2
King Torus (IRE) 2
Lakefield Rambler (IRE)*......2
Little Buck (IRE) 2
Lord Harry (IRE)*..................2
Mr Snowman* 2
Noyan...................................2
Overflowing River (IRE) 2
Saint Joseph* 2
Silverdalesureshot.................2
Solo Gent 2
Tea Box (IRE)*......................2
Trade Dispute (IRE)..............2

The Top Horses 2000

Castle Mane (IRE)	12-2	Struggles Glory (IRE)	11-2
Cavalero	12-0	Chasing The Bride	11-1
Grimley Gale (IRE)	11-12	Fundy (IRE)	11-0
Last Option	11-11	Millyhenry	11-0
Bells Life (IRE)	11-7	Knight Of Passion	11-0
Mighty Moss (IRE)	11-7	Copper Thistle (IRE)	10-13
Lord Harry (IRE)	11-7	Joint Account	10-13
Trade Dispute (IRE)	11-7	Marching Marquis (IRE)	10-13
Gunner Welburn	11-6	Mr Branigan (IRE)	10-13
Real Value (IRE)	11-6	Acton Bank	10-12
Satchmo (IRE)	11-6	Barna Boy (IRE)	10-12
Secret Bay	11-6	Blanville (FR)	10-12
Celtic Abbey	11-5	Brambledown (IRE)	10-12
Coulton	11-5	Distinctive (IRE)	10-12
Lakefield Rambler (IRE)	11-5	Dry Highline (IRE)	10-12
Balisteros (FR)	11-4	Forest Fountain (IRE)	10-12
Father Andy (IRE)	11-4	Melnik	10-12
Key Debate	11-4	Overflowing River (IRE)	10-12
Coole Abbey (IRE)	11-3	Prominent	10-12
Gillan Cove (IRE)	11-3	Union Man	10-12
Jigtime	11-3	Victoria's Boy (IRE)	10-12
Martha's Boy (IRE)	11-3	Whatafellow (IRE)	10-12
Carley Lad (IRE)	11-2		
It's Himself	11-2		

The Handicap 2000

Aadann (IRE)	8-4	African Warrior	10-6	Al Jawwal	9-8
Abbey Flyer	9-8	Afternoon Delight (IRE)	9-1	Alkarine	9-0§
Abbey Lad	9-12	Against The Agent	10-5	Allerbank	9-11
Abbots Court (IRE)	10-9	Agassi's Ace	9-13	Aller Coombe	9-0
Aberfoyle Park (IRE)	10-2	Agent	9-12	All-Inclusive (IRE)	9-1
Abit More Business (IRE)	10-6	Agile King	10-0	All In The Game (IRE)	8-0
A Bit Of Fluff	9-0	Aherne	8-6	All Or Nothing	9-0
About Time (IRE)	9-2§	Aintgottime (IRE)	10-7	Allrite Bonny Lass	10-1
Absent Citizen (IRE)	10-0	Aint No Lady (IRE)	8-0	Allrite Pet	10-6
Absolute Limit	9-7	Airborne Blue	8-7	All Sewn Up	9-3
Abuljjood (IRE)	9-5	Air Command (BAR)	9-6	Allten (IRE)	9-1
Acetylene	9-3	Airtrak (IRE)	9-7	All Things Nice	9-6
Achill Sound	10-2	Aladdin Sane Too	9-8	All Weather	10-3
A Class Apart (NZ)	9-8	Alaskan Heir	9-12	Ally Pally	9-10
Across The Card	10-5	Albert Blake	10-1§	Almikino (IRE)	8-4
Across The Water	9-6	Albert The Lion (IRE)	8-12	Alpine Castle (IRE)	9-3
Act Of Parliament (IRE)	10-5§	Albert Woods	9-3	Alska (FR)	10-3
Acton Bank	10-12	Alena H Banks	8-7	Alstack	9-12
Admiral Villeneuve	10-0	Alex Thuscombe	10-1	Alston Antics	10-10
Adventurus	10-0	Alfion (IRE)	9-12	Alston Fanfare (IRE)	7-12
Aegean Fanfare (IRE)	10-4	Alfredo Garcia (IRE)	9-12	Always Trying	8-10
Aeolian	9-9	Alias Parker Jones	9-0	Aly Daley (IRE)	10-2
A Few Dollars More (IRE)	9-8	Alicat (IRE)	8-7	Amaranthine	9-0
Affair Of Honour (IRE)	7-13	Alice Shorelark	9-12	Amazing Hill (IRE)	9-6
		Alice Sunrise	8-5	Ambersam	10-1
		Alisha Bavard (IRE)	9-8	Amber Spark (IRE)	9-4
		Alizarine Blue	8-13	Ambrose	10-2

Mackenzie & Selby

Important Races – Hunter Chases
CHRISTIES FOXHUNTERS' CHALLENGE CUP

Cheltenham

Foxhunter Challenge Cup, 4m

Year	Owner	Horse		Rider	
1946	Mrs H. Freeman-Jackson's	ILOILO	(Owner)	H.Freeman-Jackson	16
1947	Mr S.C. Bank's	LUCKY PURCHASE	(Owner)	J. Nichols	26
1948	Lt Col H. Llewellyn's	STATE CONTROL	(Owner)	Owner	38
1949	Abandoned because of frost				
1950	Mr J. Stuart Evans'	GREENWOOD	(Owner)	Owner	25
1951	Capt R.B. Smalley's	HALLOWEEN	(W. Wightman)	Owner	26
1952	Mr A. Walton's	PARASOL II	(Owner)	I. Kerwood	19
1953	Miss P. Bruce's	DUNBOY II } d.h.	(Owner)	C. Scott	22
	Mr J.U. Baillie's	MERRY } d.h.	(A. Kerr)	G. Kindersley	22
1954	Mr A. Moralee's	HAPPYMINT	(J. Wight)	Owner	21
1955	Abandoned because of snow				
1956	Mr C.D. Scott's	THE CALLANT	(J. Wight)	J. Scott-Aiton	17
1957	Mr C.D. Scott's	THE CALLANT	(J. Wight)	J. Scott-Aiton	9
1958	Mr R. Brewis'	WHINSTONE HILL	(Owner)	Owner	16
1959	Mr T.D. Rootes'	SOME BABY	(Owner)	M.J. Thorne	15
1960	Mr R. Brewis'	WHINSTONE HILL	(Owner)	Owner	15
1961	Mr L.R. Morgan's	COLLEDGE MASTER	(Owner)	Owner	17
1962	Mr L.R. Morgan's	COLLEDGE MASTER	(Owner)	Owner	17
1963	Mr G. Shepheard's	GRAND MORN II	(Owner)	R. Bloomfield	20
1964	Mr R.R. Tweedie's	FREDDIE	(Owner)	A. Mactaggart	10
1965	Mr R.H. Woodhouse's	WOODSIDE TERRACE	(Owner)	Owner	19
1966	Mr W.J.A. Shepherd's	STRAIGHT LADY	(Owner)	R. Shepherd	21
1967	Mr I.H. Patullo's	MULBARTON	(Owner)	N. Gaselee	13
1968	Mr G.R. Dun's	BRIGHT BEACH	(Owner)	C. Macmillan	12
1969	Mr W. Wade's	QUEEN'S GUIDE	(Owner)	G. Wade	10
1970	Mr R.H. Woodhouse's	HIGHWORTH	(Owner)	Owner	13

Sun Alliance & London Foxhunter Challenge Cup, 4m

Year	Owner	Horse		Rider	
1971	Mr D. Windel's	HOPE AGAIN	(Owner)	R. Smith	18
1972	Mr C.D. Collins'	CREDIT CALL	(W.A. Stephenson)	Owner	9
1973	Mrs E. Barker's	BULLOCKS HORN	(R. Turnell)	Lord Oaksey	20

Foxhunter Challenge Cup, 4m

Year	Owner	Horse		Rider	
1974	Mrs G. Fairbairn's	CORRIE BURN	(Owner)	I. Williams	16
1975	Mrs B.L. Surman's	REAL RASCAL	(Owner)	G. Hyatt	16
1976	Mr A.E. Cowan's	FALSE NOTE	(J. Horton)	B. Smart	16
1977	Mr R.J. Shepherd's	LONG LANE	(Owner)	Owner	16

Foxhunter Challenge Cup, 3m2f

Year	Owner	Horse		Rider	
1978	Mr R.J. Shepherd's	MOUNTOLIVE	(Owner)	Owner	16

Christies Foxhunter Challenge Cup, 3m2f

Year	Owner	Horse		Rider	
1979	Mr M.J. Thorne's	SPARTAN MISSILE	(Owner)	Owner	10

Foxhunter Challenge Cup, 3m2f

Year	Owner	Horse		Rider	
1980	Mr B. Brazier's	ROLLS RAMBLER	(F. Winter)	O. Sherwood	7
1981	Mr F.H. Gilman's	GRITTAR	(Owner)	C.R. Saunders	17
1982	Mr B. Munro-Wilson's	THE DRUNKEN DUCK	(A. Smith)	Owner	19
1983	Miss C. Beasley's	ELIOGARTY	(B. Kelly, Ire)	Owner	16
1984	Mr N.E.C. Sherwood's	VENTURE TO COGNAC	(F. Winter)	O. Sherwood	21

Christies Foxhunter Challenge Cup, 3m2f

Year	Owner	Horse		Rider	
1985	Mr W. Mawle's	ELMBOY	(Owner)	A. Hill	17
1986	Mr F.H. Gilman's	ATTITUDE ADJUSTER	(M. Morris, Ire)	T.M. Walsh	14
1987	R.E.A. Bott Ltd.'s	OBSERVE	(F. Winter)	C. Brooks	14
1988	Mrs J. Campbell's	CERTAIN LIGHT	(Owner)	P. Hacking	9

1989 Miss K. Rimell's	THREE COUNTIES	(Mrs M. Rimell)	Owner	16
1990 Mr J. Clements'	CALL COLLECT	(J. Parkes)	R. Martin	15
1991 Mr E.J. O'Sullivan's	LOVELY CITIZEN	(E.M. O'Sullivan)	W. O'Sullivan	18
1992 Mr J.A. Keighley's	RUSHING WILD	(R. Barber)	J. Farthing	24
1993 Mr R.C. Wilkins'	DOUBLE SILK	(Owner)	R. Treloggen	18
1994 Mr R.C. Wilkins'	DOUBLE SILK	(Owner)	R. Treloggen	5
1995 Mr J.A. Keighley's	FANTUS	(R. Barber)	Miss P. Curling	13
1996 Mr J.P. McManus'	ELEGANT LORD	(E. Bolger, Ire)	E. Bolger	17
1997 Mr J.A. Keighley's	FANTUS	(R. Barber)	T. Mitchell	18
1998 Mr R.M. Penny's	EARTHMOVER (IRE)	(R. Barber)	J. Tizzard	11
1999 Mr C. Dixey's	CASTLE MANE (IRE)	(Caroline Bailey)	B. Pollock	24
2000 Mr H.J. Manners'	CAVELERO	(Owner)	A. Charles-Jones	24

MARTELL FOXHUNTERS' CHASE
Liverpool
Foxhunters Chase, 4m856yds

1947 Mr S.C. Banks'	LUCKY PURCHASE	(OWNER)	J. Nichols	6
1948 Mr H.W. Metcalfe's	SAN MICHELE	(Maj G. Cunard)	Maj G. Cunard	
1949 Mrs J. Makin's	BALLYHARTFIELD	(Owner)	J. Straker	5

Foxhunters Chase, 2m7f110yds

1950 Mr L.H. Dalton's	HILLMERE	(Owner)	P. Brookshaw	14
1951 Mr R. Brewis'	CANDY II	(Owner)	Owner	17
1952 Col H.T. Alexander's	PAMPEENE II	(Owner)	Owner	11
1953 Mr M.J. Brewis'	SOLO CALL	(Owner)	Owner	7
1954 Mr L.A. Colville's	DARK STRANGER	(Owner)	J. Bosley	14
1955 Mr A. Moralee's	HAPPYMINT	(J. Wight)	Owner	13
1956 Mr J.A. Keith's	MR SHANKS	(Owner)	J. Everitt	8
1957 Mr L.R. Morgan's	COLLEDGE MASTER	(Owner)	Owner	6
1958 Mrs S. Richard's	SURPRISE PACKET	(Owner)	T. Johnson	13
1959 Miss W.H.S. Wallace's	MERRYMAN II	(N. Crump)	C. Scott	10
1960 Mr M. Fear's	APRIL QUEEN	(Owner)	J. Daniell	8
1961 Mr L.R. Morgan's	COLLEDGE MASTER	(Owner)	Owner	13
1962 Mr K.J. Beeston's	DOMINION	(Owner)	C. Foulkes	12
1963 Mr F.D. Nicholson's	SEA KNIGHT	(W.A. Stephenson)	P. Nicholson	15
1964 Mr M. Fear's	AERIAL III	(R. Armytage)	J. Daniell	8
1965 Mr F.D. Nicholson's	SEA KNIGHT	(W.A. Stephenson)	P. Nicholson	14
1966 Mr C.J.T. Alexander's	SUBALTERN	(Owner)	J. Lawrence	14
1967 Miss B. Johnson's	MINTO BURN	(Owner)	J. Lawrence	14
1968 Mr P.H.J. Will's	JUAN	(Owner)	Owner	8
1969 Mr V. Hunter Rowe's	BITTER LEMON	(Owner)	Owner	15
1970 Mr P.C.R. Wate's	LISMATEIGE	(Owner)	A. Wates	5
1971 Mr G.A.C. Cure's	BRIGHT WILLOW	(Owner)	R. Chugg	15
1972 Mr C.D. Collins'	CREDIT CALL	(W.A. Stephenson)	Owner	8
1973 Mrs E. Barker's	BULLOCKS HORN	(R. Turnell)	Lord Oaksey	14
1974 Mrs J. Brutton's	LORD FORTUNE	(Owner)	D. Edmunds	10
1975 Hon Mrs R.L. Newton's	CREDIT CALL	(W.A. Stephenson)	J. Newton	10

Greenall Whitley Foxhunter Chase, 2m6f

1976 Hon Mrs R.L. Newton's	CREDIT CALL	(Owner)	J. Newton	9
1977 Mr N.J. Henderson's	HAPPY WARRIOR	(F. Winter)	Owner	20

Whisky Haig Hunters Chase, 2m6f

1978 Mr M.J. Thorne's	SPARTAN MISSILE	(Owner)	Owner	19

Haig Whisky Hunters Chase, 2m6f

1979 Mr M.J. Thorne's	SPARTAN MISILE	(Owner)	Owner	15
1980 Mr R. Barker's	ROLLS RAMBLER	(F. Winter)	O. Sherwood	24

Haig Fox Hunters Chase, 2m6f

1981 Mr F.H. Gilman's	GRITTAR	(Owner)	C.R. Saunders	25

1982	Mr J. Docker's	LONE SOLDIER	(Owner)	P. Greenall	12
1983	Mrs D. Hehir's	ATHA CLIATH	(P. Mullins, Ire)	W. Mullins	8
1984	Mr J.G. Dudgeon's	GAYLE WARNING	(Owner)	A. Dudgeon	17

R.E.A. Bott Fox Hunters Chase, 2m6f

1985	Mrs J. Mann's	CITY BOY	(Mrs A. Underwood)	T. Thomsom Jones	18
1986	Miss C. Beasley's	ELIOGARTY	(D.J.G. Murray-Smith)	Owner	20
1987	Mr J.S. Delahooke's	BORDER BURG	(G. Cook)	A. Hill	25

Seagram Fox Hunters Chase, 2m6f

1988	Mr M.A. Johnson's	NEWNHAM	(Owner)	S.R. Andrews	23
1989	Mr J.Clements'	CALL COLLECT	(J. Parkes)	R. Martin	16
1990	Mrs W. Tulloch's	LEAN AR AGHAIDH	(S. Mellor)	D. Gray	25
1991	Mr D.J. Harding-Jones's	DOUBLE TURN	(J.R. Jenkins)	P. Harding-Jones	27

Martell Fox Hunters Chase, 2m6f

1992	Mr G.A. Hubbard's	GEE-A	(F. Murphy)	Paul Murphy	29
1993	Mr R.C. Wilkins'	DOUBLE SILK	(Owner)	R. Treloggen	27
1994	Mr H.J. Manners'	KILLESHIN	(Owner)	G. Brown	28
1995	Mrs J. Wilson's	SHEER JEST	(Bill Warner)	A. Hill	26
1996	Mrs H.J. Clarke's	ROLLING BALL (FR)	(S. Brookshaw)	R. Ford	26
1997	Mr B. Graham & Mr J. Mahon's	BLUE CHEEK	(J. Mahon)	R. Thornton	14
1998	Mr H.J. Manners'	CAVALERO	(Owner)	A. Charles-Jones	30
1999	Mr J.P. McManus'	ELEGANT LORD	(E. Bolger, Ire)	P. Fenton	23
2000	Mr R. Gibbs'	BELLS LIFE (IRE) (P. Hobbs)		D. O'Meara	26

INTRUM JUSTITIA (HORSE & HOUND CUP)

Horse and Hound Cup, Stratford, 3m4f

1959	Mr V.R. Bishop's	SPEYLOVE	(Owner)	J. Jackson	15
1960	Mr H.W. Dufosee's	BANTRY BAY	(Owner)	M. Tory	17
1961	Mr H.W. Dufosee's	BANTRY BAY	(Owner)	M. Tory	8
1962	Mr J. Reade's	BAULKING GREEN	(Owner)	R. Willis	16
1963	Mr J. Reade's	BAULKING GREEN	(T. Forster)	A. Frank	17
1964	Miss M. Arden's	ROYAL PHOEBE	(R. Whiston)	M. Gifford	13
1965	Mr J. Reade's	BAULKING GREEN	(T. Forster)	G. Small	8
1966	Mr C.D. Collins'	SANTA GRAND	(W.A. Stephenson)	Owner	10
1967	Mrs C. Radcliffe's	CHAM	(F. Cundell)	J. Lawrence	16
1968	Mr A.M. Darlington's	GREEN PLOVER	(J. Ford)	A. Maxwell	8
1969	Mr G. Darlington's	TOUCH OF TAMMY	(Owner)	R. Guilding	14
1970	Mr H.S. Poole's	SOME MAN	(Owner)	R. Knipe	15
1971	Mr C.D. Collins'	CREDIT CALL	(W.A. Stephenson)	G. Macmillan	10
1972	Mr C.D. Collins'	CREDIT CALL	(W.A. Stephenson)	Owner	11
1973	Mr C.D. Collins'	CREDIT CALL	(W.A. Stephenson)	Owner	5
1974	Mr H. Counsell's	STANHOPE STREET	(Owner)	B. Venn	12
1975	Hon Mrs R.L. Newton's	CREDIT CALL	(W.A. Stephenson)	J. Newton	12
1976	Mr O.J. Carter's	OTTER WAY	(Owner)	G. Cann	10
1977	Mr M.W. Bishop's	DEVIL'S WALK	(Owner)	T. Rooney	16
1978	Mr B. Brazier's	ROLLS RAMBLER	(F. Winter)	N. Henderson	9
1979	Mr M.J. Thorne's	SPARTAN MISSILE	(Owner)	Owner	8
1980	Mr B. Brazier's	ROLLS RAMBLER	(F. Winter)	O. Sherwood	16
1981	Mr O.J. Carter's	OTTERY NEWS	(Owner)	A.J. Wilson	17
1982	Mrs L. Clay's	LOYAL PARTNER	(T. Clay)	T. Clay	10
1983	Mr O.J. Carter's	OTTER WAY	(Owner)	A.J. Wilson	17
1984	Mr T.D. Easterby's	PROMINENT KING	(M.H. Easterby)	Owner	20
1985	Mr A. Calder's	FLYING ACE	(Owner)	Miss D. Calder	10
1986	Mr M.J. Langton's	THE PAIN BARRIER	(O. Sherwood)	Miss A. Langton	10

1987 Mrs M. Rimell's	THREE COUNTIES	(Owner)	Miss K. Rimell	11
1988 Miss K. Rimell's	THREE COUNTIES	(Mrs M. Rimell)	Owner	14
1989 Miss H. Wilson's	MYSTIC MUSIC	(Mrs K. Anderson)	K. Anderson	16
1990 Miss H. Wilson's	MYSTIC MUSIC	(Mrs K. Anderson)	K. Anderson	9
1991 Mr P. Bonner's	FEDERAL TROOPER	(Mrs C. McCarthy)	T. McCarthy	16
1992 Abandoned because of waterlogged course				
1993 Mr P. Craggs'	GENERALS BOY	(Owner)	P. Craggs	6
1994 Mr M.E. Pinto's	MIGHTY FROLIC	(Miss S. Edwards)	T. Hills	12
1995 Miss B.W. Palmer's	HERMES HARVEST	(Owner)	A. Balding	16
1996 Mr S. Pike's	PROUD SUN	(Owner)	J. Culloty	14

Horse & Hound Cup, Stratford, 3m4f

1997 Mr G.J. Powell's	CELTIC ABBEY	(Miss V. Williams)	D. Jones	11
1998 Winning Line Ltd's	TEETON MILL	(Miss V. Williams)	Miss S. Vickery	9
1999 Mr & Mrs R.M. Phillips'	GRIMLEY GALE (IRE)	(M. Jackson)	Julian Pritchard	7

Intrum Justitia (Horse & Hound Cup) Champion HC, Stratford, 3m4f

| 2000 Mr C. Dixey's | CASTLE MANE (IRE) | (Mrs C. Bailey) | B. Pollock | 7 |

LAND ROVER GENTLEMEN'S POINT-TO-POINT CHAMPIONSHIP

Players Gold Leaf Trophy, Newbury, 3m2f

| 1968 Miss L. Jones' | BARTLEMY BOY | (Owner) | J. Daniell | 17 |

Haydock Park, 3m4f

| 1969 Mr R.A. Bethell's | FORTY LIGHT | (Owner) | J. Walker | 14 |

Newbury, 3m2f

| 1970 Mrs J. Brutton's | LORD FORTUNE | (Owner) | G. Hyatt | 16 |

Haydock Park, 3m4f

| 1971 Mr G.A.C. Cure's | MIGHTY RED | (Owner) | J. Chugg | 8 |

Newbury, 3m2f

| 1972 Mrs A.D. Wiseman's | DOCTOR ZHIVAGO | (Owner) | J. Docker | 10 |
| 1973 Mr J.H. Jewell's | GRAVEL PITS | (Owner) | B. Venn | 12 |

Hereford, 3m3f

| 1974 Mr H.V. Counsell's | STANHOPE STREET | (Owner) | B. Venn | 11 |

BMW Championship, Chepstow, 3m3f

1975 Mr W.G. Barker's	JAUNTY JANE	(Owner)	J. Ormston	20
1976 Mr M. Churches'	PANMURE	(Owner)	R. Treloggen	13
1977 Mr R.J. Shepherd's	MOUNTOLIVE	(Owner)	Owner	12
1978 Mr L. Worner's	MASTERSHIP	(Owner)	B Stevens	12
1979 Mr G.R. Dun's	CARNDONAGH	(Owner)	J. Dun	16

Jeep/Christies' Championship, Chepstow, 3m3f

| 1980 Mr A. Sanderson's | WHIGGIE GEO | (Owner) | N. Tutty | 11 |
| 1981 Mr R.G. Frost's | ARMAGNAC PRINCESS | (Owner) | J. Frost | 12 |

Christies'/TKM Championship, Chepstow, 3m3f

| 1982 Mr A. Sanderson's | LADY BUTTONS | (Owner) | N. Tutty | 11 |

Webster's Yorkshire Bitter Championship, Chepstow, 3m3f

| 1983 Mrs G. Spratt's | LITTLE BILSHAM | (W. Bryan) | W. Bryan | 13 |

Diners Club Championship, Chepstow, 3m3f

| 1984 Mr M.W. Easterby's | URSER | (Owner) | T. Thomson Jones | 9 |
| 1985 Mr M.W. Easterby's | URSER | (Owner) | T. Thomson Jones | 11 |

Land Rover Championship, Chepstow, 3m3f

1986 Mr G. Richards'	FIXED PRICE	(Owner)	J. Llewellyn	18
1987 Mr K.W. Dunn's	CAL MAL	(Owner)	P. Scholfield	12
1988 Mr D.J. Kellow's	ARIZONA BELLE	(R. Buckler)	R. Buckler	8

Land Rover Championship, Towcester, 3m190y

1989	Mr D. Jeffries'	CASTLE ANDREA	(Owner)	T. Illsley	9
1990	Mr J.A. Riddell's	BLUE RAVINE	(R. Lamb)	S. Bell	13
1991	Mr D.M. Forster's	GRANNY'S PRAYER	(Owner)	R. Lawther	10
1992	Mr J.D. Jemmeson's	GLEN LOCHAN	(Owner)	N. Tutty	12
1993	Mrs F.T. Walton's	MIGHTY MARK	(Owner)	P. Johnson	11
1994	Mr R.G. Russell's	AVOSTAR	(Miss C. Saunders)	Owner	9
1995	Mr G.W. Lewis's	WELSH LEGION	(Owner)	J. Jukes	14

Land Rover Championship, Cheltenham, 3m1f110y

| 1996 | Mr G. Tanner's | RYMING CUPLET | (M. Trickey) | R. White | 13 |

Land Rover Championship, Towcester, 3m1f

1997	Mrs D.B. Lunt's	MAGNOLIA MAN	(Miss D. Cole)	N. Harris	6
1998	Mr H.J. Manners'	CAVALERO	(Owner)	A. Charles-Jones	6
1999	Mr R.K. Crabb's	KNIGHT OF PASSION	(Mrs P. Tizzard)	M. Miller	6
2000	Mr R.S. Hunnisett's	COPPER THISTLE	(Mrs C. Bailey)	Owner	9

GREIG MIDDLETON LADIES POINT-TO-POINT CHAMPIONSHIP

BMW Championship, Chepstow, 3m3f

1977	Mr D.F.T. White's	HOROSCOPE	(Owner)	Mrs R. White	7
1978	Mr V.H. Welton's	ZANETTA	(Owner)	Mrs F. Belcher	8
1979	Miss P. Kerby's	HAPPY RETURNS	(Owner)	Owner	8

Jeep/Christies' Championship, Chepstow, 3m3f

| 1980 | Mrs D.M. Watkins' | STARNELLO | (Owner) | Mrs R. White | 4 |
| 1981 | Mr J.F. Weldhen's | MOONSTEP | (Owner) | Miss K. Halswell | 14 |

Christies'/TKM Championship, Chepstow, 3m3f

1982	Mr A. Hornblower's	PASTRY BRUSH	(Owner)	Miss M. Kimnell	16
1983	Mr A. Bray's	BAULKING BYWAY	(Miss R. Harper)	Miss R. Harper	14
1984	Mr B.B. Isaac's	COBLEY EXPRESS	(Owner)	Mrs J. Mills	18
1985	Mr A. Calder's	FLYING ACE	(Owner)	Miss D. Calder	10
1986	Mrs M. Rimell's	THREE COUNTIES	(Owner)	Miss G. Armytage	14
1987	Mr C.D. Dawson's	SWEET DIANA	(Owner)	Miss J. Grinyer	10
1988	Mr J. Parfitt's	TARVILLE	(Owner)	Miss H. McCaull	10

RMC Group Championship, Warwick, 3m1f

1989	Mr R. Fear's	AIR STRIKE	(Owner)	Miss J. Southcombe	7
1990	Mr J.M. Turner's	AS YOU WERE	(Owner)	Miss N. Bothway	8
1991	Mr C. Davies's	PADDY'S POND	(N. Reece)	Miss C. Thomas	7
1992	Mr J.M. Turner's	SKYGRANGE	(Owner)	Miss Z. Turner	14

Champagne Taittinger Championship, Huntingdon, 3m

1993	Mrs A. Leat's	QANNAAS	(W. Smith)	Mrs P. Nash	8
1994	no corresponding race				
1995	no corresponding race				
1996	no corresponding race				

Greig Middleton Championship, Chepstow, 3m

| 1997 | Mr R.M. Penny's | EARTHMOVER (IRE) | (R. Barber) | Miss P. Gundry | 7 |
| 1998 | Miss V. Roberts' | BOXING MATCH | (Owner) | Miss V. Roberts | 8 |

Greig Middleton Championship, Warwick, 3m2f

| 1999 | Miss T. McCurrich's | MASTER OF TROY | (Owner) | Miss T. McCurrich | 12 |

Greig Middleton Championship, Uttoxeter, 3m2f

| 2000 | Mrs B.K. Thomson's | BALISTEROS (FR) | (Owner) | Miss J. Wormall | 7 |

INTERLINK EXPRESS RESTRICTED CHAMPIONSHIP

Times Championship, Towcester, 3m 190y

| 1987 | Mr R. Morgans' | SEA EXPRESS | (B. Lavis) | P. Mathias | 15 |
| 1988 | Mr J. Tudor's | ST HELENS BOY | (Owner) | J. Tudor | 13 |

1989 Miss A. Howard-Chappell's I. Widdicombe	DARAHEEN SNIPER	(H. Widdicombe)		
	6			
1990 Miss I. Dady's	EASTERN CHANT	(Owner)	C. Stockton	10
1991 Mrs M.A. Cooke's	STRONG BOND	(Owner)	N. Mitchell	9
1992 Mr J. Perry's	ASTROAR	(Owner)	R. Lawther	11
1993 Mr R.J. Mansell's	GOLD SHOT	(P. Bowen)	T. Jones	10

Times Championship, Newbury, 3m

1994 Mr S. Pike's	SYNDERBOROUGH LAD	(Owner)	M. Felton	15
1995 Mrs P. Roberts'	WHAT A HAND	(R. Barber)	Miss P. Curling	8
1996 no corresponding race				

Interlink Express Championship, Stratford, 3m

1997 Mr G. Keirle's	ALLER MOOR (IRE)	(Mrs S. Alner)	J. Tizzard	10
1998 Mr M. Jones'	KINGSTHORPE	(Owner)	A. Phillips	10
1999 Mrs R. Gasson's	FREEDOM FIGHTER	(Owner)	A. Martin	14
2000 no corresponding race				

Important Races - Point-to-Point

LORD ASHTON OF HYDE'S CUP

Heythrop Open

Fox Farm, Stow-on-the-Wold, 4m

1953 Mr L.A. Colville's	DARK STRANGER	I. Kerwood	18
1954 Mr S.C. Turner's	NYLON	G. Morgan	11
1955 Mr H. Phillips'	CHANDIE IV	J. Jackson	15
1956 Mr H.M. Ballard's	CASH ACCOUNT	W. Foulkes	13
1957 Mr S.L. Maundrell's	STARBAR	Owner	14
1958 Mr S.L. Maundrell's	KOLPHAM	P. Dibble	11
1959 Mr R.J. Horton's	ANDY PANDY	D.J. Horton	19
1960 Mr R.I. Johnson's	MASCOT III	R. Woolley	9
1961 Maj H.P. Rushton's	HOLYSTONE OAK	A. Biddlecombe	18
1962 Mr W.H. Firkins'	EVERYTHING'S ROSY	D. Tatlow	19
1963 Mr C.D. Collins'	WILD LEGEND	Owner	10
1964 Mr W.J.A. Shepherd's	STRAIGHT LADY	R.J. Shepherd	19
1965 Mr J. Brutton's	SNOWDRA QUEEN	H. Oliver	15
1966 Miss V. Diment's	BOB SAWYER	G. Dartnell	14
1967 Mr J. Jordan's	BARLEY BREE	D. Tatlow	14
1968 Maj P. Ormrod's	WINTER WILLOW	D. Williams-Wynn	9
1969 Miss L. Jones'	BARTLEMY BOY	J. Daniell	21
1970 Mrs J. Brutton's	LORD FORTUNE	G. Hyatt	16
1971 Mr J.S. Townsend's	CREME BRULE	R. Knipe	16
1972 Mr M.H. Ings'	DUNSBROOK LASS	Owner	17
1973 Maj M.R. Dangerfield's	ALL A MYTH	R.N. Miller	27
1974 Mr A.E. Cowan's	FALSE NOTE	Owner	29
1975 (i) Mr J.W. Brown's	TAKE COVER	Owner	11
(ii) Mr M.R. Churches'	RICH ROSE	R.N. Miller	9
1976 Mrs J. Brutton's	LORD FORTUNE	D. Edmunds	10
1977 Mrs J. Brutton's	LORD FORTUNE	D. Edmunds	13
1978 Mrs P. Morris'	SPARKFORD	J.R. Bryan	8
1979 Mr E.J. Bufton's	HEADMASTER	A. James	14
1980 Mr H. Wellon's	SPARTAN SCOT	T. Houlbrooke	16
1981 Mr J.B. Sumner's	NOSTRADAMUS	I. McKie	13
1982 Mr H. Wellon's	SPARTAN SCOT	T. Houlbrooke	13

Dunthrop Farm, Heythrop, c 4m

1983 Mr J.B. Sumner's	NOSTRADAMUS	I. McKie	14
1984 Mrs E. Dowling's	LAY-THE-TRUMP	B. Dowling	17

1985 Mr J.B. Sumner's	NOSTRADAMUS		I. McKie	7
1986 Mr T. Perry & Mr J. Deutsch's 16		PADDY'S PERIL	J. Deutsch	
1987 Mr P. Hemelik's	POLITICAL WHIP		D. Naylor-Leyland	8
1988 Mr T. Perry & Mr J. Deutsch's 7		PADDY'S PERIL	J. Deutsch	
1989 Mr C. Main's	LOLLYS PATCH		Owner	13
1990 Mr J. Cullen's	POLAR GLEN		M. Felton	7
1991 Mr J. Deutsch's	DROMIN JOKER		J. Deutsch	8
1992 Mrs M.E. Terry's	SPEEDY BOY		T. McCarthy	10
1993 Mrs P.A. White's	UNCLE RAGGY		R. Lawther	14
1994 Mr E.C. Knight's	HOLLAND HOUSE		C. Vigors	6
1995 Mr G. Nock's	SEVENS OUT		E. James	3
1996 Mrs M.R. Daniell's	KETTLES		A. Phillips	10
1997 Mrs M.R. Daniell's	KETTLES		A. Phillips	7
1998 Mr C.J. Hitchings'	BETTER FUTURE (IRE)		T. Stephenson	9
1999 Mr G. Nock's	CAMP BANK		Julian Pritchard	7
2000 Mr I.K. Johnson's	RUSTY BRIDGE		R. Burton	16

LADY DUDLEY CUP

Worcestershire Open

Chaddesley Corbett (different course), 3m

1946 Mr E. Holland-Martin's	HEFTY	T. Holland-Martin	6
1847 Mr A.W. Garfield's	AROD	Dr K. McCarthy	7
1948 Mr P. Kerby's	VINTY	P.J. Kerby	13
1949 Mr G. Hutsby's	SIR ISUMBRAS	Owner	11
1950 Mr P.T. Cartridge's	MAYBE II	Owner	12

Upton-upon-Severn, 3m4f

1951 Mr A.H. Thomlinson's	PAUL PRY	W.A. Stephenson	15
1952 Mr G.R. Maundrell's	RIGHT AGAIN	D. Maundrell	15

Upton-upon-Severn, 3m2f

1953 (i) Mr G.R. Maundrell's	COTTAGE LACE	D. Maundrell	13
(ii) Mr H. Sumner's	FLINT JACK	J. Fowler	16
1954 (i) Mr C.S. Ireland's	BLENALAD	C. Hart	7
(ii) Mr H. Sumner's	FLINT JACK	J. Fowler	7
1955 (i) Mr H.M. Ballard's	CASH ACCOUNT	M. Tate	7
(ii) Mr C. Nixon's	CREEOLA II	C. Harty	8
1956 (i) Mr H.M. Ballard's	CASH ACCOUNT	W. Foulkes	13
(ii) Mr G.A. Miles'	GALLOPING GOLD	C. Nesfield	13
1957 (i) Mr H.M. Ballard's	CASH ACCOUNT	W.H. Wynn	19
(ii) Mr J.R. Hindley's	PROSPERO	P. Brookshaw	21
1958 (i) Mr C. Davies'	MASTER COPPER	Owner	19
(ii) Mr J.R. French's	DOMABELLE	Owner	12
(iii) Mr T.D. Roote's	SOME BABY	M.J. Thorne	15
1959 (i) Mr G. Llewellin's	CLOVER BUD	D. Llewellin	14
(ii) Miss L. Jones'	FLIPPANT LAD	J. Daniell	13
1960 (i) Mr K. Small's	PRECIOUS GEM	G. Small	13
(ii) Miss L. Jones'	CULLEEN PARK	J. Daniell	14
1961 (i) Miss L. Jones'	FLIPPANT LAD	J. Daniell	15
(ii) Miss L. Jones'	CORN STAR	J. Daniell	15
1962 (i) Mr T.D. Holland-Martin's	MIDNIGHT COUP	Owner	8
(ii) Maj J.L. Davenport's	POMME DE GUERRE	P. Davenport	9
1963 (i) Mr R.P. Cooper's	FOROUGHONA	Owner	13
(ii) Mr W. Shand Kydd's	NO REWARD	Owner	14
1964 Mr W.J.A. Shepherd's	STRAIGHT LADY	R. Willis	17
1965 Mrs J. Brutton's	SNOWDRA QUEEN	H. Oliver	18

1966 Mr T.G. Cambidge's	HANDSEL	Owner	13
1967 Mrs D.L. Freer's	TAILORMAN	P. Hobbs	10
1968 Mr G.A. Cure's	BRIGHT WILLOW	R. Chugg	13
1969 Abandoned because of waterlogged course			

Chaddesley Corbett, 3m500yds

1970 Mrs E.C. Gaze's	FROZEN DAWN	H. Oliver	14

Chaddesley Corbett, 3m600yds

1971 Mr D.T. Surman's	REAL RASCAL	G. Hyatt	5
1972 Mr G.A.C. Cure's	MIGHTY RED	J. Chugg	11
1973 Mr G.A.C. Cure's	MIGHTY RED	R. Woolley	10

Chaddesley Corbett, 3m520yds

1974 Mr P.A. Rackham's	LAKE DISTRICT	M. Bloom	5
1975 Mr P.T. Brookshaw's	MICKLEY SEABRIGHT	Owner	16
1976 Mrs P. Morris'	JIM LAD	J.R. Bryan	6
1977 Mr R. Wynn's	LITTLE FLEUR	J.R. Bryan	8
1978 Miss J. Hey's	SPORTING LUCK	T. Smith	9
1979 Miss P. Morris'	SPARKFORD	J.R. Bryan	8
1980 Mr W.R.J. Everall's	MAJOR STAR	S. Brookshaw	5
1981 Mr W. Price's	PETITE MANDY	N. Oliver	8
1982 Mr D.L. Reed's	NORMAN CASE	P. Mathias	8
1983 Mrs P.M. Jones'	CLEAR PRIDE	D. Trow	12
1984 Mr M.F. Howard's	DARLINGATE	T. Jackson	11
1985 Mr R.A. Phillips'	RIDGEMAN (NZ)	I.K. Johnson	8
1986 Mr P. Greenall's	HIGHLAND BLAZE	Owner	10
1987 Mr J. Harris & Mr A. Leighton's	PRIDE OF TULLOW	T. Bowen	7
1988 Mr J. Palmer's	NORTH KEY	A. Ulyet	9
1989 Mr P.A. Deal's	BORDER SUN	S. Sweeting	12
1990 Mrs S. Potter's	TURN MILL	M. Hammond	9
1991 Mr & Mrs P.R. Haley's	THE RED ONE	S. Swiers	11
1992 Mr R.J. Mansell's	BRUNICO	R. Treloggen	6
1993 Mr R.J. Mansell's	BRUNICO	R. Treloggen	11
1994 Mr R.F. Jones'	YAHOO	M. Rimell	13
1995 Mr P.K. Barber's	BOND JNR (IRE)	T. Mitchell	9
1996 Mrs J. Yeomans'	SHARINSKI	M. Jackson	15
1997 Mr R.C. Wilkins'	DOUBLE THRILLER	J. Tizzard	7
1998 Mr V.Y. Gethin & Miss F. Shone's	PERFECT LIGHT	M. Jackson	5
1999 Mrs S.L. Barber's	SOLBA (USA)	A. Dalton	8
2000 Mrs D.J. Jackson's	DISTINCTIVE (IRE)	A. Wintle	4

CORONATION CUP

United Services Mixed Open
Larkhill, 3m

1950 (i) Mr J. Tudor-Evans'	GREENWOOD	J. Evans	31
(ii) Mr R. Winslade's	TAI FORD	Owner	25
1951 (i) Mr L.G. Cottrell's	ROYAL SUN	F. Ryall	25
(ii) Mr L.A. Coville's	LUCIFER VI	Capt Wright	21
1952 (i) Lt Col J.R. Hanbury's	GREEN FROG	R. Black	38
(ii) Mr J.H. Jones'	MYTHICAL RAY	T. Rogers	26

Coronation Cup

1953 (i) Mr P. Dufosee's	LUCRATIVE	Owners	25
(ii) Mr J.H. Edgar's	PAUL PRY	Owner	18
1954 (i) Mr L.A. Coville's	RIVER HEAD	I. Kerwood	17
(ii) Miss H.C. Cross'	FAIR EPINARD	R.E. Hunt	15
1955 Abandoned because of snow			

Year		Owner	Horse	Rider	No.
1956	Miss H.C. Cross'	FAIR EPINARD		D. Windel	7
1957	(i) Mr T.D. Rootes'	SOME BABY		J. Barnett	22
	(ii) Mrs E.D. Benson's	SURPRISE PACKET II		Brig V. Street	24
1958	(i) Mr W.H.G. Sprott's	VAIN WAX		Owner	22
	(ii) Mr M. Fear's	APRIL QUEEN		G. Small	18
1959	(i) Mr H.W. Dufosee's	BANTRY BAY		A. Dufosee	17
	(ii) Mr J.D. Watney's	STAFFORDSHIRE BLUE		M.L.C. Meredith	15
1960	(i) Hon D. Rhys'	STAR PIONEER		Capt R. Smalley	24
	(ii) J.W. Davey's	OXFORD HILL		H. Davey	20
	(iii) H. Handel's	SPINNING COIN II		I. Balding	19
1961	(i) H. Handel's	SPINNING COIN II		R. Banks	13
	(ii) A. Dufosee's	LANDSHIRE LANE		M. Tory	16
	(iii) Hon D. Rhys'	STAR PIONEER		D. Moore	18
1962	(i) Mrs G. Gale's	ROKOS		D. Moore	11
	(ii) Mr T.J.S. Nicholson's	BIJOU		Owner	15
	(iii) Mr G. Harwood's	SPINSTER'S FOLLY		Owner	17
1963	Abandoned because of frost and snow				
1964	(i) Mr W.W. Hobbs'	PAY OUT		Capt B. Fanshawe	21
	(ii) Mr M. Atkinson's	PETER PIPER II		Owner	21
	(iii) Mr S. Parker's	ERIN'S LEGEND		A. Welton	17
1965	(i) Mr P.J.H. Wills'	JUAN		Owner	15
	(ii) Mr F.J. Bugg's	CHEMIN DE FER		P.J. Bugg	14
	(iii) Mr J.H. Manners'	OAKLEIGH WAY		G. Dartnall	12
1966	(i) Mrs D. Maundrell's	HUCKLEBERRY HOUND		D. Maundrell	22
	(ii) Mrs J. Brutton's	SNOWDRA QUEEN		H. Oliver	21
	(iii) Mr W.L. Pilkington's	CENTRE CIRCLE		D. Tatlow	23
1967	(i) Mrs D. Maundrell's	LIZZY THE LIZARD		D. Maundrell	19
	(ii) Mrs J. Brutton's	SNOWDRA QUEEN		H. Oliver	20
	(iii) Mr G. Guilding's	MASTER TAMMY		R. Guilding	22
1968	(i) Miss S. Abbott's	HURSTBERRY		R. Alner	25
	(ii) Mr P. Cave's	BRONZE MILLER		Owner	24
	(iii) Mr G. Guilding's	TOUCH OF TAMMY		R. Guilding	19
	(iv) Mrs C. St V. Fox's	MOON RIVER		C. Fox	23
1969	Abandoned because of frost				
1970	(i) Mr G. Guilding's	TOUCH OF TAMMY		R. Guilding	25
	(ii) Mr E.W. Bomford's	SALLY FURLONG		T.D. Holland-Martin	22
	(iii) Mr G. Guilding's	MASTER TAMMY		R. Guilding	19
	(iv) Mrs M.M. Brinkworth's	LORD UPHAM		V. Dartnall	24
1971	(i) Mr A.M. Darlington's	GREEN PLOVER		T.D. Holland-Martin	16
	(ii) Cdr G. Latham's	PROPHET IV		Capt M.A. Villiers	14
1972	(i) Mrs J. Brutton's	LORD FORTUNE		D. Edmunds	18
	(ii) Mrs A.M. MacEwan's	FOREMAN		P. Frost	19
1973	(i) Mr P. Hawksfield's	MOONVIEW		J.P. Hawksfield	2
	(ii) Mr W. Bush's	INNISFOIL	N. Bush		14
1974	(i) Mrs S.P. Pattemore's	ORIENT WAR		M. Reeves	15
	(ii) Mrs J. Brutton's	LORD FORTUNE		D. Edmunds	18
	(iii) Mrs E.W. Bomford's	LADYBANK		T.D. Holland-Martin	19
1975	(i) Dr W. Fullerton's	ALEXANGLE		C. Down	15
	(ii) Mr R.J. Shepherd's	SIR KAY		Owner	19
	(iii) Mr R.W. Draper's	DEBONAIR BOY		R.N. Miller	13
1976	(i) Mrs J. Brutton's	LORD FORTUNE		D. Edmunds	25
	(ii) Mr M. Stephen's	EARL MOUSE	Mrs S. Horton		19
	(iii) Mr G.C. Maundrell's	LAFITTE		Owner	19
1977	(i) Mr M.J. Thorne's	POPPYWEE		Owner	23
	(ii) Mr L.G. Tizzard's	BOOKIE'S OPINION		A. Tizzard	24
	(iii) Mrs J. Brutton's	LORD FORTUNE		D. Edmunds	19
	(iv) Mr C.R. Rendell's	MARSHALSLAND		Miss F. Geddes	16
1978	Abandoned because of frost and snow				

Year	Owner	Horse	Rider	
1979	Abandoned because of frost and snow			
1980	(i) Mrs I.R. McKie's	MAN OF EUROPE	I. McKie	14
	(ii) Mrs J. Gill's	GYPSY INN	J. Delahooke	16
	(iii) Mr H.S. Butt's	WOODHAY	R. Alner	19
1981	(i) Mr B. Pike's	BALLYTARTAR	J. Dufosee	21
	(ii) Mr M. Low's	ROYAL ARCHER	Owner	21
	(iii) Hon D. Sieff's	KIANI	Miss D. Yeomans	16
	(iv) Mr M.S. Tory's	MORNING HEATHER	M. Felton	23
1982	(i) Mr J. Sumner's	NOSTRADAMUS	I. McKie	16
	(ii) Mr R. West's	LOCHUS	I. McKie	15
	(iii) Mr H.S. Butt's	WOODHAY	R. Alner	17
1983	Abandoned because of snow			
1984	(i) Mr J.W. Dufosee's	BALLYTARTAR	Miss V. Mitchell	22
	(ii) Mr R.J. Cake's	TAWNY MYTH	R. Cake	18
	(iii) Mr T.D. Holland-Martin's	BALBEG	Owner	18
1985	Abandoned because of frost and snow			
1986	Abandoned because of frost			
1987	(i) Mrs J. Cooper & Mr R. Willis'	DAWN STREET	Miss A. Dare	12
	(ii) Lord Vestey's	GOLDSPUN	M. Felton	11
	(iii) Mr T. Perry & Mr J. Deutsch's	PADDY'S PERIL	J. Deutsch	13
1988	(i) Mrs S.N. Embiricos'	KING BA BA	Miss A. Embiricos	17
	(ii) Mr T.D. Holland-Martin's	HOT FEVER	Owner	17
	(iii) Mrs J. Cooper's	DAWN STREET	Mrs J. Litston	13
	(iv) Mr D. Naylor-Leyland's	CURAHEEN BOY	Owner	16
1989	(i) Mr J.S. Delahooke's	BORDER BURG	A. Hill	10
	(ii) Mr R.J. Hill's	NEARLY HANDY	Miss M. Hill	17
	(iii) Mrs J. Cooper's	DAWN STREET	Mrs J. Litston	8
1990	(i) Mr M. Chamberlayne's	WHITSUNDAY	M. Chamberlayne	20
	(ii) Mr W. Gooden's	MY MELLOW MAN	Mrs J. Litston	22
	(iii) Mr R. Waley-Cohen's	DROMORE CASTLE	N. Ridout	18
1991	Abandoned because of frost			
1992	(i) Mr J.R. Vail's	WELLINGTON BROWN	M. Batters	10
	(ii) Miss C. Gordon's	BEECH GROVE	M. Felton	9
1993	(i) Mr G. Harwood's	HURRY UP HENRY	Miss A. Harwood	11
	(ii) Mr A. Boucher & Mr G.L. Barker's	MR DIPLOMATIC	J. Farthing	14
1994	(i) Mr N.R. Freak's	BARON BOB	M. Miller	11
	(ii) Mr E.C. Knight's	HOLLAND HOUSE	C. Vigors	10
1995	Mr J.A. Keighley's	FANTUS	Miss P. Curling	10
1996	Mrs L.J. Roberts'	WHAT A HAND	Miss P. Curling	9
1997	Mrs S. Humphreys'	BRACKENFIELD	Miss P. Curling	6
1998	Mr H.J. Manners'	CAVALERO	A. Charles-Jones	9
1999	Mr M.S. Rose's	SKIP'N'TIME	M. Miller	10
2000	Mr H.D. Hill & Mr C.H. Sporborg's	RUPERTS CHOICE (IRE)	S. Sporborg	10

Jockey Club Enquiries in 2000

Cheltenham

467 Dick Woodhouse HC: The Disciplinary Committee of the Jockey Club held an enquiry on 24th August 2000 into the analysis of urine ordered to be taken from MALIHABAD (IRE), owned by Graham Gingell, by the stewards at Wincanton after the gelding had finished third in the Dick Woodhouse Hunters Chase on 9th March 2000.

The urine of the horse was found to contain phenylbutazone and oxyphenbutazone, which are prohibited substances. After considering the evidence, including statements from Mr Gingell, Mrs Jane Galpin, with whom the gelding was stabled, and his veterinary surgeon, the Committee was satisfied that the source of the substance was Equipalazone, which was being administered to another horse in the yard on veterinary advice.

The Committee accepted an admission from Mr Gingell that he was in breach of Rule 53 and imposed a fine of ú600 upon him. Under Rule 180*(ii)*, the Committee disqualified MALIHABAD (IRE) from the race, placing ALASKA (FR) third.

West Street-Tickham Point-to-Point

574 Mixed Open, 4m: The Disciplinary Committee of the Jockey Club, on 17th April 2000, considered an appeal lodged by John Farrant, the owner of PRIME COURSE (IRE) against the decision of the Local Stewards to place the gelding second in this race after dead-heating with HIGH GUARDIAN.

The Committee heard evidence from John Farrant, Chris Gordon, the rider of PRIME COURSE (IRE), and Julian Pritchard, the rider of HIGH GUARDIAN. It also viewed video recordings of the race.

The Committee found that PRIME COURSE (IRE) had interfered with HIGH GUARDIAN, that the interference was accidental but had improved PRIME COURSE (IRE)'s placing. It therefore dismissed the appeal, confirmed the placings of HIGH GUARDIAN as first and PRIME COURSE (IRE) as second, and ordered the deposit money to be returned.

West Street-Tickham Point-to-Point

578 Open Maiden 8yo&up: The Disciplinary Committee of the Jockey Club held an enquiry on 18th May 2000 to consider an objection to DREAMIN GEORGE (IRE), placed second in this race on the grounds that Colin Sherry, the rider of DREAMIN GEORGE (IRE), did not hold a current Riders Qualification Certificate. It also considered whether or not Sherry was in breach of Regulation 50*(ii)* of the Jockey Club Regulations for Point-to-Point Steeple Chases by riding the gelding when he did not hold a Riders Qualification Certificate.

Having considered the evidence, including a statement from Mr A. O'Gorman, the owner of DREAMIN GEORGE (IRE), the Committee found that Sherry did not, at that time, possess a current Riders Qualification Certificate and had only been allowed to ride by certifying on the day that he did possess one.

The Committee accepted an admission from Sherry that he was in of Regulation 50*(ii)* and imposed a fine of ú125 upon him. It disqualified DREAMIN GEORGE (IRE) from the race, placing ELL GEE second and ENVIRONMENTAL LAW third.

Fakenham

585 William Bulwer-Long Mem Nov HC: The Disciplinary Committee of the Jockey Club held an enquiry on 24th August 2000 into the analysis of urine ordered to be taken from COMMUTER COUNTRY, owned by Margaret Brightwell, by the stewards at Fakenham after the gelding had finished first in the William Bulwer-Long Memorial Novices Hunters Chase on 17th March 2000.

The urine of the horse was found to contain phenylbutazone and oxyphenbutazone, which are prohibited substances. After considering the evidence, including statements from Mrs Brightwell and other witnesses, the Committee was satisfied that the source of the substance was

Equipalazone, which was being administered to another horse in the yard.

The Committee accepted an admission from Mrs Brightwell that she was in breach of Rule 53 and imposed a fine of £600 upon her. Under Rule 180*(ii)*, the Committee disqualified COMMUTER COUNTRY from the race, placing ON THE FLY first, CHESTER BEN second, STARLIGHT FOOL third and CASTLE ARROW (IRE) fourth.

Eglinton Point-to-Point

663 Restricted: The Disciplinary Committee of the Jockey Club, on 17th April 2000, considered an appeal lodged by Mrs Lisa Ogilvie, the owner of LORD LEVI (IRE), against the decision of the Local Stewards to reverse the placings after LORD LEVI (IRE) had beaten WILL'S PERK (IRE) in this race.

The Committee heard evidence from Mrs Ogilvie, Andrew Robson, the rider of LORD LEVI (IRE), Tom Oates, the rider of WILL'S PERK (IRE), and Keith Tulloch, a Steward at the meeting. It also viewed video recordings of the race.

The Committee found that LORD LEVI (IRE) had interfered with WILL'S PERK (IRE), but that the interference was accidental and had not improved LORD LEVI (IRE)'s placing. It therefore upheld the appeal and placed LORD LEVI (IRE) first and WILL'S PERK (IRE) second.

Spooners & West Dartmoor Point-to-Point

849 Restricted (Div 2, Part 1): The Disciplinary Committee of the Jockey Club held an enquiry on 1st June 2000 to consider whether or not Neil Harris, the rider of BRICANMORE, placed second, and Richard Woollacott, the rider of THE UGLY DUCKLING, unplaced, had committed breaches of Regulation 123 of the Jockey Club Regulations for Point-to-Point Steeple Chases whilst riding in this race.

The Committee heard evidence from both riders and Richard Darke, the rider of SHAMELESS LADY. It also viewed a video recording of the race.

The Committee found that interference had taken place between BRICANMORE and THE UGLY DUCKLING between 13th and 14th fences and that Woollacott was guilty under Regulation 123 of intentionally causing interference to BRICANMORE. It also found that Harris had deliberately struck Woollacott with his whip and found him guilty of improper riding under Regulation 123. It imposed a fine of £175 on both Woollacott and Harris.

Braes of Derwent Point-to-Point

1159 Intermediate: The Disciplinary Committee of the Jockey Club held an enquiry on 1st June 2000 to consider an objection to MINELLA GOLD (IRE), placed second, on the grounds that the gelding, having previously won three Hurdle Races in Ireland was not qualified to run in an Intermediate Race in accordance with the definitions stated in the Jockey Club Regulations for Point-to-Point Steeple Chases. It also considered whether or not the owner, Mrs S. Scott, was in breach of Regulation 111*(iv)* in respect of her declaring MINELLA GOLD (IRE) to run in the Intermediate race when it was not qualified to run.

Having considered the evidence, including a written statement from Mrs Scott, the Committee accepted an admission from her that she was in breach of Regulation 111*(iv)* and imposed a fine of £150 upon her. Under Regulation 151*(iv)* the Committee disqualified MINELLA GOLD (IRE) from the race, placing HIGHLAND MONARCH second and TROPNEVAD third.

Ian Johnson

The Disciplinary Committee of the Jockey Club held an enquiry on 23rd March 2000 to consider whether or not Ian Johnson had committed a breach of Regulation 170*(v)* of the Jockey Club Regulations for Point-to-Point Steeple Chases concerning his failure to list, as required, all injuries he had ever suffered when completing the Declaration of Health which accompanied his application for a Riders Qualification Certificate for the 2000 Point-to-Point Season.

Having considered the evidence, including a statement from Johnson, the Committee accepted an admission from him that he was in breach of Regulation 170*(v)* and imposed a fine of £200.

Pip Jones

The Disciplinary Committee of the Jockey Club, on 9th March 2000, considered an appeal lodged by Pip Jones, the rider of WARREN BOY, pulled up in the Ludlow Gold Cup (Hunters Chase), against the decision of the Stewards at Ludlow to find her guilty of careless riding and suspended her from riding for two days, following an enquiry on 2nd March 2000.

The Committee heard evidence from Miss Jones and Mr Tim Jones, the trainer of WARREN BOY. It also viewed video recordings of the race.

The Committee found that WARREN BOY had interfered firstly with MENAMOUR, ridden by Mr Tom Scudamore and secondly with PRINCESS LU (IRE) ridden by Mr Neil Tucker but that the interference was accidental in that WARREN BOY had suffered an injury and it was necessary for the gelding to be pulled up as quickly as possible to avoid the next fence.

It therefore upheld Miss Jones' appeal, and quashed the suspension imposed on her.

Matthew Mackley

The Disciplinary Committee of the Jockey Club held an enquiry on 15th June 2000 to consider whether or not Mr M Mackley had committed a breach of Regulation 51*(i)* of the Jockey Club Regulations for Point-to-Point Steeple Chases in respect of him having ridden in four Hunt Members' Races during the current season.

Having considered the evidence, including a statement from Mr Mackley, the Committee accepted an admission from him that he was in breach of Regulation 51*(i)* in that he had ridden in Hunt Members' Races at the Cambridge University Draghounds Point-to-Point on 13th February, the Burton Point-to-Point on 5th March, the Cottesmore Hunt Point-to-Point on 12th March and the Belvoir Hunt Point-to-Point on 2nd April.

The Committee imposed a fine of £100 upon Mr Mackley.

Robert Walford

The Disciplinary Committee of the Jockey Club held an enquiry on 23rd March 2000 to consider whether or not Robert Walford had committed a breach of Regulation 170(v) of the Jockey Club Regulations for Point-to-Point Steeple Chases concerning his failure to list, as required, all injuries he had ever suffered when completing the Declaration of Health which accompanied his application for a Riders Qualification Certificate for the 2000 Point-to-Point season.

Having considered the evidence, including a statement from Walford, the Committee accepted an admission from him that he was in breach of Regulation 170*(v)* and imposed a fine of £200.

Index to Advertisers

Index to Point-to-Point Fixtures in 2001

Point-to-Point Fixtures in 2001
(by arrangement with the British Horseracing Board)

[G]	Gerrard Ladies Open Championship qualifier
[I]	Intervet Intermediate Series qualifier
[L]	Land Rover Gentlemen's Open Championship qualifier
[M]	Marsh UK/TBA PPORA Club Mares Series qualifier
[P]	Dodson & Horrell PPORA Members race

SUNDAY JANUARY 7th

1	[G]	[I]	**Cambridgeshire Harriers Hunt Club**	Cottenham
2			**Tweseldown Racing Club**	Tweseldown

SATURDAY JANUARY 13th

3	[L]	**Army**	Larkhill

SUNDAY JANUARY 14th

4	[G]	**Waveney Harriers**	Higham

SUNDAY JANUARY 21st

5			**East Cornwall**	Great Trethew
6	[I]	[P]	**Point-to-Point Owners & Riders Club**	Barbury Castle
7	[L]		**Suffolk**	Ampton
8			**West Percy**	Alnwick

SATURDAY JANUARY 27th

9		**Royal Artillery**	Larkhill

SUNDAY JANUARY 28th

10			**Essex Farmers & Union**	Marks Tey
11	[P]		**Lincolnshire United Hunts Club**	Market Rasen
12	[G]	[L]	**Silverton**	Black Forest Lodge
13	[G]		**South Midlands Area Club**	Mollington

SATURDAY FEBRUARY 3rd

14	[P]	**Cambridgeshire**	Horseheath
15	[I]	**North Cornwall**	Wadebridge

SUNDAY FEBRUARY 4th

16	[M]	**Jedforest**	Friars Haugh
17	[P]	**Midlands Area Club**	Thorpe Lodge
18	[I]	**Mid Surrey Farmers Draghounds**	Charing
19		**Old Raby Hunt Club**	Witton Castle
20		**South Dorset**	Milborne St Andrew
21	[P]	**Tiverton**	Chipley Park

SATURDAY FEBRUARY 10th

22		**United Services**	Larkhill
23		**Vale of Clettwr**	Erw Lon

SUNDAY FEBRUARY 11th

24	[L]	**Aldenham Harriers**	Cottenham

25	[I]	[M]	**Badsworth**	*Wetherby*
26			**Farmers Bloodhounds**	*Dunthrop*
27	[P]		**Grove & Rufford**	*Nottingham*
28	[M]		**Mid Devon**	*Black Forest Lodge*

SATURDAY FEBRUARY 17th

29	[M]		**Granta Harriers**	*Higham*
30	[L]		**Oxford University Hunt Club**	*Kingston Blount*
31	[L]		**Sinnington**	*Duncombe Park*
32			**South Pool Harriers**	*Buckfastleigh*

SUNDAY FEBRUARY 18th

33	[L]		**Burton**	*Market Rasen*
34	[I]	[P]	**College Valley & N. Northumberland**	*Alnwick*
35	[I]	[P]	**Meynell & South Staffordshire**	*Weston Park*
36	[M]		**South East Hunts Club**	*Charing*

SATURDAY FEBRUARY 24th

37			**Brocklesby**	*Brocklesby Park*
38			**Chiddingfold, Leconfield & Cowdray**	*Parham*
39	[L]		**Hursley Hambledon**	*Badbury Rings*
40			**Minehead Harriers & West Somerset**	*Holnicote*
41	[G]		**North Herefordshire**	*Whitwick Manor*
42	[I]		**Tivyside**	*Pantyderi*

SUNDAY FEBRUARY 25th

43	[I]		**Berwickshire**	*Friars Haugh*
44	[L]		**East Cornwall**	*Lemalla*
45	[P]		**Easton Harriers**	*High Easter*
46			**West of Yore**	*Hornby Castle*

SATURDAY MARCH 3rd

47			**Beaufort**	*Didmarton*
48	[I]		**Carmarthenshire**	*Erw Lon*
49	[I]		**East Devon**	*Bishops Court*
50	[G]		**Thurlow**	*Horseheath*
51	[L]		**Tynedale**	*Corbridge*

SUNDAY MARCH 4th

52			**Bicester with Whaddon Chase**	*Mollington*
53	[P]		**Blankney**	*Nottingham*
54			**Derwent**	*Charm Park*
55	[P]		**Southdown & Eridge**	*Rodmell*
56	[I]	[P]	**South Herefordshire**	*Garnons*
57			**Staff College & R M A Draghounds**	*Larkhill*
58			**Tanatside**	*Eyton-on-Severn*

SATURDAY MARCH 10th

59	[L]		**Avon Vale**	*Barbury Castle*
60			**Brecon & Talybont**	*Llanfrynach*
61	[I]		**Cumberland Farmers**	*Dalston*
62	[I]	[L]	**Flint & Denbigh**	*Eaton Hall*
63	[G]		**Harkaway Club**	*Chaddesley Corbett*

64	[P]		**Oakley** .... *Newton Bromswold*
65	[G]	[P]	**Seavington** .... *Littlewindsor*
66			**Western** .... *Wadebridge*

SUNDAY MARCH 11th

67	[L]		**Cottesmore** .... *Garthorpe*
68			**Dunston Harriers** .... *Ampton*
69	[I]		**Holderness** .... *Dalton Park*
70			**South Devon** .... *Black Forest Lodge*
71			**West Street-Tickham** .... *Detling*

SATURDAY MARCH 17th

72			**Cheshire** .... *Alpraham*
73	[L]		**Hurworth** .... *Hutton Rudby*
74	[I]	[L]	**Lanarkshire & Renfrewshire** .... *Lanark*
75	[M]		**Llangibby** .... *Howick*
76	[P]		**North Norfolk Harriers** .... *Higham*
77	[I]	[L]	**Quantock Staghounds** .... *Cothelstone*
78	[M]		**Ross Harriers** .... *Garnons*

SATURDAY MARCH 24th

79			**Bramham Moor** .... *Wetherby*
80	[L]		**Clifton-on-Teme** .... *Upper Sapey*
81			**Crawley & Horsham** .... *Parham*
82	[G]	[P]	**Duke of Buccleuch's** .... *Friars Haugh*
83			**Essex** .... *High Easter*
84			**Holcombe Harriers** .... *Whittington*
85			**Lamerton** .... *Kilworthy*
86			**Monmouthshire** .... *Llanvapley*
87	[M]		**V W H** .... *Siddington*
88	[G]		**Wilton** .... *Badbury Rings*

SUNDAY MARCH 25th

89	[M]		**Fitzwilliam** .... *Cottenham*
90	[I]		**Grafton** .... *Mollington*
91	[I]		**Mendip Farmers** .... *Ston Easton*
92	[G]	[L]	**South Wold** .... *Brocklesby Park*

SATURDAY MARCH 31st

93			**Cleveland** .... *Stainton*
94	[L]		**Curre** .... *Howick*
95			**Dart Vale & Haldon Harriers** .... *Buckfastleigh*
96			**East Essex** .... *Marks Tey*
97			**Heythrop** .... *Dunthrop*
98			**Old Surrey, Burstow & West Kent** .... *Penshurst*
99	[I]		**Teme Valley** .... *Brampton Bryan*

SUNDAY APRIL 1st

100	[I]		**Belvoir** .... *Garthorpe*
101			**Cattistock** .... *Littlewindsor*
102			**Hampshire** .... *Hackwood Park*
103	[I]		**Ledbury** .... *Maisemore Park*

104	[P]		Morpeth	Tranwell
105			Pembrokeshire	Lydstep
106	[G]	[M]	Sir W.W. Wynn's	Eaton Hall

SATURDAY APRIL 7th

| 107 | | | Puckeridge | Horseheath |

SUNDAY APRIL 8th

108			Blackmore & Sparkford Vale	Charlton Horethorne
109	[L]		Cheshire Forest	Tabley
110	[L]		Cotswold	Andoversford
111			Dumfriesshire	Lockerbie
112			East Sussex & Romney Marsh	Bexhill
113			Llandeilo Farmers	Erw Lon
114	[P]		Middleton	Whitwell-on-the-Hill
115	[P]		Pytchley	Guilsborough
116			Spooners & West Dartmoor	Cherrybrook

EASTER SATURDAY APRIL 14th

117	[L]		Ashford Valley	Charing
118	[G]	[I][L]	Bedale	Hornby Castle
119			Cambridge University Draghounds	Cottenham
120	[P]		Cotswold Vale Farmers	Maisemore Park
121	[G]		Glamorgan	Ystradowen
122	[I]	[L]	Ludlow	Bitterley
123			North Staffordshire	Sandon
124			Percy	Alnwick
125			Portman	Badbury Rings
126			Vale of Aylesbury	Kimble
127	[G]	[L]	Vale of Lune Harriers	Whittington
128	[P]		West Somerset Vale	Cothelstone
129	[L]	[P]	Woodland Pytchley	Dingley

EASTER MONDAY APRIL 16th

130			Braes of Derwent	Corbridge
131			East Kent	Aldington
132			Eggesford	Bishopsleigh
133			Essex Farmers & Union	Marks Tey
134			Four Burrow	Trebudannon
135			North Cotswold	Paxford
136			Old Berkshire	Lockinge
137	[M]		South Notts	Thorpe Lodge
138			Southdown & Eridge	Rodmell
139			South Pembrokeshire	Lydstep
140			South Shropshire	Eyton-on-Severn
141			Staintondale	Charm Park
142			Taunton Vale	Kingston St Mary
143			Vine & Craven	Hackwood Park

EASTER TUESDAY APRIL 17th

| 144 | [M] | | Croome & West Warwickshire | Upton-on-Severn |
| 145 | [L] | [P] | High Peak Harriers | Flagg Moor |

SATURDAY APRIL 21st

146	[G]		Dartmoor	Flete Park
147			Essex & Suffolk	Higham
148			Pentyrch	Bonvilston
149	[G]		South & West Wilts	Larkhill
150	[P]		United Pack	Brampton Bryan
151			Worcestershire	Chaddesley Corbett
152	[G]		York & Ainsty	Easingwold

SUNDAY APRIL 22nd

| 153 | [L] | | Atherstone | Clifton-on-Dunsmore |
| 154 | [G] | [L] | Fife | Balcormo Mains |

SATURDAY APRIL 28th

155	[G]		Berkeley	Woodford
156	[G]		Bicester with Whaddon Chase	Kingston Blount
157			Eglinton	Ayr
158			Llangeinor	Laleston
159	[P]		New Forest	Larkhill
160			North Ledbury	Bitterley
161	[L]		Old Surrey, Burstow & West Kent	Penshurst
162	[P]		Pendle Forest & Craven	Hesslaker
163			South Cornwall	Trebudannon

SUNDAY APRIL 29th

164			Axe Vale Harriers	Stafford Cross
165	[G]	[M]	Quorn	Garthorpe
166			West Norfolk	Fakenham

SATURDAY MAY 5th

167			Albrighton	Weston Park
168	[P]		Bilsdale	Easingwold
169			Cumberland	Aspatria
170			Devon & Somerset Staghounds	Holnicote
171			Modbury Harriers	Flete Park
172	[G]		Surrey Union	Peper Harow
173			Ystrad Taf Fechan	Rhydygwern

SUNDAY MAY 6th

174			Fernie	Dingley
175			Lauderdale	Mosshouses
176			Radnor & West Herefordshire	Cursneh Hill
177	[G]	[M]	Tedworth	Barbury Castle

MONDAY MAY 7th

178			Banwen Miners	Pentreclwydau
179			Cotley	Cotley Farm
180			Enfield Chace	Northaw
181	[P]		North Shropshire	Eyton-on-Severn
182			Stevenstone	Vauterhill
183			Warwickshire	Ashorne
184			West Street-Tickham	Aldington
185			Zetland	Witton Castle

Hunter Chasers & Point-to-Pointers 2001   FIXTURES 1243

		SATURDAY MAY 12th	
186		**West Somerset & Minehead Harriers**	*Holnicote*
187		**South Durham**	*Mordon*
188		**Vale of Aylesbury**	*Kingston Blount*
		SUNDAY MAY 13th	
189		**Border**	*Corbridge*
190		**Gelligaer Farmers**	*Bonvilston*
191		**Tetcott**	*Lifton*
192		**Wheatland**	*Wolverhampton*
		WEDNESDAY MAY 16th	
193		**Weston & Banwell Harriers**	*Cothelstone*
		SATURDAY MAY 19th	
194	[P]	**Dulverton West**	*Bratton Down*
195		**Golden Valley**	*Bredwardine*
		SUNDAY MAY 20th	
196		**Haydon**	*Hexham*
197		**Melton Hunt Club**	*Garthorpe*
198		**North West Hunts Club**	*Tabley*
		SATURDAY MAY 26th	
199		**Dulverton East**	*Mounsey Hill Gate*
200	[P]	**Tredegar Farmers**	*Rhydygwern*
		SUNDAY MAY 27th	
201		**Berks & Bucks Draghounds**	*Kingston Blount*
		MONDAY MAY 28th	
202	[P]	**Albrighton Woodland**	*Chaddesley Corbett*
203		**South Tetcott**	*Lifton*
		WEDNESDAY MAY 30th	
204		**14th Regiment Royal Artillery**	*Larkhill*
		SATURDAY JUNE 2nd	
205		**Exmoor**	*Bratton Down*
		SUNDAY JUNE 3rd	
206		**Countryside Alliance**	*Bonvilston*
207		**Harborough Hunt Club**	*Dingley*
		SATURDAY JUNE 9th	
208		**Tiverton Staghounds**	*Bratton Down*
		SATURDAY JUNE 16th	
209		**Torrington Farmers**	*Umberleigh*

Index to Photographs

At least a part of these horses is visible in the Plate indicated

So you still think you know about Point-to-Pointing?

Those who do not want to spend hours poring over the record books can concentrate on the first 10 questions below. All the answers are contained in this book, and the first all-correct entry drawn will win £50 and a free 2002 Annual.

For those who enjoy researching the answers to more obscure questions, there are the usual further 20 questions. A year's free subscription to *Mackenzie & Selby's Loose-Leaf Results Service 2001* awaits the Scholar who achieves the highest score to all 30 questions.

EVERY ENTRANT GOES INTO THE HAT TO BE DRAWN FOR
ONE OF FOUR FREE 2002 ANNUALS — EVEN IF ALL THEIR ANSWERS ARE WRONG

We are most grateful to Brian Armstrong for once again setting the Questions, although this is the first time he has been responsible all 30 (so you know who to blame!).

Enthusiast's Quiz

Ten questions for a £50 prize and a free 2002 Annual.
In 2000:
1. Which horse won a Point-to-Point two days after falling foul of the first in the Liverpool Foxhunters?
2. At which meeting did Rory Lawther ride four winners?
3. Which Portman horse was unbeaten in five races for Andy and Susie Old?
4. Which two riders won on Millyhenry?
5. Which horse won the most Point-to-Points?
6. Who rode his 100'th career Point-to-Point winner at the Berkeley meeting?
7. Which horse won five races for Robert Biddlecombe?
8. Which meeting staged 14 races?
9. Which mare won three races before losing her bridle when chasing Butler John?
10. At which meeting did Caroline Bailey train five winners?

Scholarship Questions

*A further 20 questions to win a free subscription to **Mackenzie & Selby's 2001 Loose-Leaf Results Service 2001** (worth £195). All questions relate to the post World War II period.*

11. Which horse won ten races in a season, including the first two races (neither of which was a walkover) at the same meeting?
12. Which prolific Point-to-Pointer has the same name as a 1953 film directed by Dick Powell?
13. In which eight horse race did four Cornishes take part?
14. Which of Arkle's conquerors came out of retirement to run in a Point-to-Point as a 16-year-old?
15. Which horse ran in just three Point-to-Points, winning his Hunt Members race each time, but collapsed and died a few minutes after completing his hat-trick?
16. Which Horse and Hound Cup winner had won on the Flat as a three-year-old for Sir Cecil Boyd-Rochfort?
17. There used to be two Hunter Chases at the Cheltenham Festival, which trainer-rider won both of them in the same year?
18. Which leading Hunter Chaser appeared in the first 10 editions of this Annual?
19. Which Point-to-Point rider appeared on the cover of Private Eye?
20. Which mare failed to complete in six Point-to-Points, but bred the winner of a 2000 French Group One race?

21. Which horse in a single season, under six different riders, was unbeaten in five Point-to-Points, second in his only Hunter Chase, and won his last race hard held at the Melton?

22. In 1999, which horse pulled up in three Point-to-Points before running at Royal Ascot?

23. Which horse, a winner at the Torrington Farmers, subsequently won a Gold Medal when owned by H.M. The Queen.

24. Which horse, the winner of seven Point-to-Points and 13 Hunter Chases, dead-heated in a Wye Handicap Chase in his final race?

25. Who rode four winners and a second at the South Pembrokeshire?

26. Which horse won five consecutive Ladies Opens at the Minehead Harriers?

27. Which Liverpool Foxhunters winner had previously won an Irish Point-to-Point when named Lover Divine?

28. Which Cheltenham Foxhunters runner-up was out of a full sister to The Callant?

29. Which horse having won 17 times under Rules and been in the frame in the Gold Cup and the King George, ran aged 14 in a single Point-to-Point and one Hunter Chase, and won both races easily?

30. What links the Atherstone, Berkeley, Bicester, Brecon, Brocklesby, Cattistock, Chiddingfold, Cottesmore, Dulverton, Hurworth, Ledbury, Middleton and Quorn, but no other Hunts?

Send your answers (including your name and address) to:
Mackenzie and Selby Quiz
Stour House, 68 Grove Road, Wimborne, Dorset, BH21 1BW
to arrive before Saturday 27th January 2001

All entrants' names (from both parts of the Quiz) will go into the hat and the first four drawn will each receive a complimentary copy of the 2002 Annual.

The winners and answers will be despatched shortly after with the Loose-Leaf Results Service and the Weekly and Fortnightly Supplements. They will also appear in the 2002 Annual.

Results of Last Years Quizzes

The overall winner was **David Potter** of Loughborough who achieved a remarkable 27 correct answers (out of a possible 29) and received the *2000 Mackenzie & Selby Loose-Leaf Service*.

The £50 Enthusiasts' Quiz Prize and a copy of *Mackenzie & Selby's Hunter Chasers & Point-to-Pointers 2001* was won by **Alan Taylor** of Taunton, Somerset.

Other 2001 Annuals were won by **Derek Boughton** of Buckingham; Richard Hall of Berwick St John, **Miss N.J. Holmes** of Goole and **Tina White** of Weymouth.

Answers to 2000 Enthusiasts' Quiz

1. Jimmy Tarry rode five winners at the **Grafton** meeting.

2. **Copper Thistle** won the most Point-to-Points with ten victories.

3. **Castle Mane** was the unbeaten horse, which started the season at Tweseldown and ended at Punchestown.

4. **Andrew Dalton** rode the Lady Dudley Cup winner, Solba.

5. **Rough Quest** was the Grand National winner who won a Newbury Hunter Chase.

6. Brother and sister Bruce and Natasha McKim won on **Tompet** at Mollington.

7. **Guy Opperman** won on Running Frau carrying 21lb overweight in the Pegasus Members.

8. There was no Holderness Open Maiden (Div 1, Part 2) at Dalton Park to be delayed.

9. Julian Pritchard rode **43** winners to break all records.

10. The rearranged **Tiverton Staghounds** fixture was the last of the season.

Answers to 2000 Scholarship Quiz

11. ***Pappa's Orphan*** only Pointing win was the Glamorgan Maiden at Penllyan on 25th April 1970, paying £54 9s 0d (2711/4-1) on the Tote.

12. ***Boxing Day II*** ran in two races on the same day winning one of them, but never left the ground. Having refused at the first in the Oxford University & Bullingdon Club Past & Present Maiden, it then walked over for the Varsity Grind.

13. Officer Cadet T.A. Forster won the ***Wilton Southern Command race*** on Credit at Wellhouse Farm on March 14th 1953. He also walked over in a similar contest on the same horse at the ***South & West Wilts*** at Cannfield Farm the following week.

14. Mr C.E. Jones' ***Conchita*** was disqualified from the Monmouthshire Adjacent Ladies at Raglan Castle on April 3rd 1948 for 'passing outside the winning posts' (if the posts were not specifically marked with red and white markers it is doubtful whether she should have been).

15. ***Amanda Harwood*** finished second to Alison Dare in the 1986 National Riders Championship in her debut season.

16. 22 horses ran in the ***Cotswold Vale Adjacent Hunts Moderate*** race at Andoversford on 17th May 1972 after four had been balloted out?

17. ***John Docker*** rode his 100th winner in the Woodland Pytchley Restricted Open (Div 2) on 22nd April 1978 on Lone Soldier, whose dam, All Alone II, had given him his first winner in the Woodland Pytchley Adjacent on 6th April 1961.

18. ***Dawn Baby*** ran in the Taunton Vale Restricted Open at Kingston St Mary on 4th April 1988, 13 years after pulling up in its last race, the Tamar Novices Hurdle at Newton Abbot on 3rd September 1975.

19. Top Hunter Chaser ***Matchboard*** is the grandam of Champion Hurdle winning brothers, Morley Street (1991) and Granville Again (1993).

20. ***Angela Covell*** shared the National Ladies title with Miss M. Coke as a 15-year-old in 1947.

21. Lady Dudley Cup winners, Arod (in his next race) and Maybe II (1950) finished first and second respectively in the ***Harkaway Club Members Maiden*** at Chaddesley Corbett on 18th April 1947.

22. The last West Country Banking meeting was the ***Tetcott*** at ***Newlands*** on 9th April 1964.

23. Fifth Of November (aka bonfire night) fell in the Cambridgeshire Members at Hemmingford Abbots on ***2nd April 1966***.

24. ***Janane*** retired undefeated by virtue of walking over in his only race - the United Pack Members at Brampton Bryan on 16th April 1960. ***Mountain Air*** did the same in the Dulverton East Members at Venford on 23rd April 1966.

25. Robert Baker's ***Catman*** lost his first 44 races and then won two on the trot to end his 1988 season. *[Yes, we know we said four on the trot!]* .

26. ***Argeles*** was the winning Point-to-Pointer (and successful Hurdler) who had won two French flat races, three Hurdles and a Chase at Farfelu, before his name was changed?

27. Gallivanter III, Gildon, In Again and Sculptor's Joy were ***all raced by Point-to-Point commentators*** ; Chris Leigh, Henry Franklin, Peter Wakeham and Jeremy Branfoot respectively.

28. ***Limber*** won three races in four days in 1946: South Wold Farmers (West) Adjacent Farmers and Adjacent Members & Farmers races (South Willingham, 20th March) and South Wold Farmers Adjacent Farmers race (Spilsby, March 23rd). ***Hazy Dream*** also performed the three-race trick more recently in 1974: Puckeridge & Thurlow Farmers Club race (Horseheath, 13th April), Essex Farmers Ladies Open (Beeleigh, 15th April), and High Peak Harriers & North East Cheshire Draghounds Open (Flagg Moor, 16th April) - he faced a total of only nine horses in doing so!

29. ***Lt Col Dick Bromley-Gardner*** won on Young Pretender in the New Forest Buckhounds United services Past & Present race at Larkhill on 15th March 1986, aged 64.

30. ***"Four Fivers"*** was the horse that appeared in Hunter Chasers & Point-to-Pointers with a name beginning with a non-alphanumeric character.